CASSELL'S
ENGLISH DICTIONARY

CASSELL'S

English Dictionary

INCLUDING WORDS & PHRASES CURRENT AMONG THE ENGLISH-SPEAKING PEOPLES OF THE WORLD, TOGETHER WITH MANY TECHNICAL & SCIENTIFIC TERMS IN COMMON USE

COMPLETELY REVISED & ENLARGED BY

ARTHUR L. HAYWARD

AND

JOHN J. SPARKES

B.Sc., A.Inst.P.

CASSELL · LONDON

CASSELL & COMPANY LTD
35 RED LION SQUARE, LONDON WC1
MELBOURNE, SYDNEY, TORONTO
JOHANNESBURG, AUCKLAND

First edition 1962
Second edition 1964
Third edition 1966
Fourth edition 1968

SBN 304 91945 4

SET IN 6 PT IMPRINT TYPE AND PRINTED IN GREAT BRITAIN BY
BUTLER AND TANNER LTD, FROME AND LONDON

1167

CONTENTS

PREFACE

For this edition of CASSELL'S ENGLISH DICTIONARY much fresh matter has been gathered. English is an universal language, spoken not only as a mother-tongue in wide-spread portions of the globe, but as the official language of other vast areas. It is, moreover, employed as a *lingua franca*, an essential medium of communication, by politicians, scientists, technicians and men of letters of all nations. The requirements of the ever-expanding knowledge and culture of mankind have rightly called for new terms to phrase needs of expression far removed from those in which the original language developed, and CASSELL'S ENGLISH DICTIONARY has collected many such words and phrases and incorporated them in their rightful place as component parts of the English tongue. In North America, Australia, New Zealand and parts of Africa conditions have, over the years, arisen that have called for new words to express new directions of thought in terms and phrases particularly adapted to the circumstances. It has been the endeavour of the compilers to collect these and insert them in the dictionary. Where the original English word has acquired a new significance, or has been replaced by a different term, this is shown clearly in the text; for example, under "curtain" is printed in brackets (*Am.* drape), indicating the word used for a curtain in North America.

CASSELL'S ENGLISH DICTIONARY contains a vocabulary of some hundred and thirty thousand words and phrases. The first aim has been to give all words in ordinary use, including scientific, technical and other specialized terms likely to be met with by the reader or student, and a large number of combining forms (e.g. **ante-, anti-, arch-, dis-, -esce, -graph, homo-, -ish, -ize, -ing, myo-, -phile, sub-**), furnishing the key to the meaning of new coinages. Particular care has been given to the definitions. They are given clearly and concisely, but fully; and are couched in such language that the annoyance of having to make recourse to other parts of the Dictionary to arrive at the exact meaning of a word is reduced to a minimum. The common or more usual meaning of a word is usually given priority of place, and obsolete meanings, as also obsolete and archaic words, have been marked with an asterisk (*).

The word itself, with its compounds and derivatives, is printed in **heavy type.** Where there are two or more words with identical spelling, the figures (1), (2), etc., are inserted immediately after the word. Otherwise the pronunciation is given immediately after the initial entry. Then follows the etymology in square brackets, and after it the meaning (parts of speech being indicated by *n.*, *v.t.*, *v.i.*, *a.*, etc.), beginning with the ordinary signification of the word. The more specialized senses are indicated by the appropriate abbreviations in italics and enclosed in round brackets. Space has been saved by indicating common derivatives ending in such terminations as **-al, -ity, -ive, -ness,** etc. (e.g. **postal, rapidly, rascality, suddenness**), the meaning of which is obvious from that of the root-word. When, however, some special force attaches to a derivative the meaning is fully set out (e.g. **exactly, readily**). Suffixes, prefixes, and other combining forms have been inserted in the body of the work in their alphabetical order. Cross-references are shown by SMALL CAPS.

The aim of the etymologies has been to show both the proximate and the remoter origins of words, when these have been ascertained or a probable derivation can be suggested. In numerous instances, especially in words of Teutonic origin (e.g. **horse, moon**), a selection of cognate words are quoted as they throw light on the history of the word in question.

The scheme of pronunciation (see page xi) is simple, and though it does not attempt to reproduce the extreme niceties of phonological exactitude it is perfectly adequate for giving a clear indication of the way in which the individual word is pronounced by the ordinary educated Englishman. It will be noticed that syllables have been separated in the statement of pronunciation, though in actual speech these tend to glide into one another. The syllable to be stressed is indicated by the accent which follows it, e.g. the noun **present** (prez′ ėnt) or the verb **present** (prė zent′).

It would be impossible to name all the books and authorities consulted in preparing this enlarged and revised edition, but every dictionary-maker must gratefully acknowledge the help he has received from the Oxford dictionaries, from Skeat's *Etymological Dictionary*, and from that mine of scientific wisdom, *Chambers's Technical Dictionary*. The compilers are indebted to many experts throughout the English-speaking world who have given advice on their own subjects and on the words and phrases current in their own countries. A great debt of gratitude is owed to the compositors who set this very difficult copy so carefully, and to the printer's readers and others who made many valuable suggestions in the course of correcting these pages.

CHIEF ABBREVIATIONS USED

For a more complete List of Abbreviations see Appendix, p. 1326.

	adjective.
	abbreviation.
	ablative.
	Aboriginal, Aborigines.
	accusative; according.
t.	adaptation.
	adjectival.
	adverb.
	Anglo-French.
	African.
	afterwards.
c.	Agriculture.
	Alchemy.
	Algebra.
	allusion.
	alternative.
	NorthAmerica: Canada & U.S.A.
Ind.	American Indian.
	analogous.
m.	Anamese.
t.	Anatomy.
.-Ind.	Anglo-Indian.
.-Ir.	Anglo-Irish.
.-Lat.	Anglo-Latin.
	Antiquities.
ar.	apparently.
b.	Arabic.
m.	Aramaic.
n.	Architecture.
hæol.	Archæology.
h.	Arithmetic.
	Artistic.
ll.	Artillery.
S.	Anglo-Saxon.
m.	assimilated, assimilation.
yr.	Assyrian.
rol.	Astrology.
ron.	Astronomy.
ib.	attribute
m.	augmentation, augmentative.
stral.	Australian.
str.-Hung.	Austro-Hungarian.
. v.	auxiliary verb.
at.	Aviation, Aeronautics.
l.	Bible, biblical.
liog.	Bibliography.
l.	Biology.
n.	Bohemian.
.	Botany.
z.	Brazilian.
t.	Breton.
ld.	Building.
g.	Bulgarian.
z.	Byzantine.
.	*circa*, about.
mb.	Cambridge.
mpan.	Campanology.
n.	Canada, Canadian.
rib.	Caribbean.
rp.	Carpentry.
t.	Catalonian.
lt.	Celtic.
rem.	Ceramics
.	Church.
em.	Chemistry.
Chin.	Chinese.
Civ. Eng.	Civil Engineering.
Class.	Classical.
coal-min.	coal mining.
cogn.	cognate.
coll.	collateral.
collect.	collective.
colloq.	colloquially.
comb.	combination.
comb. form.	combining form.
Comm.	Commerce, commercial.
comp.	comparative.
Conch.	Conchology.
cond.	conditional.
conf.	confusion.
conj.	conjunction.
conn.	connected.
contempt.	contemptuously.
contr.	contraction.
Cook.	Cooking.
Copt.	Coptic.
Corn.	Cornish.
corr.	corruption; corresponding.
cosmog.	cosmogony, cosmogonical.
cp.	compare.
Craniol.	Craniology.
Cryst.	Crystallography.
Dan.	Danish.
dat.	dative.
def.	definition.
deriv.	derivation.
dial.	dialect.
dim.	diminutive.
Diplom.	Diplomatics.
dist.	distinct; distinguished.
Dut.	Dutch.
Dynam.	Dynamics.
E.	East.
Eccles.	Ecclesiastical, ecclesiological.
Econ.	Economics, economy.
E.Fris.	East Frisian.
e.g.	*exempli gratia*, for example.
Egypt.	Egyptian.
Egyptol.	Egyptology.
E.Ind.	East Indian.
Elec.	Electricity.
ellipt.	elliptical, elliptically.
Embryol.	Embryology.
emphat.	emphatic.
Eng.	English; Engineering.
Ent.	Entomology.
erron.	erroneously.
esp.	especially.
Ethn.	Ethnology.
etym.	etymology.
euphem.	euphemistic.
Eur.	European.
Exam.	Examination.
exc.	except.
F.	French.
f.	feminine.
fam.	familiar, familiarly.
facet.	facetiously.
fem.	feminine.
Feud.	Feudal.
fig.	figuratively.
fl.	*floruit*, flourished.
Flem	Flemish.
foll.	the following.
For.	Foreign.
Fort.	Fortification.
freq.	frequentative.
Fris.	Frisian.
fut.	future.
G.	German.
Gael.	Gaelic.
gen.	genitive.
Geneal.	Genealogy.
Geog.	Geography.
Geol.	Geology.
Geom.	Geometry.
ger.	gerund, gerundive.
Goth.	Gothic.
Gr.	Greek.
grad.	gradually.
Gram.	Grammar.
Heb.	Hebrew.
Her.	Heraldry.
Hind.	Hindustani, Hindi.
Hist.	History.
Hort.	Horticulture.
Hung.	Hungarian.
Hydrostat.	Hydrostatics.
Hyg.	Hygiene.
Icel.	Icelandic.
ichthyol.	ichthyology.
ident.	identical, identified.
i.e.	*id est*, that is.
illit.	illiterate.
imag.	imaginary.
imit.	imitative.
imper.	imperative.
impers.	impersonal.
incept.	inceptive.
incorr.	incorrectly.
Ind.	India, Indian.
ind.	indicative.
indef. art.	indefinite article.
Indo-Port.	Indo-Portuguese.
inf.	infinitive.
influ.	influenced.
inst.	instinctive.
instr.	instrumental.
int.	interjection.
intens.	intensive.
Internat.	International.
interrog.	interrogative.
intr.	intransitive.
Ir.	Irish.
iron.	ironical.
irreg.	irregular.
It.	Italian.
Jap	Japanese.
Jav.	Javanese.
Jewel.	Jewellery.
Kant.	Kantian.

L.	Latin.
lat.	latitude
L.G.	Low German.
Lit.	Literature, literary.
lit.	literal, literally.
Lit. crit.	Literary criticism.
Lith.	Lithuanian.
loc.	locative.
Log.	Logic.
Mach.	Machinery.
manufact.	manufacturing.
Math.	Mathematics.
M.Dan.	MiddleDanish.
M.Dut.	Middle Dutch.
malaprop.	malapropism.
Mech.	Mechanics.
M.E	MiddleEnglish.
Med.	Medicine.
med.	mediæval.
Merc.	Mercian.
Metal.	Metallurgy.
Metaph.	Metaphysics.
Meteor.	Meteorology.
Mex.	Mexican.
M.F.	MiddleFrench.
M.G.	Middle German.
Microsc.	Microscopy.
Mil.	Military.
Min.	Mineralogy.
mistrans.	mistranslation.
mod.	modern.
Mongol.	Mongolian.
Mus.	Music.
Myth., Mythol.	Mythology.
N.	North. New.
n.	noun.
Nat. Hist.	Natural History.
Naut.	Nautical.
Nav.	Naval.
neg.	negative.
neol.	neologism.
neut.	neuter.
Newsp.	Newspaper.
nom.	nominative.
Norm.	Norman.
North.	Northern.
Northum.	Northumbrian.
Norw.	Norwegian.
N.T.	New Testament.
Numis.	Numismatics.
obj.	objective.
obs.	obsolete.
O.E.D.	the Oxford English Dictionary.
O.F.	Old French.
O.Fris.	Old Frisian.
O.H.G.	Old High German.
O.L.G.	Old Low German.
O.N.	Old Norse.
O.N.F.	Old Norman French.
onomat.	onomatopœic.
O.Pers.	Old Persian.
opp.	opposed, opposition.
Opt.	Optics.

orig.	origin, originally.
Ornith.	Ornithology.
O.S.	Old Saxon.
o.s.	old style.
O.Slav.	Old Slavonic.
O.Sp.	Old Spanish.
O.Teut.	Old Teutonic.
Palæont.	Palæontology.
paral.	parallel.
Parl.	Parliamentary.
part.	participle, participial.
pass.	passive.
Path.	Pathology.
perf.	perfect.
perh.	perhaps.
Pers.	Persian.
pers.	person; personal.
persp.	perspective.
Peruv.	Peruvian.
Petrol.	Petrology.
Phil.	Philosophy.
Philol.	Philology.
Phœn.	Phœnician.
phon.	phonetics; phonology.
Phot.	Photography.
phr.	phrase.
Phrenol.	Phrenology.
Phys.	Physics.
Phys. Sci.	Physical Science.
Physiol.	Physiology.
pl.	plural.
poet.	poetry, poetical.
Pol.	Polish.
Polit.	Political.
pop.	popular, popularly.
Port.	Portuguese.
poss.	possessive.
p.p.	past participle.
prec.	the preceding.
pred.	predicatival.
pref.	prefix.
prep.	preposition.
pres.	present.
pres.p.	present participle.
pret.	preterite.
prev.	previously.
Print.	Printing.
priv.	privative.
prob.	probably.
pron.	pronoun; pronounced.
pronun.	pronunciation.
prop.	proper, properly.
Pros.	Prosody.
Prov.	Provençal.
prov.	provincial.
Psych.	Psychology; psycho-analysis.
pubd.	published.
Pugil.	Pugilism.
r.	reflexive.
Radio.	Wireless communication, broadcasting, etc.
R.-C. Ch.	Roman Catholic Church.

redupl.	reduplica
ref.	referring, referen
reflex.	reflexive.
rel.	related.
Relig.	Religion.
rel. pron.	relative p noun.
remonstr.	remonstra
Rhet.	Rhetoric.
Rom.	Roman; Roman
Rus.	Russian.
S.	South.
Sansk.	Sanskrit.
Sc.	Scottish.
Scand.	Scandinav
Sci.	Science.
Sculp.	Sculpture
Semit.	Semitic.
Serb.	Serbian.
Shak.	Shakespea
Sic.	Sicilian.
sing.	singular.
Slav.	Slavonic.
Sp.	Spanish.
Spens.	Spenser.
Stock. Exch.	Stock Exchan
subj.	subjunctiv
suf.	suffix.
superl.	superlative
Surg.	Surgery.
Swed.	Swedish.
syl.	syllable.
Syr.	Syriac.
Teleg.	Telegraph
Teut.	Teutonic.
Theat.	Theatre, theatrica
Theol.	Theology, theologi
Therap.	Therapeut
Therm.	Thermioni
tr.	transitive.
trans.	translation
Trig.	Trigonom
Turk.	Turkish.
T.V.	Television
ult.	ultimately.
Univ.	University
U.S., U.S.A.	United Sta of Amer
usu.	usually.
v.	verb.
var.	variant.
Venet.	Venetian.
verb.a.	verbal adj
Vet.	Veterinary Surgery.
v.i.	verb intra tive.
viz.	*videlicet*, namely.
voc.	vocative.
v.r., v. refl.	verb reflex
v.t.	verb transi
vulg.	vulgar.
W.	West, Wel
W.G.	West Gern
wr.	written.
Zool.	Zoology.

KEY TO PRONUNCIATION

VOWELS

a as in far (far), father (fa′ *th*ėr), mikado (mi ka′ dō).
ă „ „ fat (făt), cant (kănt), abstinence (ăb′ stin ėns).
ā „ „ fate (fāt), wait (wāt), deign (dān), jade (jād).
aw „ „ fall (fawl), appal (ȧ pawl′), broad (brawd).
â „ „ fair (fâr), bear (bâr), where (wâr).

e „ „ bell (bel), bury (ber′ i).
ĕ „ „ her (hĕr), search (sĕrch), word (wĕrd), bird (bĕrd).
ē „ „ beef (bēf), thief (thēf), idea (ī dē′ ȧ), beer (bēr), casino (kȧ sē′ nō).

i „ „ bit (bit), lily (lil′ i), nymph (nimf), build (bild).
ī „ „ bite (bīt), analyse (ăn′ ȧ līz), light (līt).

o „ „ not (not), watch (woch), flock (flok), sorry (sor′ i).
ō „ „ no (nō), blow (blō), brooch (brōch).
ô „ „ north (nôrth), absorb (ȧb sôrb′).
oo „ „ food (food), do (doo), prove (proov), blue (bloo), strew (stroo).

u „ „ bull (bul), good (gud), would (wud).
ŭ „ „ sun (sŭn), love (lŭv), enough (ė nŭf′).
ū „ „ muse (mūz), stew (stū), cure (kūr).

ou „ „ bout (bout), bough (bou), crowd (kroud).
oi „ „ join (join), joy (joi), buoy (boi).

A dot placed over **a, e, o,** or **u** (ȧ, ė, ȯ, u̇,) signifies that the vowel has an obscure, indeterminate, or slurred sound, as in :—

advice (ȧd vīs′), breakable (brā′ kȧbl), current (kŭr′ ėnt), sailor (sā′ lȯr), notion (nō′ shu̇n), pleasure (plezh′ u̇r).

CONSONANTS

s is used only for the sibilant s (as in "toast," tōst, "place," plās); the sonant s (as in "toes," "plays") is printed z (tōz, plāz).

c (except in the combinations ch and *ch*), **q** and **x** are not used.

b, d, f, h (but see the combinations below), **k, l, m, n** (see ***n*** below), **p, r, t, v, z,** and **w** and **y** when used as consonants have their usual values.

ch as in church (chĕrch), batch (băch), capriccio (ka prē′ chō).
ch „ „ loch (lo*ch*), coronach (kor′ o na*ch*), clachan (klă*ch*′ an).

g „ „ get (get), finger (fing′ gėr).
j „ „ join (join), judge (jŭj), germ (jĕrm), ginger (jin′ jėr).

hl (in List of Proper Names only) as in Llandilo (hlăn dī′ lō).

wh See **wh** in main dictionary (see p. 1272).

n as in cabochon (ka bō sho*n*′), congé (ko*n*′ zhā).
ng „ „ sing, ring, think (thingk).

sh „ „ shawl (shawl), mention (men′ shu̇n).
zh „ „ measure (mezh′ u̇r), vision (vizh′ ȯn).

th „ „ thin (thin), breath (breth).
th „ „ thine (*th*īn), breathe (brē*th*).

The accent (′) *follows* the syllable to be stressed.

Words are the dress of thoughts, which should no more be presented in rags, tatters, and dirt, than your person should.

EARL OF CHESTERFIELD

In this work, when it shall be found that much is omitted, let it not be forgotten that much likewise is performed.

DR. SAMUEL JOHNSON,
in the Preface to his
Dictionary of the English Language

A

ENGLISH DICTIONARY

A

A, a, the first letter in the English alphabet, and in most others derived from the Phœnician. In English it has five sounds: (1) open as in *far, father, mikado*, left unmarked in this dictionary, a; (2) short as in *fat, man, ample*, marked ă; (3) long, as in *fate, fame*, marked ā; (4) broad as in *fall, appal*, spelt aw; (5) the long sound modified by the letter *r*, as in *fair, bear*, marked â. In unaccented syllables **a** is often slurred and obscured, as in *separate* (adj.), *amidst*, marked with a dot above it, ȧ. **A,** the sixth note of the diatonic scale of C major, corresponding to *la* in tonic sol-fa notation; the scale of a composition in which the keynote is **A. A1** (ā wŭn'), *a*. First class in Lloyd's Register of ships; first class. **A-bomb** (ā' bom), *n*. An atomic bomb, as distinct from a hydrogen bomb.

a (ā or ȧ), **an** (ăn) [A.-S. *an*, one], *a*. A weakened form of one, sometimes called the indefinite article, used before singular substantives to denote an individual of a class. *A* is used before words beginning with a consonant, *h* aspirate, or *eu* or *u*, with the sound of *yu*, also before *one* (wŭn). *An* is used before vowels and sometimes before *h* in an unaccented syllable, *e.g. an historian*. In such phrases as *twopence an ounce, twice a week*, it has a distributive force. Also used before collective phrases like *a hundred men, a dozen eggs, a few, a good many*, *i.e.* a hundred of men, etc.

a-, *pref.* (1) [A.-S. *on, an*] (*prep.*), as in *aboard, adying, afoot*; (2) [A.-S. *ar-* or *a-*, cp. G. *er-*] (*intens.*) away, out, as in *arise, awake*; (3) [A.-S. *of, af*] (*intens.*) of, from, as in *akin, athirst*; (4) [L. *a, ab*] (*prep.*) from, as in *avert*; (5) [L. *ad-*, to] (*prep.*) directly, as in *aspect, ascend*, or indirectly through F. *à*, as in *achieve*, from *à chef*, L. *ad caput*; (6) [L. *ex-, e-*] (*prep.*) out of, utterly, as in *amend* (F. *amender*, L. *ēmendāre* (or *exmendāre*)); (7) [Gr. *a-, an-*] not, without, as in *achromatic, amoral*.

aardvark (ard' vark) [Dut. *aarde*, earth, *varken*, pig), *n*. *Orycteropus capensis*, the Cape ant-eater or ground-hog. **aardwolf** (ard' wulf), *n*. *Proteles lalandi*, the earth-wolf of South Africa.

Aaronic (âr on' ik), *a*. Of or pertaining to Aaron, his descendants, or the Jewish priesthood; also **Aaronical. Aaron's beard,** *n*. Pop. name for *Hypercium calycinum*, or large-flowered St. John's wort, and for *Saxifraga sarmentosa*, a Chinese herb with hanging stems bearing clusters of hairy leaves. **Aaron's rod,** *n*. Pop. name for certain plants that flower on long stems, *e.g.* great mullein and golden rod.

Ab (ăb) [Heb.], *n*. The fifth ecclesiastical month, or eleventh civil month, of the Jewish year (corresponding roughly with August).

ab- (1) [L. *ab*], *pref.* Off, from away, apart, as in *abrogate, abuse* (cp. Gr. *apo*, Eng. *of, off*, G. *ab*); in L. and F. derivatives often assimilated to subsequent consonant or reduced to *a*, as in *assoil, avert, avocation, abstract*.

ab- (2) [L. *ad-*, to assim. to consonant *b*], *pref.* To, as in *abbreviate*.

aback (ȧ băk') [M.E. *abak*, A.-S. *onbæc* (*on-*, on, *bæc*, back)], *adv*. Backwards; behind; by surprise; (*Naut.*) with the sails pressed against the mast.

abactinal (ăb ăk tī' năl) [L. *ab-*, from, away, Gr. *aktis aktinos*, a ray], *a*. Pertaining to that part of a radiate animal that is opposite the mouth.

abacus (ăb' ȧ kŭs) [L. *abacus*, Gr. *abax -akos*, a tablet], *n*. A counting-frame; an apparatus made of beads sliding on wires for facilitating arithmetical calculations; (*Arch.*) a flat stone crowning the capital of a column and supporting the architrave. **abacist,** *n*. An arithmetician.

abaddon (ȧ băd' ȯn) [Heb. *ābad*, he perished], *n*. A destroyer, the angel of the Bottomless Pit, Apollyon (Rev. ix. 11); Hell, the Bottomless Pit.

abaft (ȧ baft') [*a-* on; A.-S. *beæftan*], *adv.* or *prep.* In, on, or towards the hinder part of a ship; behind.

***abalienate** (ăb ā' li ėn āt), *v.t.* **abalienation** (ăb ā li ėn ā' shŭn), *n*. [ALIENATE].

abandon (ȧ băn' dȯn) [O.F. *abandoner*, to leave at liberty, from *à bandon*, at liberty; low L. *ad-*, to, *bandum*, jurisdiction, proclamation, O.H.G. BAN], *v.t.* To give up, yield; to desert or forsake, to surrender oneself unreservedly, *e.g.* to indolence or vice. *n*. (ȧ băn' dȯn, -don). Freedom from conventional restraint, careless freedom of manner. **abandoned,** *a*. Deserted; wholly given up to wickedness, profligate. **abandonee** (-ē'), *n*. (*Law*) One to whom anything is abandoned, *e.g.* an underwriter to whom salvage is formally surrendered. **abandonment,** *n*. The act of abandoning; self-surrender to a cause, passion, or vice; relinquishment of property, desertion (of a relation, friend, servant).

à bas (a ba) [F.], *int*. Down with.

abase (ȧ bās') [O.F. *abaissier* (F. *abaisser*), to lower, from late L. *abassāre* (AD-, *bassāre*), late L. *bassus*, low], *v.t.* To lower, to humble, degrade. **abasement,** *n*. Act of abasing, state of humiliation, degradation.

abash (ȧ băsh') [O.F. *esbaïr* (F. *ébahir*), pres.p. *esbaïssant*; O.F. *es-* (L. *ex-*) *baïr*, to express amazement, BAH], *v.t.* To put to shame by exciting sense of guilt, mistake, or inferiority. **abashment,** *n*. Confusion produced by shame, consternation.

abasia (ȧ bā' zi ȧ) [Gr. *a-* not; *basis*, movement], *n*. (*Path.*) Lack of power to co-ordinate the movements of the muscles in walking.

abask (ȧ bask'), *adv*. In the sunshine, basking.

abate (ȧ bāt') [O.F. *abatre*, to beat down; *à* (L. *ad*) *batre*; late L. *batere*, L. *batuere*, beat], *v.t.* To diminish, reduce, lessen, deduct; * to beat down, destroy. *v.i.* To become less, diminish, fail. **abatement,** *n*. **abatable,** *a*. **abater,** *n*.

abatis, abattis (a ba tē, ȧ băt' is) [F. *abatis*, from O.F. *abatre*, to beat down], *n*. (*Mil.*) A defence made of felled trees with their boughs directed outwards. **abattised** (ăb' ȧ tīzd) *a*. Furnished with an abattis.

abatjour (a ba zhoor') [F.], *n*. A sky-light.

abattoir (a ba twar') [F.], *n*. A public slaughter-house.

abaxial (ăb ăx' i ăl) [AB- (1), AXIS], *a*. (*Bot.*) Facing away from the stem.

abb (ăb) [A.-S. *ab, aweb, awefan* (*a-* intens., *wefan*, to weave)], *n*. Yarn for a weaver's woof or weft, sometimes warp-yarn. **abb-wool,** *n*. Wool suitable for a weaver's warp.

abba (ăb' ȧ) [Aram. *abba*, O Father], *n*. Father (in the invocation *Abba father*); an episcopal title in the Syriac and Gothic churches.

abbacy (ăb′ ȧ si) [late L. *abbatia*, from *abbas*, ABBOT]. *n.* The office and jurisdiction of an abbot. **abbat,** *n.* [ABBOT]. **abbatial** (ȧ bā′ shi ȧl), *a.* Pertaining to an abbey or an abbot. **abbé** (ăb′ ā) [F. *abbé*, an abbot, L. *abbas -atem*], *n.* An ecclesiastic without a cure; a cleric in minor orders; generally a mere title without any definite office or responsibility. **abbess** (ăb′ ės) [O.F. *abaesse*, L. *abatissa*], *n.* The lady superior of a nunnery.

abbey (ă′ bi) [O.F. *abeie*, *abaie*, as prec.], *n.* A monastic community governed by an abbot or abbess; a building either now or formerly inhabited by a body of monks or nuns; a church attached to an abbey. **abbey land,** *n.* Land now, or formerly, attached to an abbey.

abbot (ă′ bȯt) [L. *abbas*, Gr. *abbas*, *abbatos*, Syriac *abba*, father], *n.* A monk; the superior of a monastery; the superior of an abbey. **abbot of misrule** (*Sc.* **abbot of unreason**), *n.* Leader in mediæval burlesque. **lay abbot,** *n.* A layman to whom the revenue of a monastery was assigned as a reward. **abbotship,** *n.* The state or office of an abbot.

abbreviate (ȧ brē′ vi āt) [L. *abbreviātus*, p.p. of *abbreviāre*, to shorten (*ab-*, *ad-*, *brevis*, short)], *v.t.* To shorten, abridge, reduce to a smaller compass. **abbreviate** (-ȧt), *a.* Shortened, cut short. **abbreviation** (-ā′ shŭn), *n.* Act of abridging or contracting; the abridged or shortened form, *e.g.* of a word; an abridgment. **abbreviator** (ȧ brēv′-), *n.* One who abridges or curtails; an officer in the Roman Chancery who abridges the petitions granted by the Pope. **abbreviatory,** *a.* Abbreviating or tending to abbreviate, shortening. **abbreviature,** *n.* An abbreviation, an abridgment.

A B C (ā bē sē) [the first letters of the alphabet], *n.* The alphabet; rudiments; first principles.

Abderian (ăb dēr′ i ȧn) [*Abdera*, a town of Thrace, the inhabitants of which were regarded as very stupid], *a.* Pertaining to Abdera; given to laughter. **Abderite** (ăb dēr′ īt), *n.* An inhabitant of Abdera; a stupid person. **the Abderite:** Democritus, the laughing philosopher.

abdicate (ăb′ di kāt) (L. *abdicātus*, p.p. of *abdicare* (*ab-*, from, and *dicāre*, to declare)], *v.t.* To resign, to formally renounce, to give up. *v.i.* To abandon or relinquish a throne, or other dignity or privilege. **abdicant,** *a.* Abdicating, renouncing. *n.* One who abdicates, an abdicator. **abdication** (ăb di kā′ shŭn), *n.* The act of abdicating. **abdicator** (ăb′ di kā tȯr), *n.*

abdomen (ăb dō′ mėn) [L.], *n.* That portion of the trunk which lies between the thorax and the pelvis; the belly; the posterior division of the body in the higher Arthropoda. **abdominal** (ăb dom′-), *a.* Belonging to the abdomen. Of fish having the ventral fins under the abdomen. **abdominal regions,** *n.pl.* Certain portions of the body near to or including the belly, arbitrarily marked off for convenience in anatomical study. **abdominous,** *a.* Having a large abdomen, corpulent, pot-bellied. **abdominally,** *adv.*

abduce (ăb-dūs′) [L. *abdūcere*, *ab-*, from, *dūcere*, to lead, draw], *v.t.* To draw from one part to another by an abductor; to lead away. **abducent,** *a.* Having the property of drawing back or away (applied to muscles the function of which is to draw away or pull back the parts to which they belong. The abducent muscles are opposed in their action to the adductor or adducent muscles).

abduct (ăb dŭkt′) [L. *abducere*, p.p. *abductus*], *v.t.* To take away (esp. a woman or child) by guile or force; to kidnap. **abduction,** *n.* A leading or drawing away; separation of parts of a bone after a fracture, or of sides of a wound; illegal taking away of a child, a wife, or a ward by fraud or force. **abductor,** *n.* One who, or that which, abducts; (*Physiol.*) a muscle which draws or pulls back any part of the body.

abeam (ȧ bēm′) [BEAM], *adv.* (*Naut.*) On a line at right angles to the keel.

abear (ȧ bâr′) [A.-S. *aberan*], *v.t.* To endure, put up with; to behave (oneself).

abecedarian (ā bė sē dâr′ i ȧn) [late L. *abecedarium*, alphabet, from A B C D], *n.* One who teaches or is learning the alphabet. *a.* Alphabetical; having verses distinguished by letters alphabetically arranged like the 119th Psalm; a member of an 18th-century Anabaptist sect that rejected all worldly knowledge, even of the alphabet. **abecedary** (ā bė sē′ dȧ ri), *n.* or *a.*

abed (ȧ bĕd′), *adv.* In bed, gone to bed.

abele (ȧ bēl′) [Dut. *abeel*, O.F. *abel*, *aubel*, late L. *albellum*, L. *albus*, white], *n.* The white poplar.

aber (ăb′ ėr), *n.* A Celtic term for the mouth of a river, found as a prefix in place names, *e.g.* Aberdeen.

Aberdeen (ăb ėr dēn′) [Scottish city], *n.* A rough-haired Scotch terrier. **Aberdonian,** *n.* A native or inhabitant of Aberdeen. *a.* Belonging to Aberdeen.

aberdevine (ăb′ ėr dė vīn) [etym. doubtful], *n.* The siskin.

***aberr, *aberre** (ăb er′) [L. *aberrāre*, *ab-*, from, *errāre*, wander], *v.i.* To wander; to err. **aberrance, aberrancy** (ăb er′ ȧns, -ȧn si), *n.* A wandering from the right way. **aberrant** (ăb er′ ȧnt), *a.* Wandering from the right way. Deviating from the normal type. **aberration** (ăb ėr ā′ shŭn), *n.* Deviation from the normal course or standard; departure from rule; deviation from type; (*Astron.*) difference between the true and observed position of a heavenly body; (*Optics*) deviation of focused rays preventing them from uniting in a point.

abet (ȧ bet′) [O.F. *abeter*, to instigate, deceive; AD-, *beter*, see BAIT], *v.t.* (*past & p.p.* **abetted**). To encourage or aid (a person or cause) by word or deed; to countenance, stimulate, or instigate (chiefly in a bad sense). **abetment,** *n.* The act of abetting, countenancing, or encouraging. **abetter,** (*Law*) **abettor,** *n.* One who encourages or instigates another; an accessory.

abeyance (ȧ bā′ ȧns) [O.F. *abeance* (*à*, to, *béer*, late L. *baddāre*, to gape)], *n.* The state of being held back, suspended; dormancy, quiescence. **in abeyance:** (*Law*) Waiting for an occupant or owner.

abhor (ȧb hôr′) [L. *abhorrēre*, to shrink from (AB-, *horrēre*, to bristle, shudder)], *v.t.* To hate extremely, loathe, detest; to shrink from with horror. **abhorrence** (ȧb hor′ ėns), **abhorrency,** *n.* Extreme hatred, aversion, repugnance, loathing. **abhorrent,** *a.* Exciting repugnance, loathing, hatred; opposed to, inconsistent with; *drawing back with loathing or fear. **abhorrently,** *adv.* **abhorrer** (ȧb hôr′ ėr), *n.* One who abhors or detests—nickname of the court party in reign of Charles II who signed address of abhorrence against the Whigs (1679).

Abib (ā′ bib) [Heb. *ābīb*, a full green ear of corn], *n.* The first month of the Jewish civil year, more commonly called Nisan. It included part of March and part of April.

abide (ȧ bīd′) [A.-S. *abīdan* (A-, *bīdan*, to bide)], *v.i.* To dwell or live in a place; to stay, wait; to continue, remain firm. **to abide by:** To remain beside, adhere to, act upon (terms). *v.t.* To await, encounter, withstand; to submit to; to endure, bear, tolerate. **abidance,** *n.* Continuance. **abider,** *n.* One who abides or continues. **abiding,** *a.* Continuing, permanent, durable. *n.* Continuance, residence. **abiding-place,** *n.* Place of abode. **abidingly,** *adv.*

abide [ABYE].

Abies (ăb′ i ēz) [L.], *n.* A genus of conifers, containing the silver firs, spruces, larches, and cedars. **abietic** (ăb i et′ ik), *a.* Pertaining to or derived from trees of this genus. **abiet-,** *comb. form.* Stem of various chemical terms relating to substances so derived, *e.g.* **abietin,** *n.*, **abietite,** *n.*

abigail (ăb′ i gāl) [Heb.], *n.* A waiting-maid (1 Sam. xxv); a lady's **maid**; *a waiting gentlewoman.

ability (ȧ bil′ i ti) [O.F. *ableté*, see ABLE], *n.* Physical, mental, or moral power; capacity, competence; wealth, means; (*pl.*) intellectual gifts.

abiogenesis (ăb i ō jen′ ė sis) [Gr. *a-* priv., *bios*, life, GENESIS], *n.* The theory that living matter can be produced from that which has no life; spontaneous generation. **abiogenetic** (ăb i ō jėn et′ ik), *a.* **abiogenetically,** *adv.* **abiogenist** (ăb i oj′ ėn ist), *n.* One who holds the hypothesis of abiogenesis. **abiogenous,** *a.* Produced by abiogenesis.

abject (ab′ jekt) [L. *abjectus*, cast away, p.p. of *abjicere* (AB-, from, away, *jacere*, to cast)], *a.* Cast away; sunk to a low condition; servile, degraded, morally debased; mean, low. ***n.** A person of the lowest condition, and morally despicable. ***abject** (ăb jekt′), *v.t.* To throw or cast down. **abjectedness,** *n.* **abjection,** *n.* The act of casting away; the state of being cast away; abasement. **abjectly,** *adv.* **abjectness,** *n.*

abjure (ăb jōōr′) [L. *ab-*, from *jurāre*, to swear], *v.t.* To renounce, recant, retract, or abrogate anything upon oath. *v.i.* To take an oath of abjuration. ***to abjure the realm** or **commonwealth:** To take an oath to quit the country within a given time. **abjuration,** *n.* The act of forswearing, abjuring, or renouncing on oath; a denial or renunciation on oath. **abjuratory** (ăb joor′ ȧ tȯ ri), *a.* **abjurement,** *n.* **abjurer,** *n.*

ablactate (ăb lăk′ tāt) [L. *ab-* from, away, *lactāre*, suckle (*lac lactis*, milk)], *v.t.* To wean from the breast. **ablactation** (ăb lăk tā′ shŭn), *n.* The weaning of a child from the breast; (*Hort.*) grafting by inarching.

ablation (ăb lā′ shŭn) [L. *ab-*, from, *lātus*, p.p. of *fero*, I bear], *n.* Removal, carrying away; wearing away. **ablative** (ăb′ lȧ tiv), *a.* Taking away, separating, subtractive. *n.* The case in Latin and other languages expressing separation, instrumentality, and other relations expressed in English by the prepositions from, by, with, etc. **ablative absolute,** *n.* (*L. Gram.*) A construction with noun and participle, noun and adjective, in the ablative case, expressing time or circumstances: corresponds to the English nominative absolute. **ablatival** (-tī′ vȧl), *a.*

ablator (ăb lā′ tȯr), *n.* (*Surg.*) An instrument for excising diseased parts; (*Vet.*) an instrument for removing the tails of sheep.

ablaut (ăb′ lout) [G. *ab-*, off, *laut*, sound], *n.* Vowel change in the middle of a word to indicate modification in meaning, as *sit, set*; *rise, raise*; *ring, rang, rung*.

ablaze (ȧ blāz′) (A.-S. *a-*, on, BLAZE], *adv.* or *a.* On fire, in a blaze; brilliant; excited.

able (ābl) [O.F. *hable, able* (F. *habile*), L. *habilis*, handy (*habēre*, to have, hold)], *a.* Having sufficient physical, mental, moral, or spiritual power, or acquired skill, or sufficient pecuniary and other resources to do something indicated; gifted, vigorous, active. ***v.t.** To make able, enable; to vouch for, warrant. **able-bodied,** *a.* Having a sound, strong body; experienced, skilled (applied to a sailor who is classed as A.B., and called an **able-seaman**). **ably** (āb′ li), *adv.* In an able manner; with ability.

-able [F. *-able*, L. *-abilis*], *suf.* Able, or likely, to; fit, suitable for, that may be, full of, as in *movable, comfortable, eatable, saleable, reasonable.*

ablegate (ăb′ le gāt) [L. *ablegatus*, one sent away], *n.* (*Eccles.*) Papal envoy sent with insignia to new cardinals, etc.

ablet (ăb′ lėt), **ablen** [F. *ablette*, from late L. *abula* (*albula*, dim. of L. *alba*), white], *n.* The bleak, a small fresh-water fish.

ablings (ā′ blinz), **ablins, aiblins** [*Sc.* and *North*, ABLE, with suf. -LINGS], *adv.* Possibly, perhaps.

abloom (ȧ bloom′), *a.* or *adv.* Blooming, in a state of bloom.

abluent (ăb′ lu ėnt) [L. *ab-*, away, *luere*, to wash, pres.p. *abluens -tis*)], *a.* Cleansing, washing away, detergent. *n.* That which washes off or carries off impurities.

ablush (ȧ blŭsh′), *adv.* and *pred.a.* Blushing, ruddy.

ablution (ȧ bloo′ shŭn) [ABLUENT], *n.* The act of washing, cleansing, or purifying by means of water or other liquids; a ceremonial or symbolical washing or cleansing; the state of being washed; the water used for washing. **ablutionary,** *a.*

abnegate (ăb′ nė gāt) [L. *ab-*, from, away, *negāre*, to deny (p.p. *abnegātus*)], *v.t.* To deny, to refuse, to renounce, to abjure. **abnegation** (-gā′ shŭn), *n.* Denial, renunciation; self-sacrifice. **abnegative** (ăb nė gā′ tiv), *a.* Implying denial, negative. **abnegator** (ăb′ nė gā tȯr), *n.*

abnormal (ăb nôrm′ ȧl) [F. *anormal*, assim. to L. *abnormis* (*ab-*, from, *norma*, rule); see NORMAL], *a.* Not according to rule, anomalous, departing from the ordinary type. **abnormality** (ăb nôr măl′ i ti), *n.* Irregularity, deformity. **abnormally,** *adv.* **abnormity** (ăb nôr′ mi ti), *n.* Departure from the ordinary type, rule, or standard.

abo (ăb′ ō) [*Austral.*], *n.* An aboriginal native of Australia.

aboard (ȧ bôrd′), *adv.* On board, in a ship or boat. *prep.* Into a ship. **to fall aboard:** To strike the side of. **to get aboard:** To get foul of. **to lay a ship aboard:** (*Naut.*) To place a ship alongside an enemy in order to board.

abode (1) (ȧ bōd′) [ABIDE], *past.* Dwelt, stayed. *n.* Stay; continuance for a longer or shorter period in any place; residence; a habitation. **to make abode:** To dwell, reside.

***abode** (2) (ȧ bōd′) [A.-S. *ābēodan*, to announce, to bode], *v.t.* To bode, presage, *n.* Prediction, boding. **abodement,** *n.* A foreboding; an omen.

aboil (ȧ boil′), *adv.* A-boiling, boiling, on the boil.

abolish (ȧ bol′ ish) [F. *abolir* (*aboliss-*), L. *abolescere, abolēre* (*ab-*, from, *olēre*, to grow)], *v.t.* To do away with, put an end to, destroy; to annul, cancel, or revoke (used of laws, customs, institutions, or offices). **abolishable,** *a.* **abolisher,** *n.* **abolishment,** *n.* **abolition** (ăb ȯ lish′ ŭn), *n.* The act of abolishing or doing away with; the state of being abolished. **abolitionism,** *n.* **abolitionist,** *n.* One who entertains views in favour of abolition; especially applied to those who favoured the abolition of slavery during the movement against it in the 18th and 19th centuries.

abomasus (ăb ȯ mā′sŭs), **abomasum** [L. *ab-*, from, *omāsum*, paunch], *n.* The fourth stomach in a ruminating animal.

abominate (ȧ bom′ i nāt) [L. *abōminātus*, p.p. of *abōminārī* (ab-, from, OMEN), to dislike], *v.t.* To loathe, to detest, to hate exceedingly. **abominable,** *a.* Very loathsome, hateful, or odious, physically or morally. **abominableness,** *n.* **abominably,** *adv.* **abomination** (ȧ bom i nā′ shŭn), *n.* The act of doing something hateful; the state of being greatly hated or loathed; an object of extreme hatred, loathing, or aversion.

aboon (ȧ bin′), *adv.* (*Sc.*) Above.

***abord** (ȧ bôrd′) [F. *aborder* (*à bord*; see ABOARD)], *v.t.* To approach; to accost. *n.* Approach; accosting.

aborigines (ăb ȯ rij′ i nēz) [L. *aborigines* (*ab-*, from, *origine*, the beginning)], *n.pl.* The earliest inhabitants of any continent, country, or district (used also of the fauna and flora). **aboriginal,** *a.* Original, indigenous, inhabiting a place from the earliest times. *n.* An original inhabitant (esp. of Australia); a member of the original fauna or flora. **aboriginally,** *adv.* From the beginning, from the first; originally.

abort (ȧ bôrt′) [L. *abort*, pp. stem of *aborīri* (*ab-*, off, away, *orīri*, to arise, grow)], *v.i.* *To miscarry, bring forth prematurely; to undergo partial or entire arrest of development. *v.t.* To make abortive. **aborted,** *a.* Prematurely born, imperfectly developed. **abortient,** *a.* (*Bot.*) Barren, sterile.

abortifacient (ȧ bôrt′ i fāsh′ ėnt), *n.* A device to procure abortion. **abortion,** *n.* The act of miscarrying; the production of the fœtus before the proper time; the product of a miscarriage; anything which fails instead of coming to maturity; a monster, a mis-shapen creature. **abortive** (ȧ bôr′ tiv), *a.* Brought forth in an immature state; imperfectly formed; procuring or intended to procure abortion; fruitless, ineffectual, failing in its effect. *n.* An immature birth; a drug causing or intended to cause abortion. **abortively,** *adv.* **abortiveness,** *n.* ***abortment,** *n.* An untimely birth; abortion.

abound (ȧ bound′) [O.F. *abunder, abonder,* L. *abundāre,* to overflow (*ab-,* away, *unda,* a wave)], *v.i.* To overflow; to be rich (in), to be copiously supplied (with); to be in great plenty. **abounding,** *a.* Plentiful, copious. *n.* Abundance.

about (ȧ bout′) [A.-S. *ābūtan, onbūtan* (*on-,* on, *be,* by, *ūtan,* outside)], *prep.* Around, surrounding, on the outside or surface of; near in time, space, number, quantity, or quality; on the point of; concerning, in connection with. *adv.* Around, circuitously, nearly; here and there; in different directions. **about face, right-about turn:** (*Mil.*) Turn right round, face the opposite way. **to bring about:** To cause to happen; to effect. **to come about:** To come to pass, to happen. **to go about:** To prepare to do; (*Naut.*) to change the course, to tack. **about-sledge** [SLEDGE], *n.* The largest hammer used by smiths. **right-about** [RIGHT], *adv.* The opposite way.

above (ȧ bŭv′) [A.-S. *ābūfan* (*an,* on, *be,* by, *ūfan,* over)], *prep.* Over, at, or to a higher point than; in excess of, superior to, more important than, beyond; previous, preceding. *adv.* Overhead; in a higher place or position; previously; in heaven. *n.* (elliptically) The upper part, the aforesaid, heaven. **above all:** Principally; before everything else. **above-board,** *adv.* and *pred.a.* Openly, without trickery. **above-ground,** *a.* Alive, unburied. **above par,** *a.* At a premium; of superior quality. **over and above,** *adv.* and *prep.* Besides, in addition to.

abracadabra (ăb rȧ kȧ dăb′ rȧ) [etym. doubtful], *n.* A cabbalistic word used as a charm: when written in triangular form—the first line containing the whole word, the others successively omitting first and last letters, till the last consisted only of the final A—it was worn as an amulet, and was considered to ward off or cure certain diseases; hence a word-charm, a jingle, or nonsensical phrase.

abrade (ȧ brād′) [L. *abrādere* (*ab-,* off, *rādere,* to scrape)], *v.t.* To rub or wear away by friction.

Abrahamic (ā brȧ hăm′ ik), **Abrahamitic, Abrahamitical** (-it′ ik, -ăl), *a.* Pertaining to the patriarch Abraham or the dispensation under which he lived. **Abraham man, Abramman,** *n.* Originally, a lunatic beggar from Bethlehem Hospital, London; an impostor who wandered about the country and feigned lunacy to excite compassion. **to sham Abraham:** To feign sickness, in allusion to the Abraham men.

abranchial (ȧ brăng′ ki ăl) [Gr. *a-,* priv., *branchia,* gills], *a.* Destitute of gills. **abranchiate,** *a.* Abranchial. *n.* An animal that at no period possesses gills.

abrasion (ȧ brā′ zhŭn) [L. *abrādere, abrāsio*], *n.* The act of rubbing away or wearing down; the state of being rubbed away or worn down; a superficial lesion of the skin; the substance worn or rubbed off. **abrasive,** *a.*

abraum (ăb′ roum) [G.], *n.* A red clay used to deepen the colour of mahogany.

abraxas (ȧ brăks′ ăs) [late Gr.], *n.* A word denoting a power which presides over 365 others, and used by the Basilidians (a Gnostic sect, 2nd cent.) to denote their supreme god; a gem with this word, or the mystical image corresponding thereto, engraved on it.

abreaction (ăb rē ăk′ shŭn), *n.* (*Psych.*) The ridding oneself of a complex by re-living in feeling or action repressed phantasies or experiences.

abreast (ȧ brest′) [A.-S. *a-,* on, BREAST], *adv.* Side by side with the breasts in a line; up to the standard (of).

abrégé (ȧ brā zhā) [F. p.p. of *abréger,* L. *abbreviāre,* to ABBREVIATE], *n.* An abridgment.

abreption (ăb rep′ shŭn) [L. *abreptus,* torn away], *n.* Complete severance.

abridge (ȧ brij′) [O.F. *abregier, abrigier,* L. *abbreviāre,* to shorten], *v.t.* To shorten, curtail, epitomize; to deprive (a person of). **abridger,** *n.* **abridgment,** *n.* The act of abridging; the state or process of being abridged; a condensed form, an epitome, a compend, an abstract, a summary.

abroach (ȧ brōch′), *adv.* Broached, pierced; in a position to allow the enclosed liquor to run out freely. *a.* Tapped or opened.

abroad (ȧ brawd′), *adv.* Widely, at large, far and wide; beyond the bounds of a house or country; in foreign countries; before the public generally. **all abroad:** At a loss, astray. **from abroad:** From foreign parts.

abrogate (ăb′ rŏ gāt) [L. *abrogātus,* p.p. of *abrogāre* (*ab-,* off, away, *rogāre,* to ask, propose a law)], *v.t.* To annul by an authoritative act; to repeal, make void. **abrogation** (ăb rŏ gā′ shŭn), *n.* The act of abrogating; repeal. **abrogative,** *a.* Tending to abrogate.

abrupt (ȧ brŭpt′) [L. *abruptus,* p.p. of *abrumpere* (*ab-,* off, *rumpere,* to break)], *a.* Broken, very steep, precipitous; sudden, disconnected; (*Bot.*) truncated; as if cut off below or above. **abruption,** *n.* A sudden or violent breaking off; the state of being broken off. **abruptly,** *adv.* **abruptness,** *n.*

abs- [L. AB-, away, from], *pref.* Away, off, from, as in *abstain, absterge, abstruse.*

abscess (ăb′ ses) [L. *abscessus,* p.p. of *abscēdere* (*abs-,* away, *cēdere,* to go)], *n.* A gathering of pus in any tissue or organ, attended with pain and heat.

abscind (ăb sind′) [L. *abscindere* (*ab-,* from, *scindere,* to cut)], *v.t.* To cut off. **abscission** (ăb sish′ ŭn), *n.* The act of cutting off; the state or condition of being cut off.

abscissa (ăb sis′ ȧ) [L. *abscissa linea,* from p.p. of *abscindere,* to cut], *n.* (*pl.* **abscissæ**). One of the two co-ordinates by which a point is referred to a system of fixed rectilinear axes.

abscond (ăb skond′) [L. *abscondere* (*abs-,* away, *condere,* to hide, from *con-, cum-,* with, and *-dere,* to put)], *v.i.* To go away secretly, to go out of the jurisdiction of a court, or conceal oneself to avoid legal proceedings. ***v.t.** To hide, conceal. **abscondence,** *n.* Act of absconding, concealment. **absconder,** *n.* One who absconds, a fugitive from justice.

absence [ABSENT].

absent (1) (ăb′ sėnt) [L. *absentem,* acc. of *absens,* pres.p. of *abesse,* to be away], *a.* Away from or not present in a place; wanting, not existing; inattentive to what is passing around one.

absent (2) (ăb sent′) [L. *absentāre* (*absens*)], *v.refl.* To keep oneself away. **absence,** *n.* The state of being absent. **absence of mind:** Inattention to what is passing. **absentee** (ăb sėn tē′), *n.* One who is habitually absent from his duty or home; a landlord who lives away from his estate. *a.* Habitually absent from duty or from one's estate. **absenteeism,** *n.* Usu. applied to unjustified failure of workers to report for work. **absently** (ăb′ sėnt li), *adv.* **absent-minded,** *a.* Inattentive, abstracted in mind. **absent-mindedly,** *adv.* Inattentively, abstractedly. **absent-mindedness,** *n.* Inattentiveness, abstraction of mind from immediate objects or business.

absidal [APSIDAL].

absinthe (ăb′ sinth, or F. ăb s*ant*) [F., from L. *absinthium,* Gr. *apsinthion*], *n.* Wormwood; a liqueur flavoured with wormwood. ***absinthian** (-sin′ thi ăn), *a.* Pertaining to or derived from wormwood; hence, bitter. **absinthic,** *a.* Absinthian. **absinthiate,** *v.t.* To impregnate with wormwood. **absinthin,** *n.* The bitter principle in *Artemisia absinthium* (wormwood).

absolute (ăb′ sọ loot) [O.F. *absolut*, L. *absolūtus*, p.p. of *absolvere*, to ABSOLVE], *a.* Independent, unlimited, under no restraint; self-existent; arbitrary, despotic; highly accomplished, perfect; unconditioned; (*Gram.*) applied to a case not determined by any other word in a sentence; (*Phil.*) existing independently of any other cause; (*Chem.*) free from mixture; (*Eng.*) measured from vacuum, as 'the absolute pressure of steam.' **absolute music,** *n.* Music which does not endeavour to illustrate or depict, as contrasted with programme music. **absolute temperature,** *n.* (*Phys.*) Temperature measured from the absolute zero. **absolute zero,** *n.* (*Phys.*) The zero of the absolute scale of temperature, equal to −273·1° C. **the Absolute:** The Self-existent, the First Cause or God of theism. **absolutely,** *adv.* **absoluteness,** *n.*

absolution (ăb sọ loo′ shŭn), *n.* Acquittal, remission, forgiveness; the declaration of pardon of sins by a priest to a penitent or a congregation after private or general public confession.

absolutism (ăb′ sọ lu tizm), *n.* Despotic government; the theological doctrine of absolute predestination; the doctrine of the Absolute. **absolutist,** *n.* One who is in favour of arbitrary government; a metaphysician who holds the theory of the Absolute. *a.* Pertaining to absolutism or despotism. **absolutistic,** *a.* Absolutist.

absolve (ăb zolv′) [L. *absolvere* (*ab-*, from, *solvere*, to loosen)], *v.t.* To set free, release, pardon, acquit; to pronounce forgiveness of sins to a penitent. **absolver,** *n.* One who absolves or pardons. **absolvitor,** *n.* (*Sc. Law*) A favourable verdict; an acquittal.

absonant (ăb′ sọn ȧnt) [L. *ab-*, from, *sonantem*, acc. of *sonans*, pres.p. of *sonāre*, to sound], *a.* Discordant, inharmonious, unreasonable.

absorb (ăb sôrb′) [F. *absorber*, from L. *absorbēre* (*ab-*, off, away, *sorbēre*, to suck up)], *v.t.* To suck up, drink in; to imbibe by capillarity; to incorporate, to engross. **absorbable,** *a.* **absorbability** (-bil′ i ti), *n.* **absorbent,** *a.* Absorbing, capable of or tending to absorb, absorptive. *n.* A vessel in an organism which takes nutritive matter into the system; (*Chem.*) a substance which has the power of absorbing gases or liquids. **absorbent cotton,** *n.* (*Am.*) Cotton-wool. **absorber,** *n.* That which absorbs; the part of a caloric-engine that absorbs heat. **absorption** (ăb sôrp′ shŭn) [L. *absorptio*; see ABSORB], *n.* The act of absorbing; the process of being absorbed. **absorptive,** *a.* Having power to absorb, tending to absorb, absorbent.

absquatulate (ăb skwot′ ū lāt) [*Am. slang*], *v.i.* To run away, make off quickly, scram.

abstain (ăb stān′) [F. *abstenir*, from L. *abstinēre* (*abs-*, away, *tenēre*, to hold)], *v.i.* To keep oneself away, refrain (from); to refrain from intoxicating liquors voluntarily. **abstainer,** *n.* One who withholds himself or refrains from, esp. from the use of intoxicants.

abstemious (ăb stē′ mi ŭs) [L. *abstemius* (*abs-*, from, *tēmum*, strong drink, a word extant only in derivatives, *tēmum*, *tēmulentus*)], *a.* Sparing, not self-indulgent, esp. in the use of food and strong liquors; moderate, temperate, inclined to abstinence. **abstemiously,** *adv.* **abstemiousness,** *n.*

abstention (ăb sten′ shŭn) [ABSTAIN], *n.* The act of abstaining or refraining, esp. from exercising one's right to vote. **abstinence** (ăb′ sti nĕns), *n.* The act or practice of refraining from some indulgence; continence, fasting. **total abstinence:** Abstaining completely from intoxicating liquors. **abstinency,** *n.* The habit of abstaining. **abstinent,** *a.* Practising abstinence. *n.* An abstainer. **abstinently,** *adv.* In an abstinent manner.

absterge (ăb stĕrj′) [L. *abstergēre* (*abs-*, away, *tergēre*, to wipe)], *v.t.* To wipe clean, to cleanse; to purge by medicine. **abstergent,** *a.* Wiping clean, making clean by wiping; having cleansing qualities. *n.* Something that cleanses, esp. a medicine which cleanses or purges. **abstersion,** *n.* The act of cleansing or purgation. **abstersive,** *a.* Having cleansing, purifying qualities; abstergent. *n.* That which wipes, cleanses, or purges away. **abstersiveness,** *n.*

abstinence, abstinent, etc. [ABSTENTION].

abstract (1) (ăb străkt′) [L. *abstractus*, p.p. of *abstrahere* (*abs-*, from, *trahere*, to draw)], *v.t.* To draw or take away, remove; (*euphem.*) to purloin. To separate mentally, to consider apart from other things; to epitomize, summarize; (*Chem.*) to separate by distillation; to extract.

abstract (2) (ăb′ străkt), *a.* Abstracted; separated from particular things, ideal; existing in the mind only; abstruse. *n.* An abstract term; a summary, an epitome; a geometrical or non-representational design. **abstract of quantities,** *n.* Apportionment of quantity and cost of materials in a building. **abstract of title,** *n.* An epitome of the evidences of ownership; an extract. **in the abstract,** *adv.* Without reference to individual cases, abstractly, ideally, theoretically. **abstract numbers,** *n.pl.* Numbers used without reference to particular objects. **abstract nouns** or **terms,** *n.pl.* Names of qualities, in contradistinction to concrete terms which are names of things. **abstracted,** *a.* Absent-minded, inattentive, withdrawn in thought. **abstractedly,** *adv.* Absent-mindedly, in the abstract, separately. **abstractedness,** *n.*

abstraction (ăb străk′ shŭn) [as prec.], *n.* The act of abstracting or separating; taking away; (*euphem.*) stealing; the state of being engrossed in thought; the process of considering separately the quality of an object; a mental conception so formed; an abstract idea; the faculty by which men form abstract ideas. **abstractive,** *a.* Possessing the power or quality of abstracting; tending to abstraction. **abstractively,** *adv.* **abstractly,** *adv.* **abstractness,** *n.*

abstruse (ăb stroos′) [L. *abstrūsus*, p.p. of *abstrūdere* (*abs-*, away, *trūdere*, to push)], *a.* Hidden from observation or knowledge; off the beaten track of human thought; recondite, profound. **abstrusely,** *adv.* **abstruseness, *abstrusity,** *n.*

absurd (ȧb sĕrd′) [F. *absurde*, from L. *absurdus*, (*ab-* away, *surdus*, deaf)], *a.* Incongruous; contrary to or inconsistent with reason; nonsensical, logically contradictory; ridiculous. **absurdity,** *n.* The quality or state of being absurd; folly; an absurd notion, statement, or action. **absurdly,** *adv.* **absurdness,** *n.*

abundance (ȧ bŭn′ dȧns) [O.F. *abondance*, from L. *abundantia* (*abundant-*, stem of pres.p. of *abundāre*, to ABOUND)], *n.* Fulness; plenteousness to overflowing; a more than sufficient quantity or number (of); copiousness, affluence. **abundant,** *a.* Overflowing; in great supply; plentiful, fully sufficient, more than sufficient, ample. **abundant number:** A number the sum of whose aliquot parts exceeds the number itself. **abundantly,** *adv.*

abuse (1) (a būz′) [O.F. *abuser*, L. *abūsus*, p.p. of *abūtī* (*ab-*, from, amiss, *utī*, to use)], *v.t.* To put to an improper use, misuse; to reproach coarsely; to use in an illegitimate sense, to pervert the meaning of; to maltreat, act cruelly to; to violate, to deflower; to deceive. **abusable,** *a.* Capable of being abused. **abuser,** n. One who abuses or misuses, a perverter; a ravisher, a seducer; a reviler.

abuse (2) (ȧ būs′), *n.* Improper treatment or employment; misuse; a corrupt practice or custom; insulting or scurrilous language; perversion from the proper meaning; *violation. **abusive,** *a.* Practising abuse; given to the use of harsh language or ill-treatment; opprobrious; misapplied, perverted. **abusively,** *adv.* **abusiveness, *abusion,** *n.*

abut (ȧ bŭt′) [O.F. *abouter*, *abuter*, (*à*, to, *but*, end), cp. F. *abouter*, to join end to end], *v.t.* (*past & p.p.* **abutted**). To be contiguous; to border upon; to form a point or line of contact; to lean upon (of buildings). **abutment,** *n.* The state of abutting;

that which abuts or borders; a pier or wall, or the part of a pier or wall, against which an arch rests. **abuttal,** *n.* The abutting part of a piece of land. **abutter,** *n.* One who or that which abuts; the owner of property that abuts.

***aby, abye** (ȧ bī') [A.-S. *a-*, intens., away, BUY], *v.t.* To redeem, to pay the penalty for; to endure; to atone. *v.i.* To make restitution; to expiate; to endure, to abide.

abyss (ȧ bis') [L. *abyssus*, Gr. *abussos* (*a-*, without, *bussos*, depth), bottomless], *n.* A vast physical depth, chasm, or cavity, as the depth of the sea, or the bowels of the earth; primeval chaos; anything profound and unfathomable, as (*fig.*) of ignorance or degradation; (*Her.*) the middle of an escutcheon. **abyssal,** *a.* Pertaining to an abyss; pertaining to the depths of the sea beyond 300 fathoms. **abysm** (ȧ bizm') [O.F. *abisme* (F. *abîme*), late L. *abyssimus*, *superl.* of *abyssus*], *n.* An older form of ABYSS, still used poetically. **abysmal,** *a.* Pertaining to an abyss; profound, immeasurable.

Abyssinian (ăb i sin' i ȧn, -sin' yȧn), *a.* Belonging to Abyssinia or its inhabitants. *n.* An inhabitant of Abyssinia or Ethiopia; a member of its Church. **Abyssinian gold,** *n.* An alloy of copper and zinc, plated thinly with gold. **Abyssinian pump,** *n.* A pump with well-tube attached to the suction-tube, for use in the following. **Abyssinian well,** *n.* A tube driven into strata of moderate hardness for obtaining water.

ac- [L. AD, assim. to *c*, *k*, *qu*], *pref.* (*accommodate*, *accord*, *acquire*.)

-ac [Gr. *-akos*], *suf.* Pertaining to, *e.g.* *cardiac*, *demoniac*. (Adjectives so formed are often used as nouns.)

Acacia (ȧ kā' shȧ, -shi ȧ) [L. *acacia*, from Gr. *akakia* (*akē*, a point, thorn)], *n.* An extensive genus of trees with pinnated leaves or else phyllodia, and small flowers in balls or spikes: some species yield catechu and others gum-arabic. **acacia-tree,** *n.* The North American locust-tree or false acacia, *Robinia pseudacacia.*

academic (ăk ȧ dem' ik) [as foll.], *a.* Pertaining to an academy, college, or university; scholarly, theoretic, professorial, unpractical; pertaining to the Platonic school. *n.* A member of an academy, college, or university; a person belonging to the academy of Plato, or adhering to the Academic philosophy. **academical,** *a.* Academic; unpractical. *n.pl.* Academical dress: cap and gown. **academically,** *adv.*

academy (ȧ kăd' ė mi) [F. *académie*, L. *acadēmīa*, Gr. *akadēmeia* (the gymnasium in the suburbs of Athens where Plato taught, named after the hero *Acadēmos*)], *n.* The members of the philosophical school founded by Plato; a place of study, a high school; a seminary for higher education; a society or association for promoting literature, science, or art, established by Government or by private individuals, the members of which are entitled Academicians; the Royal Academy. **academe** (ăk' ȧ dēm), *n.* (*poet.*) An academy [incorrect philologically; probably derived from a misunderstanding of Milton's "Grove of Academe" (Academos)]. **academician** (ȧ kăd ėm ish' ȧn), *n.* A person belonging to an academy or association for the promotion of science, literature, or art; a Royal Academician. **academicism** (ăk ȧ dem'-), *n.* The system of teaching in an academy or high school; academical mannerism; the professorial method. **academism,** *n.* The tenets of the Academic philosophy; Platonism. **academist** (ȧ kăd'-), *n.* An Academic philosopher, a member of an academy.

Acadian (ȧ kā' di ȧn) [F. *Acadie*, Nova Scotia], *a.* and *n.* Belonging to Nova Scotia.

acajou (ăk' ȧ zhu) [F. *acajou*, Brazil, *acaju*], *n.* The cashew-nut tree (*Anacardium occidentale*), and a gummy substance derived from it; a wood resembling mahogany; mahogany.

-acal [Gr. *akos*, -AK, -AL], *suf.* Adjectives ending in *-ac* being often used as nouns, *-al* was added to distinguish the adjective, *e.g.* *demoniacal*, *maniacal*; *-al* is also added to adjectives to show a less intimate connection with the original noun, *e.g.* *cardiacal*.

Acalephæ (ăk ȧ lē' fē) [Gr. *akalēphē*, a nettle], *n.pl.* A class of marine animals containing the sea-nettles, jelly-fish, etc. **acaleph** (ăk' ȧ lef), *n.* Any individual of the Acalephæ. **acalephan,** *a.* Belonging to the Acalephæ. *n.* An acaleph. **acalephoid,** *a.* Resembling the Acalephæ.

acalycine (ȧ kăl' i sin) [mod. L. *acalycinus*, from G. *a-*, priv., *kalyx*, cup], *a.* Without calyx or flower-cup. **acalycinous** (-is' in ůs), *a.*

Acanthopterygii (ȧ kăn thop tėr ij' i ī) [Gr. *akantha* (see foll.), *pteryx*, a wing, *pterygion*, a little wing], *n.pl.* A large order of fishes, having the dorsal fin or fins entirely, and the other fins partially, supported by spinous rays: the common perch is a good example. **acanthopterygian,** *a.* Belonging to the *Acanthopterygii*. *n.* Any individual of the *Acanthopterygii*. **acanthopterygious,** *a.*

Acanthus (ȧ kăn' thůs) [L. *acanthus*, Gr. *akanthos* (*akantha*, a thorn, *akē*, a point)], *n.* A genus of plants; the plant bear's-breech; (*Arch.*) a conventional ornament resembling the foliage of the acanthus, used to decorate the capitals of the Corinthian and Composite orders. **acanthaceous** (-ā' shė ůs), *a.* Armed with spines or prickles. **acanthine,** *a.* Pertaining to or resembling the acanthus; prickly; ornamented with the acanthus leaf. **acanthoid, acanthous,** *a.* Prickly, spinous. **acantho-,** *comb. form.* (*Bot.*) Spiny, having thorns or thorn-like processes.

acapsular (ȧ kăp' sū lȧr) [CAPSULE], *a.* Having no capsule.

acardiac (ȧ kar' di ăk) [Gr. *arkardios* (*a-*, priv., *cardia*, heart)], *a.* Without a heart. *n.* A fœtus destitute of a heart.

acarodomatium (ăk ăr ō dom ā' shi ům) [Gr. *akari*, a mite; *domation*, a little house], *n.* (*Zool.*) An abode for mites found in certain plants which benefit by their presence.

acarpous (ȧ kar' půs) [Gr. *akarpos* (*a-*, priv., *karpos*, fruit)], *a.* Producing no fruit; sterile, barren.

Acarus (ăk' ȧ růs) [Gr. *akari*, a mite (*a-*, priv., *keirein*, to cut)], *n.* A genus of Arachnida, comprising the mites and ticks. **Acarida** (ȧ kăr' i dȧ), **Acarina** (ȧ kăr' ī nȧ), *n.pl.* The order including the mites and ticks. **acaridan, acaridean,** *a.* Belonging to the Acarida. *n.* One of the Acarida. **acaroid,** *a.* **acaricide,** *n.* A substance that kills mites, a remedy for the itch.

acatalectic (ȧ kăt a lek' tik) [late L. *acatelēcticus*, Gr. *akatalēktos* (*a-*, priv., CATALECTIC)], *a.* Not breaking off short; complete; having the full number of metrical feet. *n.* A verse having the complete number of feet.

acatalepsy (ȧ kăt' ȧ lep si) [Gr. *akatalēpsia* (*a-*, priv., *kata*, down, *lēpsis*, a taking hold)], *n.* Incomprehensibleness; the sceptical doctrine that things are unknowable; (*Path.*) mental confusion. **acataleptic,** *a.* Incomprehensible; not to be known with certainty.

acauline (ȧ kawl' īn), **acaulose, acaulous** [Gr. *a-*, priv., *kaulos*, stalk, stem], *a.* (*Bot.*) Without apparent stem, stemless. **acaulescence,** *n.* The occasional apparent suppression of the stem. **acaulescent,** *a.* Acauline.

accablé (ȧ kab lā) [F., p.p. of *accabler*, to overwhelm (fem. *accablée*)], *a.* Crushed, overwhelmed.

Accadian (ȧ kād' i ȧn) [Heb. *Accad* (Gen. x. 10)], *n.* A member of one of the primitive races of Babylonia; the language of this primitive race. *a.* Belonging to this primitive race or its language.

accede (ăk sēd') [L. *accēdere* (*ac-*, *ad-*, to, *cēdere*, to come)], *v.i.* To come to (a certain view), to agree to, assent; to join, give one's adhesion to; to come to (an office or dignity). **access** (ăk' ses) [L. *accessus*, p.p. of *accēdere*], *n.* Admission to a place or person; approach; the means of approach, passage, channel; increase, addition; attack by disease or emotion. [See also **accessary.**]

accelerando (ăch el ėr ăn′ dō) [It.], *a.* and *adv.* (*Mus.*) With increasing speed.

accelerate (ăk sel′ ėr āt) [L. *accelerāre*, to hasten (*ac-*, *ad-*, to, *celer*, swift); -ATE], *v.t.* To hasten; to increase the rate of progress or velocity of; to bring nearer in point of time. **accelerating,** *a.* Increasing velocity of something progressively. **accelerated,** *a.* Having the velocity increased. **accelerated motion,** *n.* Motion continually receiving accessions of velocity: if these accessions are always equal in equal times, the motion is said to be *uniformly* accelerated; if they vary, it is said to be *variably* accelerated. **acceleratedly,** *adv.* **acceleration** (-ā′ shŭn), *n.* The act of accelerating, or the state of being accelerated; progressive increase of velocity or rate of progress; rate of increase of velocity, measured by time-units. **accelerative,** *a.* **accelerator,** *n.* That which accelerates; (*Motor.*) a device for increasing the supply of petrol into the carburettor, thus causing the engine to run at an accelerated speed; (*Phot.*) any chemical or apparatus for speeding up the appearance or development of a picture or an exposed sensitized plate or print. **particle accelerator,** *n.* An electrical appliance for accelerating charged particles such as electrons or protons to high velocities or energies. **accelerator nerve,** *n.* (*Anat.*) A nerve that accelerates the frequency of the heart-beat. **accelerometer,** *n.* An instrument for measuring acceleration. **acceleratory,** *a.*

***accend** (ăk send′) [L. *accendere* (*ac-*, *ad-*, to, *-cendere*, to kindle, cp. *candēre*, to glow)], *v.t.* To light, to set on fire. ***accendibility,** *n.* ***accendible,** *a.* Capable of being set on fire or burnt; inflammable. ***accension,** *n.* The act of setting on fire; the state of being set on fire; inflammation, heat. **accensor,** *n.* (*R.-C. Ch.*) The person who lights and trims the tapers.

accent (1) (ăk′ sėnt) [F. *accent*, L. *accentum*, acc. of *accentus* (*ad-*, to, *cantus*, singing)], *n.* A particular prominence given to a syllable by means of stress or higher musical pitch; manner of speaking or pronunciation expressive of feeling, or peculiar to an individual, a locality, or a nation; a mark used in writing or printing to direct the stress of the voice; musical stress, metrical or rhythmical stress (*in Prosody*); distinctive emphasis or intensity; (*pl.*) words, language.

accent (2) (ăk sent′), *v.t.* To lay stress upon a syllable or word, or a note or passage of music; to mark with emphasis, make conspicuous; to mark with an accent; *to utter, to pronounce. **accentual,** *a.* Pertaining to accent; rhythmical; (*Prosody*) accented verse as distinguished from that governed by quantity. **accentuate,** *v.t.* To pronounce or mark with an accent; to lay stress on, to emphasize. **accentuation** (ăk sent ū ā′ shŭn), *n.* The application of accent; stress, emphasis; mode of pronunciation.

accentor (ăk sen′ tȯr), *n.* (*Zool.*) The hedge-warbler or hedge-sparrow.

accept (ăk sept′) [F. *accepter*, L. *acceptāre*, freq. of *accipere* (*ac-*, *ad-*, to, *capere*, to take)], *v.t.* To consent to take what is offered; to view with favour; to admit the truth of, acknowledge; to agree to, to admit, to take responsibility for. **to accept a bill:** To subscribe it in legal form, and thus promise to pay it when due. **accepted mason:** An approved and admitted Freemason. **acceptable,** *a.* **acceptability,** *n.* **acceptableness,** *n.* **acceptably,** *adv.* **acceptance,** *n.* The act of receiving; favourable reception; agreement to terms or proposals; admission to favour; generally received meaning of an expression; an accepted bill of exchange; the act of subscribing, or the subscription to, a bill of exchange. **acceptancy,** *n.* Acceptance; willingness to accept. **acceptant,** *a.* Willingly receiving. *n.* One who accepts. **acceptation** (-tā′ shŭn), *n.* The act of accepting; favourable reception; the recognized sense or meaning of an expression. **accepter,** *n.* One who accepts; *one who shows partiality (*e.g.* a judge who is influenced by personal considerations), a respecter of persons. **acceptor,** *n.* One who accepts a bill of exchange.

accessary (ăk ses′ ȧ ri) [see ACCEDE], *n., a.* An accessory. **accessible,** *a.* Capable of being approached or reached; easy of access; approachable, attainable. **accessibility** (-bil′ i ti), *n.* **accessibly,** *adv.* **accession** (ăk sesh′ ŭn) [L. *accessio*, as prec.], *n.* The act of going or coming to; agreeing or consenting to; coming to the throne, an office, or a dignity; an increase, addition; an improvement or addition to property by growth or labour expended. **accession-book,** *n.* A register of additions to the stock of books in a library. **accession-number,** *n.* The serial number given to a volume in the accession-book on its arrival in the library. **accessory** (ăk ses′ ȯr i) [late L. *accessōrius*, adj.; see ACCEDE], *a.* Contributive, helpful to some effect, aiding, or acting in subordination to a principal; accompanying, additional; guilty, not as the chief actor, but *before the fact*, by counselling or commanding the act, or *after the fact*, by assisting or concealing the offender. *n.* One who abets or countenances anything that is wrong; an accomplice; something added merely for ornament; any secondary accompaniment.

acciacatura (ă chak ȧ too′ ra) [It. *acciaccare*, to crush together], *n.* (*Mus.*) A short grace note played rapidly.

accidence (ăk′ si dėns) [L. *accidentia*, pl. neuter n. or the same word taken as fem. sing; see foll.], *n.* That part of grammar which deals with the inflection (*i.e.* the accidents) of words; an elementary grammar; the rudiments of a subject.

accident (ăk′ si dėnt) [F. *accident*, L. *accidens -entis*, pres.p. of *accidere* (*ac-*, *ad-*, to, *cadere*, to fall)], *n.* An event proceeding from an unknown cause; the unforeseen effect of a known cause; something unexpected; a casualty, a mishap; a property or quality of a thing not essential to our conception of it; a mere accessory, an attribute. **accidental** (ăk si den′ tăl), *a.* Occurring by chance, unexpectedly; not according to the usual order of things; adventitious, non-essential. *n.* A non-essential property; an accident. **accidental colours,** *n.pl.* (*Opt.*) The complementary colours seen after looking fixedly on a bright-coloured object, and then on a white or light-coloured surface. **accidental lights** or **accidentals,** *n.pl.* (*Painting*) Effects of light and shade caused, not by daylight, but by the artificial introduction of light. **accidental,** *a.*, or **accidentals,** *n.pl.* (*Mus.*) Sharps, flats, or naturals (*signs*) occurring before particular notes, not in the signature. **accidental point,** *n.* (*persp.*) The point in which a straight line drawn from the eye parallel to another given straight line intersects the plane of the picture. **accidentalism,** *n.* Accidental character; accidental effect. **accidentality** (-tăl′ i ti), *n.* **accidentally,** *adv.* **accidentalness,** *n.*

accidie (ăk′ sidi) [ACEDIA].

Accipiter (ăk sip′ it ėr) [L. *accipiter* (*accipio*, to take, accept)], *n.* (*pl.* **-tres**). A genus of raptorial birds, containing the hawks. **accipitral,** *a.* **accipitrine,** *a.* Belonging to or resembling the Accipitres; rapacious, predatory; keen-sighted.

accite (ăk sīt′) [late L. *accītāre* (*ad-*, *cītāre*, to CITE)], *v.t.* To summon, to cite.

acclaim (ȧ klām′) [L. *acclāmāre* (*ac-*, *ad-*, to, *clāmāre*, to shout)], *v.t.* To applaud loudly, welcome with enthusiasm, announce with enthusiasm. *v.i.* To shout applause. *n.* A shout of joy; acclamation. **acclamation** (ăk klȧ mā′ shŭn) [L. *acclāmātiōnem*, acc. *acclāmātio*], *n.* A demonstration of joy or applause made by a multitude. **acclamatory** (ȧ klăm′ ȧ tȯr i), *a.*

acclimatize (ȧ klī′ mȧ tīz) (*Am.*), **acclimate** (ȧ klī′ māt) [F. *acclimater*], *v.t.* To habituate to a new climate; to adapt any organic being for existence and propagation in a new climate. **acclimatization** (-zā' shŭn), *n.* The act or process of acclimatizing; the state of being acclimatized; the modification of the constitution of an organic being which enables it to exist in a climate other than its own. **acclimation, acclimatation,** *n.* Acclimatization by nature, spontaneous accommodation to new conditions as distinguished from acclimatization by man.

acclivity (ȧ klĭv' i ti) [L. *acclīvitātem*, acc. of *acclīvitas* (*ac-*, *ad-*, *clīvus*, a slope)], *n.* An upward slope; the talus of a rampart. **acclivitous,** *a.* Characterized by an acclivity or acclivities. ***acclivous** (ȧ klī' vŭs), *a.* Rising with a slope, ascending.

accolade (ăk kō lād') [F. *accolade*, It. *accolata*, fem. p.p. of *accolare* (L. *ac-*, *ad-*, *collum*, neck), to embrace about the neck], *n.* The ceremony of conferring knighthood by an embrace, putting hand on neck, or a gentle stroke with the flat of a sword; (*Mus.*) a brace uniting several staves.

accommodate (ȧ kom' mō dāt) [L. *accommodāre* (*ac-*, *ad-*, *commodus*, fitting; COM-, with, *modus*, measure)], *v.t.* To make suitable, correspondent, or consistent; to fit, adapt to, settle or adjust; to bring into harmony or concord, reconcile; to supply or furnish; to provide lodging for. **accommodating,** *a.* Obliging, complying, yielding to others' desires. **accommodatingly,** *adv.* **accommodation** (ȧ kom ō dā' shŭn), *n.* The act of accommodating; adjustment, adaptation, reconciliation, compromise; the act of supplying a want; the state of being accommodated; fitness, state of adaptation; anything that supplies a want in respect of ease, convenience, food, lodging, etc.; a loan; (*Biol.*) changing the focus of the eye. **accommodation bill or note,** *n.* A bill or note drawn for the purpose of raising money, and not for value received. **accommodation ladder,** *n.* (*Naut.*) A light ladder fixed outside a vessel at the gangway. **accommodation land,** *n.* Land bought by a speculator to be leased out for building purposes. **accommodation unit,** *n.* (*Planning*) A home. **accommodative,** *a.* **accommodativeness,** *n.*

accompaniment (ȧ kŭm' pȧn i mĕnt) [ACCOMPANY], *n.* Something super-added to or attendant upon another thing; something which gives greater completeness to; (*Mus.*) the part or parts performed by instruments accompanying the voice. **accompanist,** *n.* (*Mus.*) The performer who plays the accompaniment.

accompany (ȧ kŭm' pȧ ni) [F. *accompagner*], *v.t.* To go with, escort, attend as a companion; to live with; to exist along with, to characterize; (*Mus.*) to play the accompaniment for; (*slang*) to cohabit. *v.i.* To play the accompaniment. **accompanier,** *n.*

accomplice (ȧ kom' plis) [F. *complice*, L. *complicem*, nom. *complex* (*com-*, together, *plicāre*, to fold); *ac* is either indef. art. *a* or due to erroneous assimilation to *accomplish*], *n.* A partner in crime; a partaker in guilt. **accompliceship,** *n.* **accomplicity** (ȧ kom plis' i ti), *n.* Complicity, assistance in crime.

accomplish (ȧ kŭm' plish) [O.F. *acomplir* (mod. F. *accomplir*, pres.p. *accomplisant*) from late L. *accomplēre* (*ac-*, *ad-*, *complēre*, to fill up)], *v.t.* To fill up, to complete, to finish; to carry out, fulfil, achieve. **accomplishable,** *a.* **accomplished,** *a.* Complete, finished, consummate; having the graces and attainments perfecting one for good society. **accomplisher,** *n.* **accomplishment,** *n.* The act of accomplishing or fulfilling; the state of being accomplished; acquirement, attainment, such as belongs to persons in good society.

***accompt** (ȧ kount'), *v.* and *n.* [ACCOUNT]. **accomptant,** *n.* [ACCOUNTANT].

accord (ȧ kôrd') [O.F. *acorder*, late L. *accordāre* (*ac-*, *ad-*, to, *cor*, *cordis*, heart)], *v.t.* To cause to agree; to adapt, to make consistent, to adjust, to grant. *v.i.* To agree, to be in correspondence or harmony. *n.* Agreement, harmony, assent, adjustment of a difference; harmonious correspondence; a treaty. **accordance, accordancy,** *n.* **accordant,** *a.* Agreeing, consonant, harmonious, in tune. **accordantly,** *adv.* **accorder,** *n.* **according,** *part. a.* and *adv.* Agreeing, corresponding (to), consentient, harmonious; agreeably with, precisely, just. **according as:** Agreeably, in proportion to. **according to:** Agreeably to, in relation to. **accordingly,** *adv.*

accordion (ȧ kôr' di ŏn) [It. *accordare*, to tune; -ION], *n.* A small portable keyed instrument in which the notes are produced by bellows action on metallic reeds. **accordion-pleating,** *n.* (*Dressmaking*) Pleats with very narrow folds resembling the bellows of an accordion. **accordionist,** *n.* A player on the accordion.

accost (ȧ kost') [F. *accoster*, late L. *accostāre* (*ac-*, *ad-*, to, *costa*, a rib, side)], *v.t.* *To come side by side with, to border, to adjoin; to approach, to speak to, to address; (of a prostitute) to solicit. **v.i.* To be contiguous; to sail along the coast. *n.* Address, salutation, greeting. ***accostable,** *a.*

accouchement (ăk koosh' mȧn, or ȧ koosh' mĕnt) [F. *accoucher* and -MENT], *n.* Confinement, lying-in, delivery. **accoucheur** (ă koosh ĕr). A doctor who assists women at childbirth; a man midwife. **accoucheuse** (ȧ koosh ĕrz). A midwife.

account (ȧ kount') [O.F. *aconter*, late L. *acomptāre* (*ac-*, *ad-*, to, *com-*, together, *putāre*, to reckon)], *v.t.* To reckon, compute, count, to regard as, to deem, consider. *v.i.* To give a reckoning, reason, explanation, or answer. *n.* Reckoning, counting, computation; a recital, description, narrative, explanation; statement of receipts and expenditure showing the balance; register of debit and credit; statement of goods or services supplied with calculation of money due, a bill; (*Fin.*) on the Stock Exchange the fortnightly period from one settlement to another; credit relations, business relations; profit, advantage; behalf, sake. **to account for:** To render an account of; to afford an explanation of; to tell the cause of. **in account with:** Having business relations with. **for account of:** To be sold on behalf of, to be accounted for to. **on account:** As an interim payment. **on account of:** For the sake of, because of. **of no account:** Valueless, negligible. **on no account:** By no means. **to find one's account in:** To find advantage, profit in. **account-book:** A register of business transactions. **account day:** A day of reckoning. **to give a good account of:** To be successful, do (oneself) credit. **accountable,** *a.* Liable to be called on to render an account of; responsible. **accountability,** *n.* Liability to be called on to give an account of; responsibility. **accountableness,** *n.*

accountant (ȧ koun' tȧnt), *n.* One whose occupation is the keeping of accounts; a public officer charged with the duty of keeping and inspecting accounts; one liable to render account; (*Law*) the defendant in an action of account. **accountant-general,** *n.* The principal accountant in large mercantile houses, companies, or public offices. **accountancy,** *n.* **accountantship,** *n.*

accouplement (ȧ kŭpl' mĕnt) [F.], *n.* The act of coupling together; the state of being coupled together; that which serves to connect; a tie or brace.

accoutre (ȧ koo' tĕr) [med. F. *accoustrer* (F. *accoutrer*), prob. from *à* prep. and *coustre*, *coutre*, a sacristan], *v.t.* To dress, to equip; to array in military dress; to equip for military service. **accoutrement** (ȧ koo' tĕr mĕnt), *n.* Dress, outfit, equipment (*usually in plural*); (*Mil.*) a soldier's equipment, excepting arms and dress.

accredit (ȧ kred' it) [F. *accréditer* (*à*, *crédit*; see CREDIT)], *v.t.* To confer credit on, vouch for, sanction; to send with credentials (as an ambassador). **accredited,** *a.* Recognized officially, generally accepted. **accredited milk:** Milk that has passed bacterial-content tests and has been produced by a periodically examined herd.

accrescence (á kres′ ėns) [L. *accrescere*, to grow], *n.* Continued growth, increase; something which grows on a thing, an accretion. **accrescent,** *a.*

accrete (á krēt′) [L. *accrētus*, p.p. of *accrēscere*, to grow (*ac-*, *ad-*, to, *crēscere*)], *v.i.* To grow together; to combine round a nucleus. *a.* (*Bot.*) Grown together by adhesion (of parts normally separate). **accretion,** *n.* Increase by organic growth; increase in growth by external additions; the growing together of parts naturally separate, as the fingers; the result of such growth; the part added; (*Law*) the accession or adhesion of foreign matter to something (chiefly used of land deposited from a river or the sea).

accrue (á kroo′) [O.F. *acreue*, growth, orig. p.p. of *acroître* (L. *accrescere*), to grow], *v.i.* To grow to, to increase; to arise, to fall, come to (as a natural growth).

accumulate (á kū′ mū lāt) [L. *accumulātus*, p.p. of *accumulāre*, to heap up (*ac-*, *ad-*, to, *cumulāre*)], *v.t.* To heap up, pile one thing above another; to bring together by degrees, to amass; to take several university degrees at a time. *v.i.* To grow in size, number, or quantity, by repeated additions. **accumulation** (á kū mū lā′ shŭn), *n.* The act of accumulating or amassing; the process of taking a number of university degrees; the state of being accumulated; that which is accumulated; a mass. **accumulative** (á kū′ mū lā tive), *a.* Accumulating, amassing. **accumulatively,** *adv.* **accumulator,** *n.* One who or that which accumulates; one who takes university degrees by accumulation; an apparatus for the storage of hydraulic or of electric energy.

accurate (ă′ kū rát) [L. *accūrātus*, p.p. of *accūrāre* (*ac-*, *ad-*, *cūrāre*, from *cūra*, care)], *a.* Careful, exact, in precise accordance with rule or standard of truth; without error or defect. **accurately,** *adv.* **accuracy,** *n.* Exactness; correctness resulting from care; precision; conformity to a standard; precision of fit. **accurateness,** *n.*

***accurse** (á kĕrs′) [A.-S. *a-*, intens., *cursian*, to curse], *v.* To call down curses on. **accursed** (á kĕr′ sėd), **accurst,** *a.* Lying under a curse; execrable, detestable; excommunicated; fated.

accusative (á kū′ zá tiv) [F. *accusatif*, L. *accūsātīvus* (ACCUSE), lit. trans. of Gr. *aitiatikē*, the case of accusing or of effect], *a.* Of or belonging to the objective case of declinable words in inflected languages; also applied to the word that represents the object in uninflected languages. (It in many respects agrees with the objective case in English, which is often called the accusative by modern grammarians.) *n.* The grammatical case defined above. **accusatival** (-tī′ vál), *a.* Pertaining to the accusative. **accusatively,** *adv.*

accuse (á kūz′) [O.F. *acuser*, L. *accūsāre* (*ac-*, *ad-*, to, *causa*, reason, cause, lawsuit)], *v.t.* To charge with a crime, offence, or fault, to indict; to lay the blame formally (on a person or thing). **accuser,** *n.* **accusingly,** *adv.* **accusable,** *a.* Liable to be charged with a crime or fault, blameworthy, censurable. **accusation** (ăk kū za′ shŭn), *n.* The act of accusing; the state of being accused; a charge brought against one. **accusatory** (á kū′ zá tôr i), *a.* Containing or involving an accusation. **accusatorial,** *a.* Involving accusation or indictment in a case in which judge and prosecutor are distinct (contrasted with inquisitorial). **accusatorially,** *adv.* ***accusal,** *n.*

accustom (á kŭs′ tŏm) [CUSTOM], *v.t.* To habituate (usually in *pass.* or *r.*, oneself to, or to do), to make familiar by use. **v.i.* To be used or wont. **accustomed,** *a.* Often practised, usual, wonted, familiar, ordinary, habitual. **accustomedness,** *n.* ***accustomary,** *a.*

A.C.E. mixture, *n.* (*Chem.*) An anæsthetic, consisting of one part of alcohol, two of chloroform and three of ether.

ace (ās) [O.F. *as*, L. *as*, a unit], *n.* The single point on cards or dice; a card or domino with but one mark upon it; a trifle, a very small amount; a hair's-breadth; an airman who has brought down ten or more hostile aircraft; a man of first rank in sport, etc.

-acea [L. *suf.*, pl. neut. of *-āceus* (*-āc-* and *-eus*)], *suf.* Used analogously to form names of classes or orders of animals, *e.g.* *Cetacea* [*cētus*, a whale], *Crustacea*, etc.

-aceæ [L. *suf.*, fem. pl. qualifying *plantæ*; see -ACEA], *suf.* Used to form names of orders or families of plants, *e.g.* *Rosaceæ*.

-acean [L. -ACEA, *-āceus*], *suf.* Forms singular nouns or adjectives corresponding to collective nouns in *-acea*, *e.g.* *a crustacean*, *crustacean*.

acedia (á sē′ di á) [Gr. heedlessness], *n.* An abnormal mental condition characterized by listlessness, fatigue, and lack of interest in things.

aceldama (á kel′ dá má, *or* á sel′ dá má) [Gr. *akeldama*, cp. Syr. *ōkēl damō*, the field of blood], *n.* A field near Jerusalem purchased by the chief priests with the thirty pieces of silver returned by Judas, and used as a burial-place (Acts i. 19); hence any place stained by slaughter.

acentric (á sen′ trik) [Gr. *a-*, priv., *kentron*, the centre], *a.* Without centre; not about a centre.

-aceous [L. *suf.* -ACEA and -OUS], *suf.* Of the nature of, belonging to, like: forming adjectives from nouns in natural science, *e.g.* *crustaceous*, *cretaceous*, *farinaceous*, *filaceous*.

acephal- [Gr. *akephalos* (*a-*, priv., *kephalē*, head)], *pref.* Headless: combining form to various scientific terms, chiefly botanical and zoological. **acephalous** (á sef′ á lŭs), *a.* Without a head; having no superior or head; short of the beginning (as in a verse or manuscript); (*Zool.*) with no distinct head, as in one division of the Mollusca; (*Bot.*) with lateral instead of terminal style. **acephalan,** *a.*, *n.*

Acer (ā′ ser) [L., a maple tree], *n.* (*Bot.*) A genus comprising over 100 species. including the sycamore and maples.

acerb (á sĕrb′) [L. *acerbus*, bitter], *a.* Sour, with a rough and astringent taste, as of unripe fruit. **acerbity** (á sĕr′ bi ti) [F. *acerbité*, L. *acerbitātem*, acc. of *acerbitas* (*acerbus*)], *n.* Sourness, with roughness or astringency, as of unripe fruit; bitterness of suffering; harshness of speech, action or temper.

acerose (ăs′ ėr ōs) [L. *acer*, sharp], *a.* (*Bot.*) Needle-sharp.

acervate (ăs′ ėr vāt) [L. *acervātus*, p.p. of *acervāre* (*acervus*, a heap), to heap up], *a.* Heaped up; growing into heaps or clusters. **acervation** (vā′ shŭn), *n.* The act of heaping up, accumulation.

acescent (á ses′ ėnt) [L. *acescere*, inceptive of *acēre*, to be sour], *a.* Turning sour, rather sour, subacid. **acescence,** *n.*

acet- [L. *acētum*, vinegar (*acēre*, to be sour)], *comb. form.* (*Chem.*) Of the nature of vinegar.

acetabulum (ăs ė tăb′ ū lŭm) [L. *acētābulum*, from *acētum*, vinegar, *-abulum*, dim. of *-abrum*, a vessel or holder], *n.* An ancient Roman vessel for holding vinegar; a cavity in any bone designed to receive the protuberant head of another bone, *e.g.* the socket of the hip-joint in man; the socket in which the leg of an insect is inserted; one of the suckers on the arms of a cuttlefish; (*Bot.*) the cup-shaped fructification of many lichens; the receptacle of certain fungi.

acetarious (ăs ė târ′ i ŭs) [L. *acētāria*, salad plants, neut. pl. of *acētāris*, *a.*, pertaining to vinegar], *a* Used in salads.

acetic (á sē′ tik, á set′ ik) [ACET-], *n.* Pertaining to vinegar, akin to vinegar; sour. **acetic acid,** *n.* (*Chem.*) The acid which imparts sourness to vinegar. **acetate** (ăs ė tāt), *n.* A salt of acetic acid. **acetated,** *a.* Treated with acetic acid. **acetify** (á set′ i fī), *v.t.* To convert into vinegar; to render sour. *v.i.* To become sour. **acetification,** *n.* The process of making into vinegar, or of rendering sour. **acetous** (ăs′ ė tůs), **acetose,** *a.* Having the character of vinegar, sour; causing acetification.

acetone (ăs′ ė tōn) [from prec.], *n.* An inflammable liquid obtained by distilling acetated or organic substances and used in the manufacture of chloroform and as a solvent; a ketone.

acetylene (ȧ set′ i lēn) [ACET-, -YL, -ENE], *n.* A gas composed of carbon and hydrogen, which burns with an intensely brilliant flame; ethine.

acharnement (ȧ shar nė mȧn) [F.] *n.* Bloodthirsty fury, ferocity; (*fig.*) gusto.

Achates (ȧ kā′ tēz), *n.* A trusty friend, from the *fidus* (faithful) *Achates*, the friend of Æneas, in Virgil's *Æneid*.

ache (āk) [A.-S. *acan*], *v.i.* To suffer pain or distress. *n.* Continuous pain (in contradistinction to a twinge); distress.

achene, achæne (ȧ kēn′) [Gr. *a*-, priv., *chainein*, to gape], *n.* (*Bot.*) A small dry carpel, with a single seed, which does not open when ripe. **achenial,** *a.*

Acheron (ăk′ ė rȯn) [L. from Gr. *Acheron* (*achos*, grief, *rhoos*, stream), river of sorrow], *n.* A fabled stream in the infernal regions; the infernal regions, the underworld. **Acherontic** (ăk ė ron′ tik), *a.* Of or pertaining to Acheron, infernal; gloomy; about to die, moribund.

Acheulian (ă shoo′ li ȧn) [St. *Acheul*, France], *a.* (*Anthrop.*) Of or pertaining to the period of Lower Palæolithic culture, typified by remains discovered in St. Acheul, and placed by archæologists between the Chellean and the Mousterian epochs.

achieve (ȧ chēv′) [O.F. *achever*, from phrase *venir à chef*, late L. *ad caput venīre*, to come to a head], *v.t.* To perform, accomplish, finish; to attain, acquire, or bring about by an effort. **achievable,** *a.* **achievement,** *n.* The act of accomplishing; the thing achieved; an heroic deed, an exploit; a complete heraldic composition; a funeral escutcheon. **achiever,** *n.*

Achillean (ăk i lē′ ȧn) [*Achilles*, the hero of the *Iliad*], *a.* Like Achilles; heroic, invulnerable; invincible. **Achilles' tendon:** The tendon or ligature connecting the muscles of the calf to the heel-bone, the part where Achilles was said to be vulnerable, his mother Thetis holding him by the heel when she dipped him in the river Styx, to make him invulnerable.

achilous (ȧ kī′ lůs) [Gr. *a*-, not, *cheilos*, lip], *a.* (*Bot.*) Without lips.

achlamydeous (ăk lȧ mid′ ė ůs), [Gr. *a*-, priv., *chlamus -udos*, a cloak], *a.* (*Bot.*) Having neither calyx nor corolla, as the willows.

achromatic (ăk rō măt′ ik) [Gr. *achrōmatos* (*a*-, priv., *chrōma -atos*, colour)], *a.* Colourless; transmitting light without decomposing it into its primary colours. **achromatically,** *adv.* **achromatism** (ȧ krō′ mȧ tizm), **achromaticity** (-tis′ i ti), *n.* The quality or state of being achromatic. **achromatize,** *v.t.* To deprive of colour. **achromatopsy** (-top′ si), *n.* Colour blindness.

acicular (ȧ sik′ ū lȧr) [L. *acicula*, a small needle, -AR], *a.* Resembling a needle in shape or sharpness. **acicularly,** *adv.* **aciculate, aciculated,** *a.* Having needle-like bristles; marked with fine, irregular streaks.

acid (ăs′ id) [L. *acidus*, sour (*acēre*, to be sour)], *a.* Sour, tart, sharp to the taste; (*Min.*) of rocks which have a large proportion of silica. *n.* A sour substance; a compound of hydrogen in which the hydrogen can be replaced by a metal, or with a basic metallic oxide form a salt of that metal and water. **to put on the acid:** (*Austral.*) To scrounge, to cadge. **acid test,** *n.* (*colloq.*) An absolute and definite test; a critical ordeal. **acidity** (-sid′ i ti), *n.* The quality of being acid; sourness, tartness, sharpness to the taste. **acidness,** *n.* **acidify,** *v.t.* To render acid or sour; to convert into an acid. *v.i.* To become acid. **acidifiable,** *a.* Capable of being rendered acid. **acidification** (-kā′ shůn), *n.* The act or process of acidifying; the state of being acidified. **acidimeter** [-METER], *n.* Instrument for measuring the strength of acids. **acidimetry,** *n.* **acidulous** (ȧ sid′ ū lůs) [L. *acidulus*, dim. of *acidus*], *a.* A little sour or acid, moderately sharp to the taste, subacid. **acidulate** (-lāt), *v.t.* To render slightly acid; to flavour with an acid. **acidulated,** *part.a.* Rendered slightly acid; flavoured with acid; soured, embittered in temper.

acidosis (ă si dō′ sis), *n.* (*Path.*) Condition characterized by the appearance of acetone bodies in the urine and bloodstream.

acierate (ăs′ i ėr āt) [F. *acier*, late L. *aciārium*, L. *acies*, edge], *v.t.* To turn into steel. **acierage,** *n.* The process of electroplating a metal with iron or steel.

acinus (ăs′ in ůs) [L. *acinus*, a berry growing in a cluster], *n.* A bunch of fleshy fruit, especially a bunch of grapes; a fruit consisting of several drupels, as the raspberry; (*pl.* **acini**) small stones as in grapes, strawberries, etc.; (*Anat.*) a racemose gland. **aciniform,** *a.* Clustered like grapes.

-acious [L. *-ax -ācis* and -OUS], *suf.* Abounding in, characterized by, inclined to; added to verbal stems to form adjectives, *e.g.* *loquacious, tenacious.*

-acity [F. *-acité*, L. *ācitas -tātem*], *suf.* The quality of: forms nouns of quality from adjectives in -ACIOUS.

ack-ack (ăk ăk′) [Morse names of letters formerly used by signallers], *n.* Anti-aircraft. **ack-emma,** *n.* Morning, a.m.

ack dum (ăk dŭm) [Hind.], *adv.* At once, quickly.

acknowledge (ȧk nol′ ėj) [A.-S. *on*, KNOWLEDGE, or from obs. n. *acknowledge* (*acknowe*, A.-S. *on, cnáwan*, to know)], *v.t.* To own the truth of, to own, to confess, to admit; to recognize the authority of; to give a receipt for; to express appreciation or gratitude for. **acknowledgment,** *n.* The act of acknowledging; recognition, confession, admission; receipt for money or goods; an expression of gratitude; something given or done in return for a service or message. **acknowledgable,** *a.*

-acle [L. *-āculum*], *suf.* Diminutive of nouns, *e.g.* *tabernacle, miracle.*

aclinic (ȧ klin′ ik) [Gr. *a*-, priv., *klinein*, to bend, see -IC], *a.* Not dipping, situated where the magnetic needle does not dip. **aclinic line,** *n.* The magnetic equator.

acme (ăk′ mē) [Gr. *akmē*, an edge], *n.* The top or highest point, the culmination; the maturity of life; the crisis or turning-point of a disease.

acne (ăk′ nē) [prob. Gr. *aknesis*, without itch], *n.* A pimple or tubercle; a skin disease characterized by pimples or tubercles.

acock (ȧ kok′), *adv.* In a cocked fashion; defiantly (usually said of the hat).

***acold** (ȧ kōld′) [A.-S. prob. *ācōlod*, pp. of *ācōlian*, to cool], *a.* Cold, chilly.

acolyte (ăk′ ȯ līt) [late L. *acolythus, acolitus*, from Gr. *akolouthos*, a follower], *n.* An inferior officer in the R.-C. Church; an attendant, ministrant.

aconite (ăk′ ȯ nīt) [F. *aconit*, L. *aconītum*, Gr. *akonīton*], *n.* The English name of the genus *Aconitum*, esp. *Aconitum napellus*, the common monk's-hood or wolf's-bane; a poison drug used medicinally, obtained from the root of this plant. **aconitic** (ăk ȯ nit′ ik), *a.* **aconitine** (ȧ kon′ it in), *n.* An alkaloid substance derived from the genus *Aconitum*.

acorn (ā′ kôrn) [A.-S. *æcern* (*æcer*, a field), fruit of the field, *i.e.* of the open country], *n.* The fruit of the oak. **acorn-barnacle, acorn-shell,** *n.* *Balanus crenatus*; a multi-valve cirriped allied to the barnacles. **acorned,** *a.* (*Her.*) Bearing acorns as a charge.

Acorus (ăk′ ôr ůs), *n.* (*Bot.*) An aromatic herb of the order Orontiaceæ, once used for strewing on floors, now for flavouring beer and in the manufacture of perfumes.

acosmism (ȧ koz′ mizm) [Gr. *a-*, priv., *kosmos*, the world], *n.* Denial of the existence of the universe as apart from the Creator.

acotyledon (ȧ kot i lē′ dȯn) [mod. L. *acotylēdones*, from Gr. *a-*, priv., COTYLEDON], *n.* Any plant of the class Acotyledones; a plant without distinct seed-lobes. **acotyledonous,** *a.* Having no cotyledons; pertaining to a plant without visible seed-lobes.

acoustic (ȧ koo′ stik, ȧ kou′ stik) [F. *acoustique*, from Gr. *akoustikos* (*akouein*), to hear], **acoustical,** *a.* Pertaining to the ear, constituting part of the physical apparatus for hearing; pertaining to hearing. *n.* (*Med.*) A remedy for deafness. **acoustics** [Gr. *akoustika*, neut. pl. of adj. *akoustikos*], *n.* The science of sound and its phenomena, and of the phenomena of hearing. **acoustician** (ăk oos tish′ ȧn), *n.* One who investigates the phenomena of sound; one skilled in acoustics. **acousticon** (ȧ koo′ sti kȯn), *n.* An appliance to aid hearing.

acquaint (ȧ kwānt′) [O.F. *acointer*, late L. *adcognitāre* (*ad-*, to, *cognitum*, p.p. of *cognoscere*, to know; *co-*, *cum-*, with, *gnoscere*, *noscere*, to know)], *v.t.* To make aware of, inform, to communicate intelligence. *v.r.* To give (oneself) knowledge of or acquaintance with. **acquaintance,** *n.* Knowledge of any person or thing; the state of knowing, or becoming known to, a person; a person, or the persons collectively (*usually in plural*), whom one knows, but with whom one is not intimate. **acquaintanceship,** *n.* The state of being acquainted; the relation of mutual acquaintance.

acquest (ȧ kwest′) [O.F. *acquest*, from late L. *acquīstum*); see ACQUIRE], *n.* A thing acquired, an acquisition; *the action of acquiring; (*Law*) property gained otherwise than by inheritance.

acquiesce (ăk wi es′) [Fr. *acquiescer*, L. *acquiēscere* (*ac-*, *ad-*, to, *quiēscere*, to rest, from *quies*, rest)], *v.i.* To submit to or remain passive under; to assent to, to accept tacitly, to concur in. **acquiescence,** *n.* **acquiescent,** *a.* Submissive to; resting satisfied with. **acquiescently,** *adv.*

acquire (ȧ kwīr′) [O.F. *aquerre*, *acquerre*, from L. *acquīrere* (*ac-*, *ad-*, to, *quærere*, to seek)], *v.t.* To gain, or obtain possession of, by one's own exertions or abilities; to come into possession of. **acquirable,** *a.* Capable of being acquired. **acquirability,** *n.* **acquired,** *part.a.* Gained by one's own exertions. **acquirement,** *n.* The act of acquiring; the object gained; a personal attainment of body or mind.

acquisition (ăk wi zish′ ȯn) [as prec.], *n.* The act of acquiring; the object acquired; a gain, an acquirement. **acquisitive** (ȧ kwiz′ i tiv), *a.* Capable of making, or disposed to make acquisitions. **acquisitively,** *adv.* **acquisitiveness,** *n.* The quality of being acquisitive; desire of possession; a phrenological organ supposed to denote such desire. **acquist,** *n.* [ACQUEST].

acquit (ȧ kwit′) [O.F. *acquiter*, late L. *aquitāre* (AC-, *quiētāre*, to settle)], *v.t.* (*past & p. p.* **acquitted).** To release from an obligation, suspicion, or charge; to pay (a debt); to declare not guilty. *v.r.* To discharge the duties of one's position. **acquitter,** *n.* **acquittal,** *n.* Discharge or release from a promise, debt, or other obligation; discharge of duty; performance; a deliverance from a charge by legal process. **acquittance,** *n.* The act of releasing from a charge or debt; a receipt in full; discharge of duty.

acre (ā′ kėr) [A.-S. *æcer*, a field (cp. O.Sax. *accar*, O.H.G. *achar*, L. *ager*, Gr. *agros*, Sansk. *ajras*)], *n.* A measure of land containing 4,840 square yards; a piece of tilled or enclosed land; a field (still surviving in place names). **acreage** (ā′ kėr ij), *n.* The area of any piece of land in acres; acres taken collectively or in the abstract.

acrid (ăk′ rid) [L. *ācer ācris*, sharp, pungent, probably assim. to ACID], *a.* Sharp, pungent, biting to the taste; irritating, corrosive; bitterly irritating to the feelings; of irritating temper and manners.

acridness, acridity (ȧ krid′ i ti), *n.* Sharpness, pungency, bitterness of manner or speech. **acritude,** *n.*

acriflavine (ăk ri flāv′ ēn) [L. *acer*, sharp; *flavus*, yellow], *n.* (*Med.*) An aniline dye, solutions of which form a strong antiseptic.

acrimony (ăk′ ri mȯ ni) [L. *ācrimōnia* (*ācer ācris*, -MONY), sharpness], *n.* Sharpness, bitterness of temper, manner, or speech. **acrimonious** (ăk ri mō′ ni ŭs), *a.* Bitter and irritating in temper or manner. **acrimoniously,** *adv.* **acrimoniousness,** *n.*

acro- [Gr. *akros*, outermost, at the top], *comb. form.* Situated on the outside, beginning, termination, extremity, point, or top, *e.g. acrobat, acrogenous.*

acrobat (ăk′ rȯ băt) [F. *acrobate*, Gr. *akrobatos* (ACRO-, *batos*, verb.a. of *bainein*, to go)], *n.* A performer of daring gymnastic feats; a tumbler; a rope-dancer. **acrobatic,** *a.* Pertaining to an acrobat or his performances. **acrobatically,** *adv.* After the manner of an acrobat. **acrobatism,** *n.* The feats or occupation of an acrobat.

acrogen (ăk′ rȯ jen) [Gr. ACRO-, *genēs*, born], *n.* A cryptogam, a plant increasing at the extremity of the stem; one of the higher cryptogams (mosses, club-mosses, and ferns). **acrogenous** (ȧ kroj′ ėn ŭs), *a.* Of the nature of an acrogen; increasing at the summit.

acrolith (ăk′ rȯ lith) [Gr. ACRO-, *lithos*, stone], *n.* A statue having only the head and extremities of stone.

acromegaly (ăk rō meg′ ȧl i) [Gr. *akron*, a point; *megas*, *megalou*, great], *n.* (*Path.*) A disease the chief feature of which is the extreme hypertrophy of the extremities of the face and limbs.

acronychal, acronycal (ȧ kron′ ik ȧl) [Gr. ACRO-, *nux nuktos*, night], *a.* Vespertine; happening in the evening or at nightfall. **acronychally,** *adv.* At the acronychal time; in an acronychal manner; at sunset or nightfall.

acronym (ăk′ rō nim) [ACRO-, Gr. *onoma*, name], *n.* A word formed from initials, *e.g.* NATO, UNICEF.

acropetal (ȧ krop′ et ȧl) [Gr. *akron*, a point; L. *petere*, to seek], *a.* In the direction of the apex.

acrophobia (ăk rō fō′ bi ȧ), *n.* (*Path.*) A morbid dread of high places.

acropolis (ȧ krop′ ȯ lis) [Gr. ACRO-, *polis*, city], *n.* The citadel or elevated part of a Greek town, especially that of Athens.

across (ȧ kros′) [A.-S. *a-*, on, CROSS], *adv.* or *prep.* Transversely, from side to side, cross-wise, forming a cross with, opposed to, athwart; upon (*e.g. come across*, come upon accidentally); over (*e.g. across the Channel*). **to put it across:** To get the better of.

acrostic (ȧ kros′ tik) [Gr. *acrostichis* (ACRO-, *stichos*, a row)], *n.* A composition in which the lines are so disposed that their initial letters taken in order constitute a word or short sentence; an Abecedarian poem. *a.* Relating to or containing an acrostic. **acrostical,** *a.* **acrostically,** *adv.* In the manner of an acrostic composition.

acroterium, acroterion (ăk ro tēr′ i ŭm, -i ȯn) [Gr. *akrotērion*], *n.* A pedestal on a pediment, for the reception of a figure; a pinnacle (*usually in the pl.* **acroteria). acroterial,** *a.* Pertaining to or having the character of acroteria.

act (ăkt) [F. *acte*, or directly from L. *actus*, a doing, and *actum* (pl. *acta*), a thing done, from *agere*, to do, to drive]. *n.* That which is done or being done, a deed, process of doing, operation; the exertion of physical, mental, or moral power; a thesis publicly maintained by a candidate for a degree; one of the principal divisions of a play, usually sub-divided into smaller portions called scenes; a statute, law, or edict of a legislative or judicial body; an instrument in writing proving the truth of some transaction; *real, as distinguished from possible existence, actuality, reality, *v.t.* To perform; to play the part of; to impersonate. *v.i.* To exert power, to produce an effect; to be in action or motion; to carry out a purpose or determination; to behave, to demean oneself; to perform as an actor. **in the act, in the very act:** In the actual commission of some deed. **act of God:** The operation of uncontrollable natural forces in causing an event. **actable,** *a.* Capable of being performed on the stage; practically possible. **acting,** *a.* Performing dramatically; operating; doing temporary duty. *n.* Performance, execution, action; dramatic performance. **actor,** *n.* A performer; one who represents a character on the stage; a doer. **actress,** *n.* A female actor.

actin-, actino- [Gr. *aktis aktinos*, a ray], *comb. form.* Radiate; stellate; pertaining to the rays of the sun; stem of many terms in physics and natural history, *e.g. actinal, actino-chemistry, actinograph.*

actinia (ȧk tin′ i ȧ), *n.* (*pl.* **actiniæ, actinias**). A genus of zoophytes, the *Actiniadæ*; hence, a sea-anemone, a polyp.

actinic (ȧk tin′ ik), *a.* Pertaining to rays; pertaining to the chemical rays of the sun. **actinic rays,** *n.pl.* Electro-magnetic rays capable of affecting photographic emulsions, including X rays, ultra-violet, infra-red rays, etc. **actinism** (ăk′ tin izm) [-ISM], *n.* The property in rays of light by which chemical changes are produced; the radiation of light or heat; **actinograph** (ȧk tin′ ȯ grăf) [-GRAPH], *n.* An instrument for registering the variations of chemical influence in solar rays. **actinometer** (ăk ti nom′ ė tėr) [-METER], *n.* An instrument for measuring the heating power of the sun's rays.

actinium (ăk tin′ i ŭm), *n.* A radio-active metallic element found in pitchblende. **actinotherapy,** *n.* (*Med.*) The treatment of disease by exposure to actinic radiation.

actinograph, actinometer [ACTINIC].

actinozoa (ăk tin ȯ zo′ ȧ), *n.pl.* Radiated animals, containing the sea-anemones and coral polyps. The singular, *Actinozoon*, is sometimes used for any animal of this group.

action (ăk′ shŭn) [F. *action*, L. *actiōnem*, acc. of *actio*, a doing, performance; see ACT], *n.* The state or condition of acting or doing; activity; anything done or performed; a deed, an exploit; a battle, an engagement; the mechanism or movement of a compound instrument; gesture, gesticulation; the trained motion of a horse; agency, operation, impulse; the working of an organ; the representation of passion in painting and sculpture; the things done, events, or series of events constituting the main subjects of a play, poem, or other work of fiction; a legal process or suit. **action radius,** *n.* (*Aviat.*) The distance an aircraft can cover without running short of fuel before returning to its base or starting-point. **action-taking,** *a.* Litigious. **actionable** *a.* Furnishing ground for an action at law. **actionably,** *adv.* So as to be actionable.

actionnaire (ăk si ȯn nâr′) [Fr.], *n.* A shareholder.

active (ăk′ tiv) [F. *actif -ve*, L. *activus*], *a.* Possessed of the power of acting, exerting the power of acting; communicating action or motion; exerting influence; quick in movement, nimble, agile; continually employed, busy, assiduous (opposed to idle or indolent); characterized by action, work, or the performance of business; in actual operation; (*Gram.*) applied to intransitive verbs, or transitive verbs that attribute the action expressed to the subject whence it proceeds (the *active voice* is opposed to the *passive voice,* in which the action is viewed in relation to the thing affected). **activate,** *v.t.* To make active; to make radio-active. **actively,** *adv.* In an active manner. **activism,** *n.* The policy of decisive action. **activity** (-tiv′ i ti), *n.* The quality or state of being active; exertion of energy; energy, liveliness.

***acton** (ăk′ tȯn) [O.F. *auqueton* (F. *hoqueton*), Sp. *alcoton* (*algodon*), Arab. *al-qūtun*, the cotton], *n.* A vest or jacket of quilted cotton, worn under mail; later, a jacket of leather or other material protected with plates or mail.

actor, actress [ACT].

actual (ăk′ tū ȧl) [F. *actuel*, L. *actuālis* (*actus*, verb.n. of *agere*, to act); see ACT, -AL], *a.* Existing in act or reality; real, existing, present, current. **actually,** *adv.* **actuality** (-ăl′ i ti), *n.* The state of being actual; reality; realism. **actualize** (ăk′ tū ȧl īz) [see -IZE], *v.t.* To make actual; to describe realistically. **actualization** (-zā′ shŭn), *n.* A making real or actual; realization.

actuary (ăk′ tū ȧ ri) [L. *actuārius*, amanuensis, account-keeper], *n.* An officer of a mercantile or insurance company, skilled in statistics, especially on the expectancy of life and the average proportion of losses by fire and other accidents. **actuarial** (ăk tū âr′ i ȧl), *a.* Of or belonging to actuaries or their profession.

actuate (ăk′ tū āt) [med. L. *actuātus*, p.p. of *actuāre* (*actus*)], *v.t.* To excite to action, to put in action, to furnish the motive of. **actuation,** *n.* A putting in action, communication of motion; effectual operation.

acuity (ȧ kū′ i ti) [F. *acuité*, med. L. *acuitātem* (*acus*, needle, *acuere*, to sharpen)], *n.* Sharpness, acuteness (of a point, an acid, disease, or wit).

aculeus (ȧ kū′ lė ŭs) [L. *acūleus*, a sting (dim. of *acus*, a needle)], *n.* (*Zool.*) A sting; (*Bot.*) a prickle. **aculeate** (ȧ kū′ lė ȧt) [L. *aculeātus* (ACULEUS, -ATE)], *a.* (*Zool.*) Furnished with a sting; (*Bot.*) prickly; set with prickles; (*fig.*) pointed, incisive, pungent. **aculeated,** *a.* [ACULEATE].

acumen (ȧ kū′ mėn) [L. *acūmen* (*acuere*, to sharpen)], *n.* Acuteness of mind, shrewdness, keen penetration.

acuminate (ȧ kū′ min ȧt) [L. *acuminatus*, pointed], *a.* (*Nat. Hist.*) Tapering to a point. *v.t.* (ȧ kū′ min āt). To sharpen, to point, to give keenness or poignancy to. **acuminated,** *part.a.* Brought to a point; sharp, stinging. **acumination** (ȧ kū min ā′ shŭn), *n.* The act of making sharp; termination in a sharp point. **acuminose,** *a.* (*Bot.*) Terminating gradually in a flat, narrow end: inclined to be acuminate.

acut-, acuti- [L. *acūtus*, sharp], *comb. form.* Sharp, acute, as in *acutangular, acutifoliate, acutiform.*

acute (ȧ kūt′) [L. *acūtus* (*acuere*, to sharpen)], *a.* Terminating in a sharp point; sharp, keen, penetrating; quick to perceive minute distinctions; sensitive, sharp, piercing (said of pain); shrill, high in pitch; applied also to the accent (′) marking such sounds; (*Med.*) attended with violent symptoms, and coming speedily to a crisis; (*Geom.*) less than a right angle. *n.* An acute accent. **acutely,** *adv.* **acuteness,** *n.*

-acy [L. *-ācia*, *-ātia*, Gr. *-ateia*], *suf.* Forming nouns of quality, state, condition, etc.; *e.g. fallacy* [L. *fallācia*], *infancy* [L. *infantia*], *magistracy* [L. *magistrātus*, Eng. suf. assimilated to prec. forms], *piracy* [Gr. *peirateia*].

ad (ăd) [*abbrev.* ADVERTISEMENT].

ad- [*ad*, to, at], *pref.* To, at, into; signifying motion towards, direction to, adherence, etc. *e.g. adduce, adhere, adjacent, admire.* (This prefix undergoes many alterations to assimilate it with the initial consonant of the root, examples of which will be found in their respective places.)

-ad [Gr. *-ad-*, nom. *-as*, gen. *-ados*], *suf.* Pertaining to (in collective numerals, feminine patronymics, titles of poems, names of botanical families); *e.g. monad, myriad, Iliad, naiad, liliad.*

adage (ăd′ ȧj) [F. *adage*, L. *adagium* (*ad-*, to, *agium*, a saying, from *aio*, I say)], *n.* A proverb; a pithy maxim handed down from old time.

adagio (ȧ da′ ji ō) [It. *ad agio*, at leisure], *adv.* (*Mus.*) Slowly, gracefully. *a.* Slow, graceful. *n.* A slow movement of a soft, tender, elegiac character. ***adagietto,*** *n.* A slow, graceful movement but somewhat quicker than adagio. ***adagissimo,*** *adv.* Very slowly.

Adam (ăd′ ȧm) [Heb. *ā-dām*, man], *n.* The name of the first man; the unregenerate state of man.

Adam's ale: Water. **Adam's apple:** The lime, the orange, or the shaddock, from the idea that it was the forbidden fruit; (*Anat.*) a protuberance on the forepart of the throat formed by the thyroid cartilage. **Adam's arms:** The spade. **adamic** (ȧ dăm′ ik), **adamical,** *a.* Pertaining to Adam, resembling Adam; naked. **adamically,** *adv.*

adamant (ăd′ ȧ mănt) [O.F. *adamaunt*, L. *adamas -antem*, Gr. *adamas* (*a-*, not, *damaō*, I tame)], *n.* A stone of impenetrable hardness; the loadstone, the diamond. *a.* Made of adamant, pertaining to adamant; hard, destitute or incapable of feeling. **adamantine** (ăd ȧ măn′ tin), ***adamantean,** *a.* Made of adamant; incapable of being broken.

Adamite (ăd′ ȧm īt) [ADAM], *a.* A descendant of Adam; one of a sect who professed to re-establish a state of innocence, and went naked. **adamitic, adamitical** (-mit′ i kȧl), *a.* Pertaining to the Adamites. **adamitism** (ăd′ ȧ mī tizm), *n.*

adapt (ȧ dăpt′) [F. *adapter*, L. *adaptāre* (*ad-*, to, *aptare*, from *aptus*, fit)], *v.t.* To fit to, to adjust to, to make suitable for, to remodel. **adaptable,** *a.* Capable of being adapted. **adaptability,** *n.* **adaptation** (ăd ȧp tā′ shŭn), *n.* The act of adapting; the state of being adapted; that which is adapted. **adaptedness,** *n.* **adapter,** *a.* One who adapts; (*Elec.*) an accessory for connecting a plug, etc., fitted with one size of terminals to a supply point fitted with terminals of another size. **adaptive,** *a.* Tending to adapt; suitable. **adaptively,** *adv.*

Adar (ā′ dȧr) [Heb. *ădār*], *n.* The sixth month of the Jewish civil, and the twelfth of the ecclesiastical year (*correspond. to* part of Feb. and March).

adaxial (ăd ăks′ i ȧl) [AD-, AXIS] *a.* (*Bot.*) Facing the stem.

add (ăd) [L. *addere* (*ad-*, to, *dare*, to put)], *v.t.* To set or put together; to join, to unite; to put into one total; to annex, to subjoin. *v.i.* To serve as an increment (with *to*); to perform the operation of addition. **adder** (1), An adding machine. **addible** (ăd′ ibl), *a.* Capable of being added. **addibility,** *n.* **additament** (ăd′ dit ȧ mĕnt) [L. *additāmentum* (*additus*, p.p. of *addere*)], *n.* Something added. **addition** (ȧ dish′ ŭn), *n.* The act of adding; the state of being added to; the thing added; the process of collecting two or more numbers or quantities into one sum; the title or designation given to a person beyond his name and surname; (*Her.*) anything added to a coat of arms as a mark of honour; (*Mus.*) a dot placed at the right side of a note to indicate that it is to be lengthened one half. **additional,** *a.* Added; supplementary. *n.* That which is added. **additionally,** *adv.* **additive** (ăd′ i tiv), *a.* That may be or is to be added. **additively,** *adv.*

addax (ăd′ ăks) [African]. A species of antelope, *Oryx nasomaculata.*

addendum (ȧ den′ dŭm) [L. *addendum*, ger. of *addere* (ADD)] *n.* (*pl.* **addenda**) A thing to be added, an addition; an appendix.

adder (1) [ADD].

adder (2) (ăd′ ėr) [A.-S. *nædre* (*n* has disappeared through mistaken division of *a naddre* as *an addre*)], *n.* The common viper, *Pelias berus*; applied, with epithet, to some of the foreign Viperidæ, as puff-adder, death-adder; *a serpent; *a dragon. **adder-bolt,** *n.* The dragon-fly. **adder's tongue,** *n.* The fern-genus *Ophioglossum.* **adderwort,** *n.* Bistort or snake-weed, *Polygonum bistorta.*

addict (1) (ȧ dikt′) [L. *addictus*, p.p. of *addicere* (*ad-*, to, *dicere*, to say)], *v.t.* To apply habitually, to habituate. *v.r.* To devote oneself to, to make oneself a slave to (a vice). **addicted,** *part.a.* Wholly devoted; given over to, prone. **addictedness. addiction,** *n.* The act of addicting or devoting; the state of being addicted or devoted; propensity, proclivity.

addict (2) (ăd′ ikt), *n.* One who is addicted to some habit, esp. the taking of drugs; a slave to a vice.

addition [ADD].

addle (ădl) [A.-S. *adela*, mire, filth], *a.* Putrid through having been deprived of vitality, as an egg; empty, idle, vain, muddled, confused. *n.* Foul and putrid water; the dry lees of wine. *v.t.* To make addle or addled; to confuse (mentally); to spoil. *v.i.* To grow putrid (as an egg). **addle-headed, addle-brained, addle-pated,** *a.* Terms applied to one whose brain seems muddled. **addle-plot,** *n.* A marplot. **addled,** *part.a.* Rendered or become putrid, as an egg; confused in one's wits, etc. **addlement,** *n.*

address (ȧ dres′) [F. *adresser*, late L. *addrictiare* (*ad-*, to, *drictum*, *directum*, DIRECT)], *v.t.* To direct an oral or written communication to; to accost or speak to; to write the address or direction on; to court or make suit to; to prepare (oneself) to, to apply (oneself) to. *v.i.* To present a formal address. *n.* The act of addressing oneself to a person or persons; a discourse; any speech or writing in which one person or body makes a communication to another person or body; tact, skill, adroitness; bearing in conversation; (*pl.*) courtship; the direction of a letter; the name of the place where one lives. **to address oneself to:** To speak to. **to pay one's addresses to:** To court. **addresser,** *n.* One who addresses; one who directs a communication. **addressee** (ăd dres sē′), *n.* One to whom a parcel or communication is addressed. **addressograph,** *n.* A machine for addressing envelopes, wrappers, etc.

adduce (ȧ dūs′) [L. *addūcere* (*ad*, to, *dūcere*, to lead)], *v.t.* To bring forward as a proof or illustration, to cite, to quote. **adducent,** *a.* (*Physiol.*) Bringing or drawing to a given point (used of the adductor muscles). **adducer,** *n.* **adducible,** *a.* Capable of being adduced. **adduction** (ȧ dŭk′ shŭn), *n.* The act of leading or drawing to or together, bringing forward, or citing. **adductive,** *a.* Tending to lead or draw to or together. **adductor,** *n.* (*Physiol.*) A muscle which brings one part of the body towards or in contact with another part.

-ade [F. *-ade* (cp. *-ada* in Sp. and Prov.), L. *-āta*, f. sing. p.p. of verbs in *-āre*], *suf.* Forms nouns from verbs and other words; *e.g.* *cannonade, ambuscade, brigade, lemonade, parade.*

adeem (ȧd ēm′) [L. *adimere*, to take away], *v.t.* (*Law*) To cancel a bequest.

adelphous (ȧ del′ fŭs) [Gr. *adelphos*, a brother], *a.* (*Bot.*) Having the stamens in groups or bundles.

ademption (ȧ demp′ shŭn) [L. *ademptiōnem*, n. of action, from *adimere* (*ad-*, to, *emere*, to take)], *n.* A taking away; (*Law*) the revocation of a grant.

aden-, adeni-, adeno- [Gr. *adēn*, an acorn, a gland], *comb. form.* Connected with a gland or glands; glandular; in medical terms, *e.g.* *adenitis, adenotomy.*

adenitis (ăd en ī′ tis), *n.* Inflamation of the lymphatic glands.

adenoid (ăd′ en oid), *a.* Having the form of a gland, glandular. *n.pl.* Adenoid tissue; a spongy growth at the back of the nose and throat, impeding respiration and speech.

adenoma (ăd en ō′ mȧ), *a.* A benign tumour formed of glandular tissue.

adenopathy (ăd en op′ ȧ thi), *n.* Disease of a gland or glands; a general affection attacking mainly the lymphatic glands.

adept (ȧ dept′) [L. *adeptus*, p.p. of *adipisci* (*ad-*, to, *apisci*, to attain)], *n.* One who was supposed to have obtained the elixir of life and the philosopher's stone; an occulist; one completely versed in any science or art. *a.* Thoroughly versed, well skilled. **adeption,** *n.*

adequate (ăd′ ē kwȧt) [L. *adæquātus*, p.p. of *adæquāre* (*ad-*, to, *æquāre*, to make equal, from *æquus*, equal)], *a.* Equal to, sufficient, proportionate, commensurate. **adequately,** *adv.* **adequateness,** *n.* **adequacy,** *n.* Adequateness, sufficiency.

adhere (ȧd hēr′) [L. *adhærēre* (*ad-*, to, *hærēre*, to stick)], *v.i.* To stick to; to remain firmly attached to; *to be coherent, consistent; to agree. **adherence** (ȧd hēr′ ėns) [F. *adhérence*, L. *adhærentia*, verbal n., from *adhærens -ntem*, pres.p. of *adhærēre*], *n.* The state or quality of adhering; firm attachment. **adherent,** *a.* Sticking to; tenaciously attached to. *n.* One who adheres to; a partisan, a follower.

adhesion (ăd hē′ zhŭn) [ADHERE], *n.* The act or state of sticking to (physically), attaching oneself to, or joining; (*Bot.*) the union of parts that are normally separate; (*Med.*) fusion of two surfaces, usually of the two opposing surfaces of a wound in healing. **adhesive,** *a.* Having the power of adhering; sticky, clinging. *n.* A substance used for sticking things together. **adhesiveness,** *n.* The power of sticking to; stickiness; (*Phrenol.*) propensity to form attachments. **adhesively,** *adv.*

adhibit (ȧd hib′ it) [L. *adhibit-*, stem in *adhibit -us*, p.p. of *adhibēre* (*ad-*, to, *habēre*, to hold)], *v.t.* To apply, to add, to append, to use, employ. **adhibition** (ăd hib ish′ ŭn), *n.* Application, employment, use.

adiabatic (ăd i ȧ băt′ ik) [Gr. *adiabatos* (*a-*, not, *dia*, through, *batos*, passable, from *baino*, I go); -IC], *a.* Impervious, esp. impervious to heat, without loss or gain of heat. **adiabatically,** *adv.* In an adiabatic manner.

Adiantum (ăd i ăn′ tŭm) [Gr. *adianton*], *n.* A genus of ferns, containing the maidenhair.

adiaphorism (ăd i ăf′ ȯr izm) [Gr. *adiaphoros*, not different (*a-*, not, *dia*, apart, *pherein*, to bear); -ISM], *n.* Indifference in religion or ethics, latitudinarianism. **Adiaphorist,** *n.* One who holds that dogmas or rites are matters of indifference; a moderate Lutheran; a latitudinarian. *a.* Pertaining to the Adiaphorists; theologically indifferent.

adieu (ȧ dū′) [F. *à*, to, *Dieu*, God], *int.* and *n.* (*pl.* **adieux**). God be with you; good-bye; farewell.

adipocere (ăd′ i pō sēr) [F. *adipocire* (L. *adeps -ipem*, fat, F. *cire*, L. *cera*, wax)], *n.* A greyish-white fatty or soapy substance, into which the flesh of dead bodies buried in moist places is converted. **adipocerous** (ăd i pos′ ėr ŭs), *a.* Of the nature of adipocere.

adipose (ăd′ i pōs) [L. *adeps -ipem*, fat], *a.* Pertaining to animal fat, fatty. *n.* Animal fat, esp. the fat on the kidneys. **adipescent,** *a.* Growing fat. **adipic** (ȧ dip′ ik), *a.* Derived from fat. **adipose fin:** The fatty dorsal fin in fishes, distinguishing the *Salmo* family. **adipose tissue:** The vesicular structure in which fat is deposited.

adit (ăd′ it) [L. *aditus*, approach, (*ad-*, to, *īre*, to go)], *n.* Approach, entrance, passage; a more or less horizontal entrance to a mine.

adjacent (ȧ jā′ sėnt) [L. *adjacentem*, pres.p. of *adjacēre* (*ad-*, to, at, *jacēre*, to lie)], *a.* Lying near to; situated contiguous to; neighbouring, bordering upon. **adjacently,** *adv.* **adjacency,** *n.* The state of lying adjacent or near to, that which lies near to; *(*pl.*) environs, precincts.

adjective (ă jėk tiv) [F. *adjectif -ve*, L. *adjectīvus*, *adjectus*, p.p. of *adjicere* (*ad-*, to, *jacere*, to throw); -IVE], *a.* Added to; dependent; forming an adjunct to a noun substantive. *n.* A part of speech joined to a substantive to define and limit its signification. **adjectival** (ă jėk tī′ vȧl), *a.* **adjectively** (ă jėk tiv li), *adv.*

adjoin (ȧ join′) [O.F. *ajoindre*, L. *adjungere* (*ad-*, to, *jungere*, to join)], *v.t.* To join or add, to unite; to be contiguous to. *v.i.* To be contiguous with. **adjoining,** *a.* Adjacent, contiguous to; neighbouring.

adjourn (ȧ jĕrn′) [O.F. *ajorner*, late L. *adjornāre*, appoint a day (*jurnus*, day, L. *diurnus*)], *v.t.* To put off or defer till a later period; to suspend a meeting; to postpone till a future meeting; to suspend proceedings so as to meet elsewhere, to change place of meeting. *v.i.* To cease business till a later period. **adjournment,** *n.* The act of adjourning; the time during which or to which business or a meeting (esp. of a public body) is postponed.

adjudge (ȧ jŭj′) [O.F. *ajūger*, L. *adjūdicāre*; see ADJUDICATE], *v.t.* To award by a judicial decision, to decide, pronounce, condemn. **adjudgment,** *n.* The act of judging; adjudging; the judgment or verdict given.

adjudicate (ȧ joo′ di kāt) [L. *adjūdicāre* (*ad-*, to, *jūdicāre*, to judge)], *v.t.* To judge, to determine, decide, pronounce sentence. *v.i.* To sit as a judge. **adjudication** (ȧ joo di kā′ shŭn), *n.* The act of adjudicating; the decision or judgment of a court. **adjudicator** (ȧ joo′ di kā tȯr), *n.*

adjunct (ăj′ ungkt) [L. *adjunctus*, p.p. of *adjungere* (*ad-*, to, *jungere*, to join)], *n.* Any thing joined to another without being an essential part of it; an attribute, qualifying addition; (*Gram.*) an extension of the subject or predicate; (*Logic*) a non-essential attribute; an associate. *a.* Added to, or conjoined with any person or thing. **adjunction** (ȧ jŭnk′ shŭn), *n.* A joining to; the act of joining; a thing joined. **adjunctive,** *a.* Joining, having the quality of joining. *n.* Anything joined to another. **adjunctively, adjunctly,** *adv.* By way of adjunct, in connection with.

adjure (ȧ joor′) [L. *adjūrāre*, to swear to (*ad-*, to, *jūrāre*, to swear); late L., to put to an oath], *v.t.* To charge upon oath, or upon pain of the divine displeasure; to entreat with great earnestness. **adjuration** (ă joo rā′ shŭn), *n.* The act of adjuring; an appeal under penalty of a curse; a solemn entreaty. **adjuratory** (ă joo rā′ tȯr i), *a.* Containing or characterized by an adjuration.

adjust (ȧ jŭst′) [O.F. *ajuster*, late L. *adjuxtāre*, bring together (*ad-*, to, *juxta*, near)], *v.t.* To put together, to order, arrange; to fit, adapt to, to make correspondent, to accommodate, to settle. **adjustable,** *a.* **adjuster,** *n.* One who or that which adjusts. **average adjuster,** *n.* An accountant who deals with claims for losses at sea. **adjustment,** *n.* The act of adjusting; the state of being adjusted; settlement, arrangement; (*Comm.*) a settlement of claims, liabilities, etc.

adjutage (ȧ joo′ tȧj), **ajutage** (ăj′ u tȧj) [F. *ajutage* (*ajouter*, to join on; see ADJUST)], *n.* A tube fitted as mouthpiece to a fountain or the pipe from a vessel.

adjutant (ăj′ ū tȧnt) [L. *adjutans*, pres.p. of *adjūtāre*, freq. of *adjūvāre*, see below], *n.* An assistant; (*Mil.*) an officer in each regiment who assists the commanding officer in matters of business, duty, and discipline. **adjutancy,** *n.* Office of adjutant. **adjutant bird,** *n.* (*Zool.*) A large wading bird of the stork family, native of India, where it is protected as a scavenger.

adjuvant (ăj′ u vȧnt) [L. *adjūvāre* (*ad-*, to, *jūvāre*, to help); -ANT], *a.* Helping. *n.* An assistant, helper, auxiliary; (*Med.*) an auxiliary ingredient in a prescription.

ad libitum, ad lib. (ăd lib′ it ŭm) [L.], *adv.* At pleasure, to any extent; (*Mus.*) at will to change time or omit passages.

admass (ăd′ măs) [ADVERTISEMENT, MASS], *n.* The mass viewers and listeners to whom television and radio advertising is directed.

admeasure (ȧd mezh′ ŭr) [O.F. *amesurer*, late L. *admensūrāre*], *v.t.* To measure out, to apportion. **admeasurement,** *n.* The act of measuring; the dimensions ascertained; apportionment of shares.

adminicle (ȧd min′ ikl) [L. *adminiculum*, a prop, (*manus*, hand)], *n.* An aid, support, auxiliary evidence. **adminicular** (ăd min ik′ ū lȧr), *a.* Auxiliary, corroborative.

administer (ȧd min′ is tėr) [O.F. *aministrer*, L. *administrāre*], *v.t.* To manage or conduct as chief agent; to superintend the execution of, as laws; to tender, as an oath; to dispense, to supply; (*Law*) to manage and dispose of the estate of a deceased person; (*Med.*) to give as medicine. *v.i.* To minister to; to act as administrator. **administrable,** *a.* **administration** (ȧd min is trā′ shŭn), *n.* The act of administering; the executive functions of government; the executive; (*Law*) the management and distribution of the estate of a person deceased, esp. of an intestate; (*Am.*) government. **administrative** (ȧd min′ is trȧ tiv), *a.* Pertaining to administration; executive. **administratively,** *adv.* In an administrative manner; with regard to administration. **administrator,** *n.* One who administers, manages, dispenses, or furnishes; (*Law*) one who administers the estate of an intestate. **administratorship** (ȧd min′-), *n.* **administratrix,** *n.* A female administrator. **administrant,** *a.* and *n.*

admirable (ăd′ mir ȧbl) [ADMIRE], *a.* Worthy of admiration; excellent, highly satisfactory. **Admirable Crichton** (krī′ tȯn), *n.* One who distinguishes himself in many spheres. Taken from James Crichton (1560–93), a Scottish adventurer famous for his accomplishments and attainments. **admirability,** *n.* Admirableness. **admirableness,** *n.* **admirably,** *adv.*

admiral (ăd′ mir ȧl) [O.F. *amiral*, Arab. *amir*, a prince (Latinized as *amīrālis*, and through confusion with *admīrāri*, converted into *admirālis*)], *n.* The commander of a fleet or a division of a fleet. This rank in England has four grades: Admiral of the Fleet, Admiral, Vice-Admiral, and Rear-Admiral; *the ship of an admiral; a flag-ship; the commander of a fishing-fleet; *Vanessa atalanta*, the red, and *Limenitis sibylla*, the white admiral butterfly. ***Lord High Admiral:** An officer who formerly had charge of naval affairs. ***admiral-ship,** *n.* A flag-ship, the largest and most important ship of a fleet. **admiralship,** *n.* The office or position of an admiral.

admiralty (ăd′ mi rȧl ti), *n.* The office of admiral. **The Admiralty,** *n.* The Government department that deals with the British navy; the Lords Commissioners who administer naval affairs in Great Britain; the building where they transact business. **Admiralty Court,** *n.* The chief court for the trial of maritime causes.

admire (ȧd mīr′) [F. *admirer*, L. *admīrāri* (*ad-*, at, *mīrāri*, to wonder)], *v.t.* *To wonder at; to regard with wonder, mingled with pleasing emotions; to look with pleasure on; to have a high opinion of. *v.i.* To feel admiration, to wonder, to be astonished. **admirer,** *n.* One who feels admiration; one who has a high opinion of; a suitor, lover. **admiringly,** *adv.* **admiration** (ăd mi rā′ shŭn), *n.* *Wonder; wonder excited by anything pleasing or excellent; pleased contemplation.

admissible, admission, etc. [ADMIT].

admit (ȧd mit′) [O.F. *amettre*, L. *admittere* (*ad-*, to, *mittere*, to send)], *v.t.* (*past & p.p.* **admitted**). To let in; to permit to enter a place, an office, or the mind; to accept as valid; to concede, to acknowledge; (*Am.*) to call to the Bar. **admittance,** *n.* The act of admittance; entrance given or permitted. **admissible** (ȧd mis′ ibl) [late L. *admissibilis*, from *admissus*, p.p. of *admittere*], **admittable,** *a.* Fit to be considered as an opinion or as evidence; (*Law*) allowable as evidence; qualified for entrance to an office. **admissibility** (ăd mis i bil′ i ti), *n.* The quality of being admissible. **admissibly,** *adv.* **admission** (ăd mish′ ŭn) [L. *admissio*, from *admissus*; -ION], *n.* The act of admitting; the state of being admitted; permission to enter; concession in argument; acknowledgment. **admissive,** *a.* Tending to admit, implying admission. **admittedly,** *adv.*

admix (ȧd miks′) [L. *ad-*, to, MIX (formed like L. *admiscere*, p.p. *admixtus*)], *v.t.* and *i.* To mix something with, to mingle with. **admixture** (ȧd miks′ tūr) [-URE], *n.* The act of mixing; an alloy; a foreign element.

admonish (ȧd mon′ ish) [O.F. *amonester*, late L. *admonestāre*, L. *admonēre* (*ad-*, to, *monēre*, to advise)], *v.t.* *To put in mind, exhort; to reprove gently; to warn, caution; to apprise, instruct. **admonisher,** *n.* **admonishment,** *n.* The act of admonishing; an admonition. **admonition** (ăd mŏn ish′ ŭn), *n.* Gentle reproof; friendly caution; counsel. **admonitive** (ȧd mon′ i tiv), *a.* Implying admonition. **admonitively,** *adv.* **admonitor,** *n.* **admonitory,** *a.*

adnate (ăd′ nāt) [L. *adnātus* (*agnātus*) (*ad-*, to, *nātus*, *gnātus*, born)], *a.* (*Bot.* and *Physiol.*) Growing or grown to another on its whole surface; attached to the stem. **adnation,** *n.* (*Bot.*) Adhesion to each other of different whorls of the inflorescence. **adnascence,** *n.* **adnascent,** *a.*

adnominal (ăd nom′ in ȧl) [L. *adnōmen* (var. of *agnōmen*); -AL], *a.* Pertaining to an adnoun; adjectival; attached to a noun. **adnoun** (ăd′ noun) [L. *ad-*, to, NOUN (like *adverb*)], *n.* Added to a noun; an adjective; an adjective used substantively.

ado (ȧ doo′) [Scand. *at*, to, DO], *n.* Doing, business, activity; trouble, difficulty, fuss, bustle.

-ado [Sp. and Port. *-ado*, L. *-ātus*, in p.p. of verbs in *āre*], *suf.* Forms nouns, *e.g.* *desperado*, *renegado*, *tornado* (*bravado*, *gambado*, *strappado*, and some other terms, are malformations of words in *-ade*).

adobe (a dō′ bė, ȧ dōb′) [Sp. *adobe*, from *adobar*, to daub, plaster, late L. *adobāre*], *n.* A sun-dried brick.

adolescent (ăd ȯ les′ ėnt) [F. *adolescent*, L. *adolēscens -ntem*, pres.p. of *adolēscere*, to grow up]. *a.* Growing up; advancing to maturity. *n.* A person in the age of adolescence. **adolescence, adolescency** (ăd ȯ les′ ėn si) [F. *adolescence*, L. *adolescentia*], *n.* The growing youth; the period between childhood and adulthood.

Adonai (ȧ dō′ nī, *or* -nā ī) [Heb. *ădōnāi*, my lords; see ADONIS], *n.* The Lord.

Adonis (ȧ dō′ nis) [Gr., name of a youth beloved by Venus for his beauty, Phœn. *adōn*, lord, title of a divinity], *n.* A beau, a dandy; (*Bot.*) a genus of Ranunculaceæ, popularly called pheasant's eye; (*Ent.*) a butterfly, *Polyommatus adonis*, called also mazarine, or Clifton blue. **adonize** (ăd′ ȯ nīz), *v.t.* To adorn, to dandify. *v.i.* To adorn oneself. **adonic** (ȧ don′ ik), *a.* Pertaining to Adonis; applied to a metre composed of a dactyl and spondee (– ∪ ∪ | – –).

adopt (ȧ dopt′) [F. *adopter*, L. *adoptāre* (*ad-*, to, *optāre*, to choose)], *v.t.* To take (any one) into any relationship (as child, heir, citizen, candidate, etc.); to take (a child) as one's own; to embrace, to espouse (as a principle, cause, etc.); to choose for one's own. **adopted,** *part.a.* Taken as one's own, accepted into some intimate relation such as that of one's child. ***adoptedly,** *adv.* (*Shak.*) By adoption. **adopter,** *n.* One who or that which adopts. **adoption,** *n.* The act of adopting. **adoptional,** *a.* Pertaining to adoption. **adoptionism,** *n.* The tenets of the Adoptionists. **Adoptionist,** *n.* A member of a Christian sect (of the 8th cent.) which held that Christ was the Son of God by adoption only. **adoptive,** *a.* Due to or by reason of adoption; fitted to adopt. **adoptively,** *adv.* ***adoptious,** *a.*

adorable (ȧ dôr′ ȧbl) [as foll.], *a.* Worthy of divine honours; worthy of the utmost love and respect; charming, delightful, fascinating. **adorably,** *adv.* In a manner worthy of adoration; delightfully. **adorableness,** *n.*

adore (ȧ dôr′) [O.F. *aörer*, *aourer* (F. *adorer*), L. *adōrāre* (*ad-*, to, *ōrāre*, to pray, from *os oris*, the mouth)], *v.t.* To pay divine honours to; to regard with the utmost respect and affection. *v.i.* To offer worship. **adorer,** *n.* One who adores, a worshipper, a votary, an admirer, a lover. **adoringly,** *adv.* **adoration** (ăd ôr ā′ shŭn), *n.* Divine worship; homage to one high in station or esteem.

adorn (ȧ dôrn′) [O.F. *aörner* (F. *adorner*), L. *adornāre* (*ad-*, to, *ornāre*, to deck)], *v.t.* To decorate, ornament, embellish; to add attractiveness to. **n.* Adornment. **adorned,** *part.a.* Ornamented, decorated, beautified, decked out. **adorner,** *n.* **adorning,** *a.* Ornamental, embellishing. *n.* Adornment. **adorningly,** *adv.* **adornment,** *n.* An adorning, decoration, ornament, embellishment.

adown (ȧ doun′) [A.-S. *of-dune*, off the down or hill], *adv.* Down from a higher to a lower place. *prep.* Upon or along in a descending direction.

adrenal (ăd rē′ nȧl) [L. *ad-*, to; *renes*, kidneys], *a.* (*Anat.*) Near the kidneys.

adrenalin (ȧd ren′ ȧ lin), *n.* A hormone secreted by the adrenal glands; a crystalline substance derived from the adrenal glands of cattle and sheep, used for checking bleeding.

adrift (ȧ drift′), *adv.* In a drifting condition; at the mercy of the wind and waves; wandering, at a loss.

adroit (ȧ droit′) [F. *à*, to, *droit*, right, late L. *drictum* (L. *directum*); see DIRECT], *a.* Dexterous, active, clever, ready in mental or bodily resource. **adroitly,** *adv.* **adroitness,** *n.*

adry (ȧ drī′), *adv.* and *pred.a.* Dry, athirst.

adscititious (ăd sit ish′ ŭs) [L. *adscitus* (*as-cītus*), p.p. of *adscīscere*, adopted, received from others (*ad-*, to, *scīt-*, part. stem of *scīscere*, to acknowledge, freq. of *scīre*, to know)], *a.* Assumed, adopted, derived from without, supplemental. **adscititiously,** *adv.*

adscript (ăd′ skript) [L. *adscriptus*, p.p. of *adscrībere* (*ad-*, to, *scrībere*, to write)], *a.* Written after (opposed to subscript); attached to the soil (said of feudal serfs). *n.* One held to service, a serf. **adscription** (ȧd skrip′ shŭn), *n.* Ascription; attachment, as a feudal inferior [ASCRIPTION].

adsorb (ăd sôrb′) [AD-, SORB], *v.t.i.* (*Chem.*) To concentrate and adhere to the surface of a solid. **adsorbent,** *n.* A solid substance that adsorbs gases, vapours or liquids that contact it. **adsorption,** *n.* Concentration of a substance on a surface.

adulate (ăd′ ū lāt) [L. *adūlātus*, p.p. of *adūlārī*, to flatter], *v.t.* To fawn upon, to flatter servilely. **adulation,** *n.* The act of fawning upon or flattering servilely; servile flattery. **adulator,** *n.* **adulatory,** *a.*

Adullamite (ă dŭl′ ȧm īt) [Heb. *Adullam*, the cave mentioned in 1 Sam. xxii, 1, 2], *n.* A nickname applied to certain M.P.s who seceded from the Liberal party in 1866, from dissatisfaction with Mr. Gladstone's Reform Bill. **adullamy,** *n.* Defection, ratting.

adult (ȧ dŭlt′) [L. *adultus*, p.p. of *adolescere*, to grow up (*ad-*, to, *olescere*, freq. of *olēre*, to grow)], *a.* Grown to maturity; grown up, full-grown. *n.* One grown to maturity. **adulthood, adultness,** *n.*

adulterate (1) (ȧ dŭl′ tėr āt) [L. *adulterātus*, p.p. of *adulterāre*, commit adultery, corrupt (*ad-*, to, *alterāre*, to change, from *alter*, other), cp. *adulter*, an adulterer, a debaser of the coinage], *v.t.* To corrupt or debase anything by mixing with it a baser substance. *a.* (-ȧt). Adulterated; adulterous, spurious, debased by admixture. **adulterant,** *a.* and *n.* Adulterating, that which adulterates or is used to adulterate. **adulterated,** *a.* **adulterately,** *adv.* **adulterateness,** *n.* **adulteration,** *n.* The act or result of adulterating; the state of being adulterated; an adulterated substance. **adulterator,** *n.* One who adulterates. **adulterine** (1), *a.* Spurious, counterfeit, illegal, unlicensed.

adultery (ȧ dŭl′ tėr i) [L. *adultĕrium* (superseding older *avoutrie*, from O.F. *avouterie*, L. *adulter*); see ADULTERATE], *n.* Violation of the marriage-bed; illicit sexual intercourse on the part of a married person. **adulterate** (2), *a.* Born of an adulterous union. **adulterer,** *n.* A man guilty of adultery. **adulteress,** *n.* A woman guilty of adultery. **adulterine** (2), *a.* Born of adultery; relating to adultery. *n.* A child born of adultery. **adulterous,** *a.* Pertaining to or guilty of adultery. **adulterously,** *adv.* ***adulterize,** *v.*

adumbrate (ȧ dŭm′-, ăd′ ŭm brāt) [L. *adumbrāre*, to cast a shadow (*ad-*, to, *umbrāre*, to shadow, from *umbra*, shadow)], *v.t.* To shadow forth, to indicate faintly as if by a shadow; to typify, foreshadow; to overshadow. **adumbration** (ăd ŭm brā′ shŭn), *n.* The act of shadowing forth; a faint or imperfect representation. **adumbrative** (ȧ dŭm′-, ăd′ ŭm brȧ tiv), *a.* Faintly representing. **adumbrant,** *a.*

adust (ȧ dŭst′) [L. *adūstus*, p.p. of *adūrere*, to burn (*ad-*, to, *ūrere*, burn)], *a.* Burnt, scorched, parched, sunburnt; gloomy in features or temperament.

advance (ȧd vans′) [O.F. *avancer*, pop. L. *abanteāre*, from *abante* (*ab-*, away, *ante*, before)], *v.t.* To bring or move forward or upward; *to extol; *to influence; *to impel; to promote; to supply before or on credit; to raise. *v.i.* To move forward, to progress, to rise. *n.* The act or process of moving forward; promotion, improvement; a rise (in price); the first step, movement towards; payment beforehand, a loan. *a.* Being before in time or place; beforehand. **in advance:** Beforehand; in front. **advanced,** *a.* In the front rank; far on; before one's age; extreme (opinions). **advance(d) guard,** *n.* (*Mil.*) A detachment which precedes the advance of the main body of an army. **advance note,** *n.* A draft for payment of one month's wages given to a member of a ship's crew when signing on. **advancer,** *n.* One who advances; a promoter; a moneylender.

advancement (ȧd vans′ mėnt), *n.* The act of advancing; the state of being advanced; preferment; furtherance, improvement; (*Law*) the application beforehand of property to which children are prospectively entitled; the property so applied.

advantage (ȧd van′ tȧj) [F. *avantage*], *n.* Favourable condition or circumstance; gain, profit, superiority of any kind; a consideration super-added to one going before, and giving it increased force; the victory resulting from such aids; (*Tennis*) the next point or game won after deuce points or games. *v.t.* To benefit; to further; promote the interests of. ***advantaged,** *a.* (*Shak.*) Placed at advantage. **advantageous** (ăd vȧn tā′ jŭs), *a.* Conferring advantage; profitable, beneficial. **advantageously,** *adv.* **advantageousness,** *n.*

advent (ăd′ vėnt) [O.F. *advent*, *auvent*, L. *adventus*, arrival (*ad-*, to, *venire*, to come)], *n.* The Incarnation of Christ; the Second Coming; the season including the four Sundays before Christmas; any important arrival; a coming. **Adventist,** *n.* Seventh Day Adventist [SEVEN].

adventitious (ăd vėn tish′ ŭs) [L. *adventicius*, coming from abroad], *a.* Not properly pertaining to; foreign to; accidental, casual; (*Law*) coming otherwise than by direct succession. **adventitiously,** *adv.* **adventitiousness,** *n.*

adventure (ȧd ven′ chŭr) [O.F. *aventure*, L. *adventūra*, fut.p. of *advenīre*; see ADVENT], *n.* Hazard, risk; an enterprise in which hazard or risk is incurred; any novel or unexpected event; a speculation. *v.t.* To risk, to hazard, to put in danger. *v.i.* To venture; to dare. **adventurer,** *n.* One who seeks adventures; one who seeks to gain social position by false pretences. **adventuresome,** *a.* Adventurous. **adventuresomeness,** *n.* **adventuress,** *n.* A female adventurer, a woman who seeks to gain social position by false pretences. **adventurous,** *a.* Fond of adventure; venturesome, daring, rash; involving risk; perilous, hazardous. **adventurously,** *adv.* **adventurousness,** *n.*

adverb (ăd′ vĕrb) [F. *adverbe*, L. *adverbium* (*ad-*, to, *verbum*, word)], *n.* A word or phrase qualifying a verb, an adjective, or another adverb. **adverbial** (ȧd vĕr′ bi ȧl), *a.* **adverbially,** *adv.*

adversary (ăd′ vėr sȧr i) [O.F. *aversier*, L. *adversarius*; see ADVERSE], *n.* An opponent, an enemy, a foe. *a.* (*Law*) Opposed, hostile. **adversarious,** *a.* **adversative,** *a.* Denoting opposition or antithesis. *n.* A word or proposition expressing opposition.

adverse (ăd′ vĕrs) [O.F. *avers*, *advers*, L. *adversus*, p.p. of *advertere* (*ad-*, towards, *vertere*, to turn)], *a.* Acting in a contrary direction; hostile, inimical, unpropitious; opposite in position. **adversely,** *adv.* **adverseness,** *n.* **adversifoliate** (-fō′ li ȧt), *a.* Having opposite leaves. **adversity** (ȧd vĕr′ si ti), *n.* Adverse circumstances, misfortune, calamity, trouble.

advert (ȧd vĕrt′) [F. *avertir*, late L. *advertēre*, L. *advertĕre* (*ad-*, to, *vertĕre*, to turn)], *v.t.* To attend to, to turn attention to, refer to. *v.i.* To take heed, pay heed. **advertence, advertency,** *n.* Attention, notice, regard. **advertent,** *a.* Attentive, heedful. **advertently,** *adv.*

advertise (ăd′ vėr tīz) [F. *avertiss-*, stem of *avertir*, *avertissement*, L. *advertir*; see ADVERT], *v.t.* To inform; to give public notice of; to make publicly known. *v.i.* To give public notice.

advertisement (ȧd vĕr′ tiz mėnt), *n.* A public notice; a paid announcement by journal, radio, television, etc. **advertiser** (ăd′ vėr tī zėr), *n.* One who or a journal which advertises. **advertising,** *n.* Publicity, advertisement. **advertising agent,** *n.* One who makes it his business to secure publicity. **advertising medium,** *n.* Organ of publicity, *e.g.* newspaper street hoarding, television, etc.

advice (ȧd vīs′) [O.F. *avis*, L. *ad-*, to, *visum*, seen (*vidēre*, to see)], *n.* Counsel, opinion as to course of action, esp. from a lawyer or medical man; intelligence, information; formal or official notice; (*Comm.*) information or notice (*usually in pl.*).

advise (ȧd vīz′) [O.F. *aviser*, late L. *advisāre*; see ADVICE], *v.t.* To counsel; to communicate intelligence to; to inform, to notify. *v.i.* To consult, to deliberate, to reflect. **advised,** *a.* Acting with deliberation; well considered, deliberate. **advisedly** (ȧd vī′ zėd li), *adv.* With mature deliberation. ***advisedness,** *n.* **advisable,** *a.* Capable of being advised; right, proper, befitting, expedient. **advisability,** *n.* **advisably,** *adv.* **advisableness,** *n.* ***advisement,** *n.* Consideration, deliberation. **adviser,** *n.* One who advises; (*Am.*) a superviser of studies. **advisership,** *n.* **advising,** *n.* Advice, counsel. **advisory,** *a.* Having power to advise; containing advice.

advocate (ăd′ vȯ kȧt) [L. *advocātus*, p.p. (used as n.) of *advocāre* (*ad-*, to, *vocāre*, to call)], *n.* One who defends or promotes a cause; (*Law*) one who pleads a cause in a civil or criminal court; an intercessor. *v.t.* (ăd′ vȯ kāt). To plead in favour of, recommend. **Devil's advocate:** A person appointed to oppose claims to canonization; one who argues against his own convictions. **Faculty of Advocates:** The Scottish bar. **Judge Advocate:** The prosecuting officer before a court-martial. **Lord Advocate:** The principal Crown lawyer in Scotland. **advocacy,** *n.* A pleading for; judicial pleading; office of advocate; support. **advocateship,** *n.* The office of an advocate or intercessor; advocacy. **advocatory** (ăd vȯ kā′ tȯr i), *a.* Pertaining to advocacy.

***advouter,** etc. [*obs.* form of ADULTERER].

advowee (ăd vou′ ē) [O.F. *avoué*, L. *advocātus*], *n.* A person possessed of an advowson; the patron of an ecclesiastical benefice.

advowson (ȧd vou′ zȯn) [O.F. *avoson*, L. *advocatiōnem* (ADVOCATE, -ION)], *n.* (*Eccles.*) The right of presentation to a vacant benefice.

adynamia (ā di năm′ i a) [Gr. *adunamia* (*a-*, not, *dunamis*, power)], *n.* Lack of power, nervous debility, physical prostration. **adynamic** (ā di năm′ ik), *a.* Pertaining to adynamia; weak, asthenic; (*Phys.*) without force.

adytum (ă′ di tŭm) [L. *adytum*, Gr. *aduton* (*a-*, not, *dutos*, verb.a. from *duein*, to enter)], *n.* (*pl.* **adyta**). A shrine; the innermost and most sacred part of a temple; an inner chamber.

adze (ădz) [A.-S. *adesa*], *n.* A cutting tool with an arched blade at right angles to the handle. *v.t.* To shape by means of an adze.

ae [Sc. form of A].

-æ, -ae [L.], *suf.* Forming plural of unnaturalized L. words, *e.g. laminæ, Belgæ, Rosaceæ, Homeridæ.*

ædile (ē′ dīl) [L. *ædīlis* (*ædes*, a building), -ILE], *n.* A magistrate in ancient Rome who had charge of public and private buildings; hence, a municipal officer. **ædileship,** *n.*

ægis (ē′ jis) [L. *ægis*, Gr. *aigis*], *n.* A shield (esp. that of Minerva); protection, a protective influence.

ægrotat (ē grō′ tăt) [L. *ægrotat*, he is sick (*æger*, sick)], *n.* A note certifying that a student is sick.

Æneid (ē′ nē id) [L. *Æneïda*, acc. of *Æneïs*, Gr. a., pertaining to *Æneas*], *n.* The great epic poem of Virgil which has Æneas for its hero.

Æolian (ē ō′ li ȧn) [L. *Æolius*, *a.* from *Æolis* (Gr. *Aiolis*), or *Æolus* (Gr. *Aiolos*), -AN], *a.* Of or belonging to Æolia. *a.* Pertaining to Æolus (god of the winds); aerial; formed by the action of the wind. **Æolian harp,** *n.* A stringed instrument played by a current of air. **Æolian mode,** *n.* (*Mus.*) The ninth of the church modes.

Æolic (ē ol′ ik) [Gr. *aiolikos* (*a.* from *Æolis*)], *a.* Of or belonging to Æolia. **Æolic dialect,** *n.* One of the three great dialects of the Greek language.

æolipyle, -pile (ē′ ȯ li pil, *or* ē ol′ i pil) [F. *æolipyle*, L. *Æoli pulæ*, Gr. *Aiolou pulai*, gates of Æolus], *n.* Apparatus for demonstrating the force of steam generated in a closed chamber and escaping through a small aperture.

æolotropy (ē ȯ lot′ rȯ pi) [Gr. *aiolos*, changeful, *tropia*, turning], *n.* Change of physical qualities consequent on change of position, as of the refracting properties of Iceland spar.

æon (ē′ ȯn) [L. *æon*, Gr. *aiōn*], *n.* An age of the universe; a cosmic cycle; a period of immense duration; an age personified; an emanation from or phase of the Deity. **æonian** (ē ō′ ni ȧn), *a.* Eternal, everlasting.

Æpyornis (ē pi ôr′ nis) [Gr. *aipus*, tall, *ornis*, bird], *n.* A genus of gigantic fossil birds much larger than the ostrich, found in Madagascar.

aerate (âr′ āt), *v.t.* To subject to the action of atmospheric air; to charge with carbonic acid gas; to oxygenate, to arterialize. **aerated,** *part.a.* Exposed to the action of the air, charged with air; charged with carbonic acid gas; effervescent. **aeration** (âr′ ā′ shŭn), *n.* The act of aerating. **aerator,** *n.* **aeriferous,** *a.* Bearing or carrying air.

aerial (âr′ i ȧl) [L. *aërius*, Gr. *aerios* (*āer*, air), -AL], *a.* Belonging to the air; resembling, produced by, or inhabiting the air; airy, thin, gaseous; atmospheric; high, elevated; imaginary, immaterial, refined; (*Radio.*) a collector or radiator of electromagnetic waves for radio, television, etc. **aerial-perspective,** *n.* The representation of distance and space on a plane surface. **aerial railway,** *n.* A wire or cable stretched from point to point across rivers, valleys, etc., for transporting loads. **aerial photograph:** A photograph made from an aeroplane for military or surveying purposes. **aerial surveying:** A method of surveying by the use of aerial photographs. **aerial torpedo,** *n.* A large, winged bomb for aircraft use. **aerially,** *adv.* **aeriality** (âr′ i ăl′ i ti), *n.* Airiness, unsubstantiality. **aeriform,** *a.* Of the form or nature of air; gaseous.

aerie, aery (ā′ ėr i), **eyrie, eyry** (ī′ ri) [med. L. *aeria*, F. *aire* (from L. *ārea*, a spot of level ground, or *ātrium*, an open hall)], *n.* The nest of any bird of prey, esp. of an eagle; the young of a bird of prey; a human dwelling or retreat perched on a rock; (*Shak.*) a family of children of high birth.

aero- [*aër*, *aeros*, the air], *comb. form.* Pertaining to the air or atmosphere; aerial, atmospheric; *e.g. aeroplane, aerodynamics, aeronaut.*

aerobatics (âr ō băt′ iks), *n.pl.* Aerial acrobatics; stunting in an aeroplane.

aerobiology (âr ō bī ol′ ȯ ji), *n.* The study of airborn micro-organisms.

aerobioscope (âr ō bī′ ō skōp), *n.* A mechanism for determining the number of forms of micro-organisms in a given volume of air.

aerocamera (âr ō kăm′ ėr ȧ), *n.* A special form of camera used vertically for photographing the ground from an aeroplane.

aerodensimeter (âr ō den sim′ i tėr), *n.* A pressure gauge for gases.

aerodrome (âr′ ȯ drōm) [AERO-, Gr. *dromos*, race, race-course], *n.* An area, with any buildings attached, for the operation of aircraft; an air-station.

aerodynamics (âr ō dī năm′ iks) [pref. AERO-, DYNAMICS], *n.* The science which treats of the force exerted by gases in motion.

aerodyne (âr′ ō dīn), *n.* A generic term for heavier-than-air aircraft.

aerofoil (âr′ ō foil), *n.* A wing-like structure constructed to obtain reaction on its surfaces from the air; a plane or flying surface of an aeroplane.

aerogram (âr′ ō grăm), *n.* A radiogram, a wireless message.

aerograph (âr′ ō grăf), *n.* Protected trade name of an instrument for spraying paint.

aerography (âr og′ rȧ fi), *n.* The description of the properties etc. of the air.

aerolite (âr ȯ līt), **aerolith** [pref. AERO-, Gr. *lithos*, a stone], *n.* A stone which falls through the air to the earth; a meteoric stone. **aerolitic,** *a.*

aerology (âr ol′ ȯ ji), *n.* The department of science that deals with the atmosphere.

***aeromancy** (âr ō măn′ si) [pref. AERO-, MANCY], *n.* Divination by means of aerial phenomena; forecasting the weather.

aerometer (âr om′ ė tėr), *n.* An instrument for measuring the weight and density of air and gases.

aeronaut (âr′ ȯ nawt) [pref. AERO-, Gr. *nautēs*, a sailor], *n.* One concerned with the navigation of balloons or airships. **aeronautic, -al,** *a.* Pertaining to aerial navigation. **aeronautics** [L. *aeronautica*, pl. neut. a., Gr. *nautikos*, pertaining to navigation], *n.* The science or art which treats of aerial navigation.

aerophyte (âr ȯ fīt), *n.* A plant which grows entirely in the air, as distinguished from one growing on the ground.

aeroplane (âr′ ȯ plān), (*Am.*) **airplane** (âr′ plān), *n.* A mechanically-driven heavier-than-air flying-machine with fixed wings as lifting surfaces.

aerosol (âr′ ō sol), *n.* A suspension of fine particles in air or gas, *e.g.* smoke or mist.

aerostat (âr ȯ stăt) [F. *aérostat* (AERO-, Gr. *statos*, verb. a., standing)], *n.* An aircraft supported in the air statically, i.e. lighter-than-air. **aerostatic** (âr ȯ stăt′ ik) [F. *aérostatique* (AERO-, Gr. *statikos*, causing to stand)], *a.* Of or pertaining to aerostatics; pneumatic; aeronautic. **aerostatics,** *n.* The science which treats of the equilibrium and pressure of air and gases; aeronautics.

aerostation (âr ō stā′ shůn), *n.* Aerial navigation; aeronautics.

aerotherapy (âr ō ther′ ȧ pi), *n.* (*Med.*) Treatment of disease by fresh or suitably medicated air.

æruginous (ē roo′ jin ůs) [L. *ærūginōsus*, rusty (*ærūgo -inis*, verdigris, from *æs æris*, copper)], *a.* Of the nature of or resembling verdigris, copper rust.

aery (âr i) [L. *āertus* (*āer*, the air)], *a.* (*Milton*) Aerial, ethereal, unsubstantial, visionary.

Æsculapius (ēs kū lā′ pi ůs) [L.], *n.* The Greek god of medicine; (*fig.*) a physician. **Æsculapian,** *a.* Of or belonging to Æsculapius; medicinal.

aesculin (ēs′ kū lin) [L. *æsculus*, the Italian oak], *n.* A kind of glucoside found in the bark of the horse chestnut (*Æsculus hippocastanum*).

æsthete (ēs′ thēt) [Gr. *aisthētes*, one who perceives]. *n.* One who professes a special appreciation of the beautiful, and endeavours to carry his ideas into practice. **æsthetic** (ēs thet′ ik), **æsthetical,** *a.* Pertaining to æsthetics; appreciating the beautiful in nature and art; in accord with the laws of the beautiful, or with principles of taste. **æsthetically,** *adv.* **æstheticism** (ēs thet′ is izm), *n.* The quality of being æsthetic; devotion to the study of the beautiful. **æsthetics** (ēs thet′ iks), *n.* The theory or philosophy of the perception of the beautiful.

æstho-physiology (ēs thȯ fiz i ol′ ȯ ji) [Gr. *aisth-* (stem of *aisthanomai*, I perceive), PHYSIOLOGY], *n.* The science dealing with the physical organs of sensation. **æsthesiometer** (ēs thē si om′ ėt ėr), *n.* An instrument for testing the sensibility of the skin.

æstival, estival (es′ ti vȧl, ēs tī′ vȧl) [L. *æstīvālis*, from *æstīvus* (*æstus*, heat)], *a.* Of or belonging to the summer; produced in the summer. **æstivate** (ēs′ ti vāt or ēs′ ti vāt) [L. *æstivāre*, -ATE], *v.i.* To remain in a place during the summer; (*Zool.*) to fall into a summer sleep or torpor. **æstivation,** *n.* (*Bot.*) The internal arrangement of a flower-bed, prefloration; (*Zool.*) the act of remaining torpid in the summer.

æther, etc. [ETHER, etc.].

æthrioscope (āth′ rē ȯ skōp) [Gr. *aithrios*, clear, -SCOPE], *n.* An instrument for measuring radiation towards a clear sky, and for indicating the presence of invisible aqueous vapour in the atmosphere.

ætiology (ē ti ol′ ȯ ji) [L. *ætiologia*, Gr. *aitiologia* (*aitia*, a cause, -LOGY)], *n.* An account of the cause of anything, assignment of a cause; the philosophy of causation; (*Med.*) the science of the causes of disease. **ætiological** (ēt i ȯ loj′ ik ȧl), *a.* Pertaining to ætiology. **ætiologically,** *adv.*

af- (AD-, assim. to *f*], *suf.*, *e.g. afford.*

afar (ȧ far′) [*a-*, on, FAR], *adv.* From, at, or to a distance.

***afeard** (ȧ fērd′) [A.-S. p.p. of *afæran* (*a-*, intens., *færan*, to frighten)], *part.a.* Afraid, frightened.

affable (ăf′ ȧbl) [L. *affābilis* (*af-*, *ad-*, to, *fāri*, to speak), -ABLE], *a.* Of easy access; courteous, complaisant, benign. **affability** (ăf ȧ bil′ i ti), *n.* The quality of being affable; courtesy of manners, encouraging strangers or inferiors to approach and converse with one. **affableness,** *n.* **affably,** *adv.*

affair (ȧ fâr′) [O.F. *afaire* (*à*, to, *faire*, to do, L. *facere*)], *n.* Any kind of business; that which is to be done; a thing, concern, matter, or object of slight importance; a love intrigue; (*pl.*) public or private business; finances; circumstances.

affect (1) (ȧ fekt′) [F. *affecter*, L. *affectāre*, freq. of *afficere* (*ad-*, to, *facere*, to do, act)], *v.t.* To tend towards, aim at, to be drawn towards; to be fond of, fancy, love, like; to practise, use, assume; to frequent, haunt; to feign, to pretend, to make a pretence of. **affectation** (ăf fėk tā′ shůn), *n.* An aiming at, a striving after; artificial appearance, assumption, pretence. **affected** (ȧ fek′ tėd), *a.* Given to false show; pretending to what is not natural or real. **affectedly,** *adv.* **affectedness,** *n.* **affectible,** *a.* That may be affected or influenced. **affectibility,** *n.* **affecting,** *a.* Touching, moving; fitted to excite emotion. **affectingly,** *adv.*

affect (2) (ȧ fekt′) [L. *afficere*], *v.t.* To act upon, exert an influence upon; to attack, impress, touch, move, have effect upon; *to appoint, assign specially.

affection (ȧ fek′ shůn) [F. *affection*, L. *affectiōnem*], *n.* The state of being affected, esp. in the emotions; feeling, disposition, attachment, fondness, love; a state of the body due to any cause, malady, disease; a relation, mode of being, attributes. **v.t.* To have regard for, like, love. **affectional,** *a.* Pertaining to the affections; having affections. **affectionate** (ȧ fek′ shůn ȧt), *a.* Of a loving disposition; tenderly disposed; indicating or expressing love. **affectionately,** *adv.* **affectionateness,** *n.* ***affectioned,** *a.* Disposed, inclined, partial; emotional, passionate; affectionate. **affective,** *a.* *Influencing the affections; pertaining to the affections, emotional.

***affeer** (ȧ fēr′) [O.F. *afeurer*, late L. *afforāre*, to fix the price (*ad-*, to, *forum*, market)], *v.t.* To fix or settle a fine; (*Shak.*) to confirm.

afferent (ăf′ fėr ėnt) [L. *afferre* (*ad-*, to, *ferre*, to bring), -ENT], *a.* Bringing to, conducting to or inwards (chiefly in *Med.* of vessels and nerves).

affettuoso (a fet too ō′ sō) [It.], *adv.* (*Mus.*) With feeling.

affiance (ȧ fī′ ȧns) [O.F. *afiancer*; late L. *affidare*, to trust], *v.t.* To promise solemnly in marriage. *n.* Faith, trust, confidence; plighting of faith, contract of marriage, betrothal; *affinity; implicit trust. **affianced,** *a.* Promised in marriage, betrothed.

affiche (ăf fēsh′) [F. *afficher*, to fasten (*af-*, L. *ad-*, to, *ficher*, L. *fīgicāre*, from *fīgere*)], *n.* A poster, placard.

affidavit (ăf i dā′ vit) [late L., he made oath, from *affīdāre*; see AFFIANCE], *n.* A voluntary affirmation sworn before a person qualified to administer an oath.

affiliate (ȧ fil′ i āt) [L. *affīliāre*, to adopt (*ad-*, to, *fīlius*, a son)], *v.t.* To adopt; to receive as a member or branch; to attribute to; to assign (an illegitimate child) to its father. **affiliable,** *a.* Capable of being affiliated or assigned to. **affiliation** (ȧ fil i ā′ shŭn), *n.* Adoption; the act of affiliating; the assignment of an illegitimate child to its father.

affined (ȧ fīnd′) [F. *affiné* (L. *affīnis*, related to)], *a.* Joined in affinity; bound, obliged. **affinity** (ȧ fin′ i ti) [F. *affinité*, L. *affīnitātem* (*af-*, *ad-*, to, *fīnis*, end, border)], *n.* Relationship, relationship by marriage as opposed to consanguinity or relationship by blood; connexion; resemblance due to common origin; physical attraction; the object of this attraction; chemical attraction, the property by which elements unite to form new compounds.

affirm (ȧ fĕrm′) [O.F. *afermer*, L. *affirmāre* (*af-*, *ad-*, to, *firmāre*, from *firmus*, strong)], *v.t.* To assert positively or solemnly; to allege confidently; to aver; (*Log.*) to state affirmatively. *v.i.* To make a solemn affirmation in lieu of oath. **affirmable,** *a.* **affirmance,** *n.* Confirmation, ratification, assertion (ăf fĕr mā′ shun), *n.* The act of affirming anything; that which is affirmed; (*Law*) a solemn declaration made under penalties, in lieu of oath. **affirmative** (ȧ fĕrm′ ȧ tiv), *a.* Relating to or containing an affirmation; confirmatory, positive. *n.* That which affirms. **in the affirmative:** Yes. **affirmatively,** *adv.*

affix (ȧ fiks′) [med. L. *affixāre*, freq. of L. *affīgere* (*af-*, *ad-*, to FIX)], *v.t.* To fix, fasten, attach; to annex, to subjoin. **affix** (ăf′ fiks), *n.* An addition; (*Gram.*) a word or syllable added to the beginning or the end of a word; a post-fix. **affixture,** *n.* The act of affixing; attachment.

afflation (ȧ flā′ shŭn) [L. *afflatiōnem*, from *afflāre* (*af-*, *ad-*, to, *flāre*, to blow)], *n.* The act of blowing or breathing upon; inspiration. **afflatus** (ȧ flā′ tŭs) [L. *afflātus*, verb. n., from *afflāre*], *n.* Inspiration; poetic impulse.

afflict (ȧ flikt′) [O.F. *aflit*, L. *afflictus*, p.p. of *afflīgere* (*af-*, *ad-*, to, *flīgere*, dash, strike)], *v.t.* To inflict bodily or mental pain on; to cast down; to trouble. **afflicted,** *a.* **afflicting,** *a.* **afflictingly,** *adv.* **affliction,** *n.* The state of being afflicted; calamity, trouble, misery, distress; mental or bodily ailment. **afflictive,** *a.* Causing affliction; distressing. **afflictively,** *adv.*

affluent (ăf′ flu ėnt) [F. *affluent*, L. *affluentem*, pres.p. of *affluere* (*af-*, *ad-*, to, *fluere*, flow)], *a.* Flowing, wealthy. *n.* A tributary. **affluently,** *adv.* **affluence,** *n.* The state of flowing to, abounding flow; abundance, wealth.

afflux (ăf′ flŭks) [med. L. *afluxus* (*fluere*)], *n.* A flowing to; that which flows to; a concourse of people, an accession.

afford (ȧ fôrd′) [A.S. *ge-forthian* (*ge-*, intens., *forthian*, to further)], *v.t.* To yield the means; to be able to bear the expense of; to share, furnish, supply.

afforest (ȧ for′ ėst) [med. L. *afforestāre* (*af-*, *ad-*, to, *foresta*], *v.t.* To convert into forest. **afforestation** (ȧ for ės tā′ shŭn), *n.* The act of converting waste or other land into forest.

affranchise (ȧ frăn′ chīz, -iz) [F. *affranchir* (*affranchiss-*) (*à*, to, *franchir*, to free)], *v.t.* To make free; to set at liberty physically or morally. **affranchisement** (ȧ frăn′ chiz mėnt), *n.* The act of making free; emancipation.

affray (ȧ frā′) [O.F. *effreër*, *esfreër*, late L. *exfridāre* (*ex-*, intens., O.H.G. *fridu*, cp. A.-S. *frith*, peace)], *v.t.* To frighten, to scare; *to rouse out of sleep. *n.* Commotion, tumult; a fight between two or more persons in a public place.

affreightment (ȧ frāt′ mėnt), *n.* A contract for conveyance of goods by sea, whereby the shipowner agrees to carry them for hire or "freight."

affrettando (ăf fret tan′ dō), **affrettate** (ăf fret tȧh tė), **affrettore** (ăf fret tō rė) [It. *affrettare*, to hasten], *adv.* (*Mus.*) Hastening the time.

affright (ȧ frīt′) [M.E. *afright*, p.p., A.-S. *āfyrht*, p.p. (*ā-*, intens., *fyrhtan*, to frighten)], *v.t.* To frighten, to terrify. **part.a.* Frightened. *n.* Fright, terror; a cause of fright or terror. **affrightedly,** *adv.*

affront (ȧ frŭnt′) [O.F. *afronter*, late L. *affrontāre*, *af-*, *ad-*, to, against, *frontem*, acc. of *frons*, forehead)], *v.t.* To consult openly; to confront in hostile way, *to accost; to make ashamed. *n.* A hostile encounter; an insult; contemptuous or rude treatment. **affrontingly,** *adv.*

affusion (ȧ fū′ zhŭn) [L. *affundere* (*af-*, *ad-*, to, *fundere*, *-fus-*, to pour)], *n.* A pouring on; baptism; (*Med.*) a remedy in fever.

afield (ȧ fēld′), *adv.* To or in the field; away, at a distance, abroad.

afire (ȧ fīr′), *adv.* and *pred.a.* On fire.

aflame (ȧ flām′), *adv.* and *pred.a.* Flaming; in or into flame.

afloat (ȧ flōt′), *a.* or *adv.* Floating; in a floating condition; at sea, aboard ship; out of debt, solvent, unembarrassed; in full swing; in circulation, current; moving about, adrift.

afoot (ȧ fut′), *adv.* On foot; in motion, in action.

***afore** (ȧ fôr′) [A.-S. *onforan* (ON, prep., *foran*, in front], *adv.* Before, in front; *in or towards the front part of a ship. **afore-cited,** *a.* Already cited. **afore-going,** *a.* and *n.* Preceding, the preceding. ***aforehand,** *adv.* Beforehand; previously. *a.* Provided, prepared, previously fitted, ready. **aforementioned,** *a.* Before-mentioned. **aforenamed,** *a.* Before-named. **aforesaid,** *a.* Said or mentioned before. **aforethought,** *a.* Premeditated, prepense. **aforetime,** *adv.* At a former time; previously. *n.* Time past.

a fortiori (ā fôr shi ôr′ ī) [L.], *adv.* With still more reason; much more; still more conclusively.

afoul (ȧ foul′), *a.* or *adv.* Fouled, entangled, in collision.

afraid (ȧ frād′) [p.p. of AFFRAY], *a.* Impressed with fear; terrified.

afreet, afrit, affrite (ăf′ frēt) [Arab. *ifrīt*], *n.* A demon or monster of Mohammedan mythology.

afresh (ȧ fresh′), *adv.* Again, anew, freshly.

African (ăf′ ri kȧn) [L. *Africa*], *a.* Pertaining to Africa. *n.* A native of Africa, or a person, wherever born, who belongs ethnologically to one of the African races. ***Afric,** *a.* African. **African green,** *n.* A pigment obtained from copper. **African oak,** *n.* A wood from Sierra Leone resembling oak or mahogany, sometimes called African teak or African mahogany.

Afridi (ăf rē′ dē) [native name], *a.* Of a race of Afghans living in the mountain region north of Peshawar. *n.* A member of this race.

Afrikaans (ăf ri kanz′) [Dut.]. The S. African Dutch language, Taal.

Afrikander (ăf ri kăn′ dėr) [Dut. *Afrikaender*, *Afrikaner*], *n.* and *a.* A South African breed of sheep and of cattle. **Afrikander Bond** [Dut. *Bund*]. A political association (founded 1879–80) for promotion of South African interests and eventual independence of South Africa as the United States of South Africa.

Afrikaner (ăf ri ka′ ner) [Dutch], *n.* and *a.* A person born in South Africa of white parents whose mother tongue is Afrikaans.

aft (aft, ăft) [A.-S. *æftan*], *a.* or *adv.* Towards or at the stern of a vessel; abaft. **fore and aft:** From stem to stern; lengthwise.

after (af′ tėr, ăf′ tėr) [A.-S. *æfter* (*af*, off, *ter*, comp. sup.; cp. Gr. *apo-ter-o*)], *adv.*, *prep.*, and *conj.* In the rear; behind; in pursuit of, according to; following (in time), next to; subsequently to, at the time subsequent. *a.* Later, subsequent; hinder, posterior. **a long way after:** In feeble imitation (of a painter, musician, writer, etc.). **five after four:** (*Am.*) Five minutes past four. **after-birth,** *n.* The placenta, the secundine; *a later birth; late-born offspring; posthumous birth. **after-clap,** *n.* An unexpected subsequent event. **after-crop,** *n.* A second crop in the same year. **after-damp,** *n.* Choke damp; carbon dioxide gas resulting from the combustion of fire-damp in coal-mines. **after-game,** *n.* A game played to reverse the issue of the first. **after-glow,** *n.* Glow in the western sky after sunset. **after-grass,** *n.* The grass which springs up after a first crop has been mown. **after-guard,** *n.* (*Naut.*) The seamen stationed on the poop of a ship to attend to the after-sails. **after-image,** *n.* The image that remains for a moment after looking away from an object at which one has been gazing steadily. **afterlife,** *n.* Life after death. **after-light,** *n.* Later knowledge. **after-mast,** *n.* (*Naut.*) Mast fitted aft. **aftermath** [A.-S. *mæty*, a mowing], *n.* After-grass; consequences. **aftermost** [A.-S. *æftemæst*, superlative], *a.* (*Naut.*) Nearest the stern. **afternoon,** *n.* Time between midday and evening. **afternoon-buyer,** *n.* A purchaser who waits till after the market dinner, in the hope of cheaper prices. **after-pains,** *n.pl.* The pains which follow childbirth, and by which the secundine is expelled. **after-piece,** *n.* A short piece acted after a more important play. **afters,** *n.pl.* (*colloq.*) What follows the main course at a meal. **afterthought,** *n.* Reflection after the act; a belated explanation. **afterward, afterwards** [A.-S. *æftanweard* (*æftan*, AFT, WARD)], *adv.* Subsequently; at a later period.

ag- [AD-], *pref.* To, at, *e.g. aggravate, aggrieve.*

aga, agha (a′ gȧ, ăg′ȧ, ȧ ga′) [Turk. *agha*, a master], *n.* A Turkish civil or military officer of high rank. **Aga Khan,** *n.* The nominated hereditary spiritual head of the Ismailian sect of Mohammedans.

agacerie (ȧ gas′ ėr i′) [F.], *n.* Blandishment, charm, allurement.

again (ȧ gān′, ȧ gen′) [A.-S. *ongean* (on, prep., on or in, *gagn, gegn*, in a direct line with, opposite)], *adv.* A second time, once more, moreover, in addition; on the other hand, in return, in answer. **again and again,** *adv.* With frequent repetition, repeatedly.

against (ȧ gānst′, ȧ genst′) [AGAIN], *prep.* In opposition to, opposite to, in contrast to; in contact with, in preparation or provision for. **against the grain:** Contrary to inclination, reluctantly, with aversion.

agalite (a′ gă lit) [Gr. *age*, wonder, -LITE], *n.* (*Min.*) A fine kind of talc used in the manufacture of paper.

agalmatolite (ȧ găl măt′ ō līt) [Gr. *agalma*, image, *lithos*, a stone], *n.* (*Min.*) A soft stone of greyish, greenish or yellowish tint.

agami (ăg′ ȧ mi) [native name in Guiana], *n.* The trumpeter, *Psophia crepitans*, a South American bird, allied to the crane.

agamic (ȧ găm′ ik) [Gr. *agamos* (*a-*, not, *gamos*, marriage)], *a.* (*Zool.*) Characterized by absence of sexual action. **agamogenesis** (ăg ȧ mō jen′ės is) [Gr. *agamos*, GENESIS], *n.* (*Biol.*) Asexual reproduction. **agamogenetic** (ăg ȧ mō jė net′ ik), *a.* Pertaining to agamogenesis, generated or reproduced asexually. **agamogenetically,** *adv.* Agamically. **agamous,** *a.* (*Biol.*) Without distinct sexual organs, asexual.

Agapanthus (ăg ȧ păn′ thůs) [Gr. *agape*, love; *anthos*, a flower], *n.* (*Bot.*) A genus of ornamental plants of the order Liliaceæ. It has bright-blue flowers.

agape (ȧ gāp′) *adv.* and *pred.a.* On the gape, in an attitude or condition of wondering expectation.

agape (ăg′ ȧ pē) [Gr. *agapē*, brotherly love], *n.* (*pl.* **agapæ**) A "love-feast," a kind of feast held by the primitive Christians in connexion with the Lord's Supper. **agapemone** (ăg ȧ pem′ ō nē) [Gr. *agapē*, *monē*, a dwelling), *n.* Abode of love; a religious community of men and women established 1846.

agar-agar (ā′ gȧr ā′ gȧr) [E. Ind. native], *n.* A gelatinous substance obtained from seaweeds and used for the artificial cultivation of bacteria.

agaric (ăg′ ȧ rik, ȧ găr′ ik) [L. *agaricum*, Gr. *agarikon*], *n.* A mushroom; name of several species of fungus. *a.* Fungoid.

***agast** (ȧ gast′) [A.-S. *gæstan*], *v.t.* (*Spens.*) To terrify, to frighten. *v.i.* To take fright.

agastric (ȧ găs′ trik) [Gr. *a-*, priv., *gaster*, the belly], *a.* (*Zool.*) Without a distinct alimentary canal.

agate (1) (ăg′ ȧt) [F. *agathe*, It. *ágatha*, L. *achātes*, Gr. *achatēs*], *n.* Any semi-pellucid variety of chalcedony, marked with bands or clouds, or infiltrated by other minerals, and used for seals, brooches, etc.; a dwarf, in allusion to the small figures cut in agates for seals; the American name for ruby or 5½ point type [as this]; an instrument used by those who draw gold wire, so called because there is an agate in the middle of it.

agate (2) (ȧ gāt′), *adv.* (*North.*) On the way; a-going.

Agave (ȧ gā′ vė) [L. *agave*, Gr. *agauē*], *n.* (*Bot.*) A genus comprising the American aloe.

***agaze** (ȧ gāz′), *adv.* At gaze; in a gazing attitude.

***agazed** (ȧ gāzd′) [prob. var. of *agast*, AGHAST], *part.a.* Affrighted, dumbfounded.

age (āj) [O.F. *aage*, *edage*, late L. *ætāticum* (L. *ætas -atis*, from *ævitas ævum*, an age)], *n.* A period of existence, duration of existence, a period or stage of life, the latter portion of life, senility; maturity, majority; an epoch, a generation; an æon. *v.i.* To grow old. *v.t.* To cause to grow old or to show signs of age. **aged** (ājd, ā′ jėd), *a.* Of a certain age, old. **the aged:** Old people. **agedness** (ā jėd nes), *n.* The state of being old, the state of having attained a certain age. **ageless,** *a.* Never growing aged, never coming to an end. **of age:** Having reached the age of 21. **age of consent:** (*Law*) The age at which a girl's consent is valid; beneath that age to have carnal knowledge of her is a criminal offence. In English and Scottish law the age of consent is 16. **age of discretion:** (*Law*) The age when one is judged capable of using one's discretion, in English Law, 14.

-age (O.F. *-age*, late L. *-āticum*, neut. of adj. in *-āticus*], *suf.* Appertaining to, aggregate of: forms abstract or collective nouns, *e.g. baronage, courage, foliage*; notes act of doing or thing done, *e.g. passage, voyage.*

agee (ȧ jē′) [*a-*, on, GEE, to move aside], *adv.* (*Sc.*) To one side; awry.

agency (AGENT).

agenda (ȧ jen′ dȧ) [L. pl. of *agendum*, neut. ger. of *agere*, to do], *n.pl.* Things to be done; engagements to be kept; a memorandum-book; a list of the business to be transacted.

agent (ā′ jėnt) [L. *agentem*, acc. of *agens*, pres.p. of *agere*, to do], *n.* One who or that which exerts power; the material cause or instrument; a deputy, an officer or servant who actually performs a function; (*Nat. Hist.*) the thing that produces results. **a.* Acting, in contradistinction to patient. **agency** (ā′ jėn si) [med. L. *agentia* (*agere*)], *n.* The office or business of an agent; causative action, instrumentality, active working, operation; place of business, office, a commercial organization. **free agent,** *n.* One who is free to act according to his own opinions and wishes. **agential** (å jen′ shål), *a.* Of or pertaining to an agent or agency.

agent provocateur (a′ zhon prō vok′ å tĕr) [F.], *n.* A person employed to detect suspected political offenders by leading them on to some overt action.

Ageratum (ă jĕr ā′ tům) [Gr. *ageraton*, an aromatic herb], *n.* (*Bot.*) A genus of low plants of the aster family.

agger (ăj′ ėr) [L. from *aggere* (AD-, *gerere*, to carry)], *n.* A mound; the rampart of a Roman camp.

agglomerate (å glom′ ėr āt) [L. *agglomerāre* (*ag-*, *ad-*, to, *glomus -meris*, a ball)], *v.t.* To heap up or collect into a ball or mass. *v.i.* To gather in a mass. **agglomerate** (-åt), *a.* Heaped up. *n.* (*Geol.*) A mass of volcanic fragments united by heat. **agglomeration** (-ā′ shůn), *n.* The act of agglomerating; a mass, a heap. **agglomerative** (å glom′ ėr å tiv), *a.*

agglutinate (å gloo′ tin āt) [L. *agglutināre* (*af-*, *ad-*, to, *gluten -inis*, glue)], *v.t.* To glue together; to turn into glue (also *v.i.*); to cause to adhere; to compound, *e.g.* simple words into compounds. **agglutinate** (-åt), *a.* Glued together; (*Philol.*) consisting of simple words, or roots, combined into compounds. **agglutination** (-nā′ shůn), *n.* The act of gluing or cementing; the formation of simple words or roots into compound terms. **agglutinative** (å gloo′ tin å tiv), *a.*

aggrandize (ăg′ grån dīz) [F. *agrandir* (lengthened stem *-iss-*), to greaten (L. *ad-*, to, *grandis*)], *v.t.* To enlarge; to make great in power, wealth, rank, or reputation; to exalt. **aggrandizement** (å grăn′ diz mėnt), *n.* The act of aggrandizing; the state of being aggrandized. **aggrandization,** *n.* Aggrandizement.

***aggrate** (å grāt′) [It. *aggratare*, late L. *aggrātāre*, see AGREE], *v.t.* To gratify.

aggravate (ăg′ rå vāt) [L. *aggravātus*, p.p. of *aggravāre* (*ad-*, to, *gravāre*, to make heavy, *gravis*, heavy)], *v.t.* To add weight to; to render less tolerable; to make more heinous; (*colloq.*) to exasperate, to provoke, to irritate. **aggravating,** *a.* (*colloq.*) Provoking; rendering less excusable. **aggravatingly,** *adv.* (*colloq.*) In an aggravating manner; in an exasperating manner. **aggravation** (ăg rå vā′ shůn), *n.* The act of aggravating; the state of being aggravated; that which aggravates, an addition to a burden, wrong, crime, abuse, or charge.

aggregate (ăg′ rė gāt) [L. *aggregātus*, p.p. of *aggregāre* (*ag-*, *ad-*, to, *grex gregis*, a flock)], *v.t.* To collect together; to bring together into a mass or whole. *v.i.* To form an aggregate of; to unite. **aggregate** (ăg′ rė gåt), *a.* Collected together; (*Bot.*) consisting of florets united together, collected into a mass; (*Zool.*) consisting of individuals united in a compound organism; (*Geol.*) composed of distinct minerals. *n.* A mass formed by the union of individual particles; the total, the whole; (*Eng.*) particles to be bonded together to form concrete. **in the aggregate:** Collectively. **aggregation,** *n.* The act of collecting together; the state of being aggregated; an aggregate. **aggregative,** *a.*

aggress (å gres′) [F. *aggresser*, late L. *aggressāre*, freq. of *aggredior* (*ad-*, *gradior*, I walk)], *v.i.* To begin an attack or quarrel. *v.t.* To attack, to assault. **aggression** (å gresh′ ůn), *n.* An unprovoked attack or injury. **aggressive** (å gres′ iv), *a.* Involving an act of aggression; making the first attack; offensive, pugnacious. **aggressively,** *adv.* **aggressiveness,** *n.* **aggressor,** *n.* One who begins a quarrel.

aggrieve (å grēv′) [O.F. *agrever*, L. *ad-*, *gravāre*, to weigh down (*gravis*, heavy)], *v.t.* To cause grief, annoyance, or pain to; to perpetrate injustice against.

aghast (å gast′) [p.p. of obsolete *v.* AGAST, to frighten; A.-S. *gæstan*], *a.* Terrified, frightened, appalled; struck with terror.

agile (ăj′ il, ăj′ īl) [L. *agilis*, nimble (*agere*, to do)], *a.* Having the faculty of moving quickly; quick, nimble, active. **agilely,** *adv.* **agility,** *n.*

agio (ăj′ i ō, ā′ ji ō) [It. *agio*, ease], *n.* The difference in value between one kind of currency and another; money-changing; the charge for changing notes for cash, or one kind of money for another. **agiotage** (ăj′ i ō taj), *n.* Money-changing; speculation in stocks, stock-jobbing.

agist (å jist′) [O.F. *agister* (*à*, to, *gister*, *géter*, to lodge)], *v.t.* To afford pasture to the cattle of others at a certain rate; to lay a public rate on land or land-owners. **agistment,** *n.* The action or practice of agisting; the pasture, or right to the pasture, of a forest; rate levied on, or profit made from, the agistment of cattle.

agitate (ăj′ i tāt) [L. *agitātus*, p.p. of *agitāre*, freq. of *agere*, to drive], *v.t.* To shake or move briskly; to excite, to disturb, to perturb; to consider, discuss, debate; to bring forward for public discussion. *v.i.* To keep a question under public discussion. **agitation** (-tā′ shůn), *n.* The act of agitating; state of being agitated; commotion, perturbation; excited discussion, public excitement. **agitator,** *n.* One who or that which agitates; one who excites or keeps up political agitation; a mechanical contrivance for shaking and mixing.

agitato (ăj i ta′ tō) [It.], *adv.* (*Mus.*) In an agitated manner.

aglet, aiglet (ăg′ lėt, āg′ lėt) [F. *aiguillette*, dim. of *aiguille*, needle (late L. *acūcula*, L. *acicula*, dim. of *acus*, needle)], *n.* The metal tag of a lace; a spangle; a tag-like ornament on a uniform.

agley (å glā′), *adv.* (*Sc.*) Astray, awry.

aglow (å glō′), *adv.* In a glow.

agmatology (ăg må tol′ ŏ ji) [Gr. *agma*, a fragment; *logos*, a discourse], *n.* (*Med.*) The department of surgery dealing with fractures.

agnail (ăg′ nāl) [A.-S. *angnægl* (*ang*, light, painful, *nægl*, nail)], *n.* A sore at the root of toe- or finger-nail, a whitlow; (*dial.*) **hang-nail** and (*Sc.*) **anger-nail** are terms invented by false etymology, mistaking *nægl* (a nail of iron or other hard substance, or a hard excrescence) for finger-nail.

agnate (ăg′ nāt) [F. *agnat*, L. *agnātus* (*ad-*, *gnātus*, born, p.p. of (*g*)*nascī*, to be born)], *n.* Descendant from the same male ancestor; a relative on the father's side. *a.* Related on the father's side; hence, allied, akin. **agnatic** (ăg năt′ ik), *a.* Pertaining to descent on the father's side. **agnation** (ăg nā′ shůn), *n.* Relationship on the father's side; descent from a common male ancestor, in contradistinction to cognation or descent from the same female ancestor.

agnomen (ăg nō′ men) [L. *ad-*, to, (*g*)*nōmen*, name], *n.* A surname appended to the cognomen among the Romans; an additional name or epithet; a nickname. ***agnomination** (ăg nom in ā′ shůn), *n.* The bestowal of an agnomen; paronomasia; alliteration.

agnostic (ăg nos′ tik) [Gr. *agnōstos*, ignorant of, unknown, unknowable (*a-*, not, *gno-*, know)], *n.* One who is uncertain about his belief in God; one who denies that man has any knowledge except of material phenomena. *a.* Pertaining to agnostics or their teachings. **agnostically,** *adv.* **agnosticism** (ăg nos′ tis izm), *n.* The teachings of the agnostics; the state of being agnostic.

Agnus Castus (ăg′ nůs kăs′ tůs) [L. *agnus*, Gr. *agnos*, name of tree (mistaken for adj. chaste), L. *castus*, chaste], *n.* An aromatic shrub, *Vitex agnus castus*, formerly supposed to be a preservative of chastity.

Agnus Dei (ăg′ nůs dē′ ī) [L. The Lamb of God], *n.* A figure of a lamb bearing a flag or cross; a cake of wax stamped with such figure of a lamb and blessed by the Pope; a part of the Mass beginning with the words *Agnus Dei*; a musical setting of this part of the Mass.

ago (å gō′) [M.E. *agone*, p.p. of v. *ago-* (*a-*, forth, GO)], *a.* or *adv.* Gone by, bygone, passed, passed away; since.

agog (ȧ gog′) [perhaps from O.F. *en gogues* (*gogue*, mirth, fun)], *adv.* In a state of eager expectation; astir.

agogic (ȧ goj′ ik) [Gr. *agoge*, tendency], *a.* (*Phonetics* and *Mus.*) Of or characterized by variations of stress in speech or musical rhythm by the lengthening of a syllable or note. **agogics,** *n.* Variation of stress by lengthening of duration.

-agogue [Gr. *agōgos*, leading], *comb. form.* A leader, a leading, as in *demagogue*, *pedagogue*, *synagogue.*

agoing (ȧ gō′ ing), *adv.* In a state of motion.

***agone** (ȧ gon′) [AGO].

agonic (ȧ gon′ ik) [Gr. *agōnios*, without an angle (*a-*, not, *gōnia*, angle)], *a.* Having no dip, applied to an imaginary line on the earth's surface, drawn through the two magnetic poles.

agonistic (ăg ȯ nis′ tik), **agonistical** [Gr. *agōnistikos*, of or pertaining to an *agōnistēs*, competitor in the athletic games (*agōn*, a gathering or assembly, from *agein*, to lead)], *a.* Pertaining to contests in public games or athletic exercises. **agonistically,** *adv.*

agonize (ăg′ ō nīz) [L. *agonizare*], *v.t.* To subject to extreme pain; to torture. *v.i.* To suffer agony; to make desperate or convulsive efforts. **agonizing,** *a.* Causing or suffering agony. **agonizingly,** *adv.*

agony (ăg′ ȯ ni) [L. *agōnia*, from Gr. *agōnia*, contest (from *agōn*, see AGONISTIC)], *n.* Anguish of mind; a paroxysm of pain or pleasure; the death struggle; a painful struggle or contest; the mental anguish of Christ in Gethsemane. **agony column,** *n.* The column in a newspaper devoted to advertisements for missing friends and other matters of a personal kind. **to pile on the agony:** (*slang*) To exaggerate, describe in the most sensational terms.

agora (ăg′ ȯr ȧ) [Gr. *agora*], *n.* The public square, forum, or market-place of an ancient Greek town. **agoraphobia,** *n.* (*Path.*) Dread of open spaces.

agouti, agouty (ȧ goo′ ti) [Native Indian, *aguti*], *n.* The popular name of a species, *Dasyprocta agouti*, of West Indian and South American rodent.

agraffe (ȧ grăf′) [F. *agrafe* (*à*, *grappe*, late L. *grappa*, O.H.G. *chrapfo*, hook)], *n.* A sort of hook, used as a clasp or fastening; a cramp used by builders to fix objects to walls.

agraphia (ȧ grăf′ i ȧ) [Gr. *a-*, not; *graphein*, to write), *n.* (*Path.*) Loss of the cerebral power of expressing one's ideas in writing.

agrarian (ȧ grâr′ i ȧn) [L. *agrārius*, pertaining to land (*ager*, land)], *a.* The epithet of an ancient Roman law pertaining to the division of conquered territory; hence, pertaining to landed property or cultivated land; (*Bot.*) growing wild in the fields. *n.* A person in favour of the redistribution of landed property. **agrarian crime, agrarian outrage:** Crime or outrage arising out of disputes about land. **agrarianism,** *n.* A redistribution of land; political agitation concerning land or land-tenure. **agrarianize,** *v.t.* To apportion (land) by an agrarian law; to imbue with agrarianism.

agree (ȧ grē′) [O.F. *agréer*, late L. *aggrātāre* (*ad-*, to, *grātāre*, to make agreeable, from *grātus*, pleasing)], *v.i.* To be of one mind; to live in concord; to consent, to accede; to settle by stipulation; to harmonize with, to coincide; to do well (with); to suit; to be in grammatical concord. *v.t.* To make agreeable or harmonious; to concert, to settle, to reconcile, arrange, render consistent.

agreeable (ȧ grē′ ȧbl) [as prec.], *a.* Affording pleasure, pleasing, pleasant; favourable, disposed to; corresponding, comfortable, suitable to. **agreeableness, *agreeability,** *n.* **agreeably,** *adv.*

agreement (ȧ grē′ mėnt), *n.* A coming into accord; mutual conformity, understanding, accordance; grammatical concord; a contract duly executed and legally binding.

agrestic (ȧ gres′ tik) [L. *agrestis* (*ager*, a field)], *a.* Rural, rustic, clownish, uncouth.

agreutic (ȧ groo′ tik) [Gr. *agreuein* to hunt], *a.* Skilful in hunting; subsisting by the chase.

agriculture (ăg′ ri kŭl tūr) [L. *agricultūra* (*ager agri*, field, *cultūra*, CULTURE)], *n.* The science and art of cultivating the soil, whether by pasturage, tillage, husbandry, farming, or by gardening. **agricultural,** *a.* Pertaining to the culture of the soil. **agriculturist, agriculturalist,** *n.* One engaged in agriculture; a husbandman.

agrimony (ăg′ ri mȯn i) [late L. *agrimōnia*, L. *argemōnia*, Gr. *argemōnē*], *n.* A genus of plants, one species of which (*Agrimonia Eupatoria*) was formerly valued as a tonic; also applied erroneously to other plants, *e.g.* hemp agrimony, and wild agrimony.

agrimotor (ăg ri mō′ tȯr) [L. *ager agri*, field; MOTOR], *n.* A motor tractor used in agriculture.

***agrise** (ȧ grīz′) [*a-*, intens., GRISE], *v.i.* To shudder, to fear, loathe. *v.t.* To terrify.

agrobiology (ăg rō bī ol′ ȯ ji) [Gr. *agros*, land; BIOLOGY], *n.* The study of plant nutrition, etc., in relation to soil control.

agronomy (ȧ gron′ ȯ mi) [Gr. *agronomos*, an overseer (*agros*, land, *nomos*, dispensing, from *nemein*, to dispense)], *n.* The management of land, husbandry. **agronomic** (ăg rȯ nom′ ik), **agronomical,** *a.* Of or pertaining to agronomy. **agronomics,** *n.* Science of land management as a branch of political economy. **agronomist,** *n.* A rural economist; one skilled in agronomy.

aground (ȧ ground′) [*a-*, on, GROUND], *adv.* and *pred.a.* On the ground; on the shallow bottom of any water.

agterskot (ăg′ tėr skot), *n.* (*S. Africa*) A percentage paid to fruit and other farmers after the first payment has been made.

ague (ā′ gū) [O.F. *ague*, fem. a., L. *acūta*, sharp], *n.* A malarial fever, marked by successive hot and cold paroxysms, the latter attended with shivering; hence, any fit of shaking. **ague-cake,** *n.* (*Med.*) A tumour of the spleen which sometimes accompanies ague. **agued,** *part.a.* (*Shak.*) Affected with ague; shaking with fear. **aguish** (ā′ gū ish), *a.* Of the nature of or subject to ague; quaking, shivering; intermittent. ***aguishly** (ā′ gū ish li), *adv.*

ah (a) [O.F. *a*, L. *ah*], *int.* An exclamation expressive of various emotions, according to the manner in which it is uttered—sorrow, regret, fatigue, relief, surprise, admiration, appeal, remonstrance, aversion, contempt, mockery.

aha (ȧ ha′) [*a* combined with HA], *int.* An exclamation of surprise, triumph, or mockery.

ahead (ȧ hed′), *adv.* and *pred.a.* In advance; forward, onward, at the head, in front. **to go ahead:** To make rapid progress; to start.

aheap (ȧ hēp′), *adv.* In a heap, all of a heap.

ahem (ȧ hem′), *int.* [HEM (2)]. An exclamation used to attract attention or merely to gain time.

ahoy (ȧ hoi′) [HOY (2)], *int.* (*Naut.*) A word used in hailing.

Ahriman (a′ri mȧn) [Pers.], *n.* The evil deity in the Zoroastrian system who divides the government of the universe with Ormuzd, the good deity.

ahull (ȧ hŭl′) [*a-*, prep., HULL], *adv.* With the sails furled and the helm lashed on the leeside.

ai (a′ ē) [Braz. *aī*, sound of its cry], *n.* A three-toed sloth, *Bradypus tridactylus*, from South America.

aiblins [ABLINGS].

Aich's Metal (āch) [J. Aich, inventor], *n.* (*Metal.*) An alloy of zinc, iron and copper, resistant to water and used for sheathing ships' bottoms.

aid (ād) [O.F. *aider*, L. *adjutāre*, freq. of *adjuvāre* (*ad-*, to *juvāre*, to help)], *v.t.* To assist, to help to relieve. [O.F. *aide*, *auide*, Prov. *ajuda*, fem. p.p. of *adjuvāre*], *n.* Help, assistance, succour, relief; an aide-de-camp; (*Hist.*) a contribution by a vassal for the ransom of his lord, on the occasion when the lord's eldest son was made a knight, or to furnish a dowry for his eldest daughter; a subsidy granted by Parliament to the sovereign; an exchequer loan; anything by which assistance is rendered, esp. in pl. *aids and appliances*. ***aidance** [M.F. *aidance*, from *aider* (-ANCE)], *n.* Aid, assistance, help. ***aidant** [O.F. *aiant*, *aidant*, pres.p. of *aider*], *a.* Helping, assisting, helpful. ***aider,** *n.* One who or that which aids; an assistant, helper; a help, assistance. ***aidless,** *a.* Helpless.

aide (ād) [F.], *n.* An assistant, a help. **aide-de-camp** (ā' dė con) [F.], *n.* (*pl.* **aides-de-camp**). An officer who receives and transmits the orders of a general. ***aide-memoire*** (ād' mem wawr) [F.], *n.* An aid to memory, a memorandum, a memorandum-book.

aigrette (ā' grėt) [F. *aigrette*], *n.* The egret or lesser white heron; hence, a tuft of feathers like that of the egret; a spray of gems worn on the head; any light feathery tuft or spray.

aiguille (ā' gwil) [F., see AGLET], *n.* A slender, needle-shaped peak of rock; an instrument used in boring holes for blasting. **aiguillesque** (ā gwil esk') [F. *aiguille*, -ESQUE], *a.* Shaped like an aiguille.

aiguillette [AGLET].

ail (āl) [A.-S. *eglan* (Goth. *agljan*), from *egle*, troublesome (Goth. *aglus*, difficult, hard)], *v.t.* *To trouble; to cause pain or uneasiness of body or mind to. *v.i.* To be in pain, trouble or ill-health. **ailing,** *part.a.* Affected with illness, sick, suffering. **ailment,** *n.* Sickness, indisposition.

aileron (ā' lėr on) [Fr. tip of a wing), *n.* (*Aviat.*) The hinged portion on the rear edge of the wing-tip of an aeroplane for purposes of control.

aim (ām) [O.F. *aësmer*, late L. *adæstimāre* (perhaps confused with O.F. *esmer*, L. *æstimāre*, to reckon)], *v.t.* To direct as one's course, effect, or intention; to endeavour; to point at with a missile weapon; to level a gun (at); to direct (a blow) at. *v.i.* To take aim; to form plans. *n.* The act of aiming; the point aimed at; direction of a missile; purpose, intention, design. **aimer,** *n.* One who aims, directs, or purposes. **aimful,** *a.* Full of aim or purpose. **aimfully,** *adv.* **aimless,** *a.* Purposeless, objectless. **aimlessly,** *adv.* **aimlessness,** *n.*

Aino (ī' nō) [native name], *n.* (*Ethn.*) A small uncivilized Mongolian tribe living in N. Japan, Saghalien, the Kuriles and adjacent parts.

aint [AN'T].

air (âr) [O.F. *air*, L. *āer-em*, Gr. *aēr* (*aēmi*, I blow)], *n.* The mixture of oxygen and nitrogen enveloping the earth, the atmosphere; open space; a light wind, a breeze; manner, appearance, mien, gesture; affectation, haughtiness (*chiefly in pl.*); (*Mus.*) a tune, melody, either solo or in harmony. *v.t.* To expose to open or fresh air; to ventilate, to dry (as clothes) before the fire; to show off, to parade. *v. reflex.* and *i.* To take the air; to show oneself off. **to go on the air:** (*Radio.*) To broadcast. **to take air:** To become public. **to take the air:** To go for an airing. **in the air:** Projected, dreamed-of, anticipated; chimerical. **castles in the air:** Something visionary, chimerical, impossible. **air-ball,** *n.* Inflated ball, a toy. **air base,** *n.* (*Aviat.*) A place used as a base for operations or the housing of aircraft. **air-bed,** *n.* A bed or mattress inflated with air. **air-bladder,** *n.* A vesicle containing air; esp. the swimming-bladder of fishes. **air-borne,** *a.* Carried by air (of troops, etc.). **air-brake,** *n.* A brake worked by atmospheric pressure. **air-brick,** *n.* A perforated brick or iron grating for admitting air through a wall. **air-bridge,** *n.* A service by air transport between two places. **air-brush,** *n.* A device for spraying paint by compressed air. **air-chamber,** *n.* A chamber filled with air, in an animal or plant; [AIR VESSEL]. **Air Chief Marshal,** *n.* Officer in R.A.F. corresponding in rank to general in the Army. **Air Commodore,** *n.* Officer in R.A.F. corresponding in rank to brigadier in the Army. **air-conditioned,** *a.* Term applied to a place ventilated by cleansed air. **aircraft,** *n.* Collective term for all types of flying-machines, both heavier and lighter than air. **aircraft carrier,** *n.* (*Nav.*) A ship designed for the housing and servicing of aircraft, with a deck where they can take off and alight. **air cushion,** *n.* A cushion or pillow inflated to make it resilient. **air-drain,** *n.* A dry area round a wall for preventing damp. **air eddy,** *n.* An eddy in the air-currents of the atmosphere. **air-engine,** *n.* Any engine driven by the compression and expansion of heated air. **air-field,** *n.* A field specially prepared for the landing and taking-off of aircraft. **air-force,** *n.* The strength of a country in military aircraft. **air fountain,** *n.* Mechanism for producing a jet of water by the elastic force of compressed air. **air-gun,** *n.* A gun from which missiles are projected by compressed air. **air-hole,** *n.* An opening to admit air; a flaw in a casting. **air hunger,** *n.* (*Path.*) A peculiar condition of the nostrils in certain diseases. **air-jacket,** *n.* An inflated jacket for supporting the wearer in water. **air-lift,** *n.* Transport of supplies, goods, etc. by air. **air-line,** *n.* A commercial organization operating regular transport by air; a straight line through the air; a bee-line. **air-liner,** *n.* A passenger-carrying aeroplane flying along a regular air route. **air-lock,** *n.* A pneumatic chamber allowing entrance to or exit from a caisson without loss of air-pressure; an impediment in a pipe caused by a bubble of air. **air-mail,** *n.* Air-post. **airman,** *n.* Aviator, a man who conducts an aeroplane or air-ship. **Air Marshal,** *n.* Officer in R.A.F. corresponding in rank to lieutenant-general in the Army. **air mechanic,** *n.* A mechanic employed in the repair of aircraft. **air-minded,** *a.* Conscious of an interest in facilities for air-travel. **air-pilot,** *n.* A man who steers and controls the machinery of an aircraft. **airplane** [AEROPLANE]. **air-plant,** *n.* An aerial plant. **air pocket,** *n.* (*Aviat.*) Popular term to describe areas of rarefied atmosphere where aircraft are apt to drop unexpectedly. **air-poise,** *n.* An instrument for weighing air. **airport,** *n.* (*Naut.*) A circular aperture in the side of a ship to admit light and air; (*Aviat.*) a station for passenger aeroplanes, furnished with Customs, etc. **air-pump,** *n.* An instrument for exhausting the air from a receiver. **air raid,** *n.* An attack on a town, camp, etc., by hostile aircraft. **Air Raid Precautions,** *n.pl.* Official regulations for the prevention of air raids, or for minimizing the damage caused by them. **air screw,** *n.* (*Aviat.*) The propeller of an aircraft. **air-shaft,** *n.* A vertical passage into a mine for the purpose of ventilation. **air-ship,** *n.* A lighter-than-air flying-machine driven by an engine. **air-sickness,** *n.* Nausea caused by the motion of aircraft. **air speed,** *n.* (*Aviat.*) The speed of an aeroplane or airship relative to the air, as distinct from its speed relative to the ground. **air-strip,** *n.* (*Aviat.*) A strip of even ground for taking-off and landing of aircraft. **air-thermometer,** *n.* A thermometer in which a column of air replaces a column of mercury. **air-threads,** *n.pl.* The floating threads of the gossamer spider. **air-tight,** *a.* So tight as to prevent the passage of the air. **air-trap,** *n.* A trap to prevent the escape of foul air from a sewer. **air-vessel,** *n.* A vessel in which air is compressed, in order that its elasticity may be employed as a moving or regulating power, used in a forcing pump to render the discharge of water continuous; (*Nat. Hist.*) any vessel containing air; esp. one of the respiratory tubes or tracheæ of insects or the spiral vessels of plants; an air-chamber. **Air Vice-Marshal,** *n.* Officer in the R.A.F. corresponding in rank to major-general in the Army. **air-way,** *n.* A tunnel in a mine, fitted with valve-like doors, for the passage of air in one direction; (*Aviat.*) a fully organized air route. **airing,** *n.* Exposure to the free action of the air, or to a fire; a walk or ride in the open air. **airless,** *a.* Not open to the air; close, musty; calm, still. **airworthy,** *a.* (*Aviat.*) Term used of an aeroplane examined and passed as fit for flying. **airworthiness,** *n.* **airy,** *a.* Of or belonging to the air; consisting of or open to the air; aerial, lofty, light, unsubstantial as air; gay, sprightly, visionary, unreal. **airily,** *adv.* **airiness,** *n.*

airedale (âr' dāl) [*Airedale* in Yorkshire], *n.* The largest type of terrier, often used as a police-dog.

airt (ârt) [Gael. *aird*], *n.* (*Sc.*) A point of the compass; a direction.

aisle (īl) [O.F. *ele*, L. *āla* (*axilla*), wing], *n.* A wing or lateral division of a church; hence, a passage between the seats in a place of worship; an avenue; (*Am.*) a corridor. **aisled,** *a.* Furnished with aisles.

ait (āt) [A.-S. *īggath, īgeoth* (*īg*), island], *n.* A small island, especially one in a river or lake.

aitchbone (āch' bōn) [O.F. *nache*, sing. of *naches*, the buttocks, L. *naticas -icæ*, dim. of *nates* (for loss of *n*, cp. ADDER)], *n.* The rump bone; the cut of beef over this bone (also *erroneously* EDGE-BONE).

ajar (1) (å jar') [*a-*, prep., *char* (A.-S. *on cerre, on cyrre*, on the turn)], *adv.* Partly open, as a door or (less usually) a window.

ajar (2) (å jar'), *adv.* In a jarring state, at discord.

ajee (å jē') [AGEE], *adv.* (*Sc.*) To one side, awry; ajar.

ajoupa (aj' oo pa), *n.* A West Indian hut constructed on piles and roofed with leaves.

ajutage [ADJUTAGE].

akimbo (å kim' bō) [etym. unknown], *adv.* With the hands resting on the hips and the elbows turned outwards.

akin (å kin') [*a-*, prep., KIN], *a.* Allied by blood relationship; allied in properties or character.

-al [L. *-ālis*, adj. suf., or noun ending *-ālis, -al, -āles, -ālia*], *suf.* Belonging to, capable of, like, *e.g.* *annual, equal, mortal*; forming substantives, *e.g.* *animal, canal, hospital.*

à la (a la) [F.], *prep.* In the fashion of, after the manner of, after.

alabaster (ăl' å bas' tėr) [O.F. *alabastre*, L. *alabaster -rum*, Gr. *alabastros -on, alabastos*, said to be from the name of a town in Egypt], *n.* Massive gypsum, and other kinds of sulphate or carbonate of lime, either white or delicately shaded. *a.* Made of alabaster; white and translucent like alabaster. **alabastrine** (ăl å bas' trin, -trīn), *a.* Made of or resembling alabaster.

alack (å lăk') [*a*, ah, LACK, ah! lack, or ah! loss], *int.* An exclamation of sorrow. **alackaday,** *int.* Shame on the day! Alas, the day!

alacrity (å lăk' ri ti) [L. *alacritās* (*alacer*, brisk)], *n.* Briskness, eagerness; vivacity, sprightliness, cheerful ardour.

alamode (a la mōd') [F. *à la mode*, in the fashion], *adv.* and *a.* Fashionable. *n.* A thin kind of black silk. **alamode beef,** *n.* Beef boiled down and served with a thick gravy. **alamodality** (a la mō dăl' i ti), *n.* The quality of being according to the prevailing mode or fashion.

alamort (ăl å-, a la môrt'), **all amort** (awl å môrt) [F. *à la mort*, to the death], *adv.* To the death. *a.* Sick to death; dejected.

alar (ā' lår) [L. *ālāris* (*āla*, a wing)], *a.* Of or pertaining to a wing; wing-like, shaped like a wing. **alary** (ā' lå ri) [L. *ālārius*], *a.* Of or pertaining to wings. **alate** (ā' lāt), **alated** (ā' lāt ėd), *a.* Having wings or winglike processes.

alarm (å larm') [O.F. *alarme*, It. *all'arme*, to arms!], *n.* A summons to arms; warning of approaching danger; terror mingled with surprise; a contrivance for waking persons from sleep or arousing attention; (*fencing*) a challenge. *v.t.* To rouse to a sense of danger; to inspire with apprehension of coming evil. **alarm-bell,** *n.* A bell rung to sound an alarm. **alarm-clock,** *n.* A clock so contrived as to sound a loud peal at a particular hour. **alarm-cord,** *n.* A cord pulled by passengers to stop a train. **alarm-gun,** *n.* A gun fired to give notice of danger. **alarm-post,** *n.* A rendezvous in case of alarm. **alarm-watch,** *n.* A watch fitted with an alarm; [ALARM-CLOCK]. **alarming,** *part.a.* Exciting apprehension; terrifying. **alarmingly,** *adv.* **alarmist,** *n.* One who needlessly raises alarm; a panic-monger. **alarum** (å lăr' ŭm), *n.* [ALARM]; (*poet.*) An alarm; an alarm-clock or alarm-watch.

alas (å las') [O.F. *a*, ah! *las!* wretched (L. *lassus*, wearied, wretched)], *int.* An exclamation of sorrow, grief, pity, or concern.

Alastor (å las' tôr) [Gr. *a*, not, *last* (*lathein*, to forget)], *n.* An avenging spirit, nemesis.

alate, alated, *a.* [ALAR].

alb (ălb) [O.F. *albe*, late L. *alba* (fem. a., *albus*, white)], *n.* A kind of surplice with close sleeves worn by priests when celebrating Mass, and by certain consecrated kings.

albacore (ăl' bå kôr) [Port. *albacor* (Arab. *al*, the, *bukr*, a young camel, a heifer)], *n.* A large species of tunny; loosely applied to allied species.

Albany (awl' bå ni) *n.* A city of the State of New York, named in honour of James, Duke of York and Albany, afterwards James II. **Albany-beef,** *n.* (*Am.*) The flesh of the sturgeon, caught in the Hudson as far up as Albany. **Albany doctor:** (*W. Austral.*) a sea breeze.

albata (ăl bā' tå, ăl ba'-) [L. *albāta*, fem. of *albātus*, whitened (*albus*)], *n.* An alloy like silver; German silver.

albatross (ăl' bå tros) [Port. *alcatraz, alcatruz*, Arab. *al*, the, *quadras*, bucket, the pelican (corrupted through assimilation to L. *albus*, white)], *n.* *The frigate-bird; the English name of a genus of Tubinares or petrels; *Diomedea exulans*, the largest known sea-bird, the great albatross.

albeit (awl bē' it) [M.E. *al be it*], ***albe** (awl bē') *conj.* Although, even though, notwithstanding.

albert (ăl' bėrt) [Prince Albert, consort of Queen Victoria], *n.* A short kind of watch-chain, fastened to a waistcoat buttonhole.

albescent (ăl bes' ėnt) [L. *albēscere*, to grow white (*albus*), -ENT], *a.* Becoming or passing into white; whitish. **albescence,** *n.*

Albigenses (ăl bi jen' sēz) [L. from *Albigeoi*], inhabitants of the town of Albi (L. *Albiga*), *n.pl.* A sect of reformers in Languedoc, who separated from the Church of Rome in the twelfth century. **albigensian,** *a.*

albino (ăl bē' nō) [Port. a white negro (L. *albus*, white)], *n.* A human being, or one of the lower animals, having the colour pigment absent from the skin, hair, and eyes, so as to be abnormally light in colour; a plant in which little or no chlorophyll is developed. **albiness** (ăl' bi nes), *n.* A female albino. **albinism** (ăl' bi nizm), *n.*

Albion (ăl' bi ŏn) [L. *albus*, white], *n.* An old name of England still retained in poetry.

albite (ăl' bīt) [L. *albus*, white, -ITE], *n.* White felspar, soda felspar. **albitic,** *a.* Pertaining to or of the nature of albite.

album (ăl' bŭm) [L. *album*, neut. of *albus*, white], *n.* A blank book for the insertion of autographs, poetry, drawings, or the like; (*Am.*) a visitors' book.

albumen (ăl bū' mėn) [L. *albumen -inis*, white of egg (*albus*, white)], *n.* The white of an egg; albumin; (*Bot.*) the substance interposed between the skin and embryo of many seeds; the endosperm or perisperm. **albumenize,** *v.t.* (*Photo.*) To coat with an albuminous solution.

albumin (ăl bū' min) [as prec.], *n.* One of the classes of albuminoids, existing in animals, in the white of egg, in blood serum, and in plants. **albuminize,** *v.t.* To convert into albumen. **albuminoid, albuminoidal** (ăl bū' min oid) [-OID], *a.* Resembling or of the nature of albumen. *n.pl.* Proteins, the chief constituents of animal and vegetable bodies. **albuminous, albuminose,** *a.* Consisting of, resembling, or containing albumen. **albuminuria,** *n.* The presence of albumen in the urine; the morbid condition causing this.

alburnum (ăl bĕr' nŭm), **alburn** (ăl bĕrn) [L. *alburnum* (*albus*, white)], *n.* The sapwood in exogenous stems, between the inner bark and heartwood. **alburnous** (ăl bĕr′ nŭs), *a.* Of or pertaining to alburnum.

alcade [ALCAYDE].

alcahest [ALKAHEST].

alcaic (ăl kā′ ik) [L. *alcaicus*, Gr. *alkaikos* (*Alkaios*, prop. name)], *a.* Of or pertaining to Alcæus, a lyric poet born in Mitylene, c. 600 B.C., or to a kind of verse he invented. *n.* (*chiefly in pl.*) Alcaic strophes.

alcayde (ăl kād′, al kī′ dė) [Sp. *alcaide*, *alcayde*, Arab. *al*, the, *qāīd*, leader, commander (*qāda*, lead)], *n.* The governor of a fortress in the Peninsula, Barbary etc.; the warden of a prison, a gaoler.

alchemy (ăl′ kė mi) [O.F. *alchemie*, *alquimie*, med. L. *alchimia*, Arab. *al*, the, *kimia* (late Gr. *chemeia*, prob. Egyptian art, confused with *chumeia*, a mingling, from *cheein*, to pour)], *n.* The chemistry of the Middle Ages, the search for an alkahest, the philosophers' stone, and the panacea; a metallic compound imitating gold; magic power of transmutation. **alchemic** (ăl kem′ ik), **alchemical,** *a.* Of or pertaining to alchemy. **alchemically,** *adv.* **alchemist** (ăl′ kė mist), *n.* One who studies or practises alchemy. **alchemistic, alchemistical,** *a.* **alchemize,** *v.t.* To transmute.

alchymy etc. [ALCHEMY].

alcohol (ăl′ kȯ hol) [med. L. *alcohol*, Arab. *al-koh'l* (*al*, the, *koh'l*, powder to stain the eyelids)], *n.* Pure spirit, rectified spirit, spirits of wine; any intoxicating liquor. **alcohol lamp,** *n.* (*Am.*) A spirit-lamp. **alcoholate** (ăl′ kȯ hŏl āt), *n.* A crystalline compound in which alcohol acts as water of crystallization. **alcoholic** (ăl kȯ hol′ ik), *n.* An addict to alcohol. *a.* Of or pertaining to alcohol. **alcoholism** (ăl′ kȯ hŏl izm), *n.* The action of alcohol on the human system; the state of being affected by alcohol. **alcoholize,** *v.t.* To rectify; to saturate with alcohol. **alcoholization,** *n.* The act or process of rectifying any spirit; saturation with alcohol; alcoholism. **alcoholometer** (ăl kȯ hol om′ ėt ĕr), **alcoometer** (ăl kȯ om′ ėt ėr) [-METER], *n.* An instrument for measuring the proportion of pure alcohol in a liquor. **alcoholometrical** (ăl′ kȯ hol ȯ met′ ri kăl), **alcoometrical** (ăl kȯ ȯ met′ ri kăl), *a.* Pertaining to the process of alcoholometry. **alcoholometry** (ăl kȯ hol om′ ėt ri), **alcoometry,** *n.* The act, art, or process of ascertaining the quantity of pure alcohol in a liquor.

alcoran (ăl′ kȯ ran, ăl kȯ ran′) [KORAN], *n.* The Koran. **alcoranist** (ăl′ kȯ răn ist), *n.* One who adheres to the letter of the Koran.

alcove (ăl′ kōv) [F. *alcôve*, Sp. *alcoba*, Arab. *alqobbah*, the vault], *n.* A vaulted recess; a recess in a wall; a bower, a summer-house.

alcyon [HALCYON].

alcyonarian (ăl si ȯ nâr′ i ăn) [Gr. *alkuonion*, Bastard-sponge (from resemblance to nest of *alcuōn*, the alcyon, or HALCYON)], *a.* Belonging to the Alcyonaria, a group of zoophytes. *n.* Any individual of that group.

aldehyde (ăl′ dė hīd) [abbrev. of L. *alcohol dehydrogenatum*, alcohol deprived of hydrogen], *n.* A volatile fluid obtained from alcohol by oxidation; an extensive class of compounds of the same type. **aldehydic** (ăl dė hī′ dik), *a.*

alder (1) (awl′ dėr) [A.-S. *alr*, *aler*, *alor* (cp. Icel. *ölr*, O.H.G. *elira*, L. *alnus*)], *n.* A well-known English tree (*Alnus glutinosa*) growing in moist places; applied also, with distinguishing epithet, to many plants whose leaves more or less resemble those of the alder.

alderman (awl′ dėr măn) [A.-S. *ealdor*, *alder*, a chief (cp. OLD) -MAN], *n.* A civic dignitary next in rank below the mayor; (*colloq.*) a long clay, *i.e.* a long clay pipe, a 'churchwarden.' **aldermanate** (awl′ dėr măn āt) [med. L. *aldermannātus*, from *aldermannus*], *n.* Aldermanry; aldermen collectively. **aldermanic** (-măn′ ik), *a.* Pertaining or relating to an alderman. **aldermanlike, aldermanly,** *a.* Like or befitting an alderman. **aldermanry** (awl′ dėr măn ri), *n.* A district having its own alderman, a ward; the dignity or office of alderman. **aldermanship,** *n.* The office or dignity of alderman.

alderney (awl′ dėr ni) [name of Island], *a.* Of a breed of cattle common in the Channel Islands. *n.* An animal of that breed.

aldine (awl′ dīn) [*Aldus*, -INE], *a.* Of, belonging to, or printed by Aldus Manutius (a celebrated Venetian printer of the sixteenth century) or his family; type modelled on that used by him.

ale (āl) [A.-S. *ealu*], *n.* An intoxicating liquor made from malt by fermentation; *a rural festival or merry-making, at which ale was drunk. **ale-bench,** *n.* A bench in or before a public-house. **ale-conner** [A.-S. *cunnere*, to know; see CAN], *n.* An examiner or inspector of ale. **ale-house,** *n.* A tavern licensed to sell ale. **ale-taster,** *n.* An ale-conner. **ale-wife** (1), *n.* A women who keeps an ale-house (see also ALEWIFE (2))].

aleatory (ā′ lė ȧ tȯ ri) [L. *āleātōrius*, from *āleātor*, a dice-player (*ālea*, dice)], *a.* Depending upon an uncertain event.

alecost (āl′ kost), *n.* (*Bot.*) The plant costmary formerly used to flavour ale.

alee (ȧ lē′) [O.N. *á hlé*, a sea-phrase (*á*, on, *hlé*, shelter)], *adv.* and *pred.a.* On the lee side; to leeward.

alegar (ā′ lė gȧr) [ALE, F. *aigre*, sharp, sour], *n.* Vinegar made from ale; malt vinegar.

alembic (ȧ lem′ bik) [F. *alambique*, Arab. *al-anbīq*, the still, Gr. *ambix -ikos*, a cup], *n.* A vessel made of glass or copper formerly used for distilling.

alert (ȧ lĕrt′) [F. *alerte*, *allerte*, *à l'erte*, It. *all'erta*, on one's guard (*à la*, to the, *erta*, fem. p.p. of *ergere*, L. *ērigere*, to erect)], *a.* Watchful, vigilant; brisk, sprightly. *n.* An alarm; a surprise; warning by siren or otherwise of a threatened air-raid. *v.t.* To warn; to put on guard; to arouse. **on the alert:** On the watch; on one's guard; ready, prepared. **alertly,** *adv.* **alertness,** *n.*

aleuron, aleurone (ȧ lūr′ ŏn) [Gr. *aleuron*, flour (*aleō*, I grind)], *n.* An albuminoid substance found in ripening seeds.

alewife (2) (āl′ wīf) [perhaps N. Am. Indian], *n.* A North American fish, *Clupea serrata*, resembling the shad but smaller [see also ALE].

alexandrine (ăl ėg zăn′ drin) [F. *alexandrin*, origin disputed], *n.* Iambic verse with six feet.

alexia (ȧ lek′ si ȧ) [Gr. *a-*, not; *lexis*, speech, but confused with L. *legere*, to read], *n.* (*Med.*) The loss of power to understand written or printed words; word-blindness.

alexin (ȧ lek′ sin) [Gr. *alexein*, to ward off], *n.* (*Med.*) A body present in blood serum, which, combining with an anti-serum, gives protection against disease.

alexipharmic (ȧ leks i far′ mik) [F. *alexipharmaque*, Gr. *alexipharmakon* (*alexō*, ward off, *pharmakon*, poison)], *a.* Preserving against poison. *n.* An antidote.

alfalfa (ăl făl′ fȧ) [Sp.], *n.* (*Bot.*) General term for lucerne.

alfresco (al fres′ kō) [It. *al fresco*, in the fresh], *adv.* and *a.* In the open air, open-air.

alga (ăl′ gȧ) [L.], *n.* (*pl.* **Algæ**, -ge, -jē) A seaweed, a subaquatic plant. **algal,** *a.* Pertaining to seaweed. *n.* A seaweed; a plant of the order Algæ. **alginic,** *a.* Pertaining to, or obtained from seaweed. **algist,** *n.* A botanist who specializes in Algæ. **algoid,** *a.* Of the nature of or like Algæ. **algology,** *n.* The branch of botany dealing with Algæ. **algologist,** *n.* An algist. **algous** (ăl′ gŭs), *a.* Pertaining to, resembling, or full of seaweed.

***algate, *algates** (awl′ gāt, -s) [O.N. *alla gôtu*, every way (GATE)], *adv.* Every way; any way; by all means, at any rate.

algebra (ăl' jė brȧ) [Arab. *al-jebr*, the reunion of parts], *n.* Universal arithmetic in which letters are used as symbols for quantities, and signs represent arithmetical processes. **algebraic** (ăl jė brā' ik), **algebraical,** *a.* Of or relating to algebra; involving or employing algebra. **algebraically,** *adv.* **algebraist** (ăl' jė brā ist), **algebrist** (ăl' jė brist), *n.* One who is versed in algebra. **algebraize** (ăl' jė brȧ īz), *v.t.* To reduce to an algebraic form; to solve by means of algebra.

algid (ăl' jid) [F. *algide*, L. *algidus* (*algēre*, to be cold)], *a.* (*Med.*) Cold, esp. in ague. **algidity,** *n.* A state of coldness.

algist, algoid, algology, algous [ALGA].

algometer (ăl gom' ėt ėr) [Gr. *algos*, pain, *metron*, measure], *n.* An instrument for estimating degrees of sensitiveness to pain.

alguazil (ăl gwȧ zil') [Sp. *alguazil* (*-cil*), Arab. *alwazir*, the vizier], *n.* An inferior officer of justice; a constable.

algum (ăl' gum) [Heb. *algūm* (wrongly *almug*, 1 Kings x. 11)], *n.* A tree mentioned in the Bible, probably sandalwood.

alhambra (ăl hăm' brȧ) [Arab. *al-hamra'*, the red house], *n.* The Moorish palace and citadel at Granada in Spain. **alhambraesque** (ăl hăm brȧ esk'), *a.* Resembling the Alhambra or its style of architecture.

alia (ā' li ȧ) [L. neut. pl. of a. *alius*, other], *n.pl.* Other things. **inter alia:** Among other things (not mentioned).

alias (ăl' i ăs) [L.], *adv.* Otherwise (named or called). *n.* A second name, an assumed name.

alibi (ăl' i bī) [L. elsewhere, loc. of *alius* (cp. *ibi, ubi*)], *n.* The plea (of a person accused) of having been 'elsewhere' when the offence with which he is charged was committed; (*Am. colloq.* but incorrect) an excuse for failing to do something; an excuse.

alicante (ăl i kăn' ti), *n.* A red, sweet wine from the Spanish town of this name.

alidad (ăl' i dăd), **alidade** (ăl' i dād) [F. *alidade*, med. L. *alhidada*, Arab. *al- 'idādah* (*al*, the, *'adad*, upper arm)], *n.* Arm or index showing degrees on circle in astrolabe, quadrant, theodolite, etc.

alien (ā' li ėn) [O.F. *alien*, L. *aliēnus*, a stranger, or of a stranger (*alius*, another)], *a.* Belonging to another or others; of foreign extraction; estranged from; averse, repugnant to; incongruous with. *n.* A foreigner. **v.* [ALIENATE]. **alienability,** *n.* Capable of being alienated. **alienable,** *a.* That may be alienated. **alienate** (ā' li ėn āt) [O.F. *aliéner*, L. *alienāre*], *v.t.* To estrange; to transfer to the ownership of another. **alienate** (ā' li ėn ȧt), *a.* Estranged. **alienation,** *n.* The act of alienating; the state of being alienated; mental derangement. **alienator,** *n.* **alienee,** *n.* (*Law*) One to whom the ownership of property is transferred.

alienism (ā' li ėn izm), *n.* The state of being an alien; the treatment and study of mental derangement. **alienist,** *n.* One skilled in the treatment or engaged in the study of mental derangement.

aliform (ā' li fôrm), *a.* Shaped like a wing.

alight (1) (ȧ līt') [A.-S. *ālīhtan* (*a-*, intens., *līhtan*, to jump down from a horse)], *v.i.* To get down, descend, dismount, reach the ground, to settle on; to light on, happen on, meet with; *to stop, arrive.

alight (2) (ȧ līt') [p.p. of *alīhtan*, *onlīhtan*, to shine upon, light up (confused with forms like ABLAZE, AFIRE)], *pred.a.* On fire; illuminated.

align, etc. [ALINE].

alike (ȧ līk') [A.-S. *onlīc* (*on-*, on, *līc*, like); also A.-S. *gelīc* (*ge-*, together, *līc*, like); cp. O.H.G. *gelīh* (G. *gleich*) and Icel. *ālīkr*], *a.* Similar. *adv.* Equally, in the same manner, similarly.

aliment (ăl' i mėnt) [L. *alimentum* (*alere*, to nourish, -MENT)], *n.* Nutriment, food; support, sustenance; mental nutriment. *v.t.* *To nourish; (*Law*) to make provision for the maintenance of. **alimental** (ăl i men' tȧl), *a.* Pertaining to aliment; nutritive. **alimentally,** *adv.* **alimentary,** *a.* Pertaining to aliment or nutrition; nutritious, nourishing; sustaining, supporting. **alimentary canal,** *n.* The great tube or duct conveying food to the stomach, and carrying off solid excreta from the system. **alimentation** (-tā' shŭn), *n.* The act or quality of affording nourishment; the state of being nourished. **alimentative** (ăl i men' tȧ- tiv), *a.* Connected with the function of nutrition.

alimony (ăl' i mȯ ni) [L. *alimōnia* (*alere*, to nourish)], *n.* Maintenance; payment of means of support, esp. the proportional part of a husband's income allowed a wife for her support on legal separation, or for other causes.

aline, align (ȧ līn') [F. *aligner* (*à*, to, *ligner*, from L. *līneāre*, to line, from *līnea*, a line)], *v.t.* To range or place in a line. *v.i.* To fall into line. **alinement,** *n.* The act of ranging in line or being ranged; objects arranged in a line or lines; the ground-plan of a road or earthwork.

aliped (ăl' i ped) [L. *ala*, wing; *pes*, *pedis*, foot], *n.* (*Zool.*) A wing-footed creature, *e.g.* bat.

aliphatic (ăl i făt' ic) [Gr. *aleiphar*, an unguent], *a.* (*Chem.*) Fatty. **aliphatic compounds,** *n.pl.* Methane derivatives or fatty compounds containing open chains of carbon atoms.

aliquot (ăl' i kwot) [F. *aliquote*, late L. *aliquota*, (fem. a. from *aliquot*, several, so many)], *a.* Pertaining to a number that is contained an integral number of times by a given number. *n.* An integral factor, an aliquot part. **aliquot part,** *n.* A part that is a division of the whole without remainder, as 10s. of £1, 3½ lb. of 1 cwt.

alive (ȧ līv') M.E. *on live*, A.-S. *on life* (*on*, prep., *līfe* dat. of *līf*, LIFE)], *adv.* and *pred.a.* Living, existent; in force or operation; astir, lively; sensible of (an idea). **alive and kicking:** In a very lively state, all alive. **all alive,** *pred.a.* Alive, lively, frisky. **look alive!** Look sharp, make haste. **man alive!** A colloquial term of expostulation or sarcastic address.

alizarin (ȧ liz' ȧr in) [F. *alizari* (prob. Arab. in origin)], *n.* The red colouring matter of madder.

alkahest (ăl' kȧ hest) [Imitation Arab.], *n.* A word invented, probably by Paracelsus (early 16th cent.), to signify the universal solvent of the alchemists.

alkali (ăl' kȧ lī) [F. *alcali*, Arab. *al-qalī*, the calcined ashes of saltwort], *n.* (*pl.* **alkalis**) A compound of hydrogen and oxygen with sodium, potassium, and other substances, which is soluble in water, and produces caustic and corrosive solutions capable of neutralizing acids and changing the colour of vegetable substances; (*Comm.*) alkaline products, such as caustic potash and caustic soda. **alkali-cellulose** [VISCOSE]. **alkali-flat, alkali-land,** *n.* Any one of several wide waste districts in Colorado and Nevada, covered with an alkaline efflorescence. **alkali-metals,** *n.pl.* [ALKALINE-METALS]. **alkalescent** (ăl kȧ les' ėnt), *a.* Becoming or tending to become alkaline; slightly alkaline. *n.* An alkalescent substance. **alkalescence,** *n.* The state or condition of becoming alkaline. **alkalescency,** *n.* Tendency to become alkaline. **alkalify,** *v.t.* To convert into an alkali. *v.i.* To be converted into an alkali. **alkalifiable,** *a.* Capable of being converted into an alkali. **alkalimetry** (ăl kȧ lim' ėt ri), *n.* The measurement of the strength of alkalis. **alkalimetrical** (-met' ri kȧl), *a.* **alkaline** (ăl' kȧ līn), *a.* Having the properties of an alkali. **alkaline-metals,** *n.pl.* Metals the hydroxides of which are alkalis: these are potassium, sodium, cæsium, lithium, and rubidium. **alkalize,** *v.t.* To render alkaline. **alkalization,** *n.* The act of rendering alkaline. **alkaloid,** *a.* Resembling an alkali in properties. *n.* A natural or artificial nitrogenous base, with an alkaline reaction; *e.g. vegeto-alkaloids*; organic bases derived from plants.

alkanet (ăl' kȧ net) [Sp. *alcana*, Arab. *al henna* [HENNA], *n.* A dye material obtained from *Anchusa tinctoria*; the plant itself.

alkyl (ăl′ kil) [ALC(OHOL) -YL], *n.* (*Chem.*) General name for a monovalent hydrocarbon radical of the methene series, *e.g.* methyl ethyl, butyl. **alkylation,** *n.* The introduction of an alkyl into a compound.

alkoran (ăl′ kŏ ran′) [ALCORAN, KORAN].

all (awl) [A.-S. *eal* (sing.), *ealle* (pl.), old Mercian form *alle*; (O.H.G. *al*)], *a.* The whole (quantity, duration, extent, amount, quality, or degree) of. *n.* The whole, everything, every one. *adv.* Wholly, entirely, completely. **after all:** After everything has been taken into account. **all aboard:** (*Am.*) Take your seats. **all ages:** (*Racing*) Of a race in which horses of all ages are entered. **all along:** Throughout. **all about it:** The whole of the matter. **all and some, all and sundry:** All (taken distributively). **all but:** Almost. **all in:** Inclusive of everything; (*colloq.*) exhausted. *a.* (*Sport*) Descriptive of a form of wrestling without restrictions. **all in all:** All things in all respects. **all one:** The same in all respects. **all out:** (*colloq.*) Completely, utterly. **all over:** (*colloq.*) Completely, everywhere; finished (in the phrases *all over with*, *is all over*). **all overish:** (*colloq.*) General sense of feeling unwell. **all the better:** So much the better. **all the same:** Nevertheless; in spite of what has been said. **and all:** (*prov.*) Too, withal. **and all that:** With all the rest of it. **at all:** In any respect; to the extent; in any degree; of any kind; whatever. ***all-to:** Wholly, completely. (The *to* is the A.-S. intensive pref. *to-*, corresponding to the Ger. *zer-*; and, in course of time, the fact that *to-* belonged to the verb was lost sight of, and it was incorporated with *all*.) (The compounds of *all* are exceedingly numerous, and only the more important are inserted here.) **All-father,** *n.* The Father of all: applied to Odin, Jupiter, and the Deity. **all-fired,** *a.* (*Am.*) A euphemism for 'hell-fired'; infernal. **All Fools' Day,** *n.* The 1st of April, from the custom of practising then on the credulity of one's neighbours. **all-fours,** *n.* A game of cards named from the four cards by which points are reckoned; a game of dominoes in which points are scored only when the pips at both ends make up some multiple of four; the four legs of a quadruped, the arms and legs of a human being. **to run on all fours:** To go evenly; to be analogous to. **all-hail,** *int.* A phrase expressive of respect or welcome. *n.* A salutation of respect and welcome. **All-Hallows** [HALLOW], *n.* All Saints' Day. **All-Hallows' Eve** [HALLOWE'EN], *n.* **all-round** (awl round) [ALL, ROUND], *a.* Good in all respects. **all-round man:** One whose merits, acquirements, or skill are not limited to one or two pursuits; one generally competent; versatile. **all-round traverse:** (*Mil.*) A machine gun mounted so that it can be fired in any direction. **all-standing:** (*colloq.*) Unexpectedly, taken by surprise; in one's clothes, as in *to turn in all-standing.* **All Saints,** *n.pl.* The saints collectively. **All Saints' Day,** *n.* A church festival (Nov. 1) in honour of the saints collectively. **All Souls,** *n.pl.* The souls of the pious dead. **All Souls' Day,** *n.* The day (Nov. 2) on which the Roman Catholic Church commemorates all the faithful departed. **all speed,** *n.* The greatest possible speed. **all there:** Sharp in intellect, quick. **all-time high,** *a.* A record high level. **all together,** *adv.* In a body, altogether. **all up,** *a.* (*Aviat.*) Expressing the total weight of an aircraft with its burden when in the air. **all up with:** No more hope for.

alla (ā′ lā) [Maori], *n.* (*N. Zealand*) The sea-mullet.

Allah (ăl′ ȧ) [Arab. *allah*, contr. of *al-ilāh*, the god (cp. Heb. *ĕlōah*)], *n.* The name of God among the Mohammedans.

allay (ȧ lā′) [*a-*, intens. pref., LAY (M.E. form *alleyen*; confused with *aleggen*, to alleviate, and also with *aleye*, allege, and *allay*, alloy)], *v.t.* To quiet, to still; to put down, to repress; to temper, to abate, to alleviate; *to dilute, to weaken. **v.i.* To sink, to subside, to grow calm. **allaying,** *n.* Dilution, mitigation. **a.* Diluting, tempering. ***allayment,** *n.* Mitigation, alleviation.

allegation (ăl e gā′ shŭn), *n.* The act of alleging; an assertion without proof; a specific charge; a statement of what one undertakes to prove.

allege (ȧ lej′) [*adlēgiāre*, Latinization of O.F. *esligier*, late L. *exlītigāre* (L. *lītigāre*, to contend at law); treated as if from *allēgāre*, to send, bring forward], *v.t.* To adduce as an authority, to plead as an excuse; to affirm positively.

allegiance (ȧ lē′ ji ȧns, ȧ lē′ jȧns) [M.E. *legeance*, O.F. *ligeance* (LIEGE); *a-* (L. *ad-*) prefixed through confusion with obs. *allegeance* (L. *allegātio*)], *n.* The obligation of a subject to his sovereign or government; respect, devotion, fealty.

allegory (ăl′ ė gŏ ri) [L. *allegŏria*, Gr. *allegoria*; speaking otherwise than one seems to speak], *n.* Description of one thing under the image of another; an instance of such description, an extended metaphor, an emblem, an allegorical representation. **allegoric** (ăl lė gor′ ik), **allegorical,** *a.* Pertaining to an allegory; resembling an allegory. **allegorically,** *adv.* **allegorist,** *n.* A writer of allegories. **allegorize** (ăl′ lė gŏ rīz), *v.t.* To convert into an allegory, to interpret allegorically. *v.i.* To use allegory, to speak or write in a figurative manner.

allegro (ăl lā′ grō) [It.], *a.* (*Mus.*) Brisk, lively, gay. *adv.* Briskly, quickly. *n.* A movement in allegro time or manner. **allegramente,** *adv.* Joyfully. **allegretto,** *adv.* Somewhat briskly.

allelomorph (ă lel′ ō môrf) [Gr. *allelon*, of one another; *morphe*, form], *n.* (*Biol.*) Either of a pair of contrasted characteristics, inherited alternatively with the other and assumed to depend on genes in homologous chromosomes.

alleluia (ăl le loo′ yȧ) [HALLELUJAH].

allergy (ăl′ ĕr ji) [Gr. *allos*, other; ENERGY], *n.* (*Med.*) An abnormal response or reaction to some food or substance innocuous to most people; hypersensitiveness to certain substances inhaled or touched. **allergic** (ăl ĕr′ jik), *a.*

alleviate (ȧ lē′ vi āt) [late L. *alleviātus*, p.p. of *alleviāre* (*al*, *ad-*, to, *levāre*, to lift)], *v.t.* To lighten, lessen, mitigate, extenuate. **alleviation** (-ā′ shŭn), *n.* The act of alleviating; relief, mitigation. **alleviative** (ȧ lē′ vi ȧ tiv), *n.* That which alleviates. **alleviator** (ȧ lē′ vi ȧ tor), *n.* **alleviatory,** *a.*

alley (1) (ăl′ i) [O.F. *alee* (*aller*, to go)], *n.* A passage, a walk; a bordered walk; a narrow street or lane; a narrow enclosure for playing at skittles, etc. **alleyed,** *a.* Formed into alleys, or laid out as an alley. **back alley,** *n.* (*Am.*) A mews.

alley (2) [ALLY (2)].

All-Hallows [ALL].

alliaceous (ăl i ā′ shus) [L. *allium*, garlic, -ACEOUS], *a.* Pertaining to the plant-genus *Allium*, which contains the onion and garlic; having the taste or smell of garlic.

alliance (ȧ lī′ ȧns) [O.F. *aliance*]. The state of being allied; union by marriage, affinity; union by treaty or league; a treaty or league; union or connexion of interests; the parties allied; (*Bot.*) Lindley's name for a group of a natural order.

alligation (ăl i gā′ shŭn) [L. *alligāre* (*ad-*, to, *ligāre*, to bind)], *n.* The act of binding together; an arithmetical rule or process for finding the value of a mixture of various ingredients of different qualities and prices.

Alligator (ăl′ i gā tŏr) [Sp. *el lagarto*, the lizard (L. *lacerta*)], *n.* Any animal of the crocodile genus *Alligator*; a genus of Saurians from America and China. **alligator-apple,** *n.* The fruit of *Anona palustris*, a West Indian tree. **alligator-gar,** *n.* The garpike of the Southern States of N. America. **alligator-pear** [AVOCADO], *n.* The fruit of *Persea gratissima*, a West Indian tree, allied to the laurel. **alligator-tortoise,** *n.* The snapping-turtle. **alligator-wood,** *n.* The timber of *Guarea swartzii*, a West Indian tree.

allign, etc. [ALINE].

allineation (ȧ lin ē ā′ shŭn) [L. *ad-*, to, *lineat-*, part. stem of *lineāre*, to draw a line], *n.* Alinement; (*Astron.*) the alinement of two or more objects with a certain point.

alliterate (ȧ lit′ ėr āt) [L. *ad-*, to, *litera*, a letter], *v.i.* To commence (as a word) with the same letter or sound; to practise alliteration. **alliteration** (-ā′ shŭn), *n.* Commencement of two or more words or accented syllables, in close connexion, with the same letter or sound. **alliterative,** *a.* Pertaining to alliteration. **alliteratively,** *adv.*

Allium (ăl′ li ŭm) [L.], *n.* A genus of plants containing garlic, leeks, onions, etc.

allocate (ăl′ ō kāt) [late L. *allocātus*, p.p. of *allocāre* (*ad-*, to, *locāre*, to place, *locus*, a place)], *v.t.* To assign, allot, apportion; to localize. **allocation,** *n.* The act of allocating; the admission of an item in an account; the item so admitted.

allocution (ăl ō kū′ shŭn) [L. *allocūtiōnem* (*ad-*, to, *loqui*, to speak)], *n.* A formal address, esp. one delivered by the Pope to the bishops and clergy, or to the Church generally.

allodium (ȧ lō′ di ŭm) [med. L. *allodium*, O. Frankish *alod* (*al*, all or whole, *ōd*, estate, cp. O.H.G. *ōt*)], *n.* Landed property held in absolute ownership. **allodial,** *a.* Pertaining to allodium; held independently, in contradistinction to feudal. **allodially,** *adv.* **allodialism,** *n.* The system of absolute proprietorship of land. **allodialist,** *n.* One who holds allodial land.

allogamy (ȧ log′ ȧ mi) [Gr. *allos*, other, -GAMY], *n.* (*Bot.*) Cross-fertilization.

allograph (ăl′ ō grăf) [Gr. *allos*, other, -GRAPH], *n.* A signature written by one person on behalf of another.

allonge (ăl lonzh′) [F. *allonge*, a lengthening], *n.* A slip of paper attached to a bill of exchange to hold further signatures; a fly-leaf.

allopathy (ȧ lop′ ȧ thi) [Gr. *allos*, other, -PATHY], *n.* The treatment of diseased action by inducing another action of a different kind not necessarily diseased; ordinary medical practice, as opposed to homœopathy. **allopathic** (ăl lȯ păth′ ik), *a.* Pertaining to or practising allopathy. **allopathically,** *adv.* **allopathist** (ȧ lop′ ȧ thist), *n.* One who practises allopathy.

allophylian (ăl ȯ fil′ i ȧn) [Gr. *allophulos*, alien (*allos*, other, *phulē*, tribe)], *a.* Of another race than Aryan or Semitic; (sometimes) Turanian. *n.* One of non-Aryan and non-Semitic race.

allot (ȧ lot′) [A.-F. *aloter* (*a-*, L. *ad-*, to, LOT)], *v.t.* (*past & p.p.* **allotted**) To distribute, to grant, to bestow, to assign as one's share. **allotment,** *n.* The act of allotting; the share assigned; a small plot of land let for cottage cultivation. **allottee** (ăl ot tē′), *n.* The person to whom allotment is made.

allotropy (ȧ lot′ rȯ pi) [Gr. *allotropia*, from *allotropos* (*allos*, other, *tropos*, turn, manner, from *trepein*, to turn)], *n.* Variation of physical properties without change of substance; thus, the diamond, graphite, and charcoal are allotropic variations of carbon. **allotropic** (ăl lȯ trop′ ik), *a.* Pertaining to allotropy; existing in diverse states. **allotropically,** *adv.* In an allotropic manner. **allotropism,** *n.* The principle or the process of allotropy.

allow (ȧ lou′) [O.F. *alouer*, from two verbs whose meanings were often confused, (1) L. *allaudāre*, to praise, (2) low L. *allocāre*, to place, to admit as proved], *v.t.* *To praise, sanction, approve; to admit, permit; to bestow, concede; to take into account, give credit for. **to allow for:** To make allowance or deduction for. **to allow of:** To accept, to admit. **allowable,** *a.* **allowableness,** *n.* **allowably,** *adv.* **allowance,** *n.* The act of allowing; *praise, approbation; permission, deduction; fixed quantity or sum allowed. *v.t.* To put upon allowance.

alloy (ȧ loi′, ăl′ oi) [formerly *alay* or *allay*, O.F. *alai*, from *aleier*, to combine, L. *alligāre* (*ad-*, to, *ligāre*, to bind)], *n.* An inferior metal mixed with one of greater value; a mixture of metals; an amalgam; any base admixture; the standard of purity, the quality of gold and silver. *v.t.* To mix with a baser metal; to mix metals; to mix with anything base or inferior.

allseed (awl′ sēd), *n.* Name of various many-seeded plants.

allspice (awl′ spīs), *n.* The berry of the pimento, said to combine the flavour of cinnamon, cloves, and nutmeg; other aromatic shrubs.

allude (ȧ lood′, ȧ lūd′) [L. *allūdere* (*ad-*, to, *lūdere*, to play)], *v.i.* To make indirect reference (to), to hint at; (*colloq.* and *incorrectly*) to mean, to refer to directly. **allusion,** *n.* A reference to anything not directly mentioned; a hint. **allusive,** *a.* Containing an allusion; hinting at an implied meaning, characterized by allusion. **allusively,** *adv.* **allusiveness,** *n.*

allure (ȧ lūr′) [O.F. *alurer*, *aleurrer* (*à*, to, *leurrer*, to lure)], *v.t.* To attract or tempt by the offer of some real or apparent good; to entice; to fascinate, to charm. *n.* Charm, sex appeal. **allurement,** *n.* The act of alluring or enticing; that which allures; a bait, an enticement. **alluring,** *a.* Luring, enticing, attractive. **alluringly,** *adv.*

allusion [ALLUDE].

alluvia, alluvial [ALLUVIUM].

alluvion (ȧ loo′ vi ŏn) [F. *alluvion*, L. *alluviōnem*, acc. of *alluvio*, a washing against; see ALLUVIUM], *n.* The wash of the sea against the land; (*Law*) the formation of new land by the action of flowing water.

alluvium (ȧ loo′ vi ŭm) [L., neut. of a. *alluvius* (*ad-*, to, *luere*, to wash)], *n.* (*pl.* **alluvia**) Earth, sand, gravel, stones, or other transported matter which has been washed away and thrown down by rivers, floods, or similar causes. **alluvial,** *a.* Pertaining to alluvium; deposited from flowing water.

ally (1) (ȧ lī′) [O.F. *alier*, L. *alligāre* (*ad-*, to, *ligāre*, to bind)], *v.t.* To unite by treaty, confederation, marriage, or friendship. *n.* (ȧ lī′, ăl′ ī) One united by treaty, confederation, marriage, or friendship; something akin to another in structure or properties; an auxiliary.

ally (2), **alley** (ăl′ li) [said to be dim. from ALABASTER], *n.* A superior kind of marble or taw.

alma, almah (ăl′ mȧ) [Arab. *'almah*, learned, knowing], *n.* An Egyptian dancing-girl.

almacantar (ăl mȧ kăn′ tȧr) [F. *almicantarat* or *almucantarat*, med. L. *almi-* or *almucontarath*, Arab. *al-muquantarāt*, pl. of *muquantarah*, sun-dial, from *quantarah*, a bridge], *n.* An instrument for determining time and latitude; (*Astron.*) a smaller circle of the celestial sphere parallel to the horizon, which formed the first almacantar; a parallel of altitude.

almagest (ăl′ mȧ jest) [O.F. *almageste*, Arab. *almajistī*, Gr. *megistē*, the greatest], *n.* The great astronomical treatise of Ptolemy; hence, any work on astrology or alchemy.

alma mater (ăl′ ma mā′ tėr) [L., fostering mother], *n.* Name used by an ex-student for his college or school.

almanac, almanack (awl′ mȧn ăk) [F. *almanach*, med. L. *almanac* (origin doubtful)], *n.* A register of the days of the year, with astronomical data and calculations, civil and ecclesiastical festivals, etc. **nautical almanac:** An official almanac giving in advance positions of stars and other data useful to mariners and astronomers.

almandine (ăl′ mȧn din) [formerly *alabandine*, L. *alabandina*, from *Alabanda*, a city of Caria], *n.* Precious garnet.

almighty (awl mī′ ti) [A.-S. *ealmihtig* (ALL, MIGHTY)], *a.* Omnipotent; possessed of unlimited ability, strength, or power. *a.* or *adv.* (*slang*)

Mighty, great, exceedingly. **the Almighty:** God. **almighty dollar,** *n.* (*colloq.*) Money; feverish love of money. **almightiness,** *n.*

almond (a' mŏnd, ăl' mŏnd) [O.F. *almande,* L. *amygdala,* Gr. *amygdalē*], *n.* The stone of the fruit of the almond-tree; the almond-tree; anything shaped like an almond, hence a tonsil. **almond-furnace** [corruption of *Allemand,* German], *n.* Furnace used to separate metals from cinders and other dross. **almond-tumbler,** *n.* A kind of tumbler pigeon. **almond-willow,** *n.* A British willow with almond-shaped leaves, *Salix amygdalina.*

almoner (ăl' mŏn ėr, a' mŏn ėr) [O.F. *aumoner,* late L. *almosinarius* (see ALMS)], *n.* An official distributor of alms or bounty; the hospital official who assesses the amount of payments to be made by patients for their treatment; the medico-social worker attached to a hospital. **Hereditary Grand Almoner, Lord High Almoner:** Officials who superintend the distribution of the royal alms in England.

almonry (ăl' mon ri) [O.F. *aumosnerie*], *n.* A place where alms are distributed; the residence of an almoner.

almost (awl' mōst), *adv.* Nearly, very nearly, well-nigh; (*used elliptically or colloquially as* a.) closely approaching; *e.g. almost night, his almost impudence.*

alms (amz) [A.-S. *ælmæsse,* L. *eleēmosyna,* Gr. *eleēmosunē* (*eleēmōn,* a., from *eleos,* pity)], *n.* Anything given out of charity to the poor; charity. ***alms-basket,** *n.* A basket containing alms to be distributed. ***to live on the alms-basket:** to live on charity. **alms-deed,** *n.* An act of charity. **alms-giving,** *n.* The giving of alms. **alms-house,** *n.* A house where poor persons are lodged and provided for by charitable endowment; (*Am.*) a workhouse. **almsman,** *n.* A man supported by alms.

almucantar [ALMACANTAR].

almug [ALGUM].

Aloe (ăl' ō) [L. *aloē,* Gr. *aloē*], *n.* A genus of succulent plants, with bitter juice; other plants, *e.g.* American aloe [AGAVE]; *pl.* the inspissated juice of plants of the genus *Aloe,* a purgative drug. **aloetic** (-et' ik), *a.* Pertaining to the aloe or aloes; consisting entirely or chiefly of aloes. *n.* An aloetic medicine.

aloft (ȧ loft') [Icel. *a lopt,* in the air (cp. LIFT)], *adv.* On high; above the ground; (*Naut.*) in the rigging, at the mast-head. **to go aloft:** (*slang*) To go to heaven, to die.

alogical (ȧ loj' ik ȧl), *a.* (*Phil.*) Not logical, not rational.

alone (ȧ lōn') [M.E. *al one* (ALL, ONE)], *pred.a.* Single, solitary, by oneself. *adv.* Only, merely, simply, solely.

along (1) (ȧ long') [A.-S. *andlang* (*and,* against, *lang,* long; cp. O.H.G. *ant-,* Gr. *anti*)], *adv.* Lengthwise, in a line with the length, in progressive motion; onward. *prep.* By the side of, from end to end, over or through lengthwise. **all along,** *adv.* Throughout, all the time. **along with,** *prep.* In company with. **along-ships,** *adv.* Lengthwise, fore and aft. **alongshore,** *adv.* In a line with, and nearly parallel to, the shore; along and on the shore. **alongshoreman,** *n.* A fisherman engaged in coastal fishing. **alongside,** *adv.* By the side of; side by side. **alongside of,** *prep.* Side by side with.

along (2) (ȧ long') [A.-S. *gelang* (*ge-,* intens., *lang,* long)], *adv.* Pertaining, belonging, chargeable. **along of, all along of:** Because of, owing to, attributable to.

aloof (ȧ loof') [*a-,* on, M.E. *loof* (cp. Dut. *to loef,* to windward) see LUFF], *adv.* Away at a distance from, apart; (*Naut.*) to windward. **to stand** (or **keep) aloof:** To take no part in, keep away; remain by oneself, remain unsympathetic. **aloofness,** *n.* State of keeping aloof.

alopecia (ăl ō pē' shȧ) [Gr. *alopekia,* fox-mange], *n.* (*Path.*) Baldness.

aloud (ȧ loud'), *adv.* Loudly; with a loud voice; audibly.

alow (ȧ lō'), *adv.* *Low down, downward; *in a low voice; (*Naut.*) in or into the lower part of the ship; opposed to aloft.

alp (ălp) [L. *Alpes,* pl., orig. doubtful], *n.* A high mountain; pasture ground on the side of mountain; (*fig.*) a formidable obstacle; (*pl.*) the chain of mountains separating France from Italy, etc. **alpenstock** (ăl' pen stok) [G. *Alpen,* of the Alps, *stock,* STICK], *n.* A long stick shod with iron, used in mountaineering. **Alpine,** *a.* Pertaining to the Alps, or to any high mountains; growing on the Alps or on any high mountain. **Alpinist** (ăl' pĭn ist) [F. *Alpiniste*], *n.* One devoted to Alpine climbing.

alpaca (ăl păk' ȧ) [Sp. *alpaca* (Arab. *al-,* the, Peruv. *paco*)], *n.* The domesticated llama of Peru; the wool of the domesticated llama; cloth made from this wool.

alpha (ăl' fȧ) [Gr. *alpha,* Heb. *āleph,* an ox, a leader], *n.* The first letter of the Greek alphabet, used to designate numerical sequence; (*Astron.*) the chief star in a constellation. **alpha and omega:** The beginning and the end. **Alpha particle,** *n.* (*Phys.*) A positively-charged particle emitted by certain radioactive substances, *e.g.* radium. It has been identified as a doubly-ionised helium atom. **Alpha plus,** *a.* Superlatively good. **Alpha rays,** *n.pl.* (*Phys.*) Rays consisting of Alpha particles.

alphabet (ăl' fȧ bet) [L. *alphabētum,* Gr. *alpha, bēta* (Heb. *bēth,* a house), the first two letters], *n.* The letters of a language arranged in order; rudiments, a long and complete series. *v.t.* To arrange in the order of the alphabet; to designate by letters of the alphabet. **alphabetic, alphabetical** (ăl fȧ bet' ik, -ȧl), *a.* Pertaining to the alphabet, arranged alphabetically. **alphabetically,** *adv.* **alphabetize,** *v.t.*

already (awl red' i) [ALL, *adv.,* READY], *adv.* Beforehand, before some specified time, in anticipation.

Alsatia (ăl sā' shi ȧ) [L. form of *Elsass,* F. *Alsace*], *n.* Province west of the Rhine; cant name for the precinct of White Friars, London, formerly a sanctuary for debtors and criminals; (*fig.*) an asylum for lawbreakers. **Alsatian,** *a.* Belonging to Alsace, or to old White Friars. *n.* A native of Alsatia; a large German wolfhound; an adventurer; a bohemian.

alsike (ăl' sik) [*Alsike,* place in Sweden], *n.* A species of clover, *Trifolium hybridum.*

alsirat (ăl si răt') [Arab. *al-sirat,* the road, way; prob. from L. *strāta*], *n.* The bridge over the abyss, finer than a hair or a razor's edge, which all must pass to reach the Mohammedan paradise.

also (awl' sō) [ALL, *adv.,* SO], *adv.* and *conj.* Likewise, in like manner, even as, besides; in addition, as well.

alt (ălt') [Prov. *alt.,* L. *altum,* high], *n.* (*Mus.*) High tone; the higher register of sounds; exaltation of mind.

Altaian (ăl tā' i ȧn) [F. *altīen,* from the *Altai* (mountains in Asia)], *a.* (*Ethn.*) A term applied to the peoples, and to the languages of the peoples (Turanian or Uralo-Altaic), lying near the Altai mountains and the Arctic ocean. *n.* A member of this group. **Altaic** (ăl tā' ik) [F. *altaïque*], *a.* Altaian.

altar (awl' tȧr) [L. *altāre* (*altus,* high)], *n.* A sacrificial block; a place of sacrifice, commemoration, or devotion; the communion-table; a southern constellation, also called Ara. **to lead to the altar:** To marry. **altar-bread,** *n.* Wafer bread used in the celebration of the Eucharist. **altar-cloth,** *n.* The linen cloth which covers an altar; an altar-frontal. **altar-frontal,** *n.* [ANTEPENDIUM]. **altar-piece,** *n.* A picture or ornamental sculpture over the altar (or communion-table) in a church. **altar-plate,** *n.* The plate used in the celebration of the Eucharist. **altar-rails,** *n.pl.* The low railings separating the altar from the main body of the church. **altar-screen,** *n.* The reredos wall or screen at the back of an altar [REREDOS]. **altar-slab,** *n.* The slab forming the top of an altar. **altar-stone,** *n.* An altar-slab; a portable altar on which Mass is said. **altar-table,** *n.* [ALTAR-SLAB]. **altar-tomb,** *n.* A raised funeral monument resembling an altar. **altar-wise,** *adv.* After the manner, or in the position of an altar.

altazimuth (ăl tăz′ i mŭth) [*alt-* (for ALTITUDE), AZIMUTH], *n.* An instrument for measuring altitude and azimuth.

alter (awl′ tėr) [F. *altérer*, late L. *alterāre* (*alter*, other, same root as *al-ius*)], *v.t.* To cause to vary or change in some degree; to modify. *v.i.* To undergo some change. **alterable,** *a.* Capable of being altered. **alterability,** *n.* **alteration,** *n.* The act of altering; the change made. **alterative,** *a.* Tending to produce alteration. *n.* A medicine which alters the processes of nutrition and reduces them to a healthy state.

altercate (awl′ tėr kāt) [L. *altercāt-*, part. stem of *altercāri*], *v.i.* To dispute hotly; to wrangle. **altercation,** *n.* Wrangling; a vehement dispute.

alter ego (ăl′ tĕr e′ gō) [L., another I], *n.* A second self; a trusted friend; a plenipotentiary.

alternate (1) (awl′ tėr nāt, ol′ tėr nāt) [L. *alternatus*, p.p. of *alternāre*, to do by turns (*alternus*, every other, from *alter*, other)], *v.t.* To arrange or perform by turns; to cause to succeed by turns or reciprocally; to interchange. *v.i.* To happen by turns; (*Elec.*) to change from positive to negative and back again in turns; (*Bot.*) placed on opposite sides of an axis at a different level; (*Geom.*) succeeding regularly (as angles) on opposite sides of a straight line. **alternately,** *adv.* **alternating,** *a.* (*Elec.*) Changing from positive to negative and back again. **alternating current,** *n.* An electric current that changes from positive to negative regularly and frequently. **alternation,** *n.* The act of alternating; the state of being alternate; antiphonal reading or singing. **alternant** (awl tĕr′ nȧnt), *a.* Alternating; (*Min.*) consisting of alternating layers.

alternate (2) (awl tĕr′ nȧt), *a.* Done or happening by turns, first one and then the other; reciprocal; (*Bot.*) placed on opposite sides of an axis at a different level; (*Geom.*) succeeding regularly (as angles) on opposite sides of a straight line. **alternate generation:** Double modes of reproduction in the same species, *e.g.* one generation being produced by fission, and these producing successors sexually. **alternately,** *adv.*

alternative (awl tĕr′ nȧ tiv, ol tĕr′ nȧ tiv) [as prec.], *a.* Offering a choice of two things; the other of two things open to choice. *n.* The permission to choose between two things; either of two courses which may be chosen. **alternatively,** *adv.*

alternator (ol′ tĕr nā tor), *n.* A dynamo for generating an alternating electric current.

although (awl *th*ō′) [ALL, *adv.*, THOUGH], *conj.* Though, notwithstanding, however.

alti- [L. *alto-*, etc., from *altus*, high], *comb form.* High, highly, height.

altimeter (ăl tim′ i tėr), *n.* (*Aviat.*) An instrument that indicates height above a given datum, usually sea-level.

altiscope (ăl′ ti skōp), *n.* An apparatus for enabling one to see over intervening objects by means of lenses and mirrors arranged in a telescopic tube.

altisonant (ăl tis′ ō nȧnt), *a.* Loud, noisy, high-sounding.

altissimo (ăl tis′ i mō) [It. superl. of ALTO], *adv.* (*Mus.*) In the second octave above the treble stave.

altitude (ăl′ ti tūd) [L. *altitūdo* (*altus*, high)], *n.* Vertical height; elevation of an object above its base; height above sea; the elevation of a heavenly body above the horizon.

alto (ăl′ tō) [It., high (viz. *canto*, singing)], *n.* The highest male voice; a singer possessing this voice; the part of the music sung by persons possessing the alto voice. **alto-clarinet, alto-viola,** *n.* Musical instruments of alto pitch. *a.* **alto-clef,** *n.* The C clef when on the third line of the stave.

altogether (awl tŏ ge*th*′ ėr) [ALL, *adv.*, TOGETHER], *adv.* Wholly, completely, entirely; on the whole, in view of all things. **the altogether,** *n.* (*vulg.*) The entirely nude.

alto-relievo (ăl′ tō rė lē′ vō) [It. *alto-rilievo*], *n.* (*Sculp.*) High relief; standing out from the surface by more than half the true proportions of the figures carved.

altruism (ăl′ troo izm) [F. *altruisme*, It. *altrui* (F. *autrui*), L. *alteri huic* (to this other)], *n.* Devotion to the good of others (opposed to egoism). **altruist,** *n.* One who practises altruism. **altruistic** (-is′ tik), *a.* **altruistically,** *adv.*

alum (ăl′ ŭm) [O.F. *alum* (F. *alun*), L. *alumen*], *n.* A name given to double salts of aluminium and potassium; a series of double salts including this; a family of analogous compounds; (*Min.*) name of various minerals, alums or pseudo-alums.

alumina (ȧ loo′ min ȧ) [L. *alumen*], *n.* The oxide of aluminium forming the basis of alum, and a constituent of all clays.

aluminium (ăl ū min′ i ŭm) [see prec.], *n.* A white, ductile metallic element with good resistance to corrosion, used as a basis for many light alloys. **aluminium-bronze,** *n.* A compound of aluminium and copper. **aluminous** (ȧ loo′ min ŭs), *a.* Composed of or pertaining to alum or alumina.

aluminum (ȧ loo′ mi nŭm) *n.* (*Am.*) Aluminium.

alumnus (ȧ lŭm′ nŭs) [L., foster-child], *n.* (*pl.* **alumni**) A pupil or student in relation to his place of education; (*Am.*) graduate, old scholar.

alveolus (ăl vē′ ŏ lŭs) [L. *alveolus*, dim. of *alveus*, a cavity], *n.* (*pl.* **alveoli**) A little cavity; the cell of a honeycomb; the conical chamber of a belemnite: the conical body found therein; a tooth socket. **alveolar,** *a.* Pertaining to the sockets of the teeth; socket-shaped. **alveolate** (ăl′ vė ŏ lăt) [L. *alveolātus*, see ALVEOLUS], *a.* Honey-combed; deeply pitted.

alvine (ăl′ vīn) [L. *alvīnus* (*alvus*, the belly)], *a.* Pertaining to the belly or to the instestines.

always (awl′ wāz), ***alway** (A.-S. *ealne weg*, acc. (ALL, WAY)], *adv.* All the while; without intermission; uninterruptedly, regularly; on all occasions; while one lives.

Alyssum (ȧ lis′ ŭm) [Gr. *alusson*], *n.* A genus of Cruciferous plants, comprising *Alyssum saxatile*, (*pop.*) gold dust, and *A. maritimum*, sweet alyssum.

am (ăm) [A.S. *am*, *eom*, from *es-m* (cp. Sansk. *asmi*, Gr. *eimi*, L. *sum*): from the root *es*, to be, also come *art* and *are*, A.-S. *eart*, *earth* (cp. Icel. *est*, *ert*, Sansk. *asī*, Gr. *essi*, L. *es*), and Merc. *earun* (cp. Northumb. *aron*, A.-S. *sindon*, Icel. *erum*, Gr. *eisin*, L. *sunt*); (see also BE, WAS)], *1st pers. sing. pres. ind. of the v.* TO BE.

amabile (ăm a′ bil i) [It., amiable], *adv.* (*Mus.*) Amiably, tenderly, sweetly.

amadou (ăm′ ȧ doo) [F. *amadou*, O. Prov. *amador*, L. *amātōrem*, a lover (*amāre*, to love)], *n.* German tinder, prepared from a dried fungus steeped in saltpetre, used as a match and a styptic.

amah (a′ ma) [Port.], *n.* (*Anglo-Indian*) A wet-nurse, nanny.

amain (ȧ mān′) [A.-S. *a-*, on, *mægen*, might], *adv.* Energetically, violently, in full force, at full speed, at once.

amalgam (ȧ măl′ gȧm) [F. *amalgame*, med. L. *amalgama*, prob. from Gr. *malagma*, an emollient, a plaster (*malassein*, to soften)], *n.* A mixture of any other metal with mercury; a compound of different things.

amalgamate (ȧ măl′ gȧ māt) [as prec.], *v.t.* To mix, to unite, to combine, to compound into one mixture; to combine another metal with mercury. *v.i.* To combine, to blend, to merge into one (of races, social classes, parties, etc. **amalgamation** (-mā′ shŭn), *n.* The act of amalgamating; the blending of different things; a homogeneous union. **amalgamative** (ȧ măl′ gȧ mā tiv), *a.* Tending to combine.

amanuensis (ȧ măn ū en′ sis) [L. *amanuensis*, a. (viz. *servus*), a scribe (*ā mānu*, by hand, *-ensis*, suf. pertaining to)], *n.* (*pl.* **amanuenses**) A person employed to write what another dictates; a secretary.

amaracus (ȧ măr′ ȧ kŭs) [L. *amāracus*, Gr. *amarakos*], *n.* An aromatic plant, marjoram or dittany.

Amaranth (ăm′ ȧ rănth) [L. *amarantus*, Gr. *amarantos* (*a-*, not, *marainein*, to wither)], ***amarant,** *n.* An imaginary flower supposed never to fade; a purple colour; (*Bot.*) a genus of plants to which love-lies-bleeding and prince's feather belong. **amaranthine** (ăm ȧ rănth′ īn), **amarantine,** *a.* Pertaining to amaranth; unfading.

Amaryllis (ăm ȧ ril′ is) [Gr. *Amarullis*, name of a country-girl], *n.* A genus of autumn-flowering bulbous plants.

amass (ȧ măs′) [F. *amasser* (*à*, to, *masse*, mass, L. *ad, massam*)] *v.t.* To make into a heap; to collect together, to accumulate.

amateur (ăm′ ȧ tūr, ăm′ ȧ tĕr) [F. *amateur*, L. *amatōrem* (*amāre*, to love)], *n.* One who cultivates anything as a pastime, as distinguished from one who does so professionally; one who is fond of, a devotee of (an art, pastime, etc.). Used as an adjective, *e.g. amateur gardener, amateur gardening.* **amateurish** (ăm ȧ tūr′ ish), *a.* Not up to the professional standard. **amateurishness,** *n.* The quality of being amateurish; inferior standard of execution. **amateurism** (ăm′ ȧ tūr izm), *n.* The state, condition, or practice of an amateur; dilettantism.

amative (ăm′ ȧ tiv) [L. *amāre*, to love, -IVE], *a.* Disposed to loving. **amativeness,** *n.* Disposition to loving; (*Phrenol.*) erotic propensity.

amatol (ăm′ ȧ tol) [AM(MONIUM), TOL(UENE)], *n.* An explosive consisting of a mixture of ammonium nitrate and trinitrotoluene.

amatory (ăm′ ȧ tȯ ri) [L. *amātorius* (*amātor*, a lover)], *a.* Pertaining to love; causing or designed to cause love. **amatorial** (ăm ȧ tôr′ i ȧl), *a.* Pertaining to love or courtship.

amaurosis (ăm aw rō′ sis) [Gr. *amaurōsis* (*amauroein*, to darken, from *amauros*, dark)], *n.* Partial or total blindness from disease of the optic nerve, usually without visible defect. **amaurotic** (ăm aw rot′ ik), *a.* Affected with amaurosis.

amaze (ȧ māz′) [A.-S. *āmasian* (*a-*, intens. pref.), to confound (*Skeat*); see also MAZE], *v.t.* To astound, to overwhelm with wonder, to bewilder. **n.* Extreme astonishment, wonder, bewilderment, amazement. **amazedly,** *adv.* **amazedness,** *n.* **amazement,** *n.* Overwhelming surprise; the state of being amazed. **amazing,** *a.* **amazingly,** *adv.*

amazon (ăm′ ȧ zȯn) [Gr. *amazōn* (foreign word explained by Greeks as *a-*, not, *mazos*, breast, from legend that they cut away the right breast to use the bow more freely)], *n.* One of a fabled race of female warriors; a female warrior; a tall, masculine woman; a virago. **amazon-ant,** *n. Formica rufescens*, the neuters of which enslave the young of other species. **amazonian** (ăm ȧ zō′ ni ȧn), *a.* Of or pertaining to the fabled Amazons, hence, warlike, masculine; or to the river Amazon, named from the female warriors recorded there by the early Spaniards.

***ambage** (ăm′ bȧj), **ambages** (ăm bā- jēz) [F. *ambage, ambages*, L. *ambāges* (*amb-*, about, *agere*, to drive)], *n.* Circumlocution; roundabout expression; equivocation; the use of ambiguous language intended to mystify or deceive. **ambagious,** *a.*

ambassador (ăm băs′ ȧ dȯr) [F. *ambassadeur*, O.Sp. *ambaxador*, late L. *ambaxiāre, ambactiāre*, (*ambactia*, a mission, office, from Celt. *ambactus*, a servant, from *amb-*, about, and Celt. root *ag-*, to drive, cognate with L. *agere*)], *n.* A minister of high rank, representing his country at a foreign court, being styled **ordinary** when resident, and **extraordinary** when sent on a special mission; an **ambassador plenipotentiary** is one armed with full powers to sign treaties, etc. **ambassadorial** (-dôr′ i ȧl), *a.* **ambassadress,** *n.* Female ambassador; wife of an ambassador. ***ambassage,** *n.* [EMBASSY].

amber (ăm′ bėr) [F. *ambre*, Arab. *'anbar*, ambergris], *n.* A yellowish translucent fossil resin, found chiefly on the southern shores of the Baltic, used for ornaments, mouthpieces of pipes, and in the manufacture of some varnishes; *ambergris; *a love-charm made of amber. *a.* Made or coloured like amber. **amber fauna,** *n.* Animals whose remains are found preserved in amber. **amber flora,** *n.* Plants found in amber. **amber-seed,** *n.* The seed *Abelmoschus moschatus*, used to perfume pomatum, etc. **amber-tree,** *n.* The genus *Anthospermum*, containing evergreen shrubs fragrant when bruised.

ambergris (ăm′ bėr grēs) [F. *ambre gris*, grey amber], *n.* A light, fatty, inflammable substance, ashy in colour, found floating in tropical seas, a morbid secretion from the intestines of the cachalot or spermaceti whale: used in perfumery, formerly in cookery and medicine.

ambidexter (ăm bi dek′ stėr) [med. L. *ambidexter* (*ambi-*, both, on both sides, *dexter*, right-handed)], *a.* Using both hands with equal facility; double-dealing. *n.* One who can use both hands with equal facility; a double-dealer; (*Law*) one who accepts bribes from both sides. **ambidexterity** (ăm bi dek ster′ i ti). **ambidextrous,** *a.* Ambidexter. **ambidextrously,** *adv.* **ambidextrousness,** *n.*

ambient (ăm′ bi ėnt) [L. *ambiens -entis*, pres.p. of *ambīre* (*amb-*, on both sides, about, *īre*, to go)], *a.* Surrounding, encompassing on all sides, circumfused, investing. **ambience, ambiency,** *n.*

ambiguous (ăm big′ ū ŭs) [L. *ambiguus*, doubtful, from *ambigere* (*amb-*, both ways, *agere*, to drive)], *a.* Susceptible of two or more meanings; of doubtful meaning, equivocal, obscure; of uncertain position or classification. **ambiguously,** *adv.* **ambiguousness,** *n.* **ambiguity** (ăm bi gū′ i ti) [med. L. *ambiguitas*], *n.* The state of being ambiguous; uncertainty of signification.

ambit (ăm′ bit) [L. *ambitus*, a going about (see AMBIENT)], *n.* Bounds, precincts, scope.

ambition (ăm bish′ ŭn) [F. *ambition*, L. *ambitiōnem*, soliciting for votes, *ambīre* (*amb-*, about, *īre*, to go)], *n.* A desire for power, superiority or excellence (generally in a bad sense); strong desire of anything advantageous or creditable; the object of such desire. **ambitious,** *a.* Actuated by or indicating ambition; full of or displaying ambition. **ambitiously,** *adv.* **ambitiousness,** *n.*

ambivalence, ambivalency (ăm biv′ ȧ lėns, -lėn si) [L. *ambo*, both, *valens*, being worth], *n.* (*Psych.*) The simultaneous working in the mind of two incompatible wishes.

amble (ăm′ bėl) [O.F. *ambler*, L. *ambulāre*, to walk], *v.i.* To move (as a horse or mule) by lifting the two feet on one side alternately with the two feet on the other; to ride an ambling horse; to move easily, or like an ambling horse. *n.* The pace described above; an easy pace; a pace like that of an ambling horse. **ambler,** *n.* An ambling horse; a person whose gait resembles that of an ambling horse.

amblyopia (ăm bli ō′ pi ȧ) [Gr. *ambluōpos*, a. (*amblus*, dull, *ōps ōpos*, eye)], *n.* Dimness of vision. **amblyopic** (ăm bli op′ ik), *a.* Affected with or pertaining to amblyopia.

ambo (ăm′ bō), **ambon** (ăm′ bȯn) [late L. *ambo -ōnem*, Gr. *ambōn*], *n.* (*pl.* **ambos, ambones**) A pulpit or reading-desk in early mediæval churches.

Amboyna-wood (ăm boi' nȧ-) [from name of island], *n.* The wood of *Pterospermum indicum,* which is finely variegated.

Ambrosia (ăm brō' zi ȧ, -zhi ȧ) [Gr. *ambrosia,* fem. of a. *ambrosios,* from *ambrotos* (*a-,* not, *brotos,* mortal)], *n.* The fabled food of the gods; anything very pleasant to the taste or the smell; bee-bread; (*Bot.*) a genus of composite plants, allied to wormwood. **ambrosial,** *a.* Containing the qualities of ambrosia; delicious, fragrant; ethereal, divine. **ambrosially,** *adv.*

Ambrosian (ăm brō' zi ȧn) [St. *Ambrose* (c. 340–397)], *a.* Pertaining to St. Ambrose or his teaching. **Ambrosian chant,** *n.* The plain-song of the Milanese liturgy.

***ambry, aumbry** (am' bri) [O.F. *armarie,* late L. *armāria,* chest or cupboard, L. *armārium* (*arma,* arms, tools, gear)], *n.* A cupboard, a locker, a chest; a niche or cupboard in a church for books and sacred vessels; a meat-safe, a store-closet. Also confused with *almonry, e.g. Almry* or *Ambry* Close, Westminster.

ambs-ace, ames-ace (ăm' zās) [O.F. *ambes as,* L. *ambas as*], *n.* Both aces, the lowest possible throw at dice; bad luck, misfortune, worthlessness.

ambulance (ăm' bū lȧns) [F. *ambulance,* L. *ambulans -ntem,* pres.p. of *ambulāre,* to walk], *n.* A moving hospital which follows an army in the field; a vehicle or wheeled stretcher for the transport of the wounded, or of invalids.

ambulate (ăm' bū lāt) [L. *ambulat-,* part. stem of *ambulāre,* see prec.], *v.i.* To walk about. **ambulation,** *n.* The act of walking. **ambulant,** *a.* Walking or moving about.

ambulatory (ăm' bū lȧ tȯ ri) [as prec.], *a.* Pertaining to walking; fitted for walking; movable, temporary. *n.* A place to walk in, such as a corridor or a cloister.

ambuscade (ăm bŭs kād') [F. *embuscade,* Sp. *emboscada* or It. *imboscata,* from late L. *imboscāre* (see AMBUSH)], *n.* An ambush; a lying in wait to attack an enemy; the force placed in ambush. *v.i.* To lie in ambush. *v.t.* To place in ambush.

ambush (ăm' bush) [O.F. *embusche,* from v. *embuscher,* late L. *imboscāre,* to set in ambush (*in,* in, *boscus,* a bush, thicket)], *n.* Concealment of forces to entrap an enemy; the locality chosen; the force employed; any lying in wait. *v.t.* To place in ambush; to cause to lie in wait. *v.i.* To lie in wait.

ameer, amir (ȧ mēr') [Arab. *amīr,* nobleman, prince (*amara,* he commanded)], *n.* The title of several Mohammedan rulers in India and Afghanistan.

ameliorate (ȧ mē' li ȯr āt) [F. *améliorer,* O.F. *ameillorer* (*à,* to, *meillorer,* from late L. *meliōrāre,* from *melior,* better)], *v.t.* To make better; to improve. *v.i.* To grow better. **amelioration** (-rā' shŭn), *n.* The act of making better; the state of being made better; improvement. **ameliorative,** *a.* **ameliorator,** *n.*

amen (ā men', a men') [L. *āmēn,* Gr. *amēn,* Heb. *ā-mēn,* certainty, truth, certainly, verily (*āman,* to strengthen, confirm)], *int.* Truly, verily; so be it; may it be as has been asked, said, or promised. *n.* The word 'Amen,' an expression of assent; a concluding word; (*Bible*) a title applied to Christ.

amenable (ȧ mēn' ȧbl) [F. *amener* (*à,* to, *mener,* to lead, bring, from late L. *mināre,* from L. *minārī,* to threaten)], *a.* Liable to be called to account; answerable, liable; easy to lead, tractable. **amenability** (-bil' i ti), *n.* The quality or state of being amenable; responsibility, tractableness. **amenableness,** *n.* **amenably,** *adv.*

***amenage** (ăm ėn āj') [O.F. *amenager* (*à,* to, *ménage,* see MANAGE)], *v.t.* To domesticate, to tame.

amend (ȧ mend') [O.F. *amender,* L. *ēmendāre* (*e-, ex-,* out of, *menda,* fault)], *v.t.* To alter (a person or thing) for the better; to improve; reform, correct, formally alter (a bill or resolution). *v.i.* To abandon evil courses, grow better. **amendable,** *a.*

amendment (ȧ mend' ment), *n.* A change for the better; improvement in health; reformation; something added to a bill or motion; correction of error in a writ or process.

amends (ȧ mendz') [O.F. *amendes*], *n.pl. but usu. sing. in use.* Reparation, satisfaction, compensation; *improvement in health.

amenity (ȧ me' ni ti) [L. *amœnitātem* (*amœnus,* pleasant, allied to *amāre,* to love)], *n.* The quality of being pleasant or agreeable; a feature conducive to the attractiveness of a building estate; (*pl.*) pleasing manners, civilities; attractions, charms.

amenorrhœa (ȧ men ō rē' ȧ) [Gr. *a-,* not, *men,* a month, *rhoia,* flow], *n.* (*Path.*) A morbid cessation of menstruation.

ament (ȧ ment'), **amentum** [L. *amentum,* a thong or strap], *n.* (*pl.* **amenta**) (*Bot.*) A catkin. **amentaceous** (ăm ėn tā' shŭs), *a.* (*Bot.*)

amentia (ȧ men' shi ȧ) [L. *a-, ab-,* from, *mens -tis,* mind], *n.* Dementia, idiocy; utter fatuity.

amerce (ȧ mẽrs') [A.F. *amercier, à merci,* at the mercy of the court (*à,* at, *merci,* MERCY)], *v.t.* To punish by fine; to exact something from; to punish. **amerciable,** *a.* Liable to amercement. **amercement** (ȧ mẽrs' mėnt), ***amerciament** (ȧ mẽr' si ȧ mėnt), *n.* The infliction of an arbitrary fine; the fine inflicted.

American (ȧ mer' i kȧn), *a.* Pertaining to the continent of America, esp. to the United States. *n.* *An American Indian; a native of America of European descent; a citizen of the United States. **American plan:** Inclusive terms, at hotel, etc. **Americanism,** *n.* Attachment to or political sympathy with the United States; anything characteristic of the United States, especially a word or phrase peculiar to or borrowed from the United States. **Americanize,** *v.t.* To naturalize as an American; to assimilate political customs or institutions to those of the United States. *v.i.* To become American in character, manners, or speech. **American blight,** *n.* (*Zool.*) Woolly aphis.

americium (ăm er is' i ŭm), *n.* An artificially-created radioactive element of atomic number 95.

Amerind (ăm' ẽr ind) [contr. American Indian], *n.* (*Ethn.*) Indian of either of the American continents. **Amerindian,** *a.*

ames-ace [AMBS-ACE].

amethyst (ăm' ė thist) [L. *amethystus,* Gr. *amethustos,* a remedy against drunkenness (*a-,* not *methuein,* to be drunken, from *methu,* strong drink)], *n.* A violet-blue variety of crystalline quartz, supposed by the ancients to be a preventive of intoxication. **amethystine,** *a.* Composed of, containing, or resembling amethyst.

Amharic (ăm hăr' ik) [*Amhara,* prov. of Abyssinia], *n.* The official language of Abyssinia.

amiable (ā' mi ȧbl) [O.F. *amiable,* L. *amicābilis* (AMICABLE),(confused with O.F. *amable,* L. *amābilis,* lovable (*amāre,* to love)], *a.* Friendly, kindly-disposed, lovable; possessed of qualities fitted to evoke friendly feeling. **amiably,** *adv.* **amiability** (-bil' i ti), *n.*

***amiant** (ăm' i ănt), **amiantus** (ăm i ăn' tŭs), **amianthus** [L. *amiantus,* Gr. *amiantos,* undefiled (*a-,* not, *miainein,* to stain)], *n.* A variety of asbestos; a fibrous kind of chrysolite of a greenish colour. **amianthoid,** *a.* Resembling amianthus. *n.* A kind of asbestos.

amic (ăm' ik) [AM(MONIA), -IC], *a.* Of, pertaining to, or derived from ammonia. **amide** (ăm' īd', ȧ mid'), *n.* Generic name of compounds derived from ammonia; compounds formed by substitution of another substance for the hydrogen in ammonia.

amicable (ăm' ik ȧbl) [L. *amicābilis* (*amicāre,* to make friendly, *amīcus,* friend)], *a.* Friendly; designed to be friendly; resulting from friendliness. **amicable suit,** *n.* (*Law*) A suit promoted by arrangement in order to obtain an authoritative decision on some point of law. **amicability** (-bil' i ti), *n.* **amicableness,** *n.* **amicably,** *adv.*

amice (1) (ăm′ ĭs) [early form, *amyte*, O.F. *amit*, L. *amictus*, p.p. of *amicīre* (*amb*-, around, *jacere*, to cast)], *n.* A loose wrap; a vest or flowing garment; a square piece of white linen worn on the neck and shoulders at Mass by R.C. priests.

amice (2) (ăm′ is) [O.F. *aumuce*, Sp. *almucio* (perhaps from Arab. *al*-, the, and G. *mütze*, cap)], *n.* A pilgrim's hood or cap, an ecclesiastical cape or other garment; a college badge or hood worn on the left arm by canons in France.

amicus curiæ (ăm ī′ kus kū′ ri ē) [L., friend of the court], *n.* A disinterested counsellor.

amid (1) (ȧ mid′), **amidst** (ȧ midst′) [M.E. *amiddes*, A.-S. *on middan*, in the middle (adverbial *s* is properly sign of gen. case)], *prep.* In the midst or middle; among. **amidships,** *adv.* In the middle part of a ship.

amid (2), **amide** (ăm′ īd) [AMADIN], *n.* (*Chem.*) A compound constituted as if obtained from ammonia by the substitution of univalent acid radicals for the atoms of hydrogen.

amide [AMIC].

amidin (ăm′ i din) [F. *amid*- (as in *amidon*), from L. *amylum*, starch], *n.* The soluble matter of starch; starch in solution.

amidol (ăm′ i dol) [AMID (2)], *n.* (*Phot.*) A compound of phenol used as a soluble crystalline powder in the development of bromide plates.

amidst, *prep.* [AMID].

amine (am′ īn) [AMIC], *n.* A compound derived from ammonia by the substitution of another radical for the hydrogen. **aminobutane** (ȧ mē′ nō bū′ tān), *n.* A pain-relieving drug.

amir [AMEER].

amiss (ȧ mis′) [MISS (2)], *a.* Faulty, beside the mark, unsatisfactory, wrong. *adv.* Wrongly, astray, in a faulty manner, unsatisfactorily.

amissibility (ȧ mis i bil′ i ti) [Fr. *amissibilité*], *n.* Liability to be lost. **amission,** *n.* Loss.

amity (ăm′ i ti) [F. *amitié*, late L. *amīcitātem* (*amīcus*, friendly, from *amāre*, to love)], *n.* Friendship, concord, mutual good feeling, friendly relations.

ammeter (ăm′ mė tėr) [AM(PERE), -METER], *n.* An instrument for measuring the quantity of the electric current in a circuit.

ammonal (ăm′ on ăl) [AMMONIA], *n.* (*Chem.*) An explosive composition containing aluminium mixed with charcoal and an oxidizing agent.

ammonia (ȧ mō′ ni ȧ) [adopted from L. *sal ammōniac*], *n.* A pungent volatile gas, powerfully alkaline, obtained from sal ammoniac; spirit of hartshorn; (*Chem.*) a class of analogous compounds. **ammoniac, ammoniacal** [F. *ammoniac*, L. *ammōniacum*, Gr. *ammōniakon*, after (Jupiter) Ammon], *a.* Pertaining to or possessing the properties of ammonia. **gum ammoniac,** *n.* Gum of Ammon, a gum resin, used in medicine and as cement. **sal ammoniac,** *n.* Ammonium chloride; said to have been first prepared from camel's dung near the temple of Jupiter Ammon. **ammoniated** (ȧ mō′ ni ā tėd), *a.* Combined with ammonia. **ammonium,** *n.* (*Chem.*) The hypothetical radical of ammonia.

ammonite (ăm′ on nīt) [med. L. *cornu Ammonis*, horn of Ammon (*Ammon*, -ITE)], *n.* The shell of a genus of fossil Cephalopods, curved like the ram's horn on the statue of Jupiter Ammon.

ammonium [AMMONIA].

ammunition (ăm ū nish′ ŭn) [F. *amunition* (MUNITION), formed by vulgar confusion of *la munition* with *l'amonition*], *n.* Military stores or supplies; (now only) powder, shot, shell, etc.; offensive missiles generally. **ammunitioned,** *a.* Provided with ammunition.

amnesia (ăm nē′ si ȧ, -shi ȧ) [Gr. *amnēsia*], *n.* Loss of memory.

amnesty (ăm′ nės ti) [L. from Gr. *amnēstia*, from *amnēstos*, forgotten (*a*-, not, *mna-omai*, I remember)], *n.* An act of oblivion, passed after an exciting political period; a general overlooking or pardon.

amnion (ăm′ ni ȯn) [Gr., caul, dim. of *amnos*, a lamb], *n.* The innermost membrane with which the fœtus in the womb is surrounded. **amnios,** *n.* (*Biol.*) The fluid of the rudimentary embryo-sac. **Amniota** (ăm ni ō′ tȧ), *n.pl.* A group of Vertebrates (reptiles, birds, and mammals), which possess an amnion in the fœtal state. **amniotic** (-ot′ ik), *a.* Pertaining to, characterized by, contained in, or of the nature of an amnion.

amœba (ȧ mē′ bȧ) [Gr. *amoibē*, change], *n.* A microscopic organism of the simplest structure, consisting of a single protoplasmic cell, which is extensile and contractile, so that the shape is continually changing. **amœbæan** (-bē′ ȧn), *a.* Answering alternately; antiphonal. **amœbiform** (ȧ mē′ bi fôrm), *a.* Amœba-like; varying in shape, protean. **amœboid** (ȧ mē′ boid), *a.* Amœba-like.

amok [AMUCK].

among (ȧ mŭng′), **amongst** (ȧ mŭngst′) [M.E. *amonges*, A.-S. *onmang*, *on gemange* (*on*, prep., *gemang*, crowd), in a crowd, allied to *mengan*, to mingle], *prep.* Mingled with, in the number of; in the midst of; surrounded by.

amontillado (ȧ mon′ til ya′ dō) [Sp.], *n.* A kind of sherry.

amoral (ă mor′ ȧl) [Gr. *a*-, not: MORAL], *a.* Not concerned with morals, non-moral. **amoralism,** *n.* **amoralist,** *n.* A non-moral person.

***amoret** (ăm′ ȯr et) [O.F. *amorete*, dim. of *amour*, love (L. *amōr*-, stem; *amāre*, to love)], *n.* A sweetheart; a paramour; a love-knot; a love-poem; (*pl.*) dalliance.

amorist (am′ or ist), *n.* A lover, a gallant, a philanderer; one who makes a study of love.

amorous (ăm′ ȯr ŭs) [O.F. *amoros*, L. *amōrōsus* (cp. AMORET)], *a.* Naturally inclined to love; in love; lecherous; relating to, or belonging to, love. **amorously,** *adv.* **amorousness,** *n.*

amorphous (ȧ môr′ fŭs) [Gr. *amorphos*, shapeless (*a*-, not, *morphē*, form)], *a.* Shapeless; irregularly shaped; (*Biol.*) not conforming to a normal standard; (*Chem.*) uncrystallized; ill-arranged, unsystematic, unorganized. **amorphism** (ȧ môr′ fizm), *n.* Lack of regular form; absence of crystallization. **amorphousness,** *n.* The quality of being amorphous.

***amort** (ȧ môrt′) [F. *à la mort*, to the death, corrupted to *all amort* (ALAMORT)], *a.* Lifeless, inanimate. *adv.* In a state of death or depression.

amortize (ȧ môr′ tīz) [F. *amortir*, *-iss*-, to bring to death, possibly from a late L. *admortīre* (*ad*-, to, *mortem*, death)], *v.t.* To deaden, to destroy; *to kill; to alienate in mortmain; to extinguish by a sinking fund. **amortization** (-zā′ shŭn), *n.* The act or the right of alienating lands in mortmain.

amount (ȧ mount′) [O.F. *amonter* (*a mont*, to a mountain, L. *ad mont -em*)], *v.i.* To run into an aggregate by the accumulation of particulars; to mount up to, to add up to; to be equivalent to; *to ascend (a hill). *n.* The sum total, effect, substance, result, significance; a (numerical) quantity.

amour (ȧ moor′) [O.F. *amur*, *amour*, L. *amōr -em*, love], *n.* A love affair; an affair of gallantry; an amorous intrigue. **amourette** (ăm oor et′) [F. dim. of *amour*], *n.* A petty love affair. **amour propre** (ăm oor pro′ pr) [Fr.], *n.* Self-esteem.

Ampelopsis (ăm pel op′ sis) [Gr. *ampelos*, vine; *opsis*, appearance], *n.* (*Bot.*) Genus of vine-creeper, including Virginia creeper.

ampere (ăm pâr′) [name of a French physicist (1775–1836)], *n.* A unit by which an electric current is measured; the current sent by one volt through a resistance of one ohm. **ampere-hour,** *n.* The quantity of electricity delivered in one hour by a one-ampere strength current. **amperemeter** [AMMETER]. **ampere turn,** *n.* The product of the number of turns in the coil of wire of an electromagnet and the number of amperes flowing through. **amperage,** *n.* The quantity of an electric current measured in amperes.

ampersand (ăm pėr sănd′) [a corruption of *and per se*, 'and' by itself makes 'and'], *n.* The sign '&'.

amphi- [Gr. *amphi*, prep., on both sides], *comb. form.* Both, of both kinds, on both sides, around, *e.g. Amphibia, amphibrach, amphitheatre.*

Amphibia (ăm fib′ i ȧ) [Gr. *amphibia*, sing. *amphibios*, living in both elements (AMPHI-, *bios*, life)], *n.pl.* Animals which can live either on land or water; a group of vertebrate animals, between reptiles and fishes, which in their early stage breathe by gills. **amphibian,** *a.* Pertaining to any amphibious animal or to the Amphibia; an aircraft, tank or other vehicle adapted for both land and water. *n.* Any animal of the Amphibia. **amphibious,** *a.* Capable of living both on land and in water; of mixed nature. **amphibiousness,** *n.*

amphibiology (ăm fi bī ol′ ȯ ji), *n.* The department of science which treats of the Amphibia. **amphibiological,** *a.*

amphibology (ăm fi bol′ ȯ ji) [F. *amphibologie*, late L. *amphibologia* (L. *amphibolia*), Gr. *amphibolia* (AMPHI-, *ballein*, to throw), -LOGY], *n.* Ambiguous expression, a sentence susceptible of two interpretations; ambiguity; equivocation. **amphibological** (-loj′ ik ȧl), *a.* **amphibologically,** *adv.*

amphiboly (ăm fib′ ȯ li) [AMPHIBOLOGY], *n.* A fallacy occurring when a sentence, composed of unambiguous words, is itself susceptible of a double meaning. **amphibolous,** *a.* Doubtful, ambiguous.

amphibrach (ăm′ fi brăk) [Gr. *amphibrachus*, (*brachus*, short)], *n.* A metrical foot of three syllables, the middle one long and the first and third short, as IN-HŪ-MAN.

Amphictyons (ăm fik′ ti ȯns) [Gr. *amphiktuones* (AMPHI-, *ktuones*), dwellers about, neighbours], *n.pl.* Delegates from twelve of the states of ancient Greece, forming an assembly or council. **Amphictyonic** (ăm fik ti on′ ik), *a.* Of or pertaining to the Amphictyons. **Amphictyony** (ăm fik′ ti ȯn i) [Gr. *amphiktuonia*], *n.* The council of Amphictyons; a confederation of states for common benefit.

amphigam (ăm′ fi găm) [F. *amphigame*, Gr. *gamos*, marriage], *n.* (*Bot.*) One of the lower cryptogams, having no distinct sexual organs.

amphigory (ăm fig′ ȯri), **amphigouri** (ăm fi goo′ ri) [F. *amphigouri*], *n.* A meaningless rigmarole, a verse-composition containing no sense.

amphimacer (ăm fim′ ȧ sėr) [Gr. *amphimakros* (*makros*, long)], *n.* A metrical foot consisting of three syllables, one short between two long.

amphimixis (ăm fi′ miks is) [Gr. *mixis*, a mingling], *n.* (*Biol.*) Sexual reproduction.

Amphioxus (ăm fi ok′ sủs), [Gr. *oxus*, sharp], *n.* A genus of fishes with one species, the lowest in organization [LANCELET].

Amphipoda (ăm fip′ ȯ dȧ) [Gr. *pous podos*, foot], *n.pl.* A group of sessile-eyed Crustacea, having two kinds of feet, one for walking and one for swimming. **amphipod,** *a.* Amphipodous. *n.* Any animal of the Amphipoda. **amphipodous,** *a.*

amphiprostyle (ăm fip′ rȯ stīl) [F. from L. *amphiprostylus*, Gr. *amphiprostulos* (*prostulos*, PROSTYLE)], *n.* A temple having a portico at each end.

amphisbæna (ăm fis bē′ nȧ) [Gr. *amphisbaina* (*amphis*, both ways, *bainein*, to go)], *n.* A fabled snake said by the ancients to have two heads, and to be able to move in either direction; (*Zool.*) a serpentiform genus of lizards, having the tail short and blunt.

amphitheatre (ăm′ fi thē ȧ tėr) [Gr. *amphitheatron* (see AMPHI-, THEATRE)], *n.* An oval or circular building with rows of seats rising one above another round an open space; a place of public contest; a semicircular gallery in a theatre; a valley surrounded with hills. **amphitheatrical** (ăm fi thē ăt′ rik ȧl), *a.*

amphitryon (ăm fit′ ri ȯn) [from the foster-father of Heracles in classical legend], *n.* A host; the giver of a banquet.

amphora (ăm′ fȯ rȧ) [L. *amphora*, Gr. *amphoreus* (*phoreus*, a bearer, from *pherein*, to bear)], *n.* An ancient two-handled vessel for holding wine, oil, etc.; an ancient liquid measure containing about six gallons among the Romans, and about nine among the Greeks. **amphoric** (ăm for′ ik), *a.* (*Med.*) Resembling the sound made by blowing into an amphora.

ample (ăm′ pėl) [F. *ample*, L. *amplus*], *a.* Of large dimensions; wide, great, fully sufficient, liberal. **amply,** *adv.* **ampleness,** *n.* **ampliate** (ăm′ pli āt) [L. *ampliāre*], *v.t.* To enlarge, extend, amplify. **ampliative** [-IVE], *a.* (*Log.*) Enlarging a simple conception.

amplexicaul (ăm plek′ si kawl) [L. *amplexus*, p.p. of *amplector*, to embrace, *caulis*, a stem], *a.* (*Bot.*) Embracing or clasping the stem. **amplexifoliate** (ăm plek si fō′ li ȧt) [-FOLIATE], *a.* (*Bot.*) Having leaves which embrace the stem.

amplify (ăm′ pli fī) [as prec.], *v.t.* To enlarge or dilate upon. *v.i.* To speak or write diffusely; to expatiate. **amplification,** *n.* Enlargement or extension; diffuseness; an enlarged representation. **amplifier,** *n.* (*Radio*) A complete unit which performs amplification; an electronic instrument to amplify electronic signals.

amplitude (ăm′ pli tūd) [as prec.], *n.* Extent, size, bulk, greatness, abundance, dignity; (*Astron.*) the angular distance of a heavenly body, at its rising or setting, from the east or the west point of the horizon; (*Radio*) the magnitude of the variations of an alternating current or voltage. **magnetic amplitude:** Amplitude measured by a compass needle.

ampoule (ăm′ pool) [Fr.], *n.* A sealed phial containing one dose of a drug.

ampulla (ăm pul′ ȧ) [L.], *n.* (*pl.* **ampullæ**) A nearly globular flask with two handles, used by the ancient Romans; a vessel for holding consecrated oil, wine, etc.; (*Biol.*) the dilated end of any vessel; a spongiole of a root. **ampullaceous** (ăm pul lā′ shủs), *a.* Resembling a globular flask; bottle-shaped, swelling.

amputate (ăm′ pū tāt) [L. *amputātus*, p.p. of *amputāre* (*amb-*, about, *putāre*, to prune, lop)], *v.t.* To cut off a portion from an animal body. **amputation** (-tā′ shủn), *n.* The act of amputating. **amputator,** *n.*

amrita (ăm rē′ tȧ) [*Sansk.*], *n.* The ambrosia of the gods in Hindu mythology.

amuck (ȧ mŭk′), **amok** (ȧ mok′) [Malay, *amoq*, engaging furiously in battle], *adv.* in **to run amuck:** To attack indiscriminately, actuated by a frenzied desire for blood; hence to run wild or headlong.

amulet (ăm′ ū lėt) [*F. amulette*, L. *amulētum*, a talisman], *n.* Anything worn about the person as an imagined preservative against sickness, witchcraft, etc.

amuse (ȧ mūz′) [O.F. *amuser*, to cause to muse (*à*, to, *muser*, stare), see MUSE], *v.t.* *To divert with false promises, beguile; to divert attention from serious business by anything entertaining; to please with anything light and cheerful; to entertain. **amusement,** *n.* That which amuses; play, diversion; excitement of laughter; the state of being amused. **amusing,** *a.* Entertaining, diverting, laughable. **amusingly,** *adv.* **amusive,** *a.* Affording entertainment; tending to excite laughter; tending to amusement.

amygdalic (ăm ig dăl′ ik) [L. *amygdala*, Gr. *amugdalē*, an almond, -IC], *a.* Pertaining to plants of the genus *Amygdalus*; obtained from almonds. **amygdalin** (ȧ mig′ dȧ lin), *n.* (*Chem.*) A crystalline substance extracted from bitter almonds, and found amorphous in the leaves of the cherry laurel.

amygdaloid, *a.* Almond-shaped. *n.* (*Geol.*) An igneous rock containing almond-shaped nodules of some mineral.

amyl (ăm′ il) [L. *amylum*, starch], *n.* (*Chem.*) A monatomic alcohol radical, also called Quintyl. **amylaceous** (-ā′ shŭs), *a.* Pertaining to or of the nature of starch. **amylene,** *n.* A diatomic hydrocarbon, with anæsthetic properties. **amyloid,** *a.* Resembling or containing starch; starchy. *n.* A non-nitrogenous starchy food.

an, *a.* [A, AN].

***an,** *conj.* [AND]. If.

an-, *pref.* (1) [A.-S., *an*, on], *prep.*, as in *anent, anon*; (2) [L. *ad-* assim.] before *n*, as in *annex, announce*; (3) [Gr. *ana*] [see ANA-]; (4) [Gr. *an-*, *a-*, not], as in *anæsthetic, anarchy.*

-an [L. *-ānus* (sometimes through F. *-ain*, retained in *captain, chaplain*, or F. *-en*, or through It., Sp., or Port. *-ano*)], *suf.* Of, belonging to, pertaining to, *e.g. human, pagan, publican, Christian, Unitarian, European*, etc.

ana (ā′ nȧ, a′ nȧ) [-ANA], *n.* Literary gossip, usually of a personal or local kind.

ana-, an- [Gr. *ana*, upon, up, backwards], *pref.* As in *anachronism, anagram, analogy, aneurism.*

-ana [L. *-āna*, neut. pl. of -ANUS], *suf.* Things about, sayings of, anecdotes concerning, as in *Boxiana, Tunbrigiana, Johnsoniana, Shakespeareana, Virgiliana.*

anabaptism (ăn ȧ băp′ tizm) [L. *anabaptismus*, Gr. *anabaptismos* (see ANA-, BAPTISM)], *n.* A second baptism; the doctrine of the Anabaptists. **anabaptist,** *n.* One who rebaptizes; member of a German sect which arose in the sixteenth century; applied (as a term of reproach) to the modern Baptists. *a.* Of or pertaining to anabaptism. **anabaptistical** (ăn ȧ băp tis′ tik ål), *a.*

anabas (ăn′ ȧ băs) [Gr. *anabas*, part. of *anabainein* (-ANA, *bainein*, to walk)], *n.* A genus of fishes that leave the water.

anabasis (ȧ năb′ ȧ sis) [Gr. *anabasis*, going up (*anabainein*, see prec.)], *n.* A military advance; the expedition of Cyrus the Younger into Asia, narrated by Xenophon.

anabolism (ȧn ab′ ol izm) [Gr. *anabole*, rising up], *n.* (*Med.*) Building up of living tissues by assimilation of nutriment.

anabranch (ăn′ ȧ branch), *n.* (*Austral.*) A tributary rejoining the main stream of a river and thus forming an island.

anacharis (ȧ năk′ ȧ ris) [ANA-, Gr. *charis*, grace], *n.* (*Bot.*) A North American waterweed which suddenly appeared in Britain in 1842, and spread with great rapidity.

anachronism (ȧ năk′ rŏn izm) [F. *anachronisme*, L. *anachronismus*, Gr. *anachronismos* (*anachronizein*, to refer to a wrong time)], *n.* The reference of an event, custom or circumstance to a wrong period or date; anything out of date or incongruous with the present. **anachronic** (ăn ȧ kron′ ik), *a.* Wrong in date, characterized by anachronism. **anachronistic** (-is′ tik), *a.* Pertaining to or involving an anachronism.

anaclastic (ăn ȧ klăs′ tik) [Gr. *anaklastos* (ANA-, *klaein*, to bend)], *a.* Pertaining to refraction; produced by refraction. **anaclastic glasses,** *n.pl.* Vessels with thin bottoms that spring in or out with a crackling sound as one sucks out the air or blows into them. **anaclastics,** *n.* The science which treats of refraction; dioptrics.

anacoluthon (ăn ȧ kŏ loo′ thŏn) [Gr. *anakolouthon* (*an-*, not, *akolouthos*, following, from *keleuthos*, road)], *n.* Want of sequence in a sentence; such a change of structure in a sentence as renders it ungrammatical.

anaconda (ăn ȧ kon′ dȧ) [Sinhalese, *henakandāya*], *n.* A python from Ceylon; *Eunectes murinus*, a large South American boa; any large snake which kills its prey by constriction.

anacreontic (ȧ năk rė on′ tik) [L. *Anacreonticus*, from Gr. *Anakreōn*], *a.* Pertaining to the Greek poet Anacreon, or the metre used by him; erotic, convivial. *n.* An erotic or convivial poem.

anacrusis (ăn ȧ kroo′ sis) [Gr. *anakrousis* (ANA-, *krouein*, to strike)], *n.* (*Pros.*) An upward beat at the beginning of a verse, consisting of an unstressed syllable or syllables.

anadem (ăn′ ȧ dem) [L. *anadēma*, Gr. *anadēma* (*ana-*, *deein*, to bind)], *n.* A garland or fillet; a chaplet or crown of flowers.

anadromous (ȧ năd′ rŏ mŭs) [Gr. *anadromos* (*dromos*, running)], *a.* Ascending rivers to deposit spawn.

anæmia (ȧ nē′ mi ȧ) [Gr. *anaimia* (*an-*, not, *haima*, blood)], *n.* Want of blood, deficiency or poor quality of the blood. **anæmic,** *a.* Of or relating to anæmia; ill-supplied with blood; pale.

anaerobe (ăn ā ĕr rōb′) [Gr. *a-*, not; *aer*, air; *bios*, life], *n.* (*Biol.*) A micro-organism that thrives best, or only, in the absence of oxygen. **anaerobic,** *a.*

anæsthesia (ăn ēs thē′ zi ȧ) [Gr. *anaisthēsia* (AN-, not, *aisthe-*, stem of *aisthanomai*, to feel)], *n.* Loss of feeling; insensibility.

anæsthetic (ăn ēs thet′ ik), *a.* Producing anæsthesia. *n.* A substance which produces anæsthesia (during surgical operations). **anæsthetically,** *adv.* By way of an anæsthetic, so as to cause anæsthesia. **anæsthetist** (ă nēs′ thė tist), *n.* One who administers an anæsthetic. **anæsthetize** (ȧ nēs′ thė tīz), *v.t.* To administer an anæsthetic to. **anæsthetization** (-zā′ shŭn), *n.* The process of effecting anæsthesia.

anaglyph (ăn′ ȧ glif) [Gr. *anagluphe* (ANA-, *gluphein*, to carve)], *n.* A figure cut or embossed in low relief. **anaglyphic, anaglyptic** (ăn ȧ glip′ tik) [Gr. *anagluptikos*], *a.* Of or pertaining to an anaglyph; wrought in low relief. **anaglyptics,** *n.pl.* The art of working in low relief.

anagnorisis (ăn ȧg nor′ i sis) [L., from Gr. *anagnōrisis* (ANA- *gnōrizein*, to recognize)], *n.* Recognition; the denouement in a drama.

anagoge, anagogy (ăn ȧ gō′ jė) [L., from Gr. *anagōgē* (AN-, *agein*, to lead)], *n.* *Mystical, allegorical, or spiritual interpretation; *spiritual enlightenment. **anagogical** (ăn ȧ goj′ ik ål), *a.* Pertaining to anagoge; mysterious, elevated, spiritual. **anagogically,** *adv.*

anagram (ăn′ ȧ grăm) [F. *anagramme*, Gr. *anagramma* (ANA-, *graphein*, to write)], *n.* A word or sentence formed by transposing the letters of another word or sentence; *change, transposition. **anagrammatical** (ăn ȧ grȧ măt′ ik ål), *a.* Of, pertaining to, or containing an anagram. **anagrammatically,** *adv.* **anagrammatize** (ăn ȧ gram′ ȧ tīz) [Gr. *anagrammatizein*], *v.t.* To transpose so as to form into an anagram. **anagrammatism,** *n.* The art or practice of making anagrams. **anagrammatist,** *n.* One who makes anagrams.

anal (ā′ nål), *a.* Pertaining to or situated near the anus.

analects (ăn′ ȧ lekts), **analecta** (ăn ȧ lek′ tȧ) [L., from Gr. *analekta* (ANA-, *legein*, to gather)], *n.pl.* *Crumbs which fall from the table; literary gleanings.

analeptic (ăn ȧ lep′ tik) [Gr. *analēptikos* (*lambanein*, to take)], *a.* (*Med.*) Restorative, increasing the strength. *n.* A restorative medicine.

analgesia (ăn ăl jē′ zi ȧ) [Gr., painlessness], *n.* (*Path.*) Loss of sensibility to pain. **analgesic,** *n.* A drug that relieves pain. *a.* Insensible to pain.

analogy (ȧ năl′ ŏ ji) [L. *analogia*, Gr. *analogia* (ANA-, *logos*, word, relation, proportion, whence *logia*)], *n.* Similitude of relations, conformity, similarity; (*Log.*) reasoning from parallel cases; (*Nat. Hist.*) relation between parts agreeing in function but not in origin; (*Math.*) proportion; the similitude of ratios. **analogic** (ăn ȧ loj′ ik), **analogical,** *a.* Of, pertaining to, or involving analogy. **analogically,**

adv. **analogist** (à năl′ ŏ jist), *n.* One who is occupied with analogy. **analogize** (à năl′ ŏ jīz) [-IZE], *v.t.* To represent or explain by analogy. *v.i.* To reason from analogy. **analogous** (à năl′ ŏ gŭs) [L. *analogus*, Gr. *analogos*, according to proportion], *a.* Presenting some analogy or resemblance. **analogously,** *adv.* **analogue** (ăn′ a log), [F. *analogue*, Gr. *analogon*, neut. a. (see ANALOGOUS)], *n.* An analogous word or thing; a parallel; (*Nat. Hist.*) a part which agrees with another in function, but not in origin.

analyse (ăn′ à līz) [F. *analyse*, v. from n. *analyse*, analysis (L., from Gr. *analusis* (ANA-, *luein*, to loosen); or directly from n. *analyse*)], *v.t.* To take to pieces, resolve into its constituent elements; to examine minutely; (*Chem.* and *Phys.*) to determine the elements of a compound; (*Lit.*) to examine critically; (*Gram.*) to resolve a sentence into its grammatical elements. **analysable,** *a.* **analyser,** *n.* One who or that which analyses; (*Optics*) an apparatus in the polariscope exhibiting the fact that the light has been polarized.

analysis (à năl′ i sis) [Gr. *analusis*], *n.* (*pl.* **analyses**) The process of analysing; separation into constituent elements; (*Chem.*) resolution of a compound into its elements to ascertain composition, purity, etc.; (*Math.*) resolution of problems by reducing them to equations.

analyst (ăn′ à list), *n.* One who analyses. **public analyst,** *n.* A chemical analyst appointed under the Sale of Food and Drugs Act.

analytic, analytical (ăn à lit′ ik, -ǎl), *a.* Pertaining to analysis; resolving anything into its constituent parts; (*Philol.*) using separate words instead of inflections. **analytically,** *adv.* **analytics,** *n.* The science of analysis.

anamnesis (ăn àm nē′ sis) [Gr. *anamnēsis*, remembrance (*anamimnēskein*, to remember)], *n.* Recollection; the doctrine of recollection of a previous existence.

anamorphosis (ăn à môr fō′ sis) [Gr. *anamorphōsis*, n. of *anamorphoein*, to transform (ANA-, *morphē*, form)], *n.* A distorted projection of any object so contrived that if looked at from one point of view, or reflected from a suitable mirror, it will appear properly proportioned; (*Bot.*) degeneration causing change of appearance; abnormal alteration of form.

ananas (à nā′ nàs, à na′ nàs), **anana** [Port. *ananás*, Guarani, *anānā* (*s* mistaken for pl.)], *n.* The pineapple plant or its fruit.

anandrous (à năn′ drŭs) [Gr. *anandros*, without a husband (*an-*, priv., *anēr andros*, male)], *a.* (*Bot.*) Destitute of stamens.

anapæst (ăn′ à pest, ăn′ à pēst) [L. *anapæstus*, Gr. *anapaistos*, reversed (ANA-, *paiein*, to strike)], *n.* A metrical foot consisting of three syllables, the first two short and the third long, a reversed dactyl. **anapæstic,** *a.* Composed of anapæsts. *n.* An anapæstic line or verse.

anaphora (à năf′ ŏ rà) [L., from Gr. *anaphorē*, a carrying back (ANA-, *pherein*, to bear)], *n.* The commencement of successive sentences with the same word or words; (*Astron.*) the rising of the constellations of the Zodiac by the daily course of the heavens.

anaphrodisiac (ăn ăf′ rō diz′ i ăk) [AN- (4); Gr. *aphrodisiakos*, venereal], *n.* (*Med.*) An agent abolishing or decreasing sexual desire.

anaphylaxis (ăn à fil ăk′ sis) [ANA-; Gr. *phulassein*, guard], *n.* (*Med.*) A sensitive condition resulting from the introduction, *e.g.* into the blood stream, of a foreign protein, allergy.

anaplasty (ăn à plăs′ ti) [Gr. *anaplastos*, that can be moulded], *n.* Plastic surgery.

anaptotic (ăn àp tot′ ik) [Gr. *ana-*, again, *aptōtos*, indeclinable; or *ana*, back, *ptotikos* (see APTOTE)], *a.* Becoming uninflected again (a term applied to languages, English for example, in which the inflections have been replaced by particles).

anarch (ăn′ ark) [Gr. *anarkhos*, without a ruler (*an-*, without, *archos*, ruler)], *n.* (*poet.*) A promoter of anarchy or leader of revolt.

anarchy (ăn′ ar ki) [Gr. *anarchia*, as prec.], *n.* Absence of government; want of settled government; disorder, lawlessness. **anarchic, anarchical,** *a.* **anarchically,** *adv.* **anarchism,** *n.* The principles of anarchy; a theory of government based on the free agreement of individuals rather than on submission to law and authority. **anarchist,** *n.* One who aims at producing anarchy; one opposed to all forms of government.

anarthrous (à narth′ rŭs) [Gr. *an-*, without, *arthron*, joint], *a.* Without the (Greek) article; (*Physiol.*) without joints.

anasarca (ăn à sar′ kà) [Gr. *ana*, up, *sarx sarca*, flesh], *n.* Dropsy in the cellular tissue. **anasarcous,** *a.* Puffy, affected with anasarca.

anastatic (ăn à stăt′ ik) [Gr. *anastatos*, caused to stand up (*ana*, up, *sta-*, stand)], *a.* Raised, in relief; with the characters or illustrations in relief. **anastatic-printing,** *n.* A process in which copies of engravings, etc., are printed from facsimiles produced in relief on zinc plates.

anastigmat lens (ăn ăs tig′ măt lenz) [ANA-; Gr. *stigme*, a dot], *n.* (*Phot.*) A lens free from astigmatism, which refers every point on the scene accurately to a corresponding point on the plate.

anastomose (à năs′ tŏ mōz) [F. *anastomoser*, v. from mod. L. *anastomōsis*, from *anastomoein*, to provide with a mouth (*stoma*)], *v.i.* (*Physiol.*) To communicate by anastomosis; to interosculate, to intercommunicate. **anastomosed,** *a.* Joined by anastomosis. **anastomosis** (à năs tŏ mō′ sis), *n.* (*pl.* **anastomoses**) The uniting of vessels, such as veins, arteries, sap-vessels, etc., by connecting branches. **anastomotic** (-mot′ ik), *a.* Of or pertaining to anastomosis; (*Med.*) tending to remove obstructions from vessels. *n.* (*Med.*) A medicine which removes obstructions from vessels.

anastrophe (à năs′ trŏ fē) [Gr. (*ana*, back, *strephein*, to turn)], *n.* Inversion of the natural order of the words in a sentence or clause.

anathema (à năth′ ė mà) [L., an excommunicated person, from Gr. *anathema* (*ana*, up, *tithēmi*, to put)], *n.* (*pl.* **anathemata,** ăn à thē′ mà tà) An accursed thing; the formal act by which a person or thing is cursed, excommunication; a thing consecrated to sacred use. **anathema maranatha** (măr àn ā′ thà) [Syriac *māran ethā*, the Lord has come, 1 Cor. xvi. 22 (connected by early criticism with the preceding *anathema*)]: An intensified imprecation. **anathematize** (à năth′ ė mà tīz), *v.t.* To excommunicate, to curse, to put under a ban. *v.i.* To curse.

anatomy (à năt′ ŏ mi) [F. *anatomie*, L. *anatomia*, Gr. *anatomia*, abstract n. (*anatomē*, cutting up, from *temnein*, to cut)], *n.* The art of dissecting an organized body so as to discover its structure, and the situation, economy, and inter-relation of its parts; the science of the structure of organized bodies; the act of dissecting; a subject, or any part of a subject, for dissection; a model of a dissected body; a skeleton; a withered, emaciated person; (*fig.*) a minute examination, reduction to parts or elements, analysis. **anatomic** (ăn à tom′ ik), **anatomical,** *a.* Pertaining to or connected with anatomy. **anatomically,** *adv.* **anatomize** (à năt′ ŏ mīz), *v.t.* To dissect; to make a dissection of. **anatomist,** *n.* One who practises or is skilled in anatomy.

anatta (à năt′ à) [? native Am.], *n.* An orange-red dye from Central America, used to colour cheese.

anbury, ambury (ăn′-, ăm′ bėr i) [? A.-S. *ang-*, pain (cp. AGNAIL), BERRY], *n.* A soft wart on a horse's neck; the disease called 'fingers and toes' in turnips.

-ance [F. *-ance*, L. *-antia* and *-entia*], *suf.* Noting state or action, as *distance*, *fragrance*, *parlance*, *riddance*.

ancestor (ăn′ sės tȯr) [O.F. *ancestre*, L. *antecessor*, one who goes before (*ante*, before, *cēdere*, go)], *n.* One from whom a person is descended; a progenitor; (*Biol.*) an organism of low type from which others of higher type have been developed. **ancestress,** *n.* A female ancestor. **ancestral** (ȧn ses′ trȧl), *a.* Pertaining to ancestors; derived from or possessed by ancestors. **ancestry** (ăn′ sės tri) [O.F. *ancesserie*], *n.* A line of ancestors; high birth, honourable lineage; ancient descent.

anchithere (ăng′ ki thēr) [Gr. *anki*, near, *thērion*, a wild beast], *n.* An extinct animal, between the palæothere and the horse.

anchor (ăng′ kȯr) [A.-S. *ancor*, L. *ancora*, Gr. *agkūra*, an anchor], *n.* A heavy hooked iron instrument dropped from a ship to grapple the bottom and prevent her drifting; anything shaped like an anchor; a ground or source of confidence. *v.t.* To secure by means of the anchor; to fix firmly. *v.i.* To come to anchor; to take up a position; (*slang*) to sit down. **sheet anchor:** the largest anchor carried by a ship. **bower anchor:** the next in size. **kedge anchor:** the smallest. **at anchor:** held by the anchor; at rest. **to cast anchor:** to drop the anchor into the sea; to fix one's self. **to weigh anchor:** to raise the anchor preparatory to sailing. **anchor-ground,** *n.* Ground for anchoring. **anchor-hold,** *n.* The hold which the anchor takes. **anchor-ice,** *n.* Ground ice, formed at the bottom of lakes, rivers, or sea. **anchor-watch,** *n.* A watch set on board ship while she is at anchor; the men composing such watch. **anchored,** *a.* Held by an anchor; firmly fixed; (*Her.*) applied to a cross, the extremities of which are bent back like the flukes of an anchor. **anchorless,** *a.* Without an anchor or firm hold; drifting.

anchorage (ăng′ kȯr ȧj), *n.* A place suitable for anchoring in; the hold on the sea-bottom by the anchor; duty paid for permission to anchor.

anchoret (ăng′ kȯ ret), **anchorite** (ăng′ kȯ rīt) [F. *anachorète*, L. *anachōrēta*, Gr. *anakhōrētēs* (*ana-*, *khōreein*, to withdraw, retire)], *n.* A religious recluse, a hermit; one of the early Christian recluses; a person of solitary habits. **anchoretic, anchoretical,** *a.* Pertaining to an anchorite, or his manner of life. **anchoress** (ăng′ kȯ res), **ancress** (ăng′ kres) [M.E. *ancre*, *anker* (L. *anachōrēta*), -ESS], *n.* A female anchorite.

anchovy (ȧn chō′ vi, ăn′ chō vi) [Sp. *anchova*, perhaps Basque *anchua*, a dried fish], *n.* A small fish, *Engraulis encrasicholus*, of the herring family, caught in the Mediterranean, pickled for exportation, and used in sauces, etc. **anchovy pear,** *n.* *Grias cauliflora*, a West Indian fruit, which is eaten as a pickle. **anchovy-toast:** Toast spread with anchovies.

anchylose (ăng′ ki lōz) [Gr. *ankulōsis*, stiffening of joints, from *ankuloein*, to crook (*ankulos*, crooked)], *v.t.* To stiffen (a joint), to consolidate two separate bones (usually in p.). *v.i.* To become stiff; to grow together. **anchylosis** (ăng ki lō′ sis), *n.* The formation of a stiff joint; the coalescence of two bones.

ancient (1) (ăn′ chėnt) [O.F. *ancien*, late L. *antiānus*, old (*ante*, before), -AN, assim. to -ENT], *a.* Of or belonging to long past time; past, former, esp. of the times before the Middle Ages, that is before the end of the Western Empire (1453); very old, antiquated. *n.pl.* Those who lived in former (esp. Classical) times. **ancient lights:** Windows that have acquired by long usage (not less than twenty years) the right to light from adjoining property. **the Ancient of Days:** The Deity. **anciently,** *adv.* In ancient times; of old; in a very old-fashioned manner. **ancientness,** *n.* The quality or state of being ancient. ***ancientry,** *n.* Ancientness; ancestry.

ancient (2) (ăn′ chėnt) [corr. of ENSIGN], *n.* A flag, a standard; a standard-bearer, an ensign.

ancillary (ăn sil′ ȧr i) [L. *ancillāris* (*ancilla*, a maid)], *a.* Subservient, auxiliary; pertaining to female servants.

ancipital (ăn sip′ it ȧl) [L. *anceps -ipitus*, two-headed (*an-*, AMBI-, *caput -itis*, head)], *a.* (*Physiol.*) Having two sharp edges. ***ancipitous** (ăn sip′ it ŭs) [-OUS], *a.* *Doubtful; (*Bot.*) ancipital.

ancle [ANKLE].

ancon (ăng′ kȯn) [L., from Gr. *agkōn*, a bend], *n.* (*pl.* **ancones,** -kō′ nēz) The elbow; (*Arch.*) the corner or quoin of a wall, cross-beam or rafter; a bracket, a console; a support to a cornice.

Ancona (ăn kō′ nȧ) [town in Italy], *n.* A strain of laying poultry.

ancress [ANCHORET].

-ancy [-ANCE], *suf.* Expressing quality or state; *e.g. constancy, elegancy, infancy, vacancy.*

and (ănd) [A.-S. *and, ond, end*, cp. O.H.G. *anti* (cognate with L. *ante*, before, Gr. *anti*, against); A.-S. *and-*, over against, as in *andswarian*, answer; *and*, and if, was often shortened to *an*], *conj.* The copulative which joins words and sentences; ***if,** whether, as if, though.

andante (an dan′ tē) [It.], *adv.* (*Mus.*) Moderately slow. *n.* A moderately slow movement or piece. **andante affettuoso** (an dan′ tē a fet tū ō′ sō) [It.], *adv., a.* and *n.* (*Mus.*) Slowly and tenderly. **andante con moto,** *adv.* Slowly but with movement. **andante grazioso,** *adv.* Slowly and gracefully. **andante maestoso,** *adv.* Slowly and majestically. **andante sostenuto,** *adv.* Slow, but sustained. **andantino** (an dan tē′ nō) [dim.], *adv.* Rather quicker than andante. *n.* A movement or piece of this character.

Anderson shelter (ăn′ dėr son) [Sir J. Anderson, Home Secretary (1939–40)], *n.* An air-raid shelter formed of arched corrugated steel.

andiron (ănd′ ī ėrn) [O.F. *andier*], *n.* A horizontal bar raised on short legs, with an ornamental upright in front, placed on each side of the hearth to support logs in a wood fire; a fire-dog.

Andrew (ăn′ droo) [personal name], *n.* A body-servant, a valet. **merry-andrew,** *n.* A clown or jester, usually attired in a coat of motley.

andro- [Gr. *anēr andros*, a man, a male], *comb. form.* Pertaining to the male sex, or to male flowers.

androecium (ăn dresh′ i ŭm) [Gr. *aner*, a man, *oikion*, a house], *n.* (*Bot.*) The stamens collectively.

androgen (an′ drō jen), *n.* (*Biol.*) Any substance with male sex hormone activity.

androgyne (ăn′ drȯ jin) [F. *androgyne*, L. *androgynous*, Gr. *androgunos*, male and female in one (*gunē*, woman)], *n.* *An hermaphrodite; an effeminate man; (*Bot.*) an androgynous plant. **androgynous** (ăn droj′ in ŭs), *a.* Presenting the characteristics of both sexes in the same individual; (*Bot.*) bearing both stamens and pistils in the same flower or on the same plant. **androgyny,** *n.* Hermaphroditism; presence of male and female organs in one individual.

Andromeda (ăn drom′ ė dȧ) [Gr. name of the daughter of Cepheus and Cassiopeia rescued by Perseus], *n.* One of the northern constellations; (*Bot.*) a genus of heaths. **andromed** (ăn′ drȯ mėd), **andromede,** *n.* One of a system of meteors radiating from a point in the constellation Andromeda.

andropetalous (ăn drȯ pet′ ȧ lŭs), *a.* (*Bot.*) A term applied to flowers made double by the conversion of stamens into petals.

androphagous (ăn drof′ ȧ gŭs) [Gr. *androphagos* (*phagos*, eating, from *phagein*, to eat)], *a.* Man-eating, cannibal.

-androus [L. *-andrus*, Gr. *-andros*, male (*anēr andros*, man)], *suf.* (*Bot.*) Having male organs or stamens, *e.g. diandrous, monandrous.*

ane (yin, ān) [Scot.], *n., a., pron.* One, a, an.

-ane [L. *-ānus*, cp. -AN; also formed to range with -ENE, -INE, and -ONE in chemical terminology for hydrocarbons], *suf.* Forming adjectives, *e.g. humane, mundane, urbane*; names of hydrocarbons, *methane, pentane, hexane.*

anecdote (ăn′ ėk dōt) [med. Lat. *anecdota*, Gr. *anekdota*, things unpublished (*an-*, not, *ekdotos*, published, from *ek-*, out, *didōmi*, I give)], *n.* The relation of an isolated fact or incident; a short, pithy narrative; a passage of private life. **anecdotage** (ăn′ ėk dō tāj) [-AGE], *n.* Anecdotes collectively; garrulous old age (as if from DOTAGE). **anecdotal,** *a.* Pertaining to or consisting of anecdotes. **anecdotic** (ăn ėk dot′ ik), **anecdotical,** *a.* Pertaining to anecdotes; in the habit of relating anecdotes. **anecdotist** (ăn′ ėk dō tist) [-IST], *n.* One given to relating anecdotes.

anele (ȧ nēl′) [*anelien*, A.-S. *on-*, on, *elein*, to oil (*ele*, L. *oleum*, oil)], *v.t.* To anoint with oil; to give Extreme Unction to.

anelectric (ăn ė lek′ trik), *a.* *Non-electric; parting readily with electricity. *n.* *A non-electric substance or body; a body which does not become electrified by friction.

anemograph (ȧ nem′ ȯ grăf) [Gr. *anemos*, wind], *n.* An instrument which automatically records the velocity and direction of the wind. **anemographic** (ăn ė mō grăf′ ik), *a.* Of or pertaining to an anemograph.

anemometer (ăn ė mom′ ė tėr) [Gr. *anemos*, wind], *n.* An instrument for measuring the velocity of the wind, a wind gauge. **anemometric** (-met′ rik), *a.* **anemometry,** *n.*

Anemone (ȧ nem′ ȯ ni) [Gr. *anemōnē*, wind-flower (*anemos*, wind)], *n.* A genus of plants with brilliantly-coloured flowers; esp. *Anemone nemorosa*, sometimes called the wind-flower, common in Britain. [See also SEA-ANEMONE.]

anemophilous (ăn ė mof′ i lŭs) [*anemos*, wind, *philos*, loving], *a.* Wind-fertilized; having the pollen carried away by the wind.

anent (ȧ nent′) [A.-S. *on-efen* (*on*, in, *efen*, even, equal), even with, on a level with], *prep.* Concerning, touching, in respect of.

-aneous [L. *-āneus*], *suf.* Belonging to, *e.g.* *extraneous*, *instantaneous*.

aneroid (ăn′ ėr oid) [F. *anëroïde* (Gr. *a-*, priv., *nēros*, wet, -OID)], *a.* A term applied to a barometer which measures the pressure of air by its action on a springy metallic box from which the air has been partially exhausted. *n.* An aneroid barometer.

aneurysm, aneurism (ăn′ ū rizm) [Gr. *aneurusma*, a widening (*an*, *ana*, up, *eurunein*, to widen, from *eurus*, wide)], *n.* A morbid dilatation in an artery, particularly of the aorta. **aneurysmal, aneurismal** (ăn ū riz′ măl), *a.*

anew (ȧ nū′), *adv.* Again; once again; afresh.

anfractuose (ăn frăk′ tū ōs), **anfractuous** [L. *anfractuōsus*, winding, L. *anfractus* (*an-*, *ambi-*, around, *frangere*, to break)], *a.* Winding, sinuous, tortuous. **anfractuosity** (ăn frăk tū os′ i ti) [F. *anfractuosité*], *n.* Circuitousness, tortuousness; a winding depression separating convolutions of the brain; intricacy.

angary (ăng′ gȧ ri), **angaria** (ăng găr′ i ȧ) [Gr. *angareia*, duty of a mounted courier], *n.* (*Law*) The confiscation or destruction by a belligerent of neutral property, esp. shipping, subject to claim for compensation.

angel (ăn′ jėl) [A.-S. *ængel*, *engel*, L. *angelos*, Gr. *angelos*, a messenger; soft *g* due to O.F. *angele*], *n.* A messenger from God; a ministering spirit; a guardian or attendant spirit; (*fig.*) a benign, innocent, or adorable creature; a title applied to some ministers; an old English gold coin, orig. the *angel-noble*, varying in value from 6s. 8d. upwards, and bearing the figure of the archangel Michael; (*Art*) a conventional representation of the heavenly messenger. **angel-fish,** *n.* A fish allied to the rays and sharks, named from the wing-like expansion of the pectoral fins. ***angel-gold,** *n.* Standard gold. **angel-noble,** *n.* [ANGEL]. **angel-shot,** *n.* A kind of chain shot. **angel-water,** *n.* Angelica-water, a perfume or cosmetic in which angelica was a chief ingredient. **angels on horseback,** *n.pl.* (*Cook.*) Oysters fried with bacon.

angelic (ăn jel′ ik), **angelical,** *a.* Resembling or of the nature of an angel. **angelic doctor:** Title or epithet applied to St. Thomas Aquinas. **angelically,** *adv.* **angelolatry** (ăn jėl ol′ ȧ tri), *n.* Angel-worship. **angelology,** *n.* The doctrine of angelic beings.

Angelica (ăn jel′ ik ȧ) [med. L. *herba angelica*], *n.* A genus of umbelliferous plants, including *archangelica*, used in medicine, and as a preserve or sweetmeat; candied angelica root; angelica-water.

angelus (ăn′ jė lŭs) [First word of opening, *Angelus domini*], *n.* A short devotional exercise in the Roman Catholic Church in honour of the Incarnation; the angelus-bell. **angelus-bell,** *n.* A bell rung early in the morning, at noon, and in the evening, as a signal to say the angelus.

anger (ăng′ gėr) [Icel. *angr*, grief, sorrow], *n.* Rage, fierce displeasure, passion, excited by a sense of wrong; *physical pain, inflammation. *v.t.* To make angry, to excite to wrath; to enrage. **angerly,** *adv.* Angrily; like an angry person. **angry** (ăng′ gri), *a.* Wrathful, expressing anger, (*Am.*) mad; hot-tempered, choleric; inflamed, painful. **angrily,** *adv.*

anger-nail [AGNAIL].

angina (ăn jī′ nȧ, ăn′ ji nȧ) [L. *angīna* (*angere*, to strangle)], *n.* Quinsy; angina pectoris. **angina pectoris** [L. *pectoris*, of or in the chest], *n.* A disease due to over-exertion when the heart is weak or diseased.

angio- [Gr. *angeion*, a vessel (dim. of *angos*, a chest)], *comb. form.* Vascular; pertaining to the vessels of organisms.

angiocarpous (ăn ji ō kar′ pŭs) [Gr. *karpos*, fruit], *a.* (*Bot.*) Having the fruit in an envelope not constituting part of the calyx.

angiosperm (ăn′ ji ō spĕrm) [*Gr. sperma*, seed], *n.* (*Bot.*) A plant that has its seed enclosed in a vessel or pericarp. **angiospermous** (ăn ji ō spĕr′ mŭs), *a.* Having the seeds enclosed in a pericarp.

angle (1) (ăng′ gėl) [A.-S. *angel*, *ongul*, fish-hook (cp. L. *oncus*, hook, Gr. *ankōn*, a bend)], *n.* A fish-hook; a rod and line for fishing. *v.i.* To fish with rod and line; (*fig.*) to fish for; to try to elicit; to get by craft; to steal. *v.t.* To fish (a stream) with rod and line. ***angle-rod,** *n.* A fishing rod. **angler,** *n.* One who fishes with a rod. **angler-fish,** *n.* *Lophius piscatorius*, a small British fish which attracts its prey by filaments attached to its head. **angling,** *n.* The art or practice of fishing with a rod and line; (*fig.*) trying to find out by craft.

angle (2) (ăng′ gėl) [O.F. *angle*, L. *angulum*, from same root as prec.], *n.* A corner; the inclination of two lines towards each other; the space between the lines or planes inclined to each other; an angular projection; (*fig.*) a point of view. **angle-bead,** *n.* (*Build.*) A vertical bead, usually of wood, fixed to an exterior angle, flush with the plaster. **angled,** *a.* Having an angle or angles. **angle-iron,** *n.* An angular piece of iron used to strengthen framework of any kind. **anglemeter** [-METER], *a.* An instrument for measuring angles; a clinometer. **angle of application:** The angle between the line along which a force is directed and the lever on which it acts. **angle of inclination:** The angle made by an inclined plane and the horizon. **angle of refraction:** The angle at which a ray of light is turned from its direct course in passing through a given medium. **angle of repose:** The slope at which a mass of loose material comes to rest if left to itself. **angle of vision:** (*persp.*) The angle at which objects are seen and which determines their apparent magnitudes. **angle-staff,** *n.* [ANGLE-BEAD]. **angle-tie,** *n.* A piece of timber placed across an angle in roofing. **angle-wise,** *adv.* In the manner of an angle, angularly.

Angle (3) (ăng′ gėl) [L. *anglus*, A.-S. *engle*, the people of *Angul*, district of Holstein, so-called from its shape (see ANGLE (1))], *n.* One of the Low German tribes that settled in Northumbria, Mercia, and East Anglia. **Anglian** (ăng′ li ȧn), *a.* Of or pertaining to the Angles. **East Anglian,** *n.* An inhabitant of Norfolk, Suffolk or Essex.

Anglican (ăng′ gli kȧn) [med. L. *Anglicānus*, from *Anglicus* (*Anglus*, ANGLE (3))], *a.* English (as opposed to Roman); of or belonging to the English Church; esp. High Church. *n.* A member of the High Church school in the Church of England. **Anglicanism,** *n.* The teachings and practices of the High Church party in the Church of England.

anglice (ăng′ gli sē) [L.], *adv.* In English.

Anglicism (ăng′ gli sizm) [L. *Anglicus*, English], *n.* An English idiom; English political principles. **Anglicize** (ăng′ gli sīz), *v.t.* To make English; to give an English form to; to turn into English.

Anglo- [L. *Anglus*], *comb. form.* English; of or belonging to England or the English; partially English (the meaning completed by another word). **Anglo-American,** *n.* An American of English parentage or descent. *a.* Of or belonging to such Americans, or to England and America. **Anglo-Catholic,** *a.* Catholic of the English communion; Anglican but of Catholic not Protestant tendencies. *n.* An English Catholic opposed to Romanizing principles; a High Churchman. **Anglo-Catholicism,** *n.* Anglican Catholicism; the doctrine that the English Church is a branch of the Catholic Church but not of the Roman Church. **Anglo-French,** *a.* Pertaining to England and France. **Anglo-Indian,** *n.* An Englishman born, or long resident, in India; a person of mixed British and Indian blood. *a.* Of or belonging to such people, or to England and India. **Anglo-Israelites,** *n.pl.* A sect claiming that the English are the lost Ten Tribes. **Anglomania** (ăng glō mā′ ni ȧ), *n.* Excessive fondness for English manners and customs. **Anglo-maniac,** *n.* **Anglophobe** (ăng′ glō fōb), *n.* A hater of England or of the English. **Anglophobia,** *n.* Fear or distrust of England. **Anglo-Saxon,** *a.* Of or belonging to the English race or language as distinct from Continental Saxons; of the whole English people before the Norman Conquest; of English people of Teutonic descent; and of English-speaking people generally, whether English or American. *n.* A member of the Anglo-Saxon race; their language [ENGLISH]. **Anglo-Saxondom,** *n.* Anglo-Saxons collectively, whether British or American. **Anglo-Saxonism,** *n.* Anything peculiar to the Anglo-Saxon race; belief in the superiority of the Anglo-Saxon race.

angola (ăng gō′ lȧ), **angora** (ăng gôr′ ȧ) [*Angora* (a town in Asia Minor), L. *Ancyra*, Gr. *Ankura*], *n.* A goat with long silky hair; the hair itself, and a fabric made therefrom; a long-haired variety of the domestic cat; a breed of rabbit with long, fine fur.

angostura (ăng gȯs tū′ rȧ), **angustura** (ăng gŭs tū′ rȧ) [*Angustura*, a town on the Orinoco (now called Ciudad Bolívar)], *a.* and *n.* Name of a febrifugal bark, used also in the preparation of bitters.

angry, angrily [ANGER].

Angström unit (Eng. pron. ăng′ strŭm ū′ nit) [A. J. Ångström (1814–74)], *n.* (*Phys.*) A unit of length used to express the wavelengths of different kinds of radiations, equivalent to 1/254,000,000 of an inch.

anguine (ăng′ gwin) [L. *anguīnus* (*anguis*)], *a.* Pertaining to or resembling a snake; snaky.

anguish (ăng′ gwish) [O.F. *anguisse, angoisse*, the sense of choking, L. *angustia*, tightness, narrowness (*angustus*, narrow; *angere*, to stifle, choke)], *n.* Excessive pain or distress of body or mind. *v.t.* To afflict with extreme pain or grief.

angular (ăng′ gū lȧr) [L. *angulāris* (*angulus*, ANGLE (2))], *a.* Having angles or sharp corners; forming an angle; in an angle; measured by an angle; bony, lacking in plumpness or smoothness; stiff, formal, unaccommodating, crotchety. An **angular party:** (*colloq.*) One composed of an odd number of people. **angular velocity:** (*Phys.*) Rate of rotation measured by the angle turned through per unit time, usu. radius per second. **angularly,** *adv.* **angularity** (ăng gū lăr′ i ti), *n.* **angulate** (ăng′ gū lāt), *a.* Angular, formed with angles or corners. *v.t.* To make angular. **angulation** (ăng gū lā′ shŭn), *n.* The making of angles; angular form or structure. **angulose** (ăng′ gū lōs), **angulous** (ăng′ gū lŭs), *a.* Angular, having angles or corners.

angustifoliate (ăng gŭs ti fō′ li āt) [L. *angusus*, narrow, *folium*, a leaf], *a.* (*Bot.*) Having the leaves narrow.

anharmonic (ăn har mon′ ik) [F. *anharmonique* (Gr. *an-*, not, *harmonikos*, HARMONIC)], *a.* (*Math.*) Not harmonic.

anhelation (ăn hē lā′ shŭn) [F. *anhélation*, L. *anhelātiōnem* (L. *anhēlāre*, to pant)], *n.* The act of panting; difficult respiration; (*fig.*) aspiration.

anhydride (ăn hī′ drīd) [ANHYDROUS], *n.* A chemical substance formed by substituting an acid radical for the whole of the hydrogen in one or two molecules of water.

anhydrite (ăn hī′ drīt), *n.* Sulphate of lime, anhydrous gypsum.

anhydrosis (ăn hī drō′ sis), *n.* (*Path.*) Deficiency of perspiration.

anhydrous (ăn hī′ drŭs) [Gr. *anudros* (*an-*, not, *hudor*, water)], *a.* Having no water in its composition; esp. destitute of water of crystallization.

anigh (ȧ nī′) [NIGH; formed in imitation of *adown*, *afar*, etc.], *adv.* and *prep.* Near; near to.

***anight** (ȧ nīt′), ***anights** [A.-S. *on niht*; *on niht* and *nihtes* (adv. gen. sing.) have coalesced in *a-nights*], *adv.* At night, by night, of a night.

anil (ăn′ il) [F., from Sp. *añil*, Arab. *an-nīl* (*al-*, the *nīl*, from Sansk. *nīlī*, indigo, from *nīlas*, blue)], *n.* The indigo-plant: indigo.

anile (ăn′ īl) [L. *anīlis* (*anus*, an old woman)], *a.* Of or resembling an old woman; old womanish; feeble-minded. **anility** (ȧ nil′ i ti) [L. *anīlitas*], *n.* The state of being old-womanish, dotage.

aniline (ăn′ i līn) [ANIL], *n.* A chemical base used in the production of many beautiful dyes, and originally obtained from indigo, now chiefly from coal-tar. *a.* Of, or belonging to, or obtained from this base.

animadvert (ăn i mȧd vĕrt′) [L. *animadvertere* (*animus*, the mind; *ad-*, to, *vertere*, to turn)], *v.i.* To direct the attention to; to criticize or censure (with *upon*). **animadversion** (ăn i mȧd vĕr′ shŭn), *n.* Criticism, comment, censure, reproof.

animal (ăn′ i mȧl) [L., n. from neut. a. *animāle*, having breath (*anima*, breath)], *n.* An organized being possessing life, sensation, and the power of voluntary motion; one of the lower animals as distinct from man, esp. a quadruped; a human being whose animal nature is abnormally strong, a brute (*lit.* or *fig.*). *a.* Of or belonging to animals, their nature, or functions; carnal; pertaining to animals as distinguished from vegetables. **animal charcoal,** *n.* Charcoal made from animal substances. **animal flower,** *n.* An actinozoon, *e.g.* a sea-anemone. **animal food,** *n.* Animal substances used as food. **animal heat, animal warmth,** *n.* The warm temperature characterizing the bodies of living animals. **animal kingdom,** *n.* Animals generally, viewed as one of the three great divisions of natural objects. **animal magnetism,** *n.* [MESMERISM]. **animal spirits,** *n.pl.* *Nerve-force, the principle of sensation and volitional movement; animal courage; liveliness of disposition. **animally,** *adv.* Physically, as opposed to intellectually; *with respect to the *anima*, psychically. **animalism** (ăn′ i mȧl izm) [-ISM], *n.* The exercise of the animal faculties; the theory which views mankind as merely animal; sensuality. **animality** (ăn i măl′ i ti) [F. *animalité*], *n.* Animal nature; the phenomena of animal life, animal life as distinct from vegetable life. **animalize** (ăn′ i mȧl īz) [-IZE], *v.t.* To make into an animal; to make into animal substance; to brutalize. **animalization,** *n.* The act or process of animalizing.

animalcule (ăn i măl′ kūl) [L. *animalculum*, dim. of *animal*; the L. form with pl. **animalcula** is still used, esp. in scientific works], *n.* An animal so small as to be invisible to the naked eye. **animalcular,** *a.* Pertaining or relating to animalcules. **animalculism,** *n.* The theory that animalcules are the germs of life and the cause of disease. **animalculist,** *n.* One who makes animalcules a special study; an adherent of animalculism.

animalism, animality [ANIMAL].

animate (ăn′ i māt) [L. *animātus*, p.p. of *animāre*, to give life to, -ATE], *v.t.* To give life or spirit to; to vivify, to inspire, to stir up. *a.* (ăn′ i mȧt) Living, endowed with life; lively. **animated,** *part.a.* Possessing life; full of life or spirits; vivacious, lively. **animated nature,** *n.* The animal kingdom. **animatedly,** *adv.* In a lively manner, vivaciously. **animating,** *a.* Life-giving, quickening, inspiring. **animatingly,** *adv.* **animation** (-mā′ shŭn), *n.* The act of animating; the state of being animated, vitality; life, vivacity. **animative,** *a.* Having the power to impart life or spirit. **animator,** *n.*

animé (an i mā′, ăn′ im i) [F., animated, *i.e.* alive with insects], *n.* A West Indian resin, used for varnish; other resins.

animism (ăn′ im izm) [L. *anima*], *n.* The doctrine that vital phenomena are produced by an immaterial soul distinct from matter; the attribution of a living soul to inanimate objects and to natural phenomena; a spiritual (not a materialist) theory of the universe. **animist,** *n.* A believer in animism. **animistic,** *a.*

animosity (ăn i mos′ i ti) [F. *animosité*, L. *animōsitātem* (*animōsus*, spirited, see foll.)], *n.* Enmity tending to show itself in action.

animoso (ăn i mō′ zō) [It.], *adv.* (*Mus.*) With spirit.

animus (ăn′ i mŭs) [L., mind, spirit, passion], *n.* Spirit actuating feeling, usually of a hostile character; animosity.

anion (ăn′ i on) [Gr. *ana*, up, *ion*, going], *n.* (*Elec.*) An ion in quest of the anode; an electro-negative ion.

anise (ăn′ is) [F., from L. *anīsum*, Gr. *anison*, *anēthon*, anise, or dill], *n.* An umbelliferous plant, *Pimpinella anisum*, cultivated for its seeds, which are carminative, anciently confused with the dill. **aniseed,** *n.* The seed of the anise, used as a carminative. **anisette** (ăn i zet′) [F., dim. of *anis*], *n.* A liqueur made from aniseed.

aniso- [Gr. *anisos*, unequal, uneven (*an-*, not, *isos*, equal)], *comb. form.* Odd, unequal, unsymmetrical.

anisomeric (ăn ī sō mer′ ik) [Gr. *meros*, a part], *a.* Not isomeric; not having the same proportions.

anisometric (ăn ī sō met′ rik) [Gr. *metron*, measure], *a.* Of unequal measurement.

anker (ăng′ kėr) [Dut.], *n.* A measure for wine and spirits of nearly nine imperial gallons; a keg containing that quantity.

ankh (ăngk) [Egypt., life or soul], *n.* A keylike cross being the emblem of life, or male symbol of generation.

ankle, ancle (ăng′ kėl) [A.S. *ancléow*, perhaps from Dut. *anklaauw* (cp. *klaaw*, claw); mod. *ankle* may be from O.Fris. *ankel*, Dut. *enkel* (cp. L. *ang-*, bend, crook, root of *angulus*)], *n.* The joint by which the foot is united to the leg; part of leg between foot and calf. **ankle-deep,** *a.* and *adv.* So deep as to cover the ankles. **ankle-high,** *a.* and *adv.* So high as to cover the ankles. **ankle-jacks,** *n.pl.* Boots reaching above the ankles. **anklet,** *n.* An ornament, fetter, strap, or band for the ankle; an ankle-ring.

ankus (ăng′ kŭs) [Hind.], *n.* An elephant goad.

ankylose [ANCHYLOSE].

anna (ăn′ ȧ) [Hind. *ana*], *n.* An East Indian money of account, equal to one-sixteenth of a rupee.

annals (ăn′ ȧlz) [L. *annāles*, annual (*annus*, year)], *n.pl.* A narrative of events arranged in years; historical records; (*R.-C. Ch.*) masses said for the space of a year. **annalist,** *n.* One who writes annals. **annalistic,** *a.*

annates (ăn′ āts) [F. *annate*, med. L. *annāta*, fruits of a year (*annus*, year)], *n.pl.* The first year's revenue of Roman ecclesiastics on their appointment to a benefice, paid to the Pope; (*Sc. Law*) the half-year's revenue of his incumbency due to the executors of a deceased minister.

annatto [ANATTA].

anneal (ȧ nēl′) [A.-S. *onælan* (*ælan*, to burn), whence M.E. *anelen*, later confused with O.F. *neeler*, to enamel, late L. *nigellāre*, to blacken (*nigellus*, dim. of *niger*, black)], *v.t.* *To bake, as tiles; *to enamel by encaustic process; to temper, as glass or metals, by subjecting them to intense heat, and then allowing them to cool slowly; (*fig.*) to temper; to render tough. **annealing,** *n.* The burning of metallic colours into glass, etc.; the tempering of glass or metals, etc.

annectent (ȧ nek′ tėnt) [L. *annectere*, to knit or bind to], *a.* Connecting, linking.

Annelida (ȧ nel′ i dȧ) [mod. L., F. *annelés*, ringed, O.F. *annel*, ring, L. *anellus*, dim. of *anulus*, ring]. *n.pl.* (*Zool.*) A class of invertebrate animals with elongated bodies composed of annular segments. **annelid** (ăn′ ė lid), *n.* One of the Annelida. **annelidan** (ȧ nel′ i dȧn), *a.* Belonging or pertaining to the Annelida. *n.* An annelid.

annex (ȧ neks′) [F. *annexer*, L. *annexum*, p.p. of *annectere* (*ad-*, to, *nectere*, to bind)], *v.t.* To unite to, add on to; to take possession of (as territory); to append as a condition, qualification, or consequence; (*slang*) to steal. **annexable,** *a.* Able to be annexed. **annexation** (ăn ėk sā′ shŭn), *n.* The act of annexing; something annexed (often with the idea of unlawful acquisition). **annexe, annex** (ăn′ eks), *n.* An appendix; a supplementary or subsidiary building; (*Sc. Law*) an appurtenance.

annihilate (ȧ nī′ hil āt) [L. *annihilātus*, p.p. of *annihilāre* (*ad-*, to, *nihil*, nothing)], *v.t.* To reduce to nothing; to blot out of existence; to destroy the organized existence of; to reduce to constituent elements or parts. **annihilation,** *n.* The act of annihilating; the state of being annihilated; complete destruction of soul and body. **annihilationism,** *n.* The doctrine that the wicked are annihilated after death. **annihilationist,** *n.* One who holds this doctrine. **annihilator,** *n.* [FIRE-ANNIHILATOR].

anniversary (ăn i vĕr′sȧ ri) [L. *anniversārius* (*annus*, year, *versus*, p.p. of *vertere*, to turn)], *a.* Recurring at the same date in succeeding years. *n.* The annual return of any remarkable date; the celebration of such annually recurring date.

Anno Domini (ăn′ ō dom′ in ī) [L.], *phr.* In the year of our Lord (abbr. A.D.); reckoned from the Christian era. *n.* (*colloq.*) Old age.

annotate (ăn′ ō tāt) [L. *annotātus*, p.p. of *annotāre*, (*ad-*, to, *notāre*, to mark)], *v.t.* To make notes or comments upon. *v.i.* To write notes or comments. **annotation,** *n.* The act of annotating; an explanatory note. **annotator,** *n.*

announce (ȧ nouns′) [O.F. *anoncer*, L. *annuntiāre* (*ad-*, to, *nuntiāre*, to report, bear a message, *nuntius*, messenger)], *v.t.* To make known, to proclaim; to declare officially, or with authority; to make known the approach or arrival of. **announcer,** *n.* (*Radio.*) The person who announces the items of a broadcasting programme. **announcement,** *n.*

annoy (ȧ noi′) [O.F. *anoier*, *anuier*, to molest, annoy, from *anoi*, *anui*, annoyance, vexation, L. *in odio*, in hatred], *v.t.* To tease, to molest, to trouble, to put to inconvenience by repeated or continued acts. **n.* Discomfort, vexation, annoyance. **annoyance,** *n.* The act of annoying; the state of being annoyed; that which annoys. **annoying,** *a.* **annoyingly,** *adv.*

annual (ăn′ ū ȧl) [F. *annuel*, late L. *annuālis* (L. *annālis*, years, from *annus*, year)], *a.* Returning or happening every year; reckoned by, or done or performed in a year; (*Bot.*) lasting but a single year or season. *n.* A book published every year, a year-book; a plant which lives for a year only; (*R.-C. Ch.*) an anniversary mass for the dead. ***annualist,** *n.* One who edits or writes for an annual. **annually,** *adv.* Year by year, yearly.

annuity (ȧ nū′ i ti) [F. *annuité*, med. L. *annuitātem* (*annuus*, yearly)], *n.* A sum of money payable annually; an investment insuring fixed annual payments. **annuitant,** *n.* One who receives an annuity.

annul (ȧ nŭl′) [O.F. *anuller*, late L. *annullāre* (*ad-*, to, *nullus*, none)], *v.t.* To render void, cancel, abolish; to destroy the validity of. **annulment,** *n.* The act of annulling; revocation; abolition.

annular (ăn′ ū lȧr) [L. *annulāris* (*annulus*, ring, dim. of *ānus*, a round shape)], *a.* Ring-shaped, ringed. **annular eclipse:** An eclipse of the sun in which the silhouette of the moon obscures only the central portion of the sun's surface and leaves a ring of light showing round the moon. **annular space:** The ring-like space between an inner and an outer cylinder. **annularly,** *adv.*

annulate (ăn′ ū lāt), **annulated** [L. *annulātus* (*annulus*, see prec.)], *a.* Wearing, marked, distinguished by or furnished with, rings; composed of rings or ring-like segments. **annulation,** *n.* The state of being annulate; ring-like structure or markings. **annulet** (ăn′ ū let) [-ET], *n.* A little ring; (*Arch.*) a small fillet encircling a column. **annuloid** (ăn′ ū loid), *a.* Ring-shaped; of or pertaining to the Annuloida. *n.* Any individual of the Annuloida. **Annuloida** (ăn ū loi′ dȧ), *n.pl.* (*Zool.*) One of Huxley's primary groups of animals, containing flukes, tape-worms, and rotifers. **Annulosa** (ăn ū lō′ sȧ), *n.pl.* (*Zool.*) One of Huxley's primary groups of animals, containing those whose body is enclosed in a kind of external ringed skeleton. **annulose** (ăn′ ū lōs), *a.* Ringed; of or belonging to the Annulosa. **annulus** (ăn′ ū lŭs), *n.* (*pl.* **annuli**). (*Biol.*) Any ring-shaped structure.

annulment [ANNUL].

annunciate (ȧ nŭn′ si āt) [ANNOUNCE], *v.t.* To announce, proclaim approach or arrival; to bring tidings. **annunciation** (ȧ nŭn si ā′ shŭn), *n.* The act of announcing; the announcement of the Incarnation made by the angel Gabriel to the Virgin Mary; the Church festival (Lady Day, March 25) in honour of that event. **annunciator,** *n.* One who or that which announces; an indicator for electric bells or telephones to show who has rung or spoken; an officer in the Greek Church who gives notice of holy days.

anode (ăn′ ōd) [Gr. *anodos*, a way up], *n.* (*Elec.*) The positive electrode or pole; the positive plate of an electronic valve. **anode battery** [HIGH TENSION BATTERY]. **anode circuit,** *n.* The particular circuit which carries the anode (High Tension) current as distinct from grid or filament heating circuits. **anode converter,** *n.* A rotary machine for supplying anode voltage. **anode current,** *n.* The current circulating in the anode circuit of a valve. **anode rays,** *n.pl.* (*Radio.*) Rays of positively charged particles issuing from the anode of a thermionic valve. **anodizing,** *ger.* The oxidizing of a metal to form a protective surface coating of an oxide of the metal.

anodyne (ăn′ ō dīn) [late L. *anōdynus*, Gr. *anōdunos* (*an-*, not, *odunē*, pain)], *a.* Assuaging pain; alleviating distress of mind, soothing to the feelings. *n.* A medicine which assuages pain; anything which alleviates distress of mind or soothes the feelings.

anoint (ȧ noint′) [O.F. *enoint*, anointed, p.p. of *enoindre* (L. *in-*, *ungere*, to smear, p.p. *unctus*)], *v.t.* To smear with oil or an unguent; esp. to pour oil on as a religious ceremony; to consecrate with oil; (*colloq.*) to belabour, thrash soundly. **anointed,** *a.* Smeared with oil or unguent; consecrated. *n.* A consecrated person. **the Lord's Anointed:** Christ; a king by divine right.

anomaly (ȧ nom′ ȧ li) [L. *anōmalia*, Gr. *anōmalia*, unevenness, *anōmalos* (*an-*, not, *ōmalos*, even)], *n.* Irregularity; deviation from the common or established order; abnormality; (*Astron.*) the angular distance of a planet or satellite from its last perihelion or perigee. **anomalistic** (ȧ nom ȧ lis′ tik) [-IST, -IC], *a.* Irregular, abnormal. **anomalistic month,** *n.* (*Astron.*) The time in which the moon passes from perigee to perigee. **anomalistic year,** *n.* (*Astron.*) The time occupied by the earth (or other planet) in passing from perihelion to perihelion: it is slightly longer than a tropical or sidereal year. **anomalous** (ȧ nom′ ȧ lŭs), *a.* Deviating from rule; irregular, abnormal. **anomalously,** *adv.* **anomalousness,** *n.*

anomo- [Gr. *a*, not, *nomos*, rule], *comb. form.* Irregular, as in *anomocarpous*, *anomorhomboid*.

anon (ȧ non′) [A.-S. *on ān*, in one moment], *adv.* Immediately, thereupon; soon after; in a little while. **ever and anon,** *adv.* Every now and then.

anonaceous (ăn ō nā′ shŭs) [mod. L. *anōna*, ANANAS], *a.* Pertaining to the pineapple.

anonymous (ȧ non′ i mŭs) [Gr. *anōnumos* (*an-*, not, *onoma*, name)], *a.* Nameless; having no name attached; of unknown or unavowed authorship. **anonymously,** *adv.* **anonym** (ăn′ ō nim) [F. *anonyme*, Gr. *anōnumos*], *n.* A person whose name is not made known; a pseudonym. **anonymity** (-nim′ i ti), *n.* **anonymousness,** *n.*

Anopheles (ȧ nof′ e lēz) [Gr.], *n.* (*Ent.*) A genus of mosquitoes including the malarial mosquito *Anopheles maculipennis*.

Anoplura (ăn ō plōō′ rȧ) [Gr.], *n.* (*Ent.*) An order of parasitic insects including the human louse.

anorexia (ăn ō reks′ i ȧ) [Gr. *oreksis*, longing], *n.* A loathing of food.

anosmia (ȧ noz′ mi ȧ) [mod. L., from Gr. *an-*, priv., *osmē*, smell], *n.* Absence of the sense of smell. **anosmatic** (ăn oz mă′ tik), *a.* (*Zool.*) Lacking the sense of smell.

another (ȧ nŭth′ ėr), *pron.* and *a.* An other one, one more; one of the same kind; a different one; any other. **you're another:** (*slang*) You are a liar, fool or rascal. ***another-guess** [corr. of *another-gates* or *another-gets*, of another gate or way], *a.* Of another sort or fashion. **another place:** The other House (of Parliament).

anotta [ANATTA].

anourous (ȧ nour′ ŭs, ȧ nūr′ ŭs) [Gr. *an-*, not, *oura*, tail], *a.* Destitute of a tail.

anoxia (ȧ noks′ i ȧ) [AN-, OXYGEN], *n.* (*Med.*) Deficiency of oxygen.

ansa (ăn′ sa) [L., handle], *n.* (pl. **ansæ**) A handle on a vase; (*Astron.*) the parts of Saturn's rings which appear to extend like handles beyond the sphere. **ansate,** *a.* Having a handle.

Anschluss (an′ shlus) [G., annexation], *n.* The forced union of Austria with Germany in 1938.

anserine (ăn′ sėr īn) [L. *anserīnus*, pertaining to a goose (*anser*)], *a.* Of or belonging to the goose; goose-like, stupid, silly.

answer (an′ sėr) [A.-S. *andswaru*, a reply (*and-*, against, *swar-*, stem of *swerian*, to swear)], *n.* A reply to a charge, objection, appeal, or question; a solution of a problem; something done in return; a practical reply; (*Law*) a counter-statement to a bill of charges. *v.t.* To reply or respond to; to be sufficient for or suitable to; to be opposite to; to solve. *v.i.* To reply, to respond; to suit, to correspond. **to answer for:** To be responsible or answerable for. **to answer to:** To correspond, to suit; to accord, to own. **answerable,** *a.* Liable to be called to account; capable of being answered; *correspondent. ***answerably,** *adv.* Proportionally, correspondingly, conformably. **answerer,** *n.* One who answers to a question, etc.; one who answers back.

ant (ănt) [A.-S. *æmette*, grad. contracted to *amte*, *ante*, *ant*], *n.* A small, social hymenopterous insect;

an emmet, a pismire. **ant-bear, ant-eater,** *n.* A genus of edentate mammals, with long extensile tongues, which they thrust into ant-hills and withdraw covered with ants [PORCUPINE ANT-EATER]; an ant-thrush. **ant-catcher** [ANT-THRUSH]. **ant-cow** [APHIS]. **ant-eggs,** *n.pl.* The popular name for the pupæ of ants. **ant-fly,** *n.* A winged ant; a perfect male or female. **ant-hill,** *n.* The mound or hillock raised by a community of ants. **ant-lion,** *n.* A genus of neuropterous insects, the larvæ of which construct a kind of pitfall for ants and other insects. **ant-thrush,** *n.* A tropical bird, allied to the thrush, which feeds chiefly on ants.

an't, ain't (ant, ānt) [contr. of *aren't, are not*], *v.* (*colloq.*) Are not, is not.

ant- [ANTI-], *pref.* Against, as in *antagonist, Antarctic.*

-ant [Lat. *-antem*, acc. sing. of pres.p. in *-ans*], *suf.* Forming adjectives as *distant, elegant, trenchant*; denoting an agent, one who or thing which produces effect, as in *accountant, merchant.*

antacid (ănt ăs' id), *a.* Counteracting acidity. *n.* That which counteracts acidity of the stomach.

antæ (ăn' tē) [L.], *n.pl.* Square pilasters on each side of a door, or at the angles of a building.

antagonist (ăn tăg' ŏ nist) [late L. *antagōnista*, Gr. *antagōnistēs*, an adversary, from *antagōnizesthai*, (*ant-, anti-*, against, *agōnizesthai*, to struggle)], *n.* An opponent; one who contends or strives with another; (*Physiol.*) a muscle which counteracts another, and is in turn counteracted by it. **antagonism,** *n.* Opposition; conflict, active disagreement; an opposing force or principle. **antagonistic** (ăn tăg ŏ nist' ik), *a.* **antagonistically,** *adv.* **antagonize** (ăn tăg' ŏ nīz), *v.t.* To compete with; to contend against; to counteract; to make antagonistic, put in active opposition; (*Am.*) to oppose. *v.i.* To act in opposition.

antalkali (ănt ăl' kȧ lī), *n.* Something that neutralizes an alkali. **antalkaline** (ănt ăl' kȧ līn), *a.* (*Med.*) Counteracting the effect of an alkali. *n.* A medicine that counteracts the effect of an alkali.

antaphrodisiac (ănt ăf rŏ diz' i ăk), *a.* Counteracting or preventing sexual desire. *n.* A medicine or agent that allays sexual desire.

Antarctic (ăn tark' tik) [M.E. *antartik*, O.F. *antartique*, L. *antarcticus* (ANT-, ARCTIC)], *a.* Opposite to the Arctic; southern; of or belonging to the southern pole or circle. *n.* The Antarctic regions.

antarthritic (ănt ar thrit' ik), *a.* (*Med.*) Tending to prevent or relieve gout. *n.* A medicine which prevents or relieves gout.

antasthmatic (ănt ȧs măt' ik), *a.* (*Med.*) Tending to prevent or relieve asthma. *n.* A medicine which prevents or relieves asthma.

ante (ăn' ti) [L., before], *n.* (*Cards*) The stake which a poker-player puts down after looking at his cards, but before drawing. *v.t.* To stake; to pay one's share.

ante- [L. prep. and adv.], *pref.* Before. **ante bellum:** (*Am.*) Before the American Civil War. **ante meridiem:** Before noon, abbr. a.m.

antecede (ăn tė sēd') [L. *antecēdere* (*ante-*, before, *cēdere*, to go)], *v.t.* To precede; to go before or in front of. **antecedence** (ăn tė sē' dėns), *n.* A going before in point of time; precedence, anteriority; (*Astron.*) an apparent motion contrary to the true motion. **antecedent,** *a.* Going before in time, prior, anterior, presumptive, a priori. *n.* That which goes before; the word to which a relative refers; the conditional clause of a hypothetical proposition; (*Math.*) the first term of a ratio; (*in pl.*) past circumstances. **antecedently,** *adv.* **antecessor** (ăn tė ses' ŏr), *n.* One who goes before; (*Law*) a previous possessor.

antechamber (ăn' tė chām bėr) [F. *antichambre* (*anti-*, ANTE, *chambre*, CHAMBER)], *n.* An anteroom.

antechapel (ăn' tė chăp ėl), *n.* The part of a chapel between the western wall and the choir screen.

antedate (ăn' tė dāt), *n.* A date preceding the actual date. *v.t.* To date before the true date; to cause to happen prematurely; to happen earlier, precede; to anticipate.

antediluvian (ăn tė di loo' vi ȧn) [L. *dilūvium*, flood], *a.* Of or pertaining to the period before the Flood; (*fig.*) antiquated. *n.* One who lived before the Flood; (*fig.*) a very old or old-fashioned person.

antelope (ăn' tė lōp) [O.F. *antelop*, late L. *antalopus*, late Gr. *antholops*], *n.* Common name for the genus *Antilope*, containing ruminants akin to the deer and the goat.

antelucan (ăn tė loo' kȧn) [L. *antelucānus* (*ante-*, before, *lux*, light)], *a.* Of or pertaining to the time just before daybreak.

antemundane (ăn tė mŭn' dān), *a.* Existing or occurring before the creation of the world.

antenatal (ăn tė nā' tȧl), *a.* Happening or existing before birth.

antenna (ȧn ten' ȧ) [L., sail-yard], *n.* (*pl.* **antennæ**) A sensory organ occurring in pairs on the heads of insects and crustaceans; a palp, a feeler; (*Bot.*) filaments in male flowers of orchids that eject the pollinium when touched; (*Radio.*) an aerial, etc. **antennal, antennary** (ȧn ten' ȧ ri), *a.* Pertaining to the antennæ. **antenniferous** (ăn tėn if' ėr ŭs), *a.* Bearing antennæ. **antenniform,** *a.* Shaped like antennæ.

antenuptial (ăn tė nŭp' shi ȧl), *a.* Happening before marriage.

antependium (ăn tė pen' di ŭm) [late L. (*ante-*, *pendēre*, to hang)], *n.* A covering for the front of an altar; a frontal.

antepenult (ăn tė pėn ŭlt'), **antepenultimate** (ăn tė pen ŭl' ti mȧt) [L. *antepænultimus* (L. *pæne*, almost, *ultimus*, latest, last)], *a.* Pertaining to the last syllable but two; last but two. *n.* The last syllable but two; the last but two.

anteprandial (ăn tė prăn' di ȧl) [L. *prandium*, dinner], *a.* Happening, done, or taken before dinner.

anterior (ăn tēr' i ŏr) [L. comp. of *ante*, before], *a.* Going before, more to the front, preceding, prior. **anteriority** (-or' i ti), *n.* **anteriorly,** *adv.*

antero- [ANTERIOR], *comb. form.* Front, in front; much used in the formation of technical adjectives and adverbs, as, **antero-lateral,** situated on the front side; **antero-posterior,** running or continued from the front to the back; **antero-posteriorly,** from front to back.

anteroom (ăn' tė rum), *n.* A room leading into or forming an entrance to another.

anth- [ANTI], *pref.* Against, opposite to; used before aspirates, *e.g. anthelion, anthelmintic.*

anthelion (ăn thē' li ŏn) [late Gr. neut. of *anthelios*, opposite to sun (*helios*, sun)], *n.* (*pl.* **anthelia**) A mock sun; a luminous ring projected on a cloud or fog-bank opposite the sun.

anthelmintic (ăn thėl min' tik) [Gr. *helmins -minthos*, a worm], *a.* (*Med.*) Remedial against intestinal worms. *n.* A remedy for intestinal worms.

anthem (ăn' thėm) [A.-S. *antefn*, late L. *antiphōna*, Gr. *antiphōna* (ANTIPHON)], *n.* A hymn in alternate parts; a portion of Scripture or of the Liturgy set to music; a song of gladness or triumph. **anthemwise,** *adv.* In the manner of an anthem; antiphonally.

Anthemis (ăn' the mis) [Gr. *anthos*, a flower], *n.* (*Bot.*) A genus of Compositæ including the camomile, *Anthemis nobilis.* **anthemium,** *n.* (*pl.* **-ia**) A palmette, honeysuckle, or conventional leaf or floral design.

anther (ăn' thėr) [M.F. *anthere*, L. *anthēra*, medicine made of flowers, Gr. *anthēra*, fem. a., flowery (*anthos*, a bud)], *n.* (*Bot.*) The pollen-bearing organ of plants. **anther-dust,** *n.* Pollen. **anther-valve,** *n.* The opening through which the pollen is discharged. **antheral** (ăn' thėr ȧl), *a.* (*Bot.*) Pertaining to an anther or anthers. **antheridium**

[mod. L. *anthēra*, Gr. *-idion*, dim. ending], *n.* (*pl.* **-idia**) (*Bot.*) An oblong sperm cell, analogous to an anther, found in cryptogams. **antheriferous,** *a.* (*Bot.*) Bearing anthers. **antheroid,** *a.* (*Bot.*) Having the nature or appearance of an anther. **antherozoid,** *n.* (*Bot.*) A minute mass of protoplasm furnished with vibratile cilia produced in an antheridium and forming the male fecundating body in cryptogams.

anthocyanine (ăn thō sī′ ȧn in) [Gr. *anthos*, a flower, *kyanos*, blue], *n.* (*Bot.*) The blue colouring matter in plants.

anthology (ăn thol′ ȯ ji) [Gr. *anthologia*, a gathering of flowers (*anthos*, flower, *legein*, to collect)], *n.* A collection of small choice poems from classic authors, esp. a famous Greek collection; a collection of poems of literary merit; (*fig.*) a collection of flowers or beauties. **anthological** (ăn thȯ loj′ i kȧl), *a.* **anthologist** (ăn thol′ ȯ jist), *a.* The compiler of an anthology.

Anthony (ăn′ tȯ ni) [St. *Anthony*, the patron saint of swineherds], *n.* The smallest in a litter of pigs. **St. Anthony's fire:** Popular name for erysipelas, from the tradition that those stricken by the pestilence of erysipelas, or sacred fire, in 1089, were cured through the intercession of St. Anthony.

anthracene (ănth′ rȧ sēn) [Gr. *anthrax*, coal], *n.* (*Chem.*) Crystalline substance with blue fluorescence obtained from tar; used in the manufacture of dyes.

anthracite (ăn′ thrȧ sīt) [L. *anthracītes*, Gr. *anthrakitēs*, resembling coals (*anthrax*, coal, carbon)], *n.* Stone coal; non-bituminous coal, burning with intense heat, without smoke, and with little flame. **anthracite stove:** A stove for domestic heating specially constructed to burn anthracite coal. **anthracitic** (ăn thrȧ sit′ ik), *a.* **anthracitous** (ăn′ thrȧ sī tůs), *a.* Bearing anthracite; composed of anthracite; characterized by the presence of anthracite.

anthrax (ăn′ thrăks) [L. from Gr., a carbuncle, also coal], *n.* A carbuncle; the splenic fever of sheep and cattle; malignant pustule in man derived from animals suffering from this.

anthropo- [Gr. *anthrōpos*, a man], *comb. form.* Human; pertaining to man or mankind.

anthropocentric (ăn thrȯ pō sen′ trik), *a.* Centring in man; regarding man as the measure and aim of the universe.

anthropogeny (ăn thrȯ poj′ e ni), *n.* The science or study of the origin of man.

anthropogeography (ăn thrȯ pō jē og′ rȧ fi), *n.* The geography of the distribution of the races of mankind.

anthropography (ăn thrȯ pog′ rȧ fi), *n.* The science which investigates the geographical distribution of man; ethnography.

anthropoid (ăn′ thrȯ poid), *a.* Resembling man; of human form. *n.* A creature, esp. one of the higher apes, resembling man in form.

anthropolite, anthropolith (ăn throp′ ō līt, -lith), *n.* A fossil man, a human fossil.

anthropology (ăn thrȯ pol′ ȯ ji), *n.* The science of man in the widest sense; the study of man, or mankind, as to body, mind, evolution, race, and environment. **anthropological** (ăn thrȯ pȯ loj′ ik ȧl), *a.* Of or pertaining to anthropology; dealing with the natural history of man. **anthropologically,** *adv.* In an anthropological way. **anthropologist** (ăn thrȯ pol′ ȯ jist), *n.* One versed in anthropology.

anthropometry (ăn thrȯ pom′ ė tri), *n.* The scientific measurement of the human body.

anthropomorphous (ăn thrȯ pȯ môr′ fůs) [Gr. *anthrōpomorphos* (*anthrōpos*, man, *morphē*, form)], *a.* Possessed of a form resembling that of man. **anthropomorphize** (ăn thrȯ pȯ môr′ fīz) [-IZE], *v.t.* To give a human shape or attribute human characters to. **anthropomorphism,** *n.* The attribution of a human form or character to the Deity, or of human characteristics to the lower animals. **anthropomorphist,** *n.* One who attributes the human form or human characters to the Deity, or other things. **anthropomorphic** (ăn thrȯ pȯ môr′ fik), *a.* Pertaining to anthropomorphism.

anthropophagous (ăn thrȯ pof′ ȧ gůs), *a.* Man-eating, cannibal. **anthropophagy,** *n.* The practice of eating human flesh; cannibalism.

Anthropopithecus (ăn thrȯ pō pith′ e kůs), *n.* The genus of apes, including the chimpanzee and the gorilla, which most resembles man.

anthroposophy (ănthrȯpos′ ȯ fi) [Gr. *anthropos*, a man, *sophia*, knowledge], *n.* A system of esoteric philosophy enunciated by Rudolf Steiner, who defined it as 'the knowledge of the spiritual human being . . . and of everything which the spirit man can perceive in the spiritual world.'

anti- [Gr.], *pref.* Opposite, opposed to, against, instead of, in exchange, as in *anti-bilious, antiphlogistic, antiseptic, anti-social*; in *comb.*, the opposite of, an opponent of, one of a contrary kind, the reverse of. **anti-abolitionist,** *n.* One opposed to the abolition of slavery. **anti-aircraft,** *a.* (*Mil.*) Employed against hostile aircraft. **anticlerical,** *a.* Opposed to the clergy. **anticlericalism,** *n.* Opposition to the political influence of the clergy. **anticlockwise,** *a.* and *adv.* From right to left, in the reverse direction from that taken by the hands of a clock. **anti-constitutional,** *a.* Opposed to the constitution of the country, or to sound constitutional principles. **anti-Darwinian,** *a.* Opposed to the Darwinian theory of the origin of species; hence, opposed to evolution. *n.* One who is opposed to evolution. **anti-federal,** *a.* Opposed to federalism. **anti-federalism,** *n.* **anti-federalist. antifreeze,** *n.* A substance that lowers the freezing-point when added to water in motor-car radiators. **anti-friction,** *n.* A substance that reduces friction. **anti-friction metals,** *n.pl.* (*Metall.*) Name given to various alloys used for high-speed bearings. **anti-Gallican,** *a.* Opposed to French aims or aspirations. *n.* One who is opposed to French aims and aspirations. **anti-Gallicanism,** *n.* Hatred of what is French. **anti-Jacobin,** *a.* Opposed to the principles of the Jacobins; opposed to the principles of the French Revolution. *n.* One who is opposed to those principles. **anti-Jacobinism,** *n.* Opposition to Jacobin or revolutionary principles. **anti-national,** *a.* Opposed to the interest of one's country, or to the national party. **anti-papal,** *a.* Opposed to the Pope or to papal doctrine. **antipope,** *n.* A pope elected in opposition to the one canonically chosen. **anti-revolutionary,** *a.* Opposed to political revolution. **anti-revolutionist,** *n.* One opposed to political revolution or to revolutionary parties. **anti-sabbatarian,** *a.* Opposed to sabbatarian views. *n.* One opposed to such views. **anti-scriptural,** *a.* Opposed to Scripture. **anti-Semite,** *n.* An opponent of the Jews in countries where they have settled freely. **anti-Semitism,** *n.* Opposition to the Jews. **anti-slavery,** *n.* Opposition to slavery. *a.* Opposed to slavery. **anti-social,** *a.* Opposed to social intercourse, or to the principles on which society is constituted. **anti-submarine,** *a.* (*Nav.*) Denoting vessels, weapons, or protective devices used against hostile submarines. **antitetanic,** *a.* (*Med.*) Curing or preventing tetanus. **antitetanin,** *n.* An antitoxin used for curing or preventing tetanus. **antitrade,** *a.* Blowing in a direction contrary to that of the trade-winds. *n.* A wind blowing in an opposite direction to that of the trade-winds. **anti-trinitarian,** *n.* Opposed to the doctrine of the Trinity. *n.* One opposed to the doctrine of the Trinity. **anti-trinitarianism,** *n.* **anti-vaccinationist,** *n.* One opposed to (compulsory) vaccination.

antiar (ăn′ ti ar) [Javanese, *antjar*], *n.* The Upas-tree; the poison obtained from it. **antiar resin,** *n.* A resin obtained from the Upas-tree.

antibilious (ăn ti bil′ i ůs), *a.* Counteracting biliousness.

antibiotic (ăn ti bī ot′ ik) [ANTI-, BIO-], *n.* and *a.* (Substance) inimical to life, esp. bacteria.

antibody (ăn′ ti bo di), *n.* (*Med.*) Substance produced in the blood in response to the presence of an antigen and capable of counteracting toxins.

antic (ăn′ tik) [It. *antico*, L. *antīquus*, ancient], *a.* *Grotesque, odd, ludicrous, whimsical. *n.* *A merry-andrew, a buffoon; (*usually in pl.*) anything antic or grotesque; an odd trick; a ludicrous gesture; (*Arch.*) grotesque figures placed as ornaments on a building. *v.t.* *To make antic or grotesque. *v.i.* *To perform antics.

Antichrist (ăn′ ti krīst) [O.F. *antecrist*, L. *antechristus*, Gr. *antichristos*], *n.* A personal antagonist of Christ spoken of in the N.T.; an opponent of Christ. **antichristian,** *a.* Opposed to Christ or to Christianity; pertaining to Antichrist. *n.* One opposed to Christ or to Christianity; an adherent of Antichrist. **antichristianism,** *n.*

anticipate (ăn tis′ i pāt) [L. *anticipātus*, p.p. of *anticipāre* (*ante-*, before, *capere*, to take)], *v.t.* To use in advance; to deal with or be before (another); to forestall; to cause to happen earlier; to hasten; to look forward to, consider, or deal with anything before the proper time. **v.i.* To occur in advance. **anticipant,** *a.* Anticipating, expecting. *n.* One who anticipates. **anticipation** (-pā′ shŭn), *n.* The act of anticipating; preconception, expectation, presentiment; (*Med.*) the occurrence of symptoms before the normal period; (*Mus.*) the introduction of a note before the chord about to be played. **anticipative,** *a.* Anticipating; containing an anticipation. **anticipatively,** *adv.* **anticipator** (ăn tis′ i pā tŏr), *n.* **anticipatory** (ăn tis′ i pȧ tŏr i), *a.*

anticlimax (ăn ti klī′ măks), *n.* The opposite of climax; a descent or decrease in impressiveness; bathos.

anticlinal (ăn ti klī′ nȧl) [Gr. *klinein*, to lean], *a.* (*Geol.*) Forming a ridge so that the strata lean against each other and in opposite directions; (*Anat.*) having an upright spine towards which the spines on both sides slope. *n.* An anticlinal axis, fold, or line from which the strata dip in opposite directions. **anticline,** *n.* (*Geol.*) An anticlinal fold; a saddleback.

anticyclone (ăn′ ti sī′ klōn), *n.* The rotary outward flow of air from an atmospheric region of high pressure. **anticyclonic** (ăn ti sī klon′ ik), *a.*

antidote (ăn′ ti dōt) [L. *antidotum*, Gr. *antidoton*, a remedy, neut. of *antidotos*, given against (ANTI-, *didōmi*, I give)], *n.* A medicine designed to counteract poison or disease; anything intended to counteract evil. **antidotal** (ăn′ ti dō′ tal, ăn tid′ ŏ tȧl), *a.*

antigen (ăn′ ti jen), *n.* (*Chem.*) Substance introduced into the body which stimulates the production of antibodies.

***antigropelos** (ăn ti grop′ ė lōs) [Coined from Gr. *anti*, against, *hugros*, wet, *pēlos*, mud], *n.pl.* Waterproof leggings.

antihelix (ăn ti hē′ liks), **anthelix** (ăn′ thē liks) [Gr. *anthelix* (*helix*, a spiral, the outer ear)], *n.* The curved elevation within the helix of the ear.

antilibration (ăn ti lī brā′ shŭn) [L. *librātiōnem*, balancing, weighing (*librāre*, to balance)], *n.* The weighing of one thing against another.

antilogarithm (ăn ti log′ ȧ rithm), *n.* The number represented by a logarithm. **antilogarithmic,** *a.*

antilogy (ăn til′ ŏ ji) [Gr. *antilogia* (*logia*, speaking)], *n.* Contradiction in terms or in ideas.

antimacassar (ăn ti mȧ kăs′ ȧr), *n.* A covering for chairs, sofas, etc., to prevent their being soiled by (macassar) oil on the hair, or as an ornament.

antimasque, antimask (ăn′ ti mask), *n.* A grotesque interlude between the acts of a masque.

antimony (ăn′ tim ŏ ni) [med L. *antimōnium*, prob. from Arab.], *n.* A bright bluish-white brittle metallic element, occurring native, and of great use in the arts and in medicine. **antimonial** (ăn ti mō′ ni ȧl), *a.* Pertaining to or containing antimony. *n.* A medicine containing antimony. **antimonial wine,** *n.* (*Med.*) Sherry in which tartar emetic has been dissolved. **antimoniate,** *n.* (*Chem.*) A salt of antimonic acid. **antimonic** (ăn ti mon′ ik), *a.* Of or pertaining to antimony; (*Chem.*) applied to compounds in which antimony combines as a pentavalent element. **antimonic acid,** *n.* An acid containing two equivalents of antimony and five of oxygen. **antimonious** (-mō′ ni ŭs), *a.* Containing or composed of antimony; (*Chem.*) applied to compounds in which antimony combines as a trivalent element.

Antinomian (ăn ti nō′ mi ȧn) [med. L. *Antinomi*, name of sect (Gr. *anti-*, against, *nomos*, law)], *a.* Opposed to the moral law; of or pertaining to the Antinomians. *n.* One who holds that the moral law is not binding on Christians; one of a German sect of the sixteenth century said to hold this opinion. **antinomianism,** *n.* Rejection of the moral law.

antinomy (ăn tin′ ŏ mi) [L. from Gr. *antinomia*], *n.* A contradiction between two laws; a conflict of authority; intellectual contradiction, opposition between laws or principles that appear to be equally founded in reason; paradox.

antipathy (ăn tip′ ȧ thi) [L., from Gr. *antipatheia* (*anti-*, against, *pathein*, to suffer)], *n.* Contrariety of nature or disposition; hostile feeling towards; aversion, dislike. **antipathetic** (ăn ti pȧ thet′ ik), **antipathetical,** *a.* Having an antipathy or contrariety to. **antipathetically,** *adv.* **antipathic** (ăn ti păth′ ik) [F. *antipathique* (*antipathie*, ANTIPATHY)], *a.* Of contrary character or disposition; (*Med.*) exhibiting or exciting contrary symptoms; allopathic.

antiphlogistic (ăn ti flŏ jis′ tik), *a.* Opposed to the doctrine of phlogiston; (*Med.*) allaying inflammation or excitement; cooling. *n.* (*Med.*) A remedy which allays inflammation.

antiphon (ăn′ ti fon) [late L. *antiphōna*, Gr. *antiphōna*, pl. of *antiphōnon*, an anthem (*anti-*, in return, *phōnē*, voice)], *n.* A sentence sung by one, choir in response to another; a series of such responsive sentences or versicles; a short sentence said or sung before the psalms, canticles, etc., in the R.-C. Church; an anthem; (*fig.*) an answer. **antiphonal** (ăn tif′ ŏ nȧl), *a.* Consisting of antiphons; sung alternately. *n.* An antiphonary. **antiphonally,** *adv.* **antiphonary** (ăn tif′ ŏn ȧr i) [med. L. *antiphōnārium*], *n.* A book containing a collection of antiphons. **antiphony,** *n.* Opposition of sound; alternate chanting or singing by a choir divided into two parts; an antiphon.

antiphrasis (ăn tif′ rȧ sis) [late L., from Gr. *antiphrasis* (*anti-*, contrary, *phrazein*, to speak)], *n.* The use of words in a sense contrary to their ordinary meaning. **antiphrastic** (ăn ti frăs′ tik), *a.*

antipodes (ăn tip′ ŏ dēz) [L., from Gr. *antipodes*, sing. *antipous* (*anti-*, against, *pous*, foot)], *n.pl.* Those who dwell directly opposite to each other on the globe, so that the soles of their feet occupy diametrically opposite positions; places on the surface of the globe diametrically opposite to us; (*fig.*) the direct opposite of some other person or thing. **antipode** (ăn′ ti pōd), *n.* One who lives on the opposite side of the globe. **antipodal** (ăn tip′ ŏ dȧl), *a.* Pertaining to the antipodes; situated on the opposite side of the globe. **antipodean** (ăn ti pŏ dē′ ȧn), *a.* Pertaining to the antipodes.

antipole (ăn′ ti pōl), *n.* The opposite pole; (*fig.*) the direct opposite.

antipyretic (ăn ti pī ret′ ik) [Gr. *puretos*, fever], *a.* (*Med.*) Preventing or allaying fever. *n.* A medicine to prevent or allay fever.

antiquary (ăn′ ti kwȧr i) [L. *antiquarius*], *n.* A student, investigator, collector, or vendor of antiques; a student of ancient times. **antiquarian** (ăn ti kwâr′ i ȧn), *a.* Pertaining to the study of antiquities; (*paper*) of the size 52½ ins. by 30½ ins. *n.* An antiquary. **antiquarianism,** *n.* **antiquarianize,** *v.i.*

antiquated (ăn′ ti kwāt ėd) [as prec.], *a.* Old-fashioned, out of date, obsolete.

antique (ăn tēk′) [F. *antique*, L. *antiquus*, *anticus* (*ante-*, before)], *a.* Ancient, old, that has long existed; old-fashioned, antiquated. *n.* A relic of antiquity; a piece of furniture, ornament, etc., more than 100 years old. **the antique,** *n.* The ancient style in art.

antiquity (ăn tik′ wi ti) [as prec.], *n.* The state of having existed long ago; the state of being ancient; great age; ancient times; the ancients; manners, customs, events, etc., of ancient times; (*usually in pl.*) a relic of ancient times.

Antirrhinum (ăn ti rī′ nŭm) [L., from Gr. *antirrhinon* (*anti-*, instead of, *rhis*, *rhinos*, nose)], *n.* (*Bot.*) Name of a genus of plants whose flowers resemble noses; snapdragon.

antiscorbutic (ăn ti skôr bū′ tik), *a.* (*Med.*) Of use against scurvy. *n.* A medicine efficacious in scurvy.

antiseptic (ăn ti sep′ tik) [Gr. *sēptikos*, putrefying (*sēptos*, decayed, from *sēpein*, to make rotten)], *a.* (*Med.*) Counteracting sepsis, or putrefaction. *n.* (*Med.*) A substance which counteracts putrefaction, which inhibits the growth of micro-organisms. **antisepsis** (ăn ti sep′ sis), *n.* The principle of antiseptic treatment.

antistrophe (ăn tis′ trŏ fi) [L., from Gr. *antistrophē* (*strophē*, a turning, a verse)], *n.* The returning of the Greek chorus, exactly answering to a previous strophe, except that the movement was from left to right, instead of from right to left; the poem or choral song recited during this movement; any choral response; (*Logic*) the rhetorical figure of retort; (*Gram.*) an inverted construction. **antistrophic** (ăn ti strof′ ik), *a.*

antitheism (ăn ti thē′ izm), *n.* Opposition to belief in a god. **antitheist,** *n.* **antitheistic** (ăn ti thē is′ tik), *a.*

antithesis (ăn tith′ ė sis) [Gr. (*thesis*, a setting, from *tithēmi*, I place)], *n.* (*pl.* **antitheses**) Sharp opposition or contrast between words, clauses, sentences, or ideas; a counter proposition; opposition, contrast. **antithetic** (ăn ti thet′ ik), **antithetical,** *a.* Pertaining to or marked by antithesis; contrasted; sharply opposed. **antithetically,** *adv.*

antitoxin (ăn ti tok′ sin) [Gr. *toxikon*, poison], *n.* (*Med.*) Matter formed in the body which neutralizes the action of toxins, a defence against certain diseases.

antitype (ăn′ ti tīp) [Gr. *antitupos*, answering to, as an impression to a die (*tupos*, a blow, a stamp, cognate with *tuptein*, to strike)], *n.* That which is represented by the type or symbol. **antitypal,** *a.* Of the nature of an antitype. **antitypical** (-tip′-), *a.*

antivenin (ăn ti ven′ in) [L. *venenum*, poison], *n.* (*Med.*) Serum obtained from animals immunized against snake venom, and used as an antidote against snake-bite.

antler (ănt′ lėr) [O.F. *antoillier*, late L. *antoculārem* (*ramum*), the branch (orig., the lowest or brow antler) which is in front of the eye (*ante-*, before, *oculus*, eye)], *n.* A branch of the horns of a stag or other deer; (*pl.*) the branched horns of any deer. **antlered** (ănt′ lėrd), *part.a.* Furnished with antlers: branched like stags' horns.

antonomasia (ăn tŏn ŏ mā′ zi ȧ) [L., from Gr. *antonomasia*, *antonomazein*, to name instead (*anti-*, instead, *onomazein*, to name)], *n.* The substitution of an epithet for a proper name, as *the Corsican* for Napoleon; the use of a proper name to describe one of a class, as a *Cicero* for an orator. **antonomastic,** *a.* Characterized by antonomasia. **antonomastically,** *adv.*

antonym (ăn′ tŏ nim) [Gr. *antōnumia* (*anti-*, instead of, *onuma*, a name)], *n.* A term expressing the reverse of some other term, as 'good' to 'bad'.

antrum (ăn′ trŭm) [Gr. *antron*, a cave], *n.* (*Anat.*) A cavity, particularly one in bone.

anus (ā′ nŭs) [L., a rounding, ring], *n.* The lower orifice of the intestinal tube; (*Bot.*) the inferior aperture of a monopetalous flower. **anal** (ā′ năl), *a.*

anvil (ăn′ vil) [A.-S. *onfilti* (etym. doubtful)], *n.* The iron block on which smiths hammer and shape their work; anything resembling a smith's anvil in shape or use; esp. a bone in the ear which is struck by another bone called the hammer. **on the anvil:** In preparation. ***v.t.** To fashion on an anvil. *v.i.* To work at an anvil.

anxious (ăngk′ shŭs) [L. *anxius* (*angere*, to choke)], *a.* Troubled or solicitous about some uncertain or future event; *inspiring anxiety; distressing, worrying; eagerly desirous (to do something). **anxiously,** *adv.* **anxiety** (ăng zī ė ti) [L. *anxietas*], *n.* The state of being anxious; trouble, solicitude, or mental distress.

any (en′ i) [A.-S. *ænig* (*ān*, one, *-ig*, adj. ending)], *a.* and *pron.* One indefinitely; some or any number indefinitely; whichever, whatever; *either; (*slang*) anything, in *I'm not taking any.* **anybody** (en′ i bŏd i) [cp. NOBODY], *n.* or *pron.* Any person, any one; a person of little importance; (in *pl.*) persons of no importance. **anyhow,** *adv.* and *conj.* At any rate; in any way; in any case; imperfectly, at haphazard. **anything,** *n.* and *pron.* Any thing (in its widest sense) as distinguished from any person. **anyway,** *adv.* and *conj.* Anyhow. ***anywhen,** *adv.* At any time. **anywhere,** *adv.* In any place. **anywhither,** *adv.* To or towards any place. **anywise,** *adv.* In any manner, case, or degree; anyhow.

Anzac (ăn′ zăk) [from initials of Australian (and) New Zealand Army Corps], *n.* A soldier in these forces, in the war of 1914–18. **Anzac button,** *n.* (*Austral.*) A nail used to hold up the trousers.

Anzus (ăn′ zŭs) [acronym], *n.* (*Pol.*) A pact for the security of the Pacific, formed in 1952 by Australia, New Zealand, and U.S.A.

aorist (ā′ ŏ rist) [Gr. *aoristos*, unlimited (*a-*, not, *horizein*, to limit)], *n.* A Greek tense expressing indefinite past time. *a.* Aoristic. **aoristic** (ā ŏ ris′ tik), *a.* Indefinite in point of time; pertaining to an aorist tense.

aorta (ā ôr′ tȧ) [late L., from Gr. *aortē* (*aerein*, to lift)], *n.* The largest artery in the body; the main trunk of the arterial system proceeding from the left ventricle of the heart. **aortic** (ā ôr′ tik), *a.* Of or pertaining to the aorta.

ap- [AD-, assim. before *p*], *pref.*, *e.g. appear, approve.*

apace (ȧ pās′), *adv.* At a quick pace; speedily, fast.

apache (ȧ pash′) [F., from N. Am. Indian], *n.* Popular name in Paris for a ruffian who robs and maltreats people; a hooligan.

apanage, appanage (ăp′ ȧ năj) [O.F. *apaner*, to nourish, med. L. *apānāre* (*ap-*, *ad-*, to, *pānis*, bread)], *n.* Lands or office assigned for the maintenance of a royal house; a dependency; a perquisite; a necessary adjunct or attribute.

apart (ȧ part′) [F. *à part*, to one side, singly, L. *ad partem*], *adv.* To one side; separately with regard to place, purpose, or things; independently.

Apartheid (ȧ part′ hāt) [Afrikaans, APART, -HOOD], *n.* Racial segregation.

apartment (ȧ part′ mėnt) [F. *appartement*, med. L. *appartīmentum*, from *appartīre*, to apportion (*ad-*, to, *partīre*, to divide)], *n.* A portion of a house; a single room in a house; (*pl.*) a suite of rooms; lodgings; (*Am.*) a flat.

apathy (ăp′ ȧ thi) [F. *apathie*, L. *apathia*, Gr. *apatheia* (*a-*, not, *pathein*, to suffer)], *n.* Absence of feeling or passion; insensibility; indifference; mental indolence. **apathetic** (ăp ȧ thet′ ik), *a.* Characterized by apathy; insensible, unemotional, indifferent.

ape (āp) [A.-S. *apa* (cp. Dut. *aap*, Icel. *api*, O.H.G. *affo*)], *n.* A tailless monkey; one of the Simiidæ (a gorilla, chimpanzee, orang-outan or gibbon); (*fig.*) a mimic; a servile imitator. *v.t.* To imitate or mimic. **God's ape:** An imbecile; a natural fool. **apery** (ā' pėr i), *n.* Mimicry; apish behaviour. **apish** (ā' pish), *a.* Of the nature of or befitting an ape. **apishly,** *adv.* **apishness,** *n.*

apeak (á pēk') [F. *à pic*, vertically, vertical (*à*, at, *pic*, summit)], *adv.* and *pred.a.* (*Naut.*) In a vertical or nearly vertical position; pointed upwards.

apepsy (á pep' si) [Gr. *apepsia* (*a-*, not *peptein*, to digest)], *n.* Indigestion, dyspepsia.

aperçu (a pĕr' soo) [F., p.p. of *apercevoir*, to perceive], *n.* A concise exposition, an outline, a brief summary.

aperient (á pēr' i ėnt), **aperitive** (á per' i tiv) [L. *aperīre*, to open], *a.* Laxative, purgative, deobstruent. *n.* A laxative medicine.

aperiodic (ă pēr i od' ik), *n.* (*Radio.*) An untuned circuit. **aperiodic aerial,** *n.* An aerial which has no natural or inherent tuning to any particular wavelength.

aperitif (ă per' it ēf) [F.], *n.* Short drink, usually alcoholic, taken as an appetizer.

aperitive [APERIENT].

aperture (ăp' ĕr tūr) [L. *apertura*], *n.* An opening, a hole, a gap, a passage; (*Opt.*) the space through which light passes in an optical instrument; the diameter of a lens. ***apert** (á pĕrt') [O.F. *apert*, L. *aperire*, to open], *a.* and *adv.* Open, manifest; openly, in public.

apery [APE].

apetalous (á pet' á lůs) [Gr. *apetalous*, leafless (*a-*, not, *petalon*, leaf)], *a.* (*Bot.*) Without petals.

apex (ā' peks) [L.], *n.* (*pl.* **apices** or **apexes**) The tip, top, or summit of anything. **apical** (ā' pi kál), *a.* Pertaining to an apex; placed at the summit. **apically,** *adv.* At the apex; towards the apex. **apicular** (á pik' ū lár) [mod. L. *apiculus*, dim. of *apex*], *a.* Of or belonging to a little apex; situated at the tip. **apiculate** (á pik' ū lāt), **apiculated,** *a.* (*Bot.*) Terminating abruptly in a little point.

aphæresis (á fēr' ė sis) [L., from Gr. *aphairesis* (*aph-*, *apo-*, away, *airein*, to take)], *n.* The taking away of a letter or syllable at the commencement of a word; (*Med.*) the removal of something that is noxious.

aphasia (ă fā' zhá) [Gr., speechlessness], *n.* (*Path.*) Loss of the power of articulate speech. **aphasic,** *a.*

aphelion (á fē' li ón) [L. *aphēlium*, Gr. *aph' hēlion*, away from the sun], *n.* (*pl.* **aphelia**) The point most distant from the sun in the orbit of a planet or a comet.

apheliotropic (á fē li ō trop' ik) [Gr. *tropikos*, turning], *a.* (*Bot.*) Bending or turning away from the sun. **apheliotropically,** *adv.* **apheliotropism,** *n.*

aphesis (ăf' ė sis) [Gr., from *aphienai* (*aph-*, *apo-*, away, *ienai*, to let go)], *n.* A form of aphæresis, in which an unaccented vowel at the beginning of a word is gradually lost. **aphetic** (á fet' ik), *a.* Pertaining to aphesis. **aphetize** (ăf' ė tīz), *v.t.* To shorten by aphesis.

aphis (ăf' is, ā' fis) [mod. L. (etym. unknown)], *n.* (*pl.* **aphides,** ăf' i dēz) Plant-louse; a group of minute insects very destructive to vegetation, comprising among others the green-fly, black fly, American blight, etc. **aphidian** (á fid' i án), *a.* Of or pertaining to aphides. *n.* An aphis or plant-louse.

aphonia (á fō' ni á) [Gr., from *aphōnos*, voiceless (*a-*, not, *phōnē*, voice)], *n.* Inability to speak; loss of voice.

aphorism (ăf' ó rizm) [Gr. *aphorismos*, a definition, from *aphorixein* (*aph-*, *apo-*, off, *horizein*, to mark)], *n.* A detached, pithy sentence, containing a maxim or wise precept. **aphorismic** (ăf ó riz' mik), *a.* **aphorist,** *n.* One who writes or utters aphorisms. **aphoristic** (ăf ó ris' tik), *a.* **aphoristically,** *adv.* **aphorize** (ăf' ó rīz), *v.i.* To utter or write aphorisms.

aphrodisiac (ăf rò diz' i ăk) [Gr. *aphrodisiakos*, from *aphroditios*, from *Aphroditē*, the goddess of sensual love], *a.* Exciting venereal desire. *n.* A drug provocative of sexual desire. **aphrodisian,** *a.*

aphthæ (ăf' thē) [L., from Gr. *aphthai* (prob. cogn. with *haptein*, to set on fire, inflame)], *n.pl.* The minute specks seen in the mouth and tongue in thrush.

aphyllous (á fil' ůs) [Gr. *aphullos* (*a-*, not, *phullon*, leaf)], *a.* (*Bot.*) Destitute of leaves.

apiarian (ā pi âr' i án), *a.* Relating to bees. *n.* An apiarist. **apiarist** (ā' pi ár ist), *n.* A bee-keeper; one who rears bees. **apiary** (ā' pi ár i) [L. *apiārium*, neut. of *apiārius*, pertaining to bees (*āpis*, bee)], *n.* A place where bees are kept.

apical, etc. [APEX].

apiculture (ā' pi kŭl tūr) [L. *apis*, a bee], *n.* Bee-keeping; bee-rearing.

apiece (á pēs') [*a piece*, for one piece], *adv.* For or to each, severally.

apish, etc. [APE].

aplanatic (ăp lá năt' ik) [Gr. *aplanētos* (*a-*, priv., *planaein*, to wander)], *a.* (*Opt.*) Free from spherical aberration.

aplasia (á plā' zhá) [A- (7); Gr. *plasis*, formation], *n.* (*Med.*) Defective or arrested development in a tissue or organ.

aplomb (a plon') [F. *aplomb*, perpendicular (*à plomb*, by the plummet)], *n.* The state of being perpendicular; self-possession, coolness.

aplustre (ăp' lŭs tėr) [Gr. *aphlaston*], *n.* The ornament above the stern of an ancient ship.

apnœa (ăp nē' á) [mod. L., from Gr. *apnoia*, from *apnoos*, breathless (*a-*, not, *pnoē*, breath)], *n.* (*Med.*) Cessation of respiration.

apo- [Gr. *apo-*, away, from], *pref.* Away, detached, separate; as in *apology*, *apostrophe*.

apocalypse (á pok' á lips) [L. *apocalypsis*, Gr. *apokalupsis*, from *apokaluptein*, to uncover (*apo-*, off, *kaluptein*, to cover)], *n.* The revelation granted to St. John the Divine; the book of the New Testament in which this is recorded; (*fig.*) any revelation or disclosure. **apocalyptic** (á pok á lip' tik), **apocalyptical,** *a.* Pertaining to the revelation of St. John; of the nature of a revelation. **apocalyptically,** *adv.*

apocarpous (ăp ó kar' půs) [APO-, Gr. *karpos*, fruit], *a.* (*Bot.*) Having the carpels wholly or partly distinct.

apocope (á pok' ó pē) [L., from Gr. *apocopē* (*apo-*, away, *koptein*, to cut)], *n.* A cutting off or dropping of the last letter or syllable.

apocrypha (á pok' ri fá) [Gr. *apokrupha*, neut. pl., things hidden, from *apokruptein* (*apo-*, away, *kruptein*, to hide)], *n.* A writing or statement of doubtful authority; a collection of fourteen books in the Old Testament, included in the Septuagint and the Vulgate, but not written in Hebrew originally, nor reckoned genuine by the Jews, nor inserted in the Authorized Version of the Bible. **apocryphal,** *a.* Pertaining to the apocrypha; spurious, fabulous. **apocryphally,** *adv.*

apod (ăp' ód) [Gr. *apous* (*a-*, not, without, *pous podos*, foot)], *n.* (*Zool.*) A footless creature, a bird, fish, or reptile in which the feet or corresponding members are absent or undeveloped. **apodal,** *a.* (*Zool.*) Footless; having no ventral fin.

apodictic (ăp ó dik' tik), **apodeictic** (ăp ó dīk' tik) [L. *apodīcticus*, Gr. *apodeiktikos* (*apodeiknunai*, to show)], *a.* Clearly demonstrative: established on uncontrovertible evidence. **apodictically, apodeictically,** *adv.*

apodosis (á pod' ó sis) [L., from Gr. *apodosis*, a giving (*apodidonai*, to give back)], *n.* The consequent clause in a conditional sentence, answering to the protasis.

apodyterium (á pod i tēr' i ům) [L., from Gr. *apodutērion* (*apo-*, off, *-duein*, put, dress)], *n.* The apartment in ancient baths or palæstras where the clothes were taken off.

apogamy (ȧ pog′ ȧ mi) [Gr. *apo*, away from, *gamos*, marriage], *n.* (*Bot.*) The absence of sexual reproductive power, the plant perpetuating itself by bulbs, etc. **apogamous,** *a.*

apogee (ăp′ ō jē) [F. *apogée*, late L. *apogæum*, Gr. *apogaion*, neut. a., away from the earth (APO-, *gaia*, earth)], *n.* (*Astron.*) The point in the orbit of the moon or any planet or satellite which is at the greatest distance from the earth; the most distant point in the orbit of a satellite from the planet round which it revolves; (*fig.*) the furthest point, the highest point; culmination. **apogean** (ăp o jē′ ȧn), *a.*

apolar (ȧ pō′ lȧr) [*a*-, not, without, POLAR], *a.* (*Biol.*) Without poles or fibrous processes.

apolaustic (ăp ō law′ stik) [Gr. *apolaustikos* (*apolauein*, to enjoy)], *a.* Devoted to pleasure; self-indulgent.

Apollyon (ȧ pol′ i ŏn) [L., from Gr. *apolluōn*, pres.p. of *apolluein*, to destroy], *n.* The destroyer; the Devil.

apologetic, apologize, etc. [APOLOGY].

apologia (ăp ol ō′ jȧ) [L., from Gr.], *n.* A vindication, formal defence, excuse.

apologue (ăp′ ō log) [F., from L. *apologus*, from Gr. (*apo*-, off, *logos*, speech)], *n.* A fable designed to impress some moral truth upon the mind; especially a beast-fable or a fable of inanimate things.

apology (ȧ pol′ ō ji) [L. *apologia*, from Gr. (*apo*-, off, *legein*, to speak)], *n.* A defence; vindication; an explanation; excuse; a regretful acknowledgment of offence; (*slang*) a wretched substitute for the real thing. **apologetic** (ȧ pol ō jet′ ik), **apologetical** [F. *apologétique*, L. *apologēticus*, Gr. *apologētikos* (*apologeesthai*, to speak in defence)], *a.* Excusing, explanatory, vindicatory. **apologetics,** *n.pl.* Defensive argument; esp. the argumentative defence of Christianity. **apologetically,** *adv.* **apologist** (ȧ pol′ ō jist), *n.* One who defends or apologizes by speech or writing; a professed defender of Christianity. **apologize,** *v.i.* To make an apology or excuse for.

apomecometer (ă pō mė kom′ ė tĕr) [Gr. *apo*, from, *mekos*, length], *n.* An instrument for measuring the height of buildings, etc.

apoop (ȧ poop′), *adv.* (*Naut.*) On or against or towards the poop.

apophthegm (ap′ ŏf them) [Gr. *apophthegma* (*apo*-, off, out, *phthengesthai*, to speak)], *n.* A terse pointed saying; a maxim expressed in few but weighty words. **apophthegmatic** (ăp ŏf theg măt′ ik), *a.* Pertaining to, or using apophthegms; sententious, pithy. **apophthegmatically,** *adv.*

apoplexy (ăp′ o plek si) [F. *apoplexie*, late L., from Gr. *apoplēxia* (*apoplēssein*, to cripple with a blow)], *n.* A malady involving loss of sense and of power of motion, generally caused by effusion on the brain. **apoplectic,** *a.* Pertaining to or tending to cause apoplexy; predisposed to apoplexy. *n.* A person liable to or afflicted with apoplexy.

aposiopesis (ăp ō sī ō pē′ sis) [L., from Gr., from *aposiōpaein* (*apo*-, off, away, *siōpaein*, to be silent)], *n.* A stopping short for rhetorical effect.

apositic (ăp ō zit′ ik) [Gr. *apositikos*, exciting distaste for food], *a.* (*Med.*) Causing *apositia* or aversion to food; tending to weaken appetite.

apostasy (ȧ pos′ tȧ si) [L., from Gr. *apostasia*, previously *apostasis* (*apo*-, away, *stasis*, a standing, from *sta*-, stem of *istēmi*, I stand)], *n.* Renunciation of religious faith, moral allegiance, or political principles; (*R.-C. Ch.*) renunciation of religious vows.

apostate (ȧ pos′ tȧt) [O.F. *apostate*, late L. *apostata*, Gr. *apostatēs*], *n.* One who apostatizes. *a.* Unfaithful to creed or principles; rebel, rebellious.

apostatical (ăp ō stăt′ ik ȧl), *a.* **apostatize** (ȧ pos′ tȧ tīz), *v.i.* To abandon one's creed, principles, or party; to commit apostasy.

a posteriori (ā pŏs ter i ôr′ ī) [L.], *a.* and *adv.* (*Log.*) Reasoning from consequences, effects, things observed to causes; inductive, as opposed to a priori or deductive.

apostil (ȧ pos′ til) [F. *apostille* (etym. doubtful)], *n.* A marginal note, gloss, annotation.

apostle (ȧ pos′ ėl) [O.F. *apostle, apostre*, L. *apostolus*, Gr. *apostolos*, a messenger (*apo*-, away, *stellein*, to send)], *n.* One of the twelve men appointed by Christ to preach the gospel; the first Christian missionary to any region, or one who labours among the heathen with pre-eminent success; the leader of a reform. **apostle bird,** *n.* (*Austral.*) The grey-crowned babbler. **Apostles' Creed,** *n.* The shortest of the three Christian creeds, each clause of which is said to have been contributed by one of the Apostles. **apostle-spoons,** *n.pl.* Silver spoons, the handles ending in figures of the Apostles—a frequent present of sponsors in baptism. **apostleship,** *n.* **apostolate** (ȧ pos′ tō lāt) [L. *apostolātus*], *n.* The office of apostle; leadership; propagation of a doctrine. **apostolic** (ăp ō stol′ ik), **apostolical,** *a.* Pertaining or relating to the Apostles; derived directly from or agreeable to the doctrine or practice of the Apostles; of the character or nature of an apostle; pertaining to the Pope as St. Peter's successor, papal. *n.* *The Pope; a bishop; *member of a sect who claimed to follow the doctrines of the Apostles. **Apostolic Fathers,** *n.pl.* Those Christian Fathers or writers contemporaneous with the Apostles or their immediate disciples. **Apostolic See,** *n.* The Papacy. **apostolic succession,** *n.* Uninterrupted transmission of spiritual authority through bishops, from the Apostles. **apostolically,** *adv.*

apostrophe (ȧ pos′ trō fi) [L., from Gr. *apostrophē*, a turning away (*apostrephein*, to turn away)], *n.* A rhetorical figure in which the speaker addresses one person in particular, or turns away from those present to address the absent or dead; the sign (') used to denote the omission of a letter or letters, and as the sign of the English possessive case (in the latter meaning it is really an earlier word, through the F. *apostrophe*, L. *apostrophus*, Gr. *apostrophos*, a., turned away). **apostrophic** (ăp ō strof′ ik), *a.* **apostrophize** (ȧ pos′ trō fīz), *v.t.* To address in or with apostrophe; to mark an omission of a letter or letters from a word by inserting an apostrophe.

apothecary (ȧ poth′ ė kȧr i) [O.F. *apotecaire*, late L. *apothēcārius*, from *apothēca*, a storehouse, Gr. *apothēkē* (*apo*-, away, *tithēmi*, I put)], *n.* One who prepares and sells medicines; a druggist or pharmaceutical chemist; a licentiate of the Apothecaries' Society. **apothecary's weight,** *n.* The scale of weights by which drugs are compounded.

apothecium (ăp ō thē′ shi ŭm) [mod L., from Gr. *apothēkē*, see prec.], *n.* (*Bot.*) The spore-case in lichens.

apothegm [APOPHTHEGM].

apotheosis (ăp ō thē′ ō sis, ȧ poth ė ō′ sis) [L., from Gr. *apotheōsis* (*apo*-, *theoō*, I deify, from *theos*, a god)], *n.* Deification; transformation into a god; canonization; enrolment among the saints; a deified ideal. **apotheosize** (ăp ō thē′ ō sīz, ȧ poth′ ė ō sīz), *v.t.* To deify, to exalt, to glorify.

apozem (ăp′ ō zem) [F. *apozème*, late L. *apozema*, Gr. *apozema* (from *apo*-, off or away, *zeein*, to boil)], *n.* A decoction or infusion.

appal, appall (ȧ pawl′) [O.F. *apalir*, *apallir*, to grow pale, to make pale], *v.i.* *To grow pale, to grow faint or feeble. *v.t.* *To make pale; *to enfeeble, impair; to inspire with terror; to terrify, to dismay. **appalling,** *a.* **appallingly,** *adv.*

appanage [APANAGE].

apparatus (ăp ȧ rā′ tŭs) [L. *ad*-, to, *parare*, to prepare], *n.* (*pl.* **apparatuses**) Equipments or arrangements generally; the instruments employed in scientific or other research; materials for critical study; the organs by which any natural process is carried on. ***apparatus criticus*, *n.*** Critical equipment, the materials employed in literary criticism and investigation.

apparel (á păr′ ėl) [O.F. *aparail*, n., and *apareiller*, v., to dress (*à*, L. *ad-*, to, *pareiller*, to assort, make fit, from *pareil*, like, late L. *pariculum*, dim. of *par*, equal)], *n.* Dress, attire, clothes; ornamental embroidery on ecclesiastical vestments; *the outfit of a ship. *v.t.* To dress, to clothe; to equip, to fit out; to adorn, to embellish, to ornament. ***apparelment,** *n.* Outfit; equipment.

apparent (á păr′ ėnt, á pâr′ ėnt) [O.F. *aparant*, *aparent*, L. *appārentem*, p.p. of *appārēre*, to come into sight], *a.* To be seen, visible, in sight; plain, obvious, indubitable; appearing (in a certain way), seeming. **heir-apparent,** *n.* Manifest heir, the one who will succeed on the death of the present possessor, in contradistinction to heir-presumptive. **apparently,** *adv.* *Manifestly, evidently; to external appearances; seemingly, as distinguished from actually.

apparition (ăp á rish′ ŭn) [F., from L. *appāritiōnem*, from *appārēre*, see APPEAR], *n.* The state of becoming visible; a strange appearance; a spectre, phantom, ghost; (*Astron.*) the visibility of a star, planet, or comet. **apparitional,** *a.*

apparitor (á păr′ i tŏr) [L., see APPEAR], *n.* One of the public servants of the ancient Roman magistrates; a petty officer in a civil or ecclesiastical court; a beadle, usher, or similar functionary.

appeal (á pēl′) [O.F. *apeler*, to invoke, L. *appellāre* (*ad-*, to, *pellere*, to drive)], *v.t.* *To accuse; to impeach; to challenge; to invoke as a judge. *v.i.* To refer to a superior judge, court, or authority; to refer to (some person or thing) as corroboration; to invoke aid, pity, mercy, etc.; to have recourse to; to apply to. *n.* *A calling to account; the act of appealing; the right of appeal; reference or recourse to another; entreaty; request for money for charitable purposes. **to appeal to the country:** To dissolve Parliament after an adverse vote. **appealable,** *a.* That may be appealed against; that can be appealed to. **appealing,** *a.* Of the nature of an appeal; suppliant. **appealingly,** *adv.* **appealingness,** *n.*

appear (á pēr′) [O.F. *aper-*, stem of *aparoir*, to appear (pres. subj. *apere*), L. *appārēre* (*ad-*, to, *pārēre*, come into sight)], *v.i.* To become or be visible; to present oneself; to come before the public; to be manifest; to seem. **appearance,** *n.* The act of appearing; the thing seen; the act of appearing formally or publicly; a phenomenon; a phantom; mien, aspect; (*pl.*) the aspect of circumstances. **to keep up appearances:** To keep up an outward show; to conceal the absence of (something desirable).

appease (á pēz′) [O.F. *apeser*, *apaisier* (*à*, to, *pais*, peace, L. *ad pacem*, *pax*)], *v.t.* To quiet, to pacify, to calm, to assuage; to allay. **appeasement,** *n.* The act of appeasing; the state of being appeased; the thing that appeases, satisfies, or makes peace; (*Polit.*) the endeavour to preserve peace by giving way to the demands of an aggressor power. **appeasable,** *a.*

appellant (á pel′ ánt) [F. *appellant*, see APPEAL], *a.* Appealing, challenging; relating to appeals. *n.* One who appeals to a higher tribunal or authority; one who makes an appeal. **appellate,** *a.* Pertaining to or dealing with appeals. **appellation** (ăp ėl ā′ shŭn), *n.* A name, designation; naming, nomenclature. **appellative** (á pel′ á tiv), *a.* Common as opposed to proper; designating a class. *n.* An appellation, a name; a common as opposed to a proper noun. **appellatively,** *adv.*

append (á pend′) [L. *appendere* (*ad-*, to, *pendere*, to hang)], *v.t.* To hang to or upon; to add or subjoin. **appendage,** *n.* Something added or appended; (*Nat. Hist.*) a subordinate or subsidiary organ or process. **appendant,** *a.* Attached, annexed, joined on to. *n.* That which is attached or annexed; an appendix, a corollary. **appendicle** (á pen′ dikl) [L. *appendicula*, dim. of *appendix*], *n.* A small appendage. **appendicular** (ăp ėn dik′ ū lár), *a.* Of or of the nature of an appendicle. **appendiculate,** *a.* Furnished with small appendages.

appendicectomy, appendectomy (á pen di sek′ tŏ mi, á pen dek′ tŏ mi), *n.* (*Surg.*) The excision of the vermiform appendix.

appendicitis (á pen di sī′ tis), *n.* Inflammation of the vermiform appendix or cæcum.

appendix (á pen′ diks), *n.* (*pl.* **appendixes, appendices**). Something appended; an adjunct or concomitant; a supplement to a book; (*Physiol.*) a small process arising from or the prolongation of any organ, esp. the vermiform appendix of the intestine.

apperception (ăp ėr sep′ shŭn) [F. *apperception*, mod. L. *appercipere* (*ad-*, to, *percipere*, see PERCEIVE)], *n.* Perception of one's own mental processes; self-consciousness.

appertain (ăp ėr tān′) [O.F. *apartenir*, late L. *appertinēre* (*ad-*, to, *pertinēre*, to pertain)], *v.i.* To belong to (as a part to a whole, as a possession, or as a right or privilege); to relate to; to be suitable or appropriate.

appetence, appetency (ăp′ ė tėns, -tėn si) [F. *appétence*, L. *appetentia*, see next], *n.* Instinctive desire, craving, appetite; natural propensity; affinity. **appetent** (ăp′ ė tėnt) [L. *appetent -em*, pres.p. of *appetere* (*ad-*, to, *petere*, to seek)], *a.* Longing, eagerly desirous; (*Phil.*) pertaining to desire and volition.

appetite (ăp′ ė tīt) [O.F. *apetit*, L. *appetitus*], *n.* Inclination, disposition; the desire to satisfy the natural functions; desire or relish for food. **appetitive** (á pet′ i tiv), *a.* Possessed of or characterized by appetite. **appetize** (ăp′ ė tīz), *v.t.* To give an appetite to; to make (one) feel hungry or relish one's food. **appetizer,** *n.* A whet; a stimulant to appetite.

applaud (á plawd′) [L. *applaudere* (*ad-*, together, *plaudere*, to clap)], *v.i.* To express approbation, esp. by clapping the hands. *v.t.* To approve, commend, praise in an audible and significant manner. **applause** (á plawz′) [L. *applausus*, p.p. of *applaudere*], *n.* The act of applauding; praise loudly expressed. **applausive,** *a.* Praising by acclamation, approbative. **applausively,** *adv.* In an applausive manner.

apple (ăp′ ėl) [A.-S. *æpl*, *æppel* (O.H.G. *aphul*, G. *apfel*)], *n.* The round, firm, fleshy fruit of the apple-tree; any similar fruit; the fruit of the forbidden tree; an apple-tree; (*fig.*) anything resembling an apple in shape or colour. **apple of discord:** The golden apple contended for as prize of beauty by Juno, Minerva, and Venus; (*fig.*) a cause of contention. **apple of Sodom:** A mythic fruit, said to resemble an apple, but turning to ashes, also called *Dead Sea apple* or *Dead Sea fruit*; (*fig.*) anything disappointing. **apple of the eye:** The pupil, formerly supposed to be a solid body; anything very dear or precious. **apple-brandy,** *n.* Spirit made from apples. **apple-butter,** *n.* A preserve (or sauce) made of apples stewed in cider. **apple-cart,** *n.* An apple-seller's cart; (*fig.*) order, equanimity, in **To upset one's apple-cart. apple-cheese,** *n.* Apple-pomace compressed. **apple-dumpling,** *n.* An apple covered with paste and baked or boiled. **apple-faced, apple-cheeked,** *a.* Having a chubby face or cheeks. **Apple Island,** *n.* (*Austral.*) Tasmania. **apple-jack** [*Am.* for APPLE-BRANDY]. **apple-john,** *n.* A variety of late apple, good for keeping, but shrivelling up outside. **apple-pie,** *n.* A pie consisting of apples enclosed in a crust. **apple-pie bed:** A bed whose sheets are so doubled as to prevent one stretching one's full length. **apple-pie order:** Perfect order. **apple-pomace,** *n.* Pulp left after apples have been pressed in cider-making. **apple-pudding,** *n.* A pudding consisting of apples enclosed in a paste. **apple-sauce,** *n.* Sauce made from apples; (*Am. colloq.*) insincere praise, nonsense. **apple-toddy,** *n.* (*Am.*) Toddy in which roasted apples are used instead of lemon-peel. **apple-woman,** *n.* A woman who sells apples in the street. ***apple-yard,** *n.* An orchard.

Appleton layer (ăp′ ĕl tŏn) [Sir E. Appleton], *n.* An ionized layer in the upper atmosphere, above the Heaviside layer, which reflects radio waves.

appliance, applicant, etc. [APPLY].

appliqué (ă′ pli kā) [F., p.p. of *appliquer*, to apply], *n.* Ornamental work laid on some other material. **appliquéd,** *part.a.* Treated with work of this kind.

apply (ȧ plī′) [O.F. *aplier*, L. *applicāre* (*ad-*, to, *plicāre*, fold together, fasten)], *v.t.* To put or lay on; to put close to; to administer (as an external remedy); to employ, to devote; to make suitable, adapt, conform to. *v.i.* To agree, to harmonize, to be relevant; to have recourse (to); to study. **applied,** *a.* Practical; put to practical use. **applied science,** *n.* Science of which the abstract principles are put to practical use in the arts. **appliance** (ȧ plī′ ȧns), *n.* The act of applying; anything applied as a means to an end; an apparatus, device, or contrivance. **safety appliance,** *n.* A safety device. **applicable** (ăp′ lik ȧbl), *a.* Capable of being applied; fit, suitable, appropriate. **applicability** (ăp lik ȧ bil′ i ti), *n.* **applicant** (ăp′ li- kȧnt), *n.* One who applies; a petitioner; (*Am.*) a person remarkable for application to study. **applicate,** *a.* Applied to practical use. *n.* (*Math.*) A straight line drawn across a curve so as to bisect its diameter. **application** (ăp li kā′ shŭn), *n.* The act of applying; the thing applied; petition, request; close attention; study. **applicative** (ăp′ lik ȧ tiv), *a.* Characterized by application; practical.

appoggiatura (a poj ȧ too′ rȧ) [It.], *n.* (*Mus.*) A grace-note before a significant note.

appoint (ȧ point′) [O.F. *apointer* (*à*, to, *point*, the point)], *v.t.* To decree, ordain, fix, prescribe; to nominate, designate; to make an appointment or assignation; to assign, to grant (a thing to a person); to furnish, to equip. *v.i.* To decree, ordain. **appointee** (ȧ poin tē′), *n.* One who receives an appointment; (*Law*) one in whose favour an appointment is executed. **appointment** (ȧ point′ mėnt), *n.* The act of appointing; the office or situation assigned; that which is appointed or fixed; an engagement or assignation; allowance, decree, ordinance; (*pl.*) equipment, accoutrements, apparel (of a ship); (*Law*) the official declaration of the destination of any specific property.

apport (ă pôrt′) [L. *apportare*, to bring], *n.* In spiritualistic terminology a material object brought without material agency.

apportion (ȧ pôr′ shŭn) [O.F. *apportionner* (*à*, to, *portionner*, to portion)], *v.t.* To mete out in just proportions; to divide in suitable proportion. **apportionment,** *n.* The act of apportioning; the state of being apportioned.

apposite (ăp′ ŏ zit) [L. *appositus*, p.p. of *appōnere* (*ad-*, to, *pōnere*, to place, put)], *a.* Fit, apt, appropriate. **appositely,** *adv.* **appositeness,** *n.*

apposition (ă pŏ zish′ ŭn), *n.* The act of putting together or side by side; juxtaposition, addition; (*Gram.*) the placing together of two words, esp. of two substantives, one being a complement to the other. **appositional,** *a.* Relating to apposition.

appraise (ȧ prāz′) [PRAISE], *v.t.* To set a price on; to value; to estimate the worth of. **appraisable,** *a.* **appraisal,** *n.* Authoritative valuation; estimate of worth; (*Am.*) valuation. **appraisement,** *n.* The act of appraising; estimated value or worth. **appraiser,** *n.* One who appraises; a person licensed and sworn to fix the value of property; (*Am.*) valuer.

appreciate (ȧ prē′ shi āt) [L. *appretiātus*, p.p. of *appretiāre*, to fix a price on (*ad*, to, *pretium*, a price)], *v.t.* To form an estimate of value, quality, or quantity; to estimate aright; to be sensible of delicate impressions; to esteem highly; to raise in value. *v.i.* To rise in value. **appreciable,** *a.* Capable of being appreciated. **appreciably,** *adv.* In a way that can be estimated, to an appreciable extent.

appreciation (ȧ prē shi ā′ shŭn), *n.* The act of appreciating; estimate, a critical study; adequate recognition, rise in value. **appreciative** (ȧ prē′ shi ȧ tiv), *a.* Capable of or expressing appreciation; esteeming favourably. **appreciatively,** *adv.* **appreciator** (ȧ prē′ shi ā tŏr), *n.* **appreciatory,** *a.*

apprehend (ăp rė hend′) [F. *appréhend*, L. *apprehendere* (*ad-*, to, *prehendere*, to seize)], *v.t.* To take hold of; to grasp, to seize, to arrest; to seize, grasp, or lay hold of mentally; to fear, to dread; to anticipate. *v.i.* To understand. **apprehensible,** *a.* **apprehension,** *n.* The act of laying hold of, seizing, or arresting; the mental faculty which apprehends; conception, idea; fear, dread of what may happen. **apprehensive,** *a.* Characterized by or fitted for (mental) apprehension; perceptive, sensitive, discerning; anticipative, fearful, anxious. **apprehensively,** *adv.* **apprehensiveness,** *n.*

apprentice (ȧ pren′ tis) [O.F. *aprentis*, from *apprendre*, to learn (L. *apprehendere*, see prec.)], *n.* One bound by indentures to serve an employer for a term of years in order to learn some trade or craft which the employer agrees to teach; a learner, a tyro, a novice. *v.t.* To bind as an apprentice. **apprenticeship,** *n.* The state or position of an apprentice; service or training of an apprentice; the term for which an apprentice is bound to serve.

apprise (ȧ prīz′) [F. *appris*, p.p. of *apprendre*, see APPREHEND], *v.t.* To inform, to make aware, to bring to the knowledge or notice of.

apprize (ȧ prīz′) [O.F. *aprisier*, to appraise (*à*, to, *prisier*, to prize or praise, perhaps from *à prix*, cp. *mettre à prix*)], *v.t.* To put a price on; to estimate the worth of.

approach (ȧ prōch′) [O.F. *aprochier*, late L. *appropiāre* (*ad-*, to, *propius*, compar. of *prope*, near)], *v.t.* To come, go, or draw near or nearer; to approximate. *v.t.* To come near to; to resemble; (*Mil.*) to make approaches or entrenchments; (*colloq.*) to come near or address with a view to a favour or intimate relations. *n.* The act of drawing near; approximation, resemblance; avenue, entrance, access; (*Mil., usually in pl.*) works thrown up by a besieging force to protect it in its advance; (*Golf*) a stroke that should take the ball on to the green. **to graft by approach:** To bring together branches which are to be grafted, to inarch. **approachable,** *a.* Capable of being approached. **approachability** (ȧ prōch ȧ bil′ i ti), *n.*

approbate (ăp′ rȯ bāt), *v.t.* (*Am.*) To express approval of; (*Sc. Law*) to approve formally as valid.

approbation (ăp rȯ bā′ shŭn), *n.* The act of approving; approval, commendation, praise; probation, trial. **approbatory** (ăp′ rȯ bā′ tŏr i), *a.* Containing, expressing, or implying approval of.

approof (ȧ proof′) [O.F. *aprove*, proof, trial, L. *approbāre* (cp. APPROVE)], *n.* Proof, trial, experience; approval.

appropinquate (ăp rȯ ping′ kwāt) [L. *appropinquatus*, p.p. of *appropinquāre*, to draw near (*ad-*, towards, *propinquus*, *prope*, near)], *v.i.* To draw near to, to approach. **appropinquation** (ăp rȯ ping kwā′ shŭn), *n.* The act of coming or bringing near. **appropinquity** (ăp rȯ ping′ kwi ti), *n.* Nearness, contiguity, propinquity.

appropriate (ȧ prō′ pri āt) [L. *appropriātus*, p.p. of *appropriāre* (*ad-*, to, *proprius*, one's own)], *v.t.* To take as one's own; to take possession of; to devote to a special purpose or use; (*Eccles.*) to annex the fruits of a benefice to a spiritual corporation. **appropriate** (ȧ prō′ pri ȧt), *a.* Annexed or attached to; set apart for a particular person or use; suitable, fit, becoming. **appropriable,** *a.* **appropriately,** *adv.* **appropriateness,** *n.* Fitness, suitability. **appropriation** (ȧ prō pri ā′ shŭn), *n.* The act of appropriating; the state of being appropriated; that which is appropriated; (*Fin.*) a sum of money or a portion of revenue appropriated to a specific object. **appropriative** (ȧ prō′ pri ȧ tiv), *a.* Appropriating; involving appropriation; tending to appropriate. **appropriator,** *n.* One who appropriates; a religious corporation owning a benefice.

approve (ȧ proov′) [O.F. *aprover*, L. *approbāre* (*ad*-, to, *probāre*, to test, try)], *v.t.* To esteem, accept, or pronounce as good; to commend, sanction, confirm; to demonstrate practically. *v.i.* To express or to feel approbation. **approved,** *a.* Tried, proved, tested; regarded with approval. **approved school,** *n.* A state school for juvenile offenders (boys under 15, girls under 17). **Approved Society,** *n.* An insurance company approved by the Government. **approvement,** *n.* (*Law*) The improvement of commons by enclosure for purposes of husbandry. **approver,** *n.* One who approves, sanctions, or commends; one who confesses a felony and gives evidence against his associates. **approving,** *a.* **approvingly,** *adv.* **approvable,** *a.* **approval,** *n.* Approbation, sanction. **on approval, on appro** (ăp′ rō): On trial to ascertain if suitable; (of goods) to be returned if not approved.

approximate (ȧ proks′ i māt) [L. *approximātus*, p.p. of *approximāre* (*ad*-, to, *proximus*, very near, superl. of *prope*, near)], *v.t.* To draw or bring near; to cause to approach. *v.i.* To draw near, to approach. **approximate** (ȧ proks′ i mȧt), *a.* Very close to; closely resembling; nearly approaching accuracy; (*Nat. Hist.*) set very close together. *n.* An approximate result, an approximate number or quantity. **approximately,** *adv.* **approximation** (ȧ proks i mā′ shŭn), *n.* The act of approximating; approaching; approach, proximity; (*Math.*) a coming or getting nearer to a quantity sought, when no process exists for ascertaining it exactly; (*Med.*) communication of a disease by contact. **approximative** (ȧ proks′ i mȧ tiv), *a.* Of an approximate character; drawing or coming nearer; approaching. **approximatively,** *adv.*

appui (a pwē′) [F., from *appuyer*, late L. *appodiāre*, to lean upon (*ad*-, upon, *podium*, a support, from Gr. *podion*, base, *pous podos*, foot)], *n.* The stay (of a horse) upon the bridle-hand of its rider; (*Mil.*) defensive support. **point of appui,** ***point d'appui*** (*Mil.*) Any particular point or body upon which troops are formed.

appulse (ȧ pŭls′) [L. *appulsus*, approach, *appellere* (*ad*-, to, *pellere*, to drive)], *n.* A striking against; (*Astron.*) the approach of a planet or a fixed star to the meridian, or to conjunction with the sun or the moon. **appulsion,** *n.* A driving against.

appurtenance (ȧ pĕr′ tėn ȧns) [O.F. *apurtenaunce*, late L. *appertinentia*, from *appertinēre* (APPERTAIN)], *n.* That which belongs to something else; an adjunct, an accessory, an appendage. **appurtenant,** *a.* Pertaining to, belonging to, pertinent. *n.* An appurtenance.

apricot (ā′ pri kot) [formerly *apricock*, Port. *albricoque*, Sp. *albaricoque*, Arab. *al-burqūq* (*al*, the, corr. of Gr. *praikokion*, from L. *præcoqua*, apricots, neut. pl. of *præcoquum*, from *præcox*, early ripe), assim. to F. *abricot*], *n.* A stone-fruit allied to the plum; the tree on which it grows.

April (ā′ pril) [O.F. *avrill*, L. *Aprīlis* (prob. from *aperīre*, to open)], *n.* The fourth month of the year. **April-fool,** *n.* One sportively imposed upon on the 1st of April. **April-fool day,** *n.* April 1, from the custom of sending persons on bootless errands on that day. **April shower,** *n.* A sudden, brief shower of rain (common in the month of April).

a priori (ā pri ôr′ i) [L., from what is before], *adv.* From the cause to the effect; from abstract ideas to consequences; deductively. *a.* Deductive; prior to experience; abstract and unsupported by actual evidence. **apriority** (-or′ i ti), *n.*

apron (ā′ prŏn) [O.F. *naperon*, a large cloth, dim. of *nape*, a tablecloth, L. *nappa*, a cloth (cp. formation of ADDER)], *n.* A garment worn in front of the body to protect the clothes, or as part of a distinctive dress, *e.g.* of bishops, Freemasons; anything resembling an apron in shape or function, as a leather covering for the legs in an open carriage; the fat skin covering the belly of a roast goose or duck; a covering for the vent of a cannon; a strip of lead carrying drip into a gutter; the extension of the stage in some theatres beyond the proscenium; a platform of planks at the entrance to a dock; surfaced area on an airfield. **aproned** (ā′ prŏnd), *a.* Wearing an apron. **apronful,** *n.* As much as can be held in an apron. **apron-string,** *n.* The string of an apron. **tied to the apron-strings** (of a wife, etc.): Unduly controlled (by a wife, etc.).

apropos (a′ prō pō) [F. *à propos*, L. *ad prōpositum*, to the thing proposed (*prōpōnere*, to propose)], *adv.* Opportunely, seasonably; by the way; as bearing upon the subject; as suggested by. *a.* Opportune, seasonable; appropriate; bearing on the matter in hand; to the point.

apse (ăps), **apsis** (ăp′ sis) [L. *apsis*, *absis*, Gr. *apsis*, *hapsis -idos*, fastening, felloe of a wheel, curve (*aptein*, to fasten, join)], *n.* (*pl.* **apsides,** ăp′ si dēz *or* ăp sī′ dēz, **apses,** ăp′ sēz) A semi-circular, or polygonal, and generally dome-roofed, recess in a building, esp. in a church; a tribune, a bishop's throne; a reliquary (from this being situated in the apse in ancient churches); (*Astron.*) one of two points at which a planet or satellite is at its greatest or least distance from the body round which it revolves; the imaginary line joining these points is called the **line of the apsides. apsidal** (ăp′ si dȧl), *a.* Pertaining to or of the shape of an apse or apsis.

apt (ăpt) [L. *aptus*, p.p. of obs. v. *apere*, to fasten (used as p.p. of *apiscī*, to reach)], *a.* Fit, suitable, proper; having a tendency to; quick, ready; qualified for. **aptitude** (ăp′ ti tūd) [F., from med. L. *aptitūdo*, n. of quality from *aptus*], *n.* Fitness, suitability, adaptation; tendency towards, proneness to. **aptly,** *adv.* **aptness,** *n.*

apteral (ăp′ tėr ȧl) [Gr. *apteros* (*a*-, not, without, *pteron*, a wing)], *a.* Wingless; (*Arch.*) without columns at the sides.

apterous (ăp′ tėr ŭs) [Gr. *apteros* (*a*-, not, *pteron*, a wing)], *a.* Wingless; having only rudimentary wings; (*Bot.*) without membranous wing-like expansions.

apteryx (ăp′ tėr iks) [Gr. *a*-, not, *pteron*, a wing], *n.* An almost extinct bird from New Zealand, about the size of a goose, with rudimentary wings.

aptote (ăp′ tōt) [L. *aptōtum*, Gr. *aptōtos -on* (*a*-, not, *ptōtos*, falling, cp. *ptōsis*, case, from *piptein*, to fall)], *n.* An indeclinable noun. **aptotic** (ăp tot′ ik) [-IK], *a.* Without grammatical inflexion.

apyretic (ăp i ret′ ik) [Gr. *apuretos* (*a*-, not, *puretos*, fever)], *a.* Without fever. **apyrexy** (ăp′ i rek si) [L., from Gr. *apurexia* (*a*-, not, *puressein*, to be feverish)], *n.* The intermission or abatement of a fever.

aqua (ăk′ wȧ, ā′ kwȧ) [L.], *n.* Water, liquid, solution. **aqua-fortis,** *n.* Nitric acid. **aquafortist,** *n.* (*Art*) One who etches or engraves with aqua-fortis. **aqua-regia** (ăk wȧ rē′ ji ȧ), *n.* A mixture of nitric and hydrochloric acids, capable of dissolving gold and platinum. **aqua-vitæ** (ăk wȧ vī′ tē), *n.* Unrectified alcohol; (*colloq.*) ardent spirits, brandy, etc.

aquaculture [HYDROPONICS].

aqualung (ăk′ wȧ lŭng), *n.* A portable diving apparatus, strapped on the back and feeding air to the diver as required.

aquamarine (ăk wȧ mȧ rēn′) [L. *aquamarina*, sea-water], *n.* A bluish-green variety of beryl, named from its colour. *a.* Bluish-green.

aquarelle (ăk wȧ rel′) [F., from It. *acquerella*, dim. of *acqua* (L. *aqua*), water], *n.* A kind of painting in Chinese ink and very thin transparent water-colours; the design so produced. **aquarellist,** *n.* One who paints in aquarelle.

aquarium (ȧ kwâr′ i ŭm), *n.* (*pl.* **aquariums, aquaria**) An artificial tank, pond or vessel in which aquatic plants and animals are kept alive; a place in which such tanks are exhibited.

Aquarius (ȧ kwâr′ i ŭs) [L. the water-carrier], *n.* (*Astron.*) A zodiacal constellation giving its name to the eleventh sign, which the sun enters on 21 January.

aquatic (à kwăt′ ik) [L. *aquaticus*], *a.* Of or pertaining to water; living, growing in or near water, *n.* An aquatic animal or plant. **aquatics,** *n.pl.* Sports or athletic exercises on the water.

aquatint (ăk′ wà tint) [F. *aqua-tinte*, It. *acqua tinta* (L. *aqua*, water, *tincta*, dyed, from *tingere*, to dye)], *n.* A method of etching on copper; a design so produced.

aqueduct (ăk′ wė dŭkt) [L. *aquæductus* (*aquæ*, of water, *ductus*, conveyance, from *ducere*, to lead)], *n.* An artificial channel, esp. an artificial channel raised on pillars or arches for the conveyance of drinking water from place to place; (*Physiol.*) a small canal, chiefly in the heads of mammals.

aqueous (ā′ kwi ŭs) [L. *aqueus*], *a.* Consisting of, containing, formed in or deposited from water; watery. **aqueous humour,** *n.* The watery fluid in the eye between the cornea and the lens. **aqueous rocks,** *n.pl.* (*Geol.*) Rocks deposited in water; sedimentary rocks. **aquiferous** (à kwif′ ėr ŭs) [-FEROUS], *a.* Conveying, bearing, or yielding water. **aquiform** (ā′ kwi fôrm) [-FORM], *a.* In the form or state of water; liquid. **aquosity** (à kwos′ i ti) [med. L. *aquōsitas*, from *aquōsus*, watery], *n.* Wateriness.

Aquilegia (ăk wi lē′ ji à) [L. *aquila*, an eagle], *n.* (*Bot.*) A genus of acrid plants, order Ranunculaceæ, commonly known as columbine.

aquiline (ăk′ wi lin, ăk′ wi līn) [L. *aquilinus*, eagle-like (*aquila*, an eagle)], *a.* Of or pertaining to an eagle; eagle-like (esp. of noses), hooked, curved, like an eagle's bill.

***aquilon** (ăk′ wi lŏn) [O.F., from L. *aquilo -ōnem*], *n.* The north-east wind.

ar- [AD-], *pref.*, as in *arrest, arrogate*.

-ar (1) (*a*) [L. *-ārem, -āris*], *adj. suf.* Belonging to, of the nature of; *e.g. angular, linear, lunar, regular*; (*b*) [L. *-āre, -ār*], *n. suf.* Thing pertaining to; *e.g. altar, exemplar, pillar*.

-ar (2) [O.F. *-ier* (F. *-aire*), L. *-ārius, -ārium*], *suf.* -er, -ary, the agent; *e.g. bursar, mortar, vicar*.

-ar (3) [-ER (1)], *suf.* -er, the agent, doer; *e.g. beggar, liar*.

Arab (ăr′ àb) [F. *Arabe*, L. *Arab -em* (nom. *Arabs*), Gr. *Araps -abos*], *n.* A native of Arabia; an Arabian horse. *a.* Arabian. **street arab,** *n.* An outcast, a vagrant, a gutter-child, a child without a home. **Arabian** (à rā′ bi àn), *a.* Pertaining to Arabia. *n.* An Arab, a native of Arabia. **Arabian-bird,** *n.* The phœnix; (*fig.* something unique). **Arabian Nights:** A famous collection of stories; (*fig.*) a collection of fantastic stories. **Arabic** (ăr′ à bik), *a.* Pertaining to Arabia, or to its language. *n.* The language of Arabia or of the Arabs. **gum arabic:** A gum that exudes from certain species of acacia. **Arabic numerals,** *n.pl.* The figures, 1, 2, 3, etc. **arabist,** *n.* A student of Arabic.

araba (à ra′ bà) [Arab. and Pers. *arābah*], *n.* An oriental wheeled carriage.

arabesque (ăr à besk′) [F.], *a.* Arabian in design; fantastic. *n.* Surface decoration composed of flowing line fancifully intermingled, usually representing foliage in a conventional manner, without animal forms; a posture in ballet-dancing.

Arabis (ăr′ à bis) [med. L. *Arabs -bis*, Arab; prob. from its liking for stony places], *n.* A genus of cruciferous plants largely grown on rockwork, also called rock-cress.

arable (ăr′ àbl) [L. *arābilis* (*arāre*, to plough)], *a.* Capable of being ploughed; fit for tillage.

***Araby** (ăr′ à bi) [O.F. *arabi*], *a.* Arabic. *n.* An Arab; an Arab horse; Arabia.

araceous (ă rā′ shŭs) [ARUM], *a.* (*Bot.*) Belonging to the *Arum* genus of plants.

Arachis (ăr′ à kis) [Gr. *arachos*, a leguminous plant], *n.* (*Bot.*) A small genus of low Brazilian leguminous herbs including the peanut, *Arachis hypogeæ*. **arachis oil,** *n.* Peanut oil.

arachnid (à răk′ nid) [Gr. *arachnē*, a spider], *n.* Any individual of the class Arachnida, which contains the spiders, scorpions, and mites. **arachnidan** (à răk′ ni dàn), **arachnidean** (à răk nid′ ė àn), *a.* Of or belonging to the arachnids. *n.* An arachnid. **arachnoid,** *a.* Resembling the Arachnida; (*Bot.*) cobweb-like, covered with long, filamentous hairs; (*Zool.*) of or belonging to the Arachnida. *n.* The transparent membrane lining the *dura mater* and enveloping the brain and spinal cord. **arachnology** (à răk nol′ ŏ ji), *n.* The scientific study of spiders or of the Arachnida generally. **arachnologist,** *n.* One versed in arachnology.

aræometer (âr ė om′ ėt ėr) [Gr. *araios*, thin, -METER], *n.* An instrument for determining the specific gravity of liquids; an hydrometer. **aræometry,** *n.* The measurement of specific gravity; hydrometry.

aragonite (ăr′ à gŏn īt), *n.* A carbonate of lime, dimorphous with calcite, first found in Aragon, Spain.

Arago's disk (ăr′ à gōz disk′) [name of inventor], *n.* (*Elec.*) An apparatus illustrating the action of induced currents by means of a magnet pivoted over a revolving copper disk.

aralkyl (ă răl′ kil), *n.* (*Chem.*) A monovalent arylated alkyl radical, *e.g.* benzyl.

Aramæan (ăr à mē′ àn) [L. *aramæus*, Gr. *Aramaios*], *a.* Pertaining to Aram or Syria, or its language. *n.* A Syrian; the Syrian language. **Aramaic** (ăr′ à mā′ ik), *a.* Of or belonging to Aram; applied to the northern branch of the Semitic family of languages, including Syriac and Chaldee. *n.* Syriac.

Araneida (ăr à nē′ i dà) [L. *arānea*, a spider], *n.pl.* The typical order of the class Arachnida. **araneidan,** *a.* Of or belonging to the Araneida, or spiders. *n.* A spider. **araneiform,** *a.* Shaped like a spider.

araphorostic (ăr à fŏ ros′ tik) [Gr. *arrhaphos*, unsewed (*a-*, not, *rhaptein*, to sew)], *a.* Not sewed, seamless.

Araucaria (ăr aw kâr′ i à) [*Arauco*, in Chile], *n.* A genus of coniferous plants, one species of which (*A. imbricata*), the monkey-puzzle, is common in England as an ornamental tree. **araucarian,** *a.*

***arbalest** (ar′ bà lest), ***arbalist,** ***arblast** (ar′ blast) [O.F. *arbaleste*, L. *arcuballista* (*arcus*, a bow, *ballista*, a military engine for hurling missiles)], *n.* A steel crossbow for throwing arrows and other missiles. ***arbalester,** ***arbalister,** ***arblaster** [O.F. *arbalestier*, L. *arcuballistārius*], *n.* A man armed with an arbalest.

arbiter (ar′ bi tėr) [L. *arbiter* (*ar-*, *ad-*, to, *biter*, a comer, from *bītere*, to go, go to see)], *n.* A judge; a person appointed to decide between contending parties; an umpire; one who has power to decide according to his absolute pleasure.

arbitrage (ar′ bi trij), *n.* (*Fin.*) Traffic in bills of exchange or stocks so as to take advantage of rates of exchange in different markets.

arbitrament (ar bit′ rà mėnt), *n.* Power or liberty of deciding; decision by authority; the award given by arbitrators.

arbitrary (ar′ bi trà ri), *a.* Determined by one's own will or caprice; capricious; irrational; subject to the will or control of no other; absolute. **arbitrarily,** *adv.* **arbitrariness,** *n.*

arbitrate (ar′ bi trāt) [L. *arbitrari*, to give judgment], *v.t.* To hear and judge as an arbitrator; to decide, to settle; to act as an arbitrator or umpire.

arbitration (ar bi trā′ shŭn), *n.* The hearing or determining of a dispute by means of an arbitrator. **arbitral,** *a.* Of or pertaining to arbitration.

arbitrator (ar′ bi trā tŏr), *n.* An umpire, an arbiter; a person chosen or appointed to arbitrate. **arbitratorship,** *n.* **arbitress** [O.F. *arbitresse*, fem. of *arbitre*, L. *arbiter*], *n.* A female arbiter; a woman who has absolute power.

arbor (ar′ bȯr) [F. *arbre*, L. *arbor*, tree], *n.* A tree, as distinguished from a plant or shrub; the main support or chief axis of a piece of mechanism; spindle; (*Nat. Hist.*) name for many things of a tree-like appearance. **Arbor Day:** A spring holiday in the U.S.A. **arbor-Dianæ**, *n.* Diana's tree; an arborescent precipitate made by introducing mercury into a solution of nitrate of silver. **arbor-Saturni**, *n.* Saturn's tree; the arborescent appearance presented when zinc is suspended in a solution of acetate of lead. **arbor-vitæ**, *n.* The tree of life; the popular name of several evergreens of the genus *Thuja*; (*Physiol.*) a dendriform appearance in a vertical section of the cerebellum. **arboraceous** (ar bȯ rā′ shůs), *a.* Resembling a tree; woody, wooded. **arboreal** (ar bôr′ ė ȧl), *a.* Pertaining to trees; connected with or living in trees. **arboreous,** *a.* Wooded, arboreal, arborescent. **arborescent** (ar′ bȯ res′ ėnt) [L. *arborēscent -em*, pres.p. of *arborēscere*, to grow into a tree], *a.* Having tree-like characteristics; branching like a tree; dendritic. **arborescence,** *n.* **arborescently,** *adv.* **arboretum** (ar bȯ rē′ tům) [L.], *n.* A botanical garden for the rearing and exhibition of rare trees. **arboriculture** (ar′ bȯr i kŭl′ tūr) [CULTURE], *n.* The systematic culture of trees and shrubs. **arboricultural** (ar bȯr i kŭl′ tūr ȧl), *a.* **arboriculturist,** *n.* **arborization** (ar bȯr i zā′ shůn) [-IZE, -ATION], *n.* Tree-like appearance; tree-like formation or markings in crystalline substances; (*Anat.*) tree-like appearance in distended veins caused by inflammation. **arborous** (ar′ bȯr ůs), *a.* Of or belonging to trees; formed by trees.

arbour (ar′ bȯr) [formerly *herber* or *erber*, O.F. *herbier*, L. *herbārium* (*herba*, a herb, grass), assim. to ARBOR], *n.* A bower formed by trees or shrubs closely planted or trained on lattice-work; a shady retreat.

Arbutus (ar′ bū tůs) [L.], *n.* A genus of evergreen shrubs and trees, one of which, *Arbutus unedo*, the strawberry-tree, is cultivated as an ornamental tree in Britain.

arc (ark) [O.F. *arc*, L. *arcum arcus*, a bow], *n.* A portion of the circumference of a circle or other curve; (*Astron.*) that part of a circle which a heavenly body appears to pass through above or below the horizon, and called respectively the **diurnal** and **nocturnal arcs**; (*Elec.*) the luminous arc or bridge between two electrodes when an electric current is sent through them. **arc-lamp,** *n.* An electric lamp in which such an arc or bridge is the source of illumination.

arcade (ar kād′) [F., from It. *arcata*, arched, fem. p.p. of *arcare*, to bend, arch (*arco*, a bow, L. *arcum arcus*, a bow)], *n.* A series of arches sustained by columns or piers; a walk arched over; a covered passage with shops on each side. **arcaded,** *a.* Furnished with or formed like an arcade.

Arcadian (ar kā′ di ȧn) [L. *Arcădius*], *a.* Of or pertaining to Arcadia, a district of the Peloponnesus, the ideal region of rural happiness; hence, ideally rustic or pastoral, *n.* An inhabitant of Arcadia; an ideal rustic. **arcadianism,** *n.* Ideal rustic condition; pastoral simplicity.

arcanum (ar kā′ nům) [L., neut. of a. *arcānus*, from *arcēre*, to shut up (*arca*, a chest)], *n.* (*usually in pl.* **arcana**) Anything hidden; a mystery, a secret; esp. one of the supposed secrets of the alchemists; an elixir, a miraculous remedy.

arch (1) (arch) [O.F. *arche*, L. *arca*, a chest (confused with *arc*, L. *arcus*, a bow)], *n.* A curved structure so arranged that the parts support each other by mutual pressure; anything resembling this, a vault, a curve; the vault of heaven, the sky. *v.t.* To cover with or form into an arch or arches; to overarch, to span. *v.i.* To assume an arched form. **arch-board,** *n.* (*Naut.*) The part of the stern over the counter. **arch-brick,** *n.* A wedge-shaped brick employed in building arches. ***arch-buttress,** *n.* A flying buttress. **Arches-Court, Court of Arches,** *n.* The ecclesiastical court of appeal for the province of Canterbury, formerly held in the church of St. Mary-le-Bow, or of the Arches. **arch-stone,** *n.* A wedge-shaped stone used in building arches; a key-stone. **archway,** *n.* An arched entrance or vaulted passage. **archwise,** *adv.* In the shape of an arch or vault. **arching,** *a.* Forming an arch, curved. *n.* Arched structure.

arch (2) (arch) [ARCH-, used as a separate word], *a.* Chief, pre-eminent, principal (in this sense generally in composition with a hyphen). **arch-enemy,** *n.* A principal enemy; esp. Satan, the devil. **arch-fiend,** *n.* The chief fiend; Satan, the devil. **arch-flamen,** *n.* A chief flamen or priest; an archbishop. **arch-foe,** *n.* A principal foe. **arch-heresy,** *n.* Extreme heresy. **arch-heretic,** *n.* A chief heretic; the founder of a heresy. **arch-hypocrite,** *n.* One notorious for hypocrisy. **arch-pastor,** *n.* A chief pastor. **arch-prelate,** *n.* Chief prelate, archbishop. **arch-priest,** *n.* A chief priest; a kind of dean or vicar to a bishop; a rural dean.

arch (3) (arch) [ARCH (2)], *a.* Clever, cunning, mischievous, mirthful, roguish, sly. **archly,** *adv.* **archness,** *n.*

arch-, archi- (arch, ar′ ki-) [A.-S. *erce-*, *ærce-*, *arce-*, L. *archi-*, Gr. *archi-* (*archos*, chief, *archein*, to be first, *archē*, beginning)], *pref.* Chief, principal; leading, pre-eminent; first; *e.g.* *archangel*, *archbishop*, *archchamberlain*, *archdeacon*, *archidiaconal*, *architect*, *arch-knave*, *arch-founder.*

archæan (ar kē′ ȧn) [Gr. *archaios*, ancient], *a.* Belonging to the earliest geological period.

archæo- [Gr. *archaios*, ancient, primitive], *pref.* Pertaining to past time (*archē*, beginning); primitive.

archæology (ar kē ol′ ȯ ji), *n.* The science or special study of antiquities, esp. of prehistoric remains. **archæologic** (ar kē ȯ loj′ ik), **archæological,** *a.* Of or pertaining to archæology. **archæologically,** *adv.* **archæologist,** *n.*

Archæopteryx (ar kē op′ tėr iks) [*pteron*, a wing, a bird], *n.* (*Palæont.*) A fossil genus containing the oldest known bird; the bird itself.

archæozoic (ar ki ō zō′ ik), *a.* Pertaining to the dawn of life on the earth.

archaic (ar kā′ ik) [Gr. *archaikos*, primitive, ancient (*archaios*, old, *archē*, beginning)], *a.* Pertaining to antiquity; old-fashioned, antiquated. **archaism** (ar′ kā izm), *n.* An old-fashioned habit or custom; an obsolete expression; affectation or imitation of ancient style or idioms. **archaize** [Gr. *archaizein*, to be old-fashioned, copy the ancients], *v.i.* To imitate or affect ancient manners, language, or style. *v.t.* To make archaic. **archaist** (ar′ kā ist), *n.* One who affects the archaic, an imitator of ancient style; an antiquary. **archaistic** (ar kā is′ tik), *a.* Imitating or affecting the archaic; tending to archaism.

archangel (ark′ ān jėl) [O.F. *archangel*, L. *archangelos*, Gr. *archangelos*], *n.* A chief angel; an angel of the highest rank; a kind of dead-nettle; a kind of fancy pigeon. **archangelic** (-ăn jel′ ik), *a.*

archbishop (arch bish′ ȯp) [L. *archiepiscopus*], *n.* A chief bishop; a metropolitan; the spiritual head of an archiepiscopal province. **archbishopric,** *n.*

archdeacon (arch′ dē kȯn) [L. *archidiāconus*, Gr. *archidiakonos*], *n.* A chief deacon; a church dignitary next below a bishop in the care of the diocese. **archdeaconry,** *n.* The portion of a diocese over which an archdeacon exercises jurisdiction; the rank or office of an archdeacon; an archdeacon's residence. **archdeaconship,** *n.*

archdiocese (arch dī′ ȯ sēs, -sės), *n.* The see of an archbishop.

archduke (arch′ dūk) [O.F. *archeduc*], *n.* A chief duke, esp. a son of an Emperor of Austria. **archducal** (arch dū′ kȧl), *a.* Of or pertaining to an archduke. **archduchess** (arch dŭch′ es), *n.* The wife of an archduke; a daughter of an Emperor of Austria. **archduchy,** *n.* The territory ruled over by an archduke.

archer (ar' chėr) [A.-F. *archer*, O.F. *archier*, late L. *arcārius*, archer (*arcus*, a bow)], *n.* One who uses the bow and arrow; a bowman; (*Astron.*) the constellation of Sagittarius; the archer-fish. **archer-fish,** *n.* A fish, *Toxotes jaculator*, from the East Indies, that has the power of projecting water from its mouth to a considerable distance. **archer-god,** *n.* Cupid, conventionally represented with a bow and arrows. **archeress,** *n.* A female archer. **archery,** *n.* The act or art of shooting with bow and arrow.

archetype (ar' kė tīp), *n.* The primitive type, model, or pattern on which anything is formed, or assumed to be formed. **archetypal,** *a.* Pertaining to an archetype; primitive, original. **archetypically,** *adv.*

archidiaconal (ar ki dī ăk' ŏn ăl) [L. *archidiāconus*, an archdeacon], *a.* Of, or pertaining to, or holding the office of an archdeacon. **archidiaconate,** *n.* The office or territory of an archdeacon.

archiepiscopal (ar ki ė pis' kŏ păl) [L. *archiepiscopus*, Gr. *archiepiskopos*, an archbishop], *a.* Of or pertaining to an archbishop or an archbishopric. **archiepiscopate,** *n.* The office, dignity, or jurisdiction of an archbishop; an archbishopric, an archbishop's tenure of office.

archil (ar' chil, ar' kil) [ORCHIL], *n.* A popular name for some lichens of the genus *Roccella*; a purple or violet dye prepared from these lichens.

Archilochian (ar ki lō' ki ăn), *a.* Pertaining to the Greek satiric poet Archilochus (*c.* 700 B.C.), or to the metre he introduced; severe, bitter. *n.* A verse supposed to have been invented by Archilochus.

archimage (ar' ki māj), *n.* A chief magician; a wizard, an enchanter.

archimandrite (ar ki măn drīt) [late L. *archimandrīta*, late Gr. *archimandritēs* (*archi-*, chief, *mandra*, an enclosure, a monastery)], *n.* The superior of a monastery or convent in the Greek Church, corresponding to an abbot in the Roman Catholic.

Archimedean (ar ki mē' dė an, -mė dē' ăn), *a.* Of pertaining to, or invented by Archimedes, a Greek mathematician of the third century B.C. **Archimedean screw,** *n.* An instrument for raising water, formed by winding a tube into the form of a screw round a long cylinder; (*Naut.*) a type of ship's propeller.

archipelago (ar ki pel' ă gō) [It. *arcipelago* (*arci-*, ARCHI-, *pelago*, gulf, pool, L. *pelagus*, Gr. *pelagos*, sea)], *n.* The Ægean Sea; any sea or water studded with islands; these islands collectively. **archipelagian** (ar ki pė lā' ji ăn), *a.* Of or pertaining to an archipelago.

architect (ar' ki tekt) [L. *architectus*, Gr. *architektōn* (ARCHI-, *tektōn*, a builder, allied to *technē*, art)], *n.* One who plans and draws the designs of buildings, and superintends their erection; (*fig.*) a contriver, a designer of some complex work; the Creator. **architective,** *a.* Of or pertaining to architecture. **architectonic** (ar ki tek ton' ik), **architectonical** [L. *architectonicus*, Gr. *architektonikos*], *a.* Of or pertaining to architecture; constructive; of or pertaining to an architect; directive, controlling; pertaining to the organization of knowledge. **architectonics,** *n.* The science of architecture; the systematization of knowledge; construction or systematic design in a literary or other artistic work. **architecture** [L. *architectūra*], *n.* The art of building edifices or constructions of any kind; architectural work; building; style of building; construction. **architectural** (ar ki tek' tū răl), *a.* **architecturally,** *adv.* In an architectural style; with regard to architecture.

architrave (ar' ki trāv) [L. *trabem*, nom. *trabs*, a beam], *n.* The lowest portion of the entablature of a column, immediately resting on the column itself; the ornamental moulding round a door or window. **architrave cornice,** *n.* An entablature comprising architrave and cornice only, without a frieze.

archive (ar' kīv) [F. *archive*, *archif*, late L. *archīvum*, *archīum*, Gr. *archeion*, public office (*archē*, government)], *n.* (*usually in pl.*) A place in which historical records are kept; historical records officially preserved. **archivist** (ar' ki vist), *n.* One who has charge of archives; a keeper of records.

archivolt (ar' ki vōlt) [It. *archivolto*, *arcovolta* (*arco*, L. *arcus*, arch, *volta*, vault, *volto*, arched)], *n.* The inner contour of an arch; the mouldings and ornaments on this inner contour.

archly, etc. [ARCH (3)].

archology (ar kol' ŏ ji) [Gr. *archē*, a beginning], *n.* The philosophy of the origin of things; the science of government.

archon (ar' kŏn) [Gr. *archōn*, ruler, pres.p. of *archein*, to rule], *n.* The chief magistrate of Athens; after the time of Solon one of the nine chief magistrates of Athens; a ruler, a chief; (*Gnostic theology*) a creator or demiurge. **archonship,** *n.* The office of an archon; the time during which he held office.

archway [ARCH (1)]. **arch-wise** [ARCH (1)].

Arctic (ark' tik) [O.F. *artique*, L., from Gr. *arktikos*, belonging to the Great Bear (*arktos*, bear)], *a.* Of or pertaining to the north, the North Pole, or the region within the Arctic Circle. *n.* The North Pole; Arctic regions. **Arctic Circle,** *n.* A parallel of the globe, 23° 28′ distant from the North Pole, which is its centre. **Arctic fox,** *n.* A small species of fox, with beautiful fur, found in America within the Arctic Circle.

Arcturus (ark tū' rŭs) [L., from Gr. *arktouros* (*arktos*, bear, *ouros*, guardian)], *n.* The bright star in the constellation Boötes; *the constellation Boötes; *the Great Bear.

arcuate, arcuated (ar' kū āt, -ėd) [L. *arcuātus*, p.p. of *arcuāre*, to curve like a bow (*arcus*, bow)], *a.* Curved like a bow; arched. **arcuately,** *adv.* **arcuation** (ar kū ā' shŭn), *n.* The act of bending; the state of being bent; arched work in building; the method of propagating trees by bending down twigs and pegging them into the ground.

-ard [O.F. *-ard*, *-art*, G. *-hart*, *-hard*], *suf.* Noting disposition or character, with augmentative force; *e.g. drunkard, niggard, sluggard.*

Ardea (ar' di ă) [L., a heron], *n.* A genus of birds embracing herons, bitterns, and egrets.

ardent (ar' dėnt) [O.F. *ardant*, pres.p. of *ardoir*, to burn, L. *ardēre*, to burn], *a.* Burning; on fire; glowing, fierce, intense, eager, zealous, fervid. **ardent-spirits,** *n.pl.* Alcoholic spirits (orig. meaning inflammable, combustible spirits). **ardency,** *n.* **ardently,** *adv.*

ardente (ar den' ti) [It.], *a.* (*Mus.*) Ardent, fiery.

ardour (ar' dŏr) [O.F. *ardor*, L. *ardorem*], *n.* Fierce heat; flame; heat of passion; warmth of emotion.

arduous (ar' dū ŭs) [L. *arduus*, steep, difficult], *a.* Steep and lofty; involving much labour; difficult, strenuous, laborious, energetic. **arduously,** *adv.* **arduousness,** *n.*

are (1) (ar) [F., from L. *area*], *n.* French superficial measure, a square of which the sides are ten metres in length, and contain 1076·44 square feet.

are (2) (ar) [see AM, BE], *pl. pres. ind. of the verb* To be.

area (âr' i ă) [L.], *n.* Any clear or open space; the sunken court, partly enclosed by railings, giving access to the basement of some dwelling-houses; space left open round a basement to obviate damp; superficial extent; a particular extent of surface, a region, a tract of country; (*Biol.*) a limited extent of the surface of any organism, distinguished from that which surrounds it. **area-bell,** *n.* Bell rung from handle at area-gate. **area-gate,** *n.* Gate at entrance into area giving access to basement of house. **area-sneak,** *n.* A thief who sneaks in at area-gates. **area-steps,** *n.pl.* Steps leading from the street down to the basement.

***areach** (ȧ rēch′) [A.-S. *arǣcan* (*a-*, on, *rǣcan*, REACH)], *v.t.* To reach, get at; get hold of, get into one's possession. *v.i.* To reach to.

***aread** (ȧ rēd) [A.-S. *arēdan*, *arǣdan* (*a-*, intens., *rǣdan*, READ)], *v.t.* To decree, declare, prophesy; to tell, make known, utter; to guess, divine, conjecture; to counsel, advise; to decide, to adjudge.

Areca (ăr′ ė kȧ) [Port., from Tamil *adaikāy* (*adai*, clustering, *kāy*, nut)], *n.* A genus of palms, esp. *Areca catechu*, which yields the betel-nut.

arefy (ăr′ ė fī) [L. *ārefacere*, to make dry (*ārēre*, to be dry, *facere*, to make)], *v.t.* To make dry, to dry up, to parch. **arefaction** (ăr ė făk′ shŭn), *n.* The act or process of drying; the state or condition of being dried.

arena (ȧ rē′ nȧ) [L. *arēna*, *harēna*, sand], *n.* The floor of an amphitheatre where combats took place, originally strewn with sand to absorb the blood; an amphitheatre; a field of conflict, sphere of action. **arenaceous** (ăr ė nā′ shŭs), *a.* Sandy; in the form of sand; composed partly or entirely of sand. **Arenaria** [L. fem. of a. *arēnārius*, belonging to the sand], *n.* The genus typified by the sandworts, tiny herbs allied to chickweed. **arenose** (ăr′ ė nōs) [L. *arēnosus*], *a.* Full of grit or sand.

areo- [Gr. *areos*, pertaining to *Arēs*, Mars], *comb. form.* Pertaining to the planet Mars; *e.g.* **areocentric** (ăr ė ŏ sen′ trik), *a.* Centring in Mars. **areography** (-og′ rȧ fi), *n.* Description of the physical features of Mars. **areology,** *n.* Scientific study of Mars.

areola (ȧ rē′ ŏ lȧ) [L. dim. of *area*], *n.* (*pl.* **areolæ**) A very small area; (*Biol.*) one of the interstices in organized tissue; any minute space enclosed by lines or markings; a slightly depressed spot; a dark circle round the human nipple; (*Med.*) a similar circle round a pustule; (*Bot.*) a cell-nucleus. **areolar,** *a.* Of, pertaining to, or consisting of areolæ. **areolar tissue,** *n.* Connective tissue, the cellular tissue underlying the skin. **areolate,** *a.* Marked or marked off by intersecting lines. **areolation** (ăr ė ŏ lā′ shŭn), *n.* The state of being areolate. **areole** (ăr′ ė ōl), *n.* An areola.

areometer, etc. [ARÆOMETER].

Areopagus (ăr ė op′ ȧ gŭs) [L. *arēopagus*, Gr. *Areios pagos* (*Areios*, belonging to *Ares* or Mars, *pagos*, a hill)], *n.* The highest court at Athens (which sat on Mars' Hill); (*fig.*) any important tribunal. **areopagite** (ăr ė op′ ȧ gīt), *n.* A member of the Areopagus.

***aret, arette** (ȧ ret′) [O.F. *areter*, *aretter* (*à*, to, *reter*, L. *reputāre*, to count, reckon)], *v.t.* To reckon, to count, to impute; (*Spens.*) to deliver, entrust. *v.i.* To allege.

arête (a rāt′) [F. *arête* (O.F. *areste*), L. *arista*, an ear of corn, a spine], *n.* A sharp ascending ridge of a mountain.

***argal** (ar′ gȧl) [corr. of L. *ergo*], *adv.* Therefore. *n.* A clumsy piece of reasoning.

argala (ar′ gȧ lȧ) [Hind. *hargālā*], *n.* The adjutant-bird; a gigantic stork from India.

argali (ar′ gȧ li) [Mongol.], *n.* The wild rock-sheep of Asia.

argand (ar′ gănd) [A. Argand (1755–1803), inventor], *a.* Having a circular hollow wick or gas-burner, which admits air so as to secure more complete combustion and brighter light. *n.* An argand lamp.

argent (ar′ jėnt) [F., from L. *argentum*], *n.* *Silver; (*Her.*) the white colour representing silver. *a.* Of or resembling silver; silvery-white. **argentiferous** (ar jėn tif′ ėr ŭs) [-FEROUS], *a.* Producing silver. **argentine** (ar′ jėn tīn) [F. *argentin*, L. *argentinus*], *a.* Of or containing silver; silvery. *n.* Silver, electro-plate, imitation silver; (*Zool.*) a small fish with silvery scales; (*Min.*) a pearly lamellar variety of calcite. **argentometer** (ar jėn tom′ ė tėr), *n.* (*Phot.*) An instrument for gauging the amount of silver put into a sensitizing bath.

argil (ar′ jil) [F. *argille*, L. *argilla*, Gr. *argillos*, white clay (*argēs*, white)], *n.* White clay, potter's earth. **argillaceous** (ar jil lā′ shŭs), *a.* Of the nature of clay; containing a large amount of clay. **argilliferous** (ar jil lif′ ėr ŭs), *a.* Producing or yielding clay.

Argive (ar′ jīv) [L. *Argīvus*, Gr. *Argeios* (*Argos*, city of Argolis, in the Peloponnesus)], *a.* Of or pertaining to Argos; hence, Greek. *n.* A native of Argos; a Greek.

argol (ar′ gŏl) [etym. unknown], *n.* An impure acid potassium tartrate deposited from wines; crude cream of tartar.

argon (ar′ gŏn) [Gr. *argos*, neut. *argon*, not working (*a-*, not, *ergon*, work)], *n.* One of the gaseous constituents of the atmosphere, discovered in 1894.

Argonaut (ar′ gŏ nawt) [L. *argonauta*, Gr. *argonautēs*], *n.* One of the legendary heroes who accompanied Jason in the ship *Argo* to seek the Golden Fleece; (*Zool.*) the popular name of a genus of cephalopod molluscs containing the paper-nautilus. **argonautic,** *a.* Of or pertaining to the Argonauts or their expedition. *n.* One of Jason's companions; an Argonaut; (*pl.*) a poem on the quest of the Golden Fleece.

argosy (ar′ gŏ si) [prob. It. *una Ragusea* (*nave*), a Ragusan (ship)], *n.* A large vessel for carrying merchandise; a carack; (*fig.*) a richly-laden ship; anything of great value.

argot (ar′ gō) [F.], *n.* Thieves' slang; the phraseology of a class; slang generally. **argotic** (-got′ ik), *a.* Slangy.

argue (ar′ gū) [O.F. *arguer*, late L. *argūtāre* (freq. of *arguere*, to prove, make clear)], *v.t.* To prove, to show, to evince; to exhibit by reasoning; to convince by logical methods; to discuss, debate. *v.i.* To bring forward reasons, to discuss; to reason in opposition, to dispute. **arguable,** *a.* Capable of being argued. **argufy,** *v.i.* (*Am.*) To argue. **argufier,** *n.* (*colloq.*) One who argues; a contentious person.

argument (ar′ gū mėnt), *n.* Proof, reason, demonstration; process of reasoning; debate, discussion; an abstract or summary of a book; the subject of a discourse. **argumentation** (-tā′ shŭn), *n.* The act or process of reasoning; methodical reasoning; a systematic argument. **argumentative** (-men′ tȧ tiv), *a.* Consisting of or pertaining to argument; controversial; having a natural tendency to argue, disputatious. **argumentatively,** *adv.* **argumentativeness,** *n.*

Argus (ar′ gŭs) [L., from Gr. *Argos*, the mythic guardian of Io, fabled to have a hundred eyes], *n.* A vigilant watcher or guardian; (*Zool.*) a genus of pheasants from the East Indies, having the plumage marked with eye-like spots; butterflies of the genus *Polyommatus*, which have eye-like spots on the wings. **argus-eyed,** *a.* Very observant, sharp-sighted. **argus-shell,** *n.* (*Conch.*) A porcelain shell, variegated with eye-like spots.

argute (ar gūt′) [L. *argūtus*, shrill, p.p. of *arguere*, ARGUE], *a.* Shrill, sharp; quick, keen, shrewd. **arguteness,** *n.*

argyle (ar gīl′) [?], *n.* A dinner-table receptacle for keeping gravy hot.

aria (a′ ri ȧ) [It.], *n.* An air; a song for one voice supported by instruments.

Arian (1) (âr′ i ȧn) [L. *Ariānus* (*Arīus*, *Arius*, Gr. *areios*, *Arios*, prop. name)], *a.* Pertaining to Arius or his doctrine. *n.* A follower of Arius of Alexandria (4th century) who denied that Christ was consubstantial with the Father. **Arianism,** *n.* The system of doctrine held by Arius and his followers. **Arianize,** *v.t.* To become an Arian. *v.i.* To convert to Arianism; to propagate Arianism.

Arian (2) [ARYAN].

-arian [L. *-ārius*], *suf.* Belonging to; *e.g. humanitarian, sabbatarian, sexagenarian, trinitarian.*

arid (ăr′ id) [L. *āridus* (*ārēre*, to dry)], *a.* Dry, parched, wanting in moisture; barren, bare; (*fig.*)

dry, uninteresting. **aridity** (ȧ rid′ i ti), **aridness** (ăr′ id nės), *n.* The quality or state of being dry or parched; dryness, drought; absence of moisture.

ariel (âr′ i ėl) [Arab. *aryil, ayyil,* stag], *n.* A Western Asiatic and African gazelle.

Aries (âr′ i ēz), ***Ariete** (âr′ i ēt) [L.], *n.* The Ram, the first of the zodiacal constellations, which the sun enters in the month of March.

arietta (a ri et′ tȧ) [It., dim. of ARIA], *n.* A short lively air, tune, or song. **ariette** (ăr i et′) [F., from It. *arietta*], *n.* An arietta.

aright (ȧ rīt), ***arights** [*a-*, on, RIGHT (*rights,* from *rihtes,* gen.)], *adv.* Right, rightly, properly, becomingly; without failure or mistake.

aril (ăr′ il) [mod. L. *arillus,* med. L. *arilli,* Sp. *arillos,* raisins], *n.* (*Bot.*) An accessory seed-covering, more or less incomplete, formed by a growth near the hilum. **arillate** (ȧ ril′ āt), **arilled** (ăr′ ild), *a.* Furnished with an aril. **arillode** (ȧ ril′ ōd), *n.* A false aril, proceeding from the placenta.

ariot (ȧ rī′ ȯt), *adv.* Riotously.

-arious [L. *-ārius*], *suf.* Connected with, belonging to; forming adjectives, *e.g. gregarious, vicarious.*

aripple (ȧ rip′l), *a.* Rippling.

arise (ȧ rīz′) [A.-S. *ārīsan* (*a-,* intens., *rīsan*)], *v.i.* (*p.* **arose,** *p.part.* **arisen**) To assume an upright position from an attitude of repose, to get up; to rise from the dead; to appear, to come into notoriety; to originate, to take its rise; to take place, occur (as a result).

arista (ȧ ris′ tȧ) [L.], *n.* (*Bot.*) An awn; the beard of grasses and grain. **aristate,** *a.* Awned; furnished with an awn or awns; bearded.

Aristarch (ăr′ is tark) [L. *Aristarchus,* Gr. *Aristarchos,* a Greek grammarian of the 2nd century B.C.], *n.* A severe critic. **aristarchian,** *a.* Pertaining to Aristarchus; severely critical.

aristocracy (ăr is tok′ rȧ si) [L. *aristocratia,* Gr. *aristokratia* (*aristos,* the best, *kratein,* to rule, hence *kratia,* rule)], *n.* Government by the best citizens or by the nobles; a state so governed; a ruling body of nobles; the nobility; (*fig.*) the best of any class. **aristocrat** (ăr′ is tȯ krăt), *n.* A noble; a member of an aristocracy; (*rare*) one who favours aristocratic government. **aristocratic** (ăr is tȯ krăt′ ik), **aristocratical,** *a.* Pertaining or relating to an aristocracy, grand, stylish. **aristocratically,** *adv.*

Aristophanic (ăr is tȯ făn′ ik), *a.* Of or pertaining to Aristophanes, an Athenian comic poet of the 5th century B.C.; witty, broadly comic.

Aristotelian, -ean (ăr is tȯ tē′ li ȧn, -tot ė lē′ ȧn), *a.* Of or pertaining to Aristotle, the famous Greek philosopher (384–322 B.C.), or to his philosophy. *n.* One who adheres to or is learned in the philosophy of Aristotle. **Aristotelianism,** *n.*

arithmancy (ȧ rith′ măn si) [more correctly **arithmomancy** (Gr. *arithmos,* number, -MANCY)], *n.* Divination by means of numbers.

arithmetic (ȧ rith′ mė tik) [O.F. *arismetique,* late L. *arismetica,* L. *arithmētica,* Gr. *arithmētikē techne,* art of counting (*arithmeein,* to count, *arithmos,* number)], *n.* The science of numbers; computation by figures; arithmetical knowledge; a treatise on computation by figures. **arithmetic of series,** *n.* Trigonometry. **mental arithmetic,** *n.* Arithmetic done in the head without recourse to pen and paper. **universal arithmetic,** *n.* Algebra. **arithmetical** (ăr ith met′ ik ȧl), *a.* Of or pertaining to arithmetic. **arithmetical progression,** *n.* A series of numbers that increase or decrease consecutively by a constant quantity. **arithmetically,** *adv.* In an arithmetical manner; according to the principles of arithmetic. **arithmetician** (ȧ rith mė tish′ ȧn), *n.* One skilled in arithmetic; a professor of arithmetic.

arithmocracy (ăr ith mok′ rȧ si) [Gr. *arithmos,* number, -CRASY], *n.* Government by a mere numerical majority. **arithmocratic** (-mȯ krăt′ ik), *a.* Having the nature of an arithmocracy.

arithmometer (ă rith mŏm′ ėt ėr), *n.* A calculating machine.

-arium [L., neut. of adj. in *-ārius* (-ARY)], *suf.* Thing connected with, used for, place for; as in *aquarium, herbarium, sacrarium.*

ark (ark) [A.-S. *arc* (cp. Goth. *arka,* Icel. *örka,* L. *arca*)], *n.* A chest, a box; a sacred repository; a refuge; a ship, a boat, esp. a large flat-bottomed vessel used in the U.S. for transporting produce. **ark of the Covenant,** *n.* The wooden coffer containing the tables of the Law, etc., in the Jewish tabernacle. **Noah's ark,** *n.* The vessel in which Noah and his family were saved from the Deluge; a toy model of this with toy animals. **arkite** (ar′ kīt), *a.* Pertaining to Noah's ark. *n.* An inmate of the ark.

arles (arlz) [L. *arrha* (perh. through an O.F. *erle* or *arle* from a dim. *arrhula*)], *n.pl.* (sometimes used *as sing.*) (*Sc.* and *North.*) Earnest-money; money paid at the hiring of a servant to clinch the engagement. **arles-penny,** *n.* Earnest-money.

arm (1) (arm) [A.-S. *earm* (cp. Dut. *arm,* L. *armus,* shoulder, Gr. *harmos,* joint, shoulder)], *n.* The upper limb of the human body on either side, from the shoulder to the hand; anything resembling the human arm; a sleeve; a projecting branch, as of the sea, a mountain, a river, nerve, machine, service, or the like; (*Zool.*) the fore-limb of any of the lower mammals; a flexible limb or appendage, with arm-like functions, in invertebrates; (*Naut.*) the parts of an anchor which bear the flukes; the parts of a yard on each side of the mast; (*fig.*) power, authority. *v.t.* To offer the arm to; to take by the arm; to put one's arm round; *to take in the arms. **fore-arm,** *n.* The part of the arm between hand and elbow. **arm-in-arm:** With the arms interlinked. **arm-band,** *n.* A band of material encircling the coat-sleeve, usu. black to indicate mourning. **arm-chair,** *n.* A chair with arms to support the elbows. ***arm-gaunt,** *a.* A Shakespearian adjective of uncertain meaning, *perhaps* with gaunt limbs. **arm-hole,** *n.* The armpit; the hole in a garment to admit the arm. **armpit,** *n.* The hollow under the arm at the shoulder. **arm's length,** *n.* The length of one's arm. **at arm's length:** At a distance. **armful,** *n.* As much as the arm or arms can hold. **armless** (1), *a.* Without arms or branches. **with open arms:** Cordially, enthusiastically.

arm (2) (arm) [F. *armes,* L. *arma,* weapons], *n.* A weapon; any branch of the military service; (*pl.*) war; the military profession; armour; heraldic bearings. *v.t.* To furnish or equip with offensive or defensive arms or weapons; to furnish with a protective covering; to prepare for war; (*fig.*) to equip with tools or other appliances; to furnish (a magnet) with an armature. *v.i.* To take arms; to prepare for war. **fire-arms:** Weapons in which gunpowder or other explosive is used. **small arms:** Arms that can be carried by those who use them. **stand of arms:** A set of arms for a soldier. **to arms!** Take your weapons; prepare for battle. **under arms:** Bearing arms; ready for service; in battle array. **up in arms:** In revolt; on the aggressive defensive. **King-of-Arms,** *n.* A Chief Herald. **armed,** *a.* Equipped with weapons or armour; prepared for war; furnished with claws, teeth, horns, etc., or with natural armour; furnished with thorns, prickles, etc.; equipped with anything required for action or defence; provided with an armature; (*Her.*) furnished with heraldic devices, represented with claws, teeth, etc. **arming,** *n.* The act of equipping with weapons or means of defence; equipment for any purpose; furnishing with heraldic devices. **arming-press,** *n.* A press used in stamping and lettering the covers of books. **armless** (2), *a.* Destitute of weapons of offence or defence.

armada (ar mā′ dȧ, ar ma′ dȧ) [Sp., fem. of *armado,* armed, p.p. of *armar* (L. *armāre*)], *n.* An armed fleet, esp. the fleet sent by Philip II of Spain against England in 1588; (*fig.*) any armed force.

Armadillo (ar mȧ dil′ ō) [Sp., dim. of *armado* (see ARMADA)], *n.* (*pl.* **-los**) The name of several small burrowing edentate animals, peculiar to South America, encased in bony armour, and capable of rolling themselves into a ball; a genus of isopod crustaceans, allied to the wood-louse.

Armageddon (ar mȧ ged′ on) [Battlefield described in Rev. xvi. 16], *n.* The final battle of the nations; a great and destructive battle.

armament (ar′ mȧ mėnt) [L. *armamentum*], *n.* The act of arming a fleet or army for war; the munitions of war, esp. the guns of a ship of war; an armed force.

armature (ar′ mȧ tūr) [L. *armatura*], *n.* Weapons, armour; means of defence in general; (*Elec.*) a piece of soft iron placed in contact with the poles of a magnet to preserve and increase its power; the revolving part of an electro-motor or dynamo.

Armenian (ar mē′ ni ȧn) [L., from Gr. *Armenia*, country in Western Asia], *a.* Of or pertaining to Armenia. *n.* A native of Armenia; the language spoken by the Armenians; a member of the Armenian Church. **Armenian bole,** *n.* A pale red medicinal earth from Armenia. **Armenian stone,** *n.* A blue carbonate of copper, formerly given in epilepsy.

armet (ar′ mėt) [F. *armet*, O.F. *armette*, dim. of *arme*], *n.* A kind of helmet consisting of a rounded iron cap, a spreading protection for the back of the neck, and visor, beaver, and gorget in front, which superseded the basinet in the 15th century.

armiger (ar′ mi jėr) [L. (*arma*, arms, *gerere*, to bear)], *n.* An esquire; one entitled to heraldic bearings. **armigerous** (-mij′ ėr ůs), *a.* Entitled to heraldic bearings.

armilla (ar mil′ ȧ) [L. *armilla*, bracelet (*armus*, the shoulder)], *n.* A bracelet, an armlet; (*Astron.*) an old astronomical instrument for ascertaining the recurrence of the solstices and the equinoxes; (*Anat.*) the round ligament of the wrist. **armillary** (ar′ mil ȧr i, ar mil′ ȧ ri), *a.* Pertaining to bracelets; consisting of parts resembling bracelets. **armillary sphere,** *n.* (*Astron.*) A skeleton celestial globe or sphere consisting of metallic circles mechanically fixed to represent the celestial equator, the ecliptic, the colures, etc.

Arminian (ar min′ i ȧn), *a.* Of or pertaining to Arminius, *i.e.* James Harmensen, Dutch theologian (d. 1609), who maintained the doctrine of free-will against Calvin. *n.* A follower of Arminius. **Arminianism,** *n.*

armipotent (ar mip′ ȯ tėnt) [L. *armipotent -em* (*arma*, arms, *potens*, powerful)], *a.* Powerful or mighty in arms (an epithet of Mars).

armistice (ar′ mis tis) [F. *armistice* (L. *arma*, arms, *-stitium*, from *sistere*, to stop)], *n.* A cessation of arms for a stipulated time during war; a truce. **Armistice Day,** *n.* Nov. 11, the day on which an armistice was signed in 1918. Since the 1939–45 war Remembrance Day (the Sunday nearest to Nov. 11) is solemnly observed to commemorate the fallen in both wars.

armlet (arm′ lėt), *n.* A small ornamental band worn on the arm; a badge on a band around the arm; armour for the arm.

armoire (ar′ mwar) [F., from L. *armārium* (see AMBRY)], *n.* A chest, a cupboard.

Armoric (ar mor′ ik), *a.* Of or pertaining to Brittany, the ancient Armorica. *n.* The language of Armorica. **Armorican,** *a.* Armoric. *n.* A Breton.

armory (ar′ mȯ ri) [O.F. *armoierie*, from *armoier*, a blazoner, *armoier*, to blazon], *n.* The science of heraldry. **armorial** (ar môr′ i ȧl), *a.* Pertaining or relating to heraldic arms. *n.* A book containing coats of arms. **armorist** (ar′ mȯr ist), *n.* One learned in heraldry; one skilled in blazoning arms.

armour (ar′ mȯr) [O.F. *armure*, *armeüre*, L. *armātūra* (see ARMATURE)], *n.* Defensive covering of a fighting man; (*Zool.*) protective covering of animals or plants; (*Naut.*) the iron or steel plating of a warship; the water-tight dress of a diver; heraldic bearings; steel plates used to protect a motor-car, train, tank or other vehicle from projectiles; (*Mil.*) collective term for tanks and other armoured vehicles. *v.t.* To furnish with armour; to furnish with protective covering, esp. ships with armour-plating. **armour-bearer,** *n.* One who carried the weapons of a warrior; an esquire. **armour-clad,** *a.* Ironclad. **armour-plate,** *n.* A plate of iron or steel for covering the sides of ships of war. **armour-plated,** *a.* Covered with plates of iron or steel; iron-clad. **armour-plating,** *n.* Iron or steel plates collectively. **armoured,** *a.* Clad in armour; protected; (*Nav.*) ironclad. **armoured car, train,** *n.* Motor-car or train protected by steel plates. **armoured column,** *n.* (*Mil.*) Force equipped with armoured vehicles, tanks, etc. **armoured concrete,** *n.* [FERRO-CONCRETE]. **armourer,** *n.* One who made armour; a manufacturer of arms; a non-commissioned officer in charge of the arms of a regiment, ship, etc. **armoury,** *n.* Armour or arms; a place for keeping arms, an arsenal; the craft or skill of an armourer; (*Am.*) an armourer's workshop; (*Am.*) a drill-hall.

armozeen (ar mȯ zēn′) [F. *armoisin*, O.F. *armesin*, taffeta], *n.* A thick plain silk, generally black, used for clerical robes.

armpit [ARM (1)].

Armstrong gun (arm′ strong gŭn′) [after Sir Wm. *Armstrong* (1810–1900), inventor], *n.* A gun built up of successive coils of wrought iron.

army (ar′ mi) [F. *armée*, fem. p.p. of *armer*, to arm (L. *armāre*)], *n.* A body of men organized for land warfare; a multitude, a host, an organized body (*e.g.* the *Salvation Army*). **army-broker,** *n.* A broker whose business is closely connected with the army. **army-corps,** *n.* A main division of an army. **Army Council,** *n.* A committee composed of military and civil officials of the War Office under the chairmanship of the Secretary of State for War. **army list,** *n.* An official list of the officers of an army.

Arnica (ar′ ni kȧ) [etym. unknown], *n.* A tincture prepared from *Arnica montana*, mountain tobacco, and used as an application for bruises, sprains, etc.; (*Bot.*) a genus of compositous plants including this; a plant of that genus.

***aroint, aroynt** (ȧ roint′) [etym. doubtful], *int.* or *v.* Avaunt! begone!

aroma (ȧ rō′ mȧ) [late L., from Gr. *arōma*, a spice], *n.* The fragrance in a plant, spice, fruit, etc.; an agreeable odour or smell; a subtle pervasive quality. **aromatic** (ăr ȯ măt′ ik) [F. *aromatique*, L. *arōmaticus*, Gr. *arōmatikos*], *a.* Of or pertaining to an aroma; fragrant, spicy. *n.* A fragrant drug, a spice; (*pl.*) a benzene-type additive to motor fuel. **aromatize** (ȧ rō′ mȧ tīz), *v.t.* To render aromatic or fragrant; to perfume, to scent. **aromatization** (ȧ rō mȧ tī zā′ shůn), *n.* The act of rendering aromatic; the state of being so scented.

aroo (ȧ roo′) [Austral.], *int.* Goodbye, au revoir.

arose (ȧ rōz′), *pret.* [ARISE].

around (ȧ round′), *prep.* Surrounding; round about; on all sides of; along the circuit of. *adv.* All round; in a circle; about, here and there, in all directions.

arouse (ȧ rouz′), *v.t.* To raise, stir up, awaken; to excite, stimulate.

arow (ȧ rō′), *adv.* In a row; one after the other; in succession.

arpeggio (ar pej′ ō) [It. (*arpa*, a harp)], *n.* A method of playing a chord on a keyed instrument by striking the notes in rapid succession instead of simultaneously; a chord so played.

arquebus [HARQUEBUS].

arrack (ăr′ ȧk) [Arab. *'araq*, juice, essence, sweat (*'arqua*, he sweated)], *n.* A name used in the East for native distilled spirits, especially those from the coco-nut and rice.

arrah (ăr′ ȧ) [Ir.], *int.* An expletive expressing mild excitement.

arraign (ȧ rān′) [O.F. *araisnier*, late L. *arratiōnāre* (*ad-*, to, *ratio -ōnem*, reason)], *v.t.* To cite before a tribunal to answer a criminal charge; to accuse; to charge with fault; to find fault with. **arraignment,** *n.* The act of arraigning; accusation, charge; the state of being so arraigned.

arrange (ȧ rānj′) [O.F. *arangier* (*à*, to, *rangier*, to range, from *rang*, rank or file; cp. O.H.G. *hring*)], *v.t.* To draw up in rank or ranks; to adjust, to settle, to put in proper order; (*Am.*) to fix; (*Mus.*) to adapt (a composition) for other instruments or voices; to plan or settle circumstances in readiness. *v.i.* To come to arrangement; to make a settlement. **arrangement,** *n.* The act of arranging, the state of being arranged; the manner in which things are arranged; settlement, disposition, preparation; a grouping or combination of things in a particular way; (*pl.*) dispositions in advance, preparations; (*Mus.*) the adaptation of a composition for instruments or voices for which it was not written.

arrant (ăr′ ȧnt) [var. of ERRANT (*e.g.* 'an outlawe or a theef erraunt,' *i.e.* wandering or roving thief)], *a.* Notorious, downright, unmitigated; complete, thorough. **arrantly,** *adv.* Shamelessly, infamously.

arras (ăr′ ȧs), *n.* A kind of tapestry made at Arras in Artois; a rich fabric of coloured tapestry; wall hangings. **arrased,** *a.* Furnished or hung with arras. **arrasene** (ăr ȧ sēn′), *n.* A mixed thread of wool and silk used in embroidery.

array (ȧ rā′) [S.-F. *arayer*, O.F. *araier* (Prov. *aredar*, early Rom. and It. *arredare*), from *a-*, *ad-*, to L.G. *rēde*, ready (cp. A.-S. *rǣde*)], *v.t.* To put in readiness (as troops); to marshal, to dress up, to deck; (*Law*) to set a jury in order for a trial. *n.* Order, esp. of battle; the summoning and arming of a military force, esp. of the Militia; a military force; an orderly arrangement or disposition for show; state of preparation; (*poet.*) dress, attire; (*Law*) the order of empanelling a jury; the panel.

arrear (ȧ rēr′) [O.F. *arere* (cp. F. *arrière*), backward (L. *ad-*, towards, *retro*, behind)], *adv.* *To or in the rear, backward. *n.* The state of being behindhand; that which is behindhand, unpaid, or unsatisfied (*usu.* in *pl.*). **in arrears:** Unpaid, unsatisfied. **arrearage** (ȧ rēr′ ȧj), *n.* Arrear, backwardness; that which is in arrear, outstanding, or kept back; arrears; items overdue.

arrect (ȧ rekt′) [L. *arrectus*, p.p. of *arrigere*, to erect (*ad-*, to, *regere*, direct)], *a.* Pricked up, pointed up (of the ears of an animal); alert, attentive.

arrest (ȧ rest′) [O.F. *arester*, late L. *adrestāre* (*ad-*, to, at, *restāre*, to stay, stop, from *re-*, back, *stāre*, stand)], *v.t.* To stop, check; to seize and fix (the sight, mind, etc.); to stay (legal proceedings, etc.); to apprehend to seize upon by authority. *n.* A stoppage, stay, check; seizure, detention. **arrested development,** *n.* (*Zool.*) Development arrested at some stage of its progress. **arrest of judgment:** Staying of a judgment after a verdict. **under arrest:** In custody. ***arrestation** (-tā′ shŭn), *n.* The act of arresting; arrest; stopping. **arrester,** *n.* One who or that which arrests; a contrivance for cutting off a force (*e.g.* lightning); (*Sc. Law*) the person who arrests a debt or property in another's hands (usually spelt *arrestor*). **arrestive,** *a.* Tending to arrest (*e.g.* the conj. *but*). **arrestment,** *n.* The act of arresting; stop, stay check; (*Law*) seizure of property by legal authority, esp. (*Sc. Law*) the process by which a creditor detains the effects of his debtor, which are in the hands of third parties, till the money owing him is paid. **arrestor** [ARRESTER]. **arrestor-hook,** *n.* (*Aviat.*) a device that enables an aircraft landing on a carrier-ship to check speed by catching on a cable.

****arret*** (a rā′, ȧ ret′) [O.F. *arest*, from *arester* (see ARREST)], *n.* An authoritative sentence or decision of the King or Parliament of France; an authoritative pronouncement, a decree.

arrière (ar′ ri ār) [F. (see ARREAR)], *n.* The rear; the rear of an army. ***arrière-fief,*** *n.* A fief held by a feudatory; a sub-fief. ***arrière-tenant,*** *n.* The tenant of a mesne-lord or feudatory; a subtenant. ***arrière-vassal,*** *n.* The holder of an *arrière-fief.*

arris (ăr′ is) [O.F. *areste*, ARÊTE], *n.* The line in which two straight or curved surfaces forming an exterior angle meet each other. **arris-gutter,** *n.* A wooden gutter shaped like the letter V. **arriswise,** *adv.* Diagonally, ridge-wise; so as to present a sharp edge.

arrive (ȧ rīv′) [O.F. *ariver*, late L. *arrībāre*, *arrīpāre* (*ad rīpam*, to shore)], *v.i.* To come to, reach a place, position, state of mind, etc.; to gain, to compass, to reach to, to attain, to come about, to occur; (*colloq.*) to attain notoriety, become eminent, make one's fortune. **v.t.* To reach, attain. **arrival,** *n.* The act of coming to a journey's end or destination; the coming to a position, state of mind, etc.; a person who or thing which has arrived; (*colloq.*) a new-born child; (*Comm.*) a cargo to be delivered when a ship comes into port.

arriviste (ȧ rē′ vist) [Fr.], *n.* A social climber, a parvenu; a self-seeker, esp. in politics.

arrogance (ăr′ ō gȧns), **arrogancy** (ăr′ ō gȧn si) [F. *arrogance*, L. *arrogantia* (see below)], *n.* The act or quality of being arrogant; undue assumption. **arrogant** (ăr′ ō gȧnt) [F. *arrogant*, L. *arrogantem*, pres.p. of *arrogāre* (see ARROGATE)], *a.* Claiming or assuming too much; insolent, assuming, overbearing, haughty. **arrogantly,** *adv.*

arrogate (ăr′ ō gāt) [L. *arrogātus*, p.p. of *arrogāre* (*ad-*, to, *rogāre*, to ask)], *v.t.* To put forth unduly exalted claims or baseless pretensions to a thing for oneself or for someone else. **arrogation** (ăr ō gā′ shŭn), *n.* The act of claiming or assuming unwarrantably; undue pretension.

arrondissement (a ron′ dis man′) [F.], *n.* A territorial division of a French department; a ward in Paris.

arrow (ăr′ ō) [A.-S. *arewe*, *earh* (Goth. *arhwazna*; allied to L. *arcus*, a bow)], *n.* A slender, straight missile shot from a bow; anything resembling an arrow in shape or function. **arrow-grass,** *n.* (*Bot.*) The popular name of the genus *Triglochin*; a kind of pampas grass. **arrow-head,** *n.* The head of an arrow; a mark like an arrow-head, indicating direction; (*Bot.*) the popular name of the genus *Sagittaria*, the leaves of which resemble arrow-heads. **arrow-headed,** *a.* Shaped like the head of an arrow; sagittate, cuneiform. **arrow-root,** *n.* A nutritious starch extracted from the tubers of several species of *Maranta*; the food prepared from this substance; (*Bot.*) the English name of the genus *Maranta*, which includes *M. arundinacea*, the tubers of which were used to absorb poison from wounds, especially those made by poisoned arrows. **arrow-stitch,** *n.* A triangular series of stitches for securing the ends of whalebone in stays. **arrowlet,** *n.* A little arrow; the feathery seeds of dandelion, thistle, etc. **broad arrow,** *n.* A mark like an arrow-head used by the Board of Ordnance on Government stores; a similar mark formerly stamped in large characters on the clothing of convicts. **arrowy,** *a.* Consisting of arrows; resembling an arrow or arrows in form or motion; darting, swift; sharp, piercing.

arroyo (a rō′ yō) [Sp.], *n.* A dried-up watercourse, a rocky ravine.

arse (ars) [A.-S. *ærs*, *ears* (Icel. and M.H.G. *ars*; cp. Gr. *orrhos*)], *n.* The buttocks, the rump, the hind parts; the fag-end.

arsenal (ar′ sėn ȧl) [It. *arsenale*, *arzenà*, *darsena*, Arab. *dār aççinā'ah* (*dār*, house, *al*, the, *çinā'ah*, art, trade)], *n.* A place for the manufacture and storage, or simply for the storage, of naval and military weapons and ammunition; (*fig.*) a magazine or factory for spiritual, literary, or other weapons.

arsenic (ar′ sė nik) [O.F. *arsenic*, L. *arsenicum*, Gr. *arsenikon* (a. *arrenikos -on*, male, masculine, used as n. from idea of the alchemists that this was a masculine metal), Arab. *az-zernikh* (*al*, the, *zernikh*, orpiment, Pers. *zerni*, orpiment, *zar*, gold)], *n.* A brittle, semi-metallic steel-grey element; the trioxide of this element, a virulent poison. **flowers of arsenic:** This substance sublimed. **arsenic** (ar sen′ ik), *a.* (*Chem.*) Of or belonging to arsenic, applied to compounds in which arsenic combines as a pentavalent element. **arsenical,** *a.* Pertaining to arsenic; having arsenic in its composition. **arsenious** (ar sē′ ni ŭs), *a.* (*Chem.*) Having arsenic as a constituent; esp. applied to compounds in which arsenic combines as a trivalent element. **arsine** (ar′ sēn), *n.* Hydrogen arsenide, a very poisonous gas.

arsis (ar′ sis) [L. from Gr. *arsis*, a raising, a lifting (*airein*, to lift)], *n.* The stressed syllable in metre; the stressed note in barred music.

arson (ar′ sŏn) [O.F. *arson*, late L. *arsio-ōnem* (*ardēre*, to burn, p.p. *arsus*)], *n.* The wilful setting on fire of another's house or other property, or to one's own with intent to defraud the insurers.

art (1) (art), *v.* The second pers. sing. pres. ind. of the verb TO BE.

art (2) (art) [O.F. *art*, L. *ars artem* (stem *ar-*, to fit)], *n.* Skill, human skill or workmanship, as opposed to nature; skill applied to subjects of taste, esp. the arts of representation and design; perfection of workmanship for its own sake; the practical application of science; a body of rules for putting principles into practice; an industrial pursuit; a craft, a profession; acquired skill; craft, cunning, artifice; (*pl.*) the humanities, the learning of the schools; the subjects studied in an ordinary university course; the faculty concerned with such subjects. **be** (or **have**) **art and part:** (*Sc. Law*) Accessory by contrivance or participation; participating, sharing in any way. **black art:** Magic. **fine arts:** Arts or pursuits in which the mind or imagination is chiefly engaged, as painting, music, sculpture, etc. **free** or **liberal arts:** The subjects studied in the Middle Ages by those who sought a liberal education. **mechanical arts:** Those in which the hands and body are chiefly concerned. **useful arts:** Arts or crafts pursued for the sake of utility, not for their own sake; the mechanical arts. **Bachelor of Arts, Master of Arts:** Titles conferred on those who have attained certain degrees of proficiency in the humanities. **art paper:** Paper coated with a composition of china clay, making it suitable for fine printing. **art union,** *n.* An association for the promotion and the encouragement of artists; (*Austral.*) a lottery. **artful,** *a.* Crafty, cunning; characterized by art or skill; artificial, unreal. **artfully,** *adv.* **artfulness,** *n.* **artless,** *a.* Guileless, simple, unaffected; without art; unskilful, clumsy; uncultured, natural. **artlessly,** *adv.* **artlessness,** *n.* **artsman,** *n.* *One instructed in the liberal or the fine arts; *an artist; one who has graduated in Arts. **arty,** *a.* (*colloq.*) Self-conscious or pretentiously aping the artistic. **arty crafty,** *a.* More showily artistic than functional (of furniture, etc.). **arty party,** *n.* A poseur, one who pretends to artistic taste.

artefact, artifact (ar′ ti făkt) [L. *ars*, *artis*, art, *factus*, made], *n.* (*Archæol.*) A man-made stone implement.

Artemisia (ar tė miz′ i ȧ) [L., from Gr. *artemisia* (*Artemis*, Diana)], *n.* A genus of composite plants, containing wormwood, southern-wood, etc.

arterial (ar tēr′ i ȧl) [as foll.], *a.* Pertaining to or contained in an artery or arteries; resembling an artery; ramifying. **arterial road,** *n.* A specially designed road for swift, long-distance traffic between the chief industrial centres; (*Am.*) a main road, a boulevard. **arterialize** (ar tēr′ i ȧ līz), *v.t.* To convert venous into arterial blood by exposing to the action of oxygen in the lungs; to endow with arteries. **arterialization,** *n.* The process of converting venous into arterial blood.

arteriosclerosis (ar tēr i ō skle rō′ sis), *n.* Thickening and loss of elasticity in the walls of the arteries.

arteriotomy (ar tē ri ot′ ō mi), *n.* The opening of an artery for the purpose of bleeding; the dissection of arteries.

arteritis (ar ter ī′ tis), *n.* Inflammation occurring in the arteries.

artery (ar′ tėr i) [L. *artēria*, Gr. *artēria* (prob. from *aeirein*, to raise)], *n.* A large membranous pulsating vessel, conveying blood from the heart to all parts of the body; a main channel.

Artesian (ar tē′ zhȧn) [F. *Artésien*, from *Artois*, an old province of France], *a.* Of or pertaining to Artois; resembling the wells said to have been first dug there. **Artesian well,** *n.* A well in which water is obtained by boring through an upper retentive stratum to a subjacent water-bearing stratum, the water being forced to the surface by natural pressure.

artful, etc. [ART (2)].

arthritic (ar thrit′ ik) [L. *arthrītikus*, Gr. *arthrītikos*, from *arthron*, a joint (orig. through O.F. *artetique*, afterwards corrected)], *a.* Pertaining to or affecting the joints; gouty; good for the gout. **arthritis** (ar thrī′ tis) [-ITIS], *n.* Disease of the joints, especially gout.

arthro- [Gr. *arthron*, a joint], *comb. form.* Pertaining to joints; characterized by joints; *e.g.* **arthrology,** *n.* A treatise on the joints. **arthropathy** (ar throp′ ȧ thi), *n.* Disease of the joints. **arthrosis** (ar thrō′ sis), *n.* Articulation.

Arthropoda (ar throp′ ō dȧ) [Gr. *pous podos*, a foot], *n.pl.* (also **arthropods**) (*Zool.*) Animals with jointed feet; a sub-division of the Annulosa, containing the more highly organized of that class. **arthropodal, arthropodous,** *a.* Of or belonging to the Arthropoda. **arthropod** (ar′ thrȯ pod), *n.* Animal with jointed feet.

artichoke (ar′ ti chōk) [It. *articiocco*, *articioffo* (O.Sp. *alcarchofa*); Arab. *al-kharshūf*], *n.* A composite plant, *Cynara scolymus*, somewhat like a large thistle: the receptacle and fleshy bases of the scales are eaten as a vegetable. **Jerusalem artichoke** (prob. corr. of It. *girasole articiocco*, sunflower artichoke), *n.* A species of sunflower, *Helianthus tuberosus*, the tuberous roots of which are edible.

article (ar′ ti kėl) [F. *article*, L. *articulus*, dim. of *artus*, joint], *n.* A distinct member or portion; a point of faith or duty; a prose composition, complete in itself, in a newspaper, magazine, encyclopædia, etc.; an item, a piece, a distinct detail; a distinct statement, clause, or provision in an agreement, statute, indictment, code, or other document; (*elliptically*) an item of trade, use, or property; a commodity, a thing; a name for the adjectives, *a*, *an*, *the*, when these are considered to form a separate part of speech; (*pl.*) a formal agreement; terms, conditions. *v.t.* To draw up in the form of articles; to bind an apprentice, indenture; indict. **leading article,** *n.* Article in newspaper or other periodical expressing the editorial opinion; a leader, an editorial. **articles of association:** The statutes of a limited liability company. **Articles of War:** A code of discipline for the British Army. **Thirty-nine Articles:** The thirty-nine statements subscribed to by the clergy of the Church of England. **articled** (ar′ tikld), *a.* Bound under article of apprenticeship, esp. of a lawyer's clerk.

articular (ar tik′ ū lȧr) [L. *articulāris* (see ARTICLE)], *a.* Pertaining or relating to the joints. **Articulata,** *n.pl.* Cuvier's name for the third sub-kingdom of animals, comprising insects, crustaceans, centipedes, and worms.

articulate (ar tik′ ū lāt) [as prec.], *v.t.* To connect by means of a joint; to join together in proper order; to joint; to divide sounds into words and syllables; to utter distinctly; to article. *v.i.* To form a joint with; to utter intelligible sounds; to speak distinctly. **articulate** (ar tik′ ū lȧt), **articulated** (ar tik′ ū lā tėd), *a.* Jointed; formed by the distinct and intelligent movements of the organs of speech; (*Biol.*) composed of segments; (*Zool.*) of or belonging to the Articulata. **articulately,** *adv.* **articulateness,** *n.* **articulation** (ar tik ū lā′ shŭn), *n.* The process or method of jointing; articulate sound, utterance, speech; a consonant; (*Anat.*) a joint; a jointed structure; the space between two natural joints; a segment of a jointed body; (*Bot.*) the point at which a deciduous member separates from the plant. **articulator,** *n.* One who pronounces words; one who articulates skeletons. **articulatory,** *a.* Pertaining to articulation.

artifact [ARTEFACT].

artifice (ar′ ti fis) [F. *artifice,* L. *artificium* (*ars artis,* art, *-ficium,* suf. from *facere,* to make)], *n.* Anything contrived by art; human skill; cunning, trickery; a contrivance; a trick. **artificer** (ar tif′ i sėr), *n.* One who practises any art, esp. mechanical art; a craftsman; a maker; a contriver; (*Mil.*) a mechanic employed to make and repair military stores.

artificial (ar ti fish′ ȧl) [as prec.], *a.* Made or produced by art; not natural, not real; affected in manner; factitious, feigned, fictitious. **artificial aerial:** (*Radio.*) A structure used in place of an aerial to test wireless apparatus. **artificial day,** *n.* (*Astron.*) That part of the day between sunrise and sunset. **artificial horizon:** An apparatus for observing with a sextant the altitude of a celestial body, employed in places where there is no visible horizon. **artificial insemination:** Artificial injection of semen into a female. In human beings from the husband (A.I.H.), or from an anonymous donor (A.I.D.). **artificial lines,** *n.pl.* (*Geom.*) Lines so drawn as to represent logarithmal lines and tangents. **artificial manure:** Chemical manure, manure composed of other than animal dung. **artificial respiration,** *n.* Method of reviving a person who has lost consciousness through drowning, etc. **artificial silk,** *n.* Synthetically produced filaments that resemble natural silk in appearance. Also called RAYON. **artificial sunlight:** A medium for producing sunlight effects by artificial sources of radiation. **artificial system,** *n.* (*Nat. Hist.*) A system of classification not based on natural affinity. **artificially,** *adv.* **artificiality** (-fish i ăl′ i ti), *n.* **artificialize,** *v.t.* To render artificial. **artificialness,** *n.*

artillery (ar til′ ėr i) [O.F. *artillerie, artiller,* to fortify, equip, late L. *artillātor,* a maker of machines (*articula, ars,* art)], *n.* Implements of war; engines or devices for casting missiles; guns, cannons, ordnance, with their equipment; the science and practice of gunnery; the branch of the military service in charge of the ordnance; (*fig.*) any immaterial weapon; thunder and lightning. **artillery train,** *n.* Cannon mounted and fitted with all equipment, ready for going into action. **artilleryman,** *n.* **artillerist,** *n.* An artilleryman; one practically acquainted with the principles of gunnery. **artilleryship.** *n.* The management of ordnance; artillery practice.

artiodactyl, -yle (ar ti ō dăk′ til) [Gr. *artios,* of even number, *daktulos,* finger, toe], *a.* (*Zool.*) Having an even number of toes. *n.* An ungulate with an even number of toes. **Artiodactyla,** *n.pl.* A division of the Ungulata, containing those with an even number of toes.

artisan (ar ti zăn′) [F., prob. from It. *artigiano* (L. *artītus,* p.p. of *artīre,* to instruct in arts)], *n.* One trained to practise a manual art; a handicraftsman, a mechanic.

artist (ar′ tist) [F. *artiste,* It. *artista,* late L. *artista* (*ars artis,* art)], *n.* *One skilled in the learned arts; *one proficient in any art requiring skill; a mechanic, artisan, craftsman; one who practises any of the fine arts, especially that of painting; a craftsman who applies to his craft the principles of taste; any artistic performer, an artiste. **artiste** (ar tēst′) [F.], *n.* A public performer, an actor, dancer, musician, acrobat, etc.; a highly proficient cook, hairdresser, etc. **artistic** (ar tis′ tik), **artistical,** *a.* Of or pertaining to art or artists. **artistically,** *adv.*

artless, arty, etc. [ART].

Arum (âr′ ŭm) [L., from Gr. *aron*], *n.* A genus of plants, containing the wake-robin or cuckoo-pint. **arum lily,** *n.* An ornamental plant of the same genus.

arundinaceous (ȧ rŭn di nā′ shŭs) [L. *arundo -inis,* a reed, -ACEOUS], *a.* Resembling a reed; reedy. **arundineous** (ăr ŭn din′ ė ŭs) [L. *arundineus*], *a.* Abounding in reeds; reedy.

Arunta (a run′ tȧ) [native name], *n.* A member of an aboriginal tribe of central Australia.

aruspex [HARUSPEX].

-ary (1) [L. *-ārius -ārium*], *suf.* Pertaining to, connected with; belonging to, engaged in; thing connected with, used in; a place for, as in *elementary, necessary, voluntary; antiquary, statuary; aviary, granary.*

-ary (2) [L. *-āris*], *suf.* Equivalent to -AR and sometimes to -ARY (1); *e.g. exemplary, military, contrary.*

Aryan, Arian (âr′ i ȧn) [Sansk. *ārya,* noble, a worshipper of the gods of the Brahmins; the earlier *Arian* (from L. *ariānus*) of Aria, eastern Persia (Gr. *Areia, Aria,* prob. from O.Pers. *Ariya,* a national name)], *a.* Of or belonging to an ancient race of northern Europe or Central Asia, from whom many of the Indian and most of the European races are descended; the Indo-European or Indo-Germanic race; in German (Nazi) terminology non-Semitic. *n.* The old Aryan language; a member of the Aryan race. **Aryanize,** *v.t.* To imbue with Aryan characteristics.

aryl (ăr′ il) [AR(OMATIC), -YL], *n.* (*Chem.*) A general name for a monovalent radical of the carbocyclic series, *e.g.* phenyl. **arylation,** *n.* The introduction of an aryl radical into a compound.

as (1) (ăz) [A.-S. *eal swā,* all so, quite so (M.E. *alswa, also, als, as*)], *adv.* and *conj.* In the same manner; in the same degree; equally with; thus; while, whilst; since, because, that. *rel. pron.* That, who, which.

as (2) (ăs) [L.], *n.* A Roman copper coin, originally of twelve ounces, but frequently reduced.

as- [AD-], *pref., e.g. assimilate, assume.*

asafœtida (ăs ȧ fet′ i dȧ) [med. L. *asa* (Pers. *aza,* mastic), *fœtida,* stinking], *n.* A gum, with a strong smell of garlic, procured from *Narthex asafetida* and allied plants; used in medicine and cookery.

asbestos (ăz bes′ tŏs) [Gr. inextinguishable (*a-,* not, *sbestos,* from *sbennunai,* to quench)], *n.* A variety of hornblende, of flax-like fibrous structure, practically incombustible, and woven into fireproof fabrics. *a fabulous stone, the heat of which, once kindled, was supposed to be unquenchable. *a.* Made of asbestos, or like asbestos in nature. **asbestic,** *a.* Pertaining to or of the nature of asbestos. **asbestine,** *a.* Made of or like asbestos; incombustible. **asbestoid,** *a.* Of the form of asbestos; fibrous. *n.* A fibrous mineral, also called byssolite.

Ascaris (ăs kar′ is) [Gr. *askaris*], *n.* A genus of intestinal worms, parasitic in man and the lower animals; thread-worms.

ascend (ȧ send′) [L. *ascendere* (*ad-,* to, *scandere,* to climb)], *v.i.* To go or come from a lower to a higher place, position, or degree; to rise, to be raised; to slope upwards; to proceed from a lower to a higher plane of thought, quality, degree, rank; to go back in order of time; (*Astron.*) to move towards the zenith; to come above the horizon; (*Mus.*) to rise in pitch. *v.t.* To climb or go up, to go to a higher position upon; to go to the top, summit, or source of; to mount. **ascendable,** *a.* Capable of being ascended; accessible. **ascendancy, ascendency** (ȧ send′ ȧn si) [O.F. *ascendant,* -ANCY], *n.* Controlling influence; governing power. **ascendant, ascendent** (ȧ send′ ȧnt) [O.F. *ascendant,* L. *ascendens -tem*], *a.* Moving upwards, rising; predominating, ruling; (*Astrol.*) just above the eastern horizon; (*Astron.*) moving towards the zenith. *n.* Ascent, slope, acclivity; one who precedes genealogically, an ancestor; superiority, supremacy; (*Astrol.*) the point of the ecliptic which is rising in the eastern point of the horizon at the moment of a person's birth; the horoscope. **house of the ascendant:** (*Astrol.*) The space from five degrees of the zodiac above to twenty-five degrees below the ascendant. **in the ascendant:** Dominant, predominant, supreme; (*colloq. but incorrectly*) ascending, rising. **lord of the ascendant:** (*Astrol.*) The heavenly body which rules in the ascendant or when the latter is just rising above the horizon.

ascension (å sen′ shůn) [as prec.], *n.* The act of ascending; the ascent of Christ to Heaven; Ascension Day; (*Astron.*) the rising of a celestial body. **oblique ascension:** The arc of the equator intercepted between the first point of Aries and that point of the equator which rises with the heavenly body. **right ascension:** The distance from the first point of Aries, measured upon the celestial equator. **Ascension Day,** *n.* The day on which the Ascension of Jesus Christ is commemorated—the Thursday but one before Whitsuntide, Holy Thursday. **ascensional,** *a.* Pertaining or relating to ascension. **ascensive** (å sen′ siv), *a.* Ascending; on an ascending scale; (*Gram.*) intensive.

ascent (å sent′), *n.* The act or process of ascending, upward motion; an eminence; a slope; a way by which one may ascend; (*fig.*) advancement, rise.

ascertain (ăs ėr tān′) [O.F. *acertainer, acertener* (*à*, to, CERTAIN)], *v.t.* To find out or learn by investigation, examination, or experiment; to make sure of; to find out. **ascertainable,** *a.* **ascertainment,** *n.*

ascetic (å set′ ik) [Gr. *askētikos*, given to exercises, *askētēs*, an athlete, a monk (*askeein*, to work, exercise)], *a.* Of or pertaining to the ascetics or their mode of life; severely abstinent, austere; practising rigorous self-discipline. *n.* One of the early hermits who practised rigorous self-denial and mortification; hence, any person given to rigorous self-denial and mortification; (*pl.*) asceticism; an ascetical treatise. **ascetical,** *a.* Concerned with the attainment of spiritual perfection by means of self-discipline. **ascetically,** *adv.* **asceticism** (å set′ i sizm), *n.*

Ascidium (å sid′ i ům) [L., from Gr. *askidion*, a small leather bottle (*askos*, a wine-skin)], *n.* (*pl.* **-ia**) A genus of tunicate Mollusca with an elastic and leathery tunic. **ascidian,** *a.* Of or belonging to the Ascidia. *n.* Any individual of the Ascidia.

ascites (ă sī′ tēz) [Gr. *askites*], *n.* (*Path.*) Dropsy of the belly or abdomen. **ascitic, ascitical,** *a.* Suffering from abdominal dropsy.

ascititious [ADSCITITIOUS].

Asclepiad (1) (ås klē′ pi åd), *n.* A kind of verse invented by Asclepiades, a Greek poet, consisting of a spondee, two (or three) choriambs, and an iambus. **Asclepiadean** (ås klē pi å dē′ an), ***Asclepiadic** (ås klē pi ăd′ ik), *a.* Of or pertaining to the metre called Asclepiad.

asclepiad (2) (ăs klē′ pi åd) [*asklēpias -ados, Asklēpios*, Æsculapius], *n.* Plant of the genus *Asclepias*, or order Asclepiadaceæ, containing the milkweeds, swallow worts, etc., principally from N. America.

ascorbic acid (ăs kôr′ bik ăs′ id), *n.* (*Chem.*) Vitamin C, occurring in vegetables and fruits.

ascribe (å skrīb′) [L. *ascrībere* (*ad-*, to, *scrībere*, to write)], *v.t.* To attribute, to impute, to assign, to claim (something) for (some one). **ascribable,** *a.* **ascription** (å skrip′ shůn), *n.* The act of attributing; that which is ascribed. **ascriptitious** (ăs krip tish′ ůs) [L. *ascrīptīicus* (*ascrīptus*, p.p. of *ascrībere*)], *a.* Additional; ascribed to (usually on insufficient evidence).

asdic (ăs′ dik) [initials of Allied Submarine Detection Investigation Committee], *n.* (*Nav.*) Instruments and apparatus for detecting the presence and position of submarines.

aseismatic (ă sīz măt′ ik) [SEISMIC], *a.* Proof against earthquake shocks, protecting from earthquake shocks.

asepsis (ă sep′ sis) [Gr. *a-*, not; SEPSIS], *n.* (*Path.*) Freedom from blood-poisoning; the process of asepticizing. **aseptic,** *a.* Not liable to putrefaction; free from tendency to blood-poisoning. *n.* An aseptic substance. **asepticism,** *n.* Treatment by aseptic or antiseptic principles. **asepticize,** *v.t.* To treat by these methods; to render aseptic.

asexual (å seks′ ū ål) [Gr. *a-*, not, SEXUAL], *a.* (*Biol.*) Without sex or sexual functions; (*Bot.*) agamic. **asexuality** (å seks ū ăl′ it i), *n.* **asexually** (å seks′ ū å li), *adv.*

ash (1) (ăsh) [A.-S. *æsce, asce, axe* (cp. Icel. *aska*, Goth. *azgō*)], *n.* The residuum left after the burning of anything combustible; (*pl.*) the remains of anything burnt; the remains of a cremated dead body preserved in an urn or coffin; (*fig.*) a buried corpse, a dead body; a symbol of grief or repentance. **to lay in ashes:** To destroy utterly. **volcanic ash:** (*Geol.*) Powdery matter ejected from volcanoes. **ash-bin,** *n.* A receptacle for household refuse. **ash-cake,** *n.* A corn-cake baked in hot ashes. **ash-can,** *n.* (*Am.*) A dust-bin. **ash-coloured,** *a.* Of a colour between brown and grey. **ash-fire,** *n.* A slow fire used in chemical operations. **ash-furnace,** *n.* A furnace used in glass-making. **ash-heap,** *n.* A collection of ashes and other refuse. **ash-hole,** *n.* A receptacle for ashes beneath a furnace. **ash-pan,** *n.* A pan beneath a furnace or grate for the reception of ashes. **ash-pit,** *n.* An ash-hole. **Ash Wednesday,** *n.* The first day of Lent, so called from the Roman Catholic practice of sprinkling the foreheads of the people with ashes on that day. **The Ashes,** *n.pl.* (*Cricket*) A term used by the *Sporting Times* in 1882 in a mock In Memoriam to the demise of English cricket after the successful visit of the Australians. Since then English and Australian teams visiting one another have endeavoured to 'bring back the ashes.' **ashy,** *a.* Of or composed of ashes; covered with ashes; whitish-grey; pale. **ashy-pale,** *a.* Very pale, ashen. **ashery,** *n.* A place where pearl-ash is manufactured; a receptacle for ashes.

ash (2) (ăsh) [A.-S. *æsc* (cp. Icel. *askr*, O.H.G. *asc*, cp. G. *esche*)], *n.* A forest tree, *Fraxinus excelsior*, with grey bark, pinnate leaves, and tough, close-grained wood; the wood of the ash-tree. *a.* Ashen. **ash-key,** *n.* The winged seed-vessel of the ash. **ash-leaf kidney,** *n.* An early potato with leaves like those of the ash. **mountain ash,** *n.* The rowan-tree, *Pyrus aucuparia.*

ashake (å shāk′), *adv.* On the shake.

ashamed (å shāmd′) [p.p. of *ashame*, obs. v. (*a-*, intens., SHAME), A.-S. *asceamod*], *a.* Affected with shame; abashed by consciousness of error or guilt. **ashamedly,** *adv.*

ashen (1) (ăsh′ ėn), *a.* Ash-coloured; pale; between brown and grey.

ashen (2) (ăsh′ ėn), *a.* Of or pertaining to the ash-tree; made of ash.

ashet (ăsh′ ėt) [F. *assiette*], *n.* (*Sc. and North.*) A large flat plate or dish.

ashine (å shīn′), *adv.* Shining.

ashiver (å shiv′ ėr), *adv.* In a shiver.

ashlar (ăsh′ lår) [O.F. *aiseler*, L. *axilla*, dim. of *axis*, axis, board, plank], *n.* Square-hewn stone used in building; masonry built of this; thin masonry built as a facing to rubble or brick work; rough-hewn stone as it leaves the quarry. **ashlar-work,** *n.* Masonry of hewn as opposed to unhewn stones. **ashlared,** *a.* Covered with ashlar. **ashlaring,** *n.* The quartering to which laths are nailed in garrets, in order to cut off the angle between roof and floor; ashlar masonry.

ashore (å shôr′), *adv.* To the shore; on the shore; on land.

ashram (ash′ râm) [Hind.]. In India, a hermitage, place for reflection; sanctuary.

Asian (ā′ shi ăn, -shàn) [L. *Asiānus*, Gr. *Asiānos*, from *Asia*], *a*. Asiatic. **Asiatic** (ā shi ăt′ ik) [L. *Asiāticus*, Gr. *Asiātikos*], *a*. Pertaining, relating, or belonging to Asia. *n*. A native of Asia.

aside (à sīd′) [formerly *on side*], *adv*. At, to, or towards one side; away. *n*. Something spoken aside so as to be audible only to the person addressed, esp. by an actor, which the others on the stage are not supposed to hear; an indirect effort.

***asinego** (ăs i nē′ gō) [Sp. *asnico*, dim. of *asno*, ass], *n*. A little ass; a fool, a duffer.

asinine (ăs′ in īn) [L. *asinīnus* (*asinus*, an ass)], *a*. Of or pertaining to asses; having the character of an ass; stupid, obstinate. **asininity** (ăs in in′ i ti), *n*. Asinine behaviour; obstinate stupidity.

-asis [L. *-ăsis*, Gr. *-āsis*], *suf*. Forming names of diseases; *e.g. elephantiasis*.

asitia (ă sish′ yà) [Gr., want of food], *n*. (*Path.*) Distaste for food, want of appetite.

ask (ask) [A.-S. *ascian*], *v.t*. To request; to seek to obtain by words; to question, to solicit, to demand, to state a price required; to question, to inquire of; to inquire concerning; to request to be informed about; to invite; (*pop.*) to publish the banns of marriage. *v.i*. To make a request, petition, or demand; to inquire. **asker**, *n*. One who asks or inquires; a petitioner, a suppliant, a beggar. **asking**, *n*. Petitioning; expressed wish; solicitation; (*pop.*) the publication of the banns of marriage.

askance (à skăns′, -skans), **askant** (à skănt′) [etym. doubtful], *adv*. Obliquely, sideways, askew, squintingly; (*fig.*) with mistrust. **v.t*. To turn away.

askari (ăs ka′ rē) [Ar. *askar*, an army], *n*. An E. African native soldier.

askew (à skū′) [SKEW], *adv*. Askance, asquint; in an oblique direction. *a*. Oblique, awry, skew.

***aslake** (à slāk′) [A.-S. *aslacian*], *v.t*. To cause to become slack; to assuage, to appease. *v.i*. To become slack, to be slaked, become cool.

aslant (à slant′), *adv*. Slantingly, obliquely. *prep*. Across, in a slanting direction; oblique.

asleep (à slēp′), *adv*. and *pred.a*. In or into a state of sleep; (*fig.*) dead.

aslope (à slōp′) [A.-S. *aslopen*, p.p. of *aslūpan*, to slip away; or from *a*-, on, SLOPE], *a*. Sloping, oblique. *adv*. With a slope, aslant; obliquely, crosswise.

a-smoulder (à smōl′ dėr), *adv*. Smouldering.

a-snort (à snôrt′), *adv*. Snorting.

asp (1) (ăsp, asp), **aspic** (1) (ăs′ pik) [L. *aspis*, Gr. *aspis*], *n*. A small venomous hooded serpent, *Naja haje*, the Egyptian cobra; a European viper, *Vipera aspis*; (*fig.*) any venomous serpent.

asp (2) (ăsp, asp), **aspen** (ăs′ pėn) [A.-S. *æspe* (cp. O.H.G. *aspâ*, G. *espe*)], *n*. *Populus tremula*, the trembling poplar, remarkable for its quivering leaves.

asparagus (à spăr′ à gùs) [L., from Gr. *asparagos* (etym. doubtful)], *n*. A culinary plant, the tender shoots of which are eaten.

aspect (ăs′ pekt) [L. *aspectus*, p.p. of *aspicere*, to behold (*ad*-, to, at, *spicere*, to look)], *n*. Look, view; looking, way of looking; (*Astrol.*) the situation of one planet with respect to another; the direction in which something is turned, phase; appearance, expression. ***aspectable** (à spek′ tàbl), *a*. Visible; worthy to be looked upon.

aspen (ăs′ pėn), *n*. [ASP (2)]. *a*. Belonging to the asp; made of the wood of the asp; like an asp, trembling, quaking; (*fig.*) always wagging (of a tongue).

asper (ăs′ pėr) [F. *aspre* or It. *aspero*, late Gr. *aspron*, white money (*aspros -on*, white, perh. from L. *asper*, rough)], *n*. A small Turkish silver coin, now only money of account.

***asperate** (ăs′ pėr āt) [L. *asperātus*, p.p. of *asperāre*, to roughen (*asper*, rough)], *v.t*. To roughen; to make rough. **asperation** (ăs pėr ā′ shùn), *n*. A making rough; roughness.

asperge (à spĕrj′) [F. *asperger*, L. *aspergere* (*ad*-, to, *spargere*, to sprinkle)], *v.t*. To besprinkle, esp. with holy water. *n*. An aspergillum. **asperges** [L., thou shalt sprinkle], *n*. The sprinkling of the congregation with holy water by the celebrant of High Mass. **aspergillum** (ăs pėr jil′ ùm) [-*illum*, dim. suf.], *n*. The brush used to sprinkle holy water. **aspergillus**, *n*. (*Biol.*) A genus of microscopic fungi or moulds growing on decaying organic matter, named from their resemblance to the aspergillum.

asperity (à sper′ i ti) [O.F. *asprete*, L. *asperitātem*, nom. *asperitas* (*asper*, rough)], *n*. Roughness of surface; a rugged excrescence; harshness of sound; severity, bleakness; moroseness, crabbedness, acrimony.

aspermia (à spĕr′ mi à) [as foll.], *n*. (*Path.*) Total absence of semen.

aspermous (à spĕr′ mùs) [Gr. *a*-, not, *sperma*, seed], *a*. (*Bot.*) Without seed; destitute of seed.

asperse (à spĕrs′) [L. *aspersus*, p.p. of *aspergere* (see ASPERGE)], *v.t*. To scatter or strew upon, to besprinkle; to bespatter with calumnies, to defame. **aspersive**, **aspersory** (à spĕr′ sò ri), *a*. **aspersively**, *adv*. **aspersorium** (ăs pėr sôr′ i ùm), *n*. The vessel from which holy water is sprinkled.

aspersion (à spĕr′ shùn), *n*. Calumny, slander, a false report or insinuation; the act of sprinkling; that which is sprinkled.

asphalt, asphalte (ăs′ fălt, ăs fălt′) [late L. *asphaltum*, Gr. *asphalton* (foreign in origin)], *n*. Mineral pitch, a dark brown or black form of bitumen; bituminous limestone, or an artificial substitute (often made with tar), used for paving, flooring, etc. *v.t*. To cover, pave, or line with asphalt. *a*. Pertaining to asphalt; consisting of or containing asphalt.

aspheterism (ăs fet′ ėr izm) [Gr. *a*-, not, *spheteros*, one's own, -ISM], *n*. Communism; the negation of private property. **aspheterize**, *v.i*. To practise this doctrine.

asphodel (ăs′ fò del) [Gr. *asphodelos* (etym. doubtful), see also DAFFODIL], *n*. A mythic undying flower, said to bloom in the Elysian fields; (*Bot.*) the English name of the liliaceous genus *Asphodelus*, comprising the king's spear. **bog asphodel**, *n*. A British moorland plant, *Narthecium ossifragum*, sometimes called the mountain asphodel.

asphyxia (ăs fiks′ i à), **asphyxy** (ăs fiks′ i) [Gr. *asphuxia* (*a*-, not, *sphuzein*, to throb, pulsate)], *n*. Stoppage of the pulse; suspended animation, produced by stoppage of the arterialization of the blood; suffocation. **asphyxial**, *a*. Of or pertaining to asphyxia. **asphyxiate**, *v.t*. To affect with asphyxia; to suffocate. **asphyxiation** (ăs fiks i ā shùn), *n*. The act of asphyxiating or the process of being asphyxiated; suffocation. **asphyxiator** (ăs fiks′ i ā tòr), *n*. One who or that which asphyxiates; a kind of fire annihilator employing carbonic acid gas; an apparatus for testing drains by means of smoke.

***aspic** (1) [ASP (1)].

aspic (2) (ăs′ pik) [F., etym. doubtful], *n*. A savoury dish composed of game, or hard-boiled eggs, fish, etc., embedded in jelly.

Aspidistra (ăs pi dis′ tra) [Gr. *aspis*, a shield; *astron*, star], *n*. (*Bot.*) A liliaceous genus including the parlour palm.

aspirant [ASPIRE].

aspirate (ăs′ pi rāt) [L. *aspirātus*, p.p. of *aspirāre* (see ASPIRE)], *v.t*. To pronounce with a full breath; to prefix the letter *h* or its equivalent; to draw out gas from a vessel. *a*. Aspirated; pronounced with a breathing. *n*. A letter pronounced with the sound of *h*.

aspiration (1) (ăs pi rā' shŭn), *n.* The act of breathing; the act of aspirating; an aspirated sound.

aspiration (2) (ăs pi rā' shŭn), *n.* The act of aspiring; steadfast desire; a seeking for better things.

aspirator (ăs' pi rā tŏr), *n.* One or that which aspirates; an instrument for drawing air or gas through a tube; an appliance enabling one to breathe in poison gas; (*Med.*) an instrument for evacuating a cavity by means of an exhausted receiver; a winnowing- or fanning-machine.

aspire (ȧ spīr') [L. *aspīrāre* (*ad-*, to, *spīrāre*, to breathe, blow)], *v.i.* To long, desire eagerly; to pant after; to seek to attain; (*fig.*) to rise, to mount up. **v.t.* To long for ardently; to mount up, to reach. **aspiring,** *a.* Eagerly desirous of some high object, ambitious; tapering upward, soaring. **aspiringly,** *adv.* **aspiringness,** *n.* **aspirant,** *a.* Aspiring, aiming at a higher position. *n.* One who aspires; a candidate.

aspirin (ăs' pi rin), *n.* (*Med.*) Name for acetyl-salicylic acid, used as an anodyne.

asplenium [SPLEENWORT].

a-spout (ȧ spout') [*a-*, on, SPOUT], *adv.* Spouting.

a-sprawl (ȧ sprawl'), *adv.* In a sprawling attitude.

a-spread (ȧ spred'), *adv.* Spread out.

a-sprout (ȧ sprout'), *adv.* In a sprouting state.

a-squat (ȧ skwot'), *adv.* In a squatting attitude.

a-squint (ȧ skwint') [*a-*, on, and a word corresponding to Dut. *schuinte*, slope, slant], *adv.* With a squint; obliquely; with distrust, suspicion; with crafty designs, furtively, awry.

ass (ăs) [A.-S. *assa*, *esol* (cp. Dut. *ezel*, G. *esel*, Goth. *asilus*, L. *asinus*)], *n.* (*pl.* **asses**) A quadruped, *Equus asinus*, allied to the horse, but of smaller size, with long ears and a tufted tail; (*fig.*) (also *pron.* ars) a stupid, obstinate fellow. **to make an ass of:** To treat as an ass, to render ridiculous. **to make an ass of oneself:** To stultify oneself; play the fool. ***ass head,** *n.* A person of dull intellect, a block-head. **asses' bridge,** *n.* The 5th proposition of Euclid, Bk. I.; the *pons asinorum.*

assafetida [ASAFŒTIDA].

assagai, assegai (ăs' ȧ gī) [Arab. *azzaghayah* (*al*, the, Berber *zaghayah*); either through F. *azagaye* or Port, *azagaia*], *n.* A slender lance of hard wood, chiefly applied to the missile lances of the South African tribes. *v.t.* To wound or kill with an assagai.

assai (ȧ sī') [It., enough], *adv.* (*Mus.*) Very; as *largo assai*, very slow.

assail (ȧ sāl') [O.F. *asailer*, *assailler*, late L. *adsalīre* (*ad-*, to, at, *salīre*, to leap)], *v.t.* To attack violently by physical means or with argument, abuse, censure, entreaty, or hostile influence, temptation, snares, and the like; to dash against; to approach with intent to overcome; *to tempt; *to woo. **assailable,** *a.* **assailant,** *a.* Assailing, attacking. *n.* One who assails.

assassin (ȧ săs' in) [F. *assassin* or It. *assassino*, med. L. *assassīnus*, Arab. *hashshāshin*, hashish-eaters], *n.* One of a body of Moslem fanatics, in the time of the Crusades, who were sent forth (maddened with hashish, or Indian hemp) to murder the Christian leaders; one who kills by surprise or secret assault (generally for other than private motives). **assassinate,** *v.t.* To kill by surprise or secret assault; to murder by sudden violence (usually for other than private motives). **assassination** (-nā' shŭn), *n.* The act of assassinating; murder by secret and sudden assault. **assassinator,** *n.*

assault (ȧ sawlt') [O.F. *asaut*, *assaut*, L. *ad-*, to, at, *saltus*, a leap (ASSAIL)], *n.* The act of assailing; a violent attack with material or immaterial weapons; the charge of an attacking body on a fortified post; (*Law*) a threatening word or act; an attempt at rape. *v.t.* To make a violent onset or attack on, with material or immaterial weapons; to attack (a fortified post) by sudden rush; to storm; (*Law*) to attack with threatening words or with blows; to attempt rape. **assault and battery:** (*Law*) An assault with action as well as words. **assault-at-arms:** An attack in fencing; a display of military exercises. **assaultable,** *a.*

assay (ȧ sā') [O.F. *assai*, L. *exagium*, from *exagere*, *exigere*, to weigh, try (*ex-*, out, *agere*, to drive, deal)], *n.* Trial, examination; esp. the scientific determination of the quantity of metal in an ore, alloy, bullion, or coin; the metal to be examined; a trying, attempt, endeavour. *v.t.* To try, to test; to determine the amount of metal in an ore, alloy, bullion, or coin; to try to do, attempt; *to taste food or drink before it is offered to a sovereign or noble. *v.i.* To attempt, to endeavour. **assay-balance,** *n.* A very delicate balance, used in assaying. **assay-master,** *n.* An officer of the Mint, appointed to assay bullion and coin. **assay ton,** *n.* A weight of 29,166⅔ grams. **assayer,** *n.* One who assays bullion; *an officer whose duty it was to taste food and drink before his lord. **assaying,** *n.* The act or process of determining the amount of a particular metal in a compound.

assegai [ASSAGAI].

assemble (ȧ sem' bĕl) [O.F. *assembler*, late L. *assimulāre* (*ad-*, to; *simul*, together)], *v.t.* To call together; to bring together into one mass or heap; to fit together the component parts. *v.i.* To meet or come together; to gather, to congregate. *n.* (*Mil.*) An assembly. **assemblage** (ȧ sem' blāj), *n.* A gathering, assembling; a concourse; a collection; (*Carp.*) a putting together. ***assemblance** (1), *n.* Assemblage, assembly. **assemblance** (2) [SEMBLANCE], *n.* Appearance, show.

assembly (ȧ sem' bli), *n.* The act of assembling; the state of being assembled; a body of people met together for some common purpose; a deliberative, legislative, or religious body; (*Mil.*) the second beat of the drum summoning soldiers to prepare to march. **assembly line,** *n.* A serial collection of workers and machines operating from stage to stage in assembling some product. **assemblyman,** *n.* A member of a legislative assembly. **assembly-room,** *n.* A room in which public assemblies, balls, concerts, etc., are held. **General Assembly,** *n.* The body of representatives that directs the affairs of the Church of Scotland. **Legislative Assembly,** *n.* (*Polit.*) The lower house of legislature in British colonies, etc. **Westminster Assembly,** *n.* The body of divines appointed in 1643 by the Long Parliament to assist in revising the government and liturgy of the Church of England.

assent (ȧ sent') [O.F. *asenter*, L. *assentīre* (*ad-*, to, *sentīre*, to feel)], *v.i.* To agree to or sanction (something proposed); to admit (a statement) as true, *n.* The act of admitting, agreeing to, or concurring in; sanction, agreement, acquiescence. **royal assent:** The assent of the sovereign to Bills passed by both Houses of Parliament. **assentation** (ăs ĕn tā' shŭn), *n.* The action of assenting, esp. with obsequiousness or servility. **assentient,** *a.* Assenting to. *n.* One who assents or agrees. **assentingly,** *adv.* **assentor,** *n.* One who gives assent, esp. one who signs the nomination of a Parliamentary candidate after the proposer and seconder.

assert (ȧ sĕrt') [L. *assertus*, p.p. of *asserere*, to add to, take to oneself (*ad-*, to, *serere*, to join, bind)], *v.t.* To affirm, to declare positively; to maintain; to insist on a claim, right, etc. **assertable,** *a.* **assertion,** *n.* The act of asserting a claim or right; a positive statement, an affirmation. **assertive,** *a.* Characterized by assertion, dogmatical. **self-assertive:** Insisting on one's real or supposed rights; assuming. **assertively,** *adv.* **assertiveness,** *n.* **assertor,** *n.* One who maintains or defends; an advocate; one who makes an assertion.

assess (ȧ ses') [O.F. *assesser*, late L. *assessāre*, freq. of *assidēre* (*ad-*, to, *sedēre*, to sit)], *v.t.* To fix by authority the amount of a tax, fine, etc., for a person or community; to value property for the purpose of taxation; to value, to estimate, to pay. **assessable,** *a.* Capable of being assessed; liable to be assessed. **assessably,** *adv.* **assessment,** *n.* The act of assessing; the amount assessed; a scheme of rating or taxation; an official valuation for those purposes; estimation, appraisal. **assessment-work,** *n.* (*Mining*) Work done each year on a claim, to maintain title.

assessor (á ses' ŏr), *n.* One who shares another's rank and sits beside him; one who makes an assessment; (*Law*) one who sits near and advises a judge or magistrate on technical points, commercial usage, navigation, etc. **assessorship,** *n.*

assets (ăs' ets) [A.-F. *asetz,* O.F. *asez,* enough, late L. *ad satis,* sufficiency (*satis,* enough)], *n.pl.* Goods sufficient to satisfy a testator's debts and legacies; property or effects that may be applied for this purpose; the effects of an insolvent debtor; all the property of a person or company which may be liable for outstanding debts; property in general.

asseverate (ă sev' ėr āt) [L. *asseverātus,* p.p. of *asseverāre* (*ad-,* to, *sevērus,* earnest, serious)], *v.t.* To affirm with solemnity; to assert positively. **asseveration** (-ā' shŭn), *n.* The act of asseverating; a solemn affirmation; an emphatic declaration or confirmation, an oath.

assiduous (á sid' ū ŭs) [L. *assiduus* from *assidēre* (see ASSESS)], *a.* Constant in application; diligent. **assiduously,** *adv.* **assiduousness,** *n.* **assiduity** (ăs i dū' i ti), *n.* Constant or close application to the matter in hand, perseverance, diligence; (*pl.*) persistent endeavours to please, constant attentions.

assiege (á sēj') [O.F. *asegier,* late L. *assediāre* (*ad-,* to, *sedium,* siege)], *v.t.* To besiege. *n.* A siege.

assiento (á syen' tō, ăs i en' tō) [Sp., a contract], *n.* A contract or convention between the King of Spain and other powers for furnishing slaves for the Spanish dominions in America, esp. that between Great Britain and Spain at the peace of Utrecht (1713).

assign (á sīn') [O.F. *assigner,* L. *assignāre* (*ad-,* to, *signāre,* to mark)], *v.t.* To allot, to apportion; to designate for a specific purpose; to name, to fix; to point out, to ascribe, to attribute; (*Law*) to transfer, to surrender. *n.* One to whom a property or right is transferred; *an appurtenance, an appendage. **assignable,** *a.* Capable of being transferred, designated, or pointed out as source or reason.

assignat (ăs' ig năt, a sin ya') [F.], *n.* Paper money issued by the Revolutionary Government of France (1790–96) on the security of State lands.

assignation (ăs ig nā' shŭn) [ASSIGN], *n.* Appointment of a particular time or place for a meeting, esp. illicit; the act of assigning; attribution of origin; an appointment; transference of property or right.

assignee (ăs i nē'), *n.* An agent, a representative; (*Law*) one to whom a right or property is transferred; (*Austral. hist.*) a convict assigned as a servant. **assignees in bankruptcy:** Persons to whom a bankrupt's estate is assigned and who manage it for the benefit of the creditors.

assignment (á sīn' mėnt), *n.* The act of assigning; allotment, allocation; specific task; specification of reasons; attribution; legal transference of right or property; the instrument by which such transference is effected; the right or property transferred; (*Austral. hist.*) the formal assignment of a convict to private service. **assignment in bankruptcy:** The transference of a bankrupt's estate to assignees for the benefit of his creditors.

assignor (ăs i nôr'), *n.* One who transfers a right or property.

assimilate (á sim' i lāt) [L. *assimilāre* (*ad-,* *similis,* like), -ATE], *v.t.* To make like to, to liken, to compare; to take as nutriment and convert into living tissue, to incorporate in the substance of an organism; (*fig.*) to incorporate. *v.i.* To become similar; to be incorporated in the substance of a living organism. **assimilable,** *a.* Capable of being assimilated. **assimilability** (á sim il á bil' i ti), *n.* Capability of being assimilated. **assimilation** (-lā' shŭn), *n.* The act or process of assimilating; the state of being assimilated; comparison; the process by which an organism converts nourishment into its own substance. **assimilative,** *a.* Having the power of assimilating; (*rare*) capable of being assimilated. **assimilator,** *n.* One who or that which assimilates. **assimilatory,** *a.* Tending to assimilate.

assise (á sīz') [F. (ASSIZE)], *n.* (*Geol.*) A formation consisting of parallel beds with the same organic remains throughout.

assist (á sist') [F. *assister,* L. *assistere* (*ad-,* to, *sistere,* to place, from *stāre,* to stand)], *v.t.* To help, to aid, to support, to succour; to be present (at). **assistance,** *n.* Help, aid, support, succour, furtherance; the persons present (at). **assistant,** *a.* Aiding, helping, auxiliary. *n.* One who assists another; an auxiliary. **assistor,** *n.* (*Law*) Assistant; one who aids or is accessory.

assize (á sīz') [O.F. *asise,* orig. fem. p.p. of *asseoir,* sit at (L. *assidēre,* see ASSESS)], *n.* *A formal session or sitting; *a decree or edict made at such sitting; *ordinance, regulation, esp. respecting weight and price, hence standard of quantity, price, or quality, esp. of bread and ale; (*Law*) a trial in which sworn assessors decide questions of fact; an action so tried or decided; (*pl.*) the sessions held periodically by the judges (since 1815) of the Supreme Court in each county in England for the administration of civil and criminal justice. **v.t.* To fix by a legal ordinance the weight, measure, or price of; to assess, to rate. **assizer,** *n.* *One who had charge of an assizes of weights, measures, or prices; (*Sc. Law*) a juryman.

associate (á sō' shi āt) [L. *associāre* (*ad-,* to, *sociāre,* to join, from *socius,* an ally), -ATE], *v.t.* To join (persons) for a common purpose; to unite (things); to combine, to connect; to connect oneself as partner. *v.i.* To unite or combine for a common purpose; to keep company or have familiar intercourse (followed by *with*). *a.* Connected, joined; confederate, allied; in the same group or category. *n.* A confederate, an ally; a partner, colleague, coadjutor; a member of an association or institution; something generally found with another. **associateship,** *n.* **associability** (-bil' i ti), *n.* **associable,** *a.* *Companionable; capable of being (mentally) associated; (*Physiol.*) liable to be affected by sympathy with other parts. **association** (á sō si ā' shŭn), *n.* The act of combining for a common purpose; a society formed for the promotion of some common object; fellowship, intimacy, connexion; (*Psych.*) mental connexion between an object and ideas related to it; an idea connected with some object and recalled to the mind in connexion therewith. **Association Football,** *n.* (*Sport*) Football played with a round ball which must not be touched with the hands. **deed of association:** A legal instrument in which the particulars of a limited liability company must be recorded on its formation. **associational,** *a.* **associationism,** *n.* (*Psych.*) The theory which accounts for mental and moral phenomena by association of ideas. **associationist,** *n.* **associative** (á sō' shi á tiv), *a.* Tending to associate.

assoil (á soil') [O.F. *assoile,* pres. sing. of *assonare,* L. *absolvere* (*ab-,* away, *solvere,* to loosen)], *v.t.* To pardon, to absolve from sin; to atone for, expiate; to discharge, acquit; to get rid of, to dispel; to discharge (a duty). **assoilzie** (á soil' yė), *v.t.* (*Sc. Law*) To acquit.

assonant (ăs' ŏ nănt) [F., from L. *assonānt -em,* pres.p. of *assonāre* (*ad-,* to, *sonāre,* to sound; *sonus,* sound)], *a.* Corresponding in vowel-sound, rhyming in the accented vowels, but not in the consonants. *n.* An assonant word. **assonance,** *n.* The quality of being assonant; a word or syllable answering to another in sound; correspondence or resemblance in other respects.

assort (á sôrt') [O.F. *assorter* (*à,* to, *sorte,* sort, manner, kind, L. *sors*)], *v.t.* To arrange or dispose in sorts or lots; to arrange into different classes; to furnish with articles so arranged. *v.i.* To suit, to agree, to match; to be in congruity or harmony with. **assortment,** *n.* A collection of things assorted; a collection of things of various kinds; the act of assorting; the state of being assorted.

assuage (á swāj′) [O.F. *assouagier*, L. *assuāviāre* (*ad-*, to, *suāvis*, sweet)], *v.t.* To sweeten, allay, mitigate; to soothe, to lessen the violence of; to appease, satisfy. **v.i.* To abate, to subside. **assuagement,** *n.* The act of assuaging; mitigation, abatement; a lenitive medicine or application. **assuasive,** *a.* Assuaging, mitigating, soothing. *n.* A soothing medicine or application.

***assuefaction** (ăs ū ė făk′ shŭn) [L. *assuēfacere*, to make accustomed (*assuētus*, p.p. of *assuēscere*, to accustom, *facere*, to make)], *n.* The act of accustoming; the state of being accustomed. ***assuetude** (ăs′ ū ė tūd) [-TUDE], *n.* The state of being accustomed.

assume (á sūm′) [L. *assūmere*, to take to oneself (*ad-*, to, *sūmere*, to take)], *v.t.* To take to oneself; to receive, adopt; to take upon oneself, to put on, to undertake; to arrogate, pretend to, to claim; to take for granted; to pretend, feign. *v.i.* To be arrogant or pretentious; to claim more than is one's due. **assumed,** *a.* Usurped, pretended; taken for granted. **assumedly,** *adv.* **assuming,** *a.* Arrogant, haughty. *n.* Assumption, presumption. **assumption** (á sŭmp′ shŭn) [L. *assūmptus*, p.p. of *assūmere*], *n.* The act of assuming; the thing assumed; a supposition, a postulate; arrogance; (*Eccles.*) ascent to heaven, esp. the reception of the Virgin Mary into heaven; the feast (Aug. 15) in honour of this event; (*Law*) an oral or unsealed contract. **assumptive,** *a.* Assumed; taken to oneself; taken for granted; arrogant.

assumpsit (á sŭmp′ sit) [L., he has taken upon him], *n.* (*Law*) An oral or unsealed contract, founded on a consideration; an action to enforce such a contract.

assumption [ASSUME].

assure (á shoor′) [O.F. *aseürer*, late L. *adsēcūrāre* (*ad-*, to, *sēcūrus*, safe)], *v.t.* To make safe, secure, or certain; to give confidence to, to encourage; to insure the payment of compensation in case of loss, to insure. **assurance** (á shoor′ áns), *n.* The act of assuring; a positive declaration; certainty, security; self-reliance, intrepidity; audacity, impudence; insurance; a contract to pay a given sum on a person's death in return for an annual premium; (*Law*) evidence of the conveyance of property. **assured,** *a.* Safe; made certain, confident; presumptuous, full of assurance. **assuredly** (á shoor′ ėd li], *adv.* **assuredness,** *n.* **assurer,** *n.* One who or that which gives assurance; an insurer, an underwriter; one who takes out a policy of assurance. **assuror,** *n.* (*Law*) An assurer, an underwriter. **assuring,** *a.* Creating assurance, inspiring confidence. **assuringly,** *adv.*

assurgent (á sĕrj′ ėnt) [L. *assurgere* (*ad-*, to, against, *surgere*, to rise)], *a.* Rising, ascending; rising aggressively; (*Bot.*) pointing upwards; rising upwards in a curve.

Assyrian (á sir′ i án), *a.* Of or pertaining to Assyria. *n.* A native of Assyria; the language of Assyria. **Assyriology** (á sir i ol′ ŏ ji) [-LOGY], *n.* The study of the history, language and antiquities of Assyria. **Assyriological** (-ŏ loj′ ik ál), *a.* **Assyriologist,** *n.*

assythment (á sīth′ mėnt) [Sc. *assyth, assythe*, M.E. *aseth*, O.F. *aset* (F. *assez*), enough, from late L. *ad satis* (cp. ASSETS, -MENT)], *n.* (*Sc.*) Satisfaction for an injury; compensation.

a-starboard (á star′ bŏrd), *adv.* (*Naut.*) Toward the right side of the ship (looking forward).

a-stare (á stâr′), *adv.* Staring, prominent, glaring.

astatic (á stăt′ ik) [Gr. *astatos* (*a-*, not, *sta-*, stem of verb, stand)], *a.* Not remaining fixed; not influenced by the earth's magnetism.

Aster (ăs-, as tėr) [L., from Gr. *astēr*, a star], *n.* A genus of compositous plants. **China aster:** A similar and allied flower, *Callistephus chinensis.*

-aster [L., diminutive and contemptuous termination], *suf.* After the manner of, somewhat after the manner of; as in *criticaster, poetaster.*

asteria (á stēr′ i á) [L.], *n.* A precious stone mentioned by Pliny; perhaps the 'asteriated' sapphire.

Asterias (á stēr′ i ăs) [Mod. L., from Gr. *asterias*, starry], *n.* (*pl.* **-iae**) A genus of Echinoderms, containing the common starfish. **asterid** (ăs′ tėr id), *n.* Any individual of the Asteridæ or starfish family.

asterisk (ăs′ tėr isk) [L. *asteriscus*, Gr. *asteriskos*], *n.* A mark (*) used in printing to call attention to a note, to mark omission, etc.; a star-shaped device placed over the paten in the Greek Church to prevent anything touching the Elements. *v.t.* To mark with an asterisk.

asterism (ăs′ tėr izm) [Gr. *asterismos*], *n.* (*Astron.*) A constellation; a small cluster of stars; *an asterisk; three asterisks placed thus (⁂) to draw attention to something important; (*Min.*) the star-like appearance in some crystals, as in the 'asteriated' sapphire.

astern (á stĕrn′), *adv.* (*Naut.*) In, at, or towards the stern of a ship, behind a ship; (*fig.*) in the rear, behind.

asteroid (ăs′ tėr oid), *a.* Having the figure or appearance of a star. *n.* (*Astron.*) One of the group of small planets between the orbits of Mars and Jupiter; a planetoid, a minor planet. **asteroidal** (ăs tėr oid′ ál), *a.*

Asterolepis (ăs tėr ol′ ė pis) [Gr. *astēr*, a star, *lepis*, a scale], *n.* (*Palæont.*) A genus of gigantic ganoid fishes from the Old Red Sandstone.

asthenia (ăs thē′ ni á) [mod. L., from Gr. *astheneia*, from *asthenes*, weak (*a-*, without, *sthenos*, strength)], *n.* Absence of strength; debility, diminution or loss of vital power. **asthenic** (ăs then′ ik), *a.*

asthma (ăs′ má) [Gr. *asthma -matos*, from *azein*, to breathe hard (*aein*, to blow)], *n.* Chronic shortness of breath; a disease of respiration characterized by cough, wheezing, and constriction of the chest. **asthmatic** (ăs măt′ ik), *a.* Of or pertaining to, affected with or good for asthma; (*fig.*) wheezy, puffing. *n.* A person affected with asthma. **asthmatical,** *a.* **asthmatically,** *adv.*

astigmatism (á stig′ má tizm) [Gr. *a-*, not, *stigma*, point], *n.* A defect of the eye or of a lens as a result of which a point source of light tends to be focused as a line. **astigmatic** (ăs tig măt′ ik), *a.* Of or pertaining to or characterized by astigmatism.

astir (á stĕr′) [*a*, on, STIR], *adv.* In motion; in commotion, in excitement; out of bed.

astomatous (á stom′ á tŭs) [Gr. *a-*, without, *stoma -atos*, a mouth], *a.* Mouthless; of or pertaining to the Astomata, a group of Infusoria without a determinate mouth. **astomous** (ăs′ tŏ mŭs) [Gr. *astomos*], *a.* Astomatous; (*Bot.*) without a deciduous operculum.

astonish (á ston′ ish) [earlier *astony*, M.E. *astone*, O.F. *estoner* (F. *étonner*), to amaze (L. *ex-*, out, *tonāre*, to thunder)], *v.t.* To strike with sudden surprise or wonder; to amaze, to surprise. **astonishing,** *a.* **astonishingly,** *adv.* **astonishment,** *n.* The act of astonishing; the state of being astonished; amazement; *stupefaction, stupor; an object causing amazement. ***astony** (á ston′ i) [M.E. *astone*], *v.t.* To stun, to paralyse, to astound. ***astonied,** *a.* Stunned, dazed, bewildered, astonished.

astound (á stound′) [M.E. *astoned*, p.p. of *astone*], *v.t.* *To stun, to stupefy; to strike with amazement; to shock with alarm, wonder, or surprise. **astounding,** *a.* **astoundingly,** *adv.* **astoundment,** *n.*

astraddle (á străd′ ėl), *adv.* In a straddling position; astride.

astragal (ăs′ trá gál) [L. *astragalus*, Gr. *astragalos*], *n.* The astragalus; (*Arch.*) a small semicircular moulding, or bead, round the top or the bottom of columns; a moulding round a cannon, or round a large pipe. **Astragalus** (ă străg′ ă lŭs), *n.* The ball of the ankle-joint; the bone which the tibia articulates below; (*Bot.*) a large genus of leguminous plants, containing the milk-vetch.

astrakhan (ăs tră kăn′), *n.* A fine kind of furry wool, obtained from lambs in Astrakhan, Persia, and Syria; a fabric with a pile in imitation of this.

astral (ăs′ trăl) [L. *astrālis* (*astrum*, Gr. *astron*, a star)], *a.* Of or pertaining to the stars; starry; star-shaped. *n.* An astral-lamp. **astral-body,** *n.* (*Spiritualism*) A kind of spiritual body which occultists claim to be able to project to a distance, and so to exercise the power of bilocation; the ethereal or spiritual body round which the physical body is built up; the spirit. **astral-lamp,** *n.* A lamp similar in character to an argand lamp, and throwing a shadowless light on the table. **astral-spirits,** *n.pl.* Spirits formerly believed to inhabit the heavenly bodies.

a-strand (ă strănd′), *adv.* On the strand, stranded.

astray (ă strā′) [prob. O.F. *estraié*, p.p. of *estraier*, to stray (L. *extra-*, out of bounds, *vagāre*, to wander)], *adv.* and *a.* Out of the right way.

astrict (ă strikt′) [L. *astrictus*, p.p. of *astringere* (*ad-*, to, *stringere*, to bind)], *v.t.* To bind up, to compress, to render costive; to bind by legal or moral obligation; to restrict, limit to; (*Sc. Law*) to restrict in tenure. **astriction** (ă strik′ shŭn), *n.* The act of binding or drawing closely; constriction, constipation, restriction; (*Surg.*) the result of devices to stop hæmorrhage, as styptics or ligatures; (*Sc. Law*) obligation to have corn ground at a particular mill. **astrictive,** *a.* Possessing the quality of astricting; binding; astringent. *n.* An astringent.

astride (ă strīd′), *adv.* and *pred.a.* In a striding position; with legs on either side. *prep.* Astride of.

astringe (ă strinj′) [L. *astringere*, see ASTRICT], *v.t.* To bind together, to compress, to constrict, to render costive. **astringent,** *a.* (*Med.*) Contracting muscular fibre; binding, astrictive, styptic; (*fig.*) stern, severe, harsh. *n.* An astringent medicine. **astringently,** *adv.* **astringency,** *n.* The quality of being astringent; (*fig.*) sternness, severity, harshness.

astro- [Gr. *astron*, a star], *comb. form.* Pertaining to the heavenly bodies; *e.g. astrology, astronomy.*

astrodome (ăs′ trŏ dōme), *n.* (*Aviat.*) A dome window in an aircraft to enable astronomical observations to be made.

astrography (ăs trog′ ră fi), *n.* (*Astron.*) The mapping of the heavens.

astrolabe (ăs′ trŏ lāb) [O.F. *astrelabe*, med. L. *astrolabium* (L. *lab-*, stem of v. to take)], *n.* An instrument formerly used in astrology and in astronomical observations, for taking altitudes and other purposes.

astrolatry (ă strol′ ă tri) [Gr. *latreia*, worship], *n.* Worship of the stars.

astrology (ă strol′ ŏ ji) [F. *astrologie*, L. *astrologia* (Gr. *logia*)], *n.* *Practical astronomy (the derivatives were also formerly used in corresponding senses); a spurious science that professes to establish a connexion between the changing aspects of the heavenly bodies and the changing course of human life, thence claiming to predict events and to be competent to advise on life's conduct. **astrologer,** *n.* One versed in astrology. **astrologic** (ăs trŏ loj′ ik), **astrological,** *a.* **astrologically,** *adv.*

astronautics (ăs trō naw′ tiks) [Gr. *nautes*, a sailor], *n.* The science of aerial navigation. **astronaut** (ăs′ trō nawt), *n.* One borne into space beyond the earth's atmosphere in a suitable projectile.

astronomy (ă stron′ ŏ mi) [O.F. *astronomie*, L. *astronomia*, Gr. from *astronomos*, star-arranging, *a.* (*nemein*, to distribute, arrange)], *n.* The science which treats of all the phenomena of the heavenly bodies, and of the earth in relation to them. **astronomer,** *n.* One who studies or is versed in astronomy. **astronomer-royal:** The officer in charge of a royal or national observatory in Great Britain. **astronomic** (ăs trŏ nom′ ik), **astronomical,** *a.* Of or pertaining to astronomy. **astronomical clock:** A pendulum clock which gives sidereal time. **astronomical-year,** *n.* A year determined by astronomical observations, as opposed to a civil year. **astronomically,** *adv.*

***astrophel** (ăs′ trŏ fel) [perhaps corrupted from Gr. *astrophyllum*, star-leaf], *n.* An unidentified herb mentioned by Spenser.

astrophotometer (ăs trō fŏ tom′ ĕ tĕr), *n.* An instrument for measuring the intensity of sidereal light.

astrophysics (ăs trō fiz′ iks), *n.* The study of stellar physics. **astrophysical,** *a.* Relating to stellar physics.

astrut (ă strŭt′), *adv.* In a strutting manner.

astute (ă stūt′) [L. *astūtus*, crafty, cunning (*astus*, craft, cunning)], *a.* Acute, discerning, shrewd; clever, wily, cunning. **astutely,** *adv.* **astuteness,** *n.*

astylar (ă stī′ lăr) [*a*, not, Gr. *stulos*, a pillar], *a.* (*Arch.*) Without columns or pilasters.

a-sudden (ă sŭdn′), *adv.* Suddenly.

asunder (ă sŭn′ dėr) [A.-S. *onsundran*], *adv.* Apart, separately, in different pieces or places.

asylum (ă sī′ lŭm) [L., from Gr. *asulon*, neut. of *asūlos*, inviolable (*a-*, not, *sulē*, a right of seizure)], *n.* A place of refuge for criminals and debtors, a sanctuary; a shelter, a refuge; an institution affording relief and shelter to the afflicted, unfortunate, or destitute, especially an institution for the treatment of the insane; (*fig.*) a secure place of refuge.

asymmetry (ă sim′ ĕt ri), *n.* Want of symmetry, or of proportion; (*Math.*) incommensurability. **asymmetrical** (ăs i met′ ri kăl), *a.* Out of proportion. **asymmetrically,** *adv.*

asymptote (ăs′ im tōt) [Gr. *asumptotos*, not coinciding (*a-*, not, *sum-*, *sun-*, together, *ptōtos*, falling, from *piptein*, to fall)], *n.* A straight mathematical line continually approaching some curve but never meeting it within a finite distance. **asymptotic** (ăs im tot′ ik), **asymptotical.**

asynartete (ă sin′ ăr tēt) [Gr. *asunartētos* (*a-*, not, *sun-*, with *artaein*, to knit together)], *a.* Disconnected; consisting of two members differing in rhythm. *n.* Such a verse as described above.

asynchronous (ă sin′ krŏ nŭs) [*a-*, not, SYNCHRONOUS], *a.* Not coincident in point of time. **asynchronism,** *n.* Want of coincidence in time.

asyndeton (ă sin′ dė tŏn) [Gr. *asundeton* (*a-*, not, *sun-*, with, *delin*, to bind)], *n.* A rhetorical figure by which the conjunction is omitted, as 'I came, I saw, I conquered.'

asyntactic (ăs in tăk′ tik) [Gr. *asuntaktos* (*a-*, not, *sun-*, together, *tassein*, to range)], *a.* Ill-arranged, irregular, ungrammatical.

at (ăt) [A.-S. *æt* (cp. Icel. *at*, O.H.G. *az*, L. *ad*)], *prep.* Denoting nearness in time, space, occupation, condition, quality, or degree, effect, relation, value; denoting direction to or towards. **at home:** In one's own house; accessible to visitors; in one's own country; (*fig.*) at one's ease, comfortable; conversant with. *n.* A formal reception of visitors. **at all events:** In any case. **at first:** To begin with, originally. **at it:** At work, engaged, busy. **at meat:** Eating. **at most, least:** At the highest, lowest, estimate. **at once,** *adv. phr.* *Once for all; immediately, straightway. **at one:** In harmony, of the same opinion; together. **at that:** Moreover.

at- [AD-], *pref.*, as in *attain, attend.*

atabal (ăt′ ă băl) [Sp., from Arab. *at tabl*, the drum], *n.* A Moorish kettle-drum.

ataraxia (ăt ă răk′ si ă), **ataraxy** (ăt′ ă răk si) [Gr. *ataraxia* (*a-*, not, *tarassein*, to disturb)], *n.* Impassiveness, indifference, stoicism.

ataunto (ȧ tawn′ tō) [O.F. *autant*, so much], *adv.* (*Naut.*) With all sails set. **all ataunto,** *adv.* (*fig.*) All in good shape and condition.

atavism (ăt′ ȧ vizm) [F. *atavisme*, L. *atavus*, an ancestor], *n.* Reversion to some peculiarity of a more or less remote ancestor; recurrence of a disease after the lapse of some generations. **atavistic** (ăt ȧ vis′ tik), *a.*

ataxy (ȧ tăk′ si, ăt′ ȧk si) [Gr. *ataxia* (*a-*, not, *taxis*, order, from *tassein*, to arrange)], *n.* Loss of the power of co-ordination of the muscles, resulting in irregular, jerky movements. **locomotor ataxy,** *n.* A nervous disorder characterized by inability to co-ordinate the movements of the limbs; constitutional unsteadiness in the use of the limbs. **ataxic,** *a.* Of or pertaining to ataxy; irregular.

ate (et), *pret.* [EAT].

-ate [L. *-ātus* in nouns of state, or *-ātus*, *-āta*, *-ātum*, p.p. of 1st conj., through F. *-at*, as in *prélat*, *sénat*], *suf.* (1) Forming nouns of office or function, *e.g. curate, episcopate, aldermanate*; participial nouns, *e.g. delegate, mandate*; chemical names for salts of acids, *e.g. acetate, carbonate*; (2) forming participial adjectives, *e.g. desolate, situate* (cp. *desolated, situated*, in which the p.p. gives rise to a causative verb); and other adjectives formed by analogy, *e.g. roseate, ovate*; (3) forming verbs, *e.g. desolate, separate*, corresponding to adjectives in same form, or others produced on the same model, *e.g. fascinate, isolate, felicitate.*

ateleo-, atelo- [Gr. *atelēs*, imperfect (*a-*, not, *telos*, end, completion)], *comb. form.* Indicating incomplete development or imperfection of structure. **ateleocephalous,** *a.* With an imperfect skull. **atelocardia,** *n.* Imperfect development of the heart.

atelier (ȧ tel′ yā) [F., O.F. *astelier*, from *astelle*, small plank or splint], *n.* A workshop, a studio.

athalamous (ȧ thăl′ ȧ mŭs) [Gr. *a-*, not, *thalamos*, a bed], *n.* Applied to lichens the thallus of which has no conceptacles or spore-shields.

Athanasian (ăth ȧ nā′ shi ȧn, -shȧn), *a.* Of or pertaining to Athanasius, bishop of Alexandria A.D. 326. *n.* A follower of Athanasius; one holding his views with respect to the Trinity. **Athanasian creed,** *n.* A creed stating the doctrine of the Trinity and the Incarnation, with damnatory clauses, formerly attributed to Athanasius.

athanasy (ȧ thăn′ ȧ si) [L. *athanasia*, from Gr. (*a-*, not, without, *thanatos*, death)], *n.* Deathlessness, immortality.

atheism (ā′ thē izm) [F. *athéisme*, from Gr. *atheos* (*a-*, not, *theos*, God)], *n.* Disbelief in a God; godlessness; disregard of God and His laws. **atheist,** *n.* One who disbelieves, or denies, the existence of a God. *a.* Atheistic, godless, impious. **atheistic** (ā thē is′ tik), **atheistical,** *a.* **atheistically,** *adv.*

•**atheling** (ăth′ ė ling) [A.-S. *ætheling* (*æthel*, noble family, *-ing*, one belonging to)], *n.* A member of a noble family, often restricted to a prince of the royal blood or to the heir-apparent.

Athenæum (ăth ė nē′ ŭm) [L., from Gr. *Athēnaion*], *n.* The temple of Athene in ancient Athens, where professors taught and orators and poets declaimed; hence, a literary or scientific club; a literary clubroom, a public reading-room or library.

ather (ā′ thėr) [Gr.], *n.* The prickly whiskers of barley known as the beard.

atherine (ăth′ ėr īn) [mod. L. *atherīna*, Gr. *atheinē*, some kind of smelt], *n.* A sand-smelt.

athermancy (ȧ thĕr′ mȧn si) [Gr. *athermantos* (*a-*, not, *thermainein*, to heat, from *thermē*, heat)], *n.* The power of stopping radiant heat. **athermanous,** *a.* Impermeable by radiant heat.

athirst (ȧ thĕrst′) [A.-S. *ofthyrst*, *ofthyrsted*, p.p. of *ofthyrstan*, to be thirsty], *a.* Thirsty, oppressed with thirst; (*fig.*) eager; eagerly desirous.

athlete (ăth′ lēt) [L. *athlēta*, Gr. *athlētēs*, from *athlein*, to contend (*athlon*, *aethlon*, a prize)], *n.* A competitor in the public games of ancient Greece and Rome; one trained to perform feats of strength and activity; a powerful, vigorous man. **athletic** (ăth let′ ik), *a.* Of or pertaining to contests requiring great strength and activity; possessing great strength; muscular, robust. **athletically,** *adv.* **athleticism** (-let′ i sizm), *n.* The practice of athletics; devotion (especially excessive) to athletics. **athletics,** *n.* The practice of physical exercises by which muscular strength is developed.

athwart (ȧ thwôrt′) [*a-*, on, THWART], *prep.* From side to side of, across. *adv.* Transversely, from side to side, crosswise, awry; (*fig.*) so as to thwart. **athwart-hawse:** (*Naut.*) Said of the position of a ship lying across the stem of another ship at anchor. **athwart-ships:** (*Naut.*) From side to side of the ship.

atibar (ăt′ i bar) [?], *n.* (*Comm.*) Gold dust found on the coast of S. Africa.

-atic [F. *-atique*, L. *-āticus*], *suf.* Forming adjectives, *e.g. aquatic, fanatic, lunatic.*

-atile [F. *-atile*, L. *-ātilis*], *suf.* Forming adjectives chiefly denoting possibility or quality, *e.g. fluviatile, volatile.*

a-tilt (ȧ tilt′), *adv.* Tilted up; as if thrusting at an antagonist. **to run a-tilt:** To attack.

atimy (ăt′ i mi) [Gr. *atimia* (*a-*, not, *timē*, honour)], *n.* Loss of honour; loss of civil right.

-ation [L. *-ātio -ōnis*], *suf.* Forming abstract nouns from verbs, *e.g. agitation, appreciation, ovation.*

-ative [L. *-ativus, -a, -um*], *suf.* Forming adjectives, *e.g. demonstrative, representative, talkative.*

atlantes (ȧt lăn′ tēz), *n.pl.* (*Arch.*) Colossal statues of men used to support an entablature.

Atlantic (ȧt lăn′ tik) [ATLANTIS], *n.* The ocean between Europe and Africa in the E. and America in the W.; of or pertaining to Mt. Atlas, in Libya.

Atlantic Charter, *n.* Joint declaration by Great Britain and U.S.A. laying down 'certain principles as a basis for a better future for the world.' The 8 points of the Charter cover freedom from fear, want, and aggression and ensure political and commercial liberty. The Charter was signed in 1941, and was accepted by nine other European countries.

Atlantis (ăt lăn′ tis) [Gr.], *n.* The traditional island in the west whose site is occupied by the Atlantic Ocean. **atlantean** (ăt lȧn tē′ ȧn), *a.*

atlas (ăt′ lȧs) [Gr. *Atlas -antos*, a Titan, fabled to hold up the pillars of the universe], *n.* A collection of maps in a volume; a large size of drawing paper; (*Physiol.*) the first cervical vertebra, on which the skull is supported. **atlas-beetle,** *n.* A large lamellicorn beetle (*Chalcosoma atlas*) from the East. **atlas-moth,** *n.* *Attacus atlas*, a large moth from China.

atmo- [Gr. *atmos*, vapour], *comb. form.* Pertaining to vapour or to the atmosphere. **atmology** (ăt mol′ ȯ ji), *n.* The branch of physics which treats of the laws and phenomena of aqueous vapour. **atmolysis,** *n.* The separation of gases in combination. **atmometer,** *n.* An instrument for measuring the moisture exhaled in a given time from any humid surface.

atmosphere (ăt′ mȯ sfēr) [ATMO-, Gr. *sphaira*, a ball], *n.* The gaseous envelope of any of the heavenly bodies; that surrounding the earth; a gaseous envelope surrounding any substance; the air in any given place; the pressure of the earth's atmosphere, *i.e.* a pressure of 15 lb. on the sq. in.; (*fig.*) mental or moral environment. **atmospheric** (ăt mȯ sfer′ ik), **atmospherical,** *a.* Of or pertaining to the atmosphere; of the nature of air; existing in the atmosphere, or produced by the atmosphere. **atmospherics,** *n.pl.* (*Radio.*) Electromagnetic waves generated in the ether by an electric discharge emitted by two clouds or from a cloud to earth. **atmospheric engine,** *n.* An engine the piston of which is driven down by the pressure of the atmosphere and forced up by steam. **atmospheric railway,** *n.* Pneumatic railway. **atmospherically,** *adv.*

atoll (ȧ tol′, ăt′ ol) [Maldive *atollon, atoll*], *n.* A coral island, consisting of an annular reef surrounding a lagoon.

atom (ăt′ ȯm) [Gr. *atomos*, indivisible], *n.* The smallest conceivable portion of anything; a mite, a pigmy; (*Phys. Sc.*) a body originally thought to be incapable of further division; (*Chem.*) the smallest particle taking part in chemical action, the smallest particle of matter possessing the properties of an element.

atomic (ȧ tom′ ik), *a.* Consisting of atoms; pertaining or relating to an atom or atoms; extremely small. **atomic bomb,** *n.* (*Mil.*) A bomb in which the explosion is due to atomic energy. **atomic clock,** *n.* An electrical apparatus which makes use of molecular or atomic resonances to generate precise intervals of time. **atomic energy,** *n.* (*Phys.*) The energy liberated when the forces within the nucleus of an atom are released, *e.g.* by fission of uranium or by fusion of hydrogen. **Atomic Energy Commission,** *n.* The British body responsible for the control and development of atomic energy. **atomic number,** *n.* (*Phys.*) The number of electrons rotating round the nucleus of an atom, or the number of protons in the nucleus. The atomic number determines the chemical properties of an atom. **atomic philosophy,** *n.* The doctrine of the formation of all things from atoms possessing gravity and motion. **atomic pile,** *n.* A nuclear reactor. **atomic theory,** *n.* The theory that all combinations take place between the ultimate particles of matter, either atom for atom, or in a definite proportion. **atomic volume,** *n.* (*Phys.*) The volume occupied by the mass of an element equal to its atomic weight. **atomic warfare,** *n.* Warfare with nuclear weapons. **atomic weight,** *n.* The weight of an atom of an element expressed on a scale in which the weight of an oxygen atom is 16. **atomically,** *adv.*

atomicity (ă tŏm is′ i ti), *n.* The combining capacity of an element or radical.

atomism (ăt′ ȯ nizm), *n.* The atomic philosophy; the atomic theory. **atomist,** *n.*

atomization (ăt ȯ mī zā′ shŭn), *n.* The process of reducing to atoms; (*Med.*) reducing a liquid to a spray.

atomize (ăt′ ȯ mīz), *v.t.* To reduce to atoms.

atomizer (ăt ȯ mī zer), *n.* An instrument for reducing a liquid into spray for disinfecting or other purposes.

atomy (1) (ăt′ ȯ mi), *n.* An atom; a diminutive being.

atomy (2) (ăt′ ȯ mi) [*anatomy*, first syl. mistaken for article *an*], *n.* A skeleton, an anatomical preparation; an emaciated person, a living skeleton.

at one, *at-on, aton (ăt wŭn′) [AT, ONE], *adv.* In harmony, at one in a state of reconciliation; of the same opinion; *with the same result; *together. **at-oneness,** *n.* The condition of being at one, reconcilement, harmony.

atone (ȧ tōn′) [AT ONE], *v.i.* To make expiation or satisfaction for some crime, sin, or fault. **v.t.* To make at one; to bring into concord; to conciliate, to appease; to expiate. **atonable,** *a.* Able to be expiated. **atonement,** *n.* The act of atoning; reparation, expiation, amends, reconciliation; the propitiation of God by the expiation of sin; the Redemption. **atoning,** *a.* **atoningly,** *adv.*

atonic (ȧ ton′ ik) [med. L. *atonicus*, Gr. *atonos*, without tone (*a-*, not, *tenein*, to stretch)], *a.* Without an accent, unaccented; (*Med.*) having no tone in the system. *n.* An unaccented word in Greek; a medicine to allay excitement. **atonal,** *a.* (*Mus.*) Without fixed key. **atonality,** *n.* **atony** (ăt′ ȯ ni), *n.* Lack of tone; enervation; lack of intellectual energy.

atop (ȧ top′), *adv.* On or at the top. **atop of,** *prep.* On or at the top of.

atrabilious (ăt rȧ bil′ i ŭs) [L. *ātra bīlis*, black bile], *a.* Of or affected by black bile; melancholy, hypochondriacal; splenetic, bitter-tempered. **atrabiliousness,** *n.* **atrabiliar, atrabiliary** [F. *atrabiliaire*, mod. L. *ātrabīliārius*], *a.* Atrabilious. **atrabiliary-capsules,** *n.pl.* (*Med.*) A name given to the renal glands or capsules, from the blackish fluid they contain.

***atramental** (ăt rȧ men′ tȧl) [L. *ātrāmentum*, blacking, ink (*āter*, black)], *a.* Of or pertaining to ink; inky, black.

a-tremble (ȧ trembl′), *adv.* In a trembling condition.

a-trip (ȧ trip′) [*a-*, on, TRIP], *adv.* (*Naut.*) Just drawn out of the ground at right angles to it (of an anchor); hoisted as high as possible on the masts (of the topsails).

atrium (ā′ tri ŭm) [L.], *n.* The court or portico in an ancient Roman house; a covered court or portico; (*Physiol.*) that part of the auricle into which the veins pour the blood.

atrocious (ȧ trō′ shŭs) [L. *atrox -ōcis* (*āter*, black)], *a.* Savagely and wantonly cruel, characterized by heinous wickedness; stern, fierce, violent; (*colloq.*) very bad, execrable. **atrociously,** *adv.* **atrocity** (ȧ tros′ i ti), *n.* Excessive cruelty or other flagrant wickedness; an atrocious act; (*colloq.*) a bad blunder; a barbarism.

atrophy (ăt′ rȯ fi) [F. *atrophie*, L. *atrophia*, from Gr., from *atrophos*, ill-fed (*a-*, not, *trephein*, to nourish)], *n.* A wasting of the body, or its organs, through want of nourishment or disease; (*fig.*) mental or spiritual starvation. *v.t.* To affect with atrophy, to cause to waste away. *v.i.* To waste away.

atropine (ăt′ rȯ pīn) [Gr. *atropos*, inflexible, name of one of the Fates], *n.* An organic base obtained from deadly nightshade, *Atropa belladonna.* **atropism,** *n.* (*Med.*) Poisoning by atropine.

attaboy (ăt′ ȧ boi′), *int.* (*Am. slang*) Exclamation of encouragement.

attach (ȧ tăch′) [O.F. *atachier* (F. *attacher*), from *a*, to, Genevese *tache* (cp. Port. *tacha*, nail, Eng. *tack*, L.G. *takk*)], *v.t.* To fasten on, connect; to affix; to lay hold on, arrest, indict, esp. to seize a person or goods by a writ of attachment; to join to in sympathy or feelings; to attract and cause to adhere to oneself; to attribute. *v.i.* To adhere to; (*Law*) to apply. **attachable,** *a.* Capable of being attached; liable to attachment. **attached,** *a.* Arrested; joined to, fastened to; joined in function, taste, feeling, or affection; incident, connected; (*Zool.*) stationary, as opposed to free; (*Arch.*) joined to a wall; not standing clear. **attachment,** *n.* The act of attaching; the means by which anything is attached; connexion; fidelity, affection, devotion; the thing attached; (*Law*) apprehension, esp. for contempt of court; the seizure of goods or estate to secure a debt or demand; the writ or precept by which such apprehension or seizure is effected. **foreign attachment:** (*Law*) Seizure of the goods of foreigners to satisfy creditors.

attaché (ȧ tăsh′ ā) [F.], *n.* One attached to the suite of an ambassador. **attaché case,** *n.* A leather case for carrying papers, etc.

attachment [ATTACH].

attack (ȧ tăk′) [F. *attaquer*, It. *attaccare*, to join (battle) (see ATTACH)], *v.t.* To fall upon with force of arms; to assault; to assail by hostile words, writings, etc.; (*fig.*) to begin a work with determination; to exert destructive influence on (of physical agents and disease). *v.i.* To make an attack. *n.* The act of attacking; an onset, an assault; violent abuse, injury; a fit of illness; the commencement of destructive action. **attackable,** *a.*

attain (ȧ tān′) [O.F. *ateign-*, pres. stem of *ataindre*, to reach, attain (L. *ad-*, to, *tangere*, to touch)], *v.i.* To arrive at some object. *v.t.* To reach, gain; to arrive at; to accomplish. **attainable,** *a.* **attainability** (-bil′ i ti), *n.* **attainableness,** *n.* **attainment,** *n.* The act of attaining; that which is attained; a personal acquirement.

attainder (ȧ tān′ dėr) [O.F. *ataindre,* to ATTAIN (meaning modified by confusion with *taindre,* to dye, stain)], *n.* The act or process of attainting a criminal; the forfeiture of civil rights as the legal consequence of a sentence of death or outlawry for treason or felony; an act or bill of attainder; (*fig.*) condemnation; dishonouring accusation; taint of dishonour. **Act** or **Bill of attainder:** One introduced into the British Parliament for attainting a person without judicial process. **attaint** (ȧ tānt′), *v.t.* To condemn or subject to attainder; to accuse; to infect; to taint, stain; to dim, sully. ***attaint,** *part.a.* Under an attainder, attainted; corrupted, infected; exhausted, overcome. *n.* *A hit; *a stain, blot; (*Law*) conviction of or process against a jury for returning a false verdict; attainder. **attainture,** *n.* Attainder; (*fig.*) dishonour, stain.

attar (ăt′ ȧr) [Pers. *'atar,* essence, Arab. *'utūr,* aroma], *n.* Fragrant essence, esp. of roses. ***attargul,** *n.* The essential oil obtained from roses by distillation.

attemper (ȧ tem′ pėr) [O.F. *atemprer,* L. *attemperāre* (*ad-,* to, *temperāre,* to temper, moderate)], *v.t.* To qualify or modify by admixture; to moderate temperature; to soften, mollify; to mix in just proportions; to fit or make suitable; to attune; to temper. **attemperance,** *n.* Temperance, moderation; natural temperament. ***attemperate** (ȧ tem′ pėr āt). *v.t.* To attemper. *a.* (ȧ tem′ pėr ȧt). Temperate; regulated, proportioned. **attemperment,** *n.* The act of tempering; the state of being tempered.

attempt (ȧ temt′) [O.F. *atempter,* undertake, L. *attemptāre, attentāre* (*ad-,* to, *tentāre,* strive after)], *v.t.* To try, endeavour; to try to influence; to attack; to make trial of; *to try to seduce. *n.* An endeavour, effort, undertaking; an effort as contrasted with attainment; an assault (on life, honour, etc.). **to attempt the life of:** To try to kill. **attemptable,** *a.* **attemptability** (-bil i ti), *n.*

attend (ȧ tend′) [O.F. *atendre,* to wait, L. *attendere* (*ad-,* to, *tendere,* to stretch)], *v.t.* To turn the thoughts towards; to apply the mind to; to accompany, escort; to wait upon; to be present at; to wait for, to expect. *v.i.* To pay attention, to be present, to be in attendance; to wait upon or for a person. **attendance,** *n.* The act of attending; service, presence; persons attending; train of servants. **in attendance:** Waiting, attendant on. **to dance attendance on:** To wait upon obsequiously. **attendance-officer,** *n.* An official whose duty it is to see that children attend school. **attendance register,** *n.* The list of pupils at a school read out at roll call. **attendant,** *a.* Accompanying, waiting on, ministering to; following as a consequence; present. *n.* One who or that which attends or accompanies; a servant. ***attendment,** *n.* Meaning; intent; (*pl.*) environment, surroundings. **attent** (ȧ tent′), *a.* Intent, attentive. *n.* Attention.

attention (ȧ ten′ shŭn) [as prec.], *n.* The act or state of attending; the mental faculty of attending; an act of courtesy, kindness, or love (*often pl.*); watchful care, close observation, notice; military attitude of readiness. **to pay attentions to:** To court.

attentive (ȧ ten′ tiv), *a.* Heedful, intent, regardful; polite, courteous. **attentively,** *adv.* **attentiveness,** *n.*

attenuate (ȧ ten′ ū āt) [L. *attenuātus,* p.p. of *attenuāre* (*ad-,* to, *tenuis,* thin)], *v.t.* To make thin or slender; to dilute, diminish the density of; to weaken, to belittle; to extenuate. *v.i.* To become thin or weak. **attenuate** (-ū ȧt), *a.* Slender; tapering; thin in consistency. **attenuated,** *a.* **attenuation** (-ā′ shŭn), *n.* The act of attenuating; diminution of thickness, density, or force; emaciation; (*Radio.*) diminution of wireless waves with distance. **attenuation constant,** *n.* (*Elec.*) Constant determining connexion between the current sent out and received. **attenuator,** *n.* (*Radio.*) A control device to provide attenuation.

attest (ȧ test′) [F. *attester,* L. *attestāri* (*ad-,* to, *testis,* a witness)], *v.t.* To testify (esp. in a formal manner); to vouch for; to put a person on his oath or solemn declaration. *v.i.* To bear witness. *n.* Evidence, attestation. **attestation** (ăt tės tā′ shŭn), *n.* The act of attesting; evidence, proof; formal confirmation; formal verification; the administration of an oath, esp. of the oath of allegiance. **attested,** *a.* Certified as being free from the bacillus of tuberculosis. **attestor,** *n.* One who attests or vouches for.

Attic (1) (ăt′ ik) [L. *Atticus,* Gr. *Attikos*], *a.* Of or belonging to Attica or its capital, Athens; classical, refined; witty. *n.* A native of Attica; an Athenian; the Attic dialect. **Attic base,** *n.* (*Arch.*) A base consisting of an upper torus, a scotia, and lower torus, with fillets between them. **Attic bird,** *n.* The nightingale. **Attic dialect,** *n.* The dialect of ancient Athens; the chief literary dialect. **Attic faith,** *n.* Inviolable faith. **Attic order,** *n.* (*Arch.*) An order of small square pillars at the uppermost part of a building. **Attic salt, Attic wit,** *n.* Refined, delicate wit, for which the Athenians were famous. **Atticism** (ăt′ i sizm), *n.* Attachment to Athens; idiom and style characteristic of Attic Greek; concise and elegant expression. **Atticize** (-sīz), *v.i.* To conform to the idiom of Attica or Athens, or to Greek habits or modes of thought; to side with the Athenians.

attic (2) (ăt′ ik) [F. *attique,* as prec.], *n.* A low story placed above an entablature or cornice; the top story of a house; a room in this story; (*slang*) the head, the brain, the 'upper story.' **attic story,** *n.* An upper story of a house; usually the highest story below the garret.

attire (ȧ tīr′) [O.F. *atirer* (*à,* to, *tire,* a row) (see TIER)], *v.t.* To dress; to array in apparel. *n.* Dress, clothes; *a woman's head-dress; (*Her.*) the horns of a stag or buck. **attired,** *a.* Dressed, decked, arrayed; (*Her.*) furnished with horns. **attiring,** *n.* Dress, apparel, trappings.

attitude (ăt′ i tūd) [F., from It. *attitudine,* L. *aptitūdinem* (*aptus,* fitted)], *n.* The posture in which a figure is represented in painting or sculpture; bearing or gesture, expressing action or passion; posture or disposition of things; behaviour indicating opinion and sentiment. **attitude of mind:** Habitual mode of thinking and feeling. **to strike an attitude:** To assume an exaggerated or theatrical attitude. **attitudinize** (-tū′ di nīz), *v.i.* To practise or assume attitudes; to pose; to behave or act affectedly.

attorn (ȧ tĕrn′) [O.F. *atorner* (*à,* to, *tourner,* L. *tornāre,* to turn)], *v.t.* To assign, transfer; (*Law*) to recognize a new owner. *v.i.* To transfer service or fealty to a new lord. **attorney** (1) (ȧ tĕr′ ni) [O.F. *atorné,* p.p. *atorner*], *n.* *An agent, deputy, factor; a qualified practitioner in the Common Law courts, who prepared the case for the barristers or counsel, as distinguished from a solicitor who practised in a court of equity, the title is now Solicitor of the Supreme Court; (*Am.*) a barrister, a solicitor. **District Attorney:** (*Am.*) The public prosecutor. **Attorney-General,** *n.* The functionary whose duty it is to transact all legal business in which the State is a party. **Attorney-Generalship,** *n.* The office or dignity of the Attorney-General. **attorney** (2) [O.F. *atornée,* fem. n. from p.p.], *n.* *Appointment of a legal representative; the authority or function so conceded. **power, letter,** or **warrant of attorney:** A written authority by which one person authorizes another to act in his stead. **attorneyship,** *n.* The office of an attorney; agency, proxy.

attract (ȧ trăkt′) [L. *attractus,* p.p. of *attrahere* (*ad-,* to, *trahere,* to draw)], *v.t.* To draw to or cause to approach (in a material or immaterial sense); to cause to approach by some influence; to entice, to allure; to draw the notice of. *v.i.* To exert the power of attraction, to be attractive. **attractable,** *a.* That may be attracted. **attractability** (ȧ trăk tȧ bil' i ti), *n.* Capability of being attracted. **attracting,** *a.* **attractingly,** *adv.* **attractor,** *n.* **attraction** (ȧ trăk' shŭn), *n.* The action or power of attracting; an attracting quality; that which attracts. **attraction of gravity:** The mutual action between two bodies by which they tend to approach each other; the force by which this action is exerted. **attraction of cohesion:** The attraction by which the atoms of a body are kept together. **capillary attraction:** The attractive force which causes liquids to be drawn up hair-like tubes. **magnetic attraction:** The force by which a magnet attracts other magnetic materials. **molecular attraction:** The force by which the molecules of bodies act upon each other; cohesion. **attractive** (ȧ trăk' tiv), *a.* Having the power of attracting; alluring. **attractively,** *adv.* **attractiveness,** *n.*

***attrahent** (ăt' rȧ hent) [L. *attrahentem*, pres.p. of *attrahere* (ATTRACT)], *a.* Drawing to, attracting. *n.* That which draws to or towards.

attribute (ăt' ri būt) [L. *attribūtus -um*, p.p. of *attribuere*, to assign (*ad-*, to, *tribuere*, to give)], *n.* A quality ascribed or imputed to any person or thing, as an essential characteristic; a characteristic; a symbol or other object recognized as peculiar or characteristic; an attributive word; (*Log.*) that which may be predicated of any subject. **attribute** (ȧ trib' ūt), *v.t.* To ascribe; to impute as belonging or due to; to ascribe as a consequence. **attributable,** *a.* **attribution** (ăt ri bū' shŭn), *n.* The act of attributing; that which is ascribed; function, authority formally assigned; commendation, honour; (*Log.*) predication. **attributive** (ȧ trib' ū tiv), *a.* Characterized by attributing; (*Log.*) assigning an attribute to a subject; (*Gram.*) expressing an attribute without actual predication. *n.* A word denoting an attribute, now generally restricted to adjectives. **attributively,** *adv.*

attrist (ȧ trist') [F. *attrister*, to sadden (*à*, to, *triste*, L. *tristis*, sad)], *v.t.* To cause to be sad.

attrite (ȧ trīt') [L. *attrītus*, p.p. of *atterere* (*ad-*, to, *terere*, to rub)], *a.* Rubbed down; subjected to the action of friction; penitent through fear of consequences. **attrited** (ȧ trī' tĕd), *part.a.* Worn down by friction. **attriteness,** *n.* **attrition** (ȧ trish' ŭn), *n.* The act or process of rubbing down or away; abrasion; wearing away by friction; (*Theol.*) sorrow for sin on account of the punishment due to it.

attune (ȧ tūn') [*at-*, AD-, TUNE], *v.t.* To tune to; to bring to the right pitch; to make tuneful; (*fig.*) to render accordant. *n.* (*rare*) Tuneful accord; harmony.

aubade (ō bad') [F., from Sp. *albada* (*alba*, dawn)], *n.* Music performed at daybreak; musical announcement of dawn.

auberge (ō bârzh') [F. *auberge*, O.F. *alberge*, *helberge*, O.H.G. *heri-berga*, army shelter (cp. G. *herberg*, inn, and Eng. HARBOUR)], *n.* An inn; a place of entertainment for travellers. ***aubergiste,*** *n.* A keeper of an *auberge*, an inn-keeper.

aubergine (ō bâr zhēn') [F. dim. of *auberge*, *alberge*, Sp. *alberchigo*, apricot], *n.* The egg-plant, *Solanum esculentum*; its fruit is used as a vegetable and in soups and stews.

Aubrietia (ō brē' shȧ). (*Bot.*) A genus of rock plants of the family Cruciferae.

auburn (aw' bėrn) [O.F. *auborne*, L. *alburnus*, whitish (*albus* white)], *a.* *Yellowish; ruddy brown; golden brown.

auction (awk' shŭn) [L. *auctio -ōnem*, an increase, auction (*auctus*, p.p. of *augēre*, to increase)], *n.* A public sale by a person licensed for that purpose, in which each bidder offers a higher price than the preceding; *property put up to auction. **Dutch auction:** A sale in which property is offered above its value, and the price gradually lowered till some one accepts an offer. *v.t.* To sell by auction.

auction bridge, *n.* (*Cards*) A development of bridge in which the players bid for the advantage of choosing trump suit. **auction-mart,** *n.* A place where goods are sold by public auction. ***auctionary,** *n.* Pertaining to an auction. **auctioneer** (awk shŭ nēr'), *n.* A person who sells goods by auction. *v.t.* or *i.* To sell by action.

auctorial (awk tôr' i ȧl) [L. *auctor*, -IAL], *a.* Pertaining to an author or his occupation.

aucupation (aw kū pā' shŭn) [L. *auceps*, bird-catcher], *n.* The art of bird-catching.

audacious (aw dā' shŭs) [L. *audax -acis* (*audēre*, to dare)], *a.* Bold, daring, spirited; impudent, shameless. **audaciously,** *adv.* Boldly, impudently. **audaciousness,** *n.* **audacity** (aw dăs' i ti), *n.* Courage, daring, gallantry; hardihood, effrontery.

audible (aw' dibl) [med. L. *audibilis* (*audīre*, to hear)], *a.* Capable of being heard; clear or loud enough to be heard. **audibility** (aw di bil' i ti), *n.* **audibleness,** *n.* **audibly,** *adv.*

audience (aw' di ĕns) [F. *audience*, L. *audientia* (*audiens -ntem*, pres.p. of *audīre*)], *n.* The act of hearing, attention; reception at a formal interview granted by a superior to an inferior; an assemblage of hearers, an auditory; (*fig.*) readers of a book. **audience-chamber,** *n.* A chamber in which formal audiences are granted. **audience-court,** *n.* An ecclesiastical court (now abolished), at first presided over by the archbishop, afterwards by auditors on his behalf. **audient,** *a.* Hearing, listening. *n.* A hearer, esp. one not yet admitted to the Church; a catechumen.

audile (aw' dīl) [L. *audīre*, to hear], *a.* (*Psych.*) Characterized by mental pictures of sounds. *n.* A man whose recollection is based mainly on terms of sounds.

audiometer (aw di om' ĕt ėr) [L. *audīre*, to hear], *n.* An application of the telephone for testing the sense of hearing. **audio-frequency** (aw' di ō-), *n.* (*Radio.*) A frequency of alternating current producing audible sounds with the aid of a loud-speaker or telephones.

audiphone (aw' di fōn) [L. *audīre*, to hear, Gr. *phōnē*, sound], *n.* An instrument which, when pressed against the teeth, enables deaf mutes to hear by conveying sound-waves to the auditory nerves.

audit (aw' dit) [L. *audītus*, hearing (*audīre*, to hear)], *n.* *A hearing, an audience; an official examination of accounts; a formal receipt of rents at stated periods; (*fig.*) a solemn rendering of accounts; the Day of Judgement. *v.t.* To examine officially and pronounce as to the accuracy of (accounts). **commissioners of audit:** Officers appointed to check the public accounts. **audit ale,** *n.* Ale of special quality brewed for the day of audit at English universities. **audit-house, audit-room,** *n.* A house or room appendant to cathedrals for the transaction of business. **audit-office,** *n.* The office in which public accounts are audited.

audition (aw dish' ŭn), *n.* The act or faculty of hearing; something heard, a sound; a trial in private of a singer or musician before a public performance is undertaken.

auditor (aw' di tȯr), *n.* A hearer, one of an audience; an audient, a catechumen; one appointed to audit accounts; the president of an audience court. **auditorship,** *n.* **auditorial** (aw di tôr' i ȧl), *a.* Auditory; of or pertaining to an audit of accounts. **auditorially,** *adv.*

auditorium (aw di tôr' i ŭm), *n.* The part of a building occupied by the audience; the nave of a church; the reception-room in a monastic building.

auditory (aw' di tȯr i), *a.* Of or pertaining to the organs or sense of hearing; perceived by the ear. *n.* An audience; people assembled to hear; a place for hearing; an auditorium.

Augean (aw jē' ȧn) [L. *Augeas*, Gr. *Augeias*], *a.* Pertaining to Augeas (mythic king of Elis, whose stable, containing 3000 oxen, had not been cleaned for thirty years, till Hercules, by turning the river Alpheus through it, did so in a day); filthy.

auger (aw' gėr) [A.-S. *nafugār* (*nafu*, the nave of a wheel, *gār*, a borer)], *n.* A carpenter's tool, somewhat resembling a very large gimlet, worked with both hands, for boring holes in wood; a similar instrument of larger size, for boring into soil or rock. **auger-hole,** *n.* A hole drilled with an auger. **auger-shell,** *n.* (*Zool.*) The long pointed shell of the molluscous genus *Teredra.* **auger worm,** *n.* (*Zool.*) The teredo, or boring-worm.

auges (aw' jēz) [L. summit], *n.* (*Astron.*) Two points in a planet's orbit, the apogee and the perigee.

aught (awt) [A.-S. *āwiht* (*ā*, one, *wiht*, a creature)], *n.* Anything whatever; a whit, a jot, or tittle; (*pop. and erroneously*) the figure o, a naught. *adv.* In any respect.

augite (aw' jīt) [L., from Gr. *augitēs*, prob. a turquoise (*augē*, lustre)], *n.* A greenish, brownish-black, or black variety of aluminous pyroxene. **augitic** (aw jit' ik), *a.*

augment (awg ment') [F. *augmenter*, L. *augmentum*, an increase (*augēre*, to increase)], *v.t.* To increase, to make larger or greater in number, degree, etc.; to extend, to enlarge; to prefix a grammatical augment to; (*Her.*) to make an honourable addition to (a coat of arms). *v.i.* To increase; to become greater in size, number, degree, etc. **augment** (awg' mėnt), *n.* A grammatical prefix (*a*) used in the older Aryan languages to denote past time. In Greek, when the prefix (*ĕ*) remains distinct, the augment is called *syllabic*; when it forms, with a following vowel, a long vowel or diphthong, it is called *temporal.*

augmentation (awg men tā' shŭn), *n.* The act of augmenting; the state of being augmented; the thing added; increase, addition; (*Her.*) an honourable addition to a coat of arms; (*Mus.*) the reproduction of a subject in notes of greater length than those in which it was first treated. **process of augmentation:** (*Sc. Law*) Action in the Court of Teinds by a parish clergyman for increase of stipend. **Augmentation court,** *n.* A court created by Henry VIII to deal with suits arising from his suppression of monasteries.

augmentative (awg men' tȧ tiv), *a.* Having the power or quality of augmenting; increasing the force of a word (used of an affix); extending the force of an idea (used of a word). *n.* An augmentative element or word.

augur (aw' gŭr) [L. (prob. *avis, aui*, a bird, *-gur*, telling, connected with *garrīre*, to talk, *garrulus*, talkative, Sansk. *gar*, to shout)], *n.* A religious official among the Romans who professed to foretell future events from omens derived chiefly from the actions of birds, inspection of the entrails of slaughtered victims, etc.; a soothsayer, a diviner. *v.t.* To prognosticate from signs or omens; to betoken, portend. *v.i.* To form auguries from signs or omens; to forebode, anticipate. **augural,** *a.* Pertaining to an augur or to augury. **augurship,** *n.* **augury** (aw' gū ri) [O.F. *augurie*, L. *augurium*], *n.* The art or practice of the augur; divination from the actions of birds; an augural ceremony; an omen, prognostication, foreboding.

august (aw gŭst') [L. *augustus*, honoured, venerable], *a.* Majestic, stately, inspiring reverence and admiration; dignified, worshipful. **augustly,** *adv.* **augustness,** *n.*

August (aw' gŭst), *n.* The eighth month of the year, named in honour of Augustus Cæsar.

Augustan (aw gŭst' ȧn), *a.* Of or belonging to Augustus Cæsar, or his age in which Latin literature reached its highest development; hence, classical, refined, distinguished by correct literary taste; of or belonging to Augusta Vindelicorum (Augsburg, Bavaria), where Luther and Melanchthon, in 1530, drew up their confession of the Protestant faith. *n.* A writer of the Augustan period of any literature.

auguste, august (ou goost') [G.], *n.* A clown with maladroit antics.

***Augustin, *Augustine** (aw gŭs' tin, aw' gŭs tin) [F. *Augustin*, L. *Augustīnus* (see also AUSTIN)], *n.* An Augustinian friar. **Augustinian** (aw gŭs tin' i ȧn) *a.* Of or pertaining to St. Augustine, Bishop of Hippo (5th century), or to his doctrine of grace and predestination. *n.* An adherent of these doctrines; one of an order of friars named after him.

auk (awk) [Swed. *alka*, a puffin], *n.* A northern seabird with rudimentary wings, esp. the great auk (now extinct); the little auk, and the razor-bill.

aularian (aw lâr' i ȧn) [late L. *aulārius*, from *aula*, hall (Gr. *aulē*)], *a.* Of or pertaining to a hall. *n.* (*Eng. Univ.*) The member of a hall as distinguished from the member of a college.

auld (awld), *a.* (*Sc. and North.*) Old. **auld lang syne:** Old long since, long ago. **Auld Reekie:** Old smoky, Edinburgh. **auldfarrant,** *a.* Old-favouring; old-fashioned, favouring the ways of grown-up people, precocious. **auld-warld,** *a.* Old-world, ancient.

aulic (aw' lik) [F. *aulique*, L. *aulicus*, Gr. *aulikos* (*aulē*, a court)], *a* Pertaining to a royal court; courtly. *n.* The ceremony observed in the Sorbonne in granting the degree of Doctor of Divinity. **aulic council,** *n.* The personal council of the sovereign in the old German empire; formerly also a council at Vienna in charge of the Austrian War Department.

***aumail** (aw māl') [O.F. *esmal*, *esmail* (perh. from O.H.G. *smelzan*, to smelt)], *v.t.* To enamel. *n.* Enamel.

***aumbry** [AMBRY].

aunt (ant) [O.F. *aunte*, L. *amita*; till 17th century *naunt* is common (*my naunt for mine aunt*; cp. F. *tante*, prob. *ta ante*)], *n.* The sister of one's father or mother; one's uncle's wife; a benevolent, practical, elderly woman; *a prostitute, a procuress. **Aunt Sally,** *n.* A game at fairs, in which a figure with a pipe in its mouth is set up, and the players endeavour to break the pipe by throwing sticks at it; (*fig.*) an object of ridicule. **aunthood,** *n.* **auntie, aunty** (an' ti), *n.* A familiar form of AUNT; a familiar term for an elderly woman; a kindly way of accosting an elderly woman. **auntship,** *n.*

aura (aw' rȧ) [L., from Gr. *aura*, breath, breeze], *n.* A subtle emanation from any body; (*Path.*) a sensation as of a current of cold air rising to the head in epilepsy and hysteria; (*Elec.*) the air-current caused by a discharge of electricity from a sharp point. **aural** (1), *a.* Of or pertaining to an aura.

aural (2) (aw' rȧl) [L. *auris*, the ear], *a.* Of or pertaining to the ear; received by the ear. **aurally,** *adv.* **auriform,** *a.* Having the form of an ear. **auriscope** (aw' ri skōp) [-SCOPE], *n.* (*Med.*) An instrument for examining the internal ear. **aurist,** *n.* A specialist in ear diseases.

aurated (aw' rā tėd) [L. *aurātus*, p.p. of *aurāre*, to gild (*aurum*, gold)], *a.* Containing gold; gilded or resembling gold in colour. **aureate** (aw' rė ȧt) [late L. *aureātus*, *aureus*, golden], *a.* Golden, gold-coloured; (*fig.*) brilliant, splendid.

Aurelia (aw rē' li ȧ) [It., silkworm, fem. of *aurelio*, shining, golden (L. *aurum*, gold)], *n.* *A chrysalis; a pupa; (*Zool.*) a genus of phosphorescent marine animals. **aurelian,** *a.* Of or pertaining to an aurelia; golden. *n.* One who studies entomology, esp. a lepidopterist, one who studies butterflies and moths.

aureola (aw rē' ŏ lȧ) [L., golden, fem. of *aureolus*, from *aurum*, gold (*aureola corona*, golden crown)], *n.* The crown which is the special reward of virgins, martyrs, and doctors; the glory attaching to such a crown; an aureole. **aureole** (aw' ri ōl), *n.* An aureola; the gold disk surrounding the head in early pictures, and denoting glory; a nimbus; a vesica; a glorifying halo, glory; (*Astron.*) the halo round the moon in total eclipses of the sun; an actual halo of radiating light.

aureomycin (aw ri ō mī′ sin) *n.* (*Med.*) An antibiotic against typhus and other diseases.

auric (aw′ rik) [L. *aurum*, gold], *a.* Of or pertaining to gold; (*Chem.*) applied to compounds in which gold is trivalent.

auricle (aw′ ri kėl) [L., external ear, dim. of *auris*, ear], *n.* The external ear, that part which projects from the head; any process shaped like the lobe of the ear; (*pl.*) the two upper cavities of the heart in mammals, birds, and reptiles, which receive the blood from the lungs. **auricled,** *a.* (*Nat. Hist.*) Furnished with an auricle or auricles. **auricula** (aw rik′ ū lȧ), *n.* A garden flower, *Primula auricula*, sometimes called bear's ear, from its leaves.

auricular (aw rik′ ū lȧr), *a.* Of or pertaining to the sense of hearing; whispered in the ear, hence secret; *traditionary; (*Nat. Hist.*) shaped like an auricle; (*Anat.*) of or pertaining to an auricle of the heart. *n.* An auricular organ; a tuft of feathers covering the auditory orifice in birds. **auricularly,** *adv.* By whispering in the ear; secretly; by means of the ear; by means of auricles. **auriculate,** *a.* Having ears, or appendages resembling ears.

auriferous (aw rif′ ėr ůs) [L. *aurifer* (*aurum*, gold, *-fer*, producing)], *a.* Yielding or producing gold. **aurific** (aw rif′ ik) [L. *aurum*, gold, *-ficus*, making (*facere*, to make)], *a.* (*Alch.*) Having the power of changing other substances into gold; producing gold.

Aurignacian (ō rē nyā′ shi ån) [grotto of *Aurignac*, France], *a.* (*Anthrop.*) Pertaining to the period of Upper Palæolithic culture, typified by human remains, and implements, etc., of stone, horn, and bone found in the cave of Aurignac, Haute-Garonne.

aurist [AURAL].

aurochs (aw′ roks) [G. *aurochs* (*auerochs*), O.H.G. *ur-ohso* (cp. A.-S. *ūr*), whence L. *ūrus*], *n.* The extinct wild ox *Bos urus* or *primigenius*, of Central Europe; erroneously applied to the European bison, *Bos bonasus*, strictly preserved in Lithuania.

aurora (aw rôr′ ȧ) [L. the goddess of the dawn], *n* Morning twilight; dawn; the colour of the sky at sunrise; the Roman goddess of the dawn; (*fig.*) beginning; early period; a peculiar illumination of the night sky common within the polar circles, consisting of streams of light ascending towards the zenith, called **aurora borealis** or **aurora australis,** as it is seen near the North or South Pole. **auroral,** *a.* Of or pertaining to the dawn, or to the rise or beginning of anything; rosy, roseate; eastern; of or pertaining to an aurora.

aurum (aw′ rům) [L.], *n.* Gold. **aurum fulminans,** *n.* Fulminate of gold. **aurum mosaicum,** *n.* Bisulphide of tin, bronze powder. **aurum potabile** (pō tā′ bi li), *n.* A cordial consisting of volatile oil containing gold in a minute state of subdivision. **aurous** (aw′ růs), *a.* Of or pertaining to gold; (*Chem.*) in which gold is univalent.

auscultation (aws kŭl tā′ shůn) [L. *auscultātiō -nem*, from *auscultāre*, to listen (*aus- auris*, the ear)], *n.* The act of listening; (*Med.*) listening with the ear or stethoscope to the sounds made by the internal organs, to judge their condition. **auscultator** (aws′ kůl tā tôr), *n.* **auscultatory** (aws kŭl′ tȧ tôr i), *a.* **auscultate** (aws′ kŭl tāt), *v.t.* (*Mil.*) To detect by means of an instrument where land mines have been laid.

Ausonian (aw sō′ ni ån) [L., Ausonia], *a.* (*Poet.*) Of or pertaining to ancient Italy, Italian.

***auspex** (aw′ speks) [L. (*avis*, bird, *spex*, an observer, from *specere*, to observe)], *n.* In ancient Rome, one who took the auspices; a protector, a favourer; one who saw that marriage ceremonies were rightly performed. ***auspicate** (aw′ spi kāt) [L. *auspicātus*, p.p. of *auspicāre*, to take omens], *v.t.* To betoken, to prognosticate; to inaugurate, initiate. *v.i.* To augur, to give promise of, to predict.

auspice (*usu. in pl.* **auspices**) (aw′ spis, aw′ spi siz) [F. *auspice*, L. *auspicium*], *n.* An omen drawn from the actions of birds; a prognostication; (*fig.*) patronage, protection. **under the auspices of:** Under the leadership, encouragement, or patronage of. **auspicious** (aw′ spish′ ůs), *a.* Having the omens favourable; auguring good fortune; conducive to prosperity; kind, benignant. **auspiciously,** *adv.* **auspiciousness,** *n.*

Aussie (aw′ si), *n.* Australia; an Australian.

Auster (aws′ tėr) [L.], *n.* The south wind.

austere (aw stēr′) [O.F., from L. *austērus*, from Gr. *austēros*, dry, harsh (*auein*, to dry, parch)], *a.* Harsh, tart, or rough to the taste; severe, stern, rigorous; sober, simple, unadorned. **austerely,** *adv.* **austereness,** *n.* **austerity** (aw ster′ i ti), *n.* Harshness to the taste or feelings; sternness, severity, asceticism; lack of adornment; (*pl.*) ascetic or penitential practices.

Austin (aw′ stin) [syncopated form of AUGUSTIN], *a.* and *n.* Augustin, Augustinian.

austral (aw′ strål) [L. *australis* (AUSTER, south wind)], *a.* Of or pertaining to, or situated in or towards the south; southern. **austral signs,** *n.pl.* (*Astron.*) the last six signs of the zodiac.

Australasian (aw strȧ lā′ shi ån) [F. *Australasie*, L. *australis*, *Asia*], *a.* Of or pertaining to Australasia, a general name for Australia and the surrounding islands. *n.* A native of Australasia. **Australian** (aw strā′ li ån), *a.* Of or belonging to Australia. *n.* A native of Australia. **Australian crawl:** A style of swimming popular in Australia. **Australian kelpie:** A smooth-haired breed of sheep-dog. **Australian rules:** A variety of rugby football played in Australia. **Australian terrier:** A short-legged breed of dog, small and wire-haired. **australioid** (-strā′ li oid), **australoid** (aw′ strȧ loid), *a.* Terms used by Huxley and Lubbock (Lord Avebury) respectively to denote resemblance to the type of the aborigines of Australia. **australite** (os′ trȧ līt), *n.* A lump of smooth black glass found in parts of Australia. **australorp** (os′ trȧ lôrp), *n.* An Australian utility type of Black Orpington fowl.

***austringer** (os′ trin jėr) [O.F. *ostruchier*, *austruchier* (*ostour*, mod. F. *autour*, the goshawk)], *n.* A keeper of goshawks.

autacoid (aw′ tȧ coid) [Gr. *autos*, self; *akos*, a drug; *eidos*, form], *n.* (*Physiol.*) An internal secretion including both hormone and chalone.

autarch (aw′ tark) [Gr. *archein*, to rule], *n.* Absolute sovereign, an autocrat. **autarchy,** *n.* Absolute sovereignty, autocracy. **autarchic,** *a.*

autarky (aw′ tark i) [Gr. *autarkeia*], *n.* Self-sufficiency.

authentic (aw then′ tik) [O.F. *autentique*, L. *authenticus*, Gr. *authentikos*, vouched for, *authentēs*, one who does things himself (AUTO-)], *a.* Entitled to acceptance or belief; trustworthy, credible; of undisputed origin, genuine; really proceeding from its professed source; *(*Law*) vested with all legal formalities, and legally attested; (*Mus.*) having its notes comprised between the keynote or tonic and the octave above. **authentical,** *a.* **authentically,** *adv.* **authenticalness,** *n.* **authenticate,** *v.t.* To render authentic or valid; to establish the truth or credibility of; to verify the authorship of. **authentication** (-kā′ shůn), *n.* The act of authenticating. **authenticity** (-tis′ i iti), *n.*

author (aw′ thôr) [O.F. *autour*, *auctor*, L. *auctor -em* (*auctus*, p.p. of *augere*, to make to grow)], *n.* The originator, producer, or efficient cause of anything; the composer of a literary work; the works of an author; an authority, an informant. **author-craft,** *n.* Skill in literary composition; literary work. **authoress,** *n.* A female author. **authorial** (aw thôr′ i ål), *a.* **authorism,** *n.* **authorless,** *a.* Without an acknowledged author; anonymous. **authorship,** *n.* The profession of a writer of books; the personality of an author; origin of a literary work.

authority (aw thor′ i ti) [F. *autorité*, L. *auctoritātem* (*auctor*)], *n.* Legitimate power to command or act;

a person or body exercising this power (*usu. pl.*); power, weight, or influence, derived from character, station, mental superiority, and the like; weight of testimony, credibility; the author or the source of a statement; the standard book or work of reference on any subject; an expert, one entitled to speak with authority on any subject. **authoritarian,** *n.* One who places obedience to authority above personal liberty. **authoritative,** *a.* Imperative, commanding; possessed of authority, founded on sufficient authority. **authoritatively,** *adv.* **authoritativeness,** *n.* **authorize** (aw′ thȯ rīz), *v.t.* To give authority to, to empower; to establish by authority; to sanction; to warrant legally; to justify, afford just ground for; to make or prove legitimate; to vouch for, to confirm. **authorized,** *a.* **Authorized Version,** *n.* The English translation of the Bible published in 1611. **authorizable,** *a.* **authorization** (-zā′ shŭn), *n.* The act of authorizing; establishment by authority.

auto- (aw′ tō) [Gr. *autos*, self], *comb. form.* Self, from, within, or by oneself; one's own, independently.

autobahn (aw′ tō ban) [G.], *n.* A road designed and reserved for motor traffic; a motor-way in Germany.

autobiography (aw tō bī og′ rȧ fi) [AUTO-, BIOGRAPHY], *n.* A memoir of one's life, written by oneself; the writing of one's own memoirs. **autobiographer,** *n.* One who writes an account of his own life. **autobiographic, autobiographical** (-grăf′ ik, -ăl), *a.* **autobiographically,** *adv.*

autocar (aw′ tō kar) [AUTO-, CAR], *n.* A vehicle driven by its own mechanical power; a motor-car.

autocarpous (aw tō kar′ pŭs), *a.* Consisting of pericarp only.

autocephalous (aw tō sef′ ȧ lŭs) [Gr., having an independent head], *a.* Having an independent head or chief, esp. of a church having its own bishop.

autochrome (aw tō krōm′), *a.* (*Phot.*) Of a process in which the screen plate is coated with an emulsion sensitive to all colours in an almost equal degree.

autochthon (aw tok′ thōn, -thȯn) [Gr., sprung from the land itself], *n.* (*usu. in pl.* **-ones** [L.], or **-ons**) A man sprung from the soil; one of the original or earliest known inhabitants; an aboriginal animal or plant. **autochthonal,** *a.* Native to the soil. **autochthonic** (aw tȯk thon′ ik), **autochthonous** (aw tok′ thȯ nŭs), *a.* **autochthonism,** *n.* Birth from the soil, or original occupation of a country. **autochthony,** *n.* Aboriginal occupation.

autocracy (aw tok′ rȧ si) [Gr. *autokrateia* (AUTO-, *krateein*, to rule)], *n.* Absolute government; controlling power. **autocrat** (aw′ tȯ krăt) [F. *autocrate*, G. *autokratēs*], *n.* A sovereign of uncontrolled authority. **autocratic, autocratical** (-krăt′ ik, -ăl), *a.* Pertaining to autocracy; absolute, despotic. **autocratically,** *adv.* **autocratrix** (aw tok′ rȧ triks). ***autocratrice** (-tris), *n.* A female autocrat; an Empress of Russia in her own right.

autocycle (aw tō sī′ kėl), *n.* A push-bicycle with motor attachment.

auto-da-fé (aw tō da fā′) [Port., action for the faith], *n.* (*pl.* ***autos-da-fé***) A sentence pronounced by the Inquisition; the execution of this judgment; the burning of a heretic.

autodidact (aw tō dī′ dăkt), *n.* A self-taught person.

autoerotism (aw tō er′ ot izm), *n.* (*Psych.*) Self-produced sexual pleasure or emotion, *e.g.* masturbation.

autogamy (aw tog′ ȧ mi), *n.* Self-fertilization.

autogenous (aw toj′ ė nŭs) [Gr. *autogenēs* (AUTO-genēs, produced, *gen-*, stem of *gignesthai*, to be begotten)], *a.* Self-engendered, self-produced, independent; (*Physiol.*) developed from distinct and independent centres; (*Path.*) a term applied to the distinctive elements of morbid tissues. **autogeny** (aw toj′ ė ni), *n.* (*Biol.*) A kind of spontaneous generation.

autogiro (aw tō jī′ rō), *n.* (*Aviat.*) An aircraft in which the lifting surfaces are the freely-rotating blades of a large horizontal air-screw.

autograph (aw′ tō grăf) [L. *autographus*, Gr. *autographos* (AUTO-, *graphein*, to write)], *n.* A person's own handwriting, especially his signature; a manuscript in an author's own handwriting; a copy produced by autography. *a.* Written by the author himself. *v.t.* To write with one's own hand; to reproduce by autography; to sign. **autographic, autographical** (aw tȯ grăf′ ik, -ăl), *a.* Written by one's own hand; of or pertaining to autographs or autography. **autographically,** *adv.* **autography** (aw tog′ rȧ fi), *n.* Writing with one's own hands; one's own handwriting; a process of reproducing handwriting or drawing in facsimile.

autogravure (aw′ tō grăv ūr, aw tō grȧ vūr′) [AUTO-, F. *gravure*, engraving], *n.* A process of photo-engraving.

auto-intoxication (aw tō in tok si kā′ shȯn), *n.* Re-absorption of toxic matter produced by the body.

autolatry (aw tol′ ȧ tri), *n.* Worship of self.

autolysis (aw tol′ i sis) [Gr. *lysis*, loosening], *n.* (*Biol.*) The breakdown of cells by the action of enzymes produced in the cells themselves.

automatic, automatical (aw tō măt′ ik, -ik ăl) [Gr. *automatos*, acting of itself (AUTO-, *-matos*, allied to Sansk. *matas*, thought, known)], *a.* Self-acting; acting as an automaton, having the power of movement within itself; carried on unconsciously; merely mechanical. *n.* An automatic pistol. **automat** (aw tō mat′), *n.* (*Am.*) Restaurant equipped with automatic machines for supplying food, etc. **automatically,** *adv.* **automaticity** (aw tȯ mȧ tis′ i ti), *n.* The state of being automatic. **automatic signalling:** (*Rail.*) A signalling system whereby the passing of a train automatically puts the signals behind it at danger. **automatic telephone:** A telephone system in which connexion between two subscribers is obtained by electrical means without the interposition of an operator. **automatic writing:** Writing performed without the consciousness of the writer. **automatism** (aw tom′ ȧ tizm), *n.* The quality of being automatic; involuntary action; the theory that animals are automata performing their functions as mere machines as the result of natural laws; unconscious action, automatic routine; the faculty of initiating movement. **automatist,** *n.* **automatize,** *v.t.* To reduce to the condition of an automaton.

automation (aw tō mā′ shŭn) [as prec.], *n.* The use of self-regulating or automatically programmed machines in the manufacture of goods.

automaton (aw tom′ ȧ tȯn), *n.* (*pl.* **automata**). That which has the power of spontaneous motion; a piece of mechanism simulating human or animal action; a man or lower animal whose actions are merely mechanical.

automatous (aw tom′ ȧ tŭs), *a.* Acting spontaneously; of the nature of an automaton.

automobile (aw tō mō′ bēl), [F. (AUTO-, L. *mōbilis*)], *a.* Self-moving. *n.* (-mō bēl′). An auto-car, motor-car. **automobilism,** *n.* **automobilist,** *n.*

automorphic (aw tō môr′ fik) [Gr. *automorphos*, self-formed (AUTO-, *morphē*, form)], *a.* Characterized by automorphism. **automorphically,** *adv.* **automorphism,** *n.* The attribution of one's own characteristics to another.

autonomy (aw ton′ ȯ mi) [Gr. *autonomia*, independence, *autonomos*, independent (AUTO-, *nomos*, law)], *n.* The right of self-government; an independent state or community; freedom to act as one pleases; (*Phil.*) freedom of the will (in Kantian system); (*Biol.*) organic independence. **autonomous,** *a.* Of or possessing autonomy; self-governing; independent; (*Biol.*) possessing organic independence. **autonomously,** *adv.* **autonomic**

(aw tō nom' ik), *a.* Autonomous; independent. **autonomist** (aw ton' ŏ mist), *n.* An advocate of autonomy. **autonomize,** *v.t.* To render independent; to make self-governing.

autonym (aw' tō nim) [Gr. *autos*, self, *onoma*, name], *n.* Real name, as opp. to pseudonym.

autophagy (aw tof' ȧ ji), *n.* Sustenance of life by the absorption of the tissues.

autoplasty (aw' tō plăs ti), *n.* Reparation of a lesion by healthy tissue from the same body.

autopsy (aw tŏp' si) [Gr. *autopsia* (AUTO-, *opsis*, sight)], *n.* Personal observation; dissection; post-mortem examination; (*fig.*) critical examination. **autoptic, autoptical** (aw top' tik, -tik ȧl), *a.* Seen by one's own eyes; based on personal examination. **autoptically,** *adv.*

autoschediasm (aw tō sked' i ăzm) [AUTO-, Gr. *schediasma*, from *autoschediazein*, to act or speak offhand (*autoschedios*, off-hand, on the spur of the moment)], *n.* Something hastily improvised. **autoschediastic, -al** (-sked i ăs' tik, -tik ȧl), *a.* Hastily improvised. **autoschediaze** (-sked' i āz), *v.t.* To improvise.

autostrada (aw tō stra' da) [It.], *n.* A motor-way in Italy.

autosuggestion (aw tō sŭ jes' chŭn), *n.* Suggestion arising from oneself, esp. hypnotic or morbid suggestion. **autosuggestive,** *a.*

autotheism (aw tō thē' izm) [Gr. *autotheos*, very God (Gr. *theos*, God)], *n.* *The self-subsistence of God; deification of self. **autotheist,** *n.* One who deifies himself.

autotomy (aw tot' ŏm i) [Gr. *autos*, self, *tomos*, cutting], *n.* (*Zool.*) Voluntary separation of a part of the body, *e.g.* tail, as in certain lizards; self-amputation.

autotoxic (aw tō toks' ik), *a.* Self-poisoning. **autotoxication,** *n.*

autotrophic (aw tō trof' ik), *a.* Self-nourishing; of plants capable of photo-synthesis.

autotype (aw' tō tīp), *n.* A true impress; a facsimile; a photographic printing process for reproducing photographs in monochrome pictures, *v.t.* To reproduce by the autotype process. **autotypography** (aw tō tī pog' rȧ fi), *n.* A process by which drawings on gelatine can be transferred to soft metallic plates, which are afterwards printed from. **autotypy** (aw' tō tī pi), *n.* The process of reproducing in autotype.

autovac (aw' tō văk), *n.* (*Motor.*) A vacuum device for raising petrol from a low tank to a level from which it will flow into the carburettor.

autumn (aw' tŭm) [O.F. *autompne* L., *autumnus*], *n.* The season of the year between summer and winter (astronomically, it extends from the autumnal equinox, September 21, to the winter solstice, December 21; popularly, it comprises August, September and October, and in North America, September, October, and November), (*Am.*) the Fall; (*fig.*) the decline of human life; the fruits of harvest. **autumn-bells:** The Calathian violet, *Gentiana pneumonanthe.* **autumnal** (aw tŭm' nȧl), *a.* Of or pertaining to, characteristic of or produced in autumn; (*fig.*) pertaining to the declining period of life. *n.* A plant which flowers in autumn. **autumnal equinox,** *n.* The time when the sun crosses the equator southward (this happens about September 21).

autunite (aw' tun īt) [town of *Autun*, France], *n.* (*Metall.*) A mineral consisting of a hydrous phosphate of uranium and calcium.

auxiliary (awg zil' i ȧ ri) [L. *auxiliārius*, from *auxilium*, help (*augēre*, to increase)], *a.* Helping, aiding; subsidiary to: applied to verbs used in the conjugation of other verbs. *n.* One who or that which helps or assists; a verb used in the conjugation of other verbs; (*Math.*) a quantity introduced with the view of simplifying some complex operation; (*pl.*) foreign or allied troops in the service of a nation at war. ***auxiliar,** *a.* and *n.* Auxiliary.

auxometer (awk zom' e tĕr) [Gr. *auxein*, to grow, METER], *n.* An optical instrument for measuring magnifying power.

ava (a' vȧ) [native name in the Sandwich Isles], *n.* An intoxicating drink [KAVA].

avail (ȧ vāl') [O.F. *vail*, 1st pers. pres. sing. of *valoir*, L. *valēre* to be worth], *v.i.* To be of value, use, profit, or advantage; to be helpful; to be effectual, sufficient, *v.t.* To be of use or advantage (to); (*Am.*) to inform, to assure of. **to avail oneself of,** (*Am.*) **to avail of:** To take advantage of, make use of. *n.* Worth, value, profit, advantage, use (obs. except in the following phrases); (*Am. in pl.*) profits, proceeds. **of no avail, without avail:** Ineffectual. **to little avail:** Ineffectually. **available,** *a.* Capable of being employed; at one's disposal; at hand, valid. **availability** (-bil' i ti), *n.* The quality of being available; (*Am.*) a qualification in a candidate which implies strong probability of his success. **availableness,** *n.* **availably,** *adv.*

avalanche (ăv' ȧ lanch, -sh) [Swiss-F. (F. *avalance*, descent), from *avaler*, to descend to the valley (*à val*, L. *ad vallem*, to the valley)] *n.* A snow-slip; a mass of snow, ice, and debris falling or sliding from the upper parts of a mountain.

***avale** (ȧ vāl') [F. *avaler*, see prec.], *v.t.* To cause to descend, come down, or fall; to let down, to lower; to doff; (*fig.*) to humble, to depress. *v.i.* To dismount; to come down; to sink.

avant (ȧ vant', a' van) [F., before, now principally found in the form *van-* or *vant-*], *comb. form.* Before, in front. **avant-brace,** *n.* [VAMBRACE]. **avant-courier,** *n.* A forerunner, a precursor; (*pl.*) scouts, skirmishers. **avant-guard,** *a.* As a forerunner in music, art, etc.; in advance of contemporary artistic taste or trend.

avarice (ăv' ȧ ris) [O.F., from L. *avāritia*, from *avārus*, greedy (*avēre*, to wish, desire)], *n.* An excessive craving after wealth; greediness of gain; (*fig.*) eager desire to get and keep. **avaricious** (ăv ȧ rish' ŭs), *a.* **avariciously,** *adv.*

avast (ȧ vast') [prob. from Dut. *hou' vast* or *houd vast*, hold fast], *int.* (*Naut.*) Stay! Stop! Desist!

avatar (ăv' ȧ tar, av ȧ tar') [Sansk. *avatara*, descent], *n.* The descent of a deity to the earth; the incarnation of a deity; (*fig.*) manifestation, phase.

avaunt (ȧ vawnt') [AVANT], *v.t.* To raise, to advance. *v.i.* To come forward, to depart. *adv.* To the front, forward. *int.* Be off! Away with you! Begone! *n.* A dismissal; a defiance.

ave (ā' vi) [L., hail (*avēre*, to fare well)], *int.* Hail! Welcome! Farewell! (in allusion to the classical custom of greeting the dead). *n.* An Ave Maria; one of the small beads on a rosary on which prayers are counted; a shout of welcome or adieu. **ave-bell,** *n.* The bell rung when the Ave Maria should be repeated. **Ave Maria, Ave Mary,** *n.* The Hail Mary; the angelical salutation (Luke i. 28) with that of St. Elisabeth (i. 42), to which a prayer is added, the whole being used as a form of devotion; the ave-bell.

avenaceous (ăv ē nā' shŭs) [L. *avēnāceus*, from *avēna*, oats], *a.* Of, pertaining to, or resembling oats.

avenge (ȧ venj') [O.F. *avengier* (*à* to, *vengier*, L. *vindicāre*, to claim, revenge)], *v.t.* To vindicate by punishing a wrong-doer; to exact satisfaction for (an injury, etc.); to inflict punishment on account of. *v.i.* To execute vengeance. **avengeful,** *a.* **avengement,** *n.* **avenger,** *n.* One who avenges or vindicates; a vindicator, a revenger. **avenger of blood:** The name given in the Mosaic law to the person on whom it devolved to punish murder by death.

avens (ăv' ĕns) [O.F. *avence* (etym. doubtful)], *n.* The popular English name of two plants of the genus *Geum*, the wood avens or herb bennet, *G. urbanum*, and the water avens, *G. rivale*; also of the mountain avens, *Dryas octopetala.*

aventail, aventayle (ăv′ ėn tāl) [O.F. *esventail* (L. *ex-*, out, *ventus* wind)], *n.* The movable part of a helmet in front, which may be lifted to admit fresh air.

aventre (ȧ ven′ tėr) [etym. doubtful (perh. F. *à*, to, *ventre*, belly)], *v.t.* To throw forward or thrust (a spear).

aventurine, aventurin (ȧ ven′ tū rin) [F., from It. *avventurino* (*avventura*, chance)], *n.* A gold-spangled glass made first at Murano; the process was accidentally discovered, whence the name; (*Min.*) a quartz of similar appearance spangled with scales of mica or some other mineral.

avenue (ăv′ ė nū) [F., fem. p.p. of *avenir*, to come to, L. *advenīre* (*ad-*, to, *venīre*, to come)], *n.* A way or means of access or approach (now used *fig.*); an approach to a building; a broad alley bordered with trees; the rows of trees bordering such alley; a fine wide thoroughfare.

aver (ȧ vĕr′) [F. *avérer*, late L. *āvērāre* (*ad*, to, *verum*, truth)], *v.t.* To assert positively; to declare; (*Law*) to prove; offer to prove; *to allege, declare. **averrable,** *a.* Capable of being affirmed with certainty. **averment,** *n.* The act of averring; affirmation, positive assertion; (*Law*) an affirmation alleged to be true, and followed by an offer to verify.

average (ăv′ ėr ȧj) [F. *avarie* (etym. doubtful; cp. Sp. *averia*, It. *avaria*, Dut. *avarij*, *haverij*, G. *haferei*)], *n.* Any charge payable by the owner of goods over and above the freight, often called **petty** (formerly **accustomed**) **average;** loss arising from damage to ship or cargo at sea; apportionment of such loss among the parties interested [if the damage was unavoidable, such apportionment is called a **particular average,** and falls upon the respective owners or insurers in proportion to their shares of the particular interests affected; if intentional (as by cutting away masts, etc.), it is called a **general average**]; hence, a number or quantity intermediate to several different numbers or quantities; a mean; the rate, proportion, degree, quantity, or number generally prevailing. *v.t.* To calculate the average; to take the ordinary standard; to divide proportionately to number involved; to be or consist of on an average; to do, have, or take as a mean rate. **on an average:** Taking the mean deduced from a number of examples. *a.* Ascertained by taking a mean proportion between given quantities; medium, ordinary. **averagely,** *adv.*

avernian (ȧ vĕr′ ni ȧn) [L. *Avernus*, -IAN], *a.* Of or pertaining to Lake Avernus in Campania, near which was the fabled entrance to the lower world; infernal.

averrable [AVER].

Averroist (ăv ėr rō′ ist) [*Averroes*], *n.* One of a sect named after Averroes, an Arabian physician and philosopher (12th century) who taught a kind of Pantheism. **Averroism,** *n.*

***averruncate** (ăv ėr rŭng′ kāt) [L. *āverruncātus*, p.p. of *āverruncāre*, to ward off, remove; wrongly taken as meaning to weed out, as if from *eruncāre*], *v.t.* To turn away, to avert; (*erroneously*) to weed, to root up. ***averruncation** (ăv ėr rŭng kā′ shŭn), *n.* The act of turning away or averting; (*erroneously*) the act of rooting up. **averruncator,** *n.* An instrument for pruning trees, consisting of two blades, working like shears, at the end of a rod.

averse (ȧ vĕrs′) [L. *aversus*, p.p. of *āvertere* (*a-*, *ab-* away, *vertere*, to turn)], *a.* Turned away mentally; feeling repugnance or dislike; unwilling, disinclined. **aversely,** *adv.* **averseness,** *n.* **aversion** (-shŭn), *n.* An averted state of mind or feeling; disinclination, dislike, repugnance; an object of dislike. (Used with *to* or *from.*)

avert (ȧ vĕrt′) [F. *avertir*, late L. *avertĕre*, L. *āvertere*, to turn away (*avertir* seems to have represented both *advertere* and *āvertere*, the meaning being differentiated later)], *v.t.* To turn from or away (used specially of something feared or threatened); to ward off. **avertible,** *a.*

avian (ā′ vi ȧn) [L. *avis*, a bird, -AN], *a.* Of or pertaining to birds. **aviary** (-ȧ ri), *n.* A large cage or building in which birds are kept. **aviarist,** *n.* **aviculture** (ā′ vi kŭl tūr) [-CULTURE], *n.* The breeding and rearing of birds. **avifauna** (-faw nȧ) [-FAUNA], *n.* The birds in any district taken collectively; the fauna of a district, so far as its birds are concerned.

aviation (ā vi ā′ shŭn) [L. *avis*, a bird], *n.* The art of flying or travelling in the air; all matters to do with aircraft or flying in an aircraft. **aviate** (ā′ vi āt), *v.i.* To fly, to travel in an aircraft. **aviator** (ā′vi ā tŏr), *n.* A person who flies; one skilled in managing an aircraft; *a flying-machine.

avid (ăv′ id) [L. *avidus*, greedy (*avēre*, to crave)], *a.* Greedy, covetous; ardently desirous; extremely eager; hungry. **avidly,** *adv.* **avidity** (ȧ vid′ i ti), *n.*

avifauna [AVIAN].

aviso (ȧ vī′ zō) [Sp., advice, L. *advīsum* (see ADVICE)], *n.* *Advice, intelligence; an advice-boat.

avizandum (ăv i zăn′ dŭm) [med. L., gerund of *avizāre*, to consider], *n.* Consideration. **to take** (a case) **to avizandum:** (*Sc. Law*) To consider privately with a view to judgment.

avocado (ăv ō ka′ dō) [Sp., 'advocate,' a popular substitute for Mex. *ahuacatl*], *n.* The pear-like fruit of a West Indian tree, *Persea gratissima*, also called the alligator pear.

avocation (ăv ō kā′ shŭn) [L. *āvocātiōnem*, from *āvocāre* (*ā-*, *ab-*, away, *vocāre*, to call)], *n.* The condition of being called away, diversion, distraction; a minor employment or occupation; (*pop.*) ordinary employment, calling, vocation, business.

avocet, avoset (ăv′ ȯ set) [F. *avocette*, It. *avosetta*], *n.* A wading bird allied to the snipes and stilts, having a long slender bill curved upwards.

avoid (ȧ void′) [A.-F. *avoider*, O.F. *esvuidier* (*es-*, out, *vuidier*, to void, from *vuit*, *vuide*, empty)], *v.t.* To keep at a distance from, to shun; to keep away from; to escape, evade; (*Law*) to defeat; to invalidate; to quash; *to empty by excretion. **v.i.* To become void or vacant; to depart, dismount, escape. **avoidable,** *a.* Capable of being avoided. **avoidably,** *adv.* **avoidability** (-bil′ i ti), *n.* **avoidance,** *n.* The act of making void or annulling; the act of shunning or avoiding; the becoming void or vacant. **avoidless,** *a.* (*poet.*) Incapable of being avoided; inevitable.

avoirdupois (ăv′ ėr dū poiz) [O.F. *avoir* (*aveir*) *de pois*, things of weight (*avoir*, *aveir*, goods, property, L. *habēre*, to have, *de*, of, *pois*, *peis*, L. *pensum*, weight)], *n.* The British standard system of weights for all commodities except gold and silver, gems, and drugs, based on the unit of a pound of 16 ounces, equal to 7000 grains; (*Am.*) weight, heaviness.

avoset [AVOCET].

avouch (ȧ vouch′) [O.F. *avochier*, L. *advocāre* (*ad*, to, *vocāre*, to call)], *v.t.* To affirm, vouch for, guarantee as certain; to own, acknowledge, avow; to maintain, to justify. *v.i.* To vouch, give assurance or guarantee. **n.* Evidence, testimony, guarantee. **avouchable,** *a.*

avow (ȧ vou′) [O.F. *avouer*, L. *advocāre*, to call upon, to call in as patron (*ad-*, to, *vocāre*, to call), more or less identified with sense of *a*, to, and *vouer*, L. *votāre*, to vow (*vōtum*, a vow)], *v.t.* To own, to acknowledge, to admit (of one's free will); to state, allege, declare; *to vow; promise with a vow. *n.* *Vow, solemn promise; avowal, sanction. **avowable,** *a.* **avowal,** *n.* An open declaration; free admission. **avowed,** *a.* Acknowledged; self-acknowledged. **avowedly** (ȧ vou′ ed li), *adv.* ***avoure** (ȧ vour′), *n.* Avowal, answer. **avowry** (ȧ vou′ ri) [O.F. *avoerie*, *avouerie*, office of the *avoueur* or patron], *n.* *Patronage, advocacy; a patron, a protector; (*Law*) the plea whereby a person who distrains for rent avows and justifies the act.

avulsion (ȧ vŭl′ shun) [L. *āvulsiōnem*, from *àvellere* (*a-*, *ab-*, from *vellere*, to pluck)], *n.* The act of tearing away or violently separating; a fragment torn off; (*Law*) sudden removal of land (without change of ownership) by flood, alteration in the course of a river, or the like. **avulsive,** *a.*

avuncular (ȧ vŭng′ kū lȧr) [L. *avunculus*, a maternal uncle], *a.* Of, pertaining to, or resembling an uncle.

await (ȧ wāt′) [O.N.F. *awaitier* (O.F. *agaitier*), to lie in wait for (*à*, to, *waitier*, *gaitier*, see WAIT)], *v.* *To watch for, lie in wait for; to wait for, look out for, expect; to be in store for. *v.i.* *To lie in wait; to wait. **n.* A lying in wait; ambush.

awake (ȧ wāk′) [two A.-S. verbs were early confused, *awæcnan* (*a-*, on, WAKE), *awōc*, *awacen*; and *awacian*, *awacode* (*awæcnan* gave us *awaken* and *awakened*, *awacian* gave *awake*, *awaked*). Both verbs were intr., meaning, to arise from sleep, cease sleeping; the tr. senses were supplied by *āweccan*, to rouse, which was gradually superseded by *awake*], *v.i.* To wake from sleep, cease sleeping; to become conscious of, alive to (anything); to become active or alert. *v.t.* To arouse from sleep, or from lethargy or inaction; to excite to action or new life. *a.* Not asleep; roused from sleep; active, vigilant, aware of, alive to (some object). **awakable,** *a.* **awaken** (ȧ wā′ kėn), *v.t.* To arouse, awake; (*fig.*) to arouse to a sense of sin. *v.i.* To awake. **awakenable,** *a.* **awakening,** *a.* Rising as if from sleep; fitted to inspire activity, rousing. *n.* A rising from sleep, lethargy, or moral indifference. **awakenment,** *n.* An awakening.

awanting (ȧ won′ ting) [*ā-*, on, WANTING, taken as a single word, as if from a v. *awant*], *a.* Wanting, missing, absent.

award (ȧ wôrd′) [A.-F. *awarder*, O.F. *esguarder*, from *es-* L. *ex-*, out of, O.L.G. *wardēn* (O.H.G. *wartēn*), watch, guard; (cp. WARD)], *v.t.* To adjudge, to assign by judicial sentence; *to decide authoritatively, after due deliberation and examination. *n.* The decision of judge, arbitrator, or umpire; the document embodying the terms of such decision; the penalty or other payment so determined.

aware (ȧ wâr′) [A.-S. *gewær* (*ge-*, intens., *wær*, aware, wary) (cp. O.H.G. *gawar*, G. *gewahr*)], *a.* Apprised, cognizant, conscious; *excited to caution; watchful, vigilant. **awareness,** *n.*

awash (ȧ wosh′), *adv.* On a level with the water; at the mercy of the waves.

a-waste (ȧ wāst′), *adv.* On the waste.

a-wave (ȧ wāv′), *a.* On the wave, waving.

away (ȧ wā′) [A.-S. *onweg*, on the way], *adv.* Implying motion from a place, person, cause, or condition; absent, in the other direction, at another place; continuously, constantly; straightway, directly. Used elliptically as a verb, Be off! Begone! (to) go away. **away back:** Long ago. **away with:** Take away; (with negative phrase) bear, endure, tolerate. **cannot away with:** Cannot endure. **to do away with, make away with:** To destroy, to kill. **far and away, out and away:** Beyond comparison. **fire away:** Go on without delay. **right away:** All right; go ahead; immediately.

awe (1) (aw) [Icel. *agi* (cp. A.-S. *ege*, fear, also *ōga*, terror)], *n.* Dread mingled with veneration; solemn, reverential wonder. *v.t.* To inspire with solemn fear or reverence; to restrain by profound respect or reverential fear. **to keep in awe:** To restrain by fear. **aweless,** *a.* Not feeling awe or dread; *not inspiring awe. **awelessness,** *n.* **awesome,** *a.* Full of awe; inspiring awe; weird. **awesomely,** *adv.* **awesomeness,** *n.* **awe-strike,** *v.t.* To overwhelm with awe. **awe-struck,** *a.*

awe (2) (aw) [etym. unknown], *n.* A float-board of a water-wheel.

aweary (ȧ wēr′ i), *a.* Tired, weary.

a-weather (ȧ weth′ ėr), *adv.* To the weather side, as opposed to the lee side; towards the wind. **aweather of,** *prep.* On that side of.

a-week (ȧ wēk′), *adv.* Weekly.

aweel (ȧ wēl′) [ah well (cp. F. *eh bien*)], *adv.* (*Sc.*) Well; well then.

a-weigh (ȧ wā′), *adv.* (*Naut.*) Raised vertically just off the bottom; a-trip.

awful (aw′ ful) [AWE (1)], *a.* Inspiring awe; worthy of profound reverence; sublime, majestic; dreadful, fearful, appalling; filled with awe; (*colloq.*) frightful, terrible, monstrous (often used as a mere intensive). **awfully,** *adv.* In an awful manner; (*colloq.*) exceedingly, very. **awfulness,** *n.*

awheto, aweto (ȧ wā′ tō) [Maori], *n.* (*N. Zealand*) A vegetable-eating caterpillar that, when dried, yields a tattoo dye.

awhile (ȧ wīl′) [A.-S. *āne while*], *adv.* For some time; for a little; (*incorrectly*) a while.

a-wing (ȧ wing′), *adv.* On the wing, alive with wings.

awkward (awk′ wȧrd) [M.E. *awk*, contrary, untoward (Icel. *afug*, *ofug*, turned the wrong way), -WARD], *a.* Unhandy, ill adapted for use; *froward, cross-grained; lacking dexterity, bungling, ungainly, embarrassed, ill at ease; clumsy, embarrassing; not easy to manage or deal with. **awkwardly,** *adv.* **awkwardness,** *n.*

awl (awl) [A.-S. *æl* (cp. O.H.G. *ala*, G. *ahle*)], *n.* A tool with a cylindrical tapering blade, sharpened at the end, for making holes for stitches in leather. **awl-bird,** *n.* (*prov.*) *Picus viridis*, the green woodpecker. **awl-shaped,** *a.* (*Bot.*) Subulate. **awlwort,** *n.* Genus *Subularia*, esp. *S. aquatica*, a British species, named from the shape of the leaves.

awn (awn) [Icel. *ögn* chaff, a husk (cp. O.H.G. *agana*, G. *ahne*)], *n.* The beard of corn and grasses; the bristle springing from a bract in the inflorescence of grasses. **awned** (1) *a.* **awnless,** *a.*

awning (aw′ ning) [etym. doubtful, perhaps from F. *auvent*, pent-house], *n.* A covering of tarpaulin, canvas, or other material used as a protection from sun or rain, esp. above the deck of a ship; (*Naut.*) the part of the poop-deck which is continued forward beyond the bulk-head of the cabin; a shelter. **awned** (2), *part.a.* Fitted with an awning.

awoke, *past* (AWAKE).

a-work (ȧ wĕrk′), *adv.* At work.

awrong (ȧ rong′), *adv.* Wrongly.

awry (ȧ rī′), *adv.* Wrily, obliquely, crookedly; erroneously, amiss. *a.* Crooked, distorted, oblique; wrong.

axe, ax (ăks) [A.-S. *æx* (cp. Icel. *öx*, O.H.G. *acchus*, G. *axt*, L. *ascia*, Gr. *axinē*)], *n.* (*pl.* **axes**) An instrument for cutting or chopping consisting of an iron head with a sharp edge, fitted to a wooden handle or helve; the headsman's axe; hence execution; a celt probably used as an axe. *v.t.* To dismiss staff for reasons of economy. **axe-head,** *n.* The cutting portion of the axe. **axe-man,** *n.* A woodman; a warrior armed with a battle-axe. ***axe-stone,** *n.* Jade, nephrite, from which prehistoric man used to make many stone implements. **put the axe on the helve:** Solve a doubt or a puzzle. **to have an axe to grind:** To have ulterior motives.

axial, axile, etc. [AXIS].

axil (ăk′ sil) [L. *axilla*, an armpit], *n.* (*Bot.*) The hollow where the base of a leaf joins the stem, or where a branch leaves the trunk. **axillar, axillary** (ăk′ sil ȧr, -ȧr i), *a.* Pertaining to the armpit; (*Bot.*) pertaining to or arising from the axil.

axiom (ăk′ si ŏm) [F. *axiome*, L. *axiōma*, from Gr. (*axioō*, I esteem, from *axios*, worthy)], *n.* A self-evident truth; (*Math.*) a self-evident proposition, assented to as soon as enunciated. **axiomatic, axiomatical** (ăk si ŏ măt′ ik, -ik ȧl), *a.* Self-evident, containing an axiom or axioms; full of maxims. **axiomatically,** *adv.*

axis (ăk′ sis) [L., the axle (cp. Gr. *axōn*, Sansk. *aksha*, A.-S. *eax*)], *n.* (*pl.* **axes** (ăk′ sēz)). A real or imaginary straight line round which a body revolves, round which its parts are arranged, or to which they have a symmetrical relation; (*Physiol.*) the second cervical vertebra; a process on that vertebra by which it articulates with the skull; the central stem, core, or main skeletal support of an organism; (*Bot.*) the central shaft of growth; the stem is the **ascending** and the root the **descending axis**; (*Cryst.*) an imaginary line round which the crystal can be symmetrically built up; (*Geol.*) a central ridge; (*Math.*) a straight line in a plane figure about which it is conceived to revolve to generate a solid; a line dividing a regular figure into two symmetrical parts; (*Opt.*) a ray of light passing through the centre of or falling perpendicularly on the eye or a lens; the straight line from the eye to the object seen; (*Arch.*, *pl.*) the sloping timbers of a roof, the principals. **The Axis,** *n.* The term used to describe the political collaboration (Rome-Berlin axis) between Nazi Germany and Fascist Italy from 1935 to 1943. **axis of a balance:** The line on which it turns. **axis of oscillation:** A straight line passing through the point about which a pendulum oscillates, at right angles to the plane of motion. **axis of the equator:** The polar diameter of the earth, the axis of revolution. **axial,** *a.* Pertaining to an axis; forming an axis. **axial pitch:** (*Mech.*) The pitch of a screw measured in a direction parallel with the axis. **axially,** *adv.* In the direction of the axis. **axiality** (ăk si ăl′ i ti), *n.* The quality of being axial. **axile** (ăk′ sīl), *a.* Situated in the axis of anything. **axile bodies,** *n.pl.* (*Physiol.*) The lactile corpuscles at the ends of sensory nerves.

axle (ăk′ sėl) [Icel. *öxull* (cp. Goth. *ahsuls*, O. Teut. *ahsā*, Sansk. *aksha*, L. *axis*, Gr. *axōn*)], *n.* The pin or bar on which a wheel revolves, or which revolves with the wheel; the thin ends of the axle-tree; the axle-tree; (*fig.*) axis; the pole of the earth or heavens. **axle-box,** *n.* A case in which the ends of axles revolve; a metal cover for the hub. **axle-pin,** *n.* A linchpin. **axle-tree,** *n.* The beam or bar connecting wheels, on the ends of which the wheels revolve; *a spindle, axis. **axled,** *a.* Furnished with an axle.

axolotl (ăks′ ō lotl) [Aztec *a-*, *atl*, water, *xolotl*, servant], *n.* A small Mexican batrachian, *Siredon pisciforme*, retaining its gills through life.

ay, aye (1) (ī) [etym. doubtful], *adv.*, *int.* Yes. *n.* An affirmative vote in the House of Commons; (*pl.*) those who vote in the affirmative. **Aye, aye, sir**; (*Naut.*) Yes, sir; very well, sir.

ayah (ī′ ȧ) [Hind.] A Hindu nurse for children; a lady's maid.

aye (2) (ā) [M.E. *aȝȝ*, *ai*, *ei*, Icel. *ei*, *ey* (cogn. with A.-S. *ā*, Goth. *aiw*, L. *ævum*, Gr. *aei*)], *adv.* Always, ever, in all cases, on all occasions. **for aye, for ever and aye:** For ever, to all eternity.

aye-aye (ī′ ī) [F., from Malagasy *aiay*, from its cry], *n.* A small aberrant lemur, found in Madagascar, *Cheiromys madagascariensis*.

a-yelp (ȧ yelp′), *adv.* On the yelp.

Aylesbury (ālz′ ber i) [town in Bucks], *n.* A breed of table ducks.

ayond, ayont (ȧ yond′, -yont), *prep.* (*Sc. and North.*) Beyond.

Ayrshire (âr′ shir), *n.* A breed of cattle named from the county of Ayr, Scotland, and highly prized for dairy purposes.

azalea (ȧ zā′ lė ȧ) [Gr., fem. of *azaleos*, dry (either from dry wood or its liking for dry soil)], *n.* A genus of shrubby plants with showy and occasionally fragrant flowers.

azarole (ăz′ ȧ rōl) [F. *azerole*, Arab. *az-zu'rūr*], *n.* The Neapolitan medlar, *Cratægus azarolus*, or its fruit.

Azilian (ă zil′ i ȧn) [cavern of Mas-d'*Azil*, France], *a.* (*Anthrop.*) Pertaining to the period of culture typified by the remains found in this cavern in the Pyrenees.

azimuth (ăz′ i mŭth) [F. *azimut*, Arab. *assamūt* (*al*, the, *sumut*, ways or points, sing. *samt*)], *n.* (*Astron.*) An arc of the heavens extending from the zenith to the horizon, which it cuts at right angles; horizontal angle or direction, point of the compass. **true azimuth** (of a heavenly body): The arc of the horizon intercepted between the north (or, in the southern hemisphere, the south) point of the horizon and the point where the great circle passing through the heavenly body in question cuts the horizon. **magnetic azimuth:** The arc intercepted between the true azimuth and the magnetic meridian. **azimuth-circle,** *n.* A circle passing through the zenith and cutting the horizon perpendicularly. **azimuth-compass,** *n.* An instrument for finding the magnetic azimuth. **azimuth-dial,** *n.* A dial having the gnomon at right angles to the plane of the horizon, the shadow indicating the sun's azimuth. **azimuthal** (ăz i mū′ thȧl), *a.* Of or pertaining to the azimuth; in azimuth. **azimuthally,** *adv.* In azimuth; in a circle parallel to the horizon.

azoic (ȧ zō′ ik) [Gr. *azōos*, lifeless (*a-*, not, *zoē*, life, *zaō*, I live)], *a.* Having no trace of life; (*Geol.*) destitute of organic remains.

azonic (ȧ zon′ ik) [Gr. *azōnikos* (*a-*, not, without, *zōnē*, region)], *a.* Not pertaining to a definite region, not local.

azorite (ăz′ ȯ rit) [from the place], *n.* A variety of zirconium found in the Azores.

***azote** (ȧ zōt′) [F. *azote* (Gr. *a-*, not, *zōt-*, as in *zōtikos*, fit for maintaining life)], *n.* An old name for nitrogen, from its fatal effects upon animal life. **azotic** (ȧ zot′ ik), *a.* **azotize** (ăz′ ȯ tīz), *v.t.* To render nitrogenous, to deoxygenize.

Aztec (ăz′ tek) [*Azteca*, native name of Mexican tribe], *a.* Of, pertaining to, or naming the leading Mexican tribe at the time of the Spanish invasion (1519); loosely applied to Mexican antiquities generally. *n.* A member of the Aztec tribe; its language.

azure (ăzh′ ėr, ăzh′ ūr) [O.F. *azur*, med. L. *azura*, Arab. *lazward*, Pers. *lājward*, *lāzhward*, lapis lazuli], *n.* Lapis-lazuli; the deep blue of the sky; the vault of heaven; a bright blue pigment or dye; (*Her.*) the blue of coats of arms, represented in engraving by horizontal lines. *a.* Resembling the clear bright blue of the sky; clear, unclouded; (*Her.*) blue. *v.t.* To colour azure or bright clear blue. **azure-spar, azure-stone,** *n.* Lazulite. **azurine,** *n.* The blue roach *Leuciscus cæruleus*. **azurite,** *n.* Blue carbonate of copper; *lazulite. **azurn,** *a.* (*poet.*) Azure.

azygous (ăz′ i gŭs) [Gr. *azugos*, unyoked (*a-*, not, *zugon*, a yoke)], *a.* (*Physiol.*) Unpaired; occurring singly, not as one of a pair. **azygously,** *adv.*

azyme (ăz′ im, ăz′ īm) [L. *azȳmus*, Gr. *azumos* (*a-*, not, without, *zumē*, leaven)], *n.* (*Jewish*) The Passover cake of unleavened bread. **Azymite** (ăz′ i mīt), *n.* One who uses unleavened bread in the Eucharist; a name given by the Greek Church to members of the Western Church and to Armenians and Maronites. **azymous,** *a.* Unleavened.

B

B, b, the second letter in the English, Aryan, and other alphabets, corresponding in power to the Greek Beta (β) and the Phœnician and Hebrew Beth, representing a flat labial mute; (*pl.* **Bs, B's, Bees**). Used as a symbol to denote the second of a series; (*Alg.*) the second known quantity; (*Mus.*) the seventh note of the diatonic scale of C major. **not to know B from a bull's foot:** To be grossly ignorant or illiterate.

baa (ba) [from the sound], *n.* The cry or bleat of a sheep. *v.t.* To cry or bleat as a sheep.

Baal (bā′ ăl) [Heb. *ba′al*, lord], *n.* (*pl.* **Baalim**) The chief male divinity among the Phœnicians; a false god. **Baalism** (-izm) [-ISM], *n.* Worship of Baal; idolatry. **Baalist, Baalite,** *n.* A worshipper of Baal; an idolater.

baal, bale (bāl) [Austral. abor.], *int.* No! Also expressing disapproval.

baas (bas) [Dut. S. Afr.], *n.* Boss, overseer.

babacoote (ba′ bȧ koot) [Malagasy *ba-bako-to*], *n.* The indri, a short-tailed woolly lemur. *Lichanotus brevicaudatus*, from Madagascar.

babbit metal, babbit's metal (băb′ it) [name of inventor], *n.* An alloy of tin, antimony, and copper, used in bearings to diminish friction.

babble (bă′ bĕl) [from *ba ba*, the earliest attempts of a child to speak, -LE (cp. Dut. *babbelen*, F. *babiller*, G. *pappelen*, etc.)], *v.i.* To utter indistinct sounds (esp. of inanimate things); to talk childishly or inopportunely; to prattle; to make inarticulate sounds (of streams, birds, etc.); to give tongue without reason (of hounds). *v.t.* To prate; to utter; to blab. *n.* Unmeaning prattle; shallow, foolish talk; confused murmur, as of a running brook. **babblement,** *n.* Idle, foolish talk; senseless, indiscreet talk; babble, as of streams. **babbler,** *n.* An unintermitting and shallow talker; a gossip; one who tells secrets; a name for the long-legged thrushes.

babe (bāb) [prob. from obs. *baban*, imit. from childish speech (cp. BABBLE)], *n.* A young child, a baby; a foolish or childish person.

Babel (bā′ bĕl) [Heb., confusion, Babylon (perh. from Assyr. *bab-ilu*, the Gate of God)], *n.* The city and tower described in Gen. xi., the place where the confusion of tongues is said to have taken place; a lofty structure; a visionary project; noisy confusion, tumult disorder.

babiroussa, babirussa (ba bi roos′ ȧ) [Malay *babī rūsa*, hog like a deer (*babi*, hog, *rusa*, deer)], *n.* The wild hog of eastern Asia, in the male of which the upper canines grow through the lip and turn backwards like horns.

baboo, babu (ba′ boo) [Hind. *babu*], *n.* A term used in Lower Bengal for a Hindu gentleman, corresponding to English *Mr.* or *Esquire*; an Indian clerk who writes English; a Bengali with a superficial English education.

baboon (bȧ boon′) [F. *babuin*, mod. *babouin* (etym. unknown)], *n.* *A grotesque decorative figure; the popular name of a large division of monkeys, with long dog-like snout, great canine teeth, callosities on the buttocks, and capacious cheek-pouches; (*fig.*) as an epithet of abuse. **baboonery** (-ėr i) [-ERY], *n.* An assemblage of baboons; behaviour like that of a baboon. **babuina** (băb ů ē′ nȧ, -ī′ nȧ) [fem. of mod. L. *babuinus*, F. *babouine*), *n.* A female baboon.

babouche, babouche (ba boosh′) [Ar.], *n.* A Turkish heelless slipper.

baby (bā′ bi) [dim. of BABE], *n.* An infant; a child in arms; *a grotesque decorative figure; (*fig.*) a foolish, childish person. *v.t.* To make a baby of, to treat like a baby. **to hold the baby:** (*colloq.*) To be left to bear the brunt of something; to be landed with something. **baby-carriage,** *n.* (*Am.*) A perambulator, pram. **baby-farmer,** *n.* One who takes in infants to nurse for payment. **baby grand,** *n.* A small grand piano. **babyhood,** *n.* Infancy; infants collectively; babyish conduct. **baby ribbon,** *n.* Narrow ribbon for threading through underwear. **baby-sitter,** *n.* A person who looks after a child while the parents are out. **baby-sit,** *v.i.* **babyish,** *a.* **babyishness,** *n.* **babyism,** *n.*

Babylon (băb′ i lŏn) [L. *Babylōn*, Gr. *Babulōn*, Heb. *Bābel*], *n.* The ancient capital of the Chaldæan empire; the mystical city mentioned in the Apocalypse; Rome; the papacy; a great and dissolute city. **Babylonian** (băb i lō′ ni ăn), *a.* Of or pertaining to Babylon; gigantic, magnificent, luxurious; (*fig.*) popish, scarlet [from the fancied identification of the Scarlet Woman (Rev. xvii. 4) with Rome]. *n.* An inhabitant of Babylon; (*fig.*) an astrologer; a papist. **Babylonic, Babylonish,** *a.*

bacca, baccy (băk′ ȧ, -i), *n.* (*pop.*) Colloquial abbreviations for tobacco.

baccalaureate (băk ȧ law′ ri ȧt) [med. L. *baccalaureus*, as if from *bacca lauri*, laurel berry, late L. *baccalāris*, BACHELOR], *n.* The university degree of bachelor.

baccara, baccarat (băk′ ȧ ra) [F. *baccara*], *n.* A gambling card game between banker and punters.

baccare [BACKARE].

baccate (băk′ āt) [L. *baccātus* (*bacca*, berry)], *a.* Berried, bearing berries; berry-like.

bacchanal (băk′ ȧ nȧl) [L. *bacchānālis* (*Bacchus*, Gr. *Bakchos*, the God of Wine)], *a.* Of or pertaining to Bacchus or his festivities; hence characterized by drunken revelry. *n.* A votary of Bacchus; hence, a drunken reveller; a song or dance, or (*pl.*) a festival, in honour of Bacchus; an orgy. **bacchanalia** (băk ȧ nā′ li ȧ), *n.pl.* The festival of Bacchus; bacchanals; drunken revelry; an orgy. **bacchanalian,** *a.* Of or pertaining to bacchanals; bacchanal. *n.* A bacchanal; a drunken reveller. **bacchanalianism,** *n.* **bacchant** (băk′ ȧnt) [L. *Bacchant -em*, pres.p. of *bacchāri* (Gr. *bakcheuein*, to celebrate the Bacchic rites)], *n.* A votary of Bacchus; hence, a drunken reveller. *a.* Worshipping Bacchus; (*fig.*) fond of the wine-cup. **bacchante** (băk′ ȧnt, bȧ kănt′, bȧ kăn′ ti) [F. (the last pronun. is after It. *baccante*)], *n.* A priestess of Bacchus. **bacchantic** (bȧ kăn′ tik), *a.* **bacchic** (băk′ ik), *a.* Pertaining or relating to Bacchus or his worship; hence, frenzied; riotously festive, roystering.

bacchius (bȧk ī′ ůs) [L., from Gr. *bakcheios*], *n.* Metrical foot of three syllables, two long and one short.

Bacchus (băk′ ůs) [L. from Gr. *Bakchos*], *n.* The god of wine; (*fig.*) wine, any intoxicant.

bacciferous (băk sif′ ėr ůs) [L. *baccifer* (*bacca*, berry, *-fer*, see -FEROUS)], *a.* (*Bot.*) Bearing berries. **bacciform** (băk′ si fôrm) [-FORM], *a.* (*Bot.*) Berry-shaped. **baccivorous** (băk siv′ ŏ rŭs) [-VOROUS], *a.* (*Zool.*) Berry-eating.

bach (băch), *n.* (*N. Zealand*) A small cottage or habitable hut.

bacharach (ba*ch*′ ȧ ra*ch*) [from *Bacharach*, a town on the Rhine], *n.* A wine from the Rhine.

bachelor (băch′ ĕl ŏr) [O.F. *bacheler*, late L. *baccalāris* (cp. *baccalārius*, a farm labourer, perh. from late L. *bacca*, L. *vacca*, a cow)], *n.* An unmarried man; *an unmarried woman; a man or woman who has taken the first degree of a university below master or doctor; *a young knight who followed the banner of another. **knight bachelor:** A knight of the oldest order of knighthood; one knighted but not belonging to any of the special orders. **bachelor's buttons,** *n.pl.* The double variety of *Ranunculus acris*; applied also to several other plants with button-like flowers; small biscuits; buttons that can be clipped in place and need no sewing. **bachelorhood, bachelorship,** *n.* The state or condition of a bachelor, position of bachelor of arts. **bachelorism,** *n.* A peculiarity of a bachelor.

bachle (bă′ *ch*ĕl) [Sc.], *n.* An old worn-out shoe.

bacillar (bȧ sil′ ȧr) [as foll.], *a.* Shaped like a rod. **bacillary** (bȧ sil′ ȧ ri) *a.* (*Path.*) Of, pertaining to, or consisting of little rods; of, pertaining to, or caused by bacilli. **bacilliform,** *a.* Rod-shaped.

bacillus (bȧ sil′ ůs) [late L., a little rod, dim. of *baculus*, a stick], *n.* (*pl.* **bacilli**) A genus of microscopic rod-like bacteria, found in diseased tissue in anthrax and tubercular diseases.

back (1) (băk) [A.-S. *bæc*], *n.* The hinder part of the human body, from the neck to the lower extremity of the spine; the corresponding portion in the lower Vertebrates, and the analogous part in the Invertebrates; the surface of any object opposite to the face or front; the outer surface of the hand, the convex part of a book, the thick edge of a knife, etc.; the hinder part, the rear, the part away from the actor or speaker; the ridge or upper surface of a hill; the keel of a ship; (*Mining*) a diagonal parting in coal; that side of an inclined mineral ore nearest the surface; (*Football*) one of the players whose duty it is to defend the goal; **half** and **three-quarter backs** are stationed nearer the front. *a.* Situated behind or in the rear; coming back, turned back, reversed; behind in time, in arrear; remote, distant, inferior. *adv.* In a direction to the rear; to the place from which one came; to a former state, position, or condition; behind, not advancing, behindhand; in return, in retaliation; in a position behind, away from the front; in a state of check; in time past; again; in returning. *v.t.* To furnish with a back or backing; to be at the back of; to support materially or morally, to second, to uphold; to bet in favour of; to mount or get on the back of, to write on the back of, to countersign, to endorse; to cause to move back; to push back; to reverse the action of. *v.i.* To retreat, to recede; to move in a reversed direction. **to back down; to back out:** To move backwards; to retreat from a difficult situation. **to back up:** To support materially or morally. **to back the field:** To bet against all the horses except one. **to back into:** To knock into someone with a backward motion; (*Rail.*) to run backwards into a station, or siding. **to back the wrong horse:** To make a bad choice. **to back water:** To reverse the motion of the oars. **back and belly, back and side:** All over, completely. **back and forth:** Backwards and forwards, up and down. **behind the back of:** Behind, out of sight of. **on the back of:** Weighing as a heavy burden on, in addition to. **to break the back of:** To overburden; to perform the greater part of (a piece of work). **to put** (or **get**) **the back up:** To offer resistance; to excite resentment; to feel resentment and show it. **to see the back of:** To get rid of. **to turn the back:** To turn away, to flee. **to turn the back upon:** To abandon, to forsake. **on one's back:** Floored; at the end of one's tether; laid up. **back-band,** *n.* A strap or chain put across the cart saddle of a horse to support the shafts. **back-bencher,** *n.* (*Pol.*) A member of Parliament without portfolio. **backbite,** *v.t.* and *i.* To slander, censure, or speak ill of. **back-biter,** *n.* **back-blocks,** *n.pl.* The settlements or claims in the remoter parts of a colony; lands away from a river; (*Austral.*) the interior parts of the continent; **back-blocker,** *n.* One who lives there. **back-board,** *n.* A board forming the back of anything; a board attached to the rim of a water-wheel to prevent the water running off the floats; a board strapped across the back to prevent stooping. **back-bond,** *n.* (*Sc. Law*) A deed by which a party holding a title acknowledges that he holds in trust for a certain purpose. **backbone,** *n.* The bony framework of the back; the spine; the spinal column; a main support or axis; (*fig.*) strength of character, firmness, decision. **to the backbone:** Thoroughly. **backboned,** *a.* **back-boxes,** *n.pl.* (*Print.*) The boxes on the top of the upper case, usually appropriated to small capitals. **back-cast,** *n.* A reverse; a relapse. *a.* Thrown backwards. **back-chat,** *n.* (*colloq.*) Flippant retort, answering back. **back-cloth,** *n.* (*Theat.*) The curtain at the back of the stage; background. **to back-comb:** To comb backwards with short, sharp strokes, making the hair fuzzy. **back-country,** *n.* Thinly populated districts. **back-door,** *n.* A back or private entrance; (*fig.*) an indirect or circuitous way. *a.* Clandestine. **back-draught,** *n.* A backward draught of air; a hood for producing back-draught in a fire. **back-end,** *n.* Late autumn. **backfall,** *n.* A throw or fall on the back in wrestling. **back fire,** *n.* (*Motor*) Premature combustion in the cylinder. **back-friend,** *n.* *A false or pretended friend; a reliable friend; a backer. **background,** *n.* The ground or surface behind the chief objects of contemplation; that part of a picture, stage-scene, or description which represents this; the setting; (*fig.*) inferior position; obscurity. **back hair,** *n.* The long hair at the back of a woman's head. **back-hand,** *n.* Handwriting sloped backwards; the hand turned backwards (as at tennis) to take a ball at the left. **back-handed,** *a.* With the back of the hand; directed backwards; (*fig.*) remiss, indirect; unexpected. **back-hander,** *n.* A blow with the back of the hand; an indirect attack; a drink out of one's proper turn. **back-lash,** *n.* Jarring reaction in a piece of mechanism. **back-light,** *n.* (*Cinema*) A light projected on a subject from a source behind the camera. **back-lock,** *n.* A trick in wrestling. **back-log,** *n.* (*Am.*) A large log placed at the back of the fire; (*Comm.*) reserves or arrears of unfulfilled orders; an accumulation of business. **back-number,** *n.* A past issue of a newspaper or magazine; (*fig.*) an out-of-date person or thing. **back of:** (*Am.*) Behind. **back-pages,** *n.pl.* (*Print.*) Pages on the left-hand side of an open book. **back-pay,** *n.* Arrears of pay. **back-pedal,** *v.i.* To press back the pedals of a cycle; (*fig.*) to restrain one's enthusiasm. **back-piece,** *n.* A piece of armour for the back; a piece forming the back of anything. **back-plate,** *n.* Armour for the back, corresponding to the breastplate in front; the piece forming the back of anything. **back-pressure,** *n.* (*Mech.*) Resistance to the working of the piston, caused by waste steam or atmospheric pressure. **backroom boys:** (*colloq.*) Scientists and others who work in the background unrecognized. **back-scratcher,** *n.* A hand-shaped appliance with outstretched fingers for scratching the back; a flatterer. **back-scratching,** *n.* Flattery; toadyism. **to take a back seat:** (*colloq.*) To make oneself inconspicuous; to withdraw; to admit that one is worsted. **backset,** *n.* A set back, a reverse; a counter current. *v.t.* (*Am.*) To plough again in the autumn after a spring ploughing. **back settlement,** *n.* An outlying settlement; (*pl.*) the backwoods. **back-settler,** *n.* A backwoodsman. **backside,** *n.* The back or hinder portion of anything; the buttocks. **back-sight,** *n.* A sight taken backwards in land surveying; the sight of a rifle near the stock. **back-slang,** *n.* A peculiar kind of slang in which ordinary words are pronounced backwards [as, *Cool the eslop* (or *slop*), Look, the police]. **back-slanging:** (*Austral.*) Asking for hospitality at a back-block home. **backslide,** *v.i.* To fall into wrongdoing or false opinions after conversion; to relapse. **backslider,** *n.* **back-spacer,** *n.* Typewriter key for moving the carriage backwards. **back-speed,** *n.* The second-speed gear of a lathe. **backstage,** *a.* (*Theat.*) Behind the scenes. **backstairs,** *n.pl.* Stairs at the back of a house; the private stairs in a palace for the use of servants, etc. *a.* Clandestine, underhand, scandalous. **backstays,** *n.pl.* (*Naut.*) Rope or stays extending with a slant aft from the mast-heads to the sides of the ship, and serving, with the shrouds, to support the mast under press of sail. **back-stitch,** *n.* A method of sewing with stitches that are made to overlap. *v.t.* and *i.* To sew in this manner. **back-stroke,** *n.* A return stroke; a swimming stroke. **back-string,** *n.* A string at the back; the fastener of a pinafore. ***back-sword,** *n.* A sword with only one sharp edge; a single-stick; hence, a backsword-man. ***backsword-man,** *n.* One skilled in the use of the backsword. **backveld,** *n.* (*S. Afr.*) Country far removed from towns. *a.* Remote, rural, primitive. **backwash,** *n.* The wash from the oars of a boat in front; the dragging motion of a receding wave; a backward current; eddy or swirl caused by a ship's propeller. **backwater,** *n.* Water dammed back or that has overflowed; a piece of water without current fed by the back flow of a river; a backward current of water; (*Naut.*) a creek or lagoon separated from the sea by a narrow strip of land and communicating therewith by barred outlets; the wash thrown back by a water-wheel or the paddles or screws of steamboats. **back-way,** *n.* A way leading to the back; a roundabout way; a bypath. **backwoods,** *n.pl.* Remote, uncleared forest land. **backwoodsman,** *n.* A settler in the backwoods; a back-settler; (*colloq.*) a peer who rarely attends the House of Lords. **backed,** *a.*

Provided with a back (chiefly in composition, the sense being completed by the first element); supported, seconded, betted on; endorsed, accepted. **backer,** *n.* One who backs or supports, by money or credit; one who bets on a horse or an event; a book-maker, a bookie; (*Build.*) a small slate laid on the back of a large one at certain points. **backing,** *n.* Supporting, seconding; the thing or the body of persons which forms a back or support; a piece forming the back or lining the back; putting back; backward motion, esp. of the wind in an opposite direction to that of the sun; (*Phot.*) opaque varnish put on back of a negative to obviate halation; (*Print.*) perfecting a sheet printed on one side by printing on the other; (*Bookbinding*) putting the shoulder on a book before putting the cover on; (*pl.*) refuse from wool or flax after dressing it. **backing down:** Withdrawal, retreat. **backing up:** Support; in cricket and other games, support or assistance rendered to a player.

back (2) (băk) [Dut. *bak*, trough, tub. F. *bac*, ferry-boat, punt, late L. *baccus*, ferry-boat], *n.* A large tub used in brewing, distilling, dyeing, etc.

backet (băk′ ĕt) [F. *baquet*, dim. of *bac*, BACK (2)], *n.* (*Sc.*) A shallow wooden trough or hod for carrying coals, mortar, and the like.

backgammon (băk găm′ ŏn) [BACK, GAME], *n.* A game played by two persons on a table with draughtsmen, the moves being determined by throwing dice; the highest win in backgammon. *v.t.* To defeat at backgammon.

backing [BACK].

backsheesh [BAKSHEESH].

backward, backwards (băk′ wȧrd, -z) [orig. *abackward*)], *adv.* With the back foremost; towards the back or rear; behind, towards the starting-point; towards past time; towards a worse state or condition, in reverse order; *the wrong way, perversely, contrariwise. **backward,** *a.* Directed to the back or rear; directed the way from which one has come; reversed, reluctant, unwilling; behind in time, late (esp. of the season, crops, etc.); behind in progress; toward or into past time. **n.* Time past. **backward and forward:** To and fro; (*fig.*) uncertain, vacillating. **backwardly,** *adv.* In a backward direction; in a reluctant or negligent manner. **backwardness,** *n.* **backwardation** (băk wȧr dā′ shŭn), *n.* (*Stock Exchange*) A consideration paid by a seller of stock for the privilege of delaying its delivery.

bacon (bā′ kŏn) [O.F., from O.H.G. *bacho* (M.H.G. *backe*), buttock, ham], *n.* The back and sides of a pig, cured by salting and drying with or without wood-smoke; *one who lives principally on bacon; a rustic, a chawbacon. **chawbacon, bacon-chops, bacon-slicer,** *n.* (*slang*) A rustic, a clod-hopper; a clownish fellow. **to save one's bacon:** To escape from injury or loss. **baconize,** *v.t.* and *i.* To make into bacon; to smoke like bacon. **bacony,** *a.* **bacon-like;** in a state of fatty degeneration.

Baconian (bȧ kō′ ni ȧn) [Francis *Bacon*, Baron Verulam (1561–1626)], *a.* Of or pertaining to Bacon or his inductive philosophy; experimental, inductive. *n.* A follower of the inductive system of natural philosophy; (*pop.*) a believer in the conceit that Bacon was really the author of Shakespeare's works.

Bacterium (băk tēr′ i ŭm) [Gr. *baktērion*, dim. of *baktron*, a stick], *n.* (*pl.* **bacteria**) A genus of Schizomycetæ, microscopic fission fungi, rod-shaped (whence the name) and unicellular; found in decomposing infusions of organic bodies. **bacterial,** *a.* **bactericide,** *n.* An agent that destroys bacteria. **bacteriology** (-ol′ ŏ ji), *n.* The scientific study of bacteria. **bacteriological** (-ŏ loj′ ik ȧl), *a.* **bacteriologist,** *n.* **bacteroid** (băk′ tėr oid), *a.* Of the nature of or resembling the genus *Bacterium.* **bacteriotherapy,** *n.* Treatment of disease by employing bacteria or their products.

Bactrian (băk′ tri ȧn) [*Bactria*, Central Asia], *a.* Descriptive of a camel with two humps.

baculine (băk′ ū lin) [L. *baculum*, a stick], *n.* Characterized by the stick or flogging.

bad (băd) [etym. doubtful], *a.* (comp. **worse,** superl. **worst**) Not good, worthless; defective, faulty, incorrect; ill, evil, hurtful, wicked, morally depraved; noxious, painful, dangerous, pernicious; in ill-health, sick; injured, diseased; (*Law*) invalid. *n.* That which is bad; a bad state or condition. **to the bad:** To ruin; to the wrong side of an account. **to go bad:** To decay. **to go to the bad:** To go to ruin, to go to the dogs. **bad blood,** *n.* Angry feeling, enmity. **bad debt,** *n.* A debt that cannot be recovered. **a bad egg, bad lot, bad penny,** *n.* A bad speculation; a worthless affair; a ne'er-do-well. **bad form,** *n.* Bad manners; lack of breeding. **bad grace,** *n.* Unwillingness, reluctance. **bad hat,** *n.* A rogue, ne'er-do-well. **bad lands,** *n.pl.* Tracts of arid country in the Western States of America. **bad shot,** *n.* A wrong guess. **baddish,** *a.* Rather bad. **badly,** *adv.* (comp. **worse,** superl. **worst**) In a bad manner; improperly, wickedly, evilly; unskilfully, imperfectly; defectively, faultily; dangerously, disastrously; (*colloq.*) very much, by much. **to want a thing badly:** To want it very much. **badness,** *n.* The quality of being bad; inferiority; incorrectness, faultiness; wickedness; worthlessness.

bade (băd, băd), *past* [BID].

badge (băj) [etym. unknown], *n.* A distinctive mark, sign, or token; (*Her.*) a cognizance; (*Naut.*) an ornament on the quarters of small vessels, near the stern; (*fig.*) a feature or quality that characterizes. *v.t.* To mark with or as with a badge.

badger (1) (băj′ ėr) [etym. doubtful (prob. in allusion to white mark on face)], *n.* A plantigrade animal about the size of a fox, with thick body and short legs, *Meles vulgaris*, found in Britain, Europe, and Asia; hence, a painter's brush, or angler's fly, made of badgers' hair. *v.t.* To worry, to tease, to annoy like dogs baiting a badger. **badger-baiting, badger-drawing,** *n.* The setting of dogs to draw a badger from its earth or from a barrel. **badger-dog,** *n.* The German dachshund, with long body and short legs, used to draw badgers. ***badger-legged,** *a.* Having legs of unequal length, as those of the badger were popularly supposed to be.

badger (2) (băj′ ėr) [etym. doubtful], *n.* (*Dial.*) A huckster; a corn-dealer; a travelling provision-dealer.

badging-hook [BAG (2)].

badigeon (bȧ dij′ ŏn) [F., etym. unknown], *n.* A mixture of plaster and freestone used by sculptors to repair defects in stone, and by builders to present the appearance of stone; a mixture of sawdust and glue, used to conceal defects in woodwork.

badinage (ba din azh′, băd′ in ȧj) [F., from *badiner* to jest (*badin*, silly, late L. *badāre*, to gape)], *n.* Light raillery; banter.

badminton (băd′ min tŏn) [name of country seat of Duke of Beaufort], *n.* A game resembling lawn-tennis, but played with shuttlecocks instead of balls; a kind of claret-cup.

baff (băf) [perh. from O.F. *baffe*, a blow; or merely imitative], *v.t.* (*Sc.*) A blow with something soft; (*Golf*) to strike the ground with a club and send the ball up in the air. **baffing-spoon,** *n.* (*Golf*) A baffy. **baffy,** *n.* A wooden club for lofting.

baffle (băf′ ėl) [perh. F. *beffler*, to deceive, mock, or *bafoŭer*, to hoodwink; (O.F. *befel*, mockery, It. *beffa*, Prov. *bafa*, a scoff, perh. from *baf!* an imitative int.)], *v.t.* *To disgrace; to treat with derision, scoff at; to frustrate, elude, escape, circumvent; to thwart, defeat; to confound, reduce to extremities. *v.i.* To struggle ineffectually. *n.* A defeat; (*Acous.*) a rigid appliance that regulates the distribution of sound-waves from a producer. **baffle-board,** *n.* A device to prevent the carrying of noise. **baffle-plate,** *n.* (*Eng.*) A plate used to direct the flow of fluid. **baffler,** *n.* **baffling,** Bewildering; thwarting; (*Naut.*, *of winds*) variable, shifting. **bafflingly,** *adv.*

baft (1) (băft) [prob. Pers., wrought, woven], *n.* A cheap coarse fabric, usually manufactured of cotton, for export to Africa.

baft (2) (baft) [A.-S. *beæftan* (*be*, by, *æftan*, behind)], *adv.* *Behind; (*Naut.*) abaft, astern.

bag (1) (băg) [etym. doubtful; perh. Icel. *baggi*], *n.* A pouch, small sack, or other flexible receptacle; a measure of quantity, varying with different commodities; the contents of such a measure; a game-bag, the result of a day's sport or of a hunting expedition; a purse, a money-bag; an udder; a sac or bag-like receptacle in animal bodies containing some secretion; (*pl.*) loose clothes, esp. trousers; (*pl.*) (*slang*) quantities. *v.t.* To put into a bag; to put into a game-bag; hence, to shoot, to catch; (*slang*) to take, seize, appropriate. *v.i.* To swell as a bag; to hang loosely; (*Naut.*) to drop away from the direct course. **bag and baggage:** With all belongings; entirely, completely; hence **bag and baggage policy:** Wholesale surrender. **bag of bones:** A living skeleton. **bag o' moonshine:** (*colloq.*) Nonsense. **bag of mystery:** (*slang*) A sausage. **the whole bag of tricks:** Everything; all means or expedients. **to give one the bag to hold:** To slip off, leave in the lurch. **to let the cat out of the bag:** To reveal the secret. **bag cap,** *n.* Brown paper in sheets measuring 24 × 19½ inches. **bag-fox,** *n.* A fox brought alive to the meet and turned out of a bag. **bagful,** *n.* As much as a bag will hold. **bagging,** *n.* Cloth, canvas, or other material for bags. **baggy,** *a.* Loose; bulging out like a bag; (of trousers) stretched by wear. **bagginess,** *n.* Looseness. **bag-swinger,** *n.* (*Austral.*) A book-maker. **bag-wash,** *n.* A system of laundry-work by which a comprehensive charge is made for a bagful of garments. **bag-wig,** *n.* A wig fashionable in the 18th century in which the back hair was enclosed in a bag.

bag (2) (băg) [etym. unknown; local var. *badge*], *v.t.* To cut wheat, haulm, grass, etc., with a hook.

bagging-hook [local var. BADGING-HOOK], *n.* A kind of sickle or hook used in bagging.

bagasse (bȧ găs′) [F., perh. var. for *bagage*], *n.* The refuse products in sugar-making; cane-trash. **bagasse-burner,** *n.* A furnace for burning cane-trash.

bagatelle (băg ȧ tel′) [F., from It. *bagatelle*, a trifle (perh. dim. of *baga*, baggage)], *n.* A trifle, a trumpery amount; a game played on a nine-holed board, with nine balls and a cue; a light piece of music.

baggage (băg′ ȧj) [O.F. *bagage* (*baguer*, to tie up, or *bagues*, bundles; It. *baga*, a wine-skin; see also BAG (1))], *n.* Portable belongings, esp. the tents, furniture, utensils, and other necessaries of an army; (*Am.*) luggage; *a woman of loose character; a playful arch young woman. *a.* Used for carrying or looking after or convoying baggage. **baggage-car,** *n.* (*Am.*) A luggage-van. **baggage-check,** *n.* A ticket given to passengers so that they may collect their luggage at the end of a journey. **baggage-man, baggage-master,** *n.* (*Am.*) A guard in charge of passengers' luggage. **baggage-smasher,** *n.* (*Am.*) Nickname for a railway porter. **baggage-train,** *n.* The part of an army that convoys the baggage.

baggit (băg′ it) [prob. Sc. form of BAGGED, see BAG (1)], *n.* A salmon that has just spawned.

bagman (băg′ mȧn) [BAG (1)], *n.* (*colloq.*) A commercial traveller; a bag-fox.

bagnio (băn′ yō) [It. *bagno*, L. *balneum*, a bath], *n.* A bathing-house, a bath; an Oriental prison for slaves; a brothel.

bagpipe (băg′ pīp), *n.* A musical instrument of great antiquity, now chiefly used in the Scottish Highlands, consisting of a wind-bag and several reed-pipes into which the air is pressed by the player.

bah (ba) [perh. from F. *bah!*], *int.* An expression of contempt.

bahadur (bȧ ha′ door) [Hind., brave], *n.* A ceremonious title formerly given in India to European officers.

baignoire (bā′ nwar) [F., orig. a vessel for bathing in, from *baigner*, to bathe], *n.* A box at the theatre on the lowest tier.

bail (1) (bāl) [O.F. *bail*, safe keeping, from *bailler*, L. *bājulāre*, to carry, to guard (*bājulus*, a porter)], *n.* The temporary release of a prisoner from custody on security given for his due surrender when required; the money security, or the person or persons giving security, for the due surrender of a prisoner temporarily released; security, guarantee. *v.t.* To procure the liberation of by giving sureties; to admit to or release on bail; to deliver (goods) in trust on an expressed or implied contract. **to give leg-bail:** To run away. **to bail out:** To procure release on bail from prison. **bailable,** *a.* Entitled to be admitted to bail; admitting of bail. **bail-bond,** *n.* A bond entered into by a prisoner upon release on bail, and his sureties. **bailsman,** *n.* One who gives bail.

bail (2) (bāl) [M.E. *beyl*, Icel. *beygla*, hoop, guard of a sword-hilt], *n.* A hoop or ring; the arched support for an awning or hood; the handle of a kettle.

bail (3) (bāl) [O.F. *bail* (etym. doubtful, perh. from *baillier*, to enclose)], *n.* A division between the stalls of a stable; (*Austral.*) a framework for securing the head of a cow while she is being milked; (*Cricket, pl.*) the crosspieces laid on the top of the wicket; *the outer line of fortifications, a palisade; *the wall of the outer courtyard in a feudal castle, a bailey. *v.i.* To surrender by throwing up the arms. **bailer** (1), *n.* (*Cricket*) A ball that hits off the bails. **v.t.* To confine. **to bail up:** (*Austral.*) To disarm travellers (said of bushrangers).

bail (4), **bale** (bāl) [obs. n. *bail*, a bucket, bailer, F. *baile*, a bucket (prob. from late L. *bacula*, dim. of *baca, bacca*, a shallow vessel)], *v.t.* To throw (water) out of a boat with a shallow vessel; to empty a boat of water. **bailer** (2), *n.* One who or that which bails water out of a boat, etc. **to bail out:** (*Aviat.*) [BALE (3)].

bailee (bā lē) [BAIL (1)], *n.* One to whom goods are entrusted for a specific purpose.

bailey (bā′ li) [BAIL (3) (perh. from med. L. *balium*)], *n.* The wall enclosing the outer court of a feudal castle; the outer court itself; any other courts or enclosures of courts, the *outer bailey* or the *inner bailey*. **Old Bailey:** The Central Criminal Court standing at the outer boundary of the old wall of London.

Bailey bridge (bā′ li) [name of inventor], *n.* (*Mil.*) A bridge of lattice steel construction made of standard parts for rapid erection and transport.

bailie (bā′ li) [M.E. *bailli*, O.F. *bailli* (prev. *baillis*, *baillif*), BAILIFF], *n.* * A Scottish magistrate with duties corresponding to those of an English sheriff; now a Scottish municipal magistrate corresponding to an English alderman. **water-bailies,** *n.pl.* (*Sc.*) Constables specially employed in carrying out the Tweed Fisheries Acts.

bailiff (bā′ lif) [O.F. *baillif* (nom. *baillis*), late L. *bājukīvus* (see BAIL (1))], *n.* An officer appointed for the administration of justice in a certain bailiwick or district; *a king's administrative officer (still used in *High Bailiff of Westminster, Bailiff of Dover Castle*); a foreign magistrate of similar standing (*e.g. Bailly* or first civil officer of the Channel Isles); a sheriff's officer who executes writs and distrains; an agent or steward to a land-owner.

bailiwick (bā′ li wik) [BAILIE, -WICK], *n.* The district within which a bailie or bailiff possesses jurisdiction.

bailment (bāl′ mėnt) [BAIL (1)], *n.* Delivery of goods; delivery in trust; the bailing of a prisoner.

bailor (bā′ lȯr), *n.* (*Law*) One who entrusts another person, called the bailee, with goods for a specific purpose.

bain-marie (băn ma′ rē) [F. (L. *balneum Mariæ*, the bath of Mary, *i.e.* the Virgin)], *n.* A flat vessel of boiling water into which stewpans are put to warm; a double saucepan.

bairam (bī ram′) [Turk., from Pers. *bairām*], *n.* The name of two Mohammedan festivals following the Ramadan, the Lesser lasting three days, the Greater, which falls seventy days later, lasting four days.

bairn (bârn) [A.-S. *bearn* (cp. Icel. *barn*, Goth. *barn*, O.Teut. *beran*, to bear); *bairn* is a Scots form adopted into literary English], *n.* A child of either sex.

***baisemain** (băz′ man) [F. *baiser*, to kiss, *main*, hand], *n.* (*usu. in pl.*). Kissing hands; compliments, respects.

bait (bāt) [Icel. *beita*, to cause to bite (*bita*, to bite)], *v.t.* To furnish (a hook, gin, snare, etc.) with real or sham food; to tempt, entice, allure; to give food to a horse on a journey, to feed; to set dogs to worry (an animal); to worry, harass, torment. *v.i.* To stop on a journey for rest or refreshment. *n.* An attractive morsel put on a hook, gin, snare, etc., to attract fish or animals; worms, insects, grubs, small fish, etc., so used; food, refreshment on a journey; a halt for refreshment; a temptation, allurement. **live bait:** Small fish used alive for bait. **-baiting,** *n.* (*in combination*) Worrying with dogs; *e.g. badger-baiting bear-baiting, bull-baiting.*

baize (bāz) [F. *baies*, pl. fem of a. *bai* (L. *badius*), chestnut-coloured], *n.* A coarse woollen stuff something like flannel.

bake (bāk) [A.-S. *bacan*], *v.t.* To cook by dry conducted (as opposite to radiated) heat, to cook in an oven or on a heated surface; to dry and harden by means of fire or by the sun's rays; *to harden by means of extreme cold. *v.i.* To cook food by baking; to undergo the process of baking; to become dry and hard by heat. **bakehouse,** *n.* A house or building in which baking is carried on. **bakestone,** *n.* A stone or metal plate on which muffins and cakes are baked. **bake-meat, baked-meat,** *n.* Pastry, a pie. **half-baked,** *a.* (*slang*) Raw, uncouth, half-witted, soft. **baker,** *n.* One whose occupation is to bake bread, biscuits, etc. ***baker-foot,** *n.* A distorted foot. ***baker-kneed, baker-legged,** *a.* Having the right knee-joint inclined inwards. **baker's dozen,** *n.* Thirteen. **baker's itch,** *n.* A kind of psoriasis affecting the hands of bakers. **bakery,** *n.* The trade or calling of a baker; a bakehouse; a baker's establishment. **baking,** *n.* The action of the verb **to bake;** the quantity baked at one operation. **baking-powder,** *n.* A powder of bicarbonate of soda and tartaric acid used as a substitute for yeast.

bakelite (bā′ kel īt) [L. H. *Baekeland*, inventor], *n.* (*Plastics*) The protected trade name of a synthetic resin much used for insulating purposes and in the manufacture of plastics, paints and varnishes.

baksheesh, bakhshish (băk′ shēsh) [Pers., a present], *n.* A gratuity, a tip (used without the article).

balaclava helmet (băl å kla′ va) [Balaclava in Crimea], *n.* A woollen headgear covering the ears and back of the head.

balalaika (bă lå lī′ kå) [Rus.], *n.* A three-stringed musical instrument resembling a guitar.

balance (băl′ åns) [F., from L. *bilancem* (nom. *bilanx*), two-scaled, in *libra bilanx* (*bi-*, two, *lanx*, a flat plate)], *n.* A pair of scales (*often in pl.*); other instrument used for weighing; (*Astron.*) a zodiacal constellation, Libra; the seventh sign of the zodiac, which the sun enters at the autumnal equinox; a contrivance for regulating the speed of a clock or watch; equipoise, equality of weight or power; the amount necessary to make two unequal amounts equal; an impartial state of mind; that which renders weight or authority equal; the difference between the debtor and creditor side of the account; (*Art*) harmony of design, perfect proportion; *doubt, suspense; (*colloq.*) the remainder, the residue. *v.t.* To weigh; to compare by weighing; to compare; to bring to an equipoise, equalize, to steady; to adjust an account, to make two amounts equal; to sway backwards and forwards. *v.i.* To be in equipoise, to have equal weight or force; to oscillate; in dancing, to move to and fro in an opposite direction to that of one's partner. **to hold the balance:** To have the power of deciding. **to lose one's balance:** To tumble; to be upset mentally. **balance of advantage:** The preponderance when a balance is struck. **balance of power:** A condition of equilibrium among sovereign states, supposed to be a guarantee of peace. **balance of trade:** The difference between the imports and exports of a country. **to strike a balance:** To reckon up the balance on a statement of credit and indebtedness. **balance-fish,** *n.* The hammer-headed shark. **balance-knife,** *n.* A table-knife with a handle weighted so as to keep the blade from touching the cloth. **balance-reef,** *n.* The closest reef, a lower fore-and-aft sail. **balance-sheet,** *n.* A tabular statement of accounts, showing receipts and expenditure. **balance-step,** *n.* The goose-step. **balance-wheel,** *n.* The wheel regulating the beat in watches. **balanceable,** *a.* Capable of being balanced. **balanced motor,** *n.* A single-cylinder motor fitted with two fly-wheels rotating in opposite directions so as to reduce vibration; a motor in which the explosion takes place between two pistons in one cylinder. **balancer,** *n.* One who or that which balances; an acrobat; (*Zool.*) an organ in lieu of the posterior wing on each side of the Diptera. **balancer meal,** *n.* Poultry meal mixed with various nutritive ingredients.

balanid (băl′ ån id) [Gr. *balanos*, an acorn], *n.* (*Zool.*) A member of the Balanidæ, or acorn shells. **balaniferous,** *a.* (*Bot.*) Acorn-bearing. **balanite,** *n.* A precious stone. **Balanoglossus,** *n.* (*Zool.*) A genus of worm-like animals. **balanoid,** *a.* (*Zool.*) Acorn-shaped.

balas (băl′ ås) [O.F. *balais*, low L. *balascius*, Arab. *balakhsh*, Pers. *Badakhshān* (L. *Balaxia*), name of district near Samarkand where found], *n.* A name given by lapidaries to a rose-red variety of the spinel ruby.

balata (băl′ å tå) [native name in South America], *n.* The dried gum of the bully-tree, used for insulating telegraph wires.

Balbriggan (băl brig′ ån) [*Balbriggan*, in Co. Dublin, where it is made], *n.* Knitted cotton hose and other goods.

balcony (băl′ kŏ ni) [It. *balcone*, *balco*, O.H.G. *balcho*, a scaffold (cogn. with BALK)], *n.* A gallery or platform projecting from a house or other building; (in theatres) a tier of seats between the dress-circle and the gallery; (*Am.*) dress-circle. **balconied,** *a.*

bald (bawld) [M.E. *balled*, etym. doubtful (perh. from Celt. *bal*, white mark on animal's face; cp. W. *ceffyl bàl*, a horse with white forehead, W. and Gael. *bal*, spot mark)], *a.* Without hair upon the crown of the head; applied to some rapacious birds which have the head destitute of feathers; bare, treeless, leafless; (of horses) streaked or marked with white; (*fig.*) trivial, meagre; destitute of ornament or grace; undisguised, shameless. **bald-coot, baldicoot,** *n.* The coot, *Fulica atra*, from its broad white frontal plate; (*fig.*) bald-head. **bald-faced,** *a.* Having the face marked with white. **bald-head,** *n.* One who is bald; a variety of pigeon. **bald-headed,** *a.* With a bald head. **go at it bald-headed:** Attack or undertake something regardless of consequences. **bald-pate,** *n.* One who is bald; a variety of duck and pigeon. *a.* Bald. **bald-pated,** *a.* Destitute of hair on the pate. **bald-rib,** *n.* A joint of pork cut from nearer the rump than the spare-rib; a lean person. **baldly,** *adv.* In a bald manner; nakedly, shamelessly, inelegantly. **baldness,** *n.*

baldachin, -quin, baldachino (bawld′ å chin, -kwin, -chē′ nō) [F. and Sp. *baldaquin*, It. *baldacchino* (*Baldaco*, *Bagdad*, whence it originated)], *n.* *A kind of rich brocade of silk and gold; a canopy over an altar, throne, or doorway, generally supported by pillars, but sometimes suspended from above, formerly of the material described above.

balderdash (bawl′ dėr dăsh) [etym. doubtful], *n.* Confused speech or writing; a jumble of words.

baldric (bawl′ drik) [M.E. *baudrik, baudry,* O.F. *baudrei* (cp. M.H.G. *balderich* and low L. *baldringus,* perh. from L. *balteus,* a belt)], *n.* A richly ornamented girdle or belt, passing over one shoulder and under the opposite, to support dagger, sword, bugle, etc. **baldric-wise,** *adv.* Worn like a baldric.

bale (1) (bāl) [A.-S. *bealo* (cp. O.S. and O.Fris. *balu,* O.H.G. *balo*), evil], *n.* Evil, mischief, calamity; pain, sorrow, misery. **baleful,** *a.* Full of evil or mischief; pernicious, harmful, deadly; *full of pain, misery, sorrow. **balefully,** *adv.* **balefulness,** *n.*

bale (2) (bāl) [O.F. *bale* (prob. from M.H.G. *balla, palla*)], *n.* A package, a certain quantity of goods or merchandise, wrapped in cloth or baling-paper and corded for transportation. *v.t.* To pack in a bale or bales. **bale-goods,** *n.pl.* Goods done up in bales, as distinguished from those packed in barrels, boxes, etc. **baling,** *n.* The process of putting goods into bales. **baling-paper,** *n.* (*Am.*) Stout paper for packing. **baling-press,** *n.* A press used to compress goods before putting them into bales.

bale (3) [BAIL (4)]. **to bale out:** (*Aviat.*) To abandon an aeroplane in the air and descend by parachute.

baleen (bȧ lēn′) [O.F. *baleine,* L. *balæna,* a whale], *n.* Whalebone. *a.* Of whalebone.

balefire (bāl′ fīr) [A.-S. *bæl* (cp. Icel. *bāl,* a great fire, O.Teut. *balom*)], *n.* *A great fire in the open; *a funeral pyre; a beacon-fire; a bonfire.

balistite (băl′ is tīt) [BALLISTA], *n.* A powerful explosive containing nitro-glycerine.

balistraria (băl is trâr′ i ȧ) [med. L., fem. of *ballistrārius,* as prec.], *n.* A cruciform aperture or loophole in the wall of a fortress, through which arbalesters shot.

balk, baulk (bawk) [A.-S. *balca,* a ridge (prob. cogn. with Icel. *bālkr,* a beam, partition)], *n.* A ridge of land left unploughed; *a dividing ridge; a ridge left unploughed inadvertently; a beam of timber; *a tie-beam of a house; the head-line of a fishing-net; the part of a billiard table behind a transverse line; (*Am.*) a balky horse; an obstacle, a hindrance, a check; a disappointment. *v.t.* To pass over intentionally; (*fig.*) to refuse; to avoid, let slip; to check, hinder; to disappoint; to evade, frustrate; to dispute, argue contentiously. *v.i.* To turn aside, to swerve, to refuse a leap. **to make a balk:** (*Billiards*) To leave one's own ball and the red inside the balk when the opponent's is in hand. **balked,** *a.* Foiled, disappointed. **balky,** *a.* Prone to balk or swerve (of a horse).

ball (1) (bawl) [M.E. *balle,* Icel. *böllr,* O.Teut. *balluz*], *n.* A spherical body of any dimensions, a globe; such a body, differing in size, make, and hardness, used in games; a game with a ball; a throw or cast of the ball in games; a globular body of wood, ivory, or other substance used for voting by ballot; a bullet (not now usually spherical) or larger globular projectile for ordnance, esp. a solid projectile; *a symbol of authority, an orb; a planetary or celestial body (usually with qualifying adjective); anything made, rolled, or packed into a spherical shape; things or parts of things with spherical or rounded outlines. *v.t.* To clog (as a horse's foot with a collection of snow). *v.i.* To gather into a ball; to become clogged; (of bees) to cluster round the queen when they swarm. **ball and socket:** An instrument made of brass with a universal screw, capable of being turned in any direction. **ball and socket joint:** A joint formed by a ball playing in a socket, and admitting of motion in any direction; (*Physiol.*) applied to joints like those of the human hip and shoulder. **ball of the eye:** The pupil, the apple of the eye; the eye itself. **ball of the foot:** The rounded part of the base of the great toe. **ball of the thumb:** The corresponding part of the hand. **three balls:** A pawnbroker's sign. **to keep the ball rolling:** To keep the conversation, debate, work, or game from flagging. **ball-bearing,** *n.* (*usu. in pl.*) A bearing containing loose metallic balls for lessening friction; axle-bearings of this kind. **ball-cartridge,** *n.* A cartridge containing a bullet. **ball-cock, ball-tap,** *n.* A self-acting tap which is turned off or on by the rising or falling of a hollow ball on the surface of the water in a cistern, boiler, etc. **ball-flower,** *n.* (*Arch.*) An ornament like a ball enclosed within three or four petals of a flower. **ballgame,** *n.* (*Am.*) Baseball. **ballpark,** *n.* (*Am.*) Baseball field. **ball-point pen,** *n.* A fountain pen with a tiny ball in place of a nib. **ball-proof,** *a.* Impenetrable by bullets. **ball-valve,** *n.* A valve opened or closed by the rising of a ball.

ball (2) (bawl) [F. *bal,* O.F. *baler,* to dance, late L. *ballāre* (prob. from Gr. *ballizein,* to dance)], *n.* A social assembly for dancing. **to open the ball:** To lead off in the first dance; (*fig.*) to commence operations. **ball-room,** *n.* A room used for balls.

ballad (băl′ ȧd) [O.F. *balade,* Prov. *balada,* a dancing song (late L. *ballāre,* see prec.)], *n.* Light simple song; a popular song, generally of a personal or political character, and printed as a broadside; a simple spirited poem usually narrating some popular or patriotic story; a proverb in the form of a rhymed couplet. **v.i.* To compose ballads. *v.t.* To make (some one) the subject of a ballad or ballads; to satirize ballad-wise. **ballad-maker,** *n.* A writer of ballads. **ballad-monger,** *n.* One who sells ballads; a contemptuous epithet for a composer of ballads. **ballad-farce, ballad-opera,** *n.* A play in which ballads are introduced into the spoken dialogue. **ballad-singer,** *n.* One who sings ballads, esp. in the streets. **ballad-wise,** *adv.* In the form of a ballad. ***ballader** (băl′ ȧ dėr), **balladist** (-dist), *n.* One who composes or sings ballads. **balladry,** *n.* The ballad style of composition; ballads collectively.

ballade (bȧ lad′) [F., see prec.], *n.* A poem consisting of three eight-lined stanzas rhyming a b a b b c b c, each having the same line as a refrain, and with an envoy of four lines; an old form revived in the nineteenth century. **ballade royal,** *n.* Stanzas of seven or eight decasyllabic lines, rhyme royal.

ballast (băl′ ȧst) [*ballast* in most Eur. languages; oldest form prob. O.Swed. and O.Dan. *barlast,* mere load (*bar,* bare, *last,* load)], *n.* Stones, iron, or other heavy substances placed in the bottom of a ship or boat to lower the centre of gravity and make her steady; gravel or other material laid as foundation for a railway, or for making roads; (*fig.*) that which tends to give intellectual or moral stability. *v.t.* To furnish with ballast; to lay or pack with ballast; *to load; (*fig.*) to steady. **in ballast:** (*Naut.*) Without a cargo, having only ballast in the hold; used for ballasting. **ballastage,** *n.* A toll paid for the privilege of taking ballast. **ballasting,** *n.* The act of ballasting; material for ballast; ballast.

ballerina (băl ė rēn′ ȧ) [It.], *n.* (*pl.* **ballerine, ballerinas**) A ballet-girl; a dancer taking a leading part in a ballet.

ballet (băl′ ā) [F., dim. of *bal,* BALL], *n.* A dramatic representation, consisting of dancing and pantomime; an artistic exhibition of dancing. **ballet-girl,** *n.* A girl who takes a subordinate part in a ballet. **ballet-master, -mistress,** *n.* The director of a ballet. **balletomane** (băl′ ĕt ō mān), *n.* An enthusiast for the ballet.

ballista (bȧ lis′ tȧ) [L., from Gr. *ballein,* to throw], *n.* (*pl.* **-æ, -as**) A military engine used in ancient times for hurling stones, darts, and other missiles.

ballistic (bă lis′ tik) [as prec.], *a.* Of or pertaining to the hurling and flight of projectiles. **ballistics,** *n.* The science of the flight of projectiles. **ballistic missile,** *n.* (*Mil.*) A missile guided over the first part of its course but then descending according to the laws of ballistics. **ballistic pendulum,** *n.* An instrument for measuring the velocity of projectiles. **ballistite,** *n.* A propellant explosive based on nitro-glycerine and nitro-cellulose.

balloon (bȧ loon′) [It. *ballone*, a large ball, from *balla* (see BALE (2))], *n.* A spherical or pear-shaped bag of paper, silk, or other light material, which when filled with heated air or hydrogen gas rises and floats in the air (to the larger kinds a car is attached, capable of containing several persons, and these balloons are used for scientific observations, reconnoitring, etc.); *an inflated ball driven to and fro by blows with the arm; *an old game played with such a ball; (*Arch.*) a ball or globe surmounting a pillar, cupola, etc.; (*Chem.*) a spherical glass receiver, used in distilling; (*Hort.*) a frame or trellis on which trees or plants are trained; the shape into which fruit trees are trained; (*fig.*) anything inflated or hollow. *v.i.* To go up in a balloon; (*fig.*) to swell out. **captive balloon,** *n.* A balloon held by a rope. **pilot balloon,** *n.* A small balloon sent up in advance to show the direction and strength of the wind. **balloon barrage,** *n.* A line or series of captive balloons employed as a defence against enemy aircraft. **balloon-fish,** *n.* Popular name for fishes belonging to the genus *Diodon*, which are able to distend their bodies with air. **balloon tire,** *n.* (*Motor*) A low-pressure tire large in section. **ballooner,** *n.* A balloonist; a balloon-like sail; a dress or other object that swells out like a balloon. **ballooning,** *n.* The practice of making balloon ascents; aeronautics; (*Am.*) the practice of running up stock above its value. **balloonist,** *n.* One who makes balloon ascents; an aeronaut.

ballot (1) (băl′ ŏt) [It. *ballotta*, dim. of *balla* (see BALE (2))], *n.* A ball used for secret voting; hence, a ticket, paper or other instrument used to give a secret vote; the method or system of secret voting; the total votes recorded; drawing of lots by means of balls or otherwise. *v.t.* *To vote upon by ballot; to select by drawing lots. *v.i.* To vote secretly. **ballot-box,** *n.* A box into which ballots are put in voting, or from which balls are taken in drawing lots. **ballot-paper,** *n.* The voting-paper used in voting by ballot. **to ballot for:** To choose by secret voting. **ballotage** (F., from *ballotter*, to ballot], *n.* The second ballot in French elections.

ballot (2) (băl′ ŏt) [F., dim. of *balle*, BALE], *n.* A small bale, weighing from 70 to 120 lb.

bally (băl′ i) [perh. from *Ballyhooly*], *a.* (*slang*) Very, great; awful, confounded.

ballyhoo (băl i hoo′) [?] *n.* Noisy and unprincipled propaganda; a great fuss about nothing.

ballyrag (băl′ i răg) [also *bullyrag* (etym. unknown)], *v.t.* To revile, abuse, assail with violent language; to victimize with practical jokes. *v.i.* To use violent or abusive language; to engage in horseplay.

balm (bam) [O.F. *basme*, L. *balsamum*, BALSAM (spelling gradually reassimilated to L. *bal-*)], *n.* The fragrant juice, sap, or gum of certain trees or plants; fragrant ointment or oil; (*fig.*) anything which soothes pain, irritation, or distress; perfume, fragrance; (*Bot.*) the genus *Balsamodendron*, which yields balm; the popular name of several fragrant garden herbs. *v.t.* To anoint or impregnate with balm; *to embalm; (*fig.*) to soothe, to assuage. **Balm of Gilead:** The gum of *Balsamodendron gileadense*, used as antiseptic and vulnerary; a quack imitation of this. **American Balm of Gilead,** *n.* A resin of *Icica carana*. **balm-cricket,** *n.* The cicada. **balmy,** *a.* Producing balm; impregnated with or having the qualities of balm; soft, soothing, healing; fragrant, mild; (*slang*) rather idiotic, daft, silly. **balmily,** *adv.* **balminess,** *n.*

Balmoral (băl mor′ ȧl) [a royal residence in Aberdeenshire], *n.* A kind of Scotch cap; a kind of petticoat; (*pl.*) ankle boots for men and women, laced in front.

balneology (băl nė ol′ ŏ ji) [L. *balneum* a bath -LOGY], *n.* The science of treating diseases by bathing and medicinal springs.

balsa (bol′ sa) [Sp.], *n.* An American tropical tree, *Ochroma lagopus*, with light, strong wood used for floats, etc.

balsam (bawl′ sȧm) [L. *balsamum*], *n.* A vegetable resin with a strong fragrant odour, balm; a tree yielding a resin of this kind; popular name of the genus *Impatiens*; a medicinal preparation made with oil or resin for anointing wounds or soothing pain; (*Alch.*) a preservative essence supposed to pervade all organic bodies; (*Chem.*) resins mixed with volatile oils; (*fig.*) anything that possesses healing or soothing qualities. **True Balsam** or **Balsam of Mecca,** *n.* Balm of Gilead. **Canada Balsam,** *n.* Resin of the Balm of Gilead fir, used for mounting objects for microscopes. **Balsam-apple,** *n.* A tropical plant of the gourd family bearing a highly coloured fruit; (*erroneously*) the common garden balsam. **balsam-fir,** *n.* The Balm of Gilead fir, *Abies balsamea*, which yields Canada Balsam. *v.t.* To impregnate or perfume with balsam; to heal, soothe; to embalm. **Balsamodendron,** *n.* (*Bot.*) A genus of trees which exude balm. **balsamic** (bȧl săm′ ik), **balsamous,** *a.* Having the qualities of balsam; mitigating, assuaging pain, soothing; like a warm, demulcent, oily medicine. **balsamically,** *adv.* **balsamiferous,** *a.* **balsamine** (băl′ sȧ mēn) [F., from Gr. *balsaminē*], *n.* The English name of *Impatiens balsamina*; (*erroneously*) the balsam-apple. **balsamy,** *a.* Balsam-like; balmy.

Baltimore, Baltimore bird (bawl′ ti môr bĕrd) [named after colours of Lord *Baltimore*, proprietary of Maryland], *n.* An American bird of the starling family, *Cterus baltimorii*, with black head and orange plumage; called also Baltimore oriole and Baltimore hang-nest.

baluster (băl′ ŭs tĕr) [F. *balustre*, It. *balausta*, *balaustra*, L. *balaustium*, Gr. *balaustion*, flower of the wild pomegranate (from supposed resemblance to its calyx-tube)], *n.* A small column, usually circular, swelling towards the bottom, and forming part of a series called a balustrade; a post supporting a hand-rail, a banister; (*Arch.*) a small pillar, swelling in the middle, in a two-light window. **balustered,** *a.* **balustrade** (băl ŭs trād′), *n.* A range of balusters, resting on a plinth, supporting a coping or rail, and serving as a protection, barrier, or ornament, etc.

bam (băm) [perh. abbr. from BAMBOOZLE]. (*slang*) *v.t.* To cheat, hoax, bamboozle. *v.i.* To hoax. *n.* A hoax, a mystification; a cock-and-bull story.

bambino (băm bē′ nō) [It., a baby], *n.* (*pl.* **-os**) A child, a baby; esp. an image of the infant Jesus in the crib, exhibited at Christmas in R.C. churches.

bamboo (băm boo′) [etym. doubtful; perh. from Canarese *bănbŭ*, *banwu*], *n.* (*pl.* **-oos**) A genus, *Bambusa*, of giant tropical grasses; the stem of such grass used as a stick, thatch, building material, etc. *v.t.* To beat with a bamboo. **bamboo curtain,** *n.* (*Pol.*) The barrier set up between Communist China and the rest of the world.

bamboozle (băm booz′ ėl) [etym. doubtful; cp. BAM], *v.t.* To mystify for purposes of fraud; to cheat, to swindle; to bewilder, confuse. *v.i.* To practise trickery. *n.* Bamboozlement. **bamboozlement,** *n.* The act or process of bamboozling; a tricky deception, a hoax.

ban (1) (băn) [A.-S. *bannan*, to summon, O.Teut. *bannan*, to proclaim, root *ba-* (cp. L. *fārī*, to speak, Gr. *phēmi*, I speak)], *v.t.* (*past & p.p.* **banned**) To curse, anathematize; to scold, to chide; to interdict, to proscribe. *v.i.* To utter curses. *n.* A public proclamation; an edict of excommunication, an interdict; a curse, a formal anathematization; an imprecation, execration, a formal prohibition; a proclamation of outlawry; denunciation, proscription, outlawry; (*pl., now spelt* BANNS) proclamation of intended marriage.

ban (2) (băn) [Pers., lord], *n.* A title given to the governor of certain districts in Hungary and Croatia, who takes command in time of war.

banal (bä′ nal, băn′ al) [F. *banal*, from *ban* (late L. *bannum*), BAN (1)], *a.* *Of or belonging to compulsory feudal service; commonplace, trite, petty. **banality** (bȧ năl′ i ti), *n.* A commonplace; commonplaceness, triviality.

banana (bȧ na′ nȧ) [through Sp. or Port. from native name in Guinea], *n.* A tropical and subtropical tree, *Musa sapientum*, about 20 feet high, closely allied to the plantain; the fruit of this, a large, elongated berry, growing in clusters, very nutritious. **Bananaland,** *n.* (*colloq.*) Queensland.

banausic (bȧ naw′ sik) [Gr. *banausikos*, from *banausos*, working by fire, mechanical (*baunos*, a furnace)], *a.* Mechanical, merely fit for a mechanic. **banausocracy,** *n.* (*Pol.*) Government by the uncultured, vulgar elements of society.

Banbury-cake (băn′ bėr i kāk′), *n.* A kind of cake filled with mincemeat, supposed to be made at Banbury in Oxfordshire. **Banbury-man,** *n.* An overzealous Puritan; a puritanical rogue; a hypocrite.

banc, banco (1) (băngk, băng′ kō) [L. (*in*) *banco* (*bancus*, a bench)], *n.* The Bench. **in banc, in banco:** A term applied to sittings of a Superior Court of Common Law as a full court, as distinguished from the sittings of the judges at Nisi Prius or on circuit.

banco (2) (băng′ kō) [It., bank, as prec.], *a.* A term applied to bank money of account, as distinguished from ordinary currency.

band (1) (bănd) [M.E. *band*, Icel. *band* (O.Teut. *bindan*, to bind)], *n.* That which binds, confines, or restrains; a fillet, a tie, a chain; one of the cords on which a book is sewn; (*fig.*) a bond, a tie, a uniting influence; *a pledge; *a league; (*pl.*) fetters, manacles. ***in bands:** In prison.

band (2) (bănd) [late M.E. *bande*, F. *bande*, a strip, Prov. and It. *benda*, O.H.G. *binda* (O.Teut. *bindan*, as prec.)], *n.* A flat slip or band [BAND (1)], used to bind together, encircle, or confine, or as part of an article of apparel; the collar of a shirt, a collar or ruff; (*pl.*) a pair of linen strips hanging down in front from the collar and forming part of clerical, legal, or academical dress; a bandage; (*Ent.*) a transverse stripe; (*Geol.*) a band-like stratum; (*Bot.*) a space between any two ribs on the fruit of umbellifers; (*Mech.*) a broad, endless strap for communicating motion; (*Naut.*) a slip of canvas used to strengthen the parts of a sail most liable to pressure. **bandbox,** *n.* A box of cardboard or other thin material for holding collars, hats, millinery, etc., originally used for bands or ruffs; (*fig.*) a flimsy affair. **band brake,** *n.* (*Mech.*) A flexible band that grips the periphery of a drum or wheel. **band-fish,** *n.* The English name of the genus *Cepola*, from their ribbon-like shape. **band-saw,** *n.* An endless steel saw, running rapidly over wheels. **band-wheel,** *n.* A wheel worked by means of an endless strap. **bandage,** *n.* A strip of flexible material used to bind up wounds, fractures, etc.; the operation of bandaging; a strip of flexible material used to cover up something; (*Arch.*) a tie or bond. *v.t.* To bind up with a bandage.

band (3) (bănd) [F. *bande* (Prov., Sp., and It. *banda*, a sash, ribbon), prob. from O.H.G. *bant*], *n.* An organized company; a confederation; an assemblage of men or of the lower animals; a company of musicians trained to play together; the musicians attached to a regiment or ship. **when the band begins to play:** When things get lively; when trouble begins. **band-master,** *n.* The leader of a band of musicians. **Band of Hope,** *n.* A name given about 1850 to any association of children pledged to total abstinence. **band-stand,** *n.* An elevated platform for the use of a band of musicians. **bandsman,** *n.* A member of a band of musicians. **band-wagon,** *n.* The musicians' wagon in a circus parade. **to climb on the band-wagon:** To try to be on the winning side.

band (4) (bănd) [F. *bander*, from *bande*; or from the nouns BAND], *v.t.* To bind or fasten with a band; to mark with a band; to form into a band, troop, or society. *v.i.* To unite, to assemble.

***band** (5), *v.* [BANDY].

bandanna, bandana (băn dăn′ ȧ) [Hind. *bāndhnū*, a mode of spot-dyeing], *n.* A silk handkerchief of Indian manufacture, having white or yellow spots on a coloured ground; a cotton handkerchief thus printed.

bandeau (băn′ dō) [F., from O.F. *bandel*, dim. of *bande*, BAND (2)], *n.* (*pl.* **bandeaux** (băn′ dōz)) A narrow band or fillet for the head; a bandage.

bandelet (bănd′ ė lėt) [F. *bandelette*, dim. of O.F. *bandel*, dim. of *bande*, BAND (2)], *n.* A small stripe or band; (*Arch.*) a small flat moulding round a column.

banderilla (băn dėr il′ yȧ) [Sp., dim. of *bandera*, BANNER], *n.* A little dart ornamented with ribbons, which bull-fighters stick in the neck of the bull.

banderol (băn′ dėr ōl), **banderole** (băn′ dėr ōl) [F. *banderole*, dim. of *bandière*, *bannière*, BANNER], *n.* A long narrow flag with a cleft end flying at a mast-head; any small ornamental streamer; the small square of silk hanging from a trumpet; (*Arch.*) a flat band with an inscription, used in the decoration of buildings of the Renaissance period.

bandicoot (băn′ di koot) [Telegu *pandi-kokku*, pig-rat], *n.* A large Indian rat (*Mus giganteus*); the marsupial genus *Perameles*, which has some resemblance to this.

bandit (băn′ dit) [It. *bandito*, p.p. of *bandire*, to proscribe, low L. *bandīre*, *bannīre* (see BAN (1))], *n.* (*pl.* **banditti, bandits**) One who is proscribed, an outlaw; a brigand; a member of an organized band of marauders infesting the mountainous districts of the south and south-east of Europe. **a banditti:** A company of bandits.

bandog (băn′ dog) [orig. *band-dog*, from BAND (1)], *n.* A large fierce dog, kept chained; a mastiff, a bloodhound.

bandoleer, bandolier (băn dȯ lēr′) [F. *bandouillere*, It. *bandoliera*, or Sp. *bandolera* (*bandola*, dim. of *banda*, BAND (2))], *n.* *A leather belt worn over the right shoulder and across the breast; such a belt used to support the musket and twelve charges of powder and shot in small wooden boxes; a similar belt with little leather loops to receive cartridges; (*usu. in pl.*) the cases or boxes containing charges.

bandoline (băn′ dȯ lin) [F.], *n.* A gummy substance applied to the hair to keep it smooth and flat.

bandore (băn′ dôr) [Sp. *bandurria*, *bandola*, or Port. *bandurra*, *mandore*, L. *pandūra*, Gr. *pandoura*], *n.* An old musical instrument somewhat resembling a lute.

bandy (1) (băn′ di) [etym. doubtful; cp. F. *bander*, to bandy at tennis, perh. from *bande*, *side*], *v.t.* To beat or throw to and fro as at the game of tennis or bandy; (*fig.*) to toss to and fro or toss about like a ball; to give and take, to exchange (esp. blows, arguments, etc.); to band together, make into a faction. *v.i.* To throw a ball about; to contend, to wrangle; to be factious, to strive, fight. *n.* *A game like tennis; a return stroke at tennis; the game of hockey; a club, bent and rounded at the lower end, used in this game for striking the ball. **bandy ball,** *n.* Bandy or hockey. **to bandy words:** To wrangle.

bandy (2) (băn′ di) [?], *a.* Crooked, bent. **bandy-legged,** *a.* Having crooked legs.

bane (bān) [A.-S. *bana*, a murderer (cp. Icel. *bani*, death, slayer, O.H.G. *bano*, Gr. *phonos*, murder, carnage)], *n.* Poison (chiefly in comb., as *henbane*, *rat's bane*, etc.); that which causes ruin; (*fig.*) ruin, destruction, mischief, woe. **v.t.* To kill, esp. by poison; to harm, to injure. **baneberry** (bān′ ber i), *n.* A popular name for *Actæa spicata* or herb Christopher; the black berries of this, which are very poisonous. **baneful,** *a.* Poisonous, harmful, destructive. **banefully,** *adv.* **banefulness,** *n.* **banewort,** *n.* A poisonous plant; the lesser spear-wort; the deadly nightshade.

bang (1) (băng) [Icel. *banga*, to beat (cp. L.G. *bangen*, to beat, G. *bengel*, a cudgel)], *v.t.* To beat with loud blows; to thrash, to thump; to handle roughly, to drub; to slam (a door), fire (a gun), beat (a musical instrument) with a loud noise; (*Am.*) to cut (the front hair) square across; (*fig.*) to beat, to surpass. *v.i.* To resound with a loud noise; to jump or bounce up noisily. *n.* A resounding blow, a thump; a sudden explosive noise; impulsive motion, a dash; (*Am.*) the front hair cut straight across. *adv.* With a violent blow or noise; suddenly, abruptly, all at once. **to bang away at:** To do something violently or noisily. **a banger:** (*slang*) A very fine and exceptional specimen; a sausage; a cudgel. ***bangster,** *n.* A bully; a victor. **bang-tail,** *n.* A horse with tail cut off square. **bang-up,** *a.* (*slang*) Fine, first-rate.

bang (2) [BHANG].

bangalay (băng' ga lā) [Austral. abor.], *n.* A variety of eucalyptus tree.

bangle (băng' gėl) [Hind. *bangrī*, a wrist-ring of glass], *n.* A ring-bracelet or anklet. **bangled,** *a.* Adorned with bangles.

banian [BANYAN].

banish (băn' ish) [O.F. *banir* (lengthened stem *baniss-*), late L. *bannīre* (see BAN)], *v.t.* To condemn to exile; to drive out or away, to expel. **banishment,** *n.* The act of banishing; the state of being banished; exile, expatriation, expulsion.

banister (băn' is tėr) [corr. of BALUSTER], *n.* A shaft or upright supporting a hand-rail at the side of a staircase; (*pl.*) the whole railing protecting the outer side of a staircase.

banjo (băn' jō) [Negro corr. of BANDORE], *n.* A stringed musical instrument, having a head and neck like a guitar and a body like a tambourine, and played with the fingers; (*Austral. slang*) a shoulder of mutton. **banjo-frame,** *n.* (*Eng.*) An appliance for raising and lowering a screw-propeller. **banjoist,** *n.*

bank (1) (băngk) [M.E. *banke* (Icel. *bakki*, O.Teut. *bankon*; cp. *bankiz*, a bench)], *n.* A raised shelf or ridge of ground; a mound with steeply sloping sides; a shelving elevation of sand, gravel, etc., in the sea or in a river; the margin or shore of a river; the ground near a river; *the seashore; an embankment; the sides of a road, cutting, or any hollow; an incline on a railway; a bed of shell-fish; a long flat-topped mass, as of ice, snow, cloud, or the like; (*Coalmin.*) the face of the coal; the surface of the ground at the top of the shaft. *v.t.* To form a bank to; to confine within a bank or banks; to embank; to bring to land; to fortify with earthworks; (*Aviat.*) to incline inwards at a high angle in turning; (*Watchmaking*) to confine the escapement of a watch; *to coast, to skirt. *v.i.* To rise into banks; (*Watchmaking*) to rest against the banking-pins. **bank-engine,** *n.* A locomotive employed to assist trains up inclines. **bank-fish,** *n.* Fish from the Newfoundland bank. **bankless,** *a.* Not defined or limited by a bank; boundless. **bank-side,** *n.* The sloping side of a bank; *shore of a river, lake, or sea; **Bankside,** the district bordering the Thames at Southwark. **banksman,** *n.* (*Coalmin.*) Workman who superintends unloading at a pit-mouth. **bank-martin, bank-swallow,** *n.* The sand-martin. **bank-smack,** *n.* A Newfoundland fishing smack. **to bank up:** To make up (a fire) by putting on and pressing down fuel.

bank (2) (băngk) [F. *banque*, It. *banca*, a bench, Teut. *bank*, BANK (1)], *n.* An establishment which deals in money, receiving it on deposit from customers and investing it; (*Gaming*) the money which the proprietor of the table, or player who plays against the rest, has before him. *v.i.* To keep a bank; to act as a banker; to be a depositor in a bank; (*Gaming*) to form a bank, to challenge all comers. *v.t.* To deposit in a bank; to realize, convert into money. **The Bank,** *n.* The Bank of England, established in 1694, which manages the public debt, receives the revenue when collected, and issues notes which are legal tender, having the Government as chief customer. **Bank annuities,** *n.pl.* Certain Government securities; the Consolidated Funds or Consols. **bank-bill,** *n.* A bill drawn by one bank on another, payable on demand or at some specified time; (*Am.*) a bank-note. **bank-book,** *n.* A pass-book in which the cashier enters the debts and credits of a customer. **bank-credit,** *n.* Permission to draw on a bank to a certain amount. **bank-holiday,** *n.* A day upon which all banks are legally closed; in England, Wales and N. Ireland, Easter-Monday, Whit-Monday, first Monday in August, and Boxing-Day; in Scotland, New Year's Day, first Monday in May and August, and Christmas Day. **bank-note,** *n.* A note issued by a bank and payable on demand. **bank-rate,** *n.* The rate per cent at which the Bank of England notifies that it is prepared to discount bills of exchange. **bank-stock,** *n.* The capital stock of the Bank of England. **to break the bank:** To win the amount of money that the dealer or the manager of a gaming-table is willing to risk for the time being. **banking-house,** *n.* A firm that does banking. **bankable,** *a.* Capable of being banked, receivable at a bank.

bank (3) (băngk) [O.F. *banc*, Teut. *bank*, BANK (1) (cp. BENCH)], *n.* *A long seat; a platform or stage; a seat of justice; the bench for rowers, or a tier of oars, in a galley; a bench or table used in various trades; (*Print.*) the table on which sheets are laid; the raised floor of a glass-furnace; (*Organ*) a row of keys.

banker (1) (băng' kėr) [BANK (1)], *n.* A bank-smack; a labourer employed to throw up banks of earth; a horse good at jumping on and off high banks; (*Austral.*) a swollen river.

banker (2) (băng' kėr) [BANK (2)], *n.* A proprietor or partner of a private bank; the manager of a joint-stock bank; one who keeps the bank at a gaming-table; the dealer in certain card-games.

banker (3) (băng' kėr) [prob. corr. of It. *banco*, a statuary's table], *n.* A sculptor's revolving table; a bench used by bricklayers or stonemasons.

banket (băng' ket) [S. Afr. Dut., hardbake], *n.* A gold-bearing conglomerate.

bankrupt (băngk' rŭpt) [earlier *banqueroute*, It. *banca rotta*, bank broken (BANK (2), L. *rupta*, p.p. of *rumpere*, to break), assimilated to L. *rupt-*], *n.* A person who, becoming insolvent, is judicially required to surrender his estates to be administered for the benefit of his creditors; an insolvent debtor. *a.* Judicially declared bankrupt; insolvent; (*fig.*) without credit; at the end of one's resources. *v.t.* To render (a person) bankrupt; to render insolvent; (*fig.*) to reduce to beggary, or to discredit. **bankruptcy,** *n.* The state of being bankrupt; the act of declaring oneself bankrupt; (*fig.*) utter ruin; loss of reputation. **bankruptcy laws,** *n.pl.* Laws requiring a bankrupt to surrender his property for the benefit of his creditors to ensure his discharge.

banksia (băngk' si ȧ) [Sir Joseph *Banks*], *n.* An Australian flowering shrub now cultivated in Europe.

banksman [BANK (1)].

banlieue (băn' li oo) [F., from L. *banleuca* (BAN (1), *leuca*, a league)], *n.* The territory outside the walls but within the jurisdiction of a town or city; suburbs, precincts.

banner (băn' ėr) [O.F. *baniere* (late L. *bannum*, *bandum*, standard, Goth. *bandwa*, sign, token, perh. from same root as BAND, BIND)], *n.* The standard of a feudal lord, used as a rallying-point in battle [hence (*fig.*) **to join, follow,** or **fight under the banner of**]; an ensign or flag painted with some device or emblem; (*Her.*) a flag, generally square, painted or embroidered with the arms of the person in whose honour it is borne; an ensign or symbol of principles or fellowship; (*Bot.*) the vexillum of a papilionaceous flower; *a banderole. **banner headline,** *n.* A headline in heavy type running across the entire page of a newspaper. **banner-screen,** *n.* A fire-screen suspended from a pole or mantelpiece by its upper edge. **bannered,** *a.* Furnished with banners; borne on a banner.

banneret (băn′ ėr ėt) [O.F. *baneret* (*baniere*, see prec., *-et*, *-ate*, L. *-ātus*)], *n.* *A knight entitled to lead a company of vassals under his banner, ranking above other knights and next below a baron; a title conferred for deeds done in the king's presence on a field of battle; a title borne by certain officers in Switzerland and in some of the old Italian republics.

bannerette (băn′ ėr et) [O.F. *banerete*], *n.* A small banner.

bannerol (băn′ ėr ōl) [BANDEROLE], *n.* A banner about a yard square, borne at the funeral of eminent personages and placed over the tomb.

bannock (băn′ ŏk) [Gael. *bannach* (perh. from L. *pānicium*, from *pānis*, bread)], *n.* A flat round cake made of pease- or barley-meal or flour, usually unleavened, and baked on an iron plate over the fire.

banns (bănz) [BAN (1)], *n.pl.* Proclamation in church of an intended marriage, so that any impediment thereto may be made known and inquired into. **to forbid the banns:** To allege an impediment to an intended marriage.

banquet (băng′ kwėt) [F. dim. of *banc*, bench (cp. It. *banchetto*, dim. of *banco*, table)], *n.* A sumptuous feast, usually of a ceremonial character, followed by speeches. *v.t.* To entertain at a sumptuous feast. *v.i.* To take part in a banquet, to feast luxuriously. ***running banquet:** A repast taken between meals; a snack. **banquetter,** *n.* The giver of a banquet; one entertained at a banquet; a feaster, a carouser.

banquette (ban ket′) [F., from It. *banchetta*, dim. of *banca*, a bench, BANK (1)], *n.* A bank behind a parapet on which soldiers mount to fire; (*Am.*) the footway in a thoroughfare, the side-walk, the pavement; the long seat behind the driver in a French diligence.

banshee (băn′ shē) [Ir. *bean sidhe*, O.Ir. *ben sīde*, woman of the fairies], *n.* A supernatural being, supposed by the peasantry in Ireland and the Scottish Highlands to wail round a house when one of the inmates is about to die.

bant, *v.* [BANTING].

bantam (băn′ tăm) [name from *Bantam* in Java, whence they were said (prob. wrongly) to have been first brought], *n.* A small domestic fowl, the cocks very pugnacious; (*fig.*) a small and conceited or very pugnacious person. **bantam-weight,** *n.* A boxer not exceeding 8 st. 4 lb. in weight.

banter (băn′ tėr) [etym. unknown], *v.t.* To ridicule good-humouredly; to rally, to chaff; (*Am.*) to challenge to a trial of skill. *v.i.* To indulge in good-natured raillery. *n.* Good-natured raillery, chaff.

banting (băn′ ting) [W. Banting (1797–1878), inventor], *n.* The reduction of obesity by abstinence from fat, starch, and sugar. **to bant,** *v.i.* (*colloq.*) To practise this method.

bantling (bănt′ ling) [prob. from G. *bănkling*, a bastard (*bank*, a bench, whence bench-begotten)], *n.* A little child, a brat; *bastard.

Bantu (băn too′) [native word, *people*], *a.* Belonging to the South African native stock apart from Bushmen and Hottentots. *n.* A member of the Bantu races; Bantu language.

banxring (băngks′ ring) [Javanese, *bangsring*], *n.* A Javanese squirrel-like tree-shrew, *Tupaia javanica.*

banyan, banian (băn′ yan, -i ăn) [Port. *banian*, a trader, Arab. *banyan*, Gujarātī *vaniyo*, one of the trading caste, Sansk. *vanij*, a merchant], *n.* A Hindu merchant or shop-keeper, esp. in Bengal, a native broker or hawker; a loose morning-gown or jacket; the banian-tree. **banian-day,** *n.* (*Naut.*) A day when sailors have no meat (in allusion to the vegetarian diet of Hindus). **banian-hospital,** *n.* A hospital for animals, named in reference to caste reverence for animal life. **banian-, banyan-tree,** *n.* The Indian fig-tree, *Ficus indica*, the branches of which drop shoots to the ground, which taking root support the parent branches and in turn become trunks, so that one tree covers a very large extent of ground. The name was originally given to a tree near Gombroon, on the Persian Gulf, under which banians or traders had built a pagoda.

baobab (bā′ ŏ băb) [prob. native], *n.* An African tree, *Adansonia digitata*, called also monkey-bread.

bap (băp) [etym. unknown], *n.* (*Sc.*) A large breakfast roll.

Baphomet (băf′ ŏ met) [F., corrupted from *Mahomet*], *n.* An idol or symbol which the Knights Templars were accused of worshipping. **baphometic** (băf ŏ met′ ik), *a.*

baptism (băp′ tizm) [BAPTIZE], *n.* The act of baptizing; the ceremony of sprinkling with or immersion in water, by which a person is admitted into the Christian Church; a ceremonial naming of ships, church bells, etc. **baptism of blood:** Martyrdom before baptism. **baptism of fire:** The baptism of the Holy Ghost, martyrdom; a soldier's first experience of actual war. **baptismal** (-tiz′ măl), *a.* Conferred at baptism. **baptismally,** *adv.*

Baptist (băp′ tist), *n.* One who baptizes; a special title of St. John, the forerunner of Christ; a member of a Christian body who hold that baptism should be administered only to adult believers, and by immersion [ANABAPTIST]. **baptistery** (băp′ tis tėr i), **baptistry** (-tri) [O.F. *baptisterie*, L. *baptistērium*, Gr. *baptistērion* (*baptizein*, BAPTIZE)], *n.* The place where baptism is administered, originally a building adjoining the church; the tank used for baptism in Baptist churches; (*poet.*) baptism.

baptize (băp tīz′) [O.F. *baptiser*, L. *baptīzāre*, Gr. *baptizein* (*baptein*, to dip)], *v.t.* To sprinkle with or immerse in water as a sign of purification and consecration, esp. into the Christian Church; to consecrate, purify, initiate; to christen, to give a name or nickname to. *v.i.* To administer baptism.

bar (1) (bar) [O.F. *barre*, late L. *barra* (etym. unknown)], *n.* A piece of wood, iron, or other solid material, long in proportion to breadth; a pole; a transverse piece in a gate, window, door, fire-grate, etc.; a connecting piece in various structures; a straight stripe, a broad band; an ingot of either of the precious metals cast in a mould; (*pl.*) the ridged divisions in a horse's palate; the ends of the wall of a horse's hoof; any thing that constitutes a hindrance or obstruction; a bank of silt, sand, or gravel deposited at the mouth of a river or harbour; a rail or barrier, a space marked off by a rail or barrier; (*Law Courts*) the barrier at which prisoners stand during trial; the railing separating ordinary barristers from Queen's Counsel, hence the profession of a barrister; barristers collectively; any tribunal; the barrier cutting off a space near the door in both Houses of Parliament, to which non-members are admitted; the counter in an hotel or other house or place of refreshment, across which liquors, etc., are sold; the room containing this; (*Mus.*) a vertical line drawn across the stave to divide a composition into parts of equal duration, and to indicate periodical recurrence; the portion contained between two such lines; (*Rail.*) a strip of metal mounted parallel to a rail, which holds points or makes a signal when depressed by the wheels of a train; (*Her.*) two horizontal lines across a shield; (*Law*) a plea or objection of sufficient force to stop an action; any physical or moral barrier or obstacle. *v.t.* (*past & p.p.* **barred**) To fasten with a bar or bars; to obstruct, to exclude; to take exception to; to hinder, to prevent; to mark with or form into bars; (*Law*) to stay by objection; to cancel a claim or right; (*Betting*) to exclude; (*slang*) to object to, dislike. **bar none:** None excepted. **to be called within the bar:** To be made a Queen's Counsel. **to call to the bar:** To admit as a barrister. **trial at bar:** A trial before all the judges of a court, a trial in the Queen's Bench division. **bar-bell,** *n.* A bar of iron or wood with a ball at each end, used in gymnastics. **bar-cutter,** *n.* [BAR-SHEAR]. **bar-iron,** *n.* Iron wrought into malleable bars. **bar-**

keeper, *n.* A tavern-keeper; a toll-bar keeper. **barmaid,** *n.* A woman who serves at the bar of a public-house, hotel, etc. **barman,** *n.* A man who serves at the bar of a public-house, hotel, etc. **bar-parlour,** *n.* A small room adjoining or containing a tavern-bar. **bar-posts,** *n.pl.* Posts sunk in the ground to admit movable bars serving the purpose of a gate. **bar-room,** *n.* The public room in a tavern in which the bar is situated. **bar-shear,** *n.* A machine for cutting metal bars. **bar-shoe,** *n.* A horse-shoe with a bar across the hinder part, to protect the frog. **bar-shot,** *n.* A bar with half a cannon-shot at each end, formerly used to injure masts and rigging. **bar-sinister,** *n.* [BEND SINISTER]. **bar-tracery,** *n.* (*Arch.*) Window tracery characteristic of later Gothic in which the stone-work resembles a twisted bar, as distinguished from *plate tracery*, in which the apertures were cut in solid slabs of stone. **barred,** *a.* Furnished or secured with a bar or bars; obstructed by a bar; striped, streaked. **barring-out,** *n.* A rebellion by schoolboys who shut the master out of the school, and keep him out till certain demands are conceded.

bar (2) (bar) [F.], *n.* The maigre, a large European fish.

bar (3) (bar) [Gr. *baros*, weight], *n.* (*Meteor.*) A unit of atmospheric pressure equivalent to a pressure of 75·007 cm. of mercury at 60° C., in lat. 45°.

bar (4) (bar), *prep.* Except, apart from. **bar one:** Except one. **bar none:** Without exception. **barring accidents:** Apart from accidents.

baracuda (bar à kū′ dà) [etym. unknown], *n.* (*Zool.*) A voracious fish found in tropical waters.

baralipton (băr à lip′ tŏn) [formed on L.], *n.* Second word in the mnemonic lines representing the first figure of a syllogism [cp. BARBARA].

barathrum (băr′ à thrŭm) [L., from Gr. *barathron*], *n.* A pit or chasm outside Athens into which condemned criminals were thrown; the abyss (of hell); (*fig.*) anything insatiable.

barb (1) (barb) [F. *barbe*, L. *barba*, beard], *n.* *The beard of man, or the analogous growth in the lower animals; the appendages on the mouth of the barbel and other fishes; *part of a woman's head-dress, still worn by some nuns; a recurved point, as in a fish-hook or arrow; (*fig.*) a point, a sting; one of the lateral filaments from the shaft of a feather; (*Bot.*) a hooked hair. *v.t.* *To shave, to trim; to furnish (fish-hooks, arrows, etc.) with barbs. **barbed wire:** A wire armed with sharp points, used for fences, to protect front-line trenches, to enclose prison camps. **barbate** (bar′ bāt) [L. *barbātus*], *n.* (*Bot., Zool.*) Bearded; having small tufts of hair.

barb (2) (barb) [F. *barbe* (from the country, *Barbarie*)], *n.* A fine breed of horse; a fancy breed of pigeons (both originally from Barbary).

***barb** (3) (barb) [corr. of BARD (2)], *n.* Armour for the breast and flanks of a horse. **barbed** (2), *a.* Covered with armour.

barbara (bar′ bà rà) [L., barbarous things], *n.* A mnemonic word used to designate the first mood of the first figure of syllogisms, containing three universal affirmatives, *e.g.* all A is B; all C is A; ∴ all C is B.

barbarian (bar bâr′ i àn) [F. *barbarien* (L. *barbaria*), see BARBAROUS], *n.* A savage, a person belonging to some uncivilized race; one destitute of pity or humanity; (*orig.*) one not Greek, one not Greek or Roman, one outside the Roman Empire; one outside the pale of Christian civilization; a foreigner having outlandish manners and language. *a.* Rude, uncivilized, savage; cruel, inhuman.

barbaric (bar bă′ rik) [as prec.], *a.* Of or pertaining to barbarians; rude, uncouth, uncivilized.

barbarism (bar′ bà rizm), *n.* An impropriety of speech, a foreign idiom; absence of civilization, brutality, cruelty; want of culture or refinement; a concrete instance of this defect.

barbarity (bar bă′ ri ti), *n.* Brutality, inhumanity, cruelty; an act of brutality or cruelty; the state or quality of being barbaric; a barbarism. **barbarize** (bar′ bà rīz), *v.t.* To render barbarous; to corrupt (a language). *v.i.* To utter a barbarism in speech; to grow barbarous. **barbarization** (-zā′ shŭn), *n.* The act of barbarizing; the state of being barbarized.

barbarous (bar′ bà rŭs) [L. *barbarus*, Gr. *barbaros* (prob. a word imitative of unintelligible speech)], *a.* Foreign in speech, barbarian; hence, harsh-sounding; rude, uncivilized; uncultured, unpolished; cruel; uncouth. **barbarously,** *adv.* **barbarousness,** *n.* **barbaresque** (bar bà resk′), *a.*

Barbary (bar′ bà ri) [Arab. *Berber*, a native of Barbary (perh. from Gr. *barbaria*, country of the barbarians)], *n.* An extensive region in the north of Africa; *a Barbary horse or pigeon, a barb. **Barbary ape,** *n.* A tailless ape, *Macacus inuus*, found in the north of Africa, with a colony on the rock of Gibraltar. **Barbary gum,** *n.* A gum obtained from *Acacia gummifera*. **Barbary hen,** *n.* [GUINEA-HEN]. **Barbary-horse,** *n.* [BARB (2)].

barbecue (bar′ bė kū) [Sp. *barbacoa*, Haitian, *barbàcoa*], *n.* A framework on which meat is smoked; a very large grill or gridiron; an animal broiled or roasted whole; a social picnic at which animals are roasted whole; an open floor for drying coffee-beans. *v.t.* To smoke or dry (flesh) on a framework over a fire; to broil or roast whole.

barbel (bar′ bėl) [O.F. *barbel*, late L. *barbellum* (nom. *-us*), dim. of *barbus*, barbel (*barba*, beard)], *n.* A European freshwater fish, *Barbus vulgaris*, allied to the carp, named from the fleshy filaments which hang below the mouth; the small fleshy filament hanging from the mouth of some fishes, probably organs of touch. **barbelled, barbeled,** *a.* Furnished with barbels.

barber (bar′ bėr) [A.-F. *barbour*, O.F. *barbeor* (L. *barbātōr -em*, from *barba*, beard)], *n.* One who shaves and cuts beards and hair. *v.t.* To shave or dress the hair of. ***barber-monger,** *n.* One who constantly frequented the barber's shop; a fop. ***barber-surgeon,** *n.* A barber who practised surgery, as was the custom till the reign of Henry VIII. **barber's block,** *n.* A round block on which wigs were made up and displayed; a fop. **barber's itch** or **rash,** *n.* Sycosis, an inflammation of the roots of the hair. **barber's pole,** *n.* A pole usually striped spirally, exhibited as a sign in front of a barber's shop.

barberry (bar′ bėr i), **berberry** (bĕr′-) [late L. *barbaris* or *berberis* (etym. doubtful)], *n.* A shrub of the genus *Berberis* esp. *B. vulgaris*; the red acid berry of this tree.

barbet (bar′ bėt) [prob. O.F. *barbet*, L. *barbātus*, bearded (*barba*, beard)], *n.* A tropical bird allied to the toucans, having tufts of hair at the base of its bill.

barbette (bar bet′) [F., *dim.* of *barbe*, beard], *n.* A mound of earth in a fortification on which guns are mounted to be fired over the parapet; a platform for a similar purpose on a warship. **guns en barbette:** Guns so mounted as to allow of their being fired over a parapet without embrasures or port-holes. **barbette-cruiser,** *n.* A cruiser equipped with barbettes.

barbican (bar′ bi kàn) [O.F. *barbacan* (etym. doubtful)], *n.* An outer fortification to a city or castle, designed as a cover to the inner works; esp. over a gate or bridge and serving as a watch-tower.

barbitone (bar′ bi tōn), *n.* [VERONAL].

barbituric (bar bi tū′ rik) [G. *barbitursäure*] *a.* Term applied to an acid obtained from malonic and uric acids. **barbiturates,** *n.pl.* (*Med.*) Compounds with hypnotic and sedative properties derived from this.

barbola (bar bō′ là) [?], *n.* The attachment of small flowers, etc. in paste to embellish vases, etc.

barbule (bar′ būl) [L. *barbula*, dim. of *barba*, beard], *n.* A hooked or serrated filament given off from the barb of a feather.

barcarole (bar′ kȧ rōl) [F. *barcarolle*, Venetian *barcarola*, It. *barcaruola*, a boat song (*barca*, a boat)], *n.* A song sung by Venetian gondoliers; a composition of a similar kind.

Barcoo grass (bar′ koo) [Queensland river], *n.* (*Austral.*) A pasture grass of fine quality. **Barcoo rot,** *n.* A festering sore due to bad or inadequate diet.

bard (1) (bard) [Gael. and Ir. *bàrd*], *n.* A Celtic minstrel; one of an order whose function it was to celebrate heroic achievements, and to perpetuate historical facts and traditions in verse; hence, a poet generally; (*Welsh*) a poet recognized at the Eisteddfod. **Bard of Avon,** *n.* Shakespeare. **bardic,** *a.* **bardish,** *a.* **bardism,** *n.* The sentiments, maxims or system of the bards. **bardling,** *n.* A young bard, a tyro; a poetaster. **bardolatry,** *n.* The worship of Shakespeare.

*__bard__ (2) (bard) [F. *barde*, armour for a horse (perhaps from Sp. and Port. *albarda*, a pack-saddle, Arab. *al-barda'ah*)], *n.* (*usu. in pl.*) Protective armour for a war-horse; armour for men-at-arms. *v.t.* To caparison; to adorn with trappings; to cover with slices of bacon before roasting (from an old sense of the noun).

bare (1) (bâr) [A.-S. *bær* (cp. O.H.G. *par*, G. *bar*, Dut. *baar*)], *a.* Unclothed, naked, nude; with the head uncovered as a mark of respect; destitute of natural covering, as hair, fur, flesh, leaves, soil, etc.; napless; unarmoured, unarmed, defenceless; unsheathed; poor, indigent, ill-furnished, empty; (*fig.*) simple, mere, unsupported, undisguised, open; bald, meagre; unadorned. *v.t.* To strip, to make bare; to uncover, unsheathe; (*fig.*) to make manifest. **bareback,** *a.* and *adv.* Without a saddle. **bare-backed,** *a.* With the back unclothed; without a saddle. **barefaced,** *a.* Having the face bare or uncovered; unconcealed, impudent, shameless; beardless, whiskerless. **barefacedly,** *adv.* **barefacedness,** *n.* **barefoot,** *a.* and *adv.* With the feet naked. **bare-footed,** *a.* **bare-headed,** *a.* **bare poles,** *n.pl.* Masts with no sails set. **barely,** *adv.* Nakedly, poorly; hardly, scarcely; baldly, openly, plainly, explicitly. **bareness,** *n.* The quality of being bare; poverty, meanness; *leanness. **barish** (bâr′ ish), *a.* Rather bare; poorly covered.

barège (ba räzh′), *n.* A light gauzy dress fabric originally made at Barèges, Hautes-Pyrénées, France.

baresark [BERSERK].

bargain (bar′ gȧn) [O.F. *bargaine*, *barcaigne*, a chaffering, *bargaigner*, to chaffer, late L. *barcāniāre* (perh. from *barca*, a barge)], *n.* Chaffering, discussions as to terms; an agreement between two parties, generally concerning a sale; the thing bought or sold; an advantageous purchase. **bargain-basement, -counter,** *n.* Basement or counter in a store where goods are sold which have been marked down in price. **a bad bargain:** A purchase or sale adverse to the party under consideration. **bargain and sale:** (*Law*) A method of conveyance. **Dutch bargain, wet bargain:** A bargain concluded over a glass of liquor. **into the bargain:** Over and above what is stipulated. **to be off one's bargain:** To be released from a purchase or engagement. **to make the best of a bad bargain:** To do the best one can in adverse circumstances. **to strike a bargain:** To come to terms. *__v.t.__ To agree to buy or sell, to transfer for a consideration. *v.i.* To haggle over terms; to make a contract or agreement for purchase or sale. **to bargain for:** To count on, to expect. **bargainee,** *n.* (*Law*) The person who accepts a conveyance of bargain and sale; the purchaser. **bargainer,** *n.* A trafficker, a haggler; *a bargainor. **bargainor,** *n.* (*Law*) One who transfers real property by bargain and sale; the seller.

bargan, barragan (bar′ găn, bă′ rȧ găn) [Austral. abor.], *n.* A boomerang.

barge (barj) [O.F. *barge*, late L. *barga*, var. for *barca*, BARK], *n.* A flat-bottomed freight-boat, with or without sails, used principally on canals or rivers; the second boat of a man-of-war; a large ornamental state or pleasure boat, an ornamental house-boat. *v.i.* (*slang*) To lurch (into), rush (against). **bargee** (bar jē′), *n.* A bargeman. **bargeman,** *n.* **barge-master,** *n.* **barge-pole,** *n.* The pole with which a barge is propelled or kept clear of banks, etc.; (*fig.*) the biggest stick from a bundle. **not fit to be touched with a barge-pole:** Not fit to come near on account of dirt, disease, or ill temper.

barge- [med. L. *bargus*, a kind of gallows], *comb. form.* (*Arch.*) **barge-board,** *n.* A projecting horizontal board at the gable-end of a building, concealing the barge-couples and warding off the rain. **barge-couples,** *n.pl.* Two beams mortised and tenoned together to increase the strength of a building. **barge-course,** *n.* The tiling projecting beyond the principal rafters in a building; a wall-coping formed of bricks set on edge. **barge-stones,** *n.pl.* Stones set on the sloping or stepped edge of a gable-end.

barghest (bar′ gest) [G. *berg-geist*, mountain demon, or *bahre*, bier, hearse (acc. to Scott), or G. *bär*, bear], *n.* A dog-like goblin whose apparition portends calamity or death.

baric (1) (băr′ ik) [Gr. *baros*, weight, -IC], *a.* Relating to weight, esp. that of the air; barometric.

baric (2) (bâr′ ik) [BARIUM].

barilla (bȧ ril′ ȧ, -yȧ) [Sp.], *n.* An impure alkali obtained from the ash of *Salsola soda* and allied species; an impure alkali obtained from kelp; a plant, *Salsola soda*, common on the seashore in Spain, Sicily, and the Canaries.

barish [BARE].

baritone (băr′ i tōn) [F. *baryton*, It. *baritono*, Gr. *barutonos* (*barus*, heavy, *tonos*, tone)], *n.* A male voice intermediate between a bass and a tenor; a singer having such a voice; the smaller bass sax-horn in B♭ or C; (*Gr. gram.*) a word unaccented on the last syllable. *a.* Having a compass between tenor and bass; of or pertaining to such a compass; (*Gr. gram.*) unaccented on the last syllable. **baritone-clef,** *n.* The F clef on the middle line of the bass stave.

barium (bâr′ i ŭm) [BARYTA, -IUM], *n.* A heavy metallic divalent element, the metallic base of baryta. **baric** (2) (bâr′ ik), *a.* Containing barium.

bark (1) (bark) [A.-S. *beorcan* (cp. Icel. *berkja*)], *v.i.* To utter a sharp, explosive cry, like that of a dog; to speak in a peevish, explosive manner; to cough. *__v.t.__ To burst forth with. *n.* A sharp, explosive cry; orig. of dogs, hence of other animals; report of a fire-arm; a cough. **to bark up the wrong tree:** (*fig.*) To be on a false scent; to accuse the wrong person. **barker** (1), *n.* One who or that which barks; a dog; a clamorous assailant; an auction tout; (*Am.*) a vocal advertiser for a circus, fun-fair, etc. (*slang*) a pistol, a cannon. **barking-bird,** *n.* The *Pteroptochus tarnu*, from S. America, named from its cry. **barking-iron,** *n.* (*slang*) A pistol.

bark (2) (bark) [Scand. (Swed. *bark*, Icel. *bōrkr*, etc.)], *n.* The rind or exterior covering of a tree, formed of tissues parallel to the wood; spent bark, tan; an outer covering; (*colloq.*) the human skin; Peruvian bark. *v.t.* To strip the bark from a tree; to cut a ring in the bark so as to kill the tree; to steep in a solution of bark, to tan; to graze, to abrade (the shins, elbows, etc.); to cover with or as with bark, to encrust; (*Am.*) to strike with a rifle-ball the bark of a tree immediately below a squirrel, etc., so that the concussion kills the animal without mutilating it; (*fig.*) to strip or scrape off. **bark-bed,** *n.* A hot-bed formed of spent bark. **bark-bound,** *a.* Having the bark so close as to hinder the growth. **bark-mill,** *n.* A mill for crushing bark. **bark-pit,** *n.* A pit in which hides are tanned. **bark-tree,** *n.* The popular name of the genus *Cinchona.* **barker** (2), *n.* One who strips the bark from a tree. **barky,** *a.* Covered with bark; of the nature of or resembling bark.

bark (3), **barque** (bark) [F. *barque*, Prov., Sp., or It. *barca*, a small ship or boat], *n.* (*poet.*) A ship or boat, esp. a small sailing vessel; (*usu.* **barque**) a sailing-vessel with three or more masts, square-rigged on the fore and main masts, schooner rigged on the mizzen or other masts. **barkentine** [BARQUENTINE]. **barque-rigged,** *a.* Rigged like a barque.

barley (1) (bar′ li) [A.-S. *bærlic*; *bær-* (cp. Icel. *barr*, O.Teut. *bariz*) -*lic*, -LY], *n.* The grain or the plant of the genus *Hordeum*, a hardy, awned cereal. **pearl-barley,** *n.* Barley stripped of the husk and ground to a small white lump. ***barley-break,** *n.* An old rustic game, played round stacks of grain [see also BARLEY (2)]. **barley-broth,** *n.* Broth made with barley; strong beer. **barley-corn,** *n.* A grain of barley; a measure, the third part of an inch. **John Barleycorn:** Barley personified as the grain from which malt liquor is made; malt liquor. **barley-mow,** *n.* A stack of barley. **barley-sugar,** *n.* A well-known confection, prepared by boiling down sugar, formerly with a decoction of barley. **barley-water,** *n.* A soothing drink made from pearl-barley. **barley-wine,** *n.* A kind of wine prepared by the ancient Greeks from barley; a strong kind of ale.

barley (2) (bar′ lē) [perh. corr. of F. *parlez*, speak], *int.* (*Sc. and North.*) Parley, truce (a word called out in various games, signifying 'quarter'). **barley-break** (see prec.) may be derived from this.

barm (1) (barm) [A.-S. *beorma* (cp. Dan. *bārme*, Fris. *berme*, G. *bärme*)], *n.* The frothy scum which rises to the surface of malt liquor in fermentation, used as a leaven; yeast. **barmy,** *a.* Of or full of barm or yeast; frothing, fermenting; (*fig.*) crazy, cracked, silly, giddy-headed [cp. BALMY: (slang)].

***barm** (2) (barm) [A.-S. *barm* (*beran*, to wear)], *n.* A bosom, lap. **barm-cloth,** *n.* An apron.

Barmecide (bar′ mė sīd) [name of a family who ruled at Bagdad, one of whom is said in the 'Arabian Nights' to have invited a beggar to an imaginary feast], *n.* One who gives illusory benefits. *a.* Barmecidal. **Barmecide feast:** Short commons. **barmecidal** (bar mė sī′ dȧl), *a.* Unreal, unsatisfying, illusory.

barn (barn) [A.-S. *bern*: *berern* (*bere*, barley, *ærn*, house)], *n.* A covered building for the storage of grain and other agricultural produce; a barn-like building; (*Am.*) a stable, a cowshed. **barn-burner,** *n.* A nickname for radical members of the Democratic Party in New York State (given in the 'forties with allusion to a farmer who burned his barn to get rid of rats). **barn dance,** *n.* A dance, originally American, somewhat like a schottische. **barn door,** *n.* The large door of a barn; (*fig.*) a target too big to be easily missed. *a.* Reared at the barn-door (applied to fowls). **barn-owl,** *n.* The white, church, and screech owl, *Strix flammea*. **barn-stormer,** *n.* A strolling-player, a mouthing actor. **barn-yard,** *n.* The yard adjoining a barn; a farm-yard, a barton. **v.t.* To put into a barn, to garner.

Barnaby (bar′ nȧ bi) [F. *Barnabé*, L. *Barnabas*], *n.* Barnabas. **Barnaby-Bright,** *n.* St. Barnabas' Day, 11th June; according to the Old Style, the longest day.

barnacle (bar′ nȧkl) [O.F. *bernaque* (etym. doubtful, perhaps from L. *Hibernicæ*, *Hiberniculæ*, Irish goose)], *n.* The barnacle-goose (also called *bernacle*); the popular name of the cirripedes, esp. those which are attached by a stalk; (*fig.*) a constant attendant. **barnacle-goose,** *n.* A species of wild goose, *Anas leucopsis*, formerly supposed to be produced from the fruit of a tree growing by the sea-shore, or to be developed from the common barnacle, *Lepas anatifera*; the name, however, belonged to the bird before it was applied to the cirripede.

barnacles (bar′ nȧklz) [O.F. *bernac*, flat-nosed (etym. unknown)], *n.pl.* A kind of twitch put on the nostrils of a restive horse while being shod; an instrument of torture used in a similar manner; (*slang*) a pair of spectacles, goggles.

barney (bar′ ni) [etym. unknown], *n.* (*slang*) A humbug, a cheating; an unfair contest, esp. a prize-fight of a disreputable kind; a lark, a spree.

barograph (băr′ ō grăf) [Gr. *baros*, weight], *n.* An aneroid barometer recording the variations of atmospheric pressure. **barogram,** *n.* The record produced by a barograph.

barogyroscope (bă rō jī′ rō skōp) [as prec.], *n.* (*Phys.*) A gyrostat used for demonstrating the rotation of the earth.

barology (bȧ rol′ ō ji), *n.* The science of weight.

barometer (bȧ rom′ ė tėr) [Gr. *baros* weight, -METER], *n.* An instrument used for measuring the atmospheric pressure, thus indicating probable weather change, and also for measuring altitudes reached. **barometric** (băr ō met′ rik), **barometrical** (-met′ rik ȧl), *a.* Of or pertaining to the barometer; measured or indicated by a barometer. **barometrically,** *adv.* **barometry** (bȧ rom′ ė tri), *n.* The art or practice of taking barometrical observations. **barometrography,** *n.* The branch of meteorology which deals with the measurement of atmospheric pressure. **baroscope,** *n.* A weather glass. **barothermograph,** *n.* An instrument combining a barometer and a thermometer.

baron (băr′ ōn) [O.F. *barun*, *baron*, acc. of *ber*, man, husband; late L. *baro*, a man (L. *bāro*, a simpleton)], *n.* Originally, one who held by military service from the king; a Great Baron, attending the Great Council or summoned to Parliament; a noble, a peer; a member of the lowest rank of nobility; a title of the judges of the Court of Exchequer; *a freeman of the Cinque Ports; *a member of Parliament for any of these Ports; (*Law and Her.*) a husband. **baron of beef:** A joint consisting of the two sirloins. **baronage** (băr′ ō nȧj), *n.* The whole body of barons, the peerage; the dignity of a baron; the land from which a baron derives his title, a barony; a published list of barons. **baroness** (băr′ ō nes), *n.* The wife of a baron; a lady who holds the baronial dignity in her own right. **baronial** (bă rō′ ni ȧl), *a.* **barony** (băr′ ō ni), *n.* The lordship, or fee, of a baron; the rank or dignity of a baron; a subdivision of a county of Ireland; a large manor in Scotland.

baronet (băr′ ō net) [dim. of BARON (BARON, -ET)], *n.* An hereditary titled order of commoners ranking next below barons, instituted by James I in 1611. *v.t.* To confer a baronetcy on. **baronetage** (-ȧj), *n.* Baronets collectively; the dignity of a baronet; a list of the baronets. **baronetcy** (-si), *n.* The title or rank of a baronet.

baroque (bȧ rōk′) [F., Port. *barroco*, Sp. *barrueco*, a rough or imperfect pearl (etym. doubtful)], *a.* Irregular in shape, grotesque, odd. *n.* Heavy and violent style of ornament.

barouche (bȧ roosh′) [G. *barutsche*, I. *baroccio*, L. *birotus*, two-wheeled], *n.* A double-seated four-wheeled carriage, with a movable top, and a seat outside for the driver.

barque [BARK (3)].

barquentine, barkentine (bar′ kėn tēn) [BARK (3), either after BRIGANTINE or from Sp. *bergantine*, a small ship], *n.* A three-masted vessel, with the foremast square-rigged, and the main and mizen fore-and-aft rigged.

***barracan, baracan** (băr′ ȧ kȧn) [F., from Arab. *barrakān*, a camlet cloak (Pers. *barak*, a garment made of camel's hair)], *n.* A coarse cloth resembling camlet; a thin silky material.

barrack (băr′ ȧk) [F. *baraque*, It. *baracca*, or Sp. *barraca* (etym. doubtful)], *n.* A temporary hut; (*Am.*) a straw-thatched roof supported by posts, and capable of being lowered or raised, to protect hay; (*pl.*) buildings used to house troops; any large building resembling barracks. *v.t.* To provide with barracks; to put in barracks. *v.i.* To lodge in barracks; (*slang*) to cheer ironically; to jeer. **barrack-master,** *n.* An officer in charge of barracks.

barracoon (băr å koon') [Sp. *barracon, barraca* (see prec.)], *n.* A fortified African slave-house.

barracouta (bȧ rȧ koo' tȧ), *n.* (*Austral.*) An edible fish allied to the baracuda.

barrad (băr' ȧd) [Ir. *baireud, bairread,* F. *barrette,* BARRET], *n.* An Irish conical cap.

barragan, barragon (băr' ȧ gȧn, - gȯn) [Sp. *barragan,* BARRACAN], *n.* A modern stuff supposed to be like barracan.

barrage (1) (bar' ȧj) [F., from *barre,* BAR, -AGE], *n.* The formation of an artificial bar or dam to raise the water in a river; the bar or dam so formed.

barrage (2) (bă' razh), *n.* (*Mil.*) A screen of artillery fire behind which troops can advance, or which can be laid down to hinder an enemy advance. **balloon barrage,** *n.* A disposition of anchored balloons to prevent hostile aircraft making machine-gun attacks. **box barrage,** *n.* A barrage surrounding a particular area. **creeping barrage,** *n.* A barrage that moves forward or backward at pre-arranged intervals.

barramundi, burramundi (bă rȧ mŭn' di) [Austral. abor.], *n.* A variety of perch found in Queensland rivers.

barranca (bar ang' ka) [Sp.], *n.* (*Am.*) A deep gorge, with steep sides.

barrator, -er (băr' ȧ tor, -tėr) [O.F. *barateor,* a fraudulent dealer, trickster (*barat,* fraud, perh. of Celtic origin; cp. O.Ir. *mrath, brath,* O. Bret. *brat,* W. *brad,* betrayal, treachery; sense influenced by Icel. *barātta,* strife)], *n.* One who out of malice or for his own purposes stirs up litigation or discord; *a quarrelsome person, a bully; *a buyer or seller of church benefices.

barratry (bă' rȧ tri) [as prec.], *n.* (*Law*) Fraud or criminal negligence on the part of a master of a ship to the owners' detriment; the offence of vexatiously exciting or maintaining law-suits. **barratrous,** *a.*

barrel (băr' ėl) [F. *baril* (etym. doubtful)], *n.* A cask; a cylindrical wooden vessel bulging in the middle, formed of staves held together by hoops, and with flat ends; the capacity or contents of such a vessel; anything resembling such a vessel, as the tube of a firearm, through which the bullet or shot is discharged; the belly and loins of a horse, ox, etc.; a measure of capacity for liquid and dry goods, varying with the commodity; a revolving cylinder or drum round which a chain or rope is wound; the revolving cylinder studded with pins in a musical box or barrel-organ; (*Physiol.*) the cavity behind the drum of the ear; (*Am. slang*) money to be used for political campaigning. *v.t.* To draw off into, or put or stow in barrels. **barrel-bellied,** *a.* Having a protuberant belly. **barrel-bulk,** *n.* (*Naut.*) A measure of five cubic feet used in estimating the capacity of a vessel for freight. **barrel campaign,** *n.* (*Am.*) An election fought by means of bribery. **barrel-drain,** *n.* A cylindrical drain. **barrel-organ,** *n.* A musical instrument in which the keys are mechanically acted on by a revolving cylinder (barrel) studded with pins. **barrel-vault,** *n.* (*Arch.*) A semi-cylindrical vault. **barrelled,** *a.* Packed in barrels; barrel-shaped; having a barrel or barrels. **to scrape the barrel:** (*fig.*) To get the last remaining bit; to obtain the last scrap.

barren (băr' ėn) [M.G. *barain, baraine,* O.F. *baraine* (masc.), *brahain* (etym. unknown)], *a.* Incapable of producing offspring; not producing; bearing no fruit; unfertile, producing no vegetation; (*fig.*) fruitless, unprofitable; not productive intellectually, uninventive, dull. *n.* A tract of barren land, esp. in the U.S., elevated land on which small trees grow but not timber. **barrenly,** *adv.* **barrenness,** *n.* **barren-wort,** *n.* The English name of the genus Epimedium, esp. E. alpinum, with purple and yellow flowers.

barret (băr' et) [F. *barrette, biretta*], *n.* A little flat cap; a biretta.

barrette (bȧ ret'), *n.* (*Am.*) A hair-clasp.

barretter (băr ret' ėr) [etym. unknown], *n.* (*Elec.*) An appliance for keeping current in a circuit at constant strength.

barricade (băr i kād'), **barricado** (-kā' dō) [F. *barricade,* Sp. *barricada,* p.p. of *barricare* (*barrica,* a barrel)], *n.* A hastily-formed rampart of heterogeneous materials thrown up to obstruct an enemy or an attacking party; (*Naut.*) a wooden rail across the fore-part of the quarter-deck in ships of war; any bar or obstruction. *v.t.* To block or defend with a barricade; to obstruct in any way by physical obstacles.

barrico (băr' i kō) [Sp. *barrica*], *n.* (*pl.* **-oes**) A small cask, a keg.

barrier (băr' i ėr) [A.-F. *barrere,* O.F., *barriere,* late L. *barrāria* (*barra,* bar)], *n.* That which hinders approach or attack; an enclosing fence; a limit, a boundary; the gate where customs are collected, in foreign towns; the starting-point (barred cells) in ancient races; the palisade enclosing a tournament ground, the lists; the railing across which tilters thrust with their spears; (*fig.*) any material or immaterial obstruction. *v.t.* To close (in) or shut (off) with a barrier. **barrier-gate,** *n.* A gate in a barrier. **barrier ice,** *n.* Ice-floe, ice-pack. **barrier-pillar,** *n.* A large pillar of coal supporting the roof of a mine. **barrier-reef,** *n.* A coral reef running nearly parallel to the land, with a lagoon between.

barring [BAR (1)], *prep.* (*colloq.*) Except, omitting.

barrister (băr' is tėr) [orig. *barrester,* prob. from BAR or F. *barre* (the bar was orig. a division among the Benchers in the Inns of Court)], *n.* A member of the legal profession who has been admitted to practise as an advocate at the bar; a counsellor-at-law; (*Am.*) an attorney. **revising barrister,** *n.* A barrister appointed to hold an annual court for the revision of the register of Parliamentary voters. **barristership,** *n.*

barrow (1) (băr' ō) [A.-S. *beorg* (cp. G. *berg,* O. Teut. *bergoz*)], *n.* A hill; a prehistoric grave-mound, a tumulus.

barrow (2) (băr' ō) [A.-S. *bearwe,* from *beran,* to carry (see BEAR)], *n.* A kind of stretcher for carrying a load by two men; a hand-barrow (as distinguished from wheelbarrow); a modification of this, the frame being converted into an open box, and a wheel added so that it can be pushed by one man, a wheelbarrow; a costermonger's two-wheeled truck; a conical basket used in salt-making to drain the wet salt; a barrowful; *a bier; (*Austral.*) a black-maria. **barrow-boy,** *n.* A street fruit-seller with a barrow. **barrowful,** *n.* As much as a barrow will hold.

***barrow** (3) (băr' ō) [A.-S. *bearg* (cp. Dut. *barg,* G. *barch,* O. Teut. *barguz*)], *n.* A castrated boar (later called **barrow-hog,** or **barrow-pig.**

barrow (4) (băr' ō) [perh. from A.-S. *beorgan,* to protect], *n.* A long flannel garment without sleeves, for infants. **barrow-coat,** *n.* A child's coat.

barter (bar' tėr) [O.F. *bareter,* from *baret,* cheat (see BARRATOR)], *v.t.* To give (anything except money) in exchange for some other commodity; to exchange. *v.i.* To traffic by exchanging one thing for another. *n.* Traffic by exchanging one commodity for another; a trade, a truck; (*Arith.*) the rule for reckoning quantities of a commodity in terms of another on the principle of exchange. **to barter away:** To dispose of by barter; to part with for a consideration (usually an inadequate one). **barterer,** *n.*

Bartholomew (bar thol' ȯ mū) [L. *Bartholomæus,* Gr. *Bartholomaios*], *n.* One of the twelve Apostles. **Bartholomew-day, -tide,** *n.* The festival held in his honour on 24th August (also known as ***Bartlemy**). **Bartholomew Fair,** *n.* A fair formerly held annually about this date at Smithfield, notorious for its roughness and licence. **Bartholomew pig,** *n.* Roast pig sold piping-hot at this fair. **Black Bartholomew,** *n.* Bartholomew-day in

1662 when the penal clauses of the English Act of Uniformity came into force. **Massacre of St. Bartholomew:** The slaughter of some 30,000 French Huguenots on St. Batholomew's Day, August 24, 1572.

bartizan (bar ti zăn′) [a modern formation from the spelling *bertisene* (or *bretising*) (see BRATTICE)], *n.* A battlement on top of a house or castle; a small overhanging turret projecting from the angle on the top of a tower. **bartizaned,** *a.*

barton (1) (bar′ tŏn) [A.-S. *beretūn* (*bere,* barley, *tūn,* enclosure)], *n.* The part of an estate which the lord of the manor kept in his own hand; a farm-yard.

barton (2) [BURTON].

barwood (bar′ wud), *n.* A red wood from West Africa used for dyeing.

barysphere (băr′ i sfēr) [Gr. *barus,* heavy; SPHERE], *n.* The solid, heavy core of the earth, probably consisting of iron and other metals.

baryta (bȧ rī′ tȧ) [Gr. *barutēs,* weight (*barus,* heavy)], *n.* The monoxide of barium, a heavy alkaline earth. **barytes** (bȧ rī′ tēz), *n.* Native sulphate of barium, heavy spar (used as white paint). **barytic** (bȧ rit′ ik), *a.*

barytone [BARITONE].

basal [BASE].

basalt (bȧ sawlt′, băs′ awlt) [L. *basaltes,* from an African word], *n.* A trap rock of a black, bluish, or leaden grey colour, of a uniform and compact texture, consisting of augite, felspar, and iron intimately blended, olivine also being often present; a black stone-ware first used by Wedgwood. **basaltic,** *a.* Of or of the nature of basalt; columnar, like basalt; resembling basalt. **basaltiform,** *a.*

basan, bazan, (băs′-, băz′ ȧn) [F. *basane,* prob. from Prov. *bazana,* Sp. *badana,* Arab. *bitānah,* lining; see also BASIL (2)], *n.* A sheepskin for bookbinding, tanned in oak or larch bark, as distinguished from roan which is tanned in sumach.

basanite (băs′ ȧ nīt) [L. *basanītes* (*lapis*), Gr. *basanos* touchstone], *n.* A velvet-black variety of quartz; Lydian-stone, touchstone.

bas-bleu (ba blœ̄) [F.], *n.* [BLUE-STOCKING].

bascinet [BASINET].

bascule (băs′ kūl) [F., a see-saw (*battre,* to bump, or *bas,* down, *cul,* the posteriors)], *n.* An apparatus on the principle of the lever, in which the depression of one end raises the other; a bascule-bridge. **bascule-bridge,** *n.* A kind of drawbridge balanced by a counterpoise which falls or rises as the bridge is raised or lowered.

base (1) (bās) [F. *bas,* late L. *bassus,* short, stout (a cognomen)], *a.* Low, of little height; occupying a low position; *low in the social scale; *illegitimate, bastard; low in the moral scale; unworthy, despicable; menial, inferior in quality; alloyed, debased, counterfeit; (*Law*) *by servile tenure; *by tenure at the will of a lord; *bass (3). **base-born,** *a.* Born out of wedlock; of humble birth; of base origin or nature. **base-court,** *n.* The outer court of a mansion, the servants' court, the back-yard, the farm-yard. **base-hearted,** *a.* Having a base, treacherous heart. **base-heartedness,** *n.* The quality of being base-hearted. **base metals,** *n.* Those which are not precious metals. **base-tenant,** *n.* A tenant holding land as a villein; a tenant holding at the will of his lord. **n.* Bass (3). **basely,** *adv.* In a low, selfish, unworthy, or despicable manner. **baseness,** *n.*

base (2) (bās) [F. *base,* L. and Gr. *basis* (*bainein,* to go, step, stand)], *n.* The lowest part on which anything rests; fundamental principle, groundwork; (*Arch.*) the part of a column between the bottom of a shaft and the top of the pedestal; a plinth with its mouldings constituting the lower part of the wall of a room; a pedestal; the bottom of anything; (*Bot., Zool.*) the extremity of a part by which it is attached to the trunk; (*Geom.*) the side on which a plane figure stands, or is supposed to stand; (*Mil.*) the imaginary line connecting the salient angles of two adjacent bastions; the protuberant rear portion of a gun, between the knot of the cascabel and the base-ring; that line or place from which a combatant draws reinforcements of men, ammunition, etc.; (*Her.*) the width of a bar parted off from the lower part of a shield by a horizontal line; (*Chem.*) that with which an acid combines to form a salt; the place from which a commencement is made in some ball-games; the starting-post; any substance used in dyeing as a mordant; (*Gram.*) the original stem of a word; (*Surv.*) the line from which trigonometrical measurements are calculated; (*Radio.*) the control terminal of a transistor; (*Math.*) the number on which a system of calculations depends; the datum or basis for any process of reckoning measurement or argument; an old popular game, still played by boys, and often called 'prisoner's base'; *(*pl.*) a skirt attached to a man's doublet, and reaching to the knee; armour occupying this position. *v.t.* To make a foundation for; to lay on a foundation; (*fig.*) to found, to secure. ***to bid base:** To challenge in the game of prisoner's base; to challenge. **base-ball,** *n.* The national ball-game of America, akin to English rounders, also called 'ball-game'; the ball used in this. **He never got to first base:** (*Am. fig.*) He never got anywhere. **base-burner,** *n.* An iron stove fed at the top, the fire being confined to the base or lower part. **base-line,** *n.* The base; (*Persp.*) the common section of a picture and the geometrical plane. **base-plate,** *n.* (*Mech.*) A foundation-plate. **basal,** *a.* Pertaining to, situated at, or constituting the base of anything; fundamental. *n.* A basal part. **baseless,** *a.* Without a base or foundation; groundless. **baselessness,** *n.* **basement,** *n.* The lowest or fundamental portion of a structure; the lowest inhabited story of a building, esp. when below the ground level. **basic,** *a.* Of, pertaining to, or constituting a base, fundamental; (*Chem.*) having the base in excess; (*Min.*) with little silica present in its composition (of igneous rocks); (*Metal.*) prepared by the basic process. **Basic English,** *n.* A fundamental selection of 850 English words, designed by C. K. Ogden as a common first step in English teaching and as an auxiliary language. **basic process,** *n.* A method of making steel or homogeneous iron by means of a Bessemer converter lined with non-siliceous materials. **basic slag,** *n.* (*Min.*) A by-product of the manufacture of steel, used as manure. **basicity** (bā sis′ i ti), *n.* The combining power of an acid. **basilar,** *a.* (*Bot., Zool.*) Growing from, or situated near, the base.

bash (1) (băsh) [imit. like *bang,* or Scand. (*cp.* Swed. *basa,* Dan. *baske,* to beat)], *v.t.* To strike, so as to smash. *v.i.* To strike violently. *adv.* With force; with a smash or bang. *n.* A heavy blow, a bang. **to have a bash at:** To attempt. **basher,** *n.* (*slang*) A rough, a hooligan.

bash (2) (băsh) [ABASH], *v.t.* To dismay, abash. *v.i.* *To be dismayed; to be abashed. **bashful,** *a.* *Without self-possession, daunted; shamefaced, shy; characterized by excessive modesty. **bashfully,** *adv.* **bashfulness,** *n.*

bashaw (bȧ shaw′) [PASHA].

bashi-bazouk (băsh′ i bȧ zook′) [Turk., one whose head is turned], *n.* A Turkish irregular soldier, noted for lawlessness and atrocious brutality.

basi- [L. *basis,* BASE (2)], *comb. form.* (*Physiol.*) Pertaining to or forming the base, or at the base of. **basicranial,** *a.* Of or at the base of the cranium. **basilateral,** *a.* At the side of a base. **basipetal,** *a.* Proceeding in the direction of the base. **basifugal,** *a.* Growing away from the base. **basiophil,** *a.* Having an affinity for basic stains. **basiophthalmite,** *n.* The lowest joint in the eye-stalk in Crustaceans. **basipodite,** *n.* The second segment of the leg of an arthropod. **basitemporal,** *a.* Of or pertaining to the base of the temples.

basic [BASE (2)].

basidium (bă sid′ i ŭm) [BASE], *n.* (*pl.* **-a**) (*Bot.*) A mother-cell carried on a stalk and bearing spores characteristic of various fungi. **Basidiomycetes** (ba sid′ i o mi sēt′ ēz), *n.* (Bot.) A group of fungi (including many toadstools and mushrooms) in which the spores are borne on basidia.

basil (1) (băz′ il) [O.F. *basile*, L. *basilisca* (*basiliscus* BASILISK); the botanical name *Basilicum* is from Gr. *basilikon*, royal], *n.* The popular name of the genus *Ocymum*, species of which are used as culinary herbs, *e.g.* the sweet basil, *O. basilicum.*

basil (2) (băz′ il) [prob. a corr. of F. *basane*, see BASAN], *n.* The skin of a sheep tanned in bark, used for bookbinding.

basil (3) [BESEL].

basilar [BASE].

Basilian (bă zil′ i ȧn) [St. Basil (329–379)], *a.* (*Eccles.*) Pertaining to the monastic order instituted by St. Basil in the Greek Church. *n.* A member of the order.

basilic (bȧ sil′ ik), **basilical** (-ik ȧl) [F. *basilique*, L. *basilicus*, Gr. *basilikos*, royal (*basileus*, king)], *a.* *Royal, kingly; (*Physiol.*) an epithet of the large vein which crosses the radial artery in the bend of the elbow.

basilica (bȧ sil′ i kȧ) [as prec.], *n.* (*pl.* **basilicas**) *A royal residence; a large oblong building with double colonnades and an apse, used as a court of justice and an exchange; such a building used as a Christian church; a church built on the same plan; one of the seven principal churches of Rome founded by Constantine the Great (4th cent.). **basilican,** *a.*

basilicum (bȧ sil′ i kŭm), [BASILIC], *n.* A name given to several ointments from their reputed sovereign virtues.

basilisk (băz′ i lisk, băs′-) [L. *basiliscus*, Gr. *basiliskos*, kingly], *n.* A fabulous reptile, said to be hatched by a serpent from a cock's egg—its look and breath were reputed fatal [COCKATRICE]; *a large cannon, generally of brass; an American lizard named from its inflatable crest.

basin (bāsn) [O.F. *bacin* (F. *bassin*), late L. *bacchīnus* (*bacca*, a water-vessel)], *n.* A hollow (usu. circular) vessel for holding water, esp. for washing; a bowl; the quantity contained by such a vessel, a basinful; a pond, a dock, a reservoir; a land-locked harbour; the scale-dish of a balance; a tool used in grinding convex lenses; the tract of country drained by a river and its tributaries; a hollow; (*Geol.*) a depression in strata in which beds of later age have been deposited; a circumscribed formation in which the strata dip on all sides inward. **basinful,** *n.* As much as a basin will hold; (*colloq.*) as much work or trouble as one can cope with. ***basin-wide,** *a.* As wide or large as a basin (of eyes).

basinet (băs′ i net), **basnet** (băz′ net) [O.F. *basinet*, dim. of *bacin*, basin], *n.* A light helmet, almost round, and generally without a visor.

basis (bā′ sis) [L., BASE (2)], *n.* (*pl.* **bases** (bā′ sēz)) The base or foundation; the fundamental principle, ground-work, ingredient, or support.

bask (bask) [prob. from O. Scand. *bathask* (*batha sik*, bathe oneself; cp. Icel. *bathast*)], *v.t.* To expose to natural or artificial warmth (*chiefly refl.*). *v.i.* To expose oneself to the influence of genial warmth; to sun; (*fig.*) to sun oneself in love, good fortune, etc. **basking-shark,** *n.* The sun-fish or sail-fish, the largest species of shark.

basket (bas′ kėt) [etym. doubtful], *n.* A wickerwork vessel of plaited osiers, twigs, or similar flexible material; as much as will fill a basket; a basketful; a basket-hilt; (*Arch.*) the vase of a Corinthian column with its carved foliage. *v.t.* To put in a basket. **the pick of the basket:** The best of the lot. **basket-ball,** *n.* (*Sport*) Outdoor game consisting in dropping a large ball into suspended basket goals. **basket-carriage,** *n.* A carriage with a body of basket-work. **basket-darning,** *n.* A kind of darning in which the stitches, called basket-stitches, cross each other like wicker-work. **basket-fish,** *n.* A starfish of the genus *Astrophyton.* **basket-hilt,** *n.* The hilt of a sword, so called because it is made something like a basket to defend the swordsman's hand. **basket-hilted,** *a.* Having a basket-hilt. ***basket-justice,** *n.* A justice who bought his position and took bribes to recoup himself. **basket-meeting,** *n.* (*Am.*) A picnic, generally followed by a religious service. **basket-stitch,** *n.* [BASKET-DARNING]. **basket-stones,** *n.pl.* Fragments of the stems of the fossil Crinoidea. **basket-woman,** *n.* A woman who carries about goods for sale in a basket. **basket-work,** *n.* Wickerwork. **basketful,** *n.* As much as would fill a basket. **basketry,** *n.* [BASKET-WORK].

bason (1) [BASIN].

bason (2) (bāsn) [etym. doubtful], *n.* A bench with a slab or iron plate and a fire underneath for felting hats. *v.t.* To harden the felt in hat-making.

Basque (bask) [F., from late L. *Vasco*, dweller in Vasconia, a region of W. Pyrenees], *n.* One of the races occupying both slopes of the western Pyrenees; the non-Aryan language spoken by this race. *a.* Of or pertaining to this. **basque,** *n.* A woman's jacket, extended below the waist, forming a kind of skirt. **basqued,** *a.* Furnished with a basque or short skirt.

bas-relief (bas′ rė lēf′, ba′ rė lēf′) [F., from It. *basso-rilievo*], *n.* Low relief; a kind of sculpture in which the figures project less than one-half of their true proportions above the plane forming the background; a carving in low relief.

bass (1) (băs) [BAST], *n.* The inner fibre of the lime-tree or any similar vegetable fibre; an article made from this fibre. **bass broom,** *n.* A coarse-fibred broom made from bass. **bass-wood:** The American lime-tree, *Tilia americana*; its wood.

bass (2), **basse** (băs) [A.-S. *bars* (cp. Dut. *baars*, G. *bars*, *barsch*; see BRISTLE)], *n.* *The common perch, *Perca fluviatilis*; a sea-fish, *Labrax lupus*, called also sea-wolf and sea-dace, common in European waters. **black-bass,** *n.* *Perca huro*, from Lake Huron. **sea-bass,** *n.* (*Am.*) A serranoid food-fish, *Centropristis striatus*, common on the Atlantic shores of the U.S.; also called blackfish, bluefish, rock-bass, etc. **striped-bass,** *n.* (*Am.*) The rockfish, *Roccus lineatus* and *Roccus sexatilis.*

bass (3) (bās) [earlier *base* (see BASE (1))], *n.* The lowest part in harmonized musical compositions; the deepest male voice; the lowest tones of an in-instrument; one who sings the bass part; a bass string. *a.* Of or pertaining to the lowest part in harmonized musical composition. *v.t.* To utter in a bass voice. **bass-bar,** *n.* A bar of wood fixed lengthwise in the belly of stringed instruments to enable them to resist pressure. **bass clef,** *n.* (*Mus.*) The F clef on the fourth line. **bass-viol,** *n.* A stringed instrument for playing bass; a violoncello. [DOUBLE-BASS, THOROUGH-BASS].

basset (1) (băs′ et) [F. *basette*, It. *bassetta*, *bassetto*, rather low (dim. of *basso*, low)], *n.* An obsolete game of cards, said to have been first played at Venice.

basset (2) (băs′ et) [F., dim. of *bas*, *basse*, low], *n.* A short-legged dog used to drive foxes and badgers from their earths.

basset (3) (băs′ et) [etym. doubtful], *n.* (*Geol.*) The outcrop of strata at the surface of the ground. *a.* Tending to crop out. *v.i.* To crop out at the surface.

basset-horn (băs′ et hôrn) [F. *cor de bassette*, It. *corno di bassetto*], *n.* A tenor clarinet with a recurved mouth.

bassinet (băs i net′) [F., dim. of *bassin*, BASIN], *n.* An oblong wicker basket with a hood at the end used as a cradle; a perambulator of similar shape.

basso (băs′ ō) [It.], *n.* Bass. ***basso-continuo,*** *n.* Thorough bass. ***basso-profondo,*** *n.* The lowest male voice. ***basso-ripieno,*** *n.* The bass of the grand chorus, which comes in only occasionally.

bassoon (bă soon') [F. *basson* (*bas, basse*, -ON, -OON; or perhaps *bas son*, low sound)], *n.* A wooden double-reed instrument, the bass to the clarinet and oboe; an organ-stop of similar tone, a similar series of reeds on a harmonium, etc. **bassoonist,** *n.*

basso-rilievo (băs' ō ri lyā' vō) [It., low relief], *n.* (*pl.* **-os**) Bas-relief.

bassorin (bas' ŏr in) [*Bassora*, in Asia Minor], *n.* (*Chem.*) An insoluble mucus found in Bassora gum and the gums of cherry, plum, etc.

bast (băst) [A.-S. *bæst*], *n.* The inner bark of the lime or linden-tree, used in Russia and elsewhere for making mats; any similar fibrous bark; a rope, mat, etc., made from this fibre [see also BASS (1)].

bastard (băs' tȧrd) [O.F. *bast* (F. *bât*), pack-saddle, late L. *bastum* (cp. BANTLING)], *n.* An illegitimate child; anything spurious, counterfeit, or false; *a kind of Spanish wine; an impure coarse brown sugar. *a.* Born out of wedlock, illegitimate; spurious, not genuine; having the resemblance of something of a higher quality or kind, inferior; of abnormal shape or size. **bastard-wing,** *n.* Three or four quill-like feathers placed at a small joint in the middle of a bird's wing. **bastardize,** *v.t.* To declare one a bastard; to debase. **v.i.* To beget bastards. **bastardization** (băs tȧr dī zā' shŭn), *n.* The action of declaring or of making illegitimate. ***bastardly,** *a.* Spurious, counterfeit, debased. **bastardy,** *n.* Illegitimacy; fornication. **bastard branch, bastard slip,** *n.* A sucker springing from a root. **bastard title,** *n.* A short title preceding the title-page of a book. **bastard fount, bastard type,** *n.* (*Print.*) A fount of type with a face too large or too small in proportion to its body.

baste (1) (bāst) [etym. unknown], *v.t.* To moisten (a roasting joint, etc.) with liquid fat, gravy, etc.

baste (2) (bāst) [perh. from the prec., or from Scand. (Swed. *basa*, to flog, cp. Icel. *beysta*, and see BASH)], *v.t.* To beat with a stick, to thrash, cudgel.

baste (3) (bāst) [O.F. *bastir* (F. *bâtir*), to baste (perh. from O.H.G. *bestan*, to patch, *bast*, BAST, or from late L. *bastīre*, to build, construct)], *v.t.* To sew slightly, to tack, to fasten together with long stitches.

bastille (băs tēl') [F., from late L. *bastīlia*, pl. of *bastīle* (*bastīre*, to build)], *n.* The State prison in Paris, destroyed in 1789; a fortified tower; (*Mil.*) a small wooden fort; one of a series of huts defended by entrenchments; a prison, a workhouse.

bastinado (băs ti nā' dō) [Sp. *bastonada* (*baston*, a stick)], *n.* An Oriental method of corporal punishment inflicted with a stick on the soles of the feet; a rod, a stick, a cudgel. *v.t.* To beat with a stick, esp. on the soles of the feet.

bastion (băs' ti ŏn) [F., from It. *bastione* (*bastia*, a building), from late L. *bastīre*, to build], *n.* A projecting work at the angle or in the line of a fortification, having two faces and two flanks; (*fig.*) a rampart, a defence. **bastioned,** *a.*

bat (1) (băt) [etym. doubtful; perh. from O.F. *batte*, a club (*battre*, to beat)], *n.* *A club, a stout piece of wood; a wooden instrument with a cylindrical handle and broad blade used to strike the ball at cricket or similar games; a blow with a bat or club; a batsman; a sheet of wadding used for filling quilts; (*Coal-mining*) interstratified shale; (*dial. and slang*) beat, rate of speed; condition. *v.t.* (*past & p.p.* **batted**). To strike with a bat. *v.i.* To take an innings as batsman. **off his own bat:** By his own exertions. **bat-fowling,** *n.* A method of taking birds by holding a light before a net, and beating their roosting-places with bats or clubs. **batlet,** *n.* A small bat, a flat wooden mallet used for beating linen. **batsman,** *n.* One who uses the bat at cricket and other ball games; (*Aviat.*) the man on an airfield who guides landing aircraft by waving a round, plainly-visible bat in each hand.

bat (2) (băt) [M.E. *bakke*, from Scand. (Dan. *aftenbakke*, evening-bat, Icel. *blaka*, to flutter, flap)], *n.* A small nocturnal mouse-like mammal, having the digits extended to support a wing-membrane stretching from the neck to the tail, by means of which it flies. **to have bats in the belfry:** (*fig.*) To be crazy; to suffer from delusions. **bat-blind,** *a.* Blind as a bat is by day; (*fig.*) mentally blind. **batwing, batswing,** *a.* A term applied to a gas-burner producing a flame shaped like the wing of a bat.

bat (3) (ba, băt, bat) [F. *bât*, a pack-saddle, O.F. *bast*, late L. *bastum*, perh. from Gr. *bastazein*, to carry], *n.* (*only in combination*) A pack-saddle. **bat-horse,** *n.* A sumpter-horse carrying officers' baggage during a campaign. **batman,** *n.* A man in charge of a bat-horse and its load; the military servant of an officer; *a man in charge of the cookery utensils of a company of soldiers in the field. **bat-money, bat-pay,** *n.* An allowance for carrying baggage in the field. **bat-needle,** *n.* A packing-needle.

bat (4) (băt), *v.t.* To blink. **he never batted an eyelash:** He never blinked.

***batable** (bā' tȧbl) [DEBATABLE], *a.* Debatable, subject to contention. **Batable Ground,** *n.* The Debatable Land on the Scottish Border.

batata (bȧ ta' tȧ) [Sp. and Port., from native American], *n.* A plant with a tuberous root, from the West Indies, the sweet potato.

Batavian (bȧ tā' vi ȧn) [L. *Batavia*, from *Batavi*], *a.* Of or pertaining to the ancient Batavians or the modern Dutch. *n.* One of the ancient Batavi; a Dutchman.

batch (1) (băch) [M.E. *bacche* (A.-S. *bacan*, to bake)], *n.* As much bread as is produced at one baking; hence, any quantity produced at one operation; sort, lot, set, crew.

batch (2) (băch), *n.* (*Austral.*) A holiday cottage.

bate (1) (bāt), *v.t.* To abate, diminish; let down, humble; to blunt, satiate; to reduce, moderate, restrain; to deduct; to take away, deprive, remove. *v.i.* To fall away, diminish; to decrease, dwindle, fall off in strength or intensity. **with bated breath:** With breath held in check.

bate (2) (bāt) [from Swed. *beta*, maceration, tanning (cp. G. *beizen*, to steep, tan)], *n.* Alkaline lye used in tanning; the vat containing this; the process of steeping. *v.t.* To steep in bate.

***bate** (3) (bāt) [O.F. *batre*, late L. *batere*, L. *battuere*; or abbr. of DEBATE], *v.i.* *To contend, strive; to beat the wings, flutter impatiently; to be restless or impatient. *n.* Strife, contention.

bateau (ba' tō) [F. (cogn. with BOAT)], *n.* (*pl.* ***bateaux***, -tōz) A long, light, flat-bottomed river-boat, tapering at both ends, used by French-Canadians. **bateau-bridge,** *n.* A floating bridge supported by *bateaux*.

bath (1) (bath) [A.-S. *bæth* (cp. Icel. *bath*, G. *bad*, O.Teut. *bathom*; cogn. with L. *fovere*)], *n.* (*pl.* ba' *thz*) The act of washing or immersing the body in water or other fluid; the water or other fluid used for bathing; a wash, a lotion; the vessel for containing water for bathing; a room or building for bathing in; a hydropathic establishment; a town having medicinal springs used for bathing; the action of immersing any substance in a solution for scientific, art, or trade purposes; the vessel containing such solution; the solution itself; the Order of the Bath. *v.t.* To wash or put (*usu.* a child) in a bath. **Order of the Bath:** A British order of knighthood, so called because the candidates formally bathed before installation. **bath robe,** *n.* A dressing-gown. **bathroom,** *n.* An apartment containing a bath. **bath salts,** *n.pl.* Crystals of borax or sodium carbonate used for softening bath water.

Bath (2) (bath) [as prec.], *n.* A city in Somerset, famous for its hot springs. **to go to Bath:** (*slang*) To go begging; to go to Jericho, to blazes, etc. **bath brick,** *n.* A preparation of calcareous earth in the form of a brick, used for cleaning knives and metal work. **bath bun,** *n.* A rich bun, generally without currants. **bath chair,** *n.* A wheeled chair for invalids; (*Am.*) a wheel-chair. **bath chap,** *n.* A small pig's cheek cured for the table. **Bath Oliver,** *n.* A special kind of biscuit invented by Dr. W. Oliver (1695–1764) of Bath. **bath stone,** *n.* A white building-stone quarried from the oolite near Bath.

bath (3) (băth) [Heb.], *n.* A liquid measure among the ancient Hebrews, containing about 6½ gallons.

bathe (bā*th*) [A.-S. *bathian* (from *bæth*, a bath; cp. Icel. *batha*, G. *baden*)], *v.t.* To immerse in or as in a bath; to plunge or dip; to suffuse, to moisten, to wet copiously. *v.i.* To take a bath, to go into the water. *n.* The act of taking a bath (esp. in the sea, a river, etc.). **bathing-machine,** *n.* A kind of covered carriage to bathe from. **bather,** *n.* One who bathes; esp. one who bathes in the sea, a river, or a swimming-bath.

batho-, bathy- [Gr. *bathys*, deep]. Prefixes used in compound words employed in oceanography, etc.

bathometer (bȧ thom' ė tėr) [Gr. *bathos*, depth], *n.* A spring-balance used to ascertain the depths reached in soundings.

bathos (bā' thos, băth' os), *n.* Ridiculous descent from the sublime to the commonplace in writing or speech; anticlimax; (*colloq.*) a bad come-down. **bathetic** (bȧ thet' ik), *a.* Characterized by bathos.

Bathybius (bȧ thib' i ŭs) [mod. L., from Gr. *bathus*, deep, *bios*, life], *n.* A slimy matter dredged up from the bottom of the Atlantic, formerly supposed to be amorphous living protoplasm, but now shown to be a flaky precipitate of gypsum; (*Biol.*) a genus of Mondera, founded on the above by Häckel.

bathymetry (bȧ thim' ėt ri) [Gr. *bathus*, deep], *n.* The art or method of taking deep soundings. **bathymetric, bathymetrical** (băth i met' rik, -rik ȧl), *a.* Of or pertaining to soundings or to the depth at which life is found in the sea. **bathymetrically,** *adv.*

bathyscaphe, bathysphere (băth' i scāf băth' i sfēr), [as prec.], *n.* An ocean diving-apparatus so constructed that observers and their instruments can descend to a great depth.

bating (bā' ting) [BATE (1)], *prep.* Leaving out of the question; excepting.

batiste (bȧ tēst') [F. perh. after *Baptiste* of Cambray, the original maker], *n.* A kind of cambric; a fine fabric resembling cambric. *a.* Made of batiste.

batlet [BAT (1)]. **batman** [BAT (3)].

baton (băt' ŏn), ***batoon** (bȧ toon') [F. *bâton*., O.F. *baston*], *n.* A staff or club; a truncheon used as a badge or symbol of authority, or as an offensive weapon; a staff or stick; (*Her.*) a diminutive of the bend sinister, used in English coats of arms as a badge of bastardy; (*Mus.*) the wand used by a conductor in beating time. *v.t.* *To cudgel; to strike with a policeman's baton or truncheon. **baton sinister,** *n.* (*Her.*) The baton signifying illegitimacy (pop. called the *bar sinister*; cp. BEND SINISTER).

Batrachia (bȧ trā' ki ȧ) [mod. L., from neut. pl. of a. *batrachīos*, Gr. *batracheia*, frog-like (*batrachos*, frog)], *n.pl.* An order of reptiles including those breathing by gills; an order of Amphibia containing those animals which have gills and a tail only in the larval stage; according to Brongniart the last of the four orders of reptiles. **batrachian,** *a.* Of or pertaining to the Batrachia. *n.* Any individual of the Batrachia. **batrachoid** (băt' rȧ koid), *a.*

batswing [BAT (2)].

***battalia** (bȧ ta' li ȧ, -ta' lyȧ) [It. *battaglia*], *n.* Order of battle, battle array; an army, or portions of it, arranged in order of battle. **in battalia:** In order of battle.

battalion (bȧ tăl' i ŏn, -tăl' yŏn) [F. *bataillon*, It. *battaglione* (*battaglia*, see prec.)], *n.* A main division of an army; an assemblage of companies of infantry; the tactical and administrative unit of infantry, consisting of from four to eight companies, and generally about 1000 strong on a war footing. *v.t.* To form into battalions.

battels (bătlz) [etym. doubtful], *n.pl.* (*Univ. of Oxford*) Provisions from the college buttery; the account for these; college accounts generally. **battel,** *v.i.* To have an account for battels; to get one's provisions at the college buttery. ***batteler,** *n.* One who receives his provisions from the college buttery; a name formerly applied to a class of students at Oxford below commoners.

batten (1) (bătn) [BATON], *n.* A piece of wood from 1 to 9 inches wide and from ½ to 2½ inches thick, used for flooring; a piece of wood for clamping together the boards of a door; a scantling, ledge, clamp; (*Naut.*) a thin piece of wood nailed on masts, etc., to prevent chafing, or to fasten down the edges of tarpaulins over the hatches. *v.t.* To fasten or strengthen with battens. **to batten down:** (*Naut.*) To close down the hatches. **battening,** *n.* The act of attaching battens to a wall for nailing up laths; the battens so affixed.

batten (2) (bătn) [prob. from Icel. *batna*, to get better, recover (*bati*, advantage, improvement; cp. Dut. *baten*, to avail, to profit; cp. BOOT (2))], **v.t.* To fatten up; to make fertile. *v.i.* To grow fat; to thrive, to prosper; to feed on gluttonously; to revel in.

batten (3) (bătn) [F. *battant*, pres.p. of *battre*, to strike], *n.* The movable bar of a loom which strikes the weft in.

batter (1) (băt' ėr) [O.F. *battre*, to beat, late L. *battere*, L. *battuere*], *v.t.* To strike with successive blows so as to bruise, shake, demolish; to wear or impair by beating or rough usage; (*Print.*) to deface type; to subject to hard, crushing attack; to attack with engines of war, formerly with a battering-ram, now with artillery; to bombard. *v.i.* To hammer (at) a door. *n.* (1) A mixture of several ingredients well beaten together; adhesive paste; liquid mud; a blow; (*Print.*) a bruise on the face of type. **battering-charge,** *n.* The heaviest charge for a siege-gun. **battering-engine, -machine,** *n.* An engine used for battering down walls or ramparts. **battering-gun, -piece,** *n.* A siege-gun. **battering-ram,** *n.* An ancient military engine used for battering down walls, and consisting of a heavy beam shod with iron, which was originally in the form of a ram's head. **battering-train,** *n.* A train of artillery for siege purposes.

batter (2) (băt' ėr) [etym. doubtful; perh. from F. *abattre*, to beat down, depress], *v.i.* To incline (as walls, parapets, embankments, etc.) from the perpendicular with a receding slope. *n.* (2) A receding slope (of a wall, etc.); a talus. **battering,** *a.* (*Arch.*) Sloping inwards.

battery (băt' ėr i) [F. *batterie* (battre, see BATTER (1))], *n.* An assailing by blows; (*Law*) an unlawful attack by beating, or even touching in a hostile manner; (*Mil.*) a number of pieces of artillery for combined action, with men, transport and equipment; the tactical unit of artillery; a ship's armament; the fortified work, or the part of a ship, in which artillery is mounted; (*Elec.*) an apparatus consisting of a connected series of electric cells, dynamos, or Leyden jars, forming a source of electric energy; any apparatus for providing voltaic electricity; a combined series of lenses or prisms; a combination of instruments and general apparatus for use in various arts or sciences; article of metal, esp. beaten copper and brass; an embankment; a series of nesting-boxes in which hens are confined to increase laying. **to turn one's battery against oneself:** To use a man's own arguments to confute him. **battery-piece,** *n.* A siege-gun. **battery-wagon,** *n.* A vehicle used for transporting tools and material for a battery. **cross batteries,** *n.pl.* Two batteries commanding the same point from different directions. **enfilading battery,** *n.* A battery that rakes a whole line with its fire. **floating battery,** *n.* An armoured vessel, heavily armed, for bombarding fortresses. **masked bat-**

tery, *n.* A battery concealed from the enemy's observation.

batting (băt' ing) [etym. doubtful, see BAT (1)], *n.* Cotton fibre prepared for quilting.

battle (bătl) [O.F. *batayle*, late L. *battuālia*, neut. pl. of a. *battuālis* fighting (*battuere*, to beat)], *n.* A fight or hostile engagement between opposing armies or forces of considerable dimensions; fighting, hostilities, war. *v.i.* To fight, to contend (with or against). **v.t.* To assail in battle, to fight against. **wager of battle, trial by battle:** Legal decision of a case by single combat. **line of battle:** The arrangement of troops in readiness for a general engagement; the line formed by warships in preparation for battle. **line-of-battle ship:** A ship adapted by size and armament for service in a general engagement; formerly one of not less than seventy-four guns. **pitched battle:** A general engagement the time and place of which have been settled beforehand. **half the battle:** An immense advantage. **to have the battle:** To be victorious. **to join battle:** To commence a general combat. **battle-array,** *n.* The order of troops prepared for engagement. **battle-axe, -ax,** *n.* A weapon like an axe, formerly used in battle; a halberd. **battle-cry,** *n.* A war-cry, a slogan. **battle-cruiser,** *n.* (*Nav.*) A large, heavily-armed cruiser. **battle-dress,** *n.* (*Mil.*) Comfortable, loose-fitting uniform of blouse and trousers. **battle-field,** *n.* The scene of a battle. **battle-piece,** *n.* A pictorial, rhetorical, or poetical description of a battle. **battle-plane,** *n.* (*Aviat.*) A large, fighting aircraft. **battle-royal,** *n.* A cock-fight in which more than two game cocks are engaged; a general engagement; a free fight, a general row. **battle-ship,** *n.* A warship; a ship adapted by armament for line of battle as opposed to a cruiser. **battled** (1), *a.* Drawn up in line of battle; fought, contested. **battled** (2), *a.* Embattled, protected with battlements.

battledore (bătl' dôr) [etym. doubtful; prob. from Prov. *batedor*, a washing-beetle (*batre*, to beat, *-dor*, -TOR)], *n.* A wooden bat used for washing; the light racket used to strike a shuttlecock; the game in which this is used; *a card or hornbook containing the alphabet, etc. **battledore and shuttlecock,** *n.* The game of battledore.

battlement (bătl' mėnt) [O.F. *batailles*, battlements, or temporary turrets of timber; prob. confused with O.F. *batillement*, a redoubt (*bastiller*, to fortify)], *n.* A parapet with openings or embrasures, on the top of a building, originally for defensive purposes, afterwards used as an ornament; a roof having a battlement; (*fig.*) the indented crest of mountains; the heights of the heavens. **battlemented,** *a.*

battue (ba too') [F. (fem. p.p. of *battre*, to beat)], *n.* Driving game from cover by beating the bushes; a shoot on this plan; (*fig.*) a beat up, wholesale slaughter.

battuta (ba too' ta) [It., a beat], *n.* (*Mus.*) A bar; the beating of time.

baubee [BAWBEE].

bauble (baw' bėl) [O.F. *babel*, *baubel*, a child's plaything; perh. confused with M.E. *babyll*, *babulle*, a stick with a thong (*bablyn*, to waver, oscillate, from *bab* or *bob*)], *n.* A short stick or wand having a head with asses' ears carved at the end of it, carried by the fools or jesters of former times; a gewgaw, a showy trinket; a piece of childish folly; a mere toy; a thing of no value; (*fig.*) a foolish, childish person.

baudekin, baudkin [BALDACHIN].

baudric [BALDRIC].

baulk [BALK].

bauxite (bō' zīt) [*Les Baux*, near Arles], *n.* A clay which is the principal source of aluminium.

bavin (băv' in) [etym. unknown], *n.* A bundle of brushwood; brushwood, firewood for baking bread.

bawbee (baw' bē) [etym. doubtful], *n.* An old Scots copper coin equivalent to about a halfpenny; a halfpenny.

***bawcock** (baw' kok) [F. *beau coq*], *n.* A fine fellow.

bawd (1) (bawd) [etym. doubtful], *n.* *A procurer; a go-between, a pander; a procuress, a brothel-keeper; (*fig.*) one who or that which panders to any evil design or act. **v.i.* To pander. **bawdy,** *a.* Dirty; of or befitting a bawd; obscene, unchaste. *n.* Bawdiness. **bawdy-house,** *n.* A brothel. **bawdily,** *adv.* Lasciviously; obscenely. **bawdiness,** *n.* Obscenity, lewdness. **bawdry,** *n.* The practice of a bawd; fornication, unchastity; obscene talk.

bawd (2) (bawd) [etym. doubtful], *n.* A hare.

bawl (bawl) [med. L. *baulāre*, to bark; or Icel. *baula*, to low (*baula*, a cow)], *v.i.* To cry loudly, howl, bellow; to shout at the top of one's voice. *v.t.* To shout aloud; to utter with bawling; to cry for sale. *n.* A loud, prolonged shout or cry. **to bawl out:** (*Am. colloq.*) To reprove ostentatiously.

bawley (baw' li) [etym. unknown], *n.* A small fishing-smack.

bawn (bawn) [etym. unknown], *n.* The courtyard of a castle; an enclosure for cattle.

bay (1) (bā) [F. *baie*, low L. *baia*], *n.* An arm or inlet of the sea extending into the land with a wide mouth; a recess or cirque in a range of hills; (*Am.*) an arm of a prairie extending into woods. **bay-floe, bay-ice,** *n.* New ice formed in bays or sheltered waters. **bay-salt,** *n.* Coarse-grained crystals of salt obtained by slow evaporation, originally of sea-water, now of a saturated solution of chloride of sodium. **Bay State,** *n.* (*Am.*) Massachusetts (formerly the colony of Massachusetts Bay). **baywood,** *n.* A coarse mahogany from Honduras or Campeachy Bay.

bay (2) (bā) [F. *baie*, O.F. *baée*, fem. p.p. of *baer*, to gape, late L. *baddāre* (fem. p.p. *badāta*)], *n.* An opening or recess in a wall; a main compartment or division, like the interval between two pillars; a division of a barn or other building, generally from 15 to 20 feet in breadth; an internal recess in a room formed by the outward projection of the walls; (*Rail.*) a platform with a cul-de-sac, forming the terminus of a side-line; the part of a ship between decks on each side forward of the bitts. **bay-window,** *n.* An angular window structure forming a recess in a room, distinguished from an *oriel* by having its walls carried down to the ground, and from a bow-window, which is curved, not angular, in ground-plan. **sick bay,** *n.* A ship's hospital.

bay (3) (bā) [etym. doubtful], *n.* A dam or embankment retaining water. *v.t.* To dam, hold (back) water.

bay (4) (bā) [O.F. *abai*, barking, from *abaier* (F. *aboi*, *aboyer*), to bark], *n.* Barking; the prolonged hoarse bark of a dog; the barking of a pack that have tracked down their prey; hence, the final encounter between hounds and their prey; the position of a hunted animal defending itself at close quarters. *v.i.* To bark hoarsely, as a hound at his prey. *v.t.* To bark at; to bring to bay; to express by barking. **at bay** [prob. from O.F. *tenir a bay*, It. *tenere a bada*, hold agape, hold in suspense (late L. *badāre*, to gape, expect), blended with F. *étre aux abois*, to be at the barking (O.F. *abai*)]: In a position of defence, in great straits, in the last extremity. **to stand at bay, hold (hounds) at bay:** To keep back the assailing dogs or other form of attack. **to bring** or **drive to bay:** To come to close quarters with the animal hunted; to reduce to extremities.

bay (5) (bā) [O.F. *baie*, L. *baca*, berry], *n.* The bay-tree or bay-laurel; (*Am.*) a place covered with bay trees; (*pl.*) *Laurus nobilis*, leaves or twigs of this tree, woven into a garland as a reward for a conqueror or poet; (*fig.*) fame, renown. **bayberry,** *n.* The berry of the bay; (*Am.*) the fruit of *Myrica cerifera*, or wax myrtle of North America; the plant itself. **bayberry tallow,** *n.* A kind of tallow obtained from the berries of the wax myrtle. **bay-cherry,** *n.* The cherry laurel, *Cerasus laurocerasus.* **bay-rum,** *n.* An aromatic, spiritous liquid, used by hairdressers, and prepared by distilling rum in which bay leaves have been steeped. **bay-tree,** *n.* The bay, *Laurus nobilis.* **baywood,** *n.* Wood of the mahogany tree, *Swietenia mahogani.*

bay (6) (bā) [F. *bai*, L. *badius* (cp. Gael. and Ir. *buidhe*, yellow)], *a.* Reddish-brown in colour, approaching chestnut. *n.* A horse of that colour.

bay (7) (bā) [abbr. of *bay-antler*, O.F. *besantlier* (*bes*, second, ANTLER)], *n.* The second branch of a stag's horn, the next to the brow antler.

bayadère (by yȧ dâr′, by yȧ dēr′) [F., from Port. *bailadeira*, a dancing girl (*bailar*, to dance)], *n.* A Hindu dancing-girl.

***bayard** (bā′ ard) [O.F. *baiard*, from *bai*, BAY (6)], *a.* Bay-coloured. *n.* A bay horse; name of the wondrous horse of Renaud de Montauban in the *chanson de geste* (*fig.* in allusion to proverbial sayings in which Bayard figures as a type of chivalry); one blinded with self-conceit. **bayardly,** *a.* Done in a blind or stupid manner. *adv.* Blindly, self-confidently.

bayonet (bā′ ȯ nėt) [etym. doubtful, said to be from *Bayonne*, France], *n.* A weapon for stabbing or thrusting, attached by a band to the muzzle of a rifle, so as to convert that into a kind of pike; (*pl.*) infantry; (*fig.*) military force; a kind of clutch. *v.t.* To stab with a bayonet; to compel by military force. **bayonet catch, joint,** *n.* Device for securing in place two cylindrical parts by means of a turn. **Spanish bayonet,** *n.* A species of yucca with lanceolate leaves.

bayou (bī′ oo) [Fr. *boyau*, a gut], *n.* (*Am.*) The outlet of a lake or river; a sluggish watercourse.

bazaar (bȧ zar′) [Pers. *bāzār*], *n.* An Oriental market-place, where goods of all descriptions are offered for sale; a sale of useful or ornamental articles for benevolent or religious purposes.

bazooka (bȧ zoo′ kȧ) [?], *n.* (*Artill.*) An anti-tank or rocket-firing gun.

bdellium (del′ i ŭm) [L., from Gr. *bdellion*, *bdella*, *bdolchon*, Heb. *bedōlakh*, perh. a pearl], *n.* A popular name of several species of *Balsamodendron*, which produces gum-resin; the gum-resin of these trees.

be (bē) [A.-S. *bēon* (cp. Sansk. *bhū*-, Gr. *phuein*, L. *fui*, O.Teut. *beo*-; see also AM, WAS)], *inf.*, *pres. subj.* and *imper. v.* To exist, to live, to have a real state or existence, physical or mental; to become, to remain, continue; to happen, occur, come to pass; to have come or gone to or to occupy a certain place; to have a certain state or quality; (most commonly used as a copula, asserting connexion between the subject and the predicate). **be-all,** *n.* All that is to be; the consummation, the finality. **the be-all and end-all:** The sole object or idea in view.

be- [A.-S. *be*-, *bī*, *by*], *pref.* About, by; *e.g.* (1) *besmear*, to smear all over, *bedaub*, to daub about, *before*, about the front of, *below*, on the low side of, *besiege*, to sit around; (2) making intransitive verbs transitive or reflective; *e.g. bemoan, bespeak, bethink*; (3) forming verbs from nouns or adjectives, as *befool, befriend, benumb*; (4) having a privative force, as in *behead, bereave*; (5) compounded with nouns, signifying to call this or that, as *bedevil, belady, bemadam*; (6) intensive, *e.g. becrowd, bedrug, bescorch*; (7) making adjectives, *e.g. bedaughtered, bejewelled, bewigged.*

beach (bēch) [etym. unknown], *n.* Shingle; a sandy or pebbly seashore; the strand on which the waves break; (*Geol.*) an old seashore. *v.t.* To haul or run (a ship or boat) on a beach. **beach-cadger,** *n.* A beggar frequenting seaside places. **beach-comber,** *n.* A long wave rolling in from the ocean; a settler in the Pacific Islands, living by pearl-fishing and other means; a loafer in these conditions; a wrecker, a water-rat. **beach-grass,** *n.* A coarse grass, *Arundo arenaria*, growing on the seashore. **beachhead** (bēch′ hed), *n.* (*Mil.*) A position held on the beach of a hostile coast. **beach-master,** *n.* An officer who directs the process of disembarking troops. **raised beach,** *n.* (*Geol.*) An ancient beach or shore, of lake or sea, left high and dry by elevation of the land or recession of the water. **beached,** *a.* Having a beach; *covered with beach or shingle; (*Naut.*) run aground on a beach. **beachy,** *a.* Like a beach; pebbly, shingly.

beacon (bē′ kȯn) [A.-S. *bēacen* (cp. O.S. *bōkan*. O.H.G. *bouhhan*)], *n.* A burning cresset fixed on a pole or on a building; a signal-fire on an eminence; a conspicuous hill; a watch-tower; a lighthouse; (*Naut.*) a fixed signal to give warning of a shoal or rock, or to indicate the fairway; (*Radio.*) a transmitter concentrating its radiation in a narrow beam, to act as a guide to aircraft; (*fig.*) anything which gives notice of danger. *v.t.* To light up with beacon-fires; to mark with beacons; (*fig.*) to lead, to guide. *v.i.* To shine like a beacon. **beaconage** (-āj), *n.* Money paid for the maintenance of beacons, buoys, etc.; a system of lighting shoals, etc.

bead (bēd) [A.-S. *bed*- (only in comb.), *gebed*, prayer (*biddan*, to pray)], *n.* *A prayer; *(*pl.*) prayers, formerly counted on the rosary or paternoster; a small globular perforated body of glass, coral, metal, or other material; a bead-like drop threaded on a string to form a rosary; the same used as an ornament; a bead-like drop of a liquid, a bubble; the front sight of a gun; (*Arch.*) a narrow semicircular moulding; an ornament resembling a string of beads; (*pl.*) a necklace; a rosary. *v.t.* To ornament with beads or beading; to thread beads. *v.i.* To form beads. **to draw a bead upon:** (*Am.*) To aim at. **to tell** or **say one's beads:** To count the rosary, to say one's prayers. **Baily's beads:** (*Astron.*) An appearance resembling a string of beads observed on the sun in total eclipses. **bead-frame,** *n.* An abacus. **bead-house** [cp. W. *Bettws*], *n.* A house of prayer; an almshouse. **bead-roll,** *n.* A list of names (originally of benefactors) to be prayed for. **beadsman, bedesman, beadswoman, bedeswoman,** *n.* One appointed to pray for another; an almsman or almswoman. **bead-tree,** *n.* The pride of India, *Melia azedirach*, and other trees, the seeds of which are used as rosary beads. **bead-work,** *n.* Ornamental work in beads. **beading,** *n.* The formation of beads; bead-work; a bead-moulding. **beady,** *a.* Small and bright like leads; covered with beads or bubbles, foaming.

beadle (bē′ dėl) [A.-S. *bydel*, a herald, or O.F. *bedel* (F. *beadeau*); O.Teut. *budiloz*, from *buidan*, to announce], *n.* A messenger, crier, or usher of a court; a petty officer of a church, parish, college, city company, etc. **beadledom,** *n.* Beadles collectively; the characteristics of beadles; (*fig.*) stupid officiousness. **beadleship,** *n.*

beadsman, beadswoman [BEAD].

beagle (bē′ gėl) [etym. unknown], *n.* A small dog originally bred for hunting hares by members of the hunt on foot; (*fig.*) one who scents out or hunts down; an officer of the law.

beak (bēk) [F. *bec*, low L. *beccus*, prob. of Celtic origin], *n.* The pointed bill of a bird; anything pointed like the bill of a bird, as the mandibles of a turtle or an octopus; the prow of an ancient war-galley, often sheathed with brass, and used as the modern ram; a promontory of land, etc.; a spout; (*Bot.*, *Zool.*) any beak-like process; (*slang*) a police magistrate. *v.t.* To seize or strike with the beak (esp. in cock-fighting). **beaked,** *a.* Having a beak or beak-like process; (*Bot.*) rostrate; (*Zool.*) having a beak-like process; (*Her.*) having the beak and legs of a different tincture from the body. **beak-head,** *n.* The prow of an ancient war-galley; (*Naut.*) a small platform at the fore part of the upper deck; the part of a ship in front of the fo'c'sle, fastened to the stem; (*Arch.*) a Norman moulding shaped like a bird's beak.

beaker (bē′ kėr) [Icel. *bikarr* (cp. G. *becher*, late L. *bīcārium*, from Gr. *bīkos*)], *n.* A large wide-mouthed drinking-vessel; the contents of a beaker; an open-mouthed glass vessel with a lip, used in scientific experiments.

beal, bull (bēl, bul) [Austral. abor.], *n.* A sweet honey drink.

beam (bēm) [A.-S. *bēam* (cp. O.H.G. *boum*, G. *baum*, Dut. *boom*)], *n.* A large, long piece of timber squared on its sides, esp. one supporting rafters in a building; the part of a balance from which the scales are suspended; the pole of a carriage; the part of a loom on which the warp is wound; a cylinder on which cloth is wound as it is woven; the main piece of a plough to which the handles are fixed; the main trunk of a stag's horn; a ray or collection of rays of light or (less generally) heat; (*Mech.*) the heavy iron lever which transmits motion in a beam-engine; (*Naut.*) a transverse piece of timber, supporting the deck and staying the sides of a ship; the width of a ship or boat; the shank of an anchor. *v.t.* To send forth, to radiate, to emit in rays; to send forth by beam-transmission. *v.i.* To send forth rays of light; to shine radiantly; (*fig.*) to smile brightly. **off** or **on the beam:** (*Radio.*) Off or on the course indicated by a radio beam; (*fig.*) off or on the mark. **on the beam:** (*Naut.*) At right-angles to the keel. **on the port or starboard beam:** Away upon the left or right of the ship. **abaft the beam:** Astern of an imaginary line drawn across the vessel amidships. **to kick the beam:** To fly up, as the lighter scale of a balance does; to be outweighed or beaten. **beam-compass**, *n.* An instrument for describing large circles, consisting of a beam of wood or brass, with sliding sockets bearing steel or pencil points. **beamed,** *a.* Furnished with a beam or beams; antlered. **beam-ends,** *n.pl.* (*Naut.*) The ends of the beams of a ship. **to be on her beam-ends:** To be thrown so much to one side that the beams are in the water; (*fig.*) to be penniless, quite destitute. **beam-engine,** *n.* An engine with a beam connecting piston-rod and crank, in contradistinction to one in which the piston-rod is applied directly to the crank. **beam-filling,** *n.* (*Arch.*) Masonry brought up from the level of the under to the upper sides of the beams; (*Naut.*) cargo between the beams. **beamless,** *a.* **beam transmission,** *n.* (*Radio.*) A method of short-wave transmission in which the energy radiated is concentrated by a reflector system of wires within a limited angle for reception in a particular zone. **beam-tree,** *n.* The white-beam, *Pyrus aria*, the timber of which is used for axle-trees. **beamy,** *a.* Massive, shining, radiant, brilliant; antlered; broad in the beam (of ships). **beaming,** *a.* Bright, shining.

bean (bēn) [A.-S. *bēan* (cp. Dut. *boon*, Icel. *baun*, O.H.G. *pona*, G. *bohne*)], *n.* The kidney-shaped seed in long pods of *Faba vulgaris* and allied plants; the seeds of other plants in some way resembling those of the common bean. **full of beans:** In good condition, like a horse after a fill of beans. **to give any one beans:** (*slang*) To punish; to scold. **bean-feast,** *n.* An annual dinner given by an employer to his workmen; a jolly outing. **bean-fed,** *a.* Fed on beans; in good condition. **bean-fly,** *n.* An insect of purple colour found on beans. **bean-goose,** *n.* A migratory goose, *Anser segetum.* **bean-stalk,** *n.* Stem of the bean. **bean-straw,** *n.* The haulm of bean plants. **bean-tree,** *n.* A popular name for several trees bearing seeds in pod, esp. the carob-tree, *Ceratonia siliqua.* **bean-trefoil,** *n.* A popular name for the leguminous genus *Anagyris*, the laburnum, *Cytisus laburnum*, and the buck-bean or bog-bean *Menyanthes trifoliata.* **old bean,** *n.* (*slang*) Old fellow, old chap. **beano** (bē' nō), *n.* (*colloq.*) A treat, a spree, a bean-feast. **beany,** *a.* (*slang*) Bean-fed, vigorous, fresh.

bear (1) (bâr) [A.-S. *bera* (cp. Dut. *beer*; Icel. *bera*, *björn*, G. bar)], *n.* A plantigrade mammal belonging to the genus *Ursus*; an animal belonging to certain allied genera; (*fig.*) a rough unmannerly man; (*Astron.*) either of the northern constellations, the Great or the Little Bear; (*Stock Exchange*) one who sells stock for future delivery in the expectation that prices will fall, a speculator for the fall. *v.i.* To speculate for a fall in stocks. *v.t.* To produce a fall in the price of (stock, etc.). **bear-baiting,** *n.* The sport of baiting a chained bear with dogs. **bear-berry,** *n.* The genus *Arctostaphylos*, a procumbent heath; (*erroneously*) the barberry. **bear-garden,** *n.* A place in which bears were kept and baited; hence, a rude, turbulent assembly. **bearish,** *a.* Bear-like; rough, rude, uncouth. **bear-leader,** *n.* (*colloq.*) A travelling tutor. **bear's-breech,** *n.* (*Bot.*) The genus *Acanthus.* **bear's ear,** *n.* The common auricula, *Primula auricula.* **bear's foot,** *n.* Stinking hellebore, *Helleborus fœtidus.* **bear's-grease,** *n.* The fat of bears, formerly much used as a pomade. **bearskin,** *n.* The skin of a bear; a shaggy woollen cloth, used for overcoats; the tall fur cap worn by the Foot Guards and some other regiments in the British Army. **bear-ward,** *n.* A bear-herd; (*colloq.*) a tutor, a bear-leader.

bear (2) (bâr) [A.-S. *beran* (cp. Goth *bairan*, O.H.G. *beran*, L. *ferre*, Gr. *pherein*)], *v.t.* (*past* **bore,** *p.p.* **borne**) To carry, to wear, to show or display (as armorial bearings); to bring; to sustain, to support the weight of (material or immaterial things); to be responsible for, to wield, to suffer, to endure; to thrust, to press; to bring forth, to give birth to; to produce, to yield. *v.i.* To behave; to suffer, to be patient; to imply, to take effect, to have relation to; to incline, take a certain direction (as to the point of the compass) with respect to something else. **to bear against:** To rest upon; to be in contact with. **to bear arms:** To be a soldier; (*Her.*) to be entitled to a coat of arms. **to bear a hand:** To lend assistance. **to bear away:** To carry off; to win; (*Naut.*) to change the course of a ship when close-hauled, and put her before the wind. **to bear down:** To overwhelm, to crush, to subdue; (*Obstetrics*) to use the abdominal muscles to assist in delivery. **to bear down on:** To sail in the direction of. **to bear hard:** To press, to urge; ***to** resent; to have a grudge against. ***to bear in hand:** To flatter with pretences; to deceive. **to bear on:** To press against. **to bear out:** To confirm, to justify. **to bear up:** To endure cheerfully; (*Naut.*) to put the helm up so as to bring the vessel before the wind. **to bear up for:** To sail before the wind towards. **to bear upon:** To be relevant to. **to bring to bear:** To apply, bring into operation. **to bear with:** To put up with, to endure. **borne in upon one:** Become one's firm conviction. **bearable,** *a.* **bearably,** *adv.* **bearer,** *n.* One who or that which bears, carries, or supports; one who assists to carry a corpse to the grave or to hold the pall; a native carrier; one who holds or presents a cheque; a bringer of anything; the holder of any rank or office; (*Arch.*) a support; the pieces supporting the winders of a stair; an animal or plant producing its kind; (*India*) a domestic servant. **a good bearer:** A fertile producer. **bearer-bond, -cheque,** *n.* (*Fin.*) Bond or cheque made out to bearer.

***bear** (3) [BIER].

***bear** (4) (bâr) [A.-S. *bere*, barley], *n.* (*Sc.*) Barley. **bear-bind, bear-bine,** *n.* Bindweed, the field convolvulus; the large *Polygonum convolvulus.*

beard (bērd) [A.-S.], *n.* The hair on the lower part of a man's face, esp. on the chin; analogous hairy appendage in the lower animals; (*Print.*) the part of a type above and below the face to allow for ascending and descending letters; the barb of an arrow; *the tail of a comet when it is in front of the nucleus; the hairy appendages in the mouth of some fishes, gills of some bivalves, etc.; a byssus; the bristles of a feather; the awn of grasses; hairs occurring in tufts. *v.t.* To furnish with or as with a beard; to chip or plane away; (*fig.*) to oppose with resolute effrontery; to set at defiance. **in one's beard:** To one's face, defiantly. **old man's beard,** *n.* The wild clematis or traveller's joy. **bearded,** *a.* Furnished with a beard or similar appendage; barbed, hooked, jagged. **beardie,** *n.* (*Austral.*) A variety of cod-fish. **beardless,** *a.*

Without a beard; hence, youthful, immature. **beardlessness,** *n.*

bearing (bâr′ ing) [BEAR (2)], *n.* Endurance, toleration; mien, deportment, carriage, manner, behaviour, relation, connexion; (*Arch.*) the space between the two fixed extremities of a piece of timber, or between one of the extremities and a post or wall; (*Mech., usu. in pl.*) a carrier or support for moving parts of any machine; any part of a machine that bears the friction; (*Her.*) a charge, a device; relation, relevance, aspect; (*Naut.*) the direction in which an object lies from a vessel; (*pl.*) relative position. **to lose one's bearings:** To be uncertain of one's position. **bearing-cloth,** *n.* The robe in which an infant is carried to the font. **bearing-rein,** *n.* A fixed rein for holding a horse's head up.

bearskin [BEAR (1)].

beast (bēst) [O.F. *beste*, L. *bestia*], *n.* Any of the inferior animals as distinguished from man; an irrational animal; a quadruped, esp. one of the chase; an animal to ride or drive; a domestic animal, esp. ox or cattle; (*fig.*) a brutal person; an objectionable person; an objectionable thing. **the beast:** Antichrist (Rev. xiii. 1); (*fig.*) man's carnal instincts. **beast-fable,** *n.* A story in which animals are the dramatis personæ, much prevalent in the earlier forms of literature. **beast-like,** *a.* **beastly,** *a.* Like a beast in form or nature; brutal, filthy, coarse; disgusting, offensive; disagreeable. ****adv.*** In a beastly manner; (*colloq.*) exceedingly, very. **beastliness,** *n.* ***beastlihead,** *n.* The nature or condition of a beast.

beastings [BEEST].

beat (bēt) [A.-S. *bēatan* (cp. O.H.G. *pōzan*)], *v.t.* (*past* **beat,** *p.p.* **beaten**). To strike with repeated blows, to thrash; to bruise or break by striking or pounding; to work (metal, etc.) by striking; to strike, as bushes, in order to rouse game; to mix or agitate by beating; to strike or impinge on, to dash against (of water, wind, etc.); to conquer, overcome, master; to tread, as a path. (*Mus.*) to play (an instrument or tune) by striking. *v.i.* To strike against some obstacle; to pulsate, throb; to knock; to move rhythmically; (*Naut.*) to make way against the wind. *n.* A stroke or blow; a stroke upon the drum, the signal given by such a blow; a pulsation, a throb; a certain assigned space regularly traversed at intervals by patrols, police, etc.; hence, sphere, department, range; (*Mus.*) the rise or fall of the hand or foot in regulating time; variously applied by different writers to melodic graces or ornament; (*Radio.*) a periodic variation in amplitude caused by the combination of oscillations of different frequencies. **to beat about:** To tack. **to beat about the bush:** To approach a matter in a roundabout way; to shilly-shally. **to beat a retreat:** To retire. **to beat back:** To compel to retire. **to beat down:** To throw or cast down; to force down (price) by haggling. **to beat hollow:** To excel or surpass in a great degree. **to beat in:** To crush. **to beat into:** To knock into by dint of blows: to instil. **to beat it:** (*Am. slang*) To go away. **to beat off:** To drive away by blows. **to beat one's brains:** To puzzle, to ponder laboriously. **to beat out:** To extend by beating, to hammer out. **to beat the bounds:** To mark the boundary of a parish by striking it with light rods. **to beat the general:** (*Mil.*) To give the signal for marching. **to beat the tattoo:** (*Mil.*) To beat to quarters. **to beat time:** (*Mus.*) To regulate or measure the time by a motion of the hand or foot. **to beat up:** To bring to a fluid or semi-fluid mass by beating; (*Naut.*) to make way against wind or tide; to injure seriously by beating. **to beat up for:** To make great endeavours to procure. **to beat up for recruits:** To collect recruits. **to beat up and down:** To run first one way, then another, as a hunted animal. **Beat generation:** Certain members of the generation of adolescents of 1950–60, so called because of their interest in beat music and its dances, and characterized by a self-conscious bohemianism in behaviour and dress. **Beatnik,** *n.* One of this class. **beat music:** Music (*e.g.* jazz) characterized by a continuous drum-beat. **beat of drum:** (*Mil.*) A succession of strokes on a drum, arranged as signals. *a.* A shortened form of **beaten. dead-beat:** Overcome, worn out. **beaten,** *a.* Subjected to repeated blows; defeated, vanquished, weary, exhausted; trodden smooth, plain, or bare; prostrated by the wind. **beater,** *n.* One who beats; a man employed to rouse game; an instrument for beating, pounding, or mixing. **beating,** *n.* The action of striking repeated blows; punishment or chastisement by blows; pulsation, throbbing; overthrow, defeat; (*Naut.*) sailing against the wind.

***beath** (bēth) [A.-S. *bethian*, to foment], *v.t.* To foment to heal; (*Spens.*) to bathe.

beatify (bē ăt′ i fī) [L. *beātificāre*, (*beātus*, happy, *facere*, to make)], *v.t.* To render supremely blessed or happy; (*R.-C. Ch.*) to pronounce (deceased person) to be in enjoyment of heavenly bliss. **beatific** (bē ȧ tif′ ik) [L. *beatificus* (*beātus*, p.p. of *beātificāre*, -FIC)], *a.* Making one supremely blessed or happy. **beatific vision,** *n.* The vision of the glories of heaven. **beatifically,** *adv.* **beatification** (bē ăt i fi kā′ shŭn), *n.* The act of rendering blessed; the Pope's declaration that a deceased person is enjoying supreme felicity in heaven, the first step towards canonization. **beatitude** (bē ăt′ i tūd) [F., from L. *beātitūdo -inem* (see -TUDE)], *n.* Supreme felicity; heavenly bliss; esp. the special blessedness announced in the Sermon on the Mount.

Beatnik [BEAT].

beau (bō) [O.F. *beau*, *bel*, L. *bellus*, fine, pretty (perh. *benlus*, dim. of *benus*, related to *bene*, well, *bonus*, good)], *n.* (*pl.* **beaux,** bōz) A man unduly attentive to dress and social punctilio; a fop, a dandy; a suitor, lover, sweetheart. *v.t.* To act as beau to; to escort. **beau-ideal** (bō ī dē′ ăl) [IDEAL, as adj.], *n.* *Ideal beauty; the highest conceivable type of excellence. ***beau-monde*** (bō mond) [F.], *n.* The fashionable world. **beauish,** *a.* After the manner of a beau; like a beau; foppish. ***beau-pere** (bō pâr′) [O.F. *beau*, *père*, father], *n.* A respectful term of address for a father, clergyman, or elderly man; a companion.

Beaufort scale (bō′ fôrt), *n.* A scale of wind velocity devised by Sir F. Beaufort (1774–1857) ranging from 0 = calm to 12 = hurricane.

beaujolais (bō zhō lā) [F., district in the Lyonnais, S.E. France], *n.* A red Burgundy wine.

beaune (bōn) [name of place in Côte-d'Or, France], *n.* A red Burgundy wine.

beautician (bū tish′ ȧn), *n.* One skilled in women's hairdressing, make-up, manicure, etc.

beauty (bū′ ti) [O.F. *biaute*, *beltet* (late L. *bellus*, see BEAU)], *n.* That quality or assemblage of qualities which gives the eye or the other senses intense pleasure; or that characteristic in a material object or an abstraction which gratifies the intellect or the moral feeling; a beautiful woman; beautiful women generally; a beautiful feature or characteristic; embellishment, grace, charm; a particular aspect that gives satisfaction or (*ironically*) the reverse; (*colloq.*) an egregious person; a scamp. *v.t.* To adorn; to beautify. **beauty-culture,** *n.* Improvement of women's appearance by artificial means. **beauty parlour,** *n.* A shop specializing in beauty treatments. **beauty-sleep,** *n.* Sleep before midnight. **beauty specialist,** *n.* One who makes a speciality of beauty culture. **beauty-spot,** *n.* A patch or spot placed upon the face to heighten some beauty; a foil; (*colloq.*) a beautiful place or landscape. **beauty-wash,** *n.* A cosmetic. **beauteous** (bū′ tė ŭs), *a.* (*poet.*) Endowed with beauty; beautiful. **beauteously,** *adv.* **beauteousness,** *n.* **beautiful,** *a.* Full of beauty; possessing the attributes that constitute beauty; satisfactory, palatable, delicious; (*ironically*) egregious. *n.* (*poet.*) One who or that which is beautiful. **the beautiful:** The abstract notion of the qualities constituting beauty. **beautifully,** *adv.* **beautifulness,** *n.* **beautify** (bū′ ti fī), *v.t.* To make beautiful. *v.i.* To grow beautiful. **beautifier,** *n.* One who or that which beautifies. ***beautiless,** *a.*

beaux esprits [BEL ESPRIT].

beauxite [BAUXITE].

beaver (1) (bē′ vėr) [A.-S. *beofer* (cp. Dut. *bever*, G. *biber*, L. *fiber*)], *n.* An amphibious rodent mammal, *Castor fiber*, with broad tail, soft fur, and habits of building huts and dams; the fur of this animal; a hat made of such fur; *a felted cloth for overcoats; (*slang*) a man with a beard. **beaver board,** *n.* (*Build.*) A building board of wood-fibre material. **beaver-dam,** *n.* An obstruction placed across a stream by beavers. **beaver-rat,** *n.* The musquash or musk-rat. **beaver-tree, beaver-wood,** *n.* (*Am.*) The sweet-bay or laurel-magnolia, *Magnolia glauca.* **beaverteen** (bē′ vėr tēn) [after VELVETEEN], *n.* A twilled cotton fabric with looped filling or pile.

beaver (2) (bē′ vėr) [O.F. *bavière*, bib, from *baver*, to foam, slaver (*bave*, froth, slaver)], *n.* The lower part of a visor; the visor of a helmet. **beavered,** *a.* Provided with a beaver; wearing a beaver hat.

bebop (bē′ bop) [imit. of the rhythm], *n.* A variety of jazz dancing.

becall (bė kawl′), *v.t.* To miscall, abuse, call names.

becalm (bė kam′), *v.t.* To render calm or still; to quiet, to tranquillize, to soothe; to deprive (a ship) of wind.

became, *past* [BECOME].

because (bė kawz′, -koz′) [*be-*, by, CAUSE], *conj.* By cause of, by reason of, on account of, for; for this reason, inasmuch as.

beccafico (bek ȧ fē′ kō) [It., fig-pecker (*beccare*, to peck, *fico*, fig)], *n.* A small migratory bird of the genus *Sylvia.*

béchamel (besh′ ȧ mel) [name of inventor], *n.* A white sauce made with cream.

bechance (bė chans′), *v.i.* To chance, to happen. *v.t.* To befall. **adv.* By chance.

becharm (bė charm′), *v.t.* To charm, to fascinate.

bêche-de-mer (bāsh dė mâr′) [Fr., sea-spade], *n.* The sea-slug or trepang, *Holothuria edulis*, an echinoderm eaten by the Chinese. **beching boat,** *n.* (*Austral.*) A boat engaged in this trade.

beck (1) (bek) [BECKON], *n.* A bow or curtsy; a mute signal of assent or command; a nod, a gesture of the finger or hand; (*fig.*) the slightest indication of will. *v.i.* To make a mute signal; to make obeisance, to curtsy. *v.t.* To call by a beck. **beck and call:** Absolute control.

beck (2) (bek) [Icel. *bekkr* (Swed. *bäck*, G. *bach*)], *n.* A brook, a rivulet; esp. a mountain or moorland stream.

becket (bek′ ėt) [etym. doubtful], *n.* (*Naut.*) Anything used to confine loose ropes, tackle, or spars, as a large hook, a rope with an eye at one end; a bracket, pocket, loop, etc.

beckon (bek′ ŏn) [A.-S. *bēacnian*, *bīecnian* (*beacen*, a sign, BEACON)], *v.i.* To make a signal by a gesture of the hand or a finger, or by a nod. *v.t.* To summon or signal to by a motion of the hand, a nod, etc.

becloud (bė kloud′), *v.t.* To cover with or as with a cloud; to obscure.

become (bė kŭm′) [A.-S. *becuman* (BE-, *cuman*, to come; cp. Goth. *bikwiman*, G. *bekommen*)], *v.i.* (*past* **became,** *p.p.* **become**). To pass from one state or condition into another; to come into existence; (*copulative*) to come to be. *v.t.* To be suitable to, to befit, to be proper to or for; to be in harmony with; to look well upon. **what has become of?** What has happened to? **becoming,** *a.* Befitting, suitable, proper; in harmony or keeping with; graceful in conduct, attire, etc. **the becoming:** That which is fitting. *n.* A coming into existence, a passing into a state. **becomingly,** *adv.* **becomingness,** *n.*

Becquerel rays (bek′ rėl rāz′) [Alex. *Becquerel* (1820–91), French physicist], *n.pl.* Invisible rays, analogous to the Röntgen rays, emitted by uranium, polonium, and certain other substances, and able to pass through objects impermeable to light.

becurl (bė kĕrl′), *v.t.* To curl; to deck with curls.

bed (bed) [A.-S. *bed*, *bedd* (cp. Goth. *badi*, G. *bett*; perh. from Aryan *bhodh-*, whence L. *fodere*, to dig, from idea of dug-out, lair)], *n.* An article of domestic furniture to sleep upon; hence, marriage, conjugal rights, childbirth, and, with qualifying adjective, the grave; the resting-place of an animal, the flat surface on which anything rests; a plot of ground in a garden; the channel of a river; the bottom of the sea; a horizontal course in a wall; (*Geol.*) a stratum, a layer of rock; hence, an aggregation of small animals disposed in a bed-like mass; a layer of oysters; the central portion of a gun-carriage; the foundation of a road, street, or railway; the bottom layer or support on which a mechanical structure or machine is laid. *v.t.* (*past & p.p.* **bedded**). To put in bed; to plant in a bed or beds; to copulate with; to fix in a stratum or course; to place in a matrix of any kind, to embed. *v.i.* To go to bed. **to bed out:** to plant out in beds. **bed and board:** Lodgings and food; connubial relations. **bed of justice:** [F. *lit de justice*] Orig. a state-bed round which the French king held receptions; a formal session of Parlement under the French kings, for the compulsory registration of royal edicts. **to be brought to bed:** To be delivered of a child. **to keep one's bed:** To remain in bed (from sickness, etc.). **to lie in the bed one has made:** To suffer for one's own misdeeds or mistakes. **to make a bed:** To put a bed in order after it has been used. **to make up a bed:** To prepare sleeping accommodation at short notice. **to take to one's bed:** To be confined to bed (from sickness, etc.). **bed-chair,** *n.* A chair with a movable back, to support an invalid in bed. **bed-chamber,** *n.* A sleeping apartment; a bedroom. **lord, groom, gentleman of the bedchamber:** Officers of the Royal Household who wait upon the king by turns. **ladies, women of the bedchamber:** Ladies who wait on a female sovereign. **bed-clothes,** *n.pl.* Sheets, blankets, and coverlets for a bed. **bedder,** *n.* A plant for bedding-out; (*Camb. Univ.*) a charwoman, a bedmaker. **bedding,** *n.* A bed with the clothes upon it; bed-clothes; litter for domestic animals; a bottom layer or foundation; (*Geol.*) stratification; the line or plane of stratification. **bedding-plane,** *n.* (*Geol.*) Plane of stratification; top or bottom surface of a stratum. **bedding-plants, bedding-out plants,** *n.pl.* Plants intended to be set in beds. **bed-bug,** *n.* [BUG]. **bed-fast,** *a.* Confined to bed. **bed-fellow,** *n.* One who sleeps in the same bed with another. **bed-gown,** *n.* A woman's night-dress; a kind of short jacket worn by country women in northern England. **bed-hangings,** *n.pl.* Hangings or curtains for a bed. **bed-key,** *n.* A wrench for fastening and unfastening the framework of a bedstead. **bed-linen,** *n.* Sheets and pillow-cases for a bed. **bed-maker,** *n.* One who makes beds; a person at English universities who makes the beds and sweeps the rooms. **bed-mate,** *n.* A bed-fellow. **bed-moulding,** *n.* (*Arch.*) The moulding under a projection, as the corona of a cornice. **bed-pan,** *n.* A warming-pan; a chamber-utensil for use in bed. **bed-piece, bed-plate,** *n.* (*Mech.*) The foundation piece, plate, or framing by which the other parts are held in position. **bed-plate,** *n.* (*Eng.*) The cast-iron or steel plate used as the base plate of an engine or machine. **bed-post,** *n.* One of the upright supports of a bedstead. **twinkling of a bed-post:** [BED-STAFF] A moment, a very short space of time. ***bed-presser,** *n.* A great lazy person. **bed-quilt,** *n.* A counterpane, a coverlet. **bed-rid, bed-ridden** [A.-S. *-rida*, rider (*-en* due to conf. with p.p.)], *a.* Confined to bed through age or sickness. **bed-rock,** *n.* (*Geol.*) The rock underlying superficial formations; hence, bottom, foundation, fundamental principles. **bedroom,** *n.* *Room in a bed; a sleeping apartment. **bedside,** *n.* Place by, or companionship by a bed. *a.* Pertaining to the sick-chamber. **bedside manner:** Suave manner in attending a patient. **bed-sitting-room, bed-sitter,** *n.* Bedroom and sitting-room combined. **bed-sore,** *n.* A sore produced by long lying in bed. **bed-spread,** *n.* A counterpane, a coverlet. ***bed-staff,** *n.* (*pl.* **-staffs, -staves**) A stick used in some way about a bed; often mentioned as a ready weapon, whence, prob., **twinkling of a bed-staff:** The twinkling of a bed-post. **bedstead,** *n.* The wooden or metal framework on which a mattress is placed. **bed-straw,** *n.* Straw covered with a sheet, and used as a bed or palliasse; English name of the genus *Galium.* **bed-swerver,** *n.* One unfaithful to marriage vows. **bed-tick,** *n.* A bag or oblong case into which the feathers, hair, straw, chaff, etc., of a bed are put. **bedtime,** *n.* The usual hour for going to bed. **bedward,** *adv.* In the direction of bed; towards bedtime.

bedabble (bė dăbl'), *v.t.* To sprinkle, to wet; to splash, stain.

bedad (bė dăd') [BY DAD], *int.* (*Ir.*) Begad (an attenuated *by God*).

bedaub (bė dawb'), *v.t.* To daub over, to besmear, to bedizen.

bedazzle (bė dăzl'), *v.t.* To confuse by dazzling. **bedazzlingly,** *adv.*

***bede, bedesman,** etc. [BEAD].

bedeck (bė dek'), *v.t.* To deck out, to adorn.

bedeguar (bed' ė gar) [F. *bédeguar,* Pers. and Arab. *bādāwar,* wind-brought, some thorny plant], *n.* A mossy growth on rose-briers.

bedel (bē' dėl) [BEADLE], *n.* An officer at the Universities of Oxford and Cambridge who performs ceremonial functions (Cambridge spelling, **bedell**).

bederel [BEDRAL].

bedevil (bė dev' ėl), *v.t.* To treat with diabolical violence or ribaldry; to bewitch; to torment; to confound, bemuddle. **bedevilment,** *n.* Demoniacal possession; a state of utter confusion or disorder; bewildering trouble.

bedew (bė dū'), *v.t.* To moisten or sprinkle with dew-like drops.

bedim (bė dim'), *v.t.* To render dim; to obscure.

bedizen (bė dizn', bė dīz' ėn), *v.t.* To deck out in gaudy vestments or with tinsel finery. **bedizenment,** *n.* Bedizening; gaudy attire, finery.

Bedlam (bed' lȧm) [from the priory of St. Mary of *Bethlehem,* incorporated as a royal foundation for lunatics, 1547], *n.* The Bethlehem Hospital; a lunatic asylum; a scene of wild uproar; madness, lunacy; *a madman, a lunatic. *a.* Of or belonging to a madhouse; mad, foolish, lunatic. ***bedlam-beggar,** *n.* An inmate of old Bedlam, discharged cured or relieved, furnished with a badge, and allowed to beg. **bedlamite** (bed' lȧm īt), *n.* A bedlam-beggar; a madman, a lunatic. *a.* Mad, lunatic.

Bedlington (bed' ling tȯn) [town in Northumberland], *n.* A grey, crisp-haired terrier.

Bedouin (bed' oo in) [F. *bédouin,* Arab. *badawīn,* pl. *badawīy,* wild, wandering (*badw,* a desert)], *n.* A nomadic Arab, as distinguished from one living in a town; (*fig.*) a gipsy, a wanderer. *a.* Pertaining to the wandering Arabs; nomad.

bedowrie shower (bė dou' ri), *n.* (*Austral.*) A red dust-storm.

bedraggle (bė drăg' ėl), *v.t.* To soil by trailing in the wet or mire.

bedral (bed' rȧl), **bederel** (bed' ė rėl), **betherel** (beth' ė rėl) [corr. of BEADLE], *n.* (*Sc.*) A kind of beadle in Scottish churches.

bee (bē) [A.-S. *bēo, bī* (cp. Dut. *bij,* G. *biene*; prob. from Aryan *bhi-,* to fear, quiver)], *n.* The hymenopterous genus *Apis,* social insects, partially domesticated for the sake of the wax and honey they produce; any closely allied insect, *e.g. carpenter-bee, bumble-bee, mason-bee*; (*fig.*) a busy worker; (*Am.*) a social meeting for work usually on behalf of a neighbour; **to have a bee in one's bonnet:** To have a crazy fancy or be cranky on some point. **spelling-bee:** A social contest in spelling. **bee-bird,** *n.* The spotted fly-catcher, *Muscicapa grisola*; (*Am.*) the king-bird, *Tyrannus tyrannus.* **bee-bread,** *n.* A mixture of honey and pollen, on which bees feed their larvæ; local name of several plants yielding nectar. **bee-cuckoo,** *n.* An African bird, *Cuculus indicator,* called also the honey-guide. **bee-eater,** *n.* A foreign bird of the genus *Merops,* esp. *M. apiaster.* **bee-fold,** *n.* An enclosure for beehives. **bee-glue,** *n.* The substance with which bees fill up crevices in their hives. **bee-gum,** *n.* (*Am.*) A beehive (formerly made of the wood of gum-trees). **beehive,** *n.* A receptacle (usually of straw and dome-shaped) for bees. *a.* Shaped like a beehive. **beehive-houses, beehive-huts,** *n.pl.* Dwellings in which a roof of dry-stone masonry covers a single chamber formed by stone walls, each course being set successively inward (common in Lewis). **bee-line,** *n.* The shortest route between two places, that which a bee is assumed to take. **bee-master, bee-mistress,** *n.* One who keeps bees. **bee-moth,** *n.* The wax-moth, *Galleria cereana,* which lays its eggs in hives, the larvæ feeding on the wax. **bee-orchis,** *n.* A British orchis, *Ophrys apifera,* the flower of which resembles a bee. **bee-skep,** *n.* A straw beehive. **beeswax,** *n.* The wax secreted by bees for their cells. *v.t.* To rub or polish with beeswax. **beeswing,** *n.* The second crust, a fine filmy deposit in an old port wine; old port. **bee-tree,** *n.* (*Am.*) A hollow tree in which bees have hived. **bee wine,** *n.* A liquor made from balm of Gilead.

beech (bēch [A.-S. *bēce, bōece* (cp. Dut. *beuk,* G. *buche,* Gr. *phēgos,* L. *fāgus*)], *n.* A forest tree of the genus *Fagus*; esp. *F. sylvatica,* the common beech, a well-known forest tree with smooth bark, and yielding nuts or mast; the wood of this tree. **beech-drops,** *n.pl.* (*Am.*) The popular name of several plants parasitic on the roots of the beech. **beech-fern,** *n.* Popular name of *Polypodium phegopteris.* **beech-mast,** *n.* The fruit of the beech-tree. **beech-nut,** *n.* The nut of the beech, two of which lie in the prickly capsule. **beech-oil,** *n.* Oil expressed from beech-mast. **beech-tree,** *n.* A beech, *Fagus sylvatica.* **beech-wheat** [BUCKWHEAT]. **beechen,** *a.* Of or pertaining to the beech; made of beech-wood. **beechy,** *a.* Abounding in beech-trees.

beef (bēf) [O.F. *boef,* L. *bovem* (nom. *bos,* cp. Gr. *bous,* Gael. *bō,* Sansk. *go,* cp. cow)], *n.* The flesh of the ox, cow, or bull, used as food; an ox (*usu. in pl.,* **beeves**), esp. one fatted for the market; flesh, muscle. *v.i.* (*Slang*) To grumble, to grouse. **beef-cattle,** *n.* (*Am.*) Oxen for food. **beef-dodger,** *n.* (*Am.*) Meat-biscuit. **beefsteak,** *n.* A thick slice of meat from the hindquarters of an ox. **beef-tea,** *n.* The nutritive juice extracted from beef by simmering. **beef-wood,** *n.* The popular name of the timber of the *Casuarina,* the *Stenocarpus salignus,* and *Banksia compar,* three Australian trees, and of that of a Jamaican shrub. **beef-eater** (bēf' ē tėr), *n.* One who eats beef; a well-fed menial; an African bird of the genus *Buphaga,* allied to the starling [BEEFEATER]. **beefy,** *a.* Like beef; fleshy; stolid. **beefiness,** *n.* Fleshiness; weight, stolidity.

Beefeater (bēf' ēt ėr) [? O.F. *buffetier*], *n.* A Yeoman of the Guard, instituted in 1485; a warder of the Tower of London.

beehive [BEE].

Beelzebub (bē el' zė bŭb) [L. *Beelzebūb,* Gr. *beelzeboub,* Heb. *ba' al-z'būb,* lord of flies], *n.* A god worshipped (as *Baal-zebub*) in Ekron (2 Kings i. 2); the prince of evil spirits, Satan; an evil spirit.

been, *p.p* [BE].

beer (1) (bēr) [A.-S. *bēor* (cp. Dut. and G. *bier*)], *n.* A fermented aqueous infusion of malt and hops; any malt liquor prepared by brewing, including ale and porter; other fermented liquors, as *ginger-beer, spruce beer,* etc. **small beer:** Weak beer; poor stuff; things of no account. **beer and skittles:** (*slang*) Everything pleasing; all one could wish. **beer-barrel,** *n.* A barrel used to contain beer. **beer-engine,** *n.* An engine for pumping up beer from the cellar to the bar. **beerhouse, beershop,** *n.* A house licensed for the sale of malt liquors only. **beer-money,** *n.* A money allowance to servants in lieu of beer. **beer-pull,** *n.* A handle of a beer-engine. **beery,** *a.* Abounding in beer; like beer; under the influence of beer; fuddled. **beeriness,** *n.* A condition approaching intoxication. **beerocracy,** *n.* (*political slang*) The brewing aristocracy.

beer (2) (bēr) [BIER], *n.* (*Weaving*) About forty threads gathered together from the ends of a warp, to help in opening or dividing the warp; in Scotland called the porter.

beest (bēst) [A.-S. *bēost* (O.H.G. *biost*, Dut. *biest*)], *n.* The first milk drawn from a cow after calving. **beestings** [A.-S. *bȳsting*, thick milk], *n.pl.* Beest.

beeswax, beeswing [BEE].

beet (bēt) [A.-S. *bēte*, L. beta], *n.* A plant or genus of plants, comprising red beet, used as a salad, and white beet, used in sugar-making, cultivated for its esculent root; (*Am.*) beetroot. **beet-radish, beet-rave,** *n.* The common beet, *Beta vulgaris*, when raised for salad. **beetroot,** *n.* The root of this, used as a salad.

beetle (1) (bē′ tėl) [A.-S. *bȳtel, bȳtl*, O.Teut. *bautilos*, from *bautan*, to beat (cp. A.-S. *beatan*, to beat)], *n.* A maul; a heavy wooden mallet for driving stones, stakes, or tent-pegs into the ground, hammering down paving-stones, and other ramming and crushing operations. *v.t.* To beat with a beetle. **as deaf as a beetle:** Very deaf; stupidly deaf.

beetle (2) (bē′ tėl) [A.-S. *bitela, bitula*, from *bitan*, to bite], *n.* An insect of the order Coleoptera, the upper wings of which have been converted into hard wing-cases, the under ones being used for flight, if it is able to fly; the name is popularly confined to those of black colour and large size, and applied to other insects resembling these, such as the cockroach. **beetle-crusher,** *n.* (*slang*) A large foot; a heavy boot. **to beetle along:** (*colloq.*) To plod along; to be on one's way somewhere.

beetle (3) (bē′ tėl) [prob. from BEETLE (2), but first found in the comb. *beetle-browed*], *a.* Projecting, overhanging, scowling. **beetle-brow,** *n.* A projecting brow. *v.i.* [prob. coined by Shakespeare from *beetle-browed*] To jut out, to hang over. **beetle-browed:** Having a projecting brow. **beetling,** *a.* Jutting, overhanging, prominent.

beetroot [BEET].

beeves [BEEF].

befall (bė fawl′) [A.-S. *befealtan* (BE-, *fallan*, FALL)], *v.t.* (*past* **befell,** p.p. **befallen**) To happen to. *v.i.* To happen.

befit (bė fit′), *v.t.* To be suitable to or for; to become; to be incumbent upon; *to fit. **befitting,** *a.* **befittingly,** *adv.*

befog (bė fog′), *v.t.* To involve in a fog; (*fig.*) to obscure, to confuse.

befool (bė fool′), *v.t.* To make a fool of; to dupe, delude.

before (bė fôr′) [A.-S. *beforan* (*be-, bi-*, by, *foran*, adv., before, *fore*, prep. before, above, O.Teut. *fora*, for)], *prep.* In front of, in time, space, rank, or degree; in presence or sight of; under the cognizance of; under the influence or impulsion of; in preference to. *adv.* Ahead, in front; beforehand, already, in the past. *conj.* Earlier than; sooner than, rather than. **a.* Anterior, prior. **before the mast:** (*Naut.*) In the fo'c'sle; applied to common sailors who live in the fo'c'sle in front of the foremast. **before the wind:** (*Naut.*) With the wind right aft. **before Christ:** Anterior to the birth of Christ (*e.g.* '1000 B.C.'). **before-cited,** *a.* Cited in a preceding part. **before God:** With the knowledge or in the sight of God. **before-going,** *a.* Preceding. **before-mentioned,** *a.* Mentioned before. **beforehand,** *adv.* In anticipation, in advance, before the time. **to be beforehand:** To forestall. **beforetime,** *adv.* Formerly; in the olden time.

befortune (bė fôr′ tūn), *v.i.* To befall, bechance.

befoul (bė foul′), *v.t.* To render dirty, to soil.

befriend (bė frend′), *v.t.* To favour, help; to countenance.

befringe (bė frinj′), *v.t.* To furnish or decorate with or as with a fringe.

beg (1) (beg) [etym. doubtful; perh. from O.F. *begard*, a lay brother, corr. to the BEGUINES], *v.i.* (*past & p.p.* **begged**). To ask for alms, to live by asking alms. *v.t.* To ask or supplicate in charity; to ask earnestly, to crave, entreat. **to beg the question:** To assume the thing to be proved. **to go a-begging:** To be acceptable to nobody. **beggar,** *n.* One who begs; one who lives by asking alms; one in indigent circumstances; *a suppliant, a petitioner; (*colloq.*) a fellow; youngster. **a good beggar:** A successful pleader or collector for charitable objects. *v.t.* To reduce to want; to impoverish; to exhaust, to outdo. **to beggar description:** To go beyond one's power of expression. **beggar-my-neighbour,** *n.* A childish game at cards. **beggarly,** *a.* Like a beggar; mean, poverty-stricken; (*fig.*) poor, contemptible. *adv.* In the manner of a beggar. **beggarliness,** *n.* The quality of being beggarly. **beggary,** *n.* The state or condition of an habitual beggar; extreme indigence.

beg (2) [BEY].

begad (bė găd′), *int.* (*slang*) By God.

began, *past* [BEGIN].

begem (bė jem′), *v.t.* To cover or set as with gems.

beget (bė get′), *v.t.* To engender, to generate, to procreate; (*fig.*) to cause to come into existence. **v.i.* To acquire. **begetter,** *n.* One who begets, a father; an originator.

beggar, etc. [BEG].

Beghard (beg′ ȧrd) [med. L. *Beghardus*, from F. *Beguine*, or directly from *Bègue*, see BEGUINE], *n.* A lay brother, belonging to a Flemish society like the Beguines, in France called *Beguins.*

begin (bė gin′) [A.-S. *beginnan* (cp. Dut. and G. *beginnen*, begin, A.-S. *ginan*, to yawn, Aryan *ghī*, L. *hiāre*, to gape)], *v.i.* (*past* **began,** *p.p.* **begun**) To come into existence, to arise, to start; to commence. *v.t.* To be the first to do, to do the first act of, to enter on, to commence. **to begin with:** To take first. *adv.* Firstly. **n.* A beginning. **beginner,** *n.* One who originates anything; one who is the first to do anything; a young learner or practitioner; (*Theat.*) the actor or actors who appear first on the stage at the start of a play. **beginning,** *n.* The first cause, the origin; the first state or commencement; first principles, rudiments.

begird (bė gĕrd′), *v.t.* To encircle with or as with a girdle.

begirdle (bė gĕr′ dėl), *v.t.* To encompass like a girdle or belt.

begone (bė gawn′, bė gon′), *imper.v.* Get you gone, go away, depart.

Begonia (bė gō′ ni ȧ, -gō′ nyȧ) [Michael *Begon* (1638–1710)], *n.* A genus of plants cultivated chiefly for their ornamental foliage.

begot, *past,* **begotten,** *p.p.* [BEGET].

begrime (bė grīm′), *v.t.* To blacken or soil with grime.

begrudge (bė grŭj′), *v.t.* To grudge; to envy (a person) the possession of.

beguile (bė gīl′) [BE-, *guile*, obs. v., deceive (see GUILE)], *v.t.* To deceive, cheat, to deprive of or lead into by fraud; to charm away tedium or weariness, to amuse. **beguilement,** *n.* The act of beguiling; a wile, temptation, deceit. **beguiler,** *n.* One who beguiles, a deceiver, a cheat. **beguiling,** *a.* Deceiving, charming, wiling away. **beguilingly,** *adv.* So as to beguile.

Beguine (1) (bā gēn′, beg′ in) [the founder, Lambert le *Bègue* (late 12th cent.)], *n.* A member of certain sisterhoods which arose in the Netherlands in the 12th century (some of which still exist); the members are not bound by perpetual vows, and may leave the community when they please. **beguinage** (bā gē nazh′, beg′ in ȧj), *n.* A house or establishment for Beguines.

beguine (2) (be gēn′) [F.], *n.* Music or dance in bolero rhythm, of S. American or West Indian origin.

begum (bē gŭm) [Hind. *bigam*, Turk. *bigīm*, princess, fem. of *beg*, BEY], *n.* A queen, princess, or lady of high rank in India.

begun, *p.p.* [BEGIN].

behalf (bė haf′) [A.-S. *be healfe*, by the side, blended with *on healfe*, on the side of], *n.* Interest, lieu, stead. **on his behalf, on behalf of:** On account of, for the sake of.

behave (bė hāv′) [BE- HAVE], **v.t.* To handle, to exercise, to employ. *v.r.* To conduct, to demean. *v.i.* To conduct oneself or itself; (*colloq.*) to conduct oneself well, to display good manners; to act as regards, to conduct oneself towards. **well-behaved,** *a.* Having good manners. **behaviour** (bė hā′ vyėr) [*haviour* (abbr. often used by Shakespeare) assim. to *havour*, *havyoure*, having possession; F. *avoir*], *n.* Outward deportment, carriage; manners, conduct, demeanour; the manner in which a thing acts; *good manners; *personality. **behaviourism,** *n.* (*Psych.*) The guiding principle of certain psychologists who hold that the proper basis of psychological science is the objective study of behaviour under stimuli.

behead (bė hed′) [A.-S. *behēadian* (*be-*, by, *hēafod*, head)], *v.t.* To cut the head off, to kill by decapitation; (*Geol.*) to cut off and capture the upper portion of (another stream) by gradual erosion in a backward direction.

beheld (bė held′), *pret.* and *p.p.* [BEHOLD].

behemoth (bē′ hė moth, bė hē′ moth) [Heb., from Egyp. *p-ehe-mau*, water-ox], *n.* The animal described in Job xl. 15–24, probably the hippopotamus; (*fig.*) a huge person or thing.

behest (bė hest′) [A.-S. *behæs* (*behatan*, to promise)], *n.* A command; an injunction.

behind (bė hīnd′) [A.-S. *behindan* (BE-, *hindan*, adv., at the back)], *prep.* At the back of; inferior to; after, later than; in the rear of. *adv.* At the back, in the rear; towards the rear; in the past; backwards, out of sight, on the further side of; in reserve; in arrears. *n.* The back part of a person or garment; the posteriors. **behind one's back:** Without one's knowledge. **behind the scenes:** Behind the scenery in a theatre; (*fig.*) out of sight, private. **behindhand,** *a.* Dilatory, tardy; backward, unfinished; in arrear.

behold (bė hōld′) [A.-S. *bihaldan* (BE-, *healdan*, hold, keep)], *v.t.* (*past & p.p.* **beheld**). *To fix the eyes upon; look attentively at, observe with care; to see, view; to consider. *v.i.* To look. *int.* Lo! **beholder,** *n.* One who beholds; a spectator. **beholden** [orig. p.p. of BEHOLD], *a.* Obliged, indebted, under obligation of gratitude (with *to*). ***beholding** [BEHOLDEN].

behoof (bė hoof′), ***behove** (bė hōv′) [A.-S. *behōf* (*behōflīc*, useful) (cp. Dut. *behoef*, G. *behuf*; *be-*, Goth. *hafjan*, A.-S. *hebban*, to heave, cp. L. *capere*, to take)], *n.* Advantage, use, profit, benefit.

behove (bė hōv′), ***behoove** (bė hoov′) [A.-S. *bihōvian*, *behōfian* (see BEHOOF)], *v.t.* To befit, to be due to, to suit. *v.i.* To be needful to; due to; to be incumbent. ***behoveful,** *a.* Needful, necessary.

beige (bāzh) [F.], *n.* A fabric made of undyed and unbleached wool. *a.* Grey.

bein (bēn) [etym. doubtful], *a.* (*Sc.*) Comfortable; well-off; well-fed, lazy. **beinness,** *n.* Comfort; comfortable circumstances.

being (bē′ ing) [BE, -ING], *n.* The state of existing; lifetime; existence; nature, essence; a thing or person existing. *conj.* Seeing that, since, *a.* Existing, present. **Supreme Being:** God. **in being:** In actual existence. **the time being:** The present.

bejade (bė jād′), *v.t.* To tire out.

bejan (bē′ jȧn) [F. *béjaune* (*bec jaune*, yellow beak, nestling)], *n.* (*Sc.*) A freshman at Aberdeen and St. Andrews Universities (borrowed from Paris University).

bekah (bē′ ka) [Heb.], *n.* A Hebrew weight of ½ ounce (Exodus xxxviii. 26).

bekko-ware (bek′ ō wâr) [Jap. *bekko*, tortoise-shell], *n.* Chinese pottery veined with colour like tortoise-shell.

bel (bel) [A. G. Bell (1847–1922)], *n.* (*Phys.*) A measure for comparing the intensity of noises, currents, etc. The logarithm to the base 10 of the ratio of one to the other is the number of bels.

belabour (bė lā′ bȯr), *v.t.* To cultivate with labour, to labour at; to beat, to thrash; to dwell unduly on.

belar, belah (bē′ la) [Austral. abor.], *n.* A variety of casuarina tree.

belated (bė lā′ ted), *a.* Very late; behind time; too late; benighted. **belatedness,** *n.*

belaud (bė lawd′), *v.t.* To praise excessively.

belay (bė lā′) [A.-S. *belecgan* (BE-, LAY), to lay round, envelop; (nautical use perh. from Dut. *beleggan*, to cover, belay)], *v.t.* To fasten a running rope by winding it round a cleat or belaying-pin. **belay there!** Stop! enough! **belaying-pin,** *n.* (*Naut.*) A stout pin to which running ropes may be belayed. *n.* (*Climbing*) A belaying-pin, a projection round which a rope can be tied or hitched.

belch (belch) [A.-S. *bealcan*], *v.t.* To expel from the mouth with violence; to eject, to throw out; to utter in a noisy or drunken manner. *v.i.* To eject wind by the mouth from the stomach; to eructate; *to issue out, as by eructation. *n.* An eructation; an eruption, a burst (of smoke or fire).

belcher (bel′ chėr) [Jim *Belcher*, the pugilist (1781–1811)], *n.* A blue and white spotted neckerchief.

beldam, *beldame (bel′ dȧm) [F. *belle*, *bel*, expressing relationship, DAM, mother], *n.* A grandmother, a remote ancestress; an old woman; a hag, a witch.

beleaguer (bė lē′gėr [Dut. *belegeren*, besiege (*be-*, around, *leger*, a bed, a camp)], *v.t.* To besiege, to invest. **beleaguerment,** *n.* Siege, blockade, investment.

belemnite (bel′ ėm nīt) [Gr. *belemnon*, a dart (*ballein*, to throw), *n.* (*Geol.*) The internal bone (the only part found fossil) of a genus of cephalopods, allied to the cuttle-fish; any individual of this genus. **belemnitic** (-nit′ ik), *a.* Of, pertaining to, or characterized by belemnites.

bel esprit (bel es prē′) [F., fine mind], *n.* (*pl.* ***beaux esprits*** (bōz es prē′)) A man of genius; a wit.

belfry (bel′ fri) [O.F. *berfrei*, *berfroi*, M.H.G. *bercfrit* (*berc.* protection, shelter, *fride*, O.H.G. *fridis*, peace), a protection tower, a siege tower], *n.* *A movable wooden tower formerly used in besieging a place; *a shed for cattle; a bell-tower attached to or separate from a church or other building; the chamber for the bells in a church-tower; (*Naut.*) the frame on which a ship's bell is hung.

belga (bel′ ga) [L., *Belgicus*, Belgian], *n.* (*Fin.*) Belgian unit of exchange, equivalent to 5 francs.

Belgian (bel′ jiȧn, -jȧn), *a.* Of or pertaining to the ancient Belgæ, to Belgium, or to the Belgians. *n.* A native of Belgium; a kind of canary. **Belgic** [L. *Belgicus* (*Belgæ*, -IC)], *a.* or *n.* Belgian.

Belgravian (bel grā′ vi ȧn) [*Belgrave* Square], *a.* Of or belonging to Belgravia, a fashionable district in the West End of London; fashionable. *n.* One of the aristocracy.

Belial (bē′ li ȧl) [Heb. *b'li-yaal*, worthlessness], *n.* The Devil, Satan; one of the fallen angels. **son of Belial, man of Belial,** *n.* A worthless, wicked man.

belie (bė lī') [A.-S. *belēogan* (BE-, *lēogan*, to lie)], *v.t.* To tell lies about, to calumniate; to misrepresent; to be faithless to; to fail to perform or justify; *to counterfeit, to imitate; *to fill with lies.

belief (bė lēf') [BE-, A.-S. *lēafa*, *gelēafa* (cp. G. *glaube*)], *n.* Reliance, confidence; the mental act or operation of accepting a fact or proposition as true; the thing so believed; opinion, persuasion; religion, faith, acceptance of the Christian religion. **the Belief:** The Apostles' Creed.

believe (bė lēv') [as prec.], *v.t.* To have confidence in, or reliance on; to give credence to; to accept as true; be of opinion that. *v.i.* To think; to have faith; to exercise the virtue of faith. **to believe in:** To trust in, to rely on. **to make believe:** To pretend. **believe it or not:** Although it may seem incredible, the statement is true. **believable,** *a.* Capable of being believed; credible. **believableness,** *n.* The quality of being believable. **believer,** *n.* One who believes; a convert to Christianity; a Christian. **believing,** *a.* Exercising belief or the virtue of faith. **believingly,** *adv.* In a believing manner; with faith.

belike (bė līk'), *adv.* Likely, possibly, perhaps.

Belisha beacon (be lī' shȧ) [L. *Hore-Belisha*, Minister of Transport, 1934], *n.* A yellow globe on a post to indicate a street-crossing for pedestrians.

belittle (bė lit' ėl), *v.t.* To make little; to dwarf; to depreciate.

bell (bel) [A.-S. *belle* (*bellan*, to bellow)], *n.* A hollow body of cast metal, usually in the shape of an inverted cup with recurved edge, so formed as to emit a clear musical sound when struck by a hammer; hence, used for many objects in nature and art of a similar form; the vase, basket, or cushion of a Corinthian capital; the cry of a buck at rutting time; (*Bot.*) a bell-shaped corolla; the catkin containing the female flowers of the hop; (*Naut.*) the bell struck on board ship every half-hour to indicate the time; a space of half an hour. *v.i.* To bellow (of stags in rutting time); to be in flower (of hops). *v.t.* To furnish with a bell; to utter loudly. **one to eight bells:** (*Naut.*) A watch of four hours. **to bear away the bell:** To carry off the prize. **to bear the bell:** To be first. **to curse by bell, book, and candle:** To excommunicate solemnly by a ceremony in which these objects were used symbolically. **sound as a bell, clear as a bell:** Sound or clear, free from any flaw. **bell-animalcules,** *n.pl.* (*Biol.*) The infusorial family Vorticellidæ, which have a bell-shaped body on a flexible stalk. **bell-bird,** *n.* A South American bird, *Procnias carunculata*, with a note like the toll of a bell; an Australian bird, *Myzantha melanophrys*, with a tinkling note. **bell-bottomed,** *a.* With wide, bell-shaped bottoms (of trousers). **bell-boy, bell-hop,** *n.* (*Am.*) An hotel page-boy. **bell-buoy,** *n.* A buoy to which a bell is attached, rung by the motion of the waves. **bell-cot, bell-cote,** *n.* A small turret for a bell or bells. **bell-crank,** *n.* A crank adapted to communicate motion from one bell-wire to another at right angles to it. **bell-faced,** *a.* Having a convex face (as a hammer). **bell-flower,** *n.* A bell-shaped flower, or plant with such flowers, belonging to the genus *Campanula*. **bell-founder, -founding, -foundry,** *n.* The caster, the casting, and the manufactory of bells. **bell-gable, bell-turret,** *n.* A gable or turret in which bells are hung. **bell-glass,** *n.* A bell-shaped glass for protecting plants. **bell-hanger,** *n.* One who hangs or fixes bells. **bell-hanging,** *n.* The act or process of fixing bells. **bellman,** *n.* A public crier who attracts attention by ringing a bell. **bell-metal,** *n.* An alloy of copper and tin, usually with a little zinc, used for bells. **bell-pull,** *n.* A cord or handle by which a bell is rung. **bell-punch,** *n.* A ticket punch in which a bell is rung each time it is used. **bell-ringer,** *n.* One whose business it is to ring a church or public bell at stated times. **bell-rope,** *n.* The rope by which a bell is rung. **bell-shaped,** *a.* Shaped like a bell; campanulate. **bell-telegraph,** *n.* A telegraph instrument in which needles are replaced by two bells, signals on one of which represent dots, and on the other dashes, of the Morse systêm. **bell-tent,** *n.* A conical tent. **bell-topper:** (*Austral. colloq.*) A top-hat. **bell-turret,** *n.* [BELL-GABLE]. **bell-wether,** *n.* The sheep that wears a bell and leads a flock; (*fig.*) a leader. **bell-wort,** *n.* (*Bot.*) Any plant of the family Campanulaceæ. **to bell the cat:** To be a ringleader in a hazardous movement; to grapple with a dangerous opponent (in allusion to the fable of the mice wishing to put a bell on the cat).

belladonna (bel ȧ don' ȧ) [It., a fine lady], *n.* Deadly nightshade or dwale, *Atropa belladonna*; (*Med.*) a drug prepared from the leaves and root of this plant.

belle (bel) [F., from L. *bella*, fem. of *bellus*, fine, pretty], *n.* A beautiful woman; a reigning beauty.

belles-lettres (bel' letr) [F.], *n.pl.* Polite literature, the humanities, pure literature. **belletrist** (bel-let' rist), *n.* A person devoted to belles-lettres. **belletristic** (bel let ris' tik), *a.* Pertaining to belles-lettres.

bellicose (bel' i kōs) [L. *bellicosus* (*bellum*, war)], *a.* Warlike; inclined to war or fighting. **bellicosity** (bel i kos' i ti), *n.* Inclination to war.

bellied [BELLY].

belligerent (bė lij' ėr ėnt) [F. *belligérant*, L. *belligerans -ntem*, pres.p. of *belligerāre* (*bellum*, war, *gerere*, to wage)], *a.* Carrying on war; of or pertaining to persons or nations carrying on war. *n.* A nation, party, or individual engaged in war. **belligerence,** *n.* The state of being at war. **belligerency,** *n.* Belligerence; the status of a belligerent.

Bellini-Tosi system (be lē' nē tō' zē) [names of inventors], *n.* (*Radio.*) A system of two aerials fixed at right-angles and joined to two coils placed in position, also at right-angles, inside of which a third coil rotates.

Bellona (bel lō' na) [L., the Roman goddess of war (*bellum*, war)], *n.* The goddess of war; (*fig.*) a tall, high-spirited woman.

bellow (bel' ō) [A.-S. *bellan*], *v.i.* To emit a loud hollow sound (as a bull); to raise an outcry or clamour, to bawl, to vociferate; to emit a loud hollow sound (as the sea, the wind, artillery, etc.). *v.t.* To utter with a loud hollow voice. *n.* The roar of a bull, or any similar sound.

bellows (bel' ōz) [M.E. *belu*, *belw* (pl. *belwes*, *belowes*), Icel. *belgr* (cp. A.-S. *bælig*), a bag (see BELLY)], *n.pl.* An instrument or machine for supplying a strong blast of air to a fire or a wind instrument; the expansible portion of a photographic camera; (*fig.*) the lungs. **pair of bellows:** A two-handled bellows for fanning fire. **bellows-fish,** *n.* The Cornish name of the trumpet-fish or sea-snipe, *Macrorhamphosus scolopax*; (*Am.*) the fishing-frog, *Lophius piscatorius*.

belly (bel' i) [A. S. *bælig*, *bylig*, a leather bag (O.Teut. *balgiz*), *balgan*, to swell out], *n.* That part of the human body in front which extends from the breast to the insertion of the lower limbs; the corresponding part in the inferior vertebrates; the part containing the stomach and bowels; the stomach, the womb; that part of a man which demands food; hence, appetite, gluttony; the front or lower surface of an object; anything swelling out or protuberant; a cavity, a hollow surface; the interior; (*Mus.*) the bulging part of a violin or a similar instrument. *v.t.* To cause to swell out, to render protuberant. *v.i.* To swell or bulge out, to become protuberant. **belly-ache,** *n.* The colic; *v.i.* To express discontent, to whine. **belly-band,** *n.* A band passing under the belly of a horse, ass, or other beast of burden to keep the saddle in place. **belly-bound,** *a.* (*slang*) Constipated, costive. **bellyful,** *n.* As much as fills the belly, as much food as satisfies the appetite; (*fig.*) sufficiency, more than enough. ***belly-god,** *n.* A glutton. **belly-furniture, -timber,** *n.* (*slang*) Food, provisions. **belly landing,** *n.* (*Aviat.*) Landing without using the landing-wheels. **belly-laugh,** *n.* A deep, hearty laugh. **bellied,** *a.* Having a belly (*in comb.*); corpulent; (*Bot.*) ventricose. **bellying,** *a.* Swelling, protuberant, bulging out of sails with wind.

belomancy (bel' ō măn si) [Gr. *belos*, an arrow, -MANCY], *n.* Divination by means of arrows.

belong (bė long') [M.E. *bilongen, belongen* (BE-, LONG (4))], *v.i.* To be appropriate, to pertain; to be the property, attribute, appendage, member, right, duty, concern, or business of; to be connected with; to be a native or resident of. **belonging,** *n.* Anything belonging to one (*usu. in pl.*); a quality or endowment; (*colloq., pl.*) one's possessions.

beloved (bė lŭvd', bė lŭv' ėd), *a.* Loved greatly. *n.* One greatly loved.

below (bė lō'), *prep.* Beneath; under in place; down stream from; on the inferior side of; inferior in rank, degree, or excellence; unworthy of, unsuitable to. *adv.* In or to a lower place, rank, or station, below; on earth (as opp. to heaven); in hell (as opp. to earth); downstairs; down stream; lower on the same page, or on a following page. **below one's breath:** In a whisper.

belt (belt) [A.-S. (cp. O.H.G. *balz*, L. *balteus*)], *n.* A broad, flat strip of leather or other material, worn as a girdle or baldric, esp. one worn as a badge of rank or distinction; anything resembling such a belt in shape; a broad strip or stripe; sometimes applied to a strait, as the Great and Little Belts in the Baltic; (*Astron.*) one of Jupiter's bands; a flat endless strap passing round two wheels and communicating motion from one to the other; a zone of armour on a warship. *v.t.* To encircle with or as with a belt; to fasten on with a belt; to invest with a belt; to deck with a zone of colour; to thrash with a belt. **corn-, cotton-belt,** *n.* A region where corn or cotton is grown. **to hit below the belt:** To act unfairly in contest (from the language of the prize-ring). **belted,** *a.* Wearing a belt, esp. as a mark of rank or distinction; furnished with a belt of any kind; affixed by a belt; surrounded as with a belt. **belted-cruiser,** *n.* A fast warship with a broad belt of armour-plating. **belted earl,** *n.* An earl wearing (or entitled to wear) his distinctive cincture. **belting,** *n.* Belts collectively; material for belts; a series of belts fixed round chimney-stacks to strengthen them; (*Mech.*) a belt or system of belts.

Beltane (bel' tān) [Gael. *beailtainn* (prob. conn. with A.-S. *bæl*, a blaze, Gr. *phalios*, bright)], *n.* Old May-day, one of the old Scottish quarter-days; a Celtic festival celebrated by bonfires on old May-day.

beluga (bė loo' gȧ) [Rus., white], *n.* The great or hausen sturgeon, *Acipenser huso*; the white whale, *Delphinapterus leucas.*

belvedere (bel vė dēr') [It. (*bel*, fine, *vedere*, to see)], *n.* A turret, lantern, or cupola, raised above the roof of a building to command a view; a summer-house built on an eminence for the same purpose.

belying [BELIE].

bema (bē' mȧ) [Gr.], *n.* (*Eccles.*) The sanctuary, presbytery, or chancel of a church; the platform from which Athenian orators spoke.

bemean (bė mēn'), *v.t.* To render mean, to lower or debase.

bemire (bė mīr'), *v.t.* To cover or soil with mire. **bemired,** *p.p.* To be stuck or sunk in mire.

bemoan (bė mōn') [A.-S. *bimænan* (BE-, *mænan*, MOAN)], *v.t.* To moan over, to deplore. *v.i.* To moan, to lament.

bemuddle (bė mŭdl'), *v.t.* To muddle completely.

bemuse (bė mūz'), *v.t.* To make utterly confused or dazed, as by drinking.

ben (1) (ben) [Gael. *beann*], *n.* A mountain-peak.

ben (2) (ben) [Sc., from M.E. *binne*, A.-S. *binnan* (cp. Dut. and G. *binnen*)], *prep.* (*Sc.*) In or into the inner apartment of. *adv.* Within, into, or towards the inner part of a house. *n.* The inner room. [*See* BUT (2).]

bench (bench) [A.-S. *benc* (cp. Swed. *bänk*, G. *bank*, It. *banca*, O.Teut. *bankiz*, see BANK)], *n.* A long seat or form; a seat where judges and magistrates sit in court, hence judges or magistrates collectively, or sitting as a court; a tribunal; the office of judge; (*pl.*) groups of seats in the Houses of Parliament; other official seats, and those who have a right to occupy them; (*Am.*) a level tract between a river and neighbouring hills; a terrace or ledge in masonry, quarrying, mining, earthwork, etc.; a carpenter's or other mechanic's work-table; (*Naut.*) a boat-thwart. *v.t.* To furnish with benches; *to seat upon a bench. **v.i.* To sit on a bench (as in a court of justice). **Queen's (or King's) Bench:** The court formerly presided over by the Sovereign; now one of the divisions of the Supreme Court. **the Bench of Bishops:** The Episcopate collectively, esp. those who rank as peers. **to be raised to the bench:** To be made a judge. **treasury bench, front bench, Conservative benches,** etc.: Seats appropriated to certain officers, parties, or groups in Parliament. ***bench-hole,** *n.* A privy. **bench-mark,** *n.* A mark cut in some durable material in a line of survey for reference at a future time. **bench-plane,** *n.* (*Carpentry*) The jack-plane, the trying-plane, or the smoothing plane. **bench-show,** *n.* A dog-show, in which the dogs are exhibited on benches or platforms. **bench-table,** *n.* A low seat of stone in churches and cloisters. **bench-warrant,** *n.* (*Law*) A warrant issued by a judge, as distinct from a magistrate's warrant. **bencher,** *n.* One who sits upon a bench, *esp. in a tavern, a tavern-haunter; *one who sits officially on a bench; (*Law*) one of the senior members of an Inn of Court who collectively govern the Inn, and have power of 'calling to the bar.'

bend (bend) [A.-S. *bendan* (Icel. *benda*, to join, strain, O.Teut. *bandjan*)] (*past* and *p.p.* **bent,** *exc.* in **bended knees**), *v.t.* To bring into a curved shape (as a bow) by pulling the string; to render curved or angular; to deflect; to direct to a certain point; to apply closely; bring into operation; to incline from the vertical; (*fig.*) to subdue; (*Naut.*) to fasten, to make fast; to tie into a knot; *to direct, aim (a weapon). *v.i.* To assume the form of a curve or angle; to incline from an erect position, to bow, stoop; to surrender, submit; to turn in a new direction; *to drink hard. *n.* A bending curve, or flexure; incurvation; a sudden turn in a road or river; an inclination; *a glance; (*Her.*) an ordinary formed by two parallel lines drawn across from the dexter chief to the sinister base point of an escutcheon; a similar ordinary from the sinister chief to the dexter base point is a mark of bastardy, and is called **bend sinister** (cp. BAR, BATON); (*Naut.*) a knot; (*pl.*) the crooked timbers which make the ribs or sides of a ship; (*Tanning*) a shape or size in tanned leather, half a butt. **bend-leather,** *n.* The stoutest kind of leather. **bender,** *n.* (*slang*) A sixpence. **the bends,** *n.* Caisson disease. **on bended knees,** *adv.* With the knees bent; (*fig.*) as a suppliant. **to bend a sail:** (*Naut.*) To extend or make it fast to its proper yard or stay. **to bend the brows:** To frown. **to bend the elbow:** (*colloq.*) To be fond of drinking. **to be bent:** To be inclined, addicted, prone to. **to be bent on:** To be resolved on.

beneath (bė nēth') [A.-S. *beneothan* (*be-*, by, *neothan*, adv. below, cp. *nither*, below, O.Teut. *nithar*, G. *nieden*)], *prep.* Below, under, in point of place or position; unworthy of. *adv.* In a lower place, below.

benedicite (ben ė dī' si ti) [L., bless ye! imper. of *benedicere* (*bene*, well, *dīcere* to speak)], *int.* Bless you! good gracious! *n.* The invocation of a blessing; grace before meat; the Song of the Three Holy Children, one of the canticles in the Prayer Book; (*Mus.* a setting of this.

benedick, benedict (ben' ė dik, -dikt) [L. *benedictus*, blessed (see prec.)], *n.* A newly married man (from *Benedick*, a character in *Much Ado About Nothing*).

Benedictine (ben ė dik′ tin) [F. *bénédictin*, L. *Benedictus*], *a.* Of or pertaining to St. Benedict, or to the order of monks founded by him. *n.* One of an order of monks founded (529) by St. Benedict, called also Black Monks, from the colour of their habit; a liqueur made by Benedictine monks.

benediction (ben ė dik′ shŭn) [L. *benedictio -ōnem* (see BENEDICITE)], *n.* The act of blessing or invoking a blessing; grace before or after meals; blessedness, grace, blessing; a blessing pronounced officially; R.C. devotion including a blessing with the Host. **benedictional,** *n.* A book containing the episcopal benedictions formerly in use. **benedictory,** *a.* Of or relating to or expressing benediction. **benedictus,** *n.* The hymn of Zacharias (Luke i. 68), used as a canticle in the Church of England; (*R.-C. Ch.*) a portion of the Mass following the Sanctus; (*Mus.*) a setting of either of these.

benefaction (ben ė făk′ shŭn) [L. *benefactio -ōnem*, from *benefacere* (see BENEFICE)], *n.* The conferring of a benefit; a benefit conferred; a gift or endowment for charitable purposes.

benefactor (ben′ ė făk tŏr) [L., as prec.], *n.* One who gives another help or friendly service; one who gives to a religious or charitable institution; *a well-doer. **benfactresss,** *n.* A female benefactor.

benefice (ben′ ė fis) [L. *beneficium* (*bene*, well, *-ficium*, a doing, from *facere*)], *n.* *An estate held by feudal tenure; an ecclesiastical living. **beneficed,** *a.* Possessed of a benefice.

beneficent (bė nef′ i sėnt), *a.* Kind, generous, doing good; characterized by benevolence. **beneficently,** *adv.* **beneficence,** *n.* The habitual practice of doing good; active kindness; charity. **beneficial** (ben ė fish′ ăl), *a.* Advantageous, helpful; remedial; (*Law*) of or belonging to usufruct; enjoying the usufruct of. **beneficially,** *adv.* **beneficiary,** *a.* (*Law*) Holding or held by feudal tenure. *n.* One who receives a favour; a feudatory; the holder of a benefice, one who benefits under a trust.

benefit (ben′ ė fit) [O.F. *bienfait*, L. *benefactum*, neut. p.p. of *benefacere* (see BENEFICE)], *n.* *A kindness, a favour, a benefaction; *a natural gift; profit, advantage, gain; a theatrical, music-hall, or other performance, the receipts from which, with certain deductions, are given to some person or charity; (*Law*) the advantage of belonging to some privileged order; exemption from the jurisdiction of the ordinary courts; allowance, pension, etc., to which a person is entitled under the National Insurance Act. *v.t.* To do good to; to be of advantage or profit to. *v.i.* To derive advantage. **benefit of clergy:** (*Law*) A privilege anciently granted to the clerical orders, and later to any who could read of certain exemptions from the sentences passed in secular courts. **benefit club** or **society,** *n.* A society whose members, in return for a certain periodical payment, receive certain benefits in sickness or old age.

Benelux (ben′ e lŭks) [first letters of *Be*lgium, *Ne*therlands, *Lux*embourg], *n.* Name given to the political and economic association of these three countries, 1947.

benevolent (bė nev′ ŏ lėnt) [O.F. *benevolent*, L. *bene volens -tem*, well wishing (*velle*, to wish)], *a.* Disposed to do good; kind, charitable, generous. **benevolently,** *adv.* **benevolence,** *n.* Disposition to do good; charitable feeling, goodwill; a forced loan formerly levied by English kings, but abolished by the Bill of Rights (1689).

Bengal (ben gawl′) [a province of former British India], *n.* Name of various piece goods exported thence to England. **Bengal light,** *n.* A firework giving a vivid and sustained light. **Bengal stripes,** *n.* A kind of striped gingham originally exported from Bengal. **Bengal tiger,** *n.* The royal tiger, *Felis tigris*, abundant in Bengal. **Bengali, Bengalee** (ben gaw′ li) [native name *Bangālī*], *a.* Of or pertaining to Bengal, its native race, or language. *n.* A native of Bengal; the Aryan language of Bengal.

benighted (bė nī′ tėd), *p.p.* Overtaken by night. *a.* Involved in moral or intellectual darkness; ignorant; uncivilized.

benign (bė nīn′) [O.F. *benigne*, L. *benignus*, prob. orig. *benigenus* (*bene*, well, *-genus*, born, cp. *indigenus*)], *a.* Kind-hearted, gracious, mild; favourable, propitious; genial, agreeable, salubrious; (*Med.*) not malignant, mild. **benignly,** *adv.* **benignant** (bė nig′ nănt), *a.* Gracious, kind, benevolent; favourable, propitious. **benignantly,** *adv.* **benignity,** *n.* Kindly feeling; kindness, a favour bestowed.

benison (ben′ i zŏn) [O.F. *beneison*, L. *benedictio -ōnem*, BENEDICTION], *n.* A blessing.

benjamin (1) (ben′ jă min) [corr. of BENZOIN], *n.* Benzoin. **benjamin-tree,** *n.* Name of three trees, *Styrax benzoin*, which yields the resin called benzoin, *Benzoin odoriferum*, a North American shrub, also *Ficus benjamina.*

Benjamin (2) (ben′ jă min) [alluding to Gen. xlii. 4], *n.* The youngest son; the darling of a family.

Benjamin (3) (ben′ jă min) [tailor's name; or perh. from Romany *bengari*, waistcoat], *n.* A kind of overcoat once in fashion.

bennet (1) (ben′ ėt) [M.E. *herbe beneit*, prob. from O.F. *herbe beneite*, L. *herba benedicta*, blessed herb (*benedictus*, p.p. of *benedicere*, see BENEDICITE)], *n.* Herb bennet, *Geum urbanum*; some other plants.

bennet (2) [BENT (2)].

bent (1) (bent) [BEND], *n.* Inclination, bias; disposition, propensity; tension, extent, capacity. **to the top of one's bent:** To one's utmost capacity, to one's full tension. *p.p.* [see BEND].

bent (2) (bent) [A.S. *beonet* (cp. O.H.G. *binuz*, G. *binse*)], *n.* Stiff, rush-like grass; old grass-stalks; grassy ground, unenclosed pasture; a heath; a slope, a rising ground. **take to the bent:** Flee to the open country. **bent-grass,** *n.* The genus *Agrostis.*

benthal (ben′ thăl) [Gr. *benthos*, sea-depths], *a.* Of or pertaining to the depths of the ocean beyond 1000 fathoms.

Benthamism (ben′ thăm izm) [Jeremy *Bentham* (1748–1832)], *n* The Utilitarian philosophy based on the principle of the greatest happiness of the greatest number. **Benthamite,** *n.* A follower of Jeremy Bentham; a Utilitarian.

benthon, benthos (ben′ thon, ben′ thos) [Gr. *benthos*, the depths of the sea], *n.* (*Zool.*) The sedentary animal and plant life on the ocean bed. **benthoscope** (ben′ thō skōp), *n.* A submersible sphere for studying deep-sea life, a bathysphere.

benumb (bė nŭm′) [formerly *benum*, A.-S. *benumen*, p.p. of *beniman* (BE-, *niman*, see NUMB)], *v.t.* To render torpid or numb; (*fig.*) to deaden, to paralyse. **benumbment,** *n.* The act of benumbing; the state of being benumbed; torpor.

benzene (ben′ zēn) [BENZ-OIC, -ENE], *n.* An aromatic hydrocarbon, also called benzol or phenyl hydride, used for illuminating purposes, and for removing grease-spots.

benzine (ben′ zēn), *n.* A mixture of liquid hydrocarbons of the paraffin series.

benzoin (ben′ zoin, -zō in) [F. *benjoin*, Sp. *benjui* (It. *bengivi*), Arab. *lubān jāwi*, Javanese frankincense (*lu-* mistaken for It. article *lo* and dropped)], *n.* A resin obtained from *Styrax benzoin*, used in medicine and in perfumery, called also gum benzoin, popularly corrupted to benjamin and gum benjamin; a North American genus of Lauraceæ; a camphor obtained from bitter-almond oil. **benzoic** (ben zō′ ik), *a.* Pertaining to or derived from benzoin.

benzol, benzole (ben′ zol), *n.* Benzene, esp. as a natural product. **benzoline** (ben′ zŏ lēn), *n.*

Impure benzene; other volatile inflammable liquid hydrocarbons. **benzyl,** *n.* (*Chem.*) An organic radical derived from benzene.

bequeath (bė kwēth') [A.-S. *becwethan* (BE-, *cwethan,* to say, cp. QUOTH)], *v.t.* *To transfer, hand over; to leave by will or testament; (*fig.*) to transmit to future generations. **bequeathable,** *a.* ***bequeathal, bequeathment,** *n.* The act of bequeathing; a legacy. **bequest** (bė kwest'), *n.* The act of bequeathing; that which is bequeathed; a legacy.

berate (bė rāt'), *v.t.* To rate or chide vehemently.

Berber (bĕr' bėr) [BARBARY], *n.* A member of the great North African stock; their language or languages collectively. *a.* Of or belonging to this people or their languages.

berberry [BARBERRY].

berceuse (bâr' sĕrz) [Fr., a cradle-rocker], *n.* (*Mus.*) A lullaby, cradle-song; lulling music.

bereave (bė rēv') [A.-S. *berēafian* (BE-, *rēafian,* to rob; cp. G. *berauben*)], *v.t.* (*past & p.p.* **bereaved, bereft**) To deprive, rob, or spoil of anything; to render desolate (*usu. in p.p.* **bereaved,** of the loss of near relatives by death). **bereavement,** *n.* The state of being bereaved; the loss of a near relative by death.

Berenice's hair (ber ė nī' sėz hâr) [from the myth that the hair of *Berenice,* wife of Ptolemy Euergetes, king of Egypt (3rd cent. B.C.), was placed in a constellation], *n.* *The star Canopus; a small northern constellation, near the tail of Leo.

béret, berret (bė rā', ber' ėt) [F. *béret,* Bearnais *berreto,* late L. *birretum,* BIRETTA], *n.* A round, brimless flat cap fitting the head fairly closely.

berg [ICEBERG].

Bergamask (bĕrg' á mask), *n.* A rustic dance imitating the people of Bergamo.

bergamot (1) (bĕrg' á mot) [*Bergamo,* in Italy], *n.* The bergamot orange, *Citrus bergamia,* which yields a fragrant essential oil; the oil itself; *a snuff scented with the oil; a kind of mint, *Mentha citrata,* which yields an oil somewhat similar.

bergamot (2) (bĕrg á mot) [F. *bergamotte,* It. *bergamotta,* Turk. *beg-armūdi,* prince's pear], *n.* A juicy kind of pear.

bergmehl (bĕrg' māl) [G., mountain flour], *n.* A diatomaceous earth that is used, in Norway, to be mixed with flour and eaten.

bergschrund (bârg' shroont) [G. (*berg,* mountain, *schrund,* crack, gap)], *n.* A crevasse or fissure between the base of a steep slope and a glacier or *nevé.*

berhyme, berime (bė rīm'), *v.t.* To compose rhymes about, to ridicule in rhyme; to put into rhyme.

beriberi (ber' i ber' i) [Cingalese *beri,* weakness], *n.* A disease prevalent in India and the Tropics, characterized by paralysis and dropsy.

Berkeleian (bark lē' ån) [Bishop *Berkeley* (1685–1753)], *a.* Of or pertaining to Berkeley or his philosophy, which denied that the mind, being entirely subjective, could know the external world objectively. *n.* An adherent of the Berkeleian philosophy.

berkelium (bĕr kē' li ům), *n.* An artificially-produced radioactive element of atomic number 97.

berlie (bĕr' li), *n.* (*Austral.*) Ground-bait for anglers.

Berlin (bĕr lin') [*Berlin,* capital of Prussia], *n.* *A four-wheeled carriage having a hooded seat behind. **Berlin black,** *n.* A black varnish for ironware. **Berlin gloves,** *n.pl.* Knitted gloves of Berlin wool. **Berlin iron,** *n.* A fusible iron smelted from bog ore and used for the finer sort of casts. **Berlin warehouse,** *n.* A shop or warehouse where Berlin wool and other fancy goods are sold. **Berlin wool,** *n.* A fine kind of wool used for knitting, embroidery, etc.

berm (bĕrm) [F. *berme,* G. *berme* (Dut. *berm*)], *n.* (*Fort.*) A narrow ledge at the foot of the exterior slope of a parapet; (*Am.*) the bank of a canal opposite the towing-path.

bernacle [BARNACLE].

Bernardine (bĕr' når' din), *a.* Of or pertaining to St. Bernard of Clairvaux, or the Cistercian order. *n.* A Cistercian monk.

berretta [BIRETTA].

berrigan (be' ri gån), *n.* (*Austral.*) The emu bush, seeds of which are eaten by emus.

berry (ber' i) [A.-S. *berige* (cp. Icel. *ber,* Goth. *basi,* G. *beere*)], *n.* Any smallish, round, fleshy fruit; one of the eggs of a fish or lobster; (*Bot.*) a many-seeded, inferior, indehiscent, pulpy fruit, the seeds of which are loosely scattered through the pulp (a def. excluding the strawberry). *v.i.* To bear or produce berries; to swell, to fill; to go berry-gathering. **in berry:** Bearing her eggs (of a hen lobster). **berried,** *a.* Having or bearing berries; bearing her eggs (of a hen lobster).

bersagliere (bâr sa lyâr' ā) [It., from *bersaglio,* a mark], *n.* (*pl.* **-ri**) A sharpshooter; one of a crack corps in the Italian army.

berserk, berserker (bĕr' sėrk, -ėr), **baresark** (bâr' sark) [Icel. *berserkr* (etym. doubtful, prob. bear-sark, bear-coat)], *n.* A Norse warrior possessed of preternatural strength and fighting with desperate fury and courage; a bravo. *a.* and *adv.* Frenzied; filled with furious rage. **to go berserk:** To lose control of one's actions in violent rage.

berth (bĕrth) [etym. doubtful; perh. from A.-S. *gebyrian,* to suit (cp. G. *gebühren*), or from BEAR (2)], *n.* (*Naut.*) Sea-room; a convenient place for mooring; a place for a ship at a wharf; (*Naut.*) a room in a ship where any number of officers mess and reside; a situation on board ship; a permanent job or situation of any kind; a sleeping-place on board ship; a sleeping-place in a railway carriage. *v.t.* (*Naut.*) To moor; to furnish with a berth. **to give a wide berth to:** (*Naut.*) To keep away from; to steer clear of. **berthage,** *n.* Room or accommodation for mooring ships; dock dues.

berthon boat (ber' thon) [E. L. *Berthon* (1813–99)], *n.* (*Naut.*) A collapsible, canvas lifeboat.

Bertillon (bĕr til lon', bâr tē lyon') [Alphonse *Bertillon* (1853–1914), F. anthropologist], *a.* Of or pertaining to Bertillon or his system. **Bertillon system:** A method of recording personal measurements and other characteristics, esp. for the purpose of identifying criminals.

beryl (ber' il) [O.F., from L. *bēryllus,* Gr. *bērullos* (Sansk. *vaidūrya*)], *n.* A gem nearly identical with the emerald, but varying in colour from pale green to yellow or white; (*Min.*) a silicate of aluminium and glucinum, occurring usually in hexagonal prisms. **berylline,** *a.* Resembling a beryl. **beryllium** (bė ril' i ům), *n.* The metal glucinum.

bescreen (bė skrēn'), *v.t.* To screen, to conceal, to hide from view; to envelop in shadow.

bescribble (bė skribl'), *v.t.* To scribble about or over; to write in a scribbling style.

beseech (bė sēch') [BE-, M.E. *sechen, seken* (cp. Dut. *bezoeken,* G. *besuchen*)], *v.t.* (*past & p.p.* **besought)** To ask earnestly, implore, entreat, supplicate. **beseeching,** *a.* **beseechingly,** *adv.*

beseem (bė sēm'), *v.t.* To be fit, suitable, proper for, or becoming to. *v.i.* To be seemly or proper. (*Usu. impersonal in either voice*). **beseeming,** *a.* Becoming, fitting. **n.* Appearance, look, becomingness, fitness. **beseemingly,** *adv.* **beseemingness,** *n.* **beseemly,** *a.* Seemly, suitable, becoming, proper.

beseen (bė sēn') [p.p. of obs. v. *besee,* from A.-S. *biseōn, beseōn,* to look about, to pay regard to], *p.p.* Seen, looking, appearing; dressed, furnished, accomplished. **well-beseen:** *Good-looking, of fair appearance; accomplished, well-versed.

beset (bė set') [A.-S. *bisettan*, to surround (BE-, *settan*, to SET)], *v.t.* (*past & p.p.* **beset**) To set or surround (with); to surround, to invest, to occupy; to set upon, to fall upon; (*fig.*) to encompass, to assail. **besetting sin:** A sin to which one is specially prone (Heb. xii. 1). **beset,** *p.p.* Set or encumbered (with difficulties, snares, etc.). **besetment,** *n.* The state of being beset; a besetting sin or weakness.

beshrew (bė shroo') [M.E. *bischrewen* (BE-, *schrewen*, to curse; see SHREW)], *v.t.* To deprave, to make evil; *(*playfully*) to curse. ***beshrew me, *beshrew my heart:** Devil take me! bless me!

beside (bė sīd') [A.-S. *be sīdan*, by side], *prep.* By the side of, side by side with, in comparison with; near, hard by, close to; away from, wide of. *adv.* Besides. **beside oneself:** Out of one's wits. **besides,** *prep.* In addition to, over and above; other than, except. *adv.* Moreover, further, over and above, in addition; otherwise.

besiege (bė sēj') [M.E. *bisegen*, *besegen* (BE-, *segen*, O.F. *asegier*, late L. *assediāre*, from *ad-*, to, *sedium*, sitting, from *sedēre*, to sit)], *v.t.* To sit down before a place with intent to capture it; to invest; to crowd round; to assail importunately. **besieger,** *n.* One who besieges a place. **besiegingly,** *adv.*

besmear (bė smēr'), *v.t.* To cover or daub with something unctuous or viscous; (*fig.*) to soil, to defile.

besmirch (bė smĕrch'), *v.t.* To soil, discolour; to sully, bedim.

besmoke (bė smōk'), *v.t.* To soil with smoke, to fumigate.

besom (bē zom) [A.-S. *besma* (cp. Dut. *bezem*, G. *besen*)], *n.* A broom made of twigs or heath bound round a handle; (*fig.*) anything that sweeps away impurity; (*Sc.*) a term of reproach for a woman. **v.i.* To sweep. **v.t.* To sweep; to sweep away.

besot (bė sot'), *v.t.* To make sottish; to stupefy, to muddle; to cause to dote upon. **besotted,** *a.* Intoxicated, muddled, infatuated. **besottedly,** *adv.* Blindly, infatuatedly.

besought, *p.p.* [BESEECH].

bespangle (bė spăng' gėl'), *v.t.* To powder over with or as with spangles.

bespatter (bė spăt' ėr), *v.t.* To spatter over or about; (*fig.*) to load with compliments or abuse.

bespeak (bė spēk') [A.-S. *besprecan* (BE-, *sprecan*, SPEAK), cp. O.H.G. *bisprācha*, detraction, G. *besprechen*, to talk over], **v.i.* (*past* **-spoke,** *p.p.* **-spoken**) To speak; to speak out. *v.t.* To speak for, to arrange for, to order beforehand; to ask; to request; to give evidence of; to betoken, to foreshow; *to speak to. *n.* The bespeaking of a particular play; an actor's benefit. **bespoke** [for BESPOKEN], *p.p.* Ordered beforehand, (*Am.*) custom-made. **bespoke boot-maker:** One who makes boots to order.

bespeckle (bė spek' ėl), *v.t.* To speckle over, to variegate.

bespoke, bespoken [BESPEAK].

bespread (bė spred') [M.E. *bispreden*, *bespreden* (BE-, *spreden*, to spread)], *v.t.* To spread over; to spread with; to adorn.

besprinkle (bė spring' kėl) [M.E. *besprengil* (BE-, *sprenkel*, freq. of *sprengan*, see prec.)], *v.t.* To sprinkle or scatter over; to bedew.

Bessemer process (bes' ėm ėr) [Sir Henry *Bessemer* (1813–98), engineer], *n.* A process invented by Sir H. Bessemer in 1856 for the elimination of carbon and silicon by forcing atmospheric air into melted cast iron. **Bessemer iron** or **steel,** *n.* Iron or steel manufactured by this process. **Bessemerize,** *v.t.*

best (best) [A.-S. *betst* (cp. BETTER), superlative of GOOD], *a.* Of the highest excellence; surpassing all others; most desirable. *v.t.* To get the better of; to cheat, outwit. *adv.* [superlative of WELL]. In the highest degree; to the most advantage; with most ease; most intimately. *n.* The best thing; the utmost; (*collect.*) the best people. **at best:** As far as can be expected. **to get** or **have the best of:** To get or have the advantage. **to make the best of:** To make the most of; to be content with. **to the best of:** To the utmost extent of. **best man,** *n.* A groomsman. **the best part:** The largest part, the most. **best people,** *n.pl.* Those considered the most select socially. **best-seller,** *n.* (*colloq.*) A popular book of the moment. **Sunday-best,** *n.* Best clothes.

bestead (1) (bė sted'), *v.t.* To help; to profit; to be of service to. *v.i.* To avail.

bested, bestead (2) (bė sted') [M.E. *bistad*, p.p. of *bisteden* (BE-, *stad*, from Icel. *staadr*, p.p. of *stethja*, to stop, fix, appoint)], *p.p.* Situated, circumstanced (usu. with adv. *ill*, *hard*, *hardly*, *sore*, etc.).

bestial (bes' ti ål) [O.F. *bestial*, L. *bestiālis* (*bestia*, a beast)], *a.* Of or pertaining to the inferior animals, esp. the quadrupeds; resembling a beast; brutish, sensual, obscene. *n.* (*Sc.*) Cattle. **bestiality** (bes ti ăl' i ti), *n.* **bestialize** (bes' ti å līz), *v.t.* To make bestial; to reduce to the level of a beast. **bestially,** *adv.* **bestiary** (bes' ti år i) [L. *bestiārius*, a fighter with beasts], *n.* One who fought with beasts in the Roman amphitheatre; *[med. L. *bestiārium*, a menagerie], a moralized natural history of animals.

bestick (bė stik'), *v.t.* To stick about, to bedeck; to transfix. **bestuck,** *p.p.* Adorned; pierced.

bestir (bė stĕr') [A.-S. *bestyrian* (BE-, *styrian*, STIR)], *v.t.* To rouse into activity.

bestow (bė stō'), *v.t.* To stow, to lay up; to stow away, to lodge, provide with quarters; to expend, to lay out; to give as a present. **bestowal,** *n.* Disposal, location; gift. **bestowment,** *n.* Bestowal.

bestrew (bė stroo') [A.-S. *bestrēowian* (BE-, *strēowian*, STREW)], *v.t.* To strew over; to bescatter; to lie scattered over.

bestride (bė strīd') [A.-S. *bestridan* (BE-, STRIDE)]. *v.t.* To sit upon with the legs astride; to bestraddle; (*fig.*) to span, overarch.

bet (bet) [perh. from ABET], *n.* A wager; a sum staked upon a contingent event. *v.t.* (*past & p.p.* **bet, betted**) To wager; to stake upon a contingency. *v.i.* To lay a wager. **you bet:** (*Slang*) Certainly, of course, depend upon it.

beta (bē' ta) [Gr.], *n.* The second letter of the Greek alphabet; (*Astron.*) the second star in a constellation; (*Science*) the second of a series of numerous compounds, and other enumerations. **beta particle,** *n.* (*Phys.*) A negatively-charged particle emitted by certain radioactive substances. Identified as an electron. **beta plus,** *a.* Better than second class. **beta rays,** *n.pl.* (*Phys.*) Rays consisting of a stream of beta particles or electrons.

betake (bė tāk'), *v.r.* (*past* **betook,** *p.p.* **betaken**) To take oneself to; to have recourse to.

betatron (bē' tå tron) [BETA, ELECTRON], *n.* (*Phys.*) An electrical apparatus for accelerating electrons to high energies.

bête noire (bāt nwar') [Fr., black beast], *n.* A bugbear, pet aversion.

betel (bē' tėl) [Port., from Malayālam, *vettila*], *n.* *Piper betle*, a shrubby plant with evergreen leaves, called also **betel-pepper** and **betel-vine**; its leaf, used as a wrapper to enclose a few slices of the areca nut with a little shell lime, which are chewed by the natives of India. **betel-nut,** *n.* The nut of the areca palm. **betel-tree,** *n.* *Areca catechu*, so called because its nut is chewed with betel-leaves.

bethankit (bė thăng' kit) [BE-, THANK], *n.* (*Sc.*) Grace after meat.

Bethel (beth' ėl) [Heb. *bēthēl*, house of God], *n.* A hallowed spot; a chapel; a mission-room; a seamen's church, esp. afloat. **little Bethel:** (*contempt.*) A Dissenting place of worship.

betherel [BEDRAL].

bethesda (bė thez′ dȧ) [Heb. *bethesda*, house of mercy, or place of the flowing of water], *n.* A Dissenting chapel.

bethink (bė think′) [A.-S. *bithencan* (cp. Dut. and G. *bedenken*)], **v.t.* To think, to recollect; to contrive, to plan. *v.r.* To consider, think; to collect one's thoughts; to meditate.

bethrall (bė thrawl′), *v.t.* To enslave, to bring into subjection.

betide (bė tīd′) [M.E. *betiden* (BE-, A.-S. *tīdan*, TIDE)], *v.t.* To happen to; (*erron.*) to betoken. *v.i.* To happen, to come to pass.

betimes, *betime (bė tīmz′, -tīm′) [BY, TIME, -ES], *adv.* At an early hour or period; in good time, in time; in a short time, soon.

betitle (bė tītl′), *v.t.* To entitle; to adorn with a title or titles.

betoken (bė tōkn′) [M.E. *bitacnen* (see BE-, TOKEN, A.-S. *getacnian*)], *v.t.* To be a type of; to foreshow, to be an omen of, to indicate.

beton (bā′ ton, bet′ ȯn) [F. *béton*, Port. *betun*, cement, L. *bitūmen*, mineral pitch], *n.* Concrete made with sand or stone and hydraulic lime or cement.

betony (bet′ ȯ ni) [O.F. *betonie*, late *betonia*, L. *vettonica* (*Vettones*, a Sp. tribe)], *n.* A labiate plant, *Stachys betonica*, with purple flowers.

betook, *past* [BETAKE].

betray (bė trā′) [M.E. *betraien* (BE-, *traien*, to betray), O.F. *traïr*, late L. *trādere* (*trans-*, over, *dāre*, to give)], *v.t.* To give up; to deliver up a person or thing treacherously; to be false to; to lead astray; to disclose treacherously; to disclose against one's will or intention; to reveal incidentally. **betrayal,** *n.* A treacherous giving up or violation of a trust; a revelation or divulging. **betrayer,** *n.* One who betrays; a traitor.

betroth (bė trōth′) [M.E. *bitreuthien* (BE-, *treuthe*, A.-S. *trēowth*, TRUTH)], *v.t.* To contract two persons in an engagement to marry; to engage, affiance; *to engage oneself to. **betrothal** (bė trō′ *th*ȧl), **betrothment** (-mėnt), *n.* The act of betrothing; the state of being betrothed; affiance. **betrothed,** *a.* Engaged to be married; affianced. *n.* A person engaged to be married.

better (1) (bet′ ėr) [A.-S. *bet*, *bett*, adv., *betera*, a., comparative of GOOD (Goth. *batiza*, Icel. *betri*, Dut. *beter*, G. *besser*)], *a.* Superior, more excellent; more desirable; greater in degree; improved in health. *v.t.* To make better; to excel, to surpass, to improve on. *v.i.* To become better, to improve. *adv.* [comp. of WELL]. In a superior, more excellent, or more desirable manner; more correctly or fully; with greater profit; in a greater or higher degree; more. *n.pl.* Social superiors. **the better part:** The most. **better than:** More than. **better half,** *n.* One's wife. **for the better:** In the way of improvement. **to get the better of:** To defeat, to outwit. **had better:** Should; would be advantageous to. **better off:** In better circumstances. **to better oneself:** To get on, to get a better job. **the better:** The mastery, superiority. **to think better of:** To reconsider. **betterment,** *n.* Amelioration; an improvement of property; (*Am. pl.*) improvements made on new lands. **betterment tax,** *n.* Compensation charges levied on improved property. **bettermost,** *a.* (*colloq.*) Best; of the highest quality.

better (2) ***bettor** (bet′ ėr) [BET], *n.* One who makes bets.

bettong (be′ tong) [Austral. abor.], *n.* A small prehensile-tailed kangaroo.

betty (bet′ i) [dim. of *Elizabeth*], *n.* *A burglar's jemmy; a man who busies himself with household duties.

between (bė twēn′) [A.-S. *betwēonum* (*be*, by, *twēonum*, dat. of *twēon*, twain, adj. corr. to distributive numeral *twā*, two)], *prep.* In, on, into, along, or across the place, space, or interval of any kind separating two points, lines, places, or objects; intermediate in relation to; related to both of; related so as to separate; related so as to connect, from one to another; among; in shares among, so as to affect all. *n.* An interval of time; (*pl.*) an intermediate size and quality of sewing-needles. *adv.* Intermediately; in an intervening space or time; in relation to both of; to and fro; during or in an interval. **go-between:** An intermediary. **between ourselves:** In confidence. **between-decks,** *n.* (*Naut.*) The space between any two decks of a vessel. **between-maid** [TWEENY]. **between-whiles,** *adv.* Now and then; at intervals. **far between:** At wide intervals. **betwixt and between:** Neither one thing nor the other; half and half, middling.

betwixt (bė twikst′) [A.-S. *betweox* (*be*, by, with either a dat. *tweoxum*, *tweohsum*, or an acc. pl. neut. *twiscu*, from O.Teut. *twiskjo*, twofold)], *prep.* and *adv.* (*archaic*) Between.

bevatron (bev′ ȧ tron), *n.* (*Phys.*) An electrical apparatus for accelerating protons to high energies.

bevel (bev′ ėl) [prob. from an O.F. *bevel* or *buvel* (F. *beveau*)], *a.* Oblique, sloping, slanting; at more than a right angle. *n.* A tool consisting of a flat rule with a movable tongue or arm for setting off angles; a slope from the right angle, an inclination of two planes, except one of 90°. *v.t.* To cut away to a slope, to give a bevel angle to. *v.i.* To recede from the perpendicular, to slant. **bevel-edge,** *n.* The oblique edge of a chisel or similar cutting tool. **bevel-gear, -gearing,** *n.* Gear for transmitting motion from one shaft to another by means of bevel-wheels. **bevel-wheels,** *n.pl.* Cogged wheels whose axes form an angle (usually 90°) with each other. **bevelling,** *n.* Reducing to an oblique angle; the angle so given; (*Naut.*) a bevelled surface or part. *a.* Slanting, having an obtuse angle. **bevelment,** *n.* The process of bevelling; (*Cryst.*) the replacement of the edge of a crystal by two similar planes equally inclined to the adjacent faces.

beverage (bev′ ėr ȧj) [O.F. *beverage*, from *bevre*, *beivre* (cp. F. *boire*), to drink, from L. *bibere*, to drink, -AGE], *n.* Drink; liquor for drinking.

bevy (bev′ i) [etym. unknown], *n.* A flock of larks or quails; a herd of roes; a company of women.

bewail (bė wāl′), *v.t.* To wail over, to lament for. *v.i.* To express grief. **bewailing,** *n.* Loud lamentation. *a.* That bewails or laments. **bewailingly,** *adv.* Mournfully, with lamentation. **bewailment,** *n.* The act of bewailing.

beware (bė wâr′) [M.E. *be war*, be cautious, A.-S. *wær* wary (cp. WARE, v. from A.-S. *warian*, to guard)], *v.i.* To be wary, to be on one's guard; to take care. *v.t.* To be wary of, on guard against; to look out for.

beweep (bė wēp′), *v.t.* To weep over or for; to moisten with or as with tears. *v.i.* To weep.

bewet (bė wet′), *v.t.* To wet profusely; to bedew.

bewig (bė wig′), *v.t.* To adorn with a wig. **bewigged,** *a.* (*fig.*) Perked up, bureaucratic, bound with convention or red tape.

bewilder (bė wil′ dėr) [BE-, *wilder*, *wildern*, a wilderness], *v.t.* To perplex, confuse, lead astray. **bewildering,** *a.* Causing one to lose his way, physically or mentally. **bewilderingly,** *adv.* **bewilderment,** *n.* The state of being bewildered.

bewitch (bė wich′) [M.E. *bewicchen* (BE-, A.-S. *wiccian*, to practise witchcraft, from *wicca*, a wizard)], *v.t.* To practise witchcraft against a person or thing; to charm, to fascinate, to allure. **bewitching,** *a.* Alluring, charming. **bewitchingly,** *adv.* **bewitchment,** *n.* Fascination, charm.

bewray (bė rā′) [BE-, A.-S. *wrēgan*, to accuse], *v.t.* To reveal, to disclose. **bewrayingly,** *adv.*

bey (bā), ***beg** (beg) [Turk. *bēg*], *n.* A governor of a Turkish town, province, or district. **beylic,** *n.* The district governed by a bey.

beyond (bė yond′) [A.-S. *begeondan* (BE-, *geond*, across, *-an*, from)], *prep.* On, to or towards the farther side of; past, later than; exceeding in quantity or amount, more than; surpassing in quality or degree, outside the limit of; in addition to, over and above. *adv.* At a greater distance than; farther away. *n.* That which lies beyond human experience, or after death. **the back of beyond:** An out-of-the-way place.

bezant (bė zănt′, bez′ ånt) [O.F. *besant*, L. *Byzantius nummus*, coin of Byzantium], *n.* A gold coin struck at Constantinople by the Byzantine emperors, varying greatly in value; a silver coin worth about 2s. 11d.; (*Her.*) a gold roundel borne as a charge.

bezel (bez′ ėl) [O.F. *bisel* (F. *bizeau*)], *n.* A sloping edge like that of a cutting tool; one of the oblique sides of a cut gem; the groove by which a watch-glass or a jewel is held.

bezique (bē zēk′) [F. *besigue* (etym. doubtful)], *n.* A game of cards of French origin.

bezoar (bē′ zôr, bez′ å år) [F., through Port. or Sp. from Arab. *bāzahr*, *bādizahr*, Pers. *pādzahr*, counter-poison], *n.* *An antidote; a calculous concretion found in the stomach of certain animals, and supposed to be an antidote to poisons. **bezoar-goat,** *n.* The Persian wild goat, the best-known example of an animal producing the bezoar. **bezoar-stone,** *n.*

***bezonian** (bė zō′ ni ån) [It. *bisogno*, want, poverty (etym. unknown)], *n.* A beggar, a low fellow.

***bezzle** (bezl) [M.E. *besil*, O.F. *besiler* (abbr. from *embesillier*, EMBEZZLE)], *v.t.* To plunder, rob, make away with; to squander. *v.i.* To drink, to bib; to revel. ***bezzled,** *part.a.* Drunk, tipsy.

bhang, bang (băng) [Hind.], *n.* An intoxicating or stupefying liquor or drug made from the dried leaves of hemp, *Cannabis indica.*

bheesti (bē′ sti) [Hind.], *n.* A servant who supplies water to an Indian house.

bi- [L. *bi-*, *dui-*, double (cp. *duo*, two, Gr. *di-*, *duō*, Sansk. *doi*)], *pref.* Double twice; doubly; with two; in two; every two, once in every two, lasting for two (used even with Eng. words, *e.g. bi-weekly*, *bi-monthly*, but chiefly with words from L., esp. scientific terms).

biacuminate (bī å kū′ min āte), *a.* (*Bot.*) Having two tapering points.

biangular (bī ăng′ gū lår), *a.* Having two angles; two-angled.

biannual (bī ăn′ ū ål), *a.* Half-yearly, twice a year.

biarticulate (bī ar tik′ ū late), *a.* (*Biol.*, *Zool.*) Two-jointed.

bias (bī′ ås) [F. *biais*, oblique or obliquity (perh. from L. *bifacem*, two faced)], *n.* A weight formerly placed on the side of a bowl to impart oblique motion; the motion so imparted; hence, a leaning of the mind, inclination, prejudice, prepossession. *a.* (*Dressmaking*) Slanting, oblique. *adv.* Obliquely, athwart, awry; (*Dressmaking*) on the slant. *v.t.* To cause to incline to one side; (*fig.*) to prejudice, to prepossess.

biaxial (bī ăk′ si ål), **biaxal** (bī ăk′ sål), *a.* (*Cryst.*) Having two (optical) axes.

bib (bib) [prob. from L. *bibere*, to drink], *v.t.* and *i.* To drink; to drink frequently; to tipple. *n.* A cloth put under a child's chin to keep the front of the clothes clean; (*Zool.*) the whiting-pout, *Gadus luscus.* **bibacious** (bī bā′ shůs), *a.* Addicted to drinking. **bibber,** *n.* A tippler. **bibbing,** *n.* Tippling. **bibulous** (bib′ ū lůs) [L. *bibulus* (*bibere*)], *a.* Readily absorbing moisture; given to tippling. **bibulously,** *adv.*

bibasic (bī bās′ ik), *a.* (*Chem.*) Having two bases.

bibelot (bē′ be lō) [F.], *n.* A small article of vertu, a knick-knack.

Bible (bī′ bėl) [F., from late L. *biblia* (used as fem. sing.), Gr. *biblia*, neut. pl. writings, *biblion*, dim. of *biblos*, a book (*bublos*, papyrus)], *n.* The sacred writings of the Old and New Testament; a copy of the Scriptures, a particular edition; (*fig.*) a text-book, an authority. **Breeches Bible:** The Geneva Bible of 1560 in which the word *breeches* was used for *aprons* in Gen. iii. 7. **Douay Bible:** An English version of the Vulgate made at the Roman Catholic college of Douai (1582–1609). **Geneva Bible:** An English translation, without the Apocrypha, and with the chapters divided into verses, published at Geneva (1560). **Mazarine Bible:** A Bible printed by Gutenberg (1450), the first book printed from movable types. **Bible-Christian,** *n.* A member of a sect founded (1815) by W. O. Bryan, a Cornish Wesleyan. **Bible-class,** *n.* A class for studying the Bible. **Bible-clerk,** *n.* (*Univ.*) A student who reads the Lessons in chapel. **Bible-reader, Bible-woman,** *n.* One employed as a lay missioner. **Bible Society,** *n.* A society for the distribution of the Bible. **biblical** (bib′ li kål), *a.* Of or pertaining to the Bible. **biblically,** *adv.* **biblicism** (-sizm), *n.* Strict adherence to the letter of the Bible. **biblism,** *n.* Adherence to the Bible as the only rule of faith. **biblicist,** *n.* **biblist** (bib′ list), *n.* One who takes the Bible as the only rule of faith; a biblical student.

biblico- [med. L. *biblicus*], *comb. form.* Pertaining to the Bible. **biblico-literary, biblico-poetic,** *a.* Relating to Scriptural literature or poetry.

biblio- [Gr. *biblion*, a book], *comb. form.* Pertaining to books. **biblioklept** (bib′ li ō klept) [Gr. *kleptēs*, a thief], *n.* One who steals books. **bibliology** (bib li ol′ ō ji) [-LOGY], *n.* Scientific study of books; bibliography; biblical study. **bibliological** (-loj′-), *a.* Pertaining to bibliology. **bibliomancy** (bib′ li ō măn si) [-MANCY], *n.* Divination by books or verses of the Bible. **bibliomania** (bib li ō mā′ ni å) [MANIA], *n.* A mania for collecting and possessing books. **bibliomaniac,** *n.* One who has such a mania. **bibliopegy** (bib li op′ ė ji) [Gr. *-pēgia*, from *pēgnunai*, to fix], *n.* The art of binding books. **bibliopegic** (bib li ō pej′ ik), *a.* Relating to the art of bookbinding. **bibliopegist** (-op′ ė jist), *n.* One who collects bindings; a bookbinder. **bibliophobia** (bib li ō fō′ bi å) [-PHOBIA], *n.* A dread or hatred of books. **bibliopole** (bib′ li ō pōl) [L. *bibliopōla*, Gr. *bibliopōlēs* (*pōlēs*, seller)], *n.* A bookseller. **bibliopolic, bibliopolical** (bib li ō pol′ ik, -ik ål), *a.* Of or pertaining to booksellers or to bookselling. **bibliopolist** (-op′ ō list), *n.* A bookseller. **bibliopoly** (-op′ ō li), *n.* Bookselling. **bibliotheca** (bib li ō thē′ kå) [L., from Gr. *bibliothēkē* (*thēkē*, a repository)], *n.* *The Bible; a library; a bibliography. **bibliothecal,** *a.* Of or pertaining to a library.

bibliography (bib li og′ rå fi) [Gr. *bibliographia* (BIBLIO, -GRAPHY)], *n.* The methodical study of books, authorship, printing, editions, forms, etc.; a book dealing with this; a systematic list of books of any author, printer, or country, or on any subject. **bibliographer,** *n.* One skilled in bibliography; one who writes about books. **bibliographical** (bib li ō grăf′ ik ål), *a.* Of or pertaining to bibliography.

bibliolatry (bib li ol′ å tri) [BIBLIO-, LATRY], *n.* Excessive admiration of a book or books; excessive reverence for the letter of the Bible. **bibliolater,** *n.* A person addicted to bibliolatry. **bibliolatrous,** *a.* Addicted to bibliolatry.

bibliophile (bib′ li ō fīl) [BIBLIO-, PHILE], *n.* A lover of books; a book-fancier. **bibliophilism** (bib li of′ il izm), *n.* Love of books; book-fancying. **bibliophilist,** *n.*

biblist [BIBLE]. **bibulous,** etc. [BIB].

bibulous [BIB].

bicameral (bī kăm′ ėr ål) [BI-, L. *camera*, CHAMBER], *a.* Having two legislative chambers or assemblies.

bicarbonate (bī kar′ bōn āte), *a.* A carbonate containing two equivalents of carbonic acid to one of a base.

bice (bīs) [F. *bis* (fem. *bise*), It. *bigio*, greyish], *n.* A blue pigment made from smalt.

bicentenary (bī sent' ė når i, bī sėn tē' nȧ ri) [BI-, CENTENARY], *a.* Consisting of or pertaining to two hundred years. *n.* The two hundredth anniversary. **bicentennial** (bī sėn ten' i ȧl) [BI-, CENTENNIAL], *a.* Occurring every two hundred years; lasting two hundred years. *n.* A bicentenary.

bicephalous (bī sef' ȧ lůs) [BI- Gr. *kephalē*, the head], *a.* Having two heads; two-headed.

biceps (bī' seps) [L. (BI-, *caput*, head)], *a.* Having two heads, points, or summits, esp. of muscles having two attachments. *n.* The large muscle in front of the upper arm; the corresponding muscle of the thigh; (*fig.*) muscular strength. **bicipital** (bī sip' i tȧl), *a.* Two-headed; of or pertaining to the biceps muscle.

bichloride (bī klôr' īd) [BI-, CHLORIDE], *n.* A compound in which two atoms of chlorine are combined with one atom of another element.

bichromate (bī krōm' āt), *n.* (*Chem.*) A salt containing two equivalents of chromic acid.

bicker (1) (bik' ėr) [M.E. *bickere*, prob. freq. of *biken*, to thrust], *v.i.* *To skirmish, fight; to dispute, wrangle; (*fig.*) to move rapidly to and fro; to quiver, glisten, flicker. *n.* *A quarrel, contention; strife, fighting; rattling, pattering, noise as of bickering, a skirmish; altercation, wrangling.

biconvex (bī kon' veks). Convex on both sides.

bicorporal (bī kôr' pôr ȧl), *a.* Having two bodies, bicorporate, bicorporated.

bicorporate (bī kôr' pôr ȧt), *a.* Double-headed; (*Her.*) having two bodies with a single head.

bicuspid (bī kŭs' pid), *a.* Having two points or cusps. *n.* A bicuspid tooth, one of the premolars in man. **bicuspidate,** *a.* (*Bot.*) Two-pointed.

bicycle (bī' si kėl), *n.* A two-wheeled velocipede, with the wheels one behind the other, and usually with a seat for the rider on a frame connecting these. *v.i.* To ride on a bicycle. **tandem bicycle:** A bicycle for two or more persons. **bicyclist,** *n.* One who rides a bicycle.

bid (bid) [two verbs blended (1) A.-S. *beodan*, to offer, inform, command (cp. Dut. *bieden*, G. *bieten*, Goth. *biudan*), (2) *biddan*, to press, beg, pray (cp. Dut. *bidden*, G. *bitten*, Goth. *bidjan*)], *v.t.* (*past* **bid,** *p.p.* **bid, bidden**) To command; to invite, to ask; to announce, to declare; to offer, to make a tender of (a price, esp. at an auction). *v.i.* To make an offer at an auction; (*Am.*) to tender. *n.* An offer of a price, esp. at an auction; (*Cards*) the call at bridge whereby a player contracts to make as many tricks as he names. **to bid beads:** To say the rosary, to pray with a rosary. **to bid defiance:** To defy, proclaim a challenge. **to bid farewell, welcome:** To salute at parting or arrival. **to bid fair:** To seem likely, to promise well. **biddable,** *a.* Obedient, willing. **bidder,** *n.* One who makes an offer at an auction. **bidding,** *n.* *Prayer, the act of praying, esp. with a rosary; invitation, command; a bid at an auction. **bidding-prayer:** *Praying of prayers; a prayer in which the congregation is exhorted to pray for certain objects.

biddy (bid' i) [corr. of *Bridget*], *n.* (*Am.*) An Irish servant-girl.

biddy-biddy (bi' di bi' di) [Maori *piri piri*], *n.* (*N. Zealand*) A burr.

bide (bīd) [A.-S. *bīdan* (cp. Dut. *beiden*, O.H.G. *bītan*)], *v.t.* To abide, await; to endure, suffer; (*arch. exc. in* **bide one's time:** Await an opportunity). *v.i.* To abide, stay; to continue, to remain. **biding,** *n.* Awaiting, abiding; stay, residence; abode, abiding-place.

bident (bī' dent), *n.* A two-pronged fork. **bidentate, bidentated,** *a.* Having two teeth or tooth-like processes.

bidet (bi det', bē' dā) [F.], *n.* A small horse; a vessel for bathing in, fitted on a low stool that can be straddled.

bield (bēld) [M.E. *belde*, A.-S. *bieldo*, boldness (Goth. *balthei*, O.H.G. *bald*)], *n.* (*Sc.*) Protection, shelter. *a.* (*Sc.*) Comfortable, cosy. **bielding,** *n.* (*Sc.*) Protection, shelter. **bieldy,** *a.* (*Sc.*) Protective, sheltering.

biennial (bī en' i ȧl), *a.* Happening every two years, lasting two years; (*Bot.*) taking two years to reach maturity, ripen its seeds, and die. *n.* A biennial plant. **biennially,** *adv.* **biennium,** *n.* A period of two years.

bier (bēr) [A.-S. *bær* (*beran*, to bear; cp. BARROW)], *n.* *A handbarrow; a stand or litter on which a corpse is placed, or on which the coffin is borne to the grave; *the corpse on a bier; (*fig.*) a tomb. ***bier-balk,** *n.* A path along which there is a right of way for funerals only.

bifacial (bī fā' shȧl), *a.* Having two faces.

bifarious (bī fâr' i ůs), *a.* (*Bot.*) Ranged in two rows.

biff (bif) [Onomat.], *v.t.* (*slang*) To strike, to cuff. *n.* A blow.

biffin (bif' in) [*beefing*, from BEEF, from the colour], *n.* A deep-red cooking-apple much cultivated in Norfolk; a baked apple of this kind, flattened into a cake.

bifid (bī' fid), *a.* (*Bot.*) Split partly into two; two-cleft.

biflorate (bī flôr' āte), *a.* Bearing two flowers or blooms.

bifocal (bī fō' kȧl), *a.* With two foci. **bifocal lenses:** Spectacle lenses divided for near and distant vision.

bifold (bī' fōld), *a.* Twofold, double.

bifoliate (bī fōl' i ȧt), *a.* Having two leaves.

biform, biformed (bī' fôrm, -ed), *a.* Having or partaking of two forms.

bifurcate (bī' fėr kāt) [med. L. *bifurcātus*, p.p. of *bifurcāri*, from L. *bifurcus*, two-pronged (BI-, *furca*, a fork, prong)], *v.i.* To divide into two branches, forks or peaks. **bifurcate** (bī fĕr' kȧt), *a.* Divided into two forks or branches. **bifurcation** (bī fėr kā' shůn), *n.* Division into two parts or branches; the point of such division; either of the forks or branches.

big (1) (big) [etym. doubtful], *a.* Large or great in bulk; grown up; pregnant, advanced in pregnancy; important; boastful, pompous, pretentious; (*Am.*) great, fine, excellent; (*fig.*) teeming, filled. **too big for one's boots:** Unduly self-important, conceited. **to talk big:** To boast. **big-bellied,** *a.* Corpulent; advanced in pregnancy. **Big Ben,** *n.* The great bell and clock in the Houses of Parliament, Westminster. **big boned,** *a.* Of massive frame; strong. **big bug,** *n.* (*colloq.*) A person of importance, esp. in his own estimation. **big business,** *n.* Large-scale commerce. **big end,** *n.* (*Motor.*) The crankpin end of the engine connecting-rod. **big-endian,** *n.* A frivolous controversialist (with reference to Swift's *Gulliver*). **big game,** *n.* A hunter's name for the larger mammals. **big head,** *n.* (*slang*) Conceit, swelled head; an Australian river-fish. **big-horn,** *n.* The Rocky Mountain sheep, *Ovis montana*. **big noise,** *n.* (*slang*) A person of importance. **big pot,** *n.* (*slang*) A person of consequence. **big shot,** *n.* An important person. **big talk,** *n.* Boasting, bragging. **big trees,** *n.pl.* The giant sequoias of California. **big-wig,** *n.* A man of importance (from the large wigs formerly worn). **bigness,** *n.* The quality of being big.

big (2) (big) [Icel. *byggja*, to dwell in, to build (cp. A.-S. *būian*, *būan*, to dwell, cultivate)], *v.t.* (*Sc.*) To build. **bigging,** *n.* The action of building; a building.

biga (bē' ga) [L.], *n.* A two-horse chariot.

bigamy (big' ȧ mi) [F. *bigamie*, from O.F. *bigame*, bigamist, med. L. *bigamus* (*bi-*, two, Gr. *gamos*, marriage)], *n.* Marriage with a second person while a legal spouse is living; (*Eccles. Law*) a second marriage; marriage of or with a widow or widower. **bigamist,** *n.* One who commits bigamy. **bigamous,** *a.* Pertaining to or involving bigamy. **bigamously,** *adv.*

bigeminate (bī jem′ in ăt), *n.* In two pairs.

bigg, big (3) (big) [Icel. *bygg* (A.-S. *bēow*, grain, barley, cp. Gr. *phuein*, Sansk. *bhū*, to grow)], *n.* (*Sc.*) Four-rowed barley, a variety of *Hordeum hexastichon.*

***biggin** (1) (big′ in) [F. *béguin*], *n.* A child's cap, a night-cap; the coif of a serjeant-at-law.

bigging, biggin' (2) [BIG (2)].

bight (bīt) [A.-S. *byht* (*būgan*, to bend)], *n.* A bending, a bend; a small bay, the space between two headlands; the loop of a rope.

Bignonia (big nō′ ni ȧ) [after Abbé *Bignon*, librarian to Louis XIV], *n.* A genus of plants, containing the trumpet flower.

bigot (big′ ŏt) [etym. unknown], *n.* A person unreasonably and intolerantly devoted to a particular creed, system, or party. **bigoted,** *a.* Affected with bigotry. **bigotedly,** *adv.* **bigotry,** *n.* The character, conduct, or mental condition of a bigot.

bijou (bē′ zhoo) [F., prob. Celtic (Bret. *bizou*, from *biz*, Corn. *bis*, W. *bys*, finger)], *n.* (*pl.* **bijoux,** pron. as sing.) A jewel, a trinket; anything small, pretty or valuable. **bijouterie** (bē zhoo′ tė ri), *n.* Jewellery, trinkets.

bike (1) (bīk) [Sc. and North.; etym. unknown], *n.* A wasps', bees', or hornets' nest; a swarm, a crowd, a rabble.

bike (2) (bīk), *n.* (*colloq.*) A bicycle. *v.i.* To ride a bicycle.

bike (3) (bīk), *n.* (*Austral.*) A prostitute.

bikini (bi kē′ ni) [atoll in the N. Pacific], *n.* A brief, two-piece sun-suit.

bilabiate (bī lā′ bi ȧt), *a.* (*Bot.*) Having two lips.

bilateral (bī lăt′ ėr ȧl) [BI-, L. *laterālis* (*latus -eris*, side)], *a.* Having, arranged on, or pertaining to two sides; affecting two parties. **bilaterally,** *adv.* With or on two sides.

bilberry (bil′ bėr i) [prob. from Scand. (cp. Dan. *böllebær*)], *n.* The fruit of a dwarf moorland shrub, *Vaccinium myrtillus*, called also whortleberry and blaeberry; the plant; other species of *Vaccinium.*

***bilbo** (bil′ bō) [from *Bilbao*, in Spain, where the best weapons were made], *n.* A rapier, a sword; (*fig.*) a bully, a swash-buckler.

***bilboes** (bil′ bōz) [etym. doubtful], *n.pl.* A long iron bar, with sliding shackles for the feet, used to fetter prisoners.

bilby (bil′ bi), *n.* (*Austral.*) A variety of marsupial burrowing rat.

bile (bīl) [F., from L. *bīlis*, bile, anger], *n.* A bitter yellowish fluid secreted by the liver; excess of bile; (*fig.*) anger, choler. **bile-pigment,** *n.* Colouring matter existing in bile. **bile-stone,** *n.* (*Med.*) A biliary calculus. **biliary** (bil′ i ȧ ri), *a.* Of or pertaining to the bile. **biliary calculus,** *n.* A calculus formed in the gall-bladder. **bilious,** *a.* Biliary; produced or affected by bile; (*fig.*) peevish, ill-tempered. **biliously,** *adv.* **biliousness,** *n.*

bilge (bilj) [corr. of BULGE], *n.* The bulging part of a cask; (*Naut.*) the bottom of a ship's floor; that part on which a ship rests when aground; the dirt which collects in the bottom of the hold; bilge-water; (*slang*) worthless nonsense. *v.i.* (*Naut.*) To spring a leak; to bulge or swell. *v.t.* (*Naut.*) To stave in, to cause to spring a leak. **bilge-keel,** *n.* A timber fixed under the bilge to hold a vessel up when ashore and to prevent rolling. **bilge-pump,** *n.* A pump to carry off bilge-water. **bilge-water,** *n.* The foul water that collects in the bilge of a ship.

Bilharzia (bil hâr′ tsi ȧ) [T. *Bilharz*, discoverer], *n.* (*Zool.*) A genus of trematode worms that are dangerous human parasites; the liver-fluke.

bilingual (bī ling′ gwȧl) [L. *bilinguis* (BI-, *lingua*, tongue)], *a.* Knowing, speaking, or composed of two languages; written in two languages. **bilingually,** *adv.* In two languages. **bilinguist,** *n.* One who knows or speaks two languages.

bilious, biliary, etc. [BILE].

bilirubin (bi li roo′ bin) [L. *bilis*, bile; *ruber*, red], *n.* (*Med.*) The chief pigment of the bile, a derivative of hæmoglobin.

biliteral (bī lit′ ėr ȧl), *a.* A philological term applied to roots consisting of two letters.

bilk (bilk) [etym. doubtful], *v.t.* To spoil an opponent's score at cribbage; to cheat, to defraud; to evade payment of; to escape from, to elude. *n.* Spoiling an opponent's score in cribbage; (*slang*) a swindler.

bill (1) (bil) [A.-S. *bile*], *n.* The horny beak of birds or of the platypus; a beak-like projection or promontory; (*Naut.*) the point of the fluke of an anchor. *v.i.* To lay the bills together (as doves); (*fig.*) to exhibit affection. **billed,** *a.* Furnished with a beak or bill (usually in comb., as *hard-billed, tooth-billed*, etc.). **to bill and coo:** To kiss and fondle; to make love.

bill (2) (bil) [A.-S. *bil*, *bill* (cp. G. *bille*)], *n.* An obsolete weapon resembling a halberd; a bill-hook. **bill-hook,** *n.* A thick, heavy knife with a hooked end, used for chopping brushwood, etc. **bill-man,** *n.* A soldier armed with a bill.

bill (3) (bil) [A.-F. and M.E. *bille*, late L. *billa*, corr. of *bulla*, a writing, a sealed writing; formerly, a stud or seal)], *n.* A statement of particulars of goods delivered or services rendered; a promissory note; a draft of a proposed Act of Parliament; an advertisement or public announcement printed and distributed or posted up; (*Law*) a written statement of a case; a petition to the Scottish Court of Session; (*Am.*) a bank-note; *a list, an inventory; *a document of any kind. *v.t.* To announce by bills or placards, to cover with bills or placards; to put into a programme. **billboard,** *n.* (*Am.*) A street hoarding. **to head, top the bill:** (*Theat.*) To have one's name at the top of the play-bill. **bill of credit:** A note issued on the credit of the state, and passing current as money. **bill of entry:** A written account of goods entered at the custom-house. **bill of exchange:** A written order from one person (the drawer) to another (the drawee) to pay a sum on a given date to the drawer, or to a third person (the payee); (such a bill drawn, not for value received, but to obtain credit, is called an **accommodation bill**). **bill of fare:** A list of dishes, a menu; (*fig.*) a programme. **bill of health:** (*Naut.*) A certificate to the master of a ship clearing out of an infected port, certifying the state of health of crew and passengers (hence a **clean bill, a foul bill,** often used *fig.*). **bill of lading** (*Comm.*) A master of a ship's acknowledgment of goods received; (*Am.*) a consignment note. **bill of mortality:** The official return of the deaths (and births) of a district; in London they were first published in 1592, for about 100 parishes in and round London (hence **within the bills of mortality:** Within this district, which, however, varied from time to time). **bill of rights:** A summary of rights and privileges claimed by a people, esp. the declaration by the English Parliament to the Prince and Princess of Orange (1689) on their acceptance of the crown. **bill of sale:** An instrument for the transfer of personal property, often given as security for a debt, authorizing seizure and sale in case of non-payment. **bill of sight:** (*Comm.*) Permission to a consignee to land for inspection by custom-house officers such goods as he cannot describe accurately. **bill of store:** (*Naut.*) A licence to a master of a ship to ship dutiable goods for consumption on the voyage, without payment of duty; a licence to reimport British goods formerly exported. **private Bill,** *n.* A Parliamentary Bill involving the interests of private individuals or corporations only. **public Bill,** *n.* A Bill involving the interests of the nation at large. **to find a true bill, to ignore**

a bill: (*Law*) Said of a grand jury when they decide that there is (or is not) sufficient evidence against a prisoner to warrant his trial. **bill-broker, -discounter,** *n.* One who discounts money bills. **bill-chamber,** *n.* (*Sc. Law*) A department of the Court of Session for summary proceedings on petition. **bill-head,** *n.* A ruled and printed form with the name, address, etc. of a tradesman or firm at the top. **bill-poster, -sticker,** *n.* A man who sticks up bills on walls, etc.

billabong (bil' å bong) [abor. Austral.], *n.* An effluent from a river; a creek that fills seasonally.

billet (1) (bil' ėt) [A.-F. *billette*, dim. of *bille*, see prec.], *n.* A small paper, a note; a ticket requiring a householder to furnish food and lodgings for a soldier or Government worker; the quarters so assigned; (*colloq.*) a situation, an appointment. *v.t.* To quarter soldiers or workers. ***billet-doux,*** (bil' ā doo') [F., a sweet note], *n.* (*pl.* ***billets-doux***) A love-letter.

billet (2) (bil' ėt) [F. *billete* (*billot*), dim. of *bille*, a log of wood (etym. unknown)], *n.* A small log or faggot for firing; a bar, wedge, or ingot of gold or silver; (*Arch.*) a short cylindrical piece placed lengthwise at regular intervals in a hollow moulding in Norman work; (*Her.*) a rectangle set on end.

billiards (bil' i årdz, bil' yårdz) [F. *billard*, a stick, a cue, dim. of *bille*, see prec.], *n.pl.* A game with ivory balls, which are driven about on a cloth-lined table with a cue. **billiard-cue,** *n.* A tapering stick used to drive the balls. **billiard-marker,** *n.* One who marks the points made by players; an apparatus for registering these.

Billingsgate (bil' ingz gāt) [prob. from a personal name *Billing*], *n.* One of the gates of the City of London; the fish-market near that gate, noted for abusive language; scurrilous abuse, foul language. *a.* Scurrilous, abusive.

billion (bil' i ȯn, bil' yȯn) [F., coined from *million*, with pref. BI-], *n.* A million millions, *i.e.* 1,000,000,000,000; (in France and America) a thousand millions (1,000,000,000).

billon (bil' ȯn) [F., base metal, orig. mass, from *bille*, see BILLET (2)], *n.* Mixed metal for coinage, esp. silver alloyed with copper.

billow (bil' ō) [Icel. *bylgja*, a billow (cp. A.-S. *balgan*, to swell)], *n.* A great swelling wave of the sea; (*fig.*) the sea; anything sweeping onward like a mighty wave. *v.i.* To surge; to rise in billows. **billowy,** *a.* Characterized by, of the nature of, or like billows.

billy (1) (bil' i) [etym. unknown], *n.* (*Sc.*) Fellow, comrade, mate; brother.

billy (2) (bil' i) [prob. from the personal name], *n.* The tea-pot of an Australian bushman; (*Am.*) a policeman's club. **billy-can,** *n.* (*Austral.*) A billy.

Billy Bluegum, *n.* (*Austral.*) The koala.

billy-boy (bil' i boi) [etym. unknown], *n.* (*Naut.*) A Humber or east-coast boat of river-barge build; a bluff-bowed north-country trader.

billy-cock (bil' i kok) [prob. meaning *cocked like a bully's hat*], *n.* A round, low-crowned felt hat; a wide-awake.

billy-goat (bil' i gōt), *n.* A male goat; a tufted beard like that of a he-goat, a goatee.

bilobed, bilobiate (bī lōbd, bī lō' bāt), *a.* (*Nat. Hist.*) Having or divided into two lobes.

bilocation (bī lō kā' shůn), *n.* The state or faculty of being in two places at once.

bilocular (bī lok' ū lår), *a.* (*Bot.*) Having two cells or compartments.

biltong (bil' tȯng) [S. Afric. Dut. *bil*, bullock, *tong* tongue], *n.* Strips of lean meat dried in the sun.

Bimana (bī' må-, bim' å nå) [BI-, L. *manus*, a hand], *n.pl.* Cuvier's name for his first and highest order of Mammalia, consisting of the single genus *Homo* or Man. **bimanal** (bim' å nål), **bimanous** (bim' å nůs), *a.* Two-handed; of or belonging to the Bimana. **bimane** (bī' mān), *n.* An animal with two hands; a man.

bimbashi (bim băsh' i) [Turk.], *n.* An army captain.

bimbo (bim' bō) [BUMBO], *n.* A kind of punch made with cognac.

bimensal, bimestrial (bī men' sål, bī mes' tri ål), *a.* Continuing for two months; occurring every two months.

bimeridian (bī me rid' i ån), *a.* Pertaining to or recurring at midday and midnight.

bimetal (bī met' ål) [BI-, METAL], *n.* The name given to two dissimilar metals fastened together so as to make up a composite strip.

bimetallic (bī mė tăl' ik) [F. *bimetallique*], *a.* Of or pertaining to bimetallism. **bimetallism** (bī met' ål izm), *n.* The employment of two metals (gold and silver) in the currency of a country, at a fixed ratio to each other, as standard coin and legal tender. **bimetallist,** *n.* A supporter or advocate of bimetallism.

bimillenary (bī mil en' å ri), *n.* A period of two thousand years.

bi-monthly (bī mŭnth' li), *a.* Occurring once in two months; lasting two months.

bin (bin) [A.-S. *binn* (perh. from L. *benna*, of Celtic origin)], *n.* A box or other receptacle for corn, bread, wine, etc.; wine from a particular bin; a large canvas receptacle into which hops are picked. *v.t.* To stow in a bin.

bin- [BI- (before vowels)], *comb. form.* **binoxide,** (bin ok' sīd) [OXIDE], *n.* (*Chem.*) Dioxide.

binary (bī' nå ri) [L .*bīnārius*, from *bīnī*, two each], *a.* Consisting of a pair or pairs; double, dual. **binary compound,** *n.* (*Chem.*) A compound of two elements. **binary measure,** *n.* (*Mus.*) A measure having two beats to the bar. **binary scale,** *n.* (*Math.*) A system with two as basis instead of ten. **binary stars, system:** Two stars, or suns, revolving round a common centre or round each other. **binary theory,** *n.* (*Chem.*) The theory that all acids are a compound of hydrogen with a simple or compound radical, and all salts are similar compounds in which a metal takes the place of hydrogen.

bind (bīnd) [A.-S. *bindan* (cp. Goth. *bindan*, G. *binden*, Aryan *bhendh*)], *v.t.* (*past & p.p.* **bound**) To tie, or fasten together, to or on something; to put in bonds, confine; to wrap or confine with a cover or bandage; to form a border to; to cover, secure, or strengthen, by means of a band; to sew (a book) and put into a cover; to tie up; to cause to cohere; to make costive; (*Law*) to oblige to do something by contract; to oblige, to engage, to compel; to confirm or ratify; *v.i.* To cohere; to grow stiff and hard; to tie up; to be obligatory. *n.* A band or tie; a bine; (*Mus.*) a sign which groups notes together; a tie or brace; (*Mining*) indurated clay, mixed with oxide of iron. **to bind down:** To restrain by formal stipulations. **to bind over:** (*Law*) To oblige under penalties. **to bind up:** To cover with dressings or bandages; to bind (as books) together. **binder,** *n.* One who binds; a book-binder; one who binds sheaves; that which binds or fastens; a fencing-withe; a bond-stone in a wall; a straw band for binding sheaves of corn; a cover for newspapers, correspondence, etc.; a clip; a tie-beam; (*Med.*) a bandage, esp. in obstetrics; (*Naut.*) a principal part of a ship's frame, as the keel, transom, beam, knee, etc. **bindery,** *n.* A book-binder's workshop. **binding,** *a.* Obligatory. *n.* The act of binding; that which binds; the state of being bound; the act, art, or particular style of bookbinding; a book-cover, braid or other edging. **bindingly,** *adv.* **bindingness,** *n.* **bind-weed,** *n.* A plant of the genus *Convolvulus*; several other climbing plants.

bine (bīn) [BIND], *n.* A flexible shoot or stem, esp. of the hop (cp. WOODBINE).

binervate (bī nĕrv′ ȧt), *a.* (*Bot.*) Having two nerves or leaf-ribs; (*Ent.*) having the two wings supported by two nerves.

bing (1) (bing) [Icel. *bingr* (cp. Swed. *binge*)], *n.* A heap, a pile; (*Mining*) a heap of alum or of metallic ore; a measure (8 cwt.) of lead ore.

bing (2), **binghi** (bing, bing′ gi), *n.* (*Austral.*) An Aboriginal.

binge (binj), *n.* (*slang*) The celebration of an occasion by a drinking party; a mild debauch.

bingey, bingy (bin′ jē) [Austral. abor.], *n.* The belly.

bingo (bing′ gō) [coined from B (brandy) and STINGO], *n.* (*slang*) Brandy.

bink (bingk) [M.E. *benk*, BENCH], *n.* (*Sc.*) A bench; a shelf, a dresser; a bank.

binnacle (bin′ ȧkl) [formerly *bittacle*, Sp. *bitacula*, L. *habitāculum*, a dwelling-place (*habitāre*, to dwell, freq. of *habēre*, to have, hold)], *n.* (*Naut.*) The case in which the ship's compass is kept.

binocular (bi nok′ ū lȧr), *a.* Having two eyes; suited for use by both eyes. *n.* A binocular microscope. **binoculars,** *n.pl.* A field or opera glass with tubes for both eyes.

binomial (bī nōm′ i ȧl) [L. *nomen*, a name], *a.* Binominal; of or pertaining to binomials; *n.* (*Math.*) An expression consisting of two terms united by the signs + or −. **binomial theorem,** *n.* (*Math.*) A formula discovered by Newton by which a binomial quantity can be raised to any power without actual multiplication.

binominal (bī nom′ in ȧl), *a.* Having two names, the first denoting the genus, the second the species.

bio- [Gr. *bios*, life], *comb. form.* Pertaining to life or living things.

bioblast (bī′ ō blast), *n.* (*Biol.*) A minute mass of amorphous protoplasm, with formative powers.

biochemistry (bī ō kem′ is tri), *n.* The chemistry of living things.

biodynamics (bī ō dī năm′ iks), *n.* (*Biol.*) The doctrine of vital forces or energy.

biogen (bī′ ō jen), *n.* Bioplasm; the hypothetical substance of the soul.

biogenesis, biogeny (bī ō jen′ e sis, bī oj′ ė ni), *n.* The doctrine that living matter originates only from living matter; the science of the origin of life. **biogenetic,** *a.*

biogeography (bī ō jē og′ rȧ fi), *n.* The study of the distribution of plant and animal life over the globe.

biograph (bī′ ō grăf), *n.* An early name for the cinematograph.

biography (bī og′ rȧ fi) [late Gr. *biographia*], *n.* The history of the life of a person; literature dealing with personal history; the life of an individual person, animal, or plant. **biographee** (bī og rȧ fē′), *n.* The person who is the subject of a biography. **biographer** (bī og′ rȧ fėr), *n.* A writer of biography. **biographic, biographical** (bī ō grăf′ ik, -ik ȧl), *a.* Of, pertaining to, or containing biography. **biographically,** *adv.*

biology (bī ol′ ȯ ji), *n.* The science of physical life or living matter in all its phases. **biologic, biological,** *a.* Pertaining to biology. **biological control,** *n.* The control of pests, etc. by using other organisms that destroy them. **biological warfare,** *n.* Warfare involving the use of disease germs. **biologist,** *n.*

biomagnetism (bī ō măg′ ne tizm), *n.* Animal magnetism.

biometry (bī om′ ė tri), *n.* The measurement of life for statistical or actuarial purposes. **biometrical,** *a.* **biometrically,** *adv.*

bionomic (bī ȯ nom′ ik), *a.* (*Biol.*) Relating to environment, habits, etc.

biophore (bī′ ȯ fôr), *n.* (*Bot.*) Hypothetically the smallest particle capable of growth and reproduction.

biophysics (bī ō fiz′ iks), *n.* The application of physics to living things.

bioplasm (bī′ ȯ plăzm), *n.* Protoplasm; the germinal matter whence all organic matter is developed. **bioplast,** *n.* A nucleus of germinal matter.

bioscope (bī′ ȯ skōp), *n.* A biograph, a cinematograph.

biosphere (bī′ ȯ sfēr), *n.* The portion of the earth's surface and atmosphere inhabited by living things.

biostatics (bī ȯ stăt′ iks), *n.* (*Biol.*) The science of structure as adapted and ready to act.

biotic (bī ot′ ik), *a.* Pertaining to life.

biparous (bī′ pȧr ůs) [L. *parere*, to produce], *a.* Bringing forth two at a birth; producing two at once.

bipartient (bī par′ shi ėnt) [L. *bipartire*, to bisect], *a.* That divides into two parts. *n.* (*Math.*) A number that divides another into two equal parts without remainder.

bipartite (bī part′ īt), *a.* (*Bot.*) Divided into two corresponding parts from the apex almost to the base (of leaves).

bipartition (bī par tish′ ůn), *n.* Division into two.

biped (bī′ ped) [L. *pes*, *pedis*, a foot], *a.* Having two feet. *n.* An animal having only two feet, as man and birds.

bipennate, bipennated (bī pen′ ȧt, bī pen′ ȧ ted), *a.* (*Zool.*) Having two wings, or two wing-like processes.

bipetalous (bī pet′ ȧ lůs), *a.* (*Bot.*) Having two petals in a flower.

bipinnaria (bī pin âr′ i ȧ), *n.* (*Zool.*) A larva of Asteroidea with two bands of cilia.

bipinnate, bipinnated (bī pin′ ȧt, bī pin′ ȧ ted), *a.* (*Bot.*) The term applied to pinnated leaflets of a pinnate leaf.

biplane (bī′ plān), *a.* (*Aviat.*) An aircraft with two wings one above the other. *a.* Adjustable in two different planes.

biplicate (bī′ pli kāt), *a.* (*Bot.*) Twice folded together.

bipolar (bī pō′ lȧr), *a.* Having two poles or opposite extremities.

Bipontine (bī pon′ tīn) [mod. L. *Bipontinus*, from *Bipontium*, L. name of Zweibrücken (Two-Bridges), in Bavaria], *a.* Printed at Zweibrücken (of editions of classics).

biquadratic (bī kwod răt′ ik), *a.* (*Math.*) Raised to the fourth power; of or pertaining to the fourth power. *n.* The fourth power, the square of a square. **biquadratic equation,** *n.* An equation containing the fourth power of the unknown quantity.

birch (bĕrch) [A.-S. *birce*, *beorc* (cp. O.H.G. *biricha*, Sansk. *bhurja*, Icel. *björk*, Sc. *birk*)], *n.* A genus of northern forest trees, *Betula*, with slender limbs and thin, tough bark; the wood of any of these trees; a birch-rod; (*Austral.*) a variety of beech tree; (*Am.*) a canoe made from the bark of *Betula papyracea*. *a.* Birchen. *v.t.* To chastise with a birch-rod; to flog. **birch-oil,** *n.* (*slang*) A flogging. **birch-rod,** *n.* An instrument of correction, usually made of twigs of birch. **birching,** *n.* A flogging. **birchen,** *a.* Composed of birch.

bird (bĕrd) [A.-S. *brid*, a bird, the young of any bird (etym. doubtful)], *n.* Any feathered vertebrate animal; a member of the class Aves; a game bird, esp. a partridge; (*slang*) a girl, young woman. **to get the bird:** (*slang*) To be hissed. **Arabian bird:** The Phœnix. **bird in the hand** and **a bird in the bush:** Certainty compared with possibility. **bird of Jove:** The eagle. **bird of Juno:** The peacock. **bird of night:** The owl. **bird of passage:** A migratory bird. **bird of peace:** The dove. **bird of Paradise:** One of the New Guinea Paradiseidæ, which have beautiful plumage. **bird of prey:** One of the Raptores or the Accipitres. **birds of a feather:** Persons of similar tastes or proclivities. **bird-cage,** *n.* A cage for a bird or birds. **bird-call,** *n.* An instrument for imitating the cry of birds. **bird-catching plant:** (*N. Zealand*) A shrub that catches small birds by its sticky seed-vessels. **bird-fancier,** *n.* One who collects, breeds, or rears birds; one who keeps live birds for sale. **bird-man,** *n.* (*Am. colloq.*) An airman. **bird-lime,** *n.* A viscous substance usually made from holly bark, used to snare birds. *v.t.* To smear or catch with or as with bird-lime. **bird-seed,** *n.* Special seed (hemp, canary, millet, etc.) given to cage-birds. **bird's-eye,** *a.* Of, belonging to, or resembling a bird's eye; having eye-like marking; seen from above, as by the eye of a bird. *n.* A kind of tobacco in which the ribs of the leaves are cut with the fibre; a popular name for several plants with small, round, bright flowers; the germander speedwell. **bird's-eye primrose,** *n.* An English wild plant, the mealy primrose, *Primula farinosa.* **bird's-eye view,** *n.* A view of a place or landscape seen from above; a representation of such a view; (*fig.*) a résumé. **bird's-foot,** *n.* A popular name for certain plants, etc., *e.g. Cheilanthes radiata*, a small fern widely distributed. **bird's-foot sea-star,** *n.* A British echinoderm, *Palmipes membranaceus.* **bird's-foot trefoil,** *n.* A British wild flower, *Lotus corniculatus.* **bird's-nest,** *n.* The nest of a bird; an edible bird's-nest; (*Naut.*) a cask or other shelter for the lookout man at the masthead. *v.i.* To search for birds'-nests. **bird's-nest fern,** *n.* Name of several exotic ferns. **bird's-nest orchid,** *n. Neottia nidus-avis*, a British orchid. **bird's-tongue,** *n.* A popular name for several plants, probably from the shape of their leaves. **birdie,** *n.* A little bird; (used as a term of endearment); (*Golf*) a hole done in one under bogey. ***birding,** *n.* Bird-catching; fowling. *a.* Pertaining to or used in fowling or bird-catching. **birding-piece,** *n.* A fowling-piece.

bireme (bī' rēm) [L. *birēmis* (BI-, *rēmus*, oar)], *n.* A Roman galley with two banks of oars. *a.* Having two banks of oars.

biretta (bi ret' ȧ) [It. *berretta*, late L. *birretum* (*birrus*, *byrrhus*, a mantle with a hood, prob. from Gr. *purrhos*, flame-coloured)], *n.* A square cap worn by clerics of the R.C. and Anglican Churches.

biribiri [BERIBERI]. **birk** [BIRCH].

birkie (bĕr' ki) [etym. doubtful], *n.* (*Sc.*) A man, a fellow; a card game. *a.* (*Sc.*) Gay, spirited; active.

birl (bĕrl) [prob. onomat.], *v.i.* To spin, to rotate noisily. *v.t.* To spin; to throw, toss.

***birle** (bĕrl) [A.-S. *byrelian*, to give drink (*byrele*, *byrle*, cup-bearer)], *v.t.* (*Sc.*) To ply with drink. *v.i.* To carouse. ***birler,** *n.* (*North.*) One who carries round drink. **birling,** *n.* The pouring out of drink; carousing.

birostrate, birostrated (bī ros' trȧt, bī ros' trȧ ted), *a.* (*Zool.*) Having two beaks, or beak-like processes.

***birr** (bĕr) [Icel. *byrr*, a favourable wind], *n.* Momentum, rush; strength, exertion; emphasis in pronunciation, energetic stress; a whirring sound.

birse (bĕrs) [Sc., A.-S. *byrst* (see BRISTLE)], *n.* Bristle. **to lick the birse:** To pass a bunch of hog's bristle through the mouth, as in the ceremony of being made a soutar or citizen of Selkirk. **to set up the birse:** To raise someone's anger; to put someone's back up.

birsle (bĕrsl) [Sc.; etym. doubtful], *v.t.* To scorch, to toast.

birth (bĕrth) [M.E. *byrthe*, Icel. *byrthr*, *burthr* (O. Teut. *beran*, to bear)], *n.* The act of bringing forth; the bearing of offspring; the act of coming into life or being born; that which is brought forth; parentage, extraction, lineage, esp. high extraction, high lineage; condition resulting from birth; origin, beginning, product, creation. **new birth:** Regeneration. **birth certificate,** *n.* An official document giving particulars of one's birth. **birth-control,** *n.* The artificial control of offspring, esp. by means of contraceptives. **birthday,** *n.* The day on which one was born, or its anniversary; (*fig.*) origin, commencement. *a.* Pertaining to the day of one's birth, or to its anniversary. **birthday-book,** *n.* A kind of diary with spaces for noting the birthdays of relatives and friends. **birthday honours,** *n.pl.* Knighthoods, peerages, and other honours conferred on the sovereign's birthday. **birthday present,** *n.* A present given on one's birthday. **birthless,** *a.* Without the advantages of birth. **birth-mark,** *n.* A mark or blemish formed on the body of a child at or before birth. **birth-place,** *n.* The place at which one was born. **birth-rate,** *n.* The percentage of births to the population. **birthright,** *n.* Rights belonging to an eldest son, to a member of a family, order, or people, or to a person as a human being.

bis (bis) [F., It., L. *bis*, twice], *adv.* Encore, again; twice (indicating that something occurs twice).

Biscayan (bis' kā ȧn) [*Biscay*, province of Spain], *a.* Pertaining to Biscay. *n.* A native of Biscay; *a heavy musket mounted on a pivot; *a ball from this.

biscuit (bis' kit) [O.F. *bescoit* (F. *biscuit*), L. *bis coctus*, twice cooked (*coctus*, p.p. of *coquere*)], *n.* Thin flour-cake baked until it is highly dried; pottery moulded and baked in an oven, but not glazed. *a.* Light brown in colour. **to take the biscuit:** (*colloq.*) To be the best of the lot; to be incredible. **a hot biscuit:** (*Am.*) A scone.

bise (bēz) [F. (med. L. and Prov. *bisa*, O.H.G. *bīsa*)], *n.* A keen, dry, northerly wind prevalent in Switzerland and adjacent countries.

bisect (bī sekt') [BI-, L. *sectum*, p.p. of *secāre* to cut], *v.t.* To divide into two parts; (*Math.*) to divide into two equal parts. *v.i.* To fork. **bisection,** *n.* Division into two (generally equal) parts; division into two branches. **bisector,** *n.* One who bisects; (*Math.*) a bisecting line.

biserial, biseriate (bī sēr' i ȧl, bī sēr' i ȧt), *a.* (*Bot.*) Arranged in two rows.

bisexual (bī seks' ū ȧl), *a.* Having both sexes combined in one individual; (*Bot.*) possessing stamens and pistils in the same envelope.

bishop (1) (bish' ŏp) [A.-S. *biscop*, L. *episcopus*, Gr. *episkopos*, an overlooker, an inspector], *n.* A spiritual superintendent in the early Christian Church; a dignitary presiding over a diocese, ranking beneath an archbishop, and above the priests and deacons; a beverage composed of wine, oranges, and sugar; a piece in chess, having the upper part shaped like a mitre; a child's all-round pinafore. **bishop in partibus infidelium:** (*R.-C. Ch.*) A bishop having episcopal rank and functions though having no diocese as it is in the lands of heretics or heathen. **bishop's apron,** *n.* [APRON]. **Bishop's Bible,** *n.* A version published in 1568 under the direction of Abp. Parker. **bishop's-cap,** *n.* The genus *Mitella*, or mitre-wort. **bishop's court,** *n.* An ecclesiastical court held in the cathedral of each diocese. **bishop's length,** *n.* (*Painting*) A size of canvas, 58 × 94 in.; **half bishop's length,** *n.* 45 × 56 in. **bishop's weed,** *n. Ægopodium podagraria*; the umbelliferous genus *Ammi.* **bishopric** (bish' ŏp rik) [A.-S. *bisceoprīce* (*rice*, dominion, cp. G. *reich*)], *n.* The diocese, jurisdiction, or office of a bishop.

bishop (2) (bish' ŏp) [from proper name], *v.t.* (*slang*) To murder by drowning; to tamper with the teeth (of a horse) so as to conceal its age.

bisk (bisk) [F. *bisque*], *n.* A rich soup made by boiling down fish, birds, or the like.

bismar (biz' mȧr) [Sc., from Dan. *bismer*], *n.* A steelyard used for weighing in Orkney and Shetland and N.E. Scotland.

bismillah (biz mil' ȧ) [Arab. *bi'sm-illah*, in the name of God], *int.* In the name of Allah (or God)! (a common Mohammedan exclamation).

bismuth (biz′ mŭth) [G., more commonly *wismut*], *n.* A reddish white trivalent or pentavalent element, used in the arts and in medicine.

bison (bī′ sŏn, bis′ ŏn, biz′ ŏn) [L., from O. Teut. *wisand* (cp. A.-S. *wesend*, O.H.G. *wismit*, G. *wisent*)], *n. Bos bonasus*, a wild ox still preserved in Lithuania; *B. americanus*, erroneously called the buffalo, now almost extinct.

bisque (1) (bisk) [F., etym. doubtful], *n.* (*Tennis, Croquet, etc.*) A stroke allowed at any time to the weaker party to equalize the players.

bisque (2) (bisk) [BISCUIT], *n.* A kind of unglazed white porcelain used for statuettes.

bissextile (bis sek′ stīl) [L. *bissextīlis annus*, the bissextile year (a term applied to every fourth year, because then the sixth day before the calends of March was reckoned twice)], *a.* Of or pertaining to leap-year. *n.* Leap-year.

bistort (bis′ tôrt) [L. *bistorta* (*bis*, twice, *torta tortus*, p.p. of *torquere*, to twist)], *n.* A plant with a twisted root and spike of flesh-coloured flowers, *Polygonum bistorta*, called also snakeweed.

bistoury (bis′ tŏ ri) [F. *bistouri*, etym. doubtful], *n.* (*Med.*) A small instrument used for making incisions; a scalpel.

bistre (bis′ tėr) [F., etym. doubtful (perh. from O.F. *behistre*, *beistre*, *besistre*, L. *bissextīlis*, leap-year, whence gloomy, unlucky; or from Icel. *bistr*, grim, angry, cp. Dut. *bijster*, troubled, at a loss, G. *biester*)], *n.* A transparent brown pigment prepared from soot. *a.* Coloured like this pigment. **bistred,** *a.* Coloured with or as with bistre.

bisulcate (bī sŭl′ kāt), *a.* (*Zool.*) Having cloven hoof.

bit (1) (bit) [A.-S. *bita*, a bit, a morsel (cp. O.Fris. *bita*, Dut. *beet*, bit, O.H.G. *bizzo*, biting, G. *bisse*), from *bitan*, to bite], *n.* *A bite, a piece bitten off; *as much as can be bitten off at once; hence, a small portion, a morsel, a fragment; the smallest quantity, a whit, a jot; a brief period of time; a small coin (usually with the value expressed, as a **threepenny-bit**); (*Am.*) 12½ cents; (*colloq.*) a poor little thing; somewhat or something of. **to do one's bit:** To do one's share. **a bit:** A little. **a bit of an orator:** Something of a speaker. **a bit of muslin, bit of stuff:** (*slang*) A young woman. **bits of children:** Poor little children. **bit by bit:** Gradually, piecemeal. **every bit:** Quite, entirely. **bittock** (bit′ ŏk) [North., dim. of BIT, see -OCK], *n.* A little bit; a small portion; a short distance.

bit (2) (bit) [A.-S. *bite*, bite, biting (cp. O.Fris. *bit*, *biti*, Dut. *beet*, O.H.G. *biz*, a piece bitten off, G. *bisz*, biting)], *n.* A bite, the act of biting; the iron part of the bridle inserted in the mouth of a horse; the cutting part of a tool; the movable boring-piece in a drill; the part of the key at right angles to the shank; a short sliding piece of tube in a cornet for modifying the tone, etc. *v.t.* To furnish with, or accustom (a horse) to, a bit; to restrain. **a bit and a sup:** Something to bite and drink. **to draw bit:** To stop a horse by pulling the reins; (*fig.*) to stop, to slacken speed. **to take the bit in one's teeth:** To hold the bit between the teeth; to become unmanageable.

bitch (bich) [A.-S. *bicce* (etym. doubtful)], *n.* The female of the dog; a female of allied species; an offensive woman; a wench; a lewd woman.

bite (bīt) [A.-S. *bītan* (cp. Icel. *bīta*, O.Teut. *bītan*, G. *beissen*, L. *fid- findere*, to cut)], *v.t.* (*past* **bit**, *p.p.* **bitten**) To seize, nip, rend, cut, pierce, or crush anything with the teeth; to cut, to wound; to affect with severe cold; to cause to smart; to inflict sharp physical or mental pain on; to wound with reproach or sarcasm; to hold fast, as an anchor or screw; to corrode; (*fig.*) to cheat, to trick. *v.i.* To have a habit, or exercise the power, of biting; to sting, to be pungent; to take a bait; to act upon something (of weapons, tools, etc.). *n.* The act of biting; a wound made by the teeth; a mouthful, a small quantity; a piece seized or detached by biting; a hold, a grip; (*fig.*) *a cheat, a trick, a fraud; a trickster; one who cheats. **to bite in:** To corrode or eat into by means of a chemical agent, esp. to eat out the lines of an engraving with acid. **to bite off:** To seize with the teeth and detach. **to bite off more than one can chew:** To undertake more than one can manage. **to bite someone's head off:** (*colloq.*) To snap at someone; to be irritable. **to bite the dust:** (*poet.*) To be slain in battle, to die. **to bite the lip:** To press the lip between the teeth so as to prevent the expression of one's feelings. **to bite the thumb at:** To show contempt for by putting the thumb into the mouth. **bitten with:** Infected by (a passion, mania, etc.). **biter,** *n.* One who or that which bites; (*fig.*) a trickster, a cheat. **the biter bit:** The cheater cheated. **biting,** *a.* Sharp, keen; acrid, pungent; stinging, caustic, sarcastic. **bitingly,** *adv.*

bitt (bit) [etym. doubtful], *n.* (*Naut.*) A strong post fixed in pairs in the deck of a ship for fastening cables, belaying ropes, etc. *v.t.* To put around a bitt. Hence prob. **bitter end:** The loose end of a belayed rope; (*fig.*) the last extremity.

bitten, *p.p.* [BITE].

bitter (bit ėr) [A.-S. *biter* (prob. from *bitan*, to bite)] *a.* Sharp or biting to the taste; acrid, harsh, virulent, piercing; piercingly cold; painful, distressing, mournful. *n.* Anything bitter; bitterness; (*colloq.*) bitter beer; (*pl.*) liquors flavoured with bitter herbs, etc., used as appetizers or stomachics. *v.t.* To make bitter. **to the bitter end** [BITT]. **bitter-almond,** *n.* A bitter variety of the common almond, *Amygdalus communis*. **bitter-cup,** *n.* A cup made of quassia wood which imparts a bitter taste to water poured into it. **bitter-nut,** *n.* (*Am.*) The swamp hickory, *Carya amara*. **bitter-sweet,** *a.* Sweet with a bitter after-taste; pleasant with admixture of unpleasantness. *n.* A kind of apple; woody nightshade, *Solanum dulcamara*. **bitter-sweeting,** *n.* The bitter-sweet apple. **bitter-vetch,** *n.* A popular name for some species of the genus *Vicia*. **bitterwort,** *n.* The yellow gentian, *G. lutea*; other species of *Gentiana*. *adv.* Piercingly. **bitter-cold,** *a* Piercingly cold. **bitterish,** *a.* **bitterly,** *adv.* **bitterness,** *n.*

bittern (1) (bit′ ėrn) [BITTER], *n.* The mother-liquid obtained when sea-water is evaporated to extract the salt.

bittern (2) (bit′ ėrn) [M.E. *bitore*, O.F. *butor* (etym. doubtful; prob. from the bird's cry)], *n.* A wading bird smaller than a heron; the genus *Botaurus*, esp. *B. stellaris*, the common bittern.

bittock [BIT (1)].

bitumen (bi tū′ mėn, bit′ ū mėn) [L.], *n.* Mineral pitch, asphalt; (*Chem.*) native hydrocarbon impregnated with oxygen, as naphtha, petroleum, etc.; (*Painting*) a pigment prepared from asphalt. **bitume,** *v.t.* To smear with bitumen. **bituminiferous** (bi tū mi nif′ ėr ŭs), *a.* Yielding bitumen. **bituminize** (bi tū′ mi nīz), *v.t.* To impregnate with or convert into, bitumen. **bituminization** (-nī zā′ shŭn), The art, process, or state of conversion into bitumen. **bituminous,** *a.* Of the nature of, resembling, or impregnated with bitumen.

bivalent (biv′ ȧ lėnt, bī vā′ lėnt), *a.* Having a valency of two.

bivalve (bī′ vălv), *a.* Having two shells or valves which open and shut. *n.* A mollusc which has its shell in two opposite directions connected by a ligament and hinge, as the oyster; (*Bot.*) a bivalve seed-capsule. **bivalved, bivalvular,** *a.* Bivalve.

bivious (biv′ i ŭs) [L. *via*, a way], *a.* Leading two different ways.

bivouac (biv′ u ăk) [F., from G. *beiwache*, a watch, keeping guard], *n.* *A night watch by an army against sudden attack; a temporary encampment in the field without tents, etc.; the scene of such an encampment. *v.i.* (*past & p.p.* **bivouacked**) To remain in the open air without tents or other covering.

bi-weekly, *a.* Occurring once a fortnight; (*incorrectly*) occurring twice a week.

biz (biz) [short for BUSINESS], *n.* (*slang*) Business, work, employment. **good biz:** A profitable affair.

bizarre (bi zar′) [F. (cp. Sp. *bizarro*, handsome, gallant; It. *bizzarro* choleric)], *a.* Odd, whimsical, fantastic, eccentric; of mixed or discordant style; irregular, in bad taste. **bizarrerie** (bi zar′ ė ri), *n.* Strangeness, grotesqueness, eccentricity, discordance.

blab (blăb) [history doubtful; perh. onomat. (cp. BABBLE)], *v.t.* To tell or reveal indiscreetly; to betray. *v.i.* To talk indiscreetly, to tell tales or secrets; to tattle. *n.* A chatterer, babbler; a tell-tale; babbling, tale-telling. **blabber,** *n.* One who blabs; a tell-tale, a tattler.

black (blăk) [A.-S. *blæc* (O.H.G. *blah, blach*; perh. cognate with Gr. *phlegein*, L. *flagrāre*, to burn)], *a.* Intensely dark in colour (the opposite of white); destitute of light; having an intensely dark ground; dark-skinned, of or pertaining to the Negro race; wearing black clothes, uniform, or armour; sombre, gloomy, dirty; (*Sci.*) denoting total absence of colour due to absence or entire absorption of light; (*fig.*) atrociously wicked; disastrous, dismal, mournful. *n.* The darkest of all colours (the opposite of white); a black pigment or dye; a Negro; a black dress; mourning garments; a minute particle of soot or dirt; *pl.* (*Print.*) spaces blackened with ink. *v.t.* To blacken; to blacklead. **black-out:** The temporary loss of sight or memory; the shading of all sources of artificial light that might be visible from the air. *v.t.* To effect this. **blacken,** *v.t.* To make black, to darken; (*fig.*) to sully, to defame. *v.i.* To become black. **blacking,** *n.* The action of making black; a composition for giving a shining black polish to boots and shoes, harness, etc. **black and blue:** Discoloured by beating; livid. **black and tan:** Marked with black and yellowish-brown; a terrier dog so marked; a member of the auxiliary police force employed in Ireland in 1919–20. **black and white:** Printed or written matter; drawn with pen and ink; this kind of drawing reproduced as a print. **blackamoor,** *n.* A black man, a Negro. **black art,** *n.* Magic, necromancy [from idea that NECROMANCY was connected with L. *niger*, black]. **black-ball,** *n.* Vote of rejection in a ballot. **blackball,** *v.t.* To vote against; to exclude; (*slang*) to dislike, bar. **black-band,** *n.* (*Mining*) The ironstone of the coal-measures. **black-beer,** *n.* A kind of spruce beer made at Danzig. **black-beetle,** *n.* A cockroach, *Blatta orientalis.* **blackberry,** *n.* The common bramble, *Rubus fruticosus* or *discolor*; its fruit. **blackberrying,** *n.* Gathering blackberries. **blackbird,** *n.* A British song-bird, *Turdus merula,* called also merle or black thrush; (*Am.*) *Gracula quiscala* and *Agelaius phœniceus*; a captive Negro or Polynesian. **black-birding,** *n.* The kidnapping of Negroes or Polynesian natives for slavery. **blackboard,** *n.* A board painted black used by teachers and lecturers to write and draw on. **black book,** *n.* A book on the black art; a book recording the names of persons liable to censure or punishment. **to be in someone's black books:** To be in disgrace. **black bread,** *n.* Rye bread. **black-browed,** *a.* Dark, gloomy; threatening, forbidding. **black cap,** *n.* A cap worn by judges in full dress, and put on when pronouncing sentence of death; the popular name of many English birds having the top of the head black, esp. the **black-cap warbler,** *Curruca atricapilla.* **black cattle,** *n.* Welsh and Scotch cattle; (*slang*) clergymen. **black coat,** *n.* A familiar name for a clergyman. **black-cock,** *n.* The male of the black grouse or black game; the heathcock, *Tetrao tetrix.* **black cod:** (*N. Zealand*) A local variety of cod-fish. **black coffee,** *n.* Coffee without milk or cream. **black country,** *n.* A term applied to the parts of the Midlands of England blackened by the coal and iron trades. **blackcurrant,** *n.* A well-known garden bush, *Ribes nigrum,* and its fruit. **black death,** *n.* An Oriental pestilence which ravaged Europe during the 14th century. **black diamonds,** *n.pl.* (*slang*) Coals. **black dog,** *n.* Melancholia; sulkiness, ill-temper. **black draught,** *n.* A purgative draught of an infusion of senna with sulphate of magnesia. **black drop,** *n.* (*Med.*) An infusion of opium in vinegar, flavoured with spices; (*Astron.*) an elongated appearance of the planet noticed in transit of Venus and Mercury. **black earth,** *n.* A fertile soil covering regions in southern U.S.S.R. north of the Black Sea. **black-edged,** *a.* (Of note-paper) having a black border as a sign of mourning. **black eye,** *n.* An eye of which the iris is very dark; discoloration produced by a blow upon the parts round the eye. **black-eyed,** *a.* Having black or dark-coloured eyes. **black-face,** *n.* A black-faced sheep or other animal. **black-faced,** *a.* Having a dark face; (*fig.*) dismal, gloomy. **black-fellow,** *n.* An Aboriginal of Australia. **black-fish,** *n.* A salmon just after spawning; a popular name for several species of English and American fish; in Australia, a small species of whale. **black flag,** *n.* A flag of black cloth used as a sign that no quarter will be given or taken, as an ensign by pirates, and as the signal for an execution. **black-foot,** *n.* A match-maker; a go-between in a love affair; one of a tribe of North American Indians, called Blackfeet from their dark moccasins. **black friar,** *n.* A Dominican friar; (*pl.*) the quarter of a town where the Dominicans had their convent (the name still survives in London and some other places). **Black Friday,** *n.* The 10th May, 1866, the day when Overend, Gurney & Co. suspended payment. **black frost,** *n.* Hard frost without rime. **black game,** *n.* [BLACK-COCK]. **black-head,** *n.* A kind of sea-gull; a pimple with a black head. **black-hearted,** *a.* Wicked; having a wicked heart. **black-hole,** *n.* A punishment cell; the guardroom. *v.t.* To send to the guard-room; to put in confinement. **black-jack,** *n.* A large leather jug for beer; (*Am.*) *Quercus nigra,* the barren or scrub oak; (*Am.*) a loaded stick, a bludgeon. **black-leg,** *n.* A gambler and cheat, a swindler, esp. on the turf; a workman who works for an employer when his comrades are on strike, (*Am.*) a scab. **black-letter,** *n.* The Old English or Gothic as distinguished from the Roman character; *a.* Written or printed in this character. **black-list,** *n.* A list of persons in disgrace, or who have incurred censure or punishment. *v.t.* To ban or prohibit books, etc. **black magic** [BLACK ART]. **black Maria,** *n.* (*slang*) A prison van, (*Am.*) a patrol-car. **black mark,** *n.* A note of disgrace put against one's name. **black market:** Illegal buying and selling of rationed goods. **black-martin,** *n.* The swift, *Cypselus apus.* **black mass,** *n.* A travesty of the Mass performed by modern diabolists. **Black Monday,** *n.* Easter Monday, 1360, a day of unusual cold and gloom; (*fig.*) an inauspicious day; the Monday on which boys return to school after a vacation. **black monks,** *n.pl.* The Benedictines, from the colour of their habit. **black perch:** (*Austral.*) A river-fish of N.S.W. **black prince:** (*Austral.*) A large, black cicada. **black-pudding,** *n.* A kind of sausage made with blood, rice, and chopped fat. **Black Rod,** *n.* The chief usher of the Lord Chamberlain's department, of the House of Lords and of the Garter. **black sheep,** *n.* A bad character, a vicious person. **black shirt:** The uniform of the Italian Fascists and of their English imitators. **blacksmith,** *n.* A smith who works in iron. **black-snake,** *n.* (*Am.*) A popular name for several harmless snakes. **blackstrap,** *n.* An inferior kind of port wine; a mixture of rum and treacle. **Black Thursday:** (*Austral.*) The day of the Victorian bush-fires, 6 Feb., 1851. **black tracker:** (*Austral.*) An Aboriginal used in tracking escaped criminals or lost travellers. **black vomit,** *n.* (*Med.*) A copious vomiting of dark-coloured matter, a fatal symptom in yellow fever. **blackwash,** *n.* (*Med.*) A lotion made from lime-water and mercury. **Black Watch,** *n.* The 42nd Highland Regiment, from the colour of their tartan. **blackwater fever,** *n.* (*Path.*) A trópical disease in which the urine is very dark in colour. **black-wood,** *n.* A popular name for several foreign trees and their timber. **blackish,** *a.* **blackness,** *n.* **blacky,** *n.* A Negro, a blackamoor.

blackguard (blag′ ard), *n.* *A body of menials in charge of the kitchen utensils in a royal household; (*pl.*) *a low, worthless rabble; a low, worthless fellow; a scoundrel, a rough. *a.* Of or pertaining to the lowest class; scurrilous, abusive. *v.t.* To revile in scurrilous language. *v.i.* To act the part of a blackguard; to behave in a riotous or indecent manner. **blackguardism,** *n.* The language or actions of a blackguard. **blackguardly,** *a.* Characteristic of a blackguard. *adv.* After the manner of a blackguard.

blacklead (blăk lĕd′), *n.* Plumbago or graphite, made into pencils, also used to polish ironwork. *v.t.* To colour or rub with blacklead.

blackmail (blăk′ māl), *n.* A tribute formerly exacted by free-booting chiefs in return for protection or immunity from plunder; (*fig.*) any payment extorted by intimidation or pressure. *v.t.* To levy blackmail on. **blackmailer,** *n.* One who levies blackmail.

blackthorn (blăk′ thôrn), *n.* The sloe, *Prunus spinosa*, so called from the dark colour of the bark; a walking-stick or cudgel of its wood.

blackwood (blăk′ wud′), *n.* Australian timber of a dark colour.

blad (blăd), **blaud** (blawd) [Sc.; prob. onomat.], *v.t.* To hit a thumping blow. *v.i.* To strike smartly. *n.* A thumping blow; a thumping piece.

bladder (blăd′ ėr) [A.-S. *blǣdre* (cp. O.H.G. *blātara*, G. *blatter*, a bladder, A.-S. *blāwan*, L. *flāre*, to blow)], *n.* A membranous bag in the animal body which receives the urine; any similar membranous bag (usually with distinctive epithet, as *gall-*, *swim-bladder*, etc.); *a morbid vesicle, a pustule; (*Bot.*) an inflated pericarp; a vesicle; the prepared (urinary) bladder of an animal; the membrane of this bladder used for air-tight coverings; (*fig.*) a wind-bag; anything inflated and hollow. **bladder-fern,** *n.* The genus *Cystopteris.* **bladder-kelp,** *n.* [BLADDER-WRACK]. **bladder-nut,** *n.* The fruit of the bladder-tree, *Staphylea trifoliata.* **bladder-tree,** *n.* [BLADDER-NUT]. **bladder-wort,** *n.* The genus *Utricularia.* **bladder-wrack,** *n.* The sea-weed, *Fucus vesiculosus*, which has air-bladders in its fronds. **bladdered,** *a.* Put or packed in a bladder; (*fig.*) inflated, puffed up. **bladdery,** *a.* Of the nature of a bladder; containing bladders.

blade (blād) [A.-S. *blæd* (O.H.G. *plat*, G. *blatt*, O.Teut. stem *blo-*, to blow, cp. L. *flos*, a flower)], *n.* A leaf of a plant; the culm and leaves of a grass or cereal; (*Bot.*) the expanded part of the leaf as distinguished from the petiole; the corresponding part of a petal; any broad, flattened part, as of a paddle, bat, oar, etc.; the thin cutting part of a knife, sword, etc.; the front part of the tongue; a sword; a dashing, reckless fellow. *v.i.* To put forth blades. **in the blade:** Not yet in ear (of cereals). **blade-bone,** *n.* The shoulder-blade in man and the lower mammals. **bladed,** *a.* Having a blade or blades; in blade, not yet in ear.

blaeberry, bleaberry (blā′ bėr i) [Icel. *blā*, *blār*, livid, dark blue (O.H.G. *blāo*, G. *blau*), whence *blāber*, bilberry], *n.* (*Sc. and North.*) The bilberry or whortleberry; similar fruits or plants.

blaes (blāz) [Sc. *blae*, blue], *n.* (*Mining*) A hardened shale found in coal measures, which is burned and powdered to make surface for tennis courts.

blague (blag) [F.], *n.* Pretentiousness, humbug.

blah (bla) [onomat.], *n.* Foolish talk, chatter, exaggeration.

blain (blān) [A.-S. *blegen* (cp. Dut. *blein*, Dan. *blegn*)], *n.* A pustule, a blister or sore [CHILBLAIN]. *v.t.* To affect with blains.

blame (blām) [O.F. *blasmer*, L. *blasphemāre*, BLASPHEME], *v.t.* To censure, to find fault with, to reproach; to hold responsible; *to reprove, to bring into discredit. *n.* The act of censuring; the expression of censure; responsibility, accountability, *culpability, demerit; a fault; *injury. **to be to blame:** To be culpable. **blame it:** A mild oath. **blamable,** *a.* Deserving blame; culpable. **blamableness,** *n.* **blamably,** *adv.* **blameful,** *a.* Imputing blame; blameworthy. **blamefully,** *adv.* **blamefulness,** *n.* **blameless,** *a.* **blamelessly,** *adv.* **blamelessness,** *n.* **blameworthy,** *a.* Deserving blame. **blameworthiness,** *n.*

blanch (blănch, blanch) [O.F. fem. of *blanc*, white], *a.* White; (*Her.*) argent. *v.t.* To whiten by taking out the colour; to bleach, to make pale; to take off the outward covering of (as of almonds, walnuts, etc.); to whiten (as plants) by the deprivation of light; (*fig.*) to palliate, whitewash. *v.i.* To lose colour; to become white. **blanch farm** [O.F. *blanche ferme* (*ferme*, a contract, L. *firmus*)], *n.* (*Law*) Rent paid in silver as distinguished from that paid in labour or kind; (*Sc. Law*) a nominal quit-rent. **blanch holding,** *n.* (*Sc. Law*) A tenure held on payment of a nominal quit-rent.

blancmange (blà manzh′, -monzh) [O.F. *blancmanger*, *-mangier* (*blanc*, see prec., L. *manducāre*, to chew, to eat)], *n.* A confection of dissolved isinglass, corn-flour, etc., boiled to a jelly with milk, and variously flavoured.

bland (blănd) [L. *blandus*, agreeable], *a.* Mild, soft, gentle; genial, balmy. **blandly,** *adv.* **blandness,** *n.*

blandish (blăn′ dish) [O.F. *blandiss-*, stem of *blandir*, L. *blandīri*, to flatter (*blandus*, see prec.)], *v.t.* To flatter gently; to coax, to cajole. **blandishment,** *n.* Flattering speech or action; cajolery, charm, allurement. **blandiloquence** (blăn dil′ ò kwėns) [ELOQUENCE], *n.* (*colloq.*) Smooth, ingratiating talk; a flattering speech.

blank (blăngk) [F. *blanc*, white, (It. *blanco*, L. *blancus*, O.H.G. *blanch*, O.Teut. *blankoz*, shining)], *a.* Empty, void, vacant; not written or printed on; not filled up; confused, dispirited, nonplussed; pure, unmixed, downright, sheer. *n.* The white point in the centre of a target; *the range of one's aim; a blank space in a written or printed document; a blank form; a lottery ticket that draws no prize; a piece of metal before stamping; a level range for a firearm [POINT-BLANK]; (*fig.*) aim, range; a vacant space, a void; an uneventful space of time; a meaningless thing. *v.t.* To render blank; to nonplus, confuse, dumbfounder; to block out; (*int.*) a mild execration. **blank-cartridge,** *n.* Cartridge containing no ball. ***blank charter,** *n.* A blank paper given to the agents of the Crown in the reign of Richard II, with liberty to fill it up as they pleased. **blank cheque,** *n.* A cheque with the amount left for the payee to insert. **blank credit,** *n.* Permission to draw on a person or firm to a certain amount. **blank verse,** *n.* Unrhymed verse, esp. the iambic pentameter or unrhymed heroic, the usual measure of English epic and dramatic poetry. **blankly,** *adv.* **blankness,** *n.*

blanket (blăng′ kėt) [O.F. *blankete*, *blanquette*, dim. of *blanc*, see BLANK], *n.* A coarse, loosely-woven woollen stuff, used for bed-coverings, horse-wrappers, and by savages for clothing; (*Print.*) a cloth interposed between the platen and the type. *a.* (*fig.*) Covering all conditions or cases. *v.t* To cover with or as with a blanket; to toss in a blanket; (*Naut.*) to take the wind out of the sails of (a yacht) by passing to windward. **born on the wrong side of the blanket:** Illegitimate. **wet blanket,** *n.* A person who is a damper to conversation or enjoyment. **blanketing,** *n.* Material for blankets; tossing in a blanket.

blare (blâr) [prob. imitated from the sound (cp. Dut. *blaren*, M.H.G. *blēren*, G. *plarren*)], *v.i.* To roar, bellow; to sound as a trumpet. *v.t.* To utter with trumpet-like sound. *n.* Sound as of a trumpet; roar, noise, bellowing.

blarney (blar′ ni), *n.* Smooth, flattering speech; cajolery. **blarney-stone,** *n.* An inscribed stone in the wall of an old castle at Blarney, near Cork,

Ireland, whoever kisses which will have a cajoling tongue. *v.t.* To wheedle, to cajole. *v.i.* To talk in a wheedling way.

blasé (bla' zā) [F.], *a.* Dulled in sense or emotion; worn out through over-indulgence, used-up.

blash (blăsh) [Sc. and North.; prob. onomat.], *n.* A splash or watery burst, watery stuff; (*fig.*) wishy-washy talk. *v.t.* and *i.* To splash or dash. **blashy,** *a.* Splashing, showery; watery, thin.

blaspheme (blăs fēm') [O.F. *blasfemer*, L. *blasphēmāre*, Gr. *blasphēmeein*, from *-phemos*, evil-speaking], *v.t.* To utter profane language against (God or anything sacred); to calumniate, to abuse. *v.i.* To utter blasphemy, to rail. **blasphemous** (blăs' fė mŭs), *a.* Uttering or containing blasphemy; grossly irreverent or impious. **blasphemously,** *adv.* **blasphemy** (blăs' fė mi), *n.* Profane language towards God or about sacred things; impious irreverence; (*fig.*) irreverent or abusive speaking about any person or thing held in high esteem.

blast (blast) [A.-S. *blǣst* (cp. O.H.G. *blāst*, Goth. *-blesan*, to blow)], *n.* A violent gust of wind; the sound of a trumpet or the like; (*fig.*) any pernicious or destructive influence on animals or plants; a flatulent disease in sheep; the strong current of air used in iron-smelting; a blowing by gunpowder or other explosive; the charge of explosive used; an explosion of fire-damp; a violent gust of air caused by the explosion of a bomb. *v.t.* To blow or breathe on so as to wither; to injure by some pernicious influence; to blight, to ruin; to blow up with gunpowder or other explosive; to curse (often used as an imprecation). **in blast, in full blast:** Hard at work. **blast-furnace,** *n.* A furnace into which a current of air is introduced to assist combustion. **blast-pipe,** *n.* A pipe conveying steam from the cylinders to the funnel of a locomotive to aid the draught. **blasted,** *a.* Blighted, confounded, cursed. **blasting-needle,** *n.* A long taper piece of metal used to make an aperture for a fuse or train. **blasting-oil,** *n.* Nitro-glycerine. ***blastment,** *n.* Withering or shrivelling up caused by a blast or blight.

-blast [Gr. *blastos*, a bud, a germ], *comb. form.* Used in biological terms; *e.g. mesoblast, statoblast.*

blastema (blăs tē' mȧ) [Gr., a sprout], *n.* (*Biol.*) Protoplasm; the initial matter from which any part is developed; (*Bot.*) the thallus or frond of lichens; the budding or sprouting part of a plant.

blasto- [see -BLAST], *comb. form.* Pertaining to germs or buds; germinal. **blastoderm** (blăs' tō dĕrm) [Gr. *derma*, skin], *n.* (*Biol.*) The germinal membrane enclosing the yolk of an impregnated ovum which divides into layers that develop into embryonic organs. **Blastoidea** (blăs toi' di ȧ), *n.* (*Zool.*) An order of bud-like calcareous fossil Echinoderms. **blastoid,** *a.* **blastomere** (blăs' tō mēr), *n.* (*Biol.*) One of the cells formed during the primary divisions of an egg. **blastula** (blăs' tū la), *n.* (*Biol.*) A hollow sphere composed of a single layer of cells, produced by the cleavage of an ovum. **blastophore** (blăs' tō fôr) [-PHORE], *n.* (*Biol.*) The part of the embryo which bears the bud.

blatant (blā' tȧnt) [etym. doubtful; prob. coined by Spenser (perh. from Sc. *blaitand*, bleating)], *a.* Bellowing like a beast; loud, clamorous; obvious, palpable. **blatancy,** *n.* Quality of being blatant. **blatantly,** *adv.*

blate (blāt) [Sc. and North., from A.-S. *blāt*], *a.* *Livid, pale; bashful, sheepish.

blather, blatherskite [BLETHER].

Blatta (blăt' ȧ) [L. cockroach], *n.* (*Zool.*) A genus of Orthoptera comprising the cockroach.

***blatter** (blăt' ėr) [L. *blaterāre*, to babble], *v.i.* To talk volubly and senselessly; to patter (as rain or hail); to rush in a clattering way. *n.* A clatter; a rushing noise. ***blatterer,** *n.* A babbler; a blusterer.

blaud [BLAD].

blawort (bla' wĕrt) [*blae* (see BLAEBERRY), WORT], *n.* (*Sc.*) The harebell, *Campanula rotundifolia*; the corn bluebottle, *Centaurea cyanus.*

blaze (1) (blāz) [A.-S. *blæse*, *blase*, a blaze, a torch (cp. M.H.G. *blas*, a torch, G. *blass*, pale)], *n.* A bright glowing flame; a glow of bright light or colour; (*fig.*) an outburst of display, glory, splendour; an outburst of passion; (*pl.*) the flames of hell. *v.i.* To burn with a bright flame; to shine, to glitter; to be bright with colour; (*fig.*) to be eminent or conspicuous from character, talents, etc. *v.t.* To make resplendent; *to pour forth (as flame). **like blazes:** Furiously. **Old Blazes:** (*slang*) The devil. **to blazes:** To perdition, to the devil. **to blaze away:** To fire continuously (with guns); (*fig.*) to work continuously and enthusiastically. **to blaze out:** To cause to flare away; to subside with a flare. **to blaze up:** To burst into anger. **blazer,** *n.* A flannel jacket of bright colour worn at cricket, lawn-tennis, etc; a jacket used in school uniform. **blazing,** *a.* Emitting flame or light; radiant, lustrous. **blazing indiscretion,** *n.* A glaring piece of folly or gratuitous frankness. **blazing scent,** *n.* (*Hunting*) A hot scent.

blaze (2) (blāz) [Icel. *blesi* (cp. G. *blässe*)], *n.* A white mark on the face of a horse or ox; a white mark made on a tree by chipping off bark; (*Am.*) the path or boundary indicated by a line of such marks. *v.t.* To mark (a tree); to indicate a path or boundary by such marks.

blaze (3) (blāz) [Icel. *blāsa*, to blow (cp. Dut. *blazen*, G. *blasen*), from O.Teut. *blǣsan*, to blow (cp. L. *flāre*)], *v.t.* To proclaim; to blazon; to depict, emblazon.

blazer [BLAZE (1)].

blazon (blā' zȯn) [F. *blason*, a coat of arms (some of the later senses prob. influenced by BLAZE (3))], *n.* *A shield; armorial bearings; a coat of arms; a banner bearing a coat of arms; the art of describing and explaining coats of arms; (*fig.*) renown, reputation (of virtues or good qualities), proclamation, revelation. *v.t.* To describe or depict according to the rules of heraldry; to depict in brilliant hues; to decorate with heraldic devices; to describe in fit terms; to publish vauntingly; to proclaim, to trumpet. **blazonment,** *n.* The act of blazoning; the act of diffusing abroad. **blazonry,** *n.* An heraldic device; the art of depicting or describing a coat of arms; armorial bearings; brilliant display.

-ble [-ABLE; -IBLE], *suf.* Tending to, able to, fit to (forming verbal adjectives); *e.g. conformable, durable, flexible, suitable, visible.*

bleaberry [BLAEBERRY].

bleach (blēch) [A.-S. *blæcan* (O.Teut. *blaikjan*, cp. G. *bleichen*, and A.-S. *blāc*, pale)], *v.t.* To make white by exposure to the sun or by chemical agents. *v.i.* To grow white; to become pale or colourless. **bleaching-clay,** *n.* Kaolin, used for sizing cotton goods. **bleaching-liquid,** *n.* A solution of chloride of lime. **bleaching-powder,** *n.* Chloride of lime. **bleacher,** *n.* One who or that which bleaches, a vessel used in bleaching. **bleachery,** *n.* **bleach-field,** *n.* A field in which bleaching is carried on.

bleak (1) (blēk) [A.-S. *blāc* (see prec.)], *a.* *Pale, pallid, wan; bare of vegetation; cold, chilly; (*fig.*) desolate, cheerless. **bleakish,** *a.* **bleakly,** *adv.* **bleakness,** *n.*

bleak (2) (blēk) [Icel. *bleikr* (O.Teut. *blaikjôn*, white, cp. BLEACH), or A.-S. *blǣc*, as prec.], *n.* A small British river fish, *Leuciscus alburnus*, six inches long, with silvery scales.

blear (blēr) [etym. doubtful], *a.* Dim, dim with rheum; indistinct, misty. *v.t.* To make (the eyes) dim; to blur with or as with tears. **blearedness,** *n.* Dimness, dullness; haziness; indistinctness.

bleat (blēt) [A.-S *blǣtan* (cp. Dut. *blaten*, O.H.G. *plāzan*, G. *blöken*)], *v.i.* To cry like a sheep, goat, or calf. *v.t.* To utter in a bleating tone; to say feebly and foolishly. *n.* The cry of a sheep, goat, or calf.

bleb (bleb) [cp. BLOB, BLUBBER; imit. of action of making a bubble with the lips], *n.* A small blister or bladder; a bubble in glass or anything similar.

bleed (blēd) [A.-S. *blēdan* (cp. BLOOD)], *v.i.* (*past & p.p.* **bled**) To emit, discharge, or run with blood; to emit sap, resin, or juice from a cut or wound; to be wounded; to die from a wound; to lose money; to have money extorted; (*fig.*) to feel acute mental pain. *v.t.* To draw blood from; (*fig.*) to extort money from; (*Bookbinding*) to cut margins too much and trench on the print. **bleeder,** *n.* One who bleeds; (*Path.*) one who exhibits the blood condition known as hæmophilia. **bleeding,** *n.* Hæmorrhage; the operation of letting blood, or of drawing sap from a tree. *a.* Running with blood; (*slang*) bloody; accursed. **bled-off:** (*Print.*) Illustration pages so arranged that the outside edges of the illustration are cut off in trimming when binding.

bleep (blēp) [onomat.], *n.* The sound of the radio signal from an earth satellite. *v.i.* To emit this sound.

blemish (blem' ish) [O.F. *blemir, blesmir,* from *blaisme, blesme, blême,* pale (etym. doubtful)], *v.t.* *To mar, to spoil; to impair, tarnish, sully. *n.* A physical or moral defect or stain; an imperfection, a flaw, a fault. ***blemishment,** *n.*

blench (1) (blench) [A.-S. *blencan,* to deceive (perh. causal to a v. *blinkan,* to BLINK)], *v.t.* *To elude, to shirk; to flinch from. *v.i.* To shrink back, to draw back; to turn aside, to flinch. **n.* A side-glance.

***blench** (2) (blench) [var. of BLANCH], *v.i.* To become pale. *v.t.* To make pale.

blench (3), **blench farm** [BLANCH].

***blend** (1) (blend) [A.-S. *blendan*], *v.t.* To blind, to make blind; (*fig.*) to blind the understanding.

blend (2) (blend) [A.-S. *blandan,* or Icel. *blanda*], *v.t.* To mix, to mingle (esp. teas, wines, spirits, tobacco, etc. so as to produce a certain quality). *v.i.* To become mingled or indistinguishably mixed; to form an harmonious union or compound; to pass imperceptibly into each other. *n.* A mixture of various qualities (of teas, wines, spirits, tobacco, etc.).

blende (blend) [G., from *blenden,* to deceive, because it yielded no lead], *n.* A native sulphide of zinc.

Blenheim (blen' im) [Duke of Marlborough's seat near Woodstock, Oxfordshire], *n.* A breed of spaniels; a variety of apple, called also a Blenheim orange.

blennorrhœa (blen ŏ rē' ȧ) [Gr. *blennos,* mucus, *rheein,* to flow], *n.* (*Path.*) Inordinate discharge of mucus, esp. from the genital and urinary organs.

blenny (blen' i) [L. *blennius,* Gr. *blennos,* from the mucous coating of the scales], *n.* A genus of small, spiny-finned sea-fishes.

blent (blent) [p.p. of BLEND (2)], *a.* Mingled.

blepharo- [Gr. *blepharon,* eyelid], *comb. form.* (*Path.*) Pertaining to the eyelids. **blepharitis** (blef a rī' tis), *n.* Inflammation of the eye-lids.

blesbok (bles' bok) [S. Afr. Dut.], *n.* (*Zool.*) The S. African white-faced antelope, *Alcelaphus albifrons.*

bless (1) (bles) [A.-S. *blētsian, bledsian, blædsian*; orig. to redden with blood, to bless (*blōd,* BLOOD)], *v.t.* To consecrate, to hallow; to invoke God's favour on, to render happy or prosperous, as by supernatural means; to wish happiness to; to extol, magnify, worship; (*euphem.*) to curse, to confound. **God bless me; or bless me!** An ejaculation of surprise, etc. **to bless oneself:** To make the sign of the cross (as a defence against evil spirits). **without a penny to bless oneself with:** Penniless (with allusion to the cross on a silver penny). **to bless one's stars:** To be very thankful. **blessed** (bles' ėd, blest), **blest** (blest), *a.* Consecrated by religious rites; worthy of veneration; happy, fortunate, beatified, enjoying the bliss of heaven; joyful, blissful; (*euphem.*) cursed. *n.* (*collect.*) The saints in heaven. **blessedly,** *adv.* Fortunately, happily. **blessedness,** *n.* The state of being blessed, esp. by Heaven; happiness, bliss. **single blessedness:** The state of being unmarried. **blessing,** *n.* Consecration; divine favour; an invocation of divine favour or happiness; a cause of happiness; a beneficent gift; grace before or after meat. **to ask a blessing:** To say grace before meat.

***bless** (2) (bles) [a Spenserian adaptation], *v.t.* To wave about, brandish; to brandish round (some object).

blet, blett (blet) [O.F. *blette,* soft, mellow], *v.i.* (Of fruit) to become "sleepy" or internally decayed, as a pear which ripens after being picked.

blether (bleth' ėr), **blather** (blăth' ėr) [Icel. *blathra,* to talk nonsense (*blathr,* nonsense)], *v.i.* To talk nonsense volubly. *n.* Voluble nonsense. **bletherskate** (bleth' ėr skāt), **blatherskite** (blăth' ėr skīt), *n.* One who talks blatant nonsense.

blew, *past* [BLOW (1)].

blewits (bloo' its) [prob. from BLUE], *n.* An edible mushroom with a purplish top.

blight (blīt) [etym. doubtful], *n.* Any baleful atmospheric influence affecting the growth of plants; diseases caused in plants by fungoid parasites and various insects, mildew, smut, rust, aphides, etc.; a close and overcast state of the weather; (*fig.*) any obscure malignant influence. *v.t.* To affect with blight; (*fig.*) to exert a baleful influence on; to mar, frustrate. **blight bird:** (*N. Zealand*) The white-eye or silver-eye. **blighter,** *n.* (*slang*) A nasty fellow, a blackguard. **blightingly,** *adv.*

Blighty (blī' ti) [Urdu *Bilati,* provincial, removed at some distance], *n.* (*slang*) Soldier's name for Britain, home; a wound that invalids one home.

blimey (blī' mi) [abbrev. God *blind me*], *int.* Exclamation of astonishment.

blimp (blimp) [etym. unknown], *n.* A small airship used for observation; (*Cinema.*) a sound-proof covering to drown the sound of the camera mechanism; (*colloq.*) a die-hard, a Tory of the old school who learns nothing.

blind (blīnd) [A.-S. (also Dut., Swed., G., etc.)], *a.* Unseeing; destitute of sight either naturally or by deprivation; unseen, dark, admitting no light, having no outlet; of, pertaining to, or for the use or benefit of, the sightless; (*fig.*) destitute of understanding, judgment, or foresight; undiscerning, obtuse; reckless, heedless; drunk; purposeless, random; imperfectly addressed [of letters, applied also to the Post officials (called **blind-officers, blind-readers**) who deal with such letters]; (*Bot.*) having no buds, eyes, or terminal flower; abortive (of a bud). *n.* A blind person; (*pl.*) blind persons collectively; anything which obstructs the light or sight; a blinker for a horse; (*fig.*) a pretence, a pretext; a window-screen, esp. one on rollers for coiling up, or of slats on strips of webbing, (*Am.* a shade); (*slang*) a drunken fit. *v.t.* To make blind, to deprive of sight (permanently or temporarily); to darken, make dim; (*fig.*) to deceive; to darken the understanding. *v.i.* (*Motor.*) To drive blindly and recklessly. **to fly blind:** (*Aviat.*) To fly by the use of instruments only. **blind alley,** *n.* A street, road, or alley walled-up at the end. **blind-blocking, -tooling,** *n.* (*Bookbinding*) Ornamentation done by impressing hot tools without gold-leaf. **blind-coal,** *n.* A flameless anthracite. **blind ditch,** *n.* A concealed ditch. **blind-door, -window,** *n.* Door or window that is walled-up. **blind drunk,** *adv.* Too drunk to be able to see straight. **blind-fish,** *n.* A fish without functional eyes found in underground streams, *e.g.* the *Amblyopsis spelæus* of Mammoth Cave, Kentucky. **blindfold,** *v.t.* To cover the eyes, esp. with a bandage; (*fig.*) to darken the understanding; *a.* Having the eyes bandaged; (*fig.*) devoid of foresight. **blind-lantern,** *n.* A dark lantern. **blind-man's-buff,** *n.* A game in which a player has his eyes bandaged, and has to catch and identify one of the others. **blind man's holiday,** *n.* The hour just before artificial light is employed. **blind side,**

n. The direction in which one is most easily assailed; a weakness, a foible. **blind spot,** *n.* A part of the retina insensitive to light, owing to the passage through it of the optic nerve; (*Radio.*) a point within the service area of a station where signals are received very faintly; (*fig.*) a tendency to overlook faults, etc. **blind-stitch,** *n.* Sewing that does not show, or that shows at the back only. *v.t.* and *i.* To sew in this manner. **blind-story,** *n.* A series of arches below the clerestory, admitting no light; a triforium. **blind-wall,** *n.* A wall with no opening in it. **blind-worm,** *n.* An aberrant British lizard, *Anguis fragilis*, called also the slow-worm, erroneously supposed to be blind, from the small size of its eyes. **blindage,** *n.* (*Mil.*) A screen for troops, a mantelet. **blinder,** *n.* One who or that which blinds; (*Am.*) a horse's blinker. **blindly,** *adv.* **blindness,** *n.* Sightlessness; lack of intellectual or moral perception; ignorance, folly, recklessness.

blink (blingk) [M.E. *blenken* (cp. Dut. and G. *blinken*; A.-S. *blencan*, see BLENCH (1))], *v.i.* To move the eyelids; to open and shut the eyes; to look with winking eyelids, to look unsteadily; to shine fitfully; to peep, to wink, to twinkle. *v.t.* To shut the eyes to; to evade, to shirk. *a.* Blinking, twinkling. *n.* A gleam, a glimmer, a twinkle; a glance, a twinkling (cp. ICE-BLINK]. ***blinkard,** *n.* One who blinks; a person with imperfect sight; an obtuse or foolish person. **blinked,** *a.* Affected with blinking. **blinker,** *n.* One who blinks; (*pl.*) spectacles to cure squinting, or to protect the eyes from cold, dust, etc.; leather screens to prevent a horse from seeing sideways.

blip (blip), *n.* (*colloq.*) An irregularity in the linear trace on a radar screen indicating the presence of an aircraft, vessel, etc.

blirt (blĕrt) [Sc., prob. onomat.], *v.i.* To weep violently. *v.t.* To disfigure with weeping. *n.* A violent burst of tears; a gust of wind and rain.

bliss (blis) [A.-S. *blis, bliss, blīths* (*blīthe*, happy); sense influenced by BLESS (1)], *n.* Happiness of the highest kind; the perfect joy of heaven; heaven. **blissful,** *a.* Full of bliss; causing bliss. **blissfully,** *adv.* In a blissful manner. **blissfully ignorant of:** Quite unaware of. **blissfulness,** *n.* The state of being blissful.

blister (blis' tėr) [M.E. *blister, blester*, perh. from O.F. *blestre*, Icel. *blāstr*, a blowing, a swelling (*blāsa*, to blow)], *n.* A pustule or thin vesicle raised on the skin by some injury or vesicatory, and containing a watery fluid or serum; any similar swelling on a plant, metal, a painted surface, etc.; (*Med.*) a vesicatory; anything applied to raise a blister. *v.i.* To rise in blisters; to be covered with blisters; (*Austral. colloq.*) to overcharge, to demand an exorbitant sum. *v.t.* To raise blisters on, esp. by a vesicatory; (*fig.*) to criticize spitefully; (*slang*) to bore; to damn. **blister-fly,** *n.* The Spanish fly, *Cantharis vesicatoria*, used to raise blisters. **blister-plaster,** *n.* A plaster for raising a blister. **blister-steel,** *n.* Steel having a blistered surface, the result of absorption of carbon in its conversion from iron. **blistered,** *a.* Affected with blisters; *ornamented with puffs. **blistery,** *a.* Full of blisters.

blithe (blīth) [A.-S. *blīthe* (cp. O.H.G. *blīdi*, Icel. *blīthr*, Dut. *blijde*)], *a.* Gay, cheerful, joyous; merry, sprightly. **blithely,** *adv.* **blitheness,** *n.* **blithesome,** *a.* Blithe; cheery. **blithesomeness,** *n.*

blithering (blith' ėr ing) [BLETHER], *a.* (*slang*) Nonsensical, contemptible.

blitz (blits) [G., lightning], *n.* (*colloq.*) Intense enemy onslaught, esp. an air raid.

blizzard (bliz' ȧrd) [etym. doubtful; perhaps fashioned on BLOW, BLAST, etc.], *n.* A snow-squall; a furious storm of snow and wind; (*Am.*) a poser, a knock-down blow in an argument.

bloat (blōt) [M.E. *bloat, blowt*, soft (prob. var. of *blote*, see BLOATER)], *v.t.* To cause to swell; to puff up; (*fig.*) to make vain or conceited. *v.i.* To swell; to grow turgid. ***a.** Soft, flabby; swollen, esp. with self-indulgence. *n.* A cattle disease, hoove. **bloated,** *a.* (*fig.*) swollen, inflated, pampered, puffed up with pride. **bloatedness,** *n.* The quality of being bloated.

bloater (blō' tėr) [M.E. *blote*, soft, soaked (Icel. *blautr*), whence *bloat*, to cure, *bloat* or *bloated*, herring, bloater], *n.* A herring partially cured by steeping in dry salt and smoking.

blob (blob) [BLEB], *n.* A globular drop of liquid; a spot of colour; *a pustule; (*Naut.*) the round mass forming the base of an iron post. **blobber-lipped,** *a.* Having swollen, pouting lips.

bloc (blok) [F.], *n.* (*Pol.*) A combination of parties, or of nations.

block (blok) [prob. from F. *bloc* (O.H.G. *bloh*, M.H.G. *bloch*, G. *block*)], *n.* A solid mass of wood or stone; a log, a tree-stump; the piece of wood on which criminals were beheaded; death by beheading; a compact or connected group of houses; a mould on which a thing is shaped; a piece of wood or metal on which figures are engraved for printing from; a cliché taken from such a block; a solid unshaped mass of any material; (*Cricket*) the position in which a batsman blocks balls; a block-hole; a pulley, or system of pulleys, mounted in a frame or shell; (*Parl.*) a notice of opposition to a Bill (*see below*); (*fig.*) an obstruction, a hindrance, an impediment or its effects; a blockhead; (*slang*) the head. *v.t.* To enclose, to shut up; to stop up, to obstruct; to impede progress or advance; to stop a train by a block-signal; to shape a hat on the block; to subject to a blockade; (*Bookbinding*) to emboss a cover by impressing a device; (*Cricket*) to stop a ball dead without attempting to hit it; (*Parl.*) to give notice of opposition to a Bill, thus preventing its being proceeded with at certain times; (*fig.*) to block up, to obstruct. **barber's block:** A head-shaped piece of wood for mounting wigs upon. **block-book,** *n.* A book printed from wooden blocks on which the letters or pictures have been cut in relief. **block-buster,** *n.* (*colloq.*) A very heavy and effective aerial bomb. **block-chain,** *n.* An endless chain on bicycles and other vehicles. **blockhead,** *n.* A stupid, dull person. **block-hole,** *n.* (*Cricket*) A mark made a yard in front of the wicket. **blockhouse,** *n.* A detached fort covering some strategical point; a one-storied timber building, with loop-holes for musketry; a house of squared timber. **block-letters,** *n.pl.* Wood type of large size used in printing; imitation in handwriting of printed capital letters. **block-machine,** *n.* A machine for making tackle-blocks. **block-plan,** *n.* A sketch-plan showing the outline and relative situation of buildings without detail. **block-printing,** *n.* Printing from engraved wooden blocks. **block-signal,** *n.* A signal to stop a train when the next section of the line is not clear. **block-system,** *n.* A system by which a railway line is divided into sections, and no train is allowed to pass into any section till it is signalled clear. **block-tin,** *n.* Tin cast into ingots. **to block in:** To sketch roughly the broad masses of a picture or drawing. **to block out:** To mark out work roughly. **to block up:** To confine. **blockish,** *a.* Stupid, dull; rough, clumsy. **blockishly,** *adv.* **blockishness,** *n.*

blockade (blok ād') [as prec.], *n.* The investment of a place by sea or land, so as to compel surrender by starvation or prevent communication with the outside; imprisonment by weather or other causes. **paper blockade:** A blockade that has been proclaimed but not rendered effective. **blockade-runner,** *n.* A vessel that runs or attempts to run into a blockaded port; the owner, captain, or any of the sailors of such a vessel.

bloke (blōk) [etym. unknown], *n.* (*slang*) A man, a fellow.

blond, blonde (used with fem. substantives), (blond) [F. (Sp. *blondo*, It. *biondo*, late L. *blundus*), prob. of Teut. origin], *a.* Fair or light in colour;

having light hair and a fair complexion. *n.* One who has light hair and a fair complexion (the form **blonde** is used of women). **blonde lace,** *n.* A kind of lace, orig. made of raw silk.

blood (blŭd) [A.-S. *blōd* (cp. Goth. *blōth,* G. *blut,* Icel. *blōth,* Dut. *bloed*)], *n.* The red fluid circulating by means of veins and arteries, through the bodies of man and other vertebrates; any analogous fluid in the invertebrates; (*fig.*) lineage, descent; honourable or high birth, family relationship, kinship; slaughter, murder, bloodshed; the guilt of murder; temperament, passion; vitality, mettle; a man of a fiery spirit, a rake, a dandy, a dissipated character; (*colloq.*) a penny-dreadful; the juice of anything, esp. if red; sap; the supposed seat of the emotions; the sensual nature of man; blood shed in sacrifice. *v.t.* To cause blood to flow from, to bleed; to inure to blood (as a hound); (*fig.*) to exasperate; to stain with blood; to render bloody. **bloody,** *a.* Of or pertaining to blood; stained or running with blood; attended with bloodshed; (*fig.*) cruel, murderous; (*slang*) damned, devilish; very, exceedingly (prob. from the bloods or hooligans of rank in the seventeenth or eighteenth century). **'sblood,** *int.* By God's blood. **bad blood:** Resentment, ill-feeling. **in cold blood:** Not in anger; deliberately. **blood and thunder:** Sensational literature; (*slang*) a mixture of port wine and brandy. **flesh and blood:** The carnal nature of man; human nature. **half-blood:** Connexion through one parent only; a half-breed. **the blood:** Royal blood; the royal family. **whole blood:** Connexion by both parents. **blood bank,** *n.* The place where blood for transfusion is stored. **blood-bought,** *a.* Bought or redeemed by blood, or at the expense of life. **blood-brother,** *n.* A brother by both parents. **blood-curdling:** (*fig.*) Harrowing, exciting. **blood donor,** *n.* (*Med.*) One from whom blood is taken for transfusion. **blood-feud,** *n.* A feud arising out of murder or homicide; a vendetta. **blood-frozen,** *a.* Having the blood chilled. **blood groups,** *n.pl.* (*Med.*) The four groups into which human beings have been classified for purposes of blood-transfusion. **blood-guilt, blood-guiltiness,** *n.* Murder or homicide. **blood-guilty,** *a.* Guilty of murder or homicide. **blood-heat,** *n.* The ordinary heat of blood in a healthy human body (about 98° F.). **blood-horse,** *n.* A horse of good breed or pedigree. **bloodhound,** *n.* A variety of hound remarkable for keenness of scent, used for tracking fugitives; (*fig.*) one who relentlessly pursues an opponent; a detective, a spy. ***bloodied,** *a.* Stained with blood. **bloodless,** *a.* Without blood; without effusion of blood; (*fig.*) spiritless; unfeeling. **bloodlessly,** *adv.* **blood-letting,** *n.* The act, process, or art of taking blood from the body; phlebotomy; (*facet.*) bloodshed. **blood-money,** *n.* Money paid for evidence of information leading to a conviction on a capital charge; money paid to the next of kin as compensation for the murder of a relative. **blood-orange,** *n.* An orange having pulp and juice of a reddish hue. **blood plasma,** *n.* Blood from which all red corpuscles have been removed. **blood poisoning,** *n.* A diseased condition set up by the entrance of septic matter into the blood. **blood pressure,** *n.* (*Med.*) Pressure of the blood on the walls of the containing arteries. **blood rain,** *n.* Rain tinted reddish from contact with dust particles in the air. **blood-red,** *a.* Red as blood. **blood-relation,** *n.* A relation by descent, not merely by marriage. **blood-shed,** *n.* The act of shedding blood; murder; slaughter in war. **bloodshot,** *a.* Red and inflamed; suffused with blood (of the eye). **blood-spavin,** *n.* A dilatation of the vein inside the hock of a horse. **blood sports,** *n.pl.* Sports entailing the killing of animals, such as fox-hunting. **blood-stain,** *n.* A stain produced by blood. **blood-stained,** *a.* Stained by blood; guilty of bloodshed. **blood stock,** *n.* Collective term for thoroughbred horses. **blood-stone,** *n.* Heliotrope, a variety of quartz with blood-like spots of jasper; other stones similarly spotted, which, like heliotrope, were supposed to stanch bleeding when worn as amulets; red iron-ore. **blood-sucker,** *n.* Any animal which sucks blood, esp. the leech; (*fig.*) an extortioner. **blood-tax,** *n.* Conscription; compulsory military service. **bloodthirsty,** *a.* Eager to shed blood; delighting in sanguinary deeds. **bloodthirstiness,** *n.* **blood-transfusion,** *n.* (*Med.*) Transference of blood from the vein of a healthy person to the vein of one whose blood is deficient in quantity or quality. **blood-vessel,** *n.* A vessel in which blood circulates in the animal body; an artery or a vein. ***blood-wite,** *n.* A fine for shedding blood paid to the king, in addition to the wergild paid to the family. **bloodwood, blood-tree,** *n.* A term applied to several varieties of trees that exude a bright red gum. **blood-worm,** *n.* A small red earth-worm used by anglers. **blood-wort,** *n.* A popular name for various plants, either from their red leaves or roots, or from the notion that they were efficacious in stanching blood. **bloody-bones,** *n.* A bugbear, a fright [RAWHEAD AND BLOODY BONES]. **bloody-faced,** *a.* Having the face stained with blood; (*fig.*) sanguinary. **bloody flux,** *n.* An old popular name for dysentery. **bloody-hand,** *n.* (*Her.*) The Ulster badge borne by baronets. **bloody-minded,** *a.* Of a cruel disposition. **bloody nose,** *n.* A bleeding nose. **bloody sweat,** *n.* The sweating sickness; transudation of blood through the pores, esp. used of the agony of Christ in Gethsemane. ***bloodily,** *adv.* **bloodiness,** *n.* The state or condition of being bloody; abounding with blood, as a battle-field.

bloom (1) (bloom) [Icel. *blōm,* a blossom (cp. O.H.G. *bluomo,* G. *blume*), from the root *blō-,* to blow, to flourish (cp. L. *flos florēre*)], *n.* A blossom, a flower; the delicate dust on newly gathered plums, grapes, etc.; the yellow sheen on well-tanned leather; lustre, efflorescence; (*Optics*) a lens-coating that increases its transparency; a kind of currant; (*fig.*) flush, glow, prime, perfection. *v.i.* To blossom, to come into flower; to be at the highest point of perfection or beauty. **bloomer** (1), *n.* A plant that blooms (esp. in comb., as an *early-bloomer*); (*slang*) a mistake, a foolish blunder. **in bloom:** Flowering, blossoming. **blooming,** *a.* In a state of bloom, flourishing; bright, lustrous; (*slang*) euphemistically for bloody. **bloomingly,** *adv.* **bloomless,** *a.* **bloomy,** *a.* Full of blooms, flowery.

bloom (2) (bloom) [A.-S. *blōma*], *n.* A mass of iron that has undergone the first hammering. *v.t.* To hammer or squeeze the ball, or lump of iron, from the puddling furnace into a bloom. **bloomery,** *n.* The apparatus for making blooms out of puddled iron; a furnace for making malleable iron by a direct process.

bloomer (2) (bloo' mėr) [Mrs. *Bloomer* (Am.), who introduced it (1850)], *n.* A style of dress for ladies, consisting of a short skirt, and loose trousers gathered round the ankles; a woman wearing such a dress; a broad-brimmed straw hat for women.

***blore** (blôr) [prob. onomat.], *n.* A violent gust or blast.

blossom (blos' ŏm) [A.-S. *blōstma, blōstm* (prob. cognate with BLOOM (1))], *n.* The flower of a plant, esp. considered as giving promise of fruit; a flower; the mass of flowers on a fruit-tree; (*fig.*) promise of future excellence or development; a promising person. *v.i.* To put forth flowers; to bloom. **blossomless,** *a.* **blossomy,** *a.* Full of blossoms.

blot (1) (blot) [etym. doubtful], *n.* A spot or stain of ink or other discolouring matter; a blotting out by way of correction; a dark patch; (*fig.*) blemish, disgrace, disfigurement, defect; a fault; a disgraceful action. *v.t.* (*past & p.p.* **blotted**) To spot or stain with ink or other discolouring matter; to obliterate; to dry with blotting-paper; to apply blotting-paper to; (*fig.*) to darken, to disfigure, to sully. *v.i.* To make blots, to become blotted. **to blot one's copybook,** (*colloq.*) To commit an indiscretion. **to blot out:** To obliterate, to efface. **blotter,** *n.* One who or that which blots; a scribbler; a paper pad or book for absorbing superfluous ink from paper after writing; a blotting-pad. **blottesque** (blot esk'), *a.* Characterized (as a painting) by masses of colour heavily laid on. **blotting-paper,** *n.* Absorbent paper for drying up ink. **blotting-book, -pad,** *n.* A book or pad made up of this.

blot (2) (blot) [etym. doubtful (prob. conn. with Dan. *blot*, bare, naked)], *n.* An exposed piece at backgammon; (*fig.*) a weak point, a failing; a mark, a butt. **to hit a blot:** To take an exposed piece at backgammon; (*fig.*) to detect a fault.

blotch (bloch) [prob. from BLOT (1)], *n.* A pustule, boil, botch; a blot; a patch; a clumsy daub. *v.t.* (*Sc.*) To blot. **blotched,** *a.* Marked with blotches. **blotchy,** *a.* Full of blotches.

blotto (blot' ō), *a.* (*slang*) Unconscious with drink.

blouse (blouz) [F. (etym. unknown)], *n.* A light, loose, upper garment resembling a smock-frock belted at the waist; a woman's loose bodice belted in at the waist, (*Am.*) a shirt-waist.

blow (1) (blō) [A.-S. *blāwan* (cp. O.H.G. *blāhan*, G. *blähen*, L. *flāre*)], *v.i.* (*past* **blew,** *p.p.* **blown**) To move as a current of air; to send a current of air from the mouth; to pant, to puff; to sound, to give forth musical notes (as a horn); to eject water and air from the spiracles (as Cetaceans); *(*fig.*) to boast, to talk big; (*slang*) to squander money, to spend. *v.t.* To drive a current of air upon; to inflate with air; to drive by a current of air; to put out of breath; to sound a wind instrument or a note on it; to taint by depositing eggs upon (as flies); to shatter by explosives; (*fig.*) to spread, as a report; to inflate, to puff up; (*slang*) curse, confound. *n.* A blowing, a blast of air; a breath of fresh air; an egg (of a flesh-fly); oviposition (of flesh-flies); a single operation of the Bessemer converter; (*fig.*) a boast; boastfulness. **I'll be blowed:** *int.* (*slang*) I'll be confounded, etc. **blow it!** Confound it. **to blow hot and cold:** To vacillate; to do one thing at one time, and its opposite at another. **to blow in:** To make an unexpected visit. **to blow off:** To escape with a blowing noise, as steam; to discharge (steam, energy, anger, etc.). **to blow one's own trumpet:** To boast, to sing one's own praises. **to blow out:** To extinguish by blowing; to clear by means of blowing. **to blow over:** To pass away, to subside. **to blow up:** To inflate, to scold, to censure severely; to ruin; to explode, to fly in fragments. ***to blow upon:** To make stale or common; to bring into discredit; to expose. **to blow the gaff:** (*slang*) To let out a secret. **blow-ball,** *n.* The downy head of the dandelion and allied plants. **blow-fly,** *n.* The meat-fly. **blow-hole,** *n.* An air-hole; a hole in the ice to which seals and whales come to breathe; (*pl.*) the spiracles of a Cetacean. **blow-lamp,** *n.* Lamp used in soldering, brazing, etc.; burner used to remove paint. **blow-line,** *n.* (*Angling*) A light line with real or artificial bait at the end, allowed to float over the surface of water with the wind. **blow-out** (blō' out), *n.* (*slang*) A hearty meal. **blow-pipe,** *n.* A tube used for increasing combustion by directing a current of air into a flame; a pipe used in glass-blowing; a tube used by American Indians for shooting darts by means of the breath. **blower,** *n.* One who or that which blows; a Cetacean, a whale; a contrivance for creating an artificial current of air; an escape of gas in a mine; the fissure through which this escapes; (*colloq.*) a telephone, speaking-tube, etc. **blowing-machine,** *n.* A machine for creating a current of air. **blowy,** *a.* Windy; exposed to the wind.

blow (2) (blō) [A.-S. *blōwan* (O.H.G. *bluojan*, G. *blühen*, cp. L. *florēre*, see also BLOOM (1))], *v.i.* To blossom; (*fig.*) to bloom, to flourish. *n.* The state of blossoming; bloom; a display of blossoms.

blow (3) (blō) [etym. doubtful], *n.* A stroke with the fist or any weapon or instrument; an act of hostility; (*fig.*) a severe shock; a sudden and painful calamity. **to come to blows:** To fight.

blowze (blouz) [conn. with BLUSH], *n.* *A wench, a beggar's wench; a red-faced, bloated woman; a woman with disordered hair. **blowzed,** *a.* Red-faced, bloated, dishevelled, slatternly. **blowzy,** *a.* Having a bloated face; blowzed.

blub (blŭb) [short for BLUBBER], *v.i.* (*slang*) To weep, shed tears.

blubber (blŭb' ėr) [prob. imit. in origin (cp. BABBLE, BLEB, BUBBLE)], *n.* The fat underlying the skin in whales and other Cetaceans, from which train-oil is prepared; weeping; (*Naut.*) a sea-nettle or jelly-fish. *a.* Having swollen, pouting lips; blobber-lipped. *v.i.* To weep in a noisy manner. *v.t.* To wet and disfigure with weeping; to utter with sobs and tears.

Blucher (bloo' kėr, bloo' chėr) [from the Prussian Field-Marshal von *Blücher* (1742–1819)], *n.* (*usu. in pl.*) A strong leather half-boot.

bludgeon (blŭj' ŏn) [etym. doubtful], *n.* A short, thick stick, sometimes loaded; (*Am.*) a black-jack. *v.t.* To strike with this.

blue (bloo) [O.F. *bleu* (O.H.G. *blāo*, G. *blau*, O. Teut. *blæwoz*, cp. L. *flāvus*, yellow)], *a.* Of the colour of the cloudless sky or deep sea; applied also to smoke, vapour, distant landscape, steel, skim-milk, etc.; *livid; dressed in blue; belonging to the political party which adopts blue for its colour (in England, usually the Conservative); (*fig.*) miserable, low-spirited; learned, pedantic (of women); (*slang*) obscene, smutty. *n.* A blue colour; a blue pigment; a blue powder used by laundresses; a blue jacket or cap worn as colours; a blue substance, object, or animal (as explained by context); a blue-coat boy; the sky; the sea; a man who plays for his University in sport or athletics; (*Austral.*) a summons. *v.t.* To make blue; to treat with laundress's blue; *v.i.* (*slang*) To squander money. **to burn blue:** To burn (as candles) with a blue flame, as an omen of death, or as indicating the presence of ghosts or evil spirits. **to look blue:** To look frightened or depressed. **deep blue, Navy blue, Prussian blue:** Different shades of dark blue. **true blue:** Staunch, faithful, genuine. **bluey** (bloo' i), *a.* Rather blue. **blue bell,** *n.* The blue bell of Scotland, *Campanula rotundifolia*; the wild hyacinth of England, *Scilla nutans.* **blueberry,** *n.* (*Am.*) The genus *Vaccinium*; (*Austral.*) the native currant. **blue-black,** *a.* Of a blue colour that is almost black; black with a tinge of blue. **blue-bird,** *n.* A small American bird, *Sylvia sialis*; (*fig.*) a symbol of happiness. **blue blood,** *n.* Aristocratic descent; good family. **blue-blooded,** *a.* Of aristocratic descent; of good family. **blue-bonnet,** *n.* A flat Scotch cap, or bonnet, of blue cloth; hence, a peasant or soldier wearing such a bonnet; (*Sc.*) a popular name for species of *Centaurea* and scabious. **Blue book,** *n.* A book bound in a blue cover; esp. an official report of Parliament or the Privy Council; (*Am.*) a list of Government officials with their salaries, etc. **blue-bottle,** *n.* The blue cornflower, *Centaurea cyanus*; applied also loosely to other blue flowers; the meat-fly or blow-fly, *Musca vomitoria*; *a beadle, a policeman. **blueing,** *n.* (*Am.*) Laundress's blue. **blue-cap,** *n.* A blue-bonnet; a salmon in its first year; the blue titmouse, *Parus cæruleus.* **blue cat,** *n.* A Siberian cat, valued for its slaty-blue fur. **blue-coat,** *n.* A coat of blue, formerly the dress of the poor classes; hence (often) of almoners and children in charity schools; hence, any individual of these classes. **blue-coat boy,** *n.* A boy wearing the blue coat of a charity school, esp. a scholar of Christ's Hospital. **blue-cod,** *n.* (*N. Zealand*) an edible salt-water fish. **blue devils,** *n.pl.* Low spirits; the illusions of delirium tremens. **blue eye,** *n.* *A livid contusion round the eye from a blow; *a dark circle round the eye from weeping; an eye with a blue iris; (*Austral.*) the blue-faced honey-eater. **blue fish,** *n.* (*Austral.*) A kind of bream. **blue funk,** *n.* Abject terror. **blue-gown,** *n.* The dress of an almoner or licensed beggar in Scotland; an almoner, a licensed beggar. **blue-grass,** *n.* (*Am.*) The rich grass of the limestone lands of Kentucky and Tennessee. **Blue-grass Country,** *n.* The regions just mentioned. **blue gum tree,** *n.* An Australian tree, *Eucalyptus globulus.* **bluejacket,** *n.* A sailor in the British

Navy. **blue-john** [prob. from F. *bleujaune*, blue-yellow], *n.* Blue fluorspar. **blue-light,** *n.* A composition burning with a blue flame used at sea as a night-signal. **Blue Mantle,** *n.* One of the four pursuivants in the College of Arms. **blue moon,** *n.* (*fig.*) A very rare or unknown occurrence. **blue mould,** *n.* A fungus growing in mature cheese. **blue-nose,** *n* (*Am.*) A native of Nova Scotia. **blue pencil,** *v.t.* (*colloq.*) To censor. **Blue Peter,** *n.* (*Naut.*) A small blue flag, with a white square in the centre, used as a signal for sailing. **blue pill,** *n.* An anti-bilious pill made from mercury. **blue pointer,** *n.* (*Austral.*) A voracious shark with a blue back. **blue print,** *n.* A plan or drawing printed on specially sensitized paper. The print is composed of white lines on a blue background, and is much used for scale and working drawings of engineering designs, electrical circuits, etc. **blue ribbon,** *n.* The ribbon of the Garter; hence, the greatest distinction, the first prize; a total abstainer's badge. **blue-ribbonite,** *n.* One who wears a blue ribbon as a badge of total abstinence. **blue-ribbonism,** *n.* The tenets or practice of total abstinence. **blue rock,** *n.* A kind of domestic pigeon. **blue ruin,** *n.* Bad gin. **blue stone,** *n.* Sulphate of copper. **bluestocking,** *a.* Wearing blue (worsted instead of black silk) stockings; hence, not in evening dress; applied (contemptuously) to a literary society that met at Montague House, London, in the latter part of the 18th cent.; hence (of women) affecting learning or literary tastes; *n.* A woman affecting learning or literary tastes. **bluestone,** *n.* A dark building-stone found in Australia and New Zealand. **blue vitriol:** Hydrous sulphate of copper. **blue water,** *n.* The open sea. **blue-water school,** *n.* The party of naval strategists who consider the Navy a sufficient defence for the British Isles. **old blue:** A man who was once a University athlete. **light-blue, dark blue:** The respective colours of Eton and Harrow Schools, and of Cambridge and Oxford Universities in their athletic contests. **the Blue:** One of the three former divisions of the British Navy. **the Blues:** The Royal Horse Guards; the Conservatives; form of Negro and modern music expressing gaiety and sadness at the same time. **the blues** [BLUE DEVILS]; **bluely,** *adv.* **blueness,** *n.* **bluish,** *a.* **bluishly,** *adv.* **bluishness,** *n.*

bluff (1) (blŭf) [Naut., etym. doubtful (cp. M.Dut. *blaf*, flat, broad)], *a.* Having a broad, flattened face or front; (*fig.*) abrupt, blunt, frank, outspoken. **bluff-bowed, bluff-headed,** *a.* (*Naut.*) Having vertical or nearly vertical bows. *n.* A cliff or headland with a broad, precipitous front. **bluffly,** *adv.* **bluffness,** *n.* **bluffy,** *a.* Having bold headlands; blunt, off-handed.

bluff (2) (blŭf) [etym. unknown], *n.* A blinker for a horse; a game of cards, called also poker; (*slang*) an excuse, a blind; the action of bluffing at cards; boastful language; empty threats or promises. *v.t.* To hoodwink; to impose upon one's adversary (at cards) by making him believe one's hand is stronger than it is, and inducing him to throw up the game; (*fig.*) to treat rivals, political opponents, or foreign powers in this way.

blunder (blŭn′ dĕr) [etym. doubtful], *v.i.* To err grossly; to act blindly or stupidly; to flounder, to stumble. *v.t.* To utter thoughtlessly, to mismanage. *n.* A gross mistake, a stupid error. **to blunder upon:** To find or succeed by luck. **to blunder away:** To throw away one's advantages. **blunderer,** *n.* One who habitually blunders. **blunderhead,** *n.* A dunderhead; a muddle-headed fellow. **blundering,** *a.* **blunderingly,** *adv.*

blunderbuss (blŭn′ dĕr bŭs) [Dut. *donderbus*, thunder-gun], *n.* A short gun, of large bore, widening at the muzzle.

blunge (blŭnj) [prob. onomat.], *v.t.* (*Pottery*) To mix (clay, powdered flint, etc.) in a pug-mill.

***blunket** (blŭng′ kĕt) [prob. cognate with BLANKET], *a.* Grey; sky-coloured.

blunt (blŭnt) [etym. doubtful], *a.* Dull, stupid, obtuse; without edge or point; abrupt, unceremonious; rough, unpolished; *bare, naked. *n.* A short, thick make of sewing-needle; (*slang*) ready money. *v.t.* To make less sharp, keen, or acute; (*fig.*) to deaden, to dull. *v.i.* To become blunt. **blunt-witted,** *a.* Dull of understanding. **bluntish,** *a.* **bluntly,** *adv.* **bluntness,** *n.*

blur (blĕr) [etym. doubtful], *n.* A smear, a blot, a stain; a dim, misty effect. *v.t.* To smear, to blot; to stain, to sully; to render misty and indistinct; to dim.

blurb (blĕrb) [etym. unknown], *n.* A synopsis of a book, usually printed on the dust-jacket.

blurt (blĕrt) [prob. an imitative word], *v.i.* *To puff out the lips contemptuously; to burst into tears. *v.t.* To utter abruptly (usually with *out*). *n.* An impetuous outburst.

blush (blŭsh) [A.-S. *āblisian* (cp. Dut. *blozen*, to blush, Dan. *blus*, a blaze, a torch, A.-S. *bæl-blys*, a fire-blaze)], *v.i.* To become red in the face from shame or other emotion, to assume a bright-red colour; to be ashamed; to bloom. *v.t.* *To make red; (*fig.*) to express by blushing. *n.* The reddening of the face produced by shame, modesty, or any similar cause; (*fig.*) a crimson or roseate hue; a flush of light. **at the first blush, at first blush:** At the first glance; at first sight. **to put to the blush:** To cause to blush; to make ashamed. **blush-rose,** *n.* A white rose with pink tinge. **blushful,** *a.* Full of or suffused with blushes; modest, self-conscious. **blushfully,** *adv.* **blushing,** *a.* That blushes; modest; ruddy, roseate; blooming. **blushingly,** *adv.* **blushless,** *a.*

bluster (blŭs′ tĕr) [onomat.; cp. BLAST], *v.i.* To blow boisterously; to be agitated (as water by wind); to make a loud boisterous noise; to play the bully, to swagger, to boast. *v.t.* To disarray, to dishevel. *n.* Boisterous, blowing, inflated talk, swaggering; empty vaunts and threats. **blusterer,** *n.* One who or that which blusters. **blustering,** ***blusterous, blustery,** *a.* Blowing boisterously; tempestuous; hectoring, boastful. **blusteringly,** *adv.*

bo, boh (bō) [imit.], *int.* An exclamation intended to surprise or frighten; (*Am. colloq.*) a meaningless form of address. **to say bo to a goose:** To open one's mouth, to speak. **bo-peep,** *n.* A childish game in which a player suddenly looks out from a hiding-place and cries 'bo!' to startle his or her playmates.

Boa (bō′ à) [L. (etym. unknown)], *n.* A genus of large South American serpents which kill their prey by crushing (popularly applied also to the pythons, which are from the Old World); a long fur or feather tippet worn round the neck. **boa-constrictor,** *n.* A Brazilian serpent, the best-known species of the genus Boa; any very large snake which kills its prey by constriction.

boanerges (bō à nĕr′ jēz) [Gr., from Heb. *b'ney regesh*, sons of thunder (Mark iii. 17)], *n.* A loud, vociferous preacher or orator.

boar (bôr) [A.-S. *bār* (cp. Dut. *beer*, Gr. *bār*)], *n.* The uncastrated male of the domesticated or the wild swine. **wild boar:** The male of *Sus scrofa*, wild in Europe, Asia, and Africa. **boar-spear,** *n.* A spear used in boar-hunting. **boarish,** *a.* Swinish, brutal; (*fig.*) sensual, cruel. **boar's foot,** *n.* The green hellebore, *Helleborus viridis*.

board (bôrd) [A.-S. *bord*, board, plank, table (cp. Dut. *boord*, M.H.G. and G. *bort*, Icel. *borth*); *bord*, in the sense of border, rim, ship's side, appears to be a distinct word which was early associated; and at later periods the F. *bord* (from Teut.) influenced the development of meaning], *n.* A piece of timber of considerable length, and of moderate breadth and thickness; a flat slab of wood, used as a table, for exhibiting notices, and other purposes; a table or frame on which games (as chess, draughts, etc.) are played; a thick substance formed of layers of paper, etc., pasted or squeezed together; a piece of stout pasteboard or millboard used as one of the sides of a bound book; a table, esp. for meals; a table spread for a meal; food served at table; daily provisions; one's keep, or money in lieu of keep; a council table; the members of a council; the persons who have the management of some public trust or business concern; (*Naut.*) the side of a ship; (*Mining*) a passage driven across the grain of the coal; (*pl.*) the stage; (*Austral.*) the floor of a shearing-shed, the shearers there employed. *v.t.* To furnish or cover with boards; to provide with daily meals (and now usu. with lodging); to board out; to attack and enter (a ship) by force; to go on a ship, to embark; *to border upon; (*fig.*) to accost, to make up to. *v.i.* To have one's meals (and usu. lodging) at another person's house. **above board:** Open, unconcealed, openly. **bed and board:** Conjugal relations. **board and lodging:** Meals and sleeping-quarters. **by the board:** (*Naut.*) Overboard, by the ship's side. **on board:** In or into a ship; in or into a train, tramcar, or omnibus. **board-school,** *n.* A school managed by a Board, as established by the Elementary Education Act, 1870. **board-wages,** *n.pl.* Wages given to servants in lieu of food. **board-walk,** *n.* (*Am.*) A seaside promenade made of planks. **to board out:** To place at board; to take one's meals out. **boarder,** *n.* One who has his food at the house of another; a scholar who is boarded and lodged at a school; (*Naut.*) one who boards an enemy's ship. **boarding,** *n.* The action of the verb TO BOARD; a structure of boards. **boarding-clerk,** *n.* A clerk in the Customs or in a mercantile firm, who communicates with the masters of ships on their arrival in port. **boarding-house,** *n.* A house in which board may be had. **boarding officer,** *n.* (*Naut.*) Officer who boards a ship to examine bill of health, etc. **boarding-out,** *n.* The obtaining of stated meals at another person's house; the placing of pauper children in the houses of poor people, by whom they are treated as their own. **boarding-school,** *n.* A school in which pupils are boarded as well as taught.

boast (bōst) [etym. doubtful], *n.* Proud, vainglorious assertion, a vaunt, a brag; an occasion of pride; laudable exultation. *v.i.* To brag, to praise oneself, to speak ostentatiously or vaingloriously. *v.t.* To extol, to speak of with pride; (*fig.*) to have as worthy of pride. **boaster,** *n.* One who boasts, a bragger, a braggadocio. **boastful,** *a.* Full of boasting; vainglorious. **boastfully,** *adv.* **boastfulness,** *n.* **boastingly,** *adv.*

boat (bōt) [A.-S. *bāt*; etym. obscure, prob. from Teut. (whence Icel. *bātr,* Dut. *boot,* and perh. F. *bateau,* etc.)], *n.* A small vessel, generally undecked and propelled by oars or sails; applied also to fishing vessels, packets, and passenger steamers; a vessel or utensil resembling a boat, a sauce-boat. *v.t.* To transport in a boat. *v.i.* To take boat, to row in a boat. **in the same boat:** In the same circumstances or position. **ship's boat:** A boat carried on board ship. **boat-bill,** *n.* The South American genus *Cancroma,* allied to the herons, esp. *Cancroma cochlearia,* from the shape of the bill. **boat-fly,** *n.* A boat-shaped water-bug, *Notonecta glauca.* **boat-hook,** *n.* (*Naut.*) A pole with an iron point and hook, used to push or pull a boat. **boat-house,** *n.* A house by the water in which boats are kept. **boatman,** *n.* A man who lets out boats on hire; a man who rows or sails a boat for hire. **boat-race,** *n.* A race between rowing-boats. **boat-train,** *n.* A train conveying passengers to or from a steamer. **boatable,** *a.* (*Am.*) That may be traversed by boat; navigable. **boatage,** *n.* Charges for carriage by boat. **boater,** *n.* A man's stiff straw hat. **boatful, boat-load,** *n.* As much or as many as a boat will hold.

boatswain, bos'n (bō' zŭn), *n.* (*Naut.*) The chief man or foreman of the crew (in the R.N. a warrant officer) who looks after the ship's boats, rigging, flags, cables, etc. **boatswain's mate,** *n.* His chief assistant.

bob (1) (bob) [etym. doubtful; prob. onomat.], *n.* A weight or pendant at the end of a cord, chain, plumb-line, pendulum, etc.; a knot of worms used in fishing for eels; a knot or bunch of hair, a short curl, a bob-wig; the docked tail of a horse; *a chorus or refrain; a short line at the end of a stanza; a shake, a jog; a short jerking action, a curtsy; (*slang*) a shilling; a peal of courses or set of changes in bell-ringing. *v.t.* To move with a short jerking motion; to cut short (as a horse's tail); to rap, to strike lightly; *to cheat, swindle. *v.i.* To have a short jerking motion; to move to and fro or up and down; to dance, to curtsy; to catch at cherries; to fish for eels with a bob. **to bob up:** To emerge suddenly. **treble bob, bob major, bob minor:** Peals in which the bells have a jerking or dodging action; in the first the treble bell is dominant; the others are rung on eight and six bells respectively. **bob-cherry,** *n.* A child's game with cherries suspended on a string. **bob-sled,** *n.* (*Am.*) A conveyance formed of two sleds or sleighs coupled together, used to transport large timber. **bob-sleigh,** *n.* A sleigh with two pairs of runners, one behind the other. **bob-tail,** *n.* A tail (of a horse) cut short; a horse or dog with its tail cut short; a lewd woman; a worthless fellow. **tag-rag and bob-tail:** The rabble. **bob-tail wig,** *n.* A short wig. **bob-tail, bob-tailed,** *a.* Having the tail cut short. **bob-wig,** *n.* A wig having the bottom turned up in bobs or curls, in contradistinction to a full-bottomed wig. **bobbish,** *a.* (*slang*) Well, in good health; brisk.

bob (2) (bob) [prob. from *Robert*], *n.* A person, a fellow. **dry-bob:** (*Eton*) A boy who devotes himself to cricket, tennis, etc., as opposed to a **wet-bob,** who devotes himself to boating. **light-bob:** A light infantry man.

Bobadil (bob' ȧ dil) [character in Jonson's *Every Man in His Humour*], *n.* A braggart.

bobbers (bob' erz), *n.pl.* A name given to the men who unload trawlers.

bobbery (bob' ėr i) [Hind. *bāp re!* O father!], *n.* A row; a fuss.

bobbie pin (bob' i), *n.* (*Am.*) A hair-grip.

bobbin (bob' in) [F. *bobine* (etym. unknown)], *n.* A wooden pin with a head on which thread for making lace, cotton, yarn, wire, etc., is wound and drawn off as required; a piece of wood with a string for actuating a door-latch; a reel, spool. **bobbin-lace, -work,** *n.* Work woven with bobbins. **bobbinet,** *n.* Machine-made cotton net, orig. imitated from bobbin-lace.

bobby (bob' i) [from Sir *Robert* Peel, who introduced the new police, 1828], *n.* (*slang*) A policeman.

bobby soxer, *n.* (*Amer.*) An immature girl who follows enthusiastically the latest adolescent fashions and fads.

bobolink (bob' ȯ link) [earlier *Bob Lincoln* or *Bob o' Lincoln,* from the cry], *n.* An American song-bird, *Dolichonyx oryzivorus,* called also reed-bird and rice-bird.

bobstay (bob' stā) [etym. unknown], *n.* (*Naut.*) A chain or rope for drawing the bowsprit downward and keeping it steady.

bob-tail, etc. [BOB].

Boche (bosh) [F. slang], *n.* A German. *a.*

bock (bok) [a mistaken sense, from F., the G. *bock,* goat, used to describe a strong kind of beer, being taken for a measure], *n.* A large beer-glass; a large glass of beer.

bode (1) (bōd) [A.-S. *bodian* (*bod,* a message, *boda,* a messenger), cp. Icel. *botha,* to announce], *v.t.* To foretell, to presage, to give promise of, to forebode. *v.i.* To portend (well or ill). ***bodeful,** *a.* Ominous, portentous. **bodement,** *n.* An omen, a presage; prognostication. **boding,** *a.* Presaging, ominous. *n.* An omen, presentiment, prediction. **bodingly,** *adv.* Ominously, forebodingly.

***bode** (2) [ABODE, ABIDE].

bodega (bȯ dē' gȧ) [Sp., from L. *apotheca,* Gr. *apothēkē*; see APOTHECARY], *n.* A wine-shop.

***bodge** (boj) [dial. form of BOTCH], *v.t.* To patch; to mend in a clumsy fashion; to construct clumsily. **bodger,** *n.* A botcher, a pedlar.

bodice (bod' is) [orig. *pair of bodies*], *n.* *A quilted inner garment for the upper part of the body (worn by both sexes); *a corset; *a pair of stays; an inner vest worn by women over the corset; a tight-fitting outer vest for women.

***bodikin** (bod' i kin) [BODY, KIN], *n.* A little body. **od's bodikins:** By God's dear body.

bodkin (bod' kin) [etym. unknown], *n.* *A small dagger; an instrument for piercing holes; a large-eyed and blunt-pointed needle for leading a tape or cord through a hem, loop, etc.; a pin for fastening up women's hair; (*Print.*) an awl-like tool for picking out letters in correcting set-up type; (*colloq.*) a third person wedged in between two others. **to ride** or **sit bodkin:** To ride or sit thus.

bodle (bō' dĕl) [perh. from *Bothwell*, an old mint-master], *n.* An old Scotch copper coin; (*fig.*) anything of little value.

Bodleian (bod lē' ản, bod' li ản) [Sir Thomas *Bodley* (1545–1613)], *a.* Of or pertaining to Sir T. Bodley, who in 1597 restored the Library at Oxford University which now bears his name. *n.* The Bodleian Library.

body (bod' i) [A.-S. *bodig*], *n.* The material frame of man or the lower animals; the trunk; the upper part of a dress [BODICE]; a corpse, a dead body; the main or central part of a building, ship, document, book, etc.; the part of a motor-car in which the driver and passengers sit; a collective mass of persons, things, or doctrine, precepts, etc.; matter, substance, as opposed to spirit; a human being, a person, an individual; a society, a corporate body, a corporation; a military force; (*Phil.*) matter, substance, that which has sensible properties; (*Geom.*) any substance, simple or compound; a figure of three dimensions; strength, substantial quality. *v.t.* To clothe with a body; to embody. **heavenly body:** A sun, star, planet, or other mass of matter, distinct from the earth. **of good body:** Having substantial quality, as opposed to thinness, flimsiness, transparency, and the like. **body-colour,** *n.* A pigment having a certain degree of consistence and tingeing power as distinct from a wash; a colour rendered opaque by the addition of white. **bodyguard,** *n.* A guard for the person of a sovereign or dignitary; retinue, following. **body politic,** *n.* Organized society; the State. **body-servant,** *n.* A valet. **body-snatcher,** *n.* One who steals a body from a grave for the purpose of dissection; a resurrection-man; (*slang*) a bailiff; a policeman. **to body forth:** To give mental shape to; to exhibit, to typify. **bodied,** *a.* Having a body; embodied. **bodiless,** *a.* **bodily,** *a.* Of, pertaining to, or affecting the body or the physical nature; corporeal. *adv.* Corporeally, united with matter; wholly, completely, entirely.

Bœotian (bē ō' shi ản, -shản) [*Bœotia*, a district of ancient Greece, the inhabitants of which were proverbially stupid], *a.* Stupid, dull.

Boer (bō' er) [Dut. *boer*, countryman, farmer (see BOOR)], *n.* A South African of Dutch birth or extraction.

boffin (bof' in) [uncert.], *n.* (*R.A.F. slang*) A scientist employed by the Services.

bog (bog) [Ir. *bogach*], *n.* A marsh, a morass; wet, spongy soil, a quagmire; (*slang*) a bog-house. *v.t.* To sink or submerge in a bog. **bog-asphodel,** *n.* The genus *Narthecium*, esp. Lancashire bog-asphodel, *N. ossifragum*. **bog-bean** [BUCK-BEAN]. **bog-berry,** *n.* The cranberry. **bog-butter,** *n.* A fatty hydrocarbon found in peat-bogs. **bog-house,** *n.* (*slang*) A privy. **bog-land,** *n.* Boggy soil, humorously applied to Ireland, hence **bog-lander,** *n.*, an Irishman. **bog-moss,** *n.* The genus *Sphagnum*. **bog-oak,** *n.* Oak found preserved in bogs, black from impregnation with iron. **bog-timber, bog-wood,** *n.* Timber found preserved in bogs. **bog-trotter,** *n.* A person used to traversing boggy country; an Irishman. **bog-violet,** *n.* The butterwort, the genus *Pinguicula*. **boggy,** *a.* Of or characterized by bogs; swampy. **bogginess,** *n.* **boglet,** *n.* A little bog.

bogey (1), **Colonel Bogey** (bō' gi) [imag. person], *n.* (*Golf*) A fair score or allowance for a good player, orig. an ideal opponent against whom a solitary player could pit himself.

bogey (2) [BOGY (2)].

boggard, boggart (bog' ȧrd, -ȧrt) [North. dial., conn. with BOGLE, BOGY, etc.], *n.* A hobgoblin; a ghost.

boggle (bogl) [BOGLE], *v.i.* To shrink back, start with fright; to hesitate, make difficulties; equivocate; to bungle.

bogie, bogy (1) (bō' gi) [etym. doubtful], *n.* *A long, low truck on four small wheels; a platelayer's truck or trolley; a revolving under-carriage. **bogie-car, -engine,** *n.* A railway-carriage or locomotive-engine mounted on these.

bogie, bogy (2) (bō' gē) [Austral. abor.], *v.i.* To bathe, to swim. *n.* A bathe. **bogie-hole,** *n.* A swimming-hole.

bogle (bō' gĕl) [Sc., perh. from W. *bwg*, a goblin], *n.* A hobgoblin, a spectre; a scarecrow, a bugbear.

bogus (bō' gůs) [Am., etym. doubtful], *a.* Sham, counterfeit, spurious, fictitious.

bogy (3), **bogey** (3) (bō' gi) [BOGLE], *n.* A spectre, a bugbear. **old Bogy:** Nick, the Devil.

bohea (bō hē') [Chin. *Wu-i* or *Bu-i* hills, in China], *n.* A name given in the 18th cent. to the finest kind of black tea; now applied to inferior qualities.

Bohemian (1) (bō hē' mi ản), *a.* Of or pertaining to Bohemia, or its people, or their language. *n.* A native or inhabitant of Bohemia.

bohemian (2) (bō hē' mi ản) [F. *bohémien*, gipsy (because the gipsies were supposed to come from Bohemia)], *n.* A gipsy; one who leads a free, irregular life, despising social conventionalities. *a.* Of or characteristic of the gipsies or of social bohemians. **bohemianism,** *n.* The habits or conduct of a social bohemian. **bohemianize** (bō hē' mi ȧ nīz), *v.i.* To live in an unconventional way.

boiar [BOYAR].

boil (1) (boil) [O.F. *boillir* (F. *bouillir*), L. *bullīre*, to bubble (*bulla*, a bubble)], *v.i.* To be agitated by the action of heat, as water or other fluids; to reach the temperature at which these are converted into gas; to be subjected to the action of boiling, as meat, etc., in cooking; to bubble or seethe like boiling water (also of the containing vessel); (*fig.*) to be agitated with passion. *v.t.* To cause a liquid to bubble with heat; to bring to the boiling-point; to cook by heat in boiling water; to prepare in a boiling liquid. *n.* An act of boiling; the state of boiling; boiling-point. **to boil away:** To evaporate in boiling. **to boil down:** To lessen the bulk of by boiling; (*fig.*) to condense. **to boil over:** To bubble up, so as to run over the sides of the vessel; (*fig.*) to be effusive. **boiled shirt,** *n.* (*colloq.*) A dress shirt. **boiler,** *n.* One who boils; a vessel in which anything is boiled; the large vessel in a steam-engine in which water is converted into steam; a tank for hot water attached to a kitchen grate; a vessel for boiling clothes in a laundry, a copper. **boiler-iron, -plate,** *n.* Rolled iron $\frac{1}{4}$ to $\frac{1}{2}$ inch thick for making boilers. **boiler-suit,** *n.* A combined overall garment, esp. for dirty work. **boiler-tube,** *n.* One of a system of tubes by which heat is transmitted to the water in a boiler. **boiling,** *a.* In a state of ebullition by heat; (*fig.*) inflamed, greatly agitated. *n.* The action of boiling. **the whole boiling,** *n.* (*slang*) The whole lot. **boiling-point,** *n.* The temperature at which a fluid is converted into the gaseous state; esp. the boiling-point of water at sea-level (100° C., 212° F.).

boil (2) (boil) [A.-S. *bȳl* (cp. Dut. *buil*, G. *beule*)], *n.* A hard, inflamed, suppurating tumour.

boisterous (bois' tĕr ůs), ***boistous** (bois' tůs) [etym. doubtful]. *a.* *Rough, coarse, cumbrous;

wild, unruly, intractable; stormy, roaring, noisy; tumultuous, rudely violent. **boisterously,** *adv.* **boisterousness,** *n.*

bolas (bō' lȧs) [Sp. and Port., pl. of *bola*, ball], *n.* A missile, used by the South American Indians, formed of balls or stones strung together and flung round the legs of the animal aimed at.

bold (bōld) [A.-S. *beald, bald* (cp. O.H.G. *pald*, G. *bald*, quickly)], *a.* Courageous, daring, confident, fearless; planned or executed with courage; vigorous, striking; audacious, forward, presumptuous; steep, prominent, projecting (of a cliff or headland). **to make** or **be so bold:** To venture, to presume. **bold-face,** *a.* (*Print.*) Heavy, conspicuous (of type). **bold-faced,** *a.* Impudent, shameless. **bold-spirited,** *a.* Courageous, daring. **boldly,** *adv.* Impudently; with effrontery. **boldness,** *n.* Courage, enterprise, audacity; effrontery, shamelessness.

bole (1) (bōl) [Icel. *bolr* (Dan. *bul*, log, G. *bohle*, plank, board)], *n.* The stem or trunk of a tree.

bole (2) (bōl) [late L. *bōlus*, Gr. *bōlos*, a clod of earth], *n.* A brownish, yellowish, or reddish, soft unctuous clay, containing more or less iron oxide. **bole armeniac, *armoniac** (ar mē' ni ăk, -mō'-), *n.* An astringent earth brought from Armenia, formerly used as an antidote and a styptic, etc.; *a bolus.

bole (3) (bōl) [etym. unknown], *n.* (*Sc.*) A small recess in a wall; a small unglazed window.

bolection (bō lek' shŭn) [etym. unknown], *n.* A projecting moulding.

bolero (bō lâr' ō, bō lĕr' ō) [Sp.), *n.* A lively Spanish dance; (*Mus.*) the air to which it is danced; (bol' ėr ō) a short jacket worn over a bodice.

Boletus (bō lē' tŭs) [L. and Gr. *bōlites* (perh. from *bōlos*, a lump)], *n.* A genus of fungi having the under surface of the pileus full of pores instead of gills. **boletic** (bō let' ik), *a.* Of or pertaining to the boletus.

bolide (bō' līd, -lid) [F., from L. *bolidem -lis*, Gr. *bolis*, missile (*ballein*, to throw)], *n.* A large meteor; usually one that explodes and falls in the form of aerolites.

***bolin, bowline** [see BOW (3)].

boll (1) (bōl) [BOWL], *n.* *A bowl; a rounded seed-vessel or pod. **boll-weevil,** *n.* (*Ent.*) A weevil (*Anthonomus grandis*) that infests the flowers and bolls of the cotton plant.

boll (2) (bōl), **bow** (bō) [perh. from Icel. *bolli* (cp. Dan. *bolle*, A.-S. *bolla*)], *n.* (*Sc.*) A measure of capacity (varying from six to two bushels) for grain.

Bollandist (bol' ȧn dist) [John *Bolland*, a Flemish Jesuit of the first half of the 17th cent.], *n.* One of the Jesuit continuators of the *Acta Sanctorum*, commenced by Bolland.

bollard (bol' ȧrd) [perh. from BOLE (1)], *n.* (*Naut.*) A large post or bitt on a wharf, dock, or on shipboard for securing ropes or cables.

Bologna (bȯ lō' nyȧ) [It.], *n.* A town in Italy. **Bologna-bottle, -flask,** *n.* An unannealed bottle which flies in pieces when scratched. **Bologna-phosphorus,** *n.* A phosphorescent preparation of Bologna-spar. **Bologna-sausage,** *n.* A large kind of sausage, first made at Bologna [POLONY]. **Bologna-spar, -stone,** *n.* Native sulphate of baryta, with phosphorescent properties, found near Bologna. **Bolognese** (bō lō nyēz'), *a.* Belonging or native to Bologna. *n.* A native or resident of Bologna.

bolograph (bō' lō grăf) [Gr. *bole*, a ray of light; -GRAF], *n.* An automatic record of the variations of temperature indicated by the bolometer. *v.i.* To produce such a record. **bolographic,** *a.* **bolometer,** *n.* An extremely sensitive instrument for measuring radiant heat.

boloney (bȯ lō' ni) [etym. unknown], *n.* (*slang*) Nonsense, humbug.

Bolshevism (bol' shė vizm) [Rus. *bolsheviki*, majority party], *n.* The doctrine of proletarian rule, as inaugurated in Russia under Lenin, in 1917. **Bolshevik, Bolshevist,** *n.* An adherent of this doctrine, *a.*

bolster (bōl' stėr) [A.-S. (O.H.G. *polstar*, G. *polster*, Icel. *bolstr*)], *n.* A long under-pillow, used to support the pillows in a bed; a pad, cushion, or anything resembling a pad or cushion, in an instrument, machine, ship, architecture, or engineering; a punching-tool. *v.t.* To support with or as with a bolster; to belabour with bolsters; to pad, stuff. *v.i.* To fight with bolsters. **to bolster up:** To support, to prevent from falling; to save from deserved chastisement, criticism, or disgrace; to aid, abet, countenance. **bolstering,** *n.* Prop, support; padding, stuffing; a fight with bolsters.

bolt (1) (bōlt) [A.-S. (cp. Dut. *bout*, G. *bolz*)], *n.* A short thick arrow with a blunt or thick head; a discharge of lightning; *a kind of fetter for the leg; the act of gulping food without chewing; a measured roll of woven fabric, esp. canvas (of which a bolt is 30 yards); a bundle of osiers or reeds, measuring about 3 feet in circumference; a sliding piece of iron for fastening a door, window, etc.; a metal pin for holding objects together, frequently screw-headed at one end to receive a nut; that portion of a lock which engages with the keeper to form a fastening; a sudden start, a sudden flight; the act of suddenly breaking away; (*Am.*) sudden desertion from a political party. *v.t.* To shut or fasten by means of a bolt or iron; to fasten together with a bolt or bolts; to gulp, to swallow hastily and without chewing; (*Am.*) to desert (a political party). *v.i.* To start suddenly forward or aside; to run away (as a horse); (*Am.*) to break away from a political party. **a bolt from the blue:** Lightning from a cloudless sky: (*fig.*) an unexpected sudden event. **bolt-head,** *n.* The head of a bolt; a globular flask with a long, cylindrical neck, used in distilling. **bolt-rope,** *n.* (*Naut.*) A rope sewed round the margin of a sail to prevent its being torn. **boltsprit,** *n.* Bowsprit. **bolt upright,** *a.* Straight upright. **to bolt in, bolt out:** To shut in; to exclude. **bolter** (1), *n.* One that bolts or runs; a horse given to bolting; (*Am.*) one who suddenly breaks away from his party; (*Austral. hist.*) a runaway convict. **bolting** (1), *n.* Sudden flight; (*Am.*) political desertion; fastening with bolts; a bundle of straw; swallowing without chewing. **bolting-hole,** *n.* A hole by which or into which one escapes; an escape.

bolt (2), **boult** (bōlt) [O.F. *bulter*, *buleter* (*buletel*, a sieve), It. *burattare* (*buratto*, a sieve, late L. *burra*, a coarse cloth)], *n.* A sieve for separating bran from flour. *v.t.* To pass through a bolt or bolting cloth; to examine, to try. **to bolt out:** To separate by sifting. **bolter** (2), *n.* A sieve; a bolting-cloth; a sifting-machine. **bolting** (2), *n.* The act or process of sifting; *(*Law*) private arguing of cases for practice. **bolting-cloth,** *n.* A fine cloth used in sifting meal. **bolting-hutch,** *n.* A tub or box into which flour or meal is bolted; (*fig.*) a receptacle for refuse. **bolting-machine, -mill,** *n.* A machine or mill for sifting flour or meal.

bolus (bō' lŭs) [late L. *bōlus*, Gr. *bōlos*, a clod, lump], *n.* Medicine in a round mass larger than a pill; a round lump of anything; (*fig.*) anything mentally unpalatable; (*slang*) an apothecary.

bomb (bom) [F. *bombe*, Sp. *bomba*, L. *bombus*, Gr. *bombos*, a humming noise), *v.t.* To drop a bomb or bombs, esp. from aircraft. *n.* An explosive usually dropped from the air or thrown by hand. **volcanic bomb:** A roundish solid mass of lava ejected from a volcano. **bomb crater,** *n.* Crater caused by the explosion of a bomb. **bomb-ketch, bomb-vessel,** *n.* A small strongly-built vessel formerly used to carry mortars for naval bombardments. **bomb-proof,** *a.* Applied to a shelter, etc., affording safety from the explosion of a bomb. *n.* A bomb-proof structure. **bomb-shell** [SHELL], *n.* A bomb thrown by artillery; (*fig.*) a total surprise. **bomb-sight,** *n.* (*Aviat.*) Device for aiming a bomb from an aircraft. **bomb-thrower,** *n.* (*Mil.*) A mechanical device for throwing a bomb; one who throws a bomb.

bombard (bŭm bard′, bom bard′) [see prec.], *v.t.* To attack with shot and shell; to assail with arguments or invective; to subject atoms to a stream of high-speed particles. *n.* (bŭm′ bard, bom′ bard) The earliest form of cannon; a bombardment; a bomb-ketch; a leather jug for liquor; a toper; a deep-toned wooden instrument of the bassoon family. ***bombardman,** *n.* A pot-boy. **bombardier** (bŭm-, bom bår dēr′), *n.* *An artilleryman employed in serving mortars and howitzers; a non-commissioned artillery officer ranking as corporal. **bombardier-beetle,** *n.* The genus *Brachinus*, which, when disturbed, emit fluid from the abdomen, with blue vapour and a perceptible report. **bombardment** (bŭm-, bom bard′ mėnt), *n.* The act of bombarding; an attack upon a place with shot and shell.

bombardon, bombardone (bom bar′ dȯn, bom bar dō′ ni), *n.* (*Mus.*) A brass instrument not unlike an ophicleide in tone; a bass-reed stop on the organ.

bombasine, bombazine (bŭm-, bom bȧ zēn′) [F. *bombasin*, late L. *bombācinus* (*bombax*, L. *bombyx*, Gr. *bombux*, silk, cotton, orig. silk-worm)], *n.* A twilled dress fabric of silk and worsted, cotton and worsted, or of worsted alone. **Bombax** (bom′ băks) [L. *bombyx*], *n.* A genus of West Indian silk-cotton trees.

bombast (bŭm′-, bom′ băst) [O.F. *bumbace*, cotton, late L. *bombax -ācem* (L. *bombyx*, see prec.)], *n.* *Cotton-wool, esp. used as padding; padding, stuffing; (*fig.*) inflated speech, fustian; high-sounding words. **a.* Turgid, bombastic. *v.t.* (*usu.* bŭm-, bom băst′) *To stuff out, to inflate; to fill out with imposing language. **bombastic** (-băs′ tik), *a.* Of the nature of bombast; inflated, turgid; given to inflated language. **bombastically,** *a.* In an inflated, grandiloquent style.

bombax [BOMBASINE].

Bombay duck (bom bā dŭk′) [Mahratti *bombil*, name of the fish], *n.* A small East Indian fish, *Harpodon nehereus*, when salted and dried eaten as a relish; called also bummalo. **Bombay bowler,** *n.* A small, light pith helmet.

bomber (bom′ er), *n.* (*Aviat.*) An aircraft used for bombing.

bombora (bom′ bȯ rȧ), *n.* (*Austral.*) Dangerous broken water, usu. at the base of a cliff.

Bombyx (bom′ biks) [Gr., see BOMBASINE], *n.* A genus of moths, containing the silk-worm, *Bombyx mori*. **bombycid,** *a.*

bona fide (bō′ nȧ, bon′ ȧ fī′ dē) [L.], *adv.* In good faith. *a.* Genuine. ***bona fides*** (fī′ dēz), *n.* Good faith, sincerity.

bonanza (bō năn′ zȧ) [Am., from Sp., fair weather, prosperity], *n.* A rich mine; a successful enterprise; a run of luck. *a.* Very successful; highly profitable. **bonanza farm,** *n.* A big farm in the West worked by the best modern appliances and securing large profits.

Bonapartism (bō′ nȧ part izm), *n.* Attachment to the dynasty founded in France by Napoleon Bonaparte. **Bonapartist,** *n.* An adherent of the Bonaparte dynasty. *a.* Of, pertaining to, or supporting the Bonaparte dynasty.

***bona-roba** (bō′ nȧ rō′ bȧ) [It. *buonaroba* (*buona*, good, *roba*, dress)], *n.* A showy wanton; a harlot.

bon-bon (bon′ bon, bon′ bon) [F. (*bon*, good, L. *bonus*)], *n.* A sweetmeat; a Christmas cracker.

bonce (bons) [etym. unknown], *n.* A large playing-marble; the game played with these.

bond (1) (bond) [var. of BAND], *n.* That which binds or confines, as a cord or band; (*pl.*) chains, imprisonment, captivity; a withe for tying a faggot; that which restrains or cements; a binding agreement or engagement; that which impedes or enslaves; (*pl.*) trammels; a mode of disposing bricks in a wall so as to tie the courses together by lapping over (as **English bond,** in which the bricks in alternate courses are laid length-wise and across, **Flemish bond,** in which the bricks are laid alternately length-wise and across in each course); (*Law*) a deed by which one person (the obligor) binds himself, his heirs, executors, and assigns, to pay a certain sum to another person (the obligee), his heirs, etc.; a document by which a government or a public company undertakes to repay borrowed money, a debenture. *v.t.* To put into a bonded warehouse; to mortgage; to bind or connect (as bricks or stones) by overlapping or by clamps. **in bond:** In a bonded warehouse, and liable to customs duty. **bond-creditor,** *n.* A creditor secured by bond. **bond-holder,** *n.* A person holding a bond or bonds granted by a private person, or by a government. **bond-stone,** *n.* A stone going through a wall, a bonder. **bond-timber,** *n.* Pieces of timber built into a stone or brick wall to strengthen it. **bonded,** *a.* Bound by a bond; put in bond. **bonded debt,** *n.* A debt secured by bonds issued by a corporation as distinguished from floating debts. **bonded goods,** *n.pl.* Goods stored, under the care of Custom House officers, in warehouses until the duties are paid. **bonded warehouse,** *n.* [see BONDED GOODS]. **bonder,** *n.* One who puts, or holds, goods in bond; a stone or brick reaching a considerable distance through a wall so as to bind it together. **bonding,** *n.* The storing of goods in bond; the act of strengthening by bonders.

bond (2) (bond) [A.-S. *bōnda*, *bunda*, a husbandman, Icel. *bōndi* (*būa*, to till); influenced in meaning by prec.], *a.* In serfdom or slavery. **bondmaid,** *n.* A slave-girl. **bond-servant,** *n.* A slave. **bond-service,** *n.* Villainage. **bond-slave,** *n.* An emphatic term for a slave. **bondsman, bondman,** *n.* A slave; a surety. **bondswoman, bondwoman,** *n.* A female slave. **bondage** (bon′ dȧj), *n.* Slavery, captivity, imprisonment; subjection, restraint, obligation. **bondager,** *n.* (*Sc.*) A cotter bound to render certain services to a farmer; a female worker paid by a cotter to render certain services on his behalf to a farmer.

bond (3) (bond) [Dut., from *binden*, to bind (cp. G. *bund*)], *n.* A league or confederation [see AFRIKANDER].

bone (bōn) [A.-S. *bān* (cp. Dut. *been*, O.H.G. *pein*, *bein*, G. *bein*)], *n.* The hard material of the skeleton of mammals, birds, reptiles, and some fishes; any separate and distinct part of such a skeleton; the substance of which the skeleton consists; applied to many articles made (or formerly made) of bone or ivory, whalebone, etc.; a small joint of meat; (*pl.*) dice; castanets, two pieces of bone held between the fingers of each hand, and used by nigger minstrels as accompaniment; the performer on these; the body; mortal remains. *a.* Of or pertaining to bone; made of bone. *v.t.* To take out the bones of (for cooking); (*slang*) to steal. **a bone of contention:** A subject of dispute. **body and bones:** Altogether. **to have a bone to pick with one:** To have a cause of quarrel with or complaint against one. **to make bones:** To hesitate; to make a fuss; to make scruples. **to point a bone:** (*Austral.*) Aboriginal magic to will the death of an enemy. **to the bone:** To the inmost part. **bone-breaker,** *n.* One who or that which breaks bones; the osprey. ***bone-ache,** *n.* Pain in the bones. **bone-ash,** *n.* The mineral residue of bones burnt in the air. **bone-bed,** *n.* (*Geol.*) A bed largely made up of bones of animals. **bone-black,** *n.* Animal charcoal used as a deodorizer and as a pigment. **bone-cave,** *n.* (*Geol.*) A cave, containing the remains of prehistoric or recent animals. **bone-dry,** *a.* Quite dry. **bone-dust,** *n.* Bones ground for manure. **bone-earth,** *n.* [BONE-ASH]. **bone-grafting,** *n.* (*Surg.*) Introduction of a piece of bone obtained elsewhere to replace bone lost by injury or disease. **bonehead,** *n.* (*slang*) A dolt. **bone-lace,** *n.* A kind of thread-lace originally made with bone bobbins. **bone-oil,** *n.* A fetid oil obtained in the dry distillation of bones. **bone-setter,** *n.* *A surgeon; a non-qualified practitioner who sets fractured and dislocated bones. **bone-shaker,** *n.* An old-fashioned bicycle without india-rubber tyres. **bone-spavin,** *n.* A bony excrescence on the inside of a horse's hock. **to bone up:** (*Am.*) To study hard, to swot. **boned,** *a.* Possessed of bones (*in comb.*); deprived of bones (for cooking). **big-boned,** *a.* Of large and massive build. **boneless,** *a.* Without bones; without backbone, having no stamina. **bonelessness,** *n.* **boner,** *n.* (*Am.*) A gross mistake, a howler. **boning,** *n.* The removing of bones from poultry, fish, etc.; the operation of levelling or judging of the straightness of a surface by the eye. **boning-rod,** *n.* One of a line of poles set up some distance apart, and used in judging the level of a surface by the eye. **bony,** *a.* Of, pertaining to, or of the nature of bone or bones; big-boned. **bony pike,** *n.* The American genus *Lepidosteus*. **boniness,** *n.*

bonfire (bon' fīr) [BONE, FIRE], *n.* A large fire lit in the open air on occasion of some public rejoicing; a fire for burning up garden rubbish.

bong (bong) [abor. Austral.], *a.* Dead.

***bongrace** (bon' grās) [F. *bonne-grace* (*bonne*, good, *grace*, GRACE)], *n.* A kind of sunshade worn on the front of the bonnet; a broad-brimmed hat for women; (*Naut.*) a bow-grace or junk-fender.

bonhomie (bon' ŏ mē') [F. *bon*, good, *homme*, man], Good-nature, geniality.

boniface (bon' i fās) [name of the innkeeper in Farquhar's 'Beaux' Stratagem'], *n.* A generic name for an innkeeper; mine host.

boning, etc. [BONE].

bonito (bo nē' tō) [Sp., etym. doubtful], *n.* The striped tunny, *Thynnus pelamys*; some other species of the mackerel family.

bon mot (bo*n* mō) [F., lit. good word], *n.* (*pl.* **bon mots**) A witticism.

bonne (bon) [F.], *n.* A nursemaid; a maid (of French nationality).

bonnet (bon' ėt) [O.F. *bonet*, stuff of which caps were made (whence *chapel de bonet*, abbr. into *bonet*), low L. *bonnētus*], *n.* A head-covering without a brim for men and boys; a flat Scotch cap; a brimless head-covering, of various shapes, worn by women out of doors; (*Gaming, etc.*) a confederate, a decoy; a protective covering to a machine, etc.; a chimney-cowl; the front part of a motor-car covering the engine, (*Am.*) the hood; (*Naut.*) an additional piece of canvas laced to the bottom of a sail to enlarge it. *v.t.* To put a bonnet on a person; to knock a man's hat over his eyes. *v.i.* *To take off the bonnet or cap as a salute. **Balmoral bonnet:** A flat cap like a Scotch bonnet. **Glengarry bonnet:** A pointed cap with flowing ribbons behind. **poke bonnet:** An old-fashioned bonnet that covered the sides of the face. **Scotch** or **Lowland bonnet:** A round, flat, woollen cap, like a beret, with a tassel in the middle. **bonnet-piece,** *n.* A gold coin of James V of Scotland, on which the king is represented as wearing a bonnet instead of a crown. ***bonnet rouge*** (bon ā roozh) [F. *rouge*, red], *n.* The red cap of liberty worn by revolutionaries. **bonneted,** *a.* Wearing a bonnet or cap.

bonny (bon' i) [F. *bonne*, good], *a.* Beautiful, handsome, pretty; healthy-looking. **bonnily,** *adv.* **bonniness,** *n.*

bonsella [bon sel' ȧ], *n.* (*S. Africa*). A tip, a present.

bonspiel (bon' spēl) [etym. unknown], *n.* (*Sc.*) A curling-match.

bonus (bō' nŭs) [L. *bonus*, a good (man)], *n.* Something over and above what is due; a premium given for a privilege, or in addition to interest for a loan; an extra dividend; a distribution of profits to policy-holders in an insurance company; a gratuity over and above a fixed salary or wages. **bonus share,** *n.* (*Fin.*) A share issued free to the holder of a paid-up share in a joint-stock company. *v.t.* To give a bonus to; to promote by bonuses.

bony, etc. [BONE].

bonza (bon' zȧ), *a.* (*Austral.*) Excellent.

bonze (bonz) [Jap. *bonzō*, Chin. *fan seng*, religious person (through F. *bonze*, Port. *bonzo*, or directly)], *n.* A Buddhist priest in Japan, China, and adjacent regions.

boo (boo) [onomat.], *int.* and *n.* A sound imitating the lowing of oxen, used as an expression of contempt, aversion, and the like. *v.i.* To low as an ox, to groan. *v.t.* To groan at, to hoot.

booby (boo' bi) [Sp. *bobo*, a blockhead; also, a kind of bird (prob. from L. *balbus*, stammering)], *n.* A dull, stupid fellow; a dunce; a gannet, esp. *Sula fusca*. **booby hatch,** *n.* (*Naut.*) A small kind of companion for the half-decks of merchant ships. **booby-prize,** *n.* The prize, usu. a worthless one, given in ridicule to the player who makes the lowest score, esp. in whist-drives. **booby-trap,** *n.* A practical joke consisting of placing books, or the like, on the top of a door left ajar, so that the whole tumbles on the head of the first person entering; a bomb so disposed that it will explode when some object is touched. **boobyish,** *a.* Stupid, foolish, awkward.

boodle (boodl) [etym. doubtful; perh. from Dut. *boedel*, estate, possession], *n.* (*slang*) Money, capital, stock in trade; a fund for bribery; bribery, plunder, graft; a pack, crew, lot.

boogie-woogie (boo' gi woo' gi), *n.* (*Mus. and Dancing*) A jazz piano style of a rhythmic and percussive nature based on 12-bar blues.

boo-hoo (boo hoo') [onomat.], *n.* An ejaculation of contempt; the sound of noisy weeping. *v.i.* To weep noisily; to bellow, to roar, to hoot.

book (buk) [A.-S. *bōc*, a book, document, charter (cp. O.H.G. *buoh*, G. *buch*) (possibly conn. with A.-S. *bōece*, G. *buche*, Gr. *phages*, L. *fāgus*, a beech)], *n.* *A writing, a document, a charter; a collection of sheets printed, written on, or blank, bound in a volume; a literary composition of considerable extent; one of its principal divisions; a libretto; a set of tickets, cheques, forms of receipt, stamps, or the like, fastened together; (*Turf*) bets on a race or at a meeting taken collectively; (*fig.*) anything that can be read or that conveys instruction; (*Cards*) the first six tricks gained by a side at whist, etc. *v.t.* To enter or register in a book; to obtain by payment in advance (as a seat in a conveyance, theatre, or the like); to take a railway ticket; to furnish with a railway ticket; to hand in or to receive for transmission (as a parcel, goods, etc.); (of police) to take name, etc. prior to making a charge. **The Book, The Book of God:** The Bible. **book of fate, book of life:** The record of souls to be saved. **book of reference:** A book for occasional consultation, not for continuous reading, as an encyclopædia, gazetteer, or the like. **by the book:** With exact information. **without book:** From memory; without authority. **like a book:** Formally, pedantically, as if one were reciting from a book. **to be on the books:** To have one's name on the official list. **in one's black books:** In bad favour with anyone. **to bring to book:** To convict, call to account. **book-account,** *n.* An account or register of debit or credit in a book. **bookbinder,** *n.* One who binds books. **bookbindery,** *n.* A place for binding books. **bookbinding,** *n.* **book-case,** *n.* A case with shelves for books; a book-cover. **book-club,** *n.* An association of persons who buy and lend each other books. **book-cover,** *n.* A pair of boards (usu. cloth- or leather-covered) for binding a book; case for periodicals, music, etc. **book-debt,** *n.* A debt for articles supplied, entered in an account-book. **book-ends,** *n.pl.* Props placed at the ends of a row of books to keep them upright. **book-holder,** *n.* (*Theat.*) A prompter. **book-hunter,** *n.* A collector of rare books. **book-keeper,** *n.* One who keeps the accounts in a merchant's office, etc. **book-keeping,** *n.* The art or practice of keeping accounts. **book-knowledge,** *n.* [BOOK-LEARNING]. ***bookland,** *n.* Land taken from the folcland or the common land and granted by *bōc* (see BOOK) or charter to a private person. **book-learned,** *a.* Learned, as far as books are concerned. **book-learning, -lore,** *n.* Learning derived from books; theory, not practical knowledge or experience. **book-maker,** *n.* One who makes or compiles books; (*disparagingly*) a literary man; a professional betting-man. **book-making,** *n.* The compilation of books; the making of a betting-book. **bookman,** *n.* A literary man; a lover of reading. **book-mark, book-marker,** *n.* A piece of ribbon, paper, or the like, put in a book to mark a place. ***book-mate,** *n.* A school-fellow. **book-muslin,** *n.* A kind of fine muslin, folded in the piece in a somewhat book-like form. ***book-oath,** *n.* An oath taken on the Bible. **book-plate,** *n.* A label with a name or device, pasted in a book to show the ownership. **book-post,** *n.* The former system and regulations by which books and printed matter, open at the ends, were conveyed by post. **book-press,** *n.* A book-case. **book-rest,** *n.* A support for a book in reading. **bookseller,** *n.* One whose trade it is to sell books. **book-slide,** *n.* An expanding holder or slide for holding books on a table or desk. **book-stall,** *n.* A stall at which books and periodicals are sold. **book-store,** *n.* A bookseller's shop. **bookwork,** *n.* Study of text-books, as opposed to practice and experiment. **bookworm,** *n.* Any worm or insect which eats holes in books; (*fig.*) one always poring over books. **booked,** *a,* Registered; entered in a book; (*slang*) caught, engaged. **bookful,** **a.* Full of knowledge derived from books. *n.* All that a book contains. **bookie,** *n.* (*slang*) A bookmaker, a professional betting-man. **booking,** *n.* Registry in a book. **booking-clerk,** *n.* A clerk who issues tickets to travellers, or who books goods to be forwarded. **booking-office,** *n.* An office where railway or other tickets are issued to passengers, where seats are booked for any conveyance, or goods booked to be forwarded. **booklet,** *n.* A little book. **bookish,** *a.* Learned, studious; acquainted with books only. **bookishly,** *adv.* **bookishness,** *n.* **booksie,** *a., adv.* (*colloq.*) Would-be literary.

boom (1) (boom) [imit. (cp. BOMB)], *n.* A loud, deep, resonant sound, as of artillery, a large bell, etc.; (*fig.*) a sudden demand for a thing; a rapid advance in prices; a burst of commercial activity and prosperity; a sudden outburst of popular favour. *v.i.* To make a loud, deep, resonant sound; to rush with violence, as a ship in full sail; (*fig.*) to go off with a boom; to become very popular, prosperous or active. *v.t.* To utter with a booming sound; (*fig.*) to push, to force on public attention; to force into great activity, popularity, and prosperity. **boomer, boomster,** *n.* One who forces a business or other undertaking into activity or notoriety.

boom (2) (boom) [Dut. *boom,* a tree (cp. BEAM)], *n.* A long spar to extend the foot of a particular sail; a chain or line of connected spars forming an obstruction to the mouth of a harbour; (*Am.*) a line of floating timber enclosing an area of water for lumber; (*pl.*) a space on deck where spare spars are stowed out. **boom-jigger,** *n.* (*Naut.*) A tackle for rigging a top-mast studding-sail boom out or in. **boom-sail,** *n.* A sail extended on a boom instead of a yard. **boom-sheet,** *n.* (*Naut.*) A sheet attached to a boom.

boomah, boomer (boo′ mȧ) [Austral. abor.], *n.* A large kangaroo.

boomerang (boo′ mĕr răng) [Australian abor.], *n.* A native Australian missile weapon, consisting of a curved stick from two to three feet long, so constructed that, thrown forward, it takes a whirling course upwards, returns with a swoop, and falls to the rear of the thrower; (*fig.*) an action, speech, or argument that recoils on the person who makes it.

boon (1) (boon) [Icel. *bōn* (cp. A.-S. *bēn*)], *n.* A prayer, a petition, an entreaty; a favour, a gift; a benefit, a blessing.

***boon** (2) (boon) [F. *bon,* good], *a.* *Good; *advantageous, fortunate; jolly, convivial; bounteous. **boon companion,** *n.* A good fellow; a jovial, merry fellow.

boong (boong), *n.* (*Austral.*) An Aboriginal.

boongarry (boon′ gă ri) [Austral. abor.], *n.* The N. Queensland tree-kangaroo.

boor (boor) [Dut. *boer* (G. *bauer,* from Goth. *bauan,* to till); the A.-S. *gebūr* (*būan,* to dwell, to till) gave the rare M.E. *boueer*], *n.* A peasant, a rustic; a rude, ill-bred fellow. **boorish,** *a.* Clownish, unmannerly, uncultivated. **boorishly,** *adv.* **boorishness,** *n.*

boost (boost) [etym. doubtful], *v.t.* To push, to shove; to give a lift to; to puff up, to advertise; (*Elec.*) to raise the electromotive force, to supplement the voltage of a battery. *n.* A push, a shove, a lift. **booster,** *n.* (*Elec.*) A contrivance for intensifying the strength of an alternating-current; an auxiliary motor in a rocket that breaks away when exhausted.

boot (1) (boot) [O.F. *bote* (F. *botte*), etym. doubtful], *n.* A covering (usually of leather) for the foot and part of the leg, differing from a shoe in reaching further up or above the ankle, (*Am.*) shoe (used for both boots and shoes); an instrument of torture applied to the leg and foot, formerly used in Scotland to extort confessions; a receptacle for luggage under driver's or guard's seat in a coach or other conveyance; *an outside space or compartment on a coach; a covering for the foot and part of the leg of a horse. *v.i.* To put boots on. *v.t.* To torture with the boot. **the boot is on the other leg:** The rights of the matter are the other way round. **boot and saddle** (F. *boute-selle,* put the saddle on): (*Mil. command*) Mount. **to get the boot:** (*slang*) To be dismissed; to get the sack. **like old boots:** (*slang*) Energetically; thoroughly. **boot-black,** *n.* A man who cleans and polishes shoes. **boot-closer,** *n.* A person who sews the upper leathers of boots together. **boot-hook,** *n.* A hook for pulling on long boots. **boot-hose,** *n.pl.* [BOOT-STOCKINGS]. **boot-jack,** *n.* A board with a crotch to retain the heel of a boot while it is being pulled off. **boot-lace,** *n.* A string or strip of leather for fastening boots. **boot-last, -tree,** *n.* A block inserted into a boot to stretch it or keep it in shape. **boot-legger,** *n.* (*colloq.*) A smuggler of liquor. **boot-licker,** *n.* (*colloq.*) A sycophant. **boot-maker,** *n.* An artisan who makes boots. **boot-stockings,** *n.pl.* Over-stockings somewhat resembling jack-boots. **boot-top,** *n.* The upper part of a boot, esp. of top-boots. **booted,** *a.* Having boots on. **booted and spurred:** Equipped for riding. **bootee** (boo tē′), *n.* A kind of high-low boot for ladies; a knitted boot for infants. **bootikin,** *n.* A little boot; a covering for the leg or hand, used as a cure for the gout; a knitted gaiter worn out of doors by children; the instrument of torture called the boot. **bootless** (1), *a.* **boots,** *n.* A male servant at an inn or hotel who cleans the boots; (*slang*) the youngest officer in a regiment; also, the last bishop raised to the House of Lords, whose duty it is to read prayers there.

***boot** (2) (boot) [A.-S. *bōt* (*bētan,* to amend, help, cp. Goth. *bōtjan,* to profit, G. *busse,* making good, atonement)], *n.* Profit, gain, advantage; anything given in addition to what is stipulated. *v.t.* To benefit, to profit. *v.i.* To avail, to be of use. **to boot:** Into the bargain. **bootless** (2), *a.* Profitless, unavailing. **bootlessly,** *adv.* **bootlessness,** *n.*

Bootes (bō ō′ tēz) [Gr., the ploughman, the waggoner], *n.* A northern constellation including Arcturus, situated near the tail of the Great Bear.

booth (boo*th*) [M.Dan. *bōth,* Dan. *bod* (Icel. *buth,* from *būa,* to dwell), related to Ir. and Gael. *both, bothan,* a hut, a bothy], *n.* *A temporary dwelling covered with boughs or other light material; a tent; a covered stall, tent, or other temporary erection at a fair; a sound-proof cabin. **polling-booth,** *n.* A temporary structure for voting in at elections.

booty (boo′ ti) [prob. from Icel. *býti*, barter, through F. *butin* or M.Dut. *būte* (Dut. *buit*, booty, spoil), with influence from *bot*, BOOT (2)], *n.* Spoil taken in war; property carried off by thieves; (*fig.*) gain, a prize. **to play booty:** To join with confederates so as to victimize another player; to play to lose.

booze, boose (booz) [M.E. *bousen*, to drink deeply; perh. from M.Dut. *būsen* (*buize*, a drinking-cup, cp. Dut. *buis*, O.F. *buse, buise*, a conduit)], *n.* Drink; a drinking bout. *v.i.* To drink to excess, to tipple. **boozy, boosy,** *a.* Drunk, tipsy; addicted to boozing.

bo-peep [BO].

bora (1) (bô′ rȧ) [(It. *borea*, L. *boreas*, the north wind)], *n.* A keen, dry, north-east wind in the Upper Adriatic.

bora (2) (bôr ȧ) [Austral. abor.], *n.* Ritual initiation rites and ground where they are performed.

•**borachio** (bȯ răch′ i ō) [Sp. *borracha*, wine-bag, *borracho*, drunkard, or It. *boraccia*, a goat-skin for wine], *n.* A leather wine-bag; (*fig.*) a drunkard.

boracic (bȯ răs′ ik), *a.* Of, pertaining to, or derived from borax. **boracic acid** [BORIC].

boracite (bô′ rȧ sīt), *n.* Native borate of magnesia.

borage (bŭr′ ȧj) [F. *bourrache* (O.F. *borrace*), or late L. *borrāgo*], *n.* A hairy, blue-flowered plant of the genus *Borago*, formerly esteemed as a cordial, and now much used to flavour claret-cup, etc.

borak (bôr′ ȧk) [Austral. abor.], *n.* Chaff, banter. **to poke borak at:** To ridicule, to pull someone's leg.

borate (bôr′ āt), *n.* A salt of boric acid.

borax (bôr′ ăks) [low L. (O.F. *boras*), from Arab. *būrāq*], *n.* A native salt used as a flux and a solder, and as a detergent.

borazon [BORON].

bordar (bôr′ dȧr) [med. L. *bordārius*, cottager, from *borda*, a hut (prob. from Teut. *bord*)], *n.* A villain of the lowest rank, doing manual service for a cottage which he held at his lord's will.

Bordeaux (bôr dō′) [city in S.W. France], *n.* A red French wine; claret. **Bordeaux mixture,** *n.* (*Hort.*) A preparation of sulphate of copper and lime for destroying fungi and other garden pests.

•**bordel** (bôr′ dėl) [O.F., hut, brothel], *n.* A brothel.

border (bôr′ dėr) [O.F. *bordure*, low L. *bordātūra* from *bordāre*, to edge, from *bordus* (Teut. *bord*)], *n.* Brim, edge, margin; boundary line or region; frontier, frontier region, esp. the boundary between England and Scotland with the contiguous regions; (*Am.*) the frontier of civilization; an edging designed as an ornament; an edging to a plot or flower-bed. *v.t.* To put a border or edging to; to form a boundary to. *v.i.* To lie on the border; to be contiguous. **border-plant,** *n.* A decorative plant for flower borders. **borderer,** *n.* One who dwells on a border or frontier, esp. on that between England and Scotland. **bordering,** *n.* An ornamental border. **bordering upon:** Adjoining; resembling. **borderland,** *n.* Land near the border between two countries or districts. **borderless,** *a.* Without a border, limitless. **border-line,** *n.* A line of demarcation. **border-line case,** *n.* A case of mental disturbance bordering on insanity.

bordereau (bôr′ dėr ō) [F., dim of *bord*, as prec.], *n.* (*pl.* ***-eaux***). A letter, memorandum, invoice, or other document.

•**bordrage** [BODRAGE].

bordure (bôr′ dūr) [F. (see BORDER)], *n.* •A border; (*Her.*) the border of an escutcheon, occupying one-fifth of the shield.

bore (1) (bôr) [A.-S. *borian* (*bor*, Icel, *borr*, gimlet, *bora*, Dut. *boren*, to bore, cp. L. *forāre*, to bore, Gr. *pharanx*, a chasm)]. *v.t.* To perforate or make a hole through; to hollow out. *v.i.* To make a hole; to push forward persistently; to thrust the head straight forward (of a horse); (*Racing*) to push a horse, boat, or other competitor out of the course; (*Pugil.*) to drive an adversary on to the ropes by sheer weight. *n.* A hole made by boring; the diameter of a tube; the cavity of a gun-barrel. **borer,** *n.* A person, tool, or machine that bores or pierces; a horse that bores; popular name for *Myxine glutinosa*, the glutinous hag or blind fish, the genus *Teredo* or shipworm, the annelid genus *Terebella*, and some insects that bore holes in wood. **bore-hole,** *n.* A shaft or pit cut by means of a special tool. **boring,** *n.* The action of the verb TO BORE; a hole made by boring; (*pl.*) chips or fragments made by boring.

bore (2) (bôr) [prob. from Icel. *bāra*, a billow], *n.* A tidal wave of great height and velocity, caused by the meeting of two tides or the rush of the tide up a narrowing estuary.

bore (3) (bôr) [etym. doubtful], *n.* A tiresome person, a wearisome twaddler. *v.t.* To weary with twaddle or dullness. **boredom,** *n.* The characteristic behaviour of bores; the condition of being bored; bores collectively.

bore (4) [BEAR (2)].

boreas (bôr′ ė ȧs) [L., from Gr. *Boreas, Borras*], *n.* The god of the north wind; (*poet.*) the north wind. **boreal** [L. *boreālis*], *a.* Pertaining to the north or the north wind; northern; living near the north; sub-arctic.

borecole (bôr′ kōl) [Dut. *boerenkool*, peasant's cabbage (BOER)], *n.* A curled variety of winter cabbage; kail.

boree (bȯ rē′) [Austral. abor.], *n.* A kind of wattle-tree affording firewood.

boreen (bō rēn′) [Ir. *bothar*, pron. bō′ ėr, *-een*, dim. suf.], *n.* (*Ir.*) A lane, a bridle-path; (*fig.*) an opening in a crowd.

borer [BORE (1)].

boric (bôr′ ik), *a.* Of or pertaining to boron. **boric acid,** *n.* An acid obtained from borax.

boring [BORE (1)].

born (bôrn) [orig. p.p. of BEAR (2)], *p.p.* and *a.* Brought into the world; brought forth, produced. **born again:** Regenerate. **born to:** Destined to. **born with a silver spoon in one's mouth:** Born in luxury.

borne (bôrn), *p.p.* [BEAR (2)].

bornite (bôr′ nīt) [I. von *Born* (1742–91), Austrian mineralogist], *n.* (*Min.*) A valuable copper ore found in Cornwall and elsewhere.

boron (bôr′ on) [BORAX], *n.* The element present in borax and boracic acid. **borazon** (bôr′ ȧ zon), *n.* A substance compounded of boron and nitrogen that for industrial use is harder than a diamond.

borough (bŭr′ ȯ) [A.-S. *burgh, burg*, O.Teut. *bergan*, to shelter (A.-S. *beorgan*); cp. G. *burg*, castle, Sc. *burgh*], *n.* A town possessing a municipal corporation; a town which sends a representative to Parliament. **the Borough:** Southwark. **to own or purchase a borough:** To control or purchase the control of a Parliamentary borough (before the Reform Act of 1832). **close** or **pocket borough:** A borough owned by a person or persons. **county borough:** A borough of more than 50,000 inhabitants ranking under the Local Government Act of 1888 as an administrative county. **rotten borough:** A borough (before 1832) having only a nominal constituency. **borough-English** [A.-F. *tenure en Burgh Engleys*, tenure in an English borough], *n.* A custom existent in some parts of England by which the youngest son inherits all lands and tenements. **borough-monger,** *n.* One who buys or sells the representation of a borough. **borough-reeve,** *n.* The chief municipal officer in certain unincorporated boroughs before the Municipal Corporations Act of 1835.

borrow (bor′ ō) [A. S. *borgian*, from *borg, borh*, a pledge. O.Teut. *bergan*, to protect (cp. G. *borgen*, to borrow, also BOROUGH)], *v.t.* To obtain and make temporary use of; to obtain under a promise or understanding to return; to adopt, to assume, to derive from other people; to copy, imitate, feign;

(*Golf*) to play a ball uphill in order that it may roll back. **borrowed,** *a.* Obtained on loan; (*fig.*) not genuine; hypocritical. **borrowing days,** *n.pl.* The last three days of March (Old Style), supposed in Scottish folk-lore to have been borrowed from April and to be particularly stormy.

Borstal system (bôr' stål sis' tĕm) [*Borstal,* nr. Rochester, Kent], *n.* A method of treating juvenile offenders by education and technical instruction.

borstall (bôr' stål) [A.-S. *beorh,* a hill, *steall,* place, stead, or *stigol,* stile], *n.* A steep track on a hillside.

bort (bôrt) [etym. doubtful (perh. O.F. *bort,* bastard)], *n.* Small fragments split from diamonds in roughly reducing them to shape, used to make diamond powder.

borzoi (bôr' zoi) [Rus.], *n.* A Russian wolfhound.

boscage, boskage (bos kāj) [O.F. *boscage,* late L. *boscum,* a bush], *n.* Wood, woodland; underwood or ground covered with it; thick foliage; wooded landscape.

bosey (bō' zi) [Eng. cricketer Bosanquet], *n.* (*Cricket*) A googly.

bosh (bosh) [Turk.], *n.* Empty talk, nonsense, folly *int.* Stuff! rubbish! humbug! *v.t.* (*slang*) To spoil, to humbug, make a fool of.

bosjes-man [BUSHMAN].

bosk (bosk) [M.E. *boske,* var. of *busk,* BUSH (mod. lit. *bosk,* prob. from BOSKY)], *n.* A bush, a thicket, a small forest. **bosket, bosquet** (bos' kĕt) [F. *bosquet,* It. *boschetto,* dim. of *bosco,* a wood], *n.* A grove; a plantation of small trees and underwood in a garden or park. **bosky** (bos' ki), *a.* Bushy, woody; covered with boscage; (*slang*) rather worse for drink. **boskiness,** *n.* The quality of being bosky.

bosom (buz' ŭm) [A.-S. *bōsm* (cp. O.H.G. *puosam,* G. *busen,* etym. unknown)], *n.* The breast of a human being (esp. of a woman); that part of the dress which covers this; the breast as the seat of emotions, or the repository of secrets; secret counsel or intention; embrace; intimate relations; affection; the surface of water or of ground; a hollow, a cavity, the interior of anything. *v.t.* To put into or hide in the bosom; to embosom; to receive into intimate companionship. **bosom friend:** Dearest and most intimate friend. **bosom of one's family:** Midst of one's family. **in one's bosom:** Clasped in one's embrace; in one's inmost feelings.

boss (1) (bos) [O.F. *boce* (F. *bosse*), It. *bozza,* a swelling; perh. from O.H.G. *bōzan,* to strike], *n.* A protuberant part; an ornamental stud; the knob in the centre of a shield; (*Arch.*) an ornamental projection at the intersection of the ribs in vaulting. *v.t.* To press out, emboss; to furnish with bosses. **bossed,** *a.* Embossed, ornamented with bosses. **bossy,** *a.* Having a boss or bosses, studded with bosses.

boss (2) (bos) [Dut. *baas,* master, orig. uncle], *n.* A master, a foreman, a manager; the manager or dictator of a party 'machine.' *a.* Chief, best, most highly esteemed; first-rate, excellent. *v.t.* To manage, to direct, to control. **bossy,** *a.* Managing.

boss (3) (bos) [slang], *n.* A miss, a bad shot, a bungle; a short-sighted person; one who squints. *v.t.* To miss, to bungle. *v.i.* To make a miss. **boss-eyed,** *a.* (*slang*) Having but one eye; having one eye injured; squinting. **bosser,** *n.*

boston (bos' tŏn) [after Boston, Mass., U.S.A.], *n.* A game of cards somewhat resembling whist; a slow waltz.

Boswell (boz' wĕl) [James *Boswell,* biographer of Samuel Johnson], *n.* A biographer; a minute and rather slavish biographer. **Boswellian** (boz wel' i ăn), *a.* Resembling Boswell in style. **Boswellism** (boz'wĕl izm), *n.* Boswell's style of biography. **Boswellize,** *v.i.* To write biography in Boswell's style.

bot, bott (bot) [etym. unknown], *n.* A parasitic worm, the larva of the genus *Œstrus.* **the bots, botts:** A disease caused by these in horses; an analogous disease in cattle and in sheep. **bot-fly,** *n.* A fly of the genus *Œstrus*; a gadfly.

botanic (bŏ tăn' ik), **botanical** (-ik ăl) [F. *botanique,* late L. *botanicus,* Gr. *botanikos,* pertaining to plants, from *botanē,* a plant, *boskein,* to feed], *a.* Of or pertaining to botany. **botanic garden,** *n.* A garden laid out for the scientific culture and study of plants. **botanically,** *adv.* **botanist** (bot' ă nist), *n.* **botanize** (-nīz), *v.i.* To collect plants for scientific study; to study plants. *v.t.* To explore botanically.

botany (bot' ă ni) [as prec.], *n.* The science which treats of plants and plant-life. **Botany Bay** [in New South Wales, named by Capt. Cook after the abundance of botanical specimens found there], *n.* A convict settlement established there; (*fig.*) transportation. **Botany Bay dozen:** (*Austral. hist.*) Twenty-five lashes with the cat-o'-nine-tails. **Botany-wool, -yarn,** *n.* Wool from Botany Bay, and yarn made from it.

botargo (bŏ tar' gō) [It., from Arab. *butarkhah,* Copt. *outarakhon* (*ou-,* a, Gr. *tarichion,* dim. of *tarichos,* dried fish)], *n.* A relish made of the roes of the mullet and tunny.

botch (1) (boch) [etym. doubtful (cp. PATCH)], *n.* A clumsy patch; a bungled piece of work. *v.t.* To mend or patch clumsily; to put together in an unsuitable or unskilful manner. **botcher** (1), *n.* A mender, a patcher, a bungler. **botchery,** *n.* The results of botching; clumsy workmanship. **botch-work,** *n.* Botchery. **botchy,** *a.* Characterized by botching or bungling.

botch (2) (boch) [O.F. *boce* (see BOSS (1))], *n.* An ulcerous swelling. **botchy,** *a.* Marked with botches or excrescences.

botcher (2) (boch' ĕr) [local; etym. doubtful], *n.* A young salmon, a grilse.

both (bōth) [Icel. *bāthir, bāthi* (*bā-thir,* both they or the); A.-S. *ba* gave the earlier *bo*], *a.* and *pron.* The one and also the other, the two. *adv.* As well the one thing as the other; equally in the two cases.

bother (bo*th*' ĕr) [etym. doubtful], *v.t.* To tease, to vex; to annoy, to pester. *v.i.* To make a fuss, to be troublesome; to worry oneself; to take trouble. *int.* An exclamation of annoyance. *n.* Worry, disturbance, fuss. **botheration** (-ā' shŭn), *n.* The act of bothering; bother. **bothersome,** *a.* Troublesome, annoying.

bothy, bothie (both' i) [etym. doubtful; cp. BOOTH], *n.* A rough kind of cottage; a hut, a hovel; esp. a place where unmarried labourers are lodged upon a Scotch farm.

bo-tree (bō' trē) [Cingalese *bo,* Pāli, *bodhi,* perfect knowledge], *n.* The tree, *Ficus religiosa,* under which Gautama is said to have received the enlightenment which constituted him the Buddha. It is held sacred by the Buddhists and planted beside their temples.

botryoid, botryoidal (bot' ri oid, bot ri oi' dăl) [Gr. *botruoeides* (*botrus,* a bunch of grapes, -OID)], *a.* (*Min.*) In form resembling a bunch of grapes.

bots, bott [BOT].

bottine (bot' ēn) [F., dim. of *botte,* boot], *n.* A buskin; a light kind of boot for women and children.

bottle (1) (bot' ĕl) [O.F. *boteile, botele,* late L. *buticula,* dim. of *butis, buttis,* a cask, a BUTT], *n.* A vessel with a narrow neck for holding liquids (usu. of glass); the quantity in a bottle. *v.t.* To put into bottles. **the bottle:** Drinking. **bottle-brush,** *n.* A brush for cleaning bottles; the genus *Equisetum*; *Hipparis vulgaris*; (*Austral.*) a genus of trees bearing brush-like flowers. **bottle gas,** *n.* Butane gas in liquid form supplied in containers for use in lighting, etc. **bottle-glass,** *n.* Coarse, green glass for making bottles. **bottle-green,** *n.* Dark green, like bottle-glass. **bottle-head,** *n.* A species of whale (see BOTTLE-NOSE). **bottle-holder,** *n.* One who attends upon a pugilist in a prize-fight, a supporter, a second, a backer. **bottle-imp,** *n.* An imp supposed to be sealed up in a bottle. **bottle-neck,** *n.* A constricted outlet. **bottle-nose,** *n.* The bottle-nosed whale, *Hyperoödon bidens. a.* Bottle-nosed. **bottle-nosed,** *a.* Having a large thick nose. **bottle-party,** *n.* A drinking party to which each person brings his own intoxicants. **bottle-tree,** *n.* (*Austral.*) A N. Australian tree that is narrow at the base, widens as the trunk is higher, and narrows again. **bottle-washer,** *n.* A person or machine that washes bottles; a general factotum, an understrapper. **to bottle up:** To conceal, to restrain, repress.

bottle (2) (bot′ ėl) [O.F. *botel*, dim. of *botte*], *n.* A bundle of hay or straw. **looking for a needle in a bottle of hay:** A hopeless search.

bottle (3) (bot′ ėl) [etym. doubtful (there is an old flower-name, *buddle*, and the form has been influenced by BOTTLE (1))], *n.* The name of many kinds of plant.

bottom (bot′ ŏm) [A.-S. *botm* (cp. Icel. *botn*, O.H.G. *podam*, G. *boden*, L. *fundus*, Gr. *puthmēn*, Sansk. *budhnā*)], *n.* The lowest part of anything, the part on which anything rests; the posteriors; the seat of a chair; the bed or channel of any body of water; an alluvial hollow; low-lying land; the lowest point; a deep cavity, an abyss; the inmost part, the furthest point of a recess, gulf, or inland sea; the end of a table remote from a host, chairman, etc.; the lowest rank; the keel of a ship, the part near and including the keel, the hull; a ship as receptacle for cargo; *a skein or ball of thread; (*pl.*) dregs of liquor, sediment; foundation, base; source, basis; stamina, power of endurance. *v.t.* To put a bottom to; *to wind, as a skein; to examine exhaustively, to sound, to fathom. **v.i.* To be based or founded (on). *a.* Of or pertaining to the bottom; lowest; fundamental. **at bottom:** In reality; at heart. **on one's own bottom:** Independently. **bottom dollar,** *n.* One's last coin. **bottom drawer,** *n.* A drawer in which a woman keeps her new clothes, etc. before marriage. **bottom-heat,** *n.* (*Gardening*) Heat supplied beneath the surface by decomposing manure or by means of a greenhouse furnace. **bottom-lands,** *n.pl.* (*Am.*) Rich flat lands on the banks of rivers in the Western states. **bottom-up,** *a.* and *adv.* Upside-down. **bottomed,** *a.* Having a bottom (*usu. in comb.*); based; well-grounded. **bottomless,** *a.* Without a bottom; having no seat; (*fig.*) fathomless, unfathomable. **Bottomless Pit,** *n.* Hell. **bottommost,** *a.* Lowest of all.

bottomry (bot′ ŏm ri) [as prec.], *n.* (*Naut.*) Borrowing money on the security of a ship. *v.t.* To pledge a ship in this manner.

botulism (bot′ ū lizm) [L. *botulus*, a sausage], *n.* (*Path.*) A form of food-poisoning caused by eating food, often sausages, infected by *Bacillus botulinus.*

boudoir (bood′ war) [F., from *bouder*, to sulk], *n.* A small, elegantly furnished room, used as a lady's private apartment.

bouffant (boo′ fon) [Fr.], *a.* Full, puffed out.

bouffe [OPERA BOUFFE].

bougainvillæa, -vilia (boo găn vi lē′ ȧ, -vɪl′ i ȧ) [Louis Antoine de *Bougainville*, French navigator (1729–1811)], *n.* A genus of tropical plants belonging to the *Nyctaginaceæ*, the red or purple bracts of which almost conceal the flowers.

bough (bou) [A.-S. *bōg*, *bōh* (cp. Icel. *bōgr*, Dan. *boug*, O.H.G. *buog*, G. *bog*, Dut. *boeg*, all meaning shoulder of man or quadruped; Gr. *pēchos*, forearm)], *n.* A large arm or branch of a tree.

bought (bawt), *p.p.* [BUY]. **boughten** (irreg. part. from BOUGHT), *a.* (*poet.*) Bought; (*Am.*) purchased, as distinguished from home-made, articles.

bougie (boo′ zhē) [F., from Bougie, Arab. *Bijiyah*, town in Algeria with trade in wax candles], *n.* A wax candle; (*Med.*) a smooth, flexible, slender cylinder used for exploring or dilating passages in the human body.

bouillabaisse (boo yȧ bās′) [F.], *n.* A rich fish-stew or chowder, popular in the south of France.

bouilli (boo yē′) [F., p.p. of *bouillir*, to boil], *n.* Meat gently simmered by a slow fire. ***bouillon*** (boo′ yon), *n.* Broth, soup; a fleshy excrescence on a horse's foot; (*Dressmaking*) a puffed flounce.

boulder (bōl′ dėr) [M.E. *bulderston*, Swed. dial. *bullersten*, from *bullra*, to make a noise (cp. Dan. *buldre*, to roar, rattle)], *n.* A water-worn, rounded stone, a cobble; (*Geol.*) a large rounded block of stone transported to a lesser or greater distance from its parent rock; an erratic block; (*Mining*) a large detached piece of ore. **boulder-clay, -drift,** *n.* (*Geol.*) A clayey deposit of the glacial period. **boulder-formation,** *n.* (*Geol.*) A formation of mud, sand, and clay containing boulders. **boulder period,** *n.* (*Geol.*) The Ice Age, the glacial period.

boulevard (bool′ vard) [F., perh. from G. *bollwerk*, BULWARK], *n.* A public walk on the rampart of a demolished fortification; a broad street planted with trees; (*Am.*) an arterial road, trunk road. **boulevardier, -dist,** *n.* One who haunts the boulevards.

boulter (bōl′ tėr) [etym. unknown], *n.* A fishing-line with a number of hooks attached.

bounce (bouns) [prob. imit.], *n.* A heavy, noisy blow; rebound; a leap, a spring; (*fig.*) swagger, self-assertion, impudence; a boastful lie. *v.t.* *To drive or hit against; to slam, to bang; (*fig.*) to bully; (*Am.*) to discharge suddenly from employment. *v.i.* To rebound; to bound like a ball; to come or go unceremoniously; (*fig.*) to talk big; (of a cheque) to be returned to drawer. **bouncer,** *n.* Anything large and bouncing; a boaster, a swaggerer; a bouncing lie; a fine specimen of anything; (*Am.*) a chucker-out. **bouncing,** *a.* Big, heavy; stout, strong; bustling, noisy. **bouncingly,** *adv.* With a bounce.

bound (1) (bound) [F. *bondir*, to bound, orig. to resound, L. *bombitāre*, to hum, buzz (*bombus*, see BOMB)], *n.* A leap, a spring, a rebound. *v.i.* To leap, to spring; to rebound, to bounce. **v.t.* To cause (a horse) to leap. **by leaps and bounds:** With astonishing speed. **bounder,** *n.* One who or that which leaps; (*slang*) an ill-bred person; a vulgar, pushful man.

bound (2) (bound) [O.F. *bonde*, *bodne*, late L. *bodena* (etym. doubtful)], *n.* A limit, a boundary; limitation, restriction; territory. *v.t.* To set bounds to; to confine; to form the boundary of. **boundless,** *a.* Without bounds; limitless. **boundlessly,** *adv.* **boundlessness,** *n.* **boundary,** *n.* A mark indicating limit; the limit thus marked. **boundary-rider,** *n.* (*Austral.*) A man who keeps the boundary fences of a station in repair.

bound (3) (bound) [past and p.p. of BIND], *a.* Under obligation; compelled, obliged, certain (*with inf.*); (*Books*) in a cover, esp. in a cover of leather or other permanent material as distinguished from paper covers. **bound up with:** Intimately associated with; having identical aims or interests with. **bounden,** *a.* Bound; enslaved; obliged; under obligation. **bounden duty:** Obligatory duty.

bound (4) (bound) [M.E. *boun*, Icel. *būinn*, p.p. of *būa*, to till, to get ready; *-d* added in assim. to other participles], *a.* Prepared, ready; starting, destined; directing one's course. **homeward bound:** On the way home.

bounty (boun′ ti) [O.F. *bonté*, *bontet*, L. *bonitātem -as*, goodness, from *bonus*, good], *n.* *Goodness, gracious liberality; an act of generosity, a gift; a premium for joining the army or navy, or to encourage commerce or industry. **Queen's (King's) Bounty:** A grant made to the mother of three or more children at a birth. **Queen Anne's bounty:** A provision made in the reign of Queen Anne for augmenting poor church livings. **bounteous,** *a.* Full of bounty; liberal, beneficent; generously given. **bounteously,** *adv.* **bounteousness,** *n.* **bountiful,** *a.* Full of bounty; liberal, munificent; plenteous, abundant. **Lady Bountiful,** *n.* A wealthy woman charitable in her neighbourhood. **bountifully,** *adv.* ***bountihead,** *n.* Bounteousness, goodness; virtue, generosity.

bouquet (bu kā′, bu′ kā) [F., O.F. *bosquet*, It. *boschetto*, BOSKET], *n.* A nosegay, a bunch of flowers; the perfume exhaled by wine.

bouquetin (boo′ kė tin, bu kė tăn′) [F. *bouquetin*, prob. for *bouc-estain* (G. *stein-bock*)], *n.* The ibex; an Alpine animal of the goat family.

Bourbon (boor′ bȯn) [French town], *n.* A member of the royal family that formerly ruled France; (*Am.*) an obsolete and unteachable Democrat; (*Am.*) a kind of whisky made of wheat or Indian corn. **Bourbonism,** *n.* Adherence to the Bourbon dynasty. **Bourbonist,** *n.*

bourdon (boor′ dȯn) [F., prob. imit.], *n.* *A low undersong or accompaniment; a bass stop on an organ; a bass reed in a harmonium; the drone of a bagpipe.

bourg (boorg) [F., from late L. *burgus*, W.G. *burg* (cp. A.-S. *burh*, Eng. BOROUGH)]. *n.* A town built under the shadow of a castle; a market town.

bourgeois (1) (boor′ zhwa) [as prec.], *n.* A French citizen; one of the mercantile or shop-keeping class. *a.* Of or pertaining to the bourgeoisie; middle-class or industrial as distinguished from the working-class; (*fig.*) commonplace, humdrum, unintellectual; middle-class in outlook. **bourgeosie** (boor zhwa zē′), *n.* The mercantile or shop-keeping class; the middle class as opposed to the proletariate.

bourgeois (2) (bėr jois′) [prob. from a F. printer], *n.* (*Print.*) A kind of type between brevier and long-primer.

bourgeon [BURGEON].

bourn (1) (bôrn) [var. of BURN (2)], *n.* A small stream; esp. a stream that runs periodically from springs in the chalk.

bourne, bourn (2) (bôrn) [F. *borne*, O.F. *bodne*, BOUND], *n.* A bound, a limit, a goal.

bourree (boo rā′) [F.], *n.* A folk-dance from the Auvergne and Basque provinces; a musical composition in this rhythm.

bourse (boors) [F., lit. purse], *n.* A foreign exchange for the transaction of commercial business; esp. that of Paris.

bourtree (boor′ trē) [etym. unknown], *n.* (*Sc. and North.*) The elder-tree, *Sambucus nigra.*

bouse [BOOZE].

boustrophedon (bou strȯ fē′ dȯn) [Gr., as an ox turns in ploughing (*bous*, ox, *strophē*, a turning, -*don*, adv. suf.)], *a.* Written alternately from left to right and from right to left.

bout (bout) [earlier *bought*, prob. doublet of BIGHT], *n.* A turn, a round, a set-to; trial, essay, attempt; a spell of work; a fit of drunkenness or of illness.

***boutade** (boo′ tad) [F., from *bouter*, to thrust], *n.* An outburst, a sudden fit of violence.

bouton (boo′ ton) [F., button], *n.* (*Path.*) A pimple, pustule, boil; (*Ent.*) the hollow at the end of the tongue of the honey-bee.

bouts-rimés (boo rē mā′) [F., rhymed endings], *n.pl.* A game in which a list of rhymed endings is handed to each player to fill in and complete the verse.

bovine (bō′ vīn) [L. *bovīnus* (*bos bovis*, ox)], *a.* Of or resembling oxen; sluggish; dull, stupid.

bow (1) (bō) [A.-S. *boga* (cp. O.H.G. *bogo*, G. *bogen*, O.Teut. *beugan*, to bend (see BOW (2))], *n.* A curve, a rainbow; a stringed weapon for discharging arrows; the doubling of a string in a slip-knot; a single-looped knot; an ornamental knot in which neckties, ribbons, etc., are tied; a necktie, ribbon, or the like, tied in such a knot; a name for various simple contrivances in shape like a bow; a saddle-bow, an ox-bow; the appliance with which instruments of the violin family are played. *v.t.* To play with or use the bow on (a violin, etc.). **to draw the long bow:** To exaggerate; to tell lies. **to have two strings to one's bow:** To have more resources, plans, or opportunities than one. **bow and string beam, bridge,** or **girder:** A structure in the form of a bent bow, with a horizontal beam or girder in the position of the string. **bow-bent,** *a.* Bent like a bow. ***bow-boy,** *n.* The Archer, Cupid. **bow-compasses,** *n.pl.* Compasses with the legs jointed, so that the points can be turned inwards. **bow-hand,** *n.* The hand that holds the bow in archery or in playing a stringed instrument. **bow-head,** *n.* The Greenland right whale. **bow-legged,** *a.* Having the legs bowed or bent. **bow-man** (1) (bō′ mȧn), *n.* One who shoots with the bow, an archer. **bow-net,** *n.* A cylinder of wicker-work with one narrow entrance, for catching lobsters; a net attached to a bow or arch of metal. **bow-pen, bow-pencil,** *n.* Bow-compasses fitted with a pen or pencil. **bow-saw,** *n.* A saw fitted in a frame like a bowstring in a bow. **bowshot,** *n.* The distance to which an arrow can be shot. **bowstring,** *n.* The string by which a bow is stretched; the string with which persons were executed in Turkey. *v.t.* To strangle with a bowstring. **bowyer,** *n.* A bow-maker; a setter of bows. **bow-window,** *n.* A bay-window segmentally curved.

bow (2) (bou) [A.-S. *būgan*, O.Teut. *beugan*, to bend, stem *bug-* (cp. L. *fugere*, Gr. *pheugein*, Sansk. *bhuj*)], *v.i.* To bend forward as a sign of assent, submission, or salutation; to incline the head; to kneel; to bend under a yoke; hence, to submit, to yield. *v.t.* To cause to bend; to incline, to influence; to crush; to express by bowing; to usher (in or out). *n.* An inclination of the body or head, as a salute or token of respect. **bowed** (boud), *a.* Bent, crooked; bent down.

bow (3) (bou) [cogn. with BOUGH], *n.* (*often in pl.*) The rounded fore-end of a ship or boat; the rower nearest this. **on the bow:** (*Naut.*) Within 45° of the point right ahead. **bow-cap,** *n.* (*Nav. and Aviat.*) A metal plate fitted on the nose of a submarine or an aeroplane. **bow-chaser,** *n.* A gun in the bow of a vessel pointing forward. **bow-grace,** *n.* (*Naut.*) A kind of junk fender round the bows and sides of a ship to prevent injury from floating ice or timber. **bowline** (bō′ lin, -līn), *n.* (*Naut.*) A rope fastened to the middle part of the weather side of a sail to make it stand close to the wind. **bowline knot,** *n.* A safe kind of knot. **on a bowline:** Close-hauled; sailing close to the wind. **bowman** (2) (bou′ mȧn), *n.* The rower nearest the bow. **bow-oar,** *n.* The rower nearest the bow; his oar. **bowsprit** (bō′ sprit), ***boltsprit** (prob. from Dut. *boegspriet*, see SPRIT], *n.* (*Naut.*) A spar running out from the bows of a vessel to support sails and stays.

Bow bells (bō belz), *n.pl.* The bells of St. Mary le Bow, Cheapside. **to be born within the sound of Bow bells:** To be born in the City of London; to be a true Cockney.

bowdlerize (boud′ lėr īz) [Thomas *Bowdler* who in 1818 published an expurgated Shakespeare], *v.t.* To expurgate (a book). **bowdlerism** (boud′ lėr izm), **bowdlerization** (boud lėr ī zā′ shŭn), *n.* The act or practice of expurgating.

bowel (bou′ ėl) [O.F. *boel* (It. *budello*), late L. *botellus*, dim. of *botulus*, a sausage], *n.* One of the intestines, a gut; (*pl.*) the entrails, the intestines, esp. of man; (*fig.*) the seat of tender emotions; pity, compassion; the interior, the centre. *v.t.* To disembowel.

bower (1) (bou′ ėr) [A.-S. *būr*, a chamber, a college (*būan*, to dwell); cp. Dan. *buur*, and G. *bauer*, a cage], *n.* (*poet.*) A dwelling; an inner room, a boudoir; an arbour, a shady retreat, a summer-house; the run of a bower-bird. **bower-bird,** *n.* The name given to several Australian birds of the starling family, which build bowers or runs, adorning them with feathers, shells, etc. **bowery,** *a.* Of the nature of a bower; leafy. **The Bowery,** *n.* A district in New York notorious for political graft.

bower (2) (bou′ ėr) [G. *bauer*, a peasant, the knave (cp. BOER)], *n.* (*Cards*) One of the two knaves in euchre. The knave of trumps is the **right,** and the other of the same colour the **left bower.**

bower (3) (bou′ ėr) [BOW (3)], *n.* (*Naut.*) The name given to two anchors (**best-bower** and **small-bower**) carried in the bows; the cable attached to either.

bowie-knife (bō′ i nīf) [Col. James *Bowie* (*d.* 1836)], *n.* A long knife with blade double-edged towards the point, used as a weapon in the south and south-west of U.S.A.

bowl (1) (bōl) [S.-S. *bolla*, Teut. stem *bul-*, to swell], *n.* A hollow (usually hemispherical) vessel for holding liquids, esp. for drinking; a basin; the contents of such a vessel; a drinking-vessel; a basin-shaped part or concavity.

bowl (2) (bōl) [F. *boule*, L. *bulla*, a bubble], *n.* A solid ball, generally made of wood, used to play with, either spherical or slightly biased or one-sided; (*pl.*) a game with bowls; (*dial.*) skittles. *v.i.* To play at bowls; to roll a bowl along the ground; to deliver the ball at cricket; to move rapidly and smoothly (usu. with *along*). *v.t.* To cause to roll or run along the ground; to deliver (as a ball at cricket); to strike the wicket and put a man out; *to pelt. **to bowl out:** To get a player out at cricket by bowling the bails off; (*slang*) to find out; to convict. **to bowl over:** To knock over; to throw into a helpless condition. **bowler** (1), *n.* One who plays at bowls; the player who delivers the ball at cricket. **bowling,** *n.* Playing at bowls; the act of delivering a ball at cricket. **bowling-alley,** *n.* A covered space for playing skittles. **bowling-crease,** *n.* The line from behind which the bowler delivers the ball at cricket. **bowling-green,** *n.* A level green on which bowls are played.

bowler (2) (bō′ lėr) [BOWL (1)], *n.* An almost-hemispherical stiff felt hat, (*Am.*) a derby (hat).

bowline [BOW (3)].

bowman (1) [BOW (1)]; (2) [BOW (3)].

bowsprit [BOW (3)].

Bow-street (bō′ strēt), *n.* A street in London where the principal police-court is situated. **Bow-street officer, runner,** *n.* Old name for a detective police officer.

bow-window [BOW (1)].

bow-wow (bou′ wou) [imit.], *int.* An exclamation imitating the bark of a dog. *n.* The bark of a dog; (*childish*) a dog. **bow-wow theory,** *n.* (*sarcastic*) The theory that language is developed from imitations of the cries of the lower animals.

bowyang (bō′ yăng), *n.* (*Austral.*) A strap or string below the knee to prevent trousers from dragging.

bowyer [BOW (1)].

box (1) (boks) [A.-S. *box*, L. *buxus*, Gr. *puxos*], *n.* A genus of small evergreen shrubs, *Buxus*, esp. the common box-tree; box-wood. **box-tree,** *n.* The common box, *Buxus sempervirens.* **box-wood,** *n.* The wood of the box-tree. **boxen,** *a.* Of, made of, or resembling box.

box (2) (boks) [from prec.], *n.* A case or receptacle usually with a lid and rectangular or cylindrical, adapted for holding solids, not liquids; the contents of such a case; a compartment partitioned off in a theatre, tavern, coffee-house, or for animals in a stable, railway-truck, etc.; the driver's seat on a coach; a hut, a small house; one of the compartments into which a type-case is divided; a case for the protection of some piece of mechanism from injury. *v.t.* To enclose in or furnish with a box; (*Am.*) to make an excavation in the trunk of (a tree); (*Law*) to deposit a document in court; (*Austral.*) to allow sheep that should be kept separate to run together. **Christmas-box,** *n.* A present given at Christmas in acknowledgement of continuous services rendered throughout the year. **fishing-, shooting-box,** *n.* A small country-house for these sports. **jury-, witness-box,** *n.* The compartments railed off for these persons in a court of law. **loose box,** *n.* A compartment in a stable where the horse is at liberty to move about. **money-box,** *n.* A public or private receptacle for collecting or keeping money in. **in the wrong box:** Mistaken, out of place. **box-bed,** *n.* A bedstead with sides, roof, and sliding panels of wood; a bedstead that folds up like a box. **box-car,** *n.* (*Am.*) A goods van. **box-cloth,** *n.* A tough, closely-woven cloth. **box-coat,** *n.* A heavy overcoat worn by coachmen. **box-day,** *n.* (*Sc. Law*) A day in vacation appointed for the lodgment of papers. **box-drain,** *n.* A square drain. **boxful,** *n.* The quantity of things that a box will hold. **box-hat,** *n.* A silk hat. **box-iron,** *n.* A smoothing-iron with a cavity for a heater. **box-key,** *n.* A T-shaped implement for turning a water cock. **box mattress, box spring mattress,** *n.* A mattress consisting of spiral springs contained in a wooden frame and covered with ticking. **box number,** *n.* A number in a newspaper office to which replies to advertisements may be sent. **box-office,** *n.* An office in a theatre or concert-hall for booking seats. **box-pleat,** *n.* A double fold or pleat. **box-respirator,** *n.* A gas-mask fitting over the respiratory organs drawing air through a box containing a chemical filter. **box-room,** *n.* A room for storing trunks, etc. **box-spanner,** *n.* (*Mach.*) A tubular spanner with the ends shaped to fit the nuts, and turned by a tommy-bar inserted into a transverse hole. **box-tree, box-gum,** *n.* (*Austral.*) A variety of Eucalyptus tree. **to box off:** (*Naut.*) To box-haul; to partition off. **to box the compass:** (*Naut.*) To name the points of the compass in proper order; (*fig.*) to go right round (in direction, political views, etc.) and end at the starting-point. **to box up:** To shut in; to squeeze together. **boxer** (1), *n.* One who puts or packs things up in boxes. **to box-haul,** *v.t.* (*Naut.*) To veer (a ship) in a particular manner when near the shore. **boxing-day,** *n.* The first week-day after Christmas, when Christmas-boxes are given.

box (3) (boks) [etym. doubtful (perh. imit.)], *n.* *A blow; a blow with the open hand on the ear or side of the head. *v.t.* To strike (on the ear, etc.) with the open hand. *v.i.* To fight or spar with fists or with gloves. **boxer** (2), *n.* One who boxes; a pugilist; a member of a secret society in China, ostensibly devoted to athletics, which took the leading part in the movement for the expulsion of foreigners, which came to a head in the rising of 1900; a large, smooth-haired mastiff derived from the German bulldog; (*Austral.*) one who organizes a game of two-up.

boy (boi) [etym. doubtful; perh. from E.Fris. *boi*, young gentleman (cp. Dut. *boef*, knave, M.H.G. *buobe*, G. *bube*)], *n.* A male child; a lad; a slave; a servant; a native, a native labourer; (*fig.*) one who remains a child at heart; (*pl.*) grown-up sons. **the boy:** (*slang*) Champagne. **old boy:** A familiar kind of address. **boy friend,** *n.* (*colloq.*) A man or boy in whom a girl is especially interested. **Boys' Brigade,** *n.* An organization founded in 1883 for the training and welfare of boys. **boy's love,** *n.* Southernwood. **boy's play,** *n.* Play such as boys engage in; trifling. **boyhood,** *n.* The state of being a boy; the time of life at which one is a boy. **Boy Scout,** *n.* A member of an organization founded in 1908 for the development of good citizenship, character and resourcefulness among boys. **boyish,** *a.* Characteristic of or suitable to a boy; puerile. **boyishly,** *adv.* **boyishness,** *n.*

boyar (bo̊ yar′, boi′ år), **boyard** (boi′ ård) [Rus. *boyāre*, pl. of *boyārin* (from O.Slav. *bol*, great, or Rus. *boi*, war)], *n.* A member of the old Russian nobility; a landed proprietor.

boycott (boi′ kot) [first used in 1880 to describe the action of the Land League towards Capt. Boycott, an Irish landlord], *v.t.* To combine to ostracize (a person) on account of his political opinions; to refuse to have dealings with. *n.* The action of boycotting. **boycottee** (boi ko tē′), *n.* **boycotter,** *n.* **boycottism,** *n.*

boyla (boi′ lå) [Austral. abor.], *n.* A sorcerer.

bra (bra) [BRASSIÈRE].

*__brabble__ (brăbl) [etym. doubtful; prob. imit. (cp. Dut. *brabbelen*, to stammer, jabber)], *v.i.* To quibble, to dispute in a captious way, to squabble. *n.* A noisy quarrel; a wrangle.

brace (brās) [O.F. *brace, brasse*, L. *brāchia*, the arms, Gr. *brachiōn*, the arm], *n.* *Armour for the arms; *a coat of armour; *warlike preparation; that which clasps, tightens, connects, or supports; (*pl.*) straps to support the trousers, (*Am.*) suspenders; a strap connecting the body of a coach to the springs; a sign in writing, printing, or music uniting two or more words, lines, staves, etc.; two taken together, a couple, a pair; a timber or scantling to strengthen the framework of a building; (*Naut.*) a rope attached to a yard for trimming the sail; a leather thong on the cord of a drum regulating the tension of the skin; a cord of a drum. *v.t.* To encompass; to gird; to bind or tie close; to tighten or make tense; to strengthen, to fill with energy or firmness; (*Naut.*) to trim sails by means of braces. **brace and bit:** A tool used by carpenters for boring, consisting of a kind of crank in which a bit or drill is fixed. **to splice the main brace:** (*Naut. slang*) To serve an extra rum ration. **a brace of shakes:** (*slang*) A couple of moments; an instant. **bracing,** *a.* Imparting tone or strength.

bracelet (brās′ lėt) [O.F. *bracel*], *n.* An ornamental ring or band for the wrist or arm; *pl.* (*slang*) handcuffs.

bracer (brā′ sėr) [O.F. *brasseure*, L. *brachium*, arm], *n.* A defence for the arm, used in archery, fencing, etc.

*__brach__ (brăch) [O.F. *brachet, braquet*, dim. of *brac*, O.H.G. *bracco* (G. *bracke*), a dog that hunts by scent], *n.* A bitch hound.

brachial ((brā′ ki ăl) [L. *brāchiālis* (*brāchium*, arm)], *a.* Of or belonging to the arm; resembling an arm. **brachiate** (brā′ ki ăt), *a.* (*Bot.*) Having branches in pairs, nearly at right angles to a stem and crossing each other alternately.

brachio- [Gr. *brachiōn*, an arm], *comb. form.* Having arms or arm-like processes. **brachiopod** (brăk′ i ō pod) [Gr. *pous podos*, foot], *n.* (*pl.* **-pods, brachiopoda,** -op′ ō dȧ) A bivalve mollusc with tentacles on each side of the mouth. **brachiopodous,** *a.* Of or resembling the brachiopoda.

brachy- [Gr. *brachus*, short], *comb. form.* Short. **brachycephalic** (brăk i sė făl′ ik) [Gr. *kephalē*, head], *a.* (*Palæont.*) Short-headed; having a skull in which the breadth is at least four-fifths of the length; belonging to a race distinguished by skulls of that proportion. **brachycephaly, brachycephalism** (brăk i sef′ ȧ lizm), *n.* The state of being brachycephalic. **brachylogy** (brȧ kil′ ō ji) [-LOGY] *n.* Concision of speech; abridged or condensed expression; inaccuracy caused by excess of brevity.

*__brack__ (brăk) [BREAK], *n.* A flaw or tear in a cloth or dress.

bracken (brăk′ ėn) [Swed. *bräken*, fern], *n.* A fern, esp. the brake-fern, *Pteris aquilina.*

bracket (brăk′ ėt) [formerly *bragget*, Sp. *bragueta*, dim. of *braga*, L. *brāca*, sing. of *bracæ, braccæ*, breeches (the sense affected by confusion with L. *brāchium*, arm)], *n.* A projection with horizontal top fixed to a wall, a shelf with a stay underneath for hanging against a wall; an angular support; the cheek of a gun-carriage, holding the trunnion; a lamp projecting from a wall; a mark used in printing to enclose a word or words. *v.t.* To furnish with a bracket or brackets; to place within brackets; to connect (names of equal merit) in a class-list; (*Artill.*) to find the range of a target by dropping shots alternately short of and over it. **bracketing,** *n.* (*Building*) A skeleton support for mouldings.

brackish (brăk′ ish) [formerly *brack*, Dut. *brak*], *a.* Partly fresh, partly salt; of a saline taste. **brackishness,** *n.*

bract (brăkt) [L. *bractea*, a thin plate], *n.* (*Bot.*) A small modified leaf or scale on the flower-stalk. **bracteal** (brăk′ tė ăl), *a.* (*Bot.*) Of the nature of a bract. **bracteate** (-te ȧt), *a.* Formed of metal beaten thin; (*Bot.*) furnished with bracts. **bracteole** (brăk′ tė ōl) [L. *bracteola*], *n.* (*Bot.*) A small bract. **bracteolate** (brăk′ tė ō lāt), *a.* (*Bot.*) Furnished with bracteoles. **bractless,** *a.*

brad (brăd) [M.E. *brod*, Icel. *broddr*; a spike (cp. A.-S. *brord*)], *n.* A thin, flattish nail, with a small lip or projection on one side instead of a head.

bradawl (brăd′ awl) [AWL], *n.* A small boring-tool.

brady- [Gr. *bradus*, slow], *comb. form.* Slow. **bradypeptic** (brăd i pep′ tik) [PEPTIC], *a.* Of slow digestion. **bradypod** (brăd′ i pod) [Gr. *pous podos*, foot], *n.* (*Zool.*) One of the sloth tribe.

brae (brā) [Icel. *brā*, eyelid, brow (cp. A.-S. *bræw*)] *n.* A slope bounding a river valley; a hill.

brag (brăg) [etym. doubtful], *n.* A boast; boasting; a game of cards. *v.i.* To boast. *v.t.* To boast; to challenge; to bully. *adv.* Proudly, conceitedly. *__bragly,__ *adv.* Finely, briskly, nimbly. **braggadocio** (brăg ȧ dō′ shi ō) [BRAG], *n.* The name given by Spenser to Vainglory personified; an empty boaster; empty boasting. **braggart** [F. *bragard*, from *braguer*, to brag], *n.* A boastful fellow. *a.* Given to bragging; boastful. *__braggartism,__ *n.* Boastfulness, bragging. *__braggingly,__ *adv.*

Brahma, Brahmapootra (bra′ mȧ, bra mȧ poo′ trȧ) [*Brahmapootra*, name of river], *n.* A variety of domestic fowl.

Brahmin (bra′ min) [Sansk. *brāhmana*, from *brahman*, worship], *n.* A member of the Hindu priestly caste. **Brahminic, Brahminical** (bra min′ ik, -ik ăl), *a.* Of or pertaining to Brahmins or to Brahminism. **brahminee** (1) (bra min ē′) [Sansk. *brāhminī*, fem. of *brāhmana*], *n.* A female Brahmin. **brahminee** (2) (bra′ mi nē), *a.* Pertaining to the Brahmin caste. **Brahminism** (bra′ min izm), *n.*

braid (1) (brād) [A.-S. *brægd, bræd*, trick, deceit, from *bregdan, bredan*, to move to and fro, weave (cp. Icel. *bregtha*, O.H.G. *brettan*)], *n.* Anything plaited or interwoven; a narrow band; a woven fabric for trimming or binding. **a.* Deceitful. *v.t.* To intertwine, to plait; to dress the hair in plaits or bands; to tie the hair with ribbon or bands; to trim or bind with braid. **braiding,** *n.* The action of plaiting or interweaving; embroidery.

*__braid__ (2) (brād) [BRAID (1), or from obs. v. *abraid*, upbraid], *v.t.* To upbraid, to reproach.

braid (3) (*Sc.*) [BROAD].

braidism (brā′ dizm) [Dr. James *Braid* (1795–1860), who applied and explained the system in 1842], *n.* Hypnotism, mesmerism.

brail (brāl) [O.F. *brail, braiel*, L. *brācāle*, breech-girdle (*bracæ*, breeches)], *n.* A piece of leather with which to bind up a hawk's wing; (*pl.*) ropes used to gather up the foot and leeches of a sail before furling. *v.t.* To fasten up (the wing of a hawk) with a brail; (*Naut.*) to haul up by means of the brails.

braille (brāl) [Louis *Braille* (1809–52), the inventor], *n.* A system of writing or printing for the blind, by means of combinations of points stamped in relief. **braille music, type,** *n.* Music or symbols designed on this system. **braille writer,** *n.* An instrument for stamping paper with these.

brain (brān) [A.-S. *brægen* (Dut. *brein*, perh. conn. with Gr. *brechmos*, forehead)], *n.* The soft, whitish, convoluted mass of nervous substance contained in the skull of vertebrates; any analogous organ in the invertebrates (*sing.* the organ, *pl.* the substance); the seat of intellect, thought, etc.; the centre of sensation; (*fig.*) intellectual power. *v.t.* To dash out the brains of; to kill in this way; (*fig.*) *to conceive in the brain. **to have a thing on the brain:** To be obsessed with it. **brain-coral,** *n.* Coral resembling the convolutions of the brain. **brain-fag,** *n.* Nervous exhaustion. **brain-fever,** *n.* Inflammation of the brain; fever with brain complications. **brain-pan,** *n.* The skull. **brain-sick,** *a.* Of diseased brain or mind; flighty, one-sided, injudicious; produced by a diseased brain. **brain**

storm, *n.* A sudden, violent mental disturbance. **brains trust,** *n.* (*Radio.*) A bench of persons before the microphone answering impromptu selected questions from an audience. **brain-washing,** *n.* The subjection of a victim to sustained mental pressure, or to indoctrination, in order to extort a confession or to induce him to change his views. **brain wave,** *n.* (*colloq.*) A brilliant idea. ***brainish,** *a.* Headstrong, ambitious. **brainless,** *a.* Destitute of brain; (*fig.*) silly, witless. **brainy,** *a.* Having brains; (*Am.*) acute, clever.

braird (brârd) [A.-S. *brerd,* brim, border, edge, point], *n.* The first shoots of corn or grain. *v.i.* To sprout.

braise (brāz) [F. *braiser,* from *braise,* hot charcoal], *v.t.* To cook in a tightly-closed pan (properly with a fire above and below). **braising-pan,** *n.* A pan in which meat is braised, with a tightly-fitting lid to hold live coals, so that heat is applied both above and below.

brake (1) (brāk) [BRACKEN], *n.* Bracken.

brake (2) (brāk) [M.L.G. *brake* or O.Dut. *bracke* (Dut. *braak*), a flax-brake, Dut. *breken,* to break], *n.* An instrument for braking flax or hemp; an implement like scissors for peeling the bark of withes for baskets; a heavy harrow for breaking up clods; *an instrument of torture; a framework in which restive horses are confined during shoeing; a light carriage in which horses are broken to harness; a large wagonette (in this sense also spelt BREAK). *v.t.* To crush flax or hemp.

brake (3) (brāk) [etym. doubtful; perh. from prec., or from O.F. *brac,* an arm, lever], *n.* An appliance to a wheel to check or stop motion; a brake-van; the handle of a pump. *v.t.* To retard by means of a brake. **brakeman** (*Am.*), **brakesman,** *n.* A man in charge of a brake, a railway guard. **brake-van,** *n.* A railway carriage containing a brake; a guard's van. **brakeless,** *a.* Without a brake.

brake (4) (brāk) [etym. doubtful; perh. from M.L.G. *brake,* tree-stumps, or conn. with BREAK], *n.* A mass of brushwood, a thicket. **braky,** *a.* Full of bracken or brake; rough, thorny.

bramah (bra' mȧ) [Joseph *Bramah,* an inventor (1749–1814)], *n.* A kind of lock; a key thereto. **bramah-lock,** *n.* A lock invented by Bramah. **bramah-press,** *n.* The hydraulic press invented by Bramah.

bramble (brăm' bėl) [A.-S. *brembel, brēmel,* dim. of O.Teut. word corr. to A.-S. *brom,* broom (cp. Dut. *braam,* blackberry, O.H.G. *brāma,* bramble, G. *brombeere,* blackberry)], *n.* The blackberry, or any allied thorny shrub. **bramble-net,** *n.* A net to catch birds. **brambled,** *a.* Overgrown with brambles. **brambly,** *a.* Full of brambles.

brambling (brăm' bling) [BRAMBLE, -LING], *n.* The mountain finch, *Fringilla montifringilla.*

bran (brăn) [O.F., etym. doubtful], *n.* The husks of ground corn separated from the flour by bolting. **bran-mash,** *n.* Bran soaked in water; (*colloq.*) bread sopped in tea or coffee.

brancard (brăng' kȧrd) [F., a litter, from *branche,* BRANCH], *n.* A horse-litter.

branch (branch) [F. *branche,* late L. *branca,* a paw], *n.* A shoot or limb of a tree or shrub, esp. one from a bough; any offshoot, member, part, or subdivision of an analogous kind; a child, a scion; a warrant or licence given to a pilot from Trinity House; anything considered as a subdivision or extension of a main trunk, as of mountain-range, river, road, railway, family, genus, system of knowledge, legislature, commercial organization, etc.; a rib in a Gothic vault. *v.i.* To shoot out into branches or subdivisions; to diverge from a main direction; to divide, to ramify. *v.t.* *To embroider with flowers or foliage; to divide into branches; to subdivide. **root and branch,** *a.* Thorough, complete. *adv.* Thoroughly, completely. **branch-pilot,** *n.* (*Naut.*) A pilot holding a Trinity House certificate. **branched-work,** *n.* Sculptured foliage. **brancher,** *n.* That which shoots out into branches; a young hawk or other bird when it leaves the nest and takes to the branches. **branchless,** *a.* **branchlet,** *n.* A small branch, a twig. **branchy,** *a.* Full of branches, ramifying.

branchia, branchiæ (brăng' ki ȧ, -ki' ē) [L. *branchia, -iæ,* Gr. *branchia,* pl. of *branchion*], *n.pl.* (*Zool.*) The gills of fishes and some amphibia. **branchial,** *a.* Pertaining to or of the nature of gills. **branchiate,** *a.* Characterized by gills. **branchiferous** (brăng kif' ėr ŭs), *a.* Furnished with gills. **branchiform** (brăng' ki fôrm), *a.* Shaped like gills. **branchio-** (brăng' ki ō), *comb. form.* Pertaining to gills. **branchiopod** (brang' ki ȯ pod) [Gr. *pous podos,* foot], *n.* (*pl.* **branchiopoda,** -op' ȯ dȧ) (*Zool.*) An individual of a group of molluscoid animals with gills on the feet. **branchiopodous** (brăng ki op' ȯ dŭs), *a.* Of or pertaining to the branchiopoda; having gills on the feet.

brand (brănd) [A.-S. (cp. O.Teut. *brandoz,* from *bran-,* pret. stem of *brinnan,* to burn, O.H.G. *brant,* brand, sword)], *n.* A piece of burning wood; a piece of wood partially burnt; a torch; a mark made by or with a hot iron, an instrument for stamping a mark; a trade-mark, hence, a particular kind of manufactured article; a kind of blight; a sword; a stigma; class, quality. *v.t.* To mark with a brand; (*fig.*) to imprint on the memory; to stigmatize. **a brand from the burning:** A person rescued or converted from sin or irreligion. **brand-iron,** *n.* A grid-iron, an andiron, *a trivet; (*fig.*) *a sword. **brand-new,** *a.* As if just from the furnace, quite new. **branding-iron,** *n.* An iron to brand with. **brander,** *n.* A branding-iron, a gridiron. *v.t.* To cook on a gridiron; to broil or grill. ***brandise,** *n.* A trivet.

brandish (brăn' dish) [F. *brandir* (pres.p. *brandissant*), from O.Teut. *brandoz,* see prec.], *v.t.* To wave or flourish about (as a weapon, etc.). *n.* A flourish; waving.

brandling (brănd' ling) [BRAND, -LING], *n.* A small red worm with vivid rings, used as bait in angling; a salmon parr.

brand-, bran-new [BRAND].

brandreth (brănd' rėth) [Icel. *brand-reith,* a grate (*brandr,* BRAND, *reith,* a vehicle)], *n.* A wooden stand for a barrel, a rick, etc.; a fence round a well.

brandy (brăn' di) [formerly *brandwine,* Dut. *brandewijn,* burnt or distilled wine (*brandt,* p.p. of *branden,* to burn)], *n.* A spirit distilled from wine. *v.t.* To mix with brandy; to furnish or refresh with brandy. **brandy-ball,** *n.* A kind of sweet. **brandy-pawnee** [Hind. *pānī,* water], *n.* Brandy and water. **brandy-snap,** *n.* Thin, wafer-like gingerbread. ***brandy-wine,** *n.* [BRANDY].

brangle (brăn' gėl) [F. *branler,* to shake (etym. doubtful)], *n.* A wrangle, a quarrel. *v.i.* To wrangle, to quarrel, to dispute. ***branglement,** *n.* A brangle, a squabble.

brank (brăngk) [etym. unknown], *n.* Buckwheat, *Fagopyrum esculentum.*

branks (brăngks) [Sc., etym. doubtful], *n.* A kind of gag or bridle for punishing scolds; a bridle; a muzzle.

brank-ursine (brăngk' ĕr sin) [med. L. *branca ursīna,* bear's paw], *n.* The acanthus or bear's-breech.

***bransle** (brănsl) [F., var. of *branle,* see BRAWL (2)], *n.* A kind of dance.

brant [BRENT (2)].

brash (1) (brăsh) [etym. doubtful], *n.* Loose, disintegrated rock or rubble. *a.* (*Am.*) Tender. brittle. **brash-ice,** *n.* Broken ice. **brashy,** *a,* Crumbly, rubbly.

brash (2) (brăsh) [onomat.], *n.* A slight indisposition arising from disorder of the alimentary canal. **teething-brash, weaning-brash:** Infantile disorders. **water-brash:** A belching of water from the stomach; heartburn; a dash of rain.

brash (3) (brăsh) [?], *a.* Self-assertive, cheeky.

brass (bras) [A.-S. *bræs*], *n.* A yellow alloy of copper and zinc; anything made of this alloy; a brazen vessel; an engraved sepulchral tablet of this metal; musical instruments of brass; (*slang*) money; effrontery, impudence. *a.* Made of brass. *v.t.* To coat with brass. **to part brass rags:** (*Nav. colloq.*) To break off a friendship. **brass band,** *n.* A band performing chiefly on brass instruments. **brass-bounder:** (*Naut. slang*) A midshipman; a ship's officer in the mercantile marine. **brass farthing,** *n.* (*colloq.* The lowest measure of value. **brass hat:** (*colloq.*) A staff officer. **brass plate,** *n.* A plate of brass engraved with name, trade or profession, etc. fixed at doors, etc. **brass tacks:** (*colloq.*) Details; facts and not words. **brassy,** *a.* Resembling brass; unfeeling, impudent, shameless; debased, cheap, pretentious. *n.* A wooden golf club faced with brass. **brassily,** *adv.* **brassiness,** *n.*

brassage (brăs′ ăj) [F., from *brasser*, to stir up or mix (molten metals)], *n.* The mintage fee for coining money.

brassard (brăs′ ård) [F. *bras*, arm, -ARD], *n.* A badge worn on the arm, an armband, armlet.

brasserie (brăs′ ė ri) [F., from *brasser*, O.F. *bracer* to brew, from *brace*, malt], *n.* A brewery; beer-shop and restaurant.

brassière (brăs′ ē âr) [F.], *n.* A bodice for supporting the bust.

brassy [BRASS].

brat (1) (brăt [A.-S. *bratt*, prob. from O.Ir. *brat*], *n.* An over-garment; a cloak, an apron, a pinafore.

brat (2) (brăt) [etym. doubtful; perh. from prec.], *n.* A child, an infant (usu. in a slighting sense).

brattice (brăt′ is) [M.E. *bretasce*, *brutaske*, O.F. *bretesce*, *breteske*, prob. from G. *brett*, board], *n.* *A temporary breastwork; a partition for ventilation in a mine; a partition; a lining of timber. **brattice-cloth,** *n.* A stout tarred cloth used instead of boards for bratticing. **brattice-work,** *n.* **bratticing,** *n.* (*Mining*) Brattice-work; (*Arch.*) open carved work.

brattle (brătl) [onomat.], *n.* A rattling noise; a scamper. *v.i.* To make a rattling noise; to scamper; to flow with a rattling noise.

bravado (brå va′ dō) [Sp. *bravada*], *n.* (*pl.* **-oes**) An insolent menace; ostentatious defiance; defiant behaviour.

brave (brāv) [F. *bravo*, It. *bravo*, gallant, fine (etym. unknown)], *a.* Daring, courageous; gallant, noble; showy, gay; excellent, fine. *n.* *A bully, a bravo; *a toast, a brag; a North American Indian warrior. *v.t.* To defy, to challenge; to meet with courage. *v.i.* To swagger, to show off. **to brave it out:** To bear oneself defiantly in the face of blame or suspicion. **bravely,** *adv.* **bravery,** *n.* Courage; *bravado; display, splendour; finery.

bravo (1) (bra′ vō) [It.], *n.* (*pl.* **-oes**) A hired assassin; a bandit, a desperado.

bravo (2) bra vō′) [It.], *int.* (*fem.*, **brava**; *superl.* ***bravissimo, -ma,*** (bra vis′ i mō, -ma) Capital! well done! *n.* A cry of approval; a cheer.

bravura (brå voo′ rå) [It., bravery], *n.* (*Mus.*) Brilliance of execution; a display of daring and skill in artistic execution; a piece of music that calls out all the powers of an executant.

braw (*Sc.*) [BRAVE].

brawl (1) (brawl) [etym. doubtful; prob. imit.], *v.i.* To quarrel noisily; to babble (as running water); (*Law*) to create a disturbance in a consecrated place or building. *v.t.* To utter loudly; *to overpower with noise. *n.* A noisy quarrel, a disturbance, a tumult. **brawler,** *n.* **brawling,** *a.* **brawlingly,** *adv.*

***brawl** (2) (brawl) [F. *branle* (*branler*, see BRANGLE)], *n.* A French dance like a cotillion.

brawn (brawn) [O.F. *braon*, flesh for roasting, W .G. *brâdo*, from *brâdan*, to roast (cp. A.-S. *brǣdan*, O.H.G. *prātan*, G. *braten*)], *n.* Muscle, flesh; the flesh of a boar; pig's head collared or potted; (*fig.*) strength. ***brawned,** *a.* Brawny, muscular. ***brawner,** *n.* A boar fattened for the table. **brawny,** *a.* Muscular, strong, hardy. **brawniness,** *n.*

braxy (brăk′ si) [etym. doubtful], *n.* Splenic apoplexy in sheep; the flesh of a sheep which has died of this disorder. *a.* Affected by this disease, or belonging to a sheep that has died through disease or accident. **braxied,** *a.* Braxy.

bray (1) (brā) [O.F. *breier* (F. *broyer*), perh. conn. with BREAK], *v.t.* To pound or grind small, esp. with pestle and mortar; to beat fine. **brayer,** *n.* A wooden muller used to temper printing-ink.

bray (2) (brā) [O.F. *braire*, low L. *bragīre* (cogn. with L. *fragor*, a crashing noise)], *v.i.* To make a harsh, discordant noise, like an ass. *v.t.* To utter harshly or loudly (often with *out*). *n.* A loud cry; the cry of the ass; a harsh, grating sound.

braze (1) (brāz) [O.F. *braser*, Icel. *brasa*, to harden by fire], *v.t.* To solder with an alloy of brass and zinc.

braze (2) (brāz) [BRASS], *v.t.* To cover or ornament with brass; to colour like brass.

brazen (brā′ zėn) [A.-S. *bræsen*, from *bræs*, brass], *a.* Made of brass; resembling brass; (*fig.*) shameless, impudent. *v.t.* To face impudently (often with *out*); (*fig.*) to harden, make shameless. **brazen age:** The third of the mythological ages, the age of violence. **brazen-face,** *n.* An impudent person. **brazen-faced,** *a.* Impudent, shameless. **brazenly,** *adv.* **brazenness,** *n.* **brazier** (1), *n.* A worker in brass. **braziery,** *n.* Brasswork.

brazier (2) (brā′ zi ėr) [F. *brasier*, from *braise*, live coals], *n.* A large pan to hold lighted charcoal.

brazil (brå zil′) [etym. unknown], *n.* A red dye-wood produced by the genus *Cæsalpinia*, which gave its name to the country in South America. **brazil-nut,** *n.* The triangular, edible seed of *Bertholletia excelsa*.

breach (brēch) [A.-S. *brice*, *bryce* (*brecan*, to BREAK)], *n.* The act of breaking; a break, a gap; *an inlet of the sea; violation, whether by a definite act or by omission, of a law, duty, right, contract, or engagement; a rupture of friendship or alliance; alienation, quarrel; a gap, esp. one made by guns in a fortification; (*Naut.*) the breaking of waves; a whale's leap from the water. *v.t.* To make a breach or gap in. *v.i.* To leap from the water (as a whale). **breach of faith:** Violation of trust. **breach of promise:** Failure to keep a promise to marry. **breach of the peace:** Violation of the public peace; a riot, an affray.

bread (bred) [A.-S. *brēad*, piece of a loaf (cp. O.H.G. *prōt*, G. *brod*)], *n.* A well-known food, made of flour or other meal kneaded into dough, generally with yeast, made into loaves and baked. **to break bread:** To take food; to dispense or partake of the Holy Communion. **bread-and-butter,** *n.* (*fig.*) The means of living. *a.* Boyish, girlish. **bread-and-butterhood, -butterishness,** *n.* **bread-and-buttery,** *a.* **bread and cheese,** *n.* (*fig.*) Simple fare; bare subsistence. **bread and wine:** The Lord's Supper; Holy Communion. **bread buttered on both sides:** Fortunate circumstances; ease and prosperity. **daily bread:** Means of livelihood. **bread-basket,** *n.* A basket for holding bread; (*slang*) the stomach. **bread-corn,** *n.* Corn for making bread. **bread-crumb,** *n.* A fragment of the soft part of bread; (*pl.*) bread crumbled for culinary purposes. **bread-fruit,** *n.* The farinaceous fruit of a South Sea tree, *Artocarpus incisa*. **bread-line,** *n.* A queue for obtaining bread. **bread-poultice,** *n.* A poultice made of hot soaked bread. **bread-room,** *n.* A place for keeping bread, esp. on board ship. **bread-root,** *n.* A North American plant with an edible carrot-like root, *Psoralea esculenta*. **bread-sauce,** *n.* (*Cook.*) A sauce made with bread-crumbs, milk and onions. **bread-stuff,** *n.* Material for bread. **bread-winner,** *n.* One who supports himself and his family by his earnings; (*fig.*) a trade, art, tool, or machine that supports a family. **breaded,** *a.* Dressed with bread-crumbs. **breadless,** *a.* Without bread, without food.

breadth (bredth) [A.-S. *brædu*, later *brede*, assim. to LENGTH, etc.], *n.* Measure from side to side; a piece of material of full breadth; width, extent, largeness; broad effect; (*fig.*) liberality, catholicity, tolerance. **breadthways, -wise,** *adv.* By way of the breadth, across.

break (1) (brāk) [A.-S. *brecan* (cp. Goth. *brican*, O.H.G. *prechan*, G. *brechan*, from O.Teut. stem *brek-*, cp. L. *frangere*)], *v.t.* (*past* **broke,** *earlier* **brake,** *p.p.* **broken, broke**) To part by violence; to rend apart, to shatter, to rupture, to disperse to, impair; to destroy the completeness or continuity of; to subdue, to tame, to train; to ruin financially; to cashier, to reduce to the ranks; to disable, to wear out, to exhaust the strength or resources of; to disconnect, interrupt; to intercept, to lessen the force of; to infringe, transgress, violate; *to carve (a deer). *v.i.* To separate into two or more portions; to burst, to burst forth; to appear with suddenness; to become bankrupt; to decline in health; to change direction; to twist, as a ball at cricket; to make the first stroke at billiards; to alter the pace (as a horse); to alter (as a boy's voice at the age of puberty). **to break a head:** To graze or wound a head. **to break a lance with:** To encounter, to try one's skill with. **to break a way:** To make a way by forcing obstacles apart. **to break away:** To remove by breaking; to start away. **to break bread with:** To be entertained at table by; to take Communion with. **to break bulk:** To begin to unload. **to break cover:** To start forth from a hiding-place. **to break down:** To destroy, to overcome; to collapse, to fail; to analyse costs etc. into component parts. **breakdown,** *n.* Down-fall, collapse; total failure resulting in stoppage; a wild dance (orig. Negro). **breakdown gang,** *n.* A gang of men sent to clear a railway line after an accident, (*Am.*) a wrecking-crew. **to break even:** To emerge without gaining or losing. **to break ground:** To plough, to dig (esp. uncultivated or fallow ground); to open trenches; (*fig.*) to commence operations; (*Naut.*) to begin to weigh anchor. **to break in:** To tame, to train to something. **to break into:** To enter by force; to interrupt. **to break free** or **loose:** To escape from captivity; to shake off restraint. **to break news:** To reveal gently. **to break off:** To detach from; to cease, to desist. **to break open:** To force a door or cover; to penetrate by violence. **to break out:** To burst loose; to burst forth (as a war); to appear (as an eruption on the skin; said also of the individual and of feelings, passions, etc.). **to break the back:** (*Naut.*) To break the keel; (*fig.*) to get through the greater part of. **to break the heart:** To overwhelm with grief. **to break the ice:** To prepare the way; to take the first steps. **to break up:** To disintegrate; to lay open (as ground); to dissolve, to disband, to separate; to start school holidays. **to break upon the wheel:** To torture or execute by stretching upon a wheel, and breaking the limbs with an iron bar. **to break wind:** To emit wind from the bowels. **to break with:** To cease to be friends with; to quarrel with. **break-away,** *n.* (*Austral.*) A stampede of cattle or sheep; an animal that breaks away from the herd. **break-club,** *n.* (*Golf*) An obstacle that might break a club accidentally hitting it. **break-head,** *n.* (*Naut.*) The reinforced head of a ship fitted for breaking its way through ice. **break-joint,** *n.* (*Build.*) A disposition of stones or bricks so that the joints do not fall immediately over each other. **break-neck,** *a.* Endangering the neck, hazardous. **break-up,** *n.* Disruption, dispersal into parts or elements; disintegration, decay, dissolution; dispersal. **break-through,** *n.* (*Geol.*) An outcrop; (*Mil.*) penetration of enemy lines. **breakable,** *a.* Capable of being broken.

break (2) (brāk) [from prec.]. *n.* The act of breaking; an opening, gap, breach; interruption of continuity in time or space; a line in writing or printing noting suspension of the sense; irregularity; the twist of a ball at cricket; (*Naut.*) the vertical face of forecastle head or poop; (*Billiards*) a number of points scored continuously; (*Mus.*) the point where one voice register changes to another, as bass to tenor; the corresponding point in musical instruments; (*colloq.*) a lucky opportunity. **break of day:** Dawn. [See also BRAKE (2).]

breakage (brāk′ ij) [as prec.], *n.* The act of breaking; the state of being broken; loss or damage from breaking; an interruption; change in quality of voice from one register to another.

breaker (1) (brā′ kėr) [BREAK (1)], *n.* One or that which breaks; a heavy wave breaking against the rocks or in passing over shallows.

breaker (2) (brā′ kėr) [Sp. *barrica*], *n.* A keg, a water-cask.

breakfast (brek′ fȧst) [BREAK, FAST], *n.* The first meal of the day. *v.i.* To take breakfast. *v.t.* To provide with or entertain at breakfast.

breakwater (brāk′ waw tėr), *n.* A pier, mole, or anything similar, to break the force of the waves and protect shipping.

bream (1) (brēm) [O.F. *bresme* (F. *brême*), (cp. M.H.G. *brahsem*, G. *brassen*; perh. from stem *breh-*, to glitter)], *n.* A freshwater fish of the genus *Abramis*, esp. *A. brama*, the carp-bream.

bream (2) (brēm) [etym. doubtful], *v.t.* (*Naut.*) To clear (a ship's bottom) of ooze, seaweed, shell-fish, etc., by burning.

breast (brest) [A.-S. *brēost*, O.Teut. *breustom* (G. *brust*, Dut. *borst*)], *n.* One of the organs for the secretion of milk in women; the rudimentary part corresponding to this in man; the fore-part of the human body between the neck and the abdomen; the analogous part in the lower animals; the upper fore-part of a coat or other article of dress; (*Mining*) the working coal-face; (*fig.*) source of nourishment; the seat of the affections; the affections; the front, the fore-part. *v.t.* To apply or oppose the breast to; (*fig.*) to stem, to oppose, to face. **to breast up a hedge:** To cut the face of it so as to lay bare the stems. **to give the breast:** To give suck. **to make a clean breast:** To confess all that one knows. **breast-bone,** *n.* The flat bone in front of chest to which certain ribs are attached, the sternum. **breast-deep,** *a.* and *adv.* As deep as the breast is high. **breast-drill,** *n.* A drill worked against the breast. **breast-harness,** *n.* Harness attached to a breast-band instead of a collar. **breast-high,** *a.* and *adv.* As high as the breast; (*Hunting*) so high that the hounds race with heads erect (of scent). **breast-knot,** *n.* A knot of ribbons worn on the breast. **breast-pin,** *n.* A pin worn on the breast or in a scarf; a brooch. **breast-plate,** *n.* Armour worn upon the breast; a piece of embroidered linen, adorned with precious stones, worn on the breast of the Jewish high priest; the upper part of the shell of a turtle or tortoise; an inscribed plate on a coffin. **breast-plough,** *n.* A kind of small hand-plough used in paring turf. **breast-pocket,** *n.* Inside pocket of a man's jacket. **breast-rail,** *n.* The upper rail on a balcony. **breast-summer** (bres′ ŭm ėr), **bres-summer** [SUMMER (2)], *n.* A beam supporting the front of a building after the manner of a lintel. **breast-wall,** *n.* A retaining wall. **breast-wheel,** *n.* A water-wheel which receives the water at the level of its axis. **breast-work.** *n.* A hastily constructed parapet thrown up breast-high for defence; (*Arch.*) the parapet of a building; (*Naut.*) a railing or balustrade across a ship. **breasted,** *a.* Having a breast; decorated on the breast.

breath (breth) [A.-S. *brœth*, O.Teut. *bræthoz*, steam, or from stem *bræ-* (Aryan *bhrē-*), to heat, burn], *n.* The air drawn in and expelled by the lungs in respiration; the act or power of breathing; a single respiration; a very slight breeze; (*fig.*) the time of a single respiration; respite; an instant; a whiff, an exhalation; a rumour, a whisper, a murmur. **below one's breath:** In a whisper. **to take breath:** To pause. **to take one's breath away:** To astonish.

breathful, *a.* Full of breath or wind; alive; odorous. **breathless,** *a.* Out of breath; dead, lifeless; panting; without a movement of the air; (*fig.*) excited, eager. **breathlessly,** *adv.* **breathlessness,** *n.* **breathy** (breth' i), *a.* (*Singing*) Aspirated; giving the sound of breathing. **breathiness,** *n.*

breathe (brēth) [from prec.], *v.i.* To inhale or exhale air, to respire; to live; to take breath; to move or sound like breath. *v.t.* To inhale or exhale (as air); to emit, send out, by means of the lungs; to utter; to utter with vehemence (with *out*); to express, to manifest; to allow breathing space to; to make breathe by means of exercise; to blow into (as a wind instrument). **to breathe again, breathe freely:** To be relieved from fear or anxiety. **to breathe one's last:** To die. **breathable,** *a.* That may be breathed. **breathableness,** *n.* **breather,** *n.* One who or that which breathes; exercise to try the lungs; a rest in order to gain breath. **breathing,** *a.* Living; life-like. *n.* The action of breathing; a respite; an aspirate; (*Greek Gram.*) either of the two signs [ʽ] or [ʼ] placed over the first vowel of a word to mark the presence or absence of the aspirate. **breathing-part, -place, -space,** *n.* A pause, place, or opening for breathing. **breathing-pore,** *n.* A minute aperture for the admission of air. **breathing-time,** *n.* Time for recovering one's breath; a pause. **breathing-while,** *n.* A moment, an instant.

breccia (brech' å, brech' i å) [Gr., gravel, rubble (cp. F. *brèche*, O.H.G. *brecha*, breaking, *brechan*, to BREAK)], *n.* A rock composed of angular, as distinguished from rounded, fragments cemented together in a matrix. **brecciated** (brech i ā' tėd), *a.* Formed into breccia.

bred, *p.p.* [BREED].

***brede** [BRAID (1)].

breech (brēch) [A.-S. *brēc*, pl. of *brōc* (M.H.G. *bruoch*, breeches)], *n.* (*pl.* **breeches,** brich' ėz) The buttocks, the posteriors; the hinder part of anything; the portion of a gun behind the bore; (*pl.*) a garment worn by men, covering the loins and thighs, and reaching just below the knees. *v.t.* To clothe or cover with or as with breeches; to whip upon the buttocks. **to wear the breeches:** To rule, to be master (said of a wife). **Breeches Bible** [BIBLE]. **breech-block,** *n.* A movable piece to close the breech of a gun. **breeches-buoy,** *n.* A life-saving device run on a rope stretched from a wrecked vessel to a place of safety. **breech-loader,** *n.* A fire-arm loaded at the breech. **breech-loading,** *a.* Loaded at the breech. **breeching,** *n.* A strong leather strap passing round the haunches of a shaft-horse; (*Naut.*) a stout rope securing a gun to a ship's side. **breechless,** *a.* Without breeches.

breed (brēd) [A.-S. *brēdan* (cp. G. *bruten*, A.-S. *brōd*, BROOD)], *v.t.* (*past & p.p.* **bred**) To bring forth; to give birth to; to raise (cattle, etc.), to rear; (*fig.*) to give rise to, to yield, to produce; to engender, to cause to develop; to train up, to educate, to bring up. *v.i.* To be pregnant; to produce offspring; to come into being, to arise, spread; to be produced or engendered. *n.* A line of descendants from the same parents or stock; family, race, offspring. **to breed in and in:** To breed always with or from near relatives. **to breed true:** Always to produce young in harmony with the parental type. ***breed-bate** [*bate*, contention, DEBATE], *n.* A quarrelsome person. **breeder,** *n.* One who breeds, esp. one who breeds cattle and other animals. **breeding,** *n.* The act of giving birth to; the raising of a breed; bringing-up, nurture, rearing; manners, deportment, good manners.

breeks (*Sc.*) [BREECHES, see BREECH].

breeze (1) (brēz) [Sp. *brisa*, the N.E. wind, prob. from F. BISE], *n.* A gentle gale, a light wind; (*fig.*) a disturbance, a row; a whisper, rumour. *v.i.* To blow gently or moderately; to move in a lively way. **to breeze up:** To begin to blow freshly; to sound louder on the breeze. **breezeless,** *a.* Undisturbed by any breeze; still, calm. **breezy,** *a.* Open, exposed to breezes, windy; (*fig.*) lively, brisk, jovial. **breeziness,** *n.*

breeze (2), **brize** (brēz) [A.-S. *briosa* (etym. doubtful)], *n.* A gad-fly.

breeze (3) (brēz) [F. *braise*, live coals (see BRAZIER)], *n.* Small cinders and cinder-dust; small coke, siftings of coke. **breeze block,** *n.* A brick or block made of breeze and cement.

bregma (breg' ma) [Gr. *brechein*, to moisten], *n.* (*pl.* **-ata**) (*Anat.*) The point on the skull where the coronal and sagittal sutures meet.

Brehon (brē' hòn) [O.Ir. *breitheamh*, a judge (*breith*, judgment)], *n.* An ancient hereditary Irish judge. **Brehon law,** *n.* The native Irish code of laws, abolished in the reign of James I.

breloque (brė lōk') [F. (etym. unknown)], *n.* An ornament attached to a watch-chain.

***bren, brent** (1) [obs. forms of BURN (1), BURNT].

Bren gun (bren) [2 first letters of Brno (Czechoslovakia), and Enfield], *n.* (*Mil.*) A type of light machine-gun.

brent (2), ***brant** (brent, brănt) [A.-S. *brant*], *a.* Steep, precipitous, lofty; smooth, without wrinkles.

brent-goose (brent' goos) [etym. doubtful; cp. Swed. *brandgås*, G. *brandgans*], *n.* The smallest of the wild geese, *Bernicla brenta*, which visits Britain in the winter.

brer (brĕr) [Negro contr. of BROTHER], *n.* Brother.

bressummer [BREASTSUMMER, see BREAST].

brethren, *n.pl.* [BROTHER].

bretwalda (bret wawl' då) [A.-S.], *n.* Ruler of the Britons or of Britain; a title given to some of the Anglo-Saxon kings who held supremacy or precedence over the rest.

breve (brēv) [BRIEF], *n.* *A brief; a sign (˘) used in printing to mark a short vowel; (*Mus.*) a note of time equal to two semibreves.

brevet (brev' ėt) [F., dim of *bref*, a letter (cp. BRIEF)], *n.* An official document conferring certain privileges; (*Mil.*) a warrant conferring nominal rank of an officer without the pay; (*Aviat.*) the wing-badge a flying member of the R.A.F. may put on his uniform. *a.* Conferred by brevet; honorary, nominal. *v.t.* To confer (a certain rank) by brevet.

brevi- (brev' i, brē' vi) [L. *brevis*], *comb. form.* Short.

breviary (brē' vi å ri) [L. *breviārium* (*brevis*, short)], *n.* *A brief statement; (*R.-C. Ch.*) a book containing the divine office.

***breviate** (brē' vi åt) [L. *breviātus*, p.p. of *breviāre*, to shorten, from *brevis*, short], *a.* Abbreviated, short. *n.* A short summary, an abridgment; a note; a brief. *v.t.* To abridge; to curtail.

brevier (brė vēr') [BREVIARY], *n.* (*Print.*) A size of type between bourgeois and minion, in which breviaries were formerly printed.

breviped (brev' i ped) [BREVI-, L. *pes, pedis*, foot], *a.* Short-footed, short-legged.

brevirostrate (brev i ros' trāt) [ROSTRATE], *a.* Having a short bill or beak.

brevity (brev' i ti) [L. *brevitas -tātem*], *n.* Briefness, shortness; conciseness.

brew (broo) [A.-S. *brēowan* (cp. O.H.G. *briuwan*, G. *brauen*; cp. L. *dēfrutum*, new wine boiled down)], *v.t.* To make (beer, ale, etc.) by boiling, steeping, and fermenting; to convert into (beer, ale, etc.) by such processes; to prepare other beverages by mixing or infusion; to prepare, to concoct; (*fig.*) to contrive, to plot; to bring about. *v.i.* To make beer, etc., by boiling, fermenting, etc.; to undergo these or similar processes; to be in preparation. *n.* The action, process or product of brewing; the quantity brewed at one process; the quality of the thing brewed. **brewage** (broo' åj), *n.* A mixture; a concocted beverage; the process of brewing. **brewer,** *n.* One whose trade is to brew malt liquors. **brewery, brewhouse,** *n.* A place where beer is brewed. **brewster,** *n.* *A female brewer; *a brewer. **Brewster Sessions,** *n.pl.* Sessions for granting licences to sell alcoholic liquors.

brewis (broo' is) [O.F. *brouetz*, dim. of *bro*, O.H.G. *brod*], *n.* Broth; liquor in which meat and vegetables have been boiled.

briar [BRIER].

Briareus (brī âr' ė ŭs, brī' å roos) [Gr. mythol.], *n.* A giant of Greek mythology, said to have had a hundred hands; a many-handed person. **Briarean** (bri âr' ė ån), *a.* Of or pertaining to Briareus; many-handed.

bribe (brīb) [O.F. *bribe*, a piece of bread given to a beggar], *n.* A gift or consideration of any kind offered to any one to influence his judgment or conduct; (*fig.*) an inducement; a seduction. *v.t.* To influence action or opinion by means of a gift or other inducement. *v.i.* To practise bribery. **bribable,** *a.* **bribability** (-bil' i ti), *n.* **bribee** (brī bē'), *n.* One who receives a bribe. **bribeless,** *a.* Incapable of being bribed. **briber,** *n.* One who offers or gives bribes. **bribery,** *n.* The act of giving or receiving bribes.

bric-a-brac (brik' å brăk) [F. phrase *de bric et de broc*, by hook or by crook], *n.* Fancy ware, curiosities, knick-knacks.

brick (brik) [F. *brique*, a fragment (cp. M.Dut. *brick, bricke*), from the Teut. root *brek-*, BREAK], *n.* A block of clay and sand, usually oblong, moulded and baked, used in building; a brick-shaped block of any material; a child's block for toy building; a brick-shaped loaf; (*slang*) a good fellow. *v.t.* To lay or construct with bricks; to imitate brickwork in plaster. **to brick up:** To block up with brickwork. **to drop a brick:** To say the wrong thing, to commit a blunder. **to make bricks without straw:** To perform the impossible. **brickbat,** *n.* A broken piece of brick, esp. for use as a missile. **brick-clay, brick-earth,** *n.* Clay used for making brick; (*Geol.*) a clayey earth in the London basin. **brick-dust,** *n.* Powdered brick. *a.* Tinged with this; coloured like this. **brick-field,** *n.* A field in which brick-making is carried on. **brickfielder,** *n.* (*Austral.*) A hot wind from the interior, laden with dust. **brick-kiln,** *n.* A kiln for baking bricks. **bricklayer,** *n.* One who lays or sets bricks. **brick-nogging,** *n.* Brickwork built into a timber framework. **brick-tea,** *n.* Tea compressed into bricks. **brickwork,** *n.* Builder's work in brick; bricklaying; a brickyard. **bricken,** *a.* Made of brick. **bricky,** *a.* Full of or composed of bricks; resembling bricks.

brickle (brikl) [parallel form to BRITTLE], *a.* Fragile, frail; ticklish, troublesome.

bricole (brik' ŏl, bri kōl') [F. *bricole*, late L. *briccola* (etym. doubtful)], *n.* *(*Mil.*) A kind of catapult; (*Tennis and Billiards*) the rebound of a ball from a wall or cushion; an indirect stroke.

bride (1) (brīd) [A.-S. *brȳd* (cp. O.H.G. *prut*, G. *braut*, from O. Teut. *brūdiz*)], *n.* A woman newly married or on the point of being married. **v.i.* To play the bride. **v.t.* To marry. **bride-ale** (see BRIDAL], *n.* An old English marriage feast; a bride-cup. **bride-bowl,** *n.* [BRIDE-CUP]. **bride-cake,** *n.* The cake distributed to the guests at a wedding. **bride-cup- bowl,** *n.* A cup or bowl handed round at a wedding; a cup of spiced wine or ale prepared for a newly-married couple **bridal** [A.-S. *brȳd-ealo*, wedding-ale, wedding-feast], *n.* The nuptial ceremony or festival; a wedding; marriage. *a.* Of or pertaining to a bride or a wedding. **bridegroom** [A.-S. *brȳdguma* (*guma*, man)], *n.* A man about to be married, or recently married. **bridemaid, bridesmaid,** *n.* A young unmarried woman who attends on the bride at her wedding. **bridesman,** *n.* A friend of the bridegroom, who attends him at his wedding; a best man. **bridewort,** *n.* (*Bot.*) Meadowsweet.

bride (2) (brīd) [F. *bride*, BRIDLE], *n.* The foundation net-work of lace; a bonnet-string.

bridewell (brīd' wel) [from a prison near St. Bride's (Bridget's) Well, near Fleet Street, London], *n.* A house of correction, a prison.

bridge (1) (brij) [A.-S. *brycg* (cp. O.H.G. *prucca*, G. *brücke*, from Teut. *brugj-*)], *n.* A structure thrown over a body of water, a ravine, another road, etc., to carry a road or path across; anything more or less resembling a bridge in form or function; the upper bony part of the nose; the thin wooden bar over which the strings are stretched in a violin or similar instrument; (*Billiards*) a support for a cue in an awkward stroke; (*Naut.*) a partial deck extending from side to side of a steam-vessel amidships. *v.t.* To span or cross with or as with a bridge. **bridgehead,** *n.* A fortification protecting the end of a bridge nearest the enemy. **bridge-train,** *n.* (*Mil.*) A company of engineers with appliances for bridge-building. **bridgeless,** *a.* Without a bridge. **bridge of boats,** *n.* A bridge supported on a number of boats moored abreast.

bridge (2) (brij) [etym. doubtful], *n.* A card game resembling whist. **bridge-marker,** *n.* A device for registering the points made at bridge. **bridge-scorer,** *n.* One who keeps the score at bridge. **auction-bridge, contract,** *n.* Varieties of bridge.

bridge (3) (brij), *n.* An electrical circuit used for the accurate measurement of electrical quantities, *e.g.* resistance.

bridle (brī' dėl) [A.-S. *brīdel*, cogn. with *bregdan* (see BRAID (1))], *n.* A head-stall, bit, and bearing or riding rein, forming the head-gear of a horse, or other beast of burden; (*fig.*) a curb, a check, restraint; (*Naut.*) a rope by which the bowline is fastened to the leech of a sail; a mooring-hawser; (*Physiol.*) a ligament checking the movement of a part. *v.t.* To put a bridle on; to control with a bridle; to hold in, to check, control. *v.i.* To hold up the head and draw in the chest in pride, scorn, or resentment (with *up*). **bridlebridge,** *n.* A bridge for horses, etc., not for vehicles. **bridle-hand,** *n.* The hand that holds the bridle; the left hand. **bridle-path, -road, -way,** *n.* A horse-track; a path for horsemen.

bridoon (bri doon') [F. *bridon* (see BRIDE (2))], *n.* The snaffle and rein of a military bridle.

brief (brēf) [O.F. *bref*, L. *breve, brevis* (cp. Gr. *brachus*)], *a.* Short in duration; expeditious; short, concise; curt. *n.* A papal letter of a less solemn character than a bull; (*Aviat.*) an airman's instructions before proceeding on operations; *a writ, a summons; a summary of facts and points of law given to counsel in charge of a case; (*Am.*) pleadings. (*pl. colloq.*) women's panties. *v.t.* To reduce to the form of a counsel's brief; to instruct or retain a barrister by brief; to give detailed instructions. **in brief:** Briefly. **briefless,** *a.* Having no briefs; without clients. **briefly,** *adv.* **briefness,** *n.* **brief-case,** *n.* A small leather handbag for carrying papers.

brier, briar (1) (brī' ėr [A.-S. *brēr, brǣr* (etym. doubtful)]. *n.* A thorny or prickly shrub, esp. of a wild rose; the stem of a wild rose on which a garden rose is grafted. **sweet brier,** *n.* A wild rose with fragrant leaves. **brier-rose,** *n.* The dog-rose or the field-rose. **briery, briary** (brī' ėr i), *a.* Full of briers; thorny.

brier, briar (2) (brī' ėr) [F. *bruyère*, heath], *n.* The white or tree heath, *Erica arborea*; a tobacco-pipe made from the root of this. **brier-root,** *n.* The root of the white heath.

brig (1) [Sc. and North. form of BRIDGE (1)].

brig (2) (brig) [short for BRIGANTINE], *n.* A square-rigged vessel with two masts.

brigade (bri gād') [F., from It. *brigata*, a troop, *brigare*, to quarrel, late L. *briga*, strife], *n.* A subdivision of an army, varying in composition in different countries and at different dates; a division of the Horse or Field Artillery; an organized body of workers, often wearing a uniform. *v.t.* To form into one or more brigades; to combine into a brigade; to associate as into a brigade. **Boys'**

Brigade [BOY]. **Fire Brigade,** *n.* A body of firemen. **Household Brigade:** The British Horse and Foot Guards. **brigade-major,** *n.* A staff officer who assists a brigadier in his command. **brigadier** (brig à dēr), *n.* (*Mil.*) The officer in command of a brigade; the rank below that of major-general.

brigalow (brig' à lō) [Austral. abor.], *n.* A variety of acacia tree.

brigand (brig' ànd) [F., prob. from It. *brigante*, pres.p. of *brigare*, see prec.], *n.* A robber, a bandit, an outlaw. **brigandage** (-dàj), *n.* The practices of brigands; highway robbery. **brigandish,** *a.* **brigandism,** *n.*

brigantine (brig' àn tēn) [F. *brigantin, brigandin*, It. *brigantino*, a pirate-ship, *brigante*, BRIGAND], *n.* A two-masted vessel square-rigged on both masts but with a fore-and-aft mainsail, and mainmast much longer than the foremast.

bright (brīt) [A.-S. *beorht*, O.Teut. *berhtoz*, shining], *a.* Lighted up, full of light; emitting or reflecting abundance of light; shining; unclouded; cheerful, happy, sanguine; witty, clever; *clear, evident; *illustrious, noble. *adv.* Brightly. **brighten,** *v.t.* To make bright; to make happy, hopeful, etc. *v.i.* To become bright; (*weather*) to clear up. **brightly,** *adv.* **brightness,** *n.*

Bright's disease (brīts di zēz') [Dr. R. *Bright* (1789–1858)], *n.* (*Med.*) A term including several forms of kidney disease, associated with albuminuria.

***brigue** (brēg) [F., from med. L. *briga*], *n.* Strife, intrigue. **v.t.* To ensnare; to obtain by intrigue. **v.i.* To intrigue.

brill (bril) [etym. unknown], *n.* A flat seafish, *Rhombus vulgaris*, allied to and like the turbot.

brilliant (bril' i ànt, bril' yànt) [F. *brillant*, pres.p. of *briller*, to shine; perh. from late L. *beryllāre*, to sparkle (*beryllus*, a gem)], *a.* Shining, sparkling; lustrous; illustrious, distinguished; extremely clever and successful. *n.* A diamond or other gem of the finest cut, consisting of lozenge-shaped facets alternating with triangles; the smallest type used in English printing. **brilliance, brilliancy,** *n.* **brilliantly,** *adv.* **brilliantine** (-tēn), *n.* A cosmetic for rendering the hair glossy.

brim (brim) [etym. doubtful (cp. G. *gebräme*, border, *brame*, brim, edge) (A.-S. *brim*, the sea, water, is prob. not the same word)], *n.* The upper edge, margin, or brink of a vessel, hollow, or body of water; the rim of a hat. *v.t.* To fill to the brim. *v.i.* To be full to the brim. **to brim over:** To overflow. **brimful,** *a.* **brimmer,** *n.* *A vessel filled to the brim; a bumper. **brimming,** *a.*

brimstone (brim' stòn) [M.E. *bren, brennen*, to burn, STONE], *n.* Sulphur, esp. in the Biblical sense of the lake of brimstone; the sulphur butterfly; (*fig.*) a spitfire, a termagant. **brimstone butterfly,** *n.* An early sulphur, *Gonepteryx rhamni.* **brimstone moth,** *n.* A sulphur-coloured moth, *Rumia cratægata.*

brindle, brindled (brindl, -d) [Shak. *brinded*, prob. variant of BRANDED], *a.* Tawny, with bars of darker hue; streaked, spotted.

brine (brīn) [A.-S. *brȳne* (cp. Dut. *brijn*, brine, pickle)], *n.* Water strongly impregnated with salt; (*fig.*) the sea; tears. *v.t.* To treat with brine, to pickle. **brine-pan,** *n.* A shallow vessel or pit in which brine is evaporated in the manufacture of salt. **brine-pit,** *n.* A pit or well of salt water. ***brinish,** *a.* **briny,** *a.* Full of brine; very salt. **the briny:** (*colloq.*) The sea.

bring (bring) [A.-S. *bringan* (cp. Goth. *briggan*, O.H.G. *pringan*, G. *bringen*)], *v.t.* (*past & p.p.* **brought**) To cause to come along with oneself; to bear, to carry, to conduct, to lead; to induce, prevail upon, influence, persuade; to produce, yield result in. **to bring about:** To cause, to bring to pass; (*Naut.*) to reverse the ship. **to bring back:** To recall to memory. **to bring down:** To humble, to abase; to shoot, to kill; to lower (a price); to carry on (a history) to a certain date. **to bring down the house:** (*Theat.*) To create tumultuous applause. **to bring forth:** To bear, to produce, to give birth to; to cause. **to bring forward:** To produce, to adduce; to carry on a sum from the bottom of one folio to the top of the next (in book-keeping). **to bring home to:** To prove conclusively; to convince. **to bring in:** To produce, to yield; to introduce (as an action or Bill); to return (as a verdict). **to bring off:** To bring away (from a ship, the shore, etc.); to procure the acquittal of; to accomplish. **to bring on:** To cause to begin; to introduce for discussion. **to bring out:** To express, to exhibit, to illustrate; to introduce to society; to launch (as a company); to produce upon the stage; to publish; to expose. **to bring over:** To convert; to cause to change sides. **to bring round:** To revive. **to bring to:** To restore to health or consciousness; (*Naut.*) to check the course of (a ship). **to bring to pass:** To cause to happen. **to bring under:** To subdue. **to bring up:** To educate, to rear; to lay before a meeting; to vomit; to come to a stop; to continue a further stage; (*Naut.*) to cast anchor. **to bring up the rear:** To come last.

brink (bringk) [Scand. (Icel. *brekka*, O.Norse *brenka*)], *n.* The edge or border of a precipice, pit, chasm, or the like; the margin of water; (*fig.*) the verge. **brinkmanship** (bringk' màn ship), *n.* (*Pol.*) The art of maintaining one's position on the brink of a decision or crisis.

brio (brē' ō) [It. *vivacity*], *n.* (*Mus.*) Spirit. **brioso** (brē ō' zō), *adv.* With a spirit.

brioche (brē osh'), [F.], *n.* A kind of bread; a sponge-cake.

briolet (brē' ō let) [F. *briller*, to sparkle], *n.* A pear- or drop-shaped diamond cut with long triangular facets.

briony [BRYONY].

briquette (bri ket'). **briquet** (brik' et) [F.], *n.* A block of compressed coal-dust; a slab of artificial stone. *v.t.* To compress (mineral matter, etc.) into bricks by heat.

brisk (brisk) [etym. doubtful (W. *brisg*, quick-footed, and F. *brusque* have been suggested)], *a.* Lively, animated, active; keen, stimulating, bracing; *(*fig.*) sharp-witted, fast, brief. *v.t.* To make brisk; to smarten (up). *v.i.* To dress finely; to come (up) briskly. **briskly,** *adv.* **briskness,** *n.* ***brisky,** *a.*

brisket (bris' kėt) [etym. doubtful], *n.* That part of the breast of an animal which lies next to the ribs; this joint of meat. **brisket-bone,** *n.* The breast-bone.

bristle (bris' ėl) [M.E. *bristle, brustel, berstle*, A.-S. *byrst*, O.Teut. root *bors-*], *n.* A short, stiff, coarse hair, particularly on the back and sides of swine; (*pl.*) a beard cropped short; stiff hairs on plants. *v.t.* *To cause to stand up (as hair); to cover with bristles. *v.i.* To stand erect (as hair); to show indignation or defiance (with *up*); to be thickly beset (with difficulties, dangers, etc.). **bristly,** *a.* Thickly covered with or as with bristles. **bristliness,** *n.*

bristling (brist' ling) [etym. unknown], *n.* A small fish caught in the Mediterranean and Bay of Biscay and packed in oil.

Bristol (bris' tòl). [A city of England, on the lower Avon.] **Bristol-board,** *n.* A thick smooth white cardboard. **Bristol brick,** *n.* A siliceous material made into bricks, for cleaning cutlery. **Bristol diamond, Bristol stone,** *n.* Transparent rock-crystal, found in the Clifton limestone. **Bristol fashion:** In good order. **Bristol milk,** *n.* Sherry.

brit (brit) [local dial; etym. unknown], *n.* The spawn and young of the herring and the sprat.

Britain (brit' àn) [M.E. *Bretayne*, O.F. *Bretaigne*, L. *Britannia*, A.-S. *Breten, Breoten, Brytten, Breoton-lond* (Celtic *Britto, Brython*, name of the people)], *n.* England, Wales, and Scotland. **Great**

Britain: the United Kingdom. **Greater Britain,** *n.* (*fig.*) Britain and the Colonies. **North Britain,** *n.* Scotland. **Britannia** (bri tăn′ yȧ), *n.* Britain; Britain personified; a female figure emblematic of Britain. **Britannia metal,** *n.* A white alloy of tin, copper, and antimony. **Britannic,** *a.* British. **British,** *a.* Of or pertaining to ancient Britain, to Great Britain or its inhabitants, or to the British Commonwealth. **British Thermal Unit** [THERM]. **British warm,** *n.* A short military overcoat. **the British:** British people or soldiers. **Britisher,** *n.* (*incorrect*) A Briton, a British subject or a native of Britain. **Britishism,** (*Am.*) **Briticism** (brit′ ish-, -is izm), *n.* An idiom employed in Britain and not in the United States or elsewhere. **Briton** (brit′ ȯn) [F. *Breton,* L. *Britto,* see BRITAIN], *n.* A member of the race inhabiting south Britain at the Roman invasion; a native of Britain or of the British Commonwealth. **North Briton,** *n.* A Scot.

brittle (brit′ ėl) [A.-S. *brēotan,* to break], *a.* Liable to break or be broken, fragile; not malleable. **brittleness,** *n.*

britzka (brits′ kȧ) [Pol. *bryczka,* dim. of *bryka,* a wagon], *n.* An open carriage with a calash top.

Briza (brī′ zȧ) [Gr. *brizein,* to nod], *n.* (Bot.) A genus of grasses comprising quaking-grass, maidenhair grass, etc.

broach (brōch) [F. *broche,* a spit, late L. *brocca,* a sharp stick (L. *broccus,* projecting like teeth)], *n.* A tapering iron instrument; a roasting-spit, an awl; a mason's chisel, a boring-bit; a first horn on the head of a young stag; a spire rising from a tower without a parapet. *v.t.* To pierce (as a cask), so as to allow liquor to flow; to tap; (*fig.*) to open, to moot, to make public; *to transfix, to spit; (*Naut.*) to turn suddenly to windward. **to broach to:** (*Naut.*) To veer to windward so as to present a ship's broadside to the sea.

broad (1) (brawd) [A.-S. *brād,* Teut. *braid-* (cp. G. *breit*)], *a.* Wide, large, extended across; extensive, expansive; of wide range, large, general; expanded, open, clear; tolerant, liberal; vigorous, rough, strong, rustic; coarse, obscene; bold, vigorous, free in style or effect. *n.* A large, fresh-water lake formed by the broadening of a river; the broad portion of a thing; (*Am. slang*) a woman; a prostitute; (*pl., slang*) playing-cards. **broad as long:** Equal upon the whole; the same either way. **broad arrow,** *n.* A mark resembling an arrowhead cut or stamped on British Government property. **broad-axe,** *n.* A battle-axe; (*Am.*) an axe for hewing timber. **broad-bean,** *n.* A leguminous plant with edible seeds in a pod, *Faba vulgaris.* **Broad Church,** *n.* A party in the Church of England interpreting formularies and dogmas in a liberal sense. *a.* Of or pertaining to the Broad Church. **broadcloth,** *n.* A fine, wide, dressed black cloth, used for men's coats, etc.; (*Am.*) poplin. **broad-gauge,** *n.* Any gauge for the rails of a railway line wider than 4 ft. 8½ in. **broadleaf,** *n.* (*N. Zealand*) The Maori *paukatea* tree. **broad-minded,** *a.* Tolerant, having an open mind. **broadsheet,** *n.* A large sheet printed on one side only. **broadside,** *n.* The side of a ship above the water; a volley from all the guns on one side of a ship of war; a broadsheet; a political attack on a person or policy. **broadsilk,** *n.* Silk in the piece as distinguished from ribbons. **broadsword,** *n.* A sword with a broad blade; a soldier armed with this.

broad (2) (brawd) [as prec.], *adv.* In breadth; broadly, widely. **broad-awake,** *a.* Wide-awake. ***broad-blown,** *a.* Full-blown, in full bloom. **broadcast,** *a.* Scattered by the hand (as seed); (*fig.*) widely disseminated; (*Radio.*) transmitted by radio. *n.* Broadcast sowing; (*Radio.*) anything transmitted to the public by radio. *adv.* By scattering widely. *v.t.* To sow by scattering with the hand; (*Radio.*) to transmit by radio; (*fig.*) to disseminate widely. **broad-spoken,** *a.* Plain spoken; using a dialect, or coarse language. **broaden,** *v.i.* To become broader, to spread. *v.t.* To make broader. **broadly,** *adv.* **broadness,** *n.* Coarseness, indelicacy. **broadways, -wise,** *adv.* In the direction of the breadth.

broadside, broadsword [BROAD (1)].

Brobdingnagian (brob ding nā′ ji ȧn) [*Brobdingnag,* a country of giants in Swift's 'Gulliver's Travels'], *a.* Gigantic, huge. *n.* A giant.

brocade (brō kād′) [Sp. *brocado,* It. *broccato,* p.p. of *broccare* (*brocca,* see BROACH)], *n.* Silken stuff with raised figures. *v.t.* To weave or work with raised patterns; to decorate with brocade.

brocard (brō′ kȧrd) [F., low L. *brocarda, Brocard* or *Burchard,* Bishop of Worms, compiler of *Regulæ Ecclesiasticæ*], *n.* (*Law*) An elementary principal; (F.) a sarcastic jest.

broccoli, brocoli (brok′ ȯ li) [It. pl. of *broccolo,* a sprout, dim. of *brocco,* a skewer (see BROACH)], *n.* A variety of cauliflower.

broché (bro′ shā) [F., stitched], *a.* Brocaded, woven with a raised design.

brochure (brȯ shoor′) [F., from *brocher,* to stitch], *n.* A small pamphlet.

brock (brok) [A.-S. *broc.* (W., Corn., and Bret. *broch,* Ir. *broc*; prob. from *breac,* spotted, cp. Gr. *phorkos,* grey)], *n.* A badger; a dirty fellow, a stinker. **brocked,** *a.* (*Sc.*) Speckled, black and white.

brocket (brok′ ėt) [F. *brocart,* from *broche* (see BROACH)], *n.* A stag in its second year with its first horns, which are straight and unbranched.

brodekin (brod′ ė kin), **brodkin** (brod′ kin) F. *brodequin*], *n.* A high boot: a buskin.

broderie anglaise (brō′ dri ong glāz′) [F.], *n.* Open embroidery on cambric or linen.

brogue (brōg) [Gael. and Ir. *brōg,* shoe, sandal, O.Ir. *broce* (prob. from O.Celt. *brācca,* whence L. *braccæ,* see BREECH)], *n.* A coarse, rough shoe, usually of untanned leather; dialectal pronunciation, esp. Irish; *(*pl.*) trousers, breeches. *v.t.* To utter in a brogue.

***broider,** etc. [EMBROIDER].

broil (1) (broil) [F. *brouiller,* to tumble, trouble, confound (It. *brogliare,* to disturb, *broglio,* confusion)], *n.* A tumult, disturbance, contention.

broil (2) (broil) [etym. doubtful], *v.t.* To cook on a gridiron; to scorch. *v.i.* To be very hot; to grow hot; to be in the heat; to be subjected to heat; to burn, to be inflamed. *n.* Broiled meat. **broiler,** *n.* One who or that which broils; a gridiron: a chicken 8–10 weeks old for broiling or roasting.

broke (1) (brōk), *part.a.* [BROKEN].

broke (2) (brōk) [A.-S. *broc,* affliction, *gebroc,* a fragment, affliction, from *brecan,* to break], *n.* *A piece; *broken meat; (*pl.*) short wool sorted, or broken, from the fleece. *adv.* (*slang*) ruined, penniless.

broken (brō′ kėn) [p.p. of BREAK], *a.* In pieces; not whole or continuous; weakened, infirm; crushed, humbled; transgressed, violated; interrupted, incoherent, ejaculatory; shattered, bankrupt, ruined; (*Painting*) reduced by the addition of some other colour. **broken-backed,** *a.* Having the back broken; (*Naut.*) drooping at stem and stern from injury to the keel. **broken-down,** *a.* Decayed; worn-out; ruined in health, in character, or financially. **broken English,** *n.* Defective English as spoken by a foreigner. **broken-hearted,** *a.* Crushed in spirit by grief or anxiety. **broken meat,** *n.* Remains of food. **broken water,** *n.* Choppy water. **broken-winded,** *a.* Having defective respiratory organs; habitually short of breath. **brokenly,** *adv.* With breaks, jerkily, spasmodically.

broker (brō′ kėr) [M.E. and A.-F. *brocour,* late L. *broccātor,* from *broccāre,* to BROACH], *n.* *A petty dealer, a pawnbroker; an agent, a factor, a middleman, *a pimp, a pander; one who buys and sells for others; a dealer in second-hand furniture; a person licensed to appraise and sell goods distrained for rent. **to put in the brokers:** To distrain. **brokerage** (-ȧj), *n.* The business or commission of a broker; a broker's commission on sales, etc. **broking,** *n.* The trade of broker.

brolly (brol' i) [corr. of UMBRELLA], *n.* (*slang*) An umbrella, a gamp.

bromal (brō' măl), *n.* A liquid like chloral produced by the action of bromine upon alcohol.

bromate (brō' māt), *n.* A salt of bromic acid.

brome grass (brōm) [Gr. *bromos,* a kind of oats], *n.* (*Bot.*) A grass of the genus *Bromus,* esp. *Bromus inermis,* a cultivated fodder-grass.

bromic (brō' mik), *a.* Of or pertaining to bromine; having bromine in its composition.

bromide (brō' mīd) [BROMINE], *n.* A combination of bromine with a metal or a radical, esp. bromide of potassium, which is used as a sedative; (*slang*) a commonplace remark. **bromide paper,** *n.* (*Phot.*) A sensitized paper used in printing from a negative. **bromide process,** *n.* (*Phot.*) Printing from negatives or enlarging on paper coated with silver bromide emulsion.

bromine (brō' min, brō' mīn) [Gr. *bromos,* a stench], *n.* A non-metallic, dark red, liquid element with a strong, irritating odour.

bromism (bro' mizm), *n.* The condition produced by long treatment with bromide of potassium.

bromize (brō' mīz), *v.t.* To treat with bromine; to prepare a photographic plate with a bromide.

bromo-, brom-, *comb. forms.*

bronchi, bronchia (brong' kī, -ki ă) [L., from Gr. *bronchos, bronchia*], *n.pl.* The main divisions of the windpipe; the ramifications into which these divide within the lungs. **bronchial,** *a.* **bronchial tubes,** *n.pl,* The bronchia. **bronchitis** (brong kī' tis) [-ITIS], *n.* Inflammation of the bronchia. **bronchitic** (-kit' ik), *a.* **bronchio-, broncho-,** *comb. forms.* Pertaining to the windpipe, or the tubes into which it divides beneath. **bronchocele** (-sēl) [Gr. *bronchkēlē* (-CELE)], *n.* Morbid swelling of the thyroid gland, goitre. **bronchotomy** (-kot' ŏ mi) [-TOMY], *n.* The operation of opening the windpipe, tracheotomy.

bronco (brong' kō) [Sp., rough, rude], *n.* A native half-tamed horse of California or New Mexico. **bronco-buster** [BURSTER], *n.* (*Am. slang*) A breaker-in of broncos.

Brontosaurus (bron tō saw' rŭs [Gr. *bronte,* thunder; *sauros,* a lizard], *n.* (*Palæont.*) A genus of huge fossil dinosaurian reptiles, notable for their small head and diminutive brain-cavity.

bronze (bronz) [F., from It. *bronzo,* bronze, *bronzino,* made of bronze, L. *Brundusīnium,* made at *Brundusium,* Brindisi], *n.* A brown alloy of copper and tin, sometimes with a little zinc or lead; a brown colour, like that of bronze; a work of art in bronze. *a.* Made of or the colour of bronze. *v.t.* To give a bronze-like appearance to (wood, metal, plaster, etc.); to brown, to tan. *v.i.* To become brown or tanned. **Bronze Age, Bronze Period,** *n.* A period after the Stone and before the Iron Age when weapons and implements were made of bronze. **bronze-powder,** *n.* A metallic powder used in printing, painting, etc., for imparting a metallic colour and lustre. **bronze-wing,** *n.* An Australian pigeon, *Phaps chalcoptera.* **bronzite** (bron' zīt), *n.* A bronze-like variety of diallage. **bronzy,** *a.* Like bronze; tinged with bronze.

brooch (brōch) [BROACH], *n.* An ornamental clasp with a pin, for fastening some part of a woman's dress. **v.t.* To adorn as with a brooch.

brood (brood) [A.-S. *brōd,* from Teut. root *bro-,* to warm], *n.* A family of birds hatched at once; offspring, progeny; *the act of breeding or hatching; parentage, lineage; a race, a species; (*contemp.*) a swarm, a crowd. *v.i.* To sit on eggs; to hover with outspread wings; (*fig.*) to hang close over (as clouds); to meditate moodily. *v.t.* To sit upon eggs to hatch them; to cherish under the wings; (*fig.*) to prepare by long meditation, to hatch; to cherish moodily. **brood-hen, -mare,** *n.* A hen or a mare kept for breeding. **brooder,** *n.* A cover for sheltering young chickens. **broody,** *a.* Inclined to sit on eggs; (*fig.*) sullen, morose; inclined to brood over matters. **broodiness,** *n.*

brook (1) (bruk) [A.-S. *brōc* (etym. doubtful; cp. Dut. *broek,* a marsh, a pool, G. *bruch,* a bog)], *n.* A small stream, a rivulet. **brooklime,** *n.* A kind of speedwell, *Veronica becca-bunga,* growing in watery places. **brooklet,** *n.* A little brook, a streamlet. **brooky,** *a.* Abounding in brooks.

brook (2) (bruk) [A.-S. *brūcan,* from O.Teut. root *bruk-,* to use, enjoy (cp. L. *fruī,* to enjoy)], *v.t.* To endure, to support, to put up with.

broom (broom) [A.-S. *brōm, broom,* O.Teut. *bræmoz* (cp. BRAMBLE)], *n.* A shrub with yellow flowers belonging to the genus *Sarothamnus* or *Cytisus,* esp. *C. scoparius;* the allied genus *Genista;* a besom for sweeping, orig. made of broom. *v.t.* To sweep with a broom. **broom-corn,** *n.* The common millet, *Sorghum vulgare,* and sugar millet, *S. saccharatum,* from the tufts of which brooms are made. **broom-rape,** *n.* The parasitic genus *Orobanche.* **broom-stick, -staff,** *n.* The handle of a broom. **broomy,** *a.* Broom-like; abounding in broom.

brose (brōz) [BREWIS], *n.* A kind of porridge made by pouring water on oatmeal or oatcake, with seasoning. **Athol brose:** A mixture of whisky and honey.

broth (broth) [A.-S. from Teut. root *bru-,* to boil (cp. A.-S. *brēowan,* to brew)], *n.* The liquor in which anything, esp. meat, has been boiled; thin soup. **a broth of a boy:** (*Ir.*) A high-spirited fellow.

brothel (broth' ėl) [A.-S. *brothen,* p.p. of *brēothan,* to go to ruin (confused with BORDEL)], *n.* A house of ill-fame.

brother (brŭ*th'* ėr) [A.-S. *brōthor* (cp. G. *bruder,* L. *frāter,* Gr. *phratēr,* Sansk. *bhrātr,* W. *brawd*)], *n.* (*pl.*) **brothers,** and in more solemn senses **brethren**) A son of the same parents or parent; one closely connected with another; an associate; one of the same community, country, city, church, order, profession, or society; a fellow-countryman, fellow citizen, etc.; a fellow-man, a fellow-creature; (*Bibl.*) kinsman, cousin. **half-brother:** Brother on one side only; having the same father or the same mother only. **brother-german,** *n.* Brother on both sides. **brother-in-arms,** *n.* Fellow-soldier. **brother-in-law,** *n.* The brother of one's husband or wife, one's sister's husband. **Brother Jonathan:** The United States personified. ***brother-love,** *n.* Brotherly love. **brother-uterine,** *n.* One born of the same mother, but of a different father. **brotherhood,** *n.* The relationship of a brother; a fraternity, an association for mutual service; brotherly affection or feeling. **brotherless,** *a.* **brotherlike,** *a.* **brotherly,** *a.* Becoming to a brother; fraternal. *adv.* Fraternally. **brotherliness,** *n.*

brougham (broom, broo' ăm, brō' ăm) [from Lord *Brougham,* 1778–1868], *n.* A close, four-wheeled carriage drawn by one horse.

brought, *past* and *p.p.* [BRING].

brow (1) (brou) [A.-S. *brū* (cp. Icel. *brūn,* Lith. *bruwis,* Rus. *brove,* Gr. *ophrus,* Sansk. *bhrū*)], *n.* The ridge over the eye; the forehead; the countenance generally; (*fig.*) aspect, appearance; the projecting edge of a cliff or hill; the top of a hill. *v.t.* To be at the edge of; to form a brow to. **to knit the brows:** To frown. **brow-antler,** *n.* The lowest tine of a deer's horn. **browbeat,** *v.t.* To bear down arrogantly; to bully.

brow (2) (brou) [prob. Swed. or Dan. *bru,* bridge], *n.* (*Naut.*) A gangway; (*Am.*) an inclined roadway for drawing up logs to a lumber-mill.

brown (broun) [A.-S. *brūn* (cp. Icel. *brunn,* G. *braun,* Gr. *phrūnos,* a toad; F. *brun* and It. *bruno* are from Teut.)], *a.* Of the colour produced when wood or paper is scorched; dusky, dark. *v.t.* To make brown; to give a brown lustre to (gun-barrels, etc.). *v.i.* To become brown, to get sun-burnt. *n.* A brown colour; a compound colour produced by a mixture of red, black, and yellow; pigment of this colour; a brown butterfly; brown clothes. **to do brown:** (*slang*) To take in, to deceive. **brown Bess,** *n.* The old flint-lock musket of the British Army. **brown-bill,** *n.* A kind of halberd formerly used by English foot-soldiers. **brown bomber:** (*Austral. colloq.*) A member of the N.S.W. parking police. **brown bread,** *n.* Bread made from whole meal; bread in which bran is mixed with the flour. **brown coal,** *n.* Lignite. **brown paper,** *n.* Coarse, unbleached paper for packing parcels and rough goods. **brown-shirt,** *n.* A uniformed member of the Nazi party in Germany. **brownstone,** *n.* (*Am.*) A dark-brown sandstone. **brown study,** *n.* Reverie, day-dream. **brown sugar,** *n.* Coarse, half-refined sugar. **brown ware,** *n.* A coarse, cheap kind of pottery. **browned off:** (*slang*) Disappointed; bored, fed up. **brownie,** *n.* (*Austral.*) A kind of currant loaf. **browning,** *n.* Colouring material for gravy. **brownish,** *a.* **brownness,** *n.*

Brownie (brou' ni) [as prec.], *n.* A kindly domestic elf; a junior Girl Guide, from 8 to 11 years of age.

Browning pistol [inventor's name], *n.* A type of automatic pistol.

Brownism (brou' nizm) [Robert *Browne* (*c.* 1550–*c.* 1633)], *n.* The Congregationalist scheme of Church government formed by Browne and adopted in a modified form by the Independents. **Brownist,** *n.*

browse (brouz) [F. *brouster*, *brouter* (M.H.G. *broz*, a bud, O.S. *brustian*, to bud, cp. A.-S. *brēotan*, to break)], *v.t.* To nibble and eat off (twigs, young shoots, etc.). *v.i.* To feed on twigs, young shoots, etc.; to graze; (*fig.*) to read in a desultory way. *n.* The tender shoots of trees and shrubs fit for cattle to feed on; the act of browsing.

browst (broust) [prob. from *brow-*, p.p. stem of BREW], *n.* A brewing.

brucine (broo' sīn) [James *Bruce* (1730–94)], *n.* (*Chem.*) A poisonous alkaloid found in the seed and bark of nux vomica and other species of *Strychnos.*

bruckle (brŭkl) [A.-S. *brucol* (in *scipbrucol*, shipwreck), from *bruc-*, stem of *brekan*, to break], *a.* Fragile, brittle, precarious, ticklish.

Bruin (broo' in) [Dut., lit. brown], *n.* Familiar name for the brown bear.

bruise (brooz) [A.-S. *brȳsan*, to bruise (combined later with O.F. *bruiser*, *brisier* (etym. doubtful), to break)], *v.t.* To crush, indent, or discolour, by a blow from something blunt and heavy; to injure without breaking skin or bone; to batter, pound, grind up; to hurt, disable. *v.i.* To box; to display the effects of a blow. *n.* An injury caused by something blunt and heavy; a contusion. **to bruise along:** (*Hunting*) To ride in a reckless fashion. **bruiser,** *n.* One who or that which bruises; (*fig.*) a pugilist, a prize-fighter.

bruit (broot) [F., noise, from *bruire*, to roar], *n.* Noise, tumult, rumour, report; (*Med.*) an abnormal sound heard in auscultation. *v.t.* To rumour, to noise abroad.

brulye, brulzie, bruilzie (brul' yi, brul' i) [Sc. for BROIL], *n.* An affray, a disturbance.

brumby (brŭm' bi), *n.* (*Austral.*) A wild horse.

brume (broom) [F. *brume*, fog, L. *brūma*, winter (contr. of *brevima*, *brevissima*, shortest)], *n.* Mist, fog, vapour. **brumal,** *a.* Pertaining to winter; winterly. **brumous,** *a.* Wintry, foggy.

brummagem (brŭm' ȧ jėm) [local vulgar form of the name of the city of *Birmingham*], *n.* An article manufactured there; a counterfeit coin, etc. *a.* Sham, spurious.

brunch (brŭnch), *n.* (*colloq.*) A meal like a late breakfast or an early lunch.

brunette (broo net') [F., fem. dim. of *brun*, brown], *n.* A girl or woman of dark hair and complexion. *a.* Brown-haired; of dark complexion.

Brunswick (brŭnz' wik) [G. *Braunschweig*, a province and town of Germany], *a.* From Brunswick. **Brunswick-black,** *n.* A black varnish made of lamp-black and turpentine. **Brunswick-green,** *n.* A green pigment made from oxychloride of copper.

brunt (brŭnt) [etym. doubtful; perh. conn. with Icel. *bruna*, to advance like fire], *n.* The shock, impetus, or stress of an attack, danger, or crisis.

bruscamente (broo ska men' ti) [It.], *adv.* (*Mus.*) Strongly accented; roughly.

brush (1) (brŭsh) [O.F. *broce*, *brosse*, brushwood, late L. *bruscia*, a thicket (prob. from O.H.G. *bursta*, bristle); and O.F. *brosse*, *broisse*, a brush, broom (perh. of similar origin)], *n.* (*Am. and Austral.*) Brushwood, underwood, a thicket of small trees; (*Am.*) loppings, faggots of brushwood; an instrument for sweeping or scrubbing, generally made of bristles, twigs, or feathers; an instrument consisting of hair attached to a handle, for colouring, white-washing, painting, etc.; a hair-pencil; a brushing; (*fig.*) an attack, a skirmish; a bushy tail, as of a fox; (*Elec.*) a piece of metal or carbon or bundle of wires or plates, forming a good electrical conductor; a brush-like discharge of electric sparks; (*Art*) a painter, a style in painting; (*Opt.*) a brush-like appearance produced by polarized light. *v.t.* To sweep or scrub with a brush; to remove by brushing; to touch lightly, as in passing. *v.i.* To move with a sweeping motion; to pass lightly over. **the brush:** (*fig.*) The art of painting. **brush-off,** *n.* (*colloq.*) A brusque rebuff. **brush-up,** *n.* A brushing. **brush-pencil,** *n.* An artist's brush. **brush kangaroo,** *n.* (*Austral.*) The wallaby. **brush-wheel,** *n.* A friction-wheel which turns a similar wheel by means of leather, cloth, etc., fixed on the circumference. **brushwood,** *n.* A thicket, underwood; low scrubby thicket; loppings. **brushwork,** *n.* A painter's manipulation of the brush; style of manipulation of the brush. **to brush up:** To clean by brushing; (*fig.*) to revive, to refresh one's memory. **brushy,** *a.* Resembling a brush; rough, shaggy; covered with brushwood.

brush (2) (brŭsh), *n.* (*Austral.*) A young woman, a girl.

brusque (brŭsk, brusk) [F., from It. *brusco*, sharp, sour; etym. doubtful], *a.* Rough, blunt, unceremonious. **brusquely,** *adv.* **brusqueness,** *n.* **brusquerie** (brus' kė rē), *n.*

Brussels (brŭs' ėlz) [the capital of Belgium], *a.* Made at or derived from Brussels. *n.* A Brussels carpet. **Brussels carpet,** *n.* A kind of carpet with a backing of linen and wool face. **Brussels lace,** *n.* A kind of pillow-lace. **brussels sprouts,** *n.pl.* The small sprouts springing from the stalks of a variety of the cabbage, and used as a vegetable.

brute (broot) [F. *brut*, *brute*, L. *brūtus*, stupid], *a.* Stupid, irrational; beastlike, sensual; unconscious, material. *n.* An irrational animal; a beast; (*fig.*) the animal nature in man; one resembling a brute in cruelty, want of intelligence, etc. **brutehood,** *n.* The condition of brutes. **brutal,** *a.* Resembling a brute; savage, cruel; coarse, unrefined, sensual. **brutally,** *adv.* **brutality** (-tăl' i ti), **brutalism** (broo' tȧ lizm), *n.* The quality of being brutal; a brutal action. **brutalize,** *v.t.* To render brutal; *v.i.* To become brutal. **brutalization** (-lī zā' shŭn), *n.* **brutify,** *v.t.* To brutalize; to render brutal. **brutification** (-fi kā' shŭn), *n.* **brutish,** *a.* Like a brute; animal, bestial. **brutishly,** *adv.* **brutishness,** *n.*

Brutus (broo' tŭs) [after the Roman hero], *n.* A method of dressing the hair in which it is brushed back from the forehead and the head covered with curls; a kind of wig.

bryology (brī ol' ŏ ji) [Gr. *bryon*, a mossy seaweed, -LOGY], *n.* The science of mosses; mosses collectively. **bryologist,** *n.* A student of mosses.

bryony (brī' ŏ ni) [L. *bryōnia*, Gr. *bruōnia* (*bruein*, to teem, swell)], *n.* A genus of climbing plants, esp. *B. dioica*, white or common bryony; a similar plant, black bryony, *Tamus communis.*

Bryophita (brī ō fī' tȧ) [Gr. *bryon*, moss, *phyton*, a plant], *n.* (*Bot.*) A division of the higher cryptogams consisting of the liverworts and mosses.

bryozoon (brī ō zō' on) [Gr. *bryon*, moss, *zōon*, *zōa*, animal, -als], *n.* (*pl.* **-zoa**) One of the lowest class of the mollusca, called also Polyzoa.

Brython (brith' ŏn) [W. *Brython*, BRITON], *n.* A member of the Celtic race occupying south Britain at the time of the Roman invasion, as distinguished from the Goidels, the Scoto-Irish or Gaelic race. **Brythonic** (bri thon' ik), *a.*

bub (bŭb) [prob. imit.], *n.* (*slang*) Drink; beer.

bubble (bŭb' ėl) [imit., cp. BLEB, BLUBBER], *n.* A vesicle of water or other liquid filled with air or other gas; a cavity in a solidified material, such as ice, amber, glass, etc.; (*fig.*) anything unsubstantial or unreal; a cheat, a fraud; a swindling project. *a.* Visionary, unreal; fraudulent, fictitious. *v.i.* To rise up in or as in bubbles; to make a noise like bubbling water. *v.t.* To cheat, to delude. **bubble-car,** *n.* A midget motor-car with rounded line and transparent top. **bubble-gum,** *n.* A kind of chewing-gum that can be blown up into a bubble. **to bubble over:** To boil over with laughter, anger, etc. **bubble and squeak:** Meat and vegetables fried together. **bubbler,** *n.* A cheat; (*Am.*) a fish found in the Ohio, named from the peculiar noise it makes. **bubbly,** *a.* Full of bubbles; (*colloq.*) champagne. **South Sea Bubble:** (*Hist.*) A mania of speculation which swept over England in 1720.

bubbly-jock (bŭb' li jok) [BUBBLE, *Jock*, Jack], *n.* (*colloq.*) A turkey-cock.

bubo (bū' bō) [late L., from Gr. *boubōn*, the groin, a swelling in the groin], *n.* An inflamed swelling of the lymphatic glands, esp. in the groin or armpit. **bubonic** (bū bon' ik), *a.* **bubonocele** (bū bō' nō sēl) [-CELE], *n.* Hernia of the groin. ***bubukle** (bū' bŭkl) [a comic confusion of BUBBLE and CARBUNCLE], *n.* (*Shak.*) A red pimple.

buccal (bŭk' ăl) [L. *bucca*, cheek], *a.* Pertaining to the cheek.

buccaneer (bŭk ă nēr') [F. *boucanier*, orig. a hunter of wild oxen, from *boucan* (from a Brazilian word), a gridiron or frame on which flesh was barbecued], *n.* One of the piratical rovers who formerly infested the Spanish Main; a filibuster. *v.i.* To act the part of a buccaneer.

buccinator (bŭk' si nā tŏr) [L. *buccināre*, to blow the trumpet (*buccina*, trumpet)], *n.* (*Anat.*) The flat, thin muscle forming the wall of the cheek, used in blowing.

Bucentaur (bū' sĕn tawr, bū sen' tawr) [It. *bucentoro*, etym. unknown], *n.* The state barge of the Venetian Republic; *a large decorated barge.

Bucephalus (bū sef' ă lŭs) [name of the charger of Alexander the Great], *n.* A riding-horse, a hack.

Buchmanism (bŭk' măn izm), *n.* The name applied to an undenominational evangelical religious movement of American origin, brought by F. Buchman to Britain where it is self-styled the Oxford Group, also Moral Rearmament Movement. **Buchmanite,** *n.* A member of this group.

buck (1) (bŭk) [A.-S. *bucc*, a buck, *bucca*, a he-goat (distinction between the two words doubtful) (cp. Dut. *bok*, G. *bock*, F. *bouc*, a he-goat, W. *bwch*, a buck, all from Teut.)], *n.* The male of the fallow-deer, reindeer, goat, hare, and rabbit; (*fig.*) a gay, dashing young fellow; (*Am.*) a male Indian or Negro; (*Am. slang*) a dollar; (*slang*) cheek. *v.i.* To buck-jump. **to pass the buck:** (*slang*) To shift responsibility to someone else. **bucker,** *n.* A buck-jumper. **old buck,** *n.* Old fellow; a slangy mode of address. **buck-eye,** *n.* The horse-chestnut of the United States; (*colloq.*) a native of Ohio. **buck-handled,** *a.* With a buckthorn handle. **buckhorn,** *n.* The horn of a buck; the material of a buck's horn used for knife-handles, etc. **buck-hound,** *n.* A small variety of the stag-hound. **buck-jump,** *n.* A jump by a vicious or unbroken horse, with the feet drawn together and the back arched to unseat the rider. *v.i.* To jump as described above. **buck-jumper,** *n.* A horse given to buck-jumping. **buck-shot,** *n.* A kind of shot larger than swan-shot. **buck-skin,** *n.* The skin of a buck; a soft yellowish leather made from deer and sheepskins; (*pl.*) buckskin breeches; *a.* Made of buckskin. **buckish,** *a.* *Lascivious; foppish. **buckishly,** *adv.*

***buck** (2) (bŭk) [etym. doubtful (cp. G. *beuche*, Swed. *byk*, lye, F. *buer*, to steep in lye, and perh. A.-S. *būc*, a pitcher)], *n.* A lye in which linen, etc., is soaked before washing; clothes washed at one operation. *v.t.* To soak or wash in lye; to drench, to soak. ***buck-basket,** *n.* A basket to hold dirty linen.

buck (3) (bŭk) [perh. from BUCK (1), a dandy], *v.i.* (with *up*) (*dial.*) To dress up; (*slang*) to exert oneself; to be pleased. **to buck up:** To hurry, to bestir oneself; to cheer up.

buck (4) (bŭk) [etym. doubtful], *n.* A large basket for trapping eels.

buck (5) (bŭk) [perh. A.-S. *būc*, belly, body, trunk], *n.* (*dial. and Am.*) The body of a wagon or cart. **buck-board,** *n.* A projecting board or ledge over the wheels of a cart; (*Am.*) a light four-wheeled vehicle. **buck-cart, -wagon,** *n.* Vehicles fitted with buck-boards.

buck (6) (bŭk) [Hind.], *n.* (*colloq.*) Talk, chatter; swagger. **not so much of your buck:** Don't swagger.

buckbean (bŭk' bēn) [?], *n.* A water-plant having pinkish-white flowers, of the genus *Menyanthes*, esp. *M. trifoliata.*

bucket (bŭk' ėt) [etym. doubtful (perh. A.-S. *būc*, pitcher, or O.F. *buket*, *buquet*, tub, pail)], *n.* A vessel of wood, iron, or leather, with a handle, for drawing or carrying water; a scoop or receptacle for lifting mud, gravel, coal, grain, etc., in a dredger or elevator; as much as a bucket will hold; the piston of a pump; a whip socket; a holder attached to a saddle for a carbine, rifle, etc. *v.t.* To lift or draw in buckets; (*slang*) to cheat; to ride (a horse) hard; (*Rowing*) to hurry or jerk. *v.i.* (*Rowing*) To hurry the forward swing. **bucket-seat,** *n.* A round-backed seat for one person in a motor or aeroplane. **bucket-shop** [conn. accidentally with *bucket*, from expression *bucketful* of people], *n.* The office of unofficial brokers who deal in trashy stock. **to kick the bucket** (perh. from O.F. *buquet*, a beam): (*slang*) To die. **bucketful,** *n.* As much as will fill a bucket.

buckie (bŭk' i) [etym. doubtful], *n.* A spiral shell, *e.g.* the whelk; (*fig.*) an obstinate, perverse person.

buckle (bŭk' ėl) [O.F. *bocle* (F. *boucle*, L. *buccula*, cheek-strap of helmet, buckle (*bucca*, cheek)], *n.* A link of metal, with a tongue, or catch, for fastening straps, etc.; a bow, a curl; the state of the hair crisped and curled, the state of being twisted; a twist. *v.t.* To fasten with or as with a buckle; to bend, to twist; (*fig.*) to equip, to confine; to join in matrimony; to prepare (oneself) resolutely. *v.i.* To bend, to be put out of shape; to be married. **buckle to:** To set to work, to set about energetically.

buckler (bŭk' lėr) [O.F. *bucler* (F. *bouclier*), from L. *buccula*, see prec.], *n.* A small round shield; (*fig.*) a protection, a protector; (*Biol.*) a hard protective covering; a carapace; the interior segment of a trilobite. *v.t.* To defend with or as with a buckler. **buckler-fern,** *n.* One of the shield ferns.

Buckley's chance (bŭk' liz chans') [?], *n.* (*Austral. colloq.*) No chance at all.

buckra (bŭk' ră) [Surinam dial. *bakra*, master], *n.* A Negro name for a white man.

buckram (bŭk' răm) [O.F. *boucaran*, *boquerant* (It. *bucherame*, *buchirano*); origin unknown], *n.* A strong, coarse kind of linen cloth, stiffened with gum; (*fig.*) a stiff, precise manner; appearance of strength. *a.* Made of buckram; (*fig.*) starched, stiff, precise. *v.i.* To stiffen with or as with buckram. **men in buckram:** [1 Henry IV, II. 4] Men existing only in the imagination of the speaker.

buckshee (bŭk′ shē) [BAKSHEESH], *n.* (*slang*) Something for nothing, a windfall; something in addition to the agreed allowance. *a.* Free, gratuitous.

buckthorn (bŭk′ thôrn) *n.* (*Bot.*) The genus *Rhamnus*, esp. *R. catharticus*, berries of which yield sap-green.

bucktooth, *n.* A large, projecting tooth.

buckwheat (bŭk′ hwēt) [*beechwheat*, from the shape of its seeds (A.-S. *boc*, beech)], *n.* A cereal plant, *Polygonum fagopyrum*, the three-cornered seeds of which are given to horses and poultry, and in the U.S. are used for cakes.

bucolic (bū kol′ ik) [L. *būcolicus*, Gr. *boukolikos*, from *boukolos*, a herdsman (*bous*, ox, *kol-*, stem of v. to drive)], *a.* Pastoral, rustic. *n.* A pastoral poem, a pastoral poet. **bucolically,** *adv.*

bud (bŭd) [etym. doubtful], *n.* The germ of a branch, cluster of leaves, or flower, usu. arising from the axil of a leaf; an unexpanded leaf or flower; (*Zool.*) a gemmule which develops into a complete animal; (*fig.*) something undeveloped. *v.i.* To put forth buds; to begin to grow; (*fig.*) to develop. *v.t.* To graft (on) by inserting a bud under the bark; to produce by germination. **budded,** *a.* In bud. **budding,** *n.* Grafting with a bud; asexual reproduction from a parent cell, as in yeast; (*Zool.*) gemmation. **budless,** *a.* **budlet,** *n.* A little bud. **in bud:** About to flower or put forth leaves.

Buddha (bud′ å) [Sansk. *buddha*, enlightened (p.p. of *budh*, to awake, to know)], *n.* The title given to Gautama, the founder of Buddhism, by his disciples. **Buddhism,** *n.* The religious system founded in India in the 5th cent. B.C. by Sakyamuni, Gautama, or Siddartha: its doctrines are pessimist, and it teaches that nirvana or extinction of individuality is the highest good. **esoteric Buddhism** [THEOSOPHY]. **Buddhist,** *n.* A follower of Buddha; *a.* Of or connected with Buddhism. **Buddhistic, -ical** (ist′ ik, -ål), *a.*

buddle (bŭdl) [etym. unknown], *n.* (*Mining*) An oblong inclined vat in which ore is washed. *v.t.* To wash (ore) by means of a buddle.

buddleia (bŭd′ lē a) [Adam *Buddle* (d. 1715)], *n.* (*Bot.*) A genus of shrubs of the family *Loganiaceæ*.

buddy (bŭd′ i), *n.* (*slang*) Close friend, pal.

budge (1) (bŭj) [F. *bouger*, to stir (cp. Prov. *bolegar*, to disturb oneself, It. *bulicare*, to bubble up, L. *bullīre*, to boil)], *v.i.* To stir; to move from one's place. *v.t.* To cause (something heavy) to move.

budge (2) (bŭj) [etym. doubtful], *n.* A kind of fur made of lambskin with the wool outwards. **a.* Wearing budge; pedantic, stiff, formal.

budgerigar (bŭj′ ĕr i gar) [Austral. abor.], *n.* (*Zool.*) The Australian green parrakeet, *Melopsittacus undulatus*.

budgery, budgeree (bŭj′ ĕr i) [Austral. abor.], *a.* Good, excellent.

budget (bŭj′ ėt) [F. *bougette*, dim. of *bouge*, a wallet, L. *bulga*, of Gaulish origin (cp. O.Ir. *bolg*, *bolc*, a bag)], *n.* A small leather bag, the contents of such a bag; a bundle, a collection of news; an estimate of receipts and expenditure, esp. the annual financial statement of the Chancellor of the Exchequer in the House of Commons. *v.i.* To prepare a budget or estimate (for). **budgetary,** *a.*

***buff** (1) (bŭf) [O.F. *bufe*, *buffe*, a blow], *n.* A blow, a buffet. **blindman's buff:** a game in which the players buffet one who is blinded and tries to catch them.

buff (2) (bŭf) [contr. of *buffe* or *buffle*, F. *buffle*, buffalo], *n.* Soft, stout leather prepared from the skin of the buffalo; the skins of other animals similarly prepared; *a soldier's coat of buff; the colour of buff leather, light yellow; (*fig.*) the bare skin; (*Med.*) BUFFY COAT. *v.t.* To polish with buff; to give a velvety surface to leather. **in buff:** Naked. **the Buffs:** The third regiment of the line (later the East Kent) from the colour of their facings. **buff-coat, -jerkin,** *n.* Stout garment of buff leather worn as a defence against sword-cuts. **buff-stick, buff-wheel,** *n.* A stick or wheel covered with buff leather, used for polishing metals. **buffy,** *a.* Coloured like buff; (*Med.*) having a buff or buffy coat. **buffy coat:** (*Med.*) A buff-coloured coating on coagulated blood.

buffalo (bŭf′ å lō) [Port. *bufalo* or It. *buffalo*, L. *būfalus*, *būbalus*, Gr. *boubalos*], *n.* The name of various kinds of ox, *Bos bubalus*, *B. caffer*, and the American bison. **buffalo-grass,** *n.* Prairie grass of various kinds. **buffalo-robe,** *n.* The skin of the American bison dressed with the hair on.

buffer (1) (bŭf′ ėr) [BUFF (1)], *n.* A mechanical apparatus for deadening or sustaining the force of a concussion: an apparatus fixed to railway carriages for this purpose. **buffer state:** (*Pol.*) A small state separating two larger states and tending to prevent hostilities.

buffer (2) (bŭf′ ėr) [etym. doubtful], n. (*slang*) A fellow. **old buffer:** A doddering old man.

buffet (1) (bŭf′ ėt) [O.F. *bufet*, dim. of *bufe*, BUFF (1)], *n.* A blow with the hand or fist, a cuff; (*fig.*) a blow of fate, a disaster, a misfortune. *v.t.* To strike with the hand; to thump, to cuff; to beat back, to contend with. *v.i.* To struggle, to contend.

buffet (2) (bŭf′ ėt) [F.; etym. unknown], *n.* A cupboard or sideboard for the display of plate, china, etc.

buffet (3) (bu′ fā) [F.], A refreshment bar.

buffo (buf′ ō) [It., comic, burlesque], *n.* A singer in a comic opera. *a.* Burlesque, comic.

buffoon (bŭ′ foon′) [F. *bouffon*, It. *buffone*, from *buffa*, a jest (*buffare*, orig. to puff out the cheeks)], *n.* One who indulges in low jests and antics; a merry-andrew; a mountebank. **buffoonery,** *n.*

bug (1) (bŭg) [perh. from W. *bwg*, ghost], *n.* A hobgoblin, a bugbear; (*slang*) a self-important person, a swell. **big bug:** (*colloq.*) An important, aristocratic or wealthy person. **bugaboo,** *n.* A bogy; (*slang*) a sheriff's officer; a tallyman. **bugbear,** *n.* A hobgoblin invoked to frighten naughty children; (*fig.*) an imaginary object of terror; a nuisance.

bug (2) (bŭg) [etym. doubtful (perh. A.-S. *budda*, beetle, influenced by BUG (1))], *n.* *A loose name for various insects; (*Am.*) any coleopterous insect; a blood-sucking, evil-smelling insect, *Cimex lectularius*, found in bedsteads, etc.; any individual of the order *Hemiptera*, to which this belongs. **bugbane,** *n.* A herb of the ranunculaceous genus *Cimifuga*, formerly used as a specific against insect pests. **bughouse,** *n.* (*slang*) An asylum. *a.* Mad, crazy. **buggy** (1) *a.* Infested with bugs.

bugger (bŭg′ ėr) [F. *bougre*, L. *Bulgarus*, one of a sect of Bulgarian heretics, 11th century, to whom abominable practices were attributed], *n.* (*Law*) A sodomite; (*obscene*) beast, cad; (*Am.*) fellow, chap. **to bugger about:** To muddle about, to interfere with a thing. **buggery,** *n.* (*Law*) Sodomy.

buggy (2) (bŭg′ i) [etym. doubtful], *n.* A light, four-wheeled vehicle, having a single seat.

bugle (1) (bū′ gėl) [short for BUGLE-HORN, O.F. *bugle*, a wild ox, L. *būculus*, dim. of *bos bovis*, ox], *n.* A hunting-horn, orig. made from the horn of a wild ox; a small military trumpet used to sound signals for the infantry. *v.t.* To sound by bugle; to call by bugle. *v.i.* To sound a bugle. **bugle-horn,** *n.* A bugle. **bugler,** *n.* One who plays a bugle; a soldier who transmits signals on a bugle. **buglet,** *n.* A small bugle.

bugle (2) (bū′ gėl) [etym. unknown], *n.* A long, slender glass bead, usually black, for trimming dresses.

bugle (3) (bū′ gėl) [F., from late L. *būgula*], *n.* Name of plants of the genus *Ajuga*, esp. *A. reptans*. **bugle-weed,** *n.* An American plant, *Lycopus Virginicus*, used as a remedy for blood-spitting.

bugloss (bū′ glos) [F. *buglosse*, L. *būglōssa*, Gr. *buglōssos* (*bous*, ox, *glōssa*, tongue)], *n.* Name of plants of the borage family with rough, hairy leaves; *Echium vulgare*, viper's bugloss; *Lycopsis arvensis*, small or wild bugloss.

buhl (bool) [from André *Buhl*, or *Boule* (1642–1732)], *n.* Brass, tortoise-shell, etc., cut into ornamental patterns for inlaying; work so inlaid.

build (bild) [A.-S. *bold*, a house (whence M.E. *bulden, bilden*, to build), from Teut. *bu-*, to dwell], *v.t.* (*past and p.p.* **built**) To construct, to erect, to make by putting together parts and materials; to put (into a structure); to establish. *v.i.* To erect a building or buildings; to make a nest. *n.* Form, style, or mode of construction; shape, proportions, figure. **to build on** or **upon:** To found or rely on (as a basis). **build-up,** *n.* A creation of favourable publicity; the leading to the climax in a speech, etc. **to build up:** To establish or strengthen by degrees; to block up. **builder,** *n.* One who builds; a master-builder or contractor who erects buildings under the direction of the architect. **building,** *n.* The act of constructing or erecting; an erection, an edifice. **building-lease,** *a.* A lease of land with covenant to build specified buildings which become the property of the landlord on the expiration of the lease. **building society,** *n.* An organization lending money to contributors enabling them to purchase dwelling-houses. **built,** *a.* Constructed, erected, fashioned, formed (in *comb.* as *well-built*). **built-in,** *a.* Part of the main structure, *e.g.* cupboards, wardrobe.

buirdly (boord′ li) [Sc., earlier *buirly*, BURLY], *a.* Stalwart, stout, burly.

bulb (bŭlb) [F. *bulbe*, L. *bulbus*, Gr. *bolbos*, onion], *n.* A subterranean stem or bud sending off roots below and leaves above, as in the onion or lily; a bulbil; a spherical dilatation of a glass tube, as in the thermometer; an electric-light globe; (*Anat.*) a spherical swelling of any cylindrical organ or structure. *v.i.* To take or grow into the form of a bulb. **bulbed,** *a.* Having the form of a bulb. **bulbiferous** (bŭl bif′ ėr ŭs), *a.* Producing bulbs. **bulbiform** (bŭl′ bi fôrm), *a.* **bulbil,** *a.* A small bulb developed at the side of a larger one, or in an axil. **bulbaceous** (-bā′ shŭs), **bulbous** (bŭl′ bŭs), **bulbose** (bŭl bōs′), *a.* Of or pertaining to a bulb; bulb-shaped.

bulbo-, *comb. form.* Bulb-like; pertaining to the bulb; as in **bulbo-tuber** [TUBER], *n.* A corm. **bulbo-medullary** [MEDULLARY], *a.* Pertaining to the bulb of the spinal marrow.

bulbul (bul′ bul) [Pers.], *n.* An eastern bird of the genus *Pycnonotus* belonging to the thrush family; (*fig.*) a singer, a poet.

bulge (bŭlj) [O.F. *boulge, bouge*, L. *bulga* (see BUDGET)], *n.* The protuberant part of a cask; a swelling on a flat or flattish surface; a temporary increase in volume or numbers; (*Naut.*) bilge. *v.i.* To swell irregularly; to be protuberant. *v.t.* To swell out (a bag); to push out of shape. **bulger,** *n.* (*Golf*) A brassy or driver with a convex face. **bulging,** *a.* Protuberant. **bulgy,** *a.* Swollen so as to be clumsy. **bulginess,** *n.*

bulimy (bū′ li mi), **bulimia** (bū li′ mi a) [Gr. *boulimia* (*bous*, ox, *limos*, hunger)], *n.* (*Med.*) Morbid craving for food; (*fig.*) voracity.

bulk (1) (bŭlk) [prob. from Icel. *būlki*, a heap, a cargo, confused with *bouk*, A.-S. *būc*, belly], *n.* Cargo; magnitude of three dimensions; size, great size, mass; the greater portion, the main mass. *v.i.* To appear relatively big or important; to amount. *v.t.* To pile in heaps; to pack in bulk; to measure the bulk of. **in bulk:** (*Naut.*) Loose in the hold; in large quantities. **to break bulk:** To begin to unload or unpack. **bulk buying:** The purchase of goods in large quantities in order to obtain cheaper prices; the purchase by one customer of the whole of a producer's output. **bulker,** *n.* (*Naut.*) A person employed to measure goods to ascertain the freight or duties chargeable. **bulky,** *a.* Of great bulk or dimensions; large. **bulkiness,** *n.*

***bulk** (2) (bŭlk) [etym. doubtful; Skeat proposed M.Dan. *bulk*, a balk], *n.* A framework projecting in front of a shop for displaying goods.

bulker [BULK (1)].

bulkhead (bŭlk′ hed), *n.* (*Naut.*) An upright partition dividing a ship into compartments.

bull (1) (bul) [A.-S. *bule* in *bule-hide* (see also BULLOCK, from *bulluc*) from *bellan*, to bellow], *n.* The uncastrated male of any bovine mammal, esp. of the domestic species, *Bos taurus*; the male of some other large animals, as the elk, the elephant, the whale; (*Stock Exchange*) one who speculates for a rise (see also BEAR); (*Astron.*) the constellation and sign Taurus; (*slang*) a bull's-eye, a hit in the bull's eye. *a.* Of large size; thickset; coarse; male. *v.i.* To speculate for a rise (in stocks); (of a cow) to low when in season. *v.t.* To produce a rise in (stocks, etc.). **John Bull:** The English people personified; an Englishman. **to take the bull by the horns:** To grapple with a difficulty boldly. **bull artist,** *n.* (*Austral.*) A swanker, a blow-hard. **bull-baiting,** *n.* The baiting of a bull with dogs. **bull-beef,** *n.* The flesh of a bull; coarse, stringy beef. **bull-board,** *n.* A game like quoits played on board ship with a disk thrown on to numbered squares. **bull-calf,** *n.* A male calf; (*fig.*) a stupid fellow. **bullfight,** *n.* A Spanish sport in which a bull is baited and then killed. **bull-headed,** *a.* With a massive head; (*fig.*) stupid; obstinate impetuous. **bull-puncher,** *n.* (*Austral.*) A cattle-driver. **bull-ring,** *n.* An arena for a bull-fight; a place where bulls used to be baited.

bull (2) (bul) [L. *bulla*, a knob, a seal], *n.* A leaden seal appended to a Papal edict; a Papal edict.

bull (3) (bul) [etym. unknown (cp. O.F. *boul*, fraud, trickery)], *n.* *A jest; a ludicrous contradiction in terms, supposed to be characteristic of the Irish.

bull (4) (bul) [origin unknown], *n.* Drink made by putting water into an empty spirit cask to acquire the flavour of the liquor.

bull (5) (bul), *n.* (*Mil.*) Undue fussiness over dress and cleanliness of accoutrements, etc.

bull (6) (bul) [BEAL].

bulla (bul′ ȧ) [L.], *n.* A round pendant worn by Roman children; (*Med.*) a watery vesicle; (*Zool.*) a genus of freshwater mollusca.

bullace (bul′ ȧs) [O.F. *beloce*, late L. *pilota*, L. *pila*, a ball], *n.* A wild plum, *Prunus insititia*, having two varieties, one with white, the other with dark fruit.

bullate (bul′ ȧt) [L. *bullātus* (*bulla*, a bubble)], *a.* (*Bot.*) Blistered, puckered; (*Physiol.*) having bleb-like excrescences.

bulldog (bul′ dog), *n.* A powerful breed of dogs formerly used to bait bulls; (*fig.*) one who possesses obstinate courage; one of the proctor's attendants at Oxford and Cambridge; a gun or pistol of a certain pattern. **bull-dog ant,** *n.* (*Austral.*) A large red or black ant with poisonous bite.

bulldozer (bul′ dō zėr), *n.* A power-operated machine with a large blade, employed for removing obstacles, levelling ground, and spreading material.

bullet (bul′ ėt) [F. *boulette*, dim. of *boule*, ball, L. *bulla*, a round object], *n.* A metal ball or cone used in fire-arms of small calibre; *a cannon-ball; a small round ball; a round missile; a fisherman's sinker. **bullet-head,** *n.* A round-shaped head; (*Am.*) An obstinate fellow. **bullet-headed,** *a.* **bullet-proof,** *a.* Impenetrable to bullets. **to get the bullet:** (*slang*) To be dismissed, get the sack.

bulletin (bul′ ė tin) [F., from It. *bulletino*, dim. of *bulletta*, a passport, a lottery-ticket, dim. of *bulla*, see BULL (2)], *n.* An official report of some matter of public interest, esp. of the condition of an invalid. *v.t.* To announce by bulletin. **bulletin board,** *n.* (*Am.*) A notice-board. **bulletinist,** *n.* **news bulletin,** *n.* The broadcast of current news by the B.B.C.

bullfinch (bul′ finch), *n.* An English song-bird with handsome plumage, belonging to the genus

Pyrrhula; a high, quick-set hedge with a ditch on one side.

bull-frog (bul′ frog), *n.* A large American frog with a deep voice, *Rana pipiens.*

bullhead (bul′ hed), *n.* The miller's thumb, a small river-fish, *Cottus gobio*, with a big head; (*Austral.*) a small shark; (*N. Zealand*) an edible freshwater fish.

bullion (bul′ yŏn) [perh. from F. *bouillon*, boiling, soup, med. L. *bulliōnem*, acc. of *bullio* (*bullīre*, to boil); or from F. *billon*, an ingot, influenced by this], *n.* Uncoined gold and silver in the mass; solid gold or silver; fringe made of gold or silver wire. *a.* Made of solid gold or silver. **bullionist,** *n.* An advocate for a metallic currency.

bullock (bul′ ŏk) [A.-S. *bulluc*, see BULL (1)], *n.* *A castrated bull; an ox; a bovine animal.

bull-pup, *n.* A young bulldog.

bullring [BULL (1)].

bull-roarer (bul′ rôr ėr), *n.* A thin slat of wood that produces a formidable noise when swung rapidly with a string, used for purposes of magic among the primitive peoples of Polynesia, W. Africa, and parts of America.

bull's-eye, *n.* A boss of glass in the middle of a blown sheet; a sweetmeat; (*Naut.*) a hemispherical disk of glass in the side or deck of a ship to give light below; a hemispherical lens in a lantern; a lantern with such a lens; a small round window; the centre of a target.

bull-terrier, *n.* A cross between a bulldog and a terrier, but now an acknowledged breed.

bull-trout, *n.* A variety of sea-trout, *Salmo eriox.*

bully (1) (bul′ i) [etym. doubtful; perh. from Dut. *boel*, a lover (cp. M.H.G. *buole*, G. *buhle*)], *n.* A blustering, overbearing fellow; a cowardly tyrant; a bravo, a swashbuckler, a hired ruffian; *a dashing fellow. *a.* (*Am.*) Jolly, first-rate, capital. *v.t.* To treat in a tyrannical manner; to tease, oppress, terrorize. *v.i.* To act as a bully. **bully for you:** (*Am.*) Well done! Bravo!

bully (2) (bul′ i), *n.* (*Eton football*) A scrimmage; (*Hockey*) the starting of a game.

bully (3) (bul′ i) [BULL (1) or BOUILLI], *n.* Tinned beef, also called **bully beef.**

bullyrag [BALLYRAG].

bulrush (bul′ rŭsh) [etym. doubtful; perh. BOLE (1), whence 'strong-stemmed,' or BULL (1), big (cp. BULL-FROG, etc.)], *n.* A tall rush growing in water, *Scirpus lacustris*, or *Typha latifolia*, the reed-mace or cat's-tail; (*Bibl.*) the papyrus. **bulrushy,** *a.*

bulwark (bul′ wȧrk) [formed like Dut. *bolwerk* and G. *bollwerk*, from words represented by BOLE (1), or the M.H.G. v. *boln*, to throw, and WORK], *n.* A rampart or fortification; a mole, a breakwater; (*fig.*) any shelter, protection, screen; (*Naut.*) that part of the sides of a ship which rises above the upper deck. *v.t.* To furnish with or protect as with bulwarks.

bum (1) (bŭm) [onomat.; cp. BOOM (1)], *v.i.* To make a humming noise; to boom.

bum (2) (bŭm) [etym. doubtful; cp. BUMP], *n.* The buttocks; a bumbailiff. **bummed,** *part.a.* (*slang*) Arrested, nabbed. **bumbailiff** (bŭm bā′ lif) [cp. F. *pousse-cul*], *n.* An under bailiff.

bum (3), **bummer** (bŭm, bŭm′ ėr) [G. *bummler*, a loafer], *n.* (*Am.*) An irregular forager in the American Civil War; an idler, a loafer; a rascal, a blackleg.

bumbaze (bŭm bāz′) [perh. from Dut. *bazen*, to astonish; see also BAMBOOZLE], *v.t.* (*Sc.*) To confound, to bamboozle.

Bumble (1) (bŭm′ bėl) [from *Bumble*, the beadle in Dickens's *Oliver Twist*], *n.* A beadle; a jack-in-office. **bumbledom,** *n.* Fussy officialism, esp. of parochial officers; parish officers collectively.

***bumble** (2) (bŭm′ bėl) [imit.; cp. BOOM (1)], *v.i.* To buzz, to boom. *v.t.* To grumble at. **bumble-bee,** *n.* A large bee belonging to the genus *Bombus*; a humble-bee.

***bumble** (3) (bŭm′ bėl) [onomat.], *n.* A jumble, a confused heap; a blunderer, an idler. **bumble-foot,** *n.* A club-foot. **bumble-puppy,** *n.* *A childish game with marbles; whist played unscientifically.

bumbo (bŭm′ bō) [cp. It. *bombo*, childish word for drink], *n.* Punch made with rum or gin.

bumboat (bŭm′ bōt), *n.* (*Naut.*) A boat used to carry provisions to vessels.

bumkin (bŭm′ kin), *n.* (*Naut.*) A small boom projecting from each bow to extend the foresail; a similar boom for the mainsail or the mizzen.

bummalo (bŭm′ ȧ lō) [Mahratti *bombīl*, *bombīla*], *n.* Bombay duck; a small Asiatic fish, dried and used as a relish.

bummaree (bŭm ȧ rē′) [?] *n.* A middleman in the Billingsgate and Smithfield markets; a porter at Smithfield.

bummock (bŭm′ ŏk) [?], *n.* (*Sc.*) A large brewing of ale.

bump (1) (bŭmp) [onomat.], *n.* A thump, a dull, heavy blow, an impact or collision; a swelling; a protuberance on the skull, said by phrenologists to indicate distinct faculties or affections; a touch in a bumping-race; (*Aviat.*) a sudden movement of an aircraft caused by currents. *v.t.* To cause to strike forcibly against anything hard or solid; to hurt by striking against something; to hit (against); (*Boat-racing*) to strike the boat in front with the prow of one's own boat. *v.i.* To strike heavily; to collide; to move along with a bump or succession of bumps. *adv.* [cp. BANG, *adv.*] With a bump; with a sudden shock. **bump off,** *v.t.* (*slang*) To murder. **bumpy,** *a.* Full of bumps, uneven, jolty.

bump (2) (bŭmp) [onomat.], *n.* The cry of the bittern. *v.i.* To cry like a bittern.

bumper (bŭm′ pėr), *n.* One or that which bumps; a glass filled to the brim, esp. for drinking a toast; (*Motor*) the fender of a motor-car; (*Am.*) a buffer; (*slang*) anything very large or wonderful or full; a crowded house at the theatre; (*Whist*) a score of two games to nothing; (*Austral.*) a cigarette-butt. *a.* (*slang*) Extraordinary, startling, fine.

bumpkin (bŭmp′ kin) [prob. BUMKIN], *n.* A country lout; a clumsy, thickheaded fellow; a bashful person.

bumptious (bŭmp′ shŭs) [facetious, from BUMP (1)], *a.* Self-assertive. **bumptiously,** *adv.* **bumptiousness,** *n.*

bun (1) (bŭn) [perh. O.F. (prov.) *bugne*, fritters], *n.* A small sweet cake; a compact ball of hair worn at the back of the head. **hot cross bun,** *n.* A bun marked with a cross and sold on Good Friday. **bun-fight,** *n.* A crowded tea-party.

bun (2) (bŭn) [etym. unknown; perh. from Gael. *bun*, a root], *n.* (*Sc.*) A hare's tail.

bun (3) (bŭn) [etym. unknown], *n.* Playful name for the squirrel; also for the rabbit.

bunce (bŭns) [etym. unknown], *n.* (*slang*) Extra profit, something to the good.

bunch (bŭnch) [prob. onomat.], *n.* A cluster of several things of the same kind growing or tied together; a tuft, a knot, a bow; a lot, a collection, a pack, a herd. *v.t.* To tie up or form into a bunch; to gather into folds. *v.i.* To come or grow into a cluster or bunch. **bunchy,** *a.* Forming a bunch; growing in bunches.

bunco [BUNKO].

buncombe, bunkum (bŭng′ kŭm) [from *Buncombe* County, N. Carolina, the representative of which made a speech in Congress (1820) merely to please his constituents], *n.* Political clap-trap; tall talk, humbug.

bund (bund) [Hind.], *n.* An embankment, quay.

Bundesrat (boon′ dės rat) [G. *bund*, confederation, *rat*, council], *n.* The federal council of the former German Empire, now of the W. German Republic; the federal council of Switzerland.

bundle (bŭn′ dėl) [*bund-*, p.p. stem of O.Teut. *bindan*, to BIND (cp. M.Dut. *bondel*, G. *bündel*)], *n.* A number of things or a quantity of anything bound together; a package, a parcel; a set of rods, wires, fibres, nerves, etc., bound together; twenty hanks (each of 3000 yards) of linen thread; (*fig.*) a group of characteristics. *v.t.* To tie up in a bundle; to throw hurriedly together. *v.i.* To prepare for departure, to pack up, to start hurriedly (in, off, away, or out); (*Am.*) to sleep (with a person of the opposite sex) without undressing. **to bundle off:** To send away hurriedly or unceremoniously; to dismiss.

bundook (bŭn dook′). [Hind.], *n.* A musket, gun.

bundu (bŭn′ doo), *n.* (*S. Africa*) The back of beyond, the far interior.

bung (bŭng) [cp. M.Dut. *bonghe, bonde, bonne* (Dut. *bon*), L. *puncta*, an orifice (fem. p.p. of *pungere*, to prick)], *n.* A large cork stopper for a bung-hole; (*slang*) a publican; [etym. doubtful], *a purse; a cut-purse, a pickpocket. *v.t.* To stop with a bung; (*fig.*) to close, to shut up. **to go bung:** (*Austral. colloq.*) To go bankrupt. **bung-hole,** *n.* The hole in the bulge of a cask through which it is filled.

bungalow (bŭng′ gȧ lō) [Hind. *bānglā*, of Bengal], *n.* A one-storied house.

bungle (bŭng′ gėl) [prob. imit., cp. BOGGLE, BUMBLE], *v.t.* To botch; to manage clumsily or awkwardly. *v.i.* To act clumsily or awkwardly; to fail in a task. *n.* Botching; mismanagement. **bungler,** *n.* **bungling,** *a.* Clumsy, awkward, unskilful. **bunglingly,** *adv.*

bunion (bŭn′ yŏn) [perh. from It. *bugnone*, *bugno*, a boil or blain (cp. O.F. *bugne*, see BUN (1))], *n.* A swelling on the foot, esp. of the joint of the great toe.

bunk (1) (bŭngk) [etym. unknown], *n.* A box or recess serving for a bed; a sleeping-berth; (*Am.*) a piece of timber on a sled to support heavy timber. *v.i.* (*Am.*) To sleep in a bunk.

bunk (2) (bŭngk) [etym. unknown], *v.i.* (*slang*) To make off, to bolt. *n.* A bolt; a making off.

bunk (3) (bŭngk) [BUNCOMBE].

bunker (bŭng′ kėr) [etym. doubtful], *n.* (*Sc.*) A bench, a bank; (*Naut.*) a coal-bin; (*Golf*) a sandy hollow or other obstruction.

bunko, bunco (bŭng′ kō), *n.* (*Am. slang*) A swindling game or confidence trick. *v.t.* To swindle in this or a similar manner. **bunko-steerer,** *n.* A decoy in bunko.

bunkum [BUNCOMBE].

bunny (bŭn′ i) [BUN (3), -Y], *n.* A childish name for a rabbit. **bunny-hug, bunny-hugging,** *n.* A romping kind of dance in which the partners closely embrace each other.

Bunsen (boon′-, bŭn′ sėn) [Prof. *Bunsen*, 1811–99], *a.* Invented by Bunsen. **Bunsen battery, cell,** *n.* (*Elec.*) A special kind of voltaic battery. **Bunsen burner, lamp,** *n.* A burner or lamp in which air is mingled with gas for heating and for work with the blow-pipe.

bunt (1) (bŭnt) [etym. doubtful], *n.* (*Naut.*) The middle part of a sail, formed into a cavity to hold the wind; the baggy part of a fishing-net. **buntline,** *n.* (*Naut.*) A rope passing from the foot-rope of a square sail and in front of the canvas to prevent bellying.

bunt (2) (bŭnt) [etym. doubtful], *n.* A fungus, *Tilletia caries*, which attacks wheat.

bunt (3) (bŭnt) [cp. BUTT, BOUNCE], *v.t.* and *i.* To hit, push, butt.

bunter (bun′ tėr) [G. *bunter sandstein*], *n.* (*Geol.*) New Red Sandstone.

bunting (1) (bŭn′ ting) [etym. doubtful], *n.* A group of birds, the *Emberizinæ*, allied to the larks; the grey shrimp, *Crangon vulgaris*.

bunting (2) (bŭn′ ting) [etym. doubtful], *n.* A thin woollen stuff of which flags are made; a flag; flags collectively.

bunya-bunya (bŭn′ yȧ bŭn′ yȧ) [Austral. abor.], *n.* A large conifer with edible seeds.

bunyip (bŭn′ yip) [Austral. abor.], *n.* The fabulous rainbow-serpent that lives in pools. **bunyip peerage:** A nickname for the attempt to introduce an aristocracy in Australia in 1853.

buoy (boi) [O.F. *boie* or Dut. *boei*, L. *boia*, a fetter], *n.* An anchored float indicating a fairway, reef, shoal, etc. *v.t.* To place a buoy upon, to mark with a buoy. **life-buoy,** *n.* A float to sustain a person in the water. **buoy up:** To keep afloat, to bear up, bring to the surface. **buoyage** (boi′ ȧj), *n.* The act of providing with buoys.

buoyancy (boi′ ȧn si), *n.* Ability to float; (*Hydrostat.*) loss of weight due to immersion in a liquid; (*fig.*) power or resisting or recovering from depression, elasticity; lightheartedness; tendency to rise (of stocks, prices, etc.). **buoyant,** *a.* Tending to float; tending to keep up; (*fig.*) elastic, light; easily recovering from depression. **buoyantly,** *adv.*

bur (1), **burr** (2) (bĕr) [cp. Dan. *borre*, burdock], *n.* Any prickly or spinous fruit, calyx, or involucre; the involucre of the burdock; the catkin or cone of the hop; a knot of excrescence on a tree; hence the series of markings left in the timber, which are valuable for their effect in polished veneer, etc.; the husk of the chestnut; (*colloq.*) a sponger; one hard to get rid of; a lump in the throat. **burdock,** *n.* A coarse plant with prickly flower-heads, of the genus *Arctium*, esp. *A. lappa*. **bur-thistle,** *n.* The spear-thistle, *Carduus lanceolatus*.

bur (2) [BURR (1)].

Burberry (bĕr′ bĕr i), *n.* Protected trade name of a type of weatherproof cloth or clothing.

burble (1) (bĕr′ bėl) [imit., cp. BUBBLE], *v.i.* To bubble, gurgle, *to flow with a gurgling noise.

burble (2) (bĕr′ bėl) [from prec., or a mod. coinage], *v.i.* To simmer, to bubble with mirth or other emotion; to talk inconsequently.

burble (3) (bĕr′ bėl) [Sc., perh. from F. *barbouiller*], *v.t.* To muddle, confuse. *n.* Disorder, confusion.

burbot (bĕr′ bŏt) [F. *bourbotte* (*bourbe*, late L. *borba*, Gr. *borboros*, mud)], *n.* The eel-pout, *Lota vulgaris*, a flat-headed freshwater fish.

***burd** (bĕrd) [etym. doubtful; cp. perh. BRIDE], *n.* (*poet.*) Lady, maiden. **burd-alone, burd-alane:** The last surviving child of a family.

burden, burthen (bĕr′ dėn, -*th*ėn) [A.-S. *byrthen*, O.S. *burthinnia*, from Teut. stem *bur-*, of *beran*, to BEAR], *n.* Something borne or carried; a load; a load of labour, sin, sorrow, care, obligation, duty, taxation, expense, fate, etc.; the principal theme, the gist of a composition of any kind; (*Naut.*) the carrying capacity of a vessel; tonnage; *an accompaniment; a refrain, a chorus. *v.t.* To load; to lay a burden on; to oppress, encumber. ***burdenous,** *a.* Heavy; onerous, oppressive. **burdensome,** *a.* Hard to bear; grievous, oppressive. **burdensomely,** *adv.* **burdensomeness,** *n.*

burdock [BUR (1)].

bureau (bū′ rō′, bū′ rō) [F., an office, a desk, orig. baize, O.F. *burel*, dim. of *bure*, drugget, L. *burra*, a coarse red cloth, fem. of *burrus* (perh. from Gr. *purrhos*, red)], *n.* (*pl.* **bureaux** (bū′ rōz)) A writing table with drawers for papers; a chest of drawers; an office; a public office; a Government department.

bureaucracy (bū rok′ rȧ si) [as prec.], *n.* Government by departments of State; centralization of government; officials as a body; officialism. **bureaucrat** (bū′ rō krăt), *n.* A Government official; a bureaucratist. **bureaucratic** (-krăt′ ik), *a.* Pertaining to or constituting a bureaucracy; tending towards bureaucracy. **bureaucratically,** *adv.* **bureaucratist** (bū rō′ krȧ tist), *n.* One who advocates or supports bureaucracy. **bureaucratism,** *n.*

burette (bū ret′) [F., dim. of *buire*, a vase (cp. *boire*, to drink)], *n.* A graduated glass tube for measuring small quantities of liquid.

burg (bĕrg) [G. (cp. BOROUGH)], *n.* A fortress; a walled town.

burgage (bĕr′ gȧj) [med. L. *burgāgium*, from *burgus*, G. burg], *n.* (*Law*) A tenure by which lands or tenements in towns or cities were held for a small yearly rent; property so held.

burgee (bĕr jē′) [etym. and connexion of the two senses doubtful], *n.* A kind of small coal suitable for furnaces; (*Naut.*) a triangular or swallow-tailed flag.

burgeois [BOURGEOIS (2)].

burgeon, bourgeon (bĕr′ jȯn) [O.F. *borjon*, prob. from O.Teut. stem *bur-* (*beran*, to BEAR)], *v.t.* To sprout, to bud; to begin to grow. *n.* (*poet.*) A bud, a shoot.

burgess (bĕr′ jės) [O.F. *burgeis*, see BOURGEOIS (1)], *n.* An inhabitant of a borough possessing full municipal rights, a citizen; a freeman of a borough; *a member of Parliament for a borough or a University. **burgess-ship,** *n.* The status of a burgess.

burgh (bŭr′ ů) [Sc. (see BOROUGH)], *n.* A Scottish town holding a charter; a borough. **burgh of barony:** A borough having a charter from the sovereign, but holding its land from a feudal lord. **burgh of regality:** A borough holding its charter of incorporation from the sovereign, with regal or exclusive criminal jurisdiction within its boundaries. **Parliamentary burgh:** A place delimited in 1832 which is entitled to send a representative to Parliament, and is municipally on the same footing as a Burgh Royal. **police burgh:** A burgh constituted by the sheriff and having the police commissioners for local authority. **Burgh Royal:** A burgh holding its municipal authority by royal charter. **burghal** (bĕr′ gȧl), *a.* Pertaining to a burgh. **burgher** (bĕr′ gėr) [G. or Dut. *burger* (BURG, -ER), assim. to BURGH], *n.* A citizen or inhabitant of a burgh, borough, or corporate town, esp. of a Continental town. **burghership,** *n.* The position and privileges of a burgher.

burglar (bĕrg′ lȧr) [Ang.-Lat. *burglātor*, *burgātor*, perh. from M.E. *burgh-breche*, breach of a borough], *n.* One who breaks into a house after sunset with intent to commit a felony. **burglarious** (-lâr′ i ůs), *a.* **burglariously,** *adv.* **burglary,** *n.* **burgle,** *v.i.* To commit burglary. *v.t.* To enter or rob burglariously.

burgomaster (bĕr′ gō mas tėr) [Dut. *burgemeester* (see BURG)], *n.* The chief magistrate of a municipal town in Holland or Flanders.

burgonet (bĕr′ gȯ net) [O.F. *bourguignotte*, from *Bourgogne*, Burgundy], *n.* A light helmet for foot-soldiers; a helmet with a visor.

burgoo (bůr goo′) [etym. doubtful], *n.* A kind of oatmeal porridge or thick gruel used by sailors.

burgrave (boor′ grāv) [G. (BURG, *graf*, count)], *n.* The commandant of a castle or fortified town; a hereditary noble ruling such a town and the adjacent domain.

Burgundy (bĕr′ gůn di), *n.* An old province in France; red or white wine made in Burgundy. **Burgundy mixture,** *n.* A preparation of soda and copper sulphate used for spraying potatoes in order to destroy disease germs.

burial (ber′ i ȧl) [A.-S. *byrgels*, a tomb, a burying-place (*byrgan*, to bury)], *n.* The act of burying, esp. of a dead body in the earth; interment; a funeral. **burial-place, burial-ground,** *n.* A place for burying the dead. **burial-mound,** *n.* A tumulus. **burial-service,** *n.* A religious service (esp. of the Church of England) for the burial of the dead.

burin (būr′ in) [F., prob. from O.H.G. *bora*, a borer, through It. *borino*], *n.* The cutting-tool of an engraver on copper; a triangular steel tool used by marble-workers.

burkah (bĕr′ ka) [Hind.], *n.* The long veil worn by Muslim women in India.

burke (bĕrk) [from *Burke*, an Irishman who (1828) killed many persons by smothering, to sell their bodies for dissection], *v.t.* *To kill secretly by suffocation; to smother, to hush up; to shirk publicity by suppressing.

burl (bĕrl) [O.F. *bourle* (prob. dim. of *bourre*, from late L. *burra*, a woollen pad)], *n.* A knot or lump in wool or cloth; (*Am.*) a knot in wood. *v.t.* To dress (cloth) by removing knots or lumps. **burling-comb, -iron, -machine,** *n.* Contrivances for clearing wool of burls.

burlap (bĕr′ lăp) [etym. doubtful (cp. Dut. *boenlap*, rubbing-clout)], *n.* A coarse kind of canvas used for bagging.

burlesque (bĕr lesk′) [F., from It. *burlesco* (*burla*, a trick, banter)], *a.* *Jocular, ludicrous; drolly or absurdly imitative; mock-serious or mock-heroic. *n.* Mockery, grotesque imitation; literary or dramatic representation caricaturing other work. *v.t.* To produce a grotesque imitation of; to travesty. **burlesquely,** *adv.*

burletta (bĕr let′ ȧ) [It., dim. of *burla*, see prec.], *n.* A comic opera; a musical farce.

burly (bĕr′ li) [M.E. *burliche*, prob. from an A.-S. *būrlīc*, suitable for a lady's BOWER], *a.* *Stately, dignified, imposing; *goodly, excellent; bluff, domineering; stout, lusty, corpulent. **burliness,** *n.*

burn (1) (bĕrn) [A.-S. *bærnan*, tr., and *biernan*, intr., from Teut. *brennan* (cp. G. *brennen*)], *v.t.* (*past and p.p.* **burnt,** sometimes **burned**) To consume, destroy, scorch, or injure by fire; to subject to the action of fire; to produce an effect (on anything) similar to the action of fire; to treat with heat for some purpose of manufacture, etc.; to corrode, eat into; (*Chem.*) to combine with oxygen; to make use of the nuclear energy of uranium, etc.; (*Med.*) to cauterize. *v.i.* To be on fire; to be or become intensely hot; to emit light, to shine; to act with destructive effect; to be bright, to glow with light or colour; (*fig.*) to glow, to rage, to be inflamed. *n.* The effect of burning; a burnt place. **to burn away:** To consume entirely by fire. **to burn in:** To render indelible by or as by burning. **to burn off:** To remove paint by means of softening with a lamp-flame or hot iron. **to burn one's boats:** To commit oneself to something without possibility of retreat. **to burn one's fingers:** To hurt oneself by meddling. **to burn out:** To consume the inside or contents of. **to burn the water:** To spear salmon by torch-light. **to burn up,** *v.t.* To destroy, get rid of, by fire; *v.i.* To blaze, to flash into a blaze. **burnable,** *a.* **burner,** *n.* That part of a lamp or gas-light from which the flame issues. **burning,** *a.* In a state of heat; ardent, glowing; vehement, exciting; flagrant. **burning bush,** *n.* The bush that burned and was not consumed (Exod. iii. 2), adopted as an emblem by the Scottish Presbyterian churches in memory of the persecutions; *Dictamnus fraxinella*, various species of *Euonymus*, and other shrubs with vivid foliage, fruit, etc. **burning-glass,** *n.* A convex lens used for causing intense heat by concentrating the sun's rays. **burning-mirror,** or **-reflector,** *n.* A concave mirror, or a combination of plane-mirrors arranged to act as a burning-glass. **burning-point,** *n.* The temperature at which volatile oils ignite [FLASH-POINT]. **burning question,** *n.* One that excites heated discussion or that demands immediate solution. **burning scent,** *n.* (*Hunting*) Very hot, strong scent. **burning shame,** *n.* A flagrant shame; *a shame that causes one to blush. **burnt-ear,** *n.* A disease in grain caused by a smut or fungus, *Uredo segetum*. **burnt offering, burnt sacrifice,** *n.* An offering or sacrifice to a deity by fire; esp. one offered to God by the Jews. **burnt-sienna** [SIENNA].

burn (2) (bĕrn) [A.-S. *burna* (cp. Dut. *born*, Goth. *brunna*, G. *brunnen*, Eng. BOURN (1))], *n.* A small stream, a brook.

burnet (bĕr′ nėt) [O.F. *burnete*, BRUNETTE], *n.* Brown-flowered plants of the genera *Poterium* and *Sanguisorba*. **burnet-fly, -moth,** *n.* A crimson-spotted, greenish-black moth, *Zygæna filipendulæ*. **burnet-rose**, *n*. The Scottish wild rose.

burnish (bĕr′ nish) [O.F. *burnir*, *brunir*, to brown, to polish], *v.t.* To polish, esp. by rubbing. *v.i.* To become bright or glossy. *n*. Polish, gloss, lacquer. **burnisher**, *n*. One who burnishes; a tool for burnishing.

burnous (bŭr nooz′, -noos′) [F., from Arab. *burnus*], *n*. A mantle or cloak with a hood, worn by Moors and Arabs.

burnt, *past* and *p.p.* [BURN (1)].

burp (bĕrp) [onomat.], *n*. A belch. *v.i.* To belch.

burr (1) (bĕr) [etym. doubtful], *n*. *A circle; a washer on a rivet; a nebulous disk or halo surrounding the moon; the round, knobby base of a deer's horn; a rough ridge or edge left on metal or other substance after cutting, punching, etc.; the roughness made by the graver on a copper plate; a triangular hollow chisel; a clinker, a mass of semi-vitrified brick; a rough sounding of the letter *r*; a whirring noise; a burr-stone; hence a whetstone; (*Geol.*) siliceous rock occurring in bands or masses among softer formations. *v.t.* To pronounce with a rough sounding of the *r*. *v.i.* To speak with a burr; to speak indistinctly. **burr-stone**, *n*. A coarse siliceous rock used for millstones. **burry** (bĕr i), *a*. Characterized by burrs; rough, prickly.

burr (2) [BUR (1)].

burro (bur′ ō) [Sp.], *n*. (*Am.*) A donkey.

burrow (bŭr′ ō) [prob. var. of BOROUGH], *n*. A hole in the ground made by rabbits, foxes, etc., for a dwelling-place. *v.i.* To excavate a burrow for shelter or concealment; to live in a burrow; to hide oneself; to bore or excavate. *v.t.* To make by means of excavating. **burrow-duck**, *n*. The sheldrake, *Anas tadorna*. **burrowing-owl**, *n*. An American owl, *Noctua cunicularia*. **burrows-town**, *n*. (*Sc.*) Borough town, a town which is a borough. *a*. Townish.

bursa (bĕr′ sȧ) [med. L., bag, purse, from Gr. *bursa*, wine-skin], *n*. (*Physiol.*) A synovial sac found among tendons in the body and serving to reduce friction. **bursal**, *a*.

bursar (bĕr′ sȧr) [late L. *bursārius* (*bursa*, see prec.)] *n*. A treasurer, esp. of a college; one who holds a bursary. **bursarship**, *n*. **bursary**, *n*. The treasury of a college or a monastery; an exhibition in a Scottish University; a scholarship at an English secondary school. **bursarial**, *a*. **burse**, *n*. *A purse; *an exchange or bourse; an exhibition, a bursary, or the fund for maintaining such; (*Eccles.*) a receptacle for the cloth used to cover the sacred Elements. **bursiculate** (bĕr sik′ ū lāt), *a*. **bursiform** (bĕr′ si fôrm), *a*.

burst (bĕrst) [A.-S. *berstan*, O.Teut. *brestan* (cp. Dut. *bersten*, M.H.G. *bresten*, G. *bersten*)], *v.t.* (*past & p.p.* **burst**) To break, split, or rend asunder with suddenness and violence. *v.i.* To be broken suddenly from within; to fly open; to issue or rush forth with suddenness and energy or force. *n*. A sudden and violent breaking forth; a sudden explosion; an outbreak; (*fig.*) a spurt, a vigorous fit of activity; a drinking-bout, a spree. **to burst in:** To enter suddenly; to interrupt. **to burst out:** To break out; to exclaim. **burst up**, (*colloq.*) **bust up**, *v.i.* To go bankrupt; to collapse; *n*. A collapse; a quarrel. **burster**, *n*. One who goes bankrupt or collapses.

burthen [BURDEN].

Burton (bĕr′ ton) [Burton-on-Trent], *n*. A kind of beer. **gone for a burton:** (*Aviat. slang*) Dead; absent, missing. **burtonize**, *v.t.* To harden water with a mixture of gypsum, salt, and sulphate of magnesia.

burton (bĕr′ tŏn), **barton** (bar′ tŏn) [etym. doubtful], *n*. (*Naut.*) A small tackle consisting of two or three pulleys.

bury (ber′ i) [A.-S. *byrgan* (cp. BURIAL)], *v.t.* To place (a corpse) under ground, to inter, to consign to the grave (whether earth or sea); to perform funeral rites for; to put under ground; (*fig.*) to consign to obscurity, oblivion, etc.; to hide, to cover up; to occupy deeply, engross, absorb (*used only in p.p.*). **to bury the hatchet:** To forget and forgive (in allusion to an American Indian custom of burying a tomahawk when peace was concluded). **burying**, *n*. Burial. **burying-ground, -place**, *n*. [BURIAL-GROUND].

bus, 'bus (bŭs), *n*. (*pl.* **buses** (bŭs′ ez)) An omnibus; (*Aviat. slang*) an aeroplane. *v.i.* To go by omnibus. **to miss the bus:** (*colloq.*) To miss an opportunity, to be too late. **busman**, *n*. The conductor or driver of an omnibus. **busman's holiday**, *n*. (*colloq.*) Holiday spent doing one's everyday work.

busbar (bŭs′ bar), *n*. (*Elec.*) A bar which serves as a common connector for several pieces of apparatus.

busby (bŭz′ bi) [etym. doubtful], *n*. *A kind of large bushy wig; the tall fur cap worn by hussars, artillery, and engineers in the British army.

bush (1) (bush) [M.E. *busch*, *busk*, Icel. *buskr* (cp. Dan. *busk*, O.H.G. *busc*, G. *busch*) late L. *boscus*], *n*. A thick shrub; a clump of shrubs, a thicket; a bunch of ivy used as a tavern-sign; uncleared land, more or less covered with wood, esp. in Australasia; anything resembling a bush; (*Austral.*) the hinterland, the interior; a thick growth of hair; *a fox's tail. *the sign of a tavern. *v.t.* To set with bushes in order to prevent poaching; to cover in (seed) with a bush-harrow. **good wine needs no bush:** A good wine needs no advertisement. **to beat about the bush:** To take circuitous methods. **to take to the bush:** To take refuge in the backwoods; to become a bushranger. **bush brotherhood**, *n*. (*Austral.*) An organization of the Church of England labouring in the bush. **bush-fighter**, *n*. An irregular combatant; a guerilla. **bush-fighting**, *n*. Irregular warfare in the bush. **bush-harrow**, *n*. A harrow with bushes interwoven in the bars. **bush hawk**, *n*. (*N. Zealand*) A predatory bird of the hawk family. **bush-lawyer**, *n*. (*Austral.*) An irregular legal practitioner. **bush-rope**, *n*. A wild, vine-like plant in tropical forests. **bush-telegraph**, *n*. The rapid dissemination of rumours, information, etc. **bushy**, *a*. Abounding with bushes; shrubby, thick; growing like a bush. **bushiness**, *n*.

bush (2) (bush) [prob. from M.Dut. *busse* (Dut. *bus*), late L. *buxis*, a box (cp. BOX)], *n*. The metal lining of an axle-hole or similar orifice. *v.t.* To furnish with a bush; to line with metal. **bush-metal**, *n*. An alloy of copper and tin used for bearings, etc.

bushel (1) (bŭsh′ el) [O.F. *boissel* (F. *boisseau*), late L. *boisselus*, *buscellus*, dim. of *busta* (*buxida*, *buxis*, BOX)], *n* A dry measure of capacity containing eight gallons or four pecks. **bushelful**, *n*.

bushel (2) (bŭsh′ el) [Am. (cp. G. *bosseln*)], *v.t.* To mend or alter. *v.i.* To mend or alter clothes. **bushelman, bushelwoman**, *n*. Tailors' assistants who repair or alter clothes.

bushido (bush ē dō) [Jap.], *n*. A Japanese code of honour.

bushman (bush′ mȧn) [Dut. *boschjesman*], *n*. One of a tribe of aborigines living in Cape colony; one who lives in the Australian bush. **bushmanship**, *n*.

bushmaster (bush′ ma stėr), *n*. A large and poisonous rattlesnake in S. America.

bushranger (bush′ rān jėr), *n*. One who has taken to the Australian bush and lives by robbing travellers, etc.

bushwhacker (bush′ wăk ėr), *n*. (*Am.*) A backwoodsman; a bush-fighter; an implement for cutting brushwood; (*Austral.*) an inhabitant of the outback, a country bumpkin.

busily, *adv.* [BUSY].

business (biz′ nės) [A.-S. *bisigness* (BUSY, -NESS)], *n*. *The state of being busy; employment, occupation, trade, profession; serious occupation, work; duty, concern, province; commercial, industrial, or professional **affairs**; buying and selling, bargaining; a particular matter demanding attention; a commercial establishment; a shop, with stock, fixtures, etc.; (*Theat.*) action, as distinct from speech; (*colloq.*) an affair, a matter, a concern, a contrivance. **good business:** (*slang*) Excellent! Well done! **man of business:** One engaged in mercantile transactions; one skilled in business; an agent, an attorney. **to mean business:** To be in earnest. **to mind one's business:** To attend to one's own affairs; to refrain from meddling. **business end,** *n.* The point (of a tool or weapon). **business hours,** *n.* Fixed hours of work or for transaction of business in a shop, office, etc. **business-like,** *a.* Suitable for or befitting business; methodical, practical; prompt, punctual; energetic. **business-man,** *n.* One used to dealing with matters of commerce, etc. **business suit,** *n.* (*Am.*) A lounge suit.

***busk** (1) (bŭsk) [prob. from Icel. *būask* (*būa -sk*, refl. of *būa*, to get ready), to get oneself ready], *v.t.* To prepare, to dress. *v.i.* To get ready, to dress oneself.

busk (2) (bŭsk) [M.F. *busque* (F. *busc*), etym. doubtful], *n.* A stiffening bone or plate in a corset. **busked,** *a.*

busker (bŭsk' ėr), *n.* (*Theat.*) An itinerant singer or actor.

buskin (bŭs' kin) [cp. Sp. *borcegui*, It. *borzacchino*, F. *brodequin*, O.F. *bousequin* (etym. doubtful)], *n.* A kind of high-boot reaching to the calf or knee; the thick-soled boot worn by actors in Athenian tragedy; (*fig.*) the tragic vein; tragedy. **buskined,** *a.* Wearing buskins; (*fig.*) tragic, lofty, sublime.

***buss** (1) (bŭs) [onomat. (M.E. *bass*, cp. F. *baiser*, L. *bāsiāre*, to kiss, from *bāsium*, a kiss)], *n.* A loud kiss. *v.t.* To kiss.

buss (2) (bŭs) [O.F. *busse* (cp. Dut. *buis*, med. L. *bussa*, M.H.G. *buze*, G. *büse*)], *n.* A herring-boat with two or three masts.

bust (1) (bŭst) [F. *buste*, It. *busto*, late L. *bustum*, etym. unknown], *n.* A sculptured representation of the head, shoulders, and breast of a person; the upper front part of the body, the breast, the bosom, esp. of a woman. **bust-bodice,** *n.* A silk or cotton garment worn by women to support the breasts.

bust (2) (bŭst) [dial., var. of BURST], *n.* (*slang*) A spree. **a bust up:** A quarrel. **to go bust:** To go bankrupt. **buster,** *n.* Something big, something astonishing; a spree; a dashing fellow; (*Austral.*) a gale. **to come a buster:** To come a cropper.

bustard (bŭs' tȧrd) [prob. from O.F. *bistarde*, confused with *oustarde*, both derivations from L. *avis tarda*, slow bird (adj. *slow* perh. due to perversion of Gr. *ōtis*)], *n.* A large bird allied to the plovers and the cranes, belonging to the genus *Otis*; the great bustard, *Otis tarda*, was formerly indigenous to Britain.

bustle (1) (bŭsl) [prob. onomat., or var. of *buskle*, from BUSK (1)], *n.* Activity with noise and excitement; stir, agitation, fuss. *v.i.* To be active, esp. with excessive fuss and noise; to make a show of activity. *v.t.* To hurry; to hustle, to cause to move quickly or work hard. **bustler,** *n.*

bustle (2) (bŭsl) [etym. doubtful; perh. from prec.], *n.* A pad, cushion, or framework, worn under a woman's dress to expand the skirts behind.

busy (biz' i) [A.-S. *bysig* (*bisgian*, to occupy, to worry)], *a.* Fully occupied; actively employed; closely engaged, diligent; characterized by activity, unresting, always at work; fussy, officious, meddlesome. *v.r.* To occupy oneself (about, in, etc.). *v.t.* *To make or keep busy. *n.* (*slang*) A detective. **busily,** *adv.* **busybody,** *n.* An officious person; a meddler; a mischief-maker. **busyness,** *n.* The state of being busy.

but (1) (bŭt) [A.-S. *būtan*, *būte* (BE-, *utan*, OUT), outside, beyond, except], *prep.* Except, barring; *conj.* Yet still; notwithstanding which; except that; otherwise than, not that; on the contrary, nevertheless, however. *n.* A verbal objection. *adv.* Only. *v.t.* To make a verbal objection. **all but:** Almost, very nearly. **but me no buts:** Bring forward no objections.

but (2) (bŭt) [Sc.], *n.* An outer room. *prep.* Apart from, outside of. *adv.* Outwards. **but and ben:** Out and in. **a but and ben:** A two-roomed cottage [*see* BEN].

butane (bū' tān) [L. *butyrum*, butter], *n.* (*Chem.*) An inflammable gaseous compound; a hydrocarbon of the paraffin series found in petroleum. **butadiene** (bū tȧ dī' ēn), *n.* The gas used in making synthetic rubber.

butcher (buch' ėr) [O.F. *bochier*, orig. a purveyor of goat's flesh (F. *bouchier*), *boc*, a he-goat], *n.* One whose trade it is to slaughter domestic animals for food; one who sells the flesh of such animals; (*fig.*) one who delights in killing; a salmon-fly. *v.t.* To put to death in a wanton or sanguinary fashion; (*fig.*) to spoil by bad playing, acting, reading, editing, etc.; to criticize savagely. **butcher-bird,** *n.* A shrike. **butcher-knife,** *n.* (*Am.*) A carving-knife. **butcher's-broom,** *n.* A prickly, evergreen English shrub, the knee-holly. **butcher's meat,** *n.* The flesh of animals killed for food, sold fresh by butchers, excluding fish, poultry, game, bacon, etc. **butcherly,** *adv.* **butchery,** *n.* The business of a butcher; a slaughter-house; (*fig.*) cruel and remorseless slaughter, carnage.

butler (bŭt' lėr) [A.-S. *butuiller* (O.F. *bouteillier*), med. L. *buticulārius*, from *buticula*, BOTTLE], *n.* A servant in charge of the wine, plate, etc.; a head servant. **butlership,** *n.* **butlery,** *n.* A butler's pantry; a buttery.

butment [ABUTMENT].

butomus (bū' tȯ mŭs) [Gr. *boutomus*], *n.* (*Bot.*) A genus of plants typified by the flowering rush, *Butomus umbellatus*. **butomaceous** (bū tȯ mā' shŭs), *a.*

butt (1) (bŭt) [prob. Eng. (cp. Icel. *buttr*, short, *būtr*, a log, Dan. *but*, Swed. *butt*, Dut. *bot*, stumpy)], *n.* The hinder, larger, or blunter end of anything, esp. of a tool, weapon, and the like; the stout part of tanned ox-hides; the square end of a piece of timber coming against another piece; the joint so formed; the bole of a tree, the base of a leaf-stalk. **butt-end,** *n.* The thick and heavy end; the remnant. **butt-hinge,** *n.* A kind of hinge screwed to the edge of the door and the abutting edge of the casing. **butt-joint,** *n.* A joint in which the pieces come square against each other. **butt-weld,** *n.* A weld formed by forcing together flat iron or steel bars.

butt (2) (bŭt) [O.F. *boute* (F. *botte*), late L. *butis*, *buttis*, a cask], *n.* A large cask; a measure of 126 galls. of wine, or 108 galls. of beer.

butt (3) (bŭt) [F. *but*, a goal], *n.* A goal; a target, a mark for shooting; hence the mound behind targets, the shelter for the marker, and (*pl.*) the distance between the targets, the shooting-range; (*fig.*) aim, object; a target for ridicule, criticism, or abuse.

butt (4) (bŭt) [O.F. *boter* (F. *bouter*), to push, thrust; senses modified by BUTT (1) in verbal sense and by ABUT], *v.i.* To strike, thrust, or push with the head or as with the head; to abut, to meet with the end against (of timber, planks, etc.); to meet end to end. *v.t.* To strike or drive away with or as with the head or horns.

butte (būt) [Am., prob. from F. *butte*, O.F. *bute*, fem. form of *but*, see BUTT (3)], *n.* An abrupt, isolated hill or peak.

butter (bŭt' ėr) [A.-S. *butere*, L. *būtyrum*, Gr. *bouturon* (*bous*, an ox, *turos*, cheese)], *n.* The fatty portion of milk or cream solidified by churning; applied also to various substances of the consistency or appearance of butter; (*fig.*) gross flattery. *v.t.* To spread with butter; (*fig.*) to flatter grossly. **to butter up:** (*colloq.*) To flatter. **butter-bird,** *n.* A Jamaican name for the bobolink. **butter-boat,** *n.* A vessel for sauce. **butter-bur,** *n.* The sweet colt's-foot. **buttercup, butter-flower,** *n.* Popular name for the genus *Ranunculus*, esp. those species with yellow cup-shaped flowers. **butter-fingered,** *a.* Apt to let things fall, as if the hands were greasy. **butter-fingers,** *n.* One who is butter-fingered; (*Cricket*) one who lets a ball slip through his fingers. **buttermilk,** *n.* That part of the milk which remains when the butter is extracted. **butter-muslin,** *n.* A fine, loosely-woven, cotton material used for protecting food from insects. **butter-nut,** *n.* The N. American white walnut-tree, *Juglans cinerea*, and its fruit; the S. American genus *Caryocar*. **butter-print, butter-stamp,** *n.* A piece of carved wood to mark butter. **butter-scotch,** *n.* A kind of toffee. **butter-tree,** *n.* East Indian and African trees, *Bassia butyracea*, and *B. Parkii*, which yield a sweet buttery substance. **butter-wife, butter-woman,** *n.* A woman who sells butter. **butterwort,** *n.* A British bog-plant belonging to the genus *Pinguicula*. **buttery** (1), *a.* Having the qualities or appearance of butter. **butteriness,** *n.*

butterbump (bŭt' ėr bŭmp) [earlier *bitterbump*, from *bitter*, BITTERN, -BUMP (2)], *n.* The bittern.

buttercup [BUTTER].

butterfly (bŭt' ĕr flī) [O.E. *buttor-fleoge*], *n.* An insect with erect wings and knobbed antennæ belonging to the diurnal *Lepidoptera*; (*fig.*) a showily-dressed, vain, giddy, or fickle person. **butterfly-nut, -screw,** *n.* A screw with a thumb-piece. **butterflies in the tummy:** (*colloq.*) Nervous tremors in the stomach.

butteris (bŭt' ėr is) [F. *boutoir*], *n.* A hoof-paring tool used by farriers.

buttery (2) (bŭt' ėr i) [O.F. *boterie, bouteillerie* (see BOTTLE)], *n.* A room in which liquor and provisions are kept: (*Univ.*) the room in which ale, bread, butter, etc., are kept. **buttery-hatch,** *n.* (*Univ.*) The half-door over which provisions are served out from the buttery.

buttock (bŭt' ȯk) [BUTT (1), -OCK], *n.* One of the protuberant parts of the rump (*usu. in pl.*); the posteriors; a manœuvre in wrestling. *v.t.* (*Wrestling*) To throw by means of the buttock or hip. **buttock-mail,** *n.* (*Sc.*) A fine imposed in the Church for the sin of fornication. **buttock-steak,** *n.* Rump-steak.

button (bŭt' ȯn) [O.F. *boton* (F. *bouton*), perh. from a late L. *botto -ōnem*, from *bottare* or *buttare*, to thrust, sprout], *n.* A knob or disk used for fastening or ornamenting the dress; a small bud; a small handle, knob, fastener, catch, etc., for securing doors, actuating electrical apparatus, etc.; the knob on a foil. *v.t.* To fasten or furnish with buttons; to secure by means of buttons or a buttoned garment. *v.i.* To fasten up the clothes with buttons. **buttoned up:** (*colloq.*) Arranged, satisfactorily settled. **do not care a button:** Am quite indifferent about something. **button-boot,** *n.* A boot fastened by means of buttons. **buttonhook,** *n.* A hook for drawing buttons through buttonholes. **button-mould,** *n.* A disk of metal or other substance to be covered with cloth, so as to form a button. **buttoned,** *a.* **buttonless,** *a.* **buttonlessness,** *n.* **buttons,** *n.* (*colloq.*) A page in buttoned livery. **buttony,** *a.* Like a button; having many buttons. **buttonhole,** *n.* A hole, slit, or loop to admit a button; a small bouquet for the buttonhole of a coat. *v.t.* To hold by the buttonhole; to detain in conversation; to make buttonholes. **buttonholer,** *n.* (*colloq.*) One who detains in conversation.

buttress (bŭt' rės) [prob. from O.F. *bouterez*, pl. of *bouteret*, a prop (*bouter*, to push against)], *n.* A structure built against a wall to strengthen it; (*fig.*) a prop, support; a spur or supporting ridge of a hill. *v.t.* To support by or as by a buttress.

butty (bŭt' i) [etym. doubtful; perh. a corr. of BOOTY], *n.* (*dial.*) A partner, companion, a mate; a middleman in the mining districts. **butty-gang,** *n.* A body of workmen who undertake a job and are paid in a lump sum. **butty-system,** *n.* The letting of work to a body of men who divide the proceeds.

butyraceous (bū ti rā' shŭs) [L. *būtyrum*], *a.* Of the nature or consistency of butter. **butyrate** (bū ti rȧt), *n.* A salt of butyric acid. **butyric** (bū tir' ik), *a.* Of or pertaining to butter. **butyric acid,** *n.* A colourless acid occurring in butter and other fats. **butyrine** (bū' ti rīn), *n.* An oily liquid, obtained by the action of butyric acid on glycerine. **butyro-,** *comb. form.* **butyro-acetic,** *a.* Applied to a combination of butyric and acetic acid.

***buxeous** (bŭk' sė ŭs) [L. *buxeus*, from *buxus*, box-tree], *a.* Pertaining to the box-tree. **buxine** (bŭk' sīn), **buxina** (bŭk sī' nȧ), **buxia,** *n.* A vegetable alkaloid obtained from the box-tree.

buxom (bŭk' sȯm) [M.E. *buhsum*, from A.-S. *būgan*, to bow, to bend], *a.* *Obedient, submissive; *pliant, flexible; blithe, jolly, full of health and spirits; plump and comely (of women). **buxomly,** *adv.* **buxomness,** *n.*

buy (bī) [A.-S. *bycgan* (cp. Goth. *bugjan*, O.S. *buggean*)], *v.t.* (*past & p.p.* **bought**) To purchase; to procure by means of money or something paid as a price; to gain by bribery; to redeem. **to buy in:** To buy back for the owner (at an auction); to obtain a stock of anything by purchase; (*Stock Exch.*) to purchase stock and charge the extra cost to the person who had undertaken to deliver it. **a good buy:** (*colloq.*) A bargain, a good thing to have bought. **to buy off:** To pay a price for release or non-opposition. **to buy out:** To buy an office or estate so as to turn out the owner; to get rid of by a payment; *to redeem. **to buy over:** To gain over by a bribe. **to buy the refusal of:** To buy the right of purchasing at a future time. **to buy up:** To purchase all the available stock of. **buyable,** *a.* **buyer,** *n.* One who buys; esp. one who buys stock for a mercantile house.

buzz (1) (bŭz) [onomat.], *n.* A sibilant hum, like that of a bee; a confused, mingled noise; stir, bustle, movement; (*fig.*) report, rumour. *v.i.* To make a noise like humming or whirring; to whisper, to circulate a rumour; (*Elec.*) to signal by buzzer. *v.t.* To tell in a low whisper; to spread abroad secretly; (*Aviat.*) to interfere with by flying very near to. **buzz-bomb,** *n.* A flying bomb. **buzzfly,** *n.* A fly that buzzes. **buzz-saw,** *n.* A circular saw. **to buzz about:** To hover or bustle about in an annoying manner. **buzzer,** *n.* A buzzing insect; a whisper; a steam or electric apparatus for making a loud humming noise; (*Elec.*) an electric warning apparatus that makes a buzzing sound; a morse transmitter. **buzzing,** *a.* **buzzingly,** *adv.*

buzz (2) (bŭz) [prob. onomat.], *n.* A bur; a fuzzy seed-vessel; a fuzzy beetle, *Rhizotrogus solstitialis*; an angler's fly made in imitation of this.

buzz (3) (bŭz) [etym. doubtful], *v.t.* (*slang*) To throw with some violence. **buzz off!** *int.* Go away.

buzzard (1) (bŭz' ȧrd) [BUZZ, -ARD], *n.* Any large nocturnal insect.

buzzard (2) (bŭz' ȧrd) [O.F. *busard*, L. *buteo*], *n.* A kind of falcon, esp. *Buteo vulgaris*; (*fig.*) a blockhead, a dunce. **a.* Stupid, ignorant.

by (bī) [A.-S. *be, bi* (cp. O.H.G. *bī, pī*, G. *bei*, Goth. *bi*, L. *ambi*, Gr. *amphi*)], *prep.* Near, at, in neighbourhood of, beside, along, through, via; with, through (as author, maker, means, cause); according to, by direction, authority, or example of; in the ratio of; to the amount of; during, not later than, as soon as; concerning, with regard to. *adv.* Near at hand; in the same place; aside, in reserve; past. *a.* Side, subordinate, secondary, of minor importance; private, secret, clandestine, sly. *n.* [BYE]. **by and by,** *adv.* Soon, presently; later on; *n.* The future; time to come. **by and large:** On the whole. **by oneself:** Alone, without help; of one's own initiative. **by the by, by the bye, by the way:** Casually, apart from the main subject. **to abide by:** Be faithful to; to observe. **to come by:** To obtain. **to do by:** To behave towards. **to set store by:** To value. **to stand by:** To aid, to support; (*Naut.*) to do nothing; to be ready to act. **by-bidder,** *n.* One who bids at an auction with the view of running up the price. **by-blow** (bī′ blō), *n.* A side-blow; a bastard. **by-business** (bī′ biz nis), *n.* A secondary business.

bye (bī) [BY], *n.* A subsidiary object; something of an incidental or secondary kind; (*Cricket*) a run scored when the ball passes the batsman and wicket-keeper; (*Golf*) holes left over after end of contest and played as a new game; a goal at lacrosse; an individual left without a competitor when the rest have been drawn in pairs; an odd man, the case of being odd man; an event not in the list of sports.

bye-bye (1) (bī′ bī), *n.* A childish word for sleep, bedtime, bed.

bye-bye (2) (bī′ bī′), *int.* (*colloq.*) Good-bye.

by-election (bī′ el ek shůn), *n.* (*Pol.*) An election caused by the death or resignation of a member.

by-end (bī′ end), *n.* Private interest.

bygone (bī′ gon), *a.* Past. *n.* A past event; (*pl.*) the past; past injuries. **let bygones be bygones:** Let us think no more of past injuries.

by-lane (bī′ lān), *n.* A lane leading off the main road.

by-law (bī′ law) [formerly *birlaw, burlaw,* from Icel. *bœr, byr,* village (cp. *bæjar-lög,* a town-law, Dan. *bylov,* municipal law)], *n.* A private statute made by the members of a corporation or local authority; rules adopted by an incorporated or other society.

by-pass (bī′ pas), *n.* A pipe passing round a tap or valve, so as to leave a gas-burner, etc. alight; a road for the purpose of diverting traffic from crowded areas, (*Am.*) a cut-off road; (*Radio.*) a cutting-out of undesirable frequencies.

bypath (bī′ path), *n.* A private or unfrequented path.

by-play (bī′ plā), *n.* Action carried on aside while the main action is proceeding.

by-product (bī′ prod ůkt), *n.* A secondary product.

by-purpose (bī′ pěr půs), *n.* An incidental purpose, esp. in manufacture.

byre (bī′ ėr) [A.-S. *byre,* a hut; prob. var. of *būr,* see BOWER], *n.* A cow-house.

***byrlaw** (běr′ law) [BY-LAW, see BY], *n.* The local custom or popular jurisprudence of a village, township, or district, dealing with minor matters of dispute without reference to the law courts. **byr-law-court, -man,** *n.*

by-road (bī′ rōd), *n.* A road little frequented.

Byronic (bī ron′ ik) [Lord *Byron* (1788–1824)], *a.* Like Lord Byron or his poetry; theatrical, moody; affecting volcanic passion, gloom, or remorse. **Byronically,** *adv.* **Byronism** (bīr′ ȯn izm), *n.*

byssolite (bis′ ō līt) [Gr. *bussos,* BYSSUS, -LITE], *n.* (*Min.*) Asbestoid.

byssus (bis′ ůs) [L., from Gr. *bussos,* a fine flax], *n.* A textile fabric of various substances; the fine linen of the Scriptures; (*Zool.*) the tuft of fibres by which molluscs of the genus *Pinna* attach themselves to other bodies; (*Bot.*) the thread-like stipe of some fungi. **byssiferous** (-sif′ ėr ůs), *a.* Producing a byssus. **byssine** (bis′ in), *a.* Made of fine flax; like byssus.

bystander (bī′ stănd ėr), *n.* One standing near; an onlooker, an eye-witness.

by-street (bī′ strēt), *n.* An out-of-the-way or little frequented street.

by-way (bī′ wā), *n.* A bypath; a secret or obscure way; a short cut; an out-of-the-way side of a subject.

byword (bī′ wěrd), *n.* A common saying; a proverb; an object of general contempt; a nickname.

by-work (bī′ wěrk), *n.* Work done apart from one's regular occupation.

byzant [BEZANT].

Byzantian (bī zăn′ ti ȧn), *a.* Of or pertaining to Byzantium or to Constantinople. *n.* An inhabitant of Byzantium; a bezant. **Byzantine** (bī zăn′ tīn, biz′ ȧn tīn) [L. *Byzantīnus*], *a.* Byzantian; belonging to the style of architecture developed in the Eastern Empire, characterized by the round arch, the circle, the dome, and ornamentation in mosaic. **Byzantine Church,** *n.* The Greek or Eastern Church. **Byzantine Empire,** *n.* The Eastern or Greek Empire (A.D. 395–1453). **Byzantinesque** (bī zăn tin esk′), *a.* **Byzantinism,** *n.* **Byzantinize,** *v.t.*

C

C, c, the third letter and the second consonant of the English alphabet, is borrowed in shape from the Latin. Before *a, o, u, l,* and *r* it is sounded like guttural mute *k,* and before *e, i,* and *y* like the soft sibilant *s* (when it has this sound before other letters it is marked ç). C is used as a symbol to denote the third serial order; (*Alg.*) the third quantity known; (*Mus.*) the first note of the diatonic scale, corresponding to the Italian *do*; the natural major mode; common time; (*Roman numeral*) 100. **C3:** (*Mil.*) Lowest category of a medical board; (of a person) of low physique.

Caaba (ka′ ȧ bȧ) [Arab. *ka'bah*], *n.* A sacred building at Mecca containing the famous black stone, the Mohammedan Holy of Holies and place of pilgrimage.

cab (1) (kăb) [short for CABRIOLET], *n.* A public covered carriage with two or four wheels; a taxi; the guard, or covered part, of a locomotive which protects the driver and fireman from the weather. *v.i.* To travel by cab. **cabby,** *n.* (*colloq.*) A cabman. **cabman,** *n.* A cab-driver. **cab-rank,** *n.* A row of cabs on a stand. **cab-stand,** *n.* A place where cabs are authorized to stand for hire. **cab-runner, -tout,** *n.* A person employed to fetch cabs or unload luggage. **cabless,** *a.* **to call a cab:** To hail a taxi.

cab (2) (kăb) [Heb. *qab,* a hollow vessel], *n.* A Jewish measure of capacity containing nearly three pints.

cab (3) (kăb) [short for CABBAGE (2)], *n.* (*slang*) A crib; a translation used covertly. *v.i.* To use a crib; to crib, to pilfer.

cabal (kȧ băl′) [CABBALA], *n.* A small body of persons closely united for some secret purpose; a junto, a clique; (*Hist.*) the five ministers of Charles II who signed the Treaty of Alliance in 1672, the initials of whose names (Clifford, Ashley, Buckingham, Arlington, and Lauderdale) happened to form the word *cabal.* *v.i.* To intrigue secretly with others for some private end. **caballer,** *n.*

cabala [CABBALA].

caballero (ka ba lyâr′ ō) [Sp. from L. *caballārius* (*caballus,* horse)], *n.* A Spanish gentleman; a stately kind of Spanish dance.

caballine (kăb′ ȧ līn) [L. *caballīnus,* horse], *a.* Pertaining to horses; equine.

cabaret (kăb′ ȧ rā) [F. (etym. unknown)], *n.* A public-house, a tavern; a restaurant where variety turns are given.

cabbage (1) (kăb′ ȧj) [F. *caboche,* great head, L. *caput,* head (F. *choux cabus,* cabbage cole)], *n.* The plain-leaved, hearted varieties of *Brassica oleracea*; the terminal bud of palm-trees. **cabbage-butterfly,** *n.* Two kinds of butterfly the larvæ of which cause injury to cabbages, *Pieris brassicæ, P. Rapæ.* **cabbage-leaf,** *n.* (*slang*) A bad cigar. **cabbage lettuce,** *n.* A kind of lettuce with a firm heart as a cabbage. **cabbage-moth,** *n.* A nocturnal moth, *Mammestra brassicæ,* whose larvæ feed on the cabbage. **cabbage-palm,** *n.* [CABBAGE-TREE]. **cabbage-rose,** *n.* A double red rose, *Rosa centifolia,* with large, compact flowers. **cabbage-**

stump, *n.* The stem of a cabbage. **cabbage-tree,** *n.* A palm with an edible terminal bud. **cabbage-worm,** *n.* The larva of the cabbage-moth and other insects.

cabbage (2) (kăb′ aj) [perh. from F. *cabas*, a basket (cp. Norman *cabasser*, to steal), late L. *cabātium* (L. *capax -ācem*, holding)], *n.* The shreds and clippings made by tailors, and taken by them as perquisites. *v.t.* To purloin (esp. cloth left after cutting out a garment); (*slang*) to pilfer; to crib.

cabbala (kăb′ å lå) [med. L., from Heb. *qabbālāh*, tradition, received doctrine (*qābal*, to receive)], *n.* A traditional exposition of the Pentateuch attributed to Moses; mystic or esoteric doctrine. **cabbalism,** *n.* The system of the cabbala; occult doctrine. **cabbalist,** *n.* One skilled in the Jewish cabbala, or in mystic learning. **cabbalistic, cabbalistical** (kăb å list′ ik, -ål), *a.* Pertaining to the Jewish cabbala; mysterious, occult. **cabbalistically,** *adv.*

caber (kā′ bėr) [Gael. *cabar*], *n.* A pole, the roughly-trimmed stem of a young tree, used in the Highland sport of tossing the caber.

cabin (kăb′ in) [F. *cabane*, late L. *capanna*, a hut], *n.* A small hut or house; a temporary shelter; a little room; a room or compartment in a ship for officers or passengers. *v.i.* To live in a cabin. *v.t.* To shelter or confine in or as in a cabin; to coop in. **cabin-boy,** *n.* A boy who waits on the officers of a ship or passengers in the cabin. **cabin-passenger,** *n.* One who pays for accommodation in the superior part of a ship.

cabinet (kăb′ i nėt) [dim. of CABIN, or from F. *cabinet*], *n.* A closet, a small room; a private room; a piece of furniture with drawers, shelves, etc., in which to keep curiosities or articles of value; a cabinet photograph; a council room; the secret council of a sovereign; a kind of deliberative committee of the principal members of the British Government. **Cabinet council,** *n.* A meeting of the Cabinet for consultation. **cabinet edition,** *n.* An edition of a book at a moderate price, inferior to a library edition and superior to a popular edition. **cabinet lock,** *n.* A lock suitable for a desk, drawer, box, and the like. **cabinet-maker,** *n.* One who makes the finer kinds of household furniture. **cabinet-making,** *n.* **Cabinet Minister,** *n.* A member of the Cabinet. **cabinet photograph,** *n.* (*Phot.*) A photographic print measuring about 6 × 4 in. **cabinet pudding,** *n.* A sort of bread-and-butter pudding.

Cabiri (kå bīr′ i) [L., from Gr. *Kabeiroi*], *n.pl.* Oriental divinities of Semitic origin worshipped in Lemnos, Samothrace, Imbros, and afterwards Greece, associated with fire and creative energy, and connected with Hephaestos (Vulcan). **Cabirian, Cabiric** (kå bir′ i ån, -bir′ ik), *a.*

cable (kā′ bėl) [ult. from L. *caplum, capulum*, from *capere*, to take hold of (cp. O.F. *cable*, It. *cappio*, Dut. *kabel*)], *n.* A strong rope, more than ten inches round; one-tenth of a nautical mile; (*Naut.*) the rope or chain to which an anchor is fastened; a measure of distance (100–140 fathoms); a wire rope; (*Elec.*) an electrical circuit of one or more conductors insulated and in a sheath; (*Arch.*) a cable-like moulding. *v.t.* To fasten with a cable; to send (a message) by cable; to inform by cablegram; (*Arch.*) to fill the lower part of the flutings in a column with convex mouldings. **cable railway,** *n.* A funicular railway. **cable stitch,** *n.* A plaited stitch in knitting. **cablegram** [-GRAM], *n.* A telegraphic message by submarine cable. **cablegrammic, cablegraphic** (kābl grăm′-, -grăf′ ik), *a.* **cable-laid,** *a.* Twisted like a cable. **cable-moulding,** *n.* (*Arch.*) A cable-like bead or moulding; (*Goldsmith.*) a cable-like ornament. **cablet,** *n.* A small cable, less than ten inches round. **cabling,** *n.* Decoration of columns by means of convex mouldings in the fluting.

***cabob** (kå bob′) [Arab. *kabāb*], *n.* A small piece of meat roasted with spices.

caboched, caboshed (kå bosht′), **cabossed** (kå bost′) [from obs. v. *caboche*, F. *cabocher* (L. *caput*, head; cp. CABBAGE (1))], *a.* (*Her.*) Borne full-faced and showing no other feature (as the heads of some animals).

cabochon (ka bŏ′ shon) [F. *caboche* (see prec.)], *n.* A precious stone polished, and having the rough parts removed, but without facets. **cabochon-shaped, en cabochon:** Polished, but without facets.

caboodle (kå boodl′) [BOODLE], *n.* (*colloq.*) Crowd, lot. **the whole caboodle:** All the lot.

caboose (kå boos′) [prob. from M.Dut. *kabuys* (etym. unknown; perh. from a form *kabanhuys*, cabin-house)], *n.* The cook's house or galley; (*Am.*) the guard's van in a goods train.

cabotage (kăb′ ŏ tåj) [F., from *caboter*, to coast (etym. doubtful)], *n.* Coasting; coasting-trade.

cabriole (kăb′ ri ōl) [F., a caper], *a.* Descriptive of table and chair legs shaped in a reflex curve.

cabriolet (kăb ri ō lā′) [F., dim. of *cabriole*, a caper (see CAPRIOLE)], *n.* (also erroneously **cabriole**) A covered carriage drawn by two horses.

ca' canny (ka′ kăn′ i) [Sc., CALL, CANNY], *int.* Go warily! *n.* A worker's policy of going slowly.

cacao (kå kā′ ō) [Sp., from Mex. *cacauatl*], *n.* A tropical American tree, *Theobroma cacao*, from the seeds of which chocolate and cocoa are prepared. **cacao-butter,** *n.* A fatty substance expressed from the nut of *T. cacao.*

cachæmia, cachemia (kå kē′ mi å) [Gr. *kakos*, bad, *haima*, blood], *n.* (*Med.*) A bad state of the blood.

cachalot (kăsh′ å lot, -å lō) [F., from Gascon *cachaon*, a big tooth], *n.* A genus of whales having teeth in the lower jaw, esp. the sperm whale.

cache (kăsh) [F., from *cacher*, to hide], *n.* A hole in the ground or other place in which provisions, goods, or ammunition are hidden; the hiding of stores; the stores hidden. *v.t.* To hide or conceal in a cache.

cachectic [CACHEXIA].

cachet (kă′ shā) [Fr. from *cacher*, to conceal], *n.* (*Med.*) Paper capsule in which nauseous or other drugs can be administered; a seal; (*fig.*) a stamp, a characteristic mark; a sign of authenticity; a mark of excellence, a stamp of good taste. ***lettre de cachet:*** (*Hist.*) A royal warrant for the imprisonment or exile of a person without trial, in France before the Revolution.

cachexia, cachexy (kå kek′ si å, -si) [L., from Gr. *kachexia* (*kakos*, bad, *hexis*, habit)], *n.* An unhealthy condition of body or mind. **cachectic** (kå kek′ tik), *a.*

cachinnate (kăk′ in āt)] [L. *cachinnāre* (onomat.)], *v.i.* To laugh immoderately. **cachinnation** (kăk in ā′ shŭn), *n.* Loud or immoderate laughter. **cachinnatory** (kăk′ in å tŏr i), *a.*

cacholong (kăch′ ŏ long) [Kalmuck *kaschtschilon*, beautiful stone], *n.* A white or opaque variety of the opal.

cachou (kå shoo′) [F., from Malay *cachu* (see CATECHU)], *n.* A small pill-like sweetmeat, made of cashew-nut, for perfuming the breath.

cachucha (kå choo′ chå) [Sp.], *n.* A lively kind of Spanish dance.

cacique (kå sēk′), **cazique** [Sp., from Haitian], *n.* A chief of the aborigines of the West Indies or the neighbouring parts of America.

cackle (kăk′ el) [M.E. *kakelen*; onomat. (cp. Dut. *kakelen*, G. *gackeln*)], *n.* The cackling of a hen; (*fig.*) silly chatter. *v.i.* To make a noise like a hen after laying an egg; (*fig.*) to chatter in a silly manner; to giggle. **to cut the cackle:** To get down to business. **cackler,** *n.* **cackling,** *n.*

caco- [Gr. *kako-*, *kakos*, evil, bad], *comb. form.* (*Path.*) Bad, malformed, evil to the senses.

cacodemon (kăk ŏ dē′ mŏn) [CACO-, Gr. *daimōn*, spirit], *n.* An evil spirit; a nightmare; an evil person.

cacodyl (kăk' ŏ dil) [Gr. *kakōdēs*, stinking (CACO-, *od-*, root of *ozein*, to smell), -YL], *n.* A stinking organic compound of arsenic and methyl. **cacodylic** (kăk ŏ dil' ik), *a.*

cacoepy (kă kō ep' i) [CACO-, Gr. *epos*, a word], *n.* False pronunciation of words.

cacoethes (kăk ō ē' thez) [L., from Gr. *kakoēthes*, evil habit, neut. of a. *kakoēthēs*, ill-disposed (CACO-, *ēthos*, disposition, character)], *n.* A bad habit; an irresistible propensity. ***cacoethes scribendi*** [L., of writing (*scrībere*, to write)], *n.* An itch for writing.

cacogastric (kăk ō găs' trik), *a.* Dyspeptic; characterized by a disordered stomach.

cacography (kăk og' rȧ fi), *n.* Bad spelling; bad writing.

cacolet (kăk' ŏ let, -ŏ lā) [F. dial., prob. Basque], *n.* A mule-chair used for the transport of the sick or wounded.

cacology (kȧ kol' ŏ ji) [Gr. *kakologia*, from *kakologos*, speaking evil (CACO-, *logos*, from *legein*, to speak)], *n.* Bad choice of words; incorrect pronunciation.

cacomorphia (kăk ō môr' fi ȧ), *n.* Malformation, deformity.

cacoon (kȧ koon') [prob. native African], *n.* The large, flat, polished seed of a tropical climbing plant of the bean family, having pods as much as eight feet long, used for making snuff-boxes and other small articles; a purgative seed of a climbing plant of the gourd family, also used as an antidote for poisons.

cacophony (kȧ kof' ŏ ni) [F. *cacophonie*, Gr. *kakophōnia*, from *kakophōnos*, harsh-sounding (CACO-, *phōnē*, voice)], *n.* A rough, discordant style; (*Mus.*) a discord. **cacophonous** (kȧ kof' ŏ nůs), *a.* Harsh-sounding, discordant.

cacophthalmia (kăk of thăl' mi ȧ), *n.* Malignant inflammation of the eyes.

cactus (kăk' tůs) [L., from Gr. *kaktos*, a prickly Sicilian plant], *n.* A genus of succulent spiny plants. **cactaceous** (kăk tā' shůs), *a.* **cactal,** *a.* Allied to the cactuses. **cactoid,** *a.*

cad (kăd) [prob. short for Sc. *cadie, caddie*, Engl. CADET], *n.* A low, vulgar fellow; a bounder; an ill-mannered person, a person guilty of ungentlemanly conduct; a fellow employed on odd jobs at school or university sports; *a bus conductor. **caddish,** *a.*

cadastre (kȧ dăs' tėr) [F., from late L. *capistratum*, register of *capita*, heads, for the land tax in Roman provinces], *n.* A register of property as a basis of taxation; an official register of the ownership of land. **cadastral,** *a.*

cadaver (kăd ăv' ėr) [L.], *n.* A corpse, dead body. **cadaverous,** *a.* Corpse-like; deathly pale. **cadaverously,** *adv.* **cadaverousness,** *n.* Cadaverous. **cadaveric** (kăd ȧ ver' ik), *a.* (*Med.*)

caddice [CADDIS (1)].

caddie, cadie (kăd' i) [CADET], *n.* (*Sc.*) A lad or man attending on a golfer; *a messenger or errand-boy; (*N. Zealand*) a straw-hat; (*Austral.*) a slouch hat, a trilby.

caddis (1) (kăd' is) [etym. doubtful], *n.* The larva of any species of *Phryganea*, esp. of the may-fly. **caddis-fly,** *n.*

***caddis** (2) (kăd' is) [A.-F. *cadace*, O.F. *cadaz*, the coarsest part of silk, and O.F. *cadis*, a kind of woollen serge], *n.* A kind of worsted yarn; caddis ribbon. **caddis ribbon,** *n.* A tape of this stuff used for garters, etc.

caddy (kăd' i) [Malay *kātī*, a weight of 1½ lb.], *n.* A small box in which tea is kept.

cade (1) (kăd) [F., from L. *cadus*, Gr. *kados*, a pail, jar, cask], *n.* A barrel of 500 herrings or of 1,000 sprats.

***cade** (2) (kăd) [etym. doubtful], *a.* Domesticated; brought up by hand. *n.* A pet lamb. *v.t.* To bring up tenderly, to coddle.

cadence (kā' dėns) [F., from It. *cadenza*, late L. *cadentia* (*cadere*, to fall)], *n.* The sinking of the voice, esp. at the end of a sentence; modulation of the voice, intonation; local modulation or accent; rhythm, poetical rhythm or measure; rhythmical beat or movement; (*Mus.*) close of a movement or phrase; a cadenza. *v.t.* To put into rhythmical measure. **cadenced,** *a.* **cadency,** *n.* *Cadence; (*Her. and Geneal.*) the state of a cadet; descent from a younger branch. **cadent,** *a.* *Falling; (*Astron.*) going down; having rhythmical cadence. **cadenza** (kȧ dent' sȧ) [It.], *n.* (*Mus.*) A vocal or instrumental flourish of indefinite form at the close of a movement.

cadet (kȧ det') [F., from Prov. *capdet*, late L. *capitellum*, dim. of L. *caput*, head], *n.* A younger son; the younger branch of a family; *a volunteer who served in hope to gain a commission; a pupil in a military or naval academy; a member of a reactionary party in the Russian revolution. **cadetship,** *n.*

cadge (kăj) [etym. doubtful; perh. a var. of CATCH], *v.t.* To get by begging. *v.i.* To peddle; to beg. **cadger,** *n.* One who cadges; a carrier, a man who collects farm produce for sale in town; a huckster, a street hawker; a beggar; a tramp.

cadi (ka'-, kā' di) [Arab. *qāḍī* (cp. ALCAYDE)], *n.* The judge of a Persian, Arab, or Turkish town or village.

cadie [CADDIE].

Cadmean (kăd mē' ȧn), **Cadmian** (kăd' mi ȧn), *a.* Of or belonging to Cadmus, the mythical founder of Thebes, and inventor of letters; Theban. **Cadmean victory,** *n.* A victory that ruins the victor; a moral victory.

cadmium (kăd' mi ům) [obs. *cadmia*, CALAMINE, L., from Gr. *kadmia*, *-meia*, Cadmean (earth)], *n.* A bluish-white metallic element. **cadmium-yellow,** *n.* A pigment prepared from cadmium sulphide. **cadmiferous** (-mif' ėr ůs), *a.* **cadmic,** *a.*

cadre (ka' dėr, kā' dėr) [F., from It. *quadro*, L. *quadrum*, square], *n.* A framework, a scheme; the skeleton of a regiment; the permanent establishment or nucleus of a regiment.

caduceus (kȧ dū' sė ůs) [L. *cādūceus*, Doric Gr. *karukion* (*kērux*, a herald)], *n.* (*pl.* **-cei**) The winged staff of Mercury, borne by him as messenger of the gods. **caducean,** *a.*

caduciary (ca dū' si ȧ ri) [as foll.], *a.* (*Law*) Heritable; subject to forfeiture.

caducous (kȧ dū' kůs) [L. *cadūcus*, easily falling (*cadere*, to fall)], *a.* (*Bot.*) Falling off quickly or prematurely. **caducity** (kă dū' si ti), *n.*

cæcum (sē' kům) [L. *cæcus*, blind], *n.* (*pl.* **cæca**) The blind gut, the first part of the large intestine which is prolonged into a blind pouch; any blind tube. **cæcal,** *a.* Pertaining to the cæcum; having a blind end. **cæcally,** *adv.* **cæciform** (sē' si fôrm), *a.* **cæcitis** (sē sī' tis), *n.* Inflammation of the cæcum.

Caen stone (kā' ėn stōn') [*Caen*, Normandy], *n.* A soft, yellowish, oolitic building-stone from Caen.

***cærule** [CERULEAN].

Cæsar (sē' zȧr) [L., cognomen of Caius Julius *Cæsar*), *n.* The title of the Roman emperors down to Hadrian, and of the heirs presumptive of later emperors; the Emperor (*i.e.* of the Holy Roman Empire), the German Kaiser; (*fig.*) an autocrat; the temporal (as distinguished from the spiritual) power. **Cæsarian, Cæsarean** (sē zâr' i ȧn), *a.* Of or belonging to Cæsar; imperial. *n.* A follower of Cæsar; a supporter of autocratic government. **Cæsarian birth, section,** *n.* The delivery of a child through the walls of the abdomen (as Julius Cæsar is said to have been brought into the world). **Cæsarism,** *n.* Absolute government; imperialism. **Cæsarist,** *n.*

cæsious (sē′ zi ůs) [L. *cæsius*), *a.* Bluish or greenish grey.

cæsium (sē′ zi ům) [as prec.], *n.* A highly-reactive, silvery-white metallic element, similar to sodium in many properties. Named after the bluish-green lines of its spectrum.

cæspitose, cespitose (ses′ pi tōs) [mod. L. *cæspitōsus*, from L. *cæspes -item*, turf], *a.* Growing in tufts; matted; turfy.

cæsura (sē sū′ rȧ, sē zū′ rȧ) [L., from *cæsus*, p.p. of *cæsere*, to cut], *n.* (*Classic pros.*) The division of a metrical foot between two words, esp. in the middle of a line; (*Eng. pros.*) a pause about the middle of a line. **cæsural,** *a.*

café (kăf′ ā, *vulg.* kāf) [F.], *n.* A coffee-house; a coffee-bar; a restaurant. **café chantant** (shan tan), *n.* A place of musical and other entertainment, indoors or in the open air, where refreshments are served. ***café,*** *n.* Coffee. ***café au lait*** (ō lā), *n.* Coffee with milk. ***café noir*** (nwar), *n.* Coffee without milk. **cafeteria** (kăf e tēr′ i a), *n.* A restaurant in which customers fetch their own food from the counter.

caffeic (kȧ fē′ ik), *a.* Derived from coffee.

caffeine (kăf′ ė in), *n.* A vegetable alkaloid derived from the coffee and tea plants.

Caffre [KAFIR].

caftan (kăf′ tȧn, kăf tan′) [Turk. *qaftān*], *n.* A kind of vest worn in the East.

cage (kāj) [O.F., from L. *cavea* (*cavus*, hollow)], *n.* A box or enclosure wholly or partly of wire, wicker-work, or iron bars, in which birds or other animals are kept; an open framework resembling this; a prison, a lock-up; (*Mining*) an iron structure used as a lift in a shaft; (*Carpentry*) an outer work of timber enclosing another. *v.t.* To shut up in a cage; to confine. **cage aerial,** *n.* (*Radio*) An aerial constructed like a cage by fixing a number of conductors parallel-wise to circular spreaders. **cageling,** *n.* A bird kept in a cage.

cagey (kā′ ji), *a.* (*slang*) Wary, shrewdly knowing; sly.

Cagot (ka′ gō) [perh. a proper name], *n.* One of an outcast race in the districts of France and Spain bordering on the Pyrenees; an outcast, a pariah.

cahier (ka′ i ā) [F. (O.F. *quayer*, see QUIRE)], *n.* A number of sheets of paper loosely put together; the report of a committee.

cahoots (kȧ hoots′), *n.pl.* (*slang*) Partnership, collusion.

cailleach, cailliach (ka′ lya) [Gael., from *caille*, a veil (cp. L. *pallium*)], *n.* (*Highland*) An old woman, a crone.

caiman [CAYMAN].

Cain (1) (kān) [*Cain*, brother of Abel, Gen. iv.], *n.* A murderer, a fratricide. ***Cain-coloured,** *a.* Reddish-yellow (the reputed colour of Cain's hair and beard). **Cainite** (kā′ nīt), *n.* A son of Cain; one of an heretical sect (2nd cent.) who reverenced Cain and other bad Scriptural characters. **to raise Cain:** (*slang*) To make a disturbance, to make trouble.

***cain** (2), **kain** (kān) [Celt. *cáin*, law, tribute], *n.* (*Sc.*) Rent paid in kind, esp. poultry. **to pay the cain:** To pay the penalty.

cainozoic (kī nȯ zō′ ik) [Gr. *kainos*, recent, -ZOIC], *a.* (*Geol.*) Tertiary, belonging to the third geological period.

caïque (kȧ ēk′) [Turk. *qāiq*], *n.* A light boat used on the Bosporus; a small Levantine sailing vessel.

caird (kârd) [Gael. *ceard*, an artificer], *n.* (*Sc.*) A travelling tinker; a vagrant.

cairn (kârn) [Gael., Ir., W. *carn*], *n.* A pyramidal heap of stones, esp. one raised over a grave or to mark a summit, track, or boundary.

cairngorm (kârn gȯrm′) [Gael., lit. blue stone, name of a mountain], *n.* A yellow or brown variety of rock crystal, from the Cairngorm mountains on the borders of Banff, Aberdeen, and Inverness shires.

caisson (kās′ ȯn, kā soon′) [F. (*caisse*, L. *capsa*, see CASE)], *n.* An ammunition-chest or wagon; a large, water-tight case or chamber used in laying foundations under water; a similar apparatus used for raising sunken vessels; a floating vessel used as a dock-gate; (*Arch.*) a sunken panel in ceilings, etc. **caisson disease,** *n.* (*Path.*) Symptoms resulting from a sudden return from high air pressure to normal pressure conditions; the bends.

caitiff (kā′ tif) [O.North. F. *caitif*, L. *captīvus*, CAPTIVE], *n.* *A poor wretch; a despicable wretch; a cowardly fellow. *a.* Cowardly, base, despicable.

cajole (kȧ jōl′) [F. *cajoler*; etym. doubtful], *v.t.* To persuade, beguile, or deceive by flattery or fair speech; to wheedle, to coax; to beguile (into or out of something). *v.i.* To use artful flattery. **cajoler,** *n.* **cajolement, cajolery,** *n.* **cajolingly,** *adv.*

cajuput (kăj′ ů pŭt) [Malay *kāyu, pūtih*, white wood], *n.* The genus *Melaleuca*, the species of which yield a volatile oil.

cake (kāk) [Icel. *kaka* (cp. Dan. *kåge*, Dut. *koek*, G. *kuchen*)], *n.* A small mass of dough baked; a composition of flour, butter, sugar, and other ingredients, baked usually in a tin; (*Sc.*) oatcake; a flat mass of food or any solidified or compressed substance. *v.t.* To make into a cake (*usu. in pass.*). *v.i.* To assume a cake-like form. **cakes and ale:** A good time. **to take the cake:** (*ironic slang*) To come out first; to take first prize. **like hot cakes:** With great speed; with energy. **cake-walk,** *n.* (*Am.*) A grotesque Negro dance; a sort of ballroom dance called after this.

calabar [CALABER].

calabash (kăl′ ȧ băsh) [F. *calebasse*, Sp. *calabaza* (Cat. *carabassa*, Sic. *caravazza*); perh. from Pers. *kharbuz*, a melon], *n.* A kind of gourd or pumpkin; the calabash-tree, *Crescentia Cujete*; the shell enclosing the fruit of this, used for drinking-vessels and other domestic utensils, and tobacco-pipes. **calabash-pipe,** *n.*

calaber, calabar (kăl′ ȧ bėr) [prob. from F. *Calabre*, *Calabria*], *n.* The fur of a grey squirrel, esp. the Siberian squirrel.

calaboose (kăl ȧ booz′) [Negro-French *calabouse*, Sp. *calabozo*], *n.* (*Louisiana region*) A prison.

caladium (kȧ lā′ di ům) [Malay *kélādy*], *n.* A genus of plants belonging to the Arum family, with starchy tuberous roots used in the tropics for food.

calamanco (kăl ȧ măng′ kō) [etym. doubtful; cp. Dut. *kalamink*, F. *calmande*, Sp. *calamaco*], *n.* A Flemish woollen stuff with a fine gloss, and checkered in the warp; much in use in the 18th cent.; (*usu. pl.*, **-coes**) a garment of this stuff.

calamander (kăl ȧ măn′ dėr) [etym. doubtful], *n.* A hard wood, beautifully marked, from India and Ceylon.

calamary (kăl′ ȧ mȧ ri) [L. *calamārius* (*calamus*, a pen)], *n.* A cuttle-fish of the genus *Loligo* or the family *Teuthidæ*; a squid, a pen-fish (named either from its pen-shaped skull or its inky fluid).

calamine (kăl′ ȧ mīn) [F., from med. L. *calamīna* (prob. corr. of L. *cadmīa*, see CADMIUM)], *n.* An English zinc ore used medicinally for skin affections.

calamint (kăl′ ȧ mint) [M.F. *calament*, late L, *calamentum*, Gr. *kalaminthē*], *n.* An aromatic herb. *Calamintha officinalis*, and the genus it belongs to.

calamite (kăl′ ȧ mīt) [mod. L. *calamītes*, from L. *calamus*, a reed], *n.* A fossil coal-plant, allied to the mare's tails or equisetums; (*Min.*) a variety of tremolite.

calamity (kȧ lăm′ i ti) [F. *calamité*, L. *calamitas -atem* (cp. *in-columis*, safe)], *n.* Extreme misfortune, adversity, disaster, misery; distress. **calamitous,** *a.* Causing or characterized by great or widespread distress or unhappiness. **calamitously,** *adv.* **calamitousness,** *n.*

calamus (kăl' ȧ mŭs) [L., from Gr. *kalamos*, a reed], *n.* The sweet flag, *Acorus calamus*; a fragrant Eastern plant; (*Bot.*) a genus of palm trees producing enormously long canes; (*Zool.*) a genus of fishes comprising the porgies; a pen.

calando (kȧ lan' dō) [It.], *a.* and *adv.* (*Mus.*) Gradually becoming softer and slower.

calash (kȧ lăsh') [F. *calèche*, G. *kalesche*, from Slav. (Boh. *kolésa*, Rus. *kolaska*)], *n.* A light pleasure-carriage, with low wheels and removable top; (*Canada*) a two-wheeled vehicle for two, with seat for the driver on the splash-board; a woman's silk hood supported by a framework of whalebone.

calc- (G. *kalk*, L. *calx -cis*], *comb. form.* (*Geol.*) Lime. **calc-sinter,** *n.* A hard crystalline deposit from water holding carbonate of lime in solution. **calc-spar,** *n.* Calcareous spar. **calc-tuff,** *n.* A porous deposit of carbonate of lime.

calcaneum (kăl kā' nė ŭm) [L., from *calx -cem*, the heel], *n.* (*Physiol.*) The bone of the heel. **calcaneal,** *a.*

calcar (1) (kăl' kar) [L. *calcāria*, lime-kiln, see CALC-], *n.* The reverberatory furnace in which the first calcination is made in glass-making.

calcar (2) (kăl' kar) [L., from *calx -cem*, heel], *n.* (*Bot.*) A spur-like process. **calcarate,** *a.*

calcareo- [as foll.], *comb. form.* (*Geol.*) Calcareous. **calcareo-argillaceous,** *a.* Composed of clay with a mixture of lime. **calcareo-bituminous,** *a.* **calcareo-siliceous,** *a.* **calcareo-sulphurous,** *a.*

calcareous, -ious (kăl kâr' i ŭs) [L. *calcārius*, see CALC-], *a.* Of the nature of lime or limestone. **calcareous-spar,** *n.* Crystallized carbonate of lime. **calcareous-tufa,** *n.* [CALC-TUFF]. **calcareously,** *adv.* **calcareousness,** *n.*

calceolaria (kăl sė ŏ lâr' i ȧ) [L. *calceolus*, dim. of *calceus*, a shoe (*calx -cem*, the heel)], *n.* Slipper-wort; a genus of plants with slipper-like flowers. **calceolate,** *a.* (*Bot.*) Shaped like a slipper.

calcic (kăl' sik) [CALC-, -IC], *a.* Pertaining to or composed in whole or in part of lime. **calciferous,** *a.* (*Chem.*) Yielding or containing calcium salts. **calciform,** *a.* **calcify,** *v.t.* To convert into lime. *v.i.* To become calcified. **calcific** (kăl sif' ik), *a.* **calcification** (kăl si fi kā' shŭn), *n.*

calcine (kăl' sin, -sīn) [L. *calcināre*, to reduce to a CALX], *v.t.* To reduce to quick-lime or powder by heat; to expel water and other volatile matter, to desiccate by heat; (*fig.*) to purify or refine; to burn to ashes. *v.i.* To undergo calcination. **calciner,** *n.* **calcination** (kăl si nā' shŭn), *n.*

calcite (kăl' sīt), *n.* (*Min.*) Native crystallized carbonate of lime. **calcitic** (kăl sit' ik), *a.*

calcium (kăl' si ŭm), *n.* A silver-white metallic element usually met with in the form of its oxide, lime. **calcium chloride,** *n.* Chloride of lime, bleaching-powder. **calcium-light,** *n.* Lime-light. **calcio-,** *comb. form* (*Chem. and Min.*). **calcio-ferrite,** *n.* A phosphate of calcium and iron. **calcio-thorite,** *n.* (*Min.*) A variety of thorite containing calcium.

calcography, etc. [CHALCOGRAPHY].

calculate (kăl' kū lāt) [L. *calculāre* (CALCULUS)], *v.t.* To compute, to reckon up, to estimate; to ascertain beforehand by mathematical process; to plan beforehand; to adjust, to arrange. *v.i.* To reckon, to form an estimate; to rely (upon); (*Am.*) to think, to suppose. **calculated,** *a.* Pre-arranged intended; cold-blooded; suitable, well-adapted (to). **calculable,** *a.* That may be calculated. **calculating,** *a.* **calculating machine,** *n.* A mechanical device which performs one or more of the fundamental arithmetical operations. **calculation** (-lā' shŭn), *n.* The act of reckoning or computing in numbers; the result of such process; computation, reckoning; estimate, opinion, inference. **calculative,** *a.* Pertaining to calculation; disposed to calculate. **calculator,** *n.* One who calculates; a series of tables for use in calculating; a mechanical contrivance for performing certain calculations.

calculus (kăl' kū lŭs) [L., a pebble, dim. of CALX], *n.* (*pl.* **-li**) A stony, morbid concretion formed in various organs of the body; (*Math.*) a method of calculation. [DIFFERENTIAL CALCULUS, INTEGRAL CALCULUS.] **calculous,** *a.* (*Med.*) Affected with or of the nature of calculus.

caldarium (kăl dâr' i ŭm) [L., from *calidus*, hot], *n.* A Roman hot bath or hot bath-room.

caldron [CAULDRON].

Caledonian [kăl ė dō' ni ȧn) [L. *Calēdonia*, N. Britain], *a.* (*poet.*) Of or pertaining to Scotland; Scottish. *n.* A Scotsman.

calefacient (kăl ė făsh' yėnt, -fā' shyėnt) [*calefaciens -ntem*, pres.p. of *calefacere*, to warm (*calēre*, to be warm, *facere*, to make)], *a.* (*Med.*) Causing or exciting heat or warmth. *n.* A medicine for increasing the heat of the body. **calefaction,** *n.* **calefactive** (kăl ė făk' tiv), *a.* **calefactor** (kăl ė făk' tŏr), *n.* A small cooking-stove. **calefactory,** *a.* Producing or communicating heat. *n.* A room in which monks used to warm themselves. ***calefy** (kăl' ė fī), *v.t.* To make warm; *v.i.* To grow warm. **calescence** (kȧ les' ėns) [L. *calescere*, to grow hot], *n.* Increasing warmth or heat.

calembour (ka lan bur, kăl' ėm boor) [F.], *n.* A pun.

calendar (kăl' ėn dȧr) [O.F. *calendier*, L. *calendārium*, an account-book], *n.* A register or list of the months, weeks, and days of the year, with the civil and ecclesiastical holidays, festivals, and other dates; a table giving the times of sunrise and sunset, with other astronomical phenomena, an almanac; the system by which the beginning, length, and subdivisions of the civil year are defined, esp. the Gregorian calendar adopted in England in 1752; a list or register, a roll, esp. a catalogue of documents in chronological order with digests of the contents. *v.t.* To register; to insert in a list; to arrange, digest, and catalogue documents. **calendar line** [DATE LINE]. **calendar month,** *n.* A month according to the calendar (opp. to lunar).

calender (1) (kăl' ėn dėr) [F. *calandre*, med. L. *celendra*, L. *cylindrus*, Gr. *kulindros*, a roller], *n.* A press or machine in which cloth or paper is passed between rollers to make it glossy. *v.t.* To glaze by passing between rollers. **calenderer, calendrer,** *n.* **calendry,** *n.*

calender (2) (kăl' ėn dėr) [Pers. *galandar*], *n.* One of an order of mendicant dervishes.

calends, kalends (kăl' ėndz) [L. *calendæ*, name of first day of month (old v. *calāre*, to proclaim, cp. Gr. *kalein*)], *n.pl.* The first day of any month in the old Roman calendar; *(*fig.*) the beginning. **at the Greek calends:** Never (the Greeks had no calends).

calenture (kăl' ėn tūr) [F., from Sp. *calentura* (L. *calens -ntis*, pres.p. of *calēre*, to be hot)], *n.* (*Med.*) A fever or delirium incident to sailors within the tropics; (*fig.*) fever, ardour, fury.

calescence [CALEFACIENT].

calf (1) (kaf) [A.-S. *cealf* (cp. Icel. *kālfr*, Goth. *kalbō*, G. *kalb*)], *n.* (*pl.* **calves** (kavz)) The young of any bovine animal, esp. of the domestic cow; leather made from calfskin; the young of some large animals, as of the elephant, rhinoceros, whale, etc.; a stupid, childish fellow; a small island (or iceberg) near a larger one. *v.i.* (*past & p.p.* **calved**) To give birth to a calf. **the Golden Calf:** The idol set up by the Israelites (Ex. xxxii.); Mammon-worship, the pursuit of riches. **in calf, with calf:** (*above animals*) Pregnant. **sea-calf,** *n.* A seal; (*Naut.*) a small iceberg. **calf-bound,** *a.* Bound in calfskin. **calf-love,** *n.* Attachment between a boy and a girl. **calfskin,** *n.* Calf-leather used in bookbinding and for boots and shoes. **calf's teeth,** *n.pl.* Milk teeth. **calfhood,** *n.* **calfish,** *a.* Like a calf; raw, inexperienced.

calf (2) (kaf) [Icel. *kālfi*, prob. conn. with prec.], *n.* (*pl.* **calves** (kavz)) The thick fleshy part of the leg below the knee. **calfless,** *a.* **-calved,** *a.* (*in comb. as thick-calved*).

Caliban (kăl′ i băn) [character in Shakespeare's *Tempest*], *n.* A man having bestial propensities; a savage, a boor.

calibre, caliber (kăl′ i bėr) [F. *calibre*, It. *calibro* (etym. doubtful; perh. from Arab. *qālib*, a mould)], *n.* The internal diameter of the bore of a gun or any tube; (*fig.*) quality, capacity, compass; ability, character, standing. **-calibred,** *a.* (*in comb.*). **calibrate,** *v.t.* To ascertain the calibre of; to test the accuracy of an instrument against a standard; to graduate (as a gauge). **calibration** (-brā′ shŭn), *n.* The act of calibrating; the testing by experiment of the accuracy of a graduated scale.

caliciform [CALYCIFORM, see CALYX].

calicle (kăl′ ikl) [L. *caliculus*, dim. of CALIX], *n.* (*Biol.*) A small cup-shaped body or organ. **calicular,** *a.*

calico (kăl′ i kō) [*Calicut* on the Malabar coast], *n.* Cotton cloth formerly imported from the East; white or unbleached cotton cloth, (*Am.*) muslin; print. **calico-ball,** *n.* A ball at which ladies wear cotton dresses. **calico-printing,** *n.* The business or art of printing patterns on calicoes.

calid (kăl′ id) [L. *calidus*, warm], *a.* Warm, tepid, hot. **calidity** (kă lid′ i ti), *n.* ***caliduct** [DUCT], *n.* A pipe for the conveyance of heat by means of steam, hot air, etc.

calif, califate [CALIPH].

California jack (kăl i fôr′ ni ă jăk′) [name of American State, JACK, the knave], *n.* A card game resembling all-fours.

californium (kăl i fôr′ ni ŭm), *n.* An artificially-produced radioactive element of atomic number 98.

***caliginous** (kă lij′ i nŭs) [L. *cālīginōsus*, misty (*cālīgo -inem*, mist, obscurity)], *a.* Misty, murky; obscure, gloomy.

calipash (kăl′ i păsh) [perh. var. of CARAPACE], *n.* That part of a turtle next to the upper shell, containing a dull green gelatinous substance. **calipee** [coined to jingle with prec.], *n.* That part next to the lower shell, containing a light yellow substance.

calipers [CALLIPERS].

caliph, calif (kăl′ if, kā′ lif) [F. *calife*, med. L. *calīpha*, Arab. *khalīfah*, successor], *n.* The chief ruler in certain Mohammedan countries, who is regarded as the successor of Mohammed. **caliphate, califate** (kăl′ i făt), *n.* The office or dignity of a caliph; his term of office; the dominion of a caliph.

***caliver** (kăl′ i vėr) [CALIBRE], *n.* A light kind of musket fired without a rest; a soldier armed with a caliver.

calix (kā′ liks) [L., cp. CALYX], *n.* (*pl.* **-ices**) (*Physiol.*) A cup-like cavity or organ.

Calixtin, -tine (kă liks′ tin) [F. *Calixtin*, med. L. *Calixtini*, pl. (*calix*, cup)], *n.* One of a Hussite sect who contended that the cup as well as the bread should be administered to the laity at the Sacrament, a Utraquist; one of the followers of the Lutheran George Calixtus (1586–1656), also called Syncretists.

calk (1) [CAULK].

calk (2) (kawk) [F. *calquer*, It. *calcare*, L. *calcāre*, to tread (*calx -cis*, heel)], *v.t.* To copy (a drawing, etc.) by rubbing the back with colouring matter, and tracing the lines with a style on to paper beneath.

calk (3) (kawk), *n.* A calkin. *v.t.* To furnish with a calkin; to rough-shoe; to knock down the edges of (an iron plate or the head or point of a rivet) so as to make them fit closely. **calking-iron,** *n.* An instrument used for this purpose.

calkin (kaw′ kin, kăl′ kin) [O.F. *calcain*, L. *calcāneum*, the heel (*calx*)], *n.* A sharp projection on a horseshoe to prevent slipping; irons nailed on shoes or clogs.

call (1) (kawl) [Icel. *kalla* (cp. Dut. *kallen*, A.-S. *ceallian*, O.H.G. *challōn*)], *v.t.* To name, to designate; to describe as; to regard or consider as; to summon; to cite; to invite; to command; to invoke; to appeal to; to rouse from sleep; to nominate; to lure (as birds), to attract by imitating their cry. *v.i.* To speak in a loud voice; to cry aloud, to shout; to pay a short visit; (*Cards*) to make a bid, in Bridge; in Poker to ask an opponent to show his cards; in Whist to show by special play that trumps are wanted; to ring up on the telephone. *n.* A loud cry; a vocal address or supplication; the cry of an animal, esp. of a bird; a whistle to imitate the cry of an animal; the act of calling at a house or office on one's way; a short, formal visit; a summons, an invitation; an invitation to become minister to a congregation; a summons or signal on a bugle, whistle or telephone; a requirement of duty; duty, necessity, justification, occasion; a demand for payment of instalments due (of shares, etc.); (*Stock Exch.*) the option of claiming stock at a certain time at a price agreed on. **to call back:** To revoke, to withdraw; to call later by telephone. **to call for:** To desire the attendance of; to appeal, demand; to signal for (trumps); to visit any place to bring some person or thing away. **to call forth:** To elicit; to summon to action. **to call in:** To summon to one's aid; to withdraw (money) from circulation; to collect, to pay a short visit (on, upon, at, etc.). **to call in question:** To dispute. **to call into being:** To give existence to, create. **to call into play:** To put in operation. **to call names:** To abuse. **to call off:** To summon away, to divert. **to call on:** To invoke, to appeal to; to pay a short visit to; to demand explanation, payment, etc. **to call one's own:** To regard as one's possession, to own. **to call out:** To bawl; to challenge to a duel; to summon to service (as troops, etc.); to elicit. **to call over:** To read aloud. **to call over the coals:** To scold, to call to account. **to call the roll:** To call over a list of names to ascertain that all are present. **to call to mind:** To recall. **to call up:** To bring into view or remembrance; to rouse from sleep; to require payment of; to summon by telephone; (*Mil., Nav.*) to mobilize. **to call upon:** To invoke, to appeal to; to pay a short visit to. **at call:** At command; available at once. **to call to the Bar:** To admit as a barrister. **within call:** Within hearing. **call-bird,** *n.* A bird that decoys others by its note. **call-box,** *n.* A public telephone booth. **call-boy,** *n.* A boy who calls actors when they are wanted on the stage; one who transmits the orders of the captain of a (river) steamer to the engineer. **call-day, -night:** (*Inns of Court*) Dates on which benchers are called to the Bar. **call-girl,** *n.* A prostitute who makes appointments by telephone. **call-loan, -money:** Money lent on condition that repayment may be demanded without notice. **call-note,** *n.* The call of an animal, esp. a bird, to its mate or young. **callable,** *a.* **caller,** *n.* One who calls, esp. one who pays a call or visit. **calling,** *n.* The action of the verb TO CALL; habitual occupation, trade, profession; a vocation; a solemn summons to duty, renunciation, faith, etc.; duty; the body of persons employed in a particular occupation, business, or vocation.

***call (2)** [CAUL].

calla lily (kăl′ ă), *n.* (*Bot.*) The arum lily, *Richardia* (or *Calla*) *æthiopica*.

callant (kăl′ ănt) [Dut. *kalant*, a customer, a blade], *n.* (*Sc.*) A youth, a lad.

caller (1) (kaw′ ler), *n.* One who calls; one who pays a visit.

caller (2) (kăl′ er), *n.* Cool, refreshing; freshly caught (of fish).

callid (kăl′ id) [L. *callidus*], *a.* Cunning, crafty. **callidity,** *n.*

calligraphy (kă lig′ ră fi) [Gr. *kalligraphia*], *n.* The art of beautiful handwriting; (*colloq.*) handwriting. **calligraph** (kăl′ i grăf), *n.* and *v.t.* **calligrapher,**

calligraphist, (kȧ lig′-), *n.* **calligraphic** (-grăf′ ik), *a.*

calling [CALL].

calliope (kȧ lī′ ȯ pē) [Gr.], *n.* The Ninth Muse, of eloquence and heroic poetry; (*Astron.*) one of the asteroids; (*Am.*) a series of steam-whistles toned to produce musical notes, and played by a key-board.

callipers, calipers (kăl′ i pĕrz) [short for *calibre-compasses*], *n.pl.* Compasses with bow legs for measuring convex bodies, or with points turned out for measuring calibres. *v.t.* To measure by means of callipers. **calliper-square,** *n.* A rule for measuring diameters, internal or external.

callisthenic (kăl is then′ ik) [Gr. *kallos*, beauty, *sthenos*, strength (anal. with *kallisthenes*, adorned with strength)], *a.* Promoting strength and beauty. **callisthenics,** *n.pl.* Gymnastics (esp. for girls) productive of strength and beauty.

callous (kăl′ ůs) [L. *callōsus*, hard or thick-skinned], *a.* Hardened, indurated; (*fig.*) unfeeling. **callously,** *adv.* **callousness,** *n.* **callosity** (kȧ los′ i ti), *n.* Hardened or thick skin, caused by friction, pressure, disease, or other injury; a callus; (*fig.*) insensibility, want of feeling.

callow (kăl′ ō) [A.-S. *calu*, Teut. *kalwoz*, L. *calvus* bald], *a.* Unfledged, downy; immature, like the down of a fledgeling; youthful, inexperienced; (*Land*) bare; low-lying and liable to floods. *n.* A meadow liable to floods. **callowness,** *n.*

calluna (kȧ loo′ nȧ) [Gr. *kallunein*, to beautify, to sweep (*kalos*, beautiful)], *n.* The ling, *Calluna vulgaris*.

callus (kăl′ ůs) [L.], *n.* (*Physiol.*) A hardening of the skin from pressure or friction; (*Med.*) a bony formation serving to unite a fracture; (*Bot.*) a hard formation.

calm (kam) [F. *calme*, Sp. and It. *calma*, prob. from late L. *cauma*, Gr. *kauma*, heat (*kaiein*, to burn)], *a.* Still, quiet, serene; tranquil, undisturbed. *n.* The state of being calm; (*Naut.*) entire absence of wind. *v.t.* To still, to quiet, to soothe. *v.i.* To become calm (with *down*). **calmative,** (kăl′ mȧ tiv), *a.* Tending to calm. *n.* (*Med.*) A cooling medicine, a sedative. **calmed,** *a.* Rendered calm; becalmed. **calmly,** *adv.* **calmness,** *n.* ***calmy,** *a.*

calmato (kal ma′ tō) [It.], *a.* and *adv.* (*Mus.*) Quiet, quietly.

calomel (kăl′ ō mel) [F.], *n.* Mercurious chloride, an active purgative.

Calor gas (kăl′ ȯr găs) [L. *calor*, heat], *n.* Proprietary name of a bottle gas.

calore (kal ôr′ i) [It.], *n.* (*Mus.*) Passion, warmth. **caloroso** (kal ȯr o′ zō), *a.* and *adv.* Passionately, with warmth.

caloric (kȧ lor′ ik) [F. *calorique*, L. *calor*, heat], *n.* *The supposed fluid cause of heat; heat. **caloric-engine,** *n.* Ericsson's hot-air engine. **caloricity** (kăl ȯ ris′ i ti), *n.* The faculty in living beings of developing heat. **calorescence** (kăl ȯ res′ ėns) (on anal. of CALESCENCE), *n.* The change of non-luminous into luminous heat-rays. **calorifacient** (kȧ lȯr i fā′ shi ėnt) [L. *facio*, I make], *a.* Heat-producing (used esp. of foods). **calorific** (kăl ȯr if′ ik), *a.* Producing heat; thermal. **calorifically,** *adv.* **calorify** (kȧ lor′ i fī) [-FY], *v.t.* To make hot.

calorie, calory (kăl′ ȯ ri) [as prec.], *n.* Unit of heat; amount that will raise the temperature of 1 gramme of water at 15° C. by 1° C. The large or **kilogram calorie** used for quoting the energy of foods is the amount that will raise a kilogram of water by 1° C. **calorimeter** (kă lȯr im′ i tėr) *n.* An instrument for measuring actual quantities of heat, or the specific heat of a body. **calorimetric,** *a.* **calorimetry,** *n.*

calotte (kȧ lot′) [F., perh. dim. of *cale*, CAUL], *n.* A small skull-cap worn by Roman ecclesiastics; a cap-like crest on a bird's head; anything cap-shaped; (*Arch.*) a recess hollowed out in the upper part of a room, chapel, etc., to diminish the apparent height.

calotype (kăl′ ȯ tīp) [Gr. *kalos*, beautiful, TYPE], *n.* A photographic process invented by Fox Talbot and now disused; a Talbotype.

caloyer (kăl′ ȯ yėr) [F., from It. *caloiero*, mod. Gr. *kalogēros* (*kalos*, beautiful, *-gēros*, aged)], *n.* A Greek monk, esp. of the order of St. Basil.

calp (kălp) [etym. unknown], *n.* (*Geol.*) The local name of a dark limestone common in Ireland.

calpac, calpack (kăl′ păk) [Turk. *qalpaq*], *n.* A high, triangular felt cap worn in the East.

Caltha (kăl′ tha) [L.], *n.* (*Bot.*) A genus of ranunculaceous marsh plants containing the marsh marigold, *Caltha palustris*.

caltrop (kăl′ trȯp) [A.-S. *calcatrippe, calcetreppe*, a thistle (cp. O.F. *kauketrape, cauchetrepe*), prob. from late L. (L. *calx -cem*, heel, late L. *trappa*, O.H.G. *trapo*, TRAP)], *n.* An instrument formed of four iron spikes joined at the bases, thrown on the ground to impede the advance of cavalry; a name for several trailing plants that entangle the feet; the star-thistle, the genus *Tribulus*, etc. **water-caltrops:** Water weeds—*Potamogeton densus, P. crispus, Trapa natans*.

calumba (kȧ lŭm′ bȧ) [*Colombo*, Ceylon, whence it was wrongly supposed to come], *n.* The root of *Cocculus palmatus*, of Mozambique, used as a tonic and antiseptic.

calumet (kăl′ ū met) [Norm. F. (preserved in French-Canadian); parallel to O.F. *chalemel* (F. *chalumeau*), from L. *calamellus*, dim. of CALAMUS], *n.* The tobacco-pipe of the North American Indians, used as a symbol of peace and friendship.

calumniate (kȧ lŭm′ ni āt) [L. *calumniātus*, p.p. of *calumniāri* (*calvī*, to deceive)], *v.t.* To slander; to charge falsely with something criminal or disreputable. *v.i.* To utter calumnies. **calumniation** (ā′ shůn), *n.* The act of calumniating. **calumniator,** *n.* **calumniatory,** *a.* **calumnious,** *a.* **calumniously,** *adv.* **calumniousness,** *n.* **calumny** (kăl′ ům ni) [F. *calomnie*, or directly from L. *calumnia*], *n.* A malicious misrepresentation of the words or actions of another; slander; a false charge.

Calvary (kăl′ vȧ ri) [L. *Calvāria*, a skull (*calvus*, bald); trans. of Gr. *Golgotha*, Heb. *gogolthā*, the skull], *n.* The place where Christ was crucified; a life-size representation of the Crucifixion, usually in the open air; a representation of the successive scenes of the passion. **Calvary-cross,** *n.* (*Her.*) A cross mounted on three steps.

calve (kav) [A.-S. *cealfian* (*cealf*, CALF)], *v.i.* To bring forth a calf; to bring forth young; (*Icebergs*) to detach and cast off a mass of ice. *v.t.* To bear, bring forth.

***calvered** (kăl′ vėrd) [from obs. v. *calver*, etym. unknown], *a.* (*Salmon, etc.*) Prepared in a particular way when fresh.

Calvinism (kăl′ vin izm) [John *Calvin*, 1509–64], *n.* The tenets of Calvin, esp. his doctrine of predestination and election. **Calvinist,** *n.* **Calvinistic** (kăl vin ist′ ik), **-ical,** *a.*

calvity (kăl′ vi ti) [L. *calvities*, baldness (*calvus*, bald)], *n.* Baldness.

calx (kălks) [L. *calx -cis*, lime], *n.* (*pl.* **calces** (kăl′ sēz), ***calxes**) Ashes or fine powder remaining from metals, minerals, etc., after they have undergone calcination; (*Eton*) a goal (from the goal marked with lime or chalk).

calyc- [CALYX].

calycanthus (kăl i kăn′ thůs) [CALYX, Gr. *anthos*, a flower], *n.* (*Bot.*) A genus of North American shrubs.

calycle [CALYX].

calypso (kă lip′ sō) *n.* A West Indian Negro narrative song made up as the singer goes on.

calyptra (kȧ lip′ trȧ) [Gr. *kaluptra*, a veil (*kaluptein*, to cover, conceal)], *n.* (Bot.) A hood or cover. **calyptr-,** *comb. form.* Furnished with a hood; resembling a hood. **calyptrate,** *a.* **calyptriform,** *a.*

calyx (kăl′ iks, kā′ liks) [L., from Gr. *kalux* (cp. *kaluptein*, L. *cēlāre*, to cover, conceal)], *n.* (*pl.* **calyces**) (*Bot.*) The whorl of leaves or sepals (usually green) forming the outer integument of a flower; (*Physiol. and Biol.*) a calix. **calyc-, calyci-,** *comb. forms.* **calyciferous** (-sif′ ėr ŭs), *a.* Bearing a calyx. **calycifloral, -florate, -florous,** (-flōr′ ăl, -ât, -ŭs), *a.* Having the petals and stamens growing upon the calyx. **calyciform** (kăl′ i si fôrm). **calycinal** (kă lis′ in ăl), **calycine** (kăl′ i sin), *a.* Of, belonging to, or in the form of a calyx. **calycle** (kăl′ ikl), **calyculus** (kă lik′ ū lŭs) [L. *calyculus*, dim. of CALYX], *n.* A little calyx; a row of small leaflets at the base of the calyx on the outside; the outer covering of a seed. **calycled, calycular** (kă lik′ ū lăr), **calyculate,** *a.*

cam (kăm) [var. of COMB], *n.* (*Mach.*) An eccentric projection attached to a revolving shaft for the purpose of giving linear motion to another part or follower. **camshaft,** *n.* (*Mach.*) A shaft bearing cams which operate the valves of internal-combustion engines.

camaraderie (kăm ă ra′ dėr i) [F., from *camarade*, COMRADE], *n.* Comradeship; good fellowship and loyalty among intimate friends.

camarilla (căm ă ril′ ă) [Sp. dim of *camara*, CHAMBER], *n.* *An audience chamber; a band or company of intriguers; a private cabinet; a cabal.

camber (kăm′ bėr) [F. *cambre*, from *cambrer*, L. *camerāre*, to vault (*camera*, chamber)], *n.* The condition of being slightly convex above; the curvature given to a road surface to make water run off it; a piece of timber bent with a camber; a small dock for discharging timber; the part of a dockyard where timber is cambered. *v.t.* To bend, to arch. **camber-beam,** *n.* **camber-keeled, camber-windowed,** *a.* **camber-slip,** *n.* A slightly curved strip of wood used in making flat arches. **cambered, cambering,** *a.*

Camberwell beauty (kăm′ bėr wel) [*Camberwell*, in south-east London], *n.* A butterfly, *Vanessa Antiopa.*

cambist (kăm′ bist) [F. *cambiste*, late L. *cambium*, exchange], *n.* One skilled in the science of exchange; a bill-broker; a money-changer. **cambism,** ***cambistry,** *n.*

cambium (kăm′ bi ŭm) [late L., exchange], *n.* The viscid substance consisting of cellular tissue which appears, in the spring, between the wood and bark of exogenous trees.

cambrel (kăm′ brėl) [etym. doubtful], *n.* A bent piece of wood used by butchers for hanging up carcases.

Cambrian (kăm′ bri ăn) [L. *Cambria*, *Cumbria*, Celt. *Cymry*, Welsh, *Cymru*, Wales], *a.* Of or belonging to Wales; (*Geol.*) the name given to the system of palæozoic strata lying below the Silurian. *n.* A Welshman.

cambric (kām′ brik) [orig. made at *Cambray*], *n.* A kind of very fine white linen; (*fig.*) handkerchiefs.

came (1) (kām) [Sc., earlier *calm*], *n.* (*usu. in pl.*) A strip of lead used in framing glass in lattice windows.

came (2) *past* [COME].

camel (kăm′ ėl) [A.-S., from L. *camēlus*, Gr. *kamēlos*, from Semitic (Heb. *gāmāl*, Arab. *jāmāl*)], *n.* A large, hornless, humpbacked ruminant with long neck and padded feet, used in Africa and the East as a beast of burden; two species, the Arabian camel, *Camelus dromedarius*, with one hump, and the Bactrian, *C. Bactrianus*, with two; (*fig.*) a great hulking fellow; (*Naut.*) a contrivance for floating ships over bars, etc. **to swallow a camel:** (alln. to Matt. xxiii. 24) To believe an incredibility; to accept something intolerable. **camel-backed,** *a.* Humpbacked. **camel-brown,** *n.* An angler's fly. **camel corps,** *n.* (*Mil.*) Troops mounted on camels. **cameleer** (kăm ė lēr′), *n.* A camel-driver. **camelish,** *a.* Obstinate. **camelry,** *n.* Troops mounted on camels. **camel's-hair,** *n.* Camel's hair used as a material for various fabrics; a painter's brush made of hairs from squirrels' tails.

cameleon [CHAMELEON].

cameline (kăm′ e lin), *n.* Camlet.

camellia (kă mel′ i ă, kă mē′ li ă) [G. J. *Kamel*, a Moravian Jesuit, and Eastern traveller], *n.* A genus of evergreen shrubs with beautiful flowers.

camelopard (kă mel′ ō pard, kăm′ el ō pard) [L. *camēlopardus -pardālis*, Gr. *kamēlopardis* (CAMEL, PARD)], *n.* The giraffe.

camembert (kăm′ em bâr) [F., name of village], *n.* A soft Norman cheese.

cameo (kăm′ ė ō) [It. *camméo*, late L. *cammæus*; etym. unknown], *n.* A precious stone with two layers of colours, the upper of which is carved in relief, the lower serving as background; used also of similar carvings on shells.

camera (kăm′ ėr ă) [L., vault, from Aryan *kam-*, to cover over (cp. Gr. *kamara*, anything with a vaulted roof)], *n.* (*Law* The private chamber of a judge; a camera obscura, esp. that form used in photography. **in camera:** (*Law*) In private, the public being excluded from the court. **camera lucida,** *n.* An instrument (used for copying drawings, etc.) by which the rays of light from an object are reflected by a prism, and produce an image of the object on paper placed below. **camera obscura,** *n.* A dark box, or chamber, admitting light through a pinhole or a double-convex lens, at the focus of which an image is formed of external objects on paper, glass, etc. **camerated,** *a.* Arched; (*Zool.*) divided into chambers.

Cameronian (kăm ėr ō′ ni ăn) [*Cameron*, -IAN], *n.* A follower of Richard Cameron (*d.* 1680), a noted Scottish Presbyterian Covenanter, or of his doctrines; a member of the Reformed Presbyterian Church; (*pl.*) the Cameronian Regiment, the 26th Regiment, later the 1st Batt. Scottish Rifles.

camion (kăm′ yon) [F.], *n.* A motor lorry or wagon.

***camis, camus** (kăm′ is, -ŭs) [Sp. and Port. *camisa*, late L. *camisia*, CHEMISE], *n.* A thin, loose linen dress; a shirt, a chemise.

camisade (kăm i sād′), ***camisado** (kăm i sa′ dō) [F. *camisade*, Sp. *camisada*, *camiçada*, from prec.], *n.* A night assault or surprise, in which the soldiers wore their shirts over their armour as a means of recognition.

Camisard (kăm′ i zard) [F., from prec.], *n.* One of the French Calvinist insurgents in the Cevennes after the revocation of the Edict of Nantes.

camisole (kăm′ i sōl) [F., from Sp. *camisola*, dim. of *camisa*, see CAMIS)], *n.* An under-bodice. **cami-knickers,** *n.pl.* Camisole and knickers in one piece.

camlet (kăm′ lėt) [F. *camelot*, Arab. *khamlat*, *khaml*, an Eastern fabric], *n.* A fabric orig. of camel's hair, now a mixture of silk, wool, and hair (applied at different times to various substances); a garment of camlet.

cammock (kăm′ ŏk) [A.-S. *cammoc*; etym. doubtful], *n.* The rest-harrow, *Ononis arvensis*; applied locally to other yellow-flowered plants.

camomile, chamomile (kăm′ ō mīl) [F. *camomille*, late L. *camomilla*, Gr. *chamaimēlon*, lit. earth-apple], *n.* An aromatic creeping plant belonging to the genus *Anthemis*, esp. *A. nobilis*; applied also to some other plants. **camomile tea,** *n.*

Camorra (kă mor′ ă) [It., a blouse], *n.* A lawless secret society in S. Italy, dating from the old kingdom of Naples; (*fig.*) a lawless clique. **Camorist,** *n.*

camouflage (kăm′ oo flazh) [F. *camouflet*, a smoke-puff], *n.* Disguise, esp. the concealment of guns, camps, buildings, vehicles, etc., from the enemy by means of deceptive painting, a covering of boughs, and the like; (*fig.*) concealment of one's actions. *v.t.* To disguise.

camouflet (kăm′ oo flā) [as prec.], *n.* A cavity formed underground by the exploding of a bomb.

---

n: cabosho*n*. **ng:** si*ng*. **sh:** *sh*awl. **zh:** mea*s*ure. **th:** *th*in. ***th*:** brea*th*e. *See page* xi.

camp (kămp) [F. *camp* (cp. *champ*), It. or Sp. *campo*, L. *campus*, a field], *n.* The place where an army is lodged in tents or other temporary structures; a station for training troops; a body of troops in tents; an army on campaign; military life; temporary quarters of gipsies, travellers, etc.; the occupants of such quarters; (*Austral.*) a halting-place for cattle; a body of adherents; a side. *v.t.* To encamp troops. *v.i.* To encamp. **camp-bed, -bedstead,** *n.* A light folding bedstead. **camp-ceiling,** *n.* A concave ceiling or one with sloping sides (as in a garret). **camp-chair,** *n.* A folding chair. **camp-colour,** *n.* A flag for marking out a camping ground. ***camp-fever,** *n.* An epidemic to which troops in camp are liable, esp. typhus. **camp-fire,** *n.* A gathering (esp. of soldiers) round the fire in camp. **camp-follower,** *n.* A civilian who follows an army in the field; a hanger-on. **camp-meeting,** *n.* A religious meeting in the open air or in a tent, often prolonged for days. **camp-stool,** *n.* A folding stool. **to camp out,** *v.i.* To lodge in a camp in the open; to sleep outdoors. *v.t.* To place troops in camp. **camper, camper-out,** *n.*

Campagna (kăm pa' nyȧ) [L. *Campania*], *n.* The flat country around Rome.

campaign (kăm pān') [F. *campagne*, the open country, a campaign. It. *campagna*, L. *campania*, a plain, *campus*, a field (cp. CHAMPAGNE, CHAMPAIGN)], *n.* *An open tract of country; the operations and continuance of an army in the field; (*fig.*) any analogous operations or course of action, esp. a course of political propaganda. *v.i.* To serve on a campaign. **campaigner,** *n.*

campanero (kăm pȧ nâr' ō) [Sp., bell-man (*campana*, bell)], *n.* The Brazilian bell-bird.

campanile (kăm pa nē' li, -nēl, kăm' pȧ nil, -nīl) [It., from *campana*, bell], *n.* (*pl.* **-iles, -ili**) A bell-tower, esp. a detached one; a steeple.

campanology (kăm pȧ nol' ȯ ji), *n.* The principles of bell-ringing, founding, etc. **campanologer, -gist,** *n.* **campanological** (-loj' ik ȧl), *a.*

campanula (kăm păn' ū lȧ), *n.* (*Bot.*) A genus of plants with bell-shaped flowers, containing the bluebell of Scotland, the Canterbury bell, etc. **campanulaceous** (-lā' shŭs), *a.* **campanular, campanulate,** *a.* (*Bot.* and *Zool.*) Bell-shaped.

Campbellite (kăm' bėl īt) [Alexander *Campbell* (1788–1866) of Virginia, a religious teacher], *n.* A member of a sect founded by Campbell, called the Disciples of Christ.

Campeachy wood (kăm pē' chi) [*Campeche*, on west coast of Mexico], *n.* Logwood.

***campestral** (kăm pes' trȧl) [L. *campester -tris*, pertaining to a field (*campus*, a field)], *a.* Pertaining to or growing in the fields or open country.

camphene, camphine (kăm' fēn, -fīn) [see foll.], *n.* An illuminating oil distilled from turpentine.

camphor (kăm' fȯr) [F. *camphre*, med. L. *camphora*, Arab. *kāfūr*, Malay *kāpūr*, chalk], *n.* A whitish, translucent, volatile, crystalline substance with a peculiar odour, obtained from *Camphora officinarum*, *Dryobalanops aromatica*, and other trees. **v.t.* To camphorate. **camphor-laurel, -tree,** *n.* *Cinnamomum camphora.* **camphor-wood,** *n.* The wood of this or of an Australian timber-tree, *Callitris robusta.* **camphoraceous** (-ā' shŭs), *a.* **camphorate** (kăm' fȯr ȧt), *n.* **camphorate** (kăm' fȯr āt), *v.t.* To wash or impregnate with camphor. **camphoric** (kăm fŏr' ik), *a.* Pertaining to or containing camphor.

campion (kăm' pi ȯn) [etym. doubtful; perh. from F. *campagne* or L. *campus*, a field], *n.* English flowering plants of the genus *Lychnis.*

campshed (kămp' shed) [etym. unknown], *v.t.* To line (a river bank) with piles and planks to prevent it from being worn away. **camp-shedding, -sheeting, -shot,** *n.*

campus (kăm' pŭs) [L., a field], *n.* (*Am.*) The fields or grounds of a college or school, or the court, or quadrangle.

camus [CAMIS].

camwood (kăm' wud) [perh. from native name *kambi*], *n.* Barwood, a hard red wood from West Africa.

can (1) (kăn) [A.-S. *canne* (cp. Dut. *kan*, O.H.G. *chann*, G. *kanne*)], *n.* A metal vessel for holding liquid; a vessel of tinned iron in which meat, fruit, fish, etc., are hermetically sealed up for preservation. *v.t.* (*past & p.p.* **canned**) To put up in cans for preservation. **can-buoy,** *n.* A conical buoy to mark out shoals and rocks. **can-opener,** *n.* (*Am.*) A tin-opener. **canful,** *n.* **canned,** *a.* (*slang*) Drunk. **canned-goods,** *n.pl.* Tinned meat, fruit, etc. **canned music,** *n.* (*colloq.*) Music recorded for gramophone reproduction. **canner,** *n.* **cannery,** *n.*

can (2) (kăn) [A.-S. *cunnan*, to know, **can, canst,** pl. *cunnon* (cp. Dut. *kunnen*, O.H.G. *chunnan*, G. *können*, KEN, KNOW, L. *gnoscere*, Gr. *gignōskein*)], *aux. v.* (*negative* **cannot,** *past* **could, couldst,** A.-S. *cūthe*, M.E. *coude*) To be able to; to be allowed to; to be possible to.

Canaan (kā' nyȧn, -nȧn) [Heb. *k'naan*, western Palestine], *n.* (*fig.*) The land of promise; heaven. **Canaanite,** *n.* An inhabitant of the land of Canaan; a descendant of Canaan, the son of Ham. **Canaanitish** (-nī' tish), *a.*

Canada (kăn' ȧ dȧ), *n.* A Dominion of the British Commonwealth of Nations. *a.* Of or from Canada, Canadian. **Canada balsam,** *n.* A pale resin obtained from *Abies balsamea* and *A. Canadensis*, used in medicine and to mount microscopic objects. **Canadian** (kȧ nā' di ȧn), *a.* and *n.*

canaille (kă nī') [F., from It. *canaglia*, *cane*, L. *canis*, a dog], *n.* The dregs of the people; the rabble, the mob.

canakin (CANNIKIN).

canal (kȧ năl') [F., from L. *canālis*], *n.* An artificial watercourse, esp. one used for navigation; (*Physiol.* and *Bot.*) a duct; (*Zool.*) a siphonal groove; (*Arch.*) a fluting, a groove. *v.t.* To make a canal across; to canalize. **canal rays,** *n.* (*Phys.*) Positive rays; a steady flow of positively electrified particles which take part in the electrical discharge in a rarefied gas. **canals of Mars,** *n.pl.* Linear markings on the surface of the planet Mars, supposed by some astronomers to be waterways, or zones of vegetation produced by periodical diffusion of moisture. **canalize** (kăn' ȧ līz), *v.t.* To make a canal across or through; to convert a river into a navigable waterway. **canalization** (-lī zā' shŭn), *n.* The construction of canals.

canaliculate, canaliculated, (kăn ȧ lik' ū lȧt, -lāt ėd) [mod. L. *canāliculātus* (*canāliculus*, dim. of *canālis*, see prec.)], *a.* (*Physiol.*) Minutely grooved; striated.

canalize [CANAL].

canape (kăn' ȧ pi) [Fr.], *n.* A thin piece of bread or toast spread with cheese, fish, etc.

canard (kȧ nard', ka nar') [F., lit. a duck], *n.* An absurd story, a hoax, a false report.

Canary (kȧ nâr' i) [F. *Canarie*, Sp. *Canāria*, L. *Canāria Insula*, Isle of Dogs (*canis*, a dog)], *n.* A group of islands off the west coast of Africa; *a lively dance, derived thence; a light sweet wine made there; a well-known cage-bird *Fringilla Canaria.* *a.* Bright yellow. **canary-coloured,** *a.* **canary-creeper, canariensis** (kăn âr i en' sis), *n.* A climbing-plant with yellow flowers. **canary-seed,** *n.* The seed of *Phalaris Canariensis*, the **canary-grass,** used as food for canaries.

canasta (kȧ năs' tȧ), *n.* A kind of card game.

canaster (kȧ năs' tėr) [Sp. *canastra*, through L., from Gr. *kanastron*, basket (cp. CANISTER)], *n.* A coarse kind of tobacco, so called from the rush baskets in which it was orig. brought from America; such a rush-basket.

cancan (kan kan, kăn′ kăn) [F., etym. doubtful], *n.* A rollicking kind of dance.

cancel (kăn′ sėl) [F. *canceller*, L. *cancellāre* (*cancellus*, a grating, *cancelli*, cross-bars, lattice)], *v.t.* (*past & p.p.* **cancelled**) To obliterate by drawing lines across; to annul, countermand, revoke, neutralize; to suppress; (*Math.*) to strike out common factors. *n.* The deletion and reprinting of a part of a book; (*Print.*) a page or sheet substituted for a cancelled one. **to cancel out:** To cancel one another. **pair of cancels:** A stamp for defacing tickets. **cancellate** (kăn′ sėl āt), **cancellated** (-lāt ėd), **cancellous,** *a.* (*Bot. and Zool*). Cross-barred; reticulated; (of bones) formed of *cancelli*. **cancellation** (-lā′ shŭn), *n.* **cancelli** (kăn sel′ ī) [L., see CANCEL], *n.pl.* A rail of latticework between the choir and the body of a church; (*Physiol.*) the reticulation in the spongy part of bones.

cancer (kăn′ sėr) [L. *cancer* (cp. Gr. *karkinos*), a crab], *n.* The fourth of the twelve signs of the zodiac, the Crab; (*Med.*) a malignant spreading growth affecting different parts of the human body; (*fig.*) a vice or other evil of an inveterate spreading kind. **Tropic of Cancer** [TROPIC (1)]. **canceration** (-ā′ shŭn), *n.* **cancered, cancerous,** *a.* **cancriform** (kang′ kri fôrm), *a.* Crab-like; (*Med.*) of the form of a cancer. **cancroid,** *a.* Crab-like; (*Med.*) having some of the qualities of cancer. *n.* A crustacean belonging to the crab family; (*Med.*) a disease resembling cancer.

candelabrum, candelabra (kăn dė lā′ brŭm, -brȧ) [L. (*candēla*, CANDLE)], *n.* (*pl.* **-bra, -bras**) A tall lamp-stand; a high, ornamental candlestick, usually branched.

candescent (kăn des′ ėnt) [L. *candescens -ntem*, pres.p. of *candescere*, to glow, to become white (*candēre*, to glow)], *a.* Glowing with or as with white heat. **candescence,** *n.*

candid (kăn′ did) [L. *candidus*, white (see prec.)], *a.* *White; *pure, innocent; frank, sincere, open, ingenuous; outspoken, freely critical. **candid camera,** *n.* A small camera for taking photographs of people without their knowledge. **candidly,** *adv.* **candidness,** *n.*

candidate (kăn′ di dāt) [L. *candidātus*, white-robed (see prec.)], *n.* One who seeks or is proposed for some office or appointment (so named because such persons in ancient Rome wore white togas); a person considered suitable or worthy for an office or dignity. *v.i.* (*Am.*) To be a candidate. **candidacy,** *n.* **candidature** (-dā tūr, -dā chėr), **candidateship,** *n.*

candied [CANDY].

candle (kăndl) [A.-S. *candel*, L. *candēla* (*candēre*, to glow, shine)], *n.* A cylindrical body of tallow, wax, etc., with a wick in the middle, used as an illuminant; candle-power. *v.t.* To test eggs by holding before a candle. **to burn the candle at both ends:** To expend one's energies or waste resources in two ways at once. **to sell by inch of candle:** To sell by auction, bids being received as long as a tiny bit of candle burns. **not fit to hold a candle to:** Not to be named in comparison with. **not worth the candle:** Not worth the trouble. **Roman candle,** *n.* A firework consisting of a tube from which coloured fireballs are discharged. **standard candle,** *n.* A spermaceti candle burning at the rate of two grains a minute, the standard of light-measurement. **candleberry-myrtle,** *n.* A North American shrub, *Myrica cerifera*, yielding wax used for candle-making. **candle-bomb,** *n.* A small bubble filled with water, which, when placed in the flame of a candle, bursts by the expansion of the steam. **candle-coal,** *n.* [CANNEL-COAL]. **candle-ends,** *n.pl.* (*fig.*) Fragments. ***candle-holder,** *n.* (*fig.*) One who assists or looks on. **candle-light,** *n.* The light of a candle; evening. **Candlemas,** *n.* The feast of the Purification of the Virgin (Feb. 2nd), when candles are blessed and carried in procession. **candle-nut,** *n.* The fruit of *Aleurites triloba*, which furnishes a kind of wax. **candle-power,** *n.* The unit for measuring light, the illuminating power of a standard spermaceti candle. **candle-stick,** *n.* A utensil for holding a candle. **candle-tree,** *n.* A tree growing in the Moluccas, *Aleurites tribola*, and other trees, the nuts or fruit of which yield illuminants.

candock (kăn′ dok) [CAN (1), DOCK (1)], *n.* The water-lily, esp. the yellow water-lily.

candour (kăn′ dŏr) [L. *candor*], *n.* *Whiteness, integrity, innocence, candidness, sincerity, openness; freedom from malice or bias.

candy (kăn′ di) [orig. *sugar-candy*, F. *sucre candi*, Arab. and Pers. *qand*, sugar, *qandi*, candied], *n.* Sugar crystallized by boiling and evaporation; (*Am.*) sweetmeats. *v.t.* To preserve with sugar, to coat with crystallized sugar; to crystallize. *v.i.* To become candied. **candy-store,** *n.* (*Am.*) A sweet-shop. **candied,** *a.* Preserved in or coated with sugar; crystalline, glistening; (*fig.*) flattering, honeyed.

candytuft (kăn′ di tŭft) [from the island *Candia*], *n.* A herbaceous plant, *Iberis umbellata*; the genus *Iberis*, esp. *I. sempervivum*, the perennial candytuft.

cane (kān) [O.F. *cane* (F. *canne*), L. *canna*, Gr. *kanna*, prob. Semit. (cp. Arab. *qanāh*, Heb. *qāneh*)], *n.* A slender, hollow, jointed stem of the bamboo, sugar-cane, or other reeds or grasses; the thin stem of the rattan or other palms; such a stem or a bamboo used as a walking-stick or an instrument of punishment; a slender walking-stick; (*Am.*) any walking-stick; the stem of a raspberry and other plants. *v.t.* To beat with a cane; (*fig.*) to thrash (a lesson, with *into*); to put a cane bottom to (as a chair). **cane-brake,** *n.* A thicket of canes; a genus of grasses. **cane-chair,** *n.* A chair with a seat of cane splints. **cane-mill,** *n.* A mill for grinding sugar-canes. **cane-sugar,** *n.* Sugar made from canes as distinguished from beet-sugar. **cane-trash,** *n.* The refuse of sugar-cane. **cany,** *a.* **caning,** *n.* A beating with a cane.

canella (kȧ nel′ ȧ) [med. L., dim. of *canna*, cane], *n.* A genus of West Indian plants, with aromatic bark, comprising *Canella alba*, the wild cinnamon.

canephorus (kȧ nē′ fŏr ŭs) [Gr. *kanēphoros* (*kaneon*, basket, *-phoros*, bearing, *pherein*, to carry)], *n.* (*pl.* **-ri**) (*Arch.*) A sculptured figure of a maiden or youth carrying a basket on head.

canescent (kȧ nes′ ėnt) [L. *cānēscere*, to grow grey (*cānus*, white)], *a.* Hoary, approaching to white. **canescence,** *n.*

cangue, cang (kăng) [F. *cangue*, Port. *cango* (conn. with *canga*, yoke)], *n.* A heavy wooden collar or yoke fixed round the neck of criminals in China.

canicular (kȧ nik′ ū lȧr) [L. *caniculāris* (*canīcula*, a little dog, the dog-star, dim. of *canis*)], *a.* Of or pertaining to the dog-star; excessively hot; (*colloq.*) pertaining to a dog.

canine (kā′ nīn, kăn′ īn, kȧ nīn′) [L. *canīnus* (*canis*, dog)], *a.* Of or pertaining to dogs; dog-like. *n.* A canine tooth. **canine teeth,** *n.pl.* Two pointed teeth in each jaw, one on each side, between the incisors and the molars.

canister (kăn′ is tėr) [L. *canistrum*, Gr. *kanastron*, a basket (*canna*, a reed)], *n.* A metal case or box for holding tea, coffee, etc.; canister-shot; (*R.-C. Ch.*) the box in which the eucharistic wafers are kept before consecration; *a reed basket. **canister-shot,** *n.* Bullets packed in metal cases which burst when fired, called also case-shot.

canker (kăng′ kėr) [A.-S. *cancer*, North.F. *cancre* (F. *chancre*), L. *cancrum*, acc. of CANCER], *n.* A corroding ulceration in the human mouth; a fungous excrescence in a horse's foot; a fungus growing on and injuring fruit trees; *the dog-rose; *a cancer; (*fig.*) anything which corrupts or consumes. *v.t.* To infect or rot with canker, to eat into like a canker; to infect, corrode. *v.i.* To become cankered, infected, or corrupt. ***canker-fly,** *n.* An insect preying on fruit. **canker-rash,** *n.* A form of scarlet fever in which the throat is ulcerated. **canker-weed,** *n.* Ragwort, esp. the common species, *Senecio Jacobæa.* **canker-worm,** *n.* A caterpillar that feeds on buds and leaves; (*Am.*) the larva of the geometer moths. **cankered,** *a.* Corroded by canker; cross, peevish. **cankerous,** *a.* Corroding, destroying.

canna (1) (kăn′ ȧ) [L. *canna,* CANE], *n.* A genus of ornamental plants with bright coloured flowers.

canna (2) [Sc. for CANNOT, see CAN (2)].

cannabis (kăn′ ȧ bis) [Gr. *kannabis*], *n.* A genus of plants containing the Indian hemp. **cannabin,** *n.* (*Chem.*) A narcotic resin obtained from hemp. **cannabine** (kăn′ ȧ bīn), *a.* Of or pertaining to hemp.

cannach (ka′ nȧ*ch*) [Gael. *cánach*], *n.* (*Sc.*) The cotton-grass.

canned, cannery, *a.* [CAN (1)].

cannel (kăn′ ėl), **cannel-coal** [var. of CANDLE], *n.* A hard, bituminous coal, burning with a bright flame.

cannelure (kăn′ e lūr) [F., a groove], *n.* (*Arch.*) A flute, a channel; (*Artill.*) a groove round a projectile.

cannibal (kăn′ i bȧl) [Sp. *Canibales,* var. of *Caribes,* Caribbeans], *n.* A human being that feeds on human flesh; an animal that feeds on its own kind. *a.* Pertaining to cannibalism; like a cannibal; ravenous, bloodthirsty. **cannibalism,** *n.* The act or practice of feeding on one's own kind; (*fig.*) barbarity, atrocity. **cannibalistic** (-lis′ tik), *a.* ***cannibally,** *adv.* **cannibalize,** *v.t.* To dismantle a machine for its spare parts to be built into a similar machine.

***cannikin** (kăn′ i kin), *n.* A little can or cup.

cannily, canniness [CANNY].

cannon (1) (kăn′ ȯn) [F. *canon,* a law, decree, a great gun, *It. cannone,* a great tube (*canna,* a pipe, a cane, L. *canna,* CANE)], *n.* A piece of ordnance; a heavy mounted gun; artillery, ordnance; (*Mech.*) a hollow sleeve or cylinder revolving independently on a shaft; a cannon-curl. **cannon-ball,** *n.* A solid shot fired from a cannon. **cannon-bit,** *n.* A smooth round bit for a horse. **cannon-bone,** *n.* The metacarpal or metatarsal bone of a horse, ox, etc. **cannon-curl,** *n.* A cylindrical curl worn horizontally. **cannon-fodder,** *n.* (*iron.*) Soldiers, esp. infantrymen. **cannon-proof,** *a.* Proof against artillery. **cannon-shot,** *n.* *A cannon-ball; the range of a cannon. **cannonade,** *n.* A continued attack with artillery against a town, fortress, etc.; *v.t.* To attack or batter with cannon; *v.i.* To discharge heavy artillery. **cannoneer, *cannonier,** *n.* A gunner, an artilleryman. **cannonry,** *n.* Cannon collectively; cannonading.

cannon (2) (kăn′ ȯn) [corr. of obs. *carom,* short for *carambole,* F., from Sp. *carambola* (etym. doubtful)], *n.* (*Billiards*) A stroke by which two balls are hit successively. *v.i.* (*Billiards*) To make a cannon; to come into violent contact (against or with).

cannot [CAN (2)].

cannula (kăn′ ū lȧ) [L., dim. of *canna,* CANE], *n.* (*Med.*) A small tube introduced into a cavity to withdraw a fluid. **cannular,** *a.*

canny (kăn′ i) [CAN (2)], *a.* Knowing, shrewd, wise; quiet, gentle; comely, good; artful, crafty; prudent, cautious; frugal, thrifty; safe to have dealings with (cp. UNCANNY); *lucky, prosperous; *gifted with occult power. **to ca' canny:** To go gently; not to work too well. **cannily,** *adv.* **canniness,** *n.*

canoe (kȧ noo′) [Sp. *canoa,* from Haitian], *n.* A kind of light boat formed of the trunk of a tree hollowed out, or of bark or hide, and propelled by paddles; a light narrow boat propelled by paddles. *v.i.* To go in a canoe. **to paddle one's own canoe:** To be independent. **canoeist,** *n.*

canon (kăn′ ȯn) [A.-S., from L., from Gr. *kanōn,* a rule (*kanē, kanna,* CANE)], *n.* A rule, a regulation, a general law or principle; a standard, test, or criterion; a decree of the Church; (*Print.*) the largest size of type, 4-line pica; the ring or loop by which a bell is suspended; the catalogue of canonized saints; the portion of the Mass in which the words of consecration are spoken; a list of the books of Scriptures received as inspired; the books themselves; the list of an author's recognized works; a rule of discipline or doctrine; a resident member of a cathedral chapter; a member of a religious body, from the fact that some cathedral canons lived in community; (*Mus.*) a composition in which the several parts take up the same subject in succession; the strictest species of imitation. **canon law,** *n.* Ecclesiastical law as laid down by popes and councils. ***canoness,** *n.* A member of a female community living by rule but not bound by vows. **canonic, canonical** (kȧ non′ ik, -ȧl), *a.* Pertaining to or according to canon law; included in the canon of Scripture; authoritative, accepted, approved; belonging or pertaining to a cathedral chapter; (*Mus.*) in canon form. **Canonical Epistles,** *n.pl.* The Epistles of Peter, James, John, and Jude. **canonical hours** (8 A.M. to 6 P.M.) during which marriages may legally be celebrated. **canonically,** *adv.* **canonicals,** *n.pl.* The full robes of an officiating clergyman as appointed by the canons. ***canonicate,** *n.* The dignity or office of a canon. **canonicity** (-nis′ i ti), *n.* The quality of being canonical, esp. the authority of a canonical book. **canonist** (kăn′ ȯ nist), *n.* One versed in canon law. **canonistic, canonistical** (-nis′ tik, -ȧl), *a.*

cañon [CANYON].

canonize (kăn′ ȯ nīz), *v.t.* To enrol in the canon or list of saints; to recognize officially as a saint; to recognize as canonical; to sanction as conforming to the canons of the Church. **canonization** (-nī zā′ shŭn), *n.* **canonry,** *n.* The dignity, position, or benefice of a canon.

canoodle (kȧ noodl′) [etym. unknown] (*slang*), *v.t.* To fondle. *v.i.* To bill and coo.

Canopus (kȧ nō′ pŭs) [L., from Gr. *Kanōpos*), *n.* The bright star in the constellation Argo; name of an ancient Egyptian city; a Canopic vase. **Canopic,** *a.* **Canopic vase,** *n.* An Egyptian vase for holding the viscera of embalmed bodies.

canopy (kăn′ ȯ pi) [F., *canapé,* a tent or pavilion (now, a sofa), med. L. *canōpeum,* L. *cōnōpēum,* Gr. *kōnōpeion,* a bed with mosquito-curtains (*kōnōps,* a gnat)], *n.* A rich covering of state suspended over an altar, throne, bed, etc.; or borne over some person, relics, or the Host, in procession; (*fig.*) a shelter, a covering, the sky; (*Arch.*) an ornamental projection over a niche or doorway; (*Aviat.*) the transparent roof of the cock-pit; the fabric portion of a parachute. *v.t.* To cover with or as with a canopy. **canopied,** *a.*

canorous (kȧ nôr′ ŭs) [L. *canōrus* (*canere,* to sing)], *a.* Tuneful, melodious, resonant.

canst [2nd pers. sing., CAN (2)].

***canstick** [contr. of CANDLESTICK].

cant (1) (kănt) [L. *cantāre,* to sing, freq. of *canere*], *n.* *A monotonous whining; the peculiar dialect or jargon of beggars, gipsies, and thieves; slang; a method of speech or phraseology peculiar to any sect or party (with depreciatory sense); hypocritical sanctimoniousness; hypocritical talk. *a.* Pertaining to or of the nature of cant. *v.i.* To speak whiningly or insincerely; to talk cant. **canter,** *n.* **canting,** *n.* Cant. *a.* Whining, hypocritical. **cantingly,** *adv.* **canting arms, canting heraldry,** *n.* Armorial bearings containing a punning device or other allusion to the name of the family. **canting crew,** *n.* The brotherhood or fraternity of vagabonds, thieves, sharpers, etc. **cantish,** *a.*

cant (2) (kănt) [Dut. *kant* (cp. O.F. *cant,* It. *canto,* med. L. *cantus,* corner, and perh. L. *canthus,* Gr. *kanthos,* corner of eye, felloe of a wheel; course of derivation uncertain)], *n.* A slope, a slant; an inclination; a jerk producing a slant or upset; an external angle, a bevel; a slanting position. *v.t.* To tip, to tilt; to throw with a jerk; to bevel, give a bevel to. *v.i.* To tilt or slant over; (*Naut.*) to swing round. **cant-board,** *n.* A sloping board. **cant-rail,** *n.* A bevelled plank placed along the top of the uprights in a railway carriage to support the roof. **canted,** *a.*

cant (3) (kănt) [Sc. and North.; etym. doubtful; perh. from CANT (2), edge, angle, corner (cp. Dut. *kant*, great, clever)], *a.* Strong, lusty; keen, lively, brisk. **canty,** *a.* Lively, cheerful. **cantiness,** *n.*

can't (kant) [contr. of CANNOT, see CAN (2)].

cantabile (kăn ta' bi lā) [It., able to be sung (L. *cantare*, to sing, freq. of *canere*)], *a.* (*Mus.*) In an easy, flowing style. *n.* A piece in the cantabile style.

Cantabrigian (kăn tȧ brij' i ȧn) [L. *Cantabrigia*, Cambridge], *a.* Of or relating to the University of Cambridge. *n.* A member of Cambridge University.

cantaloup (kăn' tȧ loop), *n.* A small, round, ribbed musk-melon, first raised at Cantalupo near Rome.

cantankerous (kăn tăng' kėr ŭs) [etym. doubtful; perh. from M.E. *contak*, contention], *a.* Disagreeable, cross-grained; quarrelsome, crotchety. **cantankerously,** *adv.* **cantankerousness,** *n.*

cantar (kăn' tȧr) [It. *cantaro* (Turk. *qantār*), L. *cantharus*, Gr. *kantharos*, a tankard], *n.* An Oriental measure of weight, varying from 100 to 130 lb.; a Spanish liquid measure, varying from 2½ to 4 galls.

cantata (kăn ta' tȧ) [It.], *n.* A poem or short lyrical drama set to music, with solos and choruses.

cantatore (kan ta tôr' ā) [It.], *n.* (*Mus.*) A male professional singer. ***cantatrice*** (kăn tȧ trē' chā, F. kan tȧ trēs), *n.* A female professional singer.

canteen (kăn tēn') [F. *cantine*, It. *cantina*, cellar (perh. from CANTO, a side, a corner)], *n.* A place in a barracks, factory or office where refreshments are sold at low prices to the soldiers or employees; a soldier's mess tin; a chest or box in which the mess utensils, cutlery, etc., are carried; a chest for cutlery; (*Am.*) a water-bottle. **dry, wet canteen,** *n.* Canteen where alcoholic liquors are not, or are, sold.

canter (kăn' tėr) [short for CANTERBURY], *n.* An easy gallop; a Canterbury gallop, a Canterbury pace, phrases applied to the easy, ambling pace at which pilgrims went to the shrine of St. Thomas à Becket at Canterbury. *v.t.* To cause (a horse) to go at this pace. *v.i.* To ride at a canter. **in a canter:** Easily.

Canterbury (kăn' tėr bėr i) [A.-S. *Cantwaraburh* (*Cantware*, people of Kent)], *n.* A city in Kent, seat of the metropolitan See of all England; a light stand with divisions for music portfolios, etc. **Canterbury bell,** *n.* Name of plants belonging to the genus *Campanula*, esp. the exotic *C. medium*. **Canterbury gallop, Canterbury pace** [CANTER].

cantharides (kăn thăr' i dēz) [L., pl. of CANTHARIS], *n.pl.* (*Med.*) Spanish flies dried and used as a blister or internally, also used as an aphrodisiac. **cantharidin, cantharidine** (kăn thăr' i din), *n.* The active principle of cantharides. **cantharis** (kăn' thȧ ris) [L., from Gr. *kantharis*, blistering-fly], *n.* Spanish fly, a coleopterous insect having vesicatory properties; applied to similar beetles.

canthus (kăn' thŭs) [L., from Gr. *kanthos*], *n.* (*Physiol.*) The angle made by the meeting of the eyelids.

canticle (kăn' tikl) [L. *canticulum*, dim. of *canticum*, song (*cantus*, song, *canere*, to sing)], *n.* A brief song, a chant; applied to certain portions of Scripture appointed in the Prayer Book to be said or sung in churches. **The Canticles:** The Song of Solomon.

cantilena (kăn ti lē' nȧ) [F. *cantilène*, L. *cantilēna*, a song (*cantillāre*, CANTILLATE)], *n.* A ballad; (*Church music*) plain-song.

cantilever (kăn' ti lē vėr) [perh. CANT (2) (or from CANTLE), LEVER], *n.* A projecting beam, girder, or bracket for supporting a balcony or other structure. **cantilever bridge,** *n.* A bridge formed with cantilevers, resting in pairs on piers of masonry or ironwork, the ends meeting or connected by girders. **cantilever spring,** *n.* A laminated spring supported at the middle and bearing the weight on shackles at either end.

cantillate (kăn' ti lāt) [L. *cantillāre*, to sing low (*cantare*, freq. of *canere*, to sing)], *v.t.* To chant; to intone, as in Jewish synagogues. **cantillation** (-lā' shŭn), *n.*

cantle (kăntl) [O.North.F. *cantel* (med. L. *cantellus*, dim. of *cantus*, CANT (2))], *n.* A fragment, a piece; the projection at the rear of a saddle. *v.t.* To cut into pieces, divide. ***cantlet,** *n.* A morsel, fragment.

canto (kăn' tō) [It., from L. *cantus*, CANT (1)], *n.* (*pl.* **-os**) One of the principal divisions of a poem; *a song; (*Mus.*) the upper voice part in concerted music. **canto fermo** [It.], *n.* Plain-song; the main theme, which is treated contrapuntally.

canton (1) (kăn' tȯn, kăn ton') [O.F., a corner, a district, It. *cantone*, from *canto*, CANT (2)], *n.* *A corner; a division of a country, a small district; a political division of Switzerland; (*Her.*) a small division in the corner of a shield. **canton** (kăn ton'), *v.t.* To divide into parts. **cantoned,** *a.* Having projecting corners. **cantonal** (kăn'-), *a.*

canton (2) (kăn toon'), *v.t.* To billet troops, to provide with quarters. **cantonment,** *n.*

***canton** (3) [var. of CANTO].

cantor (kăn' tȯr) [L., precentor (*cant-*, freq. stem of *canere*, to sing)], *n.* *A singer; a precentor; the Jewish religious official who sings the liturgy. **cantorial** (kăn tôr' i ȧl), *a.* Pertaining to the precentor or to the north side of the choir. **cantoris** [L., gen. of CANTOR], *a.* (Sung) by the cantorial side of the choir.

***cantrip** (kăn' trip) [etym. doubtful], *n.* (*Sc.*) A spell, an incantation, a charm; (*fig.*) a trick, a piece of mischief.

Cantuarian (kăn tū âr' i ȧn) [late L. *Cantuarius* (A.-S. *Cantware*, see CANTERBURY)], *a.* Of or pertaining to Canterbury or its archiepiscopal See. **Cantuar:** The official signature of the Archbishop of Canterbury.

canty [CANT (3)].

Canuck (kă nŭk') [N. Am. Ind.], *n.* (*Am. colloq.*) A Canadian; (*Canada*) a French Canadian; a small rough Canadian horse.

canvas (kăn' vȧs) [O.North.F. *canevas*, late L. *canabācius* (L. *cannabis*, Gr. *kannabis*, hemp)], *n.* A coarse unbleached cloth, made of hemp or flax, formerly used for sifting, now for sails, tents, paintings, etc.; sails; the sails of a ship; a sheet of canvas for oil-painting; a picture; a covering for the ends of a racing-boat. *a.* Made of canvas. **under canvas:** In a tent or tents; (*Naut.*) with sails set. **canvas-back,** *n.* A North American sea-duck. **canvas town,** *n.* A large encampment.

canvass (kăn' vȧs) [from prec., orig. to sift through canvas], *n.* Close examination, discussion; the act of soliciting votes. *v.t.* To examine thoroughly, to discuss; to solicit votes, interest, orders, etc., from *v.i.* To solicit votes, etc. **canvasser,** *n.*

cany [CANE].

canyon, cañon (kăn' yȯn) [Sp. *cañon*, a tube, a conduit, a cannon, from *caña*, L. *canna*, CANE], *n.* A deep gorge or ravine with precipitous sides, esp. of the type of those formed by erosion in the western plateaux of the U.S.A.

canzone (kant sō' nā) [It., from L. *cantio -ōnem*, singing (*cant-*, freq. stem of *canere*, to sing)], *n.* A Provençal or Italian song. **canzonet** (kăn zȯ net') [It. *canzonetta*], *n.* A short air or song; a light air in an opera.

caoutchouc (kou' chook) [Carib. *cahuchu*], *n.* India-rubber, the coagulated juice of certain tropical trees, which is elastic and waterproof.

cap (1) (kăp) [A.-S. *cæppe*, late L. *cappa*, later *cāpa* (cp. O.F. *capel*, *chapel*, F. *chapeau*, and CAPE,

COPE)], *n.* A covering for the head, a brimless head-covering for a man or a boy; a woman's head-dress, usually for indoor wear; a natural or artificial covering resembling this in form or function; a special form of head-dress distinguishing the holder of an office, membership of a sports team, etc.; a percussion cap; a particular size of paper; cap-paper; the top part of anything; a coping; (*Naut.*) a block pierced to hold a mast or spar above another; (*Arch.*) a capital. *v.t.* (*past & p.p.* **capped**) To cover the top with a cap; to put a cap on; (*Sc. Univ.*) to confer a degree upon; to put a percussion cap on (a gun); to protect or cover with or as with a cap; to be on the top of; (*fig.*) to complete, to surpass. *v.i.* To take one's cap off (to). **cap and bells:** The insignia of a jester. **cap and gown:** Full academic dress. **cap in hand:** In a humble or servile manner. **cap of liberty:** A conical or Phrygian cap given to a manumitted slave; the symbol of republicanism. **cap of maintenance,** *n.* A cap of state carried before the sovereign at the coronation, and before some mayors. **percussion cap,** *n.* A small cylinder containing detonating powder for igniting the explosive in a gun, cartridge, shell, torpedo, etc. **if the cap fits:** If the general remark applies to you, take it to yourself. **to send the cap round:** To make a collection. **to set one's cap at:** To endeavour to captivate (said of a woman). **capful,** *n.* As much as a cap will hold; **capful of wind:** (*Naut.*) A light gust. **cap-paper.** *n.* Coarse paper used by grocers for wrapping up sugar, etc. **cap-sheaf,** *n.* (*Am.*) The top sheaf of a stack of corn. **cap-stone,** *n.* The top stone; a coping; the horizontal stone of a cromlech or dolmen; (*Geol.*) the uppermost bed in a quarry; a kind of fossil echinite. **to cap a story:** To tell another story that is still more to the point. **to cap verses:** To reply to a verse quoted by quoting another that rhymes or is otherwise appropriate. **capping,** *n.* That caps or forms the cap (of); that which covers or protects anything.

cap (2) (kăp) [Sc., from A.-S. *copp*, cup, or Icel. *koppr*, cup], *n.* A wooden drinking-bowl; a measure, the fourth part of a peck.

capable (kā' pȧ bėl) [F., from late L. *capābilis* (formed from *capere*, to hold, on anal. of *capax -ācis*, see fol.)], *a.* Susceptible (of); competent, able, skilful, qualified, fitted. **capably,** *adv.* **capability** (-bil' i ti), *n.* The quality of being capable; capacity; (*pl.*) resources, abilities, intellectual attainments.

capacious (kȧ pā' shŭs) [L. *capax -ācis* (*capere*, to hold, contain), -ACIOUS], *a.* Able to contain much; wide, large, extensive; comprehensive, liberal. **capaciously,** *adv.* **capaciousness,** *n.* **capacitate** (kȧ păs' i tāt), *v.t.* To make capable of; to qualify; to render competent.

capacity (kȧ păs' i ti) [as prec.], *n.* Power of containing or receiving; room, cubic extent; power to absorb; capability, ability; opportunity, scope; relative position, character, or office; legal qualification; (*Elec.*) a term used to denote the output of a piece of electrical apparatus. **capacity coupling,** *n.* (*Radio.*) The coupling of two circuits by a condenser to transfer energy from one to the other. **capacity reaction,** *n.* (*Radio.*) Reaction from the output to the input circuit of an amplifier through a path with a condenser.

cap-à-pie (kăp' a pē) [O.F. *cap a pie*, head to foot (L. *caput*, head, *pes pedis*, foot)], *adv.* From head to foot (armed or accoutred).

caparison (kȧ păr' i zȯn) [M.F. *caparasson*, Sp. *caparazon*, med. L. *caparo*, a cowl (late L. *cāpa*, CAPE)], *n.* (*often in pl.*) Housings, often ornamental, for a horse or other beast of burden; (*fig.*) outfit, equipment. *v.t.* To furnish with trappings; to deck out.

cape (1) (kāp) [F. (through Sp. *capa* or It. *cappa*), from late L. *cappa*, CAP], *n.* A covering for the shoulders, attached to another garment or separate. **caped,** *a.*

cape (2) (kāp) [F. *cap*, It. *capo*, L. *caput*, head], *n.* A headland projecting into the sea. **The Cape:** The Cape of Good Hope; Cape Colony. **Cape ant-eater** [AARDVARK]. **Cape boy,** *n.* A South African half-breed. **Cape cart,** *n.* A hooded, two-wheeled vehicle. **Cape wine,** *n.* Wine from South Africa.

capelin, caplin (kăp' ė lin, kăp' lin) [F. and Sp. *capelan*], *n.* A small Newfoundland fish like a smelt, used as bait for cod.

caper (1) (kā' pėr) [short for CAPRIOLE], *n.* A frolicsome leap, a frisky movement; eccentric behaviour. *v.i.* To leap; to skip about. **to cut capers:** To caper; to act in a ridiculous manner. **caperer,** *n.* A person that capers; a caddis-fly.

caper (2) (kā' pėr) [L. *capparis*, Gr. *kapparis* (cp. PEA, L. *pisum*, for loss of the *s*)], *n.* A prickly shrub, *Capparis spinosa*; (*pl.*) the flower-buds of this, used for pickling. **English capers,** *n.pl.* The fruit of the nasturtium, used for pickling.

capercailzie (kăp ėr kā' lyi) [Gael. *capull coille*, the cock of the wood (*capull*, L. *caballus*, horse, Gael. *coille*, wood)], *n.* The wood-grouse, *Tetrao urogallus*, called also the mountain cock or cock of the wood.

Capernaite (kȧ pĕr' nȧ īt) [*Capernaum*, in Galilee], *n.* (*Theol. polemics*) A believer in transubstantiation. **Capernaitic** (kȧ pĕr nā it' ik), *a.*

capernoitie (kăp ėr noi' ti) [Sc., etym. unknown], *n.* The head, the noddle. **capernoited, capernoity,** *a.* Wrong-headed, cracked. **capernoitedness,** *n.*

capias (kăp' i ăs) [L., take thou, or thou mayst take], *n.* (*Law*) A judicial writ ordering an officer to arrest.

capibara [CAPYBARA].

capillaire (kăp i lâr') [F., from L. *capillāris*, see foll.], *n.* An infusion of maiden-hair syrup flavoured with orange-flower water.

capillary (kȧ pil' ȧ ri, kăp' il ȧ ri) [L. *capillāris*, relating to hair (*capillus*, hair)], *a.* Resembling a hair in tenuity; having a minute bore; pertaining to the hair, pertaining to the capillary vessels or capillary attraction, etc. *n.* (*Physiol.*) One of the minute blood-vessels in which the arterial circulation ends and the venous begins; also called **capillary vessels. capillary attraction** or **repulsion,** *n.* The cause which determines the ascent or descent of a fluid in a hair-like tube. **capillarity** (-lăr' i ti), *n.* **capillose,** (kăp' i lōs), *a.* Hairy. *n.* (*Min.*) Sulphide of nickel, capillary pyrites.

capital (1) (kăp' i tȧl) [prob. from O.North.F. *capitel* (F. *chapiteau*), late L. *capitellum*, dim. of L. *caput -itis*, head], *n.* The head of a pillar.

capital (2) (kăp' i tȧl) [F., from L. *capitālis*, *capitāle*, relating to the head, chief (*caput -itis*, head)], *a.* Principal, chief, most important; excellent, first-rate; involving or affecting the head or the life; punishable by death; fatal, injurious to life; initial (of letters), hence, of a larger size and a shape distinguishing chief letters; relating to the main fund or stock of a corporation or business firm; a capital letter; a head city or town; a metropolis; wealth appropriated to reproductive employment; a principal or fund employed in earning interest or profits. **capital goods,** *n.pl.* Raw materials and tools used in the production of consumers' goods. **capital levy,** *n.* (*Fin.*) A levy on capital. **capital murder,** *n.* (*Law*) A murder involving the death penalty. The crime must have been committed while resisting arrest, while in the actual committing of a theft, from being a second murder, or from causing the death of a police or prison officer. **capital punishment,** *n.* The death penalty. **capital sentence,** *n.* A sentence of death. **capital ship,** *n.* A warship of the most powerful kind. **fixed capital,** *n.* Buildings, machinery, tools, etc., used in industry. **floating** or **circulating capital,** *n.* Raw material, money, goods, etc. **to make capital out of:** To make profit from, turn to one's advantage. **capitalism**

(kăp′ it ål izm), *n.* The economic system under which individuals employ capital and employees to produce wealth. **capitalist** (kăp′ it ål ist, *incorr.* kȧ pit′ å list), *n.* One who possesses capital. **capitalistic** (-lis′ tik), *a.* **capitalize** (kăp′ it ål īz), *v.t.* To convert into capital; to use as capital; to calculate or realize the present value of periodical payments; to write or print with a capital letter; to use to one's advantage. **capitalization** (-li zā′ shůn), *n.* **capitally,** *adv.* Excellently.

capitan (ka pit tan′, kăp′ i tăn) [Sp., captain], *n.* The chief admiral of a Turkish fleet. **capitan pacha,** *n.* **capitan galley,** *n.* **capitano** (ka pi ta′ nō) [It.], *n.*

capitate (kăp′ i tåt), **capitated** (kăp′ i tā tėd) [L. *capitātus*, headed (*caput*, head)], *a.* (*Nat. Hist.*) Having a head; (*Bot.*) having the inflorescence in a head-like cluster.

capitation (kăp i tā′ shůn) [F., from late L. *capitātio -ōnem* (*caput -itis, head*)], *n.* *Enumeration by the head; a tax, fee, or grant per head. **capitation grant,** *n.* A subsidy calculated on the number of persons passing an examination or fulfilling specified conditions.

***capite** (kăp′ i tē) [L., abl. of *caput*, head], *n.* (*Law*) An old tenure by which land was held directly from the Crown.

Capitol (kăp′ i tol) [L. *Capitōlium*], *n.* The great national temple of ancient Rome, dedicated to Jupiter; (*U.S.A.*) the building in which Congress meets; (*Am.*) the senate-house of a state. **Capitolian** (kăp i tō′ li ån), **Capitoline** (kȧ pit′ ȯ līn), *a.* Of or pertaining to the Roman Capitol. **Capitoline games,** *n.pl.* Games in honour of Capitoline Jove.

capitular (kȧ pit′ ū lår) [med. L. *capitulāris*, relating to a *capitulum*, or chapter], *a.* Of or pertaining to an ecclesiastical chapter; (*Bot.*) growing in small heads. *n.* A member of a chapter; a statute passed by a chapter. **capitularly,** *adv.* In the form of an ecclesiastical chapter.

capitulary (kȧ pit′ ū lår i) [med. L. *capitulārium*, a book of decrees from *capitulāre*, a writing divided into chapters, *capitulāris*], *n.* A collection of ordinances, esp. those of the Frankish kings.

capitulate (kȧ pit′ ū lāt) [med. L. *capitulāre*, to divide into chapters, to propose terms], *v.i.* *To treat, to bargain; to stipulate; to make terms of surrender, to surrender on stipulated terms. *v.t.* To surrender on stipulated terms. **capitulation** (-lā′ shůn), *n.* The act of capitulating; the document containing the terms of surrender; (*pl.*) the articles under which foreigners in dependencies of Turkey and other states were formerly granted extraterritorial rights.

capitulum (kȧ pit′ ū lům) [L., dim. of *caput*, head], *n.* (*pl.* **-la**) A small head; (*Bot.*) a close cluster or head of sessile flowers; (*Anat.*) a head-shaped part; (*Zool.*) the body of a barnacle or cirriped which is carried on a peduncle.

***caple, capul** (kāpl) [ult. from L. *caballus*, horse (cp. Icel. *kapall*, Ir. and Gael. *capall*)], *n.* (*poet.*) A horse.

capnomancy (kăp′ nȯ măn si) [Gr. *kapnos*, smoke, -MANCY], *n.* Divination by smoke.

capon (kā′ pȯn) [A.-S. *capun*, L. *capo -ōnem*], *n.* A castrated cock; (*slang*) a eunuch. *v.t.* To caponize. **caponize,** *v.t.* To castrate.

caponiere (kăp ȯ nēr′) [F. *caponnière*, Sp. *caponera*- orig. a capon-coop, see prec.], *n.* A covered passage across the ditch of a fortified place.

caporal (kăp′ ȯ rål) [F., a corporal], *n.* A coarse kind of French tobacco.

capot (kȧ pot′) [F.], *n.* The winning of all the tricks at piquet by one player. *v.t.* To win all the tricks from.

capote (kȧ pōt′) [F., dim. of CAPE], *n.* A long shaggy overcoat; a long mantle for women, usually with a hood.

capric (kăp′ rik) [L. *caper -pri*, a goat], *a.* Pertaining to a goat; (*Chem.*) smelling of the goat. **capric acid,** *n.* An acid, having a slight goat-like smell, contained in butter, coco-nut oil, and other compounds.

capriccio (ka prē′ chō, -chi ō) [It., from *capro*, a goat], *n.* *A frisky movement, a prank, a caper; *a caprice; (*Mus.*) a lively composition more or less free in form. **capriccioso** (ka prē chō′ sō, -chi ō′ sō), *adv.* (*Mus.*) In a free, fantastic style.

caprice (kȧ prēs′) [F., from prec.], *n.* A sudden impulsive change of opinion or humour; a whim, a freak; disposition to this kind of behaviour; (*Mus., painting, etc.*) a freakish or playful work of art. **capricious** (kȧ prish′ ůs), *a.* Influenced by caprice; whimsical, uncertain, fickle, given to unexpected and incalculable changes. **capriciously,** *adv.* **capriciousness,** *n.*

capricorn (kăp′ ri kôrn) [L. *capricornus*, goat-horned (*caper*, goat, *cornu*, a horn)], *n.* The zodiacal constellation of the Goat; the tenth sign of the zodiac. **Tropic of Capricorn** [TROPIC (1)].

caprification (kăp ri fi kā′ shůn) [L. *caprificātio -nem*, from *caprificāre*, to ripen figs, *caprifīcus*, the wild fig (*caper*, goat, *fīcus*, fig)], *n.* The practice of suspending branches of the wild fig on the cultivated fig, that the fruit of the latter may be ripened by the puncture of insects produced on the former; (*improperly*) artificial fertilization. **capriform** (kăp′ ri fôrm), *a.* Having the form of a goat. **caprine,** *a.* Like a goat.

capriole (kăp′ ri ōl) [F. *capriole* (now *cabriole*), a caper, It. *capriola* (dim. of *capra*, she-goat)], *n.* A leap made by a horse without advancing. *v.i.* To leap or caper without advancing.

caproic (kȧ prō′ ik) [*caper*, a goat, -IC (specially differentiated from CAPRIC)], *a.* Pertaining to a goat. **caproic acid,** *n.* An acid contained, like capric and butyric acids, in butter, etc.

capsicum (kăp′ si kům) [prob. formed irregularly from L. *capsa*, a case], *n.* A genus of tropical plants with pungent fruit and seeds, from one species of which the chillies and cayenne pepper of commerce are obtained; the fruit, esp. the prepared fruit of *C. fastigiatum*. **capsicine** (-sīn, -sin), *n.* The active principle in capsicum pods.

capsize (kăp sīz′) [etym. unknown; perh. from Sp. *capuzar*, to sink by the head], *v.t.* To upset, to overturn. *v.i.* To be upset. *n.* An overturn. **capsizal,** *n.*

capstan (kăp′ stăn) [Prov. and F. *cabestan*, L. *capistrāre*, to fasten (*capistrum*, a halter, from *capere*, to hold)], *n.* A revolving pulley or drum, either power- or lever-driven, with a belt or cable running over it. Used to increase the force exerted by the cable or belt.

capsule (kăp′ sūl) [F., from L. *capsula*, dim. of *capsa*, a case], *n.* A metallic cover for a bottle; (*Physiol.*) an envelope or sac; (*Bot.*) a dry dehiscent seed-vessel; (*Chem.*) a shallow saucer; (*Med.*) a small envelope of gelatine containing medicine. **capsular,** *a.* ***capsulate, capsulated,** *a.* **capsuli-,** *comb. form.* **capsuliform,** *a.*

captain (kăp′ tån) [O.F. *capitain*, late L. *capitāneus*, chief, *capitānus*, a chief (L. *caput -itis*, head)], *n.* A leader, a commander; the commander of a company or troop, or of a man-of-war; the master of a merchant ship; the head of a gang, side, or team; a foreman; the chief boy in a school; (*Cornwall*) the manager of a mine; a general, a strategist, a great soldier, a veteran commander. *v.t.* To act as captain to; to lead, to head. **Captain Cookers:** (*N. Zealand colloq.*) Wild boars (descended from swine landed there by Capt. Cook). ***captain-general,** *n.* A commander-in-chief. **Captain of the Fleet,** *n.* The adjutant-general of a naval force. **captaincy,** *n.* **captainship,** *n.* **captainless,** *a.*

captation (kăp tā′ shůn) [L. *captātio -ōnem* (*captāre*, freq. of *capere*, to take, seize)], *n.* An endeavour to obtain by means of artful appeals to feeling or prejudice.

caption (kăp′ shŭn) [L. *captio -ōnem* (*capere*, to take)], *n.* *Seizure, capture; *a quibble, a fallacious argument; (*Law, esp. Sc.*) apprehension by judicial process; the heading or descriptive preamble of a legal document; (*Print.*) the wording under an illustration, the legend; the heading of a chapter, section, or newspaper article.

captious (kăp′ shŭs) [L. *captiōsus*, from prec.], *a.* Sophistical, quibbling; fault-finding, carping, cavilling; *capacious. **captiously,** *adv.* **captiousness,** *n.*

captivate (kăp′ ti vāt) [L. *captīvātus*, p.p. of *captīvāre* (*captīvus*, CAPTIVE)], *v.t.* *To take captive; (*fig.*) to fascinate, to charm. **captivating,** *a.* **captivation** (-vā′ shŭn), *n.* The act of fascinating; a fascination, a charm.

captive (kăp′ tiv) [F. *captif*, fem. *captive*, L. *captīvus* (*captus*, p.p. of *capere*, to take)], *n.* One taken prisoner, held in confinement or bondage, or fascinated. *a.* Taken prisoner; held in bondage; held in control; pertaining to captivity; captivated, fascinated. *v.t.* *To take prisoner, to enslave; to captivate. **captive balloon,** *n.* A balloon held by a rope from the ground. ***captivated,** *a.* **captivity** (kăp tiv′ i ti), *n.* **captor,** *n.* **captress,** *n.* **capture** (kăp′ chŭr), *n.* The act of seizing as a prisoner or a prize; the person or thing so taken. *v.t.* To make a capture of; to seize as a prize **capturer,** *n.*

capuche (kȧ poosh′) [F., from It. *capuccio*, a cowl (*cappa*, CAP)], *n.* A hood, esp. the long pointed hood of the Capuchins.

Capuchin (kăp′ ū chin) [It. *cappuccino*, dim. of *capuccio*, from prec.], *n.* A Franciscan friar of the reform of 1528; a hooded cloak and hood, like the habit of the Capuchins, worn by women. **capuchin monkey,** *n.* An American monkey, *Cebus capucinus.* **capuchin pigeon,** *n.* A sub-variety of the Jacobin pigeon.

capul [CAPLE].

caput (kăp′ ŭt) [L.], *n.* (*Anat., etc.*) The head, the top part; (*Bot.*) the peridium of some fungi. ***caput mortuum*** [L., lit. dead head], *n.* (*Alch.*) The residuum after distillation or sublimation; (*fig.*) worthless residuum.

capybara (kăp i ba′ rȧ) [Braz.], *n.* A South American mammal, *Hydrochærus Capybara*, the largest living rodent, allied to the guinea-pig.

car (kar) [O.North.F. *carre*, late L. *carra* (L. *carrus*, a four-wheeled vehicle mentioned by Cæsar, Bret. *karr*, cp. W. *car*, Ir. *carr*)], *n.* A motor-car; (*poet.*) a wheeled vehicle, a chariot; (*Ir.*) a jaunting-car; (*Am.*) a railway coach or wagon; the pendent carriage of an airship; a wheeled vehicle (*usu. in comb.*), as **dining-car, freight-car, jaunting-car, motor-car, sleeping-car, tram-car, tramway-car. carful,** *n.* As many people as a car will hold. **carman** (kar′ mȧn), *n.* One who drives a van or (*Ir.*) a jaunting-car; a carter, a carrier. **car-park,** *n.* A place where cars may be left for a limited period; (*Am.*) a parking-lot.

carabine, etc. [CARBINE]. **carabineer,** *n.* A soldier armed with a carbine. **The Carabineers:** The 6th Dragoon Guards.

caracal (kăr ȧ kȧl) [Turk. *qarah qalaq*, lit. black ear], *n.* The Persian lynx, *Felis caracal.*

carack [CARRACK].

caracol, -cole (kăr′ ȧ kol. -kōl) [F. *caracole*, It. *caracollo*, wheeling of a horse, Sp. *caracol*, a spiral shell, a snail (etym. doubtful; cp. Gael. *carach*, circling, winding)], *n.* A half turn or wheel made by a horse or horseman; (*Arch.*) a winding staircase. *v.i.* To perform a caracol or half turn; to caper. *v.t.* To make (a horse) caracol.

***caract** (kăr′ ăkt) [O.F. *caracte*, through L., from Gr. *charaktos*, graven, stamped, *n.* A mark; character.

carafe (kȧ raf′) [F., It., *caraffa* (cp. Sp. and Port. *garrafa*), Arab. *gharafa*, to draw water], *n.* A glass water-bottle.

carambole (kăr′ ȧm bōl) [F., from Sp. *carambola*, the red ball and a certain stroke at billiards], *n.* (*Billiards*) A cannon. *v.i.* To make a cannon.

caramel (kăr′ ȧ mel) [F., from Sp. *caramello*], *n.* Burnt sugar for colouring spirits; a kind of sweetmeat.

carapace (kăr′ ȧ pās) [F., from Sp. *carapacho*; etym. doubtful], *n.* The upper body-shell of the tortoise family; any analogous covering in the lower animals.

carat (kăr′ ȧt) [F., from It. *carato*, Arab. *qīrāt*, prob. from Gr. *keration*, fruit of the locust-tree (dim. of *keras -atos*, a horn)], *n.* A weight (about the 150th part of an oz. troy, or 3⅙ grains, standardized as the International Carat of 0·200 grammes) used for precious stones; a proportional measure of one 24th part, used to describe the fineness of gold: thus 22-carat gold has two parts, and 9-carat gold fifteen parts, of alloy.

caravan (kăr′ ȧ văn) [F. *caravane*, or directly from Pers. *karwān*], *n.* A company of merchants or pilgrims, travelling together (esp. in desert regions) for mutual security; a travelling house, a carriage for living in drawn by horse or motor-car; a showman's covered wagon; (*Am.*) a trailer. **caravaneer** (kăr ȧ vȧ nēr′), *n.* The leader of an Eastern caravan. **caravaning,** *n.* **caravaner,** *n.*

caravanserai, -sera, -sary (kăr ȧ văn′ sėr ī, -sėr a, -sȧ ri) [Pers. *karwān, -sarāy*], *n.* An Oriental inn with a large courtyard for the accommodation of caravans; (*fig.*) a large hotel.

caravel (kăr′ ȧ vel), **carvel** (kăr′ vėl) [F. *caravelle*, It. *caravella*, late L. *carabus*, Gr. *karabos*], *n.* A name applied at different times to various kinds of ships; *e.g.* a swift Spanish or Portuguese merchant vessel; a Turkish frigate.

caraway (kăr′ ȧ wā) [Arab. *karawiyā* (perh. through med. L. *carui*)], *n.* A European umbelliferous plant, *Carum carui.* **caraway-seeds,** *n.pl.* The small dried fruit of this.

carb-, carbo- [CARBON], *comb. forms.* (*Chem.*) Of, with, containing, or pertaining to carbon; *e.g.* **carbazotic** (kar bȧ zot′ ik) [AZOTIC], *a.* Composed of carbon and azote.

carbide (kar′ bīd), *n.* A compound of carbon with a metal, esp. **calcium carbide,** used for generating acetylene.

carbine (kar′ bīn), **carabine** (kăr′ ȧ bin) [F. *carabin* (now *carabine*); perh. from O.F. *calabrin*, late L. *Calabrīnus*, a Calabrian; or from late L. *chadabula*, a kind of ballista, Gr. *katabolē* (*kataballein*, to throw down with missiles)], *n.* A short rifle used by cavalry. **carbineer** (kar bi nēr′), **carabinier** (kăr ȧ bi nēr′), *n.*

carbo-cyclic, *a.* (*Chem.*) Denoting a compound which includes a closed ring of carbon atoms.

carbohydrate (kar bō hī′ drāt), *n.* An organic compound of carbon, hydrogen and oxygen. Usually there are two atoms of hydrogen to every one of oxygen as in starch, sugar, glucose, etc.

carbolic (kar bol′ ik) [CARB-, -OL (cp. ALCOHOL), -IC], *a.* Derived from coal or coal-tar. **carbolic acid,** *n.* An antiseptic and disinfectant acid. **carbolize** (kar′ bȯ līz), *v.t.* To impregnate with carbolic acid.

carbon (kar′ bȯn) [F. *carbone*, L. *carbo -ōnem*, a coal], *n.* A non-metallic element found in nearly all organic substances, in carbonic acid gas, and the carbonates, and uncombined in diamond, graphite, and charcoal; (*Elec.*) a pencil of fine charcoal used in arc-lamps. **carbon-copy,** *n.* A typewritten duplicate. **carbon dioxide,** *n.* (*Chem.*) A gaseous combination of one atom of carbon with two of oxygen, a normal constituent of the atmosphere and of expired breath. **carbon monoxide,** *n.* (*Chem.*) A gas containing one atom of oxygen for each atom of carbon; it is poisonous and a constituent of domestic gas and motor-car exhaust gases. **carbon-paper,** *n.* A dark-coated paper for taking impressions of writing, drawing, etc. **car-**

bon-point, *n.* (*Elec.*) A pencil of charcoal used in pairs in arc-lamps. **carbon-printing** or **process,** *n.* A permanent black and white photographic process, the shades of which are produced by lamp-black. **carbonaceous** (kar bŏ nā′ shŭs), *a.* Like coal or charcoal; (*Chem.*) containing carbon; (*Geol.*) abounding in or of the nature of coal. **carbonate** (kar′ bŏ nāt), *n.* (*Chem.*) A salt of carbonic acid. *v.t.* (kar′ bŏ nāt) To impregnate with carbonic acid; to aerate (water, etc.); (*Chem.*) to form into a carbonate. **carbonic** (kar bon′ ik), *a.* (*Chem.*) Pertaining to carbon. **carbonic acid,** *n.* A weak acid; the compound formed by carbon dioxide and water. **carbonic-acid gas,** *n.* Carbon dioxide, the gas formed by the combustion or decay of vegetable matter and given out in animal respiration. **carboniferous** (-nif′ ėr ŭs), *a.* Producing coal; (*Geol.*) applied to the strata between the Old Red Sandstone (below) and the Permian (above). **Carboniferous age** or **period,** *n.* The geological epoch during which these strata were deposited. **Carboniferous formation** or **system,** *n.* **Carboniferous strata,** *n.pl.* **carbonize** (kar′ bŏ nīz), *v.t.* To convert into carbon by the action of fire or acids; to cover with carbon-paper, charcoal, lamp-black, or the like. **carbonization** (-nī zā′ shŭn), *n.*

***carbonado** (kar bŏ nā′ dō) [Sp. *carbonada*], *n.* Flesh, fish, or fowl scored across, and grilled on the coals. *v.t.* To score and broil on the coals; (*fig.*) to hack, to slash.

Carbonari (kar bō na′ rē) [It., charcoal burners], *n.pl.* Members of a secret republican society in Italy and France in the early part of the 19th cent.; hence, republican revolutionists. **carbonarism,** *n.*

carbonate, carbonic [CARBON].

carbora (kar′ bŏ rå) [Austral. abor.], *n.* The koala.

carborundum (kar bō rŭn′ dum) [CARBO-, CORUNDUM], *n.* Protected trade name of a silicon carbide used for grinding-wheels, etc.

carboy (kar′ boi) [Pers. *qarābah*], *n.* A large globular bottle of green or blue glass, protected with wickerwork, used for holding corrosive liquids.

carbuncle (kar′ bŭng kėl) [M.E. *charbucle, carbuncle,* O.F. *charboucle* (O.North.F. *carbuncle*), L. *carbunculus,* a small coal, a gem], *n.* A precious stone of a red or fiery colour; a garnet cut in a concave cabochon; (*Her.*) a carbuncle borne as a charge; a hard, painful boil without a core, an anthrax; a pimple caused by intemperance. **carbuncled,** *a.* **carbuncular** (kar bŭng′ kū lȧr), *a.*

carburet (kar bū ret′), *n.* (*Chem.*) The compound formed by the combination of carbon with another element. *v.t.* To combine (another element) with carbon. **carburetted,** *a.* **carburize,** *v.t.* (*Chem.*) To carburet; (*Min.*) to impart carbon to (wrought iron). **carburization,** *n.* **carburettor** (kar′ bū ret ŏr), *n.* An apparatus designed to vaporize a liquid and to mix it intimately with air in proportions to ensure ready ignition and complete combustion.

carcajou (kar′ kȧ zhoo) [N.Am.F. (prob. Indian)], *n.* (*Zool.*) The glutton or wolverine.

carcake (kar′ kāk) [Sc., CARE, A.-S. *caru,* grief], *n.* A cake eaten on Shrove Tuesday in parts of Scotland.

***carcanet** (kar′ kȧ net) [*carcan,* an iron collar used for punishment, F. *carcan,* late L. *carcannum,* from Teut. (*cp.* O.H.G. *querca,* the throat)], *n.* A jewelled necklet or collar.

carcass, carcase (kar′ kȧs) [A.-F. *carcois,* med. L. *carcosium,* afterwards modified by M.F. *carquasse* (F. *carcasse*), It. *carcassa,* a shell or bomb (etym. doubtful)], *n.* The trunk of a slaughtered beast without the head and offal; the dead body of a beast; the human body dead or alive (only in contempt or ridicule); the framework of a building, ship, etc.; (*fig.*) a mere body, mere shell, or husk; *(*Mil.*) a perforated shell filled with combustibles. **carcass meat,** *n.* Raw meat as sold in a butcher's shop.

carcinology (kar si nol′ ŏ ji) [Gr. *karkinos,* a crab], *n.* That part of zoology which deals with the crustacea. **carcinological** (-loj′ ik ȧl), *a.* **carcinologist,** *n.*

carcinoma (kar si nō′ mȧ) [L., from Gr. *karkinōma,* cancer (*karkinos,* a crab)], *n.* (*pl.* **-mata**) (*Path.*) Cancer. **carcinomatous,** *a.* **carcinosis** (-nōs′ is) [-OSIS], *n.* The growth and development of cancer; cancerous disease.

card (1) (kard) [F. *carte,* It. *carta,* late L. *carta,* L. *charta,* Gr. *chartē, chartēs,* a leaf of papyrus], *n.* One of a pack of oblong pieces of pasteboard, marked with pips and pictures, used in playing games of chance or skill; a flat, rectangular piece of stiff pasteboard for writing or drawing on, or the like; a visiting-card, a ticket of admission, an invitation; a programme, a menu, a list of events at races, regattas, etc., and various other senses denoted by a prefixed substantive; *a chart, *the piece of card on which the points are marked in the mariner's compass; (*pl.*) a game or games with cards; card-playing; (*slang*) a character, an eccentric. **house of cards:** A structure built of cards; hence, any scheme or enterprise of an insecure kind. **on the cards:** Possible; not improbable. **to play one's cards well:** (*fig.*) To be a good strategist. **to show one's cards:** To reveal one's plan. **to speak by the card:** To speak with exactness. **to throw up the cards:** To give up the game. **cardboard,** *n.* Fine pasteboard for making light boxes and other articles, (*Am.*) pasteboard. **card-case,** *n.* A case to hold visiting-cards. **card catalogue, card index,** *n.* A catalogue or index in which each item is entered on a separate card. **card-rack,** *n.* A rack for visitors' cards. **card-sharper,** *n.* One who swindles by means of card games or tricks with cards. **card-table,** *n.* A table to play cards on. **card vote,** *n.* A ballot where the vote of each delegate counts for the number of his constituents. **visiting card,** *n.* A small card bearing the owner's name, etc.

card (2) (kard) [F. *carde,* a teazel, a wool-card, It. *carda,* late L. *cardus,* L. *carduus,* a thistle], *n.* An iron toothed instrument for combing wool or flax. *v.t.* To comb (wool, flax, or hemp) with a card; to raise a nap; to tear the flesh with a card by way of punishment or torture. **card-thistle,** *n.* The teazel. **carder,** *n.* One who cards wool; a species of wild bee, *Bombus muscorum.* **carding,** *a.* **carding-engine** or **-machine,** *n.* A machine for combing out and cleaning wool, cotton, etc.

cardamine (kȧr dăm′ i nē, kar′ dȧ mīn) [Gr. *kardaminē*], *n.* A genus of cruciferous plants comprising the cuckoo-flower or lady-smock.

cardamom (kar′ dȧ mŏm) [L. *cardamōmum,* Gr. *kardamōmon* (*kardamon,* cress, *amōmon,* an Indian spice-plant)], *n.* A spice obtained from the seed capsules of various species of Amomum.

cardiac (kar′ di ăk) [F. *cardiaque,* L. *cardiacus,* Gr. *kardiakos* (*kardia,* the heart)], *a.* Of or pertaining to the heart; heart-shaped; (*Anat.*) of or pertaining to the upper orifice of the stomach; cordial, strengthening. *n.* A cordial or stimulant for the heart. ***cardiac passion,** *n.* Heartburn. ***cardiacal,** *a.* **cardial,** *a.* **cardialgy** (-ăl′ ji), **-algia** (-ăl′ ji ȧ) [Gr. *algia, algos,* pain], *n.* An affection of the heart; heartburn. **cardialgic,** *a.*

cardigan (kar′ di gȧn) [7th Earl of *Cardigan*], *n.* An over-waistcoat of knitted wool.

cardinal (kar′ di nȧl) [F., from L. *cardinālis* (*cardo -inis,* a hinge)], *a.* Fundamental, chief, principal; of the colour of a cardinal's cassock, deep scarlet; (*Zool.*) pertaining to the hinge of a bivalve. *n.* One of the ecclesiastical princes of the Roman Church who elect a new Pope, usu. from among their own number; orig. one in charge of a cardinal church at Rome; a short cloak (orig. of scarlet) for women; a cardinal-bird; (*slang*) mulled red wine. **cardinal-bird,** *n.* A North American red-plumaged song-bird, *Cardinalis Virginianus.* **cardinal bishop,** *n.* The highest rank of cardinal. **cardinal church,** *n.* (*Hist.*) The name given in early ages to the principal or parish churches of Rome. **cardinal deacon,** *n.* The third rank of cardinal. **cardinal-flower,** *n.* The scarlet lobelia, *Lobelia cardinalis.* **cardinal numbers,** *n.pl.* The simple numbers 1, 2, 3, etc., as distinguished from 1st, 2nd, 3rd, etc. **cardinal points,** *n.pl.* The four points of the compass: north, south, east, and west. **cardinal priest,** *n.* The second rank of cardinal. **cardinal signs,** *n.pl.* Aries, Libra, Cancer, Capricorn; the two solstitial and the two equinoctial points of the ecliptic. **cardinal's hat,** *n.* The official emblem of the cardinalate, a flat red hat with fifteen tassels on each side. **cardinal virtues,** *n.pl.* (*Phil.*) Prudence, Temperance, Justice, and Fortitude; (*Theol.*) Faith, Hope, and Charity. **cardinalate, cardinalship,** *n.* The office or dignity of a cardinal. **cardinally,** *adv.* Fundamentally; *(*punningly*) carnally.

cardio- (kar′ di ō), *comb. form.* Pertaining to the heart.

cardiograph (kar′ di ō grăf), *n.* An instrument for registering the motions of the heart. **cardiography,** *n.* The use of this; a description of the heart.

cardioid (kar′ di oid) [Gr. *kardioeides* (*kardia,* heart, -OID)], *n.* (*Math.*) A heart-shaped curve.

cardiology (kar di ol′ ō ji), *n.* Knowledge of the heart; a treatise on the heart.

carditis (kar dī′ tis), *n.* (*Path.*) Inflammation of the heart.

cardoon (kår doon′) [F. *cardon* (It. *cardone,* or Sp. *cardon*), late L. *cardus,* L. *carduus,* thistle], *n.* A kitchen-garden plant, *Cynara cardunculus,* allied to the artichoke.

care (kâr) [A.-S. *caru* (cp. O.S. and Goth. *kara,* sorrow, O.H.G. *charōn,* to lament), from Teut. *karā-*], *n.* *Sorrow, grief, trouble; solicitude, anxiety, concern; a cause of these; caution, serious attention, heed; oversight, protection; object of regard or solicitude. *v.i.* To be anxious or solicitous; to be concerned about; to provide (for), attend (upon); to have affection, respect, or liking (for); to be desirous, willing, or inclined (to). **care-crazed,** *a.* Crazed with anxiety. **care-laden, care-worn,** *a.* **care-taker,** *n.* A person in charge of an unlet house or chambers, or other building, (*Am.*) a janitor. **care-tuned,** *a.* Tuned or influenced by care.

careen (kȧ rēn′) [F. *cariner* (now *caréner*), ult. from L. *carīna,* a keel], *v.t.* (*Naut.*) To turn (a ship) on one side in order to clean or caulk her. *v.i.* To heel over under press of sail. **careenage** (-nȧj), *n.* The act of, a place for, or the expense of careening.

career (kȧ rēr′) [F. *carière,* late L. *carrāria via,* a road for cars (L. *carrus,* CAR)], *n.* *A race-course; *the lists at a tournament; *a charge, an encounter; a running, a swift course; course or progress through life; the progress and development of a nation, party, etc.; business, professional, or artistic activity, etc. *v.i.* To move in a swift, headlong course; to gallop at full speed. **careerist,** *n.* One who makes personal advancement his main objective.

careful (kâr′ fụl) [CARE, -FUL], *a.* *Full of care, sorrowful, solicitous; watchful, cautious, circumspect; provident, painstaking, attentive, exact; done with care. **carefully,** *adv.* **carefulness,** *n.*

careless (kâr′ lės), *a.* Free from care, without anxiety, unconcerned; heedless, thoughtless, inaccurate; inattentive, negligent (of); negligently done; *neglected. **carelessly,** *adv.* **carelessness,** *n.*

caress (kȧ res′) [F. *caresse,* It. *carezza,* late L. *cāritia* (L. *carus,* dear)], *n.* An embrace, a kiss; an act of endearment. *v.t.* To fondle, to stroke affectionately; (*fig.*) to pet, to court, to flatter. **caressing,** *a.* **caressingly,** *adv.*

caret (kărėt) [L., is wanting (*carēre,* to need)], *n.* A mark (‸) used to show that something, which may be read above or in the margin, has been left out.

carex (kâr′ ėks) [L.], *n.* (*pl.* **carices,** kâr i sēz) (*Bot.*) A genus of grass-like plants of the sedge family.

cargo (kar′ gō) [Sp., a load, a loading, med. L. *carricum,* late L. *carricāre,* to load (*carrus,* CAR)], *n.* The freight of a ship or aircraft; such a load.

Carib (kăr′ ib) [Sp. *caribe* (see CANNIBAL)], *n.* One of the aboriginal race in the southern islands of the West Indies.

caribou, -boo (kăr i boo′) [French-Canadian, prob. from native Indian], *n.* The North American reindeer.

caricature, *caricatura (kăr′ i kȧ tūr, -tūr′ a) [It. *caricatura* (assim. to F. *caricature*), from *caricare,* late L. *carricāre* (see CARGO)], *n.* A representation of a person or thing exaggerating characteristic traits in a ludicrous way; a burlesque, a parody. *v.t.* To represent in this way; to burlesque. **caricaturable** (-tūr′ ȧbl), *a.* **caricatural,** *a.* **caricaturist** (-tūr′ ist), *n.*

caries (kâr′ i ēz) [L.], *n.* (*Path.*) Decay of the bones or teeth; (*Bot.*) decay of vegetable tissue. **carious,** *a.*

carillon (kȧ ril′ yǫn) [F., from med. L. *quadrilo -ōnem,* a quaternion (of four bells)], *n.* A set of bells so arranged as to be played by the hand or by machinery; an air played on such bells; a musical instrument (or part of one) to imitate such bells.

carina (kȧ rī′ nȧ) [L., a keel], *n.* (*Zool. and Bot.*) A ridge-like structure. **carinal,** *a.* **carinate, carinated,** *a.* **carino-,** *comb. form, e.g.* **carino-lateral** [LATERAL], *a.* Situated close to the carina on each side.

cariole [CARRIOLE].

***cark** (kark) [O.North.F. *carkier* (cp. O.F. *chargier*), late L. *carcāre, carricāre* (see CARGO)], *v.t.* To burden, to harass, to worry. *v.i.* To be anxious, to fret, to worry. *n.* Care, distress, anxiety. **carking,** *a.* Burdening, distressing, wearisome.

carl, carle (karl) [Icel. *karl* (cp. A.-S. *hūscarl* and CHURL)], *n.* (*Sc.*) A countryman; a man of low birth; a strong, sturdy fellow. **carline** (1) (kar′ lin) [Icel. *kerling,* fem. of prec.], *n.* (*Sc.*) An old woman, a witch.

carline (2) (kar′ lin) [F., from late L. *Carlīna, Carolīna,* fem. of *Carolīnus,* Charlemagne], *n.* A genus of plants allied to the thistle, commonest species *Carlina vulgaris.*

Carlisle system (kar līl′) [county town of Cumberland], *n.* A system of municipal ownership and management of public-houses.

Carlism (kar′ lizm) [*Carlos,* -ISM], *n.* Adherence to Don Carlos (1788–1855), 2nd son of Charles IV, and his heirs as the legitimate sovereigns of Spain. **Carlist,** *n.* and *a.*

carlock (kar′ lǫk) [Rus. *karluku*], *n.* Isinglass from the bladder of the sturgeon.

Carlovingian (kar lō vin′ ji ȧn), **Carolingian** (kar ō lin′ ji ȧn) [F. *Carlovingien*], *a.* Of or belonging to the dynasty of French kings founded by Charlemagne. *n.* A member of this dynasty.

Carlylese (kar lī lēz′), *n.* The irregular, vehement, vividly metaphorical style and phraseology of Thomas Carlyle.

carmagnole (kar ma nyōl′) [F., an upper garment worn during the Revolution, said to be named from *Carmagnola* in Piedmont], *n.* A lively song and dance popular among the French revolutionists of 1793; a French revolutionist; the bombastic style of the writings of the first French Revolution.

Carmelite (kar′ mė līt), *n.* One of an order of mendicant friars, founded in the 12th cent. on Mount Carmel; called also the *White Friars;* a nun of this order. *a.* Belonging or pertaining to this order; a fine woollen stuff, usually grey.

carminative (kar′ min ȧ tiv) [L. *carminātus,* p.p. of *carmināre,* to card wool], *a.* Expelling flatulence. *n.* A medicine that expels flatulence.

carmine (kar′ mĭn) [F. or Sp. *carmin* (med. L. *carmīnus, carmesīnus*), Sp. *carmesí*, Arab. *quirmazī*, CRIMSON], *n.* A beautiful red or crimson pigment obtained from cochineal. *a.* Coloured like this.

carnage (kar′ nàj) [F., from It. *carnaggio*, late L. *carnāticum* (L. *caro carnis*, flesh)], *n.* *Dead bodies slain in battle; butchery, slaughter, esp. of men.

carnal (kar′ nàl) [L. *carnālis* (*caro carnis*, flesh)], *a.* *Bodily; fleshly, sensual; sexual, unregenerate, opp. to spiritual; temporal, secular; *murderous. **carnal knowledge,** *n.* Sexual intercourse. **carnal-minded,** *a.* Worldly-minded. **carnal-mindedness, carnalism,** *n.* Sensualism. **carnalist,** *n.* **carnality** (kàr năl′ i ti), *n.* The state of being carnal. **carnalize** (kar′ nà līz), *v.t.* To sensualize; to materialize. **carneous** (kar′ nė ùs), **carnose** (kàr nōs′), ***carnous** (kar′ nùs), *a.* Resembling flesh; fleshy.

carnallite (kar′ nàl līt) [from the mineralogist Von *Carnall*], *n.* (*Min.*) A white or reddish hydrous chloride of magnesium and potassium found in Prussian and Persian salt-mines.

carnassial (kar năs′ i àl), *n.* (*Zool.*) In the Carnivora a large tooth adapted for tearing flesh.

carnation (1) (kàr nā′ shùn) [F., from L. *carnātio -ōnem* (*caro*, see CARNAL)], *n.* A light rose pink; (*Painting*) a flesh tint; a part of a painting representing human flesh. *a.* Of this colour. **carnationed,** *a.*

carnation (2) (kàr nā′ shùn) [perh. a corr. of INCARNATION or CORONATION], *n.* The cultivated clove-pink, *Dianthus caryophyllus.*

carnauba (ka na oo′ bà) [Braz.], *n.* A Brazilian palm, *Copernicia*; its yellow wax.

carnelian [CORNELIAN].

carnifex (kar′ ni feks), *n.* An executioner.

carnify (kar′ ni fī), *v.t.* To convert to flesh; (*Path.*) to convert (bone or tissue) into fleshy substance. *v.i.* To alter in this way. **carnification,** *n.*

carnival (kar′ ni vàl) [It. *carnevale*, the eve of Ash Wednesday, late L. *carnelevāmen* (*caro carnem*, flesh, *levāre*, to remove), altered into It. *carne vale* (flesh, farewell)], *n.* Shrovetide; the season immediately before Lent, in many Roman Catholic countries devoted to pageantry and riotous amusement; riotous amusement, revelry; (*Am.*) a fun-fair.

carnivora (kàr niv′ ò rà) [L. *carnivorus*, neut. *-um*, neut. pl. *-a* (*caro carnis*, flesh, -VOROUS)], *n.pl.* (*Zool.*) A large order of mammals subsisting on flesh. **carnivore** (kar′ ni vôr), *n.* A carnivorous animal or plant. **carnivorous** (kar niv′ ò rùs), *a.* Feeding on flesh; (*Bot.*) applied to insectivorous plants.

carnoso- (kar nō′ zō), *comb. form.* (*Physiol.*) pertaining to flesh, fleshy.

carnotite (kar′ nō tīt) [etym. unknown], *n.* (*Metal.*) A vanadate of uranium and potassium, noted as an important source of radium.

carny, carney (kar′ ni) [dial. and colloq.; etym. unknown], *v.i.* To act in a wheedling manner. *v.t.* To wheedle, coax.

carob (kăr′ òb) [F. *carobe*, Arab. *kharrūb*, bean-pods], *n.* The Mediterranean locust-tree, *Ceratonia siliqua*, or its fruit.

***caroche** (kà rōsh′) [F. *carroche*, It. *carroccia*, from *carro* (L. *carrus*, CAR)], *n.* A coach; a dignified kind of carriage.

carol (kăr′ òl) [O.F. *carole*, prob. from L. *choraula*, a dance, L. and Gr. *choraulēs*, a flute-player (Gr. *choros*, dance, *aulos*, a flute)], *n.* *A ring-dance; *a song, usu. with dancing; a joyous hymn, esp. in honour of the Nativity; joyous warbling of birds. *v.i.* (*past & p.p.* **carolled**) To sing carols; to warble. *v.t.* To celebrate in songs. **caroller,** *n.*

Caroline (kăr′ ò līn) [CAROLUS], *a.* Pertaining to Charlemagne, or to the reigns of Charles I and II of England. **Carolingian** [CARLOVINGIAN].

carolus (kăr′ ò lùs) [L., Charles], *n.* A gold coin of Charles I, orig. worth 20s., afterwards 23s.

carom [CANNON (2)].

caromel [CARAMEL].

carotid (kà rot′ id) [G. *karōtides*, the two neck-arteries (*karoein*, to stupefy, from *karos*, sleep, torpor)], *a.* (*Physiol.*) Of or related to either of the arteries (one on each side of the neck) supplying blood to the head. *n.* A carotid artery.

carouse (kà rouz′) [G. *gar aus*, completely (referring to emptying a bumper)], *n.* *A bumper; a toast; a carousal. *v.i.* To drink a bumper or toast; to drink freely. **v.t.* To drink, to quaff. **carousal,** *n.* A drinking bout. **carouser,** *n.* **carousingly,** *adv.* In a carousing manner.

carp (1) (karp) [Icel. *karpa*, to boast (confused with L. *carpere*, to pluck at, to slander)], *v.i.* To talk querulously; to find fault, to cavil. **carping,** *a.* **carpingly,** *adv.*

carp (2) (karp) [O.F. *carpe*, late L. *carpa*, from Teut. (cp. Dut. *karper*, O.H.G. *charpo*, G. *karpfen*)], *n.* A freshwater fish of the genus *Cyprinus*, esp. *C. cyprio*, the common carp, a pond-fish.

-carp [Gr. *karpos*, fruit], *suf.* (*Bot.*) The fruit or seed-vessel; *e.g. endocarp, pericarp.*

carpal [CARPUS].

carpel (kar′ pėl) [cp. F. *carpelle*, mod. dim. of Gr. *karpos*, fruit], *n.* One of the modified leaves composing a pistil; a simple pistil or seed-vessel, or one of the parts forming a compound one. **carpellary,** *a.*

carpenter (kar′ pėn tėr) [O.North.F. *carpentier* (F. *charpentier*), late L. *carpentārius*, from *carpentāre*, to work in timber (*carpentum*, a wagon, from Celt., cp. O.Ir. *carpat*, O.Bret. *cerpit*)], *n.* An artificer who prepares and fixes the wood-work of houses, ships, etc.; a wood-worker; (*Am.*) a joiner. *v.i.* To do carpenter's work. *v.t.* To make by carpentry. **carpenter-ant, -bee, -bird, -moth,** *n.* Insects and birds that bore into wood. **carpenter** or **-er's scene,** *n.* (*Theat.*) A front scene played whilst more elaborate scenery is being arranged at the back of the stage; a painted background behind this screening the stage-carpenters. **carpentry,** *n.* The trade of a carpenter; carpenter's work, esp. the kind of wood-work prepared at the carpenter's bench.

carpet (kar′ pėt [O.F. *carpite*, late L. *carpita*, *carpeta*, a thick cloth, from L. *carpere*, to pluck (cp. F. *charpie*, late L. *carpia*, lint, made by plucking rags)], *n.* A woollen or other thick fabric, usually with a pattern, for covering floors and stairs. *v.t.* To cover with or as with a carpet; (*colloq.*) to call over the coals; to reprimand. **on the carpet:** Under consideration; (*colloq.*) being reprimanded. **carpet-bag,** *n.* A travelling-bag orig. made with sides of carpet. **carpet-bagger,** *n.* (*Am.*) An adventurer (esp. political). **carpet-baggery,** *n.* **carpet-beater,** *n.* A racket-shaped cane utensil for beating carpets. **carpet-bedding,** *n.* (*Gardening*) The formal arrangement of dwarf foliage plants. **carpet-dance,** *n.* An informal dancing-party. **carpet-knight,** *n.* One who has seen no service; (*fig.*) a stay-at-home soldier. ***carpet-monger,** *n.* A carpet-knight. **carpet-slippers,** *n.pl.* Comfortable slippers made of tapestry. **carpet-snake,** *n.* An Australian snake, *Morelia variegata.* **carpet-rod,** *n.* A rod for holding down stair-carpet. **carpet-sweeper,** *n.* An apparatus equipped with revolving brushes and dustpans, used for sweeping carpets. **carpet-tack,** *n.* A nail for fastening down a carpet. **carpetless,** *a.* **carpeting,** *n.* The action of covering as with carpet; the stuff of which carpets are made; (*colloq.*) a dressing-down.

carphology (kàr fol′ ò ji) [Gr. *karphologia* (*karphos*, twig, *legein*, to pluck)], *n.* (*Med.*) Delirious plucking of the bed-clothes in fever.

carpo- (1) [Gr. *karpos*, the wrist], *comb. form.* (*Anat.*) Pertaining to the wrist. **carpo-metacarpal** [METACARPUS], *a.* Of or pertaining to the carpus and the metacarpus.

carpo- (2) [Gr. *karpos*, fruit], *comb. form.* (*Bot.*) Pertaining to fruit. **carpolite** (kar′ pò līt) [-LITE], *n.* (*Geol.*) A fossil fruit. **carpology** (kår pol′ ŏ ji) [-LOGY], *n.* That part of botany which treats of fruits. **carpophagous,** *a.* (*Zool.*) Fruit-eating.

carpus (kar′ pŭs) [L., from Gr. *karpos*, the wrist], *n.* (*pl.* *pi*) The wrist, the part of the human skeleton joining the hand to the forearm; the corresponding part in animals, in horses the knee. **carpal,** *a.*

carrack (kăr′ ăk) [O.F. *carraque*, late L. *carraca, carrica* (prob. conn. with *carricāre*, see CARGO)], *n.* A large merchant ship; a galleon.

carrageen (kăr′ ȧ gēn) [name of place], *n.* Irish moss, a nutritious seaweed, *Chrondus crispus*, found abundantly at Carragheen (Co. Waterford), Ireland.

carraway [CARAWAY].

carriage (kăr′ ăj) [O.North.F. *cariage* (F. *charriage*), from *carier*, to CARRY], *n.* Carrying, transporting, conveyance, esp. of merchandise; the cost of conveying; manner of carrying; mien, bearing, behaviour; conducting, management; carrying (of a motion, Bill, etc.); *things carried, burden, baggage, luggage, impedimenta; means of carrying; a conveyance, a wheeled vehicle, esp. one kept for pleasure; (*Machinery*) the sliding or wheeled portion of machinery carrying another part; the bed of a printing press on which a form is laid; the wheeled framework of a vehicle as distinguished from the body; the wheeled support of a cannon; (*Rail.*) a compartment of a coach. **carriage and pair,** *n.* A four-wheeled private vehicle drawn by two horses. **carriage-drive,** *n.* A road through a park or pleasure grounds. **carriage-folk,** *n.* The kind of people who own a carriage. **carriage forward,** *adv.* The cost of carriage to be paid by the receiver. **carriage free,** *a.* Carried without charge to the purchaser. **carriageful,** *n.* As many as a carriage will hold. **carriage rug,** *n.* A rug to cover the knees, (*Am.*) a lap-robe. **carriage-way,** *n.* That part of a road used for vehicular traffic. **carriageable,** *a.* Practicable for wheeled carriages. **carriageless,** *a.*

***carrick** [CARRACK], *a.* **carrick bend,** *n.* (*Naut.*) A particular knot for splicing two ropes together.

carrier (kăr′ i ėr), *n.* One who carries, esp. one who conveys goods and merchandise for hire; a frame for holding photographic plates or magic-lantern slides; a framework on a bicycle for holding luggage; applied also to various parts of machines or instruments which act as transmitters or bearers; (*Med.*) a person who transmits infectious disease germs without personally suffering from the disease. **common carrier:** (*Law*) A person or company transporting goods or merchandise for hire. **carrier bag,** *n.* A strong paper bag with string handles. **carrier pigeon,** *n.* A breed of pigeons trained to carry communications. **carrier wave,** *n.* (*Radio.*) An electromagnetic wave which is modulated with a lower-frequency wave for the transmission of speech.

carriole (kăr′ i ōl) [F., from It. *carriola* (*carro*, a cart, L. *carrus*, CAR)], *n.* A small open carriage; a light, covered cart; (*Canada*) an ornamental sledge.

carrion (kăr′ i ŏn) [M.E. and O.F. *caroigne*, late L. *carōnia*, a carcass (*caro carnis*, flesh)], *n.* Dead, putrefying flesh; (*fig.*) garbage, filth. *a.* Feeding on carrion; putrid; loathsome. **carrion-crow,** *n.* A species of crow, *Corvus corone*, that feeds on small animals and carrion; *the vulture.

carritch (kăr′ ich) [Sc., pl. *carriches*, corr. of CATECHIZE], *n.* The Catechism.

carrom [CARAMBOLE].

carronade (kăr ŏ năd), *n.* A short cannon of large bore, orig. made at Carron, near Falkirk, Scotland.

carron oil (kăr′ ŏn oil′), *n.* A mixture of linseed oil and lime-water, used at Carron ironworks for scalds and burns.

carrot (kăr′ ŏt) [F. *carrotte*, L. *carōta*, Gr. *karōton* (prob. from *kara*, head)], *n.* A plant with an edible tapering root, *Daucus carota*; (pl., *colloq.*) red hair; a person with red hair. **carroty,** *a.* Of the colour of a carrot; red, red-haired.

carrousel (kă′ roo sel) [F.], *n.* (*Am.*) A merry-go-round, a roundabout.

carry (kăr′ i) [O.North.F. *carier*, late L. *carricāre carrus*, CAR)], *v.t.* To convey, to bear, to transport from one place to another by lifting and moving with the thing carried; to transfer, as from one book, page, or column to another; to convey or take with one; to conduct; to bring, to enable to go or come; to support; to effect, to accomplish; to bear, to stand (as sail); to wear (as clothes), to bear or hold in a distinctive way; to extend in any direction in time or space (back, up, etc.); to imply, to import, to contain; to have in or on (esp. as armament); (*Mil.*) to take by assault. *v.i.* To act as bearer; to propel a projectile to a distance (as a fire-arm); to be propelled (as a missile); to bear the head in a particular manner (as a horse); (*Hunting*) to run on ground that sticks to the feet (as a hare). *n.* (*dial.*) The drift or motion of the clouds; the range of a fire-arm; (*Am.*) a portage. **to carry all before one:** To bear off all the honours; to succeed. **to carry away:** To excite, to deprive of self-control; (*Naut.*) to break or lose (as a rope or spar). **to carry coals to Newcastle:** To bring things to a place where they abound; to lose one's labour. **to carry off:** To remove; to win; to deprive of life. **to carry it off:** To brave it out. **to carry on:** To manage; to continue; to behave in a particular way, esp. to flirt outrageously. **to carry oneself:** To behave. **to carry out:** To perform; to accomplish. **to carry over** or **forward:** To transfer to another page or column, or to a future occasion. **to carry through:** To accomplish; to bring to a conclusion in spite of obstacles. **to carry weight:** To be handicapped; to be cogent (of an argument, etc.). **to carry with one:** To bear in mind, to convince. **carry-all,** *n.* A bag; (*Am.*) a four-wheeled pleasure-carriage for several persons; (*Am.*) a hold-all. **carrying,** *a.* **carrying trade,** *n.* The transport of goods, esp. by water. **carryings-on,** *n.pl.* Course of behaviour (usu. of a questionable kind).

carse (kars) [prob. pl. of obs. *carr*, fen, or boggy ground, from Icel. (cp. Dan. *kær*, Swed. *kærr*, Norw. *kjær*, pool, marsh, fen)], *n.* (*Sc.*) Low fertile land, usually near a river. **carse-land,** *n.*

cart (kart) [Icel. *kartr* (A.-S. *cræt* may be cogn.)], *n.* *A carriage, a chariot; a strong two-wheeled vehicle for heavy goods, etc.; a light two-wheeled vehicle (usually with attrib., as **dog-cart, spring-cart,** etc.). *v.t.* To carry or convey in a cart; *to expose in a cart as a punishment; (*slang*) to defeat badly. *v.i.* To use carts for cartage. **in the cart:** (*slang*) In a fix, a predicament. **cart-horse,** *n.* One of a breed of horses for drawing heavy carts. **cart-load,** *n.* As much as will fill a cart; a load of hay, etc. **cart-road, -way,** *n.* A rough road on a farm, etc. **cart-wheel,** *n.* The wheel of a cart; a large coin; a somersault taken sideways. **cart-wright,** *n.* One whose trade is to make carts. **cart-whip,** *n.* A long whip suitable for driving a team of horses. **cartage** (kar′ tăj), *n.* The act of carting; the price paid for carting. **carter,** *n.*

carte (1) (kart) [F. *carte*, see CARD]. *A card; a bill of fare; a carte-de-visite. **carte-blanche,** *n.* A signed sheet of paper given to a person to fill up as he pleases; (*fig.*) unlimited power to act. **carte-de-visite,** *n.* A visiting card; a photographic likeness on a small card.

carte (2), **quarte** (kart) [F. *quarte*, It. *quarta*, fourth], *n.* The fourth regular movement in fencing.

cartel (kar′ tėl) [F., from It. *cartella*, dim. of *carta*, CARD], *n.* A challenge in writing; an agreement between hostile states concerning the exchange of prisoners; an agreement (often international) among manufacturers to keep prices up.

Cartesian (kår tē′ zi ăn) [mod. L. *Cartesius*], *a.* Of or pertaining to the French philosopher Descartes (1596–1650), or his philosophy or mathematical methods. *n.* An adherent of his philosophy. **Cartesianism,** *n.*

Carthusian (kår thū′ zi ån) [med. L. *Cartusiānūs,* *Chartreuse,* in Dauphiné], *a.* Of or belonging to an order of monks founded by St. Bruno in 1086; of or belonging to Charterhouse School, founded on the site of a Carthusian monastery. *n.* A scholar or pensioner of the London Charterhouse; a Carthusian monk.

cartilage (kar′ ti lāj) [F., from L. *cartilāgo -āginem;* etym. unknown], *n.* An elastic, pearly-white animal tissue, gristle; a cartilaginous structure. **cartilaginoid** (kar ti lăj′ i noid), *a.* **cartilaginous,** *a.* Of, like, or pertaining to cartilage. **cartilaginous fishes,** *n.pl.* Fishes with a cartilaginous skeleton, as sharks and rays.

cartography (kår tog′ rå fi) [F. *carte,* CARD], *n.* The art or business of making maps and charts. **cartographer,** *n.* **cartographic** (-grăf ik), *a.* **cartology** (kar tol′ ō ji), *n.* The science of maps and charts.

cartomancy (kar′ tō măn si) [It. *carta,* playing-card, -MANCY], *n.* Divination or fortune-telling by cards.

carton (kar′ ton) [F., pasteboard, cardboard; It. *cartone* (*carta,* CARD)], *n.* A cardboard box; a white disk within the bull's eye of a target; a shot which hits this. **cartonnage,** *n.* (*Archæol.*) Layers of linen hardened with glue, used for the casing of mummies.

cartoon (kår toon′) [F.], *n.* A design on strong paper for painting tapestry, mosaic, stained-glass, etc.; a full-page illustration (esp. comic) dealing with a social or political subject. **cartoonist,** *n.*

cartouche (kår toosh′) [F., from It. *cartocchio* (*carta,* CARD)], *n* *A cartridge; (*Arch.*) a scroll on the cornice of a column; an ornamental tablet in the form of a scroll, for inscriptions, etc.; (*Egyptol.*), an elliptical figure containing the hieroglyphics of royal or divine names or titles. ***cartouche-box,** *n.* A cartridge-box.

cartridge (kar′ trij) [corr. of *cartouche*], *n.* A case of paper, pasteboard, metal, etc., holding the exact charge of a gun. **blank-cartridge,** *n.* Containing only the explosive; **ball-cartridge,** *n.* containing the bullet as well. **cartridge-bag,** *n.* A flannel-bag holding a charge of powder for a cannon. **cartridge-belt,** *n.* A belt with pockets for cartridges. **cartridge-box,** *n.* A box for storing or carrying cartridges. **cartridge-paper,** *n.* A stout, rough-surfaced paper, orig. used for cartridge-making, now for drawing, strong envelopes, etc.

cartulary (kar′ tū lår i) [late L. *ch-, cartulārium* (L. *cartula,* dim. of *carta,* CARD)], *n.* The register, or collection of documents, relating to a monastery or church; an officer in charge of such register.

carucate (kăr′ ū kāt) [late L. *carūcāta,* fem. p.p. of *carrūcāre,* to plough (L. *carrūca,* a plough, from *carrus,* CAR)], *n.* A measure of land, as much as could be tilled with one plough in a year.

caruncle (kăr′ ŭngkl, kå rŭng kėl) [F. *caruncule,* L. *caruncula,* dim. of *caro carnem,* flesh], *n.* A small, morbid, fleshy excrescence; a wattle, or the like; (*Bot.*) a protuberance round or near the hilum. **caruncular,** *a.* **carunculate, carunculated,** *a.*

carve (karv) [A.-S. *ceorfan,* from Teut. *kerf-* (cp. Dut. *kerven,* G. *kerben*), cogn. with Gr. *graphein,* to write], *v.t.* (p.p. **-ed** or **-en**) To cut; to cut into slices, as meat at table; to apportion; to make or shape by cutting; to cut or hew (some solid material) into the resemblance of some object; to cut (a design, inscription, representation, etc.); to adorn by cutting. *v.i.* To exercise the profession of a sculptor or carver; to carve meat; *(*fig.*) (*Shak.*) to show great courtesy and affability. **to carve out:** (*Law*) To create a small estate out of a larger one; (*fig.*) to win by the sword. **carver,** *n.* One who carves; a large table-knife for carving; (*pl.*) a carving-knife and fork. **carving,** *n.* The action of the verb TO CARVE; carved work. **carving-knife,** *n.* A knife to carve meat at table; (*Am.*) a butcher-knife.

carvel (kar′ vėl), *n.* A caravel. **carvel-built,** *a.* (*Naut.*) Having the planks flush at the edges, as opposed to clinker-built.

caryatid (kăr i ăt′ id) [L. *Caryātis,* Gr. *Karuatis -idos,* a priestess of Artemis at Caryæ, in Laconia], *n.* (*pl.* **-ids, -ides**) A figure of a woman in long robes, serving to support an entablature. **caryatic,** *a.* **caryatic-order,** *n.* (*Arch.*) An order in which the entablature is supported by caryatids.

caryo- [Gr. *karuon,* a nut], *comb. form.* **caryophyllaceous** (kăr i ō fil ā′ shŭs) [Gr. *karuophullon* (*phullon,* a leaf), -ACEOUS], *a.* (*Bot.*) Belonging to the order *Caryophyllaceæ,* typified by the clove-pink; having a corolla with five petals with long claws, as the clove-pink. **caryophyllic** (-fil′ ik), *a.* (*Chem.*) A term applied to an acid derived from oil of cloves. **caryopsis** (kăr i op′ sis) [Gr. *opsis,* appearance], *n.* (*pl.* **-sides,** -si dēz) (*Bot.*) A fruit with a single seed, to which the pericarp adheres throughout, as in grasses.

cascabel (kăs′ kå bel) [Sp., perh. from L. *scabellum,* castanet], *n.* The knob or loop at the end of a cannon.

cascade (kås kād′) [F., from It. *cascata,* p.p. of *cascare,* to fall (L. *cāsum,* CASE)], *n.* A small waterfall; anything resembling a cascade, as a loose, wavy fall of lace, a firework imitating a waterfall. *v.i.* To fall in or like a cascade. **cascade amplifier,** *n.* (*Radio.*) A series of valve amplifiers so connected that the output of each stage is amplified by the succeeding stage.

cascara (kăs ka′ rå) [Sp.], *n.* A birch-bark canoe; (*Med.*) the bark of the Californian *Cascara sagrada,* used as an aperient. **cascarilla** (kăs kå ril′ å) [Sp., dim. of prec.], *n.* (*Med.*) The aromatic bark of *Croton eleutheria.*

case (1) (kās) [O.North.F. *casse* (F. *châsse*), L. *capsa* (*capere,* to receive, to hold)], *n.* That which contains or encloses something else; a box, covering, or sheath; an oblong frame, with divisions, for type [LOWER-CASE, UPPER-CASE]; a cloth cover for a book; a glass box for exhibits; the outer cover of an instrument, seed-vessel, pupa, projectile, etc. *v.t.* To cover with or put into a case; *to skin. **case-bottle,** *n.* A bottle shaped to fit into a case. **case-harden,** *v.t.* To harden the outside surface of, esp. of iron, by converting into steel; (*fig.*) to make callous. **case-knife,** *n.* A knife carried in a sheath. **case-shot,** *n.* Small projectiles put in cases to be discharged from cannon, shrapnel. **case-worm,** *n.* The caddis-worm. **casing,** *n.* The action of the verb TO CASE; something that encases; an outside covering.

case (2) (kās) [O.F. *cas,* L. *cāsus,* p.p. of *cadere,* to fall], *n.* That which happens or befalls; an event, a condition of things, position, state, circumstances; an instance; a question at issue; (*Gram.*) change in the termination of a declinable word to express relation to some other word in the sentence; used also of such relation in uninflected languages; (*slang*) a queer character; (*Law*) a cause or suit in court; a statement of facts or evidence for submission to a court; the evidence and arguments considered collectively; a cause that has been decided and may be quoted as a precedent; (*Med.*) the condition of a sick person; the patient; a particular instance of any disease. *v.i.* (*slang*) To reconnoitre with a view to burglary. **case-history,** *n.* A record of a patient's ancestry and personal history made for clinical purposes. **in case:** If, supposing that, lest. **in case of:** In the event of. **in any case:** In any event, whatever may happen. **in good case:** In good condition. **in that case:** If that should happen. **it's a case with:** (*slang*) It's all up with. **case of conscience:** A matter in which conscience must make the decision between two principles. **case law** *n.* (*Law*) Law as settled by precedent.

casein (kā′ sē in) [L. *caseus,* cheese, -IN], *n.* (*Chem.*) The albuminoid or proteid in milk, forming the basis of cheese. **vegetable casein:** A similar albuminoid found in leguminous plants, called also legumin. **caseic** (kā sē′ ik), *a.* (*Chem.*) Obtained from cheese. **caseic acid,** *n.* Lactic acid. **caseous** (kā′ sė ůs), *a.* Resembling cheese; cheesy.

casemate (kās′ māt) [F., from It. *casamatta* (etym. doubtful)], *n.* A bomb-proof vault or chamber in a fortress, containing an embrasure. **casemated,** *a.*

casement (kāz′ mėnt) [from CASE (1) or from It. *casamento*, a building or frame of a building, med. L. *casamentum*], *n.* A window or part of a window opening on hinges; (*poet.*) a window; (*Arch.*) a hollow moulding. **casemented,** *a.* Having casements.

casern, -e (kȧ zĕrn′) [F. *caserne*, Sp. *caserna* (*casa*,) a house, L. *casa*, cottage)], *n.* One of a series of temporary buildings for soldiers between the ramparts and the houses of a fortified town; a barrack.

cash (1) (kăsh) [F. *casse*, box (see CASE (1))], *n.* Ready money; coin, specie, bank-notes. *v.t.* To turn into or exchange for cash. **cash-account,** *n.* An account of cash paid, received, or in hand. **cash-and-carry:** Cash sale, and the customer to carry away. **cash-balance,** *n.* The balance on the debtor side of a cash-account. **cash desk,** *n.* The desk in a shop where all payments are made by customers. **to cash in:** (*slang*) To die. **to cash in on:** (*colloq.*) To seize an opportunity. **cash on delivery:** A system by which goods are paid for on delivery, *abbr.* C.O.D. **cash-book,** *n.* A book in which money transactions are entered. **cash down:** Money paid on the spot. **hard cash:** Actual coin; ready money. **in cash:** Having money. **out of cash:** Having no money. **cashless,** *a.* Moneyless; without ready money. **cash-payment,** *n.* Payment by ready money. **cash-price,** *n.* The price for ready money. **cash register,** *n.* A calculating till used in a retail shop.

cash (2) (kăsh) [Tamil *kasu*, a small coin (confused with CASH (1))], *n.* A name applied by Europeans to various Eastern (esp. Chinese) coins of low value.

cashew (kăsh′ oo, kȧ shoo′) [F. *acajou*, Braz. *acaju* (see also ACAJOU)], *n.* The kidney-shaped fruit of a tropical tree, *Anacardium occidentale*. **cashew-nut,** *n.* **cashew-tree,** *n.*

cashier (1) (kȧ shēr′) [F. *caissier*], *n.* One who has charge of the cash or of money transactions.

cashier (2) (kȧ shēr) [Dut. *casseren* (cp. F. *casser*, L. *quassāre*, to shatter, later blended with senses of *cassāre*, to annul)], *v.t.* To dismiss from the service, to discharge; to get rid of; (*rare*) to deprive (a person) of his cash.

cashmere (kăsh′ mēr) [*Kashmīr*, state to the north of the Indian sub-continent], *n.* A material for shawls, made from the hair of the Cashmere goat; a shawl of this material; a fine woollen dress fabric. **cashmerette** (kăsh mė ret′), *n.* An imitation of cashmere.

casino (1) (kȧ sē′ nō) [It., dim. of *casa*, house, L. *casa*, cottage], *n.* A public dancing-room; a public saloon or building for social intercourse, gambling, music, dancing, etc.

casino (2) [CASSINO].

cask (kask) [perh. from Sp. *casco*, a cask, a skull, a potsherd], *n.* A barrel; the quantity contained in a cask; *a casket; *a casque.

casket (kas′ kėt) [etym. doubtful; perh. dim. of prec.], *n.* A small case for jewels, etc.; (*Am.*) a coffin. *v.t.* To enclose in a casket.

casque (kăsk) [F., from Sp. *casco*, CASK], *n.* (*poet.*) A helmet; (*Zool.*) a horny cap or protuberance on the head of some birds.

Cassandra (kȧ săn′ drȧ) [daughter of Priam, king of Troy, who had the gift of prophecy but was not believed], *n.* One who prophesies evil; one who takes gloomy views of the future; a prophet who is not listened to.

cassareep (kăs′ ȧ rēp) [Carib.], *n.* The inspissated juice of the cassava, used as a condiment.

cassation (kȧ sā′ shůn) [late L. *cassatiō -ōnem* (*cassāre*, to make void)], *n.* Abrogation; reversal of a judicial sentence. **court of cassation:** The highest court of appeal in France and Belgium.

cassava (kȧ sa′ vȧ) [Haitian *caçábi*], *n.* A West Indian plant, the manioc, *Manihot utilissima*; a nutritious flour obtained from its roots; bread made from this flour.

casserole (kăs′ ė rōl) [F. (*casse*, etym. obscure)], *n.* A stew-pan; an earthenware or glass cooking-dish with a lid.

cassia (kăs′ i ȧ, kăsh′ ȧ) [L., from Gr. *kasia*, Heb. *qetsī‘āh*, cassia-bark (*qātsa‘*, to bark or peel)], *n.* A coarse kind of cinnamon, esp. the bark of *Cinnamomum cassia*; a genus of leguminous plants, including the senna; an unidentified, fragrant plant. **cassia-bark,** *n.*

cassimere (kăs′ i mēr) [CASHMERE], *n.* A thin, fine-twilled cloth for men's clothes.

cassino, casino (2) (kȧ sē′ nō) [CASINO (1)], *n.* A game at cards for four players.

cassis (kăs′ ēs) [F., blackcurrant], *n.* A cordial made from blackcurrants.

cassiterite (kȧ sit′ ėr īt) [Gr. *kassiteros*, tin, -ITE], *n.* (*Min.*) Native stannic dioxide, common tin-ore.

cassock (kăs′ ȯk) [F. *casaque*, It. *casacca* (etym. doubtful; perh. from *casa*, house, L. *casa*, cottage)], *n.* *A long loose coat or gown (for either sex); a long, close-fitting garment worn by clerics, choristers, vergers, etc.; a soutane. **cassocked,** *a.* Wearing a cassock.

cassolette (kăs ȯ lėt′) [F., dim. of *cassole* (*casse*, see CASSEROLE)], *n.* A vessel in which perfumes are burned; a perfume-box with perforated lid.

cassowary (kăs′ ȯ wȧ ri) [Malay *kasuwāri*], *n.* An East Indian genus of large cursorial birds.

cast (1) (kast) [Icel. *kasta*, to throw], *v.t.* (*past & p.p.* **cast**) To throw, fling, hurl (now chiefly poet. or archaic except in certain uses); to drive, to toss; to cause to fall, to emit; to throw off, to shed, to throw by reflection; to allot, to assign (as the parts in a play); to condemn, to reject; to drop prematurely (as young); to add up, compute, calculate; (*Law*) to defeat; to found, to mould. *v.i.* To throw a fishing-line; to reckon accounts; to consider, to scheme, to contrive; to take form or shape (in a mould); to warp. **to cast about:** To look hither and thither for something; to consider; to devise a means. **to cast aside:** To reject; to give up. **to cast away:** To reject, to lavish. **to cast down:** To throw down; to deject, to depress, to destroy. **to cast forth:** To throw away; to emit. **to cast in one's lot with:** To share the fate or fortunes of. **to cast in one's teeth:** To upbraid one with. **to cast off:** To discard; (*Print.*) to estimate the number of words in a manuscript; (*Naut.*) to untie, to unmoor; (*Hunting, etc.*) to let loose (as dogs); (*Knitting*) to finish by closing loops and making a selvedge. **to cast oneself on:** To take refuge with. **to cast out:** To expel. **to cast up:** To reckon, to add; to vomit; to throw in one's teeth. **casting,** *n.* The action of the verb TO CAST; anything formed by casting or founding; esp. a metal object as distinguished from a plaster cast. **casting-net,** *n.* A net thrown into the water and drawn in again. **casting voice, casting vote,** *n.* The deciding vote of a president when the votes are equal.

cast (2) (kast) [from prec.], *n.* The act of casting or throwing; a throw; the thing thrown; the distance thrown; the allotment of parts in a play, the set of actors allotted; a throw of dice; the number thrown; chance; feathers, fur, etc. ejected from the stomach by a bird of prey; (*Angling*) the end portion of a line, usu. of gut or gimp, carrying hooks, etc.; an adding up, a computation; a motion or turn of the eye; direction of glance; a twist, a squint; *plan, design; tinge, characteristic quality or form; *a pair (of hawks); a mould; the thing moulded, the shape. *a.* Thrown; (*Law*) condemned; made by founding or casting. **cast-iron,** *n.* Iron melted and run in moulds; *a.* Made of cast-iron; (*fig.*) rigid, unyielding, unadaptable; hard, indefatigable. **cast-off,** *a.* Laid aside, rejected. **cast-steel,** *n.*

Steel melted and run into moulds. **caster,** *n.* One who or that which casts; a small vessel for holding condiments at table; a cruet-stand; a small swivelled wheel attached to the leg of a table, sofa, chair, etc. (in the last three senses also spelt **castor**). **caster-, castor-sugar,** *n.* White powdered sugar for table use.

castalian (kȧs tā' li ȧn) [L., from Gr. *Kastalia*], *a.* Of or pertaining to Castalia, a spring on Mount Parnassus sacred to the Muses; poetical.

castanet (kăs' tȧ net, kăs tȧ net') [Sp. *castaneta*, dim. of *castaña*, L. *castanea*, chestnut], *n.* (*usu. in pl.*) A small spoon-shaped concave instrument of ivory or hard wood, a pair of which is fastened to each thumb and rattled as an accompaniment to music.

castaway (kast' ȧ wā), *a.* Rejected, useless; shipwrecked. *n.* An outcast; a reprobate; a shipwrecked person.

caste (kast) [Port. *casta*, fem. of *casto*, lineage, L. *castus*, pure, unmixed (cp. CHASTE)], *n.* One of the hereditary classes of society in India; any hereditary, exclusive class; the class system; the dignity or social influence due to position; (*Zool.*) a term used to describe specialized individuals among insects, *e.g.* queen bee, worker bee, etc. **to lose caste:** To descend in the social scale; to lose favour or consideration. **casteless,** *a.*

castellan (kăs' tė lȧn) [O.North.F. *castellain* (F. *châtelain*), late L. *castellānus* (see CASTLE)], *n.* The governor of a castle. **castellany,** *n.* The lordship or jurisdiction of a castellan. **castellated** (kăs' tė lā tėd) [med. L. *castellātus*, p.p. *castellāre*, to build a castle (see CASTLE)], *a.* Having turrets and battlements; having castles; resembling a castle. **castellation** (-lā' shŭn), *n.*

caster [CAST (2)].

castigate (kăs' ti gāt) [L. *castigātus*, p.p. of *castigāre*, to chasten (*castus*, CHASTE)], *v.t.* To chastise, to punish; to correct. **castigation** (kăs ti gā' shŭn), *n.* **castigator** (kăs' ti gā tȯr), *n.* One who castigates; a corrector. **castigatory,** *a.*

Castile soap (kăs tēl' sōp) [Castile, in Spain], *n.* A fine, hard soap, whose main constituents are olive oil and soda.

casting [CAST (1)].

castle (ka' sėl) [O.North.F. *castel* (O.F. *chastel*, *château*), L. *castellum*, dim. of *castrum*, a fort], *n.* A fortified building, a fortress; a mansion that was formerly a fortress; the mansion of a noble or prince; a piece at chess in the shape of a tower, a rook. *v.i.* (*Chess*) To move the king two squares to the right or left and bring up the castle to the square the king has passed over. *v.t.* To treat (the king) thus. **The Castle:** Dublin Castle; the former centre of the governmental system. **castles in the air** or **in Spain:** Visionary projects. **castle-builder,** *n.* A dreamer, a visionary. ***castle-guard,** *n.* (*Law*) A tenure by which a tenant was bound to defend his lord's castle. **castle-nut,** *n.* (*Engin.*) A nut with notched extension for a locking-pin. ***castle-ward,** *n.* (*Law*) A tax for the maintenance of a castle, levied on those protected by it. **castled,** *a.* Having a castle. ***castelry,** *n.* The tenure or government of a castle; the territory attached to it. **castle-wise,** *adv.*

castor (1) (kas' tŏr) [F., from L., from Gr. *kastōr*, prob. Eastern in origin (cp. Sansk. *kastūrī*, musk)], *n.* A beaver hat; (*Zool.*) a mammalian genus, containing the beaver; (*Drug*) an oily compound secreted by the beaver, used in medicine and perfumery, called also **castoreum.**

castor (2) (kas' tŏr) [etym. doubtful; perh. from obs. *castane* (L. *castanea*, chestnut)], *n.* (*Farriery*) A patch of hard skin inside a horse's hock, corresponding to a similar feature inside the foreleg called the chestnut.

castor (3) [CAST (2)].

Castor and Pollux (kas' tȯr ȧnd pol' ŭks) [Gr., twin sons of Tyndarus and Leda], *n.pl.* The twins; stars in the constellation Gemini; St. Elmo's Fire, seen on ships during a storm (when two lights appear).

castoreum [CASTOR (1)].

castor-oil (ka' stėr oil), *n.* (*Med.*) An oil obtained from the seeds of Palma Christi, *Ricinus communis*, used as a cathartic.

castrametation (kăs trȧ mė tā' shŭn) [F. *castramétation* (L. *castra*, a camp, *mētāri*, to measure or lay out)], *n.* The act or art of arranging a camp.

castrate (kăs' trāt) [L. *castrātus*, p.p. of *castrāre*], *v.t.* To cut away the testicles, to geld; to deprive of generative power; to emasculate, to deprive of force or vigour; to expurgate unduly. **castration** (kȧs trā' shŭn), *n.* **castrato** (kas tra' tō) [It., p.p. of *castrare* (L. *castrāre*)], *n.* (*pl.* **castrati, -tē**) A male soprano; a male emasculated for the purpose of retaining the pitch of his voice.

casual (kăz' ū ȧl, kăzh' ū ȧl) [F. *casuel*, L. *cāsuālis* (*cāsus*, CASE)], *a.* Happening by chance; accidental, trivial; occasional, unmethodical. *n.* A tramp; a frequenter of casual wards; (*pl.*) flat-heeled shoes that slip on without lacing. **casual labourer,** *n.* A workman who lives by odd jobs. **casual ward,** *n.* A ward in a workhouse for tramps or occasional paupers. **casualism,** *n.* The doctrine that all things exist or happen by chance. **casualist,** *n.* **casually,** *adv.* **casualness,** *n.*

casualty (kăzh' ū ȧl ti, kăz' ū ȧl ti) [see prec.], *n.* An accident, esp. one attended with personal injury or loss of life; (*pl.*) the killed or wounded in war. **casualty ward,** *n.* The ward in a hospital for receiving the victims of accidents.

casuist (kăz' ū ist, kăzh' ū ist) [F. *casuiste* (L. *cāsus*, CASE)], *n.* (*Theol. and Ethics*) One who studies doubtful questions of conduct (esp. one who discovers exceptions); a sophist, a hair-splitter. **casuistic, -ical** (kăz ū-, kăzh ū is' tik, -ȧl), *a.* **casuistically,** *adv.* **casuistry** (kăzh ū is' tri), *n.* That part of ethics or theology which deals with cases of conscience.

cat (1) (kăt) [A.-S. (cp. Dut. *kat*, Icel. *köttr*, G. *kater*, *katze*, Ir. and Gael. *cat*, late L. *cāttus*)], *n.* Any species of the genus *Felis*, comprising the lion, tiger, leopard, etc., esp. *F. domestica*, the domestic cat; any cat-like animal; (*Naut.*) a strong tackle used to hoist the anchor to the cat-heads; various parts of this tackle; the game of tip-cat, the doubly-tapered stick used in this game; a cat-o'-nine-tails; a double tripod which always falls on its feet, as a cat is said to do; (*colloq.*) a spiteful woman. *v.t.* (*Naut.*) To draw to the cat-head; (*colloq.*) to vomit. *v.i.* (*colloq.*) To be sick. **cat-and-dog:** Quarrelsome. **care killed the cat:** Cheer up; don't worry (referring to the cat's proverbial nine lives). **to let the cat out of the bag:** To give away a secret, to be indiscreet. **to see which way the cat jumps:** To wait until the public has made up its mind; to sit on the fence. **to rain cats and dogs:** To pour. **to whip the cat:** (*Austral. colloq.*) To cry over spilt milk. **cat-beam,** *n.* (*Naut.*) The broadest beam in a ship. **cat-bird,** *n.* An American thrush, *Mimus Carolinesis*. **cat-block,** *n.* (*Naut.*) A block used to cat the anchor. **cat burglar,** *n.* A thief who enters a house by climbing up the outside. **catcall,** *n.* A squeaking instrument, used in theatres to condemn plays; any similar sound; one using a catcall; *v.i.* To make a noise like a catcall; *v.t.* To deride with a catcall. **cat-eyed,** *a.* Able to see in the dark. **cat-fish,** *n.* A North American river-fish belonging to the genus *Pimelodus*; applied to various other fishes. **cat-head,** *n.* (*Naut.*) A beam projecting from a ship's bows to which the anchor is secured; (*Geol.*) a kind of nodule containing a fossil. *v.t.* (*Naut.*) To cat (the anchor). **cat-holes,** *n.pl.* (*Naut.*) Two holes at the stern of a ship for a cable or hawser. **cat-ice,** *n.* Thin white ice over shallow places where the water has receded. **cat-lap,** *n.* (*colloq.*) Weak drink, slops. **cat-mint,** *n.* A European labiate plant, *Nepeta cataria*. **Cat-and-Mouse Act,** *n.* Popular name of an Act passed in 1913, permitting of the release and re-arrest of hunger-strikers. **cat-nap,**

n. A short sleep. **cat-o'-nine-tails,** *n.* A whip or scourge with nine lashes, formerly used as an instrument of punishment in the Army and Navy. **cat's brains,** *n.* Sandstone veined with chalk. **cat's cradle,** *n.* A childish game with string. **cat's-eye,** *n.* A precious stone, from Ceylon, Malabar, etc., a vitreous variety of quartz; a reflector stud on a road. **cat's-foot,** *n.* The ground-ivy, *Nepeta glechoma*; the mountain cudweed, *Antennaria dioica.* **cat's meat,** *n.* Horse-flesh, used as food for cats. **cat's paw,** *n.* A dupe used as a tool (in allusion to the fable of the monkey who used the cat's paw to pick chestnuts out of the fire); (*Naut.*) a light air which just ripples the surface of the water; a turn in the bight of a rope to hook a tackle on. **cat's-tail,** *n.* The horse-tail, *Equisetum*; several species of *Typha*; a catkin. **cat's whisker,** *n.* (*Radio.*) A very fine wire in contact with a crystal receiver to rectify current and cause audibility. **cathood,** *n.* **cattish,** *a.* **catlike,** *a.* **catty,** *a.* Spiteful, malicious.

*__cat__ (2) (kăt [from prec.], *n.* (*Naut.*) A coal and timber vessel formerly used on the north-east coast of England. **cat-rigged,** *a.* Having one large fore-and-aft mainsail.

cat-, cata-, cath- [Gr. *kata*, down, downwards], *pref.* Down; against; away; wrongly; entirely, thoroughly; according to.

catabolism (kȧ tăb' ō lizm) [KATABOLISM].

catacaustic (kăt ȧ kaw' stik), *a.* (*Opt.*) Formed by reflected rays. *n.* A caustic curve formed by reflection.

catachresis (kăt ȧ krē' sis) [L., from Gr. *katachrēsis* (CATA-, *chrēsthai*, to be used)], *n.* The abuse of a trope or metaphor; the wrong use of one word for another. **catachrestic** (kăt ȧ kres' tik), *a.* **catachrestically,** *adv.*

cataclasm (kăt' ȧ klăzm) [Gr. *kataklasma*, from *kataklân* (CATA-, *klân*, to break)], *n.* A violent disruption; a rending asunder.

cataclysm (kăt' ȧ klizm) [F. *cataclysme*, Gr. *kataklusmos*, from *katakluzein* (CATA-, *kluzein*, to wash)], *n.* A deluge, esp. the Noachian Flood; (*Geol.*) a terrestrial catastrophe; a vast and sudden social or political change. **cataclysmal** (kăt ȧ kliz' măl), **cataclysmic,** *a.* **cataclysmist,** *n.* (*Geol.*) One who ascribes changes in the earth's surface to cataclysms.

catacomb (kăt' ȧ kōm) [F. *catacombe*, It. *catacomba*, late L. *Catacumbas* (etym. doubtful; prob. a place-name, but not applied to the Roman catacombs when in use)], *n.* A subterranean burying-place, with niches for the dead; (*pl.*) the subterranean galleries at Rome; similar excavations at Syracuse, Paris, etc.; a cellar, esp. a wine-cellar.

catacoustics (kăt ȧ kou' stiks), *n.pl.* (*Phys.*) The science of reflected sounds.

catadioptric (kăt ȧ dī op' trik), *a.* (*Opt.*) Reflecting and refracting light.

catadromous (kȧ tăd' rȯ mŭs) [Gr. *katadromos* (*-dromos*, running, from *dramein*, to run)], *n.* (*Fishes*) Descending periodically to spawn (in the sea or the lower waters of a river).

catafalque (kăt' ȧ făłk), **catafalco** (kăt ȧ făl' kō) [F. *catafalque*, It. *catafalco* (etym. unknown)], *n.* A temporary stage or tomb-like structure for the coffin of distinguished persons during the funeral service; a kind of hearse.

Catalan (kăt' ȧ lăn), *a.* Of or pertaining to Catalonia. *n.* A native, or the language, of Catalonia. **Catalan forge,** *n.* A kind of blast furnace used in Catalonia.

catalectic (kăt ȧ lek' tik) [late L. *catalēcticus*, Gr. *katalēktikos*, from *katalēgein* (*lēgein*, to leave, cease)], *a.* (*Pros.*) Having the metrical foot at the end of a line incomplete.

catalepsy (kăt' ȧ lep si) [med. L. *catalēpsia*, Gr. *katalēpsis* (*lambanein*, to seize)], *n.* (*Med.*) A sudden trance or suspension of voluntary sensation; (*Phil.*) apprehension; mental comprehension. **cataleptic** (-lep' tik), *a.* (*Med.*) Affected by or subject to catalepsy; (*Phil.*) relating to mental apprehension. *n.* A person subject to attacks of catalepsy.

catallactic (kăt' ȧ lăk' tik) [Gr. *katallatikos* (*katalassein*, to exchange)], *a.* Pertaining to exchange. **catallactics,** *n.* A name proposed for the science of exchange; political economy.

catalogue (kăt' ȧ log) [F., from late L. *catalogus*, Gr. *katalogos*, from *katalegein* (*legein*, to choose, state)], *n.* A methodical list, arranged alphabetically or under class-headings. *v.t.* To enter in a list; to make a complete list of. **catalogue raisonné** (rā zon nā'), *n.* A catalogue in which a description of the items is given. **cataloguer,** *n.*

catalpa (kȧ tăl' pȧ) [Carolina Ind.], *n.* A genus of trees, chiefly North American.

catalysis (kȧ tăl' i sis) [Gr. *katalusis*, from *kataluein* (*luein*, to loosen)], *n.* (*Chem.*) The force supposed to be exerted by one substance upon a second, whereby the latter is decomposed, while the former remains unchanged; the effect so produced. **catalyst,** *n.* (*Chem.*) Any substance that changes the speed of a chemical reaction without itself being changed. **catalytic** (-lit' ik), *a.* Relating to or effected by catalysis. *n.* (*Med.*) A medicine supposed to act by the destruction of morbid agencies in the blood. **catalytic cracker,** *n.* An industrial apparatus used to break down the heavy hydrocarbons of crude oil and yield petrol, paraffins, etc.

catamaran (kăt ȧ mȧ răn', kȧ tăm' ȧ răn) [Tamil *katta-maram* (*katta*, tie, *maram*, wood)], *n.* A raft or float used as a surf-boat in the East and West Indies; a raft made by lashing two boats together; a double boat; an obsolete kind of fireship; (*colloq.*) a vixenish woman (perh. from some fancied connexion with CAT).

catamenia (kăt ȧ mē' ni ȧ), *n.pl.* (*Med.*) The menses. **catamenial,** *a.*

catamite (kăt' ȧ mīt) [L. *Catamītus*, corr. from Gr. *Ganymēdes*, Jove's cupbearer], *n.* A boy kept for unnatural purposes.

catamount (kăt' ȧ mount), **catamountain, cat-o'-mountain** (kăt ȧ (-ȯ-) moun' tȧn) [prob Eng. in orig.), *n.* (*Am.*) The puma; *the leopard, panther, etc.; *a fierce, outlandish person.

cataphonics (kăt ȧ fon' iks), *n.pl.* (*Phys.*) The science of reflected sounds. **cataphonic,** *a.*

cataphract (kăt' ȧ frăkt), *n.* (*Zool.*) A scaly plate. **cataphracted,** *a.* Covered with scaly plates, as some fishes.

cataphyllary (kăt ȧ fil' ȧ ri), *a.* (*Bot.*) Describing the brownish or colourless scales regarded as rudimentary leaves.

cataphysical (kăt ȧ fiz' i kăl), *a.* Against the laws of nature.

cataplasm (kăt' a plăzm), *n.* (*Med.*) A poultice, a plaster.

cataplexy (kăt' ȧ pleks i), *n.* Temporary paralysis or a hypnotic condition affecting animals which are supposed to be shamming dead.

catapult (kăt' ȧ pŭlt) [L. *catapulta*, Gr. *katapeltēs* (*pallein*, to hurl)], *n.* An ancient military engine for hurling darts or stones; hence, a toy for propelling small stones, (*Am.*) a sling-shot. *v.t.* To throw or shoot with or as with a catapult; (*Aviat.*) to assist the take-off of an aircraft by giving an initial acceleration with a spring or other device. *v.i.* To shoot with a catapult.

cataract (kăt' ȧ răkt) [F. *cataracte*, L. *cataracta*, Gr. *katarrhaktēs* (from *katarassein*, to dash down, or *katarrhēgnunai*, to break or rush down)], *n.* A large, rushing waterfall; a deluge of rain; a violent rush of water; (*Steam-eng.*) a kind of governor worked by a flow of water; (*Path.*) a disease of the eye in which the crystalline lens or its envelope becomes opaque and vision is impaired or destroyed. **cataractous** (-răk' tŭs), *a.* (*Med.*) Affected with cataract.

catarrh (kȧ tar′) [F. *catarrhe*, late L. *catarrhus*, Gr. *katarrhoos*, from *katarrheein* (CATA-, *rheein*, to flow)], *n.* A running or discharge of the mucous membrane, esp. from the nose; a cold in the head or chest. **catarrhal, catarrhous,** *a.*

catarrhine (kăt′ ȧ rīn) [Gr. *rhin rhinos*, the nostril], *a.* (*Zool.*) A term applied to the Old World monkeys, from the close, oblique position of their nostrils. *n.* A monkey of the Old World.

***catasta** (kȧ tăs′ tȧ) [L., from Gr. *katastasis* (CATA-, *sta-*, stem of *histani*, to stand)], *n.* A block on which slaves were exposed for sale; a stage or rack for torture.

catastasis (kȧ tăs′ tȧ sis) [see prec.], *n.* The part in the ancient drama leading up to the catastrophe; (*Rhet.*) the exordium.

catastrophe (kȧ tăs′ trȯ fi) [Gr. *katastrophē* (*strephein*, to turn)], *n.* The change which brings about the conclusion of a dramatic piece; a final event; a great misfortune; (*Geol.*) a violent convulsion of the globe, producing changes in the relative extent of land or water. **catastrophic** (kăt ȧ strof′ ik), *a.* **catastrophism,** *a.* (*Geol.*) The view that geological changes have been produced by the action of catastrophes. **catastrophist,** *n.*

catawampus (kăt ȧ wom′ pŭs) [Am. slang], *n.* Something very fierce; vermin. **catawampous,** *a.* **catawamptiously,** *adv.*

catawba (kȧ taw′ bȧ) [a S. Carolina river named after *Katahba* Indians], *n.* A grape-vine, *Vitis abrusca*; wine made therefrom.

catch (kăch) [O.North.F. *cachier* (cp. O.F. *chacier*, TO CHASE), prob. from a late L. *captiāre* (L. *captāre*, to chase, freq. of *capere*, to take)], *v.t.* (*past* and *p.p.* **caught**) To grasp, to seize, esp. in pursuit; to take in a snare, to entrap; to take by angling or in a net; to intercept (as a ball) when falling; to dismiss (a batsman) by this; to check, to interrupt, to come upon suddenly, to surprise; to detect: to take hold of (as fire); to receive by infection or contagion; to be in time for; to grasp, perceive; comprehend; (*fig.*) to attract, gain over, fascinate. *v.i.* To become fastened or attached suddenly; to communicate; to ignite, to spread epidemically; to take hold; to become entangled. *n.* The act of seizing or grasping; anything that seizes, takes hold, or checks; the basket, the amount of fish caught; seizing and holding the ball at cricket; a contrivance for checking motion; an acquisition; an opportunity; an advantage seized; (*colloq.*) a person worth capturing matrimonially; profit; trap; a surprise; a snare; a play upon words; (*Mus.*) a part-song in which each singer in turn catches up, as it were, the words of his predecessor. **to catch a tartar:** To meet with a formidable opponent unexpectedly; to get into difficulties of one's own making. **to catch at:** To attempt to seize. **to catch it:** To get a scolding. **to catch one's eye:** To attract attention. **to catch on:** To hit the public taste. **to catch on to:** To grasp, to understand. **to catch up:** To overtake. **catch-crop,** *n.* (*Agric.*) A quick-growing green crop sown between main crops; a crop which springs up on fallow land from seed dropped from the previous year's crop. **catch-drain,** *n.* An open drain along the side of a hill or canal to catch the surplus water. **catch-fly,** A book name for species of lychnis and silene, from their glutinous stems which often retain small insects. **catchment,** *n.* A surface on which water may be caught and collected. **catchment-area, -basin,** *n.* An area the rainfall in which feeds a river-system. **catch-penny,** *a.* Worthless, made only to sell. **catch-points,** *n.pl.* (*Rail.*) Points placed on an up-gradient and so set as to derail any vehicle accidentally descending the gradient. **catchweed,** *n.* Goose-grass or cleavers. **catchable,** *a.* **catcher,** *n.* **catching,** *a.* That catches; infectious; (*fig.*) taking, attractive. **catchy,** *a.* Catching; easy to catch (as a tune).

catchpole (kăch′ pōl) [med. L. *chassipullus*, chase-fowl (CHASE (1), *pullus*, fowl)], *n.* A constable; a bum-bailiff.

catchup, catsup [KETCHUP].

catchword (kăch′ wĕrd), *n.* A popular cry; an actor's cue; a word printed under the last line of a page, being the first word of the next; the first word in a dictionary entry.

***cate** [CATES].

catechize (kăt ė kīz) [L. *catēchizāre*, Gr. *katēchizein*, *katēcheein*, to din into the ears (*ēchein*, to sound, *ēcho*, ECHO)], *v.t.* To instruct by means of questions and answers; to instruct in the Church Catechism; (*fig.*) to question closely. **catechizer,** *n.* **catechetic, -al** (kăt ė ket′ ik, -ȧl) [L. *catēchēticus*, Gr. *katēchētikos* (*katēchētēs*, from *katēcheein*, as above)], *a.* Consisting of questions and answers, pertaining to catechism. **catechetically,** *adv.* **catechetics,** *n.pl.* That part of Christian theology which deals with oral instruction. **catechism,** *n.* A form of instruction by means of question and answer; esp. the authorized manuals of doctrine, the Church Catechism published by the Church of England, and the Longer and Shorter Catechisms by the Presbyterians; (*fig.*) a series of interrogations. **catechismal** (-kiz′ mal), *a.* **catechist** (kăt ė kist), *n.* One who teaches by catechizing; one who imparts elementary instruction, esp. in the principles of religion. **catechistic, catechistical** (kăt ė kis′ tik, -ȧl), *a.* **catechistically,** *adv.*

catechu (kăt ė choo, kă choo′) [Malay *kāchu*], *n.* A brown astringent gum, furnished chiefly by *Acacia catechu.* **catechuic** (kăt ė choo′ ik, kȧ choo′ ik), *a.*

catechumen (kăt ė kū′ mėn) [F. *catéchumène*, L. *catēchūmenus*, Gr. *katēchoumenos* (*katēcheein*, see CATECHIZE)], *n.* One who is under Christian instruction preparatory to receiving baptism; (*fig.*) a beginner in any art or science.

categorem (kăt′ ė gȯ rem, kȧ teg′ ôr em), *n.* A categorematic word. **categorematic** (kăt ė gȯr e măt′ ik), *a.* Applied to a word capable of being employed by itself as a logical term.

category (kăt′ ė gȯr i) [L. *catēgoria*, Gr. *katēgoria*, a statement, from *katēgoros*, an accuser (CATA-, AGORA, the assembly)], *n.* An order, a class, a division; (*Phil.*) one of the ten predicaments or classes of Aristotle, to which all objects of thought or knowledge can be reduced; one of Kant's twelve primitive forms of thought, contributed by the understanding, apart from experience. **categorical** (-gor′ ik ȧl), *a.* Pertaining to a category or the categories; absolute, unconditional; explicit, direct. **categorical imperative:** (*Kantian ethics*) The absolute command of the reason as interpreter of the moral law. **categorically,** *adv.*

catelectrode (kăt e lek′ trōd), *n.* (*Elect.*) The negative pole of an electric battery; a cathode

catena (kȧ tē′ nȧ) [L., see foll.], *n.* (*pl.* **-næ**) A chain; a connected series. ***Catena Patrum*:** A series of extracts from the writings of the Fathers. **catenate** (kăt′ ė nāt), *v.t.* To chain, to link together. **catenation** (-nā′ shŭn), *n.*

catenary (kȧ tē′ nȧr i) [L. *catēnārius* (*catēna*, a chain)], *n.* A curve formed by a chain or rope of uniform density hanging from two points of suspension not in one vertical line. *a.* Relating to a chain, or to a catena. **catenarian** (kăt ė nâr i ȧn), *a.* Of the nature of or resembling a chain.

cater (1) (kā′ tėr) [M.E. *catour*, a caterer, earlier *acatour*, O.F. *acateor* (*acat*, *achat*, a purchasing, late L. *accaptāre*, to purchase, freq. of *accipere*, to receive)], *v.i.* To supply food, amusement, etc. (for). **caterer,** *n.* **cateress,** *n.*

***cater** (2) (kā′ tėr) [F. *quatre*, L. *quatuor*, four], *n.* The number four on cards or dice; (*Campan.*) change-ringing on nine bells (four couples of bells changing places in the order of ringing). **cater-cornered,** *a.* Not square (applied to a house built at a corner, and therefore more or less oblique in plan; and to a sheet of paper not cut square).

cateran (kăt′ ėr ȧn) [Gael. *ceathairne*, peasantry], *n.* (*Sc.*) A Highland freebooter; *a Highland irregular soldier.

cater-cousin (kā′ tėr kŭz ėn) [prob. from CATER (1) (not from CATER (2))], *n.* Someone on very intimate terms with one.

caterpillar (kăt′ ėr pil ȧr) [etym. doubtful; perh. a corr. of O.North.F. *catepelose* (O.F. *chatepelose*), hairy-cat (*chate*, fem. of *chat*, cat, *pelose*, L. *pilōsus*, hairy, assim. to PILL (2)], *n.* The larva of a lepidopterous insect; (*Mach.*) a device whereby motor vehicles are fitted with articulated belts in lieu of wheels for operation on difficult ground. **caterpillar tractor,** *n.* (*Mach.*) A tractor fitted with an articulated belt. **caterpillar track,** *n.* (*Mach.*) An articulated belt revolving round two or more wheels, to propel a vehicle over soft or rough ground.

caterwaul (kăt ėr wawl) [CAT (1), WAUL], *v.i.* To make a noise as cats in the rutting season.

***cates** (kāts) [earlier *acates*, O.F. *acat*, a purchase (see CATER (1))], *n.pl.* Provisions; dainties, delicacies.

catgut (kăt′ gŭt), *n.* Cord made from the intestines of animals and used for strings of musical instruments; a kind of coarse cloth.

cath- [CAT-, CATA-].

Catharine [CATHERINE].

catharist (kăth′ ȧ rist) [med. L. *catharistæ*, Gr. *katharistai*, from *katharizein* (*katharos*, clean)], *n.* One who pretended to more purity of life than others (applied to various sects at different times).

catharsis (kȧ thar′ sis) [Gr. *katharsis* from *kathairein* (*katharos*, clean)], *n.* (*Med.*) Purgation of the body; (*Drama*) the purging of the emotions by tragedy (according to Aristotle's *Poetics*). **cathartic,** *a.* (*Med.*) Cleansing the bowels; purgative. *n.* A purgative medicine. **carthartical,** *a.* **cathartically,** *adv.* **cathartin,** *n.* (*Chem.*) The active principle of senna.

cathedra (kȧ thē′ drȧ, kăth′ ė drȧ) [L., from Gr. (CATH-, *hedra*, a seat)], *n.* The bishop's throne in a cathedral; hence, a professorial chair. **ex cathedra:** With authority.

cathedral (kȧ thē drȧl) [as prec.], *n.* The principal church in a diocese, containing the bishop's throne. **cathedral church,** *n.* A cathedral.

Catherine (kăth′ ėr in) [F. *Catherine*, mod. L. *Catharīna*, earlier *Katerina*, Gr. *Aikaterina* (assim. to *katharos*, pure)], *n.* **Catherine pear,** *n.* A small variety of pear. **catherine wheel** [referring to the martyrdom of St. Catherine], *n.* A firework that rotates like a wheel; (*Arch.*) an ornamental circular window with spoke-like mullions or shafts; a cartwheel somersault.

catheter (kăth′ ėt ėr) [L., from Gr. *kathetēr*, from *cathienai*, to let down (*ienai*, to send)], *n.* (*Med.*) A tubular instrument used to withdraw urine from the bladder.

cathetometer (kăth e tom′ ė têr), *n.* An instrument consisting of a telescope mounted on a vertical graduated support, used for measuring small vertical distances.

cathode (kăth′ ōd) [Gr. *kathodos*, descent], *n.* (*Elec.*) The negative electrode, the source of electrons in an electronic valve. **cathode ray,** *n.* A stream of electrons emitted from the surface of a cathode during an electrical discharge. **cathode ray tube,** *n.* (*Elec.*) A vacuum tube in which a beam of electrons, which can be controlled in direction and intensity, is projected on to a fluorescent screen thus producing a point of light. **cathodic,** *a.*

catholic (kăth′ ȯ lik) [F. *catholique*, L. *catholicus*, Gr. *katholikos*, from *kath′holou*, on the whole, universally (CATH-, *holou*, gen. of *holos*, the whole)], *a.* Universal, general, comprehensive; liberal, large-hearted, tolerant; (*Eccles.*) of or pertaining to the whole Church, not heretical or schismatic; of or pertaining to the Roman Church; orthodox, in accordance with the accepted principles of the Church. *n.* A Roman Catholic; an Anglo-Catholic. **Catholic and Apostolic Church,** *n.* The Irvingite Church. **Catholic Emancipation,** *n.* The removal of restrictions and penal laws from Roman Catholics in the United Kingdom. **Catholic Epistles,** *n.pl.* Certain epistles addressed to the Church at large, including those of Peter, James, Jude, and the 1st of John (sometimes also the 2nd and 3rd). **Catholic King,** *n.* The King of Spain. **Old Catholics,** *n.pl.* The German Catholics who separated from the Roman Communion in 1870. **Roman Catholic,** *n.* A member of the Roman Church. **catholicly, catholically** (kȧ thol′-), *adv.* **catholicism,** *n.* **catholicity** (kăth ȯ lis′ i ti), *n.* The quality of being catholic (in all the senses enumerated above). **catholicize** (kȧ thol′ i sīz), *v.t.* To make Catholic. *v.i.* To become Catholic. **catholico-,** *comb. form.*

***catholicon** (kȧ thol′ i kȯn) [F., from Gr. *katholikon*, neut. of *katholikos*, see prec.], *n.* (*Med.*) A universal medicine; a panacea; *a treatise of a general kind.

Catiline (kăt i līn) [L., Sergius *Catalīna*, a Roman conspirator, *d.* 63 B.C.], *n.* A profligate conspirator. **catilinarian** (-nâr′ i ȧn), *a.* **catalinism,** *n.*

cation (kā′ ti ȯn) [Gr. *katienai*, to go down], *n.* (*Elec.*) The positive ion which in electrolysis is attracted towards the cathode.

catkin (kăt′ kin) [prob. from Dut. *katteken*, kitten, dim. of *katte* (CAT (1), -KIN)], *n.* The pendulous unisexual inflorescence of the willow, birch, poplar, etc.

catling (kăt′ ling) [CAT (1), -LING (1)], *n.* A little cat; the smaller kind of catgut; hence, *a lutestring.

cat-nip (kăt′ nip), *n.* (*Am.*) Cat-mint.

Catonian (kȧ tō′ ni ȧn) [L. *Catōniānus*, from *Cato* (the Censor, and Uticensis)], *a.* Resembling either of the Catos; grave, severe.

catoptric (kȧ top′ trik) [Gr. *katoptrikos*, from *katoptron*, a mirror (CAT-, *optesthai*, to see)], *a.* (*Opt.*) Pertaining to a mirror or reflector, or to reflexion. **catoptrics,** *n.pl.* (*Opt.*) The science of reflected light. **catoptromancy** (kȧ top′ trȯ măn′ si) [-MANCY], *n.* Divination by looking into a mirror placed in a vessel of water.

catsup [KETCHUP].

cattle (kătl) [O.North.F. *catel* (O.F. *chatel*), late L. *captāle*, L. *capitāle*, neut. of *capitālis*, CAPITAL (2) (cp. CHATTEL)], *n.* Domesticated animals, esp. oxen and cows; often extended to sheep and pigs; (*slang*) horses; objectionable people. **cattle-duffer,** *n.* (*Austral.*) A cattle-thief. **cattle-feeder,** *n.* A mechanical device for regulating the supply of food to cattle. **cattle grid,** *n.* A trench in a road, covered by a grid which hinders cattle from passing over it but leaves the road free for traffic. **cattle-guard,** *n.* (*Am.*) A trench to keep cattle from straying on a railway. **cattle-leader,** *n.* A nose-grip used for leading dangerous beasts. **cattle-lifter, -reiver.** A cattle-stealer. **cattle-plague,** *n.* The name given to several diseases to which cattle are subject, such as foot-and-mouth disease, rinderpest, etc. **cattle-run,** *n.* (*Am.*) Grazing ground. **cattle rustler,** *n.* (*Am.*) A cattle-thief. **cattle-show,** *n.* An exhibition of cattle at which prizes are given. **cattle truck,** *n.* (*Rail.*) A van for conveying cattle.

cattleya (kăt′ lė ȧ) [Wm. *Cattley*, English horticulturist], *n.* (*Bot.*) A genus of beautifully-coloured epiphytic orchids.

catty (1) (kăt′ i) [Malay (cp. CADDY)], *n.* An East Indian weight of $1\frac{1}{3}$ lb. av.

catty (2) [CAT].

Caucasian (kaw kā′ sian, -shi ȧn), *a.* Of or pertaining to Mount Caucasus or the district adjoining; (*Ethn.*) belonging to the Indo-European race. *n.* A member of this race.

caucus (kaw′ kŭs) [etym. doubtful; perh. Algonkin *kaw-kaw-asu*, a counsellor], *n.* (*Am.*) A preparatory meeting of representatives of a political party to decide upon a course of action; a party committee controlling electoral organization; party policy; the system of organizing a political party as a machine. *v.i.* To hold a caucus. *v.t.* To control by means of a caucus. **caucuser,** *n.* **caucusdom,** *n.*

caudal (kaw' dȧl) [L. *caudālis* (*cauda*, tail)], *a.* Pertaining to the tail. **caudally,** *adv.* **caudate,** *a.* (*Nat. Hist.*) Having a tail or tail-like process. **caudiform,** *a.* (*Zool.*) Tail-shaped.

caudex (kaw' deks) [L., trunk or stem], *n.* (*pl.* **-ices**) (*Bot.*) The axis of a plant. **caudicle** [dim. of prec.], *n.* (*Bot.*) The strap which connects pollen masses to the stigma in orchids.

Caudillo (kou dē' lyō) [Sp.], *n.* (*Pol.*) The leader, the head of the state.

caudle (kaw dėl) [O.North.F. *caudel*, med. L. *caldellium*, dim. of *caldum* (L. *calidum*, neut. of *calidus*, warm)], *n.* A warm drink of wine and eggs for an invalid or a woman in childbed. *v.t.* To give as a caudle to; to comfort, refresh.

caught [CATCH].

caul (kawl) [O.F. *cale*, a little cap; etym. doubtful], *n.* The hinder part of a woman's cap; *a net for the hair; (*Anat.*) a membrane enveloping the intestines, the omentum; a part of the amnion, sometimes enclosing the head of a child when born.

cauldrife (cawl' drif) [Sc. *cauld*, COLD, RIFE], *a.* Cold, chilly; chilling, lifeless.

cauldron, caldron (kawl' drȯn) [O.North.F. *caudron* (F. *chaudron*), L. *caldārium*], *n.* A large kettle or deep, bowl-shaped vessel for boiling.

caulescent (kaw les' ėnt) [L. *caulis*, stalk, -ESCENT], *a.* (*Bot.*) Having a true stem or stalk.

caulicle, cauliculе (kaw' lik ėl) [L. *cauliculus*, dim. of *caulis*], *n.* (*Bot.*) A little stalk arising from the neck of the root.

cauliferous (kaw lif' er ŭs), *a.* Having a stalk.

cauliflower (kol i'-, kaw' li flou ėr) [earlier *cole-, colie-florie*, from O.North.F. *col* (cp. O.F. *chol*, F. *chou*, *chou-fleur*), from L. *caulis*, stem], *n.* A variety of cabbage with an edible flowering head.

caulis (kaw' lis) [L., a stalk], *n.* (*pl.* **caules** (kaw' lēz)) (*Bot.*) The stem or stalk; (*Arch.*) any of the four principal stalks from which spring the volutes in a Corinthian capital. **cauline,** *a.* Pertaining to the stem.

caulk, calk (kawk) [O.F. *cauquer* (L. *calcāre*, to tread, from *calc*, the heel)], *v.t.* (*Naut.*) To stuff the seams (of a ship) with oakum. **caulker,** *n.* **caulking,** *n.* The action of the verb TO CAULK. **caulking-iron,** *n.* A blunt chisel used by caulkers.

caulo- [Gr. *kaulos* (cp. L. *caulis*), stem], *comb. form* (*Bot.*) **caulo-bulb,** *n.* A stem with a bulbous base.

cause (kawz) [F., from L. *causa*], *n.* That which produces or contributes to an effect; (*Phil.*) the condition or aggregate of circumstances and conditions that is invariably accompanied or immediately followed by a certain effect; the person or other agent bringing about something; the reason or motive that justifies some act or mental state; a ground of action; a side or party; a movement, agitation, principle, or propaganda; a matter in dispute; (*Law*) the grounds for an action; a suit, an action. *v.t.* To act as an agent in producing; to effect; to produce; to make or induce (to do). **v.i.* To show cause. **efficient cause:** The power immediately producing an effect. **final cause:** The end or aim, esp. the ultimate object of the universe. **first cause:** The Creator. **to make common cause:** To unite for a definite purpose. **cause list,** *n.* (*Law*) A list of cases due to come up for trial. ***cause célèbre*** [F.], *n.* A famous or notorious law-suit. ***causable,** *a.* **causal,** *a.* Relating to or expressing cause; due to a cause or causes. **causally,** *adv.* **causality** (-zăl' i ti), *n.* The operation of a cause; relation of cause and effect; the theory of causation; (*Phrenol.*) the supposed faculty which traces events to their causes. **causation** (-zā' shŭn), *n.* The act of causing; connexion between cause and effect; (*Phil.*) the theory that there is a cause for everything. **causationism,** *n.* (*Phil.*) The doctrine that all things are due to the agency of a causal force. **causationist,** *n.* **causative** (kaw'-), *a.* That causes; effective as a cause; (*Gram.*) expressing cause. **causatively,** *adv.* **causeless,** *a.* Having no cause or creative agent; without just reason. **causelessly,** *adv.* ***causer,** *n.*

causerie (kō zėr ē') [F., from *causer*, to chat], *n.* A chatty kind of essay or article.

causeway (kawz' wā), **causey** (kaw' zi) [O.North. F. *caucié* (O.F. *chaucié*, F. *chaussée*), late L. *calciāta via* (L. *calcāre*, to tread, from *calx -cis*, heel) WAY], *n.* A raised road across marshy ground or shallow water; a raised footway beside a road; *a paved roadway; a path or road of any kind. *v.t.* To make a causeway for or across.

causidical (kaw sid' ik ȧl) [L. *causidicus*, a pleader], *a.* Pertaining to a legal advocate or advocacy.

caustic (kaw' stik) [L. *causticus*, Gr. *kaustikos* (*kaien*, to burn, fut. *kaus-*)], *a.* Burning, hot, corrosive; (*fig.*) bitter, sarcastic. *n.* (*Med.*) A substance that burns or corrodes organic matter. **caustic curve,** *n.* (*Math.*) A curve to which the rays of light reflected or refracted by another curve are tangents. **caustic soda,** *n.* Sodium hydroxide. **caustically,** *adv.* **causticity** (-tis' i ti), *n.*

***cautel** (kaw' tėl) [F. *cautèle*, L. *cautēla* (*caut-*, stem of *cavēre*, to beware)], *n.* A trick, a stratagem. ***cautelous,** *a.* Treacherous, tricky.

cauter (kaw' tėr) [F. *cautère*, L. *cautērium*, Gr. *kautērion*, *kautēr* (*kaein*, to burn)], *n.* A burning- or branding-iron.

cauterize (kaw' tėr īz) [F. *cautériser* late L. *cautērizāre*, from prec.], *v.t.* (*Med.*) To burn or sear (some morbid part) with a hot iron or caustic. **cauterization** (-zā' shŭn), *n.* **cautery** (kaw' tėr i), *n.* Burning with a hot iron, electricity, or a caustic; an instrument for effecting such burning; a caustic.

caution (kaw' shŭn) [F., from L. *cautio -ōnem* (*cautus*, p.p. of *cavēre*, to take heed)], *n.* Wariness, prudence; care to avoid injury or misfortune, providence; advice to be prudent, a warning; a reprimand and injunction; *security, pledge; (*Phrenol.*) the faculty of circumspection; (*slang*) something extraordinary, a strange person. *v.t.* To warn. **caution-money,** *n.* Money lodged by way of security or guarantee. **cautionary,** *a.* Given as security; containing a caution; cautious. **cautioner,** *n.* (*Sc. Law*) One who is bound as security for another. **cautious,** *a.* Heedful, careful, wary. **cautiously,** *adv.* **cautiousness,** *n.*

cavalcade (kăv ȧl kād) [F., from It. *cavalcata*, fem. of *cavalcato*, p.p. of *cavalcar* (late L. *caballicāre*, from L. *caballus*, a horse)], *n.* A company or train of riders on horseback.

cavalier (kăv ȧ lēr') [F., from It. *cavaliere* (L. *caballārius*, from *caballus*, horse)], *n.* A horseman, a knight; a gallant; a lady's man; a lover; (*Hist.*) a partisan of Charles I; a Royalist; *(*Fort.*) a work behind and commanding another. *a.* Knightly, warlike, gay; off-hand, haughty, supercilious. *v.i.* To play the cavalier to a lady. **cavaliering,** *a.* **cavalierly,** *adv.* In a haughty manner.

cavally (kȧ văl' i) [Sp. and Port. *cavalla*, mackerel (It. *caballo*, L. *caballus*, horse)], *n.* Species of tropical fish, known also as horse-mackerel.

cavalry (kăv' ȧl ri) [F. *cavallerie*, It. *cavalleria* (*cavaliere*, CAVALIER)], *n.* Horse soldiers trained to act as a body; one of the arms of the service.

cavass [KAVASS].

cavatina (kăv' ȧ tē' nȧ) [It.], *n.* (*Mus.*) A short, simple song or air.

cave (I) (kāv) [F., from L. *cava*, neut. pl. of *cavus*, hollow (cp. Gr. *kuar*, a cavity)], *n.* A hollow place in the earth; a den; (*Polit.*) the secession of a discontented body from their party; the body of seceders (see ADULLAMITE); (*slang*) a caving-in. *v.t.* To hollow out; to cause to cave in. *v.i.* To give way, to cave in; to secede from a political party; *to dwell in a cave. **cave-bear,** *n.* An extinct species of bear, *Ursus spelæus.* **cave-earth,** *n.* The earth forming the floor of a cave. **cave-hyæna,** *n.* An extinct species of hyæna, *H. spelæa.* **cave-lion,** *n.* A lion that used to inhabit caves, *Felis spelæa.* **cave-man,** *n.* (*facet.*) A man of primitive instincts. **cave-men, cave-dwellers,** *n.pl.* Prehistoric men who dwelt in caves. **to cave in** [perh. *calve in* (cp. Flem. *inkalven*, Dut. *afkalven*)], *v.i.* To fall in; (*fig.*) to give in, to yield. *v.t.* (*slang*) To smash in (hat, head, etc.).

cave (2) (kā' vē) [L., beware], *int.* Look out!

caveat (kā' vė ăt) [L., let him beware], *n.* (*Law*) A process to stop procedure; (*Am.*) a notice of intention to apply for a patent; (*fig.*) a warning, a caution. **caveator** (kā' vė ā tòr), *n.* (*Law*) One who enters a caveat.

cavendish (kăv' ėn dish) [perh. from the maker's name], *n.* A kind of tobacco softened and pressed into cakes.

cavern (kăv' ėrn) [F. *caverne*, L. *caverna* (*cavus*, see CAVE)], *n.* A cave; a deep hollow place in the earth. *v.t.* To shut or enclose in a cavern; to hollow out. **caverned,** *a.* **cavernous,** *a.* Hollow or huge, like a cavern; full of caverns.

cavey [CAVY].

caviar, caviare (kav' i ar, kăv yar', kăv i ăr' [etym. doubtful], *n.* The roes of various fish, esp. the sturgeon, dried and salted. **caviare to the general:** Something too refined to be generally appreciated.

cavicorn (kăv' i kôrn) [L. *cavus*, hollow, *cornu*, horn], *a.* (*Zool.*) Having hollow horns. *n.* A hollow-horned ruminant, one of the *Cavicornia.*

cavie (kā' vi) [prob. from M.Dut. *kēvie*, ult. from late L. *cavea* (L. *cavus*, hollow)], *n.* (*Sc.*) A hen-coop; a fowl-house.

cavil (kăv' il) [O.F. *caviller*, L. *cavillāri* (*cavilla*, jeer, mockery)], *n.* A frivolous objection. *v.i.* To argue captiously. *v.t.* To object to frivolously. ***cavillation** (-lā' shŭn), *n.* **caviller,** *n.* **cavilling,** *a.* **cavillingly,** *adv.*

cavitation (kăv i tā' shŭn) [as foll.], *n.* The formation of a cavity or partial vacuum between a solid and a liquid in rapid relative motion, *e.g.* on a propeller.

cavity (kăv' i ti) [F. *cavité* (L. *cavus*, CAVE)], *n.* A hollow place or part.

cavo-rilievo (ka' vō rē lyā' vō) [It., hollow relief], *n.* (*pl.* ***-vi***) Sculpture made by hollowing out a flat surface and leaving the figures standing out to the original level.

cavort (kȧ vôrt') [perh. corr. of CURVET], *v.i.* To prance about; to bustle about in an important manner.

cavy, cavey (kā' vi) [French Guiana native *cabiai*], *n.* A South American rodent; any of the genus *Cavia*, esp. *C. Cobaya*, the guinea-pig.

caw (kaw) [imit.], *v.i.* To cry like a rook. **to caw out:** To utter in a cawing tone. *n.* The cry of a rook.

cawk (kawk) [North. var. of CHALK, or perh. from Dut. *kalk*], *n.* (*Min.*) An opaque, compact variety of baryta.

cawker [CAULKER].

***caxon** (kăk' sŏn) [prob. from a pers. name], *n.* An obsolete style of wig.

Caxton (kăks' tŏn) [pers. name], *n.* A black-letter book printed by William Caxton, the first English printer (c. 1422–1491); type of the same pattern as Caxton's.

cay, key (2) (kā, kē) [Sp. *cayo*, med. L. *caium*, prob. from Celt (cp. W. *cae*, a hedge, a field, Bret. *kaé*, an enclosure, an embankment)], *n.* A reef, a shoal.

cayenne (kā en'), **Cayenne pepper** [Braz. *kýonha*, assim. to *Cayenne*, in French Guiana], *n.* The powdered fruit of various species of capsicum, used as a condiment.

cayman, caiman (kā' măn) [Carib. *acáyouman*], *n.* A tropical American alligator.

cayuse (kī ūs') [Am. Ind.], *n.* A small Indian horse.

cazique [CACIQUE].

Ceanothus (sē ă nō' thŭs) [Gr. *keanothos*, a kind of thistle], *n.* (*Bot.*) A genus of ornamental flowering N. American shrub of the buckthorn family.

cease (sēs) [F. *cesser*, L. *cessāre*, freq. of *cēdere* (p.p. *cessus*), to go, to yield], *v.i.* To come to an end, to leave off; to desist (from). *v.t.* To put a stop to; to discontinue. **n.* The end; extinction. **without cease:** Without intermission. **ceaseless,** *a.* Incessant, unceasing. **ceaselessly,** *adv.* **ceaselessness,** *n.*

cecity (sē' si ti) [L. *cæcitas*, from *cæcus*, blind], *n.* Blindness (physical or mental).

cedar (sē' dȧr) [O.F. *cedre*, L. *cedrus*, Gr. *kedros*], *n.* Evergreen coniferous trees with durable and fragrant wood, comprising the cedar of Lebanon, *Abies cedrus*, and many others. **cedared,** *a.* Covered with cedars. **cedarn,** *a.* (*poet.*) Made of cedar-wood; consisting of cedars. **cedrela** (sē drē' la) [Latinized from Sp. *cedrela*, dim. of *cedro*, CEDAR], *n.* A genus of East and West Indian and Australian trees. **cedrelaceous** (sē drė lā' shŭs), *a.* (*Bot.*)

cede (sēd) [L. *cēdere*, to yield], *v.t.* To give up, to surrender; to yield, grant.

cedilla (sė dil' ȧ) [Sp. *çedilla*, It. *zediglia*, dim. of Gr. *zēta*, Z], *n.* A mark (ͅ) placed under the *c* to show that it has the sound of *s*.

cedrela [CEDAR].

cee (sē), *n.* The letter C. **cee-spring, C-spring,** *n.* A C-shaped carriage-spring.

ceil (sēl) [prob. from F. *ciel*, heaven, L. *cælum* (influenced by L. *cælāre*, to emboss; cp. late L. *cælātūra*, a vaulted roof)], *v.t.* To line the roof of a room, esp. with plaster.

ceiling (sē' ling), *n.* The inner, upper surface of an apartment; the plaster or other lining of this; (*Aviat.*) the maximum height to which an aircraft can climb; (*Econ.*) the upper limit of prices, wages, etc. **ceiling price,** *n.* The maximum price for commodities, etc., fixed by law. **ceilinged,** *a.* Having a ceiling.

ceinture (săn' chūr) [Fr., girdle], *n.* (*Eccles.*) The belt of leather, stuff, or rope worn round the waist outside the cassock.

celadon (sel' ȧ dŏn) [F. perh. after the character of that name in D'Urfé's *Astrée*], *a.* and *n.* A soft, pale green colour.

celandine (sel' ȧn dīn) [O.F. *celindoine*, L. *chelidonia*, Gr. *chelidonion*, swallow-wort, neut. of *chelidonios* (*chelidōn*, swallow)], *n.* The name of two plants with yellow flowers, the **greater celandine,** *Chelidonium majus*, related to the poppy, and the **lesser celandine,** *Ranunculus ficaria*, also called the pile-wort or figwort.

celarent (sē lăr' ent) [L., they might hide], *n.* (*Log.*) A mnemonic word applied to the mood of the first figure in which the major premise and the conclusion are universal negatives, and the minor premise a universal affirmative.

celation (se lā' shŭn) [L. *celare*, to conceal], *n.* (*Law*) Concealment (of birth, etc.).

-cele (sēl) [Gr. *kēlē*, a tumour], *comb. form.* (*Path.*) A tumour; *e.g.* **enterocele,** a tumour or swelling arising from hernia.

celebrate (sel' ė brāt) [L. *celebrātus*, p.p. of *celebrāre* (*celeber -bris*, frequented, populous)], *v.t.* To praise, extol; to make famous; to commemorate; to observe; to perform, to say or sing (as Mass), to administer (as Communion). *v.i.* To officiate at the

Eucharist. **celebrated,** *a.* Famous, renowned. **celebration** (-brā′ shŭn), *n.* **celebrator** (sel′-), *n.* **celebrant,** *n.* The priest who officiates in any solemn office, esp. at Mass or at Holy Communion. **celebrity** (sė leb′ ri ti), *n.* Fame, renown; a celebrated personage.

celeriac (sė ler′ i ăc), *n.* A turnip-rooted variety of celery.

celerity (sė ler′ i ti) [F. *célérité*, L. *celeritas -tātem* (*celer*, swift, cp. Gr. *kelēs*, a runner)], *n.* Speed, swiftness, promptness.

celery (sel′ ėr i) [F. *céleri*, prov. It. *seleri, seleni*, from L., from Gr. *selinon*, parsley], *n.* A plant, *Apium graveolens*, the blanched stems of which are eaten cooked or as a salad. **celery fly,** *n.* (*Entom.*) A small, two-winged fly, *Acadia heraclei*, the larvæ of which destroy the leaves of celery and parsnips.

celestial (sė les′ ti ăl) [O.F., from L. *cælestis*; AL], *a.* Pertaining to heaven or the heavens; spiritual, angelic, divine. *n.* An inhabitant of heaven; a native of China. **Celestial Empire** [trans. of a native name meaning that the empire is divinely established], *n.* The old Chinese empire. **celestial sphere:** (*Astron.*) An imaginary sphere with the observer at its centre and all heavenly objects on its surface. **celestially,** *adv.*

Celestine (1) (sel′ ės tīn, sė les′ tin), **Celestinian** (-tin′ yăn) [L. *Celestīnus*], *n.* One of a monastic order founded about 1254 by Pietro di Morone, afterwards Pope Celestine V.

celestine (2) (sel′ ės tin), **celestite** (sel′ ės tīt) [perh. from It. *celestino*, sky-blue], *n.* (*Min.*) A native sulphate of strontium.

celiac [CŒLIAC].

celibate (sel′ i băt) [orig. the unmarried state, from F. *célibat*, L. *cælibātus*, celibacy (*cælebs -libem*, unmarried)], *n.* An unmarried person. *a.* Unmarried; devoted or vowed to a single life; fitted for a single life. **celibatarian** (-târ′ i ăn), *a.* **celibacy,** *n.* Single life; the unmarried state.

cell (sel) [O.F. *celle*, L. *cella* (cp. *cēlāre*, to hide)], *n.* A small room, esp. one in a monastery or prison; a small religious house dependent on a larger one; the retreat of a hermit; (*poet.*) a humble dwelling; the grave; a small cavity; a cavity in the brain, formerly supposed to be the seat of a particular faculty; a compartment in a comb made by bees; (*Biol.*) the unit-mass of living matter in animals or plants; (*Zool.*) the cup-like cavity containing an individual zoophyte in a compound organism; a subsidiary unit of a political organization or a trade union; (*Elec.*) a division of a galvanic battery, or a battery having only one pair of metallic plates. **celled,** *a.* **celliferous** (-lif′ ėr ŭs), *a.* **celliform** (sel′ i fôrm), *a.*

cella (sel′ ȧ) [L., CELL], *n.* (*Arch.*) The central chamber in a temple.

cellar (1) (sel′ ȧr) [O.F. *celier* (F. *cellier*), L. *cellārium*], *n.* A vault for stores under ground; a place for storing wine; (*fig.*) a stock of wine; underground chamber beneath a house used for storing coal, etc. *v.t.* To put in a cellar; to store in a cellar. **cellarage** (sel′ ȧr ȧj), *n.* Cellars collectively; space for or charge for storage in cellars. **cellarer,** *n.* A monk in charge of the stores; an officer of a chapter in charge of the provisions. **cellaress,** *n.* **cellaret** (sel ȧr et′), *n.* A small case with compartments for holding bottles; a sideboard for storing wine. **cellaring,** *n.* Cellars or cellar space. **cellar-man,** *n.* One employed in a wine or beer cellar.

cellar (2) [SALT-CELLAR].

’cello [VIOLONCELLO].

Cellophane (sel′ ō fān), *n.* Protected trade name of a transparent material chiefly used for wrapping.

cellule (sel′ ūl) [L. *cellula*, dim. of *cella*, CELL], *n.* A little cell. **cellular,** *a.* Of, pertaining to, or resembling a cell or cells; pertaining to a monastic cell; (*Physiol.*) composed of cells. *n.* A cellular plant having no distinct stem or leaves; a cryptogamic plant having spiral vessels. **cellular tissue,** *n.* Tissue composed of minute cells. **cellulate, cellulated,** *a.* Formed of cells. **cellulation** (-lā′ shŭn), *n.* **celluliferous** (sel ū lif′ ėr ŭs), *a.*

cellulo- *comb. form.* Composed of cells.

celluloid (sel′ ū loid), *n.* A thermoplastic made from nitro-cellulose, camphor and alcohol. Used for photographic films and as a substitute for ivory, horn, tortoiseshell, etc.

cellulose (sel′ ū lōz), *n.* (*Chem. & Biol.*) A carbohydrate of a starchy nature that forms the cell walls of all plants. *a.* Containing or consisting of cells. **cellulosity,** *n.*

Celosia (se lō′ shi ȧ) [Gr. *kelos*, burnt], *n.* (*Bot.*) A genus of plants of the amaranth family, containing *Celosia cristata*, the cockscomb.

Celt (1) (kelt, selt), **Kelt** [F. *Celte*, L. *Celtæ*, pl., Gr. *Keltoi, Keltai*], *n.* A member or descendant of an ancient race comprising the Welsh, Cornish, Manx, Irish, Gaels, and Bretons, whose descendants are still found in the Highlands of Scotland, Ireland, Wales, and the north of France. **Celtic, Keltic** (L. *Celticus*), *a.* Pertaining to the Celts. *n.* The language of the Celts. **Celtically,** *adv.* **Celticism** (-ti sizm), *n.* A custom peculiar to the Celts. **Celticize,** *v.i.* To become Celtic. *v.t.* To make Celtic. **Celto-,** *comb. form.* **Celtologist** (-tol′ ŏ jist), *n.* A student of Celtic antiquities, philology, etc. **Celtomaniac** (-mā′ ni ăk), *n.* **Celtophil,** *n.*

celt (2) (selt) [late Lat. *celtis*, a chisel, a hypothetical word from a reading *celte* (perh. *certe*) in the Vulgate book of Job], *n.* A prehistoric cutting or cleaving implement of stone or bronze.

cembalo (chem′ ba lō, sem′ ba lō) [It.], *n.* (*Mus.*) A stringed instrument played with hand-hammers on a keyboard.

cement (sė ment′) [O.F. *ciment*, L. *cæmentum* (prob. short for *cædimentum*, from *cædere*, to cut)], *n.* An adhesive substance, esp. one used in building for binding masonry and brickwork and hardening like stone; any analogous material, paste, gum, or mucilage for sticking things together; a substance for stopping teeth, the outer crust of the fangs of teeth; (*fig.*) a bond of union. *v.t.* To unite with or as with cement; to line or coat with cement; to unite firmly and closely. *v.i.* To cohere. **cementation** (-tā′ shŭn), *n.* The act of cementing; (*Min.*) the conversion of iron into steel by heating the former in a mass of charcoal.

cemetery (sem′ ė tėr i) [L. *cæmētērium*, Gr. *koimētērion*, orig. dormitory (*koimaein*, to put to sleep)], *n.* A public burial-ground that is not a churchyard.

cenacle (sen′ ăkl) [L. *cenaculum*, a dining-room], *n.* The room, or a representation of it, in which the Last Supper took place; a former French literary coterie.

cenobite [CŒNOBITE].

cenotaph (sen′ ō tăf) [F. *cénotaphe*, L. *cenotaphium*, Gr. *kenotaphion* (*kenos*, empty, *taphos*, tomb)], *n.* A sepulchral monument raised to a person buried elsewhere; (*fig.*) a tomb whence one has arisen. **The Cenotaph,** *n.* The monument in Whitehall, London, commemorating those in the British armed forces who died in the wars of 1914–18 and 1939–45.

cense (sens) [from obs. n. *cense*, incense, or short for v. INCENSE], *v.t.* To perfume with incense; to worship with incense. **censer** (sen′ sĕr) [O.F. *censier, encensier* (late L. *incensum*, incense, p.p. of *incendere*, to burn; cp. *candēre*, to glow)], *n.* A vessel for burning incense; a thurible; a vessel for burning perfumes.

censor (sen′ sŏr) [L., from *censēre*, to tax, to appraise], *n.* A Roman officer who registered the property of the citizens, imposed the taxes, and watched over manners and morals; a public officer appointed to examine books, plays, etc., before they are published, to see that they contain nothing immoral, seditious, or offensive; a public servant whose duty it is in war-time to see that nothing is published, or passes through the post, that might give information to the enemy; (*Psych.*) the superego, an unconscious mechanism in the mind that excludes disturbing factors from the conscious; one given to reproof or censure of other people; (*Univ.*) officials who issue licences, etc. *v.t.* To control any sort of publication in this way; to expurgate or delete objectionable matter from. **censorial, *censorian,** *a.* **censorious** (sėn sôr′-), *a.* Expressing or addicted to criticism or censure. **censoriously,** *adv.* **censoriousness,** *n.* **censorship,** *n.*

censure (sen′ shůr) [F., from L. *censūra* (*censēre,* see prec.)], *n.* *Opinion; disapproval, condemnation; an expression of this; blame, reproach. *v.t.* *To form or give a judgment or opinion on; to blame; to find fault with. **v.i.* To form an opinion (of). **censurable,** *a.* **censurableness,** *n.* **censurably,** *adv.*

census (sen′ sůs) [L., from *censēre* (see CENSOR)], *n.* An official enumeration of the inhabitants of a country; the statistical result of such enumeration.

cent (sent) [L. *centum*], *n.* A hundred; a coin of the value of the 100th part of a dollar; an insignificant coin. **per cent:** By the hundred. ***centage** (sen′ tȧj), *n.* Rate per hundred; percentage. **cental,** *n.* A weight of 100 lb. used for grain.

centaur (sen′ tawr) [L. *centauros,* Gr. *kentauros*; etym. doubtful], *n.* A Greek mythological figure, half man, half horse; (*fig.*) any incongruous union of diverse natures; a fine horseman; (*Astron.*) a constellation in the southern hemisphere. **centauress,** *n.* **centauromachy** (sen taw rom′ ȧ ki), *n.* A battle of centaurs.

centaury (sen′ taw ri, -tėr i) [L. *centaurēa, centaurēum,* Gr. *kentaureion* (nom. *kentaureios* after the Centaur Cheiron)], *n.* The name of various plants once used medically; the lesser centaury, *Erythræum centaurium*; *the genus *Centaurea*; (*Am.*) the genus *Sabbatia.* **yellow centaury:** *Chlora perfoliata.*

centenarian (sen tė nâr′ i ȧn), *n.* A person who has reached the age of one hundred years. **centenary** (sen tē′ nȧ ri, sen′ tė nȧr i) [L. *centēnārius,* from *centēni,* a hundred each (*centum,* CENT)], *a.* Relating to a hundred; recurring once in a hundred years. *n.* A hundred years; the hundredth anniversary of any event, or the celebration of this. **centennial** (sėn ten′ i ȧl), *a.* Pertaining to a hundredth anniversary; a hundred or more years old; completing a hundred years. *n.* A centenary.

center [CENTRE].

centering (sen′ tėr ing) [CENTRE], *n.* (*Arch.*) The woodwork or framing on which an arch or vault is constructed.

centesimal (sėn tes′ i mȧl, -tē′ si mȧl) [L. *centēsimus,* -AL], *a.* Hundredth; by fractions of a hundred. *n.* A 100th part. **centesimally,** *adv.*

centi- [L. *centum,* a hundred], *comb. form.* (*Metric system*) A hundred; a 100th part. **centifolious** (sen ti fō′ li ůs) [L. *foliōsus, folium,* leaf], *a.* (*Bot.*) Hundred-leaved.

centigram (sent′ i grăm), *n.* The hundredth part of a gramme.

centigrade (sent′ i grād), *a.* Divided into a hundred degrees; applied esp. to the thermometer of Celsius in which the freezing-point of water is marked 0° and the boiling-point 100°.

centilitre (sent′ i lēt ėr), *n.* The hundredth part of a litre.

centime (son′ tēm), A French coin worth a hundredth part of a franc.

centimetre (sent′ i mē tėr), *n.* The hundredth part of a metre, 0·394 inch.

centipede (sen′ ti pēd) [L. *centipeda* (CENTI-, *pes pedis,* foot)], *n.* An articulated animal popularly supposed to have a hundred feet.

centner (sent′ nėr) [G., from L. *centēnārius,* CENTENARY], *n.* A German weight equal to 110½ lb.; (*Am.*) 100 lb.

cento (sen′ tō) [L., a patchwork], *n.* A composition of verses from different authors, arranged in a new order; a string of quotations, scraps, and tags.

central (sen′ trȧl) [L. *centrālis* (*centrum,* CENTRE)], *a.* Relating to, containing, proceeding from, or situated in the centre; (*fig.*) principal, of chief importance. **central fire,** *a.* (*Cartridge*) Having the fulminate placed at a central point instead of being distributed near the rim. **central forces,** *n.pl.* (*Phys.*) The centrifugal and centripetal forces. **central heating,** *n.* A system of warming buildings from one furnace by steam or hot-water pipes or other devices. **centralism,** *n.* A system or policy of centralization. **Central Wages Board,** *n.* A board dealing with wage questions and demands of railway workers. **centralist,** *n.* **centrality** (sen trăl′ i ti), *n.* The quality of being central. **centralize,** *v.t.* To bring to a centre; to concentrate. *v.i.* To come to a centre. **centralization** (sen trȧ li zā′ shůn), *n.* The act of centralizing; the system or policy of carrying on the government or any administrative organization at one central spot. **centrally,** *adv.* **centralness,** *n.*

centre, center (sen′ tėr) [F. *centre,* L. *centrum,* Gr. *kentron,* a spike (*kentein,* to prick)], *n.* The middle of anything; the middle or central object; the point round which anything revolves, the pivot or axis; the principal point; the nucleus, the source from which anything radiates or emanates; the head or leader of an organization; a political party occupying a place between two extremes (**left centre,** the more radical portion; and **right centre,** the more conservative of this); (*Austral.*) Central Australia, Centralia; (*Mil.*) the main mass of troops between the wings; the framing on which an arch or vault is constructed; centering. *v.t.* To place on a centre; to collect to a point; to find the centre of. *v.i.* To be fixed on a centre; to be collected at one point. *a.* At or of the centre. **centre-bit,** *n.* A carpenter's tool consisting of a bit fixed in a brace, for boring large round holes. **centre-board,** *n.* (*Naut.*) A sliding keel which can be raised or lowered; a boat fitted with this. **centre-forward,** *n.* (*Football*) A player occupying the middle of the front line. **centre of attraction,** *n.* One who draws general attention; (*Phys.*) the point towards which bodies gravitate. **centre of buoyancy,** *n.* The centre of gravity of the liquid displaced by a floating body. **centre of gravity,** *n.* The point about which all the parts of a body exactly balance each other. **centre of inertia** or **mass,** *n.* A point through which a body's inertial force acts (coincident with the centre of gravity). **centre-piece,** *n.* An ornament for the middle of a table, ceiling, etc. **centre-second(s),** *a.* (*Clock-making*) (of a seconds hand) Fitted on its own arbor with those of the hour and minute hands. **centric,** *a.* Central; **n.* (*Astron.*) A circle concentric with the earth. **centrical,** *a.* **centrically,** *adv.* **centricity** (sen tris′ i ti), *n.*

centrepede (sen′ tėr pēd), *n.* A ladder made of a single upright with cross-pieces nailed on at intervals.

centrifugal (sen trif′ ū gȧl) [*centrum,* CENTRE, *fugere,* to fly from], *a.* Tending to fly or recede from the centre; (*Bot.*) expanding first at the summit, and last at the base (of inflorescence). **centrifugal force,** *n.* (*Phys.*) The tendency of a revolving body to fly off from the centre. **centrifugal machine,** *n.* A machine utilizing this force for drying or separating purposes. **centrifuge** (sen′ tri fūj), *n.* A centrifugal machine for separating liquids of different density, such as cream and milk. **centrifugally,** *adv.*

centripetal (sen trip′ ė tȧl) [*centrum,* CENTRE, *petere,* to seek], *a.* Tending to approach the centre; (*Bot.*) expanding first at the base, and then at the end or centre (of inflorescence). **centripetal force,** *n.* (*Phys.*) The force which draws a revolving body towards the centre. **centripetally,** *adv.*

centro- [L. *centrum,* centre], *comb. form.* Central, centrally.

centrobaric (sen trō băr′ ik), *a.* Pertaining to the centre of gravity.

centrode (sen′ trōd) [L. *centrum*, Gr. *hodos*, a path], *n.* (*Math.*) A locus traced out by the successive positions of an instantaneous centre of pure rotation.

centrolineal (sen trō lin′ i ȧl), *a.* Converging to a centre.

centumvir (sen tŭm′ vir) [L. (*centum*, hundred, *vir*, man)], *n.* (*pl.* **-viri**) One of the judges appointed by the prætor to decide common causes among the Romans. **centumviral,** *a.* **centumvirate** (-vir ȧt), *n.* The office or position of a centumvir; the rule of the centumviri.

centuple (sen′ tūpl) [F., from late L. *centuplum*, nom. *-us*, L. *centuplex* (*centum*, a hundred)], *n.* A hundredfold. *a.* Hundredfold. *v.t.* To multiply a hundredfold. **centuplicate** (sen tū′ pli kāt), *v.t.* To multiply a hundredfold. **centuplicate** (sen tū′ pli kȧt), *n.* A centuple. *a.* Centuple. **in centuplicate,** *adv.* A hundred-fold. **centuplication** (kā′ shun), *n.*

centurion (sen tū′ ri ŏn) [L. *centurio*], *n.* A Roman military officer commanding a company of a hundred men.

century (sen′ tū ri) [F. *centurie*, L. *centuria* (*centum* a hundred)], *n.* An aggregate of a hundred things; a hundred; a period of a hundred years; (*Hist.*) a division of the Roman people for the election of magistrates, etc.; a division of a legion, consisting originally of a hundred men; (*Cricket*) a hundred runs. **century plant,** *n.* The American aloe, *Agave Americanus*, erroneously supposed to flower only once in a hundred years. **centurial** (-tū′ ri ȧl), *a.*

ceorl (kyĕrl , syĕrl) [CHURL], *n.* An old English freeman, below the thane and above the serf.

cephal-, cephalo- (sef′ ȧl, -ȧ lō) [Gr. *kephalē*, the head], *comb. forms.* (*Physiol. and Anat.*) Pertaining to the head.

cephalalgia, cephalalgy (sef ăl ăl′ ji ȧ, -ji) [Gr. *algia*, pain], *n.* (*Path.*) Headache. **cephalalgic,** *a.* Pertaining to headache; *n.* A medicine for headache.

cephalaspis (sef ȧl ăs′ pis) [Gr. *aspis*, a shield], *n.* (*Geol.*) A genus of fossil Ganoids.

cephalic (se făl′ ik), *a.* Pertaining to the head. *n.* A remedy for pains in the head. **cephalic index,** *n.* (*Ethn.*) The ratio of a transverse to the longitudinal diameter of the skull.

-cephalic, -cephalous [Gr. *kephalē*, the head], *comb. forms.* (*Anat. and Ethn.*) Headed, see HYDROCEPHALOUS, MICROCEPHALOUS, BRACHYCEPHALIC, ORTHOCEPHALIC.

cephalitis (sef ȧ lī′ tis), *n.* (*Path.*) Inflammation of the brain.

cephaloid (sef′ ȧ loid), *a.* Shaped like a head.

cephalopod (se făl′ ō pod), *n.* (*Zool.*) Mollusc having a distinct head with prehensile and locomotive organs attached.

cephalothorax (sef ȧ lō thôr′ ăks), *n.* (*Zool.*) The anterior division of the body, consisting of the coalescence of head and thorax in spiders, crabs, and other arthropods.

cephalotomy (sef ȧ lot′ ō mi), *n.* (*Med.*) The dissection of the head.

cephalous (sef′ ȧ lŭs), *a.* Having a head.

ceramic, keramic (sė-, kė răm′ ik) [Gr. *keramikos* (*keramos*, potter's earth, pottery)], *a.* Of or pertaining to pottery. **ceramics,** *n.pl.* The art of pottery. **ceramist** (ser′-, ker′ ȧ mist), *n.*

cerasin (ser′ ȧ sin) [L. *cerasus*, cherry], *n.* (*Chem.*) The insoluble part of the gum of the cherry and plum trees.

cerastes (sė răs′ tēz) [L., from Gr. *kerastēs* (*keras*, horn)], *n.* A horned viper.

cerated (sēr′ āt ėd) [L. *cērātus*, p.p. of *cērāre*, to cover with wax (*cēra*, wax)], *a.* Waxed; covered with wax.

cerato- [Gr. *keras keratos*, a horn], *comb. form.* (*Zool.*) Horned; horny; having processes like horns. **ceratoid** (ser′ ȧ toid) [-OID], *a.* Horny; horn-like. **ceratophyte** (ser′ ȧ tō fīt) [-PHYTE], *n.* A coral polyp with a horny axis. **ceratotome** (ser′ ȧ tō tōm) [Gr. *-tomos*, cutting (*temnein*, to cut)], *n.* An instrument for cutting the cornea.

ceraunoscope (sė raw′ nō skōp) [Gr. *keraunoskopeion* (*keraunos*, thunderbolt, *skopeein*, to look at)], *n.* An apparatus for imitating thunder and lightning, used by the ancients in their mysteries.

Cerberus (sĕr′ bėr ŭs) [L., from Gr. *Kerberos*], *n.* A three-headed dog, fabled to guard the entrance of Hades. **a sop to Cerberus:** A propitiatory bribe.

cercaria (sėr kâr′ i ȧ) [mod. L., from Gr. *kerkos*, tail)], *n.* (*Zool.*) A trematode worm or fluke in its second larval stage.

cere (sēr) [F. *cire*, L. *cēra* (cp. *cērāre*, to wax)], *n.* (*Ornith.*) The naked, wax-like skin at the base of the bill in many birds. *v.t.* To cover with wax. **cereous,** *a.* Waxen, waxy; like wax. **cerin** (sēr′ in), *n.* A crystalline substance obtained from cork, from which it is extracted by means of ether or soluble alcohol. **cerecloth** (sēr′ kloth), *n.* A cloth dipped in melted wax, used to wrap embalmed bodies in. **cerement** (sēr′ mėnt) [F. *cirement*], *n.* A cerecloth; (*pl.*) grave-clothes.

cereal (sēr′ i ȧl) [L. *cereālis* (*Ceres*, the goddess of corn)], *a.* Pertaining to wheat or other grain. *n.* Any edible grain; a breakfast food made from a cereal. **cerealian** (sēr ė ā′ li ȧn), *a.* **cerealin** (sēr′ ė ȧ lin), *n.* (*Chem.*) A nitrogenous substance found in bran.

cerebellum, cerebel (ser ė bel′ ŭm) [L., dim. of *cerebrum*, brain)], *n.* (*pl.* **-la**) (*Physiol.*) A portion of the brain situated beneath the posterior lobes of the cerebrum. **cerebellar, cerebellous,** *a.*

cerebrum (se reb′ rŭm) [L., brain], *n.* (*pl.* **cerebra**) The chief portion of the brain, filling the upper cavity of the skull. **cerebral,** *a.* Of or pertaining to the brain. **cerebral hemisphere,** *n.* One of the two great divisions of the brain. **cerebral letter,** *n.* A consonant sounded by touching the roof of the mouth with the tip of the tongue. **cerebralism,** *n.* The theory that mental operations arise from activity of the brain. **cerebration** (-brā′ shŭn), *n.* The action of the brain, whether conscious or unconscious. **cerebric,** *a.* Cerebral. **cerebric acid,** *n.* A fatty compound obtained from nerve tissue. **cerebrin,** *n.* (*Chem.*) A name given to several substances obtained from brain matter. **cerebritis** (ser ė brī′ tis), *n.* (*Med.*) Inflammation of the brain. **cerebro-** (ser′ ė brō), *comb. form.* Relating to the brain. **cerebro-spinal** (ser ė brō′ spī′ nȧl) [SPINAL], *a.* (*Med.*) Pertaining to the brain and to the spinal cord. **cerebro-spinal meningitis,** *n.* (*Path.*) Inflammation of the brain and spinal cord, spotted fever.

cerement [CERE].

ceremonial (se ri mō′ ni ȧl) [as foll.], *a.* Relating to or performed with ceremonies or rites. *n.* The prescribed order for a ceremony or function; a polite usage or formality; observance of etiquette; (*R.-C. Ch.*) the rules for rites and ceremonies; the book containing these. **ceremonialism,** *n.* Fondness for or adherence to ceremony. **ceremonialist,** *n.* **ceremonially,** *adv.*

ceremony (ser′ ė mŏ ni) [O.F. *ceremonie*, L. *cærimōnia* (cp. Sansk. *karman*, an action, a rite)], *n.* A prescribed rite or formality; a usage of politeness; formality, punctilio. **master of ceremonies:** One whose duty it is to see that due formalities are observed on public or state occasions; person responsible for the running of a dance, etc. **to stand on ceremony:** To be rigidly conventional. **ceremonious,** *a.* Punctiliously observant of ceremony according to prescribed form. **ceremoniously,** *adv.* **ceremoniousness,** *n.*

cereous, cerin [CERE].

cerinthian (sė rin′ thi ȧn) [*Cerinthus*, -IAN], *a.* Pertaining to Cerinthus, an early heretic, who taught a mixture of Gnosticism, Christianity and Judaism.

ceriph [SERIF].

cerise (sė rēz′) [F., *cherry*, L. *cerasus*, Gr. *kerasos*], *n.* Cherry colour. *a.* Cherry-coloured.

cerium (sēr′ i ŭm) [after the planet *Ceres*], *n.* (*Chem.*) A grey metallic element found in cerite. **cerite** (sēr īt), *n.* (*Min.*) A silicious oxide of cerium.

cero- [L. *cēra* or Gr. *kēros*, wax], *comb. form.* Pertaining to or composed of wax. **cerography** (sė rog′ rȧ fi) [-GRAPHY], *n.* The art of writing or engraving on wax; painting in wax-colours; encaustic painting. **cerographical** (sēr ȯ grăf′ ik ȧl), *a.* **cerographist** (sē rog′ rȧ fist), *n.* **ceromancy** (sēr ȯ măn′ si) [-MANCY], *n.* Divination from the forms assumed by melting wax dropped into water. **ceroplastic** (sēr ȯ plăs′ tik) [PLASTIC], *a.* Modelled in wax; modelling in wax. **ceroplastics,** *n.pl.* The art of modelling in wax.

cert [CERTAIN].

certain (sěr′ tȧn) [O.F. *certein*, L. *certus*, -AN], *a.* Sure, convinced, assured, absolutely confident; established beyond a doubt, undoubtedly existing; absolutely determined, regular, fixed; sure to happen, inevitable; sure to do, reliable, unerring; not particularized, indefinite. *n.* An indefinite number or quantity. **for certain:** Assuredly. **cert:** (*slang*) A certainty. **certainly,** *adv.* Assuredly; beyond doubt; without fail; admittedly, yes. **certainty,** *n.* That which is certain; absolute assurance. ***certes** (sěr′ tėz) [O.F.], *adv.* Certainly, assuredly.

certificate (sěr tif′ i kȧt) [*as foll.*], *n.* A written testimony or voucher, esp. of character or ability. *v.t.* (sěr tif′ i kāt) To give a certificate to; to license by certificate. **certificated,** *a.* Possessing a certificate from some examining body. **certification** (sěr tif i kā′ shŭn), *n.*

certify (sěr′ ti fī) [F. *certifier*, L. *certificāre* (*certus*, certain, *facere*, to make)], *v.t.* To assure, to testify to in writing; to give certain information of or to; to certify as insane. **certifiable,** *a.* **certifier,** *n.* **certified milk,** *n.* Milk guaranteed free from tubercle bacillus.

certiorari (sěr shi ȯ râr′ ī) [L. to be certified], *n.* (*Law*) A writ issuing from a superior court calling for the records of or removing a case from a court below.

certitude (sěr′ ti tūd), *n.* The quality of being certain; certainty, conviction.

cerulean (sė roo′ lė ȧn) [L. *cæruleus* (prob. for *cælulus*, from *cælum*, the sky), -AN], *a.* Of a sky-blue colour; sky-coloured. **cerulein** (sė roo′ lė in), **cerulin** (sěr′ u lin), *n.* (*Chem.*) The colouring-matter of indigo dissolved in sulphuric acid with potash added to the solution; a colouring-matter obtained from coal-tar and other substances.

cerumen (sė roo′ mėn) [L. *cēra*, wax], *n.* The wax-like secretion of the ear. **ceruminous,** *a.*

ceruse (sěr′ oos) [F. *céruse*, or directly from L. *cērussa* (cp. *cēra*, wax), prob. from Gr. *kēroussa* (cp. *kērous*, waxy, from *kēros*, wax)], *n.* White lead; a cosmetic made from this. **v.t.* To apply ceruse to as a cosmetic. **cerusite, cerussite** (sěr′ ŭ sīt), *n.* (*Min.*) A native carbonate of lead.

cervical (sěr′ vi kȧl) [L. *cervix -īcis*, the neck, -AL], *a.* (*Physiol.*) Of or pertaining to the neck. **cervico-,** *comb. form.* (*Anat. and Physiol.*) Pertaining to or connected with the neck.

cervine (sěr′ vīn) [L. *cervīnus* (*cervus*, a hart)], *a.* Pertaining to the deer family; of or like deer.

Cesarevitch [TSAREVITCH].

cespitose [CÆSPITOSE].

cess (1) (ses) [prob. short for ASSESS], *v.t.* To tax, to assess. *n.* (*obs. exc. in Ireland*) A local rate.

cess (2) (ses) [Irish slang; perh. short for SUCCESS], *n.* Luck. **bad cess to you:** Ill luck befall you.

cessation (sė sā′ shŭn) [L. *cessātio* (*cessāre*, CEASE)], *n.* The act of ceasing; pause, rest. **cessavit** (ses ā′ vit), *n.* (*Law*) A process for the recovery of possession of lands from a tenant who has failed to pay rent for two years.

cesser (ses′ ėr) [F., from L. *cessāre*, CEASE], *n.* (*Law*) Cessation.

cession (sesh′ ȯn) [F., from L. *cessio -ōnem* (*cess-*, part. stem of *cēdere*, CEDE)], *n.* A yielding, a surrender, a ceding of territory, or of rights or property; (*Law*) the surrender of a benefice by its holder before accepting another; a *cessio bonorum.* ***cessio bonorum*** (sesh′ i ō bo nôr′ ŭm) [L., surrender of goods], *n.* (*Law*) A surrender by a debtor of his property to his creditors. **cessionary,** *n.* (*Law*) One who is the recipient of an assignment, an assign or assignee.

cesspit (ses′ pit) [formed on anal. of foll.], *n.* A pit for night-soil; a midden.

cesspool (ses′ pool) [etym. doubtful (perh. It. cesso, a privy, from L. *sēcessus*, from *sēcēdere*, to retire)], *n.* A deep hole in the ground for sewage to drain into; any receptacle for filth.

cestoid (ses′ toid) [L. *cestus*, Gr. *kestos*, a girdle, -OID], *a.* (*Zool.*) Ribbon-like. *n.* An intestinal worm of the group *Cestoidea*, a tape-worm.

cestus (1) (ses′ tŭs) [L., from Gr. *kestos*, a girdle], *n.* The girdle of Venus; the classic marriage girdle.

cestus (2) (ses′ tŭs) [L. *cæstus*, from *cæsus*, p.p. of *cædere*, to strike, or prec.], *n.* A heavy boxing-glove, made with thongs and armed with lead or iron, used by the Romans.

cesura [CÆSURA].

cet- [L. *cētus*, a whale, Gr. *kētos*, a sea-monster], *comb. form.* (*Chem.*) Of or relating to spermaceti.

Cetacea (sē tā′ shi ȧ) [see prec.], *n.pl.* (*Zool.*) A group of marine mammalia, containing the whales, manatees, etc. **cetacean,** *a.* Of or pertaining to the Cetacea. *n.* Any individual of the Cetacea. **cetaceous,** *a.*

ceteosaur, -saurus (sē′ tė ȯ sawr, -saw′ rŭs) [Gr. *kētos kēteos*, a whale, *sauros*, a lizard], *n.* (*Palæont.*) A large fossil saurian.

ceterach (set′ ė răk) [etym. doubtful], *n.* A genus of polypodiaceous ferns, the fronds of which are covered with scales on the back.

cha (cha) [Hind.], *n.* (*Anglo-Indian* and *slang*) Tea.

chablis (sha′ blē) [place-name], *n.* A white wine made at Chablis, in central France.

cha-cha, cha-cha-cha (cha), *n.* A W. Indian dance.

chacma (chăk′ mȧ [Hottentot], *n.* A South African baboon.

chaco (SHAKO].

chaconne (sha kōn′, chȧ kon′) [F., from Sp. *chacona*, prob. from Basque *chucun*, pretty], *n.* A Spanish dance in triple time; the music for this.

chæt- (kēt), **chæto-** (kē′ tō) [Gr. *chaite*, hair, mane], *comb. forms.* (*Zool.*) Characterized by bristles or a mane. **chætodon** (kē′ tō don) [Gr. *odous odontos*, *tooth*], *n.* A genus of fishes with bristly teeth and brilliant colouring. **chætopod** (kē′ tō pod) [Gr. *pous podos*, foot], *n.* A group of marine worms with bristles in foot-like appendages.

chafe (chāf) [O.F. *chaufer* (F. *chauffer*), L. *calefacere* (*calēre*, to glow, *facere*, to make)], *v.t.* *To make warm; *to inflame; to make warm by rubbing; to rub so as to make sore, to fret; to gall, to irritate. *v.i.* To be worn by rubbing; to fret. *n.* A sore caused by rubbing; irritation, a fit of rage, passion. ***chafer (1),** *n.* One who chafes; a chafing-dish. **chafery,** *n.* A forge in which iron is heated and welded into bars. **chafing,** *a.* That chafes. **chafing-dish,** *n.* A vessel for making anything hot; a small portable grate for coals. **chafing-gear,** *n.* (*Naut.*) Battens, mats, yarn, etc., put upon rigging to prevent its being chafed.

chafer (2) (chăf′ fėr) [A.-S. *ceafor*, prob. from Teut. *kaf-*, to gnaw (cp. Dut. *kever*, G. *käfer*)], *n.* A beetle, a cockchafer.

chaff (1) (chaf) [A.-S. *ceaf* (cp. Dut. *kaf*, O.H.G. *cheva*)], *n.* The husks of grain; hay or straw cut fine for fodder; (*Bot.*) the scales and bracts of grass and other flowers; winnowings; (*fig.*) anything worthless. **chaff-cutter,** *n.* A machine for cutting straw and hay for fodder. **chaffy,** *a.* Like or full of chaff; (*fig.*) light, worthless.

chaff (2), (chaf) [CHAFF (1), or from CHAFE], *n.* Banter. *v.t.* To banter. *v.i.* To indulge in banter.

chaffer (chăf′ ėr) [M.E. *chaffare*, *chapfare* (A.-S. *cēap*, bargain, *faru*, a journey)], *v.i.* To dispute about price; to haggle; to bargain; to chatter. **v.t.* To buy or sell. *n.* The act of bargaining; chaffering, haggling. **chafferer,** *n.*

chaffinch (chăf′ inch) [CHAFF (1) (from its frequenting barn-doors), FINCH], *n.* A common British small bird, *Fringilla cœlebs.*

***chaft** (chăft) [Sc. and North., from Icel. *kjaptr* (cp. Swed. *käpt*, A.-S. *ceafl*)], *n.* The jaw.

chagrin (shȧ grin′) [F., from Turk. *saghrī*, SHAGREEN (from the sense of rubbing or chafing)], *n.* Vexation, disappointment, mortification; ill-humour. *v.t.* To vex, to disappoint; to put out of humour.

chai [CHAL].

chain (chān) [O.F. *chaëne*, L. *catēna*], *n.* A series of links or rings fitted into or connected with each other, for binding, connecting, holding, hauling, or ornamenting; a measure of 100 links, or 66 ft., used in land surveying; (*fig.*) (*pl.*) bonds, fetters, bondage, restraint; a connected series, a sequence, a range; (*Chem.*) a series of atoms linked together; (*Naut.*) (*pl.*) strong plates of iron bolted to a ship's sides and used to secure the shrouds. *v.t.* To fasten or bind with or as with a chain or chains. **chain armour,** *n.* Chain mail. **chain-belt,** *n.* A chain used as a belt to transmit power. **chain-bridge,** *n.* A suspension bridge. **chain-coupling,** *n.* (*Rail.*) A coupling for luggage vans as a safeguard in case of breakage of the ordinary coupling. **chain-gang,** *n.* A gang of convicts working in chains. **chain letter,** *n.* A circular letter each recipient of which forwards a copy to friends and others. **chain-mail,** *n.* Armour of interwoven links. **chain-moulding,** *n.* (*Arch.*) An ornamental band carved with link-work. **chain-pier,** *n.* A pier on the principle of the suspension bridge. **chain-plate,** *n.* (*Naut.*) One of the flat iron bars bolted to a ship's side to secure the shrouds, also called channel plates [CHANNEL (2)]. **chain-pump,** *n.* A machine for raising water, consisting of an endless chain fitted with buckets or disks which return upwards through a tube. **chain reaction,** *n.* (*Phys.*) A self-perpetuating reaction applied particularly to nuclear reactions in the atomic bomb or pile. **chain-shot,** *n.* Two cannon-balls connected by a chain to destroy spars and rigging. **chain-smoking,** *ger.* (*colloq.*) Continuous smoking, lighting one cigarette from another. **chain-stitch,** *n.* An ornamental stitch resembling a chain; a loop-stitch (made by a sewing-machine). **chain-store,** *n.* One of a series of retail stores under the same ownership and selling the same kind of wares. **chain-wales,** *n.pl.* [CHANNEL (2)]. **chain-wheel,** *n.* A toothed wheel which receives or transmits power by means of an endless chain. **chain-work,** *n.* Needlework with open spaces like the links of a chain; sewing with chain-stitches. **chainless,** *a.* **chainlet,** *n.*

chair (châr) [O.F. *chaëre*, L. *cathedra*, Gr. *kathedra* (see CATHEDRA)], *n.* A movable seat with a back for one person; a seat of authority or office; a professorship; a chairmanship or mayoralty; the seat of the person presiding at a meeting; a Bath chair; a sedan; (*Rail.*) an iron socket to support and secure the metals. *v.t.* To carry publicly in a chair in triumph; to install as president of a meeting or society; to act as chairman. **to take the chair:** To preside at a meeting. **chair-bed,** *n.* A bed that folds up and becomes a chair. ***chair days,** *n.pl.* Old age. **chairman,** *n.* The president of a meeting or the permanent president of a society, committee, etc.; a man who draws a Bath chair; (*Hist.*) one of a pair of men who carried a sedan. **Chairman of Committees:** (*Parl.*) A member of either House who is appointed to preside over the House when it is in committee. **chairmanship,** *n.* **chairwoman,** *n.*

chaise (shāz) [F., corr. of *chaire*, CHAIR], *n.* A light travelling or pleasure carriage of various patterns. **chaise longue,** *n.* A chair with support for the legs.

chal (chăl [Gipsy], *n.* (fem. ***chai***) A man, a fellow.

chalaza (kă lā′ zȧ) [Gr., pimple], *n.* (*Biol.*) One of the two twisted albuminous threads holding the yolk in position in an egg; (*Bot.*) an analogous part of an ovule.

chalcedony, calcedony (kăl sed′ ȯ ni, -sē′ dȯ ni) [L. *chalcēdonius*, Gr. *chalkēdōn*, etym. doubtful], *n.* (*Min.*) A crypto-crystalline variety of quartz. **chalcedonic** (kăl sė don′ ik), *a.* **chalcedonyx** (kăl sed′ ȯ niks), *n.* A variety of agate.

chalco- (kăl′ kō) [Gr. *chalkos*], *comb. form.* Of or pertaining to copper or brass. **chalcography** (kăl kog′ rȧ fi) [-GRAPHY], *n.* The art or process of engraving on brass or copper. **chalcographer, -ist,** *n.* **chalcographic** (kăl kō grăf′ ik), *a.* **chalcopyrite** (kăl kō pī′ rit) [PYRITE], *n.* (*Min.*) A copper sulphoferrite, yellow or copper pyrites, a copper ore.

Chaldean, -dee (kăl dē′ ån, kăl dē′) [L. *Chaldæus*, Gr. *Chaldaios*, -AN], *a.* Of or belonging to Chaldea or its language. *n.* The language of Chaldea; a native of Chaldea. **chaldaic** (kăl dā′ ik), *a.* and *n.*

chaldron (chawl′ drŏn) [O.F. *chauderon* (F. *chaudron*), see CAULDRON], *n.* A measure (36 bushels) for coals.

chalet (shăl′ ā) [F. Swiss., prob. dim. of *casella*, dim. of It. or L. *casa*, cottage], *n.* A small house or villa on a mountain-side; a Swiss cottage.

chalice (chăl′ is) [O.F., from L. CALIX], *n.* A cup or drinking vessel; the cup used in the Eucharist; (*poet*) a flower-cup. ***chaliced,** *a.* Having a cell or cup; cup-shaped.

chalk (chawk) [A.-S *cealc* (cp. Dut., Dan., Swed., and G. *kalk*), from L. *calx -cis*, lime], *n.* Soft white limestone or massive carbonate of lime, chiefly composed of marine shells; a piece of this or of a coloured composition prepared from it, used for writing and drawing; (*fig.*) a public-house score. *v.t.* To rub, mark, or write with chalk; to manure with chalk. **a long chalk:** A great deal; a score or point in a game. **to chalk it up:** To give or take credit for something. **French chalk:** (*Geol.*) A kind of steatite or soap-stone. **red chalk:** (*Geol.*) A clay coloured with peroxide of iron; ruddle. **chalk-bed,** n. (*Geol.*) A stratum of chalk. **chalk-pit,** *n.* A chalk quarry. **chalk-stone,** *n.* (*Med.*) A chalky concretion in the joints of gouty persons. **to chalk out:** To sketch out, to plan. **chalky,** *a.* Containing or resembling chalk; (*Med.*) containing or resembling chalk-stones. **chalkiness,** *n.*

challenge (chăl′ ėnj) [O.F. *chalenge*, L. *calumnia*, CALUMNY], *n.* A summons or defiance to fight a duel; an invitation to a contest of any kind; the cry of hounds on finding scent; a calling in question; (*Law*) exception taken to a juror or voter; (*Mil.*) the call of a sentry in demanding the countersign. *v.t.* To invite or defy to a duel; to invite to a contest of any kind; to call on to answer; to demand, to invite, to claim; to object to, to dispute, contest. **challenge cup,** *n.* (*Sport*) A cup competed for annually by football teams, yacht clubs, etc. **challengeable,** *a.* **challenger,** *n.*

challis (chăl′ is) [perh. a pers. name], *n.* A light woollen fabric; formerly a fabric of silk and wool, for ladies' dresses.

chalumeau (shăl ů mō′) [F., from O.F. *chalemel*, L. *calamellus*, see CALUMET], *n.* A reed, a shepherd's pipe.

chalybeate (kȧ lib′ ė ȧt) [L. *chalybs*, Gr. *chalups -ubos*, steel, -ATE], *a.* (*Med.*) Impregnated with iron or steel; having the qualities of steel. *n.* A mineral water or spring so impregnated. **Chalybean,** *a.* Pertaining to the Chalybes, an ancient people of Asia Minor, famous as makers of steel.

***cham** (kăm) [KHAN], *n.* The ruler of Tartary; (*fig.*) an autocrat.

chamade (shȧ mad′) [F., from Port. *chamada* (*chamar*, to summon, L. *clāmāre*, to call)], *n.* The beat of a drum or sound of a trumpet demanding or announcing a surrender or parley.

chamber (chām′ bėr) [O.F., from L. *camera*, from Aryan *kam-*, to cover (cp. Gr. *kamara*, a vault, Icel. *hamr*, a covering)], *n.* A room, esp. a sleeping room; the place where a legislative assembly meets; the assembly itself; a hall of justice; an association of persons for the promotion of some common object; a hollow cavity or enclosed space; the space between the gates of a canal lock; *a kind of short cannon; that part of the bore of a gun or other fire-arm where the charge lies; a judge's private room in a court; (*pl.*) the office or apartments of a barrister in an Inn of Court; a suite of apartments; a chamber-pot. **chamber concert,** *n.* One where chamber music is given. **chamber council,** *n.* A secret council. **chamber-counsel,** *n.* A secret thought; (*Law*) a lawyer who gives opinions, etc., but does not plead. ***chamber-fellow,** *n.* One who sleeps in the same room. ***chamber-lye,** *n.* Stale urine, formerly used for washing. **chamber-maid,** *n.* A female servant in charge of the bed-rooms at a hotel. **chamber-master,** *n.* A small master who makes up materials at home and sells the goods to shops. **chamber-music,** *n.* Music adapted for performance in a room, as distinguished from that intended for theatres, churches, etc. **Chamber of Agriculture, of Commerce,** *n.* Boards or committees appointed to promote the interests of agriculture or business in a district. **chamber-pot, -utensil,** *n.* A bedroom receptacle for slops and urine. **chamber-practice,** *n.* The practice of a chamber-counsel. **chambered,** *a.* Enclosed; divided into compartments or sections. ***chamberer,** *n.* A valet; a lady's maid; a dissipated person; an intriguer. ***chambering,** *n.* Licentious behaviour; intrigue.

chamberlain (chām′ bėr lȧn) [O.F., from O.H.G. *chamberling* (L. *camera*, CHAMBER, -LING)], *n.* An officer in charge of the household of a sovereign or nobleman; a male servant in charge of suites of chambers; the treasurer of a city or corporation; *a servant at an inn with duties like those of a head waiter and a chamber-maid. **Lord Chamberlain of the Household:** One of the principal British officers of State, controlling the servants of the royal household above stairs, and the licensing of theatres and plays. **Lord Great Chamberlain of England:** A British hereditary officer of State in charge of the Palace of Westminster and performing ceremonial functions. **chamberlainship,** *n.*

Chambertin (shan′ bėr tan) [a vineyard near Dijon], *n.* A superior kind of Burgundy wine.

chameleon (kȧ mē′ lė ȯn) [L. *chamæleon*, Gr. *chamaileōn* (*chamai*, on the ground, dwarf, *leōn*, a lion)], *n.* A lizard having the power of changing colour and formerly fabled to live on air; a changeable person. **chameleonic** (kȧ mē lė on′ ik), *a.* **chameleon-like,** *a.* and *adv.*

chamfer (chăm′ fėr) [O.F. *chanfrein* (*chant*, CANT (2), L. *frangere*, to break)], *n.* (*Carp.*) An angle slightly pared off; a bevel, a groove, a fluting. *v.t.* To groove; to bevel off.

chamfron (chăm′ frȯn) [O.F. *chanfrain* (F. *chanfrein*), etym. unknown], *n.* Armour for a horse's head.

chamlet [CAMLET].

chamois (shăm′ wa) [F., prob. from Swiss Romanic (cp. It. *camozza*, G. *gemse*); prob. Teut. but etym. obscure], *n.* A goat-like European antelope, *Antilope rupicapra.* **chamois-leather** or **chamois** (shăm′ i), *n.* A soft, pliable leather, orig. prepared from the skin of the chamois.

chamomile [CAMOMILE].

champ (chămp) [earlier *cham*; prob. imit.], *v.t.* and *i.* To bite with a grinding action or noise; to chew, to crunch. *n.* Champing; the noise of champing.

champac (chăm′ păk, chŭm′ pŭk) [Hind. *champak*], *n.* A kind of magnolia, much venerated in India.

champagne (shăm pān′) [place-name], *n.* A light sparkling wine made in the province of Champagne, France. ***fine champagne*** (fēn shăm pān), *n.* Liqueur brandy.

champaign (chăm′ pān, chăm pān′) [O.F. *champaigne* (see CAMPAIGN)], *n.* Flat, open country; level country; *a field of battle. *a.* Flat; open, unenclosed.

champerty (chăm′ pėr ti) [earlier *champarty*, O.North.F. *campart*, L. *campi pars*, part of the field (prov. assim. to PARTY)], *n.* *Apportionment of land; *a partnership in power; (*Law*) maintenance of a party in a suit on condition of sharing the property at issue if recovered.

champignon (shăm pin′ yȯn) [F., prob. from late L. *campinio -ōnem* (*campus*, field)], *n.* *A mushroom; the fairy-ring agaric, *Agaricus oreades.*

champion (chăm′ pi ȯn) [O.F., from late L. *campio -ōnem*, a fighter in a duel (L. *campus*, field)], *n.* *A warrior; one who engages in single combat on behalf of another; one who argues on behalf of or defends a person or a cause; the acknowledged superior in any athletic exercise or trial of skill; the person, animal, or exhibit that defeats all competitors; *(*Law*) one who maintained a cause by wager of battle. *v.t.* To challenge to combat; to defend as a champion; to support a cause. *a.* Superior to all competitors; first-class, supremely excellent. **championless,** *a.* **championship,** *n.*

champlevé (shămp le′ vā) [F. *champ*, a field, *levé*, raised], *n.* Enamelling by the process of inlaying vitreous powders into channels cut in the metal base; a plate so treated.

chance (chans) [O.F. *cheance*, late L. *cadentia* (*cadens -tis*, pres.p. of *cadere*, to fall)], *n.* Fortune, luck, the course of events; event, issue, result; undesigned result or occurrence; accident, risk, possibility, opportunity; (*usu. pl.*) likelihood, probability; fate, the indeterminable course of events, fortuity. *v.t.* (*colloq.*) To risk. *v.i.* To happen, to come to pass. *a.* Fortuitous, unforeseen. **by chance:** As things fall out; accidentally; undesignedly. **on the chance:** On the possibility; in case. **the main chance:** The most important issue; gain; self-interest. **to stand a good chance:** To have a favourable opportunity. ***how chance?** How was it that? **to chance it:** To take the risk. **to chance upon:** To come upon accidentally. **chance-comer,** *n.* One who comes by chance. **chance-medley** [A.-F. *chance medlée* (*medler*, var. of *mesler*, to mix; cp. MEDDLE)], *n.* (*Law*) Homicide by misadventure, as accidental homicide in repelling an unprovoked attack; inadvertency; pure chance or luck. **chanceful,** *a.* Fortuitous, accidental; (*poet.*) eventful; *hazardous, risky. **chancy,** *a.* Risky, doubtful.

chancel (chan′ sėl) [O.F. (*see* CANCEL)], *n.* The eastern part of a church, formerly cut off from the nave by a screen.

chancellery, -ory (chan′ sėl ėr i) [O.F. *chancelerie*, late L. *cancellāria* (see CHANCELLOR)], *n.* A chancellor's court or council and official establishment; the building or room in which a chancellor has his office; the office or department attached to an embassy or consulate.

chancellor (chan′ sė lȯr) [O.F. *chancelier, cancelier*, late L. *cancellārius* (L. *cancellus*, a grating, see CANCEL)], *n.* The president of a court, public department, or university; an officer who seals the commissions etc. of an order of knighthood; a bishop's law-officer or a vicar-general. **Chancellor of the Exchequer:** The principal finance minister of the British Government. **Chancellor of the Duchy of Lancaster:** The representative of the Crown as holder of the Duchy of Lancaster. **Lord (High) Chancellor:** The highest officer of the British Crown, the keeper of the Great Seal, president of the Chancery division of the Supreme Court (formerly the High Court of Chancery), and Speaker of the House of Lords. **chancellorship,** *n.* **chancellory** [CHANCELLERY].

chancery (chan' sėr i) [O.F. *cancellerie*, CHANCELLERY], *n.* The court of the Lord Chancellor, before 1873; the highest English court of justice next to the House of Lords, comprising a court of common law and a court of equity, now a division of the High Court of Justice; (*Am.*) a court of equity; a court or office for the deposit of records. **to get into chancery:** To get into a hopeless predicament; (*Boxing*) to get one's head under an opponent's arm.

chancre (shăng' kėr) [F., cp CANCER, CANKER], *n.* A venereal ulcer. **chancrous,** *a.*

chancy [CHANCE].

chandelier (shăn dė lēr') [O.F. *chandelier*, candle-maker, candlestick (see foll.)], *n.* A hanging branched frame for a number of lights.

chandler (chand' lėr) [O.F. *chandelier*, L. *candēlārius* (*candēla*, CANDLE)], *n.* One who makes or sells candles; a retail dealer in oil, groceries, and other commodities. **corn-chandler,** *n.* **ship-chandler,** *n.* **chandlery,** *n.* Articles sold by a chandler.

change (chānj) [O.F. *changer*, late L. *cambiāre* (*cambium*, exchange, L. *cambire*; etym. doubtful)], *v.t.* To make different, to alter; to give up or to substitute for something else; to give or take an equivalent for in other coin; to exchange. *v.i.* To become different; to be altered in appearance; to pass from one state or phase to another; to become tainted; to deteriorate. *n.* Alteration, variation; shifting, transition, the passing of the moon from one phase to another; alteration in order, esp. of ringing a peal of bells; substitution of one thing for another; small coin or foreign money given in return for other coins; balance of money paid beyond the value of goods purchased; exchange; an exchange; (*fig.*) novelty, variety. **change of front:** (*Mil.*) A wheeling movement; (*fig.*) a change of attitude, a reversal of policy. **to get no change out of:** Not to be able to take any advantage of. **to change colour:** To turn pale; to blush. **to change one's mind:** To form a new plan or opinion. **to change one's clothes:** To put on different clothes. **to change one's tune:** To adopt a humbler attitude; to become sad or vexed. **to change sides:** To desert one's party. **on change** (not 'change): Where merchants meet or transact business. **to ring the changes:** To try all ways of doing something; to swindle by counterfeit money, or in changing a coin. **to take one's change:** To exact revenge; to get even with someone. **changeable,** *a.* Liable to change; inconstant, fickle, variable; *shot with different colours. **changeability** (-bil' i ti), *n.* **changeableness,** *n.* **changeably,** *adv.* **changeful,** *a.* Full of change; changeable. **changefully,** *adv.* **changefulness,** *n.* **changeless,** *a.* Free from change; unchanging. **changeling,** *n.* Anything substituted for another; a child substituted for another, esp. an elf-child; a waverer, a fickle person. **changer,** *n.* One who changes anything; a money-changer. **changing,** *a.* **change-over,** *n.* (*Cinema.*) The imperceptible change from one machine to another at the end of a reel and the start of another; (*Elec.*) the changing of circuit from one system of connexions to another.

channel (1) (chăn' ėl) [O.F. *chanel*, var. of CANAL], *n.* The bed of a stream or an artificial watercourse; the deep part of an estuary; a fairway; a narrow piece of water joining two seas; a tube or duct, natural or artificial, for the passage of liquids, fluids, or gases; means of passing, conveying, or transmitting; a furrow, a groove, a fluting; a gutter (*fig.*) a course, line, or direction. (*Radio.*) a band of frequencies on which radio and television signals can be transmitted without interference from other channels. *v.t.* To cut a channel or channels in; to cut (a way) out; to groove. **The Channel:** The English Channel.

channel (2) (chăn' ėl) [CHAIN, WALE], *n.* (*Naut.*) A plank fastened horizontally to the side of a ship to spread the lower rigging.

chanson (shan' son) [F., from L. *cantio -ōnem* (*cant-*, part. stem of *canere*, to sing)], *n.* A song. **chansonette** (shan sŏ net') [F., dim. of *chanson*], *n.* A little song.

chant (chant) [F. *chanter*, L. *cantāre*, freq. of *canere*, to sing], *v.t.* *To sing; to celebrate in song; to recite to music or musically, to intone. *v.i.* To sing in an intoning fashion. *n.* Song, melody; (*Mus.*) a composition consisting of a long reciting note and a melodic phrase; a psalm, canticle, or other piece sung in this manner; a musical recitation or monotonous song; (*slang*) cant, deception. **to chant a horse:** To sell it fraudulently by concealing its defects or over-praising it. **to chant the praises of:** To praise monotonously. **chanter,** *n.* *A singer; a chantry priest, a chorister; one who chants; a precentor; the drone of a bagpipe; (*slang*) a horse-coper.

chantage (shan tazh', chan' tȧj) [F., as prec.], *n.* Extorting money by threats of scandal; blackmailing.

chanterelle (1) (chan tėr el') [F., from mod. L. *catharellus*, dim. of *cantharus*, cup], *n.* An edible fungus, *Cantharellus cibarius*.

chanterelle (2) (chan tėr el') [F., from It. *cantarella* (L. *cantāre*, CHANT)], *n.* (*Mus.*) The highest string upon stringed instruments.

chantey (shăn' ti) [CHANT, -Y], *n.* A song sung by sailors whilst heaving or hauling.

chanticleer (chan' ti klēr) [O.F. *chantecler* (F. *chanteclair*), proper name of the cock (*chanter*, CHANT, *cler*, CLEAR)], *n.* A cock, esp. as the herald of day.

chantry (chan' tri) [O.F. *chanterie* (*chanter*, CHANT, -ERY)], *n.* An endowment for a priest or priests to say mass daily for some person or persons deceased; the chapel or the part of a church used for this purpose; the body of priests who perform this duty. **chantry-priest,** *n.*

chanty [CHANTEY].

chaos (kā' os) [L., from Gr. *chaos* (*chachaskein*, to gape)], *n.* Yawning, empty space, an abyss; the void, the confusion of matter said to have existed at the Creation; formless matter, confusion; a confused, mixed mass; confusion, disorder. **chaotic** (kā ot' ik), *a.* **chaotically,** *adv.*

chap (1) (chăp) [M.E. *chappen* (M.Dut. *cappen*, Dut. *kappen*, Dan. *kappe*), relations of these obscure], *v.t.* To cause to crack or open in long slits; (*Sc.*) to strike, to beat. *v.i.* To crack or open in long slits. *n.* (*usu. in pl.*) A longitudinal crack, cleft, or seam on the surface of the skin, the earth, etc. **chapped,** *a.* **chappy,** *a.*

chap (2) (chăp), **chop** [from prec.], *n.* (*pl.*) The jaws (usu. of animals), the mouth and cheeks; (*sing.*) the lower part of the cheek. **Bath chap:** This part of a pig's face cured in a special way for food. **Chops of the Channel:** The entrance to the English Channel near the Atlantic. **fat chops,** *n.* (*colloq.*) Fat face. **to lick one's chops:** To relish in anticipation. **chap-fallen,** *a.* Having the lower jaw depressed; (*fig.*) downcast, dejected, dispirited.

chap (3) (chăp) [CHAPMAN], *n.* *A buyer, a customer; (*colloq.*) a man, a fellow.

chaparral (chăp' á răl) [Sp., from *chaparra*, evergreen oak], *n.* A thicket of low evergreen oaks, or of thick bramble-bushes and thorny shrubs.

chap-book (chăp′ buk) [formed on anal. of CHAPMAN], *n.* A small book, usually of wonderful tales, ballads, or the like, formerly hawked by chapmen.

chape (chāp) [F., from late L. *căpa*, CAP], *n.* The catch or piece by which an object is attached, as the frog of a sword-belt, the back-piece of a buckle, etc.; the transverse guard of a sword; the hook or tip of a scabbard. *v.t.* *To furnish with a chape.

chapeau (sha′ pō) [F., from O.F. *chapel*, L. *cappellum*, dim. of *cappa*, CAP], *n.* (*pl.* ***chapeaux***) (*Her.*) A hat. ***chapeau bras*** (-bra) [F. *bras*, arm], *n.* A small, three-cornered, flat silk hat carried under the arm by men in full dress in the latter part of the 18th cent.

chapel (chăp′ ėl) [O.F. *chapele* (F. *chapelle*), from late L. *cappella*, dim. of *cappa*, *căpa*, CAP (after the *căpa* or cloak of St. Martin, which was preserved in the first chapel)], *n.* A place of worship connected with and subsidiary to a church; a part containing an altar in a church; a place of worship other than a church or cathedral, esp. one in a palace, mansion, or public institution; a dissenting place of worship; (*Printing*) a printing-office (from the legend that Caxton set up his printing press in Westminster Abbey); an association or meeting of journeymen in a printing-office to settle disputes, etc. **chapel of ease:** A subordinate church in a parish. **chapelry,** *n.* The district or jurisdiction of a chapel.

chaperon (shăp′ ėr ŏn) [F., a hood, dim. of *chape*, a cope (see CAP)]. *n.* *A kind of hood or cap; *an escutcheon on the forehead of horses drawing a hearse; a married or elderly woman who attends a young unmarried lady in public places. *v.t.* To act as chaperon to. **chaperonage** (shăp′ ėr ŏn ȧj), *n.* The duties or position of a chaperon.

chapiter (chăp′ i tėr) [O.F. *chapitre*, L. *capitulum*, dim. of *caput -itis*, head], *n.* (*Arch.*) The upper part of the capital of a column; *a chapter or article.

chaplain (chăp′ lȧn) [O.F. *chapelain*, late L. *cappellānus*], *n.* A clergyman who officiates at court, in the house of a person of rank, or in a regiment, ship, or public institution. **chaplaincy,** *n.* **chaplainship,** *n.*

chaplet (chăp′ lėt) [O.F. *chapelet*, dim. of CHAPE], *n.* A wreath or garland for the head; a string of beads one-third the number of a rosary; a necklace; a bird's crest; a toad's string of eggs; (*Arch.*) a round moulding carved into beads, olives, or the like.

chapman (chăp′ mȧn) [A.-S. *cēapmann* (*cēap*, CHEAP, *mann*, MAN), cp. Dut. *koopman*, G. *kaufmann*], *n.* One who buys and sells; an itinerant merchant, a pedlar, a hawker.

chaps (chăps) [Sp. *chaparajos*, *chaparral*], *n.pl.* Leather leggings with hair or wool outside worn by cowboys.

chapter (chăp′ tėr) [CHAPITER], *n.* A division of a book; (*fig.*) a subject of minor compass; a part of a subject; a piece of narrative, an episode; a division of Acts of Parliament arranged in chronological order for reference; the general meeting of certain orders and societies; the council of a bishop, consisting of the clergy attached to a cathedral or collegiate church; a meeting of the members of a religious order; a chapter-house. *v.t.* To divide into chapters. **chapter and verse:** Full and precise reference in order to verify a fact or quotation. **chapter of accidents:** A series of accidents; an unfortunate coincidence. **to the end of the chapter:** Throughout, to the end. **chapter-house,** *n.* The place in which a chapter is held.

char (1) (char) [perh. Celtic; cp. Ir. *cear*, red], *n.* A small fish of the salmon tribe, *Salmo salvelinus*, found in the Lake District and North Wales; the American brook-trout, *S. fontinalis.*

char (2) (char), **chare** (châr) [A.-S. *cierr*, *cyrr*, a gurn, from *cierran*, to turn (cp. Am. CHORE)], *n.* A turn of work, an odd job. *v.i.* To work by the day; to do small jobs. **charwoman,** *n.* A woman who does housework by the day, (*Am.*) a scrub-woman.

char (3) (char) [back-formation from CHARCOAL], *v.t.* (*past & p.p.* **charred**) To reduce to charcoal; to burn slightly, to blacken with fire. *v.i.* To become blackened with fire.

char (4) [CHA].

char-à-banc (shăr′ ȧ băng) [F., carriage with benches], *n.* A long brake or car provided with transverse benches, for excursionists.

character (kăr′ ȧk tėr) [F. *caractère* (or O.F. *characte*, see CARACT), L. *charactēr*, Gr. *charactēr* (*charassein*, to furrow, engrave)], *n.* A mark made by cutting, engraving, or writing; a letter, a sign; (*pl.*) letters distinctive of a particular language; style of handwriting; peculiar distinctive qualities or traits; the sum of a person's mental and moral qualities; moral excellence, moral strength; reputation, standing; good reputation; a certificate of capacity, moral qualities, and conduct (esp. of a servant); position, rank, capacity; a person, a personage; a personality created by a novelist, poet, or dramatist; a part in a play; an actor's part; (*colloq.*) an eccentric person; (*Nat. Hist.*) a characteristic. **v.t.* To inscribe; to engrave; to characterize. **generic characters:** (*Nat. Hist.*) Those which constitute a genus. **specific characters:** (*Nat. Hist.*) Those which constitute a species. **charactered,** *a.* Invested with definite character. **characteristic,** *n.* That which marks or constitutes the character; (*Math.*) the whole-number or integral part of a logarithm. **characteristic, characteristical** (kăr ȧk tėr ist′ ik, -ȧl), *a.* Constituting or exhibiting typical qualities. **characteristically** *adv.* **characterize** (kăr′ ȧk tėr īz), *v.t.* To give character to, to stamp, to distinguish; to describe; to be characteristic of. **characterization** (-zā′ shŭn), *n.* **characterless,** *a.* Without definite character; ordinary, commonplace; without a written character. ***charactery,** *n.* Characterization; a mark, an impression.

charade (shȧ rad′) [F., from Sp. and Port. *charrada* (*charro*, a peasant), or Prov. *charrada* (*charra*, to chatter)], *n.* A kind of riddle based upon a word the key to which is given by description or action representing each syllable and the whole word.

charcoal (char′ kōl) [etym. doubtful], *n.* Wood partially burnt under turf; (*Chem.*) an impure form of carbon prepared from vegetable or animal substances.

chard (chard) [F. *carde*; L. *carduus*, a thistle], *n.* An American artichoke.

chare [CHAR (2)].

***charet, charette** (chăr′ ėt) [O.F. *charette*, dim. of *charre*, CAR], *n.* A wheeled vehicle; a chariot.

charge (charj) [F. *charger*, L. *carricāre* (*carrus*, CAR)], *v.t.* *To lay a load or burden on; to fill; to put the proper load or quantity of material into (any apparatus), as to load (a gun), to accumulate electricity in (a battery), etc., to saturate (water) with gas; to rush on and attack; to put (weapons) in an attacking position; to lay on or impose; to enjoin, to command, to exhort; to entrust, to accuse; to debit to; to ask a price for; to give directions to (esp. of a judge to a jury, etc., or a bishop to his clergy). *v.i.* To make an attack or onset; (*colloq.*) to demand high prices or payments. *n.* A load, a burden; an office, duty, or obligation; care, custody; the thing or person under one's care, a minister's flock; command, commission; an entry on the debit side of an account; price demanded, cost; accusation; attack, onset; the quantity with which any apparatus, esp. a fire-arm, is loaded; instructions, directions (esp. those of a judge to a jury, or of a bishop to his clergy); (*Her.*) anything borne on an escutcheon; (*Elec.*) the amount or accumulation of electricity, *e.g.* in a battery. **in charge:** On duty; responsible (for). **to give in charge:** To commit to the care of another; to hand over to the custody of a policeman. **to take in charge:** To arrest, to take into custody. **to return**

to the charge: To begin again. ***charge-house,** *n.* A school. **charge-sheet,** *n.* A list of offenders taken into custody, with their offences, for the use of a police-magistrate. **chargeable,** *a.* Liable to be charged or accused; liable to a monetary demand; liable to be an expense (to); imputable; capable of being properly charged (to); burdensome, costly; rateable. **chargeability** (-bil' i ti), *n.* Chargeable expense. ***chargeful,** *a.* Involving expense; costly. **chargeless,** *a.* Free from charge. **charger,** *n.* One who charges; a war-horse; a cavalry horse; *a large dish.

chargé d'affaires (shar' zhā dȧ fâr'), **chargé** [F., charged with affairs], *n.* A diplomatic agent acting as deputy to an ambassador; an ambassador to a court of minor importance.

charily, etc. [CHARY].

chariot (chăr' i ȯt) [O.F. *chariot*, augm. of *char*, CAR], *n.* (*poet.* and *rhet.*) A car, a vehicle, a stately kind of vehicle; (18*th cent.*) a light, four-wheeled pleasure carriage; (*Hist.*) a carriage used in war, public triumphs, and racing. *v.t.* (*poet.*) To convey in a chariot. *v.i.* (*poet.*) To ride in a chariot. **chariot-race,** *n.* A race in chariots. **charioteer** (chăr i ȯ tēr'), *n.* A chariot-driver. **charioteering,** *n.* The act, art, or practice of driving a chariot.

charity (chăr' i ti) [O.F. *charité, charitet*, L. *caritas -tātem* (*carus*, dear)], *n.* Love of one's fellow, one of the theological virtues; liberality to the poor; alms-giving; alms; an act of kindness; kindness, goodwill; liberality of judgment; leniency, tolerance of faults and offences, a foundation or institution for assisting the poor, the sick, or the helpless. **Sisters of Charity:** An order of nuns devoted to the care of the sick and poor. ***charity-boy, -girl,** *n.* One brought up in a charity school or similar institution. **Charity Commissioners,** *n.pl.* Members of a board instituted in 1853 for the control of charitable foundations. ***charity school,** *n.* An endowed school for the education of poor children, who usually wore a distinctive dress. **charitable,** *a.* Full of, pertaining to, or supported by charity; kind; liberal to the poor; benevolent, kindly, lenient, large-hearted; dictated by kindness. **charitableness,** *n.* **charitably,** *adv.*

charivari (sha ri va' ri) [F., etym. doubtful], *n.* A mock serenade of discordant music, intended to insult and annoy; a confusion of sounds, a hubbub; a satirical journal.

charlatan (shar' lȧ tȧn) [F., from It. *ciarlatano* (*ciarlare*, to prattle)], *n.* An empty pretender to skill or knowledge; a quack; an impostor. **charlatanic, charlatanical** (shar lȧ tăn' ik, -ȧl), *a.* **charlatanically,** *adv.* **charlatanish** (shar'-), *a.* **charlatanism, charlatanry,** *n.*

Charles's wain (charl' zėz wān') [A.-S. *Carles wægn*, the wain of *Carl* (Charlemagne); perh. from confusion of *Arcturus* (the neighbouring constellation) with *Arturus* and association of King Arthur and Charlemagne], *n.* Seven stars in the constellation the Great Bear, also called the Plough.

Charleston (charlz' tȯn) [Charleston, S. Carolina], *n.* (*Dancing*) A strenuous American dance in four-four time.

***Charley, Charlie** (char' li) [var. of *Charles*], *n.* A night watchman; a small pointed beard like that of Charles I; a proper name of the fox. **a proper charlie:** (*slang*) An utterly foolish fellow.

charlock (char' lȯk) [A.-S. *cerlic*], *n.* The wild mustard, *Sinapis arvensis*.

Charlotte (shar' lȯt) [F. perh. from the fem. name], *n.* A kind of pudding made of fruit and thin slices of the crumb of bread. **Charlotte Russe** [F. *Russe*, Russian], *n.* Custard or whipped sillabub enclosed in sponge cake.

charm (1) (charm) [O.F. *charme*, L. *carmen*, a song], *n.* A spell, an enchantment; a thing, act, or formula having magical power; an article worn to avert evil or ensure good luck, an amulet; a power or gift of alluring, pleasing, or exciting love or desire; that which has great pleasing and attractive power; a trinket worn on a watch-chain. *v.t.* To enchant, to fascinate, to bewitch; to attract, to delight; (*colloq.*) to please; (*usu. in pass.*) to protect with occult power; to remove by charms (with *away*). *v.i.* To use charms. **charmer,** *n.* One who uses charms; one who fascinates. **charmful,** *a.* Full of charms; charming. **charming,** *a.* Highly pleasing; delightful. **charmingly,** *adv.* **charmingness,** *n.* **charmless,** *a.*

***charm** (2) (charm) [from obs. v. *chirm*, A.-S. *cirman*, to shout], *n.* A blended noise or confusion of voices, as of birds or children.

charnel-house (char' nėl hous) [O.F. *charnel*, carnal, a cemetery, late L. *carnāle*, a graveyard, neut. of *carnālis*, CARNAL], *n.* A place where dead bodies or the bones of the dead are deposited.

Charon (kâr' ȯn) [Gr. *Charōn*], *n.* The son of Erebus and Nox, who ferried departed spirits across the Styx into Hades; (*fig.*) a ferryman.

charpie (shar pi', shar' pi) [O.F. p.p. of *charpir*, to tear, to card (see CARPET)], *n.* Lint or scraped linen for dressing wounds.

charpoy (char' poi) [Urdu *chārpāī*, Pers. *chahār-pāī*, four-footed], *n.* A light Indian bedstead.

charqui (char' ki) [Peruv. *charqui*], *n.* Beef cut into strips and dried in the sun. **charqued,** *a.* [see JERKED BEEF].

chart (chart) [F. *charte*, L. *charta, carta*, Gr. *chartē*, a sheet of papyrus (cp. CARD)], *n.* A map of some part of the sea, with coasts, islands, rocks, shoals, etc., for the use of sailors; a statement of facts in tabular form; a projection of relative facts, statistics, or observations in the form of a graphic curve; a skeleton map for special purposes, *e.g. heliographic chart, magnetic chart, physical chart.* *v.t.* To make a chart; to map. **chartaceous** (-tā' shŭs), *a.* Resembling paper. **chartless,** *a.* Without a chart.

charter (char' tėr) [O.F. *chartre*, late L. *chartula*, dim. of prec.], *n.* A deed, an instrument; an instrument in writing granted by the sovereign or Parliament, incorporating a borough, company, or institution, or conferring certain rights and privileges; (*fig.*) privilege, exemption; a charter-party; (*Hist.*) the People's Charter, embodying the demands of the Chartists. *v.t.* To establish by charter; to license by charter; (*Naut.*) to hire or let by charter-party; (*colloq.*) to hire. **charter-land,** *n.* Land held by charter. **Charter of the United Nations,** *n.* A series of articles embodying the principles of the United Nations and corresponding to the Covenant of the League of Nations. **charter-party** [F. *charte partie*, divided document], *n.* (*Naut.*) An agreement in writing concerning the hire and freight of a vessel. **chartered,** *a.* Invested with privileges by or as by a charter. **charterer,** *n.*

Charterhouse (char' tėr hous) [A.-F. *chart rouse* (see CHARTREUSE)], *n.* *A Carthusian monastery; a hospital and school founded in London on the site of a Carthusian monastery, now removed.

Chartism (char' tizm) [L. *charta*, -ISM], *n.* The principles of the Chartists, an English democratic party (1838–48); briefly, universal suffrage, vote by ballot, annual parliaments, payment of members, equal electoral districts, and the abolition of property qualifications for members. **Chartist,** *n.*

chartography, etc. [CARTOGRAPHY].

chartreuse (shar trerz'), *n.* A pale green liqueur made by the monks at la Grande Chartreuse, near Grenoble, France.

chartulary [CARTULARY].

charwoman [CHAR (2)].

chary (châr' i) [A.-S. *cearig* (*cearu, caru*, care, sorrow, O.Teut. *karā*) cp. O.H.G. *charag*, G. *karg*, sparing], *a.* Wary, prudent, cautious, frugal, sparing. **charily,** *adv.* **chariness,** *n.*

Charybdis (ka rib' dis) [L., from Gr. *Charubdis*], *n.* A dangerous whirlpool off the coast of Sicily, opposite Scylla, a rock on the Italian shore; one of a pair of alternative risks.

chase (1) (chās) [O.F. *chacier*, late L. *captiāre* (see CATCH)], *v.t.* To pursue; to hunt; to drive away; to put to flight. *v.i.* To ride or run rapidly. *n.* Earnest pursuit; the hunting of wild animals; that which is chased; an open hunting-ground or preserve for game; (*Tennis*) where the ball completes its first bound. **chase-gun, chaser** (1), **bow-chaser, stern-chaser,** *n.* (*Naut.*) A gun mounted at the bow or stern, used for attack or defence; (*Am.*) water drunk after neat spirits.

chase (2) (chās) [earlier *enchase*, F. *enchâsser* (*en*, L *in*, *châsse*, L. *capsa*, CASE)], *v.t.* To engrave, to emboss; to cut the worm of (a screw). **chaser** (2), *n.* An enchaser; a tool used in screw cutting. **chasing**, *n.* The art of embossing metals; the pattern embossed.

chase (3) (chās) [F. *châsse*, L. *capsa*, CASE], *n.* A rectangular iron frame in which type is imposed for printing.

chase (4) (chās) [F. *chas*, late L. *capsum*, an enclosure (cp. *capsa*, CASE), from *capere*, to hold], *n.* A wide groove; the part of a gun in front of the trunnions.

chasm (kăzm) [L. and Gr. *chasma*, from *chaskein*, to gape]. A cleft, a fissure, a rent, a yawning gulf; (*fig.*) a break of continuity; a breach or division between persons or parties; a gap or void. **chasmed,** *a.* Having chasms. **chasmy,** *a.* Abounding with chasms.

chasse (shas) [F. *chasse-café*, chase-coffee (*chasser*, to chase)], *n.* A liqueur taken to remove the taste of coffee, tobacco, etc.

chassé (shăs' ā) [F., chasing, gliding (*chasser*, see prec.)], *n.* A gliding step in dancing. *v.i.* To perform this step. *v.t.* (*slang*) To dismiss.

chassepot (shăs' pō) [name of inventor], *n.* A breech-loading needle-gun in use in France 1866–74.

chasseur (sha' sĕr) [F., from *chasser*, to chase, hunt], *n.* A huntsman; a light-armed French soldier; an attendant on persons of rank, wearing a military uniform.

chassis (shăs' ē) [F., *châssis*, late L. *capsum* (cp. CHASE (4))], *n.* (*pl. unaltered*) The base-frame of a gun in a barbette or battery; the framework of a motor-car, aeroplane, etc.; *a window-frame.

chaste (chāst) [O.F., from L. *castus*, pure], *a.* Pure from unlawful sexual commerce; continent, virtuous; modest, innocent; free from obscenity; pure in style; simple, unadorned, unaffected. **chastely,** *adv.* **chastity** (chăs' ti ti) [O.F. *chasteté*, L. *castitās*, *-tātem*], *n.* The state of being chaste; purity of body or conduct; purity of taste and style; celibacy.

chasten (chā' sėn) [from obs. v. *chasty*, O.F. *chastier*, L. *castigāre* (*castus*, chaste), or from prec., -EN], *v.t.* To punish with a view to reformation; to correct; to discipline; to purify, to refine, to subdue. **chastener,** *n.*

chastise (chăs tīz') [M.E. *chastien*, chasten, later *chasty* (see prec.), -IZE (formation obscure)], *v.t.* To punish, esp. with corporeal pains; to correct an offence or wrong; to chasten; to refine; to revise and correct. **chastisement** (chăs' tiz mėnt), *n.* **chastiser** (-tī' zėr), *n.*

chastity (chăs' ti ti) [CHASTE].

chasuble (chăz' ū bėl) [F., from med. L. *casubla*, *casubula*, dim. of *casa*, a little house], *n.* A vestment worn by a priest over the alb while celebrating Mass.

chat (1) (chăt) [short for CHATTER], *v.i.* (*past & p.p.* **chatted**) To talk easily and familiarly; to gossip. **v.t.* To gossip about. *n.* Easy, familiar talk; gossip. chatty (1), a. chattiness, n.

chat (2) (chăt) [from prec.], *n.* The name of various birds, mostly *Sylviadæ* or warblers, *e.g. furze-chat* or *whin-chat*, *hay-chat*, *stone-chat*.

chateau (sha tō', shăt' ō) [F., from O.F. *castel*, CASTLE], *n.* (*pl.* **-eaux**) A castle; a Continental country-seat.

chatelaine (shăt' ėlān) [F., mistress of chateau], *n.* An ornament worn at her waist by a lady, having short chains attached for a watch, keys, trinkets, etc.

chatoyant (shȧ toi' ȧnt, sha twa' yan) [F., pres. p. of *chatoyer* (*chat*, cat)], *a.* Having a changeable lustre or colour, like that of a cat's eye in the dark. *n.* A stone with changing lustre like the cat's eye.

chattel (chăt' ėl) [O.F. *chatel*, CATTLE]. *n.* (*usu. in pl.*) Movable property; (*Law*) any article of property except such as is freehold.

chatter (chăt' ĕr) [onomat.], *v.i.* To utter rapid, inharmonious sounds like a magpie, jay, etc.; to make a noise by or like the rattling together of the teeth; to talk idly and thoughtlessly; to jabber, to prattle. *n.* Sounds like those of a magpie, jay, etc.; idle talk. **chatterbox,** *n.* An incessant talker. **chatterer,** *n.* One who chatters; name given to birds belonging to the genus *Ampelidæ*.

chatty (1) [CHAT (1)].

chatty (2) (chăt' i) [Hind. *chātī*], *n.* (*India*) An earthen pitcher or water-pot.

Chaucerian (chaw sēr' i ȧn) [Geoffrey *Chaucer* (1340–1400)], *a.* Pertaining or relating to the poet Chaucer; resembling his style. *n.* A student of Chaucer. **Chaucerism,** *n.* A characteristic or mannerism of Chaucer or imitated from Chaucer.

chaudron [CHALDRON].

chauffer (chaw' fėr) [CHAFER], *n.* A metal cage for holding fire; a portable stove or furnace.

chauffeur (shō' fĕr) [F. *chauffer*, to heat], *n.* A hired man employed to drive a motor-car.

chausses (shōs, shō' sėz) [F., from med. L. *calcias*, pl. of *calcia*, leggings, breeches (L. *calceus*, shoe)], *n.pl.* A kind of trunk-hose; armour for the leg. **chaussure** (shō sūr'), *n.* Boots, shoes, etc.

chauvinism (shō' vin izm) [F. *chauvinisme*, from Nicolas *Chauvin*, an old soldier of Napoleon, devotedly attached to the Emperor], *n.* Exaggerated patriotism of an aggressive kind; jingoism. **chauvinist,** *n.* and *a.* **chauvinistic** (-nis' tik), *a.*

chaw (chaw) [CHEW], *v.t.* To chew. *n.* A quid of tobacco. **chaw up:** (*Am. slang*) To defeat completely, to smash up. **chaw-bacon,** *n.* (*colloq.*) A yokel, a bumpkin.

***chawdron** (chaw' drȯn) [M.E. *chaudoun*, O.F. *chaudun*, prob. from a late L. *caldūnum* (cp. *caldūna*, perh. from L. *caldus*, *calidus*, warm)], *n.* Intestines; entrails of an animal used as food.

chay (shā) [corr. of CHAISE (taken as a pl.)], *n.* (*vulgar*) A chaise [see also SHAY].

chay root, chaya root (chă'-, chī'-, chī' ȧ root, [Tamil *saya*], *n.* The root of an Indian plant, *Oldenlandia umbellata*, which furnishes a red dye.

cheap (chēp) [M.E. phrase *good cheap* (cp. F. *bon marché*), A.-S. *ceap*, price, barter (cp. Goth. *kaupōn*, to trade, G. *kaufen*, to buy, *kauf*, a purchase)], *a.* Low in price; worth more than its price or cost; easy to get; easily got; of small value or esteem. **to get cheap:** To purchase at a low price; to obtain easily. **to hold cheap:** To despise. **to make oneself cheap:** To behave with undignified familiarity. **on the cheap:** Cheaply. **cheap-jack,** *n.* A travelling hawker, esp. one who sells by Dutch auction. **cheaply,** *adv.* **cheapness,** *n.* **cheapen,** *v.t.* To higgle; to beat down the price or value of; to depreciate. *v.i.* To become cheap; to depreciate. **cheapener,** *n.* One who bargains or haggles. **cheapish,** *a.*

cheat (chēt) [short for ESCHEAT], *n.* A fraud, an imposition; a swindle, a fraudulent card-game; a trickster, a swindler; (*Thieves' cant*) a thing, esp. the gallows. *v.t.* To defraud, to deprive of; to deceive, to impose upon. *v.i.* To act as a cheat. **cheater,** *n.* One who cheats or defrauds; *an escheator or confiscator. ***tame cheater:** (*slang*)

A decoy. ***cheatery,** *n.* Deception, cheating, fraud.

check (1) (chek) [O.F. *eschec*, Arab. *shāg*, Pers. *shāh*, a king], *n.* A sudden stoppage, arrest, or restraint of motion; the person, thing, or means of arrest; a reverse, a repulse; a pause, a halt; restraint, repression; a mark put against names or items in going over a list; a token by which the correctness or authenticity of a document etc. may be ascertained; a token serving for identification; a pass entitling to readmission to a theatre; a term in chess when one player obliges the other to move or guard his king; the situation of such a king; a bill at a restaurant, etc.; (*Am.*) a token at cards; (*Am.*) a left-luggage ticket. *v.t.* to arrest; to cause to stop; to repress, to curb; to test the accuracy of by comparison with a list; (*Chess*) to put an opponent's king in check; (*Naut.*) to ease off (as a rope). *v.i.* To pause, to halt. *int.* (*Chess*) A call when an opponent's king is exposed (see CHECKMATE). **to hand in one's checks:** To die. **Clerk of the Check:** An officer in the British royal household in charge of the Yeomen of the Guard; *an officer who keeps account of the men in a naval dockyard. **check-action,** *n.* A device for preventing the hammer in a piano from striking twice. **check-nut,** *n.* A cap screwed over a nut to keep it from working loose. **check-receiver,** *n.* (*Radio.*) A device for checking the quality of transmission. **check-rein,** *n.* A bearing-rein; a branch rein coupling horses in a team. **check-string,** *n.* A cord by which the occupant of a closed carriage signals to the driver. **check-taker,** *n.* A collector of tickets, etc. **check-up,** *n.* A general overhaul. **check-valve,** *n.* (*Mach.*) A valve that allows a flow in only one direction.

check (2) (chek) [short for *checker*, CHEQUER], *n.* A chequered pattern, a cross-lined pattern; a chequered fabric. **checked,** *a.*

check (3) (*Am.*) CHEQUE. **checking account,** *n.* (*Am.*) Banking account.

checker [CHEQUER].

checkmate (chek māt′) [O.F. *eschec mat*, Pers. *shāh māt*, the king is dead; see CHECK (1)], *n.* (*Chess*) The winning movement when one king is in check and cannot escape from that position; (*fig.*) a complete defeat; a position from which there is no escape. *int.* (*Chess*) The call when an opponent's king is put into this position. *v.t.* To give checkmate to; (*fig.*) to defeat utterly, to frustrate.

Cheddar (ched′ ȧr) [village in Somerset, near the Mendip Hills], *n.* Cheddar cheese. **Cheddar-pink,** *n.* A pink, *Dianthus cæsius*, found on the limestone rocks at Cheddar.

chee-chee (chē′ chē) [Hind.], *n.* The minced English spoken by Eurasians.

cheek (chēk) [A.-S. *cēace*, from Teut. (cp. Dut. *kaak*, Swed. *kāk*)], *n.* The side of the face below the eye; (*colloq.*) impudence, sauciness; effrontery, assurance; impudent speech; one of two corresponding sides of a frame, machine, or implement; a side-post of a door, the side of a pulley. *v.t.* To be impudent to. *v.i.* To be saucy. **cheek by jowl:** Side by side; in the closest proximity. **cheek-bone,** *n.* The prominence of the malar bone. **cheek-tooth,** *n.* A molar tooth. **cheeker,** *n.* **cheeky,** *a.* Impudent, saucy. **cheekily,** *adv.* **cheekiness,** *n.*

cheep (chēp) [onomat.], *v.i.* To chirp feebly (as a young bird). *n.* The feeble cry of a young bird. **cheeper,** *n.* A young game bird.

cheer (chēr) [M.E. and O.F. *chere*, the face, look, late L. *cara*, face, perh. from Gr. *kara*, head], *n.* Disposition, the frame of mind, esp. as shown by the face; entertainment, good fare, a state of gladness or joy; a shout of joy or applause; *the face, the countenance; the expression of the face. *v.t.* To make glad or cheerful (often with *up*); to applaud, to encourage, to incite (as dogs). *v.i.* To grow cheerful (with *up*); to utter cheers. **cheerful,** *a.* Contented, hopeful; full of good spirits; lively, animated; willing. **cheerfully,** *adv.* **cheerfulness,** *n.* **cheering,** *a.* **cheeringly,** *adv.* **cheerless,** *a.* Dull, gloomy, dispiriting. **cheerlessness,** *n.* **cheerly,** *adv.* (*Naut.*) Cheerfully, heartily. **cheery,** *a.* Lively, sprightly, full of good spirits, genial. **cheerily,** *adv.* **cheeriness,** *n.* **cheerio, cheer-ho,** *int.* Good-bye, au revoir.

cheese (1) (chēz) [A.-S. *cēse* (cp. Dut. *kaas*, G. *käse*, L. *cāseus*)], *n.* The curd of milk pressed into a solid mass and ripened by keeping; a cylindrical or spherical block of this; the unripe fruit of the mallow; anything of cheese-like form; the appearance of a woman's skirt when curtsying. **to make cheeses:** To whirl round and sink suddenly so as to make the petticoats stand out. **cheese-cake,** *n.* A sweet confection made of soft curds, sugar, and butter. **cheesecloth,** *n.* (*Textiles*) Thin cotton cloth loosely woven; butter muslin. **cheese-cutter,** *n.* A knife with broad curved blade. **cheese-fly,** *n.* A fly, *Piophila casei*, bred in cheese. **cheese-hopper,** *n.* The larva of the cheese-fly. **cheese-mite,** *n.* A minute acarid, *Acarus domesticus*, infesting old cheese and other food-stuffs. **cheese-monger,** *n.* One who deals in cheese. **cheese-paring,** *a.* Niggardly, mean, miserly; (*pl.*) scraps of cheese; (*fig.*) odds and ends. **cheese-plate,** *n.* A plate 5 or 6 inches wide used for cheese at the end of a meal; (*facet.*) a large button. **cheese-press, -wring,** *n.* The press in which the curds are pressed in making cheese. **cheese-rennet,** *n.* The lady's bedstraw, *Galium verum*, used to coagulate milk. **cheese-taster,** *n.* A gouge-like knife for scooping pieces of cheese as samples. **cheese-vat,** *n.* The vat in which curds are pressed. **cheese-wood,** *n.* (*Austral.*) Trees with a hard wood of a cheese colour. **cheesy,** *a.* Resembling or tasting like cheese; (*slang*) fine, showy, stylish. **cheesiness,** *n.*

cheese (2) (chēz) [etym. doubtful], *n.* (*slang*) The real thing, the correct thing.

cheese (3) (chēz) [etym. unknown], *v.t.* (*slang*) Stop. **cheese it:** Stop it, drop it.

cheetah (chē′ tȧ) [Hind. *chītā* (Sansk. *chitraka*, spotted)], *n.* The hunting leopard, *Cynælurus jubatus*.

chef (shef) [F., CHIEF], *n.* A head or professional cook. **chef-d'œuvre** (shā dĕrvr′) [*œuvre*, work], *n.* (*pl.* **chefs-**) A masterpiece.

cheil-, cheilo- [CHIL-, CHILO-].

cheir-, cheiro- [CHIR-, CHIRO-].

cheiroptera (kī rop′ tėr ȧ) [CHIRO-, Gr. *pteron*, wing, *ptera*, wings], *n.pl.* (*Zool.*) A group of mammals with membranes connecting their fingers and used as wings, consisting of the bats. **cheiropteran,** *n.* **cheiropterous,** *a.*

cheirotherium (kīr ō thēr′ i ŭm) [CHIRO-, Gr. *thērion*, a wild beast], *n.* (*Palæont.*) An animal whose footprints, resembling those of a hand, are found in the New Red Sandstone.

Cheka (che′ kȧ) [initials of Rus. *Chrezvichainaya Kommissiya*, extraordinary commission], *n.* (*Pol.*) Former name for the central organization of secret police in Soviet Russia.

chela (1) (kē′ lȧ) [Gr. *chēlē*], *n.* (*pl.* **-læ**) A claw (as of a lobster or crab), a modified thoracic limb. **chelate,** *a.* **chelifer** (kel′ i fėr) [L. *-fer*, bearing], *n.* A genus of Arachnids or spiders, resembling small tailless scorpions. **cheliferous** (kė lif′ ėr us), *a.* **cheliform** (kel′ i fôrm), *a.* **cheliped,** *n.*

chela (2) (chā′ lȧ) [Hind. *chēlā*, servant, pupil], *n.* A student or novice in esoteric Buddhism.

chelicer, -cere (kel′ i sĕr, -sēr) [F. *chélicère*, mod. L. *chelicera* (Gr. *chēlē*, claw, *keras*, horn)], *n.* (*Zool.*) One of the claw-like antennæ of scorpions and spiders. **cheliceral** (ke lis′ ėr ȧl), *a.*

chelidonic (kel i don′ ik) [L. *chelīdonium*, Gr. *chelidonion*, from *chelidōn*, swallow], *a.* (*Chem.*) Pertaining to the celandine or swallow-wort. **chelidonic acid,** *n.* An acid obtained from this. **chelidonate** (-li′ dō nāt) *n.* **chelidonine,** *n.*

chelifer, etc., **cheliform** [CHELA (1)].

Chellean (shel′ i ȧn) [*Chelles*, 8 m. E. of Paris, -AN], *a.* (*Anthrop.*) Of or pertaining to the period of Lower Palæolithic culture typified by the remains found at Chelles in the valley of the Marne.

chelonia (kė lō′ ni ȧ) [L., from Gr. *chelōnē*, tortoise], *n.pl.* An order of reptiles containing the turtles and tortoises. **chelonian,** *a.* and *n.*

chemical (kem′ ik ȧl), ***chemic** (kem′ ik) [F. *chimique*, or mod. L. *chymicus* (see ALCHEMY)], *a.* Pertaining to chemistry, its laws, or phenomena; of or produced by chemical process. *n.* A substance or agent produced by or used in chemical processes. **chemical change:** A change involving the formation of a new substance. **chemical reaction:** The process of changing one substance into another. **chemical symbol:** A letter or letters used to represent an atom of a chemical element. **chemically,** *adv.* **chemico-,** *comb. form.* Chemical. **chemico-electric,** *a.* Pertaining to or produced by chemistry in conjunction with electricity.

chemin de fer (she′ măn dė fẻr) [F., railway], *n.* (*Cards*) A variety of baccarat.

chemise (shė mēz′) [F., from late L. *camisia* (cp. A.-S. *ham*, Goth. *af-hamōn*, to unclothe)], *n.* A body garment of linen or cotton worn next to the skin by women. **chemisette** (shem i zet′) [F., dim. of prec.], *n.* A woman's light bodice; lace-work worn in the opening of a dress below the throat.

chemism (kem′ izm), *n.* Chemical attraction or affinity considered as a form of energy.

chemist (kem′ ist) [F. *chimiste*, mod. L. *chimista, chymista, alchimista*, ALCHEMIST], *n.* One versed in chemistry; a dealer in drugs, chemicals, etc., (*Am.*) a druggist. **chemist and druggist,** *n.* A person registered under the Pharmacy Act of 1868. **analytical chemist,** *n.* A chemist who carries out the process of analysis by chemical means. **pharmaceutical chemist,** *n.* A person qualified under the Pharmacy Act of 1852.

chemistry (kem′ is tri) [as prec.], *n.* The science which investigates the elements of which bodies are composed, the combination of these elements, and the reaction of these chemical compounds on each other; the practical application of this science; (*fig.*) any process or change conceived as analogous to chemical action (**inorganic chemistry** deals with mineral substances, **organic chemistry** with animal and vegetable substances).

chemitype (kem′ i tīp), *n.* A process by which a drawing or impression from an engraved plate is obtained in relief, to be employed in printing.

chemolysis (kė mol′ i sis) [CHEM-IC, Gr. *lusis*, loosening, from *luein*, to loosen], *n.* Chemical decomposition or analysis. **chemolytic** (-lit′ ik), *a.*

chemotaxis (kem ō tăk′ sis), *n.* (*Bot., Zool.*) The property possessed by some mobile cells of being drawn towards or repelled by certain chemical substances.

chemotherapy (kem ō ther′ ȧ pi), *n.* (*Med.*) Treatment by drugs.

chemurgy (kem′ ĕr ji) [Gr. *ergos*, working], *n.* That branch of chemistry which is devoted to the industrial utilization of organic raw material, esp. farm products.

chenille (shė nēl′) [F., hairy caterpillar, L. *canicula*, little dog, dim. of *canis*, dog], *n.* Round tufted or fluffy cord of silk or worsted.

chenopod (kē′ nȯ pod) [mod. L. *chenopodium*, Gr. *chēnopous, -podos* (*chēn chēnos*, goose, *pous podos*, foot)], *n.* A genus of herbs, containing the common goose-foot.

cheque (chek) [CHECK], *n.* A draft on a banker for money payable to bearer or order. **crossed cheque:** A cheque marked as negotiable only through a banker. **cheque-book,** *n.* A book containing forms for drawing cheques.

chequer, checker (chek′ ẻr) [O.F. *eschekier*, chess-board, late L. *scaccarium*, EXCHEQUER], *n.* *A chess-board; (*pl.*) a chess-board used as the sign of an inn; (*usu. in pl.*) a pattern made of squares in alternating colours, like a chess-board; (*pl., Am.*) the game of draughts. *v.t.* To form into a pattern of little squares; to variegate; to diversify, to fill with vicissitudes. **checker-board,** *n.* (*Am.*) A draught-board; a chess-board. **checker-work,** *n.* Work executed in diaper pattern or checkers.

cherimoya (cher i moi′ ȧ) [Peruv.], *n.* A Peruvian tree, *Anona cherimolia*, with pulpy fruit.

cherish (cher′ ish) [O.F. *cherir* (pres.p. *cherissant*), from *cher*, L. *cārus*, dear], *v.t.* To hold dear, to treat with affection, to caress; to foster, to promote; to hold closely to, cling to. **cherishingly,** *adv.* ***cherishment,** *n.* The act of cherishing.

cheroot (shė root′) [Tamil *shuruttu*, a roll of tobacco], *n.* A cigar with both ends cut square off.

cherry (cher′ i) [M.E. *chery*, O.North.F. *cherise* (O.F. *cerise*), L. *cerasus*, Gr. *kerasos*; (for loss of *s*, cp. PEA)], *n.* A small stone-fruit of the plum family; the tree, *Prunus cerasus*, on which it grows; the wood of this. *a.* Of the colour of a red cherry; ruddy. **two bites at a cherry:** A bungling attempt. **cherry-bag,** *n.* The common cherry-laurel. **cherry-bob,** *n.* A pair of cherries joined by their stems. **cherry-bounce,** *n.* Cherry brandy mixed with sugar. **cherry-brandy,** *n.* Brandy in which cherries have been steeped. **cherry-breeches,** *n.pl.* (*slang*) The 11th Hussars, from the colour of their trousers. **cherry-cheeked,** *a.* Ruddy-cheeked. **cherry-pie,** *n.* A pie made with cherries; the hairy willow-herb; the garden heliotrope. ***cherry-pit,** *n.* A childish game in which cherry-stones are pitched into a small hole. **cherry-ripe,** *n.* The cry of persons hawking cherries. **cherry-stone,** *n.* The endocarp of the cherry. **cherry-tree,** *n.* The tree, *Prunus cerasus*, on which the cherry grows. **cherry-wood,** *n.* The wood of the cherry-tree; the wood of the wild guelder-rose, *Viburnum opulus.*

chersonese (ker′ sȯ nēs) [L. *chersonēsus*, Gr. *chersonēsos* (*chersos*, dry land, *nēsos*, island)], *n.* A peninsula, esp. the Thracian peninsula.

chert (chert) [orig. unknown], *n.* (*Geol.*) Hornstone; impure flinty rock. **cherty,** *a.* Resembling or containing chert.

cherub (che′ rub) [Heb. *k'rūb, k'rūv*, pl. *k'rūvīm*], *n.* (*pl.* **-s, -im, -ims**) A celestial spirit next in order to the seraphim; (*fig.*) a beautiful child; (*Art.*) the winged head of a child. **cherubic** (chė ru′ bik), *a.* Of or pertaining to cherubs; angelic; full-cheeked and ruddy. **cherubically,** *adv.* **cherubin,** *n.* A cherub.

chervil (chĕr′ vil) [A.-S. *cærfille*, L. *chærephylla*, pl., Gr. *chairephullon* (*chairein*, to rejoice, *phullon*, leaf], *n.* A garden pot-herb and salad-herb, *Chærophyllum sativum.*

Cheshire (chesh′ ir) [English county], *a.* **to grin like a cheshire cat:** To laugh all over one's face. **Cheshire cheese,** *n.* A red cheese made in Cheshire.

chesnut [CHESTNUT].

chess (1) (ches) [O.F. *esches*, pl. of *eschec*, CHECK], *n.* A game played by two persons with sixteen pieces each on a board divided into sixty-four squares. **chess-board,** *n.* The board on which chess is played. **chess-man,** *n.* One of the pieces used in chess. **chess-player,** *n.* One who plays or is well-skilled in chess.

***chess** (2) (ches) [etym. doubtful; perh. from prec.], *n.* (*usu. pl.*) One of the parallel baulks of timber used in laying a pontoon-bridge.

chessel (ches′ ėl), *n.* A cheese-mould.

chest (chest) [A.-S. *cest*, L. *cista*, Gr. *kistē*], *n.* A large box; a case for holding particular commodities; the quantity such a case holds; (*fig.*) the coffer, treasury, or funds of an institution; the fore part of the human body from the neck to the belly. *v.t.* *To deposit in a chest; to put into a coffin; (*Horses*) to strike with the chest. **chest of drawers:**

A movable wooden frame containing drawers, (*Am.*) a dresser. **chest-note,** *n.* A deep note sounded from the chest, the lowest singing register. **chest-protector,** *n.* A thick scarf or wrap of flannel worn over the chest to prevent colds. **-chested,** *comb form.* Having a chest, the meaning completed by the first element.

Chesterfield (ches' tėr fēld) [6th Earl of *Chesterfield*], *n.* A loose kind of overcoat; a deeply upholstered sofa.

chestnut (ches' nŭt) [formerly *chesten, chesteine,* O.F. *chastaigne* (F. *châtaigne*), L. *castanea,* Gr. *kastanea* (prob. a place-name), -NUT], *n.* A tree of the genus *Castanea,* esp. the Spanish or sweet chestnut, *C. vesca,* or its edible fruit; hence, a reddish-brown colour; a horse of this colour; (*colloq.*) a stale joke or anecdote; (*Horses*) a knob on the inside of the forelegs, a castor. *a.* Reddish brown.

chetah [CHEETAH].

cheval de frise (shė val' dė frēz') [F., a Friesland horse], *n.* (*pl.* ***chevaux,*** shė vō') A kind of fence, consisting of a bar armed with two rows of long spikes, for checking attacks by cavalry, etc.

cheval-glass (shė văl') [F. *cheval,* a horse, a support, GLASS], *n.* A large swing glass mounted on a frame.

chevalier (shev å lēr') [F. (*cheval,* L. *caballus,* horse)] *n.* *A cavalier, a knight; a member of some foreign orders of knighthood or of the French Legion of Honour. **chevalier of industry** [F. *chevalier d'industrie*], *n.* An adventurer, a swindler.

chevelure (shev ė loor') [F., from O.F. *cheveleūre,* L. *capillātūra* (*capillātus,* haired, from *capillus,* a hair)], *n.* A head of hair; a luminous nebulosity round the nucleus of a comet.

cheverel (chev' ėr ėl) [O.F. *chevrele,* dim. of *chèvre,* L. *capra,* a goat], *n.* Leather made from kid-skin; (*fig.*) a soft, yielding nature. *a.* Made of kid-skin; (*fig.*) yielding, pliant.

chevet (shė vā') [F., pillow], *n.* (*Arch.*) An apse.

cheville (shė vēl') [F., a peg], *n.* (*Mus.*) A peg for a violin, guitar, lute, etc.; a meaningless word put into a sentence.

chevin (chev' in) [F. *chevin, chevanne* (cp. *chef,* head)], *n.* The chub.

cheviot (chev' i ot), *n.* A sheep bred on the Cheviot Hills; rough cloth made from the wool of such sheep.

***chevisance** (shev' i zăns) [O.F., from *chevissant,* pres.p. of *chevir,* to bring to a head, finish (*chef,* head)], *n.* A resource, a shift; provisions, booty, profit, gain; a borrowing of money; (*Spens., erroneously*), achievement, prowess.

chevrette (shev ret') [F., dim. of *chèvre,* L. *capra,* the goat], *n.* A thin goat-skin leather used for gloves.

chevron (shev' ron) [F., rafter, from L. *capreoli,* used of a pair of rafters], *n.* (*Her.*) An honourable ordinary representing two rafters meeting at the top; (*Mil.*) inverted, the distinguishing mark on the coat-sleeves of non-commissioned officers; (*Arch.*) zig-zag moulding. **chevronel,** *n.* (*Her.*) A bar like a chevron but only half the width. **chevonry,** *a.*

chevrotain, -tin (shev' rō tăn, -tin) [F., dim. of O.F. *chevrot,* dim. of *chèvre,* she-goat, L. *capra*], *n.* A small animal allied to the musk-deer.

chevy (chev' i), **chivy** (chiv' i) [prob. from the ballad of *Chevy Chase*], *v.t.* To chase about; to hunt. *v.i.* To scamper about. *n.* A hunt, a chase; the game of prisoners' base.

chew (choo) [A.-S. *cēowan,* from Teut. (cp. Dut. *kaauwen,* O.H.G. *kiuwan,* G. *kauen*)], *v.t.* To masticate, to grind with the teeth; (*fig.*) to ruminate on, to digest mentally. *v.i.* To masticate food; to chew tobacco or gum; (*fig.*) to meditate. *n.* That which is chewed in the mouth; a mouthful; a quid of tobacco. **to chew the cud:** (*Cattle*) To bring back to the mouth and chew over again. **to chew the rag:** (*slang*) To grumble, to complain. **chewing-gum,** *n.* A preparation of flavoured insoluble gum for chewing.

***chewet** (choo' ėt) [F. *chouette,* a chough, a daw], *n.* A chough; a chatterer.

Chewings fescue (choo' ingz fes' kū) [Agriculturist's name], *n.* (*N. Zealand*) A notable fodder-grass.

chiack (chī' ăk), *v.t.* (*Austral. colloq.*) To cheek, to poke fun at.

Chian (kī' ȧn), *a.* Of or pertaining to Chios. *n.* An inhabitant of Chios.

Chianti (ki an' ti) [It.], *n.* A red wine from Tuscany.

chiaroscuro (ki a' rō skoo' rō) [It. (*chiaro,* L. *clārus,* clear, bright, *oscuro,* L. *obscūrus,* dark)], *n.* (*Painting*) The treatment of light and shade; effects of light and shade; a drawing in black and white; (*fig.*) relief, contrast, variety of light and shade (in a literary work, etc.). *a.* Obscure; half-revealed.

chiasm (kī' ăsm) [Gr. *chiasma* (*chiazein,* to mark with a χ)], *n.* (*Anat.*) The crossing or decussation of the optic nerves.

chiasmus (kī ăz' mus) [Gr. *chiasmos,* crossing (as prec.)], *n.* (*Gram.*) Inversion of order in parallel phrases, as *you came late, to go early would be unreasonable.*

chiaster (ki ăs' tėr) [Gr. *chi,* χ, *astēr,* star], *n.* (*Zool.*) A species of sponge found in the West Indies; a star-like spicule in some sponges.

chibouk, chibouque (chi book') [Turk. *chibūq*], *n.* A long Turkish pipe for smoking.

chic (shik) [F., etym. unknown], *n.* Smartness, style; the best fashion or taste. *a.* Stylish; fashionable.

chica (1) (chē' kȧ) [native name from the Orinoco], *n.* A red colouring-matter used by South American Indians to stain the skin.

chica (2) (chē' ka) [Sp.], *n.* An old Spanish dance of an erotic character, forerunner of the fandango, bolero, and cachucha.

chicane (shi kān') [F., etym. doubtful (perh. from med. Gr. *tzukanion,* Pers. *chaugān,* a polo club)], *n.* The use of mean petty subterfuge; artifice, stratagem; sophistical conduct; (*Cards*) a hand containing no trumps. *v.i.* To use chicane; to cheat. **chicanery,** *n.* The employment of chicane, esp. legal dodges and quibbles; pettifogging.

chicha (chē' chȧ) [Haitian], *n.* A fermented drink made from maize.

chick (1) (chik) [see foll.], *n.* A young bird about to be hatched or newly hatched. (*colloq.*) a little child. **chickabiddy,** *n.* A term of endearment for a child. **chickweed,** *n.* A small weed, *Stellaria media.*

chick (2), **chicken** (chik' ėn) [A.-S. *cīcen,* pl. *cīcenu* (cp. Dut. *kieken,* G. *küchlein,* Eng. COCK)], *n.* The young of the domestic fowl; a fowl for the table; (*fig.*) a person of tender years. **no chicken:** Older than he appears or she makes out. **Mother Cary's chicken,** *n.* The stormy petrel. **chicken-breasted,** *a.* Pigeon-breasted, having a contracted chest through malformation of the breast-bone. **chicken-feed,** *n.* (*colloq.*) Trifling stuff, matter not worth considering. **chicken-hazard,** *n.* A game at dice for trumpery stakes. **chicken-hearted,** *a.* Timid, cowardly. **chicken-pox,** *n.* A pustulous, contagious disease, usually occurring in childhood. **chicken-snake,** *n.* (*Am.*) Any snake that preys on chickens and hen's eggs. **chicken yard,** *n.* (*Am.*) A fowl-run. **to chicken out:** (*Am.*) To lose one's nerve.

chickling (chik' ling) [formerly *chicheling,* dim. of *chiche,* O.F. *chiche,* L. *cicer*], *n.* The cultivated vetch; also commonly called the **chickling vetch.**

chick-pea (chik' pē) [earlier *chich,* later *chich-pease,* see prec. and PEA], *n.* A dwarf species of pea, *Cicer arietinum.*

chickweed [CHICK (1)].

chicle (chi′ kėl) [Mex. *tzictli*], *n.* The juice of *Achras sapota* used in the making of chewing-gum.

chicory (chik′ ŏ ri) [F. *chichorée, cichorée*, L. *cichorium*, Gr. *kichōrion, kichōrē*, succory], *n.* The succory, a blue-flowered plant, *Cichorium intybus*, or its root, which, when roasted and ground, is used to adulterate coffee; endive.

chide (chīd) (A.-S. *cīdan*], *v.t.* (*past* **chided, chid,** *p.p.* **chided, chid, chidden**) To find fault with, to reprove, to blame; *to drive by chiding; *to fret against; *to dispute with. *v.i.* To scold, to fret, to make complaints; (*fig.*) to make a complaining or brawling sound. *n.* Chiding, bickering, a reproof; (*fig.*) murmur, gentle noise. **chidingly,** *adv.*

chief (chēf) [O.F. *chef*, L. *caput*, head], *a.* Principal, first; highest in authority; most important, leading, main. *n.* A leader or commander, esp. the leader of a tribe or clan; the prime mover; the principal agent; the head of a department; the principal thing; the largest part; (*Her.*) the upper part of a shield. **to hold land in chief:** (*Law*) To hold it directly from the sovereign by honourable personal service. **chiefdom,** *n.* **chiefess,** *n.* ***chiefest,** *a.* First, most important. *adv.* Firstly, chiefly. **chiefless,** *a.* Without a chief or leader. **chiefly,** *adv.* Principally, especially; for the most part. **chiefery, chiefry,** *n.* The institution of chiefs of clans. *a small rent paid to the lord in chief.

chieftain (chēf′ tȧn) [O.F. *chevetain*, late L. *capitānus*, CAPTAIN], *n.* A general, a leader; the head of a tribe or a Highland clan. **chieftainess,** *n.* **chieftaincy -ry, -ship,** *n.*

chield (chēld) [Sc. var. of CHILD], *n.* A man; a lad; a fellow.

chiff-chaff (chif′ chăf) [onomat.], *n.* One of the warblers, *Phylloscopus rufa.*

chiffon (shif′ on) [F. (*chiffe*, a rag)], *n.* A gauzy semi-transparent fabric; (*pl.*) trimmings, esp. of dresses. **chiffonier** (shif ŏ nēr′) [F. *chiffonnier*, a rag-gatherer], *n.* A movable piece of furniture serving as a cupboard and sideboard.

chignon (shē nyon′) [F., earlier *chaignon* (*chaignon du col*, nape of the neck), var. of *chaînon*, ring or link (*chaîne*, CHAIN)], *n.* A pad over which women can dress their hair; the hair so dressed.

chigoe (chig′ ō) [perh. a negro corr. of Sp. *chico*, small], *n.* A small W. Indian and S. American flea *Pulex penetrans*, also known as a jigger.

chihuahua (chi wa′ wa) [town in Mexico], *n.* A very small dog with big eyes and pointed ears.

chilblain (chil′ blān), *n.* A blain, or inflamed state of the hands or feet caused by cold or frost. **chilblained,** *a.* **chilblainy,** *a.*

child (chīld) [A.-S. *cild*, from Teut. (cp. Goth. *kilthei*, the womb, Dan. *kuld*, Swed. *kull*, a litter)], *n.* (*pl.* **children,** chil′ drėn) A descendant in the first degree; a boy; a girl; an infant; a young person; a son or daughter; (*fig.*) one young in experience, judgement, or attainments; (*pl.*) descendants; the inhabitants of a country; disciples, followers, adherents. **v.t.* To give birth to. **v.i.* To bring forth a child or children. **with child:** Pregnant. **child-bearing,** *a.* Bringing forth children. *n.* The act of bearing children; the period of gestation. **childbed,** *n.* The state of a woman in labour, or bringing forth a child. **child-birth,** *n.* The time or act of bringing forth a child. **child's-play,** *n.* Easy work, trifling. **childe,** *n.* A scion of a noble family, esp. one not yet admitted to knighthood. ***childed,** *a.* Provided with a child. ***Childermas day** (A.-S. *cildru, mæsse*, MASS], *n.* The festival of Holy Innocents (Dec. 28). **childhood,** *n.* The state of being a child; the period from birth till puberty. **second childhood,** *n.* Dotage. ***childing,** *a.* Child-bearing, fruitful; in childbirth. **childish,** *a.* Of or befitting a child; silly, puerile. **childish-minded,** *a.* **childishly,** *adv.* **childishness,** *n.* **childless,** *a.* Without child or offspring. **childlessness,** *n.* **childlike,** *a.* Resembling or befitting a child; docile, simple, innocent. ***childly,** *a.* and *adv.* ***childness,** *n.* Childishness.

chiliad (kil′ i ȧd) [Gr. *chilias -ados* (*chilioi*, a thousand)], *n.* A thousand; a thousand years. **chiliagon** [-GON], *n.* (*Geom.*) A figure having a thousand angles. **chiliahedron** (kil i ȧ hē′ dron) (*hedra*, a seat, a base], *n.* (*Geom.*) A figure having a thousand angles and sides. ***chiliarch** [Gr. *chiliarchēs* (*chilioi*, thousand, *archos*, from *archein*, to rule)], *n.* The commander of a thousand men. ***chiliarchy,** *n.* A body of a thousand men. **chiliasm** (kil′ i ăzm) [Gr. *chiliasmos*, from *chilias*], *n.* The doctrine of the millennium. **chiliast,** *n.* **chiliastic** (-ăs′ tik), *a.*

chill (chil) [A.-S. *ciele, cele*, from Teut. (cp. Icel. *kala*, to freeze, Dut. *kil*, chilly, L. *gelu*, frost)], *n.* Coldness, a fall in bodily temperature; a cold; a cold, shivering sensation preceding fever or ague; (*fig.*) a check, a discouragement; discouragement, depression. *v.t.* To make cold; to preserve meat, etc. by cold; (*Metal.*) to cool suddenly so as to harden; (*fig.*) to depress, to dispirit, to discourage; to take the chill off wine, etc. *v.i.* To become cold. *a.* Cold; causing a sensation of coolness; (*fig.*) unfeeling; unemotional; coldly formal; depressing. **to take the chill off:** To warm slightly. **chillness,** *n.* **chilling,** *a.* Making cold; depressing, distant in manner. **chillingly,** *adv.* **chilly,** *a.* Rather cold; susceptible of cold; (*fig.*) cold or distant in manner. **chilliness,** *n.*

chilli (chil′ i) [Mex.], *n.* (*pl.* **-ies**) The dried ripe pod of red pepper, *Capsicum fastigiatum*, and other species.

chilo-, chil- [Gr. *cheilos*, a lip], *comb. form.* (*Zool.*) Lip-shaped, labiate. **chilopod** (kī′ lŏ pod) [Gr. *pous podos*, foot], *n.* A member of an order *Chilopoda* comprising the centipedes. **chilostomatous** (kī lŏ stom′ ȧ tŭs) [Gr. *stoma -atos*, mouth], *a.* Having a movable lip-like operculum.

Chiltern Hundreds (chil′ tĕrn hŭn′ drėdz) [certain Crown lands in Buckinghamshire and Oxfordshire, the nominal stewardship of which is granted to a Member of Parliament who wishes to vacate his seat], *n.pl.* **to apply for the Chiltern Hundreds:** To resign membership of the House of Commons.

chimæra [CHIMERA].

chime (1) (chīm) [M.E. *chimbe*, O.F. *chimble*, L. *cymbalum*, Gr. *kumbalon*, CYMBAL], *n.* The harmonic or consonant sounds of musical instruments or bells; a number of bells tuned in diatonic succession; the sounds so produced; harmony, accord; tune, rhythm; correspondence of relation. *v.i.* To sound in harmony or accord; (*of bells*) to ring; to strike the hour, etc.; to accord, to agree; to be in rhyme. *v.t.* To ring a series of bells; to ring a chime on bells; to cause to sound in harmony; to recite musically or rhythmically. **to chime in:** To join in; to express agreement.

chime (2), **chimb** (chīm) [M.E. *chimb* (cp. Dut. *kim*, G. *kimme*, A.-S. *cimb-īren*)], *n.* The edge of a cask or tub formed by the ends of the staves.

chimer (chim′ ėr), **chimere** (chi mēr′) [O.F. *chamarre* (etym. unknown)], *n.* The Convocation robe of a bishop.

chimera (ki-, kī mēr′ ȧ) [L. *chimæra*, Gr. *chimaira*, she-goat, a monster, fem. of *chimaros*, goat], *n.* A fabulous fire-eating monster, with a lion's head, a serpent's tail, and the body of a goat; (*fig.*) any incongruous conception of the fancy; (*Zool.*) a genus of cartilaginous fishes. **chimerical** (-mer′ ik ȧl), *a.* Purely imaginary. **chimerically,** *adv.*

chimney (chim′ ni) [O.F. *chiminée*, late L. *camīnāta* (L. *camīnus*, hearth, stove, flue)], *n.* *A fireplace, a hearth; the flue, vent, or passage through which smoke escapes from a fire into the open air; a glass tube placed over the flame of a lamp to intensify combustion; a vent from a volcano; (*Mountaineering*) a vertical or nearly vertical fissure in rock. **chimney-breast,** *n.* The projecting part of the wall of a room containing the fireplace. **chimney-cap,** *n.* A cowl. **chimney-corner,** *n.* A nook or seat beside the fire, esp. inside a wide, old-fashioned fireplace. **chimney-jack,** *n.* A rotating cap or cowl. **chimney-piece,** *n.* The ornamental frame round a fireplace, consisting of jambs and mantel. **chimney-pot,** *n.* A tube of pottery or sheet-metal carried up above the chimney-shaft to prevent smoking; (*colloq.*) a tall silk hat. **chimney-stack,** *n.* A series of chimney-stalks united in a block of masonry or brickwork. **chimney-stalk, -top,** *n.* The part of the chimney-stack carried up above the roof; a tall factory chimney. **chimney-swallow,** *n.* The common swallow, *Hirundo rustica.* **chimney-sweep,** *n.* A brush with long, jointed handle for sweeping chimneys; a chimney-sweeper. **chimney-sweeper,** *n.* One whose business is to sweep chimneys.

chimpanzee (chim păn zē′) [native name from Angola], *n.* A large African anthropoid ape, *Troglodytes niger*; also applied to *T. calvus.*

chin (chin) [A.-S. *cin* (cp. Dut. *kin,* G. *kinn,* Gr. *geneion,* chin, L. *gena,* cheek)], *n.* The front part of the lower jaw. **chin-wag,** *n.* (*slang*) Chat, talk.

China (chī′ nȧ) [English name for the Far-Eastern country], *a.* Of or belonging to China. **China aster,** A garden flower, *Callistephus Chinensis.* **china-grass,** *n.* The fibre of *Bohmeria nivea,* used for making ropes and cordage. **China ink,** *n.* A black solid which, when mixed with water, yields a black, indelible ink. **Chinaman,** *n.* A native of China, or one of Chinese blood. **China pink,** *n.* A variety of garden flower, *Dianthus Chinensis.* **china-root,** *n.* The foot of a Chinese plant, *Smilax China,* used medicinally. **China rose,** *n.* A garden name for several varieties of the rose. **Chinatown,** *n.* The Chinese quarter of a town. **Chinese,** *n.* A native of China, or one of Chinese blood. *a.* Of or belonging to China. **Chinese lantern,** *n.* A collapsible lantern made of thin paper. **Chinese white,** *n.* An opaque white paint. **Chino-,** *comb. form* Chinese, or relating to China.

china (chī′ nȧ) [as prec.], *n.* Porcelain, first brought from China; porcelain ware. *a.* Made of porcelain. **china-clay,** *n.* Fine clay for porcelain; kaolin. **china-closet,** *n.* A cupboard for storing china-ware. **china-shop,** *n.* A shop for the sale of china-ware. **china-ware,** *n.* Articles made of china.

chinch (chinch) [Sp. *chinche,* L. *cimex -icis*], *n.* (*Am.*) The bed-bug; a fetid insect, destructive to corn.

chinchilla (chin chil′ ȧ) [Sp., dim. of *chinche,* see prec.], *n.* A genus of South American rodents; the fur of these animals.

chin-chin (chin′ chin) [Chinese ts'ing ts'ing], *n.* (*colloq.*) A familiar form of salutation or health-drinking.

chinchona [CINCHONA].

chin-cough (chin′ kof) [earlier and still dial. *chink-cough, kink-cough* (CHINK (3), COUGH)], *n.* The whooping-cough.

chindit (chin′ dit) [Burmese *chinthey,* a griffin], *n.* (*Mil.*) A commando in Burma during World War II.

chine (1) (chīn) [O.F. *eschine* (F. *échine*), perh. from O.H.G. *skina,* a needle (cp. senses of L. *spīna,* a thorn, a backbone)], *n.* The backbone or spine of any animal; part of the back (of a pig) cut for cooking; a ridge. **v.t.* To cut or break the backbone of. **chined,** *a.* Having a backbone; backboned (*usu. in comb.*).

chine (2) (chīn) [A.-S. *cinu,* a chink, cleft (cp. Dut. *keen*)], *n.* (*Isle of Wight and Hants*) A deep and narrow ravine.

Chinese [CHINA].

chink (1) (chingk) [etym. doubtful; perh. from CHINE], *n.* A narrow cleft or crevice; a small longitudinal opening; a slit. *v.t.* To stuff up chinks. *v.i.* To split, to crack.

chink (2) (chingk) [onomat.], *n.* A jingling sound as of coin; (*slang*) cash, ready money. *v.t.* To cause to jingle. *v.i.* To emit a jingling sound.

chink (3) (chingk), **kink** [prob. from an A.-S. *cincian* (11th cent. *cincung,* noun of action); cp. Dut. *kinken,* to cough], *v.i.* To gasp or lose one's breath in coughing or laughing. *n.* A gasp of this kind.

Chink (4) (chingk), *n.* Familiar name for a Chinese.

Chinook (chi nook′) [native name of Indian tribe], *n.* A jargon of Indian and European words used in intercourse between traders and Indians in the region of the Columbia River; a warm west wind from the Pacific Ocean occurring in the Rocky Mountains.

chintz (chints) [formerly *chints,* pl., Hind. *chhīnt* (Sansk. *chitra,* variegated)], *n.* Cotton cloth, printed in colours with floral devices, etc., and usu. glazed.

chip (1) (chip) [dim. of CHOP (cp. *click, clack; clink, clank; drip, drop*)], *n.* A small piece of wood, stone, etc., detached or chopped off; a thin strip of wood; a thin fragment; (*pl.*) thin slices of fried potato, (*Am.*) french-fried potatoes; wood or wood-fibre cut into thin strips for making hats; a playing-counter used in card games. *v.t.* (*past & p.p.* **chipped**) To cut into chips; to cut or break chips off; to crack. *v.i.* To break or fly off in chips. **chip of the old block:** A son resembling his father. **chip-bonnet, -hat,** *n.* A bonnet or hat made of chip. **to chip at:** (*Austral.*) To jeer at, to nag. **to chip in:** (*slang*) To cut into a conversation. **to have a chip on one's shoulder:** To nourish a grievance. **chipper,** *a.* (*Am.*) Lively, full of spirits. **chippy,** *a.* (*slang*) Seedy; unwell after a bout of drinking; irritable. **chippiness,** *n.*

chip (2) (chip) [cp. Icel. *kippa,* to scratch, to pull, Dut. *kippen,* to catch], *v.t.* (*Wrestling*) To trip up. *n.* (*Wrestling*) A trip; a particular kind of throw.

chipmunk (chip′ mŭngk) [N.Am.Ind.], *n.* A North American rodent, *Tamias lysteri,* like the squirrel.

Chippendale (chip′ ėn dāl) [Thomas *Chippendale* (*d.* 1779)], *a.* Applied to furniture of the style introduced by the cabinet-maker Chippendale about the middle of the 18th cent.; also to a contemporaneous style of book-plates.

chir-, chiro- [Gr. *cheir,* hand], *comb. form.* Manual; having hands or hand-like organs. **chiragra** (kī răg′ rȧ) [L., from Gr. *cheiragra* (*agra,* a hunt, a catch)], *n.* (*Med.*) Gout in the finger-joints. **chiragrical,** *a.*

chirognomy (kī rog′ nō mi), *n.* Judgement of character from the lines in the hand.

chirograph (kī′ rō grăf) [F. *chirographe,* L. *chirographum,* Gr. *cheirographon* (CHIRO-, -GRAPH)], *n.* A written or signed document. **chirographer** (kī rog′ rȧ fer), *n.* An officer in the Court of Common Pleas who engrossed fines. **chirographic, chirographical** (kī rō grăf′ ik, -ȧl), *a.* Pertaining to or in handwriting. **chirography** (-rog′ rȧ fi), *n.* The art of writing or engrossing; character and style in handwriting.

chirology (kī rol′ ō ji), *n.* The art or practice of conversing by signs made with the hands or fingers; finger-speech. **chirologist,** *n.*

chiromancy (kī′ rō măn si) [CHIRO-, -MANCY], *n.* Divination by means of the hand; palmistry. **chiromantic,** *a.* **chiromancer,** *n.*

chiropodist (kī rop′ ȯ dist) [CHIRO-, Gr. *pous podos,* foot, -IST], *n.* One skilled in the care of the hands and feet, esp. in the removal of corns, etc. **chiropody,** *n.*

chiropractic (kī rō prăk′ tik), *n.* Spinal manipulation as a method of curing disease. **chiropractor,** *n.*

chiroptera [CHEIROPTERA].

chirp (chĕrp) [imit.], *v.i.* To make a quick, sharp sound (as birds and their young, insects, etc.); to talk cheerfully; to speak faintly. *v.t.* To utter or sing with a sharp, quick sound. *n.* A sharp, quick sound of a bird; a sound resembling this. **chirpingly,** *adv.* In a chirping manner. **chirpy,** *a.* Cheerful; vivacious. **chirpiness,** *n.*

chirr (chĕr) [imit.], *v.i.* To make a trilling monotonous sound like that of the grasshopper.

chirrup (chir′ ŭp) [CHIRP], *v.t.* (*slang*) To applaud a player or singer for a consideration. *v.i.* To chirp, to make a twittering sound; (*slang*) to applaud at a theatre or concert-hall for a consideration. **chirruper,** *n.* **chirrupy,** *a.* Cheerful, chatty.

***chirurgeon** (kī, chī rĕr′ jŏn) [O.F. *cirurgien*, from *cirurgie*, L. *chīrurgia*, Gr. *cheirourgia* (CHEIR-, *ergein*, to work)], *n.* A surgeon. ***chirurgeonly,** *adv.* ***chirurgery,** *n.*

chisel (chiz′ ĕl) [O.North.F. (O.F. *cisel*, F. *ciseau*), late L. *cīsellum*, acc. of *cīsellus*, forceps (L. *-cisum*, from *cædere*, to cut)], *n.* An edged tool for cutting wood, iron, or stone, operated by pressure or striking. *v.t.* To cut, pare, or grave with a chisel; (*slang*) to take advantage of, to cheat. **the chisel:** (*fig.*) Sculpture. **chiselled,** *a.* Cut with or as with a chisel; clear-cut.

chisleu (kis′ loo) [Heb.], *n.* The third month of the civil, and the ninth of the ecclesiastical Jewish year, corresponding roughly to December.

chit (1) (chit) [cp. KIT], *n.* A child; a young thing; (*slightingly*) a young girl.

chit (2) (chit), **chitty** (chit′ i) [Hind. *chitthī* (Sansk. *chitra*, mark)], *n.* A letter or note.

chit-chat (chit′ chăt) [CHAT], *n.* Trifling talk; chat, gossip.

chitin (kī′ tin) [F. *chitine*, Gr. *chitōn*, a tunic], *n.* (*Zool. and Chem.*) The horny substance that gives firmness to the integuments of crustaceans, arachnidans, and insects. **chitinous,** *a.*

chiton (kī′ tŏn) [Gr. *chitōn*, tunic], *n.* A robe; a lady's dress made in Greek fashion; (*Zool.*) a genus of *Mollusca* having an imbricated shell.

chitter (chit′ ĕr) [CHATTER (cp. CHIP (1), CHOP (1), etc.)], *v.i.* To shiver, to tremble, to chatter (as the teeth); to twitter (as birds).

chitterlings (chit′ ĕr lingz) [etym. doubtful, cp. G. *kutteln*, entrails], *n.pl.* The smaller intestines of animals, esp. as prepared for food.

chivalry (shiv′-, chiv′ ăl ri) [O.F. *chevalerie*, from L. *caballārius*, CHEVALIER], *n.* The knightly system of the Middle Ages; the ideal qualities which inspired it, nobleness and gallantry of spirit, courtesy, respect for and defence of the weak; gallantry, devotion to the service of women; *knights collectively; *horsemen, cavalry; *a knightly exploit. **flower of chivalry:** A pattern knight; the finest type of knighthood; the choicest in a body of armed knights. **chivalrous, -ric** (shiv′-, chiv′ ăl rŭs, -rik, -văl′ rŭs, -rik), *a.* Pertaining to chivalry; high-spirited, gallant, noble. **chivalrously,** *adv.*

chive (chīv), **cive** (sīv) [F. *cive* or North.F. *chive*, L. *cæpa*, onion], *n.* A small onion-like herb, *Allium schœnoprasum.*

chivy [CHEVY].

chlamys (klăm′ is) [Gr. *chlamus -udos*, a cloak], *n.* (*pl-* **-ydes**) A Greek cloak or mantle; (*Bot.*) the floral envelope of a plant. **chlamyd-,** *comb. form.* (*Bot. and Zool.*) Having a mantle or envelope.

chlor-, chloro- [Gr. *chlōros*, green], *comb. form.* (*Chem.*) Of a green colour (denoting a chemical compound in which chlorine has replaced some other element); green.

chloral (klôr′ ăl) [CHLOR-, AL(COHOL)], *n.* (*Chem.*) A narcotic liquid first obtained by the action of chlorine on alcohol; (*pop.*) chloral-hydrate. **chloral-hydrate,** *n.* (*Chem.*) A white crystalline substance obtained from chloral, used as a hypnotic and anæsthetic. **chloralism,** *n.* (*Med.*) The morbid effects on the system of taking chloral freely. **chloralize,** *v.t.* To treat with chloral.

chloric (klôr′ ik), *a.* Pertaining to chlorine. **chloric acid,** *n.* An acid containing hydrogen, chlorine, and oxygen.

chloride (klôr′ īd) [CHLOR-, -IDE], *n.* (*Chem.*) A compound of chlorine with another element. **chloride of lime,** *n.* A compound of chlorine with lime, used as a disinfectant and for bleaching. **chloridate, -dize,** *v.t.* To treat or prepare (as a photographic plate) with a chloride.

chlorine (klôr‚ in) [CHLOR-, -INE], *n.* (*Chem.*) A yellow-green, poisonous, gaseous element obtained from common salt, used as a disinfectant and for bleaching. **chlorination,** *n.* (*Min.*) The extraction of gold by exposure of the auriferous material to chlorine gas; the sterilization of water with chlorine.

chlorite (klôr′ īt), *n.* (*Chem.*) A green silicate mineral. **chloritic** (klôr it′ ik), *a.*

chlorodyne (klôr′ ō dīn) [CHLOR-, Gr. *odunē*, pain], *n.* (*Med.*) A popular anodyne composed of chloroform, prussic acid, and Indian hemp.

chloroform (klor′ ō fôrm) [F. *chloroforme* (CHLORO-, *form*(yl), see FORMIC], *n.* (*Med.*) A volatile limpid fluid used in surgery to produce anæsthesia. *v.t.* To administer chloroform to; to render insensible with chloroform.

chlorometer (klôr om′ ĕt ĕr) [CHLORO-, -METER], *n.* (*Chem.*) An instrument for testing the bleaching power of chloride of lime. **chlorometric** (klôr ō met′ rik), *a.* **chlorometry** (klôr om′ ĕt ri), *n.*

chlorophyll (klôr′ ō fil) [CHLORO-, Gr. *phullon*, a leaf], *n.* (*Bot.*) The green colouring-matter of plants which produces carbohydrates from water and carbon dioxide.

chlorosis (klôr ō′ sis) [CHLOR-, -OSIS], *n.* (*Bot.*) Etiolation, a blanching of plants through the non-development of chlorophyll; (*Med.*) green-sickness; a disease affecting young and delicate women, and due to deficiency of colouring-matter in the blood. **chlorotic** (klôr ot′ ik), *a.*

chock (chok) [prob. from O.North.F. *choque*, a log (prob. influenced by CHOKE)], *n.* A wood block, esp. a wedge-shaped block used to prevent a cask or other body from shifting. *v.t.* To wedge, support, make fast, with a chock or chocks; (*Naut.*) to place a boat on the chocks. *adv.* As close as possible; tightly, fully. **chock-a-block:** Chock-full. **boat chocks,** *n.pl.* (*Naut.*) Blocks for wedging up a boat on a ship's deck. **chock-full,** *adv.* Quite full; full to overflowing. **chock-stone** [CHOKE], *n.* (*Mountaineering*) A stone wedged in a chimney or crack.

chocolate (chok′ ō lăt) [F. *chocolat*, Sp. *chocolate*, Mex. *chocolatl* (*choco*, cacao, *latl*, water)], *n.* The nut of the cacao-tree; a paste or cake made from the roasted kernels of *Theobroma cacao*; the beverage made by dissolving chocolate in boiling water or milk; a dark brown colour. **milk-chocolate,** *n.* A cake of chocolate prepared with milk. **chocolate-cream,** *n.* A sweet confection enclosed in chocolate. **chocolate-nut,** *n.* The fruit of the cacao-tree.

choctaw (chok′ taw) [name of North American Indian tribe fancifully applied], *n.* (*Skating*) A change of foot and from one edge to the other.

choice (chois) [O.F. *chois*, from *choisir*, to choose, from Teut. (cp. Goth *kausjan*, to prove, test)], *n.* The power or act of choosing; the thing chosen; the things to be selected from; selection, preference; care in selecting; the best and preferable part. *a.* Selected, picked, chosen with care; of great value; careful, fastidious. **for choice:** For preference. **Hobson's choice** [*Hobson*, a Cambridge livery-stable keeper who insisted on every customer's taking the first horse inside the stable door or none at all]: No alternative. **to have no choice:** To have no option; to have no preference. ***choice-drawn,** *a.* Selected with special care. ***choiceful,** *a.* Fickle, changeable, varied. **choicely,** *adv.* **choiceness,** *n.*

choir (kwīr) [M.E. *queir*, *quere*, O.F. *cuer*, L. *chorum -us*, Gr. *choros*, a band of dancers and singers]. *n.* A band of singers, esp. in a church or chapel; the part of the church or chapel allotted to the singers; (*Arch.*) the part of a cathedral or large church where service is performed, the chancel; an organized body of singers; (*poet.*) a body of dancers or of singers and dancers. *v.i.* To sing together. *v.t.* To sing (a hymn, anthem, etc.) as in a choir. **choir organ** [properly *chair organ*], *n.* The least powerful section of a compound organ, used chiefly for accompaniments. **choir-screen,** *n.* A screen of lattice-work, wood, or other open work separating the choir from the nave.

choke (chōk) [A.-S. *ā-cēocian* (etym. doubtful)], *v.t.* To block or compress the windpipe (of), so as to prevent breathing; to suffocate (as by gas, water, etc.); to smother, to stifle; to repress; to silence; to stop up, to block; to obstruct, to clog. *v.i.* To have the windpipe stopped; to be wholly or partially suffocated; to be blocked up. *n.* The action of choking; a noise of suffocation in the throat; (*Radio*) an inductance coil constructed to prevent high-frequency currents from passing; the constriction of a choke-bore; (*Mech.*) a device to prevent the passage of too much gas, etc., to an engine. **to choke up:** To fill up until blocked. **choke-bore,** *n.* A gun-barrel the bore of which narrows towards the muzzle. **choke-damp,** *n.* Carbonic acid gas generated in mines, wells, etc.; suffocating vapour. **choke-full** [CHOCK-FULL]. **choke-pear,** *n.* A kind of pear with a rough, astringent taste; (*fig.*) a sarcasm which puts one to silence. ***choke-weed,** *n.* A species of broomrape, *Orobanche rapum*, a parasite on roots. **choker,** *n.* One who or that which chokes; (*slang*) a tie; a cravat; a clerical collar. **choky** (1), *a.* That chokes; having a sensation of choking.

choky (2) (chō' ki) [Hind. *chaukī*), *n.* A lock-up or police-station; (*slang*) a prison; a prisoner's cell.

chol-, chole- [Gr. *cholē*, gall, bile], *comb. form.* (*Med. and Chem.*) Of or pertaining to the bile. **cholæmia** (kŏ lē' mi ȧ) [Gr. *haima*, blood], *n.* (*Med.*) A morbid accumulation of bile in the blood. **cholagogue** (kol' ȧ gog) [F., from mod. L. *cholagōgum*, Gr. *cholagōgon* (CHOL-, *agōgos*, leading, from *agein*, to lead)], *n.* (*Med.*) A medicine which promotes the flow of bile.

choler (kol' ėr) [M.E. and O.F. *colere*, L. *cholera*, Gr. *cholera* (*cholē*, bile)], *n.* Bile, the humour supposed to cause irascibility of temper; anger; tendency to anger. **choleric,** *a.* Full of choler; irascible, passionate.

cholera (kol' ėr ȧ) [L., see prec.], *n.* (*Med.*) A term loosely employed for various forms of choleraic diarrhœa; cholera morbus, a disease characterized by violent vomiting and purging, with rice-water evacuations, tending to run a rapidly fatal course, and capable of being communicated by the dejecta of choleraic patients. **cholera morbus:** (*Med.*) Asiatic cholera, cholera proper. **choleraic** (kol ėr ā' ik), *a.* **cholerine** (kol' ėr īn, -ēn), *n.* Summer cholera, a mild form of cholera morbus; the first stage of cholera; the supposed cause of epidemic cholera.

choleric [CHOLER].

cholesterine (kŏ les' tėr in) [CHOL-, Gr. *stereos*, stiff, solid], *n.* (*Chem.*) A fatty substance forming the chief part of biliary calculi. **cholesteric,** *a.* **cholesterol** (kŏ les' ter ol), *n.* A white solid alcohol occurring in gall-stones, nerves, etc.

choliamb (kō' li ăm) [L. *chōliambus*, Gr. *chōliambos* (*cholos*, lame, IAMBUS)], *n.* A verse having an iambus in the fifth foot, and a spondee in the sixth or last; a scazon. **choliambic** (kō li ăm' bik), *a.*

cholic (kol' ik), *a.* Pertaining to or obtained from bile.

chondri-, chondro- [Gr. *chondros*, cartilage], *comb. form.* (*Physiol. and Med.*) Composed of or pertaining to cartilage. **chondrify** (kon' dri fī), *v.t.* To be converted into cartilage. **chondrification** (kon dri fi kā' shŭn), *n.* **chondrine,** *n.* (*Chem.*) Gelatine from the cartilage of the ribs, joints, etc. **chondritis** (kon drī' tis), *n.* (*Med.*) Inflammation of cartilage. **chondroid,** *a.* Like cartilage. **chondrography** (kon drog' rȧ fi), **-drology** (-drol' ŏ ji) [-GRAPHY, -LOGY], *n.* (*Med.*) A treatise on cartilages. **chondrometer** [-METER], *n.* A steelyard or balance for weighing grain. **chondropterygian** (kon drop tėr ij' i ȧn) [Gr. *pterux*, a fin], *n.* (*Zool.*) A cartilaginous fish, one of a section of fishes (as the sharks, lampreys, and sturgeons) in which the skeleton and fin spines are cartilaginous. *a.* Pertaining to this section. **chondrotomy** (kon drot' ŏ mi) [-TOMY], *n.* (*Med.*) The anatomy of cartilages.

choose (chooz) [A.-S. *cēosan*, from Teut. (*cp.* Dut. *kiezen*, G. *kiesen*, Icel. *kjōsa*)], *v.t.* (*past* **chose,** *p.p.* **chosen**) To take by preference, to select from a number; to feel inclined, to prefer (to do something rather than something else); to decide willingly (to do). *v.i.* To make one's choice; to have the power of choice. **cannot choose but:** Have no alternative but. **to pick and choose:** To make a careful choice, to be over particular. **chooser,** *n.* **choosey,** *adv.* (*colloq.*) Hard to please, particular. **choosingly,** *adv.*

chop (1) (chop) [var. of CHAP (1)], *v.t.* To cut off suddenly; to strike off; to cut short or into parts. *n.* The act of chopping; a cutting stroke; a piece chopped off; a rib (of a sheep or pig) chopped off and cooked separately; (*pl.*) broken waves of the sea. *v.i.* (*past & p.p.* **chopped**) To do anything with a quick motion like that of a blow. **to chop up:** To cut into small pieces, to mince. **to chop in:** To intervene suddenly in a conversation. **chop-house,** *n.* An eating-house. **chopper,** *n.* One who or that which chops; a butcher's cleaver; an axe; (*Radio*) an interrupter, usually a rotating commutator. **chopping,** *n.* The action of the verb TO CHOP. *a.* That chops; choppy. **chopping-block,** *n.* A wooden block on which anything is chopped. **chopping-knife,** *n.* A large knife for chopping or mincing. **choppy** (1), *a.* Full of cracks or clefts; of the sea, rough, with short quick waves.

chop (2) (chop) [etym. doubtful (perh. from prec. or from CHAPMAN)], *v.t.* To exchange, to barter. *v.i.* To shift suddenly, as the wind. *n.* Change. **to chop and change:** To vary continuously; to fluctuate. **to chop logic:** To wrangle pedantically. **choppy** (2), *a.* Variable, continually changing.

chop (3) [CHAP (2)].

chop (4) (chop) [Hind. *chhap*, print, stamp], *n.* (*India and China*) A seal or official stamp; a passport, a permit; (*colloq.*) brand, quality. **first chop:** (*slang*) First-rate. **chop-chop:** (*slang*) At once, quickly.

chopin (chop' in) [prob. from F. *chopine*, from *chope* (cp. G. *schoppen*, a half-litre)], *n.* A Scottish wine-quart.

***chopine** (chŏ pēn') [O.F. and Sp. *chapin* (Sp. *chapa*, a metal plate)], *n.* A high shoe or patten formerly worn by women.

***chopping** (chop' ing) [CHOP (1)], *a.* Fine, strapping.

chopsticks (chop' stiks) [rendering of Chinese *k' wâi-tsze*, quick ones (*chop*, quick)], *n.pl.* Two small sticks of wood or ivory used by the Chinese to eat with. **chop-suey** (chop soo' i), *n.* A kind of Chinese stew; Chinese food.

choragus (kŏ rā' gŭs) [L. *chorāgus*, Gr. *chorēgos* (*choros*, chorus, *agein*, to lead)], *n.* The leader or director of the chorus in the ancient Greek theatrical performances; the deputy of the professor of music at Oxford; the leader of a band or chorus; (*fig.*) a leader. **choragic** (-răj' ik), *a.* Of or pertaining to a choragus. **choragic monument,** *n.* A monument in honour of the choragus who produced the best musical or theatrical entertainment at the festival of Bacchus.

choral (kôr' ȧl) [med. L. *chorālis* (L. *chorus*, Gr. *choros*)], *a.* Belonging to or sung by a choir or chorus; chanted or sung. **chorally,** *adv.* **choralist,** *n.* A singer in a chorus. **chorale** (kȯ ral′) [G. *choral* (in *choralgesang*, choral song)], *n.* A simple choral hymn or song, usually of slow rhythm and sung in unison.

chord (1) (kôrd) [L. *chorda*, Gr. *chordē* (CORD, before 16th cent.)], *n.* The string of a musical instrument; (*Geom.*) a straight line joining the extremities of an arc or two points in a curve. **chordal,** *a.*

chord (2) (kôrd) [ACCORD], *n.* (*Mus.*) The simultaneous and harmonious union of sounds of different pitch; (*fig.*) any harmonious combination, as of colours.

chore (chôr) [CHAR (2)], *n.* A small regular task; a daily or other household job.

chorea (kȯ rē′ ȧ) [L., from Gr. *choreia* (*choros*, dance)], *n.* St. Vitus's dance, a nervous disorder characterized by peculiar convulsive movements.

choree (kȯ rē′) [L. *chorēus*, Gr. *choreios*, pertaining to a *choros*], *n.* A trochee; a metrical foot consisting of a long syllable followed by a short one. **choreic** (kȯ rē′ ik), *a.*

choreograph (kȯr rē′ ȯ grăf) [Gr. *choreia* (*choros*, dance), -GRAPH], *n.* The composer or designer of a ballet. **choreographer** (kor ė og′ rȧ fėr), *n.* **choreographic** (-grăf′ ik), *a.* **choreography** (-og′ rȧ fi), *n.*

chorepiscopal (kôr ė pis′ kȯ pȧl) [L. *chōrepiscopus*, Gr. *chōrepiskopos* (*chōra*, *chōras*, country, *episkopos*, BISHOP)], *a.* (*Eccles. Hist.*) Pertaining to a country bishop.

chori-, choris, [Gr. *chōri* (*chōris*, before a vowel), apart], *comb. form.* (*Bot.*) Separate. **choripetalous** (kôr i pet′ ȧ lůs) [PETAL], *a.* Having free petals; polypetalous. **chorisepalous** (kôr i sep′ ȧ lůs) [SEPAL], *a.*

choriamb (kor′ i ămb), **choriambus** (kor i ăm′ bůs) [L., from Gr. *choriambos* (CHOREE, IAMB, IAMBUS)], *n.* A metrical foot of four syllables, of which the first and fourth are long, and the second and third short. **choriambic,** *a.* Pertaining to or of the nature of a choriamb. *n.* A choriamb.

choric [CHORUS].

chorion (kor′ i ȯn) [Gr.], *n.* (*Anat.*) The outer membrane which envelops the fœtus in the womb; (*Bot.*) the external membrane of a seed. **choroid,** *a.* Resembling the chorion. *n.* (*Anat.*) The vascular portion of the retina.

choripetalous, chorisepalous [CHORI-].

chorister (kor′ is tėr), ***chorist** (kor′ ist) [med. L. *chorista*, from *chorus*, CHOIR], *n.* A singer; one who sings in a choir, a choirboy; one of a band or flock of singers; (*Am.*) the leader of a choir or congregation, a precentor.

chorography (kȯ rog′ rȧ fi) [F. *chorographie*, Gr. *chōrographia*, *chōra*, a land, a region], *n.* The art or practice of describing and making maps of particular regions or districts. **chorographer,** *n.* **chorographic, -al** (kōr ȯ grăf′ ik, -ȧl), *a.* **chorographically,** *adv.*

choroid [CHORION].

chorology (kȯ rol′ ȯ ji) [Gr. *chōra*, a district], *n.* (*Nat. Hist.*) The science of the geographical distribution of plants and animals. **chorological** (-loj′ ik ȧl), *a.*

chortle (chôrtl) [coined by 'Lewis Carroll' (cp. CHUCKLE and SNORT)], *v.i.* To make a loud chuckle. *v.t.* To utter with a loud chuckle.

chorus (kôr′ ůs) [L., from Gr. *choros*], *n.* A band of dancers and singers in the ancient Greek drama who were supposed to see what passed and to express sentiments in song between the acts; the song or recitative between the acts of a Greek tragedy; the speaker of the prologue and epilogue in an Elizabethan play; a band of persons singing in concert; a concerted piece of vocal music; the refrain of a song in which the company joins the singer. **choric** (kor′ ik), *a.* Pertaining to a chorus; like the chorus in a Greek play.

chose, *past*, **chosen,** *part.a.* [CHOOSE].

chota hazri (chō tȧ hăz′ ri) [Hind.], *n.* A light, early breakfast. **chota peg,** *n.* Whiskey and soda.

chough (chŭf) [imit. (*cp.* Dut. *kaauw*, Dan. *kaa*, O.F. *choue*)], *n.* A bird of the crow family, *Fregilus graculus.*

chouse (chouz) [Turk. *chiaus*, an interpreter, from an interpreter attached to the Turkish embassy in London who in 1609 perpetrated great frauds], *v.t.* To trick, to swindle, to cheat. *n.* A swindle.

Chow (chou) [Austral. slang], *a.* Chinese. *n.* A Chinaman; a Chinese variety of dog.

chow-chow (chou′ chou), *a.* [Chinese], *n.* A kind of mixed pickles. **chow,** *n.* (*Slang*) Food.

chowder (chou′ dėr) [F. *chaudière*, pot, L. *caldāria* (see CALDARIUM)], *n.* (*Am.*) A kind of stew made of fish, pork, biscuits, etc.; a picnic where chowder is eaten. *v.t.* To make a chowder of.

chowry (chou′ ri) [Hind. *chaunri*], *n.* A flapper for driving away flies.

chrematistic (krē mȧ tis′ tik) [Gr. *chrematistikos*, from *chrematizein*, to traffic, make money (*chrēmaatos*, money)], *a.* Concerning money-making. **chrematistics,** *n.* Political economy so far as it relates to the production of wealth.

chrestomathy (kres tom′ ȧ thi) [Gr. *chrēstomatheia* (*chrēstos*, good, *matheia*, learning, from *manthanein*, to learn)], *n.* A selection of passages with notes, etc., to be used in learning a language. **chrestomathic** (kres tȯ măth′ ik), *a.* Learning or teaching good and useful things.

chrism (krizm) [A.-S. *crisma*, L. and Gr. *chrisma* (Gr. *chriein*, to anoint)], *n.* Consecrated oil, used in the Roman and Greek Churches in administering baptism, confirmation, ordination, and extreme unction. **chrismal,** *a.* **chrismatory,** *n.* A vessel for holding chrism. ***chrisom,** *n.* A white cloth, anointed with chrism, formerly placed over the face of a child after baptism; hence, a child just baptized, or one that died within a month of its baptism. **chrisom-child,** *n.* One who died before a month old.

Christ (krīst) [A.-S. *Crist*, L. *Christus*, Gr. *Christos* (*chriein*, to anoint)], *n.* The Anointed One, a title given to Jesus the Saviour, and synonymous with the Hebrew Messiah. ***Christ-cross-row,** *n.* The alphabet, prob. from the cross being placed at the beginning in the horn-books. **Christ's-thorn,** *n.* Name of several shrubs identified with that from which the crown of thorns was made. **Christhood,** *n.* **Christless,** *a.* Without faith in or without the spirit of Christ. **Christlessness,** *n.* **Christlike,** *a.* **Christlikeness,** *n.* **Christly,** *a.* **Christward, -s,** *adv.*

Christadelphians (kris tȧ del′ fi ȧnz) [Gr. *Christos*, *adelphoi*, brethren], *n.pl.* A sect of Christians, calling themselves the brethren of Christ, and claiming apostolic origin.

christen (kris′ ėn) [A.-S. *cristnian*, from *cristen*], *v.t.* To receive into the Christian Church by baptism; to baptize; to name; to nickname. *v.i.* To administer baptism.

Christendom (kris′ ėn dȯm) [A.-S. *cristen* (see prec.)], *n.* *Baptism; *Christianity; that portion of the world in which Christianity is the prevailing religion; Christians collectively.

Christian (kris′ tyȧn) [L. *Christiānus*], *n.* One who believes in or professes the religion of Christ; one belonging to a nation or country of which Christianity is the prevailing religion; one whose character is consistent with the teaching of Christ; a civilized person as distinguished from a savage; a human being as distinguished from a brute. *a.* Pertaining to Christ or Christianity; professing the religion of Christ; Christlike; civilized, human as opposed to brutes. **Christian Democrats,** *n.pl.* (*Pol.*) Members of moderate R.C. Ch. parties in

Belgium, France, Italy, Germany, etc. **Christian era,** *n.* The chronological period since the birth of Christ. **Christian name,** *n.* A name given in baptism, (*Am.*) given name. **Christian Science,** *n.* A system based on the belief that diseases are the result of wrong thinking and can be healed without medical treatment. **Christianity,** *n.* The doctrines and precepts taught by Christ; faith in Christ and his teaching; Christian character and conduct; the state of being a Christian. **christianize,** *v.t.* To convert to Christianity. *v.i.* To be converted to Christianity. **christianization,** *n.* **christianlike,** *a.* **christianly,** *a.* and *adv.* **Christiano-,** *comb. form.*

Christmas (kris′ măs) [A.-S. *cristes mæsse*], *n.* The festival of the nativity of Jesus Christ celebrated on Dec. 25; Christmas-tide; (*colloq.*) holly. *a.* Pertaining or appropriate to Christmas or its festivities. *v.i.* (*colloq.*) To celebrate Christmas. *v.t.* To decorate with Christmas tokens. **Christmas-box,** *n.* *A box in which presents were collected at Christmas; a Christmas present. **Christmas bush,** *n.* (*Austral.*) A tree that comes into flower about Christmas-time, with bright red blooms. **Christmas card,** *n.* An ornamental card sent as a Christmas greeting. **Christmas carol,** *n.* A song of praise sung at Christmas. **Christmas day,** *n.* The festival of Christmas. **Christmas eve,** *n.* The day before Christmas day. **Christmas number,** *n.* A special number of a magazine or other periodical issued at Christmas-time. **Christmas pudding,** *n.* A rich pudding made at Christmas-time. **Christmas rose,** *n.* A white-flowered hellebore, *Helleborus niger*, flowering at Christmas-time. **Christmas-tide, Christmas-time,** *n.* The season of Christmas. **Christmas-tree,** *n.* A small tree brought within doors, on the branches of which presents for children are hung at Christmas; (*Austral.*) the Christmas bush. **Christmasy,** *a.*

Christo- [L. *Christus*, Gr. *Christos*], *comb. form.* (*Theol.*) Pertaining to Christ. **Christolatry** (kris tol′ ȧ tri) [-LATRY], *n.* The worship of Christ regarded as a form of idolatry. **Christology** (kris tol′ ȯ ji) [CHRIST, -LOGY], *n.* The doctrine of the person of Christ. **Christological** (-loj′ ik ăl), *a.* **Christologist,** *n.* **Christomaniac** (-mā′ ni ăk) [MANIAC], *n.*

Christy minstrels (kris′ ti min′ strĕlz) [George *Christy*, the originator], *n.pl.* A troupe of singers, banjoists, etc., with blackened faces imitating Negroes.

chromate (krō′ māt), *n.* (*Chem.*) A salt of chromic acid.

chromato-, chroma-, chromo- *comb. form.* [Gr. *chroma*, *chromatos*, colour].

chromatic (krō măt′ ik) [as prec.], *a.* Relating to colour; coloured; (*Mus.*) including notes not belonging to the diatonic scale. **chromatic printing,** *n.* Colour printing. **chromatic scale,** *n.* (*Mus.*) A succession of notes a semitone apart. **chromatic semitone,** *n.* (*Mus.*) The interval between a note and its flat or sharp; also called a half-step. **chromatically,** *adv.* **chromatics,** *n.* The science of colour.

chromatin (krō′ mȧ tin) [as prec.], *n.* (*Biol.*) The portion of the nucleus of a cell which readily takes up a stain.

chromatophore (krō măt′ ō fôr) [as prec.], *n.* (*Physiol.*) A movable pigment cell in some animals.

chromatoscope (krō măt′ ō skōp) [as prec.], *n.* (*Opt.*) An instrument for combining rays of different colours into one compound colour; (*Astron.*) a light-reflecting telescope for studying the scintillations of stars.

chromatrope (krō′ mȧ trōp), *n.* (*Opt.*) A rotating magic-lantern slide for producing a kaleidoscopic effect.

chrome (krōm) [F., from Gr. *chrōma*, colour], *n.* Chromium; a yellow pigment made from lead chromate. **chrome-colour,** *n.* A colour prepared from a chromium salt. **chrome-green,** *n.* A dark green pigment obtained from oxide of chromium. **chrome-yellow,** *n.* Chromate of lead; a brilliant yellow pigment.

chromic (krō′ mik), *a.* Pertaining to chromium.

chromite (krō′ mīt), *n.* A mineral containing chromium.

chromium (krō′ mi ŭm), *n.* A bright steel-grey metal, one of the elements, remarkable for the brilliance of colour of its compounds. Used as a protective plating.

chromo (krō′ mō) [CHROMOLITHOGRAPH].

chromogen (krō′ mō jen), *n.* (*Chem.*) An organic colouring matter; a dye obtained from naphthalene; an animal or vegetable matter which alters in colour under certain conditions.

chromograph (krō′ mȯ grăf), *n.* An apparatus for reproducing writing or drawing in colours from an impression on gelatine; a hectograph. *v.t.* To make copies in this way.

chromolithograph (krō mȯ lith′ ȯ grăf), *n.* A picture printed in colours from stone. **chromolithographic** (-grăf′ ik), *a.* **chromolithographer** (-og′ rȧ fẽr), *n.* **chromolithography,** *n.*

chromophotography (krō mō fō tog′ rȧ fi), *n.* Colour photography.

chromosome (krō′ mō sōm) [CHROMO-, Gr. *soma*, body], *n.* (*Biol.*) A rod-shaped body seen microscopically in the body cells of both sexes. Chromosomes are carriers of hereditary characteristics.

chromosphere (krō′ mȯ sfēr), *n.* (*Astron.*) The gaseous envelope of the sun through which light passes from the photosphere.

chromotypography (krō mȯ tī pog′ rȧ fi), *n.* Colour printing at an ordinary press.

chronic (kron′ ik) [F. *chronique*, L., late L. *chronicus*, Gr. *chronikos* (*chronos*, time)], *a.* Relating to time; (*Med.*) applied to diseases of long duration, or apt to recur; (*slang*) very bad, severe. *n.* A chronic invalid.

chronicle (kron′ i kĕl) [M.E. and O.F. *cronique*, late L. *chronica*, sing., from Gr. *kronika*, neut. p. (see prec.)], *n.* A register or history of events in order of time; a history, a record. *v.t.* To record in a chronicle; to register. **Chronicles,** *n.pl.* The two books of the Old Testament immediately following 1 and 2 Kings. **chronicler,** *n.*

chrono- [Gr. *chronos*, time], *comb. form.* Pertaining to time or dates.

chronogram (krŏn′ ȯ grăm), *n.* A device by which a date is given by taking certain letters of an inscription and printing them larger than the rest: thus, GEORGIVS DVX BVCKINGAMMIÆ (1 + 5 + 500 + 5 + 10 + 5 + 100 + 1 + 1000 + 1) = 1628 when the Duke was murdered by Felton. **chronogrammatic** (kron ȯ grȧ măt′ ik), *a.* Pertaining to or containing a chronogram.

chronograph (kron′ ȯ grăf) [Gr. *chronographos*], *n.* A contrivance for measuring and registering minute portions of time with great precision; a stop-watch. **chronographer** (krȯ nog′ rȧ fẽr), *n.* A chronicler; a chronologist. **chronography,** *n.* A description of past events. **chronographic** (-grăf′ ik), *a.* Pertaining to a chronograph.

chronology (krȯ nol′ ȯ ji) [Gr. *chronologia*], *n.* The science of computing time; an arrangement of dates of historical events; a tabular list of dates. **chronologer,** *n.* **chronologist,** *n.* **chronological** (kron′ ȯ loj′ ik ăl), *a.* **chronologically,** *adv.*

chronometer (krȯ nom′ ė tẽr), *n.* An instrument such as a sundial, clock, or watch that measures time, esp. one that measures time with great exactness, such as is used to determine the longitude at sea by the difference between its time and solar time. **chronometric, -rical** (kron ȯ met′ rik, -ăl), *a.* **chronometrically,** *adv.* **chronometry** (krȯ nom′ ĕt ri), *n.*

chronopher (kron′ ȯ fẽr) [Gr. *phoros*, carrying (*pherein*, to carry)], *n.* An instrument for sending time-signals to a distance by electricity.

chronoscope (kron′ ŏ skōp), *n.* An instrument for measuring the velocity of projectiles.

chrys-, chryso- [Gr. *chrusos*, gold], *comb. form.* (*Chem. and Min.*) Golden; of a bright yellow colour.

chrysalis, chrysalid (kris′ ȧ lis, -lid) [L. *chrysalis, chrȳsallis*, Gr. *chrusallis* (*chrusos*, gold)], *n.* (*pl.* **chrysalises, -ides, -ids**) The last stage through which a lepidopterous insect passes before becoming a perfect insect; the pupa, the shell or case containing the imago; (*fig.*) an undeveloped or transitional state.

chrysanthemum (kris ăn′ thė mŭm) [L. *chrȳsanthemum*, Gr. *chrusanthemon*, marigold (CHRYS-, *anthemon*, flower)], *n.* (*Bot.*) A genus of composite plants containing the ox-eye daisy, the corn-marigold, and the garden chrysanthemum, *C. sinense*; cultivated varieties of the last-named.

chryselephantine (kris el ė făn′ tin) [Gr. *chrysele-phantinos*], *a.* Made partly of gold and partly of ivory; overlaid with gold and ivory.

chryso- [CHRYS-].

chrysoberyl (kris ŏ ber′ il) [L. *chrȳsobērylus*, Gr. *chrusobērullos*], *n.* (*Min.*) A gem of a yellowish-green colour, composed of glucinum aluminate.

chrysocolla (kris ŏ kol′ ȧ) [L., from Gr. *chrusokolla* (*kolla*, glue)], *n.* (*Min.*) A green, lustrous, opaline silicate of copper; (*Anc. Hist.*) gold-solder (composition doubtful).

chrysolite (kris′ o līt) [O.F. *crisolit*, L. *chrȳsolithus* Gr. *chrusolithos* (*-lithos*, stone)], *n.* (*Min.*) A green-coloured translucent orthorhombic mineral; olivine.

chrysoprase (kris′ ŏ prāz) [M.E. and O.F. *criso-pace*, L. *chrȳsoprasus*, Gr. *chrusoprasos* (*prason*, a leek)], *n.* (*Min.*) An apple-green variety of chalcedony; (*N.T.*) a variety of beryl.

chthonian (thō′ ni ȧn) [Gr. *chthŏnios* (*chthōn chthonos*, earth)], *a.* Of or pertaining to the underworld; Tartarean.

chub (chŭb) [etym. unknown], *n.* A coarse river-fish, *Leuciscus cephalus*, also called the chevin; applied to various American fishes. **chub-faced,** *a.* Having a plump face, chubby. **chubby,** *a.* Fat, plump (esp. in the face). **chubbiness,** *n.*

chubb lock (chŭb lok) [from the inventor], *n.* Registered trade-mark name of a tumbler-lock.

chuck (1) (chŭk) [onomat.], *n.* The call of a hen to her chickens. *v.i.* To make a noise like a hen calling her chickens. *v.t.* To call (as a hen does her chickens).

chuck (2) (chŭk) [earlier *chock*; prob. imit. (cp. F. *choquer*, Dut. *schokken*)], *n.* A slight tap or blow under the chin; a toss or throw. *v.t.* To strike gently under the chin; to fling, to throw. **chuck-farthing,** *n.* A game in which a farthing or other piece of money is pitched into a hole. **to chuck away:** To discard; to waste. **to chuck out:** To eject forcibly from a public meeting, licensed premises, etc. **chucker-out,** *n.* A man employed to do this; (*Am.*) a bouncer. **to chuck up:** To abandon.

chuck (3) (chŭk) [CHOCK], *n.* An appendage to a lathe for holding the work to be turned. *v.t.* To fix by this means on the lathe.

chuck (4) [var. of CHICK], *n.* *Darling, dear; (*Sc. and North.*) a chick, a fowl.

chuckle (chŭk′ ėl) [CHUCK (1)], *v.i.* To laugh to oneself; to make a half-suppressed sound of laughter; to exult to oneself; to call (as a hen). *n.* A short half-suppressed laugh (esp. of triumph or derision); the sound made by a hen.

chuckle-head (chŭk′ ėl hed) [prob. var. of CHUCK (3)], *n.* A thick-headed fellow, a numskull. **chuckle-headed,** *a.*

***chuff** (chŭf) [etym. unknown], *n.* A dull, stupid thick-headed fellow; a churlish fellow. *a.* Chuffy. ***chuffy (1),** *a.* Rough, rude, clownish. ***chuffily,** *adv.*

***chuffy (2)** (chŭf′ i) [from obs. n. *chuff*, a fat face or muzzle], *a.* Fat or plump in the face, chubby.

chug (chŭg) [onomat.], *n.* The sound made by a steam-engine. **to chug along:** To move jerkily.

chukka (chŭk′ a) [Hind.], *n.* Name of each of the periods into which a polo game is divided.

chum (chŭm) [etym. doubtful], *n.* One who lives in the same room with another; a comrade and close companion. *v.i.* To occupy the same rooms with another. **new chum:** (*Austral.*) A new-comer to Australia, a new immigrant. **chummage,** *n.* The act or practice of chumming; money formerly demanded by prisoners of a new prison inmate to pay his footing. **chummery,** *n.* **chummy,** *a.*

chump (chŭmp) [recent; paral. to CHUNK (perh. influenced by CHOP and LUMP)], *n.* A short, thick piece of wood, a thick end-piece; (*slang*) a head; a silly fellow. **off his chump:** Crazy. **chump chop,** *n.* A thick chop from loin of mutton.

chunk (chŭngk) [prob. var. of CHUCK (3)], *n.* A short, thick lump of anything. **chunky,** *a.*

chupatty (chŭ păt′ i) [Hind. *cha-pā-ti*], *n.* A small coarse unleavened cake baked on a griddle.

church (chĕrch) [A.-S. *circe, cirice*, W.Ger. *kîrika*, Gr. *kuriakon*, neut. of a. *kuriakos* (*kurios*, lord)], *n.* A building set apart and consecrated for Christian worship; the English Established Church; a body of Christian believers worshipping in one place, with the same ritual and doctrines; Christians collectively; a section of Christians organized for worship under a certain form; the whole organization of a religious body or association; the clergy as distinct from the laity; divine service; ecclesiastical authority or influence; (*Am.*) the communicants of a congregation. *v.t.* To say the thanksgiving service for a woman after child-birth; (*Sc.*) to take or escort to church (esp. a bride on her first attendance after marriage). *a.* Of or pertaining to church; ecclesiastical. **to be churched:** To return thanks to God, as a woman after child-birth; to be presented at church. **Church Army,** *n.* An organization in the Church of England based on the Salvation Army. **Church Catholic** [CATHOLIC CHURCH]. **Church invisible:** Christians collectively in heaven and on earth. **Church militant:** Christians on earth, regarded as warring against evil. **Church of England:** The English Established or Anglican Church. **Church of Scotland:** The Established Church of Scotland. **Free Church of Scotland:** The Church formed at the disruption of the Scottish Church in 1843. **Church triumphant:** Christians in heaven. **to go into the Church:** To take Holy Orders. **church-ale,** *n.* A periodical merry-making in connexion with a church. **church-burial,** *n.* Burial according to the rites of the Church. **church-goer,** *n.* A regular attendant at church. **church-going,** *n.* The practice of regularly attending divine service. *a.* Calling to divine service; habitually attending divine service. **church-land,** *n.* Land belonging to the Church. **church-living,** *n.* A benefice. **churchman,** *n.* A cleric, an ecclesiastic; a member of the Church of England; an episcopalian. **churchmanly,** *a.* **churchmanship,** *n.* **churchwoman,** *n.* **church member,** *n.* One in communion with a Church. **church-membership,** *n.* **church mouse,** *n.* A type of extreme poverty. **poor as a church mouse:** Extremely poor. **church music,** *n.* Sacred music, such as is used in Church services. ***church-outed,** *a.* Excommunicated. **church-owl,** *n.* The barn-owl. **church-rate,** *n.* A rate (now voluntary) for the support of a parish church. **church service,** *n.* Service in a church; the Book of Common Prayer with the daily lessons added. **church-text,** *n.* Gothic or black-letter used in monumental inscriptions. **church-warden,** *n.* One of two officers, chosen annually at the Easter vestry, to protect Church property, to superintend the performance of divine worship, etc., and to act as the legal representatives of the parish generally; (*colloq.*) a long clay pipe with a large bowl. **churchward,**

-s, *adv.* Towards the church. **churchway,** *n.* A pathway leading to or round a church. **church-work,** *n.* Work on or for a church; work in connexion with the Church; religious efforts. **churchyard,** *n.* The ground adjoining the church consecrated for the burial of the dead. **churchyard cough,** *n.* One that is premonitory of death. **churching,** *n.* The act of returning public thanks in church after child-birth. **churchism,** *n.* Preference for and adherence to the principles of a Church, esp. of the Establishment. **churchless,** *a.* Without a church. **churchlike,** *a.* Befitting the Church or clerics. ***churchly,** *a.* **churchy,** *a.* Making a hobby of church-work and church matters; aggressively devoted to the Church and intolerant of Dissenters. **churchify,** *v.t.* **churchiness,** *n.*

churl (chĕrl) [A.-S. *ceorl*, from Teut. (cp. Icel. *karl*, O.H.G. *charal*, G. *kerl*)], *n.* *A serf or villein; a man of low birth; a peasant, a boor; a surly, clownish fellow; a crabbed person; a niggard. **churlish,** *a.* **churlishly,** *adv.* **churlishness,** *n.* **churly,** *a.* Churlish.

churn (chĕrn) [A.-S. *cyrin*, from Teut. (cp. Icel. *kirna*, Dut. *karn*)], *n.* A vessel in which milk or cream is agitated or beaten in order to produce butter; the block or chuck on a porcelain-turner's lathe, on which the articles are turned by thin iron tools; a large can for carrying milk long distances. *v.t.* To agitate in a churn for the purpose of making butter; to agitate with violence or continued motion. *v.i.* To perform the operation of churning; (*waves*) to foam, to swirl about. **churn-dash, -dasher,** *n.* The contrivance for agitating the milk in a churn. **churn-staff,** *n.* The staff used with the old plunge churn. **churning,** *n.* The action of the verb TO CHURN; the butter made at one operation.

churr (chĕr) [imit.], *n.* The deep, trilling cry of the night-jar. *v.i.* To make this cry.

chut (chut), *int.* Expressing impatience.

chute (shoot) [F. *chute* (late L., *caduta*, fem. of *cadūtus*, p.p., from L. *cadere*, to fall), influenced by SHOOT], *n.* An inclined trough for conveying water, timber, grain, etc., to a lower level; an inclined water-course; a toboggan-slide.

chutney (chŭt′ ni) [Hind. *chatnī*], *n.* A hot seasoned condiment.

chyle (kīl) [F., from L. *chȳlus*, Gr. *chulos* (stem *chu-*, *cheu-*, *chein*, to pour)], *n.* The milky fluid separated from the chyme by the action of the pancreatic juice and the bile, absorbed by the lacteal vessels, and assimilated with the blood. **chylaceous** (kī lā′ shŭs), *a.* **chylify,** *v.t.* To convert into chyle. *v.i.* To be turned into chyle. **chylification** (kī li fi kā′ shŭn), *n.* **chyliferous** (-lif′ ėr ŭs), *a.* **chylific,** *a.* **chylous,** *a.* **chylo-,** *comb. form.*

chyme (kīm) [L. *chȳmus*, Gr. *chumos* (as prec.)], *n.* The pulpy mass of digested food before the chyle is separated from it. **chymify,** *v.t.* To form into chyme. *v.i.* To become chyme. **chymification** (kī mi fi kā′ shŭn), *n.* **chymo-,** *comb. form.* **chymous,** *a.*

chymic, etc. [CHEMIC].

ciborium (si bôr′ i ŭm) [med. L., from Gr. *kibōrion*, cup-shaped seed-vessel of the Egyptian water-lily], *n.* (*Arch.*) A baldachin canopy or shrine; (*Eccles.*) a pyx or cup with arched cover for the reservation of the Eucharist; a shrine or tabernacle to receive this.

cicada (si kā′ dȧ) [L.], *n.* (*pl.* **-dæ**) A genus of homopterous insects with stridulating organs; any individual of the genus. **cicala** (si ka′ lȧ), **cigala** (si ga′ lȧ) [It. and Prov. (cp. F. *cigale*)], *n.* (*pl.* **-le**) A cicada.

cicatrice [CICATRIX].

cicatricle (si kăt′ rikl), **cicatricule** (si kăt′ ri kūl) [L. *cicātrīcula*, dim. of CICATRIX], *n.* (*Biol.*) The germinating point in the yolk of an egg, or the vesicle of a seed.

cicatrix (sik′ ȧ triks, si kā′ triks) [L.], *n.* (*pl.* **-trices**) (*Med.*) The mark or scar left after a wound or ulcer has healed. **cicatrice** (sik′ ȧ tris) [F., from prec.], *n.* **cicatricial** (sik ȧ trish′ ăl), *a.* **cicatricose** (si kăt′ ri kōs), *a.* **cicatrize** (sik′ ȧ trīz), *v.t.* To heal a wound or ulcer by inducing the formation of a cicatrix. *v.i.* To skin over. **cicatrization** (sik ȧ trī zā′ shŭn), *n.* **cicatrose,** *a.* Full of scars; scarry.

cicely (sis′ ė li) [L. *seselis*, Gr. *seseli*, *seselis* (perh. confused with *Cicely*, *Cecilia*)], *n.* The name of several plants of the parsley family.

cicerone (chich ėr ō′ ni) [It., from *Cicero -ōnem*, the Roman orator], *n.* (*pl.* **-oni**) A guide; one who explains the curiosities and interesting features of a place to strangers. *v.t.* (chi chė rōn′) To conduct in this manner.

Ciceronian (sis ėr ō′ ni ăn) [L., *Cicerōniānus* (see prec.)], *a.* Resembling the style of Cicero; easy, flowing. *n.* An admirer or imitator of the style of Cicero. **Ciceronianism,** *n.*

cicisbeo (chich iz bā′ ō) [It. (etym. doubtful)], *n.* (*pl.* **-bei**) The *cavalier servente* or recognized gallant of a married woman. **cicisbeism,** *n.* The system (18th cent.) that recognized this.

cicuta (si kū′ tȧ) [L.], *n.* (*Bot.*) A genus of umbelliferous plants comprising the British water-hemlock.

cid (sid) [Sp., from Arab, *sayyid*], *n.* A prince or commander; esp. the Spanish hero Ruy Diaz, Count of Bivar (*d.* 1099), champion against the Moors and theme of several epic poems.

-cide (sīd) [F., from L. *-cidium* (*cædere*, to kill)], *suf., e.g., fratricide, regicide, tyrannicide.*

cider (sī′ dėr) [O.F. *sidre* (F. *cidre*), late L. *sicera*, Gr. *sikera*, Heb. *shēkār*, strong drink (*shākar*, to drink to intoxication)], *n.* The juice of apples expressed and fermented. **cider-brandy,** *n.* Apple-brandy. **cider-mill,** *n.* A mill in which cider is made; a machine for grinding or crushing apples. **cider-press,** *n.* A press for squeezing the juice from crushed apples. ***ciderkin,** *n.* A liquor made from the crushed mass of apples, after the juice has been expressed for cider.

ci-devant (sē dė van) [F., formerly], *a.* Former, of a past time. *n.* (*Hist.*) A French aristocrat during the Revolution.

cierge (sērj) [earlier *cerge*, *serge*, O.F. *cerge* (F. *cierge*), L. *cēreus* (*cēra*, wax)], *n.* A wax candle used in religious processions in the Roman Church.

cigala [CICADA].

cigar, segar (si gar′) [Sp. *cigarro* (perh. from *cigarra*, cicada)], *n.* A roll of tobacco leaf for smoking. **cigar-holder,** *n.* A mouthpiece for a cigar. **cigar-shaped,** *a.* Cylindrical, with tapering ends. **cigar-store,** *n.* (*Am.*) A tobacconist's shop. **cigarette** (sig ȧ ret′) [dim. of prec.], *n.* Cut tobacco or a medical preparation rolled in paper for smoking. **cigarette-card,** *n.* A picture card enclosed in cigarette packets. **cigarette-holder,** *n.* A mouthpiece for holding a cigarette. **cigarette machine,** *n.* A machine for making cigarettes; an automatic machine for the sale of cigarettes. **cigarette-paper,** *n.* Thin paper, usually rice-paper, for wrapping the tobacco in cigarettes.

cilia (sil′ i ȧ) [pl. of L. *cilium*, eyelash], *n.pl.* (*Physiol.*) The eyelashes; hair-like, vibratile filaments on animals and plants; (*Bot.*) hairs like eyelashes on the margins of plants, leaves, etc. **ciliary,** *a.* **ciliate, -ated,** *a.* **ciliation** (sil i ā′ shŭn), *n.* **ciliato-, ciliati-, cilio-,** *comb. form.* (*Physiol.*) Pertaining to the eyelids; furnished with microscopic hairlike processes. **ciliform** (sil′ i fôrm), *a.*

cilice (sil′ is) [A.-S. *cilic*, Gr. *kilikion*, of Cilician goat's hair], *n.* Hair-cloth; a hair shirt. **cilicious** (si lish′ ŭs), *a.*

Cimbric (sim′ brik), *a.* Pertaining to the Cimbri, a tribe formerly inhabiting Jutland. *n.* The language of the Cimbri. **Cimbrian** (sim′ bri ȧn), *a.* and *n.*

***cimeter** [SCIMITAR].

cimex (sī′ meks) [L.], *n.* (*pl.* **cimices**) A genus of insects, containing the bed-bug.

Cimmerian (si mēr′ i ȧn) [L. *Cimmerius*, Gr. *Kimmerios*], *a.* Of or pertaining to the Cimmerii or their country, which was variously localized and fabled to be in a state of perpetual darkness; profoundly dark.

cimolite (sim′ ȯ līt) [L. *Cimōlia*, Gr. *Kimōlia*, pertaining to *Kimōlos*], *n.* (*Min.*) A friable white clay resembling fuller's earth, first found at Cimolus.

cinch (sinch) [Sp. *cincha*, L. *cingula*, from *cingere*, to gird], *n.* (*Am.*) A broad kind of saddle-girth; (*fig.*) a firm grip or hold; a certainty. *v.t.* To furnish or fasten with a cinch; to hold firmly; to put pressure on. **to cinch up:** To tighten a cinch.

cinchona (sin kō′ nȧ) [from the Countess of Chinchon, wife of a Viceroy of Peru in the 17th cent.], *n.* A genus of trees yielding Peruvian bark; Peruvian bark, the source of quinine. **cinchonaceous** (sin kō nā′ shu̇s), *a.* **cinchonia** (sin kō′ ni ȧ), **cinchonine** (sin′ kō nīn), *n.* (*Chem.*) An organic alkaloid contained in Peruvian bark. **cinchonism** (sin′ kȯ nizm), *n.* (*Med.*) The disturbed condition of the body caused by overdoses of quinine **cinchonize** (sin′ kȯ nīz), *v.t.* To treat with quinine

Cincinnatus (sin si nā′ tu̇s) [Roman dictator], *n.* (*fig.*) A great man summoned from retirement to save the State in a crisis.

cincture (singk′ tūr) [L. *cinctūra* (*cinctus*, p.p. of *cingere*, to gird)], *n.* A belt, a girdle, a band; an enclosure; (*Arch.*) the fillet at the top and bottom of a column. *v.t.* To gird, to encircle.

cinder (sin′ dėr) [A.-S. *sinder* (cp. Icel. *sindr*, G. *sinter*, slag or dross)], *n.* A coal that has ceased to burn but retains heat; a partly-burnt coal or other combustible; light slag; (*pl.*) the refuse of burnt coal or wood; the remains of anything that has been subject to combustion; scoriæ ejected from a volcano. **cinder-bed,** *n.* (*Geol.*) A loose bed of oyster-shells in the Middle Purbeck series. **cinder-path,** *n.* A race-course made up with cinders esp. for cycles. **cinder-sifter,** *n.* **cindery,** *a.*

Cinderella (sin dėr el′ ȧ) [scullery-maid who marries a prince in the fairy tale], *n.* One whose merits are unrecognized. **Cinderella dance,** *n.* A dance ending at midnight.

cinema, cinematograph, kinematograph (sin′ e ma, sin e mā′ tō grăph, kine e mā′ tō grăph) [F. *cinematographe*, from Gr. *kinema*, *-atos*, movement; GRAPH], *n.* An apparatus for projecting a series of instantaneous photographs on to a screen at high speed so as to give the effect of continuous motion. **cinema,** *n.* The theatre where such pictures are shown; material suitable for cinematography, (*colloq.* and *Am.*) the movies. **cinematographic,** *a.* **cinematography,** *n.* **cine-camera,** *n.* A camera used for taking cinematograph films. **Cinerama, Cinemascope,** *n.* Proprietary names of film projection methods with 3-dimensional effects.

cinenchyma (si neng′ ki mȧ) [Gr. *kinein*, to move, *enchuma*, infusion (*en*, in, *chu-*, *cheu-*, *cheein*, to pour)], *n.* (*Bot.*) Lactiferous tissue.

cineraria (sin ėr âr′ i ȧ) [L. *cinerārius*, ash-coloured (*cinis -eris*, ashes)], *n.* A genus of composite garden or hot-house plants.

cinerary (sin′ ėr ȧr i) [see prec.], *a.* Pertaining to ashes. **cinerary-urn,** *n.* An urn used to contain the ashes of the dead. **cinerarium** (sin ėr âr′ i u̇m), *n.* A place for the deposit of human ashes after cremation. **cineration** (sin ėr ā′ shu̇n), *n.* Reduction to ashes. **cinerious** (si nēr′ i u̇s) [L. *cinerius*], *a.* Ash-coloured, ash-grey. **cinerator,** *n.* A furnace for cremating corpses.

Cingalese (sing′ gȧ lēz′) [Sansk. *siṅhalās* (*siṅhalam*, Ceylon)], *n.* A native of Ceylon. *a.* Pertaining to Ceylon or its people.

cingulum (sing′ gū lu̇m) [L., from *cingere*, to gird], *n.* (*pl.* **-la**) (*Anat. and Zool.*) A band of various kinds; (*R.-C. Ch.*) the girdle of an alb.

cinnabar (sin′ ȧ bar) [late L. *cinnabaris*, Gr. *kinnabari* (Oriental in orig.)], *n.* A native mercuric sulphide; vermilion. *a.* Vermilion in colour.

cinnamon (sin′ ȧ mȯn) [F. *cinnamome*, L. *cinnamōmum*, Gr. *kinamōmon*, Heb. *qinnāmōn*], *n.* The aromatic bark of an East Indian tree, *Cinnamomum zeylanicum*, used as a spice; applied also to other trees and their bark. **cinnamate,** *n.* **cinnamomic** (-mō′ mik), **cinnamonic** (-mon′ ik), *a.* **cinnamon-stone,** *n.* (*Min.*) A cinnamon-red variety of garnet.

cinque, cinq (singk) [O.F. *cink* (F. *cinq*), L. *quinque*], *n.* Five; the five at cards or dice. **Cinque Ports,** *n.pl.* The five English ports: Dover, Sandwich, Hastings, Hythe, and Romney (to which Winchelsea and Rye were afterwards added), which enjoyed special privileges from the fact that they offered a defence against invasion. ***cinque-spotted,** *a.* Having five spots. **cinquecento** (ching′ kwė chen′ tō) [It. (short for *mil cinque cento*, 1500)], *n.* The revived classical style of art and literature that characterized the 16th century, esp. in Italy. **cinquecentist,** *n.*

cinquefoil (singk′ foil) [O.F. (cp. F. *quintefeuille*), L. *quinquefolium* (*quinque*, five, *folium*, leaf)], *n.* (*Bot.*) The genus *Potentilla*; (*pop.* several plants belonging to this; (*Arch.*) an ornamental foliation in five compartments, used in tracery, etc. **cinque-foiled,** *a.* (*Arch.*)

cipher, cypher (sī′ fėr) [O.F. *cifre* (F. *chiffre*), Arab. *çifr*, empty], *n.* The arithmetical symbol 0; a character of any kind used in writing or printing; a monogram, a device; a code or alphabet used to carry on secret correspondence designed to be intelligible only to the persons concerned; anything written in this; a key to it; a person or thing of no importance; the continued sounding of an organ-pipe through a defective valve. *v.i.* To do arithmetic. *v.t.* To express in cipher; to work by means of arithmetic; (*Organ*) to continue sounding when the key is not pressed. **cipher-key,** *n.* A key for reading writing in cipher.

cipolin (sip′ ȯ lin), **cipollino** (chip ȯ lē′ nō) [F. *cipolin*, It. *cipollino* (*cipolla*, onion)], *n.* A green Italian marble with white zones like the section of an onion.

cippus (sip′ u̇s) [L., a post, the stocks], *n.* (*Arch.*) A small, low, inscribed, monumental column.

circ (sěrk) [var. of CIRQUE], *n.* (*Archæol.*) A stone circle.

circa (sěr′ kȧ) [L.], *prep.* About, around. *adv.* About, nearly (often used instead of ***circiter*** with dates).

Circassian (sěr kăsh′ yȧn), *a.* Pertaining to the inhabitants, or country, of Circassia; a type of light cashmere of silk and mohair.

Circe (sěr′ sē) [L., from Gr. *Kirkē*, mythic enchantress, fabled to have turned the companions of Ulysses into swine], *n.* An enchantress; a woman who seduces. **Circean** (sěr sē′ ȧn), *a.*

***circensian** (sěr sen′ shi ȧn) [L. *circensis*], *a.* Pertaining to the Roman circus.

circinate (sěr′ sin ȧt) [L. *circinātūs*, p.p. of *circināre* (*circinus*, pair of compasses)], *a.* (*Bot.*) Rolled up (like the leaves of ferns).

circle (sěr′ kėl) [A.-S. *circul* (M.E. and O.F. *cercle*), L. *circulus*, dim. of *circus*, ring], *n.* A ring, a round figure; (*loosely*) a round body, a sphere; a round enclosure; a number of persons gathered in a ring; any series ending as it begins, and perpetually repeated; a period, a cycle; a complete series; a number of persons or things considered as bound together by some bond; a class, a set, a coterie, an association of persons having common interests; a sphere of action or influence; a territorial division (esp. in Germany); the arena of a circus; a tier of seats at a theatre; (*Geom.*) a plane figure bounded by a curved line, called the circumference, every point in which is equidistant from a point within the figure called the centre; (*Log.*) an inconclusive argument in which two or more statements are brought forward to prove each other. *v.t.* To move round; to surround. *v.i.* To form a circle; to revolve; to be passed round. **dress-circle,** *n.* The principal tier of seats in a theatre, in which evening dress is optional. **great circle:** (*Geom.*) A circle dividing a sphere into two equal parts. **lesser,** or **small circle:** (*Geom.*) A circle dividing a sphere into two unequal parts. **Polar circles,** *n.pl.* The Arctic and Antarctic parallels of latitude. **stone circle:** (*Archæol.*) A ring of prehistoric monoliths. **to come full circle:** To come round to where one started. **to square the circle:** To undertake an impossible task; to construct geometrically a square of area equal to that of a given circle. **to circle in:** To confine. **circled,** *a.* Having the form of a circle; encircled; marked with a circle or circles. **circler,** *n.* **circlet,** *n.* A little circle; a ring or circular band worn on the finger or the hand; *v.i.* To move in small circles. **circlewise,** *adv.*

circuit (sĕr′ kit) [F., from L. *circuitus*, a going round, from *circumīre* (*circum*, round, *īre*, to go)], *n.* The act of revolving or moving round, a revolution; the line enclosing a space, the distance round about; the space enclosed in a circle or within certain limits; (*Law*) the periodical visitation of judges for holding assizes; the district thus visited; the barristers making the circuit; (*Methodists*) a group of churches associated together for purposes of government and organization of the ministry; (*Elec.*) a continuous electrical communication between the poles of a battery; a series of conductors, including the lamps, motors, etc., through which a current passes. **short circuit** [SHORT]. **circuitous** (sir kū′ it ŭs), *a.* Indirect, roundabout. **circuitously,** *adv.* **circuitousness,** *n.* ***circuity,** *n.* Indirect procedure.

circulable [CIRCULATE].

circular (sĕr′ kū lăr) [M.E. and A.-F. *circuler*, O.F. *circulier*, L. *circulāris* (*circulus*, CIRCLE)], *a.* In the shape of a circle; round; pertaining to a circle; forming part of a circle; moving in a circle; cyclic; addressed in identical terms to a number of persons; (*Log.*) consisting of an argument in a circle. *n.* A letter or printed notice of which a copy is sent to many persons. **circular instruments,** *n.pl.* (*Geom.*) Instruments graduated for the whole circle. **circular letter,** *n.* A notice, advertisement, or appeal printed or duplicated for sending to a number of persons. **circular note,** *n.* A letter of credit addressed to several bankers. **circular lines,** *n.pl.* Lines of sines, tangents, secants, etc., on the plane scale and sector. **circular numbers,** *n.pl.* Those whose powers terminate in the same digits as the roots. **circular saw,** *n.* A rotating disk notched with teeth for cutting timber, etc.; (*Am.*) a buzz-saw. **circular scanning:** (*T.V.*) A method of scanning in which the spot follows a spiral path. **circular tour,** *n.* A journey to a number of places ending at the starting-point. **circular ticket,** *n.* A ticket for this. **circularity** (-lăr′ i ti), *n.* The state of being circular. **circularize,** *v.t.* To send circulars to. **circularly,** *adv.*

circulate (sĕr′ kū lāt) [L. *circulāre*], *v.i.* To move round; to pass through certain channels (as blood in the body, the sap of plants, etc.); to pass from point to point or hand to hand (as money); to be diffused, to travel. *v.t.* To cause to pass from point to point or hand to hand; to spread, to diffuse. **circulating,** *a.* That circulates; current; (*Math.*) recurring. **circulating decimal,** *n.* A decimal which cannot be expressed with perfect exactness in figures, and in which one or more figures recur continually in the same order. **circulating library,** *n.* A library from which books are lent to subscribers. **circulating medium,** *n.* The currency of a country. **circulable,** *a.*

circulation (sĕr kū lā′ shŭn), *n.* The act of circulating; the state of being circulated; (*Physiol.*) the motion of the blood in a living animal, by which it is propelled by the heart through the arteries to all parts of the body, and returned to the heart through the veins; (*Bot.*) the analogous motion of the sap; the free movement (of water, air, etc.); distribution (of books, newspapers, news, etc.); the amount of distribution, the number of copies sold; a medium of exchange, currency. **circulative** (sĕr′ kū lā tiv), *a.* Tending to circulate; promoting circulation. **circulator** (sĕr′ kū lā tŏr), *n.* One who or that which circulates; (*Math.*) a circulating decimal. **circulatory,** *a.* Circular, circulating.

circum- (sĕr′ kŭm) [L., round, round about, surrounding], *pref.* Round, round about; surrounding; indirectly; pertaining to the circumference.

circumambient (sĕr kŭm ăm′ bi ėnt) [L. *ambiens -entem*, pres.p. of *ambīre*, to go round (*ambi-*, about, *īre*, to go)], *a.* Going round about; surrounding. **circumambiency,** *n.*

***circumambulate** (sĕr kŭm ăm′ bū lāt) [L. *ambulāre*, to walk], *v.t.* To walk or go round about. *v.i.* To walk about, to beat about the bush. **circumambulation** (-lā′ shŭn), *n.* **circumambulatory** (-ăm′ bū lā tŏ ri), *a.*

circumbendibus (sĕr kŭm ben′ di bŭs), *n.* (*facet.*) A roundabout or indirect way; a circumlocution.

circumcise (sĕr′ kŭm sīz) [O.F. *circonciser*, L. *circumcīdere* (*cædere*, to cut)], *v.t.* To remove surgically or by ritual the prepuce or foreskin in the male, or the labia minora in the female; (*fig.*) to render spiritual and holy; to purify. **circumcision** (sĕr kum sizh′ ŭn), *n.* The operation of circumcising; a Jewish and Mohammedan rite in males; (*fig.*) spiritual purification; the Jews as a circumcised people; the festival of the Circumcision of Christ, on New Year's Day.

circumdenudation (ser kŭm dē nū dā′ shŭn) *n.* (*Geol.*) Denudation round a spot which remains as an elevated tract.

circumduct (sĕr′ kŭm dŭkt) [L. *circumductus*, p.p. of *circumdūcere* (*dūcere*, to lead)], *v.t.* To lead about or round; (*Law*) to nullify; (*Sc. Law*) to declare elapsed. **circumduction** (sĕr kŭm dŭk′ shŭn), *n.* The act of circumducting; a leading about; (*Law*) nullifying or cancelling.

circumference (sėr kŭm′ fėr ėns) [L. *circumferentia* (*ferre*, to bear)], *n.* The line that bounds a circle; a periphery; the distance round a space or a body; circuit. **circumferential** (sėr kŭm fėr en′ shăl), *a.*

circumflex (sĕr′ kŭm fleks) [L. *circumflexus* (*flexus*, p.p. of *flectere*, to bend)], *n.* A mark (ʌ or in Gr. ⌒) placed above a vowel to indicate accent, quality, or contraction. *a.* Marked with such accent; (*Anat.*) bent, turning, or curving round something. *v.t.* To mark or pronounce with a circumflex. **circumflexion, circumflection** (sĕr kŭm flek′ shŭn), *n.*

circumfluent (sĕr kŭm′ flu ėnt) [L. *circumfluens -entem*, pres.p. of *circumfluere* (*fluere*, to flow)], *a.* Flowing round on all sides. **circumfluence,** *n.* **circumfluous** (sĕr kŭm′ flu ŭs) [L. *circumfluus*], *a.* Flowing around; flowed round.

circumfuse (sĕr kŭm fūz′) [L. *circumfūsus*, p.p. of *circumfundere* (*fundere*, to pour)], *v.t.* To pour round, as a fluid; to surround, to bathe in or with. **circumfusion** (-fū zhŭn), *n.*

circumgyrate (sĕr′ kŭm ji rāt′, sĕr kŭm jī′ rāt), *v.i.* To turn, roll, or spin round. **circumgyration** (-rā′ shŭn), *n.* **circumgyratory** (-rā′ tŏ ri), *a.*

circumjacent (sĕr kŭm jā′ sėnt) [L. *circumjacens -entem*, pres.p. of *circumjacēre* (*jacēre*, to lie)], *a.* Lying round; bordering.

circumlittoral (sĕr kŭm lit′ ŏ răl) [L. *litus -oris*, the shore], *a.* Adjacent to the shore; pertaining to the zone immediately outside of the littoral.

circumlocution (sĕr kŭm lŏ kū′ shŭn) [L. *circumlocūtio -ōnem*], *n.* Periphrasis; the use of roundabout, indirect, or evasive language; the use of many words where few would suffice. **the Circumlocution Office** [Dickens's 'Little Dorrit'], *n.* A type of bureaucratic red-tape and roundabout procedure. **circumlocutional** (-kū' shŭn ăl), *a.* **circumlocutionary** (-kū' shŭn ăr i), *a.* **circumlocutionist,** *n.* **circumlocutory,** *a.*

circum-meridian (sĕr kŭm mė rid' i ăn) *a.* (*Astron.*) Occurring near or pertaining to what is near the meridian.

circumnavigate (sĕr kŭm năv' i gāt) [L. *circumnāvigāre, v.t.* To sail completely round. **circumnavigation** (-gā' shŭn), *n.* **circumnavigator** (-năv' i gā tŏr), *n.*

circumnutate (sĕr kŭm nū' tāt), *v.i.* (*Bot.*) To nod or turn successively to all points of the compass (as the tips of growing plants). **circumnutation** (-tā' shŭn), *n.*

circumoral (sĕr kŭm ôr' ăl) [L. *os oris,* mouth], *a.* (*Physiol.*) Surrounding the mouth.

circumpolar (sĕr kŭm pō' lăr), *a.* (*Geog.*) Situated round or near the pole; (*Astron.*) revolving about the pole (not setting).

circumscribe (sĕr' kŭm skrīb) [L. *circumscrībere* (*scrībere,* to write)], *v.t.* To write or draw around; to limit, to define by bounds, to restrict; (*Log.*) to define; (*Geom.*) to surround with a figure that touches at every possible point. **circumscriber** (-skrī' bėr), *n.* **circumscription** (-skrip' shŭn), *n.* The act of circumscribing; the imposing of limitations; a boundary line; a circular inscription; a definition; (*Geom.*) a figure that encloses and touches at every possible point. **circumscriptive,** *a.* **circumscriptively,** *adv.*

circumsolar (sĕr kŭm sō' lă), *a.* Revolving round or situated near the sun.

circumspect (sĕr' kŭm spekt) [L. *circumspectus,* prudent, p.p. of *circumspicere* (*specere,* to look)], *a.* Looking on all sides; cautious, wary. **circumspection** (-spek' shŭn), *n.* **circumspectness** (sĕr' kŭm spekt nės), *n.* **circumspective,** *a.* **circumspectly,** *adv.*

circumstance (sĕr' kŭm stăns) [O.F., from L. *circumstantia,* from *-stans -ntem,* pres.p. of *circumstāre* (*stāre,* to stand)], *n.* Something attending or relative to a fact or case; an incident, an event; a concomitant; abundance of detail (in a narrative), circumstantiality; ceremony, pomp, fuss; (*pl.*) the facts, relations, influences, and other conditions that affect an act or an event; the facts, conditions, etc., that affect one's living. *v.t.* To place in a particular situation. **circumstanced,** *a.* Situated; *conditioned by circumstances. **in the circumstances:** In the particular situation for which allowance should be made. **under the circumstances:** (*colloq.*) Under the particular conditions for which allowance should be made. **easy** or **straitened circumstances:** Prosperity; indigence.

circumstantial (sĕr kŭm stăn' shăl), *a.* Depending on circumstances; incidental, not essential; detailed, minute. **n.* Something incidental; a non-essential. **circumstantial evidence,** *n.* (*Law*) Evidence inferred from circumstances which usually attend facts of a particular nature. **circumstantiality** (-shi ăl' i ti), *n.* **circumstantially,** *adv.* **circumstantiate** (sĕr kŭm stăn' shi āt), *v.t.* To make circumstantial.

•**circumvallate** (sĕr' kŭm vă lāt, sĕr kŭm văl' āt) [L. *circumvallāre* (*vallāre,* from *vallum,* a rampart)], *v.t.* To surround or enclose with a rampart. **circumvallation** (-lā' shŭn), *n.*

circumvent (sĕr' kŭm vent) [L. *circumventus,* p.p. of *circumvenīre* (*venīre,* to come)], *v.t.* To deceive, to outwit, to cheat, to get the best of. **circumvention** (-ven' shŭn), *n.*

•**circumvolve** (sĕr kŭm volv') [L. *circumvolvere* (*volvere,* to roll)], *v.t.* To roll round or about; to encompass. *v.i.* To revolve. **circumvolution** (-vŏ loo' shŭn), *n.* The act of rolling round; a winding about, a coil, a convolution; a revolution; a winding or tortuous movement; (*Arch.*) the spiral in a volute.

circus (sĕr' kŭs) [L., a ring], *n.* A place of amusement where horsemanship, acrobatic feats, trained animals, etc. are exhibited; (*Hist.*) the Circus Maximus in ancient Rome, any similar building; a circle of buildings at the intersection of streets; a travelling troupe of performers in a circus.

ciré (sē' rā) [Fr., waxed], *n.* (*Textiles*) Satin with a waxed surface.

cirque (sĕrk) [F.], *n.* A circular space; (*poet.*) a circus or arena; (*Geol.*) a circular recess among hills.

cirrate [CIRRUS].

cirrhosis (si rō' sis) [Gr. *kirrhos,* yellow], *n.* (*Med.*) A morbid yellow matter sometimes secreted in the tissues; a disease of the liver.

cirri-, cirro- [L. *cirrus,* a curl], *comb. form.* (*Bot. and Zool.*) Having fringe-like appendages. **cirriferous** (si rif' ėr ŭs) [-FEROUS], *a.* (*Bot.*) Producing tendrils. **cirriform** (sir' i fôrm) [-FORM], *a.* **cirrigerous** (si rij' ėr ŭs) [-GEROUS], *a.* **cirriped, -pede** (sir' i ped, -pēd) [L. *pes pedis,* foot], *n.* Any individual of the *Cirripedia,* a class of marine animals related to the *Crustacea,* having cirriform feet and comprising the barnacles and acorn-shells.

cirrocumulus (sir ŏ kū' mū lŭs), *n.* (*Meteor.*) A cloud broken up into small fleecy masses. **cirrostratus,** *n.* A horizontal or slightly inclined sheet of cloud more or less broken into fleecy masses.

cirrus (sir' ŭs) [L., a curl], *n.* (*Bot.*) A tendril; (*Zool.*) a slender locomotive filament; a barbule; (*Meteor.*) a lofty feathery cloud. **cirrate, cirrose, cirrous,** *a.*

cis- (sis) [L., on this side of], *pref.* On this side of. **cisalpine** (sis ăl' pīn), *a.* On the Roman side of the Alps; south of the Alps. **cisatlantic** (sis ăt lăn' tik) [ATLANTIC], *a.* On this side of the Atlantic, as opposed to *transatlantic.* **cis-Leithan** (sis lī' thăn) [river *Leitha*], *a.* Austrian, non-Hungarian. **cismontane** (sis mon' tān), *a.* On the north side the mountains (this as regards France and Germany). **cispadane** (sis' pă dān) [*Padus,* Po], *a.* On this side the Po (as regards Rome), south of the Po. **cispontine** (sis pon' tin) [L. *pons -tem,* bridge], *a.* On the north side of the Thames, in London.

ciselure (sēz' loor) [F., from *ciseler,* to carve (*ciseau,* CHISEL)], *n.* Graving; chased work.

cismontane, cispontine [CIS-].

cissoid (sis' oid) [Gr. *kissoeides,* like ivy], *a.* (*Geom.*) Contained within two intersecting curves.

cist (sist) [L. *cista,* Gr. *kistē,* chest], *n.* (*Archæol.*) A tomb consisting of a kind of stone chest formed of rows of stones, with a flat stone for cover; a casket or chest, esp. one used for carrying the sacred utensils in the Greek mysteries.

Cistercian (sis tĕr' shi ăn, -shn) [med. L. *Cistercium,* Citeaux], *n.* A member of a monastic order founded in 1098, and named from the first convent, Citeaux, in France, sometimes called Bernardine after St. Bernard of Clairvaux. *a.* Pertaining to the Cistercians.

cistern (sis' tĕrn) [O.F. *cisterne,* L. *Cisterna* (*cista,* a chest)], *n.* A storage place for water or other liquid; a reservoir.

cistus (sis' tŭs) [L., from Gr. *kistos*], *n.* (*pl.* **-tuses -ti**) (*Bot.*) The rock-rose, a genus of plants with ephemeral flowers somewhat like a wild rose.

cistvaen [KISTVAEN].

•**cit** (sit) [short for CITIZEN], *n.* A townsman (in disparagement or contempt).

citable [CITE].

citadel (sit' ă dėl) [F. *citadelle,* It. *cittadella,* dim. of *cittade,* L. *cīvitas -tātem,* CITY], *n.* A castle or fortified place in a city; a stronghold; a final retreat.

cite (sīt) [F. *citer,* L. *citāre,* freq. of *ciēre* to rouse], *v.t.* To quote, to allege as an authority; to quote as and instance; to refer to; to summon to appear in court. **citable**, *a.* ***cital**, *n.* A summons, a citation; a reproof, a recital. **citation** (-tā′ shŭn), *n.* A summons; (*Mil.*) mention in despatches, etc.

cithara (sith′ ȧ rȧ) [L., from Gr. *kithara*], *n.* An instrument somewhat resembling a harp. **citharist**, *n.* **citharistic** (sith ȧ ris′ tik), *a.*

***cither, cithern** (sith′ ėr, -ėrn), ***cittern** (sit′ ėrn) [from prec.], *n.* A kind of guitar with wire strings; a lute.

citizen (sit′ i zėn) [M.E. *citesein*, A.-F. *citeseyn*, O.F. *citeain* (*cité*, CITY, -AN)], *n.* A member of a state in the enjoyment of political rights; a burgess or freeman of a city or town; a dweller in a town; a civilian. *a.* Having the character of a citizen; town-bred. **citizenhood**, *n.* **citizenship**, *n.* The state of being a citizen.

***citole** (si′ tōl) [O.F., prob. from L. CITHARA], *n.* A stringed musical instrument.

citr-, citro- [L. *citrus*, CITRON], *comb. form.* (*Chem.*) Citric.

citrate (sit′ rāt) [CITRON], *n.* A salt of citric acid. **citric** (sit′ rik), *a.* Derived from the citron. **citric acid**, *n.* The acid found in lemons, citrons, limes, oranges, etc.

citrine (sit′ rin), *a.* Like a citron; greenish-yellow. *n.* (*Min.*) A yellow, pellucid variety of quartz. **citrinous** (sit′ ri nŭs), *a.* Lemon-coloured.

citron (sit′ rŏn) [F., from late L. *citro -ōnem*, L. *citrus*], *n.* A tree, *Citrus medica*, bearing large lemon-like fruit.

citronella (sit rō nel′ ȧ), *n.* A fragrant oil used to drive away insects.

citrus (sit′ rŭs), *n.* (*Bot.*) A genus of trees containing the orange, lemon, citron, etc.

cittern [CITHERN].

city (sit′ i) [O.F. *cité*, L. *cīvitātem*, acc. of *cīvitas* (*cīvis*, a citizen)], *n.* A town incorporated by a charter; the inhabitants of a city; (*pop.*) a large and important town; a cathedral town. *a.* Pertaining to a city. **the City**: The part of London governed by the Lord Mayor and Corporation; hence, the business part of London. **City editor**, *n.* The editor of the financial column of a newspaper. **City man**, *n.* One engaged in commerce or finance. **City article**, *n.* An article in a newspaper dealing with these subjects. **City company**, *n.* A London livery company representing one of the mediæval guilds. **Eternal City**: Rome. **the Celestial City**: Heaven. **citied**, *a.* Containing cities (*usu. in comb.*, as *many-citied*). **citified**, *a.* Townish; having the peculiarities of dwellers in cities. **cityless**, *a.* **cityward, -s**, *adv.*

civet (siv′ ėt) [F. *civette*, Arab. *zabād*], *n.* A resinous musky substance obtained from the anal pouch of the genus *Viverra*, and used as a perfume. *v.t.* To perfume with civet. **civet-cat**, *n.* A carnivorous quadruped from Asia and Africa, belonging to the genus *Viverra*.

civic (siv′ ik) [L. *cīvicus* (*cīvis*, a citizen)], *a.* Pertaining to a city or citizens; urban; municipal; civil. **civic crown**, *n.* A garland of oak-leaves awarded to a Roman soldier who saved the life of a comrade in battle, often used in architecture. **civically**, *adv.* **civicism**, ***civism**, *n.* Citizenship; patriotism; (*Hist.*) allegiance to the doctrines of the French Revolution. **civics**, *n.* The science of citizenship and municipal government.

civil (siv′ il) [F., from L. *cīvīlis* (*cīvis*, citizen)], *a.* Relating to the community as a human society or as a body of citizens; pertaining to citizens; intestine; municipal, commercial, legislative; well-regulated; civilized, polite, courteous; *grave, sober, not showy; pertaining to social, commercial, and administrative affairs, not warlike, not military or naval; (*Law*) pertaining to private matters, not criminal. **civil architecture**, *n.* The construction of buildings for the purposes of civil life. **civil action, process**, *n.* [CIVIL LAW]. **civil day**, *n.* [CIVIL YEAR]. **civil defence**, *n.* A civilian service for the protection of lives and property in the event of enemy air-attack. **civil disobedience**, *n.* A concerted plan in a political campaign taking the form of refusal to pay taxes or perform civil duties. **civil engineer**, *n.* **civil engineering**, *n.* The science of constructing docks, railways, canals, etc. **civil law**, *n.* The law dealing with private rights, not criminal matters; Roman law. **civil list**, *n.* The yearly sum granted for the support of a sovereign or ruler; the officers of a government who are paid from the public treasury. **civil list pension**, *n.* A small pension granted by the state to selected artists, writers, musicians, etc. **civil magistrate**, *n.* (*Law*) A magistrate not dealing with ecclesiastical matters. **civil servant**, *n.* A member of the Civil Service. **Civil Service**, *n.* That branch of the public service which includes the covenanted non-military servants of the Crown; civil servants collectively. **civil state**, *n.* The entire body of the citizens, as distinct from the military, ecclesiastical, and naval establishments. **civil suit**, *n.* (*Law*) A suit for a private claim or injury. **civil war**, *n.* A war between citizens of the same country. **civil year**, *n.* The legal year (in any given state), as distinguished from the astronomical year. **civilian** (si vil′ yȧn), *n.* A person engaged in the pursuits of civil life, not belonging to the army or navy; *(*Law*) a student or professor of civil law. *a.* Engaged in civil pursuits. **civility** (si vil′ i ti), *n.* The quality of being civil; politeness, courtesy. **civilly**, *adv.*

civilize (siv′ il īz) [F. *civiliser* (CIVIL, -IZE)], *v.t.* To reclaim from barbarism; to instruct in the arts and refinements of civilized society. **civilizable**, *a.* **civilization** (-zā′ shŭn), *n.* The act or process of civilizing; the state of being civilized; refinement, social development; civilized society. **civilizer**, *n.*

***civism** [CIVIC].

civvies (siv′ iz), *n.pl.* (*Army colloq.*) Civilian clothes. **Civvy Street**, *n.* Civilian life.

clachan (klăch′ ȧn) [Gael., orig. a circle of stones (*clach*, a stone)], *n.* A small village or hamlet in the Highlands.

clack (klăk) [prob. imit. (cp. Icel. *klaka*, to twitter, F. *claquer*)], *v.i.* To make a sharp, sudden noise like a clap or crack; to chatter rapidly and noisily. *v.t.* To cause to emit a sudden, sharp noise; to knock together. *n.* A sudden, sharp sound frequently repeated; rapid and noisy chattering; a contrivance in a corn-mill that strikes the hopper and facilitates the descent of the corn; a bell that gives notice when more grain is needed to feed the hopper; a kind of ball-valve; a noisy tongue; a chatterbox. ***clack-dish**, *n.* A dish with a movable lid, formerly used by beggars to attract attention. **clack-valve**, *n.* A valve hinged by one edge. **clacker**, *n.* One who or that which clacks; a clack-valve. **clackety**, *a.*

clad, *p.p.* [CLOTHE].

clad-, clado- [Gr. *klados*, a twig, a shoot], *comb. form.* (*Bot. and Zool.*) Branching; pertaining to branches or branchlets.

claes (klāz) (*Sc.*) [CLOTHES].

claim (klām) [O.F. *claim-*, stem of *clamer*, L. *clāmāre*, to call out], *v.t.* To demand, or challenge, as a right; to assert that one has or is (something) or has done (something); to affirm, to maintain; (*fig.*) to be deserving of; *to proclaim, to call. *v.i.* *To cry out, to call; *to assert claims. *n.* A real or supposed right; a title; a piece of land allotted to one; a piece of land marked out by a settler or miner with the intention of buying it when it is offered for sale; *a loud call. **claim-jumper**, *n.* One who seizes on land claimed by another. **claim-jumping**, *n.* **claimable**, *a.* **claimant**, *n.* One who makes a claim.

clairaudience (klâr aw′ di ėns) [F. *clair*, clear, L. *clārus*; AUDIENCE], *n.* The faculty of hearing voices and other sounds not perceptible to the senses. **clairaudient**, *n.* and *a.*

clair-obscure [F. *clair-obscur*, CHIAROSCURO].

clairvoyance (klâr voi′ åns) [F. *clair*, L. *clārus*, clear, *voir*, L. *vidēre*, to see], *n.* The power possessed by persons in a mesmeric state of perceiving objects not present to the senses. **clairvoyant** (*fem.* **clairvoyante**), *n. a.* Pertaining to or having the power of clairvoyance.

clam (1) (klăm) [A.-S. *clǣman* (confused with M.E. *clam*, sticky, *see* CLAMMY)], *v.t.* To smear with anything viscous. *v.i.* To be sticky or clammy.

clam (2) (klăm) [A.-S. *clamm*, bond, fetter (allied to CLAMP (1))], *n.* A clamp or vice; a clutch; the lining of a vice.

clam (3) (klăm) [prob. from prec.], *n.* A name for several edible bivalves; esp. (*Am.*) *Venus mercenaria*, the hard, and *Mya arenaria*, the soft clam; (*colloq.*) a taciturn person. **clam-shell,** *n.* The shell of a clam.

clamant (klăm′ ånt, klā′ månt) [L. *clāmans -ntem*, pres.p. of *clāmāre*, to cry out], *a.* Crying or begging earnestly; clamorous. **clamantly,** *adv.*

clamber (klăm′ bėr) [prob. formed from A.-S. *climban*, to climb (cp., however, Icel. *clambra*, to pinch together, clamp, and G. *klammern*, to clamp)], *v.i.* To climb any steep place with hands and feet, to climb with difficulty; to grow by clinging; (*fig.*) to tower, ascend. **v.t.* To climb up with difficulty. *n.* A climb.

clamjamphrie (klåm jăm′ fri) [Sc., etym. doubtful], *n.* Rubbish; an affair of no value; nonsense; a rabble, a contemptible lot.

clammy (klăm′ i) [perh. from A.-S. *clām*, clay, confused with CLAM (1)], *a.* Moist, damp; sticky, tenacious, adhesive. **clammily,** *adv.* **clamminess,** *n.*

clamour (klăm′ ŏr) [O.F., from L. *clāmor* (*clāmāre*, to cry out)], *n.* An outcry; a loud and continuous shouting or calling out; a continued and loud expression of complaint, demand, or appeal; popular outcry. *v.t.* To shout (down); to utter or express with loud noise. *v.i.* To cry out loudly and earnestly; to demand or complain importunately; to make a loud noise. **clamorous,** *a.* **clamourously,** *adv.* **clamourousness,** *n.*

clamp (1) (klămp) [not in early use; etym. uncertain (cp. Dut. *klampe* (now *klamp*), G. *klampe*, A.-S. *clam*)], *n.* Anything rigid which strengthens, fastens, or binds; a piece of timber or iron used to fasten work together; (*Carp.*) a frame with two tightening screws to hold pieces of wood together; a back batten fastened crosswise to several boards to prevent them from warping; (*Naut.*) the internal planking under the shelf on which the deck beams rest. *v.t.* To unite, fasten, or strengthen with a clamp or clamps. **clamper** (1), *n.*

clamp (2) (klămp) [perh. from prec. (cp. Dut. *klamp*)], *n.* A pile of bricks for burning; (*Farming*) a heap, mound, or stack of turf, rubbish, or potatoes, etc. *v.t.* To pile into a heap; to store in a clamp.

clamp (3) (klămp) [imit., cp. CLUMP], *n.* A heavy footstep or tread. *v.i.* To tread heavily and noisily. **clamper** (2), *n.*

clamper (3) (klăm′ pėr) [Sc., prob. from CLAMP (1)], *v.t.* To botch; to botch up.

clan (klăn) [Gael. *clann* (perh. from L. *planta*)], *n.* (*Sc. Highlanders*) A tribe or number of families bearing the same name, descended from a common ancestor, and united under a chieftain representing that ancestor; (*fig.*) a clique, a set. **clannish,** *a.* United closely together, as the members of a clan; of or pertaining to a clan; cliquish. **clannishly,** *adv.* **clannishness,** *n.* **clanship,** *n.* The system or state of clans. **clansman,** *n.* A member of a clan.

clandestine (klăn des′ tin) [F. *clandestin*, L. *clandestīnus* (*clam*, in secret)], *a.* Secret, surreptitious, underhand. **clandestinely,** *adv.* **clandestineness,** *n.*

clang (klăng) [L. *clangere* (cp. Gr. *klangē*, a clang)], *v.t.* To strike together, so as to cause a sharp, ringing sound. *v.i.* To emit a sharp, ringing sound; to resound. *n.* A sharp, ringing noise, as of two pieces of metal struck together. **clanger,** *n.* (*colloq.*) A foolish mistake; a social blunder; an ill-timed remark. **clangour,** *n.* A sharp, ringing sound or series of sounds. **clangorous,** *a.* **clangorously,** *adv.*

clank (klăngk) [onomat., or perh. from Dut. *klank*], *v.t.* To strike together so as to make a heavy rattling sound. *v.i.* To make such a sound. *n.* A sound as of solid metallic bodies struck together; (usually denotes a deeper sound than *clink*, and a less resounding one than *clang*).

clannish, etc. [CLAN].

clap (1) (klăp) [M.E. *clappen* (perh. from A.-S.), cp. Dut. and G. *klappen*, Icel. *klappa*], *v.t.* (*past & p.p.* **clapped**) To strike together noisily; to strike quickly or slap with something flat; to shut hastily; to put or place suddenly or hastily; to applaud, by striking the hands together. *v.i.* *To knock loudly; to move quickly; to shut (as a door) with a bang; to strike the hands together in applause. *n.* The noise made by the collision of flat surfaces; a sudden loud noise; a peal of thunder; applause shown by clapping; *a heavy slap. **to clap on:** To add hastily. **to clap eyes on:** To catch sight of. ***to clap up:** To make hastily; to conclude (as a bargain) hastily; to imprison hastily. ***clap-dish,** *n.* A clack-dish. **clap-net,** *n.* A folding net for snaring birds or catching insects. **claptrap,** *n.* Showy words or deeds designed to win applause or public favour; * a contrivance for clapping or applause in theatres. *a.* Deceptive, unreal; intended merely to win applause. **clapper,** *n.* One who or that which claps; the tongue of a bell; the clack of a mill-hopper; a noisy rattle for scaring birds.

clap (2) (klăp) [prob. from prec.], *n.* Gonorrhœa.

clap-board (klăp′ bōrd) [formed from obs. *clapholt*, L.G. *klappholt*], *n.* A cask stave; (*Am.*) a feather-edged board used to cover the roofs and sides of houses. *v.t.* (*Am.*) To cover with clap-boards. **clap-boarding,** *n.*

clapperclaw (klăp′ ėr klaw) [CLAPPER (CLAP (1)), CLAW], *v.t.* To beat, to scratch, to drub, to revile.

claptrap [CLAP (1)].

claque (klăk) [F., from *claquer*, to clap], *n.* A body of hired applauders; the system of engaging applauders. **claquer,** *claqueur*, *n.*

clarabella (klăr å bel′ å) [L. *clārus*, clear, *bellus*, pretty], *n.* (*Organ*) A stop with open wooden pipes giving a powerful fluty tone.

clarence (klăr′ ėns) [Duke of *Clarence*, aft. William IV], *n.* A close four-wheeled carriage with a single seat inside, and a seat for the driver.

Clarenceaux (klăr′ ėn sū) [Duke of *Clarence*, son of Edward III, who first held this office], *n.* (*Her.*) The second King-of-arms.

clarendon (klăr′ ėn dŏn) [*Clarendon* Press, Oxford], *n.* and *a.* (*Print.*) A condensed type with heavy face (as the word **clarendon**).

clare-obscure [CHIAROSCURO].

claret (klăr′ ėt) [O.F. *clairet*, dim. of *clair*, L. *clārus*, CLEAR], *n.* A light red Bordeaux wine; any light red wine resembling Bordeaux; (*Angling*) an artificial claret-coloured fancy-fly; (*slang*) blood. **to tap the claret:** To strike the nose and make it bleed. **claret-coloured,** *a.* Reddish-violet. **claret-cup,** *n.* A beverage composed of iced claret, brandy, lemon, borage, etc.

clarify (klăr′ i fī) [O.F. *clarifier*, L. *clārificāre* (*clārus*, clear, *facere*, to make)], *v.t.* To clear from visible impurities; to make transparent; (*fig.*) to make lucid or perspicuous. *v.i.* To become transparent. **clarification** (-kā′ shŭn), *n.* **clarifier,** *n.* One who or that which clarifies; a vessel in which sugar is clarified.

clarinet (klăr′ i net, klăr i net′) [F. *clarinette*, dim. of *clarine* (L. *clārus*, clear)], *n.* A keyed reed instrument larger than a hautboy. **clarinettist** (klăr i net′ ist), *n.*

clarion (klăr′ i ŏn) [O.F. *claron*, med. L. *clārio -onem* (L. *clārus*, clear)], *n.* A kind of trumpet, with a narrow tube, and loud and clear note; sound of or as of a clarion; (*Organ*) a stop giving a similar tone. *a.* Loud and clear. *v.t.* To announce as with a clarion; to trumpet. **clarionet** (klăr i ŏ net′), *n.* A clarinet.

clarity (klăr′ i ti) [M.E. and O.F. *clarté*, L. *clāritas -tātem* (L. *clārus*)], *n.* Clearness; *glory, splendour.

clarkia (klar′ ki ȧ) [William *Clark* (1770–1838)], *n.* (*Bot.*) A genus of herbaceous annuals of the order *Onagraceæ*. It has a showy purple flower.

clarty (klar′ ti) [Sc. *clart*, sticky mud (etym. unknown)], *a.* Muddy, dirty, miry.

clary (klâr′ i) [A.-S. *slaridge*, med. L. *sclarea*], *n.* Name of several labiate plants of the genus *Salvia*, esp. *S. sclarea*, a garden pot-herb. **clary-water, -wine,** *n.* A cordial compounded of brandy, sugar, clary-flowers, cinnamon, and ambergris.

clash (klăsh) [imit., cp. CLACK, CRASH, and CRACK], *v.i.* To make a loud noise by striking against something; to come into collison; to disagree; to conflict; to interfere. *v.t.* To cause one thing to strike against another so as to produce a noise. *n.* The noise produced by the violent collision of two bodies; opposition, contradiction; conflict; disharmony of colours.

clasp (klasp) [M.E. *claspen*, *clapsen* (cp. A.-S. *clyppan*, to grasp, embrace)], *n.* A catch, hook, or interlocking device for fastening; a fastening; a buckle or brooch; a close embrace; a grasp; (*Mil.*) a metal bar attached to a ribbon carrying a medal commemorating a battle or other exploit. *v.t.* To fasten or shut with or as with a clasp or buckle; to fasten (a clasp); to cling to by twining; to embrace; to grasp. *v.i.* To cling (to). **clasp-knife,** *n.* A pocket-knife in which the blade shuts into the hollow part of the handle. **clasper,** *n.* One who or that which clasps; (*Zool.*) one of a pair of organs in some insects and fishes by which the male holds the female.

class (klas) [F. *classe*, L. *classis* (*calāre*, to call, summon)], *n.* A number of persons or things ranked together; social rank; the system of social caste; a number of scholars or students taught together, (*Am.*) grade; (*Am.*) the students taken collectively who expect to graduate at the same time; a division according to quality; a number of individuals having the same essential or accidental qualities; (*Nat. Hist.*) a division of animals or plants next above an order. *v.t.* To arrange in a class or classes. *a.* (*slang*) Of good quality. **-class,** *a.* (*in comb.*) *e.g. first-class, second-class*, etc. **no class:** (*slang*) Altogether inferior. **the classes:** The wealthy as opposed to the masses. **class-book,** *n.* A text-book used in a class. **class conscious:** Over-sensitive to social differences. **class-list,** *n.* A classified list of candidates issued by examiners; a select list of books, etc. **class-man,** *n.* One who takes honours at an examination, as opposed to a passman. **class-mate, -fellow,** *n.* One who is or has been in the same class. **class warfare:** Overt antagonism between the social classes in a community. **classable,** *a.* Capable of being classed. **classy,** *a.* (*slang*) Genteel; of superior quality.

classic (klăs′ ik) [L. *classicus* (*classis*, see prec.)], *n.* A Greek or Latin author of the first rank; an author of the first rank; a literary work by any of these; a recognized masterpiece; one versed in Greek and Latin literature; a follower of classic models as opposed to romantic; (*pl.*) ancient Greek and Latin literature; the study of these. *a.* Pertaining to the literature of the ancient Greeks and Romans; in the style of these; of the first rank in literature or art; harmonious, well-proportioned; pure, refined, restrained; of standard authority; clear-cut, regular (of the features). **classic ground:** A spot having illustrious associations. **classic orders:** (*Arch.*) Doric, Ionic, Corinthian, Tuscan, and Composite. **classic races,** *n.pl.* The five principal horse-races in England, being the 2,000 Guineas, 1,000 Guineas, Derby, Oaks, and St. Leger.

classical (klăs′ i kȧl), *a.* Pertaining to the classics, classic. **classicalism,** *n.* **classicality** (-kăl′ i ti), *n.* **classically,** *adv.* **classicism** (-sizm), *n.* A classic style or idiom; devotion to or imitation of the classics; classical scholarship; advocacy of classical education. **classicist,** *n.* **classicize,** *v.t.* To make classic. *v.i.* To affect or imitate the classic style. **classico-,** *comb. form.*

classify (klăs′ i fī), *v.t.* To distribute into classes or divisions; to assign to a class. **classifiable,** *a.* **classification** (-kā′ shŭn), *n.* **classifier,** *n.* **classificatory,** *a.*

clastic (klăs′ tik) [Gr. *klastos*, broken (*klaein*, to break)], *a.* (*Geol.*) Fragmentary; composed of materials derived from the waste of various rocks.

clat (klăt) [CLATTER], *v.i.* To chatter. *n.* A chatterbox.

clatter (klăt′ ėr) [A.-S. *clatrian* (cp. Dut. *klateren*, L.G. *klätern*)], *v.i.* To emit or make a sharp rattling noise; to fall or move with such a noise; to talk idly and noisily. *v.t.* To cause to emit a rattling sound. *n.* A continuous rattling noise; loud, tumultuous noise; noisy, empty talk.

Claude Lorraine glass (klawd lŏ rān′ glas) [after the French painter *Claude Lorraine*], *n.* A convex mirror, usually of dark or tinted glass, for giving a concentrated view of a landscape in low tones.

Claudian (klaw′ di ȧn), *a.* Pertaining to or of the period of the Roman emperors of the Claudian gens (Tiberius, Caligula, Claudius, and Nero; A.D. 14–68).

clause (klawz) [O.F., from L. *clausa*, fem. p.p. of *claudere*, to close, to enclose], *n.* A distinct part of a composition; a short sentence; a complete grammatical sentence; a subdivision of a compound or complex sentence; a separate and distinct portion of a document; a particular stipulation.

claustral (klaws′ trȧl) [late L. *claustrālis* (*claustrum*)], *a.* Pertaining to a cloister or monastic foundation; cloister-like; retired. **claustration** (-trā′ shŭn), *n.* The act of shutting up in a cloister.

claustrophobia (klaws trō fō′ bi ȧ) [L. *claustra*, a bolt, Gr. *phobos*, fear], *n.* (*Path.*) A morbid dread of being in a confined space.

claut (klawt) [Sc., etym. doubtful (perh. related to CLAW)], *n.* A kind of hoe, scraper, or rake; a rakeful. *v.t.* To rake or scrape.

clavate (klā′ vāt) [L. *clāvātus*, p.p. of *clāvāre*; or formed from *clāva*, a club], *a.* (*Bot. and Zool.*) Club-shaped; (*Anat.*) applied to a kind of articulation. **claviform** (klăv′ i fôrm), *a.* **clavigerous** (klȧ vij′ ėr ŭs), *a.* Club-bearing.

clave, *past* [CLEAVE].

clavecin (klăv′ ė sin) [F., from It. *clavicembalo* or med. L. *clavicymbalum* (L. *clāvis*, key, *cymbalum*, CYMBAL)], *n.* (*Mus.*) *A harpsichord; a set of keys for playing carillons.

clavichord (klăv′ i côrd), *n.* (*Mus.*) One of the first stringed instruments with a keyboard, a predecessor of the pianoforte.

clavicle (klăv′ i kėl) [L. *clāvicula*, dim. of *clāvis*, key (med. L., collar-bone)], *n.* (*Anat.*) The collar-bone. **clavicular** (klȧ vik′ ū lȧr), *a.*

clavicorn (klăv′ i kôrn) [L. *clāva*, club; *cornu*, horn], *n.* (*Ent.*) One of a group of pentamerous beetles with club-shaped antennæ.

clavier (klăv′ i ėr, klăv′ i ėr) [F. (L. *clāvis*, a key)], *n.* (*Mus.*) The keyboard of an organ, pianoforte, etc.

claviform, clavigerous [CLAVATE].

claw (klaw) [A.-S. *clawu* (cp. Dut. *klaauw*, G. *klaue*)], *n.* The sharp hooked nail of a bird or beast; the foot of any animal armed with such nails; the pincers of a crab, lobster, or cray-fish; anything resembling the claw of one of the lower animals; an implement for grappling or holding;

the hand; a grasp, a clutch. *v.t.* To tear or scratch with the claws; to clutch or drag with or as with claws; *to tickle, to stroke; (*fig.*) to flatter. **claw-hammer,** *n.* A hammer furnished at the back with claws to extract nails; (*slang*) a dress coat, from its shape. **to claw away** or **off:** (*Naut.*) To beat to windward off a lee shore. **to claw up:** (*dial. and slang*) To beat soundly. **clawed,** *a.* Furnished with claws; damaged by clawing. **clawless,** *a.*

clay (klā) [A.-S. *clǣg*, Teut. (cp. Dut. and G. *klei*, A.-S. *clam*, Gr. *gloios*, L. *gluten*)], *n.* Tenacious, plastic earth; (*fig.*) the human body; a corpse; the grosser part of human nature; (*Geol.*) a hydrous silicate of aluminium, with a mixture of other substances; (*colloq.*) a clay pipe. *v.t.* To cover, manure, or purify and whiten (as sugar), with clay; to puddle with clay. **clay-cold,** *a.* Cold and lifeless as clay. **clay-pan,** *n.* (*Austral.*) A hollow (often dry in summer) where water collects. **clay-pigeon,** *n.* (*Sport*) A clay disk thrown into the air as a target. **clay-pipe,** *n.* A pipe made of baked clay, usually long; a church-warden. **clay-pit,** *n.* A pit whence clay is dug. **clay-slate,** *n.* (*Geol.*) An argillaceous, easily-cloven sedimentary rock; roofing-slate. **clay-stone,** *n.* (*Geol.*) A felstone of granular texture. **clayey,** *a.* **clayish,** *a.*

claymore (klā′ môr) [Gael. *claidheamh mor*, great sword (cp. W. *cleddyf*, O.Ir. *claideb*, sword, L. *clades*, slaughter, W. *mawr*, Ir. *mor*, Corn. *maur*, great)], *n.* A two-edged sword used by the Scottish Highlanders; (*incorrectly*) a basket-hilted broadsword.

clean (klēn) [A.-S. *clǣne*, Teut. (cp. Dut. and G. *klein*, small)], *a.* Free from dirt, stain, alloy, blemish, imperfection, disease, ceremonial defilement, awkwardness, or defect; pure, holy, guiltless; (*Print.*) needing no correction (as a proof); empty, having no fish (as a whaler); smart, dexterous, unerring; clear, unobstructed; complete. *v.t.* To make clean; to cleanse, to purify. *adv.* Quite, completely; without qualification, absolutely; dexterously, cleverly. **a clean sweep:** A wholesale riddance. **to show a clean pair of heels:** To distance pursuit. **clean bill** [BILL OF HEALTH, see BILL (2)]. **clean-bred:** Thoroughbred. **to come clean:** To confess. **clean-cut,** *a.* Sharply defined; clear-cut. **clean fish,** *n.* Not unfit for food as at or about spawning time. **clean-handed,** *a.* Free from blame in any matter. **clean-limbed,** *a.* Having well-proportioned limbs. **clean potato:** (*Austral. hist.*) Convict's slang for a freed man. **clean-shaped, *-timbered,** *a.* Well-proportioned. **clean-shaven,** *a.* Without beard or moustache. **clean skin:** (*Austral.*) Unbranded horses or cattle. **to clean down:** To brush or wipe down. **to clean out:** To strip; (*slang*) to deprive of all (his) money. **to clean up:** To put tidy; to collect all the money, profits, etc. **cleanable,** *a.* **cleaner,** *n.* One who cleans; an office charwoman. **cleanly** (1) (klēn′ li), *adv.* In a clean manner. **cleanness,** *n.*

cleanly (2) (klen′ li) [A.-S. *clǣnlic*, a.], *a.* Clean; clean in person and habits. **cleanlily,** *adv.* **cleanliness,** *n.*

cleanse (klenz) [A.-S. *clǣnsian*], *v.t.* To make clean, to purge, to purify; (*Bibl.*) to cure.

clear (klēr) [O.F. *cler* (F. *clair*), L. *clārus*], *a.* Free from darkness, dullness, or opacity; luminous, bright; transparent, translucent; serene, unclouded; brightly intelligent; lucid, evident; indisputable, perspicuous, easily apprehended; irreproachable; unembarrassed, unentangled; free, unshackled; unobstructed; distinctly audible; certain, unmistaken; free from deduction, net, not curtailed. *adv.* Clearly, completely; quite entirely; apart, free from risk of contact. *v.t.* To make clear; to free from darkness, dimness, opacity, ambiguity, obstruction, imputation, or encumbrance; to empty; to remove, to liberate, to disengage; to acquit, to exonerate; to pay off all charges; to gain, to realize as profit; to pass or leap over without touching. *v.i.* To become clear, bright, or serene; *to become free from embarrassment or entanglements; (*Naut.*) to sail. **clear-cut,** *a.* Regular, finely outlined, as if chiselled. **clear-headed,** *a.* Acute, sharp, intelligent. **clear-seeing,** *a.* Clear-sighted. ***clear-shining,** *a.* Shining brightly. **clear-sighted,** *a.* Acute, discerning, far-seeing. **clear-sightedness,** *n.* **clear-starch,** *v.t.* To stiffen and dress with colourless starch. **clear-starcher,** *n.* **clear-story** [CLERESTORY]. **clear-stuff,** *n.* Boards free from knots or shakes. **clearwing,** *n.* (*Zool.*) One of the *Sesiadæ*, a genus of moths with translucent wings. **a clear day:** A complete day. **clear days:** Time reckoned apart from the first day and the last. **to clear a ship:** (*Naut.*) To pay the charges at the Custom-house and receive permission to sail. **to clear a ship for action:** (*Nav.*) To remove all encumbrances from the deck ready for an engagement. **to clear away:** To remove; to remove plates, etc., after a meal; to disappear; to melt away. **to clear land:** To remove trees and brushwood in order to cultivate. **to clear off:** To remove; to depart. **to clear out:** (*colloq.*) To eject; to depart; to melt away. **to clear the land:** (*Naut.*) To have good sea-room. **to clear up:** To become bright and clear; to elucidate; to tidy up. **clearage,** *n.* **clearer,** *n.* **clearly,** *adv.* In a clear manner; distinctly, audibly, plainly, evidently, certainly, undoubtedly. **clearness,** *n.* The state of being clear; perspicuity, distinctness to or of apprehension.

clearance (klēr′ ans), *n.* The act of clearing; the state of being cleared; clear profit; (*Banking*) the passing of cheques through the Clearing House; (*Naut.*) a certificate that a ship has been cleared at the Custom-house; (*Eng.*) the distance between the moving and the stationary part of a machine.

clearing (klēr′ ing), *n.* The act of making clear, freeing, or justifying; a tract of land cleared for cultivation; (*Banking*) the exchanging of bills and cheques and payment of the balances; the division among different railway companies of the proceeds of traffic passing over several lines. **clearing-house,** *n.* A house or office where the operation of clearing is performed, esp. the Clearing House in London for banking establishments.

clear-cole (klēr′ kōl) [F., *claire colle*, clear glue or size], *v.t.* To treat with a preparation of size and whiting.

cleat (klēt) [M.E., *clete*, a wedge (cp. Dut. *kloot*, G. *klosz*, a ball or clod)], *n.* A strip of wood secured to another one to strengthen it; a strip fastened on steps to obviate slipping; (*Naut.*) a piece of wood or iron for fastening ropes upon; *a wedge. *v.t.* To fasten or strengthen with a cleat.

cleave (1) (klēv) [A.-S. *clifian*, from Teut. *kli-* (cp. G. *kleben*, Dut. *kleven*, Swed. *klibba*)], *v.i.* (*past* **cleaved, *clave**) To stick ,to adhere; to be attached closely; to be faithful (to).

cleave (2) (klēv) [A.-S. *clēofan*, Teut. *kleuth-* (cp. Dut. *klieven*, G. *klieben*, Gr. *gluphein*, to hollow out, carve)], *v.t.* (*past* **clove, cleft,** *p.p.* **cloven, cleft**) To split asunder with violence, to cut through, to divide forcibly; to make one's way through. *v.i.* To part asunder; to split, to crack. **cleavable,** *a.* **cleavage** (klē′ vaj), *n.* The act of cleaving; (*Min.*) the particular manner in which a mineral with a regular structure may be cleft or split; (*fig.*) the way in which a party, etc., splits up. **line** or **plane of cleavage:** (*Min.*) The line or plane of weakness along which a mineral or a rock tends to split. **cleaver,** *n.* One who or that which cleaves; a butcher's instrument for cutting meat into joints.

cleavers (klē′ vėrs), **clivers** (kliv′ ėrs) [prob. from CLEAVE (1)], *n.* Goose grass, *Galium aparine*, a loose-growing plant with hooked prickles that catch in clothes.

cleek (klēk) [Sc. and North., from M.E. **cleche,** later *cleach*], *v.t.* (*past* **claucht, claught, cleekit**) To catch hold of suddenly; to seize. *n.* A large hook for hanging things up or for fishing; (*Golf*) an iron-headed club.

clef (klef) [F., from L. *clāvis*, key], *n.* (*Mus.*) A character at the beginning of a stave denoting the pitch and determining the names of the notes according to their position on the stave.

cleft (1) (kleft) *past* and *p.p.* **cleft-footed,** *a.* Having the hoof divided. **cleft stick,** *n.* A stick split at the end. **in a cleft stick:** In a situation where going forward or back is impossible; a tight place, a fix.

cleft (2) (kleft) [earlier *clift*, cogn. with CLEAVE (2) (cp. Icel., Dut., and G. *kluft*)], *n.* A split, a crack, a fissure; a morbid crack in the pastern of a horse; *the fork of the human body. **cleft palate,** *n.* (*Path.*) Congenital cleavage of the roof of the mouth.

cleg (kleg) [Icel. *kleggi*], *n.* A gadfly, a horsefly.

cleisto- [Gr. *kleistos* (*kleiein*, to close)], *comb. form.* (*Bot.*) Closed. **cleistogamic** (klīs tō găm′ ik) [*gamos*, marriage], *a.* (*Bot.*) Having flowers that never open and are self-fertilized.

***clem** (klem) [cp. CLAM (2) and Dut. and G. *klemmen*, to pinch], *v.t.* To pinch (as hunger). *v.i.* To starve, to famish.

clematis (klem′ ȧ tis) [late L., from Gr. *klēmatis*], *n.* A genus of ranunculaceous plants, comprising the common traveller's joy, old man's beard, or virgin's bower, *C. vitalba.*

clement (klem′ ėnt) [L. *clēmens -entis*], *a.* Mild, gentle; merciful. **clemency,** *n.*

Clementine (klem′ ėn tīn), *a.* Pertaining to St. Clement or to Pope Clement V (1305–14). *n.pl.* The decretals and constitutions of Clement V.

clench (klench) [M.E. *clenchen*, from A.-S. *clencan*, extant only in *be-clancan* (cp. O.H.G. *klenkan*, also CLING, CLINCH], *v.t.* To rivet; to fasten firmly by bending the point of (with a hammer); to grasp firmly; to close or fix firmly (as the hands or teeth). **clencher** [CLINCHER].

***clepe** (klēp) [A.-S. *clipian*], *v.t.* To call, to name. *v.i.* To call, to cry.

clepsydra (klep′ si drȧ) [L., from Gr. *klepsudra* (*kleptein*, to steal, *hudron*, water)], *n.* An instrument used by the ancients to measure time by the dropping of water from a graduated vessel through a small opening.

clerestory (klēr′ stôr i) [CLEAR, STORY], *n.* (*Arch.*) The upper part of the nave, choir, or transept of a large church containing windows above the roofs of the aisles.

clergy (klĕr′ ji) [O.F. *clergie* (*clerc*, late L. *clēricus*, Gr. *klērikos*, pertaining to the clergy), from *klērikos*, a lot or inheritance, with reference to Deut. xviii. 2 and Acts i. 17], *n.* The body of men set apart by ordination for the service of the Christian Church; ecclesiastics collectively; the clergy of a church, district, or country. **benefit of clergy:** (*Hist.*) The The exemption of clerics from the jurisdiction of secular courts; an immunity granted in certain cases to all who could read. **clergiable,** *a.* For which benefit of clergy might be pleaded. **clergyman,** *n.* A member of the clergy; an ordained Christian minister, esp. of the Established Church. **clergywoman,** *n.* (*colloq.*) The wife or other female relative of a clergyman, esp. one who tries to manage the affairs of the parish.

cleric (kler′ ik) [late L. *clēricus*, see prec.], *a.* Clerical. *n.* A member of the clergy; one subject to canon law. **clerico-,** *comb. form.*

clerical (kler′ ik ȧl) [late L. *clēricālis*, from prec.], *a.* Relating to the clergy, or to a clerk, copyist, or writer. **clerical error,** *n.* An error in copying. **clericalism,** *n.* Undue influence of the clergy. **clericalist,** *n.* **clericalize,** *v.t.* **clericality** (-kăl′ i ti), *n.* **clerically,** *adv.*

clerihew (klĕr′ i hū) [E. Clerihew Bentley], *n.* A satirical or humorous poem usually biographical, consisting of four rhymed lines of uneven length, *e.g.*:

It was a weakness of Voltaire's
To forget to say his prayers,
And one which, to his shame,
He never overcame.

clerk (klark) [A.-S. *clerc*, from O.F. *clerc* or late L. *clēricus* (see CLERGY)], *n.* A cleric, a clergyman; the lay officer of a parish church; one employed in an office, bank, shop, etc., to assist in correspondence, book-keeping, etc.; one who has charge of an office or department, subject to a higher authority, as a board, etc.; (*Am.*) a shopman, a salesman; *a scholar, one able to read and write. **Town clerk:** The chief officer of a corporation, usually a solicitor. **clerk in holy orders,** *n.* An ordained clergyman. **Clerk of the Peace,** *n.* An officer who prepares indictments and keeps records of the proceedings at sessions of the peace. **Clerk of the Weather,** *n.* (*colloq.*) The imaginary controller of the weather; the meteorological office. **clerk of works,** *n.* A surveyor appointed to watch over the performance of a contract and test the quality of materials, etc. **clerkdom,** *n.* **clerkly,** *a.* **clerkship,** *n.* Scholarship; the office or position of a clerk.

cleromancy (klēr′ ō măn si) [Gr. *klēros*, a lot], *n.* Divination by casting lots with dice.

cleuch, cleugh (klu*ch*, klū*ch*) [Sc. CLOUGH], *n.* A rocky gorge or ravine with steep sides.

cleve (klēv) [var. of CLIFF], *n.* (*Devon*) The steep side of a hill.

clever (klev′ ėr) [etym. doubtful; conn. with A.-S. *clifer*, a claw, *clifian*, to seize (cp. E.Fris. *klüfer*)], *a.* Dexterous, skilful; talented; very intelligent; expert, ingenious; *nice, agreeable; **cleverish,** *a.* **cleverness,** *n.*

clevis (klev′ is) [etym. doubtful; prob. conn. with CLEAVE (2)], *n.* A forked iron at the end of a shaft or beam, or an iron loop, for fastening tackle to.

clew (kloo) [A.-S. *clīwen* (cp. Dut. *kluwen*, G. *knäuel*); see also CLUE], *n.* (*Naut.*) The lower corner of a square sail; the aftermost corner of a staysail; the cords by which a hammock is suspended. *v.t.* To truss up to the yard. **clew-garnets,** *n.pl.* (*Naut.*) Tackles attached to the clews of the main and fore sails, by which they are trussed up to the yards. **clew-lines,** *n.pl.* (*Naut.*) Similar tackles for the smaller square sails.

cliché (klē′ shā) [F., p.p. of *clicher*, to stereotype (var. of *cliquer*)], *n.* (*Print.*) A stereotype, esp. a stereo or electrotype from a block; (*Phot.*) a negative; (*fig.*) a hackneyed phrase, a tag.

click (klik) [imit., cp. CLACK, Dut. *klikken*, F. *cliquer*], *v.i.* To make a slight, sharp noise, as small hard bodies knocking together; (*Horses*) to strike shoes together. *v.t.* To cause to click; (*slang*) to get what one wants; to get friendly at sight. *n.* A slight sharp sound; a kind of articulation used by some natives of South Africa; the detent of a ratchet-wheel; a catch for a lock or bolt; a latch. **clicker** (1), *n.* A horse that clicks.

clicker (2) (klik′ ėr) [from prec. or from obs. v. *click*, var. of CLEEK, to clutch, seize], *n.* *A tout; one who stood at the door to invite passers-by to enter a shop; one who cuts out the leather for shoemakers; (*Print.*) a foreman in charge of a companionship of compositors.

***clicket** (klik′ ėt) [O.F. *cliquet* (*cliquer*, to click)], *n.* A latch; a latch-key; a valve, a catch, etc., shutting with a click.

client (klī′ ėnt) [L. *cliens -ntis* (*cluere*, to hear, to obey)], *n.* (*Rom. Ant.*) A plebeian who placed himself under the protection of a noble (called his patron); one who employs a lawyer as his agent or to conduct a case; one who entrusts any business to a professional man; a dependant; a customer. **clientage** (klī′ ėn tȧj), **clientelage** (-tē′ laj), *n.* One's clients collectively; the system of patron and client; the condition of a client. **clientele** (klī′ ėn tel) [L. *clientēla* (more recently re-adopted from F. *clientèle*, pron. klē a*n* tāl)], *n.* Clients or dependants collectively; followers or adherents; customers, patients, frequenters, etc.; clientship. **clientless,** *a.* **clientship,** *n.*

cliff (klif) [A.-S. *clif* (cp. Dut. and Icel. *klif*, G.

klippe)], *n.* A steep, precipitous rock; a precipice. **cliffy,** *a.* Having cliffs; craggy.

***clift** (klift), *n.* A crag; a cliff.

climacteric (klī măk′ tėr ik, kli măk ter′ ik) [L. *clīmactēricus*, Gr. *klimaktērikos* (*klimaktēr*, the step of a ladder, a critical period in life; cp. *klimax*, CLIMAX)], *n.* A critical period in human life; a period in which some great change is supposed to take place in the human constitution, or in the fortune of an individual (the periods are said to be found by multiplying 7 by 3, 5, 7, and 9, the 63rd year being called the **grand climacteric;** to these the 81st year is sometimes added). *a.* Of or pertaining to a climacteric; critical; (*Med.*) occurring late in life. **climacterical,** *a.* Climacteric.

climactic [CLIMAX].

climate (klī′ māt) [F. *climat*, late L. *clima -atos*, Gr. *klima -atos*, a slope, a region (*klinein*, to slope)], *n.* A region, a country considered with reference to its weather; the temperature of a place or country, and its meteorological conditions generally, with regard to their influence on animal and vegetable life. **v.i.* To inhabit, to dwell. **climatic** (klī măt′ ik), *a.* **climatically,** *adv.* **climatology** (-tol′ ȯ ji) [-LOGY], *n.* The science of climate; an investigation of climatic phenomena and their causes. **climatological** (-loj′ ik ȧl), *a.* **climature,** *n.* Climate.

climax (klī′ măks) [L., from Gr. *klimax*, a ladder (*klinein*, to slope)], *n.* A rhetorical figure in which the sense rises gradually in a series of images, each exceeding its predecessor in force or dignity; (*incorrectly*) the highest point, culmination. *v.i.* To ascend in a climax. *v.t.* To bring to a culminating point. **climactic** (klī măk′ tik), *a.*

climb (klīm) [A.-S. *climban* (cp. *clifian*, CLEAVE, Dut. and G. *klimmen*)], *v.t.* (*past & p.p.* **climbed, *clomb**) To ascend (esp. by means of the hands and feet); to ascend by means of tendrils; to ascend; to slope upwards; to rise in rank or prosperity. *n.* An ascent; the act of climbing or ascending. **to climb down:** To descend (a cliff, a tree, etc.); (*colloq.*) to abate one's pretensions or claims; to make an ignominious withdrawal. **climbable** (klī′ mȧbl), *a.* **climber** (klī′ mėr), *n.* One who or that which climbs; a creeper or climbing plant; one of the *Scansores* or climbing birds. **climbing,** *n.* Mountaineering. *a.* That climbs. **climbing-boy,** *n.* A boy formerly sent up a chimney as a chimney-sweep. **climbing-irons,** *n.* (*pl.*) A set of spikes fastened to the legs to assist in climbing. **climbing-perch,** *n.* The anabas, a fish that climbs river-banks and trees.

clime (klīm) [late L. *clima*, CLIMATE], *n.* (*poet.*) A region, a country; a climate.

clinanthium (kli năn′ thi ŭm) [Gr. *klinē*, a couch, *anthos*, a flower], *n.* (*Bot.*) The receptacle of a composite flower.

clinch (klinch) [var. of CLENCH], *v.t.* To secure a nail by hammering down the point; to drive home or establish (an argument, a statement, etc.); (*Naut.*) to make a rope-end fast in a particular way. *n.* The act of clinching; (*Naut.*) a mode of fastening large ropes by a half-hitch; a grip, a hold-fast; a pun; an ambiguous word. **clinch-nail,** *n.* A nail with a malleable head adapted for clinching. **clincher,** *n.* One who or that which clinches; a conclusive argument or statement. **clincher-built** [CLINKER-BUILT].

cling (kling) [A.-S. *clingan* (cp. Dan. *klynge*, to cluster, Swed. *klänge*, to climb)], *v.i.* (*past and p.p.* **clung**) To adhere closely and tenaciously, esp. by twining, grasping, or embracing; to be faithful to. **v.t.* To shrivel up; to cause to wither away; to clasp, to embrace. *n.* (*Am.*) A clingstone. **to cling together:** To form one mass; to resist separation. **clingstone,** *n.* A kind of peach in which the pulp adheres closely to the stone.

clinic (klin′ ik) [F. *clinique*, L. *clinicus*, Gr. *klinikos* (*klinē*, a bed, *klinein*, to slope, recline)], *n.* One confined to bed by sickness; medical and surgical instruction, esp. in hospitals; a place where medical attention and advice are given; (*Eccles. Hist.*) one who received baptism on the deathbed. **clinical,** *a.* Pertaining to a patient in bed, or to instruction given by a professor to students in a hospital ward. **clinical baptism,** *n.* Baptism administered to a sick or dying person. **clinical thermometer,** *n.* One for observing the temperature of a patient. **clinically,** *adv.* **clinique** (kli nēk′) [CLINIC].

clink (1) (klingk) [imit.; cp. CLANK, Dut. *klinken*], *n.* A sharp, tinkling sound, as when two metallic bodies are struck lightly together. *v.i.* To make this sound. *v.t.* To cause to clink. **clinkstone,** *n.* (*Geol.*) Phonolite; a felspathic rock that clinks when struck.

clink (2) (klingk) [prob. from the name of a Southwark gaol (perh. from CLINCH)], *n.* (*slang*) A gaol, a lock-up; *a particularly dismal sort of cell.

clinker (1) (kling′ kėr) [M.Dut. *klinckaert* (*klinken*, to CLINK)], *n.* *A Dutch sun-baked brick; vitrified slag; fused cinders; bricks run together in a mass by heat; (*slang*) a sounding blow, a thumping lie, etc.

clinker (2) (kling′ kėr) [from obs. v. *clink*, CLINCH], *n.* (*North.*) A clinch-nail. **clinker-built** (kling′ kėr bilt), *a.* (*Naut.*) Built with overlapping planks fastened with clinched nails [cp. CARVEL-BUILT].

clinometer (klī nom′ ė tėr) [Gr. *klinein*, to slope, -METER], *n.* An instrument for measuring angles of inclination. **clinometric, clinometrical** (klī nȯ met′ rik, -ȧl), *a.*

***clinquant** (kling′ kȧnt) [F., p.p. of *clinquer*, to CLINK], *a.* Shining, resplendent; dressed in tinsel. *n.* Tinsel, gaudy finery.

Clio (klī′ ō) [Gr. *Kleiō* (*kleiein*, to celebrate)], *n.* The muse of epic poetry and history; (*Zool.*) a genus of minute *Mollusca* found in the Polar Seas.

clip (1) (klip) [Icel. *klippa*], *v.t.* (*past & p.p.* **clipped**) To cut with shears or scissors; to trim; to cut away; to pare the edges of (as coin); to cut short by omitting (letters, syllables, etc.); to cancel a ticket by snipping a piece out of it. *v.i.* To run or go swiftly. *n.* A shearing or trimming; the whole wool of a season; a blow. **to clip the wings of:** To put a check on the ambitions of. **clippie,** *n.* (*colloq.*) A bus conductress. **clipping,** *n.* A piece clipped off; the action of the verb. **clipping-bureau,** *n.* (*Am.*) A press-cutting agency.

clip (2) (klip) [A.-S. *clyppan* (cp. Icel. *klypa*, to pinch)], *v.t.* To clasp, to embrace; to encircle, to surround closely. *n.* An appliance for gripping, holding, or attaching.

clipper (klip′ er) *n.* One or that which clips; a fast-sailing vessel with a long sharp bow and raking masts; a fast-goer; (*Aviat.*) a fast trans-oceanic air-liner. **clipper-built,** *a.* (*Naut.*) Built like a clipper.

clique (klēk) [F., from *cliquer*, to CLICK], *n.* A small number of persons associated for some questionable purpose; an exclusive set; a coterie of snobs. **cliquish,** *a.* **cliquishness,** *n.* **cliquism,** *n.* **cliquy,** *a.*

clish-clash (klish′ klăsh) [redupl. of CLASH], *n.* (*Sc.*) Gossip. *v.i.* To gossip. **clish-maclaver** (klish mȧ klā′ vėr), *n.* (*Sc.*) Gossip.

clitellum (klī tel′ ŭm) [mod. L., from L. *clitellæ*, a pack-saddle], *n.* (*Zool.*) The thick central part of the body of an earthworm. **clitellar,** *a.* **clitelliferous** (-lif′ ėr ŭs).

clitoris (klī′ tȯ ris) [Gr. *kleitoris* (*kleiein*, to shut)], *n.* (*pl.* **-ides**) (*Anat.*) A small erectile body situated at the apex of the vulva and corresponding to the penis in the male.

clitter-clatter (klit′ ėr klăt′ ėr) [redupl. of CLATTER], *n.* Idle talk; noisy chatter.

cloaca (klō ā′ kȧ) [L.], *n.* A sewer; the excrementory cavity in certain animals, birds, insects, etc.; a receptacle for filth; (*fig.*) a sink of iniquity. **cloacal,** *a.*

cloak, *cloke (klōk) [M.E. and O.F. *cloke*, med. L. *cloca*, a bell, a horseman's cape (cp. CLOCK)], *n.* A loose, wide, outer garment worn by both sexes; a mantle; a covering; (*fig.*) a disguise, a blind, a pretext. *v.t.* To cover with or as with a cloak; to disguise; to hide. *v.i.* To put on one's cloak. ***cloak-bag,** *n.* A portmanteau, a travelling-bag. **cloak-room,** *n.* A room or office at places of public resort where cloaks, small parcels, etc., can be deposited; a lavatory. **cloaking,** *n.* Disguise, concealment; a rough, woollen material for cloaks.

cloam (klōm) [A.-S. *clām*, mud, clay], *n.* (*dial.*) Earthenware, clay pottery.

***clobber** (klob' ėr) [etym. doubtful; perh. from Gael. *clabar*], *n.* A kind of coarse paste used by cobblers to conceal cracks in leather; (*slang*) clothes. *v.t.* To patch up, to cobble. **clobberer,** *n.*

cloche (klosh) [F., a bell], *n.* A bell-shaped glass put over young or tender plants to preserve them from frost. **cloche hat,** *n.* A close-fitting hat shaped like a cloche.

clocher (klō' shėr) [F. *clocher*, O.North.F. *clockier*, *cloquier* (see foll.)], *n.* A bell-tower, a belfry.

clock (1) (klok) [O.North.F. *cloque*, med. L. *clocca*, *cloca*, a bell; or M.Dut. *clocke* (D. *klok*, cp. G. *glocke*, a bell, a clock); prob. orig. from Celt. (cp. O.Ir. *cloc*, W. and Corn. *cloch*, Gael. *clag*)], *n.* An instrument for measuring time, consisting of wheels actuated by a spring, weight, or electricity, and, in some cases, furnished with striking mechanism to mark the hours or smaller divisions of time. **what's o'clock? what o'clock is it?** (contr. of What hour of the clock is it?): What is the time? **to clock in, on, out, off:** To register on a specially constructed clock the times of arrival at, and departure from, work. **clock-bird,** *n.* (*Austral.*) The kookaburra. ***clock-setter,** *n.* One who regulates clocks. **clock-maker,** *n.* One who makes clocks. **clock-wise,** *adv.* As the hands of a clock, from left to right; opp. to **counter-clockwise,** from right to left (as seen by one standing in front). **clockwork,** *n.* The movements of a clock; a train of wheels producing motion in a similar fashion. **like clockwork:** With unfailing regularity: mechanically, automatically. **clock golf,** *n.* A putting game played on lawns.

***clock** (2) (klok) [etym. unknown], *n.* (*dial.*, *chiefly North.*) A beetle; the dung-beetle.

clock (3) (klok) [etym. doubtful], *n.* Embroidered work on the leg of a stocking. **clocked,** *a.*

clocking (klok' ing) [dial. v. *clock*, var. of CLUCK], *n.* (*Sc.*) Brooding, hatching. *a.* Brooding, sitting. **clocking-time,** *n.* Hatching-time. **clocking-hen.**

clod (klod) [var. of CLOT], *n.* A lump of earth or clay; a mass of earth and turf; any concreted mass; the shoulder part of the neck-piece of beef; a piece of earth, mere lifeless matter; a clod-hopper. ******v.t.* To pelt with clods. *v.i.* To clot. ***clod-breaker,** *n.* A rustic. **clod-crusher,** *n.* An instrument for pulverizing clods. **cloddish,** *a.* Loutish, coarse, clumsy. **cloddishness,** *n.* **cloddy,** *a.* Abounding in clods; (*fig.*) earthy, base, worthless. **clod-hopper,** *n.* An awkward rustic; a bumpkin. **clod-pate, -poll,** *n.* A stupid, thick-headed fellow; a dolt, a boor. **clod-pated,** *a.*

clog (klog) [etym unknown (perh. Scand., cp. Norw. *klugu*, a knotty log)], *n.* A block of wood attached to a person or animal to hinder free movement (*fig.*) anything that impedes motion or freedom; a kind of shoe with a wooden sole; a boot with a metal rim, a kind of sabot; a wooden-soled sandal or over-shoe worn by a woman in wet weather. *v.t.* (*past & p.p.* **clogged**) To encumber or hamper with a weight; to hinder; to obstruct; to choke up; *to form clots on. *v.i.* To be obstructed or encumbered with anything heavy or adhesive. **clog-dance,** *n.* A dance in which the performer wears clogs in order to produce a loud accompaniment to the music. **cloggy,** *a.* Clogging; adhesive, sticky. **clogginess,** *n.*

cloisonné (klwa zô nā') [F., partitioned, from *cloison*, a partition (ult. from L. *clausus*, p.p. of *claudere*, to close)], *a.* Partitioned, divided into compartments. *n.* Cloisonné enamel. **cloisonné enamel,** *n.* Chinese or Japanese enamel-work, in which the coloured parts are separated by metallic partitions.

cloister (klois' tėr) [O.F. *cloistre* (F. *cloître*), L. *claustrum* (*claudere*, to shut, p.p. *clausus*)], *n.* A place of religious seclusion; a religious house or convent; (*Arch.*) a series of covered passages usu. arranged along the sides of a quadrangle in monastic, cathedral, or collegiate buildings; hence, a piazza. ******v.t.* To shut up in a cloister or convent. ***cloister-garth,** *n.* A yard or grass-plot surrounded with cloisters, often used as a burial-ground. **cloistered,** *a.* (*fig.*) out of things; sheltered. ***cloisterer,** *n.* One who lives in a cloister. ***cloistress,** *n.* A nun. **cloistral,** *a.*

cloke [CLOAK].

clone (klōn) [Gr. *klon*, a shoot], *n.* A number of plants produced asexually from one original seedling.

clonus (klō' nŭs) [Gr. *klonos*, violent commotion], *n.* (*Path.*) A spasm with alternate contraction and relaxation. **clonic** (klon' ik), *a.*

cloot (kloot) [Sc. and North. (perh. from Icel. *klo*, claw)], *n.* A cloven hoof or one part of it. **Cloots, Clootie:** The Devil.

close (1) (klōz) [M.E. *closen*, O.F. *clos*, p.p. *clore*, L. *claudere*, to shut (p.p. *clausus*)], *v.t.* To shut to; to fill (up) an opening; to enclose, to shut in; to bring or unite together; *to include; to be the end of, conclude; to complete, to settle. *v.i.* To shut; to coalesce; to come to an end, to cease; to agree, to come to terms; to grapple, to come to hand-to-hand fighting. *n.* The act of closing; an end, a conclusion; a grapple, a hand-to-hand struggle. **to close down:** (of factories, works, etc.) To shut, to cease work; (*Radio.*) to go off the air. **to close in:** To shut in, to enclose; to come nearer; to get shorter. **to close on** or **upon:** To shut over; to grasp; to shut (eyes) to; to agree, to come to terms. **to close up:** To block up, fill in; to come together. **to close with:** To accede to, to agree or consent to; to unite with; to grapple with. **closing time,** *n.* The hour at which a shop, office, or other establishment is declared closed for work or business. **closed circuit:** (*Elec.*) A circuit with a complete, unbroken path for the current to flow through. **closed shop,** *n.* A form of union security under which an employer may hire only union members and retain only union members in good standing. **closer** (-z-), *n.* One who or that which closes or concludes; a workman who sews the seams in the sides of boots; (*Building*) the last stone or brick in the horizontal course of a wall.

close (2) (klōs) [as prec.], *a.* Closed, shut fast; confined, shut in; pronounced with the lips or mouth partly shut; solid, dense, compact; near together in time or space; intimate, familiar; concise, compressed, coherent; nearly alike; attentive; following the original closely; to the point, apt, accurate, precise, minute; without ventilation, oppressive, stifling; warm and damp (of the weather); restricted, limited, reserved; difficult to obtain, scarce (as money); retired, secret, reticent; parsimonious, penurious. *adv.* Near, close to; closely, tightly, thickly, or compactly. *n.* An enclosure; a place fenced in; the precincts of a cathedral or abbey; a small enclosed field; a narrow passage or street; a blind alley. **close-banded,** *a.* In close order or array; thickly ranged. **close borough,** *n.* A borough for which the right of returning a member to Parliament was practically in the hands of one person. **close breeding,** *n.* Breeding between animals closely akin. **close by, close to, close upon:** Within a short distance; very near; hard by. **close corporation,** *n.* One which fills up its own vacancies. **close-curtained,** *a.* With curtains drawn close round. **close file,** *n.* A row of people standing or moving one immediately behind the other. **close-fisted, *-handed,** *a.* Niggardly, miserly, penurious. ***close-handedness,** *n.* **close-hauled,** *a.* (*Naut.*) Kept as near as possible to the point from which the wind blows. **close-pent,** *a.* Shut close. **close quarters,** *n.pl.* (*Naut.*) Strong bulkheads formerly erected across a ship for defence against boarders; (*fig.*) direct contact. **to come to close quarters:** To come into direct contact, esp. with an enemy. **a close shave:** A narrow escape. **close-stool,** *n.* A night-stool. **close time,** *n.* The breeding season, during which it is illegal to kill deer and winged game, take certain fish, etc. **close-tongued,** *a.* Reticent, silent. **close-up,** *n.* (*Cinema.*) A view taken with the camera at very close range. **close vowel,** *n.* One pronounced with a small opening of the lips, or with the mouth-cavity contracted. **closely,** *adv.* **closeness,** *n.*

closet (kloz′ ėt) [dim. of O.F. *clos*, as prec.], *n.* A small room for privacy and retirement; a water-closet; (*Am.*) a cupboard. *v.t.* *To shut up; to admit into or receive in a private apartment for consultation, etc. **to be closeted with:** To hold a confidential conversation with. **closet play,** *n.* A play suitable for reading, not acting.

closure (klō′ zhėr) [O.F., from L. *clausūra* (*clausus*, p.p. of *claudere*, to close)], *n.* The act of shutting; the state of being closed; the power of terminating debate in a legislative or deliberative assembly. *v.t.* To apply this power to a debate, speaker, or motion.

clot (klot) [A.-S. *clott*, *clot* (cp. G. *klotz*, CLEAT, CLOD)], *n.* A clod, a lump, a ball; a small coagulated mass of soft or fluid matter, esp. of blood; (*slang*) a silly fellow. *v.t.* To make into clots. *v.i.* To become clotted. **clotted cream,** *n.* Cream produced in clots on new milk when it is simmered; Devonshire cream. **clotty,** *a.*

cloth (kloth, klawth, *pl.* kloths, klaw*thz*) [A.-S. *clāth* (cp. G. *kleid*)], *n.* A woven fabric of wool, hemp, flax, silk, or cotton, used for garments or other coverings (the name of the material is expressed except in the case of wool); a piece of this; a woollen fabric for making clothes; a table-cloth; the dress of a profession, esp. the clerical, from their usually wearing black cloth; (*Theat.*) a curtain, esp. a painted curtain, let up and down between stage and auditorium. **American cloth,** *n.* An enamelled fabric with a surface resembling that of polished leather. **cloth binding,** *n.* Book covers in linen or cotton cloth. **cloth hall,** *n.* A cloth exchange. **cloth-measure,** *n.* The measure by which cloth is sold, in which the yard is divided into quarters and nails. **cloth of gold** or **of silver,** *n.* A fabric of gold or silver threads interwoven with silk or wool. **cloth-shearer,** *n.* One who shears cloth and frees it from superfluous nap. **cloth-worker,** *n.* A maker of cloth. **cloth-yard shaft,** *n.* An arrow a yard long.

clothe (klō*th*) [A.-S. *clāthian* (CLAD is from O. Northum. *clǣthan*)], *v.t.* (*past* **clothed, clad**) To furnish, invest, or cover with or as with clothes. **v.i.* To wear clothes. **clothing,** *n.* Clothes, dress, apparel.

clothes (klō*thz*, klōz), *n.pl.* Garments, dress; bed-clothes. **clothes-basket,** *n.* A basket for linen clothes to be washed. **clothes-brush,** *n.* A brush for removing dust from clothes. **clothes-horse,** *n.* A frame for drying clothes on. **clothes line,** *n.* A line for drying clothes on. ***clothes-man,** *n.* A man who deals in clothes, esp. **old-clothes-man,** in old clothes. **clothes-moth,** *n.* The genus *Tinea*, the larvæ of which are destructive to cloth. **clothes-peg, -pin,** *n.* A cleft peg used to fasten clothes on a line, (*Am.*) clothes-pin. **clothes-press,** *n.* A cupboard for storing clothes. **clothes-prop,** *n.* A pole for supporting a clothes-line. **clothes-wringer,** *n.* A machine for wringing clothes after washing.

clothier (klō′ *thi* ėr) [orig. *clother*], *n.* A manufacturer of cloth; one who deals in cloth or clothing.

cloture (klō′ tūr) [F.], *n.* Closure of debate, the name first proposed for the closure in the House of Commons.

cloud (kloud) [prob. from A.-S. *clūd*, a rounded mass, conn. with CLOD], *n.* A mass of visible vapour condensed into minute drops or vesicles, and floating in the upper regions of the atmosphere; a volume of smoke or dust resmbling a cloud; the dusky veins or markings in marble, precious stones, etc.; a dimness or patchiness in liquid; a kind of light woollen scarf; (*fig.*) a veil which obscures or darkens; obscurity, bewilderment, confusion of ideas; suspicion, trouble; any temporary depression; a great number, a multitude of living creatures, or snow, arrows, etc., moving in a body. *v.t.* To overspread with clouds, to darken; to mark with cloud-like spots; to make gloomy or sullen; to sully, to stain. *v.i.* To grow cloudy. **in the clouds:** Of confused ideas; mystical, unreal; absent-minded. **under a cloud:** In temporary disgrace or misfortune. ***cloud-ascending,** *a.* So high as to reach almost to the clouds. ***cloud-born,** *a.* Born of a cloud. ***cloud-built,** *a.* Visionary, imaginary. **cloud-burst,** *n.* A sudden and heavy fall of rain. **cloud-capt, -capped,** *a.* With summit or summits veiled with clouds; very lofty. **cloud-castle,** *n.* A day dream, a visionary scheme. **cloud-compelling,** *a.* Having power to gather or disperse clouds. **cloud-cuckoo-land,** *n.* A utopia, a fantastic scheme for social, political or economic reform. **cloud-drift,** *n.* Floating, cloudy vapour. **cloud-eclipsed,** *a.* Hidden by clouds. **cloud-rack,** *n.* Shattered cloud. **cloud-scape,** *n.* A view or picture of clouds; picturesque cloud effects. **cloud-wrapt,** *a.* Enveloped in clouds; (*fig.*) abstracted, absent-minded. ***cloud-age,** *n.* Cloudiness; a mass of clouds. **cloudberry,** *n.* A low mountain and moorland shrub, *Rubus chamæmorus*, with strawberry-like fruit. **cloudless,** *a.* Unclouded; clear, bright. **cloudlessly,** *adv.* **cloudlessness,** *n.* **cloudlet,** *n.* A little cloud. **cloudy,** *a.* Consisting of or overspread with clouds; marked with veins or spots; (*fig.*) obscure, confused; dull, gloomy, sullen; wanting in clearness. **cloudily,** *adv.* **cloudiness,** *n.* **cloudwards,** *adv.*

clough (klŭf) [etym. doubtful, cp. CLEUCH], *n.* A ravine; a narrow valley.

clour (klour) [Sc., conn. with Icel. *klōr*], *n.* A heavy bump on the head; a blow on the head. *v.t.* To hit with such a blow.

clout (klout) [A.-S. *clūt* (cogn. with CLOT)], *n.* A piece of cloth, rag, etc., used to patch or mend; a rag; a mark for archers; an iron plate on an axle-tree to keep it from being rubbed; (*colloq.*) a blow with the open hand, esp. on the head. *v.t.* To patch, to mend roughly; to cover with a piece of cloth, etc.; to tip or plate with iron; to join clumsily; to stud or fasten with clout-nails; (*colloq.*) to strike with the open hand. **clout-nail,** *n.* A short nail with a large head for fastening wagon-clouts on, or to stud the soles of heavy boots and shoes. **clouted** (1), *a.* Patched; mended clumsily; studded with clout-nails.

clouted (2), *a.* [CLOTTED, see CLOT].

clove (1) (klōv) [F. *clou*, L. *clavus*, a nail (*clou de girofle*, a clove), prob. assim. in sound to CLOVE (2)], *n.* One of the dried, unexpanded flower-buds of the clove-tree, used as a spice; (*pl.*) a spirituous cordial flavoured with this. **clove-gillyflower** (F. *clou de girofle*, see above), **-pink,** *n.* Any sweet-scented double variety of *Dianthus caryophyllus*. **clove-tree,** *n.* The tree, *Caryophyllus aromaticus*.

clove (2) (klōv) [A.-S. *clufu* (from *cluf-*, cogn. with *clēofan*, to CLEAVE (2))], *n.* A small bulb forming one part of a compound bulb, as in garlic, the shallot, etc.

clove (3) [CLEAVE], *past.* **clove-hitch** (klōv′ hich), *n.* (*Naut.*) A safe kind of rope-fastening round a spar or another rope. **cloven,** *a.* Divided into two parts; cleft. **cloven-footed, -hoofed,** *a.* Having the hoof divided in the centre, as have the ruminants; bisulcate. **the cloven hoof:** An emblem of Pan or the Devil; an indication of guile or devilish design.

clover (klō′ vėr) [A.-S. *clāfre* (cp. Dut. *klaver*, Dan. *klöver*, G. *klee*)], *n.* A trefoil used for fodder. **to be** or **live in clover:** To be in enjoyable circumstances; to live luxuriously. **cloverleaf,** *n.* A traffic device in which one crossing road passes over the other and the connecting carriage-ways, having no abrupt turns, make the shape of a four-leaved clover.

clown (kloun) [cp. Icel. *klunni*, CLUMP or CLOT], *n.* A rustic, a countryman; a clumsy, awkward lout; a rough, ill-bred person; a buffoon in a circus or pantomime. *v.i.* To play silly jokes, to act the buffoon. **clownery,** *n.* **clownish,** *a.* **clownishly,** *adv.* **clownishness,** *n.* **clownswort,** *n.* (*Bot.*) The hedge stachys, *Stachys sylvatica*, used in herbalism.

cloy (kloi) [perh. from ACCLOY; or from O.F. *cloyer* (F. *clouer*), to nail], *v.t.* *To spike a gun; *to prick a horse in shoeing; *to wound with a sharp weapon; *to fill up; to satiate, to glut; to tire with sweetness, richness, or excess. ***cloyless,** *a.* That does not or cannot cloy. ***cloyment,** *n.* Surfeit, satiety.

club (1) (klŭb) [M.E. *clubbe, clobbe*, prob. from Icel. *klubba, klumba*, a club, a cudgel], *n.* A piece of wood with one end thicker and heavier than the other, used as a weapon; a stick bent and (usually) weighted at the end for driving a ball; one of the four suits at cards (in England denoted by a trefoil); a round, solid mass. *v.t.* (*past & p.p.* **clubbed**) To beat with a club; to gather into a clump. **club-foot,** *n.* A short deformed foot. **club-footed,** *a.* **club-grass,** *n.* Club-jointed grass of the genus *Corynephorus*. **club-haul,** *v.t.* (*Naut.*) To tack (a ship) by letting go the lee anchor as soon as the wind is out of the sails in order to escape from a lee-shore. **club-headed,** *a.* Having a club-shaped head or top. **club-law,** *n.* Government by force. **club-moss,** *n.* Species of moss belonging to the genus *Lycopodium*, with seed-vessels pointing straight upwards. **club-shaped,** *a.* Clavate, claviform. **club-rush,** *n.* (*Bot.*) Name of various species of the genus *Scirpus*. **to club the musket:** To seize by the barrel and use it as a club. **clubbing,** *n.* The action of the verb; a disease of plants of the *Brassica* (cabbage) tribe in which the lower part of the stem becomes swollen and mis-shapen owing to the attacks of larvæ.

club (2) (klŭb) [as prec.], *n.* An association of persons combined for some common object, as of temporary residence, social intercourse, literature, politics, sport, etc., governed by self-imposed regulations; the house or building in which such an association meets; the body of members collectively; share or proportion contributed to a common stock; joint charge or effort. *v.t.* To gather into a clump; to contribute for a common object; (*Mil.*) to work (troops) into an inextricable mass. *v.i.* To join (together) for a common object. **club car,** *n.* (*Am.*) A railway-coach designed like a lounge, usu. with a bar. **club-house,** *n.* The house occupied by a club, or in which it holds its meetings; the establishment maintained by the members of a social or sports club, at which they meet, dine, and lodge temporarily. **clubland,** *n.* The district round St. James's and Pall Mall where the principal London clubs are situated. **club-man,** *n.* A member of a club. **club-room,** *n.* A room in which a club or society meets. **clubbable,** *a.* Having the qualities necessary for club life; sociable. **clubber,** *n.* A member of a club; one who uses a club. **clubdom,** *n.*

cluck (klŭk) [A.-S. *cloccian*, imit.], *n.* The guttural call of a hen; any similar sound. *v.i.* To utter the cry of a hen to her chickens. *v.t.* To call, as a hen does her chickens.

clue (kloo) [CLEW], *n.* A ball of thread; a thread to guide a person in a labyrinth, like that given by Ariadne to Theseus to guide him back through the labyrinth at Crete; anything of a material or mental nature that serves as guide, direction, or hint for the solution of a problem or mystery. **I haven't a clue:** I have no idea whatever; I am quite in the dark. **clueless,** *a.*

clumber (klŭm′ bėr) [*Clumber*, Duke of Newcastle's seat, Notts.], *n.* A variety of spaniel.

clump (klŭmp) [cp. CLUB (Icel. *klubba, klumba*), also G. *klumpen*, Dut. *klomp*], *n.* A thick cluster of trees, shrubs, or flowers; a thick piece of leather fastened on to a boot-sole; a heavy blow. *v.t.* To tread in a heavy and clumsy fashion; to form or gather into a clump or clumps. **clump-boot,** *n.* A heavy boot for rough wear. **clumpy,** *a.*

clumsy (klŭm′ zi) [M.E. *clumsed*, p.p. of *clumsen*, to benumb (cp. CLAM, CLAMMY)], *a.* Awkward, ungainly, ill-constructed; rough, rude, tactless. **clumsily,** *adv.* **clumsiness,** *n.*

clunch (klŭnch) [prob. var. of CLUMP (cp. BUMP, BUNCH; HUMP, HUNCH)], *n.* A lump; (*Geol.*) the lower and harder beds of the Upper Chalk formation, occasionally used for building purposes; a local name for fire-clay occurring under a coal seam.

clung, *past & p.p.* [CLING].

Cluniac (kloo′ ni ăk) [med. L. *Cluniacus*, from *Cluny*], *n.* One of a reformed branch of Benedictines founded at Cluny, Saône-et-Loire, France, in the 10th cent. *a.* Pertaining to this order.

clupeoid (kloo′ pė oid) [L. *clupea*, a small river-fish, -OID], *n.* (*Ichthyol.*) A fish belonging to the *Clupeoidæ*, a division of fishes, including the *Clupidæ*, or herring family, and related families. *a.* Herring-like. **clupeoidean** (-oi′ dė ăn), *a.* and *n.* **clupeiform** (kloo′ pė i fôrm), *a.*

cluster (klŭs′ tėr) [A.-S. *clyster* (prob. from the same root as CLOT)], *n.* A number of things of the same kind growing or joined together; a bunch; a number of persons or things gathered into or situated in a close body; a group, a crowd. *v.i.* To come or to grow into clusters. *v.t.* To bring or cause to come into a cluster or clusters. **clustered column, pillar,** *n.* (*Arch.*) A pier consisting of several columns or shafts clustered together.

clutch (1) (klŭch) [M.E. *cloche, cloke*, a claw (A.-S. *clyccan*, to bring together, clench)], *n.* A snatch, a grip, a grasp; the paw or talon of a rapacious animal; the hands; a coupling for shafting used to transmit motion; a gripping device; (*Naut.*) the throat of an anchor; a contrivance for connecting and disconnecting machinery; (*pl.*) claws, tyrannical power. *v.t.* To seize, clasp, or grip with the hand; to snatch. **clutch shaft,** *n.* (*Motor.*) A shaft which engages or disengages a clutch. **cone clutch,** *n.* (*Mech.*) A friction clutch consisting of a cone sliding into a conical cavity in the engine flywheel. **disc, plate clutch,** *n.* (*Mach.*) A clutch which operates as a result of friction between the surfaces of discs.

clutch (2) (klŭch) [var. of obs. *clekch*, from *cleck*, to hatch], *n.* A sitting (of eggs); a brood (of chickens).

clutter (klŭt′ ėr) [var. of *clotter*, freq. of CLOT], *v.i.* To make a confused noise; to bustle. *n.* A confused noise; bustle, confusion; a mess, confusion. **to clutter up:** To fill untidily.

cly (klī) [cogn. with CLAW], *v.t.* To seize; to get hold of; to steal. *n.* Something stolen. **cly-faker,** *n.* A pickpocket.

clypeus (klip′ ė ŭs) [L., a shield], *n.* (*Zool.*) The shield-like part of an insect's head, which joins the labrum. **clypeal, clypeate, -eiform,** *a.* **clypeo-,** *comb. form.* (*Zool.*).

clyster (klis′ tėr) [L., from Gr. *klustēr* (*kluzein*, to wash out)], *n.* (*Med.*) An enema; an injection into the rectum to promote discharge of the bowels, to administer nourishment, or for various purposes. **clyster-pipe,** *n.* A pipe used for injections; the nozzle of an enema syringe; *(*fig.*) an apothecary.

cnida (nī′ dȧ) [Gr. *knidē*, a nettle], *n.* (*pl.*) **-dæ**) The stinging-cell of the *Cœlenterata* (jelly-fish, etc.). **cnido-,** *comb. form* (*Zool.*).

co- [L., the form of *cum* used before vowels, etc.], *pref.* CUM-, with, together, jointly, mutually;

joint, mutual; as in *coacervate, coalesce, co-operate; coeternal, coefficient, coequal; coheir, co-mate, copartner.*

coacervate (kō ăs' er vāt) [L. *coacervāre* (co-, *acervus*, heap)], *a.* Heaped up; accumulated; (*Bot.*) clustered. **coacervation** (-vā' shŭn), *n.*

coach (kōch) [F. *coche*, Magyar *kocsi*, belonging to *Kocz*, village in Hungary], *n.* A large, close, four-wheeled, double-seated vehicle, used for purposes of state, for pleasure, or (with regular fares) for travelling; a railway carriage; a tutor who prepares for examinations; one who trains a crew for a boat-race or other athletic contest; (*Naut.*) a room near the stern in a large ship of war; a long-distance omnibus; (*Austral.*) a decoy. *v.t.* To prepare for an examination; to train; to instruct or advise in preparation for any event. *v.i.* To travel in a coach; to read with a tutor. **coach-box,** *n.* The seat on which the driver of a coach sits. **coachee,** *n.* A coachman, a driver. ***coach-fellow,** *n.* A horse yoked in the same carriage with another; (*fig.*) a comrade, a mate. **coachful,** *n.* As many as will fill a coach. **coach-house,** *n.* An outhouse to keep a coach or carriage in. **coachman,** *n.* The driver of a coach; a livery servant who drives a carriage; (*Angling*) a kind of artificial fly. **coachmanship,** *n.* **coach-office,** *n.* The booking-office of a stage coach. **coach-whip,** *n.* A whip used by a driver of a coach; a harmless North American tree-snake, *Herpetodryas flagelliformis.* **slowcoach,** *n.* (*fig.*) A dull person, a laggard.

coact (kō ăkt') [L. *coactus*, p.p. of *coagere, cōgere*, to compel (co-, *agere*, to drive)], *v.t.* To compel, to control. **v.i.* To act in concert. **coaction,** *n.* ***co-active,** *a.* Having a restraining or impelling power; acting together or in concert. ***coactively,** *adv.*

coadapted (kō ȧ dăp' tėd), *a.* Adapted to one another; mutually adapted or suited. **coadaptation** (tā' shun), *n.*

coadjacent (kō ȧd jā' sėnt), *a.* Mutually near, contiguous. **coadjacence, -ency,** *n.*

coadjutor (kō ȧd joo' tȯr) [L., *coadjūtor* (*juvāre*, to help)], *n.* An assistant, a helper, a colleague. **coadjutorship,** *n.* **coadjutrix,** *n.* A female coadjutor.

coadunate (kō ăd' ū nāt) [L. *coadūnāre* (co-, AD-, *unus*, one)], *a.* (*Physiol.*) Joined together, connate; (*Bot.*) adnate. **coadunation** (-nā' shŭn), *n.*

coagent (kō ā' jėnt), *n.* One who acts with. *a.* Acting with. **coagency,** *n.*

coagulate (kō ăg' ū lāt) [from obs. a. *coagulate*, coagulated, or directly from L. *coāgulātus*, p.p. of *coāgulāre*, from *coāgulum*, dim. n. of *coagere* (co-, *agere*, to drive, impel)], *v.t.* To cause to curdle; to convert from a fluid into a curd-like mass. *v.i.* To become curdled. **coagulant,** *n.* A substance which causes coagulation. **coagulation** (-lā' shŭn), *n.* **coagulator,** *n.* **coagulometer** (-lom' ė tėr) [METER], *n.* **coagulum,** *n.* (*pl.* **-la**) A coagulated mass; a coagulant; (*Med.*) a blood-clot.

coaita (kō ī' tȧ) [Braz. *coatá*], *n.* The red-faced spider-monkey.

coak (kōk) [It. *cocca*, a notch], *n.* (*Carp.*) A dowel let into the end of a piece of wood to be joined to another; (*Naut.*) the metal pin-hole in a sheave. *v.t.*

coal (kōl) [A.-S. *col* (cp. Dut. *kool*, Icel. and Swed. *kol*, G. *kohle*)], *n.* A black solid opaque carbonaceous substance of vegetable origin, obtained from the strata usually below the surface, and used for fuel; a piece of wood or other combustible substance, ignited, burning, or charred; a cinder. *v.t.* To supply a ship with coals. *v.i.* To take in a supply of coals. **to blow a coal:** To fan a quarrel; to stir up strife. **to carry coals:** To put up with insults. **to carry coals to Newcastle:** To do anything superfluous or unnecessary. **to haul over the coals:** To call to account; to reprimand. **to heap coals of fire:** To return good for evil. **coal-backer,** *n.* A coal-porter. **coal-bed, -seam,** *n.* A stratum of or containing coal. **coal-black,** *a.* As black as coal; jet-black. **coal-box,** *n.* A coal-scuttle; (*slang*) a chorus. **coal-brand,** *n.* Smut in wheat. **coal-brass,** *n.* The iron pyrites of the coal-measures. **coal-bunker,** *n.* (*Naut.*) A receptacle for coals (usu. in a steamship). **coal-dust,** *n.* Very small coals. **coal-factor,** *n.* A middle-man between colliery-owners and customers, formerly between colliery-owners or shippers and coal-sellers. **coal-field,** *n.* (*Geol.*) A district where coal abounds. **coal-fish,** *n.* The black cod, *Gadus carbonarius.* **coal-flap, -plate,** *n.* An iron cover for the opening in a pavement, etc., for putting coal into a cellar. **coal-gas,** *n.* (*Chem.*) Impure carburetted hydrogen obtained from coal and used for lighting and heating. **coal-heaver,** *n.* One employed in carrying, loading, or discharging coals. **coal-hole,** *n.* A small cellar for keeping coals. **coal-master,** *n.* One who works a coal-mine. **coal-measures,** *n.pl.* (*Geol.*) The upper division of the carboniferous system. **coal-mine,** *n.* A mine whence coal is obtained. **coal-miner,** *n.* **coal-naphtha,** *n.* Naphtha produced as a by-product in the distillation of coal-gas from coal. **coal-oil,** *n.* (*Am.*) Petroleum. **coal-owner,** *n.* Owner of a colliery. **coal-pit,** *n.* A coal-mine; (*Am.*) a place where charcoal is burnt. **coal-plant,** *n.* (*Geol.*) A plant whose remains form coal; a plant of the carboniferous age. **coal-screen,** *n.* A large screen or sifting-frame for separating large and small coal. **coal-scuttle,** *n.* A utensil for holding coals for present use. **coal-scuttle bonnet,** *n.* A poke-bonnet with a projecting front, like an inverted coal-scuttle. **coal-ship,** *n.* A ship employed in carrying coals. **coal-tar,** *n.* Tar produced in the destructive distillation of bituminous coal. **coal-tit** [COALMOUSE]. **coal-vase,** *n.* (*vulg.*) A coal-scuttle. **coal-whipper,** *n.* A man or machine for raising coal out of the hold of a ship. **coaling station,** *n.* A port where steamships may obtain coal, esp. one established by a government for the supply of coal to warships. **coalless,** *a.* **coaly,** *a.*

coalesce (kō ȧ les') [L. *coalescere* (co-, *alescere*, incept. of *alere*, to nourish)], *v.i.* To grow together; to unite into masses or groups spontaneously; to combine; to fuse into one; to form a coalition. **coalescence,** *n.* Concretion. **coalescent,** *a.* **coalition** (-lish' ŭn), *n.* A union of separate bodies into one body or mass; a combination of persons, parties, or states, having different interests. **coalition government,** *n.* (*Pol.*) A government in which two or more parties of varying politics unite for a common policy. **coalitionist,** *n.*

coalmouse, colemouse (kōl' mous) [A.-S. *colmāse* (*col*, coal, *māse*; cp. O.H.G. *meisa*, W.G. *maisa*, a bird)], *n.* A small dark bird, called also the coal-tit or coal-titmouse.

coamings (kō' mings) [etym. doubtful], *n.pl.* (*Naut.*) The raised borders round hatches, etc., for keeping water from pouring into the hold.

coaptation (kō ăp tā' shŭn) [L. *coaptātio ōnem*, from *coaptāre*], *n.* The adaptation of parts to each other.

coarctate (kō ark' tāt) [L. *coarctātus*, p.p. of *coarctāre* (*artāre*, from *artus*, confined)], *a.* (*Bot. and Ent.*) Pressed together. **coarctation** (-tā' shŭn), *n.*

coarse (kôrs) [prob. from *in course*, ordinary (cp. MEAN, PLAIN)], *a.* Common; of average quality; of inferior quality; large in size or rough in texture; rude, rough, vulgar; unpolished, unrefined, indelicate; indecent. **coarse-fibred, -grained,** *a.* (*pers. or things*) Having a coarse grain; unrefined. **coarsely,** *adv.* **coarsen,** *v.t.* To make coarse; *v.i.* To grow or become coarse. **coarseness,** *n.* **coarsish,** *a.*

coast (kôst) [O.F. *coste* (F. *côte*), L. *costa*, a rib, a side], *n.* That part of the border of a country which is washed by the sea; the seashore; a toboggan-slide; a swift rush downhill on cycle or motor-car, without using motive power or applying brakes; *a side; *a side of meat; *border, limit; tract, region. *v.t.* To sail by or near to; to keep close to;

*to accost. *v.i* To sail near or in sight of the shore; to sail from port to port in the same country; to slide down snow or ice on a toboggan or sleigh; to descend an incline on a cycle or a mechanically propelled vehicle without applying motive power or brakes. **the coast is clear:** The road is free; the danger is over. **coastal,** *a.* Of, pertaining to, or bordering on a coast-line. **coaster,** *n.* A coasting-vessel. **coastguard,** *n.* (*Naut.*) One of a body of men under the Board of Trade who watch the coast to save those in danger, give warning of wrecks, and prevent the illegal landing of persons and goods. **coasting,** *a.* Pertaining to the coast; that coasts. **coasting-trade,** *n.* Trade between the ports of the same country. **coasting-vessel,** *n.* **coast-line,** *n.* **coastlander,** *n.* A dweller on the coast. **coastward, -s,** *adv.* **coastwise,** *adv.*

coat (kōt) [O.F. *cote* (F. *cotte*), med. L. *cota, cotta,* O.H.G. *chozza,* fem. *choz, chozzo,* a coarse, shaggy stuff or a garment of this], *n.* An upper outer garment with sleeves, worn by men; *a petticoat; a coat-like mantle for women; the hair or fur of any beast; the natural external covering of an animal; any integument, tunic, or covering; a layer of any substance covering and protecting another. *v.t.* To cover; to overspread with a layer of anything. **to trail one's coat** or **coat-tails:** To invite attack. **to turn one's coat:** To change sides, hence **turn-coat,** *n.* **great-coat,** *n.* A coat worn out of doors over another. **red-coat,** *n.* The old uniform coat of the British soldier; a soldier. **coat-armour,** *n.* (*Her.*) A loose vestment embroidered with armorial bearings, worn by knights over their armour; heraldic bearings. ***coat-card,** *n.* One of the figured cards in the pack, so called from the coats or dresses in which they are represented (now **court-card**). **coat-hanger,** *n.* A utensil for hanging up coats, dresses, etc. **coat of arms,** *n.* (*Her.*) A herald's tabard; an escutcheon or shield of arms; armorial bearings. **coat of mail,** *n.* Armour worn on the upper part of the body, consisting of iron rings or scales fastened on a stout linen or leather jacket. **coatee** (kō tē′), *n.* A short-tailed coat fitting tight to the body. **coating,** *n.* A covering, layer, or integument; the act of covering; a substance spread over as a cover or defence; cloth for coats. **coatless,** *a.*

coati (kō a′ ti) [Braz. (*coa,* a cincture, *tim,* a nose)], *n.* A racoon-like carnivorous animal with a long, flexible snout, from South America; also a Central American and Mexican species.

coax (kōks) [formerly *cokes,* from *cokes,* a fool, a gull], *v.t.* To persuade by fondling or flattery; to wheedle, to cajole. *v.i.* To practise cajolery in order to persuade. **coaxer,** *n.* **coaxingly,** *adv.*

coaxal, -ial (kō ăk′ sȧl, -si ȧl), *a.* Having a joint axis. **co-axial cable,** *n.* (*Elect.*) A cable with a central conductor within an outer tubular conductor.

cob (kob) [etym. doubtful], *n.* A lump or ball of anything; a spider, from its round body (cp. COBWEB); a short stout horse for riding; a kind of wicker basket; a cobnut; a sea-gull; a cob-swan; *a Spanish dollar; a kind of breakwater; the top or head of anything; the spike of Indian corn; a mixture of clay and straw used for building walls in the west of England. *v.t.* To punish by flogging on the breech with a belt or flat piece of wood. ***cob-loaf,** *n.* A small round loaf; (*fig.*) a coarse, rough, loutish fellow. **cobstone,** *n.* A rounded stone, a cobble. **cob-swan,** *n.* A male swan. **cob-wall,** *n.* A wall built of mud or clay, mixed with straw. **cobby,** *a.*

cobalt (kō′ bawlt) [prob. from G. *kobold,* a mine-demon, because the mineral was at first troublesome to the miners], *n.* A reddish-grey, or greyish-white, brittle, hard metallic element. **cobalt-bloom,** *n.* (*Min.*) Acicular arsenate of cobalt; erythrite. **cobalt-blue,** *n.* A pigment of alumina and cobalt. **cobaltic** (kō bawl′ tik), *a.* **cobaltiferous** (-tif′ ėr ŭs) [-FEROUS], *a.* **cobaltous,** *a.* **cobalto-,** *comb. form.*

cobber, *n.* (*Austral. slang*) A pal, a chum.

cobble (1) (kob′ ėl) [etym. unknown], *v.t.* To mend or patch as shoes; to make or do clumsily. **cobbler,** *n.* One who mends shoes; a mender or patcher; a clumsy workman; (*Am.*) a cooling drink of wine, sugar, lemon, and ice; (*Austral.*) a dirty sheep at shearing-time. **cobbler's wax,** *n.* A resinous substance used for waxing thread.

cobble (2) (kob′ ėl) [COB], *n.* A rounded stone or pebble used for paving; a roundish lump of coal. *v.t.* To pave with cobbles. **cobstone,** *n.* A rounded stone, a cobble.

cobbra (kob′ rȧ) [Austral. abor.], *n.* The skull, the head.

Cobdenism (kob′ dėn izm), *n.* (*Pol. Econ.*) The doctrines of Richard Cobden (1804–65), especially Free Trade, pacifism, and non-intervention. **Cobdenite,** *n.* An adherent of Cobdenism.

co-belligerent (kō bė lij′ ėr ėnt), *a.* Waging war jointly with another. *n.* One who joins another in waging war.

coble (kō′ bėl) [W. *ceubal* (*ceuo,* to hollow or excavate)], *n.* A flat, square-sterned fishing-boat with a lug-sail and six oars.

cobnut (kob′ nŭt), *n.* A variety of the cultivated hazel; an old children's game.

cobra (kō′ brȧ), **cobra de capello** (dē kȧ pel′ ō) [Port., snake of (with) a hood], *n.* A viperine snake, *Naja tripudians,* from the East Indies, which distends the skin of the neck into a kind of hood when excited.

cobstone [COBBLE (2)].

coburg (kō′ bėrg) [town in Germany], *n.* A loaf of bread with one or more cuts on top that spread out when baking; a thin worsted fabric.

cobweb (kob′ web) [COB (A.-S. *-coppe,* found in *attorcoppe,* poison-spider), WEB (COB, a spider, may, however, be from COBWEB)], *n.* The web or net spun by a spider for its prey; the material or a thread of this; anything flimsy and worthless; (*fig.*) a fine-spun argument; old musty rubbish. *a.* Light, thin, flimsy, worthless. **cobwebbed,** *a.* Covered with or full of cobwebs; (*Bot.*) covered with thick, matted pubescence. **cobwebby,** *a.* **to blow away the cobwebs:** (*fig.*) To refresh oneself in the open air.

coca (kō′ kȧ) [Sp., from Peruv. *cuca*], *n.* The dried leaf of *Erythroxylon coca,* a Peruvian plant chewed as a narcotic stimulant; the plant itself.

cocaine (kō kā′ in, kō kān′) [from prec., -INE], *n.* An alkaloid contained in coca leaves, used medicinally and as a local anæsthetic. **cocainize,** *v.t.* **cocainization** (-zā′ shŭn), *n.* **cocainism,** *n.* **cocainomania** (-mā′ ni ȧ), *n.* A morbid craving for cocaine; a form of insanity resulting from cocainism.

coccagee (kok ȧ jē′) [Ir. *cac a' ghéidh,* goose-dung], *n.* A kind of cider apple.

coccidiosis (kok sid i ō′ sis), *n.* A parasitic disease of the intestines, liver, etc., found in rabbits, fowls, etc.

cocciferous (kok sif′ ėr ŭs) [L. *coccum,* berry, -FEROUS], *a.* Bearing berries.

coccolite (kok′ ō līt) [Gr. *kokkos,* grain, -LITE], *n.* (*Min.*) A white or green variety of pyroxene.

coccolith (kok′ ō lith) [Gr. *kokkos,* grain, berry, -LITH], *n.* (*Biol.*) The name given by Huxley to minute bodies dredged in Atlantic ooze, and prob. the joints of an alga.

cocculus (kok′ ū lŭs) [mod. L., dim. of foll.], *n.* (*Bot.*) A genus of menispermaceous climbing plants. **cocculus indicus,** *n.* The fruit of *Anamirta cocculus,* an Eastern climber; it is an acrid narcotic, and is said to be used to adulterate beer.

coccus (kok′ ŭs) [mod. L., from Gr. *kokkos,* grain], *n.* (*Ent.*) A genus of hemipterous insects, including many forms hurtful to plants; (*Bot.*) one of the dry one-seeded carpels into which a fruit breaks up; a spore mother-cell in cryptogams. **coccoid,** *a.*

coccyx (kok′ siks) [L., from Gr. *kokkux -ugos*, the cuckoo (from the resemblance to a cuckoo's bill)], *n.* (*Anat.*) The lower solid portion of the vertebral column, the homologue in man of the tail of the lower vertebrates. **coccyg-, coccygeo-,** *comb. form* (*Anat.*). **coccygeal** (kok sij′ ė ål).

cochin-china (koch′ in chī′ nȧ), *n.* A breed of domestic fowls from Cochin-China.

cochineal (koch′ i nēl) [F. *cochenille*, Sp. *cochinilla*, L. *coccineus, coccinus* (*coccum*, a berry, scarlet)], *n.* A dye-stuff made from the dried bodies of the female cochineal insect, used in dyeing and in the manufacture of scarlet and carmine pigments. **cochineal-fig,** *n.* The cactus, *Opuntia cochinellifera*, on which the cochineal insect is principally found. **cochineal insect,** *n.* The insect, *Coccus cacti*, from which this dye is obtained.

cochlea (kok′ lė ȧ) [L., from Gr. *kochlias*, a snail, a screw, *kochlon*, a shell-fish], *n.* (*Anat.*) The anterior spiral division of the internal ear. **cochlean,** *a.* **cochlear,** *a.* (*Bot.*) Used of a form of æstivation, in which one large part covers all the others. **cochlearia** (-âr′ i ȧ), *n.* (*Bot.*) A genus of plants including the horse-radish and common scurvy-grass. **cochleariform** (-âr′ i fôrm), *a.* **cochleate, -ated,** *a.* Circular, spiral; (*Bot.*) twisted like a snail-shell.

cock (1) (kok) [A.-S. *cocc* (cp. F. *coq*), low L. *coccum*, acc. of *coccus*, onomat. (cp. Gr. *kokku*, cuckoo)], *n.* The male of birds, particularly of domestic fowls; a male salmon; a vane in the form of a cock; a weathercock; *cock-crowing; *a leader, a chief; a good fellow; a short spout, a tap, a valve for regulating the flow through a spout or pipe; (*vulg.*) the penis; the hammer of a gun or pistol, which, striking against a piece of flint or a percussion-cap, produces a spark and explodes the charge; the gnomon of a dial; the needle of a balance; the piece which covers the balance in a clock or watch. *v.t.* To set erect; to cause to stick up; to set (the hat) jauntily on one side; to turn up (the nose), to turn (the eye) in an impudent or knowing fashion; to raise the trigger of. *v.i.* To stick or stand up, to project; to hold up the head; to strut, to swagger, to bluster. **to cock one's eye:** To glance knowingly, to wink. **to cock a snook:** To put the thumb to the nose with the fingers spread out. **cock-a-doodle-doo:** The crow of the domestic cock; a nursery name for the bird. **old cock:** (*colloq.*) A familiar form of address. **to live like fighting cocks:** To have the best food and plenty of it. **cock-a-hoop** [orig. doubtful]: Strutting like a cock; triumphant, exultant; exultantly, with crowing and boastfulness, uppishly. **cock-and-bull:** A term applied to silly, exaggerated stories or canards. **cock-bill,** *v.t.* (*Naut.*) To hang (the anchor) from the cathead before letting go. **a-cock-bill:** With the anchor in this position. **cock-brained,** *a.* Rash, giddy, flighty. **cock-crow, cock-crowing,** *n.* The crow of a cock; early dawn. **cock-eye,** *n.* (*slang*) An eye that squints. **cock-eyed,** *a.* (*slang*) Having squinting eyes; irregular, ill-arranged; askew; eccentric. **cock-fight, -fighting,** *n.* A battle or match of game-cocks. **cock-horse,** *n.* A stick with a horse's head at the end, on which children ride. **a-cock-horse,** *adv.* On horseback; in an elevated position; (*fig.*) on the high horse. *a.* Mounted, as on horse-back; (*fig.*) proud, exultant, upstart. **cock-laird,** *n.* A landed proprietor who cultivates his own estate. **cock-lobster,** *n.* A male lobster. **cockloft,** *n.* An upper loft, a garret. ***cock-master,** *n.* An owner or breeder of game-cocks. **cock-match,** *n.* A cock-fight. **cock-nest,** *n.* One built by a male bird, as the wren, for roosting. **cock of the north,** *n.* The brambling. **cock of the walk,** *n.* A masterful person; a leader, a chief. **cock of the wood,** *n.* The capercailzie. **cock-pit,** *n.* A pit or area where game-cocks fight; (*Naut.*) a part of the lower deck of a man-of-war, used as a hospital in action; (*Aviat.*) that portion of the fuselage of an aircraft where the pilot and crew (if any) are accommodated. **cock-pit of Europe:** Belgium. **cock-robin,** *n.* A male robin; *(*slang*) an easy-going fellow. **cockscomb:** The comb of a cock; a fool's cap; the yellow-rattle, *Rhinanthus cristagalli*; a garden plant, *Celosia cristata* (also applied to other plants and shrubs) [see also COXCOMB]. **cock's-foot,** *n.* A pasture-grass, *Dactylis glomerata.* **cock's-head,** *n.* Sainfoin, from the shape of the pod. **cock-shot, -shy,** *n.* A rough-and-ready target for sticks or stones; a throw at a mark; a butt. **cock-shut** [prob. COCK, SHOOT, a glade suitable for catching woodcocks in nets], *n.* Night-fall. **cock-shy** [COCK-SHOT]. **cock-sparrow,** *n.* A male sparrow; a pert presuming fellow. **cock-spur,** *n.* The spur of a cock; (*Angling*) a kind of caddis; various plants. **cockspur-burner,** *n.* A gas-burner pierced with three holes. **cockspur-hawthorn, -thorn,** *n.* A shrub, *Cratægus crusgalli*, from North America. **cock-sure,** *a.* Perfectly sure; absolutely certain; self-confident, arrogantly certain. **cocksurely,** *adv.* **cocksureness,** *n.* **cockish,** *a.* [COCKY].

cock (2) (kok) [from prec. v.], *n.* The act of turning or sticking anything upward; the turn so given, as of a hat, a nose, a knowing turn of the eye, etc. **cocked-hat:** A pointed triangular hat; *a hat with the brim turned up. **knocked into a cocked hat:** Doubled up in a fight; thunder-struck, amazed; utterly discomfited.

cock (3) (kok) [cp. Dan. *kok*, a heap, Icel. *kokkr*, a lump, a ball], *n.* A small conical pile of hay. *v.t.* To put into cocks.

cock (4) (kok) [M.E. *cog, cogge*, O.F. *coque, cogue*], *n.* A small boat. **cock-boat,** *n.* A small ship's boat.

cockabondy (kok ȧ bon′ di) [W. *coch a bon ddu*, 'red with black trunk'], *n.* (*Angling*) An artificial fly of a fancy kind.

cock-a-bully (kok′ ȧ bul i) [Maori *kopapu*], *n.* A variety of New Zealand fish.

cockade (kŏ kād′) [F. *coquarde*, saucy, from *coq* (cp. COCK (1))], *n.* A knot of ribbons worn in the hat as a badge; a rosette worn in the hat by the male servants of naval and military officers, etc. **cockaded,** *a.*

cockaigne (kŏ kān′) [O.F. *coquaigne* (F. *cocagne*), perh. from *coquer*, to cook, or conn, with G. *kuchen*, cake], *n.* A fabled country of luxury and idleness; (*punningly*) cockneydom; London.

cock-a-leekie [COCKY-LEEKY].

cockalorum (kok ȧ lôr′ ŭm) [COCK (1)], *n.* A self-important little man; a game of leap-frog in which one side presents a chain of backs for the others to jump upon.

cockatoo (kok ȧ too′) [Malay *kakatūa*], *n.* A large crested parrot (usually white) from the Indian Archipelago and Australia. **cockatoo fence,** *n.* (*Austral.*) A fence made of logs. **cockatoo grass,** *n.* Pasture grass frequented by cockatoos. **cockatiel** (kok′ ȧ tēl), *n.* A small cockatoo or parrot.

cockatrice (kok′ ȧ trīs, -tris) [O.F. *cocatrice*, late L. *caucātrix*, the treader (trans. of Gr. *ichneumōn*, from *ichneuein*, to trace)], *n.* The basilisk; *(*fig.*) anything deadly; (*Her.*) a cock with a serpent's tail.

cockchafer (kok′ chā fėr), *n.* A large brown beetle, *Melolontha vulgaris*, that makes a whirring noise in flying.

cocker (1) (kok′ ėr) [etym. doubtful; perh. from COCK (1) (in allusion to the call of a hen to her chicken); cp. M.Dan. *kokre*, to keep on calling], *v.t.* To pamper, to fondle, to indulge. **cocker spaniel,** *n.* A small spaniel used in shooting snipe, etc.

Cocker (2) (kok′ ėr) [Edward *Cocker* (1631–75), a teacher and arithmetician], *n.* **according to Cocker,** *adv.* Properly, correctly.

cockerel (kok′ ėr ėl), *n.* A young cock; (*slang*) a spirited youth.

***cocket** (kok′ ėt) [perh. corr. of L. *quo quietus est*, 'by which he is quit,' at the end of the document], *n.* (*Law*) A custom-house seal; a customs' receipt for duty on exported goods; the entry-office in the custom house.

cockie-leckie [COCKY-LEEKY].

cockle (1) (kok' ĕl) [A.-S. *coccel*], *n.* The corn-cockle or darnel; an unidentified weed, the lolium or tares of the Bible; (*Geol.*) schorl (considered useless). **cockle-burr,** *n.*

cockle (2) (kok' ĕl) [F. *coquille*, a shell, L. *conchylia*, Gr. *konchulion*, dim. of *konchē*, a mussel], *n.* A bivalve belonging to the molluscous genus *Cardium*, esp. *C. edule*; its ribbed shell; a shallow skiff. **cockle-boat,** *n.* A small and shallow skiff. **cockle-hat,** *n.* A pilgrim's hat bearing a shell. **cockle-shell,** *n.* The shell of any species of *Cardium*, worn as the badge of a pilgrim; (*fig.*) a small boat. **cockles of the heart:** The feelings.

cockle (3) (kok' ĕl) [F. *coquiller*, to blister, to pucker], *v.i.* To pucker up. *v.t.* To curl, pucker up, crease, or make to bulge. *n.* A pucker, crease, or wrinkle (on paper). **cockly,** *a.* (*prov.*).

***cockle** (4) (kok' ĕl) [etym. doubtful; perh. from Dut. *kākel*, G. *kachel*, a stove-tile], *n.* A heating-stove with a kind of radiator, also called **cockle-stove**; the furnace of an oast-house, also called **cockle-oast.**

cockney (kok' ni) [M.E. *cokeney* (*coken*, gen. pl., *ey*, A.-S. *aeg*), a cock's egg, a term applied to small yolkless eggs, occasionally laid by fowls; hence applied to a foolish or effeminate person, a townsman], *n.* A native of London (traditionally, a person born within sound of the bells of Saint-Mary-le-Bow, Cheapside); the London accent; one who speaks with it; a city resident. *a.* Pertaining to a cockney. **cockneydom,** *n.* **cockneyese** (-ēz'), *n.* **cockneyfy,** *v.t.* **cockneyish,** *a.* **cockneyism,** *n.* **cockneyize,** *v.t.* and *i.*

cockroach (kok' rōch) [Sp. *cucaracha* (assim. to COCK, ROACH)], *n.* An orthopterous insect (familiarly known as the black beetle), *Blatta orientalis*, resembling a beetle, and a pest in kitchens.

cockswain [COXSWAIN].

cocktail (kok' tāl) [COCK (1), TAIL (a tail that cocks up, or like a cock's)], *n.* A horse with tail docked very short, usually a half-bred horse; hence, a half-bred fellow; a beetle, *Ocypus olens*; a drink taken before a meal, usually gin or other spirit with bitters and flavourings. *a.* Underbred; pertaining to cocktails. **cock-tailed,** *a.* With docked tail or tail cocked up.

cock-up (kok' ŭp) [COCK (1), v.], *n.* A turn up of the tip of the nose; *a cocked hat. *a.* (*Print.*) With the top well above that of the other letters (as in large initial letters).

cocky (ko' ki) [COCK (1)], *a.* Impudent, uppish, pert, saucy. **cockily,** *adv.* **cockiness,** *n.*

cocky-leeky (kok i lē' ki) [Sc. (COCK (1), LEEK)], *n.* Soup made from a fowl boiled with leeks.

Cockyolly bird (kok i ol' i bĕrd), *n.* (*Nursery*) Dicky-bird, chickabiddy.

coco-, cocoa (1) (kō' kō), **coker** (kō' kėr) [Port. and Sp. *coco*, a bugbear, a grimace (COKER is a commercial term to distinguish it from the foll.)], *n.* A tropical palm tree, *Cocos nucifera.* **coco-** or **cocoa-nut,** *n.* The fruit of this, a large, rough, hard-shelled nut with a white edible lining and a sweet liquid known as **coco-nut milk. coco-nut butter,** *n.* The solid oil obtained from the lining of the coco-nut. **coco-nut matting,** *n.* Coarse matting made from the fibrous husk of the nut. **cocoa-nut, cokernut shy,** *n.* A kind of skittles in which the aim is to knock coco-nuts off sticks.

cocoa (2) (kō' kō) [corr. of CACAO], *n.* A preparation from the seeds of *Theobroma cacao*; a drink made from this. **cocoa-bean,** *n.* The cacao seed. **cocoa butter,** *n.* A buttery substance extracted from the cacao nut in the manufacture of cocoa. **cocoa-nibs,** *n.pl.* The crushed cotyledons of *Theobroma cacao.* **cocoa-powder,** *n.* A brown powder formerly used in large guns.

cocoon (kŏ koon') [F. *cocon*, dim. of *coque*, a shell, L. *concha*, Gr. *konchē*], *n.* A silky covering spun by the larvæ of certain insects in the chrysalis state; any analogous case made by other animals. *v.t.* To wrap in a cocoon. *v.i.* To make a cocoon. **cocoonery,** *n.* A place for silkworms when feeding and forming cocoons.

cocotte (kŏ kot') [F.], *n.* A prostitute; a woman from the *demi-monde.*

***coction** (kok' shŭn) [L. *coctio* (*coquere*, to cook)], *n.* The act of boiling; digestion; (*Med.*) the alteration in morbid matter that fits it for elimination. **coctile,** *a.* Baked, as a brick.

cod (1) (kod) [etym. doubtful], *n.* A large deep-sea food-fish, *Gadus morrhua.* **cod-fish,** *n.* **cod-liver-oil,** *n.* (*Med.*) Oil from the liver of the cod, rich in vitamins A and D.

cod (2) (kod) [A.-S. *cod, codd*, a bag], *n.* A husk or pod; the scrotum; a testicle; a small bag; a pillow. ***cod-piece,** *n.* A baggy appendage in the front of breeches or of the tight hose worn in the fifteenth and sixteenth centuries.

cod (3) (kod) [etym. unknown], *n.* (*slang*) A man, a bloke, a fellow. *v.t.* (*slang*) To hoax, to impose upon.

coda (kō' dȧ) [It., from L. *cauda*, tail], *n.* (*Mus.*) An adjunct to the close of a composition to enforce the final character of the movement. ***codetta,*** *n.* A short coda.

***codding** (kod' ing) [A.-S. *cod, codd*, bag, *testiculus*], *a.* Lecherous.

coddle (1) (kod' ĕl) [prob. short for CAUDLE], *v.t.* To treat as an invalid or baby, to pamper, to cocker. *n.* One that coddles himself or other people.

coddle (2) (kod' ĕl) [etym. doubtful], *v.t.* To parboil, to stew gently; to roast.

code (kōd) [F., from L. *cōdex -icem*, see CODEX], *n.* A collection of statutes; a digest of law; a body of laws or regulations systematically arranged; (*Mil. and Nav.*) a system of signals; a series of characters, letters, and words used for the sake of brevity or secrecy; a collection of rules or canons; the principles accepted in any sphere of art, taste, conduct, etc. **codify** (kōd' i fī), *v.t.* To reduce to a systematic body; to put into a secret code. **codifier,** *n.* **codification** (-kā' shŭn), *n.*

codeclination (kō dĕk li nā' shŭn), *n.* (*Astron.*) The North-Polar distance of anything, the complement of its declination.

codeine (kō' dē in) [Gr. *kōdeia*, head, poppy-head], *n.* (*Chem.*) An alkaloid obtained from opium and used as a narcotic.

codex (kō' deks) [L. *cōdex, caudex*, a tree-trunk, a wooden tablet, a book], *n.* (*pl.*) **codices**) A manuscript volume, esp. of the Bible or of texts of classics; (*Med.*) a list of prescriptions.

codger (koj' ėr) [prob. var. of CADGER], *n.* (*colloq.*) A miser; an odd old person.

codicil (kod' is il) [M.F. *codicile* (now *codicille*), L. *cōdicillus*, dim. of CODEX], *n.* An appendix to a will, treaty, etc. **codicillary,** *a.*

codify, etc. [CODE].

codilla (kŏ dil' ȧ) [prob. dim. of It. *coda*, L. *cauda*, tail], *n.* The coarsest parts of hemp or flax.

codling (1) (kod' ling), *n.* A young cod.

codling (2) (kod' ling), **-lin** [M.E *querdling* (perh. Ir. *queirt*, apple-tree, -LING)], *n.* A long, tapering kind of apple; an apple for baking; a baked apple. **codlings and cream:** The hairy willow-herb, *Epilobium hirsutum.* **codling-moth,** *n.* The moth, *Carpocapsa pomonella*, whose larvæ feed on apples and cause them to fall prematurely.

codon (kō' dŏn) [Gr. *kōdōn*, bell], *n.* A small bell; the bell-shaped orifice of a trumpet. **codonostome** (kō dŏ nos' tōm) [Gr. *stoma*, mouth], *n.* (*Zool.*) The bell-shaped aperture of a medusa.

coeducation (kō ed ū kā' shŭn), *n.* Education of the two sexes together. **coeducational,** *a.*

coefficient (kō ė fish′ ėnt), *n.* Anything co-operating; (*Math.*) the co-factor of an algebraical number; in 4*ab*, 4 is the **numerical** and *ab* the **literal coefficient**; (*Phys.*) a number denoting the degree of a quality. **differential coefficient,** *n.* The ratio of the change of a function of a variable to the change in that variable.

coehorn (kō′ hôrn) [from the inventor Baron *Coehoorn* (1632–1704)], *n.* A small mortar for throwing grenades.

cœlacanth (sē′ lȧ kănth) [Gr. *koilos*, hollow, *akantha*, spine], *n.* (*Zool.*) The only known living representative of the fossil group of fish Crossopterygii, first captured off S. Africa in 1953.

cœlenterate (sē len′ tėr ȧt) [Gr. *koilos*, hollow, *enteron*, an intestine], *a.* (*Zool.*) Of or belonging to the *Cœlenterata*. *n.* Any individual of the *Cœlenterata*, a subdivision of the *Metazoa*, containing the sponges, medusas, etc.

cœliac (sē′ li ăk) [L. *cœliacus*, Gr. *koiliakos* (*koilia*, bowels, *koilos*, hollow)], *a.* Pertaining to the belly.

cœlo- (sē′ lō), **cœl-** (sēl) [Gr. *koilos*, hollow], *comb. form.* (*Zool., Bot., etc.*) Hollow.

coemption (kō emp′ shŭn), *n.* Concerted action among buyers for forestalling the market by purchasing the whole quantity of any commodity.

cœnæsthesis (sē nės thē′ sis) [CŒN-, Gr. *æsthesis*, sensation, from *aisthanomai*, I perceive], *n.* (*Psych.*) The collective consciousness of the body, as distinguished from the impressions of the separate senses.

cœno- (sē nō), **cœn-** (sēn) [Gr. *koinos*, common], *comb. form.* Common.

cœnobite (sē′ nō bīt) [late L. *cœnobīta*, from Gr. *koinobion*, a convent (CŒNO-, *bios*, life)], *n.* A monk living in community. **cœnobitic, -ical** (sē nō bit′ ik, -ăl), *a.* **cœnobitism,** *n.*

cœnogamy (sē nog′ ȧ mi), *n.* Sexual promiscuity.

coequal (kō ē′ kwăl), *a.* Equal with another; of the same rank, dignity, etc. *n.* One of the same rank. **coequality** (kō ē kwol′ i ti), *n.* **coequally,** *adv.*

coerce (kō ĕrs′) [L. *coercēre* (CO-, *arcēre*, to enclose, cp. *arca*, a chest)], *v.t.* To restrain by force; to compel to obey; to enforce by compulsion. *v.i.* To employ coercion (in government). **coercible,** *a.* **coercibleness,** *n.* **coercion,** *n.* Compulsion of a free agent; government by force. **Coercion Act,** *n.* An Act that conferred special power on the executive in Ireland in time of disturbance. **coercionary,** *a.* **coercionist,** *n.* **coercive,** *a.* Having power or authority to coerce; compulsory. *n.* A means of coercion. **coercively,** *adv.*

coessential (kō ė sen′ shal), *a.* Of the same essence. **coessentiality** (-shi ăl′ i ti), *n.* **coessentially,** *adv.*

coetaneous (kō ē tā′ nė ŭs) [L. *coætāneus* (CO-, *ætas*, *-ātis*, age)], *a.* Of the same age with another; beginning to exist at the same time; coeval.

coeternal (kō ē tĕr′ năl), *a.* Equally eternal with another. **coeternally,** *adv.* **coeternity,** *n.*

coeval (kō ē′ văl) [L. *coævus* (CO-, *ævum*, an age)], *a.* Of the same age; of the same date of birth or origin; existing at or for the same period. *n.* A contemporary. **coevality** (-văl′ i ti), *n.* **coevally,** *adv.*

coexecutor (kō ėg zek′ ū tŏr), *n.* A joint executor. **coexecutrix,** *n.*

coexist (kō ėg zist′), *v.i.* To exist at the same time with. **coexistence,** *n.* (*Pol.*) Mutual toleration by regimes with differing ideologies or systems of government. **coexistent,** *a.*

coextension (kō ėks ten′ shŭn), *n.* Equal extension. **coextensive,** *a.* **coextensively,** *adv.*

coffee (kof′ i) [Turk. *qahveh*, Arab. *qahweh*], *n.* A beverage made from the ground roasted seeds of a tropical Asiatic and African shrub, *Coffea arabica*; a luncheon with coffee; the last course at dinner consisting of coffee; the seeds of the tree; the tree itself. **coffee-bean, -berry,** *n.* A coffee seed. **coffee bush,** *n.* (*N. Zealand*) The karamu. **coffee-cup,** *n.* A cup from which coffee is drunk. **coffee-grounds,** *n.pl.* The sediment or lees of coffee-berries after infusion. **coffee-house,** *n.* A house where coffee and other refreshments are sold. **coffee-mill,** *n.* A mill for grinding coffee-seeds. **coffee-pot,** *n.* A vessel in which coffee is made. **coffee-room,** *n.* The public dining-room of an inn or hotel. **coffee-stall,** *n.* A street stall where non-alcoholic beverages and snacks are sold throughout the night. **coffee-tavern,** *n.* A temperance refreshment house.

coffer (kof′ ėr) [O.F. *cofre*, L. *cophinum*, acc. of *cophinus*, Gr. *kophinos* (doublet of COFFIN)], *n.* A chest or box for holding valuables; (*pl.*) a treasury, funds, financial resources; (*Arch.*) a sunk panel. **v.t.* To enclose in a coffer. **coffer-dam,** *n.* (*Eng.*) A water-tight enclosure used in laying foundations of piers, bridges, etc., in a river bottom. **coffered,** *a.* Enclosed in a coffer; ornamented with coffers. ***cofferer,** *n.* A treasurer; an officer of the royal household next below the controller.

coffin (kof′ in) [O.F. *cofin*, L. *cophinum*, as prec.], *n.* The box in which a corpse is enclosed for burial (*Am.*) a casket; a coffin-ship; the hoof of a horse below the coronet; (*Print.*) a frame for the imposing stone of a hand-press or the carriage of a machine. *v.t.* To put into a coffin; (*fig.*) to put out of sight. **coffin-bone,** *n.* The spongy bone in a horse's hoof around which the horn grows. **coffin-joint,** *n.* The joint above the coffin-bone. **coffin-plate,** *n.* A metal plate recording name, etc., fastened on the lid of a coffin. **coffin-ship,** *n.* An unseaworthy vessel.

coffle (kofl′) [Arab. *qāfilah*, caravan], *n.* A travelling gang, esp. of slaves.

cog (1) (kog) [from Scand. (cp. Swed. *kugge*, Norw. *kug*)], *n.* A tooth or projection in the rim of a wheel or other gear for transmitting motion to another part. *v.t.* To furnish with cogs; (*North. dial.*) to stop the revolutions of a wheel by means of a block or wedge. **hunting cog,** *n.* An extra cog in the larger member of cogged gear, securing a constant change of cogs engaging with each other. **cog-wheel,** *n.* A wheel furnished with cogs.

cog (2) (kog) [perh. conn. with prec. (cp. Norw. *kogga*, Swed. *kugga*, to dupe, cheat)], *v.t.* To handle (dice) in a fraudulent way; to wheedle; to seduce by flattery. *v.i.* To cheat at dicing; to cheat, deceive; to cajole, to wheedle.

***cog** (3), **cogge** (kog) [O.F. *cogue* (cp. COCK (4), Dut. *cogge*, G. *kock*)], *n.* A broad round-shaped vessel used in the Middle Ages both for burden and war; a small boat.

cog (4) [COGUE].

cogent (kō′ jėnt) [L. *cōgentum*, acc. pres.p. of *cōgere*, to compel (CO-, *agere*, to drive)], *a.* Powerful, constraining, convincing. **cogently,** *adv.* **cogency,** *n.*

coggie (kog′ i) [Sc., dim. of COGUE], *n.* A small wooden bowl.

coggle (kog′ ėl) [etym. doubtful; perh. onomat. (but cp. G. *kugel*, Dut. *kōgel*)], *n.* A pebble or cobble; a small boat.

cogitate (koj′ i tāt) [L. *cōgitātus*, p.p. of *cōgitāre*, to think (CO-, *agitāre*, freq. of *agere*, to drive)], *v.i.* To think, to reflect, to meditate. *v.t.* To meditate, devise; (*Phil.*) to form an idea or conception of. **cogitable,** *a.* Capable of being thought; conceivable by the reason. **cogitation** (-tā′ shŭn), *n.* **cogitative** (koj′-), *a.* Meditative. **cogitatively,** *adv.* **cogitativeness,** *n.*

cognac (kō′ nyăk) [name of place], *n.* French brandy of fine quality, esp. that distilled in the neighbourhood of Cognac.

cognate (kog′ nāt) [L. *cognātus* (CO-, *gnātus*, *nātus*, p.p. of *gnasci*, *nasci*, to be born)], *a.* Akin, related; of common origin; of the same kind or nature; (*Philol.*) derived from the same linguistic family or from the same word or root. *n.* (*Law*) A blood relation (distinguished from AGNATE, which is through the father only); (*Sc. Law*) a relative on the mother's side; (*Gram.*) a cognate word. **cognateness,** *n.* **cognation** (-nā' shŭn), *n.*

cognition (kog nish' ŭn) [L. *cognitio -ōnem*, from *cognoscere*, to learn (CO-, *gnoscere*, cognate with KNOW)], *n.* The act of apprehending; the faculty of perceiving, conceiving, and knowing, as distinguished from the feelings and the will; a sensation, perception, intuition, or conception; (*Law*) cognizance. **cognitional,** *a.* **cognitive** (kog'-), *a.*

cognizance (kog' ni zȧns, kon' i zȧns) [O.F. *conoissance* (L. *cognoscere*, see COGNITION), assim to L. *cog-*], *n.* Knowledge, notice, recognition; (*Law*) judicial notice; knowledge not requiring proof; acknowledgment; jurisdiction; (*Her.*) a badge, a coat, a crest.

cognizant (kog' ni zȧnt) [from prec.], *a.* Having cognizance or knowledge (of); (*Law*) competent to take judicial notice of.

cognize (kog nīz') [formed from COGNIZANCE], *v.t.* (*Phil.*) To have knowledge or perception of. **cognizer,** *n.* **cognizable** (kog' niz ȧbl, con' iz ȧbl), *a.* Knowable (*Law*) liable to be tried and determined. **cognizably,** *adv.*

cognomen (kog nō' mėn) [L. (CO-, *gnōmen*, *nōmen*, name, from *gno-*, stem of *gnoscere*)], *n.* A surname; the last of the three names of an ancient Roman citizen; a title, a name; a nickname. ***cognominal** (-nom' in ȧl), *a.* **cognominally,** *adv.* ***cognominate,** *v.t.* ***cognomination** (-nā' shŭn), *n.* A cognomen.

***cognosce** (kog nos') [L. *cognoscere*, to know (see COGNITION)], *v.t.* (*Sc. Law*) To examine; to decide judicially; to pronounce insane. **cognoscible,** *a.* That may be known; (*Sc. Law*) cognizable. **cognoscibility** (-bil' i ti), *n.* The quality of being cogniscible.

cognoscente (kon yō shen' tā) [It., from L. *cognoscens -tem*, pres.p. of *cognoscere*, see prec.)], *n.* (*pl.* **-ti**) A connoisseur.

cognovit (kog nō' vit) [L., he has acknowledged, perf. tense of *cognoscere*, COGNOSCE], *n.* (*Law*) An acknowledgment by a defendant of the justice of the plaintiff's claim, thus allowing judgment to go by default.

cogue (kōg), **cog** (4) (kog) [Sc., etym. unknown], *n.* A small wooden vessel for milking; a wooden cup.

cohabit (kō hăb' it) [F. *cohabiter*, L. *cohabitāre* (CO-, *habitāre*, to dwell, freq. of *habēre*, to hold)], *v.i.* To live together, esp. as husband and wife (usu. of persons not legally married). **cohabitation** (-tā' shŭn), *n.*

coheir (kō âr'), *n.* A joint heir. **coheiress,** *n.* A joint heiress.

cohere (kō hēr') [L. *cohærēre* (CO-, *hærēre*, to stick)], *v.i.* To stick together; to hold together, remain united; to be logically consistent. **coherence, -ency,** *n.* **coherent,** *a.* That coheres; remaining united; logically connected, consistent. **coherently,** *adv.* **coherer,** *n.* (*Radio.*) An early device for detecting electro-magnetic waves.

coheritor (kō her' i tôr), *n.* A coheir.

cohesion (kō hē' zhŭn) [F. *cohésion* (L. *cohæs-*, part. stem. of *cohærēre*, COHERE)], *n.* Coherence; state of cohering; consistency; (*Phys.*) the force uniting molecules of the same nature; (*Bot.*) union of organs. **cohesive,** *a.* **cohesively,** *adv.* **cohesiveness,** *n.*

cohort (kō' hôrt) [F. *cohorte*, L. *cohors -tem*, orig. an enclosure (CO-, *hort-*, cp. *hortus*, garden, Gr. *chortos*, GARTH, GARDEN)], *n.* The tenth part of a Roman legion, containing three maniples or six centuries; a body of soldiers.

cohortative (kō hôr' tȧ tiv), *a.* (*Heb. gram.*) A lengthened form of the imperfect tense, signifying *let me*, *let us*, etc.

coif (koif) [O.F. *coife*, low L. *cofia*, a cap, prob. from M.H.G. *kupfe* (*kopf*, the head)], *n.* A close-fitting cap; (*Legal*) the cap worn by sergeants-at-law. *v.t.* To cover with a coif. **coifed,** *a.*

coiffeur (kwa fĕr') [F., from *coiffer*, to dress the hair (*coiffe*, O.F. *coife*, COIF)], *n.* A hairdresser.

coiffure (kwa fūr'), *n.* A head-dress; method of dressing the hair.

coign (koin) [COIN], *n.* *A corner; a quoin. **coign of vantage:** A projecting corner affording a good view.

coil (1) (koil) [O.F. *coillir* (F. *cueillir*), L. *colligere* (COL-, *legere*, to gather)], *v.t.* To wind into rings (as a rope); to twist. *v.i.* To wind itself, as a snake or creeping plant. *n.* A series of concentric rings into which anything is coiled up, a length of anything coiled up; a single turn of anything coiled up; a coiled lock of hair; (*Elec.*) a wire wound round a bobbin to form a resistance or an inductance. **to coil up:** To twist into rings or a spiral shape; to be twisted into such a shape.

coil (2) (koil) [prob. from prec.], *n.* Noise, turmoil, confusion, bustle; a fuss.

coin (koin) [O.F., a wedge, hence a stamp on a coin, from L. *cuneum*, acc. of *cuneus*, a wedge], *n.* A piece of metal stamped and current as money; money, esp. coined money; *a corner, a coign; *a wedge, a quoin. *v.t.* To mint or stamp, as money; (*fig.*) to acquire (money) rapidly; to invent, to fabricate. *v.i.* To make counterfeit money. **false coin:** An imitation of coined money in base metal; a spurious fabrication. **coiner,** *n.* One who coins money, esp. one who makes counterfeit coin, (*Am.*) a counterfeiter.

coinage (koi' nȧj) [O.F. *coignaige* (COIN-, -AGE)], *n.* The act of coining; the pieces coined; the monetary system in use; invention, fabrication; something invented.

coincide (kō in sīd') [F. *coincider*, med. L. *coincidere* (CO-, IN- (1), *cadere*, to fall)], *v.i.* To correspond in time, place, relations, etc.; to happen at the same time; (*Geom.*) to occupy the same position in space; to agree, to concur. **coincidence** (-in' si dėns), *n.* The act, fact, or condition of coinciding; a remarkable instance of apparently fortuitous concurrence. **coincident,** *a.* That coincides. **coincidently,** *adv.* **coincidental** (-den' tȧl), *a.* Coincident; characterized by or of the nature of coincidence.

coinhere (kō in hēr'), *v.i.* To inhere together. **coinherence,** *n.* **coinherent,** *a.*

coinheritance (kō in her' it ȧns), *n.* A joint inheritance. **coinheritor,** *n.* A coheir.

coinstantaneous (kō in stȧn tā' nė ŭs), *a.* Occurring at precisely the same instant.

coir (koir) [Malay *kāyar*, cord], *n.* Coco-nut fibre; cordage manufactured therefrom.

coition (kō ish' ŭn) [L. *coitio -ōnem*, from *coīre* (CO-, *īre*, to come)], *n.* Conjunction; copulation; *(*Astron.*) said of the moon when in the same sign and degree of the zodiac as the sun. **coitus** (kō' i tŭs), *n.* The act of copulation.

coke (kōk) [prob. the same as M.E. *colke*, the core of an apple; etym. doubtful], *n.* Coal from which gas has been extracted. *v.t.* To convert into coke.

coker, cokernut [COCO].

col (kol) [F., from L. *collum*, neck], *n.* A depression in a mountain ridge; a saddle or elevated pass.

col- [COM-], *pref.* (before *l*).

cola, kola (kō' lȧ) [W. African native], *n.* A tropical African tree bearing a nut which is used as a condiment and digestive, a tonic, and an antidote to alcohol. **cola-nut, -seed,** *n.* The fruit of this.

colander, cullender (kŭl' ėn dėr) [ult. from med. L. *cōlātōrium* (*cōlāre*, to strain)], *n.* A culinary strainer having the bottom perforated with small holes; a similar contrivance used in casting small shot.

colatitude (kō lăt' i tūd), *n.* The complement of the latitude; the difference between the latitude and 90°.

colcannon (kol kăn′ ȯn) [COLE, termination obscure], *n.* An Irish dish consisting of potatoes and greens stewed together.

colchicum (kol′ ki kŭm, -chi kŭm) [L., from Gr. *Kolchikon* (*Kolchis*, on the Black Sea)], *n.* A genus of bulbous plants, containing the meadow saffron, the corm and seeds of which are used in medicine.

colcothar (kol′ kȯ thar) [Arab. *qolqotār*, perh. corr. of Gr. *chalchanthos* (*chalkos*, copper, *anthos*, a flower)], *n.* Red peroxide of iron used as a polishing powder.

cold (kōld) [A.-S. *ceald*, from Teut. *kal-* (cp. Icel. *kaldr*, Dut. *koud*, G. *kalt*)], *a.* Low in temperature, esp. in relation to normal or bodily temperature; lacking heat or warmth; chill, causing a sensation of loss of heat; suffering from a sensation of lack of heat; without ardour or intensity, indifferent; unconcerned, received with indifference, unwelcomed; sad, dispiriting, dispirited; calm, chaste; not hasty or violent, spiritless; (*Hunting*) not affecting the scent strongly; unaffected by the scent; (*Colour*) bluish in tone, as opposed to warm tones such as red, yellow, etc. *n.* Absence of warmth; the sensation produced by absence of warmth; a popular name for inflammation resulting from chills. **to have cold feet:** (*slang*) To be afraid. **in cold blood:** Without the excuse of passion or excitement. **to throw cold water on:** To discourage. **cold-blooded,** *a.* Having blood under 90° Fahr.; unfeeling, unimpassioned. **cold-bloodedly,** *adv.* **cold-bloodedness,** *n.* **cold chisel,** *n.* A chisel for cutting cold metals. **cold coil,** *n.* A tube carrying a stream of cold water round an inflamed part. **cold comfort,** *n.* Poor consolation, depressing reassurance. **cold cream,** *n.* A cooling ointment of oil and wax for chaps, used also as a cosmetic. **cold-drawn,** *a.* Drawn (as wire) in a cold state. **cold hammer,** *v.t.* To hammer (metals) in a cold state. **cold-hearted,** *a.* Unfeeling, indifferent. **cold-heartedly,** *adv.* In a cold-hearted manner. **cold-heartedness,** *n.* The quality of being cold-hearted. **cold-livered,** *a.* Unemotional. **cold pig,** *n.* Wakening a person for a joke by drenching him with cold water. **cold-served,** *a.* Served up cold. **cold shoulder,** *n.* A rebuff; studied indifference; lit., cold shoulder of mutton. *v.t.* To treat with studied coolness or neglect. **cold steel,** *n.* Cutting weapons, such as sword and bayonet, as opposed to fire-arms. **cold-storage,** *n.* A method of keeping perishable foodstuffs fresh by placing them in an artificially icy atmosphere. **cold war,** *n.* A state of psychological tension between two countries that may or may not precede hostilities. **cold without,** *n.* (*slang*) Spirits and cold water, without sugar. **coldish,** *a.* **coldly,** *adv.* **coldness,** *n.*

cold-short (kōld′ shôrt) [prob. from Swed. *kallskör* (Norw. and Dan. *koldskjör*), from *kall* or *kold*, COLD, and *skor*, brittle], *a.* (*Metal.*) Brittle when cold.

cole (kōl) [L. *caulis*, a stalk, a cabbage], *n.* *The cabbage, and other kinds of *Brassica*; the rape. **cole-rape,** *n.* A turnip. **cole-seed,** *n.* Rape-seed, the seed of *Brassica campestris*, from which colza oil is obtained. **colewort,** *n.* The common cabbage.

colemouse [COALMOUSE].

coleopter (kol ė op′ tėr) [Gr. *koleos*, a sheath, *pteron*, a wing], *n.* Any individual of the *Coleoptera* or beetles, an order of insects having the fore wings converted into sheaths for the hinder wings. **coleopterist,** *n.* **coleopterous,** *a.*

coleorhiza (kol ė ȯ rī′ zȧ) [Gr. *koleos*, sheath, *rhiza*, root], *n.* (*pl.* **-zæ**) (*Bot.*) The root-sheath in the embryo of grasses and other endogens.

cole-tit [COALMOUSE].

colibri (kol′ i bri, kȯ lē′ bri) [F., from Carib.], *n.* A kind of humming-bird.

colic (kol′ ik) [F. *colique*, L. *colicus*, Gr. *kolikos* (see COLON)], *n.* Acute pains in the bowels, gripes, stomach-ache. **colicky,** *a.*

coliseum [COLOSSEUM].

colitis (kō lī′ tis), *n.* (*Path.*) Inflammation of the colon.

coll (kol) [from F. *col*, L. *collum*, the neck, or from *acole*, see ACCOLADE], *v.t.* To embrace by taking round the neck. *n.* An embrace.

collaborate (kȯ lăb′ ȯ rāt) [COL-, L. *labōrāre*, to LABOUR (modelled on L. *collabōrātor*)], *v.t.* To work jointly with another, esp. in literary and scientific pursuit. **collaboration** (rā′ shŭn), *n.* **collaborator,** *n.* One who collaborates; one who collaborates with and aids an enemy in occupation of his own country.

collagen (kol′ ȧ jen) [Gr. *kolla*, glue, -GEN], *n.* A fibrous protein that yields gelatin when boiled.

collapse (kȯ lăps′) [L. *collapsus*, p.p. of *collābī* (COL-, *lābī*, to glide down, to lapse)], *v.i.* To fall in (as the sides of a hollow vessel); to shrink together; to break down, to suffer from physical or nervous prostration; to come to nothing. *n.* A falling in (as the sides of a hollow vessel); complete failure; (*Med.*) general prostration. **collapsed,** *a.* **collapsible,** *a.* Liable to collapse; made so as to fall together easily (for ease in packing).

collar (kol′ ȧr) [O.F. *colier*, L. *colāre*, a band for the neck (*collum*, neck)], *n.* Something worn round the neck, either as a separate article of dress, or as forming part of some garment; a leather loop round a horse's neck to which the traces are attached; a broad metal or leather ring for a dog's neck; brawn or other meat pickled and rolled; anything shaped like a collar or ring; (*Her.*) the chain or other ornament for the neck worn by the knights of an order; (*Mech.*) a ring or round flange; (*Arch.*) an astragal, a cincture; (*Naut.*) an eye in the end of a shroud or stay; a rope in the form of a wreath to which a stay is confined; (*Angling*) a cast with flies attached. *v.t.* To seize by the collar; to put a collar on; (*Football*) to grasp and hold; to capture; to pickle and roll (as meat); (*slang*) to seize; to steal. **to slip the collar:** To free oneself. **collar-beam,** *n.* A tie-beam. **collar-bone,** *n.* The clavicle. **collar-harness,** *n.* Harness attached to the collar, as opposed to BREAST-HARNESS in which the weight is borne by a breast-band. **collar of SS or esses,** *n.* A chain worn as badge by adherents of the House of Lancaster, and still a part of certain official costumes. **collar-stud,** *n.* A metal or bone stud to hold a collar to a shirt, etc. **collar-work,** *n.* Uphill work for a horse or (*fig.*) for a person; drudgery. **collared,** *a.* Wearing a collar; pickled and rolled (as meat); (*slang*) seized, arrested. **collarless,** *a.*

collard (kol′ ȧrd) [Am. and dial., COLEWORT], *n.* A kind of cabbage that does not grow into a head.

collarette (kol ȧ ret′) [F. *collerette*, dim. of *collier*, see COLLAR], *n.* A small collar worn by women.

collate (kȯ lāt′) [L. *collātus*, p.p. of *conferre*, to bring together (COL-, *latus*, orig. *tlatus*, conn. with *tollere*, to bear, Gr. *tlētos*, borne)], *v.t.* To bring together in order to compare; to examine critically (esp. old books and manuscripts in order to ascertain by comparison points of agreement and difference); to place in order (as printed sheets for binding); (*Church*) to present to a benefice (used when a bishop presents to a living in his own diocese). **collation,** *n.* The act of collating; a light repast (from treatises being read in monasteries at meal-times). **collator,** *n.* One who collates manuscripts, books, or sheets for binding; one who confers; (*Church*) a bishop who collates to a benefice.

collateral (kȯ lăt′ ėr ȧl) [late L. *collaterālis* (COL-, *laterālis*, from *latus -eris*, side)], *a.* Being by the side; side by side; parallel; subsidiary, concurrent, subordinate; having the same common ancestor but not lineally related (as the children of brothers), *n.* A collateral relation; collateral security. **collateral security,** *n.* (*Law*) Security for the performance of any contract over and above the main security. **collaterally,** *adv.*

collation [COLLATE].

colleague (1) (kol′ ēg) [F. *collègue*, L. *collēga* (COL-, *legere*, to choose)], *n.* One associated with another in any office or employment. **colleagueship,** *n.*

colleague (2) (kǒ lēg′) [O.F. *colleguer*, L. *colligāre* (COL-, *ligāre*, to bind)], *v.t.* To join as ally.

collect (1) (kol′ ėkt) [F. *collecte*, late L. *collecta*, a summing-up, fem. p.p. of *colligere*, to collect (COL-, *legere*, to gather)], *n.* (*Eccles.*) A brief comprehensive form of prayer, adapted for a particular day or occasion.

collect (2) (kǒ lekt′) [as prec.]. To gather together into one body, mass, or place; to gather (money, taxes, subscriptions, books, curiosities, etc.) from a number of sources; to concentrate, to bring under control; (*Riding*) to bring a horse under control; to gather from observation, to infer; to call for, to fetch. *v.i.* To come together; to meet together. **to collect oneself:** To recover one's self-possession. **collectable,** *a.* **collected,** *a.* Cool, self-possessed, composed. **collectedly,** *adv.* **collectedness,** *n.*

collectanea (kol ėk tā′ nė ȧ) [L., neut. pl. of *collectāneus*, gathered together (see prec.)], *n.pl.* A number of passages from various authors; a miscellany, a note or commonplace book. **collectaneous,** *a.*

collection (kǒ lek′ shǔn) [O.F., from L. *collectio -ōnem* (see COLLECT)], *n.* The act of collecting; that which is collected; an assemblage of natural objects, works of art, etc.; money contributed for religious, charitable, or other purposes; an accumulation; *deduction, inference; (*pl.*) an examination at the end of term at Oxford, Durham, etc.

collective (kǒ lek′ tiv) [COLLECT, -IVE], *a.* Tending to collect; collected, aggregated, formed by gathering a number of things or persons together; (*Bot.*) formed by the aggregation of numerous flowers (as the fruit of the mulberry, pineapple, etc.); pertaining to many persons, as opp. to individual. **collective bargaining,** *n.* The method whereby employer and employees determine the conditions of employment. **collective note,** *n.* A diplomatic note signed by all the powers concerned. **collective noun,** *n.* A noun in the singular number expressing an aggregate of individuals. **collective ownership,** *n.* Ownership of land, capital, and other means of production by those engaged in the production. **collective security,** *n.* (*Pol.*) A policy of mutual aid against aggression. **collectively,** *adv.* **collectivity,** *n.*

collectivism (kǒ lek′ tiv izm) [as prec., -ISM], *n.* The economic theory that industry should be carried on with a collective capital (opp. to individualism). **collectivist,** *n.* and *a.*

collector (kǒ lek′ tǒr), *n.* One who collects; a gatherer of rarities of art, etc.; one who collects taxes; (*Radio.*) the terminal of a transistor. **collectorate, -ship,** *n.*

colleen (kǒ lēn′) [Ir. *cailīn*, dim. of *caile*, a countrywoman], *n.* (*Ang.-Ir.*) A girl, a lass.

college (kol′ ėj) [M.F. *college*, L. *collēgium* (*collēga*, COLLEAGUE)], *n.* A body or community of persons, having certain rights and privileges, and devoted to common pursuits; an independent corporation of scholars, teachers, and fellows forming one of the constituent bodies of a University; a similar foundation independent of a University; an institution for higher education, esp. in affiliation with a University; a large and important secondary school, often applied pretentiously to a private school; *a charitable foundation, such as a hospital, a large almshouse, etc.; *(*slang*) a debtors' prison. **College of Arms** or **Herald's College:** A corporation presided over by the Earl Marshal, and including the Kings-of-Arms, the heralds, and pursuivants, for granting armorial bearings, etc. **College of Cardinals, Sacred College,** *n.* (*R.-C. Church*) The papal council of cardinals. **College of Justice:** (*Sc.*) The supreme civil courts. **college pudding,** *n.* A small baked pudding for one person. **colleger,** *n.* A pupil on the foundation of a school, esp. at Eton. **collegial** (kǒ lē′ ji ȧl), *a.* Constituted as a college. **collegian,** *n.* A member of a college; a student at a University; *(*slang*) a prisoner for debt.

collegiate (kǒ lē′ ji ȧt) [L. *collēgiātus*, member of a college (*collēgium*, COLLEGE)], *a.* Pertaining to a college; containing a college; instituted or regulated as a college. *v.t.* (kǒ lē′ ji āt) To constitute as a college or collegiate foundation. **collegiate church,** *n.* A church which, though not a cathedral, has an endowed chapter of canons; (*Sc.* and *Am.*) a Presbyterian church under a joint pastorate. **collegiate school,** *n.* A school organized to resemble a college.

collegium (kǒ lē′ ji ǔm) [L., see prec.], *n.* (*pl.* ***-gia***) An ecclesiastical body not under state control.

collenchyma (kǒ leng′ ki mȧ) [Gr. *kolla*, blue, *enchuma*, infusion (EN- *cheein*, to pour)], *n.* (*Bot.*) Tissue composed of elongated cells thickened at the angles, occurring immediately under the epidermis in leaf-stalks, stems, etc. **collenchymatous** (-kim′ ȧ tǔs), *a.*

collet (kol′ ėt) [F., dim. of *col*, L. *collum*, the neck], *n.* A band or ring; a flange or socket; the part of a ring in which a stone is set.

collide (kǒ līd′) [L. *collīdere* (COL-, *lædere*, to strike, hurt)], *v.i.* To come into collision or conflict. **v.t.* To bring into collision.

collie (kol′ i) [perh. COALY, black], *n.* A Scottish sheep-dog; a breed of show-dogs.

collier (kol′ yėr) [M.E. *col*, COAL, -IER], *n.* One who works in a coal-mine; (*Naut.*) a ship employed in the coal trade; one of her crew; *a charcoal-burner. **colliery,** *n.*

colligate (kol′ i gāt) [L. *colligātus*, p.p. of *colligāre* (COL-, *ligāre*, to bind)], *v.t.* To bind together; to bring into connexion. **colligation** (-gā′ shǔn), *n.* Alliance, union; (*Log.*) the mental process by which isolated facts are brought together into one concept.

collimate (kol′ i māt) [L. *collīmāre*, a misreading for *collīneāre*, to aim (COL-, *līneāre*, from *līnea*, a line)], *v.t.* (*Astron.*) To adjust the line of sight in a telescope; to make the axes of lenses or telescopes collinear. **collimation** (-mā′ shǔn), *n.* Adjustment to the line of sight. **line of collimation:** (*Astron.*) The correct line of sight, the optical axis (the amount of deviation from this line is called the **error of collimation**). **collimator,** *n.* (*Astron.*) An instrument for determining the error of collimation; a tube attached to a spectroscope for making parallel the rays falling on the prism.

collinear (kǒ lin′ ė ȧr), *a.* (*Geom.*) In the same straight line.

collingual (kǒ ling′ gwȧl), *a.* Having the same language.

collision (kǒ lizh′ ǔn) [L. *collisio -ōnem* (see COLLIDE)], *n.* The act of striking violently together; the state of being dashed or struck violently together; (*fig.*) opposition, antagonism, conflict; clashing of interests; harsh combination of sounds, consonants, etc. **collision mat,** *n.* (*Naut.*) A mat put over the side to cover a hole made by collision.

collocate (kol′ ō kāt) [L. *collocātus*, p.p. of *collocare*], *v.t.* To place together; to arrange; to station in a particular place. **collocation** (-kā′ shǔn), *n.*

collocutor (kol′ ō kū tǒr) [late L., from *colloquī*, to confer (*loquī*, to talk)], *n.* One who takes part in a conversation or conference.

collodion (kǒ lō′ di ǒn) [Gr. *kollōdēs* (*kolla*, glue)], *n.* A gummy solution of pyroxylin in ether and spirit, formerly used in photography and medicine. **collodioned,** *a.* **collodionize,** *v.t.* **collodio-,** *comb. form.*

collograph (kol′ ō grăf) [Gr. *kolla*, glue], *n.* A duplicator or copying machine in which the medium is a film of gelatine; a collotype.

collogue (kò lōg′) [perh. from F. *colloque*, a conference, or from L. *colloquī* (see COLLOQUY), influenced by COLLEAGUE], *v.i.* To talk confidentially or plot together. **v.t.* To wheedle, to flatter.

colloid (kol′ oid) [Gr. *kolla*, glue, -OID], *a.* Like glue; (*Chem.*) applied (1) to uncrystallizable liquids or semi-solids, (2) (*Min.*) to amorphous minerals, (3) (*Path.*) to degeneration of the albuminous substance of cells into jelly-like matter. *n.* (*Chem.*) An uncrystallizable, semi-solid substance, capable of only very slow diffusion or penetration. **colloidal** (-loi′ dȧl), *a.* **colloidize,** *v.t.*

collop (kol′ ȯp) [etym. doubtful], *n.* A slice of meat; a thick fold of flesh; *a slice of bacon; *a term of endearment. **Scotch collops,** *n.pl.* Meat chopped up and cooked with savoury ingredients.

colloquial (kò lō′ kwi ȧl) [COLLOQUY], *a.* Pertaining to or used in common or familiar conversation; not used in correct writing or in literature. **colloquialism,** *n.* **colloquially,** *adv.*

colloquy (kol′ ȯ kwi) [L. *colloquium*, from *colloquī* (COL-, *loquī*, to talk)], *n.* A conference, conversation, or dialogue between two or more persons; a court or presbytery in the Reformed Genevan and the Presbyterian Churches. **colloquist,** *n.* A collocutor.

collotype (kol′ ȯ tīp) [Gr. *colla*, glue], *n.* (*Print.*) A method of reproduction in which the film of gelatine constituting the negative is used to print from; a print obtained in this way.

***collude** (kò lood′) [L. *collūdere* (COL-, *lūdere*, to play)], *v.i.* To play into each other's hands; to act in concert, to conspire. ***colluder,** *n.*

collusion (kò loo′ zhŭn) [F., from L. *collūsio -onem* (*collūdere*, see prec.)], *n.* Secret agreement for a fraudulent or deceitful purpose, esp. to defeat the course of law. **collusive,** *a.* **collusively,** *adv.*

colluvies (kò loo′ vi ēz) [L., from *colluere* (COL-, *luere*, to wash)], *n.* Filth; a mixed mass of refuse.

***colly** (kol′ i) [prob. from an A.-S. *colgian*, from *col*, COAL], *v.t.* To besmear with smut or soot; to blacken. *n.* The smut, grime, or soot of coal or burnt wood; the blackbird.

collyrium (kò lir′ i ŭm) [L., from Gr. *kollurion*, a poultice (*kollura*, a roll of coarse bread)], *n.* (*Med.*) An eye-salve, and eye-wash.

colly-wobbles (kol′ i woblz′) [slang], *n.* A stomach-ache.

colocasia (kol ȯ kā′ zhi ȧ) [L., from Gr. *kolokasia*], *n.* (*Bot.*) A genus of plants of the arum family.

colocynth (kol′ ȯ sinth) [L. *colocynthis*, Gr. *kolokunthis*], *n.* The bitter cucumber or bitter apple, *Citrullus colocynthis*, or its fruit; (*Med.*) an extract obtained from the pulp of this plant and used as a purgative. **colocynthin** (kol ȯ sin′ thin), *n.* The bitter principle contained in colocynth.

Cologne (kò lōn′) [F., from L. *Colōnia* (Roman name *Colōnia Agrippina*)], *n.* A city of Germany. **Cologne earth,** *n.* A native pigment similar to Vandyke brown. **Cologne water** [EAU-DE-COLOGNE].

colon (1) (kō′ lȯn) [Gr. *kōlon*, a member, limb, clause], *n.* A grammatical point (:) denoting a pause greater than that of the semicolon, and less than that of a period.

colon (2) (kō′ lȯn) [L., from Gr. *kolon*], *n.* (*Anat.*) The largest division of the intestinal canal, extending from the cæcum to the rectum. **colonic,** *a.* **colonitis** (-nī′ tis), *n.* (*Path.*) Colitis, inflammation of the colon.

colonel (kĕr′ nėl) [F., from It. *colonello*, dim. of *colonna*, column (formerly *coronel*, also from F., due to confusion with *corona*, crown)], *n.* The commander of a regiment or of a battalion. **colonelcy, -ship,** *n.*

colonial (kò lō′ ni ȧl), *a.* Of or pertaining to a colony. *n.* An inhabitant of a colony. **colonial goose,** *n.* (*Austral. colloq.*) Baked leg of mutton boned and stuffed with sage, onions, etc. **Colonial Office,** *n.* The department of the State where business connected with the government of the British colonies is transacted. **colonialism,** *n.* An idiom or habit peculiar to colonials; alleged exploitation of the colonies. **colonially,** *adv.*

colonist (kol′ ȯ nist) [from foll.], *n.* A colonizer; a settler in or inhabitant of a colony.

colonize (kol′ ȯ nīz) [L. *colōnus*, orig. a farmer, -IZE], *v.t.* To found a colony in; to settle in; to people with colonists. *v.i.* To found a colony or colonies. **colonizer,** *n.* **colonization** (-zā′ shŭn), *n.* **colonizationist,** *n.* A supporter of colonization; (*Am.*) a favourer of the state-assisted settlement in Liberia of Negro emigrants from the U.S.A.

colonnade (kol ȯ nād′) [F., from It. *colonnata* (*colonna*, L. *columna*, a COLUMN)], *n.* A series or range of columns at certain intervals.

colony (kol′ ȯ ni) [F. *colonie*, L. *colōnia* (*colōnus*, a farmer, from *colere*, to till)], *n.* A settlement founded by emigrants in a foreign country, and remaining subject to the jurisdiction of the parent state; a group of people of the same nationality in a foreign town; a group of people following the same occupation in a town, esp. when they live in the same quarter; (*Biol.*) a body of organisms living or growing together. **crown colony,** *n.* (*Pol.*) A colony governed direct by the Crown; a colony administered by the Colonial Office.

colophon (kol′ ȯ fȯn) [late L., from Gr. *kolophōn*, a summit], *n.* A device or inscription at the beginning or end of a book, giving the printer's name, place, date of publication, etc.

colophony (kò lof′ ȯ ni) [L. *colophōnia*, pertaining to *Colophōn* in Asia Minor, where first obtained], *n.* A dark-coloured resin obtained from turpentine. **colophonate** (kò lof′ ȯ nȧt), *n.* **colophonic** (-fon′ ik), *a.*

***coloquintida** (kol ȯ kwin′ ti dȧ) [med. L., see COLOCYNTH].

Colorado (kol ȯ ra′ dō) [Sp.], *n.* One of the States of the American Union. **Colorado beetle,** *n.* A small yellow black-striped beetle, *Doryphora decemlineata*, very destructive to the potato.

coloration (kŭl-, kol ȯ rā′ shŭn) [F., from L. *colōrāre*, to colour (*color*, COLOUR)], *n.* (*Art*) The act of colouring; method of putting on or arranging colours; (*Zool. and Bot.*) particular marking, arrangement of colours.

coloratura (kol ȯ rȧ too′ rȧ) [It. *coloratura*, L. *colōrātura*, from *colōrāre*, see prec.], *n.* (*Mus.*) The use of variation, trills, etc., to assist the harmony.

colorific (kŭl-, kol ȯ rif′ ik) [F. *colorifique* (L. *color -ōrem*, -FIC)], *a.* Having the power of imparting colour to other bodies; (*fig.*) highly-coloured.

colorimeter (kol ȯ rim′ ėt ėr) [L. *color*, colour], *n.* An instrument for measuring the hue, brightness, and purity of colours.

colossal (kò los′ ȧl) [COLOSSUS, -AL], *a.* Pertaining to or resembling a colossus; huge, gigantic. **colossally,** *adv.*

colosseum (kol ȯ sē′ ŭm) [L., neut. a. from COLOSSUS], *n.* The Flavian amphitheatre in ancient Rome; applied to other amphitheatres and places of entertainment.

colossus (kò los′ ŭs) [L., from Gr. *kolossos*], *n.* (*pl.* **-si, -suses**) A statue of gigantic size; a gigantic statue of Apollo at Rhodes, which stood astride the harbour; a man of great power or genius. **colossuswise,** *adv.* In the manner of a colossus; astride.

colostrum (kò los′ trŭm) [L.], *n.* The first milk secreted after parturition; beestings.

colotomy (kol ot′ ōm i), *n.* (*Surg.*) Incision into the colon.

colour (kŭl′ ėr) [O.F. *color*, L. *colōrem*, acc. of *color*], *n.* The sensation produced by waves of decomposed light upon the optic nerve; that property of bodies by which rays of light are decomposed so as to produce certain effects upon the eye; any one of the hues into which light can be decomposed, or a tint (a hue mixed with white), or a shade (mixed with black); (*Art*) that which is used for colouring, a pigment, a paint; colouring, effect of colour, and of light and shade in drawings and engravings; the complexion or hue of the face, esp. a healthy hue, ruddiness; any tint or hue, as distinguished from black or white; (*Law*) appearance, or *prima facie* right; (*pl.*) a flag, standard, or ensign borne in an army or fleet; coloured ribbons, etc., worn as a badge of party, membership of a league, society, club, etc.; coloured dresses; (*fig.*) semblance, appearance, esp. false appearance; pretence, excuse, pretext; timbre, quality; of tone; general character, tone, quality; mood, temper, emotional quality; vividness, animation. *v.t.* To give colour to; to tinge, to paint, to dye; to paint with distemper; to give a new colour to; hence, to put in a false light, to misrepresent or disguise. *v.i.* To become coloured; to turn red, to blush. **to change colour:** To turn pale; to blush. **complementary colours:** Colours which together make up white; thus any of the primary colours is complementary to the other two. **false colours:** Pretence. **fast colours:** Colours that do not wash out. **man of colour:** A Negro. **off colour:** Faulty in colour (as a gem); faulty; out of sorts. **primary colours:** The fundamental colours from which others can be obtained by mixing. For paints they are red, blue, and yellow; for transmitted light they are red, blue, green. **prismatic colours:** Those into which pure white light is resolved when dispersed, for example, in a prism or raindrop. **secondary colours:** Colours produced by combinations of two primary colours. **water-colour** [WATER]. **to join the colours:** To enlist. **to show one's colours:** To throw off disguise; to reveal one's opinions, feelings, or designs. **with flying colours:** Brilliantly, successfully; with signal credit. **colour bar,** *n.* A social, political or other discrimination against the coloured races. **colour-blind,** *a.* **colour-blindness,** *n.* Total or partial inability to distinguish different colours, especially the primary colours (DALTONISM). **colour-box,** *n.* A box for holding artists' colours, brushes, etc. **colour-line,** *n.* (*Am.*) The caste distinction between white persons and those having any Negro blood. **colourman,** *n.* One who deals in colours, brushes, etc. **colour printing:** Reproduction in two or more colours. **colour-sergeant,** *n.* A non-commissioned officer in the infantry ranking above an ordinary sergeant. **colour-variation:** (*Zool.*) The range of variability of colour among animals of one species. **colourable,** *a.* Specious, plausible; apparent, not real. **colourableness,** *n.* **colourably,** *adv.* **coloured,** *a.* Having a colour; esp. marked by any colour except black or white; of Negro blood; (*fig.*) having a specious appearance; (*Bot.*) of any colour except green. **colouring,** *n.* The act of giving a colour to; the colour applied; the art or style of using colour; (*fig.*) a false appearance. **colourist,** *n.* One who colours; (*Art*) a painter distinguished for his management of colour. **colouristic,** *a.* **colourless,** *a.* Without colour; pale; neutral-tinted, subdued in tone, dull; lacking in life and vigour; bald, tame. **colourlessly,** *adv.* **colourlessness,** *n.* **coloury,** *a.* Having a good colour (of hops, certain coffees, etc.).

colporteur (kōl pŏr tĕr', kol' pŏr tėr) [F., from *colporter* (*col*, neck, *porter*, to carry)], *n.* One who travels about selling religious books, tracts, etc., for some society. **colportage** (kōl pŏr tazh', kol' pŏr tăj), *n.*

colt (1) (kōlt) [A.-S.; etym. unknown], *n.* A young horse, esp. a young male from its weaning till about the age of four; a young, inexperienced fellow; (*Naut.*) a rope's end knotted and used for punishment; (*Cricket*) one who plays for the first time for his county. ***v.i.** To frisk like a colt. ***v.t.** To make pregnant; *to cheat; to beat with a rope's end. **colt's-foot,** *n.* A coarse-leaved, yellow-flowered weed, *Tussilago farfara*, formerly much used in medicine. **colthood,** *n.* **coltish,** *a.*

colt (2) (kōlt) [inventor, S. *Colt* (1814–62)], *n.* An early type of American revolver.

colter [COULTER].

coluber (kol' ū bėr) [L.], *n.* (*Zool.*) A genus of innocuous snakes. **colubriform** (kŏ lū' bri fôrm), *a.* Shaped like the genus *Coluber*; belonging to the group *Colubriformes*, which contains the innocuous snakes. **colubrine** (kol' ū brīn), *a.* Relating to serpents; resembling snakes, esp. the genus *Coluber*; *(*fig.*) cunning.

columbarium (kol ŭm bâr' i ŭm) [L., neut. of *columbārius* (*columba*, dove)], *n.* (*pl.* **-ia**) A pigeon house; (*Archæol.*) a place of interment among the ancient Romans, fitted with niches like pigeon-holes to receive the cinerary urns; (*Arch.*) a hole left in a wall to receive the end of a timber. ***columbary** (kol' ŭm bå ri), *n.* A pigeon-house, a dove-cote.

Columbian (kŏ lŭm' bi ån) [Christopher *Columbus*], *a.* Pertaining to the United States of America. **Columbian press,** *n.* A kind of printing-press first made in America.

columbine (1) (kol' ŭm bīn) [O.F. *columbin*, late L. *columbīna* (*columba*, a dove)], *a.* Pertaining to or resembling a dove or pigeon. *n.* A plant with five-spurred flowers, supposed to resemble five doves clustered together, constituting the genus *Aquilegia*.

columbine (2) (kol' ŭm bīn) [It. *Colombina*, a comedy character], *n.* The female dancer in a pantomime, the sweetheart of Harlequin.

columbium [NIOBIUM].

columella (kol ŭ mel' å), ***columel** [L., dim. of *columna*, see foll.], *n.* (*Zool.*) The central pillar of a univalve shell, or of corals; (*Bot.*) the axis of fruit; the central column in the capsule of mosses.

column (kol' ŭm) [earlier *colompne*, F. *colompne*, *colombe*, L. *columna* (cogn. with *collis*, hill, *celsus*, high)], *n.* A pillar or solid body of wood or stone, of considerably greater length than thickness, usu. consisting of a base, a shaft, and a capital, used to support or adorn a building, or as a solitary monument; anything resembling such a column, as the mercury in a thermometer, a cylindrical mass of water or other liquid, a vertical mass of smoke, etc.; a perpendicular line of figures; a perpendicular section of a page; hence (*pl.*) the contents of a newspaper; a support; (*Bot.*) a solid body into which the filaments in some plants are combined; (*Mil.*) a body of troops in deep files; (*Nav.*) a line of ships behind each other. **column-rule,** *n.* A rule used in printing to divide columns of type. **columnar** (kŏ lŭm' når), *a.* **columned** (kol' ŭmd), *a.* **columniation** (kŭ lŭm ni ā' shŭn), *n.* (*Arch.*) The employment or the grouping of columns in a building; arrangement in columns. **columniform** (kŏ lŭm' ni fôrm), *a.* **columnist** (kol' ŭm nist), *n.* Writer on general subjects in a newspaper.

colure (kŏ loor') [L. *colūrus*, Gr. *kolouros* (*kol-os*, docked, *ouros*, tail)], *n.* (*Astron.*) One of two great circles passing through the equinoctial points, and cutting each other at right angles at the poles.

colza (kol' zå) [F. *colza*, *colzat*, L.G. *kôlsôt* (Dut. *koolsaad*)], *n.* Cole-seed, the grain of *Brassica campestris*, var. *oleifera*. **colza-oil,** *n.* Oil expressed from this, and used as an illuminant.

com- [L., the combining form *cum-* (chiefly before *b*, *f*, *m*, *p*)], *pref.* With; together; in combination; completely.

coma (1) (kō' må) [late L., from Gr. *kōma -atos* (cp. *koimaein*, to put to sleep)], *n.* (*Med.*) A state of absolute unconsciousness, characterized by the absence of any response to external stimuli or inner need. **comatose** (kom' å tōz), *a.*

coma (2) (kō' må) [L., from Gr. *komē*, the hair], *n.* (*pl.* **comæ**) (*Astron.*) The nebulous covering of the nucleus of a comet; (*Bot.*) the assemblage of branches constituting the head of a forest tree; the tuft of hairs terminating certain seeds.

•**comart** (kȯ mart′) [etym. unknown], *n.* (*Shak.*) Probably a covenant or agreement.

•**co-mate** (kō′ māt), *n.* A companion, associate, or partner.

comate, comose (kō′ māt, kō′ mōz), *a.* (*Bot.*) Bearing a tuft of hair at the end.

comb (kōm) [A.-S. *camb*, from Teut. *kambo-* (cp. Dut. *kam*, Icel. *kambr*, G. *kamm*; Gr. *gomphos*, a peg, Sansk. *gambhas*, a tooth)], *n.* A toothed instrument for separating and dressing the hair; an ornamental toothed contrivance for fastening ladies' hair when dressed; a rake-shaped instrument with a short handle for cleaning wool or flax; (*Elec.*) a row of points for collecting electricity; the red, fleshy tuft on the head of a fowl, esp. the cock; the crest of a bird; the cellular substance in which bees deposit their honey; the crest of a wave; a ridge. *v.t.* To separate, dress, or arrange with a comb; to curry a horse; to dress (flax, hemp, wool, etc); to make a thorough search; *to beat. *v.i.* To form a crest and roll over (as waves). **-combed** (*in comb.*). **comb-out,** *n.* (*colloq.*) A clearing out of men of military age working in factories, etc.; police search of a neighbourhood for bad characters. **comber** (1) (kō′ mėr), *n.* One who or that which combs; a combing-machine for dressing cotton or wool; a wave that forms a long crest and rolls over. **combing,** *n.* A cleaning or dressing with a comb; (*pl.*) hair removed by a comb.

combat (kŭm′-, kom′ băt) [O.F. *combatre* (COM-, *battre*, L. *batuere*, to fight)], *v.i.* To contend, to fight, to struggle. *v.t.* To oppose, to contend against, to fight with. *n.* A fight, a battle; *a duel. **single combat,** *n.* A duel. **trial by combat,** *n.* (*Hist.*) A legal method of settling a dispute or testing the justice of a charge by a duel. **combatable,** *a.*

combatant (kŭm′-, kom′ bȧ tȧnt) [F., as prec.], *a.* Engaged in combat; bearing arms; antagonistic; (*Her.*) borne in the attitude of fighting. *n.* One who fights or contends with another.

combative (kŭm′-, kom′ bȧ tiv), *a.* Inclined to combat; pugnacious. **combatively,** *adv.* **combativeness,** *n.* The quality of being combative; one of the affective propensities in phrenology.

combe (koom) [A.-S. *cumb* (etym. doubtful; perh. from W. *cwm*, *cumb*; or an application of A.-S. *cumb*, a hollow vessel, of Teut. origin)], *n.* A valley on the side of hills or mountains; a valley running up from the sea. (The word often occurs as an element in place names, as in Ilfra*combe*).

comber (1) [COMB].

comber (2) (kom′ bėr) [etym. doubtful], *n.* The wrasse, *Serranus cabrilla*, and the gaper, *Labrus maculatus*, var. *comber*; both British fish.

combination (kom bi nā′ shŭn) [O.F., from L. *combīnātio -ōnem* (*combīnāre*, to COMBINE)], *n.* The act or process of combining; the state of being combined; a combined body or mass; a union, an association; combined action; chemical union; (*Math., pl.*) the different collections which may be made of certain given quantities in groups of a given number; (*Law*) an assembly of workmen met to carry out a common purpose, formerly of an illegal nature; (*Motor.*) a motor-cycle and sidecar; *pl.* vest and knickers combined in one garment, (*Am.*) union-suit. **combination laws,** *n.pl.* Laws (repealed 1824) relating to combinations of masters or workmen. **combination-room,** *n.* The room in which the fellows of the colleges at Cambridge meet after dinner for dessert and conversation, elsewhere called the common-room.

combine (1) (kȯm bīn′) [L. *combīnāre* (COM-, *bini*, two by two)], *v.t.* To cause to unite or coalesce; to settle by agreement; to bring together; to have at the same time (properties or attributes usu. separate). *v.i.* To unite, to coalesce; to be joined or united in friendship or plans; (*Chem.*) to unite by chemical affinity. **combined operations:** (*Mil. etc.*) Operations in which sea, air and land forces work together under a single command.

combine (2) (kom′ bīn), *n.* A combination, esp. of persons or companies to further their own commercial interests; a ring; (*Agric.*) a combined reaping and threshing machine. **combinative** (kom′ bi nā tiv), *a.*

combo (kom′ bō) [Austral.], *n.* A white man living with an Aboriginal woman.

•**combust** (kȯm bŭst′) [O.F., from L. *combustus*, p.p. of *combūrere* (COM-, *ūrere*, to burn)], *a.* Burnt up, calcined; situated so near to the sun as to be obscured or eclipsed by his light. *v.t.* (*facet.*) To consume with fire.

combustible (kȯm bŭs′ tibl) [F., from L. *combustibilis* (*combustus*, see prec.)], *a.* Capable of being set on fire, inflammable; (*fig.*) irascible, hot-tempered. *n.* Inflammable material or thing. **combustibleness,** *n.*

combustion (kȯm bŭs′ chŭn) [F., from L. *combustio -ōnem* (as prec.)], *n.* The act of burning, the state of being on fire or destroyed by fire; (*Chem.*) the combination of a substance with oxygen, or another element accompanied by light and heat; oxidation of the tissue of organisms or of decomposing organic matter. **spontaneous combustion:** The ignition of a body by the development of heat within itself. ***combustious,** *a.* Combustible, inflammable; on fire; (*fig.*) raging, tempestuous. **combustive,** *a.*

come (kŭm) [A.-S. *cuman* (cp. Dut. *komen*, Icel. *koma*, G. *kommen*; Sansk. *gam*, Gr. *bainen*, L. *venīre*)], *v.i.* (*past* **came,** p.p. **come**) To move from a distance to a place nearer to the speaker; to approach; to be brought to or towards; to move towards (opp. to GO); to arrive; to advance or move into view; to travel (a certain distance) towards; to appear; to arrive at some state or condition; to happen, to befall; to result, to arise; to become, to get to be; to be descended (from); to bud, to shoot. *v.t.* (*slang*) To act the part of, to practise. *int.* Used to excite attention or rouse to action (when repeated it expresses remonstrance or rebuke). **to come the schoolmaster over:** To try to master, to bully; to lay down the law to. **come along:** Make haste. **come-back,** *n.* Return to a former position in society, etc. **come up:** (*imper.*) Go on; push on (to horse). **come February:** From now to February. **light come, light go:** Easily won, soon lost. **come what may:** Whatever happens. **to come:** Future, in futurity. **to come about:** To result, to come to pass. **to come across:** To meet with accidentally. **to come and go:** To appear and disappear (as the colour in the cheeks); to pass to and fro; to pay a short call. **to come at:** To reach, to attain, to gain access to. **to come away:** To move away; to become parted or separated. **to come back:** To return; to recur to memory. **to come between:** To intervene. **to come by:** To pass near; to obtain, to gain. **to come down:** To descend (to); to be humbled; (*colloq.*) to pay. **to come down handsome:** (*slang*) To pay a handsome price, compensation, or reward. **to come down upon:** To reprimand; to chastise; to pay out. **to come easy, expensive,** etc.: To prove easy, costly, etc. **to come home:** To return home; to affect nearly; to be fully comprehended. **to come in:** To enter; to arrive at a destination; to become fashionable; to yield; to become (useful, etc.); to enter (as an ingredient); to accrue; to assume power; (*colloq.*) to secure an advantage or chance of benefit. **to come in for:** To arrive in time for; to obtain, to get (share of). **to come into:** To join with; to comply with; to acquire, to inherit. **to come into the world:** To be born. **to come in unto:** To have sexual intercourse with. **to come it over a person:** (*colloq.*) To lord it over someone. **to come it strong:** (*slang*) To exaggerate, to affect. **to come near:** To approach; nearly to succeed. **to come of:** To be descended from; to proceed or result from. **to come off:** To part from; to escape; to get off free; to take place; to appear; to be accomplished. **to come on:** To advance; to prosper; to happen, to arise; (*imper.*) approach; proceed; do what you propose.

to come out: To come away; to be revealed, become public; to be introduced into society; to be published; to emerge from; to turn out; (*Am.*) to make profession of religion; to engage in a strike. **to come out of:** To issue forth, to proceed from. **to come out with:** To utter, to disclose. **to come over:** To cross over; to change sides; to prevail upon. **to come round:** To change; to cheat; to recover. **to come short:** To fail. **to come to:** To consent; to amount to; to recover from faintness; (*Naut.*) to cease moving; to sail close to the wind. **to come to an end:** To cease. **to come to a point:** To taper; to culminate; to reach a crisis. **to come to blows:** To begin fighting. **to come to harm:** To be injured. **to come to oneself:** To recover one's senses. **to come to pass:** To happen. **to come to stay:** To remain; to have qualities of a permanent nature. **to come under:** To be classed as; to be subjected to (authority, influence, etc.). **to come up:** To ascend; to spring; to become public or fashionable; to arise; to be introduced as a topic; (*Naut.*) to slacken (as a rope). **to come upon:** To attack; to befall; to find, discover; to meet with unexpectedly. **to come up to:** To amount to; to be equal to; to approach. **to come up smiling:** (*slang*) To laugh at punishment, defeat, or discomfiture. **to come up with:** To overtake. **come-by-chance,** *n.* (*colloq.*) A stray, a bastard. **come-back,** *n.* A retort; a return to popular favour. **come-down,** *n.* A fall or abasement. ***come-off,** *n.* A means of escape, an evasion. **come off it:** (*slang*) Don't put on airs; don't try to deceive.

comeatable (kŭm ăt' à bėl) [COME, AT, -ABLE], *a.* Easy to come at, accessible.

comedian (kŏ mē' di ăn) [F. *comédien*], *n.* An actor or writer of comedy.

comedienne (kom ėd i en') [F.], *n.* A comedy actress.

comedietta (kŏ mē di et' à) [It., dim. of *comedia*, COMEDY], *n.* A slight or brief comedy.

comedy (kom' ė di) [O.F. *comedie*, L. *cōmœdia*, Gr. *kōmōidia*, from *kōmōidos*, a comic actor (*kōmos*, a revel, *aoidos*, a singer)], *n.* A dramatic composition of a light and entertaining character depicting and often gently satirizing or laughing at the incidents of ordinary life, and having a happy termination; an entertaining drama of ordinary life more serious and more realistic than farce; life or any incident or situation regarded as an amusing spectacle.

comely (kŭm' li) [A.-S. *cymlic* (*cyme*, fine, beautiful, *lic*, like, -LY)], *a.* Pleasing in person, or in behaviour; becoming, decent. **comeliness,** *n.*

comer (kŭm' ėr), *n.* One who comes or arrives; a visitor. **the first comer:** The one who arrives first. **all comers:** Any one who accepts a challenge.

comestible (kŏ mes' tibl) [F., from late L. *comestibilis*, from *comest-*, stem of *comestus*, *comēsus*, p.p. of *comedere* (COM-, *edere*, to eat)], *n.* (*usu. in pl.*) An eatable.

comet (kom' ėt) [L. *comēta*, *comētēs*, Gr. *komētēs* (*komē*, the hair)], *n.* A luminous heavenly body, consisting, when perfect, of a nucleus or head, a coma, and a train or tail, revolving round the sun in a very eccentric orbit. **comet-finder, -seeker,** *n.* (*Astron.*) An equatorial telescope, with coarsely-divided circles and a large field, taking in at once a large part of the sky. **comet-wine,** *n.* Wine made in the year of a comet, popularly supposed to be of superior quality. **cometary,** *a.* **cometic** (kŏ met' ik), *a.* **cometography** (-tog' rà fi), *n.* A discourse on or description of comets. **cometology** [-LOGY], *n.* The science dealing with comets.

comether (kŭm *eth'* ėr) [dial., COME HITHER], *n.* **to put the comether on:** To attract by persuasion or guile; to bring under one's influence.

comfit (kŭm' fit) [O.F. *confit*, L. *confectum*, neut. p.p. of *conficere* (CON-, *facere*, to make)], *n.* A dry sweetmeat; a seed coated with sugar. ***comfiture** (kŭm' fi tūr) [F., from L. *confectūra* (as prec.)], *n.* A confection, a sweetmeat, a comfit.

comfort (kŭm' fȯrt) [O.F. *conforter*, L. *confortāre* (CON-, *fortis*, strong)], *v.t.* To cheer, to encourage, to console; to make comfortable; *to make strong; *(*Law*) to abet. *n.* Support or assistance in time of weakness; consolation; encouragement; that which affords consolation or encouragement; quiet enjoyment; ease, general well-being, absence of trouble or anxiety; (*pl.*) the material things that contribute to bodily satisfaction; (*Am.*) a quilted coverlet; a comforter. **comfort station,** *n.* (*Am.*) A public convenience. **creature comforts,** *n.pl.* The material sources of comfort, good food, warmth, clothes, etc. **cold comfort** [COLD].

comfortable (kŭm' fȯr tàbl) [A.-F. *confortable*, as prec.], *a.* At ease, in good circumstances, free from want, hardship, trouble, or pain; quietly happy, contented; such as to save hardship, pain, or trouble; *comforting. **comfortableness,** *n.* **comfortably,** *adv.*

comforter (kŭm' fȯr tėr), *n.* One who or that which comforts; a long, narrow, woollen scarf; (*Theol.*) the Holy Ghost. **Job's comforter:** One who makes a show of comforting but does exactly the opposite.

comfortless (kŭm' fȯrt les), *a.* Without comfort; cheerless. ***comfortlessly,** *adv.* ***comfortlessness,** *n.*

comfrey (kŭm' fri) [O.F. *confirie*, med. L. *cumfiria* (etym. doubtful)], *n.* A tall wild plant, *Symphytum officinale*, with rough leaves and yellowish or purplish flowers, formerly prized as a vulnerary.

comic (kom' ik) [L. *cōmicus*, Gr. *kōmikos* (*kōmos*, a revel)], *a.* Pertaining to comedy, laughable, absurd, provoking mirth; facetious, burlesque, intended to be laughable. *n.* A comedian; a droll; a comic paper; the comic aspect of things. **comic opera,** *n.* One largely in dialogue and comic in treatment; a musical burlesque. **comical** (kom' ik ăl), *a.* Ludicrous, laughable; exciting mirth. **to strike comical:** (*slang*) To astonish. **comicality** (-kăl' i ti), *n.* **comically,** *adv.* **comico-,** *comb. form.* **comico-tragic,** *a.* **comico-didactic,** *a.*

Cominform (kom' in fȯrm) [Rus.], *n.* (*Pol.*) The Information Bureau of the Communist Parties, founded in 1947, originally including Yugoslavia, since expelled. **Comintern** (kom' in tėrn), *n.* (*Pol.*) The Third Communist International, founded in Moscow in 1919, dissolved in June, 1943.

coming (kŭm' ing), *a.* Approaching; future, to come. *n.* The act of approaching or arriving, arrival; the act of sprouting, as malt; (*pl.*) sprouts or rootlets (of malted grain). **coming eleven:** Nearly eleven years old. **coming on,** *n.* Approach, improvement, increase. *a.* Affable, complaisant.

comingle [COMMINGLE].

comitatus (kom i tā' tŭs) [L., from *comes -item*, a companion], *n.* (*Hist.*) The retinue of a noble or chieftain; (*Law*) an English county. **posse comitatus,** *n.* A force which the sheriff of a county is empowered to raise in case of riot, etc.

comity (kom' i ti) [L. *cōmitās -tātem* (*cōmis*, courteous)], *n.* Affability, friendliness, courtesy, civility. **comity of nations:** The courtesy by which a nation allows another's laws to be recognized within its territory, so far as is practicable.

comma (kom' à) [L., from Gr. *komma*, a stamp, a clause (*koptein*, to strike, cut)], *n.* A punctuation mark (,), denoting the shortest pause in reading; (*Mus.*) a minute difference of tone. **inverted commas,** *n.pl.* (*Print.*) Raised or superior commas as thus: '—'; "—" used to indicate quotations, quotation marks, quotes. **comma bacillus,** *n.* A comma-shaped species of *Spirillum*, found by Koch, in cases of Asiatic cholera.

command (kŏ mand') [O.F. *comander*, late L. *commandāre* (COM-, *mandāre*, to entrust)], *v.t.* To order, to call for, to enforce, to govern, to hold in subjection, to exercise authority over; to dominate, to overlook; to control, to have at one's disposal; to master, to subjugate. *v.i.* To give orders; to exercise supreme authority. *n.* An order, a bidding, a mandate; power, authority; control, mastery, the power of dominating or overlooking; a naval or military force under the command of a particular officer. **at command:** Ready for orders; at one's disposal. **command-in-chief:** The supreme command. **to command-in-chief:** To be commander-in-chief. **command-night,** *n.* A theatrical performance given by royal command. **commandant** (kom ȧn dănt′) [F.], *n.* The governor or commanding officer of a place. **commandantship,** *n.* **commanding,** *a.* Giving or entitled to give commands; fitted to command; impressive; dominating, overlooking. **commandingly,** *adv.*

commandeer (kom ȧn dēr′) [Dut. *kommanderen,* from F. *commander,* to command], *v.t.* To make use of for military purposes; to seize (goods), to impress (men); *v.i.* To exercise the right to seize and impress for military purposes.

commander (kȯ man′ der), *n.* One who commands or is in authority; a general or leader of a body of men; a member of one of the higher grades in some orders of knighthood; (*Nav.*) an officer next above a lieutenant; a large wooden mallet. **commander-in-chief,** *n.* (*Mil.*) The officer in supreme command of the British army, of the military forces in a colony, or of a foreign expedition; (*Nav.*) the officer in supreme command of all the ships in a certain district. **commander-in-chiefship,** *n.* **commandership,** *n.* **commandery, -dry** (kȯ man′ dėr i, -dri), *n.* In military orders of knighthood, a district or manor, which, with its revenues, was administered by a commander; (*loosely*) a non-military priory.

commandment (kȯ mand′ ment), *n.* An order, a command, esp. a Divine command; a precept; a law, esp. of the decalogue; *authority, power. **the Ten Commandments:** The decalogue. **the Eleventh Commandment:** (*colloq.*) An additional precept, "Thou shalt not be found out."

commando (kȯ man′ dō) [Port., from *commandar,* to command], *n.* (*pl.* **-os**) A body of men called out for military service; an expedition or raid by Boers or Portuguese in S. Africa, esp. against natives; a body of men selected and trained to undertake a specially hazardous raid on or behind the enemy lines; a man thus selected; a mobile amphibious force.

commatic (kȯ măt′ ik) [COMMA], *a.* In brief clauses; concise, terse; (*Mus.*) pertaining to or entailing the use of the comma.

commemorate (kȯ mem′ ȯ rāt) [L. *commemorātus,* p.p. of *commemorāre* (COM-, *memorāre,* to mention, from *memor,* mindful)], *v.t.* To keep in remembrance by some solemn act; to celebrate the memory of; to be a memorial of. **commemorable,** *a.* **commemoration** (-rā′ shŭn), *n.* The act of commemorating; a service, ceremony, or festival in memory of some person, deed, or event; (*Oxford Univ.*) the annual festival commemorating benefactors to the University. **commemorative,** *a.* **commemoratively,** *adv.*

commence (kȯ mens′) [O.F. *comencer* (cp. It. *cominciare*), from L. COM-, *initiāre,* to begin (*initium,* a beginning, from IN-, *īre,* to go)], *v.i.* To start, to begin; to begin (to do something); to begin to be (something); to assume a character; (*Univ.*) to take the full degree in a faculty. *v.t.* To enter upon; to perform the first act of. **commencement,** *n.* Beginning, origin, rise; first instance, first existence; the day when the degrees of Master and Doctor are conferred, at Cambridge, Dublin, and American Universities; (*Am. schools*) speech day.

commend (kȯ mend′) [L. *commendāre* (COM-, *mandāre,* to entrust)], *v.t.* To commit to the charge of, to entrust; to recommend as worthy of notice, regard, or favour; to praise, to approve. **n.* Commendation; (*pl.*) kind wishes, remembrances. **commend me to:** Remember me to; give me as my choice. **commendable,** *a.* Worthy of commendation; *bestowing commendation. **commendableness,** *n.* **commendably,** *adv.* **commendation** (-dā′ shŭn), *n.* The act of commending; recommendation of a person to the consideration or favour of another; *a greeting, service, respects. **commendator** (kom′ ėn dā tȯr), *n.* One who holds a benefice *in commendam;* *the president of a commandery; a Spanish title corr. to viceroy or lieutenant. **commendatory** (kȯ men′ dȧ tȯr i), *a.* That serves to commend; holding a commendam; held as a commendam. *n.* Commendation, eulogy.

commendam (kȯ men′ dăm) [L., in trust], *n.* (*Eccles.*) Holding a vacant benefice in trust (abolished in 1836) till an incumbent was appointed; holding a benefice in the absence of the regular incumbent.

commensal (kȯ men′ sȧl) [F., from med. L. *commensālis* (COM-, *mensa,* table)], *a.* Eating at the same table, sharing the same food. *n.* (*Zool. and Bot.*) An animal that lives in intimate association with on the surface or in the substance of another, without being parasitic. **commensalism,** *n.* **commensality** (-săl′ i ti), *n.*

commensurable (kȯ men′ shėr ȧbl) [L. *commensūrābilis* (COM-, *mensūrābilis,* from *mensūrāre,* see foll.)], *a.* Measurable by a common unit; (*Math.*) applied to two magnitudes which have a common measure; proportionate (to). **commensurability,** *n.* **commensurableness,** *n.* **commensurably,** *adv.*

commensurate (kȯ men′ shėr ȧt) [L. *commensūrātus* (COM-, *mensūrātus,* p.p. of *mensūrāre,* to measure, from *mensūra,* a measure)], *a.* Having the same measure or extent; proportional. **commensurately,** *adv.* **commensurateness,** *n.*

comment (kom′ ėnt) [O.F. *comment,* L. *commentum,* invention, comment, neut. p.p. of *comminisci* (COM-, *minisci,* from the root *men-,* cp. *mens,* mind, *memini,* I remember)], *n.* A remark, a criticism; a note interpreting or illustrating a work or portion of a work. *v.i.* (kȯ ment′) To make explanatory or critical remarks or notes (on a book or writing); to criticize or make remarks (upon) unfavourably. *v.t.* To expound, to annotate. **commentary** (kom′-), *n.* A comment; a series of explanatory notes on a whole work; *(*pl.*) a historical narrative. ***commentate,** *v.* To comment. **commentation** (-tā′ shŭn), *n.* **commentator** (kom′ ėn tā tȯr), *n.* The author of a commentary; an annotator, an expositor; a radio reporter.

commerce (kom′ ĕrs) [F., from L. *commercium* (COM-, *merx -cis,* wares, merchandise)], *n.* Trade, traffic; the interchange of commodities between nations or individuals; a game at cards; (*fig.*) intercourse, esp. sexual. **v.i.* To trade; to have intercourse. **commerce-destroyer,** *n.* (*Nav.*) A cruiser employed to sink enemy merchant shipping on the high seas.

commercial (kȯ mĕr′ shȧl), *a.* Pertaining to or connected with commerce. *n.* A commercial traveller; a radio or television programme sponsored by an advertiser. **commercial room,** *n.* Hotel room reserved for commercial travellers. **commercial television,** *n.* System of television broadcasting financially dependent upon revenue obtained from advertisements. **commercial traveller,** *n.* An agent sent out by a trader to solicit orders from retailers, (*Am.*) a drummer. **commercialism,** *n.* A trading spirit; commercial practices. **commercialist,** *n.* **commerciality,** (-shi ăl′ i ti), *n.* **commercialize,** *v.t.* **commercially,** *adv.*

commerge (kȯ mĕrj′), *v.i.* To merge together.

comminate (kom′ i nāt) [L. *comminātus,* p.p. of *comminārī* (*minārī,* to threaten)], *v.t.* To threaten, to denounce. **commination** (-nā′ shŭn), *n.* A threat, a denunciation; (*Ch. of Eng.*) a service denouncing God's judgments on sinners, used on Ash Wednesday. **comminatory,** *a.* Threatening, denunciatory.

commingle (kȯ ming′ gėl) [COM-, MINGLE], *v.t.* and *i.* To mingle or mix together; to blend.

comminute (kom′ i nūt) [L. *comminūtus,* p.p. of

comminuere (*minuere*, to make smaller)], *v.t.* To make smaller; to reduce to minute particles or to powder; to divide into small portions. **comminuted fracture,** *n.* (*Surg.*) A fracture in which the bone is broken into small pieces. **comminution** (-nū′ shŭn).

commiserate (kŏ miz′ ėr āt) [L. *commiserātus*, p.p. of *commiserāri* (*miserāri*, to pity)], *v.t.* To pity, to compassionate to express pity or compassion for. **commiseration** (-rā′ shŭn), *n.* **commiserative** (kŏ miz′ ėr ă tiv), *a.* **commiseratively,** *adv.*

commissar (kom′ i sar) [Rus., a commissioner], *n.* The head of a department of government in the U.S.S.R.

commissariat (kom i sâr′ i ăt) [F., as foll.], *n.* That department of the army charged with supplying provisions and stores for the soldiers; (*Sc. Law*) the jurisdiction of a commissary.

commissary (kom′ i săr i) [late L. *commissārius*, from *commissus*, p.p. of *committere* (*mittere*, to send)], *n.* A commissioner; a deputy; (*Mil.*) an officer in charge of the commissariat; (*Eccles.*) the deputy who supplies a bishop's place in the remote parts of his diocese; (*Sc. Law*) the judge of a commissary court **commissary court:** (*Law*) A court to try cases that in mediæval times were under jurisdiction of the bishops' commissaries; (*Sc.*) a county court presided over by a sheriff. **commissary-general,** *n.* (*Mil.*) The head of the commissariat. **commissarial** (sâr′ i ăl), *a.* **commissaryship,** *n.*

commission (kŏ mish′ ŭn) [F., from L. *commissio -ōnem* (see prec.)], *n.* The act of doing or committing; entrusting a duty to another; hence, trust, charge, command; delegation of authority; a number of persons entrusted with authority; the document conferring authority, esp. that of military and naval officers; a body of commissioners; an allowance made to a factor or agent; a percentage. *v.t.* To authorize, to empower, to appoint to an office, or send upon active service by commission; to order (the painting of a picture, writing of a book, etc.). **in commission:** Entrusted with authority; (*Nav.*) prepared for active service; entrusted to a commission instead of the constitutional officer. **to put a ship in commission:** (*Nav.*) To issue a warrant to man and fit out a ship for active service. **on commission:** A percentage of the proceeds of goods sold being paid to the agent or retailer. **Royal Commission,** *n.* (*Pol.*) A commission of enquiry ordered by Parliament. **commissioned,** *a.* Holding a commission (esp. from the Crown). **commission agent, merchant,** *n.* One who acts as agent for others, and is paid by a percentage. **commission-day.** The opening day of assizes, when the judge's commission is read. **Commission of the Peace,** *n.* A warrant under the Great Seal empowering persons to serve as Justices of the Peace. **commissionaire** (kŏ mish ŏ nâr′) [F. *commissionnaire*, commissioner], *n.* One of a corps of time-expired soldiers and sailors, orig. enrolled in London in 1859, to carry messages, act as caretakers, timekeepers, etc. **commissional,** *a.* **commissioner,** *n.* One empowered to act by a commission or warrant; a member of a commission or government board; the head of some department of the public service. **commissioner for oaths:** (*Law*) A person authorized to receive affidavits and other sworn declarations. **High Commissioner,** *n.* The representative in Britain of a Dominion government. **Lord High Commissioner,** *n.* The sovereign's representative in the Church of Scotland. **commissionership,** *n.*

commissure (kom′ i sūr) [L. *commissūra*, from *commiss-us*, p.p. of *committere* (see foll.)], *n.* A joint, a seam; (*Anat.*) the point of junction of two sides of anything separated, or of two similar organs, as the great commissure of the brain; a suture; a line of closure, as of eyelids, lips, mandibles; (*Arch.*) the joint of two stones; the application of one surface to another; (*Bot.*) the line of junction of two opposite carpels. **commissural** (kom i sūr′ ăl), *a.*

commit (kŏ mit′) [L. *committere* (COM-, *mittere*, to send)], *v.t.* (*past & p.p.* **committed**) To entrust, to deposit; to consign, to perpetrate; to refer (as a Bill) to a Parliamentary committee; (*Law*) to send for trial or to prison. **to commit to memory:** To learn by heart. **to commit oneself:** To pledge oneself; to make a mistake; to compromise oneself. **committable,** *a.* **committer,** *n.* **commitment, -tal,** *n.* The action of the verb TO COMMIT; a sending for trial or to prison; the delivery of a prisoner to the charge of the prison authorities; an engagement to carry out certain duties or meet certain expenses.

committee (kŏ mit′ i) [late A.-F. (F. *commis*), p.p. of *commettre*, L. *committere*, as prec.], *n.* A board elected or deputed to examine, consider, and report on any business referred to them. **committeeman,** *n.* A member of a committee.

committor (kŏ mit′ ŏr), *n.* (*Law*) One who commits (a lunatic, etc.) to the care of a person or institution. **committee,** *n.* (*Law*) (kŏm i tē′) The person to whom the care of such an one is committed.

commix (kŏm iks′), *v.t.* and *i.* To mix together, to blend. **commixtion,** *n.* **commixture,** *n.*

commode (kŏ mōd′) [F., from L. *commodus*, convenient (*modus*, measure)], *n.* A head-dress worn by ladies in the time of William and Mary; a bureau; a night-stool.

commodious (kŏ mō′ di ŭs) [O.F. *commodieux*, late L. *commodiōsus*, for L. *commodus*, as prec.], *a.* Roomy; convenient, suited to its purpose. **commodiously,** *adv.* **commodiousness,** *n.*

commodity (kŏ mod′ i ti) [F. *commodité*, L. *commoditātem*, acc. of *commoditās* (*commodus*, see COMMODE)], *n.* An article which yields accommodation or convenience; an article of commerce; *convenience, expediency; advantage, profit.

commodore (kom′ ŏ dôr) [formerly *commandore* (derivation obscure, from L. *commandāre*, to COMMAND)], *n.* (*Naut.*) An officer ranking above captain or below rear-admiral; by courtesy, the senior captain when two or more ships of war are in company; the president of a yacht-club; a captain of pilots; the leading ship or the senior captain of a fleet of merchantmen.

common (kom′ ŏn) [O.F. *comun*, L. *commūnis* (*-mūnis*, bound, earlier *mœnis*, obliging, ready to serve)], *a.* Belonging equally to more than one; open or free to all; pertaining to or affecting the public; often met with, ordinary, usual; of low rank, position, or birth; vulgar; inferior, mean; (*Math.*) belonging to several quantities; (*Gram.*) applicable to a whole class; (*Pros.*) variable in quantity. *n.* A tract of open ground, the common property of all members of a community; (*Law*) conjoint possession. *v.i.* *To participate in; *to confer, to discuss; to have a right in common ground; to board together. **above the common:** Superior to most. **in common:** Equally with another or others. **out of the common:** Extraordinary, unusual. **right of common:** The right to pasture cattle, dig turf, cut wood, fish, etc., on the property of another. **common carrier:** A person or company undertaking to transport goods for hire. **common chord:** (*Mus.*) A note accompanied by its third and fifth. **common council:** The governing body of a city or corporate town. **common councilman. common crier:** The public or town crier. **common or garden:** (*colloq.*) Ordinary. **common gender:** Applied to a word used both for the masculine and the feminine. ***common hackneyed,** *a.* Hackneyed. **common jury:** (*Law*) A petty jury to try all cases. **common law:** The unwritten law, based on immemorial usage. **common lawyer. common market,** *n.* An association of countries with common tariffs to all other countries. **common measure** (*Math.*) A number which will divide two or more numbers exactly; (*Mus.*) common time, 2 or 4 beats to the bar, esp. 4 crotchets to the bar. **common metre:** (*Mus.*) Ordinary metre. **common noun:** The name of any one of a class of objects. **Common Pleas:** (*Law*) A division of the High Court of Justice with a civil jurisdiction only (abolished 1875). **Common Prayer:** The liturgy of the Church of England. **common room:** A room in a college or school to which teachers or students resort for social purposes. **common sense:** Sound practical judgment; the general feeling of mankind; the system of philosophy founded by Reid, based on general intuitions. **commonsense,** *a.* Marked by common sense. **Common Serjeant,** *n.* (*Law*) The judge of the City of London ranking next to the Recorder. **common time:** (*Mus.*) Time with two beats, or any multiple of two beats, in a bar. **commonish,** *a.* **commonly,** *adv.* Usually, frequently; meanly, cheaply; in an ordinary manner; *jointly. **commonness,** *n.* **commonweal,** *n.* The welfare of the community.

commonable (kom′ ȯn ȧbl), *a.* Held in common; that may be pastured on common land. **commonage,** *n.* The right of using anything in common; the right of pasturing cattle on a common; common property in land; common land; commonalty.

commonalty (kom′ ȯn ȧl ti) [O.F. *comunalté*, from *comunal*, L. *commūnālis*], *n.* The common people; mankind in general; a commonwealth; a corporation.

commoner (kom′ ȯ nėr), *n.* One of the commonalty, below the rank of a peer; a member of the House of Commons; a student at Oxford or Winchester not on the foundation; one having a joint right in common ground; *a prostitute.

commoney (kom′ ȯ ni), *n.* A clay marble.

commonplace (kom′ ȯn plās) [cp. L. *locus communis*, a common topic], *a.* Common, trivial, trite, unoriginal. *n.* A general idea; a trite remark; anything occurring frequently or habitually. **v.t.* To arrange under general heads; to enter in a commonplace-book. **v.i.* To indulge in platitudes. **commonplaceness,** *n.* **commonplace-book,** *n.* A book in which thoughts, extracts from books, etc., are entered for future use.

commons (kom′ ȯnz), *n.pl.* The common people; the House of Commons; food provided at a common table; a ration or allowance of food; fare. **Doctors' Commons:** A college near St. Paul's Cathedral, London, for professors of civil law, where they used to common together; the buildings occupied by them, which included a court, registry of wills, and office for marriage licences. **House of Commons:** The lower House of Parliament in the British and some other constitutions, the third estate of the realm. **short commons:** A scanty allowance of food.

commonty (kom′ ȯn ti) [O.F. *communeté*, COMMUNITY], *n.* (*Sc. Law*) Land belonging to two or more common proprietors; a common; *the commonalty, the commonwealth.

commonweal [COMMON].

commonwealth (kom′ ȯn welth) [cp. L. *res publica*], *n.* The whole body of citizens; the body politic; a free state; a republic; (*Hist.*) the form of government in England from the death of Charles I (1649), to the abdication of Richard Cromwell (1659); the federation of Australian States; (*fig.*) a body of persons having common interests; *the commonweal. **commonwealthsman,** *n.* (*Hist.*) One who supported the English Commonwealth. **British Commonwealth of Nations:** Autonomous communities united by a common allegiance to the British Crown.

commotion (kȯ mō′ shůn) [O.F. *comocion*, L. *commōtiōnem*, acc. of *commōtio* (*motio*, from *movēre*, to move)], *n.* Violent motion; agitation, excitement; a popular tumult.

commove (kȯ moov′) [F. *commovoir*, L. *commovēre*, as prec.], *v.t.* To disturb, to agitate, to excite.

commune (1) (kom′ ūn) [F., from late L. *commūnia*, neut. pl. of *commūnis*, COMMON], *n.* A small territorial district in France and Belgium governed by a mayor and council; the inhabitants or members of the council of a commune. **the Paris Commune:** (*Hist.*) The revolutionary committee who replaced the municipality in 1789; the communistic body who took possession of Paris in 1871 after its evacuation by the Germans. **communal** (ko mū′ nȧl, kom′ ū nȧl), *a.* Pertaining to a commune; for the common use or benefit; pertaining to the Paris Commune; pertaining to the community or to the commons. **communalism** (kȯ mū′ nȧl izm, kom′ ū-), *n.* The theory of government by communes or corporations of towns and districts. **communalist,** *n.* **communalistic** (-lis′ tik), *a.* **communard** (kom′-), *n.* An adherent of the Paris Commune; a communist.

commune (2) (kȯ mūn′, kom′ ūn) [O.F., *comunier*, L. *commūnicāre* (*commūnis*, COMMON)], *v.i.* To converse together familiarly, to hold converse with one's heart; (*Am.*) to receive the Holy Communion. *n.* (kom′ ūn) Communion; intimate converse. **communer** (2) (kȯ mū′ nėr). *n.*

communicate (kȯ mū′ ni kāt) [L. *commūnicāre* (*commūnis*, COMMON)], *v.t.* To impart, to give a share of, to transmit; to reveal; (*Eccles.*) to give Holy Communion to. *v.i.* To share; to hold intercourse, to confer by speech or writing; to be connected, to open into; (*Eccles.*) to partake of the Holy Communion. **communicable** (kȯ mū′ ni kȧbl), *a.* Capable of being communicated or imparted. **communicability** (-bil′ i ti). **communicableness,** *n.* **communicably,** *adv.* **communicant,** *a.* Communicating; (*Anat.*) branching from or communicating with. *n.* One who communicates (information, etc.); (*Eccles.*) one who partakes of Holy Communion. **communication** (-kā′ shůn), *n.* The act of communicating; that which is communicated; news; intercourse; means of passing from one place to another. **communication cord,** *n.* (*Rail.*) Device whereby a passenger can stop a train. **communication lines,** *n.pl.* (*Mil.*) The means of communication between an army and its base. **communicative** (-mū′ ni kȧ tiv), *a.* Inclined to communicate; not reserved. **communicatively,** *adv.* **communicativeness,** *n.* **communicator,** *n.* One who or that which imparts or informs; apparatus for sending a telegraphic message; apparatus on a train for communicating with the guard or driver; (*slang*) a bell. **communicatory,** *a.*

communion (kȯ mū′ nyȯn) [F., from L. *commūnio -ōnem* (*commūnis*, COMMON)], *n.* The act of communicating or communing; participation, sharing; fellowship, intercourse; union in religious faith; the act of partaking of the Eucharist; a religious body. **Holy Communion,** *n.* The administration of the Eucharist. **communion service,** *n.* The service used at the celebration of the Eucharist. **communion table,** *n.* The table (often called in the English Church the altar) used in the celebration of the Eucharist. **communionist,** *n.* One having special views upon admission to Holy Communion. **close communionist,** *n.* One who would restrict partakers to those who are members of a particular church. **fellow-communionist,** *n.* A member of the same body of communicants. **open communionist,** *n.* One who believes in free and unrestricted admission to Holy Communion.

communiqué (kom ū′ ni kā) [Fr.], *n.* An official announcement.

Communism (kom′ ū nizm) [L. *commūnis*, common], *n.* (*Pol.*) A theory of government based on the belief that true Socialism can be attained only through the violent overthrow of Capitalism and the establishment of dictatorship by the proletariat. **Communist,** *n.* and *a.* An adherent of, or pertaining to, Communism.

community (kȯ mū′ ni ti) [O.F. *communeté*, L. *commūnitātem*, acc. of *commūnitās* (*commūnis*, COMMON)], *n.* A body of people having common rights or interests; an organized body, municipal, national, social, or political; society at large, the public; a body of individuals living in a common home; a body of individuals having common interests, occupation, religion, nationality, etc.; common possession or enjoyment; fellowship; identity of nature or character. **community centre:** A hall or other building open to all residents in the locality who can come there together on an equal footing to enjoy social, recreative and educational activities. **community singing,** *n.* Organized singing by the audience at a social gathering, etc.

commute (kŏ mūt′) [L. *commūtāre, mūtāre,* to change)], *v.t.* To put one for the other; to exchange, to substitute one (payment, punishment, etc.) for another; (*Law*) to reduce the severity of. *v.i.* To travel to and fro on a season-ticket. **commutable,** *a.* **commutability** (-tă bil′ i ti), *n.* **commutation** (kom ū tā′ shŭn), *n.* The act of commuting; change, exchange; a payment made in commuting; (*Law*) the substitution of a less penalty for a greater. **Commutation Act:** An enactment passed in 1836 substituting payment in money for tithes instead of payment in kind. **commutation ticket:** (*Am.*) A railway ticket covering a fixed number of journeys, a season ticket. **commutative** (kom′ ū-, kŏ mū′ tă tiv), *a.* **commutatively,** *adv.* **commuter,** *n.* Holder of a commutation ticket, a season-ticket holder. **commutator** (kom′-), **commutor,** *n.* One who or that which commutes; an instrument which reverses an electric current without changing the arrangement of the conductors. **commutator transformer:** (*Elec.*) A device for converting from low to high voltage d.c.

comose (kō′ mōs) [L. *comōsus* (*coma,* the hair)], *a.* (*Bot.*) Hairy, filamentose.

compact (1) (kom′ păkt) [L. *compactus,* p.p. of *compascisci* (*pacisci,* to covenant)], *n.* An agreement, a bargain, a covenant; a small box with face-powder, puff, and mirror; a flap-jack.

compact (2) (kŏm păkt′) [L. *compactus,* p.p. of *compingere* (*pangere,* to fasten)], *a.* Closely packed or joined together; solid, succinct. *v.t.* To consolidate; to join closely and firmly together; to compose. **compacted,** *a.* **compactedly,** *adv.* **compactedness,** *n.* ***compactile,** *a.* ***compaction,** *n.* **compactly,** *adv.* **compactness,** *n.* **compacture,** *n.* Compact structure; close union of parts.

compages (kŏm pā′ jēz) [L., joining together (*pag-,* root of *pangere,* as COMPACT, (2)], *n.* A structure or system of many parts united. **compaginate** (kŏm păj′ i nāt) [L. *compāginātus,* p.p. of *compāgināre* (*compāgo -inem, compāges*)], *v.t.* To unite together in a structure or system. **compagination** (-nā′ shŭn), *n.*

companion (1) (kŏm păn′ yŏn) [O.F. *compaignon,* late L. *compānio -ōnem* (*pānis,* bread)], *n.* One who associates or keeps company with another; a comrade; a partner; a member of the lowest grade in some orders of knighthood; a person employed to live with another. *a.* Accompanying; going along with or matching something. *v.t.* To accompany. *v.i.* To go or consort (with). **companionable,** *a.* Fit to be a companion; sociable. ***companionage,** *n.* **companionableness,** *n.* **companionably,** *adv.* **companionate marriage,** *n.* Cohabitation with a view to marriage. **companionless,** *a.* **companionship,** *n.* Fellowship, association, company; (*Print.*) a body of compositors engaged on the same work.

companion (2) (kŏm păn′ yŏn) [ult. from L. *compānāticum,* provisions (cp. Dut. *kompanje,* O.F. *compagne,* It. *compagna, camera della compagna,* provision-room or pantry)], *n.* (*Naut.*) The raised window-frame upon the quarter-deck through which light passes to the cabins and decks below. **companion-hatch,** *n.* In small ships, a porch over the entrance to the cabin. **companion-ladder,** *n.* The ladder leading from the cabin to the quarter-deck. **companion-stairs, -way,** *n.* The staircase or porch of the ladder-way from the cabin to the quarter-deck.

company (kŭm′ pă ni) [O.F. *compaignie,* from *compaignon,* see prec.], *n.* Society, companionship, fellowship; a number of persons associated together by interest or for carrying on business; a corporation; associates, guests, visitors; a body of actors engaged at a theatre; (*Mil.*) a subdivision of an infantry regiment under the command of a captain. ***v.t.** To accompany. *v.i.* To associate (with); *to be a gay companion. **ship's company:** (*Naut.*) The crew of a ship. **to keep company with:** To court or woo.

comparative (kŏm păr′ ă tiv) [as foll.], *a.* Estimated by comparison; grounded on comparison; expressing comparison, expressing a higher or lower degree of a quality. *n.* (*Gram.*) The comparative degree or the word or inflection expressing it. **comparative anatomy,** *n.* The general phenomena of organic structure derived from the anatomy of all organized bodies. **comparatively,** *adv.* **comparator** (kom′ pă rā tŏr), *n.* An apparatus for comparing.

compare (kŏm pâr′) [O.F. *comparer,* L. *comparāre* (COM-, *par,* equal)], *v.i.* To show how one thing agrees with another; to liken one thing to another; to see how two things resemble each other or are mutually related; (*Gram.*) to inflect according to degrees of comparison. *v.i.* To bear comparison. *n.* Comparison; an equal. **beyond compare:** Peerless, unequalled. **to compare notes:** To exchange opinions. **comparable** (kom′-), *a.* Capable of being compared (with); worthy of being compared (to). **comparability** (kom păr ă bil′ i ti), *n.*

comparison (kŏm păr′ i sŏn) [O.F. *comparaison,* L. *comparātio -ōnem,* as prec.], *n.* The act of comparing; a comparative estimate; a simile, contrast, illustration; (*Gram.*) the inflection of an adjective or adverb. **v.t.* To compare.

compart (kŏm part′) [O.F. *compartir,* late L. *compartīre* (COM-, *partīre,* from *pars -tis,* part)], *v.i.* To divide into compartments; to partition. ***compartition** (-tish′ ŭn), *n.* **compartment** (kŏm part′ mĕnt) [F. *compartiment,* late L. *compartimentum* (as prec.)], *n.* A division; a portion of a railway carriage, room, etc., separated from the other part; (*Naut.*) a portion of the hold of a ship shut off by a bulkhead and capable of being made watertight.

compass (kŭm′ pås) [F. *compas,* a circle, a round, a pair of compasses, late L. *compassus,* a circle, a circuit; later, a pair of compasses (cp. *compassāre,* to pace round, encompass; relation to *compassus* obscure)], *n.* A circle, circumference, area, extent; a circuit, a roundabout course; (*fig.*) reach, capacity; (*Mus.*) the range or power of the voice or a musical instrument; an instrument indicating the magnetic meridian, used to ascertain direction, and esp. to determine the course of a ship, airplane, etc.; the mariner's compass; (*pl.*) an instrument with two legs connected by a joint for describing circles, measuring distances, etc. *v.t.* To go round; to besiege, surround, invest; to comprehend; to accomplish, to contrive; to plot. **to box the compass** [BOX (2)]. **to fetch a compass:** To make a circuit. **beam-compass** [BEAM]. **bow-compasses** [BOW (1)]. **compass-card,** *n.* The card or dial of a mariner's compass on which the points are drawn. **compass-needle,** *n.* The needle of the mariner's compass. **compass-plane,** *n.* (*Carp.*) A plane convex underneath for planing concave surfaces. **compass-signal,** *n.* (*Naut.*) A flag indicating a point of the compass. **compass-saw,** *n.* A saw which cuts circularly. **compass-timber,** *n.* Curved timber used in shipbuilding. **compass-window,** *n.* A semicircular window. **compassable,** *a.* **gyro-compass** [GYRO].

compassion (kŏm păsh′ ŏn) [O.F., from L. *compassio -ōnem,* from *compatī* (COM-, *patī,* to suffer)], *n.* Suffering with another; pity, sympathy for the sufferings and sorrows of others; an act of pity or mercy. **v.i.* To compassionate. **compassionable,** *a.* **compassionate** (kŏm păsh′ ŏ nāt), *a.* Merciful, inclined to pity; sympathetic. *v.t.* (-nāt) To feel compassion for; to commiserate. **compassionate leave,** *n.* Leave granted on account of domestic difficulties. **compassionately,** *adv.* **compassionateness,** *n.* ***compassive,** *a.* Compassionate.

compatible (kŏm păt′ i bĕl) [F., from late L. *compatibilis*, from *compatī*, see prec.], *a.* That may co-exist; congruous, consistent, harmonious. **compatibly,** *adv.* **compatibility** (-bil′ i ti), *n.*

compatriot (kŏm păt′ ri-, -pā′ tri ŏt) [F. *compatriote*], *n.* A fellow-countryman. **compatriotic** (-ot′ ik), *a.* **compatriotism,** *n.*

compear (kŏm pēr′) [F. *comparoir*, L. *compārēre* (*pārēre*, to appear)], *v.i.* (*Sc. Law*) To appear in court in person or by counsel. **compearance,** *n.*

compeer (kŏm pēr′) [prob. from an O.F. *comper*, L. *compar*], *n.* An equal, mate, peer. *v.t.* To equal, to be the peer of.

compel (kŏm pel′) [O.F. *compeller*, L. *compellere* (*pellere*, to drive)], *v.t.* (*past* and *p.p.* **compelled**) To force, to oblige; to cause by force; to drive with force; *to take by force, to extort, exact; *to call, to gather together by force. **compellable,** *a.* **compelling,** *a.* **compellingly,** *adv.*

***compellation** (kom pĕ lā′ shŭn) [L. *compellātio -ōnem*, from *compellāre* (COM-, *pellāre*, freq. of *pellere*, see prec. and cp. *appellāre*, APPELLATION)], *n.* Style of address; appellation. ***compellative** (kŏm pel′ ȧ tiv), *n.* The name by which one is addressed.

compendium (kŏm pen′ di ŭm) [L., from *compendere* (*pendere*, to hang, weigh)], *n.* (*pl.* **-diums, -dia**) An abridgment; a brief compilation; an epitome, a summary. **compend** (kom′ pend), *n.* **compendious** (kŏm pen′ di ŭs) [O.F. *compendieux*, L. *compendiōsus*, as prec.], *a.* Abridged; summed up in a short compass; summary; succinct. **compendiously,** *adv.* **compendiousness,** *n.*

compensate (kom′ pĕn sāt) [L. *compensātus*, p.p. of *compensāre* (*pensāre*, freq. of *pendere*, to weigh)], *v.t.* To counterbalance; to make amends for; to recompense; (*Mech.*) to furnish with an equivalent weight or other device forming a compensation. *v.i.* To supply an equivalent. **compensation** (-sā′ shŭn), *n.* The act of compensating; payment, recompense, amends; that which balances or is an equivalent for something else; (*Accounts*) payment of a debt by an equal credit; a set-off. **compensation balance** or **pendulum,** *n.* A watch-balance or a pendulum constructed so as to make equal time-beats notwithstanding changes of temperature. **compensational** (-sā′ shŭn ȧl), *a.* **compensative** (-pen′ sȧ tiv), *a.* Compensating. *n.* An equivalent. **compensator** (kom′ pĕn sā tŏr), *n.* **compensatory** (-pen′ sȧ tŏ ri), *a.* ***compense,** *v.t.* and *i.*

compere (kom′ pâr) [Fr.], *n.* (*Theat.*) A variety actor who introduces to the audience the actors and turns.

compesce (kŏm pes′) [L. *compescere*], *v.t.* To hold in check.

compete (kŏm pēt′) [F. *compéter*, L. *competere* (*petere*, to fall upon, aim at)], *v.i.* To contend as a rival; to strive in emulation.

competent (kom′ pĕ tĕnt) [F., from L. *competentem*, nom. *competens*, pres.p. of *competere*, to COMPETE], *a.* Qualified, sufficient; suitable, adequate; legally qualified; (*colloq.*) admissible, permissible. **competence, -tency,** *n.* The state of being competent; sufficiency; adequate pecuniary support; legal capacity or qualification; admissibility (of evidence); ability (for or to do some task). **competently,** *adv.*

competition (kom pĕ tish′ ŭn) [L. *competitio*, from *competere*, COMPETE], *n.* Emulous striving for the same object; emulation, rivalry; the struggle for existence or gain in industrial and mercantile pursuits; a competitive game or match. **competitioner,** *n.* A competitor; a person securing admission to a service by competition. **competitive** (-pet′ i tiv), *a.* Pertaining to or involving competition. **competitively,** *adv.* **competitor** (-pet′ i tŏr), *n.* One who competes; a rival. **competitory,** *a.* **competitress,** *n.*

compile (kŏm pīl′) [O.F. *compiler*, L. *compīlāre*, to plunder, to pillage (COM-, *pīlāre*, to thrust, from *pīlum*, a javelin)], *v.t.* To compose out of materials from various authors; to assemble various items as in an index or dictionary; to gather such materials into a volume; *to compose; *to comprise. ***compilement** [COMPILATION]. **compiler,** *n.* **compilation** (-lā′ shŭn), *n.* The act of compiling; that which is compiled; a book for which the materials have been drawn from various authors.

complacent (kŏm plā′ sĕnt) [L. *complacens -ntem*, pres.p. of *complacēre* (COM-, *placēre*, to please)], *a.* Satisfied, gratified, self-satisfied. **complacently,** *adv.* **complacence, -ency,** *n.* A feeling of inward satisfaction; the manifestation of such satisfaction by courtesy; *the object which produces such satisfaction; *complaisance.

complain (kŏm plān′) [O.F. *complaign-*, stem of *complaindre*, late L. *complangere* (COM-, *plangere*, to bewail)], *v.i.* To express dissatisfaction or objection; to state a grievance; to make a charge; to murmur, to find fault; to express grief or pain, hence, to ail; *to moan or wail. **v.t.* To mourn over, bewail. **complainant,** *n.* One who complains or makes complaint; (*Law*) a prosecutor; a plaintiff. **complaining,** *a.* That complains; querulous. *n.* A complaint. **complainingly,** *adv.* **complaint,** *n.* An expression of grief or pain, resentment or censure; the subject or ground of such expression; an accusation; a malady; (*Law*) a formal allegation or charge; an information.

complaisant (kŏm′ pli zănt) [F.], *a.* Courteous, obsequious, obliging. **complaisantly,** *adv.* **complaisance,** *n.*

complect (kŏm plekt′) [L. *complecti* (*plectere*, to twine)], *v.t.* To knit together. **complected,** *a.*

complement (kom′ plĕ mĕnt) [L. *complēmentum*, from *complēre* (*plēre*, to fill), *n.* Full quantity; *completeness, perfection; (*Naut.*) the full number required to man a vessel; that which is necessary to make complete; (*Gram.*) a word or phrase required to complete the sense, the predicate; (*Mus.*) the interval necessary to complete an octave. *v.t.* To supply a deficiency; to complete. **complement of an arc** or **angle:** (*Math.*) The difference between the arc or angle and 90°. **complement of a number:** (*Math.*) The difference between a number and the next higher power of ten. **complemental** (kom plĕ men′ tȧl), *a.* **complementally,** *adv.* **complementary,** *a.* That complements. **complementary colour,** *n.* A colour which produces white when mixed with another to which it is complementary.

complete (kŏm plēt′) [L. *complētus*, p.p. of *complēre*, as prec.], *a.* Fulfilled, finished; free from deficiency; entire, absolute. *v.t.* To bring to a state of perfection; to finish; to make whole, to make up the deficiencies of. **completely,** *adv.* **completeness,** *n.* **completion,** *n.* **completive,** *a.*

complex (kom′ pleks) [L. *complexus*, p.p. of *complectere*, COMPLECT], *a.* Composed of several parts; composite; complicated. *n.* A complicated whole; a collection; a complicated system; (*Psych.*) a group of emotional impressions which may be either partly or wholly repressed. **inferiority complex,** *n.* (*Psych.*) An intense conviction of inferiority, resulting either in a timid attitude or an assumed aggressiveness. ***complexed** (kŏm plekst′), *a.* Complex. **complexedness,** *n.* **complexity,** *n.* **complexly** (kom′-), *adv.* **complexus** (kŏm plek′ sŭs), *n.* (*Anat.*) A long, broad muscle lying along the back and side of the neck.

complexion (kŏm plek′ shŭn) [F., from L. *complexio -ōnem*, a comprehending; later, a bodily habit or combination of qualities (*complectere*, as prec.)], *n.* *The temperament or constitution; colour and appearance of the skin, esp. of the face; nature, character, aspect. **complexioned,** *a.* (*usu. in comb.*). **complexionless,** *a.*

complexity, complexus [COMPLEX].

compliance (kŏm plī′ ȧns), *n.* The act of complying; submission, agreement, consent. **compliant,** *a.* Yielding; tending to comply. **compliable,** *a.* Compliant. **compliantly,** *adv.*

complicate (kom′ pli kāt) [L. *complicātus*, p.p. of *complicāre* (*plicāre*, to fold)], *v.t.* To make complex or intricate; to involve. **complicated,** *a.* **complicacy**, *n.* The state of being complicated. **complicatedly,** *adv.* **complication** (-kā′ shŭn), *n.* The act of complicating; the state of being complicated; a complicated matter or circumstance; (*Med.*) a disease or morbid condition arising in the course of another disease.

***complice** (kom′ plis) [F., from L. *complicem*, acc. of *complex*, confederate, lit. intertwined (see COMPLEX)], *n.* An accomplice.

complicity (kŏm plis′ i ti) [F. *complicité*, from *complice*, as prec.], *n.* Participation, partnership, esp. in wrong-doing.

complier [COMPLY].

compliment (kom′ pli mĕnt) [F., from It. *complimento*, from L. *complēmentum*, COMPLEMENT (perh. through Sp. *complimiento*, fulfilment of courtesies)], *n.* An expression or act of courtesy, approbation, respect, or regard; delicate flattery; *a favour, a gift, a gratuity; (*pl.*) ceremonious greetings; courtesies, respects. *v.t.* To pay compliments to; to congratulate, to praise, to flatter courteously. *v.i.* To pay compliments. **complimental,** *a.* **complimentary,** *a.* **compliments of the season:** Greetings or remembrances appropriate to the season. **complimentary ticket,** *n.* A free ticket.

compline (kom′ plin) [M.E. and O.F. *complie*, L. *complēta* (*hōra*), fem. of *complētus*, COMPLETE, because it completed the hours of daily service], *n.* (*R.-C. Ch.*) The last part of the divine office of the Roman breviary, sung after vespers.

complot (kom′ plot) [F., a crowd, a struggle, a plot (etym. unknown)], *n.* A conspiracy or plot. *v.t.* and *i.* (kŏm plot′) To plot together; to combine together.

compluvium (kŏm ploo′ vi ŭm) [L., from *compluere* (*pluere*, to rain)], *n.* (*Hist.*) The opening in the roof of a Roman atrium which collected the rainwater.

comply (kŏm pli′) [It. *complire*, from Sp. *complir* (now *cumplir*), to complete (cp. COMPLIMENT)], *v.i.* To assent, to agree; to act in accordance with the wishes of another; *to fulfil; *to fulfil courtesies. **complier,** *n.*

compo (kom′ pō) [COMPOSITION], *n.* Applied to different compounds in various trades, as the material of which printers' rollers are made, a kind of stucco, etc.

component (kŏm pō′ nĕnt) [L. *compōnens -ntem*, pres.p. of *compōnere* (*pōnere*, to put)], *a.* Serving to make up a compound; a constituent. *n.* A constituent part. **componental** (-nen′ tăl), *a.*

comport (kŏm pōrt′) [F. *comporter*, late L. *comportāre* (*portāre*, to carry)], *v.t.* To conduct, to behave (oneself). *v.i.* To suit, to agree, to accord. ***comportance,** *n.* Behaviour, conduct, bearing.

compose (kŏm pōz′) [F. *composer* (*com-*, with, and *poser*, from late L. *pausāre*, to cease, to place, to pose), confused with L. *compōnere*, COMPOUND (I)], *v.t.* To make, arrange, or construct, by putting together several parts, so as to form one whole; to constitute, to make up by combination; to write, construct, or produce (as a literary or musical work); to write music for given words; to calm, to soothe; to settle, to adjust; to arrange in proper order (as type for printing). *v.i.* To practise composition. **composed,** *a.* Calm, tranquil, settled. **composedly** (kŏm pō′ zĕd li), *adv.* **composedness,** *n.* **composer,** *n.* One who composes, esp. the author of a musical composition. **composing,** *a.* That composes. *n.* The action of the verb TO COMPOSE. **composing-frame,** *n.* (*Print.*) An elevated frame on which the cases of type rest obliquely. **composing-machine,** *n.* A machine for setting type. **composing-room,** *n.* The room in a printing-office where the compositors work. **composing-stick,** *n.* An instrument in which the compositor sets the type from the cases, and adjusts the lines to the proper length.

composite (kom′ pŏ zit) [L. *compositus*, p.p. of *compōnere* (COM-, *pōnere*, to put)], *a.* Made up of distinct parts or elements; compound; (*Bot.*) pertaining to the *Compositæ*, the largest natural order of plants, so called because the heads are made up of many small flowers. *n.* A composite substance or thing; a compound; a composite term. **composite candle,** *n.* A candle made of stearin or coconut oil and stearic acid. **composite carriage,** *n.* A railway carriage containing compartments of different classes. **composite number,** *n.* (*Math.*) A number which is the product of two other numbers greater than unity. **composite order,** *n.* (*Arch.*) The last of the five orders, which partakes of the characters of the Corinthian and Ionic. **compositely,** *adv.* **compositeness,** *n.* **compositive** (-pos′ i tiv), *a.*

composition (kom pŏ zish′ ŭn) [F., from L. *compositio, -ōnem*, as prec.], *n.* The act of composing or putting together to form a whole; the thing composed (esp. used of literary and musical productions); orderly disposition of parts, structural arrangement, style; an agreement to terms or conditions for putting an end to hostilities or any contest or disagreement; a combination of several parts or ingredients, a compound; compensation in lieu of that demanded; settlement by compromise; the amount so accepted; the process of setting type; the act of forming sentences; a piece written for the sake of practice in literary expression; the formation of compound words; (*Arch.*) the arrangement of columns, piers, doors, etc., in a building; (*Art*) the arrangement of different figures in a picture. **composition of forces:** The combining of several forces or motions and determining the resultant of the whole. **composition-metal,** *n.* A kind of brass for sheathing ships.

compositor (kŏm poz′ i tŏr), *n.* (*Print.*) One who sets type, (*Am.*) type-setter.

compos mentis (kom′ pos men′ tis) [L., master of or controlling the mind], *a.* In one's right mind. ***non compos*** (*colloq.*) Not in one's right mind.

compossible (kŏm pos′ ibl) [O.F., from med. L. *compossibilis*], *a.* Capable of coexisting.

compost (kom′ post) [O.F. *composte*, L. *compositus*], *n.* A fertilizing mixture of vegetable matter, etc.; a kind of concrete used by plasterers; stucco. *v.t.* To make into or manure with compost; to plaster.

composure (kŏm pō′ zūr, -zhĕr), *n.* Calmness, tranquillity, a calm frame of mind.

compotation (kom pŏ tā′ shŭn) [*compōtātio -ōnem* (*pōtātio*, from *pōtāre*, to drink)], *n.* The act of drinking together. **compotator** (kom′ pŏ tā tŏr), *n.*

compote (kom′ pōt) [F. *compote*, O.F. *composte*, L. *composta*, *composita*, fem. of *compositus*], *n.* Fruit stewed or preserved in syrup.

compound (I) (kŏm pound′) [M.E. *compounen*, O.F. *componre*, *compondre*, L. *compōnere* (*pōnere*, to put)], *v.t.* To make into one mass by the combination of several constituent parts; to mix, to make up, to form a composite; to combine; to settle amicably; to adjust by agreement; to compromise; to pay a lump sum instead of a periodical subscription. *v.i.* To settle with creditors by agreement; *to bargain; to come to terms by abating something of the first demand. *a.* (kom′ pound) Composed of two or more ingredients or elements; composed of two or more parts; collective, combined, composite; (*Bot.* and *Zool.*) formed by all combination of parts or of several individual organisms. *n.* A combination, a mixture; a compound word; (*Chem.*) a combination of two or more elements by chemical action. **to compound a felony:** (*Law*) To forbear to prosecute a felony for some valuable consideration. **compound addition** or **subtraction,** *n.* (*Arith.*) Processes dealing with numbers of different denominations. **compound animal,** *n.* One consisting of a combination of organisms. **compound engine, locomotive,**

etc., *n.* An engine with one or more additional cylinders of larger diameter into which the steam passes and does further work after leaving the first cylinder. **compound flower,** *n.* An inflorescence consisting of numerous florets surrounded by an involucre; one of the flower-heads of any of the *Compositæ*. **compound fracture,** *n.* (*Surg.*) A fracture in which the integuments are injured, usually by the protrusion of the bone. **compound fructification,** *n.* (*Bot.*) Fructification composed of confluent florets. **compound householder,** *n.* One who compounds with his landlord for his rates. **compound interest,** *n.* Interest added to the principal and bearing interest; the method of computing such interest. **compound interval,** *n.* (*Mus.*) An interval greater than the octave. **compound leaf,** *n.* (*Bot.*) A leaf with branched petioles. **compound microscope,** *n.* A microscope with a combination of lenses. **compound quantity,** *n.* (*Math.*) An arithmetical quantity of more than one denomination; an algebraic quantity, consisting of two or more terms connected by the signs + (plus), or − (minus), or expressed by more letters than one. **compound raceme,** *n.* (*Bot.*) A raceme composed of several small ones. **compound ratio,** *n.* (*Arith.*) The ratio which the product of the antecedents of two or more ratios has to the product of their consequents. **compoundable,** *a.* Capable of being combined; capable of being compounded or commuted. **compounder,** *n.* One who compounds or mixes; one who effects a compromise; one who compounds a debt or a felony; (*Eng. Hist.*) a trimmer; one in favour of the restoration of James II under constitutional guarantees. ***grand compounder:** One who paid large fees for his degree at Cambridge.

compound (2) (kom′ pound) [prob. from Malayalam KAMPONG], *n.* The yard or space surrounding a dwelling-house in India, China, etc. **compound system:** A system of housing and feeding indentured and other labourers, as on the Rand.

comprador (kom prȧ dôr′) [Port., from late L. *comparātor -tōrem*, from *comparāre*, to provide, to purchase], *n.* (*China and Japan*) A native employed in European houses of business as general factotum and intermediary with native customers.

comprehend (kom prė hend′) [L. *comprehendere* (*prae-*, beforehand, *hendere*, obs., to seize, cogn. with Gr. *chandanein*, and GET)], *v.t.* To grasp mentally; to understand; to comprise, to include; *(*malaprop.*) to apprehend. **comprehensible,** *a.* That may be comprehended; clear, intelligible; *that may be comprised. **comprehensibly,** *adv.* **comprehensibility** (kom prė hen si bil′ i ti), *n.*

comprehension (kom prė hen′ shŭn) [L. *comprehensio -ōnem*, as prec.], *n.* The act or power of comprehending or comprising; the faculty by which ideas are comprehended by the intellect; (*Log.*) the sum of the attributes which a term implies; (*Eccles.*) inclusion of all Christians in one communion. **comprehensive,** *a.* Extending widely; including much or many things; having the power of grasping many things at once with the intellect. **comprehensive school,** *n.* A State school in which the various types of secondary school are united. **comprehensively,** *adv.* **comprehensiveness,** *n.*

compress (kŏm pres′) [O.F. *compresser*, L. *compressāre*, freq. of *comprimere* (*premere*, to press)], *v.t.* To squeeze or press together; to bring into narrower limits; to condense; *to have carnal intercourse with. *n.* (kom′ pres) (*Med.*) A soft pad used to preserve due pressure on an artery; a wet cloth for reducing inflammation. **compressible,** *a.* **compressibility** (-bil′ i ti), *n.* **compression** (kŏm presh′ ŭn), *n.* The act of compressing; the state of being compressed; condensation. **compression-spring,** *n.* A spring which opposes pressure. **compressive,** *a.* **compressor,** *n.*

comprise (kŏm prīz′) [F. *compris*, p.p. of *comprendre*, L. *comprehendere*, COMPREHEND], *v.t.* To contain, to include, to comprehend, to embrace; to bring (within certain limits). **comprisable,** *a.*

compromise (kom′ prŏ mīz) [F. *compromis*, p.p. of *compromettre*, L. *comprōmittere* (COM-, *prōmittere*, PROMISE)], *n.* A settlement by mutual concession; adjustment of a controversy or of antagonistic opinions, principles, or purposes by a partial surrender; a medium between conflicting purposes or courses of action. *v.t.* To settle by mutual concession; to place in a position of difficulty or danger; to expose to risk of disgrace. *v.i.* To make a compromise. **compromission** (kom prŏ mish′ ŭn), *n.* Compromise; submission to the decision of an arbitrator.

***compt** [COUNT (1)].

***compter** [COUNTER (1)].

comptograph (komp′ tŏ grăf) [F. *compter*], *n.* A variety of calculating machine which sets down the results on paper. **comptometer** (komp tom′ ė tėr), *n.* The registered trade-name of a calculating machine.

comptoir (koṅ twar′) [F., COUNTER], *n.* A commercial agency or factory in a foreign country.

comptroller [CONTROLLER].

compulsion (kŏm pŭl′ shŭn) [L. *compulsio -ōnem* (*compellere*, COMPEL)], *n.* The act of compelling by moral or physical force; constraint of the will. **compulsive,** *a.* ***compulsative,** *a.* Involving compulsion; tending to compel. **compulsively,** *adv.* **compulsivatively,** *adv.* **compulsiveness,** *n.* **compulsory,** *a.* **compulsatory,** *a.* Exercising compulsion; enforced, necessitated. **compulsorily,** *adv.*

compunction (kŏm pŭngk′ shŭn) [O.F., from L. *compunctio -ōnem*, from *compungere* (*pungere*, to prick)], *n.* Pricking or reproach of conscience; remorse, contrition; regret. ***compunctionless,** *a.* **compunctious,** *a.* **compunctiously,** *adv.*

compurgation (kom pėr gā′ shŭn) [L. *compurgātio -ōnem*, from *compurgāre* (*purgāre*, to purify)], *n.* Vindication; evidence clearing one from a charge; (*Eng. Hist.*) a trial in which a number of persons declared a man's innocence on oath. **compurgator** (kom′ pėr gā tŏr), *n.* **compurgatory** (kŏm pĕr′ gȧ tŏr i), *a.*

compute (kŏm pūt′) [F. *computer*, L. *computāre putāre*, to think)], *v.t.* To determine by calculation; to number, to estimate. **computable,** *a.* **computative,** *a.* **computation** (-tā′ shŭn), *n.* **computor,** *n.* A machine for carrying out difficult or lengthy calculations.

comrade (kom′ răd) [F. *camarade*, Sp. *camarada*, a chamber-mate (*camara*, L. *camera*, CHAMBER)], *n.* A mate, a companion; an intimate associate. **comradeship,** *n.*

Comtism (kom′ tizm, koṅ′ tizm), *n.* The positivist philosophy of Auguste Comte (1798–1857). **Comtist,** *n.*

Comus (kō′ mŭs) [L., from Gr. *kōmos*, a revel], *n.* (*Class. Myth.*) The god of revelry; revelry; licentiousness.

con (1) (kon) [A.-S. *cunnian*, see CAN], *v.t.* To peruse carefully; to study over, to learn; to know. **to con thanks:** To be grateful.

con (2) (kon) [prob. a form of *cond*, earlier *condue*, O.F. *conduire*, L. *condūcere*, to CONDUCT], *v.t.* (*Naut.*) To direct the steering of (a ship). **conner,** *n.* **conning-tower,** *n.* (*Naut.*) The armoured shelter in a warship or submarine from which the vessel is steered.

con (3) (kon) [short for L. *contra*, against], *n.* **pro and con:** For and against.

con- [L. *cum*, with, see COM-], *pref.*

conacre (kon′ ā kėr) [corr. of *cornacre*], *n.* (*Ir.*) The practice of sub-letting land already prepared for cropping.

conation (kŏ nā′ shŭn) [L. *cōnātio -ōnem*, from *cōnārī*, to endeavour], *n.* (*Phil.*) The faculty of desiring or willing. **conational,** *a.* **conative** (kon′ ȧ tiv), *a.* Pertaining to conation. ***conatus** (kŏ nā′

tŭs), *n.* An effort; an impulse in plants and animals analogous to human effort.

concamerate (kŏn kăm′ ėr āt) [L. *concamerātus*, p.p. of *concamerāre* (*camera*)], *v.t.* To divide into chambers (as a shell); *to vault or arch. **concameration** (-ā′ shŭn), *n.*

concatenate (kŏn kăt′ ė nāt) [late L. *concatēnātus*, p.p. of *concatēnāre* (*catēna*, a chain)], *v.t.* To join or link together in a successive series. **concatenation** (-nā′ shŭn), *n.*

concave (kon′ kāv) [F., from L. *concavus* (*cavus*, hollow)], *a.* Having a curve or surface hollow like the inner side of a circle or globe. *n.* A hollow curve; a hollow surface; an arch, a vault. *v.t.* (*poet.*) To make concave or hollow. **concavely,** *adv.* **concavity** (-kăv′ i ti), *n.* The state of being concave; the internal surface of a hollow spherical body. **concavo-,** *comb. form.* (*Opt.*) Concave; concavely. **concavo-concave,** *a.* Concave on both sides. **concavo-convex,** *a.* Concave on one side and convex on the other. **concavous,** *a.*

conceal (kŏn sēl′) [O.F. *conceler*, L. *concēlāre* (*cēlāre*, to hide)], *v.t.* To hide or cover from sight or observation; to keep secret or hidden; to keep back from publicity or utterance. **concealable,** *a.* **concealment,** *n.* The act of concealing; the state of being concealed; a hiding-place; (*Law*) a suppression of material matters.

concede (kŏn sēd′) [L. *concēdere* (*cēdere*, to yield)], *v.t.* To yield, to give up, to surrender; to admit, to grant; to allow to pass unchallenged. *v.i.* To yield; to make concessions.

conceit (kŏn sēt′) [L. *concepta*, fem. p.p. of *concipere*, CONCEIVE (on anal. of DECEIT)], *n.* A vain opinion of oneself, overweening self-esteem; a whim; a fanciful idea; *a quaint or witty notion or turn of expression; *conception, opinion, judgment; *a thought, an idea. **v.t.* To conceive; to imagine, to think; have a fancy for. **v.i.* To form a notion; to conceive. **out of conceit with:** No longer fond of, or inclined to. **conceited,** *a.* Full of conceit; inordinately vain; egotistical. **conceitedly,** *adv.* ***conceitless,** *a.* Dull, stupid, thoughtless.

conceive (kŏn sēv′) [O.F. *conceiv-*, stem of *concever*, L. *concipere* (*capere*, to take)], *v.t.* To receive into and form in the womb; to form, as an idea or concept, in the mind; to imagine or suppose as possible; to think; to formulate clearly in the mind. *v.i.* To become pregnant; to form an idea or concept in the mind. **conceivable,** *a.* Capable of being conceived in the mind. **conceivability** (-bil′ i ti), *n.* **conceivableness,** *n.* **conceivably,** *adv.*

concelebrate (kŏn sel′ ė brāt) [L. *concelebrātus* p.p. of *concelebrāre*], *v.i.* (*R.-C. Ch.*) To celebrate Mass along with the ordaining bishop (of a newly ordained priest).

***concent** (kŏn sent′) [L. *concentus*, singing together, harmony, from *concinere* (CON-, *canere*, to sing)], *n.* A concord of voices; harmony. *v.t.* To harmonize.

concentrate (kon′ sėn trāt) [CONCENTRE first in use, afterwards Latinized in form as if from a p.p. *concentrātus* (*concentrāre*)], *v.t.* To bring to a common focus, centre, or point; to bring (all one's energies) to bear; (*Chem.*) to reduce to a greater density. *a.* (kon sen′ trȧt) Concentrated. *n.* (*Mining and Chem.*) A product of concentration. **concentration** (-trā′ shŭn), *n.* **concentration camp,** *n.* A camp for housing political prisoners and interned persons. **concentrative** (kŏn sen′ trȧ tiv), *a.* **concentrativeness,** *n.* The faculty of fixing the attention or thoughts on any one subject or point. **concentrator** (kon′ sėn trā tŏr), *n.* An apparatus for concentrating solutions; (*Metal.*) a pneumatic apparatus for separating dry comminuted ores.

concentre (kŏn sen′ tėr) [F. *concentrer*], *v.t.* To draw or direct to a common centre. *v.i.* To have a common centre; to combine for a common object. **concentric,** *a.* Having a common centre; (*Mil.*) concentrated. **concentric fire.** Firing concentrated on the same point. **concentrically,** *adv.* **concentricity** (-tris′ i ti), *n.*

concentus (kŏn sen′ tŭs) [L.], *n.* Concordance, harmony; singing together or in harmony.

concept (kŏn′ sept) [L. *conceptum*, neut. p.p. of *concipere*, to CONCEIVE], *n.* (*Phil.*) A general notion; a general notion or idea comprising all the attributes common to a class of things.

conceptacle (kŏn sep′ tȧkl) [L. *conceptāculum*, dim. of *conceptum*, as prec.], *n.* That in which anything is contained; (*Bot.*) a follicle; a surface cavity in fungi and algæ in which reproductive bodies are produced; (*Biol.*) an analogous organ in animals of low organization.

conception (kŏn sep′ shŭn), *n.* The act of conceiving; the impregnation of the ovum; (*Phil.*) the cognition of classes, as distinct from individuals; concept. **conceptional,** *a.* **conceptionist,** *n.* ***conceptious,** *a.* Pregnant, fruitful. **conceptive,** *a.*

conceptual (kŏn sep′ tū ăl) [med. L. *conceptuālis*, from L. *conceptus*, CONCEPT], *a.* (*Phil.*) Belonging or relating to conception. **conceptualism,** *n.* (*Phil.*) The doctrine that universals exist only in the mind of the thinking subject; (a doctrine intermediate between nominalism and realism). **conceptualist,** *n.*

concern (kŏn sẽrn′) [F. *concerner*, L. *concernere* (*cernere*, to separate, sift), in med. L., to refer to, regard], *v.t.* To relate or belong to; to affect; to be of importance to; to interest; to disturb, to render uneasy. **v.i.* To be of importance. *n.* That which affects or is of interest or importance to a person; interest, regard; anxiety, solicitude; a business, a firm, an establishment; a matter of personal importance; (*pl.*) affairs; (*colloq.*) an affair, a thing. ***concernancy,** *n.* Concern, business, import. **concerned,** *a.* Interested, involved, engaged (with); anxious, solicitous (about); *muddled (with liquor). **concernedly** (-nėd li), *adv.* **concerning,** *pres.p. as prep.* With respect to. **concernment,** *n.* That which interests or concerns; an affair, a matter, business; importance.

concert (1) (kŏn sẽrt′) [F. *concerter*, It. *concertare*, to accord together (cp. Sp. *concertar*, to bargain), L. *concertāre*, to dispute, contend (CON-, *certāre*, to vie)], *v.t.* To plan, to arrange mutually; to contrive, to adjust.

concert (2) (kon′ sėrt) [It. *concerto*, as prec.], *n.* Harmony, accordance of plan or ideas; concord, harmonious union of sounds; a public musical entertainment. **concert grand,** *n.* (*colloq.*) A powerful grand piano for use at concerts. **concert pitch,** *n.* (*Mus.*) The pitch used at concerts, slightly higher than the ordinary, for the sake of additional brilliancy. **concerted,** *a.* Mutually planned or devised; (*Mus.*) arranged in parts.

concertina (kon sėr tē′ nȧ), *n.* A portable instrument of the seraphine family, having a keyboard at each end, with bellows between.

concerto (kŏn chĕr′ tō) [It.], *n.* (*Mus.*) A composition for a solo instrument or instruments with orchestral accompaniment.

concession (kŏn sesh′ ŭn) [F., from L. *concessio -ōnem*, from *concēdere*, to CONCEDE], *n.* The act of conceding; the thing conceded; esp. a privilege or right granted by a government for carrying out public works, etc.; a subdivision of townships in Canada. ***concessionnaire*** (kŏn ses i ŏ nâr′), *n.* One who holds a concession from the government. **concessionary,** *a.* **concessive,** *a.* Conceding; implying concession.

***concetto** (kŏn chet′ ō) [It., from L. *conceptum*, CONCEIT], *n.* (*pl.* **-ti**) Affected wit. **concettism,** *n.*

conch (kongk) [L. *concha*, Gr. *konche*, mussel, cockle], *n.* A shell-fish; a marine shell of a spiral form; a shell of this kind used as a trumpet; (*Arch.*)

the domed roof of an apse, or the apse itself. **concha** (kong' kȧ), *n.* (*Anat.*) The largest and deepest concavity in the external ear; (*Arch.*) the concave ribless surface of a vault; the dome of an apse; an apse. **conchiferous** (-kif' ėr ůs) [-FEROUS], *a.* Shell-bearing. **concho-**, *comb. form.* **conchoid** (kong' koid) [-OID], *n.* (*Geom.*) A shell-like curve. **conchoidal** (-koi' dȧl), *a.* (*Geom. and Min.*). **conchology** (-kol' ȯ ji) [-LOGY], *n.* The branch of zoology that deals with shells and the animals inhabiting them. **conchological** (-loj' ik ȧl), *a.* **conchologist,** *n.* **conchospiral** (kong kō spīr ȧl), *n.* A spiral curve characteristic of certain shells.

concierge (kon si ârzh') [F.], *n.* A door-keeper, a porter, a janitor.

conciliar (kȯn sil' i ȧr) [L. *concilium*, COUNCIL], *a.* Pertaining to a council, esp. an ecclesiastical council.

conciliate (kȯn sil' i āt) [L. *conciliātus*, p.p. of *conciliāre* (*concilium*, as prec.)], *v.t.* To win the regard or goodwill of; to gain over, to win; to reconcile conflicting views. **conciliation** (-ā' shůn), *n.* The act of conciliating; reconciliation of disputes, etc. **conciliative** (kȯn sil' i ȧ tiv), *a.* **conciliator,** *n.* **conciliatory,** *a.* **conciliatoriness,** *n.*

concinnous (kȯn sin' ůs) [L. *concinnus*, well-adjusted], *a.* Harmonious; elegant. **concinnity,** *n.* Elegance, fitness, neatness, esp. of literary style.

concise (kȯn sīs') [L. *concīsus*, p.p. of *concīdere* (*cædere*, to cut)], *a.* Condensed, brief, terse. **concisely,** *adv.* **conciseness,** *n.* **concision** (-sizh' ůn), *n.* Mutilation, a term applied by St. Paul to the Judaizing teachers who insisted on the necessity of outward circumcision as distinct from change of heart; conciseness.

conclamation (kon klȧ mā' shůn) [L. *conclāmātio -ōnem*, from *conclāmāre* (*clāmāre*, to cry out)], *n.* A united or general outcry.

conclave (kon' klāv) [F., from L. *conclāve* (*clāvis*, key)], *n.* The assembly of cardinals met for the election of a pope; the apartment where they meet; a close or secret assembly.

conclude (kȯn klood') [L. *conclūdere* (*claudere*, to shut)], *v.t.* To bring to an end, to finish; to determine, to settle; to gather as a consequence from reasoning, to infer. *v.i.* To make an end; to come to a decision; to draw an inference. **to conclude:** In short, in fine. **concluding,** *a.* That concludes; final. **concludingly,** adv. **conclusion** (kȯn kloo' zhȯn), *n.* The end, the finish, the termination; the result; an inference; settlement (of terms, etc.); a final decision; (*Log.*) the inferential proposition of a syllogism; *experiment, an attempt. **in conclusion:** To conclude. **to try conclusions:** To contest; to try which is superior. **conclusive,** *a.* **conclusively,** *adv.* **conclusiveness,** *n.* **conclusory,** *a.*

concoct (kȯn kokt') [L. *concoctus*, p.p. of *concoquere* (*coquere*, to cook)], *v.t.* To prepare by mixing together; to plot, to devise; *to digest. **concoction,** *n.* The act of concocting; the thing concocted; a plan, plot, or design. **concoctive,** *a.* **concoctor,** *n.*

concolorous (kȯn kŭl' ȯr ůs) [L. *concolor*], *a.* (*Nat. Hist.*) Uniform in colour.

concomitant (kȯn kom' i tȧnt) [L. *concomitans -ntem*, pres.p. of *concomitārī* (*comitārī*, to accompany)], *a.* Accompanying; existing in conjunction with. *n.* One who or that which accompanies. **concomitantly,** *adv.* **concomitance, -tancy,** *n.* The state of being concomitant; (*R.-C. Ch.*) the presence in each element of the Eucharist of both the body and the blood of Christ.

concord (kon'-, kong' kȯrd) [F. *concorde*, L. *concordia* (*cor cordis*, heart)], *n.* Agreement; union in opinions, sentiments, or interests; (*Gram.*) the agreement of one word with another in number, gender, etc.; (*Mus.*) a combination of notes satisfactory to the ear. **concordance** (kȯn kôr' dȧns), *n.* The state of being concordant; agreement; a list of the words in a book (esp. in the Bible), with exact references to the places where they occur.

concordant, *a.* In concord, harmony, or accord; agreeing, correspondent. **concordantly,** *adv.*

concordat (kȯn kôr' dȧt) [F., from late L. *concordātum*, p.p. of *concordāre*, to agree (as prec.)], *n.* A convention between the Pope and a secular government.

concorporate (kȯn kôr' pȯ rāt) [L. *concorporātus*, p.p. of *concorporāre* (*corpus -oris*, body)], *v.t.* To unite into one body or substance. *a.* (-rȧt) United into one body.

concourse (kon' kôrs) [O.F. *concours*, L. *concursus* (*concurrere*, see CONCUR)], *n.* A confluence, a gathering together; an assembly; *concurrence; (*Am.*) the main hall at a railway station.

***concreate** (kon' krė āt) [L. *concreātus*, p.p. of *concreāre* (*creāre*, to create)], *v.t.* To create at the same time.

concremation (kon krė mā' shůn) [L. *concremātio -ōnem*, from *concremāre* (*cremāre*, to burn)], *n.* Cremation at the same time; consumption by fire.

concrescence (kȯn kres' ėns) [L. *concrēscentia*, from *concrēscere* (see foll.)], *n.* (*Biol.*) A growing together, coalescence; union of parts, organs, or organisms of a low order.

concrete (kon' krēt) [L. *concrētus*, p.p. of *concrēscere* (*crēscere*, to grow)], *a.* Formed by the union of many particles in one mass; (*Log. and Gram.*) denoting a thing as distinct from a quality, a state, or an action; existing, real, not abstract; individual, not general; made of concrete. *n.* A mass formed by concretion; (*Build.*) cement, coarse gravel, and sand mixed with water. *v.i.* (kȯn krēt'). To coalesce; to grow together. *v.t.* To form into a solid mass. *v.t.* (kon' krēt). To treat with concrete. *v.i.* To apply concrete. **in the concrete:** In the sphere of reality, not of abstractions, or generalities. **concretely,** *adv.* **concreteness,** *n.* **reinforced concrete,** *n.* Concrete work strengthened by having steel bars or webbing embedded in it.

concreter (kȯn krē' tėr) [from prec., -ER], *n.* An apparatus used in sugar-boiling for concentrating the syrup.

concretion (kȯn krē' shůn) [L. *concrētio -ōnem* (see CONCRETE)], *n.* The act of concreting; the mass thus formed; (*Geol.*) an aggregation of particles into a more or less regular ball; (*Path.*) a morbid growth of solid matter in the body, stone. **concretionary,** *a.*

concubine (kon' kū bīn) [F., from L. *concubīna* (CON-, *cubāre*, to lie)], *n.* A woman who cohabits with a man without being married to him; a mistress; a lawful wife of inferior rank. **concubinage** (-kū' bi nȧj), *n.* The act or state of living with one of the opposite sex without being legally married; the state of a concubine. **concubinary,** *a.* Living in concubinage; pertaining to or sprung from concubinage. *n.* One living in concubinage.

concupiscence (kȯn kū' pi sėns) [L. *concupiscentia*, desire, from *concupiscere*, incept. of *concupere* (*cupere*, to desire)], *n.* Unlawful or excessive (esp. sexual) lust. **concupiscent,** *a.* ***concupiscible,** *a.*

concur (kȯn kĕr') [L. *concurrere* (*currere*, to run)], *v.i.* (*past & p.p.* **concurred)** To meet in one point, to converge, to coincide; to agree; to act in conjunction (with). **concurrence,** *n.* **concurrent,** *a.* That concurs; happening or existing at the same time; acting in union or conjunction; consistent, harmonious; contributing to the same effect or result. *n.* A concurrent person or thing; a concurrent circumstance; (*Sc. Law*) a sheriff's officer's assistant. **concurrently,** *adv.*

concuss (kȯn kŭs') [L. *concussus*, p.p. of *concutere* (CON-, *quatere*, to shake)], *v.t.* To shake or agitate violently; to force or intimidate.

concussion (kȯn kŭsh' ȯn), *n.* Shaking by sudden impact; a shock; (*Med.*) a state of unconsciousness suddenly produced by mechanical force applied to the skull, usually followed by amnesia. **concussion-fuse,** *n.* (*Artill.*) A shell-fuse that ignites on impact. **concussive, *concutient** (-kū' shi ėnt), *a.*

concyclic (kŏn sĭk′ lik), *a.* (*Geom.*) Lying (of points) upon the circumference of one circle; (of conoids) showing circular sections when cut by the same system of parallel planes.

condemn (kŏn dem′) [O.F. *condemner*, L. *condemnāre* (*damnāre*, to condemn)], *v.t.* To pronounce guilty; to give judgment against; to pass sentence on; to pronounce incurable or unfit for use; to adjudge to be forfeited; to censure, to blame. **condemned cell,** *n.* The cell in which prisoners condemned to death are confined before execution. **condemnable** (kŏn dem′ ȧbl), *a.* **condemnation** (-nā′ shŭn), *n.* The act of condemning; the state of being condemned; the ground for condemning. **condemnatory** (kŏn dem′ nȧ tŏr i), *a.* Involving or expressing condemnation.

condense (kŏn dens′) [F. *condenser*, L. *condensāre* (*densāre*, to thicken, from *densus*, thick)], *v.t.* To make more dense or compact; to compress; to concentrate; (*Chem.*) to reduce into another and denser form (as a gas into a liquid). *v.i.* To become dense or compact; (*Chem.*) to be reduced into a denser form. **a.* Condensed, compact. **condensable,** *a.* **condensability** (-bil′ i ti), *n.* **condensate** (-den′ sāt), *v.t.* and *i.* To condense. **a.* (-sȧt) Condensed. **condensation** (-sā′ shŭn), *n.* The act of condensing; the state of being condensed; a condensed mass; (*fig.*) conciseness, brevity. **condensed milk,** *n.* A thickened and usually sweetened form of preserved milk.

condenser (kŏn dens′ ĕr), *n.* One who or that which condenses; a lens for concentrating light on an object; a contrivance for accumulating or concentrating electricity; (*Steam eng.*) an apparatus for reducing steam to a liquid form; (*Elec.*) a device of two conductors separated by a non-conductor, serving to hold or store an electric charge. **condensity,** *n.*

condescend (kŏn dė send′) [F. *condescendre*, late L. *condēscendere* (*dēscendere*, to DESCEND)], *v.i.* To stoop, to yield; to stoop or lower oneself voluntarily to an inferior position; to deign. **to condescend upon:** (*Sc.*) To particularize. **condescendence,** *n.* Condescension; (*Sc.*) particularization. **condescending,** *a.* Marked by condescension; patronizing. **condescendingly,** *adv.* **condescension,** *n.* The act of condescending; gracious behaviour to imagined inferiors; patronizing behaviour.

condign (kŏn dīn′) [F. *condigne*, L. *condignus* (*dignus*, worthy)], *a.* Worthy, adequate; well-deserved. **condignly,** *adv.*

condiment (kon′ di mėnt) [F., from L. *condimentum*, from *condīre*, to pickle, to spice, from *condere*, to put together, store up (*-dere*, *-dāre*, to put)], *n.* A seasoning or sauce; anything used to give a relish to food. **condimental** (-men′ tȧl), *a.*

condition (kŏn dish′ ŭn) [O.F. *condicion*, L. *condicio -ōnem*, from *condīcere*, to talk over (*dīcere*, to speak)], *n.* A stipulation, an agreement; a term of a contract; that on which anything depends; (*Gram.*) a clause expressing this; (*pl.*) circumstances or external characteristics; state or mode of existence; *character; *rank or position in life; high social position; a good state of health. *v.t.* To stipulate, to agree on; to impose conditions on; to test, to examine; to make fit; to put in order. **conditional,** *a.* Containing, implying, or depending on certain conditions; made with limitations or reservations; not absolute; (*Gram.*) expressing condition. *n.* A limitation; a reservation; (*Log.*) a conditional proposition; (*Gram.*) a conditional conjunction, the conditional mood. **conditionality** (-năl′ i ti), *n.* **conditionally,** *adv.* ***conditionate,** *a.* Arranged on or subject to certain conditions or terms. *v.t.* To condition; to regulate. **conditioned,** *a.* Limited by certain conditions; (*usu. in comb.*) having a certain disposition, as **ill-conditioned, well-conditioned. conditional reflex,** *n.* (*Psych.*) A reflex modified by the individual's experience. **conditioned by:** Depending on; limited by.

condole (kŏn dōl′) [L. *condolēre* (CON-, *dolēre*, to grieve)], *v.i.* To sorrow, to mourn, to lament; to sympathize (with). ***condolment,** *n.* Condolence. **condolence,** *n.* **condolatory,** *a.* Expressing condolence.

condom (kon′ dŏm) [name of inventor], *n.* A contraceptive appliance, a sheath.

condominium (kon dŏ min′ i ŭm), *n.* Joint sovereignty over a state.

condone (kŏn dōn′) [L. *condōnāre* (*dōnāre*, to give)], *v.t.* To forgive, to remit (used esp. of breaches of marital duty); to atone for. **condonation** (-nā′ shŭn), *n.*

condor (kon′ dŏr) [Sp., from Peruv. *cuntur*], *n.* A large South American vulture, *Sarcorrhamphus gryphus*; a South American gold coin.

condottiere (kon dŏ tyâr′ i) [It.], *n.* (*pl.* **-ri**) An Italian soldier of fortune; a captain of mercenaries.

conduce (kŏn dūs′) [L. *condūcere* (CON-, *dūcere*, to lead)], *v.i.* To contribute (to a result); to tend (to). **conducement,** *n.* **conducive,** *a.* **conduciveness,** *n.*

conduct (1) (kon′ dŭkt) [partly directly from L. *conductus*, p.p. of *condūcere* (CON-, *dūcere*, to lead), partly through O.F. *conduit* (L. *conductus*) or O.F. *conduite* (cp. Sp. *conducta*, It. *condotta*), defence, escort], *n.* The act of leading or guiding; the way in which anyone acts or lives, behaviour; management, direction, control; (*Painting*) manner of treatment; *a safe conduct; *a guide, a guard, a conductor.

conduct (2) (kŏn dŭkt′), *v.t.* To lead, to guide; to manage, to direct; (*Phys.*) to transmit (as heat, etc.); (*Mus.*) to direct (as an orchestra); (*refl.*) to behave. *v.i.* (*Phys. and Mus.*) To act as a conductor. **conductance,** *n.* (*Elec.*) The reciprocal of electric resistance. **conductible,** *a.* Capable of conducting or of being conducted. **conductibility,** *n.* **conduction** (-duk′ shŭn), *n.* (*Phys.*) Transmission by a conductor; conveyance (of liquids, etc.). **conductive,** *a.* **conductivity,** *n.* (*Elec.*) The ease with which a substance transmits electricity. **conductor,** *n.* A leader, a guide; a director, a manager; the director of an orchestra; (*Am.*) the guard of a train; the person in charge of a bus or tramcar; (*Phys.*) a body capable of transmitting heat, electricity, etc.; *a general. **conductorship,** *n.* **conductress,** *n.* A woman who conducts; a woman conductor of a bus.

conduit (kŭn-, kon′ dit) [as prec.], *n.* A channel, canal, or pipe, usually underground, to convey water; *(*fig.*) a channel, a passage. **conduit system:** (*Elec.*) The enclosing of wiring in a steel conduit or pipe; in an electric tramway system the arrangement of the conductor rail beneath the roadway.

conduplicate (kŏn dū′ pli kȧt) [L. *conduplicātus*, p.p. of *conduplicāre*], *a.* (*Bot.*) Having the sides folded in face to face (in æstivation). **conduplication** (-kā′ shŭn), *n.*

condyle (kon′ dil) [L. *condylus*, Gr. *kondulos*, a knuckle], *n.* (*Anat.*) An eminence with a flattened articular surface on a bone. **condylar, condyloid,** *a.* **condylar process,** *n.* The condyle at the extremities of the under jaw.

cone (kōn) [F. *cône*, L. *cōnus*, Gr. *kōnos*], *n.* A solid figure described by the revolution of a right-angled triangle about the side containing the right-angle; a solid pointed figure with straight sides and circular or otherwise curved base; anything cone-shaped; (*Bot.*) a strobilus or dry multiple fruit, such as that of the pines; (*Conch.*) a marine shell of the genus *Conus*; (*pl.*) fine white flour used by bakers for dusting loaves. *v.i.* To bear cones. **cone-flower,** *n.* Any species of the genus *Rudbeckia*, belonging to the aster family.

coney [CONY].

confabulate (kŏn făb′ ū lāt) [L. *confābulātus*, p.p. of *confābulārī* (CON-, *fābulārī*, to converse, from *fābula*, a discourse)], *v.i.* To talk familiarly; to chat, to gossip. **confabulation** (-lā′ shŭn), *n.* **confabulatory,** *a.*

confarreation (kon făr ė ā′ shŭn) [L. *confarreātio ōnem*, from *confarreāre*, to join in marriage by the offering of bread (*farreus*, of grain or spelt, *far farris*, grain, spelt)], *n.* The highest form of marriage among the Romans.

confection (kon fek′ shŭn) [F., from L. *confectio -ōnem*, from *conficere* (*facere*, to make)], *n.* The act of compounding; a compound, esp. a sweet delicacy, a sweetmeat, a preserve; a drug made palatable by compounding with a sweetening agent; a ready-made dress or article of dress. *v.t.* To make confectionery; to make a confection. ***confectionary,** *a.* Prepared as a confection. *n.* A confectioner; *a confection; *a store for confectionery.

confectioner (kon fek′ shŭn ėr), *n.* One whose trade it is to prepare or sell confections, sweetmeats, etc.; a pastrycook. **confectionery,** *n.* Sweetmeats or preserves generally; confections, candies, etc.; a confectioner's shop.

confederacy (kon fed′ ėr ȧ si) [see foll.], *n.* A league or compact by which several persons engage to support each other; a number of persons, parties, or states united for mutual aid and support; a league, a confederation; conspiracy, unlawful cooperation, collusion. **confederal,** *a.* **confederalist,** *n.*

confederate (kon fed′ ėr ȧt) [L. *confœderātus*, p.p. of *confœderāre* (*fœdus -eris*, a league)], *a.* United in a league; allied by treaty; (*Hist.*) applied to the Southerners in the American Civil War (1861–65). *n.* A member of a confederation; an ally, esp. an accomplice; (*Hist.*) a Southerner. *v.t.* and *i.* (-āt) To unite in a league. **confederation** (-ā′ shŭn), *n.* **confederatism,** *n.* **confederative,** *a.*

confer (kon fĕr′) [L. *conferre* (*ferre*, to bring)], *v.t.* To bestow, to grant. *v.i.* To consult together; to compare views. **conferee** (kon fėr ē′), *n.* One who is conferred with; one on whom something is conferred. **conferment,** *n.* **conferrable,** *a.* **conferrer,** *n.* **conference** (kon′ fėr ėns), *n.* The act of conferring; a meeting for consultation or deliberation; a meeting of the representatives of various countries for deliberation; a meeting of two branches of a legislature to adjust differences; the annual meeting of the Wesleyan body to transact church business. **conferential** (kon fėr en′ shȧl), *a.*

conferva (kon fĕr′ vȧ) [L.], *n.* (*pl.* **-væ**) (*Bot.*) A genus of algæ, consisting of plants with unbranched filaments. **confervaceous** (-vā′ shŭs), *a.* **conferval,** *a.* and *n.* **confervoid,** *a.* and *n.*

confess (kon fes′) [O.F. *confesser*, late L. *confessāre*, freq. of *confitēri* (p.p. *confessus*), *fatēri*, to acknowledge, cogn. with *fāri*, to speak, *fāma*, FAME)], *v.t.* To own, to acknowledge, to admit; to declare one's adhesion to or belief in; to manifest; to hear the confession of. *v.i.* To make confession, esp. to a priest. **confessant,** *n.* One who confesses to a priest. **confessedly** (kon fes′ ed li), *adv.* Admittedly, avowedly. **confession** (kon fesh′ ŭn), *n.* The act of confessing; avowal, declaration; formal acknowledgment of sins to a priest in order to receive absolution. **confession of faith:** A formulary containing the creed of a Church. **confessional,** *n.* The place where a priest sits to hear confessions. *a.* Pertaining to confession. **confessionary,** *a.* **confessionist,** *n.* One who adopts a certain confession or creed, esp. the Augsburg Confession, a Lutheran. **confessor** (kon fes′ ŏr), *n.* One who confesses; a title applied to canonized saints who are neither apostles nor martyrs. **confessor** (kon′ fes ŏr), *n.* A priest who hears confessions. **The Confessor,** *n.* The Saxon king Edward the Confessor.

confetti (kon fet′ i) [It., pl. of *confetto*, from L. *confectum*, COMFIT], *n.pl.* Bonbons; bits of coloured paper thrown in the carnival, at weddings, etc.

confidant, fem. **confidante** (kon fi dănt′) [F. *confident, -e* (see foll.)], *n.* One entrusted with secrets, esp. with love affairs; a bosom friend.

confide (kon fīd′) [L. *confīdere* (*fīdere*, to trust; cp. *fides*, faith)], *v.i.* To have trust or confidence (in). *v.t.* To entrust (to); to reveal in confidence (to). **confidence** (kon′ fi dėns), *n.* Trust, belief; self-reliance, boldness, assurance; revelation of private matters to a friend; the matter revealed; *trustworthiness. **confidence trick,** *n.* A trick by which one is induced to part with valuable property for something worthless, to show the confidence the parties have in each other. **confident,** *a.* Full of confidence; assured; self-reliant, bold. *n.* A confidant. **confidential** (kon fi den′ shȧl), *a.* Trustworthy; entrusted with the private concerns of another; told or carried on in confidence. **confidentiality** (-shi ăl′ i ti), *n.* **confidentially** (-den′ shȧ li), *adv.* **confidentialness,** *n.* **confidently** (kon′-), *adv.*

configuration (kon fig ū rā′ shŭn) [see foll.], *n.* Form; structural arrangement; contour or outline; (*Astron.*) the relative position of the planets at any given time.

configure (kon fig′ ŭr) [L. *configūrāre* (*figūrāre*, from *figura*, form)], *v.t.* To give shape or form to.

confine (1) (kon′ fīn) [O.F. *confines* (pl.), L. *confīnes* (pl. a.), bordering upon (*fīnis*, a boundary)], *n.* (*usu. in pl.*) Boundaries, limits, frontier; (*fig.*) a border-land of thought or opinion; *region, territory; *a place of confinement; (*sing.*) confinement.

confine (2) (kon fīn′), *v.i.* *To have a common boundary (with or on). *v.t.* To shut up, to imprison, to keep within bounds; to limit in application. **to be confined:** To be in child-bed; to be delivered of a child. ***confineless,** *a.* Unbounded, unlimited. **confinement,** *n.* The act of confining; the state of being confined, esp. in child-bed; restraint, restriction, seclusion. **confiner** (kon fī′ nėr, kon′ fi nėr), *n.* One who confines; *one who lives on the borders or confines. **confinity** (-fin′ i ti), *n.* Nearness, contiguity.

confirm (kon fĕrm′) [O.F. *confermer*, L. *confirmāre* (*firmāre*, to make firm, from *firmus*, firm)], *v.t.* To give firmness to; to establish; to ratify; to make valid; to bear witness to; to strengthen (in a course or opinion); to administer confirmation to. **confirmation** (-mā′ shŭn), *n.* The act of confirming; corroborative testimony; the rite of admitting into full communion with an episcopal Church by the laying on of hands. **confirmand,** *n.* One being prepared for the rite of confirmation. **confirmative** (kon fĕr′-), *a.* **confirmatively,** *adv.* **confirmatory,** *a.* **confirmed,** *a.* Established, settled, perfect; beyond hope of recovery or help; having received confirmation. **confirmedly,** *adv.* **confirmedness,** *n.* **confirmee** (kon fir mē′), *n.* One who has received confirmation.

confiscate (kon′ fis kāt) [L. *confiscātus*, p.p. of *confiscāre* (*fiscus*, the treasury)], *v.t.* To adjudge to be forfeited, or to seize as forfeited, to the public treasury. **confiscate** (kon′ fis kȧt), *a.* Confiscated. **confiscation** (-kā′ shŭn), *n.* The act of confiscating; (*colloq.*) robbery, plunder (usu. with the sense of *legalized*). **confiscable, confiscatable** (kā′ tȧbl), *a.* **confiscator** (kon′ fis kā tor), *n.* **confiscatory,** *a.*

confiteor (kon fit′ ė ŏr) [L., I confess], *n.* A Roman Catholic formula of confession.

confiture [COMFITURE].

confix (kon fiks′) [L. *confixus*, p.p. of *confīgere* (*fīgere*, to fix)], *v.t.* To fix firmly.

conflagration (kon flȧ grā′ shŭn) [L. *conflagrātio*, from *conflagrāre* (*flagrāre*, to burn)], *n.* A general burning; a large and destructive fire. ***conflagrate,** *v.t.*

conflation (kon flā′ shŭn) [L. *conflātio*, from *conflāre* (*flāre*, to blow)], *n.* Blowing or fusing together; blending of two variant readings into one.

conflict (kon′ flikt) [L. *conflictus*, from *conflīgere* (*flīgere*, to strike)], *n.* A fight, a collision; a struggle, a contest; opposition of interest, opinions, or purposes; mental strife, agony. *v.i.* (kon flikt′). To come into collision; to strive or struggle; to differ, to disagree; to be discrepant. **conflicting** (-flik′ ting), *a.* Contradictory, irreconcilable. **confliction,** *n.* **conflictive,** *a.*

confluent (kon′ flu̇ ėnt) [L. *confluens -ntem,* pres.p. of *confluere* (*fluere,* to flow)], *a.* Flowing together; uniting in a single stream; (*Bot.*) cohering; (*Path.*) running together (as pustules). *n.* A stream which unites with another; (*loosely*) a tributary stream; *the place where two or more streams unite. **confluence,** *n.* A flowing together; the point of junction of two or more streams; a multitude, an assembly.

conflux (kon′ flŭks) [L. *confluxus,* as prec.], *n.*

confocal (kon fō′ kȧl), *a.* Having common focus or foci.

conform (kȯn fôrm′) [F. *conformer,* L. *conformāre* (*formāre,* to form, fashion)], *v.t.* To make like in form, to make similar to; to accommodate, to adapt. *v.i.* To comply, to assent; to be in harmony or agreement. **conformance,** *n.* **conformable,** *a.* Having the same shape or form; corresponding, similar; compliant, conforming; (*Geol.*) arranged (as strata) in parallel planes. **conformability** (-bil′ i ti), *n.* **conformably,** *adv.* **conformation** (-mā′ shŭn), *n.* The manner in which a body is formed; form, shape, structure; adaptation. **conformator,** *n.* A device for determining the conformation of anything that has to be fitted.

conformist (kȯn fôr′ mist), *n.* One who conforms to the worship of the Church of England. **conformity,** *n.* Resemblance, similitude; agreement, compliance, congruity; the act of conforming to the worship of the Established Church.

confound (kȯn found′) [O.F. *confondre,* L. *confundere* (*fundere,* to pour)], *v.t.* To throw into confusion; to perplex, to terrify; to put to shame; to destroy; to defeat, to overthrow; to mix up, confuse; to bring to shame or to perdition (used as a mild curse). **confoundedly,** *adv.* Exceedingly, greatly (with strong disapprobation).

confraternity (kon frȧ tĕr′ ni ti), *n.* A brotherhood associated for a common purpose; (*R.-C. Ch.*) a society of laymen living in the world, associated for religious or charitable purposes; a gang; brotherhood.

confrère (kon′ frâr) [F.], *n.* A fellow-member of a profession, religion, or association.

confront (kȯn frŭnt′) [F. *confronter,* late L. *confrontāre,* L. *confrontārī* (*frons -ntis,* forehead)], *v.t.* To face; to stand facing; to bring face to face; to be opposite to; to face defiantly; to oppose, to meet in hostility; to compare (with). **confrontation** (-tā′ shŭn), *n.*

Confucian (kȯn fū′ shȧn), *a.* Pertaining to Confucius, the Chinese philosopher, *n.* A follower of Confucius. **Confucianism,** *n.*

confuse (kȯn fūz′) [L. *confūsus,* p.p. of *confundere,* to CONFOUND], *v.t.* To mix or mingle so as to render indistinguishable; to jumble up; to confound, to perplex; to disconcert. **confusedly,** *adv.* **confusedness,** *n.* **confusion,** *n.* The act of confusing; the state of being confused; disorder, tumult; perplexity; *ruin, destruction; (*Path.*) disturbance of consciousness characterized by impaired capacity to think or to respond in any way to current stimuli.

confute (kȯn fūt′) [*confūtāre* (*fūt-,* stem of *fūtis,* a water-vessel, cogn. with *fundere,* to pour)], *v.t.* To overcome in argument; to prove to be false. ***confutant,** *n.* One who confutes or disproves. **confutation** (-tā′ shŭn), *n.* The act or process of confuting; refutation, disproof.

congé (kon′ zhā), ***congee** (kon′ ji) [O.F. *congiez,* late L. *comiātus,* corr. of L. *commeātus,* from *commeāre* (*meāre,* to go)], *n.* A bow; a courtesy before taking leave; leave, departure, farewell; dismissal. **v.i.* To bow; to take leave with the usual civilities. ***congé d'élire*:** A writ giving the Crown's permission to a dean and chapter to elect a bishop, and naming the person to be elected.

congeal (kȯn jēl′) [O.F. *congeler,* L. *congelāre* (*gelāre,* from *gelu,* frost)], *v.t.* To freeze; to convert from the liquid to the solid state by cold; to coagulate. *v.i.* To become hard with cold; to coagulate. **congealable,** *a.* **congealment,** *n.*

***congee** [CONGÉ].

congelation (kon jė lā′ shŭn), *n.* The act of congealing; the state of being congealed; a congealed mass.

congener (kon′ jėn ėr) [L. *congener* (*genus -eris,* kind)], *n.* One of the same kind or class; an organism of the same stock or family. *a.* Akin, closely allied (to). **congeneric** (kon jė ner′ ik), *a.* Of the same race or genus. **congenerous** (-jen′), *a.* Congeneric; (*Physiol.*) concurring in the same action (as muscles).

congenetic (kon jė net′ ik), *a.* Having the same cause, origin, or place or time of origin (of natural phenomena).

congenial (kȯn jē′ ni ȧl), *a.* Partaking of the same natural characteristics; sympathetic; suitable; pleasant. **congeniality** (-ăl′ i ti), *n.* **congenially,** *adv.*

congenital (kȯn jen′ i tȧl) [L. *congenitus* (*genitus,* p.p. of *gignere,* to produce)], *a.* Existing from birth; constitutional. **congenitally,** *adv.*

conger (kong′ gėr) [O.F. *congre,* L. *conger,* Gr. *gongros*], *n.* A genus of marine eels; the conger-eel, *Leptocephalus conger.* **congeroid, congroid,** *a.*

congeries (kȯn jer′ i ēz) [L., as foll.], *n.* A collection or heap of particles or bodies.

congest (kȯn jest′) [L. *congestus,* p.p. of *congerere* (*gerere,* to carry, bring)], *v.i.* To become congested. *v.t.* To overcharge (with blood). **congested,** *a.* Closely crowded; (*Med.*) unduly distended with an accumulation of blood. **congestion** (kȯn jes′ chȯn), *n.* (*Med.*) An abnormal accumulation of blood in the capillaries; (*fig.*) abnormal accumulation (of inhabitants, traffic, etc.). **congestive,** *a.* (*Med.*) Inducing or caused by congestion.

conglobate (kon′ glȯ bāt) [L. *conglobātus,* p.p. of *conglobāre* (*globus,* a GLOBE, a round mass)], *v.t.* To form into a ball. *v.i.* To assume a globular form. *a.* (-bȧt) Formed into a ball. **conglobation** (-bā′ shŭn), *n.* ***conglobe,** *v.t.* and *i.* To conglobate.

conglomerate (kȯn glom′ ėr ȧt) [L. *conglomerātus,* p.p. of *conglomerāre* (*glomus -eris,* a ball)], *a.* Gathered into a round body. *n.* (*Geol.*) A rock composed of water-worn pieces of rock cemented together; pudding-stone. **conglomerate** (-āt), *v.t.* and *i.* To gather into a ball; to collect into a mass. **conglomeration** (-ā′ shŭn), *n.* A gathering into a ball or heap; a miscellaneous collection.

conglutinate (kȯn gloo′ ti nāt) [L. *conglūtinātus,* p.p. of *conglūtināre* (*glūten -inis,* glue)], *v.t.* To glue together; (*Med.*) to unite the edges of a wound together with a glutinous substance. *v.i.* To stick together, to adhere. **conglutination** (-nā′ shŭn), *n.*

Congolese (kong gō lēz′), *n.* and *a.* A native of, or pertaining to the Congo.

congou (kong′ goo, -gō) [Chin. *king-fu,* labour], *n.* A kind of Chinese black tea.

congratulate (kȯn grăt′ ū lāt) [L. *congrātulātus,* p.p. of *congrātulārī,* to wish joy, from *grātus,* pleasing)], *v.t.* To express pleasure or joy to, on account of some event; to compliment upon, rejoice with, felicitate. *v.i.* To express congratulations. **congratulant,** *a.* Congratulating. **congratulation** (-lā′ shŭn), *n.* **congratulator,** *n.* **congratulative,** *a.* **congratulatory** (-lā′ tȯ ri), *a.* Expressing congratulations.

congregate (kong′ grė gāt) [L. *congregātus,* p.p. of *congregare* (*gregāre,* to collect, from *grex gregis,* flock)], *v.t.* To gather or collect together into a crowd. *v.i.* To come together, to assemble. **a.* (-gȧt) Assembled, collective. **congregant,** *n.* One who congregates (with); a member of a congregation, esp. of a particular place of worship. **congregation** (-gā′ shŭn), *n.* The act of gathering together; the body gathered together; an assembly of persons for religious worship; such an assembly habitually meeting in the same place; a board of ecclesiastics meeting as commissioners at Rome; the assembly of qualified members of a University. **congregational,** *a.* Pertaining to a congregation, or to Congregationalism.

Congregationalism (kong gre gā' shŭn ǎl izm), *n.* That form of church government in which each church is self-governed, and independent of any other authority. **Congregationalist,** *a.* and *n.* **congregationalize,** *v.t.*

congress (kong' gres) [L. *congressus,* p.p. of *congredī,* to meet together (CON-, *gradī,* to walk, from *gradus,* step)], *n.* A discussion, a conference; a formal meeting of delegates or of envoys for the settlement of international affairs; the legislature of the United States, consisting of a Senate and a House of Representatives; the body of Senators and Representatives during the two years for which the latter have been elected; the lower house of the Spanish Cortes and of the legislature of a South American republic. **Congress Party** [INDIAN NATIONAL CONGRESS]. **Congressman,** *n.* A member of the United States Congress. **Congressional** (kŏn gresh' ŏ nǎl), *a.*

Congreve match (kong' grēv) [inventor, Sir Wm. *Congreve* (1772–1828)], *n.* A kind of friction match. **Congreve rocket,** *n.* A war rocket, now disused.

congroid [CONGER].

congrue (kŏn groo') [L. *congruere,* to agree (CON-, *-gruere,* cp. *ingruere*)], *v.t.* To agree, to suit, to correspond. **congruence, -ency** (kong' grụ̇ ĕns, -i), *n.* **congruent,** *a.* Agreeing, suitable, correspondent. **congruism,** *n.* (*Eccles. Hist.*) The doctrine, advocated in a controversy in the R.C. Church about 1580, that the efficacy of divine grace depends upon its adaptation to the character, disposition, and circumstances of the recipient. **congruist,** *n.* **congruous** (kong' groo ŭs), *a.* Suitable, conformable, appropriate, fitting. **congruously,** *adv.* **congruity** (kŏn groo' i ti), *n.*

conic (kon' ik), *a.* Pertaining to or having the form of a cone; (*pl.*) the branch of mathematics dealing with conic sections. **conic sections,** *n.pl.* (*Math.*) Curves formed by the intersection of a cone and a plane—the parabola, the hyperbola, and the ellipse. **conical,** *a.* **conically,** *adv.* **conicalness,** *n.* **conico-,** *comb. form.* (*Math.*) Conical, or tending to be conical. **conicocylindrical,** *a.* Nearly cylindrical, but tapering at one end.

conidium (kŏ nid' i ŭm) [mod. L. from Gr. *konis,* dust)], *n.* (*pl.* **-dia**) (Bot.) An asexual reproductive cell or spore in certain fungi. **conidial, conidioid,** *a.* **conidiiferous, -ophorous** (-i if' ėr ŭs, -of' ŏ rŭs), *a.* **conidiophore** (kŏ nid' i ŏ fôr), *n.* A branch of the mycelium bearing conidia.

conifer (kō' ni fėr), *n.* A cone-bearing plant or tree; any tree or shrub of the *Coniferæ.* ***Coniferæ*** (kŏ nif' ėr ē) [L.], *n.pl.* (*Bot.*) An order of resinous trees, as the fir, pine, and cedar, bearing a cone-shaped fruit. **coniferous,** *a.* **coniform** (kō' ni fôrm), *a.*

conine (kō' nīn) [L. *conīum,* Gr. *kōneion,* hemlock], *n.* (*Chem.*) An alkaloid constituting the poisonous principle in hemlock. ***conium*** (kŏ nī' ŭm), *n.* (*Bot.*) The genus of *Umbelliferæ* containing the hemlock; (*Med.*) the fruit of the hemlock or the drug extracted therefrom.

conjecture (kŏn jek' chūr) [F., from L. *conjectūra*), *n.* A guess, surmise, or doubtful inference; opinion based on inadequate evidence; ill suspicion. *v.t.* and *i.* To guess, to surmise. **conjecturable,** *a.* That may be conjectured. **conjecturably,** *adv.* **conjectural,** *a.* Depending on conjecture. **conjecturally,** *adv.* ***conjecturer,** *n.*

conjoin (kŏn join') [O.F. *conjoign-,* stem of *conjoindre,* L. *conjungere* (*jungere,* to join)], *v.t.* To cause to unite. *v.i.* To unite, to come together.

conjoint, *a.* United, associated, co-operating. **conjointly,** *adv.*

conjugal (kon' jụ̇ gǎl) [L. *conjugālis,* from *conjugem,* acc. of *conjunx,* spouse (*jug-,* root of *jungere,* to join, *jugum,* a yoke)], *a.* Of or pertaining to matrimony or to married life. **conjugality** (-gǎl' i ti), *n.* **conjugally,** *adv.* **conjugial** (kŏn joo' ji ǎl), *a.* Pertaining to marriage, esp. as a spiritual union in the Swedenborgian sense.

conjugate (kon' jụ̇ gāt) [L. *conjugātus,* p.p. of *conjugāre* (*jug-,* as prec.)], *v.t.* (*Gram.*) To inflect (a verb) by going through the voices, moods, tenses, etc.; (*Biol.*) to combine, to become united. *a.* (-gǎt) Joined in pairs, coupled; (*Gram.*) agreeing in grammatical derivation; (*Math.*) reciprocally related so as to be interchangeable; (*Bot.*) paired. *n.* A word agreeing in derivation with another word; (*Math.*) a conjugate axis, hyperbola, etc. **conjugation** (-gā' shŭn), *n.* The act or process of conjugating; (*Gram.*) the inflection of a verb; a class of verbs conjugated alike; (*Biol.*) the fusion of two or more cells or distinct organisms into a single mass. **conjugational,** *a.*

conjugial [CONJUGAL].

conjunct (kŏn jŭngkt') [see CONJOIN], *a.* Conjoined; closely connected; in union; conjoint. *n.* A person or thing joined with another. **conjunctly,** *adv.* **conjunction** (kon jŭngk' shŭn), *n.* Union, association, connexion; combination; (*Gram.*) a word connecting sentences or clauses or co-ordinating words in the same clause; (*Astron.*) the state of being in apparent union (of two heavenly bodies). **conjunctional,** *a.* **conjunctionally,** *adv.* **conjunctive,** *a.* Serving to unite; (*Gram.*) connective, conjunctional, copulative; connective in sense as well as in construction (opp. to disjunctive); *closely united. **conjunctive mood,** *n.* A mood expressing condition or contingency, of a verb used in conjunction with another verb. *n.* (*Gram.*) A conjunctive word or mood. **conjunctively,** *adv.* **conjuncture,** *n.* A combination of circumstances or events; a crisis.

conjunctiva (kon jŭngk tī' vǎ), *n.* (*Anat.*) The mucous membrane lining the inner surface of the eyelids and the front of the eyeball. **conjunctivitis,** (kon jŭngk ti vī' tis), *n.* Inflammation of the conjunctiva.

conjure (1) (kŏn joor') [O.F. *conjurer,* L. *conjūrāre* (*jūrāre,* to swear)], *v.t.* To appeal to by a sacred name, or in a solemn manner; to bind by an oath; *to conspire, to plot. **v.i.* To conspire. **conjuration** (-rā' shŭn), *n.* *A conspiracy; the act of conjuring or invoking; a magic spell, a charm; a solemn adjuration. ***conjurator** (kon' jụ̇ rā tŏr), *n.* A conspirator. ***conjurement** (kŏn joor' mĕnt), *n.* A solemn adjuration. **conjuror** (kŏn joor' ŏr), *n.* One bound with others by a common oath.

conjure (2) (kŭn'jėr) [as prec.], *v.t.* To effect by magical influence; to raise up by or as by magic; to effect by jugglery. *v.i.* To practise the arts of a conjurer; to use anything as a charm. **a name to conjure with:** A name of great influence. **to conjure up:** To arouse the imagination about. **conjurer** (kŭn' jėr ėr), *n.* A juggler; one who performs tricks by sleight of hand.

conk (kongk) [perh. from CONCH], *n.* (*slang*) The nose. **to conk out:** (*slang*) To give out, to fail.

conker (kong' kėr [?], *n.* A horse-chestnut.

connate (kon' āt) [L. *connātus,* p.p. of *connāscī* (*nāscī,* to be born)], *a.* Innate, born with one, congenital; (*Bot. and Zool.*) united, though originally distinct; united at the base (as two opposite leaves).

connatural (kŏ nǎt' ūr ǎl), *a.* Inborn; naturally belonging (to); of the same nature. **connaturally,** *adv.*

connect (kŏ nekt') [L. *connectere* (*nectere,* to bind)], *v.t.* To join, link, or fasten together; to conjoin, to unite, to correlate; to associate (in one's mind); to associate (with) as a cause or a result. *v.i.* To join, to cohere. **connected,** *a.* United (esp. by marriage); closely related; coherent; associated (with). **connectedly,** *adv.* **connecter,** *n.* **connectible,** *a.* **connective,** *a.* Having the power of connecting; that connects. *n.* (*Gram.*) A connecting word; (*Bot.*) the part between the lobes of an anther, which holds them together. **connective tissue:** The fibrous tissue supporting and connecting the various parts throughout the body. **connectively,** *adv.*

connexion, connection (kȯ nek′ shŭn), *n.* The act of connecting; the state of being connected; relationship (esp. by marriage); one so connected; sexual intercourse; a connecting part; acquaintanceship; a party, a religious body; a body of customers or clients; the fitting of the departure and arrival of trains in a cross-country journey; (*Elec.*) the apparatus used in linking up electric current by contact. **in connexion with:** Connected with (esp. of trains, steam-packets, etc.). **in this connexion:** In relation to this matter. **connexional** *a.* Of or pertaining to a (religious) connexion; connective.

connive (kȯ nīv′) [L. *connīvēre* (and a form conn. with *nicere*, to make a sign, *nictāre*, to wink)], *v.i.* To wink (at); voluntarily to omit or neglect to see or prevent any wrong or fault. **v.i.* To wink at. **connivance,** *n.* Passive co-operation in a fault or crime; tacit consent. **connivent,** *a.* *That connives; (*Bot. and Zool.*) convergent.

connoisseur (kȯn à sěr′) [F.], *n.* One skilled in judging of the fine arts; a critic, a man of taste. **connoisseurship,** *n.*

connote (kȯ nōt′) [late L. *connotāre* (L. *notāre*, to mark, from *nota*, a mark)], *v.t.* To imply, to betoken indirectly; to signify, to mean, to involve; (*Log.*) to include in the meaning (said of a term denoting a subject and implying attributes). **connotation** (-tā′ shŭn), *n.* **connotative** (-nō′ tà tiv), *a.* **connotatively,** *adv.*

connubial (kȯ nū′ bi ȧl) [L. *connūbiālis* (*nūbere*, to veil, to marry)], *a.* Relating to marriage or the marriage state. **connubially,** *adv.* **connubiality** (-ăl′ i ti), *n.* Matrimony; (*pl.*) endearments.

conoid (kō′ noid), *a.* Resembling a cone. *n.* (*Math.*) A solid of which the surface is traced out by the revolution of any one of the conic sections about its axis; anything resembling a cone. **conoidal** (kȯ noi′ dȧl), *a.*

co-nominee (kō nom i nē′), *n.* One nominated with another.

conquer (kong′ kėr) [O.F. *conquerre*, L. *conquīrere* (*quærere*, to seek)], *v.t.* To win or gain by conquest; to vanquish, to overcome; to gain dominion, sovereignty, or mastery over; to subdue, to surmount. *v.i.* To be victorious. **conquerable,** *a.* ***conqueress,** *n.* **conqueringly,** *adv.* **conqueror,** *n.* One who conquers; a victor. **The Conqueror:** William of Normandy, who conquered England in 1066.

conquest (kong′ kwest) [O.F. *conquest* (F. *conquêt*), anything acquired by conquest, *conqueste* (F. *conquête*), the act of conquering, late L. *conquīsita*, fem. p.p. of *conquīrere*, as prec.], *n.* The act of conquering; that which is conquered; the acquisition of sovereignty by force of arms; victory, subjugation. **to make a conquest of:** To win the love or admiration of. **The Conquest:** The conquest of England by William of Normandy in 1066.

conquistador (kong kis′ tà dôr) [Sp.], *n.* (*pl.* ***-es***) One of the Spanish conquerors of America in the 16th century.

consanguine (kȯn săng′ gwin), **consanguineous** (kon săn gwin′ ė ŭs) [F. *consanguin -e*, L. *consanguineus* (*sanguis -inis*, blood)], *a.* Of the same blood; related by birth. **consanguinity** (-gwin′ i ti), *n.*

conscience (kon′ shėns) [F., from L. *conscientia*, from *conscīre* (*scīre*, to know)], *n.* Moral sense; the sense of right and wrong; consciousness; *inmost thought; *sense, understanding. **for conscience' sake:** For the sake of one's conscientious scruples; for the sake of one's religion. **in conscience:** In truth; assuredly. **in all conscience:** (*colloq.*) In all reason or fairness. **on my conscience:** Most assuredly (a strong asseveration). **to have the conscience to:** To have the assurance or impudence to. **conscience clause,** *n.* A clause in an Act of Parliament to relieve persons with conscientious scruples from certain requirements. **conscience money,** *n.* Money paid into the treasury voluntarily (and often anonymously), esp. as compensation for evaded income-tax. **conscience-proof,** *a.* Proof against the monitions of conscience. **conscience-smitten,** *a.* Stung by conscience on account of some misdeed. **conscienceless,** *a.*

conscientious (kon shi en′ shus), *a.* Actuated by strict regard to the dictates of conscience; scrupulous. **conscientiously,** *adv.* **conscientiousness,** *n.* **conscientious objector,** *n.* One who takes advantage of the conscience clause; one who refuses on principle to take part, or help in any way in war or in activities connected with it.

***conscionable** (kon′ shŭn ȧbl), *a.* Regulated by conscience; scrupulous, just. **conscionableness,** *n.* **conscionably,** *adv.*

conscious (kon′ shŭs) [L. *conscius*, aware, from *conscīre* (see CONSCIENCE)], *a.* Aware of one's own existence; self-conscious; having immediate knowledge, cognizant, aware; fully aware, with consciousness awake; present to consciousness, felt, sensible. **consciously,** *adv.* **consciousness,** *n.* The state of being conscious; immediate knowledge, sense, perception; (*Psych.*) the faculty by which one knows one's own existence, acts, affections, etc.; the intellectual faculties collectively or any class of them.

conscribe (kȯn skrīb′) [L. *conscrībere* (*scrībere*, to write)], *v.t.* To enlist compulsorily.

conscript (kon′ skript) [L. *conscriptus*, p.p. of *conscrībere* (as prec.)], *a.* Enrolled, registered, enlisted by conscription. *n.* One compelled to serve as a soldier. *v.t.* (kon skript′). To conscribe. **conscript fathers,** *n.pl.* The senators of ancient Rome; (*colloq.*) the members of a town council. **conscription** (-skrip′ shŭn), *n.* Compulsory enrolment for military, naval or air service.

consecrate (kon′ sė krāt) [L. *consecrātus*, p.p. of *consecrāre* (*sacrāre*, to consecrate, from *sacer*, holy)], *v.t.* To set apart as sacred; to devote to the service of; to dedicate, to hallow; *to canonize. *a.* Consecrated. **consecration** (-krā′ shŭn), *n.* The act of consecrating; dedication to a divine object; the state of being consecrated; *canonization; dedication to a sacred office, esp. that of bishop; the benediction of the elements in the Eucharist. **consecrator,** *n.* **consecratory,** *a.*

consectary (kȯn sek′ tà ri) [L. *consectārium*, *n.* from *consectārius*, a. (*consectārī*, freq. of *consequī*, see foll.)], *n.* A corollary; a necessary deduction.

consecution (kon sė kū′ shŭn) [L. *consecutio*, from *consequī* (CON-, *sequī*, to follow)], *n.* The state of being consecutive; a succession or series; logical or grammatical sequence.

consecutive (kon sek′ ū tiv), *a.* Following without interval or break; expressing logical or grammatical consequence. **consecutive intervals,** *n.pl.* (*Mus.*) A succession of similar intervals in harmony, esp. consecutive fifths and octaves. **consecutively,** *adv.* **consecutiveness,** *n.*

consenescence (kon sė nes′ ėns) [L. *consenēscere* (*senēscere*, to grow old, from *senex*, an old man)], *n.* A growing old together; general decay with age.

consensus (kȯn sen′ sŭs) [L., p.p. of *consentīre*, as foll.], *n.* A general agreement, unanimity; (*Physiol.*) the sympathetic agreement of the different organs for a particular purpose. **consensual,** *a.* (*Physiol.*) Happening by sympathetic action, as opp. to volition; (*Law*) existing by consent.

consent (kȯn sent′) [O.F. *consentir*, L. *consentīre* (*sentīre*, to feel)], *v.i.* To concur, to assent, to agree, to yield. **v.t.* To agree to. *n.* Acquiescence in feeling, thought, or action; compliance; permission; agreement, concurrence; *feeling, opinion. **consentable,** *a.* (*Pennsylvania Law*) Agreed to by consent. **consenter,** *n.*

consentaneous (kon sėn tā′ nė ůs) [L. *consentāneus* (as prec.)]. *a.* Mutually consenting, unanimous; accordant; simultaneous, concurrent. **consentaneously,** *adv.* **consentaneity** (-nē′ i ti), *n.* **consentaneousness,** *n.*

consentient (kȯn sen′ shi ėnt) [L. *consentiens -ntem,* pres.p. of *consentīre,* to CONSENT], *a.* Of one mind, unanimous; consenting.

consequence (kon′ se kwens) [as foll.], *n.* A result or effect; inference; importance; social importance, distinction, note. *n.pl.* A parlour game. **v.t.* To draw inferences.

consequent (kon′ sė kwėnt) [F. *conséquent,* L. *consequens -ntem,* pres.p. of *consequī* (*sequī,* to follow)], *a.* Following as a natural or logical result; consistent. *n.* The correlative to an antecedent; that which follows as a natural and logical result; (*Math.*) the second term in a ratio.

consequential (kon se kwen′ shȧl), *a.* Following as a result or a necessary deduction; resulting indirectly; self-important, pompous, conceited; *important. **consequentially,** *adv.* **consequentiality** (-shi ăl′ i ti), *n.* **consequently,** *adv.* As a consequence; accordingly, therefore.

conservancy (kȯn sěr′ vȧn si) [L. *conservans -ntem,* pres.p. of *conservāre*], *n.* Official preservation of forests, fisheries, etc.; a commission or court with jurisdiction over a particular river, its fisheries, navigation, etc. **conservant,** *a.*

conservation (kon sėr vā′ shůn) [L. *conservātio* (as prec.)], *n.* The act of conserving; preservation from waste or decay. **conservation of energy:** The theory that no energy is destroyed, but that the sum of energy in the universe remains the same although particular forces are continually being transformed.

conservative (kȯn sěr′ vȧ tiv) [F. *conservatif -ve,* L. *conservātīvus* (as prec.)], *a.* Tending or inclined to conserve what is established; disposed to maintain existing institutions; pertaining to the Conservative party; moderate, not extreme (as a *conservative estimate*). *n.* A person inclined to preserve established things. **Conservative Party,** *n.* (*Pol.*) A political party that upholds strenuously the capitalist system and opposes any form of constitutional change. Also called Unionist and, by its opponents, Tory.

conservatoire (kȯn sěr vȧ twar′) [F., from L. *conservātōrium,* see CONSERVATORY], *n.* A public school of music and declamation.

conservator (kȯn sěr′ vȧ tȯr) [F. *conservateur,* L. *conservātor -em,* as foll.], *n.* One who preserves from violence or injury; a member of a conservancy; a custodian, keeper, curator; an officer charged with maintaining the public peace.

conservatory (kȯn sěr′ vȧ tȯ ri) [L. *conservātōrius, a.,* from *conservāre,* to CONSERVE], *n.* A greenhouse for exotics; a glass-house for plants; a *conservatoire.*

conserve (kȯn sěrv′) [F. *conserver,* L. *conservāre* (CON-, *servāre,* to keep, serve)], *v.t.* To preserve from injury, decay, or loss; to preserve (as fruit), to candy. *n.* A preserve; a confection; preserved or candied fruit. **conserver,** *n.* One who protects from loss or injury; one who makes conserves.

consider (kȯn sid′ ėr) [F. *considérer,* L. *consīderāre* (*sīdus -eris,* a star), orig. to examine the stars], *v.t.* To think on, to contemplate; to ponder; to observe and examine; to look upon as of importance; to estimate, to regard; to have regard for. *v.i.* To reflect, to deliberate. **considerable,** *a.* Worth consideration or regard; important; moderately large or great. **considerably,** *adv.* ***considerance,** *n.* Reflection, deliberation. **considerate** (kȯn sid′ ėr ȧt), *a.* Characterized by consideration for others; *careful, deliberate, prudent. **considerately,** *adv.* **considerateness,** *n.*

consideration (con sid ėr ā′ shůn), *n.* The act of considering; reflection, thought; regard for others; a motive or ground for action; importance, worth; a recompense, a reward; an equivalent; (*Law*) the material equivalent given in exchange for something and forming the basis of a contract.

considering (kȯn sid′ ėr ing), *prep.* Taking into consideration; in view of.

consign (kȯn sīn′) [F. *consigner,* L. *consignāre* (*signāre,* to mark, to sign, from *signum,* a mark)], *v.t.* To commit to the care, keeping or trust of another; to send (as goods); to relegate; to devote, to set apart; *to mark with a sign. **v.i.* To consent, to submit. **consignable,** *a.* **consignation** (kon sig nā′ shůn), *n.* The act of consigning; the formal paying over of money to an authorized person, (*Sc. Law*) as a deposit during a trial or arbitration; the act of consecrating or blessing with the sign of the cross. **consignee** (kon sī nē′), *n.* One to whom goods are consigned; an agent, a factor. **consignor** (kȯn sī nôr′), *n.* One who consigns goods to another. **consignment** (kȯn sīn′ mėnt), *n.* The act of consigning; goods consigned; the document by which anything is consigned.

consilient (kȯn sil′ i ėnt) [L. *consiliens -ntem,* pres.p. (*salīre,* to leap)], *a.* Concurring, agreeing. **consilience,** *n.*

consist (kȯn sist′) [L. *consistere* (*sistere,* to make to stand, causal of *stāre,* to stand)], *v.i.* To be composed (of); to be founded or constituted (in); to be compatible (with); to subsist, to continue to exist; *to stand together, to remain fixed. **consistence, -ency,** *n.* Degree of density; cohesion, coherence; firmness, solidity; accord, harmony, congruity, compatibility. **consistent,** *a.* Congruous, harmonious; uniform in opinion or conduct, not self-contradictory; compatible; *solid, not fluid. **consistently,** *adv.*

consistory (kon′ sis tȯ ri, kȯn sis′ tȯ ri) [O. North.F. *consistorie* (F. *consistoire*), late L. *consistōrium* (see CONSIST)], *n.* The court of a bishop for dealing with ecclesiastical causes arising in his diocese; the college of cardinals at Rome; an assembly of ministers and elders in the Lutheran and Calvinistic Churches. **consistorial** (-tôr′ i ȧl), *a.*

consociate (kȯn sō′ shi ȧt) [L. *consociātus,* p.p. of *consociāre* (*socius,* a partner, a fellow)], *a.* Associated together. *n.* An associate; a confederate, an accomplice. *v.t.* (-āt) To unite; (*Am.*) to unite in a Congregational convention. *v.i.* To associate; (*Am.*) to meet in convention. **consociation** (-ā′ shůn), *n.* Association, fellowship; (*Am. Hist.*) a union of Congregational churches by means of pastors and delegates.

console (1) (kȯn sōl′) [F. *consoler,* L. *consōlārī* (*sōlārī,* to solace)], *v.t.* To comfort or cheer in trouble or distress. **consolable,** *a.* ***consolate** (kon′ sȯ lȧt), *v.t.* To console. **consolation** (lā′ shůn), *n.* That which consoles, cheers, or comforts; alleviation of misery or mental distress; a fact or circumstance that consoles. **consolation prize:** One awarded to a runner-up, **consolatory** (kȯn sol′ ȧ tȯ ri), *a.* **consolatorily,** *adv.*

console (2) (kon′ sōl) [F., etym. doubtful], *n.* A bracket or corbel to support a cornice, etc.; (*Artill.*) the carrier on which the breech-screw of a gun hinges; (*Organ*) the frame enclosing the claviers, draw-knobs, etc., when separate from the instrument. **console-table,** *n.* A table supported by a console or consoles.

consolidate (kȯn sol′ i dāt) [L. *consolidātus,* from *consolidāre* (*solidāre,* to make solid)], *v.t.* To form into a solid and compact mass; to strengthen, to bring into close union; to combine. *v.i.* To become solid. *a.* (-dȧt) Solidified, combined, hardened. **consolidated annuities, consols,** *n.pl.* The British Government securities, consolidated into a single stock in 1751, originally bearing interest at 3 per cent. **consolidated fund,** *n.* A national fund for the payment of certain public charges, first formed in 1786 by consolidating the aggregate, general, and South Sea funds, to which the Irish exchequer was added in 1816. **consolidation** (-dā' shŭn), *n.* **consolidator,** *n.* **consolidatory,** *a.*

consols [CONSOLIDATE].

consommé (kon som' ā) [F.], *n.* A soup made by boiling meat and vegetables to a jelly.

consonant (kon' sŏ nănt) [F., from L. *consonantem*, nom. *-ans*, pres.p. of *consonāre* (*sonāre*, to sound)], *a.* Agreeing or according, esp. in sound; congruous, in harmony; (*Mus.*) producing harmony. *n.* A letter of the alphabet which cannot be sounded by itself, as *b* or *p*; a sound that is combined with a vowel in order to make a syllable. **consonance, -nancy,** *n.* Accord or agreement of sound; agreement, harmony; recurrence of sounds; assonance; (*Mus.*) pleasing agreement of sounds, concord. **consonantal** (-năn' tăl), *a.* **consonantly,** *adv.* **consonous** (kŏn' sŏ nŭs), *a.* Agreeing in sound; harmonious.

consort (kon' sŏrt) [F. *consort, -e*, L. *consors -rtem*, sharer (*sors*, lot)], *n.* A companion, an associate; a mate, a partner; a husband, a wife; a vessel accompanying another; *[ob. from F. *concert*], an assembly, a company; *agreement, accord; harmony, harmonious music. *v.i.* (kŏn sŏrt'). To associate, to keep company with; to agree, to be in harmony (with). *v.t.* To associate; to unite in harmony; to attend, to escort. **queen consort:** Wife of a king. **king, prince consort:** Husband of a queen. **consortism,** *n.* (*Biol.*) The vital union of two organisms for mutual support, symbiosis. **consortship,** *n.*

consortium (kŏn sŏr' shŭm) [L., fellowship], *n.* (*Pol.*) Fellowship, coalition, union; temporary association of states or powerful interests.

conspecific (kon spĕ sif' ik), *a.* Of or relating to the same species.

conspectus (kŏn spek' tŭs) [L., from *conspicere* (*specere*, to look)], *n.* A general sketch or survey; a synopsis. ***conspectuity** (-tū' i ti), *n.* The faculty of sight; vision.

conspicuous (kŏn spik' ū ŭs) [L. *conspicuus* (*conspicere*, as prec.)], *a.* Obvious to the sight; attracting the eye; prominent, extraordinary. **conspicuously,** *adv.* **conspicuousness, conspicuity** (-kū' i ti), *n.*

conspiracy (kŏn spir' ă si) [L. *conspīrātio*], *n.* The act of conspiring; *harmonious concurrence; (*Law*) a secret agreement or combination between two or more persons to commit an unlawful act that may prejudice any third person.

conspire (kŏn spīr') [F. *conspirer*, L. *conspīrāre* (*spīrāre*, to breathe)], *v.i.* To combine secretly to do any unlawful act, esp. to commit treason, sedition, murder, or fraud; to concur, to unite. *v.t.* To plot, to concert. **conspiringly,** *adv.* ***conspirant,** *a.* and *n.* ***conspiration** (-spi rā' shŭn), *n.* A conspiracy; concurrence, agreement. **conspirator** (-spir' ă tŏr), *n.* One who conspires. **conspiratress,** *n.*

conspue (kŏn spū') [F. *conspuer*, L. *conspuere* (*spuere*, spit)], *v.t.* To spit upon; to abuse, denounce.

constable (kŭn' stă bĕl) [O.F. *conestable* (F. *connétable*), L. *comes stabulī*, count of the stable], *n.* A policeman, (*Am.*) patrol-man; an officer charged with the preservation of the peace; a warden, a governor, an officer; (*Hist.*) a high officer of state in the Roman Empire, in France, and in England. ***high constable:** A constable appointed by the court leet of a franchise, or in default by the justices. ***petty constable:** A constable appointed in parishes by the justices in petty sessions. **police constable:** A policeman. **special constable:** A citizen sworn in to aid the police-force in times of war, civil commotion, etc. **to outrun the constable:** To get into debt. **constableship,** *n.* ***constablewick,** *n.* The district over which a (high or petty) constable's power extended. **constabulary** (-stăb' ū lăr i), *n.* A body of police under one authority; *the district under a constable. *a.* Pertaining to the police.

constant (kon' stănt) [F., from L. *constans -ntem*, pres.p. of *constāre* (*stāre*, to stand)], *a.* Firm, unshaken; unmoved in purpose or opinion; unchanging, steadfast; faithful in love or friendship; continuous, unceasing; (*Math.*) unvarying. *n.* (*Phys.*) Any property or relation, expressed by a number, that remains unchanged under the same conditions; (*Math.*) a quantity not varying, or assumed not to vary, in value throughout a series of calculations. **constancy,** *n.* Fixedness; firmness of mind; faithful attachment; permanence; *certainty; *perseverance; (*Math.*) that which remains invariable. **constantly,** *adv.* In a constant manner; invariably, regularly; continually, always.

Constantia (kŏn stăn' shi ă), *n.* A South African wine from Constantia farm, near Cape Town.

constellate (kon' stĕl āt) [L. *stellātus*, p.p. of *stellāre*, to set with stars (*stella*, a star)], *v.i.* To shine with combined radiance. *v.t.* To set or adorn with or as with stars; to combine into a constellation; *(*Astrol.*) to predestine (by the stars one is born under).

constellation (kon ste lā' shŭn), *n.* (*Astron.*) A number of fixed stars grouped within the outlines of an imaginary figure in the sky; *(*Astrol.*) the star or planet one is born under; (*fig.*) an assemblage of splendours or excellences.

consternate (kon' stėr nāt) [L. *consternātus*, p.p. of *consternāre*, to affright, coll. with *consternere* (*sternere*, to strew)], *v.t.* To affright, to dismay. **consternation** (-nā' shŭn), *n.*

constipate (kon' sti pāt) [L. *constīpātus*, p.p. of *constīpāre* (*stīpāre*, to cram, to pack)], *v.t.* To confine; to make costive. **constipation** (-pā' shŭn), *n.* (*Med.*) An undue retention or imperfect evacuation of the fæces.

constituency (kon stit' ū ĕn si) [as foll.], *n.* The whole body of constituents; a body of electors; the place or body of persons represented by a member of Parliament; (*colloq.*) a body of clients, customers, etc.

constituent (kŏn stit' ū ĕnt) [L. *constituens -ntem*, pres.p. of *constituere*, as foll.], *a.* Constituting, making, composing; having power to elect or appoint, or to construct or modify a political constitution. *n.* One who or that which constitutes; a component part; one of a body which elects a representative; one who appoints another as his agent, a client. **Constituent Assembly,** *n.* (*Hist.*) The name assumed by the National Assembly of France shortly after that body had dropped the name of the Third Estate (17 June 1789); since revived in France and elsewhere as the name of an assembly entrusted with framing or voting a constitution.

constitute (kon' sti tūt) [L. *constitūtus*, p.p. of *constituere* (CON-, *statuere*, to place, to set)], *v.t.* To establish; to enact; to give legal form to; to give a definite nature or character to; to make up or compose; to elect or appoint to an office or employment. **constituted authorities,** *n.pl.* The magistrates or governors of a country, district, municipality, etc.

constitution (kon sti tū' shŭn) [F., from L. *constitūtio -ōnem*, as prec.], *n.* The act of constituting; the nature, form, or structure of a system or body; natural strength of the body; mental qualities; the established form of government in a kingdom or state; a system of fundamental rules or principles for the government of a kingdom or state; a law or ordinance made by civil or ecclesiastical authority. **constitutions of Clarendon:** Statutes defining civil and ecclesiastical jurisdiction enacted at Clarendon, near Salisbury, in 1164. **constitutional,** *a.* Inherent in the bodily or mental constitution; pertaining to or in accordance with an established form of government; legal. *n.* A walk or other exercise for the benefit of one's health. **constitutional government,** *n.* A government in which the head of the state is, in his sovereign capacity, subject to a written or unwritten constitution. **constitutionally,** *adv.* **constitutionalism,** *n.* Government based on a constitution;

adherence to constitutional government. **constitutionalist,** *n.* An upholder of constitutional government; a writer or authority on the political constitution. **constitutionality** (-năl′ i ti), *n.* **constitutionalize,** *v.t.* To render constitutional. *v.i.* To take a constitutional.

constitutive (kon′ sti tū tiv), *a.* That constitutes or composes, component, essential; that enacts or establishes. **constitutively,** *adv.* **constitutor,** *n.*

constrain (kŏn strān′) [O.F. *constreign-*, stem of *constreindre*, L. *constringere* (*stringere*, to draw tight)], *v.t.* To compel, to oblige (to do or not to do); to restrain; to keep down by force; to confine, to repress; *to force; *to strain; *to bind. **constrained,** *a.* Acting under compulsion; forced; embarrassed. **constrainedly,** *adv.* **constraint** *n.* The act of constraining; restraint, compulsion, necessity; a compelling force; a constrained manner.

constrict (kŏn strikt′) [L. *constrictus*, p.p. of *constringere*, as prec.], *v.t.* To draw together; to compress; to cause to contract. **constriction,** *n.* **constrictive,** *a.* That constricts. **constrictor,** *n.* That which constricts; (*Anat.*) a muscle which serves to contract or draw together; (*Surg.*) an instrument for constricting, a compressor; [BOA-CONSTRICTOR].

***constringe** (kŏn strinj′) [as prec.], *v.t.* To draw together; to cause to contract; to constrict. **constringent,** *a.* **constringency,** *n.*

construct (kŏn strŭkt′) [L. *constructus*, p.p. of *construere* (CON-, *struere*, to pile, to build)], *v.t.* To build up, to frame; to put together in proper order; to combine words in clauses and sentences; to form by drawing; to form mentally. **constructor,** *n.* **constructorship,** *n.* **constructure,** *n.* *Construction, structure; (*Sc. Law*) the right to materials used in the repair of one's house on payment of compensation to their owner.

construction (kŏn strŭk′ shŭn), *n.* The act or art of constructing; the thing constructed; style, mode, or form of structure; the syntactical arrangement and connexion of words in a sentence; explanation, interpretation (of words, conduct, etc.); construing. **constructional,** *a.* Pertaining to construction; structural; pertaining to interpretation of language. **constructionist,** *n.* One who puts a certain kind of construction upon the law, legal documents, etc.

constructive (kŏn strŭk′ tiv), *a.* Having ability or power to construct; tending to construct (opp. to destructive); structural; inferential, virtual, implied by construction or interpretation. **constructively,** *adv.*

construe (kon′ stroo, kŏn stroo′) [as prec.], *v.t.* To combine syntactically; to arrange (as words) in order, so as to show the meaning; to translate; to explain, to interpret. *v.i.* To apply the rules of syntax; to translate.

consubstantial (kon sŭb stăn′ shăl) [L. *consubstantiālis* (CON-, SUBSTANTIAL)], *a.* Having the same substance or essence. **consubstantiality** (-shi ăl′ i ti), *n.*

consubstantiate (kon sŭb stăn′ shi āt) [L. *consubstantiāre*, as prec.], *v.t.* To unite in one substance. *v.i.* To join into one substance. **consubstantiation** (-ā′ shŭn), *n.* The Lutheran doctrine that the body and blood of Christ are present along with the eucharistic elements after consecration (opp. to transubstantiation).

consuetude (kon′ swė tūd) [O.F., from L. *consuētūdo -inem*, from *consuētus*, accustomed, p.p. of *consuēscere* (*suēscere*, to become used, accustomed)], *n.* Custom, usage, habit; familiarity. **consuetudinary** (-tū′ din ăr i), *a.* Customary. *n.* A ritual of monastic and ecclesiastical forms and customs.

consul (kon′ sŭl) [L.], *n.* (*Hist.*) One of the two supreme magistrates of ancient Rome, invested with regal authority for one year; one of the three supreme magistrates of the French Republic (1799–1804); an officer appointed by a state to reside in a foreign country to promote its mercantile interests and protect merchants, seamen, and other subjects; a local agent appointed by the Cyclists' Touring Club. **consul-general,** *n.* The chief consul of a state, having jurisdiction over ordinary consuls. **consular,** *a.* Pertaining to a consul; (*Rom. Hist.*) of the rank of a consul. **consulate,** *n.* The official residence, jurisdiction, office, or term of office, of a consul; (*French Hist.*) the period of consular government (1799–1804); **First Consul,** *n.* Napoleon Bonaparte. **consulship,** *n.*

consult (kŏn sŭlt′) [L. *consultāre*, freq. of *consulere*, to consult, consider (prob. as CONSUL)], *v.i.* To take counsel together; to deliberate. *v.t.* To ask advice or counsel from; to refer to (a book) for information; to have regard to; *to plot, to contrive. ****n.*** The act of consulting; a deliberation; a meeting, esp. a secret cabal; (*Rom. Hist.*) a decree of the senate. **consultable,** *a.* **consultant,** *n.* A person who consults; a consulting physician. **consultation** (-tā′ shŭn), *n.* The act of consulting; deliberation of two or more persons; a meeting of experts to consider a point or case. **consultative, consultatory, consultive,** *a.* **consultee** (kon sŭl tē′), *n.* A person consulted. **consulter,** *n.* One who consults. **consultor,** *n.* A member of a consultative body. **consulting,** *a.* Giving advice; called in for consultation; used for consultation.

consume (kŏn sūm′) [L. *consūmere* (*sūmere*, to take)], *v.t.* To destroy by fire, waste, or decomposition; to use up; to dissipate, to squander; *to exterminate. *v.i.* To waste away; to be burned. **consumable,** *a.* **consumedly** (kŏn sū′ mėd li), *adv.* (*colloq.*) Unrestrainedly, excessively. **consumer,** *n.* One who or that which consumes; (*Polit. Econ.*) the person who uses a commodity. **consumers' goods,** *n.pl.* Goods ready to satisfy human requirements without further manufacture or preparation.

consummate (1) (kŏn sŭm′ ăt) [L. *consummātus*, p.p. of *consummāre* (*summa*, a sum)], *a.* Complete, perfect; of the highest quality or degree.

consummate (2) (kon′ sŭ māt), *v.t.* To bring to completion, to perfect, to finish. **to consummate a marriage:** To complete marriage by sexual union. **consummately,** *adv.* **consummation** (-mā′ shŭn), *n.* The act of consummating; the end or completion of something already begun; perfection, perfect development. **consummative** (kon′ sŭ mā tiv), *a.* **consummator,** *n.*

consumption (kŏn sŭmp′ shŭn) [L. *consumptio* (see CONSUME)], *n.* The act of consuming; the state or process of being consumed; utilization of the products of industry; the value of the products consumed; (*Med.*) a wasting disease; phthisis. **consumptive,** *a.* Consuming, destructive; (*Med.*) disposed to or affected with consumption. *n.* A person suffering from consumption. **consumptively,** *adv.* **consumptiveness,** *n.*

contabescent (kon tă bes′ ėnt) [L. *contābēscens, -ntem*, pres.p. of *contābēscere* (*tābēscere*, to waste, from *tābes*, consumption)], *a.* Wasting away; (*Bot.*) affected with contabescence. **contabescence,** *n.* (*Bot.*) An atrophied condition of the stamens and pollen; (*Med.*) wasting away.

contact (kon′ tăkt) [L. *contactus*, p.p. of *contingere* (*tangere*, to touch)], *n.* Touch, meeting, the relation of touching; (*Med.*) a person likely to carry contagion; (*Math.*) the touching of two lines or surfaces. *v.t.* To establish contact with. **point of contact:** (*Math.*) The point at which two lines, planes, or bodies touch each other. **to be in contact with:** To be in touch, close proximity, or association with. **to come into contact with:** To meet with, to come across. **to make contact:** To complete an electric circuit; to get into touch with. **contact-breaker,** *n.* A device for interrupting an electric circuit at regular intervals in order to produce a spark and explode gases in a cylinder in an internal combustion engine. **contact lens,** *n.* (*Opt.*) A lens worn in contact with the eyeball in place of spectacles. **contact man,** *n.* An intermediary. **contactual,** *a.*

contadino (kon tă dē′ nō) [It., from *contado*, a

county, the country, L. *comitātus*, COUNTY], *n.* (*pl.* ***-ni***, *fem.* ***-na***, ***-ne***) An Italian peasant.

contagion (kon tā' jŭn) [F., from L. *contāgio -onem* (*tăg-*, root of *tangere*, to touch)], *n.* Communication of disease by contact with a person suffering from it; contagious disease; transmission of social or moral qualities; deleterious influence; *venom, poison, poisonous exhalation. **contagionist,** *n.* (*Med.*) One who believes in the contagious character of certain diseases. **contagious,** *a.* Communicable by contact, communicating disease by contact; (*loosely*) infectious. **Contagious Diseases Acts:** Acts passed to prevent the spread of certain contagious diseases. **contagiously,** *adv.* **contagiousness,** *n.* ***contagium*** [L.], *n.* (*pl.* ***contagia***) The organism or substance that carries the infectious element in diseases from one person to another.

contain (kon tān') [O.F. *contenir*, L. *continēre* (*tenēre*, to hold)], *v.t.* To hold within fixed limits, as a vessel; to be capable of holding; to comprise, to include; (*Geom.*) to enclose; (*Arith.*) to be exactly divisible by; (*Mil.*) to hem in, to put out of action by investing; to restrain; *to keep, retain. **v.i.* To restrain oneself; to be continent. **containable,** *a.* **container,** *n.*

contaminate (kon tăm' i nāt) [L. *contaminātus*, p.p. of *contāmināre*], *v.t.* To defile, to sully, to pollute, to corrupt, to tarnish. **a.* (-nat) Contaminated. **contamination** (-nā' shŭn), *n.* **contaminative** (kon tăm' i nā tiv), *a.*

contango (kon tăng' gō) [prob. from Sp. *contengo*, 1st pers. sing. of *contener*], *n.* The commission paid by a buyer for the postponement of transactions on the Stock Exchange.

conte (kont) [F.], *n.* A tale, esp. a short amusing story in prose.

conteck (kon' tek) [A.-F. *contek*, *contec* (etym. doubtful)], *n.* Strife, dissension.

contemn (kon tem') [O.F. *contemner*, L. *contemnere* (*temnere*, to despise)], *v.t.* To despise, to scorn; to slight, to neglect. **contemner** (kon tem' nėr, -ėr), *n.*

***contemper** (kon tem' pėr) [L. *contemperāre* (*temperāre*)], *v.t.* To temper by admixture; to adapt by tempering. **contemperation** (-ā' shŭn), *n.* **contemperature,** *n.*

contemplate (kon' tėm plāt) [L. *contemplātus*, p.p. of *contemplāre*, to observe (*templum*, a space of the sky for observation)], *v.t.* To look at, to study; to meditate and reflect on; to purpose, to intend; to regard as possible or likely. *v.i.* To meditate. **contemplation** (-plā' shŭn), *n.* **contemplative** (-tem' plă tiv), *a.* Given to contemplation; thoughtful, studious. **contemplative life,** *n.* A life passed in prayer and meditation, as distinguished from active acts of mercy, etc. **contemplative order,** *n.* (*R.-C. Ch.*) A religious order, *e.g.* Carthusian, whose members are engaged wholly in worship and meditation. **contemplatively,** *adv.* **contemplativeness,** *n.* **contemplator** (kon' tėm plā tȯr), *n.*

contemporaneous (kon tem pō rā' nė ŭs) [L. *contemporāneus* (*tempus*, *-poris*, time)], *a.* Existing, living, or happening at the same time; lasting, or of, the same period. **contemporaneously,** *adv.* **contemporaneousness,** *n.* **contemporaneity** (-nē' i ti), *n.*

contemporary (kon tem' pō ră ri), *a.* Living at the same time; of the same age; belonging to the same period; up-to-date, modern. *n.* A contemporary person or thing.

contempt (kon tempt') [L. *contemptus*, scorn], *n.* The act of contemning; scorn, disdain; the state of being contemned: shame, disgrace; (*Law*) an act of disobedience to the rules, orders, or regulations of a sovereign, a court, or a legislative body. **contempt of court:** Disobedience or resistance to the orders or proceedings of a court of justice. **contemptible,** *a.* Worthy of contempt, despicable, mean; *contemptuous. **Contemptibles,** *n.pl.* Troops of the British Expeditionary Force in 1914, so named from the Kaiser's allusion to them as "a contemptible little army." **contemptibleness,** *n.* **contemptibly,** *adv.* **contemptuous,** *a.* Expressive of contempt; disdainful, scornful. **contemptuously,** *adv.* **contemptuousness,** *n.*

contend (kon tend') [O.F. *contendre*, L. *contendere* (*tendere*, to stretch, strive)], *v.i.* To strive in opposition; to exert oneself in defence or support of anything; to strive to obtain or keep; to compete; to dispute. *v.t.* To maintain by argument. **contender,** ***-dent,** *n.* One who contends; an antagonist; an opponent.

content (1) (con tent') [F., from L. *contentus*, p.p. of *continēre*, to CONTAIN], *a.* Satisfied, pleased, willing; the term used to express an affirmative vote in the House of Lords; hence (*n.pl.*) those who vote in the affirmative. *v.t.* To satisfy, to appease; to make easy in any situation; to gratify. *n.* Satisfaction, ease of mind; a condition or ground of satisfaction; *acquiescence. ***contentation** (-tā' shŭn), *n.* Contentment; satisfaction. **contentedly,** *adv.* **contentedness,** *n.* **contentless,** *a.* Without any content or meaning; *discontented. **contentment,** *n.* The state of being contented or satisfied; gratification, satisfaction.

content (2) (kon' tent), *n.* Capacity or power of containing; volume; capacity; meaning; (*pl.*) that which is comprised in a vessel, writing, or book; (*pl.*) a table or summary of subject-matter; (*pl.*) (*Math.*) the area or quantity contained within certain limits.

contention (kon ten' shŭn) [F., from L. *contentio -ōnem*, from *contendere*, to CONTEND], *n.* The act of contending; quarrel, strife, controversy; emulation; a point contended for. **contentious,** *a.* Disposed to or characterized by contention; quarrelsome. **contentiously,** *adv.* **contentiousness,** *n.*

conterminous (con tĕr' mi nŭs) [L. *terminus*, a boundary], *a.* Having a common boundary-line; having the same limits, coextensive (in line, range, or meaning). **conterminal,** *a.* Bordering, neighbouring, contiguous. **conterminously,** *adv.*

contest (kon test') [F. *contester*, L. *contestārī* (*testārī*, to bear witness, from *testis*, a witness)], *v.t.* To contend for or about, to strive earnestly for; to dispute, to call in question, to oppose. *v.i.* To strive, to contend, to vie. *n.* (kon' test) A struggle for victory or superiority; a dispute, a controversy; competition, rivalry. **contestable,** *a.* **contestant,** *n.* One who contests. **contestation** (-tā' shŭn), *n.* The act of contesting; disputation, controversy; something contended for, a contention; *contention; *attestation.

context (kon' tekst) [L. *contextus*, p.p. of *contexere* (*texere*, to weave)], *n.* The parts of a discourse or book immediately connected with a sentence or passage quoted; the setting, surroundings. **contextual** (kon teks' tū ăl), *a.* **contextually,** *adv.*

contexture (kon teks' tūr), *n.* A weaving together; the disposition and relation of parts in a compound body or a literary composition; structure; *context. *v.t.* To give contexture to.

contiguous (kon tig' ū ŭs) [L. *contiguus*, from *contingere* (*tangere*, to touch)], *a.* Meeting so as to touch; adjoining, neighbouring. **contiguously,** *adv.* **contiguity** (-gū' i ti), *n.* Contact; proximity in time or space; (*Psych.*) the immediate relation of two impressions, a principle of association.

continent (1) (kon' ti nent) [O.F., from L. *continēre*, to CONTAIN], *a.* Abstaining from indulgence in unlawful or undue indulgence in lawful pleasures; chaste; temperate; *restraining; *retentive; *continuous. **continence, -nency,** *n.* **continently,** *adv.*

continent (2) (kon' ti nent) [as prec.], *n.* A large tract of land not disjoined or interrupted by a sea; one of the great geographical divisions of land; the mainland of Europe; *that which contains anything; the summary, the sum total; *mainland;

*(*fig.*) a large and continuous extent of anything. **continental** (-nen′ tăl), *a.* Pertaining to a continent; European; (*U.S.A. Hist.*) belonging to the Union forces in the Civil War. **continentalism,** *n.* **continentalist,** *n.* **continentalize,** *v.t.* **continentally,** *adv.*

contingent (kŏn tin′ jĕnt) [L. *contingens -ntem*, pres.p. of *contingere* (*tangere*, to touch)], *a.* Dependent on an uncertain issue; of doubtful occurrence; accidental, not essential, conditional; (*Log.*) that may or may not be true. *n.* A fortuitous event; that which falls to one in a division or apportionment; a naval or military force furnished by a state for a joint enterprise; a quota of fighting men. **contingency,** *n.* The state of being contingent; a chance or possible occurrence; an accident; something dependent on an uncertain issue; (*pl.*) incidental expenses; money provided for these in an estimate. **contingent liability,** *n.* A liability that will arise only in a certain event. **contingently,** *adv.*

continual (kŏn tin′ ū ăl) [O.F. *continuel*, L. *continuālis*], *a.* Unbroken, incessant; without interruption or cessation; (*colloq.*) very frequent. **continually,** *adv.*

continuance (kŏn tin′ ū ăns) [O.F., from *continuer*, to CONTINUE], *n.* The act of continuing; duration; stay; (*Law*) adjournment; *perseverance; *continuity. **continuant,** *a.* Continuing; prolonged. *n.* A consonant whose sound can be prolonged as *f, v, s, r.*

continuate (kŏn tin′ ū ăt) [L. *continuātus*, p.p. of *continuāre*, to CONTINUE], *a.* Continuous, uninterrupted; long-continued.

continuation (kŏn tin ū ā′ shŭn) [as prec.], *n.* The act of continuing; that by which anything is continued or carried on; extension or prolongation in a series or line; (*Stock Exch.*) the carrying over of accounts for stock [see CONTANGO]; (*pl.*) gaiters or bands of box-cloth continuous with knee-breeches; (*slang*) trousers. **continuation class,** *n.* A class, established under the Education Act of 1918, for teaching those who have left school but are not yet eighteen. ***continuative** (kŏn tin′-), *a.* Causing or tending to continuation. **continuator,** *n.* One who continues a (literary) work begun by another.

continue (kŏn tin′ ū) [F. *continuer*, L. *continuāre* (*continuus*, CONTINUOUS)], *v.t.* To carry on without interruption; to keep up; to take up, to extend, to complete; (*Law*) to adjourn; *to suffer to remain. *v.i.* To remain, to stay; to last, to abide; to remain in existence; to persevere. **continued fraction,** *n.* One in which the denominator is a whole number plus a fraction, the denominator of which is a whole number plus a fraction, etc. **continued proportion,** *n.* A series of quantities in which the ratio is the same between each two adjacent terms. **continuable,** *a.*

continuous (kŏn tin′ ū ŭs) [L. *continuus*, from *continare* (*tinēre*, to hold)], *a.* Connected without a break in space or time; uninterrupted, unceasing; (*Bot.*) without joints; (*Arch.*) having the mullions carried on into the tracery. **continuity** (-nū′ i ti), *n.* Uninterrupted connexion; union without a break or interval; (*Cinema.*) the detailed description of a film in accordance with which the production is carried out; hence **continuity clerk, girl,** *n.* The person responsible for seeing that there are no discrepancies between the scenes. **law of continuity:** The principle that nothing passes from one state into another without passing through all the intermediate states. **solution of continuity:** (*Surg.*) Destruction of the texture or cohesion of parts of an animal body. **continuously,** *adv.*

continuum (kon tin′ ū ŭm) [as prec.], *n.* (*Phys.*) An unbroken mass, series, or course of events; a continuous series of component parts that pass into each other. **four-dimensional continuum,** *n.* The three space dimensions and the time dimension.

cont-line (kont′ līn) [etym. doubtful], *n.* (*Naut.*) The space between casks stowed side by side; the external space between the strands in a rope.

conto (kon′ tō) [Port., from late L. *computum*, COUNT], *n.* A million *reis* (money of account). worth about £220.

contorniate (kŏn tôr′ ni āt) [F., from It. *contorno*], *a.* (*Numis.*) Bordered by a deep furrow round the inside of the edge. *n.* A coin distinguished by this furrow.

contorno (kŏn tôr′ nō) [It.], *n.* Contour, outline.

contort (kŏn tôrt′) [L. *contortus*, p.p. of *contorquēre*, (*torquēre*, to turn, to twist)], *v.t.* To twist with violence, to wrench; to distort. **contorted,** *a.* (*Geol.*) Twisted obliquely so as to form folds (used of strata curved or twisted as if by lateral pressure when soft). **contortion,** *n.* The act of twisting; a writhing movement; (*Surg.*) partial dislocation, the wresting of a member out of its natural situation. **contortionist,** *n.* An acrobat who bends his body into various shapes; (*fig.*) one who twists the sense of words; an artist who paints contorted figures.

contour (kon′ toor) [F., from *contourner*, to turn (cp. CONTORNO)], *n.* The defining line of any figure or body; outline; outline of coast or other geographical feature. *v.t.* To make an outline of; to mark with contour-lines; to carry (a road) round a valley or hill. **contour-line,** *n.* A line on a map marking a particular level. **contour-map,** *n.* One exhibiting the elevations and depressions of the earth's surface by means of contour-lines. **contour ploughing,** *n.* (*Agric.*) Ploughing round sloping ground on a level instead of up and down.

contra (kon′ tră) [L., against], *prep.* Against, opposite. *n.* The opposite (usu. the credit) side of an account. **pro and contra:** For and against. **pros and cons:** The arguments for and against. **contra-,** *pref.* Against; denoting opposition, resistance, or contrariety; in music signifying extreme. **contra-bass** (kon′ tră bās) [It. *contra-basso*, BASS (3)], *n.* Double-bass. **contra-dance** [COUNTRY-DANCE]. **contra-tenor,** *n.* [COUNTER-TENOR].

contraband (kon′ tră bănd) [Sp. *contrabanda*, It. *contrabbando*], *a.* Prohibited, unlawful; forbidden by proclamation or law. **v.t.* To declare contraband. *v.i.* To deal in contraband goods. *n.* Prohibited traffic; articles forbidden to be exported or imported; smuggled articles. **contraband goods,** *n.pl.* Goods which are not allowed to be imported or exported, either by the laws of a particular state (for revenue purposes) or by the law of nations (to prevent neutrals from supplying belligerents with warlike stores). **contrabandist,** *n.* A dealer in contraband goods; a smuggler.

contraception (kon tră sep′ shŭn), *n.* Birth-control, the taking of measures to prevent conception. **contraceptive,** *n.* A device for preventing conception.

contract (1) (kŏn trăkt′) [L. *contractus*, p.p. of *contrahere* (CON-, *trahere*, to draw)], *v.t.* To draw together; to bring into smaller compass; (*Gram.*) to abbreviate, shorten, draw together; to acquire, to incur; to become liable for; to be attacked by (disease); to agree to or settle by covenant; to settle, to establish. *v.i.* To shrink; to agree (to do any act or supply certain articles for a settled price). **contracted,** *a.* Drawn together; betrothed; (*fig.*) mean, narrow, selfish. ***contractedly,** *adv.* ***contractedness,** *n.* **contractible,** *a.* Capable of being drawn together. **contractibility** (-bil′ i ti), *n.* **contractile,** *a.* Tending to contract; having the power to shorten itself. **contractility** (-til′ i ti), *n.* **contraction** (kŏn trăk′ shŭn), *n.* The act of shrinking, the state of being drawn together, confined, or shortened; an abbreviation; the shortening of a word by the omission of a letter or syllable; the act of contracting (a habit, a disease, etc.). **contractive,** *a.* Tending or serving to contract.

contract (2) (kon′ trăkt) [as prec.], *n.* An agreement, a compact; the writing by which an agreement is entered into; a formal betrothal; an undertaking to do certain work or supply certain articles for a specified consideration; (*Law*) an agreement recognized as a legal obligation; an offer or promise which has been formally accepted. **contract bridge,** *n.* (*Cards*) A form of auction bridge. **contractual,** *a.* Implying a contract; relating to a contract.

contractor (kŏn trăk′ tŏr) [as prec.], *n.* One who undertakes a contract, esp. to do or supply anything for a stipulated consideration; an employer of labour who contracts to perform building, engineering, and other undertakings, usu. on a large scale; a muscle that serves to contract an organ or other part of the body.

contradict (kon trȧ dikt′) [L. *contrādictus*, p.p. of *contrādīcere* (*dīcere*, to speak)], *v.t.* To oppose in words; to deny the truth of; to assert the opposite of; to oppose. *v.i.* To deny the truth of a statement. **contradictable,** *a.* **contradiction,** *n.* The act of opposing in words; denial; contrary statement; repugnancy, inconsistency; that which is inconsistent with itself. **contradiction in terms:** A statement that is obviously self-contradictory or inconsistent. **contradictious,** *a.* Inclined to contradiction; cavilling, disputatious. **contradictiously,** *adv.* **contradictiousness,** *n.* **contradictive,** *a.* Contradictory. **contradictively,** *adv.* **contradictiveness,** *n.* **contradictor,** *n.* **contradictory,** *a.* Affirming the contrary; inconsistent; mutually opposed, logically incompatible; disputatious. *n.* (*Log.*) A contradictory proposition; the contrary. **contradictorily,** *adv.* **contradictoriness,** *n.*

contradistinguish (kon trȧ dis ting′ gwish), *v.t.* To distinguish by contrasting opposite qualities. **contradistinction,** *n.*

contrahent (kon′ trȧ hėnt) [L. *contrahens -ntem*, pres.p. of *contrahere*, to CONTRACT], *a.* Contracting.

contrail (kon′ trāl), *n.* (*Aviat.*) The trail of condensed vapour left by an aircraft when flying high.

contraindicant (kon trȧ in′ di kȧnt), *n.* (*Med.*) A symptom which is adverse to the usual treatment. **contraindicate,** *v.i.* **contraindication** (-kā′ shŭn).

contralto (kŏn trăl′ tō) [It.], *n.* The lowest of the three principal varieties of the female voice, and that to which in choral music the part next above the alto is assigned; one who sings this part; music written for this part. *a.* Singing or arranged for contralto.

contraplex (kon′ trȧ pleks) [L. *-plex* (as in SIMPLEX, DUPLEX)], *a.* (*Teleg.*) Of or pertaining to the sending of messages in opposite directions over the same wire.

contraposition (kon trȧ pŏ zish′ ŭn) [L. *contrāpositio -ōnem*, from *contrāpōnere* (*pōnere*, to put)], *n.* A placing opposite to, or in contrast; (*Log.*) a kind of conversion by means of negation.

contraption (kŏn trăp′ shŭn), *n.* (*colloq.*) A contrivance.

contrapuntal (kon trȧ pŭn′ tȧl) [It. *contrapuntal* (now *contrappuntal*), see COUNTER-POINT], *a.* (*Mus.*) Pertaining or according to counterpoint. **contrapuntist,** *n.* (*Mus.*) One skilled in counterpoint.

contrary (kon′ trȧ ri) [O.F. *contrarie*, L. *contrārius*], *a.* Opposite; opposed, diametrically different; contradictory, repugnant; (*Log.*) opposed as regards affirmation and negation; different from the right one; (*colloq.* kon trâr′ i) antagonistic, wayward, perverse. *n.* A thing of opposite qualities; the opposite; a thing that contradicts. *adv.* Contrarily; adversely; in an opposite manner or direction. **v.t.* To contradict; to oppose. **by contraries:** By way of contrast; by negation instead of affirmation, and *vice versa.* **on the contrary:** On the other hand; quite the reverse. **the contrary:** The opposite of a motion put from the chair. **contrariant** (-trâr′ i ȧnt), *a.* Opposed, antagonistic, contrary. **contrariety** (-rī′ ė ti), *n.* The state of being contrary; opposition; disagreement; inconsistency. **contrarily,** *adv.* In a contrary manner. **contrariness** (kon′ trȧ ri nes, *pop.* kŏn trâr′ i nes), *n.* The state or quality of being contrary. ***contrarious** (kŏn trâr′ i ŭs), *a.* Inclined to oppose, perverse; adverse. ***contrariously,** *adv.* **contrariwise** (kon′ trȧ ri wīz, *pop.* kŏn trâr′ i wīz), *adv.* On the other hand, conversely; perversely.

contrast (1) (kŏn trast′) [O.F. *contraster*, late L. *contrāstāre* (CONTRA-, L. *stāre*, to stand)], *v.t.* To set in opposition, so as to show the difference between, or the superior excellence of one to another. *v.i.* To stand in contrast or opposition.

contrast (2) (con′ trast), *n.* Opposition or unlikeness of things or qualities; the presentation of opposite things with a view to comparison.

contrate (kon′ trāt). *a.* (*Watch- and clock-making*) Having teeth or cogs at right angles to the plane of the wheel.

contravallation (kon trȧ vȧ lā′ shŭn) [F. *contrevallation* (L. *vallatio -ōnem*; cp. CIRCUMVALLATION)], *n.* A chain of fortifications constructed by besiegers as a protection against sallies.

contravene (kon trȧ vēn′) [F. *contrevenir*, L. *contrāvenīre* (*venīre*, to come)], *v.t.* To violate, to transgress; to be in conflict with, to obstruct; to oppose, to be inconsistent with. **contravention** (-ven′ shŭn), *n.* Violation.

contretemps (kon′ trė ton) [F., bad or adverse time], *n.* An unexpected event which throws everything into confusion.

contribute (kon trib′ ūt) [L. *contribūtus*, p.p. of *contribuere* (*tribuere*, to pay)], *v.t.* To give for a common purpose; to pay as one's share. *v.i.* To give a part; to have a share in any act or effect; to write for a newspaper, etc. **contributable,** *a.* Liable to be contributed. **contribution** (-bū′ shŭn), *n.* The act of contributing; that which is contributed; a subscription; a levy made on a town or district by an invading force. **contributive,** *a.* Contributing, assisting, promoting. **contributiveness,** *n.* **contributor,** *n.* One who contributes; one who supplies articles to a newspaper, etc. **contributory,** *a.* Contributing to the same fund, stock, or result; promoting the same end.

contrite (kon′ trīt) [F. *contrit*, L. *contrītus*, p.p. of *conterere* (*terere*, to rub, to grind)], *a.* Deeply sorry for sin; thoroughly penitent; characterized by penitence. **contritely,** *adv.* **contrition** (kŏn trish′ ŭn), *n.* Heartfelt sorrow for sin; penitence.

***contriturate** (kŏn trit′ ū rāt), *v.t.* To grind thoroughly.

contrive (1) (kŏn trīv′) [M.E. *contreve, controve*, O.F. *controver* (*trover*, to find, from late L. *tropāre*; cp. TROVER, TROUBADOUR)], *v.t.* To devise, to invent; to bring to pass, to effect, to manage. *v.i.* To form designs, to scheme (against); *to plot, to conspire. **contrivable,** *a.* **contrivance,** *n.* The act of contriving; the thing contrived; device, plan; a trick, an artifice, a plot; invention, apparatus; inventiveness. **contriver,** *n.*

***contrive** (2) (kŏn trīv′) [prob. from L. *contrīvi*, past of *conterere* (cp. CONTRITE)], *v.t.* To wear away; to pass, to spend (the time),

control (kŏn trōl′) [O.F. *contre-rolle*, a duplicate roll or register], *n.* Check, restraint; restraining, directing, and regulating power; authority, command; a person who controls, esp. a spirit controlling a medium; a standard of comparison for checking the results of experiment; *n.pl.* (*Motor.*) the gear-lever, clutch, brake-lever, etc., of a car; *n.pl.* (*Pol.*). direction of industry, labour, etc., by the government. *v.t.* (*past & p.p.* **controlled**) To exercise power over, to govern, to command; to restrain, to regulate, to hold in check; to verify or check, orig. to check by a duplicate register. **control column,** *n.* (*Aviat.*) The lever by which the elevators and ailerons of an aircraft are operated, the joy-stick. **control experiment:** One carried out on two objects so as to have a means of checking and confirming the inferences deduced. **control room,** *n.* (*Elec.*) A room in which the engineers of an electric power supply system control and supervise the entire system. **control surface,** *n.* (*Aviat.*) A movable surface, *e.g.*, the elevators, rudder, etc., by which the movements of an aeroplane are controlled. **controllable,** *a.* **controller,** *n.* One who exercises control; a ruler, a director; an officer appointed to verify the accounts of other officers by means of a duplicate register; (*Am.*) one who keeps the public accounts. **controllership,** *n.* **controlment,** *n.* Control, regulation; the power or act of controlling.

controversy (con' trŏ vĕr si, *incorr.* con trov' ėr si) [L. *contrōversia,* a quarrel, from *contrōversus,* opposed (*versus,* p.p. of *vertere,* to turn)], *n.* Disputation, esp. a dispute carried on in writing; *resolute resistance; *variance, contention. **controversial** (kon trŏ vĕr' shăl), *a.* Inclined or pertaining to controversy. **controversialism,** *n.* **controversialist,** *n.* One who carries on a controversy; a disputant. **controversially,** *adv.*

controvert (kon' trŏ vĕrt) [L. *vertere,* to turn], *v.t.* To dispute; to call in question; to oppose or refute by argument. ***controverter,** *n.* **controvertist,** *n.*

contumacious (kon tū mā' shŭs) [L. *contumāx -ācis* (*tumēre,* to swell with pride)], *a.* Perverse, obstinate, stubborn; stubbornly opposing lawful authority; (*Law*) wilfully disobedient to the orders of a court. **contumaciously,** *adv.* **contumaciousness,** *n.* **contumacy** (kon' tū măs i), *n.*

contumely (kon' tū mė li) [O.F. *contumelie,* L. *contumēlia* (cogn. with *contumāx,* see CONTUMACIOUS)], *n.* Rude, scornful abuse or reproach; insolence, contempt; disgrace, ignominy. **contumelious** (kon tū mē' li ŭs), *a.* Contemptuous, insolent, abusive; *dishonouring, disgraceful. **contumeliously,** *adv.* **contumeliousness,** *n.*

contund (kŏn tŭnd') [see foll.], *v.t.* To bruise, to knock about.

contuse (kŏn tūz') [L. *contūsus,* p.p. of *contundere* (CON- *tundere,* to beat)], *v.t.* To bruise without breaking the skin. **contusion,** *n.* The act of contusing; the state of being contused; a bruise.

conundrum (kŏ nŭn' drŭm) [etym. doubtful], *n.* A riddle; a puzzling question.

conurbation (kon ĕr bā' shŏn) [L. *urbs,* a city], *n.* The aggregation of urban districts.

convalesce (kon vă les') [L. *convalēscere* (*valēscere,* incept. of *valēre,* to grow)], *v.i.* To recover health. **convalescence,** *n.* **convalescent,** *a.* Recovering from illness. *n.* One who is recovering health. **convalescent-hospital, home,** *n.* A hospital for convalescent patients.

convallaria (kon vă lâr' i ă) [L. *convallis* (*vallis,* valley), *-āria,* neut. pl. of *ārius,* -ARY], *n.pl.* (*Bot.*) A genus of *Liliaceæ,* containing only one species, the lily of the valley.

convection (kŏn vek' shŭn) [L. *convectio,* from *convehere* (*vehere,* to carry)], *n.* The act of conveying; (*Phys.*) the propagation of heat or electricity through liquids and gases by the movement of the heated particles.

convenance (kon' vė nans) [F.], *n.* (*usu. in pl.*) Conventional usages, the proprieties.

convene (kŏn vēn') [F. *convenir,* L. *convenīre* (*venīre,* to come)], *v.t.* To call together; to convoke; to summon to appear. *v.i.* To meet together, to assemble. **convenable,** *a.* **convener,** *n.* One who calls a committee, etc., together; (*Sc.*) the chairman of a public body or committee.

convenient (kŏn vē' ni ėnt) [L. *conveniens -ntem,* pres.p. of *convenīre* (as prec.)], *a.* Suitable; commodious; useful, handy; opportune, at hand, close by. **convenience, -ency,** *n.* The quality or state of being convenient; comfort, accommodation; a cause or source of comfort or accommodation; advantage; a thing that is useful; a water-closet or urinal; (*pl.*) things or arrangements that promote ease and comfort or save trouble. **conveniently,** *adv.*

convent (kon' vėnt) [M.E. and A.-F. *covent,* O.F. *convent,* L. *conventus,* p.p. of *convenīre,* as prec.], *n.* A community of religious persons of either sex (usu. women); the building occupied by such a community. **v.t.* (kŏn vent') To convene, to summon. *v.i.* To meet.

conventicle (kŏn ven' tikl) [L. *conventiculum,* dim. of *conventus,* as prec.], *n.* A clandestine gathering; (*Hist.*) a term of reproach applied to the meetings and places of worship of dissenters in the 16th and 17th cents.

convention (kŏn ven' shŭn) [F., from L. *conventio -ōnem* (*convenīre,* to CONVENE)], *n.* The act of coming together; a meeting; the persons assembled; a union of representatives; an agreement, a treaty; an accepted usage. **conventional,** *a.* Agreed on by compact; founded on custom or use; slavishly observant of the customs of society; (*Art*) following tradition and accepted models. **conventional arms,** *n.pl.* Weapons other than atomic. **conventionalism,** *n.* **conventionalist,** *n.* **conventionality** (-ăl' i ti), *n.* **conventionalize,** *v.t.* **conventionally,** *adv.* **conventionary,** *a.* (*Law*) Acting or holding under convention as distinguished from custom. *n.* A conventionary tenant.

conventual (kŏn ven' tū ăl), *a.* Belonging to a convent. *n.* A member of a convent; one of a branch of the Franciscans who follow a mitigated rule.

converge (kŏn vĕrj') [L. *convergere* (*vergere,* to turn, incline)], *v.i.* To tend towards one point; (*Math.*) to approach a definite limit by an indefinite number of steps. *v.t.* To cause to converge. **convergence, -ency,** *n.* **convergent,** *a.* Tending to meet in one point; used of rays of light which being continued will meet in a focus; and of a lens which will cause rays to meet in a focus.

conversant (kon' vĕr sănt) [CONVERSE (1)], *a.* Having knowledge acquired by study, use or familiarity; well acquainted, proficient; closely connected, familiar.

conversation (kon vĕr sā' shŭn) [CONVERSE (1)], *n.* The act of conversing; familiar talk; intimate fellowship or intercourse; sexual intercourse. **conversation piece:** Representation of figures in familiar groupings. **conversational,** *a.* **conversationalist,** *n.* **conversationally,** *adv.*

conversazione (kon vĕr săt si ō' nā) [It., from L. *conversātio -ōnem,* conversation], *n.* (*pl.* **-nes, ni**) A social meeting devoted to literary, artistic, or scientific subjects.

converse (1) (kŏn vĕrs') [F. *converser,* L. *conversārī,* to be conversant or keep company with, pass. of *convertere,* to CONVERT], *v.i.* To discourse easily and familiarly (with); *to hold intercourse, to have dealings (with). **conversable,** *a.* Inclined to conversation; free, sociable, agreeable. **conversableness,** *n.* **conversably,** *adv.*

converse (2) (kon' vĕrs), *n.* Close and intimate connexion, familiarity; conversation; the opposite, the counterpart or complement; (*Math.*) an inverted proposition; (*Log.*) a converted proposition. *a.* Opposite, reciprocal, complemental. **conversely,** *adv.* In a contrary order; reciprocally.

conversion (kŏn vĕr' shŭn) [F., from L. *conversio -ōnem,* from *convertere,* to CONVERT], *n.* Change from one state to another; transmutation; the act of changing to a new mode of life, religion, morals, or politics; (*Rel.*) the turning from sin to godliness; (*Math.*) the clearing an equation of fractions; (*Log.*) transposition of the terms of a proposition; (*Stock Exch.*) change of one kind of securities into another kind.

convert (kŏn vĕrt') [L. *convertere* (CON-, *vertere,* to turn)], *v.t.* To change from one physical state to another, to transmute; to cause to turn from one religion or party to another; to change one kind of securities into another kind; (*Log.*) to transpose the terms of. *v.i. To be converted or changed; to undergo a change. n. (kon' vėrt) One who is converted from one religion or party to another, esp. one who is converted to Christianity, or from a worldly to a spiritual state of mind. **convertend** (kon' vėr tend), n. (Log.) A proposition to be converted. **converter** (kȯn vĕr' tėr), n. One who converts; (Metal.) an iron retort used in making Bessemer steel; (Elec.) a device for changing an alternating current into another current of different frequency (or d.c.) or different number of phases. **convertible,** a. That may be converted or changed; transmutable; exchangeable for another kind of thing (as paper money for coin). **convertible husbandry:** That which is based on rotation of crops. **convertible terms:** (Log.) Such as can be changed for equivalents. **convertibility** (-bil' i ti), n.

convex (kon' veks) [L. *convexus*, arched, p.p. of *convehere* (*vehere*, to carry)], a. Having a rounded form on the exterior surface (opp. to concave). n. A convex body. **convexity** (-vek' si ti), n. Curvature. **convexly,** adv.

convexo-, comb. form. Convex. **convexo-concave,** a. Convex on one side and concave on the other. **convexo-convex,** a. Convex on both sides. **convexo-plane,** a. Convex on one side and plane on the other.

convey (kȯn vā') [O.F. *conveier*, *convoier*, late L. *conviāre* (CON-, *via*, way)], v.t. To carry, to transport, to transmit; to impart; (Law) to transfer (property); (slang) to remove secretly, to steal. v.i. To play the thief. **conveyable,** a. That may be conveyed. **conveyance,** n. The act, means, or instrument of conveying; a vehicle; (Law) the act of transferring real property from one person to another; the document by which it is transferred; *communication of meaning, style; *stealing, plagiarism; *trickery. **conveyancer,** n. (Law) One who draws up conveyances. **conveyancing,** n. (Law) The act or profession of drawing up deeds for the conveyance of real property. ***conveyer,** n. One who conveys; a thief; a juggler. **conveyor belt,** n. (Mach.) An endless mechanical belt or moving platform which carries work along a line of workers.

convict (kȯn vikt') [L. *convictus*, p.p. of *convincere* (CON-, *vincere*, to conquer)], v.t. To prove guilty; to return a verdict of guilty against; to convince of sin; *to prove, to demonstrate; *to confute. *a. Convicted. n. (kon' vikt) A criminal sentenced to penal servitude. **conviction** (-vik' shŭn), n. The act of convicting; the state of being convicted; the state of being convinced; strong belief, persuasion. **to carry conviction:** To be convincing. **convictive,** a.

convince (kȯn vins') [L. *convincere*, as prec.], v.t. To satisfy the mind of; to persuade to conviction; to overcome by proof; *to convict; *to conquer; *to confute. **convincement,** n. Conviction. **convincible,** a. Capable of conviction or refutation. **convincingly,** adv. **convincingness,** n.

convive (kon' vīv, kon' vīv) [L. *convīva*, from *convīvere* (later use from F. *convive*, L. *convīva*)], n. A guest at a banquet. **convivial** (kȯn viv' i ăl), a. Festive, social, jovial. **convivialist,** n. **conviviality** (-ăl' i ti), n. **convivially,** adv.

convocation (kon vō cā' shŭn), n. The act of calling together; an assembly, a meeting, a gathering; an assembly of qualified graduates of certain Universities; an assembly of the clergy of a province. **convocational,** a.

convoke (kȯn vōk') [F. *convoquer*, L. *convocāre* (CON-, *vocāre*, to call)], v.t. To call or summon together; to convene. ***convocate** (kon' vȯ kāt) [L. *convocātus*, p.p. of *convocāre*], v.t. To convoke.

convolute, -luted (kon' vȯ loot, -loo tėd) [L. *convolūtus*, p.p. of *convolvere* (CON-, *volvere*, to roll)], a. Rolled together; (Bot.) rolled up in another of the same kind (used of petals, leaves, etc.). **convolution** (-loo' shŭn), n. The act of convolving; the state of being convolved; a fold (esp. of brain matter); a winding; a winding motion. **convolve,** v.t. To roll or wind together; to wind one part over another. **convolvulus** (kȯn vol' vū lŭs) [L., as prec.], n. (pl. **-ses**) A genus of climbing plants, containing the bindweed.

convoy (kȯn voi') [F. *convoier*, CONVEY], v.t. To accompany on the way, by land or sea, for the sake of protection, esp. with a warship; *to escort (a lady). n. (kon' voi) The act of convoying or escorting; a protecting force accompanying persons, goods, ships, etc., for purposes of defence; an escort, a guard; that which is convoyed, esp. a company of merchant ships.

convulse (kȯn vŭls') [L. *convulsus*, p.p. of *convellere* (*vellere*, to pluck)], v.t. To agitate violently; to affect with convulsions; to excite spasms of laughter in. **convulsion** (-vŭl' shŭn), n. (usu. in pl.) A diseased action of the muscular tissues of the body characterized by violent contractions and alternate relaxations; hence, a violent agitation, disturbance, or commotion. **convulsionary,** a. (Med.) n. A convulsionist. **convulsionist,** n. (Hist.) One of the French Jansenists who, about 1730, claimed to have the power of working miracles, and asserted that the convulsions with which they were seized proceeded from divine agency. **convulsive,** a. Producing or attended with convulsions.

cony (kō' ni) [O.F. *conil*, *connil*; the sing. *cony* from the pl. *conys* or *conies*, from the O.F. pl. *coniz*, L. *cuniculum*, acc. of *cuniculus*, a rabbit (etym. doubtful)], n. A rabbit; (Bibl.) a small pachydermatous animal, *Hyrax Syriacus*, living in holes among rocks. ***cony-catch,** v.t. and i. To steal, to cheat, to gull. ***cony-catcher,** n. A thief, a cheat, a trickster. ***cony-fish,** n. The burbot. **cony-wool,** n. Rabbit-fur.

coo (koo) [imit.], v.i. To make a soft low sound, like a dove; to make love. v.t. To say in cooing fashion. n. The characteristic note of a dove. **to bill and coo** [BILL (1)].

cooboo (koo' boo) [Austral. abor.], n. An Aboriginal child.

cooee (koo' ē) [imit.], n. A call originally used by the Australian Aborigines, and by bushmen. v.i. To make this call.

cook (1) (kuk) [A.-S. *cōc*, L. *coquus*, a cook (*coquere*, to cook cogn. with Gr. *pessein*, Sansk. *pach*)], n. One who dresses or prepares food for the table. v.t. To prepare (as food) for the table by boiling, roasting, etc.; (fig.) to garble, to falsify; to concoct. v.i. To act as a cook; to undergo the process of cooking. **to cook his goose:** (slang) To settle him; to stop his game. **cooker,** n. A stove or other apparatus for cooking; anything that cooks (v.i.) well; one who garbles or concocts. **cookery,** n. The act or art of cooking; the occupation of a cook; a place for cooking. **cook-house,** n. (Naut.) A galley, a cook-room; also a detached kitchen in warm countries. ***cook-room,** n. A kitchen; (Naut.) a galley; a cookhouse. **cook shop,** n. An eating-house. **what's cooking?:** (colloq.) What's afoot? What's being done? **cooky,** n. (colloq.) A cook.

cook (2) (kuk) [Sc., etym. doubtful], v.i. To appear and disappear.

cookie (kuk' i) [prob. from Dut. *koekje*], n. (Sc.) A baker's plain bun; (Am.) a small sweet cake, a biscuit.

cool (kool) [A.-S. *cōl*, from Teut. *kōl-*, *kal-* (cp. Dan. *köl*, G. *kühl*, L. *gelu*)], a. Slightly or moderately cold; not retaining or causing heat; (fig.) not ardent or zealous, apathetic; chilling, frigid, aloof; calm, dispassionate; deliberate; indifferent; impudent, audacious; (Hunt.) faint (of scent). n. Coolness, moderate temperature; a cool place. v.t. To make cool; to quiet, to calm, to allay. v.i. To become cool. **a cool hundred:** (slang) A hundred without exaggeration. **to cool one's heels:** (colloq.) To be kept waiting. **cool-headed,** a. Dispassionate, self-possessed. **cool tankard,** n. An old-fashioned drink, usually made of wine and water mixed with lemon-juice, etc. **cooler,** *n.* That which cools; a vessel in which liquors are set to cool. **cooling tower:** (*Eng.*) A tower in which water is cooled, after circulation through a condenser, by trickling over wooden slats. **coolish,** *a.* **coolly,** *adv.* **coolness,** *n.*

coolabah (koo′ lȧ ba) [Austral. abor.], *n.* Name given to several species of eucalyptus trees.

coolah (koo′ la) [Austral. abor.], *n.* A bear.

coolamon (koo′ lȧ mon) [Austral. abor.], *n.* A wooden water-vessel or bowl for seeds.

coolie (koo′ li) [Hind. *qūli*], *n.* A hired labourer in or from any part of the East.

coom (1) (koom) [CULM (2)], *n.* Refuse matter, as soot, coal-dust, mould; the drip from journal boxes, wheels, etc.

coom (2) (koom) [Sc., etym. doubtful], *n.* The timber centering for an arch; perh. a dome-shaped hill or ridge (spelt also *comb, combe, coomb,* and sometimes identified with COMBE).

coomb (1) [COMBE].

coomb (2) (koom) [A.-S. *cumb,* cp. COMBE], *n.* A measure for corn, containing four bushels.

coon (koon) [short for RACOON], *n.* (*Am. slang*) A sly fellow. **coon-can,** *n.* (*Cards*) A simple card game for two or more players. **a gone coon:** (*Am.*) One hopelessly ruined.

Co-op (kō op′) [CO-OPERATIVE STORES].

coop (koop) [M.E. *cupe,* a basket, perh. from L. *cupa,* a lute, a cask], *n.* A box of boards, barred or wired on one side, for confining domestic birds; a cage for small animals; *a wickerwork trap for catching eels and other fish. *v.t.* To confine in or as in a coop.

cooper (1) (koo′ pėr) [prob. from W.G. (cp. M.Dut. *cuper,* G. *küper*), med. L. *cupārius,* from *cupa,* a cask], *n.* One whose trade is to make barrels, tubs, etc.; (*Naut.*) a mender of casks, etc.; *a bottle-basket for wine; a mixture of stout and porter (orig. prepared for the coopers in breweries). *v.t.* To make or repair (casks, etc.); (*colloq.*) to furnish, to rig (up). **coopered,** *a.* (*slang*) Done up, ruined. **cooperage** (koo′ pėr ȧj), *n.* The trade or workshop of a cooper; the price paid for cooper's work. **coopery,** *n.*

cooper (2) [COPER, see COPE (3)].

co-operate (kō op′ ėr āt) [late L. *coöperātus,* p.p. of *coöperārī* (CO-, *operārī,* to work, from *opus operis,* work)], *v.i.* To work or act with another or others for a common end; to contribute to an effect. **co-operant,** *a.* **co-operation** (-ā′ shŭn), *n.* The act of co-operating; a form of partnership or association for the production or distribution of goods. **co-operative,** *a.* Working with others for a common end or the common good. **co-operative stores,** *n.* The shop of a **co-operative society** for the production or distribution of goods and the division of profits among the members. **co-operatively,** *adv.* **co-operator,** *n.* One who co-operates; a member of a co-operative society.

co-opt (kō opt′) [L. *cooptāre* (CO-, *optāre,* to choose)], *v.t.* To elect into a body by the votes of the members. **co-optation** (-tā′ shŭn), *n.*

co-ordinate (kō ôrd′ in ȧt) [L. *ordinātus,* p.p. of *ordināre,* to arrange (*ordo -inis,* ORDER)], *a.* Of the same order, rank, or authority; (*Gram.*) terms or clauses of equal order, as distinguished from subordinate. *n.pl.* (*Math.*) Lines used as elements of reference to determine the position of any point. *v.t.* (-nāt) To make co-ordinate; to correlate, to bring into orderly relation of parts and whole. **co-ordinately,** *adv.* **co-ordination** (-nā′ shŭn), *n.* **co-ordinative,** *a.*

coot (koot) [Dut. **koet**, the sea-coot], *n.* A small black British aquatic bird, *Fulica atra*; a stupid fellow. **bald as a coot:** (Alluding to the broad base of the bill across the coot's forehead) Quite bald.

cop (1) (*kop*) [A.-S.], *n.* The top; a hill; a bird's crest; a conical roll or thread on the spindle of a spinning-machine.

cop (2) (kop) [etym. doubtful], *v.t.* (*slang*) To seize; to arrest; to catch or get (something unpleasant). *n.* A policeman.

copaiba, -va (kȯ pā′-, pī′ bȧ, -vȧ) [Sp., from Braz. *cupauba*], *n.* The balsam or gum-resin obtained from the **copaiba-plant,** *Copaifera officinalis,* or allied species.

copal (kō′ pȧl) [Sp., from Mex. *copalli,* resin, incense], *n.* A resin from a Mexican plant; a varnish made from this.

coparcener (kō par′ sė nėr), *n.* A coheir or coheiress. **coparcenary,** *n.* Joint heirship; joint ownership. *a.* Relating to coparceners.

copartner (kō part′ nėr), *n.* A partner, an associate; a partaker. **copartnership, -nery,** *n.*

copatriot [COMPATRIOT].

cope (1) (kōp) [late L. *cāpa*], *n.* An ecclesiastical sleeveless vestment worn in processions and at solemn ceremonies; (*fig.*) anything spread overhead, a cloud, the sky; (*Foundry*) the outer covering of a mould. *v.t.* To cover with or as with a cope or coping. *v.i.* To form an overhang. **cope-stone** [COPING-STONE]. **coping,** *n.* The course projecting horizontally on the top of a wall. **coping-stone:** The topmost stone of a building; a stone forming part of the coping; the sloping course on a wall or buttress to throw off the water.

cope (2) (kōp) [O.F. *couper,* to strike (see COUP)], *v.i.* To encounter, to contend successfully (with).

cope (3) (kōp) [from L.G. (cp. Dut. *koopen,* cogn. with A.-S. *cēapian, cēap,* see CHEAP)], *v.t.* To buy; to barter. *v.i.* To make a bargain, to deal. **coper,** *n.* A dealer, esp. in horses; (sometimes spelt *cooper*) a floating grog-shop for North Sea fishermen. **horse-coper,** *n.* A horse-dealer.

copeck (kō′ pek) [Rus. *kopeika*], *n.* A Russian copper coin, the 100th part of a rouble.

coper, cooper (2) [COPE (3)].

Copernican (kō pĕr′ nik ȧn) [*Copernicus,* L. form of G. *Koppernik*], *a.* Pertaining to the astronomical system of Copernicus (1472–1543) which has the sun as its centre.

copier [COPY].

copious (kō′ pi ŭs) [L. *cōpiōsus,* from *cōpia,* plenty], *a.* Plentiful, abundant, ample; profuse, prolific, rich in vocabulary. **copiously,** *adv.* **copiousness,** *n.*

copper (1) (kop′ ėr) [A.-S. *copor,* L. *cuprum Cyprium,* Gr. *Kuprios,* Cyprian], *n.* A red malleable, ductile, tenacious metallic element; a vessel, esp. a cooking or laundry boiler (formerly of copper); a copper (or bronze) coin. *a.* Made of or resembling copper. *v.t.* To sheath with copper; to deposit a coating of copper on. **hot coppers:** A parched feeling in the throat and mouth. **copper-bit,** *n.* A soldering-iron with a copper point. **copper-bottomed,** *a.* (*Naut.*) Sheathed with copper. **copper-butterfly,** *n.* The popular name for the genus *Lycæna.* **copper-faced,** *a.* Faced with copper (as type). **copper-fastened,** *a.* (*Naut.*) Fastened with copper bolts. **copperhead,** *n.* A highly venomous North American snake, *Trigonocephalus contortrix,* allied to the rattlesnake; its counterpart in Tasmania; (*Hist.*) a Northern sympathizer with the Confederates during the American Civil War. **copper-Indian,** *n.* A North American Indian. **copperplate,** *n.* A polished plate of copper on which something is engraved for printing; an impression from such a plate. *a.* Pertaining to the art of engraving on copper; (*Writing*) neat and elegant. **coppersmith,** *n.* A worker in copper. **coppery,** *a.* Made of, containing, or resembling copper. **copper-nose,** *a.* A red nose. **copper-pyrites,** *n.* (*Min.*) A compound of copper and sulphur. **copper-work,** *n.* Articles of copper.

copper (2) (kop′ ėr) [COP (2)], *n.* (*slang*) One who cops or seizes; a policeman.

copperas (kop' ėr ȧs) [M.E. and O.F. *coperose*, L. *cuprōsa*, from *cuprum*, copper], *n.* A green sulphate of iron; green vitriol.

coppice (kop' is) [O.F. *copeiz*, cut wood, from a late L. *colpāticium* (*colpāre*, to strike, to cut, see COUP)], *n.* A small wood of small trees and underwood, cut periodically for firewood.

copra (kop' rȧ) [Port. and Sp., prob. from Malay *koppara*, coco-nut], *n.* The dried kernel of the coco-nut exported for the expression of coco-nut oil.

copresent (kō prez' ėnt), *a.* Present at the same time. **copresence,** *n.*

copro- [Gr. *kopros*, dung], *comb. form.* Pertaining to or living on or among dung. **coprolite** (kop' rō līt) [-LITE], *n.* The fossil dung of various extinct animals, chiefly saurians, largely used as manure. **coprolitic** (-lit' ik), *a.* **coprology** (kȯp rol' ȯ ji) [-LOGY], *n.* Lubricity; filth in literature or art. **coprophagan** (kȯ prof' ȧ gǎn) [Gr. *koprophagos* (COPRO-, *phagein*, to eat)], *n.* (*Ent.*) Any individual of the *Coprophagi*, a section of lamellicorn beetles feeding on or living in dung. **coprophagous,** *a.*

copse (kops) [COPPICE], *n.* A coppice. *v.t.* To plant or preserve for copsewood; to clothe with copses. **copsewood,** *n.* Underwood, brushwood. **copsy,** *a.*

Copt (kopt) [F. *Copt*, Arab. *quft*, Copt. *gyptios*, *kyptaios*, Gr. *Aiguptios*, Egyptian], *n.* One of the old Egyptian race; a Coptic Christian. **Coptic,** *a.* Pertaining to the Copts, or to the old Egyptian Church. *n.* The language of the Copts.

copula (kop' ū lȧ) [L. *cōpula* (CO-, *apere*, to fasten), with dim. suf.], *n.* (*pl.* **-læ**) That which couples; (*Log. and Gram.*) the word in a sentence or proposition which links the subject and predicate together; (*Mus.*) a brief connecting passage. **copular,** *a.*

copulate (kop' ū lāt) [L. *cōpulātus*, p.p. of *cōpulāre*, as prec.], *v.t.* To couple together. *v.i.* To have sexual intercourse. **copulate** (-lȧt), *a.* Joined, connected. **copulation** (-lā' shŭn), *n.* The act of coupling; sexual intercouse; (*Log. and Gram.*) connexion. **copulative** (kop' ū lȧ tiv), *a.* Serving to unite; (*Gram.*) having two or more words, phrases, or predicates connected by a copulative conjunction; (*Physiol.*) pertaining to sexual conjunction. *n.* A copulative conjunction. **copulatively,** *adv.* **copulatory,** *a.*

copy (kop' i) [F. *copie*, L. *cōpia* abundance, med. L. a transcript], *n.* A transcript or imitation of an original; a thing made in imitation of or exactly like another; an original, a model, a pattern; (*Print.*) manuscript ready for setting; (*Journ.*) material for reporting, writing articles, etc.; a writing exercise; an example of a particular work or book. *v.t.* To transcribe, to imitate, to make a copy of; (*fig.*) to follow as pattern or model. *v.i.* To make a copy. **clean, fair copy:** Matter transcribed from a rough copy or a first draft. **to set copies:** To write a headline in a copy-book for imitation. **copy-book,** *n.* A book in which proverbs, maxims, etc. are written clearly to be copied by children learning to write. **copy-cat,** *n.* (*colloq.*) One who imitates someone else. **copier,** *n.* One who copies; an imitator, a plagiarist; a transcriber. **copying,** *a.* Pertaining to or used for copying. **copying-ink,** *n.* A viscid ink allowing copies to be taken from documents written with it. **copying-press,** *n.* A machine for taking a copy by pressure of a document written with copying-ink. **copyist,** *n.* **copywriter,** *n.* One who writes advertisements.

copyhold (kop' i hōld), *n.* (*Law*) A tenure for which the tenant has nothing to show but the copy of the rolls made by the steward of his lord's court; property held by such tenure. *a.* Held by such tenure. **copyholder,** *n.*

copyright (kop' i rīt), *n.* The exclusive right of the author of a literary or artistic production, or his heirs, to publish or sell copies of his work. *a.* Protected by copyright. *v.t.* To secure copyright for (a book, music, picture, etc.).

coquelicot (kok' li kō) [F., the poppy, orig. the cock's comb (*coq*, cock; termination onomat. from the cock's crowing)], *n.* A reddish orange colour.

coquet (kȯ ket') [F., dim. of *coq*, cock], *a.* Coquettish. *n.* A male flirt, a lady-killer. **coquet, coquette** (1) (kȯ ket'), *v.i.* To flirt (with); to make love; to trifle; to take up a task or a subject without serious intentions of carrying it on. **coquetry** (kō' kėt ri), *n.* The practices of a coquette; affectation of encouragement to an admirer; flirtation. **coquette,** *n.* A female flirt; a jilt. **coquettish,** *a.* **coquettishly,** *adv.*

coquilla (kȯ kil' yȧ) [Sp., dim. of *coca*, a shell], *n.* The nut of *Attalea funifera*, a Brazilian palm, used in turnery.

coquito (kȯ kē' tō) [Sp., dim. of *coco*, COCO-NUT], *n.* A Chilean nut-bearing palm-tree.

cor (1) (kôr) [Heb. *kor*], *n.* A Hebrew measure; a homer.

cor (2) (kôr) [F., from L. *cornū*], *n.* (*Mus.*) A horn. ***cor anglais,*** *n.* The English horn, the tenor oboe.

cor- [COM-], *pref.* (used before *r*).

coracle (kor' ȧ kėl) [W. *cwrwgl*, dim. of *cwrwg*, a trunk (cp. O.Ir. *curach*, boat)], *n.* A light boat used in Wales and Ireland, made of wickerwork covered with leather or oiled cloth.

coracoid (kor' ȧ koid) [mod. L. *coracoīdes*, Gr. *korakoeidēs* (*korax -akos*, a raven)], *n.* A hook-like process of the scapula in mammals; a separate bone in the pectoral arch in birds, reptiles, and monotremes. *a.* Hook-shaped; resembling a crow's beak.

co-radicate (kō răd' i kȧt) [CO-, L. *rādīcātus*, from *radix*, root], *a.* Derived from the same root.

***coraggio** (kȯ raj' ō) [It.], *int.* Courage! bravo!

coral (kor' ȧl) [O.F., from L. *corallum*, Gr. *korallion*], *n.* The calcareous polypidom or structure secreted by certain polyps or zoophytes, esp. those of the genus *Corallium*, and deposited in masses on the bottom of the sea; an infant's toy made of coral; the unimpregnated eggs of a lobster (from their colour). *a.* Made of or resembling coral; red, pink. **red coral:** *Corallium rubrum*, the red polypidom which is much used for ornaments. **coral-island,** *n.* An island formed by the growth and accumulation of coral. **coral-rag,** *n.* (*Geol.*) A coralliferous limestone of the Middle Oolite. **coral-reef,** *n.* A ridge or series of ridges of coral, tending to form a coral-island. **coral-snake,** *n.* (*Zool.*) Any of the genus *Elaps*. **coral-tree,** *n.* A tropical tree of the genus *Erythrina*, bearing blood-red flowers. **coralliferous** (-lif' ėr ŭs), *a.* **coralliform** (kor' ȧ li fôrm), *a.* (*Bot.*) Branching, like coral. **coralligenous** (-lij' ėn ŭs), *a.* Producing coral. **coralline** (kor' ȧ līn), *a.* Of the nature of coral; containing or resembling coral. *n.* A seaweed with calcareous fronds; popular name for the polyzoa. **coralline ware,** *n.* Red Italian pottery of the 17th and 18th centuries. **coralline-crag,** *n.* (*Geol.*) The white portion of the Suffolk crag. **coralline zone,** *n.* The stratum in the ocean-depths, where corallines abound. **corallite** [-LITE], *n.* (*Geol.*) A coral-shaped petrifaction; the skeleton or case of a polyp; coralline marble. **corallitic** (-lit' ik), *a.* **coralloid** [-OID], *a.* Resembling coral; coralliform. *n.* An organism akin to or resembling coral.

***coranto** (kȯ ran' tō) [from F. *courante* or It. *coranta*], *n.* A rapid kind of dance.

corb (kôrb) [L. *corbis*], *n.* A basket used in collieries; a basket.

corban (kôr' băn) [Heb. *qorbān*, an offering], *n.* Among the ancient Jews, a thing consecrated to God.

***corbe** [CORBEL].

corbeil (kôr' bėl, kôr bā' i) [F. *corbeille*, as foll.], *n.* A sculptured basket, esp. such as forms the ornamental summit of a pillar, etc.; (*Fort.*) a small basket filled with earth, and set upon parapets as a protection from the besiegers' fire.

corbel (kôr' bėl) [O.F., from low L. *corbellum*, from *corvellus*, dim. of *corvus*, a raven], *n.* A bracket or projection of stone, wood, or iron projecting from a wall to support some superincumbent weight. *v.t.* To support by means of corbels. **to corbel out:** To cause to project by constructing on corbels. **corbel-block,** *n.* A short timber helping to support a beam at either end. **corbel-table,** *n.* A projecting course, parapet, etc., supported by corbels.

corbie (kôr' bi) [O.F. *corbin*, dim. of *corb*, a raven], *n.* A raven, a crow. **corbie-steps,** *n.pl.* The stepped slopes of gables (common in Sc. and Flemish architecture).

corchorus (kôr' kȯr ŭs) [Gr. *korchoros*], *n.* A tropical genus of the lime-tree family, *Tiljaceæ*, some yielding jute; the Japan globe-flower, *Kerria Japonica.*

cord (kôrd) [F. *corde*, L. *chorda*, Gr. *chordē*, the string of a musical instrument], *n.* Thick string or thin rope composed of several strands; cord-like ribs on cloth, hence corduroy; (*pl.*) a measure for cut wood, 128 cub. ft.; (*Anat.*) a cord-like structure; (*fig.*) anything which binds or draws. *v.t.* To bind with a cord. **cord-wood,** *n.* Wood piled up to be sold by the cord. **corded,** *a.* Bound or fastened with cords; made with cords; ribbed or twilled (like corduroys). **cordage,** *n.* A quantity or store of ropes; (*Naut.*) the ropes or rigging of a ship collectively.

cordate (kôr' dāt) [L. *cor cordis*, heart], *a.* Heart-shaped.

cordelier (kôr dė lēr') [F., from *cordelle*, dim. of *corde*, CORD]. *n.* A Franciscan friar of the strictest rule, from the knotted rope worn round the waist; (*Hist.*) a member of a revolutionary club founded in Paris in 1790, which met in an old convent of the Cordeliers.

cordial (kôr' di ȧl) [F., from med. L. *cordiālis*, (*cor cordis*, the heart)], *a.* Proceeding from the heart; sincere, hearty, warm-hearted; cheering or comforting the heart. *n.* Anything which cheers or comforts; an aromatized and sweetened spirit used as a beverage; a medicine to increase the circulation or to raise the spirits. **cordiality** (-ăl' i ti), *n.* **cordialize,** *v.t.* To render cordial. *v.i.* To become cordial; to have the warmest relations (with). **cordially,** *adv.*

cordiform (kôr' di fôrm) [L. *cor cordis*, the heart, FORM], *a.* Heart-shaped.

cordillera (kôr dil yâr' ȧ) [Sp., from *cordilla*, a string or rope, dim. of *cuerda*, L. *chorda*, cord], *n.* A ridge or chain of mountains, esp. used (*in pl.*) of the Andes, and the continuation of these in Central America and Mexico.

cordite (kôr' dīt) [CORD, -ITE], *n.* A smokeless explosive, prepared in string-like grains.

cordon (kôr' dȯn) [F.], *n.* A ribbon or cord worn as an ornament, a mark of rank, or the badge of an order; a line or series of men, posts, or ships placed so as to guard or blockade a place; a projecting band of stones in a wall, a string-course; (*Gardening*) a fruit-tree trained and closely pruned to grow as a single stem. **sanitary cordon,** *n.* A line of military posts on the borders of an infected district to cut off communication. **to cordon off:** To protect by surrounding with a cordon.

cordovan (kôr dȯ văn'), *n.* Spanish leather originally made at Cordova; cordwain.

corduroy (kôr' dū roi) [prob. from F. *corde du roi*, king's cord], *n.* A stout-ribbed cotton fustian made with a pile; (*pl.*) corduroy trousers. *a.* Made of this material. **corduroy road,** *n.* A causeway of logs laid over a swamp.

cordwain (kôrd' wān) [O.F. *cordoan*, late L. *cordoānum*, from *Cordoa*, Cordova (see CORDOVAN)], *n.* A kind of leather, finished as a black morocco, orig. from Cordova, Spain. **cordwainer,** *n.* *A worker in cordwain; a shoemaker.

core (1) (kôr) [etym. doubtful (L. *cor*, the heart, and O.F. *cor*, horn, have been suggested)], *n.* The heart or inner part of anything; the hard middle of an apple, pear, or similar fruit, containing the seeds; the central strand of a rope; (*Elec.*) the insulated conducting wires of a cable; (*Eng.*) the round mass of rock brought up by an annular drill; a disease of sheep, or the tumour typical of this; (*fig.*) the pith, the gist, the essence. *v.t.* To remove the core from. **corer,** *n.* **coreless,** *a.*

core (2) (kôr) [Sc. prob. for CORPS], *n.* A company, a party; a crowd.

co-regent (kō rē' jėnt), *n.* A joint ruler or governor.

co-relation [CORRELATION].

coreless [CORE (1)].

coreopsis (ko rē op' sis) [Gr. *koris*, a bug; *opsis*, appearance], *n.* (*Bot.*) A genus of yellow garden plants; tick seed.

co-religionist (kō rė lij' ŭn ist), *n.* One of the same religion.

co-respondent (kō rė spon' dėnt), *n.* A joint respondent in a suit (esp. in a divorce suit).

corf (kôrf) [prob. from L.G. (cp. Dut. *korf*, G. *korb*)], *n.* (*pl.* **-ves**) A basket for carrying ore or coal in mines; a large basket or perforated box for keeping lobsters or fish alive in the water.

corgie (kôr' gi) [W.], *n.* A small, smooth-haired, Welsh dog.

coriaceous (kor i ā' shŭs)[L. *coriāceus*, from *corium*, skin, leather], *a.* Made of or resembling leather; (*Bot.*) stiff like leather, as the leaves of the box.

coriander (kor i ăn' dėr) [F. *coriandre*, L. *coriandrum*, Gr. *koriannon*], *n.* An umbellifer, *Coriandrum sativum*, with aromatic and carminative seeds.

Corinthian (kȯ rin' thi ȧn), *a.* Of or pertaining to Corinth, a city of Greece; licentious, dissipated; (*Lit.*) ornate, over-elaborate, brilliant to excess. *n.* A native of Corinth; a debauchee; a fast man, a swell, a dandy. **Corinthian order,** *n.* (*Arch.*) The most elaborate and ornate of the three Grecian orders, the capital being enriched with graceful foliated forms added to the volutes of the Ionic capital. **Corinthianesque** (kȯ rin thi ȧn esk'), *a.* (*Arch.*)

corium (kôr' i ŭm) [L., skin, leather], *n.* (*Archæol.*) A kind of body-armour, composed of scales or small plates of leather, worn by Roman soldiers; (*Physiol.*) the innermost layer of the skin in mammals.

cork (kôrk) [etym. doubtful (cp. O.Sp. *alcorque*, a cork shoe, and Sp. *corcho*)], *n.* The outer layer of bark of the cork-tree, from which stoppers for bottles, floats for fishing, etc., are made; a stopper for a bottle or cask. *a.* Made of cork. *v.t.* To stop with a cork; to blacken with burnt cork. **cork-jacket,** *n.* A jacket lined with cork, to sustain the wearer in the water. **corkscrew,** *n.* A screw for drawing corks. *v.t.* To direct or push forward in a wriggling fashion. **cork-screw curl,** *n.* Hair twisted in a spiral shape. **cork-screwy,** *a.* **cork-tree,** *n.* An oak, *Quercus suber*, much cultivated in Spain, Portugal and France for the sake of its bark. **corkwood,** *n.* Cork in quantity; a light porous wood. **corkage,** *n.* The corking or uncorking of bottles; a charge levied at hotels on wines consumed by guests but not supplied by the hotel. **corked,** *a.* Stopped with cork; blackened with burnt cork; tasting of the cork (as wine). **corker,** *n.* (*slang*) Something astounding, a whacker; a statement that puts an end to the discussion. **corky,** *a.* Resembling cork in nature or appearance; (*colloq.*) sprightly, lively.

***corking-pin** (kôr king pin') [prob. corr. of CALKIN], *n.* A large pin formerly used to fasten dresses, etc.

corm (kôrm) [Gr. *kormos*, the trimmed trunk of a

tree], *n.* (*Bot.*) A bulb-like, fleshy subterranean stem, sometimes called a solid bulb.

cormo- [as prec.], *comb. form.* (*Ethn.*) The trunk, the stem. **cormogeny** (kôr moj′ ė ni) [-GENY], *n.* The germ-history of races and other aggregates of peoples.

cormophyte (kôr′ mō fīt) [Gr. *kormos*, trunk, -PHYTE], *n.* (*Bot.*) A name formerly used for a division of plants embracing those with roots, stems, and leaves.

cormorant (kôr′ mō rȧnt) [O.F. *cormerant*, L. *corvus marīnus*, sea-crow], *n.* Any species of the genus *Phalacrocorax*, esp. *P. carbo*, a voracious British sea-bird; (*fig.*) a glutton.

corn (1) (kôrn) [A.-S. from Teut. *korno-* (cp. Dut. *koren*, Dan. and Swed. *korn*, Goth. *kaurn*, G. *korn*), Aryan *grnóm* (L. *grānum*, GRAIN)], *n.* Grain; the seed of cereals; wheat; (*Am.*) maize, Indian corn; a single seed or grain of certain plants. *v.t.* To preserve and season with salt; *to granulate; *to feed with corn. **corn-ball,** *n.* (*Am.*) A sweetmeat composed of popped corn and white of egg. **corn-bread,** *n.* (*Am.*) Bread made from Indian corn. **corn-brash,** *n.* (*Geol.*) A calcareous sandstone belonging to the Inferior Oolite. **corn-chandler,** *n.* A retail dealer in corn, etc. **corn-cob,** *n.* A spike of Indian corn. **corn-cob pipe:** A tobacco-pipe with a bowl made from this. **corn-cockle,** *n.* A purple flower of the campion tribe, *Lychnis githago.* **corn-crake,** *n.* The landrail, *Crex pratensis.* **corn-exchange,** *n.* A market where corn is sold from samples. **corn-factor,** *n.* A dealer in corn. **cornfield,** *n.* A field in which corn is growing; corn-land. **corn-flag,** *n.* A plant of the genus *Gladiolus.* **corn-flour,** *n.* The meal of Indian corn ground very fine, (*Am.*) cornstarch. **corn-flower,** *n.* A popular name for several plants that grow amongst corn, esp. the common bluebottle, *Centaurea cyanus.* **corn land,** *n.* Land suitable for or devoted to growing corn. **Corn Laws,** *n.pl.* Laws designed to regulate the price of corn (abolished in England, 1846). **corn-loft,** *n.* A store for corn. **corn-marigold,** *n.* A yellow-flowered composite plant, *Chrysanthemum segetum.* **corn meal,** *n.* (*Am.*) Meal of Indian corn. **corn-mill,** *n.* (*Am.*) A mill for grinding the cob of Indian corn. **corn-rent,** *n.* Rent paid in corn at the market-price. **corn-sheller,** *n.* (*Am.*) An instrument for rubbing the grains from the cob of Indian corn. **corn-shuck,** *n.* (*Am.*) The husk of Indian corn. **corn-stalk,** *n.* (*Austral.*) A European born in Australia. **cornstarch,** *n.* (*Am.*) Cornflour. **cornstone,** *n.* (*Geol.*) An earthy concretionary limestone forming a lower series in the Old Red Sandstone. **corned beef,** *n.* Tinned seasoned and cooked beef; bully beef. **corny** (1), *a.* [KORNY].

corn (2) (kôrn) [O.F. *corn*, L. *cornū*, horn], *n.* A horny excrescence on the foot or hand, produced by pressure over a bone. **corn-plaster,** *n.* A plaster for corns. **corny** (2), *a.*

cornea (kôr′ nė ȧ) [L., fem. of *corneus*, horny (*cornū*, horn)], *n.* (*pl.* **-eæ**) The transparent fore-part of the external coat of the eye, through which the rays of light pass.

cornel kôr′ nėl) [ult. from L. *cornus*; derivation obscure], *n.* The English name of the genus *Cornus*, which includes the cornelian cherry-tree, *C. mascula*, and the dogwood, *C. sanguinea.*

cornelian (1) (kôr nē′ li ȧn) [F. *cornaline*; etym. doubtful], *n.* (*Min.*) A variety of semi-transparent chalcedony.

cornelian (2) (kôr nē′ li ȧn) [CORNEL], *n.* The wild cornel or dogwood, or the cherry-tree, *Cornus mascula*, or its fruit.

corneous (kôr′ nė ŭs) [L. *corneus* (*cornū*, horn)], *a.* Horny; hard, like horn.

corner (kôr′ nėr) [O.F. *cornier*, late L. *cornēria*, from L. *cornū*, horn], *n.* The place where two converging lines or surfaces meet; the space included between such lines or surfaces; an angle; a place enclosed by converging walls or other boundaries; a region, a quarter, esp. a remote place; a nook; a position of difficulty or embarrassment; a combination to buy up the available supply of any commodity, in order to raise the price, a ring; (*Football*) a free kick from a corner; (*Am.*) a street-turning. *v.t.* To drive into a corner, or into a position of difficulty; to furnish with corners; to buy up (a commodity) so as to raise the price. *v.i.* To form a corner (in a commodity). **to cut off a corner:** To take a short cut. **to turn the corner:** To go round it into the next street; (*fig.*) to pass the crises of an illness; to get past a difficulty. **corner boy,** *n.* A street loafer. ***corner-cap,** *n.* A three- or four-cornered cap; (*fig.*) the chief embellishment. **corner-chisel, -punch,** *n.* One of an angular shape for cutting corners of mortises, etc. **cornerman,** *n.* A cornerer; the performer at the end of a nigger-minstrel troupe; a lounger at street corners. **corner-stone,** *n.* The stone which unites two walls of a building; (*fig.*) the principal stone; the foundation. **cornerwise,** *adv.* Diagonally, with the corner in front. **cornered,** *a.* Having corners or angles (*usu. in comb.*); (*fig.*) placed in a difficult position. **cornerer,** *n.* A member of a corner or ring.

cornet (1) (kôr′ nėt) [O.F. from late L. *cornetum*, L. *cornū*], *n.* A wind instrument not unlike a hautboy; a cornet-à-piston; *a square cap formerly worn by doctors of divinity; *a lady's head-dress, with two horn-like projections; a conical paper bag; a piece of paper twisted into a conical receptacle for small-wares; the lower part of a horse's pastern; a conical wafer containing ice-cream. **cornet-à-piston, -s,** *n.* (*Mus.*) A metallic wind-instrument of the trumpet class, but furnished with valves and stoppers.

cornet (2) (kôr′ nėt) [F. *cornette*, dim. of *corne*, as prec.], *n.* Formerly the lowest commissioned officer in a cavalry regiment; *the standard of a cavalry troop; *a troop of cavalry. **cornetcy,** *n.*

cornflower [CORN (1)].

cornice (kôr′ nis) [F. *cornice* (now *corniche*), It. *cornice* (etym. doubtful)], *n.* A moulded horizontal projection crowning a wall, entablature, pillar, or other part of a building; (*Mountaineering*) a projecting mass of snow along the top of a precipice. **cornice-pole,** *n.* A pole carried along the tops of windows to support curtains. **corniced,** *a.*

corniferous (kôr nif′ ėr ŭs) [L. *cornifer* (*cornū*, horn, -FEROUS)], *n.* (*Geol.*) Containing hornstone, a term applied to a palæozoic limestone of North America containing horn-stone. **cornific** (-nif′ ik), *a.* Producing horns or horny matter. **corniform** (kôr′ ni fôrm), *a.* Horn-shaped. **cornigerous** (-nij′ ėr ŭs) [-GEROUS], *a.* Bearing horns; horned.

Cornish (kôr′ nish), *a.* Of or pertaining to Cornwall. *n.* The ancient language of Cornwall. **Cornish chough,** *n.* The chough. **Cornish engine,** *n.* A single-acting steam pumping-engine. **Cornish granite:** A coarse-grained, whitish granite quarried in Cornwall.

corno (kôr′ nō [It., from L. *cornū*], *n.* (*Mus.*) A horn. ***corno inglese,*** *n.* *Cor anglais*, the English horn.

cornopean (kôr nō′ pė ȧn), *n.* (*Mus.*) A cornet-à-piston.

cornu (kôr′ nū) [L.], *n.* (*pl.* **-ua**) (*Anat.*) A horn-like process. **cornual,** *a.* **cornuate,** *a.*

cornucopia (kôr nū kō′ pi ȧ) [L. *cornu copiæ*], *n.* (*pl.* **-ias**) The horn of plenty; a goat's horn wreathed and filled to overflowing with flowers, fruit, corn, etc., the symbol of plenty and peace; a representation of a cornucopia; an abundant stock. **cornucopian,** *a.*

cornute (kôr nūt′) [L. *cornūtus*, horned, from *cornū*, horn], **v.t.* To cuckold. **cornuted,** *a.* Horned or having horn-like projections; horn-shaped; (*fig.*) cuckolded. ***cornuto** (kôr nū′ tō) [It., as prec.], *n.* A cuckold.

corny, *a.* (*colloq.*) Trite, stale; old-fashioned; unsophisticated; crude.

corolla (kȯ rol′ ȧ) [L., dim. of *corōna*, a crown], *n.* (*Bot.*) The inner whorl of two series of floral envelopes occurring in the more highly developed plants. **corollaceous** (kor ȯ lā′ shůs), *a.* **corollate** (kor′ ȯ lȧt), **-lated** (-lā tėd), *a.* Like a corolla; having a corolla. **corolline** (kor′ ȯ lin, -līn), *a.* Pertaining to a corolla.

corollary (kȯ rol′ ȧ ri) [L. *corollārium*, the price of a garland, a gratuity, a corollary, from *corollārius*, pertaining to a garland, as prec.], *n.* (*Log.*) An additional inference from a proposition; a natural consequence; something appended.

corona (kȯ rō′ nȧ) [L., a crown], *n.* (*pl.* **-næ**) A broad projecting face forming the principal member of a cornice; a circular chandelier hanging from the roof, esp. in churches; (*Bot.*) the circumference or margin of a compound radiated flower; a disk or halo round the sun or the moon; an anthelion or disk of light opposite the sun; the zone of radiance round the moon in a total eclipse of the sun.

coronach (kor′ ȯ na*ch*) [Ir. (cp. Gael. *corranach*), from *comh-*, together, *rànach*, an outcry, from *ràn*, to howl], *n.* A dirge, a funeral lamentation, in the Scottish Highlands and in Ireland.

coronal (kȯ rō′ nȧl) [F., from L. CORONA], *a.* Pertaining to a crown or the crown of the head; (*Bot.*) pertaining to a corona. *n.* (kor′ ȯ nal) A circlet or coronet; a wreath, a garland. **coronal suture,** *n.* (*Anat.*) The suture extending over the crown of the skull and separating the frontal and parietal bones.

coronary (kor′ ȯ nȧr i) [L. *corōnārius*, as prec.], *a.* Resembling a crown; placed as a crown. *n.* A small bone in a horse's foot. **coronary arteries,** *n.pl.* (*Anat.*) Two arteries springing from the aorta before it leaves the pericardium. **coronary thrombosis,** *n.* (*Med.*) The formation of a clot in one of the arteries of the heart. **coronary vessels,** *n.pl.* (*Anat.*) Certain vessels which furnish the substance of the heart with blood.

coronate, -nated (kor′ ȯ nȧt, -nā tėd) [L. *coronātus*, p.p. of *coronāre*, as prec.], *a.* (*Bot. and Zool.*) Having a crown, or arranged like a crown; (*Conch.*) having the whorls surrounded by a row of spines or tubercles.

coronation (kor ȯ nā′ shůn) [as prec.], *n.* The act or ceremony of solemnly crowning a sovereign. **coronation oath,** *n.* The oath taken by a sovereign at the coronation. **coronation stone,** *n.* The stone in the seat of the chair in Westminster Abbey in which British sovereigns are crowned, taken from the Scots in 1296.

coroner (kor′ ȯ nėr) [A.-F. *coruner*, from *coruna*, L. *corona*, CROWN], *n.* An officer of the Crown whose duty it is to inquire into cases of sudden or suspicious death, and to determine the ownership of treasure-trove; formerly an officer in charge of the private property of the Crown. **coroner's inquest:** An inquiry held by a coroner and jury.

coronet (kor′ ȯ nėt) [O.F., dim. of *corone*, as prec.], *n.* A little crown; an ornamental fillet worn as part of a woman's head-dress; (*Her.*) an inferior crown worn by princes and noblemen, varying according to the rank of the wearer; (*fig.*) nobility. **coroneted,** *a.* Entitled to wear a coronet; (*fig.*) of noble birth.

coronoid (kor′ ȯ noid) [Gr. *korōnē*, a crow], *a.* (*Anat.*) Resembling a crow's beak; hooked at the tip.

corozo (kȯ rō′ zō) [native name], *n.* A South American ivory-nut tree, *Phytelephas macrocarpa*, the source of vegetable ivory. **corozo nut,** *n.* The fruit of this, used by turners for making ornaments, etc.

corporal (1) (kôr′ pȯ rȧl) [F. (var. *caporal*, It. *caporale*, perh. from confusion with *capo*, head), as foll.], *n.* An army non-commissioned officer of the lowest grade. **ship's corporal:** (*Nav.*) A sailor who attends to police matters under the master-at-arms. **corporalship,** *n.*

corporal (2) (kôr′ pȯ rȧl) [O.F. *corporel*, L. *corporālis* (*corpus -oris*, the body)], *a.* Relating to the body; material, corporeal. *n.* The fine linen cloth on which the elements are consecrated in the Mass. **corporal punishment,** *n.* Punishment inflicted on the human body; flogging. ***corporal oath,** *n.* A solemn oath, taken with the hand on the corporal. **corporality** (-răl′ i ti), *n.* Materiality; *a corporation; (*pl.*) material things. bodily matters. **corporally,** *adv.*

corporate (kôr′ pȯ rȧt) [L. *corporātus*, p.p. of *corporāre* (as prec.)], *a.* United in a body and acting as an individual; collectively one; pertaining to a corporation; *united. **body corporate:** The State; the nation considered as a corporation. **corporate body,** *n.* A corporation. **corporate state,** *n.* (*Pol.*) A system of government based on trade and professional corporations. **corporate town,** *n.* One having municipal rights and privileges. **corporately,** *adv.*

corporation (kôr pȯ rā′ shůn) [L. *corporātio*, as prec.], *n.* A united body; (*Law*) a corporate body empowered to act as an individual; (*loosely*) a company or association for commercial or other purposes; an elected body charged with the conduct of civic business; (*colloq.*) a prominent abdomen. **corporation aggregate:** One consisting of many persons, as a corporation of a town. **corporation sole:** One consisting of a single individual and his successors, as a king, a bishop, etc. **corporative** (kôr′ pȯ rȧ tiv), *a.* **corporator** (kôr′ pȯ rā tȯr), *n.* A member of a corporation.

corporeal (kȯr pôr′ ė ȧl) [L. *corporeus* (*corpus -oris*)], *a.* Having a body; pertaining to the body; material, physical, as opp. to mental; (*Law*) tangible, visible. **corporeality** (-al′ i ti), *n.* **corporeally,** *adv.*

corporeity (kôr pȯ rē′ i ti) [med. L. *corporeitās*, from *corporeus*, as prec.], *n.* Material existence; corporeality.

corposant (kôr′ pȯ zȧnt) [Port. *corpo santo*, L. *corpus sanctum*, sacred body], *n.* A sailor's name for a luminous electric body often seen on the masts and rigging on dark stormy nights; also called St. Elmo's fire.

corps (kôr) [F.], *n.* [*pl.* **corps** (kôrz)] (*Mil.*) A body of troops. **army corps,** *n.* A grouping of two or more divisions. ***corps de ballet*** (dė ba lā′), *n.* A body of dancers in a ballet. ***corps-diplomatique*** (dip lō ma tēk′), *n.* The body of ambassadors, attachés, etc., accredited to a court.

corpse (kôrps) [O.F. *cors* (F. *corps*), L. *corpus*, the body], *n.* A dead body, esp. of a human being; the body. **corpse-candle, -light,** *n.* An ignis fatuus seen in churchyards and regarded as an omen of death.

corpulent (kôr′ pū lėnt) [F., from L. *corpulentus* (*corpus*, body)], *a.* Excessively fat or fleshy; *corporeal, carnal. **corpulence, -lency,** *n.* **corpulently,** *adv.*

corpus (kôr′ půs) [L.], *n.* (*pl.* **corpora**) A body; the mass of anything; a collection of writings or of literature; (*Physiol.*) the body of an organ or any part of an organism. **Corpus Christi,** *n.* The festival of the body of Christ, held in honour of the real presence in the Eucharist on the Thursday after Trinity Sunday. **corpus delicti,** *n.* (*Law*) The aggregation of facts which constitute a breach of the law.

corpuscle (kôr′ půsl), **corpuscule** (-pŭs′ kūl) [L. *corpusculum*, dim. of *corpus*, body], *n.* A minute particle of matter, a molecule, an atom; (*Physiol.*) a minute body or cell forming part of an organism; (*pl.*) those which exist free in the blood. **corpuscular** (-pŭs′ kū lȧr), *a.* Pertaining to corpuscles; atomic. **corpuscular forces,** *n.pl.* Forces acting on corpuscles, and determining the forms and relations of matter. **corpuscular theory,** *n.* The obsolete theory that light is due to the rapid projection of corpuscles from a luminous body.

corrade (kȯ rād′) [L. *corrādere* (COR- *rādere*, to scrape)], *v.t.* (*Geol.*) To wear down (rocks, etc.), as a river by mechanical force and solution. **corrasion** (kŏ rā′ zhŭn), *n.*

***corradiate** (kŏ răd′ i āt), *v.i.* To radiate together.

corral (kŏ ral′) [Sp., from *corro*, a ring of people (*correr* (*toros*), to hold a bull-fight, L. *currere*, to run)], *n.* An enclosure (orig. of emigrants' wagons in Red Indian territory) for cattle or for defence; an enclosure for capturing elephants and other animals. *v.t.* (*past & p.p.* **corralled**) To pen up; to form into a corral.

correct (kŏ rekt′) [L. *correctus*, p.p. of *corrigere* (*regere*, to rule, to order)], *v.t.* To set right; to remove faults or errors from; to mark errors for rectification; to admonish, to punish, to chastise; to obviate, to counteract; to eliminate an aberration. *a.* Free from fault or imperfection; conforming to a fixed standard or rule; right, proper, decorous; true, exact, accurate. **correctly,** *adv.* **correctness,** *n.* **corrector,** *n.* One who or that which corrects; a censor; a critic. **corrector of the press,** *n.* A proof-reader.

correction (kŏ rek′ shŭn), *n.* The act of correcting; that which is substituted for what is wrong; amendment, improvement; punishment, chastisement; animadversion, criticism. **house of correction:** A gaol, a penitentiary. **under correction:** As liable to correction; perhaps in error. **correctional,** *a.* ***correctioner,** *n.* One who administers chastisement.

corrective (kŏ rek′ tiv), *a.* Having power to correct; tending to correct; *n.* That which tends to correct or counteract; an antidote. **corrective training:** Imprisonment for persistent offenders of 21 years of age or over for periods of from two to four years during which they are trained for some useful occupation.

corregidor (kŏ rej i dôr′) [Sp. (*corregir*, L. *corrigere*, to CORRECT)], *n.* The chief magistrate of a Spanish town.

correlate (kor′ ĕ lāt), *v.i.* To be reciprocally related. *v.t.* To bring into mutual relation. *a.* Mutually related. *n.* A correlative. **correlation** (-lā′ shŭn), *n.* Reciprocal relation; the act of bringing into correspondence or interaction; (*Phys.*) interdependence of forces and phenomena; (*Biol.*) the mutual relation of structure, functions, etc., in an organism. **correlationist,** *n.* A believer in the doctrine of universal correlation of powers and forces as the outcome of one primary force. **correlative** (kŏ rel′ ā tiv), *a.* Reciprocally connected or related; (*Gram.*) corresponding to each other, as *either* and *or*, *neither* and *nor*. *n.* One who or that which is correlated with another. **correlatively,** *adv.* **correlativity** (-tiv′ i ti), *n.*

correspond (kor ĕ spond′) [F. *correspondre*, med. L. *correspondēre* (COR-, *respondēre*, to RESPOND)], *v.i.* To be congruous; to fit, to suit, to agree; to communicate by letters sent and received. **correspondence,** *n.* Mutual adaptation; congruity; intercourse by means of letters; the letters which pass between correspondents. **correspondent,** *a.* Agreeing or congruous with; answering; *obedient. *n.* A person with whom intercourse is kept up by letters; a person or firm having business relations with another; one who sends news to a journal, esp. a person employed to do this. **correspondently,** *adv.* **corresponding,** *a.* Suiting; communicating by correspondence. **correspondingly,** *adv.* ***corresponsive,** *a.* Corresponding, conformable.

corridor (kor′ i dôr) [F., from It. *corridore* (*correre*, to run, L. *currere*)], *n.* A gallery or passage communicating with the apartments of a building; (*Am.*) an aisle; (*Fort.*) a covered way encircling a place; (*Pol.*) a strip of territory not under the state through which it passes. **corridor coach,** *n.* (*Rail.*) A coach with a passage down one side leading to doors in the ends; when connected these coaches make a **corridor train.**

corrie (kor′ i) [Gael. *coire*, cauldron], *n.* A semicircular hollow or cirque in a mountain side, usually surrounded in part by crags.

corrigendum (kor i jen′ dŭm) [L., ger. of *corrigere*, to CORRECT], *n.* (*pl.* **-da**) An error needing correction, esp. in a book. **corrigent** (kor′ i jĕnt), *a.* (*Med.*) Corrective. *n.* A corrective ingredient (in a prescription, etc.).

corrigible (kor′ ij ibl) [F., from L. *corrigere*, as prec.], *a.* Capable of being corrected; punishable; submissive, docile. **corrigibly,** *adv.*

corrival (kŏ rī′ văl) [F., from L. *corrīvālis* (*rīvālis*)], *n.* A rival, a competitor; a comrade, a compeer. *a.* Emulous.

corroborate (kŏ rob ŏ rāt) [L. *corrōborātus*, p.p. of *corrōborāre* (COR-, *rōborāre*, to strengthen, from *rōbur -boris*, strength)], *v.t.* To strengthen, to confirm, to establish; to bear additional witness to. **a.* (-răt) Strengthened. **corroborant,** *a.* Strengthening; confirming. *n.* (*Med.*) A tonic. **corroboration** (-rā′ shŭn), *n.* The act of strengthening or confirming; confirmation by additional evidence. **corroborative** (kŏ rob′-), *a.* Corroborating; *n.* (*Med.*) A corroborant. **corroborator,** *n.* **corroboratory,** *a.*

corroboree (kŏ rob′ ŏ rē) [Austral. abor.], *n.* A festive or warlike dance of the Australian Aborigines.

corrode (kŏ rōd′) [L. *corrōdere* (*rōdere*, to gnaw)], *v.t.* To wear away by degrees; to consume gradually; to prey upon. *v.i.* To waste away gradually. **corrosion** (kŏ rō′ zhŭn), *n.* The act or process of corroding; a corroded state. **corrosive,** *a.* Tending to corrode; (*fig.*) fretting, biting, vexing, virulent. **corrosive sublimate,** *n.* (*Chem.*) Bichloride of mercury, a powerful irritant poison; any corrosive substance. **corrosively,** *adv.* **corrosiveness,** *n.*

corrugate (kor′ ū gāt) [L. *corrūgātus*, p.p. of *corrūgāre* (*rūgāre*, to wrinkle, from *rūga*, a wrinkle)], *v.t.* To contract or bend into wrinkles or folds. *v.i.* To become wrinkled. *a.* (-gət) Wrinkled; (*Bot.* and *Zool.*) marked with more or less acute parallel angles. **corrugated iron,** *n.* Sheet iron pressed into folds and galvanized. **corrugation** (-gā′ shŭn), *n.* The act of corrugating; a wrinkle, a fold. **corrugator** (kor′-), *n.* (*Anat.*) a muscle which contracts the brow.

corrupt (kŏ rŭpt′) [L. *corruptus*, p.p. of *corrumpere* (*rumpere*, to break)], *a.* Putrid, decomposed; spoiled, tainted; unsound; (*fig.*) depraved; perverted by bribery; vitiated by additions or alterations; not genuine. *v.t.* To change from a sound to an unsound state; to infect, to make impure or unwholesome; (*fig.*) to vitiate or defile; to debauch, to seduce; to bribe; to falsify. *v.i.* To become corrupt. **corrupt practices,** *n.pl.* (*Law*) Direct or indirect bribery in connexion with an election. **corrupter,** *n.* ***corruptful,** *a.* Corrupting; corrupt. **corruptibility** (-bil′ i ti), *n.* **corruptible,** *a.* Liable to corruption. **corruptibly,** *adv.* **corruption,** *n.* The act of corrupting; the state of being corrupt; decomposition, putrefaction; putrid matter; (*fig.*) moral deterioration; misrepresentation; bribery; a corrupt reading or version. **corruption of blood:** (*Law*) Taint in the blood arising from attainder. **corruptive,** *a.* **corruptless,** *a.* Free from or not liable to corruption; undecaying. **corruptly,** *adv.* **corruptness,** *n.*

corsac (kôr′ săk) [Turk.], *n.* A small yellowish Asiatic fox, the Tartar fox.

corsage (kôr′ saj) [O.F.], *n.* The bodice of a woman's dress; a flower worn therein.

corsair (kôr′ sâr) [F. *corsaire*, M.It. *corsaro*, late L. *cursārius* (*cursus*, a course, from *currere*, to run)], *n.* A pirate or a privateer, a pirate authorized by the government of his country; a pirate-ship.

corse (kôrs) [O.F. *cors*, CORPSE], *n.* (*poet.*) a corpse; *a human body.

corset (kôr′ sĕt) [F., dim. of O.F. *cors*, body], *n.* A close-fitting garment, stiffened with whalebone or steel, worn by women to give shape to the body; a pair of stays.

corslet (kôrs′ lėt) [F. *corselet*, double dim. (*-el* and *-et*) of *cors*, as prec.], *n.* Body armour; a light cuirass; (*Zool.*) the thorax of insects.

***corsned** (kôr′ snėd) [A.-S. *cor-snæd* (*cor*, choice, trial, *snæd*, a bit, from *snīthan*, to cut)], *n.* The bread of choosing; a piece of bread consecrated by exorcism, swallowed by a suspected person as a test of innocence, in early English times.

cortège (kôr tāzh′) [F., from It. *corteggio* (*corte*, a court)], *n.* A train of attendants, a procession.

Cortes (kôr′ tėz) [Sp. and Port., pl. of *corte*, court], *n.* The legislative assemblies of Spain and Portugal.

cortex (kôr′ tėks) [L.], *n.* (*pl.* **-ices**) Bark; (*Anat. and Zool.*) a covering more or less resembling bark; the outer layer of the brain.

cortical (kôr′ ti kȧl), *a.* Belonging to the outer part of a plant or animal; pertaining to the bark or rind.

corticata (kôr ti kā′ tȧ), *n.pl.* (*Biol.*) A group of protozoa in which the fleshy portions project from a fixed axis.

corticate, corticated (kôr′ ti kȧt -ā ted), *a.* Coated with bark or something resembling bark.

corticin (kôr′ ti sin), *n.* (*Chem.*) An alkaloid obtained from the bark of the aspen.

cortisone (kôr′ ti sōn), *n.* A crystalline hormone isolated from the adrenal cortex, used in treating rheumatoid arthritis.

corundum (kȯ rŭn′ dȯm) [Tamil *kurundam*], *n.* A rhombohedral mineral of great hardness, allied to the ruby and sapphire; (*Min.*) a class of minerals including these consisting of crystallized alumina.

coruscate (kor′ ȯs kāt) [L. *coruscātus*, p.p. of *coruscāre*], *v.i.* To gleam, to glitter in flashes. **coruscant** (kȯ rŭs′ kȧnt), *a.* **coruscation** (-kā′ shȯn), *n.*

corvee (kôr vā′) [F., from late L. *corrogāta* (*opera*), requisitioned work (COR-, *rogāre*, to ask)], *n.* An obligation to perform certain services for a feudal lord, as the repair of roads, etc.; hence, forced labour.

corvette (kôr vet′) [F., from Port. *corveta*, Sp. *corbeta*, prob. from L. *corbīta* (*navis*), a ship of burden (*corbis*, basket)], *n.* (*Nav.*) A small, fast escort vessel armed with anti-submarine devices; a flush-decked, full-rigged ship of war, with one tier of guns.

corvine (kôr′ vin) [L. *corvīnus* from CORVUS], *a.* Pertaining to the crows. **corvus** (kôr′ vȯs) [L., a raven], *n.* (*Zool.*) A genus of conirostral birds, including the raven, jackdaw, rook, and crow; (*Rom. Ant.*) a name for several ancient war-engines, from the supposed resemblance to a crow's beak.

corybant (kor′ i bănt) [F. *Corybante*, L. *Corybantem*, acc. of *Corybās*, Gr. *Korubas -anta*], *n.* (*pl.* **-ntes**) A priest of Cybele, whose rites were accompanied with wild music and dancing. **corybantian** (-băn′ shi ȧn), *a.* **corybantic,** *a.* **corybantine,** *a.*

Corydon (kor′ i dȯn) [L., from Gr. *Korudōn*], *n.* A shepherd, a rustic (in pastoral literature), from the name of characters in the eclogues of Theocritus and Virgil.

corylus (kor′ i lȯs) [L.], *n.* (*Bot.*) A genus of shrubs including the hazel.

corymb (kor′ imb) [F. *corymbe*, L. *corymbus*, Gr. *korumbos*, a cluster], *n.* (*Bot.*) A raceme or panicle in which the stalks of the lower flowers are longer than those of the upper. **corymbiate** (kȯ rim′ bi ȧt), *a.* (*Bot.*) With clusters of berries or blossoms in the form of corymbs. **corymbiferous** (-bif′ ėr ȯs), *a.* **corymbiform** (kȯ rim′ bi fôrm), *a.* **corymbose** (kor im bōs′), *a.*

coryphæus (kor i fē′ ȯs) [L., from Gr. *koruphaios* (*koruphē*, the head)], *n.* The leader of a chorus in a classic play; a chief, a leader; the assistant of the choragus at Oxford.

coryphee (kor′ i fā) [F., from prec.], *n.* A ballet-girl, esp. the chief dancer in a ballet.

coryza (kȯ rī′ zȧ) [L., from Gr. *koruza*, running at the nose], *n.* Nasal catarrh; cold in the head.

cos (1) (kos) [Gr. *Kōs*], *n.* A curly variety of lettuce introduced from the island of Cos (now Stanchio) in the Ægean.

cos (2) (koz) [abbr. of COSINE].

cosaque (kȯ sak′) [F. *cosaque*, a Cossack], *n.* A Cossack dance; a cracker bon-bon.

cosecant (kō sek′ ȧnt) [CO-, SECANT], *n.* (*Trig.*) The secant of the complement of an arc or angle.

coseismal (kō sīz′ mȧl) [CO- SEISMAL], *a.* Relating to the points simultaneously affected by an earthquake. *n.* A coseismal line. **coseismal line** or **curve,** *n.* A line drawn on a map through all the points simultaneously affected by an earthquake. **coseismic,** *a.*

***cosentient** (kō sen′ shi ėnt) [CO-, SENTIENT], *a.* Perceiving together. **cosentiency,** *n.*

cosh (kosh) [?], *n.* A bludgeon, a life-preserver.

cosher (kōsh′ ėr) [KOSHER].

***coshering** (kosh′ ėr ing) [Ir. *coisir*, a feast, feasting], *n.* An Irish custom whereby the lord was entitled to exact from his tenant food and lodging for himself and his followers; rack-rent. ***cosherer,** *n.* One who practised coshering.

cosignatory (kō sig′ nȧ tȯ ri) [CO-, SIGNATORY], *n.* One who signs jointly with others.

cosin, cosinage [COUSIN].

cosine (kō′ sīn) [CO-, SINE], *n.* (*Trig.*) The sine of the complement of an arc or angle.

cosmetic (kȯz met′ ik) [F. *cosmetique*, Gr. *kosmētikos* (*kosmein*, to adorn, from *kosmos*, order)], *a.* Beautifying; used for dressing the hair, or skin *n.* An external application for rendering the skin soft, clear, and white, or for improving the complexion. ***cosmetical,** *a.* ***cosmetically,** *adv.*

cosmic (koz′ mik) [Gr. *kosmikos*, from *kosmos*, order, the world], *a.* Pertaining to the universe, esp. as distinguished from the earth; derived from some part of the solar system other than the earth; pertaining to cosmism; of inconceivably long duration; of world-wide importance. **cosmic dust,** *n.* Minute particles of matter distributed throughout space. **cosmic radiation,** *n.* Very energetic radiation falling on the earth from outer space, consisting chiefly of charged particles. **cosmical,** *a.* Cosmic; (*Astron.*) rising or setting with the sun. **cosmically,** *adv.* In a cosmic way; (*Astron.*) with the sun at rising or setting. **cosmicism,** *n.* (*Phil.*) The evolutionary philosophy of Herbert Spencer, who conceived of the universe as a self-acting whole, the laws of which were explicable by positive science. **cosmist,** *n.*

cosmo- [Gr. *kosmos*, the universe], *comb. form.* Pertaining to the universe.

cosmogony (kȯz mog′ ȯ ni) [Gr. *kosmogonia*], *n.* A theory, investigation, or dissertation respecting the origin of the world. **cosmogonic, -ical** (koz mȯ gon′ ik, -ȧl), *a.* **cosmogonist** (kȯz mog′ ȯ nist), *n.*

cosmography (kȯz mog′ rȧ fi) [Gr. *kosmographia*], *n.* A description or delineation of the features of the universe, or of the earth as part of the universe. **cosmographer,** *n.* **cosmographic, -ical** (koz mȯ grăf′ ik, -ȧl), *n.*

cosmology (kȯz mol′ ȯ ji), *n.* The science which investigates the laws of the universe as an ordered whole; (*Phil.*) the branch of metaphysics dealing with the universe and its relation to the mind. **cosmological** (-loj′ ik ȧl), *a.* **cosmologist,** *n.*

cosmonaut (koz′ mō nawt), *n.* An astronaut.

cosmopolitan (koz mȯ pol′ i tȧn) [Gr. *kosmopolitēs* (*kosmos*, the world, *politēs*, a citizen)], *a.* Common to all the world; at home in any part of the world; free from national prejudices and limitations. *n.* A cosmopolite. **cosmopolitanism,** *n.* **cosmopolitanize,** *v.t.* and *i.* **cosmopolite** (kȯz mop′ ȯ līt), *n.* A citizen of the world; one who is at home in any part of the world. *a.* World-wide in sympathy or experience; devoid of national prejudice. **cosmopolitanism,** *n.* **cosmopolitical** (-lit′ ik ȧl), *a.* Relating to world-wide polity.

cosmorama (koz mȯ ra′ mȧ) [KOSMO-, Gr. *horama*, a spectacle, from *horaein*, to see], *n.* An exhibition of pictures from all over the world, shown through lenses.

cosmos (koz′ mos) [Gr.], *n.* The universe regarded as an ordered system; an ordered system of knowledge; order, as opp. to chaos.

cosmosphere (koz′ mȯ sfēr), *n.* An apparatus for showing the relative position of the earth and the fixed stars.

cosmotheism (koz mȯ thē′ izm), *n.* (*Phil.*) Pantheism, the identification of God with the universe.

cosmothetic (koz mȯ thet′ ik) [COSMO-, Gr. *thetikos*, putting, positing, from *tithēnai*, to put], *a.* (*Phil.*) Believing in the existence of matter, but at the same time denying that we have any immediate knowledge of it. **cosmothetical,** *a.*

cosmotron (koz′ mō tron), *n.* (*Phys.*) The name given to an electrical apparatus for accelerating protons to high energies.

Cossack (kos′ ȧk) [Rus. *kozak'*, Turk. *quzzaq*, a vagabond, an adventurer], *n.* One of a race, probably of mixed Turkish origin, living on the southern steppes of Russia, and furnishing light cavalry to the Russian army.

cosset (kos′ ėt) [etym. doubtful (perh. from A.-S. *cot-sǣta*, cot-sitter, brought up within doors)], *n.* A pet lamb; a pet. *v.t.* To pet, to pamper.

cost (kost) [O.F. *coster* (F. *coûter*), L. *constāre* (CON-, *stāre*, to stand)], *v.i.* (*past & p.p.* **cost**) To require as the price of possession or enjoyment; to cause the expenditure of; to result in the loss of or the infliction of; (*Comm.*) (*past & p.p.* **costed**) to fix prices (of commodities). *n.* The price charged or paid for a thing; expense, charge; expenditure of any kind; penalty, loss, detriment; pain, trouble; *a costly thing; (*pl.*) expenses of a lawsuit, esp. those awarded to the successful against the losing party. **cost-plus,** *a.* Used of a contract where work is paid for at actual cost, with an agreed percentage addition as profit. **cost price,** *n.* The price paid by the dealer. **prime cost,** *n.* The cost of production. **costing,** *n.* (*Comm.*) The system of calculating the exact cost of production, so as to ascertain the profit or loss entailed. **costless,** *a.* Costing nothing. **costly,** *a.* Of high price; valuable; *extravagant; *gorgeous; **adv.* In a costly manner. **costliness,** *n.*

costa (kos′ tȧ) [L.], *n.* (*pl.* **-tæ**) (*Zool. and Physiol.*) A rib; any process resembling a rib in appearance or function; (*Bot.*) the midrib of a leaf. **costal,** *a.* **costate,** *a.*

costard (kos′ tȧrd) [perh. from O.F. *coste*, a rib (as prec.), referring to apples with prominent ribs], *n.* A large, round apple; (*slang*) the head. ***costard-monger** [COSTER-MONGER].

costean (kȯs tēn′) [Corn. *cothas*, dropped, *stean*, tin], *v.i.* (*Mining*) To sink shafts down to the rock in search of a lode. **costean-pit,** *n.* A shaft sunk to find tin.

coster, costermonger (kos′ tėr mŭng′ gėr) [COSTARD, MONGER], *n.* A seller of fruit, vegetables, etc. (esp. from a street barrow), (*Am.*) huckster. **a.* Mean, petty, mercenary. **costering, costermongering,** *n.* **costermongery,** *n.* **costermongerdom,** *n.*

costive (kos′ tiv) [O.F. *costivé, costevé*, L. *constipātus*, CONSTIPATED], *a.* Having the motion of the bowels too slow; constipated; (*fig.*) reserved, reticent; niggardly. **costiveness,** *n.*

costly [COST].

***costmary** (kost′ mâr i) [A.-S. *cost* (?), L. *costum*, Gr. *kostos*, Arab. *qust*; *Mary* (St. Mary)], *n.* An aromatic plant of the aster family, cultivated for use in flavouring.

costo- [L. *costa*, a rib], *comb. form.* (*Anat. and Physiol.*) Pertaining to the ribs.

***costrel** (kos′ trėl) [O.F. *costerel*], *n.* A vessel used by labourers for drink during harvest time.

costume (kos′ tūm, kȯs tūm′) [F., from It. *costume*, late L. *costūma*, L. *consuētūdinem*, acc. of *consuētūdo*, CUSTOM], *n.* Dress; the customary mode of dressing; the dress of a particular time or country; fancy dress; the attire of an actor or actress; a set of outer garments; a lady's coat and skirt, usu. tailor-made, a suit; (*Art and Lit.*) dress and other accessories. *v.t.* To furnish or dress with costume. **costume-piece,** *n.* A play in which the actors wear an historical or foreign costume. **costumer, costumier** (kȯs tū′ mėr, kos tū′ mi ėr), *n.* A maker or dealer in costumes.

cosy (kō′ zi) [etym. doubtful], *a.* Comfortable; snug. *n.* A padded covering for a teapot, put on it to retain the heat, called also tea-cosy; a canopied seat or corner for two people. **cosily,** *adv.* **cosiness,** *n.*

cot (1) (kot) [A.-S. *cot, cote* (cp. Dut. and Icel. *kot*, G. *koth*)], *n.* A small house, a hut; a shelter for beasts. **cot-folk,** *n.* (*Sc.*) Cottar-folk. **cot-house,** *n.* A small cottage; (Sc.) the house of a cottar. **cotland,** *n.* Land held by a cottar. ***cotquean,** *n.* A man who busies himself with household affairs.

cot (2) (kot) [from Hind. *khāt*], *n.* A light bedstead; a crib; a child's bedstead in a hospital; (*Naut.*) a swing bed for officers, invalids, etc.

cot (3) (kot) [abbr. of COTANGENT].

cotangent (kō tăn′ jėnt), *n.* (*Trig.*) The tangent of the complement of an arc or angle.

cote (1) (kōt) [COT (1)], *n.* A sheepfold; a small house or shelter. **bell-cote,** *n.* A small erection for hanging a bell. **dove-cote,** *n.* A pigeon-house.

***cote** (2) (kōt) [etym. doubtful], *v.t.* (*Coursing*) To outstrip; to pass by.

***cotemporary** [CONTEMPORARY].

cotenant (kō ten′ ȧnt), *n.* A joint tenant.

coterie (kō′ tėr i) [F., from low L. *coteria*, an association of cottars for holding land, from *cota*, a COT (1) (of Teut. orig.)], *n.* A set of people associated together for friendly intercourse; an exclusive circle of people in society; a clique.

coterminous [CONTERMINOUS].

cothurnus (kȯ thĕr′ nŭs) [L., from Gr. *kothornos*], *n.* The buskin worn by actors in Greek and Roman tragedy; (*fig.*) tragedy; the tragic style.

cotidal (kō tī′ dȧl), *a.* Having the tides at the same time as some other place.

cotillion (kȯ til′ yȯn), ***cotillon*** (kȯ tē′ lyon) [F. *cotillon*, lit. a petticoat, dim. of *cotte*, coat], *n.* A dance performed by four or eight persons; the music for this.

cotoneaster (kȯ tō nė ăs′ tėr) [L. *cotonea*, quince, -ASTER], *n.* A genus of ornamental shrubs belonging to the order *Rosaceæ*.

cotswold (kots′ wōld) [a range of hills in Gloucestershire], *n.* A famous breed of sheep, formerly peculiar to the counties of Gloucester, Worcester, and Hereford.

cotta (kot′ ȧ) [med. L. (see COAT)], *n.* (*Eccles.*) A surplice.

cottage (kot′ ȧj) [COTE (1), -AGE], *n.* A small house, esp. for labourers; a cot; a small country or suburban residence. **cottage cheese,** *n.* (*Am.*) Cream cheese. **cottage hospital,** *n.* A hospital of moderate size without a resident medical staff. **cottage loaf,** *n.* A loaf of bread made with two rounded masses of dough stuck one above the other. **cottage piano,** *n.* A small upright piano. **cottager,** *n.* One who lives in a cottage; (*Am.*) a person living in a country or seaside residence; (*Hist.*) a cottar.

cottar (kot′ ȧr) [COT (1) or COTE (1), perh. through med. L. *cotārius* (*cota*, COTE (1))], *n.* A Scottish peasant living in a cottage belonging to a farm and paying rent in the form of labour; a peasant holding a cottage and a plot of land on similar terms to Irish cottier-tenure.

cotter (kot′ ėr) [etym. doubtful], *n.* A key, wedge, or bolt for holding part of a machine in place.

cottier (kot′ i ėr) [O.F. *cotier,* med. L. *cotārius* (*cota,* COTE (1))], *n.* A peasant living in a cottage; (*Ir.*) a peasant holding a piece of ground under cottier-tenure (cp. COTTAR). **cottier-tenure,** *n.* The system, now illegal, of letting portions of land at a rent fixed yearly by public competition.

cotton (kotn) [F. *coton,* from Sp. *coton,* Arab. *qutun*], *n.* A downy substance, resembling wool, growing in the fruit of the cotton-plant, used for making thread, cloth, etc;; thread made from this; cloth made of cotton. *v.t.* To wrap up. *v.i.* To get on, to agree well (with); to be drawn (to), to become attached (to); *to succeed, to prosper. **cotton-cake,** *n.* Cotton-seed pressed into cakes as food for cattle. **cotton-gin,** *n.* A device for separating the seeds from cotton. **cotton-grass,** *n.* Plants with downy heads belonging to the genus *Eriophorum,* growing in marshy ground. **cotton-lord,** *n.* A rich cotton manufacturer. **cotton-seed,** *n.* The seed of the cotton-plant, yielding oil, and when crushed made into cotton cake. **cotton-spinner,** *n.* An operative employed in a cotton mill; an owner of a cotton mill. **cotton-waste,** *n.* Refuse cotton used for cleaning machinery. **cotton-weed,** *n.* Cudweed. **cotton-wood,** *n.* (*Am.*) Several kinds of poplar, esp. *Populus monilifera* and *P. angulata*; (*Austral.*) the dog-wood of Tasmania. **cotton-wool,** *n.* Cotton in its raw state, used for surgical purposes, etc., (*Am.*) absorbent cotton. **cotton-yarn,** *n.* Spun cotton ready for weaving. **cottonocracy** (kotn ok′ rȧ si) [-CRACY], *n.* The cotton lords, the great employers in the cotton industry. **cottony,** *a.*

cotyle (kot′ i lē) [Gr. *kotulē*], *n.* (*Gr. Ant.*) A deep cup, a measure of capacity; (*Anat.*) the cavity of a bone which receives the end of another in articulation; (*Zool.*) the sucker of a cuttle-fish. **cotyliform** (kȯ til′ i fôrm), *a.* (*Bot.*) **cotyloid** (kot′ i loid), *a.* (*Anat.*) Cup-shaped (used of the socket of the hip-bone).

cotyledon (kot i lē′ dȯn) [Gr. *kotulēdōn,* a cup-shaped hollow, from prec.], *n.* The rudimentary leaf of an embryo in the higher plants, the seed-leaf; (*Bot.*) a genus of plants, chiefly greenhouse evergreens, including *C. umbilicus,* the navelwort. **cotyledonal,** *a.* (*Bot.*) Resembling a cotyledon. **cotyledonous,** *a.* (*Bot.*) Possessing cotyledons.

couch (1) (kouch) [F. *coucher,* L. *collocāre* (COL-; *locāre,* to place, from *locus,* place)], *v.t.* To cause to lie, to lay oneself on a couch (*only in p.p.*); to lay (oneself) down; to deposit in a layer or bed; (*Malting*) to spread out (*barley*) on the floor for germination; to express in words; to imply, to veil or conceal; to set (a spear) in rest; (*Surg.*) to operate upon for cataract. *v.i.* To lie down, to rest; to crouch; to stoop, to bend; to lie in concealment; to be laid or spread out. *n.* A bed, or any place of rest; a lounge or sofa; a layer of steeped barley germinating for malting; the frame or floor for this; a preliminary coat of paint, size, etc. **couch-fellow,** *n.* A bedfellow; an intimate companion. **couch-mate,** *n.* A bedfellow.

couch (2) (kooch, kouch) [QUITCH], *n.* Couch-grass. *v.t.* To clear of couch-grass, **couch-grass,** *n.* *Triticum repens,* whose long, creeping root renders it difficult of extirpation.

couchant (kou′ chȧnt) [F., pres.p. of *coucher,* to lie (see COUCH (1))], *a.* Lying in repose; lying hid; (*Her.*) lying down with the head raised.

***couchée** (ku′ shā) [F. *couché,* var. of *coucher*], *n.* A reception in the evening, orig. at the king's retirement for the night.

Couéism (koo′ ā izm) [Emil *Coué* (1857–1926), *n.* *b.* (*Med.*) A therapeutic system based on auto-suggestion.

cougar (koo′ gȧr) [F. *couguar,* adapted from Guarani name], *n.* The puma or American lion.

cough (kof, kawf) [A.-S. *cohhetan,* prob. representing an unrecorded *cohhian* (cp. Dut. *kuchen,* to cough, G. *keuchen,* to pant); imit. in orig.], *n.* A convulsive effort, attended with noise, to expel foreign or irritating matter from the lungs; an irritated condition of the organs of breathing that excites coughing. *v.t.* To drive from the lungs by a cough. *v.i.* To expel air from the lungs in a convulsive and noisy manner, with a cough. **to cough down:** To silence (a speaker) by a noise of or as of coughing. **to cough out:** To say with a cough. **to cough up:** To eject; (*slang*) to pay up. **cough-drop,** *n.* A jujube or lozenge taken to cure or relieve a cough; (*slang*) a singular person, a caution.

could, *past* [CAN (2)].

coulée (koo′ li, ku lā′) [F., fem. p.p. of *couler,* to flow], *n.* (*Geol.*) A solidified lava-flow; (*Am.*) a ravine or gully.

coulisse (koo lēs′) [F., from *couler,* to flow], *n.* A grooved timber in which a sluice-gate or a partition slides; a side-scene in a theatre; (*pl.*) the space between the side-scenes.

couloir (kool′ war) [F., from *couler,* to flow], *n.* A steep gully or long, narrow gorge on a precipitous mountain-side.

coulomb (kool′lȯm) [C. A. de *Coulomb* (1736–1806), French physicist], *n.* (*Elec.*) A unit of electrical charge.

coulter (kōl′ tėr) [A.-S. *culter,* L. *culter*], *n.* The iron blade fixed in front of the share in a plough.

coumarin (koo′ mȧ rin) [F. *coumarine*; Guiana native name *cumarú,* the Tonka bean], *n.* (*Chem.*) An aromatic crystalline substance extracted from the Tonka bean.

council (koun′ sil) [F. *concile,* L. *concilium* (CON-, *calāre,* to summon)], *n.* A number of persons met together for deliberation or advice; persons acting as advisers to a sovereign, governor, or chief magistrate; the higher branch of the legislature in some of the states of America and English colonies; an ecclesiastical assembly attended by the representatives of various churches; the governing body of a University; (*N.T.*) the Jewish Sanhedrin. **British Council,** *n.* An official organization for dissemination of British culture abroad. **common council:** The elective council of a city or corporate town. **Council of Europe,** *n.* (*Pol.*) A council set up in 1949 to discuss matters of common concern excluding defence. The countries adhering were, U.K., Belgium, Denmark, France, Ireland, Italy, Luxemburg, Netherlands, Norway, Sweden. **Council of State:** A deliberative assembly advising the sovereign in Britain and other countries. **council of war:** A council of officers called together in time of difficulty or danger. **county council:** A body of representatives elected under the Local Government Act of 1888. **Great Council:** (*Hist.*) The assembly of tenants-in-chief and great ecclesiastics which corresponded to the A.-S. *witena gemot,* and was superseded by the House of Lords. **Œcumenical Council:** An assembly of prelates and doctors representing the universal Church. **Privy Council:** A select council for advising the sovereign in administrative matters. **council-board,** *n.* The table round which a council deliberates; a council; the council in session. **council-chamber,** *n.* The room where a council meets. **council-fire,** *n.* The sacred fire kept burning by the Red Indians during their councils. **council-house,** *n.* The building in which a council meets; a small house owned and leased to tenants by the local council. **council-man,** *n.* A member of a common council. **councillor,** *n.* A member of a council. **councillorship,** *n.*

counsel (koun′ sėl) [O.F. *conseil,* L. *consilium,* from *consulere,* to consult (see CONSUL)], *n.* A consultation; advice; opinion given after deliberation; (*Law*) a barrister; (*collect.*) the advocates engaged on either side in a law-suit. *v.t.* (*past & p.p.*

counselled) To give advice or counsel to; to advise. **counsel of perfection:** A precept aiming at a superhuman standard of righteousness (ref. to Matt. xix. 21). **Queen's, King's Counsel:** Counsel to the Crown, who take precedence of ordinary barristers. **to keep one's counsel:** To keep a matter secret. ***counsel-keeper,** *n.* A confidant. ***counsel-keeping,** *a.* Keeping secret. **counsellor,** *n.* One who gives counsel or advice; an adviser; *a member of a council. **Counsellor-at-Law,** *n.* (*Ireland*) An advocate, a counsel, a barrister. **counsellorship,** *n.*

count (1) (kount) [O.F. *conter*, L. *computāre*, to COMPUTE], *v.t.* To reckon up in numbers, to compute; to call the numerals in order; to keep up a reckoning, to esteem. *v.i.* To possess a certain value; to depend or rely (upon); *to take account (of). *n.* A reckoning or numbering; the sum (of); (*Law*) a statement of the plaintiff's case; one of several charges in an indictment; *an object of interest. **a count out:** The act of counting out; (*Parl.*) an adjournment when less than forty are present. **to count out:** To reckon one by one from a number of units; to adjourn a meeting (esp. of Parliament) after counting those present and finding they are not sufficient to form a quorum; to declare a boxer defeated upon his failure to stand up within ten seconds of the referee beginning to count. **to count up:** To calculate the sum of. **to take the count:** (*Boxing*) To be counted out. **count-wheel,** *n.* A toothed wheel which regulates the striking of a clock. **countable** (1), *a.* **counting house** (koun' ting hous), *n.* The house, room, or office appropriated to the business of keeping accounts, etc. **countless,** *a.* Innumerable; beyond calculation.

count (2) (kount) [O.F. *conte*, L. *comitem*, acc. of *comes*, companion], *n.* A foreign title of rank corresponding to an English earl. **count-cardinal,** *n.* A count who is also a cardinal. **count-palatine,** *n.* A high judicial officer under the Merovingian kings; the ruler of either of the Rhenish Palatinates. **countship,** *n.*

countable (2) [ACCOUNTABLE].

countenance (koun' tė nȧns) [O.F. *contenance*, aspect, demeanour, L. *continentia* (*continēre*, to contain)], *n.* The face; the features; air, look, or expression; composure of look; favour, support, corroboration; *credit, estimation. *v.t.* To sanction, to approve, to permit; to abet, to encourage; *to favour; *to pretend, to make a show of. **in countenance:** In favour; confident, assured. **out of countenance:** Out of favour; abashed, dismayed. **to keep one's countenance:** To continue composed in look; to refrain from laughter. **to put out of countenance:** To abash; to cause to feel ashamed. **countenancer,** *n.*

counter (1) (koun' tėr) [A.-F. *counteour*, O.F. *countour*, L. *computātōrium*, from *computāre*, to COMPUTE], *n.* One who or that which counts; a calculator; a piece of metal, ivory, etc., used for reckoning, as in games; an imitation coin or token; a table or bench on which goods are displayed and money counted, and across which goods are sold. **counter-jumper,** *n.* (*colloq.*) A salesman, a shop assistant. **under the counter:** The reserving by a tradesman of black market or other goods for favoured customers.

counter (2) (koun' tėr) [F. *contre*, L. *contra*, against], *n.* The opposite, the contrary; a horse's breast; (*Naut.*) the curved part of a ship's stern; (*Fencing*) a circular parry; (*Boxing*) a blow dealt just as the opponent is striking; the part of a boot or shoe enclosing the wearer's heel. *a.* Contrary, adverse, opposed; opposing; duplicate. *adv.* In the opposite direction; wrongly; contrarily. *v.t.* To oppose, to return a blow by dealing another one. *v.i.* (*Boxing*) To give a return blow.

***counter** (3) [ENCOUNTER].

counter- [COUNTER (2)], *comb. form.* In return; in answer; in opposition; in an opposite direction. **counter-agent,** *n.* That which counteracts. **counter-approaches,** *n.pl.* (*Mil.*) A line of trenches made by the besieged outside the permanent fortifications to hinder the approach of besiegers. **counter-attack,** *v.t.* and *v.i.* To make an attack after an attack by the enemy. *n.* **counter-attraction,** *n.* Attraction in an opposite direction; a rival attraction. **counter-attractive,** *a.* **counter-brace,** *n.* (*Naut.*) The lee brace of the foretopsail yard. *v.t.* To brace in opposite directions. **counter-brand,** *v.t.* (*Am.*) To brand (cattle when sold) on the opposite side to the original brand. ***counter-caster,** *n.* A merchant, a book-keeper. **counter-ceiling,** *n.* Pugging, dry material packed between the joists of a floor to deaden sound. **counter-claim,** *n.* A claim brought forward by a defendant against a plaintiff. **counter-clockwise,** *adv.* In a direction contrary to that of the hands of a clock. **counter-espionage,** *n.* A system to detect and catch spies. **counter-gauge,** *n.* (*Carp.*) An adjustable double-pointed gauge for transferring the measurement of a mortise to the end of a stick where a tenon is to be made. **counter-irritant,** *n.* (*Med.*) An irritant applied to the body to remove some other irritation. *a.* Acting as a counter-irritant. **counter-irritate,** *v.t.* **counter-irritation,** *n.* **counter-movement,** *n.* A movement in an opposite or contrary direction. **counter-opening,** *n.* (*Surg.*) An opening on the opposite side. **counter-poison,** *n.* A poison administered as an antidote. **counter-proof,** *n.* A reversed impression taken from another just printed. **counter-reformation,** *n.* A reformation of an opposite nature to another; (*Hist.*) the attempt of the Roman Church to counteract the results of the Protestant Reformation. **counter-revolution,** *n.* A revolution opposed to a former one, and designed to restore a former state of things. **counter-seal,** *v.t.* To seal with another seal. **counter-security,** *n.* Security given to cover a person's risk as a surety. **counter-tenor,** *n.* (*Mus.*) A voice, or a person with a voice higher than tenor, an alto; a part written for such a voice. **counter-view,** *n.* A position opposite to or facing another; an opposite view of a question.

counteract (koun tėr ăkt'), *v.t.* To act in opposition to, so as to hinder or defeat; to neutralize. **counteraction,** *n.* **counteractive,** *a.*

counterbalance (koun tėr băl' ȧns), *v.t.* To weigh against or oppose with an equal weight or effect; to countervail. *n.* An equal weight or force acting in opposition.

counterblast (kount' tėr blast), *n.* An argument or statement in opposition.

counterbuff (koun' tėr bŭf) [COUNTER-, BUFF (1), a blow (onomat.)], *n.* A blow in return. *v.t.* To strike back, or in an opposite direction.

counterchange (koun' tėr chānj), *n.* Exchange reciprocation. *v.t.* To exchange, to alternate; to interchange, to chequer.

countercharge (koun' tėr charj), *n.* A charge in opposition to another; a counter-claim. *v.t.* (-charj') To make a charge against in return; to charge in opposition to (a charge of troops).

countercheck (koun' tėr chek), *n.* A check brought against another; an opposing check.

counterfeit (koun' tėr fēt) [O.F. *contrefait*, p.p. of *contrefaire* (L. *contra*, against, *facere*, to make)], *v.t.* To imitate, to mimic; to imitate or copy without right and pass off as genuine; to put on a semblance of; (*Law*) to coin, to imitate in base metal; (*fig.*) to pretend, to simulate. **v.i.* To make pretences, to feign. *a.* Made in imitation with intent to be passed off as genuine; forged. *n.* One who pretends to be what he is not, an impostor; a counterfeit thing. **counterfeiter,** *n.* One who counterfeits; (*Am.*) a coiner.

counterfoil (koun'tėr foil), *n.* That portion of the tally formerly struck in the exchequer which was kept by an officer of that court, the other part being given to the person who had lent the king money; the counterpart of a cheque, receipt, or other document, retained by the giver.

counterfort (koun′ tėr fôrt) [F. *contrefort*], *n.* A buttress, arch, or oblique wall built against a wall or terrace to retain, support, or strengthen it.

countermand (koun tėr mand′) [O.F. *contremander* (L. *contra*, against, *mandāre*, to command)], *v.t.* To revoke, to annul; to recall; to cancel; *to contradict, to oppose. *n.* An order contrary to or revoking a previous order.

countermarch (koun′ tėr march), *v.i.* (*Mil.*) To march in an opposite direction; to perform a countermarch. *v.t.* To cause to countermarch. *n.* The action of countermarching; (*Mil.*) a change in the position of the wings or front and rear of a battalion; (*fig.*) a change of measures or conduct.

countermark (koun′ tėr mark), *n.* An additional mark for identification or certification, an additional mark put upon goods belonging to several persons that they may not be opened except in the presence of all; the mark of the Goldsmiths' Company to show the standard of the metal.

countermine (koun′ tėr mīn), *n.* A gallery or mine to intercept or frustrate a mine made by the enemy; a submarine mine employed to explode the mines sunk by the enemy; a stratagem to frustrate any project. *v.t.* To oppose by a countermine. *v.i.* To make or place countermines.

countermure (koun′ tėr mūr) [F. *contremur* (COUNTER-, *mur*, L. *murus*, wall)], *n.* A wall raised before or behind another as an additional or reserve defence.

counterpane (koun′ tėr pān) [earlier *counterpoint*, O.F. *contrepointe*, corr. of *coultepointe*, L. *culcita puncta*, stitched QUILT (*puncta*, p.p. of *pungere*, to prick)], *n.* A coverlet for a bed; a quilt.

counterpart (koun′ tėr part), *n.* A correspondent part; a duplicate or copy; anything which exactly fits another, as a seal and the impression; one who is exactly like another in person or character; (*Law*) one of two corresponding copies of an instrument; (*Mus.*) a part written to accompany another.

counterplot (koun′ tėr plot), *v.t.* To oppose or frustrate by another plot. *n.* A plot to defeat another plot.

counterpoint (1) (koun′ tėr point) [F. *contrepoint*, med. L. *contrapunctum*, point against point (*contra*, against, *punctum*, p.p. of *pungere*, to prick)], *n.* (*Mus.*) A melodious part or combination of parts written to accompany a melody; the art of constructing harmonious parts; the art of harmonious composition. **double, triple,** or **quadruple counterpoint,** *n.* Counterpoint so arranged that the parts can be transposed in any way without impairing the harmony.

***counterpoint** (2) [COUNTERPANE].

counterpoise (koun′ tėr poiz) [F. *contrepois* (now *poids*), *n.* A weight in opposition and equal to another; a counterbalancing force, power, or influence; equilibrium. *v.t.* To oppose with an equal weight so as to balance; to oppose, check, or correct with an equal force, power, or influence; to bring into or maintain in equilibrium.

counterscarp (koun′ tėr skarp) [F. *contrescarpe*, It. *contrascarpa* (*contra*, against, *scarpa*, SCARP)], *n.* (*Fort.*) The exterior wall or slope of the ditch; the whole covered way with the parapet and glacis.

countershaft (koun′ tėr shaft), *n.* (*Mach.*) An intermediate shaft driven by the main shaft and transmitting motion.

countersign (koun′ tėr sīn) [F. *contresigner*], *v.t.* To attest the correctness of by an additional signature; to ratify. *n.* A password, a secret word or sign by which one may pass a sentry, or by which the members of a secret association may recognize each other. **counter-signature** (koun tėr sig′ nȧ tūr), *n.* The signature of an official to a document certifying that of another person.

countersink (koun′ tėr singk), *v.t.* To chamfer a hole for a screw or bolt head; to sink (the head of a screw, etc.) into such a hole. *n.* A chamfered hole; a tool for making such a hole.

countervail (koun tėr vāl′) [O.F. *contrevail*, stem of *contrevaloir* (*contre*, against, *valoir*, L. *valēre*, to avail)], *v.t.* To act against with equal effect or power; to counterbalance. *v.i.* To be of equal weight, power, or influence on the opposite side.

***counterweigh** (koun tėr wā′), *v.t.* To counterbalance.

counterwork (kount′ tėr wĕrk), *v.t.* To work against; to counteract. *n.* An opposing work or effort; (*Mil.*) a work constructed to oppose those of the enemy.

countess (koun′ tes) [O.F. *cuntesse*, late L. *comitissa*, fem. of *comes*, COUNT], *n.* The wife of a count or of an earl; a lady holding this rank in her own right.

counting-house [COUNT (1)].

countless [COUNT (1)].

countrified (kŭn′ tri fīd) [p.p. of *countrify*], *a.* Rustic in manners or appearance.

country (kŭn′ tri) [O.F. *cuntrée*, *contrée*, late L. *contrāta*, a region over against, from *contrā*, against], *n.* A region or state; the inhabitants of any region or state; one's native land; the rural part as distinct from cities and towns; the rest of a land as distinguished from the capital. **to appeal to the country:** To hold a general election, to appeal to the electors. **in the country:** (*Cricket*) Far from the wickets, at deep-long-off or long-on. **country club,** *n.* A sporting or social club in country surroundings. **country cousin,** *n.* A relation of countrified ways or appearance. **country-dance** [altered to *contre-danse* in French, this being often mistaken for the orig. form], *n.* A dance in which the partners are ranged in lines opposite to each other; any rural English dance. **countryman,** *n.* One who lives in a rural district; an inhabitant of any particular region; a native of the same country as another. **countrywoman,** *n.* **country note:** A bank-note issued by a provincial bank. **country party:** A political party that professes to maintain the interests of the nation as a whole, or of the agricultural interests as against the industrial. **country-seat, -house,** *n.* A gentleman's country mansion. **countryside,** *n.* A rural district; the inhabitants of this.

county (koun′ ti) [O.F. *cunté*, *conté*, L. *comitātus* (see COUNT (2))], *n.* A shire; *the country or district ruled by a count; a division of land for administrative, judicial, and political purposes; (*Brit. Isles*) the chief civil unit; the chief administrative division; (*U.S.A.*) the civil division next below a State; *a count, an earl. *a.* Pertaining to a county; (*colloq.*) affecting an air of gentility. **county borough,** *n.* A town with more than 50,000 inhabitants, ranking (under the Local Government Act of 1888) as an administrative county. **county corporate,** *n.* A city or town having sheriffs and other magistrates of its own, and ranking as a county. **county council,** *n.* The board administering the civil affairs of a county. **County court:** A local court for the recovery of small debts. **county-court,** *v.t.* To sue in a County court. **county family,** *n.* A family belonging to the nobility or gentry with an ancestral seat in the county. **county palatine,** *n.* A county of which the count or earl palatine was formerly invested with royal privileges, as Cheshire and Lancashire. **county road,** *n.* A main road maintained by a county council. **county town,** *n.* The chief town of any county.

coup (1) (koo) [F., from O.F. *colp* (It. *colpo*), late L. *colpus*, *colapus*, L. *colaphus*, Gr. *kolaphos*, a blow], *n.* A stroke, a telling or decisive blow; a victory; a successful move, piece of strategy, or revolution; (*Billiards*) a stroke putting a ball into a pocket without its touching another. ***coup d'état*** (-dā ta′) [F.], *n.* A sudden and violent change of government, esp. of an illegal and revolutionary nature. ***coup de grâce*** (-dė gras), *n.* A finishing stroke. ***coup de main*** (-dė man′) [F.], *n.* A sudden and energetic attack. ***coup d'œil*** (-du i) [F.], *n.* A quick comprehensive glance; a general view.

coup de théâtre (-de tā atr') [F.], *n.* A sensational stroke, a notable hit.

coup (2) (koup) [Sc. for COPE (2)], *v.t.* To upset, to overturn. *v.i.* To be overturned.

coup (3) (koup) [perh. from Icel. *kaupa*, to buy, to bargain, or a var. of COPE (3)], *v.t.* (*Sc.*) To exchange, to barter. **couper,** *n.*

coupé (koo' pā) [F., p.p. of *couper*, to cut (as COUP (1))], *n.* A four-wheeled closed carriage; a half compartment with glazed front at the end of a railway carriage; (*Motor.*) a two-seater car with an enclosed body.

couped (koopt) [p.p. of obs. *coop*, to cut (as prec.)], *a.* (*Her.*) Cut clean (as a head, hand, etc., on a shield), opp. to erased.

couple (kŭp' el) [O.F. *cople*, L. COPULA], *n.* That which joins two things together; two of the same kind considered together; a leash; a pair or brace; a betrothed or married pair; a pair of dancers; (*Carp.*) a pair of rafters connected by a tie; (*Dynam.*) a pair of equal forces acting in parallel and opposite directions so as to impart a circular movement. *v.t.* To connect or fasten together; to unite persons together, esp. in marriage; to associate. *v.i.* To copulate. ***couplement,** *n.* The act of coupling; the state of being coupled; a couple. **coupler,** *n.* One who or that which couples; (*Organ*) a connexion between two or more manuals or keys, or manuals and pedals. **couplet,** *n.* Two lines of running verse; *a couple. **coupling,** *n.* The action of the verb TO COUPLE; a device for connecting railway carriages, etc., together; a device for connecting parts of machinery and transmitting motion. **coupling-box,** *n.* A contrivance for connecting the ends of two shafts and causing them to rotate together. **coupling-pin,** *n.* A bolt for fastening together parts of machinery; a part of a railway coupling.

coupon (koo' pon) [F., a piece cut off, from *coupere*, to cut], *n.* A detachable certificate for the payment of interest on bonds; a portion of a railway pass printed in book form; a detachable ticket or certificate entitling to food ration, etc.; a voucher; (*Pol.*) the official recognition of a candidate as a genuine supporter of a particular party, coalition, programme, etc.

coupure (koo' pūr) [as prec.], *n.* (*Mil.*) A passage, esp. one cut through the glacis to facilitate sallies by the besieged.

courage (kŭr' ij) [O.F. *corage*, *courage*, from L. *cor*, the heart, -AGE], *n.* Bravery, boldness, intrepidity. **Dutch courage:** Valour inspired by drinking. **courageous** (kŭ rā' jŭs), *a.* **courageously,** *adv.* **courageousness,** *n.*

courant (ku rănt') [F., pres.p. of *courir*, L. *currere*, to run], *a.* (*Her.*) In a running attitude. *n.* An old dance with a running or a gliding step; the music for this.

***courb** (koorb) [F. *courber*, L. *curvāre*], *v.i.* and *t.* To bend, bow. *a.* Bent, crooked.

courbette [CURVET].

courier (kur' i ėr) [M.E. *corour*, O.F. *coreor* (F. *coureur*), late L. *curritōrem*, acc. of *curritor*, from L. *currere*, to run (coalescing later with F. *courier*, It. *corriere*, med. L. *currerius*, from It. *corre*, L. *currere*, to run)], *n.* A messenger sent in great haste, an express; a travelling servant who makes all necessary arrangements beforehand; a guide in charge of a party of tourists; a title of a newspaper.

course (kôrs) [O.F. *cours*, L. *cursum*, acc. of *cursus*, a running, from *currere*, to run], *n.* The act of moving or running, a race; the act of passing from one place to another; the track passed over, the route; the bed or the direction of a stream; the ground on which a race is run; a chase after a hare by one or a brace of greyhounds; continued progress; career; a series; one of a series of dishes served at one meal; mode of procedure; a planned programme of study; method of life or conduct; a row or tier of bricks or stones in a building; (*pl.*) behaviour; *(*pl.*) the menses; (*Hist.*) the charge of two mounted knights in the lists; (*Naut.*, *pl.*) the sails set on a ship's lower yards. *v.t.* To run after, to pursue; to traverse. *v.i.* To chase hares with greyhounds; to run or move quickly; to circulate (as the blood). **in due course:** In due, regular, or anticipated order. **matter of course:** A natural event. **of course:** By consequence, naturally. **courser,** *n.* A swift horse, a war-horse; one who practises coursing; a dog used in coursing; (*Ornith.*) a bird of the genus *Cursorius*, which are noted for swiftness in running. **coursing,** *a.* That courses. *n.* The sport of hunting hares with greyhounds. **coursing-joint,** *n.* The mortar-joint between two courses of bricks or stones.

court (kôrt) [O.F. *cort*, L. *cōrtem*, *cohortem*, acc. of *cohors*, an enclosure, a cohort (cp. Gr. *chortos*, *a* courtyard, L. *hortus*, a garden)], *n.* A place enclosed by buildings, or enclosing a house; a narrow street; a quadrangle; a subdivision of a large building; an enclosed piece of ground used for games; a subdivision of a piece so enclosed or merely marked out, the residence of a sovereign; the retinue of a sovereign; the body of courtiers; the sovereign and advisers regarded as the ruling power; a State reception by a sovereign; any meeting or body having jurisdiction; the chamber in which justice is administered; the judges or persons assembled to hear any cause; deferential attention paid in order to secure favour or regard. *v.t.* To seek the favour of; to pay court to; to seek the affections of, to woo; (*colloq.*) to county-court. *v.i.* To solicit a woman in marriage; to make love; *to act the courtier. **Court of St. James's:** (*Hist.*) The court of the British Crown. **Court of Session:** The Supreme Court in Scotland. **General Court:** (*Am.*) The state legislature in Massachusetts and New Hampshire. **out of court:** Not worth considering. **court-baron,** *n.* (*Law*) The court of a manor. **court-card,** *n.* [COAT-CARD]. (*Cards*) The king, queen and knave of a suit. **court-cupboard,** *n.* A movable kind of sideboard. **court-day,** *n.* A day on which a court of justice sits. **court-dress,** *n.* The costume proper for a royal levee. ***court-dresser,** *n.* A flatterer. **court-guide,** *n.* A directory of private residents (orig. of those entitled to be presented at court). **court hand,** *n.* The style of handwriting (based on Norman handwriting) used in records and judicial proceedings. **court-house,** *n.* A house or building containing rooms used by any court. ***court leet,** *n.* A court of record held once a year by the steward of a hundred, lordship, or manor. **court-like,** *a.* Elegant, polished. **court-martial,** *n.* A court for the trial of service offenders, composed of officers, none of whom must be of inferior rank to the prisoner. *v.t.* To try by court-martial. **drumhead court-martial:** A court held (orig.) round the drumhead in war-time. **court-plaster,** *n.* Silk surfaced with a solution of balsam of benzoin (used in the 18th cent. by fashionable ladies for patches, and since for cuts or slight wounds). ***court-roll,** *n.* The record of a manorial court. **courtyard,** *n.* An open area round or within a large building.

courteous (kĕr'-, kôr' tė ŭs) [O.F. *cortois*, *curteis*], *a.* Having court-like manners, polite, affable, considerate. **courteously,** *adv.* **courteousness,** *n.*

courtesan, -zan (kôr'-, kĕr' tė zăn) [F. *courtisane*, It. *cortĕgiana* (*corte*, court)], *n.* A prostitute; a woman of loose virtue.

courtesy (kĕr'-, kôr' tė si) [O.F. *cortesie*, from *corteis*, COURTEOUS], *n.* Courteousness, politeness; graciousness; gracious disposition; favour, as opposed to right; an act of civility; a bow, a curtsy. **by courtesy:** As a matter of courtesy, not of right. **courtesy of England:** (*Law*) A tenure by which a man having issue by a woman seized of land, after her death holds the estate for life; called also **tenure by courtesy. courtesy title,** *n.* A title to which a person has no legal right (used esp. of the hereditary titles assumed by the children of peers).

courtier (kôr′ ti ėr) [from O.F. *cortoier*, to live at court (*cort*, COURT)], *n.* One who is in attendance or a frequenter at the court of a prince; one of polished or distinguished manners; one who courts. ***courtierism,** *n.*

courtly (kôrt′ li), *a.* Of or pertaining to a court; polished, elegant, polite; flattering, obsequious. **adv.* As befits a court or courtier. **courtliness,** *n.*

courtship (kôrt′ ship), *n.* The act of soliciting in marriage; (*fig.*) the act of seeking after anything; *good breeding, courtliness; courtly state; courteous attention.

couscous, couscousou (koos′ koos, -soo) [F., from Arab. *kuskus*, from *kaskasa*, to pound], *n.* An African dish of pounded millet or flour steamed over meat or broth.

cousin (kŭzn) [F., from late L. *cosīnus*, L. *consobrīnus*, a cousin-german on the mother's side, from *soror*, a sister)], *n.* The son or daughter of an uncle or aunt; a title used by a sovereign in addressing a nobleman; *a kinsman; a familiar form of address. **a.* Allied, related, kindred. **first cousins:** The children of brothers or sisters. **second cousins:** The children of cousins. **cousin once removed:** The child of one's first cousin. **to call cousins:** To profess kinship with. **cousin-german,** *n.* A first cousin. **cousinhood,** *n.* **cousinly,** *a.* ***cousinry,** *n.* Kindred, relatives. **cousinship,** *n.*

couthie (kuth′ i) [Sc., prob. from COUTH, knowing], *a.* Friendly, kindly, genial. *adv.* In a friendly or genial way.

couture (koo tūr′) [F.], *n.* Dressmaking; dress-designing. **couturier, couturiere** (koo tū′ ri ā, koo tū′ ri âr), *m.* Man, woman dress-designer.

couvade (ku vad′) [F., from *couver*, to hatch, L. *cubāre*, to lie], *n.* A custom among primitive races, by which the father on the birth of a child performs certain acts and abstains from certain foods, etc.

covariant (kō vâr′ i ant), *n.* (*Math.*) A function standing in the same relation to another from which it is derived as any of its linear transforms do to a transform similarly derived from the latter function.

cove (1) (kōv) [A.-S. *cofa*, a chamber (cp. Icel. *kofi*, G. *koben*, a hut or cabin)], *n.* A small creek, inlet, or bay; a nook or sheltered recess; (*Am.*) a strip of prairie extending into woodland; (*Arch.*) a hollow in a cornice-moulding; the cavity of an arch or ceiling. *v.t.* To arch over; to cause to slope inwards. **coved ceiling,** *n.* One with a hollow curve at the junction with the wall.

cove (2) (kōv) [etym. doubtful], *n.* (*slang*) A man, a fellow, a chap.

coven (kŭv′ ėn) [CONVENT], *n.* An assembly of witches.

covenant (kŭv′ ė nant) [O.F. pres.p. of *convenir* (see CONVENE)], *n.* An agreement on certain terms; a compact; a document containing the terms of agreement; (*Law*) a formal agreement under seal; a clause in an agreement; (*Hist.*) the name given to certain formal agreements in favour of the Reformation, and later (esp. in 1638 and 1643) in favour of Presbyterianism; (*Bibl.*) a covenant between the Israelites and Jehovah. *v.t.* To grant or promise by covenant. *v.i.* To enter into a covenant. **Covenant of the League of Nations:** A series of articles embodying the principles of the League. **New Covenant:** The Christian relation to God; **Old Covenant:** The Jewish dispensation. **Ark of the Covenant** [ARK]. **Solemn League and Covenant:** The Presbyterian compact of 1643. **covenantal, covenanted,** *a.* Secured by or held under a covenant; bound by a covenant. **The Covenanted Service:** The former Indian Civil Service (in reference to the covenant entered into by members with the East India Company and later with the Secretary of State). **covenanter,** *n.* One who enters into a covenant; (*Hist.*) an adherent of the Scottish National Covenant of 1638 or the Solemn League and Covenant of 1643.

Coventry (kov′-, kŭv′ ėn tri) [town in Warwickshire], *n.* **to send one to Coventry:** To refuse to have communication or intercourse with one.

cover (kŭv′ ėr) [O.F. *cuvrir, covrir*, L. *coöperīre* (CO-, *operīre*, to shut)], *v.t.* To overlay; to overspread with something; to overspread with something so as to protect or conceal; to clothe; to hide, cloak, or screen; (*Cricket*) to stand behind so as to stop balls that are missed; to lie over so as to shelter or conceal; (*Bibl.*) to pardon, to put out of remembrance; to save from punishment, to shelter; to incubate; to copulate with a female (of the lower animals); to include; to be enough to defray; to have range or command over; to extend over; to hold under aim with a fire-arm; to protect by insurance; (*Journalism*) to write all that can be ascertained about an episode, subject or event; (*Mil.*) to protect with troops. *v.i.* To be spread over so as to conceal; *to put one's hat on. *n.* Anything which covers or hides; a lid; the outside covering of a book (*often in pl.*); one side or board of this; anything which serves to conceal, screen, disguise; pretence, pretext; shelter, protection; a shelter; the articles necessary for one person at table; a thicket, woods which conceal game; (*Comm.*) sufficient funds to meet a liability or ensure against loss. **coverage, cover,** *n.* The area or the people reached by an advertisement campaign. **cover-charge,** *n.* The amount added to a restaurant bill to cover service. **cover-girl,** *n.* A pretty girl whose photograph is used to illustrate a magazine cover. **under cover:** Enclosed in an envelope addressed to another person. **to cover in:** To fill in; to finish covering. **to cover up:** To conceal. **cover-point,** *n.* (*Cricket*) A fielder or the position behind point. **covered,** *a.* Sheltered, protected; concealed. **covered wagon,** *n.* A type of large wagon with a tent roof used by American settlers to transport their families and belongings. **covered-way, covert-way,** *n.* A sunken area round a fortification between the counterscarp and glacis. **covering,** *n.* That which covers; a cover. **covering letter:** A letter explaining an enclosure.

***coverchief** (kŭv′ ėr chif) [F. *couvre-chef* (*couvrir*, to cover, *chef*, head)], *n.* A head-dress; a kerchief.

coverlet (kŭv′ ėr lėt), **coverlid** (kŭv′ ėr lid) [A.-F. *coverlit* (COVER-, *lit*, bed)], *n.* An outer covering for a bed; a counterpane.

covert (kŭv′ ėrt) [O.F., *p.p.* of *covrir*, to COVER], *a.* Covered; disguised, secret, private; (*Law*) under protection. *n.* A place which covers and shelters; a cover for game. **feme-covert, femme-couvert:** (*Law*) A married woman. **covert-coat,** *n.* A short overcoat. **covert-way** [COVERED-WAY]. **covertly,** *adv.* **coverture,** *n.* Covering, shelter, a hiding-place; secrecy; (*Law*) the state of a married woman, as being under the authority of her husband.

co-vertical (kō vėr′ ti kal), *a.* (*Geom.*) Having common vertices.

covet (kŭv′ et) [A.-F. and O.F. *coveiter* (*L. cupere*, to desire)], *v.t.* To desire (something unlawful) inordinately; to long for. *v.i.* To have an inordinate desire. **covetable,** *a.* ***covetise,** *n.* Covetousness. **covetiveness,** *n.* (*Phren.*) Acquisitiveness. **covetous,** *a.* Eagerly desirous; eager to obtain and possess; avaricious; *aspiring. **covetously,** *adv.* **covetousness,** *n.*

covey (kŭv′ i) [O.F. *covée* (F. *couvée*), fem. p.p. of *couver*, to hatch, L. *cubāre*, to lie down], *n.* A brood or small flock of birds (prop. of partridges); * a small company, a party.

covin (kŭv′ in) [O.F., from late L. *covenium*, a convention (*convenīre*, to CONVENE)], *n.* (*Law*) An agreement between two or more persons to injure or defraud another.

cow (1) (kou) [A.-S. *cu*, from Teut. *kō-* (cp. Dut. *koe*, G. *kuh*, Gael. *bo*, L. *bos*, Gr. *bous*)], *n.* (*pl.* **cows** (kouz), **kine** (kīn)) The female of any bovine species, esp. of the domesticated species *Bos taurus*; a female elephant or cetacean. **cowbane,** *n.* The water-hemlock, *Cicuta virosa.* **cow-**

berry, *n.* The red whortleberry, *Vaccinium vitis-Idæa*; *Vaccinium myrtillus*, the bilberry or whortleberry. **cow-bird,** *n.* (*Am.*) Applied to several species of the genus *Molothrus*, from their haunting cattle. **cowboy,** *n.* A boy who tends cattle; a man in charge of cattle on a ranch. **cow-catcher,** *n.* (*Am.*) An inclined frame attached to the front of a locomotive, etc., to throw obstructions from the track. **cow-fish,** *n.* The sea-cow or manatee; a fish, *Ostracion quadricorne*, with horn-like protuberances over the eyes. **cow-grass,** *n.* A wild trefoil, *Trifolium medium*. **cow-heel,** *n.* The foot of a cow or ox used to make jelly. **cowherd,** *n.* One who tends cattle. **cow-hide,** *n.* The hide of a cow; a whip made of cow-hide; *v.t.* To thrash with a cow-hide. **cow-house,** *n.* A house or shed in which cows are kept. ***cow-leech,** *n.* A cow-doctor. **cow-parsley,** *n.* The cow-weed or wild chervil, *Anthriscus sylvestris*. **cow-parsnip,** *n.* Name of various umbelliferous plants of the genus *Heracleum*, esp. *H. sphondylium*. **cow-pock,** *n.* A pustule or pock of cowpox. **cow-pony,** *n.* (*Am.*) The mustang of a cowboy. **cowpox,** *n.* A vaccine disease affecting the udders of cows, capable of being transferred to human beings, and generally held to confer immunity from smallpox. **cow-puncher,** *n.* (*Am.*) A cowboy. **cow-tree,** *n.* Various milky trees, esp. *Galactodendron utile*. **cow-weed** [COW-PARSLEY]. **cow-wheat,** *n.* The melampyre, *M. pratense*, and other plants of the genus *Melampyrum*. **cowish,** *a.*

cow (2) (kou) [prob. from Icel. *kūga*], *v.t.* To intimidate, to deprive of spirit or courage, to terrify, to daunt. **cowed,** *a.*

cowage, cowhage (kou' ȧj) [Hind. *kawānch*], *n.* The sharp, stinging hairs of a tropical climbing plant, *Macuna pruriens*, used as an anthelmintic.

coward (kou' ȧrd) [O.F. *coart* (It. *codardo*), from *coe* (It. *coda*), a tail, L. *cauda*; see -ARD], *n.* A poltroon; one without courage. *a.* Timid, pusillanimous; (*Her.*) represented with the tail between the legs. **cowardice,** *n.* Extreme timidity; want of courage. **cowardlike,** *a.* **cowardliness,** *n.* The quality of being cowardly. **cowardly,** *adv.* In the manner of a coward. *a.* Craven, faint-hearted, spiritless. ***cowardry,** *n.* Cowardice.

cowboy [COW (1)].

cower (kou' ėr) [etym. doubtful (cp. Icel. *kūra*, to doze, to be quiet, Dan. *kure*, G. *kauern*)], *v.i.* To stoop, to bend, to crouch; to shrink or quail through fear.

cowl (1) (koul) [M.E. *cowle*, *cule*, A.-S. *cugele*, late L. *cucullа*, a frock, L. *cucullus*, a hood (blended with M.E. *covel*, *cuuel*, A.-S. *cufle*, cp. Dut. *keuvel*)], *n.* A hooded garment, esp. one worn by a monk; a hood-like chimney-top, usually movable by the wind, to facilitate the exit of smoke. **cowled,** *a.*

***cowl** (2) (koul) [O.F. *cuvele* (later *cuveau*), a small tub, L. *cūpella*, dim. of *cūpa*, a vat, a large cask], *n.* A water-vessel borne on a pole between two men. **cowling,** *n.* (*Aviat.*) A sheet-metal casing placed so as to direct cooling air on to the cylinders. ***cowl-staff,** *n.* The staff on which a cowl is carried.

cowlick (kou' lik), *n.* A strand of hair brushed across the forehead.

cowpox [COW (1)].

cowry, cowrie (kou' ri) [Hind. *kawrī*, Sansk. *kaparda*], *n.* A gasteropod of the genus *Cypræa*, esp. *Cypræa moneta*, a small shell used as money in many parts of southern Asia and Africa.

cowslip (kou' slip) [A.-S. *cū-slyppe*, cow-dung], *n.* A wild plant with fragrant flowers, *Primula veris*, growing in pastures in England. **cowslip-tea, -wine,** *n.* Beverages made from the flowers.

cox [COXSWAIN].

coxa (kok' sȧ) [L.], *n.* (*Anat. and Zool.*) The hip; the articulation of the leg to the body in arthropoda. **coxal,** *a.* **coxalgia** (coks ăl' jȧ), *n.* (*Path.*) Pain in the hip; hip disease. **coxitis** (kok sī' tis) [-ITIS], *n.* (*Path.*) Inflammation of the hip-joint.

coxcomb (koks' kōm), *n.* *The comb resembling that of a cock formerly worn by jesters; a conceited person, a fop, a dandy; *the head. **coxcombical** (-kō' mik-, -kom' ik-), *a.* **coxcombically,** *adv.* **coxcombly,** *adv.* **coxcombry,** *n.*

coxitis [COXA].

coxswain (koksn, kok' swān) [COCK (4), SWAIN], *n.* One who steers a boat, esp. in a race; (*Naut.*) the petty officer on board ship in charge of a boat and its crew.

coy (koi) [F. *coi* (fem. *coite*), L. *quiētus*, QUIET], *a.* Shrinking from familiarity; modest, shy, reserved; disdainful; simulating reserve, coquettish; sequestered, secluded. **v.t.* To caress. *v.i.* To be shy or reserved; *to disdain; (*fig.*) to withdraw, to recede. **coyly,** *adv.* **coyness,** *n.*

coyote (kȯ yō' ti, -yōt') [Sp., from Mex. *coyotl*], *n.* The Mexican prairie wolf.

coypu (koi poo') [Indian name], *n.* A S.American aquatic rodent, Myopotamus, yielding nutria fur, and since its introduction a pest in East Anglia.

coz (kŭz), *n.* [short for COUSIN].

cozen (kŭzn) [perh. from COUSIN (cp. F. *cousiner*, to claim kindred)], *v.t.* To deceive, to cheat. **cozenage,** *n.* **cozener,** *n.*

***cozier** (kō' zi ėr) [O.F. *cousere*, from *couder*, to sew], *n.* A cobbler.

cozy [COSY].

crab (1) (krăb) [A.-S. *crabba* (cp. Icel. *krabbi*, Dut. *kreeft*, G. *krebs*; also Dut. and L.G. *krabben*, to scratch)], *n.* A decapod crustacean of the genus *Brachyura*, esp. the common crab, *Cancer pagurus*, and other edible species; (*Astron.*) the zodiacal constellation Cancer; a kind of crane; a kind of windlass for hauling ships into dock; a portable capstan; (*pl.*) deuceace or two aces, the lowest throw at hazard. **a case of crabs:** A disagreeable conclusion; failure. **to catch a crab:** (*Rowing*) To sink an oar too deep and be pushed backwards by the resistance of the water; to miss a stroke. **crab-louse,** *n.* An insect, *Phthirius inguinalis*, found on the human body. **crab's-eyes,** *n.pl.* Concretions formed in the stomach of the crayfish. **crab-pot,** *n.* A basket or wicker trap for catching lobsters.

crab (2) (krăb) [cogn. with prec. (cp. Dut. and L.G. *krabben*)], *v.t.* (*Falconry*) To claw, to scratch; (*colloq.*) to criticize savagely, to pull to pieces; to hinder. *v.i.* (*Falconry*) To scratch and claw.

crab (3) (krăb) [etym. doubtful], *n.* A crab-apple; (*fig.*) a peevish, morose person. *a.* Sour, rough, austere. **crab-apple,** *n.* A wild apple, the fruit of *Pyrus malus*; (*Am.*) wild apples of other species. **crab-tree,** *n.*

crabbed (krăb' d) [CRAB (1) (influenced later in sense by CRAB (3))], *a.* Peevish, morose; sour-tempered; harsh, sour; intricate, perplexing, abstruse; cramped, undecipherable. **crabbedly,** *adv.* **crabbedness,** *n.*

crack (krăk) [A.-S. *cracian* (cp. Dut. *kraken* and *krakken*, G. *krachen*, imit. in orig.)], *v.t.* To break without entire separation of the parts; to cause to give a sharp, sudden noise; to say smartly or sententiously; to open and drink (as a bottle of wine); (*in p.p.*) to break with grief, to render insane; *to utter boastfully. *v.i.* To break partially asunder; to be ruined; to fail; to utter a loud sharp sound; to boast, to brag; to change (applied to the changing of voices at puberty); to chat. *n.* A sudden and partial separation of parts; the chink, fissure, or opening so made; a sharp sudden sound or report; a smart blow; *the change of voice at puberty; a chat; *(*pl.*) news; boasting; a boast; (*slang*) a burglar; a burglary; something first-rate; (*colloq.*) a sarcastic joke. *a.* Having qualities to be boasted of; excellent, superior, brilliant. **crack of doom:** The end of the world. **to crack a crib:** (*slang*) To break into a house. **to crack up:** To extol highly, to puff. **to have a crack at:** (*slang*) To have a try, to attempt. **crack-brained,** *a.* Crazy, cracked. ***crack-hemp, *rope,** *n.* One who deserves hanging. **crack-jaw,** *a.* Applied to long or unpronounceable words. **crack-pot,** *n.* A crazy person. **crackable,** *a.* **cracked,** *a.* (*colloq.*) Half-witted; insane. **cracker,** *n.* One who or that which cracks; a form of explosive firework; a thin, brittle, hard-baked biscuit; a bonbon that gives a sharp report in being torn open; an implement for cracking; (*Am.*) a biscuit; *a boaster; (*slang*) a smash; a rattling pace; a lie. **crackers,** *adv.* (*slang*) Crazy.

crackle (krăk′ ėl) [from prec.], *v.i.* To make short, sharp cracking noises. *n.* A rapid succession of slight, sharp noises like cracks; a small crack; a series of such cracks. **crackle-china, -glass, -ware,** *n.* Porcelain or glass covered with a delicate network of cracks; also called **cracklin. crackling,** *a.* Making short, sharp, frequent cracks. *n.* The browned scored skin of roast pork.

cracknel (krăk′ nėl) [corr. of F. *craquelin* (cp. dial. *crackling*)], *n.* A hard, brittle biscuit.

cracksman (krăks′ mȧn) [CRACK (slang), MAN], *n.* A burglar.

***Cracovienne** (krȧ kō′ vi ėn) [F., fem. adj., from *Cracovie*, Cracow], *n.* A light Polish dance.

-cracy [F. *-cratie*, Gr. *-kratia*, from *kratos*, power], *suf.* Government, rule of; influential or dominant by means of; as in *aristocracy, democracy, plutocracy, theocracy.*

cradle (krā′ dėl) [A.-S. *cradol* (etym. doubtful)], *n.* A baby's bed or cot, usu. rocking or swinging; (*fig.*) place of birth or early nurture; infancy; (*Surg.*) a frame to protect a broken or wounded limb in bed; (*Naut.*) a bed or framework of timbers to support a vessel out of water; the apparatus in which sailors are brought to land along a line fastened to a ship in distress; a tool resembling a chisel used for scraping and preparing the plate for mezzotints; a set of fingers in a light frame mortised into a scythe to lay the corn more evenly; (*Mining*) a gold-washing machine; the centering for an arch, culvert, etc. *v.t.* To lay or place in a cradle; to rock to sleep; to nurture or rear from infancy; to receive or hold in or as in a cradle; *to cut and lay (corn) with a cradle. **v.i.* To lie or lodge as in a cradle. **cradle-clothes,** *n.pl.* Swaddling-clothes. **cradle-scythe,** *n.* A broad scythe fitted with a cradle. ***cradle-walk,** *n.* A walk under an avenue of trees. **cradling,** *n.* The act of laying or rocking in a cradle; (*Build.*) a framework of wood or iron; the framework in arched or coved ceilings to which the laths are nailed.

craft (kraft) [A.-S. *cræft* (cp. Dut. *kracht*, Swed., Dan., and G. *kraft*, power)], *n.* Dexterity, skill; cunning, deceit; an art, esp. one applied to useful purposes, a handicraft, occupation or trade; the members of a particular trade; a vessel (*pl.* **craft**). **small craft:** Small vessels of all kinds. **the craft:** The brotherhood of Freemasons; Freemasonry. **the gentle craft:** Angling. **craft-brother,** *n.* One of the same craft or guild. **craft-guild,** *n.* An association of workmen in the same occupation or trade. **craftsman, craftswoman,** *n.* A skilled artisan. **craftsmanship,** *n.*

crafty (kraf′ ti) [see prec.], *a.* Artful, sly, cunning, wily. **craftily,** *adv.* **craftiness,** *n.*

crag (1) (krăg) [cp. W. *craig*, Gael. and Ir. *creag*], *n.* A rugged or precipitous rock. **crag-and-tail,** *n.* (*Geol.*) A rock or hill with a precipitous face on one side and a gradually sloping descent on the other. **cragsman,** *n.* A skilful rock-climber. **cragged,** *a.* **craggedness,** *n.* **craggy,** *a.* Full of crags, rugged, rough; *knotty. **cragginess,** *n.*

***crag** (2) (krăg) [cp. Dut. *kraag*, G. *kragen*], *n.* The neck; (*dial.*) the crop of a fowl.

crag (3) (krăg) [perh. from CRAG (1)], *n.* (*Geol.*) Shelly deposits, esp. in Norfolk, Suffolk, and Essex, of Pliocene age.

crake (krāk) [imit.; cp. CROAK, CROW], *n.* The corncrake; other birds of the same family; their cry. *v.i.* To cry like the corncrake. **crakeberry,** *n.* The black crowberry, *Empetrum nigrum.*

cram (krăm) [A.-S. *crammian*, from *crimman*, to insert (cp. O.H.G. *chrimman*, G. *krimmen*)], *v.t.* To stuff, push, or press in so as to fill to overflowing; to thrust in by force; to coach for examination by storing the pupil's mind with formulæ and answers to probable questions. *v.i.* To eat greedily; to stuff oneself; to get up a subject hastily and superficially, esp. to undergo cramming for examination. *n.* The system of cramming for an examination; information acquired by cramming; a crush, a crowd; (*slang*) a lie. **crammer,** *n.* One who crams; a coach who crams; (*slang*) a lie.

crambo (krăm′ bō) [L. *crambē*, in ref. to Juvenal's *crambē repetīta*, cabbage served up again, Sat. vii. 154], *n.* A game in which one selects a word to which another finds a rhyme. **dumb crambo:** A similar game in which the rhymes are expressed in dumb show.

***cramoisy** (krăm′ oi zi), **cramesy** (krăm′ ė zi) (early It. *cremesi*, and O.F. *crameisi* (later *cramoisi*), Sp. *carmesi*, see CRIMSON], *a.* Crimson. *n.* Crimson cloth.

cramp (1) (krămp) [O.F. *crampe* (cp. Dut. *kramp*; also O.H.G. *krimphan*, G. *krampfen*, to cramp)], *n.* A spasmodic contraction of some limb or muscle, attended with pain and numbness. *v.t.* To affect with cramp. *a.* Cramped, contracted; difficult to read; knotty. **cramp-fish,** *n.* The torpedo fish. **crampness,** *n.* ***cramp-ring, *-stone,** *n.* A ring or stone worn or carried as a preservative against cramp. **to cramp one's style:** (*fig.*) To spoil the effect one is trying to make. **crampedness,** *n.*

cramp (2) (krămp [Dut. *kramp*, see prec.], *n.* A cramp-iron; a clamp; (*fig.*) restraint, a hindrance. *v.t.* To confine closely; to hinder, to restrain; to fasten with a cramp-iron. **cramp-iron,** *n.* (*Masonry*) An iron with bent ends binding two stones together in a course.

crampon (krăm′ pȯn) [F., from late L. *crampo -ōnem*, from L.G. (cp. CRAMP (1 and 2))], *n.* A hooked bar of iron; a grappling-iron; (*Mountaineering*) plate with iron spikes worn on the boots to assist in climbing ice-slopes.

cran (krăn) [Sc., etym. doubtful], *n.* A measure of $37\frac{1}{2}$ gallons by which herrings are sold.

cranage (krān′ ȧj), *n.* The right to use a crane on a wharf; money paid for the use of the crane.

cranberry (krăn′ bėr i) [L.G. *kraanbere* (G. *kranbeere*), introd. by N. Amer. colonists], *n.* The American cranberry, *Vaccinium macrocarpon*; the British marsh whortleberry *V. oxycoccos*, used for tarts.

crance (krăns) [cp. Dut. *krans*, G. *kranz*, CRANTS], *n.* (*Naut.*) A boom-iron, esp. one forming a cap to the bowsprit.

crane (1) (krān) [A.-S. *cran* (cp. Dut. *kraan*, G. *kranich*, Gr. *geranos*, L. *grus*)], *n.* A bird of the genus *Grus*, esp. *G. cinerea*, a migratory wading bird. *v.i.* To stretch out the neck like a crane, esp. before a dangerous leap in hunting. **crane-fly,** *n.* The daddy-long-legs, any fly of the genus *Tipula.* **crane's-bill,** *n.* Various species of wild geranium; (*Surg.*) a pair of long-nosed forceps. **craner,** *n.* (*Hunting*) One who cranes or hesitates at a fence.

crane (2) (krān) [as prec.], *n.* A machine for hoisting and lowering heavy weights; anything similar, as an iron arm turning on a vertical axis, fixed to the back of the fireplace, on which to support a kettle, etc.; a siphon used for drawing liquors from a cask; a pipe for supplying a locomotive with water; (*Naut.*) a projecting pair of brackets in which to stow spare spars. **v.t.* To raise by a crane.

cranio- [L. *crānium*, Gr. *kranion*, the skull], *comb. form.* (*Anat. and Ethn.*) Pertaining to the skull. **craniognomy** (krā ni on′ ō mi) [Gr. *gnōmē*, knowledge], *n.* The science of the peculiarities of the cranium in different races or individuals. **cranio-**

logy (-ol' ŏ ji) [-LOGY], *n.* The scientific study of crania. **craniological** (-loj' ik ăl), *a.* **craniologist** (-ol' ŏ jist), *n.* **craniometer** (-om' ĕ tėr) [-METER], *n.* An instrument for measuring the cubic capacity of skulls. **craniometrical** (-met' rik ăl), *a.* **craniometry** (-om' ĕ tri), *n.* **cranioscopy** (-os' kŏ pi) [-SCOPY], *n.* The examination of the skull for scientific purposes. **craniotomy** (-ot' ŏ mi) [-TOMY], *n.* The operation of opening the head of the fœtus.

cranium (krā' ni ŭm) [L., from Gr. *kranion*], *n.* (*pl.* **-ia**) The skull, esp. the part enclosing the brain. **cranial,** *a.*

crank (1) (krăngk) [A.-S. *cranc*, orig. past of *crincan*, a form of *cringan*, to be bent up], *n.* An arm at right angles to an axis for converting rotary into reciprocating motion, or the converse; an iron elbow-shaped brace for various purposes; a machine formerly used in prisons for inflicting hard labour; (*Motor.*) a handle which turns the shaft of a motor until the pistons reach the maximum of compression. **crank-axle,** *n.* A shaft that turns or is turned by a crank. **crank-pin,** *n.* A cylindrical pin parallel to a shaft and fixed at the outer end of a crank. **crank-shaft,** *n.* A shaft that bears one or more cranks. **to crank up:** (*Motor.*) To start the engine with the crank-handle.

crank (2) (krăngk) [etym. doubtful; perh. conn. with prec.], *n.* (*fig.*) A whimsical turn of speech; a caprice, a whim, a crotchet; a crotchety person, an eccentric.

crank (3) (krăngk) [conn. with CRANK (1) and CRANKY], *a.* Infirm, shaky; (*Mach.*) shaky, liable to break down; (*Naut.*) liable to upset; (*Sc.*) crooked, misshapen.

crank (4) (krăngk) [etym. doubtful], *a.* Brisk, lively. ******adv.* Briskly, vigorously.

crankle (krăngkl) [CRANK (1)], *v.i.* To bend, to twist. *n.* A bend, a twist.

cranky (krăng' ki) [formed from CRANK (1–4) in the various senses], *a.* Irritable, fidgety, whimsical; full of twists; shaky, sickly; (*Naut.*) liable to upset.

crannog (krăn' ŏg) [Ir., from *crann*, a tree, a beam], *n.* (*Archæol.*) A lake-dwelling, common in Scotland and Ireland, built up from the lake bottom on brushwood and piles, and often surrounded by palisades.

cranny (krăn' i) [prob. from F. *cran*, a notch, a chink)], *n.* A crevice, a chink; a corner, a hole. **crannied,** *a.*

crap [CROP].

crape (krāp) [F., CRÊPE], *n.* A gauzy fabric of silk or other material, with a crisped, frizzly surface, usually dyed black, used for mourning; a band of this material worn round the hat as mourning. ******v.t.* To cover, dress, or drape with crape; *to curl, to frizzle. **crape-cloth,** *n.* A woollen fabric made in imitation of silk crape. **crape fern,** *n.* (*N. Zealand*) A handsome, large-fronded fern. **crapy,** *a.*

crappit-head (krăp' it head) [Sc., p.p. of a v. *crap*, not extant (cp. Dut. *krappen*, to cram)], *n.* A haddock's head stuffed with the roe, oatmeal, suet, onions, etc.

craps (krăps) [orig. unknown], *n.pl.* (*Am.*) A game of dice, also known as **crap-shooting.**

crapulent (krăp' ū lėnt) [L. *crāpulentus*, from *crāpula*, drunkenness, Gr. *kraipalē*, nausea, the effect of a debauch], *a.* Surfeited, drunken; given to intemperance. **crapulence,** *n.* **crapulous,** *a.*

crash (1) (krăsh) [imit. (cp. CRACK, CRAZE)], *v.t.* To break to pieces with violence; to dash together violently. *v.i.* To make a loud smashing noise; (*Aviat.*) to crash in landing; (*colloq.*) to go to a party uninvited, to intrude. *n.* A loud sudden noise, as of many things broken at once; a violent smash; a sudden failure, collapse, bankruptcy. **crash dive,** *n.* (*Naut.*) A submarine's sudden and rapid dive, usu. to avoid an enemy. **crash helmet:** (*Aviat.*, *Motor.*) A helmet padded with resilient cushions, to protect the head in the event of accident.

crash (2) (krăsh) [etym. doubtful], *n.* A coarse linen cloth used for towelling or packing cloth.

crasis (krā' sis) [Gr., a mixture, a blending, from *kerannunai*, to mix], *n.* (*Gram.*) The contracting of the vowels of two syllables into one long vowel or diphthong; the mixture of the constituents of the blood. **crasial** (krā' si ăl), *a.*

crass (krăs) [L. *crassus*], *a.* Thick, coarse, gross, stupid, obtuse. ***crassitude,** *n.* Crassness. **crassly,** *adv.* **crassness,** *n.*

-crat [F. *-crate*, Gr. *-kratēs* (cf. *-kratia*, -CRACY)], *suf.* A partisan, a supporter, a member, as *autocrat*, *democrat*, *plutocrat*.

cratægus (krȧ tē' gŭs) [L., from Gr. *krataigos*], *n.* (*Bot.*) A genus of thorny trees containing the hawthorns.

cratch (krăch) [O.F. *creche* (F. *crèche*), O.H.G. *chrippa*], *n.* A manger, a hay-rack, esp. for feeding animals out of doors.

crate (krāt) [L. *crātes*, or Dut. *krat*], *n.* A large wicker case for packing crockery; an open framework of wood for packing cycles, bottles, etc. **crateful,** *n.*

crater (krā' tėr) [L., from Gr. *kratēr*, a bowl for mixing wine (*kerannunai*, to mix)], *n.* The mouth of a volcano; a funnel-shaped cavity; a large cavity formed in the ground by the explosion of a shell or bomb. **crateriform,** *a.*

cravat (krȧ văt') [F. *cravate*, orig. a Croat, G. *krabate*, Croatian], *n.* A neckcloth for men (introd. into France by the Croats); a tie.

crave (krāv) [A.-S. *crafian*], *v.t.* To ask for earnestly and submissively; to beg, to beseech, to entreat; to long for; to require. *v.t.* To beg; to long (for). ***craver,** *n.* **cravingly,** *adv.*

craven (krā'vėn) [M.E. *crauant*, prob. from O.F. *cravant*, pres.p. of *craver* (*crever*), to burst, break, overcome], *n.* *One who is overcome; a word cried by the vanquished one in the ancient trial by battle; a coward, a recreant, a dastard. *v.t.* To make craven. *a.* Cowardly, faint-hearted. **cravenly,** *adv.* **to cry craven:** To surrender.

craw (kraw) [cogn. with Dut. *kraag*, the neck], *n.* The crop or first stomach of fowls or insects.

crawfish [CRAYFISH].

crawl (1) (krawl) [prob. from Scand. (cp. Icel. and Swed. *krafla*, to grop, Dan. *kravle*, to crawl)], *v.i.* To move slowly along the ground; to creep; to move slowly; to assume an abject posture or manner; to get on by meanness and servility; to have a sensation as though insects were creeping over the flesh. *n.* The act of crawling; a racing stroke in swimming. **crawler,** *n.* One that crawls, a reptile. **crawlingly,** *adv.* **crawly,** *a.*

crawl (2) [Dut. *kraal*], *n.* An enclosure in shallow water for keeping fish, turtles, etc., alive.

***crayer, crare** (krâr) [O.F. *craier*, low L. *craiera*, *creyera* (etym. unknown)], *n.* A kind of trading ship.

crayfish (krā' fish), **crawfish** (kraw' fish) [M.E. *crevice*, O.F. *crevisse*, *crevice* (F. *écrevisse*), O.H.G. *crebiz* (cp. CRAB)], *n.* The freshwater lobster, *Astacus fluviatilis*; the spiny lobster, *Palinurus vulgaris*; *any kind of crab.

crayon (krā' ŏn) [F., from *craie*, L. *crēta*, chalk], *n.* A pencil of coloured chalk or similar material; a drawing made with crayons; the carbon pencil of an electric arc-lamp. *v.t.* To draw with crayons; to sketch. **crayon-drawing,** *n.* The act, art, or result of drawing in crayons.

craze (krāz) [perh. from Swed. *krasa* (cp. F. *écraser*)], *v.t.* To derange the intellect; to make cracks or flaws in (china, etc.); *to break, to shatter. ******v.i.* To become weakened or impaired; to become cracked (as the glaze on pottery); to go mad. *n.* A mania, an extravagant idea or enthusiasm, a rage;

madness; a flaw, impaired condition. **crazed,** *a.* Deranged in intellect. **crazing-mill,** *n.* One for crushing tin-ore. **crazy,** *a.* Broken down, feeble; unsound, shaky; broken-witted, deranged. **crazy bone,** *n.* (*Am.*) The funny-bone. **crazy paving,** *n.* A pavement of irregularly-shaped flat stones. **crazily,** *adv.* **craziness,** *n.*

creagh, creach (krā*ch*) [Gael. and Ir. *creach,* plunder], *n.* A Highland raid; booty. *v.t.* To plunder.

creak (krēk) [imit. (cp. CRAKE, CRACK)], *v.i.* To make a continued sharp grating noise. **v.t.* To cause to make such a noise. *n.* A creaking sound. **creaky,** *a.*

cream (krēm) [F. *crème,* O.F. *cresme* (see CHRISM)], *n.* The oily part of milk which rises and collects on the surface; a sweet-meat or dish prepared from cream; (*fig.*) a cream-coloured horse; the best part of anything; essence or quintessence. *v.t.* To skim cream from; to add cream to; (*fig.*) to remove the best part from. *v.i.* To gather cream; to mantle or froth. **cold cream,** *n.* A cooling unguent. **cream-cake,** *n.* A cake with custard inside. **cream-cheese,** *n.* A soft cheese made of unskimmed milk and cream, (*Am.*) cottage cheese. **cream-coloured,** *a.* Yellowish white. ***cream-faced,** *a.* Pale or colourless. **cream-fruit,** *n.* A juicy fruit from Sierra Leone. **cream-laid,** *a.* Applied to laid paper of a creamy colour. **cream of lime,** *n.* A creamy mixture of slaked lime and water. **cream of tartar,** *n.* Purified potassium bitartrate. **cream-separator,** *n.* A machine for separating cream from milk. **cream-wove,** *a.* Applied to woven paper of a cream colour. **creamer,** *n.* A flat dish used for skimming the cream off milk; a separating machine. **creamery,** *n.* A shop for the sale of dairy produce and light refreshments; an establishment where cream is bought and made into butter. **creamy,** *a.* **creaminess,** *n.*

***creance** (krē' ans) [O.F., from L. (as CREDENCE)], *n.* Faith, credit; (*Falconry*) a fine line fastened to a hawk's leash when she is first lured.

crease (1) (krēs) [etym. doubtful], *n.* A line or mark made by folding or doubling; (*Cricket*) a line on the ground marking the position of bowler and batsman at each wicket. *v.t.* To make a crease or mark in; (*Am.*) to shoot in the neck (as a wild horse), so as to cut the skin without doing serious injury. *v.i.* To become creased or wrinkled. **creaser,** *n.* **creasy,** *a.*

crease (2) [CREESE].

create (krē āt') [L. *creātus,* p.p. of *creāre*], *v.t.* To cause to exist; to produce, to bring into existence; to be the occasion of; to originate; to invest with a new character, office, or dignity; (*colloq.*) to make a fuss; to cause a disturbance. **a.* Brought into existence; composed. **creative,** *a.* **creatively,** *adv.* **creativeness,** *n.*

creatine (krē' ȧ tin) [Gr. *kreas, -atos,* meat], *n.* (*Chem.*) An organic substance obtained from muscular fibre.

creation (krē ā' shŭn) [F., from L. *creātio -ōnem* (*creāre,* to CREATE)], *n.* The act of creating, esp. creating the world; that which is created or produced; the universe, the world, all created things; the act of appointing, constituting, or investing with a new character or position; a production of art, craft, or intellect. ***creational,** *a.* **creationism,** *n.* The doctrine that a human soul is created for each human being at birth; the theory that the universe was brought into existence out of nothing by God, and that new forms and species are the results of special creations. **creator,** *n.* One who or that which creates; a maker; the Maker of the Universe.

creature (krē' chėr) [F. *créature,* L. *creatūra,* as prec.], *n.* That which is created; a living being; an animal, esp. as distinct from a human being; a person (as an epithet of pity, or endearment); one who owes his rise or fortune to another; an instrument. *a.* Of or pertaining to the body. **creature comforts:** Those pertaining to the body, esp. food and drink. **the creature:** Drink, liquor, esp. whisky. **creaturely,** *a.* Of or pertaining to the creature; having the nature or qualities of a creature.

crèche (krāsh) [F.], *n.* A public nursery in which children are taken care of while their parents are at work.

credence (krē' dėns) [F., from med. L. *crēdentia* (*crēdere,* to believe)], *n.* Belief, credit; reliance, confidence; that which gives a claim to credit or confidence; a credence table. **credence-table,** *n.* A small table or shelf near the (south) side of the altar (or communion table) to receive the eucharistic elements before consecration. ***credent,** *a.* Giving credence; bearing credit. **credently,** *adv.*

credential (kre den' shȧl), *a.* Giving a title to credit; accredited. *n.* Anything which gives a title to confidence; (*pl.*) certificates or letters accrediting any person or persons.

credible (kred' ibl), *a.* Deserving of or entitled to belief. **credibility,** *n.* **credibly,** *adv.*

credit (kred' it) [F. *crédit,* It. *credito,* L. *crēditus -um,* p.p. of *crēdere,* as prec.], *n.* Belief, trust, faith; a reputation inspiring trust or confidence, esp. a reputation for solvency; anything due to any person; trust reposed with regard to property handed over on the promise of payment at a future time; the time given for payment of goods sold on trust; a source or cause of honour, esteem, or reputation; the side of an account in which payment is entered, opposed to debit; an entry on this side of a payment received. *v.t.* To believe; to set to the credit of (*to* the person); to give credit for (*with* the amount); to believe (a person) to possess something; to ascribe to. **credit squeeze,** *n.* Government restrictions imposed on banks to limit their loans to clients. **letter of credit:** An order authorizing a person to draw money from an agent. **public credit:** The faith in the honesty and financial ability of a government seeking to borrow money. ***crédit foncier*** (krā dē' fon syā') [F.], *n.* A company for promoting improvements by means of loans on real estate ***crédit mobilier*** (krā dē' mō bē' lyā') [F.], *n.* A company for banking purposes, and for the promotion of public works by means of loans on personal estate.

creditable (kred' it ȧbl), *a.* Bringing credit or honour. **creditability,** *n.* **creditableness,** *n.* **creditably,** adv.

creditor (kred' i tȯr), *n.* One to whom a debt is due; (*Book-keeping*) the side of an account on which receipts are entered.

credo (krē' dō) [L., I believe], *n.* The first word of the Apostles' and the Nicene Creed; hence either of these creeds; the Nicene Creed, said in the Mass; (*Mus.*) a setting of the Nicene Creed; (*fig.*) the statement of a belief.

credulous (kred' ū lŭs) [L. *crēdulus* (*crēdere,* to believe)], *a.* Disposed to believe, esp. without sufficient evidence; characterized by or due to such disposition. **credulity** (krė dū' li ti), *n.* **credulously** (kred'-), *adv.* **credulousness,** *n.*

creed (krēd) [A.-S. *crēda,* L. *crēdo*], *n.* A brief summary of the articles of religious belief; any system or solemn profession of religious or other belief or opinions. **v.t.* To believe.

creek (krēk) [etym. doubtful (cp. O.F. *crique,* Dut. *krēke, kreek,* Swed. *krik,* Icel. *kriki*)], *n.* A small inlet, bay, or harbour, on the coast; a backwater or arm of a river; (*Am. and Austral.*) a small river, esp. a tributary; a narrow strip of land between mountains; *a narrow winding passage. ***creeky,** *a.*

creel (krēl) [Sc., etym. doubtful], *n.* An osier basket; a fisherman's basket.

creep (krēp) [A.-S. *creōpan,* from Teut. *creup-* (cp. Dut. *kruipen,* Swed. *krypa*)], *v.i.* (*past* & *p.p.* **crept**) To crawl along the ground as a serpent; to grow along, as a creeping plant; to move slowly and insensibly, stealthily, or with timidity; to gain admission unobserved; to behave with servility; to fawn; to have a sensation of shivering or shrinking as from fear or repugnance; (*Naut.*) to drag with a creeper at the bottom of the water. *n.* Creeping; a slow, almost imperceptible movement; a place for creeping through; a low arch or passage for animals; (*pl.*) a feeling of shrinking horror. **creep-hole,** *n.* A hole into which an animal may creep to escape danger; (*fig.*) a subterfuge, an excuse. **creeper,** *n.* One who or that which creeps or crawls; any animal that creeps; a reptile; a parasitic insect; a kind of patten worn by women; a small spike attached to a boot to prevent slipping on ice; a plant with a creeping stem; (*Naut.*) a four-clawed grapnel used in dragging a harbour, pond, or well. **creeping jenny** [MONEYWORT]. **creepingly,** *adv.* **creep-mouse,** *a.* Shy, timid; sly, furtive. *n.* A childish game. **creepy,** *a.* Having the sensation of creeping of the flesh; causing this sensation; characterized by creeping. **creepy-crawly,** *a.* Creepy.

creese (krēs) [Malay *krīs*], *n.* A Malayan dagger with a wavy blade.

***creesh** (krēsh) [Sc., from O.F. *craisse*, grease], *n.* Grease, fat; a stroke, a smack. *v.t.* To grease. **creeshy,** *a.*

cremate (krė māt') [L. *cremātus*, p.p. of *cremāre*, to burn], *v.t.* To burn; to dispose of a corpse by burning. **cremation,** *n.* **cremationist,** *n.* **cremator,** *n.* One who cremates a dead body; a furnace for consuming corpses or rubbish. **crematorium** (-tôr' i ŭm), *n.* A place where bodies are cremated. **crematory** (krem'-), *a.* Employed in or connected with cremation. *n.* A crematorium.

crème (krām) [F., CREAM], *n.* ***crème de menthe,*** *n.* A liqueur made with peppermint. ***crème de la crème:*** The pick, the most select, the élite.

Cremona (1) (krė mō' nȧ) [town in the north of Italy], *n.* A violin made at Cremona, by the Stradivarii, the Amatis, or their pupils.

cremona (2) [CROMORNE].

crenate, -nated (krē' nāt, nā tėd) [late L. *crēna*, a notch], *a.* Notched; (*Bot. and Zool.*) having the edge notched. **crenation** (-nā' shŭn), *n.* **crenature** (krē' nȧ, kren' ȧ tūr), *n.* A scallop; a crenel; a small rounded tooth on the edge of a leaf. **crenato-,** *comb. form.* (*Bot. and Zool.*) Notched.

crenel (kren' ėl), **crenelle** (krė nel') [O.F. *crenel* (F. *créneau*), dim. of *cren, crena* (as prec.)], *n.* A loophole through which to discharge musketry; a battlement; (*Bot.*) a crenature. **crenellate** (kren' ė lāt) [F. *créneler* (as prec.)], *v.t.* To furnish with battlements or loopholes. **crenellation** (-lā' shŭn), *n.*

crenic (krē' nik) [Gr. *krēnē*, spring], *a.* (*Chem.*) Applied to an acid found in humus and in spirits from ferruginous springs. **crenitic** (krē nit' ĭk), *a.* (*Geol.*) Formed by or pertaining to the action of springs.

crenulate (kren' ū lȧt) [late L. *crēnula*, dim. of *crēna*, notch, -ATE], *a.* Finely crenate, notched, or scalloped (of the edges of leaves, shells, etc.). **crenulated,** *a.* **crenulation** (-lā' shŭn), *n.*

creole (krē' ōl) [F. *créole*, Sp. *criollo*, prob. a negro corr. of *criadillo*, dim of *criado*, instructed, bred, p.p. of *criar*, to create], *n.* One born of European parentage in the West Indies or Spanish America; (*Louisiana*) a native descended from French or Spanish ancestors; a Negro born in the country as distinguished from one brought from Africa. *a.* Relating to the Creoles. **creolize,** *v.t.* **creolization** (-zā' shŭn), *n.*

creophagous (krė of' ȧ gŭs) [Gr. *kreas -atos*, -PHAGOUS], *a.* Carnivorous, flesh-eating. **creophagist** (-jist), *n.* **creophagy,** *n.*

creosote (krē' ō sōt) [Gr. *kreas -atos*, flesh, *sōt* (*sōtēr*, saviour), from *sōzein*, to save, preserve], *n.* A liquid distilled from coal-tar, used for preserving wood, etc. *v.t.* To saturate (as woodwork) with creosote. **creosote-bush, -plant,** *n.* A Mexican shrub, *Larrea Mexicana*, smelling of creosote.

crêpe (krāp) [F., from L. *crispa*, curled], *n.* Crape; a crapy fabric other than mourning crape. **crêpe de Chine** (dė shēn') [F., Chinese crape], *n.* Crape manufactured from raw silk. **crêpe rubber,** *n.* Rubber with a rough surface used for shoe soles, etc. ***crêpé*** (krā pā), *a.* Frizzled. **crêpy,** *a.*

crepitate (krep' i tāt) [L. *crepitātus*, p.p. of *crepitāre*, freq. of *crepāre*, to creak], *v.i.* To crackle; to burst with a series of short, sharp reports, as salt in fire; to rattle. **crepitant,** *a.* Crackling. **crepitation** (-tā' shŭn), *n.*

crêpon (krep' on) [F., as CRÊPE], *n.* A mixed stuff of silk and wool, resembling crape.

crept, *past and p.p.* [CREEP].

***crepuscle, -cule** (krep' ŭsl, -ŭs kūl) [F. *crépuscule*, L. *crepusculum*], *n.* Morning or evening twilight. **crepuscular** (krė pŭs' kū lȧr), *a.* Pertaining to or connected with twilight; glimmering, indistinct, obscure; (*Zool.*) appearing or flying about at twilight.

crescendo (krė shen' dō) [It., pres.p. of *crescere*, to grow (see foll.)], *n.* (*Mus.*) A gradual increase in the force of sound; (*fig.*) a gradual increase in force or effect. *adv.* (*Mus.*) With an increasing volume of sound.

crescent (kre' sėnt) [L. *crēscens -ntem*, pres.p. of *crēscere*, to grow (incept. of *creāre*, to CREATE)], *a.* Increasing, growing; shaped like a new moon. *n.* The increasing moon in her first quarter; a figure like the new moon; the Turkish power; Mohammedanism; a row of buildings in crescent form; (*Her.*) a bearing in the form of a half-moon; a military order with a half-moon for a symbol. **Red Crescent:** The equivalent institution in Moslem countries to the Red Cross.

cress (kres) [A.-S. *cærse*, from Teut. *kras-* (*cp.* Dut. *kers*, G. *kresse*, F. *kresson*; O.H.G. *chresan*, to creep)], *n.* A name for various cruciferous plants with a pungent taste [see WATER-CRESS].

cresset (kres' ėt) [O.F. *cresset*, *craisset*, from *craisse*, CREESH], *n.* *A metal cup or vessel, usu. on a pole, for holding oil for a light; a frame of open ironwork to contain a fire for a beacon; a torch; a brilliant light.

crest (krest) [O.F. *criste*, L. *crista*], *n.* A plume or comb on the head of a bird; any tuft on the head of an animal; a plume or tuft of feathers, esp. affixed to the top of a helmet; the apex of a helmet; (*Her.*) any figure placed above the shield in a coat-of-arms; the same printed on paper or painted on a building, etc.; the summit of a mountain or hill; the top of a ridge; the line of the top of the neck in animals; the ridge of a wave; (*Anat.*) a ridge on a bone; (*fig.*) spirit, courage. *v.t.* To ornament or furnish with a crest; to serve as a crest to; to attain the crest of a hill; *to mark with lines or streaks. *v.i.* To rise into a crest or ridge. **crestfallen,** *a.* Dispirited, abashed. **crestfallenly,** *adv.* **crestfallenness,** *n.* **crested,** *a.* Adorned with or wearing a crest. **crestless,** *a.* Not entitled to a crest; not of gentle family. **crestlet,** *n.*

cretaceous (krē tā' shŭs) [L. *crētāceus*, from *crēta*, chalk], *a.* Of the nature of or abounding in chalk. **cretaceous formation,** *n.* (*Geol.*) The uppermost member of the Mesozoic rocks.

cretic (krē' tik) [L. *crēticus*, from *crēta*, Crete], *n.* A metrical foot consisting of a short syllable preceded and followed by a long syllable; also called an amphimacer.

cretin (krē' tin) [F. *crétin*, Swiss patois *crestin*, *creitin*, L. *Christiānum*, Christian], *n.* The name given in the Valais and other Alpine regions to one suffering from a particular kind of idiocy prevalent there; a person mentally and physically deficient. **cretinism,** *n.* **cretinize,** *v.t.* **cretinous,** *a.*

cretonne (kret' ŏn, krė ton') [F., from *Creton*, a village in Normandy], *n.* A cotton fabric with pictorial patterns, used for upholstering, frocks, etc.

crevasse (krė vȧs') [F., see foll.], *n.* A deep fissure in a glacier; (*Am.*) a break in an embankment or levee of a river.

crevice (krev′ is) [M.E. and O.F. *crevace* (F. *crevasse*), late L. *crepātia*, from *crepāre*, to crackle, to burst], *n.* A crack, a cleft, a fissure. **creviced,** *a.*

crew (1) (kroo) [from O.F. *creue*, p.p. of *croistre*, (F. *croître*), to grow; or from O.F. *acreue*, ACCRUE (*acrewe*, eventually becoming *a crew*)], *n.* The company of seamen manning a ship or boat; a number of persons associated for any purpose; a gang, a mob. **crew cut,** *n.* A close style of hair-cut.

crew (2), *past* [CROW (2)].

crewel (kroo′ ėl) [etym. unknown], *n.* Fine two-threaded worsted; embroidery worked with such thread. **crewel-work,** *n.*

*__crewels__ (kroo′ ėlz) [Sc., from F. *écrouelles*, scrofula], *n.* The king's-evil.

crib (krib) [A.-S. (cp. Dut. *krib*, O.H.G. *krippha*, G. *krippe*, Icel. and Swed. *krubba*)], *n.* A rack or manger; a stall for cattle; a child's cot; a small cottage, a hut, a hovel; a wicker salmon-trap; (*Eccles.*) a model of the Nativity scene placed in churches at Christmas; (*Mining*) a timber framework lining a shaft; (*Am.*) a bin for grain; a salt-box; cribbage; a hand at cribbage made up of two cards thrown out by each player; (*colloq.*) anything stolen; a plagiarism; a translation of or key to an author, used by schoolboys and students; a situation, place, berth. *v.t.* To shut up in a crib; *to confine; (*colloq.*) to steal, to appropriate; to plagiarize; to copy from a translation. *v.i.* To bite the crib (of horses). **crib-biting,** *n.* A bad habit in some horses of biting the crib, occasioned by uneasiness in breeding teeth or from being ill-fed. **cribbing,** *n.* The act of enclosing in a crib or narrow place; stealing, plagiarizing; (*Mining*) internal lining of a shaft to prevent caving in.

cribbage (krib′ ȧj), *n.* A game at cards for two, three, or four players. **cribbage-board,** *n.* A board on which the progress of the game is marked.

cribriform (krib′ ri fôrm) [L. *cribrum*, a sieve, -FORM], *a.* (*Anat. and Bot.*) Resembling a sieve; perforated like a sieve. **cribrate, cribrose,** *a.*

crick (krik) [prob. onomat.], *n.* A spasmodic affection from stiffness, esp. of the neck or back. *v.t.* To cause a crick to.

cricket (1) (krik′ ėt) [O.F. *criquet*, from *criquer*, to creak (imit.)], *n.* Any insect of the genus *Acheta*; the house-cricket, well known from its chirp is *A. domestica*, and the field-cricket *A. campestris*.

cricket (2) (krik′ ėt) [etym. doubtful (perh. from O.F. *criquet*, a stick serving as a mark in some game with a ball)], *n.* An open-air game played by two sides of eleven each, consisting of an attempt to strike with a ball wickets defended by the opponents with bats. *v.i.* To play cricket. **not cricket:** (*fig.*) Unfair, not straightforward. **cricketer,** *n.*

cricket (3) (krik′ ėt) [etym. unknown], *n.* A low, wooden stool.

cricoid (krī′ koid) [Gr. *krikoeidēs* (*krikos*, *kirkos*, a ring, -OID)], *a.* (*Anat.*) Ring-like. **cricoid cartilage,** *n.* The cartilage at the top of the trachea.

crier (krī′ ėr) [O.F. *criere*, *crieur*, from *crier*, to CRY], *n.* One who cries or proclaims. **town-crier,** *n.* An officer who makes public proclamation of sales, lost articles, etc.

crikey (krī′ ki) [perh. euphem. for L. *Christe*, O Christ], *int.* An expression of astonishment.

crim. con. [CRIMINAL CONVERSATION].

crime (krīm) [F., from L. *crīmen* (*cernere*, to decide, cp. Gr. *krinein*, to separate, *krīma*, a decision], *n.* A ground of accusation; a charge; an act contrary to law, human or divine; any act of wickedness or sin; wrong-doing, sin; (*Mil.*) any offence or breach of regulations. **capital crime:** A crime punishable with death. ***crimeful,** *a.* Criminal, wicked. **crimeless,** *a.*

criminal (krim′ in ȧl), *a.* Of the nature of a crime; contrary to duty, law, or right; guilty of a crime; tainted with crime. *n.* One guilty of a crime; a convict. **criminal conversation:** (*Law*) Adultery (*abbr.* **crim. con.**). **Criminal Investigation Department, C.I.D.:** The detective branch of the Metropolitan Police, Scotland Yard. **criminality** (-năl′ i ti), *n.* **criminally,** *adv.*

criminate (krim′ in āt), *v.t.* To accuse of a crime; to prove guilty of a crime; to blame, to condemn. **crimination** (nā′ shŭn), *n.* **criminative** (krim′-), *a.* **criminatory,** *a.*

criminography, criminology (krim in og′ rȧ fi, -ol′ ō ji), *n.* The science of crime.

criminous (krim′ in ŭs), *a.* Guilty of a crime, criminal. **criminousness,** *n.*

crimp (1) (krimp) [cp. CRAMP], *v.t.* To curl; to compress into ridges or folds, to frill; to corrugate, to flute, to crease; to cause to contract and become crisp and firm, as the flesh of live fish, by gashing it with a knife; to compress so as to shape or mould. **crimping-iron, -machine,** *n.* An instrument or machine for fluting cap fronts, frills, etc. **crimpy,** *a.*

crimp (2) (krimp) [etym. doubtful], *n.* One who decoys men for military, naval, or maritime service; a decoy, a disreputable agent. *v.t.* To decoy into the military or naval service.

crimson (krim′ zŏn) [Sp. *cremesin*, *carmesi*, Arab. *qirmazī*, see also CRAMOISY], *n.* A deep red colour. *a.* Of this colour. *v.t.* To dye with this colour. *v.i.* To turn crimson; to blush.

crinal (krī′ nȧl) [L. *crīnālis*, from *crīnis*, hair], *a.* Of or pertaining to the hair.

cringe (krinj) [M.E. *crengen*, causal from *cringan*, to sink, to fall], *v.i.* To bend humbly to any one; to crouch, to fawn; to pay servile court. **v.t.* To contract, to draw together, to distort. *n.* Servile court or flattery; an obsequious action. **cringer,** ***cringeling,** *n.* One who cringes.

cringle (kring′ gėl) [cp. L.G. *kringel*, dim. of *kring*, a circle, a ring; cogn, with CRANK, CRINKLE], *n.* (*Naut.*) An iron ring on the bolt-rope of a sail, for the attachment of a bridle.

crinite (krī′ nīt) [L. *crīnītus*, from *crīnis*, hair], *a.* Hairy; resembling a tuft of hair; (*Bot. and Zool.*) covered with hair in small tufts. ***crinitory,** *a.* Relating to or consisting of hair.

crinkle (kring′kėl) [A.-S. *crinkan*, cp. CRANK, CRINGE], *v.i.* To wind in and out; to make short frequent bends and turns. *v.t.* To wrinkle; to form with frequent bends or turns; to mould into inequalities. *n.* A wrinkle, a twist; a short bend or turn. **crinkly,** *a.* **crinkle-crankle,** *n.* A twisting, a wavy line, a zigzag. *a.* and *adv.* Zigzag; (twisting) in and out. **crinkum-crankum** (kring′ kŭm krăng′ kŭm), *n.* A crooked, twisted figure; a zigzag. *a.* Full of twists and turns.

crinoid (krin′ oid) [Gr. *krinoeidēs* (*krinon*, a lily, -OID)], *a.* (*Zool.*) Lily-shaped. *n.* Any individual of the *Crinoidea*. **crinoidal,** *a.* Pertaining to or containing crinoids. **crinoidal limestone,** *n.* (*Geol.*) Carboniferous limestone studded with the broken joints of encrinites. ***Crinoidea,*** *n.pl.* (*Zool.*) An order of echinoderms, containing the sea-lilies and hair-stars.

crinolette (krin ō let′) [F., dim. of foll.], *n.* A kind of bustle for distending a woman's skirts behind. **crinoletted,** *a.*

crinoline (krin′ ō lin) [F. (*crin*, L. *crīnis*, hair; *lin*, L. *līnum*, flax)], *n.* A stiff fabric of horsehair formerly used for petticoats; a petticoat of this material; any stiff petticoat used to expand the skirts of a dress; a large hooped skirt, originally worn in the mid-19th century; the whale-bone hoops for such skirt; a series of nets extended round a warship to keep off torpedoes.

crio- [Gr. *krios*, a ram], *comb. form.* **crio-sphinx** (krī′ ō sfingks) [SPHINX], *n.* A sphinx with a ram's head.

cripple (krip′ ėl) [A.-S. *crypel*, conn. with *crēopan*, to creep, from O.Teut. *kruipan*], *n.* A lame person;

one who creeps, halts, or limps; a rough staging such as is used for window-cleaning; (*Carp.*) a makeshift contrivance. *v.t.* To make lame; to deprive of the use of the limbs; to deprive of the power of action. ***v.i.** To walk like a cripple. **crippledom**, *n.* **cripplehood**, *n.*

crisis (krī′ sis) [L., from Gr. *krisis*, a separating, a decision, from *krinein*, to decide], *n.* (*pl.* **crises** (krī′ sēz)) The turning-point, esp. that of a disease indicating recovery or death; a momentous juncture in war, politics, commerce, domestic affairs, etc.

crisp (krisp) [A.-S., from L. *crispus*, curled], *a.* Firm but brittle, fragile; fresh-looking, cheerful, brisk; curt, sharp, decisive; *curled; *twisting, rippling. *v.t.* To curl, to wrinkle, to ripple, to interlace. *v.i.* To become curly; to become crisp. **crisped**, *a.* **crisper**, *n.* One who or that which curls or crisps; an instrument for crisping the nap of cloth; a crisping-iron. ***crisping-iron**, ***-pin**, *n.* An iron or pin for crisping or crimping the hair. **crisply**, *adv.* **crispness**, *n.* ***crispy**, *a.* Curled, curling; wavy; crisp. **crisps**, *n.pl.* Fried slices of potato.

crispate (kris′ pāt) [L. *crispātus*, p.p. of *crispāre*, as prec.], *a.* (*Bot. and Zool.*) Curled or wrinkled at the edges. ***crispation** (-pā′ shŭn), *n.*

crispin (kris′ pin) [L. *Crispinus*], *n.* A shoemaker, from the patron saint of the craft.

criss-cross [CHRIST-CROSS-ROW, CHRIST].

cristate (kris′ tāt) [L. *cristātus*, from *crista*, a crest], *a.* (*Nat. Hist.*) Having a crest; tufted with hairs.

criterion (krī tēr′ i ŏn) [Gr., as foll.], *n.* (*pl.* **-ia**) A principle or standard by which anything is or can be judged.

critic (krit′ ik) [L. *criticus*, Gr. *kritikos* (*kritēs*, a judge, from *krinein*, to judge)], *n.* A judge, an examiner; a censurer, a caviller; one skilled in judging of literary or artistic merit; a reviewer. **critical**, *a.* Pertaining to criticism; competent to criticize; fastidious, exacting, captious; indicating a crisis; decisive, hazardous; attended with danger or risk; (*Math.*) relating to points of coincidence or transition. **critically**, *adv.* ***criticalness**, *n.* **criticaster** [-ASTER], *n.* A petty or contemptible critic.

criticism (kri′ ti sizm), *n.* The act of judging, esp. literary or artistic works; a critical essay or opinion; the work of criticizing. **higher criticism:** (*Bibl.*) A critical study of authenticity and the literary and historical aspects of the Scriptures. **textual criticism:** A critical study of the words to test their correctness and meaning.

criticize (kri′ ti sīz), *v.t.* To examine critically and deliver an opinion upon; to censure. *v.i.* To play the critic. **criticizable**, *a.*

critico- *comb. form.* Critically; with criticism.

critique (kri tēk′) A critical essay or judgement; the art of criticism; (*Phil.*) the analysis of the basis of knowledge.

croak (krōk) [prob. imit.], *v.i.* To make a hoarse low sound in the throat, as a frog or a raven; to grumble, to forbode evil; (*slang*) to die. *v.t.* To utter in a low hoarse voice. *n.* The low harsh sound made by a frog or a raven. **croaker**, *n.* One who croaks; a querulous person; (*slang*) a dying person. **croaky**, *a.* Croaking, hoarse.

Croat (krō′ ăt) [O.Slav. *Khruvat*], *n.* A native of Croatia; one of the irregular cavalry in the Austrian service which were largely recruited from Croats. **Croatian** (krō ā′ shăn), *a.* and *n.*

croceate (krō′ sė āt, -shė āt), **croceous** (krō′ sė ŭs, -shė ŭs) [L. *croceus*, saffron], *a.* Of or like saffron; (*Bot.*) saffron-coloured.

crochet (krō′ shā) [F., dim. of *croche*, a hook], *n.* A kind of knitting performed with a hooked needle. *v.t.* To knit or make in crochet. *v.i.* To knit in this manner. **crocheting** (krō′ shā ing), *pres.p.* **crocheted** (krō′ shād), *a.*

crocidolite (krō sid′ ō līt) [Gr. *krokis -idos*, the nap of cloth, -LITE], *n.* A silky fibrous silicate of iron and sodium, also called blue asbestos; a yellow form of this used as a gem or ornament.

crock (1) (krok) [A.-S. *crocca* (cp. O.Ir. *crocan*, Gael. *crog*, Icel. *krukka*, Dut. *kruik*, G. *krug*)], *n.* An earthenware vessel; a pot, a pitcher, a jar; a potsherd; soot or black collected from combustion on pots or kettles, etc. *v.t.* To blacken with soot from a pot. **crockery**, *n.* Earthenware; earthenware vessels.

crock (2) (krok) [etym. doubtful; prob. cogn. with CRACK (cp. Norw. *krake*, a weakly or sickly animal; M.Dut. *kraecke*, E.Fris. *krakke*, a broken-down horse, house, or man)], *n.* *An old ewe; a broken-down horse; a broken-down machine or implement; (*colloq.*) a sick person; a fool, a worthless person.

crocket (krok′ ėt) [A.-F. *crocket*, var. of F. CROCHET], *n.* (*Arch.*) A carved foliated ornament on a pinnacle, the side of a canopy, etc.

crocodile (krok′ ō dīl) [F., from L. *crocodīlus*, Gr. *krokodeilos*], *n.* A large amphibian reptile having the back and tail covered with large, square scales; a string of school children walking two by two; (*Rhet.*) a captious sophism to ensnare an enemy. **crocodile bird**, *n.* (*Zool.*) An African plover-like bird which feeds on the insect parasites of the crocodile. **crocodile tears**, *n.pl.* Hypocritical tears like those with which the crocodile is fabled to attract its victims. **crocodilian** (dil′ i ăn), *a.*

crocus (krō′ kŭs) [L., from Gr. *krokos*], *n.* A genus of small bulbous plants belonging to the *Iridaceæ*, with yellow, white, or purple flowers, extensively cultivated in gardens; metal calcined to a deep red or yellow powder and used for polishing.

Crœsus (krē′ sus) [king of Lydia, 6th cent. B.C.], *n.* A very wealthy man.

croft (kroft) [A.-S.], *n.* A piece of enclosed ground, esp. adjoining a house; a small farm in the Highlands and islands of Scotland. **crofter**, *n.* One who farms a croft, esp. one of the joint tenants of a farm held by several peasants in Scotland.

***crome** (krōm) [from a non-extant A.-S. *cramb* or *cromb* (cp. M.Dut. and L.G. *kramme*, Dut. *kram*)], *n.* A hook or crook. *v.t.* To hook; to drag with a hook.

cromlech (krom′ lek) [W., from *crom*, bent, *llech*, stone, slab], *n.* A prehistoric structure in which a large flat stone rests horizontally on upright ones.

cromorne (krō môrn′), **cremona** (2) (kre mō′ nă) [F., corr. of G. *krummhorn*, crooked horn], *n.* (*Organ*) One of the reed stops.

crone (krōn) [O.North.F. *carogne*, an old woman (L. *caro carnis*, see CARRION)], *n.* An old ewe; an old woman.

cronk (krongk) [CRANK (3)], *a.* (*Austral. colloq.*) Unwell, poorly. **to cronk up:** To go sick, to be ill.

crony (krō′ ni) [etym. unknown], *n.* An intimate friend.

crood (krood) [Sc., imit.], *v.i.* To coo, like a dove.

crook (kruk) [prob. from Icel. *krōkr* (cp. Swed. *krok*, Dan. *krog*, O.H.G. *kracho*)], *n.* A bent or curved instrument; a shepherd's or bishop's hooked staff; a curve, a bend, a meander; *a bending, a genuflexion; *a trick, a wile; (*slang*) a thief, a swindler; (*Mus.*) a short tube for altering the key on a brass wind instrument. *v.t.* To make crooked or curved; to pervert, to misapply. *v.i.* To be bent or crooked; *to go astray. **by hook or by crook:** By fair means or foul. **crook-back**, *n.* One who has a deformed back. **crook-backed**, *a.* ***crook-kneed**, *a.* With crooked or bent knees. **crook-neck**, *n.* (*Am.*) A curved species of squash. **crooked** (kruk′ ėd), *a.* Bent, curved; turning, twisting, winding; deformed; not straightforward; perverse. **crookedly**, *adv.* **crookedness**, *n.*

crool (krool) [imit.], *v.i.* To make a low inarticulate sound like a baby.

croon (kroon) [Sc., imit. (cp. Dut. *kreunen*, to groan)], *v.i.* To sing in a low voice. *v.t.* To mutter. *n.* A hollow, continued moan; a low hum. **crooner,** *n.* One who sings mawkishly sentimental songs in affected low tones.

crop (krop) [A.-S., a bird's crop, a swelling, a head or bunch sticking out (cp. L.G. and Dut. *krop*, G. *kropf*, W. *cropa*)], *n.* The craw of a fowl, constituting a kind of first stomach; an analogous receptacle in masticating insects; the top or highest part; the upper part of a whip, a fishing-rod, etc.; a short whipstock with a loop instead of a lash; that which is cut or gathered; the harvest yield; an entire hide; a close hair-cut; *hair worn short and without powder; a piece chopped off; a name for various cuts of meat; (*Mining and Geol.*) the outcrop of a lode, a seam, or a stratum of rock. *v.t.* To cut off the ends of; to mow, to reap; to pluck, to gather; to cut off, to cut short; to sow, to plant and raise crops on; to reduce the margin of (a book) unduly, in binding. *v.i.* To yield a harvest, to bear fruit. **neck and crop:** Altogether. **to crop out:** To come to light; (*Geol.*) to come out at the surface by the edges (as an underlying stratum of rock). **to crop up:** To come up unexpectedly. **crop-ear,** *n.* A horse with cropped ears. **crop-eared,** *a.* ***crop-sick,** *a.* Sick from excess. ***cropful,** *a.* Having a full crop; satiated. **cropper,** *n.* One who or that which crops; a grain or plant which yields a good crop; *a pigeon with a long crop, a pouter; (*colloq.*) a fall on the head; a collapse. **croppy,** *n.* One with hair cropped short; a Roundhead; an Irish rebel of 1798.

croquet (krō′ kā) [O.North.F. *croket*, var. of F. CROCHET], *n.* An open-air game played on a lawn with balls and mallets; the act of croqueting an opponent's ball. *v.t.* To drive an opponent's ball away in this game by placing one's own ball against it and striking. *v.i.* To play croquet. **croqueting** (krō′ kā ing), *n.* **croqueted** (krō′ kād), *p.p.*

croquette (krō ket′) [F., from *croquer*, to crunch], *n.* A fried ball of forcemeat, made from chicken, meat, butter, etc.

crore (krôr) [Hind. *kror*], *n.* Ten millions, a hundred lakhs of rupees (about = £1,000,000).

crosier (krō′ zhyėr [O.F. *crossier*, *crocier*, from *croce*, a bishop's staff, late L. *crocia* (cp. O.F. *croc*, a crook, a hook); confused with F. *crosier*, from *crois*, L. *crux crucis*, CROSS], *n.* The pastoral staff of a bishop or abbot; (*erron.*) an archbishop's staff, which bears a cross instead of a crook.

croslet [CROSSLET].

cross (1) (kros) [A.-S. *cros*, L. *crux crucis*], *n.* An ancient instrument of torture made of two pieces of timber set transversely at various angles; a monument, emblem, staff, or ornament in this form; a sign or mark in the form of a cross; a market-place; a cross-shaped monument erected there; the mixture of two distinct stocks in breeding animals; the animal resulting from such a mixture; a mixture; a compromise; *money (from the cross formerly on the reverse); *the reverse of a coin; anything that thwarts or obstructs; trouble, affliction; the Christian religion, Christianity; (*slang*) a swindle, a preconcerted fraud. *a.* Transverse, oblique, lateral; intersecting; adverse, contrary, perverse; peevish; (*slang*) dishonest; ill-gotten. **cross as two sticks:** Very peevish; in very bad humour. **cross of St. Anthony:** One shaped like a **T. fiery cross:** Two sticks dipped in blood sent out as a signal to rouse the inhabitants of a district. **Greek cross:** An upright beam with a transverse beam of the same length. **Latin cross:** One with a long upright below the cross-piece. **Maltese cross:** One with limbs of equal size widening from the point of junction towards the extremities. **on the cross:** Diagonally; (*slang*) unfairly, fraudulently. **St. Andrew's cross:** One formed by two slanting pieces like an **X. St George's cross.** A Greek cross used on the British flag. **Southern Cross:** A cross-shaped constellation visible in the southern hemisphere. **to take up the cross:** To sacrifice self for some pious object. **Victoria Cross:** A decoration in the form of a Maltese cross awarded for military valour. **cross-action,** *n.* (*Law*) A case in which the defendant in an action brings another action against the plaintiff on points arising out of the same transaction. ***cross-arrow,** *n.* The arrow of a cross-bow. **cross-banded,** *a.* A term used of veneer when its grain is contrary to the general surface. **cross-bar,** *n.* A transverse bar. ***cross-barred,** *a.* Secured by cross-bars. **cross-beam,** *n.* A large beam running from wall to wall. **cross-bearer,** *n.* One who bears a processional cross, esp. before an archbishop. **cross-bench,** *n.* (*Parl.*) One of the benches for those independent of either recognized party; hence **cross-bench,** *a.* Impartial. **cross-bill,** *n.* A bird of the genus *Loxia*, the mandibles of the bill of which cross each other when closed; esp. *L. curvirostra*, an irregular British visitor. ***cross-bite,** *n.* A cheat; *v.i.* To swindle, to gull. **cross-bond,** *n.* Brick-laying in which points of one course fall in the middle of those above and below. **cross-bones,** *n.pl.* The representation of two thigh-bones crossed as an emblem of mortality. **cross-bow,** *n.* A weapon for shooting, formed by placing a bow across a stock. **cross-bowman,** *n.* **cross-bred,** *a.* Of a cross-breed, hybrid. **cross-breed,** *n.* A breed produced from a male and female of different strains or varieties; a hybrid. *v.t.* To produce a cross-breed; to cross-fertilize. **cross-bun,** *n.* A bun marked with a cross (eaten on Good Friday). **cross-buttock,** *n.* (*Wrestling*) A throw over the hip. **cross-country,** *a.* Across fields, etc., instead of along the roads. **cross-cut,** *n.* A cut across; a step in dancing; a figure in skating; (*Mining*) a drift from a shaft. *v.t.* To cut across. **cross-cut saw,** *n.* A saw for cutting timber across the grain. **cross-entry,** *n.* (*Book-keeping*) An entry to another account; a cancelling of a former entry. **cross-examine,** *v.t.* To examine systematically for the purpose of elicitating facts not brought out in direct examination, or for confirming or contradicting the direct evidence. **cross-examiner,** *n.* **cross-examination,** *n.* **cross-eye,** *n.* A squinting eye. **cross-eyed,** *a.* With both eyes squinting inwards. **cross-fertilize,** *v.t.* and *i.* To apply the pollen of one flower to the pistil of a flower of another species. **cross-fertilization,** *n.* **cross-fire,** *n.* Firing in directions which cross each other. **cross-grain,** *n.* The grain or fibres of wood running across the regular grain. **cross-grained,** *a.* Having the grain or fibres running across or irregular; perverse, peevish; intractable. **cross-hatch,** *v.t.* To shade with parallel lines crossing regularly in drawing or engraving. **cross-head,** *n.* (*Steam-eng.*) The block at the head of a piston-rod communicating motion to the connecting rod; a heading printed across the page or a column. **cross-jack** (kroj′ ėk, kros′ jăk), **cross-jack yard,** *n.* (*Naut.*) The yard of a square-sail occasionally carried by a cutter in running before the wind; the lower yard on the mizzen-mast. **cross-legged,** *a.* Having one leg over the other. **cross-light,** *n.* A light falling at an angle or crossing another; a view of a subject under a different aspect. **cross-patch,** *n.* (*colloq.*) A cross, ill-tempered person. **cross-piece,** *n.* A transverse piece; (*Ship-building*) the flooring-piece resting upon the keel; a bar connecting the bitt-heads. **cross-purpose,** *n.* A contrary purpose; contradiction, inconsistency, misunderstanding; (*pl.*) a game carried on by question and answer. **to be at cross-purposes:** To misunderstand or act unintentionally counter to each other. **cross-question,** *n.* One put in cross-examination. *v.t.* To cross-examine. **cross-questions and crooked answers:** A game in which questions and answers are connected at random with ludicrous effect. **cross-reference,** *n.* A reference from one part of a book to another. **cross-road,** *n.* A road that crosses another or connects two others; a by-way; (*pl.*) the crossing of two roads. **cross-row** [CHRIST-CROSS-ROW]. **cross-ruff,** *n.* (*Whist*) The play in which partners trump different suits and lead accordingly. **cross-sea,** *n.* Waves setting in contrary directions. **cross-section,** *n.* A cutting across the grain, or at right angles to the length; a cutting which shows all the strata; a comprehensive representation, a representative example. **cross-springer,** *n.* (*Arch.*) A rib which extends from one pier to another in groined vaulting. **cross-staff,** *n.* An archbishop's staff; *an instrument for taking altitudes or offsets in surveying. **cross-stitch,** *n.* A kind of stitch crossing others in series; needle-work done thus. **cross-stone** [HARMOTOME]. **cross-tie,** *n.* (*Arch.*) A connecting band. **cross-trees,** *n.pl.* (*Naut.*) Timbers on the top of masts to support the rigging of the mast above. **cross-trump** [CROSS-RUFF]. **cross-vaulting,** *n.* (*Arch.*) The intersecting of two or more simple vaults of arch-work. ***cross-way,** *n.* A cross-road. **cross-wind,** *n.* An unfavourable wind; a side-wind. **crossword puzzle,** *n.* A puzzle in which a square divided into blank chequered spaces is filled with words corresponding to clues provided.

cross (2) (kros) [from prec.], *v.t.* To draw a line across; to erase by cross lines, to cancel; to make the sign of the cross on or over; to pass across, to traverse; to intersect; to pass over or in front of; to meet and pass; to bestride; to cause to interbreed; to cross-fertilize; to write across the face of (a cheque) in order to render payable through another bank; to thwart, to counteract; to be inconsistent with. *v.i.* To lie or be across or over something; to pass across something; to move in a zigzag; to be inconsistent; to interbreed. **to cross** (a fortune-teller's) **hand:** To give money to. **to cross one's mind:** To occur to one's memory or attention. **to cross off, to cross out:** To strike out; to cancel. **to cross the floor:** (*Parl.*) Used of a member leaving one political party to join another. **to cross the path of:** To meet with; to thwart. **crossing,** *n.* The action of the verb TO CROSS; a place of crossing; the intersection of two roads, railways, etc.; contradiction, opposition. **crossing-sweeper,** *n.* A person who sweeps a street-crossing. **crossly,** *adv.* In an ill-humoured manner. **crossness,** *n.* **crosswise,** *adv.* Across; in the form of a cross.

crosse (kros) [F., from O.F. *croce*, a crook or hook], *n.* The long, hooked, racket-like stick used in the game of lacrosse.

crossing, crosswise [CROSS (2)].

crosslet (kros' lėt), *n.* A small cross. **crossleted,** *a.*

crotch (kroch) [etym. doubtful (cp. CRUTCH)], *n.* A forking; the parting of two branches; a hook or crook; *a curved weeding tool; (*Billiards*) a small space in the corner of a billiard-table; (*Naut.*) [see CRUTCH]. **crotched,** *a.* Having a crotch; forked.

crotchet (kroch' ėt) [F. *crochet*, dim. of *croc*, a hook], *n.* A peculiar turn of mind; a whimsical fancy, a conceit; (*Printing*) a square bracket; (*Mus.*) a note, double of a quaver. **crotchet-monger,** *n.* A crotcheteer. **crotcheteer,** *n.* A crochety person; a faddist. **crotchety,** *a.* Having crochets; whimsical. **crotchetiness,** *n.*

croton (krō' tŏn) [Gr. *krotōn*, a tick], *n.* A genus of euphorbiaceous medicinal plants from the warmer parts of both hemispheres. **croton-oil,** *n.* A drastic purgative oil expressed from *Croton tiglium.*

crottle (krotl) [Gael. *crotal*, a lichen], *n.* A name for several species of lichens used for dyeing.

crouch (krouch) [etym. doubtful], *v.i.* To stoop, to bend low; to lie close to the ground; to cringe, to fawn. *n.* The action of crouching.

crouchware (krouch' wâr) [etym. doubtful], *n.* A collector's name for old salt-glazed Staffordshire pottery.

croup (1) (kroop) [F. *croupe* (cp. CROP)], *n.* The rump, the buttocks (esp. of a horse); the part behind the saddle.

croup (2) (kroop) [imit.], *n.* Inflammation of the larynx and trachea, characterized by hoarse coughing and the difficulty of breathing, common in infancy.

croupier (kroo' pēr) [F., orig. one who rides on the CROUP (1)], *n.* A vice-chairman; one who superintends a gaming-table and collects the money won by the bank.

crouse (krooz) [Sc. and North., from M.E. *crūs* (cp. G. *kraus*, Dut. *kroes*)], *a.* Bold, forward; lively, pert. *adv.* Boldly, with plenty of confidence. **crousely,** *adv.*

crow (1) (krō) [A.-S. *crāwe*, from *crawan* (see foll.)], *n.* A large black bird of the genus *Corvus*, esp. *C. cornix*, the hooded crow, and *C. corone*, the carrion crow; *a crow-bar; *a grappling-iron; (*slang*) a confederate who keeps watch while another steals. **as the crow flies:** In a direct line. **to have a crow to pluck with any one:** To have some fault to find with or an explanation to demand from one. **to pluck or pull a crow:** To contend for trifles. **crow-bar,** *n.* A bar of iron bent at one end (like a crow's beak) and used as a lever. **crow-bill,** *n.* (*Surg.*) A forceps for extracting bullets, etc., from wounds. **crow-flower** [CROWFOOT]. **crow-keeper,** *n.* A boy employed to scare away crows; a scarecrow. **crow-quill,** *n.* A fine pen for sketching (orig. made from the quill of a crow). **crow-stone,** *n.* The top stone of a gable; (*Geol.*) a local name for sandstone in Yorkshire and Derbyshire. **crow's-foot,** *n.* A wrinkle at the corner of the eye in old age; (*Mil.*) a caltrop. **crow's nest,** *n.* (*Naut.*) A tub or box for the look-out man on a ship's mast.

crow (2) (krō) [A.-S. *crāwan* (cp. Dut. *kraaijen*, G. *krähen*), imit.], *v.i.* (*past* **crew, crowed**) To make a loud cry like a cock; to make a cry of delight like an infant; to exult; to brag, to boast. *v.t.* To proclaim by crowing. *n.* The cry of a cock; the cry of delight of an infant.

crowberry (krō' be ri), *n.* (*Bot.*) A heathlike plant, *Empetrum nigrum*, with black berries.

crowd (1) (kroud) [A.-S. *crūdan*], *v.t.* *To drive, to push; to press or squeeze closely together; to fill by pressing; to throng or press upon; to press (into or through). *v.i.* To press, to throng, to swarm; to collect in crowds. *n.* A number of persons or things collected closely and confusedly together; the mass, the mob, the populace; (*colloq.*) a set, a party, a lot; a large number (of things); (*Cinema.*) any group of persons photographed in a film but not playing definite parts. **a crowd of sail:** (*Naut.*) A press of sail. **to crowd out:** (*Newsp.*) To omit in order to make room for other matter. **to crowd sail:** (*Naut.*) To carry an extraordinary force or press of sail.

***crowd** (2) (kroud) [W. *crwth*], *n.* An instrument somewhat like a violin, but with six strings (in early times three), four played with a bow and two with the thumb. *v.i.* To play a crowd or fiddle. ***crowder,** *n.* One who plays upon a crowd; a fiddler.

crowdy, -die (krou' di) [Sc., etym. unknown], *n.* Meal and water (or milk) stirred together cold, so as to form a thick gruel.

croweater (crō' ē tėr), *n.* (*Austral. colloq.*) A native of South Australia, a resident there.

crowfoot (krō' fut), *n.* (*Bot.*) Name for several species of buttercup, *Ranunculus bulbosus*, *R. acris*, and *R. repens*; (*Mil.*) a caltrop; (*Naut.*) a contrivance for suspending the ridge of an awning.

crown (kroun) [A.-F. *coroune*, O.F. *corone*, L. *corōna*, a garland, a crown (cogn. with Gr. *korōnē*, the curved end of a bow)], *n.* A garland of honour worn on the head; the ornamental circlet worn on the head by emperors, kings, or princes as a badge of sovereignty; an ornament of this shape; royal power; the sovereign; a five-shilling piece; a foreign coin of certain values; a size of paper, 15 in × 20 in. (formerly with a crown for a water-mark); the top of anything, esp. of the head, a hat, a mountain, etc; the head; the top of the head; the vertex of an arch; the upper member of a cornice; the highest part of a road, bridge, or causeway; the portion of a tooth above the gum; (*Naut.*) the part of an anchor where the arms join the shank; the culmination, glory; reward, distinction. *a.* Belonging to the Crown or the sovereign. *v.t.* To invest with a crown, or regal or imperial dignity; (*fig.*) to surround, or top, as with a crown; to form a crown, ornament, or top to; to dignify, to adorn; to consummate; (*Dentist.*) to put a crown or cap on (a tooth); (*Draughts*) to make a king; *to fill so as to brim over. **Crown-agent,** *n.* (*Sc. Law*) The solicitor who under the Lord Advocate takes charge of criminal prosecutions. **crown-antler,** *n.* The topmost antler of a stag's horn. **Crown-Colony,** *n.* A colony administered by the home Government. **Crown-court,** *n.* (*Law*) The court in which criminal business is transacted at an assize. **crown-glass,** *n.* The finest kind of window glass, made in circular sheets without lead or iron; glass used in optical instruments, containing potassium and barium in place of sodium. **Crown Imperial,** *n.* A garden flower from the Levant, *Fritillaria imperialis,* with a whorl of florets round the head. **Crown jewels,** *n.pl.* The regalia and other jewels belonging to the sovereign for the time being. **Crown-lands,** *n.pl.* Lands belonging to the Crown as the head of the Government. **crown law,** *n.* Common law, as applicable to criminal matters. **crown lawyer,** *n.* A lawyer in the service of the Crown. **Crown Office,** *n.* A section of the Court of King's Bench which takes cognizance of criminal cases; the office which now transacts the common law business of the Chancery. **crown-post,** *n.* A king-post. **Crown prince,** *n.* The name given in some countries to the heir apparent to the Crown; **Crown princess,** *n.* His wife. **crown-side,** *n.* The Crown office. **crown-solicitor,** *n.* (*Law*) The solicitor who prepares the cases when the Crown prosecutes. **crown-wheel,** *n.* A contrate wheel. **crown-witness,** *n.* A witness for the Crown in a criminal prosecution. **crown-work,** *n.* (*Fort.*) An extension of the main work, consisting of a bastion between two curtains. **crowned,** *a.* Having a crown; invested with a crown. **high-crowned, low-crowned,** *a.* High or low in the crown (of hats). **crownless,** *a.* Destitute or deprived of a crown.

***crowner** [CORONER].

croydon (kroi' dȯn) [town in Surrey], *n.* A light two-wheeled gig.

croze (krōz) [perh. from F. *creux,* O.F. *croz,* a hollow], *n.* The groove in barrel staves near the end to receive the head; a cooper's tool for making this. *v.t.* To make this groove in.

crozier [CROSIER].

crucial (krooshl, kroo' shi ȧl) [F., from L. *crux crucis,* a cross], *a.* Decisive; searching; (*Anat.*) in the form of a cross; intersecting.

crucian (krooshn, kroo' shyȧn) [L.G. *karusse,* perh. from L. *coracīnus,* Gr. *korakīnos*], *n.* The German or Prussian carp, a small fish without barbels.

cruciate (kroo' shi āt) [med. L. *cruciātus* (L. *crux crucis,* cross)], *n.* (*Nat. Hist.*) Cruciform.

crucible (kroo' sibl) [late L. *crucibulum,* perh. from *crux,* see prec.], *n.* A melting-pot of earthenware, porcelain, or of refractory metal, adapted to withstand high temperatures without sensibly softening, and sudden and great alterations of temperature without cracking; a basin at the bottom of a furnace to collect the molten metal; (*fig.*) a searching test or trial.

crucifer (kroo' si fėr) [L. *crucifer* (*crux crucis,* a cross, *-fer,* a bearer)], *n.* A cross-bearer; one of the Cruciferæ. ***Cruciferæ*** (-sif' ėr ē), *n.pl.* (*Bot.*) A natural order of plants, the flowers of which have four petals disposed crosswise. **cruciferous,** *a.* Bearing a cross; (*Bot.*) belonging to the *Cruciferæ.*

crucifix (kroo' si fiks) [O.F. *crucefix,* L. *cruci fixus,* fixed to a cross], *n.* A cross bearing a figure of Christ. **crucifixion** (-fik' shŭn), *n.* The act of crucifying; punishment by crucifying; (*Hist.*) the death of Christ on the cross; a picture of this; torture; mortification. **cruciform** (kroo' si fôrm), *a.* Cross-shaped; arranged in the form of a cross.

crucify (kroo' si fī) [O.F. *crucifier,* late L. *crucifīgere* (L. *cruci fīgere,* fix to a cross)], *v.t.* To inflict capital punishment by affixing to a cross; (*fig.*) to torture; to mortify, to destroy the influence of.

crude (krood) [L. *crūdus,* raw], *a.* Raw; in a natural state, not cooked; unripe; not digested; imperfectly developed, immature, inexperienced, rude; coarse, rough, unfinished; (*Gram.*) uninflected. **crude form,** *n.* The original form of an inflected substantive divested of its case ending. **crudely,** *adv.* **crudeness,** *n.* **crudity,** *n.*

***crudy** (CURDY (I)).

cruel (kroo' ėl) [F., from L. *crūdēlis* (cogn. with *crūdus,* CRUDE)], *a.* Disposed to give pain to others; inhuman, unfeeling, hard-hearted; causing pain to others, painful. **cruel-hearted,** *a.* Delighting in cruelty. **cruelly,** *adv.* ***cruelness,** *n.* **cruelty,** *n.* Cruel disposition or temper; a barbarous or inhuman act.

cruet (kroo' ėt) [A.-F., dim. of O.F. *crue, cruie,* prob. from O.L.G. *crûca* (cp. O.H.G. *kruog*), a pot], *n.* A small bottle for vinegar, oil, etc.; a small bottle for holding the wine or water in the Eucharist. **cruet-stand,** *n.* A frame or stand for holding cruets.

cruise (krooz) [Dut. *kruisen,* to cross, from *kruis,* L. *crux crucis,* a cross], *v.i.* To sail to and fro for pleasure or in search of plunder or an enemy. *n.* Such a voyage. **cruiser,** *n.* A person or ship that cruises; (*Nav.*) a warship designed primarily for speed, faster and lighter than a battleship. **armoured cruiser,** *n.* Such a vessel armed like (usually not so heavily as) a battleship.

cruisie [CRUSIE].

cruiskeen (kroos' kēn) [Ir.], *n.* A small vessel for liquor; a measure of whisky.

cruive (kroov) [Sc., etym. doubtful], *n.* *A cabin; a sty; a wickerwork enclosure on a tidal flat for catching fish.

cruller (krŭl' ėr) [Dut. *cruller,* from *crullen,* to curl], *n.* (*Am.*) A cake, often ring-shaped, cut out of dough made of flour, sugar, sour cream, etc.

crumb (krŭm) [A.-S. *crūma* (cp. Dut. kruim, G. *krume*)], *n.* A small piece, esp. of bread; the soft inner part of bread; (*fig.*) a tiny portion, a particle. *v.t.* To break into crumbs; to cover with crumbs (for cooking). **v.i.* To crumble. **crumb-brush,** *n.* A curved brush for sweeping crumbs from the table. **crumb-cloth,** *n.* A cloth laid over a carpet to receive the crumbs that fall from the table. **crumby** (krŭm' i), *a.*

crumble (krŭm' bėl) [as prec.], *v.t.* To break into small particles. *v.i.* To fall into small pieces; to fall into ruin. **crumbly,** *a.* Apt to crumble.

crummy (krŭm' i), *a.* (*slang*) Plump, well-developed (of women); comely; plump in the pockets, well off; lousy.

crump (krŭmp) [onomat.], *n.* The sound of the explosion of a heavy shell or bomb.

crumpet (krŭm' pėt) [etym. doubtful], *n.* A thin, light, spongy tea-cake; (*slang*) the head.

crumple (krŭm' pėl) [from obs. *crump,* to bend or curl up], *v.t.* To draw or press into wrinkles. *v.i.* To become wrinkled, to shrink (as cloth, paper, etc.). **crumplet,** *n.* **crumpling,** *n.* The action of the verb TO CRUMPLE; *a small apple with a wrinkled skin.

crunch (krŭnch) [imit.], *v.t.* To crush noisily with the teeth; to grind with the foot. *v.i.* To make a noise, as of crunching; to advance with crunching. *n.* A noise of or as of crunching.

cruor (kroo' ŏr) [L., blood, gore], *n.* Coagulated blood.

crupper (krŭp' ėr) [O.F. *cropiere* (as CROUP (I))], *n.* A strap with a loop which passes under a horse's tail to keep the saddle from slipping forward; the croup or hindquarters of a horse. *v.t.* To put a crupper on.

crural (kroo' răl) [L. *crūrālis* (*crūs crūris*) the shank], *a.* Belonging to the leg; shaped like a human leg.

crusade (kroo sād') [F. *croisade* (O.F. *croisée* and Sp. *cruzada*, med. L. *cruciāta*, p.p. of *cruciāre*, to mark with a CROSS)], *n.* One of several expeditions undertaken in the Middle Ages under the banner of the Cross to recover possession of the Holy Land, then in the power of the Saracens; any hostile enterprise conducted in an enthusiastic or fanatical spirit. *v.i.* To engage in a crusade. **crusader** (kroo sā' dėr), *n.*

*__crusado__ (kroo sā' dō) [Port. *crusado*, as prec.], *n.* A Portuguese coin (stamped with a cross), worth about 2s. 4d.

cruse (krooz) [cp. Icel. *krūs*, Dut. *kroes*, G. *krause*], *n.* A small pot, cup, or bottle.

crush (krŭsh) [O.F. *cruisir*, *croissir*, from Teut. (cp. Dan. *kryste*, Swed. *krossa*)], *v.t.* To press or squeeze together between two harder bodies so as to break or bruise; to crumple; (*fig.*) to overwhelm by superior power; to oppress, to ruin. *v.i.* To be pressed into a smaller compass by external force or weight; to make one's way by crushing. *n.* The act of crushing; a crowd; (*colloq.*) a crowded meeting or social gathering; (*Austral.*) the funnel of a stock-yard where the cattle are got in hand. **to crush a cup** or **pot**: To crack a bottle, to drink it. **to crush out**: To extinguish. **to have a crush on**: (*slang*) To have a violent liking for. **crush-hat**, *n.* A soft hat collapsing with a spring, so as to be carried under the arm without injury; an opera-hat. **crush-room**, *n.* A large room or hall at a theatre, opera-house, etc., in which the audience may promenade during the intervals. **crusher**, *n.* One who or that which crushes.

crusie (kru' zi) [Sc., prob. from F. *creuset*, a crucible], *n.* A small iron lamp burning oil or tallow.

crust (krŭst) [O.F. *crouste*, L. *crusta*], *n.* The hard outer part of bread; the crusty end of a loaf; any hard rind, coating, layer, deposit, or surface covering; a hard piece of bread; the pastry covering a pie; a scab; a deposit from wine as it ripens; (*Geol.*) the solid outer portion of the earth; a film deposited on the inside of a bottle of wine. *v.t.* To cover with a crust; to make into crust. *v.i.* To become encrusted. **crust of the earth**: The solid exterior of the earth. **crusted**, *a.* Having a crust; antiquated, hoary, venerable; describing port or other wine from a bottle with a crust. **crusty**, *a.* Resembling or of the nature of crust; (*fig.*) harsh, peevish, morose. **crustily**, *adv.* **crustiness**, *n.*

crustacea (krŭs tā' shi ȧ) [mod. L., neut. pl. of *crustāceus*, a. (L. *crusta*, see prec.)], *n.pl.* (*Zool.*) A class of *Articulata*, containing lobsters, crabs, shrimps, etc., named from their shelly covering, cast periodically. **crustacean**, *a.* and *n.* **crustaceology** (-ol' ȯ ji), *n.* The branch of science dealing with the crustacea. **crustaceologist**, *n.* **crustaceous**, *a.* Of the nature of shell; (*Zool.*) crustacean, (*Bot.*) hard, thin, and brittle. **crustation** (-tā shŭn), *n.* An incrustation.

crutch (krŭch) [A.-S. *cryce*, from Teut. *kruk-* (cp. Dut. *kruk*, Dan. *krukke*, G. *krücke*)], *n.* A staff, with a cross-piece to fit under the arm-pit, to support a lame person; a support; (*Naut.*) various appliances for spars, timbers, etc. **v.t.* To support on or as on crutches. *v.i.* To go on crutches.

*__crutched__ (krŭcht) [M.E. *crouch*, to cross], *a.* Wearing a cross as a badge. **Crutched** (krŭch' ėd) **Friars**, *n.pl.* A minor order of friars who wore a cross as badge; the site of their convent in London.

crux (krŭks) [L. CROSS], *n.* The real essential; anything exceedingly puzzling.

crwth [CROWD (2)].

cry (krī) [F. *crier*, L. *quīritāre*, lit. to cry for the help of the *Quīrites* or Roman citizens], *v.i.* To call loudly, vehemently, or importunately; to make utterance in a loud voice; to make proclamation; to exclaim; to lament loudly; to weep; to squall; to call (of animals), to utter inarticulate sounds; to yelp. *v.t.* To utter loudly; to proclaim, to declare publicly; to announce for sale; *to demand. *n.* A loud utterance, usually inarticulate, expressive of intense joy, pain, suffering, astonishment, or other emotion; an importunate call or prayer; proclamation, public notification; a catchword or phrase; a bitter complaint of injustice or oppression; weeping, lamentation; inarticulate noise; yelping; *a pack of dogs; *a pack of people, a company. **a far cry**: A long way off. **to cry against**: To exclaim loudly by way of threatening or censure. **to cry down**: To decry, to depreciate; *to overbear. **to cry halves**: To demand a share of something. **to cry in church**: To publish the banns of marriage. **to cry mercy**: To beg pardon. **to cry off**: To withdraw from a bargain. **to cry out**: To vociferate, to clamour. **to cry out against**: To exclaim loudly, by way of censure or reproach. **to cry quits**: To declare matters equal. **to cry shame upon**: To protest against. **to cry stinking fish**: To decry or condemn, esp. one's own wares. **to cry up**: To extol, to praise highly. **cry-baby**, *n.* A child or person easily provoked to tears. **crying**, *a.* That cries; calling for notice or vengeance, flagrant.

cryo- [Gr. *kruos*, frost], *comb. form* (*Chem.*) **cryogen** (krī' ȯ jėn) [-GEN], *n.* (*Chem.*) A freezing mixture. **cryolite** (krī' ȯ līt) [-LITE], *n.* (*Min.*) A brittle fluoride of sodium and aluminium from Greenland. **cryophorus** (krī of' ȯ rŭs) [Gr. *-phoros*, bearing, bearer], *n.* An instrument for freezing water by its own evaporation.

crypt (kript) [L. *crypta*, Gr. *kruptē*, fem. of *kruptos*, hidden (*kruptein*, to hide)], *n.* A vault, esp. one beneath a church, used for religious services or for burial. **cryptic**, *a.* Hidden, secret, occult. **cryptically**, *adv.*

crypt-, **crypto-**, *comb. form.* Secret; inconspicuous; not apparent or prominent. **crypto-crystalline** (krip tȯ kris' tȧ līn) [CRYSTALLINE], *a.* (*Min.*) Having a crystalline structure which cannot be resolved under the microscope.

cryptogam (krip' tȯ găm) [Gr. *-gamos*, married (*gamein*, to marry)], *n.* (*Bot.*) A plant destitute of pistils and stamens. **cryptogamia** (-găm' i ȧ), *n.pl.* A Linnæan order of plants in which the reproductive organs are concealed or not distinctly visible, containing ferns, lichens, mosses and seaweeds, fungi, etc. **cryptogamic**, *a.* **cryptogamist** (-tog' ȧ mist), *n.* **cryptogamous**, *a.* **cryptogamy**, *n.* Concealed or obscure fructification.

cryptogram (krip' tȯ grăm), *n.* A cipher; cipher-writing. **cryptograph** (krip' tȯ grăf), *n.* A system of writing in cipher; secret writing. **cryptographer**, **-raphist** (-tog' rȧ fėr, -fist), *n.* **cryptographic** (-grăf' ik), *a.* **cryptography** (-tog' rȧ fi), *n.*

cryptonym (krip' tō nim) [Gr. *onuma*, a name], *n.* A secret name; the name one bears in a secret society or brotherhood.

crystal (kris' tăl) [O.F. *cristal*, L. *crystallum*, Gr. *krustallos*, ice, rock-crystal, from *krustainein*, to freeze (*kruos*, frost)], *n.* A clear transparent mineral; transparent quartz, also called rock crystal; (*Chem. and Min.*) an aggregation of atoms arranged in a definite pattern which often assumes the form of a regular solid terminated by a certain number of smooth plane surfaces; (*fig.*) anything clear as crystal; a very pellucid kind of glass; (*Radio.*) a crystal with a wire connected to it to form a rectifier. Also a crystal which vibrates and gives rise to electrical voltages at a particular frequency. *a.* Clear, transparent, as bright as crystal; made of crystal. **watch crystal**, *n.* (*Am.*) A watch-glass. **crystal detector** (*Radio.*) A crystal arranged in a circuit so that the modulation on a radio carrier wave becomes audible in earphones, etc. **crystal gazer**, *n.* One who pretends to foresee the future by gazing into a crystal sphere. **crystalline** (kris' tȧ līn, -lin), *a.* Consisting of crystal; resembling crystal; clear, pellucid. **crystalline heavens** or **spheres**: Two transparent spheres which, according to the Ptolemaic cosmogony, were situated between the *primum mobile*, which carried with it in its revolution all that lay within it, and the firmament in which were the fixed stars. **crystalline humour** or **lens**, *n.* (*Anat.*) A lenticular, white, transparent solid body enclosed in a capsule behind the iris of the eye. **crystallite**, *n.* (*Geol.*) One of the particles of definite form observed in thin sections of igneous rock cooled slowly after fusion. **crystallize** (kris' tȧ līz), *v.t.* To cause to form crystals. *v.i.* To assume a crystalline form; (*fig.*) to assume a definite form (of views, etc.). **crystallizable**, *a.* **crystallization** (-zā' shůn), *n.*

crystallo- [Gr. *krustallos*, CRYSTAL], *comb. form.* (*Chem. and Min.*) Forming, formed of, pertaining to crystal, crystalline structure, or the science of crystals. **crystallogeny** (kris' tȧ lŏj' ė ni) [-GENY], *n.* That branch of science which treats of the formation of crystals. **crystallogenic** (-jen' ik), *a.* **crystallographer** (-log' rȧ fėr), *n.* One who describes or investigates crystals and their formation. **crystallography** [-GRAPHY], *n.* The science which deals with the forms of crystals. **crystallographic** (-grăf' ik), *a.* **crystallographically**, *adv.* **crystalloid** (kris' tȧ loid), *a.* Like a crystal. *n.* A body with a crystalline structure. ***crystallomancy** (kris' tȧ lō măn si) [-MANCY], *n.* Divination by means of a crystal or other transparent body. **crystallometry** (-lom' ėt ri) [-METRY], *n.* The art or process of measuring the forms of crystals.

crystoleum (kris tō' lė ům) [L. *oleum*, oil], *n.* The process of transferring photographs to glass and painting with oil colours.

ctenoid (tē' noid) [Gr. *ktenoeides* (*kteis ktenos*, a comb)], *a.* Comb-shaped; pectinated; (*Zool. and Palæont.*) belonging to the *Ctenoidei*. **ctenoid scales**, *n.pl.* Scales pectinated on the lower edge. *n.* A ctenoid fish. ***Ctenoidei*** (tē noi' dė ī), *n.pl.* (*Zool.*) One of Agassiz's artificial orders of fishes, founded on scales, now merged in the *Teleostei*, though the name is retained in palæontology.

ctenophora (tē nof' ȯ rȧ) [Gr. *kteis ktenos*, a comb, *-phoros*, bearing, a bearer], *n.pl.* (*Zool.*) A division of the *Cœlenterata*, characterized by fringed or comb-like locomotive organs. **ctenophoral**, *a.*

cub (kŭb) [etym. doubtful], *n.* The young of certain animals, as of a lion, bear, fox; a whelp; (*colloq.*) an uncouth, mannerless youth; a young Boy Scout. *v.i.* To bring forth cubs. ***cub-drawn**, *a.* Sucked by cubs. **cub-hunting**, *n.* Hunting young foxes. **cubhood**, *n.* **cubbing**, *n.* Cub-hunting. **cubbish**, *a.* **cub reporter**, *n.* An inexperienced newspaper reporter.

cubage (kū' bȧj), **cubature** (kū' bȧ tūr) [CUBE], *n.* The process of finding the solid contents of any body.

cubby (kŭb' i) [cp. obs. *cub*, a stall or pen, L.G. *kübbung*, *kübje*, a shed], *n.* A cubby-hole; (*Orkney and Shetland*) a straw basket. **cubby-hole**, *n.* A narrow or confined space; a cosy-place.

cube (kūb) [F., from late L. *cubum*, acc. of *cubus*, Gr. *kubos*], *n.* A solid figure contained by six equal squares, a regular hexahedron; the third power of a number (as 8 is the cube of 2). *v.t.* To raise to the third power; to find the cube of a number or the cubic content of a solid figure. **cube estimate**, *n.* A builder's or architect's estimate based on the cubic dimensions of a building. **cube-powder**, *n.* Gunpowder made in coarse cubical grains. **cube-root**, *n.* The number which, multiplied into itself, and then into the product, produces the cube: thus $3 \times 3 \times 3 = 27$, 3 being the cube-root of 27, which is the cube of 3; the rule for the extraction of the cube-root. **cube sugar**, *n.* (*Am.*) Lump sugar. **cubic, -bical**, *a.* Having the properties or form of a cube; being or equalling a cube the edge of which is a given unit; (*Math.*) of the third degree. **cubic-equation**, *n.* (*Math.*) An equation involving calculation to the third degree. **cubic foot**, *n.* A volume equal to a cube every edge of which measures a foot. **cubically**, *adv.* **cubiform**, *a.*

cubeb (kū' beb) [F. *cubèbe* (Sp. and It. *cubeba*). Arab, *kabābah*], *n.* The small spicy berry of *Cubeba officinalis*, a Javanese shrub used in medicine and cookery. **cubebic** (kū beb' ik), *a.* **cububin**, *n.* (*Chem.*) A vegetable principle found in the seeds of the cubeb.

cubic [CUBE].

cubicle (kū' bi kėl), **cubicule** (kū' bi kūl) [L. *cubiculum* (*cubāre*, to lie)], *n.* A portion of a bedroom partitioned off as a separate sleeping apartment; a compartment.

cubiform [CUBE].

cubist (kū' bist), *n.* (*Art*) One of an early 20th cent, school of painters who depict surfaces, figures, tints, light and shade, etc., on canvas, etc., by a multiplicity of representations of cubes.

cubit (kū' bit) [L. *cubitus*, a hand, an elbow], *n.* A measure of length, from the elbow to the tip of the middle finger, but varying in practice at different times from 18 to 22 in. **cubit-arm**, *n.* An arm cut off at the elbow. **cubital**, *a.* *Containing or of the length of a cubit; (*Anat. and Zool.*) pertaining to the forearm or corresponding part of the leg in animals.

cuboid (kū' boid) [Gr. *kuboeidēs*], *a.* Resembling a cube. *n.* (*Geom.*) A solid like a cube but with the sides not all equal, a rectangular parallelepiped; (*Anat.*) a bone on the outer side of the foot. **cuboidal**, *a.*

cububin [CUBEB].

cucking-stool (kŭk' ing stool) [prob. from obs. *cuck*, to void excrement (cp. Icel. *kúka*)], *n.* A kind of chair, used for ducking scolds or refractory women, dishonest tradesmen, etc.

cuckold (kŭk' ȯld) [O.F. *cucualt*, from *cucu*, CUCKOO (cp. F. *coucou*, cuckoo, *cocu*, cuckold)], *n.* One whose wife is unfaithful. *v.t.* To make (a man) a cuckold. ***cuckoldly**, *a.* Like a cuckold; mean, sneaking. ***cuckoldom**, *n.* ***cuckoldry**, *n.*

cuckoo (kuk' oo) [F. *coucou*, imit. (cp. L. *cuculus*, Gr. *kokkuks*)], *n.* A migratory bird, *Cuculus canorus*, which visits Britain in the spring and summer and lays its eggs in the nests of other birds; (*fig.*) a foolish fellow; a fool. *a.* (*slang*) Crazy. **cuckoo-clock**, *n.* A clock which announces the hours by emitting a sound like the note of the cuckoo. **cuckoo-flower**, *n.* A local name for many plants, esp. for the lady's smock, *Cardamine pratensis*. **cuckoo-pint** (kuk' oo pint), *n.* The common arum. **cuckoo-spit**, *n.* An exudation on plants from the frog-hopper.

cucullate, cucullated (kū' ků lȧt, -lā tėd) [late L. *cucullātus*, p.p. of *cucullāre* (L. *cucullus*, a hood)], *a.* (*Bot. and Zool.*) Hooded; resembling a hood; formed like a hood. **cuculliform** (ků kŭl' i fôrm), *a.*

cucumber (kū' kŭm bėr) [orig. *cucumer*, L. *cucumeren*, acc. of *cucumis* (later influenced by F. *cocombre*, now *coucombre*)], *n.* A trailing plant, *Cucumis sativus*; its elongated fruit, extensively used as a salad and pickle. **cucumber fish**, *n.* (*Austral.*) A variety of grayling. **cucumiform** (kū kū mi fôrm), *a.*

cucurbit (kū kėr' bit) [F. *cucurbite*, L. *cucurbita*], *n.* A gourd; a gourd-shaped vessel used in distillation. **cucurbitaceous** (-tā' shůs), *a.*

cud (kŭd) [A.-S. *cudu*, *cwidu* (cp. Icel. *kwatha*, resin, O.H.G. *chuti*, *quiti*, glue)], *n.* Food deposited by ruminating animals in the first stomach, thence drawn and chewed over again. **to chew the cud:** To ruminate; (*fig.*) to reflect.

cudbear (kŭd' bâr) [named by the inventor, Dr. Cuthbert Gordon], *n.* A crimson dye obtained from *Lecanora tartarea* and other lichens.

cuddle (kŭdl) [etym. doubtful], *v.i.* To lie close or snug together; to join in an embrace. *v.t.* To embrace, to hug, to fondle. *n.* A hug, an embrace. **cuddlesome,** *a.* Attractive to cuddle.

cuddy (1) (kŭd′ i) [Sc.; etym. doubtful (perh. an abbreviation of *Cuthbert*)], *n.* A donkey, an ass; a blockhead, a lout; a young coal-fish; a jack or lever for hoisting.

cuddy (2) (kŭd′ i) [etym. doubtful], *n.* (*Naut.*) A cabin in a ship where officers and passengers take their meals; a small cabin in a boat; a closet or cupboard.

cudgel (kŭ′ jėl) [A.-S. *cycgel*; etym. doubtful], *n.* A short club or thick stick, a bludgeon. *v.t.* (*past & p.p.* **cudgelled**) To beat with a cudgel. **to cudgel one's brains:** To try to recollect or find out something. **to take up cudgels:** To strike in and fight; to defend vigorously. **cudgel-play,** *n.* Fighting with cudgels. **cudgel-proof,** *a.* Able to resist a blow with a cudgel.

cudweed (kŭd′ wēd), *n.* Popular name for the genus *Gnaphalium*, esp. *G. sylvaticum*, a plant formerly administered to cattle that had lost their cud.

cue (1) (kū) [etym. doubtful], *n.* The last words of a speech, which the player who follows waits for as an intimation to begin; (*Mus.*) a similar signal; (*fig.*) a hint; the right course of action.

cue (2) (kū) [O.F. *cue* (F. *queue*), L. *cauda*, a tail], *n.* A long straight rod used by billiard-players. **cueist,** *n.*

cuff (1) (kŭf) [cp. Swed. *kuffa*, to thrust, to push], *v.t.* To strike with the open hand. *n.* A blow of this kind.

cuff (2) (kŭf) [etym. doubtful], *n.* The fold or band at the end of a sleeve; a linen band worn round the wrist.

cuirass (kwi răs′, kū răs′) [F. *cuirasse*, It. *corazza*, late L. *corācium*, L. *coriācea*, fem. *coriāceus*, leathern (*corium*, leather)], *n.* Armour for the body, consisting of a breast-plate and a back-plate strapped or buckled together; a woman's close-fitting, sleeveless bodice; (*Nat. Hist.*) any analogous protective covering; a sheathing of iron plates on ironclads. **cuirassier** (kwir-, kūr å sēr′), *n.* A soldier wearing a cuirass.

cuisine (kwi zēn) [F.], *n.* The kitchen; style of cooking; cookery.

Culdee (kŭl′ dē) [O.Gr. *céle dé*, a servant of God], *n.* One of an ancient Scoto-Irish Christian fraternity, founded about the eighth century.

cul-de-sac (kul′ dė săk) [F., bottom of a bag], *n.* A street or lane open only at one end; (*Mil.*) a situation with no exit except in front; (*Anat.*) a vessel, tube, or gut open only at one end.

-cule [F. *-cule*, L. *-culus -cula -culum* (which is fully anglicized in *-cle*)], *dim. suf.*, as in *animalcule*, *corpuscule*.

culex (kū′ leks) [L., a gnat], *n.* (*Zool.*) A genus of dipterous insects, containing the gnat and the mosquito. **culiciform** (-lis′ i fôrm), *a.*

culinary (kū′ lin år i) [L. *culīnārius* (*culīna*, a kitchen)], *a.* Relating to the kitchen or cooking; used in kitchens or in cooking.

cull (kŭl) [O.F. *cuillir*, L. *colligere*, to COLLECT], *v.t.* To pick; to select, to choose. *n.* (*usu. in pl.*) An animal picked out as inferior or too old for breeding, and usually fattened for killing; (*Am. pl.*) defective logs or planks picked out from lumber. **culler,** *n.* **culling,** *n.* The act of picking or choosing; that which is rejected; an under-sized oyster.

cullender [COLANDER].

cullet (kŭl′ ėt) [COLLET], *n.* Broken glass for re-melting.

***cullion** (kŭl′ i ŏn) [F. *couillon*, ult. from L. *cōleus*, bag, Gr. *koleos*, sheath], *n.* *A testicle; (*fig.*) a mean, base wretch. ***cullionly,** *a.* Mean, cowardly, base.

***cullis** (kŭl′ is) [F. COULISSE], *n.* A gutter; a groove or channel.

***cully** (kŭl′ i) [etym. doubtful], *n.* (*slang*) A dupe; one easily imposed upon.

culm (1) (kŭlm) [L. *culmus*], *n.* Stems, esp. of corn and grasses. **culmiferous** (1) (-mif′ ėr ůs), *a.*

culm (2) (kŭlm) [prob. cogn. with COAL], *n.* Stone-coal; anthracite coal, esp. if in small pieces; coal-dust; soot, smut. **culmiferous** (2) (-mif′ ėr ůs), *a.* Abounding in anthracite.

culmen (kŭl′ mėn) [L., the top], *n.* (*Ornith.*) The ridge on the top of a bird's bill.

culminate (kŭl′ mi nāt) [late L. *culminātus*, p.p. of *culmināre* (see prec.)], *v.i.* To reach the highest point; (*Astron.*) to come to the meridian. **culminant,** *a.* At the highest point; (*Astron.*) on the meridian; (*fig.*) supreme, predominant. **culmination** (-nā′ shůn), *n.* The highest point; the end of a series of events, etc.

culpable (kŭl′ påbl) [O.F. *culpable* (F. *coupable*), L. *culpābalis* (*culpa*, a fault)], *a.* Blameable; blameworthy; guilty. **culpability,** *n.* **culpableness,** *n.* **culpably,** *adv.* **culpatory,** *a.* Involving or expressing blame.

culprit (kŭl′ prit) [from the A.-F. legal abbrev. *cul. prit* or *prist* (prob. in full *culpable*: *prist* or *prest d'averrer*, guilty: I am ready to confess)], *n.* An offender; one who is in fault; one who is arraigned before a judge on a charge.

cult (kŭlt) [L. *cultus*, from *colere*, to till, to worship], *n.* Worship; homage; a system of religious belief; the rites and ceremonies of any system of belief.

culter [COULTER].

cultism (kŭl′ tizm) [Sp. *cultismo*, F. *cultisme* (CULT, -ISM)], *n.* An affected style of literary elegance cultivated in Spanish literature about the end of the sixteenth century, Gongorism. **cultist,** *n.*

cultivate (kŭl′ ti vāt) [late L. *cultīvātus*, p.p. of *cultivāre* (cp. *cultus*, CULT)], *v.t.* To till; to prepare for crops; to raise or develop by tilling; to improve by labour or study, to civilize; to cherish, to foster, to seek the friendship of. **cultivation,** *n.* The art or practice of cultivating; the state of being cultivated; a state of refinement or culture. **cultivation paddock,** *n.* (*Austral.*) A cultivated field. **cultivator,** *n.* One who cultivates; an improved harrow. **cultivable,** *a.*

cultrate (kŭl′ tråt) [L. *cultrātus* (*culter*, knife)], *a.* (*Nat. Hist.*) Shaped like a knife; having a sharp edge. **cultriform,** *a.* **cultrirostral** (kŭl tri ros′ trål) [ROSTRAL], *a.* (*Ornith.*) Having a knife-shaped bill.

culture (kŭl′ tyůr, -chėr) [F., from L. *cultūra* (cp. *cultus*, CULT)], *n.* The act of tilling; husbandry, farming; breeding and rearing; (*Microsc.*) a set of microscopic organisms produced by artificial development; intellectual or moral discipline and training; a state of intellectual and artistic development. **v.t.* To cultivate. **cultural,** *a.* **cultured,** *a.* In a state of intellectual development. ***cultureless,** *a.* **culturist,** *n.*

cultus [CULT].

culver (kŭl′ vėr) [A.-S. *culfre*], *n.* A wood-pigeon; *a pigeon, a dove. ***culver-house,** *n.* A dove-cot. ***culver-keys,** *n.pl.* A bunch of ash-keys; a dialect name for the columbine, squill, cowslip, and male orchis.

culverin (kŭl′ vėr in) [O.F. *coulevrine*, fem. of *coulevrin*, adder-like (*couleuvre*, L. *colubra*, snake, whence *colubrīnus*, COLUBRINE)], *n.* A long cannon or hand-gun, usually an 18-pounder so called because like a serpent.

culvert (kŭl′ vėrt) [etym. unknown], *n.* A waterway, usually in the form of an arch or barrel of masonry or brickwork, beneath a road or canal; (*Elec.*) an underground channel for wires or cables.

cumber (kŭm′ bėr) [O.F. *combrer*, to hinder, late L. *cumbrus*, a heap (cp. G. *kummer*, trouble, prov. rubbish)], *v.t.* To hamper, to clog; to hinder, to impede; to perplex; to embarrass. *n.* A hindrance; an impediment. **cumberless,** *a.* Free from care or encumbrance. **cumbersome,** *a.* Unwieldy, unmanageable; burdensome, troublesome. **cumbersomely,** *adv.* **cumbersomeness,** *n.* ***cumbrance,** *n.* An encumbrance. **cumbrous,** *a.* **cumbrously,** *adv.*

Cumbrian (kŭm′ bri ȧn) [L. *Cumbria*, Celt. *Cymry*, Welsh, or *Cymru*, Wales], *a.* Belonging to Cumberland or to Strathclyde, the ancient British kingdom between the Clyde and the Ribble. *n.* A native of Cumberland. **Cumbrian system** or **group,** *n.* (*Geol.*) The slate or greywacke system, remarkably developed in Cumberland.

cumin (kŭm′ in) [A.-S. *cymen*, L. *cuminum*, Gr. *kuminon*], *n.* A plant of the parsley family, the *Umbelliferæ*, with aromatic and carminative seeds; the name of a genus containing this, together with the caraway and other plants. **cumin-oil,** *n.* A volatile extract from the seeds of cummin. **cumene** (kū′ mēn), *n.* An aromatic hydrocarbon obtained from cumin oil. **cumic** (kū′ mik), *a.*

cummer (kŭm′ ėr), **kimmer** (kim′ ėr) [Sc., from F. *commere*, late L. *commāter* (COM-, *mater*, mother)], *n.* A godmother; a close woman friend; a gossip.

cummerbund (kŭm′ ėr bŭnd) [Hind. *kamarband* (Pers. *kamar*, the waist, *band*, a band)], *n.* A waistband or sash worn in India.

cummin [CUMIN].

cumquat (kŭm′ kwot) [Chin. *kin keu*, golden orange], *n.* A small orange, fruit of *Citrus Aurantium*, var. *Japonica.*

cumshaw (kŭm′ shaw) [Chin. pigeon English], *n.* A present, a tip, a douceur. *v.t.* To make a present.

cumulate (kū′ mū lāt) [L. *cumulātus*, p.p. of *cumulāre*, to heap up (*cumulus*, a heap)], *v.t.* and *i.* To accumulate. *a.* (-lȧt) Heaped up, accumulated. ***cumulation,** *n.* **cumulative,** *a.* Increasing by additions; tending to accumulate; (*Law*) enforcing a point by accumulated proof; (*Med.*) used of drugs which, after remaining quiescent, exert their influence suddenly. **cumulative preference shares,** *n.pl.* Shares on which arrears of interest are paid before ordinary shareholders are paid any on the current year. **cumulative vote,** *n.* A method of voting by which the votes of the elector can be all given to a single candidate instead of being given singly to several candidates. **cumulatively,** *adv.* **cumulativeness,** *n.*

cumulus (kū′ mū lŭs) [L., see prec.], *n.* (*pl.* **-li**) A heap, a pile; a series of round masses of cloud, like bales of wool; (*Anat.*) the thickened portion of a cellular layer containing the ovum. **cumulo-,** *comb. form* (*Meteor.*) **cumulo-nimbus,** *n.* (*Meteor.*) Great masses of cloud resembling mountains or towers. **cumulo-stratus,** *n.* Cumulus clouds with a stratified appearance. **cumulo-cirro-stratus,** *n.* A combination of cirrus and stratus with or into cumulus, a common form of rain-cloud. **cumulous,** *a.*

Cunarder (kū nar′ dėr) [Sir Samuel *Cunard* (1787–1865) founder of the line], *n.* One of a line of steamers between England and America, and other countries.

***cunctation** (kŭnk tā′ shŭn) [L. *cunctātio* (*cunctārī*, to delay)], *n.* Cautious delaying; delay, dilatoriness. ***cunctative** (kŭnk′ tȧ tiv), *a.* ***cunctator** (kŭnk tā′ tȯr), *n.*

cuneate (kū′ nė ȧt) [L. *cuneus*, a wedge, -ATE], *a.* Wedge-shaped. ***cuneal,** *a.* **cuneatic** (-ȧt′ ik), *a.* [CUNEIFORM].

cuneiform (kū′ nė i fôrm, kū nē′ fôrm) [as prec.], *a.* Wedge-shaped. **cuneiform writing,** *n.* Inscriptions in the characters resembling wedges or arrow-heads, covering the surfaces of Babylonian, Hittite, Ninevite, and Persian sculptures.

cunning (kŭn′ ing) [pres.p. of M.E. *cunnen*, A.-S. *cunnan*, to know], *a.* Knowing, skilful; ingenious; artful, crafty; (*Am.*) amusingly interesting, piquant. *n.* Skill, knowledge acquired by experience; artfulness, subtilty. **cunning-man** or **-woman,** *n.* One who pretends to tell fortunes, or how to recover stolen goods, etc. **cunningly,** *adv.*

cup (kŭp) [A.-S. *cuppe*, late L. *cuppa*, a cup, L. *cūpa*, a vat, a cask], *n.* A vessel to drink from; the liquor contained in it; an ornamental drinking-vessel, usu. of gold or silver, awarded as a prize or trophy; anything shaped like a cup, as an acorn, the socket for a bone; (*fig.*) the lot one has to endure; (*Med.*) a cupping-glass; (*Naut.*) the step of the capstan spindle; (*Eccles.*) the chalice used in the Holy Communion; (*usu. in comb. as claret-cup*) a drink made from wine, cider, etc., with flavouring; (*Am. cooking*) Half an Am. pint. *v.t.* (*past & p.p.* **cupped**) (*Med.*) To bleed by means of a cupping-glass; (*Golf*) to strike the ground when hitting the ball; *to supply with liquor. *v.i.* (*Bot.*) To form a cup or cups. **a bitter cup:** A hard fate; a heavy retribution. **in one's cups:** Intoxicated. **cup-and-ball,** *n.* A child's game consisting in throwing up a ball and catching it in a socket. **cup-and-ball joint,** *n.* A ball-and-socket joint. **cup-bearer,** *n.* A person who serves wine, esp. in royal or noble households. **cup-final,** *n.* (*Sport*) The final match of the football season to decide which club shall be awarded the League cup. **cup-gall,** *n.* A cup-like gall on oak leaves. **cup-lichen, -moss,** a lichen *Scyphophorus pyxidatus*, with cup-shaped processes rising from the thallus. **cup-tie,** *n.* (*Sport*) A football match in a round of knock-out competition. **cupful,** *n.*

cupboard (kŭb′ ȯrd), *n.* *A shelf on which cups were placed; a sideboard; an enclosed case with shelves to receive plates, dishes, food, etc.; a wardrobe, (*Am.*) a closet. **v.t.* To keep in or as in a cupboard; to hoard. **cupboard-love,** *n.* Interested love.

cupel (kū′ pėl) [late L. *cūpella*, dim. of *cūpa*, a cask], *n.* A small shallow vessel used in assaying precious metals. *v.t.* To assay in a cupel. **cupellation** (-lā′ shŭn), *n.*

cupid (kū′ pid) [L. *Cupīdo* (*cupere*, to desire)], *n.* The Roman god of Love; a picture or statue of Cupid; a beautiful boy.

cupidity (kū pid′ i ti) [F. *cupidité*, L. *cupiditās -tātem*, from *cupidus*, desirous, as prec.], *n.* An inordinate desire to possess; covetousness, avarice.

cupola (kūp′ ȯ lȧ) [It., from L. *cūpula*, CUPEL], *n.* A little dome; a lantern or small apartment on the summit of a dome; a spherical covering to a building, or any part of it; a cupola-furnace; a revolving dome or turret on a warship; (*Anat. and Zool.*) a dome-like organ or part, esp. the extremity of the canal of the cochlea. **cupola-furnace,** *n.* A furnace for melting metals.

cuppa (kŭp′ ȧ), *n.* (*colloq.*) A cup of tea.

cupping (kŭp′ ing) [CUP], *n.* The act of bleeding with a cupping-glass. **cupper,** *n.* One who does this. **cupping-glass,** *n.* An exhausted glass vessel placed over a (usually) scarified place to excite the flow of blood.

cupreous (kū′ pri ŭs) [L. *cupreus*, copper], *a.* Of, like, or composed of copper. **cupric** (kū′ prik), *a.* Having bivalent copper in its composition. **cupriferous** (kū prif′ ĕr ŭs), *a.* Copper-bearing. **cuprite** (kū′ prīt), *n.* Red oxide of copper, a mineral with cubic crystal structure. **cuproid** (kū′ proid), *a.* Resembling copper; *n.* A crystal of the tetrahedal type, with twelve equal angles. **cuprous,** *a.* Having monovalent copper in its composition. **cupro-nickel,** *n.* An alloy of copper and nickel.

cupressus (kū pres′ ŭs) [L.], *n.* (*Bot.*) A genus of conifers, containing the cypress.

cupule (kūp′ ūl) [L., CUPOLA], *n.* (*Bot.*) An inflorescence consisting of a cup, as in the oak or hazel; (*Zool.*) a cup-like organ. **cupular, cupulate,** *a.* **cupuliferous** (-lif′ ėr ŭs), *a.*

cur (kĕr) [mit. (cp. Icel. *kurra*, to murmur, grumble, L.G. *kurren*, to snarl)], *n.* A mongrel, worthless dog; an ill-conditioned, surly fellow. **currish,** *a.* **currishly,** *adv.* **currishness,** *n.*

curable [CURE].

curaçao (kū rä sō′) [island, north of Venezuela (often misspelt *Curaçoa*)], *n.* A liqueur flavoured with orange-peel, sugar, and cinnamon, orig. from Curaçao.

curacy [CURATE].

curare (kū ra′ ri) [Guiana Ind. *courali*], *n.* The dried extract of the vine *Strychnos toxifera* used by the Indians of South America for poisoning arrows, and employed in physiological investigations as an anæsthetic; it paralyses the motor nerves and ultimately causes death by suffocation. **curarine,** *n.* **curarize,** *v.t.*

curassou (kū′ rà sō) [CURAÇAO], *n.* Name of a tribe of turkey-like birds found in South and Central America.

curate (kū′ ràt) [med. L. *cūrātus* (L. *cūra*, a care, charge, cure)], *n.* One with a cure of souls; a clergyman of the Church of England who assists the incumbent. **perpetual curate** [PERPETUAL]. **curacy,** *n.* The office of a curate; the benefice of a perpetual curate.

curative (kū′ rà tiv), *a.* Tending to cure. *n.* Anything that tends to cure.

curator (kū rā′ tòr) [L., from *cūrāre*, to CURE], *n.* One who has charge of a library, museum, or similar establishment; (*Sc. Law*) (kūr′ à tòr) a trustee for the carrying out of any purpose, a guardian; a member of a governing body in some British and foreign Universities. **curatorial** (-tôr′ i àl), *a.* **curatorship,** *n.* **curatrix,** *n.*

curb (1) (kĕrb) [F. *courbe*, from L. *curvus*, bent, curved], *n.* A chain or strap passing behind the jaw of a horse in a curb-bit; a kerb-stone; an injury to the hock-joint of a horse; (*fig.*) a check, a restraint. *v.t.* To put a curb on; (*fig.*) to restrain, to keep in check. **curb-bit,** *n.* A stiff bit forming a leverage upon the jaws of a horse. **curb-roof,** *n.* A mansard roof. ***curbless,** *a.* Without any curb or restraint. **curby,** *a.*

***curb** (2) (kĕrb) [F. *courber*, to bend], *v.i.* To bow, to cringe.

curb (3) [KERB].

curch (kĕrch) [Sc., cp. KERCHIEF], *n.* A piece of linen formerly worn by women; a kerchief.

curculio (kėr kū′ li ō) [L.], *n.* The corb weevil; (*Ent.*) the genus of insects comprising this.

curcuma (kĕr′ kū mà) [Arab. *kurkum*, saffron (cp. CROCUS)], *n.* (*Bot.*) A genus of tuberous plants of the ginger family; turmeric, which is obtained from its root, and used as an ingredient in curry-powder, and for chemical, medicinal, and other purposes.

curd (kĕrd) [perh. from A.-S. stem *crud-*, *crūdan*, to CROWD], *n.* The coagulated part of milk, used to make cheese; the coagulated part of any liquid; the fatty matter found in the flesh of boiled salmon. **v.t.* To curdle. **curd-breaker,** *n.* An instrument used to break the cheese-curd into small pieces. **curd-cutter, -mill,** *n.* An instrument with knives to cut the curd. **curd-soap,** *n.* A white soap manufactured of tallow and soda. **curdy** *a.* Full of curds; curdled, congealed. *v.i.* To congeal.

curdle (kĕr′ dėl), *v.t.* To break into curds; to coagulate; to congeal. *v.i.* To become curdled.

cure (1) (kūr) [O.F., from L. *cūra*, care, whence *cūrāre*, to take care of], *n.* The act of healing or curing; a remedy; anything which acts as a remedy or restorative; the state of being cured or healed; the care or spiritual charge of souls. *v.t.* To heal, to restore to health, to make sound or whole; to preserve or pickle; to correct a habit or practice. *v.i.* To effect a cure; to be cured or healed. **cure of souls:** A benefice to which parochial duties are annexed. ***to do no cure:** To take no care. **cure-all,** *n.* A panacea, a universal remedy; a name for *Geum rivale*. **curable,** *a.* **curability** (-bil′ i ti), *n.* **cureless,** *a.* Without cure or remedy. **curer,** *n.* One who cures or heals; one who prepares preserved food (*often in comb.*, as *fish-curer*). **curing,** *n.* The act of curing or healing; the act or process of preparing articles of food for preservation. **curing-house,** *n.* A building in which sugar is drained and dried; a house in which articles of food are cured.

cure (2) (kūr) [slang; perh. abbrev. of CURIOUS], *n.* An odd or funny person, an eccentric.

curé (kū′ rā) [F.], *n.* A parish priest, a French rector or vicar.

curette (kū ret′) [F.], *n.* (*Surg.*) An instrument used for scraping the throat, ear, or other cavity.

curfew (kĕr′ fū) [A.-F. *coeverfu*, O.F. *couvrefeu* (*couvrir*, to COVER, *feu*, L. *focum*, acc. of *focus*, fire)], *n.* A regulation in the Middle Ages to extinguish fires at a stated hour; the bell announcing or the hour for this; a military or civil regulation to be within doors between stated hours. **curfew-bell,** *n.* The bell announcing curfew; a bell rung at a stated hour in the evening, still customary in certain places in France and the United States. **curfew-time,** *n.*

curia (kū′ ri à) [L.], *n.* (*pl.* **curiæ**) One of the ten subdivisions of the three Roman tribes, as instituted by Romulus; the building in which they met; the Roman senate-house; the senate of an ancient Italian town; a mediæval court of justice; the Roman See, including Pope, cardinals, etc., in their temporal capacity. **curial,** *a.* Pertaining to a curia, esp. the Papal curia. **curialism,** *n.*

curie (kū′ ri) [Mme. *Curie* (1867–1934)], *n.* The standard unit of radioactivity.

curio (kū′ ri ō) [short for CURIOSITY], *n.* (*pl.* **-os**) A curiosity, esp. a curious piece of art; a bit of bric-à-brac.

curious (kū′ ri ùs) [O.F. *curios*, L. *cūriōsus* (*cūra*, care)], *a.* Inquisitive, desirous to know; given to research; extraordinary, surprising, odd; *careful; *anxious, solicitous; *fastidious. **curiosity** (-os′ i ti), *n.* A desire to know; inquisitiveness; a rarity, an object of curiosity; (*colloq.*) a strange personage. **curiously,** *adv.* ***curiousness,** *n.*

curium (kū′ ri ùm), *n.* An artificially-produced radioactive element of atomic number 96.

curl (kĕrl) [earlier *crul*, *crulle* (cp. Dut. *krul*, G. *krolle*)], *n.* A ringlet or twisted lock of hair; anything coiled, twisted, or spiral; a contemptuous curving of the lip; a disease in potatoes of which curled shoots and leaves are a symptom. *v.t.* To twine; to twist into curls; to dress with ringlets; to raise (breaking waves); to curve up (the lip) in contempt. *v.i.* To twist, to curve up; to rise in curves or undulations; to play at the game of curling. **to curl one's hair:** (*colloq.*) To chastise. **curl-cloud,** *n.* Cirrus. **curl-paper,** *n.* Paper round which hair is wound to form a curl. ***curled pate,** *a.* Having curly hair. **curling-irons, curling-tongs,** *n.pl.* An instrument for curling the hair. **curlingly,** *adv.* In curls or waves. **curly,** *a.* Having curls; wavy, undulated; (*Bot.*) having curled or wavy margins. **curliness,** *n.*

curlew (kĕr′ lū) [O.F., *courlieus* (imit. of the cry)]. *n.* A migratory wading bird, esp. the European *Numenius arquatus*.

curlicue (kĕr′ li kū) [CURLY, CUE (from either F. *queue*, a tail, or the letter Q)], *n.* A fantastic curl; a flourish in writing.

curling (kĕr′ ling), *n.* A Scottish game on the ice in which contending parties slide smooth stones towards a mark. **curler,** *n.* A player of this game. **curling-stone,** *n.* The stone used in the game.

curmudgeon (kùr mŭj′ òn) [etym. unknown], *n.* A miserly, niggardly person. **curmudgeonly,** *adv.*

curmurring (kùr mŭr′ ing) [Sc., verbal noun of *curmur* (imit.), to make a low purring sound], *n.* A low rumbling, esp. a sound in the bowels from flatulence.

curr (kĕr) [imit.], *v.i.* To make a low murmuring or whirring sound like that made by an owl. *n.* A curring sound.

currach (kŭr′ ȧ, -ȧch) [Ir. *curach*], *n.* A skiff made of wickerwork and hides, a coracle.

currant (kŭr′ ȧnt) [formerly *raisins of corauns*, F. *raisins de Corinthe* (L. *Corinthus*, Gr. *Korinthos*, Corinth)], *n.* The dried fruit of a dwarf seedless grape from the Levant; the fruit of shrubs of the genus *Ribes*, containing the black, red, and white currants.

currency (kŭr′ ėn si) [L. *currere*, to run], *n.* A continual passing from hand to hand, as of money; the circulating monetary medium of a country, whether in coin or paper; the period during which anything is current; the state of being current; *running, rapid motion. **currency note,** *n.* Paper money of the value of ten shillings, one pound, etc.

current (kŭr′ ėnt) [O.F. *curant*, pres.p. of *currere*, to run (as prec.)], *a.* Passing at the present time; belonging to the present week, month, year; in circulation (as money); generally received or acknowledged; in general circulation among the public; *running, flowing, fluent. *n.* A flowing stream, a body of water, air, etc., moving in a certain direction; general drift or tendency; (*Elec.*) electrical activity regarded as the rate of flow of electrical charge along a conductor; (*Build.*) the fall or slope of a platform or roof to carry off the water. **currently,** *adv.* With a constant progressive motion; commonly, generally. **currentless,** *a.*

curricle (kŭr′ i kėl) [from foll.], *n.* A two-wheeled chaise for a pair of horses. **v.i.* To drive in a curricle.

curriculum (kŭ rik′ ū lŭm) [L., a race-course, dim. from *currere*, to run], *n.* (*pl.* **-la**) A fixed course of study at a school, etc.

currier (kŭr′ i ėr) [O.F. *corier*, L. *coriārius* (*corium*, hide, leather)], *n.* One who curries, dresses, and colours leather after it has been tanned. **curriery,** *n.* The trade of a currier; the place where the trade is carried on.

currish, etc. [CUR].

curry (1) (kŭr′ i) [O.F. *correier*, *conreder* (CON-, *reder*, cp. ARRAY)], *v.i.* To dress a horse with a comb; to dress leather; (*fig.*) to thrash; to flatter. *v.i.* To use flattery. **to curry favour** [corr. of M.E. *to curry favel*, to rub down a fallow-coloured horse]: To seek favour by officiousness, or flattery. **curry-comb,** *n.* A comb used for grooming horses.

curry (2) (kŭr′ i) [Tamil *kari*], *n.* A highly-spiced Indian dish of stewed fowl, meat, fish, fruit, etc., seasoned with turmeric, etc.; a hash or stew flavoured with curry-powder. *v.t.* To season or dress with curry. **curry-paste, -powder,** *n.* A condiment of ginger, turmeric, and other strong spices.

curse (kĕrs) [A.-S. *cursian*; etym. unknown], *v.t.* To invoke harm or evil upon; to blast, to injure, vex, or torment; to excommunicate. *v.i.* To swear, to utter imprecations. *n.* A solemn invocation of divine vengeance (upon); a sentence of divine vengeance; an oath; an imprecation (upon); the evil imprecated; anything which causes evil, trouble, or great vexation; a sentence of excommunication. **don't care a curse:** Regard it as worthless or as too contemptible to trouble about. **cursed, curst** (kĕr′ sėd, kĕrst), *a.* Execrable, accursed, deserving of a curse; blasted by a curse, execrated; vexatious, troublesome; *shrewish. **cursedly,** *adv.* **cursedness,** *n.* The state of being under a curse; *shrewishness. **curser,** *n.* One who curses; a blasphemer.

***cursitor** (kĕr′ si tŏr) [med. L. (cp. *cursitāre*, freq. of *currere*, to run)], *n.* A clerk of Chancery, whose office was to make out original writs; *a courier; a vagrant.

cursive (kĕr′ siv) [late L. *cursīvus* (from *cursus*, p.p. of *currere*, to run)], *a.* Written in a running hand. *n.* Cursive writing; manuscript written in a running hand, as opp. to uncial.

cursores (kĕr sôr′ ēz) [L. pl. of *cursor*, a runner, as prec.], *n.pl.* (*Ornith.*) An order of birds with rudimentary wings and strong feet well adapted for running, containing the ostrich, the emu, cassowary, and apteryx. **cursorial** (-sôr′ i ȧl), *a.*

cursory (kĕr′ sȯ ri) [L. *cursōrius*, as prec.], *a.* Hasty, superficial, careless. **cursorily,** *adv.* **cursoriness,** *n.*

curst [CURSE].

curt (kĕrt) [L. *curtus*, docked], *a.* Short, concise, abrupt; esp. rudely terse and abrupt. ***curt-hose,** *n.* Short hose or short boot, a nickname of Robert, eldest son of William the Conqueror. **curtly,** *adv.* **curtness,** *n.*

curtail (kĕr tāl′) [CURTAL], *v.t.* To shorten; to cut off the end or tail of; to lessen; to reduce. **curtail-step** [connexion with CURTAIL doubtful], *n.* The bottom step of a flight of stairs, finished at its outer extremity in a scroll. **curtailment,** *n.*

curtain (kĕr′ tȧn) [O.F. *cortine*, L. *cortīna* (etym. doubtful)], *n.* A cloth hanging beside a window (*Am.* drape) or door, or round a bed, which can be drawn across at pleasure; a screen, a cover, a protection; the screen in a theatre separating the stage from the spectators; (*Fort.*) a wall or rampart extending between two bastions; a partition or cover of various kinds; a shifting plate in a lock. *v.t.* To enclose with or as with curtains; to furnish or decorate with curtains. **curtain!** Call to engage hearers' attention at the conclusion of a dramatic episode. **curtain call,** *n.* (*Theat.*) Applause for an actor which calls for him to re-appear before the curtain falls. **curtain fire,** *n.* (*Mil.*) A form of artillery barrage. **curtain-lecture,** *n.* A reproof or lecture from a wife to a husband after they have retired. **curtain-pole,** *n.* A pole for hanging curtains on. **curtain-raiser,** *n.* (*Theat.*) A short piece given before a regular play. **curtain-rings,** *n.pl.* Rings running along the curtain-pole, by which the curtains can be drawn backwards or forwards. **curtainless,** *a.*

***curtal** (kĕr′ tȧl) [O.F. *cortald*, *courtault* (*court*, short, L. *curtus*, CURT; with suf. *-ald*, *-ault*, from Teut.)], *n.* A horse with a cropped tail; anything docked or cut short. *a.* Having a cropped tail; (*fig.*) concise; niggardly. **curtal friar,** *n.* (*prob.*) A friar with a short frock.

***curtal-ax, -axe** (kĕr′ tȧl ăks) [corr. of CUTLASS], *n.* A heavy sort of cutting sword.

curtana (kŭr ta′ nȧ, -tā′ nȧ) [Ang.-Lat. *curtana* (prob. *urtana spada*, curtailed sword), cp. CURTAL], *n.* The pointless Sword of Mercy carried before the English sovereigns at their coronation.

curtilage (kĕr′ ti lȧj) [O.F. *courtillage*, dim. of *courtil*, a little court (*cort*, a COURT)], *n.* A piece of ground lying near and belonging to a dwelling-house and included within the same fence.

curtsy, curtsey (kĕrt′ si) [COURTESY], *n.* A bow; an act of respect or salutation, performed by slightly bending the body and knees at the same time (of women only). *v.i.* To make a curtsy.

curule (kū′ rul) [L. *curūlis* (perh. from *currus*, a chariot)], *a.* (*Rom. Ant.*) Having the right to a curule chair; (*fig.*) of high civic dignity. **curule chair,** *n.* The chair of honour of the old Roman kings, and of the higher magistrates of senatorial rank under the republic, originally ornamented with ivory, and in shape like a camp-stool with crooked legs.

curvate (kĕr′ vāt) [L. *curvātus*, p.p. of *curvāre* (from foll.)], *a.* Curved, bent. **curvative,** *a.* (*Bot.*) Having the margins slightly curved. **curvature,** *n.* Deflexion from a straight line; a curved form; (*Geom.*) the continual bending of a line from a rectilinear direction.

curve (kĕrv) [L. *curvus*, bent], *n.* A bending without angles; that which is bent; a flexure; (*Math.*) a line of which no three consecutive points are in a straight line. *v.t.* To cause to bend without angles. *v.i.* To form or be formed into a curve.

curvet (kĕr vet′, kĕr′ vėt) [It. *corvetta*, dim. of *corvo*, a curve, as prec.], *n.* A particular leap of a horse raising his fore-legs at once, and, as his forelegs are falling, raising his hind-legs, so that all four are off the ground at once. *v.i.* To make a curvet; to frolic, to frisk.

curvi- [L. *curvus*, bent], *comb. form.* Curved. **curvicaudate** (kĕr vi kaw′ dât) [CAUDATE], *a.* Having the tail curved. **curvicostate** (kĕr vi kos′ tât) [COSTATE], *a.* (*Bot.*) Marked with small bent ribs. **curvifoliate** (kĕr vi fō′ li ât) [FOLIATE], *a.* (*Bot.*) Having revolute leaves. **curviform** (kẽr′ vi fôrm), *a.* Of a curved form. **curvilinear** (kĕr vi lin′ ė år) [LINEAR], *a.* Bounded by curved lines; consisting of curved lines. **curvilinearity** -ăr′ i ti), *n.* **curvilinearly,** *adv.* **curvirostral** (kĕr vi ros′ trål) [ROSTRAL], *a.* Having a curved beak.

cuscus (kŭs′ kŭs) [Hind. *khas khas*], *n.* The fibrous, aromatic root of an Indian grass, used for making fans, baskets, etc.

cusec, cu.-sec, (kū′ sek) [abbr. cubic feet per second], *n.* (*Eng.*) Unit of rate of flow of water, one cubic foot per second.

cushat (kush′ åt) [A.-S. *cūsceote*], *n.* (*Sc. and North.*) The woodpigeon or ringdove.

cushion (kush′ ȯn) [F. *coussin*, prob. O.F. *coissin* (prob. from L. *coxa*, hip)], *n.* A kind of pillow or pad for sitting, kneeling, or leaning on, stuffed with feathers, wool, hair, or other soft material; anything padded, as the lining at the side of a billiard-table which causes the balls to rebound; a flat leather bag filled with sand, used by engravers to support the plate or block; a pad on which gilders and binders spread gold-leaf; (*Bot., Zool., etc.*) a cushion-like organ, part, or growth; (*Steam-engine*) the elastic body of steam left in the cylinder and acting as a buffer to the piston. *v.t.* To seat or support on a cushion; to protect or pad with cushions; to furnish with cushions; (*Billiards*) to place or leave (a ball) close up to the cushion; (*fig.*) to suppress or quietly ignore. **lady's cushion:** The sea-pink, or thrift, *Armeria maritima*; the moss saxifrage, *Saxifraga hypnoides*. **pin-cushion,** *n.* A pad for keeping pins in. **sea cushion,** *n.* The thrift, *Armeria maritima*. **cushion-capital,** *n.* (*Arch.*) A capital shaped like a cushion pressed down by a weight. **cushion-tire,** *n.* A cycle tire made of rubber stuffed with rubber shreds. **cushiony,** *a.*

cushy (ku′ shi) [Hind. *khushi*, pleasant; also CUSHIONY], *a.* (*slang*) Soft, easy, comfortable; well paid and little to do.

cusp (kŭsp) [L. *cuspis -idis*, a point], *n.* A point, an apex, a summit; (*Arch.*) a Gothic ornament consisting of a projecting point formed by the meeting of curves; (*Geom.*) the point in a curve at which its two branches have a common tangent; (*Bot.*) the pointed end of a leaf or other part; a projection on a molar tooth. **cusped,** *a.* **cuspidal,** *a.* (*Geom.*) Ending in a point. **cuspidate, -dated** (kŭs′ pi dāt, -dā tėd), *a.* (*Nat. Hist.*) Furnished with small eminences; (*Bot.*) tapering to a rigid point; abruptly acuminate. **cuspidate teeth,** *n.pl.* Canine teeth.

cuspidor (kŭs′ pi dôr) [Port., a spitter, from *cuspir*, to spit, L. *conspuere*, CONSPUE]. *n.* (*Am.*) A spittoon.

cuss (kŭs) [CURSE], *n.* A curse; a worthless fellow. **cussedness,** *n.* Perverseness; obstinacy, resolution.

custard (kŭs′ tård) [prob. from M.E. *crustade*, a pie with crust, O.F. *croustade*, L. *crustāta*, fem. p.p. of *crustāre* (see CRUST)], *n.* A composition of milk and eggs (or substitutes), sweetened and flavoured; orig., an open pie. **custard-apple,** *n.* A West Indian fruit, *Anona reticulata*, with a soft pulp. ***custard-coffin,** *n.* The raised crust of a pie.

custodian (kŭs tō′ di ån), *n.* One who has the custody or guardianship of anything. **custodial,** *a.* Pertaining to custody or guardianship. *n.* (*Hist.*) A portable shrine or relic-case.

custody (kŭs′ tȯ di) [L. *custōdia* (*custos -todis*, a guardian)], *n.* Guardianship, security; imprisonment, confinement. **to take into custody:** To arrest.

custom (kŭs′ tȯm) [O.F. *costume*, L. *consuītūdinem*, acc. of *consuētūdo*, custom, from *consuētus*, p.p. of *consuescere* (CON-, *suescere*, inceptive of *suēre*, to be accustomed)], *n.* An habitual use or practice; established usage; familiarity, use; buying of goods, business; a frequenting a shop to purchase; (*pl.*) custom-duties on imports, etc.; (*Law*) long established practice constituting common law. **v.t.* To accustom; to give custom to; to pay duty on. **v.i.* To be accustomed. **custom-duties,** *n.pl.* Duties imposed on goods imported or exported. **custom-house,** *n.* The office where vessels enter and clear, and where custom-duties are paid. **custom made,** *a.* (*Am.*) Made to measure. **custom suit,** *n.* (*Am.*) A bespoke suit. ***customable,** *a.* Customary; liable to duty. **customed,** *a.* Usual, accustomed.

customary (kŭs′ tȯ må ri), *a.* Habitual, usual, wonted: (*Law*) holding or held by custom, liable under custom. *n.* A written or printed record of customs. **customarily,** *adv.* **customariness,** *n.*

customer (kŭs′ tȯ mẽr), *n.* One who deals regularly at a particular shop; a purchaser; (*fig.*) a person one has to do with, a fellow.

custos (kŭs′ tos) [L.], *n.* A keeper, a custodian. ***custos rotulorum,*** *n.* The chief civil officer or Lord Lieutenant of a county and keeper of its records.

cut (kŭt) [origin doubtful], *v.t.* (*past & p.p.* **cut**) To penetrate or wound with a sharp instrument; to divide or separate with a sharp-edged instrument; to sever, to detach, to hew, to fell, to mow or reap; to carve, to trim or clip; to form by cutting; to reduce by cutting; to mutilate or shorten a play, article, or book; (*Cinema.*) to edit a film; to intersect, to cross; to divide (as a pack of cards); (*Cricket*) to hit (a ball) with a downward stroke and make it glance to one side; to wound deeply; to leave, to give up; to renounce the acquaintance of; to reduce as low as possible. *v.i.* To make a wound or incision with or as with a sharp-edged instrument; to have a good edge; to come through the gums; to divide a pack of cards; (*slang*) to move away quickly, to run; (*Med.*) to perform an operation by cutting, esp. in lithotomy. *a.* Subjected to the act or process of cutting; severed; shaped by cutting; castrated. *n.* The action of cutting; a stroke or blow with a sharp-edged instrument; an opening, gash, or wound made by cutting; anything done or said that hurts the feelings; the omission of a part of a play; a slit, a channel, a groove, a trench; a part cut off; a gelding; a stroke with a whip; a particular stroke in various games with balls; the act of dividing a pack of cards; the shape in which a thing is cut, style; the act of ignoring a former acquaintance; *a dupe; a degree (from count being formerly kept by notches); an engraved wood block or an electrotype therefrom; an impression from such block or electrotype; (*Cinema.*) the place where one strip of film ends in a picture and another begins. *int.* (*Cinema.*) The order for cameras to stop. **to be a cut above:** (*fig.*) To be superior to. **cut-and-cover:** A tunnel made by excavating an open cutting and covering it in. **cut and dry** or **dried:** Prepared for use; ready-made; unoriginal, trite. ***cut and long tail:** All kinds of dogs; hence, everybody. **cut and thrust:** Cutting and thrusting; a hand-to-hand struggle. **short cut:** A near way or path; the readiest means to an end. ***to draw cuts:** To draw lots. **to cut a caper:** To frisk about. **to cut across:** To pass by a shorter course so as to cut off an angle. **to cut a dash:** To make a show or display. **to cut a figure, a flourish,** etc.: To look, appear, or perform (usually qualified by an adjective, and perhaps derived from the practice of cutting figures on ice in skating). **to cut and come again:** To help oneself and take more if one will. **to cut away:** To detach by cutting; to reduce by cutting. **to cut down:** To fell; to compress, to reduce. **to cut in:** (*Motor.*) To drive in front of another person's car so as to affect his driving; (*Dancing*) to take a lady away from her partner; to interrupt, to intrude. **to cut it fine:** To reduce to the minimum. **to cut no ice:** (*colloq.*) To have no effect, to make no impression. **to cut off:** To remove by cutting, to eradicate; to intercept; to prevent from access. **to cut one's losses:** To write off as lost, to abandon a speculation. **to cut one's teeth:** To have the teeth come through the gums. **to cut one's stick:** (*colloq.*) To go away; to run; to escape. **to cut out:** To shape by cutting; to remove or separate by cutting, to excel, to outdo; to supplant; (*Naut.*) to enter a harbour and seize and carry off (as a ship) by sudden attack; to relinquish a game as the result of cutting the cards. **to cut short:** To hinder by interruption; to abridge. **to cut to pieces:** To exterminate, to massacre. **to cut under:** To undersell. **to cut up:** To cut in pieces; to criticize severely; to distress deeply. **to cut up well:** (*colloq.*) To leave plenty of money. **to cut up rough:** (*slang*) To become quarrelsome or savage. **cut-away,** *a.* Having the skirts rounded off. *n.* A coat with the skirts rounded off. **cut-glass,** *n.* Flint glass in which a pattern is formed by cutting or grinding. **cut-grass,** *n.* *Leersia oryzoides*, the leaves of which are so rough as to cut the hands. **cut-price,** *n.* The lowest price possible; reduced price. **cutpurse,** *n.* One who stole purses by cutting them from the girdle to which they were fastened; a highwayman, a thief. **cut-throat,** *n.* A murderer, an assassin. *a.* Murderous, barbarous. **cut-off,** *n.* A passage cut by a river, affording a new channel; (*Eng.*) a mode of using steam by which it is admitted to the cylinder only during a portion of the piston-stroke; a valve to stop discharge. **cut-off road,** *n.* (*Am.*) A bypass. **cut-out:** (*Motor.*) A device for disconnecting the exhaust from the silencer, so as to gain extra power in racing, etc.; (*Motor.*) a device which automatically disconnects the battery from the dynamo; (*Elec.*) a device for automatic severance of an electric circuit in case the tension becomes too high for the wiring. *n.* (*Elec.*) A switch for shutting off a light or a group of lights from a circuit. **cutter,** *n.* One who or that which cuts; one who cuts out men's clothes to measure; a cutting tool; (*Cinema.*) a film editor; (*Am.*) a light sledge; a soft brick adapted to be rubbed down for ornamental work or arching; *a cut-throat; (*Naut.*) a man-of-war's boat smaller than a barge, with from four to eight oars; a one-masted vessel with fore-and-aft sails. **cutter-bar,** *n.* The bar of a cutting-machine in which the cutters are fixed. **cutting,** *a.* Dividing by a sharp-edged instrument; sharp-edged; wounding the feelings deeply; sarcastic, biting. *n.* The action of the verb TO CUT; underselling, keen competition by means of reduced prices; a piece cut off or out (of a newspaper, etc.); (*Gardening*) a slip; (*Eng.*) an excavation for a road, railway, or canal; lithotomy; (*Cinema.*) the selection of those portions of a film that are finally to be shown. **cutting-bench,** *n.* (*Cinema.*) Table on which a cutter assembles and edits a film. **cuttingly,** *adv.* In a cutting manner.

cutaneous (kū tā' nė ŭs) [L. *cutāneus*, from *cutis*, skin], *a.* Belonging to or affecting the skin.

cutch (kŭch) [Malay *cachu*], *n.* (*Comm.*) Catechu, used in tanning.

cute (kūt) [ACUTE], *a.* (*slang*) Cunning, sharp, clever; (*Am.*) piquant, delightful, attractive, amusing; pretty. **cutie,** *n.* (*Am. slang*) A bright, attractive girl. **cutely,** *adv.* **cuteness,** *n.*

Cuthbert's duck (kŭth' bĕrts dŭk) [St. *Cuthbert*]. *n.* The eider duck, so called because it breeds on the Farne Islands, and is connected with the legend of St. Cuthbert, the apostle of Northumbria.

cuticle (kū' ti kėl) [L. *cutīcula*, dim. of *cutis*, skin], *n*, (*Physiol.*) The epidermis or scarf-skin; the outer layer of the integument in the lower animals; (*Bot.*) the thin external covering of the bark of a plant. **cuticular,** *a.* **cuticularize,** *v.t.*

cutikin (kū' ti kin) [Sc., from obs. *coot*, the ankle-joint (cp. Dut. *koot*, L.G. *kote*, *köte*), -KIN], *n.* A long gaiter, a spatterdash.

cutin (kū' tin), *n.* (*Bot.*) A form of cellulose existing in the cuticle of plants.

cutis (kū' tis) [CUTICLE], *n.* (*Physiol.*) The true skin beneath the epidermis; (*Bot.*) the peridium of certain fungi.

cutlass (kŭt' lȧs) [F. *coutelas*, augm. of O.F. *coutel* (F. *couteau*), a knife, L. *cultellum*, acc. of *cultellus*, COULTER], *n.* A broad curved sword, esp. that used by sailors.

cutler (kŭt' lėr) [O.F. *coutelier*, *cotelier*, from *coutel* (see prec.)], *n.* One who makes or deals in cutting instruments. **cutlery,** *n.* The business of a cutler; knives and other edged instruments or tools.

cutlet (kŭt' lėt) [F. *côtelette*, dim. of *côte*, O.F. *coste*, L. *costa*, rib], *n.* A small slice of meat, usually from the loin or neck, for cooking.

cutter, cutting [CUT].

cuttle (1) (kŭtl) [A.-S. *cudele*; etym. doubtful], *n.* A cuttle-fish. **cuttle-fish,** *n.* The octopus, *Sepia officinalis*; other members of the genus *Sepia*.

***cuttle** (2) (kŭtl) [prob. from O.F. *coutel* (F. *couteau*), L. *cultellum*], *n.* (*Shak.*) A knife, or one too ready to use a knife; a bravo.

cutty (kŭt' i) [Sc. and North., from CUT], *a.* Short, cut short; hasty, quick, *n.* A cutty pipe; a short girl; a hare. **cutty pipe,** *n.* A short clay tobacco-pipe. **cutty-stool,** *n.* A bench in old Scottish churches on which women guilty of unchastity were compelled to sit and undergo public rebuke.

cutwater (kŭt' waw tėr), *n.* (*Naut.*) The fore part of a ship's prow which cuts the water.

cutworm (kŭt' wĕrm), *n.* A caterpillar, esp. (*Am.*) the larvæ of the genus of moths *Agrotis*, which cuts off plants near the roots.

cuvette (kū vet') [F., dim. of *cuve*, L. *cūpa*, a cask, a vat], *n.* A little scoop; a clay crucible.

-cy [L. *-cia*, *-tia*; Gr. *-keia*, *-kia*, *-teia*, *-tia* (cp. -ACY)], *suf.* Forming nouns of quality from adjectives, and nouns of office (cp. -SHIP) from nouns.

cyan-, cyano- [Gr. *kuanos*, a dark-blue mineral], *comb. form.* Of a blue colour; pertaining to or containing cyanogen.

cyanate (sī' ȧ nāt), *n.* (*Chem.*) A salt of cyanic acid.

cyanic (sī ăn' ik), *a.* Derived from cyanogen. **cyanic acid,** *n.* A compound of cyanogen and hydrogen.

cyanide (sī' ȧ nīd), *n.* A compound of cyanogen with a metallic element.

cyanine (sī' ȧ nīn), *n.* A blue colouring matter used for dyeing calico.

cyanite (sī' ȧ nīt), *n.* (*Min.*) A hard, translucent mineral, often blue, occurring in flattened prisms in gneiss and mica-schist.

cyanogen (sī ăn' ŏ jen), *n.* (*Chem.*) Colourless, poisonous gas composed of carbon and nitrogen, burning with a peach-blossom flame, and smelling like prussic acid.

cyanometer (sī ȧ nom' e tėr), *n.* (*Opt.*) An instrument for determining the depth of the tint of the atmosphere.

cyanosis (sī ȧ nō' sis), *n.* (*Med.*) A disease in which the skin becomes blue or leaden-coloured owing to defective circulation.

cyanotype (sī ăn' ō tīp), *n.* A photographic process in which a cyanide is employed.

cyathiform (sī ăth' i fôrm) [Gr. *kuathos*, cup], *a.* (*Bot.*) Cup-shaped; resembling a drinking cup.

cybernetics (sī bĕr net' iks) [Gr. *kubernetes*, a steersman], *n.* The study of control and communication mechanisms in machines and living creatures.

cycad (sī' kȧd) [mod. L. *cycas -adis* (from a supposed Gr. *kukas*, now recognized as an error for *koïkas*, acc. pl. of *koïx*, the Egyptian doum-palm)], *n.* (*Bot.*) A cycadaceous plant. **cycadaceous** (sī kȧ dā' shi ŭs), *a.* Belonging to the *Cycadaceæ*, an order of gymnosperms, allied to the conifers.

cyclamen (sik' lȧ mėn) [late L., from Gr. *kuklaminos* (perh. from *kuklos*, a circle, with reference to the bulbous root)], *n.* The sowbread, a genus of tuberous plants with beautiful flowers.

cycle (sī' kėl) [L. *cyclus*, Gr. *kuklos*, a circle], *n.* A series of years, events, or phenomena recurring in the same order; a series that repeats itself; a complete series or succession; the period in which a series of events is completed; a long period, an age; a body of legend connected with some myth; a bicycle or tricycle; *(*Astron.*) an imaginary circle in the heavens. *v.i.* To revolve in a circle; to ride a bicycle or tricycle. **cycle of the moon, lunar** or **Metonic cycle:** A period of nineteen years, after which the new and full moon recur on the same days of the month. **cycle of the sun** or **solar cycle:** A period of 28 years, after which the days of the month recur on the same days of the week. **cyclic, -al,** *a.* Pertaining to, or moving or recurring in, a cycle; (*Bot.*) arranged in whorls. **cyclic chorus** (*Gr. Ant.*), *n.* The chorus which performed the songs and dithyrambs round the altar of Bacchus. **cyclic poets,** *n.pl.* Poets dealing with the subject of the Trojan war, or with the cycle of legend that has grown up round any myth, *e.g.* King Arthur. **cyclist,** *n.* One who rides a bicycle or tricycle.

cyclo- [Gr. *kuklos*, a circle], *comb. form.* Circular; pertaining to a circle or circles.

cyclograph (sī' klō grăf), *n.* An instrument for describing the arcs of large circles.

cycloid (sī' kloid) [as prec.], *n.* The figure described by a point in the plane of a circle as it rolls along a straight line till it has completed a revolution (**common cycloid:** When the point is on the circumference; **curtate cycloid:** When the point is without the circumference; **protate cycloid:** When the point is within the circumference). **cycloidal** (-kloi' dål), *a.* Resembling a circle; (*Zool.*) having concentric striations; pertaining to the Cycloidei. **Cycloidei** (sī kloi' dė ī), *n.pl.* (*Ichthyol.*) An artificial order of fishes, founded by Agassiz, consisting of those with cycloid scales.

cyclometer (sī klom' ė tĕr), *n.* An instrument for recording the revolutions of a wheel, esp. that of a bicycle. **cyclometry,** *n.* The art or process of measuring circles.

cyclone (sī' klōn) [Gr. *kuklos*, a circle], *n.* (*Meteor.*) A disturbance in the atmosphere caused by a system of winds blowing spirally towards a central region of low barometric pressure; a violent hurricane. **cyclonic** (sī klon' ik), *a.*

cyclopædia, etc. [ENCYCLOPÆDIA].

cyclopean (sī klō pē' ån, sī klō' pė ån) [L. *Cyclōpēus*, *Cyclōpius*, Gr. *Kuklōpeios*, *Kuklōpios* (see foll.)], *a.* Of or pertaining to the Cyclops; immense, gigantic. **cyclopean masonry:** A style of architecture of great antiquity, in which massive blocks are accurately fitted together, or rough blocks laid one on another, and the interstices filled up with small stones, no mortar being used in either form.

cyclops (sī' klops) [L., from Gr. *Kuklops* (*kuklos*, a circle, *ops*, an eye)], *n.* (*pl.* **-opes**) A mythical one-eyed giant supposed to have dwelt in Sicily; (*fig.*) a one-eyed person; (*Zool.*) a genus of *Entomostraca* with a single eye.

cyclorama (sī klō ra' må) [Gr. *horama*, a view], *n.* A panorama painted on the inside of a large cylinder and viewed by the spectator from the middle.

cyclosis (sī klō' sis) [Gr. *kuklōsis*, an encircling (*kukloein*, to move in a circle)], *n.* (*Biol.*) Circulation, as of blood, the latex in plants, or protoplasm in certain cells; (*Math.*) the occurrence of cycles.

cyclostomata (sī klō stom' å tå), *n.* (*Zool.*) A sub-class of fishes, with a circular suctorial mouth, containing the lampreys and hags. **cyclostomatous** (-stom' å tůs), **cyclostomous** (sī klos' tō můs), *a.* **cyclostome** (sī' klō stōm), *n.*

cyclostyle (sī' klō stīl), *n.* A machine for printing copies of handwriting or typewriting by means of a sheet perforated like a stencil.

cyclotron (sī' klō tron), *n.* (*Phys.*) A particle accelerator designed to accelerate protons to high energies.

cyder [CIDER].

cygnet (sig' nėt) [dim. of O.F. *cygne* or L. *cygnus*, a swan], *n.* A young swan.

cylinder (sil' in dėr) [L. *cylindrus*, Gr. *kulindros* (*kulindein*, to roll)], *n.* A straight roller-shaped body, solid or hollow, and of uniform circumference; (*Geom.*) a solid figure described by the revolution of a right-angled parallelogram about one of its sides which remains fixed; a cylindrical member of various machines, esp. the chamber in a steam-engine in which the piston is acted upon by the steam; the roller used in machine-printing. **cylinder-press,** *n.* A printing-press in which the type is secured on a cylinder, or in which the impression is given by a cylinder. **cylindrical** (si lin' drik ål), *a.* Having the form of a cylinder. **cylindriform,** *a.* **cylindroid** (sil' in droid) [Gr. *kulindroeidēs* (-OID)], *n.* (*Geom.*) A solid body differing from a cylinder in having the bases elliptical instead of circular.

cyma (sī' må) [Gr. *kûma*, anything swollen, a wave, an ogee moulding, a sprout], *n.* (*Arch.*) A convex and a concave curve forming the topmost member of a cornice; (*Bot.*) a cyme. **cymagraph,** *n.* An apparatus for tracing the outline of mouldings. ***cyma recta,*** *n.* A curve convex above and concave below. ***cyma reversa,*** *n.* Concave above and convex below, ogee. **cymatium** (sī măt' i ům, -mā' shi ům) [L., from Gr. *kumation*, dim. of *kûma*], *n.* A cyma.

cymar (si mar') [F. *simarre*, O.F. *chamarre* (see CHIMER)], *n.* A woman's light loose robe or under-garment.

cymbal (sim' bål) [L. *cymbalum*, Gr. *kûmbalon* (*kumbē*, hollow)], *n.* One of a pair of disks of brass or bronze more or less basin-shaped, clashed together to produce a sharp, clashing sound. **cymbalist,** *n.*

cymbalo (sim' bå lō) [It. *cembalo*, as prec.], *n.* The dulcimer, a stringed instrument played by means of small hammers held in the hands.

cymbiform (sĭm' bi fôrm) [L. *cymba*, a boat, -FORM], *a.* (*Anat. and Bot.*) Boat-shaped; navicular (of certain bones and grasses).

cyme (sim) [F., from L. *cȳma*, Gr. *kûma*, see CYMA)], *n.* An inflorescence in which the central terminal flower comes to perfection first, as in the guelder-rose. **cymoid,** *a.* Resembling a cyme. **cymose** (sī mōs'), *a.*

cymophane (sī' mō fān) [Gr. *kûma*, a wave, *-phanēs*, appearing (*phainein*, to appear)], *n.* (*Min.*) A variety of chrysoberyl. **cymophanous** (sī mof' å nůs), *a.*

Cymric (kim'-, sim' rik) [W. *Cymru*, Wales], *a.* Pertaining to the Welsh. *n.* The Welsh language.

cynanthropy (sī năn' thrō pi) [Gr. *kunanthropos* (*kun-*, stem of *kuōn*, a dog, *anthrōpos*, a man)], *n.* Madness in which a person fancies he is changed into a dog, and imitates the habits of that animal.

cynic (sin' ik) [L. *cynicus*, Gr. *kunikos* (*kun-*, stem of *kuōn*, a dog)], *n.* (*Hist.*) One of a rigid sect of Greek philosophers (of which Diogenes was the most distinguished member) founded at Athens by Antisthenes, a pupil of Socrates, who insisted on the complete renunciation of all luxury and the subjugation of sensual desires; a morose, sarcastic, sneering person. **cynical,** *a.* Bitter, sarcastic, misanthropical; (*Hist.*) of or belonging to the cynics. **cynically,** *adv.* **cynicism** (sin' i sizm), *n.*

cynocephalus (sī nō sef' å lůs) [L., from Gr. *kunokephalos* (Gr. *kuōn kunos*, dog, *kephalē*, head)], *n.* A dog-headed man in ancient mythology; the dog-faced baboon. **cynophobia** (sī nō fō byå), *n.* (*Path.*) A morbid fear of dogs; a neurosis resembling rabies.

cynosure (sin' ō-, sī' nō shūr) [F., from L. *cynosūra*, Gr. *kunosoura*, the dog's tail, the Lesser Bear (*kuōn kunos*, dog, *oura*, tail)], *n.* (*Astron.*) The constellation of the Lesser Bear (*Ursa Minor*), containing the north star; (*fig.*) a centre of interest or attraction.

cypher [CIPHER].

cy près (sē prā') [A.-F. (F. *si près*, so near)], *adv.* and *a.* (*Law*) As near as practicable (referring to the principle of applying a bequest to some object as near as may be to the testator's aim when that is impracticable). *n.* An approximation.

cypress (1) (sī' pres) [O.F. *cyprès*, late L. *cypressus*, Gr. *kupressos*], *n.* A genus of coniferous trees, esp. *Cupressus sempervirens*, valued for the durability of its wood; a branch of this as emblem of mourning.

***cypress** (2) (sī' pres) [prob. from O.F. *Cipré*, *Cypre*, Cyprus], *n.* A kind of satin that was highly valued, also known as *satin of Cypres*; a piece of this worn as a token of mourning. ***cypress-lawn,** *n.* A thin, transparent black fabric, a kind of lawn or crape, worn as mourning.

Cyprian (sip' ri ȧn), *a.* Of or belonging to Cyprus, where the worship of Venus especially flourished. *n.* A Cypriot; (*fig.*) a lewd woman, a prostitute. **Cypriot,** *n.* An inhabitant of Cyprus.

cyprine (sī' prin, -prīn) [L. *cyprīnus*, Gr. *kuprīnos*, carp], *n.* (*Ichthyol.*) Of or belonging to the fish genus *Cyprinus*, containing the carp.

cypripedium (sī pri pē' di ŭm) [Gr. *Kupris*, Venus, and *podion*, a slipper], *n.* (*Bot.*) Lady's slipper, a genus of orchids, possessing two fertile stamens, the central stamen (fertile in other orchids) being represented by a shield-like plate.

Cyrenaic (sī rė nā' ik), *a.* Of or pertaining to Cyrene, a Greek colony in the north of Africa, or to the hedonistic or eudæmonistic philosophy founded at that place by Aristippus.

Cyrillic (si ril' ik) [St. *Cyril*], *a.* A term applied to the alphabet of the Slavonic nations who belong to the Greek Church, from the fact that it was introduced by Clement, a disciple of St. Cyril.

cyrto- [Gr. *kurtos*, curved], *comb. form.* Curving; bent. **cyrtometer** (sėr tom' ė tėr) [-METER], *n.* An apparatus used to measure and record the curves of a chart.

cyst (sist) [L. *cystis*, from Gr. *kustis*, a bladder], *n.* (*Biol.*) A bladder, vesicle, or hollow organ; a cell; a receptacle; (*Path.*) a sac containing morbid matter.

cyst-, cysti-, cysto- [Gr. *kustē*, *kustis*, a bladder], *comb. form.* (*Anat.*, *Zool.*, *etc.*) Pertaining to the bladder; bladder-shaped. **cystic** (sis' tik), *a.* Pertaining to or enclosed in a cyst, esp. the gall bladder or the urinary bladder; having cysts, or of the nature of a cyst. **cystic worms,** *n.pl.* Immature tapeworms encysted in the tissues of their host. **cystiform,** *a.* **cystine** (sis' tīn), *n.* (*Chem.*) An organic, crystalline substance found in a rare kind of urinary calculus. **cystitis** (sis tī' tis) [-ITIS], *n.* Inflammation of the bladder. **cystocele** (sis' tȯ sēl) [-CELE], *n.* Hernia caused by protrusion of the bladder. **cystopteris** (sis top' tėr is) [Gr. *pteris*, a fern], *n.* (*Bot.*) A genus of ferns containing the bladder-ferns. **cystoscope** (sis' tȯ skōp) [-SCOPE], *n.* An instrument or apparatus for the exploration of the bladder. **cystose** (sis tōs'), **cystous** (sis' tŭs), *a.* Containing cysts. **cystotomy** (sis tot' ȯ mi) [-TOMY], *n.* The act or practice of opening cysts; the operation of cutting into the bladder to remove calculi.

-cyte [Gr. *kutos*, a hollow, a receptacle], *suf.* (*Biol.*) A cell; as in *leucocyte*. **cytology,** *n.* (*Biol.*) The study of cells. **cytoplasm,** *n.* The protoplasm of a cell.

cytherean (sith ėr ē' ȧn), *a.* Pertaining to Venus, the goddess of love, who was connected with Cythera (the modern Cerigo).

cyto- [Gr. *kutos*, a hollow], *comb. form.* (*Biol.*) Cellular; pertaining to or composed of cells. **cytoblast** (sī' tȯ blast) [Gr. *blastos*, a sprout], *n.* A cell-nucleus. **cytology** (si tol' ȯ ji), *n.* The study of cells. **cytolysis** (sī tol' i sis), *n.* The dissolution of cells. **cytoplasm** (sī' tō plăzm), *n.* The protoplasm of a cell apart from the nucleus.

Czar, etc. [TSAR].

czardas (char' dosh) [Hung.], *n.* A Hungarian national dance.

Czech (chek) [Boh. *Cech*; Pol. *Czech*], *n.* A Bohemian; the Bohemian language. *a.* Pertaining to the Czechs or their language. **Czechoslovakia** (che' kō slō văk' i ȧ), *n.* The country inhabited by the Czechs and the Slovaks, whose independence was acknowledged by the Allied governments in 1918. **Czechoslovak,** *a.*

D

D, d, the fourth letter in the English alphabet, represents a dental sound formed by placing the tip of the tongue against the roots of the upper teeth, and then passing up vocalized breath into the mouth. After a non-vocal or surd consonant it takes a sharper sound, nearly approaching that of *t*, especially in the past tenses and past participles of verbs in *-ed*. D is a symbol for the second note of the musical scale of C, corresponding to the Italian *re*; the fourth in numerical series; (*Roman numeral*) 500. **D-day,** *n.* The code name for the date of the invasion of France, 6 June, 1944.

-d [A.-S. *-de* (see -ED)], *suf.* Forming past tense and p.p. of weak verbs, as *died, heard, loved, proved.*

da [DAD, etc.].

dab (1) (dăb) [etym. doubtful; prob. imit. (cp. TAP)], *v.t.* (*past & p.p.* **dabbed**) To strike gently with some moist or soft substance; to pat; to rub with a dabber; to press with a soft substance. *n.* A gentle blow; a light stroke or wipe with a soft substance; a lump; *a rap, a blow; (*slang*) a dabster. **dabber,** *n.* One who or that which dabs.

dab (2) (dăb) [perh. from DAB (1)], *n.* A small flatfish, *Pleuronectes limanda.*

dabble (dă' bėl) [freq. of DAB (1) (cp. Norw. *dabla*, Dut. *dabbelen*)], *v.t.* To keep on dabbing; to wet by little dips; to besprinkle, to moisten, to splash. *v.i.* To play or splash about in water; (*fig.*) to do or practise anything in a superficial manner; to dip into a subject. **dabbler,** *n.* One who dabbles with any subject. **dabblingly,** *adv.* Superficially, shallowly.

dabchick (dăb' chik) [earlier *dap-chick*, *dop-chick* (*dap*, cogn. with DIP)], *n.* The little grebe, *Podiceps minor.*

dabster (dăb' stėr) [DAB (1), -STER], *n.* (*colloq.*) One who is expert at anything.

da capo (da ka' pō) [It., from the beginning], *Mus. direction.* The player is to begin again.

dace (dās) [M.E. *darse*, O.F. *darz*, DART], *n.* A small river fish, *Leuciscus vulgaris.*

dachshund (daks'-, da*chs*' hunt) [G., badger-hound], *n.* A short-legged breed of dog.

dacker (dăk' ėr), **daiker** (dā' kėr) [Sc. and North. (cp. M.Flem. *daeckeren*)], *v.i.* To toddle, to saunter; to vacillate.

dacoit (dȧ koit') [Hind. *ḍakait* (*ḍākā*, robbery by a gang)], *n.* One of an Indian or Burmese band of armed robbers. **dacoity,** *n.*

dacryops (dăk' rē ops) [Gr. *dakru*, a tear; *ops*, face], *n.* (*Path.*) A cyst of the lachrymal gland; watery eye.

dactyl (dăk' til) [L. *dactylus*, as foll.], *n.* A metrical foot consisting of one long followed by two short syllables. **dactylic** (-til' ik), *a.*

dactyl-, dactylio-, dactylo- [Gr. *daktulos*, a finger], *comb. form.* Having fingers or digits; pertaining to fingers or digits. **dactylioglyph** (dăk til' i ȯ glif)

[Gr. *daktulioglupkos* (*gluphos*, carver, from *gluphein*, to carve)], *n.* An engraver of rings or gems; the engraver's name on rings or gems. **dactylioglyphy** (-og' li fi), *n.* **dactyliography** (dăk til i og' rȧ fi) [-GRAPHY], *n.* The art of engraving gems. **dactyliology** (-l' ŏ ji) [-LOGY], *n.* A treatise on finger-rings. ***dactyliomancy** (dăk til' i ŏ măn si) [-MANCY], *n.* Divination by finger-rings. **dactylogram,** *n.* A finger-print.

dactylology (dăk ti lol' ō ji), *n.* The art of conversing with the deaf and dumb by means of the fingers.

dad (1) (dăd), **da** (da), **dada** (dăd'a), **daddy** (dăd' i) [cp. W. *tad*, Gr. *tata*, Sansk. *tata-*], *n.* A child's name for father. **daddy,** *n.* A form of address for an old man. **daddy-long-legs,** *n.* Various species of crane-fly.

dad (2) (dăd), **daud** (dawd) [Sc. and North., onomat.], *v.t.* To strike with a blow that shakes; to thrash. *v.i.* To fall; to tumble about. *n.* A thumping blow; a thumping piece.

daddle (1) (dădl) [etym. obscure (cp. DODDER)], *v.i.* To walk totteringly; to toddle.

daddle (2) (dădl) [dial.], *n.* The hand; the fist.

dadism (da' dizm) [Fr. *aller à dada*, ride a cock-horse], *n.* A school of art and literature that aims at suppressing any correlation between thought and expression.

dado (dā' dō) [It., a die, a cube], *n.* The cube of a pedestal between the base and the cornice; an arrangement of wainscoting or decoration round the lower part of the walls of a room.

dædal (dē' dȧl) [L. *dædalus*, Gr. *daidalos*], *a.* Dædalian; mazy, intricate; wonderfully wrought; skilful; deceitful; complicated. **Dædalian, -ean** (dē dā' li ȧn) [L. *Dædaleus*, pertaining to *Dædalus*, the Greek artificer (cp. Gr. *daidaleos*, cunningly wrought)], *a.* Curiously wrought; maze-like.

dæmon, etc. [DEMON].

daff (1) (dăf) [DOFF], *v.t.* To throw off; to thrust away; to put off.

daff (2) (dăf) [Sc.; cp. DAFT], *v.i.* To play the fool.

daffodil (dăf' ŏ dil), **daffodilly** (dăf ŏ dil' i), **daffadowndilly** (dăf ȧ doun dil' i) [M.E. *affodill*, O.F. *asphodile*, L. *asphodelus*, Gr. *asphodelos*], *n.* The Lent lily or yellow narcissus, *Narcissus pseudo-narcissus*; other species and garden varieties of the genus *Narcissus*.

daft (daft) [A.-S. *gedæfte*, mild, gentle], *a.* Weak-minded, imbecile; foolish, silly, thoughtless; frolicsome. **daftly,** *adv.*

***dag** (dăg) [etym. unknown], *n.* A heavy pistol or hand-gun used in the 16th and 17th centuries.

dagger (dăg' ėr) [F. *dague*, influenced by M.E. *daggen*, to pierce], *n.* A short two-edged weapon adapted for stabbing; (*Print.*) a reference mark (†). **at daggers drawn:** On hostile terms; ready to fight. **to look daggers:** To look with fierceness or animosity. **dagger-plant,** *n.* The yucca.

daggle (dă' gėl) [freq. of obs. verb *dag*, etym. doubtful], *v.t.* To trail through mud or wet; to bemire, as the bottom of a garment. *v.i.* To run through wet or mire. **daggle-tailed,** *a.* Slatternly, sluttish.

dago (dā' gō) [Sp. *Diego*, James], *n.* (*slang*) A contemptuous term for a Spaniard, Italian, or Portuguese.

dagoba (da' gŏ bȧ) [Singh. *dāgaba*], *n.* A dome-shaped Buddhist shrine containing relics.

daguerreotype (dȧ ger' rō tīp), *n.* The process of photographing on polished metal plates used by Daguerre (1789–1851), of Paris; a photograph by this process. *v.t.* To photograph by this process; (*fig.*) to picture exactly. **daguerreotyper, -ist,** *n.* One who produced daguerreotypes. **daguerreotypic, -al** (-tip' ik, -al), *a.* Pertaining to daguerreotype. **daguerreotypism,** *n.*

dahabeeyah (da ha bē' ya) [Arab. *dhahabīyah*, the golden (*dhahab*, gold)], *n.* A native sailing-boat on the Nile.

dahlia (dā' li ȧ) [*Dahl*, a pupil of Linnæus), *n.* A genus of composite plants from Mexico, cultivated for their beautiful flowers.

Dail Eireann (dal ā' ri ėn) [Ir.], The House of Representatives in the parliament of Eire.

daily (dā' li) [A.-S. *dæglic* (found only in comb.), *a.* Happening, done, or recurring every day; published every weekday; necessary for every day; ordinary, usual. *adv.* Day by day; often; continually, always. *n.* A newspaper published every week-day; woman employed daily for house-work. **daily dozen:** (*colloq.*) Daily physical exercises.

daimio (dī' myō) [Jap. (Chin. *dai*, great, *myo*, name)], *n.* The official title of a former class of feudal lords in Japan.

dainty (dān' ti) [O.F. *dainté*, L. *dignitātem*, acc. of *dignitās* (*dignus*, worthy)], *n.* A delicacy; a choice morsel; a choice dish; *fastidiousness. *a.* Pleasing to the taste, choice; pretty, delicate, elegant; fastidious, nice; luxurious; over-nice. ***daint,** *a.* Dainty. **daintily,** *adv.* **daintiness,** *n.*

dairy (dâr' i) [A.-S. *dǣge*, a maid-servant (cp. DAY-WOMAN), -ERY], *n.* The place or building or department of a farm where milk is kept and converted into butter or cheese; a place where milk, cream, and butter are sold; a dairy-farm; a herd of milch cattle. *a.* Belonging to a dairy or its business. **dairy-farm,** *n.* **dairying,** *n.* Dairy-farming. **dairy-maid,** *n.* **dairy-man,** *n.*

dais (dās) [A.-F. *deis*, O.F. *dois*, L. *discum*, acc. of *discus*, a quoit, late L. a table], *n.* The raised floor at the upper end of a mediæval dining-hall; the principal table on such a raised floor; the chief seat at the high table; a chair of state; a platform.

daisy (dā' zi) [A.-S. *dæges ēage*, day's eye], *n.* A small composite flower, *Bellis perennis*; other flowers resembling this; (*slang*) a first-rate person or thing. **daisy-chain,** *n.* A string of daisies made by children. **daisy-cutter,** *n.* A trotting horse; a ball at cricket bowled so low that it rolls along the ground. **daisied,** *a.* Covered, or adorned, with daisies.

dak, dawk (dăk, dawk) [Hind.], *n.* Post or transport in India by relays of men.

dakoit [DACOIT].

Dalai-lama [LAMA].

dalbergia (dăl bėr' ji ȧ) [Nicholas *Dalberg*], *n.* (*Bot.*) A genus of tropical leguminous trees and climbing shrubs yielding valuable timber.

dale (dāl) [A.-S. *dæl*, a valley (cp. Icel. *dalr*, Dan. *dal*, Goth. *dal*, G. *thal*)], *n.* A valley, esp. from the English midlands to the Scottish lowlands. **dalesman,** *n.* A native or inhabitant of a dale, esp. in the northern counties of England.

dally (dăl' i) [O.F. *dalier*, to chat], *v.i.* To trifle, to toy; to exchange caresses; to sport coquettishly (with); to idle, to delay, to waste time. *v.t.* To consume or waste (away). **dalliance,** *n.*

Dalmatian (dăl mā' shi ȧn), *a.* Belonging to Dalmatia. *n.* A Dalmatian dog; a native or inhabitant of Dalmatia. **Dalmatian dog,** *n.* A variety of hound, white with numerous black spots, formerly kept chiefly as a carriage dog.

dalmatic (dăl măt' ik) [F. *dalmatique*, L. *dalmatica*, orig. adj., of Dalmatia], *n.* An ecclesiastical vestment worn by bishops and deacons in the Roman and Greek churches at High Mass; a similar robe worn by monarchs at coronation and other ceremonies.

dal segno (dal sā' nyō) [It. from the sign], *adv.* (*Mus.*) Repeat from point indicated.

dalt (dawlt) [Sc., from Gael. *dalta*], *n.* A foster-child.

daltonism (dawl' ton izm) [John *Dalton* (1766–1844), an English chemist, who suffered from this], *n.* Colour-blindness, esp. inability to distinguish between red and green.

D

dam (1) (dăm) [DAME], *n.* A female parent (chiefly of quadrupeds); used of a human mother in contempt; (*Sc.*) a crowned man in the game of draughts [see DAMBROD].

dam (2) (dăm) [cp. O.Fris. *dam, dom,* Dut. *dam,* M.H.G. *dam,* G. *damm,* Swed. and Dan. *dam*; also A.-S. *fordemman,* to stop up], *n.* A bank or mound raised to keep back water; the water so kept back; a causeway. *v.t.* (*past & p.p.* **dammed**) To keep back or confine by a dam; to obstruct, to hinder.

damage (dăm′ ȧj) [F., from *dam,* L. *damnum,* cost, loss], *n.* Hurt, injury, mischief, or detriment to any person or thing; loss or harm incurred; (*pl.*) value of injury done; (*slang*) cost; (*Law, pl.*) reparation in money for injury sustained. *v.t.* To cause damage to. *v.i.* To receive damage. ***damage feasant,** *n.* (*Law*) The injury sustained by the cattle of another coming upon a man's land and damaging the crops. **damageable,** *a.* Susceptible of damage; causing damage.

damascene (dăm ȧ sēn′) [F. *damasquiner* (from L. *Damascēnus,* Gr. *Damaskēnos,* of Damascus)], *v.t.* To ornament by inlaying or incrustation, or (as a steel blade) with a wavy pattern in welding. *a.* Pertaining to Damascus. *n.* A native of Damascus; a damson. **Damascus blade,** *n.* A sword of fine quality the blade of which is variegated with streaks or veins.

damask (dăm′ ȧsk) [It. *damasco,* as prec.], *n.* A rich silk stuff with raised figures woven in the pattern, orig. made at Damascus; a linen fabric, with similar figures in the pattern, used for table-cloths, dinner-napkins, etc.; the colour of the damask rose; steel made with a wavy pattern by forging iron and steel together. *a.* Made of damask; red, like the damask rose; of or resembling damask steel. *v.t.* To work flowers on; to damascene, to give a wavy appearance to (as steel work); (*fig.*) to variegate. **damask plum,** *n.* The damson. **damask rose,** *n.* An old-fashioned rose, *Rosa gallica,* var. *damascena.* **damask steel,** *n.* A laminated metal of pure iron and steel, used for Damascus blades.

***damaskeen** [DAMASCENE].

***damassin** (dăm′ ȧ sin) [F. *damas,* damask], *n.* Silk damask with a raised pattern in gold or silver.

dambrod (dăm′ brod), **damboard** (dăm′ bôrd), *n.* (*Sc.*) A draught-board.

dame (dām) [O.F., from L. *domina,* fem. of *dominus,* lord], *n.* A lady; a title of honour (now applied to the widows of knights and baronets); a female member of the Order of the British Empire; mistress of a house; a woman advanced in years; (*Eton*) the matron or master of a boarding-house for boys at the school. **dame-school,** *n.* An elementary school kept by a woman.

dammar (dăm′ ȧr) [Malay *damar*], *n.* A resin of various kinds from eastern conifers.

damn (dăm) [O.F. *damner,* L. *damnāre,* from *damnum,* loss, a fine], *v.t.* To condemn; to call down curses on; (*Theat.*) to ruin by expressing disapprobation; to condemn to eternal punishment; to receive with disapprobation, to reject. *v.i.* To swear profanely. *n.* A profane oath; a negligible amount. **don't care a damn:** Don't care a farthing. **damnable** (dăm′ nȧ bėl), *a.* Deserving damnation or condemnation; odious. **damnably,** *adv.* **damnation** (dăm nā′ shŭn), *n.* Condemnation to eternal punishment; eternal punishment; condemnation; the damning of a play; a profane oath. **damnatory** (dăm′-), *a.* Causing or implying condemnation. **damnatory clauses,** *n.pl.* Clauses in the Athanasian Creed implying the condemnation of those who do not accept various dogmas. **damned** (dămd), *a.* Condemned; condemned to eternal punishment; hateful, execrable; damnable, infernal. *adv.* Confoundedly, infernally. **damnify** (dăm′ ni fī), *v.t.* (*Law*) To cause damage to. **damnification** (-kā′ shŭn), *n.* **damning** (dăm′ ing), *a.* Involving damnation; damnable; cursing.

Damoclean (dăm ō klē′ ȧn), *a.* Of or relating to Damocles, who having grossly flattered Dionysius of Syracuse was placed by that tyrant at a magnificent banquet with a sword suspended over his head by a single hair, to show the dangerous nature of such exalted positions; hence, perilous, anxious. **sword of Damocles,** *n.*

damoiseau (dăm′ i zō) [O.F., late L. *domicellus, dominicellus,* double dim. of L. *dominus,* lord], *n.* A squire, a young man of gentle birth not yet knighted.

***damosel** [DAMSEL].

damp (dămp) [cp. Dut. and Dan. *damp,* G. *dampf*], *a.* Moist, humid; admitting moisture; clammy; dejected, depressed. *n.* Humidity, moisture in a building or article of use or in the air; dejection, discouragement, chill; depression; subterranean gases met with in mines. *v.t.* *To stifle; to moisten; to check, to depress; to discourage, to chill, to deaden. **to damp down:** To fill (as a furnace) with coke to prevent the fire going out. **to damp off:** To rot off, as the stems of plants, from damp. **damp-course,** *n.* A layer of impervious material put between the courses of a wall to keep moisture from rising. **damp-proof,** *a.* Impenetrable to moisture. **dampen,** *v.t.* To make damp; to dull, to deaden, to deject. *v.i.* To become damp. **damper,** *n.* One who or that which damps; a valve or sliding plate in a flue for regulating a fire; (*Austral.*) bread or cake baked in hot ashes; (*Mus.*) a padded finger in a piano for deadening the sound; a mute in brass wind instruments. **damping,** *n.* (*Motor.*) The deadening of the shock of sudden movement; (*Radio.*) the rate at which an electrical oscillation dies away. **damping off,** *n.* (*Hort.*) The killing of plants from excess of moisture. **dampish,** *a.* **damply,** *adv.* **dampness,** *n.*

damsel (dăm′ zėl) [O.F. *damoisele,* late L. *dominicella* (cp. DAMOISEAU)], *n.* (*Archaic*) A young unmarried woman; a female attendant.

damson (dăm′ zȯn) [M.E. or A.-F. *damascene,* L. *Damascēnum,* of Damascus], *n.* A small black plum, *Prunus domestica,* var. *damascena*; the tree that bears this. *a.* Damson-coloured. **damson-cheese,** *n.* A conserve of damsons, pressed to the consistency of cheese. **damson plum,** *n.* A large kind of damson.

***dan** (dăn) [O.F. *dans,* nom. *dan.* acc., from L. *dominus -um,* lord], *n.* The title formerly given to monks; a title of respect placed before personal names (and before mythological names in the archaic poets).

dance (dans) [O.F. *danser,* O.H.G. *dansōn,* to draw as in a dance], *v.i.* To move or trip, usu. to music with rhythmical steps, figures, and gestures; to skip, to frolic; to move in a lively or excited way; to bob up and down; to be dangled; to exult, to triumph. *v.t.* To express or accomplish by dancing; to perform (a particular kind of dance); to toss up and down, to dandle; to cause to dance. *n.* A rhythmical stepping with motions of the body, usu. adjusted to the measure of a tune; the tune by which such movements are regulated; a figure or set of figures in dancing; a dancing-party, a ball. **a dance of death:** (*fig.*) An allegorical representation of the universal power of death. **St. Vitus's dance:** Chorea, a nervous disorder characterized by rhythmic nervous movements of an involuntary kind. **to dance attendance on:** To pay assiduous court to; to be kept waiting by. **to lead one a dance:** To cause one trouble or delay in the pursuit of an object. **dancer,** *n.* One who dances, esp. one who earns money by dancing in public. **dancing-girl,** *n.* A professional female dancer; a nautch-girl. **dancing-master,** *n.* One who teaches dancing. ***dancing-rapier,** *n.* A light sword worn for ornament. **dancing-school,** *n.* A place where dancing is taught.

dancette (dan set′) [prob. corr. from O.F. *dant,* L. *dens, dentem,* a tooth], *n.* (*Arch.*) The chevron or zigzag moulding in Norman work; (*Her.*) a fesse with three indentations. **dancetté,** *a.* (*Her.*)

dandelion (dăn′ de lī ȯn) [F. *dente de lion,* lion's tooth], *n.* A well-known composite plant, *Taraxa-*

cum dens leonis, with a yellow flower and toothed leaves.

dander (1) (dăn′ dėr) [Sc. and dial.; perh. conn. with DANDLE], *v.i.* To wander about idly; to maunder.

dander (2) (dăn′ dėr) [etym. doubtful], *n.* (*Am. colloq.*) Temper, anger. **to get one's dander up, to have one's dander raised:** To get into a passion.

dander (3) (dăn′ dėr) [Sc.; etym. unknown], *n.* A cinder, a piece of slag.

dandify (dăn′ di fī) [DANDY, -FY], *v.t.* To make smart, or like a dandy. **dandification** (-kā′ shŭn), *n.*

dandle (dăn′ dl) [cp. L.G. *dand-* (W.Flem. *danderen*, to bounce up and down); and It. *dandolare*, from *dandola, dondola*, a doll or puppet], *v.t.* To dance up and down on the knees or toss in the arms (as a child); to pet; *to trifle or toy with. *v.i.* To trifle or toy (with). **dandler,** *n.*

dandruff (dăn′ drŭf) [prob. a comb. of Yorks. *dander*, scurf on the skin, and *hurf* (cp. Icel. *hrufa*, scab)], *n.* Scurf on the head.

dandy (1) (dăn′ di) [Sc. var. of *Andrew*], *n.* One extravagantly fond of dress; a fop, a coxcomb; (*Irish*) a small jug or glass of whisky; (*Naut.*) a sloop or cutter with a jigger-mast aft, on which a lug-sail is set. *a.* Fond of dress, foppish; neat, spruce, smart; (*Am.*) very good, superior. **dandy-brush,** *n.* A hard whalebone brush for cleaning horses. **dandy-cart,** *n.* A spring-cart. **dandy-cock, -hen,** *n.* A bantam cock or hen. **dandiacal** (dăn di′ ȧ kăl), *a.* **dandyish,** *a.* **dandyism,** *n.*

dandy (2) (dăn′ di) [Negro corr. of DENGUE], *n.* Dengue, also called dandy-fever.

dandy (3) (dăn′ di) [Hind. *ḍāṇḍī* from *ḍāṇḍ*, an oar], *n.* A Ganges boatman; a kind of hammock slung on a staff and carried by two or more bearers, used in the Himalayas.

Dane (dān) [Dan. *Daner*, O.Teut. *Daniz*, pl.], *n.* A native of Denmark; (*Hist.*) one of the Northmen who invaded Britain in the Middle Ages. **Great Dane,** *n.* A Danish breed of large, short-haired dogs. **danegeld** [O.Dan. *Danegjeld* (*gjeld*, payment, tribute, cogn. with A.-S. *gield*)], *n.* An annual tax formerly levied on every hide of land in England to maintain forces against or furnish tribute to the Danes (finally abolished by Stephen). **Danelagh** (dān′ law) [A.-S. *Denalagu*, Danish law], *n.* The portion of England allotted to the Danes by the treaty of Wedmore (A.D. 878), extending north-east from Watling Street; *the Danish law which held over this. **dane-hole** [DENE-HOLE].

danewort (dān′ wert), *n.* (*Bot.*) The dwarf elder, *Sambucus ebulus*, the flowers, bark and berries of which are used medicinally.

danger (dān′ jėr) [O.F. *dangier, dongier*, ult. from L. *dominium*, from *dominus*, lord], *n.* Risk, peril, hazard; exposure to injury or loss; anything that causes peril; (*Railway*) risk in going on owing to obstruction; the signal indicating this; *servitude, power, jurisdiction. **danger-signal,** *n.* A signal on railways directing stoppage or cautious progress. **dangerous,** *a.* **dangerously,** *adv.*

dangle (dăng′ gėl) [etym. doubtful; cp. DING, also Dan. *dangle*], *v.i.* To hang loosely; to swing or wave about, to hang about, esp. to obtain some favour; to hover. *v.t.* To cause to dangle; to hold out (as a temptation, bait, etc.). **dangler,** *n.* One who dangles after anything, esp. after women.

Daniel (dăn′ yėl) [from *Dan.* i.-vi. and *Merchant of Venice*, IV. SC. I], *n.* An upright judge; an infallible judge.

Danish (dā′ nish) [A.-S. *Denisc*], *a.* Pertaining to Denmark or the Danes. *n.* The Danish language.

dank (dăngk) [cp. Swed. dial. *dank*, a marshy place, Dan. dial. *dunkel*, moist], *a.* Damp, moist; chilly with moisture; soaked with cold moisture. *n.* A wet or marshy place; dampness. **dankish,** *a.* **dankly,** *adv.*

danseuse (dan serz′) [F., fem. of *danseur*], *n.* A female professional dancer.

Dantean (dăn tē′ ȧn), *a.* Relating to Dante; in the style of Dante, esp. of his *Inferno*; sombre, sublime. *n.* A student of Dante. **Dantesque** (dăn tesk′), *a.*

dap (dăp) [cp. DIP, DAB], *v.t.* (*past & p.p.* **dapped**) To fish by letting the bait fall gently into the water. *v.t.* To let fall lightly; to cause to bounce on the ground. *n.* A bounce (of a ball, etc.).

daphne (dăf′ ni) [Gr.], *n.* One of Diana's nymphs, fabled to have been changed into a laurel; (*Bot.*) a genus of shrubs, partly evergreen, allied to the laurel. **daphnin,** *n.* (*Chem.*) The bitter principle obtained from species of daphne.

dapper (dăp′ ėr) [cp. Dut. *dapper*, G. *tapfer*, brave], *a.* Spruce, smart, brisk, active. **dapperly,** *adv.* **dapperness,** *n.* ***dapperling** [-LING], *n.*

dapple (dă′ pėl) [cp. Icel. *depill*, a spot, dim. of *dapi*, pool], *n.* A spot on an animal; a mottled marking; a horse or other animal with a mottled coat. *a.* Spotted; variegated with streaks or spots. *v.t.* To spot, to streak, to variegate. *v.i.* To become dappled. **dapple-grey,** *n.* A horse with a mottled grey coat.

darbies (dar′ biz) [etym. doubtful], *n.pl.* (*slang*) Handcuffs.

Darbyites (dar′ bi īts) [J. N. *Darby* (1800–82)], *n.pl.* Name given to the stricter adherents of the sect of Plymouth Brethren.

dare (1) (dâr) [A.-S. *durran*, to dare, pres. *dearr, durron*, past *dorste* (cp. Gr. *tharsein*, to be bold); the present is an old past tense, and consequently *dare* survives as 3rd sing. along with *dares*], *v.i.* (*past and conditional* **durst, dared**) To venture; to have the courage or impudence; to be able, willing, or ready; to be bold or adventurous. *v.t.* To attempt, to venture on; to challenge, to defy. *n.* Daring, defiance; a challenge. **I dare say:** I suppose. **dare-devil,** *n.* A fearless, reckless fellow. **daring** (1), *a.* Courageous, bold; fearless, presumptuous. *n.* Boldness, bravery; presumption. **daringly,** *adv.*

dare (2) (dâr) [etym. doubtful], *v.t.* To frighten, to terrify; to daze (birds) so as to catch. *n.* A contrivance made with mirrors or bits of glass for daring and catching larks. **daring** (2), *n.* The act or process of catching birds by means of a mirror or a hawk. ***daring-glass,** *n.* A mirror used to dare larks; hence, any fascination. ***daring-net,** *n.* A net thrown over birds which have been dared.

darg (darg) [Sc.; corr. of *day work*]. The quantity of work done in a day; a task.

daric (dăr′ ik) [Gr. *Dareikos*, adj.], *n.* A gold coin of Darius I of Persia.

dark (dark) [A.-S. *deorc*], *a.* Destitute of light; approaching black; shaded; swarthy, brown-complexioned; opaque; gloomy, sombre; (*fig.*) blind, ignorant; obscure, ambiguous; hidden, concealed; without spiritual or intellectual enlightenment; wicked, evil; cheerless; sad, sullen, frowning; unknown, untried (esp. used of a horse that has never run in public). **v.i.* To become dark, to be eclipsed. *v.t.* To make dark; to obscure. *n.* Darkness; absence of light; night, nightfall; shadow, shade; dark tint, the dark part of a picture; lack of knowledge; doubt, uncertainty. **to keep dark:** To keep silence about. **dark ages,** *n.pl.* The Middle Ages (from an incorrect view of the ignorance then prevailing). **Dark Blues:** (*Sport*) The representatives of Oxford University in sporting events. **Dark Continent,** *n.* Africa, esp. in the period before it was explored. **dark-browed,** *a.* Stern of aspect. **dark-eyed,** *a.* Having dark-coloured eyes. **dark horse:** (*fig.*) One who keeps his own counsel; a person of unknown capabilities. **dark lantern,** *n.* A lantern that can be obscured at pleasure. ***dark-minded,** *a.* Treacherous, revengeful. **dark room,** *n.* A room from which actinic light is shut out for photographic work. **darkish,** *a.* **darkly,** *adv.*

darken (dar′ kėn) [as prec.], *v.i.* To become dark or darker; to become obscure; to become darker in colour; to become gloomy or displeased. *v.t.* To make dark or darker; (*fig.*) to deprive of vision; to render gloomy, ignorant or stupid; to perplex, to obscure; to sully. **to darken one's door:** To appear as a visitor.

darkle (dar′ kėl), *v.i.* To lie in the dark, to lie hid; to grow dark; to become gloomy or dark with anger. *v.t.* To obscure. **darkling,** *adv.* In the dark. *a.* Gloomy, dark; in the dark; obscure.

darkness (dark′ nes), *n.* The state or quality of being dark; (*fig.*) blindness; obscurity; ignorance; wickedness; the powers of hell. **Prince of Darkness:** Satan.

darksome (dark′ sŏm), *a.* Dark, gloomy.

darky (dar′ ki), *n.* (*colloq.*) A Negro; a dark lantern.

darling (dar′ ling) [A.-S. *dēorling* (*dēor*, DEAR, -LING)], *n.* One who is dearly beloved; a favourite, a pet. *a.* Dearly beloved; (*colloq.*) charming, delightful.

Darling pea (dar′ ling pē) [Darling Downs], *n.* (*Austral.*) Popular name of a poisonous plant and bush. **Darling shower,** *n.* (*Austral.*) A cyclone and dust storm.

darn (1) (darn) [cp. A.-S. *gedyrnan*, to hide, to stop up a hole], *v.t.*. To mend by imitating the texture of the stuff (used in the article and of the hole). *n.* A place mended by darning. **darner,** *n.* One who darns; a needle for darning. **darning-needle,** *n.* A needle used in darning.

darn (2) (darn) [DAMN], *v.t.* A mild form of imprecation.

darnel (dar′ nėl) [etym. doubtful (cp. Walloon *darnelle*)], *n.* A kind of grass, *Lolium temulentum*, formerly believed to be poisonous, which grows among corn; the genus *Lolium*.

dart (dart) [O.F. *dart* (F. *dard*), prob. from L.G. (cp. A.-S. *daroth*, a javelin, O.H.G. *tart*, a dart)], *n.* A short-pointed missile weapon thrown by the hand; a small pointed missile used in the game of darts; a javelin; the act of throwing; a sudden leap or rapid movement; a sting; (*Dressmaking*) a V-shaped tuck. (*Austral. colloq.*) A plan, a project. *v.t.* To throw; to shoot or send forth suddenly; *to pierce with a dart. *v.i.* To run or move swiftly; to throw darts or other missiles. **darter,** *n.* One who throws or hurls; one who moves with great rapidity; (*Zool.*) any species of *Plotus*, a genus of long-necked swimming birds; (*pl.*) the order *Jaculatores*, comprising the kingfishers and bee-eaters; the archer-fish. **dart-board,** *n.* A marked target used in the game of darts. **darts,** *n.pl.* An indoor game of throwing small darts at a marked target.

dartre (dar′ tėr) [etym. doubtful], *n.* A name for several skin diseases, esp. herpes; the scab characterizing these.

Darwinian (dar win′ i ȧn), *a.* Pertaining to Charles Darwin (1809–82), or to Darwinism. *n.* A believer in Darwinism. **Darwinianism, Darwinism** (dar′ win izm), *n.* The teaching of Charles Darwin, esp. the doctrine of the origin of species by natural selection. **Darwinist,** *n.* **Darwinistic,** *a.* **Darwinite,** *n.* **Darwinize,** *v.t.* and *i.*

dash (dăsh) [cp. Dan. *daske*, to slap, Swed. *daska*, to beat, L.G. *daschen*, to thrash], *v.t.* To break by collision (usu. with *to pieces*); to smite, to strike, to knock (usu. with *out, down, away*, etc.); to cause to come into collision; to throw violently or suddenly; to throw away suddenly; to bespatter, to besprinkle; to cause to rise; to dilute or adulterate by throwing in some other substance; to compose or sketch hastily (off); to obliterate with a stroke; to destroy; to frustrate; to confound, to abash, to discourage, to daunt; (*slang*) to confound (as a mild imprecation). *v.i.* To rush, fall, or throw oneself with violence; to strike against something and break; to run, ride, or drive smartly (usu. with *up, off,* or *away*); to move or behave showily or spiritedly. *n.* A sharp collision of two bodies; the sound of this, the sound of water in commotion; a rapid movement; a rush, an onset; a slight admixture; a sudden stroke; a blow; activity, daring; brilliancy, display, ostentation; a sudden check; a mark (—) denoting a break in a sentence, a parenthesis, or omission; a hasty stroke with a pen, etc.; (*Mus.*) a line drawn through a figure in thorough-bass, to raise the interval a semitone; a short stroke placed above notes or chords, directing that they are to be played staccato. **to cut a dash:** To make an impression. **dash-board,** *n.* A splashboard; the float of a paddle-wheel; (*Motor.*) indicator-board in front of the driver of a car. **dasher,** *n.* One who or that which dashes; a float, a plunger; a contrivance for agitating the contents of a churn; (*fig.*) a dashing person. **dashing,** *a.* Daring, spirited; showy, smart. **dashingly,** *adv.* **dashy,** *a.* Ostentatious, showy, smart.

dassie (da′ si) [S. African], *n.* A hare.

dastard (dăs′ tȧrd) [prob. from DAZE, -ARD], *n.* A coward, a poltroon; a cowardly villain. *a.* Cowardly; basely shrinking from danger. ***dastardize,** *v.t.* **dastardly,** *a.* **dastardliness,** *n.*

dasymeter (dȧ sim′ ė tėr) [Gr. *dasus*, dense, -METER], *n.* An instrument for measuring the density of gases.

Dasypodidæ (dăs i pod′ i dē) [Gr. *dasypous*, hairy-footed], *n.* (*Zool.*) The South American family of armadillos.

Dasyure (dăs′ i ūr) [Gr. *dasus*, hairy, rough; *oura*, a tail], *n.* (*Zool.*) A genus of small marsupials found in Australia, Tasmania, and New Guinea.

data [DATUM].

dataria (dȧ târ′ i ȧ) [L. *datārius*, giveable], *n.* The papal chancery at Rome whence all bulls are issued. **datary** (dā′ tȧ ri), *n.* An officer of the papal chancery who affixes *datum Romæ* (given at Rome) to the papal bulls.

date (1) (dāt) [F., from late L. *data*, given, fem. p.p. of *dāre*, to give (referring to the time and place at which a letter was given)], *n.* A fixed point of time; the time at which anything happened or is appointed to take place; the specification of this in a book, inscription, document, or letter; (*colloq.*) a social or other engagement (usu. with one of the opposite sex); the person thus concerned; period, age, duration; conclusion. *v.t.* To affix a date to; to note or fix the date of. *v.i.* To reckon; to begin; to be dated. ***date-broke,** *a.* Not provided for on the appointed day. **to make, to have a date:** (*colloq.*) To make or have an appointment. **out of date:** Obsolete. **up to date:** (*colloq.*) Recent, modern. **date-line,** *n.* The line on either side of which the date differs, running meridionally across the western hemisphere from the poles and theoretically 180° from Greenwich; line with date and place of sending printed above a newspaper despatch. **datable,** *a.* **dateless,** *a.* **dater,** *n.* One who dates; a stamp for marking dates.

date (2) (dāt) [O.F., from L. *dactylus*, Gr. *daktulos*, a finger, a date], *n.* The fruit of the date-palm, an oblong fruit with a hard seed or stone; (*Bot.*) any species of the genus *Phœnix*. **date-palm, -tree,** *n.* *Phœnix dactylifera*, the palm-tree of Scripture, common in North Africa and Asia Minor.

dative (dā′ tiv) [L. *datīvus*, pertaining to giving (*dāre*, to give)], *a.* (*Gram.*) Denoting the grammatical case used to represent the remoter object, or the person or thing interested in the action of the verb; (*Law*) that may be parted with at pleasure; removable (from an office); appointed by a court. *n.* The dative case. **datival** (dȧ tī′ vȧl), *a.* **datively,** *adv.*

datum (dā′ tŭm) [L., neut. p.p. of *dāre*, to give], *n.* (*pl.* **data**) A quantity, condition, fact, or other premise, given or admitted, from which other things or results may be found. **datum-line,** *n.* The horizontal line, such as sea-level, from which calculations are made in surveying, etc.

datura (dȧ tū′ rȧ) [Hind. *dhatūra*], *n.* A genus of solanaceous plants, containing the thorn-apple, *D. stramonium*, which yields a powerful narcotic. **daturine,** *n.* An alkaloid obtained from the thorn-apple.

daub (dawb) [O.F. *dauber*, to plaster, L. *dealbāre*, to whitewash (DE-, *albāre*, from *albus*, white)], *v.t.* To smear or coat with a soft adhesive substance; to paint coarsely; to stain, to soil; (*fig.*) to whitewash, to cloak, to disguise; *to flatter grossly. *v.i.* To paint in a crude or inartistic style; (*fig.*) to indulge in gross flattery; to play the hypocrite. *n.* A smear; a coarse painting. **dauber,** *n.* ***daubery,** *n.* Daubing; (*fig.*) specious colouring; false pretence. **daubing,** *n.* Coarse painting; gross flattery. **daubster,** *n.*

daughter (daw′ tėr) [A.-S. *dohtor* (cp. Dut. *dochter*, G. *tochter*, Gr. *thugatēr*, Sansk. *duhitā*)], *n.* A female child with relation to its parents; a female descendant; a female member of a family, race, city, etc.; a female in a child-like relation, as a penitent to her confessor. **daughter-in-law,** *n.* A son's wife; (*loosely*) a step-daughter. **daughterhood,** *n.* **daughterly,** *a.*

daunt dawnt) [O.F. *danter* (F. *dompter*), L. *domitāre* (freq. of *domāre*, to tame)], *v.t.* To intimidate, to dishearten; to check by frightening; to discourage; *to daze. **dauntless,** *a.* Fearless, intrepid. **dauntlessly,** *adv.* **dauntlessness,** *n.*

dauphin (daw′ fin) [O.F. *daulphin*, L. *dephīnus*, DOLPHIN], *n.* The title of the heir-apparent to the French throne, from the fact that the principality of Dauphiné was an appanage of his. **dauphiness,** *n.* The wife of the dauphin.

daur [Sc., DARE].

daut, dawt (dawt) [Sc.; etym. unknown], *v.t* To caress; to cherish. **dautie, dawtie,** *n.* A darling, a pet.

davenport (dăv′ ėn pôrt) [prob. from the first maker], *n.* A small writing-desk with drawers on both sides; (*Am.*) a large sofa, a couch.

davit (dăv′ it) [formerly *david*, prob. from the Christian name], *n.* A spar used as a crane for hoisting the anchor; one of a pair of beams projecting over a ship's side, with tackles to hoist or lower a boat.

davy (dā′ vi) [short for AFFIDAVIT], *n.* (*slang*) **to take one's solemn davy:** To swear.

Davy Jones (dā′ vi jōnz) [origin unknown], *n.* An imaginary malign spirit with power over the sea. **Davy Jones's locker:** A sailor's name for the sea as the tomb of the drowned.

Davy lamp [the inventor, Sir Humphry *Davy* (1778–1829)], *n.* A miner's wire-gauze safety-lamp.

daw (1) (daw) [cp. O.L.G. *dāha*, O.H.G. *tāha*, G. *dohle* (imit. in origin)], *n.* A jackdaw; (*fig.*) an empty-headed fellow.

daw (2) (daw) [obs. exc. in Sc., from A.-S. *dagian*], *v.i.* To dawn. *v.t.* To awaken.

dawdle (daw′ dl) [prob. a recent var. of DADDLE], *v.i.* To trifle; to idle about; to waste time. *n.* A dawdler; the act of dawdling. **dawdler,** *n.*

dawk (dawk), **dâk** (dak) [Hind. *ḍāk* (prob. conn. with Sansk. *drāk*, quickly, from *drā*, to run)], *n.* The Indian post or transport by relays of runners, horses, etc. **dawk-bungalow,** *n.* An inn or house for travellers at a dawk station.

dawn (dawn) [M.E. *dawnen*, earlier *dawen*, DAW], *v.i.* To grow light, to break (as day); (*fig.*) to begin to open, expand, or appear. *n.* The break of day; the first rise or appearance. **to dawn upon:** To be realized gradually by. **dawning,** *n.* Dawn; the time of dawn; (*fig.*) the east; the first beginning or unfolding.

dawt [DAUT].

day (dā) [A.-S. *dæg* (cp. Dut., Dan., and Swed. *dag*, G. *tag*)], *n.* The time the sun is above the horizon; daylight; the space of twenty-four hours, commencing at midnight, a practice borrowed from the ancient Romans, and called the **civil day,** as distinguished from a **mean solar day** which begins at noon; the average time interval between two successive returns of the sun to the meridian. An **astronomical day** is the time in which the earth rotates on its axis relative to the stars (about 4 minutes less than the mean solar day), also called **the sidereal** or **natural day;** daylight, light, dawn, day-time; any specified time; the day in the week or month for receiving visitors; an age; (*often in pl.*) life, lifetime, period of vigour, activity, or prosperity; a day appointed to commemorate any event; a contest, a battle, the victory; to-day. **all day, all the day:** Throughout the day. **better days, evil days:** A period of prosperity or of misfortune. **let's call it a day:** That's all we can do to-day. **day and night:** Throughout both day and night; always; by or in both day and night. **day by day:** Daily. **days of grace:** (*Law*) Days granted by a court for delay at the prayer of a plaintiff or defendant; a customary number of days (in England three) allowed for the payment of a note, or bill of exchange, after it becomes due. **every day:** Daily. **one day, one of these days:** Shortly; in the near future. **present day:** Modern times; modern. **some day:** In the future. **the other day:** On a day recently. **this day week:** A week ago or a week forward from to-day. **to-day:** This day, now. **to gain or win the day:** To come off victor. **day-bed,** *n.* A couch, a sofa. **day-blindness,** *n.* Indistinct vision by day. **day-boarder,** *n.* A pupil who has meals but does not sleep at a school. **daybook,** *n.* A book in which the mercantile transactions of the day are recorded. **day-boy,** *n.* A boy attending a day-school, but differing from a **day-boarder** in not taking his dinner there. **day-break,** *n.* The first appearance of daylight. **day coach,** *n.* (*Am.*) A railway carriage. **day of doom:** The Last Judgement as described in Rev. xx. 11–15. **day-dream,** *n.* A reverie, a castle in the air. **day-dreamer,** *n.* One who indulges in day-dreams. **day-dreaming,** *n.* **day-fly,** *n.* Insects of the genus *Ephemera*. **Day of Judgment:** The end of the world, the Last Day. **day-labour,** *n.* Work done by the day. **day-labourer,** *n.* One who is hired by the day. **day-lily,** *n.* A liliaceous plant of the genus *Hemerocallis*, the flowers of which last one day. **day-long,** *a.* Lasting all day. *adv.* The whole day. **to name the day:** To settle the marriage date. **day-nursery,** *n.* Children's playroom in the daytime; a crèche. **day-owl,** *n.* The hawk-owl which hunts by day. ***day-peep,** *n.* The break of day. **day-room,** *n.* A room used in daylight only; a common living-room in a school; a ward where prisoners are confined during the day. ***day-rule, *-writ,** *n.* A rule or order of court allowing a prisoner of the King's Bench to leave prison for one day. **day-school,** *n.* A school held in the day-time, distinguished from evening-school, Sunday school, or boarding-school. **day-sight,** *n.* Vision clear by day, but indistinct at night. ***days-man,** *n.* An umpire (from appointing a day for arbitration); a mediator, a day-labourer. **day-spring,** *n.* The dawn; day-break. **day-star,** *n.* The morning star; *the sun. **day-ticket,** *n.* A ticket entitling one to return the same day only. **day-time,** *n.* Day as opposed to night. **day-times,** *adv.* (*Am.*) By day. ***day-wearied,** *a.* Wearied with the occupation of the day. **day-work,** *n.* Work done by the day. **day's-work,** *n.* The work of one day; (*Naut.*) the reckoning of a ship's course for 24 hours, from noon till noon.

daylight (dā′ līt), *n.* The light of day as opposed to that of the moon or artificial light; dawn; light visible through an opening; hence, an interval, a gap, a visible space; (*fig.*) openness, publicity. **to let daylight in:** (*slang*) To stab or shoot. **daylight reflector,** *n.* A reflector placed near a window to throw in more light. **daylight saving,** *n.* A system [see SUMMER TIME] of advancing the clock by one hour in Spring and setting back the hands by one hour in Autumn. Summer time was introduced into Great Britain in 1919.

daze (dāz) [M.E. *dasen*, v.t. and i (cp. Icel. *dasask*, to become weary, refl. of *dasa*)], *v.t.* To stupefy, to confuse, to dazzle, to overpower with light. *n.* The state of being dazed; mica (from its glitter). **dazedly,** *adv.*

dazzle (dă′ zĕl) [freq. of prec.], *v.t.* To overpower with a glare of light; to daze or bewilder with rapidity of motion, brilliant display, stupendous number, etc. *v.i.* To be dazzled; to be excessively bright. *n.* Anything which dazzles; a method of painting ships for purposes of camouflage. **dazzlement,** *n.* **dazzling,** *a.* That dazzles; brilliant, splendid. **dazzlingly,** *adv.*

de- [L. *de*, prep., and *de-*, pref.; or from F. *dé-* (L. *dis-*, *de-*)], *pref.* From; down; away; out; (*intens.*) completely, thoroughly; (*priv.*) UN- (expressing undoing, deprivation; reversal, or separation).

deacon (dē′ kŏn) [A.-S., from L. *diăconus*, Gr. *diakonos*, a servant], *n.* One of a class entrusted with the care of the sick and the distribution of alms to the poor in the early Church; a cleric in orders next below a priest; one who superintends the secular affairs of a Presbyterian church; one who admits persons to membership, and assists at communion in the Congregational Church; (*Sc.*) the master of an incorporated guild of craftsmen. *v.t.* (*Am. colloq.*) To read aloud a line or two of a hymn for the congregation to sing; (*slang*) to put the finest (fruit, etc.) on the top. **to deacon land:** (*Am.*) To extend one's fence so as to take in part of the highway. **to deacon off:** To give the cue to; to lead in debate. **deaconess,** *n.* A female deacon; a member of a Lutheran sisterhood. **deaconship, -ry,** *n.*

dead (ded) [A.-S. *dēad*, from Teut. stem *dau-*, to die (cp. Dut. *dood*, Dan. and Swed. *död*, G. *tot*)], *a.* Having ceased to live; having no life, lifeless; benumbed, insensible, temporarily deprived of the power of action; (*fig.*) resembling death; unconscious or unappreciative; without spiritual feeling; cooled, abated; obsolete, effete, useless; inanimate or inorganic as opp. to organic; extinct; lustreless, motionless, inactive, soundless; flat, vapid, dull, opaque; certain, unerring. *adv.* Absolutely, quite, completely; profoundly. *n.* A dead person; the time when things are still, stillness; (*Mining, pl.*) non-metalliferous rock excavated round a vein, or in forming levels, shafts, etc. **v.i.* To die. **v.t.* To kill. **dead against:** Immediately against or opposite; also **dead on end. dead of night:** The middle of the night. **dead on the mark:** Absolutely straight. **the dead.** Dead persons. **dead-alive,** *a.* Spiritless, **dead-beat,** *a.* Quite exhausted. *n.* (*Am.*) A worthless, lazy fellow; (*Austral.*) a ruined man, one down on his luck. **dead-beat escapement:** (*Horol.*) An escapement which gives no recoil to the escape wheel. **dead-born,** *a.* Still-born; (*fig.*) falling flat or spiritless. **dead-broke,** *a.* (*slang*) Penniless, ruined. **dead-centre** [DEAD-POINT]. **dead certainty,** *n.* Something sure to occur; also (*slang*) **dead cert. dead colouring,** *n.* The first layer of colour in a picture, usually of some shade of grey. ***dead-doing,** *a.* Death-dealing. **dead-drunk,** *a.* Helpless from drink. **dead-end,** *n.* A cul-de-sac. *a.* (*Radio.*) Describing the portion of a coil not connected into circuit. **dead-eye,** *n.* (*Naut.*) One of the flat round blocks having eyes for the lanyards, by which the rigging is set up. **dead-fire,** *n.* St. Elmo's fire, an augury of death. **dead-freight,** *n.* A sum paid for space reserved in a vessel but not made use of for cargo. **deadhead,** *n.* (*Am.*) One who has a free pass. **Dead Heart:** (*Austral.*) The land of the Central Australian Desert. **dead heat,** *n.* An equally run race. **dead-hedge** or **fence,** *n.* A hedge of dead wood. **to flog a dead horse:** To seek to revive a dead and worn-out controversy. **dead-house,** *n.* A mortuary. **dead language,** *n.* A language no longer spoken, as classical Latin. ***dead latch,** *n.* A kind of latch the bolt of which may be so locked that it cannot be opened from within by the handle, or from without by the key. **dead letter,** *n.* A letter which cannot be delivered by the post office, and is sent to the Returned Office to be opened and returned to the sender; (*fig.*) a law or anything that has become inoperative. **Dead-Letter Office:** Now the Returned Office, a department in the Post Office. **dead level,** *n.* A perfect level; flat country that offers no difficulty to making a railway or road. **dead lift** or **pull,** *n.* A lift or pull at a dead weight; a thankless effort. **dead-lights,** *n.pl.* (*Naut.*) Shutters placed over port-holes or cabin windows in rough weather; the luminous appearance sometimes seen over putrescent animal bodies; corpse candles. **dead-line,** *n.* (*Print.*) The time of going to press; a fixed time or date terminating something. **dead-lock,** *n.* A lock worked on one side by a handle, and on the other by a key. **deadlock,** *n.* A complete standstill, a position whence there is no exit. **dead loss,** *n.* A loss with no compensation whatever. **dead man,** *n.* (*slang*) An empty wine bottle; a loaf charged for but not delivered. **dead man's** or **men's fingers,** *n.pl.* Various species of orchis, the wild arum, and other flowers; the zoophyte *Alcyonium digitatum*, also called **dead man's hand** or **dead man's toes. dead march,** *n.* A piece of solemn music played at funerals (esp. of soldiers). **dead man's handle,** *n.* (*Mach.*) Device for automatically cutting off the current of an electrically-driven vehicle if the driver releases his pressure on the handle. **dead men's shoes,** *n.pl.* Inheritances, legacies. **dead-nettle,** *n.* A non-stinging labiate plant, like a nettle, of several species belonging to the genus *Lamium*. **dead-pan,** *a.* (Of the face) expressionless. ***dead pay,** *n.* Pay drawn and appropriated by officials for subordinates who are dead or discharged. **dead point,** *n.* Either of the two points at which a crank assumes a position in line with the rod which impels it. **dead reckoning,** *n.* (*Naut.*) The calculation of a ship's position from the log and compass, when observations cannot be taken. **dead-ropes,** *n.pl.* (*Naut.*) Ropes which do not run in any blocks. **dead set,** *n.* A determined attack. **dead shot,** *n.* A marksman who never misses. **dead spot,** *n.* (*Radio.*) An area of low wave intensity caused by interference, or because sound-waves are focused by curved surfaces in the configuration of the land. **dead stand,** *n.* Determined opposition; a standstill. **dead stock,** *n.* Unsaleable goods left on hand. **dead wall,** *n.* A blank wall. **dead-water,** *n.* Water that is absolutely still; (*Naut.*) the eddy under the stern of a ship or boat. **dead weight,** *n.* A mass of inert matter, a burden that exerts no relieving force; an advance by the Bank of England to the Government for officers' half-pay and pensions. **dead window,** *n.* A sham window. **dead wire,** *n.* (*Elec.*) A wire that has been cut off from communication with the source of electrical energy. **dead-wood,** *n.* (*Naut.*) The built-up timbers fore and aft above the keel. **dead-wood fence:** (*Austral.*) A high fence built of fallen or felled timber. **deadness,** *n.*

deaden (dedn) [from prec.], *v.t.* To diminish the vitality, brightness, force, or power of; to make insensible, to dull; to blunt. *v.i.* To lose vitality, strength, feeling, spirit, etc.

deadly (ded′ li) [A.-S. *dēadlic*], *a.* Causing or procuring death; fatal; like death; (*fig.*) implacable, irreconcilable; intense; very excessive. *adv.* As if dead; extremely, excessively, intensively; to death, mortally. **deadly-carrot,** *n.* Southern European plants of the genus *Thapsia*. **deadly nightshade,** *n.* A shrub with dark purple berries, *Atropa belladonna*; wrongly applied to the woody nightshade, *Solanum dulcamara*. ***deadly-standing,** *a.* With a dull, fixed stare. **deadliness,** *n.*

deaf (def) [A.-S. *dēaf* (cp. Dut. *doof*, Dan. *döv*, G. *taub*; also Gr. *tuphlos*, blind)], *a.* Incapable or dull of hearing, unwilling to hear; disregarding, refusing to listen, refusing to comply; insensible (to). **v.t.* To deafen. **deaf-and-dumb alphabet** or **language:** A system of signs for holding communication with deaf people. **deaf-aid,** *n.* A hearing-aid.

deafly, *adv.* **deafness,** *n.* **deaf-mute,** *n.* One who is deaf and dumb. **deaf-mutism,** *n.* ***deaf-nut,** *n.* A nut with a rotten kernel.

deafen (defn), *v.t.* To make wholly or partially deaf; to stun with noise; to render impervious to sound by pugging (as a floor, partition, etc.).

deal (1) (dēl) [A.-S. *dæl*, a share, a portion (*cp.* Dut. and Dan. *deel*, O.H.G. *teil*, G. *theil*), whence *dælan*, to divide], *n.* An indefinite quantity; the distribution of cards to the players; a share, a part, a portion; a bargain, a piece of business; an underhand transaction; (*Am. polit.*) a policy of economic administration. *v.t.* (*past & p.p.* **dealt** (delt)) To distribute; to award as his proper share to some one; to distribute or give in succession (as cards). *v.i.* To have business or traffic (with); to associate, occupy oneself, take measures (with); to distribute cards to the players. **a great** or **good deal:** A large quantity; to a large extent; by much, considerably. **a deal:** (*colloq.*) A good amount. **a raw deal:** Harsh, unfair treatment. **to deal by:** To act towards. **to deal in:** To be engaged in; to trade in. **to deal with:** To have to do with; to consider judicially; to behave towards. **dealer,** *n.* A trader, a merchant; one who deals the cards. **dealing,** *n.* Conduct towards others; intercourse in matters of business; traffic.

deal (2) (dēl) [cp. A.-S. *thille*, THILL (prob. through L.G. *dele* or Dut. *deel*)], *n.* A plank of fir or pine not more than 3 in. thick, 7 in. wide, and 6 ft. long; fir or pine wood.

deambulation (dē ăm bū lā′ shŭn) [L. *deambulātio*, from *deambulāre* (DE-, *ambulāre*, to walk)], *n.* Walking abroad. **deambulatory,** *n.* A place for walking about in; a cloister; the passage round the screen enclosing the choir in a cathedral or other large church.

dean (1) (dēn) [O.F. *deien*, L. *decānum*, acc. of *decānus*, one set over ten (*decem*, ten)], *n.* An ecclesiastical dignitary presiding over the chapter of a cathedral or collegiate church; a rural dean, a clergyman charged with jurisdiction over a part of an archdeaconry; a title applied to the head of the establishment of a chapel royal, and to the Bishop of London (as Dean of the Province of Canterbury); (*Eng. Univ.*) a resident fellow with disciplinary and other functions; the head of a faculty; (*Am.*) the secretary of a faculty. **Dean of Faculty:** (*Sc.*) The president of the Faculty of Advocates. **Dean of Guild:** (*Sc.*) A magistrate with jurisdiction over buildings, weights and measures, etc. **deanery,** *n.* The office, district, or official residence of a dean. **deaness,** *n.* (*facet.*) The wife of a dean. **deanship,** *n.* The office or personality of a dean.

dean (2), **dene** (1) (dēn) [A.-S. *denu*], *n.* A valley; a deep and narrow valley (chiefly in place-names).

deaner, deener (dē′ nėr) [uncert.], *n.* (*Austral. colloq.*) A shilling.

dear (dēr) [A.-S. *dēore* (cp. Dut. *dier*, O.H.G. *tiuri*, G. *teuer*)], *a.* Beloved, cherished; precious, valuable; costly, of a high price; characterized by high prices; *characterized by scarcity; *grievous, dire. *n.* A darling, a loved one; a cherished person, a favourite. *adv.* Dearly, at a high price. *v.t.* To address as dear. *int.* Expressing distress, sympathy, or mild astonishment and protest. **dear-bought,** *a.* Dearly bought. **dearly,** *adv.* **dearness,** *n.* **deary,** *n.* Dear one.

dearborn (dēr′ bôrn) [name of inventor], *n.* (*Am.*) A light four-wheeled family carriage.

dearth (dĕrth) [M.E. *derthe*, from A.-S. *dēore*, DEAR], *n.* Scarcity, causing high price; dearness, lack; want, privation.

deasil [DEISEAL].

deaspirate (dē ăs′ pi rāt), *v.t.* To remove the aspirate from.

death (deth) [A.-S. *dēadh*, from Teut. stem *dau-*, to die (cp. Dut. *dood*, G. *tod*)], *n.* Extinction of life; the act of dying; the state of being dead; decay, destruction; a cause or instrument of death; a skull or skeleton as the emblem of mortality; spiritual destruction, annihilation; capital punishment; *an imprecation. **to be in at the death:** (*fig.*) To be present at the finish. **to be the death of someone:** (*colloq.*) To make someone "die of laughing"; to be a source of great worry to someone. **Black Death:** A mediæval pestilence. **civil death:** Extinction of one's civil rights and privileges. **death on:** (*slang*) Deadly to; skilful at killing; skilful at anything. **unto death:** To the last, forever. **to do to death:** To kill. **death-adder,** *n.* A genus of venomous snakes. **death-bed,** *n.* The bed on which a person dies; a last illness. *a.* Of or pertaining to a death-bed. **death-bell,** *n.* A passing-bell; a ringing in the ears supposed to forebode death. **death-blow,** *n.* A mortal blow; (*fig.*) utter ruin, destruction. ***death-boding,** *a.* Foreboding death. ***death-divining,** *a.* Presaging death. **death duties,** *n.* A tax levied on property when it passes to the next heir. **death-feud,** *n.* A feud that is brought to an end only by the death of one of the parties. ***death-marked,** *a.* Doomed to perish. **death-mask,** *n.* A plaster cast of the face after death. ***death-practised,** *a.* Threatened with death by conspiracy. **death-rate,** *n.* The proportion of deaths in a given period in a given district. **death-rattle,** *n.* A gurgling sound in the throat of a person just before death. **death's-door,** *n.* A near approach to death. **death's-head,** *n.* A human skull, or a representation of one, as an emblem of mortality. **death's-head moth,** *n.* *Acherontia atropos*, the largest European moth, with markings on the back of the thorax faintly resembling a human skull. **death-stroke,** *n.* A fatal stroke. **death-struggle, -throe,** *n.* The agony of death. **death-token,** *n.* A token of approaching death. **death-trap,** *n.* A place unsuspectedly dangerous to life through insanitary or other conditions. **death-warrant,** *n.* An order for the execution of a criminal; an act or measure putting an end to something. **death-watch,** *n.* Any species of *Anobium*, a genus of wood-boring beetles that make a clicking sound formerly thought to presage death. **deathful,** *a.* Fraught with death; mortal. **deathfully,** *adv.* **deathfulness,** *n.* A resemblance to death. **deathless,** *a.* Immortal, imperishable. **deathlessly,** *adv.* **deathlessness,** *n.* **deathlike,** *a.* Resembling death. **deathly,** *a.* Like death; deadly; pertaining to death. *adv.* So as to resemble death. **deathsman,** *n.* An executioner. **deathwards,** *adv.* Towards death.

deave (dēv) [A.-S. *-dēafian* (in *ādēafian*), from *dēaf*, DEAF], *v.t.* (*Sc. and North.*) To deafen; to stun with noise.

deb (deb) abbrev. [DEBUTANTE].

debacle (dā bakl′) [F. *débâcle*, n., from *débâcler*, to unbar (DE-, *bâcler*, to bar)], *n.* A breaking up of ice in a river; (*Geol.*) breaking up and transport of rocks and gravel by a sudden outburst of water; a rout, a complete overthrow.

debar (dė bar′), *v.i.* (*past & p.p.* **debarred**) To hinder or exclude from approach, enjoyment, or action; to prohibit, to forbid.

debark (dė bark′) [F. *débarquer*], *v.t.* and *i.* To disembark. **debarkation,** *n.*

debarrass (dė băr′ ȧs) [F. *débarrasser* (DE-, *barrasser*, from *barrer*, to BAR)], *v.t.* To disembarrass.

debase (dė bās′), *v.t.* To lower in condition, quality, or value; to adulterate; to degrade. **debasement,** *n.* **debasingly,** *adv.* So as to debase.

debate (dė bāt′) [O.F. *debatre* (DE-, low L. *battere*, from L. *batuere*, to beat)], *v.t.* To contend about by words or arguments; to contend for; to discuss; to consider. *v.i.* To discuss or argue a point; to engage in argument; to fight. *n.* A discussion of a question; an argumentative contest; contention; battle, strife. **debatable,** *a.* **debatement,** *n.* **debater,** *n.* One who takes part in a debate. **debating society,** *n.* A society established for holding debates, and to improve the extempore speaking of the members.

debauch (dė bawch') [F. *débaucher*, O.F. *desbaucher* (DE-, perh. *bauche*, a workshop)], *v.t.* To corrupt, to pervert; to lead into sensuality or intemperance; to seduce from virtue; to vitiate, to deprave; *to vilify. **v.i.* To revel; to engage in riotous living. *n.* An act of debauchery; a carouse. **debauchable,** *a.* **debauchee** (deb o shē'), *n.* A profligate. **debaucher,** *n.* A corrupter, a seducer. **debauchery,** *n.* Vicious indulgence of the sensual appetites; seduction from duty.

debenture (dė ben'-chŭr) [L. *dēbenter*, they are due (*dēbēre*, to be due)], *n.* (*Fin.*) A written acknowledgment of a debt; a deed or instrument issued by a company or a public body as a security for a loan of money on which interest is payable till it is redeemed; a certificate issued by a customhouse to an importer entitling him to a drawback or bounty; *a voucher given by the royal household or a Government office entitling payment for goods supplied. **debenture-stock,** *n.* Debentures consolidated or created in the form of stock, the interest on which constitutes the first charge on the dividend. **debentured,** *a.* Secured by debenture, entitled to drawback.

debilitate (dė bil' i tāt) [L. *dēbilitātus*, p.p. of *dēbilitāre*, to weaken, from *dēbilis*, weak], *v.t.* To weaken, to enfeeble; to enervate, to impair. **debility,** *n.* Weakness, feebleness.

debit (deb' it) [L. *dēbitum*, DEBT], *n.* An amount set down as a debt; the left-hand side of an account, in which debits are entered. *v.t.* To charge to as a debt; to enter on the debit side. ***debitor,** *n.* A debtor.

debitumenize (dē bi tū' mė nīz), *v.t.* To deprive of bitumen.

debonair (deb ō nâr') [O.F. *debonaire* (*de bon aire*, of good disposition)], *a.* Courteous, genial, pleasing in manner and bearing. ***debonairly,** *adv.* ***debonairness,** *n.*

***deboshed** [DEBAUCHED].

debouch (dė boosh') [F. *déboucher*, lit. to unstop (DE-, *bouche*, the mouth)], *v.i.* To march out from a confined place into open ground; to flow out from a narrow ravine. ***debouchment,** *n.* ***debouchere,** *n.* The mouth of a river or channel.

debris (deb' rē) [F. *débris*, fragments, from *débriser* (DE-, *briser*, to break)], *n.* Broken rubbish, fragments; (*Geol.*) fragmentary matter detached by a rush of water.

debruise (dė brooz') [O. North. F. *debruisier*, O.F. *debrisier* (DE-, *brisier*, to break)], *v.t.* (*Her.*) To cross so as to hide. **debruised,** *a.* Crossed or folded so as to be partly covered.

debt (det) [M.E. and O.F. *dette*, L. *dēbitum*. neut. p.p. of *dēbēre*, to owe (*b* the result of acquaintance with the L. word)], *n.* That which is owing from one person to another, esp. a sum of money that is owing; (*fig.*) obligation, liability. **action of debt:** (*Law*) An action to recover a sum of money. **debt of honour:** A debt which cannot be recovered at law; a gambling debt. **debt of nature:** Death. **in debt:** Under obligation to pay something due. **bad debt,** *n.* An irrecoverable debt. **National Debt:** The debt of a nation in its corporate capacity; (**funded debt:** The portion of this converted into bonds and annuities; **floating debt:** The portion repayable at a stated time or on demand). ***debted,** *a.* Indebted; under obligation. **debtless,** *a.* **debtor,** *n.* One who is indebted to another; the left hand or debit side of an account.

debunk (dē bŭngk'), *v.t.* To dispel false sentiment, to destroy pleasing legends.

debus (dē bŭs'), *v.t.* and *i.* (*Mil.*) To cause to alight, or to alight, from a motor vehicle.

debut (dė bu') [F., from *débuter*, to make a first stroke (DE-, *buter*, to throw at, from *but*, BUTT)], *n.* A first appearance before the public; a first attempt. **debutant** (deb ū tan'), fem. **debutante** (-tant'), *n.* One who makes a debut at court.

deca-, dec- [Gr. *deka*, ten], *comb. form.* **decachord** (dek' å kôrd) [L. *decachordus*, Gr. *dekachordos* (*chordē*, string)], *n.* A Greek instrument with ten strings.

decade (dek' åd) [F., from L. *decadem*, acc. of *decas*, Gr. *dekas -ados*, from *deka*, ten], *n.* A group of ten; a period of ten years. **decadal,** *a.* **decadic** (dė kăd' ik), *a.*

decadence (dek' å dėns) [F. *décadence*, late L. *dēcadentia* (DE-, *cadere*, to fall)], *n.* Decay, deterioration; declension from a high standard of excellence. **decadent** (dek' å dėnt) [F. *décadent*], *a.* In a state of decay. *n.* A decadent writer or artist, esp. one having weaknesses, vices, and affectations indicating lack of strength and originality.

decagon (dek' å gon) [Gr. *gonos*, angled], *n.* (*Geom.*) A plane figure with ten sides and ten angles.

decagram (dek' å grăm), *n.* A weight of ten grammes, 0·353 oz.

decagynia (dek å jin' i å) [DECA-, Gr. *gunē*, a female], *n.pl.* (*Bot.*) A Linnæan order of plants, containing those with ten pistils. **decagynian, decagynous** (dė kăj' i nŭs), *a.*

decahedron (dek' å hē' drón) [DECA-, Gr. *hedra*, a base], *n.* (*Geom.*) A solid figure with ten sides. **decahedral** (-hē' drål), *a.*

decalcify (dē kăl' si fī), *v.t.* To clear (bone, etc.) of calcareous matter. **decalcification** (-kă' shŭn), *n.*

decalitre (dek' å lē tĕr), *n.* A liquid measure of capacity containing 10 litres, nearly 2½ gallons.

decalogue (dek' å log) [F. *décalogue*, L. *decalogus*, Gr. *dekalogos* (DECA-, -LOGUE)], *n.* The Ten Commandments. **decalogist** (dė kăl' ō jist), *n.* One who treats of the decalogue.

Decameron (dė kăm' ėr ón) [It. *Decamerone* (DECA-, Gr. *hēmera*, day; on anal. of *hexāmeron*, corr. of Gr. *hexaēmeron*)], *n.* A collection of a hundred tales told in ten days (the title of such a collection by Boccaccio).

decametre (dek' å mē tĕr), *n.* A measure of length, containing 10 metres or 393·7 in.

decamp (dė kămp') [F. *décamper* (DE-, CAMP)], *v.i.* To break camp; to depart quickly; to take oneself off. ***decampment,** *n.*

decanal (dė kā' nål) [L. *decānus*, DEAN], *a.* Pertaining to a dean or a deanery, or to the south side of the choir, where the dean has his seat. **decani** (dė kā' nī) [L., of the dean's (side)], *a.* Of the dean or the dean's side; of the side to the right of one facing the altar.

decandria (dė kăn' dri å) [DEC-, Gr. *anēr andros*, a male], *n.pl.* (*Bot.*) A Linnæan class of plants characterized by ten stamens. **decandrian, -drous,** *a.* Having ten stamens.

decangular (dek ăng' gū lår), *a.* (*Geom.*) Having ten angles.

decant (dė kănt') [F. *décanter*, med. L. *décanthāre* (DE-, *canthus*, Gr. *kanthos*, corner of the eye, lip of a cup, CANT)], *v.t.* To pour off by gently inclining, so as not to disturb the sediment; to pour from one vessel into another (as wine). **decantation** (dē kăn tā' shŭn), *n.* The act of decanting. **decanter,** *n.* A vessel for decanted liquors; an ornamental glass bottle for holding wine or spirit.

decaphyllous (dė kăf' i lŭs) [DECA-, Gr. *phullon*, a leaf], *a.* (*Bot.*) Having ten leaves in the perianth.

decapitate (dė kăp' i tāt) [late L. *dēcapitātus*, pp. of *dēcapitāre* (DE-, *caput*, head)], *v.t.* To behead; (*Am.*) to cashier. **decapitable,** *a.* **decapitation** (-tā' shŭn), *n.*

decapod (dek' å pod) [F. *décapode*, Gr. *dekapous* (DECA-, *pous podos*, a foot)], *n.* Any individual of the Decapoda; a locomotive having ten driving-wheels. *a.* Pertaining to the Decapoda; having ten limbs. **Decapoda** (dė kăp' ō då) [mod. L., from Gr. pl. of prec.], *n.pl.* (*Zool.*) A section of cephalopods, with two tentacles and four pairs of arms, containing the cuttle-fishes, squids, etc.; an order of crustaceans with five pairs of ambulatory limbs, the first pair chelate, comprising crabs, lobsters, etc. **decapodal, odous,** *a.*

decarbonize (dē kar′ bŏ nīz), **decarburize** (dē kar′ bū rīz) [CARBURIZE], *v.t.* To clear of carbon or carbonic acid (as in the process of converting cast-iron into malleable iron or steel); (*Motor.*) to remove the solid carbon deposited in the combustion chamber and on the piston crown. **decarbonate** (dē kar′ bŏ nāt) [DE-, CARBONATE], *v.t.* To decarbonize. **decarbonization** (-zā′ shŭn), *n.*

decastich (dek′ ȧ stik) [Gr. *deka*, ten; *stichos*, a verse], *n.* A poem consisting of ten lines.

decastyle (dek′ ȧ stīl) [med. L. *decastylus*, Gr. *dekastulos* (DECA-, *stulos*, column)], *a.* (*Arch.*) Having ten columns. *n.* (*Arch.*) A portico with ten columns in front.

decasualize (dē kăz′ ū ȧ līz), *v.t.* To make less casual, to promote the regular employment of workmen.

decasyllabic (dek ȧ si lăb′ ik), *a.* Having ten syllables. *n.* A line of ten syllables. **decasyllable** (-sil′ ȧbl), *n.* and *a.*

decatholicize (dē kȧ thol′ i sīz), *v.t.* To deprive of catholicity or of Catholicism.

decay (dė kā′) [O.F. *decair*, folk L. *decadēre* (DE-, *cadēre*, L. *cadere*, to fall)], *v.i.* To fall away, to deteriorate; to decline in excellence; to waste away. *v.t.* To impair, to cause to fall away. *n.* Gradual failure or decline; deterioration; a state of ruin; wasting away, consumption, gradual dissolution; decomposition of dead tissue, rot; decayed matter.

decease (dė sēs′) [O.F. *deces*, L. *dēcessus*, p.p. of *dēcēdere* (DE-, *cēdere*, to go)], *n.* Death; departure from this life. **v.i.* To die. **deceased,** *a.* Dead. *n.* One lately dead.

deceit (dė sēt′) [O.F. *deceite*, orig. fem. p.p. of *deceveir*, to deceive, L. *dēcipere* (DE-, *capere*, to take)], *n.* The act of deceiving; propensity to deceive; trickery, deception, duplicity; delusive appearance; a stratagem; (*Law*) any trick or craft to defraud another. **deceitful,** *a.* **deceitfully,** *adv.* **deceitfulness,** *n.*

deceive (dė sēv′) [O.F. *deceveir*, as prec.], *v.t.* To mislead; to impose upon; to cheat, to delude; to disappoint; to be unfaithful (of husband or wife). *v.i.* To act deceitfully. **deceivable,** *a.* **deceiver,** *n.*

decelerate (dē sel′ ĕr āt) [DE-, L. *celer*, swift], *v.t.* (*Mach.*) To reduce speed, to slow down. **deceleration,** *n.* The rate of diminution of speed, measured, for example, in feet per second per second.

decem- [L. *decem*, ten], *comb. form.* (*Bot.*) Ten; in or having ten parts. **decemfid** (dė sem′ fid) [L. *fid-*, stem of *findere*, to cut], *a.* (*Bot.*) Ten-cleft (applied to perianths with ten divisions). **decemlocular** (dē sem lok′ ū lȧr) [LOCULAR], *a.* Having ten receptacles for seeds.

December (dė sem′ bėr) [L. (*decem*, ten)], *n.* The twelfth and last month of the year; (*Rom. Ant.*) originally the tenth and afterwards the twelfth month of the Roman year. **Decemberly,** *a.* **Decembrish,** *a.* **Decembrist,** *n.* One of the conspirators against the Tsar Nicholas, at his accession in Dec. 1825.

decemfid, decemlocular [DECEM-].

decemvir (dė sem′ vir) [L. *decem viri*, ten men], *n.* (*pl.* **-viri, -virs**) One of the various bodies of ten magistrates appointed by the Romans to legislate or rule, esp. the body appointed in 451 B.C. to codify the laws in the Twelve Tables; a member of any governing council of ten. **decemviral,** *a.* **decemvirate,** *n.* The office, or term of office, of the decemviri; a governing body of ten persons.

decency (dē′ sėn si) [L. *decentia* (*decēre*, to become)], *n.* Propriety; that which is becoming in words or behaviour; freedom from immodesty or obscenity; decorum.

decennary (dė sen′ ȧ ri) [L. *decennis* (*decem*, ten, *annus*, year)], *n.* A period of ten years. *a.* Pertaining to a period of ten years. **decenniad** (dė sen′ i ȧd), **decennium** (-ŭm), *n.* (*pl.* **-iads, -ia**) A period of ten years. **decennial,** *a.* Lasting ten years; occurring every ten years. **decennially,** *adv.*

decent (dē′ sėnt) [L. *decens -ntem*, pres.p. of *decēre*, to become], *a.* Becoming, seemly; modest; decorous; respectable; passable, tolerable. **decentish,** *a.* (*slang*) Moderately good; passable. **decently,** *adv.*

decentralize (dē sen′ trȧ līz), *v.t.* To break up (as a centralized administration); to organize on the principle of local management. **decentralization** (-zā′ shŭn), *n.*

deception (dė sep′ shŭn) [F. *déception*, L. *dēceptio -ōnem* (*dēcipere*, DECEIVE)], *n.* The act of deceiving; the state of being deceived; that which deceives; a deceit, a fraud. ***deceptible,** *a.* Liable to be deceived. ***deceptibility** (-bil′ i ti), *n.* ***deceptious,** *a.* Deceitful, deceiving. **deceptive,** *a.* Tending or apt to deceive, easy to mistake. **deceptively,** *adv.* ***deceptiveness,** *n.* ***deceptivity** (dē sep tiv′ i ti), *n.*

decern (dė sĕrn′) [F. *décerner*, L. *dēcernere* (DE-, *cernere*, to separate, to distinguish)], *v.t.* (*Sc. Law*) To decree; *to discern.

dechristianize (dē kris′ tyȧ nīz), *v.t.* To pervert from Christianity; to divest of Christian sentiments and principles.

deci- [L. *decimus*, tenth], *pref.* A tenth part of.

decibel (des′ i bel), *n.* A unit to compare levels of intensity, esp. of sound.

decide (dė sīd′) [F. *décider*, L. *dēcīdere* (DE-, *cædere*, to cut)], *v.t.* To determine; to adjudge; to settle by adjudging (victory or superiority); to bring to a decision. *v.i.* To come to a decision. **decidable,** *a.* **decided,** *a.* Settled; clear, evident, unmistakable; determined, resolute, unwavering, firm. **decidedly,** *adv.* **decider,** *n.* One who or that which decides; a deciding heat or game.

deciduous (dė sid′ ū ŭs) [L. *dēciduus*, from *dēcidere* (DE-, *cadere*, to fall)], *a.* Falling off, not permanent; having only a temporary existence; (*Zool.*) shed (as wings) during the life-time of an animal; (*Bot.*) falling, not perennial (applied to leaves, etc., which fall in autumn, and to trees which lose their leaves annually). **deciduous teeth,** *n.pl.* Milk teeth. **decidua,** *n.* (*Physiol.*) The membrane lining the internal surface of the uterus, coming away after parturition. **deciduate,** *a.* (*Physiol.*) Having a decidua; thrown off after birth. **deciduousness,** *n.*

decigramme (des′ i grăm), *n.* A weight equal to one-tenth of a gramme, 1·54 grain.

decilitre (des′ i lē tĕr), *n.* A fluid measure of capacity of one-tenth of a litre, 0·176 pint.

decillion (dė sil′ yŏn) [F., from L. *decem*, ten, comb. with million, cp. BILLION], *n.* A million raised to the tenth power, represented by 1 followed by 60 ciphers. **decillionth,** *a.*

decimal (des′ i mȧl) [late L. *decimālis*, from L. *decima*, tithe, fem. of *decimus*, tenth (*decem*, ten)], *a.* Of or pertaining to ten or tenths; counting by tens. *n.* A decimal fraction. **decimal arithmetic,** *n.* Arithmetic in which quantities are expressed by tens or tenths; arithmetic based on decimal notation. **decimal coinage:** A monetary system in which the coins represent the value of a given unit in multiples of ten. **decimal fraction,** *n.* A fraction having some power of 10 for its denominator, esp. when it is expressed by figures representing the numerator of tenths, hundredths, etc., following a dot (the **decimal point**) to the right of the unit figure. **decimal notation,** *n.* The Arabic system of numerals. **decimal system,** *n.* A system of weights and measures in which the values proceed by multiples of ten. **decimalist,** *n.* **decimalize,** *v.t.* To reduce or adapt to the decimal system. **decimalization** (-zā′ shŭn), *n.* **decimally,** *adv.*

decimate (des′ i māt) [L. *decimātus*, p.p. of *decimāre* (*decimus*, tenth)], *v.t.* To take the tenth part of; to destroy a tenth or a large proportion of; (*Mil.*) to punish every tenth man with death. **decimation** (-mā′ shŭn), *n.*

decimetre (des′ i mē tĕr), *n.* The tenth part of a metre, 3·937 in.

decipher (dė sī′ fĕr), *v.t.* To turn from cipher into ordinary language; to discover the meaning of (something written in cipher); to discover, to detect; to read or explain (as bad or indistinct writing). *n.* A translation of a cipher. **decipherable,** *a.* **decipherment,** *n.*

decision (dė sizh′ ŭn) [F. *décision*, L. *dēcisio -ōnem* (*dēcīdere*, DECIDE)], *n.* The act or result of deciding; the determination of a trial, contest, or question; (*fig.*) resolution, firmness of character. **decisive** (dė sī′ siv), *a.* Having the power of deciding; conclusive, final; characterized by decision. **decisively,** *adv.* **decisiveness,** *n.*

deciso (de chē′ zō) [It.], *adv.* (*Mus.*) Energetically, decidedly.

decivilize (dē siv′ i līz), *v.t.* To render less civilized; to divest of civilization.

deck (dek) [cp. Dut. *decken*, to cover, O.Teut. *thakjan* (cp. A.-S. *theccan*, to THATCH)], *v.t.* To adorn, to beautify; to cover, to put a deck to. *n.* The plank or iron flooring of a ship; a pack (of cards), a heap, a pile (of cards); the floor of an omnibus or tramcar. **main deck** [MAIN]. **lower** and **middle deck:** Below the main deck. **lower deck:** (*Naut.*) Naval ratings and petty officers. **upper** or **spar deck:** Above the main deck. **orlop deck:** Below the lower deck. **poop** and **forecastle decks:** Short decks at the ends of a vessel. **hurricane deck:** A partial deck over the saloon, or above the central part of some war-ships. **to clear the decks:** (*Naut.*) To prepare for action; (*fig.*) to make tidy. **to sweep the decks:** (*Naut.*) To clear the decks of boarders by a raking fire; to win all the stakes. **deck-chair,** *n.* A collapsible chair, camp-stool, or long chair for reclining in. **deck-hand,** *n.* (*Naut.*) A seaman who works on deck, but is allowed to go aloft. **deck-house,** *n.* A room erected on deck. **deck-passenger,** *n.* A steerage passenger; one who has no right in the cabins. **decked** (dekt), *a.* Adorned; (*Naut.*) furnished with a deck or decks; (*Her.*) edged with another colour, as the feathers of a bird. **-decker** (with number, etc. prefixed); **double-decker,** *n.* An omnibus, etc. with two decks.

deckle (dek′ ėl) [G. *deckel*, dim. of *decke*, a cover], *n.* A frame used in paper-making to keep the pulp within the desired limits. **deckle-edge,** *n.* The rough, untrimmed edge of paper. **deckle-edged,** *a.* Uncut (of paper or books).

declaim (dė klām′) [L. *dēclāmāre* (DE-, *clāmāre*, to cry out)], *v.t.* To utter rhetorically; *to cry down. *v.i.* To speak a set oration in public; to inveigh; to speak rhetorically or passionately (as opp. to reasoned speech). **declaimer,** *n.* **declamation** (dek lȧ mā′ shŭn), *n.* The act or art of declaiming according to rhetorical rules; practice in declaiming; a formal oration; impassioned oratory. **declamatory** (dė klăm′ ȧ tȯ ri), *a.*

declaration (dek lȧ rā′ shŭn) [as foll], *n.* The act of declaring or proclaiming; that which is declared or proclaimed; the document in which anything is declared or proclaimed; a manifesto, an official announcement, esp. of constitutional or diplomatic principles, laws, or intentions; (*Law*) a statement reduced to writing; an affirmation in lieu of oath.

declare (dė klâr′) [F. *déclarer*, L. *dēclārāre* (DE-, *clārus*, clear)], *v.t.* To make known; to announce publicly, to proclaim formally; to pronounce, to assert or affirm positively. *v.i.* To make a declaration, to avow; to state the possession of (dutiable articles); (*Law*) to make an affirmation in lieu of oath; to recite the cause of action; (*Cards*) to name the trump suit; (*Cricket*) to announce an innings as closed. **to declare against** or **for:** To side against or with. **to declare off:** To refuse to proceed with any engagement or contract. **to declare oneself:** To avow one's intentions; to disclose one's character or attitude. **declarant,** *n.* (*Law*) One who makes a declaration. **declarative** (dė klăr′ ȧ tiv), *a.* Explanatory, declaratory. **declaratively,** *adv.* **declaratory,** *a.* Making declaration; expressive, affirmatory. **declaredly,** *adv.*

déclassé (dė klăs′ ā), fem. **-ée**[F., p.p. of *déclasser* (DE-, *classe*, L. *classis*, CLASS)], *a.* Sunk in social position or estimation.

declassify (dē klăs′ i fī), *v.t.* To remove from the security list.

declension (dė klen′ shŭn) [O.F. *declinaison*, DECLINATION], *n.* Declining, descent, deterioration, falling-off; a state of inferiority; (*Gram.*) the case-inflection of nouns, adjectives, and pronouns; the act of declining a noun, etc.; a number of nouns declined in the same way.

declinable [DECLINE].

declinate (dė klī′ nȧt) [L. *dēclīnātus*, p.p. of *dēclīnāre*, to DECLINE], *a.* (*Bot.*) Bending or bent downwards in a curve, as the stamens of amaryllis.

declination (dek li nā′ shŭn) [O.F., from L. *dēclīnātio -ōnem*, from *dēclīnāre*, to DECLINE], *n.* The act of bending or moving downwards; deviation from a straight line or fixed point; deviation from moral rectitude; (*Astron.*) the angular distance of a heavenly body north or south of the celestial equator. **declination of the needle** or **compass:** The angle between the geographic and the magnetic meridians, also called **magnetic declination. declination-compass,** *n.* A declinometer. **declinational,** *a.* **declinator** (dek′ li nā tȯr), *n.* An instrument for taking the declination and inclination of a plane. **declinature** (dė klī′ nȧ tūr), *n.* (*Sc. Law*) Refusal to acknowledge the jurisdiction of a court; *a refusal or declining.

decline (dė klīn′) [F. *décliner*, L. *dēclīnāre* (DE-, *clīnāre*, to lean, cp. Gr. *klinein*, to bend)], *v.i.* To incline from a right line; to slope downwards; to droop, to stoop; to deviate from rectitude; to sink, to fall off, to deteriorate, to decay; to approach the close. *v.t.* To depress, to lower; to direct to one side; to refuse, to turn away from; to reject; (*Gram.*) to inflect (as a noun); to recite the cases of a noun in order. *n.* A falling-off; deterioration, decay, diminution; fall in prices; gradual failure of strength; consumption; setting; gradual approach to extinction or death. **to go into a decline:** To develop consumption. **declinable,** *a.*

declinometer (dek li nom′ ė tėr) [L. *declīno*, I decline, -METER], *n.* An apparatus for measuring the declination of the needle of the compass; (*Astron.*) an instrument for registering declinations.

declivity (dė kliv′ i ti) [L. *dēclīvitās*, from *declīvis* (DE-, *clīvus*, a slope)], *n.* An inclination, slope, or gradual descent of the surface of the ground; an inclination downward. **declivitous,** *a.* **declivous** (dė klī′ vŭs), *a.*

declutch (dē klŭch′), *v.t.* (*Motor.*) To release the clutch; to disconnect the drive.

decoct (dė kokt′) [L. *dēcoctus*, p.p. of *decoquere* (DE-, *coquere*, to COOK)], *v.t.* To boil down or digest in hot water; to extract the virtue of by boiling; *to heat, to cook. **decoction,** *n.* The act of boiling or digesting a substance to extract its virtues; the liquor or substance obtained by boiling.

decode (dē kōd′), *v.t.* To translate from code symbols into ordinary language.

decohere (dē kȯ hēr′), *v.t.* (*Radio.*) To put an end to coherence; to separate or disconnect. **decoherence,** *n.* **decoherer,** *n.* A mechanical device for restoring a coherer to a condition of high resistance. **decohesion,** *n.*

decollate (dė kol′ āt) [L. *dēcollātus*, p.p. of *dēcollāre* (DE-, *collum*, the neck)], *v.t.* To behead. **decollated,** *a.* Beheaded; (*Conch.*) having lost the apex (of spiral shells). **decollation** (-lā′ shŭn), *n.* The act of beheading, esp. the beheading of St. John the Baptist.

décolleté (dė kol' ė tā), fem. **-ée** [F., p.p. of *décolleter* (DE-, *collet*, a collar)], *a.* Wearing a low-necked dress; low-necked (of a dress).

decolour (dē kŭl' ŏr), *v.t.* To deprive of colour. **decolorant** (dē-,) *a.* Bleaching, blanching. *n.* A bleaching substance. **decolorate** (dē-), *v.t.* **decoloration** (-ā' shŭn), *n.* **decolorize,** *v.t.* **decolorization** (-zā' shŭn), *n.* **decolorizer,** *n.*

decomplex (dē' kŏm pleks) [DE-, COMPLEX], *a.* Of complex constituents; doubly complex.

decompose (dē kŏm pōz') [F. *décompose* (DE-, COMPOSE)], *v.t.* To resolve into constituent elements; to separate the elementary parts of, to analyse; to cause to rot. *v.i.* To become decomposed; to putrefy. **decomposable,** *a.* **decomposer,** *n.* **decomposition** (dē kŏm pŏ zish' ŭn), *n.* **decomposite** (-poz' it), *a.* Doubly compound; compounded of compounds. *n.* A substance or word compounded of compound parts.

decompound (dē kŏm pound'), *a.* (*Bot.*) Decomposite. **decompound flower,** *n.* A flower composed of compound flowers. **decompound leaf,** *n.* A leaf which is twice or thrice pinnated.

decompress (dē kŏm pres'), *v.t.* Gradually to relieve pressure on an under-water worker. **decompressor,** *n.* (*Motor.*) A contrivance for relieving pressure on the engine.

deconsecrate (dē kon' sė krāt), *v.t.* To deprive of consecration; to secularize.

decontaminate (dē kon tam' in āt), *v.t.* To clear of poison gas or liquid. **decontamination,** *n.*

decontrol (dē kon trōl'), *v.t.* To terminate government control of a trade, etc.

decor (dā côr) [F.], *n.* The setting, arrangement and decoration of a scene on the stage, or of a room.

decorate (dek' ŏ rāt) [L. *decorātus*, p.p. of *decorāre* (*decor-*, stem of *decus*, an ornament)], *v.t.* To adorn, to beautify; to be an embellishment to; to confer a badge of honour on; to paint, paper, etc. (a house). **decorated,** *a.* Adorned, ornamented, embellished; possessing a medal or other badge of honour; (*Arch.*) an epithet applied to the middle pointed architecture in England (*c.* 1300–1400). **decoration** (-rā' shŭn), *n.* The act of decorating; ornamentation, ornament; a badge of honour; (*pl.*) flags, flowers, and other adornments put up at a church festival or on an occasion of public rejoicing. **Decoration Day,** *n.* (*U.S. Hist.*) 30 May, appointed for the decoration of the graves of those who fell in the Civil War (1861–65). **decorative** (dek' ŏ rȧ tiv), *a.* **decorativeness,** *n.* **decorator,** *n.* One who adorns or embellishes; one whose business it is to paint and paper rooms or houses.

decorous (dė kôr' ŭs, dek' ŏ rŭs) [L. *decōrus* (*decor*, seemliness, from *decēre*, to befit)], *a.* Becoming, seemly; befitting, decent. **decorously,** *adv.* ***decorousness,** *n.* **decorum** (dė kôr' ŭm), *n.* Decency and propriety of words and conduct; etiquette, polite usage.

decorticate (dė kôr' ti kāt) [L. *dēcorticātus*, p.p. of *dēcorticāre* (DE-, *cortex -icem*, bark)], *v.t.* To strip the bark, skin, or husk from. **decortication** (-kā' shŭn), *n.* **decorticator,** *n.* A machine for stripping the hull from grain.

decoy (dė koi') [formerly *coy*, Dut. *kooi*, M.Dut. *koye*, *kouwe*, late L. *cavea*, CAGE], *v.t.* To lure into a trap or snare; (*fig.*) to entrap, to allure, to entice. *n.* A pond or enclosed water into which wild-fowl are decoyed; a place for entrapping wild-fowl; a decoy-duck; a person employed to lure or entrap; a tempter; a bait, an attraction. **decoy-duck,** *n.* A tame duck or an imitation of one; a duck used to lure wild-fowl into the decoy. **decoy-man,** *n.* A man employed to attend to a decoy.

decrassify (dē krăs' i fī), *v.t.* To render less crass or gross.

decrease (dē krēs') [A.-F. *decreiss-*, stem of *decreistre* (O.F. *descreiss-*, *descreistre*), L. *dēcrēscere* (DE-, *crēscere*, to grow)], *v.i.* To become less, to wane, to fail. *v.t.* To make less; to reduce in size gradually. **decrease** (dē' krēs), *n.* Lessening, diminution; the waning of the moon. **decreasingly,** *adv.*

decree (dė krē') [O.F. *decret*, L. *dēcrētum*, neut. of *dēcrētus*, p.p. of *dēcernere* (DE-, *cernere*, to sift, to decide)], *n.* An edict, law, or ordinance made by superior authority; (*Law*) the decision in Admiralty cases; an order in Divorce cases [NISI]; the predetermined purpose of God; a law of nature, the will of Providence; (*Eccles.*) an edict, law, or ordinance of a council; the award of an umpire. *v.t.* To command by a decree; to ordain or determine; to decide by law or authoritatively; *to resolve. *v.i.* To make an edict; to resolve, to determine.

decrement (dek' rė mėnt) [L. *dēcrēmentum* (*dēcrē-*, stem of *dēcrēscere*)], *n.* Decrease, diminution; the quantity lost by diminution; (*Astron.*) the wane of the moon; (*Radio.*) a measure of the speed of damping out of damped waves. **decremeter,** *n.* An instrument for measuring this. **equal decrement of life:** The equal annual decrease of a given number of lives within a given period.

decrepit (dė krep' it) [L. *dēcrepitus* (DE-, *crepitus*, p.p. of *crepāre*, to crackle)], *a.* Broken down by age and infirmities; feeble, decayed. **decrepitude,** *n.*

decrepitate (dė krep' i tāt), *v.t.* To calcine in a strong heat, so as to cause a continual crackling of the substance. *v.i.* To crackle, as salt in a strong heat. **decrepitation** (-tā' shŭn), *n.*

decrescendo (dā krė shen' dō) [It., decreasing], *a.*, *n.* and *adv.* (*Mus.*) Diminuendo.

decrescent (dė kres' ėnt) [L. *decrescens -ntem*, pres.p. of *dēcrēscere* (see DECREASE)], *a.* Waning; (*Bot.*) decreasing gradually from base to summit.

decretal (dė krē' tȧl) [F. *décrétal*, late L. *dēcrētāle*, neut. of *dēcrētālis* (L. *dēcrētum*, DECREE)], *a.* Pertaining to a decree. *n.* A decree, esp. of the Pope; (*pl.*) a collection or body of papal decrees on points of ecclesiastical law or discipline. **decretalist,** *n.* **decretist,** *n.* One versed in decretals. **decretive,** *a.* Having the force of a decree. **decretory,** *a.* Judicial, deciding; determining.

***decrew** (dė kroo') [O.F. *décreu*, p.p. of *décreistre*, to DECREASE], *v.i.* To decrease.

decrown (dė kroun'), *v.t.* To discrown.

decry (dė krī') [F. *decrier*, O.F. *descrier* (DE-, CRY)], *v.t.* To cry down; to clamour against; to depreciate. **decrial,** *n.* **decrier,** *n.*

decuman (dek' ū mȧn) [L. *decumānus*, var. of *decimānus* (*decimus*, tenth)], *a.* The epithet of the principal gate of a Roman camp, near which the tenth cohorts were stationed; (*fig.*) huge, applied to waves, the tenth being said to be much larger than the other nine.

decumbent (dė kŭm' bėnt) [L. *decumbens -ntem*, pres.p. of *decumbere* (DE-, *cumbere*, to lie)], *a.* Lying down, reclining; prostrate; (*Bot.*) lying flat by its own weight. **decumbence, -bency,** *n.*

decuple (dek' ūpl) [F. *décuple*, L. *decuplus* (*decem*, ten, *-plus*, as in *duplus*, double)], *a.* Tenfold. *n.* A tenfold number. *v.t.* and *i.* To increase tenfold.

decurion (dė kū' ri ŏn) [L. *decurio*, from *decem*, ten (cp. *centurio*)], *n.* (*Rom. Ant.*) A Roman officer commanding ten men; a member of a colony or municipal town; a member of the council of a town in Fascist Italy. **decurionate,** *n.*

decurrent (dė kŭr' ėnt) [L. *dēcurrens -ntem*, pres.p. of *dēcurrere* (DE-, *curre*, to run)], *a.* (*Bot.*) Attached along the side of a stem below the point of insertion (as the leaves of the thistle). **decurrence,** *n.* (*Bot.*) **decurrently,** *adv.* **decursive** (dė kėr' siv), *a.* Running down; (*Bot.*) decurrent. **decursively,** *adv.* (*Bot.*)

decussate (dė kŭs' āt) [L. *decussātus*, p.p. of *decussāre* (*decussis*, number 10, X)], *v.t.* and *i.* (*Bot.*) To intersect (as nerves, lines, or rays) at acute angles—*i.e.* in the form of an X. *a.* (-ȧt) Having this form; (*Bot.*) arranged in this manner. **decussated,** *a.* Crossed, intersected; (*Bot.*) crossing each other in pairs at right angles (of leaves); (*Rhet.*) in the form of chiasmus. **decussately,** *adv.* **decussation** (-sā′ shŭn), *n.*

dedal, dedalian [DÆDAL, DÆDALIAN].

dedicate (ded′ i kāt) [L. *dēdicātus*, p.p. of *dēdicāre* (DE-, *dicāre*, to proclaim, to devote)], *v.t.* To apply or give up wholly to some purpose, person, or thing; to inscribe or address (as a literary work to a friend or patron); to set apart and consecrate solemnly to God or to some sacred purpose. *a.* (-kȧt) Dedicated, consecrated. **dedication** (-kā′ shŭn), *n.* The act of dedicating; the words in which a book, building, etc., is dedicated. **dedicator,** *n.* **dedicatee** (ded i kȧ tē′), *n.* The person to whom a thing is dedicated. **dedicative,** *a.* **dedicatory,** *a.* Of the nature of or containing a dedication. ***n.** A dedication.

deduce (dė dūs′) [L. *dēdūcere* (DE-, *dūcere*, to lead)], *v.t.* To draw as a conclusion by reasoning, to infer; to trace down step by step; to trace the descent (from); *to derive. ***deducement,** *n.* **deducible,** *a.*

deduct (dė dŭkt′) [L. *dēductus*, p.p. of *dēdūcere*, as prec.], *v.t.* To take away, to subtract; *to reduce. **deduction,** *n.* The act of deducting; that which is deducted; abatement; the act of deducing; an inference, a consequence. **deductive,** *a.* Deduced, or capable of being deduced, from premises. **deductive reasoning,** *n.* (*Log.*) That process of reasoning by which we arrive at the necessary consequences, starting from admitted or established premises. **deductively,** *adv.* A priori.

dee (dē), *n.* The letter D; a D-shaped loop or link in harness.

deed (1) (dēd) [A.-S. *dæd* (cp. Dut. *daad*, Icel. *dāth*, O.H.G. *tat*, G. *that*)], *n.* An action, a thing done with intention; an illustrious exploit, an achievement; fact, reality [see INDEED]; (*Law*) an instrument comprehending the terms of a contract, and the evidence of its due execution. *v.t.* (*Am.*) To transfer or convey by deed. ***deed-achieving,** *a.* Performing noble deeds. ***deed of saying:** The performance of what has been promised. **deed-poll,** *n.* (*Law*) A deed made by one person only; so called because the paper is cut or polled evenly, and not indented. **deedful,** *a.* **deedless,** *a.* **deedy,** *a.* (*dial.*) Industrious, active.

deed (2) (dēd) [short for INDEED], *adv.* (*chiefly Sc.*) Indeed.

deem (dēm) [A.-S. *dēman*, from Teut. *dōm-*, DOOM (cp. Dut. *doemen*, O.H.G. *tuomian*)], *v.t.* To suppose, to think; to judge, to consider; *to sit in judgment; *to estimate; *to distinguish between. *v.i.* To come to a decision; to think; to think (of). ***n.** Judgment, sentence; idea. **deemster,** *n.* *A judge, an umpire; one of two officers who officiate as judges, one in the north and the other in the south part of the Isle of Man.

deep (dēp) [A.-S. *dēop*, from Teut. *deup-*, cogn. with DIP (cp. Dut. *diep*, O.H.G. *tiuf*, G. *tief*)], *a.* Extending far down; extending far in from the surface or away from the outside; having a thickness or measurement back or down; dark-coloured, intensely dark; profound, abstruse, penetrating; heartfelt, grave, earnest; intense, extreme, heinous; from far down, low in pitch, sonorous, full in tone; well-versed, sagacious; (*colloq.*) artful, scheming, secretive; *weighty. *adv.* Deeply, far down; far on; profoundly, intensely. *n.* Anything deep; the sea; (*usu. in pl.*) the deep parts of the sea; a deep place, an abyss, a gulf, a cavity; the abyss of space; the lower regions; the bottom of the heart, the mysterious region of personality; (*Naut., pl.*) the estimated fathoms between the marks on the hand lead-line. **to go off the deep end:** To give way to one's anger. ***deep-contemplative,** *a.* Given up to meditation. ***deep-drawing,** *a.* (*Naut.*) Requiring great depth of water. **deep-drawn,** *a.* Drawn from the depths. **deep-freeze,** *n.* The storage of foods and perishable goods at a very low temperature. **deep-laid,** *a.* Profoundly, secretly, or elaborately schemed. **deep-mouthed,** *a.* Having a sonorous note. **deep-read,** *a.* Deeply versed. **deep-rooted,** *a.* Firmly established. **deep-sea,** *a.* Pertaining to the open sea. **deep-sea fauna,** *n.* (*Zool.*) Fauna living at a depth below 200 fathoms. **deep-sea line,** *n.* (*Naut.*) A line of 200 fathoms used for soundings. **deep-seated,** *a.* Profound; situated far in; firmly seated. **deep therapy,** *n.* (*Med.*) The method of treating disease by gamma rays. **deep-toned,** *a.* Emitting a low, full sound. **deepen,** *v.t.* To make deeper. *v.i.* To become deeper. **deeply,** *adv.* **deepmost,** *a.* **deepness,** *n.*

deeping (dē′ ping), *n.* One of the strips of twine-netting, a fathom deep, of which a fishing-net is constructed.

deer (dēr) [A.-S. *dēor* (cp. Dut. *dier*, Icel. *dȳr*, O.H.G. *tior*, G. *thier*)], *n.* Any of the *Cervidæ*, ruminant quadrupeds, only the males horned, except in the one domesticated species, the reindeer. ***small deer:** (*Shak.*) Small, insignificant animals. **deer-forest,** *n.* A tract of wild land on which red deer are bred or allowed to breed for stalking. **deer-hound,** *n.* A large greyhound with rough coat, formerly used for hunting deer. **deer-lick,** *n.* A wet or marshy spot impregnated with salt where deer come to lick. **deer-neck,** *n.* A thin, ill-formed neck in a horse. **deer-skin,** *n.* The skin of a deer, leather made therefrom. *a.* Of this material. **deer-stalker,** *n.* One who hunts deer by stalking; a cap peaked in front and behind.

deeve [DEAVE].

deface (dė fās′), *v.t.* To disfigure; to spoil the appearance or beauty of; to erase, to obliterate; *to defeat. **defaceable,** *a.* **defacement,** *n.* **defacer,** *n.*

defæcation [DEFECATION].

defalcate (dē′ fȧl kāt) [late L. *dēfalcātus*, p.p. of *dēfalcāre* (DE-, *falcāre*, to cut with a sickle, from *falx falcis*, sickle)], *v.t.* To take away fraudulently; to misappropriate (money, etc.) held in trust, to embezzle; *to curtail, to reduce. *v.i.* To commit embezzlement. **defalcation** (-kā′ shŭn), *n.* **defalcator,** *n.*

defame (dė fām′) [O.F. *defamer*, *diffamer*, L. *diffāmāre* (*dif-*, DIS-, *fāma*, report)], *v.t.* To speak evil of maliciously; to slander, to libel; to asperse the character of; *to disgrace; *to accuse. ***n.** Infamy. **defamation** (def ȧ mā′ shŭn), *n.* **defamatory** (dė făm′ ȧ tŏr i), *a.*

default (dė fawlt′) [O.F. *defaute* (DE-, late L. *fallita*, fem. p.p. of L. *fallere*, to fail)], *n.* Want, lack, absence; omission or failure to do any act; neglect; (*Law*) failure to appear in court on the day assigned; failure to meet liabilities; *a fault, a defect. *v.i.* To fail in duty; to fail to meet liabilities, to break; (*Law*) to fail to appear in court. *v.t.* (*Law*) To enter as a defaulter and give judgment against, in case of non-appearance; *to omit, to neglect. **in default of:** Instead of (something wanting). **judgment by default:** (*Law*) Decree against a defendant who does not appear. **to make default:** To fail to appear in court, or to keep any engagement. **defaulter,** *n.* One who defaults; one who fails to account for moneys entrusted to him; one who is unable to meet his engagements (esp. on the Stock Exchange or turf); (*Law*) one who makes default; (*Mil.*) a soldier guilty of a military offence.

defeasance (dė fē′ zȧns) [O.F. *defesance*, from *defaire*, *desfaire* (*des-*, DE-, L. *facere*, to do)], *n.* The act of annulling a contract; (*Law*) a condition relating to a deed which being performed renders the deed void; *defeat. **defeasible,** *a.* That may be annulled or forfeited. **defeasibility** (-bil′ i ti), *n.*

defeat (dė fēt′) [O.F. *defait*, p.p. of *defaire*, *desfaire* (as prec.)], *v.t.* To overthrow, to discomfit; to resist successfully, to frustrate; to render null; to baffle; *to disappoint; *to disfigure. *n.* Overthrow, discomfiture, esp. of an army; a rendering null; disappointment; *ruin. **defeatism,** *n.* Persistent belief in defeat in a war, and a consequent advocacy of a policy of surrender. **defeatist,** *n.* A person who contemplates or desires defeat in a war, or advocates measures that would bring about defeat.

defeature (dė fē' chŭr), *v.t.* To disfigure; to disguise.

defecate (dē' fė kāt, def' ė kāt) [L. *dēfæcātus*, p.p. of *dēfæcāre* (DE-, *fæx fæcis*, dregs)], *v.t.* To purify from lees, dregs, or other impurities; to purify, to clarify. *v.i.* To become clear by depositing impurities, excrement, etc. **defecation** (-kā' shŭn), *n.* The ejection of fæces from the body. **defecator,** *n.* One who or that which defecates; an apparatus to remove feculent matter from a saccharine liquid such as sugar.

defect (dė fekt') [L. *dēfectus*, a want, p.p. of *dēficere*, to fail (DE-, *facere*, to do)], *n.* Absence of something essential to perfection or completeness; blemish, failing; moral imperfection; the degree to which one falls short; *default, faultiness. **defects of one's qualities:** (*colloq.*) Shortcomings that usually correspond to the particular abilities or good points one possesses. **defection,** *n.* A falling away from allegiance; desertion, apostasy. **defective,** *a.* Imperfect, incomplete, faulty; wanting in something physical or moral; (*Gram.*) lacking some of the forms or inflections. **defectively,** *adv.* **defectiveness,** *n.*

defence (dė fens') [M.E. and O.F. *defens*, L. *defensum*, forbidden, neut. p.p. of *dēfendere*, to defend; M.E. and O.F. *defense*, defence, L. *dēfensa*, fem. p.p. of *dēfendere*], *n.* The state or act of defending; that which defends; (*Mil.*, *pl.*) fortifications, fortified posts; (*Cricket*) batting as opp. to bowling; justification, vindication; excuse, apology; (*Law*) defendant's reply to the plaintiff's declaration, demands, or charges; *prohibition, a decree forbidding something. **v.t.* To fortify. **defence mechanism,** *n.* (*Psychol.*) A usually unconscious mental adjustment for excluding from the consciousness matters the subject does not wish to receive. **line of defence:** (*Mil.*) A succession of fortified places, forming a continuous line. **Defence of the Realm Act:** An Act of Parliament in force from 1914 to 1921 giving the Government wide powers over most forms of national activity, usually known as D.O.R.A. **science** or **art of self-defence:** Boxing or fencing. **defenceless,** *a.* **defencelessly,** *adv.* **defencelessness,** *n.* The state of being undefended.

defend (dė fend') [O.F. *defender*, L. *dēfendere* (DE-, *fendere*, to strike)], *v.t.* To protect, to guard; to shield from harm; to keep safe against attack; to support, to maintain by argument, to vindicate; (*Law*) to plead in justification of; *to forbid, to prohibit. *v.i.* To plead on behalf of the defendant; to contest a suit. **defendable,** *a.* **defender,** *n.* One who defends; (*Hist.*) one of a society formed in Ireland late in the 18th century to defend Roman Catholic interests against the Orangemen; (*Law*) a lawyer who appears for the defence; (*Sc. Law*) a defendant. **Defender of the Faith:** A title bestowed by Pope Leo X on Henry VIII, in 1521, for his defence of the Roman Church against Luther, and since borne by English sovereigns. **defensible,** *a.* **defensibility** (-bil' i ti), *n.* **defensibly,** *adv.* **defensive,** *a.* Serving to defend; entered into or carried on in self-defence; protective, not aggressive. *n.* An attitude or condition of defence; *a safeguard, a protection. **to be, act,** or **stand on the defensive:** To be, act, or stand in a position to repel attack. **defensively,** *adv.* **defensor,** *n.* (*Rom. Law*) An advocate for a defendant; (*Rom. Hist.*) a magistrate in a provincial city appointed to keep watch against acts of oppression by the governor.

defendant (de fend' ănt), *n.* (*Law*) One summoned into court to answer some charge; one sued in a law-suit. *a.* Holding this relationship.

defense, defensible, defensive [DEFENCE, DEFEND].

defer (1) (dė fĕr') [O.F. *differer*, L. *differre* (*dif-*, DIS-, *ferre*, to bear)], *v.t.* To put off; to postpone. *v.i.* To delay; to procrastinate. **deferred pay:** Wages or salary, esp. of a soldier, held over to be paid at his discharge or death. **deferment,** *n.*

defer (2) (dė fĕr') [F. *déférer*, L. *dēferre* (DE-, *ferre*, to bring)], **v.t.* (*past & p.p.* **deferred**) To offer, to refer; to submit. *v.i.* To yield to the opinion of another. **deference** (def' ĕr ĕns), *n.* Submission to the views or opinions of another; compliance; respect, regard; courteous submissiveness. **deferent** (1), *a.* Deferential. **deferential** (def ĕr en' shăl), *a.* **deferentially,** *adv.*

deferent (2) (def' ĕr ĕnt) [from F. *déférent*, or directly from L. *dēferens -ntem*, pres.p. of *deferre*, as prec.], *n.* That which carries or conveys; (*Physiol.*) a vessel or duct conveying fluids. *a.* (*Physiol.*) Conveying fluids.

defervescence (dē fĕr ves' ĕns) [L. *dēfervēscens -ntem*, pres.p. of *dēfervēscere* (DE-, *fervēscere*, incept. of *fervēre*, to be hot)], *n.* (*Med.*) A cooling down; an abatement of feverish symptoms. **defervescent,** *a.*

defeudalize (dē fū' dȧ līz), *v.t.* To deprive of feudal character or form.

defiance (dė fī' ăns) [DEFY], *n.* Challenge to battle, single combat, or any contest; contemptuous disregard; opposition; open disobedience; *declaration of hostilities. **defiant,** *a.* Challenging; openly disobedient; hostile in attitude; suspicious, distrustful. **defiantly,** *adv.*

deficiency (dė fish' ĕn si) [late L. *dēficientia*, from L. *dēficiens -ntem*, pres.p. of *dēficere* (see DEFECT)], *n.* A falling short; deficit, lack, want, insufficiency; the amount lacking to make complete or sufficient. **deficiency bills,** *n.pl.* A monetary advance made by the Bank of England to the Government to meet a temporary deficiency. **deficiency disease,** *n.* (*Path.*) A disease due to lack or insufficiency of one or more of the essential food constituents. **deficient** (dė fish' ĕnt) [L. *deficiens, -ntem*, as prec.], *a.* Wanting, defective; falling short; not fully supplied; mentally defective. **deficiently,** *adv.* **deficit** (def' i sit, dē' fis it), *n.* A falling short (of estimated receipts); the amount of this deficiency; the amount required to make assets balance liabilities.

defier [DEFY].

defilade (def' i lād), *v.t.* (*Mil.*) To arrange the defences so as to shelter the interior works when they are in danger of being enfiladed. *n.* Defilading. **defilement** (1), *n.*

defile (1) (dė fīl') [M.E. *defoulen*, O.F. *defouler*, to trample on (L. DE-, late L. *fullāre*, to full cloth), afterwards assimilated to BEFOUL and the obs. *befile*, A.-S. *fȳlan*, from *fūl*, FOUL], *v.t.* To make foul or dirty; to soil, to stain; to corrupt the chastity of, to violate; to pollute, to desecrate, to make ceremonially unclean. **defilement** (2), *n.*

defile (2) (dė fīl') [F. *défiler* (DE-, *filer*, to FILE (3))], *v.i.* To march in a file or by files. *n.* A long, narrow pass or passage, as between hills along which men can march only in file; a gorge.

define (dė fīn') [O.F. *definer* (superseded by F. *définir*) for *definir*, L. *dēfīnīre* (DE-, *fīnīre*, to set a bound, from *fīnis*, bound)], *v.t.* To determine the limits of; to mark out, to fix with precision (as duties, etc.); to give a definition of, to describe a thing by its qualities and circumstances. *v.i.* To give a definition. **definable,** *a.* **definably,** *adv.* ***definement,** *n.* Definition, description.

definite (def' i nit) [L. *dēfīnītus*, p.p. of *dēfīnīre*, as prec.], *a.* Limited, determinate, fixed precisely; exact, distinct, clear; positive; (*Gram.*) indicating exactly, limiting, defining. **definite article:** The. **past** or **preterite definite:** (*French Gram.*) The tense corresponding to the Greek aorist and the English past. **definitely,** *adv.* **definiteness,** *n.*

definition (def i nish' ŭn) [O.F. *definicion*, *diffinicion*, L. *dēfīnītio -ōnem*, from *dēfīnīre*, to DEFINE], *n.* The act of defining; an exact description of a thing by its qualities and circumstance; (*Log.*) an expression which explains a term so as to distinguish it from everything else; an enumeration of the constituents making up the logical essence; distinctness, clearness of form, esp. of an image transmitted by a lens.

definitive (dė fin′ i tiv) (O.F. *definitif*, L. *definītīvus*, as prec.], *a.* Decisive, conclusive, positive; *peremptory. *n.* A word used to limit the application of a common noun, as an adjective or pronoun. **definitively,** *adv.*

deflagrate (dē′ flȧ grāt) [L. *dēflāgrātus*, p.p. of *dēflāgrāre* (DE-, *flāgrāre*, to burn)], *v.t.* To consume by means of rapid combustion. *v.i.* To be consumed by means of rapid combustion. **deflagration** (-grā′ shŭn), *n.* **deflagrator,** *n.* An instrument for producing rapid combustion, usu. a form of the voltaic battery.

deflate (dė flāt′) [L. *dēflātus*, p.p. of *dēflāre* (DE-, *flāre*, to blow)], *v.t.* To let down (a pneumatic tire, balloon, etc.) by allowing the air to escape; (*Fin.*) to reduce the inflation of currency. **deflation,** *n.* Reduction of size by allowing air to escape; (*Fin.*) the reduction and control of the issue of paper money, causing prices to fall.

deflect (dė flekt′) [L. *dēflectere* (DE-, *flectere*, to bend), p.p. *deflexus*], *v.i.* To turn or move to one side, to deviate. *v.t.* To cause to turn or bend. **deflector,** *n.* **deflexed,** *a.* (*Bot. and Zool.*) Deflected, bent downwards. **deflection, deflexion, deflexure,** *n.*

***deflorate** (dė flôr′ ȧt, def′ lō rȧt) [L. *dēflōrātus*, p.p. of *dēflōrāre*, as foll.], *a.* (*Bot.*) Having shed its pollen; having the flowers fallen. **defloration** (-rā′ shŭn), *n.*

***deflower** (dė flou′ ėr) [O.F. **desfleurer** (F. *déflеurer*), L. *dēflōrāre* (DE-, *flos floris*, flower)], *v.t.* To deprive of virginity, to ravish; to cull the best parts from; to ravage, to despoil; to strip of its bloom. ***deflowerer,** *n.*

defluent (dē′ flü ėnt) [L. *dēfluens -ntem*, pres.p. of *dēfluere* (DE-, *fluere*, to flow)], *a.* Flowing down. *n.* That which flows down (as the lower part of a glacier).

defluxion (dė flŭk′ shŭn) [L. *dēfluxio*, from *dēfluxus*, p.p. of *dēfluere*, as prec.], *n.* A flowing or running down; (*Path.*) a flowing down of humours, esp. from the inflamed mucous membrane of the air-passages, in catarrh.

defoliation (dė fō li ā′ shŭn) [L. *dēfoliāre* (DE-, *folium*, a leaf)], *n.* The fall or shedding of leaves.

***deforce** (dė fôrs′) [O.F. *deforcier*, late L. *difforciāre* (*dif-*, DIS-, *fortia*, power, L. *fortis*, strong)], *v.t.* To withhold with violence; (*Law*) to withhold the possession of from its rightful owner (as an estate); (*Sc. Law*) to oppose (an officer of the law) in the execution of his duty. ***deforcement,** *n.* ***deforcer,** *n.*

deforest (dė for′ ėst) [O.F. *desforester*, DISFOREST], *v.t.* To clear of forest.

deform (dė fôrm′) [O.F. *deformer*, L. *dēformāre* (DE-, *forma*, beauty, form)], *v.t.* To render ugly or unshapely; to disfigure, to distort; to mar, to spoil. **a.* Disfigured, distorted, unshapely. **deformation** (-mā′ shŭn), *n.* The act or process of deforming; a disfigurement, perversion, or distortion; a change for the worse as opp. to reformation; (*Geol.*) alteration in the structure and external configuration of the earth's crust through the action of internal forces. **deformed,** *a.* Disfigured, ugly, misshapen; *causing deformity. **deformer,** *n.* **deformity,** *n.* The state of being deformed; a disfigurement, a malformation; that which mars or spoils the beauty of a thing.

defraud (dė frawd′) [O.F. *defrauder*, L. *dēfraudāre* (DE-, *fraus -dis*, FRAUD)], *v.t.* To deprive of what is right by deception; to cheat. ***defrauder,** *n.*

defray (dė frā′) [O.F. *défrayer* (DE-, *frai*, sing. of *frais*, cost, expense, prob. from low L. *fredum*, a fine, O.H.G. *fridu*, peace)], *v.t.* To pay; to bear the charge of; to settle. **defrayable,** *a.* ***defrayal,** *n.*

defrock (dė frok′), *v.t.* To unfrock (a priest, etc.).

deft (deft) [A.-S. *gedæfte*, see DAFT], *a.* Neat in handling; dexterous, clever. **adv.* Deftly. **deftly,** *adv.* **deftness,** *n.*

defunct (dė fŭngkt′) [L. *dēfunctus*, p.p. *dēfungī* (DE-, *fungī*, to perform)], *a.* Dead, deceased; *no longer in operation. *n.* A dead person. ***defunction,** *n.* Death, decease. ***defunctive,** *a.* Funereal.

defy (dė fī′) [O.F. *defier*, late L. *diffidāre* (*dif-* DIS-, *fīdus*, faithful)], *v.t.* To challenge to a contest of any kind; to dare, to brave; to challenge to do or substantiate; to disregard openly, to make light of; to resist, to baffle. **n* A defiance. **defier,** *n.*

dégagé (dā ga zhā′), fem. ***ée*** [F., p.p. of *dégager*, to disengage (DE-, GAGE)], *a.* Easy, unembarrassed, unconstrained.

de-gauss (dē gous′), *v.t.* (*Elec.*) To neutralize the magnetization of, e.g., a ship, by the installation of a current-carrying conductor.

degenerate (dė jen′ ėr ȧt) [L. *dēgenerātus*, p.p. of *dēgenāre*, from *dēgener*, base (DE-, *genus -eris*, race)], *a.* Fallen off from a better to a worse state; sunk below the normal standard; declined in natural or moral growth. *n.* A person or animal that has sunk below the normal type. *v.i.* (-āt) To fall off in quality from a better to a worse physical or moral state; to deteriorate; (*Biol.*) to revert to a lower type; to become wild. **degeneracy,** *n.* **degenerately,** *adv.* **degeneration,** *n.* The act or process of degenerating; the state of being degenerated; the return of a cultivated plant to the wild state; (*Bot.*) transition to an abnormal state; (*Path.*) gradual deterioration of any organ or class of organisms.

degerm (dė jĕrm′), *v.t.* To remove the germ from (wheat). **degerminator,** *n.*

deglutition (dē glü tish′ ŭn) [F. *déglutition* (DE-, down, L. *glūtītus*, p.p. of *glūtīre*, to swallow)], *n.* The act or power of swallowing.

degradation (deg rȧ dā′ shŭn), *n.* The act of degrading; the state of being degraded; debasement, degeneracy; diminution or loss of strength, efficacy, or value; (*Painting*) a lessening and obscuring of the appearance of objects in a picture to convey the idea of distance; (*Geol.*) the wearing away of higher lands, rocks, etc.

degrade (dė grād′) [O.F. *degrader*, late L. *dēgradāre* (DE-, *gradus*, a step)], *v.t.* To reduce in rank; to remove from any rank, office or dignity; to debase, to lower; to bring into contempt; (*Biol.*) to reduce from a higher to a lower type; (*Geol.*) to wear away; to disintegrate. *v.i.* To degenerate; (*Camb. Univ.*) to postpone entering for the honours degree to a year later than the normal time. **degraded,** *a.* Reduced in rank, position, value or estimation; low, mean, base; (*Her.*) furnished with steps. ***degradement,** *n.* Deprivation of rank. **degrading,** *a.* Lowering the level or character. **degradingly,** *adv.*

degree (dė grē′) [O.F. *degre* (DE-, L. *gradus*, a step)], *n.* *A step, a stair; a step or stage in progression, elevation, quality, dignity, or rank; relative position or rank; a certain distance or remove in the line of descent determining proximity of blood; social, official, or Masonic rank; a rank or grade of academic proficiency conferred by Universities after examination, or as a compliment to distinguished persons; relative condition, relative quantity, quality, or intensity; (*Geom.*) $\frac{1}{90}$th part of a right angle; (*Geog.*) the 360th part of the circumference of the earth; (*Therm.*) the unit of measurement of temperature; (*Gram.*) one of the three grades of comparison of adjectives and adverbs (POSITIVE, COMPARATIVE, SUPERLATIVE). **by degrees:** Gradually, step by step. **honorary degrees:** Those conferred by a University without examination. **to a degree:** (*colloq.*) Exceedingly. **degree-day,** *n.* The day on which degrees are conferred at a University, (*Am.*) commencement. **degreeless,** *a.* **third degree,** *n.* A long and gruelling cross-examination.

degust (dė gŭst') [L. *dēgustāre* (DE-, *gustāre*, to taste)], *v.t.* To taste so as to relish. *v.i.* To relish. **degustate,** *v.t.* To degust. **degustation** (-tā' shŭn), *n.*

dehisce (dė his') [L. *dēhiscere* (DE-, *hiscere*, to yawn)], *v.i.* (*Bot. and Physiol.*) To gape, to burst open (of the capsules or anthers of plants). **dehiscence,** *n.* **dehiscent,** *a.*

***dehort** (dė hôrt') [L. *dēhortārī* (DE-, *hortārī*, to exhort)], *v.t.* To dissuade from anything; to advise to the contrary. ***dehortation** (-tā' shŭn), *n.* **dehortative,** *a.* **dehortatory,** *a.*

dehumanize (dē hū' mȧ nīz), *v.t.* To divest of human character, esp. of feeling or tenderness; to brutalize.

dehydrate (dē hī' drāt), *v.t.* To liberate or remove water or its elements from. **dehydration** (-drā' shŭn), *n.*

dehypnotize (dē hip' nō tīz), *v.t.* To awaken from a hypnotic condition.

de-ice (dē īs'), *v.t.* (*Aviat.*) To disperse ice which has formed on the wings and control surfaces of an aircraft. **de-icer,** *n.* Apparatus or composition to effect this.

deicide (dē' i sīd) [L. *deus*, god, -CIDE], *n.* The putting of Christ to death; one concerned in putting Christ to death.

deictic (dīk' tik) [Gr. *deiktikos*, from *deiktos* (*deiknunai*, to show)], *a.* (*Gram. and Log.*) Proving directly; demonstrative, as distinguished from indirect or refutative.

deid (dēd) [Sc., DEAD, DEATH].

deify (dē' i fī) [O.F. *deifier*, late L. *deificāre* (*deus*, god, *facere*, to make)], *v.t.* To make a god of; to make godlike; to adore as a god; to idolize. **deific** (dē if' ik), *a.* Making divine. **deification** (-kā' shŭn), *n.* **deifier,** *n.* **deiform,** *a.* Of godlike form; conformable to the will of God.

deign (dān) [O.F. *degnier*, L. *dignārī*, to deem worthy], *v.i.* To condescend, to vouchsafe. *v.t.* To condescend to allow or grant.

deil (dēl) [Sc., DEVIL], *n.* The devil; a devil or evil sprite.

deiparous (dē ip' ȧ rŭs) [L. *deus*, god, *parus*, bearing, from *parere*, to bear], *a.* Bringing forth a god (an epithet applied to the Virgin Mary).

deipnosophist (dīp nos' ō fist) [Gr. *deipnosophistēs* (*deipnon*, dinner, SOPHIST)], *n.* A table philosopher; a philosopher of eating and drinking, after the title of a work by Athenæus in which a company of ancient Greek philosophers discourse learnedly at meals.

deiseal (dē' shēl, dē' zėl), **deasil** (dē' shėl) [Gael. *deiseil*, righthandwise, cogn. with L. *dexter*, Gr. *dexios*], *n.* Motion towards the right, in the direction of the hands of a clock or of the apparent motion of the sun.

deism (dē' izm) [F. *déisme* (L. *deus*, god, -ISM)], *n.* The belief in the being of a god as the governor of the universe, on purely rational grounds, without accepting divine revelation. **deist,** *n.* **deistic, -ical** (dē is' tik, -ȧl), *a.* **deistically,** *adv.*

deity (dē' i ti) [F. *déité*, L. *deitās -tātem*, from *deus*, god], *n.* Divine nature, character, or attributes; the Supreme Being; a fabulous god or goddess; the divinity ascribed to such beings.

deject (dė jekt') [L. *dejectus*, p.p. of *dējicere* (DE-, *jacere*, to throw)], *v.t.* To cast down; to depress in spirit; to dishearten. **a.* Dejected. **dejectedly,** *adv.* ***dejecta,*** n.pl. Excrements of man or animal. **dejection,** *n.* The act of casting down; the state of being dejected; lowness of spirits; (*Med.*) evacuation of the bowels, excrement.

déjeuner (dāzh' u nā) F. [DE-, *jeun*, L. *jejūnus*, fasting)], *n.* Breakfast, luncheon.

dekad (dek' ăd) [Gr. *deka*, ten], *n.* An interval of ten days.

dekko (dek' ō) [Hind. *dekhna*, a look], *n.* (*slang*) A look at.

delaine (dė lān') [F. *mousseline de laine*, woollen muslin], *n.* A kind of untwilled wool muslin; a fabric of wool and cotton.

delapse (dė lăps') [L. *dēlapsus*, p.p. of *dēlābī* (DE-, *lābī*, to slip, to fall)], *v.i.* To descend, to sink.

delate (dė lāt') [late L. *dēlātāre*, to accuse (DE-, *lātus*, p.p. of *ferre*, to bring)], *v.t.* To accuse, to inform against; to cite before an ecclesiastical court. **delation,** *n.* **delator,** *n.*

delay (1) (dė lā') [O.F. *delaier*, prob. from L. *dīlātāre*, freq. of *differre* (*dif-*, DIS-, *ferre*, cp. prec.)], *v.t.* To postpone, to put off; to hinder, to retard. *v.i.* To put off action; to linger. *n.* A stay or stopping; postponement, retardation; detention; hindrance. **delayed-action bomb,** *n.* (*Mil.*) A bomb timed to explode some time after striking its objective. ***delayer,** *n.* **delayingly,** *adv.*

***delay** (2) (dė lā') [O.F. *desleier*, to unbind, to disunite (L. DIS-, *ligāre*, to bind)], *v.t.* To temper, to mitigate.

dele (dē' lē) [L., 2nd pers. sing. imper. of *dēlēre*, to DELETE], *v.t.* (*Print.*) Take out, omit, expunge.

delectable (dė lek' tȧ bėl) [O.F., from L. *dēlectābilis* (*dēlectāre*, to DELIGHT)], *a.* Delightful, highly pleasing. **delectability** (-bil' i ti), **delectableness,** *n.* **delectation** (-tā' shŭn), *n.* Delight, pleasure, enjoyment.

delectus (dė lek' tŭs) [L., selection, from *deligere* (DE-, *legere*, to gather, to choose)], *n.* A text-book containing select passages for translation.

delegate (del' ė gȧt) [O.F. *delegat*, L. *dēlēgātus*, p.p. of *dēlēgāre* (DE-, *lēgāre*, to send, to depute)], *n.* One authorized to transact business as a representative; a deputy, an agent; (*U.S.A.*) a deputy from a territory in Congress. *v.t.* (-gāt). To depute as delegate, agent, or representative, with authority to transact business. **delegation,** *n.* The act of delegating; a body of delegates; (*Law*) the assignment of a debt; a share certificate; (*Am.*) a deputation.

delete (dė lēt') [L. *dēlētus*, p.p. of *dēlēre* (DE-, *lēre*, conn. with *linere*, to smear)], *v.t.* To strike out, to erase. ***delenda,*** *n.pl.* Things to be deleted. **deletion,** *n.* **deletitious** (-tish' ŭs), *a.* Such that anything may be erased (of paper, etc.). **deletory** (del' ė tȯr i), *n.* That which deletes.

deleterious (del ė tēr' i ŭs) [late L. *dēlētērius*, Gr. *dēlētērios*, from *dēlētēr*, a destroyer (*dēleesthai*, to destroy)], *a.* Noxious; injurious to health or mind.

delf (delf), *n.* Glazed earthenware, orig. made at Delft, Holland.

Delian (dē' li ȧn) [L. *Dēlius*, Gr. *Dēlios*, from *Dēlos*], *a.* Of or pertaining to Delos. **Delian problem,** *n.* (*Gr. Ant.*) The duplication of the cube.

deliberate (dė lib' ėr ȧt) [L. *dēlīberātus*, p.p. of *dēlīberāre* (DE-, *lībrāre*, to weigh, from *lībra*, a balance)], *a.* Weighing matters or reasons carefully; circumspect, cool, cautious; done or carried out intentionally; leisurely, not hasty. *v.i.* (-āt) To weigh matters in the mind, to ponder; to estimate the weight of reasons or arguments; to consider, to discuss, to take counsel. *v.t.* To weigh in the mind. **deliberately,** *adv.* **deliberateness,** *n.* **deliberation** (-ā' shŭn), *n.* Calm and careful consideration; discussion of reasons for and against; freedom from haste or rashness; leisurely, not hasty, movement. **deliberative,** *a.* Pertaining to, proceeding from, or acting with, deliberation. **deliberatively,** *adv.*

delicacy (del' i kȧ si), *n.* The quality of being delicate; anything that is subtly pleasing to the senses, the taste, or the feelings; a luxury, a dainty; fineness of texture, design, tint, or workmanship; subtlety and sensitiveness of construction and action; weakness, fragility, susceptibility to injury; nicety of perception; fineness, sensitiveness, shrinking from coarseness and immodesty; gentleness, consideration for others.

delicate (del′ i kȧt) [L. *dēlicātus* (cp. *deliciæ*, delight)], *a.* Highly pleasing to the taste; dainty, palatable; fine, smooth, not coarse; exquisite in form or texture; fastidious, tender, soft, effeminate; sensitive, subtly perceptive or appreciative; subtle in colour, form, or style; requiring acuteness of sense to distinguish; easily injured, fragile, constitutionally weak or feeble; requiring careful treatment; critical, ticklish; refined, chaste, pure; gentle, considerate; *luxurious, voluptuous, sumptuous; skilful, ingenious, dexterous. *n.* Anything choice, esp. food, a dainty; a dainty or fastidious person. **delicately,** *adv.* **delicateness,** *n.*

delicatessen (del i kȧt es′ ėn) [G.], *n.pl.* Cooked meats and preserves.

***delice** (dė lēs′) [O.F. *delices*, L. *deliciæ*, see foll.], *n.* Pleasure, delight.

delicious (dė lish′ ŭs) [O.F., from late L. *dēliciōsus*, from L. *deliciæ*, delight, from *dēlicere* (DE-, *lacere*, to entice)], *a.* Yielding exquisite pleasure to the senses, to taste, or to the sense of humour. **deliciously,** *adv.* **deliciousness,** *n.*

delict (dė likt′) [L. *dēlictum*, a fault, a crime, from *dēlinquere* (DE-, *linquere*, to omit)], *n.* An offence, a delinquency; the actual commission of an offence. ***delictum,*** *n.* (*pl.* ***-ta***).

deligation (del i gā′ shŭn) [L. *dēligāre*], *n.* (*Surg.*) A binding; tying up with a ligature.

delight (dė līt′) [O.F. *deliter*, L. *dēlectāre*, freq. of *dēlicere*], *v.t.* To please greatly, to charm. *v.i.* To be highly pleased; to receive great pleasure (in). *n.* A state of great pleasure and satisfaction; a source of great pleasure or satisfaction. **delightedly,** *adv.* **delightful,** *a.* **delightfully,** *adv.* **delightfulness,** *n.* ***delightless,** *a.* ***delightsome,** *a.* ***delightsomely,** *adv.* ***delightsomeness,** *n.*

Delilah (dė lī′ lȧ) [the Philistine woman who betrayed Samson (Judges xvi)], *n.* A temptress; a light woman.

delimit (dė lim′ it) [F. *délimiter*, L. *dēlīmitāre* (DE-, *līmitāre*, to bound, from *līmes līmitem*, a boundary)], *v.t.* To fix the boundaries of. **delimitate** (dė lim′ i tāt), *v.t.* To delimit. **delimitation** (-tā′ shŭn), *n.*

delineate (dė lin′ ė āt) [*dēlīneātus*, p.p. of *dēlīneāre* (DE-, *līneāre*, to mark out, from *līnea*, a LINE)], *v.t.* To draw in outline; to sketch out; to describe, to depict, to portray. **delineation** (-ā′ shŭn), *n.* **delineator,** *n.* **delineatory,** *a.*

delinquent (dė ling′ kwėnt) [L. *dēlinquens -ntem*, pres.p. of *dēlinquere* (DE-, *linquere*, to omit)], *a.* Offending, failing, neglecting. *n.* One who fails in his duty; an offender, a culprit. **delinquency,** *n.* A failure or omission of duty; a fault, an offence; guilt. **juvenile delinquent:** An offender under 17 years of age.

deliquesce (dē li kwes′) [L. *dēliquēscere* (DE-, *liquēscere*, incept. of *liquēre*, to be liquid)], *v.i.* To liquefy, to melt away gradually by absorbing moisture from the atmosphere; (*fig.*) to melt away (as money). **deliquescence,** *n.* **deliquescent,** *a.*

deliquium (dė lik′ wi ŭm) [L., from *dēlinquere* (see DELINQUENT)], *n.* (*Astron.*) A failure of the sun's light without an eclipse; (*Med.*) faintness, a swoon; (*fig.*) a maudlin mood.

***deliration** (dē li rā′ shŭn) [L. *dēlīrātio*, see DELIRIUM], *n.* Delirium, dotage. **deliriant** (dė lir′ i ȧnt), *a.* (*Med.*) Producing or tending to produce delirium. *n.* A drug or poison that has this effect. **delirifacient** (-fā′ shi ėnt), *a.* and *n.*

delirious (dė lir′ i ŭs) [see foll.], *a.* Suffering from delirium, wandering in mind; raving, madly excited; frantic with delight or other excitement. **deliriously,** *adv.*

delirium (dė lir′ i ŭm) [L., from *dēlīrāre* (DE-, *līra*, a furrow)], *n.* A wandering of the mind; (*fig.*) frantic excitement or enthusiasm, rapture, ecstasy; (*Med.*) perversion of the mental processes, the results of cerebral activity bearing no true relation to reality, characterized by delusions, illusions, or hallucinations. **delirium tremens,** *n.* An acute phase in chronic alcoholism.

delitescent (dē li tes′ ėnt) [L. *dēlitēscens -ntem*, pres.p. of *dēlitēscere* (DE-, *litēscere*, incept. of *latēre*, to lie hid)], *a.* Concealed, latent; (*Surg.*) disappearing, subsiding. **delitescence,** *n.*

deliver (dė liv′ ėr) [F. *délivrer*, late L. *dēlīberāre* (DE-, L. *līberāre*, to set free)], *v.t.* To free from danger or restraint; to save, to rescue; to disburden of a child; to discharge, to send forth; to utter, or pronounce formally or officially; to surrender, to give up; to give over, to hand over or on; to distribute, to present; (*Law*) to hand over to the grantee. **v.i.* To speak, to deliver oneself. **to deliver out:** To distribute. **to deliver over:** To put into the hands of; to transmit. **to deliver the goods:** (*fig.*) To fulfil a promise, to carry out an undertaking. **to deliver up:** To surrender possession of. **deliverable,** *a.* **deliverance,** *n.* The act of delivering; the state of being delivered; (*Law*) the acquittal of a prisoner; (*Sc.*) the decision of a judge or arbitrator. **deliverer,** *n.* One who delivers; one who releases or rescues; a saviour, a preserver.

delivery (dė liv′ ėr i) [A.-F. *delivrée*, n. from fem. p.p. of *délivrer*], *n.* The act of delivering; setting free; rescue, transfer, surrender; a distribution of letters from the post-office; the utterance of a speech; style or manner of speaking; child-birth; discharge of a blow or missile; (*Cricket*) the act or style of delivering a ball, style of bowling; (*Law*) the act of putting another in formal possession of property; the handing over of a deed to the grantee.

dell (del) [A.-S., cp. DALE], *n.* A hollow, or small valley, usually wooded.

Della Cruscan (del′ ȧ krŭs′ kȧn), *a.* Pertaining to the Accademia della Crusca, at Florence, which was established to purify the Italian language and published an authoritative dictionary; pertaining to the Della Cruscan school; hence, artificial, affected in style. **Della Cruscan school,** *n.* A name applied to some English writers residing at Florence about 1785.

Della Robbia ware (del′ ȧ rob′ yȧ wâr) [Luca *della Robbia*, It. sculptor (*c.* 1400–82)], *n.* A kind of earthenware founded on terra cotta.

delouse (dē lous′), *v.t.* To rid a person or place of personal vermin.

delph [DELF].

Delphian (del′ fi ȧn), **Delphic** (del′ fik), *a.* Of or belonging to Delphi, a town of Greece, where was a celebrated oracle of Apollo; (*fig.*) susceptible of two interpretations, ambiguous.

Delphin (del′ fin) [L., from Gr., dolphin, see DAUPHIN], *a.* A title given to an annotated edition of the Latin classics, prepared for the Dauphin, son of Louis XIV.

delphin (del′ fin), *n.* (*Chem.*) A natural fat found in the oil of the dolphin.

delphinine (del′ fi nīn) [L. *Delphīnium*, Gr. *delphinion*, the larkspur, dim. of *delphin*, DOLPHIN], *n.* (*Chem.*) A vegetable alkaloid obtained from stavesacre, *Delphinium staphysagria*. **delphinium,** *n.* (*Bot.*) The genus comprising the larkspurs.

delphinus (del fī′ nŭs) [L., as prec.], *n.* (*Zool.*) A genus of cetaceans containing the dolphins. **delphinoid** (del′ fi noid) [-OID], *a.* and *n.*

delta (del′ tȧ) [Gr.], *n.* The fourth letter of the Greek alphabet (δ, Δ), corresponding to the English *d*; the delta-shaped alluvial deposit at the mouth of the Nile; any similar alluvial deposit at the mouth of a river. **delta rays,** *n.pl.* Electrons moving at relatively low speeds. **delta-leaved,** *a.* Having leaves resembling a delta. **deltaic** (del tā′

ik), *a.* **deltoid,** *a.* Shaped like a delta; triangular. *n.* (*Anat.*) A triangular muscle of the shoulder which moves the arm.

delude (dė lood') [L. *dēlūdere* (DE-, *lūdere,* to play)], *v.t.* To deceive, to impose upon. **deluder,** *n.*

deluge (del' ūj) [F. *déluge,* L. *dīluvium,* from *dīluere,* DILUTE], *n.* A general flood or inundation, esp. the general flood in the days of Noah; (*fig.*) a heavy downpour of rain; a torrent of words; a torrent or flood of anything liquid, as lava; an overwhelming calamity. *v.t.* To flood, to inundate; to overflow with water.

delusion (dė loo' zhŭn) [L. *dēlūsio,* from *dēlūdere,* to DELUDE], *n.* The act of deluding; a cheat, an imposition; the state of being deluded; an error, a fallacy; an erroneous idea in which the subject's belief is unshaken by facts. **delusional,** *a.* **delusive,** *a.* Deceptive, misleading, unreal. **delusively,** *adv.* **delusiveness,** *n.* **delusory,** *a.*

delve (delv) [A.-S. *delfan* (cp. Dut. *delven,* M.H.G. *telben*)], *v.t.* To dig, to open up with a spade; (*fig.*) to fathom, to get to the bottom of. *v.i.* To work with a spade; (*fig.*) to carry on laborious research; to dip, to descend suddenly. *n.* *A pit, a cavity, a depression; work with a spade; a cave, a den. ***delver,** *n.*

demagnetize (dē măg' nė tīz), *v.t.* To deprive of magnetism; to free from mesmeric influence. **demagnetization** (-zā' shŭn), *n.*

demagogue (dem' å gog) [Gr. *dēmagōgos* (DEMOS, *agōgos,* leading, from *agein,* to lead)], *n.* A leader of the people; an agitator who appeals to the passions and prejudices of the people; a facetious orator; an unprincipled politician. **demagogic** (-gog' ik, -goj' ik), *a.* **demagogism,** *n.* ***demagoguery,** *n.* **demagogy,** *n.*

***demain** [DEMESNE].

demand (dė mand') [F. *demande,* from *demander,* L. *dēmandāre* (DE-, *mandāre,* to entrust, to order)], *n.* An authoritative claim or request; the thing demanded, esp. price; a claim; a peremptory question; desire to purchase or possess; a legal claim. *v.t.* To ask or claim with authority or as a right; to question, to interrogate; to seek to ascertain by questioning; to need, to require; to ask in a peremptory or insistent manner. *v.i.* To ask something as a right; to ask. **demand and supply:** (*Polit. Econ.*) A phrase used to denote the relations between consumption and production: if the demand exceeds the supply, the price rises; if the supply exceeds the demand, the price falls. **demand note,** *n.* The final notice served for payment of rates, taxes, etc. **in demand:** Much sought after. **demandable,** *a.* **demandant,** *n.* (*Law*) A plaintiff in a real action; a plaintiff generally; one who demands. **demander,** *n.*

demarcate (dē' mar kāt) [Sp. *demarcacion,* from *demarcar,* to demarcate], *v.t.* To fix the limits of. **demarcation** (-kā' shŭn), *n.* The fixing of a boundary or dividing line; the division between different branches of work done by members of trade unions on a single job.

demarche (dā' marsh) [F.], *n.* A diplomatic approach; method of procedure; announcement of policy.

dematerialize (dē må tēr' i å līz), *v.t.* To deprive of material qualities or characteristics; to spiritualize.

deme (dēm) [Gr. *dēmos*], *n.* A sub-division or township in Greece; (*Biol.*) an undifferentiated aggregate of cells.

demean (dė mēn') [O.F. *demener* (DE-, *mener,* lead, late L. *mināre,* to drive cattle, L., to threaten)], *v.t.* To manage, to treat; to conduct (oneself), to behave; to debase, to lower (in this sense the meaning has been altered to suit an erroneous popular etymology). *n.* Behaviour, demeanour. **demeanour,** *n.* Conduct, carriage, behaviour, deportment; *management.

dement (dė ment') [L. *dēmentāre* (DE-, *mens mentis,* mind)], *v.t.* To madden; to deprive of reason. **demented,** *a.* Insane. **dementedly,** *adv.* **dementedness,** *n.*

dementi (dā mon' tē) [F.], *n.* An official contradiction (of a rumour, etc.).

dementia (de men' shi å), *n.* Idiocy; infatuation; loss or feebleness of the mental faculties. **dementia præcox,** *n.* (*Path.*) A mental disorder resulting from a turning inwards into self away from reality, schizophrenia.

demerara (dem ė rār' å) [river in British Guiana], *n.* A kind of brown sugar.

demerit (dē mer' it) [L. *dēmeritum,* neut. p.p. of *dēmerēre,* to deserve (DE-, *merēre,* to deserve)], *n.* Ill-desert, that which merits punishment; *merit, desert.

demersal (de mĕr' sål) [L. *demersus,* submerged, plunged into], *a.* (*Zool.*) Found in deep water or on the ocean bed.

demesne (dė mēn, -mān) [O.F. *demeine,* as DOMAIN], *n.* An estate in land; the manor-house and the lands near, which a lord keeps in his own hands; (*Law*) possession as one's own; the territory of the Crown or State; a region, territory.

demi- [F., from L. *dimidius,* half], *pref.* Half, semi-, partial, partially. **demi-Atlas,** *n.* One who supports half the world. **demi-bastion,** *n.* (*Fort.*) A single face and flank, resembling the half of a bastion. **demi-cadence,** *n.* (*Mus.*) A half-cadence ending on the dominant. ***demi-cannon,** *n.* A cannon carrying a ball of from 30 to 36 pounds. ***demi-culverin,** *n.* A cannon carrying a ball of 9 or 10 pounds. ***demi-deify,** *v.t.* To deify in part. ***demi-devil,** *n.* One who is in nature half a devil. ***demi-ditone,** *n.* (*Mus.*) A minor third. **demigod,** *n.* One who is half a god; an inferior deity; the offspring of a god and a human being. **demi-gorge,** *n.* (*Fort.*) The line formed by the prolongation of the curtain to the centre of a bastion. ***demi-lance,** *n.* A light lance; a half-pike; a light horseman armed with a lance. **demi-monde,** *n.* Persons not recognized in society, women of dubious character. **demi-mondaine,** *n.* A prostitute. **demi-puppet,** *n.* A diminutive puppet. **demi-relief,** *a.* (*Sculp.*) A term applied to sculpture projecting moderately from the face of a wall; between high and low relief. **demi-rep** [DEMI-, REPUTABLE], *n.* A woman of doubtful chastity. **demi-semiquaver,** *n.* (*Mus.*) A note of the value of the half of a semi-quaver or one-fourth of a quaver. **demi-tint,** *n.* (*Painting*) A half-tint, or medium shade. **demi-toilette,** *n.* Morning dress. **demi-tone** [SEMITONE]. **demivolte,** *n.* An artificial motion of a horse in which he raises his legs in a particular manner. ***demi-wolf,** *n.* A cross between a wolf and a dog.

demijohn (dem' i jon) [corr. of F. *damejeanne,* Dame Jane], *n.* A glass vessel or bottle with a large body and small neck, enclosed in wicker-work.

demise (dė mīz') [O.F., p.p. of *desmettre,* to DISMISS], *n.* Death, decease, esp. of the sovereign or a nobleman; (*Law*) a transfer or conveyance by lease or will for a term of years or in fee simple. *v.t.* To bequeath; (*Law*) to transfer or convey by lease or will. **demise of the Crown:** Transference of sovereignty upon the death or abdication of the monarch. **demisable,** *a.*

***demiss** (dė mis') [L. *dēmissus,* p.p. of *dēmittere* (DE-, *mittere,* to send)], *a.* Submissive; abject. ***demission** (1) (dė mish' ŭn), *n.* Degradation; diminution of dignity.

demit (dė mit') [F. *démettre* (DIS-, *mettre,* L. *mittere,* to send)], *v.t.* and *i.* To resign. **demission** (2) (dė mish' ŭn), *n.* The act of resigning or abdicating.

demiurge (dem' i ĕrj) [L. *dēmiūrgus,* Gr. *dēmiourgos* (*dēmios,* public, from DEMOS, *ergos,* worker)], *n.* (*Gr. Hist.*) The name of a magistrate in some of the Peloponnesian states; (*Phil.*) a name given by the Platonists to the creator of the universe; the

Logos of the Platonizing Christians. **demiurgic** (-ĕr′ jik), *a.*

demivolte [DEMI-].

demob (dē mob′), *v.t.* (*past & p.p.* **demobbed**) (*colloq.*) To demobilize.

demobilize (dē mō′ bi līz), *v.t.* To disband, to dismiss (as troops) from a war footing. **demobilization** (-zā′ shŭn), *n.*

democracy (dė mok′ rȧ si) [F. *démocratie*, L. *dēmocratia*, Gr. *dēmokratia* (DEMOS, -CRACY)], *n.* The form of government in which the sovereign power is in the hands of the people, and exercised by them directly or indirectly; a democratic State; the people, esp. the unprivileged classes. **democrat** (dem′ ȯ krăt), *n.* One in favour of democracy; (*U.S.A.*) a member of the Democratic party. **democratism** (dė mok′ rȧ tizm), *n.* **democratic** (dem ȯ krăt′ ik), *a.* Pertaining to a democracy; governed by or maintaining the principles of democracy. **Democratic party,** *n.* The alternative political party to the Republican in the government of the U.S.A. **democratically,** *adv.* **democratize** (dė mok′ rȧ tīz), *v.t.* and *i.* **democratization** (-zā′ shŭn), *n.* The inculcation of democratic views and principles.

démodé (dā mod′ ā) [F.], *a.* Out of fashion.

demogorgon (dē′ mȯ gôr gȯn) [late L., from Gr. (DEMOS, GORGON)], *n.* A mysterious divinity, first mentioned by a scholiast on the *Thebaid* of Statius as one of the infernal gods; a personage of mysterious origin and attributes in poems by Ariosto, Spenser, Shelley, etc.

demography (dė mog′ rȧ fi), *n.* The department of science which deals with statistics of health and disease, as bearing on anthropology, ethnology, etc. **demographer,** *n.* **demographic** (-grăf′ ik), *a.* **demographically,** *adv.*

demoiselle (dem wȧ zel′) [F.], *n.* The Numidian crane, *Anthropoides virgo*, from its graceful form and bearing; an unmarried woman.

demolish (dė mol′ ish) [F. *démoliss-*, stem of *démolir*, L. *dēmōlīrī* (DE-, *mōlīrī*, construct, from (*mōles*, mass)], *v.t.* To pull or throw down; to raze; to ruin, to destroy. **demolition** (dem ȯ lish′ ŭn), *n.*

demon, dæmon (dē′ mȯn) [L. *dæmōn*, Gr. *daimōn*, a deity, a genius], *n.* (*Gr. Myth.*) A supernatural being, lesser divinity, genius, or attendant spirit supposed to exercise guardianship over a particular individual, in many respects corresponding to the later idea of a guardian angel; an evil spirit having the power of taking possession of human beings; a fallen angel, a devil; (*fig.*) a very cruel or malignant person; (*slang*) an extremely clever person (*usu. in comb.*, as *demon-bowler*). **demoness,** *n.* **demoniac** (dė mō′ ni ăk), *a.* Pertaining to or produced by demons; possessed by a demon; devilish; frantic, frenzied. *n.* One possessed by a demon. **demoniacal** (dė mȯ nī′ ȧ kȧl), *a.* Devilish; pertaining to possession by a devil. **demoniacally,** *adv.* ***demonian** (dė mō′ ni ȧn), *a.* Pertaining to or possessed by a demon; devilish. **demonic** (de mon′ ik), **dæmonic** (dē-), *a.* **demonism** (dē′ mȯ nizm), *n.* Belief in demons or false gods. **demonist,** *n.* **demonize,** *v.t.* To make into a demon; to make devilish; to bring under demonic influence. **demono-,** *comb. form.* The power or government of demons. **demonolatry** (-nol′ ȧ tri) [-LATRY], *n.* The worship of demons or of evil spirits. **demonology** (-nol′ ȯ ji) [-LOGY], *n.* A treatise on demons or evil spirits. **demonomania** (-mā′ ni ȧ) [Gr. *daimonomania* (MANIA)], *n.* A kind of mania in which the sufferer believes himself possessed by devils.

demonetize (dė mon-′ de mŭn′ ė tīz) [DE-, MONETIZE], *v.t.* To deprive of its character as money; to withdraw (a metal) from currency. **demonetization** (-zā′ shŭn), *n.*

demoniac, demonism etc. [DEMON].

demonstrate (dem′ ȯn strāt) [L. *dēmonstrātus*, p.p. of *dēmonstrāre* (DE-, *monstrāre*, to show)], *v.t.* To show by logical reasoning; to prove beyond the possibility of doubt; to exhibit, describe, and prove by means of specimens and experiments; to display, to indicate. *v.i.* To organize or take part in a military or public demonstration. **demonstrant** (dė mon′ strȧnt), *n.* **demonstrable,** *a.* That may be proved beyond doubt; *apparent, evident. **demonstrability** (-bil′ i ti), *n.* **demonstrably,** *adv.*

demonstration (de mon strā′ shŭn), *n.* The act of demonstrating; clear, indubitable proof; an outward manifestation of feeling, etc.; a public exhibition or declaration of principles, etc., by any party; exhibition and description of objects for the purpose of teaching; (*Log.*) a series of syllogisms the premises of which are definitions, self-evident truths or propositions already established; (*Mil.*) a movement of troops as if to attack.

demonstrative (de mon′ strȧ tive), *a.* Having the power of exhibiting and proving; proving; conclusive; pertaining to proof; serving to show and make clear; manifesting the feelings strongly and openly. **demonstratively,** *adv.* **demonstrativeness,** *n.*

demonstrator (dem′ ȯn strā tȯr), *n.* One who demonstrates; one who teaches by means of exhibition and experiment; one who takes part in a public demonstration of political, religious, or other opinions. **demonstratorship,** *n.*

demoralize (dė mor′ ȧ līz) [F. *démoraliser* (DE-, MORAL, -IZE)], *v.t.* To subvert and corrupt the morals and principles of; to corrupt the discipline or morale of. **demoralization** (-zā′ shŭn), *n.*

Demos (dē′ mos) [Gr., the people], *n.* The people, as distinguished from the upper classes; the mob; democracy.

Demosthenian, Demosthenic (dem os thē′ ni ȧn, -then′ ik) [Gr. *Dēmostheneios*, *-nikos*], *a.* Of or pertaining to Demosthenes, the famous Greek orator (385–322 B.C.), or to the style of his oratory; eloquent, fervid, patriotic.

demote (dē′ mōt) [DE-, L. *movere*, to move]. *v.t.* (*colloq.*) To reduce in status, to degrade from rank.

demotic (dė mot′ ik) [Gr. *dēmotikos*, from *dēmotēs*, one of the people (see DEMOS)], *a.* Of or belonging to the people; popular, common, vulgar. **demotic alphabet:** The alphabet used by the laity and people of Egypt as distinguished from the hieratic on which it was based.

dempster [DEEMSTER].

***dempt,** *past* and *p.p.* [DEEM].

***demulce** (dė mŭls′) [L. *dēmulcēre* (DE-, *mulcēre*, to stroke)], *v.t.* To soothe, to pacify, to soften. **demulcent,** *a.* Softening, mollifying, lenitive. *n.* A medicine which allays irritation.

demur (dė mĕr′) [O.F. *demeurer*, L. *dēmorārī* (DE-, *morārī*, to delay, from *mora*, delay)], *v.i.* (*past & p.p.* **demurred**) *To tarry; *to delay, to loiter, to hesitate; to have or express scruples; (*Law*) to take exception to any point in the pleading as insufficient. **v.t.* To hesitate about; to take exception to; to put off. *n.* *Hesitation, pause, delay; the act of demurring; scruple, objection.

demure (dė mūr) [O.F. *de (bons) murs*, of good manners], *a.* Staid; modest; affectedly modest.

demurrable (de mŭ′ rȧ bėl), *a.* Liable to exception, esp. legal objection. **demurrant,** *n.*

demurrage (de mŭ′ rij), *n.* An allowance by the freighter of a vessel to the owners for delay in loading or unloading beyond the time named in the charter-party; the period of such delay; a charge for the detention by one company of trucks, etc., belonging to another; a discount of 1½d. an oz. paid to the Bank of England in exchanging notes or coin for bullion.

demurrer (de mŭr′ er), *n.* (*Law*) An objection made to a point submitted by the opposing party on the score of irrelevance or legal insufficiency.

demy (dė mī'), *n.* (*pl.* **demies,** dė mīz') A particular size of paper, 22½ × 17½ in. for printing, 20 × 15½ in. for drawing or writing (*Am.* 21 × 16 in.); a scholar of Magdalen College, Oxford. **demyship,** *n.*

den (den) [A.-S. *denn,* cp. *denu,* a valley, DEAN (2) (Dut. *denne,* G. *tenne*)], *n.* The lair of a wild beast; a retreat, a lurking-place; a hovel; a miserable room; (*colloq.*) a study, a sanctum, a snuggery. ***v.i.** and *r.* To live in a den.

denarius (dė nâr' i ŭs) [L. *dēnārius,* containing ten (*dēnī,* pl., ten by ten, from *decem,* ten)], *n.* (*pl.* **-rii**) A Roman silver coin, worth ten asses or 7¾d.; a penny.

denary (dē' nȧ ri) [from prec.], *a.* Containing ten; based on the number ten, decimal.

denationalize (dē năsh' ŭn ȧ līz), *v.t.* To deprive of the rights, rank, or characteristics of a nation; to make cosmopolitan; to transfer to another State; to deprive of citizenship; to divest of its character as a national institution. **denationalization** (-zā' shŭn), *n.*

denaturalize (dē năt' ū rȧ līz, -năch' rȧ līz), *v.t.* To render unnatural; to alter the nature of; to deprive of naturalization or citizenship. **denaturalization** (-zā' shŭn), *n.*

denature (dē nā' tūr, -chŭr) [F. *dénaturer,* O.F. *desnaturer*], *v.t.* To divest of essential nature or character (by adulteration, etc.). **denatured alcohol:** Alcohol which has been rendered unfit according to law for human consumption; (*Am.*) methylated spirit.

denazify (dē năts' i fī), *v.t.* To purge of Nazism and its evil influence on the mind.

dendr-, dendri-, dendro- [Gr. *dendron,* a tree.] *comb. form.* Resembling a tree; branching. **dendriform** (den' dri fôrm) [-FORM], *a.* (*Zool.*) Arborescent. **dendrite** (den' drīt) [-ITE], *n.* (*Min.*) A stone or mineral with arborescent markings. **dendritic, -al** (-drit' ik, -ȧl), *a.* Resembling a tree; arborescent; with tree-like markings **dendrodentine** (-drȯ den' tin) [DENTINE], *n.* (*Zool.*) A modification of the fundamental tissue of the teeth, produced by the blending of several teeth into one mass, the whole presenting a dendritic appearance. **dendrodont** (den' dro dont), *a.* (*Palaeont.*) Applied to a group of ganoid fishes from the Devonian, from the labyrinthine microscopic structure of their teeth. **dendrograph,** *n.* (*Bot.*) An instrument for measuring the swelling of tree-trunks. **dendroid** (den' droid) [-OID], *a.* Tree-like, arborescent. **dendrolite** (den' drȯ līt) [-LITE], *n.* A fossil plant, or part of a plant; fossilized wood. **dendrology** (den drol' ȯ ji) [-LOGY], *n.* A treatise on trees; the natural history of trees. **dendrologist,** *n.* **dendrometer** (den drom' ė tėr) [-METER], *n.* An instrument for measuring the height and diameter of trees.

dene (1) [DEAN (2)].

dene (2) (dēn) [etym. doubtful; cp. L.G. and G. *düne,* Dut. *duin,* F. *dune*], *n.* A sandy down or low hill, a tract of sand by the sea.

denegation (dē nė gā' shŭn) [F. *dénégation,* L. *dēnegātio -ōnem,* from *dēnegāre,* to DENY], *n.* Contradiction, denial.

dene-hole (dēn' hōl) [etym. doubtful; perh. DANE or A.-S. *denu* DEAN (2)], *n.* An excavation consisting of a shaft, from 2 ft. 6 in. to 3 ft. in diameter and 20 ft. to 90 ft. in depth, ending below in a cavern in the chalk; made originally to obtain chalk (in Essex called DANE-HOLE).

dengue (deng' gā) [W. Indian Sp., prob. from Swahili], *n.* A continued fever common in the East and West Indies, Africa, and America, characterized by severe pains, an eruption like erysipelas, and swellings.

deniable (dė nī' ȧ bėl), *a.* That may be denied. **denial,** *n.* The act of denying, contradicting, or refusing; a negation; abjuration, disavowal; self-denial. **denier** (1) (dė nī' ėr), *n.* One who denies.

denier (2) (dė nēr') [O.F., from DENARIUS], *n.* A small French coin, the twelfth part of a sou; a coin of insignificant value; the unit for weighing and grading silk and rayon yarn.

denigrate (dē' ni grāt) [L. *dēnigrātus,* p.p. of *dēnigrāre* (DE-, *niger,* black)], *v.t.* To blacken; to defame. **denigration** (-grā' shŭn), *n.* **denigrator** (dē'-), *n.*

denim (dė nim', den' im) [short for F. *serge de Nim* (*Nîmes*), serge of Nîmes], *n.* A coarse, twilled cotton fabric used for overalls, etc.

denitrate (dē nī' trāt), *v.t.* To set free nitric or nitrous acid or nitrate from. **denitrify** (dē nī' tri fī), *v.t.* To denitrate. **denitrification,** *n.* (*Agric.*) The liberation of nitrogen from the soil by the agency of bacteria.

denizen (den' i zėn) [A.-F. *denizein,* from *deniz* (F. *dans*), within (L. DE-, *intus,* within), -AN], *n.* A citizen, an inhabitant, a dweller, a resident; (*Eng. Law*) an alien who has obtained letters patent to make him an English subject; (*fig.*) a foreign word, plant, or animal, that has become naturalized. *v.t.* To naturalize; to make a denizen of. **denizenship,** *n.*

***dennet** (den' ėt) [prob. a personal name], *n.* An open two-wheeled vehicle like a gig.

denominate (dė nom' i nāt) [L. *dēnōminātus,* p.p. of *dēnōmināre*], *v.t.* To name; to give a name, epithet, or title to; to designate. **denomination** (-nā' shŭn), *n.* The act of naming; a designation, title, or appellation; a class, a kind, esp. of particular units (as coins, weights, etc.); a particular body or sect. **denominational,** *a.* Pertaining to a particular denomination, sectarian. **denominational education,** *n.* A system of education recognizing the principles of a religious denomination. **denominationalism,** *n.* **denominationalist,** *n.* **denominationally,** *adv.* **denominationalize,** *v.t.*

denominative (dė nom' i nȧ tiv) [L. *dēnōminātīvus,* as prec.], *a.* That gives or constitutes a distinctive name. **denominator,** *n.* One who or that which denominates; (*Arith.*) the number below the line in a fraction which shows into how many parts the integer is divided, while the numerator, above the line, shows how many of these parts are taken.

denote (dė nōt') [F. *dénoter,* L. *dēnotāre* (DE, *notāre,* to mark, from *nota,* a mark)], *v.t.* To mark, to indicate, to signify; to mark out, to distinguish; (*Log.*) to be a name of, to be predicable of (distinguished from CONNOTE). **denotable,** *a.* **denotation** (-tā' shŭn), *n.* The act of denoting; separation or distinction by means of a name or names; meaning, signification; a system of marks or symbols. **denotation of a term:** (*Log.*) The extent of its application. **denotative** (dė nō' tȧ tiv), *a.* Signifying, pointing out; designating, without implying attributes. **denotatively,** *adv.* **denotement,** *n.* A sign, an indication.

dénouement (dā noo' man) [F., from *dénouer* (DIS-, L. *nodāre,* to knot, from *nodus,* knot)], *n.* The unravelling of a plot or story; the catastrophe or final solution of a plot.

denounce (dė nouns') [O.F. *denoncer,* L. *dēnuntiāre* (DE- *nuntiāre,* to announce, from *nuntius,* a messenger)], *v.t.* To accuse publicly; to charge, to inform against; to declare in a solemn or threatening manner; to declare (war); to give formal notice of termination of (a treaty or convention). **denouncement,** *n.* Denunciation.

dense (dens) [L. *densus*], *a.* Thick, compact; having its particles closely united; (*fig.*) stupid, obtuse; (*Phot.*) opaque, strong in contrast. **densely,** *adv.* **denseness,** *n.* **densimeter** (den sim' ė tėr) [-METER], *n.* An apparatus for measuring density or specific gravity. **densimetry,** *n.* **density,** *n.* Denseness; (*Phys.*) the mass per unit volume of a substance measured, for example, in grammes per cubic centimetre; a crowded condition; (*fig.*) stupidity.

dent (1) (dent) [DINT], *n.* A depression such as is caused by a blow with a blunt instrument; an indentation; *a stroke or blow. *v.t.* To make a dent in; to indent.

dent (2) (dent) [F., tooth, from L. *dens dentis*], *n.* A tooth of a wheel, a cog; (*Carding*) the wire staple that forms the tooth of a card; (*Weaving*) a wire of the reed-frame of a loom.

dental (den' tȧl) (L. *dens dentis*, as prec.], *a.* Pertaining to or formed by the teeth; pertaining to dentistry. *n.* A letter or articulation formed by placing the end of the tongue against the upper teeth. **dental formula:** (*Zool.*) A formula used to describe the dentition of a mammal. **dentalize,** *v.t.* To pronounce as a dental; to alter to a dental sound. **dentary,** *a.* Pertaining to the teeth. *n.* (*Anat.*) The bone in the lower jaw of fishes and reptiles carrying the teeth.

dentate, dentated (den' tȧt, den tā' ted), *a.* (*Bot., Zool.*) Toothed; indented. **dentately,** *adv.* **dentation,** *n.*

dentato-, *comb. form.* Toothed; having tooth-like processes. **dentato-sinuate,** *a.* (*Bot.*) Having the margin scalloped and slightly toothed.

dentelle (den tel') [F., lace], *n.* A style of angular decoration like saw-teeth; a lace edging resembling a series of small teeth.

denti- [L. *dens dentis*, a tooth], *comb. form.* Pertaining to or of the teeth.

denticle (den' ti kėl) [L. *denticulus*, dim. of *dens dentis*, tooth], *n.* A small tooth; a projecting point, a dentil. **denticular** (-tik' ū lȧr), *a.* **denticulate, -lated** (-tik' ū lȧt, -lā' tėd), *a.* Finely toothed; formed into dentils. **denticulately,** *adv.* **denticulation** (-lā' shŭn), *n.*

dentiform (den' ti fôrm), *a.* Having the form of a tooth or teeth.

dentifrice (den' ti fris) [F., from L. *dentifricium* (DENTI-, *fricāre*, to rub)], *n.* Powder, paste, or other material for cleansing the teeth.

dentil (den' til) [obs. F. *dentille*, from *dent*, a tooth], *n.* (*Arch.*) One of the small square blocks or projections under the bed-moulding of cornices.

dentilingual (den ti ling' gwȧl), *a.* Formed by the teeth and the tongue. *n.* A consonant so formed.

dentine (den' tin), *n.* The ivory tissue forming the body of a tooth.

dentiroster (den ti ros' tėr), *n.* (*Ornith.*) One of a tribe of passerine birds, *Dentirostres*, having a tooth or notch near the top of the upper mandible. **dentirostral,** *a.*

dentist (den' tist) [F. *dentiste*, from *dent*, tooth], *n.* A dental surgeon. **dentistry,** *n.* **dentition** (den tish' ŭn), *n.* Teething; the time of teething; the arrangement of the teeth in any animal. **denture,** *n.* Set of teeth, esp. artificial.

denude (dė nūd') [L. *dēnūdāre* (DE-, *nūdāre*, to strip, from *nūdus*, bare)], *v.t.* To make bare or naked; to strip of clothing, attributes, possessions, rank, or any covering; (*Geol.*) to lay bare by removing whatever lies above. **denudate** (dē' nū dāt), *v.t.* To denude. *a.* (-dȧt) Made naked, stripped; (*Bot.*) appearing naked. **denudation** (-dā' shŭn), *n.*

denunciate (dė nŭn' si āt) [L. *dēnuntiātus*, p.p. of *dēnuntiāre*, DENOUNCE], *v.t.* To denounce. **denunciation** (dė nŭn si ā' shŭn), *n.* **denunciative** (dė nŭn' si ȧ tiv), *a.* **denunciator** (dė nŭn si ā tȯr), *n.* **denunciatory,** *a.*

deny (dė nī') [F. *dénier*, L. *dēnegāre*, (DE-, *negāre*, to deny)], *v.t.* To assert to be untrue or non-existent; to disown, to reject, to repudiate; to refuse to grant, to withhold from; to refuse admittance to; to refuse access to; *to contradict; to say 'no' to. *v.i.* To say 'no'; to contradict. **to deny oneself:** To refrain or abstain from; to practise self-denial.

deobstruent (dė ob' strŭ ėnt) [DE-, *obstruere*, to OBSTRUCT], *a.* (*Med.*) Removing obstructions; aperient; having the quality of opening and clearing the ducts of the body. *n.* A deobstruent medicine.

deodand (dē' ȯ dănd) [A.-F. *deodande*, L. *Deo dandum*, to be given to God (*dandum*, from *dare*, to give)], *n.* (*Hist.*) A personal chattel which had been the immediate cause of the death of any person, and on that account forfeited to be sold for some pious use.

deodar (dē' ȯ dar) [Hind. *dē'odar*, *dēwdār*, Sansk. *deva-dāra*, timber of the gods (*dēva-*, a deity, *dāru*, a kind of pine)], *n.* A large Himalayan tree, *Cedrus deodara*, allied to the cedars of Lebanon.

deodorize (dė ō' dȯr-, dė od' ȯr īz), *v.t.* To deprive of odour; to disinfect. **deodorant,** *n.* An agent which counteracts unpleasant smells. **deodorization** (-zā' shŭn), *n.* The act of deodorizing. **deodorizer,** *n.*

deontology (dē ȯn tol' ȯ ji) [Gr. *deon deontos*, duty, neut. pres.p. of *dei*, it is binding; -LOGY], *n.* The science of duty, the Benthamite doctrine of ethics. ***deontological** (-loj' ik ȧl), *a.* ***deontologist,** *n.*

deoxidize (dē ok' si dīz), *v.t.* To deprive of oxygen; to extract oxygen from. **deoxidization** (-zā'shŭn), *n.* **deoxygenate** (dē ok' si jėn āt), *v.t.* To deoxidize. **deoxygenation** (-nā' shŭn), *n.* **deoxygenize** (dē ok' si jėn īz), *v.t.* To deoxidize.

depart (dė part') [O.F. *departir*, DE-, L. *partīre*, to PART, to divide], *v.i.* To go away, to leave; to diverge, to deviate, to pass away; to die. *v.t.* To go away from, to quit; *to divide, to distribute; *to separate. ***departal,** *n.* **departed,** *a.* Past, bygone; dead. **the departed:** The dead.

department (dė part' mėnt) [F. *département* (as prec., -MENT)], *n.* A separate part or branch of business, administration, or duty; a branch of study or science; one of the administrative divisions of a country, as in France; (*U.S.A. polit.*) a ministry, *e.g.* War Department. **department store,** *n.* A shop selling a great variety of goods. **departmental** (dē part men' tȧl), *a.* **departmentalism,** *n.* A too-rigid adherence to regulations, red tape. **departmentalize,** *v.t.* **departmentally,** *adv.*

departure (dė par' tyŭr, -chŭr) [O.F. *departeure*], *n.* The act of departing; leaving; starting; quitting; death; divergence, deviation; (*Law*) a deviation from ground previously taken in pleading; (*Naut.*) distance of a ship east or west of the meridian she sailed from; the position of an object from which a vessel commences her dead reckoning;* separation, severance. **new departure:** A new course of thought or ideas; a new enterprise.

depasture (dė pas' tūr), *v.t.* To graze upon; to put to graze. *v.i.* To graze. **depasturage,** *n.*

depauperate (dė paw' pėr āt) [med. L. *dēpauperātus*, p.p. of *dēpauperāre* (DE-, *pauperāre*, to make poor)], *v.t.* To make poor; to deprive of fertility or vigour; to impoverish, to stunt. *a.* (-ȧt) Impoverished; (*Bot.*) imperfectly developed. **depauperation** (-ā' shŭn), *n.* **depauperize** (dē paw' pėr īz), *v.t.* To raise from pauperism, to dispauperize; *to make poor, to depauperate.

depend (dė pend') [O.F. *dépendre*, L. *dēpendēre* (DE-, *pendēre*, to hang)], *v.i.* To hang down; to be contingent, as to the issue or result, on something else; to rely, to trust, to reckon (upon); to rely for support or maintenance; to be pending. **depend upon it:** You may rely upon it, you may be certain. **that depends:** That is conditional; perhaps. **dependable,** *a.* That may be depended upon. **dependableness,** *n.* **dependably,** *adv.* **dependant,** *n.* One depending upon another for support or favour; that which depends upon something else; a retainer. **dependence,** *n.* The state of being dependent; that on which one depends; connection, concatenation; reliance, trust, confidence; a dependency; (*Law*) pendency, waiting for settlement; *a subject of dispute or quarrel. **dependency,** *n.* Something dependent, esp. a country or state subject to another; an accident, a quality. **dependent,** *a.* Hanging down; depending on another; subject to, contingent (upon), relying on for support, benefit, or favour; *impending. **dependently,** *adv.*

depersonalize (dē pĕr′ sȯn ȧ līz), *v.t.* To divest of personality; to regard as without individuality. **depersonalization,** *n.* The divesting of personality; (*Psych.*) the experience of unreality feelings in relation to oneself.

***dephlogisticate** (dē flȯ jis′ ti kāt) [DE-, PHLOGISTICATE], *v.t.* To deprive of phlogiston; to relieve of inflammation. ***dephlogisticated air:** Priestley's name for oxygen.

depict (dė pikt′) [L. *dēpictus*, p.p. of *dēpingere* (DE-, *pingere*, to paint)], *v.t.* To paint, to portray; to describe or represent in words. **depicter,** *n.* **depiction,** *n.* **depictive,** *a.* **depicture** (dė pik′ tyŭr, -chŭr), *v.t.* To depict, to represent, to paint.

depilate (dep′ i lāt) [L. *dēpilātus*, p.p. of *dēpilāre* (DE-, *pilāre*, to pluck away, from *pilus*, a hair)], *v.t.* To pull out, or strip off (hair). **depilation** (-lā′ shŭn), *n.* **depilator** (dep′ i lā tȯr), *n.* **depilatory** (dė pil′ ȧ tȯr i), *a.* Having the power of stripping off hair. *n.* An application for removing superfluous hair without injuring the skin.

deplenish (dė plen′ ish), *v.t.* To deprive of stock, furniture, etc.; to empty of contents.

deplete (dė plēt′) [L. *dēplētus*, p.p. of *dēplēre* (DE-, *plēre*, to fill)], *v.t.* To empty, to exhaust; (*Med.*) to empty or relieve (as in blood-letting). **depletion,** *n.* **depletive,** *a.* Causing depletion. *n.* A depleting agent. **depletory,** *a.*

deplore (dė plōr′) [L. *dēplōrāre* (DE-, *plōrāre*, to wail)], *v.t.* To lament over; to grieve; to regret; to regard with concern and resentment; *to complain of. **deplorable,** *a.* **deplorableness,** *n.* **deplorably,** *adv.* ***deploring,** *a.* **deploringly,** *adv.*

deploy (dė ploi′) [F. *déployer*, O.F. *desployer*, L. *displicāre*, to unfold (DIS-, *plicāre*, to fold)], *v.t.* (*Mil.*) To open out; to extend from column into line. *v.i.* To form a more extended front. **deployment,** *n.*

deplume (dė ploom′) [F. *déplumer* (DE-, L. *plūma*, feather)], *v.t.* To strip of plumage; (*fig.*) to strip (of honour, money, ornaments, etc.). **deplumation** (dē ploo mā′ shŭn), *n.*

depolarize (dē pō′ lȧ rīz), *v.t.* (*Elec.*) To free from polarization (as the gas-filmed plates of a voltaic battery); to deprive of polarity; (*fig.*) to divest of ambiguity; (*Opt.*) to remove the polarization of a ray of light. **depolarization** (-zā′ shŭn), *n.* **depolarizer,** *n.*

depone (dė pōn′) [L. *dēpōnere* (DE-, *pōnere*, to put)], *v.t.* To give evidence upon oath; to testify; *to lay down, to deposit. *v.i.* To testify, esp. on oath. **deponent,** *a.* *Laying down; deposing. *n.* A deponent verb; (*Law*) a witness; one who makes an affidavit to any statement of fact. **deponent verb:** A Latin verb with a passive form and active meaning.

depopulate (dė pop′ ū lāt) [L. *dēpopulātus*, p.p. of *dēpopulāre*, to lay waste, late L., to divest of inhabitants (DE-, *populus*, people)], *v.t.* To clear of inhabitants; to reduce the inhabitants of. *v.i.* To become less populous. **depopulation** (-lā′ shŭn), *n.*

deport (dė pôrt′) [O.F. *deporter*, L. *dēportāre* (DE-, *portāre*, to carry)], *v.t.* To carry away, esp. from one country to another; to conduct, to demean, to behave (oneself, etc.). **n.* Deportment. **deportation** (dē pôr tā′ shŭn), *n.* The act of transporting to a foreign land; the state of being banished. **deportee,** *n.* One who is deported.

deportment (dė pôrt′ mėnt), *n.* Conduct, demeanour, carriage, manners; (*fig.*) the behaviour of a substance (as in an experiment).

depose (dė pōz′) [F. *déposer* (DE-, *poser*, L. *pausāre*, to PAUSE, late L., to place, by confusion with *ponere*, to DEPONE)], *v.t.* To remove from a throne or other high office; to bear witness, to testify on oath; *to lay down, to deposit, *to take away; *to examine on oath. *v.i.* To bear witness. **deposable,** *a.* **deposal,** *n.*

deposit (dė poz′ it) [M.F. *depositer*, L. *depositum*, neut. p.p. of *dēpōnere*, to DEPONE], *v.t.* To lay down, to place; to let fall or throw down; to entrust; to lodge with any one for safety or as a pledge; to lay (as eggs); to leave behind as precipitation; to bury. *n.* Anything deposited or laid down; that which is entrusted to another; a pledge, an earnest or first instalment, a trust, a security; money lodged in a bank; matter accumulated or precipitated and left behind. **on deposit:** Entrusted to some one for safety, or on interest. **depositary,** *n.* One with whom anything is deposited for safety; a trustee.

deposition (dep ȯ-, dē pȯ zish′ ŭn) [O.F., from L. *depositio -ōnem*, as prec.], *n.* The act of depositing; the act of deposing, esp. from a throne; a statement, a declaration; an affidavit; the act of bearing witness on oath; the evidence of a witness reduced to writing. **the Deposition:** The taking down of Christ from the Cross; a picture of this.

depositor (de poz′ i tȯr), *n.* One who makes a deposit, esp. of money; an apparatus for depositing anything.

depository (de poz′ i tȯr i), *n.* A depositary; a place where anything, esp. furniture, is placed for safety.

depot (dep′ ō) [F. *dépôt*, L. *dēpositum*, DEPOSIT], *n.* A place of deposit, a magazine, a storehouse; (*Am.*) a railway station; (*Mil.*) a magazine for stores; a station for recruits; the headquarters of a regiment; that portion of the battalion at headquarters while the rest are abroad; (*Fort.*) a particular place at the end of the trenches out of reach of fire from the besieged place.

deprave (dė prāv′) [O.F. *depraver*, L. *dēprāvāre* (DE-, *prāvus*, crooked, depraved)], *v.t.* To make bad or corrupt; to vitiate; to deteriorate; *to defame. **v.i.* To utter calumnies. **depravation** (-vā′ shŭn), *n.* The act of depraving; the state of being depraved; deterioration; *censure, detraction. **depravity** (dė prăv′ i ti), *n.* A state of corruption; viciousness, profligacy; perversion, degeneracy.

deprecate (dep′ rė kāt) [L. *dēprecātus*, p.p. of *dēprecārī* (DE-, *precārī*, to pray)], *v.t.* To endeavour to avert by prayer; to argue or plead earnestly against; to express regret or reluctance about; to express disapproval of or regret for; *to implore mercy of. **deprecatingly,** *adv.* **deprecation** (-kā′ shŭn), *n.* **deprecative** (dep′-), *a.* **deprecatory,** *a.*

depreciate (dė prē′ shi āt) [L. *dēpretiātus*, p.p. of *dēpretiāre* (DE-, *pretium*, price, value)], *v.t.* To lower the value of; to disparage, to undervalue, to decry; to reduce the price of; to lower the exchange value of (money, etc.). *v.i.* To fall in value. **depreciatingly,** *adv.* **depreciation** (de prē shi ā′ shŭn), *n.* The act of depreciating; the state of becoming depreciated; fall in value; (*Comm.*) allowance for wear and tear. **depreciatory** (dė prē′ shi ā tȯr i), *a.*

depredation (dep rė dā′ shŭn) [F. *déprédation*, L. *dēprædātio -ōnem*, form *dēprædārī* (DE-, *prædārī*, to rob, from *præda*, booty)], *n.* Plundering, spoliation. **depredator** (dep′ rė dā tȯr), *n.* A pillager, a plunderer.

depress (dė pres′) [L. *depressus*, p.p. of *dēprimere* (DE-, *premere*, to PRESS)], *v.t.* To press down; to lower; to bring down; to humble, to abase; to reduce or keep down the energy or activity of; to cast down; to dispirit. **depressant,** *a.* (*Med.*) Lowering. *n.* (*Med.*) A sedative. **depressed area,** *n.* An area of very serious unemployment. **depressed classes** [UNTOUCHABLES]. **depressible,** *a.* **depressing,** *a.* **depressingly,** *adv.* **depression** (dė presh′ ŭn), *n.* The act of depressing; the state of being depressed; lowering of the spirits, dejection; lowering of energy or activity, slackness of business; an economic crisis; (*Path.*) reduced vitality; (*Surg.*) operation for cataract; the reduction of an obtruding part; a hollow place on a surface; (*Astron.*) the angular distance of a heavenly body below the horizon; (*Meteor.*) a low state of the barometer indicative of bad weather; the centre of low pressure in a cyclone; (*Mil.*) the lowering the muzzle of a gun; (*Mus.*) lowering in pitch; flattening. **depressive,** *a.* **depressor,** *n.* One who or that which depresses; (*Anat.*) a muscle which depresses the part to which it is attached; (*Surg.*) an instrument for reducing or pushing back an obtruding part.

deprive (dė prīv') [O.F. *depriver*, late L. *dēprīvāre* (DE-, *prīvāre*, to deprive, from *prīvus*, single, peculiar)], *v.t.* To take from; to debar; to dispossess, to bereave; to divest of an ecclesiastical dignity or preferment. **deprivable,** *a.* **deprival,** *n.* **deprivation** (de pri vā' shŭn), *n.* The act of depriving; the state of being deprived; loss, dispossession, bereavement; the act of divesting a clergyman of his spiritual promotion or dignity.

de profundis (dē prō fŭn' dis) [L., 'Out of the depths,' Ps. cxxx], *n.* A cry from the depths of penitence or affliction; the title of the 130th Psalm.

depth (depth), *n.* Deepness; measurement from the top or surface downwards or from the front backwards; a deep place, an abyss; the deepest, innermost part; the middle or height of a season; (*pl.*) the sea, the deep part of the ocean, deep water; abstruseness, profundity, mental penetration; intensity of colour, shade, darkness, or obscurity; profundity of thought or feeling; (*pl.*) the extremity, the extreme or inmost part; (*Mil.*) the number of men in a file. **depth of a sail:** The extent (of a square sail) from the head-rope to the foot-rope. **out of one's depth:** In deep water; (*fig.*) puzzled beyond one's knowledge or ability. **depth-charge,** *n.* (*Nav.*) A mine or bomb exploded under water, used for attacking submarines. **depthless,** *a.* Without depth; *unfathomable.

depurate (dep' ū rāt) [med. L. *dēpūrātus*, p.p. of *dēpūrāre* (DE-, L. *pūrus*, PURE)], *v.t.* To purify. *v.i.* To become pure. **depuration** (-rā' shŭn), *n.* **depurative** (dė pū' rȧ tiv), *a.* **depurator,** *n.* One who or that which purifies; (*Med.*) an apparatus to assist the expulsion of morbid matter by the excretory ducts of the skin.

depute (dė pūt') [F. *députer*, L. *dēputāre* (DE-, *putāre*, to think, to consider, to allot)], *v.t.* To appoint or send as a substitute or agent; to give as a charge, to commit. *n.* (*Sc.*) A deputy. **deputation** (dep ū tā' shŭn), *n.* The act of deputing; an authority or commission to act; the person or persons deputed to act as representatives for others, (*Am.*) a delegation. **deputational,** *a.* **deputationist,** *n.* **deputize** (dep' ū tīz), *v.t.* To appoint or send as deputy. *v.i.* To act as deputy.

deputy (dep' ū ti), *n.* One who is appointed or sent to act for another or others; a delegate, a member of a deputation; a member of the French and other legislative chambers; (*Law*) one who exercises an office in another's right; (*in comb.*) acting for, vice-; acting. **deputy-governor,** *n.* **deputy-speaker,** *n.* **deputize** (dep' ū tīz), *v.t.* To appoint or send as deputy. *v.i.* To act as deputy.

***deracinate** (dė răs' i nāt) [F. *déraciner* (DE-, *racine*, ult. from L. *rādix -īcem*, root)], *v.t.* To tear up by the roots; (*fig.*) to destroy.

***deraign** (dė rān') [O.F. *desraisnier*, prob. from a late L. *dērationāre* (DE-, *ratio -ōnem*, reckoning, account)], *v.t.* To prove, to vindicate; to set (a battle) in array; to array.

derail (dė rāl') [F. *dérailler*], *v.t.* To throw off the rails. *v.i.* To run off the rails. **derailer,** *n.* **derailment,** *n.*

derange (dė rānj') [F. *déranger*], *v.t.* To put out of line or order; to disorganize; to disturb, to unsettle, to disorder (esp. the intellect). **deranged,** *a.* Insane; slightly insane. **derangement,** *n.*

deration (dē răsh' ŏn), *v.t.* To remove from the rationed category.

Derby (dar' bi), *n.* A race for three-year-old horses, held at Epsom in May or June, founded by the twelfth Earl of Derby in 1780; a stout kind of boot; (*Am.*) a bowler hat. **Derby day,** *n.* The day on which the Derby is run. **Derby Scheme,** *n.* A form of voluntary military conscription devised by the Earl of Derby in 1915.

Derbyshire neck (dar' bi shėr nek), *n.* Goitre; so called because of its prevalence in parts of Derbyshire. **Derbyshire spar,** *n.* Fluor-spar.

derelict (der' ė likt) [L. *derelictus*, p.p. of *dērelinquere* (DE-, *relinquere*, to RELINQUISH)], *a.* Left, forsaken, abandoned. *n.* Anything abandoned (esp. a vessel at sea), relinquished, or thrown away; land left dry by the sea. **dereliction** (-lik' shŭn), *n.* Abandonment; the state of being abandoned; omission or neglect (as of a duty); the abandonment of land by the sea; land left dry by the sea. **dereliction of duty:** Reprehensible neglect or shortcoming.

derequisition (dē rek wi zi' shŏn), *v.t.* To free requisitioned property.

deride (dė rīd') [L. *dērīdēre* (DE-, *rīdēre*, to laugh)], *v.t.* To laugh at, to mock. *v.i.* To indulge in mockery or ridicule. **deridingly,** *adv.* **derision** (dė rizh' ŭn), *n.* The act of deriding; the state of being derided; ridicule, mockery, contempt. **in derision:** In contempt, made a laughing-stock. **derisive, -sory,** *a.* Scoffing, deriding, ridiculing; ridiculous. **derisively,** *adv.*

derive (dė rīv') [F. *dériver*, L. *dērīvāre*, to draw off water (DE-, *rīvus*, a stream)], *v.t.* To obtain as by logical sequence; to deduce; to draw, as from a source, root or principle; to trace (an etymology); (*Math.*) to deduce or determine from data; *to conduct, convey, transmit. *v.i.* To come, to proceed, to be descended; to originate. **derivable,** *a.* That may be derived; deducible. **derivation** (der i vā' shŭn), *n.* The act of deriving; deduction, extraction; the etymology of a word, the process of tracing a word to its root; (*Math.*) the process of deducing a function from another; (*Med.*) the drawing off of inflammation or congestion; (*Biol.*) the theory of evolution as an explanation of the descent of organisms from other forms of life; *a drawing off or turning aside of anything from its natural course. **derivationist,** *n.* **derivative** (dė riv' ȧ tiv), *a.* Derived; taken from something else; secondary, not original. *n.* Anything derived from a source; a word derived from or taking its origin in another; (*Math.*) a differential coefficient. **derivatively,** *adv.*

derm, dermis (dĕrm, dĕr' mis) [Gr. *derma*, from *derein*, to flay], *n.* Skin; (*Anat.*) true skin or corium lying beneath the epidermis. **derm-, dermo-, dermato-** [Gr. *derma dermatos*, the skin], *comb. form.* Pertaining to the skin. **-derm,** *noun suf.* (see ENDODERM, PACHYDERM). **dermal,** *a.* **dermalgia** (dĕr măl' ji ȧ), **dermatalgia** (dĕr mȧ tăl' ji ȧ) [Gr. *algos*, pain], *n.* (*Path.*) Neuralgia of the skin. **dermatic** (dĕr măt' ik), *a.* Of or pertaining to the skin. **dermatitis** (-tī' tis) [-ITIS], *n.* Inflammation of the skin. **dermatoid,** *a.* Skin-like. **dermatology** (tol' ŏ ji) [-LOGY], *n.* The science of the skin and its diseases. **dermatologist,** *n.* **dermatosis** (dĕr mȧ tō' sis), *n.* (*Path.*) Any disease of the skin. **dermic,** *a.* **dermophyte** (dĕr' mō fīt) [-PHYTE], *n.* (*Path.*) Any parasitic plant infesting the cuticle and causing various skin diseases. **dermoskeleton** (dĕr mō skel' ė tŏn) [SKELETON], *n.* The exoskeleton; the external bony shell of crabs, tortoises, and other animals, both vertebrates and invertebrates.

***dern** (dĕrn) [A.-S. *derne* (cp. O.S. *derni*, O.Fris. *dern*, O.H.G. *tarni*)], *a.* Secret, reserved; dark, sombre; gloomy, dire, dreadful. *n.* Secrecy. ***dernful,** *a.* Solitary, sad, mournful. ***dernly,** *adv.*

derogate (der' ŏ gāt) [L. *dērogātus*, p.p. of *dērogāre* (DE-, *rogāre*, to ask, to propose a law)], *v.i.* To detract, to withdraw a part (from); to become inferior, to lower oneself, to degenerate; *to withdraw a part. *v.t.* To lessen the effect of; to detract from, to disparage; *to repeal or annul partially. *a. (-gȧt) Debased, degenerate. **derogation** (-gā′ shŭn), *n.* The act of derogating; the act of detracting from worth, name, or character; disparagement; deterioration. **derogatory** (-rog′ ȧ tŏr i), *a.* Tending to detract from honour, worth, or character; disparaging, depreciatory.

derrick (der′ ik) [the name of a Tyburn hangman in the 17th cent.], *n.* A hoisting machine with a boom stayed from a central post, wall, floor, deck, etc., for raising heavy weights; the framework over an oil-well. **derrick-crane**, *n.*

derring-do (der′ ing doo) [Chaucer, *dorring don*, daring to do, mistaken by Spenser], *n.* Courageous deeds; bravery.

derringer (der′ in jėr) [from the inventor], *n.* A short-barrelled pistol carrying a large ball.

derris (der′ is), *n.* (*Chem.*) An extract of the root of the *Derris*, a tropical species of tree, which forms an effective insecticide.

derv (dĕrv) [initials Diesel Engine Road Vehicle], *n.* Diesel engine fuel oil.

dervish (dĕr′ vish) [Pers. *darvīsh*, poor], *n.* A Mohammedan friar who makes a vow of poverty and austerity; one of the Sudanese followers of the Mahdi or Khalifa.

descant (des′ kănt) [O.North.F. *descant*, O.F. *deschant*, med. L. *discantus* (DIS-, L. *cantus*, singing, song)], *n.* A song, a melody; *a song or tune with modulations or in parts; a variation; a counterpoint above the plainsong, an accompaniment; the upper part, esp. the soprano, in part music; *a discourse branching into parts; a series of comments. *v.i.* (des kănt′) To comment or discourse at large, to dilate (on); to sing in parts; (*Mus.*) to compose music in parts; to add a part or parts to a melody or subject.

descend (dė send′) [F. *descendre*, L. *dēscendere* (DE-, *scandere*, to climb)], *v.i.* To come or go down, to sink, to fall, to slope downwards; to make an attack, to fall upon suddenly; to have birth, origin, or descent; to be derived; to be transmitted in order of succession; to pass on, as from more to less important matters, from general to particular, or from more remote to nearer times; to stoop; to condescend; to lower or abase oneself morally or socially; *to retire. *v.t.* To walk, move, or pass along downwards. **descendable, -ible**, *a.* That may be transmitted from ancestor to heir. **descendant**, *n.* One who descends from an ancestor; offspring, issue. **descended**, *p.p.* Derived, sprung (from a race or ancestor). ***descension**, *n.* The act of falling, moving, or sinking downwards; descent. ***descensional**, *a.* Of or pertaining to descent. ***descensive**, *a.* Tending downwards.

descent (dė sent′) [F. *descente*, as prec.], *n.* The act of descending; a declivity, a slope downwards; a way of descending; downward motion; decline in rank or prosperity; a sudden attack, esp. from the sea; a fall; pedigree, lineage, origin, evolution; issue of one generation; transmission by succession or inheritance; (*Mus.*) a passing to a lower pitch; *the lowest part; *offspring, issue. **descent theory**, *n.* The theory of evolution.

describe (dė skrīb′) [O.F. *descrire*, L. *dēscrībere* (DE-, *scrībere*, to write (afterwards assim. to L.))], *v.t.* To draw, to trace out; to form or trace out by motion; to set forth the qualities, features, or properties of in words; *to descry. *v.i.* To give a description. **describable**, *a.* **description** (dė skrip′ shŭn), *n.* The act of describing; an account of anything in words; a kind, a sort, a species; (*Log.*) an enumeration of properties or accidental attributes. **descriptive**, *a.* Containing description; capable of describing; given to description. **descriptively**, *adv.* ***descrive** [O.F. *descrivre*, F. *décrire*, see above], *v.t.* To describe.

descry (dė skrī′) [O.F. *descrire*, as prec.], *v.t.* To make out, to espy; *to reveal; to bewray; *to explore, to spy out.

desecrate (des′ ė krāt) [L. *dēsecrātus*, p.p. of *dēsecrāre* (DE-, *sacrāre*, to make sacred, *sacer*, SACRED)], *v.t.* To divert from any sacred purpose; to profane; to divert from a sacred to a profane purpose. *a. Desecrated. **desecration** (-krā′ shŭn), *n.* **desecrator** (des′-), *n.*

desert (1) (dez′ ert) [O.F., from L. *dēsertus*, p.p. of *dēserere* (DE-, *serere*, to bind, to join)], *a.* Uninhabited, waste; untilled, barren. *n.* A waste, uninhabited, uncultivated place, esp. a waterless and treeless region; solitude, dreariness. **desert-bird**, *n.* The pelican. **desert oak**, *n.* (*Austral.*) A variety of casuarina. **Desert Rat**, *n.* (*colloq.*) A soldier of the 7th Armoured Division in N. Africa (1941–2).

desert (2) (dė zĕrt′) [F. *déserter*, late L. *dēsertāre*, as prec.], *v.t.* To forsake, to abandon; to quit, to leave; to fail to help; to fail. *v.i.* (*Mil., etc.*) To abandon the service without leave. **deserter**, *n.* **desertion**, *n.*

desert (3) (dė zĕrt′) [O.F. *deserte*, p.p. of *deservir*, see foll.], *n.* What one deserves, either as reward or punishment; merit or demerit, (*unconditional*) merit; state of deserving; (*pl.*) deserved reward or punishment. **desertless**, *a.* Without merit.

deserve (dė zĕrv′) [O.F. *deservir*, L. *dēservīre* (DE-, *servīre*, to serve)], *v.t.* To be worthy of, to merit by conduct or qualities good or bad, esp. to merit by excellence, good conduct, or useful deeds; *to earn. *v.i.* To be worthy or deserving. **deservedly**, *adv.* **deserver**, *n.* **deserving**, *a.* Merited, worthy, having deserved. *n.* The act or state of meriting. **deservingly**, *adv.*

deshabille (des ȧ bēl′) [F. *déshabillé*, p.p. of *déshabiller* (DIS-, *habiller*, to dress)], *n.* Undress, being partly or carelessly attired; a loose morning dress.

desiccate (des′ i kāt, dė sik′ āt) [L. *dēsiccātus*, p.p. of *dēsiccāre* (DE-, *siccāre*, to dry, from *siccus*, dry)], *v.t.* To dry, to exhaust of moisture. *a.* (-kȧt) Dried up. **desiccant** (dė sik′ ȧnt), *a.* Drying up; *n.* (des′ i kȧnt). **desiccation** (-kā′ shŭn), *n.* **desiccative** (dĕ sik′ ȧ tiv), *a.* **desiccator** (des′ i kā tŏr), *n.* (*Chem.*) An apparatus for drying substances liable to be decomposed by moisture; an apparatus for drying food and other commercial substances.

desiderate (dė zid′ ėr āt) [L. *dēsiderātus*, p.p. of *dēsiderāre*, to DESIRE], *v.t.* To feel the loss of; to want, to miss. ***desideration** (-ā′ shŭn), *n.* **desiderative**, *a.* Expressing desire. *n.* (*Gram.*) A verb formed from another, and expressive of a desire to do the action implied in the primitive verb.

desideratum (de zid ĕr ā′ tŭm), *n.* (*pl.* **desiderata**) Anything desired, esp. anything to fill a gap; a state of things to be desired.

design (dė zīn′) [F. *désigner*, to denote, to signify, L. *dēsignāre* (DE-, *signāre*, to mark, from *signum*, a sign)], *v.t.* To contrive, to formulate, to project; to draw, to plan, to sketch out; to purpose, to intend; to appropriate, to devote or apply to a particular purpose; *to point out, to specify, to appoint. *v.i.* To draw, esp. decorative figures. *n.* A plan, a scheme; a purpose, an object, an intention; thought and intention as revealed in the correlation of parts or adaptation of means to an end; an arrangement of forms and colours intended to be executed in durable material; a preliminary sketch, a study; a working plan; the art of designing; artistic structure, proportion, balance, etc.; plot, construction, general idea; artistic invention. **designed**, *a.* Intentional. **designedly** (dė zī′ nėd li), *adv.* **designer**, *n.* One who designs, esp. artistic patterns for execution in various materials by manufacturers. **designing**, *a.* Crafty, scheming. **designingly**, *adv.*

designate (dez′ ig nāt) [L. *dēsignātus*, p.p. of *dēsignāre* (as prec.)], *v.t.* To point out, to specify by a distinctive mark or name; to cause to be known; to indicate, to mark; to describe (as); to select, to nominate, to appoint. *a.* Nominated (to an office). **designation** (-nā′ shŭn), *n.* The act of designating; appointment, nomination; name, appellation, title, description. **designative, -tory** (dez′ -), *a.*

desilverize (dē sil′ vėr īz), *v.t.* To extract the silver from (as lead).

***desipient** (dė sip′ i ėnt) [L. *dēsipiens -ntem*, pres.p. of *dēsipere* (DE-, *sapere*, to be wise)], *a.* Foolish, childish, nonsensical. **desipience,** *n.*

desire (dė zīr′) [O.F. *desirer*, L. *dēsīderāre*, to long for], *v.t.* To wish (to do); to wish for the attainment or possession of; to express a wish to have, to request, to beseech, to command; *to need, to require; *to invite. *v.i.* To have desire. *n.* An eagerness of the mind to obtain or enjoy some object; a request, an entreaty; the object of desire; sensual appetite, lust. **desirable,** *a.* Worthy of being desired; agreeable. **desirability** (-bil′ i ti), *n.* **desirableness,** *n.* **desirably,** *adv.* **desireless,** *a.* **desirous,** *a.* Desiring, wishful; characterized by desire, covetous. **desirously,** *adv.*

desist (dė zist′) [O.F. *desister*, L. *dēsistere* (DE-, *sistere*, to put, to stop)], *v.i.* To cease, to forbear; to leave off. **desistance,** *n.*

desk (desk) [med. L. *desca*, L. *discus*, a DISK], *n.* A table, frame, or case for a writer or reader, often with a sloping top; the place from which prayers are read; a pulpit; the occupation of a clerk. **desk-work,** *n.* Writing, copying. **deskful,** *n.*

desmid (des′ mid) [mod. L. *desmidium*, Gr. *desmos*, a bond, a chain], *n.* (*Bot.*) Any individual of the *Desmidiaceæ*, a group of microscopic conjugate freshwater algæ, differing from the diatoms in their green colour, and the absence of a siliceous covering.

desmine (des′ min) [Gr. *desmē*, a bundle], *n.* (*Min.*) Stilbite, a zeolitic mineral occurring in bundles of crystals.

desmography (des mog′ rȧ fi) [Gr. *desmos*, a bond, -GRAPHY], *n.* A description of the ligaments of the body.

desmoid (des′ moid), *n.* (*Path.*) Morbid tissue of a fibrous character.

desmology (des mol′ ō ji), *n.* A branch of anatomy which treats of the ligaments and sinews.

desmotomy (des mot′ ō mi), *n.* The anatomy or dissection of the ligaments and sinews.

desolate (des′ ȯ lȧt) [L. *dēsōlātus*, p.p. of *dēsōlāre* (DE-, *sōlāre*, to make lonely, from *sōlus*, alone)], *a.* Forsaken, solitary, lonely; uninhabited, deserted, neglected, ruined; barren, forlorn, comfortless; *destitute. *v.t.* (-lāt) To deprive of inhabitants; to lay waste; to make wretched. **desolately,** *adv.* **desolateness,** *n.* **desolator,** *n.* **desolating,** *a.* Wasting, ruining, ravaging. **desolation** (-lā′ shŭn), *n.* The act of desolating; the state of being desolated; neglect, ruin; loneliness; bitter grief, affliction.

despair (dė spâr′) [O.F. *despeir-*, stem of *desperer*, L. *dēspērāre* (DE-, *spērāre*, to hope)], *v.i.* To be without hope; to give up all hope. **v.t.* To lose all hope of. *n.* Hopelessness; that which causes hopelessness. **despairer,** *n.* **despairful,** *a.* **despairfully,** *adv.* **despairing,** *a.* Hopeless, desperate. **despairingly,** *adv.*

despatch [DISPATCH].

desperado (des pėr a′ dō) [O.Sp., desperate, L. *dēsperātus*, as foll.], *n.* A desperate or reckless ruffian.

desperate (des′ pėr ȧt) [L. *dēspērātus*, p.p. of *dēspērāre*, to DESPAIR], *a.* Hopeless, reckless, lawless, regardless of danger or consequences; fearless; affording little hope of success, recovery, or escape; tried as a last resource; extremely dangerous; very bad, awful. *adv.* (*colloq.*) Extremely, awfully. **n.* A desperado, a wretch. **desperately,** *adv.* In a desperate manner; awfully, extremely. **desperateness,** *n.* **desperation** (-ā′ shŭn), *n.*

despicable (des′ pik ȧbl) [*dēspicābilis*, from *dēspicārī* (DE-, *specārī*, cogn. with *specere*, see DESPISE)], *a.* Meriting contempt; vile, worthless, mean. **despicably,** *adv.*

despise (dė spīz′) [O.F. *despis-*, stem of *despire*, L. *dēspicere* (DE-, *specere*, to look at)], *v.t.* To look down upon; to regard with contempt; to scorn. ***despisedness,** *n.* **despisingly,** *adv.*

despite (dė spīt′) [O.F. *despit*, L. *dēspectus*, contempt, p.p. of *dēspicere*, to DESPISE], *n.* Spite, malice; aversion, vexation; contemptuous treatment, outrage, contumely; *an act of contempt or malice. *prep.* Notwithstanding; in spite of. **v.t.* To vex, to spite; to treat with despite. **despite, despite of, in despite of:** In spite of. ***to do despite to:** To dishonour. **despiteful,** *a.* Spiteful, malicious, malignant. **despitefully,** *adv.* ***despiteous** (des pit′ ē ŭs), *a.* Despiteful. ***despiteously,** *adv.*

despoil (dė spoil′) [O.F. *despoiller* (F. *dépouiller*), L. *dēspoliāre* (DE-, *spoliāre*, to SPOIL)], *v.t.* To strip or take away from by force; to plunder; to deprive. **n.* Plundering, robbery. **despoiler,** *n.* ***despoilment, despoliation** (dė spō li ā′ shŭn), *n.*

despond (dė spond′) [L. *dēspondēre* (DE-, *spondēre*, to promise)], *v.i.* To be cast down in spirits; to lose hope. *n.* Despondency. **despondency,** *n.* **despondent,** *a.* **despondently,** *adv.* **despondingly,** *adv.*

despot (des′ pȯt) [O.F., from late L. *despotus*, Gr. *despotēs*], *n.* An absolute ruler or sovereign; a tyrant, an oppressor. **despotic** (dė spot′ ik), *a.* Absolute, irresponsible, uncontrolled; arbitrary, tyrannical. **despotically,** *adv.* **despotism** (des′ pȯ tizm), *n.* Absolute authority; arbitrary government, autocracy; tyranny. **despotist,** *n.* An advocate of autocracy. **despotize,** *v.i.*

desquamate (des′ kwȧ māt) [L. *dēsquāmātus*, p.p. of *dēsquāmāre* (DE-, *squama*, a scale)], *v.t.* (*Surg.*) To scale, to peel. *v.i.* (*Surg.*) To scale or peel off, to exfoliate. **desquamation** (-mā′ shŭn), *n.* The separation of the skin in scales. **desquamative** (dė skwăm′ ȧ tiv), **-atory** (dė skwăm′ ȧ tȯr i), *a.*

dessert (dė zërt′) [F. from *desservir*, to clear the table (*des-*, L. DIS-, *servir*, to SERVE)], *n.* The last course at dinner, consisting of fruit and sweetmeats; (*Am.*) the sweet course. **dessert-spoon,** *n.* A medium-sized spoon holding half as much as a tablespoon and twice as much as a teaspoon.

destemper [DISTEMPER].

***destinate** (des′ ti nȧt) [L. *dēstinātus*, p.p. of *dēstināre*, to DESTINE], *a.* Fixed by destiny or fate. *v.t.* (-nāt) To destine, to appoint.

destination (des ti nā′ shun), *n.* The act of destining; the purpose for which a thing is appointed or intended; the place to which one is bound or to which a thing is sent.

destine (des′ tin) [F. *destiner*], *v.t.* To appoint, fix, or determine to a use, purpose, duty, or position. **destinism,** *n.* Fatalism.

destiny (des′ tin i), *n.* The purpose or end to which any person or thing is appointed; fate, fortune, lot, events as the fulfilment of fate; invincible necessity; the power which presides over the fortunes of men. **the Destinies:** The three Fates.

destitute (des′ ti tūt) [L. *dēstitūtus*, p.p. of *dēstituere* (DE-, *statuere*, to place, from *status*, p.p. of *stāre*, to stand)], *a.* In want, devoid of the necessities of life; forsaken, forlorn; bereft (of). **n.* A destitute person. **v.t.* To forsake; to deprive; to make destitute. **destitution** (-tū′ shŭn), *n.*

***destrier** (dė strēr′) [M.E. and A.-F. *destrer* (O.F. *destrier*), late L. *dextrārius*, from *dextra*, right hand], *n.* A war-horse, a charger.

destroy (dė stroi′) [O.F. *destruire* (F. *détruire*), late L. *destruere* (DE-, *struere*, to build)], *v.t.* To pull down or demolish; to pull to pieces; to undo, to nullify; to annihilate; to lay waste; to kill; to extirpate; to sweep away; to consume; to overthrow; to disprove; to put an end to. ***destroyable,** *a.* **destroyer,** *n.* One who destroys; (*Nav.*) a fast warship armed with torpedoes. **destructible,** *a.* **destructibility** (dė strŭk ti bil′ i ti), *n.*

destruction (dė strŭk′ shŭn), *n.* The act of destroying; the state of being destroyed; demolition, ruin; death, slaughter; that which destroys. **destructionist,** *n.* A believer in the annihilation of the wicked. **destructive,** *a.* Causing or tending to destruction; ruinous, mischievous, wasteful; serving or tending to subvert or confute (arguments or opinions); negative, not constructive. *n.* A destroyer, esp. of existing institutions; a radical reformer. **destructive distillation** [DISTILLATION]. **destructively,** *adv.* **destructiveness,** *n.* **destructor,** *n.* A furnace for burning up refuse.

desuetude (dez′ wė tūd) [F. *désuétude,* L. *dēsuētūdo,* from *dēsuētus,* p.p. of *dēsuēscere* (DE-, *suēscere,* incept. of *suēre,* to be used)], *n.* Disuse; cessation of practice or habit.

desulphurize (dē sŭl′ fėr īz), *v.t.* To free from sulphur (used of ores). **desulphurization (-zā′ shŭn),** *n.*

desultory (des′ ŭl tȯr i) [L. *dēsultōrius,* from *dēsultor,* a circus horse-leaper, from *dēsilere* (DE-, *salīre,* to jump)], *a.* Passing quickly from one subject to another; following no regular plan; loose, disjointed, discursive. **desultorily,** *adv.* **desultoriness,** *n.*

desynonymize (dē si non′ i mīz), *v.t.* To differentiate; to make distinctions between synonymous terms.

detach (dė tăch′) [F. *détacher*], *v.t.* To disconnect, to separate; to disengage; (*Mil. and Nav.*) to separate from the main body for a special service; (*usu. in pass.*) to free from prejudice, personal considerations, etc. ***v.i.** To become disconnected. **detachable,** *a.* **detached,** *a.* Separated; a term applied to figures standing out from one another or from the background; free from prejudice; disinterested. **detachedly** (dė tăch′ ėd li), *adv.* **detachedness,** *n.* **detachment,** *n.* The act of detaching; the state of being detached; a body of troops or a number of ships detached from the main body and sent on a special service or expedition; freedom from prejudice, self-interest, or worldly influence; independence, isolation.

detail (dė tāl′) [F. *détailler*], *v.t.* To set forth the particular items of; to relate minutely; (*Mil.*) to appoint for a particular service. *n.* (dē′ tāl) An item; a minute and particular account; (*pl.*) a number of particulars; (*Mil.*) a list of names detailed for particular duties; a body of men selected for a special duty; a minor matter; (*Painting, etc., pl.*) minute parts of a picture, statue, etc., as distinguished from the work as a whole. **in detail:** Minutely; item by item. **beaten in detail:** (*Mil. and Nav.*) Defeated by detachments or in a series of partial engagements. **detailed,** *a.* Related in detail; minute, complete.

detain (dė tān′) [O.F. *detenir,* L. *dētinēre* (DE-, *tenēre,* to hold)], *v.t.* To keep back or from; to withhold; to delay, to hinder; to restrain; to keep in custody. ***n.** Detention. **detainer,** *n.* One who detains; (*Law*) the holding possession of what belongs to another; the holding of a person in custody; a writ of detainer. **forcible detainer:** (*Law*) A violent taking or keeping possession of lands without legal authority. ***writ of detainer:** (*Law*) A writ commanding a governor of a prison to detain a prisoner on another suit. ***detainment,** *n.*

detant (dė tănt′) [var. of DETENT], *n.* (*Gun-making*) An attachment on a pivot for preventing the sear from catching in the half-cock notch.

detect (dė tekt′) [L. *dētectus,* p.p. of *dētegere* (DE-, *tegere,* to cover)], *v.t.* To discover or find out; to bring to light; *to expose. ***a.** Detected, exposed. **detectable,** *a.* **detection,** *n.* The act of detecting; the discovery of crime, guilt, etc., or (*Sci.*) of minute particles. **detective,** *a.* Employed in or suitable for detecting. *n.* A police officer employed to investigate special cases of crime, etc. (*in full,* **detective officer**). **amateur detective:** A person with theories supposed to explain police problems. **private detective:** A private person or an agent of a detective bureau employed privately to investigate cases. **detectophone,** *n.* An instrument for tapping and listening-in on telephone wires. **detector,** *n.* One who detects; (*Radio.*) the part of a radio receiver which demodulates the radio waves.

detent (dė tent′) [F. *détente,* from *détendre,* L. *dētinēre* (DE-, *tenēre,* to hold)], *n.* A pin, catch, or lever forming a check to the mechanism in a watch, clock, lock, etc.

détente (dā tant′) [F., as prec.], *n.* Relaxation of international tension.

detention (dė ten′ shŭn) [DETAIN], *n.* The act of detaining; the state of being detained; hindrance; arrest; confinement, compulsory restraint; keeping in school after hours. **house of detention:** A place where offenders are kept while under remand. **detention camp,** *n.* An internment camp. **detention centre,** *n.* A place where young offenders (aged 14 to 20) are detained for periods up to six months.

detenu (dā tė nū′) [F., p.p. of *detenir,* to DETAIN], *n.* (*fem.* **-nue**) One kept in custody, a prisoner.

deter (dė tĕr′) [L. *dēterrēre* (DE-, *terrēre,* to frighten)], *v.t.* To discourage or frighten (from); to hinder or prevent. **determent, deterrence,** *n.* The act of deterring; a deterrent. **deterrent,** *a.* Tending to deter. *n.* That which deters; (*colloq.*) a nuclear weapon the possession of which is supposed to deter the use of a similar weapon by another power.

detergent (dė tĕr′ jėnt) [L. *detergens -ntem,* pres.p. of *dētergere* (DE-, *tergere,* to wipe)], *a.* Cleansing, purging. *n.* (*Med.*) A medicine or application which has the property of cleansing; a chemical cleansing agent.

deteriorate (dė tēr′ i ȯr āt) [L. *dēteriorātus,* p.p. of *dēteriorāre* (*deterior,* worse, from *dē,* away, down)], *v.t.* To make inferior; to reduce in value. *v.i.* To become worse; to degenerate. **deterioration** (dė tēr i ȯr ā′ shŭn), **deteriorative** (dė tēr′ i ȯr ā tiv), *a.*

determinant (dė tĕr′ mi nȧnt), *a.* Determinative, decisive. *n.* One who or that which determines or causes to fix or decide; (*Math.*) the sum of a series of products of several numbers, the products being formed according to certain laws, used in the solution of equations and other processes; (*Biol.*) a conditioning element or unit of germ-plasm in the development of cells.

determinate (dė tĕr′ mi nȧt) [DETERMINE], *a.* Limited, definite; specific, distinct, predetermined, positive; determined, resolute. *v.t.* (-nāt) To determine. **determinate equation,** *n.* An equation which admits of a finite number of solutions. **determinate inflorescence,** *n.* (*Bot.*) Centrifugal flowering beginning with the terminal bud. **determinate problem,** *n.* (*Math.*) A problem which admits of a finite number of solutions. **determinately,** *adv.* **determinateness,** *n.*

determination (dė tĕr′ mi nā′ shŭn) [DETERMINE], *n.* The act of determining or settling; that which is determined on; a conclusion; fixed intention, resolution, strength of mind; direction to a certain end, a fixed tendency; ascertainment of amount, etc.; (*Law*) settlement by a judicial decision; final conclusion; (*Log.*) definition, delimitation; (*Nat. Hist.*) reference of an object to its proper genus and species. **determinative,** *a.* That limits or defines; directive, decisive; (*Log.*) defining, serving to limit; (*Nat. Hist.*) tending to determine the genus, etc., to which a thing belongs. *n.* That which decides, defines, or specifies; (*Gram.*) a demonstrative pronoun; (*Hieroglyphics*) a sign indicating the exact signification. **determinator,** *n.* One who or that which determines.

determine (dė tĕr′ min) [O.F. *determiner*, L. *dētermināre* (DE-, *termināre*, to bound, from *terminus*, a boundary)], *v.t.* To terminate, to conclude; (*Law*) to bring to an end; to fix the limits of, to define; to fix, to settle finally, to decide; to direct, to condition, to shape; to ascertain exactly; to cause to decide; *to put an end to; *to destroy, to kill. *v.i.* To end, to reach a termination; to decide, to resolve. **determinable,** *a.* That may be determined. **determinable freehold:** (*Law*) An estate for life which may expire upon future contingencies before the life for which it was created ends. **determinability** (-bil′ i ti), *n.* **determined,** *a.* Resolute; having a fixed purpose; ended; limited, conditioned. **determinedly,** *adv.* **determiner,** *n.*

determinism (dė tĕr′ mi nizm) [DETERMINE], *n.* The doctrine that the will is not free, but is determined by antecedent causes, whether in the form of internal motives or external necessity, the latter being the postulate of fatalism. **determinist,** *a.* Pertaining to determinism. *n.* One who believes in determinism. **deterministic** (-nist′ ik), *a.*

detersive (dė tĕr′ siv) [F. *détersif -ive*, from *dētersus*, p.p. of *detergēre* (DE-, *tergēre*, to wipe)], *a.* Cleansing. *n.* A cleansing agent or substance.

detest (dė test′) [F. *détester*, L. *dētestārī* (DE-, *testārī*, to testify, from *testis*, a witness)], *v.t.* To hate exceedingly, to abhor. **detestable,** *a.* **detestableness,** *n.* **detestability** (-bil′ i ti), *n.* **detestably,** *adv.* **detestation** (dē tes tā′ shŭn), *n.* Extreme hatred; abhorrence, loathing.

dethrone (dė thrōn′), *v.t.* To remove or depose from a throne; (*fig.*) to drive from power or pre-eminence. **dethronement,** *n.*

detinue (det′ i nū) [O.F. *detenue*, p.p. of *detenir*, to DETAIN], *n.* (*Law*) Unlawful detention. **action of detinue:** An action to recover property illegally detained.

detonate (dē′ tō-, det′ ō nāt) [L. *dētonātus*, p.p. of *dētonāre* (DE-, *tonāre*, to thunder)], *v.t.* To cause to explode with a report. *v.i.* To explode with a report. **detonating bulb,** *n.* A Prince Rupert's drop. **detonating powder,** *n.* A compound powder which explodes by a blow or when heated. **detonating tube,** *n.* A graduated glass tube used for the detonation of gases by means of electricity, a eudiometer. **detonation,** *n.* The act or process of detonating; an explosion with a loud report; a noise resembling this; a violent and noisy outburst of anger; (*Motor.*) the spontaneous combustion in a petrol engine of part of the compressed charge after sparking; the knock that accompanies this. **detonator,** *n.* (*fig.*) One who or that which detonates; a device for causing detonation, a fog-signal.

detour (dė toor′) [F. *détour*, from *détourner*, to turn aside], *n.* A roundabout way; a deviation, a digression; (*Am.*) a road-diversion.

detract (dė trăkt′) [L. *dētractus*, p.p. of *dētrahere* (DE-, *trahere*, to draw)], *v.t.* To take (something) away from; to take (a part) away from; to take away from the reputation or credit of. **v.i.* To speak disparagingly. ***detractingly,** *adv.* **detraction,** *n.* The act of detracting; depreciation, slander. **detractive,** *a.* **detractor,** *n.* One who detracts; a defamer, a slanderer; (*Anat.*) a muscle which draws one part from another.

detrain (dė trān′), *v.t.* To cause to alight from a train. *v.i.* To alight from a train.

detriment (det′ ri mėnt) [F. *détriment*, L. *dētrīmentum*, from *dētrī-* (*dētrītus*, p.p.), from *dēterere* (DE-, *terere*, to rub)], *n.* Loss; harm, injury, damage; (*Her.*) the decrement of the moon in her wane or eclipse. **v.t.* To damage. **detrimental,** *a.* Causing detriment. **detrimentally,** *adv.*

detrited (dė trī′ tėd) [L. *dētrītus*, p.p. of *dēterere*, as prec.], *a.* (*Geol.*) Worn away; disintegrated. **detrital,** *a.* (*Geol.*) **detrition** (dė trish′ ŭn), *n.* A wearing down or away by rubbing. **detritus** (det′ ri tŭs), *n.* (*Geol.*) Accumulated matter produced by the disintegration of rock; debris, gravel, sand, etc.

***detrude** (dė trood′) [L. *dētrūdere* (DE-, *trūdere*, to thrust)], *v.t.* To thrust or force down; to expel from.

***detruncate** (dė trŭng′ kāt) [L. *dētruncātus*, p.p. of *dētruncāre* (DE-, *truncāre*, to cut off)], *v.t.* To lop or cut off; to shorten by cutting. ***detruncation** (-kā′ shŭn), *n.*

deuce (1) (dūs) [F. *deux*, L. *duos*, acc. of *duo*], *n.* Two; a card or die with two spots; (*Tennis*) a score of 40 all, requiring two successive points to be scored by either party to win. **deuce-ace,** *n.* The one and two thrown at dice.

deuce (2) (dūs) [prob. from prec. (G. *daus*, L.G. *duus* is used similarly)], *n.* Mischief, trouble, ruin, confusion; the devil, invoked as a mild oath. **play the deuce with:** Spoil completely, to ruin. **the deuce to pay:** The consequences will be serious. **deuced,** *a.* Confounded, devilish; very great. **deucedly,** *adv.*

deuteragonist (dū tėr ăg′ ō nist) [Gr. *deuteragōnistēs* (*deuteros*, second, *agōnistēs*, actor)], *n.* The second actor in a classical Greek play; the next actor in importance to the protagonist.

deuterium (dū tēr′ i ŭm) [Gr. *deuteros*, second], *n.* (*Chem.*) Heavy hydrogen.

deutero-, deuto- [Gr. *deuteros*], *comb. form.* Second, secondary. **deuterocanonical** (dū tėr ō kȧ non′ ik ȧl) [CANONICAL], *a.* Belonging to a second and inferior canon (of certain books of the Bible).

deuteron (dū′ tĕr on), *n.* (*Chem.*) A heavy hydrogen nucleus.

Deuteronomy (dū tėr on′ ō mi) [L. *Deuteronomium*, Gr. *Deuteronomion* (DEUTERO-, *nomos*, law)], *n.* The fifth book of the Pentateuch, named from its containing a recapitulation of the Mosaic law. **deuteronomic, -al** (-nom′ ik, -ȧl), *a.* **Deuteronomist** (-on′ ō mist), *n.* The supposed writer or one of the supposed writers of Deuteronomy.

deuteroscopy (dū tĕr os′ kō pi), *n.* Second sight.

deutoplasm (dū′ tō plăzm), *n.* (*Biol.*) That portion of the yolk that nourishes the embryo, the food yolk of an ovum or egg-cell.

deutzia (doit′-, dūt′ si ȧ) [J. *Deutz*, Dutch botanist], *n.* A genus of Chinese or Japanese shrubs of the saxifrage family.

devall (dė vawl′) [F. *dévaler* (DE-, L. *vallis*, a VALLEY)], *v.i.* *To sink; (*Sc.*) to ease, to leave off.

devaluate (dē văl′ ū āt), *v.t.* (*Fin.*) To reduce the value of currency; to stabilize currency at a lower level.

Devanagari (dā vȧ na′ gȧ ri) [Sansk., Hind., Marithi (Sansk. *dēva*, god, *nāgarī*, alphabet, script)], *n.* The formal alphabet in which Sanskrit and certain vernaculars are usually written, also called simply Nagari.

devastate (dev′ ȧ stāt) [L. *dēvastātus*, p.p. of *dēvastāre* (DE-, *vastāre*, to waste)], *v.t.* To lay waste, to ravage. **devastation** (-stā′ shŭn), *n.* **devastating,** *a.* (*colloq.*) Overwhelming. **devastator,** *n.*

develop (dė vel′ ŏp) [F. *développer*; etym. doubtful (cp. It. *viluppare*, to enwrap, *viluppo*, a wrapping, a bundle)], *v.t.* To unfold or uncover, to bring to light gradually; to work out; to bring from a simple to a complex state, to bring to completion; to evolve; to bring to completion or maturity by natural growth; (*Mil.*) to carry out the successive stages of an attack; (*Phot.*) to render visible (as the picture latent in the sensitized film). *v.i.* To expand; to progress; to be evolved; to come to light; to come to maturity. **developable,** *a.* **developer,** *n.* **development,** *n.* The act of developing; the state of being developed; growth and advancement; the gradual advance of organized bodies from the embryonic to the perfect state; evolution; maturity, completion; (*Phot.*) the process of bringing into distinctness the picture latent in the sensitized film.

development area, *n.* A region where new industries are being encouraged by Government to combat unemployment. **development theory,** *n.* The theory of evolution. **developmental** (dė vel ŏp men′ tăl) *a.* Pertaining to development or growth; evolutionary. **developmentally,** *adv.*

***devest** (dė vest′) [DIVEST], *v.t.* To undress; to strip; to denude, deprive; (*Law*) to alienate (as a right or title).

deviate (dē′ vi āt) [L. *dēviātus*, p.p. of *deviāre*, from *dēvius*, out of the way (DE-, *via*, way)], *v.i.* To turn aside; to stray or swerve from the path of duty; to err. *v.t.* To cause to stray or err. **deviation** (-ā shŭn), *n.* The act of deviating; error; the deflexion of a compass from the true magnetic meridian; the divergence of a plumb-line or a falling body from the true vertical, caused by surface inequalities or differences of density in the earth's crust, or by the rotation of the earth; (*Path.*) the divergence of one of the optic axes from the normal position. **deviationist,** *n.* (*Pol.*) One who departs from orthodox Communist doctrine. **deviator,** *n.*

device (dė vīs′) [O.F. *devis*, fem. *devise*, late L. *dīvīsa*, a division, mark, device, fem. of L. *dīvīsum*, neut. p.p. of *dīvīdere*, to DIVIDE (cp. DEVISE)], *n.* A plan, a scheme, a contrivance; a stratagem, a trick; an invention; inventive skill; (*pl.*) will, inclination; a design, a figure, a pattern; (*Her.*) an emblem or fanciful design, a motto; a fanciful idea, a conceit; *a dramatic entertainment, a masque; *an opinion, a suggestion. ***deviceful,** *a.* Full of devices; ingenious. ***deviceless,** *a.*

devil (dev′ il) [A.-S. *dēoful*, L. *diabolus*, Gr. *diabolos*, from *diaballein*, to slander (*dia*, through, *ballein*, to throw)], *n.* Satan, the chief of the fallen angels, the spirit of evil, the tempter; any evil spirit; an idol or false god; the spirit possessing a demoniac; a wicked person; a malignant or cruel person; a person of extraordinary energy, ingenuity, and self-will directed to selfish or mischievous ends; an unfortunate person, a wretch; a personification of evil; energy, dash, unconquerable spirit; an expletive to express surprise or vexation; a printer's errand-boy; a hot grill highly seasoned; a kind of firework; a tackle for catching a number of fish at once; a device for tearing fishing-nets; one who does literary work for which another takes the credit; a barrister who prepares a case for another, or who takes the case of another without fee in order to gain reputation; a spiked mill for tearing rags; a Tasmanian marsupial, *Dasyurus ursinus*; various other animals, fish, etc. *v.t.* To make devilish; to grill with pepper; to tear up rags with a devil. *v.i.* To act as a literary or legal devil; to do the hard spade-work. **devil a bit:** Not any. **devil a one:** Not a single one. **the devil:** A nuisance; a dilemma, an awkward fix; (*int.*) an expression of surprise or annoyance. **the devil on two sticks:** An early kind of diabolo. **the devil to pay:** The consequences will be serious. **to give the devil his due:** To allow the worst man credit for his good qualities. **to go to the devil:** To go to ruin; (*imper.*) be off! **to play the devil:** To worry, to ruin. **you little** or **young devil:** A playful, semi-ironical address. **devil-fish,** *n.* The octopus; various other fish, as (*Am.*) *Lophius piscatorius* and *Cephalopterus vampyrus*. **devil-may-care,** *a.* Reckless. **devil-may-careness,** *n.* **devil-may-carish,** *a.* **devil-may-carishness,** *n.* **devil-worship,** *n.* Homage paid by primitive tribes to conciliate the spirit of evil. **Devil's advocate** [ADVOCATE]. **devil's bit,** *n.* A small dark-blue scabious, *Scabiosa succisa*. **devil's bones,** *n.pl.* Dice. **devil's coach-horse,** *n.* A large cocktail beetle, *Ocypus olens*. **devil's darning-needle,** *n.* Various species of dragon-fly; Venus's comb, *Scandix pecten-Veneris*. ***devil's dirt, *devil's dung,** *n.* Asafœtida. **devil's dust,** *n.* Flock torn out of wool and made into cheap cloth, shoddy. **Devil's Own,** *n.* The 88th Regiment of the line; the Inns of Court Officers Training Corps. **devil's playthings,** *n.pl.* Playing-cards. **devil's tattoo,** *n.* A drumming with the fingers upon a table, etc., by persons when vacant or impatient. ***devildom,** *n.* **devilhood,** *n.* ***devilet, *-kin,** *n.* A little devil; the deviling or swift. **deviling,** *n.* *A young devil, an imp; a local name for the swift. **devilish** (dev′ il ish), *a.* Befitting a devil; diabolical; damnable. *adv.* (dev′ lish) Extraordinarily, damnably, infernally, awfully. **devilishly,** *adv.* **devilishness,** *n.* ***devilism** (dev′ il izm), *n.* Devilry; devil-worship. **devilment** (devl′ mėnt), *n.* Mischief, roguery, devilry. **devilry, -iltry** (devl′ ri, -tri), *n.* Diabolical wickedness, esp. cruelty; dealings with the devil; diabolism, black magic, demonology; devils collectively; wild and reckless mischief, revelry, or high spirits. ***devilship,** *n.* **devilward, -s,** *adv.*

devious (dē′ vi ŭs) [L. *dēvius* (DE-, *via*, way)], *a.* Out of the way, sequestered; wandering out of the way; circuitous; erring, rambling. **deviously,** *adv.* **deviousness,** *n.*

devise (dė vīz′) [O.F. *deviser*, late L. *dēvīsāre*, to divide, to devise, to think, freq. of L. *dīvīdere* (p.p. *dīvīsus*), to DIVIDE], *v.t.* To invent, to contrive; to form in the mind, to scheme, to plot; (*Law*) to give or assign (real property) by will; *to guess; *to emblazon. **v.i.* To consider, to plan. *n.* (*Law*) The act of bequeathing landed property by will; a will or clause of a will bequeathing real estate. **devisable,** *a.* **devisee** (dev ī zē′), *n.* (*Law*) One to whom anything is devised by will. **deviser** (dė vī′ zėr), *n.* One who devises. **devisor,** *n.* (*Law*) One who bequeaths by will.

devitalize (dē vī′ tă līz), *v.t.* To deprive of vitality or of vital power. **devitalization** (-zā′ shŭn), *n.*

devitrify (dē vit′ ri fī), *v.t.* To deprive of vitreous quality; to deprive glass or vitreous rock of transparency by making it crystalline. **devitrification** (-kā′ shŭn), *n.*

devocalize (dē vō′ kă līz), *v.t.* To make voiceless or non-sonant. **devocalization** (-zā′ shŭn), *n.*

devoid (dė void′) [short for *devoided*, p.p. of obs. *devoid*, to empty, O.F. *devuidier*, from *vuide*, empty, VOID], *a.* Vacant, destitute, empty (of). **v.t.* To avoid; to make devoid.

***devoir** (dėvwar′) [M.E. *dever*, O.F. *deveir*, L. *debēre*, to owe], *n.* A service, a duty; (*usu. in pl.*) politeness, courtesy.

devolute (dē′ vŏ loot) [L. *dēvolūtus*, p.p. of *dēvolvere* (DE-, *volvere*, to roll)], *v.t.* To transfer power or authority; to depute.

devolution (dē vŏ lū′ shŭn), *n.* Transference or delegation of authority (as by Parliament to its committees); passage from one person to another; descent by inheritance; descent in natural succession; (*Biol.*) degeneration of species; lapse of a right, privilege, or authority through desuetude.

devolve (dė volv′) [L. *devolvere*, as prec.], *v.t.* To cause to pass to another, to transfer; *to cause to roll down. *v.i.* To be transferred, delegated, or deputed (to); to fall by succession, to descend. ***devolvement,** n.

Devonian (dė vō′ ni ăn), *a.* Pertaining to Devonshire. *n.* A native of Devon; (*Geol.*) the Old Red Sandstone formation, well displayed in Devonshire.

devonport [DAVENPORT].

devote (dė vōt′) [L. *dēvōtus*, p.p. of *dēvovēre* (DE-, *vovēre*, to vow)], *v.t.* To consecrate, to dedicate; to apply; to give wholly up (to); to doom, to consign (to ruin, etc.); *to curse. **devoted,** *a.* Dedicated, consecrated, doomed; wholly given up, zealous, ardently attached. **devotedly,** *adv.* **devotedness,** *n.* **devotee** (dev ŏ tē′), *n.* A votary, a person devoted (to); a bigot, an enthusiast. ***devotement, devotion,** *n.* The act of devoting; the state of being devoted; (*pl.*) prayer, religious worship; deep, self-sacrificing attachment, intense loyalty; *purpose, object; *disposal. **devotional,** *a.* Pertaining to or befitting religious devotion. **devotionalism,** *n.* **devotionalist,** *n.* **devotionality** (năl′ i ti), *n.* **devotionally,** *adv.*

devour (dė vour′) [O.F. *devorer*, L. *dēvorāre* (DE-, *vorāre*, to swallow)], *v.t.* To eat up ravenously or swiftly; to consume as a beast consumes its prey; to destroy wantonly, to waste; to swallow up, to engulf; to take in eagerly with the senses; to absorb, to overwhelm. **to devour the way:** (*poet.*) To move with extreme swiftness. **devouring,** *a.* That devours; consuming, wasting. **devouringly,** *adv.*

devout (dė vout′) [O.F. *devot*, L. *dēvōtus*, p.p. of *dēvovēre*, to DEVOTE], *a.* Pious, filled with devotion; expressing devotion; heartfelt, earnest, genuine. **devoutly,** *adv.* **devoutness,** *n.*

dew (dū) [A.-S. *dēaw* (cp. Dut. *daaw*, Icel. *dögg*, Dan. *dug*, G. *thau*)], *n.* Moisture condensed from the atmosphere upon the surface of bodies at evening and during the night; (*fig.*) anything falling cool and light, so as to refresh; an emblem of freshness; dewy moisture, tears, sweat. *v.t.* To wet with dew. *v.i.* To form as dew; to fall as dew. **mountain-dew:** Whisky distilled illicitly. **dewberry,** *n.* A kind of blackberry, *Rubus cæsius.* ***dew-besprent,** *a.* Sprinkled with dew. ***dew-burning,** *a.* Glistening like dew in the sun. **dew-claw,** *n.* One of the bones behind a deer's foot; the rudimentary upper toe often found in a dog's foot. **dewdrop,** *n.* A drop of dew; a drop at the end of one's nose. **dew-dropping,** *a.* Wetting, rainy. **dewfall,** *n.* The falling of dew; the time when dew falls. **dewpoint,** *n.* The temperature at which dew begins to form. **dew pond,** *n.* A shallow, artificial pond formed on high land where water collects at night through condensation. **dew-rake,** *n.* A rake used for the surface of grass or stubble. **dew-retting,** *n.* The softening of flax by exposure to dew and rain. **dew-worm,** *n.* A large earth-worm. **dewless,** *a.* **dewy,** *a.* **dewiness,** *n.*

dewan (dė wan′) [Arab. and Pers. *dīwān* (cp. DIVAN)], *n.* Chief financial minister of an Indian state; prime minister of such a state. **dewani** (dė wa′ ni), *n.* The office of a dewan.

dewlap (dū′ lăp) [etym. of *dew* uncertain; *lap* from A.-S. *læppa*, a skirt, a LAP (1) (cp. Dan. *doglæb*, Norw. *doglæp*)], *n.* The flesh that hangs loosely from the throat of an ox or cow; (*fig.*) the flesh of the throat become flaccid through age; the wattle of a turkey, etc. **dewlapped,** *a.*

dexter (deks′ tėr) [L., a comparative from the root *dex-* (cp. Gr. *dexios*, *dexiteros*, Goth. *taihswa*, Sansk. *daksha*)], *a.* Pertaining to or situated on the right-hand side; (*Her.*) situated on the right of the shield (to the spectator's left), etc.

dexterity (dek ster′ it i), *n.* Physical or mental skill, expertness; readiness and ease; cleverness, quickness, tact; *righthandedness.

dexterous (dek′ stėr ŭs), *a.* Expert in any manual employment; quick mentally; skilful, able; done with dexterity; *right-handed. **dexterously,** *adv.*

dextral (dek′ strål), *a.* (*Conch.*) Having the whorls (of a spiral shell) turning towards the right, dextrorse. **dextrality,** *n.*

dextrin (deks′ trin) [F. *dextrine*, from L. *dextra*, fem. of DEXTER], *n.* A gummy substance obtained from starch, so called from its dextro-rotatory action on polarized light.

dextro- (deks′ trō) [L. *dexter*, the right hand], *comb. form.* (*Chem.*) Turning the plane of a ray of polarized light to the right, or in a clockwise direction (as seen looking against the oncoming light). **dextro-glucose,** *n.* Dextrose. **dextro-gyrate,** *a,* Causing to turn towards the right-hand. *v.t.* To cause to rotate clockwise. **dextro-rotary, dextro-rotatory,** *a.* Causing to rotate clockwise.

dextrorse (deks trôrs′) [L. *dextrorsum*, *-sus* (DEXTRO, *-vorsum*, *-versum*, turned)], *a.* Rising from left to right in a spiral line.

dextrose (deks′ trōs) [DEXTER, -OSE], *n.* A form of glucose which rotates polarized light clockwise; (*Comm.*) grape-sugar.

dextrous [DEXTEROUS].

dey (dā) [F., from Turk. *dāī*, lit. a maternal uncle, a title in the janizaries], *n.* The title of the old sovereigns of Algiers, Tripoli, and Tunis. **dey-ship,** *n.*

***dey-woman** (dā′ wum ån) [A.-S. *dæge*, a maid-servant, later, a dairywoman or dairyman], *n.* A dairywoman. ***dey-girl,** *n.*

dhobi (dō′ bi) [Hind. *dhōbī*, from *dhōb*, washing, Sansk. *dhāv-*, to wash], *n.* An Indian washerman.

dhole (dōl) [etym. unknown], *n.* The wild dog of India, *Canis dukhunensis.*

dhoti (dō′ ti) [Hind.], *n.* A loin-cloth worn by male Hindus.

dhow (dou) [etym. unknown], *n.* A native vessel with one mast, a very long yard, and a lateen sail, used on the Arabian Sea; an Arab vessel, esp. one used in the slave-trade.

dhurrie (dŭr′ i) [Hind. *darī*], *n.* A coarse cotton fabric, made in squares, and used in India for carpets, curtains, coverings for furniture, etc.

di- (1) [see DIS-], *pref.*, used before *b, d, g, l, m, n, r, s, v,* and sometimes *j.*

di- (2) [Gr. *di-*, double, two], *pref.* Twice, two, dis-, double.

di- (3) [see DIA-], *pref.*, before a vowel.

dia- [Gr. *dia*, through], *pref.* Through; thorough, thoroughly; apart, across.

diabase (dī′ å bās) [F.], *n.* (*Min.*) An igneous rock which is an altered form of basalt; it includes most greenstone and trap. **diabasic** (dī å bā′ sik), *a.*

diabetes (dī å bē′ tēz) [L., from Gr., from *diabainein* (DIA-, *bainein*, to go)], *n.* A disease marked by excessive discharge of urine containing glucose, insatiable thirst, and great emaciation. **diabetic,** *a.* Pertaining to diabetes. *n.* A person suffering from diabetes.

diablerie (di ab′ lėr i) [F., from *diable*, L. *diabolus*, DEVIL], *n.* Dealings with the devil; diabolism, magic, or sorcery; rascality, devilry.

diabolic, -ical (dī å bol′ ik, -ål) [F. *diabolique*, L. *diabolicus*, Gr. *diabolikos*, from *diabolos*, DEVIL], *a.* Pertaining to, proceeding from, or like the devil; outrageously wicked or cruel; fiendish, devilish, satanic, infernal. **diabolically,** *adv.* **diabolism** (dī ăb′ ŏ lizm), *n.* Devil-worship; belief in the Devil or in devils; black magic; devilish conduct or character, devilry. **diabolize,** *v.t.* To make diabolical; to represent as a devil.

diabolo (di-, dī ăb′ ŏ lō) [a recent formation from L. *diabolus*, devil], *n.* A game with a double cone spun in the air by a cord on two sticks; an adaptation of the old game of the devil on two sticks.

diacaustic (dī å kaw′ stik) [DIA-, Gr. *kaustikos*, burning, from *kaiein*, to burn], *a.* Formed by refracted rays. **diacaustic curve,** *n.*

diachylon (dī ăk′ i lŏn), **diaculum** (dī ăk′ ū lŭm) [late L. *diachylōn*, Gr. *dia chulōn*, lit. by means of juices (*chulōn*, gen. pl. of *chulos*, juice)], *n.* A plaster made by boiling hydrated oxide of lead with olive oil; sticking-plaster.

diachyma (dī ăk′ i må) [DIA-, Gr. *chuma*, liquid, juice], *n.* (*Bot.*) Parenchyma of leaves.

diaconal (dī ăk′ ŏ nål) [F., from late L.], *a.* Pertaining to a deacon. **diaconate** (dī ăk′ ŏ n åt), *n.* The office, dignity, or tenure of the office, of a deacon; deacons collectively.

diacoustic (dī å kou′ stik), *a.* Pertaining to diacoustics. **diacoustics,** *n.* The science of refracted sounds.

diacritic, -al (dī å krit′ ik, -ål) [Gr. *diakritikos*], *a.* Distinguishing, distinctive; discerning, able to perceive distinctions. **diacritical mark, diacritic** *n.* A mark used to distinguish letters or sounds which resemble each other as written.

diactinic (dī ăk tin′ ik), *a.* Transparent to or capable of transmitting actinic rays.

diaculum [DIACHYLON].

diadelph (dī' à delf) [DI- (2), Gr. *adelphos*, brother], *n.* (*Bot.*) A plant of the Linnæan order *Diadelphia*, in which the stamens are united into two bodies or bundles by their filaments. **diadelphous** (-del' fŭs), *a.* (*Bot.*)

diadem (dī' à dem) [O.F. *dyademe*, L. and Gr. *diadema* (DIA-, Gr. *deein*, to bind)], *n.* A fillet or band for the head, worn as an emblem of sovereignty; a crown, a wreath, a reward; a crown of glory or victory; supreme power, sovereignty. *v.t.* To adorn with a diadem. **diadem-spider,** *n.* The garden spider, *Epeira diadema*, so called from its markings.

diæresis (dī ĕr' e sis) [L., from Gr. *diairesis*, from *diaireein*, to divide (DI- (3), *haireein*, to take)], *n.* (**diæreses** (dī ĕr' ė sēz)) The resolution of one syllable into two; a mark placed over the second of two vowels to show that it must be pronounced separately, as *Laïs*.

diaglyph (dī' à glif) [from Gr. *diagluphein* (DIA-, *gluphein*, to carve)], *n.* A piece of sculpture in which the figures are sunk into the general surface; an intaglio. **diaglyphic** (dī à glif' ik), *a.*

diagnosis (dī àg nō' sis) [L., from Gr. *diagnōsis* (DIA-, *gnōsis*, inquiry, knowledge, from *gignōskein*, to learn, to recognize)], *n.* (*pl.* **diagnoses** (dī àg nō' sēz)) Determination of diseases by their symptoms; a summary of these; (*Bot. and Zool.*) a summary of the characteristics by which one species is distinguished from another; differentiation of character, style, etc., by means of distinctive marks. **diagnose** (dī àg nōz'), *v.t.* To distinguish, to determine; (*Med.*) to ascertain the nature and seat (of a disease) from the symptoms. *v.i.* To make a diagnosis of a disease. **diagnostic** (-nos' tik), *a.* That serves to distinguish; characteristic. *n.* A sign or symptom by which anything is distinguished from anything else; a characteristic; (*pl.*) diagnosis. **diagnostically,** *adv.* **diagnostician** (-tish' ǎn), *n.*

diagometer (dī à gom' ė tėr) [F. *diagomètre* (Gr. *diagein*, to carry across, -METER)], *n.* An instrument for measuring the relative conductivity of substances, originally used to detect adulteration in olive oil.

diagonal (dī ăg' ò năl) [[L. *diagōnālis*, Gr. *diagōnios* (DIA-, *gōnis*, an angle)], *a.* Extending from one angle of a quadrilateral or multilateral figure to a non-adjacent angle, or from one edge of a solid to a non-adjacent edge; oblique, crossing obliquely; marked by oblique lines, ridges, etc. *n.* A right line or plane extending from one angle or edge to a non-adjacent one; a diagonal row, line, beam, tie, etc.; a fabric with diagonal twills or ridges. **diagonal scale,** *n.* (*Math.*) A scale in which small divisions are marked by oblique lines, so as to make minute measurements. **diagonally,** *adv.*

diagram (dī' à grăm) [F. *diagramme*, L. and Gr. *diagramma*, from Gr. *diagraphein* (DIA-, *graphein*, to write)], *n.* (*Geom.*) A drawing made to demonstrate or illustrate some proposition, statement, or definition; an illustrative figure drawn roughly or in outline; a series of marks or lines representing graphically the results of meteorological, statistical, or other observations, or symbolizing abstract statements. **diagrammatic** (-măt' ik), *a.* **diagrammatically,** *adv.* **diagrammatize** (-grăm' à tīz), *v.t.* **diagraph** (dī' à grăf) [F. *diagraphe*], *n.* An instrument used for drawing mechanically outline sketches, enlargements of maps, etc.

diaheliotropic (dī à hē li ò trop' ik), *a.* (*Bot.*) Growing or turning transversely to the light. **diaheliotropism** (dī à hē li ot' rò pizm), *n.* (*Bot.*) Tendency to grow transversely to the light.

dial (dī' ăl) [med. L. *diālis*, daily, from *diēs*, day], *n.* An instrument for showing the time of the day by the sun's shadow; the graduated and numbered face of a time-piece; a similar plate on which an index finger marks revolutions, indicates steam-pressure, etc.; an instrument used by lapidaries; (*Radio.*) the device for adjusting the tuning controls; *a time-piece, a watch; (*slang*) the human face. *v.t.* (*past & p.p.* **dialled**) To measure or indicate with or as with a dial; to survey with a dial; to indicate on the dial of an automatic telephone the number one wishes to call up. **dialling tone,** *n.* The sound given by an automatic telephone to show that the line is clear. **dial-plate,** *n.* The face of a time-piece or other instrument with a dial.

dialect (dī' à lekt) [L. *dialectus*, Gr. *dialektos*, from *dialegesthai*, to discourse (DIA-, *legein*, to speak)], *n.* A form of speech or language peculiar to a limited district or people. **dialectal** (dī à lek' tăl), *a.* **dialectally,** *adv.* **dialectology** (-tol' ò ji), *n.* **dialectologist,** *n.*

dialectic (dī à lek' tik) [O.F. *dialectique*, L. *dialectica*, Gr. *dialektikē* (*technē*), the dialectic (art), as prec.], *a.* Dialectal; pertaining to logic; logical, argumentative. *n.* (*often in pl.*) Logic in general; the rules and methods of reasoning; discussion by dialogue; the investigation of truth by analysis; the logic of probabilities; (*Kant*) critical analysis of knowledge based on science; (*Hegel*) the philosophic process of reconciling the contradictions of experience in a higher synthesis, the world-process which is the objective realization of this synthesis; a person skilled in logical reasoning and analysis. **dialectical materialism,** *n.* The Marxian theory that reveals nothing but the class-struggle between opposites, the haves and the have-nots. **dialectically,** *adv.* In a logical manner; dialectally. **dialectician,** *n.* One skilled in dialectics; a logician; a reasoner.

diallage (1) (dī ăl' à jē) [Gr. *diallagē*, from *diallassein* (DIA-, *allassein*, to change)], *n.* (*Rhet.*) A rhetorical figure by which arguments, having been considered from various points of view, are brought to bear on one point.

diallage (2) (dī' à lăj) [F., from prec.], *n.* (*Min.*) A dark to bright-green non-aluminous variety of pyroxene, common in serpentine rock. **diallagic** (-lăj' ik), *a.*

dialogue (dī' à log) [M.E. and O.F. *dialoge*, L. *dialogus*, Gr. *dialogos* (DIA-, *logos*, discourse, from *legein*, to speak)], *n.* A conversation or discourse between two or more persons; a literary composition in conversational form; the conversational part of a novel, etc. **v.i.* To hold a dialogue. *v.t.* To put into the form of a dialogue. **dialogic** (dī à loj' ik), *a.* Of the nature of a dialogue. **dialogically,** *adv.* **dialogist** (dī ăl' ò jist), *n.* One who takes part in a dialogue; a writer of dialogues. ***dialogistic** (-jis' tik), *a.* ***dialogize** (dī ăl' ò jīz), *v.i.* To discourse in dialogue. **dialogue-wise,** *adv.*

dialysis (dī ăl' i sis) [Gr. *dialusis* (DIA-, *luein*, to loose)], *n.* (*Rhet.*) A figure by which connectives are omitted; (*Gram.*) a diæresis mark; (*Chem.*) the process of separating the crystalloid from the colloid ingredients in soluble substances by passing through moist membranes; a method of detecting poisons most of which are crystalloids. **dialyse** (dī à līz), *v.t.* (*Chem.*) **dialyser** (dī à lī' zėr), *n.* The apparatus in which the process of dialysis is performed. **dialytic** (-lit' ik), *a.* (*Chem.*)

diamagnetic (dī à măg net' ik), *a.* Pertaining to or exhibiting diamagnetism. *n.* A diamagnetic body or substance. **diamagnetically,** *adv.* **diamagnetism** (-măg' nė tizm), *n.* The force which causes certain bodies, when suspended freely and magnetized, to assume a position at right angles to the magnetic meridian, and point due east and west; the branch of magnetism treating of diamagnetic substances and phenomena. **diamagnetize,** *v.t.*

diamantiferous (dī à măn tif' ėr ŭs) [DIAMOND, -FEROUS], *a.* Yielding diamonds.

diameter (dī ăm' ė tėr) [O.F. *diametre*, L. and Gr. *diametros* (DIA-, *metrein*, to measure, cp. METER)], *n.* A straight line passing through the centre of any object from one side to the other; (*Geom.*) a straight line passing through the centre of a circle or other curvilinear figure, and terminating each way in the circumference; the length of such a line; the length of a straight line extending from side to side of anything; transverse measurement, width, thickness; (*Opt.*) the unit of measurement of magnifying power. **diametral,** *a.* **diametrally,** *adv.* **diametrical** (dī à met′ ri kȧl), *a.* Pertaining to a diameter, diametral; along a diameter, direct; (*fig.*) directly opposed; as far removed as possible. **diametrically,** *adv.*

diamond (dī′ à mȯnd) [O.F. *diamant*, late L. *diamas -antem*, L. *adamas -antem*, Gr. *adamas*, ADAMANT], *n.* The hardest, most brilliant, and most valuable of the precious stones, a transparent crystal of pure carbon, colourless or tinted; a facet of this when cut; a figure resembling this, a rhomb; a playing-card with figures of this shape; a glazier's cutting tool with a diamond at the point; a very small type for printing; a small rhomboid sheet of glass used in old-fashioned windows; (*fig.*) a glittering point or particle; *adamant, a hard and impenetrable substance. *a.* Made of, or set with, diamonds; resembling a diamond or lozenge. *v.t.* To adorn with or as with diamonds. **black diamonds:** Dark-coloured diamonds; coal. **rough diamond:** A diamond in the native state, not yet cut; (*colloq.*) a worthy, good-hearted, but uncouth person. **diamond-back,** *n.* The salt-marsh turtle or terrapin; a kind of moth. **diamond-cement,** *n.* Cement used for setting diamonds. **diamond-drill,** *n.* An annular drill the cutting edge of which is set with diamonds for boring very hard substances. **diamond-field,** *n.* A region yielding diamonds. **diamond jubilee,** *n.* The sixtieth anniversary of a sovereign's accession. **diamond-point,** *n.* A stylus or cutting tool with a point tipped with a diamond, used by etchers, engravers, lapidaries, etc.; (*pl.*) an oblique crossing of railway lines. **diamond-snake,** *n.* Diamond-marked snakes of southern Australia and Tasmania. **diamond-wedding,** *n.* The sixtieth anniversary of a marriage. **diamondiferous** (-dif′ ėr ůs), *a* **diamond-wise,** *adv.*

Diana (dī ăn′ ȧ) [Latin name of the Greek Artemis. the goddess of hunting], *n.* A fine horsewoman; a woman who hunts; (*Astron.*) the 78th asteroid. **diana-monkey,** *n.* A large African monkey, *Cercopithecus diana*, named from the white crescent-shaped band on its forehead.

diandria (dī ăn′ dri ȧ) [mod. L. (DI- (2), Gr. *andr-*, stem of *aner*, man, male)], *n.pl.* (*Bot.*) A Linnæan order of plants the flowers of which have only two stamens. **diandrous,** *a.*

dianoetic (dī à nō et′ ik) [Gr. *dianoētikos*, from *dianoētos*, conceived in the mind, from *dianoeisthai* (DIA-, *noein*, to think)], *a.* Pertaining to the rational or discursive faculty; intellectual. *n.* Logic as treating of reasoning; the science that deals with the laws of conception, judgment, and reasoning.

dianthus (dī ăn′ thůs) [Gr. *Dios*, of Zeus, *anthos*, flower], *n.* A genus of caryophyllaceous plants, including the pinks and carnations.

diapason (dī à pā′ zȯn), ***diapase** (dī′ à pāz) [L. *diapāsōn*, Gr. *diapasōn* (short for *dia pasōn*, *chordōn*, through all the chords)], *n.* An harmonious combination of notes; a melodious succession of notes; the foundation stops of an organ; an harmonious burst of music; a recognized standard of pitch amongst musicians; harmony, concord; range, pitch.

diaper (dī′ à pėr) [O.F. *diapre*, *diasper*, Byz. Gr. *diaspros* (DIA-, *aspros*, white)], *n.* A silk or linen cloth woven with geometric patterns; a towel or napkin made of this; a baby's napkin, a nappy; a surface decoration consisting of square or diamond reticulations. *v.t.* To decorate or embroider with this. **diaper-work,** *n.* (*Arch.*)

diaphanometer (dī à fà nom′ e tėr), [as foll.], *n.* An instrument for measuring the transparency of the atmosphere.

diaphanoscope (dī à făn′ ō skōp), *n.* A dark box for exhibiting transparent positive photographs.

diaphanous (dī ăf′ à nůs) [med. L. *diaphanus*, Gr. *diaphanēs* (DIA-, *phan-*, stem of *phainein*, to show)], *a.* Transparent, pellucid; having the power of transmitting light. ***diaphane** (dī′ à făn) [F.], *n.* A transparent substance; a transparency. ***diaphaneity** (dī à fà nē′ i ti), *n.* Transparency; perviousness to light. **diaphanie** [F.], *n.* A process for imitating stained glass by transparencies.

diaphoretic (dī à fō ret′ ik) [L. *diaphorēticus*, Gr. *diaphorētikos*, from *diaphorēsis*, sweat, from *diaphorein* (DIA-, *phorein*, to carry)], *a.* Having the power of promoting perspiration. *n.* A medicine having this property.

diaphragm (dī′ à frăm) [L., from Gr. *diaphragma*, from *diaphrēgnunai* (DIA-, *phrassein*, to fence)], *n.* The large muscular partition separating the thorax from the abdomen; the straight calcareous plate dividing the cavity of certain shells into two parts; (*Teleph. and Radio.*) the vibrating disk in the mouthpiece and earpiece of a telephone, or in the loudspeaker of a radio receiver; a dividing membrane or partition; (*Opt.*) an annular disk excluding marginal rays of light. **diaphragmatic** (-măt′ ik), *a.* **diaphragmatitis** (-tī′ tis), *n.* (*Path.*) Inflammation of the diaphragm.

diaphysis (dī ăf′ i sis) [Gr. *diaphusis* (DIA-, *phuein*, to bring forth)], *n.* (*Anat.*) The shaft of a bone as distinct from the ends; (*Bot.*) an abnormal elongation of the inflorescence.

***diarchy** (dī′ ar ki) [DI (2), Gr. *archia*, rule], *n.* A government by two rulers.

diarist, etc. [DIARY].

diarrhœa (dī à rē′ ȧ) [L., from Gr. *diarrhoia* (DIA-, *rheein*, to flow)], *n.* The excessive discharge of fæcal matter from the intestines. **diarrhœal, diarrhœic,** *a.*

diarthrosis (dī ar thrō′ sis), *n.* An articulation of the bones permitting them to act upon each other; free arthrosis.

diary (dī′ à ri) [L. *diārium*, from *diēs*, a day], *n.* An account of the occurrences of each day; the book in which these are registered; a daily calendar with blank spaces for notes; (*Sc.*) a railway time-table. **diarial** (dī âr′ i ȧl), *a.* **diarian,** *n.* **diarist** (dī′ à rist), *n.* One who keeps a diary. **diaristic** (dī à ris′ tik), *a.* **diarize,** *v.t.* and *i.*

diaskeuast (dī à skū′ ȧst) [Gr. *diaskeuastēs*, a reviser, from *diaskeuuzein* (DIA-, *skeuazein*, to make ready)], *n.* A reviser, esp. one of those who brought the old Greek epics into their present shape. **diaskeuasis** (-skū′ à sis), *n.*

Diaspora (dī ăsp′ ȯr ȧ) [DIA-, Gr. *spora*, scatter], *n.* (*Hist.*) The historical dispersion of the Jews.

diastaltic (dī à stăl′ tik) [Gr. *diastaltikos*, from *diastellein*, to separate (DIA-, *stellein*, to set, to send)], *a.* (*Physiol.*) A term applied to reflex action and the nerves governing this.

diastase (dī′ à stās) [F., from Gr. *diastasis*, separation (DIA-, *stasis*, placing, from the root *sta-*, to stand)], *n.* (*Chem.*) A nitrogenous substance produced during the germination of all seeds, and having the power of converting starch into dextrine, and then into sugar. **diastasic** (-stās′ ik), *a.*

***diastasis** (dī ăs′ tà sis) [as prec.], *n.* (*Path.*) Separation of bones without fracture, or of the pieces of a fractured bone.

diastema (dī à stē′ mȧ) [L., from Gr. *diastēma* (as DIASTASE)], *n.* (*pl.* **-ata**) (*Zool. and Anat.*) A space between two adjacent teeth, as in most mammals except man.

diastole (dī ăs′ tȯ lē) [med. L., from Gr. *diastolē*, from *diastellein* (DIA-, *stellein*, to send)], *n.* Dilatation of the heart and arteries alternating with systole. **systole and diastole:** The pulse; (*fig.*) regular reaction; fluctuation. **diastolic** (-stol′ ik), *a.*

diastyle (dī′ à stīl) [L. *diastylos*, Gr. *diastulos* (DIA-, *stulos*, a pillar)], *n.* (*Arch.*) An arrangement of columns in which the space between them is equal to three or four diameters of the shaft. *a.* Arranged on this plan.

diatessaron (dī ȧ tes′ ȧ rŏn) [O.F., from L. *diatessarōn*, Gr. *dia tessarōn*, by four], *n.* A harmony of the four Gospels; *(*Mus.*) the interval of a fourth, composed of a greater and lesser tone and a greater semitone.

diathermancy (dī ȧ thĕr′ măn si) [F. *diathermansie* (DIA-, Gr. *thermansis*, heating, from *thermainein*, to heat)], *n.* The property of being freely pervious to heat. ***diathermal**, *a.* **diathermanous, diathermous**, *a.* **diathermaneity** (-nē′ i ti), *n.* **diathermometer** (-mom′ ė tėr), *n.*

diathermy (dī ȧ thĕrm′ i), *n.* (*Med.*) The employment of high-frequency currents for the production of localized heat in the tissues.

diathesis (dī ăth′ ė sis) [Gr., from *diatithenain* (DIA-, *tithenain*, to put)], *n.* (*pl.* **-theses**) (*Med.*) A constitution of body predisposing to certain diseases.

diatom (dī′ ȧ tŏm) [Gr. *diatomos*, cut through, from *diatemnein* (DIA-, *temnein*, to cut)], *n.* An individual of the genus *Diatoma* or of the order *Diatomaceæ*, a group of microscopic algæ with siliceous coverings which exist in immense numbers at the bottom of the sea, multiplying by division or conjugation, and occurring as fossils in such abundance as to form strata of vast area and considerable thickness. **diatomaceous** (-mā′ shŭs), *a.* **diatomist** (dī ăt′ ŏ mist), *n.* **diatomite**, *n.* (*Geol.*) Any diatomaceous deposit.

diatomic (dī ȧ tom′ ik) *a.* (*Chem.*) Containing only two atoms; containing two replaceable univalent atoms.

diatomous (dī at′ ŏ mŭs) [Gr. *diatomos*, as DIATOM], *a.* (*Min.*) Having crystals with one distinct diagonal cleavage.

diatonic (dī ȧ ton′ ik) [F. *diatonique*, L. *diatonicus*, Gr. *diatonikos*, from *diatonos* (DIA-, *tonos*, TONE)], *a.* (*Mus.*) Of the regular scale without chromatic alteration; applied to the major and minor scales, or to chords, intervals, and melodic progressions. **diatonically**, *adv.*

diatribe (dī′ ȧ trīb) [F., from L. *diatriba*, Gr. *diatribē*, a wearing away, a discussion, a discourse, from *diatribein* (DIA-, *tribein*, to rub)], *n.* An invective discourse; a strain of harsh criticism or denunciation.

dib (1) (dib) [var. of DAB], *v.i.* To tap; to dap; to dibble. **dibber**, *n.* A dibble.

dib (2) (dib) [prob. from prec.], *n.* A sheep's knuckle-bone; (*pl.*) a children's game in which these are thrown into the air and caught on the back of the hand; counter used with card games; *pl.* (*slang*) money.

dibasic (dī bā′ sik), *a.* (*Chem.*) Containing two bases or two replaceable atoms.

dibber [DIB (1)].

dibble (dib′ ėl) [perh. from DIB (1)], *n.* A pointed instrument used to make a hole in the ground to receive seed. *v.t.* To make holes with a dibble; to plant with a dibble. *v.i.* To use a dibble; to dap as in angling. **dibbler**, *n.* One who dibbles; a machine for dibbling.

dibranchiata (dī brăng ki ā′ tȧ) [DI-, Gr. *branchia*, gills], *n.pl.* (*Zool.*) An order of cephalopods, having only two gills, the shell rarely external and never chambered. **dibranchiate** (di brăng′ ki ȧt), *a.* and *n.*

***dicacity** (di kăs′ i ti) [L. *dicāx dicācem*, from *dīcere*, to speak], *n.* Talkativeness; fluency, pertness.

dice (dīs) (*pl.* of DIE (2)), *v.i.* To play at dice. *v.t.* To gamble (away) at dice; to weave into a pattern with squares; to trim or ornament with such a pattern; (*Book-binding*) to ornament with squares or diamonds by pressure. **dice-box**, *n.* The case out of which dice are thrown. **dicer**, *n.*

dicephalous (dī sef′ ȧ lŭs) [Gr. *dikephalos* (DI- (2), *kephalē*, head)], *a.* Having two heads on one body.

dichlamydeous (dī klȧ mid′ ė ŭs) [DI- (2), Gr. *chlamus -udos*, a cloak], *a.* (*Bot.*) Having both corolla and calyx.

dichogamous (dī kog′ ȧ mŭs) [Gr. *dicho-*, asunder, *gamos*, wedded], *a.* (*Bot.*) Having stamens and pistils maturing at different times, so that self-fertilization is prevented. **dichogamy**, *n.*

dichotomy (dī kot′ ŏ mi) [Gr. *dicho-*, as prec., -TOMY], *n.* A separation into two; (*Log.*) distribution of ideas into two mutually exclusive classes; (*Astron.*) the moon's phase when half the disk is illuminated; (*Bot. and Zool.*) a continued bifurcation or division into two parts. **dichotomic**, *a.* **dichotomist**, *n.* **dichotomize**, *v.t.* and *i.* **dichotomous**, *a.*

dichroic (dī krō′ ik) [Gr. *dichroos* (DI- (2), *chrōs*, colour, complexion)], *a.* (*Min.*) Assuming two or more colours, according to the direction in which light is transmitted. **dichroism** (dī′ krō izm), *n.* **dichroitic** (dī krō it′ ik), *a.* **dichroscope** (dī′-), *n.*

dichromate (dī krō′ măt), *n.* (*Chem.*) A double chromate.

dichromatic (dī krō măt′ ik), *a.* Characterized by or producing two colours, esp. of animals. **dichromatism** (dī krō′ mȧ tizm), *n.* (*Optics*) Inability to distinguish more than two colours.

dichromic (dī krō′ mik) [Gr. *dichromos*, as prec.], *a.* Having or perceiving only two colours. **dichromism** (dī′ krō mizm), *n.* A form of colour-blindness in which only two of the three primary colours are distinguished.

dicht (di*ch*t) [DIGHT], *v.t.* (*Sc.*) To wipe, to clean up.

dick (dik) [prob. short for DECLARATION], *n.* (*Am. slang*) A detective. **to take one's dick:** To swear; to make a solemn affirmation. **up to dick:** Up to the mark, quite satisfactory; artful, wide-awake.

dickens (dik ėnz) [perh. from *Dickon*, Richard], *n.* (*colloq.*) The devil, the deuce.

dicker (dik′ ėr) [M.E. *dyker*, late L. *dicora*, L. *decūria*, a set of ten, from *decem*, ten], *n.* Half-a-score, esp. of hides. *v.i.* To barter, to haggle; to carry on a petty trade. *v.t.* To barter or exchange.

dicky (1) (dik′ i) [etym. doubtful], *n.* (*colloq.*) An ass, a donkey; a pinafore or bib; a front separate from the shirt; a seat behind the body of a carriage or a motor-car; a driver's seat, (*Am.*) rumble-seat; a bird. **dicky-bird**, *n.* (*colloq.*) A little bird.

dicky (2) (dik′ i) [etym. unknown], *a.* Doubtful, questionable; queer, unwell.

diclinic (dī klin′ ik) [Gr. DI- (2), *klinē*, a bed], *a.* (*Cryst.*) Having two of the axes obliquely inclined.

diclinous (dī′ klin ŭs) [as prec.], *a.* (*Bot.*) Having the stamens and the pistils on separate flowers. **diclinism**, *n.*

dicotyledon (dī kŏt i lē′ dŏn), *n.* (*Bot.*) A plant with two cotyledons. ***dicotyledones*** [mod. L.], *n.pl.* The largest and most important class of flowering plants containing all those with two cotyledons. **dicotyledonous**, *a.*

dicrotic (dī krot′ ik) [Gr. *dikrotos* (DI- (2), *krotos*, a beat)], *a.* (*Physiol.*) Double-beating (of a pulse in an abnormal state).

Dictaphone (dik′ tȧ fōn), *n.* Protected trade name of an apparatus for recording sounds, used for taking down correspondence, etc., to be afterwards transcribed.

dictate (1) (dik tāt′) [L. *dictātus*, p.p. of *dictāre*, freq. of *dīcere*, to say], *v.t.* To read or recite to another words to be written or repeated; to prescribe, to lay down with authority, to impose, as terms. *v.i.* To give orders; to utter words to be written or repeated by another. **dictation**, *n.*

dictate (2) (dik′ tāt), *n.* An order, an injunction; a direction; a precept.

dictator (dik tā′ tŏr), *n.* One who dictates; one invested with supreme authority; (*Hist.*) a Roman magistrate created in time of emergency, and invested with absolute power; a ruler with similar authority appointed in a time of civil disorder or securing the supremacy after a revolution. **dictatorate, dictature**, *n.* **dictatorial** (-tȧ tŏr′ i ȧl), *a.* Pertaining to a dictator; imperious, overbearing. **dictatorially,** *adv.* **dictatorship,** *n.* **dictatress** (dik tā' tres), *n.* ***dictatory** (dik'-), *a.* Dictatorial, dogmatical.

diction (dik' shŭn) [L. *dictio*, from *dīcere*, to say], *n.* The use of words; manner of expression; style; *verbal description.

dictionary (dik' shŭn ăr i) [med. L. *dictiōnārium*, from prec.], *n.* A book containing the words of any language in alphabetical order, with their definitions, or with their equivalents in another language; a work of information on any subject under words arranged alphabetically.

dictum (dik' tŭm) [L., neut. p.p. of *dīcere*, to say], *n.* (*pl.* **-ta**) A positive or dogmatic assertion; a judge's personal opinion on a point of law as distinguished from the decision of a court; a maxim, an adage.

dictyogen (dik' ti ŏ jen, dik tī' ŏ jen) [Gr. *diktuon*, a net, -GEN], *n.* (*Bot.*) A sub-class (proposed by Lindley) of monocotyledonous plants with reticulated leaves often articulated with the stem.

dicynodont (dī sin' ŏ dont) [DI- (2), *kun-* (stem of *kuōn*), dog, *odont-*, tooth], *n.* (*Palæont.*) A large fossil reptile of a lizard-like form with turtle jaws.

did, *past* [DO (1)].

Didache (did' ă kē) [Gr. *didachē*, teaching, first word of title, 'Teaching of the Twelve Apostles'], *n.* A Christian manual written in the second century. **Didachist,** *n.*

didactic (di dăk'-, dī dăk' tik) [Gr. *didaktikos*, from *didaskein*, to teach], *a.* Adapted or tending to teach; containing rules or precepts; in the manner of a teacher. *n.pl.* The science or art of teaching. **didactically,** *adv.*

didactyl (dī dăk' til), **-tylous** (-ŭs) [DI- (2), Gr. *daktulos*, finger], *a.* (*Zool.*) Having only two toes, fingers, or claws.

didapper (dī' dăp ėr) [earlier *dive-dapper*, A.-S. *dūfe-doppa* (*dūfan*, to dive, *doppa*, dapper, dipper)], *n.* A small diving-bird, the dab-chick.

diddle (did' ėl) [?], *v.t.* To cheat, to overreach; to swindle; to jog, to jerk to and fro. *v.i.* To fritter away, to waste time; to totter, to walk unsteadily. **diddler,** *n.*

didelphia (dī del' fi ă) [DI- (2), Gr. *delphus*, a womb], *n.pl.* A family of marsupials, including the opossums. **didelphian,** *a.* **didelphic,** *a.* **didelphoid,** *a.*

didgeridoo (dij' ė ri doo) [Austral. abor.], *n.* A long, hollow wooden tube that gives a deep booming sound when blown.

dido (dī' dō) [Slang; origin doubtful], *n.* An extravagant doing, an antic, a caper. **to cut up didoes:** To behave extravagantly; to behave rowdily.

didst, *2nd sing. past* [DID].

didymous (did' i mŭs), *a.* (*Bot.*) Twin, growing in pairs.

didynamia (did i nā' mi ă) [DI- (2), Gr. *dunamis*, power], *n.pl.* (*Bot.*) A Linnæan class, containing plants with four stamens. **didynamian, didynamous** (-din' ă mŭs), *a.*

die (1) (dī) [M.E. *degen*, *deghen*, Icel. *deyja* (cp. O.S., *dōian*, O.H.G. *touwan*, from Teut. *tāu-*)], *v.i.* To lose life, to expire; to depart this life; to come to an end; to cease to exist; to wither, to lose vitality, to decay; to fail, to become useless; to go out, to disappear, to be forgotten; to cease or pass away gradually; to faint, to fade away, to languish with affection; to suffer spiritual death; to perish everlastingly. **to die away:** To become gradually less distinct. **to die of laughing:** (*fig.*) To laugh at something immoderately. **to be dying to do:** (*fig.*) To be eager to do. **to die for:** To sacrifice one's life for; to pine for. **to die off:** To die in large numbers; to languish. **to die out:** To become extinct. **to die unto:** To cease to be affected by (sin). **die-away,** *a.* Fainting or languishing. **die-hard,** *n.* An obstinate Tory; *n.pl.* The old 47th Foot (from the colonel's rallying cry at Albuera); (*fig.*) stubborn, uncompromising persons.

die (2) (dī) [O.F. *de*, *det*, late L. *datum*, neut. of L. *datus*, p.p. of *dare*, to give], *n.* (*pl.* **dice, dies**) A small cube marked with figures on the sides, used in gaming, being thrown from a box; hazard, chance, lot; (*pl.* **dice**) the game played with these; (*in foll. senses pl.* **dies**) (*Arch.*) the cube or plinth of a pedestal; a machine for cutting out, shaping, or stamping; a stamp for coining money, or for impressing a device upon metal, paper, etc. **die-sinker,** *n.* One who cuts or engraves dies for coins, medals, etc. **die-stock,** *n.* A handle or stock to hold the dies in screw-cutting.

dielectric (dī ė lek' trik), *n.* Any medium, such as glass, through or across which electric force is transmitted by induction; a non-conductor; an insulator. *a.* Non-conductive, insulating.

diesel engine (dē' zel) [R. *Diesel* (1858–1913)], *n.* (*Mach.*) A type of reciprocating internal-combustion engine which burns heavy oil. **diesel-electric,** *a.* (*Eng.*) Employing power from a diesel-operated electric generator. **diesel train,** *n.* (*Rail.*) A train drawn by a diesel engine.

diesis (dī' ė sis) [L., from Gr., from *dihienai* (DIA-, *hienai*, to send)], *n.* (*pl.* **-eses**) The double dagger (‡); a reference mark; (*Mus.*) the difference between three true major thirds and one octave.

Dies iræ (dī' ēz ī' rē) [L., day of wrath], *n.* The Last Day, the Day of Judgment; a Latin hymn opening thus (written *c.* 1250).

dies non (dī' ēz non) [L., short for *dies non juridicus*, a day not for judicial business], *n.* (*Law*) A Sunday, holiday, or other day on which the courts are not open; a day on which business cannot be transacted; a day that does not count.

diet (1) (dī' ėt) [O.F. *diete*, late L. *diēta*, Gr. *diaita*, mode of life (prob. conn. with *zaein*, to live)], *n.* A prescribed course of food, a regimen; the food and drink usually taken; an allowance of food; *an allowance for board, or for living expenses. *v.t.* To feed according to the rules of medicine; to feed in a restricted way as a punishment; to feed. *v.i.* To take food, esp. according to a prescribed regimen. ***to take diet:** To be under regimen for a disease. **dietary** (dī' ė tăr i), *a.* Pertaining to a rule of diet. *n.* A regimen; a prescribed course of diet; a fixed daily allowance of food (esp. in prisons, workhouses, etc.). ***dieter,** *n.* One who prescribes or prepares food according to rules. **dietetic, -ical** (dī ė tet' ik, -ăl), *a.* Pertaining to diet. **dietetically,** *adv.* **dietetics,** *n.pl.* The science of diet; rules of diet. **dietician, dietitian,** (dī ė tish' ăn), *n.* A professional adviser on dietetics.

diet (2) (dī' ėt) [L. *diēta* (as prec.), confused with *diēs*, a day], *n.* A legislative assembly or federal parliament holding its meetings from day to day (esp. as an English name for Continental parliaments); a conference or congress, esp. on international affairs; (*Sc.*) a session of a court or any assembly. **dietine** (dī' ė tin), *n.* A subordinate or local diet; a cantonal convention.

dietetic, dietician [DIET (1)].

dif- [DIS-], *pref.*, before *f* in words from Latin.

differ (dif' ėr) [F. *différer*, L. *differre* (DIF-, *ferre*, to bear)], *v.i.* To be dissimilar; to disagree in opinion; to dissent; to be at variance; to quarrel. **v.t.* To make different or distinct; to set at variance. *n.* (*Sc.*) Difference. **to agree to differ:** To give up trying to convince each other.

difference (dif' ĕr ėns) [as prec.], *n.* The state of being unlike or distinct; the quality by which one thing differs from another; disproportion between two things; the remainder of a quantity after another quantity has been subtracted from it; the alteration in the price of stock from one date to another; a distinction, a differential mark, the specific characteristic or differentia; a point or question in dispute, a disagreement in opinion, a quarrel, a controversy; (*Her.*) a figure on a coat-of-arms which distinguishes one family from another, or shows how distant a younger branch is from the elder. *v.t.* To distinguish between; to make different; (*Her.*) to mark with a difference. *v.i.* To serve as a distinguishing mark. **with a difference:** With something distinctive added; differently; (*Her.*) as a mark of distinction.

different (dif′ ĕr ėnt), *a.* Unlike, dissimilar, distinct, not the same. **differently,** *adv.*

differentia (dif ėr en′ shi ȧ) [L., as prec.], *n.* That which distinguishes one species from another of the same genus; an essential attribute, which when added to the name of the genus distinctly marks out the species; thus the attribute of rationality is the differentia of the species 'man' from all other animals.

differential (dif ĕr en′ shȧl), *a.* Differing; consisting of a difference; making or depending on a difference or distinction; relating to specific differences; pertaining to differentials; (*Phys. and Mech.*) relating to the difference between sets of motions acting in the same direction, or between pressures, etc. *n.* (*Math.*) An infinitesimal difference between two consecutive states of a variable quantity. **differential calculus,** *n.* (*Math.*) The method of finding an infinitely small quantity, which, being taken infinite times, shall equal a given quantity. **differential car axle:** (*Motor.*) The driving axle of a car (usu. the rear axle) in which the motive power is transmitted through a differential gear. **differential coefficient,** *n.* (*Math.*) The measure of the rate of change of a function relatively to its variable. **differential duties,** *n.pl.* Duties levied unequally upon the productions of different countries. **differential gear,** *n.* (*Mach.*) A device of bevelled planetary and other wheels which permits of the relative rotation of two shafts driven by a third. Applied to a motor-car it enables the rear (driving) wheels to rotate at different speeds when rounding a corner. **differential motion,** *n.* A mechanical movement in which a part moves with a velocity equal to the difference between the velocities of two other parts. **differential screw,** *n.* A screw with two threads of unequal pitch on the same shaft, one unwinding as the other winds up. **differential winding,** *n.* The combination of two insulated wires in an electric coil, through which currents pass in opposite directions, employed in telegraphy as a resistance coil.

differentiate (dif ėr en′ shi āt) [mod. L. *differentiātus*, p.p. of *differentiāre*, from prec.], *v.t.* To make different; to constitute difference between, of, or in; to discriminate by the differentia, to mark off as different; (*Math.*) to obtain the differential coefficient of; (*Biol.*) to develop variation in; to specialize. *v.i.* To develop so as to become different, to acquire a distinct character. **differentiation** (-ā′ shŭn), *n.*

difficile (dif′ i sēl) [F., from L. *difficilis* (DIF-, *facilis*, easy)], *a.* Awkward, hard to deal with; uncompliant, uncompromising.

difficult (dif′ i kŭlt) [from *difficulty*, O.F. *difficulté*, L. *difficultās -tātem*, from *difficilis*, as prec.], *a.* Hard to do or carry out; troublesome; hard to please; not easily managed; hard to understand; cantankerous. **difficultly,** *adv.* **difficulty,** *n.* The quality of being difficult; anything difficult; an obstacle; objection, reluctance, scruple; (*pl.*) pecuniary embarrassment.

diffident (dif′ i dėnt) [L. *diffidens -entem*, pres.p. of *diffidere* (DIF-, *fidere*, to trust, from *fidēs*, faith)], *a.* Distrustful of oneself or of one's powers; bashful, modest, shy; *distrustful. **diffidence,** *n.* Distrust of oneself; bashfulness, shyness; *distrust of others. **diffidently,** *adv.*

diffluent (dif′ lu ėnt) [L. *diffluens -entem*, pres.p. of *diffluere* (DIF-, *fluere*, to flow)], *a.* Flowing apart or away, dissolving; deliquescing, becoming fluid. **diffluence,** *n.*

diffract (di frăkt′) [L. *diffractus*, p.p. of *diffringere* (DIF-, *frangere*, to break)], *v.t.* To break in parts; (*Opt.*) to bend or deflect a ray of light by passing it close to an opaque object. **diffraction,** *n.* **diffraction grating,** *n.* An array of fine, closely-spaced opaque lines on glass which disperses light into its component colours since the amount of diffraction differs for different-coloured rays of light.

diffuse (1) (di fūz′) [L. *diffūsus*, p.p. of *diffundere* (DIF-, *fundere*, to pour)], *v.t.* To pour forth; to spread abroad by pouring out; to circulate; to cause to intermingle; to dissipate; *to confuse. *v.i.* To be diffused; to intermingle by diffusion. **diffusedly,** *adv.* **diffused lighting:** A form of illumination in which the light is softened and spread over an area instead of being concentrated in one spot. **diffuser,** *n.* One who or that which diffuses or circulates. **diffusible,** *a.* **diffusibility** (-bil′ i ti), *n.*

diffuse (2) (di fūs′) [as prec.], *a.* Diffused, scattered, spread out; copious, prolix, not concise; (*Bot.*) diverging or spreading widely. **diffusely,** *adv.* Copiously, verbosely, fully. **diffuseness,** *n.* **diffusion** (di fū′ zhŭn), *n.* The act of diffusing a liquid, fluid, etc.; a spreading abroad of news, etc.; the state of being widely dispersed. **diffusion-tube,** *n.* (*Chem.*) An instrument for determining the rate of diffusion of different gases. **diffusive** (di fū′ siv), *a.* Diffusing; tending to diffuse; spreading, circulating, widely distributed. **diffusively,** *adv.* **diffusiveness,** *n.*

dig (dig) [prob. from F. *diguer*, to make a dike (*digue*)], *v.t.* (*p.* **dug,** *past p.* **dug**) To excavate or turn up with a spade or similar instrument, or with hands, claws, etc.; to thrust or push into something; to obtain by digging; to make by digging; to poke, to pierce. *v.i.* To work with a spade; to excavate or turn up ground with a spade or other implement; to search, make one's way, thrust, pierce, or make a hole by digging. *n.* A piece of digging (esp. archaeological); a thrust, a poke; (*Am. colloq.*) a plodding student. **to dig oneself in:** (*fig.*) To take up permanent quarters; to refuse to budge; to make oneself indispensable. **to dig out:** To obtain by digging; (*fig.*) to obtain by research. **to dig through:** To open a passage through. **to dig up:** To excavate; to extract or raise by digging; to break up (ground) by digging; (*fig.*) to obtain by research. **to have a dig at:** (*fig.*) To make a cutting or sarcastic remark. **digger,** *n.* One who digs, esp. a gold-miner; an implement, machine, or part of a machine that digs; one of a tribe of North American Indians who live chiefly on roots; (*Austral.*) a fellow, a man. **digging,** *n.* The act of opening the ground with a spade; (*pl.*) a gold-mine or gold-field. **diggings, digs,** *n.pl.* (*colloq.*) Lodgings.

digamma (dī găm′ ȧ) [L., from Gr. (DI- (2), *gamma*, the letter *g*)], *n.* A letter in the oldest Greek alphabet (F) which had the sound of *w*, named from its resemblance to two gammas placed one above the other.

digamy (dig′ ȧ mi) [L. and Gr. *digamia*, from Gr. *digamos* (DI- (2), *gamos*, marriage)], *n.* Marrying a second time. **digamist,** *n.* **digamous,** *a.*

digastric (dī găs′ trik) [DI-, Gr. *gaster*, belly], *a.* Having a double belly or protuberance. **digastric muscle,** *n.* A double muscle which depresses the lower jaw.

digest (di jest′) [L. *dīgestus*, p.p. of *dīgerere* (DI-, (1), *gerere*, to carry)], *v.t.* To arrange under proper heads or titles, to classify; to reduce to system or order; to arrange methodically in the mind; to think over; to soften and prepare by heat; to concoct in the stomach in order to assimilate; to promote the digestion of; to assimilate; (*fig.*) to receive and enjoy; to put up with. *v.i.* To be digested; to be prepared by heat. *n.* (dī′ jėst) A compendium or summary arranged under proper heads or titles; a magazine containing summaries of articles, etc., in current literature; (*Law*) a collection of Roman laws arranged under proper heads, as the pandects of Justinian. **digestible,** *a.* **digestibility** (-bil′ i ti), *n.* **digestibly,** *adv.* **digester,** *n.* One who digests; anything which helps to promote digestion; an apparatus for cooking food by exposing to a heat above boiling point.

digestion (di jes′ chŭn, di jes′ tyŭn), *n.* The act or process of assimilating food in the stomach; the conversion of food into chyme; the power of digesting; concoction for the purpose of extracting the essence from a substance, stewing; (*Bot.*) the absorption of carbonic acid by plants under the influence of light; mental reduction to order and method. **digestive,** *a.* Pertaining to or promoting digestion. *n.* Any substance which aids or promotes digestion; (*Med.*) an application disposing to suppurate.

digger, digging [DIG].

***dight** (dīt) [A.-S. *dihtan*, L. *dictāre* (cp. G. *dichten*, to make poetry)], *v.t.* To dress, array, to adorn; to equip, to prepare (*usu. in p.p.*). *a.* Dressed, adorned, embellished.

digit (dij′ it) [L. *digitus*], *n.* A finger; the measure of a finger's breadth, or three-quarters of an inch; any integer under ten, so called from the primitive habit of counting on the fingers; (*Astron.*) the twelfth part of the diameter of the sun or moon (used to express the quantity or magnitude of an eclipse); (*Anat. and Zool.*) a finger or toe. **digital,** *a.* and *n.*

digitalin, digitalia (di jit′ ȧ lin, di ji tā′ li ȧ), *n.* (*Chem.*) An alkaloid obtained from the foxglove.

digitalis (dij i tā′ lis) [mod. L., pertaining to the fingers, alluding to G. *Fingerhut*, thimble], *n.* (*Bot.*) A genus of scrophulariaceous plants, containing the foxglove (*D. purpurea*); (*Med.*) the dried leaves of the foxglove, which act as a cardiac sedative.

digitate, -tated (dij′ i tāt, -ėd) [L. *digitātus*, from *digitus*, DIGIT], *a.* (*Zool.*) Having finger-like processes; (*Bot.*) branching into distinct leaves or lobes like fingers. **digitately,** *adv.* **digitation** (-tā′ shŭn), *n.* **digitato-,** *comb. form.*

digitiform (di jit′ i fôrm), *a.* Finger-shaped (used of the corolla of digitalis).

digitigrade (dij′ it i grād) [F., from L. *digitus*, DIGIT, *-gradus*, walking], *a.* Belonging to the *Digitigrada*, a section of the carnivora (according to Cuvier's classification) comprising the families of cats, dogs, hyenas, and weasels, in which the heel is raised above the ground, so that these animals walk on their toes. *n.* A digitigrade animal.

diglyph (dī′ glif) [Gr. *digluphos* (DI- (2), *gluphein*, to carve)], *n.* (*Arch.*) A projection like a triglyph, with only two channels instead of three.

dignify (dig′ ni fī) [O.F. *dignifier*, late L. *dignificāre* (*dignus*, worthy, -FY)], *v.t.* To make worthy; to invest with dignity; to make illustrious; to exalt. **dignified,** *a.* Invested with dignity; stately; gravely courteous.

dignity (dig′ ni ti) [O.F. *dignité*, L. *dignitās -tātem* (*dignus*, worthy)], *n.* Worth, nobility; estimation, rank; the importance due to rank or position; elevation of mien or manner, stateliness; a high office, a position of importance or honour. **dignitary** (dig′ ni tȧr i), *n.* One who holds a position of dignity, esp. ecclesiastical.

digraph (dī′ grăf), *n.* A combination of two letters to represent one simple sound, as *ea* in *mead*, *th* in *thin*. **digraphic** (-grăf′ ik), *a.*

digress (di-, dī gres′) [L. *dīgressus*, p.p. of *dīgredī* (DI- (1), *gradī*, to step, from *gradus*, a step)], *v.i.* To turn aside from the direct path; to deviate, to wander from the main topic. **digression** (di-, dī gresh′ ŭn), *n.* A deviation from the direct course; *a departure from the path of virtue; a part of a discourse, etc., which wanders from the main subject. ***digressional,** *a.* **digressive** (-gres′), *a.* **digressively,** *adv.* **digressiveness,** *n.*

digynia (dī jin′ i ȧ), [DI- (2), *gunē*, a female], *n.pl.* (*Bot.*) A Linnæan order of plants with two free pistils, or a single style deeply cleft into two parts. **digynian, digynous** (dī′ jin ŭs), *a.*

dihedral (dī hē′ drȧl) [DI- (2), Gr. *hedra*, seat], *a.* (*Cryst.*) Having two sides or faces; (*Math.*) of the nature of a dihedron. **dihedron,** *n.* (*Geom.*) A figure with two sides or surfaces.

dihexagonal (dī hek săg′ ȯ nȧl), *a.* (*Cryst.*) Twelve-sided; consisting of two hexagonal parts combined.

dihexahedron (dī hek sȧ hē′ drȯn), *n.* (*Cryst.*) A six-sided prism with three planes at the extremities. **dihexahedral,** *a.*

dike (dīk) [A.-S. *dīc* (cp. Dut. *dijk*, G. *teich*)], *n.* A ditch, a moat, a water-course or channel, natural or artificial; a mound or dam to protect low-lying lands from being flooded; (*Sc.*) a wall or fence of turf or stone without cement; a causeway; (*fig.*) a barrier, a defence; (*Geol.*) a wall-like mass of cooled and hardened volcanic or igneous rock, occupying rents and fissures in sedimentary strata; (*Mining*) a fissure filled with mineral matter. *v.t.* To defend with dikes or embankments; *to dig. **dike-reeve,** *n.* An officer in charge of dikes, drains, and sluices in fen districts.

***dilacerate** (dī lăs′ ėr āt) [L. *dilacerātus*, p.p. of *dilacerāre*], *v.t.* To tear in pieces, to rend asunder. ***dilaceration** (-ā′ shŭn), *n.*

dilapidate (di lăp′ i dāt) [L. *dīlapidātus*, p.p. of *dīlapidāre* (DI (1), *lapid-*, stem of *lapis*, stone)], *v.t.* To damage, to bring into decay or ruin. *v.i.* To fall into decay or ruin. **dilapidation** (-da′ shŭn), *n.* Decay for want of repair; a state of partial ruin, decay; the action of an incumbent in suffering ecclesiastical buildings, etc., to fall into disrepair; charge for making this good; the falling down or wasting away of rocks, cliffs, etc.; the debris resulting. **dilapidator** (di lăp′ i dā tŏr), *n.*

dilate (di-, dī lāt′) [F. *dilater*, L. *dīlātāre* (DI-, *lātus*, broad)], *v.t.* To expand, to widen, to enlarge in all directions; *to spread abroad; to enlarge upon. *v.i.* To be extended or enlarged; to expand, to swell; (*fig.*) to expatiate, to speak fully and copiously (upon a subject). **a.* Extended, expanded. **dilatable,** *a,* Capable of dilatation; elastic. **dilatant,** *a.* and *n.* **dilatancy,** *n.* **dilatability** (-bil′ i ti), *n.* **dilatation** (-tā′ shŭn), *n.* The act of dilating; the state of being dilated; a dilated or expanded form or part; amplification, diffuseness; *extension, expansion. **dilation** [DILATATION]. **dilatometer** (-tom′ ė tėr), *n.* **dilator,** *n.* (*Anat.*) A muscle that dilates the parts on which it acts; (*Surg.*) an instrument for dilating the walls of a cavity.

dilatory (dil′ ȧ tŏr i) [L. *dīlātōrius*, from *dīlātōr -em*, a delayer (from *dīlāt-*, p.p. stem of *differre*, to DEFER)], *a.* Causing or tending to cause delay; addicted to or marked by procrastination; slow, tardy; wanting in diligence. **dilatorily,** *adv.* **dilatoriness,** *n.*

dilemma (di-, dī lem′ ȧ) [L., from Gr. *dilēmma* (DI- (2), *lēmma*, an assumption, from *lambanein*, to take)], *n.* (*Log.*) An argument in which a choice of alternatives is presented, each of which is fatal; (*fig.*) a position in which one is forced to choose between alternatives equally unfavourable. **the horns of a dilemma:** The alternatives presented to an adversary in a logical dilemma. **dilemmatic** (-măt′ ik), *a.* **dilemmist** (di lem′ ist), *n.*

dilettante (dil ė tăn′ ti) [It., from *dilettare*, L. *dēlectāre*, to DELIGHT], *n.* (*pl.* **-ti**) A lover or admirer of the fine arts; a superficial amateur, a would-be connoisseur, a dabbler. *a.* Art-loving; amateurish, superficial. **dilettantish,** *a.* **dilettantism,** *n.*

diligence (1) (dil′ i jėns, dē′ li zhans) [F.], *n.* A public stage-coach, used in France and adjoining countries.

diligence (2), (dil′ i jėns), *n.* Steady application or assiduity in business of any kind; *care, heedfulness; *officiousness; *a diligent person; *speed, dispatch.

diligent (dil′ i jėnt) [F., from L. *dīligens -ntem*, pres.p. of *dīligere* (DI-, *legere*, to choose)], *a.* Assiduous in any business or task; persevering, industrious, painstaking. **diligently,** *adv.*

dill (dil) [A.-S. *dile* (cp. Dut. *dille*, Swed. and G. *dill*)], *n.* An annual umbellifer, *Anethum graveolens*, cultivated for its carminative seeds. **dill-water,** *n.* A popular remedy for flatulence in children, prepared from the seeds of the dill.

dilly-bag (dil' i băg) [Queensland native name *dilli*], *n.* An Australian native basket or bag made of rushes or bark.

dilly-dally (dil' i dăl' i) [redupl. of DALLY], *v.i.* To loiter about; to waste time; to hesitate.

dilute (dī-, di lūt') [L. *dīlūtus*, p.p. of *dīluere* (DI- (1), *luere*, to wash)], *v.t.* To make thin or weaken (as spirit, acid, or colour) by the admixture of water; to reduce the strength or brilliance of; to water down. *a.* (dī' lūt) Diluted; weakened, washed out, faded, colourless. ***dilutedly,** *adv.* ***diluent** (dil' ū ėnt), *a.* Making thin or liquid; diluting. *n.* That which dilutes; (*Med.*) a substance tending to increase the proportion of fluid in the blood. **dilution** (di lū' shŭn), *n.* **dilution of industry:** The employment of unskilled workers in positions hitherto held by skilled workers.

diluvial (di loo'-, di lū' vi ăl), **-vian** (-vi ăn) [L. *dīluviālis*, from *dīluvium*, a deluge, from *dīluere*, as prec.], *a.* Pertaining to the Noachian deluge; (*Geol.*) produced by or resulting from a flood; pertaining to the diluvium or glacial drift. **diluvial clay,** *n.* (*Geol.*) The boulder clay. **diluvial theory,** *n.* (*Geol.*) The theory that explains many geological phenomena as the result of a catastrophic deluge. **diluvialist,** *n.* (*Geol.*) One who regards certain physical phenomena as the result of the Noachian deluge or a series of catastrophic floods. **diluvium,** *n.* (*pl.* **-via**) (*Geol.*) An accumulation of deposits apparently the result of water-action on a vast scale, formerly attributed to the Noachian deluge, now referred to the drift or boulder formation.

dim (dim) [A.-S. (cp. Icel. *dimmr*, M.H.G. *timmer*, *timbar*)], *a.* Lacking in light or brightness; somewhat dark; obscure; not clear, not bright; faint, indistinct, misty; devoid of lustre, tarnished, dull; not clearly seen; imperfectly heard; indistinctly, not clearly understanding or understood; (*fig.*) mentally obtuse. *v.t.* (*past & p.p.* **dimmed**) To render dim. *v.i.* To become dim. **to take a dim view of:** (*colloq.*) To regard pessimistically, to view with suspicion or disfavour. **dim-eyed,** *a.* Having indistinct vision. **dim-out,** *n.* A less rigorous form of black-out. **dim-shining,** *a.* Giving a dim light. **dim-sighted,** *a.* Dull, obtuse. **dim-twinkling,** *a.* Twinkling or shining feebly. **dimly,** *adv.* **dimmer,** *n.* (*Elec.*) A device whereby an electric lamp can be switched on and off gradually. **dimmish,** *a.* **dimness,** *n.*

dime (dīm) [O.F. *dime disme*, L. *decima*, fem. or *decimus* (*decem*, ten)], *n.* A silver coin of the U.S.A., worth ten cents or one-tenth of a dollar. **dime novel,** *n.* A sensational story, the equivalent of the penny dreadful.

dimension (di-, dī men' shŭn) [F., from L. *dīmensio -onem*, from *dīmensus*, p.p. of *dīmetīrī* (DI- (1), *metīrī*, to measure)], *n.* Measurable extent or magnitude, length, breadth, height, thickness, depth, area, volume, etc. (*usu. in pl.*); (*Alg.*) the number of unknown or variable quantities contained as factors in a given product (thus ab^2c^3 is a term of 6 dimensions). **of large dimensions:** Very large. **three dimensions:** Length, breadth and thickness; a line, a surface, a volume, constituting the three degrees of measurement. **fourth dimension:** (*Math.*) A property that is to volume what volume is to area, or to solids as solids to planes. **dimensional,** *a.* (*usu. in comb.*) **fourth-dimensional,** *a.* **dimensioned,** *a.* Having dimensions; proportional (*usu. in comb.*). **four-dimensioned,** *a.* **dimensionless,** *a.*

dimerous (dim' ėr ŭs), *a.* (*Bot., Entom.*) Having two parts, joints, divisions, etc.; arranged in pairs.

dimeter (dim' ė tėr) [L. *dimetrus*, Gr. *dimetros* (DI- (2), *metron*, measure)], *n.* A verse of two prosodial measures.

dimethyl (dī meth' il), *n.* Ethane, an organic compound in which two equivalents of methyl take the place of two of hydrogen. **dimethylaniline,** *n.* One of the aniline bases, an oil liquid from which various dyes are obtained.

dimidiate (di mid' i ăt) [L. *dīmidiātus*, p.p. of *dīmidiāre*, from *dīmidium*, half (DI- (1), *medius*, middle)], *a.* Divided into two halves; (*Bot.*) divided or split into parts; (*Zool.*) a term used when corresponding organs have different functions.

diminish (di min' ish) [DI- (1), MINISH (formed on anal. of obs. *diminue*, F. *diminuer*, L. *diminuere*, to break into small pieces)], *v.t.* To make smaller or less; to reduce in quantity, power, rank, etc.; to disparage, to degrade; to take away or subtract from; (*Mus.*) to lessen by a semitone. *v.i.* To become less, to decrease; to taper. **diminishable,** *a.* **diminished,** *a.* Made less or smaller; reduced in size or quality; (*Mus.*) lessened by a semitone. **diminisher,** *n.* One who or that which diminishes. **diminishingly,** *adv.* **diminution** (dim i nū' shŭn), *n.* The act of diminishing; subtraction; amount subtracted; the state of becoming less or smaller; (*Arch.*) the gradual decrease in the diameter of the shaft of a column from the base to the capital.

diminuendo (di min ū en' dō) [It., pres.p. of *diminuire*, L. *dīminuere*; see prec.], *Mus. direction.* Gradually decrease in loudness. *n.* A gradual decrease in loudness; a passage characterized by this.

diminutive (di min' ū tiv), *a.* Small, tiny; (*Gram.*) expressing diminution. *n.* Anything of a small size; (*Gram.*) a word formed from another to express diminution in size or importance. **diminutival** (-tī' văl), *a.* Expressing diminution; pertaining to a diminutive word. **diminutively,** *adv.* **diminutiveness,** *n.*

dimissory (dim' i sŏr i) [L. *dīmissōrius*, from *dimittere* (DI- (1), *mittere*, to send)], *a.* Dismissing, discharging; giving leave to depart. **dimissory letter,** *n.* Letter addressed by one bishop to another, giving leave for the bearer to be ordained by the latter.

dimity (dim' i ti) [It., pl. of *dimito*, late L. *dimitum*, Gr. *dimitos* (DI- (2), *mitos*, a thread)], *n.* A stout cotton fabric with stripes or patterns, chiefly used for bed-hangings.

dimorphic (dī mŏr' fik) [Gr. *dimorphos* (DI- (2), *morphē*, form)], *a.* Having or occurring in two distinct forms. **dimorphism,** *n.* (*Cryst.*) The power of assuming or crystallizing into two distinct forms; (*Biol.*) a difference of form between members of the same species; (*Bot.*) a state in which two forms of flower are produced by the same species; (*Philol.*) the existence of a word in more than one form. **dimorphous,** *a.*

dimple (dim' pėl) [M.E. *dympull*; etym. doubtful (cp. G. *tümpel*, a pool, O.H.G. *dumphilo*)], *n.* A little depression or hollow; a small natural depression on the cheek or chin; a ripple; a shallow dell or hollow in the ground. *v.t.* To mark with dimples. *v.i.* To form dimples; to sink in slight depressions. **dimply,** *a.*

dimyaria (dim i âr' i ă) [DI- (2), *mus*, a muscle], *n.pl.* (*Zool.*) A group of conchiferous bivalves having the shells closed with two distinct adductor muscles, as in the common mussel. **dimyarian** (dim i âr' i ăn), *a.*

din (din) [A.-S. *dyn*, *dyne* (whence *dynnan*, to make a loud noise) (cp. Icel. *dynr*, Sansk. *dhūni*)], *n.* A loud and continued noise; a rattling or clattering sound. *v.t.* (*past & p.p* **dinned**) To harass with clamour; to stun with a loud continued noise; to repeat or impress with a loud continued noise. *v.i.* To make a din. **to din into:** (*fig.*) To teach by constant repetition.

dinar (dī nar') [Arab. and Pers. *dīnār*, late Gr. *dēnarion*, L. *denārius*, DENARIUS], *n.* An Eastern coin; a Persian money of account; the monetary unit of Yugoslavia.

dinarchy [DIARCHY].

dine (dīn) [F. *dîner*, prob. from a late L. *disjūnāre* or *disjējūnāre* (DIS-, L. *jējūnus*, fasting)], *v.i.* To take dinner. *v.t.* To give or provide a dinner for; to afford accommodation for dining. **to dine with Duke Humphrey:** To go dinnerless (said to allude to *Duke Humphrey's Walk*, a part of old St. Paul's where people were supposed to stroll whilst others were dining). **diner,** *n.* One who dines; a railway dining-car. **diner-out,** *n.* One who habitually dines away from home; one who is frequently invited out to dinner. **dining-chamber, -hall, -room, -table,** *n.* A place or table for taking dinner at. **dining-car,** *n.* (*Rail.*) A coach in which meals are cooked and served.

ding (ding) [M.E. *dingen* (cp. Icel. *dengja*, Swed. *dänga*)], *v.t.* To strike; to beat violently; to beat, to surpass; to knock or drive with violence; to damn or confound (as an imprecation). *v.i.* To knock or thump; to fall heavily; to be impressed or moved.

ding-dong (ding′ dong) [onomat.], *n.* The sound of a bell; a jingle, a jingling rhyme or tune. *a.* Sounding like a bell; jingling. *adv.* In a hammering way; like the sound of a bell. *v.i.* To ring; to jingle; to read, speak, or recite in a jingling or ding-dong fashion. **a ding-dong race:** A neck-and-neck race.

dinghy (ding′ gi) [Hind. *ḍēṅgī* or *ḍiṅgī*], *n.* Orig. a row-boat on the Hugly; a small ship's boat; any small boat.

dingle (ding′ gėl) [etym. doubtful], *n.* A dell, a wooded valley between hills.

dingo (ding′ gō) [Austral. abor.], *n.* The Australian wild dog, *Canis dingo.*

dingy (din′ ji) [perh. from DUNG], *a.* Soiled, grimy; of a dusky, soiled, or dun colour; faded. **dingily,** *adv.* **dinginess,** *n.*

dink (dingk) [Sc.; etym. unknown], *a.* Fine, braw, trim. *v.t.* To dress finely; to deck. **dinky,** *a.* (*fam.*) Charming, dainty, pleasing.

dinkum (ding′ kŭm), *a.* (*Australian colloq.*) Good, genuine, satisfactory.

dinmont (din′ mŏnt) [etym. doubtful], *n.* (*Sc. and North.*) A wether between the first and the second shearing. **Dandie Dinmont,** *n.* A Scottish terrier.

dinner (din′ ėr) [F. *dîner*, to DINE], *n.* The principal meal of the day; a feast, a banquet. **dinner dance,** *n.* A dinner followed by dancing. **dinner-hour,** *n.* The time set apart for dinner. **dinner-jacket,** *n.* A less formal dress coat, without tails and worn with black tie and waistcoat. **dinner party,** *n.* Invitation of guests to dinner; the guests so invited. **dinner service, set,** *n.* The china plates, etc., used for serving dinner. **dinner-table,** *n.* A dining-table. **dinner-time,** *n.* The hour for dinner. **dinner-wagon,** *n.* A tray or set of trays or shelves on castors. **dinnerless,** *a.*

dinoceras (dī nos′ ėr ăs) [Gr. *deinos*, terrible, *keras*, horn] *n.* (*Palæont.*) An extinct genus of gigantic mammals found in Wyoming, apparently armed with three pairs of horns.

dinornis (dī nôr′ nis) [Gr. *deinos*, terrible, *ornis*, bird], *n.* (*Palæont.*) A genus of gigantic fossil birds, with rudimentary wings, found in New Zealand.

dinosaur (dī′ nō sawr) [Gr. *deinos*, terrible, *sauros*, lizard], *n.* (*Palæont.*) A gigantic mesozoic reptile. **dinosaurian** (dī nō saw′ ri ăn), *a.* Pertaining to the group *Dinosauria. n.* A dinosaur.

dinotherium (dī nō thēr′ i ŭm) [mod. L., from Gr. *deinos*, terrible, *thērion*, wild beast], *n.* (*Palæont.*) A genus of gigantic fossil pachyderms, having enormous tusks projecting from the lower jaw, and a trunk.

dint (dint) [A.-S. *dynt* (cp. Icel. *dyntr*)], *n.* A blow, a stroke; the mark or dent caused by a blow; *violence, force. *v.t.* To mark with a dint. *v.i.* To make a dint. **by dint of:** By force of, or by means of.

diocese (dī′ ō ses, -sēs) [O.F., from L. *diœcēsis*, Gr. *dioikēsis* (DI-, *oikeein*, to keep house, to inhabit)], *n.* The district under the jurisdiction of a bishop. **diocesan** (dī os′ ė săn), *a.* Pertaining to a diocese. *n.* One who has ecclesiastical jurisdiction over a diocese; a bishop or archbishop; a member of a diocese.

diodon (dī′ ō don) [DI- (2), Gr. *odous odontos*, a tooth], *n.* (*Palæont.*) A genus of teleostean fishes with inflatable bodies and undivided jaws which exhibit one piece of bony substance above and another below.

diœcia (dī ē′ shi ă) [mod. L. (DI- (2), Gr. *oikos*, house)], *n.pl.* (*Bot.*) A Linnæan class of plants, having the stamens on one individual and the pistils on another. **diœcious,** *a.* (*Bot.*) Belonging to the *diœcia*; (*Zool.*) having the sexes in separate individuals.

diopside (dī op′ sīd) [F. (DI- (2), *opsis*, appearance)], *n.* (*Min.*) Pyroxene, esp. the transparent variety.

dioptase (dī op′ tās) [F. (DI- (3), *optos*, visible)], *n.* (*Min.*) An emerald-green ore of copper.

dioptric (dī op′ trik) [Gr. *dioptrikos*, from *dioptra*, an optical instrument (DI- (3), *op-*, stem of verb, to see, *-tra*, instr. suf.)], *a.* Affording a medium for assisting the sight in the view of distant objects; refractive; pertaining to dioptrics. *n.pl.* That part of optics which treats of the refraction of light in passing through different mediums, esp. through lenses. **dioptric light,** *n.* Light produced in lighthouses by refraction through a series of lenses. **dioptric system,** *n.* Illumination by this method. **dioptre** (dī op′ tėr), *n.* The unit of refractive power, being the power of a lens with a focal distance of one metre. **dioptrically,** *adv.*

diorama (dī ō ra′ ma) [DI- (3), Gr. *horama* (*horaein*, to see)], *n.* A scenic representation viewed through an aperture by means of reflected and transmitted light, various alterations of colour and lighting imitating natural effects; a building in which dioramic views are shown. **dioramic** (-răm′ ik), *a.*

diorite (dī′ ō rīt) [F., from Gr. *diorizein*, to distinguish (DI- (3), *horos*, a boundary)], *n.* (*Geol.*) A granite-like rock, consisting principally of hornblende and feldspar.

Dioscuri (dī os kū′ rī) [Gr. *Dioskouroi* (*Dios*, gen. of *Zeus*, *kouroi koroi*, pl. of *koros*, a lad)], *n.pl.* The twins Castor and Pollux.

diosmose (dī os′ mōs), *n.* The gradual passage of a fluid through a permeable wall.

diothelism, etc. [DYOTHELISM].

dioxide (dī ok′ sīd, -sid), *n.* (*Chem.*) One atom of a metal combined with two of oxygen.

dip (dip) [A.-S. *dyppan*, cogn. with *dēop*, DEEP (cp. Dut. *doopen*, G. *taufen*)], *v.t.* (*past & p.p.* **dipped**) To plunge into a liquid for a short time, to immerse; to baptize by immersion; to wash, to dye, to coat by plunging into a liquid; to lower for an instant; to put the hand or a ladle into liquid and scoop out; *to mortgage, to pledge, to implicate; (*Motor.*) to lower the headlights; (*Naut.*) to salute by lowering the flag and hoisting it again. *v.i.* To plunge into liquid for a short time; to sink, as below the horizon; to bend downwards, to bow; to slope or extend downwards, to enter slightly into any business; to read a book cursorily; to choose by chance. *n.* The act of dipping in a liquid; bathing, esp. in a river, sea, etc.; a candle made by dipping wicks in melted tallow; the quantity taken up at one dip or scoop; a preparation for washing sheep; sauce, gravy, etc., into which anything is to be dipped; depth or degree of submergence; (*Geol.*) the angle at which strata slope downwards into the earth; a curtsy; (*slang*) a pickpocket. **dip of the horizon:** The apparent angular depression of the visible horizon below the horizontal plane through the observer's eye, due to his elevation. **dip of the needle:** The angle which a magnetic needle makes with the horizontal, also called **magnetic dip.** **to dip deep:** To plunge far in; to investigate. **dip-chick,** *n.* The dabchick. **dip-net,** *n.* A small fishing-net with a long handle. **dip-pipe, -trap,** *n.* A pipe bent down from a gas-main with its end plunged into liquid to form a seal. **dipper,** *n.* One who dips; a vessel used for dipping; (*Phot.*) a contrivance for lifting negatives out of the developer; a contemptuous name for the Baptists or Anabaptists; (*Am.*) the seven stars of the Great Bear; popular name for several birds, esp. the water-ousel; (*Am.*) a pannikin, a ladle. **dipping compass, dipping-needle,** *n.* A magnetized needle which, when mounted on an axis passing at right angles through its centre of gravity, will point downwards indicating the inclination of the lines of magnetic force. **dipping-tube,** *n.* A tube for taking microscopic objects out of a liquid.

dipetalous (dī pet′ ȧ lŭs), *a.* (*Bot.*) Having two petals.

diphtheria (dif thēr′ i ȧ) [F. *diphthérie*, Gr. *diphthera*, leather, skin], *n.* An infectious disease characterized by acute inflammation and the formation of a false membrane, chiefly on the pharynx, nostrils, tonsils, and palate. **diphtherial, diphtheric** (-ther′ ik), *a.* **diphtheritis** (-thėr ī′ tis), *n.* **diphtheritic** (-it′ ik), *a.* **diphtheroid** (dif′ thėr oid), *a.*

diphthong (dif′ thong) [F. *diphthongue*, L. *diphthongus*, Gr. *diphthongos* (DI- (2), *phthongos*, voice)], *n.* The union of two vowels in one syllable; a digraph or combination of two vowel characters to represent a vowel sound; (*pop.*) the vowel ligatures, *æ*, *œ*. **diphthongal** (-thong′ gȧl), **-gic** (-thon′ jik), *a.* **diphthongally,** *adv.* **diphthongize,** *v.t.*

diphyllous (dī fil′ ŭs) [DI- (2), Gr. *phullon*, a leaf)], *a.* (*Bot.*) Having two leaves or sepals.

diphyodont (dī′ fi ȯ dont) [Gr. *diphuēs*, of double nature, *odous odontos*, tooth], *a.* (*Anat.* and *Zool.*) A term applied to those mammals which have two sets of teeth, one deciduous, the other permanent.

diphysite, etc. [DYOPHYSITE].

dipl-, diplo- [Gr. *diplous*, double], *comb. form.*

dipleidoscope (dip lī′ dō skōp) [Gr. *eidos*, form, -SCOPE], *n.* An instrument for determining the moment of transit of a heavenly body over the meridian by the coincidence of two images produced by single and double refraction.

diploblastic (dip lō blăs′ tik) [Gr. *blastos*, a sprout], *a.* (*Bot.*) Having two germ-layers.

diplocardiac (dip lō kar′ di ăk), *a.* (*Anat. Zool.*) Having the heart double or the two sides separated.

diplodocus (di plod′ ō kŭs), *n.* (*Palæont.*) A genus of sauropod dinosaurs characterized by a large tail and a small head.

diploe (dip′ lō ē) [Gr. double], *n.* (*Anat.*) The spongy tissue between the plates of the skull; (*Bot.*) the tissue of a leaf between the two layers of epiderm.

diploma (di plō′ mȧ) [L., from Gr. *diplōma* (*diploos*, double, folded)], *n.* (*pl.* **-as,** rarely **-ata**) A document conveying some authority, privilege, or honour; a charter, a state paper; a certificate of a degree, licence, etc. **diplomaed** (-măd), *a.* **diplomaless,** *a.* **diplomate** (dip′-), *n.* **diplomatics** (-măt′ iks), *n.* The art or science of ascertaining the authenticity, date, genuineness, etc., of ancient literary documents; *diplomacy.

diplomacy (di plō′ mȧ si) [F. *diplomatie*, from *diplomate*, from *diplomatique*, mod. L. *diplōmaticus*, from prec.], *n.* The art of conducting negotiations between nations; the act of negotiating with foreign nations; skill in conducting negotiations of any kind; adroitness, tact. **diplomat** (dip′ lȯ măt), *n.* A professional diplomatist, one skilled or trained in diplomacy. **diplomatic** (-măt′ ik), *a.* Pertaining to diplomacy or to ambassadors. **diplomatic corps,** *n.* The body of diplomatic representatives accredited to any government. **diplomatically,** *adv.* **diplomatics** [see DIPLOMA]. ***diplomatism** (di plō′ mȧ tizm), *n.* **diplomatist,** *n.* One skilled or engaged in diplomacy. **diplomatize,** *v.i.* To act as a diplomatist; to exert the arts of a diplomatist.

diplopia (dip lō′ pi ȧ) [Gr. *ops*, an eye], *n.* A disease of the eyes in which the patient sees objects double.

diplozoon (dip lō zō′ on), *n.* (*pl.* **diplozoa**) A trematode or flat-worm composed of two individual organisms fused together in the shape of a cross, parasitic on the gills of fishes.

dipnoi (dip′ noi) [mod. L., from Gr. *dipnoos* (DI- (2), *pnoē*, breathing, breath)], *n.pl.* (*Zool.*) An order of fishes, of very ancient type, breathing both by gills and true lungs, exhibiting a transition to the amphibia. **dipnoid,** *a.* and *n.* **dipnoous,** *a.*

dipody (dip′ ȯ di) [L. and Gr. *dipodia* (DI- (2), Gr. *pous podos*, foot)], *n.* (*Pros.*) A double foot.

dipolar (dī pō′ lȧr), *a.* (*Elec. and Opt.*) Having two poles. **dipolarize,** *v.t.* **dipolarization** (-zā′ shŭn), *n.*

dipper, dipping [DIP].

dippy (dip′ i), *a.* (*Slang*) Slightly mad, cracked.

dipsas (dip′ sȧs) [L., from Gr. *dipsas* (*dipsa*, thirst)], *n.* A serpent whose bite was said to produce unquenchable thirst; (*Zool.*) a genus of non-venomous tree-snakes.

dipsomania (dip sō mā′ ni ȧ) [as prec., -MANIA], *n.* Alcoholism; an irresistible morbid craving for stimulants. **dipsomaniac,** *n.* **dipsomaniacal** (-nī′ ăk ȧl), *a.* **dipsopathy** (dip sop′ ȧ thi), *n.* (*Med.*) Treatment of dipsomania by enforced abstinence. **dipsosis** (dip sō′ sis), *n.* (*Path.*) Morbid craving for drink.

diptera (dip′ tėr ȧ) [mod. L., from Gr. *diptera* (DI- (2), *pteron*, wing)], *n.pl.* (*Entom.*) An order of insects, such as flies and gnats, that have two wings and two small knobbed organs called poisers. **dipteran,** *a.* **dipterous,** *a.* (*Entom.*) Two-winged; belonging to the **diptera;** (*Bot.*) having two wing-like appendages.

dipteral (dip′ tėr ȧl) [as prec.], *a.* (*Arch.*) Applied to a temple having a double row of columns all round.

diptych (dip′ tik) [late L. *diptycha*, Gr. *diptucha*, neut. pl. of *diptuchos*, folding (DI- (2), *ptuchē*, a fold)], *n.* An ancient writing-tablet of two hinged leaves, made of carved ivory waxed on the inner side; an altar-piece or other painting with hinged sides closing like a book.

dire (dīr) [L. *dīrus*], *a.* Dreadful, fearful, dismal, lamentable, sad. **direful,** *a.* **direfully,** *adv.* **direfulness,** *n.* **direly,** *adv.*

direct (di-, dī rekt′) [L. *dīrectus*, p.p. of *dīrigere* (DI- (1), *regere*, to rule)], *a.* Straight; in a straight line from one body or place to another; not curved or crooked; not reflected or refracted; nearest, shortest; tending immediately to an end or result; not circuitous; not collateral in the line of descent; diametrical; not contrary or retrograde; immediate; personal, not by proxy; (*Mus.*) not inverted; (*Gram.*) as spoken, not in oblique oration; plain, to the point, straightforward, upright; (*Astron.*) from east to west, applied to the motion of a planet when in the same direction as the movement of the sun amidst the fixed stars. *v.t.* To point or turn in a direct line towards any place or object; to show the right road to; to inscribe with an address or direction; to address, to speak or write to some one; to guide, to prescribe a course to, to advise; to order, to command; to manage, to control, to act as leader or head of; to compel work-people in time of emergency to engage in certain occupations. *v.i.* To give orders or instructions. *adv.* (*colloq.*) Directly; immediately; absolutely. **direct action,** *n.* The use of the strike as a weapon to force political or social measures on a government. **direct chord,** *n.* (*Mus.*) A chord in which the fundamental note is the lowest. **direct circuit,** *n.* (*Teleg.*) A circuit going from one station to another without using relays. **direct current,** *n.* (*Elec.*) A current which flows in one direction only. **direct interval,** *n.* (*Mus.*) An interval which forms any kind of harmony with the fundamental sound that produces it. **direct pickup,** *n.* (*T.V.*) The transmission of television images directly, without photographic medium. **direct speech,** *n.* A report of actual words spoken. **direct tax,** *n.* A tax levied on the persons who ultimately bear the burden. ***directitude,** *n.* A ludicrous formation in Shakespeare (*Coriolanus*, iv. 5), perh. difficulties. **directive,** *n.* An authoritative instruction or direction. *a.* Having the power of directing; capable of being directed; directory. **directly,** *adv.* In a direct or straight line; in a direct manner; as an immediate step; without any intervening space; at once; *openly, without ambiguity; *conj.* (*colloq.*) As soon as, directly that. **directness,** *n.*

direction (dī rek′ shůn), *n.* The act of directing; the end or object aimed at; the course taken; the point towards which one looks; the act of inscribing with an address; (*often in pl.*) the superscription of a letter or parcel; an order or instruction; a directorate; sphere, subject. **direction finder,** *n.* (*Radio.*) An apparatus for finding the bearings of a transmitting station. **directional aerial,** *n.* (*Radio.*) An aerial that transmits or receives wireless waves from one direction.

directoire (dē rek′ twar) [F.], *a.* Term applied to the costume and furniture of the Directory period in France, 1795–99.

director (di rek′ tȯr) [F. *directeur* (as prec., -OR)], *n.* One who directs or manages; an instructor, a counsellor; anything which controls or regulates; one appointed to direct the affairs of a company; a spiritual adviser, a confessor; a device for controlling the application of a knife, an electric current, etc.; (*Cinema.*) the person responsible for the acting, etc., in a film play; (*Am.*) a theatrical producer; (*F. Hist.*) a member of the Directory. **directorate,** *n.* The position of a director; a body or board of directors. **directorial** (-tôr′ i ål), *a.* **directorship,** *n.* **directress,** *n.* A female who directs or superintends.

directory (di rek′ tȯ ri), *a.* Directing, commanding advising; (*Law*) directive, not coercive. *n.* A board of directors; a book containing the names and addresses of the inhabitants, etc., of a district; a book of direction for public worship; (*F. Hist.*) the executive council of the French Republic in 1795–99.

directrix (di rek′ triks), *n.* (*pl.* **directrices** (di rek′ tri sēz)] (*Geom.*) A line determining the motion of a point or another line so that the latter describes a certain curve or surface.

dirge (děrj) [L. *dīrige*, direct thou, imper. of *dīrigere*, to DIRECT (first word of antiphon in the office for the dead)], *n.* A funeral song or hymn; a mournful tune or song; a lament.

dirhem (dir′ hėm) [Arab. *dirham*, *dirhim*, L. *drachma*, Gr. *drachmē*, DRACHM], *n.* An Eastern measure of weight; a small silver coin still used in Morocco, worth about 3¾d.

dirigible (dir′ ij i bėl) [L. *dīrigere*, to DIRECT, -IBLE], *a.* That may be directed or steered. *n.* A balloon or airship that can be steered.

diriment (dir′ i mėnt) [L. *dirimens -ntem*, pres.p. of *dirimere* (DIR-, DIS-, *emere*, to take)], *a.* (*Law*) Nullifying, rendering a marriage null and void.

dirk (děrk) [earlier *dork* (cp. Dut. *dolk*, G. *dolch*)], *n.* A dagger or poniard, esp. that worn by a Highlander; the short sword of a midshipman. *v.t.* To stab with a dirk.

dirl (děrl) [Sc.; cp. THRILL (Sc. *thirl*), DRILL], *v.t.* To thrill; to cause to vibrate or ring. *v.i.* To vibrate. *n.* A thrill; a tingling sensation from a blow.

dirt (děrt) [M.E. *drit*, prob. from Icel. *drit*, dirt, excrement (cp. A.-S. *drītan*, to void excrement)], *n.* Foul or unclean matter, matter that soils; mud, mire, dust; a worthless thing, trash, refuse; dirtiness; earth, soil; (*contempt.*) land; foul talk, scurrility; (*Mining*) the material put into the cradle to be washed; (*fig.*) meanness, sordidness. *v.t.* To make dirty or filthy. **to eat dirt:** To put up with insult and abuse. **dirt-beds,** *n.pl.* (*Geol.*) Loam-like beds occurring interstratified with the oolitic limestones and sandstones of Portland. **dirt-cheap,** *a.* Very cheap. **dirt-eating,** *n.* A disease of the nutritive functions among Negroes causing an irresistible craving to eat dirt. **dirt road,** *n.* (*Am.*) An unmade-up road. **dirt-track,** *n.* A racing-track with a soft, loose surface, for motor-cycle racing; a speedway. **dirty,** *a.* Full of, mixed, or soiled with dirt; foul, nasty, unclean; (*fig.*) base, obscene; sordid, mean; contemptible; (*weather*) sloppy, rough, gusty. *v.t.* To make dirty, to soil; to sully, to tarnish. *v.i.* To become dirty. **Dirty Allan,** *n.* A seabird, *Stercorareus crepidatus*, that eats food which it has forced gulls, etc., to disgorge. **Dirty Shirts,** *n.pl.* The 101st Regiment of Foot, from their fighting in their shirtsleeves at Delhi in 1857. **dirtily,** *adv.* **dirtiness,** *n.* **dirtyish,** *a.*

dis- [direct from L. *dis-* (conn. with *bis*, twice, orig. *duis*, Gr. *dis*, and *duo*, two; or F. *dés-*, *dé-*, O.F. *des-*, L. *dis-*, *di-*; or late L. *dis-*, L. *dē-*)], *pref.* Asunder, apart, away; between, separating, distinguishing; separately; (*intensively*) utterly, exceedingly; (*forming negative compounds*) not, the reverse of; undoing, depriving or expelling from.

disability (dis å bil′ i ti) [from obs. *disable*, unable], *n.* Want of physical or intellectual power, or pecuniary means; weakness, incapacity, inability; legal disqualifications.

disable (dis ā′ bėl), *v.t.* To render unable; to deprive of adequate, physical or intellectual power, to incapacitate; to disqualify legally; to injure so as to incapacitate, to cripple. **disablement,** *n.*

disabuse (dis å būz′), *v.t.* To free from error or misapprehension, to undeceive.

disaccord (dis å kôrd′), *v.i.* To disagree; to refuse assent. *n.* Disagreement; lack of harmony, incongruity.

disaccustom (dis å kŭs′ tȯm), *v.t.* To do away with a habit; to free from the force of custom.

disacknowledge (dis åk nol′ ėj), *v.t.* To disown, to deny acquaintance with.

disadvance (dis åd vans′) [O.F. *desavancer*], *v.t.* To draw back, to lower (as a weapon).

disadvantage (dis åd van′ tåj), *n.* Injury, detriment, hurt; an unfavourable position or condition. *v.t.* To cause disadvantage to. **disadvantageous** (-tā′ jůs), *a.* Prejudicial, detrimental; unfavourable to one's interests; disparaging, depreciative. **disadvantageously,** *adv.*

disadventurous (dis åd ven′ tyur ůs, -chur ůs), *a.* Unfortunate, unprosperous. **disadventure,** *n.* Misadventure, misfortune.

disaffect (dis å fekt′), *v.t.* (*chiefly in pass.*) To estrange, alienate the affection or loyalty of. **disaffected,** *a.* Alienated in affection, estranged; disloyal. **disaffectedly,** *adv.* **disaffection,** *n.* Alienation of feeling or affection, esp. from those in authority; disloyalty.

disaffirm (dis å fěrm′), *v.t.* To deny what has been affirmed; (*Law*) to reverse, to repudiate. ***disaffirmance,** *n.* **disaffirmation** (-mā′ shůn), *n.*

disafforest (dis å for′ ėst) [med. L. DIS-, *afforestāre*, to AFFOREST], *v.t.* To reduce from the legal status of forest to that of ordinary land; to strip of forest. **disafforestation** (-ta′ shůn), *n.*

disaggregate (dis ăg′ rė gāt), *v.t.* and *i.* To separate into components, parts, or particles. **disaggregation** (-gā′ shůn), *n.*

disagree (dis å grē′) [F. *désagréer*], *v.i.* To differ; to be different or unlike; to differ in opinion; to quarrel, to fall out; to be unsuitable or injurious (to health, digestion, etc.). **disagreeable,** *a.* Not in agreement or accord; offensive, unpleasant, repugnant; ill-tempered. *n.* (*usu. in pl.*) Annoyances, troubles, worries. **disagreeableness,** *n.* **disagreeably,** *adv.* **disagreement,** *n.* Want of agreement; unsuitableness, unfitness; difference of opinion; a quarrel, a falling out, dissension.

disallow (dis ȧ lou′) [O.F. *desalouer*], *v.t.* To refuse to sanction or permit; to refuse assent to; to disavow, to reject; to prohibit. *v.i.* To refuse allowance (of). ***disallowance,** *n.*

***disally** (dis ȧ lī′), *v.t.* To cancel the alliance of; to separate.

disanchor (dis ăng′ kôr), *v.t.* To weigh the anchor of. *v.i.* To weigh anchor, to depart.

***disanimate** (dis ăn′ i māt) [F. *désanimer*], *v.t.* To deprive of vitality, to discourage, to depress. ***disanimation** (-mā′ shŭn), *n.*

disannul (dis ȧ nŭl′), *v.t.* To annul, to abrogate. **disannulment,** *n.*

***disanoint** (dis ȧ noint′), *v.t.* To annul the consecration of.

***disapparel** (dis ȧ păr′ ėl), *v.t.* To disrobe, to strip.

disappear (dis ȧ pēr′), *v.i.* To go out of sight; to become invisible; to be lost; to cease to exist. **disappearance,** *n.*

disappoint (dis ȧ point′) [F. *désappointer*], *v.t.* To defeat of expectation, wish, hope, or desire; to frustrate, to hinder, to belie; to fail or neglect to keep an appointment with; *to annul the appointment of. **disappointed,** *a.* Frustrated, thwarted, deceived, or defeated in one's desires or expectations; *unfurnished, unprepared. **disappointedly,** *adv.* **disappointing,** *a.* **disappointingly,** *adv.* **disappointment,** *n.*

disapprobation (dis ăp rȯ bā′ shŭn), *n.* Disapproval, condemnation. **disapprobative** (dis ăp′ rȯ bā tiv), *a.* **disapprobatory,** *a.*

***disappropriate** (dis ȧ prō′ pri āt), *v.t.* To remove from individual possession; to sever, as an appropriation.

disapprove (dis ȧ proov′), *v.t.* To condemn or censure as wrong; to reject, as not approved of. **disapproval,** *n.* **disapprovingly,** *adv.*

disarm (dis arm′) [F. *désarmer*], *v.t.* To take the weapons away from; to deprive of weapons; to disband; to reduce to a peace footing; to dismantle; (*fig.*) to render harmless; to subdue, to tame. *v.i.* To lay aside arms; to be reduced to a peace footing; to reduce or abandon military and naval establishments. **disarmament,** *n.* Reduction of armaments by mutual agreement between nations. **disarmer,** *n.*

disarrange (dis ȧ rānj′), *v.t.* To put out of order; to derange. **disarrangement,** *n.*

disarray (dis ȧ rā′), *v.t.* To throw into confusion, to rout; *to undress, disrobe. *n.* Disorder, confusion; disorderly attire.

disarticulate (dis ȧr tik′ ū lāt), *v.t.* To separate the joints of, to disjoint. *v.i.* To become disjointed or separated at the joints. **disarticulation** (-lā′ shŭn), *n.*

disassimilation (dis ȧ sim i lā′ shŭn), *n.* The conversion of assimilated substances into such as are less complex or waste substances; catabolism.

disassociate (dis ȧ sō′ shi āt) [F. *désassocier* (DIS-, **associer,** ASSOCIATE)], *v.t.* To separate, to disjoin.

disaster (di zas′ tėr) [F. *désastre* (DIS-, *astre*, L. *astrum*, Gr. *astron*, a star)], *n.* A sudden misfortune, a calamity; misfortune, ill luck; *(*astrol.*) the influence of an unfavourable planet; an evil omen. **v.t.* To blast by the influence of an unfavourable planet; to injure, to disfigure. **disastrous,** *a.* Occasioning or threatening disaster; ruinous, calamitous. **disastrously,** *adv.*

disavow (dis ȧ vou′) [F. *désavouer* (DIS-, *avouer*, to AVOW)], *v.t.* To deny the truth of, to disown; to disapprove; to disclaim; to repudiate. **disavowal,** *n.*

disband (dis bănd′) [F. *desbander* (DIS-, O.F., BAND (4))], *v.t.* To break up (as a body of men in military service). *v.i.* To be disbanded; to separate, to disperse. **disbandment,** *n.*

disbar (dis bar′), *v.t.* (*past & p.p.* **disbarred**) To deprive of status as a barrister; to expel from membership of the bar.

disbelieve (dis bė lēv′), *v.t.* To refuse credit to, to refuse to believe in. *v.i.* To be a sceptic. **disbelief,** *n.* **disbeliever,** *n.*

***disbench** (dis bench′), *v.t.* To deprive of status as a bencher, to dismiss from senior membership of the Inns of Court; *to unseat.

disbody (dis bod′ i), *v.t.* To disembody.

disbosom (dis buz′ ŭm), *v.t.* To unbosom, to confess.

disbowel (dis bou′ ėl), *v.t.* To disembowel.

disbranch (dis branch′), *v.t.* To strip of branches; to sever (as a branch).

disbud (dis bŭd′), *v.t.* To cut away (esp. the superfluous) buds from.

disburden (dis bėr′ dėn), *v.t.* To remove a burden or encumbrance from; to relieve, to get rid of. *v.i.* To unload; to ease one's mind.

disburse (dis bėrs′) [O.F. *desbourser* (DIS-, BURSE)], *v.t.* To pay out, to expend; to defray. **disbursement,** *n.* **disburser,** *n.*

disc [DISK].

discalced (dis kăl′ sėd) [L. *discalceātus*, p.p. of *discalceāre* (DIS-, *calceāre*, to shoe, from *calceus*, a shoe)], *a.* Unshod, barefoot (of friars, nuns, etc.). *n.* A barefoot friar or nun. **discalceated,** *a.* **discalced,** *a.*

discandy (dis kăn′ di), *v.t.* To melt away, to dissolve.

discant [DESCANT].

discapacitate (dis kȧ păs′ i tāt), *v.t.* To incapacitate.

discard (dis kard′), *v.t.* To throw aside or away as useless; to get rid of, to reject; to cast aside; to dismiss; (*Whist, etc.*) to play (a particular card) that does not follow suit. *v.i.* To play a non-trump card that does not follow suit. *n.* The playing of useless cards; the card or cards so played; rejection as useless.

discarnate (dis kar′ nāt) [DIS-, L. *caro, carnis*, flesh], *a.* Having no flesh, disembodied.

discern (di zėrn′, -sėrn′) [F. *discerner*, L. *discernere* (DIS-, *cernere*, to separate)], *v.t.* *To discriminate, to perceive the difference between, to distinguish (from); to perceive distinctly with the senses, to make out; to recognize clearly or perceive mentally; to judge or decide between. *v.i.* To make distinction (between); to discriminate; to see. **discernible,** *a.* **discernibleness,** *n.* **discernibly,** *adv.* **discerning,** *a.* Having power to discern; discriminating, acute, penetrating. *n.* Discernment. **discerningly,** *adv.* **discernment,** *n.* The act, power, or faculty of discerning; clear discrimination, accurate judgment.

discerptible (di sėrp′ tibl) [L. *discerptus*, p.p. of *discerpere* (DIS-, *carpere*, to pick, to pluck), -IBLE], *a.* Separable, capable of being torn apart. **discerptibility** (-bil′ i ti), *n.* **discerption,** *n.* Severance, division into parts or pieces; a severed portion.

discharge (dis charj′) [O.F. *descharger*], *v.t.* To unload (from ship, vehicle, etc.); to take out or away, as a load; to get rid of; to emit, to let fly; to dismiss, to release from confinement; to relieve of a load; to set free from something binding; to fire off; to empty (as a cistern); to pay off; to settle; to perform; (*Dyeing*) to remove colour from by process of bleaching; *to cancel, to annul. *v.i.* To discharge a cargo; to unload or empty itself (as a river). *n.* The act of discharging; unloading, release, emission, firing off; payment, satisfaction; dismissal, release, acquittal, liberation, performance; a document certifying any of these; that which is discharged; (*Elec.*) neutralization or loss of electrical charge. **discharge in gases:** The passage of electricity through a tube containing gas at low pressure, used in fluorescent lighting. **discharge-valve,** *n.* A valve covering the top of the air-pump in marine engines, opening only to discharge. **discharger,** *n.* One who or that which discharges; (*Elec.*) a discharging rod. **discharging arch,** *n.* An arch in a wall (*e.g.* over a window) to relieve the part below from undue pressure. **discharging rod,** *n.* (*Elec.*) An instrument to discharge an electrical jar or battery by opening a communication between the two surfaces.

***discide** (di sīd′) [L. *discīdere* (DIS-, *cædere*, to cut)], *v.t.* To cut in two or in pieces.

disciple (di sī′ pėl) [A.-S. *discipul* and O.F. *deciple* (L. *discipulum*, acc. of *discipulus*, from *discere*, to learn), both assim. to L. spelling], *n.* A pupil or adherent of a philosopher, leader, or public teacher; one of the early followers, esp. one of the twelve personal followers of Christ. **v.t.* To teach; to make a disciple of; to discipline. **discipleship,** *n.* **discipular,** *a.*

discipline (dis′ i plin) [F., from L. *dīsciplīna*, as prec.], *n.* Instruction, training, exercise, or practice of the mental, moral, and physical powers to promote order, regularity, and efficient obedience; correction, chastisement; training supplied by adversity; military training; order, systematic obedience, methodical action, the state of being under control; (*R.-C. Ch.*) penitential chastisement, the instrument by which this is applied corporeally; (*Eccles.*) control over the members of a church, the rules binding on the members of a church, penal or reformatory action against a transgressor of these; *a branch of instructions; *military skill, generalship. *v.t.* To bring into a state of discipline; to teach, to train, to drill, esp. in obedience, orderly habits, and methodical action; to chastise, to chasten, to bring into a state of order and obedience. **disciplinal** (dis′ i plin ȧl, -plī′ nȧl), *a.* ***discipliner,** *n.* **disciplinable,** *a.* ***disciplinant,** *n.* One of a Spanish religious body of the Middle Ages who used to take discipline in public. **disciplinarian** (-nâr′ i ȧn), *a.* Pertaining to discipline. *n.* One who rigidly enforces discipline; one skilled in maintaining discipline; *a Puritan, a Presbyterian, esp. one of those who in the Elizabethan period endeavoured to introduce the Genevan or Presbyterian ecclesiastical system. **disciplinary** (dis′ i plin ȧr i), *a.* Pertaining to or promoting discipline; tending to promote efficient mental action.

disclaim (dis klām′) [A.-F. *desclamer*], *v.t.* To deny, to repudiate; to refuse to acknowledge, to disown, to disavow; to reject; (Law) to renounce, to relinquish or to disavow; *to decline, to refuse. **v.i.* To deny all claim or participation. **disclaimer,** *n.* The act of disclaiming; renunciation, disavowal, repudiation.

disclose (dis klōz′) [O.F. *desclore* (DIS-, L. *claudere*, to shut, p.p. *clausus*)], *v.t.* To uncover; to lay bare or open; to make known, to reveal, to divulge. **n.* A discovery, a coming to light. **disclosure** (dis klō′ zhŭr), *n.* The act of disclosing; that which is disclosed.

discobolus (dis kob′ ȯ lŭs) [L., from Gr. *diskobolos* (*diskos*, a quoit, *-bolos*, -thrower, from *ballein*, to throw)], *n.* (*pl.*) **-li**) (*Class. Ant.*) A quoit-thrower; a statue by Myron of an athlete throwing the discus.

discography (dis kog′ rȧ fi) [DISK, -GRAPH], *n.* The literature and study of gramophone records.

discoid, discoidal (dis′ koid, -koi′ dȧl) [L. *discoīdēs*, Gr. *diskoeidēs* (as prec., -OID)], *a.* Having the shape of a disk. **discoid flowers,** *n.pl.* (*Bot.*) Composite flowers not radiated but having the corollas tubular, as in the tansy. **discoidal shells,** *n.pl.* Univalve shells in which the whorls lie in the same plane.

discolour (dis kŭl′ ėr) [O.F. *descolorer*, med. L. *discolōrāre* (DIS-, L. *colōrāre*, in place of L. *dēcolōrāre*)], *v.t.* To alter the colour of; to give an unnatural colour to; to stain; to tarnish; to give a wrong colour to. *v.i.* To become stained or tarnished in colour; to fade, to become pale. **discoloration** (-ā′ shŭn), *n.* The act of discolouring; the state of being discoloured; a discoloured appearance, a spot, a stain. **discolourment,** *n.*

discomfit (dis kŭm′ fit) [O.F. *desconfit*, p.p. of *desconfire*, late L. *disconficere* (DIS-, *conficere*, to finish, to preserve)], *v.t.* To defeat, to rout; to scatter in fight; to thwart, to frustrate; to disconcert, to confound. **n.* Discomfiture. **discomfiture** (-tyŭr, -chŭr), *n.* Defeat, overthrow; disappointment, frustration.

discomfort (dis kŭm′ fȯrt) [O.F. *desconforter*], *v.t.* To deprive of comfort; to cause pain or uneasiness to. *n.* Deprivation of ease or comfort; uneasiness, disquietude, distress. ***discomfortable,** *a.* Causing or suffering discomfort; causing disquiet or discouragement.

***discommend** (dis kȯ mend′), *v.t.* To blame, to censure; to disapprove; to disparage. ***discommendable,** *a.* ***discommendation** (-dā′ shŭn), *n.*

discommode (dis kȯ mōd′) [DIS-, obs. v. *commode*, L. *commodāre*, to suit, from *commodus*, suitable], *v.t.* To incommode. ***discommodious,** *a.* Inconvenient, troublesome. ***discommodity** (-mod′ i ti), *n.*

***discommon** (dis kom′ ȯn), *v.t.* To appropriate from being common land; to deprive of the use of a common; to deprive of a privilege (esp. tradesmen in a University town who may be debarred from serving undergraduates).

discommons (dis kom′ ȯnz), *v.t.* (*Eng. Univ.*) To deprive of commons; to deprive (a tradesman) of the right to serve undergraduates.

discommunity (dis kȯ mū′ ni ti), *n.* Lack of community; absence of common properties or relations.

discompose (dis kȯm pōz′), *v.t.* To disturb, to destroy the composure of; to agitate, to vex, to disquiet; *to disarrange, to disorder. **discomposedly,** *adv.* **discomposingly,** *adv.* **discomposure** (-zhŭr), *n.* Want of composure; agitation, perturbation, disquiet; disorder.

disconcert (dis kȯn sĕrt′) [M.F. *disconcerter*], *v.t.* To derange, to disorder, to throw into confusion, to baffle, to foil, to defeat; to discompose, to disquiet. **disconcertment,** *n.* ***disconcertion** (-sĕr′ shŭn), *n.*

***disconformity** (dis kȯn fôr′ mi ti), *n.* A want of conformity of agreement; inconsistency.

***discongruity** (dis kȯn groo′ i ti), *n.* A want of congruity.

disconnect (dis kȯ nekt′), *v.t.* To separate; to disunite, to sever. *a.* Separated; incoherent, ill-connected. **disconnectedly,** *adv.* **disconnectedness,** *n.* **disconnecting-pit,** *n.* A pit in which a house-drain is separated from direct discharge into a main sewer. **disconnexion** (-nek′ shŭn), *n.* The act of disconnecting; the state of being separated, ill-connected, or incoherent.

disconsolate (dis kon′ sȯ lȧt) [late L. *disconsōlātus*, p.p. of *disconsōlārī* (DIS-, *consōlārī*, to CONSOLE)], *a.* Inconsolable, dejected, cheerless, forlorn; without hope or consolation; that cannot be consoled or comforted; not affording comfort or consolation. **disconsolately,** *adv.* **disconsolateness,** *n.* ***disconsolation** (-lā′ shŭn), *n.*

discontent (dis kȯn tent′), *n.* Want of content; dissatisfaction; cause of dissatisfaction, a grievance; (*pl.*) a feeling of dissatisfaction or annoyance; *a discontented person. *a.* Not content, dissatisfied. *v.t.* To make discontented, dissatisfied, or uneasy. **discontented,** *a.* Dissatisfied, uneasy, disquiet. **discontentedly,** *adv.* **discontentedness,** *n.* **discontentment,** *n.*

discontiguous (dis kȯn tig′ ū ŭs), *a.* Not contiguous; having the parts not in contact.

discontinue (dis kȯn tin′ ū) [F. *discontinuer*, late L. *discontinuāre* (DIS-, L. *continuāre*], *v.t.* To break off, to interrupt; to leave off, to cease to use; to give up. *v.i.* To cease; to lose continuity. **discontinuance,** *n.* Interruption of continuance; a break in succession; cessation, interruption, intermission; (*Law*) an interruption or breaking-off of possession. **discontinuance of a suit:** (*Law*) Failure on the part of a plantiff to carry on a suit, by not continuing it as the law requires. ***discontinuation** (-ā' shŭn), *n.* **discontinuous,** *a.* Not continuous, disconnected; incoherent; intermittent, *gaping. **discontinuity** (-nū' i ti), *n.* **discontinuously,** *adv.*

discord (dis' kôrd) [O.F. *descord,* from *descorder,* L. *discordāre* (DIS-, *cor cordis,* the heart)], *n.* Want of concord or agreement; disagreement, contention, strife; disagreement or opposition in quality, esp. in sounds; (*Mus.*) a lack of harmony in a combination of notes sounded together; the sounding together of two or more inharmonious or inconclusive notes; the interval or the chord so sounded; a note that is out of harmony with another. *v.i.* (dis kôrd') To be out of harmony (with); to disagree; to be inconsistent, to clash (with). **discordance,** *n.* **discordant,** *a.* Disagreeing, not in accord, unpleasing, esp. to the ear; opposite, contradictory: inconsistent; causing discord. **discordantly,** *adv.* ***discordful,** *a.* Quarrelsome, contentious.

discorporate (dis kôr' pŏ răt), *a.* Not incorporated, disunited.

***discounsel** (dis koun' sĕl), *v.t.* To dissuade, disadvise.

discount (1) (dis kount') [O.F. *desconter,* late L. *discomputāre* (DIS-, L. *computāre,* to COMPUTE)], *v.t.* To deduct a certain sum or rate per cent from (an account or price); to lend or advance the amount of; deducting interest at a certain rate per cent from the principal; to leave out of account; to anticipate, to enjoy beforehand; to make allowance for, to make little account of, to disregard. *v.i.* To advance money on bills and other documents due at some future date, deducting the interest at the time of the loan.

discount (2) (dis' kount), *n.* A deduction from the amount of a price or an account for early or immediate payment; a deduction at a certain rate from money advanced on a bill of exchange which is not yet due; the deduction of a sum for payment in advance; the act of discounting; the rate of discount; allowance for exaggeration. **at a discount:** Depreciated; below par; not in much esteem. **discount-broker,** *n.* One who cashes bills of exchange; a bill-broker. **discount-day,** *n.* The day of the week on which the bank discounts bills and notes. **discountable,** *a.*

discountenance (dis koun' tĕ năns) [M.F. *descontenancer*], *v.t.* To discourage; to set one's face against; to express disapprobation of; to put out of countenance, to abash. **n.* Discouragement, disfavour.

discourage (dis kŭr' ăj) [O.F. *descoragier*], *v.t.* To deprive of courage; to dishearten, to dispirit; to discountenance; to deter (from). **discouragement,** *n.* **discourager,** *n.* **discouraging,** *a.* **discouragingly,** *adv.*

discourse (dis' kôrs) [F. *discours,* L. *discursus,* p.p. of *discurrere* (DIS-, *currere,* to run)], *n.* Talk, conversation, exchange of ideas; a dissertation, a lecture or sermon; a formal treatise; *the process of reasoning; *familiar intercourse. (dis kôrs'), *v.t.* To utter, to give forth; to pass (time) in conversation; to tell, to narrate; to discuss. *v.i.* To talk, to speak, to converse; to talk formally, to hold forth (upon). ***discourse of reason,** *n.* Use or exercise of the faculty of reason.

discourteous (dis kĕr'-, -kôr' tĕ ŭs), *a.* Uncourteous, uncivil, rude. **discourteously,** *adv.* **discourteousness,** *n.* **discourtesy,** *n.*

discover (dis kŭv' ĕr) [O.F. *descovrir,* med. L. *discooperīre* (DIS-, L. cooperīre, to COVER)], *v.t.* To disclose, to reveal, to make known, to betray; to gain the first sight of; to find out by exploration; to ascertain, to realize suddenly; to detect; *to explore; *to uncover. **discoverable,** *a.* **discoverer,** *n.* One who discovers; *an explorer, *a spy, a scout.

discovert (dis kŭv' ĕrt) [O.F. *descovert,* p.p. of prec.], *a.* Uncovered, exposed, unprotected; (*Law*) not covert, not protected by a husband, unmarried or widowed. ***at discovert:** Uncovered or exposed. **discoverture,** *n.* (*Law*) The state of an unmarried woman or a widow; freedom from coverture.

discovery (dis kŭv' ĕr i), *n.* The act of discovering; that which is made known for the first time; something that is found out; revelation, disclosure, manifestation; the unravelling of the plot of a play; (*Law*) compulsory disclosure of facts and documents essential to the proper consideration of a case.

discredit (dis kred' it), *n.* Want or loss of credit; disrepute, disgrace; the cause of disrepute or disgrace; disbelief; lack of credibility; loss of commercial credit. *v.t.* To disbelieve; to bring into disrepute; to deprive of credibility. **discreditable,** *a.* Tending to discredit; disreputable, disgraceful. **discreditably,** *adv.*

discreet (dis krēt') [F. *discret,* L. *discrētus,* p.p. of *discernere,* to DISCERN (differentiated from DISCRETE by late L. sense, discerning, distinguishing, judicious)], *a.* Prudent, wary, circumspect; judicious, careful in choosing the best means of action; (*Sc.*) polite, well-spoken, decently behaved; *discrete; *needing discretion. **discreetly,** *adv.* **discreetness,** *n.*

discrepant (dis krep' ănt) [L. *discrepans -antem,* pres.p. of *discrepāre* (DIS-, *crepāre,* to sound)], *a.* Differing, disagreeing, inconsistent. **discrepancy,** *n.*

discrete (dis krēt') [L. *discrētus,* DISCREET], *a.* Distinct, discontinuous, detached, separate; (*Mus.*) applied to a movement in which the successive notes vary considerably in pitch; (*Phil.*) not concrete, abstract. **discrete proportion,** *n.* A proportion in which the ratio of the first term to the second = that of the third to the fourth, but does not = that of the second to the third, as, for example, 5 : 10 :: 9 : 18. **discreteness,** *n.* **discretive,** *a.* Disjunctive, separate. **discretive proposition,** *n.* A proposition in which some opposition or contrariety is noted by the use of a discretive particle. **discretively,** *adv.*

discretion (dis kresh' ŭn) [O.F. *discrecion*], *n.* The power or faculty of distinguishing things that differ, or discriminating correctly between what is right and wrong, useful and injurious; discernment, judgment, circumspection; freedom of judgment and action; *separation, distinction. **at discretion:** At the judgment or pleasure (of). **to surrender at discretion:** To surrender unconditionally. **years of discretion:** The age when one is capable of exercising one's own judgment, (*Eng. Law*) the age of 14. ***discretional,** *a.* ***discretionally,** *adv.* **discretionary,** *a.*

discriminate (dis krim' i năt) [L. *discrīminātus,* p.p. of *discrīmināre* (*discrīmen,* separation, distinction, from *discernere,* to DISCERN)], *v.t.* To distinguish; to mark or observe the difference or distinction between; to distinguish by marks of difference, to differentiate. *v.i.* To make a distinction or difference; to mark the difference between things. *a.* (-năt) Distinctive; having the difference clearly marked. **to discriminate against:** To distinguish or deal with unfairly or unfavourably. **discriminately,** *adv.* **discriminating,** *a.* Distinguishing clearly, distinctive; exercising discrimination, discerning. **discriminating duties, rates,** *etc.*: Such as fall unequally on different parties according to their country, position, etc.; differential duties, etc. **discriminatingly,** *adv.* **discrimination** (-nā' shŭn), *n.* The power or faculty of discriminating; discernment, penetration, judgment; the act of discriminating; a distinguishing mark or feature. **discriminative,** *a.* Serving to distinguish; observing distinctions or differences. ***discriminatively,** *adv.* **discriminator,** *n.* **discriminatory** (dis krim' i nā tòr i), *a.*

discrown (dis kroun'), *v.t.* To divest or deprive of a crown; to depose.

disculpate (dis kŭl' pāt) [L. *disculpātus*, p.p. of *disculpāre* (DIS-, *culpāre*, to blame)], *v.t.* To exculpate.

discumber (dis kŭm' bėr), *v.t.* To disencumber.

discursive (dis kĕr' siv) [L. *discurs-*, p.p. stem of *discurrere*, see DISCOURSE], *a.* Passing from one subject to another; rambling, desultory; (*Psych. and Log.*) rational, argumentative, ratiocinative as opp. to intuitive. **discursively,** *adv.* **discursiveness,** *n.*

discus (dis' kŭs) [L., from Gr. *diskos*], *n.* (*Class. Ant.*) A metal disk thrown in athletic sports, a quoit.

discuss (dis kŭs') [L. *discussus*, p.p. of *discutere*, to shake asunder, late L., to discuss (DIS-, *quatere*, to shake)], *v.t.* To debate; to consider or examine by argument; (*fig.*) to try the flavour of (as a dish, wine, etc.); (*Med.*) to break up, to disperse (as a tumour); (*Sc. Law*) to proceed against by discussion; to put aside, shake off; *to make known. **discussible,** *a.* **discussion** (dis kŭsh' ŭn), *n.* The act of discussing; consideration or investigation by argument for and against; the enjoyment of food; (*Med.*) scattering, dispersion; (*Sc. Law*) the proceeding against a principal debtor before proceeding against his surety or sureties, or against an heir for a debt due from his ancestor in respect of the subject inherited before proceeding against the other heirs. **discussion group:** A group (in school, club, etc.) formed to discuss current political and other topics.

discutient (dis kū' shi ėnt), *a.* (*Med.*) Having power to disperse morbid matter. *n.* A discutient preparation.

disdain (dis dān') [O.F. *desdein*, from *desdaigner* (F. *dédaigner*), to scorn, from L. *dēdignārī* (DE-, *dignārī*, to deem worthy, from *dignus*, worthy)], *n.* Scorn, a feeling of contempt combined with haughtiness and indignation; *shame, disgrace; *that which is worthy of disdain. *v.t.* To regard as unworthy of notice; to despise or repulse as unworthy of oneself; to scorn, to contemn. *v.i.* To feel or manifest scorn. **disdained,** *a.* Treated with disdain; *disdainful. **disdainful,** *a.* **disdainfully,** *adv.* ***disdainfulness,** *n.*

dis-ease (dis ēz'), *n.* Lack of ease, discomfort. **v.t.* To deprive of ease; *to disturb.

disease (di zēz') [O.F. *desaise*], *n.* Any alteration of the normal vital processes of man, the lower animals, or plants, under the influence of some unnatural or hurtful condition; any disorder or morbid condition, habit, or function, mental, moral, social, etc. **diseased,** *a.* Affected with disease; morbid, unhealthy, deranged. ***diseaseful,** *a.* Troublesome; affected with disease.

disedify (dis ed' i fī), *v.t.* To shock, to scandalize; to weaken the faith of. **disedification** (kā' shŭn), *n.*

disembark (dis ėm bark') [F. *désembarquer*], *v.t.* To put on shore. *v.i.* To come on shore. **disembarkation** (-kā' shŭn), *n.*

disembarrass (dis ėm băr' ȧs), *v.t.* To free from embarrassment or perplexity; to disencumber (of); to liberate (from). **disembarrassment,** *n.*

disembellish (dis ėm bel' ish), *v.t.* To divest of ornament.

disembody (dis ėm bod' i), *v.t.* To divest of body or the flesh; to free from the concrete; to disband. **disembodiment,** *n.*

disembogue (dis ėm bōg') [Sp. *desembocar* (*des-*, DIS-, *em-*, IN-, *boca*, the mouth, L. *bucca*, cheek, mouth)], *v.t.* To pour out or discharge at the mouth, as a stream; (*fig.*) to pour forth, to empty itself. **v.i.* To flow out; to be discharged at an outlet, as at the mouth; *(*Naut.*) to pass out at the mouth of a river, bay, gulf, etc. ***disemboguement,** *n.*

disembosom (dis ėm buz' ŭm), *v.t.* To unbosom (oneself); to reveal. *v.i.* To make confidences.

disembowel (dis ėm bou' ėl), *v.t.* To take out the bowels of, to eviscerate; to lacerate so as to let the bowels protrude; *to draw from the bowels (as a spider does its web).

disembroil (dis ėm broil'), *v.t.* To free from confusion or perplexity.

disemburden (dis ėm bĕrd' ėn), *v.t.* To disburden.

disenable (dis ė nābl'), *v.t.* To disable, to incapacitate (from).

disenchain (dis ėn chān'), *v.t.* To set free from restraint.

disenchant (dis ėn chant') [F. *désenchanter*], *v.t.* To free from enchantment or glamour, to free from a spell; to disillusion. **disenchanter,** *n.* **disenchantment,** *n.*

disencumber (dis ėn kŭm' bėr) [F. *désencombrer*], *v.t.* To free from encumbrance.

disendow (dis ėn dou'), *v.t.* To strip of endowments. **disendowment,** *n.*

disenfranchise (dis ėn frăn' chīz), *v.t.* To disfranchise. **disenfranchisement,** *n.*

disengage (dis ėn gāj'), *v.t.* To separate; to loosen, to detach; to withdraw (oneself); to release; to disentangle; to set free from any engagement; (*Fencing*) to pass the point of one's foil to the other side of one's adversary's. *n.* (*Fencing*) The act of disengaging. **disengaged,** *a.* Separated, disjoined; at leisure, having the attention unoccupied; free from any engagement. ***disengagedness,** *n.* **disengagement,** *n.* The act of disengaging; extrication; (*Chem.*) liberation of a component; the state of being disengaged; freedom from mental occupation or care; detachment; ease, freedom of manner; dissolution of a matrimonial engagement; (*Fencing*) a disengage.

disentail (dis ėn tāl'), *v.t.* (*Law*) To free from or break the entail of.

disentangle (dis ėn tăng' gėl), *v.t.* To unravel, to free from entanglement; to disengage, to disembarrass. *v.i.* To come clear (from). **disentanglement,** *n.*

disenthral (dis ėn thrawl'), *v.t.* To set free from thraldom, to emancipate. **disenthralment,** *n.*

disestablish (dis ės tăb' lish), *v.t.* To annul the establishment of, esp. to deprive a Church of its connexion with the State; to depose from established use or position. **disestablishment,** *n.*

disesteem (dis ės tēm'), *n.* A lack of esteem or regard. *v.t.* To look upon without esteem; to slight, despise.

diseur (dē' zĕr) [F.], *n.* A reciter (fem. **diseuse**).

disfame (dis fām'), *n.* Ill-fame, dishonour.

disfavour (dis fā' vòr), *n.* A feeling of dislike or disapprobation; disesteem; displeasure, odium; *an ungracious or disobliging act. *v.t.* To treat or regard with disfavour, to discountenance.

disfeature (dis fē' tyŭr, -chŭr), *v.t.* To deprive of a feature; to deface, disfigure.

disfellowship (dis fel' ō ship), *n.* Lack of fellowship. *v.t.* (*Am.*) To exclude from fellowship, esp. of a church.

disfigure (dis fig' ŭr) [O.F. *desfigurer* (*des-*, DIS-, *figurer*, L. *figūrāre*, the fashion; from *figūra*, FIGURE)], *v.t.* To injure the beauty or appearance of; to deform, to mar, to spoil, to sully. **disfigurement,** *n.* **disfiguration** (ā' shŭn), *n.* **disfigurer,** *n.*

disforest (dis for' ėst) [O.F. *desforester*], *v.t.* To disafforest, to clear of forest.

disform (dis fôrm'), *v.i.* To alter in form.

disfranchise (dis frăn' chīz), *v.t.* To deprive of electoral privileges; to withdraw the rights of citizenship from. **disfranchisement,** *n.*

disfrock (dis frok'), *v.t.* To strip of clerical attire; to depose from the clerical office.

disfurnish (dis fĕr′ nish) [O.F. *desfourniss-*, stem of *desfournir* (DIS-, *fournir* to FURNISH)], *v.t.* To strip of equipments, apparatus, or furniture; to strip, to deprive.

disgarnish (dis gar′ nish) [O.F. *desgarniss-*, *desgarnir* (DIS-, *garnir*, to GARNISH)], *v.t.* To disfurnish, to despoil.

disgorge (dis gŏrj′) [O.F. *desgorger* (DIS-, GORGE)], *v.t.* To eject from the mouth or stomach; to vomit; to empty (as a river); (*fig.*) to give up (esp. what has been unjustly acquired). *v.i.* To yield, give up, surrender; to disembogue, to discharge.

disgrace (dis grās′) [F. *disgrâce*, It. *disgrazia*, med. L. *disgrātia* (DIS-, L. *grātia*, GRACE)], *n.* The state of being out of favour; disesteem, discredit, ignominy, shame, a fall from honour or favour; infamy; the cause or occasion of discredit or shame; *opprobrium, reprobation, *a loss or lack of grace or of decency. *v.t.* To dismiss from favour; to degrade; to dishonour; to bring disgrace on. **disgraceful,** *a.* **disgracefully,** *adv.* **disgracefulness,** *n.* ***disgracious,** *a.* Ungracious; out of favour.

disgruntled (dis grŭnt′ ėld) [DIS-, *gruntle*, obs. freq. of GRUNT], *a.* (*colloq.*) Disgusted, offended, disappointed, discontented.

disguise (dis gīz′) [O.F. *deguisier*], *v.t.* To conceal or alter the appearance of, with a mask or unusual dress; (*fig.*) to hide by a counterfeit appearance; to alter, to misrepresent; (*slang*) to intoxicate. *n.* A dress, mask, or manner put on to disguise or conceal; a pretence or show; *a masque, an interlude, a mummery; *the state of intoxication. **disguisement,** *n.* **disguiser,** *n.* One who or that which disguises; a masquer, a mummer. **disguising,** *n.* The act of concealing with or wearing a disguise; *a masque; mummery.

disgust (dis gŭst′) [M.F. *desgouster* (DIS-, L. *gustāre*, to taste)], *v.t.* To excite loathing or aversion in; to offend the taste of. *n.* A strong disrelish or distaste; aversion, loathing, repulsion. **disgustedly,** *adv.* ***disgustful,** *a.* Causing disgust, disgusting; full of or inspired by disgust. **disgusting,** *a.* **disgustingly,** *adv.*

dish (dish) [A.-S. *disc*, L. *discus*, DISK], *n.* A broad, shallow, open vessel for serving up food at table; the food so served; any particular kind of food; *a deep, hollow vessel for liquors; *a cup; any dish-like utensil, receptacle, or concavity; (*Mining*) a box, containing 672 cub. in., for measuring ore. *v.t.* To put into or serve in a dish; (*fig.*) to prepare; to make concave; (*colloq.*) to foil, to disappoint, to frustrate. *v.i.* To assume a concave form. **made dish:** A dish compounded of various ingredients. **side-dish:** An extra dish at a meal. **standing dish:** A dish that is brought in day after day; a familiar topic, grievance, etc. **to dish up:** To prepare, to serve up; to present in an attractive way. ***dish of tea:** A tea-drinking; whence, **dish of gossip:** A chat; tittle-tattle. **dish-cloth, -clout,** *n.* A cloth used for washing up dishes, plates, etc. **dish-cover,** *n.* A cover of metal or earthenware for keeping food warm in a dish. **dish-mat,** *n.* A mat on which dishes are placed. **dish-pan,** *n.* (*Am.*) A washing-up bowl. **dish-towel,** *n.* (*Am.*) A tea-cloth. **dish-wash, -water,** *n.* Water in which dishes have been washed. **dishwasher,** *n.* (*Zool.*) The pied wagtail, *Motacilla lugubris*. **dished wheel,** *n.* One that has been made concave, the spokes slanting outward from the nave.

dishabille [DESHABILLE].

dishabit (dis hăb′ it), *v.t.* To move from its place; to expel from a habitation.

dishabituate (dis hȧ bit′ ū āt), *v.t.* To make unaccustomed (to).

dishallow (dis hăl′ ō), *v.t.* To make unholy; to profane.

dishallucination (dis hȧ lū si nā′ shŭn), *n.* Release from hallucination; disillusion.

disharmony (dis har′ mȯ ni), *v.t.* Lack of harmony; discord incongruity. **disharmonious** (-mō′ ni ŭs), *a.* **disharmonize** (dis har′ mȯ nīz), *v.t.* and *i.*

dishearten (dis har′ tėn), *v.t.* To discourage, to dispirit. **disheartenment,** *n.*

***disherit** (dis her′ it) [O.F. *desheriter* (*des-*, DIS-, *heriter*, L. *hērēditāre*, to inherit, from *hērēditās*, heirship)], *v.t.* To disinherit; to dispossess. ***disherison,** *n.* The act of disinheriting.

dishevel (di shev′ ėl) [O.F. *descheveler* (*des-*, DIS-, *chevel*, L. *capillum*, acc. of *capillus*, hair)], *v.t.* To disorder (the hair); to let (the hair) down. *v.i.* To be spread in disorder. **dishevelled,** *a.* Flowing in disorder; hanging loosely and negligently; with disordered hair; untidy, unkempt. **dishevelment,** *n.*

dishonest (dis on′ ėst) [O.F. *deshoneste*, L. *dehonestus* (DE-, *honestus*, HONEST)], *a.* Destitute of honesty, probity, or good faith; fraudulent, deceitful, insincere, untrustworthy; *dishonourable, disgraced; disgraceful; *unchaste, lewd. **dishonestly,** *adv.* **dishonesty,** *n.* Want of honesty or uprightness; fraud, cheating, violation of duty or trust; *disgrace, dishonour; *unchastity, lewdness.

dishonour (dis on′ ȯr) [O.F. *deshonneur* (DIS-, L. *honor -em*, HONOUR)], *n.* Lack of honour; disgrace, discredit, ignominy; reproach, disparagement; the cause of this; refusal to honour a cheque, etc. *v.i.* To bring disgrace or shame on; to damage the reputation of; to treat with indignity; to violate the chastity of; to refuse to accept or pay (as a bill or draft). **dishonourable,** *a.* Causing dishonour; disgraceful, ignominious; unprincipled, mean, base; destitute of honour. **dishonourableness,** *n.* **dishonourably,** *adv.* **dishonourer,** *n.* One who dishonours; a debaucher.

dishorn (dis hôrn′), *v.t.* To deprive of horns.

dishorse (dis hôrs′), *v.t.* To unhorse.

dishwasher [DISH].

disilluminate (dis i loo′ mi nāt), *v.t.* To deprive of light; to obscure.

disillusion (dis i loo′ zhŭn), *v.t.* To free or deliver from an illusion; to undeceive. *n.* Disenchantment; release from an illusion. **disillusionize,** *v.t.* **disillusionment,** *n.*

disimpassioned (dis im păsh′ ȯnd), *a.* Dispassionately, tranquillized.

disimprison (dis im priz′ ȯn), *v.t.* To release from captivity; to liberate.

disincline (dis in klīn′), *v.t.* To make averse or indisposed (to). **disinclination** (-nā′ shŭn), *n.* A want of inclination, desire, or propensity; unwillingness.

disincorporate (dis in kôr′ pȯ rāt), *v.t.* To deprive of the rights, powers, or privileges of a corporate body; to dissolve (such a body). **disincorporation** (-rā′ shŭn), *n.*

disindividualize (dis in di vid′ ū ȧ līz), *v.t.* To take away the individuality of.

disinfect (dis in fekt′), *v.t.* To free or cleanse from infection. **disinfectant,** *n.* That which removes infection by destroying its causes. **disinfection,** *n.* **disinfector,** *n.*

disinfest (dis in fest′), *v.t.* To rid of vermin, rats and insects, esp. lice. **disinfestation,** *n.*

disingenuous (dis in jėn′ ū ŭs), *a.* Not ingenuous; wanting in frankness, openness, or candour; underhand, insincere. **disingenuously,** *adv.* **disingenuousness,** *n.*

disinherit (dis in her′ it), *v.t.* To cut off from an hereditary right; to deprive of an inheritance; (*fig.*) to dispossess. ***disinherison,** *n.* **disinheritance,** *n.*

disinhume (dis in hūm′), *v.t.* To exhume, to disinter.

disintegrate (dis in′ tė grāt), *v.t.* To separate into component parts; to reduce to fragments or powder. *v.i.* To fall to pieces, to crumble, to lose cohesion.

disintegrable, *a.* **disintegration** (-grā′ shŭn), *n.* The separation of a solid body into its component parts; (*Geol.*) the wearing down of rocks by the action of the weather. **disintegrator,** *n.* One who or that which causes disintegration; a machine for grinding bones, etc.

disinter (dis in tĕr′) [F. *désenterrer*], *v.t.* To dig up, esp. from a grave; (*fig.*) to unearth. **disinterment,** *n.*

disinterest (dis in′ tėr ėst), *n.* Impartiality, disinterestedness; *disadvantage, prejudice. *v.t.* *To divest of personal interest, to make disinterested. **disinterested,** *a.* Without personal interest or prejudice; unbiased, impartial, unselfish. **disinterestedly,** *adv.* **disinterestedness,** *n.*

disjasked (dis jăsk′ ėd) [Sc.; probl corr. of DEJECTED], *a.* Broken-down, worn-out; jaded.

disjoin (dis join′) [O.F. *desjoign-*, *desjoindre*, L. *disjungere* (DIS-, *jungere*, to JOIN)], *v.t.* To separate, to put asunder. **v.i.* To be separated, to part.

disjoint (dis joint′) [O.F. *desjoint*, p.p. of *desjoindre*, as prec.], *v.t.* To put out of joint, to dislocate; to separate at the joints; (*fig.*) to derange, to put out of working order; to break the connexion of. **v.i.* To fall in pieces. *a.* Disjointed, disconnected, out of order. **disjointed,** *a.* Out of joint; broken up, incoherent. **disjointedly,** *adv.* **disjointedness,** *n.*

disjunction (dis jŭngk′ shŭn) [L. *disjunctio*, from *disjungere*, as prec.], *n.* The act of disjoining; separation; (*Log.*) a disjunctive proposition. **disjunct,** *a.* Disjoined (in various technical applications). **disjunctive,** *a.* Separating, disjoining; marking separation. *n.* A disjunctive particle; (*Log.*) a disjunctive proposition. **disjunctive conjunction,** *n.* A conjunction (as *or*, *but*, *though*, etc.) which unites sentences or clauses in composition, but divides them in sense. **disjunctive proposition,** *n.* (*Log.*) A proposition with alternate predicates united by the conj. *or*. **disjunctive syllogism,** *n.* (*Log.*) A syllogism in which the major is a disjunctive proposition. **disjunctively,** *adv.*

***disjune** (dis joon′) [Sc., from O.F. *desjun*, *déjeuner*], *n.* Breakfast.

disk (disk) [L. *discus*, Gr. *diskos*], *n.* A flat circular plate or surface; a gramophone record; (*Astron.*) the face of a celestial body, any round luminous and apparently flat object; (*Bot.*) the central part of a radiate compound flower; (*Zool.*) a round flattish part of an animal organism; (*Anat.*) a layer of fibro-cartilage between vertebræ. **slipped disk,** *n.* (*Med.*) A displacement of this. **disk brake,** *n.* Brake comprising a metal disk attached to the axle, on the opposite surfaces of which the pads press. **disk harrow,** *n.* (*Agric.*) A harrow consisting of sharpened saucer-shaped disks for cutting clods of soil. **disk jockey,** *n.* (*Radio.*) The compère of a programme of gramophone records. **disk scanner,** *n.* (*T.V.*) A rotating disk carrying the picture-scanning elements.

***disleal** (dis lēl′) [prob. from It. *disleale* (DIS-, LEAL)], *a.* Disloyal.

dislike (dis līk), *v.t.* To regard with repugnance or aversion; *to displease; *to express aversion towards. *n.* A feeling of repugnance; aversion. ***dislikeful,** *a.* Disagreeable, unpleasant. **disliker,** *n.* **disliking,** *n.* and *a.*

disload (dis lōd′), *v.t.* and *i.* To unload.

dislocate (dis′ lȯ kāt) [late L. *dislocātus*, p.p. of *dislocāre* (DIS-, *locāre*, to place, from *locus*, place)], *v.t.* To put out of joint; to disturb, derange; (*Geol.*) to break the continuity of strata, to displace. **dislocation** (-kā′ shŭn), *n.*

dislodge (dis loj′) [O.F. *desloger*], *v.t.* To eject from a place of rest, retirement, or defence; to drive out, to expel. *v.i.* To quit a place, to remove. **dislodgement,** *n.*

disloyal (dis loi′ ȧl) [O.F. *desloial*], *a.* Not true to allegiance; unfaithful to the sovereign, disaffected towards the government. **disloyally,** *adv.* **disloyalty,** *n.*

dismal (diz′ mȧl) [O.F. *dis mal*, L. *diēs mali*, evil days, unlucky days], *a.* Dark, cheerless, depressing, doleful, dreary; *unlucky, unpropitious, sinister, bodeful, disastrous. *n.pl.* Low spirits, the blues. **dismally,** *adv.* **dismalness,** *n.*

***disman** (dis măn′), *v.t.* To unman; to divest of men.

dismantle (dis măn′ tėl) [M.F. desmanteller (DIS-MANTLE)], *v.t.* To strip of covering, equipment, or means of defence; to take to pieces; to unrig (as a ship); to remove the defences (of a fortress). **dismantlement,** *n.*

***dismask** (dis mask′) [O.F. *desmasquer*], *v.t.* To unmask.

dismast (dis mast′), *v.t.* To deprive a ship of a mast or masts.

dismay (dis mā′) [prob. O.F. *des-*, DIS-, *mayer*, O.H.G. *magan*, to be able, to have power, cogn. with A.-S. *magan*, MAY (I) (cp. *esmayer*, to lose power, to faint, also Sp. *desmayer*, to DISMAY)], *v.t.* To deprive of courage; to dispirit; to terrify, to daunt; *to vanquish. **v.i.* To be dismayed. *n.* Utter loss of courage or resolution; a state of terror or affright; *ruin, destruction. ***dismayful,** *a.*

***dismayd** (dis mād′) [perh. DIS-, MADE], *a.* (*Spens.*) Misshapen, deformed (?).

dismember (dis mem′ bėr) [O.F. *desmembrer*], *v.t.* To separate limb from limb; to divide, to distribute, to partition; (*fig.*) to tear asunder. **dismemberment,** *n.*

dismiss (dis mis′) [L. *dīmittere* (DI, *mittere*, to send), *dis-*, due to influence of O.F. *desmettre* (p.p. *dismit*)], *v.t.* To send away; to dissolve, disband; to allow to depart; to discharge from office or employment; to put aside, reject; to cast off, discard; to pass on to something else; (*Law*) to discharge from further consideration; (*Mil. command*) Break ranks! Disperse! **dismissal,** *n.* **dismissible,** *a.* ***dismission,** *n.* ***dismissive,** *a.*

dismount (dis mount′) [prob. from O.F. *desmonter*], *v.i.* To alight from a horse; *to descend. *v.t.* To throw down or remove from a carriage or support (as cannon); to unhorse; to take down or to pieces; *to get down from; *to bring down, to lower; *to withdraw a sheathed sword from its frog. *n.* The act of dismounting, the mode of dismounting.

disnature (dis nā′ chŭr) [O.F. *desnaturer*], *v.t.* To render unnatural; to divest of essential nature. **disnaturalize** (dis năt′ ū rȧ līz), *v.t.* To denaturalize.

disobedience (dis ȯ bē′ di ėns) [O.F. *desobedience*], *n*, Refusal to obey; wilful neglect or violation of duty; non-compliance. **disobedient,** *a.* Refusing or neglecting to obey; refractory. **disobediently,** *adv.*

disobey (dis ȯ bā′) [F. *désobéir*], *v.t.* To neglect or refuse to obey; to violate, transgress. *v.i.* To be disobedient. **disobeyer,** *n.*

disoblige (dis ȯ blīj′) [F. *désobliger*], *v.t.* To act in a manner contrary to the wishes or convenience of; to inconvenience, to incommode; *to release from an obligation. ***disobligation,** *n.* A disobliging act; freedom from obligation. ***disobligement,** *n.* The act of disobliging; the state of being released from an obligation. **disobliging,** *a.* Not obliging, not disposed to gratify the wishes of another; churlish, ungracious. **disobligingly,** *adv.* **disobligingness,** *n.*

disorb (dis ôrb′), *v.t.* *To unsphere, to remove from its orbit; to deprive of the orb of sovereignty.

disorder (dis ôr′ dėr) [F. *desordre* (DIS-, ORDER)], *n.* Want of order; confusion, irregularity; tumult, commotion; neglect or infraction of laws or discipline; discomposure of mind; derangement of the animal economy, disease, illness. *v.t.* To throw into confusion; to derange the natural functions of. **disorderly,** *a.* Confused, disarranged; unlawful, irregular; turbulent, causing disturbance, unruly. **disorderly house,** *n.* (*Law*) A term including brothels, gaming-houses, betting-houses, and certain unlicensed places of entertainment. **disorderliness,** *n.* ***disordinate,** *a.* Inordinate, excessive; disorderly, irregular, vicious. ***disordinately,** *adv.*

disorganize (dis ŏr′ gȧ nīz) [F. *désorganizer*], *v.t.* To throw into confusion; to destroy the systematic arrangement of. **disorganization** (-zā′ shŭn), *n.*

disorient (dis ôr′ i ėnt) [F. *désorienter* (DIS-, *orienter*, to ORIENT)], *v.t.* To turn from the east; to throw out of one's reckoning. **disorientate,** *v.t.* To disorient; to place (a church) with the chancel not pointing due east. **disorientation** (-tā′ shŭn), *n.*

disown (dis ōn′), *v.t.* To refuse to own; to disclaim, to renounce, to repudiate. **disownment,** *n.*

disoxygenate [DEOXYGENATE].

dispace (dis pās′) [formation obscure], *v.i.* (*Spens.*) To wander to and fro.

disparage (dis păr′ ȧj) [O.F. *desparagier* (*des-*, DIS-, *parage*, lineage, rank, late L. *parāgium, parāticum*, from *par*, equal)], *v.t.* To think lightly of, to undervalue; to treat or speak of slightingly; to depreciate; to injure by unjust comparison. **disparagement,** *n.* The act of disparaging; depreciation, detraction; diminution of value or excellence; *an unequal marriage, the disgrace due to this. **disparagingly,** *adv.*

disparate (dis′ pȧ rȧt) [L. *disparātus*, p.p. of *disparāre* (DIS-, *parāre*, to make ready), assimilated in sense to *dispar*, unequal], *a.* Dissimilar, discordant; incommensurable; having nothing in common, not co-ordinate. *n.* (*usu. pl.*) Things so unlike that they admit of no comparison with each other. **disparately,** *adv.* **disparateness,** *n.*

disparity (dis păr′ i ti) [F. *disparité*], *n.* Inequality; difference in degree; unlikeness.

dispark (dis park′), *v.t.* To throw open park-land; to employ it for other purposes.

dispart (1) (dis part′) [L. *dispartīre*, to distribute], *v.t.* To part; to separate, to dissolve; to divide, to distribute. *v.i.* To separate.

dispart (2) (dis part′) [etym. doubtful], *n.* The difference between the external semi-diameter of a gun at the muzzle and at the breech. **dispart-sight,** *n.* A sight allowing for the dispart, and bringing the line of sight parallel to the axis.

dispassionate (dis păsh′ ȯ nȧt), *a.* Free from passion; calm, temperate; impartial. **dispassionately,** *adv.* **dispassioned,** *n.*

dispatch (dis păch′) [Sp. *despachar* (DIS-, late L. *pactāre*, to make an agreement, from L. *pactum*, an agreement, neut. p.p. of *pangere*, to fasten)], *v.t.* To send off to some destination, esp. to send with haste and celerity; to transact quickly; to settle, to finish; to put to death; *to deliver (from), to relieve (of); *to deprive; *to get rid of. *v.i.* *To conclude an affair with another; to go quickly, to hurry; to hasten. *n.* The act of dispatching or being dispatched; prompt execution; promptitude, celerity, quickness, expedition; a message or letter dispatched, esp. an official communication on State affairs; a putting to death; *dismissal, deliverance, riddance; *management, care; *transaction of business. **dispatcher,** *n.* ***dispatchful,** *a.* **dispatch box,** *n.* A box for carrying dispatches and other state papers. **dispatch case,** *n.* A leather case for carrying papers. **dispatch-rider,** *n.* (*Mil.*) A motor-cyclist who carries dispatches. **mentioned in dispatches:** Cited for bravery or valuable services.

dispauper (dis paw′ pėr), *v.t.* To deprive of public support as a pauper; (*Law*) to deprive of the privilege of suing *in forma pauperis*. **dispauperize,** *v.t.* To relieve (a community) of paupers; to free from pauperism.

dispel (dis pel′) [L. *dispellere* (DIS-, *pellere*, to drive)], *v.t.* To dissipate, to disperse; to drive away, to banish. **dispeller,** *n.*

dispensable (dis pen′ sȧbl), *a.* (*Eccles.*) For which a dispensation may be granted, pardonable; that may be dispensed with, inessential.

dispensary (dis pen′ sȧr i), *n.* A place where medicines are dispensed; an establishment where medicines and medical advice are given gratis to the poor. **dispensatory,** *a.*

dispensation (dis pėn sā′ shŭn) [L. *dispensātio*, as foll.], *n.* The act of dispensing; distribution; (*fig.*) scheme, plan, economy; the government of the universe; the management of the world by Providence; God's dealings with man, esp. the divine relation to man at a particular period (as the Mosaic dispensation); a system of principles, rights, and privileges enjoined; (*R.-C. Ch.*) a licence to omit or commit something enjoined or forbidden by canon law; the act of dispensing with or doing without; *management, administration.

dispense (dis pens′) [O.F. *dispenser*, L. *dispensāre*, freq. of *dispendere* (DIS-, *pendere*, to weigh)], *v.t.* To deal out, to distribute; to administer, to prepare and give out medicine; to grant a dispensation to; to grant exemption (from). *v.i.* To dispense medicines, *to make amends. **to dispense with:** To forgo, to do without; to render unnecessary; to suspend, to waive the observance of; *to set aside, disregard; to excuse, condone. **n.* The act of dispensing or spending; a dispensation. **dispenser,** *n.* One who dispenses; (*Med.*) one who dispenses medicines; *a steward. **dispensing-power,** *n.* The power claimed by the Stuart kings to dispense with or suspend the operation of any law.

dispeople (dis pē′ pėl), *v.t.* To depopulate.

dispermatus (dī spĕr′ mȧ tŭs), **dispermous** (dī spĕr′ mŭs) [DI- (2), Gr. *sperma -tos*, seed], *a.* (*Bot.*) Having only two seeds.

disperse (dis pĕrs′) [F. *disperser*, from L. *dispersus*, p.p. of *dispergere* (DIS-, *spargere*, to scatter)], *v.t.* To scatter; to send, drive, or throw in different directions; to dissipate, to cause to vanish; to distribute, to diffuse; to disseminate; (*Opt.*) to distribute with its component colours; *to publish. *v.i.* To be scattered abroad; to break up, to vanish; to become spread abroad. **dispersal,** *n.* **dispersedly,** *adv.* **dispersive,** *a.* **dispersively,** *adv.* **dispersiveness,** *n.*

dispersion (dis pĕr′ shŭn) [L. *dispersio*, as prec.], *n.* The act of dispersing; the state of being dispersed; (*Med.*) the removal of inflammation from a part. **The Dispersion,** *n.* (*Hist.*) The scattering of the tribes of Israel, *esp.* the Babylonish captivity. **dispersion of heat, light,** etc.; (*Opt.*) The separation produced by the refraction at different angles of rays of different wave-lengths.

dispirit (dis pir′ it), *v.t.* To deprive of spirit or courage; to discourage, to dishearten, to deject. **dispiritedly,** *adv.* In a dispirited manner. ***dispiritment,** *n.*

dispiteous (dis pit′ ė ŭs), *a.* Pitiless. **dispiteously,** *adv.* **dispiteousness,** *n.*

displace (dis plās′), *v.t.* To remove from the usual or proper place; to remove from a position or dignity; to dismiss; to take the place of, to put something in the place of, to supersede; *to banish. **displaced persons:** (*Pol.*) Refugees who for any reason cannot be repatriated. **displacement,** *n.* The act of displacing; the state of being displaced; removal by supersession; change of position; supersession by something else; (*Hydrostat.*) the water displaced by a floating body (as a ship), the weight of which equals that of the floating body at rest; (*Phys.*) the amount by which anything is displaced; (*Meteor.*) alteration of the zero in a thermometer; (*Elec.*) the movement of electricity in a dielectric acted upon by an electric force; (*Geol.*) a fault.

***displant** (dis plant′) [O.F. *desplanter*], *v.t.* To pluck up; to remove (as plants, trees, etc.); to displace; to strip of inhabitants. ***displantation,** (-tā′ shŭn), *n.*

display (dis plā′) [O.F. *despleier* (*dis-*, DIS-, *pleier*, L. *plicāre*, to fold)], *v.t.* To exhibit, to expose, to show; to exhibit ostentatiously, to parade; to make known, to unfold, to reveal; (*Printing*) to make prominent; *to discover. **v.i.* To make a show, to parade. *n.* Displaying, show, exhibition; ostentatious parade; (*Printing*) setting in prominent type.

displease (dis plēz′) [O.F. *desplaisir*], *v.t.* To dissatisfy, to offend; to vex, to annoy; to be disagreeable to. *v.i.* To cause displeasure or offence. **to be displeased at or with:** To be annoyed or vexed (at or with); to disapprove. ***displeaser,** *n.* One who displeases. **displeasing,** *a.* **displeasingly,** *adv.* ***displeasance,** *n.* Displeasure, vexation.

displeasure (dis plezh′ ůr) [O.F. *desplaisir*, as prec. (assim. to PLEASURE)], *n.* A feeling of annoyance, vexation, irritation, or anger; a state of disgrace or disfavour; *injury, offence. **v.t.* To displease, to annoy.

displume (dis ploom′), *v.t.* To strip of plumes, feathers, or decorations.

dispone (dis pōn′) [L. *dispōnere* (DIS-, *pōnere*, to place)], *v.t.* *To dispose, or dispose of; (*Sc. Law*) to make over or convey (as property). **disponee** (dis pȯ nē′), *n.* (*Sc. Law*) One to whom property is disponed. **disponer,** *n.* (*Sc. Law*) One who dispones property.

disport (dis pôrt′) [O.F. *desporter* (*des-*, DIS-, *porter*, *portāre*, to carry)], *v.t.* To amuse, to divert (oneself); to enjoy (oneself); to display, to sport; *to remove, to carry away. *v.i.* To play, to amuse or divert oneself; to gambol. *n.* Sport, play, diversion, relaxation.

disposal (dis pō′ zȧl), [as foll.], *n.* The act of disposing; distributing, bestowing, giving away, or dealing with things in some particular way; disposition; sale or assignment; control, management, command; order or arrangement in which things are disposed. **at the disposal of:** In the power of, at the command of.

dispose (dis pōz′) [O.F. *disposer* (DIS-, *poser*, L. *pausāre*, to cease, to POSE, substituted for *pōnere*, to place)], *v.t.* To arrange, to set in order; to place; to settle; to adjust, to direct, to incline; to regulate, to fix, to determine; *to control, to manage; *to hand over, to bestow. **to dispose of:** To apply to any purpose; to put into the hands of another; to get rid of; to sell, to alienate; to finish, to settle, to kill; to use up; to dismiss, to put away, to stow away. *v.i.* To determine or arrange affairs; *to come to terms. **n.* Disposal, control; disposition, turn of mind; inclination, behaviour. **disposable,** *a.* **disposedness,** *n.* Disposition, inclination. **disposer,** *n.*

disposition (dis pȯ zish′ ůn) [F., from L. *dispositio* -*ōnem*, from *dispositus*, p.p. of *dispōnere* (DIS-, *pōnere*, to place)], *n.* The act of disposing, ordering, arranging, or bestowing; disposal; the state or manner of disposal; arrangement in general; fitness, aptitude; inclination, temperament, propensity, bent, natural tendency; humour, caprice, fancy; (*Arch.*) the arrangement of the whole design of a building; (*Painting*) composition in regard to general effect; (*Sc. Law*) the disposal of property; any unilateral writing by which a person makes over to another a piece of heritable or movable property; (*usu. in pl.*) arrangement, plan, preparation; the posting of troops in the most advantageous position.

dispossess (dis pȯ zes′) [O.F. *despossesser* (DIS-POSSESS)], *v.t.* To oust from possession, esp. of real estate; to disseize, to eject, to dislodge; to deprive; to rid; **to exorcise. dispossession,** *n.* ***dispossessor,** *n.*

dispraise (dis prāz′) [O.F. *despreisier*, L. *dēpretiāre*, to DEPRECIATE], *v.t.* To censure, to express disapprobation of. *n.* Blame, disapprobation, disparagement. ***dispraiser,** *n.* ***dispraisingly,** *adv.*

***dispread** (dis pred′) [DIS-, SPREAD], *v.t.* To spread in different directions. *v.i.* To be spread out.

disproof (dis proof′) [DIS-, PROOF], *n.* Refutation; proof of error or falsehood.

disproportion (dis prȯ pôr′ shůn), *n.* Want of proportion between things or parts; inadequacy, disparity; lack of symmetry. *v.t.* To make out of proportion; to spoil the symmetry of, to disfigure, deform; *to make inconsistent. ***disproportionably,** *adv.* ***disproportional,** *a.* Disproportionate. ***disproportionality** (-năl′ i ti), *n.* ***disproportionally,** *adv.* **disproportionate,** *a.* Not duly proportioned; unsymmetrical; too large or too small in relation to something. **disproportionately,** *adv.* ***disproportionateness,** *n.*

disprove (dis proov′) [O.F. *desprover* (DIS-, PROVE)], *v.t.* To prove to be erroneous or unfounded; to refute; *to disapprove. **disprovable,** *a.* **disproval,** *n.*

***dispurse** (dis pěrs′), *v.t.* To disburse, to pay.

dispute (dis pūt′) [O.F. *desputer*, L. *disputāre* (DIS-, *putāre*)], *v.i.* To contend in argument; to argue in opposition to another; to quarrel, to wrangle; to strive against another, to compete; *to debate, to discuss. *v.t.* To contend about in argument; to oppose, to question, to challenge or deny the truth of; to reason upon, to discuss, to argue; to contend or strive for, to contest; *to strive against, to resist. *n.* Contention or strife in argument; debate, controversy; a difference of opinion; a falling out, a quarrel; contest, strife, struggle; the possibility of being disputed. **disputer,** *n.* **disputable** (dis′-, dis pū′ tȧbl), *a.* Open to dispute, controvertible; questionable, uncertain; *given to argument or controversy; disputatious. **disputably,** *adv.* **disputant** (dis′ pū tȧnt), *a.* Engaged in disputation or controversy. *n.* One who disputes; one who engages in controversy. **disputation** (-tā′ shůn), *n.* The act of disputing; controversy, discussion; an exercise in arguing both sides of a question for the sake of practice; *conversation. **disputatious,** *a.* Given to dispute or controversy; cavilling, contentious. **disputatiously,** *adv.* **disputatiousness,** *n.* ***disputative** (dis pūt′ ȧ tiv), *a.*

disqualify (dis kwol′ i fī), *v.t.* To render unfit, to disable, to debar; to render or declare legally incompetent for any act or post; (*Sport.*) to disbar from competition on account of an irregularity. **disqualification** (-kā′ shůn), *n.* The act of disqualifying; that which disqualifies.

disquiet (dis kwī′ ėt), *v.t.* To disturb, to make uneasy, to harass, to vex, to fret. *a.* Uneasy, disquieted, restless. *n.* Want of quiet or peace; uneasiness, restlessness, anxiety. **disquietness,** *n.* **disquietous,** *a.* **disquietude,** *n.* The state of being disquiet; anxiety, uneasiness.

disquisition (dis kwi zish′ ůn) [L. *disquīsītio*, from *disquīsitus*, p.p. of *disquīrere* (DIS-, -*quærere*, to seek)], *n.* A formal and systematic inquiry into, an investigation; a formal discourse or treatise. **disquisitional,** *a.* **disquisitive** (dis kwiz′ i tiv), *a.* Disquisitional; fond of inquiry; inquisitive.

disrate (dis rāt′), *v.t.* (*Naut.*) To degrade or reduce in rating or rank.

disregard (dis rė gard′), *n.* Want or omission of attention or regard; slight, neglect. *v.t.* To take no notice of; to neglect; to ignore as unworthy of regard. **disregarder,** *n.* **disregardful,** *a.* Negligent, careless, heedless, regardless. **disregardfully,** *adv.*

disrelish (dis rel′ ish), *n.* A distaste or dislike, aversion, antipathy. *v.t.* To dislike the taste of; to make unpleasant or nauseous; to feel dislike or or aversion (to).

disremember (dis rė mem′ bėr), *v.t.* (*dial. and colloq.*) To be unable to remember; to forget.

disrepair (dis rė pâr′), *n.* A state of being out of repair; dilapidation.

disreputable (dis rep′ ū tȧ bėl), *a.* Not reputable; of bad repute, not respectable; discreditable, mean. **disreputableness,** *n.* **disreputably,** *adv.* ***disreputation** (-tā′ shůn), *n.* Disgrace, dishonour, discredit. **disrepute** (dis rė pūt′), *n.* A loss of, want of reputation; discredit.

disrespect (dis rė spekt′), *n.* Want of respect or reverence; rudeness, incivility; an act of rudeness. **v.t.* To treat with disrespect. ***disrespectable,** *a.* Not respectable. **disrespectful,** *a.* Wanting in respect; uncivil, rude. **disrespectfully,** *adv.* **disrespectfulness,** *n.*

disrobe (dis rōb′), *v.t.* To strip of a robe or dress; to undress (oneself). *v.i.* To undress. **disrober,** *n.*

disroot (dis root′), *v.t.* To tear up by the roots; to tear from the foundations.

disrupt (dis rŭpt′) [see DISRUPTION], *v.t.* To tear asunder, to break in pieces. *a.* Disrupted. **disruption** (dis rŭp′ shŭn) [L. *disruptio*, from *disruptus*, p.p. of *disrumpere* (DIS-, *rumpere* to break)], *n.* The act of tearing or bursting asunder; the state of being torn asunder; breach, rent, split; (*Hist.*) the great secession from the Established Church of Scotland in 1843. **disruptive,** *a.* **disrupture,** *v.t.* To tear or rend asunder; *n.* Disruption.

dissatisfy (di săt′ is fī), *v.t.* To fall short of the expectations of; to make discontented, to displease. **dissatisfaction** (-făk′ shŭn), *n.* **dissatisfactory,** *a.*

disseat (dis sēt′), *v.t.* To remove from a seat.

dissect (di sekt′) [L. *dissectus*, p.p. of *dissecāre* (DIS-, *secāre*, to cut)], *v.t* To cut in pieces; to anatomize; to cut up (an organism) so as to examine the parts and structure; to analyse, to criticize in detail; to apportion the items of (an invoice, etc.) to different departments. **dissectible,** *a.* **dissecting-clerk,** *n.* A clerk employed to dissect invoices, etc. **dissection,** *n.* **dissector,** *n.*

disseise (dis sēz′) [A.-F. *disseiser*, O.F. *dessaisir*], *v.t.* To deprive of possession (of estates, etc.); to dispossess wrongfully. **disseisee** (di sē zē′), *n.* One who is deprived unlawfully of the possession of an estate. **disseisin,** *n.* Unlawful dispossession. **disseisor,** *n.*

dissemble (di sem′ bėl) [O.F. *dissimuler*, L. *dissimulāre* (DIS-, *simulāre*, to simulate), assim. to RESEMBLE], *v.t.* To hide under a false appearance; *to disguise; to pretend, to feign, to simulate; *to ignore, to shut the eyes. *v.i.* To give a false appearance to, to cloak, to conceal; to hide one's feelings, opinions, or intentions; to play the hypocrite. **dissembler,** *n.* **dissemblingly,** *adv.* ***dissemblance,** *n.* The act of dissembling; unlikeness, dissimilarity.

disseminate (di sem′ i nāt) [L. *dissēminātus*, p.p. of *dissēmināre* (DIS-, *sēmināre*, to sow, from *sēmen*, seed)], *v.t.* To scatter abroad, as seed, with a view to growth or propagation; to diffuse, to circulate. **v.i.* To spread; to be dispersed. **dissemination** (-nā′ shŭn), *n.* **disseminator,** *n.*

dissension (di sen′ shŭn) [F., from L. *dissentio -ōnem*, as foll], *n.* Disagreement of opinion; discord, contention, strife. ***dissensious, *-tious,** *a.*

dissent (di sent′) [L. *dissentīre* (DIS-, *sentīre*, to feel)], *v.i.* To differ or disagree in opinion; to hold opposite views; to withhold assent or approval; to differ from an established Church, especially from the Church of England. *n.* Difference or disagreement of opinion; refusal of assent; a declaration of disagreement or nonconformity; the principles of Dissenters from the established Church; Dissenters collectively. ***dissentaneous,** *a.* Disagreeing, discordant. **Dissenter,** *n.* One who dissents or disagrees, esp. one who dissents from an established Church; a member of a sect that has separated from the Church of England. ***dissenterism,** *n.*

dissentient (di sen′ shi ėnt) [L. *dissentiens -ntem*, pres.p. of *dissentīre*, as prec.], *a.* Disagreeing or differing in opinion; holding or expressing contrary views. *n.* One who holds or expresses contrary views; a dissenter from the views of a political or other party. **Dissentient Liberals,** *n.pl.* A name formerly applied to Liberal Unionists.

dissepiment (di sep′ i mėnt) [L. *dissæpīmentum*, *dissæpīre* (DIS-, *sæpīre*, to hedge off, from *sæpes*, a hedge)], *n.* (*Bot. and Zool.*) A division or partition in an organ or part.

dissert (di sĕrt′), ***dissertate** (dis′ ėr tāt) [*dissertus*, p.p. and *dissertāre*, freq. of *disserere* (DIS-, *serere*, to join)], *v.i.* To discourse in a formal manner; to write a dissertation. **dissertation** (-tā′ shŭn), *n.* A formal discourse on any subject; a disquisition, treatise, or essay. ***dissertational,** *a.* ***dissertationist,** *n.*

disserve (dis sĕrv′), *v.t.* To do a disservice to; to injure. **disservice,** *n.* An injury, detriment, or ill service.

dissever (di sev′ ėr), *v.t.* To sever, to separate. ***disseverance, *disseveration** (-ā′ shŭn), *n.* Disseverment. **disseverment,** *n.*

dissident (dis′ i dėnt) [L. *dissidens -ntem*, pres.p. of *dissidēre* (DIS-, *sedēre*, to sit)], *a.* Not in agreement; disagreeing, dissenting. *n.* One who dissents from or votes against any motion; a dissenter. **dissidence,** *n.*

dissilient (di sil′ i ėnt) [L. *dissiliens -ntem*, pres.p. of *dissilīre* (DIS-, *salīre*, to leap)], *a.* (*Bot.*) Starting asunder; separating with force and elasticity. **dissilience,** *n.*

dissimilar (di sim′ i lȧr) *a.* Not similar; unlike in nature, properties, or appearances; discordant. **dissimilarity** (-lăr′ i ti), *n.* **dissimilarly,** *adv.* **dissimilitude** (-mil′ i tūd), *n.* Unlikeness, dissimilarity.

dissimilate (di sim′ i lāt) [DIS-, L. *similis*, after ASSIMILATE], *v.t.* (*Philol.*) To make unlike. **dissimilation** (-lā′ shŭn), *n.* (*Philol.*) The rendering two similar sounds unlike, or two dissimilar sounds identical, when such sounds come together.

dissimulate (di sim′ ū lāt) [L. *dissimulātus*, p.p. of *dissimulāre* (DIS-, *simulāre*, to SIMULATE)], *v.t.* To dissemble, to conceal, to disguise. **dissimulation** (-lā′ shŭn), *n.* The act of dissimulating; concealment under a false pretence; hypocrisy. **dissimulator,** *n.*

dissipate (dis′ i pāt) [L. *dissipātus*, p.p. of *dissipāre* (DIS-, obs. *sipāre*, to throw)], *v.t.* To scatter; to drive in different directions; to disperse, to dispel; to squander, to waste, to fritter away. *v.i.* To be dispersed, to vanish; to indulge in dissolute or frivolous enjoyment. **dissipated,** *a.* Scattered, dispersed; given to dissipation, dissolute; wasted in dissipation. **dissipation** (-pā′ shŭn), *n.* The act of dissipating or scattering; the state of being dispersed or scattered; distraction of energy; lack of concentration or perseverance; excessive indulgence in luxury, frivolity, or vice; dissoluteness; wasteful expenditure, extravagance; (*Phys.*) insensible loss or waste; disintegration, dispersion, diffusion.

***dissociable** (di sō′ shȧ bėl) [DIS-, SOCIABLE], *a.* Incongruous, discordant; separable, unsociable. **dissociableness,** *n.* ***dissocial,** *a.* Unfitted for society. ***dissocialize,** *v.t.* To make unsocial; to disunite.

dissociate (di sō′ shi āt) [L. *dissociātus*, p.p. of *dissociāre* (DIS-, *sociāre*, to associate, from *socius*, a comrade)], *v.t.* To separate, to disconnect; (*Chem.*) to decompose, esp. by the action of heat. **dissociation** (-ā′ shŭn), *n.* Separation, disconnexion; (*Psych.*) a loosening of control over consciousness in which the personality is temporarily taken control of by unconscious complexes. **dissociative,** *a.*

dissoluble (di sol′ ū bėl) [L. *dissolūbilis*, from *dissolvere*, to DISSOLVE], *a.* That can be dissolved, decomposed, or disconnected. **dissolubility** (-bil′ i ti), *n.*

dissolute (dis′ ȯ lūt) [L. *dissolūtus*, p.p. of *dissolvere*, to DISSOLVE], *a.* Given to dissipation, loose in conduct; licentious, debauched; *relaxed, negligent, remiss. **n.* A dissolute person. **dissolutely,** *adv.* **dissoluteness,** *n.*

dissolution (dis ȯ lū′ shŭn) [L. *dissolūtio*, as prec.], *n.* The act or process of dissolving, separating, disintegrating, decomposing; liquefaction; the destruction of any body by the separation of its parts;

death, the separation of soul and body; separation of a meeting, assembly, or body; (*Chem.*) resolution into the elements or components; *a solution; *dissoluteness, corruption, depravity; *melting by the action of heat. **Dissolution of the Monasteries:** (*Hist.*) The suppression of the monasteries by Henry VIII. **dissolution of Parliament:** The end of a parliament to be followed by a general election.

dissolve (di zolv′) [L. *dissolvere* (DIS-, solvere, to loosen)], *v.t.* To diffuse the particles of a substance in a liquid; to convert from a solid to a liquid state by heat or moisture; to decompose; to separate; to break up; to put an end to (as a meeting, etc.); to dismiss, to disperse; to relax; to rescind, to annul; *to part, to sunder. *v.i.* To become liquefied; to decompose, to disintegrate; to break up, to separate; to fade away, to melt away; *to become weak or powerless; to melt by the action of heat; to vanish. **dissolvable,** *a.* **dissolvent,** *a.* Having power to melt or dissolve. *n.* Anything which has the power of dissolving or melting, a solvent. **dissolver,** *n.* **dissolving views,** *n.pl.* Pictures projected on a screen and made to fade one into another by a special magic-lantern apparatus.

dissonant (dis′ ŏ nănt) [L. *dissonans -ntem*, pres.p. of *dissonāre*, to be unlike in sound, from *dissonus*, discordant], *a.* Discordant, inharmonious; harsh, incongruous. **dissonantly,** *adv.* **dissonance,** *n.*

dissuade (di swād′) [L. *dissuādēre* (DIS-, *suādere*, to persuade)], *v.t.* To seek to persuade not to do some act; to advise against; to divert from a purpose by argument; *to represent as unadvisable. **dissuader,** *n.* **dissuasion,** *n.* **dissuasive,** *a.* Tending to dissuade; dehortatory. *n.* A dissuasive argument or reason. **dissuasively,** *adv.*

dissyllable, etc. [DISYLLABLE].

dissymmetry (di sim′ ė tri), *n.* Absence of symmetry between objects or parts. **dissymmetrical** (-met′ rik ǎl), *a.* **dissymmetrically,** *adv.*

distaff (dis′ taf) [A.-S. *dīstæf* (cp. L.G. *diesse*, a bunch of flax)], *n.* A cleft stick about three feet long, on which wool or carded cotton was wound for spinning; (*fig.*) an emblem of woman; women collectively. **distaff-side,** *n.* The female side of a family or descent. ***distaff-woman,** *n.* A spinner.

distal (dis′ tǎl) [formed from DIST-ANCE, -AL], *a.* (*Anat. and Bot.*) Applied to the extremity of a bone or organ farthest from the point of attachment or insertion; situated at the farthest point from the centre. **distally,** *adv.*

distance (dis′ tǎns) [O.F., from L. *distantia* (see foll.)], *n.* The space between two objects measured along the shortest line; extent of separation however measured; the quality of being distant, remoteness; a set interval; the length of a course run in a competition; reserve, coolness; avoidance of familiarity; constraint, unfriendliness, alienation; remoteness in time (past or future); separation in rank or relationship; ideal space or separation; the remoter parts of a view or the background of a picture; (*Mus.*) a tone interval; *discord, dissension. *v.t.* To place far off; to leave behind in a race; to outstrip, to outdo; to cause to seem distant; to give an appearance of distance to. **angular distance:** (*Opt.*) The space included between the lines drawn from two objects to the eye. **line of distance:** A straight line drawn from the eye to the principal point in the plane. **middle distance:** The central portion of a picture between the foreground and the distance. **point of distance:** (*persp.*) That point of a picture where the visual rays meet. **to keep one's distance:** To behave respectfully; to behave with reserve or coldness. **distance-rod:** (*Motor.*) A rod for keeping different parts (as chains, axle-arms, etc.) at a proper distance from each other. **distance-signal,** *n.* (*Rail.*) A signal reached before the home-signal and indicating whether that is at danger or not.

distant (dis′ tǎnt) [F., from L. *distans -ntem*, pres.p. of *distāre* (DIS-, *stare*, to stand)], *a.* Separated by intervening space; remote in space, time (past or future), succession, consanguinity, resemblance, kind, or nature; at a certain distance (specified numerically); not plain or obvious; faint, slight; reserved, cool. **distant signal** [DISTANCE-SIGNAL]. **distantly,** *adv.*

distaste (dis tāst′), *n.* Disrelish, aversion of the taste; dislike, disinclination (for); *unpleasantness, discomfort. **v.t.* To dislike the taste of; to make distasteful; to offend. **v.i.* To be distasteful. **distasteful,** *a.* Unpleasant to the taste; offensive, displeasing; *repulsive; *exhibiting dislike. **distastefulness,** *n.*

distemper (1) (dis tem′ pėr) [DIS-, L. *temperāre*, to TEMPER, to mix in due proportions (cp. O.F. *destempré*, immoderate)], *v.t.* To derange (the mental or bodily functions of); to disturb, to vex. *n.* A derangement of the health; a catarrhal disorder affecting young dogs; mental derangement or perturbation; ill-humour; undue predominance of a passion or appetite; dissatisfaction, discontent; want of due balance or proportion of parts; political disturbance; *intoxication. **distempered,** *a.* Disordered in mind or body; intemperate, immoderate.

distemper (2) (dis tem′ pėr) [O.F. *destemprer*, as prec.], *v.t.* To paint or colour with distemper; *to dilute, to weaken. *n.* A method of painting with colours soluble in water, mixed with chalk or clay, and diluted with size instead of oil: the coloured preparation used in this style of painting; a painting done by this method or with this preparation; tempera.

distend (dis tend′) [L. *distendere* (DIS-, *tendere*, to stretch)], *v.t.* To spread or swell out; to inflate; to cause to open. *v.i.* To swell out. **distensible,** *a.* **distensibility** (-bil′ i ti), *n.* **distension,** *n.* The act of distending; the state of being distended; breadth, expansion. **distent,** *a.* Spread out, extended; expanded, swollen.

disthrone (dis thrōn′), *v.t.* To dethrone.

distich (dis′ tik) [L. *distichus*, *distichon*, Gr. *distichon* (DI- (2), *stichos*, a row)], *n.* A couplet; two lines of poetry making complete sense.

distichous (dis′ ti kŭs) [L. *distichus*, as prec.], *a.* (*Bot.*) Having two rows (of leaves, etc.); arranged in two rows.

distil (dis til′) [L. *distillāre* (DI- (1), *stillāre*, to trickle, from *stilla*, a drop)], *v.i.* (*past & p.p.* **distilled**) To fall in drops; to trickle; to flow forth gently, to exude; to undergo the process of distillation. *v.t.* To extract by means of vaporization and condensation; to extract the essence of; to make or obtain by this process; to purify by this process; to let fall in drops, to shed; *to melt. **distillable,** *a.* **distillate** (dis til′ ǎt), *n.* The product of distillation.

distillation (dis til ā′ shŭn), *n.* The act of distilling; the act or process of heating a solid or liquid in a vessel so constructed that the vapours thrown off from the heated substance are collected and condensed; the product of this process, a distillate. **destructive distillation:** Distillation at a temperature sufficiently high to decompose the substance, and evolve new products possessing different qualities. **dry distillation:** The distillation of a solid substance without the addition of water. **fractional distillation:** The separation of liquids having different boiling-points. **distillatory** (di stil′-), *a.* **distiller,** *n.* One who distils, esp. a manufacturer of spirits by distillation.

distillery (dis til′ ė ri), *n.* A building where spirits are produced by distillation.

distinct (dis tingkt′) [L. *distinctus*, p.p. of *distinguere*, to DISTINGUISH], *a.* Clearly distinguished or distinguishable, different, separate; standing clearly apart, not identical; unmistakable, clear, plain, evident, definite; (*colloq.*) decided, positive; *adorned, variegated; *marked off, specified. **n.* A distinct or individual person. **distinction,** *n.* A mark or note of difference; a distinguishing quality, a characteristic difference; the act of distinguishing, discrimination; that which differentiates; honour, title, rank; eminence, superiority; (*Lit. crit.*) individuality; *variety of detail. **without distinction:** Promiscuously, indiscriminately. **distinctive,** *a.* Serving to mark distinction or difference; separate, distinct. **distinctively,** *adv.* **distinctiveness,** *n.* **distinctly,** *adv.* **distinctness,** *n.* ***distincture,** *n.* Distinctness.

distingué (dis tăn' gā) [F., p.p. of *distinguer*, to DISTINGUISH], *a.* (*fem.* ***-guée***) Having an air of distinction.

distinguish (dis ting' gwish) [L. *distinguere* (DI- (1), *stinguere*, prob. cogn. with Gr. *stizein*, to prick)], *v.t.* To discriminate, to differentiate; to indicate the difference of from others by some external mark; to classify; to tell apart, to discriminate between; to perceive the existence of by means of the senses; to recognize; to be a mark of distinction or characteristic property; to separate from others by some token of honour or preference; to make eminent, prominent, or well known. *v.i.* To differentiate; to draw distinctions. **distinguishable,** *a.* **distinguishably,** *adv.* **distinguished,** *a.* Marked by some distinctive sign or property; eminent, celebrated, remarkable; conspicuous, specially marked. **Distinguished Conduct Medal (D.C.M.):** (*Mil.*) Medal awarded to warrant officers and other ranks for gallantry in the field. **Distinguished Flying Cross (D.F.C.):** (*Aviat.*) Medal for gallantry awarded to officers and warrant officers of R.A.F. **Distinguished Service Cross, Medal (D.S.C., D.S.M.):** (*Nav.*) Medals awarded for gallantry to R.N. officers and warrant officers, and C.P.O.s and other ratings. **Distinguished Service Order (D.S.O.):** Medal for meritorious service awarded to officers in the three Services. **distinguishedly,** *adv.* In a distinguished manner; eminently. **distinguisher,** *n.* One who distinguishes one thing from another by marks of difference; a critical observer. **distinguishing,** *a.* Constituting a difference or distinction; peculiar. **distinguishingly,** *adv.* With some mark of distinction; markedly. ***distinguishment,** *n.* Distinction; observation of difference.

distoma (dis tō' mȧ) [Gr. *distomos -on*, double-mouthed (DI- (2), *stoma*, mouth)], *n.pl.* (*Zool.*) A genus of *Trematoda*, parasitic worms or flukes, typified by the liver-fluke, the cause of sheep-rot.

distort (dis tôrt') [L. *distortus*, p.p. of *distorquēre* (DIS-, *torquēre*, to twist)], *v.t.* To twist or alter the natural shape or direction; to pervert from the true meaning. **a.* Distorted. **distortedly,** *adv.* **distortion,** *n.* The act of distorting; the state of being distorted; a writhing, a contortion; a distorted part of the body, a deformity; a perversion of meaning, a misrepresentation; (*Radio.*) deviation from strict reproduction in a receiver or loudspeaker. **distortional,** *a.* **distortionist,** *n.* A caricaturist; one who distorts his body for public entertainment. **distortive,** *a.*

distract (dis trăkt') [L. *distractus*, p.p. of *distrahere* (DIS-, *trahere*, to draw)], *v.t.* To draw or turn aside, to divert the mind or attention (from); to draw in different directions, to confuse, bewilder, perplex; to drive mad, to craze (*usu. in p.p.*); *to tear asunder. **a.* Separated, divided; deranged, distracted. **distracted,** *a.* Disturbed mentally, crazed, maddened; confounded, harassed, perplexed; *divided, separated. **distractedly,** *adv.* **distractingly,** *adv.* **distraction,** *n.* Diversion of the mind or attention; the thing that diverts; an interruption, a diversion, relaxation, relief, amusement; confusion, perplexity, agitation, violent mental excitement arising from pain, care, etc.; mental aberration, madness, frenzy; *separation, a division; *disorder, dissension, tumult. **distractive,** *a.* **distractively,** *adv.*

distrain (dis trān') [O.F. *destreign-*, stem of *destreindre*, L. *distringere* (DI- (1), *stringere*, to STRAIN, compress)], *v.t.* To seize for debt; to take the personal chattels of, in order to satisfy a demand or enforce the performance of an act; *to rend asunder; to oppress, to compel; *to take possession of, to seize. *v.i.* To levy a distress. **distrainable,** *a.* **distrainee** (dis- trā nē'), *n.* One whose goods are distrained. **distrainer, -or** (dis trā' nȯr), *n.* **distrainment,** *n.* **distraint,** *n.* The act of seizing goods for debt.

distrait (dis trā') [F., p.p. of *distraire*, to DISTRACT], *a.* (*fem.* **-aite,** -āt) Absent-minded, abstracted, inattentive.

distraught (dis trawt') [DISTRACT, *a.*, distracted, assim. to CAUGHT, TAUGHT, etc.], *a.* Torn asunder, bewildered, agitated, distracted.

distress (dis tres') [O.F. *destrece*, from *destrecier*, late L. *districtiāre*, from *districtus*, p.p. of *distringere*, to DISTRAIN, late L. to punish], *n.* Extreme anguish or pain of mind or body; misery, poverty, destitution; exhaustion, fatigue; calamity, misfortune; a state of danger; (*Law*) the act of distraining; goods taken in distraint. *v.t.* To afflict with anxiety, unhappiness, or anguish, to vex; to exhaust, to tire out; *to constrain, to compel by pain or suffering; (*Law*) to distrain. **in distress:** (*Naut.*) In a disabled or perilous condition (of a ship). **distress-gun, -rocket,** *n.* A signal for help from a ship in imminent danger. **distress sale,** *n.* A sale of goods under a distress warrant. **distress warrant,** *n.* A writ authorizing the seizure and compulsory sale of household effects, etc., in settlement of a debt. **distressed,** *a.* Afflicted with pain or anxiety; destitute, exhausted; in a position of danger, **distressed areas:** Industrial areas where there is wide unemployment and poverty. ***distressedness,** *n.* **distressful,** *a.* Painful, afflictive; attended by distress; *gained by toil. **distressfully,** *adv.* **distressing,** *a.* Painful, afflicting; awakening pity or compassion. **distressingly,** *adv.*

distribute (dis trib' ūt) [L. *distribūtus*, p.p. of *distribuere* (DIS-, *tribuere*)], *v.t.* To divide or deal out amongst a number, to spread abroad, to disperse, to give in charity; (*Print.*) to separate and return (as type) to the cases; to arrange, to allocate, to classify; (*Log.*) to employ (a term) in its fullest extent, so as to include every individual of the class. **distributable,** *a.* **distributary,** *a.* Distributive. **distributing-machine,** *n.* A machine for distributing type. **distributor,** *n.* One who or that which distributes.

distribution (dis tri bū' shŭn), *n.* The act of distributing; apportionment, division; the apportionment of wealth among the various classes of the community; the dispersal of commodities among the consumers; dispersal, arrangement of a number of scattered units; an assigning to different positions; the act of dividing or arranging into classes, etc.; (*Log.*) the application of a term to all the members of a class individually, as distinguished from collective application; the manner, degree, and extent in which the flora and fauna of the world are distributed over the surface of the earth. **distributional,** *a.*

distributive (dis trib' ū tiv) [F., from late L. *distribūtīvus*, as prec.], *a.* Distributing or allotting the proper share to each; pertaining to distribution; (*Gram.*) expressing distribution, separation, or division; (*Log.*) indicating distribution, as distinguished from collective terms. *n.* A distributive word, *e.g. each, every, either*, and *neither*. **distributively,** *adv.*

district (dis' trikt) [F., from late L. *districtus*, p.p. of *distringere*, to DISTRAIN], *n.* A portion of territory specially defined for judicial, administrative, fiscal, or other purposes; a division having its own representative in a legislature, its own district council, a church or chapel of its own, or a separate magistrate; a separate sphere of organization or operation; a region, a tract of country. *v.t.* (*Am.*) To divide into districts. **district-attorney,** *n.* (*Am.*) The prosecuting officer of a district. **district commissioner,** *n.* A magistrate or official exercising semi-judicial authority over a district in a Crown Colony. **district-court,** *n.* (*Am.*) A court having cognizance of cases arising within a defined district. **district-judge,** *n.* (*Am.*) The judge of a district-court. **district nurse,** *n.* A nurse employed by a local authority to visit and tend patients in their own homes. **District Railway,** *n.* A railway serving various parts of London and the suburbs. **district-surveyor,** *n.* A local officer, usually a civil engineer, appointed to examine buildings, roads, etc., superintend repairs, etc. **district-visitor,** *n.* A person employed to visit the sick, distribute alms, and give religious instruction in a section of a parish.

distrust (dis trŭst'), *v.t.* To have no confidence in; to doubt, to suspect; to question the reality, truth, or sincerity of; *to be anxious about. *n.* Want of confidence, reliance, or faith (in); suspicion, *discredit. ***distruster,** *n.* **distrustful,** *a.* Inclined to distrust; suspicious, without confidence, diffident. **distrustfully,** *adv.* **distrustfulness,** *n.*

distune (dis tūn'), *v.t.* To put out of tune.

disturb (dis tĕrb') [O.F. *destourber,* L. *disturbāre* (DIS-, *turbāre,* to trouble, from *turba,* a crowd, a tumult)], *v.t.* To agitate, to disquiet; to move from any regular course; to discompose, unsettle; to make uneasy, to hinder, to interrupt, to interfere with; (*Law*) to put out of possession. **n.* Disturbance. **disturbance,** *n.* Interruption of a settled state of things; agitation, public agitation or excitement, tumult, disorder, uproar, an outbreak; (*Law*) the interruption of a right; the hindering and disquieting of a person in the lawful and peaceable enjoyment of his right; (*Radio.*) any interruption from unwanted stations, atmospherics, etc., in the reception of a signal. ***disturbant,** *a.* Causing disturbance.

distyle (dī' stīl) [DI- (2), Gr. *stulos,* a pillar], *n.* A portico having two columns.

disulphate (dī sŭl' fȧt), *n.* (*Chem.*) A salt of sulphuric acid, containing two equivalents of the acid to one of the base. **disulphide,** *n.* (*Chem.*) A compound in which two atoms of sulphur are united to another element or radical.

disunion (dis ū' nyȯn), *n.* The state of being disunited; disagreement, discord; (*U.S.A.*) secession from the Union. **disunionist,** *n.*

disunite (dis ū nīt'), *v.t.* To disjoin, to divide, to put at variance. *v.i.* To become divided. **disunity** (-ū' ni ti), *n.* Disunion; a state of variance.

disuse (dis ūs'), *n.* A cessation of use, practice, or exercise: the state of being disused; desuetude *v.t.* (dis ūz') To cease to use; *to disaccustom (*usu. in p.p.*). **disused,** *a.* No longer in use; obsolete; unaccustomed.

***disvalue** (dis văl' ū), *v.t.* To undervalue; to depreciate, to disparage.

disyllable (dī sil' ȧbl) [F. *dissyllabe* (DI- (2), SYLLABLE)], *n.* A word or metrical foot of two syllables. *a.* Disyllabic. **disyllabic** (-lăb' ik), *a.* **disyllabically,** *adv.* **disyllabism** (-sil'-), *n.* **disyllabize,** *v.t.*

disyoke (dis yōk'), *v.t.* To unyoke.

dital (dī' tȧl) [It. *dito,* -AL], *n.* (*Mus.*) A thumb stop on a guitar or lute for raising the pitch of a string's semitone.

ditch (dich) [A.-S. *dīc,* cp. DIKE]. A trench made by digging to form a boundary or for drainage; (*Fort.*) a trench or fosse on the outside of a fortress, serving as an obstacle to assailants. *v.t.* To make a ditch, trench, or drain in; to surround with a ditch. *v.i.* To dig or repair ditches. **to die in the last ditch:** To resist to the uttermost. ***ditch-delivered,** *a.* Brought forth in a ditch. ***ditch-dog,** *n.* A dead dog thrown in a ditch, or, perhaps, the water-vole. **ditch-water,** *n.* Stagnant water in a ditch, whence **dull as ditch-water:** Very uninteresting or unentertaining. **ditcher,** *n.* One employed in making ditches.

***dite** [DIGHT, or DITTY].

ditetragonal (dī tė trăg' ŏ nȧl), *a.* (*Cryst.*) Twice tetragonal. **ditetrahedral** (dī tet rȧ hē' drȧl), *a.* (*Cryst.*) Twice tetrahedral.

ditheism (dī' thė izm), *n.* The theory of two co-equal gods or opposing powers of good and evil, the basic principle of Zoroastrianism and Manichæism. **ditheistic** (-ist' ik), *a.*

dither (di*th*' ėr) [rel. to DODDER (2)], *v.t.* To be distracted or uncertain; to quiver, thrill.

dithyramb (dith' i rămb, -răm) [L. *dīthyrambus,* Gr. *dithurambos* (etym. unknown)], *n.* A choric hymn in honour of Bacchus, full of frantic enthusiasm; hence, any wild, impetuous poem or song. **dithyrambic** (-răm' bik), *a.* Of the nature of a dithyramb; wild, enthusiastic. *n.* A dithyramb.

ditriglyph (dī trī' glif) [F. *ditriglyphe*)], *n.* (*Arch.*) The interval between two triglyphs; an interval between Doric columns allowing the insertion of two triglyphs in the frieze between those over the columns.

ditrochee (dī trō' kē) [L. *ditrochæus,* Gr. *ditrochaios*], *n.* A metrical foot of two trochees.

dittany (dit' ȧ ni) [O.F. *ditain,* L. *diktamnum,* Gr. *diktamnon,* from *Diktē,* in Crete], *n.* A herb, *Origanum dictamnus,* which was prized by the ancients as a vulnerary; (*Am.*) a small herb, *Cunila mariana,* growing in the Eastern U.S.A.; *Dictamnus fraxinella,* the bastard dittany.

dittay (dit' ā, -i) [Sc., from O.F. *dité,* DITTY], *n.* (*Sc. Law*) An indictment, a charge.

ditto (dit' ō) [It., from L. *dictum,* acc. of *dictus,* p.p. of *dīcere,* to say], *n.* (*pl.* **-os**) That which has been said before; the same thing, a similar thing. *a.* Similar. **suit of dittos:** A suit of clothes of the same stuff. **to say ditto:** To repeat, endorse a view; to coincide in opinion. **dittography** (di tog' rȧ fi), *n.* Repetition of words or letters in copying. **dittographic** (-grăf'), *a.* **dittology** (di tol' o ji), *n.* A twofold reading of a text.

ditty (dit' i) [O.F. *dité,* L. *dictātum,* a thing dictated, neut. p.p. of *dictāre,* to DICTATE], *n.* A little poem, a song, an air; anything sung; *a saying, a refrain. *v.i.* To sing verses, to fit to music.

ditty-bag (dit' i băg) [etym. doubtful], *n.* (*Naut.*) A sailor's bag for needles, thread, and odds and ends. **ditty-box,** *n.* A box similarly used by fishermen.

diuretic (dī ū ret' ik) [L. *diūrēticus,* Gr. *diourētikos,* from *diourein,* to void urine], *a.* (*Med.*) Provoking the secretion of urine. *n.* A diuretic medicine.

diurnal (dī ĕr' nȧl) [L. *diurnālis,* from *diurnus,* daily (*diēs,* day)], *a.* Of or pertaining to a day or the day-time; performed in a day; daily, of each day; of common occurrence; (*Zool.*) of the day as opp. to nocturnal. *n.* *A journal, a day-book; *(*R.-C. Ch.*) a book containing the little hours of the divine office. **diurnal arc:** (*Astron.*) The arc described by a heavenly body from rising to setting. **diurnally,** *adv.*

***diuturnal** (dī ū tĕr' nȧl) [L. *diūturnus,* from *diū,* long], *a.* Of long continuance. ***diuturnity,** *n.* Lastingness, long duration.

diva (dē' vȧ) [It., from L. *dīva,* a goddess, fem. of *dīvus,* divine, a deity], *n.* A famous female singer, a prima donna.

divagate (dīv' ȧ gāt) [L. *dīvagātus,* p.p. of *dīvagārī* (DI- (1), *vagārī,* to wander)], *v.t.* To ramble, to diverge, to digress. **divagation** (-gā' shŭn), *n.*

divalent (div' ȧ lent) [DI- (2), L. *valens -ntem,* pres.p. of *valēre,* to be worth], *a.* (*Chem.*) With a valency of two.

divan (di văn') [Turk. *divān,* Pers. *dīvān,* a brochure, a collection of poems, a tribunal, a custom-house (cp. DOUANE)], *n.* In Oriental countries a court of justice, the highest council of state; a council, a council-chamber; a restaurant; a smoking-saloon; a thickly-cushioned seat or sofa against the wall of a room; *a collection of poems by one author. **divan bed,** *n.* A mattress bed that can be converted into a sofa by day.

divaricate (di-, dī văr' i kāt) [L. *dīvāricātus,* p.p. of *dīvāricāre* (DI- (1), *vāricāre,* to spread apart, to straddle, from *vāricus,* straddling)], *v.i.* To diverge into branches or forks; (*Bot.*) to branch off from the stem at a right or obtuse angle. **v.t.* To divide into two branches. *a.* (-kāt) Spreading irregularly and widely asunder; branching off at a right or obtuse angle. **divarication** (-kā' shŭn), *n.*

dive (dīv) [A.-S. *dūfan*, to dive, to sink, and *dyfan*, to dip (eventually combined)], *v.i.* To plunge, esp. head first, under water; to descend quickly; to descend quickly and disappear; to thrust one's hand rapidly into something; (*fig.*) to enter deeply into any question, science, or pursuit. *v.t.* To explore by diving; to dip, to duck. *n.* A sudden plunge head foremost into water; a sudden plunge or dart; a drinking-saloon of a low type; an underground room in a restaurant or bar; (*Aviat.*) a steep descent with the nose down. **dive-dapper** [DI-, DAPPER]. **dive-bombing,** *n.* (*Aviat.*) Diving suddenly on a target to release bombs. **diver,** *n.* One who dives; esp. one who dives for pearls, or to work on sunken vessels, etc.; (*Ornith.*) any member of the family *Colymbidæ*, remarkable for their habit of diving. **diving-bell,** *n.* A hollow vessel originally bell-shaped, in which persons may remain for a time under water, air being supplied through a flexible tube. **diving-dress,** *n.* Waterproof clothing and breathing-helmet for divers working at the bottom of the sea.

diverge (di-, dī vĕrj') [DI- (1), L. *vergere*, to VERGE], *v.i.* To tend in different directions from a common point or from each other; to branch off; to vary from a normal form; to deviate, to differ. *v.t.* To cause to diverge. ***divergement,** *n.* **divergence, -ency,** *n.* **divergent,** *a.* **divergent series,** *n.* An infinite series the sum of which becomes indefinitely greater as more are taken. **divergingly,** *adv.*

divers (dī' vĕrz) [O.F., from L. *dīversus*, various, p.p. of *dīvertere*, to DIVERT], *a.* Several, sundry; *different.

diverse (di-, dī vers') [as prec.], *a.* Different, unlike, distinct; varying, changeable, multiform; *divers. **v.t.* To diversify. **v.i.* To turn aside, to diverge. **diversely,** *adv.* **diverseness,** *n.* **diversiform,** *a.* Of divers or varied forms; (*Bot.*) applied to organs of the same nature but of different forms. **diversify,** *v.t.* To make different from others; to give variety to; to variegate. **diversification** (-kā' shŭn), *n.*

diversion (di vĕr' shŭn) [med. L. *dīversio*, from *dīvertere*, to DIVERT], *n.* The act of diverting or turning aside; that which tends or serves to divert the mind or attention from care, business, or study; a relaxation, distraction, amusement; a re-direction of traffic owing to the temporary closing of a road; (*Mil.*) the act of diverting the attention of the enemy from any design by demonstration or feigned attack. **diversity,** *n.* Difference, unlikeness; variance; variety, distinctness or non-identity; variegation; (*Law*) plea by a prisoner that he is not the person charged.

divert (di vĕrt') [M.F. *divertir*, L. *dīvertere* (DI-, (1), *vertere*, to turn), to turn aside, *dēvertere* (DE-, *vertere*), to turn away], *v.t.* To turn from any course or direction, to turn aside, to deflect; to turn in another direction, to avert; to draw off, to distract; to entertain, to amuse; *to turn away. **v.i.* To go out of the way, to go astray. ***diverter,** *n.* **divertible,** *a.* **diverting,** *a.* Entertaining, amusing. **divertingly,** *adv.* **divertisement,** *n.* Diversion; source of amusement. **divertissement,** *n.* (*Theat.*) An interlude, ballet, light entertainment.

Dives (dī' vēz) [L., rich], *n.* The popular name for a wealthy man (after the parable of Lazarus and the rich man in Luke xvi. 19–31). **Dives costs:** (*Law*) Costs on a higher scale.

divest (di-, dī vest') [formerly *devest*, O.F. *devestir*, *desvestir*, late L. *disvestīre*, *dīvestīre* (DI- (1), *vestīre*, from *vestis*, a garment)], *v.t.* To strip of clothing; to deprive, to rid (of). **divestiture,** *n.* Divestment; the state of being divested; (*Law*) deprivation or alienation of property. **divestment,** *n.* The act of divesting.

divide (di vīd') [L. *dīvidere* (DI- (1), *-videre*, cp. *vidua*, WIDOW)], *v.t.* To cut or part asunder; to sever, to partition; to cause to separate, to break into parts; to distribute, to deal out; to make an opening or passage through; to form the boundary between; to sunder; to part or to mark divisions on (as on mathematical instruments, etc.); to distinguish the different kinds of, to classify; to distribute as a dividend; to share, to take a portion of with others; to separate (as Parliament, a meeting) by taking opinions on, for and against; to draw or attach to different sides; to destroy unity amongst, to disunite in feelings; (*Math.*) to separate into factors, to perform the operation of division on. *v.i.* To be parted or separated; to share; to diverge; to express decision by separating into two parts, as a legislative house; (*Math.*) to be an exact division of; (*fig.*) to be disunited in feelings, opinions, etc. ***dividable,** *a.* ***dividant,** *a.* Divided, separated. **divider,** *n.* One who or that which divides; one who causes division or disunion; (*pl.*) compasses used to divide lines into a given number of equal parts; (*Am.*) a watershed. **dividedly,** *adv.*

dividend (div' i dend) [F. *dividende*, L. *dividendum*, gerund of *dīvidere*, as prec.], *n.* The share of the interest or profit which belongs to each shareholder in a company, bearing the same proportion to the whole profit that the shareholder's capital bears to the whole capital; (*Law*) the fractional part of the assets of a bankrupt paid to a creditor, in proportion to the amount of his debt; (*Math.*) a number to be divided by a divisor. **dividend-warrant,** *n.* The authority on which shareholders receive the amount of a dividend from the bankers of a company.

dividivi (div' i div' i) [native Carib. name], *n.* A tropical American tree, *Cæsalpinia coriaria*; the seedpods of this, used for tanning and dyeing.

***dividual** (di vid' ū ăl) [L. *dividuus*, as DIVIDE], *a.* Divided; shared with others; separate, distinct, particular. ***dividually,** *adv.* ***dividuous,** *a.* Dividual; separable, accidental, not essential.

divine (1) (di vīn') [F. *deviner*, L. *dīvīnāre*, from *dīvīnus*, as foll.], *v.t.* To find out by inspiration, magic, or intuition; to foresee, to presage; to conjecture, to guess; to feel a presentiment of. *v.i.* To practise divination; to have a presentiment; to guess. **diviner,** *n.* One who divines; a dowser. **divination** (-nā' shŭn), *n.* The act of predicting or foretelling events, or of discovering hidden or secret things by real or by alleged supernatural means; an omen, an augury; a prediction or conjecture as to the future. ***divinator,** *n.* **divinatory,** *a.* **divining-rod,** *n.* A forked twig or other staff used by dowsers to discover subterranean waters or minerals.

divine (2) (di vīn') [O.F. *devin*, L. *dīvīnus*, cogn. with *dīvus*, *deus*, god], *a.* Pertaining to, proceeding from, or of the nature of God, a god, or gods; appropriated to the service of the Deity, religious, sacred; above the nature of man, superhuman, godlike, celestial; pertaining to theology; *prescient; *(of the soul) beatified; *immortal; *holy, pious; divining, presaging. *n.* A clergyman, an ecclesiastic; a theologian; *a priest, a soothsayer. **divine office,** *n.* The office of the Roman breviary, consisting of matins with lauds, prime, tierce, sext, none, vespers, and compline, the recitation of which is obligatory on all clerics holding a benefice, on all persons in Holy Orders, and on all monastics of both sexes professed for the service of the choir. **divine right,** *n.* The claim of kings to hold their office by divine appointment, and hence to govern absolutely without any interference on the part of their subjects. **divine service,** *n.* The worship of God according to established forms. **divinely,** *adv.* ***divineness,** *n.* The quality of being divine; perfection, excellence. **divinify** (di vin' i fī), *v.t.* To make divine to deify.

diving-bell [DIVE].

divinity (di vin' i ti), *n.* The quality of being divine, deity, godhead; the Divine Being; God; a deity, a god; a being who partakes of the divine nature; a supernatural power or influence; the science of divine things; theology; (*Univ.*) the faculty of theology. **divinity-calf,** *n.* Dark brown calf, ungilded and with blind stamping, used for binding theological works. **divinize,** *v.t.* To treat as divine; to deify. **divinization** (-zā' shŭn), *n.*

divisible (di viz' i bėl) [L. *dīvīsibilis*, from *dīvīsus*, p.p. of *dīvidere*, to DIVIDE], *a.* Capable of division; (*Math.*) able to be divided into equal parts by a divisor without a remainder. **divisibility** (-bil' i ti), *n.*

division (di vizh' ŭn) [DIVIDE], *n.* The act of dividing; the state of being divided; separation; distribution; that which divides or separates; a boundary, a partition; a separate or distinct part; a district, an administrative unit; a separate body of men; a distinct sect or body; disunion, disagreement, variance; (*Nat. Hist.*) a separate class, species, variety, or kind; a distinction; (*Parl.*) the part of a county or borough returning a Member; (*Parl.*) the separation of members for the purpose of voting; (*Math.*) the process of dividing one number by another; (*Log.*) the separation of a genus into its constituent species; classification; analysis of meaning; (*Mil.*) a body of men, usually three brigades, under the command of a general officer, applied loosely to smaller bodies; (*Nav.*) a number of vessels under one command; *arrangement, disposition; *(*Mus.*) variation. **division of labour:** Distribution of parts of industrial and other work among different persons in order to secure specialization on particular processes and to save time. **long division:** (*Arith.*) The process of dividing a number by another number greater than 12, the stages being fully set forth. **short division:** (*Arith.*) Division by a number less than 12, the successive steps being performed mentally. **divisional, -sionary,** *a.* **divisionally,** *adv.* ***divisive,** *a.* Forming or noting division, analytical; tending to division or dissension. ***divisiveness,** *n.* **divisor** (di vī' zŏr), *n.* (*Math.*) That number by which a dividend is divided; a number that divides another without a remainder. **divisural** (di viz' ū răl), *a.* Divisional (used of the dividing line in the peristome of mosses).

divorce (di vôrs') [F., from L. *dīvortium*, from *dīvortere*, old form of *divertere*, to DIVERT], *n.* The dissolution of the marriage tie by competent authority; the separation of husband and wife by judicial sentence of a secular or ecclesiastical court; (*fig.*) a separation of things closely connected. *v.t.* To dissolve by legal process the bonds of marriage between; to separate (a married pair) by divorce; to obtain a divorce from; to put away (a spouse) by divorce; (*fig.*) to dissolve (a union); to disunite things closely connected; to remove, to separate. ***divorceable,** *a.* **divorcee** (di-, dī vôr sē'), *n.* One who has been divorced. ***divorcement,** *n.* A divorce; a dissolution of the marriage contract. **Bill of Divorcement:** An Act of Parliament as formerly required, setting forth the grounds for a divorce. **divorcer,** *n.* One who procures a divorce; one who or that which produces separation. ***divorcive,** *a.*

divot (div' ŏt) [Sc. and North., etym. unknown], *n.* A turf, a sod used for roofing or capping dry walls; (*Golf*) a piece of turf torn up by the head of a club when driving.

***divulgate** (di vŭl' gāt) [L. *dīvulgātus*, p.p. of *dīvulgāre*, as foll.], *v.t.* To spread or publish abroad; to make public. **divulgation** (-gā' shŭn), *n.*

divulge (di vŭlj') [prob. from F. *divulguer* or directly from L. *dīvulgāre* (DI- (1), *vulgāre*, to publish, from *vulgus*, the people)], *v.t.* To make known; to reveal, disclose; to publish; *to proclaim publicly. **v.i.* To become known. **divulgence,** *n.* **divulger,** *n.* **divulgement,** *n.*

***divulsion** (di-, dī vŭl' shŭn) [F., from L. *dīvulsio -ōnem*, from *dīvellere* (DI- (1), *vellere*, to pluck, pull)], *n.* The act of tearing away or asunder; a rending asunder; laceration. ***divulsive,** *a.*

divvy (div' i), *n.* (*colloq.*) A dividend.

dixie (diks' i) [Hind. *degshi*, a pot], *n.* A field-service kettle, a pot for cooking over an outdoor fire.

dizen (dī' zėn, diz' en) [cp. L.G. *diesse*, A.-S. *distæf*, DISTAFF], *v.t.* To dress up; to deck out gaudily.

dizzy (diz' i) [A.-S. *dysig*, foolish, stupid, *dysigian*, to be foolish], *a.* Giddy, dazed, vertiginous; causing dizziness, confusing; high; whirling; reeling; *foolish, stupid. *v.t.* To make dizzy; to confuse, to confound. **dizzily,** *adv.* **dizziness,** *n.*

djinn [JINN].

do (1) (doo) [A.-S. *dōn*, past, *dyde*, p.p. *gedōn*, from Teut. *dō-* (Dut. *doen, deed, gedaan*, G. *tun, tat, taten, getan*)] (*2nd sing.* **doest;** *aux.* **dost,** dŭst; *3rd sing.* **does,** dŭz; ***doth,** dŭth; *past*, **did, didst;** *p.p.* **done,** dŭn; **don't,** dōnt, **didn't,** colloq. for *do not, did not*; **doesn't,** dŭznt, for *does not*), *v.t.* To execute, perform, effect, transact, carry out (a work, thing, service, benefit, injury, etc., or the action of any verb understood); to bring about as a result; to produce, to make; to bring to an end, to complete, finish, accomplish; to produce, to cause, to render (good, evil, honour, justice, injury, etc.) to; to work, act, operate, deal with; hence, to translate, to prepare, to cook, to play the part of; (*colloq.*) to cheat, to swindle, to humbug; (*colloq.*) to injure, to kill; (*slang*) to entertain, feed; (*colloq.*) to undergo (as a punishment); to tire out, fatigue, exhaust; (*colloq.*) to visit and see the sights of; to employ, exert, put forth (as effort). *v.i.* To act, behave, conduct oneself; to strive, to work or act vigorously; to perform deeds; to finish, to make an end, to cease; to fare, to get on (in an undertaking or in health, etc.); to serve, to suffice, to be enough (for), to answer the purpose. *aux.v.* (in neg. and in interrog. sentences), as *I do not play, do you not play?*; with inf. for special emphasis, as *I do believe, they do love him*; in the imper., as *do give it him, do but ask*; in inverted sentences, as *seldom did it occur*; also poetically, *it did appear*; substitute (for a verb expressing any action, usu. to avoid repetition), as *I walked there in the same time as he did; you play whist as well as he does; did he catch the train? I did; he often comes here, I seldom do.* *n.* A swindle, a fraud; a party, a jollification. **to-do:** Bustle, confusion. **to do away with:** To put out of sight or mind; to abolish; to make away with, to kill. **do-nothing,** *n.* An idler. *a.* Lazy, idle. **to do by:** To treat, to deal with. **to do for:** To suit; to put an end to; to ruin, to kill; (*colloq.*) to attend upon. **to do one's best** or **diligence:** To exert one's best efforts. **to do in:** (*slang*) To kill. **to do over:** To perform a second time; to cover with a coating. **to do time:** (*slang*) To serve a prison sentence. **to do to:** To do by. **to do to death:** To put, or cause to be put, to death; to kill. **to do up:** To put in repair; to paint and paper (as a house); to pack in a parcel; to tire out. **to do with:** To have business or connexion with; to dispose of, to employ; to make shift with. **to do without:** To dispense with. **to have to do with:** To have business or intercourse with; to deal with. **well-to-do:** Well off; prosperous. ***do-all,** *n.* A factotum. **anything doing:** Anything going on. **nothing doing:** (*Comm.*) No business; (*colloq.*) no offers; no acceding to a request. **doable,** *a.* **doer,** *n.*

do (2) (dō) [arbitrary], *n.* (*Mus.*) The first of the syllables used for the solfeggio of the scale; the note C.

dobbin (dob' in) [a familiar form of *Robert*, cp. ROBIN], *n.* A draught horse.

dobby (dob' i) [cp. prec.], *n.* A brownie; (*Weaving*) an attachment to a loom for weaving small figures.

dobchick [DABCHICK].

Docetæ (dō sē' tē) [Gr. *Dokētai*, from *dokeein*, to see], *n.pl.* A sect in the early Church who maintained that Christ had not a natural but only a phantasmal or celestial body. **Docetic,** *a.* **Docetism,** *n.* **Docetist,** *n.*

doch-an-dorris (*Eng. pron.* dok an dor' is) [Gael.], *n.* A stirrup cup; a farewell drink.

dochmius (dok' mi ŭs) [L., from Gr. *dochmios*, pertaining to a *dochmē*, a hand's-breadth], *n.* (*pl.* **-mii**) A metrical foot of five syllables, one short, two long, one short, and one long: ◡ -- ◡ -. **dochmiac,** *a.* Pertaining to or consisting of dochmii. *n.* (*usu. in pl.*) A line composed of such feet.

docile (dō' sīl, dos' il) [F., from L. *docilis*, from *docēre*, to teach], *a.* Teachable; willing or ready to learn; tractable; easily managed. **docility** (dŏ sil' i ti), *n.*

docimasy (dos' i mȧs i) [Gr. *dokimasia*, from *dokimazein*, to examine], *n.* (*Min.*) The act or process of assaying metals; (*Chem. and Med.*) act or process of testing, esp. in materia medica and forensic medicine. **docimastic** (-mȧs' tik), *a.* **docimology** (-mol' ŏ ji), *n.* A treatise on metallurgy, or the art of assaying metals, etc.

dock (1) (dok) [A.-S. *docce*], *n.* A common name for various species of the genus *Rumex*, perennial herbs, most of them troublesome weeds, esp. the common dock, *R. obtusifolius.*

dock (2) (dok) [cp. Icel. *dockr*, a short, stumpy tail, L.G. *dokke*, a bunch, a stump, G. *docke*, a plug, a peg], *n.* The solid fleshy part of an animal's tail; the tail after being cut short; *a leather case for a docked tail; the divided part of the crupper through which a horse's tail is put. *v.t.* To cut the tail off; to cut short; to abridge, to curtail; to deduct a part from; to deprive of a part of.

dock (3) (dok) [cp. M.Dut. *docke*, *dokke* (mod. Dut. *dok*), also prov. Engl. *doke*, a hollow], *n.* An artificial basin in which ships are built or repaired; (*often in pl.*) an artificial basin for the reception of ships to load and unload; a dockyard; a wharf; (*Railway*) an enclosure between platforms where lines terminate; (*Am.*) a wharf. *v.t.* To bring into dock; to place in a dry dock; to equip with docks. **dry, graving dock:** A dock from which the water can be pumped out for building and repairing vessels. **floating dock:** A capacious iron or wooden structure into which a vessel can be floated, the internal water then being pumped out to result in a floating dry dock. **wet dock:** A dock with the water kept at high-tide level, in which vessels load or unload. **dock-charges, -dues,** *n.pl.* Dues payable by vessels using docks. **dock-glass,** *n.* A large glass, orig. used for sampling wine at the docks. **dock-master,** *n.* The officer in charge of docks or of a dockyard. **dockyard,** *n.* A large enclosed area with wharves, docks, etc., where vessels are built or repaired, usually in connexion with the Navy. **dockage,** *n.* Accommodation in docks; dock-dues. **docker,** *n.* A labourer at the docks. **dockize,** *v.t.* To convert a river into a floating harbour or range of docks. **dockization** (dok i zā' shŭn), *n.*

dock (4) (dok) [perh. through thieves' cant from *dok*, a hutch, a pen], *n.* The enclosure for prisoners in a criminal court. **dock brief,** *n.* (*Law*) A brief undertaken without a fee for a prisoner who would not otherwise be defended.

docket (dok' ėt) [etym. doubtful], *n.* A summary or digest; a register of judgments; an alphabetical list of cases for trial; a similar summary of business to be dealt with by a committee or assembly; an endorsement of a letter or document summarizing the contents; a warrant certifying payment of duty, issued by a custom-house; a certificate from the Clearing House entitling to delivery of cotton goods; a ticket or label showing the address of a package, etc.; a form of rationing coupon. *v.t.* (*Law*) To make an abstract, digest, or summary of judgments and enter in a docket; to make an abstract or note of the contents of (a document) on the back.

dockize [DOCK (3)].

doctor (dok' tŏr) [O.F. *doctour*, L. *doctōrem*, acc. of *doctor*, from *docēre*, to teach], *n.* A qualified practitioner of medicine or surgery; *a teacher, a learned man; one who has taken the highest degree in a faculty at a University either for proficiency or as a compliment; a name for various mechanical devices; an artificial fly for salmon; (*slang*) a loaded die; brown sherry, from its being doctored; a ship's cook; (*Austral.*) a camp cook. *v.t.* To administer medicines to; to treat medically; to confer the degree of doctor on; to patch up, to mend; to adulterate; to falsify. *v.i.* To practise as a physician. **Doctors' Commons** [COMMONS]. **Doctors of the Church:** A name applied to certain early Fathers, esp. Ambrose, Augustine, Jerome, and Gregory, in the Western Church, and Athanasius, Basil, Gregory of Nazianzen, and Chrysostom, in the Eastern. **doctor's stuff,** *n.* Physic. **doctoral,** *a.* **doctorial,** *a.* **doctorate,** *n.* The degree, rank, or title of a doctor; doctorship. **doctorhood,** *n.* **doctoring,** *n.* Medical treatment; adulteration, falsification. **doctorless,** *a.* **doctorship,** *n.* Doctorate; the personality of a doctor. ***doctress,** *n.*

doctrinaire (dok tri nâr') [F., from L. *doctrīna*, DOCTRINE], *n.* One who theorizes in politics without regard to practical considerations; a theorizer, an ideologist; (*Hist.*) one of a party of French politicians, who, under the Restoration (1814–30), advocated a limited monarchy with representative institutions. *a.* Visionary, theoretical, impractical. **doctrinairian,** *a.* and *n.* **doctrinairism, doctrinarianism,** *n.*

doctrine (dok' trin) [F., from L. *doctrīna*, from DOCTOR], *n.* That which is taught; the principles, tenets, or dogmas of any church, sect, literary or scientific school, or party; *a lesson; *learning, erudition. **Monroe doctrine,** *n.* The view that non-American powers should not intervene in American affairs, first set forth by President Monroe in 1823. **doctrinal** (dok' tri nȧl), *a.* *Pertaining to the act, art, or practice of teaching; pertaining to doctrine; of the nature of or containing a doctrine. **doctrinally,** *adv.* **doctrinism, doctrinist,** *n.* **doctrinize,** *v.i.*

document (dok' ū mėnt) [F., from L. *documentum*, from *docēre*, to teach], *n.* A written or printed paper containing information for the establishment of facts; (*loosely*) any mark, fact, deed, or incident furnishing evidence or illustration of a statement or view; *a precept, a dogma; *an example, a warning; *a lesson. *v.t.* To furnish with documents necessary to establish any fact; to prove by means of documents; *to teach. **documental** (-men' tȧl), *a.* **documentary** (dok ū men' tȧ ri), *a.* **documentary film,** *n.* (*Cinema.*) A film which represents real events or phases of life. **documentation** (-tā' shŭn), *n.*

dodder (1) (dod' ėr) [M.E. *doder*, cp. Dan. *dodder*, G. *dotter*], *n.* A plant of the genus *Cuscuta*, which consists of slender, twining leafless parasites, involving and destroying the plants on which they grow.

dodder (2) (dod' ėr) [etym. doubtful; cp. TOTTER], *v.i.* To shake, to tremble, to totter; to be feeble and worn out. **doddering-grass,** *n.* Quaking-grass.

doddered (dod' ėrd) [prob. from obs. *dod*, to poll or top], *a.* Having lost their top or branches (of aged oaks, etc.); *(*erroneously*) overgrown with dodder.

doddy (dod' i) [Sc. from Gael. *dod*, peevishness], *a.* Cross-grained, crabbed.

dodec-, dodeca- [Gr. *dōdeka*], *pref.* Twelve. **dodecagon** (dō dek' ȧ gŏn) [Gr. *dōdekagōnon* (-GON)], *n.* (*Geom.*) A plane figure of 12 equal angles and sides. **dodecagyn** (dō dek' ȧ jin), *n.* (*Bot.*) A plant having 12 separate styles. ***dodecagynia*** (-jin' i ȧ) [*gunē*, a woman, a female], *n.pl.* (*Bot.*) A Linnæan order of plants containing those having from 12 to 19 free styles. **dodecagynian, dodecagynous** (-kăj' i nŭs), *a.* **dodecahedron** (-hē' drŏn, -hed' rön) [Gr. *dōdekaedron* (*hedra*, a seat)], *n.* (*Geom.*) A solid figure of 12 equal sides, each of which is a regular pentagon. **dodecahedral,** *a.* ***dodecandria*** (dō dė kăn′ dri å) [*anēr andros*, a male], *n.pl.* (*Bot.*) A Linnæan class of plants, comprising those having 12 to 19 free stamens. **dodecandrian, -drous,** *a.* **dodecapetalous** (dō dek å pet′ å lůs), *a.* (*Bot.*) Having 12 petals. **dodecasyllable** (dō dek å sil′ åbl), *n.* (*Pros.*) A verse of 12 syllables; an alexandrine.

dodge (doj) [etym. doubtful], *v.i.* To start aside suddenly; to change place by a sudden movement; to move rapidly from place to place so as to elude pursuit, etc.; to act trickily, to prevaricate, to quibble. *v.t.* To escape from by starting aside; to evade by craft; to baffle by playing fast and loose with, to cheat; to dog. *n.* A sudden start or movement to one side; a trick, an artifice; an evasion; a skilful contrivance or expedient; a particular change or order in bell-ringing. **dodger,** *n.* One who dodges or evades; a trickster, a cheat; (*Am.*) a hard-baked cake or biscuit. **dodgery,** *n.* **dodgy,** *a.* Full of dodges; crafty, artful, tricky.

dodo (dō′ dō) [Port. *doudo*, silly, foolish], *n.* (*pl.* **-oes, -os**) A large bird, *Didus ineptus*, allied to the pigeons, with rudimentary wings, found in Mauritius in great numbers when that island was colonized in 1644 by the Dutch, but soon totally exterminated, the last record of its occurrence being in the year 1681.

dodonæan (dō dō nē′ ån) [L. *Dōdōnæus*, Gr. *Dōdōnaios*], *a.* An epithet of Jupiter, worshipped in the temple of Dodona, where there was a famous oracle.

doe (dō) [A.-S. *dā*, cp. L. *dāma*], *n.* The female of the fallow deer; the female of the rabbit, hare, and sometimes of other animals. **doeskin,** *n.* The skin of a doe; an untwilled fine woollen cloth resembling this.

doer, does, doest [DO (1)].

doff (dof) [contr. of DO OFF], *v.t.* To take off (as clothes); to lay aside, to discard. *v.i.* To take off the hat as a mark of respect. **doffer,** *n.* A part of a carding-machine for stripping the cotton or wool from the cylinder; a person who removes the full bobbins or spindles.

dog (dog) [A.-S. *docga*], *n.* A wild or domesticated quadruped of numerous breeds classed together as *Canis familiaris*, derived from crossing of various species living and extinct; the male of the wolf, fox, and other animals; a surly fellow; a contemptible person; a gay young fellow; (*Astron.*) one of two southern constellations; a name given to various mechanical contrivances acting as holdfasts; a device with a tooth which penetrates or grips an object and detains it; an andiron or fire-dog; *the hammer of a fire-arm. *v.t.* To follow like a dog; to track the footsteps of; (*fig.*) to follow or attend closely; (*Naut.*) to fasten, to secure. **the dogs,** *n.pl.* (*colloq.*) Greyhound races. ***a dead dog:** A thing of no worth. **dog in the manger:** One who prevents other people from enjoying what is useless to him; a churlish person. **hot dog,** *n.* (*colloq.*) A hot sausage sandwich. **lucky dog:** A lucky fellow. **sea-dog:** A jack-tar, an old sailor, esp. one of the Elizabethan adventurers; a luminous appearance on the horizon presaging storm. **sly dog:** An artful fellow. **sun-dog,** *n.* A parhelion. **to die a dog's death:** To perish miserably or shamefully. **to go to the dogs:** To go to ruin. **to lead a dog's life:** To live a life of continual worry; to be continually bickering. **to rain cats and dogs:** To rain in torrents. **to throw** or **give to the dogs:** To throw away. ***dog-ape,** *n.* A male ape. **dog-bane,** *n.* A plant with a bitter root, belonging to the genus *Apocynum*, supposed to be poisonous to dogs. **dog-belt,** *n.* A belt with a chain attached, worn by those who draw sledges in mines. **dog-biscuit,** *n.* Coarse biscuit, often mixed with greaves for feeding dogs. ***dog-bolt,** *n.* A wretch, a villain. **dog-box,** *n.* A railway van for dogs. **dog-cart,** *n.* A light, two-wheeled, double-seated, one-horse vehicle. **a dog's chance:** The slightest chance. **dog-cheap,** *a.* [according to Prof. Skeat, from Swed. dial. *dog*, very.] Extremely cheap, dirt-cheap. **dog-collar,** *n.* A leather or metal collar worn by dogs; (*fig.*) a high, straight shirt-collar; a stiff, white collar fastening at the back, as worn by clergymen. **dog-days,** *n.pl.* The period in July and August during which the dog-star rises and sets with the sun, a conjunction formerly supposed to account for the great heat usual at that season. **dog-eared,** *a.* Dog's-eared. **dog-faced,** *a.* Applied to a kind of baboon. **dog-fall,** *n.* (*Wrestling*) A fall in which both wrestlers touch the ground together. **dog-fancier,** *n.* One who keeps and breeds dogs for sale. **dog-fennel,** *n.* The stinking camomile, *Anthemis cotula*, an acrid emetic. **dog-fight,** *n.* A fight between dogs; a wrangle; (*Aviat.*) a duel in the air between two aircraft. **dog-fox,** *n.* A male fox; *(*fig.*) a crafty fellow. **dog-fish,** *n.* Any species of the genus *Scyllium*, sometimes extended to the family *Scylliidæ*, comprising small sharks which follow their prey in packs, whence their popular name. **dog-grass,** *n.* Couch-grass, *Triticum repens*. **dog-head,** *n.* The hammer of a gun-lock. **dog-hearted,** *a.* Cruel, pitiless, malicious. **dog-hole,** *n.* A place fit only for dogs. **dog-house, -hutch,** *n.* A dog-kennel; (*fig.*) a miserable room. **dog-kennel,** *n.* A house or hut for a dog. **dog-Latin,** *n.* Barbarous, ungrammatical Latin. **dog-lead,** *n.* A string or thin chain for leading a dog. ***dog-leech,** *n.* A dog doctor; used as a term of reproach or contempt. **dog-leg,** *a.* Bent like a dog's hind leg, applied to a crook-shanked chisel. **dog-leg fence:** (*Austral.*) A fence made of logs laid horizontally on X-shaped supports. **dog-legged,** *a.* Applied to staircases constructed in zigzags without a well-hole. **dog-power,** *n.* A mechanical device worked by a dog; (*Am.*) a churn worked by a dog. **dog-rose,** *n.* The wild brier, *Rosa canina*. **dog's-ear,** *n.* A corner of a leaf of a book turned down like a dog's ear. *v.t.* To turn the corners of (a book) by careless handling. **dog's-eared,** *a.* **dog's grass** [DOG-GRASS]. **dog-shore,** *n.* One of two struts that hold the cradle of a ship from sliding on the slipways when the keel-blocks are taken out. **dog-sick,** *a.* Exceedingly sick; vomiting. **dog-skin,** *n.* The skin of a dog tanned for gloves; an imitation of this. *a.* Made of dog-skin. **dog-sleep,** *n.* A light, fitful sleep. **dog's letter,** *n.* The letter *r*, from its snarling sound. **dog's meat,** *n.* Coarse meat, given as food to dogs; (*fig.*) refuse, rubbish. **dog's mercury,** *n.* *Mercurialis perennis*, a common poisonous plant. **dog's-nose,** *n.* A mixture of gin and beer. **dog-star,** *n.* Sirius, the principal star in the constellation *Canis major* [DOG-DAYS]. **dog's-tail,** *n.* A pasture-grass, *Cynosurus cristatus*. **dog-tired,** *n.* Worn out. **dog's-tongue,** *n.* The hound's tongue, *Cynoglossum officinale*. **dog's-tooth,** *n.* A canine tooth; (*Arch.*) a kind of ornament used in Early English mouldings. **dog-tooth,** *a.* Dog's tooth. **dog-tooth spar:** A kind of calcareous spar crystallizing in pointed rhombohedral forms. **dog-trot,** *n.* A gentle easy trot; a jog-trot. **dog-vane,** *n.* (*Naut.*) A small vane of cork and feathers, placed on the weather-rail as a guide to the man at the wheel. **dog-violet,** *n.* The scentless wild violet, *Viola canina*. **dog-watch,** *n.* (*Naut.*) One of two watches of two hours each between 4 and 8 p.m. **dog-wolf,** *n.* A male wolf. **doggish,** *a.* **doggishly,** *adv.* **doggishness,** *n.* **doggy, doggie,** *n.* Pet term for a dog. *a.* Pertaining to a dog; (*fig.*) smart, chic, with an air; flashy, raffish. **doghood,** *n.* **dogless,** *a.* **doglike,** *a.* Like a dog; unquestioningly obedient. **to lie doggo:** (*colloq.*) To wait silently and motionlessly.

Dogberry [pers. name], *n.* An ignorant, conceited, but good-natured constable in *Much Ado about Nothing*; an officious constable or policeman; an incapable and overbearing magistrate.

dogberry (dog′ be ri), *n.* (*Bot.*) The fruit of the wild cornel or dogwood, *Cornus sanguinea*; also *Viburnum opulus*, *Arctostaphylos uva ursi*, and the fruit of *Rosa canina*. **dogberry tree** [DOGWOOD].

doge (dōj) [It. *doge* (dō′ jā), L. *ducem*, acc. of *dux*, leader (cp. DUKE)], *n.* The title of the chief magistrate of the republics of Venice and Genoa. **dogate** (dō′ gāt), *n.* The position, office, or rank of a doge.

dogged (dog′ ėd), *a.* Stubborn like a dog, obstinate, persistent, tenacious; *ill-conditioned, malignant. **doggedly,** *adv.* **doggedness,** *n.*

dogger (dog′ ėr) [A.-F. *doggere*; etym. unknown], *n.* A Dutch fishing-vessel with bluff bows like a ketch, employed in the North Sea in the cod and herring fishery.

doggerel (dog′ ėr ėl) [etym. unknown], *a.* and *n.* Originally applied to loose, irregular verses, such as those in Butler's *Hudibras*; now to verses written with little regard to rhythm or rhyme.

dogma (dog′ mȧ) [L., from Gr. *dogma -atos*, from *dokein*, to seem, to think, cogn. with L. *docēre*, to teach], *n.* (*pl.* **-as, -ata**) An established principle, tenet, or system of doctrines put forward to be received on authority, esp. that of a Church, as opposed to one deduced from experience or reasoning; a positive, magisterial, or arrogant expression of opinion. **dogmatic, *-al** (dog măt′ ik, -ȧl), *a.* Pertaining to dogma, doctrinal; based on theory not induction; asserted with authority, positive, authoritative; magisterial, arrogant, dictatorial. **dogmatically,** *adv.* **dogmatics,** *n.* Doctrinal theology, the science which deals with the statement and definition of Christian doctrine. **dogmatism** (dog′ mȧ tizm), *n.* Dogmaticalness; arrogance or undue positiveness in assertion; the rule of dogma in the realm of thought. **dogmatist,** *n.* **dogmatize,** *v.i.* To make dogmatic assertions; to lay down principles with undue positiveness and confidence. *v.t.* To lay down as a dogma. **dogmato-,** *comb. form.* **dogsbody** (dogz′ bod i), *n.* (*colloq.*) A useful person of little importance, a drudge; (*Nav.*) a concoction of pea soup, biscuit, scraps, etc.

dogwood (dog′ wud), *n.* (*Bot.*) The genus *Cornus*, esp. *C. sanguinea*, the wild cornel; also applied to *Euonumus europaeus* and *Rhamnus frangula*.

doh (dō) [DO (2)].

doiled (doild), **doilt** (doilt) [Sc. and North.], *a.* Crazy, foolish.

doily (doi′ li) [name of maker], *n.* A small ornamental mat or napkin on which to place bottles, glasses, etc.

doings (doo′ ingz), *n.pl.* (*colloq.*) Things done or performed; events, transactions, proceedings, affairs, goings-on; objects; behaviour, conduct.

doit (doit) [Dut. *duit*; perh. conn. with A.-S. *thwitan*, to cut], *n.* A small Dutch copper coin worth about half a farthing; a small Scots copper coin; any small piece of money, a trifle.

doited (doi′ tėd) [perh. a var. of DOTED, see DOTE], *a.* Crazed; mentally affected, esp. by old age.

dolabra (dȯ lā′ brȧ) [L.], *n.* (*pl.* ***-brae***) A kind of mattock or pickaxe used by Roman soldiers in making entrenchments and destroying fortifications. **dolabriform,** *a.* Having the form of an axe; (*Bot.*) hatchet-shaped as the leaves of *Mesembryanthemum dolabriforme*; (*Ent.*) applied to joints of the antennæ.

doldrums (dol′ drŭmz) [prob. a slang deriv. from DULL], *n.pl.* Low spirits, the dumps; (*Naut.*) that part of the ocean near the equator between the regions of the trade-winds where calms and variable winds prevail. **in the doldrums:** In low spirits, in the dumps; (*Naut.*) becalmed.

dole (1) (dōl) [O.F. *doel* (F. *deuil*), late L. *dolium*, L. *dolor*], *n.* Sorrow, lamentation; a cause of grief. **doleful,** *a.* Sorrowful, sad; afflicted, lamentable; dismal, gloomy. **dolefully,** *adv.* **dolefulness,** *n.* ***dolesome,** *a.* Doleful, cheerless, dispiriting. ***dolesomely,** *adv.* **dolesomeness,** *n.*

dole (2) (dōl) [A.-S. *dāl*, var. of *dæl*, DEAL (1)], *n.* A share, a lot, a portion; distribution, esp. in charity; alms, money, or food distributed in charity; *fortune, lot; *dealing, delivery (of blows, death, etc.); unemployment relief. *v.t.* To distribute. **on the dole:** In receipt of unemployment relief. **to dole out:** To distribute in small quantities. **dolesman, -woman,** *n.* One who receives a small charitable gift.

dolerite (dol′ ėr īt) [F. *dolérite*, Gr. *doleros*, deceptive, from the difficulty of discriminating the compounds], *n.* (*Min.*) A variety of trap-rock consisting of feldspar and pyroxene.

dolichocephalic, -cephalous (dol i kō sė făl′ ik, -sef′ ȧ lŭs) [Gr. *dolichos*, long, CEPHALIC], *a.* Long-headed; an epithet applied to skulls in which the width from side to side bears a less proportion to the width from front to back than 80 per cent. **dolichocephalism** (-sef′ ȧ lizm), *n.*

dolichos (dol′ i kŏs) [Gr., long], *n.* (*Bot.*) A genus of papilionaceous plants with long pods, allied to the kidney bean.

dolichosaurus (dol i kō saw′ rŭs) [Gr. *dolichos*, as prec., *sauros*, a lizard], *n.* (*Palæont.*) A small snake-like lacertilian reptile from the chalk.

dolichurus (dol i kū′ rŭs) [Gr. *dolichouros* (*dolichos*, long, *oura*, a tail)], *n.* (*Pros.*) A verse having a redundant foot.

dolium (dō′ li ŭm) [L., a cask, a jar], *n.* (*Zool.*) A genus of gastropodous molluscs from warm seas.

doll (dol) [pet name for *Dorothy*], *n.* A child's toy representing a human figure; a pretty but silly woman. **to doll up:** (*colloq.*) To dress up, to make oneself look smart. **dollish,** *a.* **dollishly,** *adv.* **dollishness,** *n.*

dollar (dol′ ȧr) [L.G. *daler*, G. *thaler*, abbr. of *Joachimsthaler*, coins of silver from a mine in the *Joachimsthal*], *n.* A silver coin, unit of currency in Canada and U.S.A. equivalent to 100 cents; applied to coins of different values; (*slang*) five shillings; a crown piece. **dollar area,** *n.* (*Fin.*) The area in which currency is linked to the U.S. dollar. **dollar gap,** *n.* (*Fin.*) The excess of imports over exports in trade with a dollar-area country.

dollop (dol′ ŏp) [etym. doubtful], *n.* (*colloq.*) A shapeless lump; a heap, quantity. **all the dollop:** (*slang*) The whole thing.

dolly (dol′ i), *n.* A pet name for a doll; (*Mining*) a perforated board placed over a tub to wash ore in; the tub itself; a hoisting platform; an appliance used in pile-driving; a stick or club with which dirty clothes are agitated in the wash-tub; *a mistress. *a.* Dollish. **dolly-shop,** *n.* An unlicensed pawnshop; a marine-store (from a black-doll being used as a sign). **dolly-tub,** *n.* A washing-tub.

Dolly Varden (var′ dėn) [a character in Dickens's 'Barnaby Rudge'], *n.* A large-patterned print dress; a wide-brimmed woman's hat with one side bent down.

dolman (dol′ mȧn) [F., from G., from Hung. *dolmany*, Turk. *dōlāmān*], *n.* A long Turkish robe, open in front, and with narrow sleeves; a woman's loose mantle with hanging sleeves; a hussar's jacket or cape with sleeves hanging loose.

dolmen (dol′ mėn) [F. prob. from Corn. *dolmēn*, *tolmēn* (*doll*, *toll*, hole, *mēn*, stone)], *n.* A cromlech; the megalithic framework of a chambered cairn, consisting usually of three or more upright stones supporting a roof-stone.

dolomite (dol′ ō mīt) [*Dolomieu* (1750–1801), French geologist. Nothing to do with the Dolomite Mountains in Tyrol.], *n.* A brittle, subtransparent or translucent mineral consisting of the carbonates of lime and magnesia. **dolomitic** (-mit′ ik), *a.* **dolomitize, dolomize,** *v.t.* **dolomitization** (zā′ shŭn), *n.*

***dolorous** (dol′ ŏr ŭs) [O.F. *dolerus* from DOLOUR], *a.* Full of pain or grief; causing or expressing pain or grief, dismal, doleful. ***dolorously,** *adv.* ***dolourousness,** *n.*

dolose (dȯ lōs′) [L. *dolōsus*, from *dolus*, deceit], *a.* (*Law*) With criminal intent.

***dolour** (dol′ ȯr) [O.F., from L. *dolōrem*, acc. of *dolor*, from *dolēre*, to grieve], *n.* Pain, suffering, distress; grief, sorrow, lamentation. **Our Lady of Dolours:** (*R.-C. Ch.*) A title given to the Virgin Mary on account of her sorrows at the Passion. **Feast of the Dolours:** A festival in commemoration of these on the Friday after Passion Sunday.

dolphin (dol′ fin) [M.E. *delfyn*, L. *delphīnus*, see DAUPHIN, O.F. *daulphin*, which affected the later spelling], *n.* The cetacean genus *Delphinus*, esp. *D. delphis*, the common dolphin; the dorado, *Coryphæna hippuris*, which takes a series of brilliant colours in dying; (*Naut.*) a mooring-post; an anchored spar with rings, serving as a mooring-buoy; (*Her., etc.*) a conventional representation of a curved fish; *a ponderous mass of metal let fall suddenly from the yard-arm of a vessel upon an enemy's ship; *the Dauphin. **dolphin fly,** *n. Aphis fabæ*, an insect infesting bean-plants. ***dolphin-like,** *a.* Showing the back above the surface of the sea, etc. **dolphinet,** *n.* *A female dolphin.

dolt (dōlt) [prob. *dult*, DULLED, see DULL], *n.* A stupid fellow; a numskull. **doltish,** *a.* **doltishly,** *adv.* **doltishness,** *n.*

dom (1) (dom) [abbr. of L. *dominus*, lord], *n.* (*R.-C. Ch.*) A title given to members of the Benedictine and Carthusian orders.

dom (2) (dom) [G., cathedral, L. *domus*, DOME], *n.* A Continental cathedral.

-dom [A.-S. *dōm*, judgment, cogn. with G. *-tum*], *suf.* Noting power, jurisdiction, office, or condition, as in *earldom, kingdom, officialdom, popedom.*

domain (dō mān′) [F. *domaine*, late L. *dominicum* L. *dominium*, from *dominus*, lord], *n.* Territory district, or space over which authority, jurisdiction or control is or may be exercised; one's landed property, demesne, estate; (*fig.*) sphere, province, field of influence, thought, or action; *lordship, authority. **eminent domain:** (*Am. and Internat. Law*) The sovereign power of the State to exercise control over private property for public purposes on payment of compensation to owners. **domainal,** *a.*

domboc [DOOM-BOOK, see DOOM].

domdaniel (dom dăn′ i ėl) [F., prob. from Gr. *dōma Daniēl*, the house or hall of Daniel], *n.* A fabulous submarine hall in the continuation of the *Arabian Nights* by Chaves and Cazotte; an 'infernal cave', a 'den of iniquity' (*Carlyle*).

dome (1) (dōm) [M.F. *dome*, It. *duomo*, L. *domus*, a house], *n.* A roof, usually central, the base of which is a circle, an ellipse, or a polygon, and its vertical section a curved line, concave towards the interior; a cupola; a natural vault, arching canopy, or lofty covering; a rounded hill-top; a mansion, temple, or other building of a stately kind; any dome-shaped object or structure; (*Cryst.*) a termination of a prism by two planes meeting above in a horizontal edge. **domed,** *a.* Furnished with a dome; dome-shaped. **domic, domical,** *a.* **domelike,** *a.* **domy,** *a.*

***dome** (2) [DOOM].

Domesday Book (doomz′ dā buk) [M.E. DOOMS-DAY], *n.* A register of the lands of England compiled (1084–86) by order of William the Conqueror, from the results of a Great Inquisition or survey, forming a basis for all historical accounts of the economic state of the country at that epoch.

domestic (dȯ mes′ tik) [F. *domestique*, L. *domesticus*, from *domus*, home], *a.* Pertaining to the home or household; made, done, or performed at home; employed or kept at home; fond of home; tame, not wild; relating to the internal affairs of a nation; not foreign; made in one's own country; (*Am.*) inland (as for postage, etc.), native grown (as for wine, etc.). *n.* A household servant; *a fellow-countryman; (*pl.*) articles of home (as opp. to foreign) manufacture, esp. (*Am.*) cotton cloth. **domestic economy,** *n.* The economical management of household affairs. **domestically,** *adv.* **domesticate** (dȯ mes′ ti kāt), *v.t.* To make domestic or familiar; to naturalize (foreigners, etc.); to accustom to domestic life and the management of household affairs; to tame; to bring into cultivation from a wild state; to civilize. **domesticable,** *a.* **domestication** (-kā′ shŭn), *n.*

domesticity (do mės tis′ i ti), *n.* The state of being domestic; domestic character, homeliness; home life; the tone of home; (*pl.*) domestic affairs, family matters.

domett (dom′ ėt) [etym. unknown], *n.* A plain cloth made of cotton and wool.

domicile (dom′ i sīl, -sil) [F., from L. *domicilium*, from *domus*, home], *n.* A house, a home, a place of abode; (*Law*) a place of permanent residence; length of residence (differing in various countries) necessary to establish jurisdiction in civil actions; the place at which a bill of exchange is made payable. *v.t.* To establish in a place of residence; to make payable at a certain place. *v.i.* To dwell. **domiciliary,** *a.* Pertaining to a domicile or residence. **domiciliary visit,** *n.* A visit under legal authority to a private house, to search for suspected persons or things. **domiciliate,** *v.t.* and *i.* To domicile. **domiciliation** (-ā′ shŭn), *n.*

dominant (dom′ i nănt) [F., from L. *dominans -ntem*, pres.p. of *dominārī*, from *dominus*, lord], *a.* Ruling, governing; predominant, overshadowing, supereminent; (*Mus.*) pertaining to the fifth note of a scale. *n.* (*Mus.*) The fifth note of the scale of any key, counting upwards; the reciting note of Gregorian chants. **dominant chord,** *n.* A chord formed by grouping three tones rising from the dominant by intervals of a third. **dominance,** *n.* **dominantly,** *adv.*

dominate (dom′ i nāt) [L. *dominātus*, p.p. of *dominārī*, as prec.], *v.t.* To predominate over; to be the most influential or the chief or most conspicuous; to overlook (as a hill); to influence controllingly, to rule, to govern. *v.i.* To predominate, to prevail. **domination** (-nā′ shŭn), *n.* The exercise of power or authority; rule, sway, control, dominion, ascendency; (*pl.*) the fourth order of angels. ***dominative** (dom′-), *a.* ***dominator,** *n.*

domineer (dom i nēr′) [M.Dut. *domineren*, O.F. *dominer*, L. *dominārī*, as prec.], *v.i.* To exercise authority arrogantly and tyrannically; to assume superiority over others; to hector, to bluster; *to roister, to revel. *v.t.* To tyrannize over. **domineeringly,** *adv.*

dominical (dȯ min′ ik ȧl) [med. L. *dominicālis*, L. *dominicus*, from *dominus*, lord], *a.* Pertaining to the Lord or the Lord's Day. *n.* The Lord's Day; one who observes the Lord's Day as distinguished from the Jewish Sabbath; a dominical letter. **dominical letter,** *n.* The letter (one of the seven A–G in the calendar) which denotes Sunday in any particular year. **dominical year,** *n.* The year of our Lord, A.D.

Dominican (dȯ min′ ik ȧn) [med. L. *Dominicānus*, from *Dominicus, Domingo*], *n.* One of an order of preaching friars, founded in 1216 by Domingo de Guzman (canonized as St. Dominic); a Black Friar; a native of the island of Dominica. *a.* Pertaining to the Dominicans.

dominie (dom′ i ni) [Sc., from L. *domine*, sir, voc. of *dominus*, lord], *n.* A pedagogue, a schoolmaster.

dominion (dȯ min′ yȯn) [O.F., from late L. *dominio -ōnem*, L. *dominium*, from *dominus*, lord], *n.* Sovereign authority, lordship; control, rule, government; (*Law*) uncontrolled right of possession or use; the domain of a feudal lord; a district, region, or country under one government; (*Pol.*) a self-governing country of the British Commonwealth, esp. Canada.

domino (dom′ i nō) [Sp. or F., from L. *dominus*, lord (orig. perh. the hood worn by a master)], *n.* A masquerade dress worn for disguise by both sexes, consisting of a loose cloak or mantle with a small mask; a kind of half mask; a person wearing a domino; one of twenty-eight oblong dotted pieces of bone or ivory used in playing **dominoes;**

(*slang*) an employee's check handed in to the time-keeper on entering the works or factory. **dom-inoed,** *a.* Wearing a domino.

don (1) (don) [Sp., from L. *dominus*, lord], *n.* A title formerly restricted to noblemen and gentlemen, now common to all classes in Spain; a Spanish gentleman; a Spaniard; a fellow or tutor of a college; a person of distinction; one who assumes airs of importance; (*slang*) an adept, an expert. **Don Juan** (don joo' ȧn) [Byron's poem], *n.* (*fig.*) A lady-killer; a male flirt; a would-be rake. **donnish,** *a.* **donnishness,** *n.*

don (2) (don) [contr. of DO ON], *v.t.* (*past & p.p.* **donned**) To put on, to assume.

dona (dō' nȧ) [Sp. or Port., from L. *domina*, lady], *n.* Lady; madam; (*slang*) a woman; a sweetheart.

donate (don āt') [L. *dōnāre*, to give], *v.t.* To bestow as a gift, esp. on a considerable scale for public or religious purposes. **donator,** *n.* A donor.

donation (dȯ nā' shŭn) [F., from L. *dōnātio -ōnem*, from *dōnāre*, to give, from *dōnum*, a gift], *n.* The act of giving; that which is given, a gift, a presentation, a contribution, esp. to a public institution; (*Law*) an act or contract by which any thing, or the use of and the right to it, is transferred as a free gift to any person or corporation. **donation-party,** *n.* (*Am.*) A party or number of persons assembling at the house of one person (usu. a pastor), each bringing a present.

Donatism (don' ȧ tizm) [med. L. *Donatismus*], *n.* The doctrine of an Arian sect, founded in A.D. 311 by Donatus, a Numidian bishop who denied the infallibility of the Church and insisted on individual holiness as a condition of membership. **Donatist,** *n.* **Donatistic, -tical** (-tis' tik, -ȧl), *a.*

donative (dō' nȧ-, don' ȧ tiv) [L. *dōnātivus*, from *dōnāre*, to give], *n.* A gift, a present, a gratuity, esp. an official donation; a benefice directly given by a patron without presentation to or institution by the ordinary. *a.* Vested or vesting by this form of presentation. **donatory** (don' ȧ-, dō nā' tȯr i), *n.* The recipient of a donation.

done (dŭn) [DO (1)], *p.p.* Performed, executed; (*colloq.*) cheated, baffled; cooked. *int.* Accepted (used to express agreement to a proposal, as a wager, or a bargain). **done brown:** (*slang*) Cheated or over-reached thoroughly. **done for:** Ruined, killed, exhausted. **done up:** Worn our or exhausted from any cause. **to have done:** To have finished. **to have done with:** To have no further concern with.

donee (dō nē') [L. *dōnum*, a gift, -EE], *n.* The person to whom anything is given; (*Law*) the person to whom lands or tenements are given gratuitously or conveyed in fee-tail.

donga (dong' gȧ) [S. African native name], *n.* A gully, a watercourse with steep sides.

***donjon** (don'-, dŭn' jȯn) [DUNGEON], *n.* The grand central tower or keep of esp. a mediæval Norman castle, the lower story generally used as a prison.

donkey (dong' ki) [perh. a double dimin. of DUN, from the colour], *n.* An ass; (*fig.*) a stupid person. **donkey-engine,** *n.* An auxiliary engine for light work on board steamships. **donkey-pump,** *n.* A steam-pump, worked independently of the main engine, for supplying boilers with water and for other purposes. **donkey's years:** (*facet.*) A long time. **donkey-work,** *n.* Drudgery, routine work.

donna (don' ȧ) [It., from L. *domina*, lady], *n.* A lady; madam; a prima donna.

donnered, donnard (don' ėrd) [Sc. v., *donner*, to stupefy, to din], *a.* Stunned, stupefied.

donor (dō' nȯr) [A.-F. *donour*, O.F. *doneur*, L. *dōnātōr -em*, from *dōnāre*, to give], *n.* A giver; (*Law*) one who grants an estate; one who gives blood for transfusion.

do-nothing (doo' nŭth ing), *a.* Idle, indolent, lazy. *n.* An idle person. **do-nothingness,** *n.*

donsie (don' si) [Sc., etym. unknown], *a.* Neat, trim; luckless, unfortunate; stupid, dull.

don't (dōnt), *imper.* (*colloq.*) Do not. *n.* (*facet.*) A prohibition. **don't care,** *adj. phr.* Careless, reckless.

***donzel** (don' zėl) [O.F., cp. DAMOISEAU], *n.* A young gentleman following arms, but not yet knighted.

doodah (doo' da), *n.* **to be all of a doodah:** (*slang*) To be flustered, in a state of confusion.

doodle (1) (doo' dėl) [*onomat.*], *n.* To draw pictures or designs semi-consciously while thinking or listening.

doodle (2) (doo' dėl) [Sc.; cp. G. *dudeln* (*dudelsack*, bagpipe)], *v.t.* To play (the bagpipes). *v.i.* To drone (as a bagpipe). **doodlebug,** *n.* (*colloq.*) The earliest type of flying bomb used by the Germans in the war of 1939–45.

doolally (doo lăl' i) [Indian place-name], *a.* Insane, eccentric.

doolie (doo' li) [Hing. *dōlī*], *n.* A covered litter of bamboo.

doom (doom) [A.-S. *dōm*, from O.Teut. *dōmo* (Dan. and Swed. *dom*, O.H.G. *tuom*, cp. G. *themis*, law)], *n.* Judgment; judicial decision or sentence; condemnation, penalty; *the Day of Judgment; fate or destiny (usu. in an evil sense); ruin, destruction, perdition; *an enactment, statute, or law; *an opinion; *decision. *v.t.* *To judge, to decide; to pass sentence upon; to condemn to punishment; to condemn (to do something); to predestine; to consign to ruin or calamity. **crack of doom:** The dissolution of all things at the universal Judgment. ***doom-book,** *n.* A book of laws, customs, and usages, esp. one compiled under King Alfred. **doomsday,** *n.* The Day of Judgment; the end of the world; a day of judgment or dissolution. **Doomsday Book** [DOMESDAY BOOK].

door (dôr) [A.-S. *dor*, fem. *duru* (cp. Dan. *dor*, Icel. *dyrr*, G. *thür*, Gr. *thura*, L. *fores*)], *n.* A frame of wood or metal, usually on hinges, closing the entrance to a building, room, safe, etc.; an opening for entrance and exit; entrance, exit, access, means of approach; (*fig.*) a house, a room; the entrance or beginning; means of access. **front door:** The principal entrance from the street. **in** or **within doors:** Inside the house. **next door:** In the next house or room. **next door to:** Closely bordering on, nearly, almost. **out of door, doors:** Outside the house; in the open air; done away with. **to lie at one's door:** To be chargeable to. **to show the door:** To turn out; to send away unceremoniously. **to turn from the door:** To refuse to admit; to refuse a beggar or petitioner. **door-bell,** *n.* A bell inside a building actuated by a handle outside a door. **door-case, -frame,** *n.* The structure in which a door swings. **door-keeper,** *n.* A porter, a janitor. **door-mat,** *n.* A mat for removing dirt from the boots, placed inside or outside a door. **door-money,** *n.* Payments taken at a place of entertainment. **door-nail,** *n.* A large nail formerly used for studding doors. **door-plate,** *n.* A metal plate on a door bearing the name of the occupant. **door-post,** *n.* Side-piece or jamb of a doorway. **door-step,** *n.* A step leading up to an outer door. **door-stone,** *n.* A slab in front of a door; the threshold. **doorway,** *n.* An opening in a wall fitted with a door. **doored,** *a.* (usu. with adj. prefixed.) **doorless,** *a.*

dope (dōp) [Dut. *doop*, dipping, sauce, from *doopen*, to dip], *n.* Any thick liquid or semi-fluid used for food or as a lubricant; axle-grease; opium paste; (*colloq.*) a drug given to a horse or greyhound to make it win a race; (*slang*) a stupefying drink; an absorbent material used for holding liquid; the material used to hold nitro-glycerine and other explosives; (*Aviat.*) a varnish used for waterproofing, protecting and strengthening the fabric parts of an aircraft; (*slang*) inside information, particulars. *v.t.* To stupefy with drink, to drug. **dope-fiend,** *n.* A drug addict. **dopey,** *a.* (*colloq.*) Stupid; drugged; sluggish.

Dopper (dop' ėr) [Dut. *Dooper*, Baptist], *n.* (*S. Afr.*) A member of the Reformed Church of South

Africa, a religious sect characterized by extreme simplicity of manners and dress.

Doppler's principle (dop′ lĕrz) [C. *Doppler* (1803–53)], *n.* (*Phys.*) When the source of any wave motion is approached the frequency appears greater than it would to an observer moving away. **Doppler sound effect:** The apparent change of pitch of sound produced by a body when approaching and passing with considerable velocity.

dor (dôr) [A.-S. *dora*, prob. onomat.], *n.* Name of several insects that make a loud humming noise in flying, esp. the black dung-beetle, *Geotrupes stercorarius*; the cockchafer; the rose-beetle. **dor-hawk,** *n.* The goat-sucker or night-jar.

D.O.R.A. [DEFENCE OF THE REALM ACT].

dorado (dō ra′ dō) [Sp., gilded, from L. *deaurātus*, p.p. of *deaurāre* (DE-, *aurum*, gold)], *n.* A fish, *Coryphæna hippuris*, of brilliant colouring, sometimes called a dolphin; (*Astron.*) a southern constellation.

Dorcas (dôr′ kȧs) [Gr. transl. of *Tabitha* (Acts ix. 36)], *n.* A meeting of women for making clothes for the poor. **Dorcas Society,** *n.* A charitable association for providing clothes for the poor.

doree [DORY].

Dorian (dôr′ i ȧn), *a.* Of or relating to Doris, in ancient Greece, or its inhabitants. *n.* An inhabitant of Doris; a member of one of the four great ethnic divisions of the ancient Greeks. **Dorian mode,** *n.* (*Mus.*) A simple, solemn form of music, the first of the authentic Church modes. **Doric** (dor′ ik), *a.* Dorian. *n.* (*Arch.*) Doric order; a broad rustic dialect. **Doric dialect,** *n.* The broad, hard dialect of the natives of Doris; (*fig.*) any broad, hard dialect, esp. the Scottish. **Doric order,** *n.* (*Arch.*) The earliest, strongest, and most simple of the three Grecian orders.

Dorking (dôr′ king) [town in Surrey], *n.* Name of a breed of domestic fowls, orig. from Dorking.

dorlach (dôr′ la*ch*) [Gael.], *n.* A bundle carried by the Highlanders instead of a knapsack.

dormant (dôr′ mȧnt) [F., pres.p. of *dormir*, L. *dormīre*, to sleep], *a.* In a state resembling sleep, torpid, inactive (of animals hibernating); undeveloped, inoperative, not asserted or claimed; in abeyance; *fixed, stationary. **dormant partner,** *n.* A sleeping partner. **dormancy,** *n.*

dormer (dôr′ mėr) [O.F. *dormeor*, L. *dormītōrium*, as prec.], *n.* *A sleeping chamber; a dormer-window. **dormer-window,** *n.* A window piercing a sloping roof and having a vertical frame and a gable (orig. used in sleeping chambers, whence the name).

dormeuse (dôr mĕrz′) [F., fem. of *dormeur*, sleeper, from *dormir*, as prec.], *n.* A travelling-carriage for sleeping in; a kind of couch or settee.

dormitive (dôr′ mi tiv) [L. *dormit*, p.p. stem of *dormīre*, to sleep, -IVE], *a.* Promoting sleep; narcotic, soporific. *n.* An opiate, a soporific.

dormitory (dôr′ mi tȯr i) [L. *dormītōrium*, DORMER], *n.* A sleeping-chamber, esp. in a school or public institution, containing a number of beds; (*fig.*) a resting-place; *a burial-place.

dormouse (dôr′ mous) [prov. Eng. *dorm*, to sleep, F. *dormir* (see DORMANT), MOUSE], *n.* (*pl.* **-mice**) A small British hibernating rodent; *Myoxus avellanarius*; others of the genus *Myoxus*, animals between the mouse and the squirrel. **a.* Dormant.

dormy (dôr′ mi) [Sc., etym. doubtful, said to be from F. *dormi*, p.p. of *dormir*, to sleep], *a.* (*Golf*) Applied to a player when he is as many holes ahead of his opponent as there remain holes to play.

dornic (dôr′ nik) [Flem. *Doornik*, Tournai, in Flanders], *n.* A stout damask linen cloth, orig. made at Tournai.

dorp (dôrp) [Dut.], *n.* A South African small town.

dorsal (dôr′ sȧl) [F., from late L. *dorsālis*, from *dorsum*, the back], *a.* Of or pertaining to the back; situated on the back; shaped like a ridge. *n.* A dorsal fin.

dors-, dorsi-, dorso- [L. *dorsum*, back], *comb. form.* **dorsabdominal** (dôr sȧb dom′ i nȧl), *a.* Relating to the back of the abdomen. **dorsibranchiate** (dôr si brăng′ ki ȧt), *a.* Belonging to the *Dorsibranchiata*, a group of annelids in Cuvier's classification. **dorsiferous, -siparous** (dôr sif′ ėr ŭs, -sip′ ȧ rŭs) [-FEROUS; L. *-parus*, bringing forth], *a.* (*Bot.*) An epithet applied to ferns which have the seeds at the back of the frond. **dorsispinal** (dôr si spī′ nȧl), *a.* Belonging to the spine and the back.

dorsum (dôr′ sŭm) [L., the back], *n.* (*Zool. and Anat.*) The back; (*Bot.*) the part of a carpel farthest from the axis; (*Conch.*) the surface of the body of a shell opposite the opening.

***dortour** (dôr′ tȯr) [O.F., L. *dormītōrium*, DORMITORY], *n.* A dormitory.

dory (1) (dôr′ i) [F. *dorée*, fem. p.p. of *dorer*, to gild (cp. DORADO)], *n.* A golden-yellow sea-fish, *Zeus faber*, called also John Dory.

dory (2) (dôr′ i) [unknown], *n.* A small, flat-bottomed boat.

dose (dōs) [F., from med. L. and Gr. *dosis*, a giving, from *didonai*, to give], *n.* So much of any medicine as is taken or prescribed to be taken at one time; (*fig.*) a quantity or amount of anything offered or given; anything nauseous or unpleasant which one has to take; a share. *v.t.* To administer doses to; to give anything unpleasant to; to adulterate, to mix (as spirits with wine). **dosage,** *n.* The process or method of dosing; the application of doses (as of spirits to wine). **dosimeter** (-sim′ ė tėr), *n.* **dosimetric** (-met′ rik), *a.*

doss (dos) [prob. from F. *dos*, back, L. *dorsum*], *n.* (*slang*) A bed or a sleeping-place in a common lodging-house. *v.i.* To sleep in this. **dosser,** *n.* **doss-house,** *n.*

dossal (dos′ ȧl) [med. L. *dossāle*, L. *dorsum*], *n.* An ornamental hanging at the back of an altar or a stall, or round the sides of a chancel.

dossier (dos′ yā, -i ėr) [F., from *dos*, L. *dorsum*, back (from its bulging shape)], *n.* A collection of papers and other documents relating to a person, a thing or an event.

dossil (dos′ il) [O.F. *dosil*, late L. *duciculus*, dim. of *dux ducis*, a leader], *n.* A plug for stopping a wound; a cloth for wiping the face of a copper-plate.

dost [DO (1)].

dot (1) (dot) [A.-S. *dott*, the head of a boil (cp. Dut. *dot*, a little bundle, L.G. *dutte*, a plug)], *n.* A little mark, spot, or speck made with a pen or pointed instrument; a period mark, a full point, a point over *i* or *j*, or used as a diacritic; (*Mus.*) a point used as a direction, in various senses; a tiny thing, a little child. *v.i.* (*past & p.p.* **dotted**) To make dots or spots. *v.t.* To mark with dots; to mark or diversify with small detached objects like dots. **to dot one's i's and cross one's t's:** To be precisely exact. **dot and carry one:** A school-child's phrase for putting down the units and transferring the tens to the next column; (*colloq.*) a lame person. **dot and dash:** The system of symbols in Morse telegraphy. **dot-, dotting-wheel,** *n.* A wheel used for making dotted lines. **dotter,** *n.*

dot (2) (dot) [F., from L. *dōtem*, acc. of *dōs*], *n.* A dowry. *v.t.* To dower. ***dotal** (dō′ tȧl), *a.* Pertaining to a dowry; constituting or comprised in a dowry. ***dotation** (-tā′ shŭn), *n.*

dotage (dō′ tij) [F. *radoter*, to talk nonsense], *n.* Impairment of the intellect by age; silliness, infatuation. **dotard** (dō′ tȧrd), *n.* A man in his dotage; one who is foolishly and excessively fond.

dote (dōt), *v.i.* To be silly, to be deranged, infatuated or feeble-minded. **to dote on:** To be foolishly fond of.

***doth** [DO (1)].

dotterel (dot′ ėr ėl) [from DOTE], *n.* A small migratory plover, *Endromias morinellus*, said to be so foolishly fond of imitation that it mimics the actions of the fowler, and so suffers itself to be taken; a dupe a gull, a dotard.

dottle (dotl) [prob. from DOT (1)], *n.* A plug of tobacco left unsmoked in a pipe.

dotty (dot′ i) [DOT (1), -Y], *a.* Marked with dots, dot-like; (*slang*) unsteady of gait; shaky, imbecile.

douane (doo an′) [F., from Arab. *dīwān*, DIVAN], *n.* A Continental custom-house. ***douanier*** (doo a nyā′), *n.* A custom-house officer.

Douay (doo ā′) [*Douai*], *n.* An ancient town in N. France. **Douay** (dou′ ā) **Bible,** *n.* An English version of the Vulgate, made by the students of the Roman Catholic college at Douai and published 1582–1609, still in general use.

double (1) (dŭb′ ėl) [O.F., from L. *duplus* (*duo*, two, *-plus*, cogn. with Gr. *-plos*, -fold)], *a.* Composed of two, in a pair or in pairs; forming a pair, twofold; folded, bent back or forward; twice as much, as great, or as many; of twice the strength or value; of two kinds, aspects, or relations; ambiguous; (*fig.*) hypocritical, treacherous, deceitful; (*Mus.*) an octave lower in pitch; (*Bot.*) applied to flowers when the stamens become more or less petaloid. *adv.* Twice; in two ways; in twice the number, quantity, amount, strength, etc.; two together. **double-acting,** *a.* Exerting power in two directions. **double-action,** *n.* In a pianoforte movement, an arrangement of a jointed upright piece at the back end of the key, used to lift the hammer. **double ale:** Ale of double strength. **double-banked,** *a.* Used of a boat or galley which has two men to work the same oar, or two tiers of oars. **double bar,** *n.* (*Mus.*) Two single bars put together, to denote the end of a part. **double-barrel,** *a.* Double-barrelled. *n.* A double-barrelled gun. **double-barrelled,** *a.* Having two barrels, as a gun; (*fig.*) producing a double effect, serving a double purpose. **double-bass,** *n.* (*Mus.*) The largest and lowest-toned of the stringed instruments played with a bow, a contra-basso. **double-bearing,** *a.* Producing twice in one season. **double-bedded,** *a.* Having two beds or a double bed. **double-bitt,** *v.t.* (*Naut.*) To pass twice round a bitt or round two bitts (of ropes). **double-breasted,** *a.* Lapping over and buttoning on either side, as a coat or waistcoat. ***double-charge,** *v.t.* To entrust with a double share; to charge (a gun) with a double quantity. **double chin,** *n.* Two chins, due to obesity, etc. **double-cross,** *v.t.* (*colloq.*) To betray to both sides. **double-crown,** *n.* A size of printing paper, 20 × 30 in. **double-dagger,** *n.* A reference mark (‡). **double-dealer,** *n.* One who acts two parts at the same time or in the same business. **double-dealing,** *a.* Deceitful, tricky. *n.* The conduct of a double-dealer. **double diapason,** *n.* (*Mus.*) An organ stop of 16-foot tone. **double-drummer,** *n.* (*Austral.*) A large cicada with swollen drums. **double-Dutch,** *n.* Gibberish, jargon; a language not understood by the hearer. ***double-dye,** *v.t.* To dye with double intensity. **double-dyed,** *a.* Stained or tainted with infamy; doubly infamous. **double-eagle,** *n.* An American gold coin worth 20 dollars; a representation, as in the imperial arms of Russia and Austria, of an eagle with two heads. **double-edged,** *a.* Having two edges; (*fig.*) telling for and against; cutting both ways. **double-ender,** *n.* A kind of gunboat, round at both ends, used in the American Civil War (1861–1865). ***double-entendre*** (doobl′ an tandr′) [F. (*sometimes double entente*)], *n.* A word or phrase with two interpretations, one of which is usually indelicate. **double entry,** *n.* A method of book-keeping in which every transaction is entered twice, once on the credit side of the account that gives, and once on the debit side of the account that receives. **double event:** The winning of two races or matches by a horse or a team in the same race or season. **double-face,** *n.* A double-dealer. **double-faced,** *a.* Double-dealing; insincere. ***double-fatal,** *a.* Fatal in two ways. **double first,** *n.* One who comes out first in two subjects in an examination for a degree. **double-ganger** [G. *doppel-gänger*, double-goer], *n.* A wraith; a double, the apparition of a living person. ***double-gild,** *v.t.* To gild with a double coating; (*fig.*) to excuse. **double-handed,** *a.* Deceitful, treacherous. **double-headed,** *a.* Having two heads; (*Bot.*) having the flowers growing one to another. **double-hearted,** *a.* False-hearted, deceitful, treacherous. **double-hung,** *a.* A term applied to the sashes of a window when both are movable and fitted with lines and weights. **double-jointedness,** *n.* (*Anat.*) Abnormal mobility of joints not associated with injury or disease, nor causing symptoms. **double-leaded,** *a.* (*Print.*) Having spaces of double width between the lines for the sake of display. **double-lock,** *v.t.* To fasten by shooting the lock twice; to fasten with extra security. **double-manned,** *a.* Furnished or equipped with twice the number of men. ***double-meaning,** *a.* Saying one thing and meaning another; speaking equivocally. **double-minded,** *a.* Unsettled, wavering; fickle, undetermined. ***double-mouthed,** *a.* Deceitful or untrustworthy in statement. **double-natured,** *a.* Having a double or twofold nature. **double-octave,** *n.* (*Mus.*) An interval of two octaves or fifteen notes. **double-quick,** *n.* (*Mil.*) The quickest pace next to a run; (*U.S.*) a marching step at the rate of 165 steps a minute. *adv.* At the rate of this marching step. **double-reef,** *v.t.* (*Naut.*) To reduce (the spread of sail) by two reefs. **double-refine,** *v.t.* To refine twice over. ***double-shade,** *v.t.* To make doubly dark or shady. **double-shuffle,** *n.* A kind of clog-dance, jig, or hornpipe. **double-stars,** *n.pl.* Stars so near each other that they appear to be one when seen with the naked eye. **double-stop,** *v.i.* (*Mus.*) To play chords on a violin on two stopped strings. **double summer time,** *n.* The time indicated by clocks advanced one hour more than summer time, or two hours in front of Greenwich mean time. **double-talk,** *n.* Talk that sounds sensible though it is actually a compound of sense and gibberish. **double-time:** A marching step at the rate of 165 steps (of 33 in.) to the minute, or (*U.S.*) of 180 steps (of 36 in.) to the minute. **double-tongue,** *v.i.* (*Mus.*) To apply the tongue rapidly to the teeth and the palate alternately, as in staccato passages played on the flute or cornet; to play with double-tonguing. **double-tongued,** *a.* Giving contrary accounts of the same thing at different times; deceitful, double-dealing. **double-vantage,** *v.t.* To benefit doubly. **doubleness,** *n.* **doubly,** *adv.*

double (2) (dŭbl) [as prec.], *n.* Twice as much or as many, a double quantity; a fold, a plait; a bend or twist (in a road or river); a wraith, a double-ganger; a person exactly resembling someone else; (*Theat.*) an understudy; (*Mil.*) running, the pace for charging; a turn in running to escape pursuit; (*fig.*) *a trick, an artifice; (*Lawn Tennis, etc.*) a game between two pairs; (*Whist*) the score when one side has scored five before the other scores three; (*Racing*) a bet on two races, the stake and winnings on the first being applied to the second race; (*Darts*) a throw between the two outer circles. *v.t.* To increase by an equal quantity, amount, number, value, etc.; to multiply by two; to make twice as thick; to fold down or over, to bend, to turn upon itself; to be twice as much as; (*Mus.*) to add the upper or lower octave to; (*Acting*) to play two (parts) in the same piece; (*Naut.*) to sail round or by; *to copy, to make a duplicate of. *v.i.* To become twice as much or as great; to enlarge a wager to twice the previous amount; (*Bridge*) On the strength of one's own hand to double the number of points an opponent may gain or lose; to turn or wind to escape pursuit; (*fig.*) to use tricks or artifices; (*Mil.*) to march at the double, to run. **double or quits:** A game such as pitch and toss to decide whether the person owing shall pay twice his debt or nothing. **to double and twist:** To add one thread to another and twist them together. **to double up:** To bend one's body into a stooping or folded posture; to collapse; to make another person do this; to clench; (of paper, etc.) to become folded or crumpled. **to double upon:** (*Mil.*) To shut in between two fires; to turn back on a parallel course so as to elude (pursuers). **doubler,** *n.*

doublet (dŭb′ lĕt) [F., dim. of prec.], *n.* One of a pair; one of two words from the same root, but differing in meaning; (*Print.*) a word or passage printed twice by mistake; (*Opt.*) a combination of two lenses; (*Shooting*) a pair of birds brought down at once with a double-barrelled gun; (*pl.*) the same number on both dice; (*Hist.*) a close-fitting garment covering the body from the neck to a little below the waist, introduced from France in the 14th cent., and worn by all ranks until the time of Charles II; a counterfeit gem made of two pieces of crystal with a coloured substance between them. **doublet and hose:** Regular masculine attire in the Tudor period; an undress attire suitable for active exertion (implying the absence of a cloak).

doubloon (dŭb loon′) [F. *doublon*, or Sp. *doblon* (*doble*, DOUBLE)], *n.* A Spanish and South American gold coin, orig. the double of a pistole (whence the name), worth about a guinea.

doublure (du bloor′) [F., lining, from *doubler*, to DOUBLE, to line], *n.* (*Bookbinding*) An ornamental lining for a book cover.

doubt (dout) [O.F. *douter*, L. *dubitāre*, from *dubius*, doubtful], *v.i.* To be in uncertainty about the truth, probability, or propriety of anything; to hesitate, to waver; *to be afraid, to be apprehensive; *to suspect. *v.t.* To hold or think questionable; to hesitate to believe or assent to; *to be undecided about; *to distrust, suspect, or fear. *n.* Uncertainty of mind upon any point, action, or statement; an unsettled state of opinion; indecision, hesitation, suspense; distrust, inclination to disbelieve; a question, a problem, an objection; *fear, dread, apprehension, suspicion. **beyond a doubt, no doubt, without doubt:** Certainly, admittedly, unquestionably. **doubter,** *n.* **doubtful,** *a.* Liable to doubt; uncertain, admitting of doubt; ambiguous, not clear in meaning; uncertain, undecided, hesitating; suspicious; characterized by fear or apprehension. **doubtfully,** *adv.* **doubtfulness,** *n.* **doubtingly,** *adv.* **doubtless,** **a.* Free from fear; sure, confident, certain. *adv.* Assuredly, certainly, admittedly. **doubtlessly,** *adv.*

douce (doos) [O.F. *doux*, fem. *douce*, *dolz*, L. *dulcis*, sweet], *a.* (*Sc.*) Sober, sedate, peaceable, *sweet, pleasant. **doucely,** *adv.* **douceness,** *n.*

douceur (doo sĕr′) [F., as prec.], *n.* A small present; a gift, a bribe; *mildness, gentleness; *a courtesy, a compliment.

douche (doosh) [F., from It. *doccia*, a conduit, from L. *ductus*, p.p. of *ducere*, to lead], *n.* A jet of water or vapour directed upon some part of the body; an instrument for applying this. *v.t.* To apply a douche, esp. to flush out the vagina or other cavity. *v.i.* To take a douche.

dough (dō) [A.-S. *dāh* (cp. Dut. *deeg*, Dan. *deig*, G. *teig*, also Sansk. *dih-*, to smear, L. *fingere*, to shape, Gr. *teichos*, a wall, orig. of earth)], *n.* The paste of bread, etc., yet unbaked; a mass of flour or meal moistened and kneaded; anything resembling this in appearance or consistency; (*slang*) money. ***dough-baked,** *a.* Not perfectly baked; hence imperfect, unfinished; deficient in intellect. **dough-boy,** *n.* (*Naut.*) A flour dumpling boiled in salt water (see also DUFF (1)); (*Am.*) a private soldier in the U.S. army. **dough-faced,** *a.* (*Am.*) Cowardly, weak, pliable. **dough-nut,** *n.* A cake made of sweetened dough and fried in fat. **dough-kneaded,** *a.* Soft like dough. **doughy,** *a.* Like dough; soft, half-baked; (*fig.*) soft, unsound. **doughiness,** *n.*

doughty (dou′ ti) [A.-S. *dohtig* (cp. *dugan*, to be strong, G. *taugen*, to be worth, whence *tüchtig*, able)], *a.* Brave, valiant, stout, redoubtable. ***doughty-handed,** *a.* Strong-handed, mighty. **doughtily,** *adv.* **doughtiness,** *n.*

doum-palm (doum′-, doom′ pam) [Arab. *daum*, *dūm*], *n.* An Egyptian palm, *Hyphæne Thebaïca*, remarkable for the dichotomous division of the trunk and branches.

doup (doup) [Sc., cp. Icel. *daup*], *n.* The bottom, the posteriors; the end (as of a candle).

dour (door) [Sc. and North., from L. *dūrus*], *a.* Hard, bold, sullen; stern, severe, obstinate, pertinacious. **dourly,** *adv.* **dourness,** *n.*

douse (dous) [etym. doubtful], *v.t.* To plunge into water, to dip; to throw water over, to drench; (*Naut.*) to strike or slacken suddenly (as sails); to extinguish. *v.i.* To be plunged into water. **to douse the glim:** (*slang*) To put out the light.

douser [DOWSE].

dout (dout) [contr. of DO OUT], *v.t.* To extinguish. **douter,** *n.* One who or that which extinguishes; (*Gas-making*) a man employed to throw water over flaming coke from the retorts.

dove (dŭv) [A.-S. *dūfe* (only in *dūfe-doppa*), from *dūfan*, to dive (cp. G. *taube*, and for sense L. *columba*, dove, Gr. *kolumbos*, diver)], *n.* One of several kinds of pigeon, a bird of the genus *Columba*; an emblem of gentleness and innocence; the symbol of the Holy Ghost; a messenger of peace or deliverance (in allusion to the dove sent by Noah, Gen. viii. 8–12); a term of endearment. **dove-coloured,** *a.* Grey with a tinge of pink. **dove-cot,** *n.* A small house or box for domestic pigeons. **to flutter the dove-cots:** To throw peaceful people into alarm; to scandalize conventional circles. **dove-eyed,** *a.* Having eyes like a dove; meek, gentle-looking. ***dove-feathered,** *a.* Disguised in feathers like those of a dove. **dove-hawk,** *n.* The dove-coloured falcon, *Circus cyaneus*, also called the hen-harrier. **dove-kie,** *n.* An Arctic bird, *Uria grylle*, the black guillemot. **dove's-foot,** *n.* One of the crane's-bills, *Geranium molle*, and some other plants. **dovelike,** *a.* **dovelet,** *n.* A young dove.

***dover** (dō′ vĕr) [Sc. and North.], *v.i.* To slumber lightly, to doze. *v.t.* To stupefy. *n.* A light slumber.

dovetail (dŭv′ tāl), *n.* A mode of fastening boards together by fitting tenons, shaped like a dove's tail spread out, into corresponding cavities; a tenon or a joint of this kind. *v.t.* To fit together by means of dovetails; to fit exactly. *v.i.* To fit into exactly. **dovetail-moulding,** *n.* (*Arch.*) Moulding consisting of a series of projections somewhat like doves' tails.

dowager (dou′ ȧ jĕr) [O.F. *douagere*, from *douage*, dowry, *douer*, to DOWER], *n.* A widow in possession of a dower or jointure; a title given to a widow to distinguish her from the wife of her husband's heir; (*slang*) an old lady.

dowdy (dou′ di) [M.E. *dowd*, a shabby or untidily dressed person, etym. doubtful], *n.* An awkward, shabby, badly or vulgarly dressed woman. *a.* Awkward, shabby, unfashionable. **dowdily,** *adv.* **dowdiness,** *n.* **dowdyish,** *a.* **dowdyism,** *n.*

dowel (dou′ ĕl) [perh. from F. *douille*, a socket (but cp. L.G. *dovel*, G. *döbel*, plug or tap, O.F. *douelle*, a barrel-stave)], *n.* A pin or peg for connecting two stones or pieces of wood, being sunk into the side of each; a thin wooden rod for hanging light curtains. *v.t.* To fasten by dowels. **dowel-joint,** *n.* A junction by means of a dowel. **dowel-pin,** *n.* A dowel.

dower (dou′ ĕr) [O.F. *doaire*, late L. *dōtārium*, from *dōtāre*, to endow (*dōs dōtis*, cp. Gr. *dōs*, a gift)], *n.* The property which a wife brings to her husband in marriage; that part of the husband's property which his widow enjoys during her life; dowry, endowment, natural gifts, talents. *v.t.* To endow; to give a dower or portion to. **dower house,** *n.* A house on an estate reserved for the widow of the late owner. **dowerless,** *a.*

dowf (douf) [Sc. and North., cp. Icel. *daufr*, deaf], *a.* Dull, flat, spiritless. *n.* A stupid or spiritless fellow.

dowie (dou′ i) [Sc. and North., prob. from A.-S. *dol*, DULL], *a.* Dull, low-spirited, dreary.

dowlas (dou′ lȧs) [*Daoulas*, near Brest, in Brittany], *n.* A kind of coarse linen or calico.

***dowle** (doul) [etym. doubtful (Skeat suggests O.F. *doulle, douille*, soft, L. *ductilis*, DUCTILE)], *n.* One of the filaments of a feather; wool-like down.

down (1) (doun) [A.-S. *dūn* (cp. O.Dut. *dúna*, whence Dut. *duin*, L.G. *düne*, F. *dune*)], *n.* A tract of upland, esp. the chalk uplands of southern England, used for pasturing sheep; a bank of sand, etc., cast up by the sea. **the Downs:** The downs in the south of England; a roadstead between the North and South Forelands. **downland,** *n.*

down (2) (doun) [Icel. *dūnn* (cp. L.G. *dûne*, G. *daune*)], *n.* The fine soft plumage of young birds or that found under the feathers; fine soft hair, esp. the first hair on the human face; the pubescence of plants; the feather-like substance by which seeds are transported to a distance; any soft, fluffy substance. **downy,** *a.* Covered with down; made of down; resembling down; (*fig.*) soft, placid, soothing; (*slang*) cunning, knowing, artful. **downily,** *adv.* **downiness,** *n.*

down (3) (doun) [M.E. *adown*, A.-S. *of-dūne*, ADOWN], *adv.* (*superl.* **downmost)** Towards the ground; from a higher to a lower position; on the ground; from the sky upon the earth; below the horizon; (*fig.*) from former to later times; from north to south; away from the capital or a University; with a stream or current; (*Naut.*) to leeward; into less bulk; to finer consistency; to quiescence; to or in a state of subjection, disgrace, or depression; at a low level, prostrate, in a fallen posture or condition; downstairs, out of bed; reduced in price. *prep.* Along, through, or into, in a descending direction; from the top or the upper part to the bottom or a lower part of; at a lower part of; along (a river) towards the mouth. *a.* Moving, sloping, or directed towards a lower part or position; downcast. *v.t.* (*colloq.*) To put, strike, or throw down, to overcome. *v.i.* To descend. *n.* A reverse (*esp. in pl.*); (*colloq.*) a grudge, dislike; (*slang*) suspicion, alarm. **be down on:** Severe towards; pounce upon. **down!** *imper.* (*ellipt.*) Get, lie, put, or throw down. **down in the mouth:** Discouraged. **down town:** (*Am.*) At, or near the business centre of the town. **down on one's luck:** (*slang*) Hard-up. **to down with:** To pull or throw down. **to bear** or **bear down:** (*Naut.*) To sail from windward. **to get down:** To alight; to swallow (something). **to go down:** To sink; to leave the University for the vacation, or at the end of one's term; to prove acceptable. **to have a down on:** (*colloq.*) To have a grudge against. **to put a down on:** (*slang*) To peach, to give information about. **to put, set, take** or **write down:** To write on paper, etc.; hence **down for Tuesday:** Announced to take place on Tuesday. **to ride** or **hunt down:** To overtake by pursuit; to bring to bay. **to send down:** (*Univ.*) To expel or suspend an undergraduate. **to shout down:** To silence with noise. **up and down:** Here and there; altogether; throughout. **ups and downs:** Vicissitudes (of fortune, life, etc.). **down and out:** Utterly destitute and without resources. **down at heel:** Shabby, disreputably dressed. **down-draught,** *n.* A current of air downwards. **down-easter,** *n.* (*Am.*) A person from New England. **down-grade,** *n.* (*Rail.*) A downward gradient; (*fig.*) decadence. **down-haul,** *n.* (*Naut.*) A rope for hauling down a sail. *v.t.* (*Naut.*) To pull down. **down-hearted,** *a.* Dispirited, dejected. **down line,** *a.* The line of railway from the main terminus. **down-looked,** *a.* Having a downcast countenance; gloomy. **down-lying,** *n.* (*prov.*) Lying down or going to bed; (*Sc.*) childbed, confinement. **down platform,** *n.* The platform adjoining the line of railway from the main terminus. ***down-roping,** *a.* Hanging down in filaments. **down-sitting,** *n.* The act of sitting down, repose, rest. **to down tools:** To go on strike. **down train,** *n.* A train proceeding from the main terminus. **down under:** (*colloq.*) Australia.

downcast (doun′ kast), *a.* Cast downward; dejected, sad. *n.* (*Mining*) A ventilating shaft; (*Geol.*) a downthrow.

downcome (doun′ kŭm), *n.* A sudden fall; an overthrow.

downfall (doun′ fawl), *n.* A fall of rain, snow, etc.; a sudden loss of prosperity, rank, or reputation, ruin, overthrow; *that which falls suddenly downwards; *a precipice. **downfallen,** *a.* Ruined, fallen, fallen down.

downgrowth (doun′ grōth), *n.* Growth in a downward direction.

downhill (doun′ hil), *a.* Descending, sloping downwards, declining. *n.* A declivity, a downward slope; a decline. *adv.* (doun hil′) On a descending slope; (*fig.*) towards ruin or disgrace.

downpour (doun′ pôr), *n.* A heavy persistent fall of rain.

downright (doun′ rīt, *when used predicatively* doun′ rīt′), *a.* Directed straight downwards; directly to the point; plain, unequivocal; outspoken, artless, blunt. *adv.* Straight downwards; thoroughly, absolutely; *plainly, definitely. **downrightness** (doun rīt′ nės), *n.*

downstairs (doun stârz′), *adv.* Down the stairs; on or to a lower floor. *n.* The lower part of a building. **downstair, -s,** *a.* Pertaining to a lower floor.

downstream (doun strēm′), *a.* In the direction of the current of a river.

downthrow (doun′ thrō), *n.* (*Geol.*) The casting down, by earthquake or other action, of the strata on one side of a fault to a lower level.

downtrodden (doun′ trodn), *a.* Trodden under foot; oppressed; tyrannized over.

downward (1), **-s,** *adv.* From a higher to a lower position, level, condition, or character; from earlier to later; from superior to inferior, etc. **downward** (2), *a.* Moving, directed, or tending from higher, superior, or earlier to lower, inferior, or later.

downy [DOWN].

dowry (dou′ ri) [A.-F. *dowarie*, as DOWER], *n.* The property which a wife brings to her husband; an endowment, gift, or talent.

dowse (dous) [etym. unknown], *v.t.* To use the divining rod for the discovery of subterranean waters or minerals. **dowser,** *n.* **dowsing-rod,** *n.*

doxology (dok sol′ ŏ ji) [late L. and Gr. *doxologia* (*doxa*, glory, -LOGY)], *n.* A brief formula or hymn of praise to God. **doxological** (-loj′ ik ȧl), *a.*

***doxy** (1) (dok′ si) [etym. doubtful], *n.* A jade, a trull, a paramour; a loose woman.

doxy (2) (dok′ si) [from ORTHODOXY, etc.], *n.* (*facet.*) Opinion, esp. in religious matters.

doyen (dwa′ yen) [F., from L. *decānus*, DEAN], *n.* The senior member of a body.

doyley [DOILY].

doze (dōz) [cp. Dan. *döse*, Icel. *dūsa*, L.G. *dussen*], *v.i.* To sleep lightly; to be drowsy. *v.t.* To spend in drowsy inaction; *to stupefy, to muddle. *n.* A light sleep; a nap. **dozer,** *n.* **dozily,** *adv.* ***doziness,** *n.* **dozy,** *a.*

dozen (dŭz′ ėn) [O.F. *dozaine* (*doze*, L. *duodecim*, twelve, *-aine*, L. *-ēna*, as in *centēna*)], *n.* An aggregate of twelve things; an indefinite number. *a.* Twelve. **baker's** or **devil's dozen:** Thirteen. **to talk nineteen to the dozen:** To talk incessantly.

drab (1) (drăb) [cp. Irish *drabog*, Gael. *drabach*], *n.* A prostitute, a slut, a slattern. *v.i.* To associate with loose women. **drabber,** *n.* **drabbish,** *a.*

drab (2) (drăb) [F. *drap*, cloth], *a.* Of a dull brown or dun colour; (*fig.*) dull, commonplace, monotonous. *n.* Drab colour; a group of moths. **drabbet,** *n.* A coarse drab linen used for smock-frocks. **drably,** *adv.* **drabness,** *n.*

draba (drā′ bȧ) [Gr. *drabē*], *n.* (*Bot.*) A genus of low cruciferous herbs, the whitlow-grasses.

drabble (drăb′ ėl) [M.E. *drabelen*, cp. L.G. *drabbeln*], *v.t.* To draggle; to make wet and dirty, as by dragging through filth. **drabble-tail,** *n.* A slattern.

Dracaena (drȧ sē′ nȧ) [mod. L., from Gr. *drakaina* fem. of *drakōn*, dragon], *n.* (*Bot.*) A genus of tropical plants of the lily family, comprising the dragon-tree, *D. draco*, of the Canaries.

drachm (drăm) [F. *drachme*, L. *drachma*, Gr. *drachmē* (*drassesthai*, to grasp), cp. *dragma*, a grasp, full], *n.* A drachma, a dram (*Apoth. wt.*) 60 gr., ⅛ oz.; (*Avoirdup.*) 27⅓ gr., $\frac{1}{16}$ oz. **drachma** (drăk′ mȧ), *n.* An Attic weight, about 60 gr. avoirdupois; the principal silver coin of the ancient Greeks, worth six obols, nearly 9¾d. English; the standard coin of modern Greece, equivalent to about 3d.

draconian, draconic (drȧ kō′ ni ȧn, -kon′ ik) [*Dracon*, an Athenian legislator (about 621 B.C.), whose laws were extremely severe], *a.* Inflexible, severe, cruel.

***draff** (draf) [M.E. *draf* (cp. Dut., Icel., and Swed. *draf*)], *n.* Refuse, lees, esp. of malt after brewing or distilling; hog's-wash; (*fig.*) anything vile and worthless. ***draffish,** *a.*

draft (draft) [DRAUGHT], *n.* The first outline of any writing or document; a rough copy; a rough sketch of work to be executed; a written order for the payment of money; a cheque or bill drawn, esp. by a department or a branch of a bank upon another; a number of men selected for some special purpose, a detachment, a contingent; (*Am.*) conscription for army, etc. *v.t.* To draw up an outline, of, to compose the first form, or make a rough copy of; to draw off (a portion of a larger body of men) for some special purpose; (*Austral.*) to separate and sort out cattle. **drafter,** *n.* One who drafts; (*Austral.*) a man engaged in drafting cattle. **drafting-gate:** (*Austral.*) A gate whereby cattle are sorted out. **drafting-yard:** Yard where cattle or sheep are herded into separate groups. **draftsman,** *n.* One who draws up documents; a draughtsman.

drag (drăg) [prob. a var. of DRAW], *v.t.* (*past & p.p.* **dragged**) To pull along the ground by main force; to draw by force; to haul; to draw along with difficulty; to break the surface with a harrow; to search (a river, etc.) with a grapnel; to search or rack (as the brains); to put a drag on (a wheel); to perform too slowly. *v.i.* To trail along the ground (as a dress); to search a river, etc., with a grapnel, nets, etc.; (*Mus.*) to move slowly or heavily; to keep behind in singing. *n.* Anything which retards movement; an iron shoe or skid fastened on a wheel of a vehicle to check the speed; a rough, heavy sledge; a kind of open four-horse coach; a dredge; a low cart; a four-clawed grapnel for dragging or dredging under water; a drag-net; a heavy kind of harrow; an implement to spread manure; (*Aviat.*) the total resistance of an aeroplane along its line of flight; (*Hunting*) an artificial scent; the trail of a fox; a drag-hunt; the action of dragging; laborious movement, slow progress; a clog; an impediment; a drawback. **to drag in:** To introduce (a subject) gratuitously or out of season. **to drag one's feet:** (*colloq.*) To go slow deliberately. **to drag out:** To protract. **to drag up:** To bring up or rear in a careless fashion; to pull along contemptuously, as unworthy to be carried. **to drag the anchor:** (*Naut.*) To trail it along the bottom when it will not take firm hold (said of a ship). **drag-anchor,** *n.* (*Naut.*) A sail stretched by spars and thrown overboard to lessen the lee-way of a drifting vessel. **drag-chain,** *n.* A chain for clogging a wheel in descending steep roads. **drag-hunt,** *n.* A hunt in which a drag is used; a club devoted to this kind of hunting. **dragman,** *n.* A fisherman who uses a drag-net. **drag-net,** *n.* A net dragged along the bottom of a river, etc., for catching fish; a net drawn over a field to enclose game. **drag-sheet,** *n.* (*Naut.*) A drag-anchor. **dragsman,** *n.* The driver of a drag or coach.

dragger (drăg′ ėr), *n.* One who or that which drags; a street hawker.

draggle (drăg′ el), *v.t.* To make wet and dirty by dragging on the ground; to wet, to drabble. *v.i.* To become dirty by being trailed along the ground; to trail along the ground; (*fig.*) to lag, to straggle. **draggletail,** *n.* A slut. **draggle-tailed,** *a.* Sluttish; draggling.

dragoman (drăg′ ȯ mȧn) [F., from It. *dragomanno*, med. Gr. *dragoumanos*, O.Arab. *targumān*, interpreter], *n.* (*pl.* **-mans**). One who acts as guide, interpreter, and agent for travellers in the East.

dragon (drăg′ ȯn) [F., from L. *draco -ōnem*, Gr. *drakōn*, serpent (*drak-*, stem of *derkesthai*, to see)], *n.* A fabulous monster found in the mythology of nearly all nations, generally as an enormous winged serpent with formidable claws, etc.; (*Astron.*) a constellation in the northern hemisphere; any species of the lacertilian genus *Draco*, comprising the flying lizard; a kind of pigeon; a violent, spiteful person; a guardian, a duenna; (*Bibl.*) various formidable animals, such as the crocodile, serpent, whale, and shark; ***a musket of large bore with a figure of a dragon on the muzzle. **the Old Dragon:** Satan. **dragon-fly,** *n.* An anisopterous insect belonging to the *Libellulidæ*, having a long brilliant body and two pairs of large wings. **dragon-tree,** *n.* *Dracæna draco*, a liliaceous tree from West Africa and the adjacent islands [see DRACÆNA]. **dragon's-blood,** *n.* A red resin exuding from various trees, much used for staining and colouring. **dragon's-tail,** *n.* (*Astron.*) The descending node of the moon's orbit with the ecliptic. **dragon's teeth:** (*fig.*) Seeds or causes from which wars and disputes spring. **dragonet,** *n.* *A little dragon; (*Zool.*) a fish of the genus *Callionymus*. **dragonish,** *a.* Shaped or otherwise like a dragon.

dragonnade (drăg ȯ nād′) [F., from *dragon*, DRAGOON], *n.* (*usu. in pl.*) The persecutions of Protestants in France during the reign of Louis XIV by means of dragoons who were quartered upon them; a persecution by means of troops. *v.t.* To persecute by this means.

dragoon (drȧ goon′) [F. *dragon*, orig. a kind of musket, DRAGON], *n.* A cavalry soldier, orig. a mounted infantryman armed with a short musket or carbine called a dragon; in the British army the name is applied to certain regiments that were formerly mounted infantry; a kind of pigeon. *v.t.* To abandon to the mercies of soldiers; to subdue by military force; to compel to submit by violent measures.

dragsman [DRAG].

drain (drān) [A.-S. *dreahnian*, cogn. with *drȳge*, DRY], *v.t.* To draw off gradually; to cause to run off by tapping, etc.; to empty by drawing away moisture from, to exhaust; to drink up; to deprive (of vitality, resources, etc.). *v.i.* To flow off gradually; to be emptied of moisture. *n.* The act of draining; a strain, a heavy demand, exhaustion; a channel for conveying water, sewage, etc.; (*Surg.*) a tube for drawing off pus, etc.; (*slang*) a drink. **drain-cock,** *n.* A tap for emptying a tank or other vessel. **drain-pipe,** *n.* A pipe for draining superfluous or waste water, particularly from a roof or gutter. *a.* (*colloq.*) (of) trousers with very tight legs. **drain-trap,** *n.* A device for preventing the escape of foul gases from drains. **drainage,** *n.* The act, practice, or science of draining; the natural or artificial system by which land or a town is drained; that which is carried away through drains; the surface drained. **drainage-area,** *n.* The region drained by a river and its tributaries. **drainage-tube,** *n.* (*Surg.*) A tube introduced into a suppurating wound or chronic abscess to allow free discharge of putrid accumulations. **drainer,** *n.* One who or that which drains; one who constructs drains; a vessel in which wet things are put to drain. **draining-board,** *n.* A board beside a sink on which washed-up crockery is put to dry.

draining-engine, *n.* A pumping-engine for removing water from mines, etc. **draining-plough,** *n.* A plough for cutting drains.

drake (1) (drāk) [etym. doubtful (cp. prov. G. *draak*, O.H.G. *antrahho*, G. *enterich*, dial. *endedrach*, from *ente*, *ende*, duck)], *n.* The male of the duck. **drake-fly,** *n.* An artificial fly made with drake's feathers. **drake-stone,** *n.* A flat stone thrown so as to skim over water [cp. DUCKS AND DRAKES].

drake (2) (drāk) [A.-S. *drăca*, L. *draco*, DRAGON], *n.* The May-fly, an ephemeral insect common in meadows in early summer; *a dragon; *a kind of small cannon.

dram (drăm) [DRACHM], *n.* The eighth part of an ounce, or 60 gr., in apothecaries' weight; the sixteenth part of an ounce in avoirdupois weight; (*fig.*) a small quantity; as much spirit as is drunk at once. *v.i.* To drink drams. *v.t.* To ply with stimulants. **dram-drinker,** *n.* One who habitually drinks spirits. **dram-shop,** *n.* A tavern where spirits are sold.

drama (dra' mȧ) [late L. *drāma*, Gr. *drâma -atos*, (*drân*, to do, to act)], *n.* A poem or composition representing life and action, usually intended for performance by living actors on the stage; a series of events invested with the unity and interest of a play; dramatic art, the composition and presentation of plays; the dramatic literature or theatrical art of a particular country or period. **dramatic, -ical** (drȧ măt' ik, -ȧl), *a.* Pertaining to or of the nature of drama; pertaining to the stage, theatrical; intended or suitable for representation on the stage; striking, catastrophic, impressive; meant for effect; (*Lit. crit.*) expressing the personalities of different characters. **dramatically,** *adv.*

dramatis personæ (drăm' ȧ tis pėr sō' nē) [L., characters of the play], *n.pl.* The set of characters in a play; a list of these.

dramatist (drăm' ȧ tist), *n.* A writer of plays.

dramatize (drăm' a tīz), *v.t.* To set forth in the form of a drama; to describe dramatically; to exaggerate; to convert a story, novel, etc. into a play. **dramatization,** *n.*

dramaturge (drăm' ȧ tĕrj) [F., from Gr. *dramatourgos* (*drâma -atos*, DRAMA, *ergein*, to work)], *n.* A dramatist, a playwright. **dramaturgic** (-tĕr' jik), *a.* **dramaturgist,** *n.* **dramaturgy** (drăm' ȧ tĕr ji), *n.*

drammock (drăm' ŏk) [Sc., prob. from Gael. *dramag*], *n.* Oatmeal and water mixed without cooking.

drank, *past* [DRINK].

drant (drant) [Sc., prob. onomat., cp. DRAWL, RANT], *v.t.* and *i.* To drawl; to drone. *n.* A droning tone.

drape (drāp) [F. *draper*, from *drap*, cloth], *v.t.* To cover, clothe, or decorate with cloth, etc.; to adjust or arrange the folds of a dress, curtains, etc. *n.* (*Am.*) A curtain, a hanging.

draper (drā' pĕr) [as prec.], *n.* One who deals in cloth and other fabrics. **Drapers' Company:** The third of the twelve great London livery companies, whose charter was granted by Edward III. **drapery,** *n.* The trade of a draper; cloth and other fabrics; (*Am.*) dry-goods; articles of dress, etc., made of these materials; that with which an object is draped, curtains, hangings, tapestry, etc.; the arrangement of dress in sculpture, painting, etc. **draperied,** *a.* ***drapet,** *n.* A cloth, a coverlet.

drastic (drăs' tik) [Gr. *drastikos*, from *drasteos*, to be done (*drân*, to do)], *a.* Acting vigorously; effective, efficacious; (*Med.*) strongly purgative. **drastically,** *adv.*

drat (drăt) [said to be a corr. of GOD ROT], *v.t.* (*slang*) Confound, bother, dash (as a mild form of imprecation). **dratted,** *a.*

draught (draft) [M.E. *drahte*, as if from A.-S. *dragan*, to DRAW (cp. Dut. *dragt*, G. *tracht*)], *n.* The act of drawing; the capacity of being drawn; the act of dragging with a net; the quantity of fish taken in one sweep of a net; the act of drinking; the quantity of liquor drunk at once; a dose; a current of air; the depth to which a ship sinks in water; a draft, a preliminary drawing, design, or plan for a work to be executed; the drawing of liquor from a vessel; *a privy, a cess-pool; (*pl.*) a game played by two persons on a chess-board with twelve round pieces of different colours on each side, (*Am.*) checkers. *v.t.* To draw out or off; to sketch; to draft. **beast of draught:** An animal for drawing loads. **black draught:** A purgative medicine. **forced draught:** A strong current of air in a furnace, maintained by means of an exhaust or an apparatus for driving. **on draught:** Able to be obtained by drawing off (from a cask, etc.). **draught beer,** *n.* Beer drawn from the cask, as distinguished from bottled beer. **draught-board,** *n.* A board on which draughts are played. **draught-engine,** *n.* An engine for raising ore, water, etc. **draught-hole,** *n.* A hole for supplying a furnace with air. **draught-hook,** *n.* An iron hook on the cheeks of a gun-carriage to manœuvre it. **draught-horse,** *n.* A horse for drawing heavy loads. ***draught-house,** *n.* A house where filth is deposited; a privy.

draughtsman (drafts' mȧn), *n.* One who draws, designs, or plans; one skilled in drawing; a piece used in the game of draughts. **draughtsmanship,** *n.* **draughtswoman,** *n.*

draughty (draf' ti), *a.* Full of draughts or currents of air; (*Sc.*) artful, crafty. **draughtiness,** *n.*

***drave,** *past* [DRIVE].

Dravidian (drȧ vid' i ȧn), *a.* Of or pertaining to Dravida, an old province of India. *n.* One of the supposed primitive non-Aryan races of India, comprising the peoples speaking Tamil, Telegu, Canarese, and Malayalam.

draw (draw) [A.-S. *dragan*, cp. Dut. *dragen*, G. *tragen*], *v.t.* (*past* **drew,** *p.p.* **drawn**) To drag or pull; to pull after one, to haul; to pull out or up from; to extract or remove by pulling; to cause to flow or come forth, to elicit; to take, to receive, to derive; to infer, deduce; to take in, to inhale; to draft, to picture, to portray; to lengthen, to pull out, to stretch, to protract; to extract, to disembowel; to take out of a box or wheel (as tickets); to unsheathe (as a sword); to allure, attract, to cause to follow one; to cause to come out; (*Hunting*) to search for game; (*Banking*) to write (cheque, draft, order) on a banker, etc.; (*Naut.*) to require a specified depth of water to float; *to withdraw; *to draw aside (as a curtain); *to muster; *to track; to leave undecided, as a match. *v.i.* To pull, to haul; to attract; to allow a free motion, current, etc. (as a chimney, pipe, etc.); to unsheathe a sword; to draw lots; to extract the essence, to extract humour, etc. (as a poultice); to move, to approach (as if drawn towards); to come together, to contract; to come out or away (as if pulled); to practise the art of delineation; to write out a draft for payment; (*Naut.*) to require a certain depth of water. *n.* The act or power of drawing; a pull, a strain; an attraction, a lure; the act of drawing lots; a lot or chance drawn; the act of drawing a covert; a drawn game or contest; a feeler, a device to elicit information. **to draw a bead:** [BEAD]. **to draw away:** To get further in front. **to draw back:** To move back; to withdraw; to be unwilling to fulfil a promise. **to draw blank:** To find nothing. **to draw in:** To collect, to contract; to entice, to inveigle; (of days) to close in, to shorten. **to draw it mild:** To draw beer from the cask of mild; (*colloq.*) to state, describe, or ask moderately, not to exaggerate or be exorbitant. **to draw near** or **nigh:** To approach. **to draw off:** To withdraw, retire, retreat; to rack wine, etc.; **to draw on:** To lead to as a consequence; to allure, attract, entice; to approach. **to draw out:** To lengthen; to set in order for battle; to induce to talk, to elicit; to write out; to protract; (of days) to become longer. **to draw over:** To bring over; to induce to change parties. **to draw stumps:**

(*Cricket*) To stop playing for the day. **to draw the long bow:** To tell incredible stories. **to draw the line at:** To refuse to go any farther. **to draw up:** To range in order, or in line of battle; to compose, to put into proper form; to put (oneself) into a stiff erect attitude. **to draw up with:** To overtake. **drawn and quartered:** (*Hist.*) Penalty of disembowelling and dismembering after hanging. **draw-bar,** *n.* A bar to connect a locomotive with a tender. **draw-gear,** *n.* Harness for horses drawing wagons, etc.; railway-carriage couplings. **draw-head,** *n.* A device in spinning, by which the slivers are lengthened and receive an additional twist; the projecting part of a draw-bar in which the coupling-pin connects with the link. **draw knife,** *n.* (*Carp.*) A cutting blade with a handle at each end, for shaving wood. ***draw-latch,** *n.* A thief. **draw-link,** *n.* A connecting link for railway carriages. **draw-net,** *n.* A net with wide meshes for catching large birds; a seine. **draw-plate,** *n.* A drilled steel plate through which wire is drawn to reduce and equalize its thickness. **draw-sheet,** *n.* (*Med.*) An extra sheet doubled lengthwise and placed across the bed so that it may be pulled beneath the patient as required. **draw-well,** *n.* A deep well from which water is drawn by means of a rope and bucket.

drawback (draw′ băk), *n.* Money paid back, esp. excise or import duty remitted or refunded on goods exported; a deduction, a rebate; a disadvantage; an inconvenience; an obstacle. **drawback lock,** *n.* One having a spring-bolt that can be drawn back by a knob inside the door.

drawbridge (draw′ brij), *n.* A bridge that may be raised on hinges at one or both ends to allow vessels to pass or to prevent passage across; a game of bridge for two.

***Drawcansir** (draw kăn′ sėr) [character in *The Rehearsal*], *n.* A bully, a braggart, a swashbuckler. *a.* Blustering, bullying.

drawee (draw ē′), *n.* The person on whom a bill of exchange or order for payment in money is drawn.

drawer (draw′ ėr), *n.* One who draws; a tapster, a barman; a sliding receptacle in a table, etc.; one who draws a bill or order for the payment of money; one who or that which has the quality of attracting; (*pl.*) an undergarment worn on the lower limbs. **chest of drawers:** [CHEST]. **drawerful,** *n.*

drawing (draw′ ing), *n.* The action of the verb TO DRAW; the art of representing objects on a flat surface by means of lines drawn with a pencil, crayon, etc.; a delineation of this kind; a sketch in black and white, or monochrome; the distribution of prizes in a lottery; (*pl.*) takings, receipts. **out of drawing:** Incorrectly drawn. **drawing-block,** *n.* A number of sheets of drawing-paper adhering at the edges so that the uppermost sheet can be detached. **drawing-board,** *n.* A rectangular frame for holding a sheet of paper while drawing. **drawing-compass, -es,** *n.* A pair of compasses with a pencil or pen at one of the points. **drawing-knife,** *n.* A blade having a handle at each end, used by coopers, etc.; a tool used for cutting a groove as a starting-point for a saw. **drawing office,** *n.* The department in an engineering works where designs and plans are set out. **drawing-pin,** *n.* A flat-headed tack for securing drawing-paper to a board, (*Am.*) a thumb-tack.

drawgate (draw′ gāt), *n.* The valve or door of a sluice or lock.

drawing-room (draw′ ing rum) [formerly *withdrawing*], *n.* A room for the reception of company; a formal reception by a sovereign or person of high official rank; the company assembled in a drawing-room; (*Am.*) a private compartment in a railway coach.

drawl (drawl) [prob. from DRAW (cp. Dut. *dralen*)], *v.t.* To utter in a slow, lengthened tone; to protract, drag (out). *v.i.* To speak with a slow, prolonged utterance; *to dawdle. *n.* A slow, lengthened manner of speaking. **drawling,** *a.* **drawlingly,** *adv.*

drawn (drawn) [DRAW], *p.p.* Pulled out (as a sword); depicted, sketched, composed; pulled to one side, distorted; eviscerated (as a fowl). **drawn game, battle,** *n.* A game or battle in which neither side can claim any decided advantage. **drawn-thread work,** *n.* Fancy work in which the threads of a fabric are some pulled out and some fastened so as to form a pattern.

dray (drā) [from A.-S. *dragan*, to DRAW (cp. *dræge*, a draw-net)], *n.* A low cart, generally of strong and heavy construction, used by brewers, etc. **dray-horse,** *n.* A strong, heavy horse for drawing a dray. **drayman,** *n.* A driver in charge of a dray. **drayage,** *n.* The use of a dray or the charge for its use.

dread (dred) [A.-S. *drǣdan* (in *on-drǣdan*, *of-drǣdan*, etc.)], *v.t.* To fear greatly; to anticipate with terror and shrinking; *to be apprehensive or anxious about, to doubt. *v.i.* To be in great fear. *n.* Great fear or terror; apprehension of evil; awe, reverence; the person or thing dreaded. *a.* Exciting great fear or terror, frightful; awe-inspiring, to be reverenced. **dreadful,** *a.* Inspiring dread; terrible; awe-inspiring; *full of dread; (*colloq.*) annoying, disagreeable, troublesome, frightful, horrid; (*vulg.*) very, exceedingly. **penny dreadful,** *n.* A journal or story-book dealing with crude sentiment and horrors. **dreadfully,** *adv.* **dreadless,** *a.* Free from dread; undaunted; secure. **dreadlessly,** *adv.* ***dreadless,** *n.*

dreadnought (dred′ nawt), *n.* One totally devoid of fear; a heavy, woollen, felted cloth; a heavy overcoat made of this material; (*Nav.*) a type of battleship, first built 1905–6, with its main armament composed of big guns.

dream (drēm) [M.E. *dream*, A.-S. *drēam*, music, joy, mirth, appear to be distinct and to have caused a non-extant *drēam*, vision, to be avoided in favour of *swefn*, sleep (cp. O.S. *drōm*, a dream, G. *traum*)], *n.* A vision; thoughts and images that pass through the mind of a sleeping person; the state of mind in which these occur; a visionary idea, a fancy, reverie; something beautiful or enticing; a chimerical scheme, a castle in the air. *v.i.* (*past* **dreamt** (dremt) or **dreamed**) To have visions; to think, to imagine as in a dream; to conceive as possible; to waste time in idle thoughts. *v.t.* To see, hear, feel, etc., in a dream; to imagine or conceive in a visionary fashion, to picture in hope or imagination. **day-dream,** *n.* A romantic scheme or vain fancy voluntarily indulged in. **waking-dream,** *n.* A waking experience of involuntary vision; an hallucination. **dreamland,** *n.* The region of fancy or imagination. **dream-reader,** *n.* A person who professes to reveal the meanings of dreams. **to dream away:** To spend (time) idly or vainly. **dreamer,** *n.* ***dreamery,** *n.* **dreamful,** *a.* **dreamingly,** *adv.* **dreamless,** *a.* **dreamlessly,** *adv.* **dreamlike,** *a.* **dreamy,** *a.* Full of or causing dreams; visionary; addicted to dreaming. **dreamily,** *adv.* **dreaminess,** *n.*

dream-hole (drēm′ hōl) [perh. from A.-S. *drēam*, music, mirth], *n.* A hole in the wall of a steeple (perh. one of the holes in belfries through which the sound passed out).

dreary (drēr′ i), **drear** (drēr) [A.-S. *drēorig*, from *drēor*, gore], *a.* Dismal, gloomy; cheerless, tiresome, dull. **n.* Dreariness. **drearily, drearly,** *adv.* **dreariment,** *n.* **dreariness,** *n.* **drearness,** *n.* **drearisome,** *a.* ***drearihead,** *n.* Dreariness.

dredge (1) (drej) [Sc. *dreg*, M.E. *drege*, prob. from A.-S. *dragan*, to DRAW, to DRAG], *n.* A drag-net for taking oysters; an apparatus for dragging under water to bring up objects from the bottom for scientific purposes; a bucket or scoop for scraping mud, etc. from the bed of a pond, etc. *v.t.* To gather or bring up with a dredge; to remove or clear away by means of a dredge; to clean or deepen (as a river) with a dredging machine. *v.i.* To use a dredge. **dredger** (1), *n.* One who fishes with a dredge; a ballast-lighter; a dredging-machine. **dredging-machine,** *n.* A floating machine for raising silt, etc., from the bottom of a river, harbour, channel, etc., to deepen it or obtain ballast.

dredge (2) (drej) [M.E. *dragie*, later *dredge*, a comfit, from O.F. *dragee*, late L. and Gr. *tragēmata*, spices, condiments], *v.t.* To sprinkle (flour, etc.) upon or over; to sprinkle with flour, etc. **dredger** (2), *n.* A box with perforated lid for sprinkling. **dredging-box,** *n.*

***dree** (drē) [A.-S. *drēogan*, to perform, to endure], *v.t.* To suffer, to endure. **to dree one's weird:** To abide by one's lot.

dreg (dreg) [cp. Icel. *dregg*, pl. *dreggjar*, Swed. *dragg*], *n.* (*usu. in pl.*) The sediment or lees of liquor; feculence; the end, the bottom; worthless refuse; vile matter; the lowest class. **not a dreg:** Not a drop, not the least part (left). **dreggy,** *a.*

dreich (drēch) [DREE], *a.* (*Sc.*) Tedious, wearisome, long.

drench (drench) [A.-S. *drencan*, causal of *drincan*, to drink], *v.t.* To wet thoroughly; to soak, to saturate; to cause to swallow (a medicinal draught); (*Tanning*) to bate; *to submerge, to drown; *to overwhelm; to purge violently. **v.i.* To be drowned. *n.* A liquid medicine for horses or cattle; a soaking, a flood; (*Tanning*) a solution for bating, etc.; *a large draught, a potion. **drencher,** *n.* One who or that which drenches; an apparatus for drenching cattle; (*colloq.*) a heavy downpour.

dress (dres) [O.F. *dresser*, ult. from L. *dīrectus*, DIRECT], *v.t.* To make straight; (*Mil.*) to form (ranks) into a straight line; to order, arrange, array; to clothe, to attire; to adorn, to deck; (*Naut.*) to decorate with flags, etc.; to furnish with costumes; to cleanse, trim, brush, comb, etc.; to curry or rub down (as a horse); to cleanse and apply remedies to; to prepare for use, to cook; to cover with dressing (as a salad); to prune, to cut; to manure; to square and give a smooth surface to (as stone); (of a shop window) to arrange goods attractively; to size (as yarn); to smooth and give a nap to (as cloth); *to address, to apply; *to put right, to adjust; *to train, to break in; *to direct ones course. *v.i.* To clothe oneself; to put on evening clothes; to attire oneself elaborately; to pay great attention to dress; (*Mil.*) to arrange oneself in proper position in a line; *to direct one's course. *n.* That which is worn as clothes, esp. outer garments; garments, apparel; a lady's gown, a frock; the art of adjusting dress; an external covering, as plumage; external appearance, outward form. **to dress down:** To chastise, to thrash; to reprimand severely. **to dress to death:** To overdress. **to dress up or out:** To clothe elaborately; to deck, to adorn; to invest with a fictitious appearance. **evening dress:** Clothes worn at dinners, evening receptions, etc. **full dress:** That worn on state or important occasions. **morning dress:** Ordinary attire. **dress-circle,** *n.* The first tier of seats above the pit in a theatre, in *Am.* the balcony. **dress-coat,** *n.* A man's coat with narrow pointed tails, worn as evening dress. **dress-goods,** *n.pl.* Fabrics for women's and children's outer garments. **dress-guard,** *n.* A wire or thread guard over a bicycle wheel to keep the dress from becoming entangled. **dress-improver,** *n.* A bustle. **dress-preserver, -shield,** *n.* A protector, usu. of waterproof material, fitted under the armpits of a woman's dress to prevent staining of this by perspiration. **dress rehearsal,** *n.* (*Theat.*) The final rehearsal, with costumes and effects. **dressmaker,** *n.* One who makes women's dresses. **dressmaking,** *n.* **dressy,** *a.* Fond of showy dress; wearing rich or showy dress; showy, stylish, smart. **dressiness,** *n.*

dressage (dres' azh) [F.], *n.* The training of a horse in deportment and obedience.

dresser (1) (dres' ėr), *n.* One who dresses another, esp. an actor for the stage; a surgeon's assistant in operations, etc., who dresses wounds, etc.

dresser (2) (dres' ėr) [O.F. *dresseur*, from *dresser*, as prec.], *n.* A kitchen sideboard; a set of shelves or an open cupboard for plates, etc.; (*Am.*) a chest of drawers; *a bench or table on which meat was prepared or dressed for use.

dressing (dres' ing), *n.* The action of the verb TO DRESS; gum, starch, etc., used in sizing or stiffening fabrics; stuffing, sauce, salad-dressing; manure applied to a soil; ointment, liniment, bandages, etc., applied to a wound or sore; a thrashing, a scolding; any stuff used for stiffening fabrics; (*pl.*) the mouldings and sculptured decorations on a wall or ceiling. **dressing-bag, -case,** *n.* A bag or case fitted with articles for the toilet. **dressing-bell,** *n.* A bell rung as a signal to dress for dinner. **dressing-gown,** *n.* A light, loose gown worn during the toilet or in deshabille. **dressing-room,** *n.* A room appropriated to dressing. **dressing-station,** *n. Mil., etc.*) A first-aid post. **dressing-table,** *n.* A table with conveniences for the toilet.

dressmaker, etc. [DRESS].

drew, *past* [DRAW].

drey (drā), [?], *n.* A squirrel's nest.

***drib** (drib) [prob. onomat., or from A.-S. *drepan*, to hit], *v.t.* To cut off by bits; to cheat by petty tricks; to entice by degrees. *v.i.* To dribble; to shoot at short distances. *n.* A driblet, a petty amount or quantity. **in dribs and drabs:** Little bits at a time.

dribble (drib' el) [freq. of prec.], *v.i.* To fall in a quick succession of small drops; to drip, to trickle; to fall or run slowly; to slaver, to drivel; to fall weakly, like a drop; *to want energy or vigour; (*Football*) to manœuvre the ball in a forward direction by slight kicks from alternate sides; (*Billiards*) to cause the ball just to roll into a pocket; *to fly (as an arrow) so as to fall short. *v.t.* To allow to drip; to give out slowly by drops. *n.* Drivelling; drizzle; (*Football, etc.*) a piece of dribbling. **dribbler,** *n.* **driblet,** *n.* A small or petty portion or sum.

drier [DRY].

drift (drift) [from A.-S. *drīfan*, DRIVE (cp. Dut., Icel., Swed. *drift*, G. *trift*)], *n.* That which is driven along by a wind or current; a driving, a current, a driving or compelling force; the course of drifting or movement; tendency, purpose, aim, tenor; a mass (of snow, leaves, sand, etc.) driven together; (*Geol.*) a loose accumulation of sand and debris deposited over the surface by the action of water or ice; (*Naut.*) deviation from a direct course caused by currents, the tendency of a current; (*Mining*) a horizontal passage following a lode or vein; a drive of cattle, esp. (*Forest Law*) to a particular place on a given day for determination of ownership, etc.; (*Fishing*) a drift-net; (*S.Afr.*) a ford; (*Arch.*) the horizontal thrust of an arch upon its abutments; *a shower, a storm; *a scheme. *v.i.* To be driven into heaps; to float or be carried along by or as by a current; to be carried along by circumstances; (*Mining*) to make a drift. *v.t.* To drive along or into heaps; to carry along (of a current); to cover with drifts or driftage; to shape or enlarge (a hole). **drift-anchor,** *n.* A drag-anchor. **drift-bolt,** *n.* A steel rod used to drive out a bolt. **drift-ice,** *n.* Floating masses of ice drifting on the sea. **drift-land,** *n.* A yearly rent paid by some tenants for driving cattle through a manor. **drift-net,** *n.* A large fishing net. **drift-way,** *n.* (*Mining*) A drift; (*prov.*) a common way for driving cattle; (*Naut.*) the course of a ship drifting. **drift-wood,** *n.* Wood carried by water to a distance from its native locality.

driftage (drift' ij), *n.* Drifting, or drifted substances; (*Naut.*) the distance to which a ship drifts in bearing up against wind and currents.

drifter (drif' tėr), *n.* (*Naut.*) A trawler or fishing-boat using a drift-net to fish esp. for enemy mines.

driftless (drift' lės), *a.* Without clear meaning or aim.

drifty (drif' ti), *a.* Forming snow-drift.

drill (1) (dril) [cp. M.Dut. *drillen*, to bore, to turn round, to form to arms, to exercise], *v.t.* To bore or pierce with a pointed tool, to perforate; to make holes by this means; to train by repeated exercise, to train to the use of arms, to exercise in military exercises; *to draw on, to decoy. *v.i.* To go through a course of military exercise. *n.* A metal tool for boring holes in hard material; a boring shell-fish; constant practice or exercise in any art or business; the act of drilling soldiers or sailors, the series of exercises by which they are rendered efficient; rigorous training or discipline; (*colloq.*) correct procedure, the right way to do something. **drill-bow,** *n.* A bow by the string of which a drill is rotated. **drill hall,** *n.* A hall for physical exercises or social functions, (*Am.*) an armory. **drill-press,** *n.* An upright drilling-machine. **drill-serjeant,** *n.* A non-commissioned officer who drills soldiers or schoolboys; (*fig.*) a martinet, a narrow-minded devotee of routine. **drill-stock,** *n.* A handle or holder for a metal drill. **drilling-machine,** *n.* A machine for drilling holes in metal.

drill (2) (dril) [etym. doubtful; perh. from prec.], *v.t.* To sow (seed) or plant in rows. *v.i.* To sow or plant in this manner. *n.* A small trench or furrow, or a ridge with a trench along the top, for seeds or small plants; a row of plants in such a furrow; a machine for sowing grain in rows. **drill-barrow,** *n.* A manual machine for drilling and sowing. **drill-harrow,** *n.* A harrow for crushing the earth and extirpating weeds between the rows of plants. **drill-husbandry,** *n.* The practice of sowing in drills by a machine. **drill-plough,** *n.* A plough for sowing grain in drills.

drill (3) (dril) [earlier *drilling*, corr. of G. *drillich*, corr. of L. *trilix trilīcem* (*tri-*, three, *līcium*, a thread)], *n.* A heavy cotton twilled cloth used for trousers, etc.

***drill** (4) (dril) [perh. from native name], *n.* A baboon from the coast of Guinea, *Cynocephalus leucophæus.*

drily [DRY].

drink (dringk) [A.-S. *drincan*, from Teut. *drenk-* (cp. Dut. *drinken*, G. *trinken*)], *v.t.* (*past* **drank,** *p.p.* **drunk**) To swallow (a liquid); to imbibe, absorb, suck in; to swallow up, to empty; to take in by the senses; to pledge, to toast; to waste (money, wages, property) on indulgence in liquor; *to inhale. *v.i.* To swallow a liquid; to take intoxicating liquors to excess. *n.* Something to be drunk; a draught, a potion; intoxicating liquor; excessive indulgence in intoxicating liquors, intemperance; (*slang*) the sea. **in drink:** Intoxicated. **to drink deep:** To take a long draught; to drink to excess. **to drink down:** To destroy the memory of by drinking; to beat another in drinking. **to drink in:** To absorb readily; to receive greedily, as with the senses; to gaze upon, listen to, etc., with delight. **to drink off:** To swallow at a single draught. **to drink the health of:** To wish health to one in drinking; to pledge. **to drink to:** To salute in drinking; to drink the health of. **to drink up:** To swallow completely. **drink-money,** *n.* Money given to buy liquor; a tip. **drink-offering,** *n.* A Jewish offering of wine; a libation. **drinkable,** *a.* That may be drunk; fit for drinking. *n.* A liquor that may be drunk; (*pl.*) the beverages provided at a meal. **drinkably,** *adv.* **drinkableness,** *n.* **drinker,** *n.* One who drinks; a tippler, a drunkard. **drinking-bout,** *n.* A set-to at drinking; a revel. **drinking-fountain,** *n.* A fountain erected in a public place to supply water. **drinking-horn,** *n.* A drinking-vessel made of horn. **drinking-house,** *n.* An ale-house, a tavern. ***drinking-money,** *n.* Drink-money. **drinking-song,** *n.* A song in praise of drinking or to be sung at drinking parties. **drinkless,** *a.*

drip (drip) [A.-S. *dryppan* (cp. O.Sax. *driopan*, G. *triefen*)], *v.i.* (*past & p.p.* **dripped**) To fall in drops; to throw off moisture in drops. *v.t.* To let fall in drops. *n.* The act of dripping, a falling in drops; that which falls in drops; (*Arch.*) the projecting edge of a moulding or corona over a door or window. **drip-drop:** A persistent dripping. **drip dry,** *a.* Of clothing made of such a material that it dries quickly without wringing and needs no ironing. **drip-moulding, drip-stone,** *n.* (*Arch.*) A corona or projecting tablet or moulding over the heads of doorways, windows, etc., to throw off rain; a filtering-stone. **dripping,** *n.* The act of falling in drops; the fat which falls from roasting meat; (*pl.*) water, grease, etc., falling or trickling from anything. **dripping-pan,** *n.* A pan for receiving the fat which drips from roasting meat. **drippy,** *a.*

drive (drīv) [A.-S. *drīfan* (cp. Dut. *drijven*, Goth. *dreiban*, G. *treiben*)], *v.t.* (*past* **drove,** *p.p.* **driven**) To push or urge by force; to urge in a particular direction, to guide, to direct (as a horse, an engine, a ship); to convey in a carriage; to constrain, to compel; to prosecute, to carry on; to chase, hunt, esp. to frighten into an enclosure or towards guns; to distress, straiten, overwork; to throw, to propel; (*Golf*) to propel the ball with the driver; (*Cricket*) to hit the ball to or past the bowler with a swift free stroke; to force (a nail, etc.) with blows; to propel (machinery, etc.); to bore (a tunnel, etc.); to delay, defer; to press (as an argument); *to distrain (cattle). *v.i.* To be urged forward by violence; to dash, to rush violently, to hasten; to drift, to be carried; to travel in a carriage, esp. under one's own direction or control; to control or direct a vehicle, engine, etc.; to aim a blow, to strike furiously; to tend, to aim, to intend; (*Golf*) to hit the ball with the driver; *to distrain goods. *n.* A ride in a vehicle; the distance one is driven; a road for driving on, esp. a private carriageway to a house; a forward stroke at cricket, etc.; a driving of game, cattle, or of an enemy; (*Am.*) an annual gathering of cattle for branding; push, energy; (*slang*) a blow, a violent stroke; (*Cards*) a series of competitive games of whist or bridge. **drive-in,** *n.* A roadside café, cinema, etc. where a motorist can be catered for without alighting from his car. **to drive away:** To force to a distance; to scatter; to go away in a carriage, etc. **to drive a good bargain:** To make a good bargain. **to drive a hard bargain:** To be hard in making a bargain. **to drive at:** (*fig.*) To hint at. **what are you driving at?:** What exactly do you mean? **to drive in:** To hammer in; (*Mil.*) to force to retreat on their supports. **to drive off:** To compel to move away; *to put off, to defer. **to drive out:** To expel; to oust; to take the place of; in printing, to space widely. **to let drive:** To strike furiously, to aim a blow (at). **driver,** *n.* One who or that which drives; one who drives a vehicle or an engine; one who conducts a team; a tool used by coopers in driving on the hoops of casks; an overseer on a plantation; that which communicates motion to something else, as a wheel; the piece of wood which impels the shuttle in weaving through the shed of the loom; (*Golf*) a wooden-headed club used to propel the ball from the tee. **driver-ant,** *n.* A West African ant, *Anomma arcens.* **driverless,** *a.* **driving-band, -belt,** *n.* The strap or belt for connecting and communicating motion to parts of machinery. **driving-band,** *n.* (*Artil.*) A soft metal band at the end of a projectile which engages with the rifling of the gun and causes the fired shell to rotate. **driving licence,** *n.* (*Motor.*) A permit to drive, granted to one who has passed a **driving test,** or examination in the driving and handling of a motor-car. **driving-shaft,** *n.* A shaft transmitting motion from the driving-wheel. **driving-wheel,** *n.* The wheel which communicates motion to other parts of the machinery; a large wheel of a locomotive, a cycle-wheel or motor-wheel to which motive force is applied directly.

drivel (driv′ el) [A.-S. *dreflian*, from same stem as DRAFF], *v.i.* To slaver; to allow spittle to flow from the mouth, as a child, idiot, or dotard; to be weak or silly; to dote. *v.t.* To utter childishly or foolishly; to fritter (away). *n.* Slaver; spittle flowing from the mouth; silly, nonsensical talk, twaddle. **driveller,** *n.* A slaverer, an idiot, a dotard, a fool.

driver [DRIVE].

drizzle (driz′ el) [freq. of M.E. *dresen*, A.-S. *drēosan*, to fall in drops], *v.i.* To fall, as rain, in fine drops; to rain slightly. *v.t.* To shed in small fine drops; to wet with fine drops. *n.* Fine small rain. **drizzly,** *a.*

drogher (drō' gėr) [obs. F. *droguer*, Dut. *drogher*, from *droogen*, to dry (herrings, etc.)], *n.* A slow W. Indian coasting-vessel for carrying heavy burdens, as timber, etc.

drogman, -oman [DRAGOMAN].

drogue (drōg) [prob. var. of DRAG], *n.* (*Naut.*) A bag drawn behind a boat to prevent her broaching to; (*Whale-fishing*) a drag attached to a harpoon line to check the progress of a whale when struck; (*Aviat.*) a wind-sock.

droguet (drō gā') [F., DRUGGET], *n.* A kind of rep.

***droil** (droil) [etym. doubtful; cp. Dut. *druilen*, to loiter], *n.* A drudge, a slave; drudgery. *v.i.* To drudge, to toil, to moil.

droit (droit, drwa) [F., from late L. *drictum*, L. *dīrēctum*, DIRECT, late L., a right, a law], *n.* A right, a due; a legal right; *(*Law*) a writ of right; (*pl.*) legal perquisites. **droits of Admiralty:** Rights to the property of enemies, proceeds of wrecks, etc., which go into the public treasury.

droll (drōl) [F. *drôle*, etym. doubtful (whence *drôler*, to play the wag)], *a.* Odd, merry, facetious, ludicrous, comical, laughable, queer. *n.* A merry fellow, a jester, a buffoon. *v.i.* To play the wag or buffoon; to jest, to joke, to trifle. **drollery,** *n.* Idle sportive jocularity, buffoonery; *a puppet; *a puppet-show; *a lively or comical sketch. **drollness,** *n.* **drolly,** *adv.*

dromedary (drom'-, drŭm' ė dăr i) [O.F. *dromedaire*, late L. *dromedārius*, L. *dromas -adem*, Gr. *dromas -ada*, running, runner, from *dramein*, to run], *n.* The Arabian camel, *Camelus dromedarius*, distinguished from the Bactrian camel by its single hump; a swift variety of the species used for riding on. ***dromedarian,** *n.* The rider or driver of a dromedary.

***dromond** (drom' ŏnd) [A.-F. *dromund*, O.F. *dromon*, late L. *dromōn -em*, Gr. *dromōn*, from *dromos*, racing, a course], *n.* A large mediæval ship.

drone (drōn) [A.-S. *drān*, *drǣn*, a bee, cogn. with M.E. *drounen*, Sansk. *dhran*, to sound], *n.* The male of the bee, larger than the worker by which the honey is made; an idler, a lazy person who lives on the industry of others; a deep humming sound; the humming sound made by a bee; the unchanging bass produced from the three lower pipes of the bagpipe; any of these lower pipes. *v.i.* To make a monotonous humming noise, as a bee or as a bagpipe; to talk in a monotonous tone; to live in idleness. *v.t.* To read or speak in a monotonous tone. **drone-pipe,** *n.* The drone of a bagpipe. **droningly,** *adv.*

drool (drool) [contr. of DRIVEL], *v.i.* To drivel, to slaver.

droop (droop) [cp. Icel. *drūpa*, cogn. with foll.], *v.i.* To hang, lean, or bend down; to sink as if languishing; to fail, to flag, to languish, to decline; to be dejected, to despond, to lose heart. *v.t.* To let (the head, eyes, face) fall or hang down. *n.* The act of drooping; a drooping attitude. **droopingly,** *adv.*

drop (drop) [A.-S. *dropa*, whence *dropian*, to drop (cogn. with DRIP, DROOP)], *n.* A globule or small portion of liquid in a spherical form, which is falling, hanging, or adhering to a surface; a very small quantity of a fluid; (*Med.*) the smallest quantity separable of a liquid, (*pl.*) a dose or doses measured by such units; (*fig.*) a minute quantity, an infinitesimal particle; (*colloq.*) a glass or drink of liquor; anything resembling a drop, or hanging as a drop, as an earring, or other pendent ornament; a sugar plum, (*pl.*) various sweetmeats; the act of dropping, a fall, a descent, a collapse; a thing that drops or is dropped; a drop-curtain; a falling trap-door; the part of a gallows contrived so as to fall from under the feet of persons to be hanged, the distance they are allowed to fall; a machine for lowering anything heavy into the hold of a vessel; an abrupt fall in a surface, the amount of this; a drop-kick. *v.t.* (*past & p.p.* **dropped**) To allow or cause to fall in drops, as a liquid; to cause to fall, to fell; to lower, to let down; to dismiss, to give up; to set down from a carriage; to let fall, to utter casually; to write to in an informal manner; to bear a foal, calf, etc.; to omit; to stop (doing something), to have done with; to let go; to sprinkle with drops; (*colloq.*) to bring down, to kill; (*colloq.*) to lose. *v.i.* To fall in drops; to drip, to discharge itself in drops; to fall; to collapse suddenly, to sink as if exhausted, to faint; to kneel; to disappear; to die; to die suddenly; to be uttered; to cease, to lapse, to come to an end; to fall (behind); *to submerge. **a drop too much:** Said of a person who is slightly drunk. **drop-curtain,** *n.* (*Theat.*) A drop-scene. **drop-drill,** *n.* A contrivance for simultaneously manuring and sowing in drills. **drop-handle,** *n.* A handle or knob of a drawer, door, etc., that hangs down when not in use. **drop-kick,** *n.* (*Football*) A kick made by letting the ball drop and kicking it on the rise; whence **drop-off, drop-out. to drop off:** (*fig.*) To fall gently asleep. **drop-letter,** *n.* (*Am.*) A letter posted for delivery in the same district. **drop-press,** *n.* A machine for embossing, punching, etc., by means of a weight made to drop on an anvil. **drop-scene,** *n.* (*Theat.*) A painted curtain suspended on pulleys which is let down to conceal the stage. **drop-shutter,** *n.* (*Phot.*) A shutter in a camera for making instantaneous exposures. **drop-sulphur, -tin,** *n.* Sulphur or tin granulated by being dropped in a molten state into water. **drop-wort,** *n.* A plant with tuberous root-fibres, *Spiræa filipendula*; other species of spiræa; various species of *Œnanthe*, esp. *Œ. fistulosa*. **to drop anchor:** To let down the anchor. **to drop across:** To meet with accidentally; to reprimand. **to drop astern:** To move or pass towards the stern; to reduce speed so as to allow another to pass ahead. **to drop away:** To depart; to desert a cause. **to drop down:** To sail down a river towards the sea. **to drop in:** To make an informal visit; to call unexpectedly. **droplet,** *n.* **dropper,** *n.* One who or that which drops; (*Angling*) an artificial fly set at some distance from the end of a cast. **dropping-bottle,** *n.* An apparatus for supplying small quantities to test-tubes, etc. **dropping fire,** *n.* An irregular discharge of small arms. **dropping-tube,** *n.* A tube for allowing liquid to exude in drops. ***droppingly,** *adv.* **droppings,** *n.pl.* That which falls or has fallen in drops; the dung of beasts or birds.

dropsy (drop' si) [M.E. *dropesie*, *ydropesie*, M.F. *hydropisie*, L. *hydrōpisis*, Gr. *hudrōps -ōpos* (*hudōr*, water)], *n.* An accumulation of watery fluid in the areolar tissues or serous cavities; (*Bot.*) a disease in plants caused by an excess of water; (*fig.*) a swollen or bloated condition. **dropsical,** *a.* **dropsically,** *adv.* **dropsied,** *a.* Suffering from dropsy; *inflated.

Drosera (dros' ėr ȧ) [Gr. *droseros*, fem. *-ra*, dewy, from *drosos*, dew], *n.* (*Bot.*) A genus of insectivorous plants comprising the sundew.

droshky (drosh' ki) [Russ. *drozhki*, dim. of *drozi*, a wagon], *n.* A Russian open four-wheeled vehicle in which the passengers ride astride a bench, their feet resting on bars near the ground; a public cab in Berlin and other German towns.

drosometer (drŏ som' ė tėr) [Gr. *drosos*, dew, -METER], *n.* An instrument for measuring the quantity of dew collected on the surface of a body during the night.

dross (dros) [A.-S. *drōs* (cp. M.Dut. *droes*, G. *drusen*, lees, dregs)], *n.* The scum or useless matter left from the melting of metals; (*fig.*) anything utterly useless, refuse, rubbish; anything impure. **drossy,** *a.* **drossiness,** *n.*

drought (drout), ***drouth** (drouth) [A.-S. *drūgath*, from *drūgian*, to dry (*drȳge*, DRY)], *n.* Dryness, dry weather; an absence of rain or moisture; long-continued rainless weather; thirst. **droughty,** *a.* ***drouthy,** *a.*

drouk (drook) [Sc. and North.; etym. doubtful (cp. Icel. *drukna*, to be drowned, DRUNK)], *v.t.* To drench; to duck. **droukit,** *part.a.*

drove (1) (drōv) [A.-S. *drāf*, from *drīfan*, to DRIVE], *n.* A collection of animals driven in a body; a road for driving cattle on; a shoal, a crowd, a mass of people, esp. as moving together; (*Fens*) a narrow channel for draining or irrigation; a stone-mason's broad chisel. *v.t.* To dress (stone) with a drove. *v.i.* To drive cattle in droves. **drover,** *n.* One who drives cattle or sheep to market; a cattle-dealer; a boat used for fishing with a drift-net.

drove (2), *past* [DRIVE].

drow (drou) [Sc.], *n.* A drizzling mist.

drown (droun) [A.-S. *druncnian*, to become intoxicated, to drown, from *druncen*, p.p. of *drincan*, to DRINK], *v.i.* To be suffocated in water or other liquid; to perish in this manner. *v.t.* To suffocate by submersion in water or other liquid; to submerge, to drench, to overwhelm with water, to overflow, to deluge; (*fig.*) to overpower (as by a volume of sound); to overwhelm, to quench, to put an end to. **to drown out:** To drive out by a flood. **drowner,** *n.* One who is drowning.

drowse (drouz) [A.-S. *drūsian*, to become languid (prob. through **drowsy**)], *v.i.* To be sleepy or half-asleep; to be heavy and dull; to doze. *v.t.* To make drowsy; to spend (time) in an idle or sluggish way. *n.* The state of being half-asleep; a nap, a doze; drowsiness, heaviness. **drowsy,** *a.* Inclined to sleep, sleepy; disposing to sleep; sluggish, stupid. **drowsy-head,** *n.* A sleepy person. **drowsy-headed,** *a.* Sleepy, sluggish in disposition; dull. ***drowsihead, drowsiness,** *n.* **drowsily,** *adv.*

drub (drŭb) [prob. from Arab. *darb*, a beating], *v.t.* To beat with a stick; to cudgel; to beat thoroughly in a fight or contest. **drubber,** *n.* **drubbing,** *n.* A cudgelling, a heavy beating.

drudge (drŭj) [prob. cogn. with A.-S. *drēogan*, to DREE], *v.i.* To perform menial work; to work hard with little reward; to slave. *v.t.* To spend or pass laboriously. *n.* One employed in menial work; one who toils at uncongenial work and is ill-paid; a slave, a hack. **drudger** (1), *n.* A drudge. **drudgery,** *n.* ***drudgingly,** *adv.*

drudger (2) [DREDGER].

drug (drŭg) [F. *drogue*, etym. doubtful], *n.* Any substance, mineral, vegetable, or animal, used as the basis or as an ingredient in medical preparations; a poison, a potion. *v.t.* (*past & p.p.* **drugged**) To mix drugs with, esp. to make narcotic; to administer drugs to, esp. narcotics; to render insensible with drugs; (*fig.*) to deaden; to surfeit, to cloy. **drug addict, fiend,** *n.* One addicted to the use of narcotics. **drugstore,** *n.* (*Am.*) A chemist's shop where other small articles are sold. **drug traffic,** *n.* Illicit trading in narcotic drugs. **drug in the market:** So common as to be unsaleable.

drugget (drŭg′ ėt) [F. *droguet*, etym. doubtful], *n.* A coarse woollen fabric, felted or woven, used as a covering or as a substitute for carpet.

druggist (drŭg′ ist), *n.* One who deals in drugs; a pharmaceutical chemist; (*Am.*) a chemist.

druid (droo′ id) [F. *druide*, L. *druidæ*, *-des*, pl., from O.Celt. (cp. O.Ir. *druid-*, Gael. *draoi*, *draoidh*, *druidh*, a magician, a sorcerer)], *n.* The name commonly given to the priests and teachers of the early Gauls and Britons or perh. of pre-Celtic peoples, who taught the transmigration of souls, frequently celebrated their rites in oak-groves, and are stated by Cæsar to have offered human sacrifices; a member of the Ancient Order of Druids, a benefit society, estab. 1781; an officer of the Welsh Gorsedd. **druidess,** *n.* **druidic, -ical** (droo id′ ik, -ȧl), *a.* **druidism,** *n.*

drum (1) (drŭm) [cp. M.Dut. *tromme* and Dut. *trom*, M.H.G. *trumme*, orig. a trumpet], *n.* A musical instrument made by stretching parchment over the head of a hollow cylinder or hemisphere; (*Anat.*) the tympanum or hollow part of the middle-ear; the membrane across this; (*Zool.*) the hollow hyoid bone of a howling monkey; applied to certain resonant organs in birds, fishes, and insects; the drum-like cry of the bittern and other animals; anything drum-shaped, esp. a small cylindrical box for holding fruit, fish, etc.; the quantity contained in such a box; (*Austral. colloq.*) a swag, a bundle, a tramp's roll, a bluey; the solid part of the Corinthian and composite capitals; the upright part of a cupola, either above or below a dome; a cylindrical block forming part of a column; (*Mach.*) a revolving cylinder over which a belt or band passes; the drum-fish; *an evening or afternoon party at which card-playing was carried on. *v.i.* (*past & p.p.* **drummed**) To beat or play a tune on a drum; to beat rapidly or thump, as on a table, the floor, or a piano; to make a sound like the beating of a drum (as certain insects, birds, etc.); (*Am.*) to tout for customers. *v.t.* To perform on a drum; to summon; to beat (up) recruits by the sound of a drum; to din (into) a person, to drive a lesson (into) by persistence. **drum-fish,** *n.* The American genus *Pogonias*, the two species of which emit a drumming or grunting noise. **drum-head,** *n.* The membrane stretched at the top of a drum; the membrane across the drum of the ear; the top of the capstan. **drum-head court-martial** [COURT]. **drum-major,** *n.* A non-commissioned officer in charge of the drums of a regiment, or who leads the band on the march. **drum scanner:** (*Television*) A rotating drum carrying the picture-scanning elements. **drum-stick,** *n.* The stick with which a drum is beaten; anything resembling such a stick, as the leg of a fowl. **to drum out:** To expel from a regiment with disgrace; to cashier. **to drum upon:** To beat or thump repeatedly.

drum (2) (drŭm) [Gael. and Ir. *druim*], *n.* A narrow hill or ridge; (*Geol.*) a long narrow ridge of drift or alluvial formation; also called a **drumlin.**

***drumble** (drŭm′ bel) [etym. doubtful (cp. Swed. and Norw. *drumla*, to be half asleep)], *v.i.* To be sluggish; to move sluggishly. **drumble-dore,** *n.* A dor-beetle; a stupid, heavy fellow.

drumlin [DRUM (2)].

drumly (drŭm′ li) [Sc., prob. var. of obs. *drubly*], *a.* Muddy, turbid; troubled, cloudy, overcast.

drummer (drŭm′ ėr), *n.* One who performs on a drum, esp. a soldier whose office is to beat the various calls, etc. on his drum; the member of an orchestra in charge of the percussion instruments; a commercial traveller.

Drummond light (drŭm′ ȯnd līt) [Capt. *Drummond*, (1797–1840) the inventor], *n.* The lime-light or oxy-hydrogen light.

drunk (drŭngk) [p.p. of DRINK], *pred.a.* Intoxicated, stupefied or overcome with alcoholic liquors; (*fig.*) inebriated, highly excited (with joy, etc.). *n.* (*slang*). A drunken person; a fit of drunkenness. **drunkard,** *n.* One addicted to the excessive use of alcoholic liquors; one who is habitually or frequently drunk. **drunken** [A.-S. *druncen*, p.p. of *drincan*, to DRINK], *p.p.* and *a.* Intoxicated; given to drunkenness; caused by drunkenness; characterized by intoxication. **drunkenly,** *adv.* **drunkenness,** *n.*

Drupaceæ (droo pā′ sė ē) [L. *drūpa*, Gr. *druppa*, an over-ripe olive], *n.pl.* (*Bot.*) A sub-order of *Rosaceæ*, including the plum, cherry, peach, olive, and other trees bearing stone-fruit. **drupaceous** (droo pā′ shŭs), *a.* (*Bot.*) Belonging to the *Drupaceæ*; bearing drupes; pertaining to or of the nature of drupes.

drupe (droop), *n.* (*Bot.*) A fleshy fruit containing a stone with a kernel, as the peach, plum, etc. **drupel, drupelet,** *n.* A succulent fruit formed by an aggregation of small drupes, as the raspberry.

druse (droos) [G., from Boh. *druza*], *n.* (*Cryst.*) A cavity in a rock lined or studded with crystals; the crystalline lining of this. **drusy,** *a.*

Druse (drooz) [Arab. *Durūz*, said to be from Ismail al-*Darazi*, or the Tailor, founder of the sect in 1040], *n.* A member of a politico-religious sect of

Mohammedan origin, inhabiting the region of Mount Lebanon in Syria.

dry (drī) [A.-S. *drȳge* (cp. Dut. *droog*, G. *trocken*)], *a.* Devoid of moisture; arid; without sap or juice, not succulent; lacking rain, having an insufficient rainfall; thirsty; dried up, removed by evaporation, draining or wiping; not giving milk, not yielding juice; not under water (of land, a shore, etc.); not sweet (of wines, etc.); without butter (as bread); prohibited by law for sale of alcoholic liquors; (*fig.*) lifeless, insipid lacking interest, dull; meagre, bare, plain; sarcastic, cynical, ironical, sly; without sympathy or cordiality, cold, discouraging, harsh; (*Art*) exhibiting a sharp, frigid preciseness in execution or the want of a delicate contour in form. *n.* (*Austral.*) The rainless season. *v.t.* To free from or deprive of water or moisture; to deprive of juice, sap, or succulence; to drain, to wipe; to cause to cease yielding milk; to exhaust. *v.i.* To lose or be deprived of moisture; to grow dry; to cease to yield moisture; *to become withered; *to be thirsty. **to go dry:** (*Pol.*) To prohibit the sale of alcoholic liquors. **the Dry,** *n.* (*Austral.*) The dry season; the inland desert. **to dry up:** To deprive totally of moisture; to deprive of energy; to lose all moisture; to cease to flow, to cease to yield water; to become withered; (*Theat.*) to forget one's lines; (*slang*) to leave off talking or doing something. **dry-beat,** *v.t.* To beat severely. **dry-bob,** *n.* (*School slang*) One who plays cricket and football, as distinguished from a boy who rows. **dry-bulb thermometer,** *n.* One of a pair of thermometers the other of which is always kept moist, the two together indicating the degree of humidity of the air. **dry canteen,** *n.* A canteen where no alcoholic drinks are served. **dry cell,** *n.* (*Elec.*) A battery cell in which the electrolyte is a paste and not a fluid. **dry-clean,** *v.t.* To clean with petrol or other detergent. **dry-cooper,** *n.* A maker of casks for dry goods. **dry-cure,** *v.t.* To cure by drying and salting, as distinguished from pickling. **dry-eyed,** *a.* Without tears. **dry-fly,** *n.* An angler's fly that floats on the surface, as distinguished from one that is allowed to sink. **dry-foot,** *adv.* Dry-shod, without wetting the feet; *following game by the scent of the foot. **dry-footed,** *a.* Dry-shod. **dry-goods,** *n.pl.* Cloths, silks, drapery, haberdashery, etc., as distinguished from grocery; sometimes extended to include any non-liquid goods. **dry-goods store,** *n.* (*Am.*) A draper's shop. **dry ice,** *n.* Solid carbon dioxide used in refrigeration. **dry lodging,** *n.* (*slang*) Accommodation without board. **dry-measure,** *n.* A measure for dry goods, as a bushel. **dry-nurse,** *n.* A nurse who rears a child without the breast; (*colloq.*) one who looks after and instructs another; (*Mil. slang*) a subordinate officer who coaches a superior. *v.t.* To rear without the breast; (*Mil.*) to act as instructor to (a superior officer). **dry-pile,** *n.* A voltaic battery in which the plates are separated by layers of dry substance. **dry-plate,** *n.* A photographic plate with a hard, dry, sensitized film, adapted for storing and carrying about. **dry-point,** *n.* A needle for engraving on a copper plate without acid. *v.i.* To engrave by this process. *n.* An engraving so produced. **dry-rot,** *n.* Decay in timber caused by fungi which reduce it to a dry brittle mass. **dry-salt,** *v.t.* To dry-cure. **dry shaver,** *n.* An electric razor. **dry ship,** *n.* Ship in which no alcoholic liquor is permitted. **dry-shod,** *a.* and *adv.* Without wetting the feet. **dry wall,** *n.* A wall built without mortar. **dryish,** *a.* **drily, dryly,** *adv.* **dryness,** *n.* **drier, dryer,** *n.* A desiccative; a material added to oil paints and printers' ink to make them dry quickly; an apparatus for drying the hair after shampoo, etc.

dryad (drī' ăd) [L. *dryas*, pl. *-ades*, Gr. *druas -ades* (*drūs*, a tree)], *n.* (*pl.* **-ades)** A nymph of the woods.

dry-as-dust (drī' az dŭst), *n.* A dull, prosy, plodding historian; an antiquary who carries on his researches in a mechanical spirit (from the name of the imaginary person to whom Scott dedicated some of his novels). *a.* Dull, prosy; dry, uninteresting.

drysalter (drī sol' tėr), *n.* A dealer in dried and salted meat, pickles, etc.; a dealer in dye-stuffs, chemical products, etc. **drysaltery,** *n.* The goods sold by a drysalter; the shop or business of a drysalter.

duad [DYAD].

dual (dū' ăl) [L. *duālis*, from *duo*, two], *a.* Consisting of two; twofold, binary, double; expressing two; (*Gram.*) applied to an inflexion of a verb, adjective, pronoun, or noun, which, in certain languages, expresses two persons or things, as distinct from the plural which expresses more than two. *n.* (*Gram.*) The dual number. **Dual Monarchy,** *n.* The former union of Austria-Hungary. **duality,** *n.* **dualize,** *v.t.* **dually,** *adv.*

dualin (dū' ȧ lin), *n.* An explosive compound, composed of nitro-glycerine, fine sawdust, and nitre.

dualism (dū' ȧ lizm), *n.* Duality, the state of being twofold; a system or theory based on a radical duality of nature or animating principle, as mind and matter, good and evil in the universe, divine and human personalities in Christ, independence of the cerebral hemispheres. **dualist,** *n.* **dualistic** (-lis' tik), *a.*

duan (dū' ăn) [Gael.], *n.* A song; a canto.

dub (1) (dŭb) [late A.-S. *dubbian*, perh. from O.F. (cp. *adober*, *adouber*, It. *addobare*), etym. unknown], *v.t.* (*past & p.p.* **dubbed**) To confer knighthood upon by a blow of a sword on the shoulder; to confer any dignity, rank, character, or nickname upon; to dress or trim; to smear with grease; *to invest, to clothe. **to dub a cock:** To trim the hackles, and cut off the comb and gills for cock-fighting. **to dub a fly:** To dress an artificial fly for fishing. **to dub cloth:** To raise a nap on by striking it with teasels.

dub (2) (dŭb) [prob. onomat.], *v.i.* To strike, to poke (at); to make a noise of beating (as a drum). **dub-a-dub,** *adv.* With the sound of or as of a beaten drum.

dub (3) (dŭb) [Sc. and North.; etym. doubtful], *n.* A deep pool in a stream; a puddle.

dub (4) (dŭb), *v.t.* (*Cinema.*) To give a new sound-track (esp. in a different language) to a film.

dubbin (dŭb' in), *n.* A preparation of grease for preserving and softening leather.

dubious (dū' bi ŭs) [L. *dubiōsus*, from *dubius*, doubtful (*duo*, two)], *a.* Undetermined; doubtful; wavering in mind; of uncertain result or issue; obscure, vague, not clear; questionable; open to suspicion. **dubiety** (-bī' ė ti), *n.* ***dubiosity** (-os' i ti), *n.* **dubiously,** *adv.* **dubiousness,** *n.*

dubitation (dū bi tā' shŭn) [F., from L. *dubitātio -ōnem*, from *dubiāre*, to DOUBT], *n.* The act of doubting; doubt, hesitation, uncertainty. **dubitative** (dū' bi tā tiv), *a.* Tending to doubt; expressing doubt. **dubitatively,** *adv.*

ducal (dū' kăl) [F., from late L. *ducalis*, from *dux ducis*, DUKE], *a.* Of or pertaining to a duke. **ducally,** *adv.*

ducat (dŭk' ăt) [F., from It. *ducato*, late L. *ducātus*, a DUCHY], *n.* A coin first minted in the Duchy of Apulia about A.D. 1140, afterwards current in several European countries; when of gold, worth about 9s. 4d., and of silver, about 3s. 6d.; (*slang pl.*) money, cash. **ducatoon** (dŭk ȧ toon'), *n.* An old silver coin, originally Venetian, worth about 5s. 4d., formerly circulating in the Netherlands.

Duce (doo' chā) [It., leader], *n.* The official title of Benito Mussolini (1883–1945) when head of the Fascist state in Italy.

duchess (dŭch' es) [F. *duchesse*], *n.* The wife or widow of a duke; a lady who holds a duchy in her own right; (*colloq.*) a woman of imposing appearance; (*Build.*) a size of roofing slate; (*Comm.*) a kind of fancy blind with ornamental edging. **duchy** (dŭch' i), *n.* The territory, jurisdiction, or dominions of a duke; the royal dukedom of Cornwall or Lancaster. **duchy-court,** *n.* The court of a duchy, esp. that of Lancaster in England.

duck (1) (dŭk) [prob. from Dut. *dock* (cp. Dan. *dug*, Swed. *duk*, G. *tuch*)], *n.* A kind of untwilled linen or cotton fabric lighter and finer than canvas, used for jackets, aprons, etc., (*pl.*) trousers or a suit made of this.

duck (2) (dŭk) [A.-S. *dūce*, cogn. with foll.], *n.* A web-footed bird of the genus *Anas*, esp. the domestic duck, a variety of *A. boschas*, the wild duck or mallard; the female of this species (as distinguished from a drake); a stone made to skip along the surface of water; (*colloq.*) darling; (*Cricket*) a duck's egg, a score of nothing; (*Mil.*) popular name for an amphibious motor vehicle. **Bombay-duck:** [BUMMALO]. **ducks and drakes:** A game of making a flat stone skip along the surface of water. **to make ducks and drakes of:** To squander. **lame duck:** A crippled person; a defaulter on the Stock Exchange. **duck-billed,** *a.* Having a bill like a duck, esp. applied to the duck-billed platypus or ornithorhynchus. **duck-board,** *n.* Planking used to cover muddy roads or paths. **duck-hawk,** *n.* The marsh-harrier, *Circus æruginosus*. **duck-meat, duck's-meat,** *n.* **duck-weed,** *n.* A popular name for several floating water-weeds of the genus *Lemna*, esp. *L. minor*, which is eaten by ducks and geese. **duck's-egg,** *n.* (*Cricket*) No score. **duck-shot,** *n.* Small shot for shooting wild duck. **ducker** (1), *n.* A breeder of ducks. **duckling,** *n.* A young duck. **ducky, ducks,** *n.* (*fam.*) A term of familiarity or endearment.

duck (3) (dŭk) [M.E. *duken*, *douken*, as from an A.-S. *dūcan* (cp. Dut. *duiken*, Dan. *dukke*, G. *tauchen*)], *v.i.* To dive, dip, or plunge under water; to bob the head; to bow, to cringe. *v.t.* To dip under water and suddenly withdraw; to throw into water; to wet thoroughly. *n.* A quick plunge or dip under water; a bob or sudden lowering of the head. **ducker** (2), *n.* A diving-bird, esp. the dabchick or little grebe, and the water ouzel. **ducking,** *n.* Immersion in water; a thorough wetting. **ducking-pond,** *n.* A pond wherein petty offenders were ducked. **ducking-stool,** *n.* A kind of stool or chair on which scolds were tied and ducked.

duct (dŭkt) [L. *ductus*, a leading, p.p. of *ducere*, to lead], *n.* A tube, canal, or passage by which a fluid is conveyed; (*Anat.*) a tubular passage for conveying chyle, lymph, and other fluids; (*Bot.*) a canal or elongated cell holding water, air, etc. **ductless,** *a.* **ductless glands:** (*Med.*) Endocrine glands.

ductile (dŭk′ til, -tīl) [F., from L. *ductilis*, as prec.], *a.* That may be drawn out into threads or wire; malleable, not brittle; capable of being moulded, plastic; (*fig.*) pliant, tractable, yielding to persuasion or advice. **ductility** (til′ i ti), *n.*

dud (dŭd) [etym. doubtful], *n.* (*colloq.*) A useless thing; bad coin; a shell that has failed to explode. *a.* Useless, worthless. **duds,** *n.pl.* Clothes, old clothes, rags.

dude (dūd) [L.G. *duden-dop*, *dudenkop*, a lazy fellow], *n.* A fop, an exquisite, an affected person; a swell, a masher; an æsthete; (*Am.*) a city-bred person. **dude ranch,** *n.* (*Am.*) A ranch run as a pleasure resort by city people. **dudette** (dū det′), **dudine** (dū dēn′), *n.* A female dude. **dudish,** *a.*

dudeen (doo dēn′) [Ir., etym. unknown], *n.* A short clay tobacco pipe.

***dudgeon** (1) (dŭj′ ȯn) [etym. unknown], *n.* The root of the box-tree; the handle of a dagger formerly made of this wood; a small dagger.

dudgeon (2) (dŭj′ ȯn) [etym. doubtful], *n.* Anger, sullen resentment, indignation.

due (1) (dū) [O.F. *deü*, p.p. of *devoir*, to owe, L. *debēre*], *a.* Owed, owing, that ought to be paid, rendered, or done to another; claimable, proper, suitable, appropriate; expected, appointed to arrive, calculated to happen; ascribable, that may be attributed (to); *punctual, exact. *adv.* Exactly, directly; *punctually; *duly. *n.* That which is owed or owing to one; that which one owes; a debt, an obligation, a tribute, toll, fee, or other legal exaction; *a debt; *just right or title; (*pl.*) (*Am.*) a club subscription. **dock-, harbour-dues:** Charges levied by corporate bodies for the use of docks or harbours. **to fall due:** To become payable; to mature (as a bill). **to give the devil his due** [DEVIL]. ***dueful,** *a.* Due, bounden, suitable. **dueness,** *n.*

***due** (2) (dū) [var. of obs. *dow*, F. *douer*, L. *dōtāre*, to endow (*dōs dōtis*, a gift)], *v.t.* To endow; to endue, invest.

duel (dū′ ėl) [F., from It. *duello*, med. L. *duellum*, archaic form of *bellum*, war (cp. *duo*, two)], *n.* A combat between two persons with deadly weapons to decide a private quarrel; any contest or struggle between two persons, parties, causes, animals, etc. *v.i.* To fight in a duel; to contest. **duellist,** *n.* ***duello*** (dū el′ ō) [It.], *n.* A duel; the rules of duelling.

duenna (dū en′ ȧ) [Sp. *dueña*, L. *domina*, lady], *n.* An elderly female employed as companion and governess to young women, a chaperon.

duet, duetto (dū et′, -ō) [It. *duetto*, dim. of *duo* (L. *duo*, two)], *n.* A composition for two performers, vocal or instrumental; a dialogue; any performance by two persons. **duettino** (dū ė tē′ nō), *n.* A short duet.

Dufaycolor (dū fā′ kŭl ȯr) [name of inventor], *n.* (*Photo.*) A colour process employing a specially designed colour screen separate from the sensitive plate.

duff (1) (dŭf) [DOUGH], *n.* (*dial. and colloq.*) A stiff, flour pudding boiled in a bag. **plum duff:** Such a pudding made with raisins.

duff (2) (dŭf) [slang; perh. from DUFFER], *v.t.* To fake up (rubbishy articles) for sale; (*Austral.*) to steal cattle by altering the brands; to cheat. **duffing,** *a.* Counterfeit, rubbishy; faked up for sale.

duffel (dŭf′ ėl) [*Duffel*, town in Brabant], *n.* A thick, coarse kind of woollen cloth, having a thick nap or frieze; (*Am.*) a camper-out's change of clothes, outfit, kit. **duffel bag,** *n.* (*Nav.*) A sort of kit-bag.

duffer (dŭf′ ėr) [etym. doubtful (cp. DUFF (2))], *n.* A pedlar, a hawker of women's dress, or of cheap and flash jewellery, sham smuggled goods, etc.; a stupid, awkward, or useless person.

dug (1) (dŭg) [etym. obscure (cp. Sansk. *duh*, to milk)], *n.* A teat, a nipple (now used only of the lower animals.

dug (2) (dŭg) [DIG, *past & p.p.*] **dug-out,** *n.* A canoe formed of a single log hollowed out, or of parts of two logs thus hollowed out and afterwards joined together; a rough cabin cut in the side of a bank or hill; a cellar, cave, or shelter used as a protection against enemy shelling; (*contemp.*) a retired officer recalled for service; (*Am.*) the enclosure at baseball occupied by the trainer and men waiting to bat.

dugong (doo′ gong) [Malay *dūyōng*], *n.* A large herbivorous aquatic mammal, *Halicore dugong*, with two fore limbs only, belonging to the *Sirenia*, and inhabiting the Indian seas.

duke (dūk) [F. *duc*, L. *dux ducis*, a leader], *n.* A noble holding the highest hereditary rank outside the royal family; the sovereign prince of a duchy; (*Rom. Hist.*) a provincial military commander under the later emperors; *a commander, a leader, a chieftain; (*pl.*) (*slang*) fists; hands. **dukedom,** *n.* The territory, title, rank, or quality of a duke. **dukeling,** *n.* A petty duke; a little duke. **dukeship,** *n.*

Dukeries (dū′ kėr iz) [from prec.], *n.pl.* A district in Nottinghamshire formerly comprising five ducal seats.

Dukhobors (doo′ kō bôrz) [Rus., spirit-wrestlers], *n.pl.* A Russian mystical sect who were oppressed for their passive resistance to militarism and migrated in large numbers from their homes in the Caucasus to Canada.

dulcamara (dŭl kȧ mar′ ȧ) [med. L. (*dulcis*, sweet, *amāra*, fem. of *amārus*, bitter)], *n.* The bitter-sweet *Solanum dulcamara*.

dulcet (dŭl′ sėt) [O.F. *doucet*, dim. of *doux*, L. *dulcis*, sweet; assim. to L.], *a.* Sweet to the ear; sweet to the senses; *luscious.

dulcify (dŭl′ si fī) [L. *dulcificāre*, as prec.], *v.t.* To sweeten; to free from acidity, acrimony, or saltness. **dulcification** (-kā′ shŭn), *n.*

dulcimer (dŭl′ si mėr) [O.F. *doulcemer*, Sp. *dulcemele*, perh. from L. *dulce melos*, a sweet song], *n.* A musical instrument with strings of wire, which are struck with rods.

Dulcinea (dŭl si nē′ ȧ, -sin′ ė ȧ) [Don Quixote's lady-love], *n.* A sweetheart; an idealized mistress.

dule-tree (doo̅l′ trē) [DOLE (2)], *n.* (*Sc.*) The gallows.

dulia (dū′ li ȧ, dū li′ ȧ) [med. L., from Gr. *douleia*, slavery, servitude, from *doulos*, slave], *n.* The lowest of the three degrees of adoration recognized in the Roman Catholic Church, the reverence paid to angels, saints, etc.

dull (dŭl) [M.E. *dul* (cp. A.-S. *dol*, stupid, Dut. *dol*, G. *toll*, mad)], *a.* Slow of understanding; stupid, not quick in perception; without sensibility; blunt, obtuse, not sharp or acute; wanting keenness in any of the senses; sluggish, inert, slow of movement; stagnant; not brisk or active (as trade); not bright, dim, tarnished; cloudy, overcast, gloomy, depressing; uninteresting, tedious, wearisome; hard of hearing, deaf. *v.t.* To make dull or stupid; to stupefy; to make blunt of edge, to render less acute, sensitive, interesting or effective; to make heavy or sluggish, to deaden; to tarnish, to dim. *v.i.* To become dull, blunt, stupid, or inert. **dull-brained,** *a.* Stupid; of dull intellect. **dull-eyed,** *a.* Having a listless or gloomy look. ***dull-head,** *n.* A stupid, silly fellow. **dull-sighted,** *a.* Not sharp-sighted; having dim vision. **dull-witted,** *a.* Stupid. **dullard,** *n.* A blockhead; a dunce. *a.* Stupid, doltish, inert. **dullish,** *a.* **dully,** *adv.* **dullness,** *n.*

dulse (dŭls) [Ir. and Gael. *duileasg*], *n.* An edible kind of seaweed, *Rhodymenia palmata.*

duly (dū′ li), *adv.* In suitable manner; properly; becomingly; regularly; punctually; sufficiently.

Duma (doo′ mȧ) [Rus., originally, an elective municipal council], *n.* The old Russian parliament or chamber of representatives, a legislative and revising body whose authority was limited by the veto of the Tsar, first summoned in 1906.

dumb (dŭm) [A.-S.; cp. Dut. *dom*, Swed. *dumb*, Dan. *dum*, O.H.G. *tump*, G. *dumm*, mute, stupid], *a.* Unable to utter articulate sounds; unable to speak; mute, silent, speechless, refraining from speaking, reticent, taciturn; soundless; (*colloq.*) stupid, unintelligent. *v.t.* To make dumb; to silence; *to confound. **to strike dumb:** To confound; to astonish; to render speechless by astonishment. **dumb-barge, -craft,** *n.* A heavy boat or hopper without means of propulsion, used for lifting matter from the bottom of the water, and similar purposes. **dumb-bells,** *n.pl.* Pairs of weights connected by short bars or handles, swung in the hands for exercise. *v.i.* To perform exercises with these. **dumb crambo** [CRAMBO]. **dumb-iron,** *n.* A carriage-spring consisting of two half-elliptical springs joined at the ends; (*Motor.*) the curved forward end of the frame to which a front spring is made fast. **dumb-piano,** *n.* A keyboard for exercising the fingers. **dumb-show,** *n.* Gestures without speech; pantomime. **dumb-waiter,** *n.* A dining-room apparatus with (usu. revolving) shelves for holding dishes, etc.; (*Am.*) a movable framework for conveying food, etc., from one room to another, a service-lift. **dumb-well,** *n.* A well for carrying off drainage. **dumbly,** *adv.* **dumbness,** *n.*

dumbfound (dŭm′ found), *v.t.* To strike dumb; to confound, confuse, perplex, to astound.

dumbledore (dŭm′ bėl dôr) [*dumble* prob. conn. with DUMB, DOR], *n.* (*prov.*) The humble bee; the brown cockchafer.

dumdum bullet (dŭm′ dŭm) [*Dumdum*, town and military station near Calcutta], *n.* A soft-nosed expanding bullet that lacerates the flesh.

dummy (dŭm′ i), *n.* One who is dumb; any sham article; a sham package displayed in a shop; a lay-figure, for showing off dress, etc.; the fourth exposed hand when three persons are playing at whist, etc.; a game so played; a person who appears on the stage without speaking; a mere tool; a doll; a stupid fellow; a mallet; a rubber teat for a baby to suck. **double dummy:** A game at whist, etc., with only two players, the two other hands being exposed.

dump (1) (dŭmp) [M.E. *dumpen*, to fall flat, prob. from Scand. (cp. Norw. *dumpa*, to thump, Swed. dial. *dompa*, Dan. *dumpe*, to fall plump)], *v.t.* To throw into a heap; to unload (as dirt) from wagons by tilting them up; to shoot, to deposit; to send surplus produce, esp. manufactured goods that are unsaleable at home, to a foreign market for sale at a low price; to get rid of superfluous or objectionable things or people (*e.g.* emigrants) by sending elsewhere. *v.i.* To sit down heavily and suddenly. *n.* A pile of refuse; a place for shooting rubbish; a mean house or room; an Army storage depot; (*Am.*) a refuse-tip. **dump-car, -cart, -wagon, -truck,** *n.* A vehicle that tips up in front and so dumps its load. **dumpage,** *n.* (*Am.*) The right of shooting loads of earth, rubbish, etc., in a certain spot; money paid for such right. **dumper,** *n.* **dumping-ground,** *n.*

dump (2) (dŭmp) [etym. doubtful; perh. from DUMPY], *n.* A leaden counter used in playing chuck-farthing; a small coin formerly current in Australia, worth about 1s. 3d.; (*slang*) a small coin; a short, thick, and heavy object of various kinds; a kind of nail or bolt; a kind of sweetmeat; a stocky person.

dumper (dŭm′ pėr) [Austral.], *n.* A heavy wave dangerous to swimmers.

dumpling (dŭmp′ ling) [prob. dim. of DUMP (2)], *n.* A mass of dough or pudding, boiled or baked, often enclosing fruit, etc.

dumps (dŭmps) [etym. doubtful; cp. DAMP], *n.pl.* Sadness, depression, melancholy. **in the dumps:** Low-spirited, depressed. ***dumpish,** *a.* Sad, gloomy, melancholy; depressed in spirits.

dumpy (dŭm′ pi) [etym. doubtful; cp. DUMP (2)], *a.* Short and thick. *n.* A short-legged Scottish breed of domestic fowls; (*pl.*) the 19th Hussars. **dumpy level,** *n.* A spirit level with a short telescope and a compass attached, used in surveying. **dumpiness,** *n.*

dun (1) (dŭn) [A.-S. *dunn*, cp. Ir. and Gael. *donn*, W. *dwn*], *a.* Of a dull brown or brownish-grey colour; (*poet.*) dark, gloomy. *n.* A dun-fly; a dun-horse. *v.t.* *To darken; (*Am.*) to preserve or cure (as codfish), so as to impart a dark colour to. **dun-bird,** *n.* The pochard. **dun-diver,** *n.* The female and young male of the goosander or merganser. **dun-fish,** *n.* (*Am.*) Codfish cured by dunning. **dun-fly,** *n.* A kind of artificial fly used by anglers; a local name for a horse-fly.

dun (2) (dŭn) [perh. a var. of DIN], *v.t.* (*past & p.p.* **dunned**) To demand payment from with persistence; to press, to plague, to pester. *n.* A creditor who presses persistently for payment; a debt-collector; an importunate demand for the payment of a debt.

dun (3) (dŭn) [Ir. and Gael.], *n.* A hill, a mound, an earthwork (largely used in place-names).

dunce (dŭns) [a word introduced by the Thomists or disciples of Thomas Aquinas, in ridicule of the followers of John *Duns* Scotus (d. 1308)], *n.* A dullard; one slow in learning; *a sophist, a hair-splitter. ***duncedom,** *n.* The realm of dunces; dunces collectively. **duncehood,** *n.* ***duncery,** *n.* Stupidity, dullness of intellect. **Dunciad,** *n.* The epic of dunces, title of a satire (1728) by Alexander Pope.

dunch (dŭnch) [Sc. and North.; etym. unknown], *v.t.* To push with the elbow; to gore. *n.* A jog, a smart push or blow.

dunderhead (dŭn′ dėr hed) [etym. doubtful], *n.* A blockhead, a numskull, a dolt, a dunce. **dunderpate,** *n.*

dundreary whiskers (dŭn drēr′ i) [Lord *Dundreary*, character in a play], *n.pl.* Long side-whiskers worn without a beard.

dune (dūn) [F., from M.Dut. *dûne*, cogn. with A.-S. *dūn*], *n.* A hill, mound, or ridge of sand on the sea-shore. **duny,** *a.*

dung (dŭng) [A.-S. (cp. O.Fris. and G. *dung*, Swed. *dynga*, Dan. *dynge*)], *n.* The excrement of animals; manure. *v.t.* To manure or dress with dung; to immerse (as printed calico) in a dung-bath to fix the colour. *v.i.* To void excrement. **dung-bath,** *n.* A bath used in calico-printing works. **dung-beetle,** *n.* A beetle, *Geotrypes stercorarius*, and other species the larvæ of which develop in dung. **dung-fly,** *n.* A two-winged fly of the genus *Scatophaga* that feeds upon dung. **dung-fork,** *n.* A fork for spreading manure. **dung-worm,** *n.* A worm or larva found in dung and used as bait for fish. **dunghill,** *n.* A heap of dung; an accumulation of dung and refuse in a farmyard; (*fig.*) a mean, filthy abode; any vile or contemptible situation, position, or condition; *one meanly born. *a.* Of low, mean, or vile extraction; mean, poor. **dunghill cock,** *n.* The common barn-door cock as distinguished from the spirited game-cock. **dungy,** *a.* Full of dung; filthy, base, mean, vile.

dungaree (dŭng gȧ rē′) [Hind. *dungrī*], *n.* A coarse kind of calico used for overalls; (*pl.*) overalls made of this.

dungeon (dŭn′ jȯn) [F. *donjon*, late L. *domniōnem*, acc. of *domnio*, L. *dominio*, from *dominus*, lord (cp. DOMINION)], *n.* *A donjon or keep of a mediæval castle; a close prison or place of confinement, esp. one that is dark and underground. **v.t.* To confine in or as in a dungeon.

dunghill [DUNG].

dunite (dŭn′ īt) [Mt. Dun, New Zealand], *n.* (*Geol.*) A rock consisting essentially of olivine, frequently accompanied by chromite.

duniwassal (doo ni wăs′ ȧl) [Gael. *duine vasal* (*duine*, a man, *vasal*, noble, cp. W. *uchel*)], *n.* A Highland gentleman of inferior rank, a yeoman.

Dunker (dŭng′ kėr) [G. *tunker*, from *tunken*, to dip], *n.* A member of a sect of German-American Baptists, more properly called Tunkers.

dunlin (dŭn′ lin) [DUN (1), -LING], *n.* The red-backed sand-piper, *Tringa alpina*, a common shore-bird.

dunlop (dŭn lop′) [*Dunlop* in Ayrshire], *n.* A kind of rich, white cheese made in Scotland of un-skimmed milk.

dunnage (dŭn′ ȧj) [formerly *dinnage*; etym. doubtful], *n.* (*Naut.*) Loose wood, faggots, boughs, etc., laid in the hold to raise the cargo above the bilge-water, or wedged between the cargo to keep it from rolling when stowed.

dunning (1) (dŭn′ ing) [DUN (1)], *n.* The process of curing codfish, so as to give them a dun colour.

dunning (2) (dŭn′ ing), *n.* (*Cinema.*) A process for superimposing action on a separately-taken picture.

dunnock (dŭn′ ȯk), *n.* The hedge-sparrow, from its colour.

dunny (dŭn′ i) [etym. doubtful (perh. conn. with DIN)], *a.* Hard of hearing.

dunt (1) (dŭnt) [etym. doubtful], *n.* (*dial.*) Staggers, a disease of yearling lambs.

dunt (2) (dŭnt) [Sc.; perh. a var. of DINT], *n.* A blow or stroke; a dint or wound; a bump, a jolt. *v.t.* To knock. *v.i.* To heal (of the heart).

duo (dū′ ō) [It., DUET], *n.* A duet.

duo- [L., two], *pref.* Two. **duodecagon** (dū ȯ dek′ ȧ gȯn) [DODECAGON]. **duodecahedron** (dū ȯ dek ȧ hē′ drȯn) [DODECAHEDRON].

duodecimal (dū ȯ des′ i mȧl) [L. *duodecimus*, twelfth, *duodecim*, twelve (DUO-, *decem*, ten)], *a.* Proceeding in computation by twelves; applied to a scale of notation in which the local value of the digits increases twelvefold as they proceed from right to left. *n.pl.* A method of cross-multiplying units of feet, inches, etc., without reduction to a common denominator, so as to find areas or cubic contents. **duodecimally,** *adv.* **duodecimo,** *a.* Consisting of twelve leaves to the sheet. *n.* A book consisting of sheets of twelve leaves or twenty-four pages; the size of such a book (written 12mo and called 'twelve-mo.').

duodenary (dū ȯ dē′ nȧ ri) [L. *duodēnārius*, from *duodēnī*, twelve apiece, as prec.], *a.* Pertaining to the number twelve; proceeding by twelves. **duodene** (dū′ ȯ dēn), *n.* (*Mus.*) A group of twelve notes having fixed relations of pitch, taken as a base for determining exact intonation and exhibiting harmonic relations.

duodenum (dū ȯ dē′ nŭm) [med. L., as prec.], *n.* (*Anat.*) The first portion of the small intestine, so called from being about the length of twelve fingers' breadths. **duodenal,** *a.* **duodenitis** (-nī′ tis), *n.*

duologue (dū′ ȯ log), *n.* A dialogue for two persons; a dramatic composition for two actors.

duomo (dwō′ mō) [It. (see DOME)], *n.* An Italian cathedral.

dupe (dūp) [F., etym unknown], *n.* One who is easily deceived; a credulous person; a gull. *v.t.* To trick, to cheat, to make a dupe of, to gull. **dupable,** *a.* **dupability** (-bil′ i ti), *n.* ***duper,** *n.* ***dupery,** *n.*

dupion (dū′ pi ȯn) [F. *doupion*, from It. *doppione*, from *doppio*, L. *duplus*, DOUBLE], *n.* A double cocoon formed by two or more silkworms.

duple (dū′ pėl) [L. *duplus*, double (*duo*, two, *-plus*, -fold)], *a.* Double, twofold; duplicate; (*Mus.*) having two beats to the bar. **duple-ratio,** *n.* The ratio of 2 to 1, 6 to 3, etc.; (*Mus.*) duple measure.

duplex (dū′ pleks) [L. (*duo*, two, *plic-*, see foll.)], *a.* Double, twofold; compounded of two. *v.t.* (*Teleg.*) To make (a wire, cable, or system) duplex, so that two messages can be sent at once in opposite directions. **duplex escapement,** *n.* So called from the double character of its scape-wheel, which has spur and crown teeth. **duplex gas-burner,** *n.* One with two jets that coalesce into a single flame. **duplex-lamp**, *n.* A lamp with two wicks.

duplicate (dū′ pli kȧt) [L. *duplicātus*, p.p. of *duplicāre* (*duo*, two, *plicāre*, to fold)], *a.* Double, two-fold, existing in two parts exactly corresponding; corresponding exactly with another. *n.* One of two things exactly similar in material and form; a reproduction, replica, copy; (*Law*) a copy of an original document having equal binding force; a copy made in lieu of a document lost or destroyed; the second copy of a bill drawn in two parts; a pawn-ticket; complete similarity between two things. *v.t.* (dū′ pli kāt) To make a reproduction of; to double; to make in duplicate; to make copies of on a machine; (*Biol.*) to divide and form two parts or organisms. **duplicate ratio** or **proportion,** *n.* The ratio or proportion of squares. **duplication,** *n.* **duplication of the cube:** The impossible problem of finding a cube whose volume shall be double that of a given cube. **duplicative,** *a.* **duplicator,** *n.* A machine for duplicating typescript.

duplicity (dū plis′ i ti) [F. *duplicité*, L. *duplicitās -tātem*, from DUPLEX], *n.* Doubleness of speech or action; double-dealing, dissimulation.

durable (dūr′ ȧbl) [F., from L. *dūrābilis*, from *dūrāre*, to last, from *dūrus*, hard], *a.* Having the quality of endurance or continuance; lasting, permanent, firm, stable. **durability** (-bil′ i ti), *n.* **durableness,** *n.* **durably,** *adv.*

duralumin (dūr ă lū′ min) [L. *durus*, hard, ALUMINIUM], *n.* (*Metall.*) An alloy of aluminium, copper and other metals. It has great strength and lightness.

dura mater (dūr′ à mā′ tėr) [med. L., the hard mother, a trans. of an Arabic phrase], *n.* (*Anat.*) The first of three lining membranes of the brain and spinal column.

duramen (dū rā′ mėn) [L., hardness, from *dūrāre*, to harden], *n.* (*Bot.*) The heart-wood or central wood in the trunk of exogenous trees.

durance (dūr′ àns) [F., from *durer*, to last, as prec.], *n.* Imprisonment; endurance, durability.

duration (dū rā′ shŭn) [O.F., from late L. *dūrātio -ōnem*, from L. *dūrāre*, to last], *n.* Continuance; length of time of continuance; power of continuance. **for the duration:** (*slang*) So long as the war lasts.

durbar (dĕr′ bar) [Pers. and Hind. *darbār*, a court], *n.* An Indian ruler's court; a state-reception by an Indian ruler or formerly by a British governor; a hall of audience.

***dure** (dūr) [F. *durer*, from L. *dūrāre*, to endure, from *dūrus*, hard], *v.i.* To last, to endure, to continue. **dureful,** *a.*

duress (dū′ res, dū res′) [O.F. *duresce*, L. *dūritia*, from *dūrus*, hard], *n.* Constraint, compulsion, restraint of liberty, imprisonment; (*Law*) restraint of liberty or threat of violence to compel a person to do some act of exculpation by one who has been so restrained or threatened.

durian (dū′ ri àn) [Malay *durian*, from *durī*, prickle], *n.* The globular pulpy fruit of a tree, *Durio zibethinus*, cultivated in the Malay Archipelago.

during (dū′ ring) [orig. pres.p. of DURE], *prep.* In or within the time of; throughout the course or existence of.

durmast (dĕr′ mast) [etym. doubtful], *n.* A European oak, *Quercus sessiliflora.*

durra (dur′ à) [Arab. *durah, durrah*], *n.* Indian millet, *Sorghum vulgare.*

durst, *past* [DARE].

dusk (dŭsk) [M.E. *dose*, dark, dim, A.-S. *dox* (cp. Swed. *dusk*, a shower, Norw. *dusk*, mist)], *a.* Tending to darkness or blackness; darkish, shadowy, dim, obscure; swarthy. *n.* A tendency to darkness; shade, gloom; partial darkness, twilight. ****v.t.*** To make somewhat dark; to obscure. *v.i.* To grow or to appear dark. **duskish,** *a.* **dusky,** *a.* Swarthy. **duskily,** *adv.* **duskiness,** *n.*

dust (dŭst) [A.-S. *dūst* (cp. Dut. *duist*, G. *dunst*)], *n.* Earth or other matter reduced to such small particles as to be easily raised and carried about by the air; a stirring of such fine particles; household refuse; pollen; the decomposed bodies of the dead; the human body; the grave; a low or despised condition; turmoil, excitement, confusion, commotion, a row; (*slang*) money. *v.t.* To brush or sweep away the dust from; to sprinkle or cover with or as with dust; to make dusty; to clean by brushing or beating, hence **to dust one's jacket:** To give one a drubbing. **dust and ashes:** Extreme penitence and humility. **to bite the dust:** (*fig.*) To be beaten; to be humiliated. **to raise, make,** or **kick up a dust:** To make a disturbance. **to throw dust in one's eyes:** To mislead, to deceive, to delude. **to turn to dust and ashes:** To become utterly worthless. **dustbin, -hole,** *n.* A receptacle for household refuse, (*Am.*) a garbage-can. **dust-bowl,** *n.* (*Geog.*) An area reduced to aridity by drought and over-cropping. **dust-brand,** *n.* Smut, a disease of corn. **dust-cart,** *n.* A cart for removing refuse from houses, streets, etc. **dust-cloth,** *n.* A dusting sheet. **dust-coat,** *n.* A light overcoat. **dust-colour,** *n.* A light greyish brown. **dust-cover, -jacket,** *n.* A paper book-jacket. **dust-guard,** *n.* A fitting on a machine to protect a worker, rider, etc., from dust. **dustman,** *n.* One whose occupation is to remove refuse from dust-bins [SANDMAN]. **dust up,** *n.* A row, a heated quarrel. **dustpan,** *n.* A domestic utensil into which dust is swept. **dust-shot,** *n.* Shot of the smallest size, also called mustard seed. **duster,** *n.* A cloth or brush used to remove dust; a person who dusts; a machine to remove particles of flour from bran; (*Naut. colloq.*) a flag; (*Am.*) a dust-coat. **dust-sheet,** *n.* A sheet thrown over furniture while a room is being dusted. **dustward,** *a.* and *adv.* **dusty,** *a.* Covered with or full of dust; like dust; dull, uninteresting. **not so dusty:** (*slang*) Pretty good. **dusty miller,** *n.* The auricula, from the dusty appearance of the leaves and flowers; (*Angling*) an artificial fly. **dustily,** *adv.* **dustiness,** *n.*

Dutch (1) (dŭch) [M.Dut. *Dutsch*, Hollandish, or G. *Deutsch*, German], *a.* Pertaining to Holland, its people, or language, Hollandish; (*Hist.*) pertaining to the Low Germans, or to the German or Teutonic race; from Holland; made or invented by the Dutch; (*Am.*) of German extraction. *n.* The language of Holland and the Netherlands; the German language, esp. Low German; the Low Germans, esp. the Hollanders. **to talk like a Dutch uncle:** To be sternly candid. **double Dutch** [DOUBLE]. **High Dutch:** The southern Germans; their language. **Low Dutch:** The Germans of the coast, esp. of the Netherlands; their language. **Dutch auction** [AUCTION]. **Dutch cheese,** *n.* A small round cheese manufactured in Holland from skim milk. **Dutch clinker,** *n.* A yellow hard brick made in Holland. **Dutch-clover,** *n.* White clover, *Trifolium repens.* **Dutch courage,** *n.* False or fictitious courage, esp. inspired by stimulants. **Dutch foil, gold, leaf, metal,** *n.* A highly malleable copper alloy with zinc, used instead of gold-leaf. **Dutchman,** *n.* A native of Holland; (*Am. colloq.*) a Dutchman or German. **if not, I'm a Dutchman:** An emphatic negative. **the Flying Dutchman:** A legendary mariner condemned to sail against the wind till the Day of Judgment; his spectral ship. **Dutch oven,** *n.* A cooking-chamber suspended in front of a fire so as to cook by radiation. **Dutch-rush,** *n.* The scouring rush, *Equisetum hyemale*, used for cleaning and polishing wood. **Dutch School,** *n.* A school of painters distinguished for minute realism and for the artistic treatment of commonplace subjects. **Dutch tile,** *n.* A variegated or painted glazed tile made in Holland, formerly used for lining their capacious fireplaces. **dutch treat,** *n.* (*colloq.*) Each paying his own score.

dutch (2) (dŭch) [perh. short for DUCHESS], *n.* (*Cockney slang*) A wife.

duty (dū′ ti) [A.-F. *dueté*], *n.* That which is bound or ought to be paid, done, or performed; that which a particular person is bound morally or legally to do; moral or legal obligation; the course of conduct prescribed by ethics or religion, the binding force of the obligation to follow this course; obedience or submission due to parents or superiors; an act of reverence, respect, or deference; any service, business, or office; toll, tax, impost, or custom charged by a government upon the importation, exportation, manufacture, or sale of goods; office, function, occupation, work; the various acts entailed in these; the obligations and responsibilities implied in one's engagement to perform these; the useful work actually done by an engine or motor, measured in units against units of fuel. **off duty:** Not engaged in one's appointed duties. **on duty:** Engaged in performing one's appointed duties. **to do duty for:** To serve in lieu of someone or something else; to serve as a makeshift. **duty-free,** *a.* Not liable to duty, tax, or custom. **duteous** (dū′ tė ŭs), *a.* Obedient, obsequious, dutiful. **duteously,** *adv.* **duteousness,** *n.* **dutiable,** *a.* Liable to the imposition of a duty or custom. **dutied,** *a.* Charged with duty. **dutiful,** *a.* Careful in performing the duties required by law, justice, or propriety; reverential, deferential. **dutifully,** *adv.* **dutifulness,** *n.*

duumvir (dū ŭm' vir) [L. (*duo*, two, *viri*, men)], *n.* (*pl.* **viri, virs**) One of two officers or magistrates in ancient Rome appointed to carry out jointly the duties of any public office. **duumvirate,** *n.* The association of two officers or magistrates in the carrying out of any public duties; a government of two; their term of office.

duvet (du vā) [F., down, earlier *dumet*, dim. of O.F. *dum* (cp. Icel. *dūnn*)], *n.* A quilt stuffed with down.

dux (dŭks) [L., leader], *n.* (*Sc.*) The head boy of a school.

***dwale** (dwāl) [M.E. *dwale* (cp. Dan. *dvale*, Swed. *dwala*, a trance, A.-S. *dwala*, an error, stupefaction)], *n.* The deadly nightshade, *Atropa belladonna.*

dwalm, dwam (dwam) [Sc. and North.; cp. A.-S. *dwolma*, confusion], *n.* A swoon. *v.i.* To faint; to sicken. **dwaminess,** *n*

dwarf (dwôrf) [A.-S. *dweorg*, *dweorh*, from O.Teut. *dwerg-* (Dut. *dwerg*, Swed. and Dan. *dverg*, G. *zwerg*)], *n.* A human being, animal, or plant much below the natural or ordinary size; a supernatural being of small stature. *a.* Below the ordinary or natural size; stunted, puny, tiny. *v.t.* To stunt; to cause to look small by comparison; to check the physical or mental development of. *v.i.* To become stunted. **dwarf tree,** *n.* A tree whose branches have been made to shoot near the root. **dwarf wall,** *n.* A low wall serving to surround an enclosure; such a wall as that on which iron railing is commonly set. **dwarfish,** *a.* **dwarfishly,** *adv.* **dwarfishness,** *n.*

dwell (dwel) [A.-S. *dwellan*, to lead astray (later, *dwelian*, to lead astray, to err, to be delayed, to tarry)], *v.i.* (*past & p.p.* **dwelt**) To reside, to abide (in a place); to live, spend one's time; to linger, pause, tarry; *to delay; *to continue in any state. **v.t.* To inhabit. *n.* (*Mech.*) A pause; a slight regular stoppage of a movement whilst a certain operation is effected. **to dwell on** or **upon:** To occupy a long time with; to fix the attention upon; to be absorbed with; to expatiate. **dweller,** *n.* A resident, an inhabitant. **dwelling,** *n.* The action of the verb TO DWELL; residence, abode, habitation. **dwelling-house,** *n.* A house for residence, in contradistinction to a house of business, office, warehouse, etc. **dwelling-place,** *n.* A place of residence.

dwindle (dwin' dėl) [A.-S. *dwinan*], *v.i.* To shrink, to diminish, to become smaller; to waste or fall away; to degenerate, to decline.

dyad (dī' ad) [L. *dyas dyadis*, Gr. *duas duados* (*duo*, two)], *n.* Two units treated as one; a group of two, a pair, a couple; (*Chem.*) a diatomic element, atom, or radical. **dyadic** (dī ăd' ik), *a.*

Dyak (dī' ăk) [native name], *n.* An individual of the aboriginal race inhabiting Borneo, probably related to the Malays.

dye (dī) [A.-S. *dēagian*, from *dēag*, a dye], *v.t.* To stain, to colour; to impregnate with colouring-matter; to cause (a material) to take a certain colour. *v.i.* To follow the business of a dyer; to take a colour (of a material that is being dyed). *n.* A fluid used for dyeing, colouring-matter; colour, tinge, hue, produced by or as by dyeing; (*fig.*) stain. **dye-house, works,** *n.* A building where dyeing is carried on. **dye-stuffs,** *n.pl.* The materials used in dyeing. **dye-wood,** *n.* Any wood from which a dye is extracted. **dyeing,** *n.* **dyer,** *n.* One whose business is dyeing. **dyer's-weed,** *n.* Name of various plants yielding dye-stuff, as dyer's green-weed or dyer's broom, *Genista tinctoria*, dyer's rocket, *Reseda luteola*, which yields a yellow dye, and dyer's woad, *Isatis tinctoria.* **dyster,** *n.* (*Sc.*) A dyer.

dying (dī' ing) [DIE (1), -ING], *a.* About to die; mortal, perishable; done, given, or uttered just before death; associated with death; drawing to an end, fading away; perishing. *n.* The act of expiring, death. **dyingly,** *adv.*

dyke [DIKE].

dynam (dī' năm) [short for Gr. *dynamis*, see DYNAMIC], *n.* A foot-pound, as a unit of measurement.

dynameter (dī năm' ė tėr), *n.* An instrument for measuring the magnifying powers of a telescope. **dynametric, -rical** (-met' rik, -ål), *a.*

dynamic (dī năm' ik) [F. *dynamique*, Gr. *dunamikos*, from *dunamis*, power, *dunamai*, I am strong], *a.* Of or pertaining to forces not in equilibrium, as distinguished from static; motive, active, energetic, as opp. to potential; pertaining to dynamics; involving or dependent upon mechanical activity, as the dynamic theory of Kant; (*Med.*) functional, as opp. to organic. *n.* The motive force of any action. **dynamical,** *a.* Dynamic; pertaining to dynamism; (*Theol.*) inspiring or animating, not impelling mechanically. **dynamically,** *adv.*

dynamics (dī năm' iks), *n.* The branch of mechanics which deals with the behaviour of bodies under the action of forces which produce changes of motion in them.

dynamism (dī' nȧ mizm), *n.* A system or theory explaining phenomena as the ultimate result of some immanent force, as the doctrine of Leibnitz that all substance involves force. **dynamist,** *n.*

dynamite (dī' nȧ mīt) [Gr. *dunamis*, as prec., -ITE], *n.* A powerful explosive compound, extremely local in its action, consisting of nitro-glycerine mixed with an absorbent material. *v.t.* To smash or destroy with dynamite. **dynamite-gun,** *n.* A pneumatic gun for hurling shells filled with dynamite. **dynamiter, -ard,** *n.* A revolutionary or criminal employing dynamite. **dynamitic** (-mit' ik), *a.* **dynamitism,** *n.* **dynamitist,** *n.*

dynamize (dī' nȧ mīz), *v.t.* (*Med.*) To increase the power of medicines by trituration, etc. **dynamization,** *n.*

dynamo- [Gr. *dynamis*, power], *comb. form.* Pertaining to force or power.

dynamo (dī' nȧ mō) [short for foll.], *n.* (*pl.* **-os**) A dynamoelectric machine. **dynamoelectric** (dī nȧ mō ė lek' trik), *a.* Pertaining to current electricity; pertaining to the conversion of mechanical into electric energy or the reverse. **dynamoelectric machine,** *n.* A machine for converting mechanical energy into electric by means of electromagnetic induction (usu. applied only to d.c. generators).

dynamograph (dī năm' ō grăf), *n.* A dynamometer used for recording speed, power, adhesion, etc., on electric railways; a recording telegraphic instrument; an instrument for testing muscular strength, esp. by means of gripping.

dynamometer (dī nȧ mom' e tĕr), *n.* An instrument for the measurement of power, force, or electricity.

dynast (dī' năst, din' ăst) [late L. *dynastēs*, Gr. *dunastēs*, a lord, from *dunatos*, able (*dunamai*, I am strong)], *n.* A ruler, a monarch; a member or founder of a dynasty. **dynastic** (dī năs' tik, di năs' tik), *a.* **dynastically,** *adv.* **dynasty** (din' ȧ sti), *n.* A line, race, or succession of sovereigns of the same family.

dyne (dīn) [F., from stem of Gr. *dunamai*, see prec.], *n.* A unit for measuring force, the amount that, acting upon a gramme for a second, generates a velocity of one centimetre per second.

dyophysite (dī of' i zīt) [late Gr. *diophusitai*, pl. (*duo*, two, *phusis*, nature)], *n.* (*Theol.*) One who held that two natures were combined in the personality of Christ, a divine and a human. **diophysitic** (-sit' ik), *a.* **dyophysitism** (dī of' iz i tizm), *n.*

dyothelete (dī oth' ė lēt) [Gr. *duo*, two, *thelētēs*, willer, from *thelein*, to will], *a.* (*Theol.*) Holding that Christ had two wills, a human and a divine. *n.* An adherent of this creed. **dyothelism,** *n.*

dys- [Gr. *dus-*, badly, with difficulty], *pref.* Bad, badly, depraved; difficult, working badly, painful.

dysæsthesia (dis es thē′ zi ȧ), *n.* (*Path.*) Insensibility; derangement of sensation or the senses.

dyscrasia (dis krā′ si ȧ) [Gr. *duskrasia* (DYS-, *krasis*, mixing)], *n.* (*Path.*) A morbid condition of the blood or fluids of the body.

dysentery (dis′ ėn tėr i) [O.F. *dissenterie*, L. *dysenteria*, Gr. *dusenteria* (DYS-, *hentera*, bowels)], *n.* An infectious tropical febrile disease, seated in the large intestines, accompanied by mucous and bloody evacuations. **dysenteric** (-ter′ ik), *a.*

dyslogistic (dis lȯ jis′ tik), *a.* Disparaging, disapproving, censuring. **dyslogistically,** *adv.*

dysmenorrhœa (dis men ō rē′ ȧ), *n.* (*Path.*) Difficult or painful menstruation.

dysorexia (dis ȯ rek′ si ȧ) [Gr. *dusorexia* (DYS-, Gr. *orexis*, a longing, from *oregein*, to long, yearn)], *n.* (*Path.*) Want of appetite; a bad or depressed appetite.

dyspepsia, dyspepsy (dis pep′ si ȧ, -si) L., from Gr. *duspepsia*, from *duspeptos*, hard to digest (DYS-, *peptein*, to cook)], *n.* Indigestion arising from functional derangement of the stomach. **dyspeptic,** *a.* Pertaining to, of the nature of, or suffering from dyspepsia. *n.* One subject to dyspepsia.

dysphagia (dis fā′ ji ȧ) [Gr. *phagein*, to eat], *n.* (*Path.*) Difficulty of swallowing.

dysphonia (dis fō′ ni ȧ) [Gr. *dusphōnia*, harshness of sound (DYS-, *phonē*, sound)], *n.* (*Path.*) A difficulty in speaking arising from disease or malformation of the organs.

dyspnœa (disp nē′ ȧ) [L., from Gr. *duspnoia* (DUS-, *pnoē*, breathing)], *n.* (*Path.*) Difficulty of breathing. **dyspnoic** (-nō′ ik), *a.*

dysprosium (dis prō′ zi ŭm) [Gr. *dysprositos*, difficult of access] *n.* (*Metall.*) A rare metallic element of the rare earth group.

dysthymic (dis thīm′ ik) [Gr. *dusthumos*, desponding (DYS-, *thumos*, spirit)], *a.* (*Path.*) Depressed in spirits; dejected.

dysuria, dysury (dis ū′ ri ȧ, dis′ ū ri) [O.F. *dissurie*, L. *dysūria*, Gr. *dusouria* (DYS-, *ouron*, urine)], *n.* (*Path.*) Difficulty and pain in passing urine; morbid condition of the urine. **dysuric** (dis ū′ rik), *a.*

***dyvour** (dī′ voor) [Sc.; etym. unknown], *n.* A debtor; a bankrupt who has made a *cessio bonorum* to his creditors.

dziggetai (dzig′ ė tī) [Mongol.], *n.* A species of wild ass, *Equus hemionus*, somewhat resembling the mule, native to Central Asia.

E

E, e, the second vowel, has three principal sounds, long as in *me* (marked ē), short as in *men*, *set* (left unmarked), and short with a modification caused by a subsequent *r*, as in *her* (marked ĕ). There is also the indeterminate *e* in *camel*, *garment* (marked ė), and in many words, like *there*, it is pronounced as long **a** (marked â). At the end of words it is usually silent as in *mane*, *cave*, where it also indicates that the preceding syllable is long. It is employed after *c* and *g* to denote that those letters are to be sounded as *s* and *j* respectively. (*Mus.*) The third note of the diatonic scale; (*Naut.*) a second-class ship in Lloyd's register; (*Math.*) symbol for the base of Napierian logarithms, approximately equalling 2·718. **E-boat,** *n.* (*Nav.*) A small, fast motor-boat of the German navy armed with guns and torpedoes.

e- [EX-], *pref.*, as in *elocution*, *emend*, *evade*, *evolve*.

each (ēch) [A.-S. *ælc* (*ā*, *ge-*, *līc*, aye-like or ever-like)], *a.* and *pron.* Every one (of a number) considered separately. ***eachwhere,** *adv.* Everywhere.

eager (ē′ gėr) [A.-F. *egre*, O.F. *aigre*, L. *ācrem*, acc. of *ācer*, keen], *a.* Excited by an ardent desire to attain, obtain, or succeed in anything; keen, ardent, vehement, impatient; *sharp, acrid; *biting, pungent, cutting, severe. **eagerly,** *adv.* **eagerness,** *n.*

eagle (ē′ gėl) [A.-F. *egle*, O.F. *aigle*, L. *aquila*], *n.* A large bird of prey, the larger species of the *Falconidæ*; any bird of the genus *Aquila*, esp. the golden eagle; a figure representing this, a lectern in the form of an eagle with expanded wings, a Roman or French military ensign bearing such a device; (*Her.*) one of the nobler armorial bearings, emblematic of fortitude and magnanimity, and adopted as a national emblem by U.S.A., Prussia, Austria, Russia, and France; hence, used as the name of various coins stamped with an eagle, esp. for a gold coin of the U.S. worth ten dollars; (*Astron.*) the constellation Aquila in the northern hemisphere. **eagle-eyed,** *a.* Sharp-sighted as an eagle; quick to discern. **eagle-flighted,** *a.* Mounting to a great height. **eagle-hawk,** *n.* A South American hawk of the genus *Morphuus*. **eagle-owl,** *n.* Name of large European and American owls, esp. the European *Buvo maximus*. **eagle-stone,** *n.* An argillaceous oxide of iron occurring in nodules of various sizes, which often contain a loose kernel or nucleus, from the ancient belief that the eagle carried such a nodule to her nest to facilitate the laying of her eggs. **eagle-winged,** *a.* Having wings like those of the eagle; soaring high like an eagle. **eaglet,** *n.* A young eagle.

eagre (ē′ gėr) [etym. unknown], *n.* A tidal wave or bore in an estuary (as of the Humber, Trent, and Severn).

ealdorman [ALDERMAN].

***ean** (ēn) [A.-S. *ēanian* (prob. cogn. with A.-S. *eown*, EWE)], *v.i.* To bring forth lambs, to yean. **eaning-time,** *n.* The time or season of bearing young. ***eanling,** *n.* A lamb just brought forth.

-ean, -æan, -eian [-AN, embodying the end of the stem in L. words in *-æus*, *-eius*; Gr. words in *-aios*, *-eios*; and E. words in *-ey* and *-y*], *suf.* Belonging to; like.

ear (1) (ēr) [A.-S. *ēare* (cp. Dut. *oor*, Icel. *eyra*, G. *ohr*, L. *auris*, Gr. *ous*)], *n.* The organ of hearing; the external part of this organ; the sense of hearing; a delicate perception of the differences of sounds, and judgment of harmony; notice or attention (esp. favourable consideration); a small ear-like projection from a larger body, usually for support or attachment; judgment, opinion, taste. **all ear:** Deeply attentive. **bring about one's ears:** To involve oneself in (trouble, etc.). **middle ear:** The ear drum. **over head and ears, up to the ears:** Completely, so as to be overwhelmed. **to be by the ears, to fall together by the ears:** To be at loggerheads, to disagree; to quarrel, to scuffle. **to prick up one's ears:** To begin to listen attentively. **to send away with a flea in his ear:** To dismiss a man angrily or with contumely. **to give, lend an ear:** To listen. **to set by the ears:** To incite or cause strife between. **ear-cap,** *n.* A cover to protect the ears against cold. ***ear-drop,** *n.* (*vulg.*) A jewel hanging from the ear, an ear-ring. **ear-drum,** *n.* The tympanum; the membrane of the tympanum. **ear-lap,** *n.* The lobe of the ear. ***ear-lock,** *n.* A curl worn near the ear by dandies early in the 17th century. **ear-mark,** *n.* A mark on the ear by which a sheep can be identified; (*fig.*) any distinctive mark or feature. *v.t.* To mark (as sheep) by cutting or slitting the ear; (*fig.*) to set a distinctive mark upon; to allocate (funds, etc.) for a particular purpose. **ear-pick,** *n.* A small scoop to extract hardened wax from the ear. **ear-piercing,** *a.* Shrill. **ear-ring,** *n.* A pendant or ornamental ring worn in the lobe of the ear. **earshot,** *n.* Hearing distance. **ear-trumpet,** *n.* A tube to aid the sense of hearing by the collection and conduction of sounds. ***ear-witness,** *n.* One who can attest anything as heard with his own ears. **eared**

(1), *a.* Having ears; (*Bot.*) auriculate. **earless,** *a.* **earlet,** *n.* A little ear.

ear (2) (ēr) [A.-S. *ēar*, pl. (cp. Dut. *aar*, Icel., Dan. and Swed. *ax*, G. *ähre*; cogn. with L. *acus*, *aceris*, husk of corn)], *n.* A spike or head of corn. *v.i.* To form ears, as corn. **eared** (2), *a.* **ear-cockle,** *n.* A disease of wheat and other corn.

*__ear__ (3) (ēr) [A.-S. *erian* (cp. Icel. *erja*, Goth. *arjan*, L. *arāre*, Gr. *aroein*)], *v.t.* To plough, to till, to cultivate.

earache (ēr′ āk), *n.* A pain in the drum of the ear.

earing (ēr′ ing), *n.* (*Naut.*) A small line for fastening a reef or the corner of a sail to the yard, gaff, etc. [see also EAR-RING, EAR (1)].

earl (ĕrl) [A.-S. *eorl*, a warrior (cp. Icel. *jarl*, *earl*, O.S. *erl*, a man)], *n.* An English nobleman ranking next below a marquess and next above a viscount [cp. COUNT]. **Earl Marshal,** *n.* An English officer of state, head of the College of Arms, with whom resides the determination of all questions relating to arms and grants of arms; the office is now hereditary, and held by the Dukes of Norfolk. **earldom,** *n.* The rank, title, or position of an earl; *the seigniory or jurisdiction of an earl.

early (ĕr′ li) [A.-S. *ǣrlīce* (*ǣr*, sooner, *līc*, like, *līce*, -LY)], *adv.* **(earlier, earliest)** In good time; soon, betimes; towards, in, or near the beginning. *a.* Soon; in advance, as compared with something else; coming before or in advance of the usual time; situated in or near the beginning. **early door,** *n.* (*Theat.*) Admission before the official time for opening on payment of an extra charge. **Early English,** *n.* and *a.* The first of the pointed or Gothic styles of architecture employed in England, characterized by lancet windows, clustered pillars, and vaulted roofs with moulded groins on the ribs only. **earlies,** *n.pl.* (*Hort. colloq.*) Early potatoes. **earliness,** *n.*

earn (1) (ĕrn) [A.-S. *earnian* (cp. O.H.G. *arnōn*, also G. *ernten*, to reap, from *ernte*, harvest)], *v.t.* To gain as the reward of labour; to merit, deserve, or become entitled to as the result of any action or course of conduct. **earnings,** *n.pl.* That which is earned, gained, or merited; wages, reward.

*__earn__ (2) (ĕrn) [YEARN], *v.i.* To long; to grieve.

earnest (1) (ĕr′ nėst) [A.-S. *eornost*, whence *eorneste*, a. and adv. (cp. Dut. and G. *ernst*)], *n.* Seriousness; reality, not a pretence; a serious object or business, not a jest. *a.* Serious, important, grave; ardent, eager, or zealous in the performance of any act or the pursuit of any object; heartfelt, sincere. **in earnest**: Seriously; with sincerity. **earnestly,** *adv.* **earnestness,** *n.*

earnest (2) (ĕr′ nėst) [M.E. *ernes*, prob. a corr. of *erles*, ARLES], *n.* A pledge, an assurance of something to come; earnest-money. **earnest-money,** *n.* An instalment paid to clinch a bargain.

earphone (ēr′ fōn), *n.* (*Radio.*) An instrument which is held close to the ear and converts electrical signals into audible speech, music, etc.

earth (ĕrth) [A.-S. *eorthe* (cp. Dut. *aarde*, Icel. *jörth*, Goth. *airtha*, G. *erde*)], *n.* The ground, the visible surface of the globe; the globe, the planet on which we live; dry land, as opposed to the sea; this world, as opposed to other scenes of existence; soil, mould, as distinguished from rock; dead, inert matter; clay, dust, the body; the hole of a fox, badger, etc.; (*Elec.*) the part of the ground completing an electrical circuit; a connexion to ground; (*Radio.*) plates or wires buried in the earth which provide a path to ground for currents flowing in the aerial; (*Chem.*) an earth-like metallic oxide, such as alumina. *v.t.* To cover (usu. with *up*) with earth; to drive (fox, etc.) to his earth; *to hide or place under the earth; to complete a circuit by connecting with the earth. *v.i.* To retire to an earth (as a fox). **earth-bath,** *n.* (*Med.*) A kind of bath in which the patient is partially covered with loose earth. **earth-board,** *n.* A mould-board of a plough. **earth-born,** *a.* Born of the earth, terrigenous; relating to or arising from earthly things or objects; human, mortal; of mean birth. **earth-bound,** *a.* Fixed or fastened in or to the earth; (*fig.*) fixed on earthly objects. *__earth-bred__, *a.* Low-born, abject, grovelling. **earth circuit,** *n.* (*Radio.*) That portion of a radio receiver or transmitter which includes the earth lead. **earth-closet,** *n.* A convenience in which earth is used instead of water. **earth-created,** *a.* Created of the dust of the earth. **earth-fall,** *n.* A land-slide. **earth-hunger,** *n.* An inordinate desire to possess land. **earth-light,** *n.* (*Astron.*) Light reflected from the earth upon the dark part of the moon, when the latter is either very young or has waned considerably. **earth-nut,** *n.* The pig-nut or ground-nut; the truffle, the heath-pea, and other plants. **earth-plate,** *n.* (*Elec.*) A plate buried in the earth connected with a terminal or return wire, so as to utilize the earth itself as a part of the circuit. **earth satellite** [SATELLITE]. **earth-shine** [EARTH-LIGHT]. **earth-wolf** [AARDWULF]. **earth-worm,** *n.* A burrowing worm, esp. belonging to the genus *Lumbricus*; (*fig.*) a grovelling, a sordid person. **earthward, -s,** *adv.* **rare earths** [RARE].

earthen (ĕr′ thėn), *a.* Made of earth, baked clay, or similar substance. **earthenware,** *n.* Ware made of baked clay; pottery, esp. the lower and coarser forms of ceramic work.

*__earthling__ (ĕrth′ ling), *n.* An inhabitant of the earth; an earthly-minded person.

earthly (ĕrth′ li), *a.* Of or pertaining to this world; mortal, human; carnal, as opposed to spiritual; pertaining to this life, as opposed to a future life; corporeal, not mental; (*colloq.*) possible, conceivable; *in the earth. **earthly-minded,** *a.* Having a mind fixed on this earth; destitute of spirituality. **earthly-mindedness,** *n.* **earthliness,** *n.* **not an earthly:** (*slang*) Not a chance.

earthquake (ĕrth′ kwāk), *n.* A movement of a portion of the earth's crust produced by volcanic forces; (*fig.*) a social, political, or other disturbance.

earthwork (ĕrth′ wĕrk), *n.* Mounds, ramparts, etc., used for defensive purposes; embankments, cuttings, etc.

earthy (ĕr′ thi), *a.* Consisting or composed of earth or soil; resembling earth; cold and lifeless as earth; gross, carnal, material; dull, lustreless. **earthiness,** *n.*

earwig (ēr′ wig) [A.-S. *ēar-wicga*, ear-runner (*wicga*, from *wegan*, to move, allied to L. *vehere*, *vec-*, to carry), from the erroneous belief that it crept into the ear], *n.* An insect, *Forficula auricularia*, having curved forceps at its tail; (*fig.*) a whisperer; a prying, insinuating informer or talebearer.

ease (ēz) [O.F. *aise*, etym. doubtful (cp. It. *agio*)], *n.* A state of freedom from labour, trouble, or pain; quiet, tranquillity; freedom from constraint or formality; facility, readiness; absence of effort. *v.t.* To free from pain, anxiety, labour, or trouble; to relieve or free from a burden; to make easier or lighter; to assuage, to mitigate; to render less difficult; to make looser, to relax, to adjust; (*Naut.*) to slacken (a rope, sail, speed, etc.); (*colloq.*) to despoil, to rot. *v.i.* To relax one's efforts or exertions. **at ease:** In a state free from anything likely to disturb, annoy, or cause anxiety. **ill at ease:** In a state of mental or bodily disquiet, trouble, or pain. **to ease oneself:** To empty the bowels; to urinate. **stand at ease:** (*Mil.*) A command to stand with the legs apart and hands behind the back. **ease her:** (*Naut.*) The command to reduce the speed of the engines of a steamer. **to ease away** or **off:** (*Naut.*) To slacken gradually (as a rope); to become less oppressive. **easeful,** *a.* Promoting ease, quiet, or repose; comfortable; indolent. **easefully,** *adv.* **easefulness,** *n.* **easeless,** *a.* **easily,** etc. [EASY].

easel (ē′ zėl) [Dut. *ezel*, a little ass (cp. G. *esel*)], *n.* A wooden frame used to support a picture, blackboard, open book, etc. **easel-picture,** *n.* A picture of small dimensions suitable for standing on an easel.

easement (ēz′ mėnt), *n.* The act of easing; alleviation, mitigation; a convenience; (*Law*) a liberty, right, or privilege, without profit, which one proprietor has in or through the estate of another, as a right of way, light, air, etc.

east (ēst) [A.-S. *ēast*, adv., in the east, eastwards, *ēastan*, from the east (cp. Dut. *oost*, Icel. *austr.* G. *osten*)], *a.* Situated towards the point where the sun rises when in the equinoctial; coming from this direction. *n.* The point of the compass where the sun rises at the equinox; 90° to the right of north; the eastern part of a country; the countries to the east of Europe; the east wind. *adv.* Towards, at, or near the quarter of the rising sun. *v.i.* To move towards the east; to veer from the north or south towards the east; (*reflex.*) to find one's east, to orientate oneself. **East End,** *n.* The east and unfashionable end of London. **East-Ender,** *n.* **Far East:** The regions east of India. **Middle East:** Irak, Iran, Mesopotamia, etc. **Near East:** Turkey, the Levant, etc. **East Indiaman,** *n.* (*Naut. hist.*) A ship sailing to and from the E. Indies. **easting,** *n.* (*Naut.*) Distance traversed on an easterly course; distance east of a given meridian; movement to the east. **eastward,** *a.* and *n.* **eastwards,** *adv.* **east wind,** *n.* A wind coming from an easterly direction.

Easter (1) (ēs′ tėr) [*ēastre*, *Ēastre*, *Ēostre* (Teutonic dawn-goddess)], *n.* The festival in commemoration of the resurrection of Christ, taking place on the Sunday after the full moon that falls on or next after 21 March. **Easter-dues, -offerings,** *n.pl.* Payments or offerings to the parson of a parish at Easter. **Easter-eggs,** *n.pl.* Eggs boiled hard and stained or gilded, to symbolize the resurrection; egg-shaped presents given at Easter. **Easter-eve,** *n.* The day before Easter day. **Easter sepulchre,** *n.* (*Eccles.*) A canopied recess in a choir or chancel for the reception of the elements of the Eucharist consecrated on Maundy Thursday. **Easter week,** *n.* The week beginning with Easter Day.

***easter** (2) (ēs′ tėr) [perh. comp. of EAST], *a.* Eastern.

***easterling** (ēs′ tėr ling) [prob. from prec., after Dut. *oosterling*], *n.* A native of eastern Germany or the Baltic, esp. a citizen of the Hanse towns; a native or inhabitant of the east; an inhabitant of the eastern part of a country.

easterly (ēs′ tėr li), *a.* Situated or in the direction of the east; looking towards the east; coming from the east, or parts lying towards the east. *adv.* In the direction of the east; in or from the east.

eastern (ēs′ tėrn) [A.-S. *ēasterne*], *a.* Situated in the east; pertaining to the east; blowing from the east. *n.* An inhabitant of the East, an Oriental; a member of the Eastern or Greek Church. **Eastern Church:** Term for the Greek, as distinguished from the Latin or Western Church. **Eastern question,** *n.* (*Hist.*) The political question in the late 19th and early 20th centuries as to the distribution of political power in Eastern Europe, esp. those parts under the actual or nominal rule of Turkey. **Easterner,** *n.* (*U.S.A.*) An inhabitant of the eastern or New England States. **easternmost,** *a.*

easting [EAST].

easy (ē′ zi) [O.F. *aisié* (F. *aisé*), p.p. of *aiser*, to EASE], *a.* At ease; free from pain, trouble, care or discomfort; in comfortable circumstances, well-to-do; not strict; free from embarrassment, constraint, or affectation; smooth, flowing, fluent; not difficult, not requiring great labour, exertion, or effort; easily persuaded, compliant; indulgent, not exacting; (*Comm.*) not straitened, not hard to get (opp. to tight); *fitting loosely; slight, trivial. *adv.* In an easy manner. *n.* A relaxation of effort or a pause in rowing. **in easy circumstances:** Well-to-do, affluent. **easy!** Move or go gently. **take it easy!** Take your time! **easy ahead!** Move or steam at a moderate speed. **easy all!** Stop rowing. **honours easy:** (*Cards, colloq.*) Honours equally divided. **easy chair,** *n.* An arm-chair stuffed and padded for resting or reclining in. **easy-going,** *a.* Moving easily; taking things in an easy manner; indolent. **easy mark,** *n.* (*colloq.*) A gullible fellow. **easily,** *adv.* **easiness,** *n.* **easy-osy,** *a.* Indolent, easy-going.

eat (ēt) [A.-S. *etan* (cp. Dut. *eten*, G. *essen*; also L. *edere*, Gr. *edein*)], *v.t.* (*past* **ate** (et), *p.p.* **eaten** (ētn) To masticate and swallow as food; to devour; to destroy by eating; (*fig.*) to corrode; to consume; to wear away, to waste. *v.i.* To take food; to be eaten; to taste, to relish. **eaten up with pride:** Absorbed with self-conceit. **to eat away:** To destroy, to rust, to corrode. **to eat dirt:** To retract. **to eat into:** To corrode. **to eat one's heart out:** To pine away. **to eat one's terms:** To study for the English bar (from the fact that the student has to eat so many dinners each term in the public hall of the Inn to which he belongs). **to eat one's words:** To retract what one has said. **to eat out of house and home:** To ruin (some one) by consuming all he has. **eatable,** *a.* Fit to be eaten; proper for food. *n.* Anything fit or proper for food; (*pl.*) the solid materials of a meal. ***eatage,** *n.* Pasturage, esp. that obtained from the aftermath. **eater,** *n.* One who eats; fruit suitable for eating uncooked. **eating-house,** *n.* A shop where provisions are sold ready for eating; a restaurant.

eau (ō) [F.], *n.* Water (used in compounds to designate various spirituous waters and perfumes). **eau-de-Cologne** (ō dĕ kŏ lōn′), *n.* A scent consisting of a solution of volatile oils in alcohol, orig. made in Cologne. **eau de luce** (ō dĕ lūce′), *n.* A mixture of oil of amber, alcohol, and ammonia, used as an antidote to snake-bites. **eau-de-Nil** (ō dĕ nēl′), *n.* A greenish colour, said to be like Nile water. **eau de vie** (ō dĕ vē), *n.* Brandy.

eaves (ēvz) [A.-S. *efes*, sing., prob. cogn. with OVER (now taken as pl. and *eave* sometimes used as sing.)], *n.pl.* The lower edge of the roof which projects beyond the wall, and serves to throw off the water which falls on the roof. **eavesdrop,** *n.* The water which drops from the eaves of a house. *v.i.* To listen under the eaves of a house in order to catch what may be said indoors; to listen so as to surprise confidences. **eavesdropper,** *n.*

ebb (eb) [A.-S. *ebba*, the ebb, whence *ebbian*, to ebb (cp. Dut. *ebbe*, *eb*)], *n.* The reflux of the tide; (*fig.*) decline, failure, decay. *v.i.* To flow back; (*fig.*) to recede, to decline, to decay. **ebb-tide,** *n.* The retiring tide. **to ebb and flow:** To rise and fall; (*fig.*) to increase and decrease.

Ebenezer (eb ė nē′ zėr) [Heb. *eben hā′ ēzer*, the stone of help, a memorial set up by Samuel after the victory of Mizpah (1 Sam. vii. 12)], *n.* A dissenting chapel.

Ebionite (eb′ i-, ē′ bi ŏ nīt) [L. *Ebionita* (Heb. *ebiōnīm*, the poor)], *n.* A Christian sect of the 1st and 2nd centuries consisting of those Jewish converts who considered the Mosaic law as still binding, and sought to Judaize Christianity. **Ebionitic** (nit′ ik), *a.* **Ebionitism** (ē′ bi on it izm), *n.*

Eblis (eb′ lis) [Arab. *Iblīs*], *n.* (*pl.* **Iblees**) The chief of the jinn who were cast out of heaven. **hall of Eblis:** Pandemonium.

ebony (eb′ ŏ ni) [O.F. and L. *ebenus*, Gr. *ebenos* (prob. of Oriental orig.)], *n.* The wood of various species of *Diospyros*, noted for its solidity and black colour, capable of a high polish, and largely used for mosaic work and inlaying. *a.* Made of ebony; intensely black. ***ebon,** *a.* Consisting of or like ebony; black. *n.* Ebony. ***ebon-coloured,** *a.* Black, dark. ***ebonist,** *n.* A worker in ebony. **ebonite,** *n.* Vulcanite. **ebonize,** *v.t.* To make the colour of ebony.

éboulement (ā bool′ man) [F., from *ébouler*, to crumble], *n.* (*Fort.*) The crumbling of a wall; (*Geol.*) a sudden fall of rock in a mountainous district.

ebracteate (ē brăk′ tė ăt) [E-, BRACT, -ATE], *a.* (*Bot.*) Without bracts.

ebriety (ē brī′ ė ti) [F. *ébriété*, L. *ēbrietās -tātem*, from *ēbrius*, drunk], *n.* Drunkenness, intoxication. **ebriate** (ē′ bri āt) [L. *ēbriātus*, p.p. of *ēbriāre*, to intoxicate], *v.t.* To intoxicate. **ebriosity** (-os' i ti), *n.* Habitual drunkenness; (*fig.*) exhilaration. **ebriose, ebrious,** *a.* Drunk; addicted to drink; characteristic of drunkenness.

ebullient (e bŭl' i ėnt) [L. *ēbulliens -ntem*, pres.p. of *ēbullīre* (E-, *bullīre*, to boil)], *a.* Boiling over; (*fig.*) overflowing (with high spirits or enthusiasm). **ebullience, -ency,** *n.* **ebullition** (eb ŭ lish' ŭn), *n.* The boiling or bubbling of a liquid caused by the action of heat, by the escape of gases on the removal of pressure, or by chemical action; effervescence; (*fig.*) sudden outburst (of feeling).

eburnation (eb ėr nā' shŭn), **eburnification** [L. *eburnus*, ivory, -ATION], *n.* (*Path.*) An excessive deposition of osseous matter, sometimes found in a diseased state of the joints.

eburnean, -ian (ė bĕr' ni ȧn), **eburnine** (ė bĕr' nīn) [as prec.], *a.* Of ivory; ivory-like.

écarté (ā kar' tā) [F., from *écarter*, to discard], *n.* A game of cards played by two persons with 32 cards.

ecaudate (ē kaw' dāt) [E-, L. *cauda*, a tail], *a.* (*Zool.*) Without a tail; (*Bot.*) spikeless; without a stem.

ecbasis (ek' bȧ sis) [Gr. *ekbasis* (*ekbainein*, to go out)], *n.* (*Rhet.*) An argument dealing with probable consequences. **ecbatic** (ek băt' ik), *a.*

ecbole (ek' bō li) [Gr. *ekbole*, a throwing-out], *n.* (*Rhet.*) A digression. **ecbolic** (ek bol' ic), *n.* (*Med.*) A drug which stimulates uterine contractions and promotes the expulsion of the fœtus.

ecce homo (ek' si hō' mō, -hom' ō) [L., behold the man], *n.* A name given to paintings representing Christ crowned with thorns, as He appeared before Pilate (John xix. 5).

eccentric (ek sen' trik) [late L. *eccentricus*, Gr. *ekkentros* (*ek*, out, *kentron*, CENTRE)], *a.* Deviating from the centre; departing from the usual practice or established forms or laws; erratic, irregular, anomalous; peculiar or odd in manner or character; (*Geom.*) not having the same centre, a term applied to circles and spheres which are not concentric. *n.* A person of odd or peculiar habits; an oddity; a mechanical contrivance for converting circular into reciprocating rectilinear motion, esp. that operating the slide-valve of a steam-engine. **eccentric-rod,** *n.* A rod transmitting the motion of an eccentric-wheel. **eccentric-strap,** *n.* The iron band within which an eccentric-wheel revolves. **eccentric-wheel,** *n.* A wheel whose axis of revolution is different from its centre. **eccentrically,** *adv.*

eccentricity (ek sen tris' i ti), *n.* The state of not being concentric; deviation from the centre; departure from what is usual, regular or established; whimsical conduct or character; oddity, peculiarity; (*Astron.*) a measure of the departure from circularity of the orbit of a planet.

ecchymosis (ek i mō' sis) [Gr. *ek*, out; *chumos*, CHYME], *n.* (*Path.*) A bruise; a discoloration of the skin due to the effusion of blood from blood-vessels ruptured by a blow.

ecclesia (ė klē' zi ȧ) [med. L., from Gr. *ekklēsia*, from *ekkalein* (*ek*, out, *kalein*, to call)], *n.* (*Gr. Hist.*) An assembly of free citizens, esp. the legislative assembly of ancient Athens; (*Eccles.*) a church; a religious assembly, a congregation. ***ecclesiarch,** *n.* A ruler of the church. ***ecclesiast,** *n.* A member of a Greek ecclesia; Solomon regarded as the preacher or author of the Book of Ecclesiastes.

ecclesiastic (ė klē zi ăs' tik) [Gr. *ekklēsiastikos*, as prec.], *a.* Ecclesiastical. *n.* A person in holy orders, a clergyman. **ecclesiastical,** *a.* Pertaining to the Church or the clergy. **Ecclesiastical Commissioners,** *n.pl.* Members of a permanent commission established in 1836 to administer the revenues of the Church of England. **ecclesiastical courts,** *n.pl.* Courts for administering ecclesiastical law and for maintaining the discipline of the Established Church; courts in the Presbyterian Church for deciding matters of doctrine and discipline. **ecclesiastical modes,** *n.pl.* (*Mus.*) The Ambrosian and Gregorian scales in which plain song and plain chant are composed. **ecclesiastical states,** *n.pl.* The territory formerly under the temporal rule of the Pope. **ecclesiastically,** *adv.* **ecclesiasticism,** (-ăs' ti sizm), *n.*

ecclesiography (e klē zi og' rȧ fi), *n.* Descriptive history of the Church or of Churches.

ecclesiolatry (e klē zi ol' ȧ tri), *n.* Excessive reverence for ecclesiastical forms and traditions. **ecclesiolater,** *n.*

ecclesiology (ė klē zi ol' ō ji), *n.* The science which treats of all matters connected with churches, esp. church architecture, decoration, and antiquities. **ecclesiological** (-loj' ik ȧl), *a.* **ecclesiologist,** *n.*

ecdysis (ek' di sis) [Gr. *ekdusis*, from *ekduein* (*ek*, off, *duein*, to put)], *n.* The casting of the skin, as by snakes, insects and crustacea.

***eche** (ēk) [A.-S. *ēcan*, *īecan*, to increase, to add, cogn. with L. *augēre*, Gr. *auxanein*], *v.t.* To increase, to augment; to eke (out).

echelon (esh' ė lȯn, esh' lȯn) [F., from *échelle*, L. *scāla*, a ladder], *n.* The arrangement of troops as in the form of steps, with parallel divisions one in advance of another. *v.t.* To form in echelon.

echidna (ė kid' nȧ) [Gr., viper], *n.* (*Zool.*) A genus of mammals from Australia, Tasmania, and New Guinea, popularly known as porcupine ant-eaters, which lay eggs instead of bringing forth their young alive like other mammals.

echinate, -nated (ė kī' nāt, -ėd) [L. *echinātus*, from *echīnus*, a hedgehog], *a.* (*Bot.*) Furnished with numerous rigid hairs or straight prickles; (*Zool.*) bristly or spiny like a hedgehog or sea-urchin. **echinid, -nidan,** *n.* A sea-urchin. **echinite,** *n.* (*Geol.*) A fossil echinoderm or sea-urchin. **echinoid,** *a.*

echinoderm (ė kī' nō dĕrm) [Gr. *echīnus*, as prec., *derma*, skin, pl. *dermata*], *a.* (*Zool.*) Having a prickly skin; pertaining to the *Echinodermata*. *n.* Any individual of the *Echinodermata*. ***Echinodermata,*** *n.pl.* A class of animals containing the sea-urchins, starfish, and sea-cucumbers. **echinodermatous,** *a.* **echinus** (ė kī' nŭs), *n.* A sea-urchin; (*Arch.*) the ovolo moulding below the abacus of an Ionic column and in the cornices of Roman architecture.

echo (ek' ō) [L., from Gr. *ēchō* (cp. *ēchos*, *ēchē*, sound)], *n.* The repetition of a sound caused by its being reflected from some obstacle; the personification of this phenomenon or its cause; (*fig.*) close imitation in words or sentiment; a hearty reponse; (*Mus.*) repetition of a phrase in a softer tone; (*Pros.*) repetition of the last syllables of a verse in the next line, so as to give a continuous sense; (*Whist*) a response to a partner's call for trumps. *v.i.* To give an echo; to resound; to be sounded back. *v.t.* To return or send back (as a sound); (*fig.*) to repeat with approval; to imitate closely. **echo sounder,** *n.* (*Naut.*) An apparatus for sounding the depth of water beneath the keel. **echogram,** *n.* A recording of this. **echoer,** *n.* **echoism,** *n.* Onomatopœia. **echoless,** *a.* **echometer** (ė kom' ė tėr), *n.* An instrument for measuring the duration of sounds.

eclair (ā' klâr) [F., lightning], *n.* An iced, finger-shaped cream cake.

éclaircissement (ė klâr' sis man) [F., from *éclaircir*, to clear up], *n.* An explanation or clearing up of a subject of dispute or misunderstanding.

eclampsia (ek lămp' si ȧ) [Gr. *ek*, out, *lampein*, to shine], *n.* (*Path.*) Convulsions or fits, particularly the type that may occur as a complication of pregnancy.

eclat (ė kla') [F., from *éclater*, O.H.G. *skleizan*, to burst into fragments], *n.* Brilliant success; acclamation, applause; splendour, striking effect.

eclectic (ek lek' tik) [Gr. *eklektikos* (*eklegein*, see ECLOGUE)], *a.* Selecting, choosing, picking out at will from the doctrines, teachings, etc., of others;

containing or consisting of selections from the works of others. *n.* A philosopher who borrows doctrines from various schools; a person who derives his opinions, tastes, or practical methods from various sources. **eclectically,** *adv.* **eclecticism,** *n.*

eclipse (ė klips′) [O.F., from L. *eclipsis*, Gr. *ekleipsis*, from *ekleipein* (*ek*, out of, *leipein*, to leave)], *n.* The total or partial obscuration of the light from a heavenly body by the passage of another body between it and the eye or between it and the source of its light; a temporary failure or obscuration; loss of brightness, glory, honour, or reputation. *v.t.* To cause an eclipse of (a heavenly body) by passing between it and the spectator or between it and its source of light; to intercept the light of, to obscure; to outshine, surpass, excel. *v.i.* To suffer an eclipse; to be eclipsed.

ecliptic (ek lip′ tik) [L. *eclipticus*, Gr. *ekleiptikos*, as prec.], *a.* Constituting or pertaining to the sun's apparent path in the sky; pertaining to an eclipse. *n.* The apparent path of the sun round the earth; the plane passing through the sun's centre which contains the orbit of the earth; a great circle on the terrestrial globe answering to, and falling within, the plane of the celestial ecliptic.

eclogue (ek′ log) [L. *ecloga*, Gr. *eklogē*, from *eklegein* (*ek*, out of, *legein*, to pick)], *n.* An idyll or pastoral poem, esp. one containing dialogue.

ecology (ē kol′ ȯ ji) [Gr. *oikos*, house; -LOGY], *n.* The branch of biology dealing with the relations between organisms and their environment. **ecological** (ē kō loj′ i kȧl), *a.* **ecologist** (ē kol′ ō jist), *n.*

economic (ē kȯ nom′ ik) [L. *œconomicus*, Gr. *oikonomikos*, see foll.], *a.* Relating to the science of economics; pertaining to industrial concerns or commerce; maintained for the sake of profit or for the production of wealth; economical. **economic warfare:** Measures taken in war-time against an enemy's trade, finance, etc. **economical,** *a.* Characterized by economic management; careful, frugal, thrifty; economic. **economically,** *adv.*

economics (ē kȯ nom′ iks), *n.* The science of the production and distribution of wealth, political economy; the condition of a country, community, or individual, with regard to material prosperity; *domestic economy.

economist (ē kon′ ō mist), *n.* One who manages with economy; one skilled in the science of economics.

economize (ē kon′ ō mīz), *v.i.* To manage domestic or pecuniary affairs with economy. *v.t.* To use, administer, or expend with economy; to use sparingly, to husband, to turn to the best account. **economization** (-zā′ shŭn), *n.*

economy (ė kon′ ȯ mi) [L. *œconomia*, Gr. *oikonomia*, from *oikonomein*, to manage a household (*oikos*, house, *nemein*, to deal out)], *n.* The management, regulation, and government of a household or household affairs; a frugal and judicious use or expenditure of money; carefulness, frugality; a saving or reduction of expense (*usu. in pl.*); cheapness of operation; a careful and judicious use of anything, as of time; the disposition, arrangement, or plan of any work; the operations of nature in the generation, nutrition, and preservation of animals and plants; the administration of the internal affairs of a State, nation, or department; organization, system; an organized body or system; a system of laws, principles, doctrines, rites, etc. **political economy,** *n.* The science of the production and distribution of wealth.

écorché (ā kôr′ shā) [F., p.p. of *écorcher*, to flay], *n.* An anatomical figure with the muscular system exposed for the purpose of study.

écossaise (ā kos āz′) [F., fem. of *écossais*, Scottish], *n.* A Scottish dance or the music to it.

ecostate (ė kos′ tāt) [E-, L. *costa*, a rib], *a.* (*Bot.*) Having no central rib (as some leaves).

écraseur (ā kra′ zur) [F., crusher, from *écraser*, to crush], *n.* (*Surg.*) An instrument for removing tumours, etc., without effusion of blood.

ecru (ek′ roo, ā kru′) [F., raw, unbleached], *a.* and *n.* The colour of unbleached linen.

ecstasy (ek′ stȧ si) [O.F. *extasie*, med. L. *ecstasis*, Gr. *ekstasis* (*ek*, out, *stasis*, a standing, from *histanai*, to place)], *n.* A state of mental exaltation; excessive emotion, rapture, excessive delight, or excessive grief, distress, or pain; prophetic or poetic frenzy; a trance; (*Med.*) a morbid state of the nervous system in which the mind is completely absorbed by one idea; *madness, distraction. **ecstasize,** *v.t.* To fill with ecstasy, to enrapture. *v.i.* To go into ecstasies. **ecstatic** (ek stăt′ ik), *a.* Pertaining to or producing ecstasy; ravishing, entrancing, rapturous; subject to ecstasy; ravished, entranced. **ecstatically,** *adv.*

ecthyma (ek thī′ mȧ) [Gr. *ekthuma*, from *ekthuein* (*ek*, out, *theuin*, to boil)], *n.* (*Path.*) A skin disease characterized by an eruption of pimples.

ecto- [Gr. *ektos*, outside], *comb. form.* (*Biol. and Zool.*)

ectoblast (ek′ tō blast) [Gr. *blastos*, a sprout], *n.* The membrane composing the walls of a cell.

ectocyst (ek′ tō sist), *n.* The external investment of a polyzoon.

ectoderm (ek′ tō dĕrm), *n.* The outer layer of the ectoblast; the external integument of the *Cœlenterata.*

ectopia (ek tō′ pi ȧ), *n.* (*Path.*) Congenital displacement of an organ or part. **ectopic,** *a.* Out of place.

ectoplasm (ek′ tō plăzm), *n.* The outer layer of protoplasm or sarcode of a cell.

ectosarc (ek′ tō sark), *n.* The outer transparent sarcode-layer of certain protozoa, as the amœba.

ectozoon (ek tō zō′ on), *n.* (*pl.* **ectozoa**) An animal parasitic on the outside of other animals.

ectropium, -pion (ek trop′ i ŭm, -ŏn) [Gr. *ektropion* (*ek*, out, *trepein*, to turn)], *n.* (*Path.*) An everted eyelid, so that the red inner surface becomes external. **ectropic,** *a.*

ectype (ek′ tīp) [Gr. *ektupon* (*ek*, out, *tupos*, figure)], *n.* A copy as distinguished from an original. **ectypal,** *a.* **ectypography** (-pog′ rȧ fi), *n.* A mode of etching which leaves the design in relief.

écu (ā′ kū) [F., from L. *scutum*, a shield], *n.* A French silver coin of varying value, usually considered as equivalent to the English crown; the old five-franc piece.

ecumenical [ŒCUMENICAL].

eczema (ek′ zė mȧ) [Gr., a pustule, from *ekzeein* (*ek*, out, *zeein*, to boil)], *n.* An inflammatory disease of the skin; a skin disease. **eczematous** (ek zem′ ȧ tŭs), *a.*

-ed [A.-S. *-ed*, *-ad*, *-od*], *suf.* Forming the past tense and p.p. of regular verbs; used also (representing A.-S. *-ede*) to form adjectives, as in *cultured*, *moneyed*, *talented*.

edacious (ė dā′ shŭs) [L. *edax edācis*, from *edere*, to eat], *a.* Greedy, voracious, ravenous. **edacity** (e dăs′ i ti), *n.*

Edam (ē′ dăm) [town in Holland], *n.* A kind of pressed, yellow cheese.

edaphic (e dăf′ ik) [Gr. *edaphos*, ground], *a.* Relating to the soil.

Edda (ed′ ȧ) [Icel.], *n.* The title of two Icelandic books, the *Elder or Poetic Edda* (*c.* 1200), ascribed to *Sæmund*, a collection of ancient poems dealing with the Norse mythology and heroic traditions, and the *Younger or Prose Edda*, partly written by Snorri Sturluson (*c.* 1230), a handbook of prosody, grammar, and rhetoric for the training of young poets.

eddish (ed′ ish) [etym. doubtful], *n.* Aftermath, or the crop of grass which grows after mowing; a stubble field; eatage.

eddy (ed′ i) [etym. doubtful], *n.* A small whirlpool; a current of air, fog, smoke, etc., moving in a circle, whirling. *v.i.* and *v.t.* To whirl in an eddy. **eddy current,** *n.* (*Elec.*) Electrical current circulating in the mass of a conductor caused by a change in the magnetic field.

edelweiss (ādl′ vīs) [G. *edel*, noble, *weiss*, white], *n.* A small composite plant, *Gnaphalium leontopodium*, growing in rocky places in the Alps.

edema, etc. [ŒDEMA].

Eden (ē′ dėn) [Heb. *'ēden*, pleasure, delight], *n.* The region in which Adam and Eve were placed at their creation; a region or abode of perfect bliss; a state of complete happiness. **Edenic** (ē den′ ik), *a.* **Edenization** (-zā′ shůn), *n.*

edentate (ė den′ tāt) [L. *ēdentātus*, p.p. of *ēdentāre*, to render toothless (E-, *dens dentem*, a tooth)], *a.* Having no incisor teeth; belonging to the *Edentata.* **edental,** *a.* Edentate. *n.* An edentate animal. ***edentata*** (-tā′ tȧ), *n.pl.* An order of mammals quite or nearly destitute of teeth, containing the armadillos, sloths, and ant-eaters. **edentulous,** *a.* [EDENTATE].

edge (ej) [A.-S. *ecg* (cp. Dut. *egge*, G. *ecke*; also L. *aciēs*, Gr. *akis*, a point)], *n.* The sharp or cutting part of an instrument, as a sword; the sharpness of this; anything edge-shaped, the crest of a ridge, the line where two surfaces of a solid meet; a boundary-line; the brink, border, margin, or extremity of anything; sharpness, keenness, of mind or appetite; acrimony, bitterness. *v.t.* To sharpen, to put an edge on; to make an edge or border to; to be a border to; (*fig.*) to incite, to egg on, to instigate; to move or put forward by little and little. *v.i.* To move forward or away by little and little; to move sideways, to sidle (up). **to be on edge:** To be irritable. **to edge away from:** (*Naut.*) To sail gradually away from. **to edge in with:** (*Naut.*) To approach gradually and not directly towards. **to set the teeth on edge:** To cause a tingling or grating sensation in the teeth. **edge-bone** [AITCH-BONE]. **edge-rail,** *n.* A form of rail which bears the rolling stock on its edge; a rail placed by the side of the main rail at a switch. **edge-, edged-tool,** *n.* A general name which includes the heavier varieties of cutting-tools; (*fig.*) anything dangerous to deal or play with. **edgeless,** *a.* **edge-ways, -wise,** *adv.* With the edge turned up, or forward in the direction of the edge; sideways. **edging,** *n.* That which forms the border or edge of anything, as lace, trimming, etc., on a dress; a border or row of small plants set along the edge of a bed. **edgy,** *a.* Having or showing an edge; (*Art*) too sharply defined; (*fig.*) sharp or keen in temper; irritable.

edible (ed′ i bėl) [late L. *edibilis*, from *edere*, to eat], *a.* Fit for food, eatable. *n.* Anything fit for food; an eatable. **edible birds'-nests:** The nests of the esculent swallow, *Collocalia esculenta.* **edibility** (-bil′ i ti), *n.*

edict (ē′ dikt) [L. *ēdictum*, neut. p.p. of *ēdīcere* (E-, *dīcere*, to speak)], *n.* A proclamation or decree issued by authority. **edictal** (ė dik′ tȧl), *a.* **edictal citation,** *n.* (*Sc. Law*) A citation by proclamation when personal citation was impossible.

edifice (ed′ i fis) [F. *édifice*, L. *ædificium* (*ædes*, a building, *-ficium*, from *facere*, to make)], *n.* A building, esp. one of some size and pretension. ***edificial** (-fish′ ȧl), *a.*

edify (ed′ i fī) [F. *édifier*, L. *ædificāre* (as prec.)], *v.t.* *To build, to construct; *to build in or upon, to inhabit; *to organize, to establish; to build up spiritually; to improve, to instruct; to enlighten. **edification** (-kā′ shůn), *n.* **edificatory,** *a.*

edile [ÆDILE].

edit (ed′ it) [L. *ēditus*, p.p. of *ēdere* (E-, *dare*, to give)], *v.t.* To prepare for publication by compiling, selecting, revising, etc.; (*fig.*) to censor, to alter, to garble; to conduct or manage, as a periodical, by selecting and revising the literary matter.

edition (e dish′ ůn), *n.* The form in which a literary work is published; the whole number of copies published at one time. **editio princeps** (ed ish′ yō prin′ seps), *n.* The first printed edition of a book. **edition de luxe** (ed is′ yon de luks), *n.* A handsomely printed and bound edition of a book.

editor (e′ di tȯr), *n.* One who prepares the work of others for publication; one who conducts or manages a newspaper or periodical; (*Cinema.*) One who cuts and makes up the shots for the final sequence of a film. **editorial** (ed i tôr′ i ȧl), *a.* Of or pertaining to an editor. *n.* An article written by or proceeding from an editor; a leading article. **editorially,** *adv.* **editorship,** *n.* **editress,** *n.*

educate (ed′ ū kāt) [L. *ēducātus*, p.p. of *ēducāre*, rel. to *ēdūcere*, to EDUCE], *v.t.* To bring up (a child or children); to train and develop the intellectual and moral powers of; to provide with schooling; to train or develop (an organ or a faculty); to train (an animal). **educable,** *a.* **educability** (-bil′ i ti), *n.*

education (ed ū kā′ shůn), *n.* The process of educating, systematic training and development of the intellectual and moral faculties; instruction; a course of instruction; the result of a systematic course of training and instruction. **educational,** *a.* **educationally,** *adv.* **educationalist, educationist,** *n.* An advocate of education; one who is versed in educational methods. **educative,** *a.* **educator,** *n.*

educe (ė dūs′) [L. *ēdūcere* (E-, *dūcere*, to lead)], *v.t.* To bring out, evolve, develop; to deduce, infer; (*Chem.*) to extract. **educible,** *a.* **educt** (ē′ dŭkt), *n.* That which is educed; an inference, a deduction; (*Chem.*) a body separated by the decomposition of another body in which it previously existed. **eduction,** *n.* The act of educing. **eduction-pipe,** *n.* The pipe which carries off the exhaust steam from the cylinder.

edulcorate (ė dŭl′ kȯ rāt) [L. *ēdulcorātus*, p.p. of *ēdulcorāre* (E-, *dulcor*, sweetness)], *v.t.* To sweeten; to remove acidity from; (*Chem.*) to free from acids, salts, or impurities, by washing. **edulcoration** (-rā′ shůn), *n.* **edulcorator,** *n.* One who or that which sweetens or removes acidity; a dropping-tube for applying small quantities of water to test-tubes, watch-glasses, etc.

Edwardian (ed wôrd′ i ȧn), *a.* Referring to the periods of any of the kings of England named Edward, but usu. to that of Edward VII (1901–10). **Edwardian prayer book:** The prayer-book authorized by Edward VI in 1549.

-ee [A.-F. *-é*, p.p. used as noun (*e.g. apelé*, summoned, corr. to *apelour*, summoner)], *suf.* Denoting the recipient, as in *grantee*, *legatee*, *payee*, *vendee*; or [F. *-é*, fem. *-ée*] the direct or indirect object, as in *addressee*, *employee*; also used arbitrarily, as in *bargee*, *devotee*.

eel (ēl) [A.-S. *æl* (cp. Dut. and G. *aal*, Icel. *āll*)], *n.* A snake-like fish, the genus *Anguilla*, esp. the common European species, *A. anguilla*; an eel-like fish; (*fig.*) a slippery person; an eel-worm, as the vinegar-eel. **eel-buck, -pot,** *n.* A basket trap for catching eels. **eel-fare,** *n.* The passage of young eels up streams; a brood of young eels. **eel-fork, -spear,** *n.* A pronged instrument or fork for spearing eels. **eel-grass** [GRASS-WRACK]. **eel-pout,** *n.* A burbot; a blenny. **eel-worm,** *n.* A minute eel-like worm found in vinegar, sour paste, etc. **eely,** *a.*

e'en [EVEN (1, 4)].

-eer [F. *-ier*, L. *-iārius*, or F. *-air*, L. *-ārius*], *suf.* Denoting an agent or person concerned with or who deals in, as *charioteer*, *musketeer*, *pamphleteer*, *sonneteer*.

e'er (âr) [EVER].

eerie (ēr′ i) [M.E. *eri*, prob. from A.-S. *earg*, *earh*, timid, cowardly], *a.* (*chiefly Sc.*) Superstitiously frightened; causing fear; strange, weird. **eerily,** *adv.* **eeriness,** *n.*

ef- [EX-], *pref.* Used before *f*, as in *efface, effigy.*

efface (ė fās′) [F. *effacer* (EF-, L. *facies*, face)], *v.t.* To rub out, to wipe out, obliterate; to cast into the shade; to render negligible; *to erase, expunge. **effaceable,** *a.* **effacement,** *n.*

effect (ė fekt′) [O.F. *effect*, L. *effectus*, p.p. of *efficere* (EF-, *facere*, to make)], *n.* The result or product of a cause or operation, the consequence; efficacy, power of producing a required result; accomplishment, fulfilment; purport, aim, purpose; the impression created by a work of art; a combination of colours, forms, sounds, rhythm, etc., calculated to produce a definite impression; *a sign, a symptom; (*pl.*) goods, movables, personal estate; (*Radio.*) characteristic sounds, etc., artificially produced in order to create illusion. *v.t.* To produce as a consequence or result; to bring about, to accomplish; *to effect; *to give effect to. **in effect:** In reality, substantially; practically. **for effect:** In order to produce a striking impression. **of no effect:** Without validity or force; without result. **to give effect to:** To carry out; to make operative. **to no effect:** In vain, uselessly. **to take effect:** To operate, to produce its effect. **without effect:** Invalid, without result. **effective,** *a.* Producing its proper effect; producing a striking impression; fit for duty or service; real, actual. *n.* One who is fit for duty. **effectively,** *adv.* **effectiveness,** *n.* **effectless,** *a.* **effector,** *n.* (*Biol.*) An organ that effects response to stimulus, *e.g.* muscle, gland, cila. **effectual,** *a.* Productive of an intended effect; adequate, efficacious; *conclusive, pertinent, definitive. **effectuality** (ė fek tū ăl′ i ti), *n.* **effectually,** *adv.* **effectualness,** *n.* **effectuate,** *v.t.* To effect, to bring to pass, to accomplish. **effectuation,** *n.*

effeminate (ė fem′ i nȧt) [L. *effēminātus*, p.p. of *effēmināre* (EF-, *fēmina*, woman)], *a.* Womanish; soft and delicate; unmanly, weak; voluptuous; *gentle, tender. **effeminacy,** *n.* **effeminately,** *adv.* **effeminize,** *v.t.*

Effendi (ė fen′ di) [Turk. *efendī*, sir, lord (corr. of Gr. *authentēs*)], *n.* Master, as a title of respect, bestowed on civil dignitaries and learned men.

efferent (ef′ ėr ėnt) [L. *efferens -ntem*, pres.p. of *efferre* (EF-, *ferre*, to carry)], *a.* (*Physiol.*) Conveying outwards; discharging. *n.* An efferent vessel or nerve; a stream carrying off water from a lake, etc.

effervesce (ef ėr ves′) [L. *effervescere* (EF-, *fervescere*, incept. of *fervēre*, to boil)], *v.i.* To bubble up, from the escape of gas, as fermenting liquors; to escape in bubbles; (*fig.*) to boil over with excitement. **effervescence,** *n.* **effervescent,** *a.*

effete (ė fēt′) [L. *effētus*, weakened by bringing forth young (EF-, *fētus*, FŒTUS)], *a.* Worn out or exhausted; having lost all vigour and efficiency; sterile, barren. **effeteness,** *n.*

efficacious (ef i kā′ shŭs) [L. *efficax -ācis*, from *efficere*, to EFFECT], *a.* Producing or having power to produce the effect intended. **efficaciously,** *adv.* **efficaciousness,** *n.* **efficacy** (ef′ i kȧ si), *n.*

efficiency (e fish′ ėn si) [as foll.], *n.* Adequate fitness; power to produce a desired result; (*Eng.*) the ratio of the output of energy to the input of energy.

efficient (ė fish′ ėnt) [F., from L. *efficiens -ntem*, pres.p. of *efficere*, to EFFECT], *a.* Causing or producing effects or results; competent, capable. *n.* *An efficient agent or cause; a member of the auxiliary forces who has attended a prescribed number of drills, so as to earn the Government grant. **efficient cause:** The power or agency producing a thing or event. **efficiently,** *adv.*

effigy (ef′ i ji), ***effigies** (ė fij′ i ēz) [L. *effigiēs* (EF-, *fingere*, to fashion)], *n.* The representation or likeness of a person, as on coins, medals, etc. **to burn or hang in effigy:** To burn or hang an image of a person, to show hatred, dislike, or contempt.

effloresce (ef lȯ res′) [L. *efflōrescere*, incept. of *efflōrēre*, to blossom (EF-, *flōrēre*, to blossom, from *flōs, flōris*, a flower)], *v.i.* To burst into flower, to blossom; (*Chem.*) to crumble to powder through loss of water or crystallization on exposure to the air; (of salts) to form crystals on the surface; (of a surface) to become covered with saline particles; (*fig.*) to display itself, to blossom forth. **efflorescence,** *n.* **efflorescent,** *a.*

effluent (ef′ lū ėnt) [L. *effluens -ntem*, pres.p. of *effluere* (EF-, *fluere*, to FLOW)], *a.* Flowing or issuing out; emanating. *n.* A river or stream which flows out of another or out of a lake; the liquid that is discharged from a sewage tank. **effluence,** *n.* The act or state of flowing out; that which flows out, an emanation.

effluvium (ė floo′ vi ŭm) [late L., as prec.], *n.* (*pl.* **-via**) An emanation affecting the sense of smell, esp. a noxious or disagreeable exhalation as from putrefying substances, etc.

efflux (ef′ lŭks) [L. *effluxus*, as prec.], *n.* The act of flowing out or issuing; outflow, effusion; an emanation, that which flows out; a passing away, lapse, expiry. **effluxion** (ė flŭk′ shŭn), *n.*

effort (ef′ ȯrt) [F., as prec.], *n.* An exertion of physical or mental power, a strenuous attempt, an endeavour; a display of power, an achievement. **effortless,** *a.*

effrontery (ė frŭn′ tėr i) [F. *effronterie*, from *effronté*, shameless (EF-, *frons, -ntis*, forehead)], *n.* Impudence, shamelessness, audacious insolence.

effulge (ė fŭlj′) [L. *effulgēre* (EF-, *fulgēre*, to shine)], *v.i.* (*poet.*) To shine forth; (*fig.*) to become famous or illustrious. **effulgence,** *n.* **effulgent,** *a.* Shining brightly; diffusing radiance. **effulgently,** *adv.*

effuse (ė fūz′) [L. *effūsus*, p.p. of *effundere* (EF-, *fundere*, to pour)], *v.t.* To pour out, to emit; to diffuse, shed abroad. *a.* (ė fūs′) (*Bot.*) Spreading loosely (of an inflorescence); (*Conch.*) having the lips separated by a groove. **n.* Effusion, outpouring. **effusion,** *n.* The act of pouring out; that which is poured out; (*fig.*) a shedding, as of blood; an outpouring of genius or emotion (usu. in contempt); frank expression of feeling, effusiveness; (*Path.*) the escape of any fluid out of the proper vessel into another part.

effusive (e fūz′ iv), *a.* Gushing, exuberant, demonstrative. **effusively,** *adv.* **effusiveness,** *n.*

eft (eft) [A.-S. *efete* (etym. doubtful)], *n.* The common newt.

***eftsoon, -s** (eft soon′, -z) [A.-S. *eftsōna*, again (AFT, SOON)], *adv.* Soon after, speedily, forthwith; *presently, by and by.

egad (ė găd′) [prob. *a*, AH, GOD], *int.* By God (a minced oath).

egalitarian (e găl i târ′ i ȧn), *a.* Believing in the principle of human equality. *n.* **egality,** *n.*

egence (ē′ jėns) [L. *egens- ntem*, pres.p. of *egēre*, to be in need], *n.* The state of being needy.

***eger** [EAGRE].

***egest** (ė jest′) [L. *ēgestus*, p.p. of *ēgerere* (E-, *gerere*, to carry)], *v.t.* To eject; to void as excrement. ***egestion,** *n.* **egesta,** *n.* Waste matter thrown out; excreta.

egg (1) (eg) [A.-S. *æg* (cp. Icel. *egg*, Dan. *æg*, Dut. and G. *ei*)], *n.* The ovum of birds, reptiles, fishes, and many of the invertebrates, usually enclosed in a spheroidal shell, and containing the embryo of a new individual; the egg of a bird, esp. of domestic poultry, largely used as food; (*Biol.*) an ovum or germ-cell; (*fig.*) the early stage of anything; the germ, the origin. *v.t.* (*Am.*) To pelt with rotten eggs. *v.i.* To collect eggs. **bad egg:** (*slang*) A worthless person; a bad or risky speculation. **good egg!** *int.* (*slang*) Excellent! **egg and anchor, egg and dart, egg and tongue:** (*Arch.*) Various kinds of moulding carved alternatively with egg-shapes. **egg and spoon race:** A race in which the runners carry eggs in spoons. **to egg and crumb:** To cover with yolks of egg and crumbs. **egg-bird,** *n.* A sea-bird the eggs of which are collected for food, etc., esp. a West Indian tern,

Hydrochelidon fuliginosum. **egg-bound,** *a.* Term applied to the oviduct of birds when obstructed by an egg. **egg-cleavage,** *n.* The first process of germination, in which the fertilized cell of the ovum becomes divided. **egg-cup,** *n.* A cup-shaped vessel used to hold an egg at table. **egg-dance,** *n.* A dance by a blindfold person among eggs; (*fig.*) a task of extreme intricacy. **egg-flip, -nog,** *n.* A drink compounded of eggs beaten up, sugar, and beer, cider, wine, or spirits. **egg-head,** *n.* (*Am. slang*) An intellectual. **egg-plant,** *n.* Popular name for the *Solanum esculentum*, an edible plant of the nightshade family. **egg-shape,** *n.* An egg-shaped object. **egg-shaped,** *a.* Having the form of an egg, oval, esp. with one end smaller than the other. **egg-shell,** *n.* The calcareous envelope in which an egg is enclosed. **egg-shell china:** Very thin porcelain. **egg-slice,** *n.* A kitchen utensil for removing eggs or omelets from the pan. **egg-spoon,** *n.* A small spoon used for eating eggs. **egg-tooth,** *n.* A hard point or knob on the bill-sheath or snout of an embryo bird or reptile for cracking the containing shell. **egg-whisk,** *n.* A kind of wire brush used for beating up eggs. **egger,** *n.* One who gathers eggs. **eggar-moth,** *n.* Various British moths of the genera *Lasiocampa* and *Ereog aster.*

egg (2) (eg) [Icel. *eggja*, to EDGE], *v.t.* To incite, to urge (*on*).

egis [ÆGIS].

eglandulose (ė glăn′ dū lōs), **eglandular,** *a.* (*Bot.*) Without glands.

eglantine (eg′ lȧn tīn, -tin) [F. *églantine*, from O.F. *aiglant*, prob. from L. *acus*, needle, *-lentus*, -LENT], *n.* The sweet brier. ***eglatere** (eg lȧ tēr′) [O.F. *esglantier*, *aiglantier*, as prec.], *n.* Eglantine.

ego (eg′ ō) [L., I], *n.* Individuality, personality; the self-conscious subject, as contrasted with the non-ego, or object; (*Psych.*) the conscious self, which resists on the one hand the threats of the super-ego, and on the other the impulses of the id. **ego-altruistic,** *a.* (*Phil.*) A term introduced by Herbert Spencer to denote sentiments which, while they imply self-gratification, also imply gratification in others. **egocentric,** *a.* Self-centred. **egocentricity** (-tris′ i ti), *n.*

egoism (eg′ ō izm), *n.* (*Ethics*) The theory that man's chief good is the complete development and happiness of self, and that this is the proper basis of morality; pure self-interest, systematic selfishness; (*Phil.*) the doctrine that man can be absolutely certain of nothing but his own existence and the operations of his own mind; egotism. **egoist,** *n.* **egoistic, -ical** (eg ō is′ tik, -ȧl), *a.* **egoistically,** *adv.* **egomania,** *n.*

egotism (eg′ ō tizm), *n.* The habit of too frequently using the word I in writing or speaking: hence a too frequent mention of oneself in writing or conversation; self-glorification, self-conceit. **egotist,** *n.* **egotistic, -ical** (eg ȯ tis′ tik, ȧl), *a.* **egotistically,** *adv.* **egotize,** *v.i.*

egregious (ė grē′ jŭs) [L. *ēgregius* (E-, *grex gregis*, flock)], *a.* Extraordinary, out of the common, remarkable, exceptional; notable, notorious. **egregiously,** *adv.* **egregiousness,** *n.*

egress (ē′ gres) [L. *ēgressus*, p.p. of *ēgredī* E-, *gradī*, to go)], *n.* The act or power of going out; departure; a means or place of exit; (*Astron.*) the end of a transit or eclipse. **egression** (ē gresh′ ŭn), *n.*

egret (ē′ grėt, eg′ rėt) [O.F. *egrette*, *aigrette*, AIGRETTE], *n.* A heron, esp. the lesser white heron, of those species that have long and loose plumage over the back; the feathery or hairy down of seeds; an aigrette.

Egyptian (ė jip′ shȧn), *a.* Of or pertaining to Egypt or the Egyptians; *gipsy. *n.* A native of Egypt; a gipsy; (*Print.*) type with thick stems. **Egyptian pebble, jasper,** *n.* A variety of jasper with zones of brown and yellow, found between Cairo and Suez. **Egyptian lotus,** *n.* *Nymphœa lotus.* **Egyptian thorn,** *n.* The tree *Acacia vera*, which yields gum-arabic. **Egyptology** (ē jip tol′ ȯ ji) [-LOGY], *n.* The study of the antiquities, language, etc., of ancient Egypt. **Egyptological,** *a.* **Egyptologist,** *n.*

eh (ā) [M.E. *ey*, A.-S. *ēa*), *int.* An exclamation expressive of doubt, inquiry, surprise, etc.

eident (ī′ dėnt) [Sc., prob. from M.E. *ithen*, cp. Icel. *ithinn*], *a.* Diligent, attentive.

eider (ī′ dėr) [Icel. *æthar*, gen. of *æthr*, an eider duck (as in *ærhar-dūn*, eider-down)], *n.* A large Arctic sea-duck, *Somateria mollissima.* **eider-down,** *n.* The soft and elastic down from the breast of this bird; a quilt filled with eider-down.

eidograph (ī′ dȯ grăf) [Gr. *eidos*, form, -GRAPH], *n.* An instrument for copying plans or drawings on an enlarged or reduced scale.

eidolon (ī dō′ lȯn) [Gr., see IDOL], *n.* An image, likeness, or representation; an apparition, a spectre.

eight (āt) [A.-S. *eahta* (cp. Dut. and G. *acht*, L. *octo*, Gr. *oktō*, Gael. *ochd*, Sansk. *ashtau*)], *n.* The sum of one and seven; the cardinal number next above seven; the figure 8 or viii, representing eight units; (*Rowing*) a crew of eight in a boat; (*Skating*) a curved outline resembling the figure 8. *a.* Consisting of one more than seven. **one over the eight:** (*colloq.*) Slightly drunk. **eight-day,** *a.* Going for eight days (of clocks). **eight-fold,** *a.* **eighth** (ātth), *a.* Coming next in order to the seventh; denoting one of eight equal parts into which anything has been divided. *n.* One of eight equal parts of anything; (*Mus.*) the interval of an octave. **eighthly** (āt′ thli), *adv.* **eightsome,** *n.* (*Dancing*) A form of Scottish reel for eight dancers.

eighteen (ā tēn′) [A.-S. *eahtatȳne*], *a.* Eight more than ten. *n.* The sum of eight and ten. **eighteenmo,** *n.* (*colloq.*) An octodecimo, a book whose sheets are folded to form eighteen leaves, written 18mo. **eighteenth,** *a.*

eighty (ā′ ti) [A.-S. *eahtatig*], *a.* Consisting of eight times ten. *n.* Eight times ten; the cardinal number representing this; the numeral 80 or lxxx. **eightieth,** *a.*

eikon [ICON].

eild (ēld) [Sc.; prob. a var. of YELD], *a.* Not yielding milk.

***eine,** *pl.* [EYE].

eirenicon (ī rē′ ni kȯn) [Gr. *eirēnikon*, neut. of *eirēnikos*, from *eirēne*, peace], *n.* A measure or proposal intended to make or restore peace.

eisteddfod (ā steth′ vod) [W., a sitting, from *eistedd*, to sit], *n.* (*Welsh*) A congress of bards held annually to encourage native poetry and music.

either (ī′-, ē′ thėr) [A.-S. *ægther*, contr. of *æghwæther* (*ā*, aye, *ge-*, pref., *hwæther*, WHETHER)], *a.* and *pron.* One or the other of two; each of two. *a.*, *adv.*, or *conj.* In one or the other case (as a disjunctive correlative); (*colloq.*) any more than the other (with neg. or interrog., as *If you don't I don't either*).

ejaculate (ė jăk′ ū lāt) [L. *ējaculātus*, p.p. of *ējaculārī* (E-, *jaculārī*, to cast, from *jaculum*, a dart, as foll.)], *v.t.* To utter suddenly and briefly; to exclaim; to eject. *v.i.* To utter ejaculations. **ejaculation** (-lā′ shŭn), *n.* An abrupt exclamation; emission of seminal fluid. **ejaculative,** *a.* **ejaculatory** (ė jăk′ ū lȧ tȯr i), *a.*

eject (ė jekt′) [L. *ējectus*, p.p. of *ējicere* (E-, *jacere*, to throw)], *v.t.* To discharge, to emit; to drive away, to expel; (*Law*) to oust or dispossess. *n.* (ē′ jėkt) (*Psych.*) Something that is not an object of our own consciousness but inferred to have actual existence. **ejection,** *n.* **ejective,** *a.* Tending to eject; pertaining to an eject. ***ejectively,** *adv.* **ejectment,** *n.* The act of casting out or expelling; ejection, expulsion; dispossession; (*Law*) an action to recover possession.

ejector (e jek′ tȯr) *n.* One who ejects, drives out, or dispossesses; an appliance by which a jet of elastic fluid, such as steam or air, is made to exhaust a fluid of the same or a different kind; a contrivance for removing a spent cartridge from a breech-loader gun. **ejector seat,** *n.* (*Aviat.*) A seat that can be shot clear of the plane in an emergency.

eke (1) (ēk) [A.-S. *īecan* (cp. Goth. *aukan*, L. *augēre*)], *v.t.* To make up for or supply deficiencies in (with *out*); (*colloq.*) to produce, support, or maintain with difficulty; *to augment, to protract, to lengthen.

***eke** (2) (ēk) [A.-S. *ēac*, cogn. with prec.], *adv.* Also, besides, likewise.

-el [-LE].

elaborate (ė lăb′ ŏ rȧt) [L. *ēlabōrātus*, p.p. of *ēlabōrāre* (E-, *labōrāre*, to work (*labor*, LABOUR))], *a.* Carefully or highly wrought; highly finished. *v.t.* (-rāt) To produce by labour; to develop in detail; to work up and produce from its original material (as the food of animals or plants, so to adapt it for nutrition). **elaborately,** *adv.* **elaborateness,** *n.* **elaboration** (ė lăb ŏ rā′ shŭn), *n.* **elaborative,** *a.*

elæo- [Gr. *elaion*, olive-oil], *comb. form.* Relating to oil. **elæometer** (el i om′ ė tėr) [-METER], *n.* An instrument for determining the specific gravity and hence the purity of oils.

élan (ā′ lan) [F., prob. from foll.], *n.* Ardour; dash.

eland (ē′ lȧnd) [Dut., an elk (cp. G. *elend*, also W. *elain*, a hind)], *n.* A large ox-like antelope, *Oreas canna*, from South Africa.

elapse (ė lăps′) [L. *ēlapsus*, p.p. of *ēlābī* (E-, *lābī*, to glide)], *v.i.* To glide or pass away.

elasmobranch (ė lăz′ mŏ brăngk) [Gr. *elasmos*, a metal plate, *branchia*, gills], *n.* One of a class of fishes, the *Elasmobranchii*, having plate-like gills, containing the sharks, rays, and chimæras. **elasmobranchiate,** *a.*

elastic (ė lăs′ tik) [Gr. *elastikos*, propulsive, from *ela-*, stem of *elaunein*, to drive], *a.* Having the quality of returning to that form or volume from which it has been compressed, expanded, or distorted; springy, rebounding; flexible, adaptable; admitting of extension; readily recovering from depression or exhaustion, buoyant. *n.* A strip of elastic substance, a string or cord woven with india-rubber threads. **elastic bitumen, pitch,** *n.* Elaterite. **elastic tissue,** *n.* (*Anat.*) Yellow fibrous tissue occurring in the ligaments of the vertebræ, the jaw, etc. **elastically,** *adv.* **elasticity** (-tis′ i ti), *n.* **elasticin, elastin,** *n.* (*Chem.*) The substance forming the fibres of elastic tissue.

elate (ė lāt′) [L. *ēlātus* (E-, *lātus*, p.p. of *ferre*, to bear, to raise)], *v.t.* To raise the spirits of, to stimulate; to make exultant; *to raise, to elevate. *a.* Lifted up, in high spirits, exultant. **elation** (ė lā′ shŭn), *n.*

elater (el′ ȧ tėr) [ELASTIC], *n.* A genus of coleopterous insects, called click-beetles or skip-jacks, from their ability to spring up and alight on their feet; (*Bot.*) an elastic spiral filament attached to spores; *a spring.

elaterin [ELATERIUM].

elaterite (ė lăt′ ėr īt), *n.* A soft elastic mineral, elastic bitumen.

elaterium (el ȧ tēr′ i ŭm) [L., from Gr. *elatērion*, as prec.], *n.* A powerful purgative obtained from the fruit of the squirting cucumber. **elaterin** (ė lăt′ ėr in), *n.* The active principle of elaterium.

elbow (el′ bō) [A.-S. *elboga*, *elnboga* (*eln*, ELL, *boga* BOW)], *n.* The joint uniting the forearm with the upper arm; an elbow-shaped (usu. obtuse) angle, bend, or corner. *v.t.* To push or thrust with the elbows, to jostle; to force (a way or oneself into, out of, etc.) by pushing with the elbows. *v.i.* To make one's way by pushing with the elbows; to jostle; to go out of one's way; to zig-zag. **at one's elbow:** Near at hand. **out at elbows:** Shabby in dress; in needy circumstances. **to crook** or **lift the elbow:** To drink. **to jog the elbow:** (*fig.*) To give a reminder. **up to the elbows:** Deeply engaged in business. **elbow-chair,** *n.* An arm-chair. **elbow-grease,** *n.* Hard and continued manual exercise. **elbow-pipe,** *n.* A pipe with an end resembling an elbow. **elbow-room,** *n.* Ample room for action.

***eld** (eld) [A.-S. *ield*, *ieldo*, from *eald*, OLD], *n.* Old age; *an old man; *people of old times; former ages; antiquity. **a.* Old; former. **v.t.* To make old or aged.

elder (1) (el′ dėr) [A.-S. *ieldra*, comp. of *eald*, OLD], *a.* Older; senior in position; pertaining to former times; in card-playing, having the right to play first. *n.* A senior in years; one whose age entitles him to respect; (*pl.*) persons of greater age; a member of a senate, a counsellor; an officer in the Jewish synagogue, in the early Christian, and in the Presbyterian and other churches. **Elder Brethren,** *n.pl.* The masters of Trinity House, London. **Elder Statesmen,** *n.pl.* (*Pol.*) Confidential advisers of the Emperor of Japan, *genro*. **elderly,** *a.* Bordering on old age. **eldership,** *n.* **eldest,** *a.* Oldest; first born of those surviving; *of earliest date, of longest standing.

elder (2) (el′ dėr) [A.-S. *ellen*, *ellern*], *n.* A tree of the genus *Sambucus*, esp. *S. nigra*, the common elder, a small tree bearing white flowers and dark purple berries. **elder-gun,** *n.* A pop-gun made of the hollow stem of the elder. **elder-wine,** *n.* A wine made from elder-berries and elder-flowers.

El Dorado (el dŏ ra′ dō) [Sp., the gilded], *n.* An imaginary land of gold in South America, between the Orinoco and Amazon; (*fig.*) an inexhaustible mine; a country for making money in.

eldritch (el′ drich) [Sc., etym. doubtful], *n.* Strange, weird, ghastly, frightful.

Eleatic (el ė ăt′ ik) [L. *Eleāticus*], *a.* Pertaining to Elea, a town of Magna Græcia; relating to the school of philosophy founded by Xenophanes at Elea. *n.* A follower of the philosophy of Xenophanes, Parmenides, and Zeno. **Eleaticism** (-ăt′ i sizm), *n.*

elecampane (el ė kȧm pān′) [F. *enule-campane*, L. *inula campāna* (*enule*, assim. to A.-S. *eolone*, *elene*, a perversion of L. *inula*; *campāna*, either growing in the fields or Campanian)], *n.* A composite plant, *Inula helenium*; the candied root-sticks of this used as a sweetmeat.

elect (ė lekt′) [L. *ēlectus*, p.p. of *ēligere* (E-, *legere*, to choose)], *a.* Chosen, picked out; designated to an office, but not yet in possession of it; chosen by God for everlasting life. *v.t.* To choose for any office or employment; to choose by vote; to choose to everlasting life; to determine on any particular course of action; *to pick out. **the elect:** Those chosen by God, etc.; highly select or self-satisfied people.

election (ė lek′ shŭn) [as prec.], *n.* The act of choosing out of a number, esp. by vote; the ceremony or process of electing; power of choosing or selection; (*Theol.*) the selection of certain individuals from mankind to be eternally saved (the characteristic doctrine of Calvinism). **by-election** [BY]. **general election:** An election of members of Parliament in all constituencies in the United Kingdom. **election-auditor,** *n.* An official who examines and publishes the accounts of the expenses of parliamentary elections. **electioneer** (ė lek shŭ nēr′), *v.i.* To work at an election in the interests of some particular candidate. **elective,** *a.* Appointed, filled up, or bestowed by election; pertaining to election or choice; having or exercising the power of choice. **elective affinity:** (*Chem.*) The tendency of substances to unite with particular substances rather than with others. **electively,** *adv.*

elector (e lek′ tŏr), *n.* One who has the right, power, or privilege of electing; (*Hist.*) one of the princes of Germany who were entitled to vote in the election of the Emperor. **electoral,** *a.* **electorate,** *n.* Electorship; the whole body of electors; (*Hist.*) the dignity or territory of an elector of the

German Empire. **electorship,** *n.* **electress,** *n.* A female elector; (*Hist.*) the wife of a German elector.

Electra complex (ėl ek' tra kom' pleks) [in Gr. mythol. Electra incited her brother Orestes to murder their mother who had already murdered their father, Agamemnon], *n.* (*Psych.*) Attraction of a daughter for her father accompanied by hostility to her mother.

electric (ė lek' trik) [L. *ēlectrum*, Gr. *ēlektron*, amber, conn. with *ēlektor*, shining], *a.* Containing, generating, or operated by electricity; (*fig.*) resembling electricity, magnetic, spirited. *n.* A non-conductor, in which electricity can be excited by means of friction. **electric battery** [BATTERY]. **electric bell,** *n.* A bell in which the hammer is operated electrically by means of a solenoid. **electric blanket,** *n.* A blanket containing an electrically-heated element. **electric blue,** *n.* Trade name for a steely blue. **electric cable,** *n.* An insulated wire or flexible conductor for conveying a current. **electric cautery,** *n.* (*Med.*) Cauterization by means of electrically heated instruments. **electric chair,** *n.* A chair in which persons condemned to death are electrocuted. **electric charge,** *n.* The accumulation of electric energy in an electric battery. **electric circuit,** *n.* The passage of electricity from a body in one electric state to a body in another by means of a conductor; the conductor. **electric clock,** *n.* A clock worked by electricity, esp. one operated by a synchronous motor working off a.c. mains. **electric cooker,** *n.* An assembly of electrically-heated boiling-plates, grill, and oven for commercial or domestic cooking. **electric current,** *n.* Continuous transition of electricity from one place to another. **electric eel,** *n.* (*Zool.*) A large S. American eel, *Gymnotus electricus*, able to give an electric shock. **electric field,** *n.* A region in which forces are exerted on any electric charge present in the region. **electric furnace,** *n.* A furnace used for industrial purposes heated by electricity. **electric hare,** *n.* An artificial hare made to run by electricity used in greyhound racing. **electric jar,** *n.* A Leyden jar. **electric light,** *n.* A light produced by the passage of an electric current. **electric locomotive,** *n.* A locomotive in which the power is derived from a battery, a generator, or a contact wire or rail. **electric railway,** *n.* (*Rail.*) A system employing electricity to drive trains. **electric ray,** *n.* (*Zool.*) A flat fish of the genus *Torpedo*. **electric razor, electric shaver,** *n.* An appliance for removing bristles, hair, etc. by the rapid movement of a protected blade actuated by electricity. **electric shock,** *n.* The sudden pain felt from the passing of an electric current through the body. **electric storm,** *n.* A disturbance of electric conditions of the atmosphere. **electric strength,** *n.* The maximum electric field strength that can be applied to an insulator without causing breakdown. **electric telegraph,** *n.* An apparatus for transmitting signals to a distance by means of an electric current over metallic wires. **electrical,** *a.* Relating to electricity; electric. **electrical recording,** *n.* (*Gramophone*) A device for making records by operating the cutting stylus by electromagnetic means. **electrical reproduction,** *n.* (*Gramophone*) Reproduction from a record by a tracking needle which operates an electromagnetic device or other transducer instead of the diaphragm of a sound-box. **electrically,** *adv.*

electrician (e lek trish' ŭn), *n.* One skilled in the science and application of electricity.

electricity (el ėk tris' i ti) [prec.], *n.* A powerful physical agent which makes its existence manifest by attractions and repulsions, by producing light and heat, chemical decomposition, and other phenomena; the science of the laws and phenomena of this physical agent. **Electricity Bill,** *n.* (*Pol.*) The measure by which all electricity undertakings were nationalized in 1947–48.

electrify (ė lek' tri fī), *v.t.* To charge with electricity; to give an electric shock to; (*fig.*) to thrill with joy, surprise, or other exciting emotion. **electrification,** *n.* The act or process of electrifying; the state of being electrified; conversion of a steam or other mechanical system into one worked by electricity.

electrize (ė lek' trīz), *v.t.* To electrify. **electrization** (-zā' shŭn), *n.*

electro (ė lek' trō), *n.* An electro-type; electroplate.

electro- [Gr. *ēlektron*, amber], *comb. form.* Having electricity for its motive power; resulting from, or pertaining to electricity. **electro-bath,** *n.* A solution of a metallic salt used in electrotyping and electro-plating. **electro-biology,** *n.* Electrophysiology, the science of the electric phenomena of living organisms. **electro-biologist,** *n.* **electrocardiograph,** *n.* (*Med.*) An instrument which indicates and records the manner in which the heart muscle is contracting. **electro-cardiagram,** *n.* A record so produced. **electro-chemistry,** *n.* The science of the chemical effects produced by electricity. **electro-chemical,** *a.* **electro-copper,** *v.t.* To give copper coating by electrolysis. **electro-culture,** *n.* The application of electricity to tillage. **electro-dynamics,** *n.* The science of electricity in motion. **electro-dynamic,** *a.* **electrodynamometer,** *n.* An instrument for measuring the strength of an electric current. **electro-engraving,** *n.* Engraving by means of electricity. **electro-kinetics,** *n.* Electro-dynamics. **electro-magnet,** *n.* A bar of soft iron rendered magnetic by the passage of a current of electricity through a coil of wire surrounding it. **electro-magnetic,** *a.* **electro-magnetism,** *n.* Magnetism produced by an electric current; the science which treats of the production of magnetism by electricity, and the relations between magnetism and electricity. **electro-metallurgy,** *n.* The act of separating metals from their alloys by means of electrolysis. **electro-motion,** *n.* The passage of an electric current in a circuit; mechanical motion produced by means of electricity. **electro-motive,** *a.* **electro-motor,** *n.* A machine for converting electric into mechanical energy. **electro-muscular,** *a.* Pertaining to the action of the muscles under electric influence. **electro-negative,** *a.* Passing to the positive pole in electrolysis; pertaining to or producing negative electricity. *n.* An electro-negative element. **electro-plate,** *v.t.* To cover with a coating of silver or other metal by exposure in a solution of a metallic salt, which is decomposed by electrolysis. *n.* Articles so produced. **electro-polar,** *a.* Applied to a conductor positively electrified at one end and negatively at the other. **electro-positive,** *a.* Having a tendency to pass to the negative pole in electricity; pertaining to or producing positive electricity. *n.* An electro-positive element. **electro-static,** *a.* Pertaining to electro-statics; produced by electricity at rest. **electro-statics,** *n.* The science of statical electricity. **electro-therapeutics,** *n.* Electropathy, also called **electro-therapy. electro-thermancy,** *n.* The science of the relations of electric currents and the temperature of bodies. **electro-thermic,** *a.*

electrocute (e lek' trō kūt), *v.t.* To kill by an electric shock; to carry out a judicial sentence of death by administering a powerful electric shock. **electrocution,** *n.*

electrode (e lek' trōd), *n.* One of the poles of a galvanic battery, or of an electrical device; an anode, cathode, grid, collector, base, etc.

electrograph (e lek' trō grăph), *n.* The record of an electrometer.

electrolier (e lek trō lēr'), *n.* A pendant or bracket for supporting an electric lamp in a building.

electrology (e lek trol' ō ji), *n.* The science of electricity.

electrolysis (e lek trol' i sis), *n.* The decomposition of chemical compounds by the passage of an electric current through them; the science dealing with this process and its phenomena.

electrolyte (e lek′ trō līt), *n.* A compound which may be decomposed by an electric current.

electrolyze (e lek′ trō līz), *v.t.* To decompose by direct action of electricity.

electrometer (e lek trom′ e tĕr), *n.* An instrument for measuring the amount of electrical force, or for indicating the presence of electricity. **electrometrical,** *a.*

electromobile (e lek′ trō mō bil), *n.* A motor-car propelled by batteries.

electron (ėl ek′ tron) [ELECTRO], *n.* (*Phys.*) A particle bearing a negative electric charge, the most numerous constituent of matter and probably the cause of all electrical phenomena. **electron camera,** *n.* (*Television*) A device which converts an optical image into an electric current by electronic means. **electron microscope,** *n.* A thermionic tube in which a stream of electronics is focused on to a cathode and thence casts a magnified image of the cathode on to a screen. It is capable of very high magnification. **electron volt,** *n.* A unit of energy in atomic physics. It is the increase in energy of an electron when its potential is raised by 1 volt.

electronics (el ek tron′ iks), *n.* The science of applied physics that deals with the conduction of electricity in a vacuum, or a semi-conductor, and with other devices in which the movement of electrons is controlled. **electronic brain,** *n.* Popular term for a type of calculating machine that is worked by thermionic valves, transistors, etc.

electropathy (e lek′ trō păth i), *n.* The treatment of disease by electricity.

electrophorus (e lek trof′ ȯr ŭs), *n.* An instrument for generating statical electricity by induction.

electroscope (e lek′ trō skōp), *n.* An instrument for detecting the presence and the quality of electricity.

electrotonus (e lek trot′ ō nŭs), *n.* The alteration in the activity of a nerve or muscle under the action of a galvanic current. **electrotonic,** *a.*

electrotype (e lek′ trō tīp), *n.* The process of producing copies of medals, wood-cuts, type, etc., by the electric deposition of copper upon a mould; the facsimile so produced. *v.t.* To copy by this process. **electrotyper,** *n.* **electrotypist,** *n.*

electrum (ė lek′ trŭm) [L. *ēlectrum,* Gr. *ēlektron,* amber, conn. with *ēlektōr,* shining], *n.* An alloy of gold and silver in use among the ancients; native gold containing silver; an alloy of copper, zinc, and nickel, also called German silver.

electuary (ė lek′ tū ȧr i) [late L. *ēlectuārium,* prob. from Gr. *ekleikton* (*ekleichein,* to lick away, cp. LICK)], *n.* A purgative medicine compounded with some sweet confection.

eleemosynary (el ė ē moz′ in ȧr i) [med. L. *eleēmosynārius,* Gr. *eleēmosunē,* ALMS], *a.* Given or done by way of alms; devoted to charitable purposes; supported by or dependent on charity. **n.* One who subsists on charity.

elegant (el′ ė gȧnt) [F. *élégant,* L. *ēlegantem,* acc. of *ēlegans,* conn. with *ēligere,* to choose, see ELECT], *a.* Pleasing to good taste; graceful, well-proportioned, delicately finished, refined; *having a fine sense of beauty or propriety; (*vulg.*) excellent, first-rate, capital. **elegant extracts,** *n.pl.* A collection of choice passages in prose and verse from various authors; (*Mil. slang*) the 85th Foot. **elegance,** *n.* **elegantly,** *adv.*

elegiac (el ė jī′ ȧk) [L. *elegiacus,* Gr. *elegeiakos,* as ELEGY], *a.* Pertaining to or of the nature of elegies; (*Pros.*) suited to elegy; mournful. *n.pl.* Verse consisting of alternate hexameters and pentameters, in which the elegies of the Greeks and Romans were commonly written.

elegy (el′ ė ji) [F. *élégie,* L. *elegīa,* Gr. *elegeia* (*elegos,* a lament)], *n.* A lyrical poem or a song of lamentation; a poem of a plaintive, meditative kind; a poem written in elegiac verse. **elegize,** *v.t.* To compose an elegy upon. *v.i.* To compose an elegy; to write in a plaintive strain. **elegist,** *n.*

eleme (el′ ė mi) [Turk.], *a.* Applied to a superior kind of dried figs from Turkey. **eleme figs,** *n.pl.*

element (el′ ė mėnt) [O.F., from L. *elementum* (etym. doubtful)], *n.* One of the fundamental parts of which anything is composed; (*Chem.*) a substance which cannot be resolved by chemical analysis; (*pl.*) earth, air, fire, and water, formerly considered as simple elements; the natural habitat of any creature, as water of fish; the proper or natural sphere of any person or thing; anything necessary to be taken into account in coming to a conclusion; the rudiments of any science or art; (*Eccles.*) the bread and wine used in the Eucharist; (*Elec.*) the resistance wire of an electric heater; one of the electrodes of a primary or secondary cell.

elemental (el e men′ tȧl), *a.* Pertaining to or arising from first principles; pertaining to the four elements of which the world was supposed to be formed; hence, pertaining to the primitive forces of nature; ultimate, simple, uncompounded. **elemental spirits,** *n.pl.* Those identified with natural forces, as salamanders, sylphs, gnomes, and undines, said to inhabit respectively fire, air, earth, and water. **elementalism,** *n.* The theory which resolves the gods of antiquity into the forces and aspects of nature. **elementally,** *adv.* In an elemental manner; literally.

elementary (el ė men′ tȧr i), *a.* Consisting of one element; primary, uncompounded; rudimentary, treating of first principles, introductory. **elementary substance,** *n.* An element. **elementary-schools,** *n.pl.* Primary schools. **elementarily,** *adv.* **elementariness,** *n.*

elemi (el′ ė mi) [etym. unknown], *n.* A gum resin obtained from the Manila pitch-tree, *Canarium commune,* used in pharmacy. **elemin,** *n.* (*Chem.*)

elenchus (ė leng′ kŭs) [L., from Gr. *elenchos,* cross-examination], *n.* (*pl.* **-chi**) An argument by which an opponent is made to contradict himself; a refutation. **elenctic,** *a.*

elephant (el′ ė fȧnt) [M.E. *olifaunt,* O.F. *olifant,* L. *elephantem,* acc. of *elephas,* Gr. *elephas* (etym. doubtful)], *n.* A large pachydermatous animal, four-footed, with flexible proboscis and long curved tusks, of which two species now exist, *Elephas indicus* and *E. africanus,* the former partially domesticated and used as a beast of draught and burden; a size of paper (28 × 23 in.; double, 40 × 26¾ in.). **to see or show the elephant:** (*Am.*) To see or show life, esp. the sights of a great city. **white elephant:** A useless and expensive possession (alluding to the cost of an elephant's keep). **elephant-beetle,** *n.* A large West African beetle, *Goliathus giganteus* or *G. cacicus.* **elephant fish,** *n.* The southern chimera, *Callorhyncus antarcticus,* found off N. Zealand, S. Australia, and Tasmania, so called from its prehensile snout. **elephantiasis** (el ė fȧn tī′ ȧ sis), *n.* A cutaneous disease occurring in tropical countries, in which the skin of the patient becomes hardened and the part affected greatly enlarged. **elephantine** (el ė făn′ tīn), *a.* Pertaining to or resembling an elephant; huge, immense; unwieldy, clumsy. **elephantine epoch,** *n.* (*Palæont.*) That period during which the large pachydermata abounded. **elephantoid,** *a.* and *n.*

Eleusinian (el ū sin′ i ȧn) [L. *Eleusīnius,* Gr. *Eleusinios*], *a.* Relating to Eleusis, in ancient Attica, or to the mysteries in honour of Ceres annually celebrated there; (*fig.*) darkly mysterious.

eleuthero- [Gr. *eleutheros,* free], *combining form.* Free; not adherent. ***eleutheromania** (ė lū thĕr ō mā′ ni ȧ), *n.* A mad passion or enthusiasm for freedom. ***eleutheromaniac,** *a.* and *n.* **eleutheropetalous** (-pet′ ȧ lŭs), *a.* (*Bot.*) Composed of distinct or separate petals.

elevate (el′ ė vāt) [L. *ēlevātus,* p.p. of *ēlevāre* (E-, *levāre,* to lift, from *levis,* light)], *v.t.* To lift up; to raise aloft; to raise from a lower to a higher place;

to exalt in position or dignity; to make louder or higher; to raise in character or intellectual capacity; to refine, to improve; to elate, to animate, to exhilarate; (*colloq.*, *p.p.*) to make slightly intoxicated. **elevated railway,** *n.* A city railroad raised on pillars above the street-level. **elevation** (-vā′ shŭn), *n.* The act of elevating; the state of being elevated; an elevated position or ground; height above sea-level; the height of a building; a side or end view of an object or building drawn with or without reference to perspective; (*Astron.*) the angular altitude of a heavenly body above the horizon; (*Gunnery*) the angle of the line of fire with the plane of the horizon; (*fig.*) exaltation, grandeur, dignity. **elevation of the Host:** (*R.-C. Ch.*) The part of the Mass in which the celebrant raises the Host above his head, to be adored. **elevator** (el′ ė vā tôr), *n.* One who or that which elevates; (*Anat.*) a muscle whose function it is to raise any part of the body; a machine to raise grain from a car or ship to a high level, whence it can be discharged into any other receptacle; a lift; (*Aviat.*) a hinged flap on the tail plane to provide vertical control. **elevatory,** *a.*

eleven (ė lev′ ėn) [A.-S. *endlufon, endleofan,* from O.Teut. *ainlif-* (cp. Dut. and G. *elf,* Goth. *ainlif,* Icel. *ellifu*)], *a.* Ten with one added. *n.* The sum of ten with one added; a symbol representing the sum of ten and one, as 11 or xi; (*Cricket, Assoc. Football*) the eleven men selected to play for a particular side. **the eleven:** The disciples of Christ without Judas. **eleven plus exam.:** A school examination taken by children of about 11 to determine the particular type of secondary education they are suited for. **eleven year period:** (*Astron.*) The cycle of periodic changes in the occurrence of sun-spots. **eleventh,** *a.* The next in order after the tenth; forming one of eleven equal parts. *n.* One of eleven equal parts; (*Mus.*) the interval of an octave and a fourth. **at the eleventh hour:** At the last moment (in allusion to the parable of the labourers, Matt. xx). **elevenses,** *n.pl.* (*colloq.*) A snack taken in the middle of the morning.

elf (elf) [A.-S. *ælf* (cp. Icel. *ālfr,* G. *elf,* also *alp,* a nightmare)], *n.* (*pl.* **elves**) A tiny supernatural being supposed to inhabit groves and wild and desolate places, and to exercise a mysterious power over man; a fairy; a mischievous person; an imp; a tiny creature, a dwarf; a pet name for a child. **v.t.* To twist or tangle (the hair) in an intricate manner. **elf-arrow, -bolt, -dart,** *n.* A flint arrow-head used by the men of the Stone Age, popularly thought to be shot by fairies. **elf-child,** *n.* A child supposed to be left by fairies in exchange for one taken away by them. **elf-lock,** *n.* Hair twisted in a knot, as if done by elves. **elf-struck,** *a.* Bewitched by elves. **elfin,** *a.* Elfish. *n.* A little elf; a sprite, an urchin. **elfish, elvish,** *a.* Like an elf; of the nature of an elf; proceeding from or caused by elves; mischievous.

Elgin Marbles (el′ gin), *n.pl.* Ancient sculptured marbles brought to England in 1812, by the Earl of Elgin (1766–1841), from the Parthenon or temple of Athene, etc. at Athens.

elicit (ė lis′ it) [L. *ēlicitus,* p.p. of *ēlicere* (E-, *lacere,* to entice)], *v.t.* To draw out, evoke; to educe, extract.

elide (ė līd′) [L. *ēlīdere* (E-, *lædere,* to dash)], *v.t.* To strike out, omit; (*esp. in Gram.*) to cut off (as the last syllable); (*Law*) to annul; *to destroy.

eligible (el′ i jibl) [F. *éligible,* L. *ēligibilis,* from *ēligere,* see ELECT], *a.* Fit or deserving to be chosen; desirable, suitable; fit or qualified to be chosen to any office or position; (*colloq.*) desirable for marriage. **eligibility** (-ji bil′ i ti), *n.* **eligibly,** *adv.*

eliminate (ė lim′ i nāt) [L. *ēlimīnātus,* p.p. of *ēlimīnāre* (E-, *līmīn-* stem of *līmen,* threshold)], *v.t.* To cast out, expel; to cast aside, remove, get rid of; to exclude, to ignore (certain considerations); (*Math.*) to cause to disappear from an equation, (*incorrectly*) to disengage, to isolate. **eliminable,** *a.* **elimination** (-nā′ shŭn), *n.* The act of eliminating; expulsion, ejection; leaving out or passing over; (*Math.*) removal of a quantity from an equation. **eliminator,** *n.* (*Radio.*) A device for supplying a battery receiving-set with electricity from the mains.

eliquation (el i kwā′ shŭn) [L. *ēliquatio-ōnem*], *n.* Liquefaction; (*Metal.*) the separation of a fusible substance from another less fusible by heating to a degree sufficient to melt the former but not the latter.

elision (ė lizh′ ŭn) [L. *ēlīsio -ōnem* (ELIDE)], *n.* The suppression of a letter or syllable for the sake of euphony, metre, etc.; the suppression of a passage in a book or a discourse.

elisor (e lī′ zôr), *n.* (*Law*) A sheriff's substitute for selecting a jury.

élite (ā lēt′) [F., from L. *ēlecta,* fem. of *ēlectus,* ELECT], *n.* The pick, the flower, the best part.

elixir (ė lik′ sėr) [med. L., from Arab. *al-iksīr* (*al,* the, Gr. *xērion,* dry powder for wounds)], *n.* The alchemists' liquor for transmuting metals into gold; a potion for prolonging life, usu. called **elixir vitæ** or **elixir of life**; a cordial, a sovereign remedy; *the essential principle or quintessence; *a distillation or concentrated tincture.

Elizabethan (ė liz ȧ bē′ thȧn), *a.* Pertaining esp. to Queen Elizabeth I or her time; in the style characterizing the literature, architecture, dress, etc., of her time. *n.* A personage or writer of that time.

elk (elk) [A.-S. *elh,* elch (cp. Icel. *elgr.* O.H.G. *elaho,* L. *alces,* Gr. *alkē*)], *n.* The largest animal of the deer family, *Alces malchis,* a native of northern Europe and of North America, where it is called the moose; applied also to the wapiti, *Cervus Canadensis,* and the eland. **Irish elk:** An extinct animal, *Cervus megaceros.* **elk-nut,** *n.* The buffalo nut, *Hamiltonia oleifera.* **Elks,** *n.pl.* A fraternal society.

ell (el) [A.-S. *eln* (cp. Dut. *el,* G. *elle,* Goth. *aleina,* Swed. *aln,* Gr. *ōlenē,* L. *ulna,* whence F. *aune*)], *n.* A measure of length, varying in different countries, for measuring cloth; the (obsolete) English ell is 45 in. **give him an inch he'll take an ell:** He will take liberties if possible. **ell-wand,** *n.* A measuring rod an ell long; (*Sc.*) the belt of Orion.

ellagic (ė lăj′ ik) [F. *ellagique,* from *ellag,* anagram of galle, gall-nut], *a.* Pertaining to gall-nuts or to gallic acid. **ellagic acid,** *n.* An acid obtained from gallic acid, bezoars, certain barks, etc.

elleborin [HELLEBORE].

ellipse (1) (ė lips′) [L. *ellipsis,* Gr. *elleipsis,* from *elleīpein* (*el-, en,* in, *leipein,* to leave)], *n.* A regular oval, a plane curve of such a form that the sum of two straight lines, drawn from any point in it to two given fixed points called the foci, will always be the same; a conic section formed by a plane intersecting a cone obliquely. **ellipsograph,** *n.* An instrument for describing ellipses. **elliptic, -al** (ė lip′ tik, -ăl), *a.* Pertaining to an ellipse; (*Gram. and Rhet.*) pertaining to ellipsis. **elliptically,** *adv.* **ellipticity** (el ip tis′ i ti), *n.* The quality of being elliptic; the extent to which any ellipse differs from a circle, or any ellipsoid from a sphere.

ellipsis, ellipse (2) (ė lip′ sis, ė lips′) [as prec.], *n.* (*pl.* **-ses**) Omission of one or more words necessary to the complete construction of a sentence; *a mark denoting the omission of one or more words or letters, as in *d——d* for 'damned'; *an ellipse.

ellipsoid (ĕl lip′ soid), *n.* A solid figure of which every plane section through one axis is an ellipse and every other section an ellipse or a circle; *a solid figure produced by the revolution of an ellipse about its axis. *a.* Ellipsoidal. **ellipsoidal** (-soi′ dăl), *a.* Pertaining to an ellipsoid.

elliptic [ELLIPSE].

elm (elm) [A.-S. (*cp.* Icel. *ālmr,* Swed. and Dan. *alm,* G. *ulm,* L. *ulmus*)], *n.* A tree of the genus

Ulmus; the common English elm, *U. campestris*. ***elmen**, *a*. Pertaining to the elm. **elmy**, *a*.

Elmo's, St. Elmo's fire (el′ mōz fīr) [perh. corr. of *Helena*, sister of Castor and Pollux, or after It. *Elmo* or *Ermo*, *St. Erasmus*, a Syrian martyr of the 3rd cent.], *n*. The corposant.

elocution (el ō-, e lō kū′ shūn) [L. *ēlocūtio -ōnem*, from *ēloquī* (*ō-*, *loquī*, to speak)], *n*. The art, style, or manner of speaking or reading; effective oral delivery; *eloquence, oratory; *rhetoric, literary expression; appropriate language in speaking or writing. **elocutionary**, *a*. **elocutionist**, *n*.

eloge (ā lōzh′) [F. *éloge*, L. *ēlogium*, a short saying (Gr. *logos*, a saying, a word), confused with *eulogium*, EULOGY], *n*. An encomium, a panegyric, esp. a discourse in honour of a deceased person.

Elohim (ė lō′ him) [Heb. *elōhim*, pl. used in sing. sense, God], *n*. The ordinary name of God in the Hebrew Scriptures. **Elohist**, *n*. A Biblical writer or one of the writers of parts of the Hexateuch, where the word *Elohim* is habitually used for *Yahveh*, Jehovah. **Elohistic** (el ō his′ tik), *a*.

***eloin** (ė loin′) [O.F. *esloignier* (F. *éloigner*), late L. *exlongāre*, *ēlongāre*, as foll.], *v.t.* To remove; to remove or seclude (oneself); to carry off; (*Law*) to remove beyond the jurisdiction of a court or sheriff.

elongate (ē′ long gāt) [late L. *ēlongātus*, p.p. of *ēlongāre*, to remove (*ō-*, *longus*, long)], *v.t.* To extend; to make longer; *to remove to a distance. *v.i.* To grow longer; (*Bot.*) to increase in length, to taper; *to depart; to recede. *a*. Lengthened, extended; (*Bot. and Zool.*) very slender in proportion to length. **elongation** (-gā′ shūn), *n*. The act of lengthening or extending; the state of being elongated; a prolongation, an extension; (*Astron.*) the angular distance of a planet from the sun or of a satellite from its primary.

elope (ė lōp′) [A.-F. *aloper*, perh. from a M.E. *alope* or *ilope*, p.p. of *aleapen* or *leapen*, to LEAP (cp. the later M.Dut. *ontlōpen* and G. *entlaufen*)], *v.i.* To run away with a lover, with a view to clandestine marriage, or a paramour in defiance of social or moral restraint; to run away in a clandestine manner, to abscond. **elopement**, *n*.

eloquence (el′ ō kwėns) [F. *éloquence*, L. *ēloquentia*, *ēloquens -ntem*, pres.p. of *ēloquī* (E-, *loquī*, to speak)], *n*. Fluent, powerful, and appropriate verbal expression, esp. of emotional ideas; eloquent language; rhetoric. **eloquent**, *a*. Having the power of expression in fluent, vivid, and appropriate, language; full of expression, feeling, or interest. **eloquently**, *adv*.

else (els) [A.-S. *elles*, gen. sing. used as adv. (cp. O.H.G. *elles*, *alles*, also L. *alius*, other)], *adv*. Besides, in addition, other; instead; otherwise, in the other case, if not. **elsewhere**, *adv*. In or to some other place.

elsin (el′ sin) [perh. from M.Dut. *elssene* (Dut. *els*), cp. AWL], *n*. (*Sc. and North.*) An awl.

elucidate (ė loo′ si dāt) [late L. *ēlūcidātus*, p.p. of *ēlūcidāre* (*ō-*, *lūcidus*, bright)], *v.t.* To make lucid, throw light on; to render intelligible; to explain. **elucidation** (-dā′ shūn), *n*. **elucidative**, *a*. **elucidator**, *n*. **elucidatory**, *a*.

***elucubration** [LUCUBRATION].

elude (ė lood′) [L. *ēlūdere* (E-, *lūdere*, to play, p.p. *lūsus*)], *v.t.* To escape from by artifice or dexterity; to evade, to dodge, to shirk; to remain undiscovered or unexplained by; to baffle (search or inquiry); *to delude. ***eludible**, *a*. **elusion**, *n*. **elusive**, *a*. **elusively**, *adv*. **elusiveness**, *n*. **elusory**, *a*.

Elul (ē′ lŭl) [Heb. *ālal*, to reap], *n*. The sixth month of the Jewish ecclesiastical, and the twelfth of their civil year, beginning with the new moon of our September.

***elutriate** (ė loo′ tri āt) [L. *ēlutriātus*, p.p. of *ēlutriāre*, to wash out], *v.t.* To purify by straining or washing so as to separate the lighter and the heavier particles; to decant liquid from. ***elutriation** (-ā′ shūn), *n*.

elvan (el′ vȧn) [etym. doubtful (perh. Corn. *elven*)], *n*. Intrusive igneous rock penetrating sedimentary strata in Cornwall, Devon, and Ireland; a vein or dike of this. **elvanite**, *n*. **elvanitic** (-nit′ ik), *a*.

elver (el′ vėr) [EELFARE], *n*. A young eel, especially a young conger.

elvish (el′ vish), *a*. Pertaining to elves; elfish; mischievous. ***elvish-marked**, *a*. Marked by the fairies. **elvishly**, *adv*.

Elysium (ė liz′ i ŭm, -lizh′ i ŭm) [L., from Gr. *Ēlusion* (*pedion*), the plain of the blessed], *n*. The abode of the souls of Greek heroes after death; (*fig.*) a place or state of perfect happiness. **Elysian**, *a*. **the Elysian Fields**: The Greek Paradise.

elytron (el′ i trŏn) [Gr. *elutron*, a sheath, from *eluein*, to roll round], *n*. (*pl.* **-tra**) One of the horny sheaths which constitute the anterior wings of beetles; (*Anat.*) the vagina. **elytriform** (ė lit′ ri fôrm), *a*.

Elzevir (el′ zė vēr) [name of a celebrated family of printers, of Amsterdam (1595–1680)], *n*. A book printed by the Elzevirs. *a*. Printed by the Elzevirs; pertaining to or resembling the type used by them.

em (em), *n*. (*Print.*) The letter *m*; the square of the body of any size of type, used as the unit of measurement for printed matter; a printers' general measure of 12 points or one-sixth of an inch.

'em (ėm) [M.E. *hem*], *pron*. A colloquial contraction of THEM.

em- [EN-, before *b*, *p*, and sometimes *m*], *pref*. As in *embank*, *empanoply*.

emaciate (ė mā′ shi āt) [L. *ēmaciātus*, p.p. of *ēmaciāre* (E-, *maciēs*, leanness, from *macer*, lean)], *v.t.* To cause to lose flesh or become lean; to reduce to leanness, to impoverish (soil, etc.). **v.i.* To waste or pine away. **emaciation** (ė mās i ā′ shūn), *n*.

emanate (em′ ȧ nāt) [L. *ēmānātus*, p.p. of *ēmānāre*], *v.i.* To issue or flow as from a source, to originate; to proceed (from). **emanation** (-nā′ shūn), *n*. The act of emanating from something, as from a source; that which emanates, an efflux, an effluence; the theory that all things are outflowings from the essence of God; any product of this process. **emanative** (em′-), *a*.

emancipate (ė măn′ si pāt) [L. *ēmancipātus*, p.p. of *ēmancipāre* (E-, *mancipāre*, to transfer property, from *manceps*, from *manus*, hand, *capere*, to take)], *v.t.* To release from bondage, slavery, oppression, or legal, social, or moral restraint; to set free, to liberate; (*Roman Law*) to liberate from parental authority. **emancipation** (-pā′ shūn), *n*. The releasing from slavery, oppression, restraint, or legal disabilities; the state of being freed from any bond or restraint. **emancipationist**, *n*. An advocate of emancipation of slaves. **emancipator**, *n*. **emancipatory**, *a*. **emancipist**, *n*. (*Austral. hist.*) A convict who had served his term.

emarginate (ė mar′ ji nāt) [L. *ēmarginātus*, p.p. of *ēmargināre* (E-, *margināre*, to furnish with a border, from *margo -ginis*, MARGIN)], *v.t.* To take away the edge or margin of; (*Opt.*) to emphasize the contour lines of (a microscopic object embedded in jelly) through unequal refraction. **emarginate** (-nȧt), **-ginated** (-nā tėd), *a*. With the margin notched; (*Bot.*) notched at the apex. **emargination** (-nā′ shūn), *n*.

emasculate (ė măs′ kū lāt) [L. *ēmasculātus*, p.p. of *ēmasculāre* (E-, *masculus*, male)], *v.t.* To castrate; to deprive of masculine strength or vigour; to make effeminate, to weaken; to deprive (as language) of force or energy; to enfeeble (a literary work) by undue expurgation or excision; to remove coarse expressions from a literary production. *a*. (-lȧt) Castrated; enfeebled, effeminate, weak. **emasculation** (-lā′ shūn), *n*. **emasculative**, *a*. **emasculatory**, *a*.

***embale** (em bāl′) [EM-, BALE (2)], *v.t.* To make up in a pack or bale.

embalm (em bam′) [F. *embaumer*], *v.t.* To preserve (as a body) from putrefaction by means of spices and aromatic drugs; to imbue with sweet scents; (*fig.*) to preserve from oblivion. **embalmer,** *n.* **embalmment,** *n.*

embank (em băngk), *v.t.* To confine or defend with a bank or banks, dikes, masonry, etc. **embankment,** *n.* The act or process of embanking; a bank or stone structure for confining a river, etc.; a raised mound or bank for carrying a road, etc.

***embar** (em bar′) [F. *embarrer* (EM-, *barre*, BAR (1))], *v.t.* To shut in, confine, imprison; to hinder, to stop; (*Law*) to forbid, to bar; to put under embargo.

***embarcation** [EMBARKATION].

embargo (em bar′ gō) [Sp., from *embargar*, to arrest, hinder, prob. from a late L. *imbarricāre* (*im-*, IN-, *barra*, BAR (1))], *n.* A prohibition by authority upon the departure of vessels from ports under its jurisdiction; a complete suspension of foreign commerce or of a particular branch of foreign trade; a hindrance, check, impediment. *v.t.* To lay an embargo upon; to seize for purposes of State; to requisition, seize, confiscate; to prohibit, to forbid. ***embargement,** *n.* A putting under embargo.

embark (em bark′) [F. *embarquer*, late L. *imbarcāre* (*im-*, IN-, *barca*, BARK (3))], *v.t.* To put on board ship; (*fig.*) to invest (as money) in any business. *v.i.* To go on board ship; (*fig.*) to engage or enter (upon any undertaking). **embarkation** (-kā′ shŭn), *n.* The act of putting or going on board a ship or vessel; *a cargo, anything that is embarked; *a vessel, a craft. ***embarkment,** *n.*

embarrass (em băr′ ȧs) [F. *embarrasser*, from *embarras*, conn. with *embarrer*, to EMBAR], *v.t.* To encumber, hamper, entangle, impede, hinder; to confuse, perplex, disconcert; to complicate, render difficult; to involve in pecuniary difficulties. *n.* (*Am.*) A place where navigation is rendered difficult by accumulations of drift-wood, etc. **embarrassing,** *a.* Causing embarrassment. **embarrassingly,** *adv.* **embarrassment,** *n.* Perplexity of mind, discomposure, uneasiness, perturbation arising from bashfulness; confusion or intricacy of affairs; pecuniary difficulties; an impediment, a hindrance.

***embase** (em bās′), *v.t.* To lower; (*fig.*) to debase, degrade, humiliate; to impair, to corrupt. ***embasement,** *n.*

embassy (em′ bȧ si) [O.F. *ambassée*, late L. *ambactiāta*, *ambasciāta*, orig. fem. p.p. of *ambactiāre*, to go on a mission (see AMBASSADOR)], *n.* The function, office, or mission of an ambassador; the body of persons sent as ambassadors; an ambassador and his suite; the official residence of an ambassador; *the message sent by an ambassador. ***embassade** (em′ bȧ sād), *n.* Embassy. ***embassador** (em băs′ ȧ dȯr), *n.* An ambassador. ***embassadorial** (-dôr′ i ȧl), *a.* ***embassadress,** *n.* ***embassage** (em′ bȧ sȧj), *n.* Embassy.

***embathe** (em bā*th*′), *v.t.* To imbathe, immerse, suffuse.

embattle (1) (em bătl′) [O.F. *embataillier*], *v.t* To array in order of battle; to prepare for battle; (*fig.*) to fortify. *v.i.* To be drawn up in battle array.

embattle (2) (em bătl′), [BATTLEMENT], *v.t.* To furnish with battlements.

embay (em bā′), *v.t.* To enclose (a vessel) in a bay, to landlock; to force (a vessel) into a bay; to shut in, confine, enclose, surround. **embayment,** *n.*

embed (em bed′), *v.t.* (*past & p.p.* **embedded**) To lay as in a bed; to set firmly in surrounding matter; to enclose firmly (said of the surrounding matter). ***embedment,** *n.*

embellish (em bel′ ish) [O.F. *embellir* (EM-, *bel*, L. *bellus*, handsome)], *v.t.* To beautify, to adorn; to add incidents or imaginary accompaniments so as to heighten a narrative. **embellishment,** *n.*

ember (1) (em′ bėr) [A.-S., *ǣmerge* (cp. Dan. *emmer*, O.H.G. *eimurja*)], *n.* A live coal, an unextinguished brand; (*pl.*) smouldering remnants of a fire.

ember (2) (em′ bėr) [A.-S. *ymbren*, prob. corr. of *ymbryne*, a period, revolution (*ymb*, about, *ryne*, running)], *n.* An anniversary, a recurring time or season. **Ember days,** *n.pl.* Certain days set apart for fasting and prayer; the Wednesday, Friday, and Saturday next following the first Sunday in Lent, Whit-Sunday, Holy Cross Day (14 Sept.), and St. Lucy's Day (13 Dec.). **Ember-tide,** *n.* The season at which Ember days occur. **Ember weeks,** *n.pl.* The weeks in which the Ember days fall. ***emberings,** *n.pl.* The Ember days; called also **embering days.**

ember-goose (em′ bėr-goos′) [Norw. *emmer-gaas*], *n.* The northern diver or loon, *Colymbus glacialis*, also called **ember-diver.**

embezzle (ėm bez′ ėl) [A.-F. *enbeseler*, O.F. *besillier*, to maltreat, to ravage, prob. from *bes-*, late L. *bis-*, a pejorative pref. (cp. O.F. *besil*, ill-treatment, torture), influenced by L. *imbecillāre*, to weaken], *v.t.* To appropriate fraudulently what is committed to one's care; *to squander, waste, dissipate. *v.i.* To commit embezzlement. **embezzlement,** *n.* **embezzler,** *n.*

embitter (em bit′ ėr), *v.t.* To make bitter, or more bitter; to render harder or more distressing, to aggravate; to add poignancy or sharpness to; to exasperate. **embitterment,** *n.*

***emblaze** (em blāz′), *v.t.* To set in a blaze, to kindle; (*fig.*) to light up, to cause to glitter; to emblazon, to set forth by heraldic devices; to glorify.

emblazon (em blā′ zȯn), *v.t.* To blazon; to adorn with heraldic figures or armorial designs; to decorate; to make brilliant; to celebrate, to render illustrious. **emblazoner,** *n.* **emblazoning,** *n.* Emblazonment. **emblazonment,** *n.* The act or art of blazoning; blazonry. **emblazonry** [BLAZONRY].

emblem (em′ blėm) [L. and Gr. *emblēma*, from *emballein* (EM-, *ballein*, to throw)], *n.* *Inlaid or mosaic work; a symbolical figure; a picture, object, or representation of an object symbolizing some other thing, class, action, or quality, as a crown for royalty or a balance for justice; a symbol, a type, a personification; an heraldic device. *v.t.* To symbolize, to represent or show forth by an emblem. **emblema** (em blē′ mȧ), *n.* (*usu. in pl.* **-mata**) Figures with which the ancients decorated golden, silver, and copper vessels, and which could be fixed on or taken off at pleasure. **emblematic, -ical** (-măt′ ik, -ȧl), *a.* **emblematically,** *adv.* **emblematist** (em blem′ ȧ tist), *n.* A writer of allegories or inventor of emblems. **emblematize,** *v.t.* To represent by or as an emblem; to symbolize. **emblematology** (-tol′ ȯ ji), *n.*

emblement (em′ blė mėnt) [O.F. *emblaement*, from *emblaer* (F, *emblaver*), to sow with corn, med. L. *imbladāre* (IN-, *bladum*, L. *ablatum*, the gathered-in harvest, hence corn)], *n.* (*usu. in pl.*) (*Law*) The produce of land sown or planted; growing crops annually produced by the cultivator's labour, which belong to the tenant, though his lease may terminate before harvest, and in the event of his death fall to his executors; sometimes extended to the natural products of the soil.

emblossom (em blos′ ȯm), *v.t.* To cover with blossoms.

embody (em bod′ i), *v.t.* To incarnate or invest with a material body; to express in a concrete form; to be a concrete expression of, to form into a united whole; to incorporate, include. **v.i.* To unite, coalesce, come into a body. **embodier,** *n.* **embodiment,** *n.*

embog (em bog′), *v.t.* To plunge into a bog; to encumber in or as in a bog.

***embogue** (em bōg′) [Sp. *embocar* (EM-, *boca*,

mouth)], *v.i.* To disembogue, to discharge (as a river into the sea).

embolden (em bōl′ dėn), *v.t.* To give boldness to; to encourage.

embolism (em′ bȯ lizm) [L. *embolismus*, late Gr. *embolismos*, from *embolē*, a throwing in (EM-, *ballein*, to throw)], *n.* An intercalation; the insertion of days, months, or years, in the calendar in order to produce regularity; anything intercalated, such as a period of time, a prayer in the order of public worship, etc.; (*Path.*) partial or total blocking-up of a blood-vessel by a clot of blood, occasioning apoplexy or paralysis, and in many cases death. ***embolismic** (liz′ mik), *a.*

embolus (em′ bō lůs) [as prec.], *n.* A thing inserted in another and moving therein, as a piston; (*Path.*) the clot which causes embolism.

embonpoint (an bon pwan′) [F., orig. *en bon point*, in good condition], *n.* Plumpness of person or figure, esp. in women. *a.* Plump, well-nourished; stout; (*euphem.*), fat.

emborder (em bôr′ dėr), *v.t.* To adorn or furnish with a border.

***embosom** (em buz′ ům), *v.t.* To place or hold in or as in the bosom of anything; to enclose, surround; to embrace, to cherish.

emboss (em bos′) [O.F. *embosser* (EM-, *bosse*, BOSS (1))], *v.t.* To engrave or mould in relief; to decorate with bosses or raised figures; to cause to stand out in relief. **embossment,** *n.*

embouchure (an boo shoor′) [F., from *emboucher*, to put in the mouth, to discharge by a mouth (EM-, *bouche*, mouth)], *n.* The mouth of a river, etc.; (*Mus.*) the mouthpiece of a wind instrument; the shaping of the lips to the mouthpiece.

***embound** (em bound′), *v.t.* To hem or shut in, to enclose.

***embow** (em bō′), *v.t.* To bend, to curve like a bow; to arch, to vault.

embowel (em bow′ ėl) [O.F. *enboweler* (EM-, *bouel*, BOWEL)], *v.t.* To disembowel; *to put or convey into, to enclose, to embed. **embowelment,** *n.* The act of disembowelling; the inward parts of anything.

embower (em bou′ ėr), *v.t.* To enclose in or as in a bower; to shelter, to surround (as with trees or shrubs).

embox (em boks′), *v.t.* To set or shut in or as in a box.

embrace (1) (em brās′) [O.F. *embracer* (EM-, *brace*, L. *bracchia*, pl., the arms)], *v.t.* To enfold in the arms; to clasp and hold fondly; to clasp or twine round (as a creeping plant); to enclose, encircle, surround; to include, contain, comprise; to receive, adopt, accept eagerly; to take in with the eye, to comprehend; *to have sexual intercourse with. *v.i.* To join in an embrace; * to join in sexual intercourse. *n.* A clasping in the arms; sexual intercourse; a hostile struggle or grapple. **embraceable,** *a.* **embracement,** *n.* **embracer** (1), *n.* **embracingly,** *adv.* **embracingness,** *n.* **embracive,** *a.*

***embrace** (2) (em brās′), *v.t.* To fasten or fix with a brace.

embracer (2) (em brā′ sėr) [O.F. *embraceor*, from *embraser*, to set on fire (EM-, *braise*, hot charcoal)], *n.* (*Law*) One who endeavours to corrupt a jury by embracery. **embracery,** *n.* (*Law*) An attempt to influence a jury corruptly.

embranchment (em branch′ mėnt), *n.* A branching out; that part of the tree where the branches diverge; a ramification.

embrangle (em brăng′ gėl), *v.t.* To entangle, to complicate; to confuse, perplex. **embranglement,** *n.*

embrasure (em brā′ zhůr) [M.F., from *embraser* (F. *ébraser*), to splay or chamfer (EM-, *braser*, to splay or chamfer)], *n.* An opening in a parapet or wall to fire guns through; the inward enlargement, bevelling, or splaying of the sides of a window or door.

***embrave** (em brāv′), *v.t.* To inspire with courage, to embolden; to adorn, beautify, embellish.

embreathe (em brēth′), *v.t.* To breathe into, inspire, to breathe in, inhale.

embrocate (em′ brȯ kāt) [med. L. *embrocātus*, p.p. of *embrocāre*, from *embrocha*, Gr. *embrochē*, from *embrechein* (EM-, *brechein*, to wet)], *v.t.* To moisten, bathe, or foment (as a diseased part of the body). **embrocation** (-kā′ shůn), *n.* A preparation for application by rubbing or painting; the act of bathing or fomenting; the liquid used.

embroglio [IMBROGLIO].

embroider (em broi′ dėr). [A.-F. *enbroyder* (O.F., EM-, *broder*, prob. rel. to *bord*, edge, border)], *v.t.* To ornament with figures or designs in needlework; to variegate, to diversify; (*fig.*) to embellish with additions, esp. a narrative with exaggerations or fiction. **embroiderer,** *n.* **embroidery,** *n.* The act, process, or art of embroidering; ornamentation done with the needle; the fabric ornamented; additional embellishment; exaggeration or fiction added to a narrative.

embroil (em broil′) [F. *embrouiller* (EM-, *brouiller*, see BROIL (1))], *v.t.* To throw into confusion; to entangle, to confuse; to involve (some one) in a quarrel or contention (with another). **embroilment,** *n.*

embrown (em broun′), *v.t.* To make brown; to darken, obscure.

embrue [IMBRUE].

embryo (em′ bri ō) [med. L. *embryo -ōnis*, Gr. *embruon* (EM-, *bruon*, neut. of *bruōn*, pres.p. of *bruein*, to be full of a thing, to swell with it)], *n.* (*pl.* **-os**) The unborn offspring; the germ, the undeveloped fœtus; the vitalized germ; the rudimentary plant in the seed after fertilization; the beginning or first stage of anything. *a.* In the germ, undeveloped; rudimentary. **in embryo:** In the first or earliest stage: in a rudimentary or undeveloped state. **embryonic** (-on′ ik), *a.*

embryo- [as prec.], *comb. form.* Of or pertaining to the embryo or embryos. **embryectomy** (em bri ek′ tȯ mi) [Gr. *ektomē*, a cutting out (*ek-*, out, *temnein*, to cut)], *n.* (*Surg.*) The operation of removing the fœtus through an incision in the abdomen. **embryoctony** (-ok′ tȯ ni) [Gr. *embruoktonos* (*ktenein*, to kill)], *n.* (*Surg.*) The destruction of the fœtus in the womb. **embryogenesis** (-jen′ ė sis), **embryogeny** (-oj′ ė ni) [GENESIS], *n.* The formation of an embryo. **embryogony** (-og′ ȯ ni) [Gr. *-gonia*, production], *n.* The formation of an embryo. **embryology** (-ol′ ȯ ji) [-LOGY], *n.* The science of the embryo and the formation and development of organisms. **embryological** (loj′ ik ål), *a.* **embryologist** (-ol′ ȯ jist), *n.* **embryotomy** (-ot′ ȯ mi) [-TOMY], *n.* A cutting up of an embryo or fœtus in the uterus.

embus (em bŭs′), *v.t.* (*past & p.p.* **embussed**) (*Mil.*) To put troops into omnibuses for transport. *v.i.* (Troops) to mount an omnibus or lorry.

***eme** (ēm) [A.-S. *ēam* (? maternal) uncle (cp. Dut. *oom*, O.H.G. *ôheim*, G. *oheim*, *ohm*], *n.* An uncle; a neighbour, friend, gossip.

emend (ė mend′) [L. *ēmendāre* (E-, *menda*, a fault)], *v.t.* To correct, remove faults; to improve (as the result of criticism). **emendable,** *a.* **emendals,** *n.pl.* A term in old accounts, signifying the sum total in the bank or in stock (orig. prob., set aside for making up losses), still used in the books of the Society of the Inner Temple. **emendation** (-dā′ shůn), *n.* **emendator** (ē′ mėn dā tȯr), *n.* **emendatory** (ė men′ dȧ tȯr i), *a.*

emerald (em′ ėr åld) [O.F. *emeraude*, *esmeralde*, L. *smaragdum -dus*, Gr. *smaragdos* (Sansk. *asmā*, a stone, *marakata*, emerald)], *n.* A variety of beryl, distinguished by its beautiful green colour; the colour of this; (*Her.*) the green colour in coat armour, vert; (*Print.*) old name for a small type, between nonpareil and minion. *a.* Of a bright-green colour. **emerald-copper,** *n.* Dioptase, an emerald-green crystallized mineral. **emerald-green,** *n.* A light-green pigment, produced from arsenate of copper. **the Emerald Isle,** *n.* Ireland.

emerge (ė mĕrj') [L. *ēmergere* (E-, *mergere*, to dip)], *v.i.* To rise up out of anything in which a thing has been immersed or sunk; to appear in sight (from below the horizon or from a place of concealment); to appear, to come out (as facts on an enquiry); to crop up, become apparent; to issue from a state of depression, suffering, or obscurity. **emergence,** *n.* **emergent,** *a.* Emerging. **emergent year,** *n.* The epoch or date from which any people begin to compute their time.

emergency (ė mĕr' jėn si) [late L. *ēmergentia*, as prec.], *n.* A sudden occurrence or situation demanding immediate action; a crisis. **emergency-man,** *n.* One employed in a pressing necessity; a bailiff's officer temporarily employed on land in Ireland from which tenants had been evicted. **emergency exit,** *n.* (*Theat., etc.*) A door specially provided for exit in case of fire or other contingency. **emergency landing,** *n.* (*Aviat.*) A forced descent due to engine trouble, etc.

emeritus (e mer' i tŭs) [L., p.p. of *ēmerēri* (E-, *merēri*, to earn)], *a.* A term applied in ancient Rome to one who had served his time and retired from the public service; having served one's term of office (used esp. of professors). *n.* (*pl.* **-ti**) One who has served his time and retired from any office.

emerods (em' ėr ods) [HÆMORRHOIDS], *n.pl.* (I *Sam.* v. 6–7) Hæmorrhoids.

emersion (ė mĕr' shŭn), *n.* The action of emerging; (*Astron.*) the reappearance of a heavenly body from behind another at the end of an eclipse or occultation.

emery (em' ėr i) [F. *émeri*, M.F. *emeril*, *esmeril*, It. *smeriglio* (or late L. *smericulum*), Gr. *smēris*], *n.* A coarse variety of corundum, of extreme hardness, and black or greyish-black colour, used for polishing hard substances. **emery-cloth, emery-paper,** *n.* Cloth or paper brushed with liquid glue and dusted with powdered emery. **emery-wheel,** *n.* A wheel faced with emery, used for grinding and polishing metal articles.

emetic (ė met' ik) [L. *emeticus*, Gr. *emetikos*, from *emeein*, to vomit], *a.* Inducing vomiting. *n.* A preparation for causing vomiting. **emetically,** *adv.* **emesis** (em' ė sis), *n.* (*Path.*) The action of vomiting. **emetine,** *n.* An alkaloid obtained from ipecacuanha, of which it forms the chief active principle. **emetocathartic** (em' ė tŏ kă thar' tik) [CATHARTIC], *a.* Producing vomiting and purging. **emetology** (-tol' ŏ ji) [-LOGY], *n.*

émeute (ė mut') [F., from *émouvoir*, L. *ēmovēre* (E-, *movēre*, to move)], *n.* A seditious or revolutionary outbreak; a riot or popular disturbance.

emiction (ė mik' shŭn) [L. *ēmictio*, from *ēmict-*, p.p. stem of *ēmingere* (E-, *mingere*, to make water)], *n.* (*Physiol.*) The discharge of urine; urine. **emictory,** *a.* and *n.*

emigrate (em' i grāt) [L. *ēmigrātus*, p.p. of *ēmigrāre* (E-, *migrāre*, to MIGRATE)], *v.i.* To leave one's country in order to settle in another; (*colloq.*) to leave one's place of abode for another. *v.t.* To send emigrants out of the country. **emigrant,** *a.* Emigrating; pertaining to emigration. *n.* One who emigrates. **emigration** (-grā' shŭn), *n.* **emigrationist,** *n.* An advocate for or promoter of emigration. **emigratory** (em i grā' tŏr i), *a.*

emigré (ā' mē grā), *n.* An emigrant, esp. one of the royalists who left France at the time of the French Revolution.

eminent (em' i nėnt) [L. *ēminens -ntem*, pres.p. of *ēminēre*, to stand out, project (E-, *minæ*, threats, projections)], *a.* Rising above others; high, lofty, prominent; (*fig.*) distinguished; remarkable (of services, qualities, etc.). **eminence, -nency,** *n.* Loftiness, height; a part rising above the rest, or projecting above the surface; high rank, superiority; distinction, celebrity; *supreme degree; a title of honour applied to cardinals. **eminence grise** (ā' mi nans grēz), [F.], *n.* A man in the background exercising power unofficially. ***to have the eminence of:** To be better than. **eminently,** *adv.*

emir (ė mēr') [Arab. *amīr*, AMEER (*amara*, he commanded)], *n.* A Saracen or Arab prince, chieftain, governor, or commander; a title given to the descendants of Mohammed through Fatima his daughter.

emissary (em' i sȧr i) [L. *ēmissārius*, from *ēmiss-*, p.p. stem of *ēmittere*, to EMIT], *n.* A messenger or agent, esp. one sent on a secret or odious mission; *an outlet for water; (*Physiol.*) an excretory vessel. *a.* Of or pertaining to a messenger or agent; serving as an outlet.

emission (ė mish' ŭn) [L. *emissio*, as prec.], *n.* The act or process of emitting or being emitted; the thing given off or out; the act of issuing bank-notes, etc.; the number and value of the notes, etc., sent out; (*Radio.*) a stream of electrons radiated from the filament of a thermionic valve; radiating power. **theory of emission:** The theory of Newton that light consists of particles emitted by luminous bodies. **emissive, emissory,** *a.* **emissivity** (em i siv' i ti), *n.*

emit (ė mit') [L. *ēmittere* (E-, *mittere*, to send)], *v.t.* To give out, to send forth; to give vent to, to issue, to discharge; to print and send into circulation (as bank-notes). **emitter,** *n.* (*Elec.*) An electrode of a transistor.

emmarble (ė marbl'), *v.t.* To turn into marble; to decorate with marble.

emmenagogue (ė men' a gog) [Gr. *emmēna*, menses of women, *agōgos*, drawing forth], *n.* (*Med.*) A medicine that promotes the catamenial flow. **emmenology** (-nol' ŏ ji) [-LOGY], *n.*

emmet (em' ėt) [A.-S. *æmete*, see ANT], *n.* An ant, a pismire.

emollient (ė mol' i ėnt) [L. *ēmolliens -ntem*, pres.p. of *ēmollīre*, to soften (E-, *mollis*, soft)], *a.* Softening, relaxing; making soft or supple. *n.* A substance which softens the part to which it is applied, and soothes and diminishes irritation; (*fig.*) anything intended to soothe or comfort.

emolument (ė mol' ū mėnt) [O.F., from L. *ēmolumentum*, profit, from *ēmolere* (E-, *molere*, to grind) or *ēmōlīrī* (E-, *mōlīrī*, to work)], *n.* The profit arising from any office or employment; remuneration; *gain, profit. **emolumentary,** *a.*

emotion (ė mō' shŭn) [L. *ēmōtio -ōnem*, from *ēmovēre* (E-, *movēre*, to move)], *n.* Agitation of the mind; a state of excited feeling of any kind, whether of pain or pleasure; excitement. **emotional,** *a.* Pertaining to emotion; easily affected with emotion. ***emotionalism,** *n.* **emotionalist,** *n.* **emotionality** (-năl' i ti), *n.* **emotionally,** *adv.* **emotionless,** *a.* **emotive,** *a.* Emotional; tending to produce emotion. **emotively,** *adv.*

empacket (em păk' ėt) [F. *empaqueter*], *v.t.* To pack up.

empanel (em păn' ėl), *v.t.* To enter on the list of jurors; to enrol as a jury.

***empanoply** (em păn' ŏ pli), *v.t.* To invest in complete armour.

empathy (em' pȧ thi) [Gr. *empathes*, in a state of emotion], *n.* The capacity for reacting to the experience of, or appreciating things or emotions outside, ourselves; the losing one's identity in, *e.g.*, a work of art.

***empeople** (em pēpl'), *v.t.* To populate; to establish as inhabitants.

emperor (em' pėr ŏr) [O.F. *empereor*, nom. *emperere*, L. *imperātor -ōrem*, from *imperāre*, to command (IM-, *parāre*, to prepare, order)], *n.* The sovereign of an empire; the sovereign of the Holy

Roman Empire; the highest dignity (superior to king). **purple emperor,** *n.* *Apatura iris,* a large and handsome British butterfly. **emperor-moth,** *n.* *Saturnia pavonia,* a large and beautiful British moth. **emperor penguin,** *n.* The large penguin, *Aptenodytes Forsteri.* **emperorship,** *n.* ***empery,** *n.* Sovereignty, empire; the territory of an emperor.

emphasis (em' fă sis) [L., from Gr. (EM-, *phasis,* from *phainein,* to show)], *n.* (*pl.* **-ses**) A particular stress laid upon a word or words, to indicate special significance; force or intensity of expression, language, feeling, gesture, etc.; accent, stress, prominence, sharp definition. **emphasize,** *v.t.* To pronounce with emphasis; to lay stress upon; to make more distinct, prominent, or impressive. **emphatic, -ical** (em făt' ik, -ăl), *a.* Bearing emphasis or special stress; accentuated, forcible, striking; positive, earnest. **emphatically,** *adv.*

emphractic (em frăk' tik) [Gr. *emphraktikos,* from *emphrattein* (EM-, *phrattein,* to block)], *a.* (*Med.*) Having the quality of closing the pores of the skin. *n.* An emphractic medicine.

emphysema (em fi sē' mă) [Gr. *emphusēma,* from *emphusaein* (EM-, *phusaein,* to blow, puff)], *n.* (*Med.*) The pressure of air causing distension in the cellular tissue. **emphysematous,** *a.*

empire (em' pīr) [O.F., from L. *imperium,* conn. with *imperāre* (see EMPEROR)], *n.* Supreme and extensive dominion; absolute power; the region over which an emperor rules; a State in which the sovereign is an emperor; (*fig.*) supreme control, rule, sway. *a.* Indicating the style of costume and furniture of the First or Second French Empire. **British Empire:** Former name of the British Commonwealth of Nations, the association of self-governing dominions, colonies, dependencies, etc. acknowledging the sovereignty of the King or Queen of Great Britain, Ireland and the Dominions beyond the seas. **Eastern Empire:** The Greek or Byzantine Empire formed by the division of the Roman Empire at the death of Theodosius the Great. **the Empire:** the British Empire; the first Napoleonic Empire (1804–15); the Holy Roman Empire. **the Second Empire:** (*Hist.*) The empire of Napoleon III (1852–70). **Western Empire:** The Latin Empire, the part of the Roman Empire which fell to Honorius at the death of his father Theodosius. **Empire Day, Commonwealth Day:** A British celebration held annually on May 24, Queen Victoria's birthday. **empire gown,** *n.* A high-waisted gown after the style of those worn during the first French Empire. **Empire Marketing Board:** A body set up to foster the employment in the Mother Country of the produce of the Dominions. **empire preference,** *n.* (*Pol.*) The policy of granting favourable tariffs to countries within the British empire. **Empire State:** (*U.S.A.*) The State of New York.

empiric (em pir' ik) [F. *empirique,* L. *empīricus,* Gr. *empeirikos,* from *empeiros,* experienced (EM-, *peira,* trial)], *a.* Founded on experience or observation, not theory; acting on this; of the nature of a quack, charlatanic; pertaining to quackery. *n.* One who relies solely on experience or observation, esp. a medical practitioner without scientific training; a quack, a charlatan; *one of an ancient medical sect who considered observation and experiment the only true method of obtaining knowledge. **empirical,** *a.* **empirically,** *adv.* **empiricism** (-sizm), *n.* **empiricist,** *n.* ***empiricutic** (em pir i kū' tik) [assim. to PHARMACEUTIC], *a.* (*Shak.*) Empiric. **empirism** (em' pi rizm), *n.* A conclusion attained on empirical grounds; empiricism. **empiristic** (-ris' tik), *a.*

emplacement (em plās' mĕnt), *n.* Location, situation, position; a setting in position; (*Fort.*) a platform for guns.

emplane (em plān'), *v.i.* (*Aviat.*) To go on board an aeroplane. *v.t.* To place in an aeroplane.

employ (em ploi') [O.F. *employer,* L. *implicāre* (IM-, *plicāre,* to fold)], *v.t.* To use, to exercise; to set at work; to keep in one's service; to spend or pass (time, oneself, etc.) in any occupation. *n.* Occupation, business, profession. **in the employ of:** Employed by. **employable,** *a.* **employé** (om ploi' ā, an plwa' ā) [F., p.p. of *employer*], *n.* (*fem.* **-ée**) One who is employed regularly in some task or occupation for salary or wages, an employee. **employee** (em ploi ē'), *n.* **employer,** *n.* **employment,** *n.* The act of employing; the state of being employed; regular occupation, trade, or profession.

emplume (em ploom') [F. *emplumer* (EM-, PLUME)], *v.t.* To adorn with or as with plumes; *to tar and feather.

empoison (em poizn') [F. *empoisonner* (EM-, POISON)], *v.t.* To mix poison with; to envenom; to taint, vitiate, corrupt; to render hostile; *to administer poison to; *to kill with or as with poison. ***empoisonment,** *n.*

emporium (em pôr' i ŭm) [L., from Gr. *emporion,* neut. of *emporios,* commercial, from *emporos,* a passenger, a merchant. (EM-, *poros,* a way)], *n.* (*pl.* **-ia**) A commercial centre; a mart; (*colloq.*) a large shop where many kinds of goods are sold.

empoverish [IMPOVERISH].

empower (em pou' ėr) [EM-, POWER], *v.t.* To authorize; to enable.

empress (em' pres) [O.F. *emperesse,* fem. of *empereor,* EMPEROR], *n.* The consort of an emperor; a female ruler of an empire.

empressement (an pres' man) [F., from *empresser,* to urge, *s'empresser,* to be eager], *n.* Cordiality, goodwill, eagerness.

***emprise** (em prīz') [O.F., orig. fem. of *empris,* p.p. of *emprendre* (EM-, *prendre,* L. *prehendere,* to take)], *n.* An adventurous or chivalrous undertaking. *v.t.* To undertake.

***emption** (emp' shŭn) [L. *emptio -ōnem,* from *emere,* to buy], *n.* The act of buying; a purchase. **emptor,** *n.* A purchaser.

empty (emp' ti) [A.-S. *æmtig,* from *æmetta,* leisure], *a.* Void, containing nothing; devoid (of); vacant, unoccupied; unloaded; destitute, desolate; meaningless, unsubstantial, shadowy; senseless, inane; without intelligence, ignorant; hungry, unsatisfied. *n.* An empty packing-case, truck, barrel, crate, etc. *v.t.* To remove the contents from, to make vacant; to remove from a receptacle (into another); to pour out, discharge. *v.i.* To become empty; to discharge (as a river). **empty-handed,** *a.* Bringing nothing; carrying away nothing. **empty-headed,** *a.* Silly, witless. **empty-hearted,** *a.* Heartless. **emptyings,** *n.pl.* (*Am.*) The lees of beer, cider, etc., used as yeast. **emptier,** *n.* **emptiness,** *n.*

***empurple** (em pĕrpl'), *v.t.* To tinge or colour with purple.

empyema (em pī ē' mă) [G. *empuēma,* from *empueein* (EM-, *pueein,* to suppurate)], *n.* (*Path.*) A collection of pus consequent on pleurisy.

empyrean (em pi rē' ăn) [med. L. *empyræus,* Gr. *empuros,* fiery (EM-, *pur,* fire)], *n.* The highest and purest region of heaven, where the element of fire was supposed by the ancients to exist without any admixture of grosser matter; the upper sky. *a.* Pertaining to the highest heaven or to the upper sky. **empyreal** (em pir' ė ăl), *a.*

empyreuma (em pi roo' mă) [Gr. *empureuma,* from *empureuein,* to set on fire (EM-, *pur,* fire)], *n.* (*pl.* **-ata**) The disagreeable smell and taste produced when animal or vegetable substances in closed vessels are submitted to considerable heat. **empyreumatic, -ical** (-măt' ik, -ăl), *a.* **empyreumatize** (-roo' mă tīz), *v.t.*

emu (ē' mū) [Port. *ema,* ostrich], *n.* A large Australian cursorial bird of the genus *Dromæus,* esp. *D. Novæ-Hollandiæ,* resembling the cassowary but different in having no casque. **emu-wren,** *n.* A small Australian bird, *Stipiturus malachurus,* having the tail feathers loose-webbed, and somewhat resembling those of the emu.

emulate (em′ ū lāt) [L. *æmulātus*, p.p. of *æmulārī*, from *æmulus*, EMULOUS], *v.t.* To try to equal or excel; to rival; to imitate with intent to equal or excel. ***a.** (-lȧt) Ambitious, emulous. **emulation** (-lā′ shŭn), *n.* The act of emulating; ambition to equal or excel the action of others; rivalry, envy, jealousy. **emulative** (em′ ū lā tiv), *a.* **emulatively,** *adv.* **emulator,** *n.* One who emulates; a rival; *a disparager. ***emulatress,** *n.* ***emule,** *v.t.* To emulate.

emulgent (ė mŭl′ jėnt) [L. *ēmulgens -ntem*, pres.p. of *ēmulgēre* (E-, *ēmulgēre*, to milk)], *a.* Milking or draining out; (*Physiol.*) applied to the renal arteries and veins, the ancients assuming that they milked out the serum by means of the kidneys.

emulous (em′ ū lŭs) [L. *æmulus*], *a.* Desirous of equalling or excelling others; engaged in rivalry or competition; desirous of fame or honour; envious, factious, contentious. **emulously,** *adv.* **emulousness,** *n.*

emulsify (ė mŭl′ si fī) [L. *ēmuls-*, p.p. stem of *ēmulgēre*], *v.t.* To convert into an emulsion. **emulsification** (-kā′ shŭn), *n.* **emulsin,** *n.* A neutral fermenting substance found in almonds.

emulsion (ė mŭl′ shŭn) [as prec.], *n.* A colloidal suspension of one liquid in another; (*Phot.*) a light-sensitive substance held in suspension in collodion or gelatine used for coating plates or films. **emulsionize,** *v.t.* **emulsive,** *a.*

emunctory (ė mŭngk′ tȯr i) [L. *ēmunct-*, p.p. stem of *ēmungere*, to wipe the nose], *a.* Serving to wipe the nose; (*Physiol.*) serving to carry noxious or useless particles out of the body. *n.* (*Physiol.*) An excretory duct.

emys (em′ is) [Gr. *emus*], *n.* (*pl.* **emydes** (em′ i dēz)). (*Zool.*) The freshwater tortoise.

en- [F. *en-*, *em-*, L. *in-*, *im-*, in ; also Gr. *en-*, *em-*], *pref.* In, on, into, upon; as in *enambush, encamp, encourage, engulf, enjewel, enslave, enlighten, encomium, energy, enthusiasm.*

-en (1) [A.-S., from O.Teut. *-īnom*], *suf.* Diminutive; as in *chicken, maiden.* (2) [A.-S., from O. Teut. *-inī* (G. *-inn*)], *suf.* Noting the feminine; as in *vixen.* (3) [A.-S., from O.Teut. *-īno-* (cp. Gr. and L. *-ino-*)], *suf.* Pertaining to, made of, of the nature of; as in *earthen, flaxen, golden, woollen.* (4) [A.-S. *-an*, pl. of weak decl.], *suf.* Forming pl.; as in *oxen.* (5) [A.-S. *-nan, -nian*], *suf.* Forming verbs from adjectives: as *deepen, fatten, heighten, moisten, sweeten.* (6) [A.-S. *-en*] *suf.* Forming p.p. of strong verbs; as *bounden, spoken.*

en, *n.* (*Print.*) The unit of measurement for casting-off copy, an en being the average width of a letter.

enable (en a′ bėl), *v.t.* To make able; to authorize, empower (to); to supply with means (to do any act).

enact (en ăkt′), *v.t.* To decree; to pass, as a bill into a law; to represent, act, play; *to accomplish, perform. ***n.** That which is enacted; (*fig.*) a purpose, a resolution. **enacting clauses:** Clauses in a bill which contain new enactments, in contradistinction to declaratory clauses. **enaction,** *n.* **enactive,** *a.* **enactment,** *n.* **enactory,** *a.* ***enacture,** *n.* (*Shak.*) Action, fulfilment.

enallage (en ăl′ ȧ jē) [L., from Gr., conn. with *enallassein* (EN-, *allassein*, to change)], *n.* (*Gram.*) A change of words, or a substitution of one mood, tense, number, case, or gender of the same word for another.

enamel (en ăm′ ėl) [M.E. *enamayl*, O.F. *esmail*, med. L. *smaltum*, from Teut. (*cp.* O.H.G. *smalzjan*, Dut. *smelten*, to SMELT)], *n.* A vitreous, opaque, or semi-transparent material with which metal, porcelain, and other vessels, ornaments, etc., are coated by fusion, for decorative or preservative purposes; any smooth, hard, glossy coating; a lacquer, a varnish, a paint, a cosmetic; the ivory-like substance which covers the surface of the teeth; a bright smooth surface; *gloss, **polish.** *v.t.* (*past and p.p.* **enamelled**) To coat with enamel; to paint, encrust, or inlay with enamel; to form a smooth glossy surface upon; to decorate with various colours. *v.i.* To practise the art of enamelling. **enamelier,** *n.* **enamelist,** *n.*

enamour (ė năm′ ȯr) [O.F. *enamorer*], *v.t.* To captivate, to charm; to inflame with love. **to be enamoured:** To be in love.

enantiosis (ė năn ti ō′ sis) [Gr., from *enantioesthai*, from *enantios*, contrary], *n.* (*Rhet.*) A figure of speech by which one says (usually ironically) the reverse of what one means.

enarch (en arch′), *v.t.* To arch over; (*Her.*) to arch with a chevron; (*Hort.*) to inarch.

***enarration** (ē nȧ rā′ shŭn) [L. *ēnārrātio -ōnem*, *īnārrāre* (E-, *nārrāre*, to NARRATE)], *n.* A narration or description.

enarthrosis (en ar thrō′ sis) [Gr., from *enarthros*, jointed (EN-, *arthron*, a joint)], *n.* A ball-and-socket joint. **enarthrodial,** *a.*

enation (e nā′ shŭn) [L. *enatus*, born], *n.* (*Bot.*) The production of outgrowths upon the surface of an organ.

encænia (en sē′ ni ȧ) [L., from Gr. *enkainia* (EN-, *kainos*, new)], *n.pl.* A festival to commemorate the dedication of a church, the founding of a city, etc.; the annual commemoration of founders and benefactors of Oxford University.

encage (en kāj′), *v.t.* To shut in or as in a cage; to confine.

encamp (en kămp′), *v.i.* To form an encampment; to settle down temporarily in tents. *v.t.* To settle (troops) in an encampment; to lodge (troops) in tents. **encampment,** *n.* The act of encamping; a camp; the place where troops are encamped.

encarnalize (en kar′ nȧ līz), *v.t.* To make carnal; to make fleshly; to embody in the flesh.

encase (en kās′) [F. *encaisser* (EN-, *caisse*, CASE (1))], *v.t.* To put into a case; to enclose in a case; to protect with a case. **encasement,** *n.*

encash (en kăsh′), *v.t.* To cash, to convert (bills, etc.) into cash; to realize, to obtain in the form of cash. **encashable,** *a.*

encaustic (en kaw′ stik) [F. *encaustique*, L. *encausticus*, Gr. *enkaustikos*, from *enkaiein* (EN-, *kaiein*, to burn)], *n.* A mode of painting in which the colours are fixed by heat (now chiefly of painting on vitreous or ceramic ware in which the colours are burnt in). *a.* Pertaining to or executed by this method. **encaustic brick** or **tile:** Such as are inlaid with clay patterns burnt in.

encave (en kāv′) [O.F. *encaver*, a cellar)], *v.t.* To hide in a cellar.

-ence [F. *-ence*, or directly from L. *-entia*, from pres.p. in *-ens -entis* (rarely from neut. pl. of adjectives)], *suf.* Forming abstract nouns as *consistence, corpulence.*

enceinte (an sănt′) [F., fem. of *enceint*, L. *incinctus*, p.p. of *incingere* (IN- (1), *cingere*, to girdle)], *a.* Pregnant; with child. *n.* The space within the ramparts of a fortification.

encephalon (en sef′ ȧ lon) [Gr. *enkephalon* (EN-, *kephalē*, the head)], *n.* (*pl.* **-la**) (*Anat.*) The brain; the contents of the skull. **encephalic** (-făl′ ik), *a.* **encephalitis** (-lī′ tis), *n.* (*Path.*) Inflammation of the brain. **encephalitis lethargica,** *n.* (*Path.*) Acute inflammation of the brain, commonly called sleepy sickness. **encephalocele** (en sef′ ȧ lȯ sēl) [-CELE, a tumour], *n.* (*Path.*) Hernia of the brain. **encephaloid,** *a.* Pertaining to or resembling brain matter. *n.* (*Path.*) A kind of cancer in which the parts affected resemble the medullary parts of the brain. **encephalopathy** (-lop′ ȧ thi), *n.* (*Path.*) Disease referable to disorder of the brain. **encephalopathic** (-păth′ ik), *a.* **encephalotomy** (-lot′ ȯ mi), *n.* (*Surg.*) The operation of cutting into the brain; dissection of the brain. **encephalous** (en sef′ ȧ lŭs), *a.* Having a distinct brain or head, used of certain *Mollusca* called the *Encephala.*

enchafe (en chāf′) [M.E. *enchaufe*, O.F. *eschaufer*], *v.t.* To make hot; to excite, to irritate.

enchain (en chān′) [O.F. *enchainer*], *v.t.* To bind with chains; to chain up; to hold fast, to rivet (attention, etc.). **enchainment,** *n.*

enchant (en chant′) [F. *enchanter*, L. *incantāre* (IN- (1), *cantāre*, to sing)], *v.t.* To influence by magic, to bewitch; to endow with magical powers; to fascinate, to charm; to delight in the highest degree. **enchanter,** *n.* One who practises enchantment; a magician; one who delights or fascinates. **enchanter's nightshade,** *n.* A woodland plant of the genus *Circæa*, esp. *C. lutetiana*. **enchantingly,** *adv.* **enchantment,** *n.* **enchantress,** *n.*

encharge (en charj′) [O.F. *encharger*], *v.t.* To enjoin, to give (something) in charge; to commission (with).

***enchase** (en chās′) [F. *enchâsser* (EN-, *châsse*, shrine, L. *capsa*, CASE (1))], *v.t.* To set or encase within any other material, as a gem in precious metal; to serve as a setting, to encircle; to adorn with embossed work; to decorate with figures; to enshrine, to enclose.

enchiridion (en kī rid′ i ŏn) [Gr. *encheiridion* (EN-, *cheir*, hand, *-idion*, dim. suf.)], *n.* A handbook or manual, a small guide or book of reference.

enchorial (en kôr′ i ȧl) [Gr. *enchorios* (EN-, *chora*, country)], *a.* Belonging to or used in a country; popular, common; applied to the demotic characters formed from Egyptian hieroglyphics. **enchoric** (-kor′ ik), *a.*

encincture (en singk′ tūr) [EN-, CINCTURE], *v.t.* To surround with or as with a ring or girdle. *n.* A girdle; a surrounding or enclosing.

encircle (en sẽr′ kėl) [EN-, CIRCLE], *v.t.* To enclose or surround (with); to take up a position round; to embrace, to encompass. **encirclement,** (*Pol.*) A German phrase to describe the formation of an alliance between her neighbouring countries to prevent her expansion.

en clair (ong klâr′) [F.], *a.* (of telegrams, etc.) Not in code or cipher.

enclasp (en klasp′), *v.t.* To enfold in a clasp, to embrace.

enclave (en klāv′) [F., from *enclaver*, late L. *inclāvāre* (IN- (1), *clāvus*, nail, or *clāvis*, key)], *n.* A territory completely surrounded by that of another power. *a.* (*Her.*) Shaped like a dovetail; dovetailed. **enclavement,** *n.*

enclitic (en klit′ ik) [L. *encliticus*, Gr. *enklitikos* (EN-, *klinein*, to lean)], *a.* (*Gr. Gram.*) Applied to a word which cannot, as it were, stand by itself, but is pronounced as part of the preceding word, on which it throws its accent, *e.g.* "thee" in "prithee". *n.* An enclitic word or particle. **enclitically,** *adv.*

***encloister** (en klois′ tėr), *v.t.* To shut up in a cloister; to immure.

enclose (en klōz′), *v.t.* To shut in; to surround or hem in on all sides; to surround by a fence; to put one thing inside another for transmission or carriage; to contain. **encloser,** *n.* **enclosure** (ĕn klō′ zhůr), *n.* The act of enclosing, esp. the act of enclosing common land so as to make it private property; that which is enclosed; a space of ground enclosed or fenced in; that which encloses, as a fence; anything enclosed in an envelope, wrapper, etc.

encode (en kōd′), *v.t.* To translate a message into code.

encolure (en kȯ loor′) [F. (EN-, *col*. L. *collum*, neck, -URE)], *n.* (*Browning*) A horse's mane.

encomiast (en kō′ mi ăst) [Gr. *enkōmiastēs*, from *encomiazein*, to praise, as foll.], *n.* One who composes an encomium, a panegyrist; a flatterer. **encomiastic** (-ăs tik), *a.* Bestowing praise; laudatory, panegyrical. **n.* An encomium. ***encomiastical,** *a.* **encomiastically,** *adv.*

encomium (en kō′ mi ům) [L., from Gr. *enkōmion*, neut. of *enkōmios*, laudatory (EN-, *kōmos*, revelry)], *n.* (*pl.* **-ums**) A formal eulogy or panegyric; high commendation; high-flown praise.

encompass (en kŭm′ pȧs), *v.t.* To surround, to invest; to go round, to encircle; to include, contain; *to get in one's power, circumvent. **encompassment,** *n.*

encore (on kôr′) [F., again, L. (*in*) *hanc horam*, to this hour], *adv.* Again, once more; used as a call for a repetition at a concert, theatre, etc. *n.* A demand for a repetition of a song, etc.; the repetition itself. *v.t.* To call for a repetition of. *v.i.* To call for an encore.

encounter (en koun′ tėr) [O.F. *encontrer*, late L. *incontrāre* (IN- (1), *contra*, against)], *v.t.* To meet face to face; to meet in a hostile manner; to confront resolutely; to attack and endeavour to refute; to meet with, come across. *n.* A meeting face to face; a hostile meeting, a skirmish, a battle; an undesigned meeting; *address, manner of accosting. **encounterer,** *n.* An adversary, an opponent; *one who is quick to accost another.

encourage (en kŭr′ ȧj) [O.F. *encoragier* (EN-, COURAGE)], *v.t.* To give courage or confidence to; to animate, embolden; to urge, to incite (to do); to stimulate, to promote, to foster (trade, opinion, etc.). **encouragement,** *n.* **encourager,** *n.* **encouragingly,** *adv.*

encradle (en krā′ dėl), *v.t.* To place in a cradle.

encraty (en′ krȧt i) [Gr. *egkrateia*, mastery], *n.* Mastery over the senses, self-control.

encrimson (en krim′ zȯn), *v.t.* To make crimson, redden.

encrinite (en′ kri nīt) [Gr. EN-, *krinon*, lily; -ITE], *n.* (*Geol.*) A fossil crinoid. **encrinal** (en′ kri nȧl), **encrinic** (en krin′ ik), **encrinital** (en kri nī′ tȧl), *a.* Pertaining to or containing encrinites.

encroach (en krōch′) [O.F. *encrochier* (EN-, *croc*, hook, cp. M.Dut. *kroke*, Icel. *krōkr* crook)], *v.i.* To intrude (upon) what belongs to another; to infringe (upon); to get possession of anything gradually or by stealth. **encroacher,** *n.* **encroachingly,** *adv.* **encroachment,** *n.* The act of encroaching; that which is taken by encroaching; (*Law*) the act of unlawfully trespassing upon or interfering with the rights, property, or privileges of another.

encrust (en krŭst′) [prob. through F. *incruster*, from L. *incrustāre* (IN-, *crusta*, CRUST)], *v.t.* To cover with a crust or hard coating; to form a crust upon the surface of; to apply a decorated layer or lining to the surface of. **encrustment,** *n.* [see also INCRUSTATION].

encumber (en kŭm′ bėr) [O.F. *encombrer*, late L. *incumbrāre* (IN-, *cumbrus*, an obstacle, see CUMBER)], *v.t.* To hamper, impede, or embarrass by a weight, burden, or difficulty; to burden; to weigh down with debt; to perplex; *to fold (the arms). **encumberment,** *n.* **encumbrance,** *n.* A hindrance to freedom of action or motion; a burden, a hindrance, a clog; (*Law*) a liability upon an estate, such as a mortgage, a claim, etc. **encumbrancer,** *n.* (*Law*) One who holds an encumbrance upon another person's estate.

encurtain (en kẽr′ tȧn), *v.t.* To enwrap or veil with or as with a curtain.

-ency [-ENCE], *suf.* Forming nouns of state or quality.

encyclic, -al (en sik′ lik, -ȧl) [late L. *encyclicus*, Gr. *enkuklios* (EN-, *kuklos*, a ring, a circle)], *a.* Sent about to many persons or places. *n.* A circular letter, esp. a letter from the Pope to the bishops or to the Church at large.

encyclopædia (en sī klȯ pē′ di ȧ) [late L., from pseudo-Gr., *enkuklopaideia*, a false reading for *enkuklios paideia*, general instruction (as prec., and *paideia*, from *paideuein*, to educate, from *pais paidos*, a boy)], *n.* A book containing information on all branches of knowledge, or on a particular branch, usually arranged alphabetically, esp. the great French Encyclopædia (see below); a general system of knowledge or instruction. **encyclopædian,**

encyclopædic, -al, *a.* **encyclopædism,** *n.* The compilation of an encyclopædia; the possession of a large range of knowledge and information; the doctrines of the French Encyclopædists. **encyclopædist,** *n.* A compiler of an encyclopædia; one who has acquired an extensive range of knowledge or information; (*pl.*) Diderot, D'Alembert, and their associates, who produced the great French Encyclopædia between 1751 and 1772.

encyst (en sist'), *v.t.* To enclose in a cyst, bladder, or vesicle. **encystation** (-tā' shŭn), *n.* **encystis,** *n.* (*Path.*) An encysted tumour. **encystment,** *n.*

end (end) [A.-S. *ende* (cp. Dut. *einde*, Icel. *endi*, Dan. and G. *ende*)], *n.* The extreme point or boundary of a line or of anything that has length; the termination, limit, or last portion; the last part of a period; the conclusion of a state or action; a ceasing to exist; the final lot or doom; abolition; death; the cause of death; a result, a natural consequence, a necessary outcome; a purpose, an object, a designed result; a reason for (a thing's) existence, a final cause; (*usu. in pl.*) a remnant. *a.* Final; farthest; last. *v.i.* To come to an end, to cease; to result (in). *v.t.* To bring to an end; to put to an end, to destroy; *(*fig.*) to harvest, to get in (corn). **at a loose end:** (*colloq.*) Temporarily disengaged. **at one's wits' end:** Bewildered, utterly perplexed, nonplussed. **at the end of his tether:** Unable to do anything more. **in the end:** Finally; after all. **no end:** Plenty, much, many. **odds and ends:** Odd remnants. **on end:** Upright, erect. **rope's end:** The end of a rope whipped with cord; such a piece cut off and used for flogging. **shoemaker's end:** A waxed thread armed with a bristle. **the ends of the earth:** The remotest parts of the earth. **to come to an end:** To end, to be finished, to be exhausted. **to go off the deep end:** To lose one's temper. **to keep one's end up:** (*colloq.*) To stand one's ground. **to make both ends meet:** To keep the expenditure within the income. **to put an end to:** To terminate, to stop; to abolish. **to that end:** For that purpose. **be all and end all:** The sole aim, ambition. **endiron,** *n.* A movable plate in a kitchen range for enlarging or contracting the fire space. **end-paper,** *n.* (*Bookbinding*) One of the blank pages placed between the cover and the body of a book. **end-stopped,** *n.* (*Pros.*) Having a pause in sense at the end of a line of poetry, opp. to enjambment. **end on:** With the end pointing towards one. **end to end:** With the ends touching; lengthwise. **without end:** Everlasting; very long; inexhaustible. **wrong end of the stick:** The contrary to what is meant. **ending,** *n.* A conclusion, a termination; the latter part of a story, an occurrence, etc.; the terminating syllable of a word in grammar. **endlong** [ENDLESS]. **endmost,** *a.* The nearest to the end, the furthest.

end- [ENDO-].

endamage (en dăm' ȧj), *v.t.* To damage; to prejudice.

endanger (en dān' jėr), *v.t.* To expose to danger, to put in hazard. ***endangerment,** *n.*

endear (en dēr'), *v.t.* To make dear (to); to cause to be loved; *to secure the affections of; *to bind (to) by gratitude, etc.; *to make dear or costly. **endearing,** *a.* **endearingly,** *adv.* **endearment,** *n.*

endeavour (en dev' ŏr), *v.i.* To strive (after) a certain end; to try, to make an effort (to). **v.t.* To attempt or essay. *n.* An effort, an attempt; exertion for the attainment of some object. ***endeavourment,** *n.*

endeca [HENDECA].

endeictic (en dīk' tik) [Gr. *endeiktikos*, from *endeiknunai* (EN-, *deiknunai*, to show)], *a.* Showing, exhibiting. **endeixis,** *n.* (*Path.*) A symptom.

endemic (en dem' ik) [EN-, Gr. *dēmos*, people (*cp. endēmios*)], *a.* Peculiar to a particular locality or people. *n.* An endemic disease. **endemic disease,** *n.* One common from local causes in a particular district or among a particular people or class, beyond which it shows no tendency to spread. **endemically,** *adv.* **endemicity** (-mis' i ti), *n.* **endemeology** (en dē mi ol' ŏ ji), *n.* The study of endemic diseases.

endermic (en dĕr' mik), *a.* Acting upon or through the skin, as an unguent applied after blistering. **endermically,** *adv.*

enderon (en' dėr ŏn) [EN-, Gr. *deros*, *derma*, skin], *n.* (*Physiol.*) The inner derm or true skin.

endive (en' div) [F., from L. *intibus*], *n.* A kind of chicory, *Cichorium endivia*, much cultivated for use in salads, or *C. Intybus*, the wild endive.

endless (end' les), *a.* Having no end; infinite, unlimited, perpetual; incessant. **endless band, cable, or chain,** *n.* A band with ends fastened together for conveying mechanical motion. **endless screw,** *n.* A screw conveying motion to a wheel in the teeth of which the threads engage. **endlessly,** *adv.* **endlessness,** *n.*

endlong (end' long), *adv.* Lengthwise as distinguished from crosswise; straight along; *continuously. **a.* Standing on end, vertical. **endmost** [END].

endo-, end- [Gr. *endon*, within], *comb. form.*

endocardium (en dō kar' di ŭm) [Gr. *kardia*, heart], *n.* (*Phys.*) A membrane lining the interior of the human heart. **endocardiac,** *a.* **endocarditis,** *n.* Inflammation of the endocardium.

endocarp (en' dō karp) [Gr. *karpos*, fruit], *n.* (*Bot.*) The inner layer of a pericarp.

endochrome (en' dō krōm), *n.* (*Bot.*) A colouring matter found in the cells of plants.

endocrane (en' dō krān), *n.* (*Phys.*) The inner surface of the cranium.

endocrine (en' dō krīn), *n.* (*Med.*) The internal secretion of a gland. **endocrine gland,** *n.* An organ of a glandular structure possessing no duct but yielding an internal secretion which is poured into the blood stream. **endocrinology,** *n.* The study of the secretions of the endocrine glands.

endoderm (en' dō dĕrm), *n.* (*Biol.*) The inner layer of the blastoderm; the membrane lining the internal cavity of certain organisms, esp. the *Cœlenterata*; (*Bot.*) an inner layer of cells beneath the liber; the inner layer of the wall of a cell.

endogamous (en dog' ȧ mŭs) [Gr. *gamos*, marriage], *a.* Necessarily marrying within the tribe. **endogamy,** *n.* The custom of taking a wife only within the tribe; (*Bot.*) pollination between two flowers on the same plant.

endogen (en' dō jen), *n.* (*Bot.*) An endogenous plant; (*pl.*) one of the divisions of the vegetable kingdom, in which the plants increase by internal layers and elongation at the summit, instead of externally, and have no distinction of bark and pith, as in the palm, the sugar-cane, etc. **endogenous,** *a.* Growing from within.

endolymph (en' dō limf), *n.* The serous fluid in the membranous labyrinth of the ear.

endometrium (en dō met' ri ŭm) [Gr. *metra*, womb], *n.* The membrane lining the cavity of the womb. **endometritis,** *n.* (*Path.*) Inflammation of this.

endomorph (en' dō mŏrf), *n.* A mineral enclosed inside another.

endoparasite (en dō păr' ȧ sīt), *n.* (*Zool.*) A parasite living in the interior of its host. **endoparasitic,** *a.*

endophyllous (en dof' i lŭs), *a.* (*Bot.*) Applied to leaves evolved from a sheath.

endoplasm (en' dō plăzm), *n.* (*Biol.*) The partially fluid inner layer of protoplasm. **endoplast** (en' dŏ plăst) [Gr. *plastos*, formed], *n.* (*Biol.*) The nucleus in the protoplasm of some of the protozoa.

endopleura (en dō ploo' rȧ), *n.* (*Bot.*) The internal tegument of a seed.

endorhiza (en dō rī′ zȧ) [Gr. *rhiza*, root], *n.* (*Bot.*) The sheath-enclosed radical of the embryo in many monocotyledonous plants. **endorhizal, -ous,** *a.*

endorse (en dôrs′) [M.E. *endosse*, O.F. *endosser*, med. L. *indorsāre* (IN-, L. *dorsum*, the back)], *v.t.* To write (one's name, a note of contents, etc.) on the back of (a document); (*fig.*) to assign by indorsement; to ratify, confirm, approve; *to load the back (with); *to take upon one's back. **to endorse over:** To transfer one's rights in (a bill, etc.) to another person. **endorsee** (en dôr sē′), *n.* The person to whom a bill, etc., is assigned by indorsement. **endorsement,** *n.* **endorser,** *n.*

endosarc (en′ dō sark), *n.* (*Biol.*) Endoplasm.

endoscope (en′ dō skōp), *n.* An instrument for inspecting internal parts of the body.

endoskeleton (en dō skel′ e tȯn), *n.* (*Anat.*) The internal bony and cartilaginous framework of the vertebrates.

endosmose, endosmosis (en doz′ mōs, en doz mō′ sis), *n.* (*Biol.*) The passage of a fluid from outside inwards through a porous diaphragm. **endosmotic** (-mot′ ik), **endosmic** (-doz′ mik), **endosmosmic** (-moz′ mik), *a.*

endosperm (en′ dō spĕrm), *n.* (*Bot.*) The albumen of a seed, **endospermic,** *a.*

endospore (en′ dō spôr), *n.* (*Bot.*) The inner layer of the wall of a spore.

endostome (en′ dō stōm), *n.* (*Bot.*) The aperture in the inner integument of an ovule.

endothelium (en dō thē′ li ŭm), *n.* (*Physiol.*) A membrane lining blood-vessels, tubes, cavities, etc.

endow (en dou′) [EN-, F. *douer*, L. *dōtāre*, to DOWER], *v.t.* To invest with goods, estate, privileges, etc.; to invest (with qualities, etc.); to bestow a permanent income upon; to give a dowry to. **endowment,** *n.* The act of settling a dower or portion upon a woman; the act of making permanent provision for the support of any person, institution, etc.; the fund or property so appropriated; (*pl.*) natural gifts, qualities, or ability. **endowment assurance,** *n.* An assurance to provide a fixed sum at a specified age or on death before that age.

endozoic (en dō zō′ ik), *a.* Living inside an animal, a term applied to the method of seed-dispersal by being swallowed by an animal and then passed out in its excreta.

endue (en dū′) [O.F. *enduire*, L. *indūcere* (IN-, *dūcere*, to lead, draw), in certain senses confused with prec. and also with L. *induere*, to put on], *v.t.* To put on (as clothes); to clothe, to invest (with); (*usu. in p.p.*) to endow, to furnish.

endure (en dūr′) [O.F. *endurer*, L. *indūrāre* (IN-, *dūrus*, hard)], *v.t.* To bear, to stand (a test or strain); to undergo, to suffer; to submit to. *v.i.* To last; to abide in the same state; to bear sufferings with patience and fortitude. **endurer,** *n.* **enduring,** *a.* Bearing; durable, permanent. **enduringly,** *adv.* **enduringness,** *n.* **endurability** (-bil′ i ti), *n.* **endurable,** *a.* **endurableness,** *n.* **endurance,** *n.* The act or state of enduring or suffering; the capacity of bearing or suffering with patience; continuance, duration.

endways (end′ wāz), *adv.* On end; with the end foremost or uppermost; end to end; lengthwise. **endwise,** *adv.*

***ene** (ēn) [A.-S. *ǣne*, instrumental of *ān*, one], *adv.* Once.

-ene [L. *-ēnus*, adj. suf.], *suf.* (*Chem.*) Denoting a hydrocarbon, such as *benzene*, *naphthalene*.

enema (en′ ė mȧ, ė nē′ mȧ) [Gr. *enema*, from *enienai* (EN-, *hienai*, to send)], *n.* An injection; a liquid or gaseous substance injected into the rectum; the apparatus with which an injection is made.

enemy (en′ ė mi) [O.F. *enemi*, L. *inimīcus* (*in*, UN-, *amīcus*, friend)], *n.* One hostile to another; an adversary, one opposed to any subject or cause; a hostile army, military force, or ship; a member of a hostile force or nation. **the Enemy:** The Devil. **how goes the enemy?** (*colloq.*) What is the time?

energetic (en ĕr jet′ ik) [ENERGY], *a.* Forcible, powerful; active, vigorously operative. **energetically,** *adv.* **energetics,** *n.* Physical, as distinct from vital, dynamics. ***energic** (ė nĕr′ jik), *a.* Energetic. **energize** (en′ ėr jīz), *v.i.* To act energetically and vigorously. *v.t.* To give energy to.

energumen (en ėr gū′ mėn) [late L. *energūmenus*, Gr. *energoumenos*, p.p. *energeein*, to work in or upon, as foll.], *n.* One possessed by a spirit, esp. an evil spirit, a demoniac; an enthusiast, a fanatic.

energy (en′ ėr ji) [late L. *energīa*, Gr. *energeia* (EN-, *ergon*, work)], *n.* Internal or inherent power; force, vigour; capability of action or performing work; active operation; emphasis; (*Phys.*) a body's power of performing mechanical work. **actual, kinetic,** or **motive energy:** The energy of a body in actual motion (measured by the product of half the mass and the square of the velocity). **conservation of energy:** (*Phys.*) The doctrine that no energy is destroyed, but that it is transformed into some equivalent capable of doing the same amount of work that it could have done if unchanged. **latent, potential,** or **static energy:** The energy possessed by virtue of the relative condition of parts of a body or of bodies to each other.

enervate (en′ ėr vāt) [L. *ēnervātus*, p.p. of *ēnervāre* (E-, *nervus*, sinew)], *v.t.* To deprive of force or strength; to weaken; to render effeminate. *a.* (e nĕr′ vȧt) Weakened; wanting in spirit, strength, or vigour. **enervation** (-vā′ shŭn), *n.*

enface (en fās′), *v.t.* To write, print, or stamp on the face of.

enfant terrible (on fon târ ēbl′) [F., terrible child], *n.* A child who makes embarrassing remarks; a person who embarrasses his party.

enfeeble (en fē′ bėl), *v.t.* To make feeble or weak. **enfeeblement,** *n.*

enfeoff (en fef′) [A.F. *enfeoffer*, O.F. *enfeffer* (EN-, FIEF)], *v.t.* (*Law*) To invest with a fief; to bestow or convey an estate in fee-simple or fee-tail; (*fig.*) to surrender, to give (oneself) up. **enfeoffment,** *n.* (*Law*) The act of enfeoffing; the deed by which the fee simple is conveyed.

enfetter (en fet′ ėr), *v.t.* To fetter; to enslave (to).

enfilade (en fi lād′) [F., from *enfiler*, to thread (EN-, *fil*, L. *fīlum*, a thread)], *n.* *A straight passage or suite of apartments; a position liable to a raking fire; a fire that may rake a position, line of works, or body of troops, from end to end. *v.t.* To pierce or rake with shot from end to end.

enfold (en fōld′), *v.t.* To wrap up, to enwrap, to enclose; to clasp, to embrace; to arrange or shape in folds. ***enfoldment,** *n.*

enforce (en fôrs′) [O.F. *enforcer*, late L. *infortiāre* (IN-, L. *fortis*, strong)], *v.t.* To carry out vigorously, to execute strictly; to compel obedience to; to give force to; to press or urge forcibly; *to force, to compel; *to ravish; *to prove; to strengthen, to fortify. **v.i.* To strive, to endeavour, to struggle. **n.* Power, strength; effort. **enforceable,** *a.* **enforced,** *a.* Forced, not voluntary. **enforcedly,** *adv.* **enforcement,** *n.* **enforcement officer:** A government official employed to report on infringements of regulations.

enframe (en frām′), *v.t.* To set in or as in a frame; to be a frame to.

enfranchise (en frăn′ chīz) [O.F. *enfranchiss-*, stem of *enfranchir* (EN-, *franc*, FRANK)], *v.t.* To set free; *to release from custody; *to release from anything which exercises power or influence; to give (a town, constituency, etc.) full municipal or parliamentary rights and privileges; to give (a person) the right to vote. ***enfranch,** *v.t.* **enfranchisement,** *n.* The act of enfranchising; the state of being enfranchised; admission to the municipal or the parliamentary franchise. **enfranchisement of copyhold lands:** (*Law*) The conversion of such lands into freeholds. **enfranchiser,** *n.*

engage (en gāj′) [F. *engager* (EN-, *gage*, a pledge)], *v.t.* To bind by a promise or contract, esp. by promise of marriage; to hire, order, bespeak; to employ, to occupy the time or attention of; to attack, to come into conflict with. *v.i.* To pledge oneself (to do something); to undertake; to enter into, embark (in); to begin to fight, to enter into conflict (with); to interlock (with), *n.* *An engagement, pledge, or bargain; (*Fencing*) the order to interlock (swords or foils). **engaged column:** (*Arch.*) A column fastened into a wall so that it is partly concealed. **engaged couple:** Two persons who have exchanged promises of marriage. **engaged wheels:** Wheels interlocking with each other by means of cogs, etc. **engagement,** *n.* The act of engaging; an obligation, a contract; a mutual promise of marriage; employment or occupation of time or attention; an appointment; a hiring, a contract to employ; the state of being hired; an enterprise embarked in; an action or battle between armies or fleets; (*pl.*) the contracts entered into by a trader. **engagement ring,** *n.* A ring worn by a woman on the third finger of the left hand to show that she is engaged to be married. **engaging,** *a.* Winning, pleasing, attractive (used of manners or address). **engagingly,** *adv.*

engarland (en gar′ lȧnd), *v.t.* To invest with a garland, to wreathe (with).

engender (en jen′ dėr) [F. *engendrer*, L. *ingenerāre* (IN-, *genus*, a race, a brood)], *v.t.* To beget; to give birth to (*now usu. fig.*); to be the cause of, to bring about. **v.i.* To come into existence.

engine (en′ jin) [O.F. *engin*, L. *ingenium*, genius (see INGENIOUS)], *n.* A machine consisting of a complication of parts for applying mechanical power, esp. one that converts energy into motion; a machine or instrument used in war; an instrument, a tool; means to effect a purpose; *native wit; understanding. *v.t.* *To torture by means of an engine; to furnish (a ship) with engines. **engine-driver, -man,** *n.* One who drives or manages a locomotive, (*Am.* engineer). **engine-lathe,** *n.* One driven by machinery. **engine plane,** *n.* (*Mining*) An underground passage along which an endless chain or rope worked by an engine hauls tubs and trucks. **engine-sized,** *a.* Sized by machinery (of paper). **engine-turning,** *n.* Complex ornamental turning, as on the outside of watch-cases, done by machinery. ***enginery,** *n.* Engines; apparatus, mechanism, machinery; (*fig.*) artful contrivances; *engines of war, artillery.

engineer (en ji nēr′) [O.F. *engigneor*, late L. *ingeniātor -ōrem*, from *ingeniāre*, as prec.], *n.* One who designs or carries out construction work of mechanical, electrical, or civic nature; (*Am.*) One who manages or attends to an engine, an engine-driver; a member of that part of an army which attends to engineering work; (*fig.*) one who carries through any undertaking. *v.t.* To direct or carry out, as an engineer, the formation or execution of (as railways, canals, etc.); (*colloq.*) to contrive, to manage by tact or ingenuity. **civil engineering,** *n.* The construction of works of public utility, esp. bridges, canals, railways, etc. **electrical engineering,** *n.* Construction of electrical engines and equipment. **electronic engineering,** *n.* Construction of electronic equipment and apparatus. **hydraulic engineering,** *n.* The construction of waterworks, the application of water-power, the construction of dams, docks, etc. **mechanical engineering,** *n.* The construction of engines and machinery. **military engineering,** *n.* The construction of fortification, and of roads, bridges, etc., used for military purposes.

***engird** (en gĕrd′), *v.t.* (*past* and *p.p.* **engirt**) To encircle, to encompass, as with a girdle.

engirdle (en gĕr′ del), *v.t.* To surround with or as with a girdle.

English (ing′ glish) [A.-S. *Englisc*, *Ænglisc*, from *Engle*, the Angles], *a.* Pertaining to England or its inhabitants; spoken or written in the English language; characteristic of or becoming an Englishman. *n.* The language of the British Isles, N. America, Australasia, parts of S. Africa, and other parts of the British Commonwealth; in printing, a size of type between great primer and pica; the people of England; the soldiers fighting on the English side. *v.t.* To translate into the English language; to express in plain English. **Basic English** [BASIC]. **Queen's, King's English:** Correct English as spoken by educated people. **Middle English:** The English language in use from about 1150 to 1500. **Old English:** The English language in use before 1150, also called Anglo-Saxon; (*Print.*) [BLACK-LETTER]. **plain English:** Plain, unmistakable terms. **English bond:** (*Bricklaying*) Bonding by means of alternate courses of headers and stretchers. **Englishism,** *n.* **Englishman, -woman,** *n.* A native or a naturalized inhabitant of England; one of English blood. **Englishness,** *n.* ***Englishry,** *n.* The quality or state of being an Englishman; *the part of the population of a country that is of English blood, esp. the English settlers in Ireland and their descendants; *the English population, the English quarter.

***englut** (en glŭt′) [O.F. *englotir*, L. *ingluttīre* (IN-, *gluttīre*, to swallow); and in later senses formed from EN-, GLUT], *v.t.* To swallow; to gulp down, to glut, to satiate.

engorge (en gôrj′) [F. *engorger* (EN-, *gorge*, GORGE)], *v.t.* To swallow up, to devour; (*in p.p.*) to fill to excess; (*Path.*) to congest (with blood). **engorgement,** *n.*

engraft (en graft′), *v.t.* To graft upon, to insert (a scion of one tree) upon or into another; to incorporate; to implant, instil; to superadd.

engrail (en grāl′) [O.F. *engresler*, perh. from *gresle* (F. *grêle*), hail], *v.t.* (*chiefly in Her.*) To indent in curved lines, to make ragged at the edges as if broken with hail; (*poet.*) to adorn. **engrailment,** *n.*

engrain (en grān′), *v.t.* *To dye in fast colours; to dye deeply; (*fig.*) to implant (qualities, esp. vices) ineradicably.

engrave (en grāv′), *v.t.* To cut figures, letters, etc., on, with a chisel or graver; to represent on wood, metal, etc., by carving with a graver; to inscribe or decorate (a surface) with figures, etc.; to imprint; to impress deeply. *v.i.* To practise the art of engraving. **engraver,** *n.* **engraving,** *n.* The act, process, or art of cutting figures, letters, etc., on wood, stone, or metal; that which is engraved; an impression from an engraved plate, a print.

engroove (en groov′), *v.t.* To make a groove in; to set in a groove.

engross (en grōs′) [A.F. *engrosser* (EN-, *grosse*, late L. *grossa*, large writing)], *v.t.* To write in large, bold letters; to write out in legal form; to buy up the whole or large quantities of in order to enhance the price; to monopolize, to occupy entirely, to absorb; *to make gross or fat. **to be engrossed in:** To be absorbed in (as in reading a book). **engrosser,** *n.* **engrossment,** *n.* Exorbitant appropriation or acquisition; the act of engrossing documents; the state of having one's attention wholly taken up.

enguard (en gard′), *v.t.* To guard or defend.

engulf, *-gulph (en gŭlf′), *v.t.* To swallow up, as in a gulf or whirlpool; to cast, as into a gulf. **engulfment,** *n.*

engyscope (en′ ji skōp) [Gr. *engus*, close at hand, -SCOPE], *n.* (*Opt.*) A reflecting microscope; *any kind of compound microscope.

enhalo (en hā′ lō), *v.t.* To encircle with or as with a halo.

enhance (en hans′) [A.-S. *enhauncer*, O.F. *enhaucer* (IN-, late L. *altiāre*, to heighten, from *altus*, high)], *v.t.* To raise in importance, degree, etc.; to augment, to intensify; to heighten (in price); to exaggerate; *to advance, to exalt. *v.i.* To be raised; to grow larger, to increase. **enhancement,** *n.* **enhancive,** *a.*

enharmonic (en har mon′ ik) [L. *enharmonicus*, Gr. *enarmonikos* (EN-, *harmonia*, HARMONY)], *a.* (*Mus.*) Having intervals less than a semitone, as between G sharp and A flat. *n.* Enharmonic music. **enharmonic modulation,** *n.* Change as to notation, but not as to sound. **enharmonically,** *adv.*

enhearten (en har′ tėn), *v.t.* To encourage, cheer, strengthen.

Eniac (en′ i ăk) (acronym Electronic Numeral Integrator And Calculator), *n.* One of the first electronic computors.

enigma (ė nig′ mȧ) [L. *ænigma*, Gr. *ainigma -tos*, from *ainissesthai*, to speak obscurely or allusively, from *ainos*, fable], *n.* A dark saying in which the meaning is concealed under obscure language, a riddle; any inexplicable proceeding. **enigmatic, -al** (en ig măt′ ik, -ȧl), *a.* **enigmatically,** *adv.* **enigmatist** (ė nig′ mȧ tist), *n.* A maker of or dealer in enigmas or riddles. **enigmatize,** *v.i.* To speak or write enigmatically; to deal in enigmas.

enjambment (en jămb′ mėnt) [F. *enjambement*, from *enjamber* (EN-, *jambe*, leg)], *n.* (*Pros.*) The continuation of a sentence or clause, without a pause in sense, from one verse or couplet into the next.

enjoin (en join′) [O.F. *enjoindre*, L. *injungere* (IN-, *jungere*, to join)], *v.t.* To direct, prescribe, impose (an act or conduct); to direct or command (a person to do something); to instruct (that); *to prohibit or restrain. ***enjoinment,** *n.*

enjoy (en joi′) [O.F. *enjoier*], *v.t.* To take pleasure or delight in; to have the use or benefit of; to experience or have; to have sexual intercourse with. **to enjoy oneself:** (*colloq.*) To experience pleasure or happiness. **enjoyable,** *a.* **enjoyableness,** *n.* **enjoyably,** *adv.* **enjoyment,** *n.*

enkindle (en kin′ dėl), *v.t.* To kindle, to set on fire; (*fig.*) to inflame, to rouse into passion, action, etc.

enlace (en lās′) [F. *enlacer* (EN-, *lacer*, ult. from L. *laqueāre*, to ensnare, from *laqueus*, a noose)], *v.t.* To encircle tightly, to surround; to embrace, enfold, entwine; to entangle. **enlacement,** *n.*

enlard (en lard′), *v.t.* To dress with lard or grease; to baste; to fatten.

enlarge (en larj′) [O.F. *enlarger*], *v.t.* To make greater; to extend in dimensions, quantity, or number; to expand, to widen; to make more comprehensive; to set free from confinement. *v.i.* To become bigger; to expatiate (upon). **to enlarge the heart:** To expand or extend the affections. **enlargement,** *n.* The act or process of extending or increasing; increase in size or bulk; something added on, an addition; release from confinement; diffuseness of speech or writing; (*Phot.*) a print or negative of a larger size taken from another. **enlarger,** *n.*

enlighten (en lī′ tėn), *v.t.* To give mental or spiritual light to, to instruct; to give (a person) information (on); to supply with light; (*poet.*) to shed light upon; to release from ignorance, prejudice, or superstition. **enlightener,** *n.* **enlightenment,** *n.*

enlink (en lingk′), *v.t.* To join together as with a link, to connect closely.

enlist (en list′), *v.t.* To enrol, esp. to engage for military service; to gain the interest, assistance, participation, or support of. *v.i.* To engage oneself for military service. **enlisted man,** *n.* (*U.S.A.*) A private soldier, not a conscript. **enlistment,** *n.*

enliven (en lī′ vėn), *v.t.* To give spirit or animation to; to impart life to, to stimulate; to brighten, render cheerful in appearance. **enlivener,** *n.*

enlumine (en loo′ min) [O.F. *enluminer*, late L. *inlūmināre* (L. *illūmināre*) (IN-, *lūmen -inis*, light)], *v.t.* To light up, to illuminate.

enmesh (en mesh′), *v.t.* To entangle or catch in or as in a net; to entrap. **enmeshment,** *n.*

enmity (en′ mi ti) [A.-F. *enemité*, O.F. *enemistié*, late L. *inimīcitas -tātem*, from L. *inimīcus*, enemy], *n.* The quality of being an enemy; hatred, hostility.

ennea- [Gr., nine], *comb. form.* **enneagynous** (en ė ăj′ i nŭs) [Gr. *gunē*, woman], *a.* (*Bot.*) Having nine pistils. **enneandria** (en ė ăn′ dri ȧ) [Gr. *anēr andros*, man], *n.pl.* (*Bot.*) A Linnæan class of plants distinguished by the nine stamens of the flowers. **enneandrian, -drous,** *a.* **enneapetalous** (en ė ȧ pet′ ȧ lŭs) [Gr. *petalon*, leaf], *a.* (*Bot.*) Having nine petals. **enneaphyllous** (en ė ȧ fil′ ŭs) [Gr. *phullon*, leaf], *a.* (*Bot.*) Having nine leaflets composing a compound leaf.

ennead (en′ ė ăd) [Gr. *enneas- ados*, as prec.], *n.* A set of nine, esp. of nine books or discourses.

enneahedral (en ė ȧ hē′ drȧl) [Gr. *hedra*, base], (*Geom.*) Having nine sides.

ennoble (ė nō′ bėl) [O.F. *ennoblir* (EN-, NOBLE)], *v.t.* To make noble; to make a noble of; to elevate in character or dignity; to make famous or illustrious. **ennoblement,** *n.*

ennui (on′ nwē, an nwē) [F., from O.F. *enui*, L. *in odio* (cp. ANNOY)], *n.* Listlessness; want of interest in things; boredom. **ennuyé** (an nwē′ yā) (*fem.* **ennuyée**), **ennuied** (on′ wēd, an wēd), *a.* Affected with ennui.

enormity (e nôr′ mi ti), *n.* The state or quality of being enormous, inordinate, outrageous, esp. of being excessively wicked; a monstrous crime, an outrage, an atrocity.

enormous (ė nôr′ mŭs) [earlier *enorm*, M.F. *enorme*, L. *enormis* (E-, *norma*, pattern, NORM)], *a.* *Out of all rule; exceedingly great in size, number, or quantity; huge, immense; *extraordinary, extravagant; *monstrous, outrageously wicked, heinous, atrocious. **enormously,** *adv.* **enormousness,** *n.*

Enosis (en′ ō sis) [Gr.], *n.* (*Pol.*) The union of Cyprus to Greece.

enough (ė nŭf′) [A.-S. *genōh*, *genōg*, allied to impers. *geneah*, it suffices (cp. Goth. *ganohs*, enough, *ganah*, it suffices, also Icel. *gnogr*, Dan. *nok*, G. *genug*, enough, Sansk, *naç*, to attain, L. *nancisci*, to obtain, p.p. *nactus*)], *a.* Sufficient for or adequate to need or demand (usu. placed after a noun). *n.* A sufficiency; a quantity or amount which satisfies requirement or desire; that which is equal to the powers or abilities. *int.* An exclamation denoting sufficiency or satisfaction. *adv.* Sufficiently, tolerably, passably. **well enough:** Tolerably well.

enounce (ė nouns′) [F. *énoncer*, L. *ēnuntiāre*, to ENUNCIATE], *v.t.* To enunciate, state definitely; to pronounce. **enouncement,** *n.*

***enow** (1) [ENOUGH].

enow (2) (ė nou′) [prob. short for *e'en now*], *adv.* (*Sc.*) Just now; soon.

enquire [INQUIRE].

enrage (en rāj′) [O.F. *enrager*], *v.t.* To put in a rage; to exasperate; to provoke to fury. ***enragement,** *n.*

***enrange** (en rānj′), *v.t.* To arrange; to set in place or order; to range, or wander over.

enrapture (en răp′ tūr), *v.t.* To fill with rapture; to transport with delight.

***enravish** (en răv′ ish), *v.t.* To throw into ecstasy; to enrapture.

enregiment (en rej′ i mėnt) [F. *enrégimenter*], *v.t.* To form into a regiment; to organize and discipline.

***enregister** (en rej′ is tėr) [F. *enregistrer*], *v.t.* To enrol; to enter in a register.

enrich (en rich′) [F. *enrichir*], *v.t.* To make rich or wealthy; to fertilize; to add to the contents of; to make richer. **enrichment,** *n.*

enring (en ring′), *v.t.* To encircle, to surround (with); to put a ring upon, to adorn with a ring.

enrobe (en rōb′), *v.t.* To put a robe upon, to attire.

enrol (en rōl′) [O.F. *enroller*], *v.t.* (*past and p.p.* **enrolled**) To write down on or enter in a roll; to record, to register, to celebrate; to include as a member, to record the admission of. **enroller,** *n.* One who enrols or registers. **enrolment,** *n.*

enroot (en root′), *v.t.* To fix by the root; to implant deeply; to entangle by or as by the roots.

ens (enz) [late L. *ēns*, neut. pres.p. of *esse*, to be], *n.* (*pl.* ***entia***) (*Phil.*) Entity, being, existence; any existing being or thing.

Ensa (en′ sa) [initials of Entertainment National Service Association], *n.* An official organization for entertaining men and women in the armed services and war-workers.

ensample (en sam′ pėl) [A.-F., corr. of O.F. *essample*, EXAMPLE], *n.* An example, a pattern, a model. *v.t.* To exemplify; to show by example.

ensanguine (en săng′ gwin) [EN-, L. *sanguis -inis*, blood], *v.t.* (*now only in p.p.*) To smear or cover with blood; to make crimson.

ensate (en′ sāt) [L. *ensis*, a sword, -ATE], *a.* (*Bot.*) Shaped like a sword with a straight blade.

ensconce (en skons′), *v.t.* To hide; to settle (oneself) comfortably or securely as in a sconce or fort.

enseam (en sēm′) [etym. doubtful; cp. M.E. *in same*, *inseme*, together], *v.t.* To bring together, to contain.

ensemble (a*n* sa*n*bl′) [F., from late L. *insimul* (*in simul*, at the same time)], *n.* All the parts of anything taken together; (*Mus.*) the joint effort of all the performers. ***tout ensemble***: The general effect.

ensepulchre (en sep′ ŭl kėr), *v.t.* To place in a sepulchre.

***ensew** [ENSUE].

enshield (en shēld′), *v.t.* To shield, guard, protect. **a.* Protected, covered.

enshrine (en shrīn′), *v.t.* To place in or as in a shrine; to enclose and cherish as if sacred. **enshrinement,** *n.*

enshroud (en shroud′), *v.t.* To cover with or as with a shroud; to conceal.

ensiform (en′ si fôrm) [L. *ensis*, a sword, -FORM], *a.* Sword-shaped, as the leaf of an iris. **ensiform cartilage** or **process,** *n.* The cartilaginous part at the end of the sternum or breast-bone.

ensign (en′ sīn) [O.F. *enseigne*, late L. *insignia*, orig. neut. pl. of *insignis*, remarkable, from *signum*, a SIGN], *n.* A national banner, a standard, a regimental flag, the flag with distinguishing colours carried by ships; a badge of rank or office; a sign or symbol; formerly, the lowest rank of commissioned officers in an infantry regiment, by the senior of whom the colours were carried. *v.t.* To distinguish by a badge; to be the distinguishing mark of; (*Her.*) to distinguish by any mark or ornament, borne on or over a charge. **naval ensign:** A flag with a field of white, blue, or red, with the union in the upper corner next the staff (white ensign carried by Royal Navy and Royal Yacht Squadron, blue by naval reserve, and red by merchant service). ***ensign-bearer,** *n.* The soldier who carries the colours; an ensign. **ensigncy, ensignship,** *n.*

ensilage (en′ sī lăj) [F., from *ensiler*, Sp. *ensilar*, to preserve grain in a pit, see SILO], *n.* A method of preserving forage crops whilst moist and succulent, without previously drying, by storing them in mass in pits or trenches; fodder so preserved. *v.t.* To preserve by the process of ensilage. **ensile** (en sīl′), *v.t.* To put into a silo for this purpose; to ensilage.

enslave (en slāv′), *v.t.* To make a slave of, to reduce to bondage; (*fig.*) to bring under the domination of some influence, habit, vice, etc.

enslavement, *n.* Servitude. **enslaver,** *n.* One who or that which enslaves, esp. a woman who dominates a man by her charms.

ensnare (en snâr′), *v.t.* To entrap; to overcome by treachery.

ensorcell (en sôr′ sėl) [O.F. *ensorceler* (EN-, *sorceler*, from *sorcier*, SORCERER)], *v.t.* To bewitch, to fascinate.

ensphere (en sfēr′), *v.t.* To place in or as in a sphere; to form into a round body.

ensue (en sū′) [O.F. *ensu-*, stem of *ensuivre*, late L. *insequere*, L. *insequī* (IN-, *sequī*, to follow)], *v.i.* To follow in course of time, to succeed; to result (from). **v.t.* To pursue, to practise. **ensuing,** *a.* Coming next after.

ensure (en shoor′) [A.-F. *enseurer*, from O.F. *seur*, SURE], *v.t.* To make certain (that); to make safe (against or from any risk); to assure or guarantee (something to or for); *to insure.

enswathe (en swā*th*′), *v.t.* To enwrap, to bandage. **enswathement,** *n.*

-ent [L. *-entem*, acc. of *-ens*, pres.p.], *suf.* Forming adjectives, *e.g. consistent*, *frequent*; noting an agent, *e.g. student*.

entablature (en tăb′ lȧ tūr) [ult. from late L. *intabulāre*, to form an *intabulātum* or flooring (cp. It. *intavolatura*)], *n.* (*Arch.*) That part of an order supported upon the columns, consisting in upward succession of the architrave, frieze, and cornice.

entablement (en tā′ bėl mėnt) [F., from *entabler*], *n.* The platform or series of platforms supporting a statue, above the dado and base; an entablature.

entail (en tāl′) [EN-, F. *taille*, TAIL (2)], *v.t.* To bestow or settle a possession inalienably on a certain person and his heirs; to restrict an inheritance to a particular class of heirs; to impose (certain duties, expenses, etc., upon some one); to involve, to necessitate. *n.* An estate in fee limited in descent to a particular heir or heirs; the limitation of inheritance in this way; (*fig.*) anything that is inherited as an inalienable possession; *carved or inlaid work; *shape, form. **to cut off the entail:** To put an end to the limitation of an inheritance to a particular class of heirs. **entailment,** *n.*

entangle (en tăng′ gėl), *v.t.* To twist together so that unravelling is difficult; to ensnare, as in a net; to involve in difficulties, obstacles, contradictions, etc.; to perplex, to embarrass. **entanglement,** *n.*

entasis (en′ tȧ sis) [Gr., from *enteinein* (EN-, *teinein*, to strain)], *n.* (*Arch.*) The almost imperceptible convex curvature given to a shaft or a column.

entelechy (en tel′ ė ki) [Gr. *entelecheia* (EN-, *telei*, dat. of *telos*, the end, perfection, *echein*, to have)], *n.* (*Phil.*) Aristotle's term for complete realization or full expression of a function or potentiality; a monad in the system of Leibnitz.

entellus (en tel′ ŭs) [name of a person in *Aeneid* v. 437–72], *n.* (*Zool.*) An East Indian monkey.

***entender** (en ten′ dėr), *v.t.* To make tender, to soften (as the heart).

entente (on tont′) [F.], *n.* A friendly understanding. **Entente Cordiale,** *n.* Understanding between France and Britain reached in 1904. **Little Entente,** *n.* Between Czechoslovakia, Yugoslavia and Rumania. **Triple Entente,** *n.* Between Britain, France, and Russia, 1907.

enter (en′ tėr) [F. *entrer*, L. *intrāre*, from *intrā* within], *v.t.* To go or come into; to pierce, to penetrate; to associate oneself with, become a member of; to insert, to set down in a writing, list, book, etc.; to put down the name of as a competitor for a race, etc.; to initiate into a business, etc.; to admit into the regular pack (said of a young dog); to cause to be inscribed upon the records of a court or legislative body; to admit as a pupil or member, to procure admission as such; (*Law*) to take possession of; to report a vessel's arrival at the custom-house; *to initiate, to introduce. *v.i.* To go or come in; to become a competitor; (*Theat.*) to appear on the scene. **to enter an appearance:** To show oneself. **to enter a protest:** To make a protest. **to enter into:** To form a part of; to join; to engage or take an interest in, to sympathize with; to become a party to (an agreement, treaty, recognizances, etc.). **to enter up:** To set down in a regular series; to complete a series of entries. **to enter upon:** To begin, set out upon; to begin to treat of (a subject, etc.); to take legal possession of. **enterable,** *a.*

nteric (en ter′ ik) [Gr. *enterikos*, from *enteron*, ntestine (comparative of *in*, in)], *a.* Pertaining to the intestines. **enterectomy,** *n.* (*Surg.*) Resection of part of the small intestine. **enteric fever,** *n.* (*Path.*) Typhoid fever. **enteritis** (-ī′ tis), *n.* (*Path.*) Inflammation of the bowels, esp. of the small intestines. **entero-,** *comb. form* (*Path.*). **enterocele** (en′ tėr ȯ sēl), *n.* A hernia containing part of the intestines. **enterolite** (en′ tėr ȯ līt), *n.* A stony calculus. **enterology** (-ol′ ȯ ji), *n.* A treatise or discourse on the intestines, often extended to all the internal parts of the human body. **enteropathy** (-op′ ȧ thi), *n.* Disease of the intestines. **enterotomy** (-ot′ ȯ mi), *n.* Dissection of the intestines.

nterprise (en′ tėr prīz) [O.F. *enterprise*, from *nterpris*, p.p. of *entreprendre*, late L. *interprendere*, to undertake (L. *inter*, among, *prendere, prehendere*, to take in hand)], *n.* An undertaking, esp. a bold or difficult one; spirit of adventure, boldness, readiness to attempt. *v.t.* To undertake, to venture on. *v.i.* To attempt a difficult undertaking. ***enterpriser,** *n.* **enterprising,** *a.* Ready to undertake schemes involving difficulty or hazard; energetic, adventurous; full of enterprise. **enterprisingly,** *adv.*

ntertain (en tėr tān′) [F. *entretenir*, late L. *intertenēre* (*inter*, among, *tenēre*, to hold)], *v.t.* To receive and treat as a guest; to occupy agreeably; to divert, to amuse; to harbour; to hold in mind, cherish; to consider favourably; *to keep or maintain in one's service; *to maintain, to keep up; to take into one's service, to hire, to retain; *to while away time; *to engage (as an enemy's forces). *v.i.* To exercise hospitality; to receive company. **entertainer,** *n.* One who entertains, esp. one who performs amusingly at an entertainment. **entertaining,** *a.* Amusing. **entertainingly,** *adv.* **entertainment,** *n.* The act of entertaining; receiving guests with hospitality; accommodation for a traveller or guest; a banquet; the art of entertaining, amusing, or diverting; the pleasure afforded to the mind by anything interesting; amusement; a dramatic or other performance intended to amuse; *hospitality. ***entertake,** *v.t.* To receive, to entertain.

thalpy (en′ thȧl pi) [EN-, Gr. *thalpos*, heat], *n.* (*Phys.*) Heat content of a substance per unit mass.

thral (en thrawl′), *v.t.* (*past & p.p.* **enthralled**) To reduce to the condition of a thrall; to enslave, to captivate. **enthralment,** *n.*

throne (en thrōn′), *v.t.* To place on a throne or place of dignity; to invest with sovereign power; to induct or instal (as an archbishop or bishop) into the powers or privileges of a see. **enthronement,** *n.*

thronize (en thrō′ nīz) [O.F. *intronizer*, late L. *thronīzāre*, Gr. *enthronizein* (EN-, *thronos*, THRONE)], *v.t.* To enthrone, to induct. **enthronization** (-zā′ shŭn), *n.*

thusiasm (en thū′ zi ăzm) [late L. *enthūsiasmus*, Gr. *enthousiasmos*, from *enthousiazein*, to be inspired, from *enthousia*, from *entheos*, possessed by a god (EN-, *theos*, god)], *n.* Intense and passionate zeal; ardent admiration; fervour; *ecstatic feeling arising from supposed inspiration or possession by a divinity. **enthusiast,** *n.* One filled with or prone to enthusiasm; one whose mind is completely possessed by any subject; a visionary; *one who believes himself possessed or inspired. **enthusiastic** (-ăs′ tik), *a.* and **n.* **enthusiastically,** *adv.*

enthuse (en thūz′), *v.i.* (*colloq.*) To manifest enthusiasm; to gush.

enthymeme (en′ thi mēm) [L. *enthȳmēma*, Gr. *enthumēma -tos*, from *enthumeesthai*, to think (EN-, *thumos*, mind)], *n.* (*Log.*) A syllogism of which one premise is suppressed, and only an antecedent and a consequent expressed in words. **enthymematic** (-măt′ ik), *a.*

entice (en tīs′) [O.F. *enticier*, prob. from a late L. *initiāre*, to kindle, set on fire (EN-, L. *titio*, a firebrand)], *v.t.* To allure, especially into evil or to do evil; to tempt, seduce (from). **enticement,** *n.* **enticer,** *n.* **enticing,** *a.* Alluring, seductive. **enticingly,** *adv.*

entire (en tīr′) [O.F. *entier*, L. *integrum*, acc. of *integer* (*in-*, not, *tăg-*, root of *tangere*, to touch)], *a.* Whole, complete, perfect; unbroken, undivided; unmixed, pure; unqualified, unreserved; not castrated (of a horse); (*Bot.*) having the edges (as of a leaf) unbroken or unserrated; *honest, sincere; unfeigned, earnest; *unimpaired, fresh. *n.* A kind of porter. **entirely,** *adv.* Wholly, in every part; fully, completely; exclusively. **entireness,** *n.* **entirety** (en tīr′ ti), *n.* Entireness, completeness; the entire amount, quantity, or extent. **in its entirety:** Completely, as a whole. **possession by entireties:** (*Law*) Joint possession by two persons, neither of whom can alienate without the other's consent.

entitle (en tītl′) [O.F. *entiteler*, L. *intitulāre* (IN- (1), *titulus*, TITLE)], *v.t.* To give a certain name or title to, to designate; to dignify (a person) by a title; to give a right, title, or claim to anything.

entity (en′ ti ti) [late L. *entitās -tātem*, from ENS], *n.* Essence, existence, as distinguished from qualities or relations; anything that has real existence, a being; the essential nature of a thing, that which constitutes its being. **entitative,** *a.*

ento- [Gr. *entos*, within], *comb. form.*

entoblast (en′ tō blast) [Gr. *blastos*, a sprout], *n.* (*Biol.*) The nucleus of a cell.

entoil (en toil′) *v.t.* To entrap. **entoilment,** *n.*

entomb (en toom′) [F. *entomber* (EN-, *tombe*, TOMB)], *v.t.* To place in a tomb, to bury; to be a grave or tomb for. **entombment,** *n.*

entomo- [Gr. *entomon*, an insect, neut. of *entomos*, cut into, from *entemnein* (EN-, *temnein*, to cut)], *comb. form.* Pertaining to insects. **entomic** (en tom′ ik), *a.* Relating to insects. **entomoid** (en′ tȯ moid) [-OID], *a.* Resembling an insect. *n.* Anything resembling an insect. **entomolite** (en tom′ ȯ līt) [-LITE], *n.* A fossil insect. **entomology** (en tȯ mol′ ȯ ji) [-LOGY], *n.* The science which treats of insects. **entomologic, -al** (-loj′ ik, -ȧl), *a.* **entomologically,** *adv.* **entomologist,** *n.* **entomophagous** (-mof′ ȧ gŭs) [-PHAGOUS], *a.* Feeding on insects. **entomophilous** (-mof′ i lŭs) [-PHILOUS], *a.* Attractive to insects. **entomophilous flowers:** Flowers in which the pollen is carried by insects from the male to the female flowers. **entomostracous** (-mos′ trȧ kŭs) [Gr. *ostrakon*, shell], *a.* Belonging to the *Entomostraca*, a division of crustacea, small in size, with the body segments usually distinct, and gills attached to the feet or organs of the mouth.

entonic (en ton′ ik) [Gr. *entonos* (EN-, *tonos*, a straining)], *a.* (*Path.*) Exhibiting abnormal tension.

entoparasite (en tō pă′ rȧ sīt) [ENTO-], *n.* (*Zool.*) An internal parasite.

entophyte (en′ tō fīt), *n.* (*Bot.*) Any parasitic plant growing in the interior of animal or vegetable structures.

entourage (an′ too razh) [F., from *entourer*, to surround, from *entour* (EN-, *tour*, circuit)], *n.* Surroundings, environment; retinue, attendant company.

entozoon (en tō zō′on) [Gr. *zōon*, animal], *n.* (*pl.* **entozoa**) (*Zool.*) Animal living within the body of another animal. **entozoal, entozoic,** *a.* **entozoology,** *n.* The study of the entozoa. **entozoologist,** *n.*

entr'acte (an' trakt) [F. *entre,* between, *acte,* act], *n.* The interval between the acts of a play; music, dancing, or other performances between the acts of a play.

entrails (en' trālz) [O.F. *entraile,* late L. *intrālia,* from *inter,* among], *n.pl.* The internal parts of animals; the intestines; the internal parts (as of the earth).

entrain (1) (en trān') [F. *entraîner* (en-, L. *inde,* away, *traîner,* to drag, see TRAIN)], *v.t.* To draw after, to bring as a consequence.

entrain (2) (en trān'), *v.t.* To put into a railway train. *v.i.* To get into a train.

entrammel (en trăm' ėl), *v.t.* To entangle, hamper, fetter.

entrance (1) (en' trȧns), *n.* The act of entering; the power, right, or liberty of entering; the passage or doorway by which a place is entered; the means of entering into; the act of coming upon the stage; entering into or upon; the right of admission; entrance-fee, or fee paid for admission, as to an entertainment, club, race, etc.; the entering of a ship or goods at the custom-house; (*Naut.*) the bow of a vessel. **entrance-fee, -money,** *n.* Money paid for entrance or admission.

entrance (2) (en trans') [EN-, TRANCE], *v.t.* To throw into a state of ecstasy; to carry away, transport, enrapture; to overwhelm (with some strong emotion). **entrancement,** *n.*

entrant (en' trȧnt), *n.* One who enters; one entering upon or into a new profession, sphere, competition, etc.

entrap (en trăp') [O.F. *entraper* (EN-, *trape,* a trap)], *v.t.* To catch in or as in a trap; to entangle in contradictions, difficulties, etc.

entreasure (en trezh' ŭr), *v.t.* To lay up in or as in a treasury.

entreat (en trēt') [O.F. *entraiter* (EN-, *traiter,* to TREAT)], *v.t.* To beseech, to ask earnestly; *to obtain by solicitation; to treat, to act towards; to treat of, to discuss. *v.i.* To make entreaties; *to discourse; *to negotiate. **entreatingly,** *adv.* ***entreative,** *a.* Of the nature of an entreaty; entreating. ***entreatment,** *n.* Conversation, interview; treatment; entreaty. **entreaty,** *n.* An urgent solicitation; importunity; *treatment, usage; *handling, discussion, *negotiation.

entrechat (antr' sha) [F.], *n.* A caper in dancing, esp. a striking of the heels together several times in a leap from the ground.

entrée (on' trā, an' trā) [F., entry], *n.* Freedom or right of entrance; a made dish served between the fish and the joint.

entremets (an' tr mā) [F., from O.F. *entremès* (*entre,* between, *mès,* viands)], *n.pl.* Side dishes.

entrench (en trench'), *v.t.* To surround with trenches; to defend (oneself) as if with trenches; to trespass, encroach (upon); to make furrows in. **entrenchment,** *n.*

entrepôt (an' tr pō) [F., from L. *interpositum,* neut. p.p. of *interpōnere* (*inter,* between, *pōnere,* to put)], *n.* A warehouse or magazine for the temporary deposit of goods; a free port where foreign merchandise is kept in bond till re-exported; a commercial centre to which goods are sent for distribution.

entrepreneur (antr pren ur') [F., from *entreprendre,* to undertake (see ENTERPRISE)], *n.* A contractor, an organizer, esp. of entertainments for the public.

entresol (antr' sōl) [F. (*entre,* between, *sol,* the ground)], *n.* A low storey between two higher ones, usually between the first and the ground floor.

entrochite (en' trȯ kīt) [mod. L. *entrochus* (EN-, Gr. *trochos,* wheel), -ITE], *n.* (*Palæont.*) A wheel-like joint or segment of an encrinite. **entrochal,** *a* Pertaining to or containing entrochites.

entropion (en trō' pi ŏn) [Gr. *entropē,* rel. to *entre pein* (EN-, *trepein,* to turn)], *n.* Introversion of th eyelids.

entropy (en' trȯ pi) [EN-, Gr. *tropē,* a transforma tion or turning, from *trepein,* to turn], *n.* (*Phys* The property of a substance, expressed quantita tively, which remains constant when the substanc changes its volume or does work with no heat pass ing into or from it, thus forming an index of th availability of the thermal energy of a system fo mechanical work.

entrust (en trŭst'), *v.t.* To commit or confide to person's care; to charge with (a duty, care, etc.).

entry (en' tri) [F. *entrée,* late L. *intrāta,* fro *intrāre,* to ENTER], *n.* The act of entering; ceremonial entrance into a place; the passage, gat opening, or other way by which anything entered; the act of entering or inscribing in a boo etc.; an item so entered; the exhibiting of a ship papers at the custom-house to procure leave t land goods; (*Law*) the act of taking possession b setting foot upon land or tenements; the depositin a document in the proper office; the formal puttin upon record; unauthorized entrance into premise thus one of the acts necessary to constitute burgla or trespass; (*pl.*) a list of competitors, etc. **doub entry, single entry:** Systems of accounts i which each item is entered twice or once in th ledger, etc.

entwine (en twīn'), *v.t.* To twine or twist togethe (*fig.*) to interlace, to mingle together; to embrac clasp, enfold. *v.i.* To become twined or twiste together. **entwinement,** *n.*

entwist (en twist'), *v.t.* To twist around; to for into a twist; to twist (with something else).

enucleate (ē nū' klė āt) [L. *ēnucleātus,* p.p. *ēnucleāre*], *v.t.* To bring to light, elucidate, solv (*Surg.*) to extract (a tumour) from its coverin **enucleation** (-ā' shŭn), *n.*

enumerate (ė nū' mėr āt) [L. *ēnumerātus.* p.p. *ēnumerāre*], *v.t.* To reckon up one by one, count; to specify the items of. **enumeration** (- shŭn), *n.* **enumerative** (ė nū' mėr ȧ tiv), *a.* **enu merator** (ė nū' mėr ā tŏr), *n.*

enunciate (e nŭn' shi āt) [L. *ēnuntiātus,* p.p. *ēnuntiāre* (E-, *nuntius,* a messenger)], *v.t.* To pr nounce distinctly, articulate clearly; to expre definitely, state or announce with formal precisio *v.i.* To pronounce words or syllables; to spea **enunciation** (-si ā' shŭn), *n.* A declaring or a nouncing; the manner of pronunciation or utte ance; statement, formal expression; the stateme of a proposition; a proposition, esp. one that has n been proved or disproved. **enunciative** (ė nŭ shi ȧ tiv), *a.* **enunciatively,** *adv.* **enunciator** nŭn' shi ā tŏr), *n.* **enunciable,** *a.*

enure [INURE].

enuresis (en ū rē' sis) [Gr. *en,* in, *ouron,* urine], (*Path.*) Involuntary micturition, incontinence urine.

enveigle [INVEIGLE].

envelop (en vel' ŏp) [O.F. *enveloper* [etym. doub ful; cp. DEVELOP)], *v.t.* To enwrap, to enclose, surround so as to hide, to enshroud; to wrap in as in an envelope or covering; to surround wi troops or offensive works. **envelopment,** *n.*

envelope (en' vė lōp, on' vė lōp) [F. *enveloppe,* prec.], *n.* A wrapper, a covering, esp. a paper ca to contain a letter; (*Astron.*) the nebulous coveri of the head of a comet; (*Bot.*) a whorl of alter leaves surrounding the organs of fructificatio (*Aviat.*) the gas-bag of a balloon. **windo envelope** [WINDOW].

envenom (en ven' ŏm) [O.F. *envenimer*], *v.t.* make poisonous, to impregnate with poison; (*fi* to make bitter or spiteful; *to poison; *(*fig.*) corrupt.

envermeil (en vĕr′ mil) [O.F. *envermeiller* (EN-, VERMEIL)], *v.t.* To tinge with vermilion.

enviable, etc. [ENVY].

environ (en vī′ rŏn) [F. *environner*, from *environ*, round about (EN-, *virer*, to veer, to turn)], *v.t.* To surround, to be or extend round, to encompass; to surround so as to attend or protect, to beset; to surround (with persons or things); *to travel round. **environage,** *n.* Environment. **environment,** *n.* The act of environing or surrounding; that which encompasses surrounding objects, scenery, circumstances, etc.; (*Nat. Hist.*) the sum of external influences affecting an organism. **environs** (en vī′ rŏnz, en′ vi rŏnz), *n.pl.* The parts or districts round any place.

envisage (en viz′ åj) [F. *envisager*], *v.t.* To look into the face of, to look directly at; to face, confront; to contemplate, esp. a particular aspect of; (*Phil.*) to perceive by intuition. **envisagement,** *n.*

envoy (1) (en′ voi) [O.F. *envoié*, properly, a message, p.p. of *envoyer*, to send (*en voie*, L. *in via*, on the way)], *n.* A postscript to a collection of poems, or a concluding stanza to a poem.

envoy (2) (en′ voi) [as prec.], *n.* A diplomatic agent, next in rank below an ambassador, sent by one government to another upon some special occasion; a messenger, a representative. **envoyship,** *n.*

envy (en′ vi) [O.F. *envie*, L. *invidia*, from *invidus*, rel. to *invidēre*, to envy (IN-, *vidēre*, to see)], *n.* Ill-will at the superiority, success, or good fortune of others, a grudging sense of another's superiority to oneself; the object of this feeling; *odium, hatred, malice. *v.t.* To regard with envy; to feel jealous of; to covet. *v.i.* To have envious feelings. **enviable,** *a.* Capable of exciting envy; of a nature to be envied; greatly to be desired. **enviably,** *adv.* **envious,** *a.* Infected with envy; instigated by envy; *enviable. **enviously,** *adv.*

enwind (en wīnd′), *v.t.* To wind or coil around.

enwrap (en răp′), *v.t.* To wrap or enfold; to envelop; to engross, to absorb; to involve, implicate.

enwreathe (en rēth′), *v.t.* To encircle with or as with a wreath.

enzootic (en zō ot′ ik) [EN-, Gr. *zōon*, animal], *a.* Pertaining to a disease which affects animals in a certain district either constantly or at periodical intervals, endemic among animals. *n.* An enzootic disease.

enzyme (en′ zīm) [Gr. *enzumos*, unfermented (cp. AZYME)], *n.* (*Chem.*) A catalyst produced by living cells, esp. in the digestive system. **enzymic** (-zim′ ik), **enzymotic** (-mot′ ik), *a.* **enzymosis** (-mō′ sis), **enzymation** (-mā′ shŭn), *n.* **enzymology** (-mol′ ŏ ji), *n.*

eoan (ē ō′ ăn) [L. *ēōus*, Gr. *ēōos*, from *ēōs*, dawn], *a.* Pertaining to the dawn; eastern.

Eocene (ē′ ō sēn) [Gr. *ēōs*, dawn, *kainos*, new], *a.* (*Geol.*) Pertaining to the lowest division of the Tertiary strata.

Eolian, etc. [ÆOLIAN].

eolipyle [ÆOLIPYLE].

eolith (ē′ ŏ lith) [Gr. *ēōs*, dawn, -LITH], *n.* (*Palæont.*) A supposed stone implement of rude construction anterior in date to the Palæolithic age, found abundantly in parts of the North Downs, but not accepted as artificial by many archæologists. **eolithic** (-lith′ ik), *a.*

eon [ÆON].

-eous [L. *-eus*, pertaining to, of the nature of], *suf.* Forming adjectives, as *arboreous*, *ligneous*, *righteous*.

eozoon (ē ō zō′ ŏn) [Gr. *ēōs*, dawn, *zōon*, animal], *n.* (*Palæont.*) A hypothetical genus of protozoa found in the Laurentian strata in Canada, the supposed remains of which are now believed to be inorganic. **eozoic,** *a.*

ep- [EPI-], *pref.* (*before a vowel*) as in *epact*, *epoch*.

epact (ē′ păkt, ep′ ăkt) [M.F. *epacte*, late L. *epacta*, Gr. *epaktē*, from *epagein*, to intercalate (EP-, *agein*, to bring)], *n.* The moon's age at the beginning of the year; the excess of the solar year above the lunar year.

epagoge (ep å gō′ jē) [Gr. *epagōgē*, from *epagein* (EP-, *agein*, to bring)], *n.* (*Log.*) The bringing forward of particular examples to prove a universal conclusion; the argument or induction.

epana-, epan- [Gr. EP-, *ana*, up, again], *comb. form* (*Rhet.*). **epanadiplosis** (ep ăn å di plō′ sis) [Gr. *diplōsis*, a doubling], *n.* A figure by which a sentence ends with the same word with which it begins. **epanalepsis** (-lep′ sis) [Gr. *lēpsis*, from *lambanein*, to take], *n.* A figure of speech by which the same word or clause is repeated after other words intervening. **epanastrophe** (ep ăn ăs′ trŏ fi), *n.* A figure of speech by which the end word of one sentence becomes the first word of the following sentence. **epanados** (ėp ăn′ ŏ dos) [Gr. *hodos*, way], *n.* A figure in which the second member of a sentence is an inversion of the first; resumption after a digression. **epanorthosis** (-thō′ sis) [Gr. *orthōsis*, a setting straight, from *orthos*, straight], *n.* A figure by which a person recalls what he has said for the purpose of putting it more forcibly.

epanthous (ė păn′ thŭs) [EP-, Gr. *anthos*, flower], *a.* (*Bot.*) Growing upon a flower, as certain fungi.

eparch (ep′ ark) [Gr. *eparchos* (EP-, *archos*, a ruler)], *n.* A governor or prefect of an eparchy; (*Russ. Ch.*) the bishop of an eparchy. **eparchy,** *n.* A province of modern Greece; (*Hist.*) a prefecture; (*Russ. Ch.*) a diocese.

epaulement (ė pawl′ mėnt) [F., *épaulement*, from *épauler*, to protect by an *épaule*, shoulder], *n.* (*Fort.*) A breastwork, short parapet, or bank of earth, to defend the flank of a battery, etc.

epaulet (ep′ ŏ let) [F. *épaulette*, from *épaule*, shoulder], *n.* An ornamental badge worn on the shoulder in military, naval, and certain civil full dress uniforms; (*fig.*, *pl.*) the rank of officer. **epauletted** (-let′ ėd), *a.*

épée (ep′ ā) [Fr., a sword], *n.* A duelling sword; fencing foil.

epeirogenesis (e pī rō gen′ e sis) [Gr. *epeiros*, mainland, GENESIS], *n.* (*Geol.*) The making of a continent.

epencephalon (ep ėn sef′ å lon) [EP-, ENCEPHALON], *n.* (*Anat.*) The hindmost division of the brain.

epenthesis (ė pen′ thė sis) [late L., from Gr. (EP-, *en-*, in, *thesis*, a placing, from *tithenai*, to place)], *n.* (*Gram.*) The addition of a letter or letters in the middle of a word, as in *alitium* for *alitum*; (*Philol.*) the phonetic change resulting from the transference of a semi-vowel to the preceding syllable. **epenthetic** (ep ėn thet′ ik), *a.*

epergne (ė pârn′, -pĕrn′) [etym. doubtful], *n.* An ornamental stand, usu. branched, for the centre of a table, etc.

epexegesis (ėp ek sė jē′ sis) [*epexēgēsis* (EP-, EXEGESIS)], *n.* Further elucidation of something which has gone before; further statement. **epexegetical,** *a.*

eph- [EPI-], *pref.* Before *h*, as in *ephemera*, *ephor*.

ephah (ē′ fâ) [Heb. *ēyphāh*, said to be of Egyptian origin], *n.* A Jewish measure of capacity for dry goods.

ephebe (ė fēb′) [L. *ephēbus*, Gr. *ephēbos* (EPI-, *hēbe*, early manhood)], *n.* (*Gr. Ant.*) A freeborn youth between the ages of 18 and 20, qualified for citizenship. **ephebic** (ė fē′ bik), *a.* (*Zool.*) Adult, mature, at the maximum of development.

ephemera (ė fem′ ėr å) [Gr. *ephēmeros* (EPI-, *hēmera*, day)], *n.* (*pl.* -ræ) A genus of ephemeropterous insects, containing the May-fly; the May-fly; a fever of only one day's continuance; anything short-lived. **ephemeral,** *a.* Beginning and ending in a day; short-lived, transient. **ephemerality** (-ăl′ i ti), *n.* **ephemeric,** *a.* Ephemeral. **ephemeris** (ė fem′ ėr is) [Gr., calendar], *n.* A journal, an account of daily transactions; (*Astron.*) a collection of tables or data showing the daily position of the planets; an astronomical almanac; ephemera. **ephemeron,** *a.* (*pl.* **-ra**) Ephemera.

Ephesian (ė fē′ zhȧn) [L. *Ephesius*, Gr. *Ephesios*], *a.* Of or pertaining to Ephesus. *n.* An inhabitant of Ephesus; *a jolly companion.

ephod (ef′ od) [Heb. *āphad*, to put on], *n.* An emblematic short coat covering the shoulders and breast of the Jewish High Priest; a similar but less splendid garment worn by the ordinary priests.

ephor (ef′ ȯr) [Gr. *ephoros* (EPI, *horaein*, to see)], *n.* (*pl.* **ephori**). One of the five magistrates chosen at Sparta and invested with the highest power, controlling even the kings. **ephoralty** (ef′ ȯr ȧl ti), *n.*

epi- [Gr. *epi*, upon, at, to, besides, in addition], *pref.*, as in *epigram*, *episode*.

epi (ā′ pē) [F.], *n.* A tuft of hair, esp. on a horse's forehead; a cow-lick.

epiblast (ep′ i blăst) [EPI-, Gr. *blastos*, sprout], *n.* (*Biol.*) The outermost of the layers in the blastoderm.

epic (ep′ ik) [L. *epicus*, Gr. *epikos*, from *epos*, a word], *a.* Narrating some heroic event in a lofty style. *n.* A poem narrating the history, real or fictitious, of some notable action or series of actions, accomplished by a hero or heroes. **epic dialect,** *n.* The Greek dialect in which the *Iliad* and the *Odyssey* were composed. **national epic,** *n.* An heroic poem embodying a nation's traditional history. **epical,** *a.* **epically,** *adv.*

epicalyx (ep′ i kăl iks), *n.* (*Bot.*) A whorl of leaves forming an additional calyx outside the true calyx.

epicarp (ep′ i karp) [EPI-, Gr. *karpos*, fruit], *n.* (*Bot.*) The integument of fruits; peel, rind, skin.

epicedium (ep i sē′ di ŭm), **epicede** (ep′ i sēd) [L. *epicēdīum*, Gr. *epikēdeion* (EPI-, *kēdos*, care)], *n.* (*pl.* **-dia, -diums**) A dirge; a funeral ode. **epicedial** (-sē′ di ȧl), *a.*

epicene (ep′ i sēn) [L. *epicœnus*, Gr. *epikoinos* (EPI-, *koinos*, common)], *a.* (*Gram.*) Of common gender, having only one form for both sexes; pertaining to both sexes; hermaphrodite; sexless. *n.* A noun common to both genders, as *sheep*; a person having the characteristics of both sexes.

epicentrum (ep i sen′ trŭm) [Gr. *epikentron*, nom. *-ros* (EPI-, *kentron*, centre)], *n.* The point over the focus of an earthquake.

epichirema (ep i kī rē′ mȧ) [Gr. *epicheirēma*, from *epicheireein*, to undertake (EPI-, *cheir*, hand)], *n.* (*Log.*) A syllogism in which the proof of the premises is introduced with the premises themselves.

epicure (ep′ i kūr) [*Epicūrus*, Gr. *Epikouros*], *n.* One devoted to sensual pleasures, esp. those of the table; *an Epicurean. **epicurism,** *n.* **Epicurean** (ep i kū rē′ ȧn), *a.* Pertaining to Epicurus or his system of philosophy, which taught that pleasure is the supreme good and the basis of morality; devoted to pleasure, esp. the more refined varieties of sensuous enjoyment. *n.* A follower of Epicurus; a person devoted to pleasure; a sensualist, a gourmand. **epicureanism,** *n.*

epicycle (ep′ i sī′ kėl) [L. *epicyclus*, Gr. *epikuklos* (EPI-, *kuklos*, circle)], *n.* A small circle the centre of which is carried round upon another circle. **epicyclic** (-sik′ lik), *a.* **epicycloid** (-sik′ loid), *n.* A curve generated by the revolution of a point in the circumference of a circle rolling along the exterior of another circle. **epicycloidal** (-kloi′ dȧl), *a.*

epideictic (ep i dīk′ tik) [Gr. *epideiktikos*, from *epideiknunai* (EPI-, *deiknunai*, to show)], *a.* Showing off; displaying (applied to set orations).

epidemic (ep i dem′ ik) [F. *épidémique*, from *épidémie*, late L. and Gr. *epidēmia*, from *epidēmios* (EPI-, *demos*, people)], *a.* Affecting at once a large number in a community. *n.* A disease attacking many persons at the same time, and spreading with great rapidity. **epidemical,** *a.* **epidemically,** *adv.* **epidemiology** (-ol′ ȯ ji), *n.* The study and treatment of epidemic diseases. **epidemiologist,** *n.*

epidermis (ep i dĕr′ mis) [L., from Gr. (EPI-, *derma*, skin)], *n.* The cuticle or skin constituting the external layer in animals; (*Bot.*) the exterior cellular coating of the leaf or stem of a plant. **epidermal, -mic,** *a.* Pertaining to the epidermis. **epidermoid, epidermoidal,** *a.*

epidiascope (ep i dī′ ăs kōp) [Gr. *epi*, upon; *dia*, through; *skopein*, view], *n.* A magic lantern which may be used for opaque objects or transparencies.

epidote (ep′ i dōt) [F. *épidote*, formed from Gr. *epididonai* (EPI-, *didonai*, to give)], *n.* (*Min.*) A brittle mineral, a silicate of alumina and lime, of vitreous lustre and of various colours, mostly found in crystalline rocks. **epidotic** (-dot′ ik), *a.*

epigastrium (ep i găs′ tri ŭm) [Gr. *epigastrion* (EPI-, *gastēr*, stomach)], *n.* The upper part of the abdomen, esp. that part above the stomach. **epigastric,** *a.*

epigene (ep′ i jēn) [F. *épigène*, Gr. *epigenēs* (EPI-, *genēs*, born)], *a.* (*Geol.*) Originating on the surface of the earth; (*Cryst.*) having undergone an alteration in its chemical character while retaining the same crystalline form as before; pseudomorphous.

epigenesis (ep i jen′ ė sis), *n.* (*Biol.*) The theory that in reproduction the organism is brought into being by the union of the male and female elements. **epigenesist,** *n.* **epigenetic** (-net′ ik), *a.* **epigenous** (ė pij′ ė nŭs), *a.* (*Bot.*) Growing upon the surface of a part, as do many fungi.

epiglottis (ep i glot′ is) [Gr. *epiglōttis* (EPI-, *glōssa*, tongue)], *n.* A leaf-like cartilage at the base of the tongue which covers the glottis during the act of swallowing. **epiglottic,** *a.*

epigone (ep′ i gōn) [Gr.], *n.* One belonging to a later and less noteworthy generation.

epigram (ep′ i grăm) [F. *épigramme*, L. and Gr. *epigramma* (EPI-, -GRAM)], *n.* A short poem or composition of a pointed or antithetical character; a pithy or antithetical saying or phrase. **epigrammatic** (-măt′ ik), *a.* **epigrammatically,** *adv.* **epigrammatist** (-grăm′ ȧ tist), *n.* **epigrammatize,** *v.t.* To write or express by way of epigrams.

epigraph (ep′ i grăf) [Gr. *epigraphē* (EPI-, *graphein*, to write)], *n.* A sentence placed at the beginning of a work, or of divisions in a work, as a motto; an inscription placed on buildings, statues, tombs, and the like, denoting their use and appropriation. **epigraphic, -al** (-grăf′ ik, -ȧl), *a.* **epigraphically,** *adv.* **epigraphist** (ė pig′ rȧ fist), *n.* **epigraphy,** *n.* The deciphering and explanation of inscriptions; inscriptions taken collectively.

epigynous (ė pij′ i nŭs) [EPI-, Gr. *gunē*, woman], *a.* (*Bot.*) Growing on the top of the ovary, with only the upper portions free (of the stamens or corolla).

epilepsy (ep′ i lep si) [M.F. *epilepsie*, L. and Gr. *epilēpsia*, from *epilambanein* (EPI-, *lambanein*, to take)], *n.* A nervous disease, formerly called the falling sickness from the suddenness of its attacks which involve convulsions and loss of consciousness. **epileptic** (ep i lep′ tik), *a.* Afflicted with epilepsy; pertaining to or indicating the presence of epilepsy. *n.* One afflicted with epilepsy. **epileptical,** *a.* **epileptoid,** *a.*

epilogue (ep′ i log) [F., from L. *epilogus*, Gr. *epilogos* (EPI-, *logos*, speech)], *n.* A short speech or poem addressed to the spectators at the end of a play; the concluding part of a book, essay, or speech, a peroration. **epilogist** (ė pil′ ȯ jist), *n.* **epilogize, *-guize** (ė pil′ ȯ jīz, -gīz), *v.i.* To pronounce or deliver an epilogue. *v.t.* To put an epilogue to.

epinasty (ep′ i năs ti) [EPI-, Gr. *nastos*, from *nassein*, to squeeze close], *n.* (*Bot.*) Curving of an organ through more rapid growth of the upper surface.

epiperipheral (ep i pĕr if′ ėr ȧl), *a.* Originating at the periphery.

epipetalous (ep i pet′ å lůs), *a.* (*Bot.*) Growing separately on the corolla (of stamens).

Epiphany (ė pif′ å ni) [F. *épiphanie*, from late L., from Gr. *epiphania*, neut. pl., from *epiphainein* (EPI-, *phainein*, to show), used as equivalent to *epiphaneia*, appearance, manifestation, from *epiphanēs*, manifest], *n.* The manifestation of Christ to the Magi at Bethlehem; the annual festival, held on January 6, the twelfth day after Christmas, to commemorate this; the appearance or manifestation of a divinity.

epiphenomenon (ep i fen om′ en on), *n.* A phenomenon that is secondary and incidental, a mere concomitant of some effect.

epiphragm (ep′ i frăm) [Gr. *epiphragma*, a lid, from *epiphrassein* (EPI-, *phrassein*, to fence)], *n.* (*Zool.*) The disk-like secretion with which snails and other molluscs close their shells during hibernation; (*Bot.*) a membrane closing the aperture of the sperm-case in urn-mosses and fungi.

epiphyllous (ep i fil′ ůs) [EPI-, Gr. *phullon*, leaf], *a.* (*Bot.*) Growing upon a leaf; (of stamens) growing upon the perianth.

epiphysis (ep i fis′ is) [Gr. (EPI-, *phusis*, growth)], *n.* (*pl.* **-ses**) (*Anat.*) A process formed by a separate centre of ossification.

epiphyte (ep′ i fīt), *n.* A plant growing upon another, usu. not deriving its nourishment from this; a fungus parasitic on an animal body. **epiphytal** (-fī′ tål), **epiphytic** (-fit′ ik), *a.*

epiploon (ė pip′ lō ŏn) [Gr., from *epipleein* (EPI-, *pleein*, to sail or float)], *n.* The fatty membrane enwrapping the entrails; the omentum. **epiploic** (-plō ik), *a.*

epirhizous (ep i rī′ zůs) [EPI-, Gr. *rhiza*, root], *a.* (*Bot.*) Growing on a root.

episcopacy (ė pis′ kō på si) [late L. *episcopātus*, *episcopus*, BISHOP, -ACY], *n.* Government of a Church by bishops, the accepted form in the Latin and Greek communions and the Church of England, prelacy; the bishops taken collectively. **episcopal,** *a.* Appertaining to a bishop; constituted on the episcopal form of government. **episcopal church:** A Church, like the Anglican, constituted on this basis. **episcopalian** (-pā′ li ån), *n.* A member of an episcopal Church; a supporter of episcopal Church government and discipline. *a.* Episcopal. **episcopalianism,** *n.* **episcopalism** (ė pis′ kŏ på lizm), *n.* **episcopally,** *adv.* **episcopate** (-påt), *n.* The office or see of a bishop; the term during which any bishop holds office; bishops collectively. **v.i.* (-pāt) To fill the office of a bishop; to discharge episcopal functions. ***episcopy** (ė pis′ kŏ pi), *n.* Oversight, superintendence; episcopacy; episcopate.

episcope (ep′ i skōp), *n.* (*Opt.*) A projection lantern used for throwing on a screen an enlarged image of an opaque object.

episode (ep′ i sōd) [Gr. *epeisodion*, adventitious, episodic (EPI-, *eisodos*, entering)], *n.* Originally the parts in dialogue between the choric parts in Greek tragedy, which were primarily interpolations; an incident or series of events in a story, separable though arising out of it; an incident or closely connected series of events in real life; (*Mus.*) a portion of a fugue deviating from the main theme. **episodic, -al** (ep i sod′ ik, -ål), *a.* **episodically,** *adv.*

epispastic (ep i spăs′ tik) [Gr. *epispastikos* (EPI-, *spaein*, to draw)], *a.* Drawing, exciting action in the skin; blistering. *n.* Any preparation for producing counter-irritation, a blister.

episperm (ep′ i spĕrm), *n.* (*Bot.*) The outer integument of a seed. **epispermic,** *a.*

epistemology (ep i stē mol′ ŏ ji) [Gr. *epistēmē*, knowledge, -LOGY], *n.* The science which deals with the origin and method of knowledge.

episternum (ep i stĕr′ nům), *n.* (*Anat.*) The upper part of the sternum or breast-bone in mammals, or that portion of an articulate animal immediately adjoining the sternum. **episternal,** *a.*

epistle (ė pis′ ėl) [O.F., from L. *epistola*, Gr. *epistolē*, from *epistellein* (EPI-, *stellein*, to send)], *n.* A written communication, a letter (now only in a formal or facetious sense); a literary work (usu. in verse) in the form of a letter; (*pl.*) letters written by Apostles to the Churches, now forming part of the New Testament; a lesson in the Church service, so called as being taken from the apostolic Epistles. **v.t.* To write or communicate by a letter; to write an introduction or preface. **epistle-side,** *n.* The (right facing) side of the altar at which the epistle is read. **epistler** (ė pis′-, -pist′ lėr), **-toler,** *n.* A writer of letters; the person who reads the epistle in the Church service. **epistolary** (ė pis′ tŏ lår i), *a.* Pertaining to or suitable for letters; contained in or carried on by means of letters. *n.* A book containing the Epistles. ***epistolet,** *n.* A short letter or epistle. ***epistolist,** *n.* ***epistolize,** *v.i.* ***epistolizer,** *n.* ***epistolographic** (-grăf′ ik), *a.* Pertaining to the writing of letters, demotic. ***epistolography** (-log′ rå fi) [-GRAPHY], *n.*

epistrophe (ė pis′ trŏ fi), *n.* (*Rhet.*) A figure in which several sentences or clauses end with the same word; (*Bot.*) the return of a variegated form to the normal condition.

epistyle (ep′ i stīl) [L. *epistӯlium*, Gr. *epistulion* (EPI-, *stulos*, pillar)], *n.* (*Arch.*) The architrave.

epitaph (ep′ i taf) [L. *epitaphium* (directly or through F. *épitaphe*), Gr. *epitaphion*, neut. of *epitaphios*, a., over a tomb (EPI-, *taphos*, tomb)], *n.* An inscription on a tomb; an inscription in prose or verse, as for a tomb or monument. *v.t.* *To commemorate in an epitaph. **epitaphial** (-tăf′ i ål), *a.* ***epitaphian, -taphic,** *a.* **epitaphist** (ep′ i tåf ist), *n.*

epitasis (ė pit′ å sis) [Gr., from *epiteinein* (EPI-, *teinein*, to stretch)], *n.* The portion of a play in which the plot is developed, between the protasis or introduction and the catastrophe.

epithalamium (ep i thå lā′ mi ům) [L., from Gr. *epithalamion*, neut. of *epithalamios*, a. (EPI-, *thalamos*, bridal chamber)], *n.* (*pl.* **-mia**) A nuptial song or poem. **epithalamial,** *a.* **epithalamic** (-lăm′ ik), *a.*

epithelium (ep i thē′ li ům) [mod. L. (EPI-, Gr. *thēlē*, teat)], *n.* (*pl.* **-lia**) The cell-tissues lining the alimentary canal; the outer layer of the mucous membranes; (*Bot.*) the thin epidermis lining inner cavities, the stigma, etc., of plants.

epithem (ep′ i them) [Gr. *epithema*, from *epitithenai* (EPI-, *tithenai*, to place)], *n.* (*Med.*) Any external application, except ointment or plasters.

epithet (ep′ i thet) [L. and Gr. *epitheton*, from *epitithenai* (as prec.)], *n.* An adjective or phrase denoting any quality or attribute; (*colloq.*) an abusive expression; a nickname; *a term, phrase, or expression. **v.t.* To describe by epithets; to entitle. **epithetic, -al** (-thet′ ik, -ål), *a.* **epithetically,** *adv.* ***epitheton,** *n.* Epithet.

epithymetic (ep i thi met′ ik) [Gr. *epithumētikos*, from *epithumeein*, to desire (EPI-, *thumos*, soul, appetite)], *a.* Pertaining to desire.

epitome (ė pit′ ŏ mi) [L., from Gr. *epitomē* (EPI-, *temnein*, to cut)], *n.* A brief summary of a book, document, etc.; a condensation, abridgment, abstract; (*fig.*) a representation in little. **epitomist,** *n.* **epitomize,** *v.t.* To make an abstract, summary, or abridgment of; to represent in miniature; *to cut down, curtail. *v.i.* To make epitomes.

epitonic (ep i ton′ ik) [Gr. *epitonos*, from *epiteinein* (EPI-, *teinein*, to stretch)], *a.* Overstrained.

epitrite (ep′ i trīt) [L. and Gr. *epitritos* (EPI-, *tritos*, third)], *n.* (*Pros.*) A metrical foot consisting of three long syllables and a short one, in any order.

epizoon (ep i zō′ ŏn) [EPI-, *zōōn*, animal], *n.* (*pl.* **-zoa**) (*Zool.*) An animal parasitic upon the exterior surface of another. **epizootic** (-ot′ ik), *a.* Pertaining to diseases epidemic among animals;

(*Geol.*) containing fossil remains, and therefore posterior to the advent of organic life. *n.* An epizootic disease; a murrain or epidemic among cattle.

epoch (ē′ pok, ep′ ok) [late L. *epocha*, Gr. *epochē*, a stop, check, pause, from *epechein* (EP-, *echein*, to have, to hold)], *n.* A fixed point from which succeeding years are numbered, a memorable date; a period characterized by momentous events, an era; (*Geol.*) a subdivision of geological time; (*Astron.*) the moment when a certain event takes place or a certain position is reached; the longitude of a planet at any given time. **epoch-making,** *a.* Of such importance as to mark an epoch. **epochal** (ep′ ŏ kȧl), *a.*

epode (ep′ ōd) [O.F., from L. *epōdos*, Gr. *epōdos*, from *epadein* (EP-, *adein*, *aeidein*, to sing)], *n.* In lyric poetry the part after the strophe and antistrophe; a chorus; lyric poetry in which a shorter line follows a longer one. **epodic** (ė pod′ ik), *a.*

eponym (ep′ ŏ nim) [Gr. *epōnumos* (EP-, *onoma*, Æolic *onuma*, name)], *n.* A name given to a people, place, or institution, after some person; the name of a mythical person made to account for the name of a country or people. **eponymic** (-nim′ ik), **eponymous** (ė pon′ i mŭs), *a.*

epopee (ep′ ŏ pē), **epopœia** (ep ŏ pē′ yȧ) [F. *épopée*, Gr. *epopoiia*, from *epopoios* (*epos*, word, song, *poios*, maker, from *poiein*, to make)], *n.* An epic or heroic poem; epic poetry, the series of events forming the material for an epic.

epos (ep′ os), *n.* An epopee; epic poetry; primitive, unwritten narrative poetry embodying heroic traditions.

eprouvette (ep ru vet′) [F., from *éprouver*, to try, test], *n.* An apparatus for determining the strength of gunpowder; a spoon used in assaying.

Epsom salts (ep′ sŏm sawlts), *n.* Sulphate of magnesia, a saline purgative, formerly prepared from a mineral spring at Epsom, Surrey. **epsomite,** *n.* (*Min.*) Native sulphate of magnesia.

equable (ek′ wȧbl, ē′ kwȧ bėl) [L. *æquābilis*, from *æquāre*, to make level, from *æquus*, equal], *a.* Characterized by evenness or uniformity; smooth, level, even; not varying, not irregular; not subject to irregularities or disturbance. **equability** (-bil′ i ti), *n.* **equableness,** *n.* **equably,** *adv.*

equal (ē′ kwȧl) [L. *æquālis*, as prec.], *a.* The same in magnitude, number, quality, degree, etc.; even, uniform, not variable; impartial, unbiased, fair, just; having adequate power, ability, or means (to). *n.* One not inferior or superior to another; one of the same or similar age, rank, office, talents, or the like; a match; (*pl.*) equal things; *equality. *v.t.* (*past & p.p.* **equalled**) To be equal (to); *to make equal; *to make level or even; *to become equal to, to match; *to return a full equivalent for; *to compare. **equality** (ė kwol′ i ti), *n.* The state of being equal; *evenness; *equability. **on an equality with:** On equal terms with. **equalize** (ē′ kwȧ līz), *v.t.* To make equal (to, with). **equalization** (-zā′ shŭn), *n.* **equally,** *adv.* **equalness,** *n.*

equanimity (ē kwă nim′ i ti) [F. *equanimité*, L. *æquanimitās -tātem*, from *æquanimis* (*æquus*, equal, *animus*, mind)], *n.* Evenness or composure of mind; temper not easily disturbed; resignation. ***equanimous,** *a.* Of an even frame of mind; not easily elated or depressed. ***equanimously,** *adv.* ***equanimousness,** *n.*

equate (ė kwāt′) [L. *æquatus*, p.p. of *æquāre*, from *æquus*, equal], *v.t.* To equalize; to reduce to an average or common standard.

equation (ė kwā′ shŭn) [L. *æquātio -ōnem*, from *æquāre*, as prec.], *n.* The act of making equal; equality; (*Math*) two algebraic expressions equal to one another, and connected by the sign =; (*Astron.*) a sum added or subtracted to allow for any special circumstance affecting the exactness of a calculation. **personal equation:** (*Astron.*) The quantity of time by which a person is in the habit of noting a phenomenon wrongly; (*fig.*) aberration from strict accuracy, logical reasoning, or absolute fairness, due to personal characteristics. **equation of light:** (*Astron.*) The allowance made in determining the position of a heavenly body for the time occupied in the transmission of its light to the eye of the observer. **equation of payments:** A rule for ascertaining at what time a person should pay the whole of a debt contracted in different portions to be repaid at different times. **equation of time:** (*Astron.*) The difference between mean and apparent time. **equational,** *a.* **equationally,** *adv.*

equator (ė kwā′ tŏr) [late L., as prec.], *n.* A great circle on the earth's surface, equidistant from its poles, and dividing it into the northern and southern hemispheres; (*Astron.*) a great circle of the heavens, dividing it into a northern and a southern hemisphere, constituted by the production of the plane of the earth's equator. **equatorial** (-tôr′ i ȧl), *a.* Pertaining to the equator; situated on or near the equator. **equatorial telescope,** *n.* A telescope mounted on an axis parallel to that of the earth, used for noting the course of the stars as they move through the sky. **equatorially,** *adv.*

equerry (ek′ wėr i) (F. *écurie*, med. L. *scūria*, a stable, O.H.G. *scūr*, *sciura*, a shed (G. *scheuer*, barn), confused with L. *equus*, horse], *n.* An officer having the care of the horses of nobles or princes; an officer of a royal household.

equestrian (ė kwes′ tri ȧn) [L. *equestris*, from *eques*, horseman, from *equus*, horse], *a.* Pertaining to horses or horsemanship; mounted on horseback; *given to or skilled in horsemanship; (*Rom. Ant.*) pertaining to the Equites or Knights. *n.* A rider on horseback; one who performs feats of horsemanship; a circus-rider. **equestrianism,** *n.* **equestrienne** (ė kwes tri en′), *n.* A female equestrian.

equi- (L. *æquus*, equal], *comb. form.* **equiangular** (ē kwi ăng′ gū lȧr) [ANGULAR], *a.* (*Math.*) Having or consisting of equal angles.

equidifferent (ē′ kwi dif′ ėr ėnt), *a.* Having equal differences; arithmetically proportional.

equidistant (ē kwi dis′ tȧnt), *a.* Equally distant from some point or place; separated from each other by equal distances. **equidistance,** *n.* **equidistantly,** *adv.*

equilateral (ē kwi lăt′ ėr ȧl), *a.* Having all the sides equal. *n.* A figure having all its sides equal. **equilaterally,** *adv.*

equilibrate (ē kwi lī′ brāt), *v.t.* To balance (tw things) exactly; to counterpoise. *v.i.* To balanc (each other) exactly; to be a counterpoise (to). **equilibration** (-brā′ shŭn), *n.*

equilibrist (ė kwil′ i brist) [EQUILIBRIUM], *n.* On who keeps his balance in unnatural positions, rope-dancer, an acrobat.

equilibrium (ē kwi lib′ ri ŭm) [L. *æquilībriun* (EQUI-, *lībrāre*, to balance, from *lībra*, a balance)], *n* A state of equal balance, equipoise; equality o weight or force; the equal balancing of the min between conflicting motives or reasons; due propor tion between parts; (*Mech.*) a state of rest or balanc due to the action of forces which counteract eac other.

equimultiple (ē kwi mŭl′ ti pėl), *a.* Multiplied b the same number. *n.pl.* (*Math.*) The product obtained by multiplying quantities by the sam quantity; numbers having a common factor.

equine (ēk′ wīn) [L. *equīnus*, from *equus*, a hors (cp. Gr. *hippos*, *hikkos*, A.-S. *eoh*)], *a.* Pertainin to a horse or horses; resembling a horse. **equini** (ė kwin′ i ȧ), *n.* (*Path.*) A contagious disease which equine animals are subject, horse-pox glanders.

equinoctial (e kwi nok′ shȧl) [EQUINOX], *a.* Of pertaining to the equinoxes, or the regions climates near the terrestrial equator; designatin an equal length of day and night; happening at about the time of the equinoxes. *n.* The equinocti line; (*pl.*) equinoctial gales. **equinoctial gale**

n.pl. Gales happening at or near either equinox. **equinoctial line,** *n.* (*Astron.*) The celestial equator, a circle the plane of which is perpendicular to the axis of the earth and passes through the terrestrial equator. **equinoctial points,** *n.p.* The two points wherein the equator and ecliptic intersect each other. **equinoctial time,** *n.* Time reckoned from the moment when the sun passes the vernal equinox. **equinoctially,** *adv.* In the direction of the equinoctial line.

equinox (ek′ wi-, ē′ kwi noks) [F. *équinoxe,* L. *æquinoctium* (EQUI-, *nox -ctis*)], *n.* The moment at which the sun crosses the equator and renders day and night equal throughout the world, now occurring (vernal equinox) on 21st Mar. and (autumnal equinox) on 23rd Sept.; (*Astron.*) one of two points at which the sun in its annual course crosses the celestial equator; *an equinoctial gale.

equip (e kwip′) [F. *équiper, esquiper* (A.-F. *eskiper*), prob. from Icel. *skipa,* to arrange, to man (a ship), from *skip,* ship], *v.t.* (*past & p.p.* **equipped**) To furnish, accoutre, esp. to supply with arms and military apparatus; to fit out (as a ship), to prepare for any particular duty; to qualify.

equipage (ek′ wi pȧj), *n.* That with which one is equipped; arms and general outfit of a body of troops, including baggage, provisions, etc; the outfit of a ship for a voyage; a carriage with horses and attendants; *retinue, attendance, train of followers. **camp-equipage:** (*Mil.*) Tents, cooking-utensils, etc. **field-equipage:** *(*Mil.*) Saddle-horses, bat-horses, baggage-wagons, and other things for the movements of an army. **siege-equipage:** The train of siege-guns, ammunition, etc. **equipaged,** *a.*

equipedal (ē kwi pē′ dȧl) [L. *æquipedus* (EQUI-, *pes pedis,* foot)], *a.* (*Zool.*) Having the pairs of feet equal.

equipment (e kwip′ ment), *n.* The act of equipping; the state of being equipped; that which is used in equipping or fitting out; outfit, furniture, apparatus required for work, intellectual and other qualifications.

equipoise (ē′ kwi poiz), *n.* A state of equality of weight or force, equilibrium; that which counterbalances. *v.t.* To counterbalance; to hold in equilibrium; (*fig.*) to hold (a person) in mental suspense.

equipollent (ē kwi pol′ ėnt) [O.F. *equipolent,* L. *æquipollens -ntem* (EQUI-, *pollens,* pres.p. of *pollēre,* to be strong)], *a.* Having equal force, power, significance, etc.; equivalent. **equipollence, -lency,** *n.* Equality of force, etc.; (*Log.*) equivalence between two or more propositions. **equipollently,** *adv.*

equiponderate (ē kwi pon′ dėr āt) [med. L. *æquiponderātus,* p.p. of *æquiponderāre* (EQUI-, *ponderāre,* to weigh, from *pondus,* weight)], *v.t.* To counterpoise; to put into equipoise. ***equiponderance,** *n.* **equiponderant,** *a.*

equipotential (ek wi pō ten′ shȧl), *a.* (*Phys.*) Having the same or at the same potential at all points (of a line, surface, or region).

equisetum (ek wi sē′ tŭm) [L. (*equus,* horse, *sæta,* bristle)], *n.* (*pl.* **-ta, -tums**) (Bot.) A genus of cryptogams containing the horse-tails and constituting the order *Equisetaceæ.* **equisetaceous** (-tā′ shŭs), *a.* **equisetic** (-set′ ik), *a.* Pertaining to or derived from any species of Equisetum. **equisetic acid,** *n.* An acid obtained from some species of Equisetum, identical with aconitic acid. **equisetiform,** *a.*

equisonance (ē kwi sō′ nȧns), *n.* The concord between octaves.

equitable (ek′ wi tȧbl) [F. *équitable*], *a.* Acting or done with equity; fair, just; (*Law*) pertaining to a court or the rules of equity. **equitableness,** *n.* **equitably,** *adv.*

equitant (ek′ wi tȧnt) [L. *equitans -ntem,* pres.p. of *equitāre,* as foll.], *a.* Riding on horseback; (*Bot.*) overlapping, astride, or overriding (of leaves, etc.).

equitation (ek wi tā′ shŭn) [L. *equitātio -ōnem,* from *equitāre,* from *eques -itis,* horseman, from *equus,* horse], *n.* The act or art of riding on horseback; horsemanship. **equitative** (ek-′), *a.*

Equites (ek′ wi tēz) [L., pl. of *eques,* see prec.], *n.pl.* (*Rom. Ant.*) The Knights, the equestrian order of nobility.

equity (ek′ wi ti) [O.F. *equité,* L. *æquitās -tātem,* from *æquus,* fair], *n.* Justice, fairness; the application of principles of justice to correct the deficiencies of law; (*Law*) the system of law, collateral and supplemental to statute law, administered by courts of equity; (*Fin.*) the net value of mortgaged property. **equity of redemption:** (*Law*) The right allowed to a mortgagor to a reasonable time within which to redeem his estate when mortgaged for a sum less than it is worth. **equities,** *n.pl.* (*Fin.*) Stocks and shares not bearing a fixed rate of interest.

equivalent (ė kwiv′ ȧ lėnt) [M.F., from late L. *æquivalens -ntem* (EQUI-, *valēre,* to be worth)], *a.* Of equal value, force, or weight; alike in meaning, significance, or effect; interchangeable, corresponding; having the same result; (*Geom.*) having equal areas or dimensions; (*Chem.*) having the same combining power; (*Geol.*) corresponding in position, and, within certain limits, in age. *n.* Anything which is equal to something else in amount, weight, value, force, etc. **equivalently,** *adv.* **equivalence, -alency,** *n.*

equivocal (ė kwiv′ ȯ kȧl) [late L. *æquivocus* (EQUI-, *voc-,* root of *vocāre,* to call)], *a.* Doubtful of meaning, ambiguous, capable of a twofold interpretation; of uncertain origin, character, etc.; open to doubt or suspicion; *equivocating. **equivocality** (-kăl′ i ti), *n.* **equivocally,** *adv.* **equivocalness,** *n.*

equivocate (ė kwiv′ ȯ kāt) [late L. *æquivocātus,* p.p. of *æquivocāre,* as prec.], *v.i.* To use words in an ambiguous manner; to speak ambiguously so as to deceive; to prevaricate. **v.t.* To render equivocal. **equivocation** (-kā′ shŭn), *n.* **equivocator** (ė kwiv′ ȯ kā tȯr), *n.* **equivocatory** (ė kwiv′ ȯ kā tȯr i), *a.* **equivoque** (ek′ wi-, ē′ kwi vōk) [late L. *æquivocus,* EQUIVOCAL], *n.* An ambiguous term or phrase, an equivocation; a pun or other play upon words.

-er (1) [A.-S. *-ere,* from O.Teut. *-ărjoz* (*cp.* L. *-arius*)], *suf.* Denoting an agent or doer, as *hatter, player, singer*; sometimes doubled, as in *caterer, poulterer*; denoting residence, etc., as *Lowlander, Londoner*; (2) [O.F. *-er,* L. *-ar -ārem*; A.-F. *-er,* O.F. *-ier,* L. *-arius*; or O.F. *-eüre,* L. *-ātūram*] denoting a person or thing connected with, as *butler, draper, officer, sampler*; (3) [M.E. *-er, -ere, -re,* A.-S. *-ra*] denoting comparison, as *richer, taller*; (4) [F. *-er, -re,* indicating the infinitive] denoting an action, as *disclaimer, user*; (5) [A.-S. *-rian,* O.Teut. *-rôjan*) frequentative, as *chatter, slumber, twitter.*

era (ēr′ ȧ) [late L. *æra,* a number, orig. pl. of *æs,* money], *n.* An historical period or system of chronology running from a fixed point of time marked by an important event such as the birth of Christ, the Hegira, etc.; the date from which this is reckoned.

eradiate (ė rā′ di āt), *v.i.* To shoot out, as rays of light. *v.t.* To emit (as rays). **eradiation** (-ā′ shŭn), *n.*

eradicate (ė răd′ i kāt) [L. *ērādīcātus,* p.p. of *ērādīcāre* (E-, *rādix,* root)], *v.t.* To root up; to extirpate. **eradicable,** *a.* **eradication** (-kā′ shŭn), *n.*

erase (ė rāz′, -rās) [L. *ērāsus,* p.p. of *ērādere* (E-, *rādere,* to scrape)], *v.t.* To rub out; to obliterate, to expunge; (*fig.*) to raze. **erasable** (ė rā′ zăbl), *a.* ***erasement,** *n.* **eraser,** *n.* ***erasion,** *n.* **erasure** (ė rā′ zhŭr), *n.*

Erasmian (ė răz′ mi ȧn) [Desiderius *Erasmus* (1466–1536), Dutch humanist], *a.* Pertaining to Erasmus or his teaching, esp. with regard to the pronunciation of Greek. *n.* A follower of Erasmus; one who pronounces Greek in the manner taught by Erasmus.

Erastian (ė răs′ ti ȧn), *n.* One holding the opinions on ecclesiastical matters attributed to Erastus, a German physician (1524–83); one holding that the State has supreme authority over the Church. *a.* Pertaining to Erastus or holding his doctrines. **Erastianism,** *n.* **Erastianize,** *v.t.* To imbue with Erastian doctrines; to organize (a Church system) on these principles. *v.i.* To hold Erastian views.

erbium (ĕr′ bi ŭm) [*Ytterby*, in Sweden], *n.* (*Chem.*) A rare metallic element, forming a rose-coloured oxide, one of three formerly known together as Yttria.

ere (âr) [A.-S. *ǣr* (cp. Dut. *eer*, O.H.G. *ēr*, G. *eher*, sooner) from O.Teut. *airiz*, orig. comparative of *air*, early], *prep.* Before, sooner than. *conj.* Before that, sooner than. **ere long:** Before long; soon. **erewhile,** *adv.* Some time ago, formerly.

Erebus (er′ ė bŭs) [L., from Gr. *Erebos*], *n.* (*Class. Myth.*) A deity of hell, the son of Chaos and Night; the lower world; the region between earth and Hades.

erect (ė rekt′) [L. *ērectus*, p.p. of *ērigere* (E-, *regere*, to rule, to set)], *a.* Upright; standing up straight; not bending or stooping; vertical; (*Bot.*) pointing straight up (as leaves); (*fig.*) uplifted, undismayed, firm; attentive, alert. *v.t.* To set upright; to raise; to construct, to build; (*fig.*) to elevate, to exalt; to set up; *to establish, to found; *to animate, to cheer. **v.i.* To rise upright; to become erect. **to erect a perpendicular:** (*Geom.*) To draw a line at right angles to another line or plane. **erectile** (ė rek′ tīl), *a.* Susceptible of erection. **erectile tissue,** *n.* Tissue formed of blood-vessels intermixed with nervous filaments, and capable of dilatation under excitement. **erection,** *n.* The act of setting upright, building, constructing, establishing, etc.; the state of being erected; a building, a structure; the distension of a part consisting of erectile tissue, esp. the penis. **erectly,** *adv.* **erectness,** *n.* **erector,** *n.*

eremite (er′ ė mīt) [late L. *erēmīta*, HERMIT], *n.* A hermit or anchorite. **eremitic, -al** (-mit′ ik, -ȧl), *a.*

eremurus (er ė mūr′ ŭs) [Gr. *erēmos*, solitary; *oura*, tail], *n.* (*Bot.*) A genus of liliaceous plants flowering in tall scapes, natives of Central Asia.

erethism (er′ ė thizm) [F. *éréthisme*, Gr. *erethismos*, from *erethizein*, to irritate], *n.* Undue excitation of an organ or tissue.

erewhile [ERE].

erg (ĕrg), **ergon** (ĕr′ gon) [Gr. *ergon*, work], *n.* The unit of work done in moving a body through one centimetre of space against the resistance of one dyne. **ergograph,** *n.* **ergometer** (-gom′ ė tėr), *n.*

ergal (ĕr′ gȧl), *n.* A function expressing potential energy.

ergo (ĕr′ gō) [L.], *adv.* Therefore; consequently.

ergot (ĕr′ gȯt) [F., from O.F. *argot*, a cock's spur, hence spurred rye; etym. doubtful], *n.* A disease in various grains and grasses, esp. in rye, caused by the presence of a fungus; (*Med.*) a preparation of ergot of rye used in midwifery to produce contraction of the uterus. **ergotine,** *n.* A slightly bitter substance, forming the active principle of ergot of rye.

ergotism (1) (ĕr′ got izm) [ERGO], *n.* Arguing, wrangling.

ergotism (2) (ĕr′ got izm) [ERGOT], *n.* The disease of ergot in grasses; (*Path.*) an epidemic disease produced by eating grain affected with ergot.

erica (e rī′ kȧ) [L., from Gr. *ereikē*], *n.* (*Bot.*) A genus of shrubby plants forming the heath family. **ericaceous** (er i kā′ shŭs), *a.*

erigeron (ė rij′ ėr ŏn) [Gr. *ērigerōn* (*ēri*, early, *gerōn*, old man)], *n.* (Bot.) A genus of plants resembling the aster, and including the flea-bane.

eringo (e ring′ gō) [L. *Eryngium*], *n.* (*Bot.*) Sea holly, a species of the genus *Eryngium.*

erinite (er′ in īt) [*Erin*, old name of Ireland], *n.* (*Min.*) A native emerald-green arseniate of copper from Cornwall, Giant's Causeway, etc.

eriometer (er i om′ ė tėr) [Gr. *erion*, wool, -METER], *n.* An optical instrument for measuring the diameters of small fibres, such as wool, etc.

eristic (ė ris′ tik) [Gr. *eristikos*, from *erizein*, to contend, from *eris*, strife], *a.* Controversial. *n.* A controversialist; the art of disputation.

erk (ĕrk), *n.* (*Aviat. slang*) An aircraftsman.

erlking (ĕrl′ king) [G. *erl-kōnig*, alder-king, after Dan. *ellerkonge*, king of the elves], *n.* In German and Scandinavian folklore a goblin harmful to children.

***ermelin** (ĕr′ mė lin) [conn. with ERMINE; etym. uncertain], *n.* Ermine.

ermine (ĕr′ min) [O.F. (F. *hermine*, cp. Prov. *ermini*), etym. uncertain], *n.* An animal of the weasel tribe, *Mustela erminea*, the stoat, hunted in winter for its fur, which then becomes snowy white, with the exception of the tip of the tail which is always black; the fur of this used for the robes of judges, peers, etc.; (*fig.*) the office of judge; an emblem of purity; (*Her.*) a fur represented by triangular black spots on white. **ermined** (ĕr′ mind), *a.* Clothed with or wearing ermine.

-ern [A.-S., from O.Teut. *-rônjo-* (*-ro-*, *-ônjo-*, cp. L. *-āneus*)], *suf.* as in *northern, southern.*

erne (ĕrn) [A.-S. *earn* (cp. Dut. *arend*, Icel. *orn*; also Gr. *ornis*, bird)], *n.* An eagle, esp. the golden eagle or the sea-eagle.

Ernie (ĕr′ ni) [acronym Electronic Random Number Indicator Equipment], *n.* The device employed for drawing the prize-winning numbers of Premium Bonds.

erode (ė rōd′) [F. *éroder*, L. *ērōdere* (E-, *rōdere*, to gnaw, p.p. *rōsus*)], *v.t.* To eat into or away; to corrode; (*Geol.*) to wear away; to eat out a channel, etc. **erose** (ė rōs′), *a.* Gnawed; (*Bot.*) irregularly indented, as if bitten away. **erosion** (ė rō′ zhŭn), *n.* **erosionist,** *n.* (*Geol.*) One who holds that geological changes are due to denudation rather than to subterranean agencies. **erosive,** *a.*

Eros (ē′ ros, e′ ros) [Gr. myth. *Eros*, god of love], *n.* (*Astron.*) One of the asteroids, or a minor planet, nearer the Earth than Mars.

erotic (ė rot′ ik) [Gr. *erōtikos*, from *erōs erōtos*, love], *a.* Pertaining to or caused by sexual love; amatory. *n.* An amatory poem. **eroticism** (e rot′ i sizm), *n.* Sexual excitement; an exaggerated display of sexual feelings. **erotomania** (ė rō tȯ mā′ ni ȧ), *n.* Melancholia or insanity caused by sexual love.

err (ĕr) [O.F. *errer*, L. *errāre* (cogn. with Goth. *airzjan*, whence G. *irren*)], *v.i.* To blunder, to miss the truth, right, or accuracy; to be incorrect; to deviate from duty; to sin. **v.t.* To miss, to mistake. ***errable,** *a.* Liable to error; fallible.

errand (er′ ȧnd) [A.-S. *ǣrende* (cp. O.S. *ārundi*, Icel. *eyrindi*, *ōrindi*, *erindi*, O.H.G. *ārunti*); etym. obscure], *n.* A short journey to carry a message or perform some other commission for a superior; the object or purpose of such a journey; *a message. **errand-boy,** *n.* A boy kept to run on errands. **a fool's errand:** A useless or foolish undertaking.

errant (er′ ȧnt) [O.F., wandering, pres.p. of *errer*, low L. *iterāre*, L. *iter*, a journey; or L. *errantem*, acc. of *errans*, pres.p. of *errāre*, to wander, to ERR], *a.* Wandering, roving, rambling, esp. roaming in quest of adventure as a knight-errant; erring; *complete, unmitigated, arrant. **errancy, errantry,** *n.* **knight errant** [KNIGHT].

erratic (ė răt′ ik [L. *errāticus*, from *errāre*, see ERR], *a.* Irregular in movement, eccentric; wandering, straying (formerly applied to the planets in contradistinction to the fixed stars); (*Path.*) shifting from one place to another; (*Geol.*) transported from their original situation (of boulders). *n.* *A rogue, a vagabond; (*Geol.*) an erratic block, a transported boulder. **erratically,** *adv.*

erratum (ė rā′ tŭm) [L. neut. p.p. of *errāre*, as prec.], *n.* (*pl.* **-ta**) An error or mistake in printing or writing; (*pl.*) a list of corrections appended to a book.

erroneous (ė rō′ nė ŭs) [L. *errōneus*, from *erro -ōnis*, a vagabond (see ERR)], *a.* Mistaken, incorrect; *straying from the right course, faulty, criminal. **erroneously,** *adv.* **erroneousness,** *n.*

error (er′ ŏr) [O.F. *errour*, L. *errōrem*, acc. of *error*, a wandering, from *errāre* (see ERR)], *n.* A mistake in writing, printing, etc.; deviation from truth or accuracy; wrong opinion; false doctrine or teaching; a transgression, a sin of a venial kind; (*Astron.*) the difference between the positions of the heavenly bodies as determined by calculation and by observation; *a wandering or roving course. **writ of error:** (*Law*) A writ or order for reviewing the proceedings of an inferior court on the ground of error. ***errorist,** *n.* One who is in error, or who encourages or promotes error. **errorless,** *a.*

ersatz (âr′ sats) [G.], *n.* A substitute in a pejorative sense. *a.*

Erse (ĕrs) [early Sc. var. of *Irish*], *n.* The Gaelic dialect of the Scottish Highlands. *a.* Gaelic; (*erroneously*) Irish.

erst (ĕrst) [A.-S. *ǣrest*, superl. of *ǣr*, soon], *adv.* Once, formerly, of yore. ***at erst:** At earliest, at once. **erstwhile,** *adv.* Some while ago.

erubescent (er ū bes′ ėnt) [L. *ērubescens -ntem*, pres.p. of *ērubescere* (E-, *rubescere*, incept. of *rubēre*, to be red)], *a.* Reddening, blushing; reddish. **erubescence,** *n.*

eruciform (er oo′ si fôrm) [L. *eruce*, a caterpillar], *a.* (*Zool.*) Resembling a caterpillar; term applied to certain larvæ, such as the saw-fly, with fleshy, cylindrical body.

eructation (ē rŭk tā′ shŭn) [L. *ēructātio -ōnem*, from *ēructare* (E-, *ructāre*, to belch)], *n.* The act of belching; that which is ejected by belching; any sudden ejection of gases or solid matter from the earth.

erudite (er′ oo dīt) [L. *ērudītus*, p.p. of *ērudīre* (E-, *rudis*, rude)], *a.* Learned; well-read, well informed. **eruditely,** *adv.* **eruditeness,** *n.* **erudition** (er ū dish′ ŭn), *n.* Learning, extensive knowledge gained by study; scholarship.

erupt (ė rŭpt′) [L. *ēruptus*, p.p. of *ērumpere* (E-, *rumpere*, to break)], *v.t.* To emit violently, as a volcano, geyser, etc.; to force through (as teeth through the gums). *v.i.* To burst out; to break through. **eruptive,** *a.*

eruption (ė rŭp′ shŭn), *n.* The act of bursting forth; a sudden emission; that which breaks out; (*Path.*) the breaking out of vesicles, pimples, rash, etc., upon the skin; the breaking through of teeth; an outburst of lava, etc., from a volcano or other vent.

-ery, -ry [F. *-erie* (L. *-ārio-*, *-ia*; or L. *-ātor -ōrem*)], *suf.* Used with nouns and adjectives, and sometimes with verbs to form nouns, generally abstract or collective, meaning a business, place of business, cultivation, etc., conduct, things connected with or of the nature of, etc.; originally confined to Romance words, but now used with those of Teutonic origin, *e.g.*, *foolery*, *grocery*, *pinery*, *rockery*, *tannery*, *witchery*.

eryngo (ė ring′ gō) [L. *ēryngion*, Gr. *ērungion*, dim. of *ērungos*, goat's beard], *n.* *A sweetmeat prepared from eryngo-root; (*Bot.*) any plant of the genus *Eryngium*. **eryngo-root,** *n.* The root of *Eryngium maritimum*, a reputed aphrodisiac, prepared as a sweetmeat. **eryngium** (ē rin′ ji ŭm), *n.* (*Bot.*) A genus of umbelliferous plants, including the sea-holly.

erysipelas (er i sip′ ė lăs) [L., from Gr. *erusipelas* (*erusi-*, rel. to *eruthros*, red, *pella*, skin)], *n.* An inflammation of the skin in which the affected parts are of a deep red colour, with a diffused swelling of the underlying cutaneous tissue and cellular membrane; popularly called the rose, or St. Anthony's fire.

erythema (er i thē′ ma) [Gr. *eruthēma*, from *eruthainein*, to be red, from *eruthros*, red], *n.* A superficial skin-disease characterized by redness in patches. **erythematic** (-măt′ ik), **erythematous** (-thē′ mȧ tŭs), *a.*

erythism [ERETHISM].

erythrite (ė rith′ rīt) [Gr. *eruthros*, red, -ITE], *n.* (*Min.*) A red or greenish-grey variety of feldspar.

erythrocytes (e rith′ rō sīts) [Gr. *eruthros*, red, -CYTE], *n.* Red blood cells or red corpuscles of vertebrata.

erythromycin (er ith rō mī′ sin) [Gr. *eruthros*, red, *mykes*, fungus], *n.* (*Med.*) An antibiotic.

erythrophobia (er ith rō fō′ bi ȧ) [Gr. *eruthros*, red, PHOBIA], *n.* (*Path.*) A morbid fear of blushing.

escalade (es kȧ lād′) [F., from Sp. *escalada*, fem. p.p. of *escalar*, med. L. *scalāre*, to scale, from *scāla*, ladder], *n.* An attack on a fortified place in which scaling-ladders are used to mount the ramparts etc. *v.t.* To storm by means of scaling-ladders.

escalator (es′ kȧ lā tŏr) [F. *escalader*, to scale, to climb], *n.* A conveyor for passengers consisting of a continuous series of steps on an endless chain, ascending or descending and arranged to give facilities for mounting or leaving at either end; a moving staircase.

escallonia (es kȧ lō′ ni ȧ) [*Escallon*, a Spanish traveller], *n.* A genus of South American flowering trees or shrubs of the saxifrage family.

escallop [SCALLOP].

escapade (es kȧ pād′) [F., from Sp. or Prov. *escapada*, from *escapar*, to escape (as foll.)], *n.* A wild freak or prank; an escape from restraint; a wild fling of a horse.

escape (es kāp′) [A.-F. *escaper*, O.F. *eschaper* (F. *échapper*), prob. from a late L. *excappāre* (EX-, *cappa*, cloak], *v.t.* To get safely away from; to flee so as to be free from; to evade, to avoid (a thing or act); to slip away from, elude attention or recollection of; to find an issue from; to slip from unawares or unintentionally. *v.i.* To get free; to get safely away; to find an issue, to leak; to evade punishment, capture, danger, annoyance, etc. *n.* The act of escaping; the state of having escaped, a means of escaping; evasion, flight, deliverance; a leakage (from a gas or water-pipe, electric-main, etc.); a plant from a garden apparently growing wild; (*Law*) violent or privy evasion out of lawful restraint. **fire-escape** [FIRE]. **escape-pipe, -valve,** *n.* An outlet for steam, water, etc., in case of necessity. **escape-shaft,** *n.* A shaft provided in case of emergency for the escape of miners. **escape warrant,** *n.* (*Law*) A warrant addressed to sheriffs etc. to retake an escaped prisoner. **escapee** (es kȧ pē′), *n.* One who has escaped, esp. an escaped prisoner.

escapement (es kāp′ mėnt), *n.* A device in a clock or watch for checking and regulating the movement of the wheels; a vent, an escape.

escapism (es kāp′ izm), *n.* (*Psychol.*) Shirking unpleasant facts and realities by filling the mind with pleasing irrelevancies.

escapologist (es kȧ pol′ ō jist), *n.* A performer whose stage turn is escaping from locked handcuffs, chains, boxes, etc.

escarp (es karp′) [F. *escarper*, from *escarpe*, SCARP], *v.t.* (*Fort.*) To cut or form into a slope; to scarp. *n.* The slope on the inner side of a ditch, below a rampart, opposite the counterscarp; a scarp. **escarpment,** *n.* The precipitous face of a hill or ridge; (*Fort.*) ground cut away precipitously so as to render a position inaccessible.

-esce [L. *-esco.*], *suf.* Forming inceptive verbs, as *acquiesce*, *coalesce*, *effervesce*. **-escent** [L. *-escens*

-*ntis*, pres.p. of inceptive verbs], *suf.* Forming adjectives from inceptive verbs, as *acquiescent, coalescent, iridescent, opalescent.* **-escence,** *suf.* Forming abstract nouns from inceptive verbs, as *acquiescence, coalescence, opalescence.*

eschalot (esh' à lot) [SHALLOT].

eschatology (es kà tol' ȯ ji) [Gr. *eschatos*, last, -LOGY], *n.* The doctrine of the final issue of things, death, the last judgment, the future state, etc. **eschatological** (-loj' ik ȧl), *a.*

escheat (es chēt') [O.F. *eschete*, fem. p.p. of *escheoir* (F. *échoir*), late L. *excadere* (EX-, L. *cadere*, to fall)], *n.* The reverting of property to the lord of the fee, or to the Crown or (*U.S.A.*) the State, on the death of the owner intestate without heirs; property so reverting; *a plunder, booty. *v.t.* To confiscate; to forfeit (to). *v.i.* To revert by escheat. **escheator,** *n.* An officer formerly appointed in every county to register the escheats of the Crown.

eschew (es choo') [O.F. *eschiver*, O.H.G. *sciuhan* (G. *scheuen*), cogn. with A.-S. *sceoh*, SHY], *v.t.* To flee from; to avoid; to shun; to abstain from. **eschewal,** *n.* ***eschewance,** *n.* **eschewer,** *n.*

Eschscholtzia (esh sholt' si ȧ) [J. F. von *Eschscholtz* (1793–1831), German naturalist], *n.* (*Bot.*) A genus of flowering herbs comprising the California poppy.

escort (es' kôrt) [F. *escorte*, It. *scorta*, fem. p.p. of *scorgere*, to guide, conduct (EX-, L. *corrigere*, to CORRECT)], *n.* An armed guard attending a person or persons, baggage, munitions, etc., which are being conveyed from one place to another, as a protection against attack or for compulsion or surveillance; a guard of honour; a person or persons accompanying another for protection, guidance, or company; guidance, protection, guardianship. *v.t.* (es kôrt') To act as escort to; to attend upon.

escribe (es krīb') [E-, L. *scrībere*, to write], *v.t.* (*Math.*) To draw (a circle) so as to touch one side of a triangle exteriorly and the other two produced.

escritoire (es kri twa') [F., now *écritoire*, L. *scriptōrium*, from *scriptus*, p.p. of *scrībere*, to write], *n.* A writing-desk, with drawers etc. for papers and stationery, a bureau.

escrow (es krō') [O.F. *escroue*, a scroll], *n.* (*Law*) A fully-executed deed or engagement to do or pay something put into the custody of a third party until some condition is fulfilled.

Esculapian [ÆSCULAPIAN].

esculent (es' ku lėnt) [L. *esculentus*, from *esca*, food], *a.* Fit or good for food; edible. *n.* A thing suitable for food.

escutcheon (es kŭch' ȯn) [A.-F. and O.North.F. *escuchon*, O.F. *escusson*, prob. from a late L. *scūtiōnem*, from L. *scūtum*, a shield], *n.* A shield or shield-shaped surface charged with armorial bearings; any similar surface or device; an ornamental name-plate on a coffin; a perforated plate to finish an opening, as a keyhole etc.; part of a ship's stern bearing her name; (*Zool.*) a depression behind the beak of a bivalve. **a blot on the escutcheon:** A stain on the reputation of a person, family, etc.

-ese [O.F. *-eis*, L. *enis*, pl. *-enses*], *suf.* Belonging to a city or country as inhabitant(s) or language, also (*fig.*) pertaining to a particular writer (of a style or diction); as *Bolognese, Chinese, Johnsonese, journalese.*

esemplastic (es em plăs' tik) [Gr. *es*, into, *hen*, neut. of *heis*, one, *plastikos*, from *plassein*, to mould], *a.* Moulding, shaping, or fashioning into one, unifying.

eskar (es' kâr) [Ir. *eiscir*], *n.* (*Geol.*) A bank or long mound of glacial drift such as are found abundantly in Irish river-valleys.

Eskimo (es' ki mō) [N.Amer.Indian, eaters of raw flesh], *n.* (*pl.* **-mos**) A member of a race inhabiting Greenland and the adjacent parts of North America. **Eskimo-dog,** *n.* A wolf-like variety of the domestic dog, used by the Eskimos to draw sledges.

esophagus [ŒSOPHAGUS].

esoteric, -ical (es ȯ ter' ik, -ȧl) [Gr. *esōterikos*, from *esōteros*, inner, compar. from *esō*, within, from *eis*, into], *a.* Meant for or intelligible only to the initiated (of philosophical doctrines, religious rites, etc.); recondite, secret, confidential; initiated (of disciples etc.); arising from internal causes. **esoterically,** *adv.* **esoterism** (e sot' ėr izm), *n.* ***esotery,** *n.*

espagnolette (es păn yȯ let') [F., from *espagnol*, Spanish], *n.* A bolt used for fastening a french window, one turn of the knob securing the sash both at top and bottom.

espalier (es păl' i er) [F., from It. *spalliera*, from *spalla*, a shoulder, L. *spatula*, a blade], *n.* Lattice-work on which to train shrubs or fruit-trees; a tree so trained.

esparto (es par' tō) [Sp., from L. *spartum*, Gr. *spartan*, a rope made of a plant called *spartos*], *n.* A kind of coarse grass or rush, *Macrochloa tenacissima*, growing in the sandy regions of northern Africa and Spain, largely used for making paper, mats, etc.

especial (es pesh' ȧl) [O.F., from L. *speciālis*, SPECIAL], *a.* Distinguished in a certain class or kind; pre-eminent, exceptional, particular; pertaining to a particular case, not general or indefinite. **especially,** *adv.*

***esperance** (es' pėr ans) [F., ult. from L. *sperans -ntis*, pres.p. of *sperāre*, to hope], *n.* Hope.

Esperanto (es pėr ăn' tō) [Esp., hopeful], *n.* An artificial language invented by L. L. Zamenhof (1887), based on the chief European languages. **Esperantist,** *n.*

espial (es pī' ȧl) [O.F. *espialle*, from *espier*, to ESPY], *n.* Spying, observation; *a spy, a scout.

espiègle (es pi āgl) [F., corr. of G. *Eulenspiegel*, a German peasant with a traditionary reputation for impish practices], *a.* Roguish, frolicsome. **espièglerie,** *n.*

espionage (es' pi on azh) [F., from *espionner*, from *espion*, spy], *n.* The act or practice of spying; the employment of spies.

esplanade (es plȧ nād') [M.F., from *esplaner*, to level (as Sp. *esplanada* and It. *spianata*), L. *explānāre* (EX-, *plānus*, level)], *n.* A level space, esp. a level walk or drive by the seaside, etc.; a clear space between the citadel and the houses of a fortified town.

espouse (es pouz') [O.F. *espouser*, from *espouse*, SPOUSE, wife, L. *sponsa*, fem. p.p. of *spondēre*, to promise], *v.t.* To marry; to give in marriage (to); (*fig.*) to adopt, to support, defend (a cause etc.). **espousal,** *n.* (*usu. in pl.*) The act or ceremony of contracting a man and woman to each other; betrothal, marriage; (*fig.*) adoption (of a cause etc.).

espressivo (es pres' ē vō) [It.], *a.* (*Mus.*) With expression.

espresso (es pres' ō) [It.], *n.* A coffee-making machine using pressure for high extraction. **espresso, espresso bar,** *n.* A coffee-bar where such coffee is served.

esprit (es prē') [F., from L. *spīritus*, SPIRIT], *n.* With sprightliness. **esprit de corps** (dė kôr'): The spirit of comradeship, loyalty, and devotion to the body or association to which one belongs. **esprit fort** (fôr), *n.* (*pl.* **esprits forts**) A strong-minded person, esp. a determined free-thinker in religious matters.

espy (es pī') [O.F. *espier*, O.H.G. *spehōn* (G. *spähen*), to SPY], *v.t.* To catch sight of; to detect, to discern; *to watch, to spy upon. *v.i.* To watch or look narrowly.

-esque [F., from It. *-esco*, med. L. *-iscus* (cp. O.H.G. *-isc*, G. *-isch*, -ISH)], *suf.* Like, in the manner or style of; as *arabesque, burlesque, Dantesque, picturesque.*

Esquimau [ESKIMO].

esquire (es kwīr') [O.F. *escuyer*, L. *scūtārius*, from *scūtum*, shield], *n.* The armour-bearer or attendant on a knight, a squire; a title of dignity next in degree below a knight; a title properly belonging to the eldest sons of baronets and the younger sons of noblemen, and to officers of the king's courts, barristers, justices of the peace, etc., but commonly given to all professional men, and used as a complimentary adjunct to a person's name in the addresses of letters. *v.t.* To attend upon as an escort; to dignify with the title of esquire.

ess (es) [A.-S.], *n.* The name of the letter S; an S-shaped thing. **collar of esses:** A chain or collar composed of S-shaped links.

-ess [Fr. *-esse*, L. *-issa*], *suf.* Noting the feminine; as *empress*, *murderess*, *seamstress*, *songstress* (the last two are double feminines formed on the A.-S. fem. *-ster*, as in *spinster*).

essay (1) (es' ā) [O.F. *essai*, ASSAY], *n.* An attempt; an informal literary composition or disquisition, usu. in prose. **essayist** (es' ā ist), *n.* A writer of essays.

essay (2) (e sā'), *v.t.* To try, to attempt; to test; to test the quality or nature of. *v.i.* To make an endeavour.

essence (es' ėns) [F., from L. *essentia*, from *essens -ntis*, pres.p. of *esse*, to be], *n.* That which constitutes the nature of a thing; that which makes a thing what it is; that which differentiates a thing from all other things, or one thing of a kind from others of the same kind; being, existence; an ethereal or immaterial being, a solution or extract obtained by distillation; the essential oil or characteristic constituent of a volatile substance; perfume, scent. *v.t.* To perfume, to scent.

Essene (ė sēn') [L. *Essēni*, pl., Gr. *Essēnoi* (etym. doubtful)], *n.* A member of an ancient Jewish sect of religious mystics who cultivated poverty, community of goods, and asceticism of life. **Essenism** (es' ė nizm), *n.*

essential (ė sen' shȧl) [late L. *essentiālis*], *a.* Of or pertaining to the essence of a thing; necessary to the existence of a thing, indispensable (to); important in the highest degree; real, actual, distinguished from accidental; containing the essence or principle of a plant etc.; (*Path.*) idiopathic, not connected with another disease. *n.* That which is fundamental or characteristic; an indispensable element; a point of the highest importance; *essence, being. **essential character,** *n.* The quality which serves to distinguish one genus, species, etc., from another. **essential harmony,** *n.* (*Mus.*) One belonging to one particular key. **essential oil,** *n.* A volatile oil containing the characteristic constituent or principle, usually obtained by distillation with water. **essential proposition,** *n.* One that predicates of a subject something entailed in its definition. **essentiality** (-shi ăl' i ti), *n.* **essentially,** *adv.*

Essex board (es' eks), *n.* Protected trade name of a building-board made of layers of wood-fibre cemented together with fire-resisting material.

***essoign, essoin** (ė soin') [A.-F. *essoigne*, O.F. *essoine*, from *essoignier*, *essoinier*, to excuse, from *essoyne*, med. L. *exsoniāre* (EX-, *sonia*, O.H.G. *sunna*, excuse, cogn. with Goth. *sunja*, truth, cp. A.-S. *soth*, true)], *n.* An excuse; an exemption; (*Law*) an excuse offered for non-appearance in a court of law. *v.t.* (*Law*) To make an excuse or to excuse for non-appearance. ***essoiner,** *n.* (*Law*) One who makes an excuse for the non-appearance of another in a court of law.

-est (A.-S. *-est*, *-ast*, *-ost*, *-st*, O.Teut. *-isto-* (cp. Gr. *-isto-*)], *suf.* Forming the superlative degree of adjectives and adverbs, as *richest*, *tallest*, *liveliest*.

establish (es tăb' lish) [O.F. *establiss-*, stem of *establir*, L. *stabilīre* (*stabilis*, firm)], *v.t.* To set upon a firm foundation, to found, institute; to settle or secure firmly (in office, opinion, etc.); to make firm or lasting (as a belief, custom, one's health, etc.); to substantiate, verify, put beyond dispute; to ordain officially and settle on a permanent basis (as a Church). **to establish a suit:** (*Cards*) To exhaust all the higher cards of a particular suit that are in the hands of opponents.

establishment (es tăb' lish mėnt), *n.* The act of establishing; the state of being established; a permanent organization such as the army, navy, or civil service, a staff of servants, etc.; a public institution, business organization, or large private household with the body of persons engaged in it; (*iron.*) a phrase of journalistic use to suggest the unconscious association of the respectable and conventional leaders in education and public affairs. **established church:** The church established by law, the State Church. **peace** or **war establishment:** The reduced or the augmented military and naval forces in time of peace or of war. **a separate establishment:** A household maintained for a paramour. **establishmentarian** (-târ' i ȧn), *n.* An advocate or supporter of an established Church. *a.* Advocating or supporting an established Church.

estafette (es tȧ fet') [F., from It., *staffetta*, dim. of *staffa*, stirrup, O.H.G. *stapho*, step], *n.* A military courier; an express, a messenger.

estaminet (es tam' i nā) [F., etym. doubtful], *n.* A café in which wine, etc. is sold; a wine-shop.

estancia (es tan' thi ȧ) [Sp., from med. L. *stantia*, from *stare*, to stand], *n.* (*Sp. Am.*) A cattle-farm, ranch, or country estate; the residence on this. ***estanciero*** (es tan thi âr' ō), *n.* A Spanish-American cattle-raiser.

estate (es tāt') [O.F. *estat*, L. *statum*, acc. of *status*, STATE], *n.* Property, esp. a landed property; (*Law*) a person's interest in lands and tenements (**real estate**) or movable property (**personal estate**); a person's assets and liabilities taken collectively; state, condition, circumstances, standing, rank; a class or order invested with political rights (in Great Britain the Three Estates are the Lords Spiritual, the Lords Temporal, and the Commons). **fourth estate:** The newspaper press. **third estate:** The bourgeoisie of France before the Revolution, as distinguished from the nobles and the clergy. **estate car,** *n.* (*Motor.*) A car for carrying passengers and luggage.

esteem (es tēm') [O.F. *estimer*, L. *æstimāre*, to ESTIMATE], *v.t.* To hold in high estimation, to regard with respect; to prize; to consider, to reckon. *n.* Opinion or judgment as to merit or demerit, esp. a favourable opinion; respect, regard. **estimable,** *a.* Worthy of esteem or regard. **estimably,** *adv.*

ester (es' tėr) [coined word], *n.* (*Chem.*) An organic compound derived by the replacement of hydrogen in an acid by an organic radical.

esthete, etc. [ÆSTHETE].

estimable [ÆSTEEM].

estimate (es' ti māt) [L. *æstimātus*, p.p. of *æstimāre*, to value], *v.t.* To compute the value of, to appraise; to form an opinion about; *to esteem. *n.* (-mȧt) An approximate calculation of the value, number, extent, etc., of anything; the result of this; a contractor's statement of the sum for which he would undertake a piece of work; (*pl.*) statement of probable expenditure submitted to Parliament or other authoritative body; a judgment respecting character, circumstances, etc.; *repute, reputation. **estimation** (-mā' shŭn), *n.* The act of estimating; opinion or judgment; esteem; *conjecture. **estimative,** *a.* **estimator,** *n.*

estival, etc. [ÆSTIVAL].

estop (es top') [A.-F. *estopper*, O.F. *estouper* (late L. *stuppāre*, to stuff with tow, from L. *stuppa*, tow)], *v.t.* (*past & p.p.* **estopped**) (*Law*) To bar, preclude, prevent. **estoppage,** *n.* **estoppel,** *n.* (*Law*) An act or statement that cannot legally be denied; a plea alleging such an act or statement.

estovers (es tō' vėrz) [O.F. *estover*, *estovoir*, to be necessary], *n.pl.* (*Law*) Necessaries or supplies allowed by law, esp. wood which a tenant can take from a landlord's estate for repairs etc.; allowance to a person out of an estate for support.

estrade (es trad') [F., from Sp. *estrado*, L. *strātum*, neut. p.p. of *sternere*, to spread], *n.* A slightly raised platform, a dais.

estrange (es trānj') [O.F. *estranger*, L. *extrāneāre*, from *extrāneus*, STRANGE], *v.t.* To alienate, to make indifferent or distant in feeling; to make (oneself) a stranger to. **estrangement,** *n.*

estray (es trā') [A.-F., from *estraier*, to stray, see ASTRAY], *n.* A domestic animal, as a horse, ox, etc., found straying or without an owner. ***v.i.** To stray.

estreat (es trēt') [A.F. *estrete*, O.F. *estraite*, fem. p.p. of *estraire*, L. *extrahere*, to EXTRACT], *n.* (*Law*) A true copy or an original writing, esp. of penalties set down in the rolls of a court. *v.t.* (*Law*) To extract or copy from the records of a court; to levy a fine under estreat.

estuary (es' tū å ri) [L. *æstuārium*, from *æstuāre*, to surge, from *æstus*, heat, surge, tide], *n.* The mouth of a river etc. in which the tide meets the current; a firth. **estuarine,** *a.*

esurient (ė sū' ri ėnt) [L. *ēsuriens -ntem*, pres.p. of *ēsurīre*, desiderative from *ēsus*, p.p. of *edere*, to eat], *a.* Hungry; needy. **esurience,** *n.* **esuritis** (es ū rī' tis), *n.* (*Path.*) Ulceration of the stomach from want of food.

-et [O.F. *et*, *-ette*, etym. doubtful (cp. It. *-etto*, *-etta*)], *suf.* Diminutive, as *chaplet*, *circlet*, *coronet*, *dulcet*, *russet*, *violet*.

etacism (ē' tå sizm) [Gr. *eta*, e, the seventh letter of the Gr. alphabet], *n.* The Erasmian pronunciation of the Gr. letter eta as ā.

eta patch (ē' tå păch), *n.* (*Aviat.*) A fan-shaped patch of fabric whereby the rigging is secured to the envelope of a balloon.

etcetera (et set' ėr å) [L., and the rest], *phrase.* And the rest; and others of like kind; and so forth, and so on, usually written *etc.* or *&c.* **etceteras,** *n.pl.* Sundries, extras; things unspecified.

etch (ech) [Dut. *etsen*, G. *ätzen*, O.H.G. *ezjan*, O.Teut. *atjan* (causal), to make eat], *v.t.* To produce or reproduce (figures or designs) on metallic plates, for printing copies, by biting with an acid through the lines previously drawn with a needle on a coated surface. *v.i.* To practise this art. **etcher,** *n.* **etching,** *n.* The act of etching; an impression taken from an etched plate. **etching-ground,** *n.* The coating of the plate for etching. **etching-needle,** *n.* A sharp-pointed instrument for making lines in the etching-ground.

eternal (e tĕr' nål) [O.F. *eternel*, late L. *æternālis*, from *æternus* (*æviternus*, from *ævum*, age)], *a.* Without beginning or end; everlasting, perpetual; (*colloq.*) incessant, unintermittent. **Eternal City,** *n.* Rome. **the Eternal:** The everlasting God; the Deity. ***eterne,** *a.* ***eternalize, eternize,** *v.t.* To make eternal; to prolong indefinitely; to immortalize. **eternally,** *adv.*

eternity (ē tĕr' ni ti), *n.* Eternal duration; endless past or future time; unchangeableness of being; the future life; immortality of fame; (*pl.*) the eternal realities.

etesian (ė tē' zhi ån) [L. *etēsius*, Gr. *etēsios*, from *etos*, year], *a.* Annual; blowing periodically. **etesian winds,** *n.pl.* Periodical winds, esp. north-westerly winds blowing for about six weeks in summer in the Mediterranean.

-eth [-TH].

ethane (eth' ān) [*eth-*, first syl. of ETHER, -ANE], *n.* (*Chem.*) A colourless and inodorous gaseous compound of the paraffin series.

ether (ē' thėr) [L. *æther*, Gr. *aithēr*, from root of *aithein*, to burn], *n.* A fluid of extreme subtlety and elasticity assumed to exist throughout space and between the particles of all substances, forming the medium of transmission of light and heat; the upper air, the higher regions of the sky, the clear sky; (*Chem.*) a light, volatile, and inflammable fluid, produced by the distillation of alcohol with an acid, esp. sulphuric acid and used as an anæsthetic. **ether waves,** *n.pl.* (*Radio.*) Electromagnetic waves. ***ethereous,** *a.* Ethereal. **etheric** (ė ther' ik), *a.* **etherify** (ē' thėr i fī), *v.t.* (*Chem.*) To make or convert into an ether. **etherification** (-kā' shŭn), *n.* **etheriform** (ē' ther i fôrm), *a.*

ethereal (e thēr' i ål), *a.* Of the nature of ether; resembling celestial ether, light, airy, tenuous, subtle, exquisite, impalpable, spiritual; (*Phys.*) pertaining to the ether; (*Chem.*) pertaining to the liquid known as ether. **ethereal oil,** *n.* (*Chem.*) An essential oil produced by distillation. **ethereality** (-ăl' i ti), *n.* **etherealize,** *v.t.* To convert into ether; (*fig.*) to render spiritual. **etherealization** (-zā' shŭn), *n.* **ethereally,** *adv.*

etherism (ē' thėr izm), *n.* (*Med.*) The effects produced by the administration of ether as an anæsthetic.

etherize (ē' thė rīz), *v.t.* (*Chem.*) To convert into ether; (*Med.*) to subject to the influence of ether. **etherization,** *n.*

etheromania (ē thėr ō mān' ĭ å), *n.* An uncontrolled desire and use of ether.

ethic, ethical (eth' ik, -ål) [L. *ēthicus*, Gr. *ēthikos*, from ETHOS], *a.* Treating of or relating to morals; dealing with moral questions or theory; conforming to a recognized standard. **ethic dative:** (*Gram.*) The dative of a personal pronoun indicating indirect interest in the fact stated, *e.g.* 'I will buy *me* a hat.' **ethic,** *n.* (*usu. in pl.*) The science of morals; a treatise on this subject; a system of principles and rules of conduct; the whole field of moral science, including political and social science, law, jurisprudence, etc. **ethically,** *adv.* **ethicize** (-sīz), *v.t.* To make ethical; to treat ethically. **ethicism,** *n.* **ethics** [ETHIC].

ethine (eth' īn) [*eth*, first syl. of ETHER, -INE], *n.* (*Chem.*) Acetylene.

Ethiopian (ē thi ō' pi ån) [L. *Æthiops -is*, Gr. *Aithiops -os* (etym. doubtful)], *a.* Pertaining to Ethiopia or Abyssinia or its inhabitants; (*Ethn.*) belonging to one of the main groups into which the human race is divided. *n.* A native of Ethiopia or Abyssinia; (*now only facet.*) a Negro. ***Ethiop,** *n.* **Ethiopic** (-op' ik), *a.* Ethiopian. *n.* The language of Ethiopia.

ethmoid, -moidal (eth' moid, -moi' dål) [Gr. *ēthmoeidēs* (*ēthmos*, sieve, -OID)], *a.* Resembling a sieve. *n.* The ethmoid bone. **ethmoid bone,** *n.* (*Anat.*) A cellular bone situated between the orbital processes at the root of the nose, through which the olfactory nerves pass. **ethmoiditis** (-dī' tis) [-ITIS], *n.* (*Path.*) Inflammation of this.

ethnarch (eth' nark) [Gr. *ethnos*, nation, *arkho*, rule], *n.* The governor of a people or district.

ethnic (eth' nik) [L. *ethnicus*, Gr. *ethnikos*, from *ethnos*, nation], *a.* Pertaining to or characteristic of a race or people; racial, ethnological; *heathen, pagan, not Jewish nor Christian. **n.* A Gentile, a heathen or pagan. **ethnical,** *a.* **ethnically,** *adv.* ***ethnicism** (-sizm), *n.* Heathenism, paganism; a non-Jewish and non-Christian religion.

ethnography (eth nog' rå fi) [Gr. *ethnos*, -GRAPHY], *n.* The science which describes the races of men and their peculiarities. **ethnographer,** *n.* **ethnographic, -al** (-grăf' ik, -ål), *a.* **ethnographically,** *adv.*

ethnology (eth nol' ŏ ji) [Gr. *ethnos*, -LOGY], *n* The science which treats of the varieties of the human race, and attempts to trace them to their origin. **ethnologic, -al** (-loj' ik, ål), *a.* **ethnologically,** *adv.* **ethnologist,** *n.* A student of ethnology.

ethology (ē thol' ŏ ji) [L. and Gr. *ēthologia*], *n* The science of character, or of the formation of character, either national or individual. **ethologic, -al** (loj' ik, 'ål), *n.*

ethos (ē′ thos) [Gr., character, disposition], *n.* The characteristic spirit, disposition, or genius of a people, community, institution, system, etc.

ethyl (eth′ il) [*eth-*, first syl. of ETHER, -YL], *n.* (*Chem.*) A monovalent fatty hydrocarbon radicle of the paraffin series, forming the base of common alcohol and ether, acetic acid, etc. **ethyl alcohol,** *n.* The ordinary alcohol of commerce.

etiolate (ē′ ti ō lāt) [F. *étioler*, Norm. *s'étieuler*, to grow into haulm, from *éteule*, O.F. *esteule*, L. *stipula*, straw], *v.t.* To blanch (used of a plant kept in the dark); to render pale and unhealthy (of persons). *v.i.* To become blanched by deprivation of light. **etiolation** (-lā′ shŭn), *n.*

etiology [ÆTIOLOGY].

etiquette (et′ i ket) [F. *étiquette*, a TICKET], *n.* The conventional rules of behaviour in polite society; the established rules of precedence and ceremonial in a court, or a professional or other body; *a rule of etiquette; *a label.

etna (et′ nȧ) [Mt. *Etna*, in Sicily], *n.* An apparatus for heating small quantities of liquid by means of burning spirit. **Etnean** (et nē′ ȧn), *a.* Pertaining to Mount Etna.

Etonian (ē tō′ ni ȧn), *n.* A person educated at Eton College. **Eton collar,** *n.* A wide, starched collar worn outside the jacket. **Eton crop,** *n.* A fashion of cutting a woman's hair short like a man's. **Eton jacket,** *n.* A boy's untailed dress-coat.

Etrurian (e troor′ i ȧn), *a.* Pertaining to Etruria, an ancient country in central Italy. *n.* A native of Etruria. **Etruscan** (L. *Etruscus*), *a.* Etrurian. **Etruscan vases,** *n.pl.* Vases found in Etruscan tombs, but of Grecian design.

et seq. (et sek) [abbr. L. *et sequentes, et sequentia*]. And the following (passage).

-ette [O.F. *-ette*, fem. of *-et*], *suf.* Diminutive, as in *brunette, leatherette, roulette, palette.*

ettle (et′ ėl) [Icel. *ætla, etla*, to think, intend (cogn. with A.-S. *eaht*, council, *eaht an*, to watch over)], *v.t.* *To purpose, intend; (*Sc.*) to design, intend (for). *v.i.* (*Sc.*) To aim at. *n.* (*Sc.*) Aim, object.

étude (ā′ tūd) [Fr., a study], *n.* (*Mus.*) A short musical composition.

etui (ė twē′) [F., etym. doubtful], *n.* A pocket-case for pins, needles, etc.

etymology (et i mol′ ō ji) [O.F. *ethimologie*, L. *etymologia*, Gr. *etumologia* (*etumos*, real, rel. to *eteos*, true, -LOGY)]. *n.* The science that treats of the origin and history of words; the history of the origin and modification of a particular word; derivation; that part of grammar which relates to individual words, their formation, inflexion, etc. **etymologer, etymologist,** *n.* **etymologic, -al** (-loj′ ik, -ȧl), *a.* **etymologically,** *adv.* ***etymologicon,** *n.* A book on etymologies; an etymological dictionary. **etymologize** (-mol′-), *v.t.* To give or trace the etymology of. *v.i.* To study etymology; to search into the source of words; to propose etymologies for words.

etymon (et′ i mon) [L. from Gr., neut. of *etumos* as pres.], *n.* The primitive or root form of a word.

eu- [Gr., well], *comb form.* Good, well, pleasant, as in *eulogy, euphony.*

eucaine (ū′ cān), *n.* (*Med.*) A form of local anæsthetic.

eucalyptus (ū kȧ lip′ tŭs) [EU-, *kaluptos*, covered, from *kaluptein*, to cover (the flower being protected by a cap)], *n.* (*pl.* **-ti**) An Australasian genus of evergreen myrtaceous trees comprising the gum-trees.

eucharis (ū′ kȧ ris) [Gr. *eucharis* (EU-, *charis*, grace)], *n.* A bulbous plant from South America, cultivated in hot-houses for the sake of its pure white bell-shaped flowers.

Eucharist (ū′ kȧ rist) [O.F. *eucariste*, late L. and Gr. *eucharistia*, from *eucharistos*, grateful (EU-, *charizesthai*, to show favour to, from *charis*, grace)], *n.* The sacrament of the Lord's Supper; the elements, bread and wine, given in this sacrament. **eucharistic, -al** (-is′ tik, -ȧl), *a.* **Eucharistic Congress,** *n.* (*Eccles.*) A congress of Roman Catholic clergy and laity for public worship of the Real Presence in the sacrament of the altar.

euchlorine (ū klôr′ in) [EU-, Gr. *chlōros*, green, -INE (on anal. of CHLORINE)], *n.* A yellow explosive gas with bleaching properties, obtained from a mixture of chlorate of potash and dilute hydrochloric acid.

euchology (ū kol′ ō ji) [earlier *euchologion*, Gr. (*euchē*, prayer, -LOGY)], *n.* The liturgy of the Greek Church; a formulary of prayers.

euchre (ū′ kėr) [etym. doubtful], *n.* An American card game for several persons, usu. four, with a pack from which the cards from the twos to the nines have been excluded. *v.t.* To beat by taking three of the five tricks at euchre; (*colloq.*) to beat thoroughly, to ruin; to outwit.

euclase (ū′ klāz) [F. (EU-, Gr. *klasis*, breaking, from *klaein*, to break)], *n.* (*Min.*) A monoclinic green, blue, or white transparent silicate of aluminium and glucinum.

Euclidean (ū klid′ ė ȧn), *a.* Of or pertaining to Euclid, Alexandrian mathematician (fl. 300 B.C.); according to the axioms and postulates of Euclid's geometry.

eudemonism (ū dē′ mō nizm) [Gr. *eudaimōn*, happy (EU-, *daimōn*, guardian genius), -ISM], *n.* The system of ethics which makes the pursuit of happiness the basis and criterion of moral conduct. **eudemonic** (-mon′ ik), *a.* **eudemonics,** *n.pl.* **eudemonist** (ū dē′ mō nist), *n.* **eudemonistic** (-nis′ tik), *a.*

eudiometer (ū di om′ ė tėr) [Gr. *eudios* (EU-, *Di-*, stem of *Zeus*, gen. *Dios*, the God of the sky), -METER], *n.* An instrument for ascertaining the quantity of oxygen in a given bulk of air. **eudiometric, -al** (-met′ rik, -ȧl), *a.* **eudiometrically,** *adv.* **eudiometry** (-om′-), *n.* The measurement of the purity of the air, or the composition of a gaseous mixture, by means of the eudiometer.

eugenic (ū jen′ ik) [EU-, Gr. *gen-*, stem, to produce, as in *eugenēs*, well-born], *a.* Pertaining to the development and improvement of offspring, esp. human offspring, through judicious breeding. *n.pl.* The science relating to this. **eugenism** (ū′ jė nizm), *n.*

eugenin (ū′ jė nin) [*eugen-*, first part of *eugenia*, name of a genus of trees in honour of *Eugene*, Prince of Savoy, -IN], *n.* (*Chem.*) Clove camphor; a crystallized substance deposited from water distilled from cloves.

euharmonic (ū har mon′ ik), *a.* (*Mus.*) Producing perfect harmony.

euhemerism (ū hē′ mėr izm), *n.* The theory formulated by Euhemerus of Messenia in Sicily (about 300 B.C.), that the classic gods are merely deified national kings and heroes, and their miraculous feats exaggerated traditions of actual events. **euhemerist,** *n.* **euhemeristic** (-is′ tik), *a.* **euhemerize,** *v.i.* To follow euhemerism. *v.t.* To treat or explain (myths) rationalistically.

eulogy (ū′ lō ji) [late L. *eulogium*, Gr. *eulogia* (EU-, LOGY)], *n.* Praise, encomium, panegyric; a writing or speech in praise of a person. **eulogist,** *n.* **eulogistic, -al** (-jis′ tik, -ȧl), *a.* **eulogistically,** *adv.* ***eulogium** (ū lō′ ji ŭm), *n.* (*pl.* **-ums**) Eulogy. **eulogize** (ū′ lō jīz), *v.t.* To speak or write of in praise; to commend, to extol.

Eumenides (ū men′ i dēz) [Gr., the kind ones, from *eumenēs*, friendly (EU-, *menos*, disposition)], *n.pl.* (*Gr. Myth.*) A euphemism for the Furies.

eunuch (ū′ nŭk) [L. *eunūchus*, Gr. *eunouchos*, one in charge of a bed-chamber (*eunē*, bed, *och-*, stem of *echein*, to hold)], *n.* A castrated man, esp. an attendant in a harem, or a state functionary in Oriental palaces and under the Roman emperors. *a.* Castrated; emasculate; unproductive. **v.t.* To make into a eunuch. **eunuchal,** *a.* **eunuchize,** *v.t.*

euonymus (ū on′ i mŭs) [L., from Gr. *euonumos*, of good name, luck (EU-, *onoma*, Æolic, *onuma*, name)], *n.* (*Bot.*) A genus of shrubs containing the spindle-tree.

eupatrid (ū păt′ rid) [Gr. *eupatridēs* (EU-, *patēr*, father)], *n.* (*pl.* **-ids, -idæ**) A member of the hereditary aristocracy of Attica, a patrician.

eupeptic (ū pep′ tik) [Gr. *eupeptos* (EU-, *peptein*, to digest)], *a.* Having a good digestion; pertaining to or characteristic of good digestion. **eupepsia,** *n.* **eupepticity** (-tis′ i ti), *n.*

euphemism (ū′ fė mizm) [Gr. *euphēmismos*, from *euphēmos* (EU-, *phēmē*, speaking, fame)], *n.* The use of a soft or pleasing term for one that is harsh or offensive; a softened expression. **euphemistic** (mis′ tik), *a.* **euphemistically,** *adv.* **euphemize** (ū′ fė mīz), *v.t.* To speak of euphemistically; to express in euphemism. *v.i.* To speak in euphemism.

euphonium (ū fō′ ni ŭm) [as foll.], *n.* (*Mus.*) A bass brass instrument of the same kind as the saxhorn but more powerful.

euphony (ū′ fŏ ni) [F. *euphonie*, Gr. *euphōnia* (EU-, *phōnē*, voice)], *n.* An agreeable sound; smoothness or agreeableness of sound in words and phrases; a pleasing pronunciation; (*Philol.*) the tendency towards greater ease of pronunciation shown in phonetic changes. **euphonic, -al** (ū fon′ ik, -ăl), *a.* **euphonically,** *adv.* **euphonious** (ū fō′ ni ŭs), *a.* **euphoniously,** *adv.* **euphonize,** *v.t.*

euphorbia (ū fôr′ bi ȧ) [L. *euphorbea*, from *Euphorbus*, Greek physician], *n.* (*Bot.*) A genus of plants known as the spurges, comprising about 700 species, many of which are poisonous while others have medicinal qualities. **euphorbiaceous** (-ā′ shŭs), *a.* **euphorbium,** *n.* An acrid poisonous, inflammable resin flowing from some African species of *Euphorbia*.

euphoria (ū fôr′ i ȧ) [Gr.], *n,* A feeling of well-being, supreme content.

euphrasy (ū′ frȧ si) [med. L. and Gr. *euphrasia*, cheerfulness, from *euphrainein* (EU-, *phrēn*, mind)], *n.* The eye-bright; (*fig.*) something that cheers.

euphuism (ū′ fū izm) [Gr. *euphuēs*, well-grown or well-endowed (EU-, *phuein*, to produce)], *n.* A pedantic affectation of elegant and high-flown language (from *Euphues* (1578–80), a work by John Lyly, which brought the style into vogue). **euphuist,** *n.* **euphuistic,** *a.* **euphuistically,** *adv.* ***euphuize,** *v.i.*

Eurasian (ū rā′ zhăn), *a.* Of mixed European and Asiatic blood; a term applied to those born of a European father and a Hindu or Mohammedan mother; pertaining to both Europe and Asia. *n.* One of European and Asiatic blood.

Euratom (ūr ăt′ ŏm), *n.* (*Pol.*) The European Atomic Energy Community of 1958 in which France, Belgium, Western Germany, Italy, the Netherlands and Luxemburg united for the peaceful development of nuclear energy.

eureka (ū rē′ kȧ) [Gr. *heurēka*, I have found it], *int.* and *n.* A discovery, an invention; exultation over a discovery (Archimedes' exclamation on discovering a test for the purity of the gold in Hiero's crown).

eurhythmics (ū rith′ miks), *n.* The science or art of rhythmical movement, esp. as applied to dancing and gymnastic exercises. **eurhythmical,** *a.* **eurhythmy,** *n.*

euro (ū′ rō) [Austral. abor.], *n.* A kangaroo, the wallaby of S. and Central Australia.

***euroclydon** (ū rok′ li dŏn) [Gr. (in Acts xxvii. 14), *eurokludōn* (*euros*, east wind, *kludōn*, surge)], *n.* A stormy north-east wind in the Mediterranean in the early spring.

Euromart (ū′ rō mart), *n.* (*Pol. Fin.*) A trading union of 1959 comprising France, Italy, Belgium, Western Germany, the Netherlands, Luxemburg.

European (ū rō pē′ ăn), *a.* Of, pertaining to, happening in, or extending over Europe; native to Europe. *n.* A native of Europe; one of European race. **European plan:** (*Am.*) A la carte meal. **Europeanism,** *n.* **Europeanize,** *v.t.* **Europeanization** (-zā′ shŭn), *n.*

europium (ū rōp′ i ŭm), *n.* An extremely rare metallic element, discovered in 1901.

Eurovision (ū′ rō vizh ŭn), *n.* (*T.V.*) The network of European television.

Eurus (ū′ rŭs) [L., from Gr. *Euros*], *n.* The east wind; the god of the east wind.

Eusebian (ū sē′ bi ăn), *a.* Pertaining to Eusebius; (*Bibl.*) pertaining to Eusebius of Cæsarea (whence **Eusebian Canons:** A classified arrangement of the four Gospels). *n.* A member of a semi-Arian sect, named after Eusebius of Nicomedia, a bishop of the 4th cent., who held that there was a subordination among the persons of the Godhead.

Euskarian (ū skâr′ i ăn) [*Euskara*, the name applied by the Basques to their own language], *a.* Basque. *n.* The Basque language; a Basque.

Eustachian (ū stā′ ki ăn) [*Eustachius*, -AN], *a.* (*Anat.*) Of or pertaining to Eustachius, an Italian physician of the 16th cent. **Eustachian tube,** *n.* A duct leading to the cavity of the tympanum from the upper part of the pharynx.

eutectic (ū tek′ tik) [Gr. *eu*, well, *tektos*, molten], *a.* (*Chem.*) Applying to the mixture of two or more substances with a minimum melting-point.

Euterpe (ū tĕr′ pi) [Gr. (EU-, *terpein*, to please)], *n.* (*Gr. Myth.*) The Muse of music, figured with a flute; (*Bot.*) a genus of graceful palms, all South American; (*Astron.*) the 27th asteroid. **Euterpean** (ū tĕr′ pė ăn), *a.* Pertaining to music.

euthanasia (ū thȧ nā′ zi ȧ) [Gr., from *euthanatos* (EU-, *thanatos*, death)], *n.* Easy, painless death; a method of producing this; putting to death in this manner.

evacuate (ė văk′ ū āt) [L. *ēvacuātus*, p.p. of *ēvacuāre* (E-, *vacuus*, empty)], *v.t.* To make empty, esp. to eject from or to empty the excretory passages; to form a vacuum; to withdraw from (esp. of troops); to remove inhabitants from a danger zone; (*fig.*) to divest of its meaning; *to nullify. **evacuant,** *a.* Producing evacuation; purgative. *n.* A medicine producing this effect. **evacuation** (-ā′ shŭn), *n.* The act of evacuating; also, the transfer of people from a danger zone. **evacuee,** *n.* Person, esp. a child, thus evacuated.

evade (ė vād′) [F. *évader*, L. *ēvādere* (E-, *vādere*, to go)], *v.t.* To avoid or elude by artifice, stratagem, or sophistry; to avoid (doing something), to shirk; to defeat, baffle, foil. **v.i.* To escape; to practise sophistry; to act evasively. **evadable,** *a.*

evaginate (ė văj′ i nāt) [L. *ēvaginātus*, p.p. of *ēvagināre* (E-, *vagina*, sheath], *v.t.* To turn inside out, to unsheathe (as a tubular organ). **evagination** (-nā′ shŭn), *n.*

evaluate (ė văl′ ū āt) [F. *évalure*], *v.t.* To determine the value of, to appraise; (*Math.*) to find a numerical expression for. **evaluation** (-ā′ shŭn), *n.*

evanesce (ev ȧ nes′) [L. *ēvānescere* (E-, *vānescere*, from *vānus*, vain)], *v.i.* To disappear; to be dissipated in vapour; to vanish. **evanescence,** *n.* **evanescent,** *a.* Disappearing gradually; fading, fleeting; (*Math.*) approaching zero, infinitesimal; imperceptibly minute. **evanescently,** *adv.*

***evangel** (ė văn′ jėl) [O.F. *evangile*, eccl. L. *ēvangelium*, Gr. *euangelion* (EU-, *angellein*, to announce)], *n.* The Gospel; one of the four Gospels; (*pl.*) the Gospels; (*fig.*) a gospel, a doctrine of political or social reform.

evangelical (ē văn jel′ ik ăl) [late L. *ēvangelicus*, Gr. *euangelikos*, as prec.], *a.* Pertaining to the Gospel; according to the doctrine of the Gospel; proclaiming or maintaining the truth taught in the Gospel; accepting for gospel only what Protestants consider the fundamental teaching of Scripture, the doctrines of the Fall, Christ's atonement, and salvation by faith not works. *n.* A member of this party in the Church, esp. in the Church of England, where it corresponds to the Low Church Party. **evangelicalism,** *n.* **evangelically,** *adv.* **evangelicity** (-lis' i ti), *n.*

evangelist (ė văn' jė list) [F. *évangeliste*, L. *ēvangelista*, Gr. *euangelistēs*, from *euangelizesthai*, from *euangelos*, see EVANGEL], *n.* One of the four writers of the Gospels (Matthew, Mark, Luke, and John); a preacher of the Gospel; a lay preacher. **evangelism,** *n.* Preaching of the Gospel; evangelicalism. ***evangelistary,** *n.* A book containing a selection of passages from the Gospels, as for lessons in divine service. **evangelistic** (-lis' tik), *a.* Pertaining to the four Evangelists; pertaining to preaching of the Gospel; evangelical.

evangelize (ė văn' jė līz) [eccl. L. *ēvangelizāre*, Gr. *euangelizesthai*, as prec.], *v.t.* To preach the Gospel to; to convert to Christianity. **evangelization** (-zā' shŭn), *n.*

evanish (ė văn' ish) [O.F. *evaniss-*, stem of *evanir*, L. *ēvānescere*, to EVANESCE], *v.i.* To vanish, to disappear. **evanishment, n.**

evaporate (ė văp' ŏ rāt) [L. *ēvaporātus*, p.p. of *ēvaporāre*], *v.t.* To convert into vapour; to vaporize; to drive off the moisture from by heating or drying. *v.i.* To become vapour; to pass away in vapour; to exhale moisture; (*colloq.*) to disappear, to vanish. **evaporable,** *a.* **evaporation** (-rā' shŭn), *n.* **evaporative,** *a.* **evaporator,** *n.* **evaporimeter** (-rim' ė tėr), *n.*

evasion (ė vā' zhŭn) [F. *évasion*, late L. *ēvāsio -ōnem*, from *ēvādere*, to EVADE], *n.* The act of evading or escaping (as from a question, argument, or charge), a subterfuge, an equivocation. **evasive** (ė vā' siv), *a.* **evasively,** *adv.* **evasiveness,** *n.*

Eve (1) (ēv) [A.-S. *Efe*, L. *Eva, Heva*, from Heb. *Hawwah*], *n.* (*Bibl.*) The wife of Adam and mother of mankind; the personification of womankind. **a daughter of Eve:** (*fig.*) A woman, usu. with an implication of curiosity, vanity, etc.

eve (2) (ēv) [A.-S. *ǣfen*, *ēfen* (cp. O.H.G. *ābant*, G. *abend*)], *n.* The evening before a holiday or other event or date; the period immediately preceding some important event; *evening.

evection (ė vek' shŭn) [L. *ēvectio*, from *ēvehere* (E-, *vehere*, to carry, p.p. *vectus*)], *n.* An inequality in the longitude of the moon, due to the action of the sun.

even (1) (ē' vėn), *n.* Evening. **evenfall,** *n.* (*Poet.*) Early evening. **evensong,** *n.* A form of worship for the evening; the time for evening prayer. **eventide,** *n.* Evening.

even (2) (ē' vėn) [A.-S. *efen, efn* (cp. Dut. *even*, O.H.G. *eban*, G. *eben*)], *a.* Level, smooth, uniform; on the same level, in the same plane (with); parallel; capable of being divided by the number 2 without any remainder; opposed to odd; equal; equally balanced, fair, impartial; unvarying, equable, unruffled; *plain, clear; *without blemish, pure; *equal in rank. **to even up:** To balance, to make equal. **even date:** (*Comm.*) To-day. **odd or even:** A game of chance. **on an even keel:** (*Naut.*) Said of a ship when she draws the same water fore and aft. **to be even with:** To retaliate upon, to pay out. **to make even:** *To square accounts with; (*Print.*) to space out the lines, so that a given passage may end with a full line. **even-handed,** *a.* Impartial, equitable, fair. **even-handedly,** *adv.* **even-handedness,** *n.* **evenly,** *adv.* **even-minded,** *a.* **even-mindedly,** *adv.* **evenness,** *n.* ***even-pleached,** *a.* Smoothly or evenly intertwined. **even-tempered,** *a.*

even (3) (ē' vėn) [A.-S. *efnan*, as prec.], *v.t.* To make smooth or level; to place on a level; *to treat as equal, to compare; *to make quits (with); to act up to, to satisfy. **v.i.* To be equal. **evener,** *n.*

even (4) (ē' vėn) [A.-S. *efne*, as prec.], *adv.* To a like degree, equally; as much as, so much as (expressing unexpectedness, surprise, concession, or emphasis, a comparison being implied); evenly; exactly, just, simply, neither more nor less than. **even so:** Exactly; yes.

evening (ēv' ning) [A.-S. *ǣfnung*, from *ǣfnian*, to grow towards evening, from *ǣfen*, EVEN (1)], *n.* The close or latter part of the day; the period from sunset to dark, or from sunset to bed-time; (*fig.*) the close or decline, as of life; the latter part. **evening dress,** *n.* The dress prescribed by convention for wearing in the evening. **evening primrose,** *n.* A plant belonging to the genus *Œnothera*, the yellow flowers of which usually open in the evening. **evening star,** *n.* (Also called Hesperus or Vesper) Jupiter, Mercury, or Venus when visible in the west in the evening.

event (ė vent') [O.F., from L. *ēventus*, p.p. of *ēvenīre*, to happen (E-, *venīre*, to come)], *n.* Anything that happens, as distinguished from a thing that exists; an occurrence, esp. one of great importance; the contingency or possibility of an occurrence; the consequence of any action; the issue or conclusion; (*theory of probabilities*) any of several possible occurrences regarded as having a probability of its own; (*Sport*) any item in a programme of games, contests, etc., esp. one on which money is wagered; *fate. **at all events:** In any case, at any rate. **a double event:** The coincidence of two occurrences. **in the event of:** If so, if it so happens. **eventful,** *a.* Full of events; attended by important changes. **eventless,** *a.*

eventide (ēv' ėn tīd), *n.* Evening.

eventual (ė ven' tū ăl) [EVENT], *a.* Happening as a consequence of something else; finally resulting, ultimate, final. **eventuality** (-ăl' i ti), *n.* **eventually,** *adv.* **eventuate,** *v.i.* To happen, to come to pass, to result; to turn out (well or ill).

ever (ev' ėr) [A.-S. *æfre* (etym. doubtful, perh. rel. to A.-S. *ā, āwa*, AYE, cp. Gr. *aiōn*, L. *ævum*)], *adv.* At all times; always; continually; at any time; in any degree. **ever and anon:** Now and then; at one time and another. **ever after or since:** Continually after a certain time. **ever so:** To any degree or extent conceivable. **for ever:** For all future time, eternally; incessantly. **seldom or ever:** (*incorrectly*) Seldom if ever; seldom or never. **or ever** [OR (2)]. ***ever-during,** *a.* Everlasting. **ever-living,** *a.* Living without end; immortal, unceasing.

everglade (ev' ėr glād), *n.* (*U.S.A.*) A low, marshy, tract of country, interspersed with patches covered with high grass; (*pl.*) the region of this character in Florida.

evergreen (ev' ėr grēn), *a.* Always green; retaining its verdure throughout the year; (*fig.*) always young or fresh. *n.* A plant which retains its verdure through the year.

everlasting (ev ėr las' ting), *a.* Lasting for ever, eternal, perpetual; continual, unintermittent; (*fig.*) interminable, tiresome; (of flowers) not changing colour when dried. *n.* Eternity; a plant whose flowers retain their colour when dried. **the Everlasting:** The Deity, the Eternal Being. **everlastingly,** *adv.* **everlastingness,** *n.*

evermore (ev ėr mōr'), *adv.* Always, eternally, continually.

evert (ė vĕrt') [L. *ēvertere* (E-, *vertere*, to turn)], *v.i.* To turn outwards, to turn inside out; *to overthrow. **eversion,** *n.*

every (ev' ri) [M.E. *everi, everich* (A.-S. *æfre*, ever, *ælc*, each)], *a.* Each of a number, all separately; each. **every bit:** Quite; the whole. **every now and then, every now and again, every so often:** From time to time; at brief intervals. **every one:** Each one. **everyone,** *n.* Everybody. **every other:** Every second or alternate (day, week, etc.). **everybody,** *n.* Every person. **everybody else:** (*collect.*) All other persons. **everyday,** *a.* Met with or happening daily; worn or used on ordinary occasions; common, usual; commonplace. *adv.* On each or every day; continually. **everything,** *n.* (*collect.*) All things; all of the things making up a whole;

(*fig.*) something of the highest importance. **everyway,** *adv.* In every way; in every respect. **everywhere,** *adv.* In every place.

evict (ė vikt′) [L. *ēvictus*, p.p. of *ēvincere* (E-, *vincere*, to conquer)], *v.t.* To dispossess by legal process; to eject from lands or tenements by law; *to prove, to evince. **eviction,** *n.* **evictor,** *n.*

evidence (ev′ i dėns) [F. *évidence*, L. *ēvidentia*, from *ēvidens -ntem*, pres.p. of *ēvidēre* (E-, *vidēre*, to see)], *n.* Anything that makes clear or obvious; ground for knowledge, indication, testimony; that which makes truth evident, or renders evident to the mind that it is truth; (*Law*) information by which a fact is proved or sought to be proved, or an allegation proved or disproved; such statements, proofs, etc., as are legally admissible as testimony in a court of law. *v.t.* To make evident, to attest. **in evidence:** Received or offered as tending to establish a fact or allegation in a court of law; (*colloq.*) plainly visible, conspicuous. **to turn King's** or **Queen's evidence:** To bear witness against one's accomplice in return for a free pardon.

evident (ev′ i dėnt) [as prec.], *a.* Open or plain to the sight; manifest, obvious; *conclusive. **evidential** (ev i den′ shȧl), *a.* Affording evidence; proving conclusively. **evidentially,** *adv.* **evidentiary,** *a.* Of, pertaining to, or of the nature of evidence. **evidently,** *adv.*

evil (ē′ vil) [A.-S. *yfel* (cp. Dut. *euvel*, O.H.G. *upil*, G. *übel*)], *a.* Bad, injurious, mischievous, worthless, morally bad, wicked; calamitous, troublous, sorrowful; unlucky, producing disastrous results; malicious, slanderous. *adv.* In an evil manner; maliciously, abusively, harmfully, injuriously; unfortunately, cruelly. *n.* An evil thing; that which injures or displeases, calamity, harm; sin, depravity, malignity; *a malady, a disease. **King's evil:** Scrofula. **the Evil One:** The Devil. **evil-disposed, -affected, -minded,** *a.* Unkindly and injuriously disposed. **evil eye,** *n.* A supposed power of fascinating, bewitching, or materially injuring by the look. **evil-eyed,** *a.* Malicious; looking malicious; having the power of the evil eye. **evil-doer,** *n.* One who does evil, a wrongdoer, a malefactor. **evilly,** *adv.* **evil-speaking,** *n.* Slander, calumny, defamation.

evince (ė vins′) [L. *ēvincere* (E-, *vincere*, to conquer)], *v.t.* To show clearly; to indicate, to make evident; to demonstrate. **v.i.* To furnish proof. **evincive,** *a.*

evirate (ē′ vī-, ev′ i rāt) [L. *ēvirātus*, p.p. of *ēvirāre* (E-, *vir*, man)], *v.t.* To emasculate; to divest of strength or virility.

eviscerate (ė vis′ ėr āt) [L. *ēviscerātus*, p.p. of *ēviscerāre* (E-, *viscera*, bowels)], *v.t.* To disembowel; (*fig.*) to empty of all that is vital; to empty, to gut. **evisceration** (-ā′ shŭn), *n.*

evite (ė vīt′) [F. *éviter*, L. *ēvitāre* (E-, *vītāre*, to shun)], *v.t.* (*chiefly Sc.*) To avoid, to shun.

evoke (ė vōk′) [F. *évoquer*, L. *ēvocāre* (E-, *vocāre*, to call)], *v.t.* To call up, to summon forth; (*Law*) to remove from one tribunal to another. ***evocate** (ev′ ȯ kāt), *v.t.* **evocation** (-kā′ shŭn), *n.* **evocative** (ė vok′ ȧ tiv), *a.* **evocator** (ev′ ȯ kā tȯr), *n.*

evolute (ev′ ȯ lūt) [L. *ēvolūtus*, p.p. of *ēvolvere*, to EVOLVE], *n.* (*Geom.*) A curve from which another is described by the end of a thread gradually wound upon or unwound from the former, thus forming the locus of the centres of curvature of the other, which is called the INVOLUTE. **evolutility** (-til′ i ti), *n.* (*Biol.*) Capability of manifesting change as the result of nutrition.

evolution (ē vȯ-, ev′ ȯ loo′ shŭn) [L. *ēvolūtio -ōnem*, as prec.], *n.* The act of unrolling, unfolding, opening, or growing; a series of things unrolled or unfolded; development, as of an argument, plot, design, organism, political, social, or planetary system, etc.; (*Biol.*) the process by which a germ develops into a complex organism; the derivation of all forms of life from early forms of a simpler character or from a single rudimentary form; the theory based on this principle, opp. to that of special creation (see CREATIONISM); the theory that the germ is not produced by fecundation, but pre-exists in the parent, having all the characters of the mature species in embryo; development of this germ, opp. to epigenesis; (*Math.*) the opening or unfolding of a curve; the extraction of roots from any given power, the reverse of involution; the evolving of gas, heat, etc.; (*Mil. and Nav.*) doubling of ranks or files, countermarching, or other changes of position, by which the disposition of troops or ships is changed; (*pl., fig.*) movements, changes of position, etc., in dancing etc. **evolutional, -tionary,** *a.* Produced by or pertaining to evolution. **evolutionism,** *n.* The theory or doctrine of evolution. **evolutionist,** *n.* One who holds the doctrine of evolution; one skilled in evolutions. **evolutionistic** (-nist′ ik), *a.* **evolutive** (ev ȯ loo′ tiv), *a.* Tending to or promoting evolution; evolutionary.

evolve (ė volv′) [L. *ēvolvere* (E-, *volvere*, to roll)], *v.t.* To unfold, to expand; to develop, to bring to maturity; to give off (gas, heat, etc.); to bring forth, work out, set forth (an argument etc.) in an orderly manner. *v.i.* To open; to develop. **evolvable,** *a.* **evolvement,** *n.* **evolver,** *n.*

evulsion (ė vŭl′ shŭn) [L. *ēvulsio -ōnem*, from *ēvulsus*, p.p. of *ēvellere* (E-, *vellere*, to pluck)], *n.* The act of forcibly plucking or extracting.

ewe (ū) [A.-S. *eowu* (cp. Dut. *ooi*, O.Ir. *oi*, Gr. *ois*, L. *ovis*, Sansk. *avi*)], *n.* A female sheep. **ewe lamb,** *n.* (*fig.*) A dearest possession.

ewer (ū′ ėr) [A.-F., from O.F. *aiguier*, L. *aquārium*, from *aqua*, water], *n.* A kind of pitcher or large jug for water; a toilet-jug with a wide mouth.

ex (eks) [L., out of], *prep.* (*Comm.*) From, out of, sold from; without. **ex dividend:** Not including the next dividend (abbr. *ex div.* or *x.d.*).

ex- [L. *ex-*, *ex*, out of, from, or Gr. *ex*, *ek*], *pref.* Out, forth, out of; thoroughly; without, -less; formerly, previously occupying the position of; as *exceed, exclude, exit, extend, extol*; *exacerbate, excruciate*; *exonerate, expatriate*; *exalbuminous, exstipulate*; *ex-chancellor, ex-president.*

exacerbate (eg zăs′-, ek săs′ ėr bāt) [L. *exacerbātus*, p.p. of *exacerbāre* (EX-, *acerbus*, bitter)], *v.t.* To irritate, to exasperate, to embitter; to aggravate, to increase the violence of (as a disease). **exacerbation** (-bā′ shŭn), **exacerbescence,** *n.*

exact (1) (eg zăkt′) [L. *exactus*, p.p. of *exigere* (EX-, *agere*, to drive)], *a.* Precisely agreeing in amount, number, or degree; accurate, strictly correct; precise, strict, punctilious; consummate, perfect. **exact sciences:** Those in which mathematical accuracy is attainable. **exactitude,** *n.* Exactness, precision. **exactness,** *n.* The quality of being exact.

exact (2) (eg zăkt′), *v.t.* To compel to be paid or surrendered; to demand as of right, to insist upon, to require authoritatively. *v.i.* To practise extortion. **exactable,** *a.* **exacting,** *a.* Severe or excessive in demanding; urgently requiring. **exactingly,** *adv.* **exaction,** *n.* The act of exacting; a forcible, illegal or exorbitant demand; extortion; that which is exacted; a compulsory or oppressive impost or service. **exactor,** *n.*

exactly (eg zăkt′ li), *adv.* In an exact manner; quite so; precisely, just so (in answer to a question or affirmation); in express terms.

exaggerate (eg zăj′ ėr āt) [L. *exaggerātus*, p.p. of *exaggerāre* (EX-, *agger*, a heap, rel. to AD-, *gerrare*, to carry)], *v.t.* To heighten, to overstate, to represent as greater than truth warrants; to increase, intensify, aggravate; to represent (features, colours, etc.) in a heightened manner; *to accumulate, heap up. *v.i.* To use or be given to exaggeration. **exaggeratedly,** *adv.* **exaggeration** (ā′ shŭn), *n.* **exaggerative,** *a.* **exaggeratively,** *adv.* **exaggerator,** *n.*

exalbuminous (ek săl bū′ mi nŭs), *a.* (*Bot.*) Destitute of albumen (used of seeds).

exalt (eg zawlt´) [L. *exaltāre* (EX-, *altus*, high)], *v.t.* To raise in dignity, rank, power, or position; to elevate in character, spirits, diction, or sentiment, to ennoble, to dignify; to elate; to praise, extol, glorify; to increase in force, to intensify. **exaltation** (-tā´ shŭn), *n.* The act of exalting; elevation in power, rank, dignity, or position; elation, rapture, ecstasy; intensification, augmentation; *(*Astrol.*) the position of a planet in the zodiac where it exerts the maximum of influence. **exaltedly,** *a.* **exaltedness,** *n.* ***exalter,** *n.*

examination (eg zăm i nā´ shŭn) [as foll.], *n.* The act of examining; careful inspection, scrutiny, or inquiry; the process of testing the capabilities or qualifications of a candidate for any post, or the progress, attainments, or knowledge of a student; (*Law*) a careful inquiry into facts by taking evidence. **examination-paper,** *n.* A paper containing questions for candidates, pupils, etc.; a series of answers to such questions by an examinee. ***examinational,** *a.*

examine (eg zăm´ in) [F. *examiner*, L. *exāmināre*, from *exāmen* (*exagmen*, the tongue of a balance, conn. with *exigere*, to weigh out (EX-, *agere*, to drive))], *v.t.* To inquire into, to investigate, scrutinize; to consider critically, to weigh and sift (as arguments for and against); to inspect, to explore; to question (as a witness); to test the capabilities, qualifications, knowledge of, etc., by questions and problems. *v.i.* To make inquiry or research. **examinable,** *a.* That may be examined. **examinant,** *n.* An examiner, *an examinee. ***examinate** (-nȧt), *n.* ***examen,** *n.* **examinee** (ex zăm i nē´), *n.* **examiner,** *n.* **examinator,** *n.* (*Sc.*) **examinatorial-** (itôr´ i ȧl), *a.*

example (eg zam´ pėl) [O.F., from L. *exemplum* (EX-, *emere*, to take, to buy, see EXEMPT)], *n.* A sample, a specimen; a copy, model, or pattern; any person, fact, or thing illustrating a general rule; a warning; a precedent, an instance; a problem or exercise (in mathematics etc.) for the instruction of students. *v.t.* To exemplify; to serve as an example to; to give a precedent for.

exanimate (eg zăn´ i mȧt) [L. *exanimātus*, p.p. of *exanimāre* (EX-, *anima*, life)], *a.* Lifeless, dead; without animation, depressed, spiritless.

exarch (ek´ sark) [L. *exarchus*, Gr. *exarchos* from *marchein*, to rule (EX-, *archein*, to begin)], *n.* A governor of a province under the Byzantine Empire; (*Gr. Ch.*) a grade in the ecclesiastical hierarchy instituted by Constantine the Great, formerly equivalent to patriarch or metropolitan, later a bishop in charge of a province, and also a legate of a patriarch. **exarchate,** *n.*

exasperate (eg zăs´ pėr āt) [L. *exasperātus*, p.p. of *exasperāre* (EX-, *asper*, rough)], *v.t.* To aggravate, to embitter; to irritate to a high degree; to provoke; *to incite. **exasperation** (-ā´ shŭn), *n.*

Excalibur (eks kăl´ i bėr) [O.F. *Escalibor*, prob. corr. of *Caliburn*, med. L. *Caliburnus* (in Geoffrey of Monmouth)], *n.* The magic sword of King Arthur, which only he could wield.

excavate (eks´ kȧ vāt) [L. *excavātus*, p.p. of *excavāre* (EX-, *cavus*, hollow)], *v.t.* To hollow out; to form by digging or hollowing out; to remove by digging; to uncover by digging, to dig out, esp. for archæological research. **excavation** (-vā´ shŭn), *n.* **excavator** (eks´-), *n.*

exceed (ek sēd´) [F. *excéder*, L. *excēdere* (EX-, *cēdere*, to go)], *v.t.* To go or pass beyond; to be more or greater than; to do more than is warranted by; to surpass, to outdo, to excel. *v.i.* To go too far, to go beyond bounds; to be greater; to excel, to be pre-eminent. **exceeding,** *a.* Very great in amount, duration, extent, or degree. **adv.* Exceedingly. **n.* Excess; superfluity. **exceedingly,** *adv.* Very much.

excel (ek sel´) [F., from L. *excellere* (EX-, *-cellere*, in *antecellere*, rel. to *celsus*, high)], *v.t.* (*past & p.p.* **excelled**) To surpass in qualities; to exceed, to outdo; *to be too much or too great for. *v.i.* To be superior, distinguished, or pre-eminent (in or at).

excellence (ek´ sel ėns) [as prec.], *n.* The state of excelling; superiority, pre-eminence; surpassing virtue, goodness, or merit; that in which any person or thing excels; an excellent quality, feature, or trait. **excellency,** *n.* Excellence; a title of honour given to a governor, an ambassador, a commander-in-chief, and certain other officers.

excellent (ek´ sel ėnt), *a.* Surpassing others in some good quality; of great virtue, worth, etc.; *exceeding, remarkable; superior or pre-eminent in bad or neutral qualities. **excellently,** *adv.*

excelsior (ek sel´ si ôr) [L. comp. of *excelsus*, lofty (EX-, *celsus*, high)], *a.* Higher, loftier. *n.* (*Am.*) Packing material composed of thin wood-shavings. **Excelsior State:** New York (from use of the word as a motto on the State seal).

except (ek sept´) [O.F. *excepter*, L. *exceptāre*, freq. of *excipere* (EX-, *capere*, to take)], *v.t.* To leave out, to omit, to exclude. *v.i.* To make objection (to or against). *prep.* Not including, exclusive of, omitting, but. *conj.* Unless. **excepter,** *n.* An objector, a caviller. **excepting,** *prep.* (*usu. after* not) Omitting, with the exception of. **exception,** *n.* The act of excepting; that which is excepted; an instance of that which is excluded from or is at variance with a rule, class, or other generalization; an objection, disapproval. **to take exception:** To object, to find fault; to express disapproval. **exceptionable,** *a.* Liable to objection; objectionable; unusual. ***exceptionableness,** *n.* **exceptional,** *a.* Forming an exception; unusual, extraordinary, unprecedented. **exceptionality** (-năl´ i ti), *n.* **exceptionally,** *adv.* **exceptionary,** *a.* Indicating an exception. ***exceptioner,** *n.* One who takes exception, an objector. ***exceptious,** *a.* Peevish; given to cavilling or taking exception; censorious. ***exceptiousness,** *n.* **exceptive,** *a.* Forming an exception; excepting. ***exceptless,** *a.* Extending to all; with no exception.

excerpt (ek´ sĕrpt, ek sĕrpt´) [L. *excerptus*, p.p. of *excerpere*, to select (EX-, *carpere*, to pluck)], *v.t.* To make an extract of or from; to cite, to quote. *n.* (*pl.* **excerpts, excerpta**) An extract or selection from a writing or book, esp. an article printed off separately from the proceedings of a learned society. **excerptible,** *a.* **excerption,** *n.*

excess (ek ses´) [O.F. *exces*, L. *excessum*, acc. of *excessus*, a going out, from *excēdere*, to EXCEED], *n.* That which exceeds what is usual or necessary; the quality, state, or fact of exceeding the ordinary measure, proportion, or limit; the amount by which one number or quantity exceeds another; (*usu. pl.*) transgression of due limits; intemperance, over-indulgence, extravagance; outrage. **excess fare:** (*Railway*) The amount paid for travelling beyond the point for which a ticket has been taken or in a higher class. **excess luggage:** A quantity above the weight allowed free carriage. **Excess Profits Tax,** *n.* (*Fin.*) A tax levied in wartime upon the excess of net profits earned in any trade or business over a specified pre-war standard. **excessive,** *a.* **excessively,** *adv.*

exchange (eks chānj´) [O.F. *eschangier*, late L. *excambiāre* (EX-, *cambiāre*, L. *cambīre*, to CHANGE)], *v.t.* To give or receive in return for something else; to hand over for an equivalent in kind; to give and receive in turn, to interchange; to give, resign, or abandon (as one state or condition for another). *v.i.* To be given or received in exchange; to be received as of equal value; (*Mil.*) to pass from one regiment to another by taking the place of another officer. *n.* The act of exchanging; a parting with one article or commodity for an equivalent in kind; the act of giving and receiving reciprocally, interchange; the act of resigning one state for another; that which is given or received in exchange; exchanging of coin for its value in coins of the same or another country; the system by which goods or property are exchanged and debts settled, esp. in different countries, without the transfer of money; the place where merchants, brokers, etc., meet to transact business; the central office where telephone connections are made. **bill of exchange** [BILL (3)]. **course** or **rate of exchange:** The rate at which bills drawn upon drawees in a foreign country may be sold where they were drawn. **par of exchange:** The value of a given amount of the currency of one country in terms of another currency. **exchange-cap,** *n.* A fine quality of paper used for printing bills of exchange. **exchangeable,** *a.* That may be exchanged (for); rateable by what can be procured in exchange. **exchangeability,** *n.* **exchanger,** *n.*

exchequer (eks chek′ ėr) [M.E. *eschekere,* O.F. *eschequier,* med. L. *scaccārium,* a chess-board, see CHECK], *n.* The State treasury; the Government department dealing with the public revenue; finances or pecuniary resources; the Court of Exchequer; *a chess-board. **v.t.* To institute a process against a person in the Court of Exchequer. **Chancellor of the Exchequer** [CHANCELLOR]. **Court of Exchequer:** A court originally intended for the recovery of debts due to the king and to vindicate his proprietary rights etc., but afterwards developed into an ordinary law-court with a jurisdiction in equity, which was transferred to the Court of Chancery, the Court itself being made in 1873 one of the divisions of the High Court of Justice, and this in 1881 merged into the Queen's (King's) Bench Division. **exchequer bill,** *n.* A bill for money, or a promissory bill, issued from the Exchequer by authority of Parliament. **exchequer bond** [TREASURY BOND].

excide (ek sīd′) [L. *excīdere* (EX-, *cædere,* to cut)], *v.t.* To cut out; to extirpate.

excise (1) (ex sīz′) [prob. from M.Dut. *excijs,* O.F. *acceis,* late L. *accēnsum,* from *accensāre,* to tax (*ac-,* AD-, *census,* tax)], *n.* A tax or duty on certain articles produced and consumed in a country (in the United Kingdom on spirits, beer, and tobacco); the branch of the Civil Service which collects and manages the excise duties, usually called the Inland Revenue; *a tax of any kind. *v.t.* To impose an excise duty on; (*fig.*) to impose upon, to overcharge. **excisable,** *a.* Subject or liable to excise duty. **excise laws:** (*U.S.A.*) Licensing laws. **excise-officer, exciseman,** *n.* An officer who collects the excise duties, and prevents any evasion of the excise laws.

excise (2) (ek sīz′) [L. *excīsus,* p.p. of *excīdere,* to EXCIDE], *v.t.* To cut out (part of a book or of the body). **excision** (ek sizh′ ŭn), *n.*

excite (ek sīt′) [O.F. *exciter,* L. *excitāre,* freq. of *exciēre* (EX-, *ciēre,* to summon)], *v.t.* To rouse, to stir into action, energy, or agitation; to stimulate, to bring into activity; to inflame the spirits of; to provoke, to bring about by stimulating; (*Elec.*) to set up electric activity in; to magnetize the poles of an electric machine. **excitable,** *a.* Susceptible of excitement; characterized by excitability. **excitability** (-bil′ i ti), *n.* **excitant** (ek′ si tȧnt), **a.* Stimulating; tending to excite. *n.* That which excites increased action in an organism; (*Med.*) a stimulant. **excitation** (-tā′ shŭn), *n.* ***excitative** (ek sī′ tȧ tiv), *a.* ***excitatory** (ek sī′ tȧ tȯr i), *a.* **excitedly,** *adv.* **excitement,** *n.* **exciter,** *n.* One who or that which excites; (*Med.*) a stimulant. **exciting,** *a.* Stimulating; producing excitement. **excitingly,** *adv.* **excitive,** *a.*

excitor (ek sī′ tȯr), *n.* (*Anat.*) An afferent nerve belonging to the spinal group. **excitomotory,** *a.* (*Physiol.*) Causing muscular contraction or movement independently of volition (applied to the spinal group of nerves).

exclaim (eks klām′) [F. *exclamer,* L. *exclāmāre* (EX-, *clāmāre,* to cry aloud)], *v.i.* To cry out abruptly or passionately; *to inveigh (against). *v.t.* To utter in an abrupt or passionate manner. **n.* Exclamation; clamour.

exclamation (eks klȧ mā′ shŭn), *n.* The act of exclaiming; an expression of surprise, pain, etc. **note of exclamation:** A sign (!) indicating emotion etc. **exclamatory** (-klăm′ ȧ tȯr i), *a.* Containing or expressing exclamation; using exclamation.

exclave (eks′ klāv) [L. *ex,* out; *clavis,* a key], *n.* (*Pol.*) Part of a country disjoined from the main part and surrounded by foreign territory, where it is considered an enclave.

exclude (eks klood′) [L. *exclūdere,* p.p. *exclūsus* (EX-, *claudere,* to shut)], *v.t.* To shut out, to prevent from coming in; to prevent from participating; to debar; to expel and keep out; to reject, to except, to leave out. **exclusion,** *n.* ***exclusionary,** *a.* Tending to exclude. ***exclusionism,** *n.* **exclusionist,** *n.* One who would exclude another from any privilege, position, etc.; one who supported the Bill, introduced in the reign of Charles II, to exclude the Duke of York (afterwards James II) from the throne: (*Austral. hist.*) the free settlers of Australia who opposed the granting of the franchise to ex-convicts.

exclusive (eks kloo′ siv) [med. L. *exclūsīvus* (as prec., -IVE)], *a.* Shutting out or tending to shut out; desiring to shut out; fastidious in the choice of associates, snobbish; not inclusive (of); excluding all else; excluding all that is not specified. *adv.* Not taking into account or not inclusively (of). *n.* One who is exclusive in his manners or tastes; one who excludes all but a very few from his society, a snob; (*Log.*) an exclusive proposition. **exclusively,** *adv.* **exclusiveness,** *n.* **exclusivism,** *n.* The act or practice of excluding; systematic exclusiveness.

excogitate (eks koj′ i tāt) [L. *excōgitātus,* p.p. of *excōgitāre* (EX-, *cōgitāre,* to COGITATE)], *v.t.* To think out; to devise by thinking. **excogitation** (-tā′ shŭn), *n.*

excommunicate (eks kȯ mū′ ni kāt) [late L. *excommūnicātus,* p.p. of *excommūnicāre* (EX-, *commūnis,* COMMON)], *v.t.* To exclude from the communion and privileges of the Church; (*fig.*) to expel. **excommunication** (-kā′ shŭn), *n.* **greater excommunication:** Total exclusion from the Church. **lesser excommunication:** A debarring from the sacraments. **excommunicative,** *a.* **excommunicatory,** *a.*

excoriate (eks kôr′ i āt) [L. *excoriātus,* p.p. of *excoriāre* (EX-, *corium,* skin, hide)], *v.t.* To strip the skin from; to gall or tear off the skin by abrasion. **excoriation** (-ā′ shŭn), *n.* The act of excoriating; an abrasion; *(*fig.*) robbery, spoliation.

excrement (1) (eks′ krė mėnt) [F. *excrément,* L. *excrēmentum,* from *excernere,* as EXCRETE], *n.* Refuse matter discharged from the body after digestion, fæces; excretion. **excremental,** *a.* **excrementitious** (-tish′ ŭs), *a.*

***excrement** (2) (eks′ krė mėnt) [L. *excrēmentum,* from *excrescere* (EX-, *crescere,* to grow)], *n.* An outgrowth, such as hair, feathers, nails, etc.

excrescence (eks kres′ ėns) [L. *excrescentia,* as prec.], *n.* An unnatural, useless, or disfiguring outgrowth; *a natural outgrowth. **excrescent,** *a.* Growing abnormally or redundantly, superfluous, redundant.

excrete (eks krēt′) [L. *excrētus,* p.p. of *excernere* (EX-, *cernere,* to sift)], *v.t.* To separate and discharge superfluous matter from the organism. **excreta** [L., pl. of *excrētum,* neut. of *excrētus*], *n.pl.* Matter discharged from the body, esp. fæces and urine. **excretion,** *n.* The ejection of waste matter from the body; that which is excreted. **excretive,** *a.* Having the quality or power of excretion. **excretory,** *a.* Pertaining to excretion, or conveying excreted matter.

excruciate (eks kroo′ shi āt) [L. *excruciātus,* p.p. of *excruciāre* (EX-, *crux, crucis,* CROSS)], *v.t.* To torture, to inflict severe pain or mental agony upon. **excruciatingly,** *adv.* **excruciation** (-si ā′ shŭn), *n.*

exculpate (eks′ kŭl pāt) [L. *exculpātus,* p.p. of *exculpāre* (EX-, *culpa,* fault)], *v.t.* To clear from a charge; to free from blame, exonerate; to vindicate. **exculpation** (-pā′ shŭn), *n.* **exculpatory** (eks kŭl′ pȧ tȯr i), *a.*

excurrent (eks kŭr′ ėnt) [L. *excurrens -ntem*, pres.p. of *excurrere* (see foll.)], *a.* Running or passing out; flowing out (as blood from the heart); forming a passage outward; (*Bot.*) projecting beyond the edge or point.

***excurse** (eks kěrs′) [*excurs-*, p.p. stem of *excurrere* (EX-, *currere*, to run)], *v.i.* To make a digression; to make an excursion. **excursive,** *a.* Rambling, deviating, exploring. **excursively,** *adv.* **excursiveness,** *n.*

excursion (eks kěr′ shŭn) [as prec.], *n.* A journey or ramble for health or pleasure; a short tour, a trip by an individual or a body of persons; a wandering from the subject, a digression; (*Astron.*) a deviation from the fixed course; *a sally, a sortie, an expedition. **excursion train,** *n.* A train carrying excursionists at a reduced fare. **excursional, -ary,** *a.* Of or pertaining to an excursion. **excursionist,** *n.* One who goes on an excursion; one who organizes excursions.

excursus (eks kěr′ sŭs) [L., verbal n. of *excurrere*, as prec.], *n.* A dissertation appended to a work, containing an exposition of some point raised or referred to in the text.

excuse (1) (eks kūz′) [O.F. *excuser*, L. *excūsāre* (EX-, *causa*, CAUSE)], *v.t.* To free from blame or guilt; to pardon, to acquit; to ask pardon or indulgence for; to serve as a vindication or apology for, to justify; to relieve of or exempt from an obligation or duty; to remit, not to exact (as a debt); to dispense with. **v.i.* To make excuses. **excusable,** *a.* **excusableness,** *n.* **excusably,** *adv.* ***excusator,** *n.* **excusatory,** *a.* **excuser,** *n.*

excuse (2) (eks kūs′), *n.* A plea offered in extenuation of a fault or for release from an obligation, duty, etc.; an apology, a justification; the ground or reason for excusing; a pretended reason; the act of excusing, an exculpation.

exeat (ek′ sė ăt) [L., let him go out, 3rd sing. subj. of *exīre*, to go out], *n.* Leave of absence, as to a student at the Universities; permission granted by a bishop to a priest to go out of his diocese; permission by a Roman Catholic bishop to one of his subjects to take orders in another diocese. **exeant** [L., let them leave], *n.* Leave of absence to several persons.

execrate (ek′ sė krāt) [L. *execrātus*, p.p. of *execrārī*, *exsecrārī* (EX-, *sacrāre*, to consecrate, from *sacer*, sacred, accursed)], *v.t.* To curse, to imprecate evil upon; to detest; *to denounce as accursed. *v.i.* To utter curses. **execrable,** *a.* Detestable, accursed; abominable; very bad; *lamentable. **execrably,** *adv.* **execration** (-krā′ shŭn), *n.* **execrative,** *a.* **execratory,** *a.*

execute (ek′ sė kūt) [O.F. *executer*, med. L. *execūtāre*, L. *execūtus*, *exsecūtus*, p.p. of *exsequī* (EX-, *sequī*, to follow)], *v.t.* To carry into effect, to put in force; to perform, to accomplish, complete; (*Law*) to perform what is required to give validity to any legal instrument, as by signing and sealing; to discharge (a duty, functions, office, etc.); to play or perform (a piece of music, a part in a play); to inflict capital punishment on. *v.i.* To perform, accomplish, or discharge (a piece of music, one's part, etc.). **executable** (eks′ ė kū tȧbl), *a.* **executant** (ėg zek′ ū tȧnt), *n.* One who performs; (*Mus.*) a performer on any instrument.

execution (ek sė kū′ shŭn) [O.F., from L. *execūtio -ōnem*, as prec.], *n.* The act of executing; performance, accomplishment; the act of carrying into effect; the infliction of capital punishment; destruction, destructive effect, slaughter; the mode of performing a work of art, skill, dexterity; (*Law*) the act of giving validity to a legal instrument, as by signing; the carrying into effect of the judgment of a court; the warrant empowering an officer to carry a judgment into effect, esp. one authorizing the seizure of a debtor's goods in default of payment.

executioner, *n.* One who inflicts capital punishment; one who kills; one who tortures; *one who performs or carries into effect.

executive (eg zek′ ū tiv) [as prec., -IVE], *a.* Having the function or power of executing; pertaining to performance or carrying into effect; carrying laws, decrees, etc., into effect. *n.* The person or body of persons carrying laws, ordinances, sentences, etc., into effect; the administrative branch of a government. **executive order:** (*U.S.A. pol.*) The equivalent to an Order in Council.

executor (eg zek′ ū tȯr) [A.-F. *executour*, L. *exsecūtor -ōrem*, as prec., -OR], *n.* One who executes, esp. a person appointed by a testator to carry out the provisions of his will; *an executioner. **literary executor,** *n.* A person appointed to deal with the copyrights and unpublished works of a deceased author. **executorial** (tôr′ i ȧl), *a.* **executorship,** *n.* **executrix,** *n.* (*pl.* **-trices**).

exedra (ek′ sė drȧ, ek sē′ drȧ) [L., from Gr. (EX-, *hedra*, a seat)], *n.* (*Gr. Ant.*) The portico of the Grecian palæstra in which disputations were held; a hall for conversation; (*Arch.*) an elevated seat, a bishop's throne, a porch, a projecting chapel; a recess.

exegesis (ek sė jē′ sis) [Gr. *exēgēsis*, from *exēgeisthai* (EX-, *hēgeisthai*, to lead)], *n.* (*pl.* **-geses**) Exposition, interpretation, esp. of the Scriptures. **exegete,** *n.* One who is skilled in the exegesis of the Scriptures. **exegetic** (-jet′ ik), *a.* Pertaining to exegesis, expository; *n.pl.* Scientific interpretation, esp. of Scripture; hermeneutics. **exegetical** (ek sė jet′ i kȧl), *a.* **exegetically,** *adv.* **exegetist** (-jē′ tist), *n.*

***exeme** (eks ēm′) [L. *eximere* (EX-, *emere*, to take)], *v.t.* (*Sc. Law*) To release, exempt.

exemplar (eg zem′plȧr) [O.F. *exemplaire*, L. *exemplārium*, from *exemplāris*, from *exemplum*, an EXAMPLE], *n.* A pattern or model to be copied; a noted example; a typical example; an instance, a parallel; a copy, as of a book. **a.* Exemplary.

exemplary (eg zem′ plȧ ri) [L. *exemplāris*, as prec.], *a.* Serving as a pattern or model; worthy of imitation; typical, serving to exemplify, illustrative; serving as a warning. **exemplarily,** *adv.* **exemplariness,** *n.*

exemplify (eg zem′ pli fī) [med. L. *exemplificāre*], *v.t.* To illustrate by example; to be an example of, to prove by an attested copy; to make an authenticated copy of. **exemplifiable,** *a.* **exemplification** (-kā′ shŭn), *n.*

exempt (eg zempt′) [O.F., from L. *exemptus*, p.p. of *eximere* (EX-, *emere*, to take)], *a.* Free (from); not liable or subject to; *cut off, removed. *n.* One who is exempted or freed (from); one of four officers of the Yeomen of the Guard, ranking as corporals, now usu. called exons. *v.t.* To free or allow to be free; to grant immunity (from); *to take away (from or out of); *to single out. **exemption,** *n.* The state of being exempt; immunity; freedom from the obligation of doing compulsory military service.

exenterate (ek sen′ tėr āt) [L. *exenterātus*, p.p. of *exenterāre* (EX-, Gr. *enteron*, intestine)], *v.t.* To disembowel, eviscerate (*now only fig.*). **exenteritis** (-ī′ tis), *n.* (*Path.*) Inflammation of the outer coating of the intestines.

exequatur (ek sė kwā′ tŭr) [L., he may perform, 3rd sing. subj. of *exequī*, see EXECUTE], *n.* A written recognition of a consul or commercial agent, given by the government to which he is accredited; official authority or permission to execute some act; an authorization by a sovereign or government for the exercise of episcopal functions under papal authority or the promulgation of a papal bull.

exequies (ek′ sė kwiz) [O.F. *exeques*, L. *exequias*, acc. of *exequiæ* (EX-, *sequī*, to follow)], *n.pl.* Funeral rites; the ceremony of burial; obsequies. **exequial** (ek sē′ kwi ȧl), *a.*

exercise (ek′ sėr sīz) [O.F. *exercice*, L. *exercitium*, from *exercitus*, p.p. of *exercēre*, to keep at work

(EX-, *arcēre*, to shut up)], *n.* The act of using, employing, or exerting; practice (of a function, virtue, occupation, art, etc.); systematic exertion of the body for the sake of health; exertion for the training of the body or mind; a task set for this purpose; a composition for the improvement of a player or singer; (*pl.*) drill, athletics; a devotional observance, an act of public or private worship; *a discourse; (*Sc.*) a meeting of the Presbytery for holding a discussion on a passage of Scripture; the Presbytery itself; *exertion, action. *v.t.* To employ, to exert, to put in practice or operation; to perform the duties of, to fulfil; to train; to keep employed or busy; to make anxious or solicitous, to perplex, worry; to exert (muscles, brain, memory, etc.) so as to develop their power. **v.i.* To use action or exertion (upon). **exercisable,** *a.* **exerciser,** *n.* **I am greatly exercised about:** I am deeply anxious regarding.

exercitation (ek sĕr si tā' shŭn) [L. *exercitātio -ōnem*, from *exercitāre*, freq. of *exercēre* (as prec.)], *n.* Exercise, practice; a dissertation, a literary or rhetorical display of skill.

exergue (eg zĕrg', eks' ĕrg) [F., prob. from Gr. EX-, *ergon*, work], *n.* The small space beneath the base line of a subject engraved on a coin or medal; the name, date, or inscription placed there.

exert (eg zĕrt') [L. *exertus*, p.p. of *exserere*, to put forth (EX-, *serere*, to bind, to put)], *v.t.* To put forth (as strength, power, or ability); to put in action or operation. **to exert oneself:** To strive, to use effort. **exertion,** *n.*

exeunt (ek' sė ŭnt) [L., they go out], *v.i.* (*Stage direction*) They go off the stage, they retire. ***exeunt omnes*:** They all go off the stage.

exfoliate (eks fō' li āt) [L. *exfoliātus*, p.p. of *exfoliāre* (EX-, *folium*, a leaf)], *v.i.* (*Min.*) To split into scales (of bone, bark, etc.); to fall or come off in scales or flakes. **exfoliation** (-ā' shŭn), *n.*

exhalation (ek sȧ lā' shŭn), *n.* The act or process of exhaling; evaporation; that which is exhaled; a breathing out; vapour, mist; effluvium, an emanation; *a meteor.

exhale (eks hāl') [F. *exhaler*, L. *exhālāre* (EX-, *hālāre*, to breathe)], *v.t.* To breathe forth; to emit, or cause to be emitted, in vapour; to draw up in vapour; to breathe out; *to draw (as a sword). *v.i.* To be given off as vapour; (*fig.*) to pass off as an emanation; to make an expiration, as distinct from inhaling. ***exhalant,** *a.* Having the quality of exhaling or evaporating.

exhaust (eg zawst') [L. *exhaustus*, p.p. of *exhaurīre* (EX-, *haurīre*, to draw)], *v.t.* To draw off; to empty by drawing out the contents; to use up the whole of, to consume; to wear out by exertion; to drain of resources, strength, or essential properties; to study, discuss, treat the whole of a subject. *n.* The discharge or escape of steam, gas, vapour, etc., from an engine after it has performed its work; apparatus for withdrawing vitiated air by means of a partial vacuum. **exhaust-pipe,** *n.* A pipe conducting spent steam etc. from the cylinder. **exhaust silencer,** *n.* (*Motor.*) A chamber fitted in the exhaust pipe where the noise of the exhaust is reduced by baffles. **exhaust-steam,** *n.* Steam which passes out of the cylinder after having performed its function in moving the piston. **exhausted receiver,** *n.* The receiver of an air-pump after the air has been pumped out. **exhauster,** *n.* **exhaustible,** *a.* **exhaustibility** (-bil' i ti), *n.* **exhausting,** *a.* Tending to exhaust or tire out completely.

exhaustion (eg zaws' chŭn), *n.* The act of exhausting; the state of being exhausted; a complete loss of strength; a method of proving a point by showing that all alternatives are absurd or impossible.

exhaustive (eg zaw' stiv), *a.* Tending to exhaust (esp. a subject), comprehensive. **exhaustively,** *adv.* So as to exhaust; by the process of exhaustion. **exhaustiveness,** *n.*

exhibit (ėg zib' it) [L. *exhibitus*, p.p. of *exhibēre* (EX-*habēre*, to have)], *v.t.* To offer to public view; to present for inspection; to show, to display, to manifest; to furnish an instance of; (*Law*) to bring forward officially; (*Med.*) to administer. *n.* Anything exhibited; an article or collection of articles sent to an exhibition; (*Law*) a document or other voucher produced in court and used as evidence. ***exhibiter, exhibitor,** *n.* **exhibitory,** *a.*

exhibition (ek si bish' ŭn) [O.F. *exhibicion*, late L. *exhibitio -ōnem*, as prec.], *n.* The act of exhibiting; a display; the act of allowing to be seen, as temper; the production of documents, etc. before any tribunal in proof of facts; a public display of works of art or manufacture, natural products, etc.; an allowance to a student in college, school, etc., originally maintenance, support, pecuniary assistance; (*Sc. Law*) an action for compelling delivery of documents; *a gift, present. **to make an exhibition of oneself:** To behave so as to appear contemptible. **exhibitioner,** *n.* One who has obtained an exhibition at a college or school. **exhibitionism,** *n.* (*Psych.*) A tendency to show off, to attract attention to oneself; a tendency to indecent exposure in public. **exhibitionist,** *n.*

exhilarate (eg zil' ȧ rāt) [L. *exhilarātus*, p.p. of *exhilarāre* (EX-, *hilaris*, glad, cheerful)], *v.t.* To gladden, to enliven, to animate. **exhilarant,** *a.* **exhilaratingly,** *adv.* **exhilaration** (-rā' shŭn), *n.* **exhilarative,** *a.*

exhort (eg zôrt') [O.F. *exhorter*, L. *exhortārī* (EX-, *hortārī*, to urge)], *v.t.* To incite by words (to good deeds); to admonish; to urge, to stimulate; to advise or encourage by argument; *to recommend. *v.i.* To deliver an exhortation. **n.* An exhortation. **exhortation** (-tā' shŭn), *n.* The act or practice of exhorting; an admonition, earnest advice; a formal address. **exhortative,** *a.* **exhortatory,** *a.*

exhume (eks hūm') [F. *exhumer*, late L. *exhumāre* (EX-, *humus*, the ground)], *v.t.* To disinter; (*fig.*) to unearth, to discover. **exhumation** (-mā' shŭn), *n.*

exigeant (ek si zhan) [F., p.p. of *exiger*, L. *exigere*, as foll.], *a.* (*fem.* **-nte**) Exacting.

exigence, -gency (eks' i jėns, -jėn si) [F. *exigence*, L. *exigentia*, from *exigere* (EX-, *agere*, to drive)], *n.* Urgent need, demand, necessity; a state of affairs demanding immediate action or remedy, an emergency.

exigent (ek' si jėnt), *a.* Urgent, pressing, demanding more than is reasonable, exacting. **n.* A pressing need; an emergency, a crisis, *the extremity, the end. **exigible,** *a.* That may be exacted (from or against).

exiguous (eg zig' ū ŭs) [L. *exiguus*, small, as prec.], *a.* Small, slender, scanty. **exiguity** (ek si gū' i ti), *n.* **exiguousness,** *n.*

exile (ek' sīl) [O.F. *exil*, L. *exilium*, *exsilium* (EX-, *salīre*, to leap)], *n.* Banishment, expatriation; long absence from one's native country, whether voluntary or enforced; one who is banished, or has been long absent from his native country. *v.t.* To banish from one's native country. ***exilement,** *n.* **exilian** (ek sil' i ȧn), **exilic** (ek sil' ik), *a.* Pertaining to exile or banishment, esp. to that of the Jews in Babylon.

exility (eg zil' i ti) [L. *exilitās*, from *exīlis*, thin], *n.* Thinness, scantiness; (*fig.*) tenuity, subtlety.

eximious (eg zim' i ŭs) [L. *eximius*, select, from *eximere*, to EXEMPT], *a.* Excellent, illustrious.

exist (eg zist') [F. *exister*, L. *existere*, *exsistere* (EX-, *sistere*, causal of *stare*, to stand)], *v.i.* To be, to have actual being; to live; to continue to be; to live or have being under specified conditions. **existible,** *a.* **existibility** (bil' i ti), *n.*

existence (eg zist' ėns), *n.* The state of being or existing; continuance of being; life; mode of existing; a thing that exists; all that exists; *a being, an entity; *reality. **existent,** *a.* Having being or existence, existing, actual.

existential (eg zis ten' shal), *a.* Pertaining to or consisting in existence. **Existentialism,** *n.* (*Phil.*) A philosophy largely deriving from Kierkegaard, implying a special conception of the idea of existence, in effect substituting 'Sentio ergo sum' for Descartes' 'Cogito ergo sum'. "It considers self as a unity of finiteness and freedom, of involvement in natural process and transcendence over process" (R. Niebuhr). ***existentially,** *adv.*

exit (1) (ek' sit) [L. *exitus*, a going out, from *exīre* (EX-, *īre*, to go)], *n.* The departure of an actor from the stage; departure, esp. from this life; death, decease; a going out; freedom to go out; a passage, a way out. *exit* (2) [L., he goes out, 3rd sing. of *exīre*], *v.i.* (*Stage direction*) Goes off the stage.

ex-libris (eks lī' bris) [L. *ex librīs*, out of books, from the library (of), *n.* (*often as pl.*) A book-plate, a label bearing an owner's name, crest, device, etc.

exo- [Gr. *exō*, without, outside], *comb form.*

exoderm (eks' ō dĕrm), *n.* (*Anat.*) The epidermis, the outer layer of the blastoderm.

exodus (eks' ō dŭs) [Gr. *exodos*], *n.* A departure, esp of a large body of persons; the departure of the Israelites from Egypt under Moses; the second book of the Old Testament narrating this event.

ex officio (ek sȯ fish' i ō) [L. *ex*, out of, *officiō*, abl. of *officium*, duty, OFFICE], *adv.* By virtue of one's office. *a.* Official.

exogamy (ek sog' ȧ mi) [EXO-, Gr. *gamos*, marriage], *n.* The custom prevalent among some tribes forbidding a man to marry a woman of his own tribe. **exogamic** (-găm' ik), **exogamous** (-sog' ȧ mŭs), *a.*

exogen (ek' sō jėn) [EXO-, Gr. *gen-*, root of *gignesthai*, to be born or produced], *n.* (*Bot.*) A plant whose stem increases by an annual layer growing on the outside of the wood, opposed to endogen; a dicotyledon. **exogenous** (ėk soj' ė nŭs), *a.*

exon (ek' sŏn) [prob. representing F. pron. of EXEMPT], *n.* One of four officers of the Yeomen of the Guard [see EXEMPT].

exonerate (eg zon' ėr āt) [L. *exonerātus*, p.p. of *exonerāre* (EX-, *onus oneris*, a burden)], *v.t.* To free from a charge or blame; to exculpate; to relieve from a duty, obligation, or liability; *to relieve of a weight or burden. **exoneration** (-ā' shŭn), *n.* **exonerative** (ėg zon' ėr ȧ tiv), *a.*

exopathic (eks ō păth' ik), *a.* Originating from causes outside the organism (of diseases).

exophagy (eks of' ȧ ji), *n.* Cannibalism in which only persons of a different tribe are eaten. **exophagous,** *a.*

exophthalmia, exophthalmos (eks of thăl' mi ȧ, -mŭs), *n.* (*Path.*) Protrusion of the eyeball. **exophthalmic,** *a.*

exoplasm (eks' ō plăzm), *n.* (*Biol.*) The denser outer layer of the cuticular protoplasm of certain protozoa.

exorbitant (eg zôr' bi tȧnt) [L. *exorbitans -ntem*, pres.p. of *exorbitāre*, to fly out of the track (EX-, *orbita*, a track)], *a.* Out of all bounds, grossly excessive, inordinate, extravagant. **exorbitance,** *n.* **exorbitantly,** *adv.*

exorcize (ek' sôr sīz) [late Latin *exorcizāre*, Gr. *exorkizein* (EX-, *horkos*, oath)], *v.t.* To expel (as an evil spirit) by adjurations, prayers, and ceremonies; to free or purify from unclean spirits; *to call upon, to conjure up. **exorciser,** *n.* **exorcism,** *n.* **exorcist,** *n.* One who exorcizes; (*Eccles.*) one of the minor orders in the Roman Catholic Church, to the members of which the function of exorcism (now restricted to priests) was formerly committed.

exordium (eg zôr' di ŭm) [L., from *exordīrī* (EX-, *ordīrī*, to begin)], *n.* (*pl.* **-ums**) The beginning of anything, esp. the introductory part of a literary work or discourse. **exordial,** *a.*

exoskeleton (eks ō skel' e tŏn), *n.* (*Anat.*) An external skeleton formed by a hardening of the integument.

exosmose (ek' soz mōs), **exosmosis** (ek soz mō' sis) [EXO-, Gr. *ōsmos*, a pushing], *n.* (*Physl.*, *Physiol.*, *etc.*) Passage of a liquid through a porous membrane from within outwards to mix with an external fluid. **exosmotic** (ek soz mot' ik), *a.*

exostome (eks' os tōm), *n.* (*Biol.*) The aperture in the outer integument of an ovule.

exostosis (eks os tō' sis), *n.* (*pl.* **exostoses**), *n.* (*Path.*) A tumour of a bony nature growing upon and arising from a bone or cartilage; (*Bot.*) a morbid growth of hard wood projecting like warts or tumours from the stem or roots of a plant.

exoteric, -al (ek sȯ ter' ik, -ȧl) [Gr. *exōterikos*, from *exōterō*, comp. of *exō*, outward, from *ex*, out], *a.* External, public, fit to be imparted to outsiders; comprehensible to the vulgar, opposed to esoteric; (of disciples) not admitted to esoteric doctrines; ordinary, popular. *n.* One of the uninitiated; (*pl.*) truths or doctrines suitable for popular instruction. **exoterically,** *adv.*

exotic (ek zot' ik) [L. *exōticus*, Gr. *exōtikos*, from *exō*, as prec.], *a.* Foreign; introduced from a foreign country; (*colloq.*) rare, unusual. *n.* Anything foreign; anything introduced from a foreign country, as a plant. **exoticism,** *n.*

expand (ek spănd') [L. *expandere* (EX-, *pandere*, to spread (p.p. *expandus*), rel. to *patēre*, see PATENT)], *v.t.* To open or spread out; to distend, to cause to increase in bulk; to widen, to extend, to enlarge; to write out in full (what is condensed or abbreviated); (*Math.*) to develop into a series, to state in a fuller form. *v.i.* To become opened or spread out, distended, or enlarged in bulk, not mass. **expanding universe:** (*Astron.*) The theory that the universe is ever expanding, based on the Doppler effect in the light from stars and galaxies. **expansible,** *a.* **expansibility** (-bil' i ti), *n.* **expansile** (ek spăn' sil, -sīl), *a.* Capable of expanding; expansible.

expanse (ek spăns') [as prec.], *n.* That which is expanded; a wide, open extent or area; expansion.

expansion (ek spăn' shŭn) [late L. *expansio -ōnem*, as prec.], *n.* The act of expanding; the state of being expanded; enlargement, extension, distension; (*Comm.*) extension of business, increase of liabilities, extension of the currency; increase of volume, as of steam in a cylinder. **expansion-engine:** A steam-engine in which the latter part of the stroke of the piston is performed by expansion of the steam already admitted. **double-, triple-expansion engine:** Steam-engines in which the steam passes into a second and third cylinder so that its expansive force is utilized in two, or three, stages. **expansionist,** *n.* One who advocates territorial expansion; (*U.S.A.*) one who advocates extension of the national domain. **expansion-gear,** *n.* The apparatus by which access of steam to the cylinder is cut off at a given part of the stroke.

expansive (ek spăn' siv) [as prec., -IVE], *a.* Having the power of expanding; able or tending to expand; extending widely, comprehensive; frank, effusive. **expansively,** *adv.* **expansiveness,** *n.*

ex parte (eks par' ti) [L., from one side], *adv.* (*Law*) Proceeding from one side only; in the interests of one side. ***ex-parte***, *a.* One-sided.

expatiate (ek spā' shi āt) [L. *expatiātus*, p.p. of *expatiārē* (EX-, *spatiārī*, to roam, from *spatium*, space)], *v.i.* To dilate; to speak or write copiously on a subject; (*fig.*) to wander at large. **expatiation** (-ā' shŭn), *n.* **expatiatory** (ek spā' shi ȧ tȯr i), *a.*

expatriate (ek spā' tri āt) [L. *expatriātus*, p.p. of *expatriāre* (EX-, *patria*, one's native land)], *v.t.* To exile; to drive into banishment; to expatriate oneself. *v.i.* To emigrate; to renounce one's citizenship in one's country. *n.* One living away from his own country. **expatriation** (-ā' shŭn), *n.*

expect (ek spekt') [L. *expectāre* (EX-, *spectāre*, freq. of *specere*, to see)], *v.t.* To look forward to; to regard as certain or likely to happen, to anticipate; to require as due; (*colloq.*) to think, to suppose; *to await. *v.i.* To wait. **n.* Expectation. **expectancy, -ance,** *n.* The act or state of expecting, expectation; the state of being expected; (*Law*) abeyance, suspense; prospect of possessing, enjoying, etc.; that which is expected. **expectant,** *a.* Expecting, waiting in expectation (of); anticipating, presumptive; (*Law*) existing in expectancy, reversionary; (*Med.*) relying on the efforts of nature, without using active medicines. *n.* One who waits in expectation of something, as a candidate for an office etc. **expectant mother,** *n.* A pregnant woman. **expectantly,** *adv.* **expectation** (-tā′ shŭn), *n.* The act or state of expecting, anticipation, a confident awaiting (of); (*pl.*) prospects (of); the ground for confident anticipation (of); the probability of a future event; something expected; (*Med.*) the treatment of a disease by leaving it to the efforts of nature. **expectation of life:** The number of years which a person of a given age may, on the average of chances, expect to live. **expectative** (ek spek′ tȧ tiv), *a.* Of, pertaining to, or giving rise to expectation; (*Eccles. Law*) reversionary, pertaining to the reversion of benefices. *n.* The object of expectation; (*Eccles. Hist.*) a mandate nominating to a benefice. **expecter,** *n.* One who expects; an expectant. **expecting,** *ger.* (*of a woman*) Pregnant. **expectingly,** *adv.*

expectorate (ek spek′ tȯ rāt) [L. *expectorātus*, p.p. of *expectorāre* (EX-, *pectus -oris*, the breast)], *v.t.* To discharge from the lungs or air-passages by coughing, hawking, or spitting. *v.i.* To discharge matter from the lungs or air-passages by coughing, etc.; to spit. **expectorant,** *a.* (*Med.*) Having the quality of promoting expectoration. *n.* A medicine promoting expectoration. **expectoration** (-rā′ shŭn), *n.* **expectorative,** *a.*

expedient (ek spē′ di ėnt) [F. *expédient*, L. *expediens -ntem* (pres.p. of *expedīre*, as foll.)], *a.* Promoting the object in view; advantageous, convenient; conducive to personal advantage; politic as opposed to just; *speedy, expeditious. *n.* That which promotes an object; an advantageous way or means; a shift, a contrivance. **expedience, -ency,** *n.* **expediential** (ek sped i en′ shȧl), *a.* **expediently,** *adv.*

expedite (ek′ spė dīt) [L. *expedītus*, p.p. of *expedīre* (EX-, *pēs pedis*, the foot)], *v.t.* To facilitate, to assist or accelerate the progress of; to dispatch. **a.* Easy, disencumbered; speedy, ready, expeditious, active, light-armed. **expeditious,** *a.* Speedy, ready, active; done with dispatch. **expeditiously,** *adv.*

expedition (ek spė dish′ ŭn) [as prec.], *n.* Speed, promptness, dispatch; a march or voyage of an army or fleet to a distance with hostile intentions; any journey or voyage by an organized body for some definite object; the persons with their equipment engaged in this. **expeditionary,** *a.* Relating to or constituting an expedition.

expel (ek spel′) [L. *expellere* (EX-, *pellere*, to drive, p.p. *pulsus*)], *v.t.* (*past & p.p.* **expelled**) To drive or force out; to eject, to banish; to turn out formally (as from a school, college, or society); *to discharge; *to reject, to refuse. **expellable,** *a.* **expellent,** *a.*

expend (ek spend′) [L. *expendere* (EX-, *pendere*, to weigh, p.p. *pensus*)], *v.t.* To spend, to lay out; to consume, to use up; *to consider. **expendable,** *a.* Likely to be or intended to be wasted. **expenditure** (ėk spen′ di tūr, -chŭr), *n.* The act of expending; disbursement, consumption; the amount expended.

expense (ėk spens′) [A.-F., from late L. *expensa*, fem. of *expensus*, p.p. of *expendere*, see prec.], *n.* A laying out or expending; cost, charge, outlay, price paid; (*pl.*) outlay in performance of a duty or commission; (*colloq.*) money reimbursed for this. **at the expense of:** At the cost of; (*fig.*) to the discredit or detriment of. **expenseless,** *a.* **expensive,** *a.* Costly, requiring a large expenditure; extravagant, lavish. **expensively,** *adv.* **expensiveness,** *n.*

experience (ek spēr′ i ėns) [O.F., from L. *experientia*, from *experīri*, to go through, to try, as in p.p. *perītus*, skilled)], *n.* Practical acquaintance with any matter; knowledge gained by observation or trial; a particular instance of such knowledge; something undergone of an affecting or impressive nature; (*usu. pl.*) a phase of religious emotion; *experiment. *v.t.* To make trial or proof of; to gain a practical knowledge of by trial or observation; to train; to undergo, to feel, to meet with; to practise, to train (oneself in). **to experience religion:** (*Am.*) To be converted. **experienced,** *a.* Taught by experience; practised, skilled; known from personal trial or observation.

experiential (ek spēr i en′ shȧl) [L. *experientia*], *a.* Pertaining to or derived from experience. **experientialism,** *n.* (*Phil.*) The doctrine that all our ideas are derived from experience, and that there are no intuitions. **experientialist,** *a.* **experientially,** *adv.*

experiment (ek sper′ i mėnt) [O.F., from L. *experīmentum*, from *experīri*, to EXPERIENCE], *n.* A trial, proof, or test of anything; an act, operation, or process designed to discover some unknown truth, principle, or effect, or to test an hypothesis; *experience. *v.i.* To make an experiment or trial (on or with); to investigate by this means; to search by trial. **v.t.* To make trial or proof of. **experimental** (-men′ tȧl), *a.* Pertaining to, derived from, or founded upon experiment; practising experiments; empirical. **experimental philosophy,** *n.* Philosophy based on induction and insisting on experiment and observation as indispensable to reasoned knowledge. **experimentalism,** *n.* **experimentalist,** *n.* **experimentalize,** *v.i.* **experimentally,** *adv.* **experimentation** (-tā′ shŭn), *n.* The act or practice of making experiments. **experimentative** (-men′ tȧ tiv), *a.* **experimenter, experimentist,** *n.*

expert (ek spĕrt′) [O.F., from L. *expertus*, p.p. of *experīri*, as prec.], *a.* Experienced, dexterous from use and experience; practised, skilful (at or in). **expert** (ek′ spĕrt), *n.* One who has special skill or knowledge; (*Law*) a scientific or professional witness. **v.t.* (ek spĕrt′) To make trial of; to experience. **expertise** (eks pĕr tēz′), *n.* Expert skill, opinion or knowledge. **expertly,** *adv.* **expertness,** *n.*

expiate (ek′ spi āt) [L. *expiātus*, p.p. of *expiāre* (EX-, *piāre*, to propitiate, from *pius*, devout)], *v.t.* To atone for; to make reparation or amends for; to pay the penalty of; *to avert. **expiable,** *a.* **expiation** (-ā′ shŭn), *n.* **expiator,** *n.* **expiatory,** *a.*

expire (ek spīr′) [F. *expirer*, L. *expīrāre* (EX-, *spīrāre*, to breathe)], *v.t.* To breathe out from the lungs; to send forth, to emit, to exhale; *to bring to an end. *v.i.* To breathe out; to emit the last breath; to die; to die out (as a fire); to come to an end; (*Law*) to cease, to come to an end, to become extinct; *to be shot out. **expiration** (ek spi rā′ shŭn), *n.* The act of breathing out; cessation, termination; *exhalation, evaporation. **expiree** (eks pī rē′), *n.* (*Austral. hist.*) A time-expired convict. **expiratory** (ek spīr′ ȧ tȯr i), *a.* Pertaining to the emission of breath from the lungs. **expiry,** *n.* Expiration, termination.

episcate (ek spis′ kāt) [L. *expiscātus*, p.p. of *expiscārī* (EX-, *piscis*, fish)], *v.t.* (*Sc.*) To fish out, to discover as if by fishing. **expiscation** (-kā′ shŭn), *n.* **expiscator,** *n.* **expiscatory,** *a.*

explain (ek splān′) [M.F. *explaner*, L. *explānāre* (EX-, *plānāre*, to flatten, from *plānus*, flat)], *v.t.* To make clear, plain, or intelligible; to expound and illustrate the meaning of; to account for; *to make plane, to flatten. *v.i.* To give explanations. **to explain away:** To get rid of (difficulties) by explanation; to modify or do away with (a charge, etc.) by explanation. **to explain oneself:** To make one's meaning clear; to give an account of one's motives, intentions, conduct, etc. **explainable,** *a.* **explainer,** *n.*

explanate (ek′ splȧ nāt), *a.* (*Zool.*) Spread out flat.

explanation (ek splȧ nā′ shŭn) *n.*, The act of explaining; the sense or definition given by an interpreter or expounder; the process of arriving at a mutual understanding or reconciliation; that which accounts for anything. **explanatory** (ek splăn′ ȧ tŏr i), *a.* Containing an explanation; serving to explain. **explanatorily,** *adv.*

expletive (ek′ splė tiv, ėk splē′ tiv) [L. *explētīvus*, from *explētus*, p.p. of *explēre* (EX-, *plēre*, to fill)], *a.* Serving to fill out or complete; introduced merely to fill a gap or vacancy. *n.* A word not necessary to the sense introduced to fill up; an interjection or word added for emphasis, esp. a profane exclamation. **expletory** (ek′ splė tŏr i), *a.*

explicate (eks′ pli kāt) [L. *explicātus*, p.p. of *explicāre* (EX-, *plica*, a fold)], *v.t.* To unfold the meaning of; to free from obscurity or difficulty; to develop (the contents of an idea, proposition, etc.). **explicable,** *a.* **explication** (-kā′ shŭn), *n.* **explicative, -plicatory** (eks′-), *a.* Serving to explain or interpret.

explicit (1) (ek splis′ it) [F. *explicite*, L. *explicitus*, old form of *explicātus*, as prec.], *a.* Plainly expressed, distinctly stated, opposed to implied; definite; unreserved, outspoken. **explicitly,** *adv.* **explicitness,** *n.*

***explicit** (2) (ek splis′ it) [med. L., here ends, orig. abbr. of *explicitus*, see prec.], *n.* A word formerly written at the end of manuscript books, and equivalent to 'finis,' 'the end.'

explode (ek splōd′) [M.F. *exploder*, L. *explōdere*, p.p. *explōsus* (EX-, *plaudere*, to clap)], *v.t.* To cause to burst with a loud report; to refute, expose, discredit (a theory, fallacy, etc.); *to drive off the stage; *to cry down, to hoot or hiss away. *v.i.* To burst with a loud report; to break forth with violence; (*fig.*) to come to an end as if by bursting, to collapse. **explodent,** *n.* An explosive consonant. **exploder,** *n.* One who explodes or rejects.

exploit (ek′ sploit) [O.F. *esploit*, profit, achievement, L. *explicitum*, neut. p.p. of *explicere*, see EXPLICATE], *n.* A feat, a great or noble achievement. *v.t.* (ėk sploit′) To turn to account; to utilize, esp. to make use of for one's own profit; *to perform, to achieve. **exploitable,** *a.* **exploitage,** *n.* **exploitation** (-tā′ shŭn), *n.*

explore (ek splôr′) [F. *explorer*, L. *explōrāre*, to search out (prob. EX-, *plōrāre*, to make to flow, from *pluere*, to flow)], *v.t.* To search or inquire into; to investigate, to examine; to travel over in order to examine; to travel into unknown country; (*Surg.*) to probe a wound. **exploration** (-ā′ shŭn), *n.* **explorative** (ek splôr′ ȧ tiv), *a.* ***explorator,** *n.* An explorer. **exploratory,** *a.* **exploratory operation,** *n.* (*Surg.*) An operation carried out for purposes of diagnosis. **explorer,** *n.* One who explores; a traveller into unknown or little-known parts.

explosion (ek splō′ zhŭn) [L. *explōsio -ōnem*, from *explōdere*, EXPLODE], *n.* A bursting or exploding with a loud report; a sudden and violent noise; (*fig.*) a sudden and violent outbreak, as of physical forces, anger, etc. **explosive** (ek splō′ siv), *a.* Bursting or driving forth with great force and noise; liable to explode or cause explosion; (*of consonants*) produced by a sudden expulsion of breath, as *p, b, t, d, k, g*, discontinuous, forming a complete vocal stop. *n.* An explosive agent or substance, as gunpowder, dynamite, etc.; a mute or non-continuous consonant. **explosively,** *adv.* **explosiveness,** *n.*

exponent (ek spō′ nėnt) [L. *expōnens -ntem*, pres.p. of *expōnere* (EX-, *pōnere*, to put, p.p. *positus*)], *a.* Setting forth or explaining; exemplifying. *n.* One who sets forth or explains; one who or that which represents a party, principle, or character; a type, a representative; (*Alg.*) a number or quantity written to the right of and above another number or quantity, to show how many times the latter is to be taken as a factor (thus, in the expression a^3, ^{3} is an exponent, and shows that a is to be taken three times as a factor thus, $a \times a \times a$). **exponential** (-nen′ shȧl), *a.* Pertaining to an exponent or exponents; involving variable exponents. **exponential curve:** A relationship between two quantities such that as one quantity increases by equal steps the other increases by equal percentages of its previous value. **exponential equation:** An equation into which the unknown quantity enters as an exponent. **exponential horn:** A horn-shaped loud-speaker in which the sides of the horn follow an exponential curve. **exponential quantity:** A quantity with a variable exponent. **exponible** (ek spō′ nibl), *a.* Capable of or requiring explanation; (*Log.*) requiring restatement in regular logical form. *n.* An exponible proposition.

export (ek spôrt′) [L. *exportāre* (EX-, *portāre*, to carry)], *v.t.* To carry or send (goods) to foreign countries. *v.i.* To send out commodities to foreign countries. *n.* (ek′ spôrt) The act of exporting, exportation; a commodity sent to a foreign country; (*pl.*) the quantity or value of goods exported. **export duty:** A duty paid on goods exported. **exportable** (-spôr′ tȧbl), *a.* **exportation** (-tā′ shŭn), *n.* The act or practice of exporting goods. **exporter,** *n.*

expose (ek spōz′) [F. *exposer* (EX-, *poser*, L. *pausāre*, to rest, to lay down), confused with L. *expōnere*, to put out (cp. COMPOSE)], *v.t.* To lay bare or open; to leave unprotected; to subject (to any influence or action); to turn out and abandon (as a child); to exhibit, to display, esp. for sale; to disclose, lay bare, reveal; to unmask.

exposé (eks pō′ zā) [F.], *n.* A formal declaration or recital of facts; a disclosure, an exposure.

exposition (eks pō zish′ ŭn), *n.* The act of exposing; an explanation or interpretation of the meaning of an author or a work, a commentary; exposure; a public exhibition. **expositive** (ek spoz′ i tiv), *a.* **expositor,** *n.* One who expounds or explains; a commentator. **expository,** *a.*

expostulate (ek spos′ tū lāt) [L. *expostulātus*, p.p. of *expostulāre* (EX-, *postulāre*, to demand)], *v.i.* To reason earnestly (with a person), to remonstrate. **v.t.* To demand, to claim; to argue, to discuss; to call in question. **expostulation** (-lā′ shŭn), *n.* **expostulative,** *a.* **expostulator,** *n.* **expostulatory,** *a.*

exposure (ek spō′ zhŭr) [EXPOSE, -URE], *n.* The act of exposing; the state of being exposed to view, inconvenience, danger, etc.; abandonment (of a child, aged person, etc.); display, esp. of goods for sale; a disclosure, revelation, unmasking; situation with respect to the points of the compass, or free access of light and air; outlook, aspect; (*Phot.*) the act of allowing light from an object to fall upon a sensitized plate; the duration of this exposure. **indecent exposure:** Public uncovering of the privy parts.

expound (ek spound′) [M.E. *expounen*, O.F. *espondre*, L. *expōnere* (see EXPONENT)], *v.t.* To set forth the meaning of; to explain, to interpret. **expounder,** *n.*

express (1) (ek spres′) [O.F. *expres*, L. *expressus*, p.p. of *exprimere* (EX-, *primere*, to press)], *a.* Set forth or expressed distinctly; direct, explicit, definitely shown or stated, not merely implied; intended, prepared, done, made, sent for a special purpose. *adv.* With speed; by express messenger; *specially, on purpose. *n.* An express train; an express messenger; an express rifle. **express bullet:** A bullet with hollow point causing it to spread on striking. **express delivery:** Delivery by special postal messenger. **express rifle:** A sporting rifle with a high muzzle-velocity and low trajectory. **express train:** A fast train with few intermediate stops. **expressly,** *adv.*

express (2) (ek spres′) [O.F. *expresser* (as prec.)], *v.t.* To squeeze or press out; to emit, to exude; to set forth, to make manifest to the understanding, to put into words; to reveal, to exhibit; (*Alg.*) to represent (by symbols, in terms, etc.); (*Am.*) to send by express; *to denote, to betoken; to resemble, to be like. **to express oneself:** To declare one's opinions or feelings in words (usu. with *well, strongly*, etc.). **expressible,** *a.*

expression (ek spresh' ůn) [F., from L. *expressio -ōnem*, as prec.], *n.* The act of expressing; that which is expressed, an utterance, saying, statement of a thought; a word, a phrase; (*Alg.*) a combination of symbols representing a quantity or meaning; mode of expression; the aspect of the face as indicative of feeling and character, purpose, etc.; intonation of voice; (*Art*) the exhibition of character and feeling (in a picture, statue, etc.); (*Mus.*) the mode of execution that expresses the spirit and feeling of a passage; expressiveness. **expression mark:** (*Mus.*) A word or sign indicating the way in which a passage is to be expressed. **expression stop:** (*Harmonium*) A stop regulating the wind-pressure and force of the notes. **expressional,** *a.* Of or pertaining to expression; having the power of expression, esp. in language, painting, etc. **expressionist,** *n.* An artist who devotes himself to the expression of feeling, character, etc. **expressionless,** *a.*

expressive (ek spres' iv) [F. *expressif -ive*, as prec., -IVE], *a.* Serving to express; significant; vividly indicating any expression or emotion. **expressively,** *adv.* **expressiveness,** *n.* **expressure,** *n.* The act of expressing; expression; a mark, impression; an image, a picture.

exprobration (eks prȯ brā' shůn) [L. *exprobrātio -ōnem*, from *exprobrāre* (EX-, *probrum*, a shameful deed)], *n.* Reproachful language; upbraiding, censure.

expropriate (eks prō' pri āt) [late L. *expropriātus*, p.p. of *expropriāre* (EX-, *proprium*, property, neut. of *proprius*, own)], *v.t.* To take from an owner, esp. for public use; to dispossess. **expropriation** (-ā' shůn), *n.*

expulsion (ek spŭl' shůn) [L. *expulsio -ōnem*, from *expellere*, to EXPEL], *n.* The act of expelling; the state of being expelled; ejection. ***expulse,** *v.t.* To expel. **expulsive,** *a.* Serving or tending to expel. *n.* An expulsive drug.

expunge (ek spŭnj') [L. *expungere* (EX-, *pungere*, to prick, p.p. *punctus*)], *v.t.* To blot or rub out; to efface, to erase. **expunction** (ek spŭngk' shůn), *n.*

expurgate (ek' spěr gāt) [L. *expurgātus*, p.p. of *expurgāre* (EX-, *purgāre*, to cleanse)], *v.t.* To free from anything offensive, obscene, or noxious (used esp. of books); to remove such parts; *to purge, to clear (as of guilt). **expurgation** (-gā' shůn), *n.* **expurgator** (ek' spěr gā tȯr), *n.* **expurgatorial** (-tôr' i ǎl), *a.* **expurgatory** (ek spěr' gȧ tȯr i), *a.* Serving to expurgate. **expurgatory index** [INDEX EXPURGATORIUS].

exquisite (ek' skwi zit) [L. *exquīsītus*, choice, p.p. of *exquīrere* (EX-, *quærere*, to seek)], *a.* Fine, delicate, dainty; delicately beautiful; delicate or refined in perception, keenly sensitive, nice, fastidious; acute; poignant; intensely pleasurable or painful; *far-fetched, abstruse. *n.* A fop; one who dresses or behaves finically. **exquisitely,** *adv.* **exquisiteness,** *n.*

exsanguinate (ek săng' gwi nāt) [L. *exsanguinātus*, p.p. of *exsanguināre* (EX-, *sanguis -inis*, blood)], *v.t.* To drain off blood. **exsanguine,** *a.* Bloodless; suffering from poorness of blood. **exsanguinity** (-gwin' i ti), *n.* Destitution of blood. **exsanguinous,** *a.*

exscind (ėk sind') [L. *exscindere* (EX-, *scindere*, to cut)], *v.t.* To cut off or out, to sever, to excise.

exsect (ėk sekt') [L. *exsectus*, p.p. of *exsecāre* (EX-, *secāre*, to cut)], *v.t.* To cut out.

exsequies [EXEQUIES].

exsert (ėk sěrt') [L. *exsertus*, p.p. of *exserere*, to put forth], *v.t.* To thrust out, protrude. **exserted,** *a.* (*Biol.*) Protruding, thrust out, unsheathed; (*Bot.*) applied to stamens longer than the corolla. **exsertile,** *a.* That may be thrust out.

exsiccate (ek' si kāt, ek sik' āt) [L. *exsiccātus*, p.p. of *exsiccāre* (EX-, *siccus*, dry)], *v.t.* To dry up; to evaporate; to drain dry. **exsiccation** (-kā shůn), *n.* **exsiccator** (ek' si kā tȯr), *n.* An apparatus for drying moist substances.

exstipulate (ek stip' ū lāt) [EX-, L. *stipula*, a stalk], *a.* (*Bot.*) Devoid of stipules.

extant (ek' stȧnt, ėk stănt') [L. *extans, -ntem*, pres.p. of *exstāre* (EX-, *stāre*, to stand)], *a.* Still in existence; surviving; *publicly known; *standing out, protruding.

extasy [ECSTASY].

extemporal (eks tem' pȯ rȧl), *a.* Extemporaneous, unpremeditated. **extemporally,** *adv.*

extemporaneous, extemporary (eks tem pȯ rā' ni ůs, eks tem' pȯ rȧ ri), *a.* Uttered, made, composed, or done without preparation. **extemporaneously, extemporarily,** *adv.* **extemporaneousness,** *n.*

extempore (ėk stem' pȯ ri) [L. *ex tempore*, from the time], *adv.* Without premeditation or preparation. *a.* Unstudied, delivered without preparation. **extemporize,** *v.t.* To compose or produce without preparation. *v.i.* To speak without notes or previous study. **extemporization** (-zā' shůn), *n.*

extend (ėk stend') [L. *extendere*, p.p. *extensus* (EX-, *tendere*, to stretch)], *v.t.* To stretch out; to make larger in space, time, or scope; to prolong (as a line, a period, etc.); to amplify, to expand, to write out in full; to cause to reach (to, over, or across); to enlarge; to put forth; to hold out, offer, grant; (*Law*) to value, to assess, to seize under a writ of extent; (*Physiol.*) to stretch out, to unbend (of muscles); *to praise, to magnify, to exaggerate; *to seize. *v.i.* To stretch, to reach (in space, time or scope). **to extend a welcome** (to): To welcome cordially. **extended,** *a.* Spread out; (*Print.*) having a broad face (of type). **extendedly,** *adv.* **extendible, extensible,** *a.* **extensibility** (-bil' i ti), *n.* **extensile,** *a.* Capable of being stretched out or protruded.

extension (ėk sten' shůn) [L. *extentio -ōnem, -sio -ōnem*, as prec.], *n.* The act or process of extending; the state of being extended; extent, range, space; prolongation, enlargement; an increase of dimension, an addition, an additional part; (*Am.* electric flex); words amplifying the subject or predicate of a sentence; (*Phys.*) the property by virtue of which every body occupies a limited portion of space in three dimensions; (*Surg.*) the pulling of the broken part of a limb in a direction away from the trunk, to bring the ends of the bone into their proper position; (*Log.*) the extent of the application of a general term, opposed to intension. **University Extension:** A system by which University instruction is extended to non-members of Universities by means of lectures, classes, and examinations. **extensionist,** *n.* A promoter of University Extension; a student connected with this.

extensive (ėk sten' siv) [late L. *extensīvus*, as prec., -IVE], *a.* Widely spread or extended; large; comprehensive; (*Agric.*) depending on amplitude of area, opposed to intensive. **extensively,** *adv.* **extensiveness,** *n.*

extensor (ek sten' sȯr) [late L., as prec., -OR], *n.* (*Anat.*) A muscle which serves to extend or straighten any part of the body.

extent (ėk stent') [A.-F. *extente, estente*, p.p. of *estendre*, L. *extendere*], *n.* The space, dimension, or degree to which anything is extended; size, width, compass, scope, comprehension, distribution, degree; a large space; (*Law*) a writ of execution against the body, lands, and goods of a debtor; seizure of lands, etc., execution; (*Log.*) extension; *fact of extending, offering, or granting. **extent-in-aid,** *n.* (*Law*) A writ issued at the suit of a Crown debtor against a person indebted to him.

extenuate (ėk sten' ū āt) [L. *extenuātus*, p.p. of *extenuāre* (EX-, *tenuis*, thin)], *v.t.* To lessen, to diminish the gravity of, to palliate; to offer excuses for; *to make thin, meagre, or lean; *to make less dense; *to disparage, to degrade; *to underrate, to belittle; (*incorrectly*) to diminish the apparent guilt or impropriety of. ***extenuatingly,** *adv.* **extenuation** (-ā' shŭn), *n.* **extenuator,** *n.* **extenuatory,** *a.* Extenuating, palliating.

exterior (ėk stēr' i ŏr) [L. comp. of *exter* or *exterus,* outer], *a.* External, outer; situated on the outside; coming from without, extrinsic; outward, visible. *n.* The outer surface; the external features; the outward or visible aspect, dress, conduct, deportment, etc. **exterior angle,** *n.* (*Geom.*) An angle between any side of a rectilinear figure and the adjacent side produced. **exteriority** (ek stēr i or' i ti), *n.* **exteriorly,** *adv.* **exteriorize,** *v.t.* To realize in outward form; to externalize. **exteriorization** (zā' shŭn), *n.*

exterminate (ėk stĕr' mi nāt) [L. *exterminātus,* p.p. of *extermināre* (EX-, *terminus,* a boundary)], *v.t.* To extirpate, to eradicate, to destroy utterly; *to put an end to. **extermination** (-nā' shŭn), *n.* **exterminator** (ek stĕr' mi nā tŏr), *n.* **exterminatory,** *a.* **extermine,** *v.t.* To exterminate.

extern (ek' stĕrn), *a.* External. *n.* A student or pupil who does not reside in a college or seminary; the outward appearance.

external (ek stĕr' năl) [L. *externus,* from *exter,* see EXTERIOR], *a.* Situated on the outside; pertaining to the outside, superficial; derived from outside; belonging to the world of phenomena as distinguished from the conscious mind, objective; (*Theol.*) consisting in outward acts; (*Med.*) applied to the outside of the body; pertaining to foreign countries; extraneous, extrinsic. *n.* An exterior or outer part; (*pl.*) outward features, symbols, rites, circumstances; non-essentials. **externalism,** *n.* **externality** (-năl' i ti), *n.* **externalize,** *v.t.* To give external shape or objective existence to; to treat as consisting of externals. **externalization** (-zā' shŭn), *n.* **externally,** *adv.*

exterrestrial (ek stė res' tri ăl), *a.* Of or from outside the earth.

exterritorial (ek ster i tôr' i ăl), *a.* Beyond the jurisdiction of the laws of the country in which one resides. **exterritoriality** (-ăl' i ti), *n.* Immunity from the laws of a country, such as that enjoyed by ambassadors.

extinct (ek stingkt') [L. *extinctus,* p.p. of *extinguere*], *a.* Extinguished, put out; that has ceased eruption; worn out, ended, finished; come to an end, that has died out (as a family, species, etc.); obsolete. **v.t.* To extinguish.

extincteur (ek stingk' tėr, ek stan tĕr) [F., from L. *extinctor* (as prec.)], *n.* A fire-extinguisher or annihilator.

extinction (ek stingk' shŭn) [L. *extinctio -ōnem,* as prec.], *n.* The act of extinguishing; the state of being extinguished; extermination, destruction, annihilation. **extinctive,** *a.* ***extincture,** *n.* Extinction.

extine (ek' stin, -stīn) [L. *ext-erus,* -INE], *n.* (*Bot.*) The outer coat of a grain of pollen.

extinguish (ėk sting' gwish) [L. *extinguere* (EX-, *stinguere,* to quench)], *v.t.* To put out, to quench (as a light, hope, passion, life, etc.); to eclipse, to cloud, to obscure, to throw into the shade; to destroy, to annihilate; to suppress; to pay off (a debt, mortgage, etc.). **extinguishable,** *a.* **extinguisher,** *n.* One who or that which extinguishes; a conical cap for extinguishing a candle (or, formerly, a link). **extinguishment,** *n.*

extirpate (ek' stir pāt) [L. *extirpātus,* p.p. of *extirpāre, exstirpāre* (EX-, *stirps, -pis,* a stem)], *v.t.* To root out, to destroy utterly, to exterminate; (*Surg.*) to cut out or off. ***extirp,** *v.t.* To extirpate. **extirpation** (-pā' shŭn), *n.* **extirpator,** *n.*

extol (ėk stol') [L. *extollere* (EX-, *tollere,* to raise)], *v.t.* To praise in the highest terms, to glorify.

extort (ėk stôrt') [L. *extortus,* p.p. of *extorquēre,* to twist)], *v.t.* To wrest or wring (from) by force, threats, importunity, etc.; (*Law*) to exact illegally under colour of a public office; (*fig.*) to extract (a meaning, esp. an arbitrary one, from a passage, data, etc.). **extorter,** *n.* An extortioner. **extortion** (ek stôr' shŭn), *n.* The act of extorting; oppressive or illegal exaction; that which is extorted; a gross overcharge. ***extortionary,** *a.* **extortionate,** *a.* Characterized by extortion; oppressive; (of prices) exorbitant. **extortioner,** *n.* **extortive,** *a.*

extra (ek' strȧ) [L. *extrā,* beyond, from outside, or short for EXTRAORDINARY], *a.* Beyond what is absolutely necessary; larger, or better than is usual; supplementary, additional; of superior quality. *adv.* Over and above what is usual; more than usually; additionally. *n.* Something beyond what is absolutely necessary or usual, esp. something not covered by the ordinary fee; an addition; (*Cricket*) a run scored otherwise than off the bat; (*Cinema.*) an actor temporarily engaged as one of a crowd, etc. **extra-special,** *a.* Latest (edition of an evening paper).

extra- [L., on the outside, without], *comb. form.* **extra-atmospheric,** *a.* Of or pertaining to the space beyond the atmosphere. **extra-cosmical,** *a.* Acting outside the universe. **extra-cranial,** *a.* (*Anat.*) Lying outside the skull. **extra-essential,** *a.* Not included in the essence of a thing. **extra-essentially,** *adv.* **extra-foraneous** [med. L. *forāneus,* from *foris,* a door], *a.* Out-door. **extramural** (ek strȧ mū' răl) [MURAL], *a.* Situated beyond or outside the walls or boundaries of a place. **extra-official,** *a.* Outside the proper duties of an office. **extra-parochial,** *a.* Beyond, outside of, or not reckoned within the limits of, any parish. **extra-physical,** *a.* Not subject to or bound by physical laws or processes. **extra-professional,** *a.* Not coming within the ordinary duties of a profession. **extra-sensory,** *a.* Beyond the ordinary senses, e.g. telepathic perception. **extra-spectral,** *a.* Lying outside the visible spectrum. **extra-terrestrial** [EXTERRESTRIAL]. **extra-territorial** [EXTERRITORIAL]. **extra-tropical,** *a.* Beyond or outside of the tropics, north or south. **extravascular** (ek strȧ văs' kū lăr) [VASCULAR], *a.* Outside the vascular system.

extract (ėk străkt') [L. *extractus,* p.p. of *extrahere* (EX-, *trahere,* to draw)], *v.t.* To draw or pull out; to draw out by mechanical or chemical means; to select a part from, to copy out or quote (as a passage from a book, etc.); to derive (from); to deduce (from). **to extract the root of:** (*Math.*) To find the root of (a number or quantity). *n.* (ek' străkt) That which is extracted by distillation, solution, etc.; a passage quoted from a book or writing; an essential obtained from a substance; a preparation containing the essence of a substance. **extractable,** *a.* **extraction,** *n.* The act of extracting; descent, family, lineage, derivation; the act of drawing anything from a substance by chemical or mechanical process. **extractive,** *a.* Tending or serving to extract; capable of extraction. *n.* An extract; (*Chem.*) the principle forming the basis in extracts. **extractive industries:** Those (*e.g.* mining, agriculture, fishing) concerned with obtaining natural productions. **extracter,** *n.*

extradition (ek strȧ dish' ŭn) [F. (EX-, L. *traditio -ōnem,* TRADITION)], *n.* The surrender of fugitives from justice by a government to the authorities of the country where the crime was committed; (*Psych.*) in perception, the localizing of sensations at a distance from the centre of sensation. **extraditable** (-dī' tȧbl), *a.* Subject to extradition, rendering one liable to extradition. **extradite** (ek' strȧ dīt), *v.t.* To surrender under a treaty of extradition; to secure the extradition of.

extrados (ėk strā' dos) [F. (EXTRA-, *dos,* L. *dorsum,* the back)], *n.* (*Arch.*) The exterior curve of an arch, esp. measured on the top of the voussoirs (cp. INTRADOS).

extrajudicial (ek strȧ jū dish' ăl), *a.* Taking place outside the court, not legally authorized; outside the ordinary course of law or justice. **extrajudicially,** *adv.*

extramundane (ek strȧ mŭn′ dān), *a.* Existing in or pertaining to a region outside our world or outside the universe.

extraneous (ėk strā′ ni ŭs) [L. *extrāneus*, from *extrā*, outside], *a.* Foreign, not belonging to a class, subject, etc.; not intrinsic, external; not essential. **extraneously,** *adv.* **extraneousness, extraneity** (-nē′ i ti), *n.*

extraordinary (ėk strôr′-, ėk strȧ ôr′ di nȧr i) [L. *extraordinārius* (*extrā ordinem*, outside the usual order)], *a.* Beyond or out of the ordinary course, unusual; of an uncommon degree or kind, remarkable, rare, exceptional, surprising; additional, extra; sent or appointed for a special purpose or occasion. *n.* An extraordinary thing; *(*pl.*) extra allowances or receipts, esp. to troops. **envoy extraordinary,** *n.* Formerly a minister sent on a special mission, now one of the second class of diplomatic ministers ranking next below ambassadors. **extraordinarily,** *adv.* **extraordinariness,** *n.*

extravagant (ėk străv′ ȧ gȧnt) [L. *extrāvagans -ntem*, pres.p. of *extrāvagārī* (EXTRA-, *vagārī*, to wander)], *a.* Exceeding due bounds, unrestrained by reason, immoderate; visionary, fantastic; prodigal in expenditure, wasteful; (of prices, etc.) exorbitant; *wandering out of bounds, straying, vagrant. **extravagance,** *n.* The state or quality of being extravagant; an extravagant act, statement, or conduct; excessive expenditure, prodigality; *a digression, a vagary. **extravagantly,** *adv.* **extravaganza** (ek străv ȧ găn′ zȧ) [It. *estravaganza*], *n.* A fantastic composition in drama, fiction, poetry, music, or other literary form; a fantastic piece of conduct, sentiment, or imagination. **extravaganzist,** *n.* **extravagate,** *v.i.* To wander or roam at will; to go beyond reasonable bounds; to go to extremes.

extravasate (ek străv′ ȧ sāt) [EXTRA-, L. *vās*, a vessel, -ATE], *v.t.* To force or let out of the proper vessels (as blood). *v.i.* To flow out of the proper vessels. **extravasation** (-sā′ shŭn), *n.*

***extreat** (ek strēt′) [var. of ESTREAT], *n.* (*Spens.*) Extraction.

extreme (ek strēm′) [O.F., from L. *extrēmus*, superl. of *exterus*, outward], *a.* Outermost, farthest; at the utmost limit, at either end; last, final; of the highest degree, most intense; very strict or rigorous; going to great lengths, immoderate; (*Mus.*) the highest and lowest (parts), augmented (of intervals). *n.* The utmost or farthest point or limit, the extremity; the utmost or highest degree; (*Math.*) the first or the last term of a ratio or series; (*Log.*) the subject or the predicate of a proposition as distinguished from the copula, the major or the minor term in a syllogism as distinguished from the middle; (*pl.*) things or qualities as different or as far removed from each other as possible; (*Mus.*) the highest and lowest parts; *an excessive degree, extremity. **in the extreme:** In the highest degree; extremely. **to extremes:** (Resorting) to the most severe or drastic measures. **extreme and mean ratio:** (*Geom.*) The ratio of a line to its two parts when the whole is to the greater part as the greater to the less. **extreme unction:** (*R.-C. Ch.*) A sacrament in which those believed to be dying are anointed with holy oil. **extremely,** *adv.* Very, greatly, to a great degree. **extremeness,** *n.* **extremist,** *n.* One ready to go to extremes; one holding extreme opinions and ready to undertake extreme actions.

extremity (ek strem′ i ti) [as prec.], *n.* The utmost point, side, or limit; the greatest degree; the remotest part, the end; a condition of the greatest difficulty, danger, or distress; (*pl.*) the limbs; extreme measures.

extricate (ek′ stri kāt) [L. *extrīcātus*, p.p. of *extrīcāre* (EX-, *trīcæ*, impediments)], *v.t.* To disentangle, to set free from any perplexity, difficulty, or embarrassment; to cause to be given off (as a gas from a state of combination). **extricable,** *a.* **extrication** (-kā′ shŭn), *n.*

extrinsic (ek strin′ sik) [F. *extrinsèque*, L. *extrinsecus*, adv., from without (*extrin*, from *exter*, outward, *secus*, beside)], *a.* Being outside or external; proceeding or operating from without; not inherent or contained in a body; not essential. **extrinsicality** (-kăl′ i ti), *n.* **extrinsically,** *adv.*

extrorse (ėk strôrs′) [F., from L. *extrorsus* (EXTRA-, *versus*, towards)], *a.* (*Bot.*) Turned outwards from the axis of growth (of anthers).

extrovert (eks′ trō vėrt) [L. *extra*, outside; *vertere*, to turn], *n.* (*Psych.*) A term to denote a type of temperament which is predominantly engaged with the external world; (*Psych.*) an hysterical person who expresses emotion freely.

extrude (ėk strood′) [L. *extrūdere*, p.p. *extrūsus* (EX-, *trūdere*, to thrust)], *v.t.* To thrust or push out or away; to expel. **extrusion** (ėk stroo′zhŭn), *n.* **extrusive** (ėk stroo′ siv), *a.* Thrusting out or tending to thrust out; (*Geol.*) poured out on the surface (as volcanic rocks).

exuberant (eg zū′ bėr ȧnt) [L. *exūberans -ntem*, pres.p. of *exūberāre* (EX-, *ūber*, fertile, cp. *ūber*, an udder)], *a.* Exceedingly fruitful; luxuriant in growth; characterized by abundance or richness; overflowing, copious, superabundant; (*fig.*) effusive, overflowing with vitality, spirits, or imagination. **exuberance,** *n.* **exuberantly,** *adv.* **exuberate,** *v.i.* To abound, to overflow; to indulge freely (in.)

exude (ėk zūd′) [L. *exūdāre* (EX-, *sūdāre*, to sweat)], *v.t.* To emit or discharge through pores, as sweat, moisture, or other liquid matter; to give out slowly. *v.i.* To ooze or flow out slowly through pores etc. **exudation** (-dā′ shŭn), *n.* **exudative** (ek sū′ dȧ tiv), *a.*

***exulcerate** (ek sŭl′ sėr āt) [L. *exulcerātus*, p.p. of *exulcerāre* (EX-, *ulcerāre*, to ULCERATE)], *v.t.* To cause or raise sores or ulcers on; (*fig.*) to afflict, to vex, to exasperate. **exulceration** (-ā′ shŭn), *n.*

exult (ėg zŭlt′) [F. *exulter*, L. *exultāre*, *exsultāre*, freq. of *exsilere* (EX-, *salire*, to leap)], *v.i.* To rejoice exceedingly; to triumph (over). **exultant,** *a.* Rejoicing, triumphing; feeling or displaying exultation. **exultantly,** *adv.* **exultancy, exultation** (-tā′ shŭn), *n.* **exultingly,** *adv.*

exuviæ (eg zū′ vi ē) [L., cast skins of animals, spoils of an enemy, from *exuere*, to put off], *n.pl.* The cast or shed skin, shells, teeth, etc., of animals; fossil remains of animals in a fragmentary state; (*fig.*) things cast off or relinquished. **exuvial,** *a.* **exuviate,** *v.t.* To cast off, to shed. *v.i.* To cast the old shell, skin, etc. **exuviation** (-ā′ shŭn), *n.*

ex-voto (eks vō′ tō) [L. *ex vōtō*, out of a vow], *adv.* In pursuance of a vow. *n.* Anything offered to a divinity in gratitude for an exemplary favour. **exvotive,** *a.*

eyas (ī′ ȧs) [earlier *nyas*, F., *niais*, a nestling, ult. from L. *nīdus*, nest], *n.* An unfledged hawk; (*Falconry*) one taken from the nest for training or whose training is not complete. **a.* Unfledged. ***eyas-musket** [MUSKET], *n.* An unfledged sparrow-hawk; (*fig.*) a pet name for a young boy.

eye (I) (ī) [A.-S. *ēage* (cp. Dut. *oog*, Icel. *auga*, Goth. *augō*, G. *auge*, also L. *oculus*)], *n.* The organ of vision; the eyeball, iris, or pupil; the socket or part of face containing this organ; (*fig.*) sight, ocular perception, view, public observation; the power of seeing, discernment, acuteness of vision; careful observation, oversight, care, attention; look, mien, expression; mental perception, way of regarding; (*pl.*) estimation, judgment (of conduct, etc.); anything more or less eye-shaped; the bud of a plant; a spot on some feathers, as those of the peacock and argus pheasant; the centre of a target, a bull's-eye; a small opening or perforation; the thread-hole of a needle; the loop or catch in which the hook of a dress is fastened; the hole in the head of an eye-bolt; (*Arch.*) a circular or oval window; the circular aperture at the summit of a dome, the central point or circle in an Ionic volute; (*Naut.*) the face (of the wind), direct opposition;

*a slight tinge, a shade. **all my eye and Betty Martin:** All humbug, rubbish. **eye for an eye:** Strict retaliation. **to catch the Speaker's eye:** To succeed in being called on to speak in the House of Commons. **eye of day:** The sun. **eyes front, right, left:** (*Mil.*) Turn the head and eyes in front, to right, or to left. **if you had half an eye:** If you were not blind or stupid. **in the eye** or **eyes of:** In the regard, estimation, or judgment of; from the point of view of. **in the wind's eye:** (*Naut.*) In the face of the wind, directly against the wind. **mind your eye:** Take care, look out. **mind's eye:** Mental view or perception. **my eye:** (*slang*) Expressing astonishment. **to be all eyes:** To watch intently. **to find favour in the eyes of:** To be graciously received and treated by. **to give the glad eye:** (*slang*) To ogle. **to have an eye for:** To pay due regard to; to appreciate; to be on the look-out for. **to have an eye to:** To regard, to have designs on. **to keep an eye on:** To watch carefully or narrowly. **to make eyes at:** To regard amorously. **to open one's eyes:** To be greatly astonished. **to pipe the eye:** (*slang*) To weep. **to see eye to eye:** To be in complete agreement (with). **to see with half an eye:** To see at a glance. **to set, lay,** or **clap eyes on:** To have sight of. **to view with a friendly** or **jealous eye:** To regard with these feelings. **to wipe the eye of:** To show up the foolishness of; to shoot what someone has missed. **up to the eyes:** Deeply (immersed, engaged, in debt, etc.). **eye-bath,** *n.* A small utensil for bathing the eyes. **eye-bolt,** *n.* (*Naut.*) A bolt having an eye or loop at one end for the reception of a ring, hook, etc. **eyebright,** *n.* The euphrasy, *Euphrasia officinalis*, formerly much used as a remedy for diseases of the eye. **eye-brightening,** *a.* Clearing the sight. **eye-drop,** *n.* A tear. **eyeful,** *n.* As much as the eye can take in at a look; (*fam.*) an attractive woman. **eye-offending,** *a.* Offending to the sight. **eye-opener,** *n.* Something that furnishes enlightenment or astonishment. **eye-pit,** *n.* The pit or socket of the eye. **eye-salve,** *n.* Salve or ointment for the eyes. **eye-servant,** *n.* One who works or attends to his duty only while watched. **eye-service,** *n.* Service performed only while under supervision. **eye-splice,** *n.* (*Naut.*) A splice made by turning the end of a rope back on itself, and interlacing the strands of this with those of the standing part, leaving a loop. **eyestrings,** *n.pl.* The tendons by which the eye is moved. **eye-teeth,** *n.pl.* The upper canine teeth of man. **eye-wash,** *n.* (*colloq.*) Deception, humbug, a fraudulent pretence, a covering up of unpleasant facts. **eye-water,** *n.* A medicated bath or water for the eyes; tears; humour of the eye. **eye-wink,** *n.* A wink of the eye given as a hint; (*fig.*) an instant.

eye (2) (ī) [from prec.], *v.t.* To watch, to observe (fixedly, suspiciously, jealously, etc.). **v.i.* To appear (in a particular aspect). **to eye askance:** To look at with suspicion or distrust.

eyeball (ī′ bawl), *n.* The pupil, apple, or globe of the eye.

eyebrow (ī′ brow), *n.* The fringe of hair above the orbit of the eyes. **eyebrow pencil,** *n.* A pencil applied to the eyebrows to alter their shape or colour.

eyeglass (ī′ glas), *n.* A lens to aid the sight; (*pl.*) a pair of these fastened over the nose or held in the hand; the lens nearest the eye in an optical instrument; a glass for applying lotion to the eyes; *the lens of the eye.

eyehole (ī′ hōl), *n.* A hole to look through; the cavity containing the eye.

eyelash (ī′ lăsh), *n.* The row of hairs edging the eyelids; a single hair from the edge of the eyelid.

eyeless (ī′ les), *a.* Destitute of eyes; blind, sightless.

eyelet (ī′ lėt) [M.E. *oilet*, O.F. *œillte*, dim. *œil*, L. *oculum*, acc. of *oculus*, eye], *n.* A small hole or opening, an aperture like an eye; a loophole; a small eye. **eyelet-hole,** *n.* A hole made as an eyelet for looking or shooting through or for fastening a hook, etc.

eyelid (ī′ lid), *n.* One of the movable folds of skin for covering the eye. **to hang on by the eyelids:** To maintain oneself in a dangerous position.

eyepiece (ī′ pēs), *n.* The lens or combination of lenses at the end nearest the eye in an optical instrument.

eyeshot (ī′ shot), *n.* Sight, range of vision, view.

eyesight (ī′ sīt), *n.* Vision; view, observation.

eyesore (ī′ sôr), *n.* Anything offensive to the sight; an object of disgust or dislike.

eyewitness (ī′ wit nes), *n.* One who sees a transaction with his own eyes and is able to bear witness.

***eyne,** *pl.* [EYE (1)].

eyot [AIT].

eyre (âr) [O.F. *eire*, *erre*, from *errer*, late L. *iterāre*, to journey, from L. *iter*, a journey], *n.* A journey or circuit; a court of itinerant justices. ***justices in eyre:** Judges who travelled in circuit to hold courts in the different counties; judges of assize.

eyrie [AERIE].

F

F, f, the sixth letter, is a labiodental spirant, formed by the emission of breath between the lower lip and the upper teeth; (*Mus.*) the fourth note of the diatonic scale of C major.

fa (fa) [It.], *n.* The fourth note in the sol-fa notation.

fabaceous (fȧ bā′ shŭs) [late L. *fabāceus*, from L. *faba*, a bean], *a.* Leguminous, bean-like.

Fabian (fā′ bi ȧn) [L. *Fabiānus*], *a.* Of or pertaining to Fabius Maximus Cunctator, who harassed Hannibal in the second Punic war by his cautious and dilatory strategy; hence, cautious, avoiding open conflict. *n.* A member of the Fabian Society, an organization of Socialists, relying entirely on moral force.

fable (fā′ bėl) [F., from L. *fābula*, from *fārī*, to speak], *n.* A story, esp. one in which lower animals are represented as endowed with speech in order to convey some moral lesson; a legend, a myth; the plot of a drama or epic poem; a fabrication, a falsehood; gossip. *v.i.* To write fables or fictitious tales; to romance; to tell falsehoods. *v.t.* To feign, to invent; to describe or narrate fictitiously or falsely. **fabled,** *a.* Mythic, legendary, fictitious; celebrated in fable. **fabler,** *n.* One who composes fables.

fabliau (făb′ li ō) [F., from O.F. *fablel*, through the pl. *fabliaux* (dim. of FABLE)], *n.* (*pl.* **-aux**) A metrical tale, dealing usually with ordinary life composed by the trouvères in the 12th and 13th centuries, and intended for recitation.

fabric (făb′ rik) [F. *fabrique*, L. *fabrica*, rel. to *faber*, artificer], *n.* Something put together, a system of correlated parts; a building, an edifice; a frame or structure; woven, felted, or knitted material; mode of construction or manufacture, workmanship, texture. **textile fabric:** A fabric made in a loom or a felting or knitting machine. **fabricant,** *n.* A manufacturer.

fabricate (făb′ ri kāt) [as prec.], *v.t.* To build, to construct; to form by art or manufacture; to forge, to invent, to trump up. **fabrication,** *n.* Forgery, a forgery, a falsehood; manufacture, construction. **fabricator,** *n.*

fabulist (făb′ ū list) [F. *fabuliste* (see FABLE, -IST)], *n.* A writer or inventor of fables; a liar. **fabulize,** *v.i.* To write or speak in fables. **fabulous,** *a.* Feigned, fictitious, invented; given to fabling; related or described in fables; mythical, legendary, unhistorical; exaggerated, absurd; beyond belief, incredible. **fabulous age,** *n.* The age of myths and legends preceding the dawn of authentic history. **fabulously,** *adv.* **fabulosity** (-los' i ti), **fabulousness,** *n.*

façade (fȧ sad') [F., from *face*, after It. *facciata*, from *faccia*, FACE], *n.* The front of a building, the principal face; outward appearance.

face (fās) [F., from pop. L. *facia*, L. *facies*], *n.* The front part of the head, the visage, the countenance; that part of anything which presents itself to the view; the dial of a watch, clock, etc.; the working side of a tool or instrument; the printing surface of type; (*Golf*) the striking part of a club; the plane surface of a solid; the exposed surface of coal etc. in a mine; expression of the countenance, look, show, appearance, aspect; the visible state of things; effrontery, audacity, assurance; (*slang*) impudence, cheek. *v.t.* To turn the face towards; to meet in front; to confront boldly; to stand opposite to; to put a coating or covering on; to put facings on (a garment); to mix (as tea) with colouring matter, so as to make it appear of better quality; to cause to turn in any direction; (*Golf*) to strike (the ball) with the face of the club full in the middle, in driving from the tee. *v.i.* To look in a certain direction; to be situated with a certain aspect; to turn the face in a certain direction; *to present a false appearance, to play the hypocrite. **about face, left** or **right face:** (*Mil. order*) Turn right-about, left, or right, without moving from the same spot. **face to face:** In the immediate presence of each other; clearly, without anything interposed. **face to face with:** Immediately confronting. **in face of:** Opposite to. **in the face of:** In spite of. **on the face of it:** To judge by appearances. **to face down:** To withstand with boldness and effrontery. **to face out:** To persist in unblushingly. **to face the enemy:** To meet the enemy with determination. **to face the music:** To meet an emergency without quailing; to meet consequences boldly. **to face up to:** To meet courageously. **to fly in the face of:** To withstand, to defy openly. **to have the face:** To be impudent, cool, or composed enough (to). **to look in the face:** To confront steadily and unflinchingly. **to lose face:** To be humiliated; to suffer loss of personal prestige. **to make** or **pull a face** or **faces:** To distort the features; to grimace. **to one's face:** Openly; in plain words. **to save one's face:** To save oneself from manifest disgrace or discomfiture. **to set the face against:** To oppose, to withstand firmly. **to show one's face:** To appear. **face-ache,** *n.* Neuralgia. **face-card,** *n.* A court-card. **face-cloth,** *n.* A cloth with a smooth satiny surface, (*Am.* a wash-rag). **face-guard,** *n.* A mask to protect the face in fencing, in metallurgical operations, etc. **face-lifting,** *n.* A method of enhancing facial beauty by an operation by which the skin is tightened and wrinkles are removed. **face-value,** *n.* The nominal value shown on coin, bank-notes, etc. **faced,** *a.* Dressed (as tea); smoothed on the surface (as stone); having a face of a certain kind. **-faced,** *comb. form.* **faceless,** *a.* Destitute of a face. **facer,** *n.* A blow in the face; (*fig.*) a sudden check, a dilemma.

facet (făs' ėt) [F. *facette*, dim. of *face*, FACE], *n.* A small face or surface; one of the small planes which form the sides of a crystal, a cut diamond or other gem; a flat surface with a definite boundary as a segment of a compound eye; (*Arch.*) a flat projection between the flutings of a column. *v.t.* To cut a facet or facets on.

facetiæ (fȧ sē' shi ē) [L., pl. of *facētia*, wit, from *facētus*, elegant, urbane], *n.pl.* Humorous or witty sayings; (*Bibliog.*) curious, comic, esp. indecent books.

facetious (fȧ sē' shŭs) [F. *facétieux*, from *facétie*, L. *facētia*, see prec.], *a.* Given to or characterized by pleasantry; waggish, jocular. **facetiously,** *adv.* **facetiousness,** *n.*

facia (fā' shi ȧ) [var. of FASCIA], *n.* A tablet or board over a shop-front bearing the occupier's name.

facial (fā' shȧl, -shi ăl) [F., from med. L. *faciālis*], *a.* Of or pertaining to the face. *n.* A face massage. **facial angle:** The angle formed by lines drawn from the nostrils to the ear and to the forehead, used as an index in the comparison of different races.

-facient [L. *faciens -ntem*, pres.p. of *facere*, to make], *comb. form.* Added to L. infinitive and Eng. words to give sense of producing the action expressed in the verb, as *calefacient, liquefacient.*

facies (fā' shi ēz) [L., face], *n.* (*Nat. Hist.*) The general aspect of an assembly of organisms characteristic of a particular locality or period of the earth's history.

facile (făs' īl) [F., from L. *facilis*, from *facere*, to do], *a.* Easy to be done; easily surmountable; easily led, pliant, yielding; dexterous, skilful, handy; ready, fluent; easy-tempered, gentle.

facilitate (fȧ sil' i tāt) [as prec.], *v.t.* To make easy or less difficult; to further, to help forward. **facilitation** (-tā' shun), *n.* **facility** (fȧ sil' i ti), *n.* Easiness in performing or in being performed; freedom from difficulty; opportunity, means, or advantage for the performance of any act or the attainment of any object; ease, readiness, fluency (of speech, etc.); quickness, dexterity, aptitude; readiness to be persuaded or led, pliability.

facing (fā' sing), *n.* The action of the verb TO FACE; a covering in front for ornament or other purposes; a coating of a different material, on a wall, etc.; (*pl.*) the trimmings on the collar, cuffs, etc., of a uniform serving to distinguish one regiment from another; the process of adulterating inferior tea, coffee, etc., by mixing it with colouring matter and other substances; (*pl.*) the movements of a soldier in turning or wheeling in the course of drill. **to put through one's facings:** (*colloq.*) To be called to account; to be made to show what one is made of.

***facinorous** (fȧ sin' ŏr ŭs) [L. *facinorōsus*, from *facinus -oris*, a deed, a crime], *a.* Criminal, atrocious, abominably wicked.

facsimile (făk sim' i li) [L. (*fac*, imper. of *facere*, to make, *simile*, neut. of *similis*, like)], *n.* An exact copy of handwriting, printing, a picture, etc. *v.t.* To make a facsimile of. **in facsimile:** Exactly like. **facsimilist,** *n.*

fact (făkt) [L. *factum*, a thing done, orig. neut. p.p. of *facere*, to do], *n.* An act or deed; something that has really occurred or been done; something known to be true or existing as distinct from an inference or conjecture; reality, actuality, the concrete basis of experience; the occurrence of an event, the actual doing of a deed. **as a matter of fact:** Actually, in fact. **before** or **after the fact:** Before or after the actual event. **in fact, in point of fact:** In reality, actually, independently of theory or argument. **factual,** *a.* **factually,** *adv.*

faction (făk' shŭn) [F., from L. *factio -ōnem*, a doing, a way of making (cp. FASHION), a class, a party, from *facere*, to do, p.p. *factus*], *n.* A body of persons combined or acting in union, esp. a party within a party combined to promote their own views or purposes at the expense of order and the public good; party spirit, discord, dissension; (*Rom. Ant.*) one of the companies who supplied horses, charioteers, etc., for the chariot-races in the Roman circus. **faction fight:** (*Irish*) A fight between factions or parties of different religions, politics, or family connexions. **factional,** *a.* ***factionary,** *a.* Adhering to a faction; active as a partisan. ***factionist,** *n.* One who promotes or supports factions. **factious,** *a.* Given to faction or party; opposed to the established government; seditious, turbulent. **factiously,** *adv.* **factiousness,** *n.*

-faction [L. *-factio -ōnem*, n. of action of verbs in *-facere*; or, occasionally, from verbs in *-ficāre*, as in *petrifaction*], *comb. form.* Denoting making, turning, or converting, as in *rarefaction, satisfaction, tumefaction.*

factitious (făk tish' ŭs) [L. *facticius*, from *factus*, p.p. of *facere*, to make], *a.* Made by art, artificial;

unnatural, conventional, affected. **factitiously,** *adv.* **factitiousness,** *n.*

factitive (făk′ ti tiv) [L. *factus*, as prec.], *a.* Causing, effecting; (*Gram.*) applied to that relation existing between two words, as between an active verb and its object, when the action expressed by the verb causes a new state or condition in the object, as in *The people made him a king.*

factor (făk′ tȯr) [F. *facteur*, L. *factōr -em*, as prec.], *n.* An agent, a deputy; (*Sc.*) a steward or agent of an estate; an agent employed to sell goods on commission; (*Math.*) one of the quantities that multiplied together make up a given number or expression; (*fig.*) any circumstance, fact, or influence which contributes to a result. *v.t.* To act as factor for or to look after (property); to manage. **factor of safety:** The ratio of the breaking stress to the greatest stress likely to be applied. **factorage,** *n.* The commission given to a factor by his employer. **factorial** (-tôr′ i ăl), *a.* Pertaining to a series of mathematical factors; pertaining to a factor or land agent; (*rare*) of or pertaining to a factory. *n.* The product of a series of factors in arithmetical progression as $(x - 2)(x + 4)(x + 6)$; the product of an integer multiplied into all its lower integers, *e.g.* the factorial of $4 = 4 \times 3 \times 2 = 24$. **factorship,** *n.*

factory (făk′ tȯr i) [med. L. *factōria*, as prec.], *n.* A trading station established in a foreign place by a company of merchants; a building in which any manufacture is carried on; a manufactory, a workshop, a mill; *manufacture. **Factory Acts:** Acts to provide for the health and safety of those employed in factories. **factory-cotton:** (*Am.*) Unbleached cotton goods. **factory-hand,** *n.* A person employed in a factory. **factory ship,** *n.* A vessel in a whaling fleet which processes the catches.

factotum (făk tō′ tŭm) [med. L. (L. *fac*, imper. of *facere*, to do, *totum*, neut. a., all)], *n.* A person employed to do all sorts of business, a man of all work, a handy-man; a servant who manages all his employer's concerns.

factual [FACT].

factum (făk′ tŭm) [L., FACT], *n.* (*pl.* **-ta**) A thing done; an act or deed; (*Law*) a deed, a sealed instrument; a memorial reciting facts or points in a controversy.

***facture** (făk′ tyŭr) [F., from L. *factūra*, as prec.), *n.* Making, manufacture; manner of making, construction, workmanship.

facula (făk′ ū lă) [L., dim. of *fax facis*, a torch], *n.* (*pl.* **-læ**) (*Astron.*) A luminous spot or streak upon the sun's disk.

faculty (făk′ ŭl ti) [F. *faculté*, L. *facultās -tātem*, contr. from *facilitās*, see FACILE], *n.* Power or ability of any special kind; (*Psych.*) a natural power of the mind, as the will, reason, sense, etc.; capacity for any natural action, as seeing, feeling, speaking; (*Am.*) the ability to do or manage; the members collectively of any of the learned professions; one of the departments of instruction in a University; the masters and doctors in such department; an authorization or licence to perform certain functions, esp. ecclesiastical; *personal quality or disposition; *efficacy, active quality; *an art, trade, profession. **Court of Faculties:** A court under an archbishop, having power to grant faculties or dispensations in certain cases. **Faculty of Advocates:** The college or incorporated body of barristers in Scotland. **the Four Faculties:** Theology, Law, Medicine Arts. **the Faculty:** (*pop.*) The medical profession and its members. **facultative,** *a.* Imparting a faculty or power; empowering, permissive, as opposed to compulsory, optional; pertaining to a faculty. **facultize,** *v.t.*

fad (făd) [etym. doubtful], *n.* A crotchet, a whim, a passing fancy, taste, or fashion, a craze; a hobby; a favourite theory or idea. **faddish,** *a.* **faddishness,** *n.* **faddism,** *n.* **faddist,** *n.* **faddy,** *a.* **faddiness,** *n.*

fade (fād) [O.F. *fader*, from *fade*, dull, tasteless, L. *vapidum*, acc. of *vapidus*], *v.i.* To wither, as a plant, to lose freshness, brightness, vigour, or beauty; to languish; to grow pale, dim, or indistinct; to disappear gradually. **v.t.* To cause to wither or decay. **fade (fade out),** *v.t.* (*Cinema.*) To cause a picture gradually to disappear from the screen. **fade in,** *v.t.* (*Cinema.*) To cause a picture to become gradually clearer until it assumes its normal density. **fade-in, -out,** *n.* (*Radio.*) (of signals) Fluctuation in strength. *v.t.* To cause one item to be effaced by another. **fadeless,** *a.* Unfading. **fadelessly,** *adv.* **fadingly,** *adv.*

***fadge** (făj) [etym. unknown], *v.i.* To suit, to fit; to agree; to get on, to prosper.

fæces (fē′ sēz) [L., pl. of *fæx*, etym. unknown], *n.pl.* Sediment, lees, dregs; excrement from the bowels. **fæcal** (fē′ kăl) *a.* **fæcula** [FECULA].

***faerie, *faery** (fā′ ėr i) [var. of FAIRY], *n.* Fairyland, esp. the imaginary realm depicted in Spenser's *Faerie Queene*. *a.* Visionary, beautiful but unsubstantial.

fag (făg) [etym. doubtful (perh. corr. of FLAG (1))], *v.i.* (*past & p p.* **fagged**) To toil wearily; to work till one is weary; to act as a fag in a public school. *v.t.* To tire, to exhaust, to weary out; to use as a fag or drudge in a public school. *n.* Laborious drudgery, toil; fatigue, exhaustion; a tiresome or unwelcome task; a junior at a public school who has to perform certain duties for some senior boy; (*slang*) a cigarette. **to fag out:** (*Cricket*) To field. **fag-end,** *n.* The loose end of a web of cloth, generally of coarser texture; the latter or meaner part of anything; the fringed or untwisted end of a rope.

faggot (făg′ ŏt) [F. *fagot*, etym. doubtful (perh. from Norw. *fagg*, a bundle)], *n.* A bundle of sticks or small branches of trees, used for fuel, filling ditches, road-making, etc.; a bundle of steel or wrought-iron rods; as a definite quantity of this, 120 lb.; a cake or ball of chopped liver, herbs, etc.; *a bundle of any material; *a person hired to take the place of another at the muster of a military company. *v.t.* To bind or tie up in a faggot or bundle; *to collect together. *v.i.* To make faggots. **faggot-vote,** *n.* A vote manufactured by the transfer of property to an unqualified person. **faggot-voter,** *n.*

fagotto (fă got′ ō) [It.], *n.* The bassoon.

fah (fa) [FA].

Fahrenheit (fa′ rėn hīt) [inventor, Gabriel Daniel *Fahrenheit* (1686–1736)], *a.* Pertaining to the thermometer on the scale of which the freezing-point of water is marked at 32° and the boiling-point at 212°.

faience (fă yans′) [Fr. *faience*; It. Faenza, town in Romagna], *n.* (*Build.*) Glazed blocks of terra-cotta used as facings; (*Ceram.*) tin-glazed earthenware of a particular kind.

fail (1) (fāl) [Sc., prob. from Gael. *fàl*, a sod], *n.* A turf, a sod. **fail-dyke,** *n.* A wall of sods.

fail (2) (fāl) [O.F. *faillir*, to miss, pop. L. *fallīre*, to be wanting, to disappoint, L. *fallere*, to deceive], *v.i.* To be or become deficient or wanting; to run short; to come short of the due amount or measure; not to succeed (in); not to succeed in the attainment (of); to lose strength or spirit, to sink, to decline; to die away; to be ineffective or inoperative; to become bankrupt or insolvent; not to pass an examination *v.t.* To be wanting to; to be insufficient for; to come short of; *to deceive, *to disappoint, to neglect. *n.* Failure, default; *death, extinction. **without fail:** Assuredly, certainly, in spite of all hindrances. **failing,** *n.* Deficiency, failure; the act of becoming insolvent or bankrupt; an imperfection, a weakness, a foible. *prep.* or *pres.p.* In default of. **failing this:** If this does not happen. **failure,** *n.* A failing or coming short; an omission, non-performance, non-occurrence; decay, breaking down; insolvency, bankruptcy; want of success; an unsuccessful person or thing.

fain (fān) [A.-S. *fægen*, rel. to *gefēan*, to rejoice], *a.* Glad, well-pleased; contented, in default of something better; *desirous. *adv.* Gladly, readily. **v.i.* To rejoice; to wish.

faineant (fā' nā an) [F., as if formed of *fait-* (*nēant*, do nothing; actually from O.F. *faignant*, sluggard, pres.p. of *faindre*, to skulk, see FAINT], *a.* Do-nothing; idle, sluggish; an epithet applied to the later Merovingian kings of France, who were puppets in the hands of the Maires du Palais. *n.* A do-nothing, an idler.

fains, fens (fānz, fenz) [orig. uncertain], *int.* A children's formula for claiming exemption, for whoever says it first, from a task, *e.g.* "Fains I batting".

faint (fānt) [O.F. *feint*, p.p. of *feindre*, *faindre*, to FEIGN], *a.* Weak, feeble; languid, giddy, inclined to swoon; timid, fearful; dim, indistinct, slight, feeble of sound or brightness); (of smells) sickly, oppressive. *v.i.* To swoon; *to lose courage, to give way. *n.* A swoon, a fainting fit. **faint-ruled,** *a.* (*Paper*) Ruled with faint lines to guide writing. ***faint-heart, faint-hearted,** *a.* Cowardly, timid, spiritless. **faint-heartedly,** *adv.* **faint-heartedness,** *n.* **faintish,** *a.* **faintly,** *adv.* **faintness,** *n.*

faints (fānts) [from prec.], *n.pl.* Crude spirit that distils over at the beginning and end in the manufacture of whisky, sold as spirit of an inferior grade.

fair (1) (fâr) [A.-S. *fæger* (cp. Icel. *fagr*, O.H.G. *fagar*)], *a.* Beautiful, comely, pleasing to the eye; pleasing to the mind; satisfactory, specious; just, equitable, legitimate; not effected by unlawful or underhand means, above-board; passably good, not bad, of moderate quality; clear, pure, clean; free from spot, blemish, or cloud, serene; favourable, auspicious, promising; open, unobstructed; civil, obliging, polite; legible, plain; *orderly, neat; *liberal, mild. *adv.* Courteously, civilly, plausibly; openly, honestly, justly; on equal terms; according to the rules, straight, clean. *n.* A beautiful woman; beauty. **v.t.* To make fair or beautiful. *v.i.* To become fair (of the weather). **by fair means:** Without deception or compulsion. **fair and square,** *a.* and *adv.* Honourable, straightforward, without finesse, above-board. **to be in a fair way:** To stand a good chance. **to bid fair:** To promise well. **to hit fair:** to hit straight or clean. ***fair-boding,** *a.* Auspicious. **fair copy:** A copy (of a document etc.) not defaced by corrections. ***fair-faced,** *a.* Having a fair or handsome face; of bright complexion; (*fig.*) fair to the eye, specious. **fair-haired,** *a.* Having hair of a light colour, blond. ***fair-head,** *n.* Beauty. **fair-minded,** *a.* Honest-minded, impartial, just. **fair play,** *n.* Equitable conduct; just or equal conditions for all. **fair-seeming,** *a.* Superficially favourable or equitable; plausible, specious. **fair sex,** *n.* (*fig.*) Women. **fair-spoken,** *a.* Using courteous language; bland, polite, plausible. **fair trade:** Reciprocity, the granting of free trade only to such nations as allow it in return; *open and legal trade; *(*euphem.*) contraband trade, smuggling. **fairway,** *n.* The navigable part of a river, channel, or harbour; (*Golf*) the smooth passage of turf between holes. **fair-weather,** *a.* Appearing only in times of prosperity; not good at need. **fairing** (1), *n.* (*Aviat.*) The stream-lining of an aircraft. **fairish,** *a.* Pretty fair; tolerably large. **fairly,** *adv.* In a fair manner; completely, absolutely, utterly; moderately, passably; *softly, gently. **fairness,** *n.*

fair (2) (fâr) [O.F. *feire* (F. *foire*), L. *fēria* or pl. *fēriæ*, a holiday], *n.* A market or gathering for trade in a particular town or place, usually held annually, with shows and entertainments. **fancy fair:** A sale of fancy goods for the benefit of a religious or philanthropic institution, a bazaar. **fairing** (2), *n.* A present bought at a fair.

Fair Isle (fâr' īl) [one of the Shetland Islands], *a.* Applied to woollen articles knitted in coloured patterns typical of this island.

fairy (fâr' i) [O.F. *faerie*, enchantment (F. *féerie*), from *fée*, a fairy], *n.* A small supernatural being having magical powers, supposed to assume human form and to meddle for good or for evil in the affairs of men; *an enchantress; *enchantment, magic; *fairyland; fairies taken collectively. *a.* Pertaining to or connected wih fairies; fairy-like; fanciful, imaginary. **fairy-land,** *n.* The imaginary abode of the fairies; a region of enchantment. **fairy-ring,** *n.* A circular band of turf greener than the rest caused by the growth of fungi, but formerly supposed to be caused by the dancing of fairies. **fairy-stones,** *n.pl.* The fossil remains of sea-urchins; recent concretions of hardened clay occurring near the source of some chalybeate springs. **fairy-tale,** *n.* A tale about fairies; a fanciful or highly improbable story. **fairily,** *adv.* **fairydom,** *n.* **fairyhood,** *n.* **fairyism,** *n.*

fait accompli (fāt å kom' plē) [F.]. An accomplished fact.

faith (fāth) [O.F. *fei*, *feid*, L. *fides fidem* (cp. Gr. *pistis*, faith, *peithein*, to persuade)], *n.* The assent of the mind to what is stated or put forward by another; firm and earnest belief, conviction, complete reliance, trust; spiritual apprehension or voluntary acceptance of divine revelation apart from absolute proof; operative belief in the doctrines and moral principles forming a system of religion; a system of religious belief; a philosophical, scientific, or political creed or system of doctrines; fidelity, constancy, loyalty; a promise, pledge, or engagement; credibility, reliability, trustworthiness. *int.* In faith; verily, indeed. **v.t.* To give faith or credence to; to believe, to credit. **bad faith:** Intent to deceive. **in faith:** In deed, in truth. **in good faith:** With honest intentions. **on the faith of:** In reliance on; on the warrant of. **Punic faith:** Bad faith, faithlessness, treachery. **the faith:** The Christian religion; the true religion. **to keep faith with:** To be loyal to. ***faith-breach,** *n.* A breach of faith or honour. **faith-cure, -healing,** *n.* Curing of disease by means of prayer and faith, without the use of drugs, etc. **faith-curer, -doctor, -healer,** *n.*

faithful (fāth' ful) [as prec.], *a.* Loyal to one's promises, duty, or engagements; conscientious, trustworthy; upright, honest; truthful, worthy of belief; exact, accurate. **the faithful:** True believers in a particular creed or religious system. **faithfully,** *adv.* In a faithful manner. **to deal faithfully with, by:** To treat frankly, conscientiously, uncompromisingly; to tell the truth to without shirking. **to promise faithfully:** (*colloq.*) With the most emphatic assurances. **yours faithfully:** A conventional mode of subscribing a letter. **faithfulness,** *n.*

faithless (fāth' lės), *a.* Destitute of faith, unbelieving; disloyal, unfaithful, not true to promises or duty, unreliable; perfidious, treacherous. **faithlessly,** *adv.* **faithlessness,** *n.*

***faitour** (fā' tor) [A.-F., from O.F. *faitor*, L. *factōr -em*, FACTOR], *n.* A lazy, disreputable fellow; an impostor; a vagabond.

faix (fāks) [corr. of FAITH], *int.* (*Irish and dial.*) In faith, verily.

fake (1) (fāk) [etym. doubtful], *v.t.* To do up, to cover up defects and faults, so as to give a presentable appearance to, to doctor; to contrive, to fabricate, to make up from defective material; to cheat, to defraud, to deceive. *n.* A thing thus prepared for deception, esp. a manufactured antique (furniture, etc.); a swindle, a dodge. **fakement,** *n.* **faker,** *n.*

fake (2) (fāk) [etym. doubtful], *n.* (*Naut.*) One of the coils in a rope or cable when laid up. *v.t.* To coil (a rope).

fakir (få kēr') [Arab. *faqīr*, orig. poor, indigent], *n.* A Mohammedan religious mendicant; often used for a native mendicant of any faith; a very holy man.

Falangist (få lănj' ist) [L. *falanga*, a band of persons, from Gr. *phalanx*], *n.* Name adopted by General Franco and his supporters in the revolution against the republican government of Spain (1936–39).

falbala (făl′ bȧ lȧ) [etym. unknown, cp. FURBELOW], *n.* A trimming, a flounce; a furbelow.

falcate (făl′ kāt) [L. *falcātus*, from *falx falcem*, a sickle], *a.* (*Nat. Hist.*) Hooked; bent or curved like a sickle or scythe. **falcated,** *a.* (*Astron.*) Sickle-shaped, applied to the moon in her first and fourth quarters.

falchion (fawl′ shȯn) [O.F. *fauchon*, late L. *falcio -ōnem*, L. *falx falcis*, a sickle], *n.* A short, broad sword with a slightly curved blade.

falciform (făl′ si fôrm) [L. *falx falcis*, sickle, -FORM], *a.* Having the form of a sickle.

falcon (fawl′ kȯn, faw′ kȯn) [O.F. *faucon*, late L. *falco -ōnem*, perh. as prec.], *n.* A small diurnal bird of prey, esp. the peregrine falcon and others trained to hawk game; (*Falconry*) a female falcon, esp. the peregrine (cp. TIERCEL); *a small cannon. **falconer,** *n.* One who keeps and trains hawks for hawking; one who hunts with hawks. **falconet,** *n.* A species of shrike; *a small cannon. **falconry,** *n.* The art of training falcons to pursue and attack game; the sport of hawking.

falderal (făl′ dė răl) [refrain to a song], *n.* A trifle, a gewgaw.

faldstool (fawld stool) [O.F. *faldestoel*, med. L. *faldistolium*, O.H.G. *faldstuol* (*faldan*, to fold, *stuol*, cp. G. *stuhl*, a chair)], *n.* A portable folding seat, stool, or chair, used by a bishop officiating out of his own cathedral; a desk at which the Litany is said; a desk or stool to kneel at during one's devotions.

Falernian (fȧ lěr′ ni ȧn) [L. (*vīnum*) *Falernum*], *n.* Wine made in ancient times from grapes grown on Mount Falernus, in Campania.

fall (fawl) [A.-S. *feallan*, cp. Dut. *vallen*, Icel. *falla*, G. *fallen*, also L. *fallere*, to deceive], *v.i.* (*past* **fell,** *p.p.* **fallen**) To descend from a higher to a lower place or position by the force of gravity; to descend suddenly, to drop; to sink, to flow down, to be poured down, to become lower in level of surface; to come down, to be overthrown, to become prostrate, to be killed, to die; to decline; to decrease or be diminished in power, dignity, value, amount, weight, etc.; to subside, to abate, to ebb, to languish, to die away; to fail, to be degraded or disgraced; to sink into sin, vice, error; to be transferred by chance, lot, inheritance, or otherwise; to turn out, to result, to happen; to be uttered or dropped (as a chance remark); to be born (said of some of the lower animals); to hang down, to droop. *v.t.* To cut down, to fell, *to let fall, to drop; *to lower, to depress; *to bring forth, to drop. *n.* The act of falling; a bout at wrestling, a throw in this; a cataract, a cascade, a waterfall; the degree of inclination, the gradient or slope; a declivity; the amount of descent, the distance through which anything falls; the disemboguing of a river; the fall of the leaf, (*Am.*) autumn; the act of felling or cutting down; the amount of timber cut down; the amount of rain, snow, etc., in a district; the number of lambs born; downfall, degradation, declension from greatness or prosperity, ruin, disgrace; death, destruction, overthrow; the surrender or capture of a town; a lapse from virtue; a yielding to temptation; a veil; that part of the rope in hoisting-tackle to which the power is applied; (*Mus.*) a cadence. **to fall aboard of:** (*Naut.*) To strike against, as one vessel in collision with another. **to fall among:** To come among accidentally. **to fall astern:** (*Naut.*) To drop behind. **to fall away:** To desert; to revolt; to apostatize; to fall into wickedness; to decay, to languish; to pine, to become thin. **to fall back:** To recede, to give way, to retreat. **to fall back upon:** To have recourse to. **to fall behind:** To be passed by, to lag behind. **to fall by the ears:** To quarrel. **to fall down:** To be thrown down, to drop; to prostrate oneself. **to fall down on (a job):** To fail to carry out. **to fall flat:** To be a failure; to fail to arouse interest. **to fall for:** (*colloq.*) To be impressed by, to fall in love with. **to fall foul of:** To collide with, to dash against; to attack; to reprimand, to use severe language to; to quarrel with; (*Naut.*) to fall aboard of. **to fall from:** To drop away from, to desert, to forsake. **to fall from grace:** To fall into sin. **to fall home:** (*Naut.*) To curve inwards (as timbers or sides of a ship). **to fall in:** To give way inwards; to become due; to become the property of a person by expiration of time; to run out, to lapse; (*Mil.*) to take one's place in line. **to fall in with:** To meet with accidentally; to agree to, to concur in; to coincide with. **to fall off:** To withdraw, to recede; to prove faithless; to become depreciated, to decrease in quality, quantity, or amount; to revolt; (*Naut.*) to fail to keep her head to the wind. **to fall on:** To make an attack, to join battle; to set to, to begin eagerly. **to fall out:** To happen, to befall, to turn out, to result; to quarrel; (*Mil.*) to leave the ranks. **fall-out,** *n.* (*Phys.*) The deposit of radioactive dust after a nuclear explosion. **to fall short:** To be deficient; to drop before reaching the mark. **to fall short of:** To fail to attain. **to fall through:** To fail, to miscarry, to come to nothing. **to fall to:** To begin hastily or eagerly, to set to; to begin eating. **to fall under:** To be subject to; to come within the range of; to be classed with or reckoned with or under. **to fall upon:** To come across; to attack; (of eyes) to take the direction of. **to fall within:** To be included in. **the Fall:** The lapse of Adam and, through him, of his posterity from a state of primeval innocence. **to try a fall:** To have a bout at wrestling; (*fig.*) to engage in a contest of any kind. **fall-trap,** *n.* A trap with a door which falls and imprisons. **falling away,** *n.* Apostasy. **falling off,** *n.* Declension. ***falling-sickness,** *n.* Epilepsy. **falling star,** *n.* A meteor appearing to fall rapidly to the earth.

fallacy (făl′ ȧ si) [L. *fallācia*, from *fallax*, deceptive, from *fallere*, to deceive], *n.* An unsound argument or mode of arguing, anything that misleads or deceives the mind; (*Log.*) a delusive mode of reasoning, an example of such; an error, a sophism; sophistry, delusiveness, unsoundness of reasoning or of belief. **fallacious** (fȧ lā′ shŭs), *a.* **fallaciously,** *adv.* **fallaciousness,** *n.*

fal-lal (făl′ lăl) [cp. KNICK-KNACK, GEWGAW; perh. conn. with FALBALA], *n.* A gaudy ornament or trinket, a gewgaw.

fallible (fal′ i bėl) [late L. *fallibilis*, from *fallere*, to deceive], *a.* Liable to err or be mistaken. **fallibility** (-bil′ i ti), *n.*

Fallopian tubes (fȧ lō′ pi ȧn tūbz) [from *Fallopius* (*d.* 1562), a famous Italian anatomist, incorrectly credited with their discovery], *n.pl.* (*Physiol.*) Two ducts or canals by which ova are conveyed to the uterus.

fallow (1) (făl′ ō) [A.-S. *fealu* (cp. Dut. *vaal*, G. *fahl*, also L. *pallidus*, pale, Gr. *polios*, grey)], *a.* Of a pale brownish or reddish-yellow colour. **fallow deer:** A small species of deer, *Dama vulgaris*, preserved in a semi-domesticated state in many English parks.

fallow (2) (făl′ ō) [M.E. *falwe*, ploughed land, A.-S. *fælging*; *fealga*, harrows for breaking crops], *n.* Land ploughed and harrowed but left unsown; land left uncultivated for a period. *a.* Ploughed and tilled but not sown; (*fig.*) uncultivated, unused, neglected. *v.t.* To plough and harrow and leave unsown.

false (fawls) [A.-S. and O.F. *fals*, L. *falsus*, p.p. of *fallere*, to deceive], *a.* Not true, contrary to truth, not conformable to fact; deceptive, misleading; erroneous, wrong, incorrect; uttering untruth, lying, deceiving; deceitful, treacherous, faithless (to); feigned, sham, spurious, counterfeit, not genuine; (*Mus.*) out of tune. *adv.* Falsely; wrongly; (*Mus.*) out of tune. **n.* Falsehood; untruth. **v.t.* To deceive, to mislead; to feign, to counterfeit; to betray. **to play one false:** To deceive. **false bedding,** *n.* (*Geol.*) Strata in which the layers are not parallel through disturbance by currents whilst they were being laid down. **false-boding,** *a.* Prophesying amiss. **false colours,** *n.pl.* Flags to which she has no right hoisted on a ship to deceive an enemy. **to sail under false colours:** To assume a false character. **false concord,** *n.* (*Gram.*) A breach of the rules of agreement in number, gender, tense, etc. **false creeping,** *a.* Moving insidiously and imperceptibly. **false face,** *n.* A mask. ***false-faced,** *a.* Hypocritical. ***false-hearted,** *a.* Treacherous, perfidious. ***false-heartedness,** *n.* **false imprisonment:** Illegal imprisonment. **false position,** *n.* An awkward position that may lead to misrepresentation or misunderstanding. **false pretences,** *n.pl.* (*Law*) Misrepresentations made with intent to deceive or defraud. **false quantity,** *n.* Incorrect length of syllable in pronunciation, scansion, etc. **false roof:** A roof-shaped ceiling below the actual roof. **falsehood,** *n.* Untruthfulness, falseness; a lie, an untruth; lying, lies; deceitfulness, unfaithfulness; a counterfeit, an imposture. **falsely,** *adv.* **falseness,** *n.* **falsity,** *n.* ***falser,** *n.* One who falsifies; a deceiver, a liar.

falsetto (fawl set′ ō) [It., dim. of *falso,* FALSE], *n.* A pitch or range of voice higher than the natural register. *a.* Pertaining to or produced by such voice; (*fig.*) artificial, affected.

falsify (fawl′ si fī) [F. *falsifier,* late L. *falsificāre,* from *falsificus* (*falsus,* FALSE, *ficus,* rel. to *facere,* to make)], *v.t.* To make false; to give a false or spurious appearance to (a document, statement, etc.); to misrepresent; to counterfeit, to forge; to disappoint (expectations), to confute, to disprove. **falsification** (-kā′ shŭn), *n.*

Falstaffian (fawl staf′ i ȧn) [*Falstaff,* a character in *Hen. IV* and *V* and *Merry Wives of Windsor*], *a.* Fat, coarsely humorous, convivial; ragged and nondescript, like Falstaff's troops.

falter (fawl′ tėr) [etym. unknown], *v.i.* To stumble, to totter, to waver, to be unsteady; to stammer, to stutter; to hesitate in action; to act with irresolution; to tremble, to flinch. *v.t.* To utter with hesitation or stammering. **falteringly,** *adv.*

fame (fām) [F., from L. *fāma* (*fārī,* to speak), cp. Gr. *phēmē*], *n.* Public report or rumour; reputation, esp. good reputation, renown, celebrity. *v.t.* To make famous or renowned; to celebrate. **ill fame,** *n.* Evil reputation. **house of ill fame:** A brothel. **famed,** *a.* Much talked of; renowned, celebrated. ***fameless,** *a.*

familiar (fȧ mil′ yȧr) [O.F. *familier,* L. *familiāris* from *familia,* FAMILY], *a.* Of one's own acquaintance, well-known, intimate; closely acquainted, intimate (with); unduly or unlawfully intimate; usual, common, ordinary, not novel; easily understood, not abstruse; unconstrained, free, unceremonious; *pertaining to one's family. *n.* An intimate or close friend or companion; a demon or spirit supposed to attend at call; (*R.-C. Ch.*) a confidential servant in the household of the Pope or a bishop; *the assistant of a magician or witch. **familiarity** (-ăr′ iti), *n.* Use, habitude; close friendship, intimacy; freedom from constraint, unceremonious behaviour, esp. towards superiors or inferiors; a liberty. **familiarize,** *v.t.* To make familiar; to habituate, to accustom; to make well acquainted (with). **familiarization** (-zā′ shŭn), *n.* **familiarly,** *adv.* ***familiary,** *a.* Of or pertaining to a household or family; domestic.

family (făm′ i li) [L. *familia,* from *famulus,* a servant], *n.* Those that live in the same house, including parents, children, and servants; father and mother and children; such a group including other relations; children, as distinguished from their parents; those who can trace their descent from a common ancestor, a house, kindred, lineage; a race, a group of peoples from a common stock; a brotherhood of persons or peoples connected by bonds of civilization, religion, etc.; genealogy, lineage; honourable descent, noble lineage; a group of genera; (*Zool.*) a subdivision of an order; (*Bot.*) an order; (*Chem.*) a group of compounds having a common basic radical. **Holy Family:** Joseph, Mary, and the child Jesus; a painting of these. **in a family way:** In a domestic way; without ceremony. **in the family way:** Pregnant. **family Bible:** A large Bible in which the names and dates of birth of members of a family are entered. **family butcher, grocer,** etc.: Tradesmen who supply families, as distinct from those who supply ships, the army, etc. **family coach:** A large closed carriage; a game of forfeits. **family likeness:** Physical or other resemblance between near relations. **family living:** A benefice in the gift of the head of a family. **family man:** One who has a (large) family; one who is fond of home life. **family name:** (*Am.*) Surname. **family tree:** A genealogical chart.

famine (făm′ in) [F., from late L. *famīna,* L. *famēs,* hunger, whence F. *faim*], *n.* Distressing scarcity of food; extreme scarcity of anything; (*fig.*) hunger, starvation.

famish (făm′ ish) [obs. v. *fame,* L. *famēs,* as prec., -ISH], *v.i.* To suffer extreme hunger; to die of hunger; *(*fig.*) to faint. *v.t.* To starve; to reduce to extreme hunger. **famishing,** *a.* Feeling extremely hungry.

famous (fā′ mŭs) [A.-F., from O.F. *fameus,* L. *famōsus,* from *fama,* FAME], *a.* Renowned, celebrated; illustrious; noted; (*colloq.*) first-rate, very good, excellent; *defamatory. **famously,** *adv.* **famousness,** *n.*

famulus (făm′ ū lŭs) [L., a servant], *n.* (*pl.* **-li**) An assistant or servant, esp. of a magician. **famulary,** *a.*

fan (1) (făn) [A.-S. *fann,* L. *vannus,* a winnowing-fan], *n.* An instrument, usually flat, with radiating sections opening out in a wedge-shape for agitating the air and cooling the face; an implement shaped like an open fan; a winnowing implement or machine; a small sail or vane for keeping the sails of a windmill to the wind; (*Naut.*) the blade of a screw-propeller; a bird's tail, a wing, a leaf shaped like a fan; a rotatory apparatus for causing a current of air for ventilation; a fan-shaped talus; *a quintain. *v.t.* (*past & p.p.* **fanned**) To agitate the air with a fan; to cool with a fan; to move or stimulate with or as with a fan; to winnow; to winnow or sweep away (as chaff). *v.i.* To move or blow gently; to spread out like a fan. **fan-blast,** *n.* The blast produced by a rotatory fan in a furnace, etc. **fan-blower,** *n.* An apparatus in which a series of vanes fixed on a rotating shaft create a blast of air. **fanlight,** *n.* A window with divisions in the shape of an open fan; the light placed over a doorway, (*Am.* transom). **fan-palm,** *n.* A name applied to all palms having fan-shaped leaves, as *Chamærops humilis,* esp. the genus *Corypha* typified by the talipot, *C. umbraculifera,* from Ceylon and Malabar. **fantail,** *n.* A variety of the domestic pigeon; an Australian flycatcher of the genus *Rhidipura*; a form of gas-burner giving a broad, flat flame; a fan-shaped joint or mortise; a coal-heaver's hat with a large flap behind, a sort of sou'wester. **fan-tailed,** *a.* **fan-tracery,** *n.* (*Arch.*) Vaulting in which the tracery spreads out like a fan from springers or corbels. **fanner,** *n.* One who or that which fans; a winnowing-machine. **fanning-machine, -mill,** *n.* A winnowing-machine.

fan (2) (fan) [abbr. FANATIC], *n.* (*colloq.*) An enthusiastic admirer; a devotee.

***fanal** (fā′ nȧl) [F., from It. *fanale,* med. L. *fanāle,* Gr. *phanos,* a lantern (*phainein,* to shine)], *n.* A small lighthouse; a beacon; a ship's lantern.

fanatic (fȧ năt′ ik) [F. *fanatique,* L. *fānāticus,* from *fānum,* a temple], *a.* Wild or extravagant in opinions, esp. on religious matters; enthusiastic in the extreme; extravagant, bigoted. *n.* A person affected with fanaticism. **fanatical,** *a.* **fanatically,** *adv.* **fanaticism** (-sizm), *n.* **fanaticize,** *v.t.* To render fanatical. *v.i.* To become a fanatic.

fancy (făn′ si) [corr. of FANTASY], *n.* The faculty or the act of forming images, esp. those of a playful, frivolous, or capricious kind; imagination as an inventive and comparative power, distinguished from creative imagination; a mental image; a visionary idea or supposition; a delusion, a baseless impression, a caprice, a whim; a personal inclination, liking, or attachment; a fad, a hobby; *artistic invention, fantasy; *taste, æsthetic feeling; *fantasticalness; *love; *a short piece of music, esp. of an impromptu kind. *v.t.* To form as a conception in the mind, to picture to oneself; to be inclined to think, to suppose; to imagine or believe erroneously; to think a good deal of (oneself, etc.); to like, to take a fancy to; to breed as a hobby or sport. **v.i.* To love. *a.* Adapted to please the fancy rather than for use; ornamental, decorative; not plain. **the fancy:** Sporting characters generally, esp. pugilists, pugilism, dog-fanciers, etc. **fancy! Just fancy!** *int.* An expression of surprise. **to fancy oneself:** To have a good opinion of oneself. **fancy ball,** *n.* A ball at which the guests appear in fancy dresses. **fancy dress,** *n.* Masquerade costume. **fancy fair** [FAIR]. ***fancy-free,** *a.* Not in love. **fancy-goods,** *n.pl.* Articles of a showy rather than a useful kind; ornamental fabrics such as ribbons, coloured silks, etc., (*Am.* notions). **fancy man,** *n.* (*slang*) A sweetheart; a prostitute's bully, a ponce. **fancy price,** *n.* A capricious or extravagant price. ***fancy-sick,** *a.* Distempered in mind; love-sick. **fancy stocks,** *n.pl.* (*Am.*) Stocks having no intrinsic or determinate value, and therefore affording an opportunity for stock-gambling. **fancy-store,** *n.* (*Am.*) A store or shop where fancy-goods are sold. **fancy-woman,** *n.* (*slang*) A kept mistress. **fancy work,** *n.* Ornamental knitting, embroidery, crocheting, etc. **fancier,** *n.* One who breeds or sells birds, dogs, rabbits, etc., for their special points; a connoisseur, an amateur (*usu. in comb. as bird-fancier*). **fanciful,** *a.* Dictated by or arising in the fancy; baseless, unreal, imaginary; indulging in fancies; whimsical, fantastical. **fancifully,** *adv.* **fancifulness,** *n.* ***fanciless,** *a.* Without fancy; unimaginative.

fandangle (făn dăng′ gėl) [prob. coined from foll.], *n.* A gaudy trinket, a gewgaw; a nonsensical idea or behaviour.

fandango (făn dăng′ gō) [Sp. prob. from native African], *n.* A lively Spanish dance in triple time, for two persons who beat time with castanets; the accompaniment of such dance.

fane (fān) [L. *fānum*], *n.* (*poet.*) A temple; a place of worship; a sanctuary.

fanfare (făn′ fâr) [F., prob. onomat.], *n.* A flourish of trumpets or bugles; *(*fig.*) ostentation, parade; (*Mus.*) a certain flourish in opera; any short, prominent passage of the brass.

fanfaronade (făn fâr ŏ nād′) [F. *fanfaronnade*, from *fanfaron*, as prec.], *n.* Swaggering, blustering, or boasting; ostentation; *a fanfare. *v.i.* To make a flourish or noisy display. ***fanfaron,** *n.* A boaster, a bully.

fang (făng) [A.-S., a taking or seizing (cp. Dut. *vangen*, G. *fangen*, to catch)], *n.* A tusk or long pointed tooth; the canine tooth of a dog, wolf, or boar; the venom-tooth of a serpent; a curved spike, the point of any device for seizing or holding; the part of a tooth embedded in the gum; *a grip, a clutch. *v.t.* *To catch, to snare; *to seize; to strike the fangs into; (*Sc.*) to put water into (a pump) to make it work. **fanged,** *a.* Furnished with fangs. **fangless,** *a.*

***fangle** (făng′ gėl) [NEWFANGLE], *n.* A trifle, a fancy, a gewgaw; a fashion, a crotchet. **v.t.* To trick out fancifully. ***fangled,** *a.* Crotchety, fantastical. **fanglement,** *n.*

fanlight [FAN (1)].

fanon (făn′ ŏn) [F., from med. L. *fanō fanōnem*, a napkin, O.H.G. *fano*], *n.* (*R.-C. Ch.*) A maniple or napkin used by the officiating priest at Mass; later an embroidered band attached to the wrist of the celebrant.

fan-tan (făn′ tăn) [Chin.], *n.* A Chinese gambling game.

fantasia (fan tȧ zē′ a, făn tā′ zi ȧ) [It., FANTASY], *n.* (*Mus.*) A composition in which form is subservient to fancy.

***fantasm** [PHANTASM].

fantastic (făn tăs′ tik) [as foll.], *a.* Fanciful, whimsical, capricious; odd, grotesque; uncertain, fickle, capricious, arbitrary; extravagant; *fabulous, illusory, imaginary. *n.* A fanciful, extravagant, or absurd person; a fop. **fantastical,** *a.* **fantasticality** (-kăl′ i ti), *n.* **fantastically,** *adv.* **fantasticalness,** *n.* **fantasticism** (-sizm), *n.* ***fantastico,** *n.* A fantastic.

fantasy (făn′ tȧ si) [O.F. *fantasie*, L., from Gr. *phantasia*, from *phantazein*, to make visible, from *phainein*, to show], *n.* An extravagant or whimsical fancy, image, or idea; the faculty of inventing or forming fanciful images; a fanciful or whimsical invention or design; (*Mus.*) a fantasia; a visionary idea or speculation; *an hallucination, a delusive vision; a caprice, a whim. **fantast,** *n.* One who indulges in fantasies; a visionary; a fantastic writer.

Fantee (făn tē′), *n.* A native of a Gold Coast (Ghana) Negro tribe.

fantoccini (făn tō chē′ nē) [It. pl. of *fantoccino*, dim. of *fantoccio*, a puppet, from *fante*, a lad], *n.pl.* Puppets or marionettes made to perform by concealed wires or strings; dramatic representations at which such puppets are made to perform.

fantom [PHANTOM].

faquir [FAKIR].

far (far) [A.-S. *feor* (cp. Dut. *ver*, Icel. *fjarri*, G. *fern*, also Gr. *peran*, beyond)], *a.* (**farther, -est, further, -est**) Distant, a long way off; separated by a wide space; extending or reaching a long way: remote from or contrary to one's purpose, intention, or wishes; *remote in affection; alienated. *adv.* At or to a great distance in space, time, or proportion; to a great degree, very greatly, by a great deal; by a great interval, widely. *n.* A long distance, a distant place; a large amount, a great degree. **as far as:** Right to (a certain point); to the extent that. **by far:** In a very great measure; very greatly; exceedingly. **far and away,** *adv.* By a great amount. **far and wide:** To a great distance in all directions. **so far as:** As regards; to such an extent or degree as. **far-away,** *a.* Remote in time, place, or relationship, distant; dreamy, absent-minded. **far be it from me:** I would not even consider; I repudiate the intention (of doing something). **far-between,** *a.* At long intervals, infrequent. **far cry,** *n.* A long way. **Far East** [EAST]. **far-famed,** *a.* Widely celebrated, renowned. ***far-fet,** *a.* Subtle, deep. **far-fetched,** *a.* Forced, unnatural, fanciful, fantastic (of reasons or arguments). **far-flung,** *a.* Extended to afar. **far-forth,** *adv.* To a great degree; to a (specified) extent. **far-gone,** *a.* Advanced a long way (towards). **far other:** Very different. **from far:** From a great distance. **far-off,** *a.* Distant, remote. *adv.* At or to a great distance. **far-seeing, -sighted,** *a.* Seeing to a great distance; (*fig.*) looking far ahead; provident for remote issues. **far-sightedly,** *adv.* **far-sightedness,** *n.* **Far West,** *n.* That part of the United States lying west of the Mississippi. *a.* Lying to the west of the Mississippi; pertaining to the Far West.

farad (făr′ ȧd) [Michael *Faraday* (1791–1867), chemist and physicist], *n.* (*Elec.*) The practical unit of capacity, the capacity of a condenser in which the electrical potential is raised one volt by the addition of one coulomb. **faradic** (fȧ răd′ ik), *a.* Inductive (of an electric current). **faradize,** *v.t.* To stimulate the muscles with faradic currents. **faradization** (-zā′ shŭn), *n.*

***farandine** [FERRANDINE].

farce (1) (fars) [F., orig. stuffing, hence, an interlude or an inserted jest, from *farcer*, L. *farcire*, to stuff], *n.* A short dramatic work in which the action is trivial and the sole purpose to excite mirth; drama of this kind; an absurd proceeding; pretence, mockery. **farcical,** *a.* Of or pertaining to farce; ludicrous, droll, comical. **farcicality** (-ikăl′ i ti), *n.* **farcically,** *adv.*

farce (2) (fars) [O.F. *farcir*, as prec.], *v.t.* To cram, to stuff; to season (of cookery or literary composition). **farcing,** *n.* Stuffing; forcemeat.

farceur (far sĕr′) [F., as prec.], *n.* (*fem.* **-euse**) A joker, a jester, a wag.

farcy, -cin (far′ si, -sin) [F. *farcin*, L. *farcīminum*, from *farcīre*, to stuff], *n.* A disease in horses, closely allied to glanders. **farcy-bud, -button,** *n.* A little tumour on the face, neck, or inside of the thigh in horses, generally the first indication of farcy.

fard (fard) [F., prob. from or rel. to O.H.G. *gifarwit*, p.p. of *farwjan*, to paint], *n.* Paint or rouge for the face, esp. white paint. *v.t.* To paint (the face) with this; to beautify; to hide the blemishes of.

***fardel** (far′ dėl) [O.F., dim. of *farde*, a burden (F. *fardeau*), perh. from Arab. *fardah*, a package], *n.* A bundle, a pack, a burden.

***fardingale** [FARTHINGALE].

fare (fâr) [A.-S. *faran* (cp. Dut. *varen*, O.H.G. *faran*, G. *fahren*, also Gr. *poros*, a way, L. *portāre*, to carry)], *v.i.* To go, to travel; to get on, to be in any state, to happen, to turn out (well or ill); to be entertained; to live as regards food and drink; to feed or be fed (well, etc.). *n.* The sum paid for conveyance on a journey, passage-money; the person or persons conveyed in a vehicle for hire; food provided; *a going, a journey; *condition, hap, welfare; the quantity of fish taken in a fishing-boat.

farewell (fâr wel′) [as prec.], *int.* Adieu, good-bye; orig. and properly addressed to one about to start on a journey, now a common formula of leave-taking; used also as expression of simple separation, and in the sense of 'No more of,' 'good-bye to'. *n.* A good-bye, an adieu. *a.* Valedictory.

farina (fȧ rī-, -rē′ nȧ) [L., from *far*, corn, spelt], *n.* Flour or meal; the powder obtained by grinding the seeds of gramineous and leguminous plants, nuts, roots, etc.; any powdery substance; (*Bot.*) pollen; (*Chem.*) starch. **farinaceous** (făr i nā′ shus), *a.* **farinaceously,** *adv.* **farinose** (făr′ i nōs), *a.* Producing farina; (*Nat. Hist.*) covered with a meal-like dust, floury, meally.

farl (farl) [Sc., corr. of obs. *fardel*, A.-S. *fēortha*, FOURTH], *n.* Orig. the quarter of a cake of oatmeal or flour; a cake of this kind and size.

farm (farm) [A.-F. and O.F. *ferme* (*à ferme*, on lease), med. L. *firma*, orig. a fixed payment (cp. FIRM (1)), L. *firmus*, firm, durable], *n.* A tract of land used under one management for agriculture (orig. used only of land under lease); a farm-house; a place where children are farmed; *the system of letting out revenues or taxes; *an annual sum paid as composition by a collector or by a town or district in respect of taxes; *a district farmed out for the collection of revenue; *a lease. *v.t.* To till, to cultivate, to take (land) on lease for cultivating; to lease or let out (as taxes, offices, etc.) at a fixed sum or rate per cent.; to take the proceeds of (taxes, offices, etc.) for such a fixed sum or rate; to let out (labourers) on hire; to contract for (as one who engages to feed or lodge children) at so much per head. *v.i.* To be a farmer. **farm labourer,** *n.* An agricultural labourer employed on a farm. **home-farm:** A farm kept in his own occupation and cultivated by the owner of a larger estate. **farming,** *n.* The business of cultivating land.

farmer (far′ mėr), *n.* One who farms or cultivates land; one who contracts to collect taxes, imposts, etc., at a certain rate per cent. **farmer-general,** *n.* One of a company who, under the French monarchy, contracted for the right of levying certain taxes in a particular district.

farmhouse (farm′ hous), *n.* A dwelling-house attached to a farm.

farmstead (farm′ sted), *n.* A farm with the dwelling and other buildings on it.

faro (fâr′ ō) [*Pharaoh*], *n.* A game at cards in which persons play against the dealer.

farouche (fa roosh′) [F., from L. *ferox*, ferocious], *a.* Wild, untamed; (*colloq.*) unsociable, unmannerly, brutal.

farrago (fȧ rā′ gō) [L., mixed fodder, a medley, from *far*, spelt], *n.* A confused mixture, a medley. **farraginous** (-rā′ ji nus), *a.*

farrier (făr′ i ėr) [O.F. *ferrier*, L. *ferrārius*, from *ferrum*, iron], *n.* One who shoes horses; a shoeing smith who is also a horse-doctor; a non-commissioned officer in charge of the horses in a cavalry regiment. *v.i.* To practise as a farrier. **farriery,** *n.* The occupation of a farrier; a farrier's shop, a smithy.

farrow (făr′ ō) [A.-S. *fearh*, a pig (cp. Dut. *varken*, O.H.G. *farah*, also L. *porcus*)], *n.* A litter of pigs; the act of bringing forth a litter of pigs. *v.t.* To bring forth (as pigs). *v.i.* To bring forth pigs.

***farse** (fars) [FARCE], *n.* (*Eccles. Ant.*) The explanation in the vernacular inserted between the Latin sentences of the epistle. *v.t.* To furnish (an epistle, etc.) with such passages; to insert (such a passage).

far-sighted [FAR].

fart (fart) [A.-S. *feortan*, cp. O.H.G. *verzen*, G. *farzen*, also Gr. *perdein*], *v.i.* To break wind. *n.* A discharge of wind from the anus.

farther (far′ *th*ėr) [var. of FURTHER], *a.* More distant or remote; more extended; additional. *adv.* At or to a greater distance, extent, or degree; in addition, moreover, besides, also (now usu. *further* in this sense). *v.t.* To further. **farthest,** *a.* The most distant. *n.* The greatest distance, the latest, the most. *adv.* At or to the greatest distance.

farthing (far′ *th*ing) [A.-S. *fēorthing*, *fēortha*, FOURTH], *n.* The fourth part of a penny, the smallest British copper coin (withdrawn in 1961); the smallest possible amount; *an old division of land. **farthingsworth,** *n.* As much as was sold for a farthing; a matter of trifling moment.

farthingale (far′ *th*ing gāl) [O.F. *verdugale*, corr. of Sp. *verdugado*, from *verdugo*, a rod], *n.* A hooped skirt used to extend the wide gown and petticoat of the 16th cent.

fasces (făs′ ēz) [L., pl. of *fascis*, a bundle (see foll.)], *n.pl.* The ancient insignia of the Roman lictors, consisting of a bundle of elm or birch rods, in the middle of which was an axe; (*fig.*) an emblem of authority.

fascia (făsh′ i ȧ) [L., a band, conn. with *fas*, that which is binding], *n.* (*pl.* **iæ**) A thin, tendon-like sheath surrounding the muscles and binding them in their places; a band, belt, sash, fillet; the name-board above a shop; (*Arch.*) a flat surface in an entablature or elsewhere; a facia; (*Astron.*) the belt of a planet; (*Surg.*) a bandage or ligature; (*Motor.*) the instrument board of a car. **fasciated,** *a.* (*Bot.*) Flattened by the growing together of several parts; striped. **fasciation** (-ā′ shun), *n.* (*Bot.*) Union of stems or branches in a ribbon-like form; (*Surg.*) binding up of diseased or injured parts; a bandage.

fascicle, fascicule (făs′ i kėl, -i kūl) [FASCICULUS], *n.* A small bundle, cluster, or group; (*Bot.*) a cluster of leaves, flowers, etc., a tuft; (*Anat.*) a bundle of fibres; a serial division of a book sold separately. **fascicled,** *a.* Clustered together in a fascicle. **fascicular** (fȧ sik′ ū lȧr), *a.* **fasciculate, -lated,** *n.* (*Nat. Hist.*) Collected in clusters, small bundles, or bunches. **fasciculation** (-lā′ shun), *n.*

fasciculus (fȧ sik′ ū lus) [L., dim. of *fascis*, see FASCES], *n.* (*pl.* **-li**) A bundle or package; a division of a book sold separately.

fascinate (făs′ i nāt) [L. *fascinātus*, p.p. of *fascināre*, from *fascinum*, a spell], *v.t.* To exercise an irresistible influence over; to deprive of volitional power by magic or by means of look or presence (esp. of serpents); to captivate, to attract irresistibly, to enchant, to charm. **fascinating,** *a.* Irresistibly attractive, charming, bewitching. **fascinatingly,** *adv.* **fascination** (-nā′ shun), *n.* **fascinator** (făs′ i nā tȯr), *n.* One who or that which fascinates; a light covering for the head worn by women.

fascine (fă sēn') [F., from L. *fascīna*, a bundle of sticks, from *fascis*], *n.* A cylindrical faggot of brushwood bound with withes, and used in building earthworks, for filling trenches, protecting river-banks, etc.

Fascism (făsh' izm) [It. *Fascismo*, from *fascio*, L. *fascis*, a bundle], *n.* (*Pol.*) A theory of government introduced into Italy by Benito Mussolini in 1922. Its object was to oppose socialism and communism by controlling every form of national activity. It was anti-democratic in principle, permitting no other party to exist and tolerating no opposition. **Fascist** (făsh' ist), *n.*

fash (făsh) [O.F. *fascher* (F. *fâcher*), Prov. *fastigar*, ult. from L. *fastidium*, from *fastus*, arrogance], *v.t.* (*chiefly Sc.*) To vex, to annoy; to trouble, to bother. *v.i.* To take trouble; to be vexed. *n.* Trouble, pains, inconvenience, vexation.

fashion (făsh' ŏn) [O.F. *faceon*, L. *factiōnem*, nom. *-tio*, a making, from *facere*, to make (cp. FACTION)], *n.* The form, make, style, or external appearance of any thing; mode, manner, way, pattern; the prevailing style or mode of dress; custom, usage, prevailing practice, esp. in dress; the conventional usages of polite society; the usages prevailing at a given period; genteel or fashionable society; *kind, sort. *v.t.* To give shape and form to; to frame, to mould; to fit, to adapt; *to make or form according to the rules prescribed by custom; *to counterfeit, to pervert; *to contrive. **after a fashion, in a fashion:** In a way; middling, rather badly; somehow or other. **after the fashion of:** In the same way as; like. **in** or **out of fashion:** Conforming or not conforming to the prevailing mode. **to set the fashion:** To set the example in a new style of dress or behaviour. ***fashion-monger,** *n.* One who affects the fashion; a fop, a dandy. **fashion-plate,** *n.* A picture illustrating a style in dress; (*colloq.*) an ultra-fashionably dressed woman. **fashionable,** *a.* Conforming to or observant of the fashion or established mode; made according to the fashion; characteristic of, approved by, or patronized by people of fashion. **n.* A person of fashion. **fashionableness,** *n.* **fashionably,** *adv.* **fashioned,** *a.* (*in comb.*) Made or shaped (in a certain way). ***fashioner,** *n.* One who fashions or gives shape to anything. ***fashionist,** *n.* **fashionless,** *a.* Without shape or fashion.

fast (1) (fast) [A.-S. *fæst* (cp. Dut. *vast*, Icel. *fastr*, G. *fest*, and fol.)], *a.* Firmly fixed, firm, tight; firmly adhering, faithful, steady, close; lasting, durable, permanent, unfading, not washing out; swift, rapid, moving quickly; promoting quick motion (as a billiard-table, cricket-pitch, etc.); dissipated, rakish, pleasure-seeking. *adv.* Firmly, tightly, securely; quickly, swiftly, in rapid succession; in a dissipated manner, so as to expend one's energies quickly. *n.* Anything which fastens or holds; (*Naut.*) a hawser securing a vessel to the shore. **fast and loose** [PLAY]. **fast asleep:** Sound or firmly asleep. ***fast beside** or **by:** Close, very near. **to make fast:** To fasten securely, to tie. ***fast-handed,** *a.* Close-fisted, avaricious. **fast train,** *n.* An express train. **fastish,** *a.* Rather fast or dissipated.

fast (2) (fast) [A.-S. *fæstan* (cp. Dut. *vasten*, Icel. *fasta*, G. *fasten*, from Goth. *fastan*, in the sense of to be firm, strict)], *v.i.* To abstain from food; to abstain entirely or partially from food voluntarily for a certain time for the mortification of the body or as a token of grief, affliction, or penitence. *n.* Total or partial abstinence from or deprivation of food, esp. from religious motives; doing without food; a time set apart for fasting; any holy time or season. **fast day,** *n.* A day appointed as a fast; (*Sc.*) a day of humiliation and prayer in preparation for Holy Communion.

fasten (fa' sėn) [A.-S. *fæstnian* (prec., -EN)], *v.t.* To fix firmly; to make fast, to attach; to secure, as by a bolt, a lock, a tie, knot, etc.; to fix or set firmly or earnestly; to affix, to fix (a stigma, nickname, etc., upon). *v.i.* To become fast; to seize, to lay hold (upon). **fastener,** *n.* One who or that which fastens, makes fast, or secures. **fastening,** *n.* The act of making fast or secure; anything which makes fast or secure, as a bolt, bar, strap, catch, etc.

fasti (făs' tī) [L., pl. of *fastus* (*dies*), lawful day], *n.pl.* (*Rom. Ant.*) The calendar of days when legal business might be transacted; the register of events during the official year; hence, annals, chronological records of events.

fastidious (fås tid' i ŭs) [L. *fastīdiōsus*, from *fastīdium*, loathing, from *fastus*, arrogance], *a.* Difficult to please; squeamish, easily disgusted; *disgusting, loathsome. **fastidiously,** *adv.* **fastidiousness,** *n.*

fastigiate (fås tij' ȧt) [L. *fastīgium*, the apex of a gable], *a.* (*Bot.*) Tapering to a point like a pyramid. **fastigium,** *n.* (*pl.* **-ia**) The pediment of a portico; the ridge of a roof; (*Path.*) the period of highest temperature in a fever or illness.

fastness (fast' nes), *n.* The quality or state of being fast or secure; *firmness, strength, security; a fortress, a stronghold, esp. in a place difficult of access.

fat (1) (făt) [A.-S. *fæt*, *fætt*, O.Fris. *fat*, Dut. *vet*, G. *fett* (orig. p.p. of a v. to fatten)], *a.* Plump, fleshy, corpulent, full-fed; (of animals) fed up for killing; oily, greasy, unctuous; resinous, bituminous (of coal), sticky, plastic (of clay etc.), thick, broad-faced (of printing type); prosperous, thriving, rich, affluent; producing a large income; fertile, fruitful, rich; (*Print.*) applied to a page having many blank spaces or lines, hence to any work that pays well; (*fig.*) dull, stupid, lazy, sluggish; *close (of a room). *n.* An animal substance of a more or less oily character, deposited in vesicles in adipose tissue; the fat part of anything; (*fig.*) the best or choicest part of anything; (*Print.*) matter profitable to the compositor; (*Theat.*) a part that gives an actor opportunity to display his powers; (*Chem.*) an organic compound of glycerine with one of a group of acids. *v.t.* To make fat or plump; to fatten. *v.i.* To become fat, to gain flesh. **the fat is in the fire:** (*colloq.*) There's going to be trouble. **fat-brained,** *a.* Dull of apprehension. **fat-faced,** *a.* Having a plump round face. **fat-head,** *n.* A dull, stupid fellow. **fat-hen,** *n.* Kinds of goosefoot or *Chenopodium*, esp. Australian varieties used for food. ***fat-kidneyed,** *a.* Gross, corpulent, obese. **a fat lot,** *n.* (*slang iron.*) Very little. **fat-witted,** *a.* Stupid, dull, slow. **fatling,** *n.* A young animal fattened for slaughter; a fattened animal. **a.* Fat, plump. **fatness,** *n.* **fatten,** *v.t.* To make fat, to feed for the table; to make (ground) fruitful, to fertilize. *v.i.* To grow or become fat, to gain flesh. **fattish,** *a.* Somewhat fat. **fatty,** *a.* Consisting of or having the qualities of fat; greasy, unctuous; adipose. *n.* (*slang*) A fat person. **fatty degeneration,** *n.* The abnormal conversion of the protein elements into a granular fatty matter.

***fat** (2) (făt) [VAT], *n.* A vat, tub, barrel; a measure of capacity differing for different commodities.

fatal (fā' tål) [O.F., from L. *fatālis*, from *fātum*, FATE], *a.* Proceeding from or decreed by fate; inevitable, necessary; fateful, fraught with heavy consequences, important, decisive; foreboding ruin or destruction; causing death (to); deadly, mortal; (*fig.*) unfortunate, unlucky, mischievous. **fatally,** *adv.*

fatalism (fā' tål izm) [as prec.], *n.* The doctrine that all events are ordered by the arbitrary decrees of God or by inevitable necessity; physical determinism, the doctrine that the human will is so controlled; submission to all that happens as the work of fate. **fatalist,** *n.* One who holds the doctrine of fatalism. *a.* Fatalistic. **fatalistic** (-lis' tik), *a.* **fatalistically,** *adv.*

fatality (fȧ tăl' i ti), *n.* A fixed and unalterable course of things; supremacy of fate; predetermination by fate, esp. to disaster, necessity, doom; deadliness, calamity; a fatal occurrence, esp. a death by accident or violence.

fata Morgana (fa′ tȧ môr ga′ nȧ) [It., *fata*, a fairy, *Morgana*, the legendary sister of King Arthur, famed for her magical powers], *n.* A mirage observed from the harbour of Messina and adjacent places, and supposed by the Sicilians to be the work of the fairy Morgana; objects reflected in the sea, and sometimes in a kind of aerial screen high above it.

fate (fāt) [L. *fātum*, orig. neut. p.p. of *fārī*, to speak], *n.* The power by which the course of events is unalterably predetermined; destiny, lot, fortune; one's ultimate condition as brought about by circumstances and events; what is destined to happen; death, destruction; (*pl.*) the Parcæ or Destinies, three Greek goddesses supposed to preside over the birth, life, and fortunes of men—Clotho held the spindle, Atropos drew out the thread of man's destiny, and Lachesis cut it off. *v.t.* (*usu. in p.p.*) To decree by fate or destiny; to destine to destruction. **fated,** *a.* Decreed by fate, predetermined; doomed to destruction; fatal, fateful; *exempted by fate; *invested with the power of determining fate or destiny. **fateful,** *a.* Fraught with fate, full of fatal import, decisive; bringing death or destruction; fatal. **fatefully,** *adv.* ***fatefulness,** *n.*

father (fa′ thĕr) [A.-S. *fæder* (cp. Dut. *vader*, G. *vater*, L. *pater*, Gr. *patēr*)], *n.* A male parent; he who begets a child; a male ancestor, a patriarch; (*fig.*) the first to practise any art; an originator, author, contriver, an early leader; a respectful mode of address to an old man or any man deserving great reverence; the title of the senators of ancient Rome; one who exercises paternal care; a stepfather; a father-in-law; the senior member of any profession or body; the First Person of the Trinity; a priest, a confessor, the superior of a convent, a religious teacher, etc.; (*pl.*) elders, senators, the leading men (of a city, etc.). *v.t.* To beget; to be or act as father of; to adopt as a child; to originate; to adopt or assume as one's own child, work, etc.; to accept responsibility for; to ascribe to any one as his offspring or as his production. **adoptive father:** One who adopts the child or children of another. **Fathers of the Church:** The ecclesiastical writers of the early Church. **Conscript Fathers:** The Roman senators. **the Holy Father:** The Pope. **putative father:** The supposed father. **Right** or **Most Reverend Father in God:** Formal title of a bishop or an archbishop. **father confessor,** *n.* (*R.-C. Ch.*) A priest who hears confessions. **father of lies,** *n.* Satan. **father superior,** *n.* (*Eccles.*) Head of a religious house. **father-in-law,** *n.* The father of one's husband or wife. **fatherhood,** *n.* The state or condition of being a father; the character or authority of a father. **father of the Chapel:** (*Print.*) The person chosen from among themselves by printers in an establishment to represent them with the employers and watch over their interests. **fatherland,** *n.* One's native country. **fatherless,** *a.* Destitute of a living father; (*fig.*) without any known author. **fatherlessness,** *n.* **fatherly,** *a.* Like a father; proper to or becoming a father; kind, tender, loving. *adv.* In the manner of a father. **fatherliness,** *n.* **fathership,** *n.*

fathom (făth′ ŏm) [A.-S. *fæthm*, the space enclosed by the arms outstretched (cp. Dut. *vadem*, G. *faden*, also L. *patēre*, to extend, Gr. *petannunai*)], *n.* A measure of length, 6 ft. (used principally in nautical and mining measurements); 6 ft. square (as a measure of wood in section independently of length); *(*fig.*) depth; penetration. *v.t.* *To embrace, to encompass with the extended arms; to ascertain the depth of; (*fig.*) to get to the bottom of, to penetrate, to comprehend. **fathom-line,** *n.* (*Naut.*) A sounding-line. **fathom-wood,** *n.* Waste timber sold by fathom lots. ***fathomable,** *a.* **fathomless,** *a.* Not to be fathomed. **fathomlessly,** *adv.* **fathometer** (făth om′ e tĕr), *n.* Instrument for measuring the depth of the sea by sound waves.

***fatidic, -al** (fȧ tid′ ik, -ȧl) [L. *fātidicus* (*fātum*, FATE, *dic-*, root of *dīcere*, to speak)], *a.* Having the power to foretell future events; prophetic. **fatidically,** *adv.*

fatigue (fȧ tēg′) [O.F. *fatiguer*, L. *fatīgāre*, prob. cogn. with *fatiscere*, to gape], *n.* Weariness, exhaustion from bodily or mental exertion; toil or exertion causing weariness or exhaustion; labour not of a military nature performed by soldiers; a weakening in metals due to prolonged strain or repeated blows. *v.t.* To tire, to weary; to exhaust the strength of by bodily or mental exertion; to harass, to importune. **fatigue-dress,** *n.* The dress worn by soldiers on fatigue-duty. ***fatigate** (făt′ i gāt), *v.t.* To weary, to tire out, to exhaust. *a.* (-gȧt) Tired out, wearied, exhausted. **fatigueless,** *a.* **fatiguing,** *a.*

fatness, fatten, etc. [FAT].

fatuous (făt′ ū ŭs) [L. *fatuus*], *a.* Stupid, imbecile, foolish; meaningless, inane, silly. **fatuity** (-tū′ i ti), *n.* **fatuitous,** *a.* **fatuously,** *adv.* **fatuousness,** *n.*

faubourg (fō′ boorg) [F.], *n.* A suburb of a town; a part now within a city, but formerly outside the walls.

fauces (faw′ siz) [L.], *n.pl.* The hinder part of the mouth, terminated by the pharynx and larynx; (*Bot.*) the orifice or opening of a monopetalous flower; (*Conch.*) the opening into the first chamber of a shell. **faucal** (faw′ kȧl), *a.* Pertaining to the fauces or gullet; deeply guttural.

faucet (faw′ sėt) [F. *fausset*; etym. doubtful], *n.* (*chiefly Am.*) A tap; a beer-tap.

faugh (faw) [onomat.], *int.* An exclamation of disgust or abhorrence.

fault (fawlt) [M.E. and O.F. *faute*, pop. L. *fallita*, a defect, fem. p.p. of *fallere*, to FAIL], *n.* Defect, blemish, imperfection; an error, failing, mistake, or blunder; a slight offence or deviation from right or propriety; responsibility for a mistake or mishap, blame; loss of the scent in hunting; an improper service at tennis; (*Teleg.*) a leak through broken insulation etc.; (*Geol.*) the sudden interruption of the continuity of strata till then upon the same plane, this being accompanied by a crack or fissure, usually filled with broken stone, clay, or similar material. **v.i.* To commit a fault, to blunder. *v.t.* (*Geol.*) To break the continuity of (*usu. in p.p.*); *to charge with a fault, to blame. **at fault:** At a loss, puzzled, embarrassed. **in fault:** To blame. **to find fault with:** To complain of, to blame, to censure. **fault-finder,** *n.* One given to fault-finding. **fault-finding,** *a.* Censorious. *n.* Censoriousness. ***faulter,** *n.* An offender; one who is in fault. ***faultful,** *a.* Faulty, guilty, criminal. **faultless,** *a.* **faultlessly,** *adv.* **faultlessness,** *n.* **faulty,** *a.* **faultily,** *adv.* **faultiness,** *n.*

Faun (fawn) [L. *Faunus*, a Latin rural deity whose attributes bear a strong analogy to those of Pan, with whom he is sometimes identified], *n.* One of a kind of demigods, or rural deities, bearing a strong resemblance in appearance and character to the satyrs, with whom they are generally identified.

fauna (faw′ nȧ) [L., a Roman goddess, sister of Faunus], *n.* (*pl.* **-næ**) The animals found in or peculiar to a certain region or epoch; a treatise upon these. **faunal,** *a.* **faunist,** *n.* **faunistic** (-nis′ tik), *a.*

fauteuil (fō′ tu i) [F., from M.F. *fauldeteuil*, low L. *faldistolium*, see FALDSTOOL], *n.* An easy, upholstered arm-chair; the chair or seat of a president; (*fig.*) membership of the French Academy; an upholstered stall in a theatre, etc.

fauvette (fō vet′) [F., from *fauve*, fallow], *n.* Bewick's generic name for the warbler family, adopted from the French.

faux pas (fō pa) [F.], *n.* A blunder, a slip.

faveolate (fȧ vē′ ŏ lāt) [from FAVUS, on anal. with F. *faveole*], *a.* (*Bot.*) Honeycombed, cellular.

favonian (fȧ vō′ ni ȧn) [L. *favōniānus*, from *Favōnius*, the west wind], *a.* Of or pertaining to the west wind; hence, mild, auspicious.

favour (fā′ vòr) [O.F., from L. *favōr-em*, from *favēre*, to show goodwill to], *n.* Friendly regard, kindness, goodwill; countenance, approval; partiality, preference, excessive kindness or indulgence; a kind of indulgent act; aid, support, furtherance, facility, convenience for doing something; behalf, advantage (of); leave, consent; (*Comm.*) a letter, a communication; a token of love or affection, esp. something given by a lady to her lover; a knot of ribbons worn on any festive occasion; *aspect, appearance, looks. *v.t.* To regard or behave toward with kindness; to befriend, to support; to facilitate; to promote; to oblige (with); to be propitious or fortunate for; to approve, to countenance, to show partiality to; to resemble in features. **in favour, out of favour:** Approved, disapproved. **in favour of:** On the side of; to the account of; on behalf of. **to curry favour** [CURRY (1)]. ***favourless,** *a.* Not regarded with favour; unfavourable; not propitious. **favoured,** *a.* Featured, having a certain look or appearance (*usu. in comb.* as *ill-favoured, well-favoured*). **favouredness,** *n.* **favouredly,** *adv.* **favouring,** *a.* Countenancing, supporting; resembling in features. **favouringly,** *adv.*

favourable (fā′ vòr àbl) [F., from L. *favōrābilis* (as prec.)], *a.* Friendly, well-disposed, encouraging; propitious; approving, commending, consenting; tending to promote or to encourage; convenient, advantageous; *well-favoured. **favourableness,** *n.* **favourably,** *adv.*

favourite (fā′ vòr it) [O.F. *favorite*, fem. p.p. of *favorir*, to FAVOUR], *n.* A person or thing regarded with special affection, predilection, or partiality; one chosen as a companion and intimate by a superior and unduly favoured; (*Sport*) the competitor considered to have the best chance, and against whom or which the shortest odds are offered. *a.* Regarded with special favour; beloved; preferred before all others. **favouritism,** *n.*

favus (fā′ vŭs) [L., honeycomb], *n.* (*Path.*) A disease of the scalp, characterized by pustules succeeded by cellular crusts bearing some resemblance to a honeycomb.

fawn (1) (fawn) [O.F. *fan, faon*, through low L. from L. *fœtus*, FŒTUS], *n.* A young deer; a buck or doe in its first year; the colour of a young deer. *a.* Like a fawn in colour, yellowish-brown. *v.t.* To bring forth (of deer). *v.i.* To bring forth a fawn. **fawn-colour,** *n.* **fawn-coloured,** *a.*

fawn (2) (fawn) [A.-S. *fahnian*, from *fægen*, see FAIN], *v.i.* To show affection by cringing, licking the hand, etc. (of animals, esp. dogs); (*fig.*) to court in a servile manner, to grovel, to cringe (usu. with *upon*). **n.* A cringe, a bow; servile flattery. ***fawner,** *n.* **fawning,** *a.* Courting servilely; flattering by cringing or meanness. *n.* Servile flattery. **fawningly,** *adv.*

fay (1) (fā) [O.F. *fae* (F. *fée*), L. *fata*, the FATES], *n.* A fairy.

***fay** (2) (fā) [O.F. *fei, feid*, FAITH], *n.* Faith; religious belief; allegiance. **by my fay:** A kind of oath or asseveration.

fay (3) (fā) [A.-S. *fēgan*, to join, unite (cp. Dut. *voegen*, G. *fügen*)], *v.i.* (*Am.*) To fit; (*prov.*) to suit, to get on well; (*Naut.*) to fit closely. *v.t.* (*Naut.*) To fit accurately.

fayence [FAIENCE].

***feague** (fēg) [cp. G. *fegen*, Dut. *vogen*], *v.t.* To whip; (*fig.*) to confound, to settle the hash of. **to feague it away:** To work at high pressure.

fealty (fē′ àl ti) [O.F. *fealte*, L. *fidēlitās -tātem*, FIDELITY], *n.* Fidelity of a vassal or feudal tenant to his lord; fidelity, loyalty, allegiance.

fear (1) (fēr) [A.-S. *fǣr*, danger, calamity (cp. G. *gefahr*, also L. *periculum*)], *n.* A painful apprehension of danger or of some impending evil; dread, a state of alarm; anxiety, solicitude; awe, reverence; an object of fear. *v.t.* To be afraid of, to dread; to shrink from, to hesitate (to do); to reverence, to venerate; to suspect, to doubt; *to terrify. *v.t.* To be afraid; to feel anxiety or solicitude; to doubt, to mistrust. **for fear:** In dread (that or lest); lest. **no fear:** (*slang*) Not likely; certainly not. **fear-naught** (fēr′ nawt) [NAUGHT], *n.* A heavy, shaggy, woollen fabric, used for seamen's coats, for lining port-holes, doors of powder magazines, etc. **fear-palsied, -shaken, -struck,** *a.* Overwhelmed with fear. ***fear-surprised,** *a.* Suddenly overcome by fear. **feared,** *a.* Regarded with fear; *afraid. **fearful,** *a.* Timid, timorous; apprehensive, afraid (lest); *anxious, solicitous; *produced by or indicating fear; *full of fear (or reverence; terrible, awful, frightful; (*colloq.*) extraordinary, unusual, annoying. **fearfully,** *adv.* **fearfulness,** *n.* **fearless,** *a.* **fearlessly,** *adv.* **fearlessness,** *n.* **fearsome,** *a.* Fearful, terrible, alarming. **fearsomely,** *adv.* **fearsomeness,** *n.*

***fear** (2) [FERE (1)].

feasible (fē′ zibl) [O.F. *faisable*, from *fais*, stem of *faire*, L. *facere*, to do], *a.* That may or can be done; practicable, possible; (*colloq.*) manageable; likely, plausible. **feasibility** (-bil′ i ti), *n.* ***feasibleness,** *n.* **feasibly,** *adv.*

feast (fēst) [O.F. *feste* (F. *fête*), late L. *festa*, orig. neut. pl. of L. *festus*, joyful], *n.* A sumptuous meal or entertainment of which a large number of persons partake, esp. a public banquet; an anniversary or periodical celebration of some great event or personage, esp. a religious anniversary; (*fig.*) anything giving great enjoyment to body or mind. *v.t.* To entertain sumptuously; (*fig.*) to gratify or please greatly, as with something delicious or luscious. *v.i.* To feed sumptuously; (*fig.*) to be highly gratified or pleased. **immovable** or **movable feasts:** Festivals or anniversaries occurring on a fixed date as Christmas, or on varying dates as Easter. **feast-day,** *n.* A day of feasting; a festival. ***feast-rites,** *n.pl.* The rites or customs observed at a feast. ***feast-won,** *a.* Gained or bribed by feasting. **to feast away:** To pass (time) away in feasting. **feaster,** *n.* One who fares sumptuously; a guest, a partaker of a feast; *the giver of a feast.

feat (1) (fēt) [O.F. *fait*, L. *factum*, FACT], *n.* A notable act or performance, esp. one displaying great strength, skill, or daring; an exploit, an achievement; a surprising trick.

***feat** (2) (fēt) [O.F. *fait*, made, L. *factus*, p.p. of *facere*, to make], *a.* Dexterous, skilful; nimble; smart, neat, trim. ***featly,** *adv.* ***featliness,** *n.* ***featness,** *n.* ***featous,** *a.* Neat, comely, handsome. ***featously,** *adv.*

feather (feth′ ėr) [A.-S. *fether* (cp. Dut. *veder*, G. *feder*, L. *penna*, Gr. *pteron*, wing, *petesthai*, to fly)], *n.* A plume or quill, one of the dermal appendages forming collectively the covering of a bird; such a plume worn as an ornament, esp. in the hat; a strip of a feather attached to an arrow-shaft; a hairy fringe on a dog's tail or legs, a patch of rough hair on a horse's coat; (*Carp.*) a tongue on the edge of a board fitting into a groove on the edge of another board; (*Rowing*) the act of feathering; (*fig.*) something extremely light. *v.t.* To dress, cover, or furnish with feathers; to adorn with or as with feathers; (*Rowing*) to turn (oar) so that the blade passes horizontally through the air; *to adorn; *to tread (as a cock). *v.i.* To move as feathers; to have a feathery appearance; (*Rowing*) to turn the oar and carry through the air edgeways; (*Hunting*) to set hounds directly on the trail; (of hounds) to make a quivering movement with the tail when searching for traces of deer, etc. **a feather in one's cap:** An honour, a distinction. **birds of a feather:** People of the same sort, taste, disposition, etc. **fur and feather:** Beasts and birds suitable for sport. **to be in high feather:** To be in high spirits, to be elated. **to cut a feather:** (*Naut.*) To leave a foamy ripple, as a ship moving rapidly; (*fig.*) to move briskly; to make oneself conspicuous; to cut a dash. **to feather one's nest:** To accumulate wealth; to make provision for oneself. **to show the white feather:** To show signs of cowardice or timidity (said to be derived from the belief that a white feather in the tail of a game-cock was a sign of cowardice). **feather-bed,** *n.* A mattress stuffed with feathers. **to feather-bed,** *v.t.* To pamper, to spoil. **feather-boarding,** *n.* A roof or other covering of boards that thin off at the top and overlap like a bird's feathers. **feather-edge,** *n.* An edge like a feather; the thinner edge of a wedge-shaped board or plank. **feather-edged,** *a.* Having one edge thinner than the other (said of boards). **feather-fern,** *n.* A branching plant, *Astilbe Japonica*, of the saxifrage family. **feather-few** [corr. of FEVERFEW]. **feather grass,** *n.* A perennial grass, *Stipa pennata*, with graceful, feathered awns. **feather-head, -brain, -pate,** *n.* A silly, frivolous person. **feather-headed, -brained, -pated,** *a.* **feather-stitch,** *n.* An embroidery stitch producing a zigzag line somewhat like feathers. **feather-weight,** *n.* Something as light as a feather; (*Racing*) a jockey of the lightest weight allowed to be carried by a horse in a handicap, 4 st. 7 lb.; (*Boxing*) a boxer not above 9 st. **feathered,** *a.* Covered with feathers (*also in comb.*, as *well-feathered*); winged; fitted, fringed, or adorned with a feather or feathers; having feather appendages; feathery, feather-like; swift, rapid. **feathered game,** *n.* (*collect.*) Game birds. **feathering,** *n.* The action of the verb TO FEATHER; plumage; feathers on an arrow; a feathery fringe or coat (of setters, etc.); (*Arch.*) an arrangement of small arcs or foils separated by projecting points or cusps. **featherless,** *a.* Destitute or deprived of feathers; unfledged. **featherlet,** *n.* **feathery,** *a.* Covered, fringed, or adorned with or as with feathers; feather-like, resembling feathers; (*fig.*) light, flimsy, fickle; (*Bot.*) plumose. **featheriness,** *n.*

feature (fē′ tyůr, -chůr) [O.F. *faiture*, L. *factūra*, from *facere*, to make], *n.* A part of the face, esp. such as gives individual expression and character (*usu. in pl.*); a prominent or distinctive part of anything, a salient point, a striking incident, a mark of individuality; (*Cinema.*) a film of considerable length and special quality or interest; *shape, form, figure; *general appearance; *handsomeness of form or figure. *v.t.* (*colloq.*) To resemble in features, to favour; to be a characteristic feature of; to sketch, to portray; (*Theat.*, *Cinema.*) to exhibit as a special attraction or 'feature.' **featured,** *a.* Having a certain cast of face (*usu. in comb.*). **featureless,** *a.* Without any distinct or distinctive features; shapeless. ***featurely,** *a.* Handsome, shapely; having distinctive features.

febricula (fė brik′ ū lȧ), **febricule** (feb′ ri kūl) [L. *febrīcula*, dim. of *febris*, FEVER], *n.* (*Path.*) A slight fever of no specific type and of short duration. **febriculose,** *a.* Slightly feverish. ***febriculosity** (-los′ i ti), *n.*

febrifacient (feb ri fā′ shi ėnt) [as prec., -FACIENT], *a.* (*Path.*) Causing fever. *n.* Anything which causes fever. ***febriferous** (fė brif′ ėr ůs) [-FEROUS], *a.* Inducing fever. **febrific,** *a.* Productive of fever; feverish.

febrifuge (fē′ bri-, feb′ ri fūj) [F. *fébrifuge* (L. *febris*, FEVER, *fugāre*, to drive away)], *n.* (*Med.*) A medicine which has the property of dispelling or mitigating fever. **febrifugal** (fė brif′ ū gȧl), *a.*

febrile (fē′ bril) [F., from L. *febrīlis*, as prec.], *a.* Pertaining to, proceeding from, or indicating fever.

Febronian (fė brō′ ni ȧn) [Justinus *Febronius*, pseud. of J. N. von Hontheim, coadjutor bishop of Treves], *a.* Of or pertaining to Febronius or his doctrines (pubd. 1763), which maintained the independence of national churches against the claims of the Pope. **Febronianism,** *n.*

February (feb′ rů ȧ ri) [L. *Februārius*, from *februa*, pl., a festival of purification, sing. *februum*, purification], *n.* The second month of the year, containing in ordinary years 28 days, and in the bissextile or leap-year 29.

fecal, etc. [FÆCAL]. **fecial** [FETIAL].

feck (fek) [Sc.; etym. doubtful; perh. corr. of EFFECT], *n.* Efficacy, strength, vigour; space, value, quantity, number; the bulk, the greatest part. **feckless,** *a.* Puny, weak, feeble in mind; improvident. **feckly,** *adv.* Mostly, chiefly; almost.

***fecks, fegs** [FAY (2)].

fecula (fek′ ū lȧ) [as foll.], *n.* Lees, sediment, from vegetable infusions, esp. starch.

feculent (fek′ ū lėnt) [F. *féculent*, L. *fæculentus*, from *fæx*, *fæces*, FÆCES], *a.* Full of dregs, lees, or sediment; muddy, turbid; filthy, fetid. **feculence, *-lency,** *n.*

fecund (fek′ ůnd, fē′ kůnd) [F. *fécond*, L. *fēcundus*], *a.* Fruitful, prolific, fertile. **fecundate** (fek′ ůn dāt, fē′ kůn dāt), *v.t.* To make fruitful or prolific; to impregnate. **fecundation** (-dā′ shůn), *n.* **fecundity** (fė kŭn′ di ti), *n.* The quality of being fruitful or prolific; the power or property of producing young or germinating; (*fig.*) power of production or creation; richness of invention. **fecundize** (fek′ ůn dīz), *v.t.*

fed, *past or p.p.* [FEED]. **fed up!** (*slang*) Surfeited, sick or tired (of). **to be fed up with:** To have had more than enough of, to be sick of.

***fedarie** (fed′ ȧ ri) [var. of *feodary*, FEUDARY], *n.* (*Shak.*) A confederate.

federal (fed′ ėr ȧl) [F. *fédéral*, from L. *fædus -eris*, a treaty, covenant, cogn. with *fidēs*, FAITH], *a.* Pertaining to or based upon a treaty, league, or contract; (*Theol.*) arising from or based upon the doctrine of a covenant between God and man; (*Polit.*) relating to, arising from, or supporting a polity formed by the union of several states; relating to such a Government as distinguished from the separate states; supporting the cause of the Union in the American Civil War. *n.* A supporter of the principle of federation, esp. a supporter of the American Union in the Civil War. **Federal Bureau of Investigation (F.B.I.):** (*U.S.A.*) A branch of the Department of Justice concerned with internal security, espionage and sabotage. **Federal Party,** *n.* (*U.S. Hist.*) A party existing from 1787 to *c.* 1830, originally under the leadership of Alexander Hamilton, supporting the Federal constitution and centralization of government. **federacy,** *n.* A federation of states. **federalism,** *n.* **federalist,** *n.* **federalize,** *v.t.* To bring together in a political confederacy. *v.i.* To combine into a political confederacy. **federally,** *adv.*

federate (fed′ ĕr āt) [as prec.], *v.t.* To organize as a federal group of states; to federalize; to bring together for a common object. *v.i.* To combine and form a federal group; to league together for a common object. *a.* (-ȧt) United under a federal government; leagued together.

federation (fed ĕ rā′ shůn), *n.* The act of uniting in a confederacy; a confederated body; a federal government. **Imperial Federation:** (*Polit.*) The doctrine that the colonies in the British Empire should combine to share the control and expense of the whole Empire. **Social Democratic Federation:** The earliest British socialist party, intended especially for the promotion of a reform movement among the middle classes. **federationist,** *n.* **federative,** *a.* **federatively,** *adv.*

fedora (fe dôr′ ȧ), *n.* (*Am. colloq.*) A soft felt hat with a curled brim.

fee (fē) [A.-F. *fee*, O.F. *fé*, *fieu*, *fief*, prob. through med. L. *feodum*, *feudum*, or *fevum*, from O.H.G. *fehu*, payment, wages, money, property, cattle (cp. A.-S. *feoh*, Dut. *vee*, L. *pecus*, cattle, *pecunia*, money)], *n.* (*Feudal Law*) Land and estate held of a superior; (*Law*) a freehold estate of inheritance; *ownership, property; payment or remuneration to a public officer or a professional man for the execution of official functions or for the performance of a professional service; a charge paid for a privilege, such as admission to an examination, society, public building, etc.; charge, payment; gratuity; *perquisite; (*Sc.*) wages; *property, estate, esp. cattle. *v.t.* To pay a fee or reward to; to engage for a fee, to hire; *to bribe; (*Sc.*) to hire oneself out. **to hold in fee:** (*Law*) To own absolutely. **retaining fee:** A payment made to a lawyer, doctor, or other professional man engaging his services for a case, etc. ***fee-grief,** *n.* A private sorrow. **fee-simple,** *n.* (*Law*) An estate held by a person in his own right, without limitation to any particular class of heirs. **fee-tail,** *n.* (*Law*) An estate entailed to the possessor's heirs. **feeless,** *a.*

feeble (fē′ bel) [A.-F. *feble*, O.F. *foible* (F. *faible*), L. *flēbilis*, mournful, from *flēre*, to weep], *a.* Weak, destitute of physical strength; infirm, debilitated; lacking in force, vigour, or energy; lacking in moral or intellectual power; (*fig.*) ineffective, pointless, insipid; dim, faint; *worthless, poor. **n.* A feeble person; weakness; (*Fencing*) the foible of a sword. *v.t.* To weaken. **feeble-minded,** *a.* Intellectually deficient, imbecile; wanting in resolution. **feebleness,** ***feebless,** *n.* **feeblish,** *a.* **feebly,** *adv.*

feed (1) (fēd) [A.-S. *fēdan* (cp. Dut. *voeden*, Goth. *fōdjan*, O.H.G. *fuotan*, see also FOOD], *v.t.* To give food to; to put food into the mouth of; to supply with that which is necessary to existence, continuance, or development; to cause (cattle) to graze; to supply with material (as a machine); to keep well supplied; to serve as food or nourishment for; to nourish, to cause to grow or develop; to fatten; to cause (land) to be grazed; to gratify; *to entertain, to edify. *v.i.* To take food; to eat; to subsist (on or upon); to grow fat; (*fig.*) to support oneself; to indulge or gratify oneself mentally. *n.* Food, fodder, pasturage; the act of feeding or giving food; amount of food or provender given to horses, cattle, etc., at a time; (*colloq.*) a meal, a feast; the operation of supplying a machine with material, or of bringing a tool into operation; the machinery for this; the amount supplied; the charge for a gun. **to feed down:** To supply (material) continuously; to bring down (a tool) into continuous operation; (of cattle, etc.) to eat away by pasturing. **at feed:** Eating, grazing. **off one's feed:** Without appetite. **on the feed:** Feeding, eating; (of fish) taking or looking out for food. **feed-pipe,** *n.* The pipe carrying water to the boilers of steam-engines. **feed-pump,** *n.* A force-pump for supplying water to boilers. **feed-tank, -trough,** *n.* A cistern or trough holding a water-supply for locomotives.

feeder (fē′ dėr), *n.* One who supplies food or nourishment; one who fattens cattle; one who eats, esp. one who eats in a certain manner as a *quick* feeder; a feeding-bottle; a child's bib; a tributary stream; an artificial channel supplying a canal, etc.; a branch railway; (*Elec.*) a wire, usu. in pairs, carrying electricity to various points in a system; the apparatus feeding a machine; one who nourishes, encourages, or supports; *a dependant, a parasite. **feeding,** *n.* That which is eaten; food. **feeding-bottle,** *n.* A bottle for supplying liquid nutriment to infants. **feeding-cup,** *n.* (*Med.*) A specially shaped cup for feeding a patient in bed. **feeding-ground,** *n.* A place where animals or fish resort for food.

feed (2), *past or p.p.* [FEE].

fee-faw-fum (fē faw fŭm′) [spoken by the Giant in *Jack the Giant-Killer*], *int.* A sham bloodthirsty exclamation. *n.* Nonsense or mummery to frighten the ignorant or childish.

feel (fēl) [A.-S. *fēlan* (cp. Dut. *voelen*, O.H.G. *fuolan*, G. *fühlen*, also A.-S. *folm*, L. *palma*, Gr. *palamē*, palm of the hand)], *v.t.* To perceive by the touch; to have the sense of touch; to have a sensation of, otherwise than by the nerves of sight, hearing, taste, or smell; to be conscious of; to have the emotions stirred by; to experience, to undergo; to be affected by; to know in one's inner consciousness, to be convinced (that); to examine or explore by the touch; to touch, to handle, to try, or find out by handling or groping. *v.i.* To have perception by the sense or act of touching; to be conscious of a certain sensation (as cold, wet, hungry, or tired); (*refl.*) to be conscious of (oneself) as in a certain state (as afraid, anxious, busy, etc.); to be stirred in one's emotions; to seem to the sense of touch, to produce a certain sensation (as *the air feels damp or cold*). *n.* The sense of touch; characteristic sensation of something, esp. one related to that of touch; perception, esp. of an emotional kind. **to feel after:** To try to find out by the sense of touch, to search for as by groping. **to feel for:** To feel after; to have sympathy or compassion for.

feeler (fē′ lėr), *n.* One who feels; (*fig.*) any device to ascertain the designs, wishes, or opinions of others; a scout; (*Zool.*) a generic term for various organs of touch in invertebrate animals.

feeling (fē′ ling), *a.* Perceiving by the touch; easily affected or moved, sensitive, of great sensibility; expressive of or manifesting great sensibility; affecting. *n.* The sense of touch; the sensation produced when a material body is touched; a physical sensation of any kind; a mental impression, consciousness, conviction; emotion, sentiment; sensitiveness, sensibility; (*pl.*) susceptibilities, sympathies; (*Psych.*) a mental state involving pleasure or pain, the emotional faculty, intuitive belief; (*Art*) qualities expressing emotion. **feelingly,** *adv.*

feet [FOOT].

***fegs** [FAY (2)].

feign (fān) [O.F. *feindre*, L. *fingere*], *v.t.* To invent, to pretend, to simulate, to counterfeit; *to imagine, to represent in fiction; *to dissemble, to hide. *v.i.* To dissimulate; to make pretences. **feigned issue,** *n.* (*Law*) An action arranged so as to try a question of right. **feignedly,** *adv.* **feignedness,** *n.*

feint (1) (fānt) [F. *feinte*, from *feindre*, see prec.], *n.* A feigned or sham attack; a pretence of aiming at one point while another is the real object; a pretence. *v.i.* To make a feint or pretended attack (upon, against, or at). **a.* Feigned, counterfeit.

feint (2), *a.* and *adv.* [FAINT].

feldspar (feld′ spar) [G. *feldspath* (*feld*, field, *spath*, spar)], *n.* (*Min.*) A name including several minerals found abundantly in igneous rocks, varying in colour, crystalline form, and chemical composition, but chiefly silicates of alumina combined with some other mineral. **feldsparization** (-zā′ shŭn), *n.* (*Geol.*) Alteration of other material into feldspar. **feldspathic** (feld spăth′ ik), **feldspathoid, feldspathose** (feld spăth′ ōz), *a.* Pertaining to feldspar; having feldspar in its composition.

felicide (fē′ li sīd) [L. *fēlis*, cat, -CIDE], *n.* Killing of a cat.

felicific (fē li sif′ ik) [L. *fēlīcificus*, from *fēlix -īcis*, happy, -FIC], *a.* Producing happiness.

felicitate (fė lis′ i tāt) [L. *fēlīcitāt-*, p.p. stem of *fēlīcitāre*, from *fēlix -īcis*, happy], *v.t.* *To confer happiness upon; to congratulate. **a.* (-tȧt) Made happy. **felicitation** (-tā′ shŭn), *n.* Congratulation. **felicitous,** *a.* Happy, delightful, prosperous; well-suited, apt, well-expressed; charming in manner, operation, etc. **felicitously,** *adv.* **felicitousness,** *n.*

felicity (fe lis′ i ti) [as prec.], *n.* Happiness, blissfulness, a source of happiness, a blessing; appropriateness, neatness; a happy turn or expression; a happy way or faculty of expressing, behaving, etc.

felid (fē′ lid) [L. *fēlis*, a cat], *n.* (*Zool.*) One of the *Felidæ*, a genus of fissiped carnivora, containing lions, tigers, leopards, pumas, and cats.

feline (fē′ līn), *a.* Belonging to the *Felidæ*; of or pertaining to cats, cat-like; (*fig.*) sly, stealthy; cruel. *n.* One of the *Felidæ*. **felinity** (fė lin′ i ti), *n.*

fell (1) (fel) [A.-S. *fiellan*, casual, from *feallan*, to FALL (cp. Dut. *vellen*, Icel. *fella*, G. *fällen*, all causatives)], *v.t.* To knock down; to bring to the ground; to hew or cut down; (*Sewing*) to finish with a fell. *n.* A quantity of timber felled; (*Sewing*) a seam or hem in which one edge is folded over another and sewed down. **feller,** *n.* One who fells or cuts down trees.

fell (2) (fel) [A.-S. *fel*, skin (cp. Dut. *vel*, G. *fell*, also L. *pellis*, Gr. *pella*)], *n.* The hide or skin of an animal, esp. if covered with hair; a fleece; a thick woolly or hairy covering; a dense, matted growth (of hair, etc.). **fellmonger** (fel′ mŭng gėr), *n.* A dealer in hides and skins.

fell (3) (fel) [Icel. *fjall*, prob. conn. with G. *fels*, a rock], *n.* A rocky hill; a lofty tract of barren moorland.

fell (4) (fel) [O.F. *fel*, late L. *fello*, *felo*, FELON], *a.* Cruel, savage, fierce; terrible, deadly, dire; (*Sc.*) huge; *keen, spirited, eager, angry, enraged. **adv.* Cruelly; (*Sc.*) hugely, greatly. **felly** (1), *adv.*

***fell** (5) (fel) [L. *fel*, gall], *n.* Bitterness, anger, resentment, rancour.

***fell** (6), *past* [FALL].

fellah (fel′ å) [Arab. *fellāh*, pl. *fellahin*], *n.* (*pl.* **fellaheen**) An Egyptian agricultural labourer or peasant.

fellic (fel′ ik), **fellinic** (fė lin′ ik) [L. *fel*, gall, see -IN, -IC], *a.* Of or pertaining to gall.

felloe (fel′ i, -ō) [A.-S. *felg* (cp. Dut. *velg*, G. *felge*)], *n.* One of the curved segments of a wheel, joined together by dowels to form the rim; the whole rim of a wheel.

fellow (fel′ ō) [Icel. *fēlagi*, a partner, one who lays down fee or goods in partnership, from *fē*, property, cogn. with A.-S. *feoh*, cattle, see FEE], *n.* An associate, a comrade; a partner; a companion; a contemporary; one of the same kind or species; an equal in rank, a peer, a compeer; one of a pair; a person or thing like or equal to another, a counterpart, a match; a member of an incorporated society; an incorporated member of a college; the holder of a fellowship or stipendiary position endowed for purposes of research; (*Am.*) one of the trustees of a college; a man, a boy; a person of little estimation; *a partaker, a sharer; (*in comb.*) one associated with oneself or of the same class or relationship. *v.t.* To match, to pair with, to suit; *to partake with, share (in); *to accompany. **fellow-commoner,** *n.* (*Univ.*) One who has the right to dine with the fellows. **fellow-craft,** *n.* A Freemason of the second degree. **fellow-creature,** *n.* One of the same race, the work of the same Creator. **fellow-feeling,** *n.* Sympathy; joint interest. **fellow traveller,** *n.* One who without declaring himself a Communist sympathizes with the aims of the Communist Party.

fellowship (fel′ ō ship), *n.* The condition or state of being a fellow; companionship, association, close intercourse, friendliness, cordiality of feeling, community of interest, participation; a body of associates; a brotherhood, a fraternity; a company, a corporation; the dignity of fellow in a college or learned society; an endowment for maintaining a graduate engaged in research; (*Relig.*) membership of a community partaking of Holy Communion together; (*Arith.*) the rule by which profit or loss is divided among partners in proportion to the capital invested. *v.t.* (*Relig.*) To admit to fellowship. *v.i.* (*Relig. chiefly Am.*) To associate with, to unite with.

felly (2) [FELLOE].

felo-de-se (fel′ ō dė sē) [A.-L., felon upon himself (see foll.)], *n.* (*pl.* ***felos-***) One who commits felony by self-murder; self-murder, suicide.

felon (fel′ ǒn) [O.F. from late L. *fellōnem*, nom. *fello*, *felo* (perh. from L. *fel*, gall)], *n.* One who has committed a felony; *a villain; a whitlow or abscess close to the nail. *a.* Cruel, malignant, malicious; wicked, murderous. **feloness,** *n.* **felonious** (fė lō′ ni ǔs), *a.* Of the nature of a felony; (*Law*) done with deliberate purpose to commit a crime; that has committed felony; villainous, malignant, malicious; (*colloq.*) thievish. **feloniously,** *adv.* ***feloniousness,** *n.* ***felonious,** *a.* Wicked, malicious; savage, fierce. ***felonry,** *n.* A body of felons; (*Austral. hist.*) British convicts. **felony,** *n.* An offence of a heinous character, conviction for which formerly involved loss of lands and goods; an offence of graver character than that of a misdemeanour; *crime, wickedness, sin.

felsite (fel′ sīt) [from *fels-*, corr. form, see FELDSPAR], *n.* (*Min.*) Felstone. **felsitic** (-sit′ ik), *a.*

felspar, etc. [FELDSPAR].

felstone (fel′ stōn) [G. *felsstein* (*fels*, rock, *stein*, stone)], *n.* (*Min.*) Feldspar occurring in compact masses.

felt (1) (felt) [A.-S., cp. Dut. *vilt*, G. *filz*], *n.* A kind of cloth made of wool or wool and cotton compacted together by rolling, beating, and pressure, with lees or size; a piece of this stuff; an article made of it, a felt hat. *v.t.* To make into felt; to cover with felt; to press into a compact mass. *v.i.* To become matted together. **felt-grain,** *n.* The grain of wood whose direction is from the pith to the bark. **felt hat,** *n.* A hat made of felt. ***felt-lock,** *n.* A matted and unkempt lock of hair. **felt-maker,** *n.* **felter** (1), *n.* A maker of or worker in felt; a bird that makes its nest with or as with felt. ***felter** (2), *v.t.* and *i.* To mat or clot together like felt. **felting,** *n.* The act or process of making felt. **felty,** *a.*

felt (2), *past & p.p.* [FEEL].

felucca (fė lŭk′ å) [It., prob. from Arab.], *n.* A small vessel used in the Mediterranean, propelled by oars or lateen sails or both.

female (fē′ māl) [O.F. *femelle*, L. *fēmella*, dim. of *fēmina*, a woman], *a.* Denoting the sex which brings forth young or lays eggs from which new individuals are developed; (*Bot.*) having a pistil, but no stamens, capable of being fertilized and producing fruit; of, pertaining to, or characteristic of woman or womanhood; womanly, feminine; (*Mech.*) fitted to receive the corresponding male part (as a FEMALE SCREW). *n.* A female person; (*vulg.*) a woman or girl; (*Zool.*) an individual of the female sex. **female die,** *n.* The concave die, into which the male or convex die is struck. **female rhymes,** *n.pl.* (*Pros.*) Rhymes in which two syllables, one accented and the other unaccented, correspond at the end of each line, as *fable, table*; *notion, motion.* **female screw,** *n.* The spiral-threaded cavity into which another (male) screw works.

feme covert (fem′ kuv′ ėrt) [A.-F. and O.F. (F. *femme couverte*)], *n.* (*Law*) A married woman. **feme sole** (sōl) [A.-F.], *n.* (*Law*) An unmarried woman, spinster, or widow; a married woman having rights of property or trade independent of her husband.

feminine (fem′ i nin) [O.F. *feminin*, L. *fēminīnus*, from *fēmina*, woman], *a.* Of, pertaining to, or characteristic of women or the female sex; womanly; effeminate; soft, tender, delicate; of the female sex; (*Gram.*) belonging to the gender denoting females; (*Pros.*) having two syllables, the first accented (of rhymes). **feminine cæsura,** *n.* A cæsura following an unstressed syllable, as in 'And eat our pot of honey on the grave.' **femininely,** *adv.* **feminineness,** *n.* **femininity** (-nin′ i ti), **feminity,** *n.* The qualities or manners becoming a woman. **feminality** (-năl′ i ti), *n.* The quality of being female; the characteristic nature of woman or the female sex; something characteristic of female nature. **femineity** (-nē′ i ti), *n.* Womanliness; womanishness. **feminize,** *v.t.* To make feminine. *v.i.* To become feminine.

feminism (fem′ in izm), *n.* Advocacy of the claims of women to political, economic and social equality with men. **feminist,** *n.*

femme de chambre (fam′ dė shanbr′) [F., bedroom woman], *n.* (*pl.* ***femmes***) A chambermaid; a lady's-maid.

femur (fē′ mŭr) [L. *femur -oris*, the thigh], *n.* (*pl.* **femora**) The thigh-bone; (*Ent.*) the third joint of the leg in insects. **femoral** (fem′ ŏr ål), *a.* Of or belonging to the thigh. *n.* The femoral artery.

fen (fen) [A.-S. *fenn* (cp. Dut. *ven*, *veen*, G. *fenne*)], *n.* Low, flat, and marshy land, esp. the low-lying districts in the east of England, partially drained and abounding in broads or lakes; a marsh, a bog. **fen-berry,** *n.* The cranberry, *Vaccinium oxycoccos.* **fen-duck,** *n.* The shoveller. **fen-fire,** *n.* The will-o'-the-wisp. **fenlander, -man,** *n.* An inhabitant of the fens. **fen-pole,** *n.* A pole used in the fens for jumping ditches. **fen-reeve,** *n.* An officer in charge of the common lands in the fens. **fen-runners,** *n.pl.* A long kind of skates suitable for high speed. **fenny,** *a.* **fenland,** *n.* A fen; the fens.

fence (fens) [short for DEFENCE], *n.* A structure serving to enclose and protect a piece of ground, or to keep cattle from straying, as a wall, a hedge, a paling, a bank, a line of rails or posts, etc.; a guard-plate, guide, or gauge of various kinds in machinery, etc.; the art of fencing or sword-play; (*fig.*) skill in debate; repartee; equivocation; (*slang*) a purchaser or receiver of stolen goods, or a place where such are purchased or deposited. *v.t.* To defend, shield, or protect; to ward (off); to enclose, encircle, or protect with or as with a fence; to parry. *v.t.* To practise the art of sword-play; to use a sword skilfully; to defend oneself or repel attack skilfully; (*fig.*) to argue adroitly, to equivocate; (*slang*) to deal in stolen goods. **dog-leg fence** [DOG]. **master of fence:** A skilled fencer or swordsman; an expert debater or dialectician. **ring-fence:** A fence encircling a whole estate. **sunk fence:** A fence set along the bottom of a ditch; a ditch forming a fence. **to sit on the fence:** To remain neutral in respect to opposing policies. **over the fence:** (*Austral. colloq.*) Unreasonable, utterly indecent. **Virginia fence, worm fence:** (*Am.*) A zigzag fence of split rails without posts. **fence-month, -season, -time,** *n.* The fawning month (about 9 June to 9 July), during which deer-hunting is forbidden; a close time for fish. **fenced,** *a.* Enclosed with a fence; fortified. **fenceless,** *a.* Unenclosed; undefended, defenceless. **fencer,** *n.* One skilled in fencing; a builder of fences; a horse good at leaping fences. **fencing,** *n.* The act of making fences; (*collect.*) fences, a railing or railings; materials for fences; the act or art of using a sword or foil in attack or defence; a protection or guard round any dangerous piece of machinery; (*fig.*) equivocation, parrying of argument. **fencing-cully,** *n.* (*slang*) A receiver of stolen goods. **fencing-crib, -ken, -repository,** *n.* (*slang*) A place for receiving stolen goods.

fencible (fen' sibl) [short for DEFENSIBLE], *n.* A soldier enlisted for home defence. *a.* (*chiefly Sc.*) Capable of defence or of being defended; belonging to the Fencibles.

fend (fend) [short for DEFEND], *v.t.* To keep off, ward off; *to defend; (*Sc.*) to provide for, to support. *v.i.* To provide or to get a living (for); (*Sc.*) to strive, to resist, to offer opposition.

fender (fen' dėr) [from prec.], *n.* One who or that which serves to defend, protect, or ward off anything hurtful or dangerous; a piece of furniture, usually of iron or brass, placed on the hearth to confine the ashes; a piece of timber or mass of rope to protect the side of a vessel from injury by collision; (*Am.*) the wing or mudguard of a motor-car. **fender-beam,** *n.* A beam hung over the side of a vessel to protect her from injury by ice. **fender-pile,** *n.* A piece of timber placed in front of dock walls and similar structures to protect against blows from vessels. **fender-stool,** *n.* A long stool placed close to the fender before a fire. **fenderless,** *a.*

fenestella (fen ės tel' å) [L. dim. of *fenestra*, see foll.], *n.* (*Arch.*) A niche on the south side of the altar containing the piscina, and often the credence.

fenestra (fė nes' trå) [L., a window], *n.* (*pl.* **-træ**) (*Anat.*) A window-like aperture in a bone; (*Ent., Bot., etc., pl.*) transparent spots or apertures in wings, leaves, etc. **fenestral** (fė nes' trål), *a.* *Of or pertaining to a window; (*Biol.*) having small transparent spots or *fenestræ*. **fenestral bandage:** (*Surg.*) One having openings through which matter can discharge. **fenestrate** (fė nes' trāt), *a.* (*Bot.*) Applied to leaves in which there is only a net-work of filamentous cells formed; (*Ent.*) applied to the naked hyaline transparent spots on the wings of butterflies. **fenestrated,** *a.* (*Arch.*) Furnished with windows; (*Anat.*) fenestral. **fenestration** (-trā' shůn), *n.* (*Arch.*) The construction, arrangement, or mode of design of windows; (*Nat. Hist.*) the formation of *fenestræ*; the condition of having *fenestræ*.

Fenian (fē' ni ån) [O.Ir. *Fēne*, a name of the ancient Irish, confused with *Fīann*, the warriors who defended Ireland in the time of Finn], *n.* A member of an Irish secret society which was formed in America about 1858, having for its object the overthrow of the British Government in Ireland, and the establishment of an independent republic. *a.* Pertaining to this society or to Fenianism. **Fenianism,** *n.*

fenks (fenks) [etym. unknown], *n.pl.* Refuse of whale-blubber, used for manure.

fennec (fen' ėk) [Arab. *fenek*], *n.* A small fox-like animal, *Canis zerda*, common in Africa.

fennel (fen' ėl) [A.-S. *finol*, *finugl*, L. *fæniculum*, dim. of *fænum*, hay], *n.* A fragrant umbelliferous plant with yellow flowers, *Fæniculum vulgare*. **fennel-flower,** *n.* A herb of the genus *Nigella*, such as ragged lady, *N. damascena*, or the nutmeg-flower, *N. sativa*.

fens [FAINS].

fent (fent) [F. *fente*, from *fendre*, L. *findere*, to cleave], *n.* The opening left in a garment (as in a shirt-sleeve) for convenience of putting it on; a crack, a rift; a remnant.

fenugreek (fen' ū grēk) [F. *fenugrec*, L. *fænugræcum* (*fænum*, hay, *Græcum*, neut. a., Greek)], *n.* A leguminous plant, *Trigonella fænum-Græcum*, the seeds of which are used in animal condiments.

***feod** [FEUD (2)].

feoff (fef) [O.F. *feoffer*, *fieffer*, from *fief*, FEE], *v.t.* (*Law*) To grant possession, to enfeoff; *to endow. *n.* A fief. **feoffee** (fef ē'), *n.* One who is invested with an estate by feoffment. **feoffor,** *n.* One who grants a fief. **feoffment,** *n.* The conveyance of any corporeal hereditament to another, accompanied by actual delivery of possession; the mode of such conveyance.

feracious (fė rā' shůs) [L. *fērāx -ācis*, fruitful, from *ferre*, to bear], *a.* Fruitful, fertile. **feracity** (-răs' i ti), *n.*

feræ naturæ (fēr' ē nā tū' rē) [L., of a wild nature]. *a.* Of a wild nature or state (applied to deer, hares, pheasants, etc., as distinguished from domesticated animals). **feral** (fēr' ål), *a.* Wild, savage; lapsed from a domesticated into a wild state; uncultivated; (*fig.*) brutal, savage.

fer-de-lance (fâr dė lans) [F., lance-head (*fer*, iron)], *n.* The yellow viper of Martinique, *Bothrops lanceolatus*.

***fere** (1) (fēr) [M.E. *fere*, A.-S. *gefēra*, cogn. with *faran*, to go, to FARE], *n.* A mate, a companion; a consort, a spouse.

***fere** (2) [Icel. *færr*, or prec.], *a.* Able, strong, whole.

feretory (fer' ė tŏr i) [O.F. *fiertre*, L. *feretrum*, Gr. *pheretron*, from *pherein*, to bear], *n.* The bier or shrine in which relics of saints were borne in procession, a reliquary, a chapel or place in a church in which shrines were kept.

ferial (fēr' i ål) [F. *férial*, L. *fēriālis*, from *fēria*, a holiday, see FAIR (1)], *a.* (*Eccles.*) Pertaining to ordinary week-days, such as are not festival or fast days; pertaining to holidays; formerly used in Scotland of days on which the courts did not sit.

ferine (fēr' īn) [L. *ferīnus*, from *fera*, wild animal], *a.* Wild, savage, untamed; bestial, brutish. ***ferinely,** *adv.*

Feringhee (fėr ing' gē) [corr. of FRANK (1)], *n.* The name given by the Hindus to the English and other Europeans, formerly more especially to Portuguese settlers and their descendants.

***ferly** (fēr' li) [A.-S. *fǣrlic*, sudden, from *fǣr*, see FEAR], *a.* Sudden; strange; marvellous. *n.* A marvel, a wonder. *v.i.* (*Sc.*) To wonder, to be amazed (at).

ferment (fĕr′ mėnt) [F., from L. *fermentum*, from root of *fervēre*, to boil], *n.* Any substance, organic or inorganic, which causes fermentation; leaven; fermentation, internal motion of the constituent parts of a fluid; (*fig.*) commotion, tumult, agitation. *v.t.* (fėr ment′) To excite fermentation in; to rouse, to agitate, to excite. *v.i.* To be in a state of fermentation, to effervesce; (*fig.*) to be agitated, as by violent emotions. **fermentable,** *a.* ***fermentability** (-bil′-), *n.*

fermentation (fĕr mėn tā′ shủn) [L. *fermentātio -ōnem*, as prec.], *n.* A process excited in certain substances or liquids by living organisms or chemical agents, with evolution of heat, effervescence, and chemical decomposition; (*fig.*) commotion, agitation, excitement. **fermentative** (fėr men′ tȧ tiv), *a.* Causing, produced by, or of the nature of fermentation. **fermentescible** (-tes′ ibl), *a.* Able to cause fermentation; capable of fermentation.

fermeture (fĕr′ mė tyủr, -chủr) [F., from *fermer*, to shut], *n.* The mechanism for closing the breech of a gun or other fire-arm.

fern (fĕrn) [A.-S. *fearn* (cp. Dut. *varen*, G. *farn*, also Sansk. *parna* and Gr. *pteron*, wing, feather)], *n.* A cryptogamic plant springing from a rhizome, and having the reproductive organs on the lower surface of fronds or leaves, which are often divided in a graceful, feathery form. **fern bird,** *n.* (*N. Zealand*). The grass-bird or N.Z. pipit. **fern-owl,** *n.* The goat-sucker or nightjar, *Caprimulgus Europæus*. **fern-seed,** *n.* The seeds or spores of ferns, formerly supposed to render a person invisible. **fernshaw,** *n.* A fern-brake. **fern-tree** (*Austral.*) [TREE-FERN]. **fernery,** *n.* A place where ferns are cultivated. **fernless,** *a.* **ferny,** *a.*

ferocious (fė rō′ shủs) [L. *ferōci-*, stem of *ferox*, cogn. with *ferus*, wild], *a.* Fierce, savage, cruel, barbarous. **ferociously,** *adv.* ***ferociousness,** *n.* **ferocity** (fė ros′ i ti), *n.* The state or quality of being ferocious, savageness, fierceness, wildness, fury; a ferocious act.

-ferous [L. *fer-*, stem of *ferre*, to bear, -OUS], *suf.* Bearing, producing, having, as in *auriferous*, *fossiliferous*.

ferox (fer′ oks) [mod. L. *Salmo ferox*, the fierce salmon], *n.* The great lake-trout.

***ferrandine** (fĕr′ ȧn din), **farandine** (făr′-) [prob. from F. *Ferrand*, name of inventor], *n.* A mixed stuff of silk and other materials.

ferrara (fė ra′ rȧ) [perh. from native of It. town *Ferrara*, or from It. *ferrajo*, cutter, L. *ferrārius*, from *ferrum*, iron], *n.* A broadsword of special excellence, often called an *Andrew Ferrara* after Andrea Ferrara, one of a famous family of swordsmiths in the 16th century.

ferrate (fer′ āt) [L. *ferrum*, iron], *n.* (*Chem.*) A salt of ferric acid. **ferreous** (fer′ ė ủs) [L. *ferreus*, as prec.], *a.* Of or pertaining to iron; of the nature of iron; made of iron.

ferret (1) (fer′ ėt) [O.F. *furet*, late L. *fūrētus*, identified with *fūrō -ōnem*, L. *fūr*, robber], *n.* A partially tamed variety of polecat, *Putorius fœtidus*, used for killing rats and driving rabbits out of their holes; (*fig.*) a sharp-eyed searcher or detective. *v.t.* To drive out of a hole or clear (ground) with ferrets; to hunt or take with ferrets; (*fig.*) to search (out) by persevering means; *to worry. *v.i.* To hunt rabbits, etc. with a ferret; (*fig.*) to search or rummage about (for). **ferreter,** *n.* One who ferrets. **ferrety,** *a.*

ferret (2) (fer′ ėt) [prob. from It. *fioretti*, a kind of silk, pl. of *fioretto*, dim of *fiore*, flower, L. *flōrem*, nom. *flōs*], *n.* A tape made of silk or cotton. ***ferret-silk,** *n.* Floss-silk.

ferri- [L. *ferrum*, iron], *comb. form.* (*Chem.*) Denoting a compound of iron in the ferric state (cp. FERRO-). **ferriferous** (fė rif′ ėr ủs) [-FEROUS], *a.* Yielding iron. **ferricyanic** [CYANIC], *a.* Of or pertaining to a compound of iron in its ferric state with cyanogen.

ferriage (fer′ i ȧj), *n.* The fare paid for conveyance by a ferry.

ferric (fer′ ik) [L. *ferrum*, iron], *a.* Of, pertaining to, or extracted from iron; containing trivalent iron.

ferrite (fe′ rīt), *n.* A sintered ceramic consisting of a mixture of ferric oxide and other metallic oxides, which possesses magnetic properties.

ferro- [L. *ferrum*, iron], *comb. form.* (*Min.*) Denoting a substance containing iron; (*Chem.*) denoting a compound of iron in the ferrous state (cp. FERRI-). **ferro-calcite** (fer ȯ kăl′ sīt), *n.* Calcite containing carbonate of iron and turning brown on exposure. **ferro-concrete,** *n.* Concrete strengthened by incorporation of iron bars, strips, etc.; reinforced concrete. **ferrocyanic** (fer ȯ sī ăn′ ik), *a.* (*Chem.*) Iron in the ferrous state and cyanogen. **ferrocyanic acid,** *n.* A white crystalline powder called also **ferrocyanhydric acid**, derived from iron and cyanogen. **ferrocyanide,** *n.* A salt of ferrocyanic acid. **ferrocyanogen** (fer ȯ sī ăn′ ȯ jen), *n.* A radical supposed to be contained in ferrocyanides. **ferromagnetic,** *a.* Acting magnetically like iron. *n.* A substance acting thus. **ferro-silicon,** *n.* (*Chem.*) A compound of silicon and iron added to molten iron to give it a larger proportion of silicon. **ferrotype** (fer′ ȯ tīp), *n.* A positive photograph on a sensitized film laid on a thin iron plate; the iron plate used in this process.

ferrous (fer′ ủs) [as prec.], *a.* (*Chem.*) Of, pertaining to, or containing divalent iron.

ferruginous (fė roo′ ji nủs) [L. *ferrūginus*, from *ferrūgo -inis*, from *ferrum*, iron], *a.* Containing iron or iron-rust; of the colour of iron-rust. **ferruginous deposits:** (*Geol.*) Rocks containing sufficient iron ore to make it worth mining. ***ferrugo** (fė roo′ gō), *n.* The rust, a disease of plants. **ferruginate** (-ji nāt), *v.t.*

ferrule (fer′ ủl) [formerly *verrel*, O.F. *virelle* (F. *virole*), late L. *virola*, L. *viriola*, dim. of *viriæ*, bracelets], *n.* A metallic ring or cap on the handle of a tool, the end of a stick, the joint of a fishing rod, a post, etc., to strengthen it; a short piece of pipe screwed into a main to form a connexion with a service-pipe. **ferruled,** *a.*

ferry (fer′ i) [A.-S. *ferian*, from *faran*, to FARE], *v.t.* To transport over a river, strait, or other narrow water, in a boat, barge, etc. *v.i.* To pass across narrow water in a boat, etc. *n.* The passage where a ferry-boat plies to carry passengers and goods across a river, etc.; the provision of such a method of transport; the right of ferrying and charging toll for so doing; a ferry-boat. **ferry-boat,** *n.* A boat used at a ferry. **ferry-bridge,** *n.* A large vessel used for carrying trains across a ferry; (*Am.*) the landing-stage at a ferry, esp. on a tidal river where it rises and falls with the tide. **ferryman,** *n.*

fertile (fĕr′ tīl, -til) [O.F. *fertil*, L. *fertilis*, from *ferre*, to bear], *a.* Productive, fruitful, prolific; having abundant resources; quick, ready; *abundant. **fertility** (-til′ i ti), *n.*

fertilize (fĕr′ ti līz), *v.t.* To make fertile or productive; to make rich (as soil); (*Bot., etc.*) to impregnate, fecundate. **fertilizable,** *a.* **fertilization** (-zā′ shủn), *n.* **fertilizer,** *n.* A fertilizing agent; (*Agric.*) a chemical applied to the soil to improve its growth-promoting qualities and modify its acidity or alkalinity.

ferula (fer′ ủ lȧ) [L., a rod, orig. giant fennel], *n.* (*pl.* **-læ**) The sceptre of the emperors of the Eastern Empire; (*Bot.*) a genus of umbelliferous plants, from the shores of the Mediterranean and Persia, yielding gum-resin, typified by the giant fennel; a ferule. **ferulaceous** (lā′ shủs), *a.* Of or pertaining to canes or reeds; having a reed-like stem. **ferule** (fer′ ủl), *n.* A rod or cane used to punish children in school. *v.t.* To punish with a ferule.

fervent (fĕr′ vėnt) [O.F., from L. *fervens, -ntem*, pres.p. of *fervēre*, to boil], *a.* Hot, boiling, glowing; ardent, earnest, zealous, vehement. **fervently,** *adv.* **fervency,** *n.* ***fervescent** (fėr ves′ ėnt) [L. *fervescens, -ntem*, pres.p. of *fervescere*, incept. of *fervēre*], *a.* Growing hot.

fervid (fĕr′ vid) [L. *fervidus*, as prec.], *a.* (*Poet.*) Burning, very hot, fervent; impassioned. **fervidly,** *adv.* **fervidness,** *n.* **fervour** (fĕr′ vŏr) [O.F. *fervor*, L. *fervōr -em*], *n.* Heat, warmth; ardour, intensity of feeling, vehemence; zeal.

fescennine (fes′ ė nīn) [L. *Fescennīnus*], *a.* Of or pertaining to the ancient festivals of *Fescennia*, a town of Etruria; hence scurrilous, licentious. **fescinnine verses,** *n.pl.* Extempore dialogues in verses, characterized by broad and licentious satire.

fescue (fes′ kū) [M.E. and O.F. *festu*, L. *festūca*, a stalk, a stem], *n.* A twig, a branch; a small rod or pin with which a teacher pointed out the letters to a child learning to read; a genus of grasses, *Festuca*. **fescue-grass,** *n.* *Festuca ovina*, an important pasture grass.

fesse (fes) [O.F., from L. *fascia*, see FASCIA], *n.* (*Her.*) A broad band of metal or colour crossing the shield horizontally, and occupying one-third of it; one of the nine honourable ordinaries, representing a knight's girdle. **fesse-point,** *n.* The centre of an escutcheon.

festal (fes′ tăl) [O.F., from L. *festum*, FEAST], *a.* Pertaining to a feast or holiday; festive, joyous, gay, merry. **festally,** *adv.*

fester (fes′ tĕr) [O.F. *festre* (whence *festrir*, to fester), L. *fistula*, see FISTULA], *v.i.* To ulcerate or suppurate; to form purulent matter; (*fig.*) to rankle; to become corrupted or rotten. *v.t.* To cause to fester or rankle. *n.* A purulent tumour or sore; the act or state of festering or rankling.

***festinate** (fes′ ti nāt) [L. *festīnātus*, p.p. of *festīnāre*, to hasten], *a.* Hasty, hurried. *v.i.* (-nāt) To hasten. *v.t.* To hurry, accelerate. ***festinately,** *adv.* **festination** (-nā′ shŭn), *n.*

festino (fės tī′ nō), *n.* (*Log.*) A mnemonic name for the third mode of the second figure of syllogisms, where the middle term is the predicate of both premises.

festival (fes′ ti văl) [O.F., from late L. *festīvālis*, L. *festīvus*, see foll.], *a.* Pertaining to or characterizing a feast; festal. *n.* A festal day or time, a joyous celebration or anniversary; a merry-making; a musical entertainment on a large scale, usually periodical; (*Am.*) an entertainment or fair where fruit and other eatables are sold.

festive (fes′ tiv) [L. *festīvus*, from *festum*, FEAST], *a.* Of or befitting or used for a feast or festival; joyous, gay, mirthful; (*Am.*) fast, loud. **festively,** *adv.* **festivity** (fes tiv′ i ti), *n.* A feast, a festival, a joyous celebration or entertainment; gaiety, mirth, joyfulness; (*pl.*) merry-making.

festoon (fės toon′) [F. *feston*, It. *festone*, prob. from *festum*, see prec.], *n.* A chain or garland of flowers, foliage, drapery, etc., suspended by the ends so as to form a depending curve; (*Arch.*) a carved ornament in the form of a garland or wreath. *v.t.* To form into or adorn with or as with festoons.

fetal, fetus [FŒTUS].

fetch (1) (fech) [A.-S. *feccan, fetian*, prob. rel. to *fæt*, step, journey], *v.t.* To go for and bring; to cause to come; to draw forth, to heave (as a sigh); to derive, to elicit; to bring in, to sell for (a price); to bring to any state, condition, or position; to reach, to arrive at, to accomplish; (*colloq.*) to delight, to charm; (*colloq.*) to strike. *v.i.* (*Naut.*) To reach a place, to bring up. *n.* A stratagem, a trick, a dodge, a striving after, a powerful effort; a deep breath, a sigh. **to fetch about, to fetch a compass:** To take a circuitous route or method. **to fetch and carry:** To go to and fro with things; to perform menial offices. **to fetch a pump:** To pour water into it to make it draw. ***to fetch off:** To get the better of. **to fetch out:** To bring out, to cause to appear. **to fetch to:** To revive, as from a swoon. **to fetch up:** To recall, to bring to mind; to vomit; to come to a stand; to recover, to make up (lost time, etc.); *to overtake; *to bring up, raise, elevate. **to fetch up all standing:** (*Naut.*) To stop suddenly with sails set. **fetcher,** *n.* **fetching,** *a.* (*colloq.*) Fascinating, charming, taking.

fetch (2) (fech) [etym. unknown], *n.* A wraith or double. **fetch-candle, *-light,** *n.* A light appearing at night, believed by the superstitious to portend the death of some person.

fête (fāt) [F. *fête*, O.F. *feste*, L. *festum*, FEAST], *n.* A festival, an entertainment; the festival of the saint after whom a person is named (in R.-C. countries). *v.t.* To entertain, to feast; to honour with festivities. ***fête champêtre,*** *n.* An open-air festival. **fête-day,** *n.* A festival day.

fetial (fē′ shăl) [L. *fetiālis* (etym. unknown)], *a.* Of or pertaining to the Fetials; ambassadorial, heraldic. *n.* One of a college of priests in ancient Rome, who presided over the ceremonies connected with the ratification of peace or the formal declaration of war.

feticide [FŒTUS].

fetid (fet′ id, fē′ tid) [L. *fētidus*, from *fētēre*, to stink], *a.* Having an offensive smell; stinking. **fetidly,** *adv.* **fetidness,** *n.* **fetor** (fē′ tŏr) [L.], *n.* A strong or offensive smell; a stench.

fetish (fet′ ish, fē′ tish) [F. *fétiche*, Port. *feitiço*, sorcery, L. *factītius*, artificial], *n.* Any material object supposed to be the vessel, vehicle, or instrument of a supernatural being, the possession of which gives to the possessor or joint possessors power over that being; (*fig.*) an object of devotion, an idol. **fetisheer** (fet′ i shėr, fet i shēr′), *n.* A sorcerer, a medicine-man. **fetishism,** *n.* Belief in fetishes; worship of them; (*Psych.*) a form of perversion in which sexual gratification is obtained from other than the genital parts of the body. **fetishist,** *n.* **fetishistic** (-shis′ tik), *a.*

fetlock (fet′ lok) [etym. obscure (cp. L.G. *fitlock*, G. *fiszloch*)], *n.* A tuft of hair behind the pastern joint of a horse; the pastern joint; a fetterlock.

fetor [FETID].

fetter (fet′ ėr) [A.-S. *fetor* (cp. Dut. *veter*, race, G. *fesser*, from O.Teut. *fet-*, rel. to *fōt-*, *foot*, also L. *pedica*, Gr. *pedē*, fetter)], *n.* A chain for the feet; a shackle, a bond (*usu. in pl.*); (*fig.*) anything which restrains or confines. *v.t.* To put fetters upon, to bind with fetters; (*fig.*) to confine, restrain; to hamper, impede. **fettered,** *a.* Chained, bound; hampered, impeded; (*Zool.*) a term applied to the feet of animals when they stretch backwards so as to be unfit for walking, as in the seals. **fetterless,** *a.* **fetterlock,** *n.* A shackle for a horse when turned out to grass; (*Her.*) a figure of a shackle and padlock.

fettle (fetl) [perh. from A.-S. *fetel*, a girdle, belt], *v.t.* To clean or put right; to work with activity or zeal. *v.i.* To fuss about, to be busy. *n.* Condition, order, trim. **in good fettle:** In good form or trim.

***fetus** [FŒTUS].

fetwa (fet′ wȧ) [Arab.], *n.* A declaration, interpretation, or decision by a mufti on a point of Moslem law.

feu (fū) [var. of FEE], *n.* (*Sc. Law*) Orig. tenure on condition of the performance of certain services or certain returns in money or kind; now, a perpetual lease at a fixed rent; the land, houses, or other real estate so held. *v.t.* (*Sc. Law*) To give or take in feu. **feu-duty,** *n.* The annual rent for such a holding. **feu-holding,** *n.* **feu-right,** *n.* **feuar,** *n.* One who holds real estate on feu.

feud (1) (fūd) [M.E. *fede*, O.F. *faide*, O.H.G. *fēhida*, cogn. with A.-S. *fæhth*, enmity], *n.* Hostility between two tribes or families in revenge for an injury, often carried on for several generations; enmity, quarrel, contention, animosity.

feud (2) (fūd) [med. L. *feudum*, see FEE], *n.* A fief; the right to lands or hereditaments held in trust, or on condition of performing certain services.

feudal (fū′ dȧl) [as prec.], *a.* Pertaining to, consisting of or founded upon a feud or fief; according to or resembling the feudal system. **feudal system,** *n.* A system of social polity prevailing in Europe during the Middle Ages, by which the ownership of land inhered in the lord, possession or tenancy being granted to the vassal in return for military service. **feudalism,** *n.* **feudalist,** *n.* A supporter of feudalism; one versed in feudal law. **feudalistic** (-lis′ tik), *a.* **feudality** (dăl′ i ti), *n.* The quality or state of being feudal; feudal principles; a fief, a feudal holding. **feudalize,** *v.t.* To reduce to feudal tenure. **feudalization** (-zā′ shŭn), *n.* **feudally,** *adv.* **feudary,** *a.* Held by or pertaining to feudal tenure. *n.* A feudatory; a retainer, a servant; *an officer in the ancient Court of Wards. **feudatory,** *a.* Holding or held by feudal tenure; subject; under foreign overlordship. *n.* One who holds lands of another by feudal tenure; a vassal; a fief, a dependent lordship.

feu de joie (fu dė zhwa) [F., fire of joy], *n.* (*pl.* ***feux***) The firing of guns in token of public rejoicing.

feuilleton (fu yė ton) [F., from *feuillet*, dim. of *feuille*, L. *folia*, pl. of *folium*, leaf], *n.* That part of a French newspaper which is devoted to light literature, criticism, or fiction; a light article or a serial story in a newspaper.

feuter [FEWTER].

fever (fē′ vėr) [A.-S. *fēfor*, L. *febris*], *n.* A disease or group of diseases usually characterized by high temperature, quickened pulse, nervous and muscular prostration, and destruction of tissues; (*fig.*) a state of nervous excitement; agitation. *v.t.* To put or throw into a fever. *v.i.* To become feverish. **fever-heat,** *n.* The abnormally high temperature of the body characteristic of fever. **fever-trap,** *n.* A place where fever germs are supposed to abound. **fever-tree,** *n.* The blue-gum tree, *Eucalyptus globulus*; also other trees with febrifugal properties. **feverish,** *a.* Suffering from or affected with fever; indicating fever; resembling a fever; infested with fever; (*fig.*) excited, restless, inconstant. **feverishly,** *adv.* **feverishness,** *n.* **feverous,** *a.*

feverfew (fē′ vėr fū) [corr. of A.-S. *fēferfuge*, L. *febrifuga* (*febris*, *fugāre*, to put to flight)], *n.* A common British plant, *Pyrethrum parthenium*, supposed to act as a febrifuge.

few (fū) [A.-S. *fēa*, *fēawe* (cp. O.H.G. *fao*, L. *paucus*, Gr. *pauros*)], *a.* Not many; small, limited, or restricted in number. *n.* A small number (of). **a good few:** (*colloq.*) A considerable number. **every few days, hours:** Once in every series of a few days or hours. **in few:** Shortly, briefly. **not a few:** A good many. **some few:** Not a great number. **the few:** The minority; the elect. **fewness,** *n.*

fewter (fū′ tėr) [O.F. *feutre*, med. L. *filtrum*, cogn. with FELT, see FILTER], *n.* A rest for the lance attached to the saddle (orig. lined with felt).

fewtrils (fū′ trilz) [FATTRELS], *n.pl.* (*prov.*) Trifles, odds and ends.

fey (fā) [A.-S. *fæge* (cp. Icel. *feigr*, Dut. *veeg*, about to die, G. *feige*, cowardly)], *a.* Fated, doomed, on the verge of death (implying both the proximity of this event and the impossibility of avoiding it); unfortunate, unlucky; disordered in mind; in unnaturally high spirits.

fez (fez) [F., prob. from *Fez*, the chief town of Morocco, where they are manufactured], *n.* (*pl.* **fezes**) A red cap without a brim, fitting close to the head, with a tassel of silk, wool, etc., worn in the Near East.

fiacre (fē akr′) [F., said to be named after an innkeeper at the Hotel de St. *Fiacre*], *n.* A French hackney-coach invented about 1640.

fiancé (fē an′ sā) [F., p.p. of *fiancer*, to betroth], *n.* (*fem.* **fiancée**) One who is betrothed.

fiar (fē′ ȧr) [Sc., perh. from FEE, -ER], *n.* (*Sc. Law*) One who has the fee-simple or reversion of property.

fiars (fē′ ȧrz) [Sc., from M.E. and O.F. *feor*, L. *forum*, market], *n.pl.* The prices of grain legally fixed by the sheriff of a county for the current year, as a basis for certain rates.

fiasco (fi ăs′ kō) [It., a flask, a bottle (sense obscure)], *n.* (*pl.* **-os**) A failure in a public performance; a ridiculous breakdown, an ignominious sequel.

fiat (fī ăt) [L., let it be done], *n.* An order, command, decree; (*Law*) the order or warrant of a judge or other constituted authority sanctioning or allowing certain processes. ***fiant** [L., 3rd pers., pl., let (documents or letters patent) be made out], *n.* A warrant to the Irish Chancery.

fib (1) (fib) [perh. from FABLE or obs. redupl. *fible-fable*, nonsense], *n.* A harmless or venial lie; a white lie. *v.i.* To tell fibs. **fibber, fibster,** *n.* One who tells fibs.

fib (2) (fib) [etym. unknown], *n.* (*Pugil.*) A blow. *v.t.* To pummel. *v.i.* To deal short, smart blows.

fibre (fī′ bėr) [F., from L. *fibra*], *n.* A slender filament; a thread, string, or filament, of which the tissues of animals and plants are constituted; the substances composed of animal or vegetable tissue forming the raw material in textile manufactures; a structure composed of filaments; (*fig.*) essence, nature, material, character, nerve, strength. **fibreboard,** *n.* A building-board composed of fibrous material. **fibre-glass,** *n.* Very fine filaments of molten glass worked into a synthetic fibre. **fibred,** *a.* Composed of or having fibres (*esp. in comb.*, *as finely-fibred*). **fibreless,** *a.* **fibriform,** *a.* **fibrous,** *a.* **fibrously,** *adv.* **fibrousness,** *n.* **fibro-,** *comb. form.*

fibril (fī′ bril), **fibrilla** (fī bril′ ȧ) [dim. of L. *fibra*, as prec.], *n.* (*pl.* **fibrillæ**) A little fibre; (*Bot.*) one of the minute subdivisions in which a branching root terminates; (*Physiol.*) a minute subdivision of a fibre in a nerve, muscle, etc. **fibrillar, fibrillary** (fī′ bri lȧr, -i), **fibrillate, -ated** (fī bril ăt, -ėd), *a.* **fibrillate** (-āt), *v.i.* **fibrillation** (-lā′ shŭn), *n.* **fibrilliform** (fī bril′ i fôrm), *a.* **fibrillose** (fī′ bri lōs), *a.*

fibrin (fī′ brin) [as prec., -IN], *n.* An albuminoid substance contained in the blood, causing it to clot. **vegetable fibrin:** A similar substance left as a residue when gluten is boiled with alcohol. **fibrination** (-nā′ shŭn), *n.* The production of an excess of fibrin in the blood, as in inflammatory diseases. **fibrino-,** *comb. form.* **fibrinous,** *a.* Composed of or of the nature of fibrin. **fibrinogen,** *n.* A protein entering into the formation of fibrin and into coagulation.

fibro- [FIBRE] *prefix.* Denoting a substance consisting of or characterized by fibres.

fibroid (fī′ broid), *a.* Of the nature or form of fibre. *n.* (*Path.*) A fibroid tumour.

fibroin (fī′ brō in), *n.* (*Chem.*) The chief constituent of silk, cobweb, the horny skeleton of sponges, etc.

fibroline (fī′ brō lēn), *n.* A yarn spun from waste in hemp, flax and jute work, for backing carpets, rugs, etc.

fibroma (fī brō′ mȧ) [mod. L., as FIBRE], *n.* (*pl.* **-ta**) (*Path.*) A benign fibrous tumour. **fibrosis** (-brō′ sis), *n.* **fibrositis** (fī brō sī′ tis), *n.* (*Path.*) Muscular rheumatism.

fibrous, etc. [FIBRE].

fibula (fib′ ū lȧ) [L., a brooch, from *fīvere*, var. of *fīgere*, to fix], *n.* (*pl.* **-læ, -las**) The outer and smaller bone of the leg; (*Ant.*) a clasp, buckle, or brooch. **fibular,** *a.*

-fic [L. *-ficus*, from weakened root of *facere*, to make], *suf.* Forming adjectives from nouns, verbs, etc., as *honorific*, *horrific*, *malefic*.

-fication [L. *-ficātio -ōnem*, from *-ficāre*, see -FY], *suf.* Forming nouns from verbs in -FY, as *purification.*

ficelle (fi sel') [F., pack-thread], *a.* Of the colour of pack-thread.

fichu (fish' u) [F., from *ficher*, to fix, to put on], *n.* A light covering worn by women over the neck, throat, and shoulders.

fickle (fi' kėl) [A.-S. *ficol*, rel. to *befician*, to deceive], *a.* Changeable, inconstant. **fickleness,** *n.* ***fickly,** *adv.*

***fico** (fē' kō) [It., from L. *ficus*, FIG], *n.* A fig; a gesture of contempt shown by a snap of the fingers.

fictile (fik' til) [L. *fictilis*, from *fingere*, to fashion], *a.* Capable of being moulded; moulded by art; made of earth or clay; manufactured by or suitable for the potter.

fiction (fik' shŭn) [F., from L. *fictio -ōnem*, as prec.], *n.* The act or art of feigning or inventing; that which is feigned, imagined, or invented; an invented statement or narrative; a story, a romance; literature, esp. in prose, consisting of invented narrative; any point or thing assumed for the purposes of justice or convenience. **legal fiction,** *n.* An accepted falsehood which averts the raising of an awkward issue. **fictional,** *a.* **fictionist,** *n.* A writer of fiction; a novelist.

fictitious (fik tish' us), *a.* Feigned, imaginary, counterfeit, false, assumed; of or pertaining to novels; having no real existence; accepted by a conventional or legal fiction. **fictitiously,** *adv.* **fictitiousness,** *n.*

fictive (fik' tiv) [F. *fictif, -ive*, as prec.], *a.* Imaginative, creative; imaginary, fictitious, feigned, counterfeit.

fid (fid) [etym. doubtful], *n.* (*Naut.*) A bar of wood or iron to support a top-mast; a pointed wooden pin used to open the strands of a rope in splicing; a wooden or metal bar used as a support, etc.; a plug of oakum for the vent of a cannon.

fiddle (fid' el) [A.-S. *fithele*, etym. doubtful (cp. Dut. *vedel*, G. *fiedel*)], *n.* A violin (*now used only in a contempt. or fam. sense*); (*Naut.*) a frame of bars and strings, to keep things from rolling off the cabin table in bad weather; (*slang*) a swindle. *v.i.* To play upon a fiddle; to trifle; to shift the hands about as if playing the fiddle. *v.t.* To play (as a tune) on a fiddle; (*fig.*) to worry, to fritter away; (*slang*) to cheat, to gamble. **fit as a fiddle:** In good condition, ready for anything. **to play first** or **second fiddle:** To take a leading or a subordinate part or position. **fiddle-block,** *n.* (*Naut.*) A block with two sheaves. **fiddle-bow,** *n.* The bow with which a fiddle is played. **fiddle-case,** *n.* A case for holding a fiddle. **fiddlededee,** *int.* and *n.* Nonsense. **fiddle-faddle,** *n.* Trifling talk; nonsense. *a.* Trifling; making a fuss about trifles. *v.i.* To trifle; to make a fuss about trifles. **fiddle-faddler,** *n.* **fiddle-head,** *n.* Ornamental carving at the bows of a ship, in the form of a volute. **fiddle-pattern,** *n.* A fiddle-shaped pattern in vogue for the heads of spoons and forks. **fiddlestick,** *n.* A fiddle-bow; (*pl., fig.*) rubbish, something absurd; *int.* (*pl.*) Fiddlededee. **fiddle-wood,** *n.* One of several tropical American trees yielding hard wood. **fiddler,** *n.* One who plays the fiddle; a small crab, *Gelasimus vocans*, having one large claw and one very small one; (*Austral.*) a variety of ray. (*fig.*) one who makes a fuss about trifles; (*slang*) a sixpence. **fiddler-fish,** *n.* A West Indian ray; *Rhinobatus percellens*, also called the guitar fish. **fiddling,** *a.* Playing the fiddle; trifling, fussy; petty, contemptible.

fiddley (fidl' i) [etym. unknown], *n.* (*Naut.*) The iron framework enclosing the deck-hatch leading to the stoke-hole of a steamer; the space below this.

fidei-commissum (fī dė ī kō mis' ŭm), ***fidei-commiss*** [L., neut. p.p. of *fidei-committere* (*fidei*, dat. of *fidēs*, faith, *committere*, to entrust, COMMIT)], *n.* A testator's bequest to trustees; a trust or trust estate. ***fidei-commissary*** (-kom' i sȧr i), *n.* A beneficiary by such a bequest or trust. ***fidei-commissor,*** *n.* One who creates a *fidei-commissum.*

fidelity (fi del' i ti) [F. *fidélité*, L. *fidēlitās -tātem*, from *fidēlis*, from *fidēs*, faith], *n.* Careful and loyal observance of duty; faithful adherence to a bond, covenant, engagement, or connexion; loyalty, faithfulness; honesty, veracity, reliability, accurate correspondence (of a copy, description, picture, etc.) to the original.

fidget (fij' ėt) [from prec.], *n.* A state of nervous restlessness; one who fidgets; one who worries or makes (others) uncomfortable; (*pl.*) restless movements. *v.i.* To move about restlessly; to worry, to be uneasy. *v.t.* To worry or make (others) uncomfortable. **fidgety,** *a.* **fidgetiness,** *n.*

fidibus (fid' i bŭs) [etym. unknown], *n.* A paper match or spill for lighting pipes, candles, etc.

fiducial (fi dū' shȧl) [L. *fīdūciālis*, from *fīdūcia*, trust, from *fīdere*, to trust, *fidēs*, faith], *a.* Confident, sure, firm; of the nature of a trust; (*Phys., Surv.*, etc.) denoting a fixed point or line used as a basis for measurement or comparison. **fiducially,** *adv.* **fiduciary** (fi dū' shȧr i), *a.* Pertaining to or of the nature of a trust or a trusteeship; held in trust; confident, trustful, unwavering. *n.* A trustee.

fidus Achates (fī dŭs ȧ kā' tēz) [L., the faithful Achates, the devoted follower of Æneas in the *Æneid*], *n.* A trusty friend, a faithful henchman.

fie (fī) [M.E. and O.F. *fi*, L. *fī*], *int.* An exclamation indicating contempt, irony, disgust, shame, or impatience.

fief (fēf) [O.F., from L. *fevum*, see FEE], *n.* An estate held of a superior under feudal tenure; feudal tenure.

field (fēld) [A.-S. *feld* (cp. Dut. *veld*, G. *feld*)], *n.* A piece of land, esp. one enclosed for tillage or pasture; a region yielding some natural product abundantly (as an oil- or coal-field); the place where a battle is fought; the battle itself; the scene of military operations; the ground on which cricket, football, or other games are played; the fielders or the players taken collectively; all the competitors in a race, or all except the favourite; the participants in a hunt; the sphere of any contest, operation, observation, etc.; the open country; a wide expanse, as of sea or sky; the surface on which the figures in a picture are drawn; (*Her.*) the surface of a shield or one of its divisions. *v.t.* (*Cricket, etc.*) To catch or stop (the ball) and return it to the wicket-keeper. *v.i.* To act as fielder in cricket and other games; (*Sporting*) to back the field against the favourite. **field of force:** (*Phys.*) The space within which a certain force is present, as a magnetic field. **field of view** or **vision:** The space visible in an optical instrument at one view. **ice-field,** *n.* A large expanse of floating ice. **snow-field,** *n.* An area covered with accumulated snow above the glaciers in a high mountain range. **to bet** or **lay against the field:** To bet on one or more horses, dogs, etc., against all the others in a race. **to hold the field:** To maintain one's ground against all comers; (*fig.*) to surpass all competitors. **to take the field:** To commence active military operations; to begin a campaign. **field-allowance,** *n.* An extra payment to officers on a campaign to meet the increased cost of living, etc. **field-artillery,** *n.* Light ordnance suitable for use in the field. **field-bed,** *n.* A folding bed; a camp-bed; *a bed in the open air. **field-book,** *n.* A book used by surveyors, engineers, etc., in which the memoranda of surveys are set down. ***field-colours,** *n.pl.* (*Mil.*) Camp colours, small flags for marking out the ground for squadrons and battalions; the colours used by troops on a campaign. **field-cornet,** *n.* The magistrate of a township in South Africa. **field-cricket,** *n.* A large cricket, *Acheta* (*Gryllus*) *campestris*, found in hot sandy localities. **field-day,** *n.* (*Mil.*) A day on which troops are exercised in field evolutions; (*fig.*) a day of unusual importance, excitement, or display. **field-dressing,** *n.* Ambulance appliances for use on the battlefield. **field-duck,** *n.* The little bustard, *Otis tetrax.* **field-equipage,** *n.* (*Mil.*) Equipage, accoutrements, etc., for service in the field. **field events,** *n.pl.* (*Sport*) Athletic events other than racing, *e.g.* running, jumping, etc. **field-botanist, -geologist, -naturalist,** *n.* One used to observing, testing and demonstrating the principles of his science by means of practical study of outdoor nature. **field-glass,** *n.* A binocular telescope in compact form; a small achromatic telescope; the lens of an eyepiece which is nearest to the object-glass. **field-gun** [FIELD-PIECE]. **field-hospital,** *n.* An ambulance or temporary hospital near a battle-field. **field-ice,** *n.* Ice formed in the polar regions in fields or floes, as dist. from icebergs. **field-marshal,** *n.* An officer of highest rank in the British Army. **field-meeting,** *n.* An open-air meeting for worship or preaching, a conventicle. **field-mouse,** *n.* One of several species of mice living in fields, etc. **field-night,** *n.* An evening or night marked by some important meeting, business, or event. **field-notes,** *n.pl.* Notes made on the spot when surveying. **field-officer,** *n.* (*Mil.*) An officer above the rank of captain, but below that of general; as a major, a colonel, etc. **field-piece,** *n.* A light piece of artillery for service in the field. **field-preacher,** *n.* One who preaches at religious meetings in the open air. **field-sports,** *n.pl.* Outdoor sports, such as hunting, shooting, coursing, etc. **field-strength,** *n.* The power of an electric (magnetic) field at some precise point. **field-telegraph,** *n.* A movable telegraph system for use on campaign, manœuvres, etc. **field-train,** *n.* A department of the Royal Artillery for the supply of ammunition to the army at the front. **field-winding,** *n.* A coil of wire wound on iron in order to make a strong electro-magnetic field when the current is passing. **field-work,** *n.* The various outdoor operations necessary in surveying, etc.; (*pl.*) temporary fortifications thrown up by besiegers or besieged. ***fielded,** *a.* Engaged in the field or in action; encamped. **fielder, fieldsman,** *n.* One who fields at cricket, etc. **fieldwards,** *adv.*

fieldfare (fēld′ fâr) [A.-S. *feldefare*; prob. field-goer], *n.* A species of thrush, *Turdus pilaris,* a winter visitant in England.

fiend (fēnd) [A.-S. *fēond,* from *fēogan,* to hate (cp. G. *feind*)], *n.* *An enemy; a demon, a devil, an infernal being; a person of diabolical wickedness or cruelty. **the fiend:** Satan. **fiendish,** *a.* **fiendishly,** *adv.* **fiendishness,** *n.* **fiendlike,** *a.*

fierce (fērs) [O.F. *fers, fiers,* nom. of *fer, fier,* L. *ferus,* wild], *a.* Savage, furiously hostile or combative; raging, violent; vehement, ardent, eager, impetuous; *strong; *great. **fiercely,** *adv.* **fierceness,** *n.*

fieri-facias (fī ėr ī fā′ si ȧs) [L., cause it to be done], *n.* (*Law*) A writ to the sheriff to levy of the goods and chattels of the defendant the sum or debt to be recovered.

fiery (fī′ er i), *a.* Consisting of fire, on fire, flaming with fire; hot, like fire; glowing or red, like fire; flashing, ardent, inflaming, inflamed; highly inflammable, liable to explosions (as a mine); (*fig.*) vehement, ardent, eager; passionate, hot-tempered, irascible; pugnacious, mettlesome, untamed. **fiery cross,** *n.* A wooden cross, the ends of which had been set on fire, and extinguished in the blood of an animal slain for the purpose, formerly sent round in the Highlands to summon a clan to war. **fiery-footed,** *a.* Swift, rapid, impetuous. ***fiery-new,** *a.* Brand-new. ***fiery-pointed,** *a.* Emitting rays pointed with fire. **fiery-red,** *a.* Red as fire. **fiery-wheeled,** *a.* Having wheels of or like fire. **fierily,** *adv.* **fieriness,** *n.*

fife (fīf) [either from F. *fifre* or through G. *pfeife,* pipe, from O.H.G. *pfīfa,* a PIPE, from *pfīfan,* to PIPE], *n.* A small flute-like pipe, chiefly used in martial music. *v.i.* To play upon a fife. *v.t.* To play (tunes) on the fife. ***fife-major,** *n.* A non-commissioned officer who formerly superintended the fifers of a regiment. **fife-rail,** *n.* (*Naut.*) A rail on the quarter-deck and poop or around the mast of a vessel, said to be so called because a fifer sat on this whilst the anchor was being weighed. **fifer,** *n.*

fifish (fī′ fish) [county of *Fife*], *a.* (*Sc.*) Queer, cranky, not quite right mentally.

fifteen (fif′ tēn, fif tēn′) [A.-S. *fīftȳne*], *a.* Amounting in number to five and ten; one more than fourteen. *n.* The number made up of five and ten, or the symbol representing this, viz. 15, xv; a set of fifteen players, pips on a card, or other things; a Rugby football team. **the Fifteen:** The Jacobite rising of 1715. **fifteenth,** *a.* Next in order after the fourteenth; being one of fifteen equal parts into which a whole is divided. *n.* A fifteenth part; (*Mus.*) the interval of a double octave; an organ-stop sounding two octaves above the open diapason.

fifth (fifth) [A.-S. *fīfta* (cp. G. *fünfte,* Gr. *pemptos,* L. *quinctus*)], *a.* Next in order to the fourth; being one of five equal parts into which a whole is or may be divided. *n.* A fifth part; (*Mus.*) a diatonic interval of five notes, equal to three tones and a semitone; two notes separated by this interval sounded together; the resulting concord. **fifth column,** *n.* Persons in a country who, whether as individuals or as members of an organization, are ready to give help to an enemy. Origin of the phrase is attributed to Gen. Mola who, in the Spanish Civil War, said that he had four columns encircling Madrid and a fifth column in the city, being sympathizers ready to assist the attacking party. **Fifth Monarchy:** The last of the five great empires referred to in Dan. ii. 44, identified with the millennial reign of Christ prophesied in the Apocalypse. **Fifth-monarchy man:** One of a sect of enthusiasts in the time of Cromwell, who declared themselves 'subjects only of King Jesus,' and believed that a fifth universal monarchy (after those of Assyria, Persia, Greece, and Rome) would be established shortly on earth under the personal reign of Christ, and that no government ought to rule mankind until His coming. **fifthly,** *adv.* In the fifth place. **fifth part:** One of five equal parts into which a whole is or may be divided.

fifty (fif′ ti) [A.-S. *fīftig* (cp. G. *fünfzig*)], *a.* Five times ten; (*colloq.*) a great many, a very large number (of things). *n.* A set of fifty persons or things; the number amounting to five times ten, or the symbol representing this, viz. 50 or L. **fifty-fifty,** *n.* (*colloq.*) Equal shares. **the fifties:** The sixth decade of a century, as the years between 1949 and 1960. **fiftieth,** *a.* Next in order after the forty-ninth; being one of fifty equal parts into which a whole is or may be divided. *n.* One such part. **fiftyfold,** *a.* and *adv.*

fig (1) (fig) [F. *figue,* L. *fīcus*], *n.* The pear-shaped fleshy fruit of the genus *Ficus,* esp. *F. Carica*; the tree bearing this, noted for its broad and handsome leaves; other trees bearing similar fruit; the fruit of these; (*fig.*) anything valueless, a trifle; (*colloq.*) a raisin; a spongy excrescence on a horse's frog, consequent on a bruise; (*Am. slang*) a small piece of tobacco; *a fico; *(*pl.*) the piles. **v.t.* To insult with ficoes or contemptuous motions of the fingers. **fig-leaf,** *n.* The leaf of a fig-tree; (*fig.*) a flimsy covering, from the use made of the fig-leaf in statuary to conceal nakedness. **fig-tree,** *n.* *Ficus Carica,* a native of Western Asia, which produces the edible fig; other trees bearing similar fruit. **fig-wort,** *n.* Plants of the genus *Scrophularia,* esp. *S. aquatica* and *S. nodosa* (from their being popular remedies for piles); the pilewort, *Ranunculus ficaria.*

fig (2) (fig) [var. of FEAGUE], *v.t.* To dress, deck, rig (up or out). *n.* Dress, array, outfit, equipment. **in full fig:** In full dress. **in good fig:** In good form or condition. **to fig out** (a horse): To make lively. **figgery,** *n.* Elaborate ornament.

fight (fīt) [A.-S. *feohtan* (cp. Dut. *vechten,* O.H.G. *fehtan,* G. *fechten*)], *v.i.* (*past & p.p.* **fought**) To contend in arms or in battle, or in single combat (with, against); to strive for victory or superiority, to war; to oppose, to offer resistance. *v.t.* To contend with, to struggle against; to maintain by conflict; to contend over; to engage in; to carry on or wage (a contest, battle, etc.); to gain or win by conflict; to manage, lead, or manœuvre in battle; to set on or cause to fight (as cocks). *n.* A struggle between individuals or armies, to injure each other or obtain the mastery; a battle, a combat; a pugilistic contest; a contest of any kind, contention; power of or inclination for fighting; *(*usu. in pl.*) a kind of screen or bulwark for protecting the crew on shipboard. **running fight:** A fight in which one party flees and the other pursues, the contest being continued during the chase. **sham fight:** A series of manœuvres carried out for practice or display. **stand-up fight:** An open encounter according to the rules. **to fight off:** To repel. **to fight out:** To decide (a contest or wager) by fighting. **to fight shy of:** To avoid from a feeling of mistrust, dislike, or fear. **fighter,** *n.* One who fights; a combatant; a warrior; (*Aviat.*) an aeroplane equipped for fighting. **fighting chance,** *n.* A chance of success if every effort is made. **fighting-cock,** *n.* A game-cock. **fighting-fish,** *n.* An artificial variety of *Betta pugnax*, a small Siamese freshwater fish, kept for fighting. **fighting-man,** *n.*

figment (fig′ mėnt) [L. *figmentum* (*fig-*, base of *fingere*, to feign, -MENT)], *n.* A fiction, an invented statement, something that exists only in the imagination, a fabrication, a fable.

***figo** [FICO].

figuline (fig′ ū lin) [L. *figulīnus*, from *figulus*, a potter], *a.* Produced by or suitable for the potter; fictile. *n.* Pottery; potter's clay.

***figurable** (fig′ ū-, -ŭr ȧbl), *a.* That may be brought to a definite figure or shape; that may be represented figuratively. ***figural,** *a.* Represented by a figure or delineation; (*Mus.*) figurate.

figurant (fig ū ran) [F., pres.p. of *figurer*, to FIGURE], *n.* (*fem.* ***-ante***) A ballet-dancer; an actor who merely appears on the stage with others and says nothing. **figurante** (fig ū ran′ ti) [It., pres.p. of *figurare*, to FIGURE], *n.* (*pl.* **-ti**, -tē) A figurant.

***figurate** (fig′ ū rȧt, -ŭr ȧt) [L. *figūrātus*, p.p. of *figūrāre*, to form, fashion, see FIGURE], *a.* Of a fixed and determinate form; resembling anything of a distinctive form; (*Mus.*) florid, figured; figurative, metaphorical.

figuration (fig ū rā′ shŭn) [F., from L. *figūrātio -ōnem*, as prec.], *n.* The act of giving a certain determinate form to; determination to a certain form; form, shape, conformation, outline; a figurative representation; ornamentation; (*Mus.*) florid or figured counterpoint.

figurative (fig′ ūr ȧ tiv) [F. *figuratif -tive*, late L. *figūrātīvus*, from *figūrāre*, as foll.], *a.* Representing something by a figure or type, typical; emblematic, symbolic, metaphorical, not literal; full of figures of speech; flowery, ornate; pictorial or plastic. **figuratively,** *adv.* **figurativeness,** *n.*

figure (fig′ ŭr) [F., from L. *figūra*, from *fig-*, stem of *fingere*, see FEIGN], *n.* The external form or shape of a person or thing; bodily shape; the representation of any form, as by carving, modelling, painting, drawing, embroidery, weaving, or any other process; a statue, an image: a combination of lines or surfaces enclosing a space, as a triangle, sphere, etc.; a diagram, an illustrative drawing, a pattern; an emblem, a type, a simile; a fancy, a creation of the imagination, an idea; a personage, a character; the sensible or mental impression that a person makes, appearance, distinction; a symbol representing a number, esp. one of the ten Arabic numerals; the several steps or movements which a dancer makes in accord with the music; a certain movement or division in a set dance; (*Skating*) a movement or combination of movements beginning and ending at a fixed point; (*Rhet.*) any mode of speaking or writing in which words are deflected from their literal or ordinary sense, such as metaphor, ellipsis, hyperbole; (*Gram.*) a recognized deviation from the ordinary form or construction; (*Mus.*) a phrase, a short series of notes producing a single impression; (*Log.*) the form of a syllogism with respect to the position of the middle term; (*Astrol.*) a horoscope; (*colloq.*) value, a price. *v.t.* To form an image, likeness, or representation of; to represent, to picture, to imagine; to symbolize, to typify; to cover, adorn, or ornament with figures; to work out in figures, to cipher, to reckon; to mark with numbers or prices; to express by a metaphor or image; (*Mus.*) to mark with figures indicating the harmony. *v.i.* To cipher; to appear, to be conspicuous; to make or cut a figure. **a high** or **low figure:** High or low price. **double, three,** or **four figures:** Number, price, or income between 9 and 100, 99 and 1000, or 999 and 10,000. **to cut** or **make a figure:** To present a (certain) appearance; to make a (certain) impression. **to figure out:** To ascertain by computation. **to figure up:** To add up, to reckon. ***figure-caster,** *n.* An astrologer, a fortune-teller. **figure-dance,** *n.* A dance or dancing with elaborate figures. **figure-dancer,** *n.* **figure-head,** *n.* The ornamental bust or full-length carving on the prow of a ship above the cutwater, and immediately below the bowsprit; a nominal leader or chief personage without real authority; (*slang*) a person's face. **figure-weaving,** *n.* The process of weaving figured fabrics. **figured,** *a.* Adorned with figures or devices; represented by figures, pictured; with variegated or ornamental grain (of wood); shaped in a (certain) fashion (*usu. in comb.*); ***figurative;** ***figurate.** **figured bass,** *n.* (*Mus.*) A bass having the accompanying chords indicated by numbers above or below the notes. **figured muslin,** *n.* Muslin in which a pattern is worked. **figureless,** *a.* Shapeless. ***figurial** (fi gūr′ i ȧl), *a.* Represented by a figure. **figurine** (fig ū rēn′, -ŭr ēn′), *n.* A statuette in clay or metal. ***figurist,** *n.* One who makes use of or interprets figures.

fike (fīk) [Sc., etym. doubtful; cp. FIDGE], *v.i.* To fidget, to be fussy or restless. *v.t.* To trouble, to worry. *n.* Fuss, trouble. **the fikes:** The fidgets.

***filaceous** (fi lā′ shŭs) [L. *fīlum*, a thread, -ACEOUS], *a.* Consisting of threads.

filacer (fil′ ȧ sėr), **-zer** (-zėr) [from A.-F. *filaz*, med. L. *filacium*, prob. from L. *fīlum*, thread], *n.* An officer who filed original writs, and issued processes, attachments, etc., in connexion with the Court of Common Pleas, the King's Bench, and the Court of Exchequer.

filament (fil′ ȧ mėnt) [F., from late L. *fīlāmentum*, from *fīlāre*, to spin, L. *fīlum*, a thread], *n.* A slender, thread-like process, a fibre or fibril, such as those of which animal and vegetable tissues are composed; the thread of carbon or metal in an incandescent electric lamp; the heater wire of a thermionic valve; (*Bot.*) that part of the stamen which supports the anther. **filamentary** (-men′ tȧ ri), *a.* Of the nature of or formed by a filament or filaments. **filamented,** *a.* Furnished with filaments. **filamentose, -tous** (-men′ tōs, -tŭs), *a.* Like a filament; composed of filaments; bearing filaments.

filar (fī′ lȧr) [L. *fīlum*, a thread], *a.* Of or pertaining to a thread; furnished with threads. **filatory,** *n.* A machine for forming or spinning threads.

filaria (fil ar′ ia) [L. *fīlum*, a thread], *n.* (*Zool.*) Genus of parasitic nematode worms producing live embryos which find their way into the bloodstream of the human host. **filariasis** (fil ar′ i ȧs is), *n.* (*Med.*) Elephantiasis and other manifestations of filarial infection.

filasse (fi las′) [F., as prec.], *n.* Prepared fibre as distinguished from the raw material.

filature (fil′ ȧ tyŭr, -chŭr) [F., from L. *fīlāre*, to spin, as prec.], *n.* The reeling of silk from cocoons; the apparatus used; floss-silk; an establishment for reeling silk.

filazer [FILACER].

filbert (fil′ bėrt) [F. *noix de filbert*, from St. *Philibert*, whose feast is on 22 Aug. (o.s.), when they are ripe], *n.* The nut of the cultivated hazel, *Corylus avellana.*

filch (filch) [etym. doubtful], *v.t.* To steal, to pilfer. *n.* That which is filched; a filcher; the act of filching. **filcher,** *n.* A petty thief, a pilferer.

file (1) (fīl) [F. *fil*, L. *fīlum*, a thread], *n.* A string, wire, or other device on which documents are kept in order, for preservation and convenience of reference; the papers so strung; a collection of papers arranged in order of date or subject for ready reference, esp. in a court of law in connexion with a case; a set of periodicals arranged in order of publication; a row of soldiers ranged one behind the other from front to rear; a row of persons or things arranged in this way; (*Chess*) a line of squares extending from player to player; *a roll, list or catalogue; *a rank, series, or class. *v.t.* To place or fasten on a file; to arrange in order and endorse; (*Law*) to place on the records of a court. *v.i.* To march in file or line, as soldiers. **a file of men:** A small body, now usu. two, told off for a specific duty. **in file:** Drawn up or marching in a line or lines of men one behind another. **Indian, single file:** A single line of men drawn up or marching thus. **on file:** In orderly and systematic preservation. **rank and file:** All the privates and corporals of a regiment who take their places in the ranks, and are arranged in files; the general body, as distinguished from the leaders. **to file off, away:** To wheel off by files and march at right angles to the former direction. ***to file with:** To keep pace with. **file-leader,** *n.* The soldier placed in front of a file; *a captain of a troop.

file (2) (fīl) [A.-S. *fēol* (cp. Dut. *vijl*, G. *feile*)], *n.* A steel instrument with ridged surface, used for cutting and smoothing metals, ivory, wood, etc.; (*fig.*) anything used to polish or refine; (*slang*) a sly, cunning, or artful person; a cove. *v.t.* To smooth or polish; to cut (the surface) away with a file; (*fig.*) to polish, to elaborate. **close file:** A miser. **to gnaw a file:** To attempt obstinately a task that ends only in vexation. **file-cutter,** *n.* A maker of files. **file-fish,** *n.* Any fish of the family *Balistidæ*, from the toothed character of the dorsal spine; (*N. Zealand*) an edible, thick-skinned fish.

***file** (3) (fīl) [A.-S. *-fȳlan* (in *gefȳlan*), to make foul, from *fūl*, FOUL], *v.t.* To defile, to taint, to pollute.

***filemot** (fil' ė mot) [corr. of F. *feuille morte*, dead leaf], *a.* Coloured like a dead leaf; russet-yellow. *n.* This colour.

filet [FILLET].

filial (fil' i ǎl, fil' i ǎl) [late L. *fīliālis*, from *fīlius*, son, *fīlia*, daughter], *a.* Pertaining to a son or daughter; befitting a child in relation to parents; *bearing the relation of a son or daughter. **filiality** (-ǎl' i ti), *n.* **filially,** *adv.* ***filiate,** *v.t.* [AFFILIATE]. **filiation** (-ā' shŭn), *n.* The relation of a child to its father, the correlative of paternity; descent, transmission (from); genealogical relation; (*Law*) affiliation.

filibeg (fil' i beg) [Sc., from Gael. *feileadh-beag* (*feileadh*, fold, *beag*, little)], *n.* A kilt of the modern kind, dist. from the great kilt of olden times, which covered the body.

filibuster (fil' i bŭs tėr) [Sp., corr. from Dut. *vrijbuiter*, a freebooter (*frij*, free, *buit*, booty)], *n.* A lawless military adventurer, esp. one in quest of plunder, a freebooter, a buccaneer; one who takes part in an unauthorized military expedition into a foreign state; (*Pol.*) a parliamentary obstructionist, one who seeks to hinder legislation by prolonged speeches. *v.i.* To act as a filibuster. **filibusterism,** *n.* **filibusterous,** *a.*

Filices (fil' i sēz) [L., pl. of *filix*, fern], *n.pl.* (*Bot.*) The order or group containing the ferns, more recently called **Filicales** (fil i kā' lēz). **filical** (fil' i kǎl), *a.* Pertaining to the ferns or Filicales. **filiciform** (fi lis' i fôrm [-FORM], *a.* Having the shape of a fern. **filicite** (fil' i sīt), *a.* (*Palæont.*) A fossil fern or fern-like plant. **filicoid** (-koid) [-OID], *a.* Filiciform. *n.* A fern-like plant.

filiform (fī' li fôrm) [L. *fīlum*, a thread], *a.* Having the form of a thread; long, slender, round, and equally thick throughout.

filigree, ***filigrane** (fil' i grē, -grǎn) [F. *filigrane*, It. *filigrana* (*filo*, L. *fīlum*, a thread, *grano*, L. *grānum*, GRAIN)], *n.* Ornamental work, executed in fine gold or silver wire, plaited, and formed into delicate open-work or tracery; any ornamental tracery or open-work; anything delicate and fantastic, showy and fragile. *a.* Pertaining to filigree; composed of or resembling filigree. **filigreed,** *a.* Ornamented with filigree.

filings (fī' lingz), *n.pl.* The fine particles cut or rubbed off with a file.

Filioque (fil i ō' kwē) [L., and from the Son], *n.* (*Ch. Hist.*) The clause in the Nicene Creed asserting the procession of the Holy Ghost from the Son as well as from the Father, which is rejected by the Eastern Church. *a.* Pertaining to this.

Filipino (fil i pē' nō) [Sp., from *Felipe*, *Philip II*, of Spain], *n.* (*fem.* **-pina**) An inhabitant of the Philippine Islands.

fill (1) (fil) [A.-S. *fyllan*, O.S. *fullian*, cogn. with FULL], *v.t.* To put or pour into till no more can be admitted; to make full (with); to occupy the whole capacity or space of, to pervade, to spread over or throughout; to block up (cracks with putty, hollow tooth with stopping, etc.); to satisfy, to glut; to stock or store abundantly; to cause to be filled or crowded; to appoint an incumbent or person to discharge the duties of; to hold; to discharge the duties of; to occupy (time); to distend (as sails); (*Am.*) to make up a prescription. *v.i.* To become or grow full; to be distended; to be satisfied; to pour out liquor, to give to drink; *to become satisfied or replete. *n.* As much as will satisfy; a full supply; as much as will fill. **to fill an order:** To execute a trade order. **to fill in:** To insert, so as to fill a vacancy; to complete (anything that is unfinished, as an outline). **to fill out:** To become distended; to enlarge, to complete; to pour out liquor. **to fill the bill:** (*colloq.*) To be the chief item in; to do or be all that is required. **to fill up:** To fill or occupy completely; to make up the deficiencies in, to supply what is wanting in; to supply, to discharge; to fulfil, to satisfy; to stop up by filling; to become full. **to have one's fill of:** To have rather too much of. ***fill-belly,** *n.* A glutton. **filler,** *n.* One who or that which fills; a funnel used in filling casks, bottles, etc.; (*Motor.*) the filling orifice of a petrol tank, gear-box, crank-case, etc. **filling,** *a.* Occupying the whole space or capacity; satisfying. *n.* Anything serving to fill up; gold or other material used to fill up a cavity in a tooth; substances used to fill up holes, cavities, or defects; inferior material used to fill up space in goods of better quality; rubble and other rough material filling up the interior of a stone- or brick-faced wall; the woof of a woven fabric; (*Am.*) stuffing for cookery. **filling-station,** *n.* (*Motor.*) A roadside establishment supplying petrol, oil, etc. **filling-in pieces,** *n.pl.* Timbers occurring in partitions, groins, and roofs, of less length than those with which they range.

***fill** (2) (fil) [*var.* of THILL], *n.* (*pl.*) Thills or shafts. ***fill-horse,** *n.* A shaft-horse.

fillet (fil' ėt) [M.E. and O.F. *filet*, dim. of *fil*, L. *fīlum*, a thread], *n.* A band of metal, a string, or ribbon for binding the hair or worn round the head; a ribbon, a narrow band or strip; a bandage; a fleshy portion or slice of meat; the fleshy part of the thigh (used chiefly of veal); portions of meat or fish removed from the bone and served either flat or rolled together and tied round; a raised rim or moulding; a plain liner band on the back of a book; (*pl.*) the loins of a horse; (*Arch.*) a narrow, flat band between mouldings; the projection between the flutes of a column; (*Carp.*) any small scantling less than a batten; (*Her.*) a small horizontal division of a shield. *v.t.* To bind with a fillet or bandage; to adorn with a fillet or fillets; to make into fillets (as meat or fish).

fillibeg [FILIBEG].

fillip (fil' ip) [prob. var. of FLIP], *v.t.* To strike with the nail of the finger by a sudden jerk from under the thumb; to propel with such a blow; (*fig.*) to stimulate, incite, encourage. *n.* A sharp, sudden blow with the finger jerked from under the thumb; (*fig.*) a stimulus, an incentive; anything of small moment, a trifle.

fillister (fil' is tėr) [etym. unknown], *n.* The rabbet on the outer edge of a sash-bar; a plane for making a rabbet.

filly (fil' i) [cogn. with FOAL], *n.* A female foal; (*fig.*) a young, lively girl. **filly-foal,** *n.*

film (film) [A.-S. *filmen*, membrane, prepuce, cogn. with *fel*, FELL (2)], *n.* A thin pellicle, skin, coating, or layer; a fine thread or filament; a thin, slight covering or veil; a cinema picture; (*Phot.*) a thin coating of sensitized material spread over a plate for receiving a negative or positive image; a thin plate or strip of celluloid or other material supporting such a coating. *v.t.* To cover with a film; to record on a cinematographic film. *v.i.* To become covered with or as with a film. **film fan,** *n.* A person excessively interested in the cinema. **film-pack,** *n.* (*Phot.*) A packet of photographic films arranged so as to be exposed in rotation. **film recorder:** (*Cinema.*) The apparatus which records sound on film. **film recording:** (*Cinema.*) The process whereby sound is recorded on the edge of a film for synchronous reproduction. **film star,** *n.* Leading cinema actor or actress. **filmy,** *a.* **filmy fern,** *n.* The widely-distributed genus *Hymenophyllum.* **filmily,** *adv.* **filminess,** *n.*

filoplume (fī' lȯ ploom) [mod. L. *fīloplūma* (L. *fīlum*, a thread, *plūma*, a feather)], *n.* A thread feather, one having an almost invisible stem. **filoplumaceous** (-mā' shủs), *a.*

filose (fī' lōs) [L. *fīlum*, a thread], *a.* (*Bot. and Zool.*) Ending in a thread-like process.

filoselle (fil' ȯ sel) [F., from It. *filosello* (L. *follis*, a bag, or *fīlum*, a thread)], *n.* Floss-silk.

filter (fil' tėr) [O.F. *filtre*, med. L. *filtrum*, O.L.G. *filt*, FELT (1)], *n.* An apparatus for straining liquids and freeing them from impurities, usu. by means of layers of sand, charcoal, or other material through which they are passed; the layer of porous material through which the liquids are passed; the material so used; an apparatus for purifying air by a similar process; (*Phot.*) a device for altering the relative intensity of the wave-lengths in a beam of light; (*Radio.*) a circuit for altering the relative intensity of different frequencies of an alternating current. *v.t.* To pass (liquid) through a filter; to strain, to purify, to defecate by passing through a filter. *v.i.* To pass through a filter; to percolate. **filter-bed,** *n.* A reservoir with a layer of sand or other filtering material at the bottom through which water is allowed to flow. **filter-paper,** *n.* Paper used for filtering liquids.

filth (filth) [A.-S. *fȳlth*, from *fūl*, FOUL], *n.* Anything dirty or foul; foulness, corruption, pollution; (*fig.*) anything that defiles morally; foul language, obscenity. **filthy,** *a.* Dirty, foul, unclean; morally impure. **filthy lucre:** Gain obtained by base methods; (*facet.*) money. **filthily,** *adv.* **filthiness,** *n.*

filtrate (fil' trāt), *n.* Any liquid that has passed through a filter. *v.t.* and *i.* (fil' trāt) To filter.

filtration (fil trā' shủn), *n.* The act or result of filtering; the absorption of traffic from a secondary road into the traffic of a main road; the holding-up of main-road traffic while this is done.

fimbria (fim' bri å) [L., a thread, fibre, or fringe], *n.* (*pl.* **fimbriæ**) (*Anat.*) The radiated fringe of the Fallopian tube; (*Bot.*) an elastic-toothed membrane situated beneath the operculum of the urn mosses. **fimbriate,** *a.* Fringed. **fimbriated,** *a.* Fringed; (*Bot. and Zool.*) having fimbriæ or fringes; (*Her.*) ornamented (as an ordinary) with a narrow border or hem of another tincture. **fimbricate, fimbricated,** *a.* Fimbriate.

fin (fin) [A.-S. *finn* (cp. Dut. *vin*, also L. *pinna*)], *n.* The organ by which fishes propel and steer themselves, consisting of a membrane supported by rays, named according to position on the body, as **anal, caudal, dorsal, pectoral,** or **ventral fin;** anything resembling a fin, the flipper of a seal, whale, etc.; a ridge left in casting; (*Aviat.*) a fixed aerofoil usually inserted in or parallel to the plane of symmetry, generally constituting part of the tail structure; (*slang*) the hand. *v.t.* To carve or cut up (used of serving a chub). *v.i.* To beat the water with the fins (as a whale). **fin-back** [FINNER]. **fin-footed,** *a.* Web-footed. **fin-keel,** *n.* A fin-shaped keel; a vessel with such a keel. **fin-ray, -spine,** *n.* A spinous ray in the fin of a fish. **fin-toed,** *a.* Web-footed. **finless,** *a.* **finlike,** *a.* **finned,** *a.* Having fins; (*in comb.*) having a certain kind of fins, as *prickly-finned, red-finned*; having broad edges on either side. **finner, finner-whale,** *n.* A whale with an adipose fin on its back, as those of the genus *Balænoptera*, esp. the rorqual. **finny,** *a.* Having fins; like a fin; abounding in fish.

finable [FINE (1)].

final (fī' nȧl) [O.F., from L. *fīnālis*, from *fīnis*, the end], *a.* Pertaining to the end or conclusion; ultimate, last; finishing, conclusive, decisive; concerned with the end or purpose. *n.* The deciding heat of an athletic contest; the last of a series of public examinations (*usu. in pl.*). **final cause:** (*Phil.*) The end or aim contemplated in the creation of the universe. **final clause:** (*Gram.*) A clause expressing the object or purpose. **finality** (fī năl' i ti), *n.* The state or quality of being final; the state of being finally and completely settled; the end of everything, completeness; the final and decisive act or event; (*Phil.*) the doctrine that everything exists or was created for a determinate cause. **finally,** *adv.* **finalist,** *n.* A competitor in the finals of exams., sports, etc. **finalize,** *v.t.* To bring to an end, to complete.

finale (fi na' li) [It., as prec.], *n.* The last part, piece, scene, or action in any performance or exhibition; the last piece in a programme; (*Mus.*) the last movement of a musical composition; (*fig.*) the close, end, the final catastrophe.

finality, finalize [FINAL].

finance (fi-, fī năns') [O.F., from late L. *fīnancia*, from *fīnāre*, to pay a fine or tax, from *fīnis*, a final payment, L., the end], *n.* The science or system of management of revenue and expenditure, esp. public revenue and expenditure; (*pl.*) monetary affairs, the income of a state, sovereign, firm, or individual; revenue, income. *v.t.* To manage the financial arrangements of; to provide with capital. *v.i.* To manage financial operations; to obtain capital by borrowing. **financial,** *a.* Pertaining to finance or revenue; monetary, fiscal. **financial year:** The period for which public or official accounts are made up. **financialist,** *n.* A financier. **financially,** *adv.* **financier** (fi năn' sēr), *n.* One who is skilled in finance, esp. the management of public revenues; one engaged in large-scale monetary dealings; a capitalist; *a receiver or farmer of the public revenues. *v.i.* To manage financial affairs; to raise money by negotiation. *v.t.* To manage the financial affairs of; to finance; (*chiefly Am.*) to get rid of or swindle (away or out of) by financial operations.

finch (finch) [A.-S. *finc* (cp. Dut. *vink*, G. *fink*)], *n.* A popular name for various small birds, many of them of the family *Fringillidæ*; the genus *Fringilla* [see also BULLFINCH, CHAFFINCH, GOLDFINCH]. **finch-backed, finched,** *a.* Striped or spotted on the back (used of cattle).

find (find) [A.-S. *findan* (cp. Dut. *vinden*, Swed. and Icel. *finna*, G. *finden*)], *v.t.* (*past & p.p.* **found**) To chance on, to meet with, to come across; to discover, learn, or acquire by search, study, or other effort; to ascertain by experience or experiment; to perceive, to recognize; to reach, to arrive at; to succeed in obtaining; to reach the feelings of, to come home to; to supply, to furnish, to provide;

to maintain, to support; (*Law*) to decide, to determine; to declare by verdict; to invent. *v.i.* To discover anything by searching or seeking; (*Am.* to locate); (*Law*) to arrive at a decision in a cause; to start a fox. *n.* The discovery of anything valuable; the thing so found; the finding of a fox. **to find a bill:** (*Law*) To remit a case for trial by judge and ordinary jury (said of the grand jury). **to find a ship's trim:** (*Naut.*) To ascertain how she will sail best. **to find fault with:** To blame, to censure. **to find in:** To provide with. **to find oneself:** To be or feel as regards health; to provide oneself (with) the necessaries of life. **to find one's feet:** To learn the use of the feet; (*fig.*) to ascertain or to make full use of one's powers and opportunities. **to find out:** To discover; to unravel, to solve; to invent; to detect, to catch tripping. **findable,** *a.* **finder,** *n.* One who finds; a discoverer, an inventor; (*Opt.*) a small telescope fixed to the tube and parallel to the axis of a larger one, for finding objects to be examined by the larger telescope; a contrivance for the same purpose attached to a microscope or to a camera. ***finder-out,** *n.* ***find-fault,** *n.* A censorious, cavilling person. **finding,** *n.* The action of the verb TO FIND; a discovery; (*Law*) the act of returning a verdict; a verdict; (*pl.*) tools and materials which some workmen have to furnish at their own expense; (*Am.*) shoemaker's tools and other requisites; (*colloq.*) things found. **finding-store,** *n.* (*Am.*) A shop where shoemaker's tools are sold.

fin de siècle (fan dė syākl′) [F., end of the age], *a.* Pertaining to or characteristic of the close of the 19th cent.; progressive, advanced, ultra-modern.

findon [FINNAN].

fine (1) (fīn) [O.F. *fin*, L. *fīnis*, end], *n.* A sum of money imposed as a penalty for an offence; a fee paid by an incoming tenant to the landlord; (*Feud. Law*) a fee paid by a tenant or vassal on the transfer or alienation of the tenant-right; (*fig.*) any sort of penalty; *an end, cessation, conclusion; *decrease, death; *(*pl.*) borders, boundaries, extreme limits. *v.t.* To impose a pecuniary penalty upon; to punish by fine; *to pay as a fine or composition; *to bring to an end, to finish. *v.i.* To pay a fine or monetary consideration; *to pay a penalty or ransom. **in fine:** In conclusion, in short, finally; to sum up. **to fine down** (1) or **off:** To pay a fine to secure a reduction of rent. **finable,** *a.* Deserving or liable to a fine. ***fineless,** *a.* Endless, boundless, limitless.

fine (2) (fīn) [O.F. *fin*, late L. *fīnus*, prob. from L. *fīnītus*, well-rounded, finished, from *fīnīre*, to end, *fīnis*, as prec.], *a.* Excellent in quality, form, or appearance; refined, pure, free from dross or extraneous matter; delicate, subtle, nice, fastidious, dainty (of feelings, taste, etc., also of differences, distinctions, etc.); in small grains or particles; thin, small, slender, tenuous; keen, sharp; of delicate texture or material; finished, consummate, accomplished, brilliant; handsome, beautiful; showy, smart, pretentious; good, satisfactory, enjoyable, pleasant; free from clouds or rain, sunshiny, complimentary, euphemistic; (*ironically*) anything but pleasant or satisfactory. *adv.* (*colloq.*) Finely. *v.t.* To refine, purify, clear from impurities; to make finer, to sharpen, to taper; to make less coarse. *v.i.* To become finer, purer, clarified; to taper, to dwindle (away). **fine!** *int.* Good! Satisfactory! Well done! **to fine down** (2): To clear or to become clear of grossness, opacity, or impurities. **one of these fine days:** At some unspecified date in the future. **fine arts:** The arts, such as poetry, music, painting, sculpture, and architecture, that appeal to our sense of the beautiful. **fine-draw,** *v.t.* To draw together the edges of and mend a rent so that no trace remains visible. **fine-drawn,** *a.* Drawn out finely (as wire); (*fig.*) excessively subtle; (*Athletics*) reduced by training. ***fine-fingered,** *a.* Skilful, dexterous; delicate, fastidious. **fine-spoken,** *a.* Using fine phrases. **fine-spun,** *a.* Drawn or spun out to minuteness; hence, over-refined or elaborate; unpractical; delicate, flimsy. **fine-stuff,** *n.* Slaked lime for the second coat of plaster. **finely,** *adv.* **fineness,** *n.* The quality or state of being fine; (*Metal.*) the quantity of pure metal in an alloy expressed in fractions or in carats. ***finer,** *n.* A refiner of metals. **finery,** *n.* Fine clothes, showy decorations; *the quality of being fine or showy; (*Metal.*) a furnace in which cast-iron is made malleable; the art of refining iron. **fines,** *n.pl.* (*Metal.*) Ores that are too fine or powdery for smelting in the ordinary way. **finish** (fī′ nish), *a.* **fining,** *n.* The process of refining metals, esp. of making cast-iron malleable; the clarifying of wines, malt liquors, etc.; the preparation, generally a solution of gelatine or isinglass, used to fine or clarify liquors. **fining-pot,** *n.* A crucible in which metals are refined.

finesse (fi nes′) [F., as prec.], *n.* Artifice, stratagem, or artful manipulation; a subtle contrivance to gain an end; skill, dexterity, artfulness; (*Whist, etc.*) an attempt to take a trick with a lower card, so as to retain a higher one for later tricks. *v.i.* To use artifice to gain an end; (*Whist, etc.*) to try to win a trick with a lower card than one possibly in your opponent's hand, while you have a higher card in your own. *v.t.* To play (a card) in this manner; to manipulate, to manage by means of trickery or stratagem.

finger (fing′ gėr) [A.-S. (cp. Dut. *vinger*, Icel. *fingr*, Dan., Swed., G., *finger*)], *n.* One of the five digits or terminal members of the hand; one of the four longer digits as distinguished from the thumb; anything resembling or serving the purpose of a finger, an index, a gripper, a catch, a guide shaped like a finger; the part of a glove that covers a finger; the width of a finger, a measure of length; (*pl.*) the hand, the instrument of work or art; (*fig.*) skill in using the fingers as in playing on a keyed instrument. *v.t.* To touch with or turn about in the fingers; to meddle or interfere with; to touch thievishly, to pilfer; to perform with the fingers; to play with the fingers (as a musical instrument); to mark a piece of music so as to indicate which fingers should be used. *v.i.* To use the fingers skilfully in playing an instrument. **to have a finger in:** To be concerned in or mixed up with. **to have at one's finger-tips** or **-ends:** To know familiarly, to be well versed in. **to lay** or **put a finger upon:** To touch, to interfere with in the slightest. **to lay one's finger upon:** To detect or point out precisely (the cause, meaning, etc.). **to the finger-tips:** Completely. **finger-alphabet, language,** *n.* Signs made on the fingers for talking to the deaf. **finger-board,** *n.* The board at the neck of a stringed instrument, where the fingers act on the strings; a keyboard, a manual. **finger-bowl, -glass,** *n.* A glass or bowl in which to rinse the fingers after dessert. **finger-fern,** *n.* One of the spleenworts, *Asplenium Ceterach.* **finger-fish,** *n.* The starfish. **finger-grass,** *n.* A genus of grasses, *Digitaria*, two of which, cock's-foot finger-grass and smooth finger-grass, are British. **finger-plate,** *n.* A plate on the side of a door, near the handle, to preserve the paint from finger-marks. **finger-post,** *n.* A sign-post where roads cross or divide, pointing out direction. **finger-print,** *n.* An impression of the whorls of lines on fingers, used for purposes of identification. **fingers and toes,** *n.pl.* [ANBURY]. **fingers all thumbs,** *adv.* Clumsily. **finger-stall,** *n.* A cover for protecting a finger during dissections, or when injured or diseased. **fingered,** *a.* Having fingers; (*in comb.*) having a certain kind of fingers (as *light-fingered*); (*Bot.*) digitate. **fingerer,** *n.* One who fingers; a pilferer. **fingering,** *n.* The act of touching with the fingers; delicate work done with the fingers; a thick, loose, woollen yarn used for knitting stockings and the like; (*Mus.*) the management of the fingers in playing upon a keyed, string, or holed instrument; marks upon a piece of music to guide the fingers in playing. **fingerless,** *a.* **fingerling,** *n.* The young of the salmon or trout when no longer than a finger; *the finger of a glove.

finial (fin′ i ȧl) [var. of FINAL], *n.* (*Arch.*) A terminal ornament surmounting the apex of a gable, pediment, roof, canopy, etc.

finical (fin′ i kăl) [prob. from FINE (2)], *a.* Affecting great nicety, precision, or delicacy; over-nice, fastidious; particular about trifles; crotchety. **finicality** (-kăl′ i ti), *n.* **finically,** *adv.* **finicalness,** *n.* **finicking,** (*colloq.*) **finicky,** *a.* Finical.

fining [FINE (2)].

finis (fī′ nis) [L.], *n.* (*Printed at end of book*) The end, finish, conclusion; (*fig.*) the end of all things, death.

finish (1) (fin′ ish) [O.F. *finiss-*, base of *finir*, L. *fīnīre*, to end, see FINIS], *v.t.* To bring to an end; to complete; to arrive at the end of; to perfect; to give the final touches to, to trim, to polish; to consume, to get through; to kill, to defeat, to render powerless. *v.i.* To come to the end, to cease, to expire; to leave off. *n.* The act of finishing; the termination, the final stage, the end of a race, when the competitors are close to the winning-post; the last touches, that which gives the effect of perfect completeness; the final stage of any work, as the last raw coat of plaster on a wall; grace, elegance, polish, refinement. **finisher,** *n.* One who or that which finishes; a workman or a machine that performs the final operation in a process of manufacture; a blow that settles a contest. **finishing-coat,** *n.* The last coat in painting or plastering.

finish (2) (fīn′ ish) [FINE (2)], *a.* Rather fine, fairly fine.

finite (fī′ nīt) [L. *fīnītus*, p.p. of *fīnīre*], *a.* Having limits or bounds, opposed to infinite; (*Gram.*) applied to those moods of a verb which are limited by number and person, as the indicative, subjunctive, imperative. **finitely,** *adv.* In a finite manner. **finiteness, finitude,** *n.*

Finn (fin) [A.-S. *Finnas*, pl. (Icel. *Finnr*, Swed., Dan., and G. *Finne*)], *n.* The Teutonic name for the Finlanders, or as they call themselves Suomi, who inhabit parts of north-west Russia and north-east Scandinavia; a native or naturalized inhabitant of Finland. **Finlander** (fin′ lăn dėr), *n.* **Finnic,** *a.* Belonging to this group of peoples. **Finnish,** *a.* Pertaining to Finland, the Finns, or their language. *n.* The language of the Finns.

finnan (fin′ ăn) [etym. doubtful; perh. corr. of *Findhorn*, a fishing-village near Forres], *n.* A kind of smoke-dried haddock, also called **finnan-haddock.**

finned, finner, etc. [FIN].

finnicking, etc. [FINICAL].

Finsen Rays (fin′ sėn rāz) [N. R. *Finsen* (1860–1904)], *n.* (*Med.*) Ultra-violet rays used in the treatment of skin diseases such as lupus.

fiord (fyôrd) [Norw.], *n.* A long, narrow inlet of the sea, bounded by high cliffs, as on the coast of Norway.

fiorin (fī′ ŏr in) [Ir. *fiorthan*], *n.* White bent-grass, *Agrostis alba.*

fiorite (fī′ ŏr īt) [from Santa *Fiora* in Tuscany, where it is found], *n.* (*Min.*) A siliceous incrustation formed by the decomposition of volcanic rocks.

fioritura (fyo rē toor′ a) [It., FLOURISH], *n.* (*pl.* **fioriture**) (*Mus.*) A decorative phrase or turn, a flourish.

fir (fĕr) [M.E. *firre*, prob. from Scand. (cp. Icel. *fyri-*, Dan. *fyr*), perh. cogn. with A.-S. *furh*, O.H.G. *forha*, G. *föhre*, and also L. *quercus*, oak], *n.* The popular name for many coniferous timber trees of the genus *Abies* or allied genera; the wood of these. **Scotch fir:** A European pine, *Pinus sylvestris*, prob. indigenous in N. Britain. **silver fir:** A European mountain fir, *Abies pectinata*; the silver fir of Canada, *Abies balsamea*, which yields Canada balsam. **spruce fir:** The Norway spruce, *Picea excelsa.* **fir-apple, -ball, -cone,** *n.* The cone-shaped fruit of the fir. **fir-needle,** *n.* The spine-like leaf of the fir. **firry** (fĕr′ i), *a.* Consisting of or containing firs.

fire (1) (fī′ ėr) [A.-S. *fȳr* (cp. Dut. *vuur*, Dan. and Swed. *fyr*, G. *feuer*, also Gr. *pûr*)], *n.* The production of heat and light by combustion; combustion, flame, incandescence; fuel in a state of combustion, as in a furnace, grate, etc.; anything burning; a conflagration; a light, glow, or luminosity resembling fire; a spark or sparks emitted when certain substances are struck violently; intense heat, fever; the discharge of fire-arms; (*fig.*) ardent emotion, fervour; liveliness of imagination, vigour of fancy, poetic inspiration; a severe affliction, torture, persecution. **cross-fire** [CROSS]. **Greek fire:** An artificial combustible used by the Greeks in their wars with the Saracens for setting hostile ships on fire. **on fire:** Burning, in flames; (*fig.*) excited, ardent, eager. **running fire:** A discharge of fire-arms in rapid succession by a line of troops. **St. Anthony's fire:** Erysipelas. **St. Elmo's fire:** The corposant. **to catch** or **take fire:** To ignite. **to set fire to, on fire,** or **a-fire:** To kindle; (*fig.*) to excite, to inflame. **to set the Thames on fire:** To do something clever or remarkable. **under fire:** Exposed to the enemy's fire-arms. **fire-alarm,** *n.* An automatic apparatus for communicating warning of a fire. **fire-annihilator,** *n.* A vessel charged with a chemical composition for extinguishing fires. **fire-arm,** *n.* (*usu. in pl.*) A weapon that projects a missile by the explosive force of gunpowder, esp. a rifle or pistol. **fireback,** *n.* The rear wall of a furnace or fire-place; a pheasant of the genus *Euplocamus* found in Sumatra. **fire-ball,** *n.* (*Mil.*) A ball or sack filled with combustible composition, a grenade; globular lightning; a large meteor or shooting star. **fire-balloon,** *n.* A balloon filled with heated air from a fire beneath its open mouth; a balloon sent up at night with fireworks. **fire-bar,** *n.* One of the bars in a furnace on which the fuel rests. **fire-basket,** *n.* A small portable grate. **fire-bird,** *n.* The Baltimore oriole. **fire-blast, -blight,** *n.* A disease in plants, esp. in hops. **fire-board,** *n.* A chimney-board used to close up a fire-place in summer. **fire bomb,** *n.* An incendiary bomb. **fire-box,** *n.* The chamber in which the fuel is burned in a locomotive, etc. **fire-brand,** *n.* A piece of wood kindled or on fire; (*fig.*) an incendiary; one who inflames passions or kindles strife. **a.* Brand new. **fire-branded,** *a.* Carrying fire-brands (in allusion to the story of Samson destroying the corn of the Philistines, Judges xv). **fire-brick,** *n.* A brick capable of withstanding fire used for fire-places, furnaces, and all kinds of work exposed to intense heat. **fire-brigade,** *n.* A body of men organized by a public authority, etc., for the extinction of fires. **fire-bucket,** *n.* A bucket (usu. filled with water) kept in readiness in case of fire. **fire-bug,** *n.* (*colloq.*) An incendiary. **fire-clay,** *n.* A kind of clay consisting of nearly pure silicate of alumina, capable of standing intense heat, used in the manufacture of fire-bricks. **fire-cock,** *n.* A street plug for attachment of hose for extinguishing fire, etc. **fire-company,** *n.* (*Am.*) A fire-brigade; a fire-insurance company. **fire-cross** [FIERY-CROSS]. **fire-damp,** *n.* The explosive carburetted hydrogen which accumulates in coal-mines. **fire-dog,** *n.* An andiron. **fire-drake,** *n.* A fiery dragon or serpent; an ignis fatuus; a firework. **fire-drill,** *n.* An instrument used by the Australians and Tasmanians for producing fire, consisting of two pieces of soft dry wood, one of which is made to revolve quickly upon the other till they ignite; practice in the routine to be observed in case of fire. **fire-eater,** *n.* A juggler who pretends to swallow fire; (*fig.*) a bully, a duellist, a lover of fighting. **fire-engine,** *n.* A machine for throwing water to extinguish fires. **fire-escape,** *n.* An apparatus for enabling persons to escape from the upper parts of buildings that are on fire. **fire-extinguisher,** *n.* A portable apparatus for extinguishing fires by cutting off the air necessary for combustion. **fire-flair,** *n.* The sting ray, *Trygon pastinaca.* **fire-fly,** *n.* A small luminous winged insect, chiefly of the families *Elateridæ* and *Lampyridæ.* **fire-guard,** *n.* A wire frame placed before an open fire as a safeguard against accidental fire or injury to children, etc.; person entrusted with watching for and guarding against incendiary bombs. **fire-hose,** *n.* Hose-pipe employed for extinguishing fires. **fire-insurance,** *n.* Insurance against loss by fire. **fire-irons,** *n.pl.* The implements for tending a fire—poker, tongs, and shovel. **fire-light,** *n.* The light from a fire. **fire-lighter,** *n.* An inflammable substance for kindling fuel. **fire-lock,** *n.* An old-fashioned musket or other gun having a lock with a flint and steel, by means of which the priming was ignited. **fireman,** *n.* One who is employed to extinguish fires; a member of a fire-brigade; a stoker; (*Coal-mining*) a man employed to examine the workings to see that no fire-damp is present. **fire-master,** *n.* (*Local*) The chief of a fire-brigade; *(*Mil.*) an officer who directed the making of fireworks. ***fire-new,** *a.* Brand-new. **fire-office,** *n.* A fire-insurance office. **fire-opal** [GIRASOL]. **fire-pan,** *n.* A pan for holding fire, a brazier; *the receptacle for the priming in a fire-lock. **fire-place,** *n.* A grate; a hearth. **fire-plug,** *n.* A hydrant for connecting a fire-hose with a water-main. **fire-policy,** *n.* A policy or certificate guaranteeing compensation up to a stated limit in case of damage by fire. **fire-pot,** *n.* The pot or receptacle in a stove for holding the fuel; (*Metal.*) a crucible; *(*Mil.*) a small earthen pot filled with combustibles. **fire-proof,** *a.* Proof against fire; incombustible. *v.i.* To render proof against fire. **fire-proof curtain** [SAFETY-CURTAIN]. **fire-proofing,** *n.* The process of rendering fire-proof; material used for this purpose. **fire-raising,** *n.* The act of setting on fire; incendiarism, arson. **fire risk,** *n.* Risk of accidental damage by fire. ***fire-robed,** *a.* Robed in fire. **fire-screen,** *n.* A fire-guard; a screen placed between a person and the fire to intercept the direct rays. **fire-ship,** *n.* A vessel freighted with combustibles and explosives, and sent among an enemy's ships in order to set them on fire. **fire-shovel,** *n.* A shovel for putting coals on a fire. **fireside,** *n.* The space around a fire-place, the hearth; hence home, home life. *a.* Home, domestic. **fire-stick,** *n.* (*Austral.*) An Aboriginal torch. **firestone,** *n.* A stone capable of bearing a high degree of heat, used in furnaces, etc.; a stone used for striking fire, as a flint or iron pyrites. **fire-trap,** *n.* (*colloq.*) A building without adequate means of exit in case of fire. **fire-tree,** *n.* The Queensland tulip-tree. **fire-water,** *n.* The name given by the native Indians of North America to ardent spirit. **fire-weed,** *n.* (*Austral.*) Any weed springing up after a forest fire. **firewood,** *n.* Wood for burning; fuel, (*Am.* kindling). **firework,** *n.* A preparation of various kinds of combustibles and explosives for producing a brilliant display at times of public rejoicing, etc.; similar preparations used for illumination, signalling, incendiary purposes, or in war. ***fire-worker,** *n.* An officer of artillery in charge of fireworks or explosives, subordinate to the fire-master. **fire-worship,** *n.* Worship of fire as a living being or deity. **fire-worshipper,** *n.* One who worships fire, a Parsee. **fireless,** *a.* Destitute of or without fire (a term applied to races said to be ignorant of any method of producing fire).

fire (2) (fī′ ėr) [from prec.], *v.t.* To set on fire, to kindle, to ignite; to discharge, to cause to explode; to bake (as pottery); (*Vet.*) to cauterize; to supply with fuel (as a furnace); (*fig.*) to inflame, to irritate, to excite, to illuminate strongly; (*slang*) to dismiss, to discharge from employment. *v.i.* To take fire, to be kindled; to discharge fire-arms; to shoot (at) with fire-arms; to ring (as a peal of bells) simultaneously. **fire-control,** *n.* (*Nav., Mil.*) The system of controlling gun-fire from one spot. **Fire!** (*Mil.*) A word of command for soldiers to discharge their fire-arms. **fire away:** Begin, proceed. **to fire out:** To expel forcibly, to chuck out. **to fire up:** To be inflamed with passion, to be irritated. **fire-step, firing-step,** *n.* A raised ledge inside a trench on which soldiers stand to fire. **firer,** *n.* One who or that which fires; (*in comb.*) a gun with one or more barrels (as a *single-firer*). **firing,** *n.* The adding of fuel to a boiler furnace; (*Mach.*) the ignition of an explosive mixture in an internal combustion cylinder; the act of discharging fire-arms; fuel; the act of cauterizing; the application of a cautery to a horse. **firing-charge,** *n.* The explosive used for detonating the charge in a torpedo, mine, etc. **firing-iron,** *n.* A veterinary's cautery. **firing-line,** *n.* A line of troops engaging the enemy with fire-arms. **firing-party,** *n.* A detachment told off to fire over a grave at a military funeral, or to shoot a condemned man. **firing-pin,** *n.* A sliding pin in fire-arms that strikes upon the detonator and explodes the charge. **firing-point** [FLASH-POINT].

firk (fĕrk) [A.-S. *fercian*, prob. from *fær*, journey, see FARE], *v.t.* To drive or rouse (up, out, or off); *to whip, to beat.

firkin (fĕr′ kin) [formerly *ferdekyn*, prob. from M.Dut. (*vierde*, fourth, *ken*, -KIN)], *n.* A measure of capacity; the fourth part of a barrel or nine gallons; a small wooden cask used for butter, tallow, etc., of no fixed capacity.

***firlot** (fĕr′ lot) [perh. corr. of FOUR or FOURTH and LOT], *n.* (*Sc.*) A dry measure; the fourth part of a boll.

firm (1) (fĕrm) [O.F. *ferme*, L. *firmus*], *a.* Fixed, stable, steady; difficult to move or disturb; solid, compact, unyielding; securely established, immutable; steadfast; stanch, enduring, resolute; constant, unwavering, not changing in level (as prices). *adv.* Firmly. *v.t.* To fix firmly; to make firm, to consolidate; *to confirm. *v.i.* To become firm; to solidify. **firm offer,** *n.* A definite offer. **firmly,** *adv.* **firmness,** *n.*

firm (2) (fĕrm) [late L. *firma*, a signature, L. *firmāre*, to confirm, as prec. (cp. FARM)], *n.* A partnership or association of two or more persons for carrying on a business; the business itself. **long firm,** *n.* A gang of swindlers who get hold of goods for which they do not pay.

firmament (fĕr′ må mėnt) [O.F., from L. *firmāmentum*], *n.* The sky regarded as a solid expanse, the vault of heaven; *a foundation, a basis. **firmamental** (-men′ tål), *a.* Of or pertaining to the firmament; celestial; of the upper regions.

firman (fĕr′ mån) [Pers. *fermān*], *n.* A decree, mandate, or order of an Eastern monarch, issued for any purpose, as a passport, grant, licence, etc.

firn (fĕrn) [G., last year's snow (*firne*, of last year)], *n.* *Névé*, snow on the higher slopes of lofty mountains, not yet consolidated into ice.

first (fĕrst) [A.-S. *fyrst* (cp. Icel. *fyrstr*, Dan. *förste*, also G. *fürst*, prince), superl. from stem *fur-*, *for-*, see FORE, FORMER], *a.* Foremost in order, time, place, rank, importance, or excellence; earliest in occurrence; nearest, coming next (to something specified); chief, highest, noblest. *adv.* Before all others in order, time, place, rank, importance, or excellence; before some time, act, or event (specified or implied); sooner, rather, in preference, for the first time. *n.* That which or the person who comes first; the first mentioned; the beginning; (*Exam.*) a place in the first class, a candidate winning this; (*Racing*) the first place in a race, the winner of this; (*pl.*) the best quality of a commodity (such as flour); (*Mus.*) the upper part in a duet, trio, etc. **at first, at the first:** At the beginning; originally. **at first blush,** *adv.* On first appearance, at first consideration. **first of exchange:** The first of a set of bills of exchange of even date. **first or last:** At one time or another. **from first to last:** Throughout; altogether. **first aid,** *n.* Assistance rendered to an injured person before a doctor comes. **first-begot, first-begotten,** *a.* First-born among offspring (applied esp. to Christ as the offspring of the Father). *n.* The eldest child. **first-born,** *a.* Born first, eldest. *n.* The first in order of birth. **first-class,** *a.* First-rate; of the highest quality or degree. *n.* The highest division in an examination list; a place in this; the first or best class of railway carriage or other accommodation. **first cost,** *n.* The original cost, as dist. from the price which includes profit. **first day,** *n.* Sunday, as being the first day of the week. **First Fleet,** *n.* (*Austral. hist.*) The ships that brought the original convicts to Australia in 1788. **First Fleeter,** *n.* One of these convicts. **first floor,** *n.* The floor or story of a building next above the ground-floor; (*Am.*) the ground-floor (the first floor in Eng. is Am. second floor). **first-foot,** *n.* (*Sc.*) The first caller at a house on New Year's Day; the first person met in setting out on some important business. **first form,** *n.* The lowest class in schools. **first-fruits,** *n.pl.* The fruit or produce first gathered in any season and offered to God by the Jews; the first effects or results; the first profits of any office, paid to a superior; (*Feud. Law*) a year's profit on land after the death of a tenant, payable to the king; (*Eccles. Law*) the first year's income of a spiritual benefice, orig. paid to the Pope, but appropriated by Henry VIII, and afterwards transferred to Queen Anne's Bounty. **first-hand,** *a.* Obtained directly from the first or original source; direct. **at first hand:** Directly; by personal knowledge or observation. **first mate,** *n.* The chief officer of a merchant-vessel, next in rank to the captain. **first-nighter,** *n.* One who makes a point of attending first performances of plays. **first offender,** *n.* One not previously convicted. **first-rate,** *a.* Of the first or highest class or quality; of the highest excellence. *adv.* Excellently, very well. *n.* (*Naut.*) A warship of the most powerful class. **first water,** *n.* The purest quality (of diamonds, etc.). **firstling,** *a.* *That is first produced or brought forth. *n.* The first-born, the first-born in a season; (*pl.*) the first-fruits. **firstly,** *adv.* In the first place, to begin with.

firth (fĕrth) [Sc., prob. from Icel. (cp. Norw. FIORD)], *n.* An estuary, an arm of the sea.

fisc (fisk) [L. *fiscus*, a basket, a purse, the treasury], *n.* The treasury of the State, the public purse or exchequer; the Crown Treasury of Scotland; (*facet.*) one's purse. **fiscal,** *a.* Pertaining to the public revenue or exchequer, financial. *n.* A public functionary with legal or financial duties in Scotland and various foreign countries; *a treasurer; a procurator-fiscal. **fiscally,** *adv.*

fisgig [FIZGIG].

fish (1) (fish) [A.-S. *fisc* (cp. Dut. *visch*, Icel. *fiskr*, G. *fisch*, also L. *piscis*)], *n.* (*pl.* in general **fish**; in particular **fishes**) An aquatic, oviparous, cold-blooded vertebrate animal, provided with permanent gills, usually covered with scales, and progressing by means of fins, the homologues of the limbs of the higher vertebrates; the flesh of fish used as food; (*fig.*) one who is being angled for; (*Naut.*) a strip of wood for mending or strengthening a spar; (*colloq.*) a certain kind of person (as an odd fish). *v.i.* To try to catch fish, by angling, netting, etc.; to search for something under water; (*fig.*) to seek to learn or obtain anything by indirect means or finesse. *v.t.* To attempt to catch fish in; to lay hold of and drag up from under water; to search (water, etc.) by sweeping, dragging, etc.; (*Naut.*) to strengthen (as a piece of timber or a sprung mast or yard) by securing a piece of timber or a spar on each side of the weak part. **to feed the fishes:** To be seasick. **to fish for compliments:** To lead people to pay compliments. **to fish out:** To catch or draw out of water; (*fig.*) to ascertain by cunning inquiry. **to fish the anchor:** (*Naut.*) To draw up the flukes to the bulwarks after the anchor has been catted. **a fish out of water:** Anyone out of one's element, in a strange or bewildering situation. **neither fish, flesh, nor fowl,** or (*colloq.*) **nor good red herring:** Nondescript; of a vague indefinite character. **other fish to fry:** More important matters to attend to. **fish and chips:** (*colloq.*) Fried fish and fried potato chips. **fish-ball, -cake,** *n.* A fried cake of chopped fish and mashed potatoes. **fish-basket,** *n.* A basket for carrying fish. **fish-carver,** *n.* A large flat knife for serving fish. **fish-curer,** *n.* One who salts or smokes fish. **fish-day,** *n.* A day on which fish is eaten instead of meat. **fish-garth,** *n.* A staked or dammed enclosure on a river for taking or preserving fish. **fish-gig,** *n.* A spear with several barbed prongs used in taking fish. **fish-globe,** *n.* A small globular aquarium for gold-fish, etc. **fish-glue,** *n.* A glue made of the entrails and skin of fish; isinglass. **fish-hawk,** *n.* The osprey. **fish-hook,** *n.* A barbed hook for catching fish; (*Naut.*) the hook in tackle for raising an anchor. **fish-joint,** *n.* A joint made with fish-plates on a railway-line. **fish-kettle,** *n.* A long oval pan for boiling fish. **fish-knife,** *n.* A silver or silver-plated knife for eating fish. **fish-louse,** *n.* A small crustacean parasitic upon fishes and other aquatic animals. **fish-oil,** *n.* Oil obtained from fish and other marine animals, as whales, etc. **fish-plate,** *n.* (*Rail.*) A plate used to fasten rails end to end. **fish-pond,** *n.* A pond in which fish are kept; (*facet.*) the sea. ***fish-room,** *n.* (*Naut.*) A room or compartment in a ship, between the after-hold and the spirit-room. **fish-slice,** *n.* A broad-bladed knife, usually of silver, for serving fish at table; a similar instrument used by cooks for turning or taking fish out of the pan, etc. **fish-sound,** *n.* The swimming-bladder of a fish. **fish-spear,** *n.* A spear or dart, usu. with barbs, for striking fish. **fish-strainer,** *n.* A metal colander with handles, used for taking fish out of the fish-kettle; a perforated slab at the bottom of a dish to drain cooked fish. **fish-tackle,** *n.* (*Naut.*) A tackle used for raising an anchor to the gunwale for stowage after being catted. **fish-tail,** *a.* Shaped like the tail of a fish. **fish-tail burner,** *n.* A gas-burner producing a jet like a fish's tail. **fish-tail wind,** *n.* (*Rifle-shooting*) A variable wind blowing down the range from behind the firers. **fish-torpedo,** *n.* A fish-shaped, self-propelled torpedo. **fish-wife,** *n.* A woman that sells fish; (*colloq.*) a coarse, foul-mouthed woman.

fish (2) (fish) [F. *fiche*, a peg, from *ficher*, prob. L. *figere*, to fix], *n.* A counter used in various games.

fisher (fish' ĕr), *n.* One who is employed in fishing; a fisherman; an animal that fishes; a fishing-boat.

fisherman (fish' ĕr măn), *n.* One whose employment is to catch fish; an angler; a boat or vessel employed in catching fish. **fisherman's bend:** A kind of knot.

fishery (fish' ĕr i), *n.* The business of catching fish; any place where fishing is carried on; (*Law*) permission to fish in reserved water.

fishing (fish' ing), *n.* The action of the verb TO FISH; the sport of angling; a place where angling is carried on; a fishery. **fishing-boat,** *n.* A boat employed in catching fish. **fishing-frog,** *n.* The angler-fish. **fishing-line,** *n.* A line with hook attached for catching fish. **fishing-net,** *n.* A net for catching fish. **fishing-rod,** *n.* A long, slender, tapering rod, usu. in sections jointed together, for angling. **fishing-tackle,** *n.* All the apparatus required by a fisherman.

fishmonger (fish' mŭng gėr), *n.* A retail dealer in fish, (*Am.* a fish-dealer).

fishy (fish' i), *a.* Like, consisting of, pertaining to, or suggestive of fish; inhabited by or abounding in fish; (*fig.*) of a doubtful character, questionable, dubious. **fishily,** *adv.* **fishiness,** *n.*

***fisk** (fisk) [perh. from A.-S. *fȳsan*, to hurry], *v.i.* To bustle; to frisk (about).

***fisnomy** [PHYSIOGNOMY].

fissi-, fisso- [L. *fissus*, p.p. of *findere*, to split, cleave], *comb. form.* (*Anat., Biol., etc.*) Divided; dividing; by division. **fissidactyl** (fis i dăk' til) [Gr. *daktulos*, finger], *a.* Having the digits divided.

fissile (fis' il) [L. *fissilis*, from *findere*, to cleave], *a.* That may be cleft or split, esp. in the direction of the grain, as wood, or along natural planes of cleavage, as rock. ***fissility** (-sil' i ti), *n.*

fission (fish' ŭn), *n.* The act or process of cleaving, splitting or breaking up into parts, particularly of uranium or plutonium to liberate nuclear energy; (*Biol.*) a form of asexual reproduction in certain simple organisms, the individual cell dividing into new cells. **nuclear fission:** (*Phys.*) The splitting of the nucleus of an atom into two parts.

fissiparous (fi sip' ȧ rŭs), *a.* Propagating by fission. **fissiparously,** *adv.* **fissiparity** (fis i păr' i ti), *n.*

fissiped (fis' i ped), *a.* (*Zool.*) Having the toes separate. *n.* An individual of the carnivorous group *Fissipedia.*

fissirostral (fis i ros' trȧl), *a.* (*Zool.*) Having a deeply cleft beak; belonging to the tribe of insessorial birds *Fissirostres.*

fissure (fish' ŭr) [F., from L. *fissūra*, as FISSILE], *n.* A cleft or opening made by the splitting or parting of any substance; (*Anat., etc.*) a slit or narrow opening, as the deep narrow depression between the anterior and middle lobes of the cerebrum on each side. *v.t.* To cleave, to split. *v.i.* To become split or cleft.

fist (fist) [A.-S. *fyst* (cp. Dut. *vuist*, G. *faust*)], *n.* The clenched hand, esp. in readiness to strike a blow; (*colloq.*) the hand; (*facet.*) handwriting; (*Typog.*) a hand pointing, as ☞; *the talons of a bird of prey. *v.t.* To strike or grip with the fist; (*Naut.*) to handle (ropes, sails, etc.). **fisted,** *a.* (*usu. in comb.*) Having a certain kind of fist (as *close-fisted*, miserly). **fistic, -al,** *a.* Pertaining or relating to pugilism. **fisticuffs,** *n.pl.* A fight with the fists; a boxing-match.

fistula (fis' tū lȧ) [L., a pipe, a flute], *n.* (*Path.*) A kind of ulcer or suppurating swelling, in form like a pipe; (*Zool.*) a narrow pipe-like passage, duct, or spout, in insects, whales, etc.; (*Rom. Ant.*) a kind of flute made of reeds. **fistular, fistulate,** *a.* Hollow like a reed; (*Path.*) pertaining to fistula. **fistuliform** (-fôrm), *a.* Of a fistular form; (*Min.*) in round hollow columns, as minerals. **fistulose, -lous,** *a.* Hollow like a pipe or reed; (*Path.*) of the form or nature of a fistula.

fit (1) (fit) [A.-S. *fitt*, etym. and sense doubtful (perh. as foll.)], *n.* A violent seizure or paroxysm; a sudden transitory attack of illness; a sudden attack of epilepsy or other disease characterized by convulsions, swooning, and hysteria; a spasm, a seizure; a transient state of impulsive action, a mood, a caprice. **by fits and starts:** Intermittently. **fitful,** *a.* Spasmodic, capricious, wavering; acting by fits and starts. **fitfully,** *adv.* **fitfulness,** *n.*

***fit** (2), ***fytte** (fit) [A.-S. *fitt*, a song, part of a poem], *n.* A short canto or division of a poem.

fit (3) (fit) [M.E. *fyt*, etym. doubtful], *a.* Adapted, suitable, appropriate; becoming, proper, meet; qualified, competent; ready, prepared, in a suitable condition (to do or for); (*colloq.*) in good bodily condition; (*colloq.*) as if, in such a mood or condition as (to cry, to do something violent, etc.). *v.t.* (*past & p.p.* **fitted**) To adapt to any shape, size, or measure; to make suitable, to accommodate; to try on a garment; to supply, to furnish, to equip; to qualify, to prepare; to be adapted, suitable, or proper for; to be of the right size, measure, and shape for; to correspond to exactly. *v.i.* To be adjusted or adapted to the right shape, measure, form, etc.; to be proper, suitable, convenient, or becoming. *n.* Exact adjustment, as of a dress to the body; the manner in which anything fits, the style in which a garment fits. **to fit in:** To find room for; to prove accommodating or suitable. **to fit out:** To equip, to furnish with the necessary outfit, stores, armament, etc. **to fit up:** To furnish with the things suitable or necessary. **to think fit to:** To decide to (do something). **fitly,** *adv.* **fitment,** *n.* A piece of furniture; (*usu. in pl.*) fittings; *that which is fit or proper, a duty; *preparation, a making fit. **fitted,** *a.* Adapted, suitable (for); (*in comb.*) fitted in a particular way (as *well-fitted*).

***fitch** (1) [var. of VETCH].

fitch (2) (fich) [cp. M.Dut. *fisse*, a polecat], *n.* The fur of the polecat; a brush made of this. **fitch-brush,** *n.*

fitchew (fich' oo) [as prec.], *n.* A polecat.

fitness (fit' nes), *n.* Suitability, good health.

fitter (fit' er), *n.* One who or that which fits; one who puts together the several parts of machinery; one who fits certain kinds of apparatus (*e.g.* gas-fitter).

fitting (fit' ing), *a.* Suitable, appropriate, right, proper. *n.* The act of making fit; (*pl.*) fixtures, apparatus, furniture employed in fitting up a house, shop, etc.; (*Dressmaking*) preliminary trying on of a garment. **fitting-shop,** *n.* A workshop in which machinery is fitted up. **fitting-up,** *n.* The act or process of furnishing with the necessary fittings or fixtures. **fittingly,** *adv.*

five (fīv) [A.-S. *fīf* (cp. Dut. *vijf*, G. *fünf*, Gr. *pente*, L. *quinque*)], *a.* Amounting to one more than four. *n.* The number amounting to one more than four; a symbol representing such number, as 5 or v; a set of five things; a card, counter, etc., with five pips; (*pl.*) articles of attire, such as boots, gloves, etc., of the fifth size; bonds bearing five-per-cent interest. **a bunch of fives:** The fist. **five-eighth,** *n.* (*Football*) Player in Rugby posted between the half-backs and three-quarter backs. **five-figure tables,** *n.pl.* Tables of five-figure logarithms. **five-finger,** *n.* A name for various plants, esp. *Potentilla reptans*, *Lotus corniculatus*; species of starfish, *Uraster rubens* and *Solaster papposus.* **five-finger exercises,** *n.pl.* Exercises to improve the touch in playing the piano. ***five-finger tied:** Tied by the whole hand; securely or strongly tied. **five-penny** (fīv' pėn i, fip' ėn i), *a.* Priced at five pence. **five-per-cents,** *n.pl.* Stocks or shares paying five per cent. **fivefold,** *a.* and *adv.* Five times as much or as great. **five-leaf,** *n.* Cinquefoil. **five-shooter,** *n.* A five-chambered revolver. **Five Power Treaty,** *n.* Treaty adopted at the Washington Conference in 1922, whereby the British Empire, U.S.A., France, Italy, and Japan agreed upon definite limitations of naval armaments. **fiver,** *n.* (*colloq.*) A five-pound note; anything that counts as five, as a stroke for five at cricket, etc.

fives (1) (fīvz) [from prec.], *n.* A game in which a ball is struck against a wall by the open hand or a small wooden bat. **fives-court,** *n.* A court with two, three, or four walls where the game of fives is played.

***fives** (2) (fīvz) [F. *vives*, *avives*, Sp. *avivas*, *adivas*, Arab. *ad-dībah* (*al-*, the, *dībah*, she-wolf)], *n.pl.* A disease in horses, the strangles.

fix (fiks) [orig. an adj., from O.F. *fixe*, L. *fixus*, p.p. of *fīgere*, to fix], *v.t.* To make fast, firm, or stable; to fasten, attach, secure firmly; to establish; to deprive of volatility, to make permanent or stable (as colours, a photographic picture, etc.); to solidify; to arrest and hold (as eyes, attention, etc.); to direct steadily; to settle, to determine, to decide (on); to adjust, to appoint a definite position for; (*colloq.*) to adjust, to arrange properly, to set to rights. *v.i.* To become fixed; to settle down permanently; to lose volatility; to become congealed. *n.* An awkward predicament, a dilemma. **to fix on** or **upon:** To determine on; to choose, to select. **to fix up:** (*colloq.*) To arrange, to organize; to make arrangements or preparations for. **fixable,** *a.* **fixed,** *a.* Fast, firm; established, settled, unalterable. ***fixed air:** Carbonic-acid gas. **fixed alkalies** or **oils,** *n.pl.* Alkalies or oils not easily volatilized. **fixed idea,** *n.* A rooted idea, one tending to become a monomania. **fixed point,** *n.* A place where a police-constable is permanently stationed. **fixed property,** *n.* Landed estate, houses, etc. **fixed stars,** *n.pl.* Stars which apparently maintain the same relative positions to each other in the sky, as distinct from planets. **fixedly,** *adv.* Steadfastly, firmly; intently. **fixedness,** *n.* The quality or state of being fixed; immobility, steadfastness; absence of volatility. **fixer,** *n.*

fixate (fiks' āt), *v.t.* and *i.* To render fixed; (*Psych.*) to direct upon an object with the eyes.

fixation (fik zā' shŭn), *n.* The act of fixing; the process of making nonvolatile, as causing a gas to combine with a solid; the process of ceasing to be fluid and becoming firm; (*Psych.*) an emotional arrest of development of the personality.

fixative (fik' zȧ tiv), *a.* Serving to fix. *n.* A substance used to make colours permanent or prevent crayon or pastel drawings from becoming blurred.

fixature (fik' zȧ chůr), *n.* A preparation for fixing the hair, as bandoline.

fixings (fik' zingz), *n.pl.* Equipment, apparatus, outfit, adjuncts of any kind.

fixity (fik' zi ti), *n.* Coherence of parts; fixedness, stability, permanence; (*Phys.*) the quality of being able to resist the tendency to lose weight or become volatilized through heat.

fixture (fiks' chůr), *n.* Anything fixed in a permanent position; (*Law*) articles of a personal nature fitted in a house.

fizgig (fiz' gig) [etym. obscure (perh. foll. and GIG)], *n.* A gadding, flirting girl; a firework of damp powder that fizzes.

fizz (fiz) [imit.], *v.i.* To make a hissing or sputtering sound. *n.* A hissing, sputtering sound; (*slang*) champagne, from its effervescence; ginger-beer, lemonade.

fizzle (fiz' ėl) [freq. of prec.], *v.i.* To fizz; (*Am. slang*) to fail ignominiously (at an examination). *v.t.* To cause to fail (at an examination). *n.* The sound or action of fizzing or fizzling; (*slang*) a lame ending, a fiasco. **to fizzle out:** To come to a lame conclusion, to make a fiasco.

fjord [FIORD].

flabbergast (flăb' ėr gast) [etym. doubtful], *v.t.* To strike with wonder and amazement; to astound, to stagger with surprise.

flabby (flăb' i) [var. of obs. *flappy* (FLAP)], *a.* Hanging loosely, limp, flaccid; lacking in fibre or nerve, languid, feeble. **flabbily,** *adv.* **flabbiness,** *n.*

flabellate (flȧ bel' ȧt), *a.* Fan-shaped. **flabellation** (flăb ė lā' shůn), *n.* (*Med.*) Cooling with a fan or similar contrivance. **flabelliform** [-FORM].

flabellum (flȧ bel' ům) [L., a fan], *n.* (*pl.* ***la***) A fan, esp. one used (*Gr. Ch.*) to drive away flies from the chalice or (*R.-C. Ch.*) to carry in religious processions; (*Nat. Hist.*) a fan-shaped part or organ.

flaccid (flăk' sid) [F. *flaccide*, L. *flaccidus*, from *flaccus*, flabby], *a.* Lacking firmness or vigour; limp, flabby, drooping; relaxed, feeble. **flaccidity** (flăk sid' i ti), *n.* **flaccidly,** *adv.* **flaccidness,** *n.*

flack (flăk) [M.E. *flacken*, onomat. (cp. FLAP, FLICK)], *v.t.* To flap, flick, or flourish (as a whip); to flap or flick (with).

***flacket** (flăk' ėt) [O.N.F. *flaquet*, O.F. *flaschet*, dim. of *flasque*, see FLASK], *n.* A little flask or flagon.

flacon (fla kon) [F., see FLAGON], *n.* A small bottle, esp. a scent-bottle.

flag (1) (flăg) [prob. imit. in origin (cp. M.E. *flakken*, to waver, flutter, O.F. *flaquir*, to hang down, become flaccid, L. *flaccus*, limp; also FLABBY, FLICKER)], *v.i.* To hang loosely, to droop; to become limp; to lose strength or vigour; to become spiritless or dejected; to lose interest. **v.t.* To allow to droop; *to tire out, to enfeeble; *to slacken, to cease to fly vigorously (as wings).

flag (2) (flăg) [perh. imit. (cp. prec., also Dut. *vlag*, Dan. *flag*, Norw. and Swed. *flagg*, G. *flagge*)], *n.* A piece of bunting or other cloth, usu. square or oblong, and plain or bearing a device, attached by one edge to a staff or halyard by which it can be hoisted on a pole or mast, and displayed as a banner, ensign, or signal; (*Naut.*) a flag carried by a flagship to show that the admiral is in command; the flagship itself; the bushy part of a dog's tail, as of a setter; the uncut tuft of hair on a brush; the long quill-feathers of a bird's wing; *a bird's wing. *v.t.* (*past & p.p.* **flagged**) To put a flag over; to decorate with flags; to mark out with flags; to signal by means of a flag or flags. **black flag:** A flag indicating piracy, or that no quarter will be given; a flag hoisted over a prison to signalize an execution. **Black Flags:** Chinese irregular soldiers. **flag of convenience:** A foreign flag under which a vessel is registered to escape taxation, etc., in its real country of origin. **flag of truce:** A white flag indicating that the enemy has some pacific communication to make; (*fig.*) an offer of peace. **red flag:** The symbol of revolution; a sign of defiance. **to dip the flag:** (*Naut.*) To lower and then raise it as a salute. **to hang the flag half-mast high:** To fly it halfway up the staff as a token of mourning. **to hoist one's flag:** (of an admiral) To take up the command of a squadron. **to strike** or **lower the flag:** To pull the flag down in token of surrender or submission; (of an admiral) to relinquish the command. **white flag:** [FLAG OF TRUCE]. **yellow flag:** A flag hoisted by a hospital ship, a ship in quarantine, or a ship with infectious disease on board. **flag captain,** *n.* (*Nav.*) The commanding officer of a flagship. **flag day,** *n.* A day on which street collections are made for a specific charity, a small flag being worn as a token of having given money. **flag-lieutenant,** *n.* An officer in immediate attendance upon a flag-officer. **flag-list,** *n.* The roll or register of flag-officers. **flag-man,** *n.* One who makes signals with flags; *a flag-officer. **flag-officer,** *n.* A commander of a squadron; an admiral, vice-admiral, or rear-admiral. **flagship,** *n.* The ship which carries the admiral, and on which his flag is displayed. **flag-staff,** *n.* (*pl.* **-staffs, -staves**) The pole or staff on which a flag is displayed. **flag-station,** *n.* A railway station at which trains stop only when signalled. **flag-wagging,** *n.* (*Mil. slang*) Signalling or signalling-drill.

flag (3) (flăg) [prob. rel. to prec., from its waving or fluttering (cp. Dut. *flag*, mod. Dan. *flæg*)], *n.* One of various herbaceous plants with long blade-like leaves growing in moist places, chiefly belonging to the genus *Iris*; (*pl. or collect. sing.*) a coarse, reedy kind of grass. **flag-basket,** *n.* A basket made of reeds for carrying tools. **flag-worm,** *n.* A worm or grub found in the roots of flags and used as bait by anglers. **flaggy,** *a.*

flag (4) (flăg), **flagstone** [prob. a form of FLAKE (1)], *n.* A broad flat stone used for paving; (*pl.*) a pavement made of such stones; (*Geol.*) a fine-grained rock which can be split into slabs for paving. *v.t.* To pave with flags. **flagging,** *n.* The act of paving with flagstones; flagstones; a pavement of flagstones.

flagellate (flăj' ė lāt) [L. *flagellātus*, p.p. of *flagellāre*, to scourge, from *flagellum*, dim. of *flagrum*, a scourge], *v.t.* To whip, to beat, to scourge. *a.* (-lȧt) (*Zool., Bot., etc.*) Having whip-like processes or flagella. **flagellant** (flăj' ė lȧnt, flȧ jel' ȧnt), *n.* One of a sect of fanatics which arose in Italy about 1260 who sought to avert the divine wrath by scourging themselves till the blood came; (*Psych.*) one who thrashes (himself or others) for sexual gratification. *a.* Given to scourging. **flagellation** (-lā' shůn), *n.* A scourging or flogging. **flagellator** (flăj'-), *n.* **flagellatory,** *a.* **flagelliform** (flȧ jel' i fôrm) [-FORM], *a.* **flagellum** (flȧ jel' ům), *n.* (*pl.* **-la**) (*Zool., Biol.*) A minute whip-like appendage; (*Bot.*) a trailing shoot; a runner.

flageolet (1) (flăj ō let', flăj'-) [F., dim. of O.F. *flageol*, etym. doubtful], *n.* A small wind instrument blown from a mouthpiece at the end, and producing a shrill sound similar to but softer than that of the piccolo; a tin-whistle. **flageolet-tones,** *n.pl.* (*Mus.*) The natural harmonics of stringed instruments.

flageolet (2) (flăj ō let', fla jō lā) [F., corr. of *fageolet*, dim. of *fageol*, L. *faseolus*], *n.* The green pod of the haricot bean, *Phaseolus vulgaris*.

flagitate (flăj' i tāt) [L. *flāgitātus*, p.p. of *flāgitāre*], *v.t.* To demand with importunity. ***flagitation** (-tā' shůn), *n.*

flagitious (flȧ jish' ůs) [L. *flāgitiōsus*, from *flagitium*, a disgraceful act (rel. to prec.)], *a.* Heinous, flagrant, villainous; deeply criminal. **flagitiously,** *adv.* **flagitiousness,** *n.*

flagon (flăg′ ŏn) [O.F. *flacon*, late L. *flasco -ōnem*, *flasca*, FLASK], *n.* A vessel with a narrow mouth or spout, used for holding liquors; a flat bottle holding the contents of nearly two bottles, used in the wine-trade.

flagrant (flā′ grȧnt) [L. *flāgrans -ntem*, pres.p. of *flāgāre*, to blaze], *a.* Glaring, notorious, outrageous, scandalous; *burning, blazing; *eager. **flagrancy,** *n.* **flagrantly,** *adv.*

flagstone [FLAG (4)].

flail (flāl) [A.-S. *fligel*, prob. from L. FLAGELLUM (form influenced by the cognate O.F. *flael*, whence F. *fléau*)]. A wooden instrument consisting of a staff or swingle hinged to a longer staff or handle, used for threshing grain by hand.

flair (flâr) [F., from *flairer*, to smell, pop. L. *flāgrāre*, L. *frāgrare*], *n.* A keen sense of smell; (*fig.*) keen perception, discernment; a natural aptitude or gift.

flak (flăk) [initials of G. *flug abwehr kanone*, anti-aircraft gun], *n.* Fire from anti-aircraft guns.

flake (1) (flāk) [etym. obscure (O.E.D. suggests Aryan *plag-*, as in Gr. *plēgnunai*, to beat)], *n.* A thin scale-like fragment; a thin piece peeled off; a chip (as of flint); a loosely cohering mass, a fleecy particle (as of snow); a carnation with petals striped on a white ground; *a flash, a gleam of light. *v.t.* To form into flakes or loose particles; to chip flakes off or in flakes; to sprinkle with flakes, to fleck. *v.i.* To peel or scale off in flakes. **flake-white,** *n.* English white lead in the form of scales, used as a pigment. **flaky,** *a.* **flakiness,** *n.*

flake (2) (flāk) [perh. from Icel. *flake*, *fleke*, a hurdle, rel. to L. *plectere*, and Gr. *plekein*, to plait], *n.* A light platform or rack; a frame for storing provisions, esp. oatcake; a rack for drying fish; (*Naut.*) a stage hung over a ship's side, for the use of painters, etc.; (*prov.*) a hurdle, esp. one used for a fence.

flam (flăm) [etym. doubtful], *n.* A false pretext, a sham, a deception, a lie. **a.* Lying, false, deceitful. *v.t.* To deceive, to impose upon.

flambeau (flăm′ bō) [F., dim. of O.F. *flambe*], *n.* A torch, esp. one made of thick wicks covered with wax or pitch.

flamboyant (flăm boi′ ȧnt) [F., pres.p. of *flamboier*, as prec.], *a.* (*Arch.*) A term applied to the decorated French Gothic (contemporary with the Perpendicular style in England), from the flame-like tracery; florid, highly decorated; gorgeously coloured; wavy or flame-like (as hair).

flame (flām) [O.F. *flambe*, L. *flamma*, prob. from the base *flag-*, to burn (*flagrāre*, to blaze), or *flāre*, to blow], *n.* A mass or stream of vapour or gas in a state of combustion; a blaze; fire; a glow, a bright light; a blaze of colour; (*fig.*) ardour, excitement, passion; the object of one's affection, a sweetheart. **v.t.* To burn; to inflame, to excite; to send with or as with flame. *v.i.* To burn with a flame; to send out flame, to blaze, to burst into flames; (*fig.*) to break (out) or blaze (up) in violent passion; to shine, to glow, to flash. **flame-colour,** *n.* A bright yellow colour. **flame-coloured,** *a.* ***flame-eyed,** *a.* Having eyes burning like fire. **flame-flower,** *n.* A plant of the genus *Tritoma* or *Kniphofia*, pop. called the red-hot poker. **flaming onion,** *n.* (*Artill.*) An anti-aircraft projectile having the appearance of a string of yellow fire-balls. **flame-projector,** *n.* (*Mil.*) An apparatus for projecting 'liquid fire' against the enemy. **flame-tree,** *n.* The Australian fire-tree. **flameless,** *a.* **flamelet,** *a.* **flaming,** *a.* Burning, blazing; (*fig.*) intensely hot; intensely bright; inflaming, exciting; vehement, violent; exaggerated, florid, extravagant. **flamingly,** *adv.* **flamy,** *a.*

flamen (flā′ mėn) [L., prob. as prec.], *n.* An ancient Roman priest devoted to some special deity. **flaminical** (-min′ i kȧl), *a.*

flamenco (fla men′ kō) [Sp.], *n.* A Gipsy song or dance from Andalusia.

flamingo (flȧ ming′ gō) [Port. *flamengo*, Sp. *flamenco*], *n.* A long-necked bird, with small body and very long legs, its feathers rose or scarlet in colour, belonging to the genus *Phœnicopterus*.

flan (flăn) [F.], *n.* An open fruit tart.

flanch (flanch) [perh. a var. of FLANGE or FLANK], *n.* A flange; (*Her.*) a sub-ordinary or part of a shield enclosed by an arc from the upper corners to the base, and always borne in pairs.

flanconnade (flăng kō nād′) [F., from *flanc*], *n.* (*Fencing*) A thrust in the flank.

Flanders (flan′ dėrz) [Dut. *Vlaanderen*, pl., a district of the Netherlands], *n.* Flanders lace; Flanders horse, a carriage horse formerly imported from Flanders. **Flanders brick,** *n.* A soft brick used for cleaning knives, the same as Bath brick.

flaneur (fla′ nûr) [F., from *flaner*, to saunter], *n.* A lounger, an idler. ***flanerie,*** *n.* The practice or habit of sauntering or idling.

flange (flănj) [prob. from O.F. *flanche*], *n.* A projecting rib or rim affixed to a wheel, tool, pipe, etc., for strength, as a guide, or for attachment to something else. *v.t.* To supply with a flange. **flange-rail,** *n.* A rail having a bent-up flange to keep the wheel on the metals.

flank (flăngk) [F. *flanc*; perh. from Teut. (cp. O.H.G. *hlanca*, the loin, the side, also A.-S. *hlanc*, slender)], *n.* The fleshy or muscular part of the side between the hips and the ribs; either side of a building, mountain, etc.; the side of an army or body of troops; (*Fort.*) the portion of a bastion reaching from the curtain to the face; (*Mech.*) the acting surface of a cog within the pitch-line. *v.t.* To stand or be at the flank or side of, to border; to attack, turn, or threaten the flank of; to secure or guard the flank of. *v.i.* To border, to touch; to be posted on the flank or side. **flank-company,** *n.* (*Mil.*) The company posted on the extreme right or left of a body of troops. **flank-files,** *n.pl.* (*Mil.*) The first two men on the right and the last two men on the left. **flank-movement,** *n.* (*Mil.*) A manœuvre directed at turning the enemy's flank. **flanker,** *n.* One who or that which flanks, or is posted, stationed, or placed on the flanks; (*Mil., pl.*) skirmishers thrown out on the flanks of an army when marching; (*Fort.*) a work projecting so as to command the flank of an assailing body.

flannel (flăn′ ėl) [from W. *gwlanen*, from *gwlan*, wool (Skeat), or from O.F. *flaine*, blanket, coverlet], *n.* A soft woollen stuff of open texture, with a light nap; (*pl.*) garments made of this material, esp. underclothing, also trousers for cricketers, etc.; a piece of flannel used for washing the face, etc. (*Am.* a wash-rag); *(*Shak.*) a Welshman. *v.t.* To wrap in or rub with flannel or a flannel. **flannel-flower,** *n.* The mullein. **flannel-weed,** *n.* A water plant that covers stones and the surface of water with woolly fibres, esp. in time of drought. **flannelled,** *a.* Covered with or wrapped up in flannel. **flannelly,** *a.* **to receive one's flannels:** (*School*) To be promoted to the cricket or football eleven.

flannelette (flăn ė let′), *n.* A cotton fabric made to imitate flannel.

flap (flăp) [prob. imit.], *v.t.* To beat, strike, or drive away with anything broad and flexible; to move rapidly up and down or to and fro (as wings); to let fall (as the brim of a hat). *v.i.* To move the wings rapidly up and down or to and fro; to be moved loosely to and fro, to flutter, swing about, or oscillate; to hang down, as the brim of a hat; to strike a loose blow or blows, to beat (as with the wings). *n.* Anything broad and flexible, hanging loosely, or attached by one side only; the hinged leaf of a table or shutter; the motion or act of flapping; a light stroke or blow with something broad and loose; a slap; an implement for driving flies away; (*slang*) a state of anxiety, or confusion; (*pl.*) a disease in the lips of horses. ***flap-eared,** *a.* Having broad, pendulous ears. **flap-jack,** *n.* A kind of pancake; an apple-puff or apple-jack; a flattish circular case for holding a powder-puff and a mirror.

flapdoodle (flăp doodl'), *n.* Rubbish, nonsense, bunkum.

flapper (flăp' ėr), *n.* One who or that which flaps; a partridge or wild duck not yet able to fly; a flap, a part, or organ loosely attached or hanging; a young girl in her early teens.

flare (flâr) [cp. Norw. *flara*; also G. *flattern*, to flicker], *v.i.* To blaze, to flame up, or to glow, esp. with an unsteady light; (*fig.*) to be gaudy, glaring, or too showy in dress; (*slang*) to bounce, to swagger; (*Naut.*) to open or spread outwards (as a ship's bows). *n.* A large unsteady light, a glare; (*fig.*) a sudden outburst; (*Dressmaking*) material cut on the cross to give additional fulness; (*Naut.*) the widening or spreading out upwards (as of a ship's bows); a torch-like night-signal. **to flare up:** To blaze out; (*fig.*) to fly into a passion. **flare-up:** A sudden outbreak into flame; a showy but transient display; an outburst of anger, excitement, merry-making, etc.; a row, a spree. **flaring,** *a.* Flaming, dazzling; gaudy, too showy or ostentatious. **flaringly,** *adv.* **flary,** *a.* Gaudy, showy.

flash (flăsh) [prob. onomat. in sense of dashing or flapping like water], *v.i.* To appear with a sudden and transient gleam; to burst suddenly into flame or light; to send out a rapid gleam; to reflect light, to glitter, to burst forth, appear, or occur suddenly; to rush swiftly (as surf), to dash, break, or splash (as water, or waves). *v.t.* To emit or send forth in flashes or like flashes; to cause to gleam; to convey or transmit instantaneously (as news by telegraph); (*Glass-making*) to expand into a dish or sheet, to cover (plain glass) with a thin coating of coloured glass; (*fig.*) to send swiftly along; to send a rush of water down (a river, weir, etc.); *to strike or throw up in glittering spray. *n.* A sudden and transitory blaze or gleam of bright light; the space of time taken by this, an instant; a body of water driven along with violence; a sluice or lock just above a shoal, to raise the water while boats are passing; a preparation of capsicum, burnt sugar, etc., used for colouring and giving a fictitious strength to rum and brandy; (*Mil.*) a label with regimental name, etc., sewn on the uniform shoulder; (*fig.*) a sudden outburst, as of anger, wit, merriment, etc.; show, ostentation; thieves' jargon, cant, slang; *a showy person, a fop. *a.* Gaudy, vulgarly showy; counterfeit, forged; slang, cant; pertaining to thieves or vagabonds. **a flash in the pan:** A flash produced by the hammer of a gun upon a flint which fails to explode the powder; hence, an abortive attempt. **flash-board,** *n.* A hatch for releasing water in a mill-leat. ***flash-pipe,** *n.* A perforated gas-pipe for lighting burners. **flashing-point** [FLASH-POINT]. **flash-light,** *n.* (*Phot.*) A brilliant light for taking (usu. indoor) photographs, usu. produced by the ignition of an illuminating powder mixed with an explosive; an electric battery torch; a flashing-light. ***flashman,** *n.* A rogue; a fancy man; a sporting character. **flash-notes, -money,** *n.* Counterfeit notes or coin. **flash-point,** *n.* The degree of temperature at which the vapour from oil or spirit ignites. **flash-house,** *n.* A house frequented by thieves, and in which stolen goods were received. **flasher,** *n.* One who or that which flashes; a shallow wit, a pretentious person. **flashing,** *n.* A lap-joint used in roofing with sheet metal, a strip of lead carrying the drip of a wall into a gutter. **flashing-light,** *n.* A light exhibited from some lighthouses in which brilliant flashes alternate with periods of entire obscuration. **flashy,** *a.* Showy but empty, brilliant but shallow; gaudy, tawdry, cheap and showy; *insipid, vapid; *impulsive, fickle. **flashily,** *adv.* **flashiness,** *n.*

flask (flask) [F. *flasque* or It. *flasco* (cp. G. *flasche*, O.H.G. *flasca*, A.-S. *flasce*, *flaxe*), ult. perh. from L. *vasculum*, dim. of *vas*, a vessel], *n.* A small bottle or similar vessel; a leather or metal case for powder or shot (usu. POWDER-FLASK); a flat bottle, usu. mounted in metal, for carrying spirits in the pocket; a thin, long-necked bottle, encased in wicker, for wine or oil; an iron vessel holding about 75 lb. of quicksilver.

flasket (flas' kėt) [O.F. *flasquet*, dim. of *flasque*, as prec.], *n.* A long shallow basket with two handles; a small flask.

flat (1) (flăt) [Icel. *flatr*, etym. doubtful], *a.* Having a level and even surface; horizontal, level; even, smooth, having few or no elevations or depressions; level with the ground, lying prone, prostrate, overthrown, ruined; depressed, dejected; monotonous, dull, uninteresting, vapid, insipid, pointless, spiritless; having lost sparkle or freshness; plain, positive, absolute, downright; dull (as sales); low (as prices); (*Painting*) wanting relief or prominence of the figures; uniform, without variety of tint or shading; (*Mus.*) below the true pitch; minor (applied to intervals); (*Arch.*) having only a small rise, as some arches. *adv.* Flatly, positively; prostrate, level with the ground; (*Mus.*) below the true pitch. *n.* A flat, plain surface; a level plain or low tract of land; a plot of ground laid down level; a shoal, a shallow, a low tract flooded at high tide; a flat part of anything; anything that is flat; a broad, flat-bottomed boat; (*Am.*) a broad-brimmed straw hat; the palm of the hand; (*Theat.*) scenery on a wooden frame pushed on to the stage from the sides; (*Mus.*) a note a semitone lower than the one from which it is named, the sign indicating this lowering of pitch; (*slang*) one easily duped, a duffer. *v.i.* (*chiefly manufact.*) To flatten, to make flat and smooth. **flat-boat,** *n.* A large boat with a flat bottom, used for transport on rivers in the U.S. **flat cap,** *n.* A size of writing paper, 14 × 17 in.; *a cap with a low, flat crown, formerly worn by all classes in England. **flat-fish,** *n.* Any fish (such as the sole, plaice, turbot, etc.) of the *Pleuronectidæ*, distinguished by their laterally compressed body, absence of coloration on the under side, and the position of both eyes on the upper side. **flat-footed,** *a.* With the feet not arched; (*slang, esp. Am.*) downright, resolute, determined. **flat-head,** *n.* (*Austral.*) An edible fish with flattened head and body. **flat-iron,** *n.* An instrument for smoothing clothes, etc. **flat-race,** *n.* A race on level ground without obstacles. **flat rate,** *n.* A rate of payment not varying with the amount supplied, as for electric energy. **flattish,** *a.* **flatways, flatwise,** *adv.* ***flat-long,** *adv.* With the flat side (of a sword), not edgewise. **flatly,** *adv.* **flatness,** *n.*

flat (2) (flăt) [A.-S. *flet*, a floor, cogn. with prec.], *n.* A floor or storey of a house; a suite of rooms on one floor forming a separate residence; (*Am.* an apartment).

flatten (flăt' en), *v.t.* To make flat, to level; to lay flat; (*fig.*) to make vapid, dull, or insipid; to deject, to dispirit; (*Mus.*) to depress or lower in pitch. *v.i.* To become flat or level; (*fig.*) to lose force or interest, to pall; (*Mus.*) to depress the voice, to fall in pitch. **to flatten a sail:** (*Naut.*) To extend it fore and aft so as to catch the side wind. **to flatten out:** (*Aviat.*) To change from the gliding approach to the position to alight, when approaching to land.

flattie (flăt' i), *n.* (*slang*) A detective.

flatting (flăt' ing), *n.* The act or process of flattening; a covering of size over gilding; the process of rolling out metal into sheets; a style of inside house-painting in which the colours are not glossy. **flatting-mill,** *n.* A mill for rolling out metal by cylindrical pressure.

flatter (flăt' ėr) [etym. obscure; prob. from O.F. *flater*, to flatten, smooth, caress, cogn. with FLAT (1) (*-er* not from O.F. infin., but from the derivative *flaterie*, or from assim. to or substitution for the obs. v. *flatter*, to flutter or float)], *v.t.* To court, cajole, or gratify by compliment, adulation, or blandishment; to praise falsely or unduly; to raise false hopes in; to persuade (usu. oneself of some favourable contingency); to represent too favourably. *v.i.* To use flattery. **flatterer,** *n.* **flatteringly,** *adv.* **flattery,** *n.* The act or practice of flattering; false or venal praise; adulation, cajolery.

flatulent (flăt' ū lĕnt) [F., from late L. *flātulens*

-*ntem*, from *flātus*, a blowing, from *flāre*, to blow], *a.* Affected with or troubled by wind or gases generated in the alimentary canal; generating or likely to generate wind in the stomach; (*fig.*) inflated, empty, vain; pretentious, turgid. **flatulence, -ulency,** *n.* **flatulently,** *adv.* **flatus** (flā′ tŭs), *n.* Wind in the stomach or bowels; flatulence.

flaught (fla*cht*) [Sc., var. of FLIGHT], *n.* A flapping, a commotion; a flight (as of birds); a flash (as of lightning).

flaunt (flawnt) [etym. doubtful], *v.i.* To make an ostentatious or gaudy show; to behave pertly or saucily. *v.t.* To display ostentatiously or impudently; to parade, to show off; to wave or flutter in the wind. *n.* The act of flaunting; impudent parade; finery; a boasting or vaunting; (*pl.*) finery. **flauntingly,** *adv.* **flaunty,** *a.* Flaunting, ostentatious.

flautist (flaw′ tist) [It. *flautista*, from *flauto*, a flute], *n.* A flutist, a player on the flute.

flavescent (flȧ ves′ ėnt) [L. *flāvescens -ntem*, pres.p. of *flāvescere*, to become yellow, from *flāvus*, yellow], *a.* Yellowish; turning yellow.

flavin, *-ine (flā′ vin) [L. *flāvus*, yellow, -IN], *n.* (*Chem.*) A yellow dye-stuff obtained from quercitron bark.

flavour (flā′ vŏr) [M.E. *flauor*, *flavoure*, prob. from O.F. *flaur*, *fraar*, smell (L. *frāgrāre*, to smell sweet or *flāre*, to blow)], *n.* That quality in any substance which affects the taste, or the taste and smell; (*fig.*) the quality of any thing that affects the æsthetic taste, esp. pleasingly. *v.t.* To impart a flavour to; to render pleasing to the palate; to season. **flavoured,** *a.* Having a distinct flavour; (*in comb.*) having a particular flavour (as *full-flavoured*). **flavourless,** *a.* **flavourous, flavoursome,** *a.* Pleasing to taste or smell. **flavouring,** *n.* Something that flavours; seasoning.

flaw (1) (flaw) [perh. from Icel. *flaga*, a slab (cp. Swed. *flaga*, flake, flaw)], *n.* A crack, a slight fissure; a defect, an imperfection; (*Law*) a defect in an instrument, evidence, etc., rendering it invalid; *a flake; *a fragment. *v.t.* To break, to crack; to mar; to render invalid. *v.i.* To crack; *to flake (off). **flawless,** *a.* **flawlessly,** *adv.* **flawlessness,** *n.* **flawy** (1), *a.* Full of flaws; defective.

flaw (2) (flaw) [perh. cogn. with prec. or with FLAY (cp. Dut. *vlaag*)], *n.* A sudden puff or gust; a squall, a violent but transient storm; *a tumult; *a mental commotion. **flawy** (2), *a.* Gusty.

***flawn** (flawn) [O.F. *flaon* (F. *flan*), med. L. *fladō -ōnem*, O.H.G. *flado*, a broad flat cake], *n.* A kind of custard.

flax (flăks) [A.-S. *fleax* (cp. Dut. *vlas*, G. *flachs*; perh. cogn. with Gr. *plekein*, and L. *plectere*, to weave)], *n.* A plant of the genus *Linum*, esp. *L. usitatissimum*, the common flax, the fibre of which is made into yarn, and spun into linen cloth; the fibrous part of the plant prepared for manufacture; one of various kinds of similar plants, as white flax, false flax, or toad-flax. **New Zealand flax:** A textile fibre obtained from the flax-bush, *Phormium tenax*, a native of New Zealand. **flax-comb,** *n.* A comb or hackle for dressing flax. **flax-dresser,** *n.* One who prepares flax for the spinner. **flax-mill,** *n.* A mill or place where flax is spun. **flax-seed,** *n.* Linseed. **flax-weed,** *n.* The toad-flax, *Linaria vulgaris*. ***flax-wench,** *n.* A woman who dresses flax. **flaxen,** *a.* Made of flax; like flax in softness, silkiness, or colour; light yellow or straw-coloured. **flaxen-haired, -headed,** *a.* **flaxy,** *a.*

flay (flā) [A.-S. *flēan* (cp. Icel. *flā*, M.Dut. *vlaen*; cogn. with Gr. *plēssein*, to strike)], *v.t.* To strip the skin from; to peel; to pare; to strip; (*fig.*) to plunder; to criticize savagely. **flay-flint,** *n.* A skinflint, a miser.

flea (flē) [A.-S. *flēah* (cp. Dut. *vloo*, G. *floh*; prob. cogn. with FLEE)], *n.* An insect belonging to the genus *Pulex*, esp. *P. irritans*, which is parasitic on man, and remarkable for its leaping powers. **sand-flea,** (*Am.*) **beach-flea, water-flea** *n.* Small crustaceans with similar leaping powers. **flea-bane, -wort,** *n.* Compositous plants of the genus *Pulicaria*, *Erigeron*, or *Conyza*, from their supposed efficacy in driving away fleas. **flea-beetle,** *n.* A small leaping beetle of the family *Halticidæ*, very destructive to hops and other plants. **flea-bite,** *n.* The bite of a flea; the red spot caused by the bite; (*fig.*) a tiny amount; the smallest trifle; a trifling inconvenience. **flea-bitten,** *a.* Bitten by a flea; full of fleas; coloured (as some horses) with small red spots on a lighter ground. **flea-dock,** *n.* The burdock, *Petasites vulgaris*. **flea-louse,** *n.* A jumping plant-louse of the genus *Psythidæ*.

fleam (flēm) [O.F. *flieme*, med. L. *flētoma*, abbr. of L. *phlebotomum*, Gr. *phlebotomon*, see PHLEBOTOMY], *n.* A lancet for bleeding horses and cattle.

flèche (flāsh) [F., orig. an arrow], *n.* (*Arch.*) A spire, esp. a slender one, usu. of wood covered with lead, over the intersection of nave and transepts; (*Fort.*) a simple kind of redan, usually constructed at the foot of the glacis, consisting of a parapet with faces.

fleck (flek) [cp. Icel. *flekkr*, Dut. *vlek*, G. *fleck*], *n.* A spot, a freckle, a stain, a speck; a dot, stain, or patch of colour or light. *v.t.* To spot, to streak, to dapple, to variegate with spots or flecks. **fleckless,** *a.* Spotless, stainless, blameless. **flecker,** *v.t.* To fleck, to spot, to dapple; to scatter (light) in flakes or patches.

flection [FLEXION].

fled, *past & p.p.* [FLEE].

fledge (flej) [A.-S. *flycge* (found in *unflycge*, unfledged), cp. Dut. *vlug*, G. *flügge* (cogn. with FLY (2))], *v.t.* To furnish with feathers or plumage; (*fig.*) to wing for flight; to feather (an arrow); to deck or cover with anything resembling feathers. *v.i.* To acquire feathers or plumage for flight. **fledged,** *a.* Feathered; able to fly. **fledgeless,** *a.* **fledgeling,** *n.* A young bird just fledged; (*fig.*) a raw and inexperienced person. *a.* Newly fledged.

flee (flē) [A.-S. *flēon*, cp. G. *fliehen*, Goth. *thliuhan*], *v.i.* (*past & p.p.* **fled**) To run away, as from danger; to vanish, to disappear; (*fig.*) to pass away. *v.t.* To run away from; to shun.

fleece (flēs) [A.-S. *flēos* (cp. Dut. *vlies*, G. *fliess*)], *n.* The woolly covering of a sheep or similar animal; the quantity of wool shorn from a sheep at one time; (*fig.*) anything resembling a fleece, as a woolly head of hair, a fleecy cloud or fall of snow; a web of carded fibres of cotton or wool; *a snatch. *v.t.* To shear the wool from; to furnish with a fleece; to cover with anything fleecy; (*fig.*) to rob, to plunder, to strip. **fleeced,** *a.* Furnished with a fleece (*usu. in comb.*, as *well-fleeced*). **fleeceable,** *a.* **fleeceless,** *a.* **fleecer,** *n.* One who fleeces or plunders. **fleecy,** *a.* Woolly, wool-bearing; resembling a fleece in appearance or qualities.

fleech (flēch) [Sc.; etym. doubtful], *v.t.* To flatter; to beg, to entreat.

fleer (flēr) [cp. Norw. *flira*, Swed. *flissa*, to titter], *v.i.* To grin or laugh in contempt or scorn; to gibe, to sneer; *to leer, to smirk. *v.t.* To laugh or sneer at. *n.* Mockery or scorn expressed by words or looks; *a leer, a smirk. **fleeringly,** *adv.*

fleet (1) (flēt) [A.-S. *flēot*, a ship, from *flēotan*, to float], *n.* A number of ships or smaller vessels in company with a common object or destination, esp. a body of warships under one command; the entire body of warships belonging to one government, a navy; a collection of road vehicles used for a common purpose and usu. under one ownership. **First Fleet** [FIRST].

fleet (2) (flēt) [A.-S. *flēot* (cp. Dut. *vliet*, G. *fliess*, Icel. *fljōt*; cogn. with prec.)], *n.* A creek, an inlet. **the Fleet:** A stream or ditch, now a sewer, emptying into the Thames east of Fleet Street; the prison that stood near this. **Fleet marriage:** A clandestine marriage performed by disreputable clergymen in the Fleet Prison and recorded in the Fleet

Books (prohibited 1753). **Fleet-street,** *n.* The centre of newspaper offices in London; journalism. **Fleet-Streeter,** *n.* A journalist. **fleet-dike,** *n.* An embankment to prevent inundation.

fleet (3) (flēt) [A.-S. *flēotan* (cp. Dut. *vlieten*, G. *fliessen*, Icel. *fljōta*; also Gr. *plēssein*, to sail)], *v.i.* To move swiftly; to pass swiftly; (*fig.*) to glide away, to vanish; *to flow away. *v.t.* (*Naut.*) To change the position of, to shift; *to pass (the time) quickly or pleasantly. *a.* Swift of pace, nimble, rapid, speedy. **fleet-footed,** *a.* Able to run with great speed. **fleetness,** *n.* **fleeting,** *a.* Passing quickly, transient. **fleetingly,** *adv.*

fleet (4) (flēt) [prob. cogn. with prec. (cp. Dut. *vloot*)], *a.* (*prov.*) Shallow. *adv.* At no great depth. **fleetly** (2), *adv.*

Fleming (flem′ ing) [M.Dut. *Vlâming*, whence *Vlaemisch*, from *Flân-*, whence FLANDERS], *n.* A native of Flanders; one of Belgian or Dutch descent. **Flemish,** *a.* Pertaining to Flanders. *n.* The Flemish language. **Flemish bond** [BOND (1)]. **Flemish bricks,** *n.pl.* A kind of brick used for paving, of a yellowish colour, and harder than ordinary bricks.

flench (flench), **flinch** (2) (flinch), **flense** (flens) [Dan. *flense*], *v.t.* To strip the blubber or the skin from (a whale or seal).

flesh (flesh) [A.-S. *flæsc* (cp. Dut. *vleesch*, G. *fleisch*; also Icel. and Dan. *flesk*, pork, bacon)], *n.* The soft part of an animal body, esp. the muscular tissue, investing the bones, and covered by the skin; animal tissue used as food, as distinct from vegetable, fish, and sometimes from fowl meat; the body, as distinguished from the soul; animal nature; the human race; carnal appetites; the present state of existence; kindred; the soft pulpy part of a fruit or plant; that which is carnal; a carnal, unrenewed state. *v.t.* To encourage by giving flesh to, to make eager (from the sportsman's practice of giving hawks, dogs, etc., the flesh of the first game they take); (*fig.*) to initiate; to exercise or use for the first time; to harden, to inure or accustom to any practice or habit. **an arm of flesh:** Human strength or aid. **in the flesh,** *adv.* In bodily form. **flesh and blood:** The body; human nature, esp. as alive not imaginary, or as liable to infirmities; one's children or near relations. **flesh and fell:** The entire body; completely. **proud flesh:** A granular growth resembling flesh growing over a wound. **to be made flesh:** To become incarnate. **to be one flesh:** To be closely united as in marriage. **to lose flesh:** To lose plumpness, to become thin. **flesh-brush, -glove,** *n.* A brush or glove for stimulating the action of the skin by friction. **flesh-colour,** *n.* The colour of flesh; yellowish pink. **flesh-coloured,** *a.* **flesh-eater, -feeding,** *a.* Living or feeding on flesh. **flesh-fly,** a carnivorous insect of the genus *Sarcophaga*, esp. *S. carnaria*, the larvæ of which feed on decaying flesh. **flesh-hook,** A hook to take meat out of a pot. **flesh-meat,** *n.* The flesh of animals used or prepared for food. ***flesh-monger,** *n.* One who deals in meat; (*fig.*) a sensualist, a profligate. **flesh-pot,** *n.* A pot in which flesh is cooked; (*fig.*) sumptuous living. **the flesh-pots of Egypt:** Material welfare, sordid considerations (ref. to Exodus xvi. 3). **flesh-pottery,** *n.* **flesh-tints,** *n.pl.* (*Painting*) The colours which best represent the human skin. **flesh-worm,** *n.* The flesh-eating larva of an insect. **flesh-wound,** *n.* A wound not reaching the bone or any vital organ. **flesher,** *n.* (*Sc.*) A butcher. **fleshhood,** *n.* Corporeal existence. **fleshlings,** *n.pl.* Light flesh-coloured tights to represent the skin, worn by actors, dancers, etc. **fleshless,** *a.* Destitute of flesh, lean, scraggy. **fleshling,** *n.* One devoted to carnal pleasures. **fleshly,** *a.* Pertaining to the flesh, corporeal, sensual, lascivious; human, as distinct from spiritual, mortal, material; worldly. **fleshly-minded,** *a.* Addicted to sensual pleasures. **fleshliness,** *n.* ***fleshment,** *n.* Eagerness consequent on an initial success. **fleshy,** *a.* Fat, plump, corpulent; pulpy (as fruit). **fleshiness,** *n.* Like flesh.

***fletch** (flech) [corr. of FLEDGE], *v.t.* To feather (as an arrow). **fletcher,** *n.* One who feathered arrows, a maker of bows and arrows.

fleur de lis (flĕr dė lē) [F., lily flower], *n.* (*pl.* **fleurs de lis**) Various species of iris; (*Her.*) the heraldic lily, a charge borne in the French royal arms. **fleury** (floor′ i), **flory** (flôr′ i), *a.* Adorned with fleurs de lis.

fleuret (floor′ ėt) [F. *fleurette*, dim. of *fleur*], *n.* An ornament like a small flower; *a fencing-foil.

fleuron (flu ron) [F., from *fleur*], *n.* A flower-shaped ornament, used for a tailpiece, in architecture, on coins, etc.

fleury [FLEUR DE LIS].

flew, *past* [FLY (2)].

flews (flooz) [etym. doubtful], *n.pl.* The large chaps of a deep-mouthed hound.

flex (1) (fleks) [*flexus*, p.p. of *flectere*], *v.t.* To bend or cause to bend; (*Geol.*) to subject (strata) to fracture or distortion.

flex (2) [short for FLEXIBLE], *n.* (*Elec.*) Flexible insulated wire, or a piece of this.

flexible (flek′ si bėl), *a.* Pliant, easily bent; tractable; easily persuaded, manageable, plastic, supple, versatile. **flexibility** (-bil′ i ti), *n.* **flexibly,** *adv.* In a flexible manner. **flexile,** *a.* Easily bent; pliant, tractable; supple, versatile. **flexility** (sil′ i ti), *n.* **flexion** (flek′ shŭn), *n.* The act or process of bending; a bend, a curve; (*Gram.*) inflexion; (*Physiol.*) bending movement of a joint or limb; (*Math.*) flexure. **flexional,** *a.* **flexionless,** *n.* **flexor,** *n.* A muscle that causes a limb or part to bend. **flexuose,** *a.* Winding, serpentine; crooked, zigzag. **flexuoso-** (flek sū ō′ sō), *comb. form.* **flexuosity** (-os′ i ti), *n.* **flexuous,** *a.* Full of bends or turns, winding; wavering, unsteady; (*Bot., Zool., etc.*) presenting alternating curvatures in opposite directions. **flexuously,** *adv.* **flexure** (flek′ shŭr), *n.* The act, process, or manner of bending; the state of being bent; a bend, a curve, a turn, curvature; (*Math.*) curving of a line, surface or solid; (*Geol.*) bending or folding of strata under pressure. **flexure of a curve:** The bending of a curve towards or from a straight line.

fley (flā) [A.-S. *flȳgan* (found in *a-flȳgan*), causative of *flēogan*, to FLY (2)], *v.t.* (*Sc. and North.*) To frighten; to affright.

flibbertigibbet (flib′ ėr ti jib′ ėt) [onomat., or meaningless jargon], *n.* A chatterer; a flighty, thoughtless person; an impish knave (in allusion to Scott's *Kenilworth*); a fiend.

flick (flik) [onomat.], *n.* A smart, light blow or flip, as with a whip. *v.t.* To strike with such a stroke; to jerk or flip (dust, etc., away). **flick-knife,** *n.* A knife with a blade that springs out when a button in the handle is pressed.

flicker (flik′ ėr) [A.-S. *flicerian*, onomat.], *v.i.* To flutter, to flap the wings; to quiver, to burn unsteadily, to waver. *n.* The act of flickering; an unsteady or dying light; (*Cinema.*) discontinuity of projection caused by too few flashes of the pictures per second. **flickeringly,** *adv.* **flick, flicks,** *n.* (*colloq.*) A cinematograph film.

flickermouse [FLITTERMOUSE].

flier [FLYER].

flight (1) (flīt) [A.-S. *flyht*, from O.Teut. *fleugan*, to FLY (2)], *n.* The act or power of flying through the air; swift movement or passage, as the motion of a projectile, the passing away of time; a soaring, a sally, an excursion, a sustained effort; the distance to which anything can fly; a number of birds or insects moving together; a migration; a volley (of arrows, spears, etc.); a series of steps mounting in one direction; (*Aviat.*) R.A.F. unit, usually consisting of three aeroplanes; (*Racing*) the alinement of hurdles on a course; (*Angling*) a device for causing the bait to spin rapidly. *v.t.* To shoot at wildfowl flying overhead; *to put to flight. **flight-arrow,** *n.* A light, blunt, well-feathered arrow for long-distance shooting. **flight-deck,** *n.* (*Aviat.*) An aircraft-carrier's deck from which planes take off and land. **flight-engineer** (*Aviat.*) Member of the crew of an aeroplane in charge of the motors. **flight-feather,** *n.* One of the large wing-quills used in flying. **Flight Lieutenant,** *n.* Commissioned rank in R.A.F. equivalent to captain in the Army. **flight-muscle,** *n.* One of the muscles working the wings of a bird. **flight-path,** *n.* (*Aviat.*) The path of the centre of gravity of an aeroplane relative to the air. **Flight Sergeant,** *n.* Non-commissioned rank in R.A.F. **flight-shooting,** *n.* (*Archery*) Shooting with flight-arrows; (*Fowling*) shooting at flocks of wild-fowl on the wing. ***flight-shot,** *n.* The distance to which a flight-arrow can be shot. **flighty** (flī′ ti), *a.* Capricious, volatile; wild, fickle; *fleeting, swift. **flightily,** *adv.* **flightiness,** *n.*

flight (2) (flīt) [M.E. *fliht*, *fluhte*, O.H.G. *flucht*, from O.Teut. *thliuhan*, to FLEE], *n.* The act of fleeing or running away; a hasty departure, retreat, or evasion.

flimflam (flim′ flăm) [prob. onomat.], *n.* Nonsense, bosh; humbug, deception; a piece of deception.

flimsy (flim′ zi) [etym. doubtful, prob. onomat.], *a.* Thin, slight, frail; without strength or solidity; unsubstantial; easily torn; ineffective, unconvincing; frivolous, trivial, paltry. *n.* Thin paper used for manifolding; (*Journalism*) copy for the press written on this; (*slang*) an old-style £5 bank-note. **flimsily,** *adv.* **flimsiness,** *n.*

flinch (1) (flinch) [O.F. *flenchir*, etym. doubtful], *v.i.* To shrink from (an undertaking, suffering, etc.); to wince, to give way, to fail. **flincher,** *n.* **flinchingly,** *adv.*

flinch (2) [FLENCH].

flinder (flin′ dėr) [Norw. *flindra*, a chip, a splinter, Dut. *flenter*], *n.* (*usu. in pl.*) A fragment, a piece, a splinter.

Flinders grass (flin′ derz gras) [M. *Flinders* (1774–1814) explorer], *n.* Native pasture grass, chiefly in E. Australia.

fling (fling) [cp. Icel. *flengja*, Swed. *flänga*], *v.i.* (*past & p.p.* **flung**) To rush violently, to flounce; (*of horses*) to kick, struggle, plunge (out); to flout, sneer, throw invective or aspersions (at); *to dash, to rush, to fly. *v.t.* To cast or throw with sudden force; to hurl; to send forth, to emit; to throw to the ground, to defeat. *n.* A cast or throw from the hand; a gibe, a sneer; unrestrained enjoyment; a lively Highland dance; a kick, plunge, jump, or flounce. **to fling away:** To discard, to reject. **to fling down:** To cast or throw to the ground, to demolish, to ruin. **to fling off:** To abandon, discard, disown; to baffle in the chase. **to fling open:** To throw open suddenly or violently. **to fling out:** To be violent or unruly; to make violent or insulting remarks; to utter hastily or violently. **to fling to:** To shut violently. **to fling up:** To abandon. **to have a fling at:** To make a passing attempt at; to gibe or scoff at. **to have one's fling:** To give oneself up to unrestrained enjoyment; to have one's own way.

flint (flint) [A.-S. (cp. Dan. *flint*, Swed. *flinta*); perh. Gr. *plinthos*, brick], *n.* A variety of quartz, usually grey, smoke-brown or brownish-black and encrusted with white, easily chipped into a sharp cutting edge; a nodule of flint, a flint pebble; a piece of flint shaped for use in a gun, a tinder-box, lighter, or as an implement used by savages or prehistoric man; (*fig.*) anything extremely hard; extreme hardness. **to skin a flint:** To be excessively mean or stingy. **flint age** [STONE AGE]. **flint and stone work:** Architectural decoration with stone on a ground of flints, frequent in East Anglian churches. **flint and tinder, steel:** The old means of making fire by lighting tinder from a spark made by striking a flint against a piece of steel. **flint-glass,** *n.* A very pure and lustrous kind of glass, orig. made with calcined flints. ***flint-heart, -hearted,** *a.* Hard-hearted, unfeeling. **flint implements,** *n.pl.* A generic name for flint tools or weapons, etc., made by prehistoric man. **flint-knapper,** *n.* One who makes flints for guns or strike-a-lights. **flint-lock,** *n.* A lock for fire-arms, in which the cock holds a piece of flint, and comes down upon the steel cap of the pan containing the priming, which is ignited by the spark thus caused. **flinty,** *a.* Composed of flint; of the nature of or resembling flint; (*fig.*) cruel, pitiless, hard-hearted. **flintiness,** *n.* **flintwood,** *n.* (*Austral.*) The black-butt tree.

flip (1) (flip) [prob. onomat.], *v.t.* (*past & p.p.* **flipped**) To fillip, flick, or jerk; to strike lightly; to move (about or away) with a light blow. *v.i.* To strike lightly, to flap or flick (at). *n.* A quick light blow or stroke.

flip (2) (flip) [prob. from prec. v., to beat up], *n.* A mixture of beer and spirits, sweetened and heated up [cp. EGG-FLIP]. ***flip-dog,** *n.* An iron heated to warm egg-flip.

flip-flap (flip′ flăp) [onomat., perh. redup. of FLAP], *n.* A flapping noise; something that makes such a noise, as a tongue in a valve; a kind of firework, a cracker; (*slang*) a somersault; a machine for lifting people high in the air in cars attached to huge arms which revolve through a semicircle. *adv.* With a noise as of repeated flapping.

flip-flop (flip′ flop) [cp. prec.], *n.* The sound of a regular footfall. **flipperty-flopperty,** *a.* Flopping, dangling.

flippant (flip′ ȧnt) [perh. from FLIP (1)], *a.* Pert, trifling, lacking in seriousness; impertinent, disrespectful. **flippancy,** *n.* **flippantly,** *adv.*

flipper (flip′ ĕr) [FLIP (1)], *n.* The broad fin of a fish; the limb or paddle of a turtle, penguin, etc.; (*slang*) the hand.

flirt (flĕrt) [prob. imit.], *v.t.* To jerk or fillip (away); to wave or jerk to and fro rapidly (as a fan); *to jeer or gibe at. *v.i.* To make love for amusement or self-gratification; to play at love-making, to coquet; to move with jerks, short flights, or springs; *to flit about. *n.* A flirting motion, a jerk, a fling; a person, esp. a woman, who plays at courtship. **flirtation** (-tā′ shŭn), *n.* Coquetry; a playing at courtship. **flirtatious,** *a.* ***flirtgill,** *n.* A light woman. **flirtingly,** *adv.* **flirtish,** *a.* **flirty,** *a.*

***flisk** (flisk) [onomat., cp. WHISK], *v.i.* To frisk; to be restive. *n.* A whim, a freak.

flit (flit) [cogn. with FLEET (4), cp. Icel. *flytja*, Swed. *flitta*], *v.i.* (*past & p.p.* **flitted**) To move, to pass from place to place; to fly about lightly and rapidly; to depart; to leave one's house, usu. secretly; (*Sc.*) to move from one place of abode to another; *to flutter.

flitch (flich) [A.-S. *flicce* (cp. Icel. *flikki*, Dan. *flik*)], *n.* The side of a pig salted and cured; a steak from a fish, esp. halibut; a board or plank from a tree-trunk, usu. from the outside. *v.t.* To cut into flitches. **Dunmow flitch:** A flitch of bacon formerly given at Dunmow, in Essex, to any married couple proving that they lived in harmony for a year and a day.

flite (flīt) [A.-S. *flītan*], *v.i.* *To contend; to wrangle; (*Sc.*) to brawl, to scold. *n.* (*Sc.*) A scolding, a heated dispute. ***flyting:** (*Sc. poet.*) A poetical dispute or abusive dialogue in alternate tirades of verse.

flitter (flit′ ėr), *v.i.* To flit about; to flutter. **flitter-mouse,** *n.* A bat.

***flittern** (flit′ ėrn) [etym. doubtful], *n.* A young oak; the wood or the bark of young oak-trees, as distinguished from that of old ones.

flivver (fli′ ver), *n.* (*Am. slang*) A cheap small motor-car; (*Naval slang*) a small destroyer.

flix (fliks) [etym. unknown], *n.* Fur, esp. the down of the beaver.

float (1) (flōt) [A.-S. *flotian*, cogn. with FLEET (4); influenced by O.F. *flotter* (F. *floter*)], *v.i.* To be supported on the surface of or in a fluid; to swim on water; to hover in the air; to move or glide without effort; to move with a fluid, to drift. *v.t.* To support on the surface of or in a fluid; to bear up or bear along (of water); to convey, to carry on or as on water; to set afloat, to launch; to flood with a liquid; (*fig.*) to put into circulation; to waft through the air; (*Fin.*) to be or become current; to form a limited company with a view to making a public issue of shares. **floatable,** *a.* Able to float; navigable. **floatage,** *n.* Anything found floating, flotsam; floating power, buoyancy. **floatation** [FLOTATION]. **floater,** *n.* One who or that which floats; (*Stock Exch.*) a Government stock certificate, bond, etc., accepted as a recognized security. **floating,** *a.* Resting on the surface of a fluid; at sea; unattached, free, disconnected; circulating, not fixed or invested; fluctuating, variable, of uncertain amount. **floating assets,** *n.pl.* (*Comm.*) Assets held for the purpose of being subsequently converted into money. **floating axle,** *n.* (*Mach.*) A live axle in which the revolving part turns the wheels, while the weight of the vehicle is supported on the ends of a fixed axle-housing. **floating battery,** *n.* An armoured vessel employed to defend harbours, etc. **floating bridge,** *n.* A bridge of rafts and timber floating on the surface of the water; a kind of double bridge for enabling troops to pass narrow moats; a large steam-ferry. **floating capital** [CAPITAL (2)]. **floating debt** [DEBT]. **floating dock** [DOCK (3)]. **floating harbour,** *n.* A breakwater of heavy timbers, fastened together and anchored, so as to form a protection for shipping. **floating kidney,** *n.* (*Path.*) Malformation in which the kidney is entirely surrounded by peritoneum; condition in which the kidney is displaced. **floating-light,** *n.* A lightship; a life-buoy to which a light is attached, to attract the attention of a person in the water, and to direct the boat's crew coming to the rescue. **floating pier,** *n.* A landing-stage which rises and falls with the tide. **floating ribs,** *n.pl.* (*Anat.*) Lowest two pairs of ribs, which are not attached to the sternum. **floatingly,** *adv.*

float (2) (flōt) [A.-S. *flota*, a ship, as prec.], *n.* Anything buoyed up on the surface of a liquid; the cork or quill on a fishing-line; a cork on a fishing-net; the bladder supporting fish, animals, etc., in the water; the wall of a ball-cock regulating a supply-tap; a timber-raft, a floating wharf; (*Aviat.*) the gear of an aircraft for alighting on water; a kind of dray for heavy goods; (*usu. in pl.*) the footlights of a theatre; a kind of trowel for smoothing the plastering on walls; a float-board. **float-board,** *n.* One of the boards of an undershot water-wheel or a paddle-wheel. **float-bridge,** *n.* A bridge of boats or rafts. **float-carburettor,** *n.* (*Mech.*) A carburettor in which the feed is controlled by a float. **float-feed,** *n.* (*Mech.*) A feed regulated by a float. **float roll calender,** *n.* (*Laundry*) An ironing machine in which articles with buttons can be ironed and pressed without damage. **float seaplane,** *n.* (*Aviat.*) An aeroplane equipped with floats instead of wheels, for alighting on water. **float-stone,** *n.* A spongy variety of opal light enough to float on the surface of water.

floccillation (flok si lā′ shŭn) [FLOCCULUS, -ATION], *n.* (*Path.*) A picking of the bed-clothes by a delirious patient, a very unfavourable symptom.

floccose (flok′ ōs) [late L. *floccōsus*, from L. FLOCCUS], *a.* Covered with little woolly tufts. **floccosely,** *adv.*

floccule (flok′ ūl) [FLOCCULUS], *n.* A loose tuft; a small woolly or tuft-like portion. **flocculent** (flok′ ū lent), *a.* In small flakes, woolly, tufted. **flocculose, flocculous,** *a.*

flocculus (flok′ ū lŭs) [dim. of foll.], *n.* (*pl.* **-li**, -lī) A lobe on the under surface of the human cerebellum. ***floccus*** (flok′ ŭs) [L.], *n.* (*pl* ***-ci***, flok′ sī, -sī) A long tuft of hair terminating the tail in some mammals; the down of unfledged birds.

flock (1) (flok) [A.-S. *flocc* (cp. Icel. *flokkr*)], *n.* A company or collection of animals, esp. sheep, goats, or birds; a crowd, a large body; a congregation, considered in relation to their minister. *v.i.* To come together in a flock; to congregate, to assemble in crowds. *v.t.* To crowd; to press by crowding. **flock-master,** *n.* A sheep-farmer.

flock (2) (flok) [prob. from O.F. *floc*, L. *floccus*], *n.* A lock or tuft of wool, cotton, hair, etc.; (*usu. in pl.*) wool-dust used in coating certain portions of the patterns in some wall-papers [FLOCK-PAPER]; fibrous material, made by tearing up woollen rags by machinery, used to stuff upholstery, mattresses, etc.; (*Chem.*) matter in woolly or loose floating masses precipitated in a solution. **flock-bed,** *n.* A bed stuffed with flocks of wool, hair, or torn-up rags. **flock-paper,** *n.* Wall-paper, to which flock is attached with size. **flocky,** *a.*

floe (flō) [prob. from Norse *flo*, a layer], *n.* A large sheet of floating ice.

flog (flog) [perh. corr. of L. *flagellāre*, see FLAGELLATE], *v.t.* (*past & p.p.* **flogged**) To thrash, esp. with a whip or birch rod; to whip, to lash (as the water in fly-fishing); to urge or drive by beating; (*slang*) to push the sales of; to sell; to pawn. **to flog a dead horse:** To try to revive interest in something stale; to pursue a hopeless task. **flogger, *-ster,** *n.* **flogging,** *n.* Punishment by whipping.

flong (flong) [F. *flan*, FLAWN], *n.* (*Print.*) Prepared paper used for the matrices in stereotyping.

flood (flŭd) [A.-S. *flōd* (cp. Icel. *flōd*, Dut. *vloed*, G. *flut*), cogn. with FLOW], *n.* An abundant flow of water; a body of water rising and overflowing land not usually covered with water, an inundation; the inflow of the tide; a downpour, a torrent; (*poet.*) a river, the sea; (*fig.*) an overflowing, abundance; excessive menstrual discharge. *v.t.* To overflow, to inundate, to deluge; to supply copiously (with). *v.i.* To be at the flood (of the sea); to rise and overflow; (*Path.*) to have uterine hæmorrhage, to have excessive menstrual discharge. **the Flood:** The Deluge recorded in Genesis. **flood-gate,** *n.* A gate in a waterway arranged to open when the water attains a certain height, and so allow it to escape freely to prevent floods, a sluice; the lower gate of a lock. **flood-lighting,** *n.* Artificial lighting of the exteriors of buildings by light from projectors at some distance. **flood-mark,** *n.* High-water mark. **floodometer** (flŭ dom′ ė tėr), *a.* An instrument for registering the height of floods. **flood-tide,** *n.* The rising tide. **flooding,** *n.* The act of inundating; the state of being flooded, an inundation; (*Path.*) a morbid discharge of blood from the uterus.

floor (flôr) [A.-S. *flōr* (cp. Dut. *vloer*, G. *flur*)], *n.* The bottom surface of a room, on which the inmates walk and which supports the furniture; the boards or other material of which this is made; a storey in a building; a suite of rooms on the same level; the part of the house assigned to members of a legislative assembly; any level area corresponding to the floor of a room; the flat portion of a vessel's hold; the bottom of a coal seam; the low limit of prices. *v.t.* To furnish with a floor; to be or serve as a floor (to); (*fig.*) to knock down; to put to silence (as in argument); to pose (a difficult question); to get the better of, to defeat. **to take the floor:** To rise to speak, to take part in a debate; (*Ir.*) to get up to dance. **floor-cloth,** *n.* A piece of soft fabric used for washing floors; a substitute for a carpet. **floor-lamp,** *n.* A lamp, usu. portable, that stands on the floor. **floor-show,** *n.* (*Theat.*) A performance on the floor of a restaurant, etc. **floor-timbers,** *n.pl.* The main timbers on which a floor is laid. **floor-walker,** *n.* A shop-walker. **floorer,** *n.* (*colloq.*) That which floors or defeats; a knock-down blow; a poser, a baffling question; a decisive report. **flooring,** *n.* Material for floors; a floor, a platform; (*Malting*) the process of spreading and turning grain to restrict germination. **floorless,** *a.*

flop (flop) [var. of FLAP], *v.i.* To tumble about or fall loosely and heavily; to sway about heavily, to flap (as wings); to make a dull sound as of a soft body flapping; to move or walk about (in an ungainly manner). *v.t.* To let fall negligently or noisily; to cause to strike with a heavy dull sound. *n.* The act or motion of flopping; the noise of a soft outspread body falling suddenly to the ground; (*slang*) a complete failure. *adv.* With a flop; suddenly. **flop-house,** *n.* (*Am.*) A doss-house, a cheap lodging-house. **floppy,** *a.* **floppily,** *adv.* **floppiness,** *n.*

flora (flôr′ ȧ) [L., Flora, the Roman goddess of flowers and gardens, from *flōs flōris*, FLOWER], *n.* The whole vegetation of a country or geological period; a book dealing with the vegetation of a country or district. **floral,** *a.* Of or pertaining to floras; of or pertaining to flowers. **floral envelope,** *n.* (*Bot.*) The perianth or parts surrounding the stamens and pistils, generally consisting of calyx and corolla. **florally,** *adv.*

Florence (flor′ ėns) [F., from L. *Flōrentia* (It. *Firenze*)], *n.* A kind of red wine from Florence, the chief city of Tuscany, in northern Italy. **Florence flask,** *n.* A thin glass flask, with large globular body and long narrow neck. **Florence oil,** *n.* A superior olive oil.

Florentine (flor′ ėn tīn) [L. *Flōrentīnus*, from *Flōrentia*, see prec.], *a.* Of or pertaining to Florence. *n.* A native or inhabitant of Florence; a kind of silk stuff; a kind of pie or tart, esp. a meat pie without under-crust; *a Florentine ship. **Florentine iris,** *n.* A white or pale-blue iris, *I. Florentina*, also called the Florentine flower de luce.

florescence (flȯ res′ ėns) [L. *flōrescens -ntem*, pres.p. of *flōrescere*, incept. of *flōrēre*, see FLOURISH, -ENCE], *n.* The flowering of a plant; the season when a plant flowers. **florescent,** *a.*

floret (flor′ ėt) [O.F. *florete*, dim. of *fleur*], *n.* A small flower; (*Bot.*) a small flower forming part of a composite one.

floriate (flor′ i ȧt), **floriated** (-ā tėd) [L. *flōs flōris*], *a.* Adorned with floral ornaments or designs. **floriation** (-ā′ shŭn), *n.*

floricomous (flȯ rik′ ȯ mŭs) [late L. *flōricomus*, as prec., *coma*, hair], *a.* Having the head or top adorned with flowers; (*Zool.*) applied to sponges having a terminal bunch of curved branches.

floriculture (flor′ i kŭl tūr), *n.* The cultivation of flowers or flowering plants. **floricultural** (-kŭl tū rȧl), *a.* **floriculturist,** *n.*

florid (flor′ id) [L. *flōridus*], *a.* Covered with or abounding in flowers; bright in colour; flushed with red, ruddy; (*fig.*) flowery, highly embellished, elaborately ornate; showy; (*Arch.*) applied to the richly ornamented architecture of the latest stages of the pointed style in England about 1400–1537. **floridity** (flȯ rid′ i ti), *n.* **floridness,** *n.* **floridly,** *adv.*

Florida (flor′ i dȧ) [Sp. *Florida* (flō rē′ dȧ), orig. *Pascua florida*, or flowery Easter, because, it is said Ponce de Leon discovered the country on Easter Day, 1513], *n.* A Southern State in the U.S.A. **Florida water:** A perfume like eau-de-Cologne, much used in the U.S. **Florida wood:** A hard, close-grained wood used for inlaying.

floriferous (flȯ rif′ ėr ŭs) [L. *flōrifer*], *a.* Bearing flowers.

floriform (flôr′ i fôrm), *a.* Having the shape of a flower.

florilegium (flôr i lē′ ji ŭm) [L. *flōs flōris*, *legere*, to cull], *n.* An anthology.

florin (flor′ in) [O.F., from It. *fiorino*, dim. of *fiore*, L. *flōrem*, as prec.], *n.* A British silver coin, worth 2s.; a foreign gold or silver coin, of various values according to country and period; *an English gold coin of Edward III, worth 6s. 8d.; orig. a Florentine coin, stamped with the lily flower, the national badge of Florence.

florist (flor′-, flôr′ ist), *n.* A cultivator of flowers; one who sells flowers; one skilled in flowers.

floruit (flôr′ ŭ it) [L., he flourished, 3rd sing. perf. of *flōrēre*, see FLOURISH], *n.* The period of a person's eminence; the date at which he was known to be alive (in the absence of exact dates of birth and death).

flory [FLEURY].

floscular, -lous (flos′ kū lȧr, -lŭs) [L. *flōsculus*, dim. of *flōs*, FLOWER], *a.* Having little flowers; (*Bot.*) bearing many florets (as the composites). **floscule,** *n.* (*Bot.*) A floret.

flos ferri (flos fer′ i) [L., flower of iron], *n.* (*Min.*) A spicular variety of aragonite.

floss (flos) [perh. from O.F. *flosche*, down, cp. FLOCK (2)], *n.* The exterior soft envelope of a silkworm's cocoon; the downy substance on the husks of certain plants, as the bean. **floss-silk,** *n.* Untwisted filaments of the finest silk, used in embroidery, etc. **floss-thread,** *n.* Soft flaxen yarn or thread for embroidery. **flossy,** *a.*

flotage [FLOATAGE].

flotant (flō′ tȧnt) [F. *flottant*, pres.p. of *flotter*, see foll.], *a.* (*Her.*) Floating, as a flag, bird, or anything swimming.

flotation (flō tā′ shŭn), *n.* The act or state of floating; the science of floating bodies; (*Fin.*) the floating of a company. **centre of flotation:** The centre of gravity in a floating body. **flotative** (flō′-), *a.* Capable of floating; tending to float.

flotilla (flȯ til′ ȧ) [Sp., dim. of *flota*, a fleet], *n.* A small fleet; a fleet of small vessels.

flotsam (flot′ sȧm) [A.-F. *floteson*, O.F. *flotaison*, from *floter*, to FLOAT (1)], *n.* Goods lost in shipwreck and found floating. **flotsam and jetsam:** Wreckage or any property found floating or washed ashore.

flounce (1) (flouns) [prob. cogn. with Norw. *flunsa*, to hurry, Swed. dial. *flunsa*, to plunge], *v.i.* To throw oneself about; to make violent or agitated movements of the limbs; to plunge, to flounder. **v.t.* To throw violently. *n.* A flinging about of the body or limbs; the act of plunging or floundering.

flounce (2) (flouns) [M.E. *frounce*, O.F. *fronce*, from *froncer*, to wrinkle, L. *frons*, the forehead], *n.* A gathered or plaited strip of cloth sewed to a petticoat, dress, etc., with the lower border hanging loose. *v.t.* To attach flounces to; to deck or trim with flounces.

flounder (1) (floun′ dėr) [O.F. *flondre* (cp. Norw. *flundra*, Dan. *flynder*)], *n.* A flat-fish, *Pleuronectes flesus*, resembling the plaice, but with paler spots; (*Boot-making*) a tool to stretch leather for a boot-front.

flounder (2) (floun′ dėr) [prob. cogn. with Norw. *flundra*, Dut. *flodderen*], *v.i.* To struggle or stumble about violently, as when stuck in mire; (*fig.*) to struggle along with difficulty; to blunder along, to do things badly. *n.* A stumbling or blundering effort; the motion or act of floundering.

flour (flou′ er, flour) [var. of FLOWER (M.E. *flour of whete*, the finest meal)], *n.* The finer part of meal, esp. of wheat-meal; fine soft powder of any substance. *v.t.* To sprinkle flour upon; (*Am.*) to grind and bolt flour. **flour-bolt, -dresser,** *n.* A machine for bolting or bolting and dressing flour. **flour-box,** *n.* **-dredge, -dredger,** *n.* A perforated tin for sprinkling flour. **flour-mill,** *n.* A mill for grinding and sifting flour. **floury,** *a.* Covered with flour; like flour.

***flouret, *flourette** [FLOWERET].

flourish (flŭr′ ish) [O.F. *floriss-*, stem of *florir*, L. *flōrēre*, from *flōs flōris*, FLOWER]. *v.i.* To grow luxuriantly; to thrive, to prosper, to increase in wealth, honour, or happiness; to be in a state of complete development; to be alive or at work (at or about a certain date); to use florid language; to make bold and fanciful strokes in writing; to move about fantastically; (*Mus.*) to play in a bold, dashing style, with ornamental notes; to sound a fanfare; *to brag; *to blossom. *v.t.* To brandish, fling, or wave about; to flaunt, to show ostentatiously; to embellish with ornamental or fantastic figures; *to cause to thrive or bloom; *to varnish over. *n.* A flourishing condition, prosperity; a figure formed by strokes or lines fancifully drawn; rhetorical display, florid diction, a florid expression; a brandishing or waving of a weapon or other thing; (*Mus.*) a passage played for display, a fanfare of trumpets, etc., an improvised prelude or other addition. **flourish of trumpets:** The sounding of trumpets when receiving any person of distinction; (*fig.*) ostentatious announcement. **flourished,** *a.* Adorned with flourishes; (*Her.*) fleury. **flourishing,** *a.* Thriving, prosperous; making a show. **flourishingly,** *adv.* **flourishy,** *a.*

flouse, floush (flous, floush) [prob. onomat.; cp. FLUSH (2)], *v.i.* To splash.

flout (flout) [prob. var. of FLUTE (cp. M.Dut. *fluyten*, to play the flute, to jeer)], *v.t.* To mock, to insult; to treat with contempt. *v.i.* To sneer; to behave with contempt or mockery. *n.* A word or act of contempt; a sneer, an insult. **flouter,** *n.* **floutingly,** *adv.*

flow (flō) [A.-S. *flōwan* (cp. Dut. *vloeijen*, Icel. *flōa*), cogn. with Gr. *pleein*, to sail, L. *pluere*, to rain (not *fluere*, to flow)], *v.i.* To move, run, or spread, as a fluid; to circulate, as the blood; to rise, as the tide; to issue, to spring, to gush out; to sway, glide, or float, to move easily or freely, to undulate; to be poured out abundantly, to abound, to come or go in abundance or great numbers; (*Path.*) to discharge blood in excess from the uterus; *to melt, to become liquid; *to issue, to be descended (from); to overflow. **v.t.* To overflow, to flood; to cover with varnish. *n.* The act, state, or motion of flowing; the quantity that flows; a flowing liquid, a stream; a copious stream, abundance, a plentiful supply; the rise of the tide; an overflowing; undulation (of drapery, etc.); a wet or marshy tract; a quicksand. **flow-lines,** *n.pl.* (*Geol.*) Lines in igneous rocks resulting from the flow of the material before consolidation. ***flowage,** *n.* The act or state of flowing.

flower (flou' ėr, flour) [O.F. *flour*, L. *flōrem*, nom. *flōs*, cogn. with BLOW (2)], *n.* The organ or growth comprising the organs of reproduction in a plant; a flowering plant; the blossom, the bloom; (*fig.*) the finest, choicest, or best individual, part, period, etc., an embellishment; a figure of speech; the prime; the period of youthful vigour; (*Chem. pl.*) substances of a powdery consistence or form, esp. if produced by sublimation; (*vulg., pl.*) the menstrual discharge. *v.i.* To produce flowers, to bloom, to blossom; *to flourish; to be in the prime; *to froth, to ferment gently. *v.t.* To embellish with flowers; (*Hort.*) to cause to blossom. **flower-bearing,** *a.* Producing flowers. **flower-bed,** *n.* A plot of ground in which flowering-plants are grown. **flower-bud,** *n.* A bud which develops into a flower. **flower-de-luce** [FLEUR-DE-LIS]. **flower-garden,** *n.* A garden devoted to the cultivation of flowers. **flower-girl,** *n.* A girl or woman selling flowers. **flower-head** [CAPITULUM], *n.* **flower-piece,** *n.* A picture of flowers. **flowerpot,** *n.* An earthenware pot to hold plants. **flower-show,** *n.* A horticultural exhibition, usu. competitive. **flower-stalk,** *n.* The peduncle supporting the flowers of a plant. **flowers of sulphur,** *n.* (*Chem.*) A form of sulphur obtained by distillation from other forms. **flowerage,** *n.* The state of being in flower; flowers in general. **flowered,** *a.* Embellished with flowers or figures of flowers; bearing flowers (*usu. in comb.*, as *blue-flowered, six-flowered*). **flowerer,** *n.* A plant that flowers (at a particular time or in a particular way), as *spring-flowerer*. **floweret,** *n.* **flowering,** *a.* That flowers; flowery. **flowering-fern,** *n.* The king-fern, *Osmunda regalis*. **flowering-rush,** *n.* A water-plant, *Butomus umbellatus*, with an umbel of pink flowers. **flowerless,** *a.* **flowerlessness,** *n.* **flowery,** *a.* Abounding in flowers or blossoms; highly figurative, florid. **flowery-kirtled,** *a.* Adorned with garlands of flowers.

flowing (flō' ing) [FLOW], *a.* Moving as a stream; copious, fluent, easy; smooth, unbroken, not abrupt or stiff; hanging loose and waving; (*Naut.*) slackened, with the wind across the vessel's course (of fore-and-aft sail). **flowingly,** *adv.* **flowingness,** *n.*

flown, *p.p.* [FLY (2)].

flu (floo) [short for INFLUENZA], *n.* (*colloq.*) Influenza.

fluctuate (flŭk' tū āt) [L. *fluctuātus*, p.p. of *fluctuāre*, from *fluctus*, a wave], *v.i.* To rise and fall like waves; to vary, to change irregularly in degree, to be unsettled; to hesitate, to waver. **v.t.* To cause to move or roll about like waves. ***fluctuant,** *a.* *Undulating, moving like a wave; unsteady, wavering. **fluctuating,** *a.* Unsteady, wavering. **fluctuation** (-ā' shŭn), *n.*

flue (1) (floo) [etym. doubtful, perh. from obs. *flue*, shallow, or from FLUE (4)], *n.* A passage or tube by which smoke can escape or hot air be conveyed; *a chimney. **flue-pipe,** *n.* An organ pipe in which the sound is produced by air passing through a fissure and striking an edge above. **flue-work,** *n.* The flue-stops of an organ as distinct from the reed-stops.

flue (2) (floo) [etym. unknown, perh. cogn. with FLY (cp. Norw. *flu*, G. *flug*, flight)], *n.* Light down or fur; fluff. **fluey,** *a.*

flue (3) (floo) [etym. doubtful, cp. Dut. *flouw*], *n.* A fishing-net, of various kinds.

flue (4) (floo) [prob. from obs. a. *flue*, see FLUE (1)], *v.i.* To widen or spread out; to splay. *v.t.* To cause (a window, jambs, etc.) to splay.

fluent (floo' ėnt) [L. *fluens -ntem*, pres.p. of *fluere*, to flow], *a.* *Flowing, liquid; fluid, mobile, changeable; moving or curving smoothly, graceful; ready in the use of words; eloquent, copious, voluble. *n.* (*Math.*) The variable quantity in fluxions. **fluency,** *n.* The quality of being fluent; readiness and easy flow (of words or ideas). **fluently,** *adv.*

fluff (flŭf) [prob. from FLUE (2)], *n.* Light down or fur; flocculent matter; the nap of anything; (*Theatrical slang*) lines half learned or not properly delivered. *v.t.* To cover with fluff or give a fluffy surface to; to shake or spread (feathers out, as a bird); (*Theatrical slang*) to forget one's part or deliver it badly. **a little bit of fluff,** *n.* (*slang*) A flirtatious girl. **fluffy,** *a.* **fluffiness,** *n.*

fluid (floo' id) [O.F. *fluide*, L. *fluidus*, from *fluere*, to flow], *a.* Composed of particles that move freely in relation to each other; capable of flowing, as water; liquid, gaseous; not rigid or stable. *n.* A liquid, not a solid; a substance whose particles readily move and change their relative positions. **fluid drive,** *n.* (*Eng.*) A system of transmitting power through a change in the momentum of oil. **fluid measure,** *n.* Apothecaries' measure of capacity of the British Pharmacopœia. **fluidify** (floo id' i fī), **fluidize,** *v.t.* **fluidity** (floo id' i ti), *n.*

fluke (1) (flook) [A.-S. *flōc*; cogn. with G. *flach*, flat], *n.* A flounder; applied, with distinctive epithet, to other flat-fish; a parasitic worm belonging to the *Trematoda*, found chiefly in the livers of sheep; a kind of potato. **fluky** (1), *a.* Infested with flukes (as sheep).

fluke (2) (flook) [prob. from prec.], *n.* The broad holding portion of an anchor; one of the flat lobes of a whale's tail; a barb of a lance, harpoon, etc.; a tool for cleansing a hole previous to blasting.

fluke (3) (flook) [etym. doubtful], *n.* An accidentally successful stroke, esp. in billiards; any lucky chance. *v.i.* To score by luck, esp. in billiards. *v.t.* To hit or obtain in this way. **fluky** (2), *a.* Obtained by chance, not skill. **flukily,** *adv.* **flukiness,** *n.*

flume (floom) [O.F. *flum*, L. *flumen*, a river, from *fluere*, to flow], *n.* *A river; an artificial channel for conveying water to a mill or for some other industrial use; a chute; (*Am.*) a deep ravine traversed by a torrent. *v.t.* To carry down a flume; to drain by means of a flume. *v.i.* To make flumes. **to go or be up the flume:** (*Am. slang*) To come to grief; to be done for.

flummery (flŭm' ėr i) [W. *llymru*], *n.* A food made

of oatmeal or bran boiled to a jelly; a kind of blancmange; (*fig.*) anything insipid or out of place; nonsense, humbug; empty compliment.

flummox (flŭm' ȯks) [slang; prob. onomat.], *v.t.* To perplex, confound; to abash, to silence; to best, to cheat.

flump (flŭmp) [imit.], *v.i.* To fall down heavily; to flop; to sit down with a flop. *v.t.* To throw down with a dull, heavy noise. *n.* A dull, heavy noise, as of something let fall.

flung, *past & p.p.* [FLING].

flunkey (flŭng' ki) [Sc., prob. from FLANKER (cp. F. *flanquer*, to run at the side of)], *n.* A servant in livery, a footman; a lackey; a toady, a snob. **flunkeydom,** *n.* **flunkeyish,** *a.* **flunkeyism,** *n.*

fluor (floo' ȯr) [L., flow, from *fluere*, to flow], *n.* An isometric, transparent or subtranslucent, brittle mineral, having many shades of colour, composed of fluoride of calcium, also called fluor-spar and fluorite; formerly applied to any mineral containing fluorine; *a fluid state; *a menstrual flux.

fluor-, *comb. form* as prec.

fluorate (floo' ôr āt), *n.* A salt of fluoric acid.

fluorescence (floo ôr es' ėns), *n.* A quality existing in certain substances of giving out light of a different colour from their own or that of the light falling upon them; the coloured luminosity thus produced, esp. the visible light produced by the action of ultraviolet rays. **fluoresce,** *v.i.* To exhibit fluorescence.

fluorescein (floo ôr es' in), *n.* A colouring matter or dye used only for certain purposes because the colours produced are not fast.

fluorescent (floo ôr es' ėnt), *a.* Having the quality of fluorescence. **fluorescent lamp,** *n.* A lamp consisting of a glass tube with a fluorescent coating inside, which emits light on the passage through the tube of an electric discharge.

fluorhydric [HYDROFLUORIC].

fluoric (floo ŏr' ik), *a.* (*Chem.*) Containing fluorine. **fluoric acid,** *n.*

fluoride (floo ôr' īd), *n.* (*Chem.*) A compound of fluorine with an element or radical.

fluorine (floo' ôr in), *n.* (*Chem.*) A non-metallic gaseous element, forming with chlorine, bromine, and iodine the halogen group.

fluoroscope (floo ôr' ō skōp), *n.* An apparatus consisting of a light-proof box with a fluorescent screen, for observing the effects of Röntgen Rays. **fluoroscopy,** *n.*

fluorotype (floo ŏr' ō tīp), *n.* A photographic process in which sodium fluorate is used.

fluosilicic (floo ō sil is' ik), *a.* (*Chem.*) Obtained from fluorine and silica.

flurry (flŭr' i) [onomat.; cp. HURRY], *n.* A squall; a sudden and violent shower of rain, snow, etc.; commotion, agitation, bustle, confusion; nervous excitement; the death-struggle of a harpooned whale. *v.t.* To agitate, to fluster, to upset, to bewilder with noise or excitement.

flush (1) (flŭsh) [prob. imit.; cp. *flisk*, var. of FRISK, RUSH], *v.i.* To take wing; to start up suddenly (of game-birds). *v.t.* To cause to take wing; to put up. *n.* The flushing of a bird; a flock of birds put up at once.

flush (2) (flŭsh) [perh. from prec., or a form of FLASH], *v.i.* To flow swiftly; to rush; to become filled (as pipes) with a sudden rush of water; to become suffused. *v.t.* To cleanse by a rush of water; to flood. *n.* A sudden flow of water; the run or race from a mill-wheel; the cleansing of a drain with a rush of water; a morass, a bog. **flusher,** *n.* One who flushes drains, etc. **flushing-box, -cistern, -tank,** *n.* A cistern for supplying water-closets or urinals with a rush of water.

flush (3) (flŭsh) [perh. the same as prec., influenced by BLUSH (but cp. Swed. dial. *flossa*, to blaze, to flare)], *v.i.* To colour as with a rush of blood, to redden up, to blush, to glow. *v.t.* To cause to colour or become red; to redden; to inflame; to encourage, to excite (as with passion). *n.* A sudden flow or rush of blood to the face causing a redness; any warm colouring or glow; a sudden access of emotion, elation, excitement; a hot fit in fever; vigour; bloom, blossoming.

flush (4) (flŭsh) [prob. from FLUSH (2)], *a.* Full to overflowing; copious, abounding; plentifully supplied, esp. with money; abundant; filled up even; level, even, on the same plane (with). *v.t.* To make even; to level (up); to fill in (a joint) so as to make even with the surface. **flush-deck,** *n.* A deck with a level floor from stem to stern. **flushness,** *n.* Fullness; abundance.

flush (5) (flŭsh) [perh. from F. *flux*, L. *fluxus*, from *fluere*, to flow], *n.* (*Cards*) A hand of cards all of one suit. **four-flusher,** *n.* (*Am. slang*) A bluffer, a deceiver, humbug. **royal flush:** Cards in a sequence headed by the ace. **straight flush:** Cards in a sequence.

fluster (flŭs' tėr) [conn. with Icel. *flaustra*, to be flustered (cp. E.Fris. *flostern*, *flustern*, to rustle)], *v.t.* To flurry or confuse; to agitate, to make nervous; to befuddle, to make tipsy. *v.i.* To be in an agitated or confused state. *n.* Flurry, confusion of mind, agitation.

flustra (flŭs' trȧ) [mod. L., substituted by Linnæus for *eschara*], *n.* (*pl.* **-træ**) (*Zool.*) A sea-mat, an individual of the genus of polyzoa called *Flustridæ*.

flute (floot) [O.F. *fleute*, *flaute*, *flahute* (prob. imit.; perh. conn. with L. *flāre*, to blow)], *n.* A tubular wind-instrument with blow-hole near the end and holes stopped by the fingers or with keys for producing variations of tone; an organ-stop with a similar tone; (*Arch.*) a long vertical groove semicircular in section, esp. in the shaft of a column; a similar groove or corrugation in a dress, etc.; a long thin French roll of bread. *v.i.* To play a flute; to whistle or sing with a flute-like sound. *v.t.* To play, sing, or utter with flute-like tones; to play (an air) on a flute; to form flutes or grooves in. **fluted,** *a.* (*Arch.*) Channelled, furrowed; (*Mus.*) clear and mellow, applied to the upper notes of a soprano. **flutina** (floo tē' nȧ), *n.* A kind of accordion resembling the concertina. **fluting,** *n.* A groove, a channel; fluted work in pillars, etc. **flutist,** *n.* One who plays upon the flute, a flautist. **fluty,** *a.* Resembling a flute in tone.

flutter (flŭt' ėr) [A.-S. *flotorian*, from *flēotan*, to FLEET (4)], *v.i.* To flap the wings rapidly; to hover, flit, or move about in a fitful, restless way; to move with quick, irregular motions; to quiver, to vibrate; to beat spasmodically (as the pulse); to be agitated or uncertain; to wander; to act frivolously. *v.t.* To cause to move about with quick vibrations; to vibrate, to cause to quiver or flap about rapidly; to agitate or alarm. *n.* The act of fluttering; quick, short, and irregular vibration; a state of excitement, anxiety, or agitation; disorder, stir; (*slang*) a gamble; a toss or spin (as of a coin); a venture or speculation. **flutteringly,** *adv.*

fluvial (floo' vi ȧl), **fluviatic** (-ăt' ik), **fluviatile** (floo' vi ȧ tīl, -til) [F. *fluvial*, L. *fluvialis*; F. *fluviatile*, L. *fluviātilis*; from *fluvium*, river], *a.* Of or belonging to a river; (*Geol.*) caused by a river; (*Bot. and Zool.*) living in rivers. **fluvio-,** *comb. form.* **fluvio-marine** (floo' vi ō mȧ rēn'), *a.* (*Geol.*) Pertaining to or produced by the joint action of a river and the sea (as deposits at a river-mouth). **fluviometer** (-om' ė tėr), *n.* An apparatus for measuring the rise and fall in a river.

flux (flŭks) [O.F., from L. *fluxus*, from *fluere*, to flow], *n.* The act or state of flowing; the motion of a fluid; a state of movement or continual change; an issue or flowing out, a discharge; the flow of the tide, as opposed to the ebb; (*Path.*) an abnormal discharge of fluid matter from the body; *dysentery; (*Chem. and Min.*) any substance which assists the fusion of minerals or metals; fusion; (*Phys.*) the quantity of light falling on an area; (*Elec.*) the strength of a magnetic field; (*Math.*) continuous motion (as a line considered as the flux of a point). *v.t.* To melt, to fuse; to facilitate fusion with a flux; (*Med.*) to purge; *to overflow or cause to overflow. *v.i.* To flow; to rise (as the tide); to issue in a flux; to melt. **flux-spoon,** *n.* A small ladle for dipping out molten metal. ***fluxation,** *n.* A flowing or passing away, and giving place to others. ***fluxible,** *a.* **fluxibility** (-bil' i ti), *n.* ***fluxive,** *a.* Flowing, running, as tears; fickle.

fluxion (flŭk' shŭn) [F., from L. *fluxio -ōnem* as prec.], *n.* The act or state of flowing; that which flows; fusion of metals; continuous variation; (*Path.*) an unnatural flow of blood or humour towards any organ; (*Math.*) the rate of variation of a fluent quantity; (*pl.*) the Newtonian method now known as the differential calculus. **fluxional, -ionary,** *a.* Pertaining to fluxions. ***fluxionist,** *n.* One skilled in fluxions.

fly (1) (flī) [A.-S. *flēoge*, from foll.], *n.* (*pl.* **flies**) A two-winged insect, esp. of the genus *Musca*, of which the house-fly, *M. domestica*, is the type; (*loosely*) any winged insect; a disease in turnips, hops, etc., caused by various flies; an artificial fly for fishing; *a familiar spirit, orig. in the shape of a fly or louse; *an unimportant or valueless thing. **to have no flies on one:** (*slang*) To be no fool. **fly-agaric,** *n.* A scarlet mushroom, *Agaricus muscarius*, growing in woods. **fly-bane,** *n.* A popular name for the catch-fly and other plants. **fly-bitten,** *a.* Marked by the bites of flies. **fly-blister,** *n.* (*Med.*) A blister prepared from cantharides. **fly-block,** *n.* (*Naut.*) A block which moves with the tackle from one position to another. **fly-blow,** *v.t.* To deposit eggs in, as the blow-fly in meat; (*fig.*) to corrupt, to taint. *n.* The egg of a blow-fly. **fly-blown,** *a.* Tainted by maggots; (*fig.*) impure, corrupt, tainted. **fly-book,** *n.* A book or case for anglers' flies. **fly-case,** *n.* An elytron. **fly-catcher,** *n.* A fly-trap; a bird of the genus *Muscicapa*. **fly-fish,** *v.i.* To angle with natural or artificial flies for bait. **fly-fisher,** *n.* **fly-flap,** *n.* An instrument to drive away flies. **fly-net,** *n.* A net to protect (a horse, etc.) from flies. **fly-paper,** *n.* Paper prepared to catch or poison flies. **fly-powder,** *n.* A powder usu. consisting of arsenic mixed with sugar, used to kill flies. **fly-rod,** *n.* A flexible, resilient rod used in fly-fishing. **fly-trap,** *n.* A trap for catching flies; the spreading dog-bane, *Apocynum androsæmifolium*, a sensitive plant; also Venus's fly-trap, *Dionæa muscipula*. **fly-water,** *n.* A solution of arsenic, etc., for killing flies. **fly weight,** *n.* (*Boxing*) 8 stone or less in weight. **fly-whisk,** *n.* A whisk for driving away flies.

fly (2) (flī) [A.-S. *flēogan* (cp. Dut. *vliegen*, Icel. *fljūga*, G. *fliegen*), not conn. with FLEE], *v.i.* (*past* **flew,** *p.p.* **flown**) To move through the air with wings; to ride in an air-ship, esp. an aeroplane; to flutter or wave in the air; to pass or be driven through the air with great speed or violence; to flee, to run away, to try to escape, to depart (*chiefly colloq. or in ordinary prose, with p.p.* **fled**); to burst or break violently (in pieces); to start, to pass suddenly or violently, to spring, to hasten, to burst (as to arms or into a rage). *v.t.* To cause to fly or float in the air; to flee from, to avoid, to quit by flight; to hunt with a hawk; to make (a hawk, pigeon, etc.) fly; to set or keep (a flag) flying. **to fly a kite:** (*comm. slang*) To obtain money on accommodation bills; (*fig.*) to launch a project tentatively to see how the wind blows. **to fly at:** To attack suddenly, to rush at with violence or fierceness; (*Hawking*) to soar at and attack. **to fly high:** To be ambitious. **to fly in the face of:** To act in direct opposition to. **to fly off:** To become suddenly detached; *to revolt, to desert. **to fly open:** To open suddenly and violently. **to fly out:** To burst into a passion; to break out into licence or extravagance. **fly-over, fly-under:** A line of railway, or road, carried over or under another at an intersection. **to let fly:** To shoot or throw out; to direct a violent blow (at); to use violent language; (*Naut.*) to let go suddenly and entirely. **fly-away,** *a.* Streaming, loose; (*fig.*) flighty, volatile. *n.* A runaway. **fly-by-night,** *n.* One given to nocturnal excursions; a runaway debtor; *a kind of sedan-chair on wheels, introduced at Brighton in 1816.

fly (3) (flī) [from prec.], *n.* The act or state of flying; the distance that something flies; (*pl.* **flys**) a one-horse carriage, a hackney coach [perh. from FLY-BY-NIGHT]; a flywheel or a regulating device acting on the same principle; the portion of a vane that shows the direction of the wind; the length of a flag from the staff to the outer edge; the part of a flag farthest from the staff; a flap covering buttonholes; a loose flap for covering the entrance to a tent; (*pl.*) a gallery over the proscenium in a theatre where the curtains or scenes are controlled. **fly-cutter,** *n.* (*Mach.*) A machine for shaping the ends of metal rods, cutting the teeth of wheels, etc. **fly-drill,** *n.* (*Mach.*) A hand drill with a fly-wheel on its shank which gives it the requisite momentum to rewind the cord that gives its reciprocating motion. **fly-leaf,** *n.* A blank leaf at the beginning or end of a book. **flyman,** *n.* The driver of a fly; the man who works the ropes of scenes, etc., in a theatre. **fly-posting,** *n.* Unauthorized affixing of posters. **fly-sheet,** *n.* A handbill; a prospectus; a two- or four-page tract. **fly-wheel,** *n.* A heavy-rimmed wheel attached to a machine for regulating the speed by its inertia.

fly (4) (flī) [etym. doubtful], *a.* (*slang*) Sharp, wide-awake.

flyer (flī' ėr), *n.* One who flies or flees; (*in comb.*) one who or that which flies in a particular way (as a *high-flyer*); a flying jump; (*colloq.*) a horse, vehicle, train, etc., that goes with exceptional speed; (*Mech.*) a fly-wheel; (*Print.*) a vibratory rod with fingers to carry the sheet from the tapes to the delivery table; (*pl.*) a straight flight of stairs; (*Austral.*) the kangaroo.

flying (flī' ing), *a.* Moving with or as with wings; moving or adapted to move swiftly; brief, hurried. **flying army, column, squadron,** *n.* A body of troops kept moving from one place to another, either to protect its own garrisons and posts, or to harass the enemy. **flying bedstead,** *n.* A framework resembling a bedstead raised vertically from the ground by jet-propulsion. **flying bomb,** *n.* A jet-propelled, pilotless aeroplane with a charge of explosive in the head which is detonated when the plane falls with the failure of the propelling jet. **flying bridge,** *n.* A temporary bridge for military purposes. **flying buttress,** *n.* An arched or slanting structure springing from solid masonry and serving to support another part of a structure. **flying colours** [COLOUR]. **flying dog,** *n.* A variety of vampire-bat. **Flying Dutchman** [DUTCHMAN]. **flying fish,** *n.* A fish which has the power of sustaining itself in the air for a time by means of its fins. **flying fox,** *n.* An East Indian frugivorous bat belonging to the genus *Pteropus*; (*Austral.*) a conveyor on a suspended wire. **flying-gurnard,** *n.* A fish with large pectoral fins, *Dactylopterus volitans*. **flying jib,** *n.* A sail extending beyond the standing jib. **flying jib-boom,** *n.* An extension of the jib-boom. **flying jump,** *n.* A jump taken with a running start. **flying machine,** *n.* A machine for flying through the air. **flying man,** *n.* A man who works a flying machine, aeroplane, or airship. **flying-lemur,** *n.* Any individual of the genus *Galeopithecus*, esp. *G. volans*, whose fore and hind limbs are connected by a fold of skin enabling the animal to take flying leaps from tree to tree. **Flying Officer,** *n.* (*Aviat.*) Junior commissioned rank in R.A.F. equivalent to lieutenant in the Army. **flying party,** *n.* A detachment of men employed in skirmishing round an enemy. **flying-phalanger,** *n.* A popular name for the marsupial genus *Petaurus*. **flying saucer,** *n.* A large, luminous disk reported as having been seen in the air by various persons. **flying squad,** *n.* (*Police*) Mobile detachment of police. **flying-squadron,** *n.* (*Mil. and Nav.*) A squadron kept distinct from a main force to carry out a special manœuvre. **flying-squirrel,** *n.* A squirrel with a patagium or fold of skin like that of the flying-lemurs, by which it makes flying leaps.

foal (fōl) [A.-S. *fola* (cp. Dut. *veulen*, G. *fohlen*), cogn. with L. *pullus*, Gr. *pōlos*], *n.* The young of an equine animal, as of the horse, ass, etc.; a colt, a filly. *v.i.* To bring forth young (as a mare or she-ass). *v.t.* To bring forth (a foal). **foal-foot,** *n.* The coltsfoot, *Tussilago farfara.*

foam (fōm) [A.-S. *fām* (cp. G. *feim*); prob. cogn. with L. *spūma*], *n.* The aggregation of bubbles produced in liquids by violent agitation or fermentation; the similar formation produced by saliva in an animal's mouth; froth, spume; (*poet.*) the sea. *v.i.* To gather, produce, or emit foam; to be covered or filled with foam; to move (along, against, etc.) with production of foam; to pass (away) in foam. **v.t.* To cause to foam; to throw out or express with violence. **foam-rubber,** *n.* Rubber of foamlike consistency largely used in upholstery, etc. ***foam-crested,** *a.* Crested with foam. **foamingly,** *adv.* **foamless,** *a.* **foamy,** *a.*

fob (1) (fob) [etym. doubtful (cp. G. dial. *fuppe*)], *n.* A watch-pocket, formerly in the waistband of breeches. *v.t.* To put into one's pocket.

fob (2) (fob) [prob. from L.G. *foppen* (cp. G. *foppen*, to befool)], *v.t.* To cheat, to impose upon; *to beat, to ill-treat. **to fob off:** To put off, to shift off; to delude (into accepting) by a trick.

focal [FOCUS].

fo'c'sle [FORECASTLE].

focus (fō' kůs) [L., hearth], *n.* (*pl.* **foci** (fō' sī), **focuses** (fō' kůs ėz) A point at which rays of light, heat, electrons, etc., meet after reflection, deflection, or refraction; relation between the eye or lens and the object necessary to produce a clear image; the point from which any activity (such as a disease or an earthquake wave) originates; (*Geom.*) one of two points having a definite relation to an ellipse or other curve. *v.t.* (*past & p.p.* **focused, focussed**) To bring (rays) to a focus or point; to adjust (eye or instrument) so as to be at the right focus; to bring into focus. **focal,** *a.* Of, pertaining to, or situated at a focus. **focal distance or length:** The distance between the centre of a lens and the point where initially parallel rays converge. **focal plane:** A plane containing the foci of the systems of parallel rays passing through a lens. **focalize,** *v.t.* To focus. **focalization** (-zā' shůn), *n.* **focimetry** (fō sim' ėt ri), *n.* The measurement of focal distances.

fodder (fod' ėr) [A.-S. *fōdor*, from *fōda*, FOOD (cp. Dut. *voeder*, G. *futter*)], *n.* Food served to cattle, as hay, etc., distinguished from pasture. *v.t.* To feed or supply with fodder; *to feed. **fodderer,** *n.* One who fodders cattle. **fodderless,** *a.*

foe (fō) [A.-S. *fāh, fāg*, hostile (*gefā*, an enemy, *fēon, fēogan*, to hate)], *n.* A personal enemy; an opponent, an adversary; an enemy in war; an ill-wisher. **v.t.* To treat as a foe. **foe-like,** *a.* Like a foe. *adv.* As a foe. **foeman,** *n.* An enemy in war.

fœtus (fē' tůs) [L. *fētus*, offspring, rel. to *fu-*, *fuī*, I was, *futurus*, to be, Gr. *phuein*, to beget], *n.* (*pl.* **fœtuses** (fē' tůsėz)) The young of viviparous animals in the womb, and of oviparous vertebrates in the egg, after the parts are distrinctly formed. **fœtal,** *a.* Pertaining to a fœtus. **fœtation** (fē' tā' shůn), *n.* The formation of a fœtus. **fœticide** (fē' ti sīd), *n.* The destruction of a fœtus; abortion.

fog (1) (fog) [etym. doubtful], *n.* Coarse, rank grass which has not been eaten off in summer, aftermath; coarse grass remaining through the winter; (*Sc.*) moss. *v.t.* To feed (cattle) with fog. **v.i.* To grow mossy. **foggy** (1), *a.* Full of coarse, rank grass; consisting of or resembling rank grass; (*Sc.*) covered with moss, mossy.

fog (2) (fog) [etym. doubtful], *n.* A dense watery vapour rising from land or water and suspended near the surface of land or sea; (*Phot.*) a cloudiness on a negative; (*fig.*) a state of confusion or perplexity. *v.t.* To surround with or as with a fog; (*fig.*) to becloud, to perplex, to bewilder; (*Phot.*) to make (a negative) cloudy. *v.i.* To become foggy; (*Phot.*) to become cloudy; (*Railway*) to lay fog-signals on a line. **fog-bank,** *n.* A dense mass of fog at sea resembling land at a distance. **fog-bell,** *n.* A bell rung by waves as a warning to mariners. **fog-bow,** *n.* A faint bow, resembling a rainbow, produced by light on a fog. **fog-horn, -trumpet, -whistle,** *n.* An instrument to give warning to ships in a fog. **fog-signal,** *n.* A detonator placed on a railway for the guidance of engine-drivers. **fogger,** *n.* One who lays fog-signals on railway lines. **foggy** (2), *a.* Thick, murky; full of or abounding in fog; (*fig.*) beclouded, obscure, perplexed, indistinct. **foggily,** *adv.* **fogginess,** *n.* **not the foggiest:** (*slang*) Not the slightest notion of.

fogle (fōgl) [thieves' slang], *n.* A pocket-handkerchief.

fogy, fogey (fō' gi), *n.* An old-fashioned eccentric person. **fogydom,** *n.* **fogyish,** *a.* **fogyism,** *n.*

föhn (fōn) [G., perh. ult. from L. *Favōnius*], *n.* The warm south wind in the Alps.

foible (foi' bėl) [F., now *faible*, FEEBLE], *n.* A weak point in one's character; (*Fencing*) the part of a sword-blade between the middle and point.

foil (1) (foil) [O.F. *foil* (F. *feuille*), L. *folium*, a leaf (cp. Gr. *phullion*)], *n.* An amalgam of quicksilver and tin at the back of a mirror; very thin sheet metal; a thin leaf of metal put under gems to increase their lustre or brighten or alter their colour; (*fig.*) that which serves to set off something else to advantage; (*Arch.*) a rounded leaf-like space or arc in window tracery. *v.t.* To back (glass, crystal, etc.) with foil; (*fig.*) to set off by contrast; (*Arch.*) to decorate or design with foils. **foiling** (1), *n.* (*Arch.*) Decoration with or consisting of foils.

foil (2) (foil) [O.F. *fouler*, to tread, to stamp or full (cloth), late L. *fullāre*, from L. *fullo*, a fuller (perh. influenced by M.E. *fylen*, to make foul)], *v.t.* To baffle, to frustrate; to throw off the scent; to defeat, to repulse, to parry; *to foul, to dishonour. *n.* The trail of hunted game; *a defeat, a frustration, a failure when success seems certain. **foilable,** *a.* **foiling** (2), *n.* The track of a deer on the grass.

foil (3) (foil) [etym. doubtful, perh. from foll., or from FOIL (1 or 2)], *n.* A straight thin sword, blunted by means of a button on the point, used in fencing.

***foin** (foin) [O.F. *foine*, *foisne*, L. *fusana*, a fish-spear], *v.t.* To thrust at. *v.i.* To lunge or thrust. *n.* A thrust or lunge; a stroke, as in fencing. ***foiningly,** *adv.*

***foison** (foi' zůn) [O.F., from L. *fūsio -ōnem*, from *fundere*, to pour], *n.* Plenty, abundance; power, strength; (*pl.*) resources.

foist (foist) [orig. to palm or conceal in the hand, prob. from Dut. prov. *vuisten*, from *vuist*, fist], *v.t.* To introduce surreptitiously or wrongfully; to insert fraudulently; to palm off (on or upon) as genuine; *to cheat. **n.* A swindle, an imposition; a foister, a cheat, a sharper. ***foister,** *n.* One who foists.

fold (1) (fōld) [A.-S. *fald* (cp. Dut. *vaalt*, Dan. *fold*)], *n.* A pen or enclosure for sheep; a flock of sheep; (*fig.*) the Church, the flock of Christ; *a boundary. *v.t.* To put or enclose in or as in a fold. **foldless** (1), *a.*

fold (2) (fōld) [A.-S. *fealdan* (cp. Icel. *falda*, G. *falten*, also Gr. *plassein, plekein*, L. *plicāre*)], *v.t.* To double or lay one part of (a flexible thing) over another; to clasp (arms, etc.) round; to clasp, to embrace, to enfold, to envelop; *to enswathe, to conceal. *v.i.* To become folded or doubled; to shut in folds; (*Geol.*) to be doubled up; *to fail to give way. *n.* A part doubled or laid on another; a bend or doubling, a plait; a hollow between two parts (as of a fabric); a coil, a folding, an embrace; (*Geol.*) a flexure in strata. **folding-chair,** *n.* A collapsible chair. **folding-doors,** *n.pl.* Two doors hung on opposite side-posts, and meeting in the middle. **folding-machine,** *n.* A machine for folding printed sheets for newspapers or books; a machine which shapes pans and tin-ware by pressure. **folding-stool,** *n.* A portable collapsible stool. **foldless** (2), *a.*

-fold [A.-S. *feald*, cogn. with prec. (cp. Gr. *-plasios*, L. *-plex*)], *suf.* Forming adjectives and adverbs denoting multiplication, as *fourfold*, *manifold.*

folder (fōl′ dĕr), *n.* One who or that which folds; a holder for loose papers; a bone or ivory blade used in folding papers.

foldstool [FALDSTOOL].

foliaceous (fō li ā′ shŭs) [L. *foliāceus*, from *folium*, a leaf], *a.* Having the texture, structure, or organs of or as of leaves; leaf-shaped; furnished with leaves; (*Cryst.*) consisting of thin laminæ; splitting into thin laminæ; (*Zool.*) *shaped or arranged like leaves.

foliage (fō′ li aj) [M.F., *fueillage*, *foillage* (F. *feuillage*), from *fueille*, L. *folia*, leaves], *n.* Leaves in the aggregate; (*Art*, *esp. Arch.*) the representation of leaves or clusters of leaves, as ornament. *v.t.* To work or ornament with representation of foliage.

foliar (fō′ li ār) [L. *folium*, a leaf], *a.* Consisting of or pertaining to leaves; of the nature of leaf.

foliate (fō′ li āt) [as prec., -ATE], *v.i.* To split or disintegrate into thin laminæ. *v.t.* To decorate with leaf-patterns, foils, leaf-like tracery, etc.; *to beat into a leaf or thin plate; *to cover over with a thin coat or sheet of tin, quicksilver, etc. (as a mirror). *a.* (-āt) Leaf-shaped; furnished with leaves. **foliation** (-ā′ shŭn), *n.* Foliating; (*Arch.*) ornamentation by trefoil, quatrefoil, cinquefoil, and similar tracery based on the form of a leaf. ***foliature,** *n.* Foliage; the state of being beaten into foil. **foliferous** (fō lif′ ėr ŭs) [-FEROUS], *a.* (*Bot.*) Bearing leaves. **foliose, -ous,** *a.* Leafy, abounding in or of the nature of leaves.

folio (fō′ li ō) [abbr. of L. *in foliō*, in the form of a sheet folded once], *n.* (*pl.* **-os**) A sheet of paper folded once; a book of the largest size, whose sheets are folded once, hence, any large volume or work; a page of manuscript; a leaf of paper or other material for writing, etc., numbered on the front; (*Book-keeping*) a page in an account book, or two opposite pages numbered as one; (*Print.*) the number of a page; (*Law*) seventy-two words of manuscript in legal documents, ninety words in Parliamentary proceedings.

foliole (fō′ li ōl) [F., from L. *foliolum*, dim. of *folium*, a leaf], *n.* A leaflet; one of the separate parts of a compound leaf. **folio-late,** *a.*

foliose, -ous [FOLIATE].

folk (fōk) [A.-S. *folc* (cp. Icel. *fōlk*, Dan. and Swed. *folk*, Dut. and G. *volk*)], *n.* People; people collectively; a particular class of people, as old folk (*sometimes pl.*); a people, nation, or race. **folk-custom,** *n.* A custom of the people. **folk dance,** *n.* A traditional dance of countryfolk. **folk-etymology,** *n.* A popular but often erroneous derivation of a word. ***folkland,** *n.* (*Feud. Law*) The land of the people as distinguished from land held by deed. **folk-lore,** *n.* Popular superstitions, tales, traditions, or legends; the systematic study of such superstitions, etc. **folklorism,** *n.* **folklorist,** *n.* One versed in the study of folklore. **folkloristic** (-is′ tik), *a.* ***folkmoot,** *n.* An assembly of the people of a shire, city, or town; a courtleet or local court. **folk-right,** *n.* Common law, the right of the people. **folk-song,** *n.* A song or ballad, supposed to have originated among the people and to have been handed down by tradition. **folk-tale,** *n.* A popular myth.

follicle (fol′ i kl) [F., from L. *folliculus*, a little bag, dim. of *follis*, bellows], *n.* A small cavity, sac, or gland; (*Bot.*) a fruit formed by a single carpel dehiscing by one suture, usually the ventral; (*Entom.*) a cocoon; (*pl. pop.*) roots of the hair. **follicular** (fŏ lik′ ū lăr), **folliculated,** *a.* **folliculous,** *a.* Abounding in follicles; having or producing follicles.

follow (fol′ ō) [M.E. *folwan*, A.-S. *folgian* (cp. Dut. *volgen*, G. *folgen*)], *v.t.* To go or come after; to move behind; to pursue, as an enemy; to accompany, to attend upon, to serve; to adhere to, to side with, to espouse the cause of; to initiate, to pattern oneself upon; to go after as an admirer or disciple; to go along (a path, road, etc.); to engage in, to practise, as a profession; to conform to, act upon (a rule, policy, etc.); to come or happen after in point of time, order, rank, or importance; to watch the course of; to keep the mind or attention fixed on; to understand, to grasp the meaning of; to result, to be the consequence of; to seek after, to try to attain; *to follow up, to prosecute (an affair). *v.i.* To come or go after another person or thing; to pursue; to be the next thing to be done or said; to be a natural consequence, to ensue; to be the logical consequence, to be deducible. **as follows:** A prefatory formula to a statement, enumeration, etc. **to follow on:** To continue without break. **to follow the plough:** To be a ploughman or peasant. **to follow suit:** To play a card of the same suit as that first played, hence, to follow the same course of action. **to follow through:** (*Golf*) To continue the swing after hitting the ball. **to follow up:** To pursue closely and steadily; to prosecute an advantage; to make further efforts. **a follow-up,** *n.* A reminding circular sent by an advertiser.

follower (fol′ ō ĕr), *n.* One who follows; a disciple, an imitator or adherent, an attendant; a companion; a subordinate, a servant; one of the same party; an admirer; a Victorian maidservant's sweetheart.

following (fol′ ō ing), *a.* Coming next after, succeeding, now to be mentioned; a body of followers or adherents.

folly (fol′ i) [O.F. *folie*, from *fol*, FOOL], *n.* Foolishness, want of understanding or judgment, senselessness; a foolish act, idea, or conduct; an object of foolish attention or imitation; a costly structure apparently built for fantastic reasons; *wantonness, immorality, depravity.

foment (fō ment′) [F. *fomenter*, L. *fōmentāre*, from *fōmentum* (for *fovimentum*), from *fovēre*, to warm, cherish], *v.t.* To apply warm or medicated lotions to; to warm; to poultice; (*fig.*) to nourish, to foster, to encourage, to promote. **fomentation** (-tā′ shŭn), *n.* The act of fomenting; the lotion, poultice, warm cloths, etc., applied. **fomenter,** *n.*

fomes (fō′ mēz) [L., touchwood], *n.* (*pl.* ***fomites,*** fō′ mi tēz) A substance of a porous kind liable to absorb and retain contagious effluvia and thus propagate disease.

***fon** (fon) [etym. doubtful], *n.* A fool, an idiot. *a.* Foolish. *v.i.* To play the fool, to be foolish. ***fonly,** *adv.*

fond (1) (fond) [M.E. *fonned*, p.p. of prec. v.], *a.* Foolish, tender, or loving; doting on, delighting in; *trivial; *foolish, silly, simple. **v.t.* To fondle, to caress. **v.i.* To be fond or doting. **to be fond of:** To like very much, to love. **fondly,** *adv.* **fondness,** *n.*

***fond** (2) [FAND (1)].

***fond** (3) [FOUND (2)].

fondant (fon′ dănt) [F., from *fondre*, to melt, L. *fundere*, to pour], *n.* A soft kind of sweetmeat.

fondle (fondl) [freq. of FOND (1)], *v.t.* To caress; *to treat with great kindness or indulgence. *v.i.* To indulge in caresses (with). **fondler,** *n.* **fondling,** *n.* A person or thing fondled; *a fool, an idiot.

font (1) (font) [A.-S. *fant*, *font*, L. *fontem*, nom. *fons*, a FOUNT], *n.* The vessel or basin to contain water for baptism; the oil-reservoir for a lamp; *a spring; *a fountain. ***font-stone,** *n.* A baptismal font. ***fontal,** *a.* Of or pertaining to a fount or source, to a baptismal font, or to baptism.

font (2) [FOUNT (2)].

fontanel, -nelle (fon tȧ nel') [F. *fontanelle*, dim. of *fontaine*, FOUNTAIN], *n.* (*Anat.*) An interval between the bones of the infant cranium; an issue for the discharge of humours from the body.

fonticulus (fŏn tik' ū lŭs) [L., dim. of *fons*, see FONT (1)], *n.* (*Surg.*) A small ulcer produced artificially; (*Anat.*) the depression just above the breast-bone.

food (food) [A.-S. *foda*, from root *fōd-*, *fad*, cp. Gr. *pateesthai*, L. *pāscere*, to feed, *pānis*, bread], *n.* Any substance which, taken into the body, is capable of sustaining or nourishing, or which assists in sustaining or nourishing the living being; aliment, nutriment; victuals, provisions, esp. edibles as distinguished from drink; nutriment for plants; that which nourishes, sustains, or is material for; *feeding, eating. **food preservative:** (*Chem.*) A substance added to food to prevent its fermentation or putrefaction. **foodstuff,** *n.* Any thing or material used for food. **food-yolk,** *n.* (*Biol.*) The part of the yolk of an egg which nourishes the embryo. ***foodful,** *a.* Furnishing food; fruitful, fertile. **foodless,** *a.*

fool (1) (fool) [O.F. *fol* (F. *fou*), L. *follem*, acc. of *follis*, bellows, wind-bag, late L. fool], *n.* A person without common sense or judgment; a silly person; a dupe; *a jester, a buffoon; *an idiot, an imbecile; *a wicked person. *a.* (*colloq.*) Foolish, silly. **v.i.* To play the fool; to trifle, to idle. *v.t.* To make a fool of; to dupe, to cheat, to impose upon, to play tricks upon; to disappoint; to waste (time away); *to make foolish. **to fool away:** To waste on objects of little or no value; to fritter away. **to fool with:** To meddle with in a careless and risky manner. **to make a fool of:** To cause to appear ridiculous; to deceive, to disappoint. **to play the fool:** To act like a fool; to act the buffoon. ***fool-begged,** *a.* Foolish, idiotic. ***fool-born,** *a.* Born of or sprung from folly. ***fool-happy,** *a.* Fortunate; lucky by chance. **fool-proof,** *a.* and *adv.* Secure against any ignorant mishandling. **fool's-errand,** *n.* An absurd or fruitless errand or quest; the pursuit of what cannot be found. **fool's paradise,** *n.* A state of unreal or deceptive joy or good fortune. **fool's-parsley,** *n.* A poisonous umbelliferous herb, *Æthusa cynapium*. **foolery,** *n.* Habitual folly; the act of playing the fool; folly; absurdity. **fooling,** *n.* Buffoonery. **foolish,** *a.* **foolishly,** *adv.* **foolishness,** *n.*

fool (2) (fool) [prob. from prec.], *n.* A dish made of fruit, esp. gooseberries, stewed and crushed with cream, etc.

foolhardy (fool har' di) [O.F. *folhardi* (*fol*, fool, *hardi*, bold)], *a.* Daring without sense or judgment, foolishly bold; rash, reckless. **foolhardily,** *adv.* **foolhardihood, foolhardiness,** *n.*

foolscap (foolz' kăp), *n.* A pointed cap with bells, formerly worn by professional jesters; a size of writing-paper 17 × 13½ in. or of printing paper, folio, 13½ × 8½ in., quarto, 8½ × 6¾ in., octavo, 6¾ × 4¼ in., named from its original watermark of a fool's cap and bells.

foot (fut) [A.-S. *fōt* (cp. Dut. *voet*, Icel. *fōtr*, G. *fuss*, also Gr. *pous podos*, L. *pes pedis*)], *n.* (*pl.* **feet**) The part of the leg which treads on the ground in standing or walking, and on which the body is supported; the part below the ankle; (*Zool.*) the locomotive organ of invertebrate animals, the tube-foot of an echinoderm; that which serves to support a body; that part of an article of dress which receives the foot; a measure containing 12 in., named as being roughly the length of a man's foot; the lowest part, the base, the lower end; the bottom; foot-soldiers, infantry; (*Pros.*) a set of syllables forming the rhythmical unit in verse; (*pl.* **foots**) sediment, dregs, oil refuse, etc.; *basis, footing, status. *v.i.* To walk, to dance; to pace; to go or travel on foot. *v.t.* To travel over by walking; to add a new foot to (as to stockings); to add up figures and set the total at the foot; *to kick, spurn with the foot. **on foot:** Walking; in motion, action, or process of execution. **on one's feet:** Standing up; (*fig.*) in good health; thriving, getting on well. **to carry one off one's feet:** To send wild with delight, excitement, etc. **to fall on one's feet:** To emerge safely or successfully. **to foot a bill:** (*colloq.*) To pay a bill, to acknowledge payment. **to foot it:** To go on foot. **to foot up to:** To mount or total up to (of items in an account). **to keep one's feet or footing:** Not to fall. **to put one's foot down:** To be firm, determined. **to put one's foot in it:** To blunder, to get into a scrape. **to set on foot:** To put in motion; to originate. **wet under foot:** Wet on the ground. **foot-and-mouth disease,** *n.* A contagious eczematous disease chiefly affecting cattle. **foot-barracks,** *n.* Barracks for infantry. **foot-bath,** *n.* A vessel in which to wash the feet; the act of washing the feet. **foot-board,** *n.* A platform for a footman behind a carriage; a step for getting into or out of a vehicle; a foot-plate; a treadle; a board at the foot of a bed. **foot-boy,** *n.* A page, a boy in livery. **foot-bridge,** *n.* A narrow bridge for foot-passengers. ***foot-cloth,** *n.* The housings of a horse, reaching down to the ground. **foot-drill,** *n.* A drill worked by a treadle. **footfall,** *n.* The sound of a footstep. **foot-fault,** *n.* (*Lawn tennis*) The act of overstepping the base-line when serving. **foot-guards,** *n.pl.* Regiments of infantry, the Grenadier, Coldstream, Scots, Welsh and Irish Guards. **foot-hill,** *n.* A hill lying at the base of a range of mountains. **foot-hold,** *n.* That which sustains the foot; support at the foot; (*fig.*) a position of stability or security; a basis of operations. ***foot-hot,** *adv.* In hot haste; immediately. ***foot landraker,** *n.* A footpad. **foot-licker,** *n.* A sycophant, a mean flatterer. **foot-loose,** *a.* Free, unbound by ties. **foot-muff,** *n.* A covering lined with fur, to keep the feet warm. **foot-pace,** *n.* A pace no faster than a walk. **foot-page,** *n.* A foot-boy. **foot-pan,** *n.* A vessel for washing feet. **foot-passenger,** *n.* One who travels on foot. **foot-path, -road, -way,** *n.* A narrow path or way for foot-passengers only. **foot-pound,** *n.* The unit of energy, the amount that will raise one pound avoirdupois one foot. **foot-race,** *n.* A running-match on foot. **foot-rope,** *n.* (*Naut.*) A rope beneath a yard upon which the seamen stand in reefing and furling sails; a rope at the foot of a sail. **foot-rot,** *n.* A disease in the feet of sheep and cattle, characterized by an abnormal growth. **foot-rule,** *n.* A measure twelve inches long. **foot-slogger,** *n.* (*slang*) An infantry-man, a foot-soldier. **foot-soldier,** *n.* An infantry soldier. **footsore,** *a.* Having the feet sore or tender. **foot-stalk,** *n.* (*Bot.*) The petiole of a leaf; the peduncle of a flower; (*Zool.*) the attachment of a crinoid, etc.; (*Mech.*) the lower portion of a mill spindle. **foot-stall,** *n.* A woman's stirrup. **foot-stick,** *n.* (*Print.*) A bevelled piece of wood or iron placed against the foot of the page to lock up the type. **foot-stone,** *n.* A stone placed at the foot of a grave, distinguished from the headstone. **footstool,** *n.* A stool for the feet. **foot-warmer,** *n.* A metal vessel containing hot water for warming the feet; a hot-water bottle. **foot-worn,** *a.* Foot-sore. **footage,** *n.* (*Mining*) Payment of miners by the running foot of work; (*Cinema.*) the length of a film in feet. **footed,** *a.* Having feet; (*usu. in comb.*) having a particular kind of feet (as *swift-footed*).

football (fut' bawl), *n.* An inflated bladder encased in leather used in the game of football; a game between two teams in which a football is kicked, or handled and kicked, to score goals or points. There are many different varieties of the game. **footballer,** *n.* **Football Association,** *n.* The body founded in 1863 to make rules, supervise and preside over Association football in Britain. **Football League,** *n.* An organized collection of Association Football clubs founded in 1888 to arrange matches and supervise the business arrangements of its constituents.

footer (fut' er), (*colloq.*) The game of football.

footing (fut' ing), *n.* Place for standing or putting the feet on; foothold; a firm or secure position; relative position, status, or condition; (*colloq.*)

entrance into a new sphere, society, profession, trade, etc.; the adding up of a column of figures and putting the total at the foot; (*Arch.*) a course at the base or foundation of a wall; (*pl.*) foundations, bases; *a footprint, a track. **to pay one's footing:** To pay a sum of money on doing anything for the first time, as on being admitted to a trade, etc.

footle (footl) [slang; etym. doubtful], *v.i.* To trifle; to potter about aimlessly. *n.* Rubbish, twaddle; nonsense, foolery. **footling,** *a.*

footlights (fut' līts), *n.pl.* A row of lights, screened from the audience, in front of the stage of a theatre.

footman (fut' mán), *n.* A male domestic servant in livery; a foot-soldier; a stand for holding a kettle before the fire.

footmark (fut' mark), *n.* A footprint.

footnote (fut' nōt), *n.* A note at the bottom of the page of a book.

footpad (fut' păd), *n.* A highwayman who robs on foot.

footplate (fut' plāt), *n.* A platform for the driver and fireman on a locomotive.

footprint (fut' print), *n.* The mark or print of a foot; any sign of the presence of a person.

footstep (fut' step), *n.* The act of stepping or treading with the feet; tread; a footprint; the sound of the step of a foot; (*fig.pl.*) traces of a course pursued or actions done.

***footy** (foo' ti) [earlier *foughty*, prob. from A.-S. *fūht*, damp], *a.* *Musty; paltry, contemptible, worthless.

foozle (foo' zėl) [cp. G. prov. *fuseln*, to work slowly], *v.i.* To waste time, to fool about. *v.t.* To make a mess of; (*Golf*) to boggle. *n.* A fogy; (*Golf*) a bungled stroke. **foozler,** *n.* **foozling,** *a.*

fop (fop) [M.E. *foppe* (cp. Dut. and G. *foppen*, to cheat, to hoax)], *n.* A man over-fond of dress; a dandy, a coxcomb. ***fopling,** *n.* A petty fop. **foppery,** *n.* **foppish,** *a.* **foppishly,** *adv.* **foppishness,** *n.*

for (fôr, fȯr) [A.-S., prob. abbr. from *fore* (cp. Dut. *voor*, G. *vor*, also L. *prō*, Gr. *pro*)], *prep.* In the place of, instead of; in exchange against, as the equivalent of; as the price or requital or payment of; in consideration of, by reason of; because of, on account of, in favour of, on the side of; in order to, with a view to; appropriate or suitable to; toward, tending toward, conducive to; to fetch, to get, to save; to attain, to reach, to arrive at; (*slang*) against; on behalf of, for the sake of; with regard to, in relation to; as regards; so far as; as, as being, in the character of; to the amount or extent of; at the cost of; in spite of, notwithstanding; in comparison of, contrast with; during; to prevent; because of. *conj.* Since, because; seeing that; in view of the reason that; *on this account that; *in order that. **to be for it:** (*colloq.*) To be marked for reprimand or punishment. **for all that:** Nevertheless; in spite of all that. **for all the world:** Exactly, completely. **for as much as** [FORASMUCH]. **for good:** For ever, once for all, permanently. **for short:** As an abbreviation or contraction. **once for all:** Finally.

for- [A.-S. *for-* (cp. Icel. and Dan. *for-*, Dut. and G. *ver-*), cogn. with Gr. *peri-*, *pro-*, *para-*, L. *per-*, *pro-*], *pref.* Away, off, as in *forget*, *forgive*; negative, prohibitive, or privative, as in *forbear*, *forbid*, *forfend*, *forsake*; amiss, badly, as in *fordo*, *forshapen*; intensive, as in *forlorn*, *forspent*, *forwearied.*

forage (for' ȧj) [O.F. *fourrage*, from *forre* (F. *feurre*), low L. *fōdrum*, from Teut., cogn. with FODDER], *n.* Food for horses and cattle, esp. for the horses of an army; the act of foraging. *v.i.* To seek for or to collect forage; to hunt for supplies, to rummage (about); *to raven. *v.t.* To overrun in order to collect forage; to ravage, to plunder; to obtain for forage; to supply with forage or food. **forage-cap,** *n.* A military undress cap. **forager,** *n.*

foramen (fȯ rā' mėn) [L., from *forāre*, to bore], *n.* (*pl.* **foramina**) A small natural opening, passage, or perforation in parts of plants and animals. **foraminate** (fȯ răm' i nȧt), *a.* **foraminated,** *a.* **foraminifer** (for ȧ min' i fėr) [L. *-fer*, bearing], *n.* One of the *Foraminifera.* **Foraminifera** (-nif' ėr ȧ), *n.pl.* (*Zool.*) A large group of *Protozoa*, esp. an order of *Rhizopoda*, the body of which is contained within a calcareous shell, many-chambered, the outer surface presenting a punctate appearance, produced by numerous *foramina.* **foraminiferal, -erous,** *a.* **foraminous** (fō răm' i nŭs), *a.*

forane (fō rān') [F. *forain*, L. *foraneus*, out of doors], *a.* (*Eccles.*) Pertaining to things remote. **vicar forane** [VICAR].

forasmuch (for ȧz mŭch'), *conj.* (*foll. by* as) Seeing that; since; in consideration that.

foray (for' ā) [Sc., prob. from M.E. *forreyer*, a forager, O.F. *forrier*, from *forre*, FORRAGE], *v.t.* To pillage, to ravage; to make a raid on. *v.i.* To make a raid; to go foraging or pillaging. *n.* A predatory expedition, a raid.

forbear (1) (fôr' bâr, fȯr bâr'), *n.* (*usu. pl.*) A forefather, an ancestor.

forbear (2) (fȯr bâr') [A.-S. *forberan*], *v.t.* (*past* **-bore,** *p.p.* **-borne**) To refrain or abstain from; to bear with, to treat with patience. *v.i.* To refrain or abstain (*usu. with* from); to be patient, to refrain from feelings of resentment. **forbearance,** *n.* **forbearingly,** *adv.*

forbid (fȯr bid') [A.-S. *forbēodan*], *v.t.* (*past* **-bad, -bade** (-băd), *p.p.* **-bidden**) To order not to do; to interdict, to prohibit; to exclude, to oppose; *to defy. **forbiddance,** *n.* The act of forbidding. **forbidden,** *a.* Prohibited, interdicted. **forbidden fruit:** The fruit of the tree of the knowledge of good and evil, which Adam was commanded not to eat (Gen. ii. 17); (*fig.*) anything desired but pronounced unlawful; the Adam's apple, a name applied to various species of *Citrus*, esp. *C. Paradisi* and *C. decumana.* ***forbiddenly,** *adv.* **forbidder,** *n.* **forbidding,** *a.* Repulsive, disagreeable; giving rise to aversion or dislike. **forbiddingly,** *adv.* **forbiddingness,** *n.*

forbore, *past*, **-borne,** *p.p.* [FORBEAR (2)].

forby (fȯr bī'), *prep.* (*Sc. and prov.*) Besides, in addition to; *near, past. *adv.* Besides; moreover.

force (1) (fōrs) [O.F., from late L. *fortia*, from L. *fortis*, strong], *n.* Strength, energy, active power; military or naval strength; an organized body, esp. an army or part of an army; (*pl.*) troops; power exerted on a person or object; violence, coercion, compulsion; unlawful violence; efficacy, validity; significance, weight, import, full meaning; persuasive or convincing power; (*Rhet.*) energy, vigour, animation, vividness; (*Phys.*) that which produces or tends to produce a change of velocity in a body at rest or in motion. *v.t.* To constrain by force (to do or to forbear from); to compel, to constrain; to use violence to, to ravish; to strain, to distort; to impose or impress (upon) with force; to bring about, to accomplish, or to make a way by force; to stimulate artificially, to cause to grow or ripen by artificial heat; to cause to ripen prematurely; (*Cards*) to compel (a player) to play in a certain way, to compel (a certain card) to be played; *to enforce; *to care for. **to force the pace:** To hasten excessively or unnecessarily. **by force:** By compulsion. **in force:** In operation, valid, enforced; (*Mil.*) in large numbers. **in great force:** (*colloq.*) Lively, in excellent form. **of force:** Of necessity. **to come into force:** To become valid; to be enforced or carried out. **the Force:** The police. **to force from:** To elicit by force; to wrest from. **to force one's way:** To push through obstacles by force. **to force out:** To drive out. **force-pump,** *n.* A pump which delivers water under pressure, so as to raise it to an elevation above that attainable by atmospheric pressure. **forced,** *a.* Constrained, affected; unnatural. **forced draught** [DRAUGHT]. **forced march:** (*Mil.*) A march in which the physical capacity of troops is exerted to the utmost. **forcedly,** *adv.* **forceful,** *a.* Full of or possessing force, forcible; impelled with force; violent, impetuous. ***forcefully,** *adv.* **forcefulness,** *n.* **forceless,** *a.* **forcing-house,** *n.* A hot-house. **forcing-pit,** *n.* A sunk hot-bed containing fermenting materials to produce bottom heat for forcing plants. **forcing-pump** [FORCE-PUMP].

force (2) (fôrs) [Icel. and Norw. *foss*], *n.* (*North.*) A waterfall.

***force** (3) (fôrs) [FARCE (2)], *v.t.* To stuff. **force-meat,** *n.* Meat chopped fine and highly seasoned, used as stuffing or served up alone.

force majeure (fôrs ma zhĕr') [F.], *n.* Superior power; circumstances not under one's control.

forceps (fôr' seps) [L. *forceps -cipis*], *n.* A pair of tongs, pincers, or pliers for holding or extracting anything; (*Anat.* and *Zool.*) an organ shaped like a pair of forceps. **forcipate, -pated,** *a.* Formed like a forceps, to open and enclose, as the chelæ of a lobster, etc.

forcible (fôr' si bėl), *a.* Done or brought about by force; having force, powerful, efficacious, impressive; *valid, binding. **forcible detainer:** (*Law*) The keeping of houses, land, etc., from the owner by force. **forcible entry:** (*Law*) A violent taking possession of or entering into or upon houses or lands. ***forcible-feeble,** *a.* Feeble but making a show of vigour; *n.* One who tries to appear vigorous. **forcibleness,** *n.* **forcibly,** *adv.*

forcite (fôr' sīt) [FORCE (1), -ITE], *n.* A kind of dynamite.

forclose [FORECLOSE].

ford (fôrd) [A.-S., cogn. with FARE (cp. G. *furt*; also L. *portus*, a harbour)], *n.* A shallow part of a river where it may be crossed by wading. *v.t.* To cross (as water) by wading. *v.i.* To cross water by wading. **fordable,** *a.* **fordless,** *a.*

fordo (fôr doo') [A.-S. *fordōn*], *v.t.* (*past* **-did,** *p.p.* **-done**) To destroy, to ruin; to kill, to put an end to; (*usu. in p.p.*) to wear out, to exhaust.

fore (1) (fôr) [A.-S., for, before, prep., beforehand, adv. (see FOR, with which it is radically identical)], *prep.* Before; for, in the presence of (chiefly now in asseverations as *fore God*); *in preference to. *adv.* *Previously; in the front part; (*Naut.*) in or towards the bows. **fore-and-aft:** (*Naut.*) At, along, or over the whole length of a ship from stem to stern. **fore-and-aft rigged,** *a.* Having sails set lengthwise to the ship, as opposed to square sails set on yards.

fore (2) (fôr), *a.* Being in front; being in front of some other thing; being the front part; front; anterior, prior, former, first. *n.* The front part; (*Naut.*) the bow; the foremast. **at the fore:** (*Naut.*) Displayed on the foremast. **to the fore:** To the front; ready, available, forthcoming; (*Sc.*) still surviving.

fore (3) (fôr) [short for BEFORE], *int.* (*Golf*) Before, beware in front (warning to persons standing in the direction of a drive).

fore-, *pref.* Before, in front, beforehand (*chiefly with verbs*), as *foreconceive, foreordain*; in front, the front or front part of; (*Naut.*) of, near, or at the bow or the foremast; (*with nouns*) as *forecourt, forearm, forecastle, forepeak, forerunner.*

fore-advise (fôr ȧd vīz'), *v.t.* To advise beforehand.

forearm (fôr arm'), *v.t.* To prepare beforehand for attack or defence.

fore-arm (fôr' arm), *n.* The anterior part of the arm, between the wrist and elbow.

forebode (fôr bōd'), *v.t.* To foretell, predict; to prognosticate, to portend; to feel a presentiment of. *v.i.* To prognosticate, esp. evil. ***forebodement,** *n.* **foreboder,** *n.* **foreboding,** *n.* Prophecy, presage, or anticipation, esp. of evil. **forebodingly,** *adv.*

fore-body (fôr' bod i), *n.* (*Naut.*) That part of a vessel's hull forward of midship.

forebrace (fôr' brās), *n.* (*Naut.*) A rope on the fore yard-arm for shifting the sail.

fore-cabin (fôr' kăb in), *n.* A forward cabin, usu. for second-class passengers.

fore-carriage (fôr' kăr ij), *n.* A carriage in front; a seat in front of a motor-cycle.

forecast (fôr kast'), *v.t.* (*past and p.p.* **forecast,** *erron.* **forecasted**) To calculate beforehand; to foresee, to predict. *v.i.* To form a scheme beforehand. *n.* (fôr' kast) A previous contrivance; provision against the future, or calculation of probable events, esp. regarding future weather; foresight, prevision.

forecastle, fo'c'sle (fôr' kasl, fōksl) [FORE-, CASTLE], *n.* The part of the upper deck forward of the after-shroud; a short upper deck forward, formerly raised to command the enemy's decks; in merchant-ships, a forward space below deck where the crew live.

fore-cited (fôr' sī tėd), *a.* Cited before or above.

foreclose (fôr klōz') [O.F. *forclos*, p.p. of *forclore* (for-, L. *foris*, outside, *clore*, to CLOSE (1))], *v.t.* To shut out, exclude, or bar; to preclude; to put an end to or settle beforehand (as an arguable matter). *v.i.* To foreclose a mortgage. **to foreclose a mortgage:** To deprive the mortgager of his equity of redemption on failure to pay money due on a mortgage. **foreclosure,** *n.* The act of foreclosing.

forecourt (fôr' kôrt), *n.* The first or outer court, that immediately inside the entrance to the precincts of a building.

fore-deck (fôr' dek), *n.* The forepart of a deck; the deck in the forepart of a ship.

foredoom (fôr doom'), *v.t.* To doom beforehand; to predestinate. *n.* (fôr' doom) Doom or judgment previously delivered; destiny.

fore-edge (fôr' ej), *n.* The front or outer edge of a book or of a leaf in a book.

fore-end (fôr' end), *n.* The fore-part (*chiefly Naut.*); *the beginning, the early part; *spring.

forefather (fôr' fa thėr), *n.* An ancestor. **Forefather's Day:** (*U.S.A.*) The anniversary of the landing of the Pilgrim Fathers in America on 21 December, 1620.

forefeel (fôr fēl'), *v.t.* To feel beforehand; to have premonition of. **forefeelingly,** *adv.*

forefend [FORFEND].

forefinger (fôr' fing gėr), *n.* The finger next to the thumb, also called the first or index finger.

fore-foot (fôr' fut), *n.* A front foot of a quadruped; (*Naut.*) the forward end of a vessel's keel.

forefront (fôr' frŭnt), *n.* The extreme front, the foremost part or position.

foregather [FORGATHER].

foregift (fôr' gift), *n.* (*Law*) A premium paid by a tenant for the renewal of a lease.

forego (1) (fôr gō'), *v.t.* and *i.* (*past* **-went,** *p.p.* **-gone**) To go before, to precede in time, order, or place. **foregoer,** *n.* One who goes before another, a predecessor; *an ancestor; *a royal purveyor. **foregoing,** *a.* Preceding, previously mentioned. **foregone** (fôr gon'), *a.* Past; preceding; determined before. **foregone conclusion,** *n.* A conclusion determined on beforehand or arrived at in advance of evidence or reasoning; a result that might be foreseen.

forego (2) [FORGO].

foreground (fôr' ground), *n.* The nearest part of a view; the part of a picture which seems to lie nearest the spectator.

fore-hammer (fôr' hăm ėr) [Sc.], *n.* A sledge-hammer.

forehand (fôr' hănd), *n.* That part of a horse before the rider; *(*fig.*) the chief part, the mainstay the upper hand, superiority, advantage. *a.* Foremost, leading; (*Tennis, etc.*) not backhanded (of a stroke); *anticipative, in advance; *(*Archery*) for a point-blank shot (of an arrow). **forehanded,** *a.* (*Am.*) Done in good time; timely; thrifty, well-off; formed in the forehand or fore-parts (of horses).

forehead (for' ėd) [A.-S. *forhēafod* (FORE-, HEAD)], *n.* That part of the face which reaches from the eyebrows upwards to the hair; (*fig.*) the front part, the brow; assurance, impudence.

fore-hold (fôr' hōld), *n.* The fore-part of a ship's hold.

fore-horse (fôr' hôrs), *n.* The foremost horse in a team.

foreign (for' in) [O.F. *forain,* late L. *forāneus,* from L. *forās,* out of doors, conn. with *foris,* a door], *a.* Belonging to, connected with, or derived from another country or nation; alien, strange, extraneous, dissimilar, not belonging (to); having no connexion with, irrelevant, impertinent, inappropriate. **adv.* (*Naut.*) (To sail) to foreign parts. **foreign-built,** *a.* (*Naut.*) Built in a foreign country. **foreign body,** *n.* (*Path.*) A substance occurring in an organism or tissue where it is not normally found. **foreign correspondent,** *n.* A representative of a newspaper sent to a foreign country to report on its politics, etc. **Foreign Office,** *n.* The Government department for foreign affairs; the building occupied by this. **foreigner,** *n.* A person born or belonging to a foreign country or speaking a foreign language, an alien; a foreign ship, an import or production from a foreign country; a stranger, an outsider. **foreignism, foreignness,** *n.* **foreignize,** *v.t.* and *i.*

forejudge (fôr jŭj'), *v.t.* To judge before trial or decide before hearing the evidence. **forejudgment,** *n.*

foreknow (fôr nō'), *v.t.* (*past* **-knew,** *p.p.* **-known**) To know beforehand. ***foreknowable,** *a.* **foreknower,** *n.* ***foreknowingly,** *adv.* **foreknowledge** (-nol' ėj), *n.* Prescience; knowledge of a thing before it happens.

forel (for' ėl) [O.F. *forrel* (F. *fourreau*), dim. of *forre,* a sheath], *n.* A kind of parchment used for book-covers.

foreland (fôr' lȧnd), *n.* A point of land extending into the sea, a promontory; a strip of land outside of or in front of an embankment, etc.; (*Fort.*) a space between a fortified wall and the moat.

forelay (fôr lā'), *v.t.* To contrive beforehand.

foreleg (fôr' leg), *n.* A front leg of an animal, chair, etc.

***forelie** (fôr lī'), *v.t.* To lie before.

forelock (1) (fôr' lok), *n.* A lock of hair growing over the forehead. **to take by the forelock:** To seize at the earliest opportunity.

forelock (2) (fôr' lok), *n.* A pin or wedge passing through the end of a bolt to prevent this from being withdrawn. *v.t.* To secure by a forelock.

foreman (fôr' mȧn), *n.* A head or chief man; the chief man of a jury, who acts as their spokesman; a workman supervising others.

foremast (fôr' mȧst), *n.* The mast nearest the bow of a vessel. **foremastman, -hand, -seaman,** *n.* A common sailor.

***fore-mean** (fôr mēn'), *v.t.* (*past* and *p.p.* **-meant**) To intend beforehand.

forementioned (fôr men' shŭnd), *a.* Already mentioned.

foremost (fôr' mōst) [A.-S. *foremost, fyrmest,* double superlative from *forma,* first, old superlative of *fore,* before, above; assim. to MOST], *a.* First in time, place, order, rank, or importance; chief, most notable. *adv.* In the first place; first, before anything else.

forename (fôr' nām), *n.* A name preceding the surname; a Christian name. **forenamed,** *a.* Named or mentioned before.

forenight (fôr' nīt), *n.* (*Sc.*) The evening.

forenoon (fôr' noon), *n.* The early part of the day, from morning to noon.

forensic (fō ren' sik) [L. *forensis,* pertaining to the forum, see FORUM], *a.* Pertaining to courts of judicature, or to public debate; used in debates or legal proceedings. *n.* (*Am.*) An argumentative thesis at a college. **forensic medicine,** *n.* The science of medicine in its relation to law; medical jurisprudence. **forensically,** *adv.*

fore-ordain (fôr ȯr dān'), *v.t.* To ordain beforehand, to predestinate. **fore-ordination** (ȯr di nā' shŭn), *n.*

fore-part (fôr' part), *n.* The first or most advanced part; the earlier part.

forepast (fôr' past), *a.* Already past (of time).

forepeak (fôr' pēk), *n.* (*Naut.*) The part of a vessel's hold in the angle of the bow.

fore-plane (fôr' plān), *n.* (*Carp.*) A plane intermediate between the jack-plane and the smoothing-plane; sometimes applied to the jack-plane, the first used after saw or axe.

***fore-point** (fôr point'), *v.t.* To appoint beforehand; to foreshadow. *v.i.* To point beforehand.

fore-rank (fôr' rănk), *n.* The foremost rank; the front.

fore-reach (fôr rēch'), *v.t.* (*Naut.*) To gain upon; to get ahead of. *v.i.* To shoot ahead (on), esp. on a ship going in stays.

***fore-read** (fôr rēd'), *v.t.* To tell beforehand; to signify by tokens. **fore-reading,** *n.* A previous perusal.

***fore-run** (fôr rŭn'), *v.t.* (*past* **-ran,** *p.p.* **-run**) To precede; to betoken, to usher in. **forerunner,** *n.* A messenger sent before; a precursor, herald, harbinger; a predecessor, an ancestor; *an omen, a prognostic.

foresail (fôrsl, fôr' sāl), *n.* The principal sail on the foremast.

***fore-say** (fôr sā') [A.-S. *fore-secgan*], *v.t.* To say beforehand; to predict; to prognosticate.

foresee (fôr sē'), *v.t.* (*past.* **-saw,** *p.p.* **-seen**) To see beforehand; to know beforehand, to have prescience of. ***foreseer,** *n.* **foreseeing,** *a.* Exercising foresight. **foreseeingly,** *adv.*

foreshadow (fôr shăd' ō), *v.t.* To shadow beforehand; to typify beforehand, to prefigure. *n.* A foreshadowing or prefiguration of something.

fore-sheet (fôr' shēt), *n.* (*Naut.*) The rope holding the lee corner of a foresail; (*pl.*) the space in a boat forward of the foremost thwart, usu. covered with a grating.

foreship (fôr' ship) [A.-S. *forscip* (as FORE-, SHIP)], *n.* The fore-part of a ship; the prow.

foreshore (fôr' shôr), *n.* The part of the shore lying between high- and low-water marks; the ground between the sea and land that is cultivated or built upon; (*Eng.*) the slightly inclined portion of a breakwater, projecting seaward.

foreshorten (fôr shôr' tėn), *v.t.* In drawing or painting to represent (figures or parts of figures that project towards the spectator) so as to give a correct impression of form and proportions.

foreshow (fôr shō') [A.-S. *fore-scēawian* (as FORE-, SHOW)], *v.t.* (*p.p.* **-shown**) To predict, to represent beforehand; to foreshadow.

***foreside** (fôr' sīd), *n.* The front side; a specious outside.

foresight (fôr' sīt), *n.* Prescience, forethought; provident care for the future, prudence, precaution; the muzzle-sight of a gun. ***foresighted,** *a.* ***foresightful,** *a.*

foresignify (fôr sig' ni fī), *v.t.* To betoken beforehand; to typify; to foreshow.

foreskin (fôr' skin), *n.* (*Anat.*) The prepuce, the loose skin covering the end of the penis.

***foreskirt** (fôr′ skĕrt), *n.* The loose hanging portion of a coat in front.

foresleeve (fôr′ slēv), *n.* That part of a sleeve between the wrist and elbow.

***forespeak** (fôr spēk′), *v.t.* (*past* **-spoke,** *p.p.* **-spoken**) To predict, to foretell; (*Sc.*) to bespeak.

fore-spur (fôr′ spĕr), *n.* A foreleg of bacon or pork.

forest (for′ ėst) [O.F. (F. *forêt*), from late L. *foresta*, a wood, *forestis* (*silva*), the outside or open (wood), from L. *foris*, outside], *n.* An extensive wood or tract of wooded country; a wild uncultivated tract of ground partly covered with trees and underwood; a large tract of country set apart for game and hunting, in many cases orig. a royal hunting-ground. *v.t.* To plant with trees; to convert into a forest. ***forest-born,** *a.* Born in a forest; wild. **forest-fly,** *n.* A fly frequenting woodlands, *Hippobosca equina*, troublesome to horses. **forest-laws,** *n.pl.* Laws for the regulation of forests and preserving game, instituted by William I. **forest-marble,** *n.* A stratum of lower Oolitic age abounding in marine fossils, named from Whichwood Forest, Oxfordshire, where it is quarried. **forest-oak,** *n.* The she-oak or *Casuarina*, an Australian genus of timber-trees. ***forestage,** *n.* A tribute payable to the king's foresters; an ancient service paid by foresters to the king; the right to take estovers from a forest. ***forestal,** *a.*

forestall (fôr stawl′) [A.-S. *forsteall*, interference, interception], *v.t.* To hinder by preoccupation or anticipation; to anticipate; to be beforehand with; to buy up (commodities) beforehand so as to control the sale; *to deprive (of); *to obstruct or stop up (as a road). **to forestall the market:** To engross or buy up commodities, so as to obtain the control of the market. **forestaller,** *n.*

forestay (fôr′ stā), *n.* (*Naut.*) A strong rope, reaching from the foremast head to the bowsprit end, to support the mast.

forester (for′ es tĕr), *n.* One who has charge of a forest; an inhabitant of a forest; one who looks after the trees on an estate; (*fig.*) a bird, beast, or tree of a forester; a member of the Forester's Benefit Society; (*Austral.*) the largest variety of kangaroo.

forestry (for′ es tri), *n.* The act or art of cultivating trees and forests; the management of growing timber; (*poet.*) woodland, a multitude of trees; (*Sc. Law*) the privileges of a royal forest.

foretaste (fôr′ tāst), *n.* Experience or enjoyment (of) beforehand; anticipation. *v.t.* (**fôr tāst′**) To taste beforehand; to anticipate enjoyment (of).

foretell (fôr tel′), *v.t.* (*past* and *p.p.* **-told**) To predict, to prophesy; to foreshadow. **foreteller,** *n.*

forethought (fôr′ thawt), *n.* Consideration beforehand; premeditation; foresight, provident care. **forethoughtful,** *a.*

foretime (fôr′ tīm), *n.* Time past; early times.

foretoken (fôr tō′ kėn), *v.t.* To foreshadow, to prognosticate. *n.* (fōr′ tō′ ken) A token beforehand, an omen.

foretooth (fôr′ tooth), *n.* (*pl.* **-teeth**) A front tooth.

foretop (fôr′ top), *n.* (*Naut.*) The top or platform at the head of the foremast; (*short*) fore-topgallant-masthead; (*fig.*) *the top of a periwig; *the forehead; *an erect tuft of hair, esp. a horse's forelock. **foretopman,** *n.* A man stationed in the foretop. **fore-topmast,** *n.* The mast at the head of the foremast, and surmounted by the fore-topgallant mast. **fore-topgallant-sail,** *n.* **fore-topsail,** *n.*

foretype (fôr′ tīp), *n.* An antitype. *v.t.* (fôr tīp′) To prefigure.

forever (fôr ev′ ĕr), *adv.* (*Am.*) For ever. *n.* (*poet.*) Eternity. **forevermore,** *adv.*

***foreward** (fôr′ wȧrd), *n.* The vanguard; the front.

forewarn (fôr wôrn′), *v.t.* To warn or caution beforehand; to give notice to beforehand.

***forewind** (fôr′ wind), *n.* A favourable wind.

forewoman (fôr′ wum ȧn), *n.* A workwoman who supervises others; the chief woman in a jury of matrons who acts as their spokeswoman.

foreword (fôr′ wĕrd), *n.* A preface, a short introduction.

foreyard (fôr′ yard), *n.* The lowest yard on a foremast.

***forfairn** (fôr fârn′) [*p.p.* of obs. v. *forfare*, A.-S. *forfaran* (FOR-, FARE)], *a.* (*Sc.*) Worn out, exhausted with travail, age, etc.

forfeit (fôr′ fit) [O.F. *forfait*, orig. p.p. of *forfaire*, late L. *foris facere*, to transgress, lit. to act beyond or outside], *n.* That which is lost through fault, crime, omission, or neglect; a penalty, a fine, esp. a stipulated sum to be paid in case of breach of contract; (*pl.*) a game in which for every breach of the rules the players have to deposit some article, which is subsequently redeemed by the performance of a playful task or ceremony; the article so deposited; *a misdeed, a crime; one condemned to capital punishment. *a.* Lost or alienated through fault or crime; *subject, liable. *v.t.* To lose the right to or possession of by fault, crime, omission, or neglect; to lose; to cause to lose, to confiscate; *to subject to loss of property, etc. ***forfeitable,** *a.* That may be forfeited; subject to forfeiture. **forfeiter,** *n.* One who incurs a penalty. **forfeiture,** *n.* The act of forfeiting; that which is forfeited; a penalty or amercement.

forfend (fôr fend′), *v.t.* To avert, to ward off.

forfex (fôr′ feks) [L., scissors], *n.* (*Ent.*) A pair of scissor-like anal appendages in earwigs; a pair of scissors. **forficate, -ed,** *a.* (*Ent.*)

forfoughten (fôr faw′ tėn), *a.* (*Sc.*) Worn out with fighting, war-worn; wearied out.

forgather (fôr găth′ ėr), *v.i.* To meet or associate (with); to meet together, to assemble; to unite (with) in marriage. *v.t.* To be friendly or intimate with.

forgave, *past* [FORGIVE].

forge (1) (fôrj) [O.F., ult. from L. *fabrica*, FABRIC], *n.* The workshop of a smith; a blacksmith's open fireplace or hearth where iron is heated by forced draught; a furnace or hearth for making wrought iron; (*fig.*) a place where anything is made; a workshop; *the working of iron or steel; *workmanship. *v.t.* To form or fabricate by heating and hammering; to make or construct; to make, invent, or imitate fraudulently, to counterfeit; to fabricate, esp. to counterfeit or alter a signature or document with intent to defraud. *v.i.* To commit forgery. **forgeman,** *n.* A forger or smith, esp. one with a hammer-man under him. **forgeable,** *a.* **forging,** *n.* That which is forged; a piece of forged metal work.

forge (2) (fôrj) [etym. doubtful], *v.i.* To move (forward or ahead) slowly or with difficulty.

forger (fôr′ jĕr), *n.* One who commits forgery; a smith, one who forges metal.

forgery (fôr′ jĕr i), *n.* The act of forging, counterfeiting, or falsifying; a fraudulent imitation; a deception.

forget (fôr get′) [A.-S. *forgitan* (FOR-, GET)], *v.t.* (*past* **-got,** *p.p.* **-gotten,** *poet.* **-got**) To lose remembrance of; to put out of mind purposely; to fail to remember through inadvertence; to neglect (to do something). **to forget oneself:** To lose one's self-control, to behave unbecomingly; to lose consciousness; to act unselfishly. **forgettable,** *a.* **forgetful,** *a.* **forgetfully,** *adv.* **forgetfulness,** *n.* **forgetter,** *n.* ***forgettingly,** *adv.*

forget-me-not (fôr get′ mė not), *n.* A small plant of the genus *Myosotis*, esp. *M. palustris*, with bright blue flowers.

forgive (fôr giv′) [A.-S. *forgifan* (FOR-, GIVE)], *v.t.* (*past* **-gave,** *p.p.* **-given**) To pardon or remit, as an offence or debt; not to exact the penalty for; to pardon, not to punish (a person or offence, or a person his offence); to cease to feel resentment towards. *v.i.* To show forgiveness. **forgivable,** *a.* **forgiveness,** *n.* The act of forgiving; a disposition to forgive; remission, pardon. **forgiver,** *n.* **forgiving,** *a.* Disposed to forgive; merciful, gracious. **forgivingly,** *adv.* **forgivingness,** *n.*

forgo (fôr gō′) [A.-S. *forgān*], *v.t.* (*past* **-went,** *p.p.* **-gone**) To go without, to refrain from; to give up, deny oneself, renounce, relinquish; to quit.

forgotten, *forgot, *p.p.* [FORGET].

forint (fôr′ int) [Hung.], *n.* The monetary unit of Hungary since 1946, worth about 8d.

***forisfamiliate** (fôr is fȧ mil′ i āt) [med. L. *forisfamiliātus, p.p.* of *forisfamiliāre* (*foris,* outside, *familia,* FAMILY)], *v.t.* (*Law*) To emancipate from parental authority; to bestow a portion of lands on (a son in his father's lifetime, and thus discharge him from the family). *v.i.* To renounce all further claim on the paternal estate. *a.* (-ȧt) Having possession of property during the father's lifetime.

forjudge (fôr jŭj′) [O.F. *forjuger*], *v.t.* (*Law*) To deprive, dispossess, or exclude by a judgment. ***forjudgment,** *n.* **forjudger,** *n.*

fork (fôrk) [A.-S. *forc,* L. *furca*], *n.* An agricultural instrument terminating in two or more prongs, used for digging, impaling, lifting, carrying, or throwing; a pronged implement used in cooking or at table; anything of a similar form; a forking or bifurcation; a diverging branch; a point where a road divides into two; the crutch, the bifurcation of the human body; *a barbed point, as of an arrow; *a point; *a gibbet. *v.t.* To raise or pitch with a fork; to dig or break up with a fork, as ground; to make sharp or pointed; (*Chess and Draughts*) to attack two pieces so that only one can escape. *v.i.* To divide into two; to send out branches. **to fork out or over:** (*slang*) To hand or deliver over; to produce the cash for. **tuning-fork,** *n.* A piece of steel with two prongs that vibrate on being struck and give a fixed musical note. **fork-chuck,** *n.* A piece of steel in a turning-lathe carrying points which enter the wood and cause it to rotate. **fork-head,** *n.* The double head of a rod which divides to form a connexion by means of a pin; *the barbed head of an arrow. **forked,** *a.* Dividing into branches, branching, cleft, bifurcated; terminating in points or prongs. ***forkedly,** *adv.* ***forkedness,** *n.* ***forkless,** *a.* **forktail,** *a.* Having a forked tail. *n.* A salmon in its fourth year's growth. **forky,** *a.* Forked, fork-like.

forlorn (fôr lôrn′) [A.-S. *forloren, p.p.* of *forlēosan* (FOR-, LOSE)], *a.* Deserted, abandoned; helpless, wretched, hopeless; *deprived, bereft (of); *lost. **forlorn hope** [after Dut. *verloren hoop,* lit. lost troop (from *hoop,* heap, see HEAP), *cp.* F. *enfans perdus*], *n.* A detachment of men selected for some service of uncommon danger; (*fig.*) a bold, desperate enterprise. ***forlornly,** *adv.* **forlornness,** *n.*

form (fôrm) [O.F. *forme,* L. *forma*], *n.* The shape or external appearance of anything apart from colour; configuration, figure, esp. of the human body; particular arrangement, disposition, organization, or constitution; established practice or method; a rule of procedure, ceremony, or ritual; the mode in which anything is perceptible to the senses or intellect; kind, specific state, species, variety, variation; (*Gram.*) a specific shape of a word as regards inflexion, spelling, or pronunciation; a shape, mould, or model upon which a thing is fashioned; a customary method or formula, a fixed order of words, a document with blanks to be filled in; (*Art*) style or mode of expression, as opp. to content or subject-matter, orderly arrangement of parts, order, symmetry; behaviour according to accepted rules or conventions; (*colloq.*) good physical condition or fitness, a good state of health or training; a long seat without a back; a class in a public or secondary school; the seat or bed of a hare; (*Print.*) a body of type composed and locked in a chase ready for printing; (*Bibliog.*) literary nature of a book as dist. from the subject; (*Math.*) the structure of a mathematical expression; (*Phil.*) that which differentiates matter and generates species; that which the mind contributes, the mode of knowing, the subjective element in perception; (*Kant*) the categories or subjective elements by which the mind apprehends objects. *v.t.* To give form or shape to; to arrange in any particular manner; to make, construct, or create; to model or mould to a pattern; to train, to instruct, to mould or shape by discipline; to conceive, devise, construct (ideas, etc.); to articulate; to become; to be the material for; to be or constitute (a part or one of); (*Mil.*) to combine into (a certain order); (*Gram.*) to make by derivation or by affixes or prefixes. **v.i.* To assume a form; (*Mil.*) to combine (into a certain order). **bad, good form,** *n.* Bad, good manners; ill, good breeding.

form- [FORMYL], *comb. form.* (*Chem.*) Containing formyl as a radical.

-form [F. *-forme,* L. *-formis,* from *forma,* FORM], *suf.* Like, having the shape of, as *cruciform, dendriform;* having a certain number of forms, as *multiform, uniform.*

formal (fôr′ măl) [L. *formālis,* from *forma,* FORM], *a.* In a set form; made, performed, or done according to established forms; orderly, regular; explicit, definite; observant of established form, ceremonious, punctilious, precise; conventional, perfunctory; of or pertaining to the outward form as opposed to reality, outward; (*Log.*) pertaining to form as opposed to matter; (*Phil.*) pertaining to the formative essence that makes a thing what it is, essential, not material. **formalize,** *v.t.* To render formal; to formulate. **formalization** (-zā′ shŭn), *n.* **formally,** *adv.*

formaldehyde (fôr măl′ de hīd), *n.* Formic aldehyde, a colourless gas generated by the partial oxidation of methyl alcohol, and used as an antiseptic and disinfectant.

formalin (fôrm′ ȧ lin), *n.* A solution of formic aldehyde used as an antiseptic, for the destruction of disease germs, and as a food preservative.

formalism (fôr′ mȧ lizm), *n.* The quality of being formal; formality, esp. in religion. **formalist,** *n.* **formalistic,** *a.*

formality (fôr măl′ i ti), *n.* The condition or quality of being formal; conformity to custom, rule, or established method; conventionality, mere form; an established order or method, an observance required by custom or etiquette; (*Art*) precision, observance of rule as opposed to originality.

format (fôr′ mȧ, fôr′ măt) [F., from L. *formātus,* from *forma,* FORM], *n.* The external form and size of a book.

formate [FORMIC].

formation (fôr mā′ shŭn) [L. *formātio -ōnem,* from *forma,* FORM], *n.* The act or process of forming or creating; the state of being formed or created; the manner in which anything is formed; conformation, arrangement, disposition of parts, structure; a thing formed, regarded in relation to form or structure; (*Geol.*) a group of rocks or strata of common origin, structure, or physical character; (*Mil.*) an arrangement of troops. **formative** (fôr′ mȧ tiv), *a.* Having the power of giving form; plastic; pertaining to formation; (*Philol.*) serving to form words (of comb. forms, prefixes, etc.), inflexional, not radical. *n.* (*Philol.*) That which serves to form, and is no part of the root; a word formed in accordance with some rule or usage.

forme (*Print.*) [FORM].

former (fôr′ mėr) [formed from M.E. *formest,* FOREMOST, double superl. from A.-S. *forma,* first], *a.* Preceding in time; mentioned before something else, the first-mentioned (of two); past, earlier, ancient, bygone. **formerly,** *adv.* In former times; of the past or earlier times; *first, beforehand; *just now.

formic (fôr′ mik) [short for *formicic,* from L. *formīca,* an ant], *a.* (*Chem.*) Pertaining to or produced by ants. **formic acid,** *n.* An acid found in the fluid emitted by ants, in stinging-nettles, etc., and now obtained from oxalic acid distilled with glycerin. **formicant,** *a.* (*Path.*) Weak, almost imperceptible, creeping like an ant (said of the pulse). **formicary,** *n.* An ant-hill. **formicate,** *a.* Resembling an ant. **formication** (-kā′ shŭn), *n.* (*Path.*) Irritation of the skin like the crawling of ants. **formate,** *n.* A salt of formic acid. **formene,** *n.* (*Chem.*) Methane. **formyl,** *n.* (*Chem.*) The radical theoretically constituting the base of formic acid.

Formica (fôr mī′ kȧ), *n.* Protected trade name of a plastic used for surfacing materials and other purposes.

formidable (fôr′ mid ȧ bėl, *incorr.* fôr mid′ ȧbl) [F., from L. *formīdābilis*, from *formīdāre*, to dread], *a.* Tending to excite fear; to be feared; dangerous to encounter; difficult to resist, overcome, or accomplish. **formidableness,** *n.* **formidably,** *adv.* **formidability** (-bil′ i ti), *n.*

formin (fôr′ min), *n.* A white crystalline powder produced from formaldehyde and ammonia, used as antiseptic and diuretic.

formless (fôrm′ lės) [FORM, -LESS], *a.* Without form, shapeless; having no regular form. **formlessly,** *adv.* **formlessness,** *n.*

formula (fôr′ mū lȧ) [L., dim. of *forma*, FORM], *n.* (*pl.* **-læ, -las**) A prescribed form of words; a formal enunciation of faith, doctrine, principle, etc.; a fixed rule, a set form, a conventional usage; a prescription, a recipe; (*Chem.*) an expression by means of symbols of the elements of a compound; (*Math.*) the expression of a rule or principle in algebraic symbols. **formularize,** *v.t.* To formulate. **formularization** (-zā′ shŭn), *n.* **formulary,** *a.* Stated, prescribed; of the nature of a formula; formal, ritual. *n.* A collection of formulas; a book containing stated and prescribed forms, esp. relating to religious belief or ritual; a formula. **formulate,** *v.t.* To express in a formula; to set forth in a precise and systematic form. **formulation** (-lā′ shŭn), *n.* **formulism,** *n.* Strict observance of or dependence upon formulas. **formulist,** *n.* **formulistic** (-lis′ tik), *a.* **formulize,** *v.t.* To formulate. **formulization** (-zā′ shŭn), *n.*

formyl [FORMIC].

fornent, -nenst (fôr nent′, -nenst′) [Sc., FORE, ANENT], *prep.* Right opposite to. *adv.* Opposite.

fornicate (fôr′ ni kāt) [L. *fornicātus*, p.p. of *fornicārī*, from *fornex -icis*, an arch, a brothel], *v.i.* To commit fornication. **fornication** (-kā′ shŭn), *n.* Sexual intercourse of unmarried persons, or of a married with an unmarried person; (*Bibl.*) applied to idolatry, incest, or adultery. **fornicator,** *n.* ***fornicatress,** *n.*

fornix (fôr′ niks) [L., an arch], *n.* (*Anat.*) The arch of the vagina; the roof of the pharynx; an arch-shaped formation in the brain; (*Bot. and Conch.*) similar parts or organs.

forpit (fôr′ pit) [Sc. and North., corr. of FOURTH PART], *n.* The fourth part of a measure, now of a peck.

forrader [corr. of FORWARDER (2), see FORWARD].

forrel [FOREL].

forrit (for′ it) [Sc., prob. corr. of FORWARD], *adv.* Forward.

forsake (fȯr sāk′) [A.-S. *forsacan* (FOR-, *sacan*, to quarrel, see SAKE)], *v.t.* (*past* **-sook,** *p.p.* **-saken**) To leave, to abandon, to withdraw from; to renounce, to cast off, to reject; *to refuse, *to deny. **forsaker,** *n.*

***forsay** (fȯr sā′), *v.t.* To renounce, to forsake; to deny, to forbid.

***forshapen** (fȯr shā′ pėn) [p.p. of obs. *forshape*, A.-S. *forsciеppen* (FOR-, SHAPE)], *a.* Misshaped, deformed; transformed.

***forslow** (fȯr slō′) [A.-S. *forslāwian* (as FOR-, *slāwian*, from *slāw*, SLOW)], *v.t.* To delay, to put off; to neglect, to omit; to render slow, to obstruct. *v.i.* To be slow.

forsooth (fȯr sooth′), *adv.* (*ironically*) In truth, certainly, doubtless.

***forspeak** (fȯr spēk′), *v.t.* To forbid, to speak against; to bewitch, to charm.

forspend (fȯr spend′), *v.t.* (*usu. in p.p.* **-spent**) To wear out, to exhaust with toil.

forswear (fȯr swâr′) [A.-S. *forswerian*], *v.t.* (*past* **-swore,** *p.p.* **-sworn**) To abjure; to renounce upon oath or with protestations; *to break (an oath, allegiance, etc.). *v.i.* To swear falsely. **to forswear oneself:** To perjure oneself. ***forswearer,** *n.* A perjurer. ***forswornness,** *n.* The state of being forsworn; perjury.

forsythia (fôr sī′ thyȧ) [W. *Forsyth* (1737–1804)], *n.* (*Bot.*) A genus of oleaceous shrubs bearing numerous yellow flowers in early spring before the leaves.

fort (fôrt) [O.F., from L. *fortis* (*domus*), strong (house)], *n.* A fortified place, esp. a detached outwork or an independent fortified work of moderate extent; (*Am. Hist.*) a trading-post. ***forted,** *a.* Guarded by forts, fortified.

fortalice (fôr′ tȧ lis) [med. L. *fortalitia*, as prec.], *n.* An outwork of a fortification; a small fort.

forte (1) (fôrt) [F. fem. adj., strong, as prec. (fem. unmeaningly adopted instead of masc.)], *n.* The strong part of a sword blade, *i.e.* from the hilt to the middle; a person's strong point; that in which one excels.

forte (2) (fôr′ ti) [It., strong, as prec.], *adv.* (*Mus.*) With loudness or force. ***forte forte,*** *adv.* Very loud. ***forte piano*** [PIANO], *adv.* Loudly, then softly.

forth (fôrth) [A.-S., from *fore*, see FORE (1) (cp. Dut. *voort*, G. *fort*)], *adv.* Forward; out; out into view; out from home; out of doors; forward in place, time, or order; indefinitely forward, in time. **prep.* Out of, away from. **and so forth:** And the rest, and so on, and the like. **back and forth:** To and fro. **forthcoming** (fôrth kŭm′ ing), *a.* Coming forth, ready to appear, or to be brought forward; *in custody; (*colloq.*) pushing, assertive. *n.* A coming forth; (*Sc. Law*) an action by which an assessment is made effectual. **forth-going,** *a.* Going forth; proceeding; (*fig.*) affable, encouraging. *n.* A going out or proceeding from; that which goes forth; an utterance. **forth-issuing,** *a.* Issuing forth. **forth-putting,** *a.* Putting forth or forward; (*Am.*) forward, pushing, obtrusive. **forth-right** (fôrth rīt′), *adv.* Straight forward; at once, straightway. *a.* (fôrth′ rīt) Going straight forward, direct; outspoken; to the point. *n.* A direct course. **forthwith** (fôrth with′), *adv.* Immediately; without delay.

***forthink** (fȯr think′) [A.-S. *forthencan* (FOR-, THINK)], *v.t.* To repent of; to be sorry for.

fortieth [FORTY].

fortify (fôr′ ti fī) [O.F. *fortifier*, L. *fortificāre* (*fortis*, strong, *ficāre*, from *facere*, to make)], *v.t.* To make strong; to give power or strength to; to invigorate; to encourage; to add alcoholic strength to; to confirm, to corroborate; (*Fort.*) to strengthen or secure by forts, ramparts, etc.; to make defensible against the attack of an enemy. *v.i.* To raise fortifications. **fortifiable,** *a.* **fortification** (-kā′ shŭn), *n.* The act, art, or science of fortifying a place or position against the attacks of an enemy; a defensive work, a fort; (*pl.*) works erected to defend a place against attack; increasing the strength of wine with alcohol; *an accession of strength, a strengthening. **fortifier,** *n.*

fortissimo (fôr tis′ i mō) [It., superl. of *forte*, see FORTE (2)], *adv.* (*Mus.*) Very loud.

fortition (fôr tish′ ŭn) [erroneously formed from L. *fors fortis*, chance, on anal. of SORTITION], *n.* Trusting to chance; selection by chance.

fortitude (fôr′ ti tūd) [F., from L. *fortitūdo*, from *fortis*, strong], *n.* Strength, esp. that strength of mind which enables one to meet danger or endure pain with calmness. **fortitudinous** (-tū′ di nŭs), *a.*

fortlet (fôrt′ lĕt), *n.* A small fort.

fortnight (fôrt′ nīt) [M.E. *fourtenight*, A.-S. *fēowertȳne niht*, fourteen nights], *n.* A period of two weeks or fourteen days. **fortnightly,** *a.* Happening once a fortnight. *adv.* Once a fortnight; every fortnight.

fortress (fôr′ tres) [O.F. *forteresse*, var. of *fortalesce*, *fortalice*], *n.* A fortified place, esp. a strongly fortified town accommodating a large garrison and forming a permanent stronghold. *v.t.* (*poet.*) To furnish with or serve as a fortress, to defend.

fortuitous (fôr tū′ i tŭs) [L. *fortuitus*, from *fors fortis*, chance], *a.* Happening by chance; casual, accidental. **fortuitously,** *adv.* **fortuitousness,** *n.* **fortuitism,** *n.* (*Phil.*) The doctrine that mere chance, not design, is the principle governing the operation of natural causes. **fortuitist,** *n.* **fortuity,** *n.* A chance occurrence; an accident; fortuitousness.

fortunate (fôr′ tū-, -chŭ nắt) [L. *fortūnātus*, p.p. of *fortūnāre*, from *fortūna*, see foll.], *a.* Happening by good luck; bringing or presaging good fortune; auspicious; lucky, prosperous. **fortunately,** *adv.* ***fortunateness,** *n.*

fortune (fôr′ tyŭn, -chŭn) [F., from L. *fortūna*, cogn. with *fors fortis*, chance, and *ferre*, to bring], *n.* Chance, luck, that which happens as if by chance; that which brings good or ill hap, a personification of this, a supernatural power supposed to control one's lot and to bestow good or evil; one's future lot; good luck, prosperity; wealth; a large property. **v.t.* To control the fortunes of; to provide with a fortune. *v.i.* To happen, to chance. **fortune-hunter,** *n.* One who seeks to marry a woman with a large portion. **fortune-hunting,** *a.* and *n.* **fortune-teller,** *n.* One who pretends to reveal future events. **fortune-telling,** *n.* **fortuneless,** *a.* *Luckless; without a dowry. ***fortunize,** *v.t.* To regulate the fortunes of; to make fortunate.

forty (fôr′ ti) [A.-S. *fēowertig* (FOUR, -TY), *cp.* Dut. *veertig*, G. *vierzig*], *a.* Four times ten. *n.* The sum of four times ten, a symbol expressing this, as 40 or xl; (*pl.*) the years of one's life between 39 and 50, the corresponding period in a century. **the roaring forties:** (*Naut.*) The stormy part of the Atlantic between 39° and 50° S. lat. **the Forty-five:** The Jacobite rebellion of 1745–6. **forty-niner,** *n.* One of the adventurers who went to California at the time of the gold-rush in 1849. **forty winks,** *n.* A nap. **fortieth,** *a.* Next in order after the thirty-ninth. *n.* One of forty equal parts.

forum (fôr′ ŭm) [L.], *n.* (*Rom. Ant.*) The public place in Rome in which were the courts of law, public offices, etc., and where orations were delivered; a market-place; a place of assembly for public discussion or judicial purposes; a tribunal, a court of law; (*R.C. Ch.*) the sphere in which the Church exercises jurisdiction.

forward (fôr′ wărd) [A.-S. *foreweard* (FORE (1), -WARD)], *a.* At or near the fore-part of anything; in front; towards the front; onward; in advance, advancing, or advanced; well advanced, progressing, early, premature, precocious; eager, prompt; pert, presumptuous. *n.* A player at football, etc., stationed at the front of his side. *v.t.* To help onward, to promote; to hasten the growth of; to send on or ahead, to send to a further destination; (*colloq.*) to send. **forwarder** (1), *n.* One who helps forward; a promoter; one who transmits goods; (*Am.*) a person or firm whose business is to send forward goods received for that purpose, a forwarding-merchant; (*Bookbinding*) one who prepares a sewed book for the finisher by plain covering. **forwarding-merchant,** *n.* (*Am.*) One who receives and forwards goods to their destination. **forwardly,** *adv.* **forwardness,** *n.* The quality or state of being forward; assurance; pertness. **forward, -s,** *adv.* Towards the front or the forepart; onward, in place or time; towards the future; in advance, ahead; to the front, to a prominent position; (*Naut.*) towards, at, or in the fore-part of the vessel. **to bring forward:** To draw attention to; (*Bookkeeping*) to bring the totals from the last page to the top of this one. **to put forward:** To advance or allege (a plea, argument, etc.); to start, to help forward; to make (oneself) too prominent. **forwarder** (2), (*slang*) **forrader,** *adv.* Further forward, in advance. **could get no forrader:** Could make no progress.

***forweary** (fôr wēr′ i), *v.t.* (*p.p.* **-wearied, -worn**) To tire out.

forwent *past* [FORGO].

fossa (fos′ ȧ) [L., a ditch, orig. fem. p.p. of *fodere*, to dig], *n.* (*pl.* -*æ*) (*Anat.*) A shallow depression, pit, or cavity. **fossiform,** *a.*

fosse (fos) [F., from L. FOSSA], *n.* A ditch, a trench, esp. around a fortification, commonly filled with water; a canal; a *fossa*. **fossette,** *n.* A dimple, a small *fossa*.

***fosset** (fos′ sĕt) [FAUCET], *n.* A faucet.

fossick (fos′ ik) [Austral., prob. of Engl. prov. orig.], *v.i.* (*Mining*) To dig about in crevices and rubbish-heaps; to rummage about. **fossicker,** *n.*

fossiform [FOSSA].

fossil (fos′ il) [O.F., from L. *fossilis*, from *fossus*, p.p. of *fodere*, to dig], *a.* Found underground; dug up; preserved in the strata of the earth's crust, esp. if mineralized; (*fig.*) antiquated. *n.* An organic body preserved in the strata of the earth's crust; an antiquated person; *anything dug up. **fossilate,** *v.t. and i.* To fossilize. **fossilation** (-lā′ shŭn), *n.* **fossiliferous** (-lif′ ĕr ŭs) [-FEROUS], *a.* **fossilify** (fŏ sil′ i fī), *v.t.* To fossilize. ***fossilism,** *n.* The study of fossils. ***fossilist,** *n.* **fossilize,** *v.t.* To convert into a fossil; (*fig.*) to render antiquated. *v.i.* To be converted into a fossil; (*fig.*) to become antiquated. **fossilization** (-zā′ shŭn), *n.* ***fossilogy** (fŏ sil′ ŏ ji), **fossilology** (fos il ol′ ŏ ji), *n.* ***fossilogist, fossilologist,** *n.*

fossor (fos′ ŏr) [late L., grave-digger, as prec.], *n.* (*Eccles. Ant.*) One of an order of inferior clergy charged with the burial of the dead. ***Fossores*** (fŏ sôr′ ēz), *n.pl.* (*Zool.*) Burrowing *Hymenoptera*, insects with legs formed for burrowing; a group of mammals containing the burrowing moles. **fossorial** (fŏ sôr′ i ăl), *a.* Adapted for digging; (*Zool.*) pertaining or relating to the *Fossores*.

foster (fos′ tĕr) [A.-S. *fōstrian*, from *fōstor*, nourishment, cogn. with *fōda*, FOOD], *v.t.* To nourish, to support, to rear, to promote the growth of; to encourage, to nurse, to cherish; to harbour (as an ill feeling). **v.i.* To be brought up together. **n.* A fosterer. **foster-brother, -sister,** *n.* A brother or sister by nursing, but not by birth. **foster-child, -daughter, -son,** *n.* A child nursed by a woman not the mother, or bred up by a man not the father. ***foster-dam,** *n.* A nurse, a foster-mother. **foster-father, -mother, -parent,** *n.* One who takes the place of a parent in rearing a child. **foster-land,** *n.* *Land allotted for the support of monks; one's adopted country. ***foster-nurse,** *n.* A nurse. **fosterage,** *n.* The act of fostering; the state of being a foster-child; the custom of fostering; the care of a foster-child; fostering or encouraging. **fosterer, fostress,** *n.* One who fosters; a nurse, a foster-parent. **fosterling,** *n.* A foster-child.

fother (1) (foth′ ĕr) [perh. from Dut. *voederen* (now *voeren*) or L.G. *fodern*, to line (cp. Icel. *fōthra*)], *v.t.* (*Naut.*) To stop (a leak) at sea by letting down a sail and putting oakum, yarn, etc., between it and the ship's sides or bottom; to use (a sail) thus.

fother (2) [A.-S. *fōther* (cp. M.Dut. *voeder*, Dut. *voer*, G. *fuder*)], *n.* *A load, a cartload; *a large quantity; a load of lead, 19½ cwt.; a large quantity, load, or weight; a heavy weight.

fou (foo) [Sc., FULL (1)], *a.* Drunk. **n.* A bushel.

foudroyant (fu droi′ ănt) [F., pres.p. of *foudroyer*, to strike with lightning, from *foudre*, ult. from L. *fulgur*, lightning], *a.* Overwhelming, thundering, or flashing, like lightning; (*Path.*) beginning in a sudden and intense form.

fougade (foo gad'), ***fougasse*** (foo găs') [F.], *n.* (*Mil.*) A small mine for blowing up assailants or abandoned works.

fought, *past* and *p.p.*; ***foughten,** *p.p.* [FIGHT].

foul (foul) [A.-S. *fūl* (cp. Dut. *vuil*, Icel. *fūll*, G. *faul*, also Gr. *puon*, stinking, L. *pus*, see PUS) whence *fūlian*, to decay], *a.* Dirty, filthy, unclean; loathsome, offensive to the senses; covered or filled with noxious matter, overgrown with weeds, clogged, choked; morally offensive, obscene, disgusting; polluted; unfair, unlawful, dishonest, against the rules; stormy, cloudy, rainy; (*Print.*) full of printer's errors, dirty, inaccurate (of a proof); *unlucky, unfavourable; *coarse, gross; *unsightly, ugly. *adv.* Irregularly, against the rules. *n.* Foul weather or fortune; (*Sport*) a foul stroke; a wilful collision, an interference, any breach of the rules of a game or contest. *v.t.* To make foul; to defile, to soil, to pollute; to dishonour; to come into collision with, to impede, block, or entangle. *v.i.* To become foul or dirty; to come into collision; to become clogged or entangled. **to fall** or **run foul of:** To come or run against with force; to come into collision with; to quarrel with. **to hit** or **play foul:** To hit or deal with an opponent or competitor in a manner forbidden by the rules. ***foul-faced,** *a.* Having a repulsive face. ***foul-feeding,** *a.* Feeding on filthy food. **foul fish,** *n.* A fish in or just after the spawning season. **foul-mouthed, -spoken, -tongued,** *a.* Addicted to profane, scurrilous, or obscene language. **foul play,** *n.* Unfair behaviour in a game or contest, a breach of the rules; dishonest or treacherous conduct. **foully** (foul' li), *adv.* In a foul manner; abominably, treacherously, wickedly. **foulness,** *n.*

foulard (fu lar, -lard') [F., etym. unknown], *n.* A soft, thin material of silk or silk mixed with cotton; a silk handkerchief.

***foulder** (foul' dėr) [O.F. *fouldrer*, from *fouldre* (F. *foudre*), ult. from L. *fulgur*, lightning], *v.i.* To flash or flame as lightning.

foumart (foo' mârt) [M.E. *fulmart*, *folmard*, A.-S. *fūl*, FOUL, *mearth*, a marten], *n.* The polecat.

found (1) (found) [F. *fondre*, L. *fundere*, to pour], *v.t.* To cast by melting (metal) or fusing (material for glass) and pouring it into a mould; to make of molten metal or glass. **founder** (1), *n.* One who casts metal. **founders'-dust,** *n.* Charcoal powder and coal or coke dust ground fine for casting purposes. **founders'-sand,** *n.* A fine sand for making founding-moulds.

found (2) (found) [F. *fonder*, L. *fundāre*, from *fundus*, bottom, base], *v.t.* To lay the foundation or basis of; to fix firmly; to begin to erect or build; to set up, to establish; to endow; to originate; to give origin to; to conduct or base (upon). *v.i.* To rest (upon) as a foundation. **founder** (2), *n.* One who founds or originates anything, esp. one who endows a permanent fund for the support of an institution. **founder's share:** A share of stock allotted to a promoter of a corporation as part payment for goodwill, plant, etc. **foundership,** *n.* **foundress,** *n.*

found (3), *past* and *p.p.* [FIND]. **all found,** *adv.* With complete board and lodging.

foundation (foun dā' shŭn) [L. *fundātio* (FOUND (2), -ATION)], *n.* The act of founding or establishing; that on which anything is established or by which it is sustained; permanent basis; the fund or endowment which supports an institution; the natural or artificial basis of a structure; (*pl.*) the part of a structure below the surface of the ground; the first set of stitches in crochet or knitting; the stiff fabric forming the basis of various articles of attire; the grounds, principles, or basis on which anything stands; the reasons on which an opinion, etc., is founded; that which is founded or endowed; an endowed institution. **foundation garment,** *n.* A woman's undergarment that supports the figure, *e.g.* corset. **foundation-muslin, -net,** *n.* Openwork, gummed fabrics for stiffening dresses and bonnets. **foundation-school,** *n.* An endowed school. **foundation-stone,** *n.* A stone laid with ceremony to commemorate the founding of a building. **foundationer,** *n.* One who derives support from the endowment of a college or school. **foundationless,** *a.* Without foundation.

founder (3) (foun' dėr) [O.F. *fondrer*, to sink in, from *fond*, L. *fundus*, the bottom], *v.i.* (*Naut.*) To fill with water and sink (as a ship); to fall lame (of a horse); to fall in, to give way; to fail, to break down; to be ruined. *v.t.* To lame, by causing soreness or inflammation in the feet of (said of a horse); to sink (a ship) by making her fill with water. *n.* Inflammation of the sensitive parts of a horse's foot from overwork. ***founderous,** *a.* Causing to founder; full of ruts and holes; (*fig.*) puzzling, perplexing.

foundling (found' ling) [FOUND (3), -LING], *n.* A deserted child of unknown parents. **foundling hospital,** *n.* A charitable institution where deserted children are reared.

foundry (foun' dri), *n.* A building where metals are cast; the act or art of casting metals.

fount (1) (fount) [F. *font*, L. *fons fontem*], *n.* A spring, a fountain, a well.

fount (2) (fount) [F. *fonte*, from *fondre*, to FOUND (1)], *n.* (*Print.*) A set of type of one face and size.

fountain (foun' tăn) [O.F. *fontaine*, late L. *fontāna*, L. *fons fontis*], *n.* A spring of water, natural or artificial; the source of a river or stream; an ornamental jet of water driven high into the air by pressure; the structure for producing such a jet; a public erection with a drinking-supply; a reservoir to contain a liquid, as in a lamp, printing-press, fountain-pen, etc.; (*fig.*) a source, a first principle; (*Her.*) a roundel divided into six spaces by waved lines across the shield. **fountain-head,** *n.* An original source or spring. **fountain-pen,** *n.* A pen with an ink reservoir. **fountained,** *a.* Having fountains (*esp. in comb.* as *many-fountained*). ***fountainless,** *a.* ***fountful,** *a.*

four (fôr) [A.S. *fēower* (cp. Dan. *fire*, Dut. and G. *vier*, W. *pedwar*, L. *quatuor*, Gr. *tessares*)], *a.* Consisting of one more than three or twice two. *n.* The sum of one and three, twice two; a symbol expressing this, as 4, iiii or iv; a set of four persons or things, a team of four horses, a four-oared boat or its crew; a card or domino with four spots; (*colloq.*) four-penny-worth of (spirits, beer, etc.); (*Mil.*, *pl.*) a marching column four men wide. **carriage and four:** A carriage drawn by four horses. **to be, go,** or **run on all fours:** To crawl on the hands and feet or knees; (*fig.*) to agree precisely with. **four-ale,** *n.* Small ale, once sold at fourpence a quart. **four-centred,** *a.* (*Arch.*) Having the curve described from four centres (of an arch). **four-coupled,** *a.* With two pairs of wheels coupled together (of a locomotive). **four-course,** *n.* (*Agric.*) A four years' series of crops in rotation. **four-eyes,** *n.* (*slang*) A person in spectacles. **four-flusher,** *n.* (*Am. slang*) A bluffer. **four-foot way:** The space between the metals (actually 4 ft. 8½ in.) on a railway. **four-footed,** *a.* Having four feet; quadruped. **four-handed,** *a.* Quadrumanous: for four players (of games); for two performers (of music). **four-horse,** *a.* Drawn by four horses. ***four-inched,** *a.* Four inches wide. **four-in-hand,** *a.* Drawn by four horses. *adv.* With four horses driven by one driver. *n.* A vehicle so drawn and driven. **four-oar,** *a.* Propelled by four oars. **four-o'clock,** *n.* The Marvel of Peru, *Mirabilis dichotoma*, so named from its flowers opening at four o'clock in the afternoon. **fourpence,** *n.* The sum of four pennies. **four-penny,** *n.* A silver coin worth 4d., no longer minted; (*slang*) four-ale. *a.* Worth fourpence; costing fourpence. **four-post,** *a.* Having four high posts at the corners to support a canopy and curtains. **four-poster,** *n.* A (usu. large) bedstead with these. **four-pounder,** *n.* A gun throwing a four-pound shot. **fourscore,** *a.* Four times twenty, eighty; eighty years old. *n.* The number of four times twenty. **four-square,** *a.* Having four sides and angles equal; square-shaped; (*fig.*) firmly established; immovable. **four-stroke,** *n.* (*Mach.*) Term applied to an internal-combustion engine which fires once every four strokes of movement of the piston. **four-away,** *a.* Allowing passage in any one of four directions. **four-wheeler,** *n.* A vehicle having four wheels, esp. a cab. **fourfold,** *a.* Four times as many or as much, quadruple. *adv.* In fourfold measure. **foursome,** *a.* Done by four persons. *n.* (*Golf*) A game between two pairs, the partners playing their ball alternately.

fourchette (foor shet′) [F., dim. of *fourche*, L. *furca*, FORK], *n.* A fork-shaped piece between the fingers of gloves; (*Surg.*) a forked instrument formerly used for cutting the frænum in tongue-tied infants.

fourgon (foor′ gon) [F., etym. unknown], *n.* A French baggage-waggon.

Fourierism (fur′ i ėr izm) [F. M. C. *Fourier* (1772–1837), French Socialist], *n.* A system of social reorganization advocated by Fourier, based on the principle of natural affinities (see PHALANSTERY). **Fourierist, -ite,** *n.*

fourteen (fôr tēn′), *a.* Amounting to four and ten. *n.* The number amounting to four and ten; a symbol denoting this, as 14 or xiv. **fourteenth,** *a.* Next after the thirteenth; being one of fourteen equal parts. *n.* One of fourteen equal parts; (*Mus.*) an interval of an octave and a seventh; a note separated from another by this interval, two such notes sounded together.

fourth (fôrth), *a.* Next after the third; being one of four equal parts. *n.* One of four equal parts, a quarter; (*Mus.*) an interval of four diatonic notes, comprising two whole tones and a semitone; two notes separated by this interval sounded together; (*pl.*) goods of fourth-rate quality. **fourth estate,** *n.* The press. **Fourth of July,** *n.* Independence Day in U.S.A., anniversary of the Declaration of Independence, 4 July, 1776. **fourth-rate,** *n.* Formerly a 50- to 70-gun vessel, later a gunboat carrying from one to four guns. *a.* Fourth best, as a grade of quality in various commodities; (*colloq.*) indifferently good. **fourthly,** *adv.* In the fourth place.

***fouter, -re** (foo′ tėr) [O.F. *foutre*, L. *futuere*, to lecher], *n.* A coarse term of contempt (in phrases, *a fouter for, not to care a fouter*).

fouth (footh) [Sc. form of obs. *fulth* (cp. LENGTH)], *n.* Fullness; plenty.

fovea (fō′ vė ȧ) [L.], *n.* (*pl.* **-veæ**) (*Anat. etc.*) A small pit or depression. **foveate,** *a.* ***foveola*** (fō vē′ ȯ lȧ) [L., dim. of prec.], *n.* **foveolate, -lated** (fō′ vė ȯ lāt, -lā tėd), *a.*

fovilla (fō vil′ ȧ) [from *fov*, root of *fovēre*, to cherish, after *favilla*], *n.* The matter contained in the pollen grain, the immediate agent in fertilization.

fowl (foul) [A.-S. *fugol* (cp. Dut. and G. *vogel*, Icel. and Dan. *fugl*), from Teut. *flug-*, to FLY], *n.* A bird; birds collectively; a cock or hen of the domestic or poultry kind; their flesh used as food. *v.i.* To hunt, catch, or kill wild birds for sport. **barn-door fowl** [BARN-DOOR]. **fowl-pest,** *n.* A contagious virus disease of birds. **fowl-run,** *n.* An enclosure in which domestic fowls can run about; a breeding-establishment for fowls. **fowler,** *n.* One who pursues wild-fowl for sport. **fowling-piece,** *n.* A light smooth-bore gun adapted for shooting wild-fowl.

fox (foks) [A.-S. (cp. Dut. *vos*, G. *fuchs*)], *n.* A quadruped, *Canis vulpes*, with a straight bushy tail, reddish-brown hair, and erect ears, notorious for its cunning, hunted in England for sport; (*fig.*) a sly, cunning fellow. *v.t.* To make sour, in fermenting; (*chiefly in p.p.*) to discolour (pages of a book, etc.); (*Am.*) to repair (boots) by adding an outer covering over the upper; to intoxicate. *v.i.* To become sour, in fermenting; to become discoloured, esp. to turn reddish (of paper, etc.); *to be crafty. **fox-brush,** *n.* The tail of a fox. **fox-case,** *n.* The skin of a fox. **fox-earth, fox's earth,** *n.* The burrow of a fox. **fox-evil, fox's-evil,** *n.* A disease in which the hair falls off. **fox-hole,** *n.* (*Mil.*) A small trench. **fox-shark,** *n.* The thresher, *Alopias vulpes*, a shark about fifteen feet long, with a long rough tail. **foxtail,** *n.* The tail of a fox; kinds of grasses, esp. *Alopecurus pratensis*; a club-moss, *Lycopodium clavatum*; (*Metal.*) the cinder obtained in the last stage of the charcoal process of refining iron. **fox-terrier,** *n.* A short-haired dog, orig. employed to unearth foxes, now chiefly as a pet. **fox-trap,** *n.* A snare to catch foxes. **fox-trot,** *n.* A kind of ballroom dance; short steps taken by a horse when changing its pace. **foxed,** *a.* Stained with spots, as a book or print; (*slang*) drunk. **fox-like,** *a.* ***fox-ship,** *n.* The character of a fox; artfulness. **foxy,** *a.* Fox-like, tricky, crafty; foxed; reddish-brown in colour; (*Painting*) having too much of this colour, hot-coloured. **foxiness,** *n.*

foxglove (foks′ glŭv), *n.* The genus *Digitalis*, esp. *D. purpurea*, with purple flowers resembling the fingers of a glove, the leaves of which are used as a sedative.

foxhound (foks′ hound), *n.* A hound trained to hunt foxes.

foxhunt (foks′ hŭnt), *n.* The chase of a fox. *v.i.* To hunt foxes with hounds. **foxhunter,** *n.* One who hunts foxes. **foxhunting,** *n.* Pertaining to, or fond of hunting foxes. *n.* The act or practice of hunting foxes with a pack of hounds.

foy (foi′) [now chiefly Sc.; from M.Dut. (Dut. *fooi*), prob. from F. *voie*, way, journey], *n.* A parting entertainment given by one setting out on a journey.

foyer (fwa′ yā) [F., from low L. *focārum*, from *focus*, see FOCUS], *n.* A large public room in a theatre; the entrance hall of an hotel; (*Metal.*) the crucible in a furnace to receive the molten metal.

fozy (fō′ zi) [Sc.; cp. L.G. *fussig*], *a.* Spongy, soft; (*fig.*) without backbone. **foziness,** *n.*

frab (frăb) [onomat.], *v.t.* (*Prov.*) To worry.

fracas (fra′ ka) [F., from *fracasser*, It. *fracassare*, to break in pieces], *n.* (*pl.* **fracas**) (fra′ kaz) A disturbance, a row; an uproar; a noisy quarrel.

***fracted** (frăk′ tėd) [L. *fractus*, as foll.], *a.* Broken. **fractile,** *a.* Liable to break; (*Geol.*) indicating breakage of cleavage.

fraction (frăk′ shŭn) [O.F. *fraccion*, from eccles. L. *fractio -ōnem*, from *fractus*, p.p. of *frangere*, to break], *n.* The act of breaking, esp. by violence; the state of being broken; a fragment, a small piece; (*Math.*) the expression of one or more parts of a unit; *dissension, a rupture; *the rite of breaking the bread in the Eucharist. **fractional, -ary,** *a.* Of or pertaining to fractions; constituting a fraction; forming but a small part, insignificant. **fractionally,** *adv.* **fractionate,** *v.t.* (*Chem.*) To separate (a mixture) into portions having different properties, by distillation or analogous process. **fractionation** (-nā′ shŭn), *n.* **fractionize,** *v.t.* To break up into fractions or divisions.

fractious (frăk′ shŭs) [from prec., in the sense of dissension], *a.* Apt to quarrel; snappish, cross, fretful, peevish. **fractiously,** *adv.* **fractiousness,** *n.*

fracture (frăk′ chŭr) [O.F., from Latin *fractūra*, as FRACTION], *n.* The act of breaking by violence; a break, a breakage; (*Min.*) the irregularity of surface produced by breaking a mineral across, as distinguished from splitting it along the planes of cleavage; (*Surg.*) the breakage of a bone (when only the bone is broken the fracture is called **simple,** when there is also a wound of the integuments it is termed **compound**). *v.t.* To break across; to separate the continuity of the parts of. *v.i.* To break or crack.

frænum, frenum (frē′ nŭm) [L., a bridle], *n.* (*pl.* **-na**) (*Anat.*) A small band or ligament restraining the action of an organ, as that of the tongue. **frænulum** [dim. of prec.], *n.*

fragaria (frȧ gâr′ i ȧ) [L. *frāga*, strawberries], *n.pl.* (*Bot.*) A genus of *Rosaceæ*, consisting of the cultivated and wild strawberries.

fragile (frăj′ il, -īl) [F., from L. *fragilis*, from *frag-*, root of *frangere*, to break], *a.* Brittle, easily broken; weak, frail, delicate. **fragility** (frȧ jil′ i ti), *n.*

fragment (frăg′ mėnt) [F., or directly from L. *fragmentum*, as prec.], *n.* A piece broken off; a small detached portion; an incomplete or unfinished portion; the surviving portion of a whole that has been destroyed; *a term of extreme contempt. **fragmental** (frăg′ mėn-, frȧg men′ tȧl), *a.* Pertaining to or consisting of fragments; disconnected. **fragmentary rocks,** *n.pl.* (*Geol.*) Rocks made up of fragments, as breccias, conglomerates, etc. **fragmentally, fragmentarily,** *adv.* **fragmentariness,** *n.* **fragmented,** *a.* **fragmentation,** *n.* The breaking into fragments; (*Biol.*) the breaking-up of a chromosome.

fragrant (frā′ grȧnt) [F., from L. *frāgrans -ntem*, pres.p. of *frāgrāre*, to emit a perfume], *a.* Emitting a pleasant perfume, sweet-smelling, odorous. **fragrance,** *n.* **fragrantly,** *adv.*

frail (1) (frāl) [O.F. *fraile*, L. *fragilis*, FRAGILE], *a.* Fragile, delicate; infirm, in weak health; perishable; (*fig.*) weak in mind or resolution, liable to be led astray; (*euphem.*) unchaste. **frailish,** *a.* ***frailly,** *adv.* **frailness,** *n.* **frailty,** *n.*

frail (2) (frāl) [O.F. *frayel*, *freēl*, acc. to Skeat from earlier *fleēl*, L. *flagellum*, a whip, a vine-shoot]. A rush basket used for packing figs, etc.; a certain quantity of figs or raisins, about 75 lb., contained in a frail.

fraise (1) (frāz) [F., a ruff], *n.* A ruff; (*Fort.*) a horizontal or sloping palisade round a rampart; a tool for enlarging a drill-hole, etc.

fraise (2) (frāz) [etym. doubtful], *n.* (*Sc. and North.*) A commotion.

frambœsia (frăm bē′ zi ȧ) [F. *framboise*, a raspberry], *n.* (*Path.*) The yaws, a contagious eruption characterized by swellings like raspberries, peculiar to the Negro.

frame (frām) [A.-S. *framian*, to avail, to further, from *fram*, adv. forward], *v.t.* To form or construct by fitting parts together; to fit, adapt, or adjust; to contrive; to devise, to invent; to compose, to express; to plan, to arrange; to form in the mind, conceive, imagine; to surround with a frame, to serve as a frame to; *to shape; *to direct (one's course); *to cause, to bring about; to put a person in an incriminating position. *n.* A fabric or structure composed of parts fitted together; a structure or fabric of any kind; the skeleton of a structure; the construction, constitution, or build of anything; the established order or system (of society or the body politic); disposition of mind; a case or border to enclose or surround a picture, a pane of glass, etc.; (*Hort.*) a glazed portable structure for protecting plants from frost; various machines in the form of framework used in manufactures, mining, building, printing, etc. **frame-up,** *n.* Evidence concocted for incriminating. *v.i.* (*prov.*) To manage, to contrive; *to move. **frame-aerial,** *n.* (*Radio.*) An aerial consisting of wire wound on a frame. **frame-bridge,** *n.* A bridge constructed of timbers so as to combine the greatest strength with the least material. **frame-house,** *n.* A house with a wooden framework covered with boards. **frame-saw,** *n.* A flexible saw-blade stretched in a frame to stiffen it. **framework,** *n.* The frame of a structure; the fabric for enclosing or supporting anything, or forming the substructure to a more complete fabric; (*fig.*) structure, arrangement (of society, etc.). **framer,** *n.* One who frames; a maker, a contriver. **frameless,** *a.* **framing,** *n.* A frame, framework; setting. **framing-chisel,** *n.* A heavy chisel used for making mortises.

franc (frăngk) [F., said to be from *Francorum Rex*, King of the Franks, the inscription on the earliest coins], *n.* A French coin, the unit of value and account in France; *a French gold coin of the 14th cent., worth about 10s. 6d.; *a French silver coin first issued in 1575.

franchise (frăn′ chīz, -chiz) [O.F., from *franchiss-*, stem of *franchir*, to free oneself, from *franc*, FRANK (2)], *n.* A right, privilege, immunity, or exemption granted to an individual or to a body; the district or territory to which a certain privilege extended; citizenship; the right of voting for a member of Parliament; the qualification for this; *a sanctuary for persons liable to be arrested; *liberty. **v.t.* To enfranchise; to give freedom or liberty to. ***franchisement,** *n.* **franchiser,** *n.* One having the elective franchise.

Franciscan (frăn sis′ kȧn) [med. L. *Franciscus*, Francis], *a.* Of or pertaining to St. Francis of Assisi (1182–1226), or the order of mendicant friars founded by him in 1209. *n.* A member of the Franciscan order, a grey friar.

Franco- [med. L. *Francus*, FRANK (1)], *comb. form.* Pertaining to the French. **Franco-Chinese,** *a.* Applied to a method of decorating pottery adopted by the French from the Chinese. **Franco-German, Prussian War:** The war between France and Germany in 1870–71. **Francophile,** *n.* **Francophobe,** *n.*

francolin (frăng′ kȯ lin) [F., from It. *franco-lino*], *n.* A bird of the genus *Francolinus*, allied to the partridges, esp. *F. vulgaris*, a richly-coloured species common in India.

franc-tireur (fran′ ti rur′) [F., free-shooter (*franc*, FRANK (2), *tirer*, to shoot)], *n.* (*pl.* ***franco-tireurs***) A French light-infantry soldier belonging to an irregular corps.

frangible (frăn′ jibl) [late L. *frangibilis*, from *frangere*, to break], *a.* That may be easily broken. **frangibleness, frangibility** (-bil′ i ti), *n.*

frangipane (frăn′ ji pān), **frangipani** (frăn ji pa′ ni) [prob. from the inventor, the Marquis *Frangipani*], *n.* A kind of pastry made with cream, almonds, and sugar; a perfume prepared from the flowers of *Plumiera rubra*, a West Indian tree.

***franion** (frăn′ i ȯn) [etym. doubtful], *n.* A boon companion; a woman of loose character.

Frank (1) (frăngk) [L. *Francus*, O.H.G. *Franko*, prob. from the name of a weapon (cp. A.-S. *franca*, a javelin)], *n.* A member of the ancient German peoples or tribes who conquered France in the 6th cent.; a name given by Turks, Greeks, Arabs, etc., to a European. **frankish,** *a.*

frank (2) (frăngk) [O.F. *franc*, low L. *francus*, free, from prec.], *a.* Open, ingenuous, sincere, candid; generous, liberal, profuse, free, unrestrained; *licentious; (*Law*) free, privileged, exempt. ***frank-fee,** *n.* (*Law*) A tenure of land in fee-simple. ***frankfold,** *n.* Liberty to fold sheep. ***frank-pledge,** *n.* The system by which freemen in a tithing were pledged for each other's good behaviour. ***frank-service,** *n.* Service performed by freemen. ***frank-tenement,** *n.* (*Law*) An estate in freehold; freehold property. **frankly,** *adv.* **frankness,** *n.*

frank (3) (frăngk) [from prec.], *v.t.* To send or cause to be sent under an official privilege, such as, formerly, the signature of a member of Parliament, so as to pass free; to secure the free passage of (a person or thing). *n.* A signature authorizing a letter to go through the post free of charge; the right to send (letters, etc.) in this manner; the letter or package thus sent.

***frank** (4) (frăngk) [O.F. *franc*], *n.* A pigsty; an enclosure in which animals are fattened. *v.t.* To shut up in a frank; to fatten up; to feed high.

frankalmoign (frăngk′ ȧl moin) [O.F. *franc*, FRANK, A.-F. *almoine*, O.F. *almosne* (F. *aumône*), alms], *n.* (*Law*) A tenure by which a religious body holds lands with no obligations except such as prayers, almsgiving, etc.

Frankenstein (frăng′ kėn stīn) [Character in the

novel by Mary Shelley], *n.* The maker of a mechanical monster that brought disaster to its author.

Frankfort (frăngk′ fŏrt) [G. *Frankfurt*], *n.* A town in Germany. **Frankfort black,** *n.* A pigment made of wine-lees, used in copper-plate engraving. **Frankfurter, Frankfurt sausage,** *n.* A highly-seasoned sausage of beef and pork.

frankincense (frăngk′ in sens) [O.F. *franc encens*], *n.* A gum or resin burning with a fragrant smell, used as incense; in the East olibanum, an exudation from trees of the genus *Boswellia*, is used.

franking (frăngk′ ing) [prob. from FRANK (2)], *n.* (*Carp.*) The notching out a portion of a sash-bar for the passage of the transverse bar, to make a mitre-joint.

franklin (frăngk′ lin) [A.-F. *fraunclein*, low L. *francus*, free, -LING], *n.* (*14th and 15th cents.*) An English freeholder, not liable to feudal service.

frantic (frăn′ tik) [O.F. *frenetique*, late L. *phrenēticus*, Gr. *phrenitikos*, from *phrenitis*, inflammation of the brain, from *phrēn*, brain], *a.* Raving, outrageously excited or demented; suffering from frenzy. **n.* One who is frantic; a lunatic. **frantically, -ticly,** *adv.* ***franticness,** *n.*

frap (frăp) [O.F. *fraper*, to strike], *v.t.* (*past & p.p.* **frapped**) (*Naut.*) To draw together by ropes crossing each other, to secure and strengthen, to bind the end of a rope with string.

frappé (fra′ pā) [F., p.p. of *frapper*, to strike, to ice], *a.* Iced.

frass (frăs) [G. *frasz*, cogn. with *fressen*, to devour], *n.* Excrement of larvæ; refuse left by a wood-boring insect.

fratch (frăch) [now chiefly North., prob. onomat.], *v.i.* To quarrel; to worry. *n.* A quarrel. **frachety, fratching, fratchy,** *a.* Quarrelsome; irritable.

frate (fra′ tā) [It., brother], *n.* (*pl.* ***frati***) A friar.

fraternal (fră tẽr′ năl) [O.F. *fraternel*, late L., *frāternālis*, L. *frāternus*, from *frāter*, brother] *a.* Brotherly; pertaining to or becoming brethren; existing between brothers. **fraternally,** *adv.*

fraternity (fră tẽr′ ni ti), *n.* The state of a brother; brotherliness; a brotherhood, a body of men associated for a common interest or for religious purposes; a body of men associated or linked together by similarity of rank, profession, interests, etc.; (*Am.*) a college association of students.

fraternize (frăt′ ĕr nīz), *v.i.* To associate or hold fellowship with others of like occupation or tastes. **fraternization,** *n.* **fraternizer,** *n.*

fratricide (frā′ tri-, frăt′ ri sīd) [O.F., from L. *frātricīda* (*frāter*, brother, -CIDE)], *n.* The murder of a brother; one who murders his brother. **fratricidal,** *a.*

fratry, fratery (frā′ tri, -tĕr i) [from obs. *frater*, O.F. *fraitur*, short form of *refreitor*, low L. *refectōrium*, REFECTORY], *n.* The refectory in a monastery; a common-room in a monastery.

frau (frou) [G.], *n.* (*pl.* **frauen**) A German woman, wife, or widow; Mrs. **fräulein** (froi′ līn), *n.* (*pl. unaltered*) A young lady, a German spinster; Miss; a German governess.

fraud (frawd) [O.F. *fraude*, L. *fraudem*, nom. *fraus*], *n.* An act or course of deception deliberately practised to gain unlawful or unfair advantage; (*Law*) such deception directed to the detriment of another; a deception, a trick, trickery; (*colloq.*) a sham, a take-in, a deceptive person, a humbug; *a plot, a snare. **v.t.* To defraud. ***fraudful,** *a.* ***fraudfully,** *adv.* **fraudulent,** *a.* Practising fraud; characterized by or containing fraud; intended to defraud, deceitful. **fraudulence,** *n.* **fraudulently,** *adv.*

fraught (frawt) [p.p. of obs. v. *fraught*, to load, from obs. n. *fraught*, cargo, from L.G. (see E.Fris. and G. *fracht*, M.Dut. and M.L.G. *vracht*), cp. FREIGHT], *a.* Freighted, laden, stored (with); involving, entailing, attended by, charged (with). **n.* A cargo, a burden; (*Sc.*) a load, two pails (of water).

fraxinella (frăk si nel′ ȧ) [dim. of L. *fraxinus*, ash], *n.* Kinds of rue or dittany, esp. *Dictamnus fraxinella* and *D. albus*, cultivated for their leaves and flowers. **fraxinus** (frăk′ si nŭs), *n.* A genus of deciduous trees containing the common ash, etc.

fray (1) (frā), *n.* An affray; a noisy quarrel, a brawl, a riot; a combat, a contest; *anxiety, fear. **v.t.* To frighten; to drive away; to fight against. **v.i.* To fight.

fray (2) (frā) [O.F. *freier*, L. *fricāre*, to rub], *v.t.* To wear away by rubbing; to fret, to chafe; *to rub. *v.i.* To become rubbed or worn, esp. so as to become unravelled or ragged at the edges (of a garment, cloth, etc.). **n.* A fret or chafe in cloth; a sore place caused by rubbing. **fraying,** *n.* The velvet off a deer's horns.

frazil (frā′ zil) [French-Canadian, perh. from F. *fraisil*, cinders], *n.* Anchor-ice.

frazzle (frăz′ ėl), *v.t.* To fray at the edge, to unravel. *v.i.* To be worn out, nervous. *n.* An exhausted state. **to beat to a frazzle:** To beat thoroughly.

freak (frēk′) [etym. doubtful (perh. conn. with A.-S. *frec*, bold, rash, or *frīcian*, to dance)], *n.* A sudden wanton whim or caprice; a humour, a vagary; (*colloq.*) a sport, a monstrosity, a living curiosity. *v.t.* (*usu. in p.p.*) To variegate, to streak. **freakful,** *a.* **freakish,** *a.* **freakishly,** *adv.* **freakishness,** *n.* **freaksome,** *a.*

freck (frek), **frack** (frăk) [A.-S. *frec*, greedy, bold (cp. Icel. *frekr*, Swed. *fräch*, G. *frech*)], *a.* (*Sc.*) Eager, ready, prompt, lusty.

freckle (frek′ ėl) [earlier *frecken*, cp. Icel. *freknur*, pl.], *n.* A yellowish or light-brown spot on the skin, due to sunburn or other causes; any small spot or discoloration. *v.t.* To mark with freckles. *v.i.* To become marked with freckles. **freckling,** *n.* Marking with freckles; a mark like a freckle. ***freckly,** *a.*

free (1) (frē) [A.-S. *frēo* (cp. Dut. *vrij*, G. *frei*, cogn. with Sansk. *priya*, beloved)], *a.* At liberty; not in bondage or under restraint; living under a government based on the consent of the citizens; not arbitrary or despotic (of a government); not under foreign domination (of a State); released from authority or control; not confined, restricted, checked, or impeded; at liberty to choose or act, permitted (to do); independent, unattached, unconnected with the State (of a Church); released, clear, exempt (from); unconstrained, not bound or limited (by rules, etc.), not literal (of a translation); unconventional, unceremonious, careless, reckless; forward, impudent; indelicate, broad; unreserved, frank, ingenuous; admitted to or invested with certain privileges (of); not subject to the ordinary restrictions, duties, fees, etc.; without restriction, open, gratuitous; liberal, generous; spontaneous, unforced; (*Chem.*) not combined with another body; (*Zool.*) unattached; (*Bot.*) not adhering, not adnate. *adv.* Freely. **free and easy:** Unconstrained, unceremonious. *n.* An unceremonious kind of smoking-concert or other entertainment. **free alongside ship:** (*Comm.*) Delivered free on the dock or wharf. **free on board:** (*Comm.*) Delivered on board or into conveyance free of charge (of goods). **to make free:** To take liberties (*usu.* with). **free agency,** *n.* The state of acting freely, or without constraint upon the will. **free agent,** *n.* **free alms:** (FRANKALMOIGN]. **free association,** *n.* (*Psych.*) The bringing to consciousness of unconscious processes. **free bench,** *n.* (*Law*) A widow's dower in a copyhold. **free-board,** *n.* The space between the water-line on a vessel and the upper side of the deck, or the uppermost full deck. **free-born,** *a.* Born free; inheriting the right and liberty of a citizen. **Free Church,** *n.* A Church exempt from State control, or one in which there are no enforced payments, esp. the ecclesiastical body founded by those who left the Scottish Presbyterian establishment at the Disruption in 1843; (*pl.*) the Nonconformist Churches. **Free Churchism,** *n.* **free city** or **town,** *n.* A city or town of the

German Empire, independent in its government and franchise, and virtually forming an independent State. **free enterprise,** *n.* The conduct of business without State interference or control. **free fight,** *n.* A fight in which anyone can join. ***free-footed,** *a.* Unrestrained. **free hand,** *n.* (To be given) complete freedom to do. **free-hand,** *a.* (*Drawing*) Executed by the hand without the aid of instruments. **free-handed,** *n.* Open-handed, liberal. **free-hearted,** *a.* Frank, open, unreserved; liberal. **free-heartedly,** *adv.* **free-heartedness,** *n.* **free house,** *n.* A public-house free to buy its goods from any supplier. **free labour,** *n.* Labour performed by freemen, not slaves; workmen not belonging to trade-unions. **free-labourer,** *n.* **free-lance,** *n.* (*Hist.*) A member of one of the free companies of mercenaries in the Middle Ages; a controversialist whose pen is used independently of party, or one who sells his pen to the highest bidder; an unattached journalist. **free-liver,** *n.* One who indulges his appetities, esp. at table. **free-living,** *a.* and *n.* **free love,** *n.* Sexual intercourse without marriage; the doctrine that the affections should be free to fix on any object to which they are drawn, without restraint of marriage obligation. **free lover,** *n.* One who advocates or practises free love. **freed man,** *n.* An emancipated slave. **free market,** *n.* (*Fin.*) A market in which there are free dealings in securities. ***free-minded,** *a.* Having the mind free from care, trouble, or perplexity. **free pass,** *n.* A ticket that has not been paid for, entitling the holder to travel or to enter an exhibition, theatre, etc. **free port,** *n.* A port where ships of all nations may load or unload free of duty. **free school,** *n.* A school where no fees are charged. **free selection:** (*Austral.*) The legal right to select Crown lands, those who did so being termed 'selectors.' **free ship,** *n.* A neutral ship, free from liability to capture. **free soil,** *a.* (*U.S. Hist.*) Applied to the principles of a party in the United States who advocated the non-extension of slavery. **free-soiler,** *n.* **free-soilism,** *n.* **free-spoken,** *n.* Speaking without reserve; blunt, candid, frank. **free-spokenness,** *n.* **Free States,** *n.pl.* Those States of the American Union in which slavery never existed, or was abolished before the Civil War. **freestone,** *n.* A stone which can be cut freely in any direction. **free-stone,** *n.* A kind of peach easily freed from its stone when ripe. **free-thinker,** *n.* A rationalist, sceptic, or agnostic; one who rejects authority in religious belief. **free-thinking,** *n.* and *a.* **free-thought,** *n.* **free-tongued,** *a.* Free-spoken. **free town** [FREE CITY]. **free trade,** *n.* The liberty of unrestricted trade with other countries; free interchange of commodities without protection by customs duties. **free-trader,** *n.* One who advocates free trade; *a smuggler. **free vote,** *n.* (*Pol.*) A vote left to the individual's choice, free from party discipline. **free-warren,** *n.* (*Law*) A royal franchise or exclusive right of killing beasts and fowls of warren within certain limits. **free-wheel,** *n.* A driving wheel on a cycle that can be disconnected from the driving gear and allowed to revolve while the pedals are at rest; a cycle with such a wheel. *v.i.* To run down a hill (on a cycle or motor-car) without employing locomotive power or brakes. **free will,** *n.* The power of directing one's own actions without constraint by any external influence; voluntariness, spontaneity. **free-will,** *a.* Given freely, voluntary. **free-wind,** *n.* (*Naut.*) A fair wind. **free-woman** [FREEMAN]. **open free:** Open freely, without charge for admission. **freely,** *adv.* **freeness,** *n.*

free (2) (frē) [from prec.], *v.t.* To set at liberty, to emancipate; to rid or relieve (of or from); to extricate, to clear, to disentangle; *to remove; *to acquit; *to frank. **freedman,** *n.* A manumitted slave.

freebooter (frē′ boo tėr) [Dut. *vrijbuiter*, from *vrijbuit* (FREE (1) BOOTY)], *n.* A pirate or buccaneer, an adventurer who makes a business of plundering. **freeboot,** *v.i.* **freebootery,** *n.* **freebooting,** *a.*

freedom (frē′ dȯm) [A.-S. *frēo-dōm* (as FREE (1), -DOM)], *n.* The state of being free, liberty, independence; personal liberty, non-slavery, civil liberty; exemption from restraint or necessity, liberty of action, free will; lack of conventionality, frankness, excessive familiarity; violation of the rules of good breeding, a liberty; ease or facility in doing anything; participation in certain privileges, exemptions, and immunities pertaining to citizenship of a city or membership of a company; free use (of); *a free, unconditional grant; *liberality, generosity. ***freedomless,** *a.*

freehold (frē′ hōld), *n.* An estate held in fee-simple or fee-tail; the tenure by which such an estate is held; also applied to an office held for life. *a.* Held in fee-simple or fee-tail; of the nature of a freehold. **freeholder,** *n.* The possessor of a freehold.

freeman (frē′ mȧn), *n.* One not a slave or serf; one who holds the franchise of a citizen or a particular privilege, esp. the freedom of a city, company, etc. **freewoman,** *n.*

freemartin (frē′ mar tin) [etym. unknown], *n.* A sexually imperfect cow, usu. born as twin with a bull-calf.

Freemason (frē′ mā sȯn), *n.* A member of an association of 'Free and Accepted Masons,' a secret order or fraternity, stated to have been traced back to the building of Solomon's Temple, but probably originating as a fraternity of skilled masons, with right of free movement, about the 14th cent. **Freemasonry,** *n.* The system, rites and principles of Freemasons; (*fig.*) a secret understanding, community of interests, or instinctive sympathy among a number of people.

freesia (frē′ zi ȧ) [etym. unknown], *n.* A genus of bulbous flowering plants allied to the iris, from the Cape of Good Hope.

freeze (frēz) [A.-S. *frēosan* (cp. Dut. *vriezen*, G. *frieren*, also L. *pruīna*, hoar-frost)], *v.i.* (*past* **froze,** *p.p.* **frozen**) To be turned from a fluid to a solid state by cold; (*impers.*) to be at that degree of cold at which water turns to ice or becomes covered with ice; to become attached (to) or fastened (together) by frost; to feel cold, to lose animation through cold; (*fig.*) to be chilled (by fear); (*Fin.*) to make credits unrealizable; to stabilize prices. *v.t.* To congeal by cold; to form ice upon or convert into ice; to injure, overpower, or kill with cold; (*fig.*) to chill, to paralyse. *n.* The act or state of freezing; a frost. **it freezes:** There is frost. **to freeze on to:** (*slang*) To seize or hold tightly. **to freeze out:** (*colloq.*) To compel the retirement of from business, competition, society, etc., by boycotting, contemptuous treatment, or similar methods. **freezer,** *n.* An apparatus for freezing (meat, etc.); (*Austral.*) a sheep bred for export as frozen lamb or mutton. **freezing,** *a.* (*fig.*) Very cold; distant, chilling. **freezing-mixture,** *n.* A mixture of salt and snow, or pounded ice, or a combination of chemicals with or without ice, for producing intense cold. **freezing-point,** *n.* The point at which water freezes, marked 32° on Fahrenheit's thermometer, and 0° on the Centigrade and Réaumur thermometers; the temperature at which a substance freezes. **freezingly,** *adv.* **frozenly,** *adv.* **frozenness,** *n.*

freight (frāt) [cp. M.Dut. *vrecht*, *vracht*, O.F. *fret*, O.H.G. *frēht*, see also FRAUGHT], *n.* The money due or paid for the transportation of goods, esp. by water; that with which a ship is loaded; a cargo. *v.t.* To load (a ship) with goods for transportation; to hire or charter for this purpose; to load, *to fill. **freight-car,** *n.* (*Am.*) A railway car for goods, distinguished from a passenger-car. **freight-note,** *n.* (*Comm.*) A statement supplied to ship-owners by dock authorities giving weights, measurements, etc., of cargo. **freight train,** *n.* (*Am.*) A goods train. **freightage,** *n.* Money paid for the hire of a ship or the transportation of goods; the transporting of goods; freight. **freighter,** *n.* One who hires or loads a ship; a cargo-boat; one who sends goods by railway; one who contracts to receive and forward goods. **freightless,** *a.*

freit (frēt) [cp. Icel. *frett*, news, A.-S. *freht*, a

oracle], *n.* (*Sc.*) An omen, a charm; superstition. **freity,** *a.*

***fremd** (fremd) [A.-S. *fremde, fremede,* cogn. with *fram,* FROM], *a.* Strange, foreign.

fremescent (frė mes′ ėnt) [L. *fremere,* to roar (as if from pres.p. of a freq. form)], *a.* Noisy, tumultuous, riotous. **fremescence,** *n.*

fremitus (frem′ i tůs) [L., a roaring from *fremere,* to roar], *n.* (*Path.*) A movement or vibration perceptible externally, as on the walls of the chest when a patient speaks.

French (french) [A.-S. *Frencisc* (FRANK (1), -ISH)], *a.* Pertaining to France or its inhabitants; belonging to or native of France. *n.* The language spoken by the people of France; (*collect.*) the people of France. **to take French leave:** To go away or do a thing without permission. **French-bean,** *n.* The kidney or haricot bean, *Phaseolus vulgaris.* **French bread,** *n.* A kind of fancy bread. **French chalk,** *n.* A variety of talc, steatite, or soap-stone used for marking cloth, and in powder as a dry lubricant for tight boots, etc. **French curve,** *n.* An instrument designed to assist in drawing curved lines. **french fried:** (*Am.*) (Potato) chips. **French grey,** *n.* A tint composed of white with ivory-black, Indian red and Chinese blue. **French horn,** *n.* A metal wind instrument of circular shape with a gradual taper from the mouthpiece to a large everted bell. **French letter,** *n.* (*colloq.*) A contraceptive sheath. **Frenchman,** *n.* A native or naturalized inhabitant of France; a French ship. **french polish,** *n.* A solution of resin or gum-resin in alcohol or wood naphtha, for polishing cabinet-work, etc.; the polish produced. *v.t.* To polish with this. **french polisher,** *n.* **French-roll,** *n.* A light kind of fancy bread. **French roof,** *n.* A mansard roof or one having portions of two different pitches. **French white,** *n.* Finely pulverized talc. **french window,** *n.* A long window opening like a folding-door. **Frenchwoman,** *n.* A woman native of or naturalized in France. **Frenchify,** *v.t.* To make French; to infect with French tastes or manners. **Frenchification** (kā′ shůn), *n.* **Frenchless,** *a.* Not knowing French. **Frenchlike,** *a.*

frenetic [PHRENETIC].

***frenne, *fren** (fren) [corr. of FREMD], *a.* Strange. *n.* A foreigner; an enemy.

frenum [FRÆNUM].

frenzy (fren′ zi) [O.F. *frenesie,* late L. and late Gr. *phrenēsis,* Gr. *phrenitis,* inflammation of the brain (cp. FRANTIC)], *n.* Delirium, madness; temporary mental derangement; a violent access of mania, delirium, or unnatural excitement; extravagant folly. **a.* Mad. frantic. *v.t.* (*usu. in p.p.*) To drive to madness; to infuriate. ***frenzical,** *a.* **frenzied,** *a.* **frenziedly,** *adv.*

frequence, frequency (frē′ kwėns, frē′ kwėn si), [as foll.], *n.* The quality of occurring frequently; common occurrence; repetition at short intervals; rate of occurrence; the comparative number of occurrences in a given time; (*Elec.*) a term referring to the speed of variations of alternating currents, alternating electro-motive forces, and electromagnetic waves; (*Phys.*) rate of repetition or recurrence; *a throng. **high frequency,** *n.* (*Elec.*) Any frequency of alternating current from about 12,000 cycles per second upwards. **frequency distortion,** *n.* (*Radio.*) The phenomenon when amplitude of modulation varies with frequency. **frequency modulation,** *n.* (*Radio.*) The varying of the frequency of the carrier wave in accordance with the frequency of speech or music, for example; the broadcasting system using this.

frequent (frē′ kwėnt) [L. *frequens, -ntem,* pres.p. of lost v. *frequēre,* allied to *farcīre,* to cram, see FARCE (1)], *a.* Occurring often, common; repeated at short intervals; occurring near together, abundant; *crowded, thronging; *currently reported. *v.t.* (frė kwent′) To visit or resort to often or habitually. **frequentage,** *n.* Frequentation. **frequentation** (-tā′ shůn), *n.* **frequentative** (frė kwen′ tȧ tiv), *a.* (*Gram.*) Expressing frequent repetition of an action; *n.* A verb which expresses frequent repetition of an action. **frequenter** (frė kwen′ tėr), *n.* One who frequents. **frequently,** *adv.* Often, commonly, at frequent intervals; *populously. **frequentness,** *n.*

fresco (fres′ kō) [It., orig. adj. FRESH], *n.* (*pl.* **-coes**) A kind of water-colour painting on fresh plaster or on a wall covered with mortar not quite dry. *v.t.* To paint (a picture) or decorate (a wall, etc.) in fresco.

fresh (fresh) [A.-S. *fersc* (cp. Dut. *versch,* G. *frisch,* O.H.G. *frisc,* assim. to the cognate O.F. *fresche,* fem. of *freis*)], *a.* New; not known, met with, or used previously, recent; other, different; newly produced, not withered or faded, not stale, decayed, or tainted; pure, not salt, drinkable; (of butter) (*Am.* sweet); not preserved with salt, or by pickling, tinning, etc.; raw, inexperienced; just arrived (from); looking young or healthy; vividly and distinctly retained in the mind; refreshed, reinvigorated; frisky (of a horse); brisk, active, vigorous, fit; refreshing, reviving, cool (of air, a breeze, etc.); cheeky, impertinent, amorously impudent; quarrelsome. *adv.* Freshly (*esp. in comb.* as *fresh-blown*); recently; coolly, refreshingly; with fresh vigour. *n.* A freshet; a day of open weather; a freshwater river or spring; (*ellipt.*) the fresh part (of the day, season, etc.); (*Sc.*) a thaw, open weather; (*pl.*) the mingling of fresh and salt water in bays or rivers; the increased current of an ebb-tide caused by a flood of fresh water flowing into the sea. **v.t.* To refresh. **v.i.* To become fresher. **to have** or **gather fresh way:** (*Naut.*) To go at increased speed. **fresh-blown,** *a.* Newly flowering. **fresh-coloured,** *a.* Having a young-looking or ruddy complexion. **fresh fish,** *n.* (*slang*) A novice. **fresh-looking,** *a.* Appearing fresh. **freshman,** *n.* A novice, a beginner, esp. a student in his first term at a University. **freshmanship,** *n.* ***fresh-new,** *a.* Unpractised. **fresh-run,** *a.* Newly come up from the sea (of salmon, sea-trout, etc.). **freshwater,** *a.* Pertaining to, found in, or produced by fresh water; used to river or coasting trade, as a sailor; *raw, *unskilled. **fresh-watered,** *a.* Supplied with fresh water; newly watered. **freshen,** *v.t.* To make fresh; to enliven, to revive; to make less salty; (*Naut.*) to relieve (as a rope) by altering the position of a part subject to friction. *v.i.* To become fresh; to lose saltness; to become brisk, to gain strength; (of cattle) to come into milk. **fresher,** *n.* (*slang*) A freshman. **freshet,** *n.* A sudden flood caused by heavy rains or melted snow; *a freshwater stream. ***freshish,** *a.* **freshly,** *adv.* **freshness,** *n.*

fret (1) (fret) [A.-S. *fretan* (cp. Dut. *vreten,* G. *fressen*), from *ētan,* to EAT, with pref. *fra-,* FOR-], *v.t.* (*past & p.p.* **fretted**) To eat away, to corrode; to wear away, to rub or chafe; to make (a way or passage) by rubbing; to grieve, to repine; to be uneasy; to irritate, vex, annoy; to make rough or disturb (as water); *to devour. *v.i.* To be worn or eaten away; to be irritated, vexed, or troubled, to chafe; to be in a state of agitation or commotion; to flow in little waves or ripples; to make way by attrition or corrosion. *n.* The act or process of fretting or rubbing away; a spot abraded or corroded; an agitation of the surface of a fluid; (*fig.*) a state of chafing or vexation; (*Path.*) a chafing of the skin; herpes. **fretful,** *a.* Angry, peevish, irritable; captious. **fretfully,** *adv.* **fretfulness,** *n.* **fretty** (1), *a.*

fret (2) (fret) [prob. from O.F. *freten,* found in p.p. *frete,* adorned with interlaced work], *v.t.* To ornament, to decorate; to ornament (esp. a ceiling) with carved work; to variegate. *n.* Fretwork; ornamental work; an ornament formed by small bands or fillets intersecting each other at right angles, used in classical architecture; (*Her.*) a figure composed of bars crossed and interlaced. **fretsaw,** *n.* A small ribbon-saw used in cutting fretwork. **fretwork,** *n.* Carved or open woodwork in ornamental patterns and devices; a variegated pattern composed of interlacing lines of various patterns. **fretted (1),** *a.* Ornamented with fretwork; having raised or sunken ornamentation in rectangular forms; (*Her.*) applied to charges or ordinaries interlaced with each other. **fretty (2),** *a.* (*Her.*) Fretted.

fret (3) (fret) [etym. doubtful; perh. from O.F. *frete*, a ferrule], *n.* A small piece of wood or ivory placed upon the finger-board of certain stringed instruments to regulate the pitch of the notes. **v.t.* To put such a fret on a musical instrument. **fretted** (2), *a.*

Freudian (froi′ di ȧn) [Sigmund *Freud* (1856–1939)], *a.* (*Psych.*) Of or pertaining to the psychological theories of Freud.

friable (frī′ ȧ bėl) [F., from L. *friābilis*, from *friāre*, to rub, to crumble], *a.* Capable of being easily reduced to powder; readily crumbled. **friability** (-bil′ i ti), **friableness,** *n.*

friar (frī′ ȧr) [M.E. and O.F. *frere*, L. *frātrem*, nom. *frāter*, brother], *n.* One belonging to a monastic order, esp. one of the four mendicant orders, Augustinians or Austin Friars, Franciscans or Grey Friars, Dominicans or Black Friars, and Carmelites or White Friars; (*Print.*) a patch in a printed sheet that has not received the ink. **friar bird,** *n.* (*Austral.*) A honey-eater with bald head and neck. **friar's balsam,** *n.* A tincture of benzoin for application to ulcers and wounds. **friar's cowl,** *n.* The wake-robin, *Arum Arisarum, A. maculatum.* **friar's lantern,** *n.* The ignis fatuus. **friarlike, -ly,** *a.* **friary,** *n.* A monastery of a mendicant order.

fribble (frib′ ėl) [prob onomat.], *v.i.* To act frivolously; *to totter. *v.t* To waste or trifle (away); (*Sc.*) to frizzle. *a.* Frivolous, silly. *n.* A trifler; a frivolous, contemptible fellow. **fribbledom,** *n.* **fribbler,** *n.* **fribblish,** *a.*

fricandeau (frik′ ȧn dō) [F., etym. unknown], *n.* A cutlet of veal or other meat, fried or stewed, and served with sauce. *v.t.* To make into a fricandeau.

fricassee (frik ȧ sē′) [F. *fricassée*, orig. fem. p.p. of *fricasser*, etym. unknown], *n.* A dish of birds, rabbits, or other small animals, cut into pieces, fried or stewed, and served with sauce. *v.t.* To cook as a fricassee.

fricative (frik′ ȧ tiv) [L. *fricāre*, to rub, -ATIVE], *n.* A consonant, such as *f, sh, th,* produced by the friction of the breath issuing through a narrow opening. *a.* Produced by this friction.

friction (frik′ shůn) [F., from L. *frictiōnem*, nom. *frictio*, from *fricāre*, to rub], *n.* The act of rubbing two bodies together; (*Phys.*) resistance which any body meets with in moving over another body; (*fig.*) conflict, disagreement, lack of harmony; (*Med.*) chafing or rubbing a part of the body to promote circulation. **friction-balls,** *n.pl.* Balls placed in bearings to relieve friction. **friction-clutch, -cone, -coupling, -gear, -gearing,** *n.* Contrivances for applying or disconnecting parts of machinery by the use of friction. **friction-rollers,** *n.pl.* A bearing formed of two rollers. **friction-wheel,** *n.* One whose motion is caused by the friction of a moving body, or which communicates motion by frictional contact. **frictional,** *a.* **frictionally,** *adv.* **frictionless,** *a.*

Friday (frī′ dā, -di) [A.-S. *frīge- dæg* (cp. O.H.G. *Frīatag*, G. *Freitag*)], *n.* The sixth day of the week, dedicated by Teutonic peoples to Frig, the wife of Odin, as a translation of the late L. *dies Veneris*, day of the planet Venus. **Black Friday:** A Friday that is the anniversary of a noted calamity, as that of the Young Pretender's advance to Derby on 6th Dec. 1745, and those of various financial panics in New York. **Good Friday:** The Friday before Easter, kept sacred by the Christian Church in memory of the Crucifixion.

fridge, frig, frij (frij), abbrev. REFRIGERATOR.

fried, *past* and *p.p.* [FRY].

friend (frend) [A.-S. *frēond*, cp. Dut. *vriend*, G. *freund*, Goth. *frijōnds*, pres.p. of *frijōn*, to love (cp. A.-S. *frēon, frēogan*, see FREE (1 and 2))], *n.* One attached to another by intimacy and affection, as distinguished from sexual love or family relationship; an acquaintance; one of the same nation or party, one who is not an enemy; one on the same side, an adherent, a sympathizer, a patron or promoter (of a cause, institution, etc.); a member of the Society of Friends; (*fig.*) anything that helps one, esp. in an emergency; a term of salutation; (*pl.*) one's near relations; *a lover. **v.t.* To befriend. **a friend at court:** One who has influence to help another. **Society of Friends:** A religious sect (commonly called Quakers), founded by George Fox in the seventeenth century, who object to taking oaths, believe the sacraments of baptism and the Lord's Supper to be symbols, and that there is an Inner Light of God in every man. **to make friends:** To become intimate or reconciled (with). ***friended,** *a.* Having friends (*esp. in comb.*, as *well-friended*). **friendling,** *n.* Friendliness. **friendless,** *a.* **friendlessness,** *n.* ***friendlike,** *a.* **friendly,** *a.* Having the disposition of a friend, good-natured; acting as a friend; characteristic of friends or of kindly feeling; amicable, not hostile; favourable, propitious. *adv.* In the manner of a friend. *n.pl.* Natives belonging to a friendly tribe. **friendly society,** *n.* A society for the purpose of mutual assurance against sickness, distress, or old age. **friendly suit,** *n.* (*Law*) A suit instituted between two parties not at variance to obtain a judicial decision upon a certain point. **friendlily,** *adv.* **friendliness,** *n.* **friendship,** *n.* Mutual attachment between persons as distinguished from sexual and family affection; the state of being friends; an act of personal kindness or goodwill; *aptness to unite or combine.

frieze (1) (frēz) [F. *frise* (cp. Sp. *friso*), perh. from It. *fregio*, a fringe, L. *Phrygium* (*opus*), Phrygian (work)], *n.* The middle division of an entablature, between the architrave and the cornice, usu. enriched by sculpture; the band of sculpture occupying this; a horizontal band or strip, either plain or decorated, elsewhere in a wall. **frieze-panel,** *n.* One of the upper panels of a six-panel door.

frieze (2) (frēz) [F. *frise* (in *drap de frise*, cloth of Friesland, from Dut. *Vries*, a Frieslander)], *n.* A coarse woollen cloth, with a rough nap on one side. **friezed,** *a.* Made rough like the nap of frieze.

frigate (frig′ ȧt) [M.F. *fregate*, It. *fregata*, etym. doubtful], *n.* A warship of the period *c.* 1650–1840, next in size and strength to a line-of-battle ship, having a main deck usu. carrying from twenty-eight to forty-four guns, and a raised quarter-deck and forecastle; a steam warship of considerably larger size and strength which preceded the ironclad; (*loosely*) a cruiser; a frigate-bird; a corvette, small destroyer; *a light, swift vessel, propelled by oars and sails, also a larger sailing vessel. **frigate-bird,** *n.* A large tropical raptorial bird, *Tachypetes aquilus*, of great swiftness, usu. found at sea near land. **frigate-built,** *a.* (*Naut.*) Having a quarter-deck and forecastle raised above the main-deck.

frigatoon (frig ȧ toon′) [It. *fregatone*, as prec.], *n.* A Venetian vessel with a square stern, and only a main- and mizzen-mast.

fright (frīt) [A.-S. *fyrhto*, cogn. with *forht*, afraid, cp. O.S. *foroht, forht*, G. *furcht*], *n.* Sudden and violent fear or alarm; a state of terror; one who presents a ridiculous appearance in person or dress. **v.t.* To frighten. **frighten,** *v.t.* To throw into a state of fright; to alarm, terrify, scare; to drive (away, out of, or into) by fright. **frightful,** *a.* Dreadful, fearful, shocking; horrible, hideous, very disagreeable; causing fright; (*colloq.*) awful, extraordinary. **frightfully,** *adv.* **frightfulness,** *n.* **frightsome,** *a.*

frigid (frij′ id) [L. *frīgidus*, from *frīgēre*, to be cold, from *frīgus*, cold], *a.* Cold; wanting heat or warmth; (*fig.*) lacking warmth of feeling or ardour; stiff, formal, forbidding; without animation or spirit, dull, flat; sexually unemotional. **frigid**

zones, *n.pl.* The parts of the earth between the Arctic Circle and the North Pole and the Antarctic Circle and the South Pole. **frigidity** (fri jid′ i ti), *n.* The state of being frigid; (*Psych.*) the decrease or absence in a woman of sexual response. **frigidly,** *adv.* **frigidness,** *n.*

frigidarium (frij i dâr′ i ŭm) [L., from *frīgidus*, cold], *n.* The cooling-room in a Roman bath; the cold bath itself.

frigorific (frig or if′ ik) [F. *frigorifique*, L. *frīgorificus*, from L. *frīgus -oris*, cold], *a.* (*Phys.*) Producing cold, from an old theory that cold is due to an imponderable substance called *frigoric* (cp. CALORIC.)

frij [REFRIGERATOR].

frijole (frē hōl′, -chōl′) [Mex.], *n.* A Mexican bean, resembling the kidney-bean.

frill (fril) [etym. doubtful; acc. to Skeat prob. from L.G. (cp. W.Flem. *frul*, *frulle*, Swed. dial. *fräll*, *fröll*)], *n.* A pleated or fluted edging, as of linen on the bosom of a shirt; a ruffle, a flounce; a ruff or frill-like fringe of hair, feather, etc., on an animal, bird, or plant; (*colloq., pl.*) airs, affectations, finery, frippery; (*Phot.*) the puckering of a film at the edge of a negative. *v.t.* (*past & p.p.* **frilled**) To furnish with a frill; to serve as a frill to. *v.i.* (*Phot.*) To pucker at the edge of a plate (of film). **frilled,** *a.* Furnished with a frill or frills. **frillery,** *n.* A quantity or mass of frills; frills taken collectively. **frilling,** *n.*

fringe (frinj) [O.F. *frenge* (F. *frange*), L. *fimbria*], *n.* An ornamental border to dress or furniture, consisting of loose threads or tassels; a border, an edging; the front hair cut short with a straight edge along the forehead; (*Bot.*) a row of long filiform processes; (*Zool.*) a border of hairs or other processes; (*Opt.*) one of the coloured bands seen when a beam of light is transmitted through a slit. *v.t.* To border with or as with a fringe. **fringe-flower,** *n.* The genus *Schizanthus*, cultivated plants from Chile with beautiful fringed and coloured flowers. **fringe-like,** *a.* **fringe-net,** *n.* A net, usu. made of hair, for confining a woman's hair. **fringing,** *n.* **fringeless,** *a.* **fringy,** *a.*

fringilla (frin jil′ ă) [L.], *n.* A genus of small singing birds, containing the finches. **fringillaceous** (-lā′ shŭs), *a.*

frippery (frip′ ĕr i) [O.F. *freperie*, from *frepe*, a rag, prob. from L. *fibra*, FIBER], *n.* Worthless, needless, or trumpery adornments; tawdry finery; mere display; knick-knacks, gewgaws; old clothes; second-hand furniture; a shop or mart for old clothes; trade in old clothes. **fripper, -perer,** *n.* A dealer in old clothes.

frisette (fri zet′) [F., from *friser*, to FRIZZ], *n.* A front or band of artificial curls worn on the forehead.

friseur (frē zĕr′) [F., as prec.], *n.* A hairdresser. ***frisure** (frē zūr′), *n.* Hairdressing.

Frisian (friz′ i ăn) [L. *Frisii*, pl., O.Fris. *Frise*], *a.* Of, pertaining to, or native of Friesland. *n.* The language of Friesland; (*pl.*) the people of Friesland.

frisk (frisk) [from obs. adj. *frisk*, O.F. *frisque*, lively, O.H.G. *frisc*, FRESH], *v.i.* To leap, skip, or gambol about; to frolic. *v.t.* (*Am. slang*) To search a person for fire-arms. *n.* A gambol, a frolic. **frisker,** *n.* One who frisks; (*slang*) a pilferer. **friskful,** *a.* **frisky,** *a.* **friskily,** *adv.* **friskiness,** *n.*

frisket (fris′ kĕt) [F. *frisquette*], *n.* (*Print.*) The light frame by which a sheet of paper to be printed is held in place.

frit (frit) [F. *fritte*, It. *fritta*, fem. p.p. of *friggere*, to FRY], *n.* A calcined mixture of sand and fluxes ready to be melted in a crucible to form glass; applied to other vitreous compositions used in manufactures. *v.t.* To expose to dull red heat so as to decompose and fuse.

frit-fly (frit′ flī) [etym. unknown], *n.* A small fly that arrests the growth of wheat by boring into the bud.

frith (1) [FIRTH].

***frith** (2) (frith) [A.-S. *frith*, *frithu* (cp. Dut. *vrede*, O.H.G. *fridu*, G. *friede*)], *n.* Peace. **frith-stool,** *n.* (*Eccles. Ant.*) A seat near the altar which was the most sacred refuge for those claiming sanctuary.

***frith** (3) (frith) [M.E., from A.-S. *gefyrhthe*, etym. doubtful], *n.* A forest for game; ground covered with underwood; a small field taken out of a common.

fritillary (frit′ i lăr i, fri til′ ă ri) [late L. *fritillāria*, from L. *fritillus*, a dice-box], *n.* The liliaceous genus *Fritillaria*, esp. *F. meleagris*, with flowers speckled with dull purple; a butterfly of the genus *Argynnis*, from their wings being marked like this flower.

fritter (1) (frit′ ĕr) [O.F. *friture*, L. *frictus*, p.p. of *frīgere*, to FRY], *n.* A light batter usually containing slices of fruit; (*pl.*) fenks.

fritter (2) (frit′ ĕr) [etym. doubtful; perh. from obs. *fitters*, n.pl., cogn. with G. *fetzen*, a rag, a scrap; or from O.F. *fretura*, L. *fractūra*, FRACTURE; or from prec.], *n.* (*pl.*) Fragments, bits, shreds. *v.t.* To break into small pieces. **to fritter away:** To waste in trifles.

frivolous (friv′ ŏ lŭs) [L. *frīvolus*, prob. cogn. with *friāre*, *fricāre*, to rub], *a.* Trifling, trumpery, of little or no moment; inclined to unbecoming levity or trifling, silly. **frivol,** *v.i.* (*colloq.*) To trifle. *v.t.* To trifle (away). **frivolity** (fri vol′ i ti), *n.* **frivolously,** *adv.* **frivolousness,** *n.*

***frize** [FRIEZE (2)].

frizz (friz) [F. *friser*, from *frise*, FRIEZE (2)], *v.t.* To curl, to crisp; to form into a curly, crinkled mass (of hair); to raise a nap on (of cloth). *n.* Frizzed hair, a mass or row of curls. **frizzy,** *a.*

frizzle (1) (friz′ ĕl) [etym. doubtful, older than but probl. conn. with prec.], *v.t.* To curl, to crisp. *n.* A curled or crisped lock of hair; frizzed hair.

frizzle (2) (friz′ ĕl) [prob. from earlier *frizz*, imit. adaptation of FRY], *v.t.* To fry (bacon, etc.) with a hissing noise. *v.i.* To make a hissing noise while being fried.

fro (frō) [Icel. *frā*, FROM; cp. A.-S. *fram*], *adv.* Away, backward. **to and fro:** Forward and backward.

frock (frok) [F. *froc*, prob. from late L. *frocus*, *floccus*, FLOCK (2)], *n.* The long upper garment worn by monks; a loose garment, formerly a loose over-garment worn by men, now a gown worn by women or children; a woman's dress; a frock-coat; a military coat of similar shape; a smock-frock; a woollen tunic or guernsey worn by sailors. **frock-coat,** *n.* A close-fitting body-coat, with broad skirts of the same length before and behind. **frocked,** *a.* **frocking,** *n.* Material for smock-frocks. ***frockless,** *a.*

Froebel (frĕr′ bĕl) [F. W. A. *Froebel* (1782–1852)]. The Froebel System, a form of kindergarten in which the child's senses are developed by handwork, etc.

frog (1) (frog) [A.-S. *frogga*, *frox* (cp. Icel. *froskr*, G. *frosch*)], *n.* An amphibious animal of any species of the genus *Rana*, esp. *R. temporaria*, the common frog, which abounds in all parts of Britain. **frog-bit,** *n.* A small aquatic plant, *Hydrocharis morsusranæ*. **frog-eater,** *n.* A contemptuous name for a Frenchman. **frog-fish,** *n.* The angler, *Lophius piscatorius*, and other fish. **froghopper,** *n.* A genus of small insects, remarkable for their leaping powers, living on plants. **frogman,** *n.* Diver equipped for under-water operations. **frog's-march,** *n.* A way of carrying a man face downwards by four men each holding a limb (sometimes employed by the police with violent drunken men). **frog-mouth,** *n.* (*Austral.*) A bird of the mopoke family, a variety of goat-sucker. **frog-spawn,** *n.* The spawn of the frog; certain freshwater algæ. **froggery,** *n.* A place where frogs are kept or abound. **froggy,** *a.* Abounding with frogs.

frog (2) (frog) [Port. *froco*, L. *floccus*, FLOCK (2)], *n.* A spindle-shaped button or toggle used for fastening military cloaks and undress coats, ladies' mantles, etc.; the loop of a scabbard. **frogged,** *a.*

frog (3) (frog) [etym. unknown; perh. corr. of FORK], *n.* A tender horny substance in the middle of the sole of a horse's foot.

frog (4) (frog) [etym. doubtful; perh. corr. of FORK], *n.* A solid piece of iron forming the portion of a railway track where lines cross or diverge, grooved so as to make the line continuous.

frolic (frol' ik) [prob. from M.Dut. *vrolick* (Dut. *vrolijk*), cp. *fröhlich* (*vrō-* or *froh-*, merry, joyous, -LIKE)], *a.* Gay, merry, sportive; full of pranks. *n.* A wild prank; an outburst of gaiety and mirth; a merry-making. *v.i.* To play pranks; to frisk; to indulge in merry-making. ***frolicful,** *a.* **frolicsome,** *a.* **frolicsomely,** *adv.* **frolicsomeness,** *n.* ***frolicky,** *a.*

from (from) [A.-S. *from*, *fram* (cp. Icel. *frā*, FRO, O.S. and O.H.G. *fram*, Goth. *framis*), orig. forward], *prep.* Away, out of (expressing separation, departure, point of view, distinction, or variation); beginning with, after (expressing the starting-point or lower limit in time or space); by means of, because of, by reason of (expressing instrumentality, cause, reason, or motive). **from out:** Out from, forth from. **from time to time:** At intervals, now and then. *adv. phrases.* **from above, from afar, from amidst, from among, from behind, from beneath, from beyond, from far, from high, from hence, from long ago, from off, from out of, from under, from where, from within, from without.** ***fromward** [A.-S. *framweard*], *prep.* From, away from.

frond (frond) [L. *frons -ndis*, a leaf], *n.* (*Bot.*) A leaf-like expansion in which the functions of stem and foliage are not entirely differentiated, often bearing the organs of fructification, as in many cryptogams, esp. the ferns; (*Zool.*) a leaf-like expansion, as in many zoophytes. **frondage,** *n.* ***frondesce,** *v.i.* To come into leaf. **frondescence,** *n.* **frondescent,** *a.* **frondiferous** (fron dif' ėr ůs), *a.* **frondlet,** *n.* **frondose** (fron dōs'), **frondous** (fron' důs), *a.*

Fronde (frond) [F., lit. a sling], *n.* (*Fr. Hist.*) The name given to a party (1648–57) who attacked Mazarin and the Court during the minority of Louis XIV; any party of malcontents. **Frondeur** (fron dur') [F.], *n.* A member of the Fronde; an opponent of the government, an irreconcilable.

front (frŭnt) [O.F., from L. *frontem*, nom. *frons*, the forehead], *n.* The forehead, *the face; (*fig.*) visage, countenance, assurance, effrontery; the forepart of anything; the most conspicuous part; a position directly before the face of a person or the foremost part of a thing; false hair or curls worn over the forehead; the part of a man's shirt covering the breast, a dicky; (*Meteor.*) the line of separation at the earth's surface between warm and cold air masses; (*Arch.*) a face of a building, esp. the principal face, usu. that containing the main entrance; (*Theat.*) the auditorium; (*Mil.*) the most advanced line or part of an army, the line of battle, the part of the field towards the enemy, the ground on which fighting is going on, the direction in which a line of troops faces; *the beginning, the first part. *a.* Relating to or situated in or at the front. *v.t.* To stand or be situated opposite to; to face, to look (to or towards); to confront, to meet face to face, to oppose; to furnish with a front. *v.i.* To face, to look, to be situated with the front (towards); *to be foremost; *to be opposed. **front!** (*Mil.*) word of command for men to turn to the front. **in front of:** Before; in advance of. **to come to the front:** To take a prominent position. **two-pair front:** A second-floor room in the front of a house. **frontsman,** *n.* A salesman standing in front of a shop. **front bench,** *n.* The foremost bench in either house of Parliament, assigned to ministers or ex-ministers. **front door,** *n.* The principal entrance to a building. **front box,** *n.* A box in a theatre from which there is a direct view on to the stage. **front piece,** *n.* (*Theat.*) A small play acted in front of the curtain. **front room,** *n.* A room in the front of a house. **fronted,** *a.* Formed with a front, as troops. **frontless,** *a.* Without a front; *full of effrontery, shameless. **frontward,** *a.* and *adv.* **frontwards,** *adv.*

frontage (frŭn' tij), *n.* The front part of a building; the extent of this; land between this and a road; land facing a road or water; the direction in which anything faces. **frontager,** *n.* The owner of a frontage, one who lives on the frontier.

frontal (frŭn' tål), *a.* Situated on or pertaining to the front; (*Anat.*) belonging to the forehead. *n.* (*Arch.*) A small pediment over a door or window; an ornamental hanging or panel in front of an altar; (*Med.*) a bandage or application for the forehead. **frontal attack.** An attack on the front of an army, distinguished from a flank attack.

frontate, frontated (frŭn' tåt, frŭn tā' ted), *a.* (*Bot.*) Increasing in breadth.

frontier (frun'-, fron' tēr) [O.F., late L. *frontēria*, *-tāria*, as prec.], *n.* That part of a country which fronts or borders upon another; *an outwork. *a.* Pertaining to or situated on the frontier. **v.i.* To lie on the frontier. **v.t.* To surround as a frontier; to oppose, to bar the advance of. **frontiersman,** *n.*

Frontignac (fron tin yăk') [erroneously for *Frontignan*], *n.* A muscat wine made at Frontignan, in the department of Hérault, France.

frontispiece (frŭn' tis pēs) [F. *frontispice*, late L. *frontispicium*, (*frons -ntis*, the forehead, *specere*, to look), assim. to PIECE], *n.* A picture fronting the title-page of a book; (*Arch.*) a façade, a decorated front or chief entrance; (*slang*) the face. *v.t.* To furnish with, to serve or put as, or to supply a frontispiece (to a book).

frontlet (frŭnt' let), *n.* A small band or fillet worn on the forehead, a phylactery; the forehead in birds.

fronto- [L. *frons -ntis*, the forehead], *comb. form.* (*Anat.*) Pertaining to the forehead, the frontal bone, or the frontal region.

fronton (frŭn' tǒn) [F., from It. *frontone*, as prec.], *n.* A pediment; a frontal.

***frore** (frôr) [A.-S. *froren*, p.p. of *frēosan*, to FREEZE], *a.* Frozen, frosty. *adv.* Frostily, keenly. ***frory,** *a.*

frost (frost) [A.-S. *forst* (cp. Dut. *vorst*, Dan., Swed., and G. *frost*); cogn. with FREEZE], *n.* The act or state of freezing, the congelation of fluids by the abstraction of heat; temperature below freezing-point; the state of the atmosphere that produces freezing; frosty weather; minute crystals of frozen dew or vapour, rime or hoar frost; (*fig.*) frigidity; (*slang*) a disappointment, a fiasco, a 'fraud.' *v.t.* To injure by frost; to cover with or as with rime; to sharpen (as the nails of a horse's shoes) in frosty weather; (*fig.*) to cover with anything like frost, to whiten (as the hair). **black-frost,** *n.* Frost without rime. **degrees of frost:** (*with number*) Degrees below freezing-point. **Jack Frost:** Frost personified. **white frost:** Frost with rime. **frost-bite,** *n.* Inflammation often resulting in gangrene, usu. of the extremities, caused by exposure to extreme cold. **frost-bitten,** *a.* **frost-bound,** *a.* Confined by frost. **frost-fish,** *n.* (*Austral.*, *N. Zealand*) A variety of thin, edible scabbard fish. **frost-nail,** *n.* A projecting nail driven into a horse's shoe to prevent slipping in frosty weather. **frost-work,** *n.* The figures formed by frost on glass, etc. **frosted,** *a.* Covered with frost or any substance resembling frost; damaged by frost. **frosting,** *n.* A mixture of powdered loaf-sugar and white of egg, used to cover cakes; a rough, granulated surface produced on glass, metal, etc., in imitation of frost. **frostless,** *a.* **frosty,** *a.* Producing frost; excessively cold; attended with frost; affected or injured by frost; covered with or as with rime; (*fig.*) cool or frigid in disposition. ***frosty-spirited,** *a.* Tame, spiritless. **frostily,** *adv.* **frostiness,** *n.*

froth (frawth, froth) [cogn. with Icel. *frotha* (cp. A.-S. *āfrēothan, to froth*)], *n.* Foam, spume, the mass of small bubbles caused in liquors by agitation or fermentation; foamy excretion, scum; (*fig.*) empty display of wit or rhetoric; light, unsubstantial matter. *v.t.* To cause to foam; to cover with froth. *v.i.* To form or emit froth. **frothless,** *a.* **frothsome,** *a.* **frothy,** *a.* **frothily,** *adv.* **frothiness,** *n.*

frou-frou (froo' froo) [F., imit.], *n.* A rustling, as of a silk dress.

***frounce** (frouns) [O.F. *froncir*, see FLOUNCE], *v.t.* To form into folds or wrinkles; to curl, to crisp; to trim with flounces. *v.i.* To frown. *n.* A wrinkle, a plait, a fold, a flounce; a disease in hawks.

frow (frou) [Dut. *vrouw*, cp. FRAU], *n.* A Dutchwoman.

froward (frō' wărd) [M.E. *fraward*], *a.* Not willing to comply, refractory, perverse, mutinous; *adverse, untoward. **prep.* (also **frowards**) Away from. **adv.* Away. **frowardly,** *adv.* **frowardness,** *n.*

frown (froun) [O.F. *frongnier* (cp. F. *renfrogner, refrogner*), from Teut. (cp. Swed. dial. *fryna*, to make a wry face)], *v.i.* To express displeasure or seriousness by contracting the brows; to look gloomy, threatening, or with disfavour; to scowl, to lower; to manifest displeasure (at or upon). *v.t.* To repress, repel, or rebuke with a frown; to express with a frown. *n.* A knitting of the brows in displeasure or mental absorption; (*fig.*) any sign of displeasure. **frowningly,** *adv.*

frowst (froust) [etym. unknown], *n.* Stuffiness; an unwholesome smell (in a room). **frowsty,** *a.*

frowzy (frou' zi) [etym. doubtful], *a.* Musty, fusty, close; slovenly, unkempt, dirty. **frowziness,** *n.*

froze, *past,* **frozen,** *p.p.* [FREEZE].

Fructidor (frŭk' ti dôr) [F., from L. *frūctus*, fruit, Gr. *dōron*, gift], *n.* The name given in the French revolutionary calendar to the twelfth month of the republican year (18 Aug. to 16 Sept.); the *coup d'état* that occurred in Fructidor 1797.

fructify (frŭk' ti fī) [F. *fructifier*, L. *fructificāre* (*fructus*, FRUIT, *-ficāre*, *facere*, to make)], *v.t.* To make fruitful or productive; to fertilize. *v.i.* To bear fruit. **fructiferous** (frŭk tif' ėr ŭs) [-FEROUS], *a.* Bearing fruit. **fructification** (-kā' shŭn), *n.* The act or process of fructifying; (*Bot.*) the organs of reproduction; the fruit and its parts. **fructiform,** *a.* **fructose,** *n.* Fruit-sugar. ***fructuary,** *a.* (*Rom. Law*) Of or pertaining to usufruct. *n.* One who enjoys the produce, fruits, or profits of anything. **fructuate,** *v.i.* To bear fruit, to come to fruit. **fructuation,** *n.* Coming to fruit; fruition. **fructule,** *n.* (*Bot.*) A drupel, or part of a compound fruit. **fructuous,** *a.* Fruitful, fertile.

frugal (froo' găl) [L. *frūgālis*, from *frūgi*, dat. of *frux*, fruit, profit], *a.* Thrifty, sparing; not profuse or lavish; economical in the use or expenditure of food, money, etc. **frugality** (frŭ găl' i ti), *n.* Economy, thrift; a sparing use of anything. **frugally,** *adv.*

***frugiferous** (frŭ jif' ėr ŭs) [L. *frūgifer*], *a.* Bearing fruit, fruitful. **frugivorous,** *a.* Feeding on fruit.

fruit (froot) [O.F., from L. *fructum*, nom. *-us*, from *fruī*, to enjoy], *n.* The edible succulent product of a plant or tree in which the seeds are enclosed; (*Bot.*) the matured ovary or seed-vessel with other parts adhering thereto; the spores of cryptogams; (*pl.*) the vegetable products yielded by the earth, serving for food to man and the lower animals; (*Bibl.*) offspring; (*fig., sing.* or *pl.*) product, result, or consequence, benefit, profit. *v.i.* To bear fruit. *v.t.* To cause to produce fruit. **fruit-bearer,** *n.* A tree or plant which produces fruit. **fruit-bearing,** *a.* **fruit-bud,** *n.* A bud which produces fruit. **fruit-cake,** *n.* A cake containing currants, etc. **fruit-clipper,** *n.* A swift sailing-vessel carrying fruit. **fruit-knife,** *n.* A knife with a silver blade for paring and cutting fruit. **fruit machine,** *n.* A coin-in-the-slot gaming device employing coloured balls. **fruit-piece,** *n.* A picture of fruit. **fruit salad,** *n.* A mixture of fruits cut up and sweetened. **fruit-spur,** *n.* A small branch the growth of which is arrested for the development of fruit-buds. **fruit-sugar,** *n.* Lævulose, fructose, or glucose, obtained from fruit or honey. **fruit-tree,** *n.* A tree cultivated for its fruit. **fruitage,** *n.* **fruitarian** (froo târ' i ăn), *n.* One that feeds on fruit. **fruiter,** *n.* A tree that bears; a fruit-ship; (*Am.*) a fruit-grower. **fruiterer,** *n.* One who deals in fruits. ***fruitery,** *n.* Fruit; a fruit crop; a fruit-loft. **fruitful,** *a.* Producing fruit in abundance; productive, fertile; bearing children, prolific. **fruitfully,** *adv.* **fruitfulness,** *n.* **fruiting,** *a.* Bearing fruit. **fruitless,** *a.* Not bearing fruit; unsuccessful, unprofitable, useless, vain, idle. **fruitlessly,** *adv.* **fruitlessness,** *n.* **fruitlet,** *n.* (*Bot.*) A drupel. **fruity,** *a.* Like fruit, in taste, etc.; (of wine) tasting of the grape; rich, full-flavoured. **fruitiness,** *n.*

fruition (froo ish' ŭn) [O.F. from *fruitiōnem*, nom. *-tio*, from *fruī*, to enjoy (cp. FRUIT)], *n.* Attainment, fulfilment; pleasure or satisfaction derived from attainment of a desire. **fruitive** (froo' i tiv), *a.* Pertaining to fruition; able to enjoy.

***frumentaceous** (froo mėn tā' shŭs) [L. *frūmentāceus*, from *frūmentum*, corn], *a.* Of the nature of, resembling, or composed of wheat or other cereal. ***frumentarious,** *a.* [Lat.] Of or pertaining to corn. ***frumentation,** *n.* (*Rom. Ant.*) A gift or largess of corn to the Roman people.

frumenty (froo' mėn ti) [O.F. *frumentée*, from *frument*, L. *frumentum*, as prec.], *n.* A dish made of wheat boiled in milk and flavoured with spices.

frump (frŭmp) [etym. doubtful], *n.* An old-fashioned, prim, or dowdy-looking woman; *a sneer, a flout; *a lie. **v.t.* To mock, to jeer; to snub. **frumpish,** *a.* **frumpy,** *a.*

***frush** (1) (frŭsh) [O.F. *fruissier* (F. *froisser*), to break in pieces, from L. *frustum*, a fragment], *v.t.* To batter, to smash; to knock down. *v.i.* To rush. *n.* A rush, an onset, an encounter; a noise, as of violent collision; splinters, fragments. *a.* (*Sc.*) Easily broken, brittle.

***frush** (2) (frŭsh) [prob. from A.-S. *frosc*, frog], *n.* A frog in a horse's foot; a discharge of fetid matter therefrom.

frustrate (frŭs trāt', frŭs' trāt) [L. *frustrātus*, p.p. of *frustrārī*, from *frustrā*, in vain], *v.t.* To make of no avail; to defeat, to thwart, to balk; to nullify, to disappoint. *a.* (frŭs' trāt) Vain; of no effect. **frustration** (-trā' shŭn), *n.* ***frustrative** (frus' tră tiv), *a.* ***frustratory,** *a.*

frustule (frŭs' tūl) [F., from late L. *frustulum*, dim. of foll.], *n.* (*Bot.*) The covering or shell, usu. in two valves, of a diatom.

frustum (frŭs' tŭm) [L., a fragment], *n.* (*pl.* **-ta**) The part of a regular solid next the base formed by cutting off the top; the part of a solid between two planes.

frutex (froo' tėks) [L.], *n.* (*Bot.*) A woody plant smaller than a tree, a shrub. **frutescent** (froo tes' ėnt), *a.* Shrubby. **frutescence,** *n.* **fruticose** (froo ti kōs'), *a.* (*Bot.*) Of the nature of a shrub, shrubby; (*Zool.*) shrub-like in appearance (as certain zoophytes). **fruticetum** (-sē' tŭm), *n.* An arboretum for fruit-trees and shrubs. **fruticulose** (froo tik' ū lōs), *a.* Resembling or branching like a small shrub.

***frutify** (froo' ti fī) [Shak., humorous word, *Merchant of Venice*, ii, 2], *v.i.* To notify.

fry (1) (frī) [O.F. *frire*, L. *frigere*, cp. Gr. *phrugein*, to parch], *v.t.* To cook with fat in a pan over the fire. *v.i.* To be cooked in a frying-pan; *to boil; *to ferment. *n.* A dish of anything fried; the liver, lights, heart, etc., of pigs, sheep, calves, and oxen; (*fig.*) a state of worry, agitation, or excitement. **fryer,** *n.* A vessel for frying fish. **frying-pan,** *n.* A shallow metal pan with a long handle, in which food is fried. **out of the frying-pan into the fire:** Out of one trouble into a worse.

fry (2) (frī) [cp. Icel. *friō*, Dan. and Swed. *frō*], *n.* Young fish, esp. those fresh from the spawn, also yearling salmon; a swarm of children, a quantity of trifling objects. **small fry:** Unimportant, insignificant, people.

fub [FOB].

fubby, fubsy (fŭb′ i, -zi) [from obs. *fub*, chubby, onomat.], *a.* Fat, squat.

fuchsia (fū′ shȧ) [L. *Fuchs*, German botanist (1501–1566)], *n.* A genus of garden plants with pendulous funnel-shaped flowers. **fuchsine** (fook′ sin) [from prec., owing to resemblance to flower], *n.* A magenta dye of the rosaniline series.

fucus (fū′ kŭs) [L., rock-lichen, red dye, rouge], *n.* (pl. **-ci**, -sī) A genus of algæ, containing some of the commonest seaweeds; any species of this genus; *a paint, a dye; (*fig.*) deceptive show. **fucivorous** (fū siv′ ȯr ŭs), *a.* Feeding on seaweed (used of the sirenians). **fucoid** (-koid), *a.* Resembling a fucus. *n.* A fossil plant, like a fucus. **fucoidal** (-koi′ dȧl), *a.*

fud (fŭd) [Sc. and North., etym. obscure], *n.* A hare's scut; the buttocks; (*Manufact.*) woollen waste.

fuddle (fŭd′ ėl) [cp. L.G. *fuddeln*, to work lazily], *v.t.* To make stupid with drink, to intoxicate; (*fig.*) to stupefy, to make stupid. *v.i.* To tipple, to get drunk. *n.* A drinking bout; the state of being muddled; *drink. **fuddler,** *n.* A drunkard, a sot.

fuddy-duddy (fŭd′ i dŭd′ i), *n.* (*colloq.*) An old fogy; a carper.

fudge (1) (fŭj) [onomat.], *int.* Nonsense, stuff, humbug. *n.* Nonsense; a made-up or nonsensical story; a soft confection of chocolate, candy, etc.

fudge (2) (fŭj) [etym. doubtful; perh. var. of FADGE], *v.t.* To patch or make up, to fake; to contrive in a makeshift, careless way. *v.i.* To work in this manner. *n.* (*Print.*) An attachment on rotary machines for the insertion of a small form giving an item of late news. **fudgy,** *a.*

fuel (fū′ ėl) [A.-F. *fewaile*, O.F. *fouaille*, low L. *focālia*, neut. pl. of *focālis*, from *focus*, a hearth], *n.* Combustible matter, such as wood, coal, peat, etc., for fires; (*fig.*) anything which serves to feed or increase passion or excitement. *v.t.* (*past & p.p.* **fuelled**) To supply or store with fuel. *v.i.* To get fuel. ***fueller,** *n.* **fuelless,** *a.* **fuelling,** *n.* Fuel, firing.

fuero (fwâr′ ō) [Sp., L. *forum*, see FORUM], *n.* (*Sp. Hist.*) A code, charter, grant of privileges, or custom having the force of law; a tribunal or a place where justice is administered.

fuff (fŭf) [Sc., onomat.], *n.* A puff, a whiff; a huff, an ebullition of temper; the spitting of a cat. *v.t.* To puff, to whiff. **fuffy,** *a.* Puffy, light.

fug (fŭg), *n.* The close atmosphere of an unventilated room. **fuggy,** *a.*

fugacious (fū gā′ shŭs) [L. *fugax -ācis*, from *fugere*, to flee], *a.* Fleeting, lasting but a short time, transitory, ephemeral; (*Bot.*) falling off early. ***fugaciousness,** *n.* **fugacity** (fū găs′ i ti), *n.* Fleetingness, transience; (*Chem.*) the tendency to expand or escape.

fugal (fū′ gȧl) [FUGUE, -AL], *n.* Pertaining to or of the nature of a fugue. **fugally,** *adv.*

fugato [FUGUE].

-fuge [L. *-fugus*, from *fugere*, to flee, but altered in meaning to *fugāre*, to put to flight], *suf.* (*Med.*) Expelling, driving out, as in *febrifuge*.

fugitive (fū′ ji tiv) [F. *fugitif -ve*, L. *fugitīvus*, from *fugere*, to flee], *a.* Fleeing, running away, having taken flight, runaway; transient, not stable or durable, volatile, easily wafted or carried away; fleeting, evanescent, ephemeral, of only passing interest; *wandering, vagabond. *n.* One who flees from danger, pursuit, justice, bondage, or duty; a runaway, a deserter, a refugee; (*fig.*) a person or thing hard to be caught or detained. **fugitive compositions,** *n.pl.* (*Lit.*, *Mus.*) Occasional pieces written for the moment or for a special purpose, and not intended to be permanent. ***fugitively,** *adv.* **fugitiveness,** *n.*

fugleman (fū′ gel mȧn) [G. *flügelmann* (*flügel*, wing, *mann*, man)], *n.* (pl. **-men**) A soldier who takes up a position in front of a company as a guide to the others in their drill; (*fig.*) one who sets an example for others to follow, a leader, a ringleader; a spokesman.

fugue (fūg) [F., from It. *fuga*, L. *fuga*, flight, cogn. with *fugere*, to flee], *n.* A polyphonic composition on one or more short subjects or themes, which are harmonized according to the laws of counterpoint, and reintroduced from time to time with various contrapuntal devices; (*Psych.*) an attempt to escape from reality; (*Psych.*) loss of memory coupled with disappearance from one's usual resorts. **fuguist** (fū′ gist), *n.* A writer or performer of fugues. ***fugato*** (fū gä′ tō) [It.], *adv.* In the fugue style but not in strict fugal form.

Führer (Eng. pronun. fū′ rėr) [G., leader], *n.* The head of the National-Socialist German government, Adolf Hitler (1889–1945). **führer prinzip** (Eng. pron. fū′ rėr prin′ tsip), *n.* The principle of subordination to a Leader.

-ful [A.-S. *full*, see FULL (1)], *suf.* Full of, abounding in, having, as in *artful, beautiful, sinful, wilful*; the quantity or number required to fill, as in *cupful, handful, houseful*.

Fulah (foo′ la) [African native], *n.* A member of one of the dominant races in the Sudan; the language of this race.

fulcrum (fŭl′ krŭm) [L., a support, from *fulcīre*, to prop], *n.* (*pl.* **-cra**) The fixed point on which the bar of a lever rests or about which it turns; (*fig.*) a means of making any kind of force or influence effective; (*Bot.*, *pl.*) additional organs, as stipules, scales, spines, etc. **fulcraceous** (fŭl krā′ shŭs), **fulcral, fulcrant,** *a.* **fulcrate,** *a.* (*Bot.*) Furnished with or supported by fulcra.

fulfil (ful fil′) [A.-S. *fullfyllan* (as FULL (1), FILL)], *v.t.* To accomplish, to carry out, to execute, to satisfy; to perform, to correspond to, to comply with, to fill out, to finish, to complete (a term of office, etc.). **fulfiller,** *n.* **fulfilment, fulfilling,** *n.*

fulgent (fŭl′ jėnt) [L. *fulgens -ntem*, pres.p. of *fulgēre*, to shine], *a.* Shining, dazzling, exceedingly bright. **fulgency,** *n.* **fulgently,** *adv.* **fulgid,** *a.*

fulgor (fŭl′ gȯr) [L., as FULGENT], *n.* Splendour, dazzling brightness. **fulgorous,** *a.* **fulguration** (fŭl gŭ rā′ shŭn), *n.* Flashing of lightning (*usu. in pl.*); *(*Assaying*) the sudden brightening of gold or silver in the crucible as the last traces of dross leave the surface.

fulgurite (fŭl′ gŭ rīt) [L. *fulgur*, lightning, as prec.], *n.* (*Geol.*) A vitrified tube in sand, supposed to be produced by the action of lightning; an explosive made from nitroglycerine.

***fulham** (ful′ ȧm) [perh. from *Fulham*, the place-name], *n.* (*slang*) A loaded die.

fuliginous (fū lij′ i nŭs) [L. *fūlīginōsus*, from *fūlīgo -inis*, soot], *a.* Sooty, smoky, soot-coloured; dusky, gloomy. **fuliginously,** *adv.* **fuliginosity** (-nos′ i ti), *n.*

full (1) (ful) [A.-S. *full* (cp. Dut. *vol*, Icel. *fullr*, Goth. *fullo*, G. *voll*, Sansk. *pūrna*, L. *plēnus*, Gr. *plērēs*)], *a.* Filled up, replete; having no space empty, containing as much as the limits will allow; well supplied, having abundance (of); filled to repletion, satisfied with; charged or overflowing (with feeling, etc.); plentiful, copious, ample; complete, perfect; visible in its entire dimensions; having the whole disk illuminated (of the moon); ample in volume or extent, swelling, plump; strong, sonorous; pregnant; high (as the tide). *adv.* Quite, equally; completely, exactly, directly; very. *n.* Complete measure or degree; the utmost or fullest extent; the highest state or point; a state of satiety. *v.t.* To fill (out), to give fullness to, to make full; *to fulfil. *v.i.* To become full. **at the full:** At the height or the highest condition; with the whole disk illuminated (of the moon). **full of the moon:** The period when it presents a perfect orb to the spectator. **in full:** Completely, without abridgment, abatement, or deduction. **keep her full:** (*Naut.*) Keep the sails filled (order to the steersman). **of full age:** Twenty-one years of age. **full-aged,** *a.* **to the full:** To the utmost extent. **full-acorned,** *a.* Full-fed with acorns. **full-armed,** *a.* Completely armed. **full-back,** *n.* (*Football etc.*) A player stationed at the back of the team. **full-blooded,** *a.* Vigorous; sensual; of pure blood. **full-blown,** *a.* Fully expanded (as a flower); mature, perfect. **full-bodied,** *a.* Full of body (as wine). **full-bottomed,** *a.* Having a large bottom, as distinguished from a bob-wig. **full-bound,** *a.* Bound entirely in leather (of books). **full-butt,** *adv.* (*slang*) With sudden violent collision. **full-cry,** *a.* Giving tongue in chorus (as a pack of hounds). **full dress,** *n.* Dress worn on ceremonious occasions; evening dress. *a.* At which full dress is to be worn. **full-dress debate:** One previously arranged on some important question, opp. to one arising casually. **full-drive,** *adv.* (*colloq.*) With great force or speed. **full-eyed,** *a.* Having prominent eyes. **full-faced,** *a.* Having a broad chubby face; facing directly towards the spectator; (*Print.*) having the heavy lines very thick (of type). **full-flavoured,** *a.* Strongly flavoured, highly spiced; (*slang*) indecent (of a story). ***full-fraught,** *a.* Fully laden. **full hand,** *n.* (*Cards*) In poker, three of a kind and a pair. ***full-hearted,** *a.* Brave, confident, courageous; deeply stirred. **full-hot,** *a.* Heated to the utmost degree. **full-length,** *a.* and *n.* Of the entire figure (of portraits). **full-manned,** *a.* Having a complete crew. ***full-orbed,** *a.* Showing a complete disk. **full pitch,** *adv.* (*Cricket*) Without touching the ground. **full-split,** *adv.* (*Am. colloq.*) With great force or impetuosity. **full stop,** *n.* A period (.), the longest pause in reading; (*fig.*) an abrupt finish. **full-swing,** *adv.* At full speed. *n.* The highest speed, efficiency, etc. **full-timer,** *n.* A child attending school the whole day, opp. to half-timer. **full up,** *adv.* Quite full; no room for more. **full-winged,** *a.* Having powerful or complete wings. **fullish,** *a.* **fully,** *adv.* Completely, entirely; quite.

full (2) (ful) [O.F. *fouler*, late L. *fullāre*, from L. *fullo*, a fuller], *v.t.* To cleanse and thicken (as cloth). **fuller** (1) (ful′ ėr), *n.* One whose occupation is to full cloth. **fuller's earth,** *n.* An argillaceous earth which absorbs grease, much used in fulling cloth. **fullery,** *n.* A place where cloth is fulled. **fulling-mill,** *n.*

fuller (2) (ful′ ėr) [etym. unknown], *n.* A blacksmith's tool for making grooves; a groove made by this. *v.t.* To form a groove or channel in with this.

fullness (ful′ nės), *n.* The state or quality of being full; completeness, satiety; largeness, richness, volume, force. **in the fullness of time:** At the destined time.

fulmar (ful′ mȧr) [prob. Scand. (cp. Icel. *fūll*, FOUL, *mar*, a MEW)], *n.* A sea-bird, *Fulmaris glacialis*, allied to the petrels, abundant in the Arctic seas.

fulminate (fŭl′ mi nāt) [L. *fulminātus*, p.p. of *fulmināre*, from *fulmen*, lightning], *v.i.* To lighten or thunder; to explode with a loud noise or report, to detonate; (*fig.*) to thunder out denunciations. *v.t.* To cause to explode; (*fig.*) to utter (threats, denunciations, or censures). *n.* (-nȧt) A salt of fulminic acid; an explosive containing this. **fulminant,** *a.* Fulminating; (*Path.*) developing suddenly (of diseases); *thundering. *n.* Something that fulminates or explodes. **fulminating,** *a.* Thundering, explosive. **fulminating powder,** *n.* An explosive compound. **fulmination** (-nā′ shŭn), *n.* **fulminatory** (fŭl′ mi nā tȯr i), *a.* ***fulmine,** *v.i.* To flash and thunder like lightning; to fulminate. *v.t.* To send forth (thunder and lightning); to thunder forth. **fulmineous** (fŭl min′ ė ŭs), *a.* **fulminic** (fŭl min′ ik), *a.* (*Chem.*) Pertaining to or capable of detonation. **fulminic acid,** *n.* An unisolated acid that unites with certain metals to form explosive fulminates.

fulness [FULLNESS].

fulsome (ful-, fŭl′ sŭm), *a.* Disgusting by excess or grossness, coarse, excessive, satiating (esp. of compliments, flattery, etc.). **fulsomely,** *adv.* **fulsomeness,** *n.*

fulvous (fŭl′ vŭs) [L. *fulvus*], *a.* (*chiefly Bot. and Zool.*) Tawny, reddish-yellow; fox-coloured. **fulvescent,** *a.* ***fulvid** (fŭl′ vid), *a.* Fulvous.

fum, fung (fŭm, fŭng) [Chin. *fung* (in *fung-whang*)], *n.* A fabulous bird, sometimes called the Chinese phœnix, a symbol of imperial dignity, much used in Chinese and Japanese decoration.

***fumacious** (fū mā′ shŭs) [L. *fūmāre*, to smoke], *a.* Smoky; addicted to tobacco or smoking.

fumade (fū mād′), ***fumado** (fū ma′ dō) [Sp. *fumado*, smoked, as prec.], *n.* A smoked pilchard.

***fumage** (fū′ māj) [med. L. *fumāgium*, L. *fūmus*, smoke], *n.* Hearth-money.

fumarium (fū mâr′ i ŭm) [late L., from *fumāre*, to smoke], *n.* (*pl.* **-ria**) A smoke-chamber in an ancient Roman house, for drying wood, seasoning meat, etc.

fumarole (fū′ mȧ rōl) [It. *fumaruolo*, L. *fūmāriolum*, dim. of *fūmārium*, as prec.], *n.* A hole in the ground in a volcanic region forming an exit for subterranean vapours; a smoke-vent. **fumarolic** (-rol′ ik), *a.*

fumatorium (fū mȧ tôr′ i ŭm) [L. *fumare*, to smoke], *n.* (*pl.* **fumatoria**) A room or apparatus for fumigating; a chamber in a conservatory etc. for destroying insects by chemical fumes.

fumatory (fū′ mȧ tôr i), *n.* A place for smoking or fumigation.

fumble (fŭm′ bel) [perh. from Dut. *fommelen* (cogn. with A.-S. *folm*, L. *palma*, the palm of the hand)], *v.i.* To grope about; to act, esp. to use one's hands, in an uncertain, aimless, or awkward manner; *to bungle in any business; *to stammer, to be confused. *v.i.* To handle or manage awkwardly; to deal with in an uncertain or hesitating manner. **fumbler,** *n.* One who acts awkwardly; a fumbling attempt. **fumblingly,** *adv.*

fume (fūm) [O.F. *fum*, L. *fūmus*, smoke], *n.* A vaporous or smoky exhalation; a narcotic vapour, esp. such as is supposed to rise from alcoholic liquors and to affect the brain (*usu. in pl.*); (*fig.*) mental agitation, esp. an angry mood; anything empty, fleeting, or unsubstantial; *vanity, emptiness; *flattery; *incense; *smoke. *v.i.* To emit smoke or vapour; to pass off in smoke or vapour; to show irritation, to fret, to chafe. *v.t.* To dry, perfume, stain, or cure with smoke, esp. to darken (oak, photographic plates, etc.) with chemical fumes, as of ammonia; to dissipate in vapour; to flatter; to perfume. ***fumeless,** *a.* ***fumid,** *a.* Smoky. ***fumingly,** *adv.* Angrily; with passion. ***fumish,** *a.* Smoky; passionate, irascible. **fumishness,** *n.* Heat of temper; passion. ***fumous, fumose** (fū mōs′), *a.* Producing fumes or vapours; fumy; (*Bot.*) smoke-coloured. **fumosity** (fū mos′ i ti), *n.* Tendency to emit fumes; fumes arising from excessive drinking. **fumy,** *a.* Full or composed of fumes; causing fumes; smoky, vaporous.

***fumet, fumette** (fū met′) [F., from *fumer*, L. *fumāre*, to FUME], *n.* The smell of game or meat when high.

fumigate (fū′ mi gāt) [L. *fūmigātus*, p.p. of *fūmigāre* (*fūmus*, smoke, *-ig-*, *ag-*, base of *agere*, to drive)], *v.t.* To subject to the action of smoke or vapour, esp. for the purpose of disinfection; to perfume. **fumigation** (-gā′ shŭn), *n.* **fumigator** (fū′ mi gā tȯr), *n.* One who or that which fumigates, esp. an apparatus for applying smoke, gas, etc., for the purpose of cleansing, disinfecting, or perfuming. ***fumigatory,** *a.*

fumitory (fū′ mi tôr i) [M.E. and O.F. *fumeterre* (*fume de terre*), late L. *fūmus terræ*, smoke of the earth], *n.* A herb belonging to the genus *Fumaria*, esp. *F. officinalis*, formerly used for skin diseases.

fumosity, fumy [FUME].

fun (fŭn) [prob. corr. of FON], *v.i.* To indulge in fun; to joke, to sport. *n.* Sport, amusement, merriment, frolic, drollery. **like fun:** (*colloq.*) Energetically; thoroughly. **to make fun of, to poke fun at:** To hold up to or turn into ridicule; to banter. **fun fair:** (*Am.*) A carnival, a fair.

funambulist (fū năm′ bū list) [earlier *funambule*, L. *fūnambulus* (*fūnis*, rope, *ambūlare*, to walk)], *n.* A performer on the tight or slack rope; a rope-walker or rope-dancer. ***funambulate,** *v.i.* To walk or dance on a rope. **funambulation** (-lā′ shŭn), *n.* ***funambulatory** (fū năm′-), *a.* Performing like a rope-dancer; narrow, like the walk of a rope-dancer.

function (fŭngk′ shŭn) [O.F. (F. *fonction*), L. *functiōnem*, nom. *functio*, from *fungi*, to perform], *n.* The specific activity, operation, or power belonging to an agent; duty, occupation, office; a public or official ceremony, esp. a religious service of an elaborate kind; hence (*colloq.*) a social entertainment of some importance; (*Physiol.*) the specific office of any animal or vegetable organ; (*Math.*) a quantity dependent for its value on another or other quantities so that a change in the second correspondingly affects the first. *v.i.* To perform a function or duty; to operate. **functional,** *a.* Pertaining to some office or function; official, formal; (*Physiol.*) pertaining to or affecting the action or functions of an organ, not its substance or structure; (*Math.*) relating to or depending on a function. **functional disease:** Derangement of some function of the body, as distinguished from organic or structural disease. **functionalism,** *n.* **functionally,** *adv.* **functionary,** *n.* One who holds any office or trust; an official. *a.* Pertaining to a function or functions; official. **functionate,** *v.i.* To function. **functionless,** *a.*

fund (fŭnd) [F. *fond*, L. *fundus*, the bottom; later assim. to L.], *n.* A sum of money or stock of anything available for use or enjoyment; assets, capital; a sum of money set apart for a specific object permanent or temporary; (*pl.*) money lent to a government and constituting a national debt; the stock of a national debt regarded as an investment; (*colloq., pl.*) money, finances, pecuniary resources; *the bottom. *v.t.* To convert into a single fund or debt, esp. to consolidate into stock or securities bearing interest at a fixed rate; to amass, collect, store; to place in a fund. **in funds:** Provided with cash, flush of money. **fund-holder,** *n.* One who has property invested in the public funds. **fundable,** *a.* **funded,** *a.* Invested in public funds; forming part of the national debt of a country, existing in the form of bonds bearing regular interest. **funded debt,** *n.* **fundless,** *a.*

fundament (fŭn′ dȧ mėnt) [M.E. and O.F. *fondement*, L. *fundāmentum*, from *fundāre*, to found (later form directly from L.)], *n.* *A foundation; the lower part of the body, the buttocks; the anus.

fundamental (fŭn dȧ men′ tȧl) [as prec.], *a.* Pertaining to or serving as a foundation or base; basal, essential, primary, original, indispensable. *n.* A principle, rule, or article forming the basis or ground-work (*usu. in pl.*). **fundamental bass,** *n.* (*Mus.*) A bass consisting of a succession of fundamental notes. **fundamental tone:** (*Mus.*) The lowest note or 'root' of a chord. **Fundamentalist,** *n.* One who believes in the verbal inspiration of the Bible and interprets it literally. **fundamentality** (-tăl′ i ti), *n.* **fundamentally,** *adv.*

funeral (fū′ nėr ȧl) [O.F., from late L. *fūnerālis*, from *fūnus fūneris*, a funeral procession], *a.* Pertaining to or connected with the burial of the dead. *n.* The solemn and ceremonial burying of the dead; interment, obsequies; a procession of persons at a burial; *a death; *a funeral sermon. **funebrial** (fū nē′ bri ȧl), **funerary** (fū′ nėr ȧr i), *a.* Pertaining to funerals. **funereal** (fū nēr′ ė ȧl), *a.* Pertaining to or suitable for a funeral; dismal, sad, mournful; gloomy, dark. **funereally,** *adv.*

***funest** (fū nest′) [F. *funeste*, L. *fūnestus*, from *fūnus*, see prec.], *a.* Portending or causing death or disaster; sad, lamentable, mournful.

fung [FUM].

fungible (fŭn′ jibl) [med. L. *fungibilis*, from *fungī*, to perform, operate, see FUNCTION], *a.* (*Law*) Of such a nature that it may be replaced by another thing of the same class. *n.pl.* Movable goods which may be valued by weight or measure.

fungus (fŭng′ gŭs) [L., prob. cogn. with Gr. *sphongos*, a SPONGE], *n.* (*pl.* **-gi,** (-ji), **-guses**) A mushroom, toadstool, mould, mildew, or other cryptogamous plant, destitute of chlorophyll and deriving its nourishment from organic matter; (*Path.*) a morbid growth or excrescence of a spongy nature; (*fig.*) something of rapid or parasitic growth. **fungal,** *a.* Of, pertaining to, or of the nature of a fungus. *n.* A fungus. **fungaceous** (fŭng gā′ shŭs), *a.* **fungic** (fŭn′ jik), *a.* Obtained from fungi. **fungic acid:** An acid contained in the juice of most fungi. **fungicide,** *n.* Anything that destroys fungi or their germs. **fungiform, fungiliform** (fŭn′ ji-, fŭn jil′ i fôrm), *a.* Having a termination like the head of a fungus. **fungin,** *n.* The cellulose of fungi and lichens. **fungivorous** (fŭn jiv′ ȯr ŭs), *a.* Feeding on fungi. **fungoid** (fŭng′ goid), *a.* Of the nature of or like a fungus. **fungology** (fŭng gol′ ȯ ji), *n.* The science of fungi. **fungological** (-loj′ i kȧl), *a.* **fungologist,** *n.* **fungous,** *a.* Like or of the nature of a fungus; excrescent, springing up suddenly, ephemeral; spongy, unsubstantial. **fungosity** (fŭng gos′ i ti), *n.* **fungusy,** *a.*

funicular (fū nik′ ū lȧr) [L. *fūniculus*, dim. of *fūnis*, a rope, -AR], *a.* Pertaining to, consisting of, or depending on a rope or cable. **funicular railway:** One worked by means of a cable, usu. a mountain railway. **funicle** (fū′ ni kėl), *n.* (*Bot.*) A *funiculus*. ***funiculus*** (fū nik′ ū lŭs), *n.* (*pl.* **-uli**) (*Anat.*) The umbilical cord; a number of nerve-fibres enclosed in a tubular sheath; (*Bot.*) a cord connecting the seed with the placenta. **funiliform** (fū nil′ i fôrm), *a.* (*Bot.*) Formed of cord-like fibres. ***funis,*** *n.* (*Anat.*) The umbilical cord.

funk (1) (fŭngk) [etym. doubtful], *n.* A state of fear or panic; a coward. *v.i.* To be in a state of terror; to flinch, to shrink in fear or cowardice. *v.t.* To be afraid of; to shirk, to try to evade through fear or cowardice; (*usu. in p.p.*) to frighten, to scare. **blue funk:** (*colloq.*) Abject terror. **funker,** *n.* **funky** (1), *a.*

funk (2) (fŭngk) [etym. doubtful (perh. from O.F. *funkier*, ult. from L. *fūmigāre*, see FUMIGATE)], *v.t.* To blow smoke upon so as to stifle or annoy. *v.i.* To smoke; to stink. *n.* A stink.

funk (3) (fŭngk) [Sc.; perh. onomat.], *v.i.* and *t.* To kick (said of a horse). **funky** (2), *a.*

funkia (fŭng′ ki ȧ) [H. C. *Funck* (1771–1839), German botanist], *n.* A genus of liliaceous plants, comprising the plantain-lilies, from China and Japan.

funnel (fŭn′ ėl) [M.E. *fonel*, prob. through O.F. (cp. Prov. *founil*, Sp. *fonil*, Port. *funil*), from late L. *fundibulum* (L. *infundibulum*), from *fundere*, to pour], *n.* A conical vessel usu. terminating below in a tube, for conducting liquids, etc. into vessels with a small opening; a tube or shaft for ventilation, lighting, etc.; the chimney of a steamship or steam-engine; the inside of a chimney, a flue. **funnel-net,** *n.* A tapering, funnel-shaped net. **funnel-form, -shaped,** *a.* (*Bot.*) Having the tube gradually enlarging upwards so as to constitute a funnel (of a calyx, corolla, etc.). **funnel-web spider,** *n.* (*Austral.*) A large venomous spider found in N.S.W. **funnelled,** *a.* Having a funnel or funnels; funnel-shaped.

funny (1) (fŭn′ i), *a.* Droll, comical, laughable; causing mirth or laughter; strange, curious, queer, puzzling. **funny-bone,** *n.* The lower part of the elbow over which the ulnar nerve passes, a blow on which causes a curious tingling sensation. **funny man,** *n.* A clown; a buffoon or wag. **funnily,** *adv.* **funniment,** *n.* **funniness,** *n.* **funnyism,** *n.*

funny (2) (fŭn′ i) [etym. doubtful, perh. from prec.], *n.* A narrow, clinker-built pleasure-boat, for a pair of sculls.

fur (fĕr) [O.F. *forrer*, to line, to sheathe (F. *fourrer*), from Teut. (cp. A.-S. *fōdor*, G. *futter*, Icel. *fōthr*)], *n.* The soft fine hair growing thick upon certain animals, distinct from ordinary hair; (*pl.*) the skins, esp. dressed skins of such animals; the skin of such animals used for lining or trimming garments; a fur-lined garment (*usu. in pl.*); the downy covering on the skin of a peach; a coat or crust deposited by a liquid; a deposit from wine; a coat of morbid matter collected on the tongue; a crust deposited on the interior of kettles, etc. by hard water. *v.t.* (*past & p.p.* **furred**) To cover, line, or trim with fur; to cover or coat with morbid matter; to nail pieces of timber to (as joists or rafters) in order to bring them into a level. *v.i.* To become encrusted with fur or scale (as the inside of a boiler). **to make the fur fly:** To create a scene, to start a row. **fur and feather:** (*Sport*) Fur-bearing animals and game birds. **furred,** *a.* Lined or ornamented with fur; coated with fur or scale. **furrier** (fŭr′ i ėr), *n.* A dealer in furs; one who prepares and sells furs. **furry,** *a.* Covered or clad in fur; made of fur; resembling fur; coated with a scale or deposit. **fur-seal,** *n.* A seal or sea-bear yielding a fur valuable commercially.

***furacious** (fū rā′ shŭs) [L. *fūrax -cis*], *a.* Inclined to steal; thievish. ***furacity** (fū răs′ i ti), *n.*

furbelow (fĕr′ bė lō) [var. of FALBALA], *n.* A piece of stuff, plaited and puckered, used as trimming on skirts and petticoats, a flounce; (*pl.*) finery; a seaweed, *Laminaria bulbosa*, with wrinkled fronds. *v.t.* To furnish or trim with furbelows.

furbish (fĕr′ bish) [O.F. *forbiss-*, stem of *forbir*, O.H.G. *furban*], *v.t.* To rub so as to brighten, to polish up; to renovate, to restore the newness or brightness of; to clean or brighten (up). **furbisher,** *n.*

furcate (fĕr′ kăt, -kȧt) [L. *furcātus*, from *furca*, a FORK], *a.* Forked, dividing into branches like the prongs of a fork. *v.i.* (fĕr kăt′) To fork, to divide into branches. **furcation** (-kā′ shŭn), *n.* **furcato-,** *comb. form.* **furciferous** (fĕr sif′ ėr ŭs), *a.* (*Ent.*) Having a forked process, as the larvæ of some butterflies; *scoundrelly, rascally. ***furcula*** (fĕr′ kū lȧ) [L., dim. of *furca*], *n.* (*pl.* **-læ**) The two clavicles of birds anchylosed together so as to form one V-shaped bone, the merrythought or wishbone. **furcular,** *a.*

furfur (fĕr′ fėr) [L.], *n.* Scurf or dandruff; (*pl.* **-fures**) particles of scurf, bran-like scales of skin. **furfuraceous** (fĕr fėr ā′ shŭs), *a.* **furfurous,** *a.* **furfuration** (-ā′ shŭn), *n.*

furfurol (fĕr′ fėr ol) [as prec., -OL], *n.* (*Chem.*) An oil formed in the dry distillation of sugar, or by distilling bran with dilute sulphuric acid.

***furibund** (fū′ ri bŭnd) [L. *furibundus*, from *furere*, to rage], *a.* Raging, furious.

furioso (fū ri ō′ sō) [It., as foll.], *adv.* (*Mus.*) With fury or vehemence. **n.* A furious or impetuous person.

furious (fū′ ri ŭs) [O.F. *furieus* (F. *furieux*), L. *furiosus*, from *furia*, FURY], *a.* Full of fury, raging, violent, frantic; rushing with vehemence or impetuosity, tempestuous; vehement, eager. **furiosity** (fū ri os′ i ti), *n.* **furiously,** *adv.* **furiousness,** *n.*

furl (fĕrl) [acc. to Skeat, prob. contr. from earlier *furdle*, corr. of *fardle*, to pack up, see FARDEL], *v.t.* To roll up (a sail) and wrap about a yard, mast, or stay; to roll, wrap, fold, or close (up). *v.i.* To become rolled or folded up.

furlong (fĕr′ long) [A.-S. *furlang* (*furh*, FURROW, *lang*, LONG)], *n.* A measure of length, the eighth part of a mile, 40 rods, or 220 yards; a group of strips of land in the open-field system of agriculture.

furlough (fĕr′ lō) [Dut. *verlof* (cp. Dan. *forlov*, G. *verlaub*), as FOR-, LEAVE (1)], *n.* Leave of absence, esp. to a soldier. *v.t.* To grant leave of absence to.

furmenty, furmety [FRUMENTY].

furnace (fĕr′ nȧs) [O.F. *fornais* (F. *fournaise*), L. *fornācem*, nom. *-nax*, *for-*, *furnus*, oven], *n.* A chamber or structure containing a chamber in which fuel is burned for the production of intense heat, esp. for melting ores, metals, etc.; a closed fire-place for heating a boiler, hot-water or hot-air pipes, etc.; (*fig.*) a time, place, or occasion of severe trial or torture. *v.t.* To cast into or heat in a furnace; *to exhale like a furnace.

***furniment** (fĕr′ ni mėnt) [O.F. *fourniment*, as foll.], *n.* Furniture, equipment.

furnish (fĕr′ nish) [O.F. *fourniss-*, stem of *fournir*, ult. from O.H.G. *frumjan*, to perform, provide (cogn. with *fruma*, profit, advantage, G. *fromm*, good, Eng. FORMER)], *v.t.* To provide or supply (with); to equip, to fit up, esp. (a house or room) with movable furniture; to supply, to afford, to yield; *to provide with what is necessary; *to decorate. *v.i.* (*Racing slang*) To fill out, to improve in strength and appearance (said of a horse). **furnisher,** *n.* **furnishings,** *n.pl.* Furniture, upholstery, apparatus; *mere externals or incidentals. ***furnishment,** *n.*

furniture (fĕr′ ni chŭr) [French *fourniture*, as prec.], *n.* Equipment, equipage, outfit; movable articles, esp. chairs, tables, etc., with which a house or room is furnished; an ornamental addition; (*Print.*) the material, either of wood or metal, which keeps the pages firmly fixed in the chase, and separates them so as to allow a uniform margin when printed; (*Carp.*) locks, door and window trimmings, etc.; (*Mil.*) the mountings of a gun; (*Naut.*) the masts and rigging of a ship; the trappings of a horse.

****furor*** (fū′ rŏr) [L., from *furere*, to rage], *n.* Rage, fury, madness.

furore (fū rŏr′ ā) [It., as prec.], *n.* Great excitement or enthusiasm; a craze, a rage.

furphy (fĕr′ fi) [*J. Furphy*, maker of the cart], *n.* (*Austral.*) A camp rumour, a false report, orig. circulated by the drivers of Furphy's military water- and sanitary-carts. **furphy merchant,** *n.* One who circulates groundless rumours.

furrier, etc. [FUR].

furring (fĕr′ ing), *n.* Trimming or lining with furs; a deposit of scale (on the inside of boilers, etc.); (*Carp.*) thin pieces fixed on the edge of timber to make the surface even; (*Building*) a lining on a brick wall to prevent dampness; (*Ship-building*) double planking on the sides of a ship.

furrow (fŭr′ ō) [A.-S. *furh* (cp. Dut. *voor*, Icel. *for*, G. *furche*)], *n.* A trench in the earth made by a plough; a narrow trench, groove or hollow; a rut; the track of a ship; a wrinkle on the face. *v.t.* To plough; to make grooves, furrows, or wrinkles in; to mark (the face) with deep wrinkles. **furrow-drain,** *n.* A deep open channel made by a plough, to carry off water. *v.t.* To make furrow-drains in. ***furrow-faced,** *a.* Having a wrinkled face or surface. **furrow-slice,** *n.* The strip of earth thrown up from a furrow by the plough. ***furrow-weed,** *n.* A weed growing on ploughed land. **furrowless,** *a.* **furrowy,** *a.*

furry [FUR].

furry dance (fĕr′ i dans) [perh. *Flora*], *n.* A festival dance through the streets of Helston and certain other Cornish towns on May 8, called Flora's day.

further (fĕr′ thėr) [A.-S. *furthra*, adv. *furthor* (cogn. with FORE, *-ther* is the comp. suf.), cp. Dut. *vorders*, G. *vorder*, Gr. *proteros*, comp. of *pro*], *a.* More remote; more advanced; going or extended beyond that already existing or stated, additional (chiefly used when distance in space is not implied, cp. FARTHER). *adv.* To a greater distance, degree, or extent; moreover, in addition, also. *v.t.* To help forward, to advance, to promote. **furtherance,** *n.* Promotion, help, assistance. **furtherer,** *n.* **furthermore,** *adv.* Moreover, besides. **furthermost,** *a.* Furthest, most remote. ***furthersome,** *a.* Advantageous. **furthest** [superl. from FURTHER], *a.* Most remote in time or place. *adv.* At or to the greatest distance or extent.

furtive (fĕr′ tiv) [F. *furtif*, fem. *furtive*, L. *furtīvus*, from *furtum*, theft (*fūr*, a thief, cp. Gr. *phōr*)], *a.* Stealthy, sly; secret, surreptitious, designed to escape attention; obtained by or as by theft; *thievish. **furtively,** *adv.*

furuncle (fū′ rŭng kėl) [L. *fūrunculus*, orig. dim. of *fūr*, thief], *n.* (*Path.*) A superficial inflammatory tumour, with a central core; a boil. **furuncular, furunculoid, furunculous** (fū rŭng′ kū lȧr, -loid, -lůs), *a.*

fury (fū′ ri) [O.F. *furie*, L. *furia*, from *furere*, to rage], *n.* Vehement, uncontrollable anger, rage; a fit of raving passion; impetuosity, violence; intense, ecstatic passion, inspiration, enthusiasm; (*pl.*) the three avenging goddesses of Classical mythology; hence, a furious woman, a virago. **like fury:** (*colloq.*) With furious energy. ***fury-like,** *a.* Raging, frenzied.

furze (fĕrz) [A.-S. *fyrs*], *n.* The gorse or whin, *Ulex Europæus*, a spinous evergreen shrub with bright yellow flowers, common on waste, stony land. **furze-chat,** *n.* The whinchat. **furzeling, furze-wren,** *n.* The Dartford warbler. **furzy,** *a.*

fusarole (fū′ zȧ rōl) [F. *fusarolle*, It. *fusaruola*, L. *fūsus*, a spindle], *n.* A moulding placed immediately under the echinus in Doric, Ionic, and composite capitals.

fuscous (fŭs′ kůs) [L. *fuscus*], *a.* Brown tinged with grey or black; dingy.

fuse (1) (fūz) [L. *fūsus*, p.p. of *fundere*, to pour], *v.t.* To melt; to reduce to a liquid or fluid state by heat, to unite by or as by melting together. *v.i.* To melt; to become fluid; to become united by or as by melting together. *n.* (*Elec.*) A device for protecting against the effect of excess of current, consisting of a piece of wire or metal inserted in a circuit so that it will interrupt the circuit by melting when an excess current flows; the melting of wire, etc. caused by a short circuit. **fuse box,** *n.* (*Elec.*) Box containing one or more fuses. ***fusile,** *a.* Fusible; fluid through heat; produced by melting or casting. **fusing-point,** *n.* The temperature at which a given substance melts.

fuse (2) (fūz) [It. *fuso*, L. *fūsus*, a spindle], *n.* A tube, cord, or casing filled or saturated with combustible material, and used for igniting a charge in a mine or projectile. *v.t.* To furnish with a fuse or fuses.

fusee (fū zē′) [F. *fusée*, L. *fūsāta*, spindleful, orig. fem. p.p. of *fūsāre*, from *fūsus*, a spindle], *n.* The cone round which the chain is wound in a clock or watch; a fuse; a match with a mass of inflammable material at its head, used for lighting pipes etc. in a wind. **fusiform,** *a.* (*Nat. Hist.*) Shaped like a spindle; tapering at both ends.

fusel oil (fū′ zėl oil) [G. *fusel*, spirits of inferior quality], *n.* A poisonous oily product, composed chiefly of amyl alcohol, formed during the manufacture of corn, potato, or grape spirits.

fuselage (fū′ zė lazh) [F. *fusele*, spindle-shaped, -AGE], *n.* (*Aviat.*) The framework of the body of an aeroplane.

fusible (fū′ zi bėl), *a.* Capable of being fused or melted. **fusible alloy or metal,** *n.* An alloy, usually of lead, tin, and bismuth, compounded in definite proportions to melt at a given temperature. **fusible plug,** *n.* A plug of fusible metal used in a steam-boiler or an electric circuit to obviate an excessive increase of temperature. **fusibility** (-bil i ti), *n.*

fusil (1) (fū′ zil), ***fusee** (fū zē′) [F. *fusil*, It. *focile* a fire-steel, ult. from L. *focus*, a hearth]. *n.* An obsolete firelock, lighter than a musket.

fusil (2) (fū′ zil) [O.F. *fusel* (F. *fuseau*), from L. *fūsus*, a spindle], *n.* (*Her.*) A bearing resembling a lozenge, longer in proportion to breadth.

fusilier (fū zi lēr′), *n.* Orig. a soldier armed with a fusil, as distinguished from a pikeman or archer still applied in the British army to certain regiments of the line.

fusillade (fū zi lād′) [FUSIL (1)], *n.* A continuous discharge of fire-arms. *v.t.* To shoot down or storm by fusillade.

fusion (fū′ zhůn) [FUSE (1)], *n.* The act of melting or rendering liquid by heat; the state of being so melted or liquefied; union by or as by melting together, blending; the combination at very high temperature of atoms of hydrogen or deuterium to form helium and liberate nuclear energy; (*fig.*) coalescence or coalition (as of political parties). **fusionism,** *n.* **fusionist,** *n.* One who advocates political fusion.

fuss (fŭs) [prob. onomat.], *n.* Excessive activity, labour, or trouble, taken or exhibited; unnecessary bustle or commotion, too much ado; undue importance given to trifles or petty details. *v.i.* To make much ado about nothing; to worry, to be nervous or restless. *v.t.* To worry, to agitate. **fussy,** *a.* **fussily,** *adv.* **fussiness,** *n.*

***fust** (fŭst) [O.F. (F. *fût*), L. *fustem*, nom. *fustis*, a stick, a log], *n.* *A wine-cask; a strong, musty smell, as of a cask; (*Arch.*) the shaft of a column. *v.i.* To grow mouldy; (of wine) to taste of the cask. **fusty,** *a.* Mouldy, musty; rank, ill-smelling. **fustiness,** *n.*

fustanella (fŭs tȧ nel′ ȧ) [It., dim. of mod. Gr. *phoustani*, It. *fustagno*, FUSTIAN], *n.* The short white skirt worn by men in modern Greece.

fustet (fŭs′ tėt) [F., Sp. *fustete* corr. of *fustoc*, FUSTIC], *n.* The wood of the Venetian sumach, *Rhus cotinus*; fustic.

fustian (fŭs′ ti ȧn) [M.E. *fustane*, O.F. *fustaigne*, It. *fustagno*, low L. *fustāneum*, neut. adj. masc. *fustāneus*, prob. from Arab. *Fustāt*, a suburb of Cairo], *n.* A coarse twilled cotton or cotton and linen cloth, with short velvety pile; applied as trade-name to velveteen, corduroy, etc.; (*fig.*) inflated or pompous writing or speaking; bombast, clap-trap, mere verbiage; *a kind of egg flip. *a.* Bombastic; pompous, pretentious, inflated; using bombastic language. **fustianed,** *a.* **fustianist,** *n.* One who uses bombastic language in writing or speaking. **fustianize,** *v.i.*

fustic (fŭs′ tik) [F. and Sp. *fustoc*, Arab. *fustuq*, Gr. *pistakē*, PISTACHIO (acc. to O.E.D., earlier traced to L. *fustis*, a cudgel)], *n.* A yellow wood used in dyeing, that of *Maclura tinctoria*, a large West Indian tree, sometimes called in distinction **old fustic,** and that of *Rhus cotinus*, a bushy shrub of southern Europe, now usu. called **young fustic.**

***fustigate** (fŭs′ ti gāt) [late L. *fūstīgātus*, p.p. of *fūstīgāre*, from *fūstis*, a cudgel], *v.t.* To beat with a cudgel; to cane. ***fustigation** (-gā′ shůn), *n.*

***fustilarian** (fŭs ti lâr′ i ȧn) [Shak., 2 *Henry VI*, ii. 1, prob. coined from FUSTY], *n.* A low fellow.

fusty [FUST].

futchel (fŭch′ ėl) [etym. unknown], *n.* One of the timbers set lengthwise in the framework of a carriage, to support the splinter-bar and the shaft or pole.

futhorc (foo′ thôrk) [from the first six letters *f u þ o r k*], *n.* The Runic alphabet.

futile (fū′ tīl, -til) [L. *fūtilis*, *futtilis*, leaky, easily poured out, prob. from root of *fundere*, to pour], *a.* Useless; of no effect; trifling, worthless, frivolous. **futilely,** *adv.* **futility** (fū til′ i ti), *n.*

futtock (fŭt' ŏk) [prob. corr. of FOOT HOOK], *n.* (*Naut.*) One of the timbers in the compound rib of a vessel. **futtock-plate,** *n.* An iron plate at the head of a lower mast, to which the futtock-shrouds and the dead-eyes of the topmast shrouds are secured. **futtock-shrouds,** *n.pl.* The short shrouds from this to a band on the mast below.

future (fū' chŭr) [O.French *futur*, fem. *future*, L. *futurus*, fut. p. of *esse*, to be], *a.* That will be; that is to come or happen hereafter; (*Gram.*) expressing action yet to happen; (*in comb.*) that will be something specified (as *our future king*). *n.* Time to come; that which will be or will have happened hereafter; prospective condition, state, career, etc.; (*Gram.*) the future tense; (*colloq.*) one's future husband or wife; (*Comm., pl.*) goods, stocks, etc., bought or sold for future delivery; whence, **to deal in futures:** To speculate for a rise or fall. **future perfect tense:** (*Gram.*) The tense expressing an action as completed in the future (as *it will have been*). **futureless,** *a.* ***futurely,** *adv.* **futureness,** *n.* **Futurism,** *n.* (*Art*) A movement in painting, poetry and sculpture aiming at visualizing the movement and development of objects, instead of the picture they present at a given moment. **Futurist,** *n.* and *a.* **Futuristic,** *a.* **futurist,** *n.* One who holds that a great part of Scripture prophecy (esp. of the Apocalypse) is still to be fulfilled. ***futurition** (-ish' ŭn), *n.* The state of being future; existence or accomplishment in the future. **futurity** (fū tūr' i ti), *n.* The state of being future; future time, esp. eternity; future events, things to come (*in sing. or pl.*).

fuze [FUSE].

fuzz (fŭz) [prob. echoic of blowing], *v.i.* To fly off in minute particles. *n.* Minute light particles of down or similar matter, fluff; fuzziness. **fuzz-ball,** *n.* A puff-ball. **fuzz-wig,** *n.* A wig of frizzed curls. **fuzzy,** *a.* **fuzzily,** *adv.* **fuzziness,** *n.* **fuzzy-wuzzies,** *n.pl.* (*Austral.*) Natives of New Guinea; (*Kipling*) Sudanese, Sudanese fighters.

fy [FIE].

-fy [F. *-fier*, L. *-ficāre, facere*, to make], *suf.* To make, to produce; to bring into a certain state (forming verbs), as in *beautify, deify, horrify, petrify, sanctify, terrify*; (*colloq.*) as in *argufy, Frenchify, speechify.*

fyke (fīk) [Am., from Dut. *fuik*], *n.* A bag-net, open at one end so as to allow fish to enter but opposing their exit.

fylfot (fil' fot) [borrowed by mod. antiquaries from a MS. (*c.* 1500) where it prob. means *fill-foot*], *n.* An ancient figure consisting of a great cross with arms continued at right angles, used heraldically, as a mystic symbol, or for decoration; called also gammadion and swastika.

fyrd (fĕrd, fērd) [A.-S., cogn. with FARE], *n.* (*Eng. Hist.*) An array, at the command of the king in Anglo-Saxon times, of all able to bear arms.

fytte [FIT (2)].

G

G, g, the seventh letter, and fifth consonant, of the Roman and English alphabets, has two sounds in modern English: one hard, a guttural stop, before *a, o, u*, as in *gate, god, gun* (except in *gaol*), and when initial, always before *e* and *i* in words of English origin, as in *get, give,* and when final as in *bag*; as also before the consonants *l* and *r*, as in *glove, grove*; the other soft, like that of *j*, in words of Gr. or L. origin before *e* or *i*; (*pl.* **Gs, G's, Gees**); (*Mus.*) the fifth note of the diatonic scale of C major; the key or scale corresponding to this; the fourth string of a violin, the third of the viola and violoncello, the first of the double-bass; the mark of the treble clef; **g,** (*Phys.*) a symbol of the acceleration on the surface of the earth due to gravity, about 32 ft. per second. **G-man** (jē' măn) [initials of Government man], *n.* U.S.A. police term for a member of the Federal Bureau of Investigation specially selected for his intrepidity as a criminal-hunter.

gab (găb) [prob. onomat.], *n.* (*vulg.*) Idle talk, chatter; (*Sc.*) the mouth. *v.i.* To talk glibly, to chatter, to prate. **the gift of the gab:** (*colloq.*) A talent for speaking, fluency. **gabby,** *a.* Talkative, loquacious. **gabster,** *n.*

gabarage (gă' bȧ rij) [etym. uncertain], *n.* A coarse kind of packing-cloth.

gabardine (găb' ȧr din) [Sp. *gabardina*, a pilgrim's frock], *n.* (*Textiles*) A cloth with a corded effect, used largely for rain-coats.

***gabbart** (găb' ȧrt) [F. *gabarre* (now *gabare*), It. *gabara*], *n.* (*Sc.*) A flat river-vessel, a lighter.

gabble (găb' ėl) [prob. imit. (cp. BABBLE)], *v.i.* To utter inarticulate sounds rapidly; to talk rapidly and incoherently. *v.t.* To utter noisily or inarticulately. *n.* Rapid, incoherent, or inarticulate talk; cackle, chatter. ***gabblement,** *n.* **gabbler,** *n.*

gabbro (găb' rō) [It.], *n.* (*Geol.*) Rock composed of feldspar and diallage, sometimes with serpentine or mica. **gabbronite,** *n.* A bluish-green or grey variety of scapolite somewhat resembling gabbro.

gabelle (gȧ bel') [F., from med. L. *gabella, gablum*, from Teut. (cp. GAVEL)], *n.* A tax or duty, esp. the tax on salt in France before the Revolution (1789).

gaberdine (găb' ėr dēn) [from Sp. *gabardina* or O.F. *gauvardine*, prob. a pilgrim's frock, from M.H.G. *wallevart* (G. *wallfahrt*), pilgrimage], *n.* A long coarse gown or cloak, worn in the Middle Ages by Jews and others.

gaberlunzie (găb ėr lŭn' zi, -yi) [Sc., etym. unknown], *n.* A strolling beggar; a beadsman; (*erroneously*) a beggar's wallet. **gaberlunzie man** or **beggar,** *n.*

gabion (gā' bi ŏn) [F., from It. *gabbione*, augm. form of *gabbia*, cage], *n.* A cylindrical basket of wicker- or iron-work, filled with earth, used for shelter against an enemy's fire while trenches are being dug, and for foundations etc. in engineering work. **gabionade** (gā bi ŏ nād'), *n.* A work formed of gabions. **gabionage** (gā' bi ŏ nāj), *n.* Gabions collectively. **gabioned,** *a.* Furnished with, formed of, or protected with gabions.

gable (gā' bėl) [O.F., from Teut. (cp. Icel. *gafl*, Dut. *gevel*, pinnacle, Gr. *kephalē*, head; also O.H.G. *gabala*, G. *gabel*, fork)], *n.* The triangular portion of the end of a building, bounded by the sides of the roof and a line joining the eaves; a wall with upper part shaped like this; a canopy or other architectural member with this shape. **gable-end,** *n.* The end wall of a building with such an upper part. **gable-roof,** *n.* A ridge roof ending in a gable. **gable-window,** *n.* A window in a gable or with a gable over it. **gabled,** *a.* Having gables. **gablet,** *n.* A small gable, esp. forming an ornamental canopy over a tabernacle or niche.

gaby (gā' bi) [perh. cogn. with GAPE], *n.* A fool, a simpleton.

gad (1) (găd) [Icel. *gaddr*, cogn. with L. *hasta*, a spear], *n.* (*Mining*) A pointed tool of iron or steel, also an iron punch with a wooden handle; an iron wedge sharply pointed for splitting stone, etc.; *a pointed bar or rod, a spike, a goad, a stylus. ***gadling,** *n.* A boss or small spike of steel on the knuckles of gauntlets. ***gadman, *gadsman,** *n.* (*Sc.*) A goadsman.

gad (2) (găd) [etym. doubtful (perh. from obs. *gad*, gad-fly, in sense of running about as if stung; or formed from obs. *gadling*, A.-S. *gædling*, a companion, from *gæd*, fellowship)], *v.i.* (*past & p.p.* **gadded**) To rove or wander idly (about, out, etc.); to ramble or straggle (as a plant). *n.* Gadding or roaming about. **gadabout,** *n.* One who gads about habitually. **gadder,** *n.* **gaddingly,** *adv.* ***gaddish,** *a.* Inclined to gad about. ***gaddishness,** *n.*

gad (3) (găd) [minced pron. of GOD], *int.* An exclamation of surprise etc. **begad** or **by gad.** Minced oaths.

gadfly (găd′ flī), *n.* An insect of the genus *Tobanidæ* or *Œstrus*, which bites cattle and other animals, a breeze-fly; (*fig.*) a person, thing, or impulse that irritates or torments; *a gadabout.

gadge (găj) [used by Browning, etym. unknown], *n.* Some instrument of torture.

gadget (gă′ jėt) [etym. doubtful], *n.* (*colloq.*) A tool, an appliance; a contrivance for making a job easier; a trick of the trade.

Gadhelic (găd el′ ik) [Ir. *Gaedheal*, pl. *Gaedhil*, Gael], *a.* Of or pertaining to the branch of the Celtic race that includes the Gaels of Scotland, the Irish, and the people of the Isle of Man, as dist. from the Cymri. *n.* The language spoken by this branch of the Celtic race.

gadoid (gā′ doid) [Gr. *gados*, -OID], *a.* Of or belonging to the family *Gadidæ*, which comprises the cod-fishes. *n.* Any fish of the family *Gadidæ*.

gadolinite (găd′ ȯ li nīt) [J. *Gadolin* (1760–1852), Finnish mineralogist], *n.* (*Min.*) A black, vitreous silicate of yttrium, formed in crystals. **gadolinic** (găd ȯ lin′ ik), *a.*

gadolinium (găd ō lin′ i ŭm), *n.* A rare metallic element.

gadroon (gȧ droon′) [F. *godron*, etym. doubtful], *n.* (*usu. pl.*) An ornament consisting of a series of convex curves, used in architecture and metal-work for edgings, mouldings, etc. **gadrooned,** *a.*

gaduin (gā′ dū in) [GADOID], *n.* A brown substance contained in cod-liver oil, and one of its essential constituents.

gadwall (găd′ wawl) [perh. corr. of *gadwell* (GAD (2), WELL (2))], *n.* A large freshwater duck, *Anas strepera*, of northern Europe and America.

gae (gā) [Sc. var. of GO].

Gael (gāl) [Gael. *Gaidheal*], *n.* A Scottish Celt; (*less commonly*) an Irish Celt. **Gaelic** (gā′-, gi′ lik, găl′ ik), *a.* Of or pertaining to the Gaels or their language. *n.* The language spoken by the Gaels; (*less commonly*) the language of the Irish and Manx Celts. **Gaelic League,** *n.* An association formed to further the revival of the Irish language and ancient culture.

gaff (1) (găf) [O.F. *gaffe* (cp. L.G. *gaffel*, G. *gabel*, a fork)], *n.* A stick with a metal hook at the end, used by anglers to land heavy fish; (*Naut.*) the spar which extends the upper edge of fore-and-aft sails not set on stays. *v.t.* To seize or land with a gaff. **gaff-topsail,** *n.* A sail spread by a gaff above the mainsail of a fore-and-aft rigged vessel.

gaff (2) (găf) [etym. doubtful], *n.* A theatre, music-hall, or other place of entertainment of the lowest class; *a fair.

gaff (3) (găf) [Slang, etym. doubtful], *n.* Outcry. **to blow the gaff:** To let out the secret; to give information.

gaff (4) (găf) [Slang, etym. unknown], *v.i.* To gamble; to toss, esp. for liquor.

gaffe (găf) [F.], *n.* A social solecism. **to make a gaffe:** To put one's foot in it.

gaffer (găf′ ėr) [corr. of GRANDFATHER], *n.* An old fellow, esp. an aged rustic (formerly a term of respect, now of familiarity); a foreman, an overseer; a schoolmaster.

gag (găg) [prob. imit.], *v.t.* (*past & p.p.* **gagged**) To stop the mouth (of a person) by thrusting something into it, so as to prevent speech; to silence; to deprive of freedom of speech; to apply the gag-bit to a horse; (*Theat.*) to put interpolations into; (*slang*) to deceive. *v.i.* (*Theat.*) To introduce interpolations into a part; (*slang*) to practise imposture. *n.* Something thrust into the mouth to prevent one from speaking; (*Surg.*) an instrument for holding the mouth open during an operation; (*Parl.*) the closure; (*Theat.*) interpolation introduced by an actor into his part; (*slang*) an imposture, a lie, a hoax. **gag-bit,** *n.* A very powerful bit used in horse-breaking. **gag-rein,** *n.* A rein used for pulling the bit upward or backward. **gagger,** *n.* One who gags; (*Metal.*) a light T-shaped lifter used in iron-founding.

gaga (ga′ ga) [Fr. slang], *a.* Foolish, senile, fatuous.

gage (1) (gāj) [O.F. *gage*, *gauge*, *wagc*, from Teut. (cp. WED, also WAGE)], *n.* A pledge, a pawn; something laid down as security, to be forfeited in case of non-performance of some act; a glove or other symbol thrown down as a challenge to combat; hence, a challenge. *v.t.* To deposit as a pledge or security for some act; to stake, to risk, to wager; to guarantee; *to engage; *to bind or entangle. ***gagelike,** *adv.*

gage (2) (gāj) [Sir William *Gage* (*c.* 1725), the introducer], *n.* A greengage.

gage (3) [GAUGE].

gaggle (găg′ ėl) [imit.; cp. GUGGLE, also CACKLE], *v.i.* To make a noise like a goose; to cackle, to chatter. *n.* A collection of geese.

gagliarda (găl yar′ da) [It.], *n.* A dance in three-four time.

gaiety (gā′ ė ti) [O.F. *gayeté*], *n.* The state of being gay; mirth, merriment; (*pl.*) amusements, festivities; gay appearance, brave show.

Gaikwar (gīk′ war) [Marathi, cowherd], *n.* The ruler of Baroda, India; formerly the monarch of the Mahrattas.

***gaillard** [GALLIARD].

gaily [GAY].

gain (1) (gān) [O.F., from *gaigner*, *gaaignier* (cp. F. *gagne gagner*), O.H.G. *weidenēn*, to pasture, to graze, from *weida*, pasturage], *n.* Anything obtained as an advantage or in return for labour; profit; increase, growth, accession; amount of this; (*pl.*) profits, emoluments; the acquisition of wealth. *v.t.* To obtain by or as by effort; to earn, to win, to acquire; to progress, to advance, to get more of; to reach, to attain to; to win (over); to obtain as a result, to incur. *v.i.* To advance in interest, possessions, or happiness; to gain ground, to encroach (upon); to get the advantage (on or upon). **to gain ground:** To advance in any undertaking; to make progress. **to gain on** or **upon:** To get nearer to (an object of pursuit); to encroach upon. **to gain ground upon:** To get nearer (to one pursued). **to gain over:** To win over to any side, party, or view. **to gain the ear of:** To secure favourable consideration from. **to gain the upper hand:** To be victorious. **to gain time:** To obtain delay for any purpose. **to gain the wind:** (*Naut.*) To get to the windward side (of another ship). **gainable,** *a.* ***gainage,** *n.* (*Law*) The gain or profit of tilled or planted land. **gainer,** *n.* One who gains profit, return, or advantage. **gainful,** *a.* Profitable, advantageous, remunerative; devoted to gain. **gainfully,** *adv.* **gainfulness,** *n.* **gainings,** *n.pl.* Profits, gains. **gainless,** *a.* Unprofitable. ***gainlessness,** *n.*

***gain** (2) (gān) [Icel. *gegn*, straight, direct], *a.* Near, straight; kindly favourable. *prep.* Against, contrary to. *adv.* Back, again. **the gainest way:** The shortest way.

gaine (gān) [F. *guine*, a sheath], *n.* (*Mech. Artill.*) A metal tube containing explosive which is screwed to a fuse.

gainly (gān′ li) [Icel. *gegn*, straight, ready, serviceable, -LY], *a.* Suitable, gracious; comely, shapely.

gainsay (gān′ sā), *v.t.* (*past and p.p.* **-said, -sed,** -săd) To contradict, to deny; to controvert, to dispute, *to hinder. **n.* Contradiction. **gain-sayer,** *n.* **gainsaying,** *n.*

gainst, 'gainst [AGAINST].

gair (gâr) [Sc., from Icel. *geire*, cogn. with GORE (2)], *n.* A strip, as of grass.

gairfowl [GAREFOWL].

gait (1) (gāt) [Icel. *gata*, GATE (2)], *n.* Manner of walking or going, carriage. **gaited,** *a.* (*usu. in comb.*) Having a particular gait.

gait (2) (gāt) [prov., etym. doubtful], *n.* A sheaf of grain tied up; charge for pasturage, etc. *v.t.* To set up in sheaves for drying.

gaiter (gā′ tėr) [F. *guêtre*, etym. unknown], *n.* A covering for the ankle or the leg below the knee, usu. fitting down upon the shoe; (*Am.*) a half-boot with a cloth top or elastic sides. *v.t.* To dress with gaiters. **gaiterless,** *a.*

gal [GIRL].

gala (gā′ lȧ) [F., from It., conn. with *galante*, gay], *n.* A festivity, a fête; *festivity, gaiety; *festive attire. **gala day,** *n.* A holiday with sports or festivities. **gala dress,** *n.* Festive attire.

galactic (gȧ lăk′ tik) [Gr. *galaktikos*, from *gala galaktos*, milk], *a.* Pertaining to milk or the secretion of milk, lactic; (*Astron.*) pertaining to the galaxy. **galactia,** *n.* (*Path.*) A morbid flow of milk. **galactin,** *n.* A nitrogenous substance obtained from milk, and existing in the juices or the seeds of certain plants. **galacto-** (*comb. form*). **galactogogue** (gȧ lăk′ tō gog) [Gr. *agōgos*, leading, from *agein*, to lead], *a.* (*Med.*) Promoting the flow of milk. *n.* A medicine which promotes the secretion of milk. **galactometer** (-tom′ ė tėr), *n.* A lactometer. **galactophagist** (-tof′ ȧ jist) [Gr. *galaktophagos* (*-phagos*, eating, from *phagein*, to eat)], *n.* One who subsists on milk. **galactophagous,** *a.* Subsisting on milk. **galactophorous** [-PHOROUS], *a.* Producing milk. **galactopoietic** (gȧ lăk tō poi et′ ik) [Gr. *poētikos*, from *poiein*, to make], *a.* Increasing the flow of milk. *n.* A substance which increases the flow of milk. **galactorrhœa** (gȧ lăk tō rē′ ȧ) [Gr. *rhoia*, a flowing], *n.* An excessive secretion of milk. **galactose** (gȧ lăk′ tōs), *n.* A sweet crystalline glucose obtained from milk-sugar by treatment with dilute acid. **galactonic** (găl ȧk ton′ ik), *a.*

galago (gȧ lā′ gō) [from African native name], *n.* An African genus of lemurs.

galah (gă′ lȧ) [Austral. abor.] The grey, rose-breasted cockatoo; (*colloq.*) a silly person, a simpleton.

Galanthus (gȧ lăn′ thŭs) [Gr. *gala*, milk, *anthos*, flower], *n.* (*Bot.*) A genus of bulbous plants, containing the snowdrop.

galantine (găl′ ȧn tēn) [F., from low L. *galatina*, corr. of *gelatina*, GELATINE (n. due to conf. with *galant*, GALLANT)], *n.* A dish of white meat, freed from bone, tied up, spiced, boiled, covered with jelly, and served cold.

galanty show (gȧl′ ȧn ti shō′) [prob. from It. *galanti*, pl. of *galante*, GALLANT], *n.* A miniature shadow pantomime.

galatea (gă lȧ tē′ ȧ) [L. *Galatea*, a sea-nymph], *n.* (*Textiles*) A blue-and-white striped cotton fabric.

Galatian (gȧ lā′ shi ȧn) [*Galatia*, in Asia Minor, -AN], *a.* Belonging to Galatia. *n.* A native or inhabitant of Galatia.

galaxy (găl′ ȧk si) [O.F. *galaxie*, L. *galaxiam*, nom. *-ias*, Gr. *galaxias*, from *gala*, milk], *n.* The Milky Way, a luminous band, consisting of innumerable stars indistinguishable to the naked eye, stretching across the sky; a nebula or large cluster of stars beyond the Milky Way; (*fig.*) a brilliant assemblage of persons or things.

galbanum (găl′ bȧ nŭm) [L., from Gr. *chalbanē*, prob. from an Oriental word], *n.* A bitter, odorous gum resin obtained from Persian species of *Ferula*, esp. *Ferula galbaniflua*, an ingredient in the anointing-oil of the Jews. ***galbanean** (găl bȧ nē′ ȧn), *a.* Derived from or resembling galbanum.

gale (1) (gāl) [cp. Dan. *gal.*, Norw. *galen*, mad, furious, Icel. *gola*, a breeze], *n.* A strong wind, one stronger than a breeze but less violent than a tempest; (*Meteor.*) a wind with a velocity of 40 m.p.h. or over, at a height of 32 ft. from the ground; (*Naut.*) a storm; (*fig.*) a quarrel, a disturbance.

gale (2) (gāl) [prob. from A.-S. *gafol*, GAVEL], *n.* A periodic payment of rent. **gale-day,** *n.* Rent-day.

gale (3) (gāl) [A.-S. *gagel* (cp. Dut. and G. *gagel*)], *n.* The bog-myrtle, *Myrica gale*, a twiggy shrub growing on marshy ground, also called sweet-gale.

galea (gā′ lė ȧ) [L., a helmet], *n.* A helmet-like organ or part; (*Anat.*) the amnion; (*Surg.*) a bandage for the head; (*Bot.*) the arched upper lip in some labiates. **galeate** (găl′ ė ȧt), **galeated** (-ā′ tėd), *a.*

galeeny (gȧ lē′ ni) [Sp. *gallina Morisca*, a Moorish fowl], *n.* (*prov.*) A guinea-fowl.

Galega (gȧ lē′ gȧ) [etym. doubtful], *n.* (*Bot.*) The goat's rue, a genus of leguminous herbs.

Galen (gā′ lėn) [Claudius *Galēnus* (A.D. 130–200), a Greek physician of Pergamos], *n.* (*fig.*) A physician. **Galenic** (1), **-al** (1) (gȧ len′ ik, -ȧl), *a.* Of or according to Galen, esp. applied to medicines prepared from vegetable substances by infusion or decoction, as opp. to chemical remedies. **Galenism** (gā′ lė nizm), *n.* **Galenist,** *n.*

galena (gȧ lē′ nȧ) [L.], *n.* (*Min.*) Native sulphide of lead or lead-ore. **galenic** (2), **-al** (2) (gȧ len′ ik, -ȧl), *a.* **galenite** (gȧ lē′ nīt), *n.* Galena. **galenoid** (gȧ lē′ noid), *a.* and *n.*

galeopithecus (găl ė ō pi thē′ kŭs) [Gr. *galeē*, weasel, *pithēkos*, an ape], *n.* (*Zool.*) A genus of flying lemurs. **galeopithecine** (-sīn), **-coid** (-koid), *a.*

galette (gȧ let′) [F., from *galet*, a pebble, Bret. *kalet*, hard as a stone], *n.* A flat, round cake.

Galician (gȧ lish′ i ȧn) [*Galicia*, a province in the north-west of Spain], *a.* Of or pertaining to Galicia. *n.* A native or inhabitant of Galicia.

Galilean (1) (găl i lē′ ȧn) [*Galileo*, the astronomer (1564–1642)], *a.* Of or according to Galileo, esp. applied to the simple telescope developed and used by him.

Galilee (găl′ i lē) [A Roman province, comprehending the north of Palestine west of the Jordan], *n.* A porch or chapel at the entrance of a church; prob. so called because, like Galilee in respect to Judea, it was less sacred than the body of the church, or in allusion to Matt. iv. 15, "Galilee of the Gentiles." **Galilean** (2) (-lē′ ȧn), *a.* Pertaining to Galilee. *n.* A native or inhabitant of Galilee; (*Eccles. Hist.*) a Christian (applied contemptuously by pagans). **the Galilean:** (*contemptuously*) Jesus Christ.

galimatias (găl i măt′ i ȧs, -mā′ shi ȧs) [F., etym. unknown], *n.* Nonsense; an absurd jumble or rigmarole.

galingale (găl′ ing gāl) [O.F. *galingal*, Arab. *khalanjān*, acc. to O.E.D. through Pers. from Chin. *Ko-liang-Kiang*, mild ginger from *Ko*, in Canton], *n.* The aromatic root-stock of certain East Indian plants of the ginger family and of the genus *Alpinia* and *Kæmpferia*, formerly used for culinary purposes; applied to a rare English sedge, *Cyperus longus*.

galiongee (găl i ŏn jē′) [Turk. *qālūnjī*, from It. *galeone*, GALLEON], *n.* A Turkish sailor, esp. a man-of-war's man.

galipot (1) (găl′ i pot) [F., etym. doubtful], *n.* A yellowish-white, viscid resin exuding from *Pinus maritimus* and hardening into a kind of turpentine, called, after refining, white, yellow, or Burgundy pitch. **galipot varnish,** *n.*

galipot (2) [GALLIPOT].

galium (găl′ i ŭm) [Gr. *galion*], *n.* (*Bot.*) Bedstraw, a genus of slender herbaceous plants, containing goose-grass, lady's bedstraw, etc.

gall (1) (gawl) [A.-S. *gealla* (cp. Dut. *gal*, Icel. *gall*, G. *galle*, also L. *fel*, Gr. *cholē*), cogn. with YELLOW], *n.* A bitter, yellowish fluid secreted by the liver, bile; the gall-bladder; (*fig.*) anything exceedingly bitter; rancour, malignity, bitterness of mind; *spirit, courage; (*Am. colloq.*) self-assurance, cheek.

gall and wormwood: A symbol for all that is hateful, exasperating, and unwelcome. **gall-bladder,** *n.* A pear-shaped membraneous sac, lodged on the under surface of the liver, which receives the bile. **gall-duct, -passage, -pipe,** *n.* A duct which conveys the bile. **gall-stone,** *n.* A morbid calcareous concretion formed in the gall-bladder. **gall-less,** *a.*

gall (2) (gawl) [O.F. *galle*, L. *galla*], *n.* A morbid excrescence on plants, esp. the oak, caused by the action of some insect. *v.t.* To impregnate with a decoction of galls. **oak-gall, gall-apple** [GALL-NUT]. **gall-fly, -insect, -louse,** *n.* An insect, chiefly belonging to the genus *Cynips*, that causes the production of galls. **gall-nut, -apple,** *n.* A gall produced on the oak, esp. by the puncture by *Cynips gallæ tinctoria* of the leaf-buds of the gall-oak, which form the galls of commerce, used in making ink and for other purposes. **gall-oak,** *n.* The oak, *Quercus infectoria*, on which the galls of commerce are produced.

gall (3) (gawl) [A.-S. *gealla*, perh. cogn. with GALL (1)], *n.* A sore, swelling, or blister, esp. one produced by friction or chafing on a horse; soreness, irritation; one who or that which causes this; a bare place in a field or a crop; *a blemish, a defect; (*U.S.A.*) a marshy lowland (in the Southern States). *v.t.* To chafe, hurt, or injure by rubbing; to make sore by friction; (*fig.*) to annoy, to harass, to vex. *v.i.* To fret; *to act in an irritating manner. **galling,** *a.* Vexing, irritating, chafing. **gallingly,** *adv.*

gallant (găl' ȧnt) [O.F. *gallant*, *galant*, pres.p. of *galer*, to make merry, from Teut. (cp. M.H.G. *wallen*, O.H.G. *wallōn*, to wander)], *a.* Gay, showy, well-dressed; fine, stately; brave, high-spirited, courageous, chivalrous; (gȧ lănt') specially attentive to women; pertaining to love. (găl' ȧnt) *n.* A man of fashion, a beau; *a bold and dashing fellow; (gȧ lănt'), a man attentive and polite to women; a lover, a wooer; a paramour. *v.t.* (gȧ lănt') To attend as a gallant or cavalier, to escort; to pay court to; to flirt with; *to handle (a fan) in a fashionable manner. *v.i.* To play the gallant; to flirt (with). **gallantly** (găl' ȧnt li, gȧ lănt' li), *adv.* **gallantry,** *n.* Bold, dashing, magnanimous courage; politeness and deference to women, with or without evil intent; amorous intrigue; *showy appearance, a brave show; *gallants collectively.

***galleass** (găl' ė ăs) [O.F. *galeace*, It. *galeazza*, late L. *galea*, GALLEY], *n.* A heavy, low-built vessel propelled both by sails and oars, usu. with three masts and about twenty guns.

galleon (găl' ė ȯn) [Sp. *galeon*, late L. *galeo -ōnem*, from *galea*, GALLEY], *n.* A large ship, with three or four decks, much used in 15th–17th cents., esp. by the Spaniards in their commerce with their American possessions.

gallery (găl' ėr i) [O.F. *galerie*, late L. *galeria*, etym. doubtful], *n.* An elevated floor or platform projecting from the wall toward the interior of a church, hall, theatre, or other large building, commonly used for musicians, singers, or part of the congregation or audience; (*Theat.*) the highest and cheapest tier of seats; the persons occupying these, hence (*fig.*) the most unrefined of the auditors; a passage open at one side, usu. projecting from the wall of a building and supported on corbels or pillars; a corridor, a passage, a long and narrow room; such a room used for the exhibition of pictures, hence, a collection of pictures; a portico or colonnade, a balcony, a veranda; (*Fort.*) a covered passage in a work, either for defence or communication; (*Mining*) an adit, drift, or heading. *v.t.* To furnish or pierce with a gallery or galleries. **to play to the gallery:** To court vulgar applause. **galleried,** *a.* **galleryful,** *n.*

gallet (găl' ėt), **garret** (2) [prob. from F. *galet*, a pebble, dim. of O.F. *gal*, a stone], *n.* A chip or splinter of a stone. *v.t.* To insert bits of stone in the joints of coarse masonry. **galleting, garreting,** *n.*

galley (1) (găl' i) [O.F. *galie*, late L. *galea*, a galley], *n.* A low, flat vessel, with one deck, navigated with sails and oars, which were usu. worked by slaves or convicts; an ancient Greek or Roman war-vessel of this type with one or more tiers of oars; a row-boat of large size, esp. one, larger than the gig, used by the captain of a man-of-war; a state barge; the cook-house on board ship. **galley-slave,** *n.* A criminal condemned to the galleys; (*fig.*) a drudge.

galley (2) (găl' i) [F. *galée*], *n.* (*Print.*) An oblong tray on which compositors place matter as it is set up. **galley-press,** *n.* A press at which galley-proofs are pulled. **galley-proof,** *n.* A proof taken from type in a galley, as dist. from that arranged in pages.

galliambic (găl' i ăm' bik) [L. *galliambus*, the metre used by the Galli or priests of Cybele in their chants], *n.* (*Pros.*) A tetrameter catalectic composed of Ionics, a minore (◡ ◡) with variations and substitutions—the metre of the *Attis* of Catullus and of Tennyson's *Boadicea*; (*pl.*) verses in this metre. *a.* In this metre.

***Gallian** [GALLIC (2)].

galliard (găl' i ȧrd) [F. *gaillard* (fem. *gaillarde*, whence the n.), etym. unknown], *a.* Merry, gay, jaunty. *n.* A merry or lively person; *a lively dance; *the music to this. **galliardise** (găl' i ȧr dīz), *n.* Merriment, liveliness.

gallic (1) (găl' ik) [GALL (1)], *a.* **gallic acid,** *n.* (*Chem.*) An acid derived from oak-galls and other vegetable sources. **gallo- (1),** *comb. form.*

Gallic (2) (găl' ik) [L. *Gallicus*, from *Gallus*, a GAUL], *a.* Of or pertaining to ancient Gaul; (*loosely*) French. **Gallice** (găl' i sē), *adv.* In French. **Gallicism,** *n.* A French expression or idiom. **Gallicize,** *v.t.* and *i.*

Gallican (găl' i kȧn) [L. *Gallicānus*, as prec.], *a.* Pertaining to the ancient Church of Gaul or France; ultramontane, claiming autonomy for the Church in France and repudiating papal control. *n.* A member of the French Church who holds these views. **Gallicanism,** *n.* **Gallicanist,** *n.*

galligaskins (găl i găs' kinz) [corr. of F. *garguesques*, corr. of *greguesques*, It. *Grechesca*, orig. fem. of *Grechesco*, Greekish], *n.pl.* Loose breeches; gaiters worn by sportsmen; orig. loose hose or breeches such as were worn in the 16th and 17th centuries.

gallimaufry (găl i maw' fri) [F. *gallimafrée*, etym. unknown], *n.* A hash, a hodge-podge; (*fig.*) an inconsistent or ridiculous medley.

gallinaceous (găl i nā' shŭs) [L. *gallīnāceus*, from *gallīna*, a hen], *a.* Of or pertaining to the *Gallinæ*, a group of birds containing pheasants, partridges, grouse, turkeys, domestic fowls, and allied forms. **gallinacean,** *a.* Gallinaceous. *n.* One of the *Gallinæ*.

gallinazo (găl i na' zō) [Sp. *gallinaza*, from *gallina*, as prec.], *n.* An American vulture.

galling [GALL (3)].

gallinule (găl' i nūl) [late L. *gallīnula*, dim. of L. *gallina*, hen], *n.* Any bird of the genus *Gallinula*, esp. *G. chloropus*, the moor-hen.

Gallio (găl' i ō) [Junius Annæus *Gallio*, pro-consul of Achaia, A.D. 53, who refused to attend to the Jewish agitation against Paul, Acts xviii. 12–17], *n.* One who pays no attention to matters, however grave or sacred, that do not directly concern him.

galliot (găl' i ȯt) [O.F. *galiote*, late L. *galeota*, from *galea*, GALLEY], *n.* A small, swift galley propelled by sails and oars; a one- or two-masted Dutch or Flemish merchant vessel.

gallipot (găl' i pot) [prob. GALLEY, POT], *n.* A small glazed earthenware pot used to contain ointments, medicines, preserves, etc.

gallium (găl' i ŭm) [from L. *gallus*, a cock, alluding to *Lecoq*], *n.* A soft, grey metallic element of extreme fusibility discovered in zinc-blende by M. Lecoq de Boisbaudren.

gallivant (găl i vănt') [prob. from GALLANT], *v.i.* To gad about, to go pleasure-seeking.

gallivat (găl' i văt) [corr. of Port. *galeota*, GALLIOT], *n.* A large swift-sailing boat used in the East Indies.

galliwasp (găl i wosp) [etym. doubtful], *n.* A small harmless West Indian lizard, *Celestus occiduus*, erroneously reputed to be venomous.

gallize (găl' īz) [the inventor, Dr. L. *Gall*, of Treves], *v.t.* To treat (unfermented grape-juice) with water and sugar, so as to produce a larger quantity of wine.

gallo- (1) [GALLIC (1)]. **gallo-bromol** (găl' ō brō' mōl) [BROMINE, -OL], *n.* A grey crystalline powder obtained from gallic acid and bromine, used as a sedative, astringent, antiseptic, etc.

Gallo- (2) [L. *Gallus*, a Gaul], *comb. form.* French. **Gallomania** (găl ō mā' ni ȧ), *n.* A mania for French fashions, habits, or practices, literature, etc. **Gallomaniac,** *n.* **Gallophil** (găl' ō fil) [-PHIL], *n.* A devotee of French customs, etc. **Gallophobe** [-PHOBE], *n.* One who hates French ways or fears the French. **Gallophobia** (găl ō fō' bi ȧ), *n.*

galloglass (găl' ō glas) [Ir. *gallóglách* (*gall*, a foreigner, *óglách* a youth, a warrior)], *n.* An armed soldier or retainer of an ancient Irish chieftain.

gallon (găl' ŏn) [O.F. *galon*, *jalon*, prob. cogn. with F. *jale*; etym. unknown], *n.* An English measure of capacity; a dry measure equal to one-eighth of a bushel. **imperial gallon,** *n.* A British measure for liquids, containing 277¼ cubic inches. **Winchester gallon,** *n.* A measure for wine forming the standard in the United States, containing 231 cubic inches.

galloon (gȧ loon') [F. *galon*, prob. from O.F. *gall*, see GALA], *n.* A narrow braid of silk, worsted, or cotton, with gold or silver thread interwoven, for binding uniforms, dresses, etc.; other materials used for binding or edging.

gallop (găl' ŏp) [O F. *galoper*, prob. from Teut. (cp. Flem. *walop*, gallop, O.S. *hlōpan*, to LEAP)], *v.i.* To run in a series of springs, as a horse at its fastest pace; to ride at a gallop; (*fig.*) to go or do anything at a very rapid pace. *v.t.* To make (a horse) gallop. *n.* The motion of a horse at its fastest speed, with all the feet off the ground at one point in the progressive movement of the four limbs; the act of riding or a ride at this pace; a galop. **gallopade** (găl ŏ pād'), *n.* A sidelong or curvetting kind of gallop; a brisk dance, of Hungarian origin. *v.i.* To dance this. **galloper,** *n.* A horse that gallops; a man who gallops on a horse, or who makes great haste; (*Mil.*) an aide-de-camp; a light field-gun attached to cavalry. **galloping consumption,** *n.* A rapid consumption or phthisis.

Gallovidian (găl ō vid' i ȧn) [med. L. *Gallovidia*, W. *Gallwyddel*, Galloway], *a.* Of or belonging to Galloway. *n.* A native of Galloway.

***gallow** [GALLY].

galloway (găl' ō wā) [*Galloway*, in S.W. Scotland], *n.* A small, hardy variety of horse, bred in Galloway.

gallows (găl' ōz) [A.-S. *galga* (cp. Icel. *gālgi*, Dut. *galg*, G. *galgen*)], *n.* (*pl. used as sing.*) A framework, usu. consisting of timber uprights and a cross-piece, on which criminals are executed by hanging; execution by hanging; a similar framework used for gymnastics, for hanging things on, in printing, cookery, etc.; *a wretch who deserves the gallows; (*Am. colloq., pl.* **gallowses**) braces, suspenders. **gallows-bird,** *n.* One who deserves hanging. **gallows-bitts,** *n.pl.* (*Naut.*) A strong frame erected amidships on the deck to hold spare spars. **gallows-free,** *a.* Saved from hanging. **gallows-ripe,** *a.* Ready to be hanged. **gallows-top,** *n.* (*Naut.*) A crosspiece of timber placed at the top of the gallows-bitts. **gallows-tree,** *n.* (*poet.*) The gallows.

Gallup Poll (găl' ŭp pōl) [inventor G. *Gallup*], *n.* Protected name of a method of ascertaining the trend of public opinion by interrogating a cross-section of the population.

***gally** (găl' i) [A.-S. *gælwan* (in the form *agælwan*), to astonish, to alarm], *v.t.* To frighten, to scare; (*Whaling*) to startle or disturb (a whale). **gally-beggar, -crow,** *n.* (*prov.*) A scarecrow.

galoche [GALOSH].

galoot (gȧ loot') [slang; etym. doubtful], *n.* (*Naut.*) A clumsy soldier; an awkward, uncouth fellow.

galop (găl' ŏp) [F., see GALLOP], *n.* A lively dance in 2–4 time; the music to the dance. *v.i.* To dance this.

galore (gȧ lôr') [Ir. *go leor* (*go*, to, *leor*, sufficient)], *n.* Plenty, abundance. *adv.* In plenty, abundantly.

galosh (gȧ losh') [F. *galoche*, prob. through L. from Gr. *kalopodion*, dim. of *kalopous*, a shoemaker's last (*kalon*, wood, *pous podos*, foot)], *n.* (*usu. pl.*) An overshoe, usu. of vulcanized rubber, for protecting one's boots or shoes in wet weather, (*Am.* rubbers); (*Boot-making*) a piece of leather or other material sewn round the lower part of uppers. *v.t.* To furnish (boots or shoes) with this.

galt [GAULT].

galumph (gȧ lŭmf') [coined by 'Lewis Carroll,' prob. from GALLOP and TRIUMPH], *v.i.* To prance exultantly.

galvanic (găl văn' ik) [L. *Galvani* (1737–98), Italian physician and its discoverer], *a.* Of, pertaining to, or produced by galvanism; (*fig.*) forced, spasmodic (of movements, expression, etc.). **galvanic battery** or **pile,** *n.* A number of connected galvanic cells for producing an electric current. **galvanic belt,** *n.* A galvanic apparatus in the form of a belt for applying electricity to the body. **galvanic electricity,** *n.* **galvanically,** *adv.*

galvanism (găl' vȧ nizm) [as prec.], *n.* Electricity produced by chemical action, esp. that of acids on metals; the branch of science dealing with this; its application for medical purposes. **galvanist,** *n.* **galvanize,** *v.t.* To apply galvanism to, esp. to stimulate muscular action, etc., by galvanism; to plate with gold or other metal by galvanism; (*fig.*) to rouse into life or activity as by a galvanic shock. **galvanization** (-zā' shŭn), *n.* **galvanizer,** *n.* **galvanized iron,** *n.* Iron coated with zinc (orig. by galvanic deposition), to protect it from moisture. **galvanography** (-nog' rȧ fi), *n.* The production of a printing-plate by electrotypy from a drawing in viscid ink on a silvered plate. **galvanograph** (găl' vȧ nŏ grăf), *n.* A plate so produced; the resulting impression, which resembles that from copper-plate. **galvanographic** (-grăf' ik), *a.* **galvanology** (-nol' ŏ ji), *n.* The science of galvanism; a treatise on its phenomena. **galvanologist,** *n.* **galvanometer** (-nom' ė tėr), *n.* A delicate apparatus for determining the existence, direction, and intensity of electric currents. **galvanometric, -al** (-met' rik, -ȧl), *a.* **galvanometry** (-nom' ė tri), *n.* **galvanoplasty** (-plăs' ti) [Gr. *-plastos*, moulded, from *plassein*, to mould], *n.* The coating of objects with a metal deposit by galvanism, electrotypy. **galvanoplastic,** *a.* **galvanoplastically,** *adv.* **galvanoscope** (găl văn' ŏ skōp), *n.* An instrument for detecting the presence and showing the direction of electric currents.

Galwegian (găl wē' ji ȧn) [*Galloway*, assim. to NORWEGIAN], *a.* and *n.* Gallovidian.

gam (1) (găm) [etym. doubtful], *n.* (*Naut.*) A herd of whales; a keeping company or exchange of visits among whalers at sea. *v.i.* To congregate or form a school (as whales); to exchange courtesies (of whalers and their crews). *v.t.* To forgather with or exchange visits with (another whaler and its crew at sea).

***gam** (2) (găm) [Sc., etym. doubtful], *n.* The mouth; (*pl.*) large teeth.

gama grass (ga' mȧ gras) [perh. var. of GRAMA], *n.* A fodder grass, *Tripsacum dactyloides*, with culms from 4 to 7 feet high, growing in the Southern U.S.A.

gamash (gȧ măsh') [F. *gamache*, perh. ult. from Arab. *ghadāmasī*, from *Ghadāmas*, in Tripoli, a place where leather was made], *n.* (*usu. pl.*) A kind of leggings, spatter-dashes, or high-boots.

gamb (găm) [O.F. *gambe* (F. *jambe*)], *n.* (*Her.*) A figure of an animal's leg on a coat-of-arms.

gamba (1) (găm' bȧ) [L.], *n.* (*Anat.*) The metacarpus or metatarsus.

gamba (2) (găm' bȧ) [for VIOLA DA GAMBA], *n.* A *viola da gamba*, an organ stop with a tone like that of the violin or violoncello.

gambade (găm bād') **gambado** (1) (găm bā' dō) [F. *gambade* or Sp. *gambada*, GAMBOL], *n.* A bound or spring of a horse; a caper, a fantastic movement; (*fig.*) a freak, a frolic.

gambado (2) (găm bā' dō) [It. *gamba*, the leg], *n.* A leather legging or large boot for equestrians.

***gambeson** (găm' bė sȯn) [O.F. *gambison*, *wambison*, prob. from Teut. (cp. O.H.G. *wamba*, WOMB)], *n.* A body-covering or tunic extending over the thighs, quilted and stuffed with wool, and usu. worn under armour, chiefly in the 14th cent.

gambet (găm' bėt) [It. *gambetta*, from *gamba*, leg], *n.* The redshank.

gambier (găm' bi ėr) [*gambir*, Malay], *n.* An extract from the leaves of *Uncaria gambir*, used in medicine as an astringent, and for dyeing and tanning.

gambit (găm' bit) [derivation obscure, ult. from It. *gambetto*, a tripping up, from *gamba*, leg], *n.* An opening in chess, in which a pawn is sacrificed in order to obtain a favourable position for attack [most of the gambits have distinctive names, as *King's gambit*, *Queen's gambit*, *Steinitz gambit*]; the opening move in a concerted plan. **gambit-pawn,** *n.* A pawn so sacrificed.

gamble (găm' bėl) [prob. from A.-S. *gamenian*, to play, from *gamen*, a GAME, with freq. suf. -LE], *v.i.* To play, esp. a game of chance, for money; (*fig.*) to risk large sums or other possessions on some contingency; to speculate financially. *n.* Gambling; a gambling venture or speculation. **to gamble away:** To squander or lose in gambling. **gambler,** *n.* **gamblesome,** *a.*

gamboge (găm boozh') [mod. L. *Gambogium*, *Cambodia*, in Annam], *n.* A gum-resin, from Cambodia, Ceylon, etc., used as a yellow pigment, and in medicine.

gambol (găm' bȯl) [earlier *gambold*, *gambalde*, O.F. *gambade*, It. *gambata*, from *gamba*, leg], *v.i.* To frisk or skip about; to frolic. *n.* A frolic; a skipping or playing about.

***gambrel** (găm' brėl) [etym. doubtful (cp. CAMBREL)], *n.* A horse's hock; a bent piece of wood used for suspending carcases; (*Am.*) a gambrel-roof. **gambrel-roof,** *n.* A curved or double-pitched roof.

gambroon (găm broon') [prob. from seaport of *Gambroon*, on the Persian Gulf], *n.* A twilled linen fabric for linings; a twilled cloth for trousers.

game (1) (gām) [A.-S. *gamen* (cp. Icel. and O.H.G. *gaman*, Dut. *gammen*)], *n.* Sport, merriment, diversion; jest, as opp. to earnest; an exercise for diversion, usu. in concert with other players, a pastime; a contest played according to specified rules and decided by chance, strength, skill, or any combination of these; (*pl.*) athletic contests, esp. such as are held at periodical dates, like the Olympian, the Caledonian Games, etc.; (*Am.*) a match, *e.g.* football; a single round in a sporting contest; the number of points required to win a game; (*fig.*) a project, plan, or scheme designed to defeat others; success in a game or contest; (*colloq.*, *pl.*) tricks, dodges, subterfuges; wild animals or birds pursued in the chase, as hares, grouse, partridges, pheasants; the flesh of these; (*fig.*) an object of pursuit; (*slang*) a lark, an amusing incident; *field sports, as hunting, coursing, falconry, etc.; *gallantry. *a.* Pertaining to game; having the spirit of a game-cock; plucky, spirited; ready, willing (to do, etc.). *v.i.* To play at games of chance; to play for a stake; to gamble. *v.t.* To gamble (away). **the game is up:** Everything has failed; the game (bird or animal) has started up. **to die game:** To maintain a resolute attitude to the last. **to have the game in one's hands:** To be sure of winning; (*fig.*) to have success (in any contest, undertaking, etc.) at one's command. **to make game of:** To turn into ridicule. **to play the game:** To abide by the rules; (*fig.*) to act in an honourable way. **game-bag,** *n.* A bag to hold the game killed or taken by a sportsman. **game-ball,** *n.* (*Tennis, etc.*) The state of the score when one point is enough to determine the game. **game-cock,** *n.* A cock bred for fighting. **game-egg,** *n.* An egg from which game-fowls are bred. **game-keeper,** *n.* One employed to look after game, coverts, etc., and to prevent poaching. **game-laws,** *n.pl.* Laws for the preservation of game; the regulation of the seasons for killing it, etc. **game-licence,** *n.* One giving the right to kill or deal in game. **game-preserver,** *n.* A landowner who strictly preserves game, and rigidly insists on his legal rights in that respect. **game-tenant,** *n.* A person renting an estate or piece of land for shooting or fishing. **gameful,** *a.* Full of sport or mirth; sportive. **gamely,** *adv.* **gameness,** *n.* **gamesome,** *a.* Inclined to play; merry, gay. **gamesomely,** *adv.* **gamesomeness,** *n.* **gamester,** *n.* One who is addicted to gaming, a gambler; *a frolicsome person, *a prostitute. **gaming-house,** *n.* A house where gambling is carried on; a house of ill-repute. **gaming-table,** *n.* A table for gambling games. **gamy,** *a.* Having the flavour or odour of game, high; abounding in game; plucky, spirited, game. **gaminess,** *n.*

game (2) (gām) [etym. doubtful], *a.* (*colloq.*) Lame, crippled; crooked (of the arm or leg). **gammy** (găm' i), *a.* Wrong, spurious; crippled, crooked; *n.* A lame person.

gamete (găm' ēt) [Gr. *gametes*, husband], *n.* (*Biol.*) A sexual reproductive cell. **gametocyte** (gȧ mēt' ō sīt), *n.* A cell which breaks up into gametes. **gametogenesis** (gȧm ēt ō jen' e sis), *n.* The formation of gametes.

gamic (găm' ik) [Gr. *gamikos*, from *gamos*, marriage], *a.* (*Biol.*) Of or pertaining to sex, sexual; capable of development after sexual fertilization (of ova) [cp. AGAMIC]. **gamete** (gȧ mēt'), *n.* (*Biol.*) A reproductive cell, a germ cell—in the male a spermatozoon, in the female the ovum.

gamin (găm' in, ga măn) [F., perh. from G. *gemein*, a common soldier], *n.* A street arab, an urchin.

gamma (găm' ȧ) [Gr.], *n.* The third letter of the Greek alphabet, Γ, γ, G, g, representing 3 in enumerations; a moth *Flusia gamma*, also called the gamma moth; an instrument for cauterizing a hernia (from its resemblance to the Greek gamma); *(*Mus.*) the gamut. **gamma plus:** Rather better than third class. **gamma-rays** (*Phys.*) Short-wave-length, penetrating electromagnetic rays emitted by radioactive substances. Used in treatment of cancer and in radiography of metals.

gammadion, gammation (gȧ mā' di ȯn, -ti ȯn) [late Gr., from prec.], *n.* (*pl.* **-ia**) An ornament composed of the gamma singly or in the combination, formerly used in sacerdotal vestments in the Greek Church; a cruciform ornament composed of four gammas, placed back to back, forming a voided Greek cross; a fylfot, swastika.

gammer (găm' ėr) [prob. a corr. of GRANDMOTHER], *n.* An old woman.

gammon (1) (găm' ȯn) [O.F. *gambon* (F. *jambon*), from *gambe*, a leg], *n.* The buttock or thigh of a hog salted and dried; a cured ham. *v.t.* To make into bacon; to salt and dry in smoke.

gammon (2) (găm' ȯn) [orig. thieves' slang, prob. from M.E. and A.-S. *gamen*, GAME (1)], *n.* Nonsense, humbug; a fraud, a hoax. *int.* Nonsense, humbug. *v.t.* To hoax, to impose upon. *v.i.* To make pretences; to talk deceptively, to chaff.

gammon (3) (găm' ŏn) [prob. from A.-S. *gamen*, GAME], *n.* A defeat at backgammon in which the winner's score is equivalent to two games; *backgammon. *v.t.* To win a gammon against (an opponent in backgammon).

gammon (4) (găm' ŏn) [etym. doubtful], *v.t.* (*Naut.*) To make fast (the bowsprit) to the stem. *n.* The lashing so used. **gammoning,** *n.* **gammoning-hole, -plate,** *n.* The hole through which or the hole to which the gammoning is fastened.

gammy [GAME (2)].

gamo- [Gr. *gamos*, marriage], *comb. form.* (*Biol.*) flexual; (*Bot.*) having certain parts united. **gamogenesis** (găm ō jen' ė sis) [GENESIS], *n.* (*Biol.*) Sexual reproduction. **gamogenetic** (găm ō jė net' ik), *a.* **gamogenetically,** *adv.* **gamopetalous** (-pet' ȧ lŭs), *a.* (*Bot.*) Having the petals united. **gamophyllous** (-fil' ŭs), *a.* (*Bot.*) Having the leaves united. **gamosepalous** (-sep' ȧ lŭs), *a.* (*Bot.*) Having the sepals united.

gamp (gămp) [Mrs. *Gamp*, the monthly nurse in Dickens's 'Martin Chuzzlewit'], *n.* (*facet.*) An umbrella, esp. a large and clumsy one.

gamut (găm' ŭt) [med. L. *gamma ut* (*gamma*, the third letter of the Greek alphabet, used by Guido of Arezzo to mark the first or lowest note in the mediæval music scale, combined with *ut*, the first word in a mnemonic stanza from a hymn beginning *Ut queant laxis resonare fibris*, containing the six names of the hexachord *Ut re mi fa sol la*)], *n.* *The first or lowest note in Guido's scale equivalent to G on the lowest line of the modern bass stave; the major diatonic scale; the whole series of notes recognized by musicians; (*fig.*) the whole range, compass, or extent.

gamy [GAME (1)].

-gamy [Gr. *gamos*, marriage], *suf.* Marriage or kind of marriage, as in *endogamy, misogamy.*

ganch (gănch) [F. *gancher*, from It. *gancio*, prob. from Turk. *ganja*, hook], *v.t.* To impale, esp. to execute by dropping on to hooks or sharp stakes.

gander (găn' dėr) [A.-S. *gandra*, earlier *ganra* (*d* inserted as in Dut. *gander*), perh. cogn. with GOOSE], *n.* The male of the goose; a simpleton, a noodle. **ganderism,** *n.* **gander-party,** *n.* A gathering of men only. **gander-pulling,** *n.* (*U.S.A.*) A barbarous sport in which horsemen try to pull the head off a gander as they ride past it at full speed.

gang (1) (găng) [A.-S. *gang* (from foll.) or Icel. *gangr* (cp. Dut. and G. *gang*)], *n.* A number of persons associated for a particular purpose (often in a bad sense); a number of workmen under a foreman, or of slaves or convicts; a set of tools operating in concert; (*Mining*) a course or vein; a gangue; (*Sc.*) a walk or pasturage (for cattle). *v.i.* To act in concert with. **to gang up against:** To join others in opposing. **gang-board, gang-plank,** *n.* A gangway for landing from a vessel. **gang-cask,** *n.* (*Naut.*) A small cask for bringing off water in boats. **ganger, gangsman,** *n.* The overseer or foreman of a gang of labourers, plate-layers, etc. **gangster,** *n.* Primarily an adherent of a political party in U.S.A.; a member of a criminal gang.

gang (2) (găng) [A.-S. *gangan* (cp. Icel. *ganga*, O.H.G. *gangan*)], *v.i.* (*Sc. past and p.p.* **gaed**) To go. **gang-days,** *n.pl.* The three days preceding Ascension Day or Holy Thursday, Rogation-days. **gang-week,** *n.* Rogation-week.

gange (gănj) [etym. doubtful], *v.t.* To cover (a fish-hook or part of fishing-line) with fine wire; to fasten (a fish-hook) to a ganging-line. **ganging** (găn' jing), *n.* Fastening a fish-hook to a line; the part of the line to which it is fastened, also called **ganging-line.**

Gangetic (găn jet' ik) [L. *Gangēticus*, from *Ganges*, Gr. *Gangēs*], *a.* Pertaining to the river Ganges or the region in which it runs.

gangling (găng' gling), *a.* Loosely built, lanky, awkward.

ganglion (găng' gli ŏn) [Gr.], *n.* (*pl.* **-glia**) An enlargement in the course of a nerve forming a local centre for nervous action; an aggregation of nerve-cells forming a nucleus in the central nervous system; a glandiform organ such as the spleen or the thyroid body; (*Path.*) a globular tumour in the sheath of a tendon. **gangliac, gangliar, ganglionic** (găng gli on' ik), *a.* Pertaining to a ganglion or ganglia. **gangliated, ganglionated,** *a.* **gangliform,** *a.* **ganglionary,** *a.* Composed of ganglia.

***gangrel** (găng' grėl) [prob. from GANG (1 or 2)], *n.* A vagrant.

gangrene (găng' grēn) [L. *gangræna*, Gr. *gangraina*], *n.* Cessation of vitality in a part of the body, the first stage of mortification, usu. followed by decay. *v.t.* To cause this in; (*fig.*) to inject with decay or vice; to corrupt. *v.i.* To mortify. ***gangrenate,** *v.t.* **gangrenescent** (-nes' ėnt), *a.* **gangrenous** (găng' grė nŭs), *a.*

gangster [GANG (1)].

gangue (găng) [F., from G. *gang*, vein, lode, cogn. with GANG (1)], *n.* The earthy matter or matrix in which ores are embedded.

gangway (găng' wā) [A.-S. *gangweg* (as GANG (1), WAY)], *n.* A passage into or out of a building or between rows of seats; (*House of Commons*) a narrow cross passage giving access to the back benches, and dividing the more independent members from the immediate supporters of the Government and the opposition; (*Naut.*) a temporary bridge affording means of passage from a ship to the shore; an opening in the bulwarks affording entrance to or exit from a vessel; a passage connecting different parts of a vessel; (*Min.*) a main level. **to bring to the gangway:** (*Naut.*) To punish by tying up and flogging. **to sit below the gangway:** To sit as a more or less independent member of the House of Commons.

ganister (găn' is tėr) [etym. doubtful], *n.* A kind of grit or hard sandstone from the lower coal-measures; (*Metal.*) a mixture of ground quartz and fire-clay used for lining Bessemer converters.

ganja (găn' jȧ) [Hind. *gānjhā*], *n.* A dried preparation of *Cannabis sativa* or Indian hemp, smoked as an intoxicant and narcotic.

gannet (găn' ėt) [A.-S. *ganot* (cp. Dut. *gent*, M.H.G. *ganze*, GANDER)], *n.* A sea-bird, *Sula bassana*, also called the solan goose.

ganoid (găn' oid) [F. *ganoïde* (Gr. *ganos*, brightness, -OID)], *a.* (*Ichthyol.*) Bright, smooth, like enamel (of fish-scales); belonging to the *Ganoidei* (of fish). *n.* Any fish of the *Ganoidei*. **ganoidal, ganoidean** (gȧ noi' dė ȧn), *a.* **Ganoidei** (gȧ noi' dė ī), *n.pl.* A division of fishes comprising the sturgeons and numerous extinct forms, so called from their shining scales.

gant (gănt), **gaunt** (1) (gawnt) [from A.-S. *gānian*, to yawn], *v.i.* (*Sc.*) To yawn.

gantlet [GAUNTLET (1)].

gantry (găn' tri) [etym. doubtful (perh. from O.F. *gantier*, also *chantier*, L. *canterium*)], *n.* A wooden frame for standing a barrel upon; a structure for carrying a travelling crane.

Ganymede (găn' i mēd) [L. *Ganymēdēs*, Gr. *Ganumēdēs*, the successor of Hebe as cup-bearer to Zeus], *n.* A cup-bearer; (*facet.*) a waiter; *a catamite; (*Astron.*) the largest satellite of the planet Jupiter.

gaol (jāl) etc. [JAIL].

gap (găp) [Icel., from *gapa*, see foll.], *n.* An opening, a breach, as in a hedge, a fence, etc.; a chasm, a break in a mountain ridge; (*fig.*) a breach of continuity, a blank, hiatus, interruption; a deficiency; a wide divergence. *v.t.* (*past & p.p.* **gapped**) To make a gap in. **to stand in the gap:** To expose oneself for the protection of others. **to stop, fill,** or **supply a gap:** To repair a defect or make up a deficiency. **gap-toothed,** *a.* Having interstices between the teeth. **gapped,** *a.* **gappy,** *a.*

gape (gāp) [Icel. *gapa* (cp. Dut. *gapen*, G. *gaffen*)], *v.i.* To open the mouth wide; to yawn; to stare with open mouth in wonder, surprise, or perplexity; to open in a fissure or chasm, to split open; *to bawl, to shout. *n.* The act of gaping; a stare with open mouth, a yawn; (*Zool.*) the width of the mouth when opened, as of birds, etc.; the part of a beak that opens; the opening between the shells of a bivalve that does not shut completely; (*pl.*) a disease in young poultry, characterized by much gaping; a fit of yawning; (*facet.*) a fit of staring. **to gape at:** To open the mouth and gaze at with astonishment. **to gape for** or **after:** To desire eagerly, to crave. **gaper,** *n.* One who or that which gapes, esp. various kinds of birds, fish, and molluscs. **gapingly,** *adv.*

gar (1), **garfish** (gar′ fish) [A.-S. *gār*, a spear, FISH], *n.* A fish with a long pointed snout, esp. *Belone vulgaris*, a European fish called also greenbone, in allusion to the bones of its spine; (*Am.*) species of Lepidosteus.

***gar** (2) (gar) [Icel. *gerua* (cp. Swed. *göra*), cogn. with A.-S. *gearwian*, to make ready, to make, do (cp. YARE)], *v.i.* To make, to cause (to do).

garage (găr′ ȧj, gă razh′) [F., from *garer*, to put into dock, from Teut. (cp. Goth. *warjan*, A.-S. *werian*, to defend)], *n.* A building for housing or repairing motor-cars; an establishment where this is done as a business.

garancin (găr′ ȧn sin) [F., from *garance*, madder], *n.* (*Chem.*) A colouring matter produced by the action of sulphuric acid upon madder.

garb (1) (garb) [through F. *garbe* (now *galbe*) or directly from It. *garbo*, grace, elegance, from Teut. (cp. O.H.G. *garwī*, *garawī*, cogn. with GEAR)], *n.* Dress, costume; distinctive style of dress; outward appearance; *appearance, demeanour. *v.t.* To put garments upon, esp. to put in a distinctive dress.

garb (2) (garb) [A.-F. *garbe* (F. *gerbe*), from Teut. (cp. O.H.G. *garba*, G. *garbe*)], *n.* (*Her.*) A sheaf of grain.

garbage (gar′ bȧj) [etym. doubtful (Skeat suggests O.F. *garbage*, *gerbage*, a tax paid in sheaves, from *garbe*, see prec.)], *n.* Animal refuse, esp. the entrails; offal; (*fig.*) anything worthless or offensive, sordid rubbish; (*Am.*) kitchen waste. **garbage can:** (*Am.*) A dustbin.

garble (gar′ bėl) [perh. through O.F. *garbeller*, from It. *garbellare*, to garble spices, from Arab. *gharbala* to sift], *v.t.* To separate the fine or valuable parts of from the coarse and worthless; to mutilate, so as to convey a false impression; to pervert, to falsify. **garbler,** *n.*

garboard (gar′ bôrd) [obs. Dut. *gaarboord*], *n.* (*Naut.*) The first plank fastened on either side of a ship's keel. **garboard-strake,** *n.* The row of planks next the keel on a ship's bottom; the row of plates corresponding to this in an iron ship.

***garboil** (gar′ boil) [O.F. *garbouil*, It. *garbuglio* (etym. doubtful; second part conn. with L. *bullīre*, to boil)], *n.* A tumult, an uproar, a broil. *v.t.* To disturb, to upset.

garçon (gar′ son) [F., dim. of *gars*, lad, etym. unknown], *n.* A waiter.

gardant [GUARDANT].

garden (gar′ dėn) [A.-F. *gardin* (F. *jardin*), from Teut. (cp. O.S. *gardo*, A.-S. *geard*, YARD, Icel. *garthr*, GARTH, G. *garten*)], *n.* An enclosed piece of ground appropriated to the cultivation of fruit, flowers, or vegetables, (*Am.* a yard); a place or region particularly fertile, well-cultivated, or delightful; (*pl.*) a public pleasure-ground adorned with trees, flower-beds, etc. *a.* Pertaining to a garden; cultivated, not wild. *v.i.* To cultivate a garden. **common or garden:** (*slang*) The ordinary (sort). **the Garden:** The philosophical school of Epicurus or their tenets. **garden city,** *n.* A planned township or suburb in rural surroundings. **garden-cress,** *n.* Pepper-grass, *Lepidium sativum*, **garden-engine,** *n.* A pump and tank on wheels for watering plants. **garden-frame,** *n.* A glazed frame for protecting plants during the winter or for forcing. **garden-glass,** *n.* A bell-glass for protecting plants. **garden-party,** *n.* A social meeting or a company entertained on a lawn or in a garden. **garden-plot,** *n.* A piece of ground used as a garden. **garden-seat,** *n.* A seat, esp. a long one for several persons, for use in a garden; a transverse seat on the top of an omnibus, etc. **garden-stuff,** *n.* Vegetables, herbs, fruit, etc. **garden-warbler,** *n.* A bird, *Sylvia hortensis*. **gardened,** *a.* Cultivated like a garden; furnished with gardens. **gardener,** *n.* One who gardens, esp. one whose occupation is to attend to or to manage gardens. **gardenesque** (gar dėn esk′), *a.* **gardening,** *n.* Horticulture; work in a garden.

gardenia (gar dē′ ni ȧ) [Dr. Alex *Garden*, Am. botanist (*d.* 1791)], *n.* A genus of tropical shrubs and trees cultivated in greenhouses for their large fragrant flowers.

***gardyloo** (gar di loo′) [incorrect F. *gare de l'eau* beware of the water (properly, *gare l'eau*)], *int.* The warning cried in old Edinburgh when slops were emptied from windows into the streets.

gare (gâr) [Sc., from Icel. *gorr*, cogn. with YARE], *a.* Covetous, miserly.

gare-fowl (gâr′ foul) [Icel. *geir-fugl*], *n.* The great auk; the razor-billed auk.

garfish [GAR (1)].

gargantuan (gar găn′ tū ȧn) [*Gargantua*, the giant of Rabelais], *a.* Immense, enormous, incredibly big. **gargantuism,** *n.*

gargarism (gar′ gȧ rism) [L. *gargarisma*, from Gr. *gargarizein*, to gargle, of imit. orig.], *n.* A gargle. **gargarize,** *v.t.* To gargle.

garget (gar′ gėt) [O.F. *gargate*, the throat (etym. doubtful; cp. GARGOYLE)], *n.* A distemper affecting the throat in cattle; an affection of the udder of cows or ewes.

gargil (gar′ gil) [O.F. *gargouille*, see GARGOYLE], *n.* *The throat; a distemper in the heads of swine, cattle, and geese; garget in cows affecting the udder.

gargle (gar′ gėl) [F. *gargouiller*], *v.t.* To rinse (the mouth or throat) with some medicated liquid which is prevented from passing down the throat by the breath; *to warble. *n.* A liquid used for washing the mouth or throat.

gargol [GARGIL, GARGLE].

gargoyle (gar′ goil) [F. *gargouille*, weasand (cp. F. *gorge*, throat, Gr. *garg-*, base of *gargarizein*, GARGARIZE)], *n.* A grotesque spout, usually carved to represent a human or animal figure, projecting from a Gothic building to throw rain-water clear of the wall.

garibaldi (găr i bol′ di) [Giuseppe *Garibaldi* (1807–82), liberator of Italy], *n.* A loose kind of blouse for women or children, like the red shirts worn by Garibaldi and his men. **garibaldi biscuit,** *n.* A sandwich biscuit with a layer of currants.

garish (1) (gâr′ ish) [earlier *gaurish*, from obs. *gauren*, to stare, etym. doubtful], *a.* Gaudy, showy, flashy; excessively or extravagantly decorated; dazzling, glaring. **garishly,** *adv.* **garishness,** *n.*

***garish** (2) [GUARISH].

garland (gar′ lȧnd) [O.F. *garlande*, etym. doubtful (F. *guirlande*, from It. *ghirlanda*)], *n.* A wreath, chaplet, or festoon of flowers, leaves, etc., a similar festoon of metal, stone, ribbons, or other material used for decoration, etc.; (*fig.*) the prize, the chief honour; a collection of choice pieces, especially of poems; *the thing most prized. *v.t.* To deck with a garland. **garlandage** (*poet.*), **garlandry,** *n.* **garlandless,** *a.*

garlic (gar′ lik) [A.-S. *gārlēac* (as GAR (1), LEEK)], *n.* A bulbous-rooted plant, *Allium sativum*, with strong odour and a pungent taste, used in cookery. **garlic-eater,** *n.* **garlicky,** *a.*

garment (gar′ mėnt) [M.E. and O.F. *garnement* from *garnir*, see GARNISH], *n.* An article of clothing, esp. one of the larger articles, as a coat or gown apparel, dress; (*pl.*) clothes. *v.t.* (*poet., usu. in p.p.*) To attire with or as with a garment. **garmentless,** *a.* **garmenture,** *n.* Dress, apparel, clothing.

garner (gar' nėr) [O.F. *gernier, grenier,* L. *grānārium,* GRANARY], *n.* A place for storing grain, a granary; (*fig.*) a store, a repository. *v.t.* To store in or as in a garner, to gather.

garnet (1) (gar' nėt) [O.F. *grenat, granat,* late L. *grānātus,* from (*mālum*) *grānātum,* POMEGRANATE, from the resemblance to its seeds], *n.* A vitreous mineral of varying composition, colour, and quality, the deep red, transparent kinds of which are prized as gems.

garnet (2) [Sir *Garnet* Wolseley (1833–1913)]. **All Sir Garnet:** (*Army slang*) All fit and proper, as it should be.

garnish (gar' nish) [O.F. *garniss-,* stem of *garnir, guarnir, warnir,* to defend, to fortify, from Teut. (cp. O.H.G. *warnōn,* G. *warnen,* to WARN)], *v.t.* To adorn; to embellish (as a dish) with something laid round it; to supply, to furnish; (*Law*) to warn, to give notice to. *n.* An ornament; a decoration, esp. things put round a dish as embellishment; (*slang*) a fee; *a fee paid by a prisoner to the jailer; *outfit. **maiden-garnish:** A fee or imposition among workmen paid by a man getting a job. **garnish-money,** *n.* Garnish paid to a jailer. **garnishee** (gar ni shē'), *n.* One who has received notice not to pay any money which he owes to a third person, who is indebted to the person giving notice. **garnisher,** *n.* One who garnishes. **garnishing,** *n.* The act of ornamenting; things used for decoration, esp. of dishes. **garnishment,** *n.* An ornament, an embellishment; (*Law*) a warning to a party to appear in court, or not to pay money, etc. to a defendant. **garnishry,** *n.* Embellishment.

***garnison** (gar' ni sòn) [as prec.], *n.* A guard, a protection, a garrison.

garniture (gar' ni chùr), *n.* Furniture, appurtenances; ornamental appendages, trimmings, ornament, embellishment; costume, dress.

garret (1) (găr' ėt) [O.F. *garite* (F. *guérite*), from *garir, warir,* to defend, from Teut. (cp. O.H.G. *warjan,* A.-S. *werian*)], *n.* An upper room or storey immediately under the roof; *a turret, a watch-tower; (*slang*) the head. **garret-master,** *n.* A maker of household furniture who sells his work to dealers. **garreteer** (găr ė tēr'), *n.* One who lives in a garret, esp. an impecunious writer.

garret (2) [GALLET].

garrison (găr' i sòn) [F. *garison,* defence, safety, from *garir,* to defend (sense influ. by GARNISON)], *n.* A body of troops stationed in a fort or fortified place; a fortified place manned with soldiers, guns, etc., a stronghold. *v.t.* To furnish (a fortress) with soldiers; to occupy as a garrison. **garrison-town,** *n.* A town in which a garrison is stationed.

garron (găr' òn) [Gael. *gearran,* a gelding], *n.* A small horse bred in Galloway, the Highlands, and Ireland.

garrot (1) (găr' òt) [F., etym. doubtful], *n.* A sea-duck, esp. the golden-eye.

garrot (2) (găr' òt) [from foll.], *n.* (*Surg.*) A tourniquet formed of a band and a stick, the former being twisted by turning the latter.

garrotte (gȧ rot') [Sp. *garrote,* a stick, etym. doubtful], *n.* The Spanish method of execution, in which the criminal is fastened by an iron collar to an upright post, and a knob operated by a screw or lever dislocates the spinal column, or a small blade severs the spinal cord at the base of the brain (orig. the method was strangulation by a cord twisted with a stick); hence, robbery by means of strangling. *v.t.* To execute by this means; to render helpless or insensible in order to rob. **garrotter,** *n.*

garrulous (găr' ū lùs) [L. *garrulus,* from *garrīre,* to chatter], *a.* Talkative, loquacious, wordy; chattering. **garrulity** (gȧ roo' li ti), *n.* **garrulously,** *adv.* **garrulousness,** *n.*

garter (gar' tėr) [O.F. *gartier* (F. *jarretiere*), from *garet* (F. *jarret*), the leg. perh. from Celt. (cp. Bret. and W. *gar,* the shank of the leg)], *n.* A band round the leg for holding the stocking up; (*Am.*) a sock-suspender. *v.t.* To fasten (a stocking) with a garter; to put a garter upon; *to invest with the Order of the Garter. **the Garter:** The badge of the highest order of British knighthood, instituted by Edward III, about 1348; the order itself; membership of this. **Garter Principal King-of-Arms,** *n.* The chief herald of this order. **garter-snake,** *n.* A harmless American snake belonging to the genus *Eutænia.*

garth (garth) [Icel. *garthr,* cogn. A.-S. *geard,* YARD], *n.* A close, a yard; a garden, croft, or paddock; the grass-plot surrounded by the cloisters of a religious house; a fish-weir.

garvie (gar' vi) [Sc., etym. unknown], *n.* A sprat, also called **garvock** [Gael. *garbhag,* perh. cogn.].

gas (găs) [Dut., invented by the chemist Van Helmont (*d.* 1644), from Gr. *chaos,* see CHAOS], *n.* (*pl.* **gases**) A substance in the form of air, possessing the condition of perfect fluid elasticity; such a fluid used for lighting and heating, esp. that obtained from coal; (*Am. colloq.*) gasolene, petrol; (*Coal-mining*) an explosive mixture of fire-damp and air; (*colloq.*) a gas-jet; (*fig.*) empty talk, frothy eloquence; bouncing, brag. *v.i.* (*past & p.p.* **gassed**) To indulge in empty talk; to boast. *v.t.* To supply gas to; to subject to the action of burning gas (as lace) in order to free from loose fibres; to attack, to stupefy, or kill by means of poison-gas. **to step on the gas:** To accelerate a motor-car; to hurry. **gas-bag,** *n.* A bag for holding gas or stopping an escape from a main; (*fig.*) a talkative person. **gas-bracket,** *n.* A pipe projecting from a wall and fitted with a burner or burners. **gas-burner,** *n.* The tube or jet at which the gas issues and is lighted. **gas-coal,** *n.* Bituminous coal from which gas for illuminating can be made. **gas-coke,** *n.* Coke left as a residuum after gas has been extracted from gas-coal. **gas-engine, -motor,** *n.* An engine in which the motive power is obtained from the explosion of gas. **gas-fire,** *n.* A device for burning gas for heating a room, etc. **gas-fitter,** *n.* A workman who lays the pipes and puts up fixtures for gas. **gas-fittings,** *n.pl.* Gas-brackets, stoves, gaseliers, and other apparatus for lighting or heating by gas. **gas-gauge,** *n.* An instrument for testing gas pressure. **gas-helmet, gas-mask,** *n.* Early device for protection against poison gas, since replaced by the box-respirator. **gas-holder,** *n.* A structure for storing gas, a gasometer. **gas-jet,** *n.* A gas-burner; a jet of flame from it. **gas-light,** *n.* The light produced by the combustion of coal-gas; a gas-jet. **gas-main,** *n.* A principal pipe leading from gas-works and having branches and distributing pipes. **gas-man,** *n.* A man employed at gas-works; a collector of money due for the supply of gas; a gas-fitter; a man controlling the lights on a stage. **gas-meter,** *n.* A machine for measuring and recording the quantity of gas consumed. **gas-ring,** *n.* An iron pipe perforated with holes for burning gas under cooking-utensils, etc.; a ring fastened on a gun for preventing the escape of gas. **gas-shell,** *n.* (*Artill.*) A shell containing a chemical mixture that produces or diffuses poison-gas on explosion. **gas-tank:** (*Am.*) A gasometer. **gas-tar,** *n.* Coal-tar. **gas-tight,** *a.* Not allowing gas to escape, not leaky (of pipes, etc.). **gas-works,** *n.pl.* A manufactory where gas is produced for illuminating purposes. **gaseous** (gā' sė ùs, găs' ė ùs), *a.* In the form of gas; like gas. **gaseity** (gȧ sē' i ti), *n.* **gasiform,** *a.* Of the nature or form of gas. **gasify,** *v.t.* To convert into gas. **gasifiable,** *a.* **gasification** (-kā' shùn), *n.* **gasless,** *a.* **gassy,** *a.* Containing gas; like gas; gaseous; (*fig.*) full of empty talk; (*slang*) quick to flare up, touchy, irascible. **gassiness,** *n.*

Gascon (găs' kòn) [F.], *n.* A native of Gascony, France; (*fig.*) a boaster. **gasconade** (găs kò nād'), *n.* Boasting, bravado, bragging. *v.i.* To boast, to brag. **gasconader, gasconism** (găs' kò nizm), *n.*

gaselier (găs ė lēr′) [GAS, (CHAND)ELIER], *n.* An ornamental metal-work pendant with branches carrying gas-burners for lighting a room, etc.

gaseous [GAS].

gash (1) (găsh) [earlier *garsh, garse*, O.F. *garser*, perh. from late L. *caraxāre*, Gr. *charassein*, to scratch, incise], *v.t.* To make a long, deep, gaping cut in. *n.* A deep, open cut, especially in flesh; a flesh-wound, a cleft.

gash (2) (găsh) [Sc., etym. doubtful (perh. corr. of SAGACIOUS)], *a.* Sagacious, shrewd; dignified, neat, trim; dignified-looking, pert.

gash (3) (găsh) [Sc., etym. obscure], *v.i.* To gossip, to tattle.

gashly (gash′ li), **gash** (4) (gash) [Sc., corr. of GHASTLY, influ. by GASH (1)], *a.* Ghastly, dismal. **gashliness,** *n.* **gashful,** *a.*

gasiform, etc. [GAS].

gasket (găs′ kėt) [etym. doubtful], *n.* (*Naut.*) A plaited cord by which the sails, when furled, are bound close to the yards or gaffs; (*Mach.*) a strip of leather, tow, or other material for packing or caulking joints in pipes, engines, etc. to make them air-tight or water-tight.

gaskin [GASKET].

gaskins (găs′ kinz), *n.pl.* Galligaskins.

gasogene [GAZOGENE].

gasolene, gasoline (găs′ ȯ lēn), *n.* A volatile inflammable product of the distillation of petroleum, used for heating and lighting; (*Am.*) petrol.

gasolier [GASELIER].

gasometer (gȧ som′ ė tėr) [F. *gazomètre* (*gaz*, GAS, *mètre*, -METER)], *n.* A large cylindrical reservoir used at gas-works for the storage of gas, a gas-holder, (*Am.* gas-tank); (*Chem.*) an apparatus for measuring, collecting, preserving, or mixing different gases; an instrument for measuring the gases used in chemical experiments, etc. **gasometric** (-met′ rik), *a.* **gasometry** (gȧ som′ ė tri), *n.* The science, act, or practice of measuring gases.

gasoscope (găs′ ō skōp), *n.* An instrument for detecting the presence of carburetted hydrogen in mines, buildings, etc.

gasp (gasp) [prob. from Icel. *geispa*, to yawn (cp. Dut. *gijpen*, A.-S. *gipian*, in *gipung*, a gaping)], *v.i.* To breathe in a convulsive manner, as from exhaustion or astonishment. *v.t.* To emit or utter with gasps. *n.* A short painful catching of the breath. **to gasp out** or **away:** To breathe out (as one's life) convulsively. **at the last gasp:** At the last extremity; at the point of death. **gasper,** *n.* (*slang*) A cigarette. **gaspingly,** *adv.*

***gast** (gast) [A.-S. *gǣstan*], *v.t.* To terrify. ***gastness,** *n.* Terror, fright, fear.

gasteral [GASTRIC].

gasteropod (găs′ tėr ȯ pod) [Gr. *gastēr -eros*, stomach, *pous podos*, foot], *n.* An individual of the Gasteropoda. *a.* Gasteropodous. **Gasteropoda,** *n.pl.* (*Zool.*) A class of molluscs, usually inhabiting a univalve shell (as the snails), of which the general characteristic is a broad muscular ventral foot. **gasteropodous** (găs tėr op′ ȯ dŭs), *a.* Belonging to or characteristic of the Gasteropoda.

gastræa (găs trē′ ȧ) [mod. L., from Gr. *gastēr -eros*, as prec.], *n.* (*Biol.*) A primordial animal organism in the form of a gastrula, supposed by Hæckel to have been the germ of all later animal life.

gastral [GASTRIC].

gastralgia (găs trăl′ ji ȧ) [Gr. *gastēr -eros*, stomach, *algos*, pain], *n.* (*Path.*) Neuralgia in the stomach. **gastralgic,** *a.* and *n.*

gastric (găs′ trik) [late L. *gastricus*, as foll.], *a.* Of or pertaining to the stomach. **gastric acid** [GASTRIC JUICE]. **gastric fever,** *n.* Inflammation of the stomach; now usu. applied to enteric or typhoid fever. **gastric juice,** *n.* A colourless pellucid acid secreted by the stomach, one of the principal agents in digestion. **gasteral, gastral,** *a.* **gastritis** (găs trī′ tis), *n.* Inflammation of the stomach.

gastro- [Gr. *gastēr -eros*, the stomach], *comb. form.* **gastrodynia** (găs trō dĭ′ ni ȧ) [Gr. *odunē*, pain], *n.* (*Path.*) Pain in the stomach; gastralgia. **gastro-enteric** (găs trō en ter′ ik) [ENTERIC], *a.* Pertaining to the stomach and the intestines. **gastro-enteritis** (-en tėr ī′ tis) [ENTERITIS], *n.* Inflammation of the stomach and of the intestines. **gastro-vascular** (găs trō văs′ kū lȧr) [VASCULAR], *a.* Pertaining both to the vascular system and to the stomach; serving both for circulation and the digestion of food.

gastrocnemius (găs trok nē′ mi ŭs) [Gr. *gastroknēmia* (as GASTRO-, *knēmē*, leg)], *n.* (*pl.* **-ii**) (*Anat.*) The large muscle in the calf of the leg which helps to extend the foot.

gastrograph (găs′ trō grăf), *n.* An instrument for recording the motions of the stomach and the food within it.

gastrology (găs trol′ ȯ ji) [GASTRO-, -LOGY], *n.* The science of matters pertaining to the stomach; the science of cookery or of eating, gastronomy. **gastrological** (-loj′ ik ȧl), *a.* **gastrologer, -logist** (-trol′-), *n.*

gastromancy (găs′ trō măn′ si) [GASTRO-, -MANCY], *n.* Divination by means of words seemingly spoken in the belly, that is, by ventriloquism; divination by means of large-bellied glasses in which magical figures were supposed to appear.

gastronomy (găs tron′ ȯ mi) [F. *gastronomie*, Gr. *gastronomia* (from *gastēr -eros*, stomach, on anal. of *astronomia*, ASTRONOMY)], *n.* The art or science of good eating, epicurism. **gastronome** (găs′ trȯ nōm), **gastronomer** (găs tron′ ȯ mėr), **gastronomist,** *n.* One given to good living; an epicure; a judge of good eating. **gastronomic, -al** (găs trō nom′ ik, -ȧl), *a.* **gastronomically,** *adv.*

gastrophile (găs′ trō fīl) [GASTRO-, -PHILE], *n.* A lover of his stomach or of good eating. **gastrophilism** (găs trof′ i lizm), *n.* **gastrophilist,** *n.* **gastrophilite,** *n.*

gastroscopy (găs tros′ kō pi), *n.* An examination of the abdomen in order to discover disease.

gastrosoph (găs′ trȯ sof) [GASTRO-, Gr. *sophos*, wise], *n.* One skilled in the art of good eating. **gastrosopher** (găs tros′ ȯ fėr), *n.* **gastrosophy,** *n.*

gastrostomy (găs tros′ tō mi), *n.* An operation to introduce food directly into the stomach in the case of stricture of the gullet.

gastrotomy (găs trot′ ō mi), *n.* The operation of cutting into or opening the abdomen. **gastrotomic,** *a.*

gastrula (găs′ trŭ lȧ) [mod. L., dim. from Gr. *gastēr -eros*, stomach], *n.* (*Biol.*) An embryonic form or stage in the development of a metazoon, consisting of a double-walled sac enclosing a cup-like cavity. **gastrular,** *a.* **gastrulation** (-lā′ shŭn), *n.* The formation of a gastrula.

gat (1) (găt) [prob. Icel.], *n.* A narrow passage between sandbanks, a strait, a channel; an opening in cliffs; (*prov.*) a track through moss-hags, etc.

gat (2) (găt) [abbr. GATLING], *n.* (*Am. slang*) A revolver.

gate (1) (gāt) [A.-S. *geat*], *n.* A movable barrier, consisting of a frame of wood or iron, usu. dist. from a door by open-work instead of solid panels, swinging on hinges or sliding, to close a passage or opening; an opening in a wall or fence affording entrance and exit to an enclosure, a gateway; an entrance, an opening, an opportunity; a natural opening, as a strait, a mountain pass, etc.; a sluice admitting water to or shutting it off from a lock or dock; (*Metal.*) a channel through which molten metal is poured into the mould; (*Sporting slang*) the number of people attending a race-meeting, football match, etc.; the amount of money taken at the gates. *v.t.* To furnish with a gate; (*Oxf. and Camb. Univ.*) to confine to college. **to gate-crash:** To attend a function or entertainment without an invitation. **gate-bill,** *n.* (*Oxf. and*

Camb. Univ.) The record of an undergraduate's lateness in returning to college; the account of fines imposed for late returns. **gate-change:** (*Motor.*) Mechanism on the gear lever in which the latter is held for change in an **H**-shaped rack. **gatehouse,** *n.* A lodge, house, or defensive structure at or over a gate; a toll-gate cottage. **gate-keeper, -man,** *n.* A man in charge of a gate; the lessee or collector of tolls at a toll-gate; a variety of butterfly. **gate-leg, gate-legged,** *a.* Descriptive of a folding table with legs that swing in to permit of the leaves being shut down. **gate-meeting,** *n.* A race-meeting or other gathering at which there is a charge for admission. **gate-money,** *n.* Entrance money taken at a sports ground, etc. **gate-post,** *n.* A post on which a gate is hung or against which it shuts. **gate-valve,** *n.* (*Mech.*) A valve which opens the full area of a pipe. **gateway,** *n.* An opening or passage that may be closed by a gate; an entrance, a means of ingress or egress. **gateage,** *n.* The gates used in controlling a flow of water; area of a gate-opening, as in the case of a turbine gate.

gate (2) (gāt) [Icel. *gata*, see GAIT], *n.* *A way, a road; (*Sc.*) one's way, manner of doing; course; a street (*usu. in comb.* as *Boargate, Friargate*). **any gate, some gate, that gate:** Anywhere, somewhere, etc.

gate (3) (gāt) [cp. A.-S. *gyte*, a pouring out, from *gēotan*, to pour], *n.* (*Metal.*) *A hole or channel for pouring molten metal into a mould; a waste piece of metal formed in this, also called **gate-piece, -shutter.**

gâteau (ga tō') [F., O.F. *gastel* (cp. O.H.G. *wastel*)], *n.* A cake. **veal gateau,** *n.* Minced veal boiled in a shape or mould, like a pudding.

gather (găth' ėr) [A.-S. *gædrian, gaderian*, from *geador*, together (cp. Dut. *gaderen*, from *gader*)], *v.t.* To bring together, to collect, to cause to assemble; to accumulate, to acquire; to cull, to pluck; to pick (up); to get in, as harvest; to deduce, to infer, to conclude; to draw together, to contract, to pucker, to draw into folds or plaits; to sum (up); (*Print.*) to arrange (pages) in their proper sequence. *v.i.* To come together, to assemble, to congregate, to unite; to grow by addition, to increase; to concentrate, to generate pus or matter; (*fig.*) to ripen. *n.* A plait or fold of cloth, made by drawing together. **to gather breath:** To recover one's wind, to have respite. **to gather head:** To gain strength; to ripen (as a fester, etc.). **to gather oneself together:** To concentrate all one's strength or faculties, as on an effort. **to gather way:** (*Naut.*) To begin to move, to gain impetus, so as to answer to the helm. **gatherable,** *a.* **gathered,** *p.p.* (*euphem.*) Dead. **gatherer,** *n.* **gathering,** *n.* The act of collecting or assembling together; an assembly, a meeting, a party; an abscess, a boil. **gathering-coal, -peat,** *n.* (*Sc.*) A large piece of coal or peat put on the fire at night to keep it alive. **gathering-cry,** *n.* A rallying-cry, a summons to war. **gathering-ground,** *n.* The region from which a river and its tributaries draw their supplies; the area feeding a reservoir.

Gatling (găt' ling), **Gatling-gun** [the inventor, Dr. R. J. *Gatling* (1818–1903), Am.], *n.* A machine-gun with a series of parallel barrels each having its own lock actuated by a crank at the breech, capable of firing more than 1000 shots a minute.

gator (gā' tȯr), *abbrev.* ALLIGATOR.

gauche (gōsh) [F., left hand, from Teut. (cp. O.H.G. *welk*, orig. awkward, weak)], *a.* Awkward, clumsy; tactless, uncouth, boorish. **gaucherie,** *n.* Awkwardness; a blunder, esp. a social mistake or awkwardness; awkward manners.

gaucho (gou'-, gaw chō) [Sp., prob. from S. Am. native], *n.* A native of the pampas of Uruguay and the Argentine Republic, a race of Spanish or mixed descent, noted for skill as horsemen and cowboys.

gaud (gawd) [O.F. *gaudir*, L. *gaudēre*, to rejoice], *n.* A showy ornament or trinket, finery; (*pl.*) gewgaws, trumperies, pomps and shows; *a trick. **gaudery,** *n.* Finery, showy ornament, show. **gaudy** (1), *a.* Vulgarly and tastelessly brilliant and ornate, garish, flashy. **gaudily,** *adv.* **gaudiness,** *n.*

gaudeamus (gaw dė ā' mŭs) [L., let us rejoice, as prec.], *n.* A students' feast or merry-making.

gaudy (1) [GAUD].

gaudy (2) (gawd' i) [L. *gaudium*, joy], *n.* A grand festival or entertainment, esp. one held annually at an English college in commemoration of some event. **gaudy-day,** *n.* The day on which this is held; a holiday.

gauffer [GOFFER].

gauge (gāj), (*Naut.*) **gage** [O.F. *gauger* (F. *jauger*), etym. unknown], *v.t.* To ascertain the dimensions, quantity, content, capacity, or power of; to test the content or capacity of (casks, etc.) for excise purposes; (*fig.*) to estimate or appraise (abilities, character, etc.); to reduce to a standard size; (*Dressmaking*) to gather into a uniform series of puckers. *n.* A standard of measurement; an instrument for regulating or determining dimensions, amount, capacity, etc., according to a fixed standard; a graduated instrument showing the height of a stream, quantity of rainfall, force of the wind, steam-pressure in a boiler, etc.; (*Naut.*) the depth to which a vessel sinks in the water; the position of a ship with reference to another and the wind, the **weather-gauge** being to windward, and the **lee-gauge** to leeward; (*Print.*) a piece of hard wood, variously notched, used to adjust the dimensions, slopes, etc., of the various sorts of letters in type-founding; a strip for regulating length of pages, width of margins, etc.; (*Carp.*) an instrument for striking a line parallel to the straight side of a board; (*Railway*) the width between the rails, the **standard gauge** being 4 ft. 8½ in., and the **broad gauge,** now disused, 7 ft. **gauge-glass,** *n.* A tube to indicate the height of water in a boiler. **gaugeable,** *a.* **gauger,** *n.* One who gauges; esp. one who gauges casks, etc., an excise-officer. **gauging-rod, -rule, -ruler, -stick,** *n.* An exciseman's measuring instrument.

Gaul (gawl) [F. *Gaule*, L. *Gallus*, prob. conn. with A.-S. *wealh*, a foreigner], *n.* A native of ancient Gaul; (*loosely*) a Frenchman. **Gaulish,** *a.* Pertaining to Gaul; hence, French. *n.* The language of ancient Gaul.

Gaullist (gōl' ist) [F.], *n.* (*Pol.*) A follower of President de Gaulle of France.

gault (gawlt) [prov., etym. doubtful], *n.* (*Geol.*) A series of beds of stiff dark-coloured clay and marl between the upper and lower Green-sand. *v.t.* To dress land with gault. **gaulter,** *n.*

gaultheria (gawl thēr' i ȧ) [Dr. *Gaultier*, Canadian botanist], *n.* A genus of evergreen aromatic shrubs of the heath family, containing the wintergreen, *G. procumbens.*

gaum (gawm) [cp. COOM (1)], *v.t.* To smear or bedaub; to put (some sticky substance) on anything. **gaumy,** *a.*

gaumless, gormless (gawm' less) [O.N., *gaumr*, care, attention], *a.* Witless, clumsy, stupid.

***gaunt** (1) [GANT].

gaunt (2) (gawnt) [etym. doubtful (cp. Norw. *gaud*, a thin stick, a tall, thin man)], *a.* Attenuated, thin, emaciated, haggard. **gauntly,** *adv.* **gauntness,** *n.*

gauntlet (1) (gawnt' lėt) [O.F. *gantelet*, dim. of *gant*, a glove, prob. from Scand. (cp. O.Swed. *wante*)], *n.* A long glove covered with plate-metal, worn with armour; a long stout glove covering the wrists. **to take up the gauntlet:** To accept a challenge. **to throw down the gauntlet:** To challenge, to defy. **gauntleted,** *a.* Wearing gauntlets.

gauntlet (2) (gawnt' lėt), ***gantlope** (-lōp) [Swed. *gatlopp* (*gata*, GATE (2), *lopp*, a course, from *löpa*, to run, cogn. with LEAP)], *n.* A military (and sometimes a naval) punishment, in which the prisoner had to run between two files of men armed with sticks, knotted cords, or the like, with which they struck him as he passed. **to run the gauntlet:** To suffer this punishment; (*fig.*) to undergo severe criticism, etc.

gauntry [GANTRY].

gaup, gawp (gawp) [prov., cogn. with YELP], *v.i.* To gape, esp. in astonishment. **gaupus, gawpus,** *n.* A simpleton. **gaupy,** *a.*

gaur (gour) [Hindustani], *n.* A large fierce ox, *Bos gaurus*, found in the mountain jungles in India.

gauss (gaws) [K. F. *Gauss* (1777–1855)], *n.* (*Elec.*) The unit of magnetic induction in magnetism, being 1 line per square centimetre.

gauze (gawz) [F. *gaze*, perh. from *Gaza*, in Palestine], *n.* A light, transparent silk or cotton stuff; any perforated material resembling this; (*fig.*) a thin veil or haze. **wire-gauze,** *n.* A textile fabric made of wire, used for very fine sieves, respirators, etc. **gauze-lamp,** *n.* A safety-lamp with gauze surrounding the flame. **gauzy,** *a.* **gauziness,** *n.*

gavage (gȧ vazh′) [pop. F., from *gaver*, from *gave*, the crop of a bird], *n.* The fattening of poultry by forced feeding; (*Med.*) the feeding of a patient unable or unwilling to feed himself.

gave, *past* [GIVE].

gavel (1) (găv′ ėl) [A.-S. *gafol*, tribute, toll, cogn. with GIVE; or from the first part of *gavelkind*], *n.* (*Hist.*) Partition of land among the whole tribe or sept at the holder's death. **gavel-act, -law,** *n.* A statute of Queen Anne's time enacting that the estates of Irish Catholics should descend to males, according to English gavelkind. **gavelkind** (găv′ ėl kīnd), *n.* (*Law*) A custom prevalent in Kent and Wales whereby the lands of a person dying intestate descend to all the sons in equal shares, or in default of sons, to all the daughters. **gavelman, *gavelkinder,** *n.* A tenant holding land by this tenure.

gavel (2) (găv′ ėl) [etym. doubtful], *n.* A mason's setting-maul; a small mallet, esp. one used by a chairman for demanding attention.

gavel (3) (*Sc. and North.*) [GABLE].

gavial (gā′ vi ȧl) [F., corr. of Hind. *ghariyāl*], *n.* The Gangetic crocodile, *Gavialis Gangeticus*.

gavotte (gȧ vot′) [F., from Prov. *gavoto*, from *Gavot*, an inhabitant of *Gap*. in Dauphiné], *n.* A dance of a lively yet dignified character resembling the minuet; the music for this; a dance-tune in common time and in two parts, each repeated.

***gawd** [GAUD].

gawk (gawk) [etym. doubtful], *n.* A simpleton, a booby. *v.i.* To stare (at or about) stupidly. **gawky,** *a.* Awkward, clownish. *n.* An awkward or clownish person; a simpleton. **gawkihood, gawkiness,** *n.* **gawkish,** *a.*

gawsy (gaw′ si) [Sc. and North., etym. unknown], *a.* Jolly-looking, portly, handsome, smart.

gay (gā) [O.F. *gai*, prob. from O.H.G. *wāhi*, fine], *a.* Full of mirth; light-hearted, lively, cheerful, merry; given to pleasure; (*euphem.*) wanton, licentious; showy, brilliant in appearance, dressed in bright colours. **gaily,** *adv.* ***gayness,** *n.* **gaysome,** *a.* Full of gaiety; merry.

gayal (gā′ ȧl, gā ăl′) [Hind. *gayāl*], *n.* An ox, *Bos frontalis*, with horns depressed at the base and extended outwards, widely domesticated in the East.

gaydiang (gā′ di ăng), *n.* An Anamese vessel with two or three masts and triangular sails, somewhat like a junk. **gay-you** (gā′ ū), *n.* A narrow, flat-bottomed Anamese boat.

gaze (gāz) [etym. unknown; cp. Swed. dial. *gasa*], *v.i.* To fix the eye intently (at or upon). **v.t.* To view steadfastly. *n.* A fixed look; a look of curiosity, attention, admiration, or anxiety; *that which is gazed at. ***at a gaze:** Gaping in wonder. **at gaze:** (*Her.*) Represented full-faced, as a deer. **to stand at gaze:** To be an intent spectator. **gaze-hound,** *n.* A hound which hunts by sight, as a greyhound. **gazement,** *n.* **gazer,** *n.* **gazing-stock,** *n.* A person gazed at with scorn or abhorrence; an object of curiosity and contempt. **gazy,** *a.*

gazebo (gȧ zē′ bō) [prob. a facetious coinage from GAZE on anal. of LAVABO], *n.* An ornamental turret, lantern, or summer-house with a wide prospect, often erected in a garden, a belvedere; a balcony or projecting window.

gazel [GHAZAL].

gazelle (gȧ zel′) [F. *gazelle*, earlier *gazel*, Arab. *ghazāl*], *n.* A swift and very graceful antelope, esp. *Gazelle dorcas*, celebrated for its large, soft black eyes.

gazette (gȧ zet′) [F., from It. *gazzetta*, prob. after Venetian coin, the price of the first newspaper or of the privilege of reading it], *n.* A newspaper; an official journal (one of these published in London and Edinburgh respectively) containing lists of appointments to any public office or commission, legal notices, lists of bankrupts, etc. *v.t.* To publish in a gazette, esp. to announce the appointment or bankruptcy of (*usu. in p.p.*). **gazetteer** (găz ė tēr′), *n.* *A writer for a gazette; a geographical dictionary. *v.t.* To describe in a geographical dictionary. **gazetteerage,** *n.* **gazetteerish,** *a.*

gazogene (găz′ ō jėn) [F. *gazogène* (*gaz*, GAS, *-gène*, -GEN)], *n.* An apparatus for manufacturing aerated beverages.

***gazon** (gȧ zon′) [F., grass, turf], *n.* (*Fort.*) A sod used as a revetment for parapets and earthen banks.

***geal** (1) (jē′ ȧl) [Gr. *gē*, earth], *a.* Pertaining to the earth as a planet.

***geal** (2) (jēl) [F. *geler*, L. *gelāre*, to freeze], *v.t.* and *i.* To congeal.

gean (gēn) [F. *guigne*, etym. unknown], *n.* (*chiefly Sc.*) The wild cherry, *Prunus avium*.

gear (gēr) [M.E. *gere*, prob. from Icel. *gervi* (cp. O.H.G. *garawī*, A.-S. *gearu*, GARE)], *n.* Apparatus, tools, mechanical appliances, harness, tackle, equipment, dress; (*Mech.*) combinations of cog-wheels, links, levers, etc.; a connexion by which an engine, motor, etc., is brought into work; the arrangement by which the driving-wheel of a cycle, motor-car, etc., performs more or fewer revolutions relatively to the pedals, piston, etc.; the state of being engaged or connected up, or of being in working order; (*Naut.*) the ropes, blocks, etc., belonging to any particular sail or spar; goods, movables; (*Sc.*) property, wealth; *worthless matters, rubbish, stuff; *proceedings, doings, business. *v.t.* To harness, to put gear on; (*Mech.*) to put into gear; to furnish with gearing. *v.i.* To come or be in gear (with); to fit (into) exactly (as a cog-wheel). **alighting gear,** *n.* (*Aviat.*) Mechanism such as wheels or skids fixed beneath an aeroplane to absorb shock on landing. **change-speed-gear,** *n.* (*Motor.*) Mechanism for changing the engine speed in relation to the speed of the vehicle. **conical gear,** *n.* (*Mach.*) A bevel gear; a gear with bevelled teeth for transmitting rotary motion at an angle. **crowning-gear,** *n.* A gear-wheel with teeth projecting at right-angles to the plane of the wheel. **differential gear** [DIFFERENTIAL]. **equalizing gear,** *n.* A gear in the mechanism of traction engines to permit the driving wheels to turn independently of each other. **free gear,** *n.* A gear engaging in one direction only, as in a free-wheel. **high** or **low gear:** (*Cycle, etc.*) Apparatus for transmitting high or low speed to the driving-wheel relatively to the motion of pedals, etc. **in gear:** (*Mech.*) Connected up and ready for work. **sliding gear,** *n.* A gear sliding along an axle or shaft, and thereby being capable of being instantly disconnected. **star-gear,** *n.* A variable-speed gear. **to throw out of gear:** To disconnect (gearing or couplings); to put out of working order; (*fig.*) to disturb, to upset. **gear-box, -case,** *n.* A case protecting the gearing of a bicycle, etc.

gear-cutter, *n.* A machine for making cog-wheels; a manufacturer of cog-wheels. **gear-wheel,** *n.* A wheel with cogs, esp. the wheel transmitting motion in a cycle. **gearing,** *n.* Gear, working parts; a series of wheels, etc., for transmitting motion; (*Naut.*) tackle. **gearing-chain,** *n.* An endless chain with rack-like projections, passing around cogged wheels and thereby transmitting motion. **gearless,** *a.*

gebbie (geb′ i, gib′ i) [Sc., etym. doubtful], *n.* The crop of a fowl; a person's stomach.

gebur (gė boor′) [A.-S. *gebūr*, cp. BOOR, NEIGHBOUR], *n.* A tenant farmer, not fully free, in the Old English village-community.

***geck** (gek) [cp. L.G. *geck*, Dut. *gek*, G. *geck*], *n.* A dupe, a fool; an object of scorn or contempt; (*Sc.*) a gesture of contempt or derision. *v.i.* (*Sc.*) To scoff (at); to toss the head.

gecko (gek′ ō) [Malay *gēkoq*, from its cry], *n.* A genus of lizards having toes furnished with adhesive disks, by means of which they can walk on a wall or ceiling.

ged (ged) [Icel. *gedda*], *n.* (*Sc.*) The pike.

gee (1) (jē), **gee-up,** *int.* Go on, move faster (command to horse); (*rarely*) turn to the off-side, or from the driver (walking on the left). **gee-gee** (jē′ jē), *n.* (*childish and colloq.*) A horse.

gee (2) (gē) [Sc. and North., etym. doubtful], *n.* A fit of ill-temper. **to take the gee:** To take offence.

gee-bung (jē′ bŭng) [Austral. abor.], *n.* The proteaceous tree Persoonia, or its fruit.

geese (gēs), *n.pl.* [GOOSE].

geezer (gē′ zėr) [slang, perh. from F. *guiser*, masquerader], *n.* An old man or woman.

gegg (geg) [Sc., perh. conn. with GAG], *n.* A hoax, a trick. *v.t.* To hoax. **gegger,** *n.* **geggery,** *n.*

Gehenna (gė hen′ ȧ) [L., from Gr. *geenna*, late Heb. *gēhinnōm*, the valley of Hinnom], *n.* A valley near Jerusalem, where (Jer. xix.) men sacrificed their children to Baal or Moloch; whence, hell, a place of torment.

Geiger counter (gī′ gĕr koun′ tĕr) [inventor H. *Geiger*], *n.* A device for the detection and counting of particles from radio-active materials.

geisha (gā′ shȧ) [Jap.], *n.* (*pl.* **-sha, -shas**) A Japanese dancing-girl.

Geist (gīst) [G., spirit], *n.* The spirit, principle, or tendency of an age, time-spirit.

gel (jel) [JELLY], *n.* (*Chem.*) The jelly-like material formed when a colloidal solution is left standing.

gelastic (gė lăs′ tik) [Gr. *gelastikos*, from *gelān*, to laugh], *a.* Causing laughter; risible.

gelatine (jel′ ȧ tin, -tēn) [F. *gélatine*, It. *gelatina*, L. *gelata*, JELLY], *n.* A transparent substance, forming a jelly in water, obtained from connective animal tissue, such as skin, tendons, bones, horns, etc. **blasting** or **explosive gelatine,** *n.* An explosive compound of nitro-glycerine. **vegetable gelatine,** *n.* Gelatine extracted from gluten. **gelatine paper,** *n.* (*Phot.*) Paper coated with sensitized gelatine. **gelatine process,** *n.* A photographic or photo-engraving process in which gelatine is used. **gelatigenous** (jel ȧ tij′ i nŭs), *a.* Producing gelatine. **gelatinate, -nize** (je lăt′ i nāt, -nīz), *v.t.* To be converted into jelly, or a substance like jelly. *v.t.* To convert into a substance like jelly. **gelatination** (jel ȧ ti nā′ shŭn), **-ization** (je lăt i nī zā′ shŭn), *n.* **gelatinizable** (jel ȧ ti nī′ zȧbl), *a.* **gelatiniform** (jel ȧ tin′ i fôrm), *a.* **gelatinify** (jel ȧ tin′ i fī), *v.t.* **gelatino-,** *comb. form.* **gelatinoid** (jė lăt′ i noid), *a.* and *n.* **gelatinous** (je lăt′ i nŭs), *a.* Of the nature or consisting of gelatine, jelly-like. **gelose** (jė lōs′), *n.* A gelatinous substance obtained from Chinese and Japanese moss and seaweeds, used for finishing cotton goods, and in the East for soups and jellies.

gelation (jė lā′ shŭn) [L. *gelātio*, from *gelāre*, to freeze], *n.* Solidification by cooling or freezing.

geld (1) (geld) [Icel. *gelda*, from *geldr* (cp. G. *gelt*), barren], *v.t.* To castrate (esp. a horse), to emasculate; (*fig.*) to deprive of any essential part; to expurgate excessively. ***geldable** (1), *a.* That may be gelded. **gelder** (1), *n.* One who gelds (*usu. in comb., a sow-gelder*). **gelding,** *n.* The act of castrating, castration; a castrated animal, esp. a castrated horse; *a eunuch.

***geld** (2) (geld) [A.-S. *gield*, from *gieldan*, see YIELD (cp. Icel. *giald*, O.H.G. *gelt*, G. *geld*)], *n.* Money, tribute, the tax paid by land-holders to the Crown under the Saxon and early Norman kings. **geldable** (2), *a.*

gelder (2), **-ders rose** [GUELDER ROSE].

gelid (jel′ id) [L. *gelidus*, from *gelu*, frost], *a.* Extremely cold; icy. **gelidity** (jė lid′ i ti), *n.* **gelidly,** *adv.*

gelignite (jel′ ig nīt) [GEL-ATINE, L. *ign-is*, fire, -ITE], *n.* An explosive containing nitro-glycerine.

gelose [GELATINE].

gelsemium (jel sē′ mi ŭm) mod. L., from It. *gelsomino*, JASMINE], *n.* (*pl.* **-iums**) A genus of climbing shrubs containing three species, of which the best known is the American yellow jasmine, *G. sempervirens*, the poisonous root of which yields a medicinal substance.

gelt (1), *p.p.* [GELD (1)].

***gelt** (2) (gelt) [G. or Dut. *geld*, money, cogn. with GELD (2)], *n.* Money, pay.

***gelt** (3) [GILT].

gem (jem) [O.F. *gemme*, L. *gemma*, a bud, a jewel], *n.* A precious stone, as the diamond, ruby, emerald, etc., esp. when cut and polished for ornamental purposes; an object of great rarity, beauty, or value; a treasure, the most prized or the choicest part; (*Zool.*) a *gemma*; (*Ent.*) a geometrid moth; *a bud. *v.t.* (*past & p.p.* **gemmed**) To adorn with or as with gems; *to put forth in buds. *v.i.* To bud. **gemless,** *a.* **gemmeous, gemmy,** *a.* Full of or set with gems; bright, glittering; (*slang*) spruce, smart, neat. **gemmily,** *adv.* **gemminess,** *n.*

Gemara (gė ma′ rȧ) [Aram.], *n.* The second portion of the Talmud, consisting of a commentary on the Mishna, or text. **Gemaric,** *a.* Of or pertaining to the Gemara. **Gemarist,** *n.*

gematria (gė mā′ tri ȧ) [Rabbinical Heb. *gēmatriyā*, Gr. *geōmetria*, GEOMETRY], *n.* A cabbalistic system of interpreting the Hebrew Scriptures by interchanging words whose letters have the same numerical value when added.

gemel (jem′ ėl) [O.F. (F. *jumeau*), L. *gemellus*, dim. of *geminus*, twin], *n.* *One of twins; (*Her.*) a pair of parallel bars; a kind of finger-ring formed of two (or more) rings, also called a **gemel-ring. gemel-hinge,** *n.* A hinge formed of a hook and loop. **gemel-window,** *n.* A window with two bays.

geminate (jem′ i nȧt) [L. *gemināt*us, p.p. of *gemināre*, to double, from *geminus*, twin], *a.* (*Nat. Hist.*) United or arranged in pairs. *v.t.* (-nāt) To double, to arrange in pairs. *v.i.* To occur in pairs. **gemination** (-nā′ shŭn), *n.* **geminative,** *a.*

Gemini (jĕm′ i nī) [L., twins, pl. of *geminus*, see prec.], *n.pl.* (*Astron.*) A constellation, the Twins, containing the two conspicuous stars, Castor and Pollux; the third sign of the zodiac; *a pair; a mild oath, (*vulg.*) **geminy** (1), **jiminy. Geminids,** *n.pl.* (*Astron.*) Meteoric bodies radiating, usu. in early December, from the constellation Gemini. ***geminous,** *a.* Double, in pairs, twin. ***geminy** (2), *n.* A couple.

gemma (jėm′ ȧ) [L., see GEM], *n.* (*Bot.*) (*pl.* **-mæ**) A leaf-bud; (*pl.*) minute green cellular bodies in the fructification of *Marchantia*, and in some mosses and *Hepaticæ*; (*Zool.*) a bud-like out-growth in polyps, ascidians, etc., which separates from the parent organism and develops into an individual. **gemmaceous,** *a.* Pertaining to or of the nature of leaf-buds.

gemmate (jem′ ȧt) [L. *gemmātus*, p.p. of *gemmāre*, to bud, from *gemma*, see GEMMA], *a.* (*Bot.*) Having buds; (*Zool.*) reproducing by gemmation. *v.i.* (jė māt′) To bud; to reproduce by gemmation. **gemmation** (jė mā′ shůn), *n.* The act of budding; vernation, or the arrangement of the leaf in the bud; the time of budding; the disposition of buds on the plant; (*Zool.*) reproduction by the development of *gemmæ* from the parent body. **gemmative** (jem′ ȧ tiv), *a.*

gemmeous, gemmy [GEM.]

gemmiferous (jė mif′ ėr ůs) [L. *gemmifer*], *a.* Producing gems; (*Nat. Hist.*) Producing or propagating by buds or *gemmæ*.

gemmiparous (jė mip′ ȧ růs), *a.* (*Bot.*) Producing buds; (*Zool.*) propagating by gemmation. **gemmiparity** (jem i păr′ i ti), *n.* **gemmiparously,** *adv.*

gemmule (jem′ ūl) [F., from L. *gemmŭla*, dim. of GEMMA], *n.* (*Biol.*) A small *gemma* or reproductive bud; (*Bot.*) the plumule or growing point of an embryo; a reproductive cell of a cryptogam; (*Zool.*) the ciliated embryo of many of the Cœlenterata; one of the small reproductive bodies thrown off by sponges. **gemmuliferous** (jem ū lif′ ė růs), *a.*

gemote (gė mōt) [A.-S. *gemōt* (*ge-*, together, MOOT)], *n.* (*Hist.*) A public meeting or assembly, esp. the court held in England in each hundred before the Norman Conquest.

gemsbok (gemz′ bok) [Dut., from G. *gemsbock* (*gemse*, chamois, *bock*, buck)], *n.* A large South African antelope, *Oryx gazella*, about the size of a donkey, with straight horns about 2 ft. long.

gen (jen) [*Gen*eral Information], *n.* (*slang*) Full particulars of, information about. **to gen up:** To read up about.

-gen [F. *-gène*, Gr. *genēs*, born of a certain kind, from *gen-*, root of *gignesthai*, to be born, *gennaein*, to beget, etc.], *suf.* Producing; produced; growth; as in *hydrogen, nitrogen, oxygen*; *acrogen, endogen, exogen.*

gendarme (zhan′ darm, jen darm′) [F., from pl. *gens d'armes*, men of arms], *n.* (*pl.* **gendarmes**) An armed policeman, on horse or on foot, belonging to a corps charged with the maintenance of the public peace in France and some other Continental countries; *(*F. Hist.*) a mounted knight or man-at-arms, later a trooper, esp. in the royal bodyguard. ***gendarmerie*** (zhan darm ri), **gendarmery** (jen dar′ mėr i), *n.* The armed police of France; a body of gendarmes.

gender (jen′ dėr) [M.E. *gendre*, O.F. *genre*, L. *genere*, abl. of GENUS], *n.* (*Gram.*) One of the classes (MASCULINE, FEMININE, and NEUTER) into which words are divided according to the sex, natural or grammatical, of the things they represent; classification of words into genders according to their forms etc.; (*facet.*) sex; *kind, sort, class. **v.t.* To beget, to produce, to cause. **v.i.* To breed, to copulate.

gene (jēn) [Gr. *genos*, born of a certain kind], *n.* (*Biol.*) The unit of heredity; the factor in a gamete which determines the appearance of an hereditary characteristic. **genetic** (je net′ ik), *a.*

genealogy (jen ė-, jē nė ăl′ ŏ ji) [O.F. *genealogie*, late L. *geneălogia*, Gr. *genealogia* (*genea*, race, -LOGY)], *n.* The history or investigation of the descent of families; a record or exhibition of a person's or family's descent in the natural order of succession; pedigree, lineage; the course of a plant's or an animal's development from earlier forms. **genealogical** (jen ė-, jē nė ȧ loj′ i kȧl), *a.* Of or pertaining to genealogy; exhibiting the successive stages of family descent. **genealogical tree,** *n.* The genealogy of a family drawn out in the figure of a tree, with the root, stem, branches, etc. **genealogically,** *adv.* **genealogize** (jen ė-, jē nė ăl′ ŏ jīz), *v.i.* To investigate descent; to trace a pedigree; to prepare a genealogy. **genealogist,** *n.*

genera [GENUS].

general (jen′ ėr ȧl) [O.F., from L. *generālis*, from GENUS], *a.* Relating to a whole genus, kind, class, or order; not special, particular, partial, or local; common, universal; ordinary, usual, widespread, prevalent; not limited in scope or application; indefinite, vague; not specialized or restricted; taken or viewed as a whole; commonly affixed to words expressive of rank or office, with the force of chief or supreme within a certain sphere. *n.* *The public, the common people; (*R.-C. Ch.*) the chief of a religious order, or of all the houses or congregations having the same rule; (*Mil.*) an officer ranking next below a field-marshal, usu. extended to lieutenant-generals and major-generals; the commander of an army; a strategist; (*colloq.*) a general servant; *the whole; the chief part, the majority; (*pl.*) general facts or principles; [var. **generale**] a general drum-call beaten in the morning to give notice to the infantry to be ready to march. **in general:** In the main, generally; in most cases or in all ordinary cases, for the most part. **General Assembly** [ASSEMBLE]. **General Certificate of Education (G.C.E.):** In England and Wales a certificate in secondary education obtainable in Ordinary, Advanced, and Scholarship levels. **general confession,** *n.* One in which the whole congregation joins. **general council,** *n.* (*Eccles.*) A council called together by the authority of the Church at large. **General Court,** *n.* The State legislature in Massachusetts and New Hampshire. **general dealer,** *n.* One who deals in many articles of daily use. **general hospital,** *n.* One taking patients whatever their disease. **general officer,** *n.* An officer above the rank of colonel. **general post,** *n.* A general postal delivery; a romping indoor game. **general post office,** *n.* A chief or head post office, esp. the head office in London. **general practitioner,** *n.* A physician or surgeon treating all kinds of cases. **general reader,** *n.* One who reads miscellaneous books, etc., as dist. from one following a course of special study. **general servant,** *n.* A female servant whose duties are not special, a maid-of-all-work. **general term,** *n.* (*Log.*) A term which is the sign of a general conception or notion. **general warrant,** *n.* (*Law*) A warrant (now illegal) to apprehend all suspected persons, without naming any particular individual. **generalism,** *n.* A general conclusion, statement, or opinion. **generally,** *adv.* In general; for the most part, in most cases; ordinarily, commonly, usually; without minute detail, without specifying. ***generalness,** *n.*

generale [GENERAL].

generalia (jen ėr ā′ li ȧ) [L., neut. pl. of *generalis*, GENERAL], *n.pl.* General principles.

generalissimo (jen ėr ȧ lis′ i mō) [It., superl. of *generale*, GENERAL], *n.* The chief commander of a force furnished by several powers, or military and naval in combination; a commander-in-chief.

generality (jen ėr ăl′ i ti) [F. *généralité*, L. *generālitātem*, nom. *-tas*], *n.* The state of being general, as opposed to specific; a general statement or principle; a vague statement, vagueness; the main body, the majority.

generalize (jen′ ėr ȧ līz), *v.t.* To reduce to a genus or genera; to deal with as a class not an individual; to apply generally, to make of wider or of universal application; to deduce or infer (as a general principle) from many particulars. *v.i.* To form general ideas; to reason inductively; to draw general inferences; to speak vaguely, to employ generalities; (*Art.*) to represent typical not particular features. **generalizable,** *a.* **generalization** (-zā′ shůn), *n.* The act or process of generalizing; the act of making general, or of bringing several objects, agreeing in some point, under one head or class; a general inference; an induction. **generalizer,** *n.*

generally [GENERAL].

generalship (jen′ ėr ȧl ship), *n.* The office or rank of a general; skill in the management of troops and the conduct of war, strategy; (*fig.*) skilful leadership, management, or organization; tactful diplomacy.

generant [GENERATE].

generate (jen′ ėr āt) [L. *generātus*, p.p. of *generāre*, from *genus generis*, kind], *v.t.* To produce or bring into existence; to cause to be; to produce, to evolve, to originate; to beget, to procreate; (*Math.*) to trace out or form by the motion of a point or a magnitude of inferior order. **generable,** *a.* **generant,** *a.* Generating, producing. *n.* That which generates; (*Math.*) a point, line, or surface conceived of as, by its motion, generating a line, surface, or solid. **generating plant:** (*Elec.*) All the equipment needed for generating electrical energy. **generatrix** (jen ėr ā′ triks), *n.* A female parent; (*Math.*) a generant.

generation (jen ĕr ā′ shŭn), *n.* The act of generating; propagation of the species; reproduction, propagation; production, creation, bringing into existence; a single succession or step in natural descent; an age or period between one succession and another; the people of the same period or age; the average time in which the child takes the place of the parent (usu. estimated at about ⅓ of a century); progeny, offspring, issue; *a family, a race; *pedigree, lineage.

generative (jen′ ĕr ȧ tiv), *a.* Having the power of generating; pertaining to generation or production; productive, fruitful.

generator (jen′ ĕr ā tŏr), *n.* One who or that which begets, generates, or produces; any apparatus for the production of gas, steam, electricity, etc.; (*Chem.*) a compound from which a more complex substance is moulded; (*Elec.*) a dynamo; (*Mus.*) the principal sound or fundamental tone of a chord, etc. **asynchronous generator,** *n.* A generator without fixed alternation. **generator unit,** *n.* An independent generator in an electrical plant capable of working or stopping without affecting the rest of the machinery.

generic, -al (jĕ ner′ ik, -ȧl) [*genus generis*, see GENUS, -IC], *a.* Pertaining to a genus, class, or kind, opp. to specific; comprehensive, applied to large classes. **generic name,** *n.* The name of a genus, as Saxifraga in *Saxifraga longifolia*. **generically,** *adv.*

generous (jen′ ėr ŭs) [F. *généreux*, L. *generōsus*, as prec.], *a.* Liberal, munificent, open-handed, bountiful; overflowing, abundant, fertile; strong, stimulating (as wine); magnanimous, high-spirited; *nobly-born. **generosity** (jen ėr os′ i ti), *n.* **generously,** *adv.* ***generousness,** *n.*

genesis (jen′ ė sis) [L., from Gr. *genesis*, from *gen-*, root of *gignesthai*, to become, to be born], *n.* (*pl.* **-ses**) The act of begetting, producing, or giving origin to; creation, beginning, origination, mode of production or formation. **Genesis,** *n.* The first book of the Old Testament, in which the story of the Creation is told.

genet (jen′ ėt) [O.F. *genete*, Sp. *jineta*, Arab. *jarnait*], *n.* A small mammal, *Genetta vulgaris*, allied to the civet; its fur, or cat-skin dressed in imitation of this fur.

***genethliac** (jė neth′ li ăk) [late L. *genethliacus*, Gr. *genethliakos*, from *genethlē*, race, birth, from *gen-*, root of *gignesthai*, to be born], *a.* Of or pertaining to nativities as calculated by astrologers. *n.* A person skilled in the calculation of nativities; (*pl.*) the science of this; a birthday poem or ode. ***genethliacal,** *a.* ***genethliacally,** *adv.* ***genethliacon,** *n.* A birthday poem. **genethlialogy** (jė neth li ăl′ ŏ ji), *n.*

genetic (jė net′ ik) [from GENESIS (cp. ANTITHETIC from ANTITHESIS)], *a.* Of or relating to the origin, generation, or creation of a thing. *n.pl.* (*Biol.*) The study of heredity and variation. **genetic affinity,** *n.* (*Biol.*) Affinity founded on resemblances existing from a very early age, and therefore presumed to imply a common origin. **genetical,** *a.* **genetically,** *adv.*

geneva (1) (jė nē′ vȧ) [Dut. *genever*, O.F. *genèvre*, L. *juniperus*, JUNIPER, assim. to foll.], *n.* A spirit distilled from grain flavoured with juniper-berries, also called Hollands. **genevrette** (jen ė vret′), *n.* A wine made on the Continent from wild fruits and flavoured with juniper-berries.

Geneva (2) (jė nē′ vȧ) [town in Switzerland], *a.* Of, originating from, or pertaining to Geneva. **Geneva bands,** *n.pl.* Clerical bands such as those worn by Swiss Calvinist clergy. **Geneva Bible,** *n.* A translation of the Bible into English, made and published at Geneva in 1560. **Geneva Convention,** *n.* A convention made between the great powers (1864–65) to ensure the neutrality of ambulances, military hospitals, and those in charge of them, in time of war. **Geneva cross,** *n.* A red Greek cross on a white ground, the distinguishing mark of military ambulances, etc. **Geneva gown,** *n.* The black preaching gown worn by Presbyterian ministers and Low Church clergymen in England. **Genevan,** *a.* Of or pertaining to Geneva. *n.* A Genevese, a Calvinist. **Genevanism,** *n.* Calvinism, from the long residence of its founder and the establishment of his doctrines at Geneva. **Genevese** (jen ė vēz′), *a.* Genevan. *n.* A native or inhabitant of Geneva.

genial (1) (jē′ ni ȧl) [from F. or directly from L. *geniālis*], *a.* Of a cheerful and kindly disposition, cordial, sympathetic, enlivening; conducive to life and growth, soft, mild; pertaining to marriage or procreation, generative; *presiding over marriage; *native, inborn; [G. *genial*, *genialisch*] of or characterized by genius. **geniality** (jē ni ăl′ i ti), *n.* **genialize,** *v.t.* To give geniality to; to render genial. **genially,** *adv.* ***genialness,** *n.*

genial (2) (jė nī′ ȧl) [Gr. *geneion*, chin, from *genus*, jaw], *a.* (*Anat.*) Of, pertaining to, or near the chin.

geniculate, -lated (jė nik′ ū lȧt, -lā tėd) [L. *geniculātus*, from *geniculum*, dim. of *genu*, knee], *a.* Kneed, knee-jointed; (*Bot.*) bent abruptly like a knee, as the stems of many grasses. *v.t.* (-lāt) To form a knot or joint in. **geniculation** (-lā′ shŭn), *n.* The quality of having knots or joints; *the act of kneeling.

genie (jē ni) [F. *génie*, L. GENIUS], *n.* (*pl.* **genii** (jē ni ī) (1)) A jinnee.

genio- [Gr. *geneion*, chin, see GENIAL (2)], *comb. form.* **genio-hyoid** (jė nī ō hī′ oid), *a.* (*Anat.*) A muscle from the hyoid bone to the chin.

genipap (jen′ i păp) [from a native name in Guiana], *n.* The fruit of *Genipa Americana*, about the size of an orange, with a vinous taste.

genista (jė nis′ tȧ) [L.], *n.* A genus of leguminous shrubs, with yellow flowers, often regarded as comprising the broom, *Cytisus scoparia*.

genital (jen′ i tȧl) [O.F., from L. *genitālis*, from *genit-*, part. stem of *gignere*, to beget], *a.* Pertaining to generation or procreation. *n.pl.* The external organs of generation.

genitive (jen′ i tiv) [L. *genetīvus*, of generation, as prec. (a mistranslation of Gr. *genikē*, generic)], *a.* (*Gram.*) Indicating origin, possession, or the like (applied to a case in inflected languages roughly corresponding to the Eng. possessive). *n.* The genitive case. **genitival** (-tī′ vȧl), *a.*

genito- *comb. form.* **genito-urinary** (jen′ i tō ū′ rin ȧ ri), *a.* (*Physiol.*) Pertaining to the genital and urinary organs.

***genitor** (jen′ i tŏr) [F. *geniteur*, L. *genitōrem*, nom. *-tor*, as GENITAL], *n.* One who begets; a sire. ***geniture,** *n.* Procreation, birth; nativity, horoscope.

genius (jē′ ni ŭs) [L., from *gen-*, root of *gignere*, to beget], *n.* (*pl.* **genii** (2)) A tutelary deity or spirit, supposed to preside over the destinies of an individual, place, nation, etc.; also one of two spirits attendant on a person through life, one good, the other evil; (*fig.*) one who exercises a powerful influence over another for good or ill; a jinnee; (*pl.* **geniuses**) natural bent or inclination of the mind; the dominant character, spirit, or sentiment (of); an extraordinary endowment of intellectual, imaginative, expressive, or inventive faculty; a person so endowed; a representative type or impersonation. ***genius loci*** [L.], *n.* The presiding deity of a place; hence, the spirit or associations predominant in a locality, community, or institution.

***gennet** [JENNET].

Genoa (jen′ ō ȧ) [L. *Genua*, It. *Genova*], *n.* A city in N. Italy. **Genoa cake,** *n.* A rich fruit-cake with almonds on the top. **Genoese** (jen ō ēz′), *a.* Of or pertaining to Genoa. *n.* A native or inhabitant of Genoa; (as *pl.*) the people of Genoa.

genocide (jen′ ō sīd) [Gr. *genos*, born of a certain kind, -CIDE], *n.* The intentional and systematic destruction of a national, racial, ethnical, or religious group, *e.g.* the Jews by the Nazi Germans.

***genouillère** (zhė nu yâr) [F., from O.F. *genouil* (F. *genou*), L. *genu*, the knee], *n.* A jointed metal cap for covering the knees of an armed man; (*Fort.*) the interior slope of the parapet below the sill of an embrasure.

-genous [L. *-genus*, born, from *gen-*, root of *gignere*, to beget], *suf.* Born; bearing, producing; as in *indigenous*, *polygenous*.

genre (zhanr) [F., kind, see GENDER], *n.* Kind, sort, class; style, manner; a painting the subject of which is some scene in every-day life; this style of painting, also called **genre-painting.**

genro (jen′ rō) [Jap.], *n.pl.* Elder statesmen in Japan who are on occasion consulted by the Emperor.

gens (jenz) [L., from *gen-*, stem of *gignere*, to beget], *n.* (*pl.* ***gentes***) A clan, house, or sept among the ancient Romans; [*Gr. genos*] a similar group of families among the ancient Greeks.

gent (jent), *n.* (*colloq.*) A gentleman; a would-be gentleman.

genteel (jėn tēl′) [earlier *gentile*, F. *gentil*, see GENTILE], *a.* (*now vulg. or iron.*) Gentlemanly or ladylike; elegant in mien, manners, or dress, stylish; well-bred, refined, free from vulgarity. **n.* A genteel person. **genteelish,** *a.* **genteelly,** *adv.*

gentian (jen′ shȧn) [L. *gentiāna*, from *Gentius*, king of Illyria], *n.* The English name of *Gentiana*, a genus of bitter herbs, usually having blue flowers, common in mountain regions, one among which, the yellow gentian, *G. lutea*, yields gentian-root, used in medicine as a tonic. **gentianella** (jen shi ȧ nel′ ȧ), *n.* A dwarf species, *G. acaulis*, with flowers of intense blue. **gentianic** (jen shi ăn′ ik), *a.* **gentianin** (jen′ shi ȧ nin), *n.* A bitter compound extracted from gentian-root, also called gentianic acid.

gentile (jen′ tīl) [O.F. *gentil*, L. *gentīlis*, from *gens gentis*, see GENS], *a.* Not a Jew; heathen, pagan; applied by the Mormons to all who are not of their faith; *pertaining to a race or tribe; (*Gram.*) denoting race, country, or locality. *n.* One who is not a Jew; a heathen, a pagan; one who is not a Mormon; (*Gram.*) a word denoting race, country, or locality. **gentiledom,** *n.* ***gentilic** (jen′ til ik), *a.* ***gentilish,** *a.* ***gentilism,** *n.* **gentilitial** (jen ti lish′ ȧl), **gentilitious,** *a.* Of or pertaining to a gens, tribe, or nation.

***gentilesse** (jen ti les′), *n.* Courtesy; gentle birth or breeding.

gentility (jen til′ i ti) [O.F. *gentilité*], *n.* The quality of being genteel, assumed social superiority; manners and habits distinctive of good society; gentle birth; genteel people; *elegance of manners, politeness; the state of belonging to a gens or clan.

***gentilize** (jen′ ti līz), *v.t.* To render gentle or gentlemanly; to make gentile, to paganize. *v.i.* To act as or set up for a gentleman; to live like a gentile or a heathen.

gentle (jentl) [O.F. *gentil*, see GENTILE], *a.* Mild, tender, kindly; not rough, coarse, violent, or stern; moderate, not severe, not energetic; not steep; *courteous, amiable, well-disposed; *of honourable birth, belonging to the gentry; (*Her.*) having the right to bear arms. *n.* *One of good family; *(*pl.*) gentlefolk; the larva of the flesh-fly, used as bait in angling. *v.t.* To make gentle, amiable, or kind; to tame (as a colt); to handle gently but firmly, *to raise to gentle rank. **the gentle craft:** Angling, also called the gentle art; *the trade of shoemaking. **the gentle** or **gentler sex:** Women. **gentlefolk,** *n.* (*earlier in pl.* **gentlefolks**) People of good position of gentle birth. **gentlehood,** *n.* Gentle birth, rank, or breeding. **gentleness,** *n.* **gently,** *adv.* **gently born:** Of gentle birth.

gentleman (jentl′ mȧn), *n.* *A man of gentle birth, a man above the rank of yeoman; a man belonging to the gentry, or following the profession of arms, the church, or the law; strictly, a man entitled to bear arms; a man of good breeding, kindly feelings, and high principles, a man of honour; (*pop.*) one who by education, occupation, or income, holds a good social position; used as a polite equivalent for man, esp. (*pl.*) in addressing the male members of an audience; (*Law*) a man of respectable position who follows no occupation; (*colloq.*) the personal attendant of a man of rank. **gentleman-at-arms,** *n.* One of a company forming a body-guard to the sovereign on state occasions. **gentleman of fortune:** (*euphem.*) An adventurer. **gentleman-commoner,** *n.* (*Oxf. and Camb. Univ.*) One of a privileged class of commoners who formerly enjoyed special privileges. **gentleman-farmer,** *n.* A man of property who occupies his own farm. ***gentleman-pensioner, gentleman-ranker,** *n.* A gentleman enlisting in the ranks, usu. with the object of working up for a commission. **gentleman's gentleman,** *n.* (*facet.*) A valet. **gentleman-usher,** *n.* A gentleman who officiates as usher to a sovereign or other person of high rank. **gentlemanhood, gentlemanship,** *n.* **gentlemanlike,** *a.* **gentlemanly,** *a.* Like a gentleman in appearance, feeling, or behaviour; pertaining to or becoming a gentleman. **gentlemanliness,** *n.* **gentlemen's agreement,** *n.* An agreement binding in honour but not legally.

gentlewoman (jentl′ wu mȧn), *n.* A woman of gentle birth or breeding; a lady; a woman who waits upon a lady of high rank. **gentlewomanhood,** *n.* **gentlewomanlike, -ly,** *a.* **gentlewomanliness,** *n.*

gentry (jen′ tri) [prob. corr. of prec.], *n.* The social class below the nobility; *high birth; the rank of gentleman; politeness, good breeding; (*colloq.*) people, folks.

genty (jen′ ti) [Sc., from F. *gentil*, see GENTILE], *a.* Neat, graceful; genteel.

genual (jen′ ū ȧl) [L. *genu*, knee], *a.* Of or pertaining to the knee.

genuflect (jen′ ū flekt) [late L. *genuflectere* (*genu*, the knee, *flectere*, to bend)], *v.i.* To bend the knee, esp. in worship. **genuflector,** *n.* **genuflectory,** *a.* **genuflexion** (-flek′ shŭn), *n.*

genuine (jen′ ū in) [L. *genuīnus*, from the root *gen-*, to beget], *a.* Belonging to or coming from the true stock; real, true; not counterfeit, false, spurious, or adulterated; (*Zool.*) true to type, not aberrant. **genuinely,** *adv.* **genuineness,** *n.*

genus (jē′ nŭs) [L., as prec.; cogn. with KIN], *n.* (*pl.* **genera,** jen′ ėr ȧ) (*Log.*) A class or kind of objects containing several subordinate classes or species; (*Zool. and Bot.*) a group or class of animals or plants differentiated from all others by certain common characteristics and comprising one or more species; kind, group, class, order, family. **subaltern genus:** A genus which may be considered as a species of some higher genus. **summum genus, highest genus:** One which cannot be considered as a species of another genus.

-geny [F. *génie*, from Gr. *geneia* or L. *gen-*, stem of *genesis*], *suf.* Production or mode of production, as in *ontogeny*, *philogeny*.

geo, gio (gyō) [Sc., from Icel. *gja*], *n.* (*Orkney and Shetland*) A narrow inlet, a creek.

geo- [Gr. *geo-*, from *gē*, earth], *comb. form.* Pertaining to the earth. **geo-botany** (jē ō bot′ å ni) [BOTANY], *n.* A branch of botany treating of plants as regards their geographical distribution.

geocentric, -al (jē ō sen′ trik, -ål), *a.* As viewed from or having relation to the earth as centre; having reference to the centre of the earth, as distinguished from any spot on its surface. **geocentrically,** *adv.* **geocentricism, geocentric system,** *n.* The obsolete doctrine that the earth is the centre of the planetary system.

geochemistry (jē ō kem′ is tri), *n.* The study of the chemical composition of the crust of the earth.

geochronology (jē ō kron ol′ ō ji), *n.* The measuring of geological time.

geocyclic (jē ō si′ klik), *a.* Pertaining to the revolutions of the earth. **geocyclic machine,** *n.* A machine for exhibiting the processes by which day and night and the seasons are produced.

geode (jē′ ōd) [F. *géode*, from L. *geōdes*, from Gr. *geōdēs*, earthy, from *gē*, earth], *n.* A hollow nodule of any mineral substance, often lined with crystals; the cavity in such a nodule. **geodic** (jē od′ ik), *a.* **geodiferous** (-dif′ ėr ůs), *a.*

geodesy (jē od′ ė si) [F. *géodésie*, from Gr. *geōdaisia* (as GEO-, *-daisia* division, from *daiein*, to divide)], *n.* The science or art of measuring the earth's surface or large portions of it, as distinguished from surveying, which deals only with limited tracts. **geodesic, geodetic** (jē ō des′-, -det′-, -ik), *a.* Pertaining to geodesy; carried out or determined by means of geodesy. *n.pl.* Geodesy. **geodetic, geodesic line:** The shortest line between two points on the earth's surface or that of a geometrical solid. **geodetically,** *adv.* **geodesist** (jė od′ ė sist), *n.*

geodynamic, -al (jē ō dī năm′ ik, -ål), *a.* Relating to the latent forces of the earth.

geogeny (jē oj′ e ni), *n.* The science or study of the formation of the crust of the earth.

geognosy (jē og′ nȯ si) [F. *géognosie* (GEO-, Gr. *gnōsis*, knowledge, from *gignōskein*, to know)], *n.* Knowledge of the structure of the earth, structural geology; knowledge of the mineral and structural character of rocks; local geology. **geognostic, -al** (jē ȯg nos′ tik, -ål), *a.*

geogony (jē og′ ō ni), *n.* The theory of the formation of the earth.

geography (jē og′ rå fi) [F. *géographie*, L. *geographia*, Gr. *geōgraphia*], *n.* The science of the surface of the earth, its physical features, natural productions, inhabitants, political divisions, commerce, etc.; a book dealing with this. **mathematical geography:** Those parts of the science involving mathematics, such as astronomical geography, geodesy, and cartography. **physical geography:** Geography treating of the physical features of the earth's surface, the distribution of land and water, climate, and the distribution of plants and animals. **political geography:** Dealing with countries, States, political, social, and economic conditions. **geographer,** *n.* **geographic, -al** (jē ȯ grăf′ ik, -ål), *a.* Of or pertaining to geography; relating to or containing a description of the earth. **geographic latitude:** The angle between the plane of the equator and a perpendicular to the surface of the earth at a given point. **geographic variation:** (*Biol.*) The alteration in form, habits, etc., of a species or variety of plant or animal due to a change of habitat. **geographical mile:** One minute of longitude measured at the equator, about 2000 yards. **geographically,** *adv.*

geology (jē ol′ ȯ ji) [med. L. *geōlogia*], *n.* The science of the earth's crust, its composition, its structure, and the history of its development; a treatise on this subject. **dynamical geology:** The study of the forces that have brought about geological changes. **economic geology:** The study of such rocks and minerals as are of use to mankind, and their geological relations. **stratigraphical geology:** The study of the stratification of the rock-masses forming the earth's crust, stratigraphy. **structural geology:** The study of the relations between these masses and of the physical causes to which they are due. **geologic** (jē ȯ loj′ ik), *a.* Forming part of the subject-matter of geology. **geological,** *a.* Pertaining to geology. **geologically,** *adv.* **geologist, *-ger** (jē ol′ ȯ jist, -jėr), *n.* **geologize,** *v.i.* To study geology; to make geological investigations, esp. in a particular district.

geomancy (jē ȯ măn′ si) [F. *géomancie*, L. *geōmantīa*, Gr. *geōmanteia*], *n.* Divination by means of lines, figures, or dots on the earth or on paper, or by particles of earth cast on the ground. **geomancer,** *n.* **geomantic** (jē ȯ măn′ tik), *a.*

geometer (jē om′ ė tėr) [L. and G. *geōmetrēs* (GEO-, *metrēs*, measurer, from *metrein*, to measure)], *n.* A geometrician; a moth or its caterpillar belonging to the tribe called *Geometræ*, on account of their seeming to measure the ground as they move along.

geometry (jē om′ ė tri) [O.F. *geometrie*, L. and Gr. *geōmetria*], *n.* The science of magnitudes, whether linear, superficial, or solid, with their properties and relations in space. **plane geometry:** The branch of geometry dealing with magnitudes and their relations in one plane. **solid geometry:** Geometry dealing with all three dimensions of space. **geometric, -al** (jē ȯ met′ rik, -ål), *a.* Pertaining to geometry; done, determined, or prescribed by geometry; disposed in mathematical figures. **geometrical pen:** An instrument for drawing geometrical curves. **geometrical progression:** A progression in which the terms increase or decrease by a common ratio, as 1, 3, 9, 27; 144, 72, 36, 18. **geometrical proportion:** One based on equal ratios in its two parts, as 2 : 4 : : 6 : 12. **geometrical stairs:** Spiral stairs of which the steps are secured into the wall at one end only. **geometrical spider:** One that spins a web in a geometrical form. **geometrical tracery:** (*Arch.*) Window tracery of which the openings are simple geometrical patterns. **geometrically,** *adv.* **geometrician** (jē ȯ mė trish′ ån), **geometrist** (jē om′ ė trist), *n.* **geometrize,** *v.i.* To work or construct according to the rules or methods of geometry; to proceed geometrically.

geonomy (jē on′ ō mi), *n.* The science of the physical laws relating to the structure and development of the earth.

geophagy (jē of′ å gi), *n.* The act or habit of eating earth. **geophagist,** *n.*

geophysics (jē ō fiz′ iks), *n.* The science that deals with the physical characteristics of the earth. **International Geophysical Year:** A scientific enterprise, starting 1 July, 1957, in which more than 60 nations began a concerted programme of research into the physical properties of the earth, the results of their discoveries being pooled for the benefit of all.

geopolitics (jē ō pol′ i tiks), *n.* The study of how the political views and aims of a nation are affected by its geographical position.

geoponics, geopony (jē ō pon′ iks, jē op′ ō ni), *n.* The art and science of agriculture.

georama (jē ȯ ra′ må) [F. *géorama* (Gr. *gē*, earth, *horama*, a view, from *horaein*, to see)], *n.* A hollow globe on the inside of which the countries, oceans, etc., of the earth are represented, the observer standing on a framework in the centre.

Geordie (jôr′ di) [Sc. and North., dim of GEORGE], *n.* A guinea, which had the figure of St. George on the reverse; (*Coal-min.*) a pitman; a safety-lamp invented by George Stephenson; a sailing collier-boat; (*fam.*) a native of Tyneside.

George (jôrj) [L. *Georgius*, Gr. *Geōrgios*, a saint said to have been martyred under Diocletian], *n.* A jewel bearing the figure of St. George, the patron saint of England, worn by the knights of the Garter;

*(*slang*) a coin bearing the figure of St. George, a half-crown or a guinea; *a kind of loaf; (*Aviat. colloq.*) an automatic aircraft pilot. **brown George:** A coarse, earthenware water-jug. **by George:** A mild oath or asseveration. **George Cross** (**G.C.**), A decoration instituted in 1940, primarily for civilians in recognition of acts performed of the greatest heroism or most conspicuous courage in circumstances of extreme danger; **George Medal** (G.M.), similarly awarded for acts of great bravery. **George noble,** *n.* A gold coin, with St. George on the reverse, worth 6s. 8d., minted in the reign of Henry VIII. **St. George's cross** [CROSS (1)].

georgette (jôr jet') [Mme *Georgette*, a Fr. modiste], *n.* (*Textiles*) A plain semi-transparent dress material.

Georgian (1) (jôr' ji ȧn), *a.* Relating to the period of George I–IV in Great Britain (1714–1830); relating to the reign of George V (1910–1936).

Georgian (2) (jôr' ji ȧn), *a.* Of or pertaining to Georgia, a region south of the Caucasus, or to Georgia, one of the Southern States of the American Union. *n.* A native or inhabitant of one of these.

georgic (jôr' jik) [L. *geōrgicus*, Gr. *geōrgikos*, from *geōrgos*, a husbandman (GEO-, *ergein*, to work)], *a.* Pertaining to agriculture; treating of rural affairs. *n.* A poem on husbandry or rural affairs; one book of Virgil's *Georgics*, a poem in four books on husbandry.

geoscopy (jē os' kō pi), *n.* Knowledge of the ground or soil gained by inspection.

geoselenic (jē ō sel en' ik), *a.* Pertaining or relating to the earth and the moon.

geostatic (jē ȯ stăt' ik) [GEO-, Gr. *statikos*, causing to stand, from *sta-*, root of *histanai*, to stand], *a.* Applied to an arch so constructed as to be in equilibrium under vertical pressure, as in an embankment.

geotaxis (jē ō tăks' is) [GEO-, Gr. *taxis*, an arranging], *n.* (*Biol., Bot.*) The response of an organism or a plant to the stimulus of gravity.

geotectonic (jē ō tek ton' ik), *a.* Pertaining to the structure of the earth.

geothermal (jē ō thĕrm' ȧl), *a.* Pertaining to the internal heat of the earth.

geothermometer (jē ō thĕr mom' e tĕr), *n.* An instrument for measuring the earth's heat at different depths, as in mines or wells.

geotropism (jē ot' rȯ pizm) [GEO-, *Gr. tropos*, turning, from *trepein*, to turn, -ISM], *n.* The tendency exhibited by the organs of a plant to turn towards the centre of the earth. **geotropic** (jē ȯ trop' ik), *a.* **geotropically,** *adv.*

gerah (gēr' ȧ) [Heb.], *n.* A unit of weight and of money equivalent to $\frac{1}{20}$ of a shekel, or about $1\frac{1}{2}$d.

geranium (jė rā' ni ŭm) [L., from Gr. *geranion*, from *geranos*, a crane], *n.* A genus, with about 100 species, of hardy herbaceous plants, rarely shrubs, natives of all temperate regions, typified by *G. maculatum*, the crane's-bill, so called from the shape of its seed-pod; a plant of this genus; a cultivated plant of the allied genus *Pelargonium.*

gérant (zhâr' an) [F., pres.p. of *gérer*, from L. *gerere*, to manage], *n.* A business-manager; an editor.

geratology (jer ȧ tol' ȯ ji) [Gr. *gēras gēratos*, old age, -LOGY], *n.* The science dealing with the phenomena of deterioration and decay. **geratologic** (-loj' ik), **geratologous** (-tol' ȯ gŭs), *a.*

gerbe (jĕrb) [F.], *n.* A wheatsheaf; (*Her.*) a figure resembling this; a firework giving the effect of a sheaf of fire.

gerent (jē' rĕnt) [L. *gerens -ntem*, pres.p. of *gere*, to manage], *n.* A manager; a ruler or controller.

gerfalcon (jĕr' faw kȯn) [O.F. *gerfaucon*, med. L. *gēro- gīrefalco*, M.H.G. *gīrvalke* (cp. G. *geier*, vulture)], *n.* A large and powerful falcon of northern regions, typified by the Iceland falcon, *Falcon Islandus*; *a large falcon used for hawking at herons, etc.

geriatrics (jer i ăt' riks) [Gr. *geras*, old age; *iatros*, a physician], *n.* The branch of medicine dealing with old age and its diseases. **geriatric,** *a.* **geriatrician,** *n.*

germ (jĕrm) [F. *germe*, L. *germen -inis*], *n.* (*Biol.*) The portion of living matter from which an organism develops; (*Bot. and Zool.*) the embryo of an animal or plant; a partially-developed organism; (*Path.*) a micro-organism, esp. such as is supposed to cause disease, a microbe; (*fig.*) that from which anything springs; the origin, source, or elementary principle. **in germ:** Existing in an undeveloped state. **germ-cell,** *n.* (*Biol.*) The parent cell from which a new individual develops, usu. distinguished as the female element in reproduction from the sperm-cell or male element. *v.i.* To sprout, to germinate. **germ-plasm,** *n.* (*Biol.*) The part of the protoplasm in which the power of reproduction is supposed to reside and which is transmitted from one generation to its offspring. **germ theory:** (*Path.*) The theory that certain diseases are caused by the development of micro-organisms introduced into the body through germs or spores. **germ-tube,** *n.* The tube-like growth issuing from a germinating spore. **germless,** *a.* **germicide** [-CIDE], *a.* Destroying germs, esp. disease-germs; *n.* A substance used for this purpose. **germicidal** (-sī' dȧl), *a.*

german (1) (jĕr' mȧn) [O.F. *germain*, L. *germānus*, having the same parents (cogn. with prec.)], *a.* Sprung from the same parents (*usu. in comb.*, as *cousin-german*); closely connected, relevant, pertinent; *genuine, true; *closely related, akin. *n.* One sprung from the same stock.

German (2) (jĕr' mȧn) [L. *Germānus*, perh. from Celt. (cp. O.Ir. *gair*, neighbour)], *a.* Pertaining or relating to Germany. *n.* (*pl.* **Germans**) A native of Germany; the language of Germany, High German. **German Empire:** (*Hist.*) The Western Empire; the empire established in 1871 by the union of the North German Confederation, Baden, Hesse, Bavaria, and Würtemberg. **German alloy,** *n.* (*Metal.*) An aluminium alloy comprising aluminium, copper and zinc. **German measles:** A mild infectious disorder resembling measles. **German millet:** An edible grain produced by a grass, *Setaria Germanica.* **German Ocean:** The North Sea. **German-paste:** A paste made of hard-boiled eggs, pea-meal, almonds, lard, sugar, etc., for feeding singing-birds. **German sausage:** A large kind of sausage stuffed with partly-cooked meat, highly spiced. **German silver:** A white alloy of nickel, copper, and zinc, used for mathematical instruments, table-ware, etc. **German text,** *n.* A black-letter closely resembling old English and modern German. **High German:** Originally the form of German spoken in the south, but since Luther's translation of the Bible (1450) adopted as the literary language all over Germany. **Low German:** German of the Netherlands, including Dutch, Frisian, Flemish, and Old Saxon. **Germanesque** (jĕr mȧ nesk'), *a.* **Germanic** (jĕr măn' ik), *a.* Of or pertaining to Germany; of or pertaining to the Teutonic race. *n.* The primitive Teutonic language. **East Germanic:** The group of Teutonic languages represented by Gothic, and some like Burgundian and Vandal of which mere vestiges survive. **North Germanic:** The Scandinavian group of languages. **West Germanic:** The group comprising High and Low German, Dutch, Frisian, English, etc. **Germanish** (jĕr' mȧ nish), *a.* **Germanism,** *n.* **Germanist,** *n.* **Germanity** (jĕr măn' i ti), *n.* **Germanize,** *v.t.* To assimilate or make to conform to German ideas, customs, idioms, etc. *v.i.* To conform to these. **Germanization** (-zā' shŭn), *n.* **Germanizer,** *n.* **Germano-,** *comb. form.* **Germanomania** (-mā' ni ȧ) [-MANIA], *n.* **Germanophil** (jĕr măn' ȯ fil) [-PHIL], *n.* **Germanophilist** (-nof' i list), *n.* **Germanophobe** (jĕr măn' ȯ fōb) [-PHOBE], *n.* **Germano-**

phobia (jĕr mȧ nô fō' bi ȧ), *n.* **Germanophobic** (-fob' ik), *a.*

germander (jĕr măn' dėr) [F. *germandrée*, late L. *germandra*, *gamandria*, late Gr. *chamandrua*, corr. of Gr. *chamaidrus* (*chamai*, on the ground, *drûs*, tree)], *n.* A plant of the genus *Teucrium*, esp. the wall germander, *T. chamædrys.* **germander speedwell,** *n.* An English wild plant with blue flowers, *Veronica chamædrys.*

germane (gĕr mān) [GERMAN (1)], *a.* Relevant to, pertaining to, relating to.

germanium (jĕr mā' ni ŭm) [L. *Germānus*, GERMAN (2)], *n.* (*Chem.*) A metallic element of a greyish-white colour used in the construction of transistors because of its electrical properties.

germen (jĕr' men) [L., *see* GERM], *n.* (*Bot.*) The ovary or rudimentary seed-vessel of a plant; *a shoot or sprout; *a germ. **germigenous** (-mij' ė nŭs) [-GENOUS], *a.* **germiniparous** (-nip' ȧ rŭs) [-PAROUS], *a.* **germinal** (1) (jĕr' mi năl), *a.* Pertaining to or of the nature of a germ; germinative; in the earliest stage of development. **germinally,** *adv.*

germicide [GERM]. **germinal** (1) [GERMEN].

Germinal (2) (zhâr' mē năl) [F., GERMINAL (1)], *n.* The name given by the French Convention to the seventh month of the republican year, 21 March to 19 April.

germinate (jĕr' mi nāt) [L. *germinātus*, p.p. of *germināre*, from *germen*, see GERM], *v.i.* To sprout, to shoot, to bud; to develop. *v.t.* To cause to sprout or bud; to put forth; to produce. **germinable,** *a.* **germinant,** *a.* Sprouting, growing, developing. **germination** (-nā' shŭn), *n.* The first act of growth in an embryo plant, ovum, etc.; the act or process of germinating. **germinator** (jĕr' mi nā tŏr), *n.* **germinative,** *a.*

germon (jĕr' mŏn) [F.], *n.* The long-finned tunny.

gerontic (jer-, ger on' tik) [as foll.], *a.* Pertaining to old men, senile.

gerontocracy (jer-, ger ŏn tok' rȧ si) [Gr. *gerōn gerontos*, an old man, -CRACY], *n.* Government by old men; a government of old men. **gerontarchical** (-tar' ki kăl) [Gr. *-archos*, ruling, from *archein*, to rule], *a.* Pertaining to government by old men.

gerontogeous (jer-, ger on tȯ jē' ŭs) [Gr. *gerōn gerontos*, an old man, *gē*, the earth], *a.* (*Bot.*) Indigenous to the Old World.

gerontology (je ron tol' ō ji, ge ron tol' ō ji) [as prec.], *n.* The science dealing with the phenomena of deterioration and decay in the aged.

geropigia, jerupigia (jer ȯ-, -ŭ pij' i ȧ) [Port., corr. of HIERAPICRA], *n.* A mixture used to adulterate port wine, made of unfermented grape-juice with brandy, sugar, and colouring-matter.

-gerous [L. *-ger*, from *gerere*, to bear], *suf.* Bearing, having; as in *armigerous*, *florigerous.*

gerrymander (ger-, jer i măn' dėr) [Elbridge *Gerry*, Governor of Massachusetts, *-mander* (SALAMANDER, which the map of one district was supposed to resemble)], *v.t.* To tamper with (an electoral district or constituency) so as to secure unfair advantages for a particular candidate, party, or class; to misconstrue or garble (a question, argument, etc.) so as to arrive at unfair conclusions. *n.* An unfair rearrangement of a constituency in this manner. **gerrymanderer,** *n.*

gerund (jer' ŭnd) [L. *gerundium*, from *gerundum*, neut. ger. of *gerere*, to do], *n.* (*Lat. Gram.*) A part of the verb used as a noun instead of the infinitive in cases other than the nominative; (*A.-S. Gram.*) a dative form of the infinitive, ending in *-e* and governed by the preposition *to*, expressing purpose or end; (*Eng. Gram.*) a verbal noun ending in *-ing*, when used as a part of the verb. **gerund-grinder,** *n.* A pedantic schoolmaster. **gerundial** (jė rŭn' di ăl), *a.* **gerundive** (jė rŭn' div), *a.* Pertaining to or of the nature of a gerund; *n.* (*Lat. Gram.*) A verbal adjective formed on the gerundial stem giving the sense of *must* or *should* (be done). **gerundival** (ger ŭn dī' văl), *a.* **gerundively,** *adv.*

gesso (jes' ō) [It., from L. GYPSUM], *n.* A prepared ground of plaster of Paris for painting, sometimes for sculpture. **gesso work,** *n.*

***gest** (1) (jest) [O.F. *geste*, from L. *gesta*, exploits, orig. neut. pl. of *gestus*, p.p. of *gerere*, to carry on, to perform], *n.* A deed, an exploit, an achievement; a tale or history of the exploits of a hero or heroes, esp. a mediæval ballad or metrical romance. *v.i.* To compose or recite gests or legendary tales.

***gest** (2) (jest) [F. *geste*, L. *gestus*, bearing, gesture, as prec.], *n.* Carriage, bearing; a gesture.

***gest** (3) (jest) [O.F. *giste* (cp. GIST), from *gestr*, to lie], *n.* (*in pl.*) The successive stages of a journey or progress; the time allotted for a stay.

gestalt (ge stalt') [G., form, pattern], *n.* (*Psych.*) An organized whole in which each part affects every other part. Its exponents have demonstrated that the mind tends to perceive events and situations as a pattern, or whole, rather than as a collection of separate and independent elements.

Gestapo (ges ta' pō) [first letters of G. *Geheime Staats Polizei*, secret state police], *n.* The body of secret police formed to secure strict obedience to the Nazi government.

gestation (jes tā' shŭn) [through F., or directly from L. *gestātiōnem*, nom. *gestātio*, from *gestāre*, freq. of *gerere*, to carry], *n.* The act of carrying; the state of being carried; the act of carrying or the process of being carried in the uterus from the time of conception to that of parturition; the period of this. ***gestant,** *a.* Laden, burdened, pregnant. **gestate** (jes' tāt), *v.t.* **gestatorial** (jes tȧ tôr' i ăl), *a.* For carrying. **gestatorial chair,** *n.* The state chair in which the Pope is carried on special occasions. ***gestatory** (jes' tȧ tŏr i), *a.* That may be carried or worn; pertaining to gestation or pregnancy.

gesticulate (jes tik' ū lāt) [L. *gesticulātus*, p.p. of *gesticulārī*, from *gesticulus*, dim. of *gestus*, gesture, see GEST (2)], *v.i.* To make expressive gestures or motions, as in speaking or instead of speaking. *v.t.* To express or represent by gestures. **gesticulation** (jes tik ū lā' shŭn), *n.* The act or art of gesticulating to express emotion or illustrate an argument; a gesture. **gesticulator** (jes tik' ū lā tŏr), *n.* **gesticulative, gesticulatory,** *a.* Pertaining to or represented by gesticulation.

gesture (jes' chėr) [late L. *gestūra*, from *gestus*, p.p. of *gerere*, to carry, to deport (oneself)], *n.* A motion of the face, body, or limbs, used to express emotion or to illustrate or enforce something that is said; the art of using such movements for rhetorical or dramatic purposes; *bearing, deportment; *posture; a significant move, usually of a friendly nature. *v.i.* To gesticulate. *v.t.* To accompany or represent with gestures or action. **gestural,** *a.* **gestureless,** *a.* **gesturer,** *n.*

get (1) (get) [Icel. *geta* (cp. A.-S. *-gietan*, in *forgietan*, *engietan*, etc., also Goth. *-gitan*, G. *vergessen*, cogn. with L. *-hendere*, in *prehendere*, to seize, Gr. *chandanein*, to seize)], *v.t.* (*p.* **got,** *p.p.* **got, gotten**) To procure, to obtain, to gain possession of by any means, to acquire; to earn, to win; to receive, to obtain; to receive as one's portion or penalty, to suffer; to learn, to commit to memory; (*colloq. in p.p.*) to have, to possess; (*colloq.*) to be obliged (to); to beget, to procreate; to succeed in obtaining, bringing, putting, etc.; to induce, to persuade (to); to betake (oneself); (*colloq.*) to catch, to outwit, to nonplus. *v.i.* To arrive at any place, condition, or posture; to go, to depart; (*colloq.*) to succeed, to find the way or opportunity (to); to be a gainer, to profit. **get!** (*slang*) Be off! **has got to be done:** Must be done. **to get about:** To be able to move or walk about (after an illness); to become known, to be reported abroad; to travel from place to place. **to get ahead:** To prosper; to come in advance of. **to get along:** To proceed, to advance; to succeed, to fare, to manage (well or badly); (*colloq.*) to go away. **to get**

among: To become one of. ***to get asleep:** To fall asleep. **to get at:** To be able to reach; to ascertain; (*slang*) to banter, to tease; (*slang*) to corrupt (a jockey, etc.), to hocus (a horse). **to get away:** To quit; to escape; to disengage oneself (from); (*imper.*) be off! **to get away with:** To make off with; to escape discovery in connexion with. **getaway,** *n.* (*colloq.*) Escape. **to get back:** To receive back, to recover; to return, to come home. **to get before:** To arrive in front (of). **to get behind:** To fall into the rear; to lag; to fall into arrears; to penetrate, to unravel. **to get behind the scenes:** To become acquainted with the intimate working of any scheme or design. **to get by:** To elude; to be good enough; to come off with impunity. **to get clear:** To disengage oneself; to be released. **to get done with:** To bring to an end, to finish with. **to get down:** To dismount, to descend. **to get down to:** To concentrate upon. **to get forward:** To make progress, to advance; to push on with work. **to get home:** To arrive at one's home or house; to arrive at the winning-post. **to get in:** To be elected; to enter; to collect and place under cover (as crops); to make room for. **to get into:** (*colloq.*) To put on (as clothes, etc.). **to get into one's head:** To be convinced of. **to get loose** or **free:** To liberate or disengage oneself. **to get near:** To approach within a small distance. **to get off:** To dismount, to alight (from); to escape, to be released (from); to be acquitted, to be let off (with or for); to start; to take off, to remove; to procure the acquittal of; (*colloq.*) to make impression on one of the opposite sex. **to get on:** To put or pull on; to move on; to advance, to succeed, to prosper; to do, fare, or manage (with or without); to mount. **to get out:** To pull out, to extract; to escape from any place or state of confinement or restraint; to be divulged; (*imper.*) be off! **to get over:** (*slang*) To persuade, to seduce, to take in; to surmount; to succeed in finishing; to recover from (illness, surprise, etc.); to make intelligible; (*slang*) to circumvent, to overdo; to coax. **to get quit** or **rid of:** To disengage oneself from. **to get round:** To evade, to circumvent. **to get the best of it:** To gain the advantage; to be victorious. **to get the hang of:** To come to understand; to acquire the knack of. **to get there:** (*slang*) To succeed; to make a hit. **to get the worst of it:** To be defeated. **to get through:** To reach a point beyond, to reach one's destination; to pass (as a Bill); to succeed in doing, to complete, to finish (with); to pass (an examination). **to get to:** To reach, to arrive at; to begin (a task, etc.). **to get together:** To meet, to assemble; to bring together, to amass. **to get under:** To subdue; to place oneself under. **to get under way:** (*Naut.*) To start a ship; to start, to begin to move (of a ship). **to get up:** To prepare, to get ready; to dress (as linen); to learn, to work up; to dress up, to disguise; to invent, to devise; to rise (as from a bed, etc.); to mount; to begin to rage or be violent (as the wind, waves, etc.). **get-up,** *n.* Dress and other accessories; the manner in which anything is presented, as on the stage; the style or format (of a book). **to get wind:** To become public, to be divulged; to recover breath. **to get wind of:** To receive information about, to hear of. **to get with child:** To make pregnant. **get-at-able,** *a.* Accessible. **gettable,** *a.* Obtainable. **getter,** *n.* **getting,** *n.* (*pl.*) Gains, profits.

get (2) (get) [from prec.], *n.* The act of begetting; that which is begotten, offspring, progeny; (*Sc.*) a brat.

geum (jē′ ŭm) [L.], *n.* (*Bot.*) A hardy genus of rosaceous plants comprising the avens or herb-bennet.

gewgaw (gū′ gaw) [perh. from M.E. *givegove,* a reduplication of GIVE], *n.* A showy trifle; a toy, a bauble. **a.* Showy without value, gaudy. **gewgawed,** *a.* Tricked out with gewgaws. **gewgawish, gewgawy,** *a.* **gewgawry,** *n.*

gey (gā) [Sc., var. of GAY], *a.* Considerable, middling (in amount). *adv.* Considerably, very.

geyser (gā′ zėr, gī′ zėr, gē′ zėr) [Icel. *geysir,* 'gusher,' name of a hot spring in Iceland, from *geysa,* to gush], *n.* A hot spring throwing up a column of water at intervals (in S.W. Iceland, the Yellowstone region in North America, and New Zealand); an apparatus for heating a stream of water supplying a bath, etc.

Ghanaian (ga nā′ yȧn), *n.* A native of Ghana. *a.* Pertaining to Ghana.

gharry (găr′ i) [Hind. *gārī*], *n.* A variety of wheeled carriage in India.

ghastly (gast′-, găst′ li) [GAST, -LY], *a.* Pale, deathlike, haggard; horrible, frightful, shocking; (*colloq.*) awful, unpleasant. *adv.* In a ghastly manner. **ghastlily,** *adv.* **ghastliness,** *n.* ***ghastful,** *a.* Frightful, horrible. ***ghastfully,** *adv.*

ghaut (gawt) [Hind. *ghāt*], *n.* A mountain pass; a range of mountains; a flight of steps descending to a river, a landing-place. **Eastern** and **Western Ghauts:** Two ranges of mountains parallel to the coasts of southern India.

ghazal (ga′ zȧl) [Arab., an ode], *n.* An Oriental lyric poem, usu. erotic, convivial, or religious in subject, having a limited number of couplets, all with the same rhyme.

Ghazi (ga′ zi) [Arab. *ghāzi,* p.p. of *ghazā,* to fight], *n.* One who has fought for Islam, a title now bestowed usually on Mohammedan fanatics devoted to the destruction of non-believers. **Ghazism,** *n.*

gheber, ghebre [GUEBRE].

ghee (gē) [Hind. *ghī*], *n.* Butter, usu. prepared from buffalo-milk, clarified into an oil, which can be kept for a long time.

gherkin (gĕr′ kin) [Dut. *agurkken* (now *agurkje*), ult. from late Gr. *angourion,* Pers. *angārah* (acc. to Skeat, but the O.E.D. prefers a Slavonic derivation)], *n.* A young and green small variety of cucumber, used for pickling.

ghetto (get′ ō) [It., perh. abbr. of *borghetto,* dim. of *borgo,* BOROUGH], *n.* The quarter of a town inhabited by Jews.

Ghibelline (gib′ ė lin) [It. *ghibellino,* said to be a corr. of *Waiblingen,* an estate in Würtemberg belonging to the Hohenstaufen family, from which sprang several Emperors during the 12th and 13th cent.], *n.* One who sided with the Emperors in their contests with the Guelphs or partisans of the Popes, in Italy during the Middle Ages. **Ghibellinism,** *n.*

ghilgai, gilgai (gil′ gī) [Austral. abor.], *n.* A saucer-shaped depression containing a pool of water.

ghost (gōst) [A.-S. *gāst* (cp. Dut. *geest,* G. *geist*), prob. cogn. with Icel. *geisa,* to rage, Goth. *usgaisjan,* to terrify], *n.* The spirit or soul of a deceased person appearing to the living, an apparition; the soul of a dead person in the other world; the soul or spirit, the vital principle; (*fig.*) a mere shadow or semblance; the remotest likelihood; (*Lit. slang*) one who does literary or artistic work for which another takes the credit; (*Opt.*) a spot, gleam, or secondary image caused by a defect in a lens. *v.i.* To play the ghost, to prowl as a ghost; *to die. *v.t.* To haunt as a ghost. **Holy Ghost:** The Third Person of the Trinity. **to give up the ghost:** To die, to expire. **ghost-moth,** *n.* A nocturnal moth, *Hepialus humuli,* the caterpillars of which wreak havoc on the roots of hop-plants. **ghost-story,** *n.* A tale concerned with the supernatural, esp. one of a terrifying character. **ghost-word,** *n.* A word having no right to existence, due to the errors of copyists, printers, etc. **ghost-hood,** *n.* **ghost-like,** *a.* **ghostly,** *a.* Pertaining to the spirit or soul, spiritual; pertaining to religious matters; pertaining to ghosts or apparitions; dismal, gloomy. *adv.* Spiritually. **ghostliness,** *n.*

ghoul (gool) [Arab. *ghūl*], *n.* An evil spirit supposed, in Eastern tales, to devour human corpses. **ghoulish,** *a.* **ghoulishly,** *adv.* **ghoulishness,** *n.*

ghyll [GILL (2)].

giallo antico (jȧl′ ō ăn tē′ kō) [It., antique yellow], *n.* A yellow marble found among ruins of ancient buildings in Italy, used for decoration.

giant (jī′ ȧnt) [O.F. *geant*, L. *gigantem*, nom. *gigas*, from Gr. *gigas -antos*, etym. doubtful], *n.* A mythical being of human form but superhuman size; (*Gr. Myth., pl.*) the offspring of Uranus and Gæa (heaven and earth) who rebelled against the gods; a man of extraordinary size; any person, animal, plant, etc., of abnormal size; a person of extraordinary powers, ability, etc. *a.* Gigantic; like a giant; *enormous, monstrous. **giant-killer,** *n.* (*Folk-lore*) One who overcomes giants. **giant-powder,** *n.* A form of dynamite, consisting of infusorial earth saturated with nitro-glycerine. ***giant-rude,** *a.* Rough or rude as a giant. **giantess,** *n.* **gianthood, giantship,** *n.* ***giantish,** *a.* **giantism,** *n.* (*Physiol., Bot., etc.*) Abnormal development in size. **giant-like,** *a.* **giantly,** *a.* and *adv.* **giantry,** *n.*

giaour (jour) [Pers. *gāwr*], *n.* An infidel, a name given by the Turks to those who disbelieve in Mohammed, esp. Christians.

***gib** (1) (gib) [short for *Gilbert*], *n.* A cat, esp. a tom-cat; (*prov.*) a cat that has been castrated. ***gib-cat,** *n.* A tom-cat.

gib (2) [JIB (1)].

gibber (jib′ ėr) [imit.], *v.i.* To jabber, to talk rapidly and inarticulately. *n.* Talk or noise of this kind. **gibberish** (gib′ ėr ish), *n.* Inarticulate sounds; unmeaning or unintelligible language, jargon. *a.* Unmeaning.

gibbet (jib′ ėt) [O.F. *gibet*, dim. of *gibe*, a staff or club; cp. JIB (1)], *n.* An upright post with a cross-piece from which criminals were formerly hanged; a gallows; the gallows, death by hanging; *the projecting arm of a crane. *v.t.* To execute by hanging; to hang or expose on or as on a gibbet; (*fig.*) to expose to public contempt and derision.

gibbon (gib′ ȯn) [F., prob. from Eng. GIB (1) (conferred by Buffon)], *n.* Any individual of the genus *Hylobates*, long-armed anthropoid apes from the Indian Archipelago.

gibbous (gib′ ŭs) [L. *gibbōsus*, from *gibbus*, a hump], *a.* Hunch-backed, humped, crook-backed; protuberant, convex, swelling into inequalities; (*Astron.*) a term used when the illuminated portion of the moon or of a planet exceeds a semicircle but falls short of a circle; (*Bot.*) very convex or tumid. **gibbose,** *a.* Gibbous. **gibbosity** (gi bos′ i ti), *n.* **gibboso-,** *comb. form.* **gibbously,** *adv.*

gibe (jīb) [etym. doubtful (cp. Icel. *geipa*, to talk nonsense, from *geip*, nonsense; also O.F. *giber*, to play rude pranks)] *v.i.* To use sneering or taunting expressions; to rail, to flout, to jeer, to scoff (at). *v.t.* To use sneering or taunting expressions towards; to mock, to taunt, to sneer at. *n.* A sneer, a scoff, a taunt. **giber,** *n.* **gibingly,** *adv.*

Gibeonite (gib′ ė ȯ nīt) [*Gibeon*, a city in ancient Palestine], *n.* One of the inhabitants of Gibeon, condemned for their duplicity to be 'hewers of wood and drawers of water' (Joshua ix. 23); (*fig.*) a drudge, the lowest of servants.

giblets (jib′ lėts) [O.F. *gibelet*, cogn. with *gibier*, game, and *gibelotte*, rabbit-stew], *n.pl.* The feet, neck, and internal eatable parts of a fowl, such as the heart, liver, gizzard, etc., which are removed before cooking. **giblet-pie, -soup,** *n.* Pie or soup made with these.

Gibraltar (jib rawl′ tȧr) [a rock, seaport, and fortified town at the southern extremity of Spain, since 1704 a British possession], *n.* An impregnable stronghold; a very hard rock-candy. **Gibraltar-monkey,** *n.* An African species of monkey, *Inuus ecaudatus*, a colony of which exists on the rock of Gibraltar.

gibus (zhē′ bŭs) [name of orig. maker], *n.* A crush-hat, an opera-hat.

gid (gid) [short for GIDDY], *n.* A disease in sheep; sturdy.

giddy (gid′ i) [A.-S. *gydig*, prob. cogn. with GOD (cp. Gr. *entheos*, possessed by the god)], *a.* Having a whirling, swimming, or dizziness in the head; reeling, tending to stagger or fall; causing this sensation (as a precipice, a dance, success, etc.); (*fig.*) inconstant, changeable, fickle, flighty; elated, excited, rash. **to play the giddy goat:** To act the fool. **giddy-brained, -headed, -pated,** *a.* Frivolous, flighty. **giddy-go-round,** *n.* A round-about or merry-go-round. ***giddy-head,** *n.* A thoughtless person. ***giddy-paced,** *a.* Moving irregularly; reeling, wavering in gait. **giddily,** *adv.* **giddiness,** *n.*

gie (gē) (*Sc.*) [GIVE].

gier-eagle (gēr′ ē′ gėl) [Dut. *gier* (cp. G. *geier*), a vulture, EAGLE], *n.* A bird mentioned in Lev. xi. 18 and Deut. xiv. 17, probably the Egyptian vulture.

gif (gif) [Sc., from M.E. *ȝif*, IF], *conj.* If.

gift (gift) [from A.-S. or Icel. *gift* (cp. Dut. and G. *gift*), from the verb GIVE], *n.* The act, right, or power of giving; that which is given, a present, a contribution; (*Law*) the voluntary bestowal of property without consideration; (*fig.*) a natural quality, talent, or endowment; *an oblation; *a bribe. *v.t.* To bestow or confer; to endow with gifts; to present (with) as a gift. **gift-book,** *n.* A book given as a present, or suitable for so giving. **must not look a gift-horse in the mouth:** Must not criticize what is given one for nothing. **gifted,** *a.* Given, bestowed; largely endowed with intellect, talented. **giftling,** *n.* A gift of trifling value.

gig (1) (gig) [from *fishgig*, earlier *fizgig*, Sp. *fisga*, harpoon], *n.* A fish-spear.

gig (2) (gig) [orig. a whipping-top (cp. Norw. *giga*, to totter)], *n.* A light two-wheeled vehicle drawn by one horse; (*Naut.*) a light clinker-built boat, 20–28 ft. long, rowed by 4, 6, or 8 alternate oars, usu. reserved for the commanding officer; a somewhat similar boat used on the Thames for racing; (*Mech.*) a machine for raising a nap on cloth by passing it over rotary cylinders furnished with wire teeth; a frolic, a romp; (*slang*) a fool, a freak; (*Am.*) a queerly-dressed person; *fun, merriment; *a whipping-top. **gig-lamps,** *n.pl.* (*slang*) Spectacles. **gig-man,** *n.* One who keeps a gig; (*Carlyle*) a respectable person (from the definition of 'a respectable man' as one who drove his own gig, given by a witness at the murderer Thurtell's trial in 1823). **gigmanity** (gig măn′ i ti), *n.* (*Carlyle*) Respectability; philistinism.

gig (3) [GIGLET].

gigantic (jī găn′ tik) [L. *gigas -ntis*, GIANT], *a.* Huge, enormous, giant-like; immense, extraordinary. **gigantean** (jī găn tē′ ȧn), **gigantesque** (jī găn tesk′), *a.* **gigantically,** *adv.* **giganticidal** (-sī′ dȧl), *a.* **giganticide,** *n.* **gigantify,** *v.t.* **gigantism** (jī′ găn tizm), *n.* **gigantology** (-tol′ ȯ ji), *n.* **giganto-,** *comb. form.* **gigantomachy** (-tom′ ȧ ki) [Gr. *gigantomachia* (*gigās -ntos*, *machē*), battle], *n.* A war of giants, esp. the fabulous war of the giants against Zeus.

gigger [JIGGER].

giggle (gi′ gėl) [imit., freq. in form (cp. Dut. *giggelen*)], *v.i.* To laugh in a silly or affected manner, to titter; to laugh in a nervous, catchy way, with attempts to restrain oneself. *n.* A laugh of such a kind. **gigglement,** *n.* **giggler,** *n.* **gigglesome,** *a.*

giglet, -lot (gig′ lėt, -lȯt) [orig. a wanton woman, prob. cogn. with GIG (2)], *n.* A light, giddy girl; a wanton. *a.* Fickle, inconstant, wanton.

gigmanity [GIG (2)].

gig-mill (gig′ mil), *n.* A gig or machine for putting a nap on cloth; a mill furnished with such machines.

gigolo (jig′ ō lō) [Fr. slang, a low fellow], *n.* A professional dance-partner; a man who battens on women's favours.

gigot (jig′ ŏt) [F., dim. of *gigue*, a leg], *n.* A leg of mutton; *a piece, a fragment. **gigot-sleeve,** *n.* A sleeve shaped like a leg of mutton.

Gila monster (hē′ lȧ mon′ stėr) [from *Gila*, on Arizona River], *n.* A large poisonous lizard, *Heloderma suspectum*, found in Arizona and New Mexico.

gilbert (gil′ bĕrt) [William *Gilbert*, 1544–1603], *n.* (*Elec.*) Unit for measuring magneto-motive force.

Gilbertian (gil bĕr′ ti ȧn) [Sir W. S. *Gilbert* (1836–1911), writer of comic operas], *a.* Absurdly topsy-turvy.

gild (1) (gild) [A.-S. *gyldan*, in *begyldan*, see GOLD], *v.t.* (*p.p.* **gilded,** *part.a.* **gilt**) To coat, overlay, or wash thinly with gold; (*fig.*) to impart a golden colour or appearance to; to make brilliant, to brighten; to give a specious or agreeable appearance to, to gloss over; *to enrich; *to flush or make red with drinking; *to besmear with blood. **Gilded Chamber:** The House of Lords. **gilded youth:** Young people of wealth and fashion. **to gild a pill:** To make disagreeable necessity acceptable. **gilder** (1), *n.* One whose occupation is to coat articles with gold. **gilding,** *n.* The act, process, or art of overlaying with gold; gilding-metal in leaf, powder, or liquid, for application to any surface; (*fig.*) outward decoration, covering, or disguise designed to give a fair appearance to anything. **gilding-metal,** *n.* An alloy of copper, brass, and tin. **gilding-size,** *n.* Sizing used for cementing gold-leaf on a surface.

gild (2) [GUILD]. **gilder** (2) [GUELDER ROSE].

gill (1) (gil) [cp. Dan. *giælle*, Swed. *gäl*, also Gr. *cheilos*, lip], *n.* (*usu. in pl.*) The organs of respiration or branchiæ of fishes and some amphibia; a double row of long slender lamellæ, extending, like the teeth of a comb, from the convex side of a branchial arch, and supported by a delicate membrane; hair or leaf-like respiratory processes projecting from the body of some aquatic insects; the vertical lamellæ under the cap of fungi; the wattles of a fowl; (*facet.*) the flesh about a person's jaws and chin. **gill-cover,** *n.* The external bony covering of a fish's gills. **gill-net,** *n.* A net, usu. set vertically, for entangling fish by the gills. **gill-opening,** *n.* The opening by which the water passes into the gills. **gilled radiator:** (*Motor.*) A radiator consisting of tubes with metal fins attached to dissipate heat.

gill (2) (gil) [Icel. *gil*], *n.* A deep and narrow ravine, often wooded; a gully or stream-bed on a precipitous hill-side.

Gill (3) (jil) [short for *Gillian*, F. *Juliane*, L. *Juliana*, from *Julius*], *n.* A girl, a lass; a sweetheart; ground-ivy; malt liquor flavoured with ground-ivy; a female ferret. **Jack and Gill:** Lad and lass. **gill-flirt,** *n.* A wanton girl, a flirt.

gill (4) (jil) [O.F. *gille, gelle*, low L. *gillo, gella*, etym. doubtful], *n.* A liquid-measure, usu. one-fourth of a pint.

gillaroo (gil ȧ roo′) [Ir. *giolla* (cp. GILLIE), *ruadh*, red], *n.* An Irish variety of the common trout, *Salmo fario*, in which the coats of the stomach are said to be thickened by feeding on shell-fish.

gillie (gil′ i) [Gael. *gille*], *n.* A Highland man-servant, esp. one who attends a sportsman in fishing or hunting.

gillyflower (jil′ i flou ėr) [earlier *gylofre*, O.F. *girofle*, late L. *caryophyllum*, Gr. *karuophullon* (*karuon*, nut, *phullon*, leaf), ending assim. to FLOWER], *n.* The clove-pink, *Dianthus caryophyllus*; also applied to the white stock, *Matthiola incana*, and the wallflower, *Cheiranthus cheiri*. ***gillyvor,** *n.*

gilpy (gil′ pi) [Sc., etym. doubtful], *n.* A frolicsome young person, male or female.

***gilravage** (gil răv′ ȧj) [etym. unknown], *v.i.* To frolic or gad about; to be riotous or extravagant. *n.* A noisy frolic or merry-making; disorder, confusion.

gilt (1) (gilt) [GILD], *a.* Gilded; adorned with gold or something resembling gold. *n.* Gold laid over the surface of a thing, gilding; money, gold. **gilt-edged,** *a.* Having the edges gilded. **gilt-edged securities:** Investments of the most reliable character. **gilt-head,** *n.* A name given to several fishes with golden spots or lines on their heads, including the dorado, the striped tunny or bonito, and the golden wrasse.

gilt (2) (gilt) [N. *gyltr*], *n.* A young sow.

gimbal (jim′ bȧl) [alt. form of GIMMAL, GEMEL], *n.* (*usu. in pl.*) A form of universal joint for securing free motion in suspension, or for suspending anything, as a lamp, a compass, a chronometer, etc., so that it may always retain a horizontal or other required position, or be in equilibrium.

gimblet [GIMLET].

gimcrack (jim′ krăk) [etym. doubtful, perh. in first sense from obs. *gim*, JIMP, spruce, and *crack*, a lively boy (O.E.D. refers 14th cent. *gibecrake* to O.F. *giber*, to shake)], *n.* *A showy person, a dandy, a fop; a pretty but useless or flimsy article, a gewgaw. *a.* Showy but flimsy and worthless. **gimcrackery,** *n.* **gimcracky,** *a.*

gimlet (gim′ lėt) [O.F. *guimbelet*, dim.; see WIMBLE], *n.* A small boring-tool with a worm or screw for penetrating wood, and a wooden cross-piece for handle. *v.t.* To bore or pierce with a gimlet; (*Naut.*) to turn round (as an anchor) with a motion like the turning of a gimlet.

gimmal (jim′ ȧl) [var. of GEMEL], *n.* (*pl.*) A pair or series of interlocking rings, as in machinery, a gimbal; a gemel-ring. **gimmal-bit,** *n.* The double bit of a bridle.

gimmer (1) (gim′ ėr) [Icel. *gymbr*], *n.* (*Sc. and North.*) A ewe between one and two years old.

gimmick (gim′ ik) [?], *n.* A personal trick, device, or oddity of behaviour consistently employed by a comedian, etc., as part of his stock in trade.

gimp (1) (gimp) [etym. doubtful, cp. Dut. *gimp*, F. *guimpe*], *n.* Silk, wool, or cotton twist interlaced with wire or coarse cord; a silk fishing-line whipped with thin wire to protect it against injury from the teeth of large fish. *v.t.* To trim or whip with gimp or with fine wire.

***gimp** (2) (jimp) [etym. unknown], *v.t.* To jag, to indent, to denticulate.

gimp (3) [JIMP].

gin (1) (jin) [short for GENEVA], *n.* An ardent spirit, Geneva. **gin-fizz,** *n.* A drink composed of gin, aerated water, and lemon. **gin-mill,** *n.* (*Am. slang*) A tippling shop. **gin-palace,** *n.* A gaudily-decorated public-house or drinking-saloon, esp. one in which spirits are largely sold. **gin rummy,** *n.* A card game. **gin-shop,** *n.* A tavern or drinking saloon where spirits are sold. **gin-sling,** *n.* A cold drink, composed of gin, soda-water, lemon, and sugar.

gin (2) (jin) [contraction of O.F. *engin*, ENGINE], *n.* A trap, a snare for small mammals and birds; (*Mech.*) a portable hoisting-machine usu. having a tripod frame, one leg being movable; a pump worked by a windmill; a machine for hoisting coal, a whin; a machine for separating cotton-fibre from the seeds; *any kind of machine; *an engine of torture. *artifice of any kind. *v.t.* To clean (as cotton) of the seeds by means of a gin; to snare, to entrap. **gin-horse,** *n.* A mill-horse. **gin-house,** *n.* A house where cotton is ginned.

***gin** (3) (gin) [M.E. *ginnen*, A.-S. *-ginnan* in *onginnan*, to begin, etc.], *v.i.* and *t.* To begin, to commence.

gin (4) (jin) [Austral. abor.], *n.* An aboriginal woman.

gin (5) (gin) [Sc., GAIN (2)], *prep.* Against.

gin (6) (gin) [prob. conn. with GIF], *conj.* (*Sc. and North.*) If.

gingal, jingall (jing′ gȧl, -gawl) [Hind. *janjāl*], *n.* An East Indian breech-loading fire-arm, carrying a ball from four to eight ounces, and fired from a rest.

ginger (jin' jėr) [earlier *gingivere*, A.-S. *gingifere*, late L. *gingiber*, L. *zingiber*, Gr. *zingiberis*, Sansk. *çṛngavera* (*çṛnga*, horn, *vera*, body)], *n.* A plant, *Zingiber officinale*, with a pungent, spicy root-stock; the root-stock of this, either whole or powdered, used in cookery, as a sweetmeat, or in medicine; (*slang*) a red-haired person; (*slang*) mettle, dash, go. *v.t.* To flavour with ginger; to treat a horse with ginger by putting it up the fundament; (*fig.*) to spirit (up). **white ginger,** *n.* Jamaica ginger, scraped. **black ginger,** *n.* East Indian ginger, unscraped. **preserved ginger,** *n.* A conserve or sweetmeat made from the immature root. **gingerade** (jin jėr ăd'), *n.* Ginger-beer. **ginger-ale,** *n.* An aerated beverage, prepared by dissolving sugar in water, flavouring with ginger or essence of ginger, and colouring with a solution of caramel. **ginger-beer, -pop,** *n.* An effervescing fermented beverage prepared from ginger, white sugar, water, and yeast. **ginger-brandy,** *n.* A cordial prepared by steeping bruised ginger in brandy. **ginger-cordial,** *n.* A cordial or liqueur made with raisins, lemon-rind, and ginger and water strengthened with spirits. **ginger-nut,** *n.* A gingerbread-nut. **ginger-wine,** *n.* A British wine made by the fermentation of sugar, water, and ginger. **gingerous,** *a.* (*slang*) Sandy, carroty (of hair). **gingery,** *a.* Spiced with ginger; (*slang*) red-haired, carroty.

gingerbread (jin' jĕr bred), *n.* A dark-coloured cake made of flour, treacle or molasses, ground ginger, and other spices. *a.* Showy, tawdry; flimsy and fantastic (in allusion to the fanciful shapes, often gilded, in which gingerbread used to be moulded). **gingerbread-nut,** *n.* A small button-like cake of gingerbread. **gingerbread-tree, -palm,** *n.* The doum-palm; a West African tree, *Parinarium macrophyllum*, with a farinaceous stone-fruit called the **gingerbread-plum. gingerbread-work,** *n.* Work cut or carved in fanciful shapes.

gingerly (jin' jėr li) [perh. from O.F. *gensor*, compar. of *gent*, see GENT (2)], *adv.* Daintily, fastidiously, cautiously, so as to move without noise or risk of hurting oneself or anything trodden upon. *a.* Dainty, fastidious, cautious. **gingerliness,** *n.*

gingham (ging' ȧm) [F. *guingan*, Malay *ginggang*, orig. striped], *n.* A kind of linen or cotton fabric woven of dyed yarn, usu. in stripes or checks; (*colloq.*) a common umbrella.

gingili (jin' ji li) [Hind. *jingalī*, ult. from Arab. *juljulān*], *n.* An East Indian herb, *Sesamum Indicum*, from the seeds of which is obtained a sweet oil.

ginging (gin' jing) [etym. doubtful], *n.* (*prov.*) The lining of a shaft with bricks or masonry.

gingival (jin jī' vȧl) [L. *gingīva*, the gum], *a.* (*Anat.*) Pertaining to the gums.

gingko (ging' kō) [Jap., from Chin. *yin-hing* (*yin*, silver, *hing*, apricot)], *n.* A Japanese tree, *Gingko biloba*, with handsome fan-shaped leaves, also called the maidenhair-tree.

***gingle** [JINGLE].

ginglymus (ging'-, jing' li mŭs) [Gr. *ginglumos*, hinge], *n.* (*Anat.*) A joint admitting only of flexion and extension in one plane, as the elbow. **ginglyform,** *a.* **ginglymoid,** *a.* **ginglymate,** *v.i.* To form a hinge.

gink (gink), *n.* (*Am colloq.*) Fellow, man.

***ginnet** [JENNET].

ginning (jin' ing) [GIN (2)], *n.* The operation by which cotton is cleared of its seeds.

ginny-, jenny-carriage (jin-, jen' i kăr' ȧj) [prob. from *Jenny*, a form of Janet, see JENNY], *n.* A strong railway car for conveying materials.

ginseng (jin' seng) [Chin. *jên shên* (*jên*, man, *shên*, meaning doubtful)], *n.* One of two herbs belonging to the genus *Arabia* or *Panax*, the root of which has a sharp, aromatic taste, and is highly esteemed as a medicine by the Chinese.

Giottesque (jot tesk') [*Giotto* di Bondone (1276–1337), Tuscan painter], *a.* In the style of or after Giotto. *n.* The style established by Giotto and his school.

gip (1) [GYP].

gip (2) (gip) [etym. unknown], *v.t.* To take out the entrails of (as herrings).

gipsy (jip' si) [earlier *gypcian*, *Egypcien*, O.F. *Egyptien*, late L. *Ægyptiānus*, from L. *Ægyptius*, an inhabitant of Egypt], *n.* One of a nomad race (calling themselves Romany), prob. of Hindu extraction, dark in complexion and hair, and speaking a corrupt Sanskrit dialect, who live largely by horse-dealing, fortune-telling, etc.; one resembling a gipsy, esp. in dark complexion; a cunning, mischievous, or erratic person. *v.i.* To picnic or camp out in the open air. **gipsy-bonnet, -hat,** *n.* A bonnet or hat with a large brim or side flaps, often tied down to the side of the head. **gipsy-cart, -van, wagon,** *n.* A large van such as gipsies live and travel in from place to place. **gipsy-flower, -rose,** *n.* The scabious. **gipsy-table,** *n.* A light round table on a tripod made orig. of sticks roughly tied together. **gipsydom, gipsyhood, gipsyism,** *n.* The habits, practices, or life of gipsies. **gipsify,** *v.t.* (*usu. in p.p.*). **gipsyish,** *a.*

giraffe (ji raf', -răf') [F. (now *girafe*), Sp. *girafa*, Arab. *zarāfah*], *n.* An African ruminant, *giraffa camelopardalis*, with an extremely long neck, and two bony excrescences on the head, light fawn in colour with darker spots, formerly called the camelopard.

girandole (jir' ȧn dōl) [F., from It. *girandola*, from *girare*, L. *gȳrare*, to turn in a circle, from *gȳrus*, Gr. *guros*, circle], *n.* A branching chandelier or candlestick; a revolving firework discharging rockets; a rotating jet of water; a pendent jewel, usu. for the ears, with a large set encircled by smaller ones.

girasol (jir' ȧ sol) [It. *girasole*, orig. sunflower; *girare*, as prec., *sole*, sun], *n.* A variety of opal with reddish refractions, also called fire-opal.

gird (1) (gĕrd) [A.-S. *gyrdan* (cp. Dut. *gorden*, G. *gūrten*), cogn. with GIRTH, GARDEN, YARD], *v.t.* (*past* and *p.p.* **girded, girt**) To bind round (usu. the waist) with some flexible band, esp. in order to secure or confine the clothes; to secure (one's clothes with a girdle, belt, etc.; to fasten (a sword on or to) with a girdle or belt; to invest or equip (with); to surround or encircle with or as with a girdle, to encompass, to besiege; *to dress, to clothe. **to gird up one's loins:** To get ready to do something; to prepare oneself for vigorous action.

gird (2) (gĕrd) [etym. unknown], *v.i.* To sneer, to mock (at). *n.* A sarcasm, a sneer.

girder (gĕr' dėr), *n.* A principal beam, esp. a compound structure of iron plates or lattice-work, wood or metal, spanning the distance from wall to wall, or pier to pier, used to support joints, walls, roof, roadway, or other superincumbent weight. **girder bridge,** *n.* A bridge consisting of girders. **girding,** *n.* That which girds; *a girdle; *a covering; (*Sc.*) a saddle-girth.

girdle (1) (gĕr' dėl) [A.-S. *gyrdel*, from A.-S. *gyrdan*, to GIRD (1)], *n.* A belt, zone, or cord for securing a loose garment round or encircling the waist; (*fig.*) anything that encircles as a belt or zone; (*Anat.*) the bones by which the limbs are united to the trunk in vertebrate animals; (*Arch.*) a small circular band or fillet round the shaft of a column; (*Jewel.*) the line of greatest marginal circumference of a brilliant, at which it is grasped by the setting; (*Bot.*) a zone-like ring on a stem, etc. *v.t.* To gird or surround with or as with a girdle, to surround, to environ; to make a cut round (the trunk of a tree) through the bark, so as to kill it or in some cases to make it fruit better. **girdler,** *n.* One who girdles; a maker of girdles.

girdle (2) (gĕr′ dėl) [Sc. and North., var. of GRIDDLE], *n.* A round flat plate of iron hung over a fire for baking cakes.

girkin [GHERKIN].

girl (gĕrl) [M.E. *gerle*, a young person, cp. L.G. *gör*, a child], *n.* A female child, a young and unmarried woman; a maid-servant; a sweetheart; *a roebuck of two years old. **old girl:** A slighting or unceremonious term for an elderly woman, mare, etc. **one's best girl:** (*slang*) One's sweetheart. **the girls:** The daughters of a family; girls collectively. **the principal** or **leading girl:** (*Theat.*) The leading actress, esp. in pantomime and musical comedy. **girlhood,** *n.* **girlie, girly,** *n.* **girlish,** *a.* **girlishly,** *adv.* **girlishness,** *n.*

***girlond** [GARLAND].

girn (gĕrn) [var. of GRIN], *v.i.* (*now chiefly Sc.*) To grin, to snarl; to be fretful.

girnel (gĕr′ nėl) [Sc., var. of *garnel*, GARNER], *n.* A granary; a large meal-chest.

Gironde (jir ond′, zhē rawnd′) [a maritime department in the south-west of France, adjacent to the Bay of Biscay], *n.* (*F. Hist.*) The name given to the moderate Republican party in the French Assembly (1791–93), from the fact that its leaders represented the department of the Gironde. **Girondin,** *n.* A member of the Gironde. **Girondist,** *n.* and *a.*

girouette (zhir ů et′) [F., from *girer*, L. *gȳrare*, to revolve, from *gȳrus*, Gr. *guros*, a circle], *n.* A weather-cock; (*fig.*) a time-serving politician.

girr (gĕr) [Sc., var. of GIRTH], *n.* A child's hoop; a barrel-hoop.

girt (1) (gĕrt), *a.* Girded, bound; (*Naut.*) moored so taut by cables fixed in opposite directions as to prevent her swinging (of a vessel).

girth (gĕrth) [Icel. *gjörth*, a girdle, cp. Goth. *gairda*], ***girt** (2) (gĕrt), *n.* The band by which a saddle or burden is made fast and kept secure on a horse's back by passing round his belly; a circular bandage or anything that encircles or girds; measure round anything, circumference, waist-measure; a small girder; one of two bands attached to the carriage of a printing press, to run it in and out. *v.t.* To measure the girth of; to measure (a certain amount) in girth; to surround, to encompass; to fit with a girth; to secure with a girth. **girt-line,** *n.* (*Naut.*) A rope through a block on a lower-mast head used to hoist the rigging.

gist (jist) [O.F. (F. *gît*), it lies, 3rd pers. sing. of *gésir*, L. *jacēre*, to lie], *n.* *A lodging-place; the essence or main point of a question.

gitano (ji ta′ nō) [Sp., ult. from L. *Ægyptiānus* (cp. GIPSY)], *n.* (*fem.* **gitana**) A gipsy.

gîte (zhēt) [F. *gîte*, O.F. *giste*, as GIST], *n.* A sleeping-place, a lodging.

***gittern** (git′ ėrn) [O.F. *guiterne*, as CITHERN], *n.* An instrument like a guitar, a cithern. **v.i.* To play upon a gittern.

giubiloso (joo bil ō′ zō) [It.], *a.* (*Mus.*) Jubilant.

giusto (joos′ tō) [It., from L. *justus*, JUST], *a.* (*Mus.*) Regular; strict, accurate.

give (1) (giv) [A.-S. *giefan* (cp. Dut. *geven*, Icel. *gefa*, Goth. *giban*, G. *geben*)], *v.t.* (*past* **gave,** *p.p.* **given**) To hand over or transfer the possession of or right to without price or compensation; to bestow, to confer, to present, to render without payment; to grant, to concede, to allow, to put in one's power; to hand over, to deliver; to commit, to consign, to put in one's keeping; to transfer as price or in exchange, to pay, to sell; to return, to render as due; to surrender, to relinquish; to yield up, to devote; to yield as product; to communicate, to impart; to be the source or author of; to occasion, to cause; to offer, to hold out, to show or exhibit; to assign, to suppose, to assume (as conditions or circumstances). *v.i.* To part with freely and gratuitously; to yield as to pressure, to collapse; to move back, to recede; to make way or room; to lead, to open (upon); *to make an attack; *to weep. **to give and take:** To be fair; (*fig.*) to play fair. **give you good day, even,** or **morrow:** (*ellipt.*) God give you good day, etc. **to give away:** To make over, to transfer; to give in marriage; (*slang*) to let out or divulge inadvertently. **give-away,** *n.* (*colloq.*) An unintentional revelation. **to give birth to:** To bring forth. **to give back:** To restore; *to retire, to retreat. **to give chase to:** To pursue. **to give ear:** To listen, to pay attention (to). **to give forth:** To publish, to tell. **to give ground:** To yield or retreat. **to give in:** To yield. **to give it anyone:** (*colloq.*) To punish. **to give it best:** (*Austral.*) To give up hope, to give in without trying further. **to give in marriage:** To permit the marriage of (a daughter). **to give into custody** or **in charge:** To hand over or consign to a police constable, etc. **to give off:** To emit; *to forbear, to cease. **to give on:** *To rush or fall (on); to afford a prospect on or into, to face. **to give out:** To emit; to publish, to proclaim; to distribute; (*colloq.*) to show, to profess; to break down; to run short. **to give over:** To hand over, to transfer; to abandon, to despair of; (*in p.p.*) to devote or addict; to cease (from), to desist; to yield. **to give place:** To give precedence; to yield; to be succeeded by. **to give one's hand:** To espouse, to accept in marriage. **to give place to:** To yield, to retire. **to give rise to:** To occasion, to cause. **to give the sack** (*colloq.*), **the boot** or **the mitten** (*slang*): To dismiss, esp. in a summary fashion. **to give tongue:** To bark. **to give up:** To surrender; to resign; to commit; to despair of. **to give way:** To yield, to fail to resist; to make room; to break down; to abandon (oneself to); to be depreciated in value; (*Naut.*) to begin to row; to row with increased energy. **to give what for:** (*slang*) To chastise, to punish severely. **given name,** *n.* (*Am.*) A baptismal name. **giver,** *n.*

give (2) (giv) [from prec.], *n.* The state of yielding or giving way; elasticity. **give and take:** Mutual concession or forbearance; fair measure on either side.

give (3) [GYVE].

gizz (jiz) [Sc., etym. unknown], *n.* A wig; the face.

gizzard (giz′ ård) [M.E. *giser*, O.F. *giser*, *gezier* (F. *gésier*), L. *gigeria*, pl. cooked entrails of poultry], *n.* A strong muscular division of the stomach, esp. the second stomach in birds; a thickened muscular stomach in certain fish, insects, and molluscs. **it sticks in one's gizzard:** (*slang*) It is very disagreeable to one.

gizzen (gizn) [Sc., from Icel. *gisna*], *v.i.* To shrink and become leaky through dryness; (*fig.*) to become dry and wizened.

glabrous (glā′ brůs) [L. *glaber*, -OUS], *a.* Smooth; devoid of hair or pubescence. **glabrate,** *a.* **glabrescent** (glā bres′ ėnt), *a.*

glacé (gla′ sā) [F., p.p. of *glacer*, to ice, from *glace*, ice], *a.* Iced, or with a surface or covering like ice (as confectionery); polished, glossy (as leather goods).

glacial (glā′ shi ål, glāshl, glăs′ i ål) [F., from L. *glaciālis*, from *glacies*, ice], *a.* Of or pertaining to ice; due to or like ice, icy; (*Geol.*) due to or characterized by glaciers, ice-sheets, or floating ice; (*Chem.*) crystallizing at ordinary temperatures. **glacial drift:** Gravel, sand, clay, and other debris transported or deposited by ice. **glacial period, epoch, era:** A period during which a large part of the northern hemisphere was covered with an ice-sheet, called also the ice age. **glacialist,** *n.* One who considers that certain geological phenomena are due to the action of ice. **glacially,** *adv.* **glaciate** (glā′ shi āt, glăs′ i āt), *v.t.* (*Geol.*) To scratch, polish, or wear down by means of ice; to cover with ice in the form of sheets or glaciers. *v.i.* To be converted into ice. **glaciation** (-ā′ shůn), *n.* The subjection of an area to glacial conditions. **glacio-,** *comb. form.* **glaciometer** (glăs i om′ ė tėr) [-METER], *n.* An apparatus or device for measuring the rate of movement of glaciers.

glacier (glăs′ i ėr) [F., from *glace*, L. *glacies*, ice], *n.* A stream-like mass of ice, formed by consolidated accumulations of snow at high altitudes, slowly descending to lower regions. **glacier-lake,** *n.* A lake held back temporarily or permanently by a glacier or its deposits. **glacier-mud, -silt,** *n.* Mud, sand, or pulverized debris formed underneath glaciers and deposited by glacier streams. **glacier-table,** *n.* A block of stone left standing on a pillar of ice which it has sheltered from the sun's rays while all around has melted away.

glacière (gla′ syâr) [F., as prec.], *n.* A natural or artificial cavity in which ice remains unmelted during the summer, esp. an ice-cave, or natural cave containing a small glacier below the snow-line.

glacio-, etc. [GLACIAL].

glacis (glā′ sis, gla sē′) [F., orig. a slippery place, from O.F. *glacer*, from *glace*, ice], *n.* (*Fort.*) A sloping bank, such as the declivity in front of a rampart, where assailants would be exposed to fire.

glad (glăd) [A.-S. *glæd* (cp. Dut. *glad*, Icel. *glathr*, also O.H.G. *glat*, G. *glatt*, L. *glaber*, smooth)], *a.* Pleased, gratified; indicating pleasure or satisfaction; affording pleasure, joy, or satisfaction; bright, gay. ***v.t.** To make glad. *v.i.* To be or become glad. **glad-eye,** *n.* (*slang*) Ogling. **glad hand,** *n.* (*slang*) A welcome. **glad rags,** *n.* (*slang*) Evening dress. **gladden,** *v.t.* To make glad or joyful; to cheer; ***v.i.** To rejoice. ***gladder,** *n.* ***gladful,** *a.* ***gladfully,** *adv.* ***gladfulness,** *n.* **gladly,** *adv.* **gladness,** *n.* **gladsome,** *a.* **gladsomely,** *adv.* **gladsomeness,** *n.*

glade (glād) [prob. from Scand. (cp. Icel. *glathr*, see prec.)], *n.* An open space in a wood or forest; (*Am.*) an opening in the ice of rivers or a tract of smooth ice; an everglade. ***gladly,** *a.*

gladiate (glăd′ i ȧt) [as foll.], *a.* (*Bot.*) Sword-shaped.

gladiator (glăd i ā′ tȯr) [L., from *gladius*, a sword], *n.* (*Rom. Ant.*) A man employed to fight in the Roman amphitheatre; (*fig.*) a political combatant; a controversialist. **gladiatorial, *-an** (-tôr′ i ȧl, -ȧn), ***gladiatory** (glăd′-), *a.* **gladiatorism** (glăd′ i ā tȯr izm), *n.* The act or practice of fighting as gladiators; prize-fighting. **gladiatorship,** *n.*

gladiolus (glăd′ i ȯ lŭs, glȧ dī′ ȯ lŭs, glăd i ō′ lŭs) [L., dim. of prec.], *n.* (*pl.* **-li**) An iridaceous genus of plants with a fleshy bulb, sword-shaped leaves, and spikes of bright-coloured flowers.

gladius (glā′ di ŭs) [L., see prec.], *n.* (*Anat.*) The cuttlebone or pen of a cuttlefish.

gladstone (glăd′ stŏn) [W. E. *Gladstone* (1809–98)], *n.* A gladstone-bag; (*Am.*) a four-wheeled, two-seated pleasure carriage; **gladstone-bag,** *n.* A light leather bag with flexible sides, opening along the middle and secured with a clasp and straps. **Gladstonian** (glăd stō′ ni ȧn), *a.* Pertaining to, resembling W. E. Gladstone; an adherent of W. E. Gladstone, esp. a supporter of his Home Rule policy.

glagol (glăg′ ol) [Slav., a word], *n.* The earliest Slavonic alphabet, principally used in Istria and Dalmatia, in the offices of the R.-C. Church. **Glagolitic** (-lit′ ik), *a.*

glaik (glāk) [Sc., prob. conn. with GLEEK (2)], *n.* (*usu. in pl.*) A trick, a hoax; a childish toy; a flash, a glance of the eye. **glaikit,** *a.* Foolish, giddy, flighty.

glair (glâr) [O.F. *glaire*, prob. from L. *clāra*, fem. of *clārus*, clear, bright], *n.* White of egg, or a preparation made with this, used as size or varnish; any similar viscous, transparent substance. *v.t.* To smear or overlay with glair. **glaireous, glairy,** *a.* **glairine,** *n.* A glairy substance on the surface of some thermal waters.

glaive (glāv) [O.F., from L. *gladius*, a sword], *n.* A broadsword, a sword, a falchion; a weapon for foot-soldiers, consisting of a cutting edge fixed to the end of a pole.

glamour (glăm′ ȯr) [corr. of GRAMMAR, introd. by Scott (cp. GRAMARYE)], *n.* The influence of some charm on the vision, causing things to seem different from what they are; magic, enchantment; witching, delusive charm or illusion. **glamour-girl,** *n.* A girl who attracts men by her strong sex appeal. **glamorous,** *a.*

glance (glans) [prob. from O.F. *glacier*, to slip, to glide, from *glace*, ice (influenced by M.E. *glenten*, to glide, to glance, cogn. with O.H.G. *glanz*, bright, clear)], *v.i.* To glide off or from (as a blow); (*fig.*) to touch, to allude, to hint (at); to dart or flash a gleam of light or brightness; to give a quick or cursory look (at); to move about rapidly. *v.t.* To shoot or dart swiftly or suddenly; to direct (a look or the eye) rapidly or cursorily; *to hint at, to allude to. *n.* An oblique impact of an object on another causing it to be deflected; (*Cricket*) a hit with the bat turned obliquely to the ball; a flash, a gleam; a quick or transient look, a hurried glimpse (at). **glance-coal,** *n.* Anthracite. **glancingly,** *adv.*

gland (glănd) [F. *glande*, O.F. *glandre*, L. *glandula*, dim of *glans -ndis*, acorn], *n.* An organ secreting certain constituents of the blood, either for extraction and specific use or for elimination as waste products; (*Bot.*) a cellular organ in plants, usu. secreting oil or aroma; (*Eng.*) a sleeve employed to press packing tight on or around a piston-rod.

glanders (glăn′ dėrz) [from O.F. *glandre*, as prec.], *n.pl.* A very dangerous and contagious disease in horses, attended with a running of corrupt matter from the nostrils, and enlargement and induration of the glands of the lower jaw. **glandered,** *a.* **glanderous,** *a.*

glandiferous (glăn dif′ ėr ŭs) [L. *glandifer* (*glans -ndis*, see GLAND)], *a.* Bearing acorns or other nut-like fruits. **glandiform** (glăn′ di fôrm), *a.* Having the form of an acorn; (*Physiol.*) resembling a gland.

glandule (glăn′ dūl) [F., from L. *glandula*, dim. of *glans -ndis*, GLAND], *n.* A small gland. **glandular,** *a.* Characterized by the presence of a gland or glands; consisting or of the nature of a gland or glands. **glandularly,** *adv.* ***glandulation** (-lā′ shŭn), *n.* (*Bot.*) The arrangement and structure of the glandules in plants. **glanduliferous** (glăn dū lif′ ėr ŭs), *a.* **glandulose** (*Bot.*), **glandulous,** *a.* (*Physiol.*) **glandless,** *a.*

glans (glans) [GLAND], *n.* (*Bot.*) The nut-like fruit of some forest trees; an acorn, a beech-nut, a chestnut, etc.; (*Physiol.*) a structure of somewhat similar form, as the extremity of the penis; (*Path.*) a strumous swelling.

glar (glar), **glaur** (glawr) [Sc., etym. doubtful], *n.* Slime, mud. *v.t.* To make muddy.

glare (glâr) [prob. cogn. with GLASS, cp. A.-S. *glær*, a transparent substance], *v.i.* To shine with a dazzling or overpowering light; to look with fierce, piercing eyes, to stare; to be obtrusively overdressed or gaudy; to be very conspicuous. *v.t.* To shoot or dart forth in or as in intense lustre. *n.* A fierce overpowering light, disagreeable brightness; tawdry splendour; an intense, fierce look or stare. **glaring,** *a.* Shining with dazzling brightness; staring; too conspicuous or overcoloured; notorious, barefaced, infamous. **glaringly,** *adv.* **glaringness,** *n.* **glary,** *a.* Of dazzling brightness.

glareous [GLAIR].

glass (glas) [A.-S. *glæs* (cp. Dut. *glas*, Icel. *gler*, G. *glas*, perh. from Teut. root rel. to A.-S. *glōwan*, to GLOW)], *n.* (*pl.* **-es**) A hard, brittle, transparent substance, formed by fusing together mixtures of the silicates of potash, soda, lime, magnesia, alumina, and lead in various proportions, according to the quality or kind required; a substance of vitreous structure or composition; an article made of glass; a mirror, a looking-glass; a drinking-vessel of glass; the quantity which such vessel will hold; a lens; an optical instrument composed partly of glass, an eye-glass, a telescope; a sand-glass, an hour-glass; an instrument for indicating atmospheric changes, a barometer; a thermometer; a window-pane; a carriage window; (*pl.*) a pair of spectacles; (*collect.*)

ornaments or utensils made of glass, greenhouses, windows. *v.t.* To mirror, to reflect (oneself or itself) in or as in a glass; to case in glass; to fit or cover with or as with glass, to glaze; to make (the eye) glassy. **glass-blower,** *n.* One whose business is to blow and mould glass. **glass case,** *n.* A case or shallow box having a glass lid or sides to show the contents. **glass-cloth,** *n.* A cloth for wiping and cleaning glasses; cloth covered with powdered glass, like sand-paper. **glass cloth,** *n.* A fabric woven of fine-spun glass threads. **glass-coach,** *n.* A kind of carriage with glass windows instead of curtains, a superior kind of hackney carriage. **glass-crab,** *n.* The flat, transparent larva of a shrimp, formerly regarded as a distinct genus. **glass-culture,** *n.* The cultivation of plants under glass. **glass-cutter,** *n.* A workman or a tool that cuts glass. **glass-cutting,** *n.* The art or process of cutting, grinding, and polishing glass-ware. **glass-dust,** *n.* Powdered glass used for grinding and polishing. **glass eye,** *n.* An artificial eye of glass; a species of blindness in horses; a Jamaican thrush, *Turdus Jamaicensis*; (*pl.*) (*slang*) a person wearing spectacles. ***glass-faced,** *a.* Reflecting, like a mirror, the looks of another. **glass-furnace,** *n.* A furnace in which the materials of glass are fused. ***glass-gazing,** *a.* Often contemplating oneself in a mirror. **glass-grinding,** *n.* Glass-cutting. **glass-house,** *n.* A house or building where glass is made; a greenhouse or conservatory; a glass-roofed photographic studio; (*slang*) a military prison. **to live in glass houses:** To be susceptible to criticism through one's pursuits or opinions. **glassing-jack, -machine,** *n.* A machine for smoothing and polishing leather. ***glass-man,** *n.* One who deals in glass-ware; a glass-maker. **glass-metal,** *n.* Glass in fusion in the pot. **glass-painting,** *n.* The art of painting designs on glass with colours which are burnt in. **glass-paper,** *n.* Paper covered with finely-powdered glass used for rubbing down and smoothing rough surfaces of wood, etc. **glass-pot,** *n.* The pot or crucible in which the material for glass-making is fused. **glass-snake,** *n.* An American lizard without limbs, *Ophisaurus ventralis*. **glass-soap,** *n.* Oxide of manganese and other substances used in the manufacture of glass to remove colour due to ferrous salts, etc. **glass-stainer,** *n.* **glass-staining,** *n.* The art or process of colouring glass during manufacture. **glass-ware,** *n.* (*collect.*) Articles made of glass. **glass-work,** *n.* Glass manufacture; glass-ware. **glass-worker,** *n.* **glass-works,** *n.* A place or building where glass is manufactured. **glassful,** *n.* As much as a glass will hold. **glassless,** *a.* **glass-like,** *a.* **glassy,** *a.* Like glass, vitreous; lustrous, smooth, mirror-like (of water); hard, dull, lacking fire, fixed (of the eye). **glassily,** *adv.* **glassiness,** *n.*

Glassite (glăs' īt) [John *Glass* (1695–1773), minister of the Church of Scotland, deposed for his 'Testimony of the King of the Martyrs' (1727), maintaining that a congregation is subject to no jurisdiction but that of Christ], *n.* A name sometimes given to the Sandemanians.

glasswort (glas' wĕrt), *n.* One of various maritime herbs containing alkali formerly used in glass-making.

Glastonbury (glăs' tȯn ber i) [town in Somersetshire, the seat of a celebrated abbey, now in ruins], *a.* Pertaining to Glastonbury. **Glastonbury chair,** *n.* An 'antique' arm-chair modelled upon the former Abbot's chair preserved at Wells. **Glastonbury thorn,** *n.* A variety of *Cratægus* or hawthorn flowering on old Christmas Day, said to have sprung from the staff of Joseph of Arimathæa planted at Glastonbury.

Glaswegian (glăs wē' ji ȧn) [mod. L. *Glaswegiānus*, from *Glasgow*], *n.* A native or inhabitant of Glasgow.

glauber's salt (glou'-, glaw' bėrz sawlt') [J. R. *Glauber* (1604–68), German chemist], *n.* Sodium sulphate, a strong purgative. **glauberite,** *n.* (*Min.*) A yellow, grey, or brick-red mineral, composed of sulphate of soda and sulphate of lime.

glaucescent (glaw ses' ėnt) [L. *glaucus*], *a.* Tending to become or becoming glaucous. **glaucescence,** *n.*

glaucoma (glaw kō' mȧ) [Gr., from *glaukos*], *n.* (*Path.*) A disease of the eye, causing opacity in the crystalline humour, tension of the globe, dimness and ultimately loss of vision. **glaucomatous,** *a.* **glaucosis,** *n.*

glauconite (glaw' kȯ nīt) [G. *glauconit*, from Gr. *glaukon*, neut. of *glaukos*, as foll.], *n.* (*Min.*) An amorphous green hydrous silicate of iron, potassium, etc.

glaucous (glaw' kůs) [L. *glaucus*, Gr. *glaukos*], *a.* Sea-green, pale greyish-blue; (*Bot.*) covered with a bloom or down of this tinge (as grapes).

glaucus (glaw' kůs) [L., some kind of fish, as prec.], *n.* (*Zool.*) A genus of nudibranchiate gasteropods found floating on seaweed in the Atlantic and Pacific; (*Ornith.*) the burgomaster gull, *Larus glaucus*.

glaum (glawm) [Sc., etym. doubtful], *v.i.* To grasp or snatch (at).

glaur, glaury [GLAR].

glaux (glawks) [Gr., from *glax*, a milky plant], *n.* (*Bot.*) A genus of plants belonging to the *Primulaceæ*, with one species, *G. maritima*, the sea-milkwort.

glave [GLAIVE].

glaze (glāz) [M.E. *glasen*, from A.-S. *glæs*, GLASS], *v.t.* To furnish, fit, or cover with glass; to fit with a sheet or panes of glass; to furnish with windows; to overlay (pottery) with a vitreous substance; to cover (a surface) with a thin glossy coating; to make smooth and glossy; *to cover (the eyes) with a film. *v.i.* To become glassy (as the eyes). *n.* A smooth, lustrous coating; such a coating, formed of various substances, used to glaze earthenware, pictures, paper, confectionery, etc. **glaze-kiln,** *n.* A kiln in which glazed biscuit-ware is placed for firing. **glazer,** *n.* A workman who glazes earthenware; a wheel for grinding or polishing cutlery; a calico-smoothing wheel; *a glazier. **glazier** (glā' zi ėr, -zhėr), *n.* One whose business it is to set glass in windows, etc. **glazier's diamond,** *n.* A small diamond fixed on a handle, used by glaziers for cutting glass. **glaziery,** *n.* **glazing,** *n.* The act or process of setting glass in window-sashes, picture-frames, etc.; covering with a glaze, or giving a glazed or glossy surface to pottery and other articles; the material used for this; glass-work; glazed-windows; (*Painting*) the process of applying semi-transparent colours thinly over other colours to tone down asperities. **glazy,** *a.*

gleam (glēm) [A.-S. *glæm* (cp. O.S. *glīma*, brightness, O.H.G. *glīmo*, a glow-worm), cogn. with GLIMMER], *n.* A flash, a beam, a ray, esp. one of a faint or transient kind. *v.i.* To send out rays of a quick and transient kind; to shine, to glitter. **gleamy,** *a.*

glean (glēn) [O.F. *glener* (F. *glaner*), etym. doubtful], *v.t.* To gather (ears of corn which have been passed over on the cornfield); to gather ears of corn from; (*fig.*) to collect bit by bit, to pick up here and there; *to strip, so as to leave nothing behind. *v.i.* To gather the ears of corn left on the ground. **n.* A collection or sheaf, as of corn, obtained by gleaning. **gleaner,** *n.* **gleaning,** *n.*

glebe (glēb) [O.F., from L. *glēba*, a clod of earth, the soil], *n.* *Land, soil, ground; *a piece of cultivated ground; the land furnishing part of the revenue of an ecclesiastical benefice; (*Mining*) land containing ore; *a lump, mass, or clod of earth, ore, etc. **glebe-house,** *n.* A parsonage-house. **glebe-land,** *n.* **glebeless,** *a.* ***glebous,** ***gleby,** *a.* Abounding in clods; fertile, rich.

glede (glēd) [A.-S. *glida*, cogn. with GLIDE], *n.* (*Sc. and North.*) The kite, *Milvus regalis*.

gledge (glej) [Sc., cp. GLEE (2), GLEY], *v.i.* To squint; to look slyly. *n.* A sly or cunning look.

glee (1) (glē) [A.-S. *glēo, glīw* (cp. Icel. *glȳ*)], *n.* Joy, mirth, gladness, delight; (*Mus.*) a composition for several voices in harmony, consisting usually of two or more contrasted movements and without instrumental accompaniment; *music, minstrelsy. **glee-craft,** *n.* Minstrelsy. ***glee-maiden, -woman,** *n.* A female singer. ***gleeman,** *n.* A minstrel or singer. **gleeful, *gleesome,** *a.* Merry, gay, joyous. **gleefully,** *adv.*

glee (2) (glē), **gley** (glī) [Sc. and North., etym. doubtful], *v.i.* To squint, to have a cast in the eye. *n.* A squint; a side-look.

gleed (glēd) [A.-S. *glēd*, cogn. with GLOW], *n.* A burning coal, an ember; a fire.

***gleek** (1) (glēk) [O.F. *glic*, prob. from M.Dut. *ghelic* (Dut. *gelijk*), cogn. with LIKE], *n.* A game of cards played by three persons; a set of three court-cards of the same rank; hence, three of the same sort of thing.

***gleek** (2) (glēk) [etym. doubtful], *n.* A scoff, a jest; an enticing glance. *v.i.* To mock, to scoff. *v.t.* To trick, to take in.

Gleep (glēp) [initials Graphite Low Energy Experimental Pile], *n.* The first British nuclear pile at Harwell.

gleet (glēt) [O.F. *glette*, slime, filth], *n.* (*Path.*) A purulent discharge from the urethra, a morbid discharge from a sore, ulcer, etc.; *slime, filth. *v.i.* To discharge humour; *to ooze, to flow slowly. **gleety,** *a.*

gleg (gleg) [Sc., from Icel. *glegger*, cogn. with A.-S. *glēaw*, sagacious, wise], *a.* Quick, sharp, alert, clever; lively; sharp-edged, keen. **glegly,** *adv.* **glegness,** *n.*

glen (glen) [Gael. *gleann* (cp. W. *glyn*)], *n.* A narrow valley, a dale.

Glendoveer (glen′ dō vēr) [altered from the F. adaptation *grandouver*, prob. from Sansk. *gandharva*], *n.* A beautiful and beneficent spirit in Southey's poems dealing with Hindu myth.

glene (glē′ nē) [Gr.], *n.* (*Anat.*) The ball or pupil of the eye; a small socket or cavity in a bone receiving a condyle to form a joint. **glenoid,** *a.* **glenoid cavity,** *n.* **glenoidal** (glė noi′ dȧl), *a.*

glengarry (glen găr′ i) [valley in Inverness-shire], *n.* A woollen cap, high in front with ribbons hanging down behind, worn by some Highland regiments; also called **glengarry bonnet.**

gliadin (glī′ ȧ din) [F. *gliadine*, from Gr. *glia*, glue], *n.* Gluten.

glib (1) (glib) [prob. imit. (cp. Dut. *glibberig*, slippery)], *a.* Smooth, slippery; moving easily; off-hand; voluble, fluent, not very weighty or sincere. **adv.* Glibly. **glibly,** *adv.* **glibness,** *n.*

***glib** (2) (glib) [Ir.], *n.* A long lock of hair; a thick mass of bushy hair hanging over the brows.

glide (glīd) [A.-S. *glīdan* (cp. Dut. *glijden*, G. *gleiten*)], *v.i.* To move smoothly and gently; to slip or slide along, as on a smooth surface; to pass rapidly, smoothly, and easily; to pass imperceptibly (away); (*Mus.*) to pass from tone to tone without a perceptible break; (*Aviat.*) to fly an engineless heavier-than-air aeroplane which is catapulted or launched from a height, and makes use of rising air currents. *n.* The act of gliding; (*Mus.*) a passage from one tone to another without a break; (*Phon.*) a continuous sound produced in passing from one position of the organs of speech to another. **glider,** *n.* One who or that which glides; a heavier-than-air flying-machine with no motive power. **gliding,** *n.* The art or sport of piloting such an aircraft. **glidingly,** *adv.*

gliff (glif) [Sc. and North., etym. doubtful], *n.* A glimpse; a moment; a fright, a scare.

glim (glim) [orig. obscure, cogn. with GLEAM and GLIMPSE], *n.* *Brightness; (*slang*) a light, a candle, etc. **douse the glim** [DOUSE].

glimmer (glim′ ėr) [as prec.], *v.i.* To emit a faint or feeble light; to shine faintly. *n.* A faint, uncertain, or unsteady light; (*fig.*) a faint gleam, an uncertain sign (as of intelligence, etc.); a glimpse; (*slang, pl.*) the eyes. **glimmering,** *n.* A glimmer, a twinkle; (*fig.*) a faint gleam (as of knowledge, sense, etc.); an inkling, a glimpse. **glimmeringly,** *adv.*

glimpse (glimps) [M.E. *glimsen*, as prec.], *n.* A momentary look, a rapid and imperfect view (of); a passing gleam, a faint and transient appearance; *a faint resemblance, a slight tinge. *v.t.* To catch a glimpse of; to see for an instant. *v.i.* To appear for an instant; to glance (at); to appear faintly, to glimmer. **glimpsing,** *n.* A glimpse.

glint (glint) [prob. from the earlier *glent*, M.E. *glenten*, cogn. with G. *glänzen*, to make bright, from *glanz*, brightness], *v.i.* To gleam, to flash; to glitter, to sparkle; *to glance aside. *v.t.* To reflect, to flash back. *n.* A gleam, a flash, a sparkle; *a glimpse.

glisk (glisk) [Sc., prob. cogn. with GLITTER], *n.* A glimpse, a gleam, a glint.

glissade (gli sad′, -săd′) [F., from *glisser*, to slip or slide. O.F. *glier*, from Teut. (cp. G. *gleiten*, GLIDE)], *n.* (*Mountaineering*) A method of sliding down a steep snow-slope, usu. with an ice-axe or alpenstock held as rudder and support; (*Dancing*) a gliding step. *v.i.* To slide down a steep snow-slope in this manner.

glist (glist) [shortened form of foll.], *n.* A gleam or glitter; *mica.

glisten (glis′ ėn) [M.E. *glistnen*, A.-S. *glisnian*, from *glisian*, to shine], *v.i.* To gleam, to sparkle, usu. by reflection. *n.* A glitter or sparkle, esp. by reflection; a gleam.

***glister** (glis′ tėr) [M.E. *glisteren*, A.-S. *glisian*, as prec.], *v.i.* To glitter, to sparkle. *n.* Glitter, lustre, brightness. ***glisteringly,** *adv.*

glitter (glit′ ėr) [Icel. *glitra*, freq. of *glita* (cogn. with G. *gleissen*, A.-S. *glitenian*), from Teut. *glis*, to shine], *v.i.* To gleam, to sparkle; to shine with a succession of brilliant gleams or flashes; to be brilliant, showy, or specious. *n.* A bright sparkling light; brilliancy, splendour; speciousness, attractiveness. **glitteringly,** *adv.*

gloaming (glō′ ming) [A.-S. *glōmung*, cogn. with GLOW], *n.* Evening twilight. **gloam,** *v.i.* To begin to grow dark; (*fig.*) to be sullen or threatening. *n.* Gloaming.

gloat (glōt) [cp. Icel. *glotta*, to grin, G. *glotzen*, to stare], *v.i.* To look or dwell (on or over) with exultant feelings of malignity, lust, or avarice. **gloatingly,** *adv.*

global (glō′ bȧl) [GLOBE], *a.* Relating to the globe as an entirety; world-wide; taking in entire groups of classes.

globate (glō′ bāt, -bȧt), **-bated** (glō′ bā tėd) [L. *globātus*, p.p. of *globāre*, to make into a ball, from *globus*, GLOBE], *a.* Spherical, spheroidal.

globe (glōb) [O.F., as prec.], *n.* A ball, a sphere, a round or spherical body; the earth; a sphere on which are represented the heavenly bodies (called **a celestial globe**), or representing the land and sea, and usually the political divisions of the world (called a **terrestrial globe**); anything of a globular or nearly globular shape; an orb borne as emblem of sovereignty; an almost spherical vessel, as an aquarium, lampshade, etc.; (*Anat.*) the eyeball; *a body of men, etc., drawn up in a circle. *v.t.* To form into a globe. *v.i.* To become globular. **globe-amaranth,** *n.* The tropical genus *Gomphrena* of the amaranth family, esp. *G. globosa.* **globe-fish,** *n.* A fish having the power of inflating the skin till it becomes nearly globular. **globe-flower,** *n.* The ranunculaceous genus *Trollius*, esp. the British *T. Europæus*, with yellow, almost spherical flowers. **globe-lightning,** *n.* A fire-ball. **globe-thistle,** *n.* Various species of *Echinops*, a thistle-like genus of composite plants belonging to the aster family. **globe-trotter,** *n.* A traveller who hurries from place to place sight-seeing or who visits many foreign countries. **globe-trotting,** *n.* **globe-valve,** *n.* (*Plumbing*) A ball-valve; one of spherical shape, usually operated by a screw stem; a valve enclosed in a globular chamber.

globigerina (glō bi jėr ī′ nȧ) [L. *globus*, GLOBE, *-ger*, bearing (see -GEROUS), *-ina*, -INE], *n.* (*pl.* **-næ**) A genus of *Foraminifera*, with a many-chambered shell. **globigerina mud,** or **ooze,** *n.* A light-coloured calcareous mud or ooze in places in the ocean 3000 fathoms deep, consisting of shells of globigerinæ.

globin (glō′ bin) [L. *globus*, a globe], *n.* (*Med.*) A colourless protein of the blood.

globoid (glō′ boid), *a.* Like a globe in shape. *n.* (*Bot.*) A globular granule or concretion of mineral matter found in aleuron.

globose (glō bōs′), *a.* Spherical, globular. **globosity** (glō bos′ i ti), *n.*

globule (glob′ ūl) [F., from L. *globulus*, dim. of *globus*, GLOBE], *n.* A particle of matter in the form of a small globe; (*Med.*) a minute drop or pill; (*Physiol.*) a blood-corpuscle. **globular,** *a.* Having the shape of a small globe or sphere; composed of globules. **globular chart,** *n.* A chart on a globular projection. **globular projection,** *n.* A kind of projection in which the eye is supposed to look from the distance of half the chord of 90°. **globular sailing,** *n.* (*Naut.*) The sailing from one point to another over an arc of a great circle, or the shortest distance between any two points. **globularly,** *adv.* **globularness,** *n.* **globulin,** *n.* (*Chem.*) An albuminous protein or class of proteins obtained from animals and plants; (*Physiol.*) such a compound obtained from the crystalline lens of the eye, the blood, etc.; (*Bot.*) the amylaceous granules in the cells of plants. **globulism,** *n.* A contemptuous term sometimes applied to homœopathy. **globulist,** *n.* **globulite,** *n.* (*Min.*) A minute globular body representing the most rudimentary stage in the formation of crystals.

glochidiate (glō kid′ i ȧt) [Gr. *glōchidion*, dim. of *glochis*, arrow-point], *a.* (*Bot.*) Barbed (of hairs, etc.).

glockenspiel (glok′ ėn spēl) [G., play of bells], *n.* (*Mus.*) An instrument consisting of hanging metal bars or tubes, to be struck with a hammer.

glome (glōm) [L. *glomus*, a ball], *n.* (*Bot.*) A roundish head of flowers, a glomerule. ***glomerous** (glom′ ėr ůs), *a.* **glomerule** (glom′ ėr ool), *n.* (*Bot.*) A flower-cluster forming a compact head; (*Anat.*) a convoluted mass of blood-vessels, tissues, etc.

glomerate (glom′ ėr āt) [L. *glomerātus*, p.p. of *glomerāre*, from prec.], *v.t.* To gather into a ball or sphere. *v.i.* To gather or come together into a mass. *a.* (-ȧt) (*Anat.*) Compactly clustered (as glands, vessels, etc.); (*Bot.*) congregated into a head. **glomeration** (-ā′ shůn), *n.*

glomerous, glomerule [GLOME].

gloom (gloom) [M.E. *gloumen*, to lour, cogn. with GLUM], *v.i.* To appear obscurely or dimly; to look dismal, sullen, or frowning; to lour, to be or become cloudy or dark. *v.t.* To fill or cover with darkness or obscurity; to render dark, sullen, or dismal. *n.* Obscurity, partial darkness; depression, dejection, melancholy; circumstances that occasion melancholy or despondency; *a dark or dismal place. ***gloomful,** *a.* ***glooming,** *a.* Dismal, gloomy, depressing. *n.* The gloaming. **gloomy,** *a.* Dark, obscure; louring, sad, melancholy, dispiriting; sullen, morose, threatening. **gloomily,** *adv.* **gloominess,** *n.*

gloria (glôr′ i ȧ) [L., glory], *n.* (*pl.* **-as**) A song or versicle of praise, forming part of the English Church service or the Mass; a doxology; the music to which one of these, esp. the *Gloria in excelsis*, is sung. ***Gloria in excelsis:*** The Greater Doxology or hymn beginning Glory to God in the highest. ***Gloria Patri:*** The Lesser Doxology or response beginning Glory be to the Father. ***Gloria Tibi:*** The sentence Glory be to Thee, O Lord.

glorify (glôr′ i fī) [F. *glorifier*, L. *glōrificāre* (*gloria*, GLORY, *-ficāre*, to make)], *v.t.* To magnify, to make glorious, to pay honour and glory to in worship, to praise, to extol; to exalt to celestial glory; to make splendid, to beautify; to trick out with resplendent qualities. ***glorifiable,** *a.* **glorification** (-kā′ shůn), *n.*

gloriole (glôr′ i ōl) [F., from L. *glōriola*, dim. of *glōria*, GLORY], *n.* A glory, halo, or nimbus.

glorious (glôr′ i ůs) [as foll.], *a.* Full of glory, illustrious; worthy of admiration or praise; entitling one to fame or honour; splendid, magnificent; (*colloq.*) hilarious, uproarious; very amusing; completely satisfactory. **gloriously,** *adv.* **gloriousness,** *n.*

glory (glôr′ i) [O.F. *glorie* (F. *gloire*), L. *glōria*], *n.* High honour, honourable distinction; fame, renown; an occasion of praise, a subject for pride or boasting; illustriousness, splendour of estate, magnificence, grandeur; brilliance, effulgence, splendour; a state of exaltation; adoration or praise ascribed in worship; the divine presence or its manifestations; the felicity of heaven; a combination of the nimbus and aureola; a halo; *arrogance, vainglory, *ambition. *v.i.* To boast, to feel pride, to exult. **v.t.* To glorify. **in glory:** Enjoying the felicity of heaven. **in his glory:** (*colloq.*) In full enjoyment of his doings, idiosyncrasies, etc. **glory flower, glory pea,** *n.* The papilionaceous genus Clianthus, known in Australia as Sturt's desert pea, in N. Zealand as the parrot-bill or kaka-bill. **glory-hole,** *n.* (*colloq.*) A room, cupboard, etc., where rubbish and odds and ends have been stowed away anyhow; an opening through which one can look into the interior of a furnace. **gloryingly,** *adv.* ***gloryless,** *a.* **glorious** (glôr′ i ůs), *a.*

glose [GLOZE].

gloss (1) (glos) [M.E. and O.F. *glose*, med. L. *glosa*, L. and Gr. *glōssa*, the tongue, a word requiring explanation], *n.* An explanatory word or note in the margin or between the lines of a book, as an explanation of a foreign or strange word; a comment, interpretation, or explanation; a superficial or misleading interpretation, etc.; a glossary, translation, or commentary. *v.t.* To explain by note or comment; to annotate; to comment upon, esp. in a censorious way. *v.i.* To make comments, to annotate, to write glosses. **glossator** (glȯ sā′ tȯr), **glosser** (1) (glos′ ėr), ***-ist,** *n.* A writer of glosses.

gloss (2) (glos) [prob. from Scand. (cp. Icel. *glossi*, a blaze, Norw. *glosa*, to glow)], *n.* The brightness or lustre from a polished surface; polish, sheen; (*fig.*) a specious or deceptive outward appearance. *v.t.* To make glossy or lustrous; (*fig.*) to render specious or plausible. **to gloss over:** To palliate, to excuse. **glosser** (2), *n.* One who puts a gloss on. **glossing,** *n.* The steaming, drying, and twisting of silk thread, so as to develop a gloss. **glossy,** *a.* Having a smooth, lustrous surface. **glossily,** *adv.* **glossiness,** *n.*

glossal (glos′ ȧl) [Gr. *glōssa*, tongue], *a.* (*Anat.*) Of or pertaining to the tongue, lingual. **glossic,** *a.* A phonetic system of writing English. **glossitis** (glȯ sī′ tis), *n.* (*Path.*) Inflammation of the tongue.

glossary (glos′ ȧ ri) [L. *glōssārium*, from *glōssa* GLOSS (1)], *n.* A list, vocabulary, or dictionary of explanations of obsolete, rare, technical, or dialectal words or forms; a collection of glosses or notes. **glossarial** (glȯ sâr′ i ȧl), *a.* **glossarist** (glos′ ȧ rist), *n.*

glosso- [Gr. *glōssa*, the tongue, language], *comb. form.* Pertaining to the tongue; linguistic. **glossocele** (glos′ ȯ sēl) [Gr. *kēlē*, tumour], *n.* (*Path.*) A protrusion of the tongue caused by swelling or inflammation. **glosso-epiglottic, -tid** (glos′ ȯ ep i glot′ ik, -id), *a.* (*Anat.*) Pertaining to the tongue and the epiglottis. **glossography** (glȯ sog′ rȧ fi), *n.* The writing of glosses or comments; a treatise on the tongue. **glossographer,** *n.* **glossographica**

(-grăf′ ik ȧl), *a.* **glossolalia** (glos ō lāl′ i ȧ), *n.* (*Psych.*) Speech in an unknown tongue, occurring in religious ecstasy, trances, etc. **glossology** (glŏs sol′ ŏ ji), *n.* The explanation of technical terms, as of a science; the science of language. **glossological** (-loj′ i kȧl), *a.* **glossologist** (glŏ sol′ ŏ jist), *n.*

glossy [GLOSS (2)].

Gloster [GLOUCESTER].

glottis (glot′ is) [Gr. *glōttis*, *glōtta*, var. of *glōssa*, GLOSS (1)], *n.* (*Anat.*) The mouth of the windpipe forming a narrow aperture covered by the epiglottis when one holds the breath or swallows, contributing, by its dilatation and contraction, to the modulation of the voice. **glottal, glottic,** *a.* **glottologic, glottologist, glottology** [GLOSSOLOGY, see GLOSSO-].

Gloucester, Gloster (glos′ tėr) [County of *Gloucester*], *n.* A rich cheese made in Gloucestershire. **double Gloucester:** A Gloucester cheese of extra thickness.

glove (glŭv) [A.-S. *glōf*, prob. from Teut. *lōf-*, cogn. with LOOF (1), the hand], *n.* A covering for the hand, usu. with a separate division for each finger; a padded glove for the hands in boxing, also called boxing-glove. *v.t.* To cover with or as with a glove. **to fight without the gloves:** To box without gloves; (*fig.*) to fight or contend in earnest, to show no mercy. **to throw down** or **take up the glove:** To make or accept a challenge. **glove-fight,** *n.* A pugilistic contest in which the men wear gloves. ***glove-money,** *n.* A gratuity (ostensibly to buy gloves), esp. money given by the sheriff to the clerk of assize and judge's officers when no offenders were left for execution. **glove-sponge,** *n.* A sponge shaped like a glove. **glove-stretcher,** *n.* An instrument for stretching the fingers of gloves so that they may be drawn on easily. **glover,** *n.* One who makes or sells gloves. **gloveress,** *n.* **gloveless,** *a.* **gloving,** *n.* The occupation of making gloves.

glow (glō) [A.-S. *glōwan* (cp. Icel. *glōa*, Dut. *gloeijen*, G. *glühen*)], *v.i.* To radiate light and heat, esp. without flame; to be incandescent; to be bright or red with heat, to show a warm colour; to feel great bodily heat; to be warm or flushed with passion or fervour; to be ardent. **v.t.* To cause to glow. *n.* Incandescence, red or white heat; brightness, redness, warmth of colour; vehemence, ardour; heat produced by exercise. **glow-worm,** *n.* A beetle, *Lampyris noctiluca* or *L. splendidula*, the female of which is phosphorescent. **glowingly,** *adv.*

glower (glou′ ėr) [etym. doubtful, cp. L.G. *gluren*], *v.i.* To scowl, to stare fiercely or angrily. *n.* A savage stare, a scowl. **gloweringly,** *adv.*

gloxinia (glok sin′ i ȧ) [B. P. *Gloxin*, German botanist (18th cent.)], *n.* A genus of plants with large bell-shaped flowers, from tropical America.

gloze (glōz) [F. *gloser*, from *glose*, GLOSS (1)], *v.t.* To palliate, to extenuate; *to explain by note or comment; *to flatter, to wheedle. *v.i.* To comment; *to use flattery. *n.* Flattery, wheedling; specious show; *a gloss, a comment; *(*pl.*) specious talk. **to gloze over:** To palliate speciously or explain away. ***glozer,** *n.* A glosser; a flatterer.

glucinum (gloo si′ nŭm) [F. *glucine*, Gr. *glukus*, sweet], *n.* A metallic element obtained from beryl, also called beryllium (the salts have a sweet taste, hence the name). **glucina,** *n.* Oxide of glucinum.

glucohæmia [GLUCOSURIA, see foll.].

glucose (gloo′ kōs) [Gr. *glukus*, sweet], *n.* A fermentable sugar, less sweet than cane-sugar, obtained from dried grapes and other fruits, dextrin, etc., and occurring in the urine of persons suffering from glucosuria; (*Chem.*) any of the group of sweet compounds including dextrose, lævulose, etc. **glucic** (gloo′ sik), **glucosic** (glu kos′ ik), *a.* (*Chem.*) Derived from or pertaining to glucose. **glucic acid:** A colourless honey-like compound obtained from glucose or cane-sugar by the action of acids or alkalis. **glucoside** (gloo′ kŏ sīd), *n.* (*Chem.*) A vegetable substance yielding glucose when decomposed. **glucosuria** (gloo kŏ sū′ ri ȧ) [Gr. *ouron*, URINE], *n.* (*Path.*) One form of diabetes, the principal characteristic of which is the occurrence of sugar in the urine. **glucosuric,** *a.*

glue (gloo) [O.F. *glu*, late L. *glūtem*, nom. *glūs*, cogn. with GLUTEN], *n.* An impure gelatine made of the chippings of hides, horns, and hoofs, boiled to a jelly, cooled in moulds, and used hot as a cement; an adhesive or sticky substance. *v.t.* To join or fasten with or as with glue; to unite, to attach firmly. **v.i.* To stick together; to be firmly attached. **glue-pot,** *n.* A vessel for heating glue, with an outer vessel to hold water and prevent burning. **gluer,** *n.* **gluey,** *a.* **glueyness,** *n.* **gluing,** *pres.p.* ***gluish,** *a.*

glum (glŭm) [var. of GLOOM], **v.i.* To look sullen or gloomy. *a.* Sullen, moody, dejected, dissatisfied. **glumly,** *adv.* **glumness,** *n.*

glume (gloom) [L. *glūma*, from *glūbere*, to peel, cp. Gr. *gluphein*, to hollow out], *n.* (*Bot.*) A chaff-like scale or bract forming part of the inflorescence in grasses; a husk. **glumaceous** (glu mā′ shŭs), *a.* **glumiferous** (-mif′ ėr ŭs), *a.* **glumose, -mous** (glu mōs′, gloo′ mŭs), *a.*

glut (glŭt) [O.F. *gloutir*, L. *glūtīre*, to swallow, to devour], *v.t.* To fill to excess, to stuff, to gorge, to sate; to fill with an over-supply (as a market); to swallow, to swallow down. *n.* A surfeit; plenty even to loathing; a superabundance; an over-supply of a market.

glutæus, gluteus (glu tē′ ŭs) [L., from Gr. *gloutos*, rump], *n.* (*pl.* **-tæi, -tei**) One of the three large muscles forming the buttock. **gluteal, -tæal, -tean** (glu tē′ ȧl, -ȧn), *a.*

gluten (gloo′ tėn) [L. *glūten -tinis*], *n.* A yellowish-grey, elastic albuminous substance, left in wheat-flour which has been washed in water; a sticky substance, glue. **animal gluten,** *n.* Fibrin. **gluten-bread,** *n.* Bread containing a large quantity of gluten, largely used in the diet of those suffering from diabetes. **glutin,** *n.* Vegetable gelatine; gliadin. ***glutinate,** *v.t.* To cement with glue; to glue. ***glutination** (-nā′ shŭn), *n.* **glutinative** (gloo′-), *a.* **glutinize,** *v.t.* To render viscous or gluey. **glutinous,** *a.* Viscous, gluey, tenacious; covered with a sticky exudation. **glutinously,** *adv.* **glutinosity** (-nos′ i ti), *n.*

glutton (glŭt′ ŏn) [O.F. *glutun*, *glouton*, L. *glūtōnem*, nom. *glūto*, from *glūtīre*, to swallow, see GLUT], *n.* One who eats to excess; a gormandizer; one who indulges in anything to excess, as a voracious reader, worker, etc.; a carnivorous animal of the weasel tribe, the wolverine, formerly supposed to be a voracious feeder. **v.i.* To gluttonize. **gluttonlike,** *a.* ***gluttonish,** *a.* **gluttonize,** *v.i.* To eat to excess, to gorge. **gluttonous,** *a.* **gluttonously,** *adv.* **gluttony,** *n.*

glycerine (glis′ ėr in) [F. *glycérine*, Gr. *glukeros*, *glukus*, sweet], *n.* A viscid, sweet, colourless liquid obtained from animal and vegetable fats and oils, used in the manufacture of soaps, medicines, confectionery, etc. **glyceral** [GLYCER-INE, ALDEHYDE], *n.* (*Chem.*) One of a series of compounds obtained by heating glycerine with aldehydes. **glycerinate,** *v.t.* To treat (esp. vaccine lymph) with glycerine. **glyceric** (gli ser′ ik, glis′ ėr ik), *a.* (*Chem.*) Of or pertaining to glycerine. **glycerate** (glis′ âr ėt), *n.* (*Chem.*) A salt of glyceric acid; a solution in glycerine. **glyceride,** *n.* **glyceroid,** *n.* **glycerol,** *n.* (*Chem.*) Glycerine. **glyceryl,** *n.* The radical of glycerine and the glycerides. **glycero-,** *comb. form.* **glycerophosphate** (glis ėr ŏ fos′ fāt) [PHOSPHATE], *n.* **glycerophosphoric** (-for′ ik), *a.*

glyco- [Gr. *glukus*, sweet], *comb. form.* Containing glycerol or compounds producing sugars.

glycocoll (glī′ kō kol), *n.* (*Chem.*) A crystalline sweetish compound found in bile.

glycogen (glī′ kō jen), *n.* A white, insoluble, starch-like compound occurring in animal tissues such as the liver and convertible into dextrose. **glycogenic,** *a.* **glycogenesis,** *n.*

glycol (glī′ kōl, glī′ kol), *n.* (*Chem.*) A diatomic alcohol of the fatty group typified by ethyl glycol, used as an antifreeze in motor-car engines and for de-icing aircraft wings. **glycolic, glycollic,** *a.* **glycollate,** *n.*

glyconic (glī kon′ ik) [*Glukōn*, a Gr. poet], *a.* (*Pros.*) Applied to varieties of classic verse consisting of three trochees and a dactyl.

glycosuria [GLUCOSURIA].

glyph (glif) [Gr. *gluphē.* from *gluphein*, to carve], *n.* (*Arch.*) A fluting or channel, usu. vertical; a hieroglyph. **glyphic,** *a.* Carved, sculptured. *n.* A hieroglyph.

glyphograph (glif′ ō grăf) [prec., -GRAPH], *n.* A plate prepared by glyphography; an impression from such a plate. *v.t.* and *i.* To engrave by glyphography. **glyphographer** (glif og′ rȧ fėr), *n.* **glyphographic** (-grăf′ ik), *a.* **glyphography** (glif og′ rȧ fi), *n.* The process of making engravings for printing in which an electrotype with the design in relief is obtained from an intaglio etching.

glyptic (glip′ tik) [Gr. *gluptikos*, from *gluptos*, carved, from *gluphein*, see GLYPH], *a.* Relating to carrying or engraving, esp. on gems; (*Min.*) figured. *n.* (*usu. pl.*) The art of engraving, esp. on gems.

glyptodon (glip′ tō don) [Gr. *gluptos*, carved, as prec., *odous odontos*, tooth], *n.* A huge fossil quadruped allied to the armadillo, from South America.

glyptography (glip tog′ rȧ fi) [Gr. *gluptos*, see prec., -GRAPHY], *n.* The art of engraving on gems; a description of this. **glyptograph** (glip′ tō grăf), *n.* An engraving on a gem. **glyptographer** (-tog′ rȧ fėr), *n.* **glyptographic** (-grăf′ ik), *a.*

glyptotheca (glip tō thē′ kȧ) [Gr. *gluptos*, see GLYPTIC, *thēkē*, a repository], *n.* A room or building for the preservation of sculpture.

G-man [G].

gnamma holes (năm′ ȧ hōlz) [Austral. abor.], *n.pl.* Entrances to large holes containing water in the W. Australian arid areas.

Gnaphalium (nȧ fā′ li ŭm) [Gr. *gnaphalion*, a downy plant], *n.* (*Bot.*) A genus of woolly plants, typified by the cudweed, having small sessile flower-heads.

gnar [KNAR].

gnarl (narl) [var. of KNURL], *v.t.* To twist or contort (*usu. in p.p.*). *n.* A protuberance, a twisted growth, or contorted knot, in a tree. **gnarled,** *a.* Rugged, lined, weather-beaten, twisted. **gnarly,** *a.* Full of knots or gnarls; (*fig.*) peevish, perverse.

gnash (năsh) [M.E. *gnasten*, onomat. in orig. (cp. Icel. *gnastan*, a gnashing, G. *knastern*, to gnash)], *v.t.* To strike or grind (the teeth) together; to grind or champ. *v.i.* To grind the teeth together, as in rage, despair, etc.; to rage. **gnashingly,** *adv.*

gnat (năt) [A.-S. *gnæt*], *n.* A small two-winged fly, the female of which has a blood-sucking proboscis, esp. *Culex pipiens* and some other species of the genus *Culex*. **to strain at a gnat and swallow a camel:** (Matt. xxiii, 24) To be scrupulous about trifles and lax in matters of great moment.

gnathic (năth′ ik) [Gr. *gnathos*, jaw], *a.* Of or pertaining to the jaw. **gnathal** (nā′ thȧl), *a.* **gnathism,** *n.* (*Ethn.*) Classification of mankind according to measurements of the jaw. **gnathitis** (nȧ thī′ tis), *n.* Inflammation of the upper jaw or cheek. **gnathoplasty** (năth′ ō plăs ti) [Gr. *-plastos*, from *plassein*, to mould], *n.* (*Surg.*) The formation of a cheek by plastic surgery. **gnathopod** (năth′ ō pod) [Gr. *pous podos*, foot], *n.* (*pl.* **gnathopoda** (nȧ thop′ ō dȧ)) (*Zool.*) The foot-jaw of crustaceans.

Gnathonic (nā thon′ ik) [L. *Gnathōnicus*, from *Gnatho*, the chief character in *The Gnatho* of Terence, from Gr. *gnathos*, jaw], *a.* Like or after the manner of Gnatho, parasitical, sycophantic. **Gnathonical,** *a.* **Gnathonism** (nā′ thō nizm), *n.*

gnathoplasty, gnathopod [GNATHIC].

gnaw (naw) [A.-S. *gnagan* (cp. Dut. *knagen*, G. *nagen*)], *v.t.* (*p.p.* **gnawed, gnawn**) To bite or eat away by degrees; to bite repeatedly or persistently; to bite in agony, rage, or despair; to corrode; (*fig.*) to consume or wear away by degrees. *v.i.* To use the teeth in biting repeatedly or persistently (at or into); to cause corrosion or wearing away. **gnawer,** *n.* **gnawingly,** *adv.*

gneiss (nīs) [G., from O.H.G. *gneistan*, to sparkle], *n.* (*Geol.*) A laminated metamorphic rock consisting of feldspar, quartz, and mica. **gneissic,** *a.* **gneissoid,** *a.* **gneissose,** *a.* **gneissy,** *a.*

gnome (1) (nōm) [F., from L. *gnomus* (used by Paracelsus), perh. from foll., or *gēnomos* (Gr. *gē*, earth, *-nomos*, dweller)], *n.* An imaginary being, a kind of misshapen sprite, supposed by the Rosicrucians to inhabit the interior of the earth, and to be the guardian of mines, quarries, etc. **gnomish,** *a.*

gnome (2) (nōm) [Gr. *gnōmē*, from *gignōskein*, to know], *n.* A maxim, an aphorism, a saw. **gnomic,** *a.* Dealing in maxims, sententious, didactic. **gnomic aorist,** *n.* (*Gr. Gram.*) A use of the aorist tense to express, not the past, but a general truth, as in proverbs, etc. **gnomology** (nō mol′ ō ji) [-LOGY], *n.* A collection of maxims or sententious reflections or sayings; the sententious element in writing and literature. **gnomologic, -al** (-loj′ ik, -ȧl), *a.* **gnomologist** (-mol′ ō jist), *n.* **gnomometry** (nō mom′ ė tri) [-METRY], *n.* A dividing or arranging according to subject.

gnomon (nō′ mŏn) [Gr. *gnōmōn*, an inspector, gnomon of a dial, as prec.], *n.* A rod, pillar, pin, or plate on a sundial, indicating the time of day by its shadow; a vertical pillar used in an analogous way for determining the altitude of the sun; the index of the hour-circle of a globe; (*Geom.*) the figure remaining when a parallelogram has been removed from the corner of a larger one of the same form. **gnomonic, -al** (nō mon′ ik, -ȧl), *a.* Pertaining to the art of dialling. **gnomonic projection:** The projection of the lines of a sphere from the centre. **gnomonically,** *adv.* **gnomonics,** *n.pl.* The art or science of making and using dials. ***gnomonology** (-nol′ ō ji), *n.* A treatise on dials.

gnosiology (nō zi ol′ ō ji) [Gr. *gnōsis*, see foll., -LOGY], *n.* The philosophy dealing with cognition, the theory of knowledge, or the operation of the cognitive faculties.

gnosis (nō′ sis) [Gr., GNOME (2)], *n.* (*pl.* **-ses**) Knowledge, esp. of mysteries; Gnostic philosophy.

gnostic (nos′ tik) [Gr. *gnōstikos*, from *gnōstos*, known, as prec.], *a.* Relating to knowledge or cognition, intellectual; (*facet.*) knowing, shrewd, worldly-wise; having esoteric knowledge; of or belonging to the Gnostics or Gnosticism. *n.* An adherent of Gnosticism. ***gnostically,** *adv.* **Gnosticism,** *n.* A system of religious philosophy flourishing in the first six centuries of the Church, that combined ideas from Greek and Oriental philosophy with Christianity, which it professed to expound as a mystical philosophy or gnosis. **gnosticize,** *v.t.* and *i.* **gnosticizer,** *n.*

gnu (nū) [Hottentot], *n.* A South African antelope, *Catoblepas gnu*.

go (1) (gō) [A.-S. *gān* (cp. Dut. *gaan*, G. *gehen*)], *v.i.* (*past* **went,** *p.p.* **gone,** gawn, gon, *2nd sing.* **goest,** *3rd sing.* **goes,** gōz, ***goeth**) To move, to move from one place, condition, or station to another; to begin to move, to start to move from a place, to depart, to pass away (opp. to come); to keep up a movement, to be moving, to be acting, operating, or working; to travel; to proceed, to advance; to end, to come out, to succeed, to turn out (well or ill); to take a certain course (as for or against); to be habitually (as hungry, naked, etc.); to be used, said, etc., habitually, to pass, to be circulated or current; to average; to extend, to reach, to point in a certain direction; to tend, to conduce; to run, to have a certain tenor; to be applicable, to fit, to suit (with); to belong, to be harmonious (with a tune, etc.); to be released, to get away; to be given up, to be abandoned, abolished, or lost; to fail, to give way, break down; (*usu. in p.p.*) to die; to pass into a certain state, to become (as wild, mad, etc.); to be sold; to be spent; (*as aux. verb*) to be about (to do), to intend, to purpose. **go ahead:** Start, proceed without hesitation. ***go to:** Come now; (*iron. and remonstr.*) come, come! **go to Jericho, Bath, Putney,** etc.: Be off! [cp. BLAZES]. **have gone and done it:** (*colloq.*) Have been foolish enough to do it. **to go about:** To get to work at; to go from place to place; to take a circuitous course; (*Naut.*) to tack, to wear. **to go abroad:** To go to a foreign country; to go out of doors; *to be disclosed. **to go against:** To march against; to be in opposition to. **to go ahead:** To proceed in advance; to make rapid progress. **to go aside:** To withdraw apart from others; to go wrong. **to go astray:** To wander from the right path. **to go at:** To attack; to work at vigorously. **to go away:** To depart. **to go back from or upon:** To fail to keep (one's word). **to go bail:** To act as bail for; (*colloq.*) to vouch. **to go behind:** To call in question; to look beyond (the apparent facts, etc.). **to go between:** To mediate between. ***to go beyond:** To cheat, to outdo. **to go bush:** (*Austral.*) To take to the bush, to go native. **to go by:** To pass by or near to; to pass by; to pass unnoticed or disregarded; to take as a criterion. **to go down:** To descend; to set; to founder (as a ship); to fall (before a conqueror); to be set down in writing; to be swallowed, to be palatable or acceptable. **to go dry:** (*colloq.*) To adopt prohibition; to give up drinking or having alcoholic liquor on the premises. **to go for nothing:** To count for nothing. **to go far:** (*colloq.*) To be very successful; to attain distinction. **to go forth:** To issue or depart from a place; to be published or spread abroad. **to go forward:** To advance. **to go hard with:** (*impers.*) To cause great trouble, danger, or difficulty to. **to go ill or well with:** (*impers.*) To happen or fare evil or well with. **to go in:** To enter; to go behind clouds; (*Cricket*) to have an innings. **to go in and out:** To be perfectly at liberty. **to go in for:** To be in favour of; to follow as a pursuit or occupation. **to go into:** To enter; to frequent; to take part in; to investigate or discuss. **to go in unto:** To enter the presence of; *to have sexual intercourse with. **to go it:** To carry on; to keep a thing up; to conduct oneself recklessly or outrageously. **to go native:** To adopt the ways and customs of the natives of a place, *esp.* of primitive or uncivilized people. **to go off:** To depart; to fall away; to die; to be discharged (as a firearm); to cease to be perceptible; to become unconscious; to be sold off; to fare, to succeed (well or ill). **to go off one's head:** (*colloq.*) To become insane. **to go on:** To proceed, to continue, to persevere; to become chargeable to (the parish, etc.); (*colloq.*) to behave (badly, etc.); to grumble, to complain; (*colloq., in imper.*) rubbish, nonsense; (*Theat.*) to appear on the stage. **to go one better:** To excel, to cap. **to go out:** To depart, to leave (a room, etc.); to be extinguished; to vacate office; to leave home and enter employment; to go into society; to go on strike; to be drawn forth in sympathy, etc. **to go over:** To cross, to pass over; to rat, to change one's party or opinions; to read, to examine; to rehearse; to retouch. **to go phut:** (*slang*) To collapse, to fall to pieces. **to go round:** To pay a number of visits; to encompass or be enough to encompass, to be enough for (the whole party, etc.). **to go the whole hog:** To go to the fullest extent; to be out-and-out; to stick at nothing. **to go through:** To pass through; to undergo; to suffer; to examine; (*colloq.*) to overhaul, to ransack, to strip; to discuss thoroughly; to perform (a duty, ceremony, etc.). **to go through with:** To perform thoroughly, to complete. **to go together:** To harmonize, to be suitable to or to match each other. **to go under:** To be known as (by a title or name); to sink; to be submerged or ruined; to perish. **to go upon:** To act upon as a principle. **to go west:** (*slang*) To die. **to go with:** To accompany; to follow the meaning of, to understand; to be with (child); to side or agree with; to suit, to match. **to go without:** To be or manage without, to put up with the want of. **go-ahead,** *a.* Characterized by energy and enterprise. **go-as-you-please,** *a.* Unceremonious, untroubled by rules, etc. **go-between,** *n.* One who acts as an intermediary between two parties. **go-by,** *n.* The act of passing without notice; intentional failure to notice; evasion, deception. **to give the go-by to:** To evade; to cut, to slight; to pass or outstrip; to dismiss as of no moment. **go-cart,** *n.* A small frame-work without a bottom, running on casters, for teaching infants to walk; a small hand-cart; a child's toy wagon. **go-getter,** *n.* A bustling, pushing person. **go-off,** *n.* The start. **go-to-meeting,** *a.* Suitable for church or chapel (of clothes).

go (2) (gō) [from prec.], *n.* (*pl.* **goes**) The act of going; spirit, life, animation; push, energy, enterprise; (*colloq.*) a fix, a scrape, an awkward turn of affairs; a turn, a bout (of doing something); one's turn in a game; (*Cribbage*) a player's turn at which he is unable to play, counting one to his opponent; (*colloq.*) fashion, the mode; a spree; a drink of liquor, especially of gin. **all** or **quite the go:** Entirely in the fashion. **great go, little go:** (*Eng. Univ.*) The final and preliminary or previous examinations for degrees. **near go:** (*colloq.*) A narrow squeak, a close shave. **no go:** Of no use; not to be done; a complete failure. **on the go:** On the move; vigorously in motion. **pretty go:** (*slang*) A startling affair.

goad (gōd) [A.-S. *gād* (cp. Lombardic *gaida,* arrow-head, O.Ir. *gai,* spear)], *n.* A pointed instrument to urge oxen to move faster; (*fig.*) anything that stings, spurs, or incites. *v.t.* To prick, drive or urge on with a goad; to stimulate, to incite; to drive (on, to, into, etc.). **goadsman, goadster,** *n.* One who drives with a goad.

goaf (gōf) [etym. doubtful], *n.* (*Coal-min.*) A waste place in a colliery, a part from which the coal has been removed.

goal (gōl) [etym. doubtful, perh. from an A.-S. *gāl,* conn. with *gælan,* to impede], *n.* The winning-post or mark indicating the end of a race; (*fig.*) the end or terminus of one's ambition; destination, purpose, aim; (*Football, hockey, etc.*) the posts connected by a cross-bar between which the ball must be driven to win a point; also the act of kicking the ball between such posts or over such bar. **goal-keeper,** *n.* A player stationed near to guard the goal. **goal-line,** *n.* A line drawn through the goal-posts to form the boundary at each end of the field of play in football.

goanna (gō ăn′ ȧ) [corr. *iguana*], *n.* (*Austral.*) A large lizard; (*N. Zealand*) the tuatara.

goat (gōt) [A.-S. *gāt* (cp. Dut. *geit,* G. *geiss,* also L. *hædus*)], *n.* A hairy, horned and bearded domesticated ruminant belonging to the genus *Capra,* esp. *C. hircus,* of which there are many varieties; (*pl.*) the genus *Capra*; (*fig.*) a lascivious person; *a lecher. **to get one's goat:** To make one angry. **to play the giddy goat:** To play the fool. **goat-god,** *n.* Pan. **goatherd,** *n.* One who tends goats. **goat-moth,** *n.* A large moth, *Cossus ligniperda,* brown and grey with black markings. **goat's-beard,** *n.* The meadow-sweet, *Spiræa ulmaria*; also *Tragopogon pratense,* and *T. porrifolius* or salsify. **goat's-rue,** *n.* A leguminous plant, *Galega officinalis.* **goatskin,** *n.* The skin of a goat. *a.* Made of goat-skin. **goat's-thorn,** *n.* Names of plants, *Astragalus tragacantha,* the great, and *A. poterium,* the small goat's-thorn. **goatsucker,** *n.* Any bird of the genus *Caprimulgus,* chiefly nocturnal and insectivorous, fabled to milk goats, esp. *C. Europæus,* a British summer visitant. **goatish,** *a.* Resembling a goat; of a rank smell; lecherous. **goatishly,** *adv.* **goatishness,** *n.* **goatling,** *n.* **goaty,** *a.*

goatee (gō tē′), *n.* A small beard like a goat's on the point of the chin.

gob (gob) [from O.F. *gobe*, mouthful (*gober*, to swallow), or perh. directly from Celt. (cp. Gael. and Ir. *gob*, beak, mouth)], *n.* The mouth; a mouthful; a clot of something slimy, as saliva. *v.i.* **(gobbed)** To spit. **gobbin, gobbins,** *n.* (*Coal-min.*) Waste material used to pack into spaces from which the coal has been removed.

gobang (gō băng′) [Jap. *goban*, chess-board], *n.* A game played on a chequer-board, with fifty coloured counters, the object being to get five into a row.

gobbet (gob′ ėt) [O.F. *gobet*, dim. of *gobe*, GOB], *n.* A mouthful, a lump, a piece, esp. of meat.

gobbin, gobbins [GOB].

gobble (gob′ ėl) [perh. from GOB, later adapt. as imit. of turkey], *v.t.* To swallow down hastily and greedily or noisily. *v.i.* To swallow food in this manner; to make a noise in the throat as a turkey-cock. *n.* A noise made in the throat like that of a turkey-cock; (*Golf*) a rapid stroke in putting which sends the ball straight into the hole. **gobble-stitch,** *n.* A stitch made too long through hurrying. **gobbler,** *n.* One who gobbles; a gormandizer; a turkey-cock.

gobelin (gō′ bė lin, gō b′lan) [*Gobelins*, factory in Paris founded by the *Gobelin* family], *a.* Applied to a superior kind of French tapestry made at the Gobelins or imitated from this. **gobelin blue,** *n.* A blue such as appears a good deal in this tapestry. **gobelin tapestry,** *n.*

gobe mouches (gōb moosh) [F., lit. fly-catcher (*gober*, to swallow, *mouches*, flies, L. *muscæ*)], *n.* A credulous person, one who swallows anything.

goblet (gob′ lėt) [O.F. *gobelet*, dim. of *gobel*, cup, etym. doubtful, but perh. from L. *cūpellum*, nom. *-us*, dim. of *cūpa*, cask], *n.* A drinking-vessel, with a stem and without a handle, usu. bowl-shaped and of glass or metal; (*poet.*) a drinking-cup.

goblin (gob′ lin) [F. *gobeline*, low L. *gobelīnus*, perh. from Gr. *kobălos*, a rogue, a goblin (but cp. KOBOLD)], *n.* A mischievous spirit of ugly or grotesque shape; an elf, a gnome. **goblinism,** *n.*

goburra [KOOKABURRA].

goby (gō′ bi) [L. *gōbius*, *cōbius*, Gr. *kōbios*], *n.* A small fish belonging to the genus *Gobius*, characterized by the union of the ventral fins into a disk or sucker.

god (1) (god) [A.-S. (cp. Dut. *god*, Dan. *gud*, G. *gott*), prob. from root *ghu-*, to worship (not conn. with GOOD)], *n.* A superhuman or supernatural being regarded as controlling natural forces and human destinies and worshipped or propitiated by man; a deity, a divinity; a personification of any of the forces of nature; a person formally recognized as divine and entitled to worship; an image, animal, etc., worshipped as an embodiment or symbol of supernatural power, an idol; (*fig.*) a person or thing greatly idolized; (*pl.*) the occupants of the upper gallery in a theatre; (*Monotheism*, **God**) the Supreme Being, the self-existent and eternal Creator and Ruler of the universe. **the blind god:** Cupid. ***God-a-mercy:** God have mercy! **God of war:** Mars. **God of wine:** Bacchus. **household gods:** (*Rom. Ant.*) The lares and penates or gods of the hearth; (*fig.*) one's household treasures. **ye gods!** (*facet.*) **ye gods and little fishes!** Grandiloquent exclamations of surprise, protest, etc. **God-fearing,** *a.* Worshipping or reverencing God, upright. **God-forsaken,** *n.* Abandoned by God; (*fig.*) wretched, miserable, forlorn, depraved. **godmother, -parent** [GODFATHER]. ***god-smith,** *n.* A maker of idols. **godson** [GODCHILD]. **God-man,** *n.* One both God and man, Jesus Christ. **God's acre:** A burial ground. **God's image:** The human body. ***God's lid:** God's eyelid (an oath). **God-speed,** *n.* The wish 'God speed you' to a person starting on a journey, undertaking, etc. **goddess,** *n.* A female deity; (*fig.*) a woman of preeminent beauty, goodness, or charm. **goddess-like,** *a.* and *adv.* **goddess-ship,** *n.* **Godhead,** *n.* Divine nature or essence; a deity. **the Godhead:** God. **Godhood,** *n.* **godkin, godlet,** *n.* **godless,** *a.* Acknowledging no god; without God; impious, irreligious; wicked. **godlessly,** *adv.* **godlessness,** *n.* **godlike,** *a.* ***godlikeness,** *n.* ***godling,** *n.* A little god; a petty deity. **godly,** *a.* God-fearing, pious, devout. ****adv.*** Piously, religiously. **godliness,** *n.* **godship,** *n.* **godward,** *adv.* and *a.* **godwards,** *adv.*

god (2) (god) [from prec.], *v.t.* To deify. **to god it:** To play the god.

godchild (god′ chīld), *n.* One for whom a person stands sponsor at baptism.

***god-den** [GOOD-EVEN, see GOOD].

goddess [GOD].

godet (gō′ dĕt) [Fr.], *n.* (*Dressmaking*) A piece of cloth inserted in a skirt, so that it may hang in folds suggestive of a flare.

godetia (gō dē′ shi ȧ) [M. *Godet*, Swiss botanist], *n.* A genus of hardy annual flowering herbs allied to the evening primroses.

godfather, godmother (god′ fa*th* ėr, -mŭ*th* ėr), *n.* One who is sponsor for a child at baptism; one who gives a name to any person or thing. *v.t.* To act as sponsor to; to give one's name to; to be responsible for.

godly [GOD].

godown (gō doun′) [Malay *godong*], *n.* An East Indian warehouse.

godroon [GADROON].

godsend (god′ send), *n.* An unlooked-for acquisition or gain.

godwit (god′ wit) [etym. unknown], *n.* A marsh or shore bird of the genus *Limosa*, resembling the curlew but having a slightly upturned bill.

goel (gō′ el) [Heb.], *n.* An avenger of blood, the next of kin of a murdered man whose duty it was to hunt down and slay the murderer. **goelism,** *n.*

goer (gō′ ėr) [GO (1), -ER], *n.* One who or that which goes (*usu. in comb.*, as a *fast-goer*, a fast horse).

Goethian (gĕr′ ti ȧn) [J. W. von *Goethe* (1749–1832), German poet], *a.* Of, pertaining to, or characteristic of Goethe. *n.* A follower or admirer of Goethe.

***goety** (gō′ ė ti) [Gr. *goēteia*, from *goēs goētos*, a wizard, lit. a howler, from *goaein*, to wail], *n.* Black magic. **goetic** (gō et′ ik), *a.*

gofer (gō′ fėr) [F. *gaufre*, honeycomb, wafer, from Teut. (cp. WAFER)], *n.* A thin butter-cake baked between two hinged plates that imprint a honeycomb pattern on both sides.

goff [GOLF].

goffer (gof′ ėr, gō′ fėr) [F. *gauffrer* (now *gaufrer*), to print with a pattern, as prec.], *v.t.* To plait, to crimp (edges of lace, etc.) with a heated iron; to raise in relief, to emboss (edges of books). *n.* A plaiting, fluting, or ruffle; a tool for goffering. **goffering,** *n.* This process; a plait or ruffle so produced; an embossed design on the edge of a book.

goggle (gog′ ėl) [etym. doubtful, perh. imit. (cp. Gael. *gog*, a nodding of the head)], *v.i.* To strain or roll the eyes; to squint; to stare; to project (of the eyes). *v.t.* To roll (the eyes) about or turn (the eyes) sideways. *a.* Prominent, staring, full; rolling from side to side. *n.* A strained or staring rolling of the eyes; a squint, a leer; (*pl.*) spectacles for protecting the eyes against dust or glare, usu. with tinted glasses; *spectacles to cure squinting; blinds for horses that are apt to take fright; (*slang*) spectacles; (*slang*) the eyes; a disease of sheep, staggers. **goggle-eyed,** *a.* **goggled,** *a.* Staring, prominent (of the eyes). **goggly,** *a.*

goglet (gog′ lėt) [Port. *gorgoleta* (cp. F. *gargoulette*)], *n.* (*Ang.-Ind.*) An earthenware vessel, a water-cooler.

Goidel (goi' dĕl) [O.Ir., a Gael, see GADHELIC], *n.* One belonging to the Gadhelic branch of the Celts. **Goidelic** (goi del' ik), *a.*

going (gō' ing), *n.* The act of moving or walking; departure; course of life; pregnancy, gestation; the condition of ground, roads, racecourse, track, etc., as regards walking, riding, etc. *a.* Working, in actual operation; (for AGOING) existing, to be had. **the best that are going:** The best to be had. **set the clock going,** (*properly*) **agoing:** Put it into action. **going down:** Setting, sunset. **a going concern:** A business, etc., in actual operation. **going order:** Order or condition suitable for working. **going-train,** *n.* The train of wheels turning the hands in a clock. **going-wheel,** *n.* A ratchet arrangement for keeping a clock going while it is being wound up. **goings-on,** *n.pl.* Behaviour, conduct (usu. in a bad sense). **go while the going's good:** Seize the chance of getting away.

goitre (goi' tėr) [F. *goître*, from *goitreux*, affected with goitre, ult. from L. *guttur*, the throat], *n.* A morbid enlargement of the thyroid gland, causing an unsightly deformity of the neck. **goitred,** *a.* Affected with goitre. **goitrous,** *a.* Pertaining to, affected with, or resembling goitre; characterized by cases of goitre (of places).

Golconda (gol kon' dȧ) [a ruined city 7 miles N.W. of Haidarabad], *n.* An inexhaustible mine of wealth.

gold (gōld) [A.-S. (cp. Dut. *goud*, Icel. *gull*, G. *gold*), cogn. with YELLOW], *n.* A precious metallic element of a bright yellow colour, the most ductile, malleable, and one of the heaviest of metals, much used for coins, jewellery, etc.; this metal in the form of coin, money; wealth, riches; (*fig.*) anything very precious or valuable and genuine or pure; this metal used as a coating or wash, gilding; the colour of gold; the corn marigold. *a.* Made of gold, consisting of gold; coloured like gold. **dead gold:** Unburnished gold. **old gold:** A dull brownish-gold colour. **old-gold,** *a.* **gold-amalgam:** Gold combined with mercury in a soft plastic state. **gold-beater,** *n.* One who beats out gold for gilding. **gold-beater's skin:** A prepared membrane of the cæcum of the ox, used for separating the leaves of gold under the hammer; used also as an application to cuts. **gold-beating,** *n.* The act or trade of beating out gold for gilding. ***gold-bound,** *a.* Surrounded with gold. **gold brick,** *n.* Something with a bogus display of value; a fraud. **gold-bug,** *n.* (*slang*) A millionaire. **gold-cloth,** *n.* Cloth interwoven with gold thread. **gold-digger,** *n.* One who mines for gold; a woman who sets out to fascinate men merely for gain. **gold-digging,** *n.* The act of digging for gold; (*usu. in pl.*) a place or district where gold is found. **gold-dust,** *n.* Gold in very fine particles. **gold-fever,** *n.* A mania for gold-seeking, esp. the gold-rush to California in 1848–49. **gold-field,** *n.* A district where gold is found. **gold-filled,** *a.* More thickly plated with gold than ordinary gold-plated articles (of watch-covers, spectacles, etc.). **gold-foil,** *n.* A thicker kind of gold leaf. **gold-lace,** *n.* Lace made of gold wire. **gold leaf:** Gold beaten into a thin leaf. **gold-mine,** *n.* A place where gold is mined; (*fig.*) a source of wealth or profit. **gold-plate,** *n.* Vessels, dishes, etc., of gold. **gold rush,** *n.* A rush to a place where gold has been discovered. **gold-size,** *n.* A size used in gilding. **goldsmith,** *n.* A worker in gold; a dealer in gold-plate; *a banker. **goldsmithy, -ery, -ry,** *n.* Goldsmiths' work. **gold standard,** *n.* A legal obligation on the part of a nation's central bank to sell gold at a fixed rate in terms of its own currency. **Gold Stick:** A court official (colonel of the Life Guards or captain of the Gentlemen-at-arms) carrying a gilt rod, attending the sovereign on state occasions. **gold thread:** A flattened silver-gilt wire, laid over a thread of silk. **gold-washer,** *n.* One who or that which washes the refuse dirt from gold ore. **gold wire:** Gold drawn to the form of wire. **goldless,** *a.*

golden (gōl' dėn), *a.* Made or consisting of gold; of the colour or lustre of gold; bright, shining, resplendent; excellent, precious, most valuable; most favourable; rich in or yielding gold. **golden age:** A fabled primeval period of perfect human happiness and innocence, in which the earth yielded her fruits without toil, and all creatures lived in peace; the most illustrious period of a nation's literature or prosperity, esp. the first part of the Classical age of Latin literature. **golden balls:** The three balls displayed as the emblem of a pawnbroker. **Golden Bull:** An edict of Charles IV settling the law of imperial elections (1356). **golden calf:** (*fig.*, see Ex. xxxii, 4) Money as an aim in itself. **golden-cup,** *n.* Various species of *Ranunculus* and other yellow-flowered plants. **golden eagle:** A large eagle, *Aquila chrysaëtos*, found in the mountainous parts of Britain, esp. Scotland. **golden-eye,** *n.* A sea-duck of the genus *Clangula.* **Golden Fleece:** The fleece of gold taken from the ram on which Phryxus was carried through the air to Colchis, and in quest of which the Argonauts sailed under Jason; an order of knighthood instituted in 1429 in Spain and Austria. **golden knop:** A ladybird. **golden maidenhair:** A British moss, *Polytrichum commune.* **golden mean:** The principle of neither too much nor too little, moderation. **golden mouse-ear:** Mouse-ear hawkweed, *Hieracium pilosella.* **golden-mouthed,** *a.* Eloquent, musical. **golden number:** The number denoting the year's place in a Metonic lunar cycle of 19 years, used in calculating the movable feasts, as Easter. **golden rain:** A kind of firework. **golden-rod,** *n.* A tall yellow-flowered plant of the genus *Solidago*, esp. *S. virgaurea.* **golden rule:** The rule that we should do as we would be done by (given Matt. vii, 12). **golden-samphire,** *n.* A herb, *Inula crithmoides*, of the aster family. **golden-syrup** [SYRUP]. **golden-tressed,** *a.* Having fair or golden hair. **golden wedding:** The fiftieth anniversary of marriage. ***goldenly,** *adv.* Splendidly, excellently. ***goldy,** *a.* Golden.

goldfinch (gōld' finch), *n.* A yellow-marked singing bird, *Carduelis elegans.*

goldfish (gōld' fish), *n.* A golden-red carp, *Cyprimus auratus*, kept in ponds, aquaria, etc.

goldilocks (gōl' di lŏks), *n.* A buttercup, *Ranunculus auricomus*; other plants with bright yellow flowers.

goldsmith [GOLD].

golf (golf, gof) [perh. from Dut. *kolf* (cp. L.G. *kulf*, G. *kulbe*, club)], *n.* A game played by two persons or couples with club-headed sticks and small hard balls, on commons, moorlands, fields, or links with short grass, consisting in driving the balls into a series of small holes in the ground in as few strokes as possible. *v.i.* To play golf. **golf-arm,** *n.* A nervous affection of the triceps due to exertion in playing golf. **golf club,** *n.* The club used in playing golf; a golfing association. **golf-links,** *n.pl.* The course of 9 or 18 holes on which golf is played. **golfer,** *n.*

Golgotha (gol' gŏ thȧ) [Gr., a place near Jerusalem, where Christ was crucified, from Aram. *gulgalta*, Heb. *gulgōleth*, skull], *n.* (*fig.*) A burial-place, a charnel-house.

***Goliard** (gō' li ȧrd) [O.F., a glutton, from *gole* (F. *gueule*), L. *gula*, gluttony], *n.* A name given to the authors of satirical and ribald Latin verses (12th–13th cent.), some of which were signed by a mythical *Golias*; a buffoon, a jester. **goliardic** (gō li ar' dik), *a.* **goliardy, -ery,** *n.*

Goliath (gŏ lī' ȧth) [the Philistine giant of Gath (1 Sam. xvii)], *n.* A giant; a gigantic person or thing. **goliath beetle:** A huge tropical beetle, *Goliathus giganteus.*

gollar (gol' ȧr) [Sc., imit.], *v.i.* To make a guggling sound; to shout or scold. *n.* A noise or utterance of this kind.

golliwog (gol' i wog) [nonsense-word], *n.* A black-faced doll of grotesque appearance; a bogy.

golly (1) (gol' i) [minced form of GOD], *int.* God; by God.

golly (2) (gol′ i) [Sc., imit.], *v.i.* To shout, esp. with a deep or husky voice.

***goloe-shoe, golosh** [GALOSH].

gombeen (gom bēn′) [Ir. *gaimbin*, said to be from same O.Celt. root as L. *cambium*, CHANGE], *n.* Usury. **gombeen-man, -woman,** *n.* A money-lender. **gombeenism,** *n.*

gombo [GUMBO].

gombroon (gom broon′) [town on Persian Gulf, cp. CAMBROOM], *n.* Persian semi-transparent white pottery imitated in Chelsea ware.

gomerel (gom′ ėr ėl) [Sc. and North., etym. obscure], *n.* A simpleton.

Gomorrah (gȯ mor′ ȧ) [Gr., from Heb. *'Amōrā*, one of the cities of the plain (Gen. xvii–xix)], *n.* A dissolute town.

gomphiasis (gom fī′ ȧ sis) [Gr., from *gomphios*, a molar], *n.* (*Path.*) Looseness of the teeth, esp. the molars.

gomphosis (gom fō′ sis) [Gr., from *gomphoein*, to bolt together, from *gomphos*, bolt], *n.* (*Anat.*) A kind of articulation by which the teeth are firmly implanted in their sockets.

gomuti (gȯ moo′ ti) [Malay], *n.* A black hair-like fibre, not decaying in water, obtained from the sago-palm, and used for cordage, thatching, etc.

-gon [Gr. *-gōnos*, angled], *suf.* Angled, as in *hexagon, octagon, pentagon.*

gonads (gon′ ădz) [Gr. *gonē*, cogn. with *gignesthai*, to become, to be born, -AD], *n.pl.* (*Biol.*) Undifferentiated sex-glands, the embryonic sexual apparatus, with rudiments of both sexes which later develop into either ovaries or testes. **gonadic** (gȯ năd′ ik), *a.*

gonagra (gȯ năg′ rȧ) [Gr. *gonu*, knee, *agra*, a catching], *n.* (*Path.*) Gout in the knee. **gonalgia,** *n.* Any painful affection of the knee. **gonarthritis** (gon ar thrī′ tis), *n.* Inflammation of the knee-joint.

gondola (gon′ dō lȧ), [It.], *n.* A long, narrow Venetian boat with peaked ends, propelled by one oar; (*Aviat.*) the car of an airship or balloon; (*Am.*) a large, light, flat-bottomed freight-boat. **gondolier** (gon dȯ lēr′), *n.* A man who rows a gondola.

gone (gawn, gon) [p.p. of GO (1)], *a.* Ruined, undone; lost, beyond hope; past, bygone. **gone on:** (*slang*) Infatuated with. **goneness,** *n.* A sensation of weakness, exhaustion, or depression. **goner,** *n.* (*slang*) One who is ruined or ill beyond recovery.

gonfalon (gon′ fȧ lon) [It. *gonfalone*, O.H.G. *gundfano* (*gund*, O.Teut. *gunthja*, war, *fano*, banner)], *n.* An ensign or bannerole, usu. displayed from a cross-yard on a pole, with streamers, as the standard of certain Italian republics. **gonfalonier** (gon fȧ lon ēr′), *n.* A gonfalon- or standard-bearer; the title of the chief magistrate in certain Italian republics. **gonfanon** [O.F., as above], *n.* A gonfalon.

gong (gong) [Malay], *n.* A tambourine-shaped metal instrument which when struck with a padded stick emits a loud sonorous note, used as a signal for meals, etc.; a flattish bell struck with a hammer; (*slang*) a medal. *v.t.* (*colloq.*) To stop a motorist who is infringing speed or other regulations by sounding a gong on a police car. **gong metal,** *n.* (*Metal.*) A sonorous metal, 100 parts copper, 25 parts tin.

Gongorism (gong′ gȯr izm) [Luis de *Góngora* y Argote (1561–1627), Spanish poet], *n.* A florid and affected style of writing somewhat analogous to euphuism, introduced by Góngora. **gongoresque** (gong gȯ resk′), *a.* **Gongorist,** *n.*

gongylus (gȯn′ ji lŭs) [Gr. *gongulos*, round], *n.* (*Bot.*) A round deciduous reproductive body produced by certain seaweeds; a spore of certain fungi; a granule in the shields of some lichens.

goniatite (gō′ ni ȧ tīt) [mod. L. *gōniatītēs*, from Gr. *gōnia*, angle], *n.* (*Palæont.*) A Palæozoic genus of ammonites.

gonidium (gȯ nid′ i ŭm) [from Gr. *gonē*, offspring, seed], *n.* (*pl.* **-dia**) (*Bot.*) A reproductive cell produced asexually in algæ; one of the green algal cells or buds in the thallus of lichens. **gonidial, gonidic, gonidioid, gonidiose** (gȯ nid′-), *a.*

goniometer (gō ni om′ ė tėr) [F. *goniomètre*], *n.* An instrument for measuring angles, especially of crystals. **goniometric, -al** (gō ni ȯ met′ rik, -ăl), *a.* **goniometry** (-om′ ė tri), *n.*

gonochorism (gon ō kôr′ izm) [Gr. *gonos*, offspring, Gr. *choris*, separately], *n.* (*Zool.*) The determination of sex.

gonophore (gon′ ȯ fôr) [Gr. *gonos*, offspring, generation, cogn. with prec., -PHORE], *n.* (*Bot.*) A stalk holding the pistil and stamens above the floral envelope in certain plants; (*Zool.*) one of the zooids containing the reproductive elements in *Hydrozoa.*

gonorrhœa (gon ȯ rē′ ȧ) [med. L., from Gr. *gonorrhoia* (*gonos*, seed, *rhoia*, a flowing, from *rheein*, to flow)], *n.* (*Path.*) A venereal disease affecting the urethra and other mucous surfaces, accompanied by inflammation and muco-purulent discharge; clap.

good (gud) [A.-S. *gōd* (cp. Dut. *goed*, Icel. *gōthr*, G. *gut*), cogn. with GATHER], *a.* (*comp.* **better,** *superl.* **best**) Having such qualities as are useful, proper, and satisfactory; fit, proper, suitable, expedient; conducive to the end desired, profitable, serviceable; adequate, satisfactory, competent; advantageous, beneficial; genuine, sound, valid, wholesome; perfect, complete, thorough; reliable, safe, sure; sound financially; ample, considerable; possessed of moral excellence, righteous, virtuous; kind, benevolent, friendly, amiable, courteous; pleasant, acceptable, palatable. *n.* That which contributes to happiness, advantage, etc.; that which is right, useful, etc.; welfare; prosperity; benefit, advantage; goodness, good qualities, virtuous and charitable deeds; (*pl.*) movable property, chattels, effects; wares, merchandise. **the goods:** (*slang*) Just what is wanted. **as good as:** Not less than, the same as, practically, virtually. **as good as his word:** Fulfilling his promises; trustworthy; not to be deterred. **the good** folk or **people:** (*euphem.*) The fairies. **in good sooth:** In very truth. **to be good for:** To be relied on to pay or bring in (a stated amount). **to make good:** To confirm, to demonstrate; to perform, to fulfil; to supply a deficiency; to replace; to compensate (for). **to stand good:** To remain valid. **to think good, to see good:** To consider good; to be pleased. **good breeding:** Courteous manners formed by nurture and education. ***good-conceited,** *a.* Well-devised; fanciful. ***good-conditioned,** *a.* Being in a good state. **good day,** *n.* and *int.* A form of salutation at meeting or parting. ***good e'en, good evening,** *n.* and *int.* A form of salutation. **good-faced,** *a.* Having a handsome face, pretty. **good fellow:** A person of a good easy nature; a genial, sociable person. **good-fellowship:** Sociability; pleasant company; conviviality. **good-for-nothing, -nought,** *a.* Of no value, worthless. *n.* An idle fellow, a vagabond. **Good Friday:** The Friday of Holy Week, kept as a fast in memory of the Crucifixion. **good humour:** A cheerful temper, amiability. **good-humoured** (-hū′ mȯrd), *a.* **good-humouredly,** *adv.* **good-lack** [see ALACK], *int.* An exclamation of wonder. **good lady,** *n.* Wife. **good-looking** (gud luk′ ing), *a.* Handsome; (gud′ luk ing) appearing to be good or virtuous. **good looks:** Handsomeness. **good luck,** *n.* and *int.* Good-fortune, prosperity. **good morning, *good morrow,** *n.* and *int.* A wish or salutation. **good nature:** Kindness of disposition; freedom from selfishness. **good-natured,** *a.* **good-naturedly,** *adv.* **good-neighbourhood, -ship, -liness,** *n.* Friendliness, kindly conduct, and intercourse, between neighbours. **good night,** *n.* and *int.* A wish at parting. ***good now,** *int.* An exclamation of wonder, entreaty, etc. **good oil:** (*Austral.*) Reliable information, true report. **Good Samaritan:** A friend in need (alluding to Luke x, 33, etc.). **good sense:** Sound judgment. **Good show!:** Well done! **good temper:** Freedom from irritability. **good-tempered,** *a.* Good-humoured. **good-temperedly,** *adv.* **Good Templar:** A member of a society pledged to teetotalism. **good thing:** A witty remark or story; a favourable bargain or speculation; (*pl.*) delicacies, good fare. **for good, for good and all:** Finally, definitely, completely. **the good:** Virtuous people. **to deliver the goods:** To carry out one's promise, to be as good as one's word. **to the good:** As a balance or profit; extra, over and above. **goods and chattels:** Personal property. **goods train:** A train conveying merchandise only, (*Am.* freight train); **goods truck:** A truck for goods. **goodish,** *a.*

good-bye (gud bī') [corr. of *God be with you!*], *int.* and *n.* Farewell.

goodletite (gud' lė tīt) [discoverer W. *Goodlet*], *n.* The matrix in which rubies are formed.

goodly (gud' li), *a.* Handsome, comely; graceful, kind; large, considerable; (*iron.*) poor, rubbishy. **adv.* Kindly. **goodliness,** *n.*

goodman (gud măn'), *n.* A rustic term of respect; the head of a family; the master of a house; a husband.

goodness (gud' nės), *n.* The quality or state of being good; that which is good; moral excellence, virtue; kindness, good nature, generosity; the virtue or essence of anything; (*euphem.*) God. **goodness gracious! goodness knows!** *int.*

goodwife (gud wīf), *n.* The mistress of a house.

goodwill (gud wil'), *n.* Kindly feeling or disposition, benevolence; favour; acquiescence, ready consent; the established popularity of custom of a business sold with the business itself.

goofy (goo' fi), *a.* (*slang*) Silly, infatuated.

googly (goo' gli), *n.* (*Cricket*) A ball bowled so as to break a different way from that expected from the apparent action of the bowler.

goon (goon) [?], *n.* A stupid fellow; (*Am.*) a racketeer who terrorizes workers.

goonda (goon' dȧ) [Hind.], *n.* A desperado, a hooligan.

goondie (goon' di) [Austral. abor.], *n.* A hut.

Goorkha [GURKHA].

goosander (goo săn' dėr) [etym. doubtful (perh. GOOSE, *-ander*, cp. Icel. *önd*, a duck, pl. *andir*)], *n.* A merganser, *Mergus merganser.*

goose (goos) [A.-S. *gōs* (cp. Dut. and G. *gans*, Icel. *gās*, L. *anser*, Gr. *chēn*, perh. conn. with *chainein*, to gape)], *n.* (*pl.* **geese,** gēs) A web-footed bird intermediate in size between the duck and the swan, belonging to the genus *Anser*, esp. the domesticated variety *A. ferus*; the female of this, dist. from gander; (*fig.*) a silly person, a simpleton; (*pl.* **gooses**) a tailor's smoothing iron. **to cook his goose** [COOK]. **goose-cap,** *n.* A silly person. **goose-club,** *n.* A society for providing subscribers with a Christmas goose paid for by instalments. **goose-corn,** *n.* A coarse rush, *Juncus squarrosus.* **goose-fish,** *n.* (*Am.*) The angler-fish, *Lophius piscatorius.* **goose-flesh, -skin,** *n.* A peculiar roughness of the human skin produced by cold, fear, etc. **goose-foot,** *n.* Herbs with leaves shaped like a goose's foot, as *Aspalathus chenopoda* and the genus *Chenopodium.* **goose-grass,** *n.* Silverweed, *Potentilla anserina*; cleavers, *Galium aparine.* **goose-grease,** *n.* The melted fat of the goose, formerly used as a remedy for various ailments. **gooseherd,** *n.* One who tends geese. **goose-neck,** *n.* (*Naut.*) A bent iron fitted at the end of a yard or boom for various purposes; a piece of iron shaped like the neck of a goose. **goose-quill,** *n.* A quill-feather of a goose, esp. used as a quill pen. **goose-skin** [GOOSE-FLESH]. **goose-step,** *n.* (*Mil.*) Marking time by raising the feet alternately, as a balancing-drill for recruits; a marching step in which the legs are raised almost parallel with the ground without bending the knees. **goose-wing,** *n.* (*Naut.*) A lower corner of a square mainsail or foresail when the middle part is furled. **goose-winged,** *a.*

goosey [childish dim. of GOOSE], *n.* **goosy,** *a.*

gooseberry (guz' bėr i) [prob. GOOSE, BERRY], *n.* The fruit of a thorny shrub, *Ribes grossularia.* **to play gooseberry:** To act as unwanted third to a pair of lovers. **gooseberry fool:** Stewed gooseberries strained through a sieve and mixed with cream.

gopher (1) (gō' fėr) [said to be from F. *gaufre*, honeycomb, see GOFFER], *n.* A name given to various American burrowing animals.

gopher (2) (gō' fėr) [Heb.], *n.* The wood of which Noah's ark was made, so far unidentified.

gopher (3) [GOFFER].

goral (gō' rȧl) [Nepaul.], *n.* A Himalayan goat-like antelope, *Nemorhædus goral.*

goramy (gō' rȧ mi) [Javanese], *n.* A nest-building Oriental fish, *Osphromenus olfax*, much valued for food.

***gorbellied** (gôr' bel id) [obs. *gor*, filth], *a.* Big-bellied, corpulent. **gorbelly,** *n.*

gorcock (gôr' kok) [Sc. and North., etym. doubtful], *n.* The moor-cock or male of the red grouse.

gorcrow (gôr' krō) [*gor*, see GORE (1), -CROW (1)], *n.* The carrion crow.

Gordian (gôr' di ȧn) [*Gordius*, see GORDIAN KNOT], *a.* Intricate, complicated. **Gordian knot:** A knot in the harness of Gordius, a king of Phrygia, which Alexander cut with his sword upon hearing the promise of the oracle that whoso could untie it should possess the empire of Asia; (*fig.*) any apparently inextricable difficulty or deadlock. **to cut the Gordian knot:** To remove a difficulty by drastic measures.

gordius (gôr' di ŭs) [as prec.], *n.* (*Zool.*) A genus of threadlike worms, endoparasitic during part of their existence.

gore (1) (gôr) [A.-S. *gor*, dirt, filth (cp. Icel. *gor*, Dut. *goor*)], *n.* Blood from a wound, esp. thick, clotted blood. **gore-blood,** *n.* **gory,** *a.* Covered with gore; bloody. **gory-dew,** *n.* A minute fresh-water alga, *Palmella cruenta*, coating damp walls in shady places with rosy gelatinous patches. **goriness,** *n.*

gore (2) (gôr) [A.-S. *gāra*, cogn. with foll.], *n.* A triangular piece sewed into a dress, a sail, balloon, etc., to widen it out at any part; a triangular piece of land; (*Her.*) a curved abatement cut from a shield, orig. denoting cowardice. *v.t.* To make into or shape as a gore; to fit with a gore.

gore (3) (gôr) [A.-S. *gār*, a spear (cp. Icel. *geirr*, and perh. O.Ir. *gār*)], *v.t.* To pierce, to stab; to pierce with or as with a horn or horn-like point.

gorge (gôrj) [O.F., etym. doubtful], *n.* The throat; the gullet; that which is swallowed or gorged; the act of gorging; a heavy meal, a surfeit; a narrow pass between cliffs or hills; (*Fort.*) the narrow entrance into a bastion or other outwork; (*Angling*) a bait to be swallowed by a fish. *v.t.* To swallow, to devour greedily; to glut, to satiate, to choke up. *v.i.* To feed greedily. **gorged,** *a.* Having a gorge or throat; (*Her.*) bearing a crown or the like round the neck.

gorgeous (gôr' jŭs) [O.F. *gorgias*, etym. doubtful], *a.* Splendid, richly decorated, magnificent: ornate. **gorgeously,** *adv.* **gorgeousness,** *n.*

gorget (1) (gôr' jėt) [O.F. *gorgete*, dim. of *gorge*, see GORGE], *n.* A piece of armour for defending the throat or neck; a metallic ornament formerly worn on the breast by officers on duty; a ruff or wimple formerly worn by women; a necklace.

gorget (2) (gôr' jėt) [F. *gorgeret*, as prec.], *n.* (*Surg.*) A tabular lithotomic cutting-instrument.

Gorgio (gôr' ji ō) [Romany], *n.* The gipsy name for one not a gipsy.

Gorgon (gôr' gȯn) [L. *Gorgō -ōnis*, Gr. *Gorgō*, pl. *ones*, from *gorgos*, terrible], *n.* (*Gr. Myth.*) One of three snake-haired female monsters of an aspect so terrible that the sight of them was fabled to turn beholders to stone; a terrible or hideous creature, esp. a repulsive-looking woman. **gorgoneion** (gôr go nī′ ŏn), *n.* (*pl.* **-neia**) A mask or other representation of the Gorgon's head, often used as a keystone. **gorgonesque** (gôr go nesk′), *a.* **gorgonize** (gôr′-), *v.t.* To gaze at so as to paralyse or turn to stone.

gorgonia (gôr gō′ ni ȧ) [from prec., in allusion to their petrified character], *n.* (*pl.* **iæ, -ias**) The sea-fan; a genus of flexible polyps growing in the form of shrubs, feathers, etc.

Gorgonzola (gôr gŏn zō′ lȧ) [village near Milan], *n.* A cheese somewhat like Stilton.

gorilla (gȯ ril′ ȧ) [Gr. form of alleged native African name for a wild man in account of Hermo the Carthaginian's travels in 5th or 6th cent. B.C.], *n.* A powerful and ferocious African anthropoid ape, *Troglodytes gorilla*, about five and a half feet in height.

gormandize (gôr′ mȧn dīz) [O.F. *gourmandise*, gluttony, from GOURMAND], *n.* Taste in the provision and appreciation of table delicacies; *indulgence in eating, gluttony. *v.t.* To eat greedily, to gorge. *v.i.* To eat food greedily. **gormandizer,** *n.* **gormandizing,** *n.*

gormless [GAUMLESS].

gorse (gôrs) [A.-S. *gorst* (cogn. with G. *gerst*, L. *hordeum*, barley, L. *horridus*, bristly)], *n.* A prickly shrub with yellow flowers, furze, whin. **gorsy,** *a.*

Gorsedd (gôr′ seth) [W.], *n.* A meeting of bards and Druids.

gosh (gosh) [GOD], *int.* A minced oath.

goshawk (gos′ hawk) [A.-S. *gos-hafuc* (as GOOSE, HAWK)], *n.* A large, short-winged hawk, *Astur palumbarius*; applied also to other species of *Astur*.

Goshen (gō′ shĕn) [the land in Egypt given by Pharaoh to the Israelites to dwell in (Gen. xlv)], *n.* A land of plenty.

gosling (goz′ ling), *n.* A young goose; a silly or inexperienced person; *a catkin.

gospel (gos′ pėl) [A.-S. *godspell*, good tidings], *n.* The revelation of the grace of God through Jesus Christ; the doctrine preached by Christ and the Apostles; one of the canonical books ascribed respectively to Matthew, Mark, Luke, and John; a selection from these books read in the Church service; (*fig.*) anything accepted as infallibly true; the principle that one adopts as a guide to life or action; the creed of a party, etc. **v.t.* To instruct in gospel precepts; to fill with sentiments of religion. **gospel-book,** *n.* A book containing the Gospels or one of them, or the New Testament for use at Holy Communion. **gospel side:** The north side of the chancel where the Gospel is read. **gospel truth:** Something as true as the Gospel. **gospel-wagon,** *n.* A vehicle used at open-air services. **gospeller,** *n.* One of the four Evangelists; the priest who reads the Gospel in the Communion service; a missionary; one who claims that his religious beliefs are based exclusively on the Gospels (often applied contemptuously to Protestants, Puritans, etc.). ***gospellize,** *v.t.* To lay down as gospel; to evangelize.

***goss** [GORSE].

gossamer (gos′ ȧ mėr) [M.E. *gossomer*, lit. goose-summer, *i.e.* St. Martin's summer (early Nov.), when geese were eaten, the time of its prevalence], *n.* The slender cobweb-like threads floating in the air in calm weather, produced by small spiders; thin, filmy gauze; anything exceedingly flimsy or unsubstantial. **gossamered,** *a.* **gossamery,** *a.*

gossan (gos′ ȧn) [Cornish dial., etym doubtful], *n.* (*Mining*) Decomposed, ferruginous rock forming the upper part of a metallic vein.

gossip (gos′ ip) [A.-S. *godsibb*, orig. related in God, a sponsor in baptism], *n.* *A sponsor; a friend, an acquaintance; one who runs about tattling; idle talk, tittle-tattle; mere rumour; informal chat or writing, esp. about persons or incidents of the day. **v.t.* To stand sponsor to. *v.i.* To tattle, to chat; to talk or write in an informal easy-going way. **gossiper,** *n.* **gossipry,** *n.* **gossipy,** *a.*

gossoon (gȯ soon′) [corr. of F. GARÇON], *n.* (*Ang.-Ir.*) A boy, a lad.

gossypium (gȯ sip′ i ŭm) [L. *gossypion*], *n.* (*Bot.*) A tropical genus of herbs and shrubs belonging to the *Malvaceæ* or mallow family, including three species whence the cotton of commerce is obtained.

got (got) [past and p.p. of GET]. **got-up,** *a.* Dressed up, disguised, or prepared for effect or to take in.

Goth (goth) [late L. *Gothī*, Gr. *Gothoi*, Goth. *Gutōs* or *Gutans*, pl.], *n.* One of an ancient tribe of Teutons which swept down upon southern Europe in the 3rd–5th centuries, establishing kingdoms in Italy, southern France, and Spain; (*fig.*) a barbarian, a rude, ignorant person. **Gothish,** *a.*

Gothamist (gōt′ ȧm ist) [*Gotham*, a village in Nottinghamshire, said to be noted for its foolish inhabitants], *n.* A foolish person, one easily taken in. **Gothamite,** *n.* A Gothamist; (*U.S.A.*, *facet.*) a New Yorker.

Gothic (goth′ ik) [GOTH], *a.* Pertaining to the Goths or their language; (*Arch.*) in the style of architecture characterized by pointed arches, clustered columns, etc.; (*fig.*) rude, barbarous; (*Print.*) black-letter. *n.* The language of the Goths; (*Arch.*) the Gothic style of architecture; (*Print.*) black-letter. **Gothic revival,** *n.* The wave of interest in Gothic culture that occurred in the late 18th and the first half of the 19th century. **gothically,** *adv.* **Gothicism,** *n.* A Gothic idiom; conformity to the Gothic style of architecture; rudeness of manners. **Gothicist,** *n.* **gothicize,** *v.t.* To make Gothic; to bring back to barbarism. *v.i.* To go back to barbarism.

gotten, *p.p.* [GET].

gouache (gu′ ash) [F., from It. *guazzo*], *n.* A method of painting with opaque colours mixed with water, honey, and gum.

Gouda (gou′ dȧ) [place-name], *n.* A cheese made at Gouda, in Holland.

gouge (gouj) [F., late L. *guvia*, etym. doubtful], *n.* A chisel with a concave blade, used to cut holes or grooves; (*slang*) a swindle, a fraud. *v.t.* To cut, force, or scoop (out) with or as with a gouge; (*Am.*) to cheat. **gouge-slip,** *n.* A hone used for sharpening gouges.

goulard (goo lard′) [Thomas *Goulard* (*d. c.* 1790), French surgeon], *n.* A lotion composed of subacetate of lead in solution. **goulard water,** *n.*

goulash (goo′ lăsh) [Hung. *gulyas*, herdsman], *n.* A stew of meat and vegetables highly seasoned with paprika.

goupen [GOWPEN].

goura (goor′ ȧ) [Papuan native name], *n.* A genus of pigeons found in New Guinea and the neighbouring islands.

gourami [GORAMY].

gourd (goord) [F. *gourde*, ult. from L. *cucurbita*], *n.* A large fleshy fruit of climbing or trailing plants belonging to the *Cucurbitaceæ*, the outer coat of which serves for vessels to hold water; a bottle, cup, etc., made of the hard rind of this; a vessel of a similar shape; (*pl.*) hollow dice employed for cheating. **gourd-worm,** *n.* A fluke-worm. **gourdful,** *n.*

gourmand (goor′ mȧnd) [F., etym. doubtful], *a.* Gluttonous, fond of eating. *n.* One who loves delicate fare, a gourmet; a glutton.

gourmet (goor′ mā) [F., orig. a wine-taster], *n.* A connoisseur in wines and meats; a dainty feeder, an epicure.

gousty (gous′ ti) [Sc. and North., etym. doubtful], *a.* Dreary, desolate, forlorn; gusty. **goustrous,** *a.* Violent, boisterous.

gout (1) (gout) [O.F. *goute*, L. *gutta*, a drop], *n.* A disease affecting the joints, esp. the great toe, with inflammation, pain and irritability being the leading symptoms; *a drop, a clot; a disease of wheat caused by the **gout-fly. gouty,** *a.* Affected with or pertaining to gout; swollen. **goutily,** *adv.* **goutiness,** *n.*

goût (2) (goo) [F., earlier *goust*, L. *gustus*], *n.* Taste, relish; good taste, artistic discernment.

govern (gŭv′ ėrn) [O.F. *governer*, L. *gubernāre*, to steer, guide, from Gr. *kubernân*, to steer], *v.t.* To direct and control; to rule with authority, esp. to administer the affairs of a State; to exercise military command over; to regulate, to sway, to influence, to determine; to conduct (oneself) in a specific way; to restrain, to curb; (*Gram.*) to require a particular case in the word following it, to have a noun or case dependent upon it (said of a verb or preposition). *v.i.* To exercise authority; to administer the law; to have the control (over). **governable,** *a.* **governability** (-bil′ i ti), *n.* **governably,** *adv.* **governance, *governail,** *n.*

governess (gŭv′ ėr nės) [earlier *governeress*, O.F. *gouverneresse*, fem. of *gouverneur*, GOVERNOR], *n.* A woman who has the care and instruction of young children, esp. in a private household; an instructress. **governess-cart,** *n.* A light two-wheeled vehicle with two seats only, facing each other. ***governante,** *n.*

government (gŭv′ ėrn mėnt) [O.F. *governement*], *n.* Control, direction, regulation, exercise of authority, esp. authoritative administration of public affairs; the form or system of such administration; the body of persons in charge of the government of a State at any particular time, an administration, a ministry; self-control, manageableness; the power of controlling; the form of policy in a State; the right of governing; the executive power; (*Am.*) State administration; the territory under a governor, a province; *deportment; (*Gram.*) the influence of a word in determining the case or mood of another. **government man,** *n.* (*Austral. hist.*) A convict, an assigned servant. **governmental** (-men′ tăl), *a.* **governmentally,** *adv.* **governmentalism,** *n.* **governmentalist,** *n.*

governor (gŭv′ ėr nŏr) [O.F. *governeur*], *n.* One who governs, esp. one invested with authority to execute the laws and administer the affairs of a State, province, etc.; a ruler, a head of the executive; the Crown representative in a colony or dependency; (*U.S.A.*) the elective chief magistrate of a State; the commander in a fortress or garrison; (*slang*) one's father, one's employer; an unceremonious mode of address; (*Mech.*) a contrivance for regulating the speed of an engine motor, etc., or the flow or pressure of a fluid or gas; *a pilot; *a tutor. **governor-general,** *n.* A chief of the executive in a large dependency, having deputy-governors under him. **governor-generalship,** *n.* **governorship,** *n.*

gowan (gou′ ăn) [Sc. and North., perh. conn. with Icel. *gulr*, YELLOW, or with A.-S. *golde*, GOLD], *n.* The daisy.

gowd (*Sc.*) [GOLD].

gowff (gouf) [Sc., conn. with GOLF], *v.t.* To strike, to cuff.

gowk (gouk) [Icel. *gaukr* (cp. G. *gauch*, A.-S. *gēak*)], *n.* *The cuckoo; a fool, a simple or awkward fellow.

gowl (goul) [Sc. and North., from Icel. *gaula*, to YAWL], *v.i.* To howl, to cry. *n.* A howl, a yell.

gown (goun) [O.F. *gaune*, *gonne*, late L. *gunna*, a skin, a fur garment; etym. doubtful], *n.* A woman's loose, long, outer garment, a dress, esp. a handsome or stylish one (now usu. a frock); a long, loose robe worn by clergymen, judges, lawyers, University men, etc.; a Roman toga. **town and gown:** The townspeople as opposed to or contrasted with the professors and students in a University town. **gown-boy,** *n.* A boy wearing a gown, as one belonging to an endowed school. ***gown-cloth,** *n.* A piece of cloth for making a gown. **gowned,** *a.* **gownsman,** *n.* One whose professional dress is a gown; a member of a University; a lawyer; *a clergyman; one wearing a gown as emblem of peace, a civilian.

gowpen (gou′ pėn) [Sc., from Icel. *gaupn*], *n.* A handful, a double handful; as much as can be held in the hollow of the two hands; a perquisite of meal allowed to a miller's man.

Goy (goi) [Heb., a nation], *n.* Yiddish name for a Gentile.

Graafian (gră′ fi ăn) [Regnier de *Graaf* (1643–1673), Dutch anatomist], *a.* Named after de Graaf. **Graafian follicle** or **vesicle:** (*Anat.*) A small sac in which the ova are matured in the ovary of mammals.

graal [GRAIL (2)].

grab (grăb) [prob. orig. Eng., perh. from GRIP (cp. Swed. *grabba*, M.Dut. and M.L.G. *grabben*)], *v.t.* (*past & p.p.* **grabbed**) To seize, snatch, or grasp suddenly; to take possession of violently or lawlessly; (*colloq.*) to capture, to arrest. *v.i.* To grasp, snatch, or clutch (at). *n.* A sudden snatch, grasping, or seizing (at); an implement for clutching, a grip; rapacious or dishonest acquisition, esp. in commerce or the foreign policy of a government. **grabber,** *n.* **land-grabber,** *n.* (*chiefly Irish*) One who gets hold of land by underhand means. **grab-bag,** *n.* (*Am.*) A bag from which articles are grabbed for on payment, at fairs, sports, etc., a lucky dip.

grabble (grăb′ ėl) [freq. of prec.], *v.i.* To grope, to feel about (for); to sprawl on all fours (after, for, etc.).

grace (grās) [O.F. *grace* (F. *grâce*), L. *grātia*, from *grātus*, pleasing], *n.* That quality which makes form, movement, expression, or manner elegant, harmonious, refined, and charming; a natural gift or endowment; an acquired accomplishment, charm, or attraction; a courteous or affable demeanour; free, unmerited favour or goodwill; clemency, mercy; a boon, a benefaction; (*Mus.*) an ornamental note or passage introduced as an embellishment; (*Theol.*) the free, unmerited favour of God; a divine, regenerating, and invigorating influence; the state of being forgiven by and reconciled to God, with participation in the favours granted through the merits of Christ; a spiritual favour or excellence; a short prayer invoking a blessing before or returning thanks after a meal; a privilege or indulgence, esp. an extension of time legally allowed after a payment falls due; (*Univ.*) a vote, decree, a licence to take a degree, a dispensation from statutes, etc.; *(*pl.*) thanks. **Act of grace:** A general pardon granted by Act of Parliament. **airs and graces:** Affectation; assumed refinement. **days of grace:** The time legally allowed for payment of a bill of exchange after it falls due, in England three days. **fall from grace:** Lapse from good behaviour. **her, his, your grace:** Courteous phrases adopted in speaking to or of an archbishop, duke, duchess, and formerly sovereigns. **the Graces:** (*Gr. Myth.*) Three goddesses embodying and conferring beauty and charm. **to be in the good graces of:** To enjoy the favour of. **with a good** or **bad grace:** To do a thing willingly or reluctantly. **year of grace:** Anno domini, A.D. **grace-cup,** *n.* A cup, usu. of wine, passed round after a meal for drinking the concluding health or healths. **grace-note,** *n.* (*Mus.*) An extra note introduced for embellishment. **grace-stroke,** *n.* A finishing stroke or *coup de grâce*. **graceful,** *a.* Full of grace, elegance, or beauty, esp. of form or movement. **gracefully,** *adv.* **gracefulness,** *n.* **graceless,** *a.* Void of grace; lacking in propriety or decency, mannerless; depraved, abandoned; ungraceful; *out of favour, unfortunate. **gracelessly,** *adv.* **gracelessness,** *n.*

gracile (grăs′ il) [L. *gracilis*], *a.* Slender, lean, thin. **gracility** (gră sil′ i ti), *n.*

gracious (grā′ shŭs) [O.F. (F. *gracieux*), L. *gratiōsus*, as prec.], *a.* Exhibiting grace, favour, or kindness; benevolent, kind; courteous, condescending, affable; graceful, pleasing, bland; proceeding from divine grace; benignant, merciful. **gracious me!**

gracious goodness! *int.* Exclamations of surprise or protest. **graciously,** *adv.* **graciousness,** *n.*

grackle (grăk′ ėl) [L. *grāculus*, a jackdaw], *n.* Any bird of the genus *Gracula*, allied to the starlings.

gradate [GRADATION].

gradatim (grȧ dā′ tim) [L., as foll.], *adv.* Gradually, by degrees.

gradation (grȧ dā′ shŭn) [L. *gradātio -ōnem*, from *gradus*, a step], *n.* An orderly arrangement, succession, or progression step by step; a step, stage, or degree in order, rank, quality, merit, etc. (*usu. in pl.*); (*Fine Art*) the gradual blending of one tint, tone, etc., with another; (*Mus.*) an ascending or descending succession of chords; (*Philol.*) ablaut. **gradate** (grȧ dāt′), *v.t.* To arrange or blend (colours, etc.) by imperceptible gradation. *v.i.* To pass from one tint to another by such gradations. **gradational,** *a.* **gradationally,** *adv.* **gradationed,** *a.* Formed by gradation. **gradatory** (grā′ dȧ tŏr i), *a.* Proceeding by gradations. *n.* A flight of steps, as from a cloister into a church.

grade (grād) [F., from L. *gradum*, nom. *-us*, see prec.), *n.* A degree or step in rank, quality, value, order, etc.; a class of people of similar rank, ability, proficiency, etc.; (*Am.*) class (at school); an animal or class of animals (as cattle or sheep) produced by crossing a common stock with some better breed; (*Zool.*) a group supposed to have branched off from a parent stem at a certain stage of development; (*Path.*) degree of intensity (of a disease); (*Civ. Eng.*) gradient, the degree of slope in a road; a road, track, etc., or part of such, inclined to the horizontal; (*Philol.*) the position of a vowel or root in an ablaut series. *v.t.* To arrange in grades; to gradate; to adjust the rate of slope in, as a road; (*Cattle*) to cross (a stock) with a better breed. **to make the grade:** To succeed. **at grade:** (*Am.*) At the same level (as of a place where two roads cross each other). **down** or **up grade:** A descending or ascending road or part of a road. **on the down** or **the up grade:** Descending or ascending a slope; (*fig.*) falling or rising. **to grade up:** To improve (stock) by crossing with a better breed. **grade-crossing,** *n.* (*Am. Rail.*) A level-crossing.

gradely (grād′ li) [M.E. *graythly*, Icel. *greithliga* (cp. GRAITH, A.-S. *gerǣde*, G. *gerade*, ready)], *a.* (*prov.*) Decent, respectable, worthy; well; proper, suitable; good-looking. *adv.* Decently, properly, well, becomingly.

gradient (grā′ di ėnt) [from GRADE, after L. *gradiens -ntem*, p.p. of *gradī*, to walk], *n.* The rate of ascent or descent in a railway or road; degree of slope, inclination, (*Am.* grade); (*Civ. Eng.*) grade; (*Meteor.*) rate of variation or increase or decrease in height of thermometer or barometer over a large area; the diagrammatic line denoting such variation.

gradin (grā′ din), **gradine** (1) (grȧ dēn′) [F. *gradin*, It. *gradino*, from *grado*, GRADE], *n.* One in a series of rising steps or a tier of seats; a shelf or step at the back of an altar.

gradine (2) (grȧ dēn′), **gradino** (grȧ dē′ nō) [as prec.], *n.* A toothed chisel used by sculptors.

gradual (grăd′ ū ȧl) [late L. *graduālis*, from *gradus*, *-ūs*, a step], *a.* Proceeding by steps or degrees; regular and slow, opp. to abrupt, steep, rapid. *n.* (*Eccles.*) An antiphon sung between the Epistle and the Gospel; a book containing such antiphons or the music for them. **gradually,** *adv.* **gradualness,** *n.*

graduate (grăd′ ū āt) [late L. *graduātus*, p.p. of *graduāre*, as prec.], *v.t.* To mark with degrees; to divide into or arrange by gradations; to apportion (a tax, etc.) according to a scale of grades; to temper or modify by degrees; (*Am.*) to confer an academic degree upon; (*Chem.*) to bring a fluid to a certain degree of consistency, as by evaporation. *v.i.* To alter, change, or pass by degrees; to take a degree in a University. *n.* (grăd′ ū ȧt) One who has received a degree in a University; (*Chem.*) a graduated vessel for measuring liquids. **graduateship,** *n.* **graduation** (-ā′ shŭn), *n.* Regular progression by successive degrees; a division into degrees or parts; the conferring or receiving of academical degrees; (*Chem.*) the reduction of a liquid to a certain consistency by evaporation. **graduation exercises:** (*Am.*) prize-day at school, etc. **graduator** (grăd′ ū ā tŏr), *n.* An instrument for dividing lines into minute equal parts.

graduction (grȧ dŭk′ shŭn) [erroneously formed from *gradus*, as prec.], *n.* (*Astron.*) The division of circular arcs into degrees, minutes, etc.

gradus (grā′ dŭs) [short for *Gradus ad Parnassum*, a step to Parnassus], *n.* A dictionary of Greek or Latin prosody formerly used in public schools.

Græcism (grē′ sizm) [F. *grécisme*, med. L. *Græcismus*, from *Græcus*, GREEK], *n.* A Greek idiom, style, or mode of expression; cultivation of the Greek spirit, style, or mode of expression. **græcize** (grē′ sīz), *v.t.* To give a Greek form or character to. *v.i.* To cultivate or follow the Greek spirit, ideas, ways of expression, etc. **græco-,** *comb. form.* **Græcomaniac** (grē kȯ mā′ ni ăk) [-MANIAC], *n.* **Græcophil** (grē′ kȯ fil) [-PHIL], *n.* **Græco-Roman,** *n.* Pertaining to both Greeks and Latins.

***graff** (grăf) [cp. M.Dut. *graft*], *n.* A ditch or trench; (*Sc.*) a grave.

graffito (gra fē′ tō) [It., from *graffio*, a scratch], *n.* (*pl.* ***-ti***, -tē) A drawing or inscription scratched on a wall or other surface, as in ancient buildings at Pompeii or Rome; decoration by means of scratches through plaster, revealing a differently coloured ground.

graft (1) (graft) [earlier *graff*, O.F. *grafe* (F. *greffe*), low L. *graphium*, Gr. *graphion*, a stylus, from *graphein*, to write], *n.* A small shoot of a tree or plant inserted into another tree of a different stock which supplies the sap to nourish it; (*Surg.*) living tissue from a person or animal transplanted to another; (*fig.*) incorporation with a foreign stock. *v.t.* To insert (a shoot or scion) in or upon another plant or tree; to inset as a graft; to insert grafts upon; to plant (a tree or stock) thus with another variety; (*Surg.*) to transplant (as living animal tissue); (*fig.*) to incorporate with another stock; to insert or implant (upon) so as to form a vital union; (*Naut.*) to cover (a ring-bolt, etc.) with spun yarn or a weaving of thin cord. *v.i.* To insert grafts or scions in or on other stocks. **grafter** (1), *n.* One who grafts; *a tree from which a graft was taken. **grafting clay** or **wax:** A plastic composition used for covering grafted parts and excluding air. **grafting scissors** (*Surg.*): Scissors used by surgeons in skin-grafting.

graft (2) (graft) [conn. with GRAVE (2)], *n.* (*prov.*) A spit of earth, the amount thrown up at one dig with the spade.

graft (3) (graft) [etym. doubtful], *n.* A swindle; acquisition of money, etc., by taking advantage of an official position; bribery; manipulation of State or municipal business in order to secure illicit profits or influence; illicit gains so obtained. **grafter** (2), *n.*

graft (4) (graft) [*colloq.*], *n.* Hard work, unremitting labour.

grail (grāl) [O.F. *graal*, *greal*, late L. *gradālis*, etym. doubtful], *n.* A dish or cup said to have been used by Christ at the Last Supper, and employed by Joseph of Arimathea to collect His blood while on the Cross; also called the Holy Grail, Saint Grail, and Sangreal.

grail (2) (grāl) [F. *grêle*, see foll.], *n.* A coarse file formerly used in making combs by hand.

***grail** (3) (grāl) [etym. doubtful, perh. from M.F. *graisle* (F. *grêle*), L. *gracilis*, slender, or a var. of GRAVEL], *n.* (*Spens.*) Fine gravel or sand.

grain (1) (grān) [O.F., from L. *grānum*, rel. to CORN], *n.* A single seed of a plant, particularly of those kinds whose seeds are used for food; (*collect.*) corn in general or the fruit of cereal plants, as wheat, barley, rye, etc.; (*Am.*) wheat; (*pl.*) the husks or refuse of malt after brewing or of any grain after distillation; any small, hard particle; the smallest particle or amount; the unit of weight in the English system, $\frac{1}{7000}$ lb. avoirdupois or $\frac{1}{5760}$ lb. troy; granular texture, degree of roughness or smoothness of surface; texture, arrangement of particles, esp. the arrangement of the fibres of wood or other fibrous substance; the body or substance of wood as modified by the fibres; the lines of fibre in wood or, in stone, of cleavage planes, forming a pattern; a red dye made from cochineal or kermes insects; any fast dye, esp. red, crimson, or purple; temper, disposition, natural tendency. *v.t.* To form into grains, to granulate; to treat so as to bring out the natural grain; to paint or stain in imitation of this; to give a granular surface to; to scrape the hair off (hides) with a grainer. *v.i.* To form grains, to become granulated. **against the grain:** Against one's natural inclination. **in grain:** Downright, thorough, absolute, inveterate. **to dye in grain:** To dye in a fast colour, esp. in kermes; to dye deeply or into the fibre. **grains of paradise** or **Guinea grains:** The seeds of *Amomum melegueta*, a tropical West African spice, used to give a pungent taste to cattle-powders and spirituous liquors. **grain leather,** *n.* Leather dressed with the grain-side outwards. **grain-side,** *n.* The side (of leather) from which the hair has been removed. **grain-sick,** *n.* A disease in cattle caused by distension of the rumen with food. **grainage,** *n.* (*Farriery*) Mangy tumours on the legs of horses. **grained,** *a.* (*esp. in comb.*, as *fine-grained*). **grainer,** *n.* One who paints or stains in imitation of the grain of wood; also the brush he uses; an infusion of pigeon's dung for giving flexibility to skins in tanning; a tanner's knife. **graining,** *n.* The act of producing a grain; milling on the edge of a coin; a process in tanning; painting in imitation of the grain of wood; *Leuciscus Lancastriensis*, a fish allied to the dace. **grainless,** *a.* **grainy,** *a.*

grain (2) (grān) [Icel. *grein*, division, branch], *n.* A fork, a tine, a prong; (*pl., usu. construed as sing.*) a forked fish-spear, a kind of harpoon.

graip (grāp) [Sc. and North. (cp. Icel. *greip*, grasp, Dan. *greb*, fork, also GRIP, GROPE)], *n.* A three- or four-pronged fork, used for lifting potatoes, etc.

graith (grāth) [Icel. *greithe*, cogn. with A.-S. *gerǣde*, trappings, gear], *n.* (*now Sc.*) Equipment, attire; apparatus, gear; armour; harness; goods, possessions. *a.* (*Sc.*) Ready. *v.t.* (*Sc. and North.*) To make ready; to array.

grakle [GRACKLE].

grallæ (grăl' ē), **grallatores** (grăl à tōr' ēz) [L. *grallātor*, one who walks on stilts, from *grallæ*, stilts], *n.pl.* (*Ornith.*) Waders, an order of birds with long bare legs and usually long necks and bills, as the crane. **grallatorial** (-tōr' i àl), **grallatory** (grăl' à tòr i), **grallic** (grăl' ik), **gralline** (grăl' īn), *a.*

gralloch (grăl' ŏ*ch*) [Gael. *grealach*, the viscera], *v.t.* To disembowel (a deer). *n.* The viscera of a deer.

gram (1) (grăm) [perh. from Port. *grão*, L. *grānum*, GRAIN (1)], *n.* The chick-pea, *Cicer arietinum*, or other kinds of pulse, used in the East Indies for fodder.

gram (2) [GRAMME].

-gram [Gr. *gramma -atos*, a letter, that which is written, from *graphein*, to write], *suf.* Forming compounds with prepositional prefixes, numerals, etc., as in *epigram, monogram, phonogram, telegram.*

grama-, gramma-grass (gra' mà-, grăm' à gras) [Sp. *grama*, L. *grāmen*, grass], *n.* Various species of low pasture grass in the western and south-western U.S.A.

***gramarye** (grăm' à ri) [O.F., *gramaire*, GRAMMAR], *n.* Magic, necromancy.

gramercy (grà mĕr' si) [O.F. *grant merci*, great thanks], *int.* Thanks; an exclamation expressive of surprise. *n.* An expression of thanks.

gramineæ (grà min' i ē) [mod. L., from *grāmen -inis*, grass], *n.pl.* (*Bot.*) An order of endogens, containing the grasses. **graminaceous** (grăm i nā' shùs), **gramineous** (grà min' ė ùs), *a.* Pertaining to grass, or the tribe of grasses. **graminifolious** (grăm in i fō' li ùs) [L. *folium*, a leaf], *a.* Having leaves like grass. **graminivorous** (grăm i niv' òr ùs) [-VOROUS], *a.* Subsisting on vegetable food.

gramma-grass [GRAMA-].

grammalogue (grăm' à log) [Gr. *gramma*, -GRAM, *logos*, word], *n.* (*Phonography*) A word represented by a single sign; a logogram, or letter or character standing for a word.

grammar (grăm' àr) [O.F. *gramaire*, L. *grammatica*, Gr. *grammatikē -kos*, pertaining to letters, from *gramma*, a letter, from *graphein*, to write], *n.* The principles or science of the correct use of language; dealing with phonology, the science of sounds, etymology, the grammar of words, accidence, the science of inflexions, and syntax, the arrangement of words in sentences; a system of principles and rules for speaking and writing a language; a book containing these principles and rules; one's manner of applying these rules, or speech or writing considered with regard to its correctness according to these rules; the elements of an art or science, a treatise on these. **grammar-school,** *n.* A school orig. established (mostly in the 16th century) for teaching Latin; a secondary school with an academic course. **grammarian** (grà mâr' i àn), *n.* One versed in grammar; a philologist; one who writes upon or teaches grammar. **grammarless,** *a.* ***grammatic, -al** (grà măt' ik, -àl), *a.* Pertaining to grammar; according to the rules of grammar. **grammatical gender:** Gender based on grammar, not sex. **grammatical sense:** The literal sense. **grammatical subject:** The literal as dist. from the logical subject. **grammatically,** *adv.* **grammaticism,** *n.* A point in grammar. **grammaticize,** *v.t.* To render grammatical.

gramme, gram (2) (grăm) [F. *gramme*, late L. and Gr. *grammā*, a small weight, see -GRAM], *n.* The standard unit of weight in the metric system, defined as the mass of one cubic centimetre of distilled water at its maximum density weight *in vacuo*, equalling $\frac{1}{1000}$ of a standard kilogram or 15·432 grains troy. **grammetre, gramme-centimetre,** *n.* A unit of work, equalling the amount done in raising one gramme vertically one centimetre.

gramophone (grăm' ò fōn) [Gr. *gramma*, a letter, *phōnē*, sound (cp. PHONOGRAM)], *n.* An instrument for recording and reproducing sounds, invented by E. Berliner (1887), (*Am.* phonograph). **gramophone pick-up,** *n.* Device on the tone arm of a gramophone whereby a record can be reproduced electrically through the loud-speaker of a radio-receiver.

grampus (grăm' pùs) [A.-F. *grampais*, O.F. *grapois*, L. *crassum piscem*, nom. *crassus piscis*, fat fish], *n.* A large delphinoid cetacean belonging to the genus *Orca*, esp. the voracious *O. gladiator*; also the inoffensive cetacean *Grampus griseus* or cow-fish.

granadilla (grăn à dil' à) [Sp., dim. of *granada*, a pomegranate, L. *grānātus*, from *grānum*, GRAIN], *n.* Various species of passion-flower, *Passiflora*; used also of their edible fruit.

granam [GRANNOM].

granary (grăn' àr i) [L. *grānārium*, as prec.], *n.* A storehouse for grain; (*fig.*) a country or district producing and exporting abundance of corn.

grand (grănd) [O.F., from L. *grandis*, great], *a.* Great or imposing in size, character, or appearance; magnificent, fine splendid; dignified, lofty, noble; morally impressive, inspiring; (*Mus.*) great, of full compass, for full orchestra, or with all accessory parts and movements; (*colloq.*) distinguished, fashionable, or aristocratic (society); (*colloq.*) highly satisfactory, excellent; pre-eminent in rank, etc., chief; (*Law*) principal, as opp. to petty, common, etc.; main, comprehensive, complete, final;

in the second degree (of relationships). *n.* (*Am. slang*) one thousand dollars. **grand air:** An air of distinction. **Grand Almoner, Chambellan, Falconer,** etc.: Titles of officers of state formerly denoting the highest in rank among several almoners, etc. ***grandam,** *n.* A grandmother; an animal's dam's dam; an old woman. **grand assize or inquest:** (*Law*) An assize or inquest of great or chief importance, as opp. to petty or common. **grand-aunt,** *n.* The sister of a grandfather or grandmother. **grand captain:** A chief captain, commander, or general. **grandchild,** *n.* The child of a son or daughter. **grand committee:** One or two standing committees of the House of Commons appointed every session to consider Bills relating to law or trade. **Grand duke:** A sovereign of lower rank than a king, the ruler in certain European states; a brother of the Tsar; hence **Grand duchess: Grand duchy: Grand-ducal,** *a.* **Grand Fleet,** *n.* Formerly that portion of the British Navy employed in British and northern seas (now Home Fleet). **grand guignol** (gro*n* gē′ nyol) [F.], *n.* A theatrical programme consisting of short, sensational and blood-curdling pieces. **grand juror:** A member of the grand jury. **grand jury:** (*Law*) A jury whose duty is to enquire if there is sufficient ground for a prisoner to be tried by a petty or ordinary jury. ***grand marnier*** (gro*n* mar′ nyā) [F.], *n.* A liqueur somewhat like curaçao. **Grand Master:** The head of a military order of knighthood, the head of the Freemasons, Good Templars, etc. ***grand monarque*** [F.]: Louis XIV, King of France. ***grand monde*** [MONDE]: Highest society; the Court and nobility. **Grand National,** *n.* (*Racing*) An annual steeplechase run at Aintree, Liverpool. **grand-nephew,** *n.* The grandson of a brother or sister. **grand-niece,** *n.* The granddaughter of a brother or sister. **grand passion,** *n.* An overwhelming love affair. **grand piano:** A large piano with horizontal framing. **Grand Prix** (gro*n* prē′) [F.], *n.* (*Racing*) An international race for three-year-olds held annually at Longchamps, Paris; certain motor races. ***grand signior*** (sē′ nyôr): A person of high rank, a title formerly given to the Sultan of Turkey. **grandsire,** *n.* A grandfather; an animal's sire's sire; a male ancestor. **grand slam,** *n.* (*Cards*) In auction bridge the winning of 13 tricks by a side; in contract bridge a fulfilled contract to take all 13 tricks. **grand stand:** The principal stand for spectators on a race-course, etc. **grand tour:** A tour through the principal Continental countries and cities, formerly undertaken as an essential part of the education of a man of quality. **grand-uncle:** The brother of a grandfather or grandmother. **Grand Turk:** The Sultan of Turkey. **Grand Vizier:** The prime minister of the Turkish Empire, or of any Eastern monarchy. **grandly,** *adv.* **grandness,** *n.*

granddaughter (grănd′ daw tėr), *n.* The daughter of a son or daughter.

grandee (grăn dē′) [Sp. and Port. *grande*, as prec.], *n.* A Spanish or Portuguese nobleman of the highest rank; a person of high rank or power. **grandeeship,** *n.*

grandeur (grăn′ dūr, -dyůr) [F., from *grand*, GRAND], *n.* The quality of being grand; greatness, nobility, impressiveness, sublimity, majesty; splendour, magnificence, dignity, splendid or magnificent appearance or effect.

grandfather (grănd′ fa *th*ėr), *n.* The father of a parent. **grandfather clock,** *n.* An old-fashioned clock worked by weights, in a tall wooden case

grandiloquent (grăn dil′ ȯ kwėnt), ***-loquous** (-kwůs) [L. *grandiloquus* (GRAND, L. *-loquus*, speaking, from *loquī*, to speak), *assim.* to ELOQUENT], *a.* Using lofty or pompous language; bombastic. **grandiloquence,** *n.* **grandiloquently,** *adv.*

grandiose (grăn′ di ōs) [F., from It. *grandioso*, L. *grandis*, GRAND], *a.* Imposing, impressive, producing the effect of grandeur; intended to produce the effect of grandeur, affecting impressiveness, pompous; great in style or scale. **grandiosely,** *adv.* **grandiosity** (-os′ i ti), *n.*

Grandisonian (grăn di sō′ ni ȧn) [Sir Charles *Grandison*, the hero of Richardson's novel of that title], *a.* Elaborately and pompously courteous and chivalrous.

grandmother (grănd′ mŭ *th*er), *n.* The mother of a parent. **grandmotherly,** *a.* Like a grandmother; fussy.

grandparent (grănd′ pâr ėnt), *n.* A grandfather or grandmother.

grandson (grănd′ sŭn), *n.* The son of a son or daughter.

grange (grānj) [O.F., from L. *grānea*, *grānica*, from L. *grānum*, GRAIN (1)], *n.* A barn; a farmhouse with the out-buildings, etc., esp. if occupied as a country residence; (*U.S.A.*) a farmers' union. **granger,** *n.* A farm-bailiff; (*U.S.A.*) a farmer; (*U.S.A.*) a member of a grange.

grangerize (grān′ jėr īz) [James *Granger* (1716–76), author of a 'Biographical History of England' (1769) published with blank leaves for illustration], *v.t.* To extra-illustrate (a book, etc.) with portraits, etc. (usu. taken from other books). *v.t.* To illustrate (a book or pamphlet) with engravings bearing on the subject matter (from the practice of so illustrating Granger's *Biographical History of England*). **grangerism,** *n.* The act or practice of grangerizing books. **grangerization** (-zā′ shůn), *n.* **grangerite, grangerizer,** *n.* One who grangerizes books.

graniferous (grȧ nif′ ėr ůs) [L. *grānifer* (as *grānum*)], *a.* Bearing grain or seed of grainlike form. **graniform** (grā′ ni fôrm) [-FORM], *a.* **granivorous** (grȧ niv′ ȯr ůs) [-VOROUS], *a.* Feeding on grain.

granite (grăn′ it) [It. *granito*, p.p. of *granire*, to speckle, from *grano*, L. *grānum*, as prec.], *n.* A granular, igneous rock consisting of feldspar, quartz, and mica, confusedly crystallized. **granite ware:** (*Ceram.*) An enamelled ironware or hard pottery with speckled surface resembling granite. **granitic, -al** (grȧ nit′ ik, -ȧl), *a.* **granitification** (-kā′ shůn), *n.* Formation into granite. **granitiform** (grȧ nit′ i fôrm), *a.* **granitoid** (grăn′ i toid), *a.* Resembling granite. **granolithic** (grăn ȯ lith′ ik) [Gr. *lithikos*, from *lithos*, stone], *n.* Applied to a kind of concrete.

grannom (grăn′ ȯm) [etym. doubtful], *n.* (*Angling*) A four-winged fly frequenting streams; an imitation of this used in fly-fishing.

granny (grăn′ i), *n.* (*fem.*) A grandmother; an old woman. **granny-knot** or **granny's bend:** A badly-tied reef-knot having the tie crossed the wrong way.

granodising (grăn′ ō dī zing), *n.* (*Metal.*) A process for preventing the corrosion of ferrous metals.

grant (grant) [O.F. *graunter*, *greanter*, *creanter*, late L. *crēantāre* for *crēdentāre*, from *crēdent-*, part. stem. of *crēdere*, to trust, see CREED], *v.t.* To bestow, concede, or give, esp. in answer to request; to allow as a favour or indulgence; (*Law*) to transfer the title to, to confer or bestow (a privilege, charter, etc.); to admit as true, to concede or allow (as premises to an argument). **v.i.* To agree, to consent. *n.* The act of granting; the thing granted; a gift, an assignment, a formal bestowal; a sum of money bestowed or allowed; a concession or admission of something as true; (*Law*) a conveyance in writing; the thing conveyed. **to be taken for granted:** To assume as admitted basis of an argument. **grant-in-aid,** *n.* A sum granted towards the maintenance of a school or other institution. **grantable,** *a.* **grantee** (-tē′), *n.* (*Law*) The person to whom a grant or conveyance is made. **granter,** *n.* One who grants. **grantor,** *n.* (*Law*) One who makes a conveyance.

granule (grăn′ ūl) [late L. *grānulum*, dim. of *grānum*, grain], *n.* A little grain; a small particle. **granular, *granulary** (grăn′ ū lȧr, -i), *a.* Composed of or resembling granules. **granularity** (-lăr′ i ti), *n.* **granularly,** *adv.* **granulate** (grăn′ ū lāt), *v.t.* To form into granules or small particles; to make rough on the surface. *v.i.* To collect or be formed into grains. *a.* (grăn′ ū lāt) Granulated. **granulation** (-lā′ shŭn), *n.* The act of forming into granules; a granulated surface; (*Metal.*) the process of rendering a metal granular, as by pouring it in a melted state on to a rapidly rotating disk; (*Med.*) healing by the formation of little grain-like bodies or projections, in sores or wounds; (*pl.*) the prominences thus formed. **granulator,** *n.* **granuliferous** (-lif′ ėr ŭs), *a.* Bearing or full of granules. **granuliform** (grăn′ ū li fôrm), *a.* **granulitic** (grăn ū lit′ ik), *a.* **granulize,** *v.t.* **granulo-,** *comb. form.* **granulous,** *a.*

grape (1) (grāp) [O.F. (F. *grappe*), a bunch of grapes, from *graper*, to gather with a hook, from *grape*, a hook, from Teut. (cp. O.H.G. *chrapho*, hook, conn. with CRAMP)], *n.* A berry constituting the fruit of the vine; (*Mil.*) grape-shot; (*pl.*) a mangy tumour on the legs of horses. **sour grapes:** Some object of desire which one disparages because it is out of reach. **grape-brandy,** *n.* Brandy distilled from grapes or wine. **grape-fruit,** *n.* The shaddock, *Citrus decumana.* **grape-house,** *n.* A glass-house for growing vines. **grape-hyacinth,** *n.* A bulbous plant belonging to the genus *Muscari.* **grape-scissors,** *n.pl.* Scissors for thinning out bunches of grapes on the vines, or for dividing bunches at the table. **grape-shot,** *n.* Shot arranged in three tiers between plates, so as to scatter when fired. **grape-stone,** *n.* A stone or seed of the grape. **grape sugar:** Glucose or dextrose. **grape-vine,** *n.* Any species of *Vitis*, esp. *V. vinifera*; (*Skating*) a figure in which the feet, which are both on the ice simultaneously, cut interlacing lines. **grapevine telegraph:** (*fig.*) News, or a rumour, conveyed by underground sources of intelligence. **grape-wort,** *n.* The baneberry, *Actæa spicata.* **grapeless,** *a.* Without grapes; wanting the strength and flavour of the grape. **grapery,** *n.* **grapy,** *a.*

grape (2) (*Sc.*) [GROPE].

graph (1) (grăf) [short for GRAPHIC], *n.* A diagram representing mathematical or chemical relationship and based on two graduated scales.

graph (2) (grăf) [colloq., short for HECTOGRAPH], *n.* A gelatine copying-apparatus or duplicator. *v.t.* To multiply copies by means of this.

-graph [Gr. *-graphos*, from *graphein*, to write], *suf.* -written, -writing, -writer, as in *autograph, lithograph, seismograph, telegraph.* **-grapher,** *suf.* A person versed in the science denoted by the suf. -GRAPHY.

graphic, -al (grăf′ ik, -ăl) [L. *graphicus*, Gr. *graphikos*, from *graphein*, to write], *a.* Pertaining to the art of writing, delineating, engraving, painting, etc.; well delineated; vividly or forcibly descriptive; having the faculty of vivid description; indicating by means of diagrams, etc., instead of numbers, statistics, etc. **graphic formula:** (*Chem.*) A formula representing the relations of the atoms of a molecule to each other. **graphic granite:** (*Min.*) A compound of quartz and feldspar, in which the quartz is disposed through the matrix roughly like Hebrew characters. **-graphic, -al,** *suf.* **graphically, *-icly,** *adv.* **graphicalness, graphicness,** *n.*

graphite (grăf′ īt) [G. *graphit*, as prec.], *n.* (*Min.*) Blacklead, plumbago. **graphitic** (gră fit′ ik), *a.* **graphitoid** (grăf′ i toid), *a.*

graphium (grăf′ i ŭm) [L., from Gr. *grapheion*, as prec.], *n.* (*pl.* **-phia**) A stylus, a pencil.

graphiure (grăf′ i ūr) [Gr. *grapheion*, as prec., *oura*, tail], *n.* A South African rodent resembling the dormouse, with a tufted tail.

grapho- [Gr., from *graphē*, writing, from *graphein*, to write], *comb. form.* Of, pertaining to, or for writing.

grapholite (grăf′ ō līt), *n.* (*Min.*) A kind of slate suitable for writing on.

graphology (grăf ol′ ō ji), *n.* The study of handwriting; the alleged art of inferring character from handwriting; graphic formulæ or notation. **graphologic, -al,** *a.* **graphologist,** *n.*

graphomania (grăf ō mā′ ni ă), *n.* (*Psych.*) An urge to write or scribble maybe senseless words.

graphometer (grăf om′ e tĕr), *n.* A surveying instrument for taking angles. **graphometric,** *a.* Pertaining to a graphometer; of a class of functions pertaining equally to graphic and metric geometry. **graphometrics,** *n.pl.* The science of such functions.

-graphy [Gr. *-graphia*, as prec.], *suf.* Description; style of writing as in *bibliography, geography, lithography, stenography.*

grapnel (grăp′ nĕl) [M.E. *grapenel*, dim., from O.F. *grapin* (F. *grappin*), from *grape*, see GRAPE], *n.* An instrument with several flukes or claws for seizing, grasping, or lifting; a grappling-iron; an anchor with flukes for mooring boats, balloons, etc.

grapple (grăp′ el) [M.F. *grappil*, a ship's grapnel, dim. of *grape*, see GRAPE (1)], *n.* A grappling-iron; a grapnel or similar clutching device; a close hold or grip in wrestling or other contest; a close struggle. *v.t.* To lay fast hold of, to seize, to clutch; to come to close quarters with. *v.i.* To contend or struggle (with or together) in close fight; (*fig.*) to get to close quarters (with a task, subject, etc.) and strive to accomplish, etc. ***grapplement,** *n.* **grappling-iron,** *n.* An iron instrument with claws or hooks for seizing and holding fast.

graptolite (grăp′ tō līt) [Gr. *graptos*, painted, marked, from *graphein*, to write, draw], *n.* (*Palæont.*) A fossil zoophite with a solid axis somewhat resembling a pencil or quill pen. **graptolitic** (-lit′ ik), *a.*

grasp (grasp) [M.E. *grapsen*, cogn. with A.-S. *grāphan*, to GROPE], *v.t.* To seize and hold fast; to lay hold of and keep possession of, esp. with eagerness or greed; (*fig.*) to comprehend with the mind. *v.i.* To clutch (at); to attempt to lay hold. *n.* A fast grip, clutch, or hold; ability to seize and hold; forcible possession, mastery; (*fig.*) intellectual comprehension. **to grasp at:** To try to seize; (*fig.*) to be eager to accept. **graspable,** *a.* **grasper,** *n.* **graspingly,** *adv.* **graspingness,** *n.* **grasping reflex,** *n.* (*Psych.*) The response by an infant's fingers or toes to grasp an object that touches them.

grass (gras) [A.-S. *gærs, græs* (cp. Dut., Icel., and G. *gras*, cogn. with GREEN, GROW, and L. *grāmen*, grass)], *n.* The green-bladed herbage on which cattle, sheep, etc., feed; (*Bot.*) any plant of the *Gramineæ*, distinguished by simple, sheathing leaves, a stem usually jointed and tubular, and flowers enclosed in glumes, including the cereals, reeds, and bamboos, as well as the plants pop. known as grasses; pasture, grazing; (*Mining*) the surface of the ground; (*pl.*) heads or spires of grass-flowers gathered. *v.t.* To cover with grass or turf; to lay on the grass to bleach; to bring to grass, to land (as a fish); (*slang*) to fall, to knock down; to discharge. *v.i.* (*Print.*) To fill a temporary vacancy (said of compositors); (*slang*) to inform against. **to bring to grass:** (*Mining*) To bring up to the pit-head. **to go or send to grass:** To be knocked or to knock down. **to go, put, send,** or **turn out to grass:** To go or send out to pasture; (*fig.*) to go or send out from work, on a holiday, into retirement, etc. **grass-blade,** *n.* A blade of grass. **grass-cloth,** *n.* A fine soft Eastern fabric made from the fibres of the inner bark of the **grass-cloth plant,** *Bœhmeria nivea.* **grass-cutter,** *n.* One who or that which cuts grass. **grass-green,** *a.* Verdant, dark green. *n.* The colour of grass. **grass-grown,** *a.* Overgrown with grass. **grass hand:** (*Print.*) A compositor who fills a temporary vacancy. **grass-land,** *n.* Land kept under grass. **grass of Parnassus:** *Parnassia palustris*, a white-flowered plant belonging to the saxifrage order, growing in moist places. **grass-oil,** *n.* A fragrant volatile oil distilled from various Indian grasses. **grass-plot,** *n.* A plot of ground covered with grass. **grass-snake,** *n.* The common ringed snake. **grass-tree,** *n.* An Australasian tree belonging to the *Xanthorrhæa* or other genera, having spear-like stalks, etc. **grass widow:** (*colloq.*) A wife temporarily separated from her husband; a divorced woman; *a discarded mistress. **grass-widower,** *n.* **grass-widowhood,** *n.* **grass-wrack,** *n.* A seaweed belonging to the genus *Zostera*, also called eel-grass. **grassed,** *a.* (*Golf*) With the face slightly filed back (of a club). **grasser,** *n.* (*Print. slang*) A jobbing printer. **grassless,** *a.* Destitute of grass. **grassy,** *a.* Covered with grass; like grass; green. **grassiness,** *n.*

grasshopper (gras' hop ėr), *n.* An orthopterous insect of various species, esp. *Locusta viridissima*, with hind legs formed for leaping. **grasshopper-beam,** *n.* (*Steam-eng.*) A working-beam pivoted at the end instead of the centre, and acting on the principle of parallel motion. **grasshopper-warbler,** *n.* A small warbler, so called from its note, esp. *Locustella nævia.*

grate (1) (grāt) [late L. *grāta*, var. of *crāta*, L. *crātes*, hurdle], *n.* A frame composed of parallel or cross bars, with interstices, a grating; a frame of iron bars for holding fuel for a fire. *v.t.* To furnish with a grate or grating. **grated,** *a.* **grateless,** *a.*

grate (2) (grāt) [O.F. *grater* (F. *gratter*), from Teut. (cp. Dan. *kratte*, G. *kratzen*, to scratch)], *v.t.* To rub against a rough surface so as to reduce to small particles; to rub, as one thing against another, so as to cause a harsh sound; to grind down; to produce (as a hard, discordant sound) by the collision or friction of rough bodies; (*fig.*) to irritate, to vex, to offend (one's nerves). *v.i.* To rub (upon) so as to emit a harsh, discordant noise; (*fig.*) to have an irritating effect (upon). **grater,** *n.* A utensil with a rough surface for reducing a substance to small particles (*often in comb.*, as *nutmeg-grater*). **grating** (1), *a.* Harsh, discordant, irritating. **gratingly,** *adv.*

grateful (grāt' fụl) [obs. *grate*, agreeable, L. *grātus*, -FUL], *a.* Pleasing, agreeable, acceptable, refreshing; thankful, marked by or indicative of gratitude. **gratefully,** *adv.* **gratefulness,** *n.*

graticulation (grȧ tik ū lā' shŭn) [F., from *graticuler*, to divide with squares, from *graticule*, L. *grāticula*, var. of *crāticula*, dim. of *crātes*, see GRATE (1)], *n.* The division of a design or drawing into squares for the purpose of reducing or enlarging it; a surface divided up in this way.

gratify (grăt' i fī) [F. *gratifier*, L. *grātificārī* (as *grātus*, pleasing, -FY)], *v.t.* To please, to delight; to humour, to satisfy the desire of; to indulge, to give free rein to; to requite, to reward; (*colloq.*) to give a present, gratuity, or bribe to. **gratifying,** *a.* **gratifyingly,** *adv.* **gratification** (-kā' shŭn), *n.* The act of gratifying; that which gratifies; an enjoyment, a satisfaction; a reward, a recompense, a gratuity. **gratifier,** *n.*

gratility (grȧ til' i ti) (*Shak.*) [facet. perversion of GRATUITY].

gratin (gra' tăn) [F., from *gratter*, to grate, see GRATE (2)], *n.* A dish prepared with bread-crumbs and grated cheese; a mode of preparing dishes with bread-crumbs and cheese, and cooking so as to make a light crust.

grating (1) [GRATE (2)].

grating (2) (grā' ting) [GRATE (1)], *n.* An open framework or lattice of metal bars or wooden slats, parallel or crossed; (*Opt.*) a series of parallel wires or lines ruled on glass or the like for producing spectra by diffraction.

gratis (grā' tis) [L., for *grātiis*, abl. of *grātia*, favour], *adv.* and *a.* For nothing; without charge, free.

gratitude (grăt' i tūd) [F., from late L. *grātitūdinem*, nom. *-tūdo*, from *grātus*, pleasing], *n.* Grateful feeling towards a benefactor; thankfulness, appreciation of kindness.

grattoir (grăt' war) [F., scraper], *n.* (*Archæol.*) A flint implement with a shaped edge, used as a scraper.

gratuitous (grȧ tū' i tŭs) [L. *grātuītus*, freely or spontaneously given, as prec.], *a.* Granted without claim or charge; free, voluntary; without cause, motive, or warrant; uncalled for, unnecessary. **gratuitously,** *adv.* **gratuitousness,** *n.*

gratuity (grȧ tū' i ti) [O.F. *gratuité*, late L. *grātuitātem*, nom. *-tas*, cogn. with prec.], *n.* A gift, a present voluntarily given in return for a service, a tip; a bonus or bounty paid to soldiers on retirement, discharge, etc.

gratulate, etc. [CONGRATULATE].

gratulatory (grăt ū lā' tȯr i) [from L. *grātulārī*, to CONGRATULATE], *a.* Congratulatory, complimentary, expressing joy.

graupel (grou' pėl) [G.], *n.* (*Meteor.*) Soft hail.

gravamen (grȧ vā' mėn) [late L., from *gravāre*, to load, from *gravis*, heavy], *n.* (*pl.* **-mina**) (*Law*) The substantial cause of an action; the most serious part of a charge; (*Eccles.*) a memorial from the Lower to the Upper House of Convocation setting forth a grievance; a motion in Convocation.

grave (1) (grāv) [etym. doubtful, perh. from O.F. *grave* (F. *grève*), a strand or shore], *v.t.* To clean by scraping or burning, and cover with pitch and tallow (as a ship's bottom). **graving-dock,** *n.* A dry dock into which vessels are floated for this purpose.

grave (2) (grāv) [A.-S. *grafan*, whence *græf*, a grave (cp. Dut. *graven*, Icel. *grafa*, G. *graben*), cogn. with GROOVE], *v.t.* *To dig; *to bury; to form or shape by cutting or carving into a surface, to engrave; to carve, to sculpture; to produce (a figure, inscription, etc.) by engraving or carving; to impress by or as by engraving or carving. *n.* A hole in the earth for burying a dead body in; a place of burial, a sepulchre; a monument over this, a tomb; (*fig.*) mortality, death, destruction; a place of destruction, extinction, or abandonment. **grave-clothes,** *n.pl.* Wrappings in which the dead are buried. **one foot in the grave:** Very ill, near death; old and ailing. **grave-digger,** *n.* One who digs graves; an insect that buries dead insects, etc., to feed its larvæ. **grave-maker,** *n.* A grave-digger. **grave-making,** *n.* **grave-mound,** *n.* A barrow, a tumulus. **gravestone,** *n.* A stone, usu. inscribed, set over or at the head or foot of a grave. **graveyard,** *n.* A burial ground. **graveless,** *a.* **graven,** *a.* Carved or inscribed. **graven image:** An idol. **graver,** *n.* An engraver; an engraving tool, a burin.

grave (3) (grāv) [F., from L. *gravis*, heavy], *a.* Important, serious, momentous; sedate, solemn, dignified; sombre, plain, not gaudy; (*Mus.*) low in pitch; slow in movement; (*Gram.*) low-pitched, not acute (of accents); *heavy, ponderous. **gravely,** *adv.* ***graveness,** *n.*

gravel (grăv' ėl) [O.F. *gravele*, dim. of *grave*, strand, gravel, cp. GRAVE (1)], *n.* Small water-worn stones or pebbles intermixed with sand, etc.; (*Geol.*) fragments of water-worn rock larger than sand, a stratum of this; (*Mining*) a bed of such material bearing gold; (*Path.*) a disease characterized by the presence of minute concretions in the urine. *v.t.* To cover, lay, or strew with gravel; *to run (a vessel) ashore on sand, gravel, etc.; (*fig.*) to embarrass, to confound, to perplex. **gravel-blind,** *a.* (*Shak.*) Worse than sand-blind. **gravel-pit,** *n.* A pit out of which gravel is dug. **gravel-walk,** *n.* A path laid with gravel. **gravelling,** *n.* The action of laying gravel; a covering of gravel. **gravelly,** *a.*

graven, etc. [GRAVE (2)].

***graveolent** (grȧ vē' ō lėnt) [L. *graveolens -ntem* (*grave*, adv., from *gravis*, GRAVE (3), *olens -ntem*, pres.p. of *olēre*, to smell)], *a.* Smelling strongly and offensively. ***graveolence,** *n.*

Graves (grav) [F.], *n.* A light wine of the claret type, pressed in the Graves district.

gravestone, graveyard [GRAVE (2)].

gravid (grăv' id) [L. *gravidus*, from *gravis*, GRAVE (3)], *a.* Pregnant; containing a fœtus.

gravigrade (grăv' i grād) [L. *gravis*, GRAVE (3), *gradī*, to walk], *a.* (*Zool.*) Walking heavily. *n.* (*Zool.*) One of the heavy-walking animals, like the elephant or the megatherium; an animal of the group *Gravigrada*.

gravimeter (grȧ vim′ ė tėr), *n.* (*Phys.*) An instrument for determining the specific gravities of bodies. **gravimetric** (-met′ rik), *a.* **gravimetry** (grȧ vim′ ė tri), *n.*

gravitate (grăv′ i tāt) [mod. L. *gravitāre*, from *gravis*, GRAVE (3)], *v.i.* To be acted on by gravity; to be attracted, to tend (towards); to tend downwards, to sink, to settle down; (*fig.*) to be powerfully drawn (towards). *v.t.* (*Diamond-digging*) To treat (gravel) by hand or machinery so as to cause the heavy particles to sift to the bottom. **gravitation** (-tā′ shŭn), *n.* The act or process of gravitating; the force of gravity. **gravitational,** *a.* **gravitative** (grăv′ i tā tiv), *a.*

gravity (grăv′ i ti) [from *gravité*, or directly from L. *gravitātem*, nom. *-tas*, from *gravis*, GRAVE (3)], *n.* Weight, heaviness; importance, seriousness, enormity; solemnity, sedateness, sobriety, grave demeanour; (*Phys.*) the force causing bodies to tend towards the centre of the earth; the degree of intensity of this force; the similar tendency towards the centre of other bodies. **specific gravity:** (*Phys.*) The relative weight or density of a solid or fluid expressed by the ratio of its weight to that of an equal volume of a substance taken as a standard, water in the case of liquids and solids, air for gases. **gravity feed:** A feed or supply in which the material (oil, grain, etc.) runs downhill.

gravure (grăv′ ūr) [F., from *graver*, to ENGRAVE], *n.* An engraving; (short for) photogravure.

gravy (grā′ vi) [etym. doubtful, perh. O.F. *grané*, L. *grānātus*, full of grains (*grānum*, GRAIN), misread *graué*], *n.* The fat and juice from meat during and after cooking; a sauce made with this or other ingredients. **gravy-beef,** *n.* A part of leg of beef cooked for its gravy. **gravy-boat,** *n.* A boat-shaped bowl or dish for holding gravy. **gravy-dish,** *n.* A meat-dish with a hollow for gravy; a dish in which gravy is served.

gray [GREY].

grayling (grā′ ling) [GREY, -LING], *n.* A fresh-water fish with a large dorsal and an adipose fin, belonging to the genus *Thymallus*, esp. the European *T. vulgaris*.

graze (1) (grāz) [A.-S. *grasian*, from *græs*, GRASS], *v.i.* To eat growing grass; to supply grass for grazing (of land, fields, etc.); to feed, to browse; (*fig.*) to move along devouring. *v.t.* To feed (cattle, etc.) on growing grass; to supply with pasturage; to tend (cattle, etc.) at pasture; to pasture; to feed on, to eat. **grazer,** *n.* An animal that grazes. **grazing** (grā′ zing), *n.* The act of pasturing or feeding on grass; a pasture.

graze (2) (grāz) [etym. doubtful, prob. from prec.], *v.t.* To touch, rub, or brush slightly in passing; to scrape or abrade in rubbing past. *v.i.* To touch some person or thing lightly in passing; to pass (along, by, past, etc.) in light or momentary contact. *n.* A slight touch or rub in passing; a slight abrasion.

grazier (grā′ zhėr), *n.* One who pastures cattle, and rears and fattens them for market. **graziery,** *n.*

grazioso (grăt zi ō′ zō) [It.], *a.* (*Mus.*) Graceful, elegant. **graziosamente,** *adv.* Elegantly.

grease (grēs) [O.F. *graisse*, L. *crassus*, adj., fat], *n.* Animal fat in a melted or soft state; oily or fatty matter of any kind; inflammation of a horse's heels. *v.t.* (grēs, grēz) To smear, lubricate, or soil with grease; (*fig*) to cause to go smoothly, hence to bribe; (*Farriery*) to infect (horses) with grease. **grease-box,** *n.* A holder on a wheel or axle for grease as a lubricant. **grease-cup,** *n.* (*Mach.*) A cup-shaped vessel through which grease is driven into machinery. **grease-gun,** *n.* A syringe for injecting grease or oil into machinery. **grease-paint,** *n.* A paste used for painting the face in theatrical make-up. **grease-trap,** *n.* A contrivance fixed in drains for catching grease from sinks, etc. **greaser** (grē′ sėr, -zėr), *n.* One who or that which greases; (*U.S.A. colloq.*) a Mexican or Spanish-American.

greasy (grē′ zi), *a.* Smeared, saturated, or soiled with grease; made of or like grease; unctuous, oily, exuding grease; slimy or slippery with something having the effect of grease; (of horses) affected with the disease called grease; corpulent, fat; gross, unpleasantly unctuous; *indelicate, indecent. **greasily,** *adv.* **greasiness,** *n.*

great (grāt) [A.-S. *grēat* (cp. Dut. *groot*, G. *gross*)], *a.* Large in bulk, number, amount, extent, or degree; very large, big, vast; beyond the ordinary, extreme; important, weighty, momentous, critical; of the highest importance, capital (of letters), pre-eminent, the chief; of exceptional ability, highly gifted, possessing genius; (*colloq.*) very skilful, experienced, or knowing (at); having lofty moral qualities, magnanimous, noble; grand, majestic, sublime; big with child, gravid; (*fig.*) teeming, pregnant (with); excessive, grievous, burdensome; notorious; denoting a step of ascending or descending consanguinity (as **great-grandfather,** the father of a grandfather; **great-grandson,** the son of a grandson, etc.). *n.* (*collect.*) Great people; (*pl.*) [GREATS]; *the mass, the bulk, the gross. **to be great at:** To be skilful at. **Great Assize, Day,** or **Inquest:** The Day of Judgment. ***great-bellied,** *a.* Far advanced in pregnancy. **great-coat,** *n.* An overcoat. **greatcoated,** *a.* **greatcoatless,** *a.* **Great Dane,** *n.* A breed of large dog. **Great Britain** [BRITAIN]. **great go:** The final examination for the degree of B.A. at Cambridge. **great gross:** 144 dozen. ***great-grown,** *a.* Increased in power or importance. **great-hearted,** *a.* High-spirited, magnanimous; brave. **great house:** The hall, mansion, or principal residence in a country place. **great organ** [ORGAN]. **Great Powers:** The leading States of the world collectively. **great primer:** (*Print.*) An 18-point type. **Great Seal** [SEAL (2)]. **Great Spirit:** The name given by the N. American Indians to their deity. **great toe:** The big toe. **greaten,** *v.t.* To make greater, to enlarge; to magnify. *v.i.* To become greater, to dilate; *to become pregnant. **greatly,** *adv.* In a great degree, much, exceedingly; nobly, magnanimously; *grandly, illustriously. **greatness,** *n.* **greats,** *n.pl.* The final examination at Oxford for B.A., esp. for honours in *Literæ Humaniores*.

greave (grēv) [O.F. *greve*, shin; etym. doubtful], *n.* (*usu. pl.*) Armour for the legs.

greaves (grēvz) [cp. L.G. *greven*], *n.pl.* Fibrous scraps or refuse of melted tallow, used for feeding dogs and by anglers as bait.

grebe (grēb) [F. *grèbe*, etym. doubtful], *n.* A diving-bird of the genus *Podiceps*, with lobed feet and no tail.

Grecian (grē′ shȧn) [L. *Græcia*, Greece, -AN], *a.* Pertaining to Greece. *n.* A Greek; one who adopted Greek manners or habits; a Greek scholar; a senior boy at Christ's Hospital. **Grecian bend:** An affected walk fashionable with women about 1870, in which the body was bent forward from the hips. **Grecian knot:** A mode of dressing women's hair with a knot at the back of the head. **Grecian nose:** A nose continuing the line of the forehead. **Grecianize,** *v.t.* and *i.*

Grecism, Grecize, etc. [GRÆCISM].

grecque (grek) [F., fem. of *grec*, GREEK], *n.* An ornamental Greek fret; a coffee-strainer or a coffee-pot fitted with a strainer.

***gree** (1) (grē) [O.F. *gré*, L. *grātum*, nom. *-tus*, pleasing], *n.* Goodwill, favour, pleasure, satisfaction. *v.i.* To come into agreement; to be in agreement. *v.t.* To reconcile.

***gree** (2) (grē) [O.F. *gré*, L. *gradum*, step, see GRADE], *n.* (*pl.* **grees, grece, greece,** often used as sing. in the sense of a staircase or a flight of steps) A step; a degree; a stage or degree of rank; degree, rank; the prize, the pre-eminence.

greed (grēd), *n.* Greediness; avarice, insatiable desire or covetousness. **greedy** [A.-S. *grǣdig* (cp. Dut. *gretig*, Dan. *graadig*)], *a.* Having an inordinate desire for food or drink, voracious, gluttonous; eager to obtain, covetous, desirous (of). **greedily,** *adv.* **greediness,** *n.*

Greek (grēk) [A.-S. *Grēcas, Crēcas*, pl., L. *Graecus*, from Gr. *Graikos*, ancient name for the Hellenes], *n.* A native of Greece; one of the Greek race; the language of Greece; (*fig.*) something one does not understand; (*slang*) a tricky fellow, a knave, a cheat. *a.* Pertaining to Greece or its people or to the Hellenic race. **when Greek meets Greek:** Describing an equal encounter of champions. **Greek Church:** The Orthodox or Eastern Church, including most of the Christians in Greece, Russia, the Balkan States, and the Turkish Empire, which separated from Rome in the 9th cent. **Greek cross** [CROSS]. **Greek fire** [FIRE]. **Greek gift:** A gift bestowed with some treacherous motive (in alln. to *Æneid* ii, 49). ***Greekish,** *a.*

green (grēn) [A.-S. *grēne* (cp. Dut. *groen*, G. *grün*, cogn. with *grōwan*, to GROW)], *a.* Having a colour like growing herbage, of the colour in the spectrum between blue and yellow; unripe, immature; undeveloped, inexperienced, easily imposed on; fresh, not withered, not dried, seasoned, cured, dressed, or tanned; (of a wound) not healed; pale, sickly. *n.* The colour of growing herbage; a colour composed of blue and yellow; a green pigment or dye; a grassy plot or piece of land (*esp. in comb.*, as *bowling-green*); (*pl.*) fresh leaves or branches of trees; (*pl.*) the young leaves and stems of plants of the cabbage kind, used for food; (*fig.*) vigour, youth, prime. *v.i.* To become or grow green. *v.t.* To make green; (*slang*) to hoax. **to get the green light:** (*colloq.*) To get permission to go ahead with a project. **greener,** *n.* (*slang*) A green or raw hand, a novice; a blackleg, a scab. **Paris Green:** A poisonous arsenical pigment of vivid green hue, used also as an insecticide. **green belt:** (*Civic planning*) An area around a city in which building is restricted. **green cheese:** Unripened cheese, whey cheese; cheese coloured with sage. **Green Cloth:** A Board in the royal household under the Master of the Household, chiefly concerned with the commissariat. **green cloth** or **table:** A gaming-table. **green-coloured,** *a.* Pale, sickly. **green-crop,** *n.* A crop of food-stuff in the green state. **green drake:** The May-fly. **green-earth,** *n.* (*Min.*) Glauconite. **green eye:** (*fig.*) Jealousy. **green-eyed,** *a.* Having green eyes; (*fig.*) seeing things with jealous eyes. **the green-eyed monster:** Jealousy. **green fat:** The green gelatinous part of the turtle, much esteemed by epicures. **green heart,** *n.* A hard-timbered West Indian tree, *Nectandra rodiæi*, which is used for dock-gates, ship-building, fishing-rods, etc., and yields a febrifuge. **greenhide,** *n.* (*Austral.*) Untanned raw hide as used for whips. **green laver:** An edible seaweed, *Ulva lactuca*, and *U. latissima*. **greenleek,** *n.* (*Austral.*) A small green parrot. **green manuring,** *n.* (*Agric.*) The cultivation and ploughing-in of a crop of vetch, rape, etc. **green-room:** (*Theat.*) A room in which actors and actresses wait during the intervals of their parts; a room in a warehouse where new or green cloth is received. **Green-sand,** *n.* (*Geol.*) Two series of beds of sandstone (largely consisting of green-earth or glauconite) called the Upper and Lower Greensand, in the Cretaceous series. **green-sickness,** *n.* Chlorosis. **green snake:** The popular name of two harmless snakes in the United States. **green stick:** (*Path.*) A form of fracture to which children are very liable in which one side of the bone is broken and the other merely bent. **green-stone,** *n.* (*Min.*) A greenish eruptive rock consisting of a crystalline granular admixture of feldspar and hornblende; a fine-grained stone used for putting a very keen edge on surgical instruments; a kind of jade. **green stuff:** Green vegetables for culinary use. **green tea:** Tea prepared by drying with steam. ***green vitriol:** Crystallized ferrous sulphate. **greenery,** *n.* **greening,** *n.* The act of becoming green; greenness; a kind of apple which is green when ripe. **greenish,** *a.* **greenishness,** *n.* **greenly,** *adv.* **greenness,** *n.* ***greenth,** *n.* **greeny,** *a.*

greenback (grēn′ băk), *n.* A legal-tender banknote first issued by the U.S.A. in 1862, the back being printed in green; a note issued by any national bank in U.S.A.

greenfinch (grēn′ finch), *n.* A common British singing-bird, *Chloris chloris*, with green and gold plumage.

greengage (grēn′ gāj) [Sir Wm. *Gage* who introduced it *c.* 1725], *n.* A green, fine-flavoured variety of *Prunus domestica*.

greengrocer (grēn′ grō sĕr), *n.* A retailer of green vegetables, fruit, etc. **greengrocery,** *n.*

greenhorn (grēn′ hôrn), *n.* A simpleton, a raw person.

greenhouse (grēn′ hous), *n.* A glass-house for cultivating and preserving tender plants.

greenkeeper (grēn′ kē pėr), *n.* The head man in charge of a golf-course.

greenshank (grēn′ shăngk), *n.* A large sandpiper, *Tringa nebularia*.

greensward (grēn′ swôrd), *n.* Turf covered with grass.

greentail (grēn′ tāl), *n.* The grannom.

greenweed (grēn′ wēd), *n.* *Genista tinctoria* and *G. pilosa*, used in dyeing.

Greenwich (grin′ ij) [borough in S.E. London, where an astronomical observatory was situated from 1646 to 1958], *a.* Pertaining to Greenwich or its meridian. **Greenwich time:** Mean time for the meridian of Greenwich, adopted as the standard time in Great Britain and several other countries.

greenwood (grēn′ wud), *n.* A wood in summer; wood which has become green in tint under the influence of the fungus *Chlorosplenium aeruginosum*. *a.* Pertaining to a greenwood.

greet (1) (grēt) [A.-S. *grētan* (cp. Dut. *groeten*, G. *grüssen*)], *v.t.* To address with a salutation at meeting; to accost, to hail; to receive at meeting or on arrival (with speech, gesture, etc.); to meet; *to congratulate. *v.i.* To exchange greetings. **greeting,** *n.* The act of saluting or welcoming; a salutation, a welcome.

greet (2) (grēt) [A.-S. *grǣtan* (cp. Icel. *grāta*, Goth. *grētan*, to weep) blended with *grēotan*, etym. doubtful], *v.i.* (*now chiefly Sc.*) To weep, to cry, to lament. *n.* Weeping, lamentation.

greffier (gref′ i ėr) [F., from *greffe*, a style, O.F. *grafe*, GRAFT], *n.* A registrar, clerk, or notary (chiefly in the Channel Isles and foreign countries).

gregarious (grė gâr′ i ŭs), ***gregarian** (-ăn) [L. *gregārius*, from *grex gregis*, flock, herd], *a.* Living or going in flocks or herds; tending to associate, not solitary; (*Bot.*) growing in clusters or in association with others. **gregariously,** *adv.* **gregariousness,** *n.*

Gregorian (grė gôr′ i ăn) [late L. *Gregōrius*, Gr. *Grēgorios*, Gregory, -AN], *a.* Pertaining to or established or produced by Gregory. *n.* A Gregorian chant; a member of a secret brotherhood established in England in the 18th century. **Gregorian calendar:** The reformed calendar introduced by Pope Gregory XIII. in 1582; hence **Gregorian epoch, style, year. Gregorian chant:** Choral music arranged by Pope Gregory I. (590–604); plain-song. **Gregorian telescope:** The first form of reflecting telescope, invented by James Gregory (*c.* 1663).

Gregory powder (greg′ ŏ ri) [James *Gregory* (1758–1822), Sc. physician], *n.* The compound powder of rhubarb, magnesium carbonate, and ginger, used as an aperient, sometimes called **Gregory.**

gremial (grē′ mi ăl) [late L. *gremiālis*, from *gremium*, the lap], *a.* Of or pertaining to the lap or bosom; (*Univ.*) dwelling in the bosom of the University, resident; intimate, confined to members. *n.* (*R.-C. Ch.*) An episcopal vestment covering the lap, orig. to prevent drops of chrism falling on the vestments during ordination, etc.

gremlin (grem' lim), *n.* (*Aviat. slang*) A sprite that accompanies an airman in the air, performing good or ill-natured tricks on him.

grenade (grė nād') [F., from Sp. *granada*, orig. POMEGRANATE], *n.* A small explosive shell thrown by hand or fired from a rifle; a glass shell containing chemicals for extinguishing fires, discovering leakages in drains, etc.

grenadier (gren å dēr'), *n.* Originally a foot-soldier armed with grenades; a member of what used to be the first company of every battalion of foot, chosen for long service and approved courage; the title is now confined in the British Army to one regiment, the Grenadier Guards; a South African weaver-bird, *Pyromelana oryx*, with vivid red and black plumage.

grenadine (1) (gren' å dēn) [F., perh. from *Granada*, city in Spain], *n.* A thin, gauzy, silk or woollen fabric for women's dresses, etc.

grenadine (2) (gren' å dēn) [F. *grenadin*, etym. doubtful], *n.* A fancy dish, usu. of fillets of veal or poultry, larded and glazed.

grenado [GRENADE].

gressorial (gres sôr' i ål) [L. *gressor*, walker, from *gradī*, to walk, -IAL], *a.* (*Zool.*) Adapted for walking, applied to the feet of birds having three toes in front (two of them connected) and one behind.

Gretna Green [see MARRIAGE].

***greve** [GREAVE (1)].

grew *past* [GROW]. **grewsome** [GRUESOME].

grey (grā) [A.-S. *grǽg* (cp. Dut. *grauw*, Icel. *grār*, G. *grau*)], *a.* Of a colour between white and black; ash-coloured; dull, clouded, dim; dark, dismal, depressing; hoary with age; old, aged, pertaining to old age; ancient; mature, experienced. *n.* A grey colour, grey pigment; grey light, twilight, cold, sunless light; grey clothes; a grey animal, esp. a horse; (*pl.*) [GREYS]. *v.t.* To make grey; (*Phot.*) to give a soft effect to by covering the negative in printing with ground glass. *v.i.* To become grey. **greyback,** *n.* (*Austral.*) A scarab beetle found in Queensland. **grey-coated,** *a.* Having a grey coat. **grey drake:** A species of *Ephemera*. **grey-eyed,** *a.* Having grey eyes. **grey falcon:** The hen-harrier; also the peregrine falcon. **grey fly:** (*Milton*) Probably a dor beetle. **Grey Friar:** A Franciscan friar. **grey goose:** The grey lag. **grey-haired, -headed,** *a.* Having grey hair; old, time-worn; of long service (in). **grey-hen,** *n.* The female of the black grouse. ***grey-hooded,** *a.* Grey; dusky. **grey lag** [LAG, from its staying long for a migrant]: The European wild goose, *Anser ferus*, the original of the domestic goose. ***grey malkin:** A grey cat. **grey matter:** (*Anat.*) Formerly applied to the masses of nerve-cells in the central nervous system. **grey nurse,** *n.* A shark found in E. Australian waters. **grey tin,** *n.* (*Metal.*) The powder into which tin crumbles when cooled to a low temperature. **grey wether:** (*usu. pl.*) Detached blocks of sarsen or sandstone occurring chiefly in south-west England, often in the form of circles. **greyish,** *a.* **greyly,** *adv.* **greyness,** *n.* **Greys,** *n.pl.* A British cavalry regiment, the 2nd Dragoons (orig. Scottish), so called from all the horses being greys.

greybeard (grā' bērd), *n.* An old man; a large earthen jar for spirit; a hydroid polyp *Sertularia argentea*, infesting oyster-beds. *a.* Having a grey beard. **greybeard lichen,** *n.* *Usnea barbata*. **grey-bearded,** *a.*

greyhead (grā' hed), *n.* A person with grey hair; an old male sperm whale.

greyhound (grā' hound), *n.* A variety of dog used for coursing, characterized by slender form, keen sight, and swiftness. **greyhound racing:** Racing greyhounds in pursuit of an electrically-propelled dummy hare. **ocean greyhound:** A swift ship.

greystone (grā' stōn), A compact volcanic grey or greenish rock, composed of feldspar and augite.

greywacke (grā' wăk ė) [G. *grauwacke* (*grau*, GREY, WACKE)], *n.* (*Geol.*) A gritstone or conglomerate, usually consisting of small fragments of quartz, flinty slate, etc., cemented together, occurring chiefly in Silurian strata.

grice (grīs) [Icel. *grīss*], *n.* (*now chiefly Sc.*) A young or sucking-pig; (*Her.*) a wild boar.

grid (grid) [short for GRIDIRON], *n.* A grating of parallel bars; a gridiron for cooking; (*Elec.*) a perforated or ridged plate used in a storage battery; a system of main transmission lines; (*Mining*) a griddle; (*Naut.*) a gridiron for docking ships; (*Therm.*) an electrode placed in a thermionic tube between two other electrodes for the purpose of controlling the flow of current between them. **grid bias,** *n.* Voltage applied to the grid of a valve. **grid circuit,** *n.* The circuit connected between grid and cathode. **grid current,** *n.* The current passing between grid and cathode. **grid leak,** *n.* A fixed resistance for the leakage of electrons from the grid circuit. **grid potentiometer,** *n.* A mechanism to facilitate critical adjustment of grid potential or grid-bias.

griddle (grid' ėl) [A.-F. *gridil*, O.F. *greil* (F. *grille*), perh. from L. *crātīcula*, dim. of *crātes*, a hurdle], *n.* A circular iron plate for baking cakes; (*Mining*) a wire-bottomed sieve or screen. *v.t.* (*Mining*) To screen with a griddle. **griddle-cake,** *n.* A cake baked on a griddle.

gride (grīd) [metathesis of GIRD (2)], *v.i.* To grind, scrape, or jar (along, through, etc.); to grate. ****v.t.*** To pierce, to cut; to cause to grate. *n.* A grating sound.

gridelin (grid' ė lin) [F. (*gris-de-lin*, flax-grey)], *n.* A colour of mixed white and red, a grey-violet or purple.

gridiron (grid' ī ėrn) [M.E. *gredire*, as GRIDDLE (assim. to IRON)], *n.* A grated iron utensil for broiling fish, flesh, etc.; (*Naut.*) a framework of parallel timbers or iron beams for supporting a ship in dry dock; (*Theat.*) a framework above the stage for supporting the apparatus for drop-scenes, etc.; (*Railway*) a series of parallel lines for shunting goods trains; (*Radio.*) wire network between cathode and anode; (*Am.*) a football field. **gridiron manœuvre:** (*Naval*) A movement in which ships in two parallel columns cross each to the opposite column. **gridiron pendulum:** A compensation pendulum constructed with parallel bars of different metals.

grief (grēf) [O.F., from *grever*, to GRIEVE], *n.* Deep sorrow or mental distress due to loss, disaster, or disappointment; regret, sadness; that which causes sorrow or sadness; bodily pain. **to come to grief:** To meet with disaster; to fail; to come to ruin. **griefless,** *a.* **grieflessness,** *n.*

grievance (grē' våns) [O.F. *grevance*, from foll.], *n.* That which causes grief; a wrong, an injustice; a ground for complaint. **to air a grievance:** To state a cause of complaint. **grievance-monger,** *n.* A confirmed grumbler.

grieve (1) (grēv) [O.F. *grever*, L. *gravāre*, to burden, from *gravis*, GRAVE (3)], *v.t.* To annoy; to cause pain or sorrow to; to lament, to sorrow over. *v.i.* To feel grief, to mourn, to sorrow. **grievingly,** *adv.* **grievous,** *a.* Causing grief or pain; hard to be borne, distressing, oppressive; hurtful, injurious; flagrant, atrocious, heinous. **grievously,** *adv.* **grievousness,** *n.*

grieve (2) (grēv) [Sc. and North., from O. Northumbrian *grǣfa*, A.-S. *gerēfa*, REEVE], *n.* An overseer, steward, or bailiff; *a sheriff.

grievous [GRIEVE (1)].

griffin (1), **-on** (1) (grif' in, -ôn) [F. *griffon*, L. *grȳphus*, *gryps*, Gr. *grups*, from *grupos*, hooked, hook-beaked], *n.* A fabulous creature, with the body and legs of a lion, the head and wings of an eagle, and listening ears, emblematic of strength, agility, and watchfulness; (*slang*) a betting tip; a hint; (*fig.*) a watchful guardian, a duenna. **griffin-like,** *a.*

griffin (2) (grif′ in) [etym. unknown], *n.* (old *Ang.-Ind.*) A new-comer from Europe, a greenhorn. **griffinage, griffinhood, griffinship,** *n.* **griffinish,** *a.*

griffon (1) (grif′ on), *n.* A vulture, *Gyps fulvus*, usu. called **griffon-vulture.**

griffon (2) (grif′ ôn) [F., ident. by Littré with *griffon*, GRIFFIN (1)], *n.* A foreign variety of dog like a terrier, with short, coarse hair.

grig (grig) [etym. doubtful (perh. the later senses distinct and onomat. in orig.)], *n.* A sand-eel or a young eel; a cricket or grasshopper; a lively or merry person.

grill (gril) [F. *griller*, from *gril*, O.F. *graïl*, prob. as GRIDDLE], *v.t.* To broil on a gridiron; (*fig.*) to bake or torture as if by fire; (*colloq.*) to interrogate severely. *n.* Meat, etc. broiled; a gridiron. **grill-room,** *n.* A room in a restaurant where meat, etc. is grilled and served. ***grillade** (gri lād′), *n.* The act of grilling; grilled meat, etc. **griller,** *n.*

grillage (gril′ ȧj) [foll., -AGE], *n.* A structure of sleepers and cross-beams forming a foundation in marshy soil for a pier, wharf, or the like.

grille (gril) [F., as GRIDDLE (cp. GRILL)], *n.* An open grating, railing, or screen of lattice-work, to enclose or shut a sacred or private place, or to fill an opening in a door, etc.; (*Tennis*) a square opening in the end wall on the hazard side of the court; (*Fish-culture*) a frame with glass tubes for fish-eggs during incubation.

grilse (grils) [etym. doubtful (perh. a corr. of O.F. *grisle*, grey)], *n.* A young salmon when it first returns from the sea, usu. in its second year.

grim (grim) [A.-S. (cp. G. *grimm*), cogn. with GRAME], *a.* Stern, relentless, severe, unyielding; of a forbidding aspect; savage, cruel; hideous, ghastly. ***grim-looked,** *a.* **like grim death:** With determination, unyieldingly. **grimly,** *a.* Grim, stern-looking. *adv.* In a grim manner. ***grimliness,** *n.* **grimness,** *n.*

grimace (gri mās′) [F., etym. doubtful], *n.* A distortion of the features, a wry face, expressing disgust, contempt, affectation, etc. *v.i.* To make grimaces. **grimaced,** *a.* Distorted. **grimacer, grimacier** (gri mā′ ser, -sēr), *n.*

grimalkin (gri măl′, -mawl′ kin) [GREY, *Malkin*, dim. of *Maud, Matilda*], *n.* An old cat, esp. a she-cat; (*fig.*) a jealous or spiteful old woman.

grime (grīm) [cp. W. Flem. *grijm*, Dan. *grim*, Swed. dial. *grima*, a spot or smut], *n.* Dirt, smut; dirt deeply engrained. *v.t.* To dirty; to begrime. **grimy,** *a.* **grimily,** *adv.* **griminess,** *n.*

Grimm's law (grimz law) [Jakob *Grimm* (1785–1863), German philologist], *n.* (*Philol.*) A law formulated by Grimm respecting the modification of consonants in the most important of the Aryan languages.

grin (1) (grin) [A.-S. *grennian*, cp. O.H.G. *grennan* to mutter (prob. the sense was influenced by the root seen in O.H.G. *grīnan*, to distort the face)], *v.i.* To show the teeth as in laughter, derision, or pain; to smile in a malicious, sickly, or affected manner; to gape, to stand wide open (as a joint). *v.t.* To express by grinning. *n.* The act of grinning; a smile with the teeth showing. **grinningly,** *adv.*

***grin** (2) (grin) [A.-S. *grīn*], *n.* A snare, a noose.

grind (grīnd) [A.-S. *grindan* (cp. Dut. *grendan*, and perh. L. *frendere*, to gnash, grind)], *v.t.* (*past & p.p.* **ground**) To reduce to powder or fine particles by crushing and friction; to produce (meal, etc.) by this process; to wear down, sharpen, smooth, or polish by friction, esp. on a grindstone; to grate; (*fig.*) to oppress with exactions; to work (a mill); to turn the handle of (various appliances); (*fig.*) to study laboriously; to teach (a pupil in a subject) laboriously. *v.i.* To perform the act of grinding; to be rubbed together; to be ground; to admit of being ground; to grate; to rub gratingly; to toil hard and distastefully, to drudge; to study laboriously. *n.* The act or process of grinding; hard and monotonous work; hard study, esp. for an examination; a turn at the handle of a machine or instrument. **grinder,** *n.* One who or that which grinds (*esp. in comb.* as *knife-grinder*); a grinding-machine; a molar tooth, a tooth generally; (*slang*) a coach, a crammer; one who studies hard. **grindery,** *n.* A place where tools, etc. are ground; materials and tools for leather-workers; a shop where these materials are sold. **grindingly,** *adv.* **grindstone,** *n.* A flat circular stone, used for grinding tools; *a millstone. **to keep one's nose to the grindstone:** To stick to one's work.

gringo (gring′ gō) [Mex. Sp.], *n.* A contemptuous name for an Englishman or Anglo-American.

grip (1) (grip) [A.-S. *gripa*, a handful, and *gripe*, a clutch, both cogn. with GRIPE], *n.* The act of seizing or holding firmly; a firm grasp, a clutch; the power of grasping; a particular mode of clasping hands; the part of a weapon, instrument, etc., that is held in the hand; a grasping or clutching part of a machine, a clutch; a grappling-tool; (*pl.*) close combat, hand-to-hand conflict; (*fig.*) power of holding the attention; (*Am.*) a suitcase. *v.t.* (*past & p.p.* **gripped**) To seize hold of; to grasp or hold tightly; (*fig.*) to hold the attention of. *v.i.* To take firm hold. **the grip** or ***grippe*** [cp. F. *la grippe*]: Influenza. **grip-brake,** *n.* A brake that is worked by gripping with the hand. **grip-sack,** *n.* (*Am.*) A traveller's hand-bag, suitcase. **gripper,** *n.*

grip (2) (grip) [A.-S. *grȳpe, grēpe*, a trench, a burrow], *n.* A small ditch or furrow. **v.t.* To trench, to drain.

gripe (grīp) [A.-S. *grīpan* (cp. Dut. *grȳpen*, Goth. *greipan*, G. *greipen*)], *v.t.* To seize and hold firmly; to clutch, to pinch; to oppress; to affect the bowels of with colic pains. *v.i.* To lay fast hold of anything; (*fig.*) to get money by extortion; (*Naut.*) to come up too close to the wind against the helm as in sailing close-hauled. *n.* A grasp, a firm hold with the hands; a pinch, a squeeze; the part by which anything is grasped; a handle or hilt; (*fig.*) clutch, power, control, bondage; pinching distress; a mean, niggardly fellow; (*Mech.*) a clutch, a brake applied to the wheel of a crane or derrick; (*pl.*) pains in the abdomen; (*Naut.*) the fore-foot of a ship, the forward end of the keel; a series of ropes, dead-eyes, and hooks, fastened to ring-bolts in the deck, for securing boats; one of a pair of bands passing round a boat when suspended from the davits. **griper,** *n.* An extortioner, an oppressor. **griping,** *a.* Grasping, greedy; pinching the bowels. **gripingly,** *adv.* ***gripple,** *a.* Griping, exacting; niggardly. **grippy,** *a.*

grippe [GRIP (1)]. **gripper** [GRIP (1)].

Griqua (grē′ kwȧ) [South African], *n.* One of a half-caste people in South Africa, descended from Dutch settlers and native women.

grisaille (gri zāl′, gri zā′ yė) [F., from *gris*, grey, O.H.G. *grīs*, etym. unknown], *n.* A style of painting or staining in grey monochrome, esp. on stained glass, representing solid bodies in relief, such as ornament of cornices, etc.

grisamber (gris ăm′ bėr), *n.* (*Milton*) Ambergris.

grise (1) [GREE (2)]. **grise** (2) [GRICE].

griseous (griz′ ė ŭs) [med. L. *griseus*, O.H.G. *grīs*, see GRISAILLE], *a.* Bluish-grey.

grisette (gri zet′) [F., from *gris*, see GRISAILLE], *n.* *A grey woollen fabric, used for dresses by women of the working classes; a girl or young woman of the French working classes, esp. one of gay life.

griskin (gris′ kin) [GRICE, -KIN], *n.* The lean part of the loin of a bacon pig.

grisled [GRIZZLED].

grisly (griz′ li) [A.-S. *grīslīc* (*grīs-* in *ā-grīsan*, to shudder, *-līc*, -LY)], *a.* Horrible, terrible, fearful, grim. **adv.* Horribly, terribly, fearfully.

grist (1) (grist) [A.-S. *grīst*, cogn. with GRIND], *n.* Corn to be ground; corn which has been ground; malt for a brewing. **to bring grist to the mill:**

To bring profitable business or gain. **grist-mill,** *n.* A mill for grinding corn.

grist (2) (grist) [etym. doubtful; perh. conn. with GIRD (1)], *n.* A size of rope as denoted by the number and thickness of the strands.

gristle (gris' el) [A.-S., etym. doubtful (cp. O.Fris. and M.L.G. *gristal*)], *n.* Cartilage, esp. when found in meat. **gristly,** *a.*

grit (1) (grit) [A.-S. *grēot* (cp. Icel. *grjōt*, G. *griess*), allied to GROUT], *n.* Coarse rough particles such as sand or gravel; gritstone, a compact sandstone of sharp siliceous grain; the character of a stone as regards texture or grain; (*colloq.*) firmness, determination, pluck. *v.i.* (*past & p.p.* **gritted**) To be ground together; to give out a grating sound; to grate. *v.t.* To grind or grate (as the teeth). **gritty,** *a.* **grittiness,** *n.*

grit (2) (*Sc.*) [GREAT].

grits (grits) [A.-S. *gryttan* (cp. M.Dut. *grutte*, barley, G. *grütze*, also GROATS)], *n.pl.* Husked and granulated but unground meal, esp. coarse oatmeal.

gritstone (grit' stōn), *n.* A coarse-grained sandstone.

grizzle (1) (griz' ėl) [O.F. *grisel*, from *gris*, grey, see GRISAILLE], *a.* Grey. *n.* A grey-haired man; grey hair; a kind of wig; a grey colour; *roan-coloured. **grizzled,** *a.* Grey, grey-haired; interspersed with grey. **grizzly,** *a.* Grey, greyish. *n.* A grizzly-bear. **grizzly-bear,** *n.* A North American bear, *Ursus ferox*, of great size and strength.

grizzle (2) (griz' ėl) [prov., etym. doubtful], *v.i.* To worry, to fret; to whimper. *n.* One who grizzles.

groan (grōn) [A.-S. *grānian* (cp. G. *greinen*, to GRIN)], *v.i.* To utter a deep moaning sound, as in pain or grief; (*fig.*) to grieve; to suffer hardship; to be burdened; to long or strive with or as with groans. *v.t.* To silence or express disapprobation of by groans; to utter with groans. *n.* A low moaning sound, as of one in pain or sorrow; such a sound simulated in derision or disapprobation. ***groanful,** *a.* **groaningly,** *adv.*

groat (grōt) [M.E. and L.G. *grote* (cp. M.Dut. *groot*), cogn. with GREAT], *n.* *A small silver coin, value 4d., coined 1357–1662; the silver fourpenny-piece coined 1836–56; any trifling sum. **not worth a groat:** Worthless. **groatsworth,** *n.* As much as can be bought for a groat.

groats (grōts) [cp. A.-S. *grūt*, coarse meal, cogn. with GRITS], *n.pl.* Husked oats or wheat.

grocer (grō' sėr) [O.F. *grossier*, one who sells in the gross, med. L. *grossārius*, from *grossus*, GROSS] *n.* A dealer in tea, sugar, coffee, spices and miscellaneous household supplies. **grocery,** *n.* (*usu. in pl.*) Grocers' wares; a grocer's shop; (*U.S.A.*) a grog-shop.

grog (grog) [said to be from a nickname 'Old Grog' of Admiral Vernon, from his wearing a GROGRAM cloak; about 1745 he ordered his sailors to dilute their rum with water], *n.* A mixture of spirit and cold water; spirituous liquor. **v.t.* To make grog by adding water to (spirits); to extract spirits (from an emptied cask) by pouring in hot water. *v.i.* To drink grog. **grog-blossom,** *n.* A redness or eruption on the nose or face, due to excessive drinking. **grog-shop,** *n.* A place where spirits are sold. **groggery,** *n.* (*U.S.A.*) A grog-shop. **groggy,** *a.* Tipsy, drunk; staggering; acting like one stupefied with drink; moving uneasily, as with tender feet or forelegs (said of a horse). **grogginess,** *n.*

grogram, *-ran (grog' răm, -răn) [F. *gros grain*, coarse grain], *n.* A coarse stuff of silk and mohair or silk and wool. *a.* Made of grogram.

groin (1) (groin) [earlier *grine*, *grynae* (supposed by Skeat to be from A.-S. *grynde*, an abyss or depression, cogn. with G. *grund*, valley, GROUND)], *n.* (*Anat.*) The hollow in the human body where the thigh and the trunk unite; (*Arch.*) the edge formed by an intersection of vaults; the fillet or moulding covering this. *v.t.* (*Arch.*) To form (a roof) into groins; to furnish with groins. **groined,** *a.* **groining,** *n.* (*Arch.*).

***groin** (2) (groin) [O.F. *grognir* (F. *grogner*), L. *grunnīre*], *v.i.* To groan, grunt, or growl; to pout, to grumble. *n.* The snout of a swine.

groin (3) [GROYNE].

Grolier (grō' lyā) [Jean *Grolier* (1479–1565), French bibliophile], *n.* A book or binding from Grolier's collection. **Grolier design:** (*Bookbinding*) Geometrical or arabesque ornament such as characterized Grolier's bindings. **Grolieresque** (grō lyăr esk'), *a.*

gromel, grommel [GROMWELL].

grommet (grom' ėt), *n.* (*Naut.*) A ring of rope.

gromwell (grom' wėl) [earlier *gromil*, O.F. (etym. doubtful)], *n.* A genus of trailing herbs of the borage family, esp. *Lithospermum officinale*, the hard stony seeds of which were formerly used in medicine.

groom (groom, grum) [perh. from O.F. *gromet*, *groumet* (F. *gourmet*, see GOURMET), dim. of *groume*, a boy, a servant], *n.* A servant who has charge of horses; one of several officers in the royal household, as *Groom in waiting*, *Groom of the privy* or *great Chamber*, *Groom of the stole*, etc.; a bridegroom. *v.t.* To tend or care for, as a groom does a horse; to curry and brush. **well-groomed,** *a.* (*colloq.*) Neatly or smartly got up, well tended, esp. as regards the hair and beard. **groomsman,** *n.* An unmarried friend who attends on the bridegroom.

groove (groov) [Dut. *groeve*, cogn. with A.-S. *grafan*, to GRAVE], *n.* A channel, furrow, or long hollow, such as may be cut with a tool for something to fit into or work in; (*fig.*) natural course or events of one's life, a rut; (*prov.*) a shaft or pit. *v.t.* To cut or form a groove or grooves in. **grooved,** *a.* **groovy,** *a.* **grooviness,** *n.*

grope (grōp) [A.-S. *grāpian* (cogn. with *grīpan*, to GRIPE)], *v.i.* To feel about with the hands; to search (after) something as in the dark, by feeling about with the hands; to feel one's way; to seek blindly. *v.t.* To seek out by feeling with the hands in the dark, or as a blind person; *to handle; *to seek into; *to inquire into. **gropingly,** *adv.*

groper [GROUPER (2)].

grosbeak, *gross-beak (grōs' bēk) [F. *grosbec* (GROSS, BEAK)], *n.* A name given to several birds having thick bills, esp. the genus *Coccothraustes*, comprising the hawfinch.

Groschen (grō' shėn), *n.* An old German silver coin, worth a little more than a penny.

groset (grō' zėt), *grossart* (grō' sărt) [Sc., earlier *groser*, F. *groseille*], *n.* A gooseberry.

gross (grōs) [O.F. *gros*, fem. *grosse*, late L. *grossus*, thick, etym. doubtful], *a.* Big, rank; fat, bloated, overfed; coarse, uncleanly; lacking fineness, dense, thick, material; (*fig.*) dull, unrefined; indelicate, obscene; flagrant, glaring; total, not net; general, not specific; *plain, palpable. *n.* Twelve dozen; the main body, the mass; the sum total. **in the gross, in gross:** In the bulk, wholesale; in a general way, on the whole. **gross-headed,** *a.* Thick-headed; stupid. **gross weight:** The weight of goods with the cask or whatever contains them. **grossly,** *adv.* **grossness,** *n.*

grossulaceous (gros ū lā' shŭs), **grossularious** (-lâr' i ŭs) [mod. L. *grossulāria*, from O.F. *groselle*, gooseberry], *a.* (*Bot.*) Of or belonging to the *Grossulariaceæ*, an order of plants containing the gooseberry and currant. **grossular,** *a.* Of or belonging to a gooseberry. *n.* (*Min.*) A Siberian variety of garnet, sometimes called the gooseberry garnet.

grot (grot) [F. *grotte*, GROTTO], *n.* A grotto.

grotesque (grȯ tesk') [O.F., from It. *grottesca*, antique work (GROTTO, -ESQUE)], *a.* Irregular, extravagant, or fantastic in form; ludicrous through these qualities, absurd, bizarre. *n.* Whimsically designed ornamentation consisting of figures of plants and animals of fanciful invention; (*pl.*) whimsical figures or scenery; (*Print.*) a square-cut type without serifs. **grotesquely,** *adv.* **grotesqueness,** *n.* **grotesquerie,** *n.*

grotto (grot′ ō) [It. *grotta*, late L. *crupta*, L. *crypta*, Gr. *kruptē*, CRYPT], *n.* A small cave, esp. one that is picturesque; an artificial cave or cave-like room decorated with rocks, shells, and the like. **grotto-work,** *n.* Ornamental rock-work, etc. in a garden to imitate a grotto. **grottoed,** *a.*

grouch (grouch), *v.i.* To grumble, to grouse. *n.* A discontented mood.

ground (1) (ground) [A.-S. *grund* (cp. Dut. *grond*, G. *grund*)], *n.* The surface of the earth as dist. from the air or the heavens; a floor, pavement, or other supporting surface; a region or tract of land; land, landed estates; (*pl.*) private enclosed land attached to a house; the firm, solid earth; the bottom of the sea; the substratum, the base or foundation; the background, the surface on which a picture or design is laid, the prevailing colour or tone; (*fig.*) the reason, motive, origin, cause; (*pl.*) basis, valid reason, pretext, the first or fundamental principles; the extent of an inquiry or survey, area, scope; (*pl.*) sediment, dregs, esp. of coffee; the position occupied by an army; (*Etching*) an acid-resisting composition spread over the surface of the metal to be etched; (*Mining.*) strata containing a mineral lode or coal-seam; (*Painting*) the first layer of paint; the flat surface from which the figures rise; (*Sport*) the area allotted to a single player or to a side; *the pit of a theatre. *v.t.* To set or place upon or in the ground; to base or establish (on); to instruct thoroughly (in) the elementary principles of; (*Naut.*) to run (a ship) aground; (*Aviat.*) to prevent an aeroplane from taking to the air. *v.i.* (*Naut.*) To take the ground. **down to the ground:** (*colloq.*) Thoroughly; in every respect. **forbidden ground:** An area or subject that must be avoided. **to break ground:** To cut the first sod; (*fig.*) to take the first step; to make a start. **to fall to the ground:** To come to naught; to fail. **to gain ground:** To advance, to meet with success, to prevail. ***to gather ground, *to get ground:** To gain ground. **to give ground:** To give way, to retire, to yield. **to lose ground:** To be driven back, to give way; to lose advantage or credit; to decline, to fall off. **to shift one's ground:** To change the basis or premises of one's reasoning; to try a different plan. **to stand one's ground:** Not to yield or give way. **ground-angling,** *n.* Angling without a float, with the weight placed a few inches from the hook. **ground-ash,** *n.* An ash sapling. **ground-bait,** *n.* Bait thrown into the water to attract fish. *v.t.* To put ground-bait into in preparation for angling. **ground-bass,** *n.* (*Mus.*) A bass passage of a few bars constantly repeated, with a varied melody and harmony. **ground-box,** *n.* Small box shrubs for edging garden plots and paths. **ground-colour,** *n.* The first coat of paint; the general colour or tone on which a design is painted. **ground control,** *n.* (*Aviat.*) Control of landing by information radioed from the ground. **ground floor:** The storey or rooms level with the exterior ground. (in America called the first floor). **ground frost:** A ground temperature on grass of 32° F. or under. **ground game:** Running game, as hares, rabbits, etc., dist. from birds. **ground-gudgeon,** *n.* The loach. **ground-hog,** *n.* The aardvark, *Orycteropus Capensis*; the American marmot, *Arctomys monax.* **ground-ice,** *n.* Ice formed at the bottom of the water before the surface freezes, also called anchor-ice. **ground-ivy,** *n.* A labiate creeping plant, *Nepeta glechoma*, with purple-blue flowers. **ground-landlord,** *n.* The owner of land let on a building lease. **ground-note,** *n.* (*Mus.*) The note or fundamental bass on which a common chord is built. **ground-nut,** *n.* The pea-nut, *Arachis hypogæa*; the edible tuber of Burnium flexuosum; the American wild bean, *Apios tuberosa*, having an edible tuber. **ground-oak,** *n.* An oak sapling. **ground-pine,** *n.* A herb, *Ajuga chamæpitys*, with a resinous odour. **ground-plan,** *n.* A horizontal plan of a building at the ground level; an outline or general plan of anything. **ground plane:** The horizontal plane of projection in perspective drawing. **ground-plot,** *n.* The ground upon which a building is placed. **ground-rent,** *n.* Rent paid to a ground-landlord for a building-site. **ground-sea,** *n.* A heavy sea or swell without apparent cause. **groundsman,** *n.* (*Cricket*) The man who looks after the pitch. **ground speed,** *n.* (*Aviat.*) The speed of an aircraft relative to a point on the earth's surface. **ground-squirrel,** *n.* Any species of *Tamias*, a genus of American burrowing squirrels, esp. the chipmunk. **ground staff,** *n.* (*Aviat.*) The non-flying staff of an aerodrome. **ground-swell,** *n.* A long, deep swell or rolling of the sea, occasioned by a past or distant storm or earthquake. **ground-tackle,** *n.* (*Naut.*) The ropes and tackle connected with the anchors and mooring apparatus. **ground-tier,** *n.* The lower range of boxes in a theatre. **ground-torpedo,** *n.* A torpedo laid at the bottom of the sea. **groundwork,** *n.* That which forms the foundation or basis; a fundamental principle; the original reason; the parts of any object not covered by decoration, etc. **groundedly,** *adv.* **grounding,** *n.* Instruction in the elements of a subject.

ground (2) (ground) [p.p. of GRIND], *a.* **ground glass:** Glass with the surface ground to make it obscure.

groundage (groun′ dȧj), *n.* Dues paid for space occupied by a ship on a beach or in port.

groundless (ground′ lĕs), *a.* Without foundation, reason, or warrant, baseless; *without bottom. **groundlessly,** *adv.* **groundlessness,** *n.*

groundling (ground′ ling), *n.* A spectator who stood on the floor of a theatre, hence one of the vulgar; a fish that keeps at the bottom, esp. *Cobitis tænia*, the spined loach, and *Gobius niger*, the black goby; a creeping plant.

groundsel (1) (ground′ sĕl) [A.-S. *gund-* or *grundeswylige* (perh. *gund*, pus, *swylige*, from *swelgan*, to SWALLOW, lit, pus-swallower, from use in poultices)], *n.* A composite plant with pinnatifid leaves and small yellow flowers, esp. the common weed, *Senecio vulgaris*, which is used for feeding cage-birds.

groundsel (2) **-sill** (ground′ sĕl) [GROUND (1), SILL], *n.* The timber of a building next to the ground; a threshold; a foundation.

groundwork [GROUND].

groundy (groun′ di), *a.* Full of sediment or dregs.

group (groop) [F. *groupe*, It. *groppo*, prob. from Teut. (cp. CROP)], *n.* The combination of several figures or objects to form a single mass; a number of persons or things stationed near each other, a cluster, an assemblage; a number of persons or things classed together on account of certain resemblances; a grade in classification not corresponding precisely to any regular division or subdivision; (*Min.*) a series of minerals agreeing essentially in chemical composition; (*Geol.*) a series of rocks or strata deposited about the same period; (*Aviat.*) in the R.A.F. the highest subdivision of a Command. *v.t.* To form into or place in a group; to put (an object) in close relation or contact (with); to bring together so as to produce a harmonious whole or effect. *v.i.* To form or fall into a group. **Group Captain,** *n.* Commissioned rank in the R.A.F. equivalent to that of Colonel in the Army. **groupage,** *n.* **Grouper** (1), *n.* A member of the Oxford Group.

grouper (2) (groo′ pėr) [Port. *garupa*, perh. from S. Am. native word], *n.* Name of certain Californian, Atlantic, and Australian fish.

grouse (1) (grous) [etym. doubtful], *n.* (*pl. unchanged*). A gallinaceous game-bird with feet more or less feathered, esp. *Lagopus Scoticus*, the red grouse, moor fowl, or moor game, *Lyrurus tetrix* the black game or heath fowl, *Tetrao urogallus*, the capercailzie, wood or great grouse, and *Lagopus mutus*, the ptarmigan or rock grouse; the flesh of these, esp. of the red grouse. *v.i.* To hunt or shoot grouse. **grousy,** *a.*

grouse (2) (grous) [cp. GRUDGE], *v.i.* To grumble. *n.* A grievance. **grouser,** n.

grout (1) (grout) [A.-S. *grūt*, cogn. with GRIT], *n.* Coarse meal; (*pl.*) dregs, grounds; a thin, coarse mortar to run into the joints of masonry and brickwork; a finishing coat of fine stuff for ceilings. *v.t.* To fill up with grout. **grouting,** *n.* The act or process of filling in or finishing with grout; the grout filled in; (*Build.*) the injection of cement grout into foundations, etc. for strengthening. **grouty** (1), *a.* Muddy, dirty.

grout (2) (grout) [perh. conn. with prec., or from ROOT], *v.t.* To turn (up) with the snout (of a pig). *v.i.* To turn up the ground with the snout.

grouter (grou' tėr), *n.* (*Austral. colloq.*) A bet in the game of two-up. **to come in on the grouter:** To get an unfair advantage.

grove (grōv) [A.-S. *grāf*, etym. unknown], *n.* A small wood; a cluster of trees shading an avenue or walk; a wood or forest sacred to a divinity; (*Bibl.*) erron. translation of Heb. *Asherah*, a goddess, or her pillar or symbol. **groved,** *a.* **groveless,** *a.* **grovy,** *a.*

grovel (grov' ėl) [erron. formed from obs. adv. *grovelling* (obs. *groof* in *on groof* or *grufe*, face downwards, Icel. *āgrūfu*, -LING (2))], *v.i.* To lie or move with the body prostrate on the earth; (*fig.*) to prostrate oneself, to be low, mean, or abject. **groveller,** *n.* **grovellingly,** *adv.*

grow (grō) [A.-S. *grōwan* (cp. Dut. *groeijen*, Icel. *grōa*), cogn. with GRASS, GREEN], *v.i.* (*past* **grew,** *p.p.* **grown**) To increase in bulk by the assimilation of new matter into the living organism; to develop; to increase in number, degree, power, etc.; to exist as a living thing; to spring up, to be produced, to arise; to pass into a certain state; to adhere; to become rooted; *to swell (as the sea). *v.t.* To cultivate; to raise by cultivation; to produce. **to grow downward:** To diminish. **to grow on one:** (*impers.*) To increase in one's estimation; to impress one more and more. **to grow together:** To become closely united, to become incorporated in each other. **to grow up:** To arrive at manhood or womanhood; to advance to full maturity; to arise, to become prevalent or common. **growable,** *a.* **grower,** *n.* One who or that which grows (*usu. in comb.*, as *free-grower*); a producer of corn, vegetables, etc.; a cultivator. **growing pains:** Incorrect term for rheumatic pains in the limbs felt by young children. **growingly,** *adv.* **grown-up,** *a.* Adult. *n.* An adult.

growl (groul) [prob. onomat.], *v.i.* To make a deep guttural sound as of anger; to murmur; to grumble; to speak angrily or gruffly; to rumble. *v.t.* To utter or express by a growl. *n.* A deep guttural sound like that made by an angry dog; a grumbling; a complaint. **growler,** *n.* One who growls; a grumbler; an American fish, *Grystis salmonides*, from the sound it emits when landed; other fishes; (*colloq.*) a four-wheeled horse-drawn cab. **growlery,** *n.* Growling, grumbling; a place to grumble in, one's private room or 'den.' **growlingly,** *adv.*

grown, etc. [GROW].

growth (grōth), *n.* The act or process of growing; increase, development, in number, extent, bulk, stature, etc.; cultivation of vegetable produce; that which grows or is grown; (*Path.*) a morbid formation; a product, a result.

groyne (groin) [etym. doubtful, perh. from GROIN (1); but cp. F. *groin*, snout, from *grogner*, L. *grunnīre*, to grunt], *n.* A structure of piles, concrete, etc., acting as a breakwater on a foreshore, and causing sand and shingle to be retained. *v.t.* To furnish with groynes.

grub (grŭb) [prob. cogn. with A.-S. *grafan*, to GRAVE (1)], *v.i.* (*past & p.p.* **grubbed**) To dig by scratching or tearing up the ground superficially; to search, to rummage; to drudge, to toil, to do manual work; (*slang*) to take one's food. *v.t.* To dig (up or out); to clear (ground) of roots, etc.; to find by searching; (*slang*) to provide with food. *n.* The larva of an insect, esp. of bees and wasps, with a distinct head but no legs; a drudge, a hack; (*Cricket*) a ball bowled along the ground; (*slang*) food; *a short thick-set person, a dwarf. **to grub along:** (*colloq.*) To plod or drudge along. **to grub up:** To dig up by the roots. **grub-axe, -hoe, -hook** [GRUBBING]. **to grub-stake:** (*Am. slang*) To supply food, etc. in return for a share of profit. **grubber,** *n.* One who or that which grubs; an instrument for stirring up the soil and clearing out weeds; a machine to pull up stumps and roots. **grubbing-axe, -hoe, -hook, -machine, -tool,** etc., *n.* Implements for grubbing up roots, stumps, etc. **grubby,** *a.* Full of grubs; dirty, grimy, **grubbiness,** *n.*

Grub Street (grŭb strēt) [a street (now Milton Street) near Moorfields, London, once much inhabited by literary hacks], *n.* (*collect.*) Poor, mean, or needy authors, or the region (*lit. or fig.*) they live in. *a.* Of or pertaining to this kind of writer.

grudge (grŭj) [M.E. *grachen*, O.F. *groucier* (low L. *groussāre*), etym. doubtful], *v.i.* *To murmur, to complain, to grumble, *to grieve, to repine; to be unwilling or reluctant; to be envious, to cherish ill-will. *v.t.* To feel discontent or envy at; to give or take unwillingly or reluctantly; *to cherish an envious and discontented spirit towards. *n.* Ill-will, a feeling of malice or malevolence; unwillingness, reluctance; *remorse; *a slight symptom of disease. ***grudgeful,** *a.* **grudger,** *n.* **grudgingly,** *adv.*

***grue** (groo') [Sc. and North., cogn. with Dan. *grue*, Dut. *gruwen*, G. *grauen*], *v.i.* To shudder; to feel horror or dread.

gruel (groo' ėl) [O.F., from late L. *grūtellum*, dim. of *grūtum*, from Teut. (cp. O.L.G. and A.-S. *grūt*, GROATS)], *n.* Semi-liquid food made by boiling oatmeal or other meal in water or milk; any food of like consistency. **to give one his gruel:** (*colloq.*) To defeat, punish severely, or kill one. **gruelling,** *n.* Severe or harsh treatment. *a.* Exacting, requiring fortitude.

gruesome (groo' sŭm) [GRUE, -SOME], *a.* Frightful, horrible, repulsive. **gruesomely,** *adv.* **gruesomeness,** *n.*

gruff (grŭf) [cp. Dut. *grof*, G. *grov*], *a.* Of a rough, surly, or harsh aspect; sour, rough, harsh, hoarse-voiced. **gruffish,** *a.* **gruffly,** *adv.* **gruffness,** *n.*

grumble (grŭm' bėl) [history doubtful (cp. F. *grommeler*, Dut. *grommelen*, freq. of *grommen*, and G. *grummelen*)], *v.i.* To murmur with discontent; to complain in a surly or muttering tone; to growl, to mutter, to rumble. *v.t.* To express or utter in a complaining manner. *n.* The act of grumbling; a complaint; (*pl.*) a discontented disposition. **grumbler,** *n.* One who grumbles; a discontented person; various species of gurnard, from the sound uttered when caught. **grumblingly,** *adv.*

grume (groom) [O.F., from late L. *grūmus*, a small heap], *n.* (*Med.*) A fluid of a thick, viscid consistence; a clot, as of blood. **grumous** (groo' mŭs), *a.* Thick; concreted; (*Med.*) clotted, coagulated (of blood); (*Bot.*) divided into little clustered grains. **grumousness,** *n.*

grummet (grŭm' ėt) [O.F. gromette (F. *gourmette*), a curb, from *gourmer*, to curb, etym. unknown], *n.* (*Naut.*) A ring formed of rope laid round and spliced, used as a rowlock, etc.; *(*Artil.*) a wad made of rope, rammed between the ball and the charge in a muzzle-loading gun.

grumous [GRUME].

grumph (grŭmf) [Sc., imit.], *v.i.* To grunt. *n.* A grunt. **Grumphie,** *n.* A name for the pig.

grumpy (grŭm' pi) [obs. n. *grump* (imit., cp. GRUNT), -Y], *a.* Surly, cross, peevish, ill-tempered. **grumpily,** *adv.* **grumpiness,** *n.* **grumpish,** *a.*

Grundyism (grŭn' di izm) [Mrs. *Grundy*, a character in Morton's 'Speed the Plough' (1798), adopted as the type of conventional respectability], *n.* The principles of Mrs. Grundy; prudishness; a slavish respect for conventions in matters of sex. **Grundified,** *a.* **Grundyish,** *a.* **Grundyist, Grundyite,** *n.*

grunsel [GROUNDSEL (1 and 2)].

grunt (grŭnt) [A.-S. *grunnettan*, freq. of *grunian* (cp. Dan. *grynte*, G. *grunzen*, also L. *grunnīre*)], *v.i.* To make a deep guttural noise like a pig; to grumble, to growl, to complain. *v.t.* To express or utter in a grunting manner. *n.* A deep guttural sound, as of a hog. **grunter,** *n.* One who grunts; a hog; the drum-fish and other fishes. **gruntingly,** *adv.* **gruntle** (grŭntl), *n.* (*Sc.*) A snout, esp. of a pig; a face or muzzle. **gruntling,** *n.* A young pig or hog.

gruyère (groo′ yâr) [town in Switzerland], *n.* A Swiss or French cheese made from cows' milk, pale-coloured, firm, and full of cavities.

grype [GRIPE].

***gryphon** [GRIFFIN (1)].

gryposis, -phosis (gri pō′-, -fō′ sis) [Gr., from *gruphos*, hooked], *n.* (*Path.*) The abnormal incurvation or growing inward of the nails.

grysbok (grīz′ bok) [Dut. *grijsbok* (*grijs*, GREY, BUCK)], *n.* A speckled, reddish-brown South African antelope, *Antilope melanotis*.

guacharo (gwa′ chȧ rō, gwa cha′ rō) [Sp., from South Am. native], *n.* The oil-bird, *Steatornis caripensis*, a South American goatsucker, feeding on fruit.

guacho [GAUCHO].

guaco (gwa′ kō) [Sp., from South Am. native], *n.* A tropical American plant, *Aristolochia guaco*, and others, said to cure snake-bites.

guaiac (gwī′ ăk), *n.* Wood of the guaiacum; the resin or drug.

guaiacol (gwī′ ȧ kol), *n.* A phenol obtained by distillation from guaiacum resin and found in wood tar.

guaiacum (gwī′ ȧ kŭm) [Sp. *guayaco*, from Haytian], *n.* (*Bot.*) A genus of West Indian and tropical North American trees and shrubs, one of which, *G. officinale*, furnishes *lignum vitæ*, while its bark, wood and resin, with those of *G. sanctum*, are used in medicine; the wood of this genus; (*Med.*) a drug made from the resin used as a stimulant and alterative.

guan (gwan) [native name], *n.* Any species of the South American genus *Penelope*, gallinaceous birds allied to the curassou.

guana (gwa′ nȧ), *n.* The iguana; (*Australasia*) a large lizard of various species.

guanaco (gwȧ na′ kō) [South Am. native *huanaco*], *n.* A wild llama, *Auchenia huanaco*, inhabiting the chain of the Andes to their most southerly point.

guano (gwa′ nō) [Sp., from Quichua *huanu*, dung], *n.* A valuable manure, composed chiefly of the excrement of sea-fowl, brought from South America and the Pacific; an artificial manure, esp. fish-manure or fish-guano. *v.t.* To manure or fertilize with guano. **guaniferous** (gwȧ nif′ ėr ŭs), *a.* Producing guano. **guanin** (gwa′ nin), *n.* (*Chem.*) A white amorphous substance found in guano and in the liver and pancreas of animals.

guarana (gwȧ ra′ nȧ) [native name], *n.* The powdered seeds of *Paullinia sorbilis*, a Brazilian shrub. **guarana-bread, -paste,** *n.* Bread or paste made from guarana by the Brazilian Indians for food and medicinal purposes.

guarantee (găr ȧn tē′) [GUARANTY (perh. the orig. sense, one who guarantees, from Sp. *garante*, WARRANT)], *n.* An engagement to see an agreement, duty, or liability fulfilled; guaranty; the act of guaranteeing; any security, warranty, or surety given; the person to whom the guarantee is given; (*incorrectly*) one who becomes surety for the performance of certain acts by another. *v.t.* To become guarantor or surety for; to undertake responsibility for the fulfilment of a promise, contract, etc.; to pledge oneself or engage (that); to assure the continuance or permanence of; to undertake to secure (to another); to assure or secure against or from risk or damage. **guarantee fund:** A sum subscribed to provide an indemnity in case of loss. **guaranteed,** *a.* Warranted. **guarantor,** *n.* One who guarantees.

guaranty (găr′ ȧn ti) [A.-F. *guarantie*, from O.F. *garantir*, to WARRANT], *n.* The act of guaranteeing, esp. an undertaking to be responsible for a debt or obligation of another person; that which guarantees, that on which a guarantee or security is based.

guard (gard) [O.F. *garder*, from Teut., see WARD], *v.t.* To secure the safety of; to watch over, to protect, to defend (from or against); to stand guard over, to prevent the escape of; to secure (against criticism, etc.); *to trim, to deck; *to gird. *v.i.* To be cautious or take precautions (against). *n.* Defence, protection, a state of vigilance, watch against attack, surprise, etc.; a state, posture, or act of defence, esp. in boxing, fencing, cricket, etc.; a protector; a man or body of men on guard; a sentry, an escort; (*Am.*) prison warder; a contrivance to prevent injury, accident, or loss; a man in charge of a railway train or a coach, (*Am.* conductor); the part of a sword-hilt which protects the hand; a watch-chain; an ornamental edging or border; a screen to prevent accident placed in front of a fire-place, etc. **to be on** or **off one's guard:** To be prepared or unprepared for attack, surprise, etc. **to mount guard:** To go on duty as a guard or sentinel. **guard-boat,** *n.* A boat patrolling a fleet in harbour; an official harbour boat for preventing infringement of customs or quarantine regulations. **guard-chain,** *n.* A chain for securing a watch, brooch, etc. ***guard-chamber,** *n.* A guard-room. **guard-house, -room,** *n.* A house or room for those on guard or for prisoners. **guard-rail,** *n.* A rail to protect against falling off a deck, etc.; (*Railway*) a rail fixed inside the inner rail at curves, points, etc., to prevent derailment. **guard-ring,** *n.* A keeper for a wedding-ring, etc. ***guardage,** *n.* Guardianship, wardship. **guardant,** *a.* *Guarding, protecting; (*Her.*) presenting the full face to the spectator. **n.* A guardian, protector. **guardedly,** *adv.* **guardedness,** *n.* **guarder,** *n.* ***guardful,** *a.* Wary, cautious. **guardfully,** *adv.* **guardless,** *a.*

guardian (gar′ di ȧn) [O.F. *gardien*, from *garde*, as prec.], *n.* One who has the charge, care, or custody of any person or thing; a protector; a guardian of the poor; the superior of a Franciscan convent; (*Law*) one who has the charge, custody, and supervision of a person not legally capable of managing his own affairs. *a.* Guarding; acting as a guardian or protector. **guardian angel:** An angel or spirit supposed to be assigned to a person as guardian and protector. **guardians of the poor:** (*Hist.*) Members of a board elected by the ratepayers to administer the Poor Laws in a particular parish or district. **guardianship,** *n.* The office of a guardian; care, protection, esp. legal tutelage.

Guards (gardz) [GUARD], *n.pl.* British household troops consisting of the Coldstream, Grenadier, Irish, Welsh and Scots Guards. **Guardsman,** *n.* An officer or private in the Guards.

guardship (gard′ ship), *n.* A vessel stationed in a port or harbour for defence.

guava (gwa′ vȧ) [Sp. *guayaba*, from native name], *n.* The luscious fruit of various species of the tropical American myrtaceous genus *Psidium*, esp. *P. pyriferum* and *P. pomiferum*; the trees on which they grow.

***gubernation** (gū bėr nā′ shŭn) [F., from L. *gubernātio -ōnem*, from *gubernāre*, to steer, to GOVERN], *n.* Government or guiding control. **gubernatorial** (-tōr′ i ȧl), *a.*

guddle (gŭd′ ėl) [Sc., etym. doubtful]. *v.i.* To grope for fish with the hands. *v.t.* To catch (fish) by groping and tickling. *n.* (*colloq.*) A muddle confusion.

gude (gid) (*Sc.*) [GOOD].

gudgeon (1) (gŭj′ ŏn) [F. *goujon*, L. *gōbiōnem*, nom. *gōbio*, GOBY], *n.* A small freshwater fish, *Gobio fluviatilis*, easily caught and largely used as bait; (*fig.*) one easily taken in.

gudgeon (2) (gŭj′ ŏn) [O.F. *gougeon*, perh. as prec.], *n.* The metallic journal-piece let into the end of a wooden shaft; the bearing of a shaft; an eye or socket in which a rudder turns.

***gue** (gū) [perh. from Icel. *gīgja*], *n.* A rude kind of musical instrument, apparently like a violin, formerly used in Shetland.

Guebre (gē′-, gā′ bėr) [F. *guèbre*, from Pers. *gabr*], *n.* A fire-worshipper, a Zoroastrian.

guelder rose (gel′ dėr rōz) [*Guelders*, town in Prussia, or *Guelderland*, province of Holland, formerly a German duchy with Guelders for capital], *n.* A shrubby plant, of the family Caprifoliaceae, *Viburnum opulus*, bearing ball-shaped bunches of white flowers, also called the snowball-tree.

Guelph, Guelf (gwelf) [It. *Guelfo*, M.H.G. *Welf*, name of the Dukes of Bavaria, a distinguished princely family now represented by the ducal house of Brunswick and the royal family of Great Britain, used as a war-cry in 1140 at the battle of Weinsberg against the Emperor Conrad III], *n.* A member of the popular party in mediæval Italy which aimed at national independence, and supported the Pope against the Ghibellines. **Guelphic,** *a.* Of or belonging to the Guelphs. **Guelphic order:** An order of knighthood instituted for Hanover in 1815.

guerdon (gėr′ dŏn) [O.F., from med. L. *widerdōnum*, O.H.G. *widarlōn* (*wider*, against, *lōn*, LOAN, assim. to L. *dōnum*, gift)], *n.* (*poet.*) A reward, a recompense. **v.t.* To reward. **guerdonless,** *a.*

guereza (ger′ i zȧ) [Africa native], *n.* A black Abyssinian monkey, *Colobus guereza*, with a fringe of white hair and a bushy tail.

guerilla [GUERRILLA].

guerite (gā′ rēt) [F., GARRET], *n.* (*Mil.*) A small loopholed tower, usually on the point of a bastion, to hold a sentinel.

Guernsey (gĕrn′ zi) [one of the Channel Islands], *n.* A close-fitting knitted or woven woollen shirt, usu. blue, worn by seamen, labourers, children, etc. **Guernsey cow:** One of the breeds of cattle from the Channel Islands also known as Alderneys and Jerseys. **Guernsey lily:** A South African or Japanese amaryllis, *Nerine sarniensis*, pink in colour, cultivated in Guernsey for the market.

guerrilla, guerilla (gė ril′ ȧ) [Sp., dim. of *guerra*], *n.* An irregular warfare carried on by small independent bands; a member of such a band; an irregular, petty war. *a.* Belonging to or consisting of guerrillas; carried on in an irregular manner (of a war).

guess (ges) [M.E. gessen (cogn. with Dut. *gissen*, Dan. *gisse*, prob. from A.-S. *gitan*, to GET)], *v.t.* To judge or estimate on imperfect grounds, to conjecture; to imagine, to suppose on probable grounds, to divine (one to be); to conjecture rightly; (*U.S.A. colloq.*) to suppose, to believe. *v.i.* To form a conjecture, to judge at random; to hazard a supposition (that). *n.* A conjecture; an opinion, estimate, or supposition based on imperfect grounds. **by guess:** At haphazard. **guessable,** *a.* **guesser,** *n.* **guessingly,** *adv.* **guess-rope** [GUEST-ROPE]. **guess-work** *n.* Action or calculation based on guess; procedure by guessing.

guest (gest) [A.-S. *gæst*, *giest* (cp. Icel. *gestr*, Dut. and G. *gast*, also L. *hostis*, foe, orig. stranger)], *n.* A person received and entertained in the house or at the table of another; one who resides temporarily at a hotel or boarding-house; a parasitic animal or vegetable. **v t.* To entertain; to treat hospitably. **v.i.* To be a guest. **paying guest:** A boarder. **guest-chamber,** *n.* A room appropriated to the entertainment of guests. **guest house,** *n.* A boarding-house, a small hotel. **guest-night,** *n.* A night when visitors are entertained by a club, etc.

***guest-rite,** *n.* The offices due towards a guest. **guesten** [assim. to obs. *gesten*], *v.i.* To stay as a guest. ***guester,** *n.* ***guestling,** *n.* An assembly, formerly annual, of representatives of the Cinque Ports; a young guest. **guestship,** *n.* ***guestwise,** *adv.* Like a guest.

guest-, guess-rope (ges′ rōp) [etym. unknown], *n.* (*Naut.*) A hawser carried by a boat to a distant object for warping a vessel towards this; a rope for making fast a boat to a ship; also called **guest-, guess-warp.**

guffaw (gŭ faw′) [imit.], *n.* A burst of loud or coarse laughter. *v.i.* To laugh loud or coarsely. *v.t.* To say with such a laugh.

guggle [GURGLE].

guide (gīd) [O.F. *guider*, earlier *guier*, prob. from Teut. (cogn. with A.-S. *wītan*, to know, whence *wīsian*, to guide)], *v.t.* To direct, lead, or conduct; to rule, to regulate, to govern; to direct the course of; to be the object, motive, or criterion of (action, opinion, etc.). *n.* One who leads another or points the way; a leader, a conductor, esp. a person employed to conduct a party of tourists, etc.; an adviser; anything adopted as a sign or mark of direction or criterion of accuracy; a guide-book; (*Mil.*) a subaltern acting as a pivot to regulate an evolution or alinement; (*pl.*) a company formed for reconnoitring, etc.; (*Naut.*) a ship by which a squadron or fleet regulate their movements; (*Mach.*) a bar, rod, bearing-surface, or other device acting as indicator or regulating motion. **guide-bars, -block,** *n.pl.* (*Mach.*) Pieces of metal on which the cross-head of a steam-engine slides, keeping it parallel to the cylinder. **guide-book,** *n.* A book for tourists, describing places of interest, means of transit, etc. **guide-post,** *n.* A finger-post to show the way. **guide-rope** [GUY (1)]. **guideway,** *n.* (*Mach.*) A groove, track, or frame directing the motion of a part. **guidable,** *a.* **guidage,** *n.* Guidance; (*Law*) pay for safe-conduct through a strange country. **guidance,** *n.* The act of guiding; direction; government. **guideless,** *a.* **guider,** *n.* ***guideship,** *n.* **guided missile,** *n.* (*Mil.*) A rocket- or jet-propelled projectile with a war-head, electronically guided to its target by remote control.

guidon (gī′ dŏn) [F., from It. *guidone*, prob. from *guida*, GUIDE], *n.* The forked or pointed flag of a troop of light cavalry; the flag of a guild or fraternity; a standard-bearer.

guignol (gē′ nyol) [GRAND].

guild (gild) [A.-S. *gild*, a payment, from *gildan*, to YIELD (cp. Dut. and G. *geld*, money)], *n.* A society or corporation belonging to the same class, trade, or pursuit, combined for mutual aid and protection of interests. **guild-brother,** *n.* A fellow-member of a guild. **guild-hall,** *n.* A hall where a guild or corporation meets; a town-hall; the hall where the corporation of a city meets. **Guild Socialism,** *n.* A form of socialism under which every industry would be organized as an autonomous guild, holding the factories, etc. from the central government, but managing its own affairs through representatives of the workers. **guildry,** *n.* (*Sc.*) A guild, the corporation of a burgh royal.

guilder (gil′ dėr) [corr. of Dut. GULDEN], *n.* A coin formerly current in the Netherlands, value about 1s. 8d.

guile (gīl) [O.F., from Teut., cp. WILE], *n.* Deceit, craft, cunning. **v.t.* To deceive, to beguile. **guileful,** *a.* **guilefully,** *adv.* **guilefulness,** *n.* **guileless,** *a.* **guilelessly,** *adv.* **guilelessness,** *n.* ***guiler,** *n.*

guillemot (gil′ ė mot) [F., dim. of *Guillaume*, O.H.G. *Wilhelm*, William], *n.* Any bird of the natatorial genus *Alca* or *Uria*, with a short tail and pointed wings.

guilloche (gi lōsh′) [F.], *n.* (*Arch.*) An ornament of intertwisted or interlaced bands.

guillotine (gil ŏ tēn′, gil′ ŏ tēn) [F., after Dr. J. I. *Guillotin* (1738–1814), who introduced it (1792) during the French Revolution], *n.* An apparatus for beheading persons at a stroke, consisting of an upright frame, down which a weighted blade slides in grooves; a machine for cutting thicknesses of paper, etc.; (*Surg.*) an instrument for cutting tonsils, uvula, etc.; (*Parl.*) the curtailment of debate by fixing beforehand the hours when parts of a Bill must be voted on. *v.t.* To execute by guillotine; to cut with a guillotine.

guilt (1) (gilt) [A.-S. *gylt*], *n.* The state of having committed a crime or offence; criminality, culpability; *an offence. **guiltless,** *a.* Free from guilt; innocent; having no knowledge (of), inexperienced; clear (of). **guiltlessly,** *adv.* **guiltlessness,** *n.* **guilty,** *a.* Having committed a crime; criminal, culpable (of); characterized by guilt. **guilty-like,** *a.* Like one guilty. **guiltily,** *adv.* **guiltiness,** *n.*

***guilt** (2) [GILT]. **guimp** [GIMP (1)].

guinea (gin′ i) [*Gnea,* Port. *Guiné,* country on west coast of Africa], *n.* A gold coin formerly current in Great Britain, coined 1663–1813, orig. of gold from Guinea, with the nominal value of 20s. until 1717, when this was fixed at 21s., and now a money of account; a sum of money equivalent to a guinea. **Guinea corn:** Indian millet *Sorghum vulgare,* called also durra. **guinea-fowl, -hen,** *n.* A gallinaceous bird of the genus *Numida,* esp. *N. meleagris,* something like the turkey, of a dark-grey colour with white spots, originally from Africa. **Guinea grains** [GRAIN (1)]. ***guinea pepper:** Cayenne pepper, *Capsicum*; also two species of *Amomum, A. grana Paradisi* and *A. grandiflorum.* **guinea-pig** [perh. corr. of *Guiana*], *n.* A small domesticated cavy, *Cavia cobaya,* a native of Brazil; (*slang*) a person rendering services more or less nominal for a guinea fee, such as a company director, a juryman, an officer on special duty, or a deputy clergyman; a person used as a subject for a medical experiment. **guinea-pigging,** *n.* **Guinea worm:** A whitish or dark-brown nematode worm *Filaria medinensis,* parasitic in the skin of the human feet, etc.

guipure (gē poor′) [F., from O.F. *guiper,* from Teut. (cp. Goth. *weipan,* to crown, G. *weifen,* to wind)], *n.* A lace without a ground or mesh, the pattern being held in place by threads; a kind of gimp.

guise (gīz) [O.F., from Teut. (cp. O.H.G. *wīsa,* WISE (2))], *n.* External appearance; semblance, pretence; manner, way, fashion; habit, dress. *v.t.* To dress up. *v.i.* To play the mummer. **guiser,** *n.* A masker, a mummer.

guitar (gi tar′) [Sp. *guitarra,* ult. from Gr. *kithara* (cp. CITHERN, GITTERN)], *n.* A (usu. six-) stringed instrument, somewhat like the violin in shape, but larger, with frets stopped by one hand, the strings being plucked with the fingers of the other. **guitar-fish,** *n.* A tropical sea-fish, one of the rays. **guitarist,** *n.*

gula (gū′ lȧ) [L], *n.* *The throat; (*Ent.*) a large plate supporting the submentum in some insects. **gular,** *a.*

gulch (gŭlch) [etym. doubtful (n. prob. from v., the latter imit.)], *n.* A deep ravine caused by the action of water. **v.t.* To swallow greedily.

gulden (gool′ dėn) [Dut. and G.], *n.* One of various gold coins of Germany or the Netherlands; a silver coin, the florin of Austria and Hungary, and the guilder of Holland, worth about 1s. 8d.

gules (gūlz) [M.E. and O.F. *goules* (F. *gueules*), med. L. *gulæ* ermine, dyed red, etym. doubtful], *n.* (*Her.*) A red colour, represented on an engraved escutcheon by vertical lines. *a.* Red. **guly,** *a.*

gulf (gŭlf) [F. *golfe,* ult. from late Gr. *kolphos,* Gr. *kolpos*], *n.* An inlet of the sea, deeper and narrower proportionately than a bay; a deep hollow, chasm, or abyss; a whirlpool, anything that swallows or engulfs; (*poet.*) a profound depth, as of the ocean; (*fig.*) an impassable chasm, interval, or difference; (*Univ. slang*) the pass or ordinary degree permitted to candidates who fail to get honours; (*Mining*) a large deposit of ore in a lode. **v.t.* To swallow up, to engulf; to form gulfs in; (*Univ. slang*) to award the 'gulf' to. *v.i.* To flow like a gulf or eddy. **Gulf Stream:** An ocean current carrying warm water from the Gulf of Mexico across the Atlantic to the British Isles and Scandinavia. **gulf-weed,** *n.* A sea-weed with berry-like air-vessels, *Sargassum bacciferum,* found in the Gulf Stream, the Sargasso Sea, etc. **gulfy,** *a.* Full of whirlpools; deep as a gulf.

gull (gŭl) [prob. Corn. *gullan,* cp. W. *gwylan,* Bret. *gwelan,* prob. from root, to wail], *n.* A long-winged, web-footed bird of the genus *Larus,* mostly marine in habitat; (*fig.*) a simpleton, a dupe. *v.t.* To fool, to trick; to impose upon. **gullery,** *n.* A breeding-place for gulls. **gullish,** *a.*

gullet (gŭl′ ėt) [O.F., dim. of *gole,* L. GULA], *n.* The throat; the œsophagus; a water-channel; a gore or gusset.

gullible (gŭl′ i bėl), *a.* Credulous, easily deceived. **gullibility,** *n.*

gully (1) (gŭl′ i) [var. of prec., or from F. *goulet,* GULLET], *n.* A channel or ravine worn by water; a ditch, drain, or gutter; a gully-hole; a tram-plate or rail. *v.t.* To wear a gully or gullies in, to furrow or channel by water action. **gully-drain,** *n.* A drain connecting a gully-hole with a sewer. **gully-hole,** *n.* An opening into a drain at the side of a street; a man-hole. **gully-hunter,** *n.* (*slang*) One who hunts for lost things in gutters. **gully-raker,** *n.* (*Austral.*) A drover's long whip. **gully-trap,** *n.* A grated trap to receive the discharge from rain-water pipes, etc.

gully (2) (gŭl′ i) [Sc. and North., perh. orig. a knife for the GULLET], *n.* A large knife.

gulosity (gū los′ i ti) [late L. *gūlōsitās,* from L. *gūlōsus,* gluttonous, from GULA], *n.* Gluttony, greediness.

gulp (gŭlp) [imit. (cp. Dut. *gulpen,* Norw. *glupa*)], *v.t.* To swallow (down) eagerly or in large draughts. *v.i.* To make a noise in swallowing or trying to swallow, to gasp or choke. *n.* The act of gulping; a large mouthful; an effort to swallow, a catching or choking in the throat. **to gulp up:** To disgorge. **gulpingly,** *adv.*

gum (1) (gum) [A.-S. *gōma* (cp. Icel. *gomr,* G. *gaumen,* palate)], *n.* The fleshy tissue investing the necks of the teeth; *arrogant talk. *v.t.* (*Am.*) To clear out or deepen the notches between the teeth in an old saw. **gumboil,** *n.* A boil or small abscess on the gums. **gum-rash,** *n.* A teething rash frequent in children.

gum (2) (gŭm) [M.E. and O.F. *gomme,* L. *gommi,* Gr. *kommi,* prob. from Egypt.], *n.* A viscid substance which exudes from certain trees, and hardens, but is more or less soluble in water, used for sticking things together, (*Am.* mucilage); a gum-tree or other plant or tree exuding this; (*colloq.*) chewing-gum. *v.t.* (*past & p.p.* **gummed**) To cover or stiffen with gum; to fasten or stick (down, in, together, up) with or as with gum. *v.i.* To exude gum; (*Am.*) to become sticky or clogged with disuse, dirt, etc. (as an axle). **gum arabic** [ARAB]. **gum-boots,** *n.pl.* Knee-high rubber boots, Wellingtons. **gum-dragon** [TRAGACANTH]. **gum-elastic,** *n.* Caoutchouc, indiarubber; (sometimes) gutta-percha. **gum-juniper,** *n.* Sandarac. **gum-resin,** *n.* A vegetable secretion consisting of a gum and a resin, *e.g.* gamboge. **gum-senegal,** *n.* A variety of gum arabic. **gum-tree,** *n.* (*Austral.*) One of several species of eucalyptus; (*Am.*) the name of various trees. **up a gum-tree:** Cornered, in a fix, brought to bay. **gummiferous** (-mif′ ėr ŭs), *a.* producing gum. **gumming,** *n.* A disease in trees bearing stone-fruit, characterized by a morbid exudation of gum. **gummous,** *a.* Of the nature of gum. **gummosity** (-mos′ i ti), *n.* **gummy,** *a.* Sticky, viscous, adhesive; productive of or covered with gum; puffy, swollen (of legs, ankles, etc.). **gumminess,** *n.*

gum (3) (gŭm) [minced form of GOD], **by gum:** A mild oath or expletive.

gumbo (gŭm′ bō) [Am. Negro], *n.* The okra, *Hibis-*

cus esculentus; a soup or a dish made of young capsules of this, seasoned, stewed, and served with melted butter; a Negro patois in Louisiana and the West Indies.

gumma (gŭm′ ȧ) [mod. L., from GUM (2)], *n.* (*pl.* **-as, -ata**) (*Path.*) A tumour with gummy contents, usu. due to syphilis. **gummatous,** *a.*

gummiferous, etc. [GUM (2)].

gummy (gŭm′ i), *n.* (*Austral.*) A sheep that has lost its teeth; a shark found off coasts of Tasmania and Victoria.

gumption (gŭmp′ shŭn) [Sc., etym. doubtful], *n.* Common sense, practical shrewdness, acuteness, tact, capacity for getting on; (*Painting*) the art of preparing colours; a medium for mixing colours. **gumptious,** *a.*

gun (gŭn) [short for Icel. *Gunnhildr* (*gunn-*, war, *hildr*, battle), a woman's name given to a war-engine (Skeat)], *n.* A tubular weapon from which projectiles are shot by means of gunpowder or other explosive force, a cannon, musket, rifle, or carbine; a person with a gun, a member of a shooting party. ***v.i.** To use a gun, esp. to go fowling. **as sure as a gun:** Undoubtedly; absolutely certain. **great gun:** A cannon; (*fig.*) a distinguished person. **to blow great guns:** To blow tempestuously. **to stick to one's guns:** To maintain an opinion in face of opposition. **son of a gun:** A rascal. **gun-barrel,** *n.* The barrel or tube of a gun. **gun-carriage,** *n.* The apparatus upon which a cannon is mounted for service. **gun-case,** *n.* A case for a sporting-gun. **gun-cotton,** *n.* A highly explosive substance made by soaking cotton in nitric and sulphuric acids, and then carefully drying. **gun-fire,** *n.* The hour at which the morning or evening gun is fired; discharge of guns. **gun-flint,** *n.* A flint used for firing an old-fashioned flint-lock gun. **gun-harpoon,** *n.* A harpoon shot from a gun, not thrown by hand. **gun-house,** *n.* A shelter for a gun and the gunners against the enemy's fire. **gun-layer,** *n.* (*Artil.*) The gunner whose duty it is to sight and elevate a gun or howitzer. **gun-lock,** *n.* The mechanism by which the charge in a gun is exploded. **gun-metal,** *n.* An alloy of copper and tin or zinc from which cannon were formerly cast. **gun-pit,** *n.* A pit in which a gun-mould is fixed for casting, or where a built-up gun is welded together; an excavation for sheltering a gun and gunners. **gun-reach,** *n.* (*Am.*) Gunshot. **gun-room,** *n.* A room on one of the lower decks of a war vessel to accommodate junior officers. **gun-runner,** *n.* One who smuggles any kind of fire-arms into a country. **gun-running,** *n.* **gun-shy,** *a.* Frightened at the report of fire-arms (of a dog, horse, etc.). **gun-stock,** *n.* The shaped block of wood to which the barrel of a gun is fixed. ***gunstone,** *n.* A shot for a cannon, round stones having been originally so used. **gun-tackle,** *n.* The ropes, pulleys, etc., attached to the sides of the ports, and to the gun-carriage on an old-fashioned war-ship. **gunless,** *a.* **gunning,** *n.* Shooting game with a gun.

gunboat (gŭn′ bōt), *n.* A warship of small size carrying heavy guns, formerly armed with a single heavy gun.

gunman (gŭn′ măn), *n.* An armed gangster; one engaged in the manufacture of arms.

gunnel (1) (gŭn′ ĕl) [etym. unknown], *n.* The butter-fish, *Centronotus gunnellus*, a blenny common on the British coasts and on the North American shores of the Atlantic.

gunnel (2) [GUNWALE].

gunner (gŭn′ ėr), *n.* (*Nav.*) A warrant officer in charge of ordnance or ordnance stores; (*Mil.*) an artilleryman, esp. a private; a person shooting game. **to kiss** or **marry the gunner's daughter:** (*Nav. slang*) To be lashed to a gun and flogged.

gunnery (gŭn′ ėr i), *n.* The art of managing heavy guns; the science of artillery; practice with heavy guns. **gunnery-lieutenant,** *n.* An officer trained on a gunnery-ship and qualified to supervise gunnery. **gunnery-ship,** *n.* A vessel for training officers and men in gunnery.

gunny (gŭn′ i) [Hind. *gōnī*, Sansk. *gōnī*], *n.* A heavy coarse sackcloth, usu. of jute or hemp, of which bags, etc. are made.

gunpowder (gŭn′ pou dėr), *n.* A mixture of saltpetre, carbon, and sulphur, reduced to a fine powder, then granulated and dried, used as an explosive; gunpowder-tea. **Gunpowder Plot:** A plot to blow up the Houses of Parliament by gunpowder on 5 Nov. 1605, and at one blow destroy King James I, the Lords, and the Commons. **gunpowder-tea,** *n.* A fine kind of green tea, each leaf of which is rolled up.

gunshot (gŭn′ shot), *n.* The range of a gun.

gunsmith (gŭn′ smith), *n.* One who makes or repairs small firearms.

Gunter (gŭn′ tėr) [Edmund *Gunter* (1581–1626), mathematician and astronomer], *n.* A Gunter's scale; (*Naut.*) an arrangement of topmast and rigging, in which the former slides up and down the lower mast on rings or hoops, so called from the resemblance to a sliding Gunter. **according to Gunter:** (*Am.*) A phrase like 'according to COCKER.' **Gunter's chain:** An ordinary surveyor's chain, 66 ft. in length, having 100 links, each 7·92 in. long. **Gunter's line:** A logarithmic line on Gunter's scale, used for performing the multiplication or division of numbers. **Gunter's scale:** A flat, two-foot rule having scales of chords, tangents, etc., and logarithmic lines, engraved on it, by which questions in navigation and surveying are solved mechanically.

gunwale, gunnel (2) (gŭn′ ĕl) [GUN-, WALE], *n.* The upper edge of a ship's side next to the bulwarks; a strip forming the upper edge of a boat.

gunyah (gŭn′ ya) [Austral. abor.], *n.* A native hut, usu. built of twigs and bark.

***gurge** (gĕrj) [L. *gurges*], *n.* A whirlpool, an eddy. *v.t.* To swallow up, to overwhelm. **gurgitation** (-tā′ shŭn), *n.* The movement of a liquid in a whirlpool or in boiling.

gurgle (gĕr′ gel) [prob. after It. *gorgogliare*, from L. *gurgulio*, the gullet], *v.i.* To make a purling or bubbling sound, as water poured from a bottle or running over a stony bottom; to run or flow with such a sound. *v.t.* To utter with such a sound. *n.* A gurgling sound; a purling noise.

gurgoyle [GARGOYLE].

Gurkha (goor′ kȧ) [Hind.], *n.* A member of the dominant race in Nepaul, of Hindu descent, expelled from Rajputana by the Mohammedan invasion; (*pl.*) Indian soldiers of this race.

gurly (gĕr′ li) [Sc., obs. n. *gurl*, imit. of sound], *a.* Rough, stormy.

gurnard, -net (gĕr′ nȧrd, -nĕt) [prob. from F. *grognard*, from *grogner*, to grunt], *n.* The popular name of any fish of the genus *Trigla*, characterized by a large angular head, covered with bony plates, and three free pectoral rays.

gurrah (gŭr′ ȧ) [Hind. *gārhā*], *n.* A plain, coarse Indian muslin.

gurry (gŭr′ i) [etym. unknown], *n.* (*Whale-fishing*) Fish-offal.

guru (goo′ roo) [Sansk., heavy, weighty], *n.* A Hindu spiritual teacher or guide.

gush (gŭsh) [cp. E.Fris. *gūsen*, L.G. *gusen*, Icel. *gusa*, G. *giessen*], *v.i.* To flow or rush out copiously or with violence; to be uttered rapidly and copiously; to be filled with water, tears, etc.; (*fig.*) to be effusive or affectedly sentimental. *v.t.* To pour (out) rapidly or copiously. *n.* A violent and copious issue of a fluid; the fluid thus emitted; an outburst; (*fig.*) extravagant affectation of sentiment. **gusher,** *n.* One who or that which gushes; an oil-well that discharges with great force or without requiring pumps. **gushingly,** *adv.* **gushy,** *a.*

gusset (gŭs′ ėt) [O.F. *gousset*, a flexible piece of armour filling up a joint, dim. of *gousse*, a nutshell], *n.* A small triangular piece of cloth inserted in a dress to enlarge or strengthen some part; an angle-iron or bracket for stiffening an angle in construction work; (*Her.*) a gore. **gusseted,** *a.*

gust (1) (gŭst) [Icel. *gustr*, cogn. with GUSH], *n.* A short but violent rush of wind; a squall; (*fig.*) an outburst of passion. ***gustful,** *a.* **gusty,** *a.* **gustily,** *adv.*

gust (2) (gŭst) [L. *gustus*, taste, whence *gustāre*, to taste, *gustātio*, tasting], *n.* The sense or pleasure of tasting; relish, taste. **v.t.* To have a relish for. ***gustable,** *a.* That may be tasted; pleasant to the taste. *n.* Anything agreeable to the taste. ***gustation** (gŭs tā′ shŭn), *n.* **gustative, gustatory** (gŭst′-), *a.* Of or pertaining to gustation. **gustatory nerve:** The lingual nerve upon which taste depends. **gusto,** *n.* Zest, enjoyment, pleasure; flavour, relish.

gusty, etc. [GUST (1)].

gut (gŭt) [A.-S. *gutt*, in pl. *guttas* (cp. G. *gosse*), prob. cogn. with *gēotan*, to pour], *n.* The intestinal canal; (*pl.*) the intestines; an intestine, or a part of the alimentary canal; (*pl., fig.*) the belly or the stomach as symbol of gluttony; catgut, the prepared intestines of animals used for the strings of musical instruments; fibre drawn from a silkworm before it spins its cocoon, used for fishing-lines; a narrow passage, esp. a sound or strait; *pl.* (*slang*) stamina, courage, persistence. *v.t.* (*past & p.p.* **gutted**) To eviscerate; to draw the entrails out of; (*fig.*) to plunder, to remove or destroy the contents of (as by fire). *v.i.* (*vulg.*) To gormandize. **gut-scraper,** *n.* (*facet.*) A fiddler. **gutty** (1), *a.* Corpulent.

gutta (gŭt′ ȧ) [L.], *n.* (*pl.* **-tæ**) A drop; (*Arch.*) an ornament resembling a drop, used in the Doric entablature. **gutta rosacea, rosea** or **rubea:** (*Path.*) Inflammation of the face, with redness and pimples. **gutta serena:** (*Path.*) Amaurosis. **guttate,** *a.* (*Bot.*) Besprinkled or speckled. **gutté** (gŭt′ ā), **guttee** (gŭt′ ē) [A.-F. *gutté* (F. *goutté*), as above], *a.* (*Her.*) Sprinkled with drops. **guttiferous** (gŭt if′ ėr ŭs), *a.* (*Bot.*) Yielding gum or resinous sap. **guttiform** (gŭt′ i fôrm), *a.* Drop-shaped.

gutta-percha (gŭt′ ȧ pĕr′ chȧ) [Malay *gatah*, gum, *percha*, name of the tree], *n.* The inspissated juice of *Isonandra gutta*, the Malayan gutta-percha tree, forming a horny substance used for insulators, etc. **gutty** (2), *n.* (*Golf.*) A gutta-percha ball.

gutté [GUTTA].

gutter (gŭt′ ėr) [O.F. *gutiere*, from *goute*, see GOUT], *n.* A channel at the side of a street or a trough below eaves for carrying away water; a channel worn by water; a trench, conduit, etc., for the passage of water or other fluid; (*Sc., usu. in pl.*) dirt, mire; *a receptacle for filth; (*Print.*) the space between the printed matter in two adjacent pages. *v.t.* To form channels or gutters in; to provide with gutters. *v.i.* To become channelled or worn with hollows, as a burning candle; to stream (down). **gutter-bird, -child,** *n.* A street arab. ***gutter-blood,** *n.* One of base birth. **gutter-man,** *n.* A street vendor of cheap articles. **gutter press,** *n.* Cheap and sensational newspapers. **guttersnipe,** *n.* A street arab; (*Am.*) a kerbstone broker. **guttering,** *n.* The act of forming gutters; a gutter or arrangement of gutters; material for gutters; the act of falling in drops.

guttiform, etc. [GUTTA].

guttle (gŭtl) [from GUT, after GUZZLE], *v.i.* To eat voraciously, to gobble. *v.t.* To devour gluttonously, to gobble up. **guttler,** *n.*

guttural (gŭt′ ŭr ȧl) [F., from L. *guttur*, throat], *a.* Pertaining to the throat; produced or formed in the throat. *n.* A sound or combination of sounds produced in the throat or the back part of the mouth, as *k, q*, hard *c* and *g, ng*, and the G. *ch*. **gutturalize, *gutturize,** *v.t.* To form in the throat. **gutturalism,** *n.* **gutturally,** *adv.* **gutturo-,** *comb. form.* **gutturo-nasal,** *a.* Pertaining to or produced by the throat and the nose. **gutturo-maxillary,** *a.*

gutty [see GUT, GUTTA-PERCHA].

guy (1) (gī) [O.F. *guie*, from *guier*, see GUIDE], *n.* A rope, chain, etc., to steady a load in hoisting or to act as a stay. *v.t.* To guide or steady by means of a guy or guys. **guy-rope,** *n.*

guy (2) (gī) [*Guy* Fawkes, the conspirator who attempted to blow up Parliament in 1605], *n.* An effigy of Guy Fawkes burnt on 5 Nov. in memory of GUNPOWDER PLOT; a fright, a dowdy, a fantastic figure. **a regular guy:** (*Am. colloq.*) a good fellow. *v.t.* To display in effigy; to quiz, to chaff, to ridicule. *v.i.* To carry a guy round on 5 Nov. **to do a guy:** To run away, decamp.

guzzle (gŭz′ ėl) [perh. from O.F. *gosiller*, to vomit, cogn. with *gosier*, the throat], *v.i.* To drink liquor greedily; to eat greedily. *v.t.* To drink or eat greedily; (*fig.*) to waste (one's income) in guzzling. *n.* A debauch; *drink. **guzzler,** *n.*

gwyniad (gwin′ i ȧd) [W., from *gwyn*, white], *n.* A salmonoid fish, *Coregonus Pennantii*, found in Bala Lake and the English Lakes.

gybe (jīb) [Naut., prob. from Dut. *gijben* (now *gijpen*)], *v.i.* To swing from one side of the mast to the other (of a fore-and-aft sail); to take the wind on the other quarter (of a vessel). *v.t.* To shift (a sail) in this way; to make (a vessel) take the wind on the opposite quarter. *n.* The act or process of gybing.

gym (jim) [GYMNASIUM].

gymkhana (jim ka′ nȧ) [Hind. *gend-khāna*, ball house, racket-court, assim. to GYMNASTICS], *n.* A meeting for athletic sports and games; orig. a place for such sports.

gymnasium (jim nā′ zi ŭm) [L., from Gr. *gumnasion*, from *gumnazein*, to exercise naked, from *gumnos*, naked], *n.* (*pl.* **-ia, -ums**) A building or room where athletic exercises are performed; (*G.*) (gim na′ zi ŭm) a school of the highest grade preparatory to the Universities. **gymnasial** (jim nā′ zi ȧl), *a.* **gymnasiarch,** *n.* (*Gr. Ant.*) A public official who superintended the Grecian athletes; a leading athlete; a head instructor in an academy. **gymnasiast,** *n.*

gymnast (jim′ năst) [Gr. *gymnastēs*, as prec.], *n.* An expert in gymnastic exercises. **gymnastic** (-năs′ tik), *a.* Of or pertaining to exercises for the development of the body; involving athletic effort; (*fig.*) involving great mental effort or discipline. *n.* (*usu. in pl.*) A course of instruction, discipline or exercise for the development of body or mind; exercises for the development of bodily strength and agility; the gymnastic art. **gymnastically,** *adv.* ***gymnic,** *a.* Gymnastic.

gymno- [Gr. *gumnos*, naked], *comb. form.* Naked; destitute of protective covering. **gymnocarpous** (jim nō kar′ pŭs) [Gr. *karpos*, fruit], *a.* (*Bot.*) Having the fruit or spore-bearing parts bare.

gymnogenous [GYMNOSPERMOUS].

gymnogynous (jim noj′ i nŭs), *a.* (*Bot.*) Having the ovary naked.

gymnorhinal (jim nō rī′ nȧl), *a.* (*Ornith.*) Having the nostrils naked or unfeathered.

gymnosophist (jim nos′ ȯ fist) [*gymnosophistæ*, pl., Gr. *gumnosophistai* (GYMNO-, SOPHIST)], *n.* One of an ancient Hindu sect of philosophic hermits who went nearly naked and used contemplation and asceticism. **gymnosophy,** *n.*

gymnosperm (jim′ nō spĕrm), *n.* (*Bot.*) One of a class of plants having naked seeds, as the pine. **gymnospermous,** *a.*

gymnospore (jim′ nō spôr), *n.* (*Bot.*) A naked spore. **gymnosporous,** *a.* Having naked spores.

gymnotus (jim nō′ tŭs) [GYMNO-, Gr. *nōtos*, the back], *n.* (*pl.* **-ti**) An electric eel.

gymp [JIMP].

gynæceum (gī-, jī nē sē′ ŭm) [L., from Gr. *gunaikeion*, from *gunē gunaikos*, woman], *n.* (*Gr. and Rom. Ant.*) The part of a house reserved for the women; (*Bot.*) the female organs in a plant. **gynæcian** (-nē′ shi ản), *a.* Relating to women. **gynæcik** (nē′ sik), *a.* Relating to the diseases of women.

gynæco- [Gr. *gunē gunaikos*, woman], *comb. form.* Pertaining to women.

gynæcocracy (gī-, jī ni kok′ rả si), *n.* Government by women. **gynæcocrat,** *n.* **gynæcocratic,** *a.*

gynæcology (gī-, jī nė kol′ ō ji), *n.* The science dealing with the functions and diseases peculiar to women. **gynæcological,** *a.* **gynæcologist,** *n.*

gynander (jī năn′ dėr) [Gr. *gunandros* (*gunē*, woman, *anēr andros*, man)], *n.* (*Bot.*) A plant of the class *Gynandria*; a masculine woman. ***Gynandria,*** *n.pl.* (*Bot.*) A Linnæan class of plants, in which the stamens and pistils are united, as in orchids. **gynandrian, -drous,** *a.* (*Bot.*) Having the stamens and pistil connate. **gynandry,** *n.* (*Biol.*) A tendency in the female towards a male body.

***gynarchy** (jī′ nar ki) [Gr. *gunē*, woman, *archia*, rule, from *archein*, to reign], *n.* Gynæcocracy.

gyniolatry (jī ni ol′ ả tri) [Gr. *gunē*, woman, -LATRY], *n.* Excessive devotion to women.

gyno-, gyn- [Gr. *gunē*, woman], *comb. form.* Distinctively feminine; pertaining to the female organs of plants.

gynobase (gī′-, jī′ nō bās), *n.* (*Bot.*) Enlargement of the receptacle of a flower, bearing the gynæceum.

gynophobia (gī nō fō′ bi ả), *n.* A morbid fear of women.

gynophore (jī′ nō fôr), *n.* (*Bot.*) The pedicel or stalk of the ovary, as in the passion-flower; (*Zool.*) one of the branches in hydrozoa bearing female gonophores.

-gynous [Gr. *-gunos*, from *gunē*, woman], *suf.* Pertaining to women; (*Bot.*) having female organs or pistils; as *androgynous, misogynous.*

gyp (jip) [perh. short for GIPSY (or for obs. *gippo*, scullion, orig. man's short tunic, from obs. F. *jupeau*, O.E.D.)], *n.* A male servant in college at Cambridge and Durham. **gyp-room,** *n.* A room used by a gyp as pantry, etc.

gypsum (jip′ sŭm) [L., from Gr. *gupsos*, chalk], *n.* A mineral consisting of hydrous sulphate of lime, which when deprived of its water by heat and calcined forms plaster of Paris. *v.t.* To manure with gypsum. **gypseous, gypsous,** *a.* **gypsiferous** (-sif′ ėr ŭs), *a.*

gypsy [GIPSY].

gyrate (jīr′ ảt) [L. *gȳrātus*, p.p. of *gȳrāre*, from GYRUS], *a.* Circular, convoluted; (*Bot.*) circinate; moving round in a circle. *v.i.* (jī rāt′) To rotate, revolve, whirl, in either a circle or a spiral. **gyration** (jī rā′ shŭn), *n.* **gyrational,** *a.* **gyratory** (jīr′ ả tỏr i), *a.* **gyre** (jīr), *n.* (*poet.*) A gyration, a revolution. *v.t.* To turn round; to whirl. *v.i.* To turn or move in a circle. **gyral,** *a.* **gyrally,** *adv.*

gyre-carline (gīr′ kar lin) [Icel. *gȳgr*, witch, *karlinna*, CARLINE (1)], *n.* (*Sc.*) A witch, a hag.

gyrfalcon [GERFALCON].

gyro- [Gr. *guros*, circle, ring], *comb. form.* Round, curved; relating to revolutions. **gyro-compass,** *n.* A navigating compass consisting of an electrically driven gyroscope the axle of which orientates the sensitive element.

gyrograph (jī′ rō grăf), *n.* An instrument for recording revolutions.

gyroidal (jī roi′ dảl), *a.* Arranged or moving spirally.

gyromancy (jī′ rō măn si), *n.* Divination performed by walking round in a circle or ring until one falls from dizziness.

gyron (jīr′ ỏn), F., *n.* (*Her.*) A triangular charge formed by two lines meeting at the fesse-point. **gyronny,** *a.*

gyroplane (jī′ rō plān), *n.* (*Aviat.*) An aeroplane deriving its lift from the reaction of the air on freely rotating rotors in a horizontal plane, a rotaplane, a helicopter.

gyroscope (jī′ rō skōp), *n.* A heavy fly-wheel rotated (usu. electrically) at very high speed and supported on an axis at right angles to the plane of the wheel. Any alteration of direction of the axis of rotation is resisted by the turning movement. It is used as a controlling or stabilizing device, or as a compass in ships, aeroplanes, etc. **gyroscopic** (-skop′ ik), *a.*

gyrose (jī′ rōz), *a.* (*Bot.*) Marked with wavy lines; circinate.

gyrostabiliser (jī rō stăb′ i lī zėr), *n.* A gyroscopic device for steadying the roll of a vessel.

gyrostat (jī′ rō stăt), *n.* Lord Kelvin's modification of the gyroscope, for illustrating the dynamics of rotating bodies. **gyrostatic,** *a.*

gyrus (jīr′ ŭs) [L., from Gr. *guros*, a ring, a circle] (*pl.* **gyri,** jī′ rī) (*Anat.*) A rounded serpentine ridge bounded by grooves or fissures, esp. a convolution of the brain.

gyte (1) (gīt) [Sc., etym. unknown], *a.* Mad, crazy.

gyte (2) (gīt) [Sc., corr. of GET], *n.* A child; A first-year boy at Edinburgh High School.

gytrash (gī′ trăsh) [North., etym. doubtful], *n.* A ghost, a spectre.

gyve (jīv) [M.E. *guive*, etym. doubtful], *n.* (*usu. in pl.*) A fetter, a shackle. ****v.t.*** To fetter, to enchain; (*fig.*) to entangle.

H

H, h, the eighth letter of the English alphabet (*pl.* **aitches, Hs, H's**), is mostly in English a simple breathing at the beginning of a word or syllable, as in *help, hard, hope,* etc. **H** is commonly joined to other consonants to form digraphs, as *ch* in *child, chill*; *sh* in *shin, ship*; *th* in *this, that, think*; joined with *p*, and sometimes with *g*, it gives the sound of *f*, as in *philosophy, enough*; sometimes the latter digraph is silent, as in *bough, plough. Ch* is common in words derived from the Greek, and in such cases is usu. sounded as *k*, as in *chemistry, chyle,* etc.; the Scottish and German *ch* (italicized in the scheme of pronunciation adopted here) is a guttural spirant corresponding to the Greek ϰ, as in *clachan, Reichstag.* **H-bomb,** *n.* A hydrogen bomb. **to drop one's hs:** To fail to give the breathing in words beginning with *h*; to speak incorrectly.

ha (ha) [onomat., common to Teut., Gr., L., etc.], *int.* An exclamation denoting surprise, joy, suspicion, or other sudden emotion; *expressing interrogation; an inarticulate sound expressive of hesitation; when repeated, **ha ha!** it denotes laughter. *n.* The exclamation so defined, or the sound of it. *v.i.* To express surprise, wonder, etc.; to hesitate.

ha' (*Sc.*) [HALL].

haaf (haf) [Icel., *haf*, the high sea], *n.* Deep-sea fishing ground (off Orkney and Shetland).

haar (har) [perh. from Icel. *hārr*], *n.* (*Sc. and prov.*) A wet mist, esp. a sea-fog.

habble (*Sc.*) [HOBBLE].

habeas corpus (hā′ bė ås kôr′ pŭs) [L., thou mayest have the body], *n.* A writ to produce a prisoner before a court, with particulars of the day and cause of his arrest and detention, in order that the justice of this may be determined. **Habeas Corpus Act:** Act 31 Charles II, c. 2 (1679), authorizing this.

Habenaria (hăb ė nâr′ i ȧ) [L. *habēna*, rein, strap, from *habēre*, to have], *n.* (*Bot.*) A large genus of low terrestrial orchids bearing spikes of brilliant flowers.

haberdasher (hăb′ ėr dăsh ėr) [from obs. *haberdash*, haberdashery, A.-F. *hapertas*, etym. unknown], *n.* A seller of small articles of apparel, as ribbons, laces, silks, etc.; *a pedlar; *a hatter. **haberdashery,** *n.* These small articles of underwear, etc.; (*Am.*) men's underwear.

***habergeon** (hăb′ ėr jȯn) [O.F. *haubergeon*, dim. of *hauberc*, HAUBERK], *n.* A sleeveless coat of mail or armour to protect the neck and breast.

habile (hăb′ il) [F. ABLE], *a.* Handy, adroit; *competent, fit. ***hability,** *n.* Ability.

habiliment (hȧ bil′ i mėnt) [O.F. *habillement*, from *habiller*, to get ready], *n.* *Attire, dress, equipment; (*pl.*) dress, garb; (*colloq.*) clothes. ***habilable** (hăb′ il ȧbl), *a.* Capable of being clothed. ***habilatory** (hȧ bil′ ȧ tȯr i), *a.* Pertaining to clothing; wearing clothes.

habilitate (hȧ bil′ i tāt) [L. *habilitātus*, p.p. of *habilitāre*, to make fit, from *habilitās*, ABILITY], *v.t.* To furnish with means (as a mine with working capital). *v.i.* To become qualified (for). **habilitation** (-tā′ shŭn), *n.* **habilitator** (hȧ bil′ i tā tȯr), *n.* One who supplies means.

habit (hăb′ it) [O.F., from L. *habitum*, nom. *-tus*, from *habēre*, to have, refl. to be constituted, to be], *n.* A permanent tendency to perform certain actions; a settled inclination, disposition, or trend of mind; manner, practice, use, or custom, acquired by frequent repetition; (*Bot.* and *Zool.*) a characteristic manner of growth; garb, dress, costume, esp. one of a distinctive kind, as of a religious order. *v.t.* To inhabit; to habituate; to dress, to clothe. **riding-habit,** *n.* A woman's dress for riding side-saddle. **habit-shirt,** *n.* A chemisette with collar, worn over the neck and breast by women.

habitable (hăb′ it ȧbl) [F., from L. *habitābilis*, from *habitāre*, to dwell, freq. of *habēre*, see prec.], *a.* That may be dwelt in or inhabited. **habitability** (-bil′ i ti), **habitableness,** *n.* **habitably,** *adv.* ***habitacle,** *n.* A dwelling-place. ***habitance,** *n.* A habitation; a dwelling. ***habitancy,** *n.* Inhabitancy. **habitant,** *n.* *An inhabitant; (a′ bē taṅ) an inhabitant of Lower Canada of French origin. **habitation** (-tā′ shŭn), *n.* The act of inhabiting; the state of being inhabited; a place of abode; natural region or locality; a lodge of the Primrose League.

habitat (hăb′ i tăt), *n.* The natural abode or locality of an animal or plant.

habited (hăb′ i tėd) [HABIT], *a.* Dressed; wearing a habit; inhabited.

habitual (hȧ bit′ ū ȧl) [late L. *habituālis*, from *habitus*, HABIT], *a.* Formed or acquired by habit; according to habit, usual; customary, constant; rendered permanent by use. **habitually,** *adv.* **habitualness,** *n.* **habituate,** *v.t.* To accustom; to make familiar by frequent repetition. **a.* (-ȧt) Given to a habit, formed by habit. **habituation,** (-ā′ shŭn), *n.* **habitude** (hăb′ i tūd), *n.* Customary manner or mode, habit, aptitude, tendency, propensity; customary relation, familiarity. **habitué** (hȧ bit′ ū ā, ȧ bē tu ā), *n.* (*fem.* **-uée**) One who habitually frequents a place, esp. a place of amusement.

haboob (ha boob′) [Ar. *habub*, blowing fiercely], *n.* A high wind charged with sand that blows from the desert in the Sudan.

hachis (ha shē) [F., as HACHURE], *n.* A hash.

hachisch [HASHISH].

hachure (ha shoor′) [F., from *hacher*, to HATCH (3)], *n.* (*usu. pl.*) Short lines employed to represent half-tints and shadows, and on maps to denote hill-slopes. *v.t.* To cover or mark with hachures.

hacienda (hă si en′ dȧ) [Sp., from O.Sp. and L. *facienda*, things to be done, neut. pl. gerund of *facere*, to do], *n.* (*Sp. Am.*) An estate; a farm or plantation, an establishment in the country for stock-raising, etc., esp. with a residence for the proprietor.

hack (1) (hăk) [M.E. *hakken*, A.-S. *-haccian* (cp. Dut. *hakken*, Dan. *hakke*, G. *hacken*)], *v.t.* To cut irregularly or into small pieces; to chop, to notch; to cut unskilfully; to kick (a player's shins) at football; *(*fig.*) to mangle in uttering. *v.i.* To cut or chop away at anything; to emit a short dry cough. *n.* An irregular cut, a gash, a notch, a dent; the result of a kick (on the shins, etc.); a mattock or large pick, a miner's pick with a chisel edge at one end; *a stammering. **hack-saw,** *n.* A hand-saw used for cutting metal. **hacking,** *a.* Slashing, chopping, mangling; short, dry, and intermittent (of a cough).

hack (2) (hăk), *n.* A hackney, a horse for hire; a horse for general purposes, esp. as dist. from a hunter or racer; (*Am.*) a hackney-carriage; a jade, a drudge, esp. a literary drudge. *v.t.* To let out for hire; to make a hack of; to make common, to hackney. *v.i.* To be let out for hire; to ride a hack or (*Am.*) in a hack; to ride at the pace of an ordinary hack; to be common or vulgar; to live as a prostitute. **hack-work,** *n.* Work done by a literary drudge.

hack (3) (hăk) [var. of HATCH (1)], *n.* A rack or grated frame, a hatch; a drying-frame for fish; a frame for drying bricks; a feeding-rack or manger; (*Hawking*) a feeding-board for hawks, also the state of partial liberty in which young hawks are kept. *v.t.* To keep young hawks at hack. **at hack:** (*Hawking*) To be at liberty but obedient to the falconer.

hackberry (hăk′ bėr i) [var. of HAGBERRY], *n.* A North American tree of the genus *Celtis*, related to the Elms; called also the nettle-tree, sugarberry, hog berry.

hackbut (hăk′ bŭt) [M.F. *haquebute*, O.F. *haquebusche*, see HARQUEBUS], *n.* A harquebus. **hackbuteer, hackbutier** (hăk bŭ tēr′), *n.*

hackee (hăk′ i) [imit. of cry], *n.* The North American ground-squirrel or chipmunk.

hackery (hăk′ ėr i) [prob. from Hind.], *n.* A rude East Indian two-wheeled car, drawn by bullocks.

hackle (1) (hăk′ ėl) [M.E. *hachele*, cogn. with M.H.G. *hachele* (G. *hechel*, cp. Dut. *hekel*)], *n.* An instrument with sharp steel spikes for dressing or combing (flax, etc.); fibrous substance unspun, as raw silk; a long shining feather on a cock's neck; a fly for angling, dressed with this. *v.t.* To dress or comb (flax or hemp) with a hackle; to tie a hackle on (an artificial fly). **with his hackles up:** (Of a dog, cock, etc.) ready to fight.

hackle (2) (hăkl), *v.t.* To hack, to mangle. **hackler** *n.* **hackly,** *a.* Broken or jagged as if hacked (*Cryst.*) breaking with a peculiarly uneven surface.

hacklet (hăk′ lėt) [etym. unknown], *n.* The kittiwake.

hackmatack (hăk′ mȧ tăk) [Am.-Ind.], *n.* The American larch; the tamarack.

hackney (hăk′ ni) [M.E. *Hakeney*, Hackney, co. of London], *n.* A horse kept for riding or driving; a horse kept for hire; a hackney-carriage. *v.i.* *To carry in a hackney-carriage; *to use much; (*usu. in p.p.*) to make stale, trite, or commonplace. **hackney-carriage, -coach,** *n.* A passenger road vehicle licensed for hire. **hackney-coachman,** *n.* ***hackney-man,** *n.* One who lets out hackneys.

had, *past* and *p.p.* [HAVE]. **you've had it:** (*colloq.*) There's no chance of your getting it now; there's an end of that; you've had your chance and lost it.

haddie (*Sc.*) [HADDOCK].

haddin', hadding (*Sc.*) [HOLDING].

haddock (hăd′ ȯk) [etym. doubtful], *n.* A sea-fish, *Gadus æglefinus*, allied to the cod.

hade (hād) [etym. doubtful], *n.* (*Geol. and Mining*) The inclination of a fault or vein from the vertical, complementary to the dip. **hading,** *n.*

Hades (hā′ dēz) [Gr. *Hadēs, Aidēs,* the god of the lower world], *n.* The lower world, the abode of the spirits of the dead.

hadith (hăd′ ith) [Arab.], *n.* Tradition, esp. the body of tradition relating to the sayings and doings of Mohammed.

hadji (hăj′ i) [Arab. *hājī*], *n.* A Mohammedan who has performed the pilgrimage to Mecca; a title conferred on such a man. ***hadj,*** *n.* A pilgrimage to Mecca.

hadrosaur (hăd′ rȯ sawr) [mod. L. *hadrosaurus* (Gr. *hadros,* thick, *sauros,* lizard)], *n.* (*Palæont.*) A genus of gigantic fossil saurians from the Cretaceous strata of North America.

hae (*Sc.*) [HAVE].

hæcceity (hek sē′ i ti) [med. L. *hæcceitas,* thisness (Duns Scotus), from *hæc,* fem. of *hic,* this], *n.* (*Phil.*) The quality of being a particular thing, individuality.

hæma-, hæmat-, hæmato- [Gr. *haima haimatos,* blood], *comb. form.* Consisting of or containing blood; pertaining to or resembling blood.

hæmal (hē′ măl) [as prec.], *a.* Of or pertaining to the blood; (*Anat.*) on or pertaining to the side of the body containing the heart and great blood-vessels.

hæmatemesis (hē mȧ tem′ ė sis), *n.* A vomiting of blood.

hæmatic (hē măt′ ik), *a.* Of or pertaining to the blood; acting on the blood; containing blood; blood-coloured. *n.* A medicine acting on the blood.

hæmatics (hē măt′ iks), *n.* The branch of physiology which treats of the blood.

hæmatin (hē′ mȧ tin), *n.* An amorphous substance associated with hæmoglobin in the blood; hæmotoxylin.

hæmatite (hem′ ȧ-, hē mȧ tīt) [O.F. *hematite,* L. *hæmatītēs,* Gr. *Laimatites,* blood-like], *n.* (*Min.*) Native sesquioxide of iron, occurring in two forms, red and brown, a valuable iron-ore. **hæmatitic** (-tit′ ik), *a.*

hæmatoblast (hē′ mȧ tȯ blast) [HÆMATO-, -BLAST], *n.* (*Physiol.*) One of the minute colourless disks, smaller than the ordinary corpuscles, found in the blood. **hæmatoblastic** (-blăs′ tik), *a.*

hæmatocele (hē′ mȧ tȯ sēl) [HÆMATO-, -CELE], *n.* (*Path.*) A tumour containing blood.

hæmatocyte (hē′ mȧ tō sīt), *n.* A blood-corpuscle. **hæmatocytometer,** *n.* An instrument for determining the number of corpuscles in a given quantity of blood.

hæmatoid (hē′ mȧ toid), *a.* Having the appearance of blood.

hæmatology (hē mȧ tol′ ō ji), *n.* The branch of physiology dealing with blood.

hæmatosin (hē mȧ tō′ sin), *n.* Hæmatin.

hæmatosis (hē mȧ tō′ sis), *n.* The formation of blood or of blood-corpuscles; the conversion of venous into arterial blood.

hæmatoxylin (hē mȧ tok′ si lin) [HÆMATO-, Gr. *xulon,* wood], *n.* (*Chem.*) A dye obtained from logwood. **hæmatoxylic** (-tok sil′ ik), *a.*

hæmatozoa (hē mă tō zō′ ȧ), *n.pl.* Parasites found in the blood.

hæmaturia (hē mȧ tū′ ri ȧ), *n.* The presence of blood in the urine.

hæmo- [shortened form of HÆMATO-], *comb. form.*

hæmochrome (hē′ mō krōm), *n.* The colouring matter of the blood.

hæmodynamics (hē mō dī năm′ iks), *n.* The dynamics of the circulation of the blood.

hæmoglobin (hē mō glō′ bin), *n.* (*Chem.*) The colouring matter of the red corpuscles of the blood.

***hæmony** (hē′ mȯ ni) [prob. from Gr. *haimōnios,* blood-red], *n.* An unidentified plant having supernatural properties, mentioned by Milton (*Comus,* I. 638).

hæmophilia (hē mȯ fil′ i ȧ), *n.* (*Path.*) A constitutional tendency to hæmorrhage.

hæmoptysis (hē mop′ ti sis), *n.* (*Path.*) A spitting or coughing up of blood from the lungs.

hæmorrhage (hem′ ȯr ăj) [M.F. *hemorrhagie,* late L. *hæmorrhagia,* Gr. *haimorrhagia* (HÆMO-, *-rhagia,* from stem of *rhēgnunai,* to break)], *n.* (*Path.*) Discharge of blood from the heart, arteries, veins, or capillaries. **hæmorrhagic** (-răj′ ik), *a.*

hæmorrhoids (hem′ ȯ roidz) [formerly *emorods, emoroydes,* O.F. *emoroyde,* L. *hæmorrhoidæ,* pl. of *hæmorrhoida,* Gr. *hæmorrhoïdēs,* pl. of *hæmorrhoïs,* adj., discharging blood (HÆMO-, *-rhoos,* flowing, from *rheein,* to flow)], *n.pl.* (*Path.*) Piles. **hæmorrhoidal** (-roi′ dăl), *a.*

hæmostatic (hē mȯ stăt′ ik), *a.* (*Med.*) Serving to stop hæmorrhage. *n.* A medicine for doing this; (*pl.*) the branch of physiology relating to the hydrostatics of blood. **hæmostasia** (-stăz′ i ȧ), *n.* (*Path.*) Congestion of blood; (*Med.*) stoppage of the flow of blood by means of constriction or compression of an artery.

haeremai (hī′ rȧ mī) [Maori], (*N. Zealand*) *int.* Welcome!

haffet (hăf′ ėt) [Sc., earlier *halfhed,* A.-S. *healfhēafod* (HALF-HEAD)], *n.* The side of the head, the temple.

hafflin [HALFLING].

hafiz (ha′ fiz) [Pers.], *n.* One knowing the Koran by heart (a Mohammedan title).

hafnium (hăf′ ni ŭm) [L. *Hafniæ,* Copenhagen], *n.* Metallic element occurring in zirconium ores.

haft (haft) [A.-S. *hæft,* from root of *hebban,* to HEAVE], *n.* A handle, esp. of a dagger, knife, or tool; (*Sc.*) a dwelling, a lodging. *v.t.* To set in or fit with a handle; *to drive in to the hilt; (*Sc.*) to establish as in a residence, to settle, to accustom to.

hag (1) (hăg) [perh. shortened from A.-S. *hægtesse*], *n.* A witch; a fury; an ugly old woman; an eel-like fish, *Myxine glutinosa,* of low organization, parasitic within the bodies of other fishes; *a kind of phosphoric light appearing on horses' manes, hair, etc. *v.t.* *To frighten, to torment; to sweat (work-people). ***hag-born,*** *a.* Born of a hag. **hag-ridden,** *a.* Suffering from nightmare. **hag-weed,** *n.* The broom, *Cytisus scoparius.* **haggish,** *a.* **haggishly,** *adv.*

hag (2) (hăg) [Sc. and North., perh. from Icel. *hogg,* a cut or gap, from *hoggva,* cogn. with A.-S. *heawan,* to HEW], *n.* A break or soft place in a bog; one of the turfy hillocks of firmer ground in a bog. *v.t.* and *i.* To hack, to chop.

hagberry (hăg′ bėr i) [from Scand. (cp. Dan. *hæggebær*)], *n.* The bird-cherry, *Prunus padus*; in America the hackberry.

***hagbut** [HACKBUT].

Haggadah (hȧ ga′ dȧ) [Heb., a tale], *n.* The legendary part of the Talmud. **Haggadic, -al** (hȧ găd′-, -gā′ dik, -ăl), *a.* **Haggadist** (hȧ gā′ dist), *n.* **Haggadistic** (-dis′ tik), *a.*

haggard (1) (hăg ȧrd) [F. *hagard* (perh. conn. with O.H.G. *haga,* HEDGE, whence *faucon hagard,* hedge-falcon)], *a.* Wild-looking; anxious, careworn, or gaunt from fatigue, trouble, etc.; wild (of a hawk). *n.* A wild or untrained hawk. **haggardly,** *adv.* **haggardness,** *n.*

haggard (2) (hăg′ ȧrd) [cp. Icel. *heygarthr* (*hey,* hay, *garthr,* GARTH)], *n.* (*Ireland and Man*) A stack-yard.

haggis (hăg′ is) [Sc., etym. doubtful], *n.* A Scottish dish, made of liver, lights, heart, etc., minced with onions, suet, oatmeal, etc., boiled in a sheep's stomach.

haggle (hăg′ ėl) [prob. freq. of HAG (2)], *v.t.* To hack, to mangle. *v.i.* To chaffer, to higgle, to wrangle (over or about a bargain); (*Sc.*) to struggle onwards. *n.* A wrangle about terms. **haggler,** *n.*

hagiarchy (hăg′ i ar ki) [foll., Gr. *archē*, rule, from *archein*, to reign], *n.* Government by priests; the order of priests or holy men.

hagio- [Gr. *hagios*, holy], *comb. form.* Pertaining to saints or to holy things. **hagiocracy** (hă gi ok′ ră si) [-CRACY], *n.* Government by priests or holy persons.

Hagiographa (hă gi og′ ră fă) [late L., from Gr. (HAGIO-, *graphē*, writing)], *n.pl.* The third and last of the Jewish divisions of the Old Testament, comprising the books not included in 'the Law' and 'the Prophets,' *i.e.* consisting of the Psalms, Proverbs, Job, Song of Songs, Ruth, Lamentations, Ecclesiastes, Esther, Daniel, Ezra, Nehemiah, and Chronicles. **hagiographical,** *a.*

hagiography (hăgi og′ ră fi), *n.* Biography of saints; a series of lives of saints; *the Hagiographa. **hagiographer, hagiographist,** *n.* **hagiographic, -al** (-grăf′ ik, -ăl), *a.*

hagiolatry (hă gi ol′ ă tri), *n.* The worship of saints. **hagiolater,** *n.*

hagiology (hă gi ol′ ŏ ji), *n.* Literature relating to the lives and legends of saints; a work on the lives of saints. **hagiologic, -al** (-loj′ ik, -ăl), *a.* **hagiologist** (-ol′ ŏ jist), *n.*

hagioscope (hă′ gi ŏ skōp), *n.* An oblique opening in the wall of a church to enable persons in the transept or aisles to see the high altar, a squint.

haglet [HACKLET].

hah, ha ha [HA].

ha-ha (ha′ ha) [F. *haha*, a sudden obstacle that laughs at one], *n.* A hedge, fence, or wall sunk between slopes.

haiduck, haiduk [HEYDUCK].

haik (1) (hāk) [Arab. *hayk*, from *hak*, to weave], *n.* A strip of woollen or cotton cloth worn as an upper garment by Arabs over the head and body.

haik (2) [HAKE (2)].

hail (1) (hāl) [A.-S. *hagol* (cp. Icel. *hagl*, Dut., Dan., and G. *hagel*)], *n.* Frozen rain or particles of frozen vapour falling in showers. *v.i.* (*impers.*) To pour down hail; to come down with swiftness or violence. *v.t.* To pour down or out, as hail. **hailstone,** *n.* A single pellet of hail. **hailstorm,** *n.* **haily,** *a.*

hail (2) (hāl) [Icel. *heill*, HALE (1), used ellipt. as a greeting (cp. A.-S. *wes hāl*, be whole, good health)], *v.t.* To call to (as a person at a distance); to greet or designate (as); to welcome, to salute. *v.i.* To come (as a ship). *int.* An address of welcome or salutation. *n.* A salutation; a shout to attract attention. ***hail-fellow,** *n.* An intimate acquaintance. **hail fellow well met:** On easy, familiar terms. **hail Mary** [AVE MARIA]. **to hail a ship:** To call to those on board. **to hail from:** To come from (a place designated). **within hail:** Within the reach of the voice.

hain (hān) [Icel. *hegna*, from Teut. *hag-*, fence (cp. HEDGE)], *v.t.* (*Sc.*) To protect; to save, to preserve. **haining,** *n.* (*Sc.*) An enclosure.

hair (hâr) [A.-S. *hǣr, hēr* (cp. Dut. and G. *haar*, Icel. *hār*)], *n.* A filament composed of a tube of horny, fibrous substance, with a central medulla enclosing pigment cells, growing from the skin of an animal; (*collect.*) the mass of such filaments forming a covering for the head or the whole body; (*Bot.*) hair-like cellular processes on the surface of plants; (*fig.*) something very small or fine, a hair's breadth; *haircloth; *course, tendency, grain. **against the hair:** Against the grain. **keep your hair on:** (*slang*) Don't lose your temper. **to get in one's hair:** To become a nuisance, to cause irritation. **to make one's hair curl:** To shock extremely. **to let one's hair down:** To talk without restraint; to forget ceremony. **not to turn a hair:** Not to show any sign of fatigue or alarm. **to a hair:** To an extreme nicety, exactly. **to split hairs:** To quibble about trifles; to be over-nice. **hair-breadth, hair's breadth,** *n.* The breadth of a hair; a very minute distance. **hairbrush,** *n.* A brush for the hair. **hair-brush,** *n.* A brush made of hair. **haircloth,** *n.* Cloth made wholly or in part of hair. **hair-compasses,** *n.pl.* Compasses that can be finely adjusted. **hair-cut,** *n.* The act or style of cutting a man's hair. **hair-do,** *n.* (*colloq.*) A woman's hairdressing. **hairdresser,** *n.* One who dresses and cuts hair. **hairdressing,** *n.* **hair-grass,** *n.* Tall, tufted grass of the genus *Aira*. ***hair-lace,** *n.* A fillet for tying up the hair. **hair-lead,** *n.* (*Print.*) A very fine lead for spacing out type. **hair-letter,** *n.* (*Print.*) A very thin-faced type. **hair-line,** *n.* The up-stroke of a letter; a fishing-line of horse-hair. **hair-net,** *n.* Net, sometimes invisible, to keep the hair in place. **hair-oil,** *n.* Oil for dressing the hair. **hair-pencil,** *n.* A fine brush made of hair for painting. **hairpin,** *n.* A pin for fastening the hair. **hair-pin bend:** A V-shaped turn in a road. **hair-pointed,** *a.* (*Bot.*) Terminating in a very fine weak point. **hair-powder,** *n.* A white powder formerly worn on the hair by fashionable men and women. **hair-shirt,** *n.* A shirt made of horse-hair, worn as a penance. **hair-space,** *n.* The thinnest space used by printers. **hair-splitting,** *n.* The practice of making minute distinctions. *a.* Quibbling. **hair-spring,** *n.* The fine steel spring regulating the balance-wheel in a watch. **hair-stroke,** *n.* A hair-line in penmanship or on type, a serif. **hair-trigger,** *n.* A secondary trigger for releasing a main trigger by very slight pressure. **hair-wave,** *n.* A wave-like appearance given to the hair. **hair-worm,** *n.* A genus of simple thread-like nematoid worms found in stagnant and slow-running water. **haired,** *a.* Having hair (*usu. in comb.* as *grey-haired*). **hairless,** *a.* **hairlike,** *n.* **hairy,** *a.* Covered with hair; consisting of or resembling hair. **hairiness,** *n.*

hairst (*Sc.*) [HARVEST].

haith (hāth) [Sc., corr. of FAITH], *int.* By my faith!

haka (ha′ kă) [Maori], *n.* A ceremonial Maori dance.

hake (1) (hāk) [etym. doubtful (cp. obs. *haked*, A.-S. *hacod*, the pike)], *n.* A fish, *Merlucius vulgaris*, allied to the cod. *v.i.* To fish for hake.

hake (2), **haik** (2) (hāk) [HACK (3)], *n.* A wooden frame for drying; a cheese-rack; a manger; a mill-hatch.

hakeem (hă kēm′) [Arab. *hakīm*, wise, from *hakama*, to exercise authority], *n.* (*Mohammedan countries*) A physician.

hakim (ha′ kim) [Arab. *hākim*, as prec.], *n.* (*Mohammedan countries*) A governor; a judge.

Halachah, Halakah (hă la′ kă) [Heb. *halākāh*, the rule one walks by, from *hālak*, to walk], *n.* A body of traditional laws, supposed to be of Mosaic origin included in the Mishna. **Halachic,** *a.* **Halachist,** *n.*

halation (hă lā′ shŭn) [HALO, -ATION], *n.* (*Phot.*) A blurring in a negative caused by the reflection of a strong light from the back of the plate during exposure.

halberd (hăl′ bĕrd) [O.F. *halebarde*, M.H.G. *helmbarde* (*helm*, helmet, or perh. *helm*, handle, *barde*, a broad axe)], *n.* A weapon consisting of a combination of spear and battle-axe, mounted on a pole five to seven feet in length. **halberdier** (hăl bĕr dēr′), *n.* One armed with a halberd.

halcyon (hăl′ si ŏn) [L., from Gr. *alkuōn*, kingfisher], *n.* The kingfisher, supposed by the ancients to make a floating nest at the winter solstice, and to have the power of calming the sea while it was breeding; (*fig.*) calm, peace; (*Zool.*) the genus of birds containing the Australasian king-fishers. *a.* (*fig.*) Peaceful, happy, pleasant. **halcyon days:** The time during which the halcyon was supposed to breed; hence, a time of peace and happiness.

hald (Sc.) [HOLD].

hale (1) (hāl) [North., from A.-S. *hāl*, WHOLE], *a.* Sound and vigorous, robust (esp. of elderly people). **haleness,** *n.*

hale (2) (hāl) [O.F. *haler*, from O.H.G. *halōn* (G. *holen*, cp. Dut. *halen*, A.-S. *ge-holian*)], *v.t.* To drag, to draw violently.

half (haf) [A.-S. *healf*, *half* (cp. Dut. *half*, Icel. *hālfr*, G. *halb*)], *n.* (*pl.* **halves**) One of two equal parts into which a thing is or may be divided; a moiety; (*School*) a half-year, a term; (*colloq.*) a half-pint; *a side, a part. *a.* Consisting of or forming a half. *adv.* To the extent or degree of a half; to a certain extent or degree; partially, imperfectly (*often in comb.*). **v.t.* To halve. **better half:** One's wife. **by halves:** Badly, imperfectly. **half past:** Half an hour past. **half three:** (*Naut.*) Three and a half fathoms. **not half:** (*slang*) Not at all; (*iron.*) rather. **to cry halves:** To claim an equal share. **to go halves:** To share equally (with or in). **too clever by half:** Far too clever. **half-and-half,** *n.* A mixture of two malt liquors, esp. of porter and ale; an insincere person. *a.* Languid, spiritless. **half-back,** *n.* (*Football, hockey, etc.*) A position behind the forwards; one who plays in this position. **half-baked,** *a.* Not quite baked; (*fig.*) inexperienced; not thorough; (*slang*) half-witted, silly. **half-binding,** *n.* Binding in which the backs and corners are of leather and the sides of paper or cloth. **half-blast,** *n.* (*Golf*) A shot played with half the force of a blast. **half-blood,** *n.* Relationship between two persons having but one parent in common; one so related; a half-breed. *a.* Born of the same father or mother; half-blooded. **half-blooded,** *a.* Born of different races; *partly of noble and partly of mean birth. **half-blown,** *a.* Having its blossom partially expanded. **half-boot,** *n.* A boot reaching high up the ankle. **half-bound,** *a.* Applied to a book bound in half-binding. **half-brassy shot,** *n.* (*Golf*) A brassy shot played with a half swing. **half-bred,** *a.* Imperfectly bred; wanting in refinement; of mixed breed, mongrel. **half-breed,** *n.* An offspring of parents of different races, esp. of a European and an American Indian. *a.* Half-blooded. **half-brother,** *n.* A brother by one parent only. **half-butt,** *n.* A billiard cue intermediate in length between an ordinary cue and a long butt. **half-calf,** *a.* Half-bound in calf. *n.* This kind of binding. **half-caste,** *n.* A half-breed, esp. one born of a Hindu and a European. ***half-checked** [probably *half-cheeked*], *a.* (*Shak.*) With only one cheek or end-piece left (of bridles). ***half-cheek,** *n.* A face in profile. **half-cloth,** *a.* Bound with cloth sides. *n.* This style of binding. **half-cock,** *n.* The position of the cock of a fire-arm when retained by the first notch, so that it cannot be moved by the trigger. **half-crown,** *n.* A British silver coin, value 2s. 6d. **half-dead:** Almost dead; (*colloq.*) nearly exhausted. **half-dime,** *n.* (*Am.*) Five cents. **half-dozen,** *n.* and *a.* Six. **half-face,** *n.* The face as seen in profile; *a miserable look. *a.* Half-faced. ***half-faced,** *a.* Showing the face in profile; half-hidden; miserable, thin-faced. **half-guinea,** *n.* An English gold coin, value 10s. 6d., not now in circulation. **half-hearted,** *a.* Lukewarm, indifferent; poor-spirited, timorous; *ungenerous. **half-heartedly,** *adv.* **half-heartedness,** *n.* **half-hitch** [HITCH]. **half-holiday,** *n.* The latter half of a working day taken as a holiday; a day on which this is allowed. **half-hour,** *n.* Thirty minutes. **half-inch,** *v.t.* (*slang*) To steal, to purloin. **half-iron shot,** *n.* (*Golf*) An iron shot played with a half swing. ***half-kirtle,** *n.* A woman's jacket or short-skirted gown. **half-length,** *n.* A portrait showing only the upper half of the body. *a.* Consisting of only half the full length. **half-life,** *n.* The time taken for the radiation from a radioactive substance to decay to half its initial value. **half mast:** The middle of or half-way up the mast, the position of a flag denoting respect for a dead person, thus, **half-mast high. half-moon,** *n.* The moon at the quarters when but half is illuminated; a crescent-shaped thing; (*Fort.*) a lunette. *a.* Crescent-shaped. **half-mourning,** *n.* A mourning costume of black relieved by grey. **half nelson,** *n.* (*Wrestling*) A grip in which one arm is driven through the corresponding arm of an opponent and the hand pressed on the back of his neck. **half-note,** *n.* (*Mus.*) A minim; a semitone. ***half-part,** *n.* A moiety; an equal share, half. **half-pay,** *n.* A reduced allowance to an officer retired or not in active service. *a.* Entitled to half-pay, on half-pay. ***half-pike,** *n.* A spear-headed weapon about half the length of the pike. **half-price,** *n.* A reduced charge to children for admission to an entertainment or for railway travelling, etc., or for persons admitted to an entertainment when half over. **half-round,** *a.* Semicircular. *n.* (*Arch.*) A semicircular moulding; ***half-rounding,** *a.* Forming into a semicircle. **half-saved,** *a.* (*slang*) Half-witted. **half-seas-over,** *a.* Slightly drunk. **half-servo,** *n.* (*Motor.*) A vacuum or mechanically aided foot-brake which still requires a certain amount of foot pressure. **half-shaft,** *n.* (*Motor.*) A small axle that connects the rear wheel to the differential (or universal joint if there is one). **half-shift,** *n.* (*Mus.*) A move of the hand upward on a violin to reach a high note. ***half-sighted,** *a.* Having short or imperfect sight. **half-sister,** *n.* A sister by one parent, but not by both. **half-speed shaft,** *n.* The cam shaft of a four-stroke cycle combustion engine, rotating at half the rate of the crank shaft. **half-starved,** *a.* Poorly fed, not having sufficient food. **half-step,** *n.* (*Mus.*) A semitone. ***half-strained,** *a.* Half-bred; imperfect. **half-sword,** *n.* Half the length of a sword. **at half-sword:** At close quarters. **half-tide,** *n.* Half the time of a tide, about six hours; the tide midway between flow and ebb. **half-timbered,** *a.* (*Build.*) Having the foundations and principal supports of timber, and the interstices of the walls filled with plaster or brickwork. **half-time:** (*Games*) The time at which the first half of the game is completed. **half-time,** *n.* Half the ordinary time allotted. **half-timer,** *n.* A child attending school for half-time and engaged in some occupation the rest of the day. **half-track,** *n.* (*Motor.*) A vehicle running on one pair of wheels and one pair of caterpillar tracks. **half-truth,** *n.* A statement suppressing part of the truth. **half-title,** *n.* (*Print.*) The short title on the leaf preceding the full title or title-page. **half-tone,** *a.* (*Photo-engraving*) Of or pertaining to a process by which printing blocks are made with the shaded portions in small dots, by photographing on to a prepared plate through a finely-ruled screen or grating; **half-tone block,** *n.* **half-way,** *adv.* In the middle; at half the distance. *a.* Equidistant from two extremes. ***half-wit,** *n.* A silly fellow. **half-witted,** *a.* Weak in the intellect, imbecile. ***half-world,** *n.* A hemisphere. **half-yearly,** *a.* Happening every six months. *adv.* Twice in every year. ***halfen,** *a.* Half. ***halfendale,** *adv.* By half, nearly all.

halfling (haf' ling) [Sc. and North.], *n.* A stripling; a witling; *half of an old silver penny. *a.* Half grown.

halfpenny (hā' pėn i) *n.* An English copper coin, half the value of a penny; *a small fragment. *a.* Of the value or price of a halfpenny; trumpery, almost worthless. **halfpennyworth** (hā' pȯrth, hā' pėn i wĕrth), **ha'p'worth** (hā' pȯrth), *n.* As much as can be bought for a halfpenny.

halibut (hăl' i bŭt) [M.E. *hali*, holy, and *butte*, a flounder, perh. cogn. with BUTT (1)], *n.* A large flat-fish, *Hippoglossus vulgaris*, sometimes weighing from 300 to 400 lb., much esteemed for food. **halibut oil,** *n.* (*Med.*) Extract from the liver of this fish, rich in vitamins A and D.

halicore (hȧ lik' ō rē) [Gr. *hals halos*, sea, *korē*, maiden], *n.* (*Zool.*) A genus of sirenians, comprising the dugong.

***halidom** (hăl' i dŏm) [A.-S. *hāligdōm* (HOLY, DOM)], *n.* A holy relic or sacred thing; a holy place, a sanctuary; lands belonging to a religious foundation. ***by my halidom:** An oath.

halieutic (hăl i ū' tik) [L. *halieuticus*, Gr. *halieutikos*, from *halieutēs*, a fisherman, from *halieuein*, to fish, from *hals halos*, the sea], *a.* Pertaining to fishing. *n.pl.* The art of fishing; a treatise on this.

halitus (hăl′ i tŭs) [L., breath, from *halāre*, to breathe], *n.* A vapour, an exhalation. **halituous** (hȧ lit′ ū ŭs), *a.* Like breath; vaporous; produced by breathing. **halitosis** (hăl′ i tō′ sis), *n.* Offensive breath.

hall (hawl) [A.-S. *heall* (cp. Dut. and Dan. *hal*, Icel. *hall*), cogn. with *helan*, to cover], *n.* A large room, esp. one in which public meetings are held, the large public room in a palace, castle, etc.; a large building in which public business is transacted; the building occupied by a guild, etc.; (*Univ., etc.*) a large room in which scholars dine in common, hence the dinner itself; a manor-house or mansion; a room or passage at the entrance of a house; (*Am.*) a connecting passage between rooms, a landing; the room in a mansion in which servants dine, etc.; (*Univ.*) a building for undergraduates or other students; (*Sc.*) a college or department of a University. **hall-mark,** *n.* An official stamp stamped by the Goldsmiths' Company and Government assay offices on gold and silver articles to guarantee the standard; (*fig.*) any mark of genuineness. *v.t.* To stamp with this. **hallmote** [A.-S. *gemōt*, meeting], *n.* The court of a lord of a manor.

hallan (hăl′ ȧn) [Sc. and North., perh. dim. of HALL], *n.* A wall or partition between the door and the fire-place. **hallan-shaker,** *n.* A sturdy beggar.

Hallelujah (hăl ė loo′ yȧ) [Heb. *halelū jāh*, praise Jehovah], *n.* An ascription of praise to God, sung at the commencement of many psalms and in hymns of praise. **Hallelujah-lass,** *n.* A female member of the Salvation Army who takes part in the public services. **Hallel** (hȧ lēl′, hăl′ ėl), *n.* A hymn of praise sung at the four great Jewish feasts, consisting of Ps. cxiii–cxviii.

halliard [HALYARD].

hallo (hȧ lō′) [imit., cp. O.F. *halloer*], *int.* An exclamation of surprise; an informal greeting; a preliminary summons and answer when telephoning; a call for attention; a call to cheer on dogs. *n.* This cry. *v.i.* (*past & p.p.* **halloed**) (*often pron.* hăl′ ō) To cry 'hallo'; to cheer dogs on with cries; to call out loudly. *v.t.* To shout loudly to; to cheer, or urge on; to chase with shouts.

hallow (hăl′ ō) [A.-S. *hālgian*, from *hālig*, HOLY]. *v.t.* To make sacred or worthy of reverence; to revere; to consecrate, to sanctify. **n.* A saint. **All-Hallows:** All-Saints (Day), November 1. **Hallowe'en,** *n.* The eve of All-Hallows. **Hallowmas,** *n.* The feast of All-Hallows or **Hallow-Day.**

Hallstattian (hawl stăt′ i ȧn) [*Hallstatt*, near Salzburg, Austria], *a.* (*Archæol.*) Denoting the first period of the Iron Age, typified by weapons found in the necropolis of Hallstatt which illustrate the transition from the use of bronze to that of iron.

hallucinate (hȧ loo′ si nāt) [L. *hallūcinātus*, p.p. of *hallūcinārī*, *alūcinārī*], **v.i.* To wander in mind; to blunder, to stumble. *v.t.* To affect with hallucination. **hallucination** (hȧ loo si nā′ shŭn), *n.* An apparent sense perception or appearance of an external object arising from disorder of the brain, an illusion. **hallucinatory** (hȧ loo′ si nā tŏr i), *a.*

hallux (hăl′ ŭks) [L. *allex*], *n.* (*pl.* **-ces**) The great toe; the digit corresponding to this (as in some birds).

halm [HAULM].

halma (hăl′ mȧ) [Gr., leap, from *allesthai*, to leap], *n.* A game for two or four played on a board with 256 squares.

halo (hā′ lō) [F., from L. *halō*, acc. of *halōs*, Gr. *halōs*, orig. a round threshing-floor], *n.* (*pl.* **-oes**) A luminous circle round the sun or moon caused by the refraction of light through mist; (*Painting*) a nimbus or bright disk surrounding the heads of saints, etc.; (*fig.*) an ideal glory investing an object. **v.t.* To surround with or as with a halo. *v.i.* To be formed into a halo. **haloscope,** *n.* An instrument for showing phenomena connected with haloes, parhelia, etc.

halogen (hăl′ ō jėn) [Gr. *hals halos*, salt, -GEN], *n.* (*Chem.*) An element or other radical which by combination with a metal forms a salt; chlorine, bromine, iodine, and fluorine. **halogenous** (hȧ loj′ ė nŭs), *a.*

haloid (hăl′ oid) [as prec., -OID], *a.* (*Chem.*) Resembling common salt. *n.* A salt formed by the union of a halogen with a metal.

halomancy (hăl′ ō măn si), *n.* Divination by salt.

haloscope [HALO].

halotrichite (hȧ lot′ ri kīt), *n.* (*Min.*) Iron alum, occurring in fibrous masses. **halotrichine,** *n.* A variety of this.

***hals** (hawls) [A.-S. *hals*, *heals* (cp. Icel. and O.H.G. *hals*, also L. *collum*)], *n.* The neck; the throat; a neck or strait. ***halse** [A.-S. *hālsian*], *v.t.* To beseech, to adjure; to salute, to greet; to embrace.

halser [HAWSER].

halt (1) (hawlt) [A.-S. *healt*, *halt* (cp. Icel. *haltr*, Dan. *halt*)], *a.* Limping, lame, crippled. *v.i.* To limp, to be lame; to doubt, to hesitate; (*fig.*) to be defective, to fall or come short; to be faulty in measure or rhyme. *n.* The act of limping; lameness; (*collect.*) lame persons generally; a disease in sheep. **haltingly,** *adv.*

halt (2) (hawlt) [G. *halt*, a stoppage, cogn. with HOLD], *n.* The act of stopping on a march; (*Rail.*) a minor stopping-place, without a siding. *v.i.* To come to a stand, esp. of soldiers; (*Mil. command*) cease marching, come to a stand. *v.t.* To cause to stop in marching or walking. **halting-place,** *n.*

halter (hawl′ tėr) [A.-S. *hælfter* (cp. G. *halfter*), cogn. with HELVE], *n.* A headstall and strap or rope by which an animal is fastened; a rope to hang malefactors; hence, death by hanging. *v.t.* To put a halter upon; to tie up with a halter. **halter-break,** *v.t.* To train (a horse) to submit to the halter.

halve (hav) [M.E. *halven*, from HALF], *v.t.* To divide into two equal parts; to share equally; to lessen by half, to reduce to half; to join (timbers) together by chopping away half the thickness of each; (*Golf*) to win the same number of holes, or to reach a hole in the same number of strokes, as the other side.

halyard (hăl′-, hawl′ yȧrd) [M.E. *halier* (HALE (1), IER) assim. to YARD (1)], *n.* (*Naut.*) A rope or tackle for hoisting or lowering yards, sails, or flags.

ham (1) (hăm) [A.-S. *hamm* (cp. Dut. *ham*, Icel. *hōm*, G. *hamme*)], *n.* The hind part of the thigh; (*usu. in pl.*) the thigh and buttock; the thigh of an animal, esp. of a hog, salted and dried in smoke, or otherwise cured. **ham actor,** *n.* A bad, inexperienced actor; amateur actor; tyro. **hammy,** *a.*

***ham** (2) (hăm) [A.-S. *hām*, HOME], *n.* (*Hist.*) A village, a town (now only in place-names, as *Cheltenham*).

hamadryad (hăm ȧ drī′ ȧd) [L. *hamadryas*, pl. *-ades*, Gr. *Hamadruades* (*hama*, with, *drus*, tree)], *n.* (*pl.* **-ads, -des**) (*Gr. Myth.*) A dryad or wood-nymph, who lived and died with the tree in which she lived; an Indian venomous snake, *Hamadryas elaps*; an Arabian and Abyssinian baboon, *Cynocephalus hamadryas.*

hamartiology (hȧ mar ti ol′ ō ji) [Gr. *hamartia*, sin, -LOGY], *n.* (*Theol.*) The doctrine of sin; a treatise on sin.

hamate (hā′ māt) [L. *hāmātus*, from *hāmus*, a hook], *a.* Hooked; furnished with a hook; hook-shaped. **hamiform,** *a.*

Hamburg (hăm bĕrg) [German city], *n.* A variety of black hothouse grape; a small black or speckled variety of domestic fowl. **Hamburg lake,** *n.* A deep purplish red. **hamburger,** *n.* A steak served with onions; a kind of sausage.

hame (hām) [cogn. with Dut. *haam*], *n.* One of the pair of curved bars of wood or metal fixed on the collar of a draught-horse, to which the traces are connected.

hamesucken (hām′ sŭkn) [A.-S. *hāmsōcn* (*hām*, HOME, *sōcn*, seeking, assault)], *n.* (*Sc. Law*) The crime or felony of assaulting a man in his own house.

Hamiltonian (hăm il tō′ ni ȧn) [surname *Hamilton*], *a.* Pertaining to a system of teaching foreign languages by means of interlinear translations, introduced by James Hamilton (1769–1831); pertaining to the philosophy of Sir Wm. Hamilton (1788–1856); pertaining to the Irish mathematician, Sir Wm. Rowan Hamilton (1805–65); pertaining to the doctrines of Alexander Hamilton (1757–1804), U.S. statesman and Federalist. *n.* A follower of any of these.

Hamite (hăm′ īt) [*Ham*, second son of Noah], *n.* A descendant of Ham; belonging to the Hamitic stock, comprising the Egyptians and other African races. **Hamitic** (hȧ mit′ ik), *a.* Of or belonging to Ham, his supposed descendants, or the languages spoken by them.

hamlet (hăm′ lėt) [O.F. *hamelet*, dim. of *hamel* (F. *hameau*), from Teut. (cp. O.Fris. and A.-S. *hām*, HOME)], *n.* A small village; a little cluster of houses in the country.

hammal (hȧ mal′) [Arab. *hammāl*, from *hamala*, to carry], *n.* An Oriental porter; a palanquin-bearer.

hammam (hȧ mam′) [Arab. *hāmmam*], *n.* An Oriental bath-house; a Turkish bath.

hammer (hăm′ ėr) [A.-S. *hamor* (cp. Dut. *hamer*, Icel. *hamarr*, G. *hammer*)], *n.* A tool for driving nails, beating metals, etc., consisting of a head, usu. of steel, fixed at right angles on a handle; a machine, part of a machine, or other appliance, performing similar functions, as a steam-hammer, the part of a gun-lock for exploding the charge; the striker of a bell, etc.; an auctioneer's mallet; (*Elec.*) the trembler of a magnetic make-and-break mechanism. *v.t.* To strike, beat, or drive with or as with a hammer; to forge or form with a hammer; (*fig.*) to work (out) laboriously in the mind; (*Stock Exch.*) to declare a defaulter. *v.i.* To work or beat with or as with a hammer; to make a noise like a hammer; to work hard (at). **hammer and sickle:** The emblem symbolic of worker and peasant adopted on the flag, etc. of U.S.S.R. **hammer and tongs:** With great noise and vigour; violently. **throwing the hammer:** An athletic contest in which the competitors throw a heavy hammer to a distance. **to bring to the hammer:** To put up for auction. **to come under the hammer:** To be sold by auction. **up to the hammer:** First-rate. **hammer-beam,** *n.* (*Arch.*) A short beam projecting horizontally from a wall, in place of a tie-beam, to support the timbers of a roof. **hammer break,** *n.* (*Elec.*) An interrupter in which the motion of an automatically vibrating hammer interrupts contact. **hammer-cloth,** *n.* The cloth covering the driver's seat in a coach. **hammer-harden,** *v.t.* (*Metal.*) To harden a metal by hammering it in the cold state. **hammer-head,** *n.* The head of a hammer; a South African bird; a shark with a head like a hammer, also called **hammer-fish. hammer-headed,** *a.* **hammer-lock,** *n.* (*Wrestling*) A grip in which one man's arm is held twisted and bent behind his back by his opponent. **hammerman, -smith,** *n.* One who works with a hammer. **hammer-toe,** *n.* (*Med.*) A malformation of the foot consisting of permanent angular fixing of one or more toes. **hammerwort,** *n.* The common pellitory (*Parietaria*). **hammerer,** *n.* **hammerless,** *a.*

hammochrysos (hăm ȯ krī′ sŭs) [Gr. *hammochrūsos* (*hammos*, sand, *chrusos*, gold)], *n.* A mineral known to the ancients, perhaps yellow micaceous schist.

hammock (hăm′ ȯk) [Sp. *hamaca*, prob. from Carib.], *n.* A swinging or suspended bed made of canvas or network, and hung by hooks or other contrivance from a roof, ceiling, tree, etc. **hammock-batten,** *n.* One of the strips of wood from which hammocks are slung. **hammock-chair,** *n.* A frame-work supporting canvas on which one may sit or recline. **hammock-netting,** *n.pl.* (*Naut.*) Orig. a row of stanchions supporting a netting, now long racks, in which the hammocks are stowed during the day. **hammock-rack** [HAMMOCK-BATTEN].

hamose (hā′ mōs), **-mous** (hā′ mŭs) [L. *hāmus*, a hook], *a.* (*Bot.*) Curved like a hook; having hooks.

hamper (1) (hăm′ pėr) [formerly *hanaper*, *hanper*, O.F. *hanapier*, HANAPER], *n.* A large, coarsely-made wicker-work basket, with a cover. *v.t.* *To put into or enclose in a hamper; (*facet.*) to load with hampers.

hamper (2) (hăm′ pėr) [etym. doubtful, cp. L.G. *hampern*, Dut. *haperen*, to stop, to fail], *v.t.* To impede the movement or free action of; to obstruct or impede (movement, etc.); to hinder, to shackle, to fetter; *to put out of order. *n.* Anything which hampers or impedes free action; (*Naut.*) rigging, equipment, or other gear of a cumbrous kind.

hamshackle (hăm′ shăk′ ėl) [etym. doubtful, perh. conn. with prec.], *v.t.* To fasten the head (of an ox, horse, etc.) to one of its forelegs.

hamster (hăm′ stėr) [G.], *n.* A rat-like rodent of the genus *Cricetus*, esp. *C. frumentarius*, with large cheek-pouches in which it carries grain for food during hibernation.

hamstring (hăm′ string) [HAM (1), STRING], *n.* One of the tendons of the thigh muscle behind the knee; (*Quadrupeds*) the large tendon at the back of the hock in the hind leg. *v.t.* To lame or disable by cutting or severing the hamstring.

hamulus (hăm′ ū lŭs) [L., dim. of *hāmus*, hook], *n.* (*pl.* **-li**, -lī) A little hook; (*Bot.*) a hooked bristle; (*Anat.*) a hook-like process; (*Surg.*) an instrument for extracting the fœtus. **hamular, hamulose** (hăm ū lōs′), *a.*

***hanap** (hăn′ ȧp) [O.F., from Teut. (cp. O.H.G. *hnapf*, Dut. *nap*. A.-S. *hnæp*)], *n.* A drinking-vessel, a goblet.

***hanaper** (hăn′ ȧ pėr) [O.F. *hanapier*, from *hanap*, see prec.], *n.* A hamper; a basket or wicker case for documents and valuables; the office of the old Court of Chancery dealing with the sealing, etc. of charters and other documents (abolished in 1842).

***hanaster, hanster** [HANSE].

hance (hans) [perh. through an A.-F. *haunce*, from O.F. *hauce*, from *haucer* (F. *hausser*), late L. *altiāre*, from *altus*, high], *n.* (*Naut.*) The curved rise or fall as in bulwarks, fife-rails, etc.; (*Arch.*) the haunch of an arch. **hanced,** *a.* (*Arch.*)

hand (1) (hănd) [A.-S. *hand*, *hond* (cp. Dut. and G. *hand*, Icel. *hönd*, *hand*)], *n.* The part serving as organ of prehension, consisting of the palm and fingers, at the extremity of the human arm; a similar member terminating the limbs of monkeys; the end of a limb, esp. a fore-limb, in other animals, when serving as a prehensile organ; (*fig.*) power of execution, skill, performance, handiwork; a pledge of marriage; possession, control, authority, power (*often in pl.*); source, person; (*pl.*) operatives, labourers, crew of a ship, players, persons engaged in a game, etc.; a part, a share, a turn, an innings; a game at cards; the cards held by a player; a part in a game of cards; one of the players in a game of cards; a player's turn to serve the ball at tennis, rackets, etc.; style of workmanship, handwriting, etc.; signature; a lineal measure of four inches, a palm (measuring horses); a handful; a handle or helve; the pointer or index finger of a watch, clock, or counter; five of any article of sale; a bundle of tobacco leaves; a shoulder (of pork); side direction (right or left). **a good hand:** Skilful, expert (at). **all hands:** (*Naut.*) The entire crew. **at** or **on all hands:** By all parties; from all quarters. ***at any hand:** At any rate. **at first** or **second hand:** As the original purchaser, owner, hearer, etc., or as one deriving or learning through another party. **at hand:** Near, close by; available. **at the hand** or **hands of:** From, through; by the means or instrumentality of. **by hand:** With the hands (as dist. from instruments or machines); by messenger or agent; by artificial rearing (of children or the young of the lower animals). **clean hands:** Innocence, freedom from guilt. **for one's own hand:** (To play or act) for one's personal advantage. **from hand to hand:** From one person to another, bandied about. **from hand to mouth:** Without provision for the future. **hand in** or **and glove:** On most intimate terms (with). **hand in hand:** With hands mutually clasped; (*fig.*) in union, unitedly. **hand over hand:** By passing the hands alternately one above or before the other, as in climbing; (*fig.*) with rapid, unchecked progress. **hand to hand:** At close quarters; in close fight. **hands off!** Stand off! don't touch! **hands up!** Show hands, those who assent, etc.; show hands to preclude resistance. **heavy on hand:** Hard to manage. **in hand:** In a state of preparation or execution; in possession; under control. **light on hand:** Easy to manage. **offhand:** Summarily, there and then, without deliberation or preparation, casually. *a.* Casual, disrespectful. **on hand:** In present possession; in stock. **on one's hands:** (Left) to one's responsibility; (left) unsold. **on the one hand, on the other:** From this point of view, from that. **out of hand:** Done, ended, completed; at once, directly, extempore; out of control. **to ask** or **give the hand of:** To ask or give in marriage. **to bear in hand:** To help. **to be on the mending hand:** (*Am.*) To be in a fair way of recovery. **to change hands:** To become someone else's property. **to come cap in hand:** To come humbly, to come seeking a favour. **to come to hand:** To be received; to arrive. **to have a hand for:** To be skilful at. **to have a hand in:** To have a share in; to be mixed up with. **to have one's hands full:** To be fully occupied. **to join hand in hand:** To act in concert. **to lay hands on:** To touch; to assault; to seize; to lay the hands on the head of (in ordination, confirmation, etc.). **to lend a hand:** To help, to give assistance. **to one's hand:** Ready, in readiness. ***to put** or **stretch forth one's hand against:** To use violence against; to attack. **to set the hand to:** To undertake; to engage in. **to shake hands:** To clasp each other's right hand in token of friendship, etc. ***to strike hands:** To make a bargain; to become surety. **to take a hand:** To take part in a game, esp. of cards. **to take by the hand:** To take under one's protection, care, or guidance. **to take in hand:** To undertake, to attempt. **to take one in hand:** To deal with, to manage; to discipline. **to wash one's hands of:** To declare oneself no longer responsible for; to renounce for ever. **to win hands down:** Without an effort, easily (of a jockey). **under one's hand:** With one's proper signature. **with a heavy hand:** Oppressively; unstintedly, without sparing. **with a high hand:** Arbitrarily, arrogantly. **hand-bag,** *n.* A small bag for carrying things with the hand. **hand-ball,** *n.* A ball played with the hand; a game played with this between goals. **handbarrow,** *n.* A kind of stretcher, having a pair of handles at each end, adapted to be carried by two men. **handbell,** *n.* A small bell rung with the hand, esp. one of a series played musically. **handbill,** *n.* A small printed sheet for circulating information. **handbook,** *n.* A small book or treatise on any subject, a compendium, a manual. **hand-brace,** *n.* A tool for boring. **hand-brake,** *n.* (*Motor.*) A brake worked by a hand lever. **handbreadth, hand's breadth,** *n.* A linear measurement equal to the breadth of the hand. **hand-canter,** *n.* A gentle canter. **hand-car,** *n.* (*Rail.*) A small hand-propelled truck running on the rails, used by workers on the line. **hand-cart,** *n.* A two-wheeled vehicle for carrying parcels or goods, pushed or drawn by hand. **handcuff,** *n.* (*usu. pl.*) A manacle for the wrists, consisting of a chain and locking-rings. *v.t.* To secure with handcuffs. **handfast,** *v.t.* To bind by a contract or engagement; to betroth, to pledge; to marry. *n.* A hold or grasp with the hand; custody, constraint, confinement; a contract, a pledge; a marriage engagement. **a.* Made fast by contract; betrothed. **hand-gallop,** *n.* A slow and easy gallop. **hand-gear,** *n.* (*Mech.*) Gear worked by hand, with a view to starting or checking some other machinery operated by power. **hand-glass,** *n.* A small mirror with a handle; a magnifying glass for holding in the hand; (*Hort.*) a bell-glass or glazed frame, for the protection of plants; (*Naut.*) a half-minute glass, used to measure time in running out the log-line. **handgrip,** *n.* Grasp or seizure with the hands. **handhold,** *n.* Something for the hand to hold on by (in climbing, etc.). **hand-lead,** *n.* (*Naut.*) A small lead for sounding. **hand-line,** *n.* A line worked by the hand, esp. a fishing-line without a rod. **hand-me-downs,** *n.pl.* (*slang*) Second-hand clothes. **hand-loom,** *n.* A loom worked by hand. **hand-made,** *a.* Produced by hand, not by machinery. ***handmaid, -maiden,** *n.* A female servant or attendant. **hand-mill,** *n.* A small mill worked by hand; a quern. **hand-organ,** *n.* A barrel-organ worked by a handle. **hand-out,** *n.* Information handed out to the press. **hand-press,** *n.* A press, esp. for printing, worked by the hand, as dist. from one worked by steam, water, etc. **hand-promise,** *n.* A solemn form of betrothal among the Irish peasantry. **handrail,** *n.* A rail protecting stairs, landings, etc. **hand-sale,** *n.* A sale confirmed by the shaking of hands. **hand-saw,** *n.* A saw riveted at one end to a handle, and adapted to be used by one hand. **hand-screw,** *n.* A jack-screw for raising heavy weights; (*Motor.*) a screw, generally for brake adjustment, which can be turned by hand. **hand-shake,** *n.* A shake of another's hand as a greeting. **hand-spike,** *n.* A bar, usu. of wood shod with steel, used as a lever for lifting, heaving, etc. **handstaves,** *n.pl.* (*Bibl.*) Probably javelins. **handwriting,** *n.* Writing done by hand; the style of writing peculiar to a person. **handed,** *a.* Having a hand of a certain kind (*in comb.*, as *free-handed*); *having the hands joined. **handful,** *n.* As much as can be held in the hand; a small number or quantity; (*colloq.*) a troublesome person or task. **handless,** *a.*

hand (2) (hănd) [from prec.], *v.t.* To give, deliver, or transmit with the hand; to assist or conduct with the hand (into, out of, etc.); (*Naut.*) to furl; *to seize, to lay hands on; *to handle. **v.i.* To co-operate; to agree. **to hand down:** To transmit, to give in succession; to pass on. **to hand in:** To deliver to an office, etc. **to hand over:** To deliver to a person.

handicap (hăn′ di kăp) [from the drawing of lots out of a hat or cap], *n.* *An old game at cards; a race or contest in which an allowance of time, distance, or weight is made to the inferior competitors; the heavier conditions imposed on a superior competitor. *v.t.* To impose heavier weight or other disadvantageous conditions on a competitor. **handicapper,** *n.*

handicraft (hăn′ di kraft) [A.-S. *handcræft*], *n.* Skill in working with the hands; manual occupation or trade; *a handicraftsman. *a.* Pertaining to manual labour. **handicraftsman,** *n.* One employed in a handicraft.

handily [HANDY].

handiwork (hăn′ di wĕrk) [A.-S. *handgeweorc* (HAND (1), *weorc*, collect. WORK)], *n.* Work done by the hands; the product of one's hands, labour, or effort.

handkerchief (hăng′ kẻr chif) [HAND (1), KERCHIEF], *n.* A piece of cloth, silk, linen, or cotton, carried about the person for wiping the nose, face, etc.; a neckcloth, a neckerchief. **to throw the handkerchief to:** To call upon a player to take a turn, esp. to pursue one (in certain games); (*fig.*) to single out patronizingly.

handle (hăndl) [A.-S. *handlian*, from HAND (1) (cp. Dut. *handelen*, G. *handeln*)], *v.t.* To touch, to feel with, to wield or use with the hands; to treat (well, ill, etc.); to deal with, to manage, to treat of; to deal in. *v.i.* To work with the hands; to be handled. *n.* That part of a vessel, tool, or instrument, by which it is grasped and held in the hand; (*fig.*) an instrument or means by which anything is done.

a handle to one's name: A title. **to give a handle:** To furnish an occasion or advantage that may be utilized. **handler,** *n.* One who handles; (*Tanning*) a tan-pit containing a weak ooze. **handling,** *n.* The action of touching, feeling, etc., with the hand; (*Art.*) the art of managing the pencil; characteristic style of painting, composing, manipulating etc.

handrail [HAND (1)].

handsel (hăn′ sel) [perh. from Scand. (cp. Icel. *handsal*, Dan. *handsel*, an earnest, A.-S. *handselen*, delivery into the hand)], *n.* A gift for luck, esp. on the first Monday in the New Year; earnest money; the first sale, present, use, etc.; (*fig.*) a foretaste. *v.t.* To give a handsel to; to use for the first time; to be the first to use. **handsel Monday:** (*Sc.*) The first Monday of the New Year, when presents were commonly given to servants, children, etc.

handshake, *etc.* [HAND (1)].

handsome (hăn′ sŭm), *a.* *Handy, convenient, suitable; well-formed, finely-featured, good-looking; noble; liberal, generous; ample, large. **handsomely,** *adv.* **handsomeness,** *n.*

handwriting [HAND (1)].

handy (hăn′ di), *a.* Ready or convenient to the hand; close at hand; dexterous, skilful with the hands; near, convenient. **handy-dandy,** *n.* A children's game, in which one child has to guess in which hand of the other some small article is held. **handy-man,** *n.* A man of all work. **handily,** *adv.* **handiness,** *n.*

handywork [HANDIWORK].

hang (1) (hăng) [from two A.-S. verbs. *hangian*, intr., and the causal *hōn*, and in North. Eng. from Icel. *hengja*, whence the p.p. *hung*], *v.t.* (*past & p.p.* **hung**; for put to death and as imprecation **hanged**) To suspend; to attach loosely to a point of support above the centre of gravity; to fasten so as to leave movable (as a bell, gate, the body of a coach, etc.); to suspend by the neck on a gallows as capital punishment; to cause to droop; to cover or decorate with anything suspended; to attach, to fasten. *v.i.* To be suspended; to depend, to dangle, to swing; to cling; to be executed by hanging; to droop, to bend forwards; to project (over), to impend; (*fig.*) to be fixed or suspended with attention; to depend (as on a basis, etc.); to be in suspense; *to be delayed. **hang! hang it! I'll be hanged!:** Forms of imprecation or exclamation. **hang on!:** Wait a moment! **to hang about:** To loiter, to loaf. **to hang around:** To loaf, to loiter. **to hang back:** To act reluctantly, to hesitate. **to hang down:** To decline, to droop. **to hang fire:** Said of a fire-arm when the charge does not ignite immediately; (*fig.*) to hesitate; to be wanting in life or spirit. **to hang heavy:** To go slowly (as time). **to hang in doubt:** To be in suspense. **to hang on** or **upon:** To adhere closely to; to be a weight or drag on; to rest, to dwell upon. **to hang on by the eyelids:** (*colloq.*) To hang by a very slight hold. **to hang out:** To suspend from a window, etc.; to protrude loosely (of a tongue); (*slang*) to live, to reside. **to hang over:** To be overhanging or impending. **hang-over,** *n.* (*colloq.*) The after-effects of a drinking-bout. **to hang together:** To be closely united; to be consistent. **to hang up:** To suspend; (*fig.*) to put aside, to leave undecided; to defer indefinitely; (*Austral.*) to tie a horse to a post. **hang-dog,** *n.* A low, base fellow; *a.* Base, sullen. **hang-nail** [AG-NAIL]. **hang-net,** *n.* A net with a large mesh hanging vertically on stakes.

hang (2) (hăng) [from prec.], *n.* A slope, a declivity; mode of hanging; (*fig.*) general tendency, drift, or bent. **to get the hang of:** To understand the drift or connexion of; to get the knack of.

hangar (hăng′ ėr) [F., etym. doubtful], *n.* A large shed, esp. for aircraft.

hangbird (hăng′ bĕrd), *n.* A bird building a hanging nest, esp. the Baltimore oriole.

hanger (hăng′ ėr) [HANG (1), -ER], *n.* One who hangs or causes to be hanged; that on which a thing is hung or suspended; a pot-hook; (*fig.*) a double curve (ʃ) in writing; a short, curved sword or cutlass, orig. hung from the belt; a sloping wood or grove (largely in place-names). **hanger-on,** *n.* One who hangs on or sticks to a person, place, etc.; a dependant, a parasite.

hanging (hăng′ ing) [HANG (1), -ING], *n.* The act of suspending; an execution by the gallows; an exhibition; (*pl.*) fabrics hung up to cover or drape a room. *a.* Suspended, dangling; steep, inclined; *foreboding death by the halter; deserving death by the halter; punishable with hanging. **hanging-bird** [HANGBIRD], **hanging buttress:** A buttress supported on a corbel. **hanging committee:** A committee appointed to arrange pictures in an exhibition. **hanging garden:** A garden rising in terraces one above the other. **hanging guard:** A position of defence with the broadsword. **hanging valve:** A hinged valve falling by the action of gravity.

hangman (hăng′ măn), *n.* A public executioner.

hangnest (hăng′ nest), *n.* A bird constructing a pendulous nest; the nest of such a bird; the hang-bird.

hank (hăngk) [cp. Icel. *hōnk*, Dan. and L.G. *hank*], *n.* A coil or skein; two or more skeins of yarn, silk, wool, or cotton, tied together (840 yds. of cotton yarn, 560 of worsted); a coil or bundle (as of fish); a withe for fastening a gate; (*Naut.*) one of the hoops or rings to which a fore-and-aft sail is bent. **v.t.* To form into hanks; to fasten.

hanker (hăng′ kėr) [etym. doubtful, prob. cogn. with Dut. *hunkeren*], *v.i.* To have an importunate desire or longing (after). **hankering,** *n.* **hankeringly,** *adv.*

hanky-panky (hăng′ ki păng′ ki) [coined on anal. of HOCUS-POCUS], *n.* Jugglery, trickery, fraud.

Hanoverian (hăn ō vēr′ i ăn) [G. *Hanover*, state and capital city], *a.* Of or pertaining to Hanover. *n.* A native or inhabitant of Hanover; an adherent of the House of Hanover, the dynasty that came to the throne of Gr. Britain and Ireland in 1714.

Hansard (hăn′ sărd) [Messrs. *Hansard*], *n.* The official report of the proceedings of the British Parliament, from the name of the compilers and printers (1774–1889). **Hansardize,** *v.t.* To produce the official record of an M.P.'s former utterances in order to confute him.

Hanse (hăns) [O.F., from O.H.G. *hansa*, a company], *n.* A corporation or guild of merchants; a celebrated confederacy formed in the 13th cent. between certain German towns for the protection of commerce; the entrance-fee of a mediæval guild. **Hanse Towns:** The towns which confederated to form this league. **Hanseatic** (hăn sė ăt′ ik), *a.* **Hanseatic League:** ***hanaster, hanster,** *n.* (*Oxford*) The ancient name for persons who paid the entrance-fee of the guild-merchant and were admitted as freemen of the city.

hansom (hăn′ sŏm) [J. A. *Hansom* (1803–82), patentee in 1834], *n.* A two-wheeled cab in which the driver's seat is behind the body, the reins passing over the hooded top. **hansom cab,** *n.*

han't (*vulg.*) [HAVE, NOT].

hant (hant) [HAUNT], *n.* (*Am. facet.*) A ghost.

hantle (han′ tėl) [Sc. and North., etym. unknown], *n.* A good many; a good deal.

hap (1) (hăp) [prob. from Icel. *happ* (cp. A.-S. *gehæp*, fit)], *n.* Chance, luck; that which happens or chances; a casual event. *v.i.* (*past & p.p.* **happed**) To befall, to happen by chance. **hapless,** *a.* Unhappy, unfortunate, luckless. **haplessly,** *adv.* **haply,** *adv.* By hap; perhaps.

hap (2) (hăp) [etym. unknown], *v.t.* (*Sc.*) To cover over; to wrap up. *n.* A covering.

hapalote (hăp′ ă lōt), *n.* (*Austral.*) A genus of non-marsupial rodents, also known as jumping mice.

haphazard (hăp hăz′ ȧrd), *n.* Mere chance, accident. **at haphazard:** By chance, casually. **haphazardly,** *adv.* **haphazardness,** *n.*

haplo- [Gr. *haploos, haplous*], *comb. form.* Single, simple. **haplodont** (hăp′ lō dont) [Gr. *odous odontos*, tooth], *a.* Having the crowns of the molar teeth simple, not ridged. *n.* (*Zool.*) One of the *Haplodontidæ*, an American family of marmot-like rodents regarded as a connecting-link between the beavers and the squirrels.

haplography (hăp log′ rȧ fi) [HAPLO-, -GRAPHY], *n.* Inadvertent writing of a word or letter once which should be written twice, as *superogatory* for *supererogatory*. **haploid** (hăp′ loid), *a.* Having half the usual number.

haply [HAP (I)].

ha'p'orth [see HALFPENNY].

happen (hăp′ ėn), *v.i.* To fall out; to hap; to chance (to); to light (upon). **happening,** *n.* (*usu. in pl.*) Something that happens, a chance occurrence.

happy (hăp′ i) [HAP (I), -Y], *a.* Lucky, fortunate; prosperous, successful; enjoying pleasure from the fruition or expectation of good; contented, satisfied; apt, felicitous; favourable; dexterous, ready, skilful. **v.t.* To make happy. **happy-go-lucky,** *a.* Careless, thoughtless, improvident. **happy dispatch** [HARA-KIRI]. **happily,** *adv.* **happiness,** *n.*

***haquebut** [HACKBUT]. ***haqueton** [ACTON].

hapuka (ha pu′ kȧ) [Maori], *n.* A N. Zealand fish, the grouper.

hara-kiri (ha′ rȧ kir′ i) [Jap. *hara*, belly, *kiri*, to cut], *n.* A Japanese method of suicide by disembowelling; happy dispatch.

haram [HAREM].

harangue (hȧ răng′) [M.F., from med. L. *harenga* or It. *aringa*, prob. from O.H.G. *hring*, a ring (of people)], *n.* A declamatory address to a large assembly; a noisy and vehement speech, a tirade. *v.i.* To make an harangue. *v.t.* To address in an harangue. **haranguer,** *n.*

harass (hăr′ ȧs) [M.F. *harasser*, perh. from O.F. *harer*, to hound a dog on], *v.t.* To torment by or as by importunity; to worry, to molest; to tire out with care or worry; (*Mil.*) to worry by repeated attacks. **n.* Harassment. **harasser,** *n.* **harassment,** *n.* The act of harassing; the state of being harassed.

harbinger (har′ bin jėr) [M.E. *herbergeour*, O.F. *herbergere*, from *herberge* (F. *auberge*), O.H.G. *heriberga* (*hari*, army, *bergan*, to shelter)], *n.* One who went before to provide lodgings for an approaching guest; a precursor; one who or that which goes before and foretells what is coming. *v.t.* To precede as harbinger; to announce the approach of.

harbour (har′ bŏr) [M.E. *hereberge*, perh. from A.-S. (*here*, army, *beorg*, shelter), cp. *prec.*], *n.* A refuge, esp. a refuge or shelter for ships; a port or haven; an asylum, shelter, security; *a lodging, an inn. *v.t.* To shelter, to entertain, to cherish, to foster; *to trace (a hart or hind) to its covert. *v.i.* *To come to anchor in a harbour; (*fig.*) to take shelter, to lodge. **harbour-dues:** Charges for mooring or accommodating a ship in a harbour. **harbour-master,** *n.* An official having charge of the berthing and mooring of ships in a harbour. **harbour-watch,** *n.* (*Naut.*) [ANCHOR-WATCH, see ANCHOR]. **harbourage,** *n.* Shelter, harbour, refuge. **harbourer,** *n.* One who harbours another; one who traces a hart or hind to its covert. **harbourless,** *a.*

hard (hard) [A.-S. *heard* (cp. Dut. *hard*, Icel. *harthr*, G. *hart*, also Gr. *kratus*, strong)], *a.* Firm, solid, compact; not yielding to pressure; difficult of accomplishment, comprehension, or explanation; laborious, fatiguing, toilsome; intricate, perplexing; harsh, severe, galling, inflexible, cruel, unfeeling; sordid, miserly, stingy; difficult to bear, oppressive, unjust; coarse, unpalatable; rough and harsh to the palate, the touch, etc.; containing mineral salts unfitting it for washing (of water); (*Phon.*) sounded gutturally (as *c* and *g* when not pronounced like *s* and *j*), aspirated (as *k, t, p*, compared with *g, d, b*); (*Art*) adhering too rigidly to the mere mechanism of art. *adv.* Forcibly, violently; strenuously, severely; with effort or difficulty; close, near; (*Naut.*) as hard as possible, to the utmost limit. *n.* Something that is hard; a firm landing-place, jetty, or roadway; (*colloq.*) hard cash; (*slang*) hard labour. **hard and fast:** Strict; that must be strictly adhered to. **hard-a-lee, a-port, a-starboard, -a-weather, down:** (*Naut.*) As far as it will go in the direction indicated (of the tiller). **hard by:** Close by; close at hand. **hard put to it:** In straits, in difficulties. **hard upon:** Close behind. **hard of hearing:** Rather deaf. **to die hard:** To die only after a struggle, or impenitent. **to go hard with:** To fare ill with. **hard-bake,** *n.* A kind of toffee in which blanched almonds are mixed. **hard-baked,** *n.* Cooked until hard. **hard-beam** [HORNBEAM, see HORN]. **hard-bitten,** *a.* Used to hard biting, tough, resolute. **hard-boiled,** *a.* Boiled until hard; (*slang*) hard, sophisticated, unemotional, callous; shrewd, hard-headed. **hard case,** *n.* (*Austral.*) An amusing fellow. **hard coal:** Anthracite, non-bituminous coal. **hard-core,** *n.* Refuse stone, brickbats, etc., crushed to form the substratum of a road. **hard currency:** (*Fin.*) Coin, metallic money; currency unlikely to depreciate suddenly or fluctuate in value. **hard doer,** *n.* (*Austral.*) A smart Alec, a tough nut. **hard drinker:** A drunkard. **hard-earned,** *a.* Earned with difficulty. ***hard-faced,** *a.* Having a harsh or stern face. **hard-favoured, -featured,** *a.* Of harsh features; ill-looking, ugly. **hard fern:** A fern of the genus *Lomaria*, esp. *L. spicant* or *L. blechnum*. **hard-fisted,** *a.* Having hard, strong hands; (*fig.*) close, miserly. **hard-fought,** *a.* Closely contested. **hard-got, -gotten,** *a.* Hard-earned. **hard-grained,** *a.* Having a close, firm grain; (*fig.*) unattractive. **hardhack,** *n.* (*Am.*) A New England shrub, *Spiræa tomentosa*. **hard-handed,** *a.* Having hard, rough hands; (*fig.*) harsh, severe. **hard-head,** *n.* A hard-headed person; the menhaden and other fishes. ***hard-heads,** *n.* A manner of fighting in which the combatants dashed their heads together. **hard-headed,** *a.* Matter-of-fact, practical, not sentimental. **hard-hearted,** *a.* Cruel, unfeeling, pitiless. **hardheartedly,** *adv.* **hardheartedness,** *n.* **hard hit:** Seriously damaged, especially by monetary losses; smitten with love. **hard labour:** Enforced labour, esp. when added to imprisonment. **hard lines:** A hard lot. **hard-mouthed,** *a.* Insensible to the action of the bit (of a horse); (*fig.*) harsh, severe in language. **hard pan:** (*Am.*) A firm subsoil of sand or gravel; a firm foundation. **hard pressed:** Closely pressed; in straits. **hard-set,** *a.* Rigid, stony, inflexible; firmly set (as an egg). **hardshell,** *a.* Having a hard shell (as a crab); (*fig.*) rigid, unyielding, uncompromising; (*Am.*) a term applied to a strict sect of Baptists. **hard-tack,** *n.* Coarse ship-biscuit. **hard-up,** *a.* In great want, esp. of money; very poor; (*Naut.*) as far as possible to windward (of the tiller). **hard-upness, hard-uppishness,** *n.* **hard-valve,** *n.* (*Radio.*) A thermionic valve which is very highly exhausted of gas. **hard-won,** *a.* Won with difficulty. **hard-working,** *a.* Working hard and diligently. **hard water:** Water which from holding mineral salts in solution is unfit for washing purposes. **hardish,** *a.* **hardly,** *adv.* With difficulty; harshly, rigorously; unfavourably; scarcely, not quite. **hardness,** *n.* **hardly-earned,** *a.* Earned with difficulty.

hardanger (har′ dang ėr) [Norwegian place-name], *n.* Decorative needlework in square and diamond patterns, originally done at Hardanger. *a.* On this pattern (of needlework designs).

hardboard (hard′ bŏrd), *n.* A form of compressed fibreboard.

harden (hardn), *v.t.* To make hard or harder; to temper (tools); to confirm (in effrontery, wickedness, obstinacy, etc.); to make firm; to make insensible, unfeeling, or callous. *v.i.* To become hard or harder; to become unfeeling or inured; to become confirmed (in vice). **hardener,** *n.* One who or that which hardens, esp. one who tempers tools; (*Phot.*) chemical placed in gelatine negatives to prevent the film melting in hot weather.

hardmetal (hard' met ål), *n.* Sintered tungsten carbide, for high-speed cutting tools.

***hardock** (har' dok) [prob. from A.-S. *hār*, hoar, DOCK (1)], *n.* (*Shak.*) A coarse kind of plant, prob. the burdock.

hards (hardz) [A.-S. *heordan* (cp. M.Dut. *heerde, herde*), not cogn. with HARD], *n.pl.* The coarse or refuse part of flax or wool.

hardship (hard' ship), *n.* That which is hard to bear, as privation, suffering, toil, fatigue, oppression, injury, injustice.

hardware (hard' wâr), *n.* Articles of metal, ironmongery, etc. **hardwareman,** *n.* One who deals in hardware; (*Am.* hardware dealer).

hardwood (hard' wud), *n.* Close-grained wood from deciduous trees, as dist. from pines, etc. **hardwooded,** *a.*

hardy (har di) [F. *hardi*, orig. p.p. of *hardir*, from Teut. (O.H.G. *hartjan*, to make strong, cp. A.-S. *heard*, HARD)], *a.* Bold, over-confident, audacious; inured to fatigue, robust; (of plants) capable of bearing exposure to winter weather. *n.* An ironsmith's chisel fixed upright, usu. in a **hardy-hole** or socket in an anvil, for cutting metal, etc. **half hardy,** *a.* Capable of bearing exposure except during the winter, when it requires shelter (of a plant). **hardy annual:** An annual plant that may be sown in the open; (*fig.*) a question that crops up annually or periodically. **hardihood, *hardiesse,** *n.* Boldness, daring; audacity, effrontery. **hardily,** *adv.* In a daring or audacious manner. ***hardiment, hardiness,** *n.*

hare (hâr) [A.-S. *hara* (cp. Dut. *haas*, Dan. and Swed. *hare*, G. *hase*)], *n.* A long-eared short-tailed rodent of the genus *Lepus*, with cleft upper lip, esp. *L. timidus*, similar to but larger than the rabbit. **hare and hounds:** A paper-chase. **to run with the hare and hunt with the hounds:** To keep in with both sides. **jugged hare** [JUG (1)]. **harebell,** *n.* The blue bell of Scotland, *Campanula rotundifolia*, the round-leaved bell-flower. ***harebrain,** *a.* Hare-brained; *n.* A hare-brained person. **hare-brained,** *a.* Rash, giddy, flighty. ***harehearted,** *a.* Timid, fearful, timorous. **hare-lip,** *n.* A congenital fissure of the upper lip. **harelipped,** *a.* **hare's-foot,** *n.* A species of clover, *Trifolium arvense*; a tropical American cork-tree, *Ochroma lagopus*.

harem (hâr' ĕm) [Arab. *haram*, from *harama*, be prohibited], *n.* The apartments reserved for the women in a Mohammedan household; the occupants of these; a Mohammedan sanctuary (usu. ***haram***).

haricot (hăr' i kō) [F., etym. doubtful], *n.* A stew or ragout of meat, usu. mutton, with beans and other vegetables; the kidney or French bean, *Phaseolus vulgaris*. **haricot-bean,** *n.*

haridan** [HARRIDAN]. ***hari-kari [HARA-KIRI].

hark (hark) [M.E. *herkien* (cogn. with O.Fris. *herkia*, M.Dut. *horken*, G. *horchen*)], *v.i.* To listen. *v.t.* To listen to (usu. in imper., listen). **hark forward! hark away!** Cries to urge hounds. **hark back!** Calling hounds back when they have passed the scent, hence to **hark back:** To return to some point or matter from which a temporary digression has been made.

harken [HEARKEN].

harl (1) (harl) [cp. M.L.G. *herle, harl*, L.G. *harl*], *n.* Filaments of flax; fibrous substance; a barb of a feather, esp. one from a peacock's tail used in making artificial flies.

harl (2) (harl) [Sc. and North., etym. unknown], *v.t.* To drag along the ground; to rough-cast (a wall) with lime. *v.i.* To drag oneself; (*Angling*) to troll. *n.* The act of harling; a small amount or quantity.

Harleian (har lē' ân) [Robert *Harley*, Earl of Oxford (1661–1724)], *a.* Of or pertaining to Robert and his son Edward Harley and the library collected by them, now in the British Museum.

harlequin (har' lė kwin) [F., from It. *arlecchino*, etym. doubtful], *n.* The leading character in a pantomime or harlequinade, adopted from Italian comedy; supposed to be invisible to the clown, he is dressed in a mask, parti-coloured and spangled clothes, and bears a magic wand; a buffoon; the harlequin duck. *v.i.* To act as a harlequin. **v.t.* To conjure away as with a harlequin's wand. **harlequin duck:** A sea-duck with variegated plumage, *Histronicus minutus*, of the northern hemisphere. **harlequina** (har lė kwi' nå), **harlequiness** (-kwi nes'), *n.* **harlequinade** (-năd'), *n.* That part of a pantomime in which the harlequin and clown play the principal parts; an extravaganza; a piece of fantastic conduct. **harlequinesque** (-nesk'), *a.*

harlot (har' lŏt) [O.F., orig. masc., vagabond, rogue, cp. It. *arlotto* (etym. doubtful)], *n.* A woman who prostitutes herself for hire. **v.i.* To play the harlot. **harlotry,** *n.* The practices or trade of a harlot; lewdness, incontinence; *ribaldry.

harm (harm) [A.-S. *hearm* (cp. Icel. *harmr*, G. *harm*)], *n.* Hurt, injury, damage, evil. *v.t.* To injure, hurt, or damage. **harmful,** *a.* Hurtful, injurious, detrimental. **harmfully,** *adv* **harmfulness,** *n.* **harmless,** *a.* Not hurtful or injurious; uninjured, unharmed. **harmlessly,** *adv.* **harmlessness,** *n.*

harmala (har' må lå), **harmel** (har' mėl) [late L. and Gr. *harmala*, from Sansk. (cp. Arab. *ḥarmil*)], *n.* Wild rue. **harmaline** (-līn), *n.* (*Chem.*) A white crystalline alkaloid obtained from the seeds of this.

***harman** (har' mån) [Slang], *n.* A policeman. ***harman-beck** [BEAK], *n.* A parish constable or beadle. ***harmans,** *n.pl.* The stocks.

harmattan (har măt' ån) [Fanti *haramata*], *n.* A dry hot wind blowing from the interior of Africa to the upper Guinea coast in December, January, and February.

harmonic (har mon' ik) [L. *harmonicus*, Gr. *harmonikos*, from *harmonia*, HARMONY], *a.* Pertaining to harmony or music; concordant, harmonious. *n.* An harmonic tone; *(*pl.*) the science of musical sounds. *n.pl.* (*Radio.*) Frequencies which are multiples of a main frequency; the waves that are incidental to the main waves of a transmitter. **harmonic progression:** A series of numbers whose reciprocals are in arithmetical progression, as $\frac{1}{5}$, $\frac{1}{7}$, $\frac{1}{9}$, etc. **harmonic quantities:** Numbers or quantities having this relation. **harmonic proportion:** The relation of three consecutive terms of a harmonic progression. **harmonic tones:** Tones produced by the vibration of aliquot parts of a string, column of air, etc. **harmonical,** *a.* **harmonically,** *adv.* **harmonica, -on** (har mon' i kå, -kŏn), *n.* A musical instrument of various kinds, as musical glasses, mouth-organ, a series of glass or metal plates of graduated lengths played on with a small mallet, etc.

harmonious (har mō' ni ŭs) [F. *harmonieux*, as HARMONY], *a.* Concordant, having harmony; having parts adapted and proportioned to each other, symmetrical; without discord or dissension; musical, tuneful. **harmoniously,** *adv.*

harmoniphon (har mon' i fŏn) [Gr. *harmonia*, HARMONY, *-phōnos*, sounding, from *phōnē*, a sound], *n.* A small musical instrument with reeds or reeds and pipes, played by means of a keyboard.

harmonist (1) (har' mŏ nist), *n.* One skilled in harmony; a musical composer; one who treats of and shows the agreement between corresponding passages of different authors. **harmonistic** (-nis' tik), *a.*

Harmonist (2), **-nite** (har' mŏ nist, -nīt) [*Harmony*, Pennsylvania], *n.* One of a communistic sect founded by the brothers Rapp, who emigrated from Würtemberg to the U.S.A. in 1803, and settled in Harmony.

harmonium (har mō′ ni ŭm) [F.], *n.* A keyed musical wind-instrument whose tones are produced by the forcing of air through free reeds.

harmonize (har′ mȯ nīz) [F., *harmoniser*], *v.t.* To make harmonious; to arrange in musical concord, to add the proper accompaniment to; to adjust in proper proportions; to cause to agree (with). *v.i.* To agree in sound or effect; to live in peace and concord; to correspond, to be congruous (with). **harmonization** (-zā′ shŭn), *n.* **harmonizer,** *n.* **harmonograph** (-mon′ ȯ grăf) [-GRAPH], *n.* An instrument for determining the resultant of two simple harmonic motions in different planes. **harmonometer** (-nom′ ė tėr), *n.* An instrument for measuring the harmonic relation of sounds.

harmony (har′ mȯ ni) [F. *harmonie,* L. and Gr. *harmonia* (*harmos*, a fitting or joining, from the root *ar-*, to fit)], *n.* The just adaptation of parts to each other, so as to form a complete, symmetrical, or pleasing whole; the agreeable combination of simultaneous sounds, music; an arrangement of musical parts for combination with an air or melody; the science dealing with musical combination of sounds; concord or agreement in views, sentiments, etc.; a literary work showing the agreement between parallel or corresponding passages of different authors, esp. of the Gospels. **harmony of the spheres:** The theory derived from Pythagoras that the revolving spheres in which the heavenly bodies were supposed to be carried round the earth emitted musical sounds varying according to their magnitude, velocity, and relative distance. **pre-established harmony:** (*Phil.*) According to Leibnitz, a harmony established between mind and matter by God at the Creation.

harmost (har′ most) [Gr. *harmostēs*, from *harmozein*, to fit, to put in order], *n.* (*Gr. Hist.*) A Spartan governor of a subject city, island, etc. **harmosty,** *n.*

harmotome (har′ mȯ tōm) [F., from Gr. *harmos*, joint, *-tomos*, cutting, from *temnein*, to cut], *n.* (*Min.*) A vitreous hydrous silicate of aluminium and barium characterized by cross-shaped crystals, sometimes called cross-stone.

harness (har′ nės) [M.G. and O.F. *harneis*, etym. doubtful], *n.* The working gear of a horse or other draught-animal; the accoutrement of a knight or man-at-arms, arms and armour; working apparatus or equipment in various mechanical operations; (*fig.*) business equipment. *v.t.* To equip with armour; to put harness on (a horse, etc.); to utilize natural forces, *e.g.* water, for motive power. **in harness:** At work. **to die in harness:** To continue to the last in one's business or profession. **harness-cask, -tub,** *n.* (*Naut.*) A large cask or tub with a rimmed cover, containing the supply of salt meat for immediate use. **harnesser,** *n.* **harnessry,** *n.*

harns (harnz) [Sc., from M.G. *hærnes*, prob. from Scand. (cp. Icel. *hjarne*, O.H.G. *hirni*, G. *hirn*)], *n.pl.* Brains.

***haro** (hăr′ ō) [O.F., etym. doubtful], *int.* A call for help or to raise a hue-and-cry; (*Channel Islands*) a cry constituting a form of legal appeal against encroachment on property.

harp (harp) [A.-S. *hearpe*, cp. Dut. *harp*. Icel. *harpa*. G. *harfe*], *n.* A musical instrument of triangular shape, with strings which are plucked by the fingers. *v.i.* To play upon a harp. **to harp on:** To dwell incessantly upon anything. **harp-shell,** *n.* A tropical genus of molluscs. **harper, harpist,** *n.* A player on the harp. **harpress,** *n.* A female harp-player.

harpings (har′ pingz) [prob. from prec.], *n.pl.* (*Naut.*) The fore parts of the wales encompassing the bow or extensions of the rib-bands of a vessel.

harpoon (har poon′) [F. *harpon*, from *harpe*, a claw, late L. and Gr. *harpē*, a sickle], *n.* A barbed, spear-like missile weapon with a line attached, used for striking and killing whales, etc. *v.t.* To strike, catch or kill with a harpoon. **harpoon-gun,** *n.* A gun for firing a harpoon. **harpoon-rocket,** *n.* A combination of bomb and lance for killing whales. **harpooner** (har poo′ nėr), ***harpooner** (har pu nēr′), *n.*

harpsichord (harp′ si kôrd) [O.F. *harpechorde* (*harpe*, HARP, *chorde*, CHORD)], *n.* A stringed instrument with a keyboard actuating quills that pluck instead of hammers that strike, similar in form to the pianoforte, by which it was superseded.

harpy (har′ pi) [O.F. *harpie*, L. *harpyiæ*, Gr. *harpuiai* (pl.), from the root *harp-*, to seize], *n.* (*Gr. Ant.*) A fabulous monster represented with the face of a woman, the body of a vulture, and fingers armed with sharp claws; (*fig.*) an extortioner, a rapacious person or animal; a harpy-eagle. **harpy-eagle,** *n.* A crested eagle, *Thrasaëtus harpyia*, from South America. **harpy-footed,** *a.* With claws like a harpy.

harquebus (har′ kwė bŭs) [F. *harquebuse*, It. *arcobugio* (*arco* bow, *bugio*, a hole), a pop. corr. of M.H.G. *hakebüsse*, see HACKBUT], *n.* An old kind of musket fired from a forked hand-rest or tripod. **harquebusade** (har kwė bŭ sād′), *n.* The discharge from a harquebus; *a vulnerary water for the cure of gunshot wounds. **harquebusier** (har kwė bŭ sēr′), *n.*

harr [HAAR].

harridan (hăr′ i dȧn) [prob. from M.F. *haridelle*, a worn-out horse], *n.* A worn-out haggard old woman; an old vixen.

harrier (1) (hăr′ i ėr) [HARE, -ER], *n.* A variety of dog, smaller than the foxhound, used for hare-hunting by mounted huntsmen; (*pl.*) a pack of such hounds, or a club of cross-country or hare-and-hounds runners.

harrier (2) (hăr′ i ėr) [HARRY (1), -ER], *n.* One who harries or plunders; a falconoid bird of the genus *Circus*.

Harrovian (hȧ rō′ vi ȧn) [*Harrow*-on-the-Hill, Middlesex], *a.* Of or pertaining to Harrow School. *n.* A person educated there.

harrow (1) (hăr′ ō) [M.G. *harwe*, etym. doubtful], *n.* A large rake or frame with teeth, drawn over ground to level it, stir the soil, destroy weeds, or cover seed. *v.t.* To draw a harrow over; (*fig.*) to torment, to lacerate (feelings, etc.). **under the harrow:** In distress or tribulation. **harrowing,** *a.* Causing anguish or torment.

***harrow** (2) (hăr′ ō) [HARRY], *v.t.* To plunder, to spoil, to harry, to pillage.

harry (1) (hăr′ i) [A.-S. *hergian*, cogn. with *here*, army], *v.t.* To plunder, to pillage, to lay waste; to harass. *v.i.* To make plundering excursions.

harry (2) (*Sc.*) [HARROW (1)].

Harry-long-legs [DADDY-LONG-LEGS].

harsh (harsh) [M.E. *harsk*, from Scand. (cp. Dan. *harsk*, Swed. *härsk*, G. *harsch*)], *a.* Rough to the touch or other senses: discordant, irritating; austere, morose, severe; rigorous, inclement; unfeeling. ***harsh-resounding,** *a.* Grating on the ear. ***harshen,** *v.t.* To make harsh. **harshly,** *adv.* **harshness,** *n.*

harslet [HASLET].

hart (hart) [A.-S. *heort*, *heorot*, from O.Teut. *herut*, horned (cp. L. *cervus*, stag, *keras -atos*, horn)], *n.* A stag, esp. a male red deer, from its fifth year onwards. **hart of ten:** A hart with ten tines on its antlers. **hart's tongue,** *n.* A fern, *Scolopendrium vulgare*, with tongue-shaped leaves.

hartal (har′ tal) [Hind.], *n.* A boycott in India, carried out by closing shops.

hartebeest (har′ tė bēst) [S. Afr. Dut. (*hert*, hart, *beest*, beast)], *n.* The South African *Alcephalus caama*, the commonest of the larger antelopes.

hartshorn (harts′ hôrn), *n.* A preparation from

shavings or chippings of the horns of the hart; spirit of hartshorn. **salt of hartshorn:** Impure carbonate of ammonia. **spirit of hartshorn:** A solution of ammonia in water, smelling-salts.

harum-scarum (hâr′ ŭm skâr′ ŭm) [prob. compounded from HARE and SCARE], *a.* Giddy, hare-brained. *n.* A giddy, hare-brained person.

haruspex (hă rŭs′ peks) [L., lit. inspector of entrails (root from Sansk. *hirā*, entrails, L. *spic-*, to behold)], *n.* (*pl.* **-pices**) An ancient Etruscan or Roman soothsayer who divined the will of the gods by inspecting the entrails of victims. **haruspicy,** *n.*

harvest (har′ vest) [A.-S. *hærfest* (cp. Dut. *herfst*, Icel. *haust*, G. *herbst*), from Teut. root *harb-* (cp. L. *carpere*, to pluck)], *n.* The season of reaping and gathering crops, esp. of corn; ripe corn or other agricultural products gathered and stored; the yield of any natural product for the season; the product or result of any labour or conduct. *v.t.* To reap and gather **in**, as corn, grain, etc.; to garner, to lay up; (*fig.*) to receive as payment, penalty, etc. **harvest-bug, -louse, -mite, -tick,** *n.* A minute tick, mite or acaridan which burrows in or attaches itself to the skin during late summer and autumn, setting up an irritating itch. **harvest feast:** A merry-making at the completion of the harvest. **harvest festival:** A religious service of thanksgiving for the harvest. **harvest home:** The close of harvesting; a merry-making in celebration of this. **harvest lord:** The leading reaper whose motions regulate the others. **harvest-man,** *n.* A labourer in the harvest. **harvest month:** The month of harvest, usually September. **harvest moon:** The moon at its full about the time of the autumnal equinox. **harvest mouse:** A very small field-mouse, *Mus messorius*, which makes a nest usually among wheat-stalks. **harvest queen:** A person or image representing Ceres, the goddess of fruits, flowers, etc., on the last day of harvest. **harvester,** *n.* A reaper; a reaping and binding machine; a harvest-bug. ***harvestless,** *a.* Barren.

harvey, harveyize (har′ vi, -īz) [H. A. *Harvey* (1824–93) of New Jersey, inventor], *v.t.* To harden (steel plates for armoured ships) by a patent process of cementation; to fit a ship with plates hardened by this process.

has [HAVE]. **has-been:** (*colloq.*) One who has seen better days; a not-so-young person.

hasard [HAZARD]. **hasel** [HAZEL].

hash (hăsh) [O.F. *hachis*, from *hacher*, to hack, mince], *n.* Meat, especially such as has already been cooked, cut into small pieces, mixed with vegetables, and stewed, etc.; (*Am.*) shepherd's pie; (*fig.*) a second preparation of old matter; a mess, a muddle. *v.t.* To cut or chop up in small pieces; to mince. **to settle one's hash:** To do for one; to defeat a person completely. **hashmagandy,** *n.* (*Austral.*) Bush stew.

hashish (hăsh′ ish) [Arab. *hashīsh*], *n.* The tender tops and sprouts of Indian hemp, *Cannabis Indica* (see BHANG), used as a narcotic for smoking, chewing, etc.

***hask** (hask) [prob. conn. with HASSOCK], *n.* A case or basket made of rushes or flags, etc.

haslet (hăs′ lĕt), **harslet** (hars′ lĕt) [M.E. and O.F. *hastelet*, from *haste*, a spit, L. *hasta*, a spear], *n.* A part of the entrails, liver, heart, etc., of an animal, usu. a hog, for roasting.

hasp (hasp) [A.-S. *hæpse* (cp. Dut. *haspel*, Icel. *hespa*, G. *haspe*)], *n.* A fastening, esp. a clamp or bar hinged at one end, the other end passing over a staple, where it is secured by a pin, key, or padlock; a skein of yarn. *v.t.* To fasten, shut, or secure with a hasp.

hassock (hăs′ ŏk) [A.-S. *hassuc*, etym. doubtful, not from W. *hesg*, sedges], *n.* A small stuffed footstool or cushion for kneeling on in church; a matted tuft of rank grass, a tussock; (*local*) soft calcareous sandstone separating the beds of Kentish rag.

hast [HAVE].

hastate (hăs′ tāt) [L. *hastātus*, from *hasta*, spear], *a.* Spear-shaped, as the leaf of sheep's sorrel.

haste (hāst) [O.F. *haste* (F. *hâte*), whence *haster*, from W.G. *haisti-*, violence (cp. A.-S. *hæst*)], *n.* Hurry, celerity of movement of action, urgency, precipitance. *v.i.* To make haste. **to make haste:** To be quick; to be in a hurry. **hasten** (hā′ sĕn), *v.t.* To cause to hurry; to urge or press on; to expedite. *v.i.* To move with haste or speed. **hastener,** *n.* **hasting,** *a.* Hurrying; moving or acting hastily; coming early to maturity. *n.* (*prov.*) A fruit coming early to maturity, esp. a kind of early pea. **hasty,** *a.* Hurried, quick; eager, precipitate; rash, inconsiderate; irritable; ripening early. ***hasty-footed,** *a.* Nimble, swift. **hasty pudding:** Flour stirred into boiling milk, and the mixture boiled quickly. **hasty-witted,** *a.* Hasty, rash, impulsive, irascible. **hastily,** *adv.* **hastiness,** *n.*

hastelet [HASLET]. **hasty,** etc. [HASTE].

hat (hăt) [A.-S. *hæt*, cogn. with HOOD], *n.* A covering for the head, usu. having a crown or top and a continuous brim; (*fig.*) the dignity of a cardinal, from the broad-brimmed scarlet hat worn by cardinals. *v.t.* To provide, fit, or cover with a hat. **to hang up one's hat:** To make oneself at home (in another's house). **to pass** or **send round the hat:** To ask for subscriptions, charity, etc. **to raise the hat to:** To salute. **to talk through one's hat:** To talk about something one does not understand. **red hat,** *n.* A cardinal's hat; a military policeman. **top** or **high hat:** (*colloq.*) A cylindrical silk hat, also called (*slang*) chimney-pot or chimney-pot hat. **hatband,** *n.* A band round a hat (esp. a black one as a sign of mourning). **hat block,** *n.* A block or mould for shaping or ironing hats. **hat-peg, -rack, -rail, -stand,** *n.* A contrivance or piece of furniture for hanging hats on. **hat trick:** (*Cricket slang*) The feat of taking three wickets with consecutive balls (from its being held to entitle the bowler to the reward of a new hat). **hatful,** *n.* **hatless,** *a.* **hat-maker, hatter,** *n.* A maker of hats; (*Austral.*) a miner who works by himself; a bush recluse

hatch (1) (hăch) [A.-S. *hæce* (cp. Dut. *hek*, Swed. *häck*), prob. conn. with A.-S. *haca*, the bolt of a door], *n.* A half-door, a wicket; an opening in a roof for access to the outside; an opening in a wall between two rooms; a flood-gate or a grated opening in a weir used for a fish-trap; (*Naut.*) a hatchway, or a trap-door or shutter to cover this. **v.t.* To fasten (a door, etc.). **to be under hatches:** (*Naut.*) To be confined below; (*fig.*) to be in a state of bondage or repression. **hatch-boat,** *n.* A kind of half-decked fishing-boat with a well for fish.

hatch (2) (hăch) [M.E. *hacchen* (cp. Swed. *häcka*, Dan. *hække*)], *v.t.* To produce from eggs by incubation or artificial heat; to produce young from (eggs); (*fig.*) to evolve, to contrive, to produce. *v.i.* To produce young (of eggs); to come out of the egg; to be developed from ova, cells of a brood-comb, etc. **hatchery,** *n.* A place where fish ova are hatched artificially.

hatch (3) (hăch) [F. *hacher*, see HASH], *v.t.* To mark with fine lines, parallel or crossing each other; *to engrave, to chase; to inlay with thin strips of another material. *n.* A fine line in drawing or engraving. **hatched moulding:** (*Arch.*) Ornamentation with a series of cuts or grooves crossing each other, common in Norman work. **hatching,** *n.* Shading produced by lines crossing each other at more or less acute angles.

***hatchel** (hăchl) [HACKLE (1)], *v.t.* To dress flax; (*fig.*) to heckle, to worry.

hatchet (hăch′ et) [F. *hachette*, dim. of *hache*, O.H.G. *happia*, a sickle], *n.* A small axe with a short handle for use with one hand. **to bury** or **take up the hatchet:** To make peace or war. **to throw the hatchet:** To tell lies or fabulous stories. **hatchet-face,** *n.* A narrow face with sharp, prominent features. **hatchet-faced,** *a.* **hatchety,** *a.* **hatchet-man,** *n.* (*Am.*) A gangster.

hatchment (hăch′ mėnt) [corr. of ACHIEVEMENT], *n.* A funeral escutcheon or panel bearing the coat of arms of a deceased person placed on the front of his house, in a church, etc.

hatchway (hăch′ wā) [HATCH (1)], *n.* A large opening in the deck of a ship for lowering cargo, etc.

hate (hāt) [A.-S. *hete*, from Teut. root *hat-*, whence *hatian*, to hate], *n.* Extreme dislike or aversion; detestation. *v.t.* To dislike exceedingly; to abhor, to detest. **hatable,** *a.* **hateful,** *a.* Causing hate; odious, detestable; feeling hatred. **hatefully,** *adv.* **hatefulness,** *n.* ***hateless,** *a.* **hater,** *n.* ***hatesome,** *a.* Hateful. **hatred,** *n.* Exceeding dislike or aversion; active malevolence, animosity, enmity.

***hath** [HAVE]. **hatred** [HATE].

hauberk (haw′ bĕrk) [O.F. *hauberc*, O.H.G. *halsberg* (*hals*, neck, cp. HALSE, *bergan*, cogn. with A.-S. *beorgan*, to protect, see BURY)], *n.* A coat of mail, sometimes without sleeves, formed of interwoven steel rings.

haugh (ha*ch*, haf) [SC. and North., prob. from A.-S. *healh*, nook, corner], *n.* A piece of low-lying land, esp. by a river.

haughty (haw′ ti) [earlier *haught*, F. *haut*, L. *altus*, high], *a.* Proud, arrogant, disdainful, supercilious; proceeding from or expressing disdainful pride; *lofty, high; *bold. **haughtily,** *adv.* **haughtiness,** *n.*

haul (hawl) [var. of HALE (2)], *v.t.* To pull or drag with force; to transport or move by dragging. *v.i.* To pull or drag (at or upon) with force; (*Naut.*) to alter the course of a ship. *n.* A hauling, a pull; the drawing of a net; the amount that is taken at once, take, acquisition. **to haul over the coals:** To take to task, to reprimand. **to haul the wind:** (*Naut.*) To turn the head of the ship nearer to that point from which the wind blows. **haulabout,** *n.* (*Naut.*) A large steel coal-barge or lighter equipped with transporters. **haulage,** *n.* **hauler, haulier,** *n.* One who hauls, esp. a workman who hauls trucks to the bottom of the shaft in a coal-mine.

haulm (hawm) [A.-S. *healm* (cp. Dut. and G. *halm*, Icel. *hālmr*, also L. *culmus*, Gr. *kalamos*, reed)], *n.* A stem, a stalk; (*collect.*) the stems or stalks of peas, beans, potatoes, etc.

haunch (hawnch) [O.F. *hanche*, from Teut. (cp. O.H.G. *anchā*, leg, orig. joint)], *n.* That part of the body between the ribs and the thigh; the buttock, the basal joint; (*butcher's meat*) the leg and loin cut in one piece; (*Arch.*) the shoulder of an arch; *the rear, the hind part. **haunch-bone,** *n.* **haunched,** *a.* Having haunches.

haunt (hawnt) [O.F. *hanter*, etym. doubtful], *v.t.* To frequent, to resort to often; to frequent the company of; to visit frequently, to recur to the mind of frequently in an irritating way; to frequent as a ghost or spirit; *to practise, to pursue. *v.i.* To stay or be frequently (about, in, etc.). *n.* A place to which one often or customarily resorts; a resort, a den, a feeding-place for animals, etc.; *practice, use; habit of frequenting a place; (*Am.*) a ghost. **haunter,** *n.* **hauntingly,** *adv.*

Hausa (hou′ sȧ) [native race], *n.* A member of the Bantu Negroid race occupying a large area of the central Sudan.

hausen (houzn) [G., from O.H.G. *hûso*, HUSO], *n.* The huso.

hausfrau (hous′ frou) [G.], *n.* A housewife.

Haussa [HAUSA].

haussmannize (hous′ mȧ nīz) [Baron *Haussmann* (1809–91), architect, Prefect of the Seine under Napoleon III], *v.t.* To reconstruct or improve (a town, suburbs, streets, etc.) by opening out and rebuilding.

haustellum (haws stel′ ŭm) [dim. from L. *haustrum*, from *haurīre*, to draw (water)], *n.* (pl. **-la**) (*Zool.*) The sucking organ of certain insects and crustaceans. **haustellate** (haw′ stė lāt), *a.*

haustorium (haw stôr′ i ŭm) [from L. *haustor*, a drawer, as prec.], *n.* (*Bot.*) A rootlet or sucker of a parasitic plant.

hautboy (hō′ boi) [F. *hautbois* (*haut*, L. *altus*, high, *bois*, late L. *boscus*, wood)], *n.* An oboe; an organ stop with a thin, soft tone; a tall species of strawberry, *Fragaria elatior*.

haute ecole (ōt′ ā kōl) [F.], *n.* Difficult feats of horsemanship; a method of teaching these.

hauteur (hō tĕr′) [F., from *haut*, high], *n.* Haughtiness, lofty manners or demeanour.

hautgoût (ō goo′) [F. *haut*, high, *goût*, taste, flavour], *n.* A strong relish, taste, or seasoning; a spice, a taint. ***haut-ton*** (ō ton′) [F. *ton*, TONE, fashion], *n.* High fashion; people of the most approved fashion.

haüyne (ha′ win) [F., from R. J. *Haüy* (1743–1822), French mineralogist], *n.* (*Min.*) A vitreous silicate of aluminium and sodium with calcium sulphate, found in igneous rocks.

Havana (hȧ văn′ ȧ), *n.* A cigar made at Havana or in Cuba.

have (hăv) [A.-S. *habban* (cp. Dut. *hebban*, Icel. *hafa*, G. *haben*, and perh. L. *habēre*)], *v.t.* (*2nd sing.* **hast,** *3rd sing.* **has, *hath;** *past* **had,** *2nd sing.* **hadst,** *p.p.* **had**) To possess, to hold as owner; to enjoy, to suffer, to experience; to receive, to get, to obtain; to require, to claim; to hold mentally, to retain; to entertain; to maintain; to hold as part, appurtenance, quality, etc., to contain, to comprise; to know, to understand, to be engaged in; to vanquish, to hold at one's mercy; to circumvent, to cheat, to bring forth, to bear. *v.i.* (*usu. in imper.*) To go, to betake oneself, to get (at, after, with, etc.). *aux.* Used with past participles to denote the completed action of verbs. *n.* (*slang*) A take-in, a do, a sell. **had I known:** If I had known. ***have after:** Follow, let us follow. ***have at:** (*imper.*) Assail, encounter. **have done:** Stop, cease. ***have with you:** I will go with you; come on, agreed. **I had as lief:** I would as willingly. **I had better:** It would be wiser or better (to do, go, etc.). **I had rather:** I would prefer to. **let him have it:** (*colloq.*) Punish, censure, or abuse him; give it him. **you've had it:** [HAD]. **the haves and the have-nots:** The propertied classes and the unpropertied. **to be had:** To be taken in. **to have a care:** To be cautious. **to have it out:** To settle a quarrel or dispute by fighting, debate, etc. **to have it that:** To maintain or argue that. **to have nothing for it:** To have no alternative. **to have on:** To wear. **to have on toast:** (*slang*) To take in; to make game of; to worst in argument. **to have pain:** To suffer. **to have pleasure:** To enjoy. **to have to do:** To be obliged to do. **haveless,** *a.* *Having little or nothing; (*Sc.*) shiftless, careless. **having,** *n.* Possession, goods, property; (*pl.*) endowments, qualities; (*Sc. usu. in pl.*) behaviour; good manners. **a.* Grasping, covetous.

havelock (hăv′ lok) [General Sir H. *Havelock* (1795–1857)], *n.* A light covering for the cap hanging over the neck, worn as a protection against sunstroke.

haven (hāv′ ėn) [A.-S. *hæfene* (cp. Dut. *haven*, Icel. *höfn*, G. *hafen*)], *n.* A port, a harbour; a station or refuge for ships; (*fig.*) a refuge, an asylum,. *v.t.* To shelter. ***havenage,** *n.* Harbour dues. **havener,** *n.* The overseer of a haven.

haver (1) (hăv′ ĕr), *n.* (*Sc. Law*) One who holds a deed or document.

haver (2) (hā′ vėr) [Sc. and North., etym. unknown], *n.* (*usu. pl.*) Nonsense, foolish talk. *v.i.* To talk nonsense. **haverel, haverer,** *n.*

haversack (hăv′ ėr săk) [F. *havresac*, G. *habersack* (*haber*, oats, *sack*, SACK)], *n.* A strong canvas bag to hold rations, etc. on march.

Haversian (hȧ vĕr′ si ȧn) [Clopton *Havers* (*d.* 1702), English physician], *a.* (*Anat.*) Applied to certain passages, etc. in the substance of the bones.

Haversian canals: A network of canals in bone conveying and protecting the blood-vessels.

havildar (hăv′ il dar) [Pers. *hawāl-dār*, from Arab. *ḥawālah*, charge, Pers. *dār*, holding], *n.* A sergeant of a regiment of infantry in India.

having [HAVE].

***haviour** (hā′ vyůr) [A.-F. *aveir* (F. *avoir*), to have], *n.* Possession, property; behaviour, manners.

havoc (hăv′ ŏk) [A.-F. *havok*, O.F. *havot*, plunder, prob. from Teut. and cogn. with HEAVE], *n.* Widespread destruction; devastation, waste. **v.t.* To lay waste; to devastate. **to cry havoc:** (*fig.*) To give the signal for violence or devastation.

haw (1) (haw) [A.-S. *haga* (cp. Icel. *hagi*, Dut. *haag*, G. *hag*)], *n.* The berry or fruit of the hawthorn; a hedge, an enclosed field or yard.

haw (2) (haw) [imit.], *int.* and *n.* A sound expressive of hesitation in speaking. *v.i.* To utter this sound, to speak with hesitation.

haw (3) (haw) [etym. unknown], *n.* (*Farriery*) The nictitating membrane or third eyelid (of a horse, etc.); (*often in pl.*) a disease of this characterized by inflammation, enlargement, etc.

Hawaiian (hȧ wā′ yȧn) [*Hawaii*, island in the North Pacific], *a.* Of or pertaining to Hawaii. *n.* A native or inhabitant of Hawaii.

hawbuck (haw′ bŭk), *n.* A clown, a rustic.

hawfinch (haw′ finch), *n.* The common grosbeak, *Coccothraustes coccothraustes.*

haw-haw. Lord Haw Haw: Name given derisively to William Joyce (hanged 1946), who broadcast anti-British propaganda from Germany during the war of 1939–45.

hawk (1) (hawk) [A.-S. *hafoc*, *heafoc* (cp. Dut. *havic*, Icel. *haukr*, G. *habicht*), prob. from Teut. root *haf-*, to seize, cp. L. *capere*], *n.* A name for many species of raptorial birds allied to the falcons; a bird of prey with short, rounded wings used in falconry; (*fig.*) a rapacious person, a sharper. *v.i.* To hunt birds, etc. by means of trained hawks or falcons; to attack on the wing, to soar (at). *v.t.* To pursue or attack on the wing. **hawk-bell,** *n.* A small bell on the foot of a hawk. **hawk-eyed,** *a.* Having sharp sight. **hawk-moth,** *n.* A moth of the family *Sphingidæ*, the flight of which is not unlike that of a hawk in quest of prey. ***hawk-nose,** *n.* One who has a hooked nose. **hawk-nosed,** *a.* **hawk's-beard,** *n.* The composite genus *Crepis*, related to the hawk-weeds. **hawking,** *n.* Falconry.

hawk (2) (hawk) [prob. imit.], *v.i.* To clear or try to clear the throat in a noisy manner. *v.t.* To force (up) phlegm from the throat. *n.* An effort to force up phlegm from the throat.

hawk (3) (hawk) [HAWKER (2)], *v.t.* To carry about for sale, to cry for sale; (*fig.*) to carry or spread about.

hawk (4) (hawk) [etym. doubtful], *n.* A plasterer's board with handle underneath, for carrying plaster, mortar, etc.

hawked (1) (hawkt) [Sc. and North., etym. unknown], *a.* Streaked, spotted. **hawkey, -kie,** *n.* A cow with a white or white-striped face; a pet name for a cow.

hawked (2) (hawd), *a.* Curved like a hawk's bill.

hawker (1) (haw′ kėr), *n.* One who practises the sport of hawking; a falconer.

hawker (2) (haw′ kėr) [prob. from G. (cp. L.G. *höker*, Dut. *heuker*, G. *höker*)], *n.* One who travels with any beast of burden or mechanically propelled vehicle licensed to carry goods for sale in the street or from house to house.

hawkweed (hawk′ wēd), *n.* Any plant of the composite genus *Hieracium.*

hawse (hawz) [prob. from Icel. *hals*, neck, cp. HALSE], *n.* (*Naut.*) That part of the bow in which are the hawse-holes; the distance between a ship's head and the anchors by which she rides; the situation of the cables when a ship is moored from the bows with two anchors. **hawse-hole,** *n.* A hole in each bow for a cable or hawser to pass through. **to come in at the hawse-holes:** To enter the naval service at the lowest grade.

hawser (haw′ zer) [O.F. *haucier* (F. *hausser*), late L. *altiāre*, to raise, from L. *altus*, high], *n.* A cable, used in warping and mooring.

hawthorn (haw′ thôrn) [A.-S. *hægthorn* (HAW (1), THORN)], *n.* A thorny, rosaceous shrub or tree belonging to the species Cratægus, bearing white or pink flowers which develop into haws. Other names are whitethorn and may.

hay (1) (hā) [M.E. *hey*, A.-S. *hīeg*, cogn. with HEW], *n.* Grass cut and dried for fodder; *growing grass. *v.t.* To make (grass, etc.) into hay; to supply or feed with hay. *v.i.* To make hay. **make hay:** To turn, toss, and expose mown grass to the sun for drying. **to make hay of:** To throw into confusion. **to make hay while the sun shines:** To take advantage of every favourable opportunity. **hay-asthma** [HAY-FEVER]. **hay-box,** *n.* (*Cookery*) An air-tight box, with a thick layer of hay, used for keeping food hot, and for continuing the process of slow cooking after the food has been removed from the fire. **haycock,** *n.* A conical heap of hay. **hay-fever,** *n.* A severe catarrh with asthmatic symptoms, frequent in summer and probably caused by the inhalation of pollen. **hayfield,** *n.* A field where hay is being made. **hay-fork,** *n.* A fork for turning over or pitching hay. **hay-knife,** *n.* A large, broad knife with a handle set crosswise, used for cutting hay out of a stack. **hayloft,** *n.* A loft for storing hay. **haymaker,** *n.* One employed in making hay; a machine for tossing hay; a kind of country dance. **haymaking,** *n.* **hay-mow,** *n.* A hayrick; a mass of hay laid up in a barn. **hayrick, haystack,** *n.* A pile of hay in the open air, built with a conical or ridged top, and thatched to keep it dry. **hayseed,** *n.* (*Am. slang*) A yokel, rustic. **haysel,** *n.* Hay harvest.

hay (2) (hā) [etym. doubtful], *n.* A country dance with a winding movement. ***hay-de-guy, -guise,** *n.* A frolicsome dance of the 16th and early 17th centuries.

***hay** (3) (hā) [A.-S. *hege*, cogn. with *haga*, HAW (1)], *n.* A hedge, a fence. ***hayward,** *n.* A parish or town officer in charge of fences, enclosures, commons, etc., and responsible for the impounding of stray cattle, etc.

hay (4) (hā) [It. *hai*, thou hast it (cp. L. *habet*)], *n.* A home-thrust in fencing.

haymaker, hayrick, haysel [HAY (1)].

hayward [HAY (3)].

haywire (hā′ wīr), *a.* (*slang*) Crazy, mad.

hazard (hăz′ ȧrd) [O.F. *hasard*, perh. from Arab. *al zahr*, the die], *n.* A game at dice; danger, risk; chance, casualty; the stake in gaming; (*Tennis*) one of the winning openings in a tennis-court; (*Golf*) difficulties, obstacles, bunkers, etc., on a golf-course; (*Billiards*) a stroke putting a ball into a pocket; a **winning hazard** is when the player pockets the object ball, a **losing hazard** when his own ball runs into a pocket off the object ball. *v.t.* To risk; to expose to chance or danger; to run the risk of; to venture (an act, statement, etc.). *v.i.* To run a risk, to venture. **at all hazards:** In spite of any risk. **to run the hazard:** To run the risk. ***hazardable,** *a.* ***hazardize,** *n.* A hazardous situation. **hazardous,** *a.* Full of hazard, danger, or risk. **hazardously.** *adv.* ***hazardousness,** *n.* ***hazardry,** *n.* Gambling, dicing; rashness, temerity. **chicken-hazard** [CHICKEN, see CHICK (2)].

haze (1) (hāz) [etym. unknown], *n.* Want of transparency in the air, a very thin mist or vapour, usu. due to heat; (*fig.*) obscurity or indistinctness of perception. *v.t.* To make hazy. **hazy,** *a.* Misty; thick with haze; (*fig.*) dim. vague, indistinct, obscure; (*slang*) rather drunk; muddled. **hazily,** *adv.* **haziness,** *n.*

haze (2) (hāz) [etym. doubtful, cp. O.F. *haser*, to irritate, to annoy], *v.t.* (*Naut.*) To harass or punish with overwork; to play practical jokes on; to harass with overwork or work of a disagreeable kind, esp. seamen. *v.i.* (*Am.*) To bully, to tease; to riot, to frolic (about). **hazing,** *n.*

hazel (hā′ zėl) [A.-S. *hæsel* (cp. Icel. *hasl*, Dut. *hazel*, G. *hasel*)], *n.* A shrub or small tree of the genus *Corylus*, esp. the European *C. avellana*, bearing the hazel-nut; a reddish-brown colour. *a.* Hazelly, light-brown. **hazel-eyed,** *a.* Having light-brown eyes. **hazel-nut,** *n.* The fruit of the hazel, the cob-nut. **hazeline,** *n.* (*Chem.*) A distilled product of wych-hazel used in medicine.

hazing [HAZE (2)]. **hazy** [HAZE (1)].

he (hē) [A.-S. *hē*, cogn. with O.Fris. and O.S. *hi*, *he*], *pron.* (*obj.* **him,** *poss.* **his;** *pl.* **they,** *obj.* **them,** *poss.* **their**) The male person or animal referred to. *n.* A male person; a children's game of chasing to touch another player. **he-cat, -goat,** etc. *n.* A male cat, goat, etc. **he-man,** *n.* (*colloq.*) A virile man. **he-oak,** *n.* An Australian tree, *Casuarina stricta*.

head (1) (hed) [A.-S. *hēafod* (cp. Dut. *hoofd*, Icel. *haufoth*, G. *haupt*)], *n.* The foremost part of the body of an animal, the uppermost in man, consisting of the skull, with the brain and the special sense-organs; any part, organ, or thing of an analogous kind; the upper part of anything, the top; the upper end of a valley, lake, gulf, etc.; the front part of a ship, plough, procession, column of troops, etc.; a promontory; the capital of a pillar, etc.; the part of a bed where the head rests; the more honourable end of a table, etc.; the obverse of a coin or medal; the knobbed end of a nail, etc.; the striking part of a tool; the globular cluster of flowers or leaves at the top of a stem; the first or most honourable place, the forefront, the place of command; a chief, a ruler, a principal, or leader; a headmaster of a school; a person, an individual; a single one (as of cattle); a main division, a topic, a category; a culmination, a crisis, a pitch; the ripened part of an ulcer or boil; froth on liquor; pressure of water available for driving mills; available steam-pressure; (*fig.*) liberty, licence, freedom from restraint; the mind, the understanding, the intellect, esp. as distinguished from the feelings; one's life; a bundle of flax about 2 ft. long. **from head to foot:** Over the whole person. **head and ears:** The whole person; completely. **head and shoulders:** By the height of the head and shoulders; *by force, by hook or by crook. **head over heels:** Turning upside down; completely (in love). **off one's head:** Out of one's mind; wildly excited, demented. **over head and ears:** Deeply (immersed). **out of one's own head:** By one's own invention; of one's own accord. **to come to a head:** To suppurate (of an ulcer or boil); hence, to ripen; to reach a crisis or culminating point. **to give one his head:** To give liberty or licence to; to let (a horse) go as he pleases. **to keep one's head:** To remain calm. **to lose one's head:** To be carried away by excitement; to lose one's presence of mind; to be decapitated. **to make head:** To push forward; to struggle (against) effectually. **head-cheese,** *n.* (*Am.*) Portions of the head and feet of swine cut up fine, boiled, and pressed into a mass, brawn. **head-dress,** *n.* Covering and ornaments for the head, esp. of a woman. **head-first, -foremost,** *adv.* With the head in front (of a plunge); (*fig.*) precipitately. **head-frame,** *n.* (*Mining*) A frame over a pit-shaft to which the hoisting pulleys are attached. **head-gear,** *n.* The covering, dress, or ornaments of the head; a bridle; (*Mining*) machinery at the top of a shaft or boring. **head-house,** *n.* (*Mining*) A house which houses the head-frame. **head-hunters,** *n.pl.* Several races or tribes, notably the Dyaks of Borneo and Celebes, so called from their practice of making hostile raids in order to secure human persons and heads as trophies. **head-hunting,** *n.* **head-knee,** *n.* (*Shipbuilding*) A timber which is laid edgeways to the cutwater and stem. **head-lugged,** *a.* Lugged, dragged, or drawn along by the head. **head-man,** *n.* A chief, a leader, a head worker. ***head-mark,** *n.* A feature of the face or head marking individuality. **head-money,** *n.* A capitation tax or payment. **headmost,** *a.* Most forward, most advanced. **head-mould, -moulding** [HOOD-MOULD, see HOOD]. **head-on,** *a.* Head to head. **head-phone,** *n.* A telephone receiver to fit to the head. **head-piece,** *n.* Armour for the head, a helmet; (*colloq.*) the head, the intellect; an ornamental engraving at the head of a chapter, etc. **head-race,** *n.* A race that leads water to a water-wheel. **head-resistance,** *n.* (*Aviat.*) Resistance offered by the air to the wings and body of an aeroplane when flying level. **head-room,** *n.* Room or space for the head in a low tunnel, etc. **head-sail,** *n.* (*Naut.*) Any of the foresails. **head sea:** A heavy sea running directly against a ship's course. **head-shake,** *n.* A significant shake of the head. **head-spring,** *n.* The source of a stream; (*fig.*) source, origin. **head-tire,** *n.* Attire for the head. **head-voice,** *n.* (*Singing, etc.*) Sounds produced above the chest register. **head-water,** *n.* (*usu. pl.*) The upper part of a stream near its source. **head-wind,** *n.* A contrary wind. **head-word,** *n.* One constituting a heading. **head-work,** *n.* Brain-work; (*Arch.*) head-like ornament on the keystone of an arch. **head-workman,** *n.* A chief workman. **headed,** *a.* Having a head; having intellect or mental faculties (*esp. in comb.*, as *hard-headed*). **headless,** *a.* Without a head; having no leader; *foolish, rash, obstinate, groundless. **headship,** *n.*

head (2) (hed) [from prec.], *v.t.* To lead, to be the leader to, to direct; to be or form a head to; to provide with a head; to put or to be a heading to a chapter, etc.; to get ahead of; to lop (as trees); to oppose, to check; *to behead. *v.i.* To go or tend in a direction; to form a head. **to head back** or **off:** To intercept, to get ahead of and turn back or aside. **heading** (hed′ ing), *n.* The action of the verb TO HEAD; an inscription at the head of an article, chapter, etc.; a running title; the pieces which compose a cask-head; (*Mining*) the end or the beginning of a drift or gallery; a gallery, drift, or adit; (*Football*) the act of hitting the ball with the head.

-head, -hood [A.-S. *-hād* (M.E. *-hod*), cogn. with Goth. *haiduz*, manner, way], *suf.* Denoting state or quality, as in *godhead*, *maidenhead*, *childhood*, *manhood*.

headache (hed′ āk), *n.* A neuralgic or other persistent pain in the head; (*colloq.*) a source of worry. **headachy,** *a.* Suffering from or tending to cause headache.

headband (hed′ bănd), *n.* A fillet or band for the hair; (*Bookbinding*) a band at the top and bottom inside the back of a book; (*Radio.*) the band connecting a pair of receivers or ear-phones.

headborough (hed′ bŭr ů), *n.* The chief man of a tithing; a petty constable.

header (hed′ ėr), *n.* One who puts or fixes a head on anything; a plunge or dive head-foremost; a brick or stone laid with its end in the face of the wall; (*Mech.*) a reaper that clips off the corn heads only; a machine for heading nails, rivets, etc.; a tube or water-chamber in a steam boiler into which either end of a stack of water tubes is secured in such a manner that the steam and water can go from one tube or coil to another.

headfast (hed′ fast), *n.* (*Naut.*) A rope to make fast the head of a vessel to some fixed object.

headland (hed′ lănd), *n.* A point of land projecting into the sea, a cape, a promontory; a ridge or strip of unploughed land at either end of a field, where the plough is turned.

headlight (hed′ līt), *n.* The lamp carried at the front of a locomotive, motor-car, etc.

headline (hed′ līn), *n.* The line at the head of a

page or paragraph giving the title, etc.; news set out in large, heavy type. **to hit the headlines:** To gain notoriety, to get notice in the press.

headlong (hed' long) [M.E. *hedling*], *adv.* Headforemost; violently, hastily, rashly. *a.* Steep, precipitous; (*fig.*) violent, precipitate; rash, thoughtless.

headmaster, headmistress (hed mas' tėr, hed mis' tres), *n.* The principal master or mistress at a school.

headquarters (hed kwôr' tĕrz), *n.pl.* The residence of the commander-in-chief of an army; the place whence orders are issued; the centre of authority. **headquarters staff:** The staff attached to the commander-in-chief of an army.

headsman (hedz' mȧn), *n.* One who cuts off heads, an executioner; (*Mining*) a labourer who conveys coal from the working to the horse-way; (*Whaling*) the man who takes charge of a boat after the whale has been struck.

headstall (hed' stawl), *n.* The bridle without the bit and reins.

headstock (hed' stok), *n.* The part supporting the end or head, esp. the end of a revolving spindle; the portion of a lathe that contains the mandrel; the part which supports the cutters in a planing-machine.

headstone (hed' stōn), *n.* A stone at the head of a grave. **head stone** (hed stōn'), *n.* The principal stone in a building; a corner-stone.

headstrong (hed' strong), *a.* Ungovernable, obstinate, intractable, obstinately self-willed. **headstrongness,** *n.*

headway (hed' wā), *n.* Motion ahead, rate of progress; head-room.

heady (hed' i), *a.* Headstrong, precipitate; violent, impetuous, intoxicating, inflaming. **headily,** *adv.* **headiness,** *n.*

heal (1) (hēl) [A.-S. *hǣlan*, cogn. with HALE, WHOLE], *v.t.* To make whole, to restore to health; to cure (of disease, etc.); to cause to cicatrize; (*fig.*) to reconcile; to free from guilt, to purify. *v.i.* To grow or become sound or whole. **heal-all,** *n.* A panacea; a plant popularly supposed to be a universal remedy. **healable,** *a.* **healer,** *n.* **healing,** *a.* Tending to heal; soothing, mollifying. **the healing art:** The art of medicine. **healingly,** *adv.* **healsome** (hāl' sŭm), *a.* (*Sc.*) Wholesome.

***heal** (2) [HELE].

heald (hēld) [etym. doubtful], *n.* A heddle.

health (helth) [A.-S. *hælth*, from *hāl*, WHOLE], *n.* A state of bodily or organic soundness, freedom from bodily or mental disease or decay; physical condition (good, bad, etc.); a toast wishing that one may be well, prosperous, etc. **health-resort,** *n.* A place where sick, delicate, or convalescent people stay for the benefit of their health. **healthful,** *a.* Promoting health, either physical or spiritual; salubrious; healthy. **healthfully,** *adv.* **healthfulness,** *n.* ***healthless,** *a.* Unhealthy, unwholesome. ***healthsome,** *a.* Healthy, wholesome. **healthy,** *a.* Enjoying good health; hale, sound; promoting health, salubrious, salutary. **healthily,** *adv.* **healthiness,** *n.*

heap (hēp) [A.-S. *hēap* (cp. Dut. *hoop*, Swed. *hop*, G. *haufe*)], *n.* A pile or accumulation of many things placed or thrown one on another; (*colloq.*) a large number, a lot, a crowd, a good many times, a good deal. *v.t.* To throw (together) or pile (up) in a heap; to load or overload (with); to pile (upon). **struck all of a heap:** (*colloq.*) Staggered, flabbergasted. ***heapy,** *a.* Lying in heaps; heaped.

hear (hēr) [A.-S. *hīeran* (cp. Dut. *hooren*, Icel. *heyra*, G. *horen*)], *v.t.* (*past & p.p.* **heard,** hĕrd) To perceive by the ear, to perceive the sound of; to listen to, to attend to; to listen to as a judge, etc.; to understand by listening; to be a hearer of; to pay regard to, to heed, to obey; to be informed of by report. *v.i.* To have the sense of hearing; to be told, to be informed (of, about, etc.). **hear! hear!** Listen! a form of applause or ironical approval. **hearable,** *a.* **hearer,** *n.* One who hears; one of an audience. **hearing,** *n.* The act of perceiving sound; the sense by which sound is perceived; audience, attention; a judicial trial or investigation; earshot. **hearing-aid,** *n.* A mechanical or electrical device for assisting the deaf to hear.

hearken (har' kėn) [A.-S. *heorcnian*, as HARK], **v.t.* To hear, to regard. *v.i.* To listen attentively (to). **hearkener,** *n.*

hearsay (hēr' sā), *n.* Common talk, report, or gossip. *n.a.* Told or given at second-hand.

hearse (hērs) [O.F. *herce*, It. *erpice*, L. *hirpicem*, nom. *hirpex*, a harrow], *n.* A carriage in which the dead are taken to the place of burial; *a framework or canopy (orig. like an ancient harrow) for candles etc. formerly placed over the bier or coffin at the funeral of a great person; *a coffin, a bier. *v.t.* To carry in or on a hearse to the grave; *to entomb; to put in or under a hearse. **hearse-cloth,** *n.* A pall. **hearselike,** *a.* Funereal.

heart (hart) [A.-S. *heorte* (cp. Dut. *hart*, Icel. *hjarta*, G. *herz*; also L. *cor -dis*, Gr. *kardia*)], *n.* The central organ of circulation, which it keeps going by its rhythmical contraction and dilatation; (*fig.*) the mind, the soul; the emotions or affections, esp. the passion of love; sensibility, tenderness, courage, spirit; zeal, ardour; the breast as seat of the affections; the central part of anything, the core; the vital or most essential part; strength, efficacy, fertility; a term of endearment; anything heart-shaped; (*pl.*) a suit of cards marked with figures like hearts. **v.t.* To hearten. *v.i.* To grow into a compact head or mass, as a plant. **after his own heart:** Exactly as he desires. **at heart:** In reality, truly, at bottom; in the inmost feelings. **by heart:** By rote, by or from memory. **heart and hand:** With enthusiastic energy. **heart and soul:** Devotedly. **from one's heart, from the bottom of one's heart:** With absolute sincerity; fervently. **in heart, in good heart:** In good spirits; in good condition, fertile. **in one's heart:** Inwardly, secretly. **near one's heart:** Very dear to one. **heart of oak:** A man of courage. **out of heart:** In low spirits, depressed; exhausted of fertility (of land). **to break the heart of:** To cause the greatest grief to. **to eat one's heart out:** To brood over or pine away through trouble. **to find in one's heart:** To be willing. **to get** or **learn by heart:** To commit to memory. **to have at heart:** To be earnestly set upon, to cherish (a design etc.). **to have one's heart in one's mouth:** To be violently frightened or startled. **to give** or **lose one's heart to:** To fall deeply in love with. **to pluck up heart:** To regain courage. **to set the heart at rest:** To tranquillize, to console. **to set the heart on:** To be very desirous of, or anxious for. **to speak to one's heart:** To comfort, to encourage, to cheer. **to take heart of grace:** To pluck up courage. **to take to heart:** To be greatly affected by. **to wear one's heart upon one's sleeve:** To be excessively frank and unreserved; to reveal one's inmost feelings and thoughts. **with all one's heart:** With thorough goodwill. **heart-ache,** *n.* Anguish of mind. **heartbeat,** *n.* A pulsation of the heart; (*fig.*) an emotion. **heart-blood** [HEART'S-BLOOD]. ***heart-break,** *n.* Overpowering sorrow. **heart-breaker,** *n.* One who or that which breaks the heart; a kind of curl; a love-lock. **heart-breaking,** *a.* **heart-broken,** *a.* **heart-burn,** *n.* A burning pain in the stomach arising from indigestion. ***heart-burned,** *a.* Having the heart inflamed; suffering from heart-burn. **heart-burning,** *a.* Inflaming or distressing the heart. *n.* Heartburn; secret enmity; envy. **heart-cam** [HEART-WHEEL]. ***heart-dear,** *a.* Sincerely beloved. **heart-disease,** *n.* A generic term for various affections of the heart. ***heart-easing,** *a.* Comforting, consoling, pacifying. **heart-felt,** *a.* Deeply felt, sincere. ***heart-grief,** *n.* Affliction of the heart. **heart-rending,** *a.*

Heart-breaking, intensely afflictive. ***heart-robbing,** *a.* Ecstatic. **heart's blood,** *n.* The life-blood; life; *soul, essence. **heart-seed,** *n.* Climbing plants of the genus *Cardiospermum.* **heart-sick,** *a.* Pained in mind; deeply afflicted. **heart-sickening,** *a.* **heart-sickness,** *n.* **heart-sore,** *n.* A cause of deep sorrow. *a.* Grieved at heart. **heart-stricken** [HEART-STRUCK], **heart-strings,** *n.pl.* (*fig.*) The sensibilities; pity, compassion; one's deepest affections. ***heart-struck,** *a.* Overwhelmed with anguish, grief, or terror; struck to the heart. ***heart-swelling,** *a.* Rankling in the heart. **heart-wheel,** *n.* A form of cam-wheel for converting uniform rotary motion into uniform reciprocating rectilinear motion. **heart-whole,** *a.* Having the affections free, not in love; undaunted; sincere. **heart-wood,** *n.* Duramen. **hearted,** *a.* Having a heart (*esp. in comb.*, as *sound-hearted*). ***heartedness,** *n.* Sincerity, zeal.

heartburn [HEART].

hearten (har′ tėn) [A.-S. *hiertan*, as prec.], *v.t.* To encourage, to inspirit, to stir up. *v.i.* To cheer (up). **heartener,** *n.*

hearth (harth) [A.-S. *heorth* (cp. Dut. *haard*, Swed. *hard*, G. *herd*)], *n.* The floor of a fire-place; (*Min.*) that part of a reverberatory furnace in which the ore is laid, or in a blast furnace the lowest part through which the metal flows; (*fig.*) the fireside, the domestic circle, the home. **hearth-broom, -brush,** *n.* A small brush for sweeping up ashes. ***hearth-money, -tax,** *n.* A tax on domestic hearths imposed 1662–89. **hearthstone,** *n.* The stone forming the hearth; a soft kind of stone for whitening hearths etc.

heartless (hart′ lės), *a.* Destitute of feeling or affection; insensible, pitiless, cruel; faint-hearted, spiritless. **heartlessly,** *adv.* **heartlessness,** *n.*

heartlet (hart′ lėt), *n.* A little heart, a nucleus.

heartsease (harts′ ēz), *n.* Peace of mind; the wild pansy, *Viola tricolour.*

***heartsome** (hart′ sŏm) [HEART, -SOME], *a.* Encouraging, inspiriting; merry, cheerful.

hearty (har′ ti), *a.* Proceeding from the heart, sincere; cordial, good-natured, kindly; healthy; of keen appetite; full, abundant, satisfying; boisterous; irritatingly cheerful. *n.* (*Naut.*) A brave, hearty fellow. **my hearties:** (*Naut.*) A friendly mode of address. ***hearty-hale,** *a.* Good for the heart. **heartily,** *adv.* **heartiness,** *n.*

***heast** [HEST].

heat (hēt) [A.-S. *hǣtu*, from *hāt*, HOT], *n.* A form of energy, probably consisting in the vibration of the ultimate molecules of bodies or of the ether, capable of melting and decomposing matter, and transmissible by means of radiation, conduction, or convection; hotness, the sensation produced by a hot body; hot weather; an inflamed condition of the skin, flesh, etc.; redness, flush, high colour; hotness or pungency of flavour; violence, vehemence, fury; anger; intense excitement; warmth of temperament; animation, fire; sexual excitement in animals, esp. in females; a single course in a race or other contest. *v.t.* To make hot; to inflame, to cause to ferment; (*fig.*) to excite. *v.i.* To become hot; (*fig.*) to become inflamed or excited. **latent heat:** The heat absorbed without change of temperature in altering the internal constitution of a body, as in melting or vaporization. **on heat:** (*Biol.*) Of a female animal when sexually excited. **prickly heat:** A skin rash prevalent in hot climates. **specific heat:** The heat required to raise the temperature of one unit of a given substance one degree. **heat-engine,** *n.* An engine driven by hot air, steam, or other agent for converting heat into mechanical energy. **heat pump,** *n.* A machine for transferring heat from a low temperature to a higher temperature, for the purpose of space or water heating. **heat-spot,** *n.* A freckle; an urticarious pimple attributed to heat. **heat stroke,** *n.* Prostration from excessive heat. **heat-unit,** *n.* The quantity of heat required to raise the temperature of one unit of water (usu. 1 lb.) through one degree. **heat-wave,** *n.* A wave of radiant heat; an unbroken spell of weather when the temperature exceeds 80° F. **heatedly,** *adv.* With passion, angrily. **heater,** *n.* One who or that which heats; a heating-apparatus; a block of iron made red-hot and then placed in an urn or a smoothing-iron. **heating,** *a.* Promoting warmth or heat; exciting; stimulating. **heating- apparatus,** *n.* An apparatus for warming buildings.

heath (hēth) [A.-S. *hǣth* (cp. Dut. and G. *heide*, Icel. *heithr*)], *n.* An open space of country, esp. if covered with shrubs and coarse herbage; any plant belonging to the genus *Erica*, or the allied genus *Calluna*, consisting of narrow-leaved evergreen shrubs with wiry stems and red or reddish flowers. **heath-bell,** *n.* A flower growing on a heath, esp. on heather. **heath-berry,** *n.* A berry growing on low shrubs common on heaths, as the bilberry, cranberry, etc. **heath-bird** [HEATH-FOWL]. **heath-cock,** *n.* The black-cock or male of the black grouse, *Lyrurus tetrix.* **heath-fowl, -game,** *n.* The black grouse. **heath-hen,** *n.* The female of the black grouse; (*Am.*) various species of grouse. **heath-pea,** *n.* A perennial herb, *Lathyrus macrorhizus*, of the bean family, with pea-like edible tubers. **heath-plant,** *n.* Heather. **heath-pout,** *n.* A heath-bird, esp. the female and the young. **heathy,** *a.*

heathen (hē′ thėn) [A.-S. *hǣthen* (cp. Dut. *heiden*, Icel. *heithimr*, G. *heide*), cogn. with prec.], *n.* A Gentile; one who is not Christian, Jew, or Mohammedan; a pagan, an idolater; (*fig.*) an unenlightened or barbarous person. *a.* Gentile; pagan; (*fig.*) unenlightened; barbarous. **the heathen:** (*collect.*) Heathen peoples. **heathendom, *heathenesse,** *n.* The portion of the world in which heathenism is dominant; heathens collectively; heathenism. **heathenish,** *a.* Of or belonging to the heathens; (*fig.*) barbarous, rapacious, cruel. **heathenishly,** *adv.* **heathenishness,** *n.* **heathenism, heathenry,** *n.* The moral or religious state or practices of heathens; (*fig.*) debased moral condition. **heathenize,** *v.t.* To render heathen.

heather (heth′ ėr) [etym. doubtful], *n.* Heath, esp. *Calluna vulgaris*, called in the north ling. **to set the heather on fire:** To create a disturbance. **to take to the heather:** To become an outlaw. **heather-ale,** *n.* A liquor formerly brewed from heather-flowers. **heather-bell,** *n.* The cross-leaved heather, *Erica tetralix*; sometimes applied to *Erica cinera.* **heather-mixture, -stockings, -tweed, -wool,** *n.* A fabric or garment of a speckled colour supposed to resemble heather. **heathery,** *a.* Abounding in heather.

***heaume** (hōm) [F., from O.F. *helme*, HELM (1)], *n.* A large helmet coming down to the shoulders.

heave (hēv) [A.-S. *hebban* (cp. Dut. *heffen*, Icel. *hefja*, G. *heben*, also L. *capere*, to take, Gr. *kōpē*, handle)], *v.t.* (*past and p.p.* **heaved, *hove**) To lift, to raise, with effort; to utter or force from the breast; (*colloq., orig. Naut.*) to throw, to cast (something heavy); (*Naut.*) to hoist (as the anchor), to haul; (*Geol.*) to fracture and displace (strata); (*fig.*) to elevate, to exalt. *v.i.* To rise; to rise and fall with alternate or successive motions; to pant; to retch, to vomit. *n.* An upward motion or swelling; the act of heaving; a sigh; an effort to vomit; (*Geol.*) amount of displacement of a vein or stratum, esp. measured in a horizontal direction. **heave ho!** (*Naut.*) Sailor's cry in hauling up the anchor. **to heave down:** (*Naut.*) To careen. **to heave in sight:** (*Naut.*) To come into sight. **to heave out:** To throw out. **to heave to:** (*Naut.*) To bring the head (of a ship) to the wind and so stop her motion; to bring a ship to a standstill. **heave-offering,** *n.* An offering in the Jewish Church which was consecrated by lifting up before the Lord. **heaver,** *n.* One who or that which heaves (*esp. in comb.*, as *coal-heaver*).

heaven (hev′ ėn) [A.-S. *heofon, hefon* (etym. doubtful)], *n.* The sky, the firmament (*often in pl.*); the atmosphere enveloping the earth regarded as the region in which the clouds float, the winds blow, etc.; the abode of God and the blessed; the place of supreme felicity; God, providence; *the pagan divinities or their abode; (*Anc. Cosmog.*) one of several revolving spheres in which the heavenly bodies were carried round the earth. **Good heavens!** An exclamation. **heaven of heavens, seventh heaven:** The highest of the seven heavens believed by the later Hebrews and the Mohammedans to be the dwelling-place of God. **in the seventh heaven:** In a state of supreme felicity. **heaven-banished,** *a.* Banished from heaven. **heaven-born,** *a.* Derived from heaven; inspired. **heaven-bred,** *a.* Of divine origin. **heaven-directed,** *a.* Pointing towards the sky; directed by heaven. **heaven-fallen,** *a.* Fallen or driven from heaven. **heaven-gifted,** *a.* Bestowed by heaven. ***heaven-hued,** *a.* Blue, azure. **heavenly,** *a.* Pertaining to the heavens, celestial; inhabiting heaven; situated in the heavens (as the planets, stars, etc.); divine; superhuman; supremely blest or excellent; (*colloq.*) highly pleasing, delicious. **adv.* In the manner of heaven; divinely, celestially. **heavenly body** [BODY]. **heavenly minded,** *a.* Having the affections set on heaven and heavenly things; pure, holy, pious. **heavenly mindedness,** *n.* **heavenliness,** *n.* **heavenward,** *a.* and *adv.* **heavenwards,** *adv.*

heaves (hēvz) [HEAVE], *n.pl.* An asthmatic disease in horses, broken wind. **heavy** (hē' vi), *a.* Affected with the heaves.

Heaviside layer (hev' i sīd lā' ėr) [O. *Heaviside* (1850–1925)], *n.* A layer in the upper atmosphere that reflects radio waves, thus enabling reception round the curved surface of the earth.

heavy (hev' i) [A.-S. *hefig*, cogn. with HEAVE], *a.* Having great weight, weighty, ponderous; of a large and ponderous kind (as metal, artillery, etc.); of great density or specific gravity, dense; not properly raised (as bread); of full body (as wines, etc.); great, powerful, forcible, violent; concerned with large amounts or dealings; unwieldy, clumsy; plentiful, abundant; large in amount; weighed down, loaded (with); not easily borne; oppressive, grievous, severe; burdensome, obstructive, clogging; difficult; (*fig.*) drowsy, dull, sluggish, stupid; tedious; doleful, depressing, depressed; (*Theat. slang*) serious, sombre; threatening, louring; *deep, loud; *pregnant. **adv.* Heavily, with great weight. **time hangs heavy:** Time passes tediously. **to be heavy:** To make its weight felt. **the Heavies:** The Dragoon Guards. **heavy-armed,** *a.* Bearing heavy armour or arms. **heavy-handed,** *a.* Clumsy, awkward; oppressive. ***heavy-headed,** *a.* Dull, stupid, drowsy. **heavy-hearted,** *a.* Dejected. **heavy laden:** Burdened with depression. **heavy spar:** Barytes. **heavy swell:** (*slang*) A person dressed in the height of fashion. **heavy water,** *n.* (*Phys.*) Deuterium oxide, a liquid similar to ordinary water, with density about 10% greater. **to make heavy weather:** To make a labour of a task. **heavy-weight:** A person or animal of more than average weight, esp. a jockey above the average or a boxer weighing over 12 stone 10 lb. **heavy wet:** (*slang*) A drink of strong malt liquor, esp. stout. **heavily,** *adv.* **heaviness,** *n.* **heavyish,** *a.*

hebdomad (heb' dŏ măd) [L. and Gr. *hebdomas -ados* (*hegdomos*, seventh, from *hepta*, seven)], *n.* A week, a period of seven days (alluding to Daniel's prophecy, Dan. ix. 27); a group of seven things; (*Gnostic Phil.*) a group of seven spirits dwelling in the seven planets, also the demiurge. **hebdomadal** (heb dom' ȧ dȧl) *a.* Consisting of seven days; meeting or occurring weekly. **Hebdomadal Council:** A board meeting weekly which virtually manages the principal affairs of the University of Oxford. **hebdomadally,** *adv.* **hebdomadary,** *a.* Hebdomadal. *n.* A member of a chapter or convent whose week it is to officiate in the choir.

Hebe (hē' bē) [Gr., youthful prime], *n.* The goddess of youth cupbearer to the gods of Olympus; (*facet.*) a waitress, a barmaid; (*Astron.*) the sixth asteroid. **hebetic** (hė bet' ik), *a.* (*Physiol.*) Pertaining to youth or pubescence.

***hebenon** (heb' ė nŏn) [Shak., a nonce-word, occurring only in *Hamlet*, I, 5], *n.* Perh. henbane.

hebetate (heb' ė tāt) [L. *hebetātus*, p.p. of *hebetāre*, from *hebes -etis*, blunt], *v.t.* To make blunt or dull; to stupefy. *v.i.* To become blunt or dull. **hebetant,** *a.* ***hebetation** (-tā' shŭn), *n.* ***hebetude,** *n.* Obtuseness, stupidity.

hebetic [HEBE].

Hebraic (hē brā' ik) [late L. *Hebraicus*, Gr. *Hebraikos*], *a.* Pertaining to the Hebrews, their mode of thought, or language. **Hebraically,** *adv.* **Hebraism** (hē' brā izm), *n.* The thought or religion of the Hebrews; a Hebrew characteristic; a Hebrew idiom or expression. **Hebraist,** *n.* One learned in the Hebrew language and literature; one who conforms or adheres to Jewish ideas or religious observances. **Hebraistic, -al** (hē brā is' tik, -ȧl), *a.* **Hebraistically,** *adv.* **hebraize,** *v.t.* To convert into a Hebrew idiom; to give a Hebrew character to. *v.i.* To become Hebrew; to act according to Hebrew manners or fashions.

Hebrew (hē' broo) [F. *hébreu*, L. *Hebræus*, Gr. *Hebraios*, Aram. *ebrai*, Heb. *'ibrī*, prob. one from the other side, an immigrant], *n.* A Jew, an Israelite; the language of the ancient Jews and of the State of Israel; (*colloq.*) unintelligible talk, gibberish. *a.* Pertaining to the Jews. **Hebrew-wise,** *adv.* In an opposite sense (from the fact that Hebrew is read from right to left).

Hebridean (hė brid' ė ȧn) [*Hebrides*, erron. for L. *Hebudes* (Pliny), *Hebudæ*, Gr. *Heboudai*], *a.* Of or pertaining to the Hebrides, islands off the west coast of Scotland.

Hecate (hek' ȧ tē) [Gr. *Hekatē*], *n.* (*Gr. Myth.*) A mysterious goddess holding sway in earth, heaven, and the under-world, and represented as triform; a hag, a witch. **Hecatæan** (hek ȧ tē' ȧn), *a.*

hecatomb (hek' ȧ tom) [L. *hecatombē*, Gr. *hekatombē* (*hekaton*, a hundred, *bous*, ox)], *n.* (*Gr. Ant.*) The sacrifice of a hundred oxen or other beasts; (*fig.*) any great sacrifice.

***hecatontome** (hek' ȧ ton tōm) [Gr. *hekaton*, a hundred, *tomos*, TOME], *n.* (*Milton*) A large quantity (lit. a hundred) of books.

hech (he*ch*) [Sc. HEIGH], *int.* An exclamation, chiefly of surprise.

***hecht** (*Sc.*) [HEIGHT].

heck (hek) [A.-S. *hæcc*, HATCH (1)], *n.* A rack for fodder; a hatch; a grated contrivance in a stream, used as a fish-trap or to obstruct the passage of fish.

heckle (hek' ėl), *v.t.* To hackle; to worry (a public speaker) by inconvenient questions. **heckler,** *n.*

hectare (hek' târ, ek tar') [F.], *n.* A French superficial measure, containing 100 ares or 2·471 acres.

hectic (hek' tik) [F. *hectique*, late L. *hecticus*, Gr. *hektikos*, from *hexis*, habit of body, from *hexein*, fut. of *echein*, to have, to hold], *a.* (*Path.*) Habitual, continual (of fever); consumptive; pertaining to consumption; (*colloq.*) full of excitement, exciting, wild. *n.* A hectic fever; a hectic patient; the morbid flush in hectic fever and consumption. **hectic fever:** A fever attendant on phthisis, dysentery, etc. ***hectical, hectoid,** *a.* **hectically,** *adv.*

hecto- [Gr. *hekaton*, a hundred], *comb. form.*

hectogram (hek' tō grăm), *n.* A French weight of 100 grams or 3·52 oz. av.

hectograph (hek' tō grăf), *n.* A machine for multiplying copies of writings or drawings. **hectographic,** *a.*

hectolitre (hek' tō lē tėr), *n.* A French liquid measure containing 100 litres or 3·531 cubic feet.

hectometre (hek' tō mē tėr), *n.* A French measure of length containing 100 metres or 109·3633 yds.

hector (hek' tŏr) [Gr. *Hectōr*, son of Priam and Hecuba, the bravest of the Trojan warriors (Homer's *Iliad*)], *n.* A bully, a blusterer. *v.t.* To bully, to treat with insolence. *v.i.* To play the bully, to bluster. **hectorer,** *n.* ***hectorism,** *n.* Bluster, bullying.

hectostere (hek′ tō stĕr), *n.* A French solid measure containing 100 cubic metres or 3531·66 cubic ft.

heddle (hedl) [perh. from an A.-S. *hęfedl*, earlier form of *hęfeld*], *n.* (*Weaving*) One of the sets of parallel cords or wires forming loops for the warp-threads.

hedera (hed′ ėr ȧ) [L.], *n.* A genus of climbing plants containing two species, the common and the Australian ivy. **hederaceous** (hed ėr ā′ shůs), ***hederal,** *a.* **hederiferous** (-if′ ėr ůs), *a.*

hedge (hej) [A.-S. *hecg* (cp. Dut. *hegge*, Icel. *heggr*, G. *hecke*), cogn. with *hāga*, HAW], *n.* A fence of bushes or small trees; (*fig.*) a barrier of any kind. *v.t.* To fence (in) with or separate (off) by a hedge; to surround or enclose with or as with a hedge; to secure oneself against loss (on a speculation, etc.) by transactions that would tend to indemnify one. *v.i.* To plant or repair hedges; to skulk in a hedge; (*fig.*) to act in a shifty way, to avoid making a decisive statement. **dead hedge:** One made with cut stems or branches. **quickset hedge:** One made with living bushes, esp. hawthorn. **hedge-bill,** *n.* A billhook for trimming hedges. **hedge-born,** *a.* Of low or mean birth. **hedge-creeper,** *n.* One who skulks under hedges for evil purposes. **hedge-hop,** *v.i.* (*Aviat.*) To fly very low over fields, etc. ***hedge hyssop:** A scrophulareous plant, *Gratiola officinalis*, having medicinal properties. ***hedge-marriage,** *n.* An irregular marriage performed by a hedge-priest; a clandestine marriage. ***hedge note:** Poor, inferior writing. **hedge-priest,** *n.* A poor, illiterate priest, or sham priest, formerly common in Ireland. **hedge-row,** *n.* A row of shrubs planted as a hedge. **hedge-school,** *n.* A low-class school such as was formerly conducted in the open air in the country parts of Ireland. **hedge-schoolmaster,** *n.* **hedge-sparrow,** *n.* A common European bird, *Accentor modularis*, one of the warblers. **hedge-stake,** *n.* A stake to support a hedge. **hedge-writer,** *n.* A poor hack-writer. **hedging-bill,** *n.* A hedge-bill. **hedgeless,** *a.* **hedger,** *n.* One who makes or trims hedges.

hedgehog (hej′ hog), *n.* A small insectivorous mammal, *Erinaceus Europæus*, covered above with spines, and able to roll itself up into a ball; a spiny fish, *Diodon hystrix*; a plant with spiny seed-vessels, *Medicago intertexta*; (*fig.*) an irritable, quarrelsome person; (*Mil.*) a line formed by a number of fortified points. **hedgehog thistle:** A spiny globular plant of the cactus family. **hedgehoggy,** *a.*

hedonic (hē don′ ik) [Gr. *hēdonikos*, from *hēdonē*, pleasure], *a.* Of or pertaining to pleasure. *n.pl.* The science of pleasure; the branch of ethics dealing with the relations of duty and pleasure. **hedonism** (hē′ dȯ nizm), *n.* (*Phil.*) The doctrine that pleasure is the chief good. **hedonist,** *n.* **hedonistic** (-nis′ tik), *a.*

hedyphane (hed′ i fān) [Gr. *hēdus*, sweet, *-phanēs*, appearing (*phainein*, to show)], *n.* A massive, colourless variety of mimetite, containing calcium; a variety of green lead-ore.

heed (hēd) [A.-S. *hēdan* (cp. Dut. *hoeden*, G. *hüten*, from *hut*, protection), prob. cogn. with HOOD], *v.t.* To regard, to take notice of. **v.i.* To take notice, to pay attention. *n.* Care, attention; careful consideration. **to take, give,** or **pay heed to:** To take notice of, pay regard to. **heedful,** *a.* Circumspect, wary; attentive, regardful (of). **heedfully,** *adv.* **heedfulness,** *n.* ***heediness,** *n.* Heedfulness. **heedless,** *a.* Careless; thoughtless; negligent (of). **heedlessly,** *adv.* **heedlessness,** *n.*

heehaw (hē′ haw) [imit.], *v.i.* To bray like an ass. *n.* An ass's bray; (*fig.*) a loud and foolish laugh.

heel (1) (hēl) [A.-S. *hēla* (cp. Dut. *hiel*, Icel. *hæll*), allied to *hōh*, HOUGH], *n.* The rounded hinder part of the foot in man; the corresponding part of the hind limb in quadrupeds, often above the foot; (*pop.*) the hinder part of a quadruped's foot; (*pl.*) the feet, esp. the hind feet of animals; the hinder part of a shoe, stocking, etc., covering the heel; a block built up of pieces of leather to raise the hinder part of a boot or shoe from the ground; a heel-like protuberance, knob, or part, such as the lower end of a mast, the hindermost part of a ship's keel, the cusp of a molar tooth, the crook in the head of a golf-club; the latter part, the fag-end of anything; (*Am. slang*) a worthless, disreputable fellow. *v.t.* To add a heel to; to arm (a game-cock) with a spur; to follow close on the heels; (*Football*) to pass the ball out from a scrimmage with the heels; (*Golf*) to hit the ball with the heel of a club. *v.i.* To dance. **come to heel,** or **to heel:** Come close behind, so as to be under control (direction to a dog). **heels over head** or **head over heels:** Upside down. **to be at heel** or **upon one's heels:** To be close behind; to follow hard. **to be down** or **out at heels:** To be trodden or worn down at the back (of shoes, etc.); (*fig.*) to be slipshod or slovenly; to be in unfortunate circumstances. **to lay** or **clap by the heels:** To arrest, to imprison. **to be made to cool one's heels:** To be made to wait. **to show the heels, to show a clean pair of heels, to take to one's heels:** To take to flight, to run away. **to tread upon one's heels:** To follow close or hard after. **to turn on one's heel:** To turn round sharply. **heel-ball,** *n.* A composition of hard wax and lamp-black, used to give a smooth surface to heels, and for taking rubbings of inscriptions, etc. **heel-piece,** *n.* A piece of leather on the heel of a shoe; *the end, the conclusion. *v.t.* To put a piece of leather upon. **heel-tap,** *n.* A thickness of leather in a shoe-heel; (*fig.*) a small quantity of liquor left in the bottom of a glass. **no heel-taps!** Empty your glasses. **heeler,** *n.* One who puts heels on boots; *a game-cock that strikes well with his heels or spurs; (*U.S.A. slang*) a hanger-on of a political boss.

heel (2) (hēl) [M.E. *helden*, A.-S. *hyldan*, cogn. with *heald*, sloping], *v.i.* (*Naut.*) To incline or cant over to one side. *v.t.* To make (a vessel) do this. *n.* An inclination to one side (of a ship, etc.).

heeze (hēz) [Sc., HOISE], *v.t.* To raise, to heave up. *n.* A lift.

heft (1) (heft) [from HEAVE], *n.* The act of heaving; a lift, a push; an effort, an exertion; weight, heaviness. *v.t.* To try the weight of by lifting.

heft (2) [HAFT].

hefty (hef′ ti) [HEFT (1)], *a.* (*colloq.*) Strong, muscular, powerful; big.

Hegelian (hā gā′ li ȧn, hė gē′ li ȧn) [George Frederick William *Hegel* (1770–1831), German philosopher], *a.* Pertaining to Hegel or his philosophy. *n.* One who accepts the teaching of Hegel. **Hegelianism,** *n.* The philosophical system of Hegel.

hegemony (hē ge′ mo ni) [Gr. *hēgemonia*, from *hēgemōn*, leader, from *hēg-*, stem of *agein*, to lead], *n.* Leadership, predominance, esp. applied to the relation of one state to another or to a confederation. **hegemonic** (-mon′ ik), *a.*

Hegira (hej′ i rȧ) [med. L., from Arab. *hijrah*, from *hajara*, to separate], *n.* The flight of Mohammed from Mecca to Medina, 19 July 622, from which the Moslem era is computed; (*fig.*) a precipitate flight.

hegumen (hė gū′ mėn) [med. L. *hēgūmenus*, Gr. *hēgoumenos*, orig. pres.p. of *hegeisthai*, to lead], *n.* The head of a monastery in the Greek Church.

heifer (hef′ ėr) [A.-S. *hēahfore*, etym. doubtful], *n.* A young cow that has not yet calved.

heigh (hā) [imit.], *int.* An exclamation calling attention or expressing inquiry or encouragement. **heigh-ho,** *int.* An expression of disappointment, weariness, or regret.

heighday [HEYDAY].

height (hīt) [A.-S. *hīehtho*, from *hēah*, HIGH], *n.* The quality or state of being high; the distance o the top of an object above its foot, basis, or foundation; altitude above the ground, sea-level, or other recognized level; an elevated position; an eminence, a summit; stature; elevation in rank, office, society, etc.; the fullest extent or degree. **at its height:** At its highest degree; at the culminating point. **the height:** The fullest extent. **heighten,** *v.t.* To make high or higher, to raise, to elevate; to increase, to enhance, to intensify, to accentuate, to emphasize; to exaggerate. *v.i.* To rise; to increase, to augment.

heinous (hā′ nŭs) [O.F. *haïnos*, from *haïne*, hate, from *haïr*, to hate], *a.* Abominable, flagrant, atrocious; wicked in the highest degree. **heinously,** *adv.* **heinousness,** *n.*

heir (âr) [O.F., from late L. *hērem*, L. *hērēdem*, acc. of *hērēs*], *n.* One who by law succeeds or is entitled to succeed another in the possession of property or rank; (*fig.*) one who succeeds to any gift, quality, etc.; *child, product. *v.t.* To be heir to, to inherit. **heir apparent** [APPARENT]. **heir-at-law,** *n.* One who inherits property by right of descent. **heir presumptive** [PRESUMPTIVE]. **heirdom,** *n.* **heiress,** *n.* A female heir. **heirless,** *a.* **heirship,** *n.*

heirloom (âr′ loom) [LOOM (I)], *n.* A chattel which descends with an estate to an heir; any possession that has remained in a family for several generations.

Hejira [HEGIRA].

helco- [Gr. *helkos*, ulcer], *comb. form.* (*Path.*) Of or relating to an ulcer or ulcers. **helcoid** (hel′ koid), *a.* Like an ulcer. **helcology** (hel kol′ ŏ ji), *n.* The branch of pathology relating to ulcers; a treatise on this subject. **helcoplasty** (hel′ kŏ plăs ti) [Gr. *plastos*, formed from *plassein*, to mould], *n.* The grafting of a strip of healthy skin on an ulcer. **helcosis** (hel kō′ sis), *n.* Ulceration. **helcotic** (hel kot′ ik), *a.*

held, *past & p.p.* [HOLD (I)].

***hele** (hēl) [A.-S. *helian*, *helan*, to cover (cp. Dut. *hēlen*, G. *hehlen*, also L. *celāre*, Gr. *kaluptein*)], *v.t.* To hide; to cover.

heli-, helio- [Gr. *hēlios*, the sun], *comb. form.* Pertaining to the sun; produced by the sun's rays.

heliacal (hė lī′ ȧ kȧl), ***heliac** (hē′ li ăk) [late L. *hēliacus*, Gr. *hēliakos*, from *hēlios*, sun], *a.* Closely connected with the sun; rising just before the sun. **heliacal rising** or **setting:** The apparent rising or setting of a star when it first becomes perceptible or is lost to sight in rays of the sun. **heliacally,** *adv.*

helianthus (hē li ăn′ thŭs) [Gr. *anthos*, flower], *n.* (*Bot.*) A genus of plants containing the sunflower.

helical (hel′ i kȧl) [from L. *helix -icis*, see HELIX], *a.* Like a helix; spiral. **helical gears:** (*Mach.*) Gear-wheels in which the teeth are set at an angle with the axis. **helically,** *adv.* **helicograph** (hel′ i kŏ grăf), *n.* An instrument for describing spirals. **helicoid,** *a.* **helicoidal,** *a.*

Heliconian (hel i kō′ ni ȧn) [L. *Helicōnius*, Gr. *Helikōnios*, from *Helikōn*, a mountain in Boeotia, the fabled seat of Apollo and the Muses], *a.* Of or pertaining to Helicon or the Muses.

helicopter (hel′ i kop tėr) [HELIX, Gr. *pteron*, a wing], *n.* An aircraft with one or more power-driven airscrews mounted on vertical axes with the aid of which it can take-off or land vertically.

heliocentric (hē li ō sen′ trik), *a.* Having reference to the sun as centre; regarded from the point of view of the sun. **heliocentrically,** *adv.*

heliochrome (hē′ li ŏ krōm) [Gr. *chrōma*, colour], *n.* A photograph representing an object in the natural colours. **heliochromic** (-krō′ mik), *a.* Pertaining to heliochromy. **heliochromotype** (hē li ŏ krō′ mŏ tīp), *n.* A heliochrome. **heliochromy** (hē li ŏ krō′ mi), *n.* A photographic process by which the natural colours of objects are reproduced.

heliogram [HELIOGRAPH].

heliograph (hē′ li ŏ grăf), *n.* An engraving obtained by a process in which a prepared plate is exposed to the light; an instrument for obtaining photographs of the sun; an apparatus for signalling by reflecting flashes of sunlight. *v.i.* To signal with this, to photograph by a heliographic process. **heliogram** (hē′ li ŏ grăm), *n.* A message transmitted by heliograph. **heliographic, -al** (-grăf′ ik, -ȧl), *a.* **heliography** (hē li og′ rȧ fi), *n.* The operation of signalling with the heliograph; the process of engraving by exposure to light; a description of the sun.

heliogravure (hē li ŏ grā′ vūr, -grăv′ ūr), *n.* Photo-engraving; an engraved plate or print obtained by this.

heliolatry (hē li ol′ a tri), *n.* Sun-worship. **heliolater,** *n.* **heliolatrous,** *a.*

heliology (hē li ol′ ŏ ji), *n.* The science of the sun.

heliometer (hē li om′ ė tėr), *n.* An instrument for measuring small angles in the heavens, such as the angular distance between stars, the diameter of stars, etc.; orig. for measuring the diameter of the sun. **heliometric, -al** (-met′ rik, -ȧl), *a.*

heliophilus (hē li of′ i lŭs) [HELIO-, -PHILOUS], *a.* Attracted by or turning towards the sunlight. **heliophobous** (hē li of′ ŏ bŭs) [-PHOBOUS], *a.* Disliking or turning away from the sunlight (of certain plants).

helioscope (hē′ li ŏ skōp), *n.* A form of reflecting telescope for viewing the sun. **helioscopic** (-skop′ ik), *a.*

heliosis (hē li ō′ sis), *n.* (*Bot.*) Spots caused on leaves, etc. by the concentration of the sun's rays shining through glass, water-drops, etc.; sunstroke.

heliostat (hē′ li ŏ stăt) [Gr. *statos*, standing, from *sta-*, stem of *histanai*, to stand], *n.* An instrument, comprising a mirror turned by clockwork, by which the rays of the sun are continuously reflected in a fixed direction.

heliotherapy (hē li ō ther′ ȧp i) [Gr. *therapeuein*, to heal], *n.* (*Med.*) Curative treatment by exposing the body to the rays of the sun.

heliothermometer (hē li ŏ thėr mom′ ėtėr), *n.* (*Meteor.*) A thermometer with a blackened bulb for registering the effect of atmospheric absorption on solar radiation.

heliotrope (hē′ li ŏ trōp) [L. *heliotropium*, Gr. *heliotropion* (*trop-*, stem of *trepein*, to turn)], *n.* A genus of tropical or subtropical plants belonging to the borage family, whose flowers turn with the sun, those cultivated being varieties of *Heliotropium Peruvianum*; formerly applied to the sunflower, marigold, etc.; a purple tint characteristic of heliotrope flowers; (*Min.*) a red-spotted variety of quartz, also called blood-stone; *an apparatus for reflecting the sun's rays, a kind of heliograph; *an ancient form of sundial. **heliotropic, -al** (-trop′ ik, -ȧl), *a.* Pertaining to or manifesting heliotropism. **heliotropism** (hē li ot′ rŏ pizm), **heliotropy** (-ot′ rŏ pi), *n.* Movement of leaves or flowers towards the sun.

heliotype (hē′ li ŏ tīp), *n.* A picture obtained by printing from a gelatine surface in the same way as from a lithographic stone; this process. **heliotypic** (-tip′ ik), *a.* **heliotypography** (-pog′ rȧ fi), **heliotypy** (hē′ li ŏ tī pi), *n.*

heliozoan (hē li ŏ zō′ ȧn) [Gr. *zōă*, pl. of *zōon*, animal], *a.* (*Zool.*) Pertaining to the *Heliozoa*, a group of protozoa with threadlike radiating processes, also called sun-animalcules. *n.* One of this class. **heliozoic,** *a.*

heliport (hel′ i pôrt), *n.* A station for the landing and departure of helicopters.

***helispheric, -al** (hel i sfer′ ik, -ȧl) [HELIX, SPHERICAL], *a.* Winding round a globe spirally.

helium (hē′ li ŭm) [Gr. *hēlios*, sun], *n.* (*Chem.*) A gaseous inert element discovered by Lockyer in the atmosphere of the sun by means of the solar spectrum, and afterwards found in the atmosphere and occluded to certain minerals.

helix (hel' iks, hē' liks) [L., from Gr.], *n.* (*pl.* **helices**) A spiral line, as of wire or rope in coil; (*Anat.*) the rim or fold of the external ear; (*Arch.*) the small volute under the abacus of a Corinthian column, and other spiral ornaments; (*Zool.*) a genus of molluscs, containing the common snails.

hell (1) (hel) [A.-S. *hel* (cp. Dut. and Icel. *hel*, O.H.G. *hella*, G. *hölle*), from *hel-*, to hide, whence A.-S. *hēlan*, see HELE], *n.* The place of punishment for the wicked after death; the place or state of the dead; a place of extreme misery, pain, or suffering; torment, torture; a gambling-house; in prisoner's base and other games, the place for those who have been caught. ***hell-black,** *a.* As black as hell. **hell-born, -bred,** *a.* (*fig.*) Of villainous origin. **hell-brewed,** *a.* Prepared in hell. ***hell-broth,** *n.* A magical composition for evil purposes. **hell-cat,** *n.* A witch, a hag. **hell-fire,** *n.* The torments of hell. **hell-fired,** *a.* Damned [cp. ALL-FIRED]. **hell for leather:** As fast as possible. **hell-gate,** *n.* The entrance to hell. ***hell-hag,** *n.* A mischievous, wicked old woman. **hell-hated,** *a.* Abhorred like hell. ***hell-hound,** *n.* A fiend of hell; an agent of hell. ***hell-kite,** *n.* A person of extreme cruelty. **hell-weed,** *n.* The dodder and other plants. **hellish, *helly,** *a.* Pertaining to hell; infernal; detestable; atrociously wicked. **hellishly,** *adv.* **hellishness,** *n.* **hell-ward,** *a.* and *adv.*

***hell** (2) [HELE].

hellebore (hel' ė bôr) [L. *helleborus*, Gr. *helleboros*], *n.* Any plant of the ranunculaceous genus *Helleborus*, containing *H. niger*, the Christmas rose, and the hellebore of the ancients, *H. officinalis*, which with other plants of the same genus or of *Veratrum* was supposed by the ancients to be a cure for insanity. ***helleborize,** *v.t.* To treat or dose with hellebore, as for madness. ***helleborism,** *n.*

Hellene (hė lēn', hel' ēn) [Gr. *Hellēn*], *n.* (*pl.* **Hellenes,** hel' ēnz) An ancient Greek, one of Greek descent whether inhabiting Europe or Asia Minor; a citizen of modern Greece. **Hellenic, *Hellenian** (hė lē' nik, -ni ȧn), *a.* **Hellenism** (hel' ė nizm), *n.* A Greek idiom, phrase, peculiarity, or custom; cultivation of Greek ideas, language, style, etc.; Greek civilization or culture; Greek nationalism. **Hellenist,** *n.* One who adopted the Greek language, dress, customs, etc., esp. a Greek Jew in the early days of Christianity; one who is learned in the Greek language and literature. **Hellenistic** (hel ė nis' tik), *a.* **Hellenistically,** *adv.* **hellenize,** *v.i.* To adopt or follow Greek habits; to use or study the Greek language. *v.t.* To permeate with Greek ideas, culture, etc.; to make Greek. **hellenization** (-zā' shŭn), *n.*

hellicat (hel' i kăt) [Sc., var. of *halok*, *halokit*, etym. unknown], *a.* Giddy-headed, flighty. *n.* A hell-cat.

hello [HALLO].

helm (1) (helm) [A.-S., Dut., G., cogn. with *helan*, see HELE], *n.* A helmet; *the upper part of a retort or alembic; (*Cumb. and Westmor.*) a cloud gathering over the northern Pennines before or during a storm. **helm-cloud,** *n.* **helm-wind,** *n.* A violent easterly wind blowing down from the Pennines. **helmed,** *a.* Helmeted. **helmless (1),** *a.*

helm (2) (helm) [A.-S. *helma* (cp. Icel. *hjalm*)], *n.* The instrument or apparatus by which a vessel is steered; the rudder and its operative parts, such as the tiller or wheel; the tiller; (*fig.*) a position of management or direction; *a helmsman. *v.t.* To guide, to steer; to manage. **to put up (down) the helm:** (*Naut.*) To bring the rudder to leeward (windward). ***helmage,** *n.* Guidance; direction; management. **helmless** (2), *a.* **helmsman,** *n.* The man who steers.

helmet (hel' mėt) [obs. F. *healmet*, dim. of *helm*, HELM (1)], *n.* A piece of defensive armour for the head; a hat of similar form made of felt, cork, pith, or metal, worn as a protection against the sun or by policemen, etc.; (*Bot.*) the hooded upper lip of some flowers; a helmet-shell. **helmet-shell,** *n.* A tropical mollusc belonging to the genus *Cassis*. **helmeted,** *a.* Wearing a helmet.

helminth (hel' minth) [Gr. *helmins -minthos*, cogn. with HELIX], *n.* A worm, esp. a parasitic intestinal worm. **helminthagogue** (hel min' thȧ gog) [Gr. *agōgos*, drawing forth, from *agein*, to lead or draw], *n.* (*Med.*) A medicine to expel worms; an anthelmintic. **helminthic,** *a.* Relating to intestinal worms. **helminthite,** *n.* (*Geol.*) A sinuous mark on sandstone supposed to be a fossil worm-track. **helminthoid,** *a.* **helminthology** (-thol' ȯ ji), *n.* A treatise on intestinal worms. **helminthological** (-loj' i kȧl), *a.* **helminthologist** (-thol' ȯ jist), *n.* **helminthous,** *a.*

helot (hel' ȯt) [L. *Hēlōtēs*, Gr. *Heilōtes*, pl. of *Hielōs*, prob. orig. an inhabitant of *Helos*, a Laconian town whose inhabitants were enslaved by the Spartans], *n.* A serf or bondsman in ancient Sparta; a slave or serf. **drunken helot:** A helot made drunk as an object-lesson to young Spartans. **helotism,** *n.* The system of serfdom in Sparta or elsewhere. **helotry,** *n.* Helots collectively; bondsmen or serfs. **helotize,** *v.t.*

help (help) [A.-S. *helpan* (cp. Dut. *helpen*, Icel. *hjālpa*, G. *helfen*)], *v.t.* (**past* **holp,** **p.p.* **holpen**) To assist, to aid; to further; to supply succour or relief to in time of distress; to remedy, to prevent; to serve (with food), to distribute (food) at table. *v.i.* To lend aid or assistance; to be of use; to avail. *n.* Aid or assistance; succour, relief; escape, remedy; a helper; a domestic servant; a helping (of food, etc.). **it cannot be helped:** There is no remedy; it cannot be prevented or avoided. **lady help:** A domestic assistant. **mother's help:** A superior nursemaid, etc. **so help me God:** A strong oath or asseveration. **to help forward:** To assist in making progress. **to help off:** To help (a person) to remove or take off (a garment, etc.); to help to get rid of. **to help on:** To forward, to advance. **to help out:** To help to complete or to get out of a difficulty. **to help over:** To enable to surmount. **to help to:** To supply with, to furnish with. **to help up:** To raise, to support. **helper,** *n.* **helpful,** *a.* Furnishing help, useful, serviceable, beneficial. **helpfully,** *adv.* **helpfulness,** *n.* **helping,** *n.* A portion of food given at table. **helpless,** *a.* Wanting power to help oneself; affording no help; irremediable, *unavailing; *destitute. **helplessly,** *adv.* **helplessness,** *n.*

helpmate (help' māt), *n.* A helper; a partner or helpful companion, esp. a spouse. **helpmeet** (help' mēt), *n.* A helpmate (formed by a misunderstanding of Gen. ii. 18, 'help meet for him').

helter-skelter (hel' tėr skel' tėr) [imit.], *adv.* In great hurry and confusion. *a.* Hurried and confused. *n.* Hurry; a fun-fair amusement.

helve (helv) [A.-S. *hielf* (cp. M.Dut. *helve*), cogn. with HALTER], *n.* The handle of a weapon or tool. *v.t.* To fit a helve to. **helve-hammer,** *n.* A trip hammer. **helver,** *n.* (*Mining*) A helve.

Helvetian (hel vē' shȧn) [L. *Helvētius*], *a.* Swiss. *n.* A Swiss; one of the ancient Helvetii. **Helvetic** (hel vet' ik), *a.* Helvetian. *n.* A Swiss Protestant, a Zwinglian.

hem (1) (hem) [A.-S. *hemm*, *hem* (cp. G. *hemmen*, to stop, to check)], *n.* The edge or border of a garment or piece of cloth, esp. when doubled and sewn in to strengthen it. *v.t.* (*past & p.p.* **hemmed**) To double over and sew in the border of; (*fig.*) to enclose or shut (in, about, or round). **hemmer,** *n.* One who or that which hems; an attachment to a sewing-machine for hemming. **hem-line,** *n.* The hemmed bottom edge of a skirt or dress. **hem-stitch,** *n.* An ornamental stitch made by drawing out parallel threads and fastening the cross threads. *v.t.* To hem with this.

hem (2) (hem) [imit.], *int.* and *n.* A voluntary short cough, uttered by way of warning, encouragement, etc. *v.i.* To cry 'hem'; to hesitate. **v.t.* To clear the throat by hemming.

***hem** (3) (hem), **'em** [A.-S. *him, hiom, heom,* dat. pl. of HE], *pron.* Them.

hema-, hemat-, hemato- [HÆMA-].

hematite [HÆMATITE].

hemeralopia (hem ėr å lō' pi å) [from Gr. *hēmeralops* (*hēmera,* day, *alaos,* blind, *ops,* eye)], *n.* (*Path.*) An abnormal condition of the sense of vision, in which the eyes see badly by daylight and better by night or artificial light; also applied to night-blindness or nyctalopia.

hemi- [Gr. *hēmi-*], *pref.* Half, halved; pertaining to or affecting one half. **hemianopsia** (hem i å nop' si å) [AN-, Gr. *opsis,* sight], *n.* (*Path.*) Half-blindness, paralysis of the optic nerve causing obscuration of half of the field of vision. **hemianoptic** (-nop' tik), **hemiopic** (-op' ik), *a.*

hemicrania (hem i krā' ni å) [L. *hēmicrānia,* Gr. *hēmikrania* (*kranion,* skull)], *n.* (*Path.*) Headache affecting only one side of the head. **hemicranial,** *a.*

hemicycle (hem' i sī kėl) [F. *hémicycle,* L. *hēmicyclium,* Gr. *hēmikuklion*], *n.* A semicircle; a semicircular arena, room, or division of a room. **hemicyclic** (hem i sik' lik), *a.* (*Bot.*) Having the parts of the inflorescence arranged in spirals or in spirals and whorls.

hemihedral (hem i hē' drål, -hed' rål) [Gr. *hedra,* seat, base], *a.* (*Cryst.*) Having only half the normal number of planes or facets. **hemihedrism,** *n.* **hemihedron,** *n.*

hemimetabola (hem i mė tăb' ŏ lå) [Gr. *metabolos,* changeable, from *metaballein,* see METABOLISM], *n.* (*Ent.*) A section of insects that undergo incomplete metamorphosis. **hemimetabolic** (-met å bol' ik), **hemimetabolous** (-mė tăb' ŏ lŭs), *a.*

hemione (hem' i ōn), **hemionus** (hė mī' ŏ nŭs) [L. *hemionus,* Gr. *hemionos* (HEMI-, *onos,* ass)], *n.* (*Zool.*) The dziggetai, a species of wild ass.

hemiopia, hemiopsia [HEMIANOPSIA, see HEMI-].

hemiplegia (hem i plē' ji a), ***hemiplegy** (hem' i plej i) [Gr. *hēmiplēgia* (*plēgē,* stroke, from *plēssein,* to strike)], *n.* (*Path.*) Paralysis of one side of the body. **hemiplegic** (-plej' ik), *a.*

hemiptera (hė mip' tėr å) [HEMI-, Gr. *pteron,* wing], *n.pl.* (*sing.* **hemipteron**) (*Ent.*) An order of insects with suctorial mouth-organ, and usually having four wings, the upper pair partly chitinous and partly membranous, comprising bugs, lice, etc. **hemipter,** *n.* One of this order of insects. **hemipteral, -terous,** *a.* **hemipteran,** *n.* **hemipterist,** *n.*

hemisphere (hem' i sfēr) [F. *hémisphère,* Gr. *hemisphaira*], *n.* The half of a sphere or globe, divided by a plane passing through its centre; half of the terrestrial or the celestial sphere; a map or projection of either of these. **Eastern Hemisphere:** Half the terrestrial sphere comprising Europe, Asia, Africa, etc. **Western Hemisphere:** The other half containing America. **Northern** and **Southern Hemispheres:** The halves separated by the equator. **Magdeburg hemispheres:** A pair of hollow brass hemispheres from which the air is exhausted to illustrate the pressure of the atmosphere by their cohesion. **hemispheric, -al** (-sfter' ik, -ål), *a.* **hemispheroid,** *n.* **hemispheroidal** (sfē roi' dål), *a.*

hemistich (hem i stik) [L. *hēmistichium,* Gr. *hēmistichion* (*stichos,* a row)], *n.* Half a verse, usu. as divided by the cæsura; an imperfect verse. **hemistichal,** *a.*

hemitrope (hem' i trōp) [F. *hémitrope* (Gr. *-tropos,* turning, from *trepein,* to turn)], *a.* (*Cryst.*) Used of a crystal looking as if the one half were turned round upon the other. *n.* A crystal of this form. **hemitropic** (hem i trop' ik), *a.* Hemitrope. **hemitropal, hemitropous** (-mit' rŏ pål, -pŭs), *a.* Hemitropic; (*Bot.*) used of a half-inverted ovule.

hemlock (hem' lok) [A.-S. *hemlic, hymlic,* etym. unknown], *n.* The poisonous umbelliferous genus *Conium,* esp. *C. maculatum,* the common hemlock; a poison obtained from it; (*Am.*) the hemlock fir or spruce. **hemlock fir, spruce,** or **tree:** A North American conifer, *Abies Canadensis.*

hemmer [HEM (2)].

hemorrhage, etc. [HÆMORRHAGE].

hemorrhoids, etc. (HÆMORRHOIDS].

hemp (hemp) [A.-S. *henep* (cp. Dut. *hennep,* Icel. *hampr,* G. *hanf,* also Gr. *kannabis*)], *n.* An Indian herbaceous plant, *Cannabis sativa*; the fibre of this, used for making ropes, coarse fabrics, etc.; applied also to other vegetable fibres used for cloth or cordage; bhang, hashish; (*colloq.*) the hangman's rope. **hemp-agrimony,** *n.* A composite plant, *Eupatorium cannabinum.* **hemp-nettle,** *n.* A coarse plant of the labiate genus *Galeopsis.* **hemp-palm,** *n.* An Indian and Chinese palm, *Chamærops excelsa,* which yields fibre for cordage. **hempseed,** *n.* The seed of hemp, much used as food for cage-birds; (*fig.*) one meant for the gallows. **hempen,** *a.* Made of or resembling hemp. ***hempen candle:** (*Shak.*) The hangman's rope. ***hempy,** *a.* Like or of the nature of hemp; (*Sc.*) deserving to be hanged, roguish, mischievous. *n.* (*Sc.*) A rogue, a mischievous young person.

hen (hen) [A.-S. *henn,* from *hana,* cock (cp. Dut. *hen,* Icel. *hæna,* G. *henne*), cogn. with L. *canere,* to sing], *n.* The female of any bird, esp. the domestic fowl; a female bird (*in comb.,* as *guinea-hen, pea-hen*). **hen and chickens:** One of the houseleeks, esp. *Sempervivum globiferum*; a cultivated variety of daisy with a large flower-head encircled by smaller ones; the ground-ivy. **henbane,** *n.* A plant of the genus *Hyoscyamus,* esp. *H. niger*; a poisonous drug obtained from *H. niger.* **henbit,** *n.* A species of dead-nettle, *Lamium amplexicaule*; the ivy-leaved speedwell, *Veronica hederifolia.* **hen-coop,** *n.* A coop or cage for fowls. ***hen-driver, hen-harrier,** *n.* The blue hawk, *Circus cyaneus.* **hen-house,** *n.* A fowl-house. **hen-mould,** *n.* Black spongy soil. **hen-peck,** *v.t.* To govern or rule (of a wife who has the upper hand of her husband). *n.* A wife who domineers over or nags at her husband. ***hen-peckery,** *n.* The condition of being hen-pecked. **hen-roost,** *n.* A place for fowls to roost in. **hen-wife, -woman,** *n.* A woman who has the charge of fowls. **hennery,** *n.* An enclosed place or run for fowls. **henny,** *a.* Hen-like. *n.* A hen-like male fowl.

hence (hens) [M.E. *hennes, henne,* A.-S. *heonan, heonane,* from *hi-,* root of HE, HIS, etc.], *adv.* From this place, time, source, or origin; in consequence of this, consequently, therefore. *int.* Away, away with, begone, depart. **henceforth, henceforward,** *adv.* From this time forward.

henchman (hench' mån) [M.E. *henxtman, henxman* (A.-S. *hengest,* horse, MAN)], *n.* A squire, a page; a male servant or attendant; a faithful follower; a political worker, esp. in the U.S.

hend (hend) [from A.-S. *gehęndan,* from HAND, or Icel. *hęnda*], *v.t.* To seize, to take, to lay hold on.

hendecagon (hen dek' å gŏn) [Gr. *hendeka,* eleven, *gōnia,* angle], *n.* (*Geom.*) A plane rectilinear figure of eleven sides or angles.

hendecasyllable (hen dek å sil' å bėl) [L. *hendecasyllabus,* Gr. *hendekasullabos* (*hendeka,* eleven], *n.* A verse or line of eleven syllables. **hendecasyllabic** (-si lăb' ik), *a.* Containing eleven syllables; *n.* A hendecasyllabic verse.

hendiadys (hen dī' å dis) [late L., from Gr. *hen dia duoin,* one by two], *n.* A rhetorical figure representing one idea by two words connected by a conjunction, *e.g.* 'by hook or crook.'

henequen (hen' ė ken) [Sp. *jehiquen,* from American Indian], *n.* Sisal hemp.

hen-harrier [HEN].

henna (hen' å) [Arab. *ḥinnā*], *n.* The Egyptian privet, *Lawsonia ermis*; a dye obtained from this plant used largely for dyeing hair, also in the East for dyeing parts of the body.

hennery, etc. [HEN].

henny [HEN].

henotheism (hen' ō thē izm) [Gr. *heis henos*, one, THEISM], *n.* Worship of or ascription of supreme power to one out of several gods, a phase intermediate between polytheism and monotheism. **henotheistic** (-thė is' tik), *a.*

hen-peck [HEN].

henry (hen' ri) [J. *Henry* (1797–1878)], *n.* (*pl.* **henries**). (*Elec.*) Unit of inductance. Inductance of a circuit in which a change of current of 1 ampere per second induces E.M.F. of 1 volt.

***hent** (hent) [A.-S. *hentan*, cp. HEND (1)], *v.t.* To take hold of; to seize, to get possession of. *n.* Seizing, seizure, grasp.

hep (hep), *adv.* (*Am. slang*) Aware of, informed of, wise to. **hep-cat,** *n.* A jazz dancer or player; a jazz fiend.

***hepar** (hē' par) [med. L., from Gr., the liver], *n.* (*Chem.*) Liver of sulphur, and other metallic sulphides, so called from their reddish-brown colour; (*Homœopathy*) calcium sulphide. **heparin,** *n.* (*Med.*) Substance extracted from this which prevents blood-clotting.

hepatic (hė păt' ik) [late L. *hēpaticus*, Gr. *hēpatikos*, from *hēpar hēpatos*, the liver], *a.* Of or belonging to the liver; resembling the liver in colour or form; (*Bot.*) pertaining to the liverworts. ***hepatic air** or **gas:** Sulphuretted hydrogen.

hepatica (hė păt' i kȧ) [as prec.], *n.* (*pl.* **-cæ**) (*Bot.*) A sub-genus of the genus *Anemone* containing the liverleaf, *Anemone* or *Hepatica triloba*; the common liverwort *Marchantia polymorpha*; (*pl.*) a sub-class of cryptogams comprising the liverworts, moss-like plants having no lid or operculum such as that characteristic of mosses.

hepatite (hep' ȧ tīt) [as prec.], *n.* (*Min.*) A variety of barytes giving out a fetid odour when heated; liverstone.

hepatitis (hep ȧ tī' tis), *n.* (*Med.*) Inflammation or congestion of the liver.

hepatize (hep' ȧ tīz), *v.t.* To convert the lungs into a substance like liver; to impregnate with sulphuretted hydrogen. **hepatization,** *n.*

hepato-, *comb. form.* Pertaining to, or resembling the liver. **hepatocele** (hep' ȧ tō sēl) [-CELE], *n.* (*Path.*) Hernia of the liver. **hepatocystic** (-sis' tik) [CYSTIC], *a.* Relating to the liver and the gall-bladder. **hepatogastric** (-găs' trik) [GASTRIC], *a.* Relating to the liver and the stomach. **hepatology** (hep ȧ tol' ō ji) [-LOGY], *n.* The branch of medical science relating to the liver. **hepatologist** (-tol' ō jist), *n.* **hepatorrhœa** (hep ȧ tō rē' ȧ) [Gr. *rhoia*, a flowing, from *rheein*, to flow], *n.* (*Path.*) A morbid flow of bile, bilious diarrhœa. **hepatoscopy** (hep ȧ tos' kō pi) [-SCOPY], *n.* Divination by inspection of an animal's liver.

hepta- [Gr. *hepta*, seven], *comb. form.* Consisting of seven. **heptachord** (hep' tȧ kôrd) [Gr. *heptachordos* (*chordē*, CHORD)], *n.* (*Mus.*) A series of seven notes; the interval of a seventh; an instrument with seven strings.

heptad (hep' tăd) [Gr. *heptas -tados*, as prec.], *n.* A sum or group of seven; a week; (*Chem.*) an atom with a valency of seven. (*Mus.*) a scheme of seven tones comprising all from which consonant triads with the tonic may be formed.

heptaglot (hep' tȧ glot) [HEPTA-, Gr. *glōtta*, tongue], *n.* A book in seven languages. *a.* In seven languages.

heptagon (hep' tȧ gȯn) [Gr. *heptagōnon* (HEPTA-, *gōnia*, angle)], *n.* A plane rectilinear figure having seven sides and seven angles. **heptagonal** (hep tăg' ō nȧl), *a.*

heptagynia (hep tȧ jin' i ȧ) [HEPTA-, Gr. *gunē*, woman, female], *n.pl.* (*Bot.*) A Linnæan order containing plants with seven pistils. **heptagyn** (hep' tȧ jin), *n.* A plant of this order. **heptagynian** (-jin' i ȧn), **heptagynous** (-tăj' i nŭs), *a.*

heptahedron (hep tȧ hē' drȯn) [HEPTA-, Gr. *hedra*, seat, base], *n.* (*Geom.*) A solid figure having seven sides. **heptahedral,** *a.* **heptahexahedral** (hep tȧ hek sȧ hē' drȧl) [HEXA-], *a.* Having seven ranges of faces, one above another, each range containing six faces.

heptamerous (hep tăm' ėr ŭs) [HEPTA-, Gr. *meros*, part], *a.* Having seven parts or members. ***heptamerede,** *n.* That which divides into seven parts.

heptandria (hep tăn' dri ȧ) [HEPTA-, Gr. *anēr andros*, man, male], *n.pl.* (*Bot.*) A Linnæan class of plants containing those with seven stamens. **heptandrous, -drian,** *a.*

heptangular (hep tăng' gū lȧr) [HEPTA-, ANGULAR], *a.* Having seven angles.

heptapetalous (hep tȧ pet' ȧ lŭs) [HEPTA-, PETALOUS], *a.* (*Bot.*) Having seven petals. **heptaphyllous** (hep tȧ fil' ŭs) [Gr. *heptaphullos phullon*, leaf], *a.* (*Bot.*) Having seven leaves or sepals.

heptarchy (hep' tȧr ki) [HEPTA-, Gr. *-archia*, government, from *archein*, to rule], *n.* A government by seven rulers; a country under seven rulers; the seven kingdoms established in Britain by the Angles and Saxons, *i.e.* Kent, Sussex, Wessex, Essex, Mercia, Northumbria, and East Anglia, which flourished for various periods from the 5th to the 8th century. ***heptarch, *heptarchist,** *n.* A governor of one division of a heptarchy. **heptarchic, -al,** *a.*

heptaspermous (hep tȧ spĕr' mŭs) [HEPTA-, Gr. *sperma*, seed], *a.* (*Bot.*) Having seven seeds.

heptastich (hep' tȧ stik) [HEPTA-, Gr. *stichos*, a row], *n.* (*Pros.*) A poem of seven verses.

heptasyllabic (hep tȧ si lăb' ik) [Gr. *heptasullabos* (HEPTA-, SYLLABLE)], *a.* Seven-syllabled. *n.* A verse of seven syllables.

Heptateuch (hep' tȧ tūk) [Gr. *heptateuchos* (HEPTA-, *teuchos*, book)], *n.* The first seven books of the Old Testament.

her (hĕr) [A.-S. *hire*, gen. and dat. of *hēo*, she], *pron.* The possessive, dative, or accusative case of the personal pronoun SHE; used in the possessive as an adj., and absolutely in the form **hers** when the noun is not expressed.

Heraclean (her ȧ klē' ȧn) [L. *Hēraclēus*, Gr. *Hērakleios*, from *Hēraklēs*], *a.* Pertaining to Heracles. **Heracleid** (her' ȧ klīd, -klid), *n.* One of the descendants of Heracles; one of the Dorian aristocracy who claimed this origin. **Heracleidan** (her ȧ klē' dȧn), *a.*

herald (her' ȧld) [O.F. *heralt*, *heraut*, prob. from Teut.], *n.* An officer whose duty was to proclaim peace or war, to challenge to battle, and to carry messages between sovereigns and princes; an officer whose duty it is to superintend State ceremonies, such as coronations, installations, etc., to grant, record, and blazon arms, trace genealogies, etc.; (*fig.*) a messenger; a harbinger, a precursor. *v.t.* To act as herald to; to proclaim; to announce; to introduce, to usher in. **herald-moth,** *n.* A noctuid moth, *Gonoptera libatrix*, which appears in the autumn and is supposed to be a forerunner of winter. **Heralds College:** A royal corporation, founded in 1483, consisting of the Earl Marshal, the Kings-of-Arms, the heralds, and pursuivants, whose duty now is to record pedigrees and grant armorial bearings.

heraldry (he' rȧl dri) [as prec.], *n.* The art and study of armorial bearings, etc.; pomp, ceremony, etc.; the office of a herald; heraldic bearings, emblazonment; *a coat of arms. **heraldic** (he răl' dik), *a.* Pertaining to heraldry or heralds. **heraldically,** *adv.*

herb (hĕrb) [M.E. and O.F. *erbe*, L. *herba*, grass], *n.* A plant producing shoots of only annual duration; herbage, grass, and other green food for cattle; a plant having medicinal, culinary, or aromatic properties, a simple. **herb beer:** A teetotal beverage made from herbs. **herb bennet:** The wood avens, *Geum urbanum.* ***herb grace, *herb of grace:*** Rue, *Ruta graveolens*; applied to other herbs. **herb Paris:** A herb, *Paris quadrifolia*, growing in woods, with four leaves in the form of a cross and a terminal green flower. **herb Robert:** A species of crane's-bill, *Geranium Robertianum.* **herbaceous** (hėr bā' shůs), *a.* Pertaining to herbs; of the nature of herbs; *herbivorous. **herbage,** *n.* Herbs collectively; grass, pasture; (*Law*) the right of pasture in the forest or on the grounds of another. ***herbaged,** *a.* Grassy, verdant. **herbal,** *a.* Pertaining to herbs. *n.* A book containing the names of plants, with a description of their properties, medicinal and other virtues, etc. **herbalist,** *n.* One skilled in the knowledge of herbs and their qualities; a collector of plants; an early botanist; a dealer in medicinal herbs. ***herbar, *-er,** *n.* A garden; a herb; an arbour. **herbarium** (hėr bâr' i ům), *n.* (*pl.* **-ia**) A systematic collection of dried plants; a case or room for the preservation of dried plants. ***herbary,** *n.* A garden of herbs; an herbarium; a herbal. **herbescent** (hėr bes' ėnt), *a.* Growing into a herb, becoming herbaceous. **herbless,** *a.* Destitute of vegetation. **herbous, herby,** *a.* Of the nature of or like herbs; abounding in herbs.

herbiferous (hěr bif' ěr ůs) [as prec.], *a.* Producing vegetation.

herbivora (hěr biv' ō rå) [L. *herbivorus*, herb-eating], *n.pl.* (*Zool.*) Animals, esp. mammals, feeding on grass or plants. **herbivore,** (hěr' bi vôr), *n.* One of the herbivora. **herbivorous,** *a.*

herborize (hěr' bō rīz), *v.t.* To search for or collect plants, to botanize. **herborist,** *n.* **herborization,** *n.* The act or practice of botanizing; *erron.* arborization.

Herculanean (hěr kū lā' nė ån) [L. *Herculāneus*], *a.* Of or pertaining to Herculaneum, a town of Campania which was overwhelmed with Pompeii and Stabiæ by the eruption of Vesuvius, in A.D. 79.

Hercules (hěr' kū lēz) [L., from Gr. *Hēraklēs*], *n.* (*Gr. and Rom. Mythol.*) A Greek hero, son of Jupiter and Alcmena, celebrated for his prodigious bodily strength, which enabled him to perform twelve labours of superhuman magnitude; (*fig.*) a man of enormous strength; (*Astron.*) one of the ancient northern constellations. **Pillars of Hercules:** Two rocks on either side of the Straits of Gibraltar beyond which the ancients thought it a feat of daring to sail; (*fig.*) a final limit; a critical stage, turning-point, etc. **Hercules beetle:** *Dynastes* or *Megasoma Hercules*, a Brazilian arboreal beetle five or six inches long, with hornlike projections on the head and thorax. **Hercules club:** The American prickly ash, or other shrubs or trees; a big cudgel. **Hercules powder:** A powerful kind of dynamite used in mining. **Herculean** (hėr kū' lė ån), *n.* Pertaining to Hercules; exceedingly strong or powerful; exceedingly great, difficult, or dangerous (as the labours of Hercules).

Hercynian (hėr sin' i ån) [L. *Hercynia* (*silva*), Gr. *Herkunios* (*drumos*)], *a.* A term applied to an extensive forest in Germany, the remains of which still exist in Swabia, the Harz Mountains, etc.

herd (1) (hěrd) [A.-S. *heord* (cp. Icel. *hjörd*, G. *herde*)], *n.* A number of beasts or cattle feeding or driven together; (*fig.*) a crowd of people, a rabble. *v.i.* To go in herds or companies; to associate; to act as a herd or shepherd. *v.t.* To tend or watch (cattle etc.); to form or bring into a herd. **herd-book,** *n.* A book containing the pedigrees of high-bred cattle. ***herd-groom,** *n.* A herd, a shepherd; a shepherd-lad. **herd instinct,** *n.* (*Psych.*) The instinct that urges men and animals to react to contagious impulses and follow their leader. **herdsman, *herdman,** *n.* One who tends domestic animals, esp. cattle.

herd (2) (hěrd) [A.-S. *hierde* (cp. Icel. *hirthir*, G. *hirte*)], *n.* A keeper of a herd (*usu. in comb.*, as *shepherd, swineherd*).

herdic (hěr' dik) [Peter *Herdic* of Pennsylvania, the inventor], *n.* (*Am.*) A two- or four-wheeled carriage, with a low-hung body, back entrance, and side seats, largely used as a public conveyance.

Herdwick (hěrd' wik) [HERD (2), WICK (2)], *n.* A hardy breed of sheep raised in the mountainous parts of Cumberland and Westmorland; *the district under the charge of a herd; *a pasture-ground.

here (hēr) [A.-S. *hēr* (Dut. and G. *hier*, Icel. *hēr*)], *adv.* In this place; to this place, hither, in this direction; in the present life or state; at this point; on this occasion; from this, hence. *n.* This place, point, or time. **here and there:** In this place and that; hither and thither. **neither here nor there:** Without reference to the point; irrelevant. **hereabouts** (hēr å bouts'), ***about,** *adv.* Somewhere about or near this place. **hereafter** (hēr af' tėr), *adv.* For the future; in a future state. *n.* A future state; the future life. ***hereat** (hēr ăt'), *adv.* At this. ***hereaway** (hēr' å wā), *adv.* Hereabouts. **hereby** (hēr bī'), *adv.* By this, by means or by virtue of this; *close by. **herein** (hēr in'), *adv.* In this; here. **herein after** (hēr in af' tėr): Later or below in this (writing, book, document, etc.). **herein before** (hēr' in bė fôr'), *adv.* ***hereof** (hēr ov'), *adv.* Of this; concerning this. ***hereon** (hēr on'), *adv.* On or concerning this. ***hereout** (hēr out'), *adv.* Out of this place. **hereto** (hēr too'), *adv.* Up to this place, point, or time; (attached) to this; *hitherto. **heretofore,** *adv.* Up to or before this time; formerly. **hereunder,** *adv.* Below in this (document etc.). **hereunto** (hēr ůn too', hēr ŭn' tů), *adv.* Up to this; hereto. **hereupon** (hēr ů pon'), *adv.* Upon this, after this, at this, in consequence of this. **herewith** (hēr with'), *adv.* With this.

hereditable (hė red' i tåbl) [F. *héréditable*, from L. *hērēditāre*, from *hērēs hērēdis*, an HEIR], *a.* That may be inherited. **hereditably,** *adv.* **hereditability** (-bil' i ti), *n.*

hereditament (her ė dit' å mėnt) [med. L. *hērēditāmentum*, as prec.], *n.* Any property that may be inherited; real property.

hereditary (hė red' i tår i) [L. *hērēditārius*, as foll.], *a.* Descending or passing by inheritance; transmitted by descent from generation to generation; holding or deriving by inheritance. **hereditarily,** *adv.* **hereditariness,** *n.*

heredity (hė red' i ti) [F. *hérédité*, L. *hērēditātem*, nom. *-tas*, from *hērēs hērēdis*, HEIR], *n.* The tendency to transmit peculiar characters to one's offspring; the tendency in an organism to resemble the parent. **hereditarian** (hė red i târ' i ån), *n.* One who believes in this tendency.

hereof, hereon, hereout [HERE].

heresy (her' ė si) [O.F. *heresie*, L. *hæresis*, Gr. *hairesis*, from *haireisthai*, to choose], *n.* Departure from what is held to be true doctrine, esp. when such opinions lead to division in the Christian Church. **heresy-hunter,** *n.* One who pries for and searches out heretical opinions in others. **heresiarch** (her' ė si ark, hė rē' si ark), *n.* A leader of a sect of heretics; a prominent or leading heretic. **heresiographer** (her ė si og' rå fėr), *n.* A writer on heresies. **heresiography,** *n.* **heresiologist,** *n.* **heresiology** (-ol' ō ji), *n.* The study of the history of heresy; a treatise on this.

heretic (her' ė tik) [F. *hérétique*, L. *hæreticus*, Gr. *hairetikos*, as prec.], *n.* One who holds unorthodox opinions, esp. in religious matters. **heretical** (hė ret' i kål), *a.* **heretically,** *adv.*

hereto, heretofore, hereunder, hereunto, hereupon, herewith [HERE].

heriot (her' i ōt) [corr. of A.-S. *heregeatwe*, military apparel (*here*, army, *geatwe*, equipments)], *n.* (*Law*) A fine, such as the best beast, payable to the lord of the manor on the decease of the tenant. **heriotable,** *a.* Subject to heriot.

***herisson** (her' i sǒn) [F. *hérisson*, var. of URCHIN], n. (*Fort.*) A beam armed with iron spikes used to block up a passage.

heritable (her′ i tȧbl) [F. *héritable*, from *hériter*, L. *hērēditāre*, see HEREDITABLE], *a.* Capable of being inherited; (*Law*) passing by inheritance, esp. of lands and appurtenances as dist. from movable property; capable of inheriting by descent. **heritably,** *adv.* By inheritance.

heritage (her′ i tȧj) [O.F., as prec.], *n.* Land or other property that passes by descent or course of law to an heir; (*Sc. Law*) heritable estate, realty; share, portion, lot; an inherited quality; (*Bibl.*) the people of God, the Israelites, the Church. **heritor** (her′ i tŏr), *n.* One who inherits; (*Sc. Law*) a landholder in a parish. **heritrix,** *n.* An heiress.

herling (hĕr′ ling) [Sc.], *n.* (*Solway*) The young of the sea-trout.

Herma (hĕr′ mȧ) [L., var. of HERMES], *n.* (*pl.* **-mæ**) (*Gr. and Rom. Ant.*) A statue of a head, usu. of Hermes, placed on a square pillar and set as a boundary, etc. **Hermæan** (-mē′ ȧn). **Hermaic** (-mā′ ik), *a.*

hermandad (ĕr man dad′) [Sp., a fraternity, from *hermano*, brother], *n.* (*Sp. Hist.*) A popular league or association formed to resist oppression, esp. by the cities of Castile against the nobles. ***Santa Hermandad:*** The Holy Brotherhood recognized by Ferdinand and Isabella in 1485 and afterwards formed into a national police.

hermaphrodite (hĕr măf′ rō dīt) [L. *Hermaphrodītus*, Gr. *-ditos* (*Hermēs, Aphroditē*), son of Hermes and Aphrodite, who grew together with the nymph Salmacis], *n.* A human being or an animal combining in itself both male and female organs; one in which the organs of both sexes are normally combined in the same individual; a plant having the stamens and pistils in the same floral envelope; (*fig.*) a person or thing in which opposite qualities are embodied; (*Naut.*) a vessel having the special rig of two kinds of craft, esp. an hermaphrodite brig. *a.* Possessing to a greater or less extent the characteristics of both sexes, or other opposite attributes, in a single individual. **hermaphrodite brig:** (*Naut.*) A vessel square-rigged on the foremast and schooner-rigged on the mainmast. **hermaphroditic, -al** (-dit′ ik, -ȧl), *a.* **hermaphroditism** (hĕr măf′ rō di tizm), *n.*

hermeneutic (hĕr mė nū′ tik) [Gr. *hermēneutikos*, from *hermēneutēs, hermēneus*, interpreter], *a.* Interpreting, explaining, explanatory. *n.pl.* The art or science of interpretation, esp. of Scripture. **hermeneutical,** *a.* **hermeneutically,** *adv.* ***hermeneutist,** *n.*

Hermes (hĕr′ mēz) (*pl.* **-mæ, -mai,** -mī) (*Gr. Mythol.*) The son of Zeus and Maia, messenger of the gods of Olympus, god of science, commerce, etc., identified by the Romans with Mercury [cp. HERMA], the Egyptian god Thoth, identified with Hermes, called by the Neo-Platonists Hermes Trismegistus or Thrice-great, and supposed to be the originator of art, magic, religion, etc.

hermetic (hĕr met′ ik) [low L. *hermēticus*, from HERMES *Trismegistus*], *a.* Of or belonging to alchemy; fitting by or as by fusion so as to be airtight. *n.pl.* Alchemy, chemistry. **hermetic art,** *n.* Alchemy; chemistry. **hermetism** (hĕr′ mė tizm), *n.* **hermetist,** *n.* **hermetically,** *adv.*

hermit (hĕr′ mit) [F. *hermite*, L. *her-, erēmīta*, Gr. *erēmitēs*, from *erēmos*, deserted], *n.* A person who retires from society to live in solitary contemplation or devotion, esp. an early Christian anchorite; *a beadsman. **hermit-crab, -lobster,** *n.* The genus *Pagurus*, esp. *P. Bernhardus*, from their living in abandoned univalve shells. **hermitage** (1), *n.* The cell or habitation of a hermit. **hermitess,** *n.* A female hermit. **hermitical** (hĕr mit′ i kȧl), *a.*

Hermitage (2) (hĕr′ mi tȧj) [name of a hill near Valence capped by the ruins of a supposed hermit's cell], *n.* A French wine, of two kinds, red and white.

hermitical [HERMIT].

***hern** (1) [HERON].

hern (2) (*prov.*) [HERS].

hernia (hĕr′ ni ȧ) [L.], *n.* (*Path.*) Rupture; the protrusion of any organ, or part of an organ, from its natural place. **hernial, herniary,** *a.* **herniology** (hĕr ni ol′ ŏ ji), *n.* The branch of science dealing with hernia; a treatise on ruptures. **herniotomy** (-ot′ ŏ mi), *n.* The operation for strangulated hernia.

***hernshaw** (hĕrn′ shaw), ***heronsew** (her′ ŏn sū) [O.F. *heronceau*, dim. of *hairon*, HERON], *n.* A young heron; a heron.

hero (hēr′ ō) [M.F. *heroë* (F. *héros*), L. *hērōem*, nom. *hērōs*, Gr. *hērōs*], *n.* (*pl.* **heroes,** hēr′ ōz) A person of extraordinary valour, fortitude, or enterprise; the principal male character in a novel, play, poem, etc.; orig. (*Gr. Mythol.*) a man of superhuman powers, often deified or regarded as a demigod after death [cp. HEROINE, see HEROIC]. **hero-worship,** *n.* The deification of a hero; excessive devotion to a person regarded as a hero. **hero-worshipper,** *n.*

Herodian (hė rō′ di ȧn) [L. *Hērōdiānus*, Gr. *Hērōdianos*], *a.* Of or pertaining to Herod the Tetrarch, his family, or the party supporting him; like Herod, blustering, swaggering [cp. OUT-HEROD]. *n.* A member of the party supporting Herod (Matt. xxii. 15–16; Mark iii. 6, xii. 13).

heroic (hė rō′ ik) [L. *hērōicus*, Gr. *hērōikos*], *a.* Pertaining to or becoming a hero; having the qualities or attributes of a hero; producing heroes; relating to or describing the deeds of heroes; bold, vigorous, attempting extreme deeds or methods. *n.pl.* Heroic verses; high-flown or bombastic language or sentiments. **heroic age:** The age in which heroes or demigods were supposed to have lived, esp. the age of Greece closing with the deeds celebrated in the *Iliad* and *Odyssey*. **heroic size:** (*Sculpture*) Between life-size and colossal. **heroic verse:** The metre of heroic or epic poetry: in English, German, and Italian poetry, the five-foot iambic; in French, the Alexandrine, and in Latin and Greek the hexameter. **to go into heroics:** To use high-flown or bombastic language. **heroical,** *a.* **heroically,** *adv.* ***heroicalness,** *n.* **heroicomic, -al** (hė rō-, her ō i kom′ ik, -ȧl), *a.* Combining the heroic and the comic; mock-heroic, burlesque. **heroify** (hė rō′ i fī). *v.t.* To make into a hero.

heroin (hė rō′ in) [prob. as prec.]. (*Chem.*) A derivative of morphine used as an anodyne and sedative.

heroine (her′ ō in), *n.* An heroic woman; the principal female character in a literary work or an episode of actual life.

heroism (he′ rō izm), *n.* The quality, character, or conduct of a hero; extreme bravery. **heroize** (he′ rō īz), *v.t.* To regard or treat as a hero, to make heroic. *v.i.* To show oneself off as a hero.

heron (her′ ŏn), ***hern** (hĕrn) [O.F. *hairon*, through pop. L. or It. from O.H.G. *hegir* (cp. Icel. *hegri*, also A.-S. *higora*, a magpie)], *n.* A long-legged, long-necked wading bird of the genus *Ardea*, esp. *A. cinerea*, the common European heron. **heronry,** *n.* A place where herons breed.

***heronsew, *heronshaw** [HERNSHAW].

herpes (hĕr′ pēz) [L., from Gr. *herpēs, -ētos*, from *herpein*, to creep], *n.* (*Path.*) A skin affection consisting of vesicles grouped on an inflamed surface, as in the lip in pneumonia, or in shingles. **herpetic** (hĕr pet′ ik), *a.* **herpetiform,** *a.* **herpetography** (-tog′ rȧ fi), *n.*

herpestes (hĕr pes′ tēz) [Gr., as prec.], *n.* A genus of small carnivorous mammals of the sub-family *Herpestinæ*, containing the ichneumons and the mongooses.

herpetology (hĕr pė tol′ ŏ ji) [Gr. *herpeton*, a reptile, from *herpein*, to creep, -LOGY], *n.* The natural history of reptiles. **herpetoid,** *a.* Serpentiform. **herpetologic, -al** (-loj′ ik, -ȧl), *a.* **herpetologist** (-tol′ ŏ jist), *n.*

herple (her′ pŭl), *v.t.* (*Sc.*) To hobble, limp.

Herr (hâr) [G.] *n.* German title corresponding to the English Mr.

herring (her′ ing) [A.-S. *hæring* (cp. Dut. *haring*, G. *häring*), etym. doubtful], *n.* A clupeoid marine fish, *Clupea harengus*, of the North Atlantic, moving in large shoals and spawning near the coast. **red herring:** One of these cured by smoking; (*colloq.*) an irrelevant fact introduced into an argument to divert attention from the point at issue. **herring-bone,** *a.* Like the spine and bones of a herring; (*Arch.*) denoting a kind of masonry in which the stones, etc. are set obliquely in alternate rows. **herring-bone stitch:** A kind of cross-stitch used in mending sails and for ornamental purposes. *v.t.* To sew or stitch with herring-bone stitch. **herring-fishery,** *n.* **herring-gull,** *n.* A large sea-gull, *Larus argentatus*, feeding on herrings. **herring-pond,** *n.* (*facet.*) The ocean, the North Atlantic, the North Sea and English Channel.

Herrnhuter (hâr′ noo tėr) [*Herrnhut*, Saxony, their first settlement] *n.* A Moravian, a member of the sect calling themselves the United Brethren.

herry (*Sc.*) [HARRY (1)].

hers [HER].

***hersall** (*Spens.*) [short for REHEARSAL].

***Herschel** (hěr′ shėl) [Sir Wm. *Herschel* (1738–1822), the discoverer], *n.* (*Astron.*) The planet Uranus. **Herschelian** (hėr shel′ i ȧn), *a.* Of or pertaining to Sir Wm. Herschel or his son, Sir John Herschel (applied to a telescope and the infra-red heat-rays of the spectrum discovered by the former).

Herschelite (hěr′ shėl īt) [Sir J. F. W. *Herschel* (1792–1871)], *n.* (*Min.*) An orthorhombic, colourless or white translucent silicate of aluminium, calcium, and sodium.

herse (hěrs) [F. *herse*, see HEARSE], *n.* (*Fort.*) A *cheval-de-frise*; *a portcullis with iron bars like a harrow placed above gates and lowered as a barrier.

herself (hėr self′) [A.-S. *hire self*], *pron.* The reflexive form of SHE, used to give emphasis in either the nominative or the objective case. **by herself:** Alone, unaided. **she is herself again:** She is in her normal state of health, mind, temper, etc.

Hertzian (hěrt′ si ȧn) [Heinrich *Hertz* (1857–1894), German physicist, -AN], *a.* (*Elec.*) Pertaining to Hertz or the phenomena of electro-magnetic vibrations discovered by him. **Hertzian telegraphy:** Wireless telegraphy. **Hertzian waves:** Radio waves, wireless waves first studied by Hertz.

hesitate (hez′ i tāt) [L. *hæsitātus*, p.p. of *hæsitāre*, freq. of *hærēre*, to stick, cling], *v.i.* To stop or pause in action; to be doubtful or undecided; to be reluctant (to); to stammer. **hesitant,** *a.* Hesitating, dubious, vacillating, undecided. **hesitance, -tancy,** *n.* **hesitantly,** *adv.* **hesitatingly,** *adv.* **hesitation** (-tā′ shŭn), *n.* **hesitative,** *a.*

Hesper, Hesperus (hes′ pėr, -ŭs) [L. *Hesperus*, Gr. *hesperos*, evening, the evening star], *n.* The evening star. **Hesperian** (hes pēr′ i ȧn), *a.* (*poet.*) Situated at or in the west, western. *n.* An inhabitant of a western country.

Hesperides (hes per′ i dēz) [L., from Gr., pl. of *hesperis*, western], *n.pl.* (*Gr. Mythol.*) The daughters of Hesperus, possessors of the garden of golden fruit watched over by a dragon at the western extremity of the earth; *the garden so watched over.

Hesperis (hes′ pėr is) [see prec.], *n.* (*Bot.*) A genus of cruciferous plants comprising the rockets and dame's violet.

Hesperornis (hes pėr ôr′ nis) [Gr. *hesperos*, see HESPER, *ornis*, bird], *n.* (*Palæont.*) A fossil genus of toothed birds from the chalk of North America.

Hessian (hesh′ ȧn, hes′ i ȧn) [*Hesse* in Germany, -IAN], *a.* Of or belonging to Hesse. *n.* A native of Hesse; a coarse cloth made of hemp and jute; (*pl.*) Hessian boots; (*Am. colloq.*) a mercenary politician, a hireling. **Hessian boot:** A high boot with tassels, fashionable early in the nineteenth century. **Hessian fly:** A small fly or midge, *Cecidomyia destructor*, the larva of which attacks wheat in the United States.

***hest** (hest) [A.-S. *hǣs*, from *hātan*, see HIGHT], *n.* A command, an injunction.

hesternal (hes těr′ nȧl) [L. *hesternus*], *a.* Of yesterday.

het (het). **het up:** (*slang*) Excited, agitated, annoyed.

hetæra (hė tēr′ ȧ) [Gr. *hetaira*, fem. of *hetairos*, companion], *n.* (*pl.* ***-ræ***) One of a class of highly educated courtesans in ancient Athens. **hetærism,** *n.* Recognized concubinage; (*Anthrop.*) community of women within the limits of the tribe. **hetærist,** *n.* **hetæristic** (-is′ tik), *a.* **hetærocracy** (-ok′ rȧ si), *n.*

heter-, hetero- [Gr. *heteros*, other], *comb. form.* Different, dissimilar; irregular, abnormal; erroneous.

heterauxesis (het ėr auk sē′ sis) [Gr. *auxesis*, growth], *n.* (*Bot.*) Irregular or unsymmetrical growth.

heteroblastic (het ėr ō blăs′ tik) [Gr. *blastos*, germ], *a.* (*Biol.*) Derived from unlike cells, dist. from homoblastic.

heterocarpous (het ėr ō kar′ pŭs) [Gr. *karpos*, fruit], *a.* Producing fruit of more than one kind.

heterocercal (het ėr ō sěr′ kȧl) [Gr. *kerkos*, tail], *a.* (*Ichthyol.*) Having the upper lobe of the tail longer than the lower. **heterocerc,** *n.* A heterocercal fish. **heterocercality,** *n.*

heterochromous (het ėr ō krōm′ ŭs) [Gr. *chroma*, colour], *a.* (*Bot.*) Of different colours.

heterochronic (het ėr ō kron′ ik), *a.* (*Biol. & Path.*) Occurring at irregular intervals or at abnormal times, irregular, intermittent. **heterochronia, heterochronism, heterochrony,** *n.* **heterochronistic, heterochronous,** *a.*

heteroclite (het′ ėr ō klīt) [Gr. *klinein*, to learn], *a.* Deviating from the ordinary rules or forms; anomalous, irregular. *n.* A word that deviates from the ordinary forms of inflexion; a person or thing deviating from the ordinary forms. **heteroclitic,** *a.*

heterocyclic (het ėr ō sī′ klik), *a.* (*Phys.*) Of organic chemical compounds with a ring structure of atoms of different kinds in the molecules.

heterodactyl (het ėr ō dăk′ til) [DACTYL], *a.* (*Zool.*) Having the toes different in number or form on the fore and hind legs. **heterodactylous,** *a.*

heterodont (het ėr ō dont′), *a.* (*Zool.*) Having teeth of different forms, dist. from homodont. *n.* A heterodont animal.

heterodox (het′ ėr ō doks) [Gr. *heterodoxos* (from *dokein*, to think)], *a.* Contrary to received or established doctrines, principles, or standards; heretical; not orthodox. **heterodoxy,** *n.*

heterodyne (het′ ėr ō dīn) [Gr. *dynamis*, power], *n.* (*Radio.*) A beat frequency caused in a radio receiver by the interplay of two alternating currents of similar frequencies.

heterœcious (het ėr ē′ shŭs) [Gr. *oikia*, dwelling], *a.* (*Bot.*) Developing at different times on different hosts (of parasitic fungi). **heterœcism,** *n.* **heterœcismal** (-siz′ mȧl), *a.*

heterogamous (het ėr og′ ȧ mŭs) [Gr. *gamos*, marriage], *a.* (*Bot.*) Having flowers or florets sexually different, as in certain *Compositæ*, where the disk-florets are male and the ray-florets neuter or female. **heterogamy,** *n.*

heterogeneous (het ėr ō jē′ nė ŭs), ***heterogene** (het′ ėr ō jēn), ***heterogeneal** [Gr. *genos*, kind], *a.* Diverse in character, structure, or composition; (*Math.*) of different kinds, dimensions, or degrees; incommensurable. **heterogeneously,** *adv.* **heterogeneousness, heterogeneity** (nē′ i ti), *n.*

heterogenesis (het ėr ō jen′ ė sis) [GENESIS], *n.* (*Biol.*) The production of offspring differing from the parent; abiogenesis, spontaneous generation;

alternation of generations. **heterogenetic** (-jė net′ ik), *a.* **heterogenist** (oj′ ė nist), *n.* A believer in heterogenesis.

heterogonous (het ėr og′ ȯ nu̇s) [Gr. *gonos*, offspring], *a.* (*Bot.*) Having stamens and pistils dimorphous or trimorphous so as to ensure cross-fertilization (of certain flowers). **heterogonism, heterogony,** *n.*

heterography (het ėr og′ rȧ fi), *n.* Heterogeneous or incorrect spelling; the employment of the same letters to represent different sounds as *g* in *go* and *gin.*

heterolith (het′ ėr ȯ lith) [-LITH], *n.* (*Min.*) A stony concretion composed of organic or other non-mineral matter.

heterologous (het ėr ol′ ȯ gu̇s) [Gr. *logos*, relation], *a.* Consisting of different elements, or of the same elements combined in different proportions; (*Path.*) differing in structure from normal tissue. **heterology** (-ol′ ȯ ji), *n.*

heteromera (het ėr om′ ėr ȧ) [mod. L., as foll.], *n.pl.* (*Ent.*) A section of *Coleoptera*, having five joints in the first four tarsi, and four in the other two. **heteromeran** (1) (het ėr om′ ėr ȧn), *n.*

heteromerous (het ėr om′ ėr u̇s) [Gr. *meros*, part], *a.* Differing in number, form, or character of parts. **heteromeran** (2), *a.*

heteromorphic, -ous (het ėr ȯ môr′ fik, -fu̇s) [Gr. *morphē*, form], *a.* Differing from the normal form; having dissimilar forms; (*Ent.*) having different forms at different stages of development. **heteromorphism, heteromorphy** (het′-), *n.* The quality of being heteromorphic; existence in different forms. **heteromorphosis** (-fō′ sis), *n.* Abnormal shape, structure, etc.; deformity; assumption by an organ of the functions properly belonging to another.

heteronomous (het ėr on′ ȯ mu̇s) [Gr. *nomos*, law], *a.* Subject to the law or rule of another, not autonomous; (*Biol.*) having different laws of growth, diverging from the type. **heteronomy,** *n.*

heteronym (het′ ėr ȯ nim) [Gr. *heterōnumos* (*onoma*, name)], *n.* A word spelt the same way as another but differing in sound and meaning, as *gill* (gil), a breathing-organ, and *gill* (jil), a measure. **heteronymous** (-on′ i mu̇s), *a.* **heteronymy,** *n.*

heteroousian (het ėr ȯ ou′ si ȧn) [Gr. *heteroousios* (*ousia*, essence)], *a.* Having a different nature or essence. *n.pl.* A sect holding that the Son was of a different essence from the Father, an Arian.

heteropathic (het ėr ȯ păth′ ik) [Gr. *pathos*, suffering], *a.* Allopathic. **heteropathy** (-op′ ȧ thi), *n.*

heterophemy (het ėr ȯ fē′ mi) [Gr. *-phēmia*, from *phēmē*, voice], *n.* The action or habit of saying or writing differently from what one intends. **heterophemism,** *n.* **heterophemist,** *n.* **heterophemistic** (-fė mis′ tik), *a.* **heterophemize** (-fē mīz), *v.i.*

heterophyllous (het ėr ȯ fil′ u̇s) [Gr. *phullon*, leaf], *a.* (*Bot.*) Having leaves of different form on the same plant. **heterophylly** (-of′ i li), *n.*

heteroplasm (het′ ėr ȯ plăzm) [F. *hétéroplasme* (Gr. *plasma*, see PLASM)], *n.* (*Path.*) A morbid formation of tissue foreign to the part where it occurs. **heteroplastic** (-plăs′ tik), *a.*

heteropod (het′ ėr ȯ pod) [Gr. *pous podos*, foot], *a.* Belonging to the *Heteropoda.* *n.* One of the *Heteropoda.* ***Heteropoda*** (het ėr op′ ȯ dȧ), *n.pl.* (*Zool.*) A group of Gasteropoda having the foot modified into a swimming-organ. **heteropodous,** *a.*

Heteroptera (het ėr op′ tėr ȧ) [Gr. *pteron*, wing], *n.pl.* (*Ent.*) A sub-order of hemiptera in which the wings are of dissimilar parts, comprising the bugs. **heteropterous,** *a.*

heterorhizal (het ėr ȯ rī′ zȧl) [Gr. *rhiza*, root], *a.* (*Bot.*) Having the root springing from any part of the spore.

***heteroscian** (het ėr osh′ i ȧn) [med. L. *heteroscius*, G. *heteroskios* (*skia*, shadow)], *a.* Used of a part of the earth's surface where the shadows fall in an opposite direction relatively to another part. *n.* A person living in such part of the globe.

heterosporous (het ėr os′ pȯ ru̇s) [Gr. *sporos*, seed], *a.* (*Bot.*) Having two kinds of spores.

heterostrophic (het ėr ȯ strof′ ik) [Gr. *strophos*, turning], *a.* (*Conch.*) Turned in a different direction (of spiral shells). **heterostrophous** (-os′ trȯ fu̇s), *a.* **heterostrophy,** *n.*

heterostyled (het′ ėr ȯ stīld), *a.* (*Bot.*) Heterogonous, the styles or pistils on different plants of the species differing in length so as to promote cross-fertilization. **heterostylism** (-stī′ lizm), *n.*

heterotaxy (het′ ėr ȯ tăk si) [Gr. *taxis*, arrangement], *n.* (*Anat. and Bot.*) Deviation of organs or parts from ordinary arrangement. **heterotaxic** (-tăk′ sik), *a.*

heterotomic (het ėr ȯ tom′ ik), **heterotomous,** (het ėr ot′ ȯ mu̇s) [Gr. *-tomos*, cut, from *temnein*, to cut], *a.* (*Min.*) Having an abnormal cleavage; (*Bot.*) having the perianth unequally or unsymmetrically divided.

heterotopy, heterotopism (het ėr ot′ ȯ pi, -pizm) [Gr. *-topia*, from *topos*, place], *n.* (*Path.*) Misplacement of an organ etc.; occurrence of a growth in an abnormal position; (*Biol.*) variation from the normal sequence of development resulting in displacement of the order or place of phenomena. **heterotopic** (-top′ ik), **heterotopous** (-ot′ ȯ pu̇s), *a.*

heterotropal, -tropous (het ėr ot′ rȯ pȧl, -pu̇s) [Gr. *-tropos*, turning, from *trepein*, to turn], *a.* (*Bot.*) Lying parallel with the hilum (as some embryos).

heterotrophy (het ėr ot′ rȯ fi) [Gr. *trophē*, from *trephein*, to feed], *n.* (*Bot.*) Abnormal mode of obtaining nourishment.

heterousian [HETEROOUSIAN].

hetman (het′ mȧn) [Pol.], *n.* A commander or leader of the Cossacks.

heuchera (hū′ kėr ȧ) [Prof. *Heucher*, G. botanist], *n.* (*Bot.*) A genus of herbaceous plants of the saxifrage family, with roundish leaves and scapes of red, white, or green flowers rising directly from the rootstock.

heugh (1) (hū*ch*) [Sc., from M.E. *hōgh*, A.-S. *hōh*], *n.* A crag; a craggy glen or gorge, a cleuch; a coal-pit, a pit.

heugh (2) (hoo) [imit.], *int.* Hallo! (an exclamation of surprise).

heulandite (hū′ lȧn dīt) [H. *Heuland*, English mineralogist], *n.* (*Min.*) A monoclinic, transparent brittle mineral, consisting chiefly of silica, alumina, and lime, occurring chiefly in amygdaloid rock.

heuristic (hū ris′ tik) [from Gr. *heuriskein*, to find], *a.* Serving or tending to find out. *n.* The branch of logic dealing with discovery and invention, also called **heuretic** (hū ret′ ik), *n.*

hew (hū) [A.-S. *hēawan* (cp. Dut. *houwen*, Icel. *höggva*, G. *hauen*)], *v.t.* (*p.p.* **hewed, hewn**) To cut (down, away, off, etc.) with an axe or similar tool; to hack, to chop; (*fig.*) to make or fashion with toil and exertion. *n.* The act of hewing; a cut or gash; destruction by hewing. **hewer,** *n.* One who hews; (*Coal-min.*) a miner who cuts coal from the seam.

hexa- [Gr. *hex*, six], *comb. form.*

hexachord (hek′ sȧ kôrd), *n.* (*Mus.*) An interval of four tones and a semitone; a scale or diatonic series of six notes with a semitone between the third and the fourth.

hexad (hek′ săd) [Gr. *hexas -ados*, from *hex*, six], *n.* A group of six: (*Chem.*) an atom with a valency of six.

hexadactylic (hek sȧ dăk til′ ik), **hexadactylous** (hek sȧ dăk′ ti lu̇s) [Gr. *daktulos*, see DACTYL], *a.* Having six fingers or toes.

hexaemeron (hek sȧ ē′ mėr ȯn) [late L., from Gr. (*hex*, six, *hēmera*, day)], *n.* A period of six days esp. the six days of the Creation; a history of this period. **hexaemerik** (-mer′ ik), *a.*

hexagon (hek′ sȧ gȯn) [Gr. *gōnia*, angle], *n.* A plane figure having six sides and six angles. **hexagonal** (hek săg′ ŏ nȧl), *a.*

hexagram (hek′ sȧ grăm), *n.* A figure formed by two equilateral triangles whose points coincide with those of a regular hexagon; (*Geom.*) one of various six-sided figures; (*Chinese Lit.*) one of sixty-four figures each formed by six parallel lines on which the *I Ching* or 'Book of Changes' is based.

hexagynia (hek sȧ jin′ i ȧ) [Gr. *gunē*, woman, female], *n.pl.* (*Bot.*) A Linnæan order of plants having six styles. **hexagyn** (hek′ sȧ jin), *n.* A plant belonging to this order. **hexagynian** (-jin′ i ȧn), **hexagynous** (-săj′ i nŭs), *a.* Having six styles.

hexahedron (hek sȧ hē′ drȯn) [Gr. *hedra*, seat, base], *n.* (*Geom.*) A solid body of six sides, esp. a regular cube. **hexahedral,** *a.*

hexahemeron [HEXAEMERON].

hexameter (hek săm′ ė tėr) [L., from Gr. *hexametros* (*metron*, see METER)], *n.* The heroic verse of the Greeks and Romans consisting of six feet, of which the first four were dactyls or spondees, the fifth normally a dactyl (though sometimes a spondee, and then the fourth was a dactyl), and the sixth a spondee or trochee. *a.* Hexametric. **hexametric, -al** (hek sȧ met′ rik, -ȧl), *a.* **hexametrist,** *n.*

hexandria (hek săn′ dri ȧ) [Gr. *anēr andros*, man, male], *n.pl.* (*Bot.*) A Linnæan class containing plants with six stamens. **hexander,** *n.* Any plant of this order. **hexandrian, -drous,** *a.* Having six stamens.

hexangular (hek săng′ gū lȧr), *a.* Having six angles.

hexapetalous (hek sȧ pet′ ȧ lŭs), *a.* (*Bot.*) Having six petals. **hexapetaloid,** *a.*

hexaphyllous (hek sȧ fil′ ŭs) [Gr. *phullon*, leaf], *a.* (*Bot.*) Having six leaves or sepals.

hexapla (hek′ sȧ plȧ) [Gr. neut. pl. of *hexaplous*, six-fold (*hex*, six, *-ploos*, fold)], *n.* An edition of a book, esp. of the Scriptures, having six versions in parallel columns (orig. the title of Origen's text of the Old Testament). **hexaplar, hexaplarian, -plaric** (-plâr′ i ȧn, -ik), *a.*

hexapod (hek′ sȧ pod) [Gr. *pous podos*, foot)], *n.* An animal having six feet; one of the *Hexapoda* or insects. *a.* Having six legs; belonging to the *Hexapoda.* **hexapodal, -podous** (hek săp′ ȯ dȧl, -dŭs), *a.* **hexapody,** *n.* A verse of six feet.

hexastich (hek′ sȧ stik) [Gr. *-stichos* (*stichos*, a row)], *n.* A poem or poetical passage of six lines or verses. **hexastichic** (-stik′ ik), *a.*

hexastyle (hek′ sȧ stīl) [Gr. *stūlos* (pillar)], *a.* (*Arch.*) Having six columns; a portico or temple having six columns.

Hexateuch (hek′ sȧ tūk) [Gr. *teuchos*, book], *n.* The first six books of the Old Testament.

hey (hā) [M.E. *hei* (cp. Dut. and G. *hei*)], *int.* An exclamation of joy, surprise, interrogation, encouragement, etc. **hey-day** (1), *int.* An exclamation of cheerfulness, wonder, etc.

hey-day (2) (hā′ dā) [perh. HIGH-DAY], *n.* The prime, the time of unexhausted spirits, vigour, prosperity, etc.

heyduck (hā′ duk, hī′ dŭk) [Boh., Pol. *hajduk*, from Magyar *hajdú*, pl. *-duk*, orig. robber, brigand], *n.* (*Hung. Hist.*) One of a class of mercenaries who were granted lands and the rank of nobles in 1605.

hey-ho [HEIGH-HO].

hi (hī) [cp. HEY], *int.* An exclamation, usu. calling attention, also expressing surprise, derision, etc.

hiatus (hī ā′ tŭs) [L., from *hiāre*, to yawn], *n.* A gap, a break, a lacuna in a manuscript, connected series, etc.; the coming together of two vowels in successive syllables or words.

hibernacle (hī′ bėr năk ėl) [L. *hībernāculum*, from *hīberna*, see foll.], *n.* Winter quarters; winter shelter, covering, etc. **hibernaculum** (hī bėr năk′ ū lŭm), *n.* (*Zool.*) The winter quarters of a hibernating animal; (*Bot.*) a bud or bulb sheltering the future plant; winter quarters, shelter, covering, etc. **hibernal** (hī bĕr′ nȧl), *a.* Pertaining to winter.

hibernate (hī′ bėr nāt) [L. *hībernātus*, p.p. of *hībernāre*, from *hīberna*, winter quarters, orig. neut. pl. of *hībernus*, wintry], *v.i.* To pass the season of winter in sleep or torpor, as some animals; (*fig.*) to live in seclusion or remain inactive at a time of stress. **hibernant,** *a.* Hibernating. **hibernation** (-nā′ shŭn), *n.*

Hibernian (hī bĕr′ ni ȧn) [L. *Hibernia, Iverna*, Gr. *Iernē*, from O.Celt., whence *Erin*], *a.* Pertaining to Ireland. *n.* A native or inhabitant of Ireland. **Hibernianism, Hibernicism,** *n.* A phrase, mode of speech, or other peculiarity of the Irish. **Hibernicize,** *v.t.* To render Irish. **Hibernization** (-zā′ shŭn), *n.* **Hiberno-,** *comb. form.* Pertaining to or connected with Ireland. **Hiberno-Celtic,** *a.* Pertaining to the Irish Celts. *n.* The native Irish language.

hibiscus (hi bis′ kŭs) [L., from Gr. *hibiskos*], *n.* (*Bot.*) A genus of mostly tropical mallows, with large showy flowers.

hic (hik) [imit.], *int.* A sound like a hiccup, denoting interruption, as in the speech of a drunken person.

hiccatee (hik ȧ tē′) [native name], *n.* A freshwater tortoise of the Antilles.

hiccup (hik′ ŭp) [imit., cp. HIC (spelling *hiccough* due to confusion with COUGH)], *n.* A short, audible catching of the breath due to spasmodic contraction of the diaphragm and the glottis; a series of sudden, rapid, and brief inspirations, followed by expiration accompanied by noise. *v.i.* To have or utter a hiccup. *v.t.* To utter with a hiccup. **hiccupy,** *a.*

hic jacet (hic jā′ sėt) [L., here lies], *n.* An epitaph, tombstone, or place of sepulture, from the first two words of a memorial inscription.

hick (hik) [etym. uncertain], *n.* (*Am. slang*) A farmer, countryman, yokel. *a.* Rustic, rural.

hickory (hik′ ȯ ri) [N. Am. Ind. *pohickery*], *n.* A name for several North American trees of the genus *Carya*, allied to the walnuts, esp. *C. alba*, the timber of which is tough and elastic. **hickory shirt:** A shirt of striped or check cotton. **Old Hickory:** Nickname of Andrew Jackson (1767–1845), President of U.S.A. 1829–37.

hickwall, hickway (hik′ wawl, -wā) [etym. doubtful], *n.* The green woodpecker, *Picus viridis.*

hid, *past & p.p.,* **hidden,** *p.p.* [HIDE (1)].

hidalgo (hi dăl′ gō) [Sp., earlier *hijodalgo*, L. *fīlius dē aliquō*, son of something], *n.* A Spanish nobleman of the lowest class, a gentleman by birth. **hidalgoish,** *a.* **hidalgoism,** *n.*

hide (1) (hīd) [A.-S. *hydan*, cogn. with Gr. *keuthein*], *v.t.* (*past* **hid,** hid, *p.p.* **hidden,** hidn, **hid**) To conceal; to put out of or withhold from sight; to secrete, to cover up; to keep secret, to withhold from the knowledge (of); to suppress. *v.i.* To lie concealed, to conceal oneself. *n.* A place of concealment for observing wild life. **hide-and-seek,** *n.* A children's game in which one hides and the others try to find; (*fig.*) evasion. **hiddenly,** *adv.* **hiddenmost,** *a.* **hiddenness,** *n.* **hider** (hī′ dėr), *n.* One who hides. **hiding** (1), *n.* Concealing, lying in concealment. **hiding-place, hidey-hole,** *n.* A secret chamber, priest's hiding-place.

hide (2) (hīd) [A.-S. *hȳd* (cp. Dut. *huid*, Icel. *hūth*, G. *haut*, also L. *cutis*, Gr. *kutos*)], *n.* The skin of any animal, raw or dressed; (*sarcastically*) the human skin. *v.t.* (*colloq.*) To flog. **hide-bound,** *a.* Said of an animal the skin of which adheres so closely to the ribs and back as to be raised with difficulty; having the bark so close and tight as to impede growth (of trees); (*fig.*) narrow-minded, bigoted, obstinate; *penurious. **hiding** (2), *n.* (*colloq.*) A thrashing, a flogging.

***hide** (3) (hīd) [A.-S. *hīd*, *higid*, from *hīw-*, family], *n.* A certain portion of land (variously estimated at from 60 to 120 acres) orig. enough to support a family and its dependants.

hideous (hid' ė ŭs) [M.E. *hidous*, O.F. *hidos* (F. *hideux*), *hisdos* (acc. to O.E.D. from *hisde*, *hide*, horror, fear; acc. to Brachet etc. from L. *hispidos*, rough)], *a.* Horrible, frightful, or shocking to eye or ear; ghastly, grim. **hideously,** *adv.* **hideousness,** *n.*

hidlings (hid' lingz) [HIDE (1)], *adv.* (Sc. and North.) Secretly, clandestinely. *a.* Hidden, clandestine, furtive. *n.* Furtiveness. **in hidlings:** On the quiet, secretly.

hidrotic (hi drot' ik) [late L. *hidrōticus*, Gr. *hidrōtikos*, from *hidrōs -drōtos*, sweat], *a.* (*Med.*) Causing perspiration. *n.* A sudorific.

hie (1) (hī) [A.-S. *hīgian* (cp. Dut. *hijgen*, to haul)], *v.i.* (*pres.p.* **hying**) To hasten, to hurry. **v.t.* To urge (on). **n.* Haste, speed.

hie (2), **high** (2) (hi) [Sc. and North., cp. HI], *int.* The call to a horse to turn to the left, opposed to hup.

hielaman (hē' lȧ mȧn) [Austral. abor.], *n.* The narrow wooden or bark shield of the Australian Aborigines.

hieland, -er [HIGHLAND, HIGHLANDER, see HIGH (1)].

hiemal (hī ē' mȧl) [L. *hiems*, winter], *a.* Wintry.

hierarch (hī' ėr ark) [med. L. *hierarcha*, Gr. *hierarchēs* (*hieros*, sacred, *-archēs*, ruling, from *archein*, to govern)], *n.* The chief of a sacred order, one who has authority in sacred things, a chief priest, prelate, or archbishop. **hierarchic, -al** (-ar' kik, -ȧl), *a.* Of or pertaining to a hierarch or hierarchy. **hierarchism,** *n.* Hierarchical principles, power, or character.

hierarchy (hī' ėr ar ki) [F. *hierarchie*, from L., from Gr. *hierarchia*, as prec.], *n.* A rank or order of sacred persons; any one of three orders of angels; government in sacred matters; priestly or ecclesiastical government; organization in grades or orders, esp. of a priesthood; the bishops collectively of a province.

hieratic (hī ėr ăt' ik) [L. *hierātikos*, Gr. *hierātikos*, from *hierasthai*, to be priest, from *hieros*, holy], *a.* Pertaining to the priesthood, priestly; applied to the written characters employed in Egyptian records and to early styles in Egyptian and Greek art.

hiero- [Gr. *hieros*, holy], *comb. form.* Sacred; pertaining to sacred things. **hierocracy** (hī ėr ok' rȧ si) [-CRACY], *n.* Government by priests, hierarchy.

hieroglyph (hī' ėr ō glif) [from HIEROGLYPHIC], *n.* The figure of an animate or inanimate object used to represent a word, sound, etc., a kind of writing practised by the ancient Egyptians, the Aztecs, and others; a character or symbol employed to convey a secret meaning; (*facet.*) illegible writing. *v.t.* To represent by or in hieroglyphs. **hieroglyphic** (hī ėr ō glif' ik) [late L. *hieroglyphikos*, Gr. *hieroglu-phikos* (HIERO-, *gluphē*, carving)], *a.* Written in or covered with hieroglyphs; (*fig.*) written in characters difficult to decipher; mysterious, emblematic, esoteric. *n.* (*usu. in pl.*) Hieroglyphs; hieroglyphic writing. **hieroglyphical,** *a.* **hieroglyphically,** *adv.* **hieroglyphist** (hī ėr og' li fist), *n.* A writer of hieroglyphs; one skilled in deciphering hieroglyphs.

hierogram (hī' ėr ō grăm), *n.* A sacred writing, character, or symbol. **hierogrammatic, -al** (-măt' ik, -ȧl), *a.* **hierogrammatist** (-grăm' ȧ tist), *n.* **hierograph** (hī' ėr ō grăf), *n.* A hierogram. **hierographer** (-og' rȧ fėr), *n.* **hierographic, -al** (-grăf' ik, -ȧl), *a.* **hierography** (-og' rȧ fi), *n.*

hierolatry (hī ėr ol' ȧ tri), *n.* The worship of sacred persons or things, esp. the worship of saints.

hierology (hī ėr ol' ō ji) [late Gr. *hierologia*], *n.* A discourse on sacred matters; the science of hieroglyphics, esp. of the ancient writings of the Egyptians; the science or study of religious or of sacred literature. **hierologic, -al** (-loj' ik, -ȧl), *a.* **hierologist** (-ol' ō jist), *n.*

***hieromancy** (hī' ėr ō măn si), *n.* Divination by observing things offered in sacrifice.

Hieronomian (hī ėr ō nō' mi ȧn) [L. *Hieronymus*, Jerome], *a.* Of or pertaining to St. Jerome. *n.* A Hieronymite. **Hieronymic** (-nim' ik), *a.* **Hieronymite** (-on' i mīt), *n.* One of a monastic order named after St. Jerome. *a.* Belonging to such an order.

hierophant (hī' ėr ō fănt) [late L. and Gr. *hierophantēs* (*phainein*, to show)], *n.* One who teaches or explains the mysteries of religion; a priest who acted as initiator to the Eleusinian mysteries. **hierophantic** (-făn' tik), *a.*

***hieroscopy** (hī ėr os' kō pi) [Gr. (*skopein*, to see)], *n.* Hieromancy.

Hierosolymitan (hī ėr ō sol i mī' tȧn) [late L. *Hīerosolymītānus*, from *Hierosolyma*, Gr. *Hierosoluma*, Jerusalem], *a.* Belonging to Jerusalem. *n.* A native or inhabitant of Jerusalem. **Hierosolymite,** *a.* and *n.*

hierurgy (hī ėr ĕr' ji) [Gr. *hierourgia*, religious worship], *n.* A holy work, sacred performance; worship. **hierurgical,** *a.*

hi-fi [HIGH FIDELITY].

higgle (hig' ėl) [prob. a form of HAGGLE], *v.i.* To chaffer; to make a fuss about trifles as in striking a bargain. **higgler,** *n.* One who higgles; a huckster, a pedlar.

higgledy-piggledy (hig' ėl di pig' ėl di) [etym. doubtful], *adv.* In confusion, topsy-turvy. *a.* Confused, jumbled about anyhow. *n.* A jumble.

high (1) (hī) [A.-S. *hēah* (cp. Dut. *hoog*, Icel. *hār*, G. *hoch*)], *a.* Lofty, elevated; situated at a great elevation; rising or extending upwards for or to a specified extent; upper, inland; (*fig.*) exalted in rank, position, or office; chief; of noble character or purpose; proud, lofty in tone or temper, arrogant; great, extreme, intense; full, complete consummate; far advanced (of time); expensive, costly (in price); lively, animated; boisterous, violent; (*Mus.*) sharp, acute in pitch; tainted, approaching putrefaction, strong-smelling (of meat etc.); chief, principal. *adv.* To a great altitude, aloft; in or to a high degree; eminently, greatly, powerfully; at a high price; at or to a high pitch. **high and dry:** (*Naut.*) Out of the water; aground; (*fig.*) left behind, stranded, of no account in affairs. **high and low:** All sorts and conditions (of people); *(*slang*) false dice loaded for throwing high or low. **high and mighty:** Arrogant. **on high:** Aloft; to or in heaven. **from on high:** From aloft, from heaven. **the Most High:** The Supreme Being, God. **on the high horse:** Arrogant, affecting superiority, giving oneself airs. **to play high:** To play or gamble for heavy amounts; to play a high card. **to run high:** To have a strong current; to be a high tide; (*fig.*) to be in a state of excited feeling. **with a high hand:** In an arrogant or arbitrary manner. **high-aimed,** *a.* Having lofty aims. **high altar:** The principal altar. **high-bailiff,** *n.* The chief officer of certain corporations. **high ball,** *n.* (*Am.*) Iced whisky and soda in a tall glass. **high-blower,** *n.* A horse that flaps his nostrils with a blowing noise; (*euphem.*) a roarer. **high-blown,** *a.* Swelled out with wind or (*fig.*) with pride. **high-born,** *a.* Of noble birth. **high-bred** *a.* Of pure blood or extraction. **high-brow,** *n.* (*colloq.*) An intellectually superior person; a person who takes an intellectual or academic line in conversation. *a.* Intellectual, superior. **high-caste,** *a.* Belonging to a high caste. **High Church:** One of the three great schools in the Anglican Church, distinguished by its maintenance of sacerdotal claims and assertion of the efficacy of the sacraments. *a.* Belonging to the High Church party, hence, **High Churchism, High Churchman. high-coloured** *a.* Having a strong deep colour; flushed; (*fig.*) repre sented in strong or forcible language. ***high constable** [CONSTABLE]. **High Court of Justice:** The Supreme Court. **high cross:** The cross formerly erected in market-places. **high day:** A feast, a festival; broad daylight, noon. **High Dutch, High German:** The language of the upper or inland parts of Germany. **high engendered,** *a.* Born or created on high. **high-explosive,** *n.* An explosive of extreme rapidity and great destructive energy. *a.* Exploding with great violence and rapidity. **high fidelity,** *a.* (*Gramophone, Radio.*) Excellent in reproducton of sound. **highfalutin,** *a.* Bombastic, fustian, affected. *n.* Bombast, fustian. **high-fed,** *a.* Pampered, luxurious. **high-flown,** *a.* Proud, turgid, bombastic. ***high-flushed,** *a.* Elated, excited. **high-flyer,** *n.* One who is extravagant in opinions or pretensions. **high-flying,** *a.* Extravagant in opinions, claims, or pretensions. **high frequency:** (*Radio.*) Any frequency of alternating current above the audible range, from about 12,000 cycles per second upward. **high-grown,** *a.* Overgrown with high corn. **high-handed,** *a.* Overbearing, domineering, arbitrary. **high hat,** *n.* (*colloq.*) One with an air of affected superiority. **highjacker, hijacker,** *n.* (*Am. slang*) One who robs bootleggers and rum-runners of their stock-in-trade. **high jinks,** *n.pl.* High festivities or revelry; great sport. **high life:** The style of living or the manners of the fashionable world; the fashionable classes. **high-lights,** *n.pl.* The most brilliantly lighted spots in a photograph or picture; (*fig.*) moments of crisis; persons of importance. **high living:** Rich food; the practice of living daintily. **high-lows,** *n.pl.* Laced boots reaching to the ankle. **High Mass:** A Mass in which the celebrant is attended by deacon and sub-deacon, usually, but not necessarily, sung at the high altar. **high-mettled,** *a.* Full of fire, spirited. **high-minded,** *a.* Magnanimous; *proud, arrogant. **high-mindedness,** *n.* **high noon:** The time when the sun is in the meridian. **high-octane,** *a.* (of petrol) Of high efficiency. **high-pitched,** *a.* Aspiring, haughty; steeply sloping (of roofs); (*Mus.*) acute, tuned high. **high pressure:** A pressure of more than about 50 lb. per sq. in. *a.* Working at such pressure; (*fig.*) working with abnormal energy. **high-priest,** *n.* A chief priest, esp. the head of the Jewish hierarchy. **high-priesthood, -ship,** *n.* **high-principled,** *a.* Having high or noble principles. **high-proof,** *a.* Highly rectified; containing much alcohol. **high-reaching,** *a.* Reaching to a great height; aspiring, ambitious. **high relief** [ALTO-RILIEVO]. ***high-resolved,** *a.* Very resolute. **high road:** A main road, a highway. **high seas:** The open sea or ocean; (*Law*) the waters beyond low-water mark. **high-seasoned,** *a.* Strongly seasoned, piquant; lewd, obscene. **high-seated,** *a.* Seated aloft, lofty. **high sheriff** [SHERIFF]. ***high-sighted,** *a.* Looking upward; supercilious. **high-souled,** *a.* High-spirited, high-minded. **high-sounding,** *a.* Pompous, ostentatious. **high-spirited,** *a.* Having a lofty or courageous spirit; bold, daring. **high spots,** *n.pl.* The outstanding characteristics of a thing. **high steel,** *n.* (*Metal.*) Steel containing a relatively high proportion of carbon. **high-stepper,** *n.* A horse that lifts its feet well off the ground in trotting; (*fig.*) a person of a dashing or showy walk or bearing. **high-stomached,** *a.* Haughty. **high street:** The principal street (often used as the proper name of a street). **high-strung,** *a.* Extremely sensitive, of acute nervous temperament. **high-swelled,** *a.* Inflated with passion. **high table:** (*College*) The table for the fellows etc. ***high tasted,** *a.* Having a strong taste; piquant. **high tea:** Tea at which meat is served. **high tension:** (*Radio.*) Steady and high voltage applied to the anode of a valve. **high-tension battery:** (*Radio.*) A battery of dry cells or accumulators used to provide high-tension supply to a valve. **high tide:** High water; the tide at its full; *a holiday. **high time:** Fully time. **high-toned,** *a.* High in pitch; strong in sound. **high treason** [TREASON]. ***high-viced,** *a.* Extremely wicked. **high-velocity,** *a.* (*Artill.*) Applied to projectiles with a low trajectory and long range; applied to guns firing such projectiles. **high water:** The utmost flow of the tide; the time when the tide is at its full. **high-water mark:** The level reached by the tide at its utmost height. **high-wrought,** *a.* Wrought with great skill; inflamed to a high degree (of feelings). **highly,** *adv.* In a high degree, extremely, intensely; honourably, favourably. ***highmost,** *a.* Highest, topmost. **highness,** *n.* The quality or state of being high; a title of honour given to princes and others of high rank (used with a possessive pronoun); height. ***hight** (1) [HEIGHT].

high (2) [HIE (2)].

highlands (hī′ lȧndz), *n.pl.* A mountainous region, esp. the northern mountainous parts of Scotland. **Highland,** *a.* Pertaining to the Highlands of Scotland. **Highland fling:** A hornpipe, peculiar to the Scottish Highlanders. **Highlander,** *n.* An inhabitant of the Highlands of Scotland.

***hight** (2) (hīt) [the only instance in English of a passive verb; from A.-S. *hātte*, I am or was called, from *hātan*, to call, to be called], *v.i.* (*3rd sing. past*) To be named or called; to promise. *v.t.* To call, to name; to promise; to mean, to purport.

highty-tighty [HOITY-TOITY].

highway (hī′ wā), *n.* A public road open to all passengers; a main route either by land or by water. **highway code,** *n.* (*Motor.*) The official guide and instructions for proper behaviour on the road to avoid accidents, etc. **highwayman** (hī′ wā mȧn), *n.* One who robs on the highway.

hijack (hī′ jăk), *v.i.* (*Am.*) To hold up at pistol-point; to steal already stolen goods.

Hijra, Hijrah [HEGIRA].

hike (hīk), *n.* A ramble, a walking-tour. *v.i.* To go for a tramp. *v.i.* To hoist, lift, jerk, toss up. **to hitch-hike,** *v.i.* To make a journey by obtaining lifts from motorists and others.

hilar (hī′ lȧr) [HIL-UM, -AR], *a.* (*Bot.*) Pertaining to the hilum.

hilarious (hi lâr′ i ŭs) [L. *hilaris, -us*, Gr. *hilaros*], *a.* Cheerful, mirthful, merry; enjoying or provoking laughter. **hilariously,** *adv.* **hilariousness, hilarity,** *n.*

Hilary Term (hil′ ȧ ri tĕrm) [(L. *Hilarius*) St. *Hilary* of Poitiers (*d.* 367), whose festival occurs on 13 Jan.], *n.* (*Law*) One of the four terms of the High Court of Justice etc. in England (from 11th Jan. to 31st Mar.), hence, **Hilary Sittings, Hilary-tide,** *n.*

hilch (hilch) [Sc.], *v.i.* To limp, to hobble. *n.* A hobble.

***hilding** (hil′ ding) [perh. from M.E. *helden*, A.-S. *hieldan*, to bend, to yield], *n.* A base, cowardly fellow; a mean wretch, a worthless person; a jade. *a.* Mean, base.

hill (hil) [A.-S. *hyll* (cp. M.Dut. *hil, hille*, L. *collis*)], *n.* A natural elevation on the surface of the earth, a small mountain; a heap, a mound; (*Am.*) a cluster of plants, roots, etc., with earth heaped round them. *v.t.* To form into hills, heaps, or mounds; to heap (up). **hill billy,** *n.* (*Am.*) A rustic from the mountain country. **hill-folk, -people,** *n.* (*collect.*) A name sometimes given to the Cameronians, who held their conventicles secretly among the hills; the fairies or elves, or a class of beings intermediate between elves and human beings. **hillock,** *n.* A little hill or mound. **hillocky,** *a.* **hill-side,** *n.* The slope or declivity of a hill. **hill-top,** *n.* **hilly,** *a.* **hilliness,** *n.*

hillo, -loa [HALLO].

hilt (hilt) [A.-S., perh. related to HELVE], *n.* The handle of a sword or dagger. **hilted,** *a.*

hilum (hī′ lŭm) [L., a trifle, a whit], *n.* (*Bot.*) The spot upon a seed where it was attached to the placenta; (*Anat.*) a small aperture or a small depression.

him (him) [HE], *pron.* The objective or accusative case of HE. **himself** (him self′), *pron.* An emphatic or reflexive form of the personal pronoun of the 3rd per. sing. masc. **by himself:** Alone, unaccompanied; unaided. **not himself:** Not in his normal condition physically or mentally.

Himalayan (hi ma′ lă ăn) [Sansk. *Himālaya* (*hima*, snow, *ālaya*, abode)], *a.* Pertaining to the Himalayas, a lofty range of mountains in the north of India; (*fig.*) vast, gigantic. **Himalayan pine:** The Nepal nutpine, *Pinus Gerardiana.* **Himalayan primrose** or **cowslip:** A large yellow primula, *P. Sikkimensis.*

himation (hi măt′ i ŏn) [Gr.], *n.* (*Gr. Ant.*) The ordinary outer garment in ancient Greece, an oblong piece of cloth thrown over the left shoulder.

himself [HIM].

Himyarite (him′ yȧ rīt) [*Himyar*, traditionary king of Yemen], *n.* One of an ancient Semitic race in southern Arabia. *a.* Pertaining to this race. **Himyaritic** (-rit′ ik), **Himyaric** (-yăr′ ik), *a.*

hin (hin) [Heb. *hīn*], *n.* A Jewish measure for liquids, containing rather more than a gallon.

hinau (hi′ nou) [Maori], *n.* A N. Zealand tree the bark of which yields a black dye.

hind (1) (hīnd) [A.-S. (cp. Dut. and G. *hinde*, Icel., Dan. and Swed. *hind*)], *n.* The female of the deer, esp. the red deer. ***hindberry,** *n.* The raspberry.

hind (2) (hīnd) [M.E. *hine*, A.-S. *hīna*, gen. pl. of *hīwa*, a domestic], *n.* An agricultural labourer, a farm-servant, esp. (*Sc. and North.*) one in charge of two horses and allotted a house on the farm; a peasant, a rustic, a boor; *a menial.

hind (3) (hīnd), **hinder** (1) (hīn′ dėr) [A.-S. *hindan*], *a.* Pertaining to or situated at the back or rear. **hind-afore, hind-foremost, hind-first,** *a.* and *adv.* Back to front. **hinder end:** The posteriors. **hindsight,** *n.* Wisdom after the event, the reverse of foresight. **hinderings,** *n.pl.* (*Sc.*) The posteriors. **hindermost, hindmost,** *a.* The last; that is or comes last of all.

hinder (2) (hin′ dėr) [A.-S. *hindrian*], *v.t.* To obstruct, to impede; to prevent from proceeding or moving. *v.i.* To cause a hindrance; to interpose obstacles or impediments. **hinderer,** *n.* **hindrance,** *n.* The act of hindering; that which hinders; an impediment, an obstacle.

Hindi (hin′ di) [Hind., from Pers. *hind*, India], *n.* The Aryan language spoken in northern India.

hindrance [HINDER (2)].

hindsight [HIND (3)].

Hindu, Hindoo (hin doo′, hin′ doo) [HINDI], *n.* A native of India, not of Parsee, Mussulman or Christian descent; an Aryan still adhering to Hinduism. *a.* Pertaining to the Hindus. **Hinduism,** *n.* The Hindu polytheistic system of Brahminism modified by Buddhism and other accretions. **Hinduize,** *v.t.* **Hindustani** (hin du sta′ ni), *a.* Of or belonging to Hindustan (properly India north of the Nerbudda), Indian. *n.* A native of Hindustan proper; the form of the Hindu language adopted by the Mohammedan conquerors of Hindustan, Urdu.

hinge (hinj) [M.E. *heng*, cogn. with HANG], *n.* The joint or mechanical device on which a door or lid turns; a natural articulation fulfilling similar functions; (*fig.*) the point on which anything depends or turns. *v.t.* To furnish with or as with a hinge; *to cause to bend. *v.i.* To turn on or as on a hinge; to depend (upon). **to be off the hinges:** To be in a state of mental or physical disorder; to be out of working order. **hinged,** *a.* **hingeless,** *a.*

hinny (1) (hin′ i) [L. *hinnus* (Gr. *hinnos*, *ginnos*)], *n.* The offspring of a stallion and a she-ass.

hinny (2) (hin′ i) [F. *hennir*, L. *hinnīre*], *v.i.* To neigh, to whinny.

hinny (3) (*Sc.*) [HONEY].

hint (hint) [prob. from HENT (1)], *n.* A slight or distant allusion; an indirect (usu. pointed) mention or suggestion. *v.t.* To mention indirectly, to suggest, to allude to. *v.i.* To make remote allusion. **to hint at:** To make slight but pointed allusion to. **hinter,** *n.* **hintingly,** *adv.*

hinterland (hin′ tėr lȧnd) [G. (*hinter-*, HINDER (1), LAND)], *n.* The region situated behind that on the coast or that along a navigable river.

hip (1) (hip) [A.-S. *hype* (cp. Dut. *heup*, Dan. *hofte*, G. *hüfte*)], *n.* The projecting fleshy part covering the hip-joint; the haunch; (*Arch.*) the external angle formed by the meeting sides of a roof; a rafter along the edge of this; a truncated gable; (*Wrestling*) a hip-lock. *v.t.* (*Wrestling*) To throw by a hip-lock; (*Arch.*) to furnish with a hip. **to catch** or **have on** or **upon the hip:** To have at a disadvantage. **to smite hip and thigh:** To overthrow completely, to slaughter without mercy. **hip-bath,** *n.* A bath in which the body can be immersed to the hips. **hip-disease,** *n.* A scrofulous disease of the hip-joint attacking the bones. **hip-joint,** *n.* The articulation of the femur and the thigh-bone. **hip-lock,** *n.* (*Wrestling*) A grip in which one tries to throw one's opponent by putting a leg or hip in front of him. **hip-roof,** *n.* A roof rising directly from the walls on every side and consequently having no gable. **hipped** (1), *a.* Having the hip dislocated or sprained; (*Arch.*) furnished with a hip; (*in comb.*) having hips (as *wide-hipped*). **hipped roof** [HIP-ROOF].

hip (2) (hip) [A.-S. *hēope*], *n.* The fruit of the dog-rose.

***hip** (3) (hip) [short for HYPOCHONDRIA], *n.* Melancholia, the blues. *v.t.* (*usu. in p.p.* **hipped** (2)) To affect with melancholia; to irritate, to provoke. **hippish,** *a.*

hip (4) (hip), *int.* An exclamation, usu. twice or three times repeated, introducing a hurrah.

hip (5) (hip) [HEP], *adv.* (*U.S.A. slang*) Aware of, in the know. **hipster,** *n.* One who knows what's what, one in the know.

hipe (hīp) [HIP (1)], *v.t.* (*Wrestling*) To throw (one's opponent) by lifting and putting the knee between his thighs. *n.* A throw of this kind; (*old Mil. slang*) a rifle.

hipp- [HIPPO-].

Hipparion (hi pâr′ i ŏn) [Gr., pony], *n.* (*Palæont.*) An extinct quadruped of the Miocene and Pliocene ages probably representing a stage in the evolution of the horse.

hippic (hip′ ik) [Gr. *hippikos*, as foll.], *a.* Pertaining to horses or to horse-racing.

hippo [HIPPOPOTAMUS].

hippo-, hipp- [Gr. *hippos*, a horse], *comb. form.* Pertaining to or resembling a horse.

hippocampus (hip ŏ kăm′ pŭs) [late L., from Gr. *hippokampos* (HIPPO-, *kampos*, sea-monster)], *n.* (*pl.* **-pi**, -pī) A genus of small teleostean fishes, with a head and neck somewhat like that of a horse, and a prehensile tail, the sea-horse; (*Anat.*) one of two eminences on the floor of the lateral ventricle of the brain. **hippocampus major:** A large white eminence extending the whole length of the cornu in the cerebrum. **hippocampus minor:** A curved and pointed longitudinal eminence on the inner side of the posterior cornu, projecting backwards into the posterior lobe of the cerebrum. ***hippocamp,** *n.* A sea-monster.

hippocentaur (hip ŏ sen′ tawr) [L. *hippocentaurus*, Gr. *hippokentauros*], *n.* A centaur.

hippocras (hip′ ŏ krăs) [earlier *ypocras*, O.F. *ipocras*, from *Hippocrătes*, Gr. physician (born about 460 B.C.), perh. from being strained through Hippocrates' sleeve, a woollen bag], *n.* A cordial made of wine and spices.

Hippocratic, -al (hip ŏ krăt′ ik, -ăl), **-cratian** (-krăt′ i ăn) [*Hippocratēs*, see prec.], *a.* Of or pertaining to Hippocrates. **Hippocratic oath:** An oath taken by a physician binding him to observe the code of medical ethics, secrecy, etc., first drawn up in the 4th or 5th century B.C., possibly by Hippocrates

hippocrepian (hip ŏ krē′ pi ȧn) [Gr. *krēpis*, shoe], *a.* (*Nat. Hist.*) Like a horseshoe in shape.

***hippodame** (hip′ ŏ dām) [Gr. *hippodamos* (HIPPO-, *damaein*, to tame, to subdue)], *n.* (*Spens.*) A hippocampus. **hippodamist** (hi pod′ ȧ mist), *n.* A horse-tamer. **hippodamous,** *a.*

hippodrome (hip′ ŏ drōm) [F., from L., from Gr. *hippodromos* (*dromos*, a course)], *n.* (*Gr. and Rom. Ant.*) A circus for equestrian games and chariot races; a circus; (*Am. slang*) a fraudulent race, the results of which are prearranged. *v.i.* (*Am. slang*) To carry on races of this kind. **hippodromic** (-drom′ ik), *a.* **hippodromist** (-pod′ rŏ mist), *n.* A circus rider or horse-trainer.

hippogriff (hip′ ŏ grif) [F. *hippogriffe*], *n.* A fabulous creature, half horse and half griffin; a winged horse.

hippology (hi pol′ ŏ ji), *n.* The study of the horse. **hippological** (-loj′ i kȧl), *a.* **hippologist** (-pol′ ŏ jist), *n.*

hippomanes (hi pom′ ȧ nēz) [Gr. (HIPPO-, *mainesthai*, to go mad)], *n.* A substance supposed to possess aphrodisiac qualities, obtained from a mare or the forehead of a recently dropped foal, formerly used in preparing love-potions.

hippopathology (hip ŏ pȧ thol′ ŏ ji), *n.* The pathology of the horse; veterinary medicine.

hippophagy (hi pof′ ȧ ji), **-agism** (-jizm) [Gr. *phagein*, to eat], *n.* The act or practice of feeding on horseflesh. **hippophagist,** *n.* **hippophagistical** (-jis′ ti kȧl), **hippophagous** (-pof′ ȧ gŭs), *a.*

hippophile (hip′ ŏ fīl), *n.* A lover of horses. **hippophobia** (-fō′ bi ȧ), *n.* Dislike or fear of horses.

hippopotamus (hip ŏ pot′ ȧ mŭs) [L., from Gr. *hippopotamos* (*potamos*, river)], *n.* (*pl.* **-es** (ez), **-mi** (mī) A gigantic African pachydermatous quadruped of amphibious habits, with a massive, heavy body, short, blunt muzzle, and short limbs and tail. **hippopotamic** (hip ŏ pŏ tăm′ ik, -pot′ ȧ mik), **hippopotamoid** (-pot′ ȧ moid), *a.*

hippuric (hi pū′ rik) [Gr. *ouron*, urine], *a.* (*Chem.*) Contained in the urine of horses (of hippuric acid).

Hippuris (hi pū′ ris) [L., from Gr. (*oura*, tail)], *n.* (*Bot.*) A genus of plants containing the mare's-tail, common in pools and marshes.

hippurite (hip′ ū rīt) [Gr. *hippouros*, as prec.], *n.* (*Palæont.*) A fossil mollusc of the genus *Hippurites*, from cretaceous strata.

hircine (hěr′ sīn) [L. *hircīnus*, from *hircus*, he-goat], *a.* Goatish; strong smelling. **hircinous,** *a.* **hircocervus** (hěr kŏ sěr′ vŭs) [L. *cervus*, stag], *n.* A fabulous creature, half goat, half stag. **hircosity** (-kos′ i ti), *n.*

hire (hīr) [A.-S. *hȳr* (cp. Dut. *huur*, Dan. *hyre*, G. *heuer*)], *n.* The price paid for labour or services or the use of things; the engagement of a person or thing for such a price; (*fig.*) a reward; a bribe. *v.t.* To procure at a certain price or consideration for temporary use; to employ (a person) for a stipulated payment; to grant the use or service of for a stipulated price; to bribe; (*Am.*) to engage (a servant, etc.). **on hire:** For hiring. **hire purchase,** *n.* A method by which payments for hire are accepted as instalments of the price and the article eventually becomes the property of the hirer (called in Am. 'instalment plan'). **hireable,** *a.* **hireless,** *a.* Gratuitous, unpaid. **hireling,** *n.* One who serves for hire; a mercenary; a prostitute. *a.* Mercenary. **hirer,** *n.* One who hires or lets on hire.

hirple (hěr′ pėl) [Sc. and North., etym. unknown], *v.i.* To walk with a limping or halting gait. *n.* Such a gait.

hirrient (hir′ i ėnt) [L. *hirriens -ntem*, pres.p. of *hirrīre*, to snarl], *a.* (*Phon.*) Trilled. *n.* A trilled sound.

hirsle (hěr′ sėl) [Sc. and North., cp. Icel. *hrista*, to shake], *v.i.* To slide or graze (along, down, etc.), *v.t.* To move (something or someone) in a rough, rubbing manner.

hirsute (hėr sūt′, hěr′ sūt) [L. *hirsūtus*], *a.* Rough, hairy, unshorn; (*Bot.*) covered with bristles. **hirsuteness,** *n.*

hirundine (hi rŭn′ dīn) [L. *hirundo*, a swallow], *a.* Like a swallow.

his (hiz) [A.-S., gen. of *hē*, HE], *pron* and *a.* Of or belonging to him; used absolutely as in **this is his:** This belongs to him. ***hisn, *his'n,** *pron.* (*prov.*) His (used absolutely).

Hispanic (his păn′ ik) [L. *Hispānicus*, from *Hispānia*, Spain], *a.* Pertaining to Spain or the Spanish people, esp. of ancient times. **Hispanicism** (his păn′ i siz ėm), *n.* A Spanish idiom. **Hispanicize,** *v.t.* **Hispanophile,** *n.* and *a.* (One) fond of Spain.

hispid (his′ pid) [L. *hispidus*], *a.* Rough, bristly; (*Nat. Hist.*) setose.

hiss (his) [imit.], *v.i.* To make a sound like that of the letter *s*, by forcing out the breath between the tongue and the upper teeth; to make a sibilant sound, vocally as do geese, or by rapid motion through the air, as an arrow, etc.; to express disapprobation by making such a sound. *v.t.* To utter with a hissing sound; to condemn by hissing; to drive (away, etc.) thus. *n.* A hissing sound; an expression of derision or disapprobation. **hissingly,** *adv.*

hist (hist) [imit.], *int.* Silence! hush! listen! *v.t.* To urge or incite with this sound.

histic (his′ tik) [as foll.], *a.* (*Physiol.*) Of or pertaining to tissue. **histioid,** *a.* **histiology,** etc. [HISTOLOGY].

histo- [Gr. *histos*, web], *comb. form.* Pertaining to organic tissues.

histochemistry (his tō kem′ is tri), *n.* The application of chemistry to organic tissue.

histogenesis (his tō jen′ e sis), *n.* The science of the origin of tissues. **histogenetic,** *a.* **histogeny** (his toj′ e ni), *n.* Histogenesis; the formation and development of the organic tissues.

histogram (his′ tŏ grăm), *n.* A pictorial method of showing the distribution of various quantities, *e.g.* rainfall month by month.

histography (his tog′ rȧ fi), *n.* A description of or treatise on organic tissues.

histology (his tol′ ō ji), *n.* The science of organic tissues. **histologic, histological,** *a.* **histologically,** *adv.* **histologist,** *n.*

histolysis (his tol′ i sis), *n.* The decay and dissolution of organic tissue. **histolytic,** *a.*

historian (his tôr′ i ȧn) [F. *historien*, from L. *historia*, HISTORY], *n.* A writer of history; one versed in history. **historiated,** *a.* Ornamented with figures (as illuminated capitals, etc.).

historic (his tor′ ik) [L. *historicus*, Gr. *historikos*, see HISTORY], *a.* Celebrated in history, associated with historical events. **historic infinitive:** (*Gr. Gram.*) The infinitive verb used for the indicative. **historic present:** (*Gr. Gram.*) The present tense used in a past sense. **historic tenses:** (*Gram.*) The tenses normally employed to express past events. **historical,** *a.* Pertaining to or of the nature of history, distinguished from legendary, fictitious, etc. **historic method:** Investigation or formation of a theory by the study of actual events. **historical picture:** A picture representing an historical event. **historically,** *adv.* **historicity** (his tôr is′ it i), *n.* Historical existence.

historiette (his tôr i et′) [F.], *n.* A short history; a tale.

historiographer (his tôr i og′ rȧ fėr) [late L. *historiographus* (HISTORY, -GRAPHER)], *n.* A writer of history, esp. an official historian. **historiographic, -al** (-grăf′ ik, -al), *a.* **historiography** (-og′ rȧ fi), *n.*

history (his′ tŏr i) [L. and Gr. *historia*, from *histōr*, knowing, cogn. with *id-*, *eidenai*, to know], *n.* A systematic record of past events, esp. those of importance in the development of men or peoples; a study of or a book dealing with the past of any country, people, science, art, etc.; past events, esp. regarded as material for such a study; an eventful past, an interesting career; an historical play. ***v.t.** To relate or record, to chronicle. **ancient history:** History to the end of the Western Empire (A.D. 476). **mediæval history:** From A.D. 476 to the Reformation (A.D. 1517). **modern history:** From A.D. 1517 to the present day. **natural history** [NATURAL].

histrion (his' tri ŏn), ***-trio** (-tri ō) [F. *histrion* or L. *histrio -ōnem*], *n.* (*usu. contempt.*) A stage-player. **histrionic** (his tri on' ik), *a.* Pertaining to actors or acting; theatrical; stagey, affected, unreal. *n.pl.* The art of theatrical representation; theatricals; (*fig.*) pretence, humbug. **histrionical,** *a.* **histrionically,** *adv.* **histrionicism** (his tri on' i sizm), **histrionism** (his' tri ŏ nizm), *n.* Stage representation; feigned representation; histrionics.

hit (hit) [prob. from Scand. (cp. Icel. and Swed. *hitta*, Dan. *hitte*)], *v.t.* (*past & p.p.* **hit**) To strike; to strike or touch with a blow or missile after taking aim; (*fig.*) to attain to; to guess; to affect, to wound. *v.i.* To strike (at, against, etc.); to come into collision (against); (*fig.*) to agree, to suit, to fall in with. *n.* A blow, a stroke; a touch with the sword or stick in fencing; (*fig.*) a lucky chance; a felicitous expression or turn of thought; a successful effort. **hit parade,** *n.* A list of songs in current popularity. **hard hit:** Hurt or injured, esp. by loss of money. **to hit off:** To represent or describe rapidly or cleverly. **to hit it off with** or **together:** To agree. **to hit on** or **upon:** To light or chance on; to discover by luck. **to hit out:** To strike out straight from the shoulder. **to make a hit:** To be a sudden success, to become popular. **hit and miss:** (*fig.*) Doing one thing or another as occasion demands. **a hit or a miss:** A chance of either success or failure. **to hit below the belt** [BELT]. **to hit the nail on the head** [NAIL].

hitch (hich) [etym. doubtful], *v.t.* To fasten loosely; to make fast by a hook, loop, etc.; to pull up with a jerk; (*fig.*) to drag (in). *v.i.* To move with jerks; to become entangled or caught; (*colloq.*) to work pleasantly together; to interfere (as horses). *n.* A catch, a stoppage; an impediment, a temporary difficulty; the act of catching, as on a hook; a pull or jerk up; (*Naut.*) various species of knot by which a rope is bent to a spar or to another rope. **to hitch-hike** [HIKE]. **half-hitch,** *n.* (*Naut.*) A knot made by passing the end of a rope round itself and through the bend. **hitchy,** *a.* **hitchily,** *adv.*

***hithe** (hīth) [A.-S. *hȳth*], *n.* A small port or haven (common in place-names, as *Rotherhithe*).

hither (hith' ėr) [A.-S. *hider* (cp. Icel. *hēthra*, L. *citrā*), from Teut. base of HE, HERE, etc.], *adv.* To this place, end, or point; in this direction. *a.* Situated on this side; the nearer (of two objects) to the speaker. **hither and thither:** To this place and that; here and there. ***hithermost,** *a.* Nearest in this direction. **hither side:** The nearer side. **hitherto,** *adv.* Up to this place, limit, or time. ***hitherward,** *adv.* In this direction.

Hitlerite (hit' lėr īt), *n.* Supporter of Adolf Hitler (1889–1945) and of German National Socialism.

Hittite (hit' īt) [Heb. *Khittīm*], *a.* Of or pertaining to the Hittites, a people of doubtful origin inhabiting parts of Asia Minor and Syria before 1000 B.C.

hive (hīv) [A.-S. *hȳf* (cp. Dut. *huif*, Icel. *hūfr*, also L. *cupa*, a tub)], *n.* An artificial structure for housing bees; a swarm of bees inhabiting a hive; (*fig.*) a place swarming with busy occupants; *a kind of bonnet or other object resembling a hive. *v.t.* To put into or secure in a hive; (*fig.*) to house as in a hive; to store up for future use. *v.i.* To enter or live in a hive; to take shelter or swarm together, as bees. **to hive off:** To assign part of a firm's work to a subsidiary company. **hiveless,** *a.* **hiver,** *n.* One who collects bees into hives. **hiveward,** *adv.*

hives (hīvz) [etym. doubtful], *n.* An eruptive disease characterized by scattered vesicles filled with a fluid; applied also to inflammation of the bowels or of the larynx.

ho, hoa (hō) [cp. Icel. *hō*, *hōa*], *int.* An exclamation to call attention, or to denote exultation, surprise, etc.; a cry used by teamsters to stop their teams. **ho! ho!** *int.* Expressing amusement, derision, etc. **eastward** or **westward ho!** *int.* (*Naut.*) Eastward or westward away.

hoactzin, hoatzin (hō ăkt' zin, -ăt' zin) [prob. native, onomat.], *n.* A South American bird, *Opisthocomus hoazin* or *O. cristatus*, with a harsh hissing cry.

hoar (hôr) [A.-S. *hār* (cp. Icel. *hārr*, also G. *hehr*, august)], *a.* White, grey or greyish-white; grey with age; ancient; white with foam. ***v.i.** To become mouldy or musty. ***v.t.** To make hoary or white; to make mouldy. *n.* Hoariness; antiquity; hoar-frost, rime. **hoar-frost,** *n.* Frozen dew, white frost. **hoar-headed** [HOARY]. **hoarstone,** *n.* A landmark; a stone marking out the boundary of an estate.

hoard (hôrd) [A.-S. *hord*, whence *hordian*, to hoard (cp. Icel. *hodd*, G. *hort*)], *n.* A stock, a store, a quantity of things, esp. money, laid by; an accumulated stock of anything. *v.t.* To collect and lay by; to store up. *v.i.* To amass and store up anything of value. **hoarder,** *n.*

hoarding (hôr' ding), ***hord** (hôrd) [from O.F. *hourd*, *hurt*, scaffold, or Dut. *horde*, hurdle], *n.* A temporary screen of boards round or in front of a building where erections or repairs are in progress; a large screen for posting bills on.

hoarhound [HOREHOUND].

hoarse (hôrs) [M.E. *hors*, *hos*, A.-S. *hās* (cp. Dan. *hæs*, G. *heiser*)], *a.* Harsh, rough (of the voice); grating, discordant; having such a voice, as from a cold. **hoarse-sounding,** *a.* **hoarsely,** *adv.* **hoarsen,** *v.t.* and *i.* **hoarseness,** *n.*

hoarstone (hôr' stōn) [HOAR], *n.* A stone marking out the boundary of an estate; a landmark.

hoary (hôr' i) [HOAR], *a.* White or whitish-grey as with age; white- or grey-headed; of great antiquity; venerable; (*Nat. Hist.*) covered with very short dense hairs, which give an appearance of whiteness to the surface; *mouldy, musty. **hoary-headed,** *a.* Grey-headed. **hoariness,** *n.*

hoast (hōst) [Sc., prob. from Icel., *hōsta* (cp. A.-S. *hwōstan*)], *v.i.* To cough.

***hoastman** (hōst' măn) [HOST, guest, MAN], *n.* A member of a merchant-guild in Newcastle-upon-Tyne, orig. charged with the duty of receiving strangers, and afterwards with the control of the trade in coal.

hoax (hōks) [perh. corr. of HOCUS], *n.* A practical joke, or a sportive deception. *v.t.* To play a practical joke upon, to take in for sport. **hoaxer,** *n.*

hob (1) (hob) [identified by Skeat with HUB (1)], *n.* The projecting side of a grate, or the top of this, on which things are placed to be kept warm; a peg or iron pin used as a mark in quoits and other games; a hardened, threaded spindle by which a comb or chasing-tool may be cut; the runner of a sledge.

hob (2) (hob) [var. of *Rob*, short for ROBIN, *Robert*], *n.* An elf, a sprite; a rustic; a male ferret. **hobbish,** *a.* **hob-job,** *n.* (*prov.*) An odd job. **hobjobbing,** *n.* **hob- jobber,** *n.*

hob-a-nob [HOB-NOB].

***hobbinoll** (hob' i nōl) [name of a rustic in Spenser's 'Shepherd's Calendar'], *n.* A rustic.

Hobbism (hob' izm) [Thomas *Hobbes* (1588–1679), English philosopher], *n.* The system of philosophy contained in or deduced from the writings of Hobbes, esp. his teachings with regard to absolute monarchy.

hobble (hob' ėl) [cp. Dut. *hobbelen*, to toss or rock about, to stammer], *v.i.* To walk lamely or awkwardly; to walk with unequal and jerky steps; to move in a halting or irregular way; (*fig.*) to run lamely (as verses). *v.t.* To cause to hobble; to shackle the legs of (horses, etc.) to prevent straying; *to perplex. *n.* An awkward, uneven, or limping gait; (*fig.*) a difficulty, a perplexity; a rope, shackle, clog, etc., for hobbling an animal. **hobble-skirt,** *n.* A skirt fitting closely round the legs and ankles, usu. confined to a wide band, worn largely about 1910. **hobbler** (1), *n.* One who hobbles; an unlicensed pilot, a hoveller; a casual dock-labourer. **hobblingly,** *adv.* **hobbly,** *a.* Causing to hobble; full of holes, rough.

hobbledehoy (hob ĕl dė hoi′) [etym. doubtful], *n.* A raw, awkward young fellow, esp. one between boyhood and manhood. **hobbledehoyhood, -ism,** *n.* **hobbledehoyish,** *a.*

hobby (1) (hob′ i) [O.F. *hobet*, prob. from *hober*, to move about (cp. Dut. *hobbelen*, see HOBBLE)], *n.* A small species of falcon, *Falco subbuteo*.

hobby (2) (hob′ i) [O.F. *hobin*, perh. var. of ROBIN], *n.* *A strong, active, middle-sized horse; an easy ambling horse; a hobby-horse; (*fig.*) one's favourite recreation or pursuit, plan, or object; *an early form of velocipede. **hobby-horse,** *n.* Orig. a figure rudely imitating a horse used in morris-dances, pantomime, etc.; a child's rocking-horse, or a horse's head on a stick for a child to bestride in play; a horse on a merry-go-round; (*fig.*) a hobby; *a buffoon. **hobbyism,** *n.* **hobbyist,** *n.* **hobbyless,** *a.*

hobgoblin (hob′ gob lin), *n.* A kind of goblin, elf, or fairy, esp. one of a frightful appearance.

hobnail (hob′ nāl), *n.* A short thick nail with a large head, used for heavy boots; (*fig.*) a clown, a clod-hopper (*often in pl.*). *v.t.* To set or stud (boots) with hobnails; (*fig.*) to trample. **hobnailed,** *a.* Set with hobnails; (*Path.*) rough and uneven, as if studded with hobnails (of the liver).

hob-nob (hob′ nob) [earlier *hab nab* (A.-S. *habban*, to HAVE, *nabban*, not to have)], *v.i.* To drink familiarly, or to associate familiarly (with). **adv.* (*Shak.*) Give it or take it.

hobo (hō′ bō) [unkn.], *n.* (*Am.*) A vagrant, a tramp.

hobhoy [HAUTBOY].

Hobson's choice [CHOICE].

hock (1) (hok) [A.-S., *hoh*, cogn. with HEEL], *n.* The joint between the knee and the fetlock in the hind leg of quadrupeds; (*Sc.*) the posterior part of the knee-joint in man. *v.t.* To hamstring.

hock (2) (hok) [formerly *hockamore*, G. *Hochheimer*], *n.* A kind of light wine, still or sparkling, made at Hochheim in Nassau.

hock (3) (hok), *v.t.* (*Am. slang*) To pawn.

***hock-day** (hok′ dā) [etym. doubtful], *n.* A festival held on the second Tuesday after Easter, when money was levied, with a good deal of horse-play, on passers-by for pious uses; it was traditionally believed to have been on that day that the English overcame the Danes.

hockey (1) (hok′ i) [perh. conn. with F. *hoquet*, a crook, or with HOOK], *n.* A game of ball played with a club having a curved end.

hockey (2) (hok′ i) [etym. unknown], *n.* (*Eastern Counties*) Harvest-home, or the feast celebrating this.

hockle (hok′ ĕl) [etym. doubtful; perh. from HOCK (1)], *v.t.* To hamstring; to hough.

hocus (hō′ kŭs) [from the mock L. *hocus pocus*], *v.t.* To take in, to impose upon; to stupefy with liquor treated with drugs; to put a drug into (liquor). *n.* A cheat, an impostor; drugged liquor. **hocus pocus:** *An expression used by jugglers in playing tricks; a juggler; a juggler's trick, a fraud, a hoax. *v.i.* To juggle. *v.t.* To cheat, to trick.

hod (hod) [prob. from obs. *hot*, O.F. *hotte*, from Teut. (cp. M.Dut. *hodde*, G. *hotte*)], *n.* A wooden holder shaped like a trough and fixed on a long handle, for carrying mortar or bricks on the shoulder; a coal-scuttle. **hodman,** *n.* A labourer who carries a hod for bricklayers, etc.; (*fig.*) a drudge, a hack; (*Univ. slang*) a scholar from Westminster School admitted to Christ Church, Oxford.

hodden (hodn) [Sc., etym. doubtful], *n.* A coarse woollen cloth such as would be produced by a handloom. *a.* Attired in this; plain, homely. **hodden grey:** Grey hodden manufactured from undyed wool.

hodge (hoj) [corr. of ROGER], *n.* A typical countryman; (*collect.*) the agricultural labouring class.

hodge-podge (hoj′ poj), *n.* A hotchpotch; a mixture or medley. ***hodge-pudding,** *n.* A pudding consisting of a medley of ingredients.

hodiernal (hō di ĕr′ năl) [L. *hodiernus*, from *hodiē*, to-day], *a.* Pertaining to the present day.

hodman [HOD].

***hodmandod** (hod′ măn dod) [var. of obs. *dodman*, a snail], *n.* A snail.

hodograph (hod′ ŏ grăf) [Gr. *hodos*, way, -GRAPH], *n.* (*Math.*) The curve traced by the end of lines, drawn from a fixed point, representing in magnitude and direction the velocity of a moving point. **hodographic** (-grăf′ ik), *a.* **hodographically,** *adv.*

hodometer (hŏ dom ė tĕr) [Gr. *hodos*, way, -METER], *n.* An instrument with a dial, attached to the axle of a vehicle, for measuring and recording the distance travelled.

hoe (1) (hō) [F. *houe*, O.H.G. *houwa*, to HEW], *n.* A tool used to scrape or stir up earth around plants, cut weeds up from the ground, etc. *v.t.* (*pres.p.* **hoeing**) To scrape or loosen (ground), cut (weeds), or dig (up) with a hoe. *v.i.* To use a hoe. **hoe-cake,** *n.* (*Am.*) A cake of Indian meal, orig. cooked on a hoe.

hoe (2) (hō) [O.E. *hoh*, a heel], *n.* (*Geog.*) A promontory, a protecting ridge.

hog (hog) [etym. doubtful], *n.* A swine, esp. a castrated boar meant for killing; (*Am.* any kind of pig); (*prov.*) a young sheep or bullock, usu. of a year old; (*fig.*) a dirty, filthy, gluttonous, or low fellow; (*Naut.*) a scrub-broom for cleaning a ship's bottom under water; (*Curling*) a stone that fails to pass the hog-score. (*past & p.p.* **hogged**) *v.t.* To cut short like the bristles of a hog; to cause (a ship, keel, etc.) to rise in the middle and droop at the ends; (*Naut.*) to clean (a ship's bottom) under water by scraping. *v.i* To droop at both ends; to carry the head down and back up (of animals). **hog in armour:** (*facet.*) An awkward or ungainly person; the nine-banded armadillo, *Tatusia novemcincta*. **to go the whole hog:** To do a job completely; to make no compromise or reservations. **to hog it:** (*slang*) To be greedy, to snatch for oneself. **hogback, hog's back,** *n.* A long ridged hill; (*Geol.*) a monocline; an eskar. **hog-backed,** *a.* **hog-fish,** *n.* A fish with dorsal spine or bristles on the head. **hog-frame,** *n.* A fore-and-aft frame forming a truss in the main frame of a vessel of light draught to prevent vertical flexure. **hog-mane,** *n.* A horse's mane cut so as to stand erect. **hog-pen,** *n.* A pigsty. **hog-plum,** *n.* A name for several species of West Indian trees and their fruit, which is used for feeding hogs. **hog-reeve,** *n.* A district official who adjudicated on the damage done by stray hogs. **hog-ringer,** *n.* One who puts rings on hogs' snouts. **hog's back** (HOGBACK]. ***hog's-bean,** *n.* Henbane. **hog's-lard,** *n.* The rendered fat of the hog. **hog-score,** *n.* (*Curling*) A line drawn across the rink which a stone must pass in order to count. ***hog-shearing,** *n.* Much ado about nothing. **hog-skin,** *n.* Tanned pig's skin. **hog's pudding:** A pudding of various ingredients stuffed like a sausage into a hog's entrail. **hog-wash,** *n.* The refuse of a kitchen or brewery, used for feeding hogs; (*slang*) bad liquor; anything worthless. **hoggish,** *a.* Having the qualities or manners of a hog; brutish, gluttonous, filthy, selfish. **hoggishly,** *adv.* **hoggishness,** *n.* **hoglike,** *a.*

hogger (hog′ ĕr) [Sc., etym. doubtful], *n.* A stocking without a foot, worn by coal-miners as an anklet; a pipe connexion of india-rubber, etc.

hogger-pipe, *n.* The upper terminal pipe of a mining pump. **hogger-pump,** *n.* The top pump in the sinking pit of a mine.

hoggerel (hog′ ĕr ėl), *n.* A sheep in its second year.

hogget (hog′ ėt), *n.* A yearling sheep; a year-old colt.

hoggin, hoggins (hog′ in, -inz) [etym. doubtful], *n.* (*prov.*) Screened gravel for footpaths.

hogmanay (hog′ mȧ nā) [acc. to O.E.D. from O.F. *aguillaneuf*, the last day of the year, from the shout with which new year's gifts were given and asked (cp. Norman *hoguinané*)], *n.* In Scotland, the last day of the year; an entertainment or a present given on that day.

hogshead (hogz′ hed) [HOG, HEAD (formation obscure)], *n.* A measure of capacity containing 52½ imperial gal.; a large cask.

hoick (hoik), *v.t.* To pull up or out of; (*Aviat.*) to force an aeroplane upwards; to pull.

hoiden [HOYDEN].

hoiho (hō ē′ hō) [Maori], *n.* A N. Zealand species of penguin.

hoist (hoist), ***hoise** (hoiz) [formerly *hysse*, perh. from M.Dut. *hyssen* (cp. Icel. *hisa*, Swed. and Norw. *hissa*, G. *hissen*)], *v.t.* To raise up; to lift by means of tackle; to run up (a sail or flag); to lift on to the back of another person for the purpose of flogging. *n.* The act of lifting or hoisting up; an apparatus for hoisting or raising; a lift or elevator; (*Naut.*) the vertical height of a yard, sail, or flag. **hoist with his own petard:** Blown up by his own petard; (*fig.*) caught in his own trap.

hoity-toity (hoi′ ti toi′ ti) [prob. from obs. *hoit*, to romp], *int.* An exclamation of astonishment mixed with disapproval and contempt. *a.* Flighty; petulant. *n.* A romp, a frolic; a rumpus.

hokey-pokey (hō′ ki pō′ ki) [corr. of HOCUS POCUS], *n.* A cheap confection like stiff ice-cream sold by street vendors.

hokum (hō′ kŭm), *n.* (*Am. slang*) Bunkum; a foolish stage or book plot; counterfeit culture.

holarctic (hȯ lark′ tik) [Gr. *holos*, whole, ARCTIC], *a.* (*Zool.*) Of or pertaining to the entire northern region of the globe.

hold (1) (hōld) [A.-S. *healdan, halden* (cp. M.L.G. *holden*, Icel. *halda*, G. *halten*)], *v.t.* (*past & p.p.* **held, *p.p. holden**) To grasp and retain; to keep in, to confine; to enclose, to contain; to be able to contain, to keep from running or flowing out; to keep back, to restrain; to keep in a certain manner or position; to retain possession or control of; to occupy, to possess; to regard, to believe; to maintain (that); to judge, to assert (that); to carry on; to celebrate; to use, to employ (as language); (*colloq.*) to lay, to wager, to accept as a bet or wager. *v.i.* To maintain a grasp or attachment; to continue firm, not to break; to adhere (to); to be valid or true, to stand; to be fit or consistent; (*usu. in imper.*) to stop, to stay, to refrain. **hold hard!** (*colloq.*) Stop. **to hold a wager:** To bet. **to hold by:** To hold to, to adhere to. **to hold forth:** To stretch or put forward; to propose, to offer; to speak in public; to harangue, to dilate. **to hold good** or **true:** To remain valid; to apply; to be relevant. **to hold in:** To restrain, to restrain oneself; to keep quiet, to keep silent. **to hold in esteem,** etc.: To regard with esteem, etc. **to hold of, from,** or **under:** To derive title from. **to hold off:** To keep at a distance; to remain at a distance; to delay. **to hold on:** To continue or proceed without interruption; (*colloq.*) to stop; to wait. **to hold on one's way:** To keep going steadily. **to hold one's own:** To maintain one's position. **to hold one's tongue:** To be silent. **to hold out:** To hold forward, to offer; to bear, to endure; to persist, not to yield. **to hold over:** To keep back or reserve, to defer; (*Law*) to keep possession of after the expiration of one's term. **to hold to:** To bind by (bail, one's statement, etc.); to adhere to. **to hold together:** To keep in union, to cause to cohere; to continue united; to cohere. **to hold up:** To raise or lift up; to support, to encourage; to sustain; to show forth, to exhibit (to ridicule, etc.); to stop on the highway and rob; to keep from falling; (*Weather*) to keep fine; to continue the same speed. **to hold one's head** or **one's head high:** To conduct oneself proudly or arrogantly. **to hold water:** (*fig.*) To be sound or valid, to stand scrutiny. **to hold with:** To approve of, to side with. **hold-all,** *n.* A hand-bag or case for carrying clothes, etc. **hold-back,** *n.* A restraint, a check, a hindrance.

hold (2) (hōld) [from prec.], *n.* The act of seizing or grasping in the hands; a grasp, a clutch; mental grasp; a support, anything to hold by or support oneself by; (*fig.*) moral influence; custody, possession; a refuge, a fortified place.

hold (3) (hōld) [HOLE (1)], *n.* The interior cavity of a ship, in which the cargo is stowed.

holder (hōld′ĕr), *n.* One who or that which holds; a tenant, occupier, or owner; a contrivance by or in which anything is kept or held; the payee of a bill of exchange or promissory note. **holder-forth,** *n.* One who harangues.

holdfast (hōld′ fast), *n.* A means by which something is clamped to another; a support.

holding (hōld′ ing), *n.* A hold, a grasp; tenure or occupation; that which is held, esp. land, property, stocks, or shares; *the burden of a song. **holding company,** *n.* (*Comm.*) A company formed to acquire the majority of shares in one or more subsidiary companies.

hole (1) (hōl) [A.-S. *hol* (cp. Dut. and Icel. *hol*)], *n.* A hollow place or cavity; (*Austral.*) a pool; an aperture, an orifice, a perforation; a wild animal's burrow; a mean habitation; a small pit or hollow into which the ball has to be driven in various games; (*Golf*) one of the points made by the player who drives his ball from one hole to another with the fewest strokes, the distance between two consecutive holes; (*fig.*) a difficulty, a fix. *v.t.* To form a hole or holes in; to tunnel; to put or drive into a hole; (*Mining*) to undercut a coal-seam. *v.i.* To go into a hole; to hibernate; (*Golf*) to drive one's ball into a hole. **to hole out:** (*Golf*) To play the ball into the hole. **to make a hole in:** To take or consume a large part of. **to pick holes in:** To find fault with. **hole-and-corner,** *a.* Secret, clandestine. **holey,** *a.* **holing-axe,** *n.* A tool for cutting holes in posts. **holing-pick,** *n.* A pick for undercutting coal.

***hole** (2) [WHOLE].

holibut [HALIBUT].

holiday (hol′ i dā) [A.-S. *hæligdæg*, holy day], *n.* A day of exemption from work; a day of amusement or pleasure; any period devoted to this; a vacation. *a.* Pertaining to or befitting a holiday. **holiday speeches:** Fine phrases with little meaning. **holiday-task,** *n.* Work or lessons to be performed during holidays.

holily, etc. [HOLY]. **holiness** [HOLY].

holism (hol′ izm) [HOLO; -ISM], *n.* (*Phil.*) The tendency in nature to evolve wholes that are more than the sum of the parts.

holk [HOWK]. **holla** [HALLO].

holland (hol′ ȧnd), *n.* Coarse unbleached linen with a glazed surface, first made in Holland. **brown holland:** Unbleached holland. **Hollander,** *n.* A native of Holland; a Dutch ship. **Hollandish,** *a.* **hollands,** *n.* A kind of gin made in Holland.

hollo, holloa, hollow (1) [HALLO].

hollow (2) (hol′ ō) [M.E. *holwe*, A.-S. *holge*, dat. of *holh*, prob. a form of *hol*, HOLE], *a.* Containing a cavity or empty space; not solid; excavated, sunken, concave; empty, vacant; deep, low (of sounds); (*fig.*) insincere, not genuine. *n.* A depression or unoccupied space; a cavity, a hole, a basin: a valley. *v.t.* To make hollow, to excavate. **hollow-eyed,** *a.* Having sunken eyes. **hollow-hearted,** *a.* Insincere, false. **hollow square:** A body of troops drawn up in the form of a square with a vacant space in the middle. **hollow-ware,** *n.* Cast-iron culinary vessels, such as pots, kettles, etc. **hollowly,** *adv.* **hollowness,** *n.*

holly (hol' i) [A.-S. *holen* (cp. Dut. and G. *hulst*), probl cogn. with W. *celyn*], *n.* A shrub or tree of the genus *Ilex*, esp. *I. aquifolium*, a tree with glossy, prickly leaves and scarlet or, more rarely, yellow berries.

hollyhock (hol' i hok) [M.E. *holihoc* (*holi*, HOLY, *hoc*, mallow)], *n.* A tall garden plant, *Althæa rosea*, with red, pink, and yellow flowers.

holm (1) (hōm) [Icel. *hōlmr*, perh. cogn. with A.-S. *holm*, sea, and L. *culmen*, mountain-top], *n.* Flat ground, liable to flooding, along the side of a river; an island in a river or estuary.

holm (2) (hōm) [corr. of A.-S. *holen*, HOLLY], *n.* The ilex or evergreen oak, *Quercus ilex*, often called **holm-oak.**

holo- [Gr. *holos*, whole], *comb. form.* Entire, complete; completely.

holoblastic (hol ō blăs' tik) [Gr. *blastos*, germ], *a.* Having the whole mass directly formative (of an ovum), undergoing segmentation throughout.

holobranchiate (hol ō brăng' ki āt), (*Ichthyol.*) *a.* Having complete gills.

holocaust (hol' ō kawst) [F. *holocauste*, L. *holocaustum*, Gr. *holokauston* (HOLO-, *kaien*, fut. *kausō*, to burn)], *n.* A sacrifice entirely consumed by fire; (*fig.*) a wholesale sacrifice of life, or general destruction, esp. by fire.

holocryptic (hol ō krip' tik), *a.* Wholly secret, unintelligible, or undecipherable.

holograph (hol' ō grăf) [late L. *holographus*, Gr. *-phos* (*graphein*, to write)], *a.* Wholly in the handwriting of the author or signatory. *n.* A document, letter, etc., so written. **holographic** (-grăf' ik), *a.*

holohedral (hol ō hē' drål) [Gr. *hedra*, seat, base], *a.* (*Cryst.*) Having the full possible number of planes symmetrically arranged. **holohedrism,** *n.* **holohedron,** *n.*

holometabola (hol ō mė tăb' ō lå) [Gr. *metabolos*, undergoing change], *n.pl.* (*Ent.*) A division containing those insects which undergo complete metamorphosis. **holometabolic** (-bol' ik), **holometabolous** (-tăb' ō lŭs), *a.* **holometabolism,** *n.*

holometer (hō lom' ė tėr), *n.* An instrument for taking all kinds of measurements.

holomorphic (hol ō môr' fik) [Gr. *morphē*, shape], *a.* (*Math.*) Having the properties of an entire function, being finite, continuous, and one-valued for all finite values of the variable; (*Cryst.*) holohedral or holosymmetrical.

Holophane (hol' ō fān) [HOLO-, Gr. *phainein*, to shine], *n.* (Protected trade name.) A globe or shade for a lamp made of clear glass with prismatic corrugations for refracting, reflecting, illuminating, or diffusing the light.

holophotal (hol ō fō' tål) [Gr. *phōs phōtos*, light], *a.* Utilizing the whole of the available light, applied to the illuminating apparatus in lighthouses. **holophot** (hol' ō fōt), *n.* An apparatus of this kind. **holophotally,** *adv.* **holophotometer** (-tom' ė tėr), *n.*

holophrasis (hō lof' råsis) [Gr. *phrasis*, see PHRASE], *n.* (*Philol.*) The expression of a whole sentence in a single word. **holophrase, holophrasm** (hol' ō frāz, -frăsm), *n.* **holophrastic** (-frăs' tik), *a.*

holorhinal (hol ō rī' nål) [Gr. *rhis rhinos*, the nose], *a.* (*Zool.*) Having the nasal bones almost or entirely uncleft.

holosymmetrical (hol ō si met' ri kål), *a.* (*Cryst.*) Wholly symmetrical, holohedral.

holothurian (hol ō thū' ri ån) [mod. L. *holothūria*, Gr. *holothouria*, pl. of *-rion*, zoophytes], *a.* Belonging to the *Holothuria*, a genus of echinoderms comprising the sea-slugs. *n.* An animal of this genus.

holotype (hol' ō tīp), *n.* (*Biol.*) The original specimen from which a new species is derived.

***holp, *holpen** [HELP].

holster (hōl' stėr) [Dut. (cp. Icel. *hulstr*, case, A.-S. *heolstor*, a hiding-place, a covering)], *n.* A leather case, usu. attached to the saddle-bow, to hold a pistol. **holstered,** *a.*

holt (1) (hōlt) [A.-S. (cp. Dut. *hout*, timbers, Icel. *holt*, a copse, G. *holz*)], *n.* A wood, a grove, a copse; (*prov.*) a plantation.

holt (2) (hōlt) [prov. corr. of HOLD (1)], *n.* A burrow a hole; a covert, a shelter; *a hold, grasp.

holus-bolus (hō' lŭs bō' lŭs) [mock L., from WHOLE (cp. HOCUS POCUS)], *adv.* All at once, at one gulp.

holy (hō' li) [A.-S. *hālig* (cp. Dut. and G. *heilig*, Icel. *heilagr*)], *a.* Sacred; set apart for the service of God or other sacred use; morally pure; free from sin or sinful affections; of high spiritual excellence. **Holy City,** *n.* Jerusalem. **holy cross:** The cross on which Christ was put to death. **Holy Cross Day:** The festival of the Exaltation of the Cross, 14 Sept. ***holy-cruel,** *a.* Cruel through being too rigidly virtuous. **holy day:** A day commemorating some religious event; *a holiday. **Holy Family** [FAMILY]. **Holy Ghost, Holy Spirit:** The third Person of the Trinity. **Holy Grail** [GRAIL]. **Holy Land:** Palestine. **holy office:** The Inquisition. **Holy of holies:** The innermost and most sacred apartment of the Jewish Tabernacle and the Temple, where the ark was kept; (*fig.*) the inmost shrine. **holy orders** [ORDERS]. **Holy Roman Empire** [ROMAN]. **holy rood:** A cross or crucifix, esp. one on the rood-beam in churches. **Holy Saturday:** The Saturday before Easter. **Holy Thursday:** In the English Church, Ascension Day; (*R.-C. Ch.*) Maundy Thursday, the Thursday in Holy Week. **holy water:** Water blessed by a priest, used in the Roman and Greek ritual. **Holy Week:** The week from Palm Sunday to Holy Saturday inclusive. **holy well:** A well reputed to be invested with miraculous qualities. **holy writ:** Sacred scriptures, esp. the Bible. **holily,** *adv.* **holiness,** *n.* The state of being holy, sanctity; moral purity or integrity; the state of being consecrated to God or His worship; that which is so consecrated. **his Holiness:** A title of the Pope, *given formerly to the Greek emperors and other sacred and ecclesiastical dignitaries.

holystone (hō' li stōn), *n.* A soft sandstone used for scrubbing the decks of vessels. *v.t.* To scrub with this.

hom- [HOMO-].

homage (hom' åj) [O.F., from late L. *homāticum*, *homināticum*, from *homo hominis*, man], *n.* The service paid and fealty professed to a sovereign or superior lord; respect paid by external action; deference, obeisance, reverence, worship. *v.t.* To pay homage or respect to. **homager,** *n.* One who does homage; one who holds a fee by homage.

Homburg (hom' bĕrg) [German city], *n.* A trilby hat.

home (1) (hōm) [A.-S. *hām* (cp. Dut. *heem*, Icel. *heimr*, G. *heim*)], *n.* One's own house or abode; the abode of the family to which one belongs; one's own country; the place of constant residence, of commonest occurrence, or where anything is indigenous; a place or state of rest or comfort; a charitable institution of rest or refuge for orphans, the destitute, or the afflicted; in various games, the goal or den. *a.* Connected with, carried on, or produced at home or in one's native country; domestic, opposed to foreign; (*fig.*) personal, touching the heart or conscience. *adv.* To one's home or country; to the point, pointedly, closely, intimately. **last** or **long home:** The grave. **at home** [AT]. **to be at home:** To be perfectly conversant or familiar with; to receive visitors. **to bring home to one:** To convince. **to come home to one:** To reach one's heart or conscience. **home-born,** *a.* Native, domestic, natural. **home-bound,** *a.* Weather bound; kept at home. **home-bred,** *a.* Bred at home, not foreign; natural, native; not polished by travel. **home-brewed,** *a.* Brewed at home or for consumption at home. *n.* Home-brewed ale. **home-brew,** *n.* A beverage brewed at home. **home circuit:** (*Law*) The circuit comprising the Home Counties. **home-coming,** *n.* and *a.* A return to, or arrival at home. **Home Counties:** The counties nearest London: Middlesex, Surrey, Kent, Essex, Herts, Bucks, Berks. **Home Department** [HOME OFFICE]. **home-farm** [FARM]. **home-felt,** *a.* Felt in one's heart, inward, private. **Home Guard,** *n.* The citizen army formed in Britain in May, 1940, under the title of Local Defence Volunteers. **home-keeping,** *a.* Staying at home, untravelled. **home-lot,** *n.* (*Am.*) A piece of land allotted for a residence as distinguished from the rest of a farm. **home-made,** *a.* Made at home; not manufactured abroad. **Home Office:** The department of the Secretary of State for Home Affairs, dealing with police administration, prisons, factories, licensing, etc.; the building occupied by this. **Home Rule:** The government of a country, esp. Ireland, by a separate parliament. **home-sick,** *a.* **home-sickness,** *n.* A vehement desire to return home, causing depression of spirits and affecting the physical health. **home signal:** (*Railway*) A signal that must on no account be passed if it is against a train, distinguished from distance signal. **home-speaking,** *n.* Plain direct speech that goes to the heart or conscience. **home-spun,** *a.* Spun or wrought at home; home-made; (*fig.*) plain, unaffected, rude. *n.* Cloth spun at home. **homestall,** *n.* A homestead; a farmyard. **homestead,** *n.* A house, esp. a farmhouse, with the buildings attached; (*U.S.A.*) a lot granted for the residence and maintenance of a family, under the Homestead Act of 1862; (*Austral.*) the owner's house on a sheep station. *v.t.* To occupy as a homestead. **homesteader,** *n.* **homesteading,** *n.* **homestretch,** *n.* The last section of a race-course before the winning-post is reached. **homeless,** *a.* **homely,** *a.* Plain, without affectation, unpretending; unadorned, unvarnished (*Am.* plain in looks). **adv.* Plainly, simply. **homeliness,** *n.* **homeward,** *adv.* Towards home. *a.* Being or going in the direction of home. **homeward-bound,** *a.* Returning home from abroad. **homewards,** *adv.* **homish, homy,** *a.*

home (2) (hōm) [from prec.], *v.i.* To fly home (of pigeons); (*fig.*) to go home; to dwell; to long for home. *v.t.* To send (pigeons) home; to provide with a home. **homer** (1), *n.* A homing pigeon. **homing device,** *n.* (*Mil.*) The mechanism for the automatic guiding of missiles.

homelyn (hō' mė lin) [etym. unknown], *n.* The spotted ray, *Raia maculata*, a European sea-fish used for food.

homeopathy, etc. [HOMŒOPATHY].

homer (1) [HOME (2)].

homer (2) (hō' mėr) [Heb. *khōmer*], *n.* A Hebrew liquid measure of 75⅝ gal; a dry measure of 11⅛ bush.

Homeric (hȯ mer' ik) [L. *Homēricus*, Gr. *Homērikos*, from *Homeros*, Homer], *a.* Pertaining to Homer or his poems; resembling Homer's poems in style. **Homeridæ** (hȯ mer' i dē), *n.pl.* The literary successors or reputed descendants of Homer; the rhapsodists who recited his poems, supposed by some critics to have been joint-authors of the Homeric poems. **Homerist** (hō' mėr' ist), *n.* **Homerology** (-ol' ȯ ji), *n.* **Homerologist,** *n.*

homestall, homestead, homestretch [HOME (1)].

homicide (hom' i sīd) [F., from L. *homicīdium*, manslaughter, *homicīda*, man-slayer (HOMO, man, -CIDE)], *n.* The act of killing a human being; one who kills another, a man-slayer. **homicidal** (-sī' dål), *a.*

homiletic (hom i let' ik) [Gr. *homilētikos*, from *homileein*, to hold converse with, from *homilos*, assembly (*homos*, like, *eilein*, to crowd together)], *a.* Pertaining to homilies. *n.pl.* The art of preaching; sacred eloquence; the art or method of presenting spiritual truths to an audience in the most effective form. **homilist** (hom' i list), *n.*

homily (hom' i li) [O.F. *omelie* (F. *homélie*), L. *homīlia*, as prec.], *n.* A religious discourse; a sermon, esp. on some practical subject; a tedious moral exhortation. **Books of Homilies:** Two books published in England by authority in 1547 and 1562, to be read in churches when no sermon was prepared.

hominid (hom' in id) [HOMO], *n.* (*Biol.*) A creature of the genus *homo*; a man-like fossil.

hominy (hom' i ni) [N. Am.-Ind.], *n.* Maize hulled and coarsely ground, boiled with water or milk for food.

homish [HOME (1)]. **hommack** [HUMMOCK].

homo (hō' mō) [L.], *n.* (*pl. homines*) (*Zool.*) Man, the genus of which man is the only species. ***homo sapiens,*** *n.* Man as a species.

homo-, hom- [Gr. *homos*, same], *comb. form.* Noting likeness or sameness.

homobaric (hō mō băr' ik) [BARIC (1)], *a.* Of uniform weight.

homoblastic (hō mō blăs' tik) [Gr. *blastos*, a germ], *a.* Derived from the same kind of cells.

homocentric (hō mō sen' trik), *a.* Concentric.

homocercal (hō mō sĕr' kål) [Gr. *kerkos*, a tail], *a.* Equally lobed, as the tail of the whiting; having an equally-lobed tail.

homochromy (hō mō krō' mi), *n.* (*Zool.*) The resemblance of an animal's colour to the colour of its surroundings.

homodermic (hō mō dĕr' mik) [DERM], *a.* (*Biol.*) Derived from the same primary blastoderm or germ-layer. **homodermatous, homodermous,** *a.* (*Zool.*) Having the skin or integument structurally uniform.

homodont (hō' mō dont) [Gr. *odontos*, tooth], *a.* (*Zool.*) Having the teeth all alike or nearly alike, opp. to heterodont.

homodromous, homodromal (hō mō drŏm' ůs, -ål) [Gr. *dromos*, running], *a.* (*Bot.*) Turning in the same direction, as leaf spirals; (*Mech.*) having the power and the weight moving in the same direction on the same side of the fulcrum. **homodromy,** *n.*

homœo- [Gr. *homoios*, of the same kind, similar], *comb form.* **homœomorphous** (hom i ȯ môr' fůs) [Gr. *morphē*, shape], *a.* Similar in form and structure (esp. of crystals differing in chemical composition). **homœomorphism,** *n.*

homœopathy (hom i-, hō mi op' å thi) [Gr. *homoiopatheia*], *n.* The system which aims at curing diseases by administering in small doses medicines which would produce in healthy persons symptoms similar to those they are designed to remove. **homœopath** (hom' i-, hō' mi ȯ păth), *n.* A homœopathist. **homœopathic** (-păth' ik), *a.* Belonging to homœopathy; (*fig.*) infinitesimally small, like a dose given in homœopathy. **homœopathically,** *adv.* **homœopathist** (-op' å thist), *n.* One who practises or believes in homœopathy.

homœoplastic (hom i ȯ plăs' tik) [PLASTIC], *a.* (*Path.*) Similar in structure to the surrounding tissue (of tumours, etc.).

homœostasis (hom i os' tå sis) [Gr. *stasis*, standing still], *n.* The keeping of an even level. **homœostatic** (hom i ō stăt' ik), *a.*

homœozoic (hom' i ȯ zō' ik) [Gr. *zōē*, life], *a.* Containing similar forms of life (of regions of the earth).

homogamous (hȯ mog' å můs) [HOMO-, Gr. *gamos*, marriage], *a.* (*Bot.*) Having all the florets of a *capitulum* hermaphrodite; having the stamens and pistils ripe at the same time.

homogeneous, homogeneal (hom ȯ jē' ni ůs, -ål) [Gr. *homogenēs* (*genos*, kind)], *a.* Composed of the same or similar parts or elements; of the same kind or nature throughout; (*Math.*) having all its terms of the same degree; commensurable. **homogeneously,** *adv.* **homogeneousness, homogeneity** (-nē′ i ti), *n.*

homogenesis (hom ō jen′ ė sis), *n.* (*Biol.*) Reproduction characterized by the likeness of the offspring to the parent and correspondence in the course of its development.

homogenetic (hom ō jė net′ ik), *a.* (*Biol.*) Pertaining to or characterized by homogenesis; corresponding in structure so as to show community of descent; (*Geol.*) similar in structural relations probably owing to community of origin. **homogenetical, homogenous** (hȯ moj′ ė nŭs), *a.* **homogenist** (hȯ moj′ ė nist), *n.* One who believes in community of origin. **homogenize,** *v.t.* **homogeny,** *n.*

homograph (hom′ ō grăf), *n.* (*Philol.*) A word which has the same form as another, but a different origin and meaning; a method of telegraphic signalling.

homoio- [HOMŒO-].

homoiousian (hom oi ou′ zi ăn) [Gr. *homoiousios* (HOMŒO-, *ousia*, essence)], *a.* Having a similar nature or substance. *n.* One who asserted that the Son of God is of a substance similar to but not the same as that of the Father [cp. HOMOOUSIAN].

homologate (hȯ mol′ ō gāt) [late L. *homologātus*, p.p. of *homologāre*, Gr. *homologein*], *v.t.* To admit, to concede; to approve, to confirm. **homologation** (-gā′ shŭn), *n.*

homologous (hȯ mol′ ō gŭs) [Gr. *homologos* (HOMO-, *logos*, ratio)], *a.* Having the same relative position, proportion, value, structure, etc. **homological** (-loj′ i kăl), *a.* Characterized by homology; homologous. **homologically,** *adv.* **homologize** (hȯ mol′ ō jīz), *v.t.* To be homologous. *v.t.* To make homologous. **homologue** (hom′ ō log), *n.* Something that is homologous; (*Biol.*) the same organ in different animals under every variety of form and function. **homology** (hȯ mol′ ō ji), *n.* Correspondence; (*Biol.*) identity of relation between parts developed from the same embryonic structures, as the arm of a man, the foreleg of a quadruped, and the wing of a bird.

homologumena (hom ō lō gū′ mė nȧ) [Gr. *homologoumena*, neut. pl. p.p. of *homologein*, see HOMOLOGATE], *n.pl.* Those books of the New Testament the canonicity of which was accepted at once.

homomorphic, homomorphous (hom ō môr′ fik, -fŭs) [Gr. *morphē*, shape], *a.* Analogous, identical or closely similar in form. **homomorphism,** *n.*

homonomous (hȯ mon′ ō mŭs) [Gr. *homonomos* (*nomos*, law)], *a.* (*Biol.*) Subject to the same law of growth. **homonomy,** *n.*

homonym (hom′ ō nim) [late L. *homōnymum*, Gr. *homōnumon* (HOMO-, *onuma*, name)], *n.* A word having the same sound and perhaps the same spelling as another, but differing in meaning. **homonymic** (-nim′ ik), **homonymous** (hȯ mon′ i mŭs), *a.* **homonymously,** *adv.* **homonymy,** *n.* The state of being homonymous; a sameness of name with difference of meaning; ambiguity.

homoousian (hom ō ou′ zi ăn) [Gr. *homoousios* (*ousia*, essence)], *a.* Consubstantial, of the same substance or essence, opposed to homoiousian. *n.* One who held the second Person of the Trinity to be of the same substance as the Father, an orthodox Trinitarian.

homophone (hom′ ō fōn) [Gr. *homophōnos* (*phonē*, sound)], *n.* A letter or word agreeing in sound with another, but having a different meaning, as *heir* and *air*. **homophonic** (-fon′ ik), *a.* (*Mus.*) Having the same pitch; in unison, opp. to polyphonic. **homophonous** (hȯ mof′ ō nŭs), *a.* Having the same sound; homophonic. **homophony,** *n.* Identity of sound; (*Mus.*) unison.

homoplastic (hom ō plăs′ tik), *a.* (*Biol.*) Similar in structure though not homogenetic. **homoplasmy** (hom ō plăz′ mi), **homoplasy** (hȯ mop′ lȧ si), *n.*

homoptera (hȯ mop′ tėr ȧ) [Gr. *pteron*, wing], *n.pl.* (*Ent.*) A sub-order of hemiptera having the wings uniform throughout.

homosexual (hom ō sek′ sū ăl), *a.* and *n.* Sexually attracted by those of the same sex. **homosexuality** (-ăl′ i ti), *n.*

homotaxis (hom ō tăk′ sis) [Gr. *taxis*, arrangement], *n.* (*Geol.*) Arrangement of strata in different localities in the same relative position in the geological series. **homotaxial, -eous, -ic,** *a.* **homotaxially,** *adv.*

homotonous (ho mot′ ō nŭs) [Gr. *tonos*, TONE], *a.* Of the same tenor or tone; equable. **homotonously,** *adv.* **homotony,** *n.*

homotopy (hȯ mot′ ō pi) [Gr. *topos*, place], *n.* (*Biol.*) Repetition of the ontogenetic changes in an organism in a sequence corresponding to that in which they occurred in the parent. **homotopic** (hom ō top′ ik), *a.*

homotropal, -ropous (hȯ mot′ rō păl, -pŭs) [Gr. *-tropos*, turning], *a.* Turning in the same direction; (*Bot.*) having the radicle turned towards the hilum (of seeds).

homotype (hom′ ō tīp) *n.* (*Biol.*) A part or organ having the same structure or relative position to that of another. **homotypal, -pic, -pical** (hom′ ō tī păl, -tip′ ik, -ăl), *a.* **homotypy** (hom′ ō tī pi, hȯ mot′ i pi), *n.*

homunculus, homuncle (hȯ mŭng kū′ lŭs, -mŭng′ kėl) [L. *homunculus*, dim. of HOMO], *n.* A little man; a dwarf, a manikin. **homuncular,** *a.*

homy [HOME (1)].

hone (1) (hōn) [A.-S. *hān* (cp. Icel. *hein*)], *n.* A stone for giving an edge to a cutting tool. *v.t.* To sharpen on a hone.

***hone** (2) (hōn) [perh. from O.F. *hogner*, from *hon*, a cry, a complaint], *v.i.* To moan, to whine; to pine.

honest (on′ ėst) [O.F. *honeste*, L. *honestus*, from *honos*, HONOUR], *a.* Upright, fair, truthful, trustworthy in dealings, business, or conduct; just, equitable; open, frank, candid, sincere, honourable; chaste, virtuous (of women); unimpeached, unstained; worthy. **to make an honest woman of:** To marry (a seduced woman). **to make, turn an honest penny:** (*colloq.*) To seize an opportunity to make profit. **honest to goodness:** Absolutely genuine. **honestly,** *adv.* **honesty,** *n.* The quality or state of being honest; integrity, sincerity, uprightness; chastity; a cruciferous garden plant, *Lunaria biennis*, bearing flat, round, semi-transparent seed-pods.

honey (hŭn′ i) [A.-S. *hunig* (cp. Dut. and G. *honig*, Icel. *hunang*)], *n.* A sweet viscid product collected from plants by bees, and largely used as an article of food; (*fig.*) sweetness; a term of endearment. **v.t.* To speak fondly to; to coax. *v.i.* To use endearing language; to talk or behave fondly. **honey-bag,** *n.* The receptacle for honey in a bee. **honey-bear,** *n.* A South American quadruped, also called the kinkajou, which destroys the nests of bees. **honey-bee,** *n.* A bee that produces honey. **honey-buzzard,** *n.* A British raptorial bird, *Pernis apivora*, which feeds on the larvæ of bees and wasps. **honeycomb,** *n.* A waxy substance formed in hexagonal cells by the hive-bee, for the reception of honey and for the eggs and larvæ; anything similarly perforated, esp. flaws in a metal casting. *v.t.* To fill with holes or cavities. **honey-dew,** *n.* A saccharine substance found on the leaves of some plants; (*fig.*) something extremely sweet, nectar; a kind of tobacco moistened with molasses and pressed into cakes. **honey-guide,** *n.* The genus *Indicator*, South African cuckoos, whose cry is supposed to indicate the nests of bees. **honey-harvest,** *n.* Honey collecting, the time for collecting honey. ***honey-heavy,** *a.* Heavy and somewhat oppressive. **honey-locust,** *n.* A large

American tree, *Gleditschia triacanthus*, of the family *Leguminosæ*. **honeymoon,** *n.* The first month after marriage; the period immediately following marriage spent by the married couple by themselves away from home. *v.i.* To spend the honeymoon (in, at, etc.). **honey-mouthed,** *a.* Sweet and smooth in speech. **honey-stalk,** *n.* The flower of clover. **honeysuckle,** *n.* The genus *Lonicera*, esp. *L. periclymenum*, the woodbine, a wild climbing plant with sweet-scented flowers; (*Austral.*) any one of the Banksia shrubs. **honey-sweet,** *a.* Very dear; sweet as honey. **honey-tongued,** *a.* Smooth in speech; honey-mouthed. **honey-wort,** *n.* Two cultivated plants of the borage family, *Cerinthe major* and *C. minor*, both attractive to bees. **honeyed,** *a.* ***honeyedness,** *n.* Sweetness. **honeyless,** *a.* Destitute of honey.

hong (hong) [Chin. *hang*, row, series], *n.* The Chinese name for a foreign factory, warehouse, or other mercantile establishment.

honied [HONEYED, see HONEY].

Honiton lace [LACE].

honk (hongk) [imit.], *n.* The cry of the wild goose; any similar cry or noise.

honorarium (on-, hon ŏ râr' i ŭm) [late L., as foll.], *n.* A fee or payment to a professional man for his services.

honorary (on' ŏr ăr i) [L. *honorārius*, from *honos*, HONOUR], *a.* Done, made, or conferred as a mark of honour; holding a title or an office without payment or without undertaking the duties; depending on honour, not enforceable by law (of duties or obligations). ***honorificabilitudinity** [see foll.].

honour (on' ŏr) [O.F. *onor*, *honur*, L. *honōrem*, nom. *honos*], *n.* Respect, esteem, reverence; reputation, glory, distinction, a mark or token of distinction; high rank; nobleness of mind, probity, uprightness; conformity to the accepted code of social conduct; chastity, reputation of chastity (in women); (*pl.*) courteous attentions paid to guests, etc.; (*Univ., pl.*) a distinction awarded for higher proficiency than that required for a pass; one who or that which confers honour, position, etc.; an ornament; a title of address given to certain officers, as a county court judge, etc.; (*Golf*) the right of driving off first; (*pl.*) the four highest trump cards; *a seigniory of several manors, held under one baron or lord-paramount. *v.t.* To treat with reverence or respect; to bestow honour upon; to dignify, to glorify, to exalt; to acknowledge; to accept and pay when due (as a bill). **birthday honours** [BIRTHDAY]. **funeral** or **last honours:** Marks of respect paid to the deceased at a funeral. **military honours:** Courtesies paid by troops to a soldier or person of high rank, at funerals, weddings, toasts, etc. **honour bright:** (*colloq.*) On one's honour. **honours easy** [EASY]. **honours of war:** A distinction or privilege granted to an enemy who has surrendered on terms. **in honour of:** To celebrate. **on or upon one's honour:** A declaration pledging one's honour or reputation to the accuracy or good faith of a statement. **to do the honours:** To perform the courtesies required of a master or mistress at a dinner, reception, etc. **honour-point,** *n.* (*Her.*) The point immediately above the centre or fesse-point of a shield. **honourer,** *n.* ***honorificabilitudinity** (on ŏr if' ik ă bil' i tū din' i ti), *n.* Honourableness (often cited as the longest word in the English language).

honourable (on' ŏ ră bĕl, on' ră bĕl), *a.* Worthy of honour; illustrious, of distinguished rank, noble; conferring honour; actuated by principles of honour, upright; consistent with honour or reputation; accompanied or performed with or as with marks of honour; proceeding from a laudable cause; not base; a title of respect or distinction borne by the children of peers below the rank of marquess, maids of honour, Justices of the High Court, etc. ***honourableness,** *n.* **honourably,** *adv.*

hooch (hooch) [Alaskan], *n.* Crude alcoholic liquor.

hood (hud) [A.-S. *hōd* (cp. Dut. *hoed*, G. *hut*)], *n.* A loose covering for the head and back of the neck, separate, or an appendage to a cloak or overcoat; (*Univ.*) an appendage to an academic gown marking a degree; anything more or less resembling a hood, as the blinding-cap on a hawk, a carriage-top, a paper cornet, etc.; (*Am.*) the bonnet of a motor-car. *v.t.* To dress in a hood; to put a hood on; to blind, to cover. **hoodman,** *n.* One blindfolded in blind-man's buff. ***hoodman-blind,** *n.* Blind-man's buff. **hood-mould, -moulding,** *n.* (*Arch.*) A band or moulding over the head of a door, window, or other opening, a drip-stone. **hood-wink,** *v.t.* To blindfold; (*fig.*) to deceive, to take in. **hooded,** *a.* Covered with a hood; blinded; (*Bot.*) hood-shaped, culcullate. **hooded snake:** A snake of the *Elapidæ* family, having the power of dilating the loose skin of the neck into a kind of cowl or hood. **hoodie, hoody-crow,** *n.* The hooded crow, *Corvus cornix.* **hoodless,** *a.*

-hood [-HEAD].

hoodlum (hud' lŭm) [Am. slang, etym. unknown], *n.* A street rowdy, a hooligan, esp. one of a gang of street ruffians who flourished in San Francisco during the 'seventies and 'eighties. **hoodlumism,** *n.*

hoodoo (hoo' doo) [Negro], *n.* Bad luck; the cause of bad luck, a Jonah. *v.t.* To bring bad luck; to cast a spell on something.

hoodwink [HOOD].

hooey (hoo' i) [Onomat.], *n.* Bosh, nonsense.

hoof (hoof) [A.-S. *hōf* (Dut. *hoef*, Icel. *hōfr*, G. *huf*)], *n.* (*pl.* **hoofs, hooves**) The horny sheath covering the feet of horses, oxen, etc.; (*fig.*) an animal with hoofs; (*facet.*) a human foot; (*Geom.*) an ungula. *v.t.* To strike or attack with the hoof; (*slang*) to kick. *v.i.* To walk, to go afoot; (*slang*) to kick (out). **to hoof it:** To walk, to tramp it. **hoof-bound,** *a.* Having a painful dryness and contraction of the hoof, causing lameness. **hoof-pad,** *n.* A pad fastened on a horse-shoe to prevent injury by interference. **hoof-pick,** *n.* A pointed or hooked instrument for removing stones, etc. from a horse's hoof. **hoofed,** *a.* Furnished with hoofs.

hooh-ha (hoo' ha) [Onomat.], *n.* (*colloq.*) Fuss, noisy excitement.

hook (huk) [A.-S. *hōc* (cp. Dut. *hoek*, Icel. *haki*, G. *haken*)], *n.* A curved piece of metal or other material by which an object is caught or suspended; a bent and pointed wire, usu. barbed, for catching fish; (*fig.*) a trap, a snare; a curved instrument for cutting grass or corn, a sickle; a sharp bend; a cape, a headland; (*slang*) a catch, an imposture; an advantage. *v.t.* To catch, grasp, or hold with or as with a hook; to fasten with a hook or hooks; (*slang*) to snatch, to steal, to pilfer; (*Golf*) to drive (the ball) widely to the left; (*Football*) to pull (the ball) in with the foot in a certain manner. *v.i.* To fit or fasten (on) with or as with hooks. **by hook or by crook** [CROOK]. **hook and eye:** A metal hook and corresponding loop for fastening a dress. **Hook of Holland:** The corner of Holland projecting into the North Sea. **off the hook:** Ready-made. **off the hooks:** In a state of upset. **to drop off the hooks:** (*slang*) To die. **on one's own hook:** (*slang*) On one's own account. **to hook it or to sling one's hook:** (*slang*) To decamp; to run away. **hook-nosed,** *a.* Having an aquiline nose. **hook-pin,** *n.* An iron pin with a hooked head used in building and carpentry. **hook-up:** (*Radio.*) A radio network, a series of connected stations. **hook-worm,** *n.* A parasite infesting men and animals. **hooked** (hukt), *a.* Bent; furnished with hooks. **hookedness** (huk' ĕd nĕs), *n.* The state of being hooked. ***hooky,** *a.*

hookah (huk' ă) [Arab. *ḥuqqah*, a casket, a bowl], *n.* A tobacco-pipe in which the smoke passes through water.

hooker (huk' ĕr) [Dut. *hoeker*, from *hoek*, HOOK], *n.* A two-masted Dutch coasting or fishing vessel; a one-masted fishing smack.

hookum (hoo′ kŭm) [Hind.], *n.* A command, an order.

Hoolee (hoo′ li) [Hind. *hōlī*], *n.* The great Hindu festival in honour of Krishna.

hooligan (hoo′ li gȧn) [prob. from the name of a rowdy family (cp. Ir. *Houlihan*) in a comic song pop. in music-halls, *c.* 1885], *n.* One of a gang of street roughs given to violent attacks on persons. **hooliganism,** *n*

hoop (1) (hoop) [A.-S. *hōp* (cp. Dut. *hoep*)], *n.* A strip of wood or metal bent into a band or ring to hold the staves of casks, etc. together; a circular strip of whalebone, etc. used to expand the skirts of women's dresses; a large iron or wooden ring for a child to trundle; a small iron arch used in croquet; (*Naut.*) a hank; a band on a wooden anchor-stock; (*Mech.*) a strap round an eccentric. *v.t.* To bind or fasten with hoops; to encircle. **hoop-iron,** *n.* Flat, thin bar-iron such as is used for hooping barrels. **hoop-la** (hoop′ la), *n.* Game of winning small objects by throwing rings over them. **hoop-petticoat, -skirt,** *n.* A woman's dress expanded by means of a hoop. **hooper,** *n.* One who hoops casks; a cooper.

hoop (2), **hooping-cough** [WHOOP].

hoopoe (hoo′ pō) [earlier *hoope*, F. *huppe*, L. *upupa*, onomat.], *n.* A bird, *Upupa epops*, a rare British visitant with large crest and fine plumage.

Hoosier (hoo′ zher) [etym. unknown], *n.* (*U.S.A.*) A native of the State of Indiana.

hoot (1) (hoot) [M.E. *houten*, perh. from Scand., or imit.], *v.i.* To shout or make loud cries in derision or contempt; to cry as an owl; to make a sound like this. *v.t.* To shout (down, out, away, etc.) in contempt or derision. *n.* A cry like that of an owl; an inarticulate shout in contempt or derision. **hooter,** *n.* One who or that which hoots; a steam-whistle or siren, esp. one used to give notice to workpeople of the beginning or end of work-time.

hoot (2), **hoots** (hoot, -s) [Sc. and North.], *int.* An exclamation of disgust, impatience.

hoove (hoov) [A.-S. *hōf-*, stem of HEAVE], *n.* A disease in cattle in which the stomach is distended with gas.

hop (1) (hop) [A.-S. *hoppian* (cp. Dut. *hoppen*, Icel. and Swed. *hoppa*, G. *hopfen*)], *v.i.* (*past & p.p.* **hopped**) To spring, leap, or skip on one foot; to skip with both feet (as birds) or with all four feet (as quadrupeds); to limp; *to dance. *v.t.* To jump lightly or skip over. *n.* A jump, spring, or light leap on one foot; (*colloq.*) a dance; (*Aviat.*) a one-way flight; (*fig.*) a short run, a quick passage; a distance easily covered in a few paces. **hop, skip** (or **step**), **and a jump:** Orig. a game or athletic feat in which as much ground as possible was covered by these three movements. **to hop the twig:** (*slang*) To die; to give one's creditors the slip. **to catch on the hop:** To catch by surprise, esp. in the midst of a prank. **hop-o'-my-thumb,** *n.* A pigmy. **hopper** (1), *n.* One who hops; a hopping insect, a flea, the larva of a cheese-fly, etc.

hop (2) (hop) [M.Dut. *hoppe* (cp. G. *hopfen*)], *n.* A perennial climbing plant, *Humulus lupulus*, the mature cones of which are used in brewing. *v.t.* To impregnate with hops. *v.i.* To pick hops. **hop-back,** *n.* (*Brewing*) A vessel to receive the infusion of malt and hops. **hop-bind, -bine,** *n.* The stem of the hop. **hop-fly, -louse,** *n.* An aphis, *Phorodon humuli*, destructive of hops. **hop-picker,** *n.* One who gathers hops; a machine for this purpose. **hop-pillow,** *n.* A pillow stuffed with hops for inducing sleep. **hop-pocket,** *n.* A coarse sack for hops; a half-sack, or 168 lb., a measure of capacity for hops. **hop-pole,** *n.* A training pole for hops. **hop-tree,** *n.* An American shrub, *Ptelea trifoliata*, the bitter fruit of which is used as a substitute for hops. **hop-yard, -garden,** *n.* A field where hops are grown. **hopper** (3), *n.* A hop-picker. **hoppy,** *a.* Tasting of hops. **hop-vine,** [HOP-BIND].

hope (1) (hōp) [A.-S. *hopa* (cp. Dut. *hoop*, Swed. *hopp*, G. *hoffe*), whence *hopian*, to hope], *n.* An expectant desire; confidence in a future event; a ground for expectation, trust or confidence; that in which one confides; the object of one's desires or expectations. *v.i.* To have confidence; to trust with confidence; to look (for) with desire or expectation, to trust (in). *v.t.* To expect with desire; to look forward to with trust; (*colloq.*) to think, to suppose; *to expect. **to hope against hope:** To cling to a slight chance. **hopeful,** *a.* Full of hope; giving rise to hope. **young hopeful:** A youth or girl regarded as the hope of a family. **hopefully,** *adv.* **hopefulness,** *n.* **hopeless,** *a.* Destitute of hope, despairing; affording no hope, desperate. **hopelessly,** *adv.* **hopelessness,** *n.* **hopingly,** *adv.*

hope (2) [FORLORN HOPE].

hope (3) (hōp) [A.-S. *-hop*, in *fennhop*, etc.], *n.* (*Local*) A small enclosed valley, the upper part of a dale (often used in place-names).

hoplite (hop′ līt)[Gr. *hoplitēs*, from *hoplon*, weapon], *n.* (*Gr. Ant.*) A heavy-armed Greek soldier.

hopper [HOP (1 and 2)].

hopper (3) (hop′ er), *n.* A funnel-shaped vessel for feeding material to a machine; a funnel or trough for passing grain, etc. through a mill into vehicles; a barge for receiving and dumping mud, sand, etc. from a dredging-machine; a tilting bottom in a barge, car, etc., for discharging refuse. **hopper-boy,** *n.* A revolving rake in a grinding-mill, drawing the meal over a discharge-opening in the floor.

hopple (hop′ ėl) [etym. doubtful, cp. the later HOBBLE], *v.t.* To fetter (a horse, cattle, etc.) by tying the feet together. *n.* A shackle or fetter used for this purpose.

hopscotch (hop′ skoch) [HOP (1)], *n.* A children's game in which a stone is driven by the foot of a player hopping from one compartment to another of a figure scotched or traced on the ground.

horal (hôr′ ȧl), **horary** (hôr′ ȧ ri) [late L. *hōrālis*, *hōrārius*, from *hōra*, HOUR], *a.* Relating to an hour; pertaining to the time by the clock; occurring every hour; *lasting for an hour.

Horatian (hȯ rā′ shi ȧn) [L. *Horātiānus*, from *Horātius*, Horace], *a.* Pertaining to or resembling the Latin poet Horace or his poetry.

***hord** [HOARDING].

horde (hôrd) [F., from Turk. *ordū*, camp (cp. URDU)], *n.* A nomadic tribe or clan; a gang, a multitude (usu. in contempt). *v.i.* To live in hordes; to gather together in gangs.

Hordeum (hôr′ dė ŭm) [L., barley], *n.* (*Bot.*) A genus of grasses typified by wild barley. **hordeaceous** (-dā′ shŭs), *a.* **hordeiform** (-dē i fôrm), *a.* **hordein** (hôr′ dė in), *n.* (*Chem.*) A protein found in barley grains.

horehound (hôr′ hound) [A.-S. *hārehūne* (*hār*, HOAR, *hūne*, etym. unknown)], *n.* A labiate herb, *Marrubium vulgare*, with woolly stem and leaves and aromatic juice, used as a tonic and a remedy for colds, etc.; applied to various allied herbs.

horizon (hȯ rī′ zȯn) [F., from late L. *horīzontem*, nom. *-zōn*, Gr. *horizōn*, from *horizein*, to bound, from *horos*, a limit], *n.* The circular line where the sky and the earth seem to meet, called the **apparent, sensible,** or **visible horizon,** as distinguished from the great circle parallel to it called the **celestial, geometrical, rational,** or **true horizon,** the centre of which is the centre of the earth; (*fig.*) the boundary of one's mental vision, experience, etc. **artificial horizon:** A small trough containing mercury, the surface of which affords a reflected image of a heavenly body, used in taking altitudes, etc. **horizonless,** *a.*

horizontal (hor i zon′ tȧl) [from prec.], *a.* Pertaining or relating to the horizon; situated at or near the horizon; parallel to the horizon, level, flat, plane; measured or contained in a plane of the horizon. *n.* A horizontal line, plane, bar, etc.;

a Tasmanian shrub with horizontal branches. **horizontality** (-tăl′ i ti), *n.* **horizontally,** *adv.*

hormone (hôr′ mōn) [from Gr. *hormaein,* to arouse, to stimulate], *n.* (*Physiol.*) A secretion from an internal gland having the property of stimulating vital and functional activity.

horn (hôrn) [A.-S. (cp. Icel., Dan., Swed., and G. *horn;* cogn. with L. *cornu,* Gr. *keras*)], *n.* A projecting bony growth, usu. pointed and in pairs on the heads of certain animals; the substance of which such growths are composed; anything made of or like a horn in shape, as a powder-flask or a drinking-vessel; an organ or growth resembling horns, as the feeler of a snail, etc.; an extremity of a curved object, as of the moon when on the wane or waxing; a wing of an army; the imaginary projection on the forehead of a cuckold; a branch of a lake, inlet of the sea or stream; (*Mus.*) a metal wind instrument, orig. of horn; (*fig.*) one of the alternatives of a dilemma. *v.t.* To furnish with horns; (*fig.*) to cuckold; to gore; (*Shipbuilding*) to square (a vessel's frame with the line of the keel). **to horn in:** (*Am. slang*) To push in, to intrude. **English horn:** A kind of oboe. **French horn:** A keyed instrument of the trumpet kind. **to draw** or **pull in one's horns:** To repress one's ardour; to curtail one's expenses; to draw back, to check oneself. **horn-bar,** *n.* A cross-bar in a carriage. **horn-beak,** *n.* The garfish. **horn-blower,** *n.* One who plays a horn. **horn-book,** *n.* An alphabet with the Lord's Prayer, etc., formerly printed on a slip of paper, fastened to a board, and covered with horn to prevent its being torn; hence, a primer. **horn-core,** *n.* A process of the frontal bone supporting permanent horns as distinct from antlers. **horn-distemper,** *n.* A disease of cattle affecting the horn-core. **horn-fish,** *n.* The garfish; the sand-pike, and other fishes. **horn-foot, -ed,** *a.* Having a hoof; hoofed. **horn-mad,** *a.* Furiously mad (like horned beasts, used by Shakespeare with allusion to cuckoldom). **horn-maker,** *n.* A maker of horns, esp. for drinking; (*fig.*) a cuckolder. ***horn-mercury,** *n.* Calomel. **horn of plenty:** A cornucopia. **horn-owl** [HORNED OWL]. **hornpipe,** *n.* An old wind instrument; a lively dance, usu. for one person, popular among sailors; the music for such a dance. **horn-plate,** *n.* An axle-guard, on a railway carriage, locomotive, etc. **horn-shavings,** *n.pl.* Scrapings from horns used for manure. ***horn-silver,** *n.* Chloride of silver, from its horn-like appearance when fused. **horned,** *a.* Furnished with horns; (*fig.*) having projections or extremities like horns. **horned horse:** The gnu. **horned owl:** One of several species of owl having large ear-tufts and called long-eared owls. **horned screamer:** A South American grallatorial bird, *Palamedea cornuta,* with a horn on its forehead, and a piercing voice. **horned snake** or **viper:** An Indian or African viper of the genus *Cerastes* with horns over the eyes. **hornedness,** *n.* **horner,** *n.* One who works or deals in horns; one who blows a horn; *a cuckold-maker. **hornful,** *n.* As much as a drinking-horn will hold. **hornish,** *a.* **hornless,** *a.* **horny,** *a.* Made of or like horn; callous; having or abounding in horns. **hornily,** *adv.* **horniness,** *n.*

hornbeam (hôrn′ bēm), *n.* A small tree, *Carpinus betulus,* yielding tough timber; other trees of the same family.

hornbill (hôrn′ bil), *n.* The genus *Bucerotidæ,* birds with bone-crested bills from India and the Indian Archipelago.

hornblende (hôrn′ blend) [G. *horn,* (HORN, BLENDE)], *n.* (*Min.*) A dark-coloured mineral consisting of silica, magnesia, lime, and iron. **hornblende schist:** A metamorphic schistose rock composed principally of hornblende.

hornet (hôr′ nėt) [A.-S. *hyrnet* (cp. G. *hornisse*)], *n.* A large social wasp, *Vespa crabro,* or the American *V. maculata,* with a formidable sting; (*fig.*) a person who makes himself very disagreeable. **to stir up a hornets' nest:** To excite (often unintentionally) the animosity of a large number of people.

Hornie (hôr′ ni), *n.* (*Sc.*) The devil. usu. **Auld Hornie.**

horning (hôr′ ning), *n.* The appearance of the moon when in the form of a crescent; (*Sc. Law*) a summons to a debtor to pay within a certain time, under pain of imprisonment.

hornito (hôr nē′ tō) [Sp., dim. of *horno,* ult. from L. *furnus,* oven, see FURNACE], *n.* A small smoking mound or fumerole produced by volcanic action.

hornslate (hôrn′ slāt), *n.* Grey siliceous stone.

hornstone (hôrn′ stōn), *n.* Chert.

hornwork (hôrn′ wĕrk), *n.* (*Fort.*) An outwork consisting of two half-bastions and a curtain.

hornwrack (hôrn′ răk), *n.* A sea-mat.

horo- [Gr. *hōra,* a season, an hour], *comb form.* Pertaining to times or seasons, or to the measurement of time. **horography** (hŏ rog′ ră fi) [-GRAPHY], *n.* The art of constructing clocks, watches, etc.

horologe (hor′ ŏ lōj) [O.F., from L. *hōrologium,* Gr. *hōrologion* (HORO-, *legein,* to tell)], *n.* An instrument for showing the hour, a time-piece. **horologer** (hŏ rol′ ŏ jėr), ***horologiographer** (-og′ ră fėr), **horologist,** *n.* One skilled in horology; a maker of horologes. **horological** (-loj′ i kăl), *a.* ***horologiography** (hor ŏ loj i og′ ră fi), *n.* The art of constructing instruments to show the hour; an account of such instruments. **horologiographic** (-grăf′ ik), *a.* **horology** (hŏ rol′ ŏ ji), *n.* The art of measuring time, or of constructing instruments to indicate time.

horometry (hŏ rom′ ė tri), *n.* The art or practice of measuring time. **horometrical** (-met′ ri kăl), *a.*

horopito (ho rō pē′ tō) [Maori], *n.* The N. Zealand pepper tree.

horoscope (hor′ ŏ skōp) [F., from L. *hōroscopus,* Gr. *hōroskopos* (*skopos,* observer)], *n.* (*Astrol.*) An observation of the sky and the configuration of the planets at the moment of one's birth, in order to foretell one's future; a scheme of the twelve houses or signs of the zodiac, in which is marked the disposition of the heavens at a particular moment. **horoscopic, -al** (hor ŏ skop′ ik, -ăl), *a.* **horoscopy** (hŏ ros′ kŏ pi), *n.* The pretended art of predicting the future by the disposition of the stars; a horoscope.

horrent (hor′ ėnt) [L. *horrens -ntem,* pres.p. of *horrēre,* to bristle, to shudder], *a.* (*poet.*) Bristling erect, as bristles.

horrible (hor′ i bėl) [O.F., from L. *horribilis,* as prec.], *a.* Causing or tending to cause horror; dreadful, shocking, harrowing; (*colloq.*) extremely unpleasant, awful. **horribleness,** *n.* **horribly** *adv.*

horrid (hor′ id) [L. *horridus,* as prec.], *a.* Causing horror; shocking; *rough, bristly; (*colloq.*) nasty, unpleasant, frightful. **horridly,** *adv.* **horridness,** *n.*

horrify (hor′ i fī) [L. *horrificāre* (*horrēre,* to bristle, *-ficāre, facere,* to make)], *v.t.* To strike with horror; (*colloq.*) to scandalize. **horrific** (hŏ rif′ ik), *a.* **horrification** (hor′ i fi kā′ shŭn), *n.*

horripilation (hŏ rip i lā′ shŭn) [late L. *horripilātio,* from *horripilāre* (as prec., *pilus, hair*)], *n.* A sensation of a creeping or motion of the hair of the body caused by disease, terror, etc. **horripilant** (hŏ rip i lănt), *a.* **horripilate** (-lāt), *v.t.* and *i.*

horrisonant (hŏ ris′ ŏ nănt) [L. *horrēre,* to bristle, *sonans -ntem,* pres.p. of *sonāre,* to sound], *a.* Having a dreadful sound.

horror (hor′ ŏr) [O.F. *horrour,* L. *horrōrem,* nom. *-or,* as prec.], *n.* A shaking, shuddering, or shivering; dread or terror, mingled with detestation or abhorrence; that which excites terror or repulsion. **Chamber of Horrors:** A room at Mme Tussaud's waxwork exhibition devoted to famous criminals; hence (*fig.*) a place full of horrifying objects. **the horrors:** The blues; delirium tremens. **horror-stricken, -struck,** *a.* Overwhelmed with horror.

hors (ôr) [F., earlier *fors*, L. *foris*], *prep.* Outside, out of. *adv.* Out of, beyond. ***hors de combat*** (ôr dė kon ba), *a.* Out of the battle, disabled. ***hors d'œuvre*** (ôr dĕrvr), *n.* (*pl.* ***hors d'œuvres***) A dish not forming part of the regular course, served as relish before or during a meal.

horse (hôrs) [A.-S. *hors* (cp. Icel. *hross*, O.H.G. *hros*, Dut. *ros*, G. *ross*)], *n.* A solid-hoofed quadruped, *Equus caballus*, with mane and tail of long coarse hair, domesticated and employed as beast of draught and burden; the adult male of the species; (*collect.*) cavalry; a frame or other device used as a support; a vaulting-block; a wooden frame on which soldiers were made to sit astride as a punishment; a currier's trestle; a slanting board on which pressmen place sheets to be printed; other appliances of analogous use in various trades, etc.; (*Mining*) a mass of rock, clay, etc., forming an obstruction; (*Naut.*) an iron bar on which slides the sheet-block of a fore-and-aft sail; a foot-rope beneath a yard or bowsprit; a breast-rope in the chains; (*slang*) work charged for before being executed; also called 'dead horse.' *v.t.* To provide with a horse or horses; to cover (said of a stallion); (*fig.*) to carry on the back; to put astride of anyone for flogging. *v.i.* To mount or ride on horseback. **clothes-horse** [CLOTHES]. **horse and foot:** Cavalry and infantry. **light horse:** Mounted soldiers lightly accoutred. **to flog a dead horse** [DEAD]. **to mount** or **ride the high horse:** To be arrogant; to put on consequential airs. **to take horse:** To mount for the purpose of riding; to travel on horseback. **horse artillery:** Field artillery with the gunners mounted. **horseback,** *n.* The back of a horse. **on horseback:** Mounted on a horse. **horse-bean,** *n.* A coarse variety of bean, *Faba vulgaris*, used for feeding horses. **horse-block,** *n.* A block or stage to assist a person in mounting on horseback. **horse-boat,** *n.* A ferry-boat drawn by horses; a boat for transporting horses across water. **horse-box,** *n.* A closed van or car for taking horses by rail; a compartment for horses on ship-board, or a box-like structure for slinging horses on board; (*facet.*) a large pew. **horse-boy,** *n.* A stable-boy. **horse-breaker,** *n.* One whose occupation it is to break in or train horses. **horse-car,** *n.* A tram-car drawn by a horse or horses. **horse-chestnut,** *n.* A large variety of chestnut, *Æsculus hippocastanum*, with coarse, bitter fruit. **horse-chanter** [CHANT], *n.* A dealer who buys up worthless horses and disposes of them by artifice. **horse-cloth,** *n.* A cloth or rug to cover a horse. **horse-coper,** *n.* A horse-dealer. **horse-coping,** *n.* **horse-dealer,** *n.* One who deals in horses. **horse-doctor,** *n.* A veterinary surgeon. **horse-drench,** *n.* A dose of liquid physic for a horse; the apparatus by which it is administered. **horse-faced,** *a.* Having a long, coarse face. **horse-flesh,** *n.* The flesh of the horse, used as food; (*collect.*) horses. **horse-fly,** *n.* Any large fly that irritates horses. **Horse Guards:** The brigade of cavalry of the English household troops, esp. the Third Regiment, the Royal Horse Guards; their barracks or headquarters; formerly, the office of the Commander-in-Chief in Whitehall; the military authorities of the War Department. **horsehair,** *n.* The long hair of the mane and tail of horses. *a.* Made of this. **horse-hoe,** *n.* A hoe drawn by horses. **horse-jockey,** *n.* A professional rider of racehorses; a trainer of horses; a horse-dealer. **horse-knacker** [KNACKER]. **horse-latitudes,** *n.pl.* The region of calms on the northern edge of the north-east trade winds, said to be so called because the old navigators frequently threw overboard there the horses they were carrying to America and the West Indies. **horse-laugh,** *n.* A loud, coarse laugh. **horse-leech,** *n.* A farrier; a large kind of leech which is often drawn in by horses and cattle when drinking; (*fig.*) a rapacious person, a blood-sucker (in alln. to Prov. xxx. 15). **horse-litter,** *n.* A litter borne by horses. **horse-load,** *n.* A load for a horse. **horse-mackerel,** *n.* The cavally, *Caranx trachurus*, and other fishes. **horseman,** *n.* One skilled in riding or the management of horses; *a horse-soldier; a variety of the domestic pigeon. **horsemanship,** *n.* **horse-marine,** *n.* One of a mythical body of troops; one out of his element. **tell it to the horse-marines:** A retort to one telling an incredible story. **horse-mill,** *n.* A mill turned by horse-power. **horse-milliner,** *n.* One who deals in fancy trappings and decorations for horses. **horse-play,** *n.* Rough, boisterous play. **horse-pond,** *n.* A pond for watering and washing horses. **horse-power,** *n.* The power a horse can exert, used as a unit of measurement of the rate of doing mechanical work, equivalent to 33,000 foot-pounds per minute; mechanical power expressed in such units; a mechanical contrivance by which a horse is made to drive machinery. **horse-race,** *n.* A race between horses with riders. **horse-radish,** *n.* A plant, *Cochlearia armoracia*, with a pungent, acrid root, used as a condiment. **horse-rake,** *n.* A rake drawn by horses. **horse-road, -way,** *n.* A road or way by which horses may travel. **horse-sense,** *n.* (*colloq.*) Rough, practical common sense. **horseshoe,** *n.* A shoe for horses; anything resembling this in shape. *a.* Shaped like this. **horse-shoeing,** *n.* The act or occupation of shoeing horses. **horse-stinger,** *n.* (*prov.*) A dragon-fly. **horse-tail,** *n.* The tail of a horse; this used as a Turkish standard or token of rank; a plant of the cryptogamous genus *Equisetum*, with whorls of branches like the hairs in a horse's tail. **horse-whip,** *n.* A whip for driving horses. *v.t.* To flog with a horsewhip; to thrash. **horsewoman,** *n.* A woman skilled in riding and managing horses. **horseless,** *a.* **horsy,** *a.* Of the nature of a horse; pertaining to or fond of horses or horse-racing; (*fig.*) coarse in behaviour. **horsily,** *adv.* **horsiness,** *n.*

hortative (hôr' tȧ tiv) [L. *hortātīvus*, from *hortārī*, to EXHORT], **hortatory** (hôr' tȧ tòr i), *a.* Giving or containing advice or encouragement. **hortation** (hôr tā' shŭn), *n.*

horticulture (hôr' ti kŭl chŭr) [L. *hortus*, garden, CULTURE], *n.* The art of cultivating or managing gardens. **horticultural** (-kŭl' tū rȧl), *a.* **horticulturist,** *n.*

hortus siccus (hôr' tŭs sik' ŭs) [L., dry garden, see prec.], *n.* A collection of dried plants arranged systematically.

hosanna (hō zăn' ȧ) [late L. and Gr., from Heb. *hōshī 'āh-nnā*, save, we pray], *n.* An acclamatory prayer for blessing; a shout of praise and adoration.

hose (hōz) [A.-S. *hosa* (cp. Dut. *hoos*, Icel. *hosa*, G. *hose*)], *n.* (*collect.*) Orig., close-fitting breeches or trousers reaching to the knees; stockings; (*as sing. with pl.* **hoses**) flexible tubing for water or other fluid, as for fire-engine service; the part of a spade, golf-club, etc., in which the handle is inserted. *v.t.* To water or drench with a hose; to provide with hose. **half-hose,** *n.* Socks. **hose-man,** *n.* A fireman who works the hose. **hose-pipe,** *n.* **hose-cart, -truck,** *n.* Vehicles for carrying hose. **hose-reel,** *n.* A drum (usu. on a cart or truck) for carrying hose; the vehicle itself. **hoseless,** *a.*

hosier (hō' zhėr), *n.* One who deals in hosiery. **hosiery,** *n.* (*collect.*) Stockings and other under-clothing; a factory for such goods; the shop or business of a hosier.

hospice (hos' pis) [F., from L. *hospitium*, from *hospes -pitis*, guest], *n.* A convent or other place for the reception and entertainment of travellers on some difficult or dangerous road or pass, as among the Alps; a home for the needy or afflicted.

hospitable (hos' pi tȧ bėl, *incorr.* hos pit' ȧbl) [F., from late L. *hospitāre*, to receive as a guest, as prec.], *a.* Entertaining or disposed to entertain strangers or guests with kindness. **hospitableness,** *n.* **hospitably,** *adv.* ***hospitage,** *n.* Hospitality; a place of hospitality. **hospitality** (hos pi tăl' i ti), *n.* Liberal entertainment of strangers or guests.

hospital (hos' pi tȧl) [O.F., from late L. *hospitāle*, from L. pl. *hospitālia*, as HOSPICE], *n.* *A place of shelter or entertainment, a hospice; an institution for the reception and treatment of the sick or injured; applied to some almshouses, orphanages, and other charitable foundations. **hospital fever:** A kind of typhus fever caused by the effluvia from diseased bodies in hospitals. **Hospital Saturday** or **Sunday:** A day set apart for the collection of money in support of hospitals. **cottage hospital,** *n.* A hospital of moderate size without a resident medical staff. **Lock hospital,** *n.* A hospital for the treatment of venereal diseases.

hospitality [HOSPITABLE].

hospitalize (hos′ pit ȧ līz), *v.t.* To send to hospital; to admit for hospital treatment. **hospitalization,** *n.*

hospitaller (hos′ pi tȧ lĕr), *n.* One residing in a hospital for the reception of the poor or strangers; (*Hist.*) one of a religious brotherhood whose office was to relieve the poor, strangers, and the sick. **Knights Hospitallers:** A military and charitable religious brotherhood established in the Middle Ages, esp. the Knights Hospitallers of St. John of Jerusalem founded *c.* 1048.

hospitium [HOSPICE].

hospodar (hos′ pȯ dar) [Slav.], *n.* Lord, a title borne by the princes or governors of Wallachia and Moldavia.

host (1) (hōst) [O.F. *hoste* (F. *hôte*), L. *hospitem*, nom. *-pes*, a host, a guest], *n.* One who entertains another; the landlord of an inn; (*Biol.*) an animal or plant on which another is parasitic. ******v.i.* To take up one's abode, to lodge. ******v.t.* To lodge, to entertain. **to reckon without one's host:** To overlook important considerations. **hostess,** *n.* A female host; the landlady of an inn or hotel. **air-hostess,** *n.* One employed to attend to the comfort of travellers on passenger planes.

host (2) (hōst) [O.F., from L. *hostem*, nom. *-tis*, stranger, enemy], *n.* An army; a great number, a multitude. **the heavenly host** or **host of heaven:** The angels and archangels; (*fig.*) the stars, planets, etc. **Lord of Hosts:** Jehovah. ***hosting,** *n.* A mustering of armed men; a military expedition, a foray.

host (3) (hōst) [M.E. *oste*, O.F. *oiste*, L. *hostia*, sacrificial victim], *n.* The consecrated bread or wafer used in the Eucharist. ***hostie,** *n.* The host.

hostage (hos′ tȧj) [O.F. (F. *otage*), ult. from L. *obsidātus*, hostageship, from *obses obsidis*, a hostage], *n.* A person given in pledge for the performance of certain conditions or for the safety of others. **hostages to fortune:** Those dearest to one, one's wife and children. **hostageship,** *n.*

hostel (hos′ tėl) [O.F., as HOSPITAL], *n.* An inn; a house or extra-collegiate hall for the residence of students, etc.; a place of residence not run commercially. ***hosteler,** *n.* An inn-keeper, an ostler; a student in a hostel. **hostelry,** *n.* An inn. **Youth Hostel,** *n.* One of a number of cheap hostels established throughout the country at which young people hiking can be accommodated for a limited period.

hostess [HOST (1)].

***hostie** [HOST (3)].

hostile (hos′ tīl) [L. *hostilis*, from *hostis*, HOST (2)], *a.* Pertaining to an enemy; showing enmity; unfriendly; inimical. **hostilely,** *adv.* **hostility** (hos til′ i ti), *n.* Enmity; antagonism; state of war; (*pl.*) acts of war.

***hosting** [HOST (2)]. **hostler** [OSTLER].

hot (hot) [A.-S. *hāt* (cp. Dut. *heet*, Icel. *heitr*, G. *heiss*)], *a.* Having a high temperature; having much sensible heat; producing a sensation of heat; burning, acrid, pungent; (*fig.*) ardent, impetuous; passionate, fierce; (*colloq.*) exciting, excited, trying, arduous; (*Hunting*) strong (of scent); (*Dancing*) highly elaborated, florid; rutty (of animals); fresh, recent (of news); (*slang*) of stolen goods easily identifiable. *adv.* Hotly; ardently, eagerly; fiercely, angrily. *v.t.* (*past & p.p.* **hotted)** To make hot. **to give it one hot:** To punish, censure, or abuse severely. **to make a place too hot to hold one:** To make it too uncomfortable for one to stay. **hot air,** *n.* (*colloq.*) Boastful, empty talk. **hotbed,** *n.* A bed of earth heated by means of fermenting manure, used for raising early and tender plants; (*fig.*) any place which favours rapid growth (of disease, vice, etc.). **hot blast:** A heated blast of air introduced into a smelting furnace. **hot-blooded,** *a.* Excitable, irritable, passionate. **hot-brained,** *a.* Violent, hot-headed. **hot cockles:** A child's game in which one covers his eyes and guesses who strikes him. **hot dog,** *n.* A hot sausage sandwiched in a roll. **hot-flue,** *n.* A heated chamber for drying printed calicoes, etc. **hot-foot,** *adv.* Very hastily, swiftly. **hot gospeller,** *n.* (*colloq.*) A tub-thumping preacher; a revivalist. **hot-head,** *n.* **hot-headed,** *a.* Fiery, impetuous, passionate. **hot-house,** *n.* A plant-house where a relatively high artificial temperature is maintained to facilitate growth. **hot-mouthed,** *a.* Headstrong, ungovernable. **hot music:** Swing or jazz music in which the performers break free from the score and interpolate variations without losing the rhythm or melody; music that excites the dancers. **hot news:** Exciting and very up-to-the-moment news. **hot-pot,** *n.* Meat cooked with potatoes in a closed pot in an oven. **hot-press,** *n.* A machine for giving a gloss to paper or linen by pressure between heated metal plates and glazed boards. *v.t.* To subject to this process. **hot-short,** *a.* Brittle when hot (of iron). **hot-spirited,** *a.* Having a fiery spirit. **hotspur,** *n.* A man of hot and hasty valour; a hot-headed person. **hot stuff,** *adv.* (*slang*) Tricky, smart, sharp, unscrupulous; (of a woman) amorous. **hot under the collar:** Indignant, worked up. **hot-wall,** *n.* A wall with included flues to assist in ripening the fruit of trees trained against it. **hot water:** Water heated nearly to boiling-point. **to be in hot water:** To be in trouble, difficulty, or disgrace. **hot well:** The reservoir for warm water from the condenser in a condensing engine; a natural warm spring. **hotly,** *adv.* **hotness,** *n.*

hotchpot (hoch′ pot) [F. *hochepot* (*hocher*, to shake, toss together, from Teut., cp. Flem. *hutsen*, POT)], *n.* (*Law*) A general commixture of property in order to secure equal division (among heirs of an intestate person, etc.).

hotchpotch (hoch′ poch) [corr. of prec.], *n.* A confused mixture, a jumble; a dish composed of various ingredients, esp. thick broth made with mutton or other meat and vegetables.

hotel (hō tel′) [F., from O.F. *hostel*, see HOSTEL], *n.* A superior inn for the entertainment of strangers and travellers; in France, a town residence or mansion. ***hôtel-de-ville,*** *n.* A town-hall. ***hôtel dieu*** *n.* (*pl.* **hôtels-dieu**) A hospital. ***hotelier*** (hō tel′ yer), *n.* A hotel-keeper.

Hottentot (hot′ ėn tot) [Dut., prob. a stammerer (cp. *hateren*, to stammer)], *n.* A member of a great aboriginal race inhabiting the region near the Cape of Good Hope; the language spoken by this race; (*fig.*) an ignorant, uncouth, or boorish person. **Hottentot cherry:** A glabrous Cape shrub, *Cassine maurocenia*, with a cherry-like fruit.

houdah [HOWDAH].

houff [HOWFF]. **hough** [HOCK (1)].

houhere, hohere (hoo hē′ rē) [Maori], *n.* The ribbon-wood tree of N. Zealand.

hound (hound) [A.-S. *hund* (cp. Dut. *hond*, Icel. *hundr*, G. *hund*), prob. allied to L. *canis*, Gr. *kuōn*], *n.* A dog used in hunting (*usu. in comb.*, as *bloodhound, deerhound, foxhound*, etc.); one of those who chase the hares in hare and hounds; (*fig.*) a mean, contemptible fellow. *v.t.* To hunt or chase with or as with hounds; to set on the chase; to incite to pursuit; to urge or cheer (on). **hound's tongue:** A coarse, hairy plant, of the borage family, with dull-red flowers; the genus *Cynoglossum*, comprising this. **hound-fish,** *n.* A dog-fish. **houndish,** *a.*

houp-la [WHOOP].

our (our) [O.F. *hure, ure*, L. and Gr. *hōra*, season, 1our], *n.* The twenty-fourth part of a natural day, the space of sixty minutes; the point of time indicated by a clock, etc.; a particular time; (*Astron.*) fifteen degrees of longitude; (*pl.*) times appointed for work, attendance at office, etc.; (*R.-C. Ch.*) certain prayers to be said at fixed times of the day; (*Myth.*) goddesses of the seasons and hours. **at the eleventh hour:** At the last moment (with alln. to the parable of the vineyard, Matt. xx). **the hour:** The present time. **to keep good** or **regular hours:** To be home at night early or punctually. **hour-angle,** *n.* (*Astron.*) The angular distance of a heavenly body east or west of the meridian. **hour-circle,** *n.* (*Astron.*) A great circle passing through the celestial poles, a meridian (24 of which are usu. marked on the globe); a circle on an equatorial telescope indicating the hour-angle of an object. **hour-glass,** *n.* A glass having two bulbs and a connecting opening through which the sand in one bulb runs into the other, used for measuring small periods of time. **hour-hand,** *n.* That hand which shows the hour on a clock or watch, dist. from minute-hand. **hour-plate,** *n.* The dial of a clock or watch. **hourly,** *a.* Happening or done every hour; continual. *adv.* Hour by hour; frequently.

ouri (hour' i, hoor' i) [F., from Pers. *ḥūrī*, from Arab. *ḥaurā*, having gazelle-like eyes], *n.* A nymph of the Mohammedan paradise; a beautiful woman.

ouse (1) (hous) [A.-S. *hūs* (cp. Dut. *huis*, Icel. *hūs*, G. *haus*)], *n.* A building for shelter or residence; a dwelling, a place of abode; a building used for a specified purpose (as *bake-house, carriage-house, coffee-house, farm-house, hen-house, public-house, warehouse*); the abode of a religious fraternity, a monastery; the fraternity itself; a household; a family or stock, esp. a noble family; an assembly, esp. one of the legislative assemblies of a country; a quorum of a legislative body; a theatre; the audience at a place of entertainment; manner of living, table; a commercial establishment; a square on a chess-board; the game of lotto; (*Astrol.*) the station of a planet in the heavens; a twelfth part of the heavens. **like a house on fire:** Very quickly and successfully. **house and home:** An emphatic expression for home. **the House:** (*Oxford Univ.*) Christ Church; (*colloq.*) the Stock Exchange; (*euphem.*) the workhouse. **house of call:** A house where journeymen of a particular trade meet when out of employment, and where they may be engaged. **house of correction:** A prison; a penitentiary. **house of God:** A church, a place of worship. **house of ill fame:** A brothel. **house of office:** A privy. **house-to-house:** Performed at every house (of an enquiry, etc.). **to bring down the house** [BRING]. **to keep house:** To maintain or manage a household. **to keep open house:** To provide hospitality for all comers. **to keep the house:** To be confined through illness. **house-agent,** *n.* One who sells and lets houses, collects rents, etc. **house-boat,** *n.* A boat or barge with a cabin or house for living in. **house-bote** [A.-S. *bōt*, BOOT (2)], *n.* (*Law*) The amount of wood for repairs and fuel which a tenant is allowed to take from the land. **house-dog,** *n.* A dog kept to guard the house. **house-flag,** *n.* (*Naut.*) The particular flag of an owner or firm. **house-fly,** *n.* The common fly, *Musca domestica.* **house-party,** *n.* A party of guests at a country house. **house-physician** [HOUSE-SURGEON]. **house-proud,** *a.* Taking a pride in the care and embellishment of a home. **house-room,** *n.* Accommodation in a house. **house-sparrow,** *n.* The common sparrow, *Passer domesticus.* **house-steward,** *n.* One who manages the internal affairs of a large establishment. **house-surgeon, -physician,** *n.* The resident surgeon or physician in a hospital. **house-tax,** *n.* A tax on inhabited houses. **house-top,** *n.* The top or roof of a house. **house-warming,** *n.* A feast or merry-making on going into a new house. **house-work,** *n.* Work connected with housekeeping. **house-wright,** *n.* One who builds houses. ***housage,** *n.* Rent or charge for housing goods. **houseful,** *n.* As many or as much as a house will hold. **houseless,** *a.* Destitute of house or shelter.

house (2) (houz) [A.-S. *hūsian*, as prec.], *v.t.* To place or store in a house; to lodge; to shelter; (*Naut.*) to put (a gun) in a secure state or position. *v.i.* To have a lodging, to dwell; to take shelter.

housebreaker (hous' brā kėr), *n.* One who breaks into and robs houses in the daytime; a workman employed to pull down houses. **housebreaking,** *n.*

household (hous' hōld), *n.* Those who live together under the same roof and compose a family; a domestic establishment; (*pl.*) flour of the second quality, seconds. *a.* Pertaining to the house and family, domestic. **household bread:** Bread made in the house; bread of the second quality. **household gods:** (*Rom. Ant.*) The lares and penates; (*fig.*) the most valued possessions of a home. **household stuff:** The furniture, vessels, and utensils of a home. **household troops:** Troops specially employed to guard the person of the sovereign. **household word:** A familiar name or saying. **householder,** *n.* The head of a household, the occupier of a house.

housekeeper (hous' kē pėr), *n.* An upper female servant who manages the affairs of a household; a person in charge of a house, place of business, etc.; *a householder; *one who keeps at home. **housekeeping,** *n.* The care of a household; domestic economy.

***housel** (hou' zėl) [A.-S. *hūsel* (cp. Icel. *hūsl*, Goth. *hunsl*, a sacrifice)], *n.* The Eucharist. *v.t.* To administer the sacrament to; to prepare for a journey. **houseling, housling,** *n.* and *a.*

houseleek (hous' lēk), *n.* A plant with thick, fleshy leaves, *Sempervivum tectorum*, growing on the tops of walls and houses in Great Britain.

housemaid (hous' mād), *n.* A female servant employed to keep a house clean etc., esp. one in charge of reception-rooms and bedrooms. **housemaid's knee:** Inflammation of the knee-cap, due to much kneeling.

housemaster (hous' ma stėr), *n.* A master in charge of a house of residence at a boarding-school. **housemistress** (hous' mis' trės), *n.*

housewife (hous' wīf), *n.* The mistress of a family; a domestic manager; (hŭz' if), a case for holding pins, needles, and the like. **housewifely,** *a.* Pertaining to a housewife or good domestic management, thrifty. *adv.* Like a housewife, thriftily. **housewifery** (hŭ' zif ri, hous' wif ri), *n.* The business of a housewife; female management of domestic affairs.

housing (1) (hou' zing), *n.* Lodging, shelter, accommodation. **housing estate,** *n.* A planned residential area; such an estate built by a local authority.

housing (2) (hou' zing) [O.F. *houce*], *n.* A cloth covering for a horse; (*pl.*) trappings for horses.

houyhnhnm (hwin' im) [imit., coined by Swift], *n.* One of the race of horses with the finer human characteristics, in Swift's *Gulliver.*

Hova (hō' vȧ) [Malagasy], *n.* One of the dominant race or class in Madagascar.

hove (1) *past* [HEAVE].

hove (2) (hōv) [Sc., prob. from HEAVE], *v.t.* To heave, to swell, to inflate.

***hove** (3) (hōv) [etym. unknown], *v.i.* To hover; to linger, to remain about (as lying in wait).

hovel (hov' ėl, hŭv' ėl) [etym. doubtful], *n.* A shed or outhouse open at the sides; a miserable dwelling-house; a conical building enclosing the ovens in a porcelain-factory. *v.t.* To shelter in or as in a hovel; to carry up the exposed sides of (a chimney) so as to prevent smoking.

hoveller (hov'-, hŭv' ė lėr) [etym. doubtful], *n.* An unlicensed boatman or pilot, esp. one who plunders wrecks; a small coaster.

hover (hov'-, hŭv' ėr) [prob. from HOVE (3)], *v.i.* To hang or remain (over or about) fluttering in the air or on the wing; to loiter (about); (*fig.*) to be irresolute, to waver. **Hovercraft,** *n.* Patented name of an aircraft supported above land or water on a cushion of air which it generates itself.

how (1) (hou) [A.-S. *hū* (cp. Dut. *hoe*), cogn. with WHO], *adv.* In what way or manner; by what means; to what extent, degree, etc.; in what proportion; in what condition; by what name; at what price. *n.* The way, manner, means (of becoming, happening, doing, etc.). **and how!** *int.* (*slang*) And how much more! **how-do-you-do?** How are you? A conventional form of greeting. **how-d'ye-do,** *n.* (*colloq.*) An awkward situation. **howbeit** (hou bē' it), ***howbe,** *adv.* Nevertheless, however it may be. **however** (hou ev' ėr), *adv.* In whatever manner or degree; *at all events; nevertheless, notwithstanding. **howsoever** (hou sō ev' ėr), *adv.* In whatsoever manner; however; to what extent or degree soever; *at all events.

how (2) (hou) [Icel. *haugr*, prob. cogn. with HIGH], *n.* (*North.*) A hill, esp. a low one; a hillock; a barrow or tumulus.

how (3) [HOWE].

howdah (hou' dȧ) [Pers. *haudah*, Arab. *haudaj*], *n.* A seat, usu. canopied, carried on an elephant's back.

howdy (1) (hou' di) [short for HOW-D'YE-DO, see HOW (1)], *n.* (*prov.*) A greeting.

howdy (2), **-die** (hou' di) [Sc., etym. doubtful], *n.* A midwife.

howe (hou) [Sc., prob. from A.-S. *hol*, HOLE], *n.* A hollow, a valley, a dell.

however [HOW (1)].

howff (houf) [Sc., etym. doubtful], *n.* A resort, a haunt. *v.i.* To frequent a place.

howitzer (hou' it zėr) [formerly *howitz*, G. *haubitze*, Boh. *haufnice*, sling], *n.* A short, light or heavy piece of ordnance with a high trajectory and low muzzle velocity.

howk (houk) [Sc., cogn. with HOLE], *v.t.* To dig (up or out). *v.i.* To burrow.

howker [HOOKER].

howl (houl) [M.E. *houlen*, imit. (cp. Dut. *huilen*, Icel. *ȳla*, G. *heulen*, also L. *ululāre*, Gr. *hulaein*)], *v.i.* To utter a protracted hollow cry; to cry as a dog or wolf; to wail; to make a wailing sound like the wind. *v.t.* To utter in wailing or mournful tones. *n.* The cry of a wolf or dog; a protracted, hollow cry, esp. one of anguish, distress, or derision. **howler,** *n.* One who howls; a South American monkey, *Mycetes ursinus*; (*colloq.*) a ludicrous blunder. **howling,** *a.* That howls; (*fig.*) wild and dreary (of a desert, etc.); (*slang*) extreme, glaring.

howlet (hou' lėt) [perh. from F. *hulotte*, or from OWL], *n.* An owlet.

howsoever [HOW (1)].

***hox** (hoks) [earlier *hoxen*, A.-S. *hōhseono* (*hōh*, HOUGH, *seono*, SINEW)], *v.t.* To hock, to hamstring.

hoy (1) (hoi) [M.Dut. *hoei*, etym. doubtful], *n.* A one-masted coasting-vessel; a barge or lighter (usu. distinguished as *anchor-hoy*, *gun-hoy*, etc.).

hoy (2) (hoi) [cp. Dut. and Dan *hui*], *int.* An exclamation to draw attention, etc.; (*Naut.*) a hail.

hoya (hoi' ȧ) [Thomas *Hoy* (*d.* 1821), gardener], *n.* (*Bot.*) A genus of tropical climbing shrubs with pink, white, or yellow flowers, called by gardeners wax-flowers.

hoyden (hoi' dėn) [etym. doubtful], *n.* A boisterous girl; a romp; *a clown, a lout. *a.* Boisterous, bold. *v.i.* To romp roughly or indecently. **hoydenhood, hoydenism,** *n.* **hoydenish,** *a.* **hoydenishness,** *n.*

hub (1) (hŭb) [etym. unknown], *n.* The central part of a wheel from which the spokes radiate, the nave; (*fig.*) a place of central importance; a mark at which quoits are thrown; (*prov.*) the hilt of a weapon.

hub (2) (hŭb), **hubby** (hŭb' i), *n.* (*colloq.*) Husban

hubble bubble (hŭb' ėl bŭb' ėl) [onomat.], *n.* tobacco-pipe in which the smoke is drawn throug water, making a bubbling noise, a kind of hookal a bubbling noise; a hubbub, an uproar; a jabbe ing or chattering.

hubbub (hŭb' ŭb) [onomat., perh. suggested by a Irish word], *n.* A confused noise; a noisy di turbance; a tumult, an uproar. **hubbuboo,** *n.* howling; a hubbub.

hubris (hū' bris) [Gr.], *n.* Insolent pride security, arrogance. **hubristic,** *a.*

huckaback (hŭk' ȧ băk) [etym. doubtful], *n.* coarse linen or cotton cloth, with a rough surfac used for table-cloths and towels.

huckle (hŭk' ėl) [prob. dim. of obs. *huck*, whic Skeat identifies with HOCK (1), see HOUGH], *n.* T hip, the haunch. **huckle-backed, -shouldered,** (*prov.*) Round-shouldered. **huckle-bone,** *n.* T hip-bone; the knuckle-bone or astragalus in quadruped.

huckleberry (hŭk' ėl ber i) [prob. corr. of HURTL BERRY], *n.* (*Am.*) The edible fruit of species *Gaylussacia*, low shrubs of the family *Vacciniace* bearing dark-blue berries; the fruit of the blu berry and other species of the allied *Vaccinium.*

huckster (hŭk' stėr) [etym. doubtful (conn. Skeat with M.Dut. *hucken*, to stoop or bow, c Icel. *hokra* and HAWKER (2))], *n.* A retailer of sm goods, a pedlar, a hawker; a mean, trickish, m cenary fellow. *v.i.* To deal in petty goods; to ba gain, to haggle. ***hucksterage,** *n.* Petty dealin higgling, bargaining. **hucksterer,** *n.* **huckste ess,** *n.* A female huckster. **hucksterу,** *n.*

huddle (hŭd' el) [cp. L.G. *hudern*, to shelter, cover up (*hûden*, to HIDE)], *v.t.* To throw or cro (together, up, etc.) promiscuously; to do or ma hastily and carelessly; to coil (oneself up) anyho to put (on) hurriedly or anyhow. *v.i.* To gather crowd (up or together) promiscuously; to hur *n.* A confused crowd; disorder, confusion.

Hudibrastic (hū di brăs' tik) [Butler's *Hudibr* (1663–78), a satire against the Puritans], *a.* F sembling *Hudibras* in style or metre.

hue (1) (hū) [A.-S. *hīw* (cp. Swed. *hy*, Goth. *hi* form, appearance)], *n.* Colour, tint; a compou colour, esp. one in which a primary predominat **hued,** *a.* Having a particular hue (*esp. in comb.*, *light-hued*). **hueless,** *a.*

***hue** (2) (hū) [O.F. *hu* (*huer*, to shout), imit.], *n.* loud shout or cry, a clamour. **hue and cry:** (*La* A cry or general summons to pursue a felon offender; a clamour or outcry (against); a great s or alarm. **huer,** *n.* (*now chiefly Cornish*) A pers stationed on a high point to give notice of t movements of a shoal of fish.

huff (hŭf) [imit.], *v.t.* *To blow or puff (*usu. u* up); (*fig.*) to bully, to hector; (*Draughts*) to remo (one's opponent's piece) from the board when omits to capture with it; (*usu. in p.p.*) to offe *v.i.* To take offence; *to be puffed up, to blus *n.* A sudden fit of anger or petulance; (*Draugh* the act of huffing; *a boaster, a braggart. **huffer** A blusterer. **huffish, huffy,** *a.* **huffily, huffish** *adv.* **huffiness, huffishness,** *n.*

hug (hŭg) [etym. doubtful], *v.t.* (*past & p* **hugged**) To embrace closely; to clasp or sque tightly; (*fig.*) to hold fast or cling to, to cherish; congratulate (oneself); (*Naut.*) to keep close to (shore). **v.i.* To cuddle, to huddle, to lie clo *n.* A close embrace, a particular grip in wrestli **hug-me-tight,** *n.* A woollen wrap or shawl.

huge (hūj) [O.F. *ahuge*, etym. unknown], *a.* V large; enormous, immense. **hugely,** *adv.* Ir huge manner; (*colloq.*) exceedingly, extreme **hugeness,** *n.* **hugeous,** *a.* **hugeously,** *a* **hugeousness,** *n.*

hugger-mugger (hŭg' ėr mŭg' ĕr) [prob. rhym redupl. of HUG], *n.* Secrecy, privacy, disorder, c fusion. *a.* Clandestine; confused, slovenly. *a*

Secretly, clandestinely; confusedly. *v.i.* To act clandestinely; to muddle. *v.t.* To hush up.

Huguenot (hū′ gė not) [F., etym. doubtful], *n.* A name formerly applied to the Protestants of France. **Huguenotism,** *n.*

huia-bird (hoo′ yȧ bĕrd) [Maori], *n.* A New Zealand bird of the starling family.

hula (hoo′ lȧ) [native word], *n.* A Hawaiian dance performed by women. **hula hoop,** *n.* A light hoop kept in motion by swinging round the waist.

hulk (hŭlk) [A.-S. *hulc* (cp. late L. *hulka*, O.F. *hulke*, Dut. *hulk*), perh. from Gr. *holkos*, a ship that is towed, from *helkein*, to draw], *n.* The hull or body of a ship, especially an unseaworthy one; an old ship used as a store, formerly as a prison, or for other purposes; a bulky and unwieldy ship; (*fig.*) any unwieldy object or person. **the hulks:** Old dismasted ships formerly used as convict prisons. **hulking,** *a.* Bulky, unwieldy, awkward.

hull (1) (hŭl) [A.-S. *hulu*, cogn. with *helan*, to HELE], *n.* The outer covering of anything, especially of a nut or seed; the pod, shell, or husk. *v.t.* To strip the hull or husk off. **hully,** *a.* Having hulls or husks.

hull (2) (hŭl) [prob. the same as prec., but confused with HOLE (1), HOLD (3)], *n.* The body of a ship. *v.t.* To pierce the hull of with a cannon-ball. *v.i.* To float or drive to and fro helplessly, like a dismasted ship. **hull down:** So far off that only the masts and sail are visible (said of a ship).

hullabaloo (hŭl′ ȧ bȧ loo′) [redupl. of HULLO], *n.* An uproar.

hullo, -loa [HALLO].

Hulsean (hŭl′ si ȧn) [Rev. John *Hulse* (1708–1790)], *a.* Pertaining to or commemorating John Hulse. **Hulsean Lectures:** Lectures on divinity established at Cambridge University under the will of John Hulse.

hum (1) (hŭm) [imit.], *v.i.* (*past & p.p.* **hummed**) To make a prolonged murmuring sound like a bee; to sing with the lips closed; to make an inarticulate sound in speaking, from embarrassment or hesitation; (*slang*) to smell unpleasant. *v.t.* To utter in a low murmuring voice, to applaud, disapprove, etc., by emitting such a sound. *n.* A low droning or murmuring sound; the act of humming; an inarticulate expression of hesitation, disapproval, etc.; *strong ale mixed with spirits. **to hum and ha:** To hesitate in speaking; to refrain from giving a decided answer. **to make things hum:** To stir (people, etc.) into activity (prob. from the humming of a top spinning rapidly).

hum (2) (hŭm) [var. of HEM (2)], *int.* Expressing hesitation, disapproval, etc.

***hum** (3) (hŭm) [identified with prec. by Skeat], *v.t.* (*slang*) To impose upon; to humbug. *n.* A hoax, a humbug.

human (hū′ mȧn) [M.F. *humain*, L. *hūmānus*, cogn. with HOMO], *a.* Pertaining to man or mankind; having the nature, qualities or characteristics of man; of or pertaining to mankind as dist. from divine, animal, or material. *n.* (*colloq.*) A human being. **humankind,** *n.* Mankind. **humanly,** *adv.* After the manner of men; according to the knowledge or capacity of men; from the human point of view. **humanness,** *n.*

humane (hū mān′) [as prec., differentiated in meaning late], *a.* Having the feelings proper to man; tender, compassionate, kind, gentle; elevating, refining; polite, elegant; relieving distress, aiding those in danger, etc. **humane killer,** *n.* An instrument for slaughtering animals painlessly. **Humane Society,** *n.* A society for encouraging the rescue of drowning persons. **humanely,** *adv.* **humaneness,** *n.*

humanism (hū′ mȧn izm), *n.* A moral or intellectual system that regards the interests of mankind as of supreme importance, in contradistinction to individualism or theism; humanitarianism; devotion to humanity or human interests; culture derived from literature, esp. the Greek and Latin classics. **humanist,** *n.* One versed in human history or the knowledge of human nature; one versed in the humanities, esp. one of the classical scholars of Renaissance times. **humanistic** (-is′ tik), *a.*

humanitarian (hū măn i târ′ i ȧn) [foll., -ARIAN], *a.* Humane; pertaining to the humanitarians. *n.* One who professes the 'Religion of Humanity'; one who believes that Christ was a mere man; one who believes in the perfectibility of humanity; a philanthropist. **humanitarianism,** *n.*

humanity (hū măn′ i ti) [F. *humanité*, L. *hūmānitātem*, nom. *-tas*, from *hūmānus*, HUMAN], *n.* Human nature; (*collect.*) mankind, the human race; kindness, benevolence, humaneness; humanism; (*Sc.*) Latin and Latin literature, in contradistinction to divinity; *good breeding, politeness. **the humanities:** Polite learning, the study of philology, rhetoric, poetry, and the Greek and Latin classics. **humanize** (hū′ mȧ nīz), *v.t.* To render human; to give human character or expression to; to render humane. *v.i.* To become human or humane. **humanization** (-zā′ shŭn), *n.*

humble (1) (hŭm′ bėl) [O.F., from L. *humilem*, nom. *-lis*, from *humus*, the ground], *a.* Having or showing a sense of lowliness or inferiority, modest; of lowly condition, kind, dimensions, etc.; submissive, deferential. *v.t.* To lower; to bring to a state of subjection or inferiority; to abase. **humble-mouthed,** *a.* Humble in speech. **humble pie** [UMBLE]: A pie made of the umbles or entrails of the deer. **to eat humble pie:** To submit oneself to humiliation or insult; to apologize humbly (the phrase is said to have arisen from the fact that at hunting-feasts humble pie was given to the menials). **humble plant:** The sensitive plant, *Mimosa pudica*. **humbleness, *humblesse,** *n.* **humbler,** *n.* **humbly,** *adv.*

humble (2) [HUMMEL].

humble-bee (hŭm bėl bē) [obs. *humble*, freq. of HUM (1), BEE], *n.* A bumble-bee.

humbug (hŭm′ bŭg) [etym. doubtful (perh. HUM (3), BUG (1))], *n.* A hoax; an imposition under fair pretences; a spirit of deception or trickery, sham; an impostor; a sweet highly flavoured with peppermint. *int.* Nonsense. *v.t.* (*past & p.p.* **humbugged**) To impose upon, to hoax; to take in; to cajole (into, out of, etc.). *v.i.* To behave in a fraudulent or misleading manner. **humbuggable,** *a.* **humbugger,** *n.* **humbuggery,** *n.*

humbuzz (hŭm′ bŭz), *n.* (*prov.*) The cockchafer; a piece of notched wood whirled swiftly round to make a humming sound, also called a bull-roarer.

humdinger (hŭm ding′ ĕr), *n.* (*colloq.*) Anything very good and efficient.

humdrum (hŭm′ drŭm), *a.* Dull, commonplace, tedious. *n.* A dull, stupid fellow; dull, tedious talk; dullness. *v.i.* To proceed or while away the time in a humdrum manner. **humdrumness,** *n.*

humdudgeon (hŭm dŭj′ ȯn), *n.* A causeless outcry; an imaginary illness.

Humean (hū′ mi ȧn) [David *Hume* (1711–76), Scottish philosopher], *a.* Of or pertaining to the philosophical doctrines of David Hume. **humism,** *n.* **Humist,** *n.*

humectant (hū mek′ tȧnt) [L. *hūmectans -ntem*, pres.p. of *hūmectāre*, from *hūmēre*, to be moist (cp. HUMID)], *a.* Moistening. *n.* (*Med.*) A diluent; a substance that increases the fluidity of the blood. ***humectate,** *v.t.* **humectation** (-tā′ shŭn), *n.* A making wet or moist. **humective,** *a.* **humefy,** *v.t.*

humeral (hū′ mėr ăl) [as foll.], *a.* Pertaining to the shoulder. *n.* A humeral veil. **humeral veil,** *n.* (*R.-C. Ch.*) An oblong scarf worn by priests and deacons at various ceremonies.

humerus (hū′ mėr ŭs) [L., shoulder (cp. Gr. *ōmos*)], *n.* (*Anat.*) The long bone of the upper arm, articulating above with the scapula and below with the radius and the ulna; the corresponding bone in the foreleg of quadrupeds.

hum-hum (hŭm' hŭm), *n.* A plain, coarse cotton Indian cloth.

Humian [HUMEAN].

humic (hū' mik) [from HUMUS], *a.* Pertaining to mould or earth. **humic acid:** (*Chem.*) An acid formed from mould by the action of an alkali. **humify,** *v.i.* To turn into mould. **humification** (-kā' shŭn), *n.*

humid (hū' mid) [L. *hūmidus*, from *hūmēre*, to be moist], *a.* Moist, damp; rather wet. **humidify** (hū mid' i fī), *v.t.* **humidity, *humidness,** *n.* **humidor** (hū' mid or), *n.* A container constructed to keep its contents in a moist state; a box for keeping cigars moist; a contrivance for keeping the air moist.

humify, etc. [HUMIC].

humiliate (hū mil' i āt) [L. *humiliātus*, p.p. of *humiliāre* (*humilis*, HUMBLE)], *v.t.* To lower in self-esteem, to mortify; to humble, to lower in condition, to abase. **humiliating,** *a.* **humiliation** (-ā' shŭn), *n.*

humility (hū mil' i ti) [F. *humilité*, L. *humilitātem*, nom. *-tas*, as prec.], *n.* The state of being humble; modesty, a sense of unworthiness; self-abasement.

humin (hū' min), *n.* (*Chem.*) A neutral substance supposed to exist in black humus.

Humism, etc. [HUMEAN].

hummel (hŭm ėl) [cp. L.G. *hummel*, hornless beast], *a.* Hornless (of cattle). *v.t.* To separate or free from the awns (said of barley). **hummeller,** *n.*

hummer (hŭm' ėr), *n.* One who or that which hums; a humming insect; a humming-bird.

humming (hŭm' ing), *a.* That hums; strong (applied to ale); (*slang*) vigorous, hard (of blows). **humming-bird,** *n.* One of the *Trochilidæ*, diminutive birds, mostly tropical, of brilliant plumage and very rapid flight. **humming-top,** *n.* A hollow top with a hole in the side, which emits a humming noise in spinning.

hummock (hŭm' ŏk) [etym. doubtful; prob. of naut. orig. earlier than HUMP], *n.* A mound or hillock, a protuberance formed by pressure in an icefield; (*Am.*) an elevation in a swamp or bog, esp. if wooded. *v.t.* and *i.* To form hummocks (of an ice-field). **hummocky,** *a.*

hummum [HAMMAM].

humoral (hū' mŏr ăl) [F., from L. *humor*, HUMOUR], *a.* (*Med.*) Pertaining to or proceeding from the bodily humours. **humoralism,** *n.* The doctrine that all diseases proceed from affections of the humours, humoral pathology. **humoralist,** *n.* **humoralistic** (-lis' tik), *a.* **humorism,** *n.* Humoralism; humorousness.

humoresque (hū mŏr esk') [G. *humoreske*], *n.* (*Mus.*) A composition of a humorous or capricious character. *a.* (*Lit.*) Humorous in style.

humorist (hū' mŏr ist) [F. *humoriste*, med. L. *hūmorista*, as prec.], *n.* One who displays humour in his conversation, writings, etc.; a facetious person, a wag, a droll; a whimsical person; (*Med.*) *a humoralist. **humoristic** (-is' tik), *a.*

humorous (hū' mŏr ŭs), *a.* Full of humour; tending to excite laughter; jocular; whimsical, capricious, crotchety; *humoral; *humid, moist. **humorously,** *adv.* **humorousness,** *n.*

humour (hū' mŏr) [A.-F., from O.F. *humor* (F. *humeur*), L. *hūmōrem*, moisture (cp. HUMID)], *n.* Mental disposition, frame of mind, mood; bias, caprice, whim; drollery, comicality; the capacity of perceiving the ludicrous elements in life or art; playful yet sympathetic imagination or mode of regarding things, delighting in the absurdity of incongruities; moisture, animal fluids; *(*pl.*) the four bodily fluids supposed to produce diversity of temperament. *v.t.* To fall in with the humour of; to indulge, to give way to, to make concessions to. **out of humour:** In an ill-temper, displeased. **humoured,** *a.* Having a certain humour (*usu. in comb*, as *good-humoured*). **humourless,** *a.* **humoursome,** *a.* Led by caprice or fancy, whimsical; humorous. **humoursomely,** *adv.* **humoursomeness,** *n.*

humous [HUMUS].

hump (hŭmp) [cp. Dut. *homp*, Norw. *hump*], *n.* A swelling or protuberance, esp. on the back; a rounded hillock; (*colloq.*) a fit of annoyance, ill-temper, or the blues. *v.t.* To make (the back) hump-shaped; (*colloq.*) to carry on the back. **humpback,** *n.* A crooked back; a person having a humpback; an American whale, *Megaptera nodosa*, also called the humpbacked whale. **humpbacked,** *a.* **humped,** *a.* Having a hump. **humpless,** *a.* **humpy** (1), *a.*

humph (hŭmf) [var. of HUM (2)], *int.* Expressing doubt, disapproval, etc.

humpty-dumpty (hŭmp' ti dŭmp' ti) [prob. HUMPY, DUMPY], *n.* A short, squat person; anyone or anything that having fallen down cannot be put back or mended (from the nursery rhyme in which the name stands for an egg); (*Gipsy cant*) ale boiled with brandy; a low stool formed by a big cushion. *a.* Short and squat; mechanical in rhythm, like nursery doggerel.

humpy (2) (hŭm' pi) [Austral. abor.], *n.* An Aborigine hut; a shack, a lean-to.

humus (hū' mŭs) [L., earth], *n.* Soil or mould, esp. that largely composed of decayed vegetation. **humous,** *a.*

Hun (hŭn) [A.-S. *Hūne*, med. L. *Hunni*, prob. from native name *Chunni*, *Chuni*], *n.* One of an ancient Tatar (Tartar) race from Asia, that overran Europe in the fourth and fifth centuries, and gave their name to Hungary; (*colloq.*) a German; (*fig.*) barbarian, destroyer, savage. **Hun-like, Hunnian, Hunnic, Hunnish,** *a.*

hunch (hŭnch) [etym. doubtful, perh. var. of HUMP], *n.* A hump; a lump, a thick piece; a push with the elbow; an intuition. *v.t.* To crook, to arch (esp. the back); to bend or thrust out into a hump; to push with the elbow, to shove. **hunchback,** *n.* A person with a humped back. **hunchbacked,** *a.* **hunchy,** *a.*

hundred (hŭn' drėd) [A.-S. *hundred* (*hund*, hundred, *-red*, a reckoning or account, cp. G. *rede*)], *n.* The cardinal number representing ten times ten; the product of ten multiplied by ten; (*colloq.*) a hundred pounds (money); an administrative division of a county in England, supposed to have originally contained one hundred families or freemen. **Chiltern Hundreds** [CHILTERN]. **Hundred Days:** The period 20 March to 22 June, 1815, from Napoleon's escape from Elba to his abdication. **hundredweight,** *n.* A weight of a 112 lb. av. **hundredfold,** *n.* **hundredth,** *a.* The ordinal of a hundred. *n.* One of a hundred equal parts. **Old Hundredth:** A well-known 17th-century psalm-tune originally set for the 100th Psalm.

hung, *past* [HANG].

Hungarian (hŭng gâr' i ăn) [late L. *Hungaria*, Hungary (from *Hungari*, *Ugri*, Magyars), -AN], *a.* Pertaining to Hungary. *n.* A native of Hungary; the Hungarian language. **Hungary water:** A distilled water formerly prepared from rosemary, etc.

hunger (hŭng' gėr) [A.-S. *hungor* (cp. Icel. *hungr*, Dut. *honger*, G. *hunger*), whence *hyngran*, to hunger], *n.* A craving for food; a painful sensation caused by the want of food; *a famine; (*fig.*) any strong desire. *v.i.* To feel the pain or sensation of hunger; to crave for food; (*fig.*) to desire or long eagerly. *v.t.* To make hungry, to starve; to compel, drive, etc. (into, out of, etc.) by hunger. **hunger-bitten,** *a.* Pinched with hunger. **hunger march,** *n.* A march of the unemployed to protest against their lot. **hunger strike,** *n.* and *v.i.* Refusal of a prisoner to take food. ***hungered, *a-hungered,** *a.* Hungry. ***hungerly,** *a.* Hungry, weak, thin. *adv.* Hungrily.

hungry (hŭng′ gri) [A.-S. *hungrig*], *a.* Feeling a sensation of hunger; having a keen appetite; showing hunger, emaciated, thin; causing hunger; (*fig.*) longing or craving eagerly; barren, poor (of soil). **hungry rice:** A grain like millet raised in West Africa. **hungrily,** *adv.*

hunker (hŭng′ kėr) [Sc., etym. doubtful; cp. Dut. *huiken*, G. *hocken*], *v.i.* To squat on the calves or heels. *n.pl.* The haunches. **on one's hunkers:** Squatting down.

hunks (hŭngks) [etym. doubtful], *n.* A stingy fellow.

hunt (hŭnt) [A.-S. *huntian*, cogn. with *hentan*, to HENT (1)], *v.t.* To chase (as wild animals) for the purpose of catching and killing; to employ (horses, dogs, etc.) in hunting; to pursue or chase in or over (a district, etc.); to search for, to seek after. *v.i.* To follow the chase; to pursue game or wild animals; to search (after or for). *n.* Hunting, the chase; a pack of hounds, an association of hunting men; a district hunted by a pack of hounds; *the game captured or killed in the chase. **to hunt down:** To bring to bay; to destroy by persecution or violence. **to hunt out:** To track out, to find by searching. **to hunt up:** To search for. **to hunt the fox, hare, slipper, squirrel:** Various games in which a player or an object is hunted out. **hunt-counter,** *n.* A dog that runs back on the scent; a blunderer. ***hunt's-up,** *n.* A tune used to rouse huntsmen in the morning; a reveille. **hunter,** *n.* One who follows the chase; a huntsman; a horse trained for hunting; one who searches or seeks for anything (*usu. in comb.*, as *fortune-hunter*); a hunting-watch. **hunting,** *a.* Chasing game or wild animals; pertaining or given to hunting; (*Am.*) shooting (birds, etc.). **hunting box, -lodge, -seat,** *n.* A temporary residence for the hunting-season. **hunting-crop,** *n.* A riding-rod with a loop at the end for attaching a thong. **hunting-ground,** *n.* Ground or region where one hunts; (*fig.*) a likely place for finding anything. **happy hunting-ground:** Heaven, as prefigured by the North American Indians. **hunting-horn,** *n.* A bugle or horn used in the chase; the second pommel of a side-saddle. **hunting-watch,** *n.* A watch with a metal cover over the face. **huntress,** *n.* A female hunter. **huntsman,** *n.* One who hunts; the servant who manages the hounds, esp. the fox-hounds. **huntsmanship,** *n.*

Hunterian (hŭn tēr′ i ȧn) [pers. name *Hunter*], *a.* Of or pertaining to John Hunter (1728–1793), Scottish surgeon, or his museum of anatomical and pathological specimens in London; or to his brother William Hunter (1718–83) or his museum of natural history at Glasgow.

huntress, huntsman [HUNT].

Huon pine (hū′ ŏn pīn′) [river *Huon*, Tasmania], *n.* A large Tasmanian yew, *Dacrydium Franklinii*, valued for its finely-marked wood, used in cabinet-making, boat-building, etc.

hup (hŭp) [Sc.], *int.* A call to a horse to turn to the right. *v.i.* To call thus to a horse.

hurcheon (hĕr′ chŏn) [O.North.F. *herichon*, O.F. *heriçun* (F. *herisson*), URCHIN], *n.* (*Sc. and North.*) A hedgehog; an urchin.

hurdies (hĕr′ diz) [Sc., etym. unknown], *n.* The buttocks, the haunches.

hurdle (hĕr′ dĕl) [A.-S. *hyrdel*, dim. (cp. Dut. *horde*, Icel. *hūrth*, G. *hürde*, also L. *crātis*)], *n.* A movable framework of withes or split timber serving for gates, enclosures, etc.; a barrier like this for jumping over in racing; (*Hist.*) a frame or sledge on which criminals were drawn to execution. *v.t.* To enclose, hedge, or barricade with hurdles. **hurdle-race,** *n.* A race over hurdles or fences. **hurdler,** *n.* One who runs in such races; a hurdle-maker.

hurds [HARDS].

hurdy-gurdy (hĕr′ di gĕr′ di) [prob. imit., cp. HIRDY-GIRDY], *n.* Orig. a stringed musical instrument like a rude violin, sounded by a rosined wheel turned by the left hand, the right playing on keys; a barrel-organ, or other instrument played with a handle.

hurl (hĕrl) [prob. imit., cp. HURTLE], *v.t.* To throw with violence; to drive or fling with great force; to utter or emit with vehemence. *v.i.* *To move rapidly, to whirl; to play the game of hurling. *n.* The act of throwing with great force; *a tumult. **hurler,** *n.* One who hurls or plays at hurling.

hurley (hĕr′ li), *n.* (*Ir.*) Hockey, hurling; a hockey-stick.

hurling (hĕr′ ling), *n.* Throwing, flinging with violence; an old game, similar to football, two parties striving in rivalry to throw or carry a ball to a goal; (*Ir.*) a form of hockey, hurley. **hurler,** *n.*

hurly-burly (hĕr′ li bĕr′ li) [perh. from prec., or from O.F. *hurlee*, a howling, from *hurler*, to howl, L. *ululāre*, imit.], *n.* A tumult, commotion, uproar. ***hurly,** *n.*

Huronian (hū rō′ ni ȧn) [Lake *Huron*, North America], *a.* (*Geol.*) Of or pertaining to Lake Huron; formerly applied to the archæan strata of Canada. **Huronite** (hū′ rŏ nīt), *n.* (*Min.*) An impure feldspar from Lake Huron.

hurrah, hurray (hu ra′, -rā′) [earlier HUZZA (cp. Swed., Dan., and G. *hurra*)], *int.* An exclamation of joy, welcome, applause, etc. *v.i.* To utter hurrahs. *v.t.* To salute with hurrahs. *n.* A shout of hurrahs.

hurricane (hŭr′ i kȧn), ***hurricano** (hur i ka′ nō) [Sp. *huracan*, from Carib.], *n.* A storm with violent wind with a mean velocity of over 75 miles an hour; an extremely violent gale, orig. a West Indian cyclone; (*fig.*) anything that sweeps along violently. **hurricane-deck,** *n.* The upper deck above the cabins of a river steamer; a raised deck on an ocean steamer. **hurricane-lamp,** *n.* A lamp designed to keep alight in a wind.

hurry (hŭr′ i) [imit.], *v.t.* To impel to greater speed, to accelerate; to push forward; to drive or cause to act or do carelessly or precipitately; (*Coal-min.*) to draw (a wagon) in a mine. *v.i.* To hasten; to move or act with excessive haste. *n.* The act of hurrying; urgency, bustle, precipitation; eagerness (to do, etc.); (*colloq.*) need for haste; a river-staging for loading vessels, or a shute for loading coal into a hold; (*Mus.*) a tremolo passage by the orchestra accompanying a dramatic situation. **not in a hurry:** (*colloq.*) Not soon, not easily. **hurry-scurry,** *adv.* In a hurry or bustle; confusedly. *n.* A confused bustle. *v.i.* To make haste, to act with disorderly haste. **hurryingly,** *adv.* **hurried,** *a.* Impelled to speed; done in a hurry; hasty. **hurriedly,** *adv.* **hurriedness,** *n.* **hurrier,** *n.*

hurst (hĕrst) [A.-S. *hyrst* (cp. M.H.G. *hurst*, L.G. and M.Dut. *horst*)], *n.* A wood, a thicket; a wooded eminence (a frequent element in place-names); a hillock, a knoll; (*local*) a sandbank in a river.

hurt (hĕrt) [prob. from O.F. *hurter* (F. *heurter*), to knock or push, etym. doubtful], *v.t.* (*past & p.p.* **hurt**) To cause pain, injury, loss, or detriment to; to damage; to grieve or distress (as the feelings). *v.i.* (*usu. impers.*) To be painful, to cause pain. *n.* A wound; an injury, damage, harm; anything that causes pain, injury, or detriment. **hurter** (1), *n.* One who hurts. **hurtful,** *a.* Causing hurt; mischievous, noxious. **hurtfully,** *adv.* **hurtfulness,** *n.* **hurtless,** *n.* **hurtlessly,** *adv.* **hurtlessness,** *n.*

hurter (2) (hĕr′ tėr) [F. *hurteoir*, as prec.], *n.* A timber placed at the foot of a slope or platform to prevent the wheels of gun-carriages from injuring the parapet; the shoulder or the reinforcing piece on an axle.

hurtle (hĕr tĕl) [prob. a freq. of HURT], *v.t.* To strike or dash against with violence; to move or whirl with great force. *v.i.* To rush with great force and noise; to make a crashing noise. *n.* A loud, crashing noise; a collision, a shock.

hurtleberry [var. of WHORTLEBERRY].

husband (hŭz′ bȧnd) [A.-S. *hūsbonda* (*hūs*, HOUSE, *bonda*, from Icel. *bōndi*, from *būa*, to dwell)], *n.* A man joined to a woman in marriage; *a good and frugal manager; (*Naut.*) a ship's husband [see SHIP]. *v.t.* To manage with frugality, to economize. *to till; *to cultivate; (*facet.*) to provide with a husband; to be a husband to, to marry. **husbandage,** *n.* Commission to the ship's husband. **husbandhood, -ship,** *n.* ***husbandless,** *a.* Having no husband. **husband-like,** *a.* ***husbandly,** *a.* Frugal, economical; husbandlike.

husbandry (hŭz′ bȧn dri) [as prec.], *n.* The business of a farmer, agriculture; the products of farming; economy, esp. domestic; frugality, careful management. **husbandman** (huz′ bȧnd mȧn), *n.* A farmer, a tiller of the soil; a good economist.

hush (1) (hŭsh) [from obs. adj. *husht*, imit., cp. HIST, WHIST (1)], *v.t.* To make silent; to repress the noise of. *v.i.* To be still or silent. *n.* Silence, stillness. *int.* Silence! be still! **a.* Silent, quiet. **to hush up:** To keep concealed, to suppress. **hushaby,** *int.* Used in lulling to sleep. **hush-hush:** (*colloq.*) Very secret. **hush-money,** *n.* A bribe to secure silence (about a scandal, etc.).

hush (2) (hŭsh) [onomat.], *n.* A smooth, swift rush of water; (*Mining*) a rush of water let out from a dam. *v.t.* (*Mining*) To let out (water) from a dam, esp. to clear away soil, stones, etc.

husk (hŭsk) [perh. from A.-S. *hūs*, HOUSE (cp. E.Fris. *hūske*, G. *häuschen*, little house)], *n.* The dry external integument of certain fruits or seeds; (*fig.*) a mere frame, shell, or worthless part; a disease in cattle. *v.t.* To strip the husk from. **husked,** *a.* Having or covered with a husk; stripped of a husk. **husker,** *n.* **husking,** *n.* The act of stripping off husks; (*Am.*) a husking-bee. **husking-bee,** *n.* (*Am.*) A gathering of friends at a farmer's house to husk maize. **husky** (1), *a.* Abounding in husks; consisting of or resembling husks; rough; dry, hoarse, rough and harsh in sound; (*Am. colloq.*) strong, stalwart. **huskily,** *adv.* **huskiness,** *n.*

husky (2) (hŭs′ ki) [perh. corr. of ESKIMO], *n.* (*Canada*) An Indian sledge-dog; an Eskimo; the Eskimo language.

huso (hū′ sō) [med. L., from O.H.G.], *n.* The beluga or great sturgeon, *Acipenser huso.*

hussar (hu zar′) [Hung. *huszar*, O.Serv. *husar*, Ital. *corsaro*, or late Gr. *choursarios*, med. L. *cursārius*, CORSAIR], *n.* Originally a light horseman, and applied to the national cavalry of Hungary; now, a soldier of a light cavalry regiment in European armies.

hussif [HOUSEWIFE].

Hussite (hŭs′ īt) [John *Hus* (1369–1415), -ITE], *n.* A follower of John Hus, Bohemian religious reformer.

hussy (hŭz′ i) [corr. of HOUSEWIFE], *n.* A pert, forward girl; a worthless woman; *a housewife.

husting (hŭs′ ting) [A.-S. *hūsting*, Icel. *hūsthing* (*hūs*, HOUSE, *thing*, an assembly)], *n.* (*Hist.*) A meeting for deliberative purposes, a council; (*pl.*) a platform from which, before the Ballot Act of 1872, candidates addressed the electors during parliamentary elections; proceedings at an election; a court held in the City of London, formerly the principal and highest court in the City.

hustle (hŭs′ ėl) [Dut. *hutselen*, freq. of *hutsen*], *v.t.* To shake together in confusion; to jostle, to push violently; to hurry or cause to move quickly. *v.i.* To press roughly; to move (along) with difficulty; to act with energy; to give the appearance of being busy; to push one's way in an unceremonious or unscrupulous way. *n.* Hustling. **hustler,** *n.*

***huswife,** etc. [HOUSEWIFE].

hut (hŭt) [F. *hutte*, from M.H.G. *hütte*], *n.* A small, rude house, a mean dwelling; a cabin, a hovel; (*Mil.*) a small temporary camp-shelter or house. *v.t.* To place (troops) in huts. *v.i.* To lodge in huts. **hutment,** *n.* (*Mil.*) A camp of huts.

hutch (hŭch) [O.F. *huche*, low L. *hūtica*, etym. doubtful], *n.* A coop or box-like pen for small animals; a chest, box, bin, or other receptacle; (*fig.*) a hut, a hovel, a small mean house; a kneading-trough; a bolting-hutch; (*Mining*) a truck, a trough for washing ore. *v.t.* To store, as in a hutch; (*Mining*) to wash in a hutch.

Hutchinsonian (hŭch in sō′ ni ȧn) [*Hutchinson*, -IAN], *a.* Of or pertaining to John Hutchinson (1674–1737), who held that the Bible furnished a basis for science, philosophy, etc., or to Anne Hutchinson (1590–1643), an Antinomian who emigrated to New England. *n.* A follower of either of these.

Huttonian (hŭ tō′ ni ȧn) [James *Hutton* (1726–1796), geologist], *a.* (*Geol.*) Of or pertaining to Hutton and his theory of the plutonic or volcanic origin of unstratified rocks. *n.* An adherent of this theory. **Huttonianism,** *n.*

huzza (hu za′) [imit.], *int.* A cry of joy, applause, etc. *v.i.* To shout 'huzza.' *v.t.* To applaud or greet with this cry. *n.* A shout of 'huzza.'

huzzy [HUSSY].

hyacinth (hī′ ȧ sinth) [F. *hyacinthe*, L. *hyacinthus*, Gr. *huakinthos*, a flower, prob. iris or larkspur], *n.* A plant of the genus *Hyacinthus*, esp. *H. orientalis*, a beautiful bulbous-rooted flowering plant of the order Liliaceæ; a flower mentioned by the ancients, said to have sprung from the blood of the youth Hyacinth, beloved of Apollo, and to bear the letters AI (alas!) on its petals; a precious stone known to the ancients; (*Min.*) a brownish, orange, or reddish variety of zircon. ***hyacine,** *n.* (*Spens.*) Hyacinth. **hyacinthian** (hī ȧ sin′ thi ȧn), **hyacinthine** (hī ȧ sin′ thin, -thīn), *a.* Resembling the hyacinth (the flower or the gem) in colour; (of hair) curling richly (after an epithet of Homer's of doubtful meaning).

Hyades (hī′ ȧ dēz), **Hyads** (hī′ ȧdz) [Gr. *Huades*, cogn. with *hus*, a sow (pop. derived from *huein*, to rain)], *n.pl.* A cluster of stars, including Aldebaran, in the head of Taurus, supposed by the ancients to bring rain when they rose with the sun.

hyæna [HYENA].

hyalescence (hī ȧ les′ ens) [HYALINE], *n.* The process of becoming transparent. **hyalescent,** *a.*

hyalin (hī′ ȧ lin) [Gr. *hualos*, glass] *n.* (*Chem.*) An opalescent nitrogenous compound similar to chitin, the chief constituent of hydatid cysts. **hyalose,** *n.* A sugar allied to glucose obtained from this.

hyaline (hī′ ȧ līn, -lin) [L. *hyalīnus*, Gr. *hualinos*, from *hualos*, glass or crystal], *a.* Glassy, transparent, crystalline; (*Sci.*) vitreous. *n.* The glassy surface of the sea; the clear sky or atmosphere; (*Biol.*) the pellucid substance determining the fission of cells.

hyalite (hī′ ȧ līt), *n.* (*Min.*) A glassy variety of opal.

hyalitis (hī ȧ lī′ tis), *n.* (*Path.*) Inflammation of the vitreous matter of the eye.

hyalo- [Gr. *hualos*, glass], *comb. form.* Colourless, transparent, crystalline; vitreous.

hyalograph (hī ăl′ ō graf), *n.* An instrument for etching on glass. **hyalography,** *n.*

hyaloid (hī′ ȧ loid), *a.* Glassy, vitriform. *n.* (*Anat.*) The hyaloid membrane. **hyaloid coat, membrane,** *n.* The transparent membrane enclosing the vitreous humour of the eye. **hyaloid humour, body,** *n.* The vitreous humour.

hyalose [HYALIN]. **hybernate** [HIBERNATE].

Hyblæan (hib lē′ ȧn), **Hyblan** (hib′ lȧn) [L. *Hyblæus*, from *Hybla*, Gr. *Hublē*], *a.* Of or pertaining to Hybla, a town in ancient Sicily, famous for its honey.

hybrid (hī′ brid) [L. *hybrida*, mongrel], *a.* Produced by the union of two distinct species, varieties, etc.; produced by cross-fertilization or interbreeding; mongrel, cross-bred; (*fig.*) derived from incongruous sources. *n.* A mongrel; an animal or plant produced by the union of two distinct species, varieties, etc.; one of mixed nationality; (*Philol.*) a word compounded from different languages; anything composed of heterogeneous parts or elements. **hybridity** (hī brid′ i ti), *n.* The state or quality of being hybrid. **hybridism** (hī′ bri-, hib′ ri dizm), *n.* Hybridity; the act or process of interbreeding, hybridization. **hybridist,** *n.* **hybridize,** *v.t.* To produce by the union of different species or varieties; to produce by cross-fertilization or interbreeding. *v.i.* To produce hybrids, to be capable of cross-fertilization or interbreeding. **hybridizable,** *a.* **hybridization** (-zā′ shun), *n.* **hybridizer,** *n.* ***hybridous,** *a.*

hydatid (hī′ dȧ-, hid′ ȧ tid) [Gr. *hydatis -tidos,* a watery vesicle, cogn. with *hudōr,* water], *n.* (*Path.*) A watery cyst occurring in animal tissue, esp. one resulting from the development of the embryo of a tapeworm. **hydatic** (hī dăt′ ik), *a.* **hydatidiform** (hī dȧ tid′ i fôrm), **hydatiform** (hī dăt′ i fôrm), *a.* Resembling a hydatid.

hydatism (hī′ dȧ tizm) [Gr. *hudatismos,* from *hudōr hudatis,* water], *n.* (*Med.*) A sound produced by the effusion of fluid in a cavity of the body. **hydato-,** *comb. form.*

hydatoid (hī′ dȧ toid), *a.* Resembling water. *n.* (*Anat.*) The membrane surrounding the aqueous humour of the eye, or the humour itself.

hydr- [HYDRO-].

hydra (hī′ drȧ) [L., from Gr. *hudra,* cogn. with *hudōr,* water], *n.* (*Gr. Myth.*) A water-serpent with many heads, each of which, when cut off, was succeeded by two, destroyed by Hercules; a water-serpent; an evil or calamity difficult to extinguish; (*Astron.*) one of the fifteen ancient southern constellations; (*Zool.*) a genus of freshwater polyps which multiply when divided. **hydra-headed,** *a.* Having many heads; hence, difficult to get rid of; spreading. **hydra-tainted,** *a.* Poisonous, deadly. **hydroid,** *a.* Hydra-like; (*Zool.*) allied to the genus *Hydra. n.* (*Zool.*) A hydrozoan; a member of the genus *Hydra.*

hydracid (hī drăs′ id), *n.* (*Chem.*) An acid containing hydrogen but no oxygen. *a.* Of or pertaining to a hydracid.

hydragogue (hī′ drȧ gog) [F., from L. *hydragōgus,* Gr. *hudragōgos* (HYDR-, *agein,* to lead)], *n.* (*Med.*) An active purgative, causing a large secretion of fluid.

hydrangea (hī drān′ jȧ) [HYDR-, Gr. *angeion, angos,* a vessel], *n.* (*Bot.*) A genus of flowering shrubs of the saxifrage family, from Asia and America.

hydrant (hī′ drȧnt), *n.* A spout or discharge-pipe, usu. with a nozzle for attaching hose, connected with a water-main for drawing water.

hydrargyrum (hī drar′ ji rŭm) [L. *hydrargyrus,* Gr. *hudrarguros* (HYDR-, *arguros,* silver)], *n.* Mercury, quicksilver. **hydrargyrate,** *a.*

hydrastine (hī drăs′ tīn) [mod. L. *Hydrastis*], *n.* (*Chem.*) A bitter alkaloid prepared from the root of a North American plant, *Hydrastis Canadensis,* used as a tonic and febrifuge.

hydrate (hī′ drȧt), *n.* (*Chem.*) A compound of water with an element or another compound. *v.t.* (-drāt) To combine with water to form a hydrate. **hydration** (hī drā′ shŭn), *n.*

hydraulic (hī draw′ lik) [L. *hydraulicus,* Gr. *hudraulikos* (HYDR-, *aulos,* pipe)], *a.* Pertaining to fluids in motion, or to the power exerted by water conveyed through pipes or channels; operating or operated by such power. *n.pl.* The science of water or other liquids both at rest and in motion, esp. the conveyance of water through pipes, etc., and the practical application of water-power. **hydraulic cement** or **mortar:** A cement or mortar which hardens under water. **hydraulic lift:** A lift worked by means of water-power. **hydraulic press:** A heavy pressing machine worked by water-power. **hydraulic ram:** A machine by which the fall of a column of water supplies power to elevate a portion of the water to a greater height than that at the source. **hydraulically,** *adv.* **hydraulician** (-lish′ ȧn), *n.* **hydraulico-,** *comb. form.*

hydria (hī′ dri ȧ) [L., from Gr. *hudria,* from *hudōr,* water], *n.* (*pl.* **-iæ**) (*Gr. Ant.*) A water-jar or pitcher. ***hydriad,** *n.* A water-nymph.

hydric (hī′ drik), *a.* (*Chem.*) Of, pertaining to, or containing hydrogen in chemical combination. **hydride,** *n.* A compound of hydrogen with another element or radical. **hydriodic** (hī dri od′ ik), *a.* Of, pertaining to, or containing hydrogen and iodine in chemical combination. **hydriodate, hydriodide** (hī drī′ ȯ dȧt, -dīd), *n.*

hydro (hī′ drō) [short for HYDROPATHIC], *n.* (*colloq.*) A hydropathic establishment.

hydro-, hydr- [Gr. *hudōr hudros,* water], *comb. form.* Pertaining to or connected with water; (*Chem.*) containing hydrogen in chemical combination; (*Min.*) containing water as a constituent; (*Path.*) dropsical; (*Zool.*) belonging to the genus *Hydra* or the class Hydrozoa. **hydro-aeroplane** (hī drō âr′ ȯ plān) [AEROPLANE], *n.* An aeroplane adapted for rising from or descending upon the surface of water. **hydro-barometer** (hī drō bȧ rom′ ė tėr) [BAROMETER], *n.* An instrument for determining the depth of the sea by its pressure.

hydrobromic (hī drō brō′ mik), *a.* Composed of hydrogen and bromine. **hydrobromate, hydrobromide,** *n.*

hydrocarbon (hī drō kar′ bȯn), *n.* A compound of carbon and hydrogen. **hydrocarbide,** *n.* **hydrocarbonaceous,** *a.* **hydrocarbonate,** *n.* **hydrocarbonic,** *a.*

hydrocele (hī′ drō sēl), *n.* (*Path.*) A watery tumour; dropsy of the testicle or of the scrotum.

hydrocephalus (hī drō sef′ ȧ lŭs) [Gr. *hudrokephalon*], *n.* (*Path.*) Dropsy of or water on the brain. **hydrocephalic, hydrocephaloid, hydrocephalous,** *a.* Pertaining to or akin to hydrocephalus.

hydrochloric (hī drō klôr′ ik), *n.* (*Chem.*) A compound of chlorine and hydrogen.

hydrocyanic (hī drō sī ăn′ ik), *a.* (*Chem.*) Formed by the combination of hydrogen and cyanogen. **hydrocyanic acid:** Prussic acid. **hydrocyanate** (-sī′ ȧ nȧt), *n.*

hydrodynamics (hī drō di-, -dī năm′ iks), *n.* The science which deals with water and other liquids in motion. **hydrodynamic, -al** (-dī-, -di năm′ ik, -ȧl), *a.* (*Phys.*) Pertaining to hydrodynamics; derived from the force of water.

hydro-electric (hī drō ė lek′ trik), *a.* Pertaining to electricity generated from water-power. **hydro-electricity** (-tris′ i ti), *n.* **hydro-electrization** (-zā′ shŭn), *n.* (*Med.*) **hydro-electrothermic** (-thĕr′ mik), *a.* Pertaining to a method of electric welding.

hydro-extractor (hī drō ek străk′ tôr), *n.* An apparatus for removing moisture from yarns and fabrics during the process of manufacture.

hydrofluoric (hī drȯ flū or′ ik), *a.* (*Chem.*) Consisting of fluorine and hydrogen.

hydrofoil (hī′ drō foil), *n.* (*Aviat.*) A hydroplane used to assist the take-off of seaplanes.

hydrogel (hī′ drō jel) [HYDRO-, *gel-,* from L. *gelāre,* to freeze], *n.* (*Biol.*) Protoplasm comprising gelatine or albumen in a jelly-like state with water filling the interstices.

hydrogen (hī′ drȯ jėn) [F. *hydrogène*], *n.* (*Chem.*) An invisible, inflammable, gaseous element, the lightest of all known bodies, which in combination with oxygen produces water. **hydrogen bomb,** *n.* An exceedingly powerful bomb in which an immense release of energy is obtained by the conversion by fusion of hydrogen nuclei into helium nuclei. **hydrogenate, -enize** (hī droj′ ė nāt, -nīz), *v.t.* (*Chem.*) To cause to combine with hydrogen; to charge with hydrogen. **hydrogenation, -genization** (-na′ shŭn, -zā′ shŭn), *n.* **hydrogenous** (hī droj′ ė nŭs), *a.*

hydrography (hī drog′ rȧ fi), *n.* The science and art of studying, surveying, and mapping seas, lakes, rivers, and other waters, and their physical features, tides, currents, etc. **hydrograph** (hī' drȯ grăf), *n.* A chart or diagram setting forth hydrographic phenomena. **hydrographer** (hī drog' rȧ fėr), *n.* **hydrographic, -al** (hī drȯ grăf' ik, -ȧl), *a.* **hydrographically,** *adv.*

hydroid [HYDRA].

hydrokinetic (hī drō kī net' ik), *a.* Relating to the motion of liquids. **hydrokinetics,** *n.* The kinetics of liquids.

hydrology (hī drol' ȯ ji), *n.* The science of water, its properties, phenomena, laws, and distribution. **hydrological** (-loj' i kȧl), *a.* **hydrologist** (-drol' ȯ jist), *n.*

hydrolysis (hī drol' i sis) [Gr. *lusis,* loosening, from *luein,* to loose], *n.* (*Chem.*) The formation of an acid and a base from a salt by the action of water. **hydrolytic** (-lit' ik), *a.*

***hydromancy** (hī' drȯ măn si), *n.* Divination by means of water. **hydromantik** (-măn' tik), *a.*

hydromania (hī drȯ mā' ni ȧ), *n.* (*Path.*) Morbid craving for water. **hydromaniac,** *n.* **hydromaniacal** (-mȧ nī' ȧ kȧl), *a.*

hydromechanics (hī drō mė kăn' iks), *n.* The mechanics of liquids. **hydromechanical,** *a.*

hydromel (hī' drō mel) [L., from Gr. *hudromeli* (HYDRO-, *meli,* honey)], *n.* A drink consisting of honey diluted with water.

hydro-metamorphism (hī drō met ȧ môr' fizm), *n.* (*Geol.*) Metamorphism of igneous rocks by the agency of water. **hydrometamorphic,** *a.*

hydrometeor (hī drȯ mē' tė ȯr), *n.* (*Meteor.*) A meteorological phenomenon produced by water-vapour, as rain, snow, etc. **hydrometeoric** (-or' ik), *a.* **hydrometeorology** (-ol' ȯ ji), *n.* **hydrometeorological** (-loj' i kȧl), *a.*

hydrometer (hī drom' ė tėr), *n.* An instrument for determining the specific gravity of liquids, or solids by means of flotation. **hydrometric, -al** (-met' rik, -ȧl), *a.* **hydrometry** (-drom' ė tri), *n.* The art or process of measuring the specific gravity of fluids, etc.

hydromotor (hī drō mō' tȯr), *n.* A motor for propelling vessels by means of a jet of water emitted at the stern.

hydromyd (hī' drȯ mid) [HYDRO-, Gr. *mus,* MOUSE], *n.* One of the Australian genus *Hydromys* comprising the water-rats and beaver-rats.

hydropathy (hī drop' ȧ thi), *n.* The treatment of disease by the internal and external application of water. **hydropath** (hī' drȯ păth), **hydropathist** (hī drop' ȧ thist), *n.* One who practises or believes in hydropathy. **hydropathic** (-păth' ik), *a.* Pertaining to hydropathy. *n.* An establishment for the hydropathic treatment of disease.

hydrophane (hī' drō fān) [Gr. *phanēs,* clear, from *phainein,* to show], *n.* (*Min.*) An opal which becomes translucent when immersed in water. **hydrophanous** (hī drof' ȧ nůs), *a.* Becoming more translucent or brighter when immersed in water.

hydrophid (hī' drō fid) [Gr. *ophis,* serpent], *n.* (*Zool.*) One of the *Hydrophidæ,* a family of small sea-snakes from Indian and Australian seas.

hydrophobia (hī drō fō' bi ȧ) [L., from Gr. *hudrophobia*], *n.* An unnatural dread of water, a symptom of rabies resulting from the bite of a rabid animal; rabies; dread of water. **hydrophobic** (-fob' ik), *a.*

hydrophone (hī' drō fōn) [Gr. *phōnē,* voice, sound], *n.* An instrument for detecting sound by water, used in naval warfare to locate submarines, etc.; an instrument for detecting the sound of running water, used to discover leaks, etc.

hydrophore (hī' drȯ fōr) [Gr. *hudrophoros*], *n.* An instrument for obtaining specimens of water from any given depth.

hydrophthalmia (hī drof thăl' mi ȧ), *n.* (*Path.*) Enlargement of the eyeball by the increase of its fluid contents. **hydrophthalmic** (-thăl' mik), *a.*

hydrophyte (hī' drō fīt), *n.* An aquatic plant. **hydrophytography** (-tog' rȧ fi), **hydrophytology** (-tol' ȯ ji), *n.* The study of these plants.

hydropic (hī drop' ik) [M.E. and O.F. *ydropique,* L. *hydrōpicus,* Gr. *hudrōpikos,* from *hudrops* (*hudōr,* water)], *a.* Dropsical; resembling dropsy. ***hydropical, *hydroptic,** *a.* Hydropic. ***hydropsy** (hī' drop si), *n.* Dropsy.

hydroplane (hī' drō plān), *n.* A light motor-boat capable of rising partially above the surface of water; a flat fin for governing the vertical direction of a submarine; a plane for lifting a boat partially from the water, so as to diminish the resistance and increase the speed [cp. HYDRO-AEROPLANE, see HYDRO-].

hydropneumatic (hī drō nū măt' ik), *a.* Pertaining to or produced by the combined action of water and air.

hydroponics (hī drō pon' iks) [Gr. *ponos,* work], *n.pl.* (*Agric.*) The cultivation of plants without soil in water containing chemicals.

hydropsy [HYDROPIC].

hydroquinone (hī drō kwī' nōn), *n.* (*Phot.*) A compound derived from quinone, employed in the development of photographs.

hydroscope (hī' drȯ skōp) [Gr. *hudroskopos*], *n.* A water-clock or clepsydra; a hygroscope.

hydrosol (hī' drȯ sol), *n.* (*Chem.*) A solution of a colloid in water.

hydrosome (hī' drȯ sōm) [HYDRA, Gr. *soma,* body], *n.* (*Zool.*) The colonial organism of a hydrozoan. **hydrosomal, hydrosomatous** (-sō' mȧl, -mȧ tůs), *a.*

hydrosphere (hī' drō sfēr), *n.* The watery envelope of the earth.

hydrostat (hī' drō stăt) [Gr. *statos,* standing], *n.* An electrical contrivance for detecting the presence of water; an apparatus to prevent the explosion of steam-boilers.

hydrostatic, -al (hī drō stăt' ik, -ȧl), *a.* Pertaining or relating to hydrostatics; pertaining to the pressure and equilibrium of liquids at rest. **hydrostatic balance:** A balance for weighing substances in water to ascertain their specific gravities. **hydrostatic paradox:** The principle that any quantity of liquid, however small, may be made to balance any weight. **hydrostatic press:** A hydraulic press. **hydrostatically,** *adv.* **hydrostatics,** *n.* The science which treats of the pressure and equilibrium of liquids at rest.

hydrosulphuric (hī drō sŭl fū' rik), *a.* (*Chem.*) Containing hydrogen and sulphur.

hydrotelluric (hī drō tė lū' rik), *a.* (*Chem.*) Composed of hydrogen and tellurium.

hydrotherapeutic (hī drō ther ȧ pū' tik), *a.* (*Med.*) Pertaining to the therapeutic application of water; hydropathic. **hydrotherapeutics, hydrotherapy** (-ther' ȧ pi), *n.*

hydrothermal (hī drō thĕr' mȧl), *a.* Relating to the action of heated water, esp. on the materials of the earth's crust.

hydrothorax (hī drō thôr' ăks), *n.* (*Path.*) Dropsy of the chest.

hydrotropism (hī drot' rȯ pizm) [Gr. *-tropos,* a turning, from *trepein,* to turn], *n.* (*Bot.*) The tendency in the growing parts of plants to turn towards or away from moisture. **hydrotropic** (-trop' ik), *a.*

hydrous (hī' drůs), *a.* (*Chem.*) Containing water.

hydroxide (hī drok' sīd), *n.* (*Chem.*) A compound formed by the union of a basic oxide with the molecules of water; *a hydrate. **hydroxy-,** *comb. form.* Containing the radical hydroxyl. **hydroxyl,** *n.* The monad radical formed by the combination of one atom of hydrogen and one of water occurring in many chemical compounds.

Hydrozoa (hī drō zō′ ȧ) [Gr. *zōon* (pl. *zōa*), an animal], *n.pl.* (*Zool.*) A class of cœlenterates, principally marine, comprising the hydra, medusa, jelly-fish, etc. **hydrozoan,** *a.* and *n.* **hydrozoic,** *a.*

***hydruret** [HYDRIDE].

***hyemal,** etc. [HIEMAL].

hyena (hī ē′ nȧ) [L. *hyæna*, Gr. *huaina*, sow-like, from *hus*, a sow], *n.* A genus of carnivorous quadrupeds allied to the dog, with three modern species, the striped *H. striata*, the spotted *H. crocuta*, and the brown hyena, *H. brunnea* (the first is also called the laughing hyena); (*fig.*) a ferocious or treacherous person; applied also to the thyacine. **hyena-dog,** *n.* A South African quadruped, also called the hunting-dog. **hyenaish,** *a.* **hyenaism,** *n.* **hyena-like,** *a.*

hyetal (hī′ ė tăl) [as foll.], *a.* Of or belonging to rain; relating to the rainfall of different countries.

hyeto- [Gr. *huetos*, rain], *comb. form.* Pertaining to rain or rainfall. **hyetograph** (hī′ ė tō grăf) [-GRAPH], *n.* A self-recording instrument that registers rainfall. **hyetographic, -al** (-grăf′ ik, -ȧl), *a.* **hyetography** (-tog′ rȧ fi), *n.* The branch of meteorology concerned with the distribution and mapping of the rainfall. **hyetology,** *n.* **hyetometer,** *n.* A rain-gauge.

Hygeia (hī jē′ ȧ) [Gr. *Hugeia, Hugieia*, from *hugiēs*, healthy], *n.* The goddess of health. **hygeian,** *a.* Relating to Hygeia, the goddess of health; pertaining to hygiene. ***hygeist** (hī′ jē ist), *n.*

hygiene (hī′ jēn, hī′ ji ēn) [F. *hygiène*, Gr. *hugienē technē*, the art of health, as prec.], *n.* The science of the prevention of disease; the art of preserving health, esp. of the community at large; sanitary science. **hygienic, -al** (hī ji en′ ik, -ē′ nik, -ȧl), *a.* **hygienics,** *n.* Hygiene. **hygienically,** *adv.* **hygienist** (hī ji ė nist), *n.* **hygiology** (hī ji ol′ ŏ ji), *n.* A treatise on hygiene; hygiene.

hygro- [Gr. *hugros*, wet], *comb. form.* Moist, pertaining to or denoting the presence of moisture.

hygrodeik (hī′ grō dīk) [Gr. *deiknunai*, to show], *n.* A hygrometer indicating the degree of atmospheric humidity by an index set according to the heights of a wet or dry bulb thermometer.

hygrograph (hī′ grō grăf), *n.* A self-recording hygrometer.

hygrology (hī grol′ ō ji), *n.* The branch of physics relating to humidity, esp. of the atmosphere.

hygrometer (hī grom′ ė tĕr), *n.* An instrument for measuring the moisture of the air, etc. **hygrometric, -al,** *a.* **hygrometry,** *n.* The branch of physics concerned with the measurement of moisture, esp. of the air.

hygrophanous (hī grof′ ȧ nŭs) [Gr. *phanein*, to appear], *a.* (*Bot.*, *Min.*, etc.) Appearing transparent when wet and opaque when dry. **hygrophaneity,** *n.*

hygroscope (hī′ grō skōp), *n.* An instrument for indicating the degree of moisture in the atmosphere. **hygroscopic, -al,** *a.* Pertaining to or indicated by the hygroscope; imbibing moisture from the atmosphere (of bodies); perceptible or liable to detection through moisture. **hygroscopicity,** *n.*

hygrostatics (hī grō stăt′ iks), *n.* Hygrometry.

hying [HIE].

hyleg (hī′ lĕg) [Pers. *hailāj*], *n.* (*Astrol.*) The planet ruling, or in the sign of the zodiac above the eastern horizon, at the hour of a person's nativity.

hylic (hī′ lik) [Gr. *hulikos*, as foll.], *a.* Of or relating to matter; material. **hylicism, hylism,** *n.* **hylicist** (hī′ li sist), *n.* A philosopher who assigns a material basis to being, as water or air.

hylo- [Gr. *hule*, matter], *comb. form.* Materialistic; pertaining to wood.

hylogenesis (hī lō jen′ ė sis), *n.* The origin of matter. **hylogeny** (hī loj′ e ni), *a.*

hyloism (hī′ lō izm), *n.* Hylotheism.

hylomorphism (hī lō môr′ fizm), *n.* The philosophy that finds the first cause of the universe in matter. **hylomorphic, -al,** *a.* **hylomorphist,** *n.*

hylotheism (hī lō thē′ izm), *n.* The system which regards God and matter as identical; pantheism. **hylotheist,** *n.*

hylotomous (hī lot′ ō mŭs) [Gr. *temnein*, to cut], *a.* (*Ent.*) Wood-cutting (of certain insects).

hylozoism (hī lō zō′ izm) [Gr. *zoe*, life], *n.* The doctrine that matter is necessarily endowed with life. **hylozoic,** *a.* **hylozoist,** *n.* **hylozoistic,** *a.*

Hymen (1) (hī′ mėn) [L., from Gr. *humēn*], *n.* The god of marriage. **hymeneal, *-an** (hī mė nē′ ăl, -ȧn), *a.* Pertaining to marriage. *n.* A marriage song. **hymeneally,** *adv.*

hymen (2) (hī′ mėn) [Gr. *humēn*, a membrane], *n.* (*Anat.*) A membrane stretched across the vaginal entrance; (*Bot.*) the fine pellicle enclosing a flower in the bud.

hymenium (hī mē′ ni ŭm) [Gr. *humenion*, dim. of *humēn*, HYMEN (1)], *n.* (*Bot.*) The spore-bearing stratum or surface in fungi. **hymeniferous** (-nif′ ėr ŭs), *a.*

hymeno- [Gr. *humēn humenos*, a membrane], *comb. form.* Membranous.

hymenogeny (hī me noj′ e ni), *n.* The production of membranes by the simple contacts of two liquids.

hymenography (hī men og′ rȧ fi), *n.* A description of membranes.

hymenoid (hī′ men oid), *a.* (*Bot.*) Of the nature or having the structure of a membrane.

hymenology (hī men ol′ ō ji), *n.* The branch of anatomical science that treats of membranes. **hymenological,** *a.*

hymenomycete (hī me nō mī sēt′) [Gr. *muketes*, mushroom], *n.* (*Bot.*) One of the *Hymenomycetæ*, an order of fungi characterized by an exposed hymenium. **hymenomycetal, -toid, tous,** *a.*

hymenophyllaceous (hī me nō fi lā′ shŭs) [Gr. *phullon*, a leaf], *a.* (*Bot.*) Belonging to or having the characteristics of the *Hymenophyllaceæ* or filmy ferns.

hymenoptera (hī men ŏp′ tėr ȧ) [Gr. *pteron*, a wing], *n.pl.* (*Ent.*) An order of insects having four membranous wings, as the bee, wasp, ant, etc. **hymenopteral, -ous,** *a.* **hymenopteran,** *a.* and *n.*

hymn (him) [O.F. *hymne*, L. *hymnus*, Gr. *humnos*], *n.* A song or ode in praise or adoration of God or some deity; a sacred or solemn song or ode, esp. a religious song not taken from the Bible. *v.t.* To praise or worship in hymns; to sing hymns to; to express in hymns. *v.i.* To sing hymns. **hymn-book,** *n.* A book of hymns. **hymnal** (him′ nȧl), *n.* A collection of hymns, esp. for public worship. **hymnary,** *n.* A hymnal. **hymnic,** *a.* **hymnist,** *n.* A composer of hymns. **hymnody,** *n.* The singing of hymns; the composition of hymns; hymns collectively; hymnology. ***hymnodist,** *n.* ***hymnography** (him nog′ rȧ fi), *n.* The art or act of writing hymns. **hymnographer,** *n.* **hymnology** (him nol′ ŏ ji), *n.* The composition or the study of hymns; hymns collectively. **hymnologic** (-loj′ ik), *a.* **hymnologist** (-nol′ ŏ jist), *n.*

hyoid (hī′ oid) [F. *hyoïde*, L. *hyoïdes*, Gr. *huoeidēs* (letter *u*, -OID)], *a.* (*Anat.*) Resembling the Greek *υ* in shape; pertaining to the hyoid bone. **hyoid bone:** The bone supporting the tongue.

hyoscyamine (hī ŏ sī′ ȧ mīn) [Gr. *huoscuamos* (*huos*, gen. of *hus*, sow, *kuamos*, bean)], *n.* A white crystalline alkaloid obtained from the seeds of henbane, *Hyoscyamus niger*, highly poisonous, used as a sedative. **hyoscine,** *n.* (*Med.*) A strong narcotic drug, scopolamine.

hyp [HIP (3)].

hypæthral (hi-, hī pē′ thrȧl) [L. *hypæthrus*, Gr. *hupaithros* (HYPO-, *aithēr*, ETHER)], *a.* Open to the sky, roofless (esp. of a temple or sanctuary not intended to be roofed). **hypæthron,** *n.* (*Arch.*) A temple with a central space open to the sky.

hypalgia (hip ăl'-, hī păl' ji ȧ) [HYPO-, Gr. *-algia algos*, pain], *n.* (*Path.*) Reduction of or freedom from pain. **hypalgic,** *a.*

hypallage (hī păl' ȧ ji) [L. *hypallagē*, Gr. *hupallagē* (HYPO-, *allagē*, change, from *allassein*, to change)], *n.* (*Gram. and Rhet.*) Interchange of natural or grammatical relations between terms in a sentence.

hyper- [L., from Gr. *huper*], *comb. form.* Above, beyond; excessive, beyond measure.

hyperacute (hī pěr ȧ kūt'), *a.* (*Path.*) Morbidly or excessively acute. **hyperacuity,** *n.*

hyperæmia (hī pěr ē' mi ȧ), *n.* (*Path.*) Morbid or excessive accumulation of blood. **hyperæmic,** *a.*

hyperæsthesia (hī pěr es thē' zi ȧ), *n.* (*Path.*) Morbid or excessive sensibility, esp. of the nerves. **hyperæsthetic,** *a.*

hyperalgesia (hī pěr ăl jē' zi ȧ), *n.* (*Path.*) A condition of exaggerated sensibility to pain.

hyperbaton (hī pěr' bȧ tǒn) [L., from Gr. *huperbaton* (*bainein*, to go)], *n.* (*Rhet.*) A figure by which words are transposed or inverted from their natural and grammatical order. **hyperbatic** (-băt' ik), *a.* **hyperbatically,** *adv.*

hyperbola (hī pěr' bǒ lȧ) [Gr. *huperbolē*, see foll.], *a.* (*Geom.*) A plane curve formed by cutting a cone when the intersecting plane makes a greater angle with the base than the side of the cone makes. **hyperbolic** (-bol' ik), *a.* (*Geom.*) Pertaining to or of the nature of an hyperbola. **hyperboliform** (-bol' i form), *a.* Having the form of an hyperbola. **hyperboloid** (hī pěr' bǒ loid), *n.* (*Geom.*) A solid formed by the revolution of an hyperbola about its axis.

hyperbole (hī pěr' bǒ lē) [L., from Gr. *huperbolē* (HYPER-, *ballein*, to throw)], *n.* (*Rhet.*) A figure of speech expressing much more than the truth; rhetorical exaggeration. **hyperbolical** (-bol' i kȧl), *a.* Of the nature of hyperbole; (*Geom.*) hyperbolic. **hyperbolically,** *adv.* **hyperbolism,** *n.* The use of hyperbole; a hyperbolic expression. **hyperbolist,** *n.* ***hyperbolize,** *v.i.* To use hyperbolical language. *v.t.* To express in hyperbolical language.

hyperborean (hī pėr bôr' ė ȧn) [late L. *hyperboreānus*, L. *hyperboreus*, Gr. *huperboreos* (HYPER-, *Boreas*, the north wind)], *a.* Belonging to or inhabiting the extreme north; (*Gr. Ant.*) of or pertaining to the Hyperboreans. *n.* One living in the extreme north; (*Gr. Ant.*) one of a people supposed to live in a land beyond the north wind, distinguished for piety and happiness. **hyperboreanism,** *n.*

hypercatalectic (hī pėr kăt ȧ lek' tik) [late L. *hypercatalēcticus*], *a.* (*Pros.*) Having a final redundant syllable.

hypercritic (hī pėr krit' ik), *n.* One unreasonably critical; a captious censor. **a.* Hypercritical. **hypercritical,** *a.* Unreasonably critical; captiously censorious, over-nice. **hypercritically,** *adv.* **hypercriticism,** *n.* **hypercriticize,** *v.t.* To criticize captiously. *v.i.* To be hypercritical.

hyperdulia (hī pėr dū li' ȧ), *n.* (*R.-C. Ch.*) The particular veneration due to the Virgin Mary, dist. from that paid to the saints and from the worship paid to God.

hyperemia [HYPERÆMIA].

hyperesthesia [HYPERÆSTHESIA].

hypericum (hī per' i kǔm) [L., from Gr. *hupereikon* (*ereikē*, heath)], *n.* (*Bot.*) A genus of herbaceous plants or shrubs typified by the St. John's wort.

hyperinosis (hī pėr i nō' sis) [Gr. *is inos*, fibre, -OSIS], *n.* (*Path.*) A morbid state of the blood characterized by excess of fibrin. **hyperinosed, hyperinotic** (-not' ik), *a.*

hypermetrical (hī pėr met' ri kȧl) [Gr. *hupermetros*], *a.* (*Pros.*) Having a redundant syllable or syllables; redundant (of such a syllable). ***hypermeter** (hī pěr' mė těr), *n.*

hypermetropia (hī pėr mė trō' pi ȧ) [Gr. *hupermetros*, as prec., *ōps ōpos*, eye], *n.* (*Path.*) An abnormal state of the eye characterized by long-sightedness, opposed to myopia. **hypermetropic** (-trop' ik), *a.* **hyperopia** (-ō' pi ȧ), *n.* **hyperopic** (-op' ik), *a.*

hyperoodon (hī pėr ō' ǒ don) [Gr. *huperōos*, upper, superior, *odous odontos*, tooth], *n.* A genus of cetaceans comprising the bottle-nosed whales.

hyperphasia (hī pėr fā' zi ȧ) [Gr. *phasis*, speaking], *n.* (*Path.*) Lack of control over the organs of speech. **hyperphasic** (-făz' ik), *a.*

hyperphysical (hī pėr fiz' i kȧl), *a.* Supernatural.

hyperplasia (hī pėr plā' zi ȧ) [Gr. *plasis*, formation, from *plassein*, to mould], *n.* (*Path.*) Excessive growth due to abnormal multiplication of cells. **hyperplasm** (hī' pėr plăzm), *n.* **hyperplasic, hyperplastic** (hī per plăz' ik, -plăs' tik), *a.*

hypersarcoma (hī pėr sȧr kō' mȧ), **hypersarcosis** (hī pėr sar kō' sis), *n.* (*Path.*) A fleshy excrescence; proud flesh.

hypersensitive (hī pėr sen' si tiv), *a.* Excessively or morbidly sensitive. **hypersensitiveness,** *n.*

hypersthene (hī' pėrs thēn) [F. *hypersthène* (Gr. *sthenos*, strength)], *n.* (*Min.*) An orthorhombic, foliated, brittle mineral allied to hornblende, with a beautiful pearly lustre. **hypersthenic** (1) (-then' ik), *a.* **hypersthenite** (-thē' nīt), *n.* (*Min.*) A variety of pyroxenite mainly composed of hypersthene.

hypersthenia (hī pėrs thē' ni ȧ) [Gr. *sthenos*, strength], *n.* (*Path.*) A morbid condition characterized by excessive excitement of the vital powers. **hypersthenic** (2) (-then' ik), *a.*

hyperthesis (hī pěr' thė sis) [Gr. *hyperthesis* (*thesis*, placing, from *tithenai*, to put)], *n.* (*Philol.*) Transposition of a letter from one syllable to another. **hyperthetic** (-thet' ik), *a.*

hypertrophy (hī pěr' trǒ fi) [Gr. *-trophia*, from *trephein*, to nourish], *n.* Excessive development or enlargement from over-nutrition. *v.t.* To affect with hypertrophy. *v.i.* To be affected by hypertrophy. **hypertrophic, -al** (trof' ik, -ȧl), **hypertrophous** (hī pěr' trǒ fŭs), *a.*

hypethral [HYPÆTHRAL].

hyphen (hī' fėn) [L., from Gr. *huphen*], *n.* A short stroke (-) joining two words or parts of words. *v.t.* To join by a hyphen. **hyphenic** (-fen' ik), *a.* **hyphenate** (hī' fė nāt), **hyphenize,** *v.t.* **hyphenation** (-nā' shŭn), **hyphenization** (-zā' shŭn), *n.*

hypno- [Gr. *hupnos*, sleep], *comb. form.*

hypnogenesis (hip nō jen' e sis), *n.* Inducement of hypnotic sleep. **hypnogeny** (hip noj' e ni), *n.* **hypnogenetic,** *a.*

hypnology (hip nol' ō ji), *n.* The study of the phenomena of sleep; a treatise on sleep. **hypnologist,** *n.*

hypnosis (hip nō' sis), *n.* (*Med.*) Inducement of sleep; a morbid state of sleep; a state resembling sleep in which the sub-conscious mind responds to external suggestions and forgotten memories are recovered.

hypnotherapy (hip nō ther' ȧ pi), *n.* (*Med.*) Treatment by hypnotism.

hypnotic (hip not' ik), *a.* Causing sleep; soporific; of, pertaining to, or inducing hypnotism. *n.* A medicine that produces sleep; an opiate.

hypnotism (hip' nō tizm), *n.* An artificial method of inducing sleep or hypnosis; sleep artificially produced. **hypnotist,** *n.* **hypnotize,** *v.t.* To affect with hypnotism. **hypnotizable,** *a.* **hypnotizability,** *n.* **hypnotization,** *n.* **hypnotizer,** *n.*

Hypnum (hip' nŭm) [Gr. *hupnon*], *n.* (*pl.* **-nums, -na**) (*Bot.*) A genus of pleurocarpous mosses known as feather-moss.

hypo (hī′ pō) [abbr. Sodium hyposulphite], *n.* (*Phot.*) Common term for Sodium thiosulphate, the normal fixing solution in photography.

hypo- [Gr. *hupo*, under], *comb. form.* Under, below; less than; (*Chem.*) denoting compounds having a lower degree of oxidation in a series. **hypoblast** (hip′ ŏ-, hī′ pŏ blăst) [Gr. *blastos*, sprout], *n.* (*Biol.*) The inmost membrane of the blastoderm. **hypoblastic** (-blăs′ tik), *a.*

hypobole (hi pob′ ŏ lē) [Gr. *hupobolē* (ballein, to throw)], *n.* (*Rhet.*) A mode of reasoning in which several things seemingly opposed to the argument are mentioned and then refuted.

hypobranchial (hip ŏ-, hī pŏ brăng′ ki ăl), *a.* (*Anat.*) Situated below the gills or branchiæ. *n.pl.* (*Ichthyol.*) The lower and inner part of the branchial arch.

hypocaust (hip′ ŏ kawst) [late L. *hypocaustum*, Gr. *hupokauston* (*kaiein*, fut. *kaus-*, to burn)], *n.* (*Rom. Ant.*) A space or series of channels under the floor by which heat was conducted from a furnace to heat a building, room, bath, etc.; a stove.

hypochondria (hip′ ŏ kon′ dri ă) [late L., pl., from Gr. *hupochondria*, pl., the soft parts below the cartilage (*chondros*, cartilage, esp. that of the breastbone)], *n.* (*Path.*) A morbid condition characterized by excessive anxiety with regard to the health, and depression of spirits [see also HYPOCHONDRIUM]. **hypochondriac,** *a.* Produced or characterized by hypochondria; having a disordered mind; causing melancholy; (*Anat.*) pertaining to, connected with, or situated in the hypochondria. *n.* A person affected with hypochondria. ***hypochondriacal,** *a.* **hypochondriacally,** *adv.* **hypochondriasis** (-drī′ ă sis), ***hypochondriacism,** *n.* ***hypochondriast** (-kon′ dri ăst), *n.* **hypochondrium,** *n.* (*pl.* **-dria**) (*Anat.*) Either of the two regions of the abdomen situated to the right and left under the costal cartilages and short ribs.

hypocist (hip′ ŏ-, hī′ pŏ sist) [F. *hypociste*, L. *hypocistis*, Gr. *hupokistis*], *n.* An astringent inspissated juice obtained from the fruit of *Cytinus hypocistis*, a plant from southern France.

hypocrisy (hi pok′ ri si) [O.F. *hypocrisie*, L. *hypocrisis*, Gr. *hupokrisis*, acting of a part, from *hupokrinesthai* (*krinein*, to judge, decide)], *n.* Dissimulation; a feigning to be what one is not; a pretence to virtue or goodness. **hypocrite** (hip′ ŏ krit), *n.* One who practises hypocrisy; a dissembler. **hypocritical** (hip ŏ krit′ i kăl), *a.* **hypocritically,** *adv.*

hypocycloid (hip ŏ-, hī pŏ sī′ kloid), *n.* (*Geom.*) A curve generated by a point on the circumference of a circle rolling round the inside of the circumference of another circle. **hypocycloidal** (-kloi′ dăl), *a.*

hypoderm (hī′ pŏ-, hip′ ŏ dĕrm), ***hypoderma*** (hī pŏ-, hip ŏ dĕr′ mă) [Gr. *derma*, skin], *n.* (*pl.* *-mata*) (*Zool.*) A layer beneath the outer integument, as the inner membrane lining the elytra of beetles; (*Bot.*) the cellular layer beneath the epidermis of leaves etc. **hypodermal** (-dĕr′ măl), *a.* Hypodermic. **hypodermic** (-dĕr′ mik), *a.* Pertaining to parts underlying the skin. *n.* A drug introduced into the system by injection under the skin; (*colloq.*) a hypodermic syringe. **hypodermic injection:** An injection (of narcotics, antitoxins, etc.) beneath the skin. **hypodermic syringe:** A small syringe with a hollow needle for giving hypodermic injections. **hypodermically,** *adv.*

hypogastrium (hip ŏ-, hī pŏ găs′ tri ŭm) [Gr. *hupogastrion* (*gastēr*, belly)], *n.* (*Anat.*) The middle part of the lowest zone into which the abdomen is divided. **hypogastric,** *a.* **hypogastrocele** [-CELE], *n.* (*Path.*) Hernia in the region of the hypogastrium.

hypogean, -ous, -geal (hip ŏ-, hī pŏ jē′ ăn, -ŭs, -ăl) [L. *hypogēus*, Gr. *hypogeios* (*gē*, earth)], *a.* Existing or growing underground; subterranean. **hypogene** (hip′ ŏ-, hī′ pŏ jēn), **hypogenic** (-jen′ ik), *a.* (*Geol.*) Applied to rocks that were formed under the surface; plutonic.

hypogeum (hip ŏ-, hī pŏ jē′ ŭm), *n.* (*pl.* **-gea**) (*Arch.*) A building or part of a building below the level of the ground.

hypoglossal (hip ŏ-, hī pŏ glos′ ăl) [Gr. *glossa*, tongue], *a.* Under the tongue. **hypoglossal nerve:** The motor nerve of the tongue. ***hypoglossus,*** *n.* (*Anat.*) The hypoglossal nerve.

hypognathous (hī pog′ nă thŭs) [Gr. *gnathos*, jaw], *a.* (*Ornith.*) Having a lower mandible longer than the upper. **hypognathism,** *n.*

hypogynous (hi-, hī poj′ i nŭs), *a.* (*Bot.*) Of stamens, growing from below the base of the ovary; of plants, having the stamens so situated.

hypomania (hi pō mā′ ni ă), *n.* The mental state of over-excitability.

hyponasty (hip′ ŏ-, hī′ pŏ năs ti) [Gr. *nastos*, solid, from *nassein*, to press], *n.* (*Bot.*) More active growth of a plant-organ on the under side causing a tendency to upward curvature.

hypophosphate (hip ŏ-, hī pŏ fos′ făt), *n.* (*Chem.*) A salt of hypophosphoric acid. **hypophosphite** (-fīt), *n.* A salt of hypophosphorous acid. **hypophosphoric** (-for′ ik), **hypophosphorous** (-fos′ fŏ rŭs), *a.* **hypophosphoric acid,** *n.* An acid formed by action of water and oxygen on phosphorus. **hypophosphorous acid,** *n.* A weak acid composed of hydrogen, phosphorus, and oxygen.

hypophysis (hi-, hī pof′ i sis) [Gr. *hupophusis* (*phusis*, from *phuein*, to grow)], *n.* (*pl.* **-physes**) (*Bot.*) A cell in the embryo, in flowering plants, from which the root and root-cap are developed; in mosses, an enlarged part of the pedicel beneath the capsule.

hypostasis (hi-, hī pos′ tă sis) [late L., from Gr. *hupostasis* (*stasis*, standing, basis)], *n.* (*pl.* **-stases**) That which forms the basis of anything; (*Metaph.*) that by which a thing subsists, substance as distinguished from attributes; the essence or essential principle; (*Theol.*) the personal subsistence, as opposed to substance, of the Godhead; one of the persons of the Trinity; (*Path.*) congestion of the blood (in an organ) by weight. **hypostatic, -al** (-stăt′ ik, -ăl), *a.* Pertaining to hypostasis; constitutive or elemental; constituting a distinct personality or substance. **hypostatic union:** The union of the divine and human natures in Christ. **hypostatically,** *adv.* **hypostasize** (hī pos′ tă sīz), *v.t.* To attribute proper personal existence to; to treat as or make into a substance. **hypostasization, -tization** (-zā′ shŭn). *n.*

hypostome (hip′ ŏ-, hī′ pŏ stōm) [Gr. *stoma*, mouth], *n.* (*Zool.*) A part or organ situated below the mouth, as the proboscis of Hydrozoa, the under lip of a trilobite etc. ***hypostoma*** (-pos′ tŏ mă), *n.* (*pl.* ***-mata,*** -stom′ ă tă).

hypostyle (hip′ ŏ-, hī′ pŏ stīl) [Gr. *stulos*, pillar], *a.* (*Arch.*) Having the roof supported by pillars. *n.* A building with a roof or ceiling supported by pillars; a covered colonnade; a pillared hall.

hyposulphite (hip ŏ-, hī pŏ sŭl′ fīt), *n.* (*Chem.*) A thiosulphate, a salt of hyposulphurous acid. **hyposulphuric acid,** *n.* Acid containing two more atoms of oxygen per molecule than sulphuric acid. **hyposulphurous acid,** *n.* An unstable acid containing one more sulphur atom per molecule than sulphuric acid.

hypotaxis (hip ŏ-, hī pŏ tăk′ sis), *n.* (*Gram.*) Subordinate construction, opp. to parataxis. **hypotactic** (-tăk′ tik), *a.*

hypotenuse (hi-, hī pot′ ė nūz) [F. *hypoténuse*, late L. *hypotenusa*, Gr. *hupoteinousa*, fem. p.p. of *hupoteinein* (*teinein*, to stretch)], *n.* (*Geom.*) The side of a right-angled triangle opposite to the right angle.

hypothec (hi-, hī poth′ ėk) [F. *hypothèque*, late L. *hypothēca*, Gr. *hupothēkē* (HYPO-, *thēkē*, from *tithenai*, to place)], *n.* (*Law, esp. Sc.*) A security in favour of a creditor over the property of his debtor, while the property continues in the debtor's possession. **hypothecary,** *a.* Of or pertaining to a pledge or hypothecation.

hypothecate (hī poth′ e kāt) [as prec.], *v.t.* To pledge or mortgage in security for some debt or liability. **hypothecation,** *n.* **hypothecator,** *n.*

hypothermia (hī pō thĕr′ mi ȧ) [Gr. *therme*, heat], *n.* (*Med.*) Subnormal body temperature, esp. when induced for surgical purposes.

hypothesis (hi-, hī poth′ ė sis) [L., from Gr. *hupothesis* (HYPO-, THESIS)], *n.* (*pl.* **-theses**) A proposition assumed for the purpose of argument; a theory assumed to account for something not understood; a mere supposition or assumption. **hypothesize,** *v.i.* To form hypotheses. *v.t.* To assume. **hypothetic, -al** (-thet′ it, -ȧl), *a.* Founded on or of the nature of an hypothesis; conjectural, conditional. **hypothetically,** *adv.*

hypotrachelium (hip ȯ-, hī pȯ trȧ kē′ li ŭm) [Gr. *hupotrachelion* (HYPO-, *trachelos*, neck)], *n.* (*Arch.*) A groove round the junction of the capital and shaft in a Doric column.

hypotyposis (hip ȯ ti-, -tī pō′ sis) [Gr. *hupotupōsis* (HYPO-, -TYPE)], *n.* (*pl.* **-oses**) (*Rhet.*) A vivid or forcible description of a scene, so as to present it attractively to the mind.

hypozoic (hī pȯ-, hip ȯ zō′ ik) [HYPO-, Gr. *zōē*, life], *a.* (*Geol.*) Situated beneath the strata that contain organic remains. **hypozoa,** *n.pl.* (*Zool.*) Protozoa. **hypozoan,** *a.* and *n.*

hypso- [Gr. *hupsos*, height], *comb. form.*

hypsography (hip sog′ rȧ fi), *n.* The branch of geography concerned with the altitudes above sea-level. **hypsographical,** *a.*

hypsometer (hip som′ e tėr), *n.* An instrument for measuring heights above sea-level by observing the boiling-point of water with a delicate thermometer and so determining the relative atmospheric pressure. **hypsometric, -al** (-met′ rik, -ȧl), *a.* **hypsometry** (-som′ ė tri), *n.* The art of measuring heights by observing differences in barometric pressures at different altitudes.

hypural (hi-, hī pū′ rȧl) [HYPO-, Gr. *oura*, tail], *a.* (*Ichthyol.*) Situated below the tail, as the bones supporting the fin-rays.

hyrax (hīr′ ăks) [Gr. *hurax*, shrew-mouse], *n.* A genus of small hare-like quadrupeds, comprising the Syrian rock-rabbit or cony of Scripture and the South African rock-badger. **hyracid** (hī răs′ id), *a.* **hyracoid** (hī′ rȧ koid), *a.* and *n.*

hyson (hī′ sȯn) [Chin. *hei-ch'un*, bright spring], *n.* A kind of green tea. **hyson-skin,** *n.* The refuse of this.

hy-spy (hī spī) [I SPY], *n.* Hide-and-seek.

hyssop (his′ ȯp) [L. *hyssōpus*, Gr. *hussōpos*, perh. from Heb.], *n.* A labiate plant, *Hyssopus officinalis*, with blue flowers; (*Bibl.*) an unidentified plant the twigs of which were used for sprinkling in Jewish rites of purification.

hysterectomy [HYSTERO-].

hysteresis (his tėr ē′ sis) [Gr. *husterēsis*, from *husteros*, late], *n.* (*Elec.*) The tendency of a magnetic substance to remain in a certain magnetic condition, 'the lag of magnetic effects behind their causes.' **hysteresial,** *a.*

hysteria (his tēr′ i ȧ) [mod. L., from Gr. *hustera*, the womb (from its having been attributed formerly to disturbance of the womb)], *n.* (*Path.*) A nervous disorder of women, occurring in paroxysms, and often simulating other diseases. **hysteriac** (his ter′ i ăk), *n.* One subject to hysteria. **hysteric** (his ter′ ik), *a.* Hysterical. *n.pl.* A fit or fits of hysteria, hysteria. **hysterical,** *a.* Pertaining to or affected with hysteria; morbidly emotional or excitable. **hysterical fit:** (*Path.*) An emotional paroxysm of crying, laughing, etc., occurring in hysteria. **hysterically,** *adv.* **hysteroid** (his′ tėr oid), *a.* Resembling hysteria.

hysteritis (his tėr ī′ tis) [as foll., -ITIS], *n.* (*Path.*) Inflammation of the uterus.

hystero-, hyster- [Gr. *hustera*, womb], *comb. form.* **hysterectomy** (his tėr ek′ tȯ mi) [G. *ektomē* (*ek-*, out, *temnein*, to cut)], *n.* (*Surg.*) The removal of the womb by excision. **hysterogenic** (1) (-jen′ ik), *a.* (*Path.*) Producing hysteria. **hysterogenous** (-oj′ ė nŭs), *a.* **hysterogeny** (-oj′ ė ni), *n.*

hysterogenetic (his tėr ȯ jė net′ ik) [Gr. *husteros*, later, GENETIC], *a.* (*Bot.*) Later in origin or development. **hysterogenic** (2), *a.*

hysteroid [HYSTERIA].

hysterology (his tėr ol′ ȯ ji) [HYSTERO-, -LOGY], *n.* The branch of medical science concerned with the uterus; a treatise on this.

hysteron proteron (his′ tėr on prot′ ėr on) [Gr. *husteron*, latter, *proteron*, former], *n.* (*Gram.* and *Rhet.*) A figure of speech in which what should follow comes first; an inversion of the natural or logical order.

hysterotomy (his tėr ot′ ȯ mi) [HYSTERO-, -TOMY], *n.* (*Surg.*) Delivery of a child through the walls of the abdomen; hysterectomy.

hythe [HITHE].

I

I (1), **i,** the ninth letter and the third vowel in the English alphabet (*pl.* **Is, I's**), has two principal sounds: long, as in *bīnd, fīnd*; short, as in *fin, bin, win*, etc.; and three minor sounds: (1) as in *dirk* (dĕrk), (2) as in *intrigue* (in trēg′), and (3) the consonantal sound of *y*, as in *behaviour* (bė hā′ vyėr), *onion* (ŭn′ yȯn); (*Maths.*) the symbol for the square root of minus one.

I (2) (ī) [A.-S. *ic* (cp. Dut. *ik*, Icel. *ek*, G. *ich*, L. *ego*, Gr. *egō*)], *nom. sing. 1st pers. pron.* (*obj.* **me,** *poss.* **my;** *pl. nom.* **we,** *obj.* **us,** *poss.* **our**) In speaking or writing denotes oneself. *n.* (*Metaph.*) The self-conscious subject, the ego.

***I** (3) [AYE (1)].

-i [L.], *suf.* Indicating plural of L. nouns in *-us* or *-er*, as *fungi, hippopotami*; also of It. nouns and adjectives in *-o* or *-e*, *banditti, literati.*

-ia [L. and Gr.], *suf.* Forming abstract nouns, as *mania, militia*; names of countries etc., as *Australia, Bulgaria, Helvetia*; names of diseases, as *hysteria, malaria, neuralgia*; names of botanical genera, etc., as *Begonia, Gaillardia, phanerogamia, Saponaria*; names of alkaloids, as *morphia, strychnia*; (*pl.* of L. *-ium*, Gr. *-ion*) *bacteria, mammalia, regalia, reptilia.*

-ial [L. *-iālis, -iāle*], *suf.* Forming adjectives, as *celestial, terrestrial.*

iambus (ī ăm′ bŭs) [L., from Gr. *iambos*, an iambic verse, a lampoon, from *iaptein*, to assail], *n.* (*pl.* **-buses**) (*Pros.*) A poetic foot of one short and one long, or one unaccented and one accented syllable. **iamb** (ī′ ămb), *n.* An iambus. **iambic** (ī ăm′ bik), *a.* Of or pertaining to the iambus; composed of iambics. *n.* An iambic foot; an iambic verse. ***iambically,** *adv.* **iambist,** *n.* **iambize,** *v.t.* **iambographer** (-bog′ rȧ fėr), *n.* A writer of iambics.

-ian [L. *-ānus*, -AN, with a euphonic or connective *-i-*], *suf.* Forming nouns or adjectives, as *Athenian, Baconian, Bristolian, Cantabrigian.*

-iasis [L., from Gr. *-iasis*, from *iāsthai*, to heal], *comb. form.* Noting a disease, as *elephantiasis, phthiriasis.*

iatric, -al (ī ăt′ rik, -ȧl) [Gr. *iātrikos*, as prec.], *a.* Pertaining to physicians or medicine. ***iatraliptic** (ī ăt rȧ lip′ tik) [Gr. *aleiptes*, anointer], *a.* Curing by the application of ointments and friction. ***iatrarchy** (ī ăt′ rår ki), *n.* The medical hierarchy.

iatrochemical (ī ăt rō kem′ i kăl) [CHEMICAL], *a.* Pertaining to the application of chemistry to medicine. **iatrochemist,** *n.* **iatrochemistry,** *n.* **iatrology** (-trol′ ō ji), *n.* The science of or a treatise on medicine.

Iberian (ī bēr′ i ăn) [L. *Ibēria*, from Gr. *Ibēres*, -AN], *a.* Of or pertaining to ancient Iberia in Europe, comprising modern Spain and Portugal, or ancient Iberia in Asia, now Transcaucasian Georgia. *n.* One of the inhabitants of ancient Iberia in Europe, or in Asia; one of an ancient race, chiefly dolichocephalic, who inhabited western Europe and probably entered the British Isles early in the Neolithic period, variously identified with the Silures, the modern Basques, etc., but not recognized as a definite ethnological group by most recent authorities; the language of ancient Iberia. **Iberian Peninsula:** Spain and Portugal.

Iberis (ī bēr′ is) [as prec.], *n.* (*Bot.*) A genus of crucifers comprising the candytufts.

ibex (ī′ beks) [L.], *n.* The name given to several species of wild goats inhabiting the mountain regions of Europe and Asia, of which the best known is the common ibex or steenbok, *Capra ibex.*

ibidem (i bī′ dem) [L. *ibi*, there, *-dem*, suf. as in *idem*, the same], *adv.* In the same place (as in a book, page, etc.) (abbrev. *ibid.*).

ibis (ī′ bis) [L. and Gr., prob. of Egyptian orig.], *n.* A genus of heron-like wading birds belonging to the family *Ibididæ*, esp. *Ibis religiosa*, the sacred ibis, which was venerated by the ancient Egyptians.

-ible [L. *-ibilis*, -ABLE], *suf.* As in *edible, risible.*

Iblees, (*pl.*) [EBLIS].

-ic [L. *icus* (sometimes through F. *-ique*), usu. from Gr. *-ikos*], *suf.* Of, pertaining to, like, as in *alcoholic, algebraic, domestic, Miltonic, plutonic*; (*Chem.*) in acids, etc., denoting a higher state of oxidation than the suffix *-ous*; forming names of sciences, arts, etc., as *arithmetic, epic, logic, music*; (*later in pl.*) as *acoustics, æsthetics, economics, metaphysics, politics*; (*recent var.*) *æsthetic, metaphysic*, etc.

-ical [IC, -AL], *suf.* Forming adjectives, as *algebraical, comical, historical, political.* **-ically,** *suf.* Forming adverbs, as *historically, politically.*

Icarian (ī kâr′ i ăn) [L. *Ikarius*, Gr. *Ikarios*, from *Ikaros*, Icarus, the son of Dædalus, who, on his flight from Crete, soared too high, the sun melting the wax which fastened his wings to his body, causing him to fall and perish in the sea], *a.* Soaring too high; rash or adventurous in flight.

ice (īs) [A.-S. *īs* (cp. Dut. *ijs*, Icel. *īss*, G. *eis*)], *n.* Water congealed by cold; a frozen confection of cream, syrup, etc., ice-cream; a confection of sugar etc. used for coating cakes, etc. *v.t.* To cover or cool with ice; to convert into ice; to coat with concreted sugar; to frost; to freeze. **to break the ice** [BREAK (1)]. **to cut no ice:** (*colloq.*) To fail to make an impression, to fall flat, to be unimportant. **ice age:** A glacial period. **ice-axe,** *n.* An axe shaped like a pickaxe, used by mountain-climbers for cutting steps on glaciers etc. **ice-bird,** *n.* An Arctic seabird, the little auk or sea-dove. **ice-blink,** *n.* A luminous reflection over the horizon from snow- or ice-fields. **ice-brook,** *n.* A frozen stream or brook. **ice-boat,** *n.* A boat for travelling on ice; a heavily-built boat for breaking a passage through ice. **ice-bound,** *a.* Completely surrounded with ice; fringed or edged with ice. **ice-box,** *n.* A refrigerator. **ice-cap,** *n.* The mass of ice and snow that covers the polar regions. **ice-cave,** *n.* A cave in which ice remains unmelted throughout the year. **ice-claw,** *n.* An apparatus for lifting blocks of ice. **ice-cream,** *n.* Cream or custard flavoured and artificially frozen. **ice-drift,** *n.* Masses of floating ice. **ice-fall,** *n.* A shattered part of a glacier where it descends a steep slope. **ice-field,** *n.* A large expanse of ice, esp. such as exist in the Polar regions. **ice-floe, -pack,** *n.* A sheet of floating ice. **ice-foot,** *n.* A hill or wall of ice along the shore in Polar regions. **ice-house,** *n.* A repository for the storage of ice during warm weather. **iceman,** *n.* One who deals in ice or ices; one skilled in traversing or navigating through ice. **ice-pack** [ICE-FLOE]. **ice-pail,** *n.* A pail filled with ice, for cooling wines, etc. **ice-plant,** *n.* A creeping plant, *Mesembryanthemum crystallinum*, whose leaves have a glistening lustre somewhat like ice. **ice-pudding,** *n.* A frozen confection. **ice-river,** *n.* A glacier. **ice-saw,** *n.* A saw for cutting through ice in order to free ships. **ice-show,** *n.* (*Theat.*) A performance on ice by actors wearing skates. **ice-spar,** *n.* A vitreous orthoclase. **ice-stream,** *n.* A stream of drifting ice-floes. **ice-wall,** *n.* A rampart of ice-blocks piled up on the shore. **ice-water, iced water:** Water from melted ice; water cooled by ice. **dry ice,** *n.* Frozen carbon dioxide. **young ice,** *n.* Ice which has formed recently. **icing,** *n.* A coating of concreted sugar. **icy,** *a.* Pertaining to or consisting of ice; like ice, frozen; (*fig.*) frigid, chilling. **icy-pearled,** *a.* Studded with spangles of ice. **icily,** *adv.* **iciness,** *n.*

-ice [O.F. *-ice*, L. *itia*, *-itius*, *-itium*], *suf.* Forming nouns, as *justice, malice, novice, service.*

iceberg (īs′ bĕrg) [prob. from Dut. *ijsberg* (*ijs*, ICE, *berg*, hill)], *n.* A large mass of ice, usu. floating on the sea at high latitudes, usu. formed by detachment from a glacier.

Iceland (īs′ lănd) [Icel. *Island* (*iss*, ICE, LAND)], *n.* An island in the North Atlantic between Scandinavia and Greenland. **Iceland lichen** or **moss:** An edible moss or lichen, *Cetraria Islandica*, growing in the northern and mountainous parts of Europe, used as a medicine. **Iceland poppy:** The yellow Arctic poppy. **Iceland spar:** A transparent variety of calcite. **Icelander,** *n.* A native of Iceland. **Icelandic** (īs lăn′ dik), *a.* Pertaining to Iceland. *n.* The language of Iceland.

ichneumon (ik nū′ mōn) [L., from Gr. *ichneumōn*, from *ichneuein*, to track, from *ichnos*, a track], *n.* A small carnivorous animal, *Herpestes ichneumon*, related to the mongoose, found in Egypt, where it was formerly held sacred on account of its devouring crocodiles' eggs; the ichneumon-fly, which lays its eggs in or upon the larvæ of other insects, upon which its larvæ will feed. **ichneumonidan** (-mon′ i dăn), *a.* Pertaining to the *Ichneumonidæ*. *n.* An insect of this family. **ichneumonid** (ik nū′ mō nid), *n.* **ichneumonology** (-nol′ ō ji), *n.* The branch of entomology dealing with the *Ichneumonidæ*. **ichneumon-fly,** *n.* An hymenopterous insect belonging to the family *Ichneumonidæ*.

ichnite [ICHNOLITE].

ichnography (ik nog′ ră fi) [Gr. *ichnos*, a track, -LOGY], *n.* The art of drawing ground-plans etc. **ichnograph** (ik′ nō grăf), *n.* A ground-plan. **ichnographic, -al** (ik nō grăf′ ik, -ăl), *a.* **ichnographically,** *adv.*

ichnolite (ik′ nō līt) [as prec., -LITE], *n.* (*Palæont.*) A stone with the impression of a footprint.

ichnology (ik nol′ ō ji) [as prec., -LOGY], **ichnolithology** (-li thol′ ō ji) [LITHOLOGY], *n.* (*Palæont.*) The department of palæontology that treats of and classifies fossil footprints. **ichnological, ichnolithological** (-loj′ i kăl), *a.*

ichor (ī′ kōr, ik′ ōr) [Gr. *ichōr*], *n.* (*Gr. Myth.*) The ethereal fluid which took the place of blood in the veins of the gods; (*Path.*) a thin watery humour like serum; a watery acrid discharge from a wound etc. **ichorology** (ī kōr ol′ ō ji), *n.* (*Path.*) **ichorous,** *a.*

ichthin, ichthulin [ICHTHYIN, ICHTHYLIN, see ICHTHY-].

ichthy- ichthyo- [Gr. *ichthus*, a fish], *comb. form.* Pertaining to fish; fish-like. **ichthyic** (ik′ thi ik) [Gr. *ichthuikos*], *a.* Pertaining to fishes; having the characteristics of a fish. **ichthydin, -in, -lin,** *n.* (*Chem.*) Albuminous substances said to be contained in the eggs of various fishes. **ichthyodorulite, -dorylite** (ik thi ō dor′ ŭ-, -i līt) [Gr. *doru*,

I

spear, -LITE], *n.* (*Palæont.*) A fossil spine of a fish or fish-like vertebrate.

ichthyography (ik thi og′ rȧ fi) [as prec., -GRAPHY], *n.* A description of or a treatise on fishes. **ichthyographer,** *n.*

ichthyoid (ik′ thi oid) [Gr. *ichthuoeides* (ICHTHY-, -OID)], *a.* Resembling fish. *n.* A vertebrate of fish-like form.

ichthyol (ik′ thi ol) [as prec., L. *oleum*, OIL], *n.* (*Med.*) A brownish-black substance, obtained by distilling a bituminous shale containing fish-remains, from the Tyrol, used as an application in skin diseases.

ichthyolatry (ik thi ol′ ȧ tri), *n.* The worship of fishes, or of a fish god such as Dagon. **ichthyolater,** *a.* **ichthyolatrous,** *a.*

ichthyolite (ik′ thi ȯ līt) [ICHTHYO-, -LITE], *n.* (*Palæont.*) A fossil fish; an impression of a fossil fish. **ichthyolitic** (-lit′ ik), *a.*

ichthyology (ik thi ol′ ȯ ji) [ICHTHYO-, -LOGY], *n.* The branch of zoology concerned with fishes; the natural history of fishes. **ichthyologic, -al** (-loj′ ik, -ȧl), *a.* **ichthyologist** (-ol′ ȯ jist), *n.* One versed in ichthyology.

ichthyomancy (ik′ thi ȯ măn si) [ICHTHYO-, -MANCY], *n.* Divination by means of the entrails or the heads of fish. **ichthyomantic** (-măn′ tik), *a.*

ichthyomorphic (ik thi ȯ môr′ fik) [Gr. *morphē*, form], *a.* Having the form of a fish; (*Zool.*) having the characteristics of fishes.

ichthyophagy (ik thi of′ ȧ ji) [through F. *ichtyophagie* or directly from Gr. *ichthuophagia* (ICHTHYO-, *-phagia*, from *phagein*, to eat)], *n.* The practice of eating fish; fish diet. **ichthyophagist,** *n.* **ichthyophagous** (-gůs), *a.*

ichthyopsida (ik thi op′ si dȧ) [Gr. *opsis*, appearance], *n.pl.* (*Zool.*) According to Huxley's terminology, the lowest of the three main divisions of vertebrates, comprising fishes, amphibians, and fishlike vertebrates, the other two divisions being *Mammalia* and *Sauropida.*

ichthyornis (ik thi ôr′ nis) [Gr. *ornis*, a bird], *n.* (*Palæont.*) An extinct bird having biconcave vertebræ and socketed teeth.

ichthyosaurus (ik thi ȯ saw′ růs) [ICHTHYO-, Gr. *sauros*, lizard], *n.* (*Palæont.*) A genus of gigantic fossil marine reptiles, chiefly from the Lias. **ichthyosaur** (ik′ thi ȯ sawr), *n.* Any species of the genus *Ichthyosaurus.*

ichthyosis (ik thi ō′ sis), *n.* (*Path.*) An hereditary skin disease, marked by thick, hard, imbricated grey scales. **ichthyotic** (-ot′ ik), *a.*

ichthyotomy (ik thi ot′ ȯ mi), *n.* The dissection of fishes. **ichthyotomist,** *n.*

ichthys (ik′ this) [Gr. *ichthus*, a fish], *n.* (*Ecclesiol.*) A symbol in the form of a fish, connected with Christ because the Greek letters *ιχθυς* gave the initials of the Greek words meaning 'Jesus Christ, Son of God, Saviour.'

icicle (ī′ sikl) [A.-S. *īses giecel* (*īses*, gen. of *īs*, ICE, *giecel*, cogn. with Icel. *jökull*, icicle, glacier, orig. dim. of *jaki*, a piece of ice)], *n.* A hanging conical point of ice, formed by the freezing of dripping water.

icily, icing, etc. [ICE].

-icle [Lat. *-iculus*, *-iculum*, *-icula*], *suf.* Diminutive, as in *particle*, *versicle.*

icon (ī′ kȯn) [late L. *īcōn*, Gr. *eikon*, image, likeness], *n.* (*Eastern Ch.*) A sacred image, picture, mosaic, or monumental figure of a holy personage, usu. regarded as endowed with miraculous attributes [see also EIKON]. **iconic** (ī kon′ ik), *a.* Pertaining to or consisting of figures or pictures; (*Art*) following a conventional pattern or type (as busts, memorial effigies, etc.).

icono- [as prec.], *comb. form.* Of or pertaining to images or idols.

iconoclasm (ī kon′ ō klăzm) [Gr. *klasma*, from *klaein*, to break], *n.* The breaking of idols; (*fig.*) attack on or disregard of established usages, opinions, etc. **iconoclast,** *n.* A breaker of images, esp. one of the religious zealots in the Eastern Empire who attacked the worship of images during the eighth and ninth centuries; (*fig.*) an assailant or contemner of established usages, etc. **iconoclastic** (-klăs′ tik), *a.*

iconography (ī kȯ nog′ rȧ fi) [Gr. *ikonographia*], *n.* A treatise on or the study of pictures, statues, engravings on gems, symbolism, etc.; the illustration of a subject by means of figures etc.; a book or other collection of figures, drawings, etc. **iconographer,** *n.* **iconographic** (-grăf′ ik), *a.*

iconolatry (ī kȯ nol′ ȧ tri), *n.* Adoration of images. **iconolater,** *n.*

iconology (ī kȯ nol′ ȯ ji), *n.* The science or study of images, pictures, etc.; the doctrine of images or emblematical representations.

iconomachy (ī kȯ nom′ ȧ ki) [late Gr. *eikonomachia* (*-machia*, from *machesthai*, to fight)], *n.* War against images or idols.

iconomatic (ī kon ȯ măt′ ik) [Gr. *onoma*, name], *a.* Denoting a kind of writing in which pictures or figures of objects represent phonetic elements, a stage of writing intermediate between picture-writing and phonetic writing.

iconophile (ī′ kȯ nȯ-, ī kon′ ȯ fīl), *n.* A connoisseur of pictures, prints, etc. **iconophilism, -ly** (ī kȯ nof′ i lizm, -li), *n.* **iconophilist,** *n.*

iconostasis (ī kȯ nos′ tȧ sis) [late Gr. *eikonostasis* (Gr. *stasis*, standing, position)], *n.* (*Eastern Ch.*) A screen on which icons are placed separating the sanctuary from the rest of the church.

icosahedron (ī kȯ sȧ hē′ drȯn) [Gr. *eikosaedron* (*eikosi*, twenty, *hedra*, seat, base)], *n.* (*Geom.*) A solid figure having twenty plane sides; a regular solid contained by twenty equilateral triangles. **icosahedral,** *a.*

Icosandria (ī kȯ săn′ dri ȧ) [Gr. *eikosi*, twenty, *anēr andros*, man, male], *n.pl.* (*Bot.*) A Linnæan class containing plants with twenty or more stamens inserted on the calyx. **icosander,** *n.* A plant of the class *Icosandria.* **icosandrous, -drian,** *a.*

-ics [-IC], *suf.* Noting arts or sciences, as *hydrostatics*, *metaphysics* (plural in form, such nouns are usually construed as singular).

icterus (ik′ tėr ůs) [L., from Gr. *ikteros*, jaundice], *n.* (*Path.*) Jaundice; (*Bot.*) a disease of plants characterized by yellowness of the leaves; (*Ornith.*) genus of American birds belonging to the *Icteridæ* and including the orioles. **icteric** (ik ter′ ik), *a.* Affected with jaundice; good against jaundice; (*Ornith.*) belonging to the *Icteridæ.* *n.* A remedy for jaundice. **icterical,** *a.* Icteric. **icterine** (ik′ tėr īn), *a.* ***icteritious** (ik tėr ish′ ůs), *a.* Yellow; resembling the skin in jaundice. **icteroid** (ik′ tėr oid), *a.*

ictus (ik′ tůs) [L., a stroke, from *icere*, to strike], *n.* (*Pros.*) The stress, beat, or rhythmical accent in metre; (*Med.*) the beat of the pulse. ***ictic,** *a.*

icy [ICE].

id (id) [from IDIOPLASM], *n.* (*Biol.*) A unit of germ-plasm (according to Weismann's theory of heredity); (*Psych.*) the instinctive impulses of the individual.

-id [F. *-ide*, L. *idus*], *suf.* Forming adjectives denoting the quality orig. expressed by a Latin verb, as *acid*, *frigid*, *morbid*, *tepid*; [ult. from Gr. *-id-*, nom. *-is*, pl. *-idēs*] (*Bot.*) denoting a member of an order, as *amaryllid* (*Amaryllidaceæ*), orchid (*Orchidaceæ*); (*Zool.*) member of a family, as *arachnid* (*Arachnida*) [see also -IDE].

Idalian (ī dā′ li an) [*Idalia*, a mountain in Cyprus sacred to Aphrodite], *a.* Pertaining to Idalia or to Aphrodite or Venus.

ide (īd) [Swed. *id*], *n.* A northern European fish, *Leuciscus idus*, of the carp family.

-ide [-ID], *suf.* (*Chem.*) Indicating chemical compounds of an element with another element or a radical, as *chloride, fluoride, oxide.*

idea (ī dē′ ȧ) [late L., from Gr. (*idein*, to see)], *n.* A mental image, form, or representation of anything; a notion, a conception, a supposition; a more or less vague opinion, belief, or fancy; a plan, an intention or design; a view, a way of thinking or conceiving (something); (*Platonic*) the archetype or perfect and eternal pattern of which actual things are imperfect copies; (*Cartesian, etc.*) the immediate object of cognition, present in consciousness as representing an actual thing; (*Kantian, etc.*) a conception or idea of the pure reason transcending mere experience. **idea'd, ideaed** (ī dē′ ȧd), *a.* **ideate** (ī dē′ āt), *n.* (*Phil.*) The actual existence correlating with an idea. *v.t.* (-āt) To form in ideas, to imagine; to apprehend and retain mentally. *v.i.* To form ideas. **ideation** (-ā′ shŭn), *n.* **ideational,** *a.* **idealess,** *a.* Destitute of ideas.

ideal (ī dē′ ȧl), *a.* Consisting of, existing in, or pertaining to ideas, mental; visionary, fanciful; reaching one's standard of perfection; (*Phil.*) of or pertaining to idealism or the Platonic ideas. *n.* An imaginary standard of perfection; an actual thing realizing this. **idealism,** *n.* The practice of forming ideals; the quest of an ideal; (*Art*) the representation of things in conformity with an ideal standard of perfection; (*Phil.*) the doctrine that in external perceptions the objects immediately known are ideas. **idealist,** *n.* **idealistic** (-lis′ tik), *a.* **ideality** (ī dė ăl′ i ti), *n.* The quality of being ideal; capacity to form ideals. ***idealness,** *n.* **idealize,** *v.t.* To make ideal; (*Art*) to portray in conformity with an ideal. *v.i.* To form ideals. **idealization** (-lī zā′ shŭn), *n.* The representing of an object in accordance with one's desires or ideals. **ideally,** *adv.* In an ideal manner; intellectually, mentally.

idée fixe (ē dā fiks) [Fr.], *n.* A fixed idea, monomania.

idem (ī′ dem) [L.], *n.* The same (word, author, book, etc.).

identical (ī den′ ti kȧl) [formerly *identic*, F. *identique*, late L. *identicus*, formed from *identitas*, IDENTITY], *a.* Absolutely the same, not different (though viewed or found under different conditions); similar in essentials; uniform in quality, appearance, etc.; (*Math.*) expressing identity. **identic,** *a.* (*Diplom.*) Identical. **identic note:** A note or expression of opinion in precisely similar terms (addressed simultaneously by the representatives of several powers to another). **identical twins,** *n.pl.* Uniovular or similar twins, having developed from a single oocyte. **identically,** *adv.* **identicalness,** *n.*

identify (ī den′ ti fī) [F. *identifier*, late L. *identificāre*, as foll.], *v.t.* To consider or represent as precisely the same (with); to determine or prove the identity of; to prove to be the same (with); to unite or associate (oneself) closely (with a party, interests, etc.). **identifiable,** *a.* **identification** (-fi kā, shŭn), *n.*

identity (ī den′ ti ti) [F. *identité*, late L. *identitātem* nom. *-tas*, from L. IDEM], *n.* The state of being identical; absolute sameness; one's individuality; (*Alg.*) absolute equality between two expressions; an equation expressing such equality. **old identity:** (*Austral.*) An old inhabitant.

ideo- [IDEA], *comb. form.* Pertaining to or expressing ideas. **ideo-metabolic** (-met ȧ bol′ ik), *a.* (*Physiol.*) Denoting the influence of psychological, esp. emotional states on the metabolic processes. **ideo-motor** (-mō′ tȯr), **ideo-muscular,** *a.* (*Psych.*) Denoting unconscious muscular movements due to the concentration of attention on an idea.

ideograph, ideogram (id′ i ō grăf, -grăm), *n.* A symbol, figure, etc., suggesting or conveying the idea of an object, without expressing its name. **ideographic, -al** (-grăf′ ik, -ȧl), *a.* **ideographically,** *adv.* **ideography** (-og′ rȧ fi), *n.* A system of or a treatise on ideographic writing. **ideology** (id i ol′ o ji), *n.* The science of ideas, esp. that enunciated by Condillac; abstract or fanciful theorizing; a national political or social philosophy. **ideological** (-loj′ i kȧl), *a.* **ideologically,** *adv.* **ideologist** (-ol′ ȯ jist), **ideologue** (ī dē′ ȯ log), *n.* A supporter of ideology; one who treats of ideas; a theorist, a visionary. **ideologize** (ī dė ol′ ȯ jīz), *v.t.*

ideopraxist (id i ō prăk′ sist) [Gr. *praxis*, doing]. One who puts ideas into practice.

Ides (īdz) [F., from L. *īdūs*], *n.pl.* (*Rom. Ant.*) In the ancient Roman calendar, the 15th of March, May, July, October, and 13th of the other months.

id est (id est) [L.], *phrase.* That is, that is to say (usu. written *i.e.*).

idio- [Gr. *idios*, peculiar to oneself], *comb. form.* Individual, peculiar. ***idiocrasy** (id i ok′ rȧ si) [Gr. *idiokrāsia* (*krāsis*, CRASIS)], *n.* Idiosyncrasy. ***idiocratic, -al** (-krăt′ ik, -ȧl), *a.* Peculiar in constitution.

idiocy [IDIOT].

***idioelectric** (id′ i-, ī di ō ė lek′ trik), *a.* Applied to substances electric by virtue of their own peculiar properties, and which are readily electrified by friction. *n.* An idioelectric substance.

idiograph (id′ i-, ī′ di ȯ grăf) [Gr. *ideographon*], *n.* A private mark or signature, esp. a trademark. **idiographic** (-grăf′ ik), *a.*

idiom (id′ i ȯm) [F. *idiome*, L. and Gr. *idiōma -ōmatos*, from *idios*, see IDIO-], *n.* A mode of expression, esp. an irregular use of words, peculiar to a language; a peculiarity of expression or phraseology; a dialect, a peculiar speech or language. **idiomatic, -al** (-măt′ ik, -ȧl), *a.* Peculiar to or characteristic of a language; dialectal, vernacular; expressed in idioms. **idiomatically,** *adv.*

idiomorphic (id i ȯ môr′ fik) [Gr. *morphē*, form], *a.* (*Min.*) Having a distinctive form of its own, esp. distinctive faces of crystallization.

idiopathy (id i op′ ȧ thi) [Gr. *idiopatheia*], *n.* (*Path.*) A primary disease, one not occasioned by another; *a characteristic affection or disposition peculiar to an individual. ***idiopathetic** (-pȧ thet′ ik), **idiopathic, -al** (păth′ ik, -ȧl), *a.* **idiopathically,** *adv.*

idioplasm (id′ i ȯ plăzm), *n.* (*Biol.*) The portion of protoplasm derived from the parent organism, and supposed to determine the character of the individual, dist. from that which is due to the development of the individual. **idioplasmatic** (-plăz măt′ ik), *a.*

idiosyncrasy (id i ȯ sin′ krȧ si) [Gr. *idiosunkrāsia* (IDIO-, SYN-, *krāsia*, CRASIS)], *n.* Individual quality, habit, or attitude of mind; a characteristic peculiar to an individual; (*Med.*) individual temperament or constitution. **idiosyncratic, -al** (-krăt′ ik, -ȧl), *a.*

idiot (id′ i ȯt) [F., from L. *idiōta*, Gr. *idiōtēs*, a private person, hence one who is ignorant or not an expert, from *idios*, see IDEO-], *n.* A person of weak or defective understanding; one belonging to the lowest grade of mental defectives; one destitute of reason or intellectual powers; a stupid, silly person. *a.* Idiotic. **idiocy, *idiotcy,** *n.* **idiotic, -al** (-ot′ ik, -ȧl), *a.* Resembling or characteristic of an idiot; foolish, silly, absurd. **idiotically,** *adv.* ***idiotism** (id′ i ȯ tizm), *n.* An idiom; an idiosyncrasy; idiocy. **idiotize,** *v.i.* To become idiotic. *v.t.* To make an idiot of; to make a fool of.

idle (ī′ dėl) [A.-S. *idel*, empty, vain (cp. Dut. *ijdel*, G. *eitel*, also Gr. *itharos*, pure)], *a.* Doing nothing; disengaged, inactive, not occupied, free; not in use; averse to work, lazy; useless, vain, ineffectual; unfruitful, barren; trifling, without foundation. *v.i.* (*pres.p.* **idling**) To spend time in idleness; *to move about aimlessly or lazily. *v.t.* To spend (time) in idleness. *n.* The act of idling, indolence. **to idle away:** To spend in idleness. ***idle-headed, *-pated,** *a.* Foolish, unreasonable; delirious, infatuated. **idle-tongs** [LAZY-TONGS]. **idle-wheel,**

n. A cogged wheel between two others for transmitting motion. ***idle-worms,** *n.pl.* Worms supposed to breed in the fingers of lazy persons. **idleness,** ***idlesse,** *n.* **idler,** *n.* One who spends his time in idleness; (*Naut.*) a person not required to keep night watch. **idly,** *adv.*

Ido (ē′ dō), *n.* An artificial international language based on Esperanto.

idocrase (ī′ dǒ krās) [F. (Gr. *eidos*, form, *krāsis*, CRASIS)], *n.* (*Min.*) Vesuvianite.

idol (ī′ dǒl) [O.F. *idole*, L. *īdōlum -lon*, Gr. *eidōlon*, from *eidos*, form], *n.* An image, esp. one worshipped as a god; a false god; a person or thing loved or honoured excessively; (*Phil.*) a false conception, a misleading tendency, a fallacy. **idolater** (ī dol′ ǎ tėr), *n.* One who worships idols; a pagan; (*fig.*) an adorer, an extravagant admirer. **idolatress,** *n.* ***idolatrize,** *v.i.* To practise idolatry. *v.t.* To adore; to worship as an idol. **idolatrous,** *a.* **idolatrously,** *adv.* **idolatry,** *n.* ***idolish** (ī′ dǒ lish), *a.* Idolatrous, pagan, heathenish. **idolism,** *n.* Idolatry; idolization; a vain opinion or fancy. ***idolist,** *n.* An idolater. **idolize,** *v.t.* To worship as an idol; to make an idol of; to love or venerate to excess. **idolization** (-zā′ shǔn), *n.* **idolizer,** *n.*

idolon, idolum (ī dō′ lon, -um), *n.* (*pl.* **idolia**). An image, an appearance; a phantom, an apparition; (*Phil.*) a fallacious appearance or misconception, classified by Bacon as *idola tribūs, specūs, fori, theatri*, idols of the tribe, the cave, the market-place, and the theatre, that is, limitations of the human mind, personal prejudices, fallacies due to the influence of words and phrases, and philosophic and logical misconceptions.

***idoneous** (ī dō′ nė ǔs) [L. *idoneus*], *a.* Proper, suitable.

idrialin (i drī′ ǎ lin), *n.* (*Chem.*) A crystalline compound which is an essential constituent of idrialite.

idrialite (id′ ri ǎ līt) [*Idria*, in Austria, -LITE], *n.* (*Min.*) A greyish crystalline hydrocarbon found in the mines of Idria, also called inflammable cinnabar.

idyll (ī′ dil) [L. *īdyllium*, Gr. *eidullion*, dim. of *eidos*, form], *n.* A short pastoral poem; a brief, artistic, and picturesque narrative or description of rustic life, either in verse or prose; a scene or episode suitable for the tone of such a composition. **idyllic** (ī dil′ ik), *a.* Pertaining to or suitable for an idyll; perfect in harmony, peace, beauty, etc. **idyllically,** *adv.* **idyllist** (ī′ dil ist), *n.* **idyllize,** *v.t.*

-ier [F. *-ier* or -EER], *suf.* Denoting occupation, profession, etc., as in *bombardier, brigadier, chevalier, financier.*

if (if) [A.-S. *gif* (cp. Dut. *of*, Icel. *ef, if*, G. *ob*)], *conj.* On the supposition that, providing that, in case that; even on the supposition, allowing that; whenever, at the time when; whether; also used in an exclamatory sense (as *if you were only here!*). **as if:** As it would be if.

igloo (ig′ loo) [Eskimo], *n.* An Eskimo hut, often built of snow.

***ignaro** (ig nâr′ ō) [It., from L. *ignārus*, IGNORANT], *n.* An ignorant person.

Ignatian (ig nā′ shi ǎn) [*Ignatius*, -AN], *a.* Pertaining to St. Ignatius, Bishop of Antioch (martyred A.D. 107 or 110), or to St. Ignatius of Loyola (1491–1556), founder of the Society of Jesus. *n.* A follower of the latter, a Jesuit. **Ignatian Epistles:** Epistles advocating episcopacy attributed to St. Ignatius of Antioch.

igneous (ig′ nė ǔs) [L. *igneus*, from *ignis*, fire], *a.* Containing or of the nature of fire; emitting fire; (*Geol.*) produced by volcanic action. ***ignescent** (ig nes′ ėnt), *a.* Emitting sparks when struck, as with steel; scintillating. *n.* A mineral emitting sparks when struck. ***igniferous** (ig nif′ ėr ǔs) [-FEROUS], *a.* Producing fire. ***ignigenous,** *a.* Produced by fire. ***ignipotent,** *a.* Ruling over fire.

ignis fatuus (ig′ nis făt′ ū ǔs) [L., foolish fire (see FATUOUS)], *n.* (*pl.* **ignes fatui**) An apparent flame probably due to the spontaneous combustion of inflammable gas, floating above the ground in marshes etc.; (*fig.*) a delusive object or aim.

ignite (ig nīt′) [L. *ignītus*, p.p. of *ignīre*, from *ignis*, fire], *v.t.* To set on fire; to render luminous or red with heat. *v.i.* To take fire; to become red with heat. **ignitable,** *a.* **ignition** (ig nish′ ǔn), *n.* The act of igniting; the state of being ignited; mechanism for igniting explosive mixture in the internal-combustion engine. **ignition-box, -chamber,** *n.* The chamber in an engine, gun, etc., in which combustion takes place. **igniter,** *n.* One who or that which sets on fire, esp. a contrivance for igniting powder in an explosive, firing the gases in an internal-combustion engine, etc.

ignoble (ig nō′ bėl) [F., from *ignōbilis* (IN- (2), *gnōbilis, nōbilis*, NOBLE)], *a.* Of humble or mean birth; mean, base, despicable, unworthy, dishonourable. ***v.t.** To make ignoble; to dishonour. **ignobility** (ig nō bil′ i ti), **ignobleness,** *n.* **ignobly,** *adv.*

ignominy (ig′ nǒ mi ni), ***ignomy** [F. *ignominie*, L. *ignōminia* (IN- (2), *gnōmen, nōmen*, name, from *gnōscere*, to know)], *n.* Public disgrace or shame; dishonour, infamy; an act deserving disgrace; (*colloq.*) contemptuous treatment. **ignominious** (ig nǒ min i ǔs), *a.* **ignominiously,** *adv.*

ignoramus (ig nǒ rā′ mus) [L., we do not know], *n.* (*pl.* **-muses**) An ignorant fellow; a stupid blockhead; *(*Law*) 'We know nothing of it,' the endorsement on a bill by the grand jury when there was not sufficient evidence to support the charge. ***a.** Ignorant.

ignorance (ig′ nǒ rǎns) [F., from L. *ignōrantia* from *ignōrans -ntem*, ignorant], *n.* The state of being ignorant; want of knowledge (of).

ignorant (ig′ nǒ rǎnt), *a.* Destitute of knowledge unconscious (of); illiterate, uninstructed, uneducated; *done inadvertently. ***n.** An ignorant person. **ignorantism,** *n.* Obscurantism. **ignorantly,** *adv.*

Ignorantine (ig nǒ răn′ tin) [F. *ignorantin*, from *ignorant*, IGNORANT], *n.* A member of a R.C. order originally founded (1495) to minister to the sick poor, later devoted to the teaching of poor children and called Brethren of the Christian Schools. *a.* Pertaining to this order.

ignore (ig nôr′) [F. *ignorer*, L. *ignōrāre* (IN- (2), *gnō-* stem of *gnoscere*, to know)], *v.t.* To pass over without notice, to disregard; (*Law*) to throw out (a Bill as unsupported by sufficient evidence. **ignoration** (ig nǒ rā′ shun), *n.*

iguana (ig wa′ nǎ) [Sp., from Carib. *iwana*], *n.* A genus of large American lizards, esp. *I. tuberculata* of South and Central America and the West Indies.

iguanodon (ig wăn′ ǒ don) [IGUANA, Gr. *odous odontos*, tooth], *n.* (*Palæont.*) A genus of extinct gigantic lizards.

il- (1) [IN- (1)], *pref.*, as in *illation, illuminate.*

il- (2) [IN- (2)], *pref.*, as in *illiberal, illicit.*

-il, -ile [O.F. *-il*, F. *-ile*, L. *īlis* (*-ilis* in O.F. became *-le*, as in *humble*, L. *humilis*, HUMBLE, *frail, fragilis* FRAIL)], *suf.* That may be, capable of being, pertaining to, etc., as in *civil, fossil, docile, fragile Gentile, puerile, senile.*

ileac, etc. [ILIAC].

ileo- [ILEUM], *comb. form.* (*Anat. and Path.*) **ileocæcal** (il ė-, ī lė ǒ sē′ kǎl) [CÆCAL], *a.* Pertaining to the *ileum* and the cæcum. **ileocæcal valve:** A membrane covering the opening of the *ileum* into the cæcum.

ileum (il ė-, ī′ lė ǔm) [late L., from L. *īlia*, pl., the flanks, the groin (modified in form by confusion with *īleus*, Gr. *eileos*, see ILIAC)], *n.* (*Anat.*) The portion of the small intestine communicating with the larger intestine.

***ileus** [ILIAC].

ilex (ī' leks) [L.], *n.* (*pl.* **-exes**) The holm-oak; (*Bot.*) a genus of trees or shrubs with coriaceous leaves, typified by the holly.

iliac (il' i ăk) [F. *iliaque*, late L. *iliacus*, from L. *īlia*, see ILIUM (meaning as if from L. *īleos*, Gr. *eileos*, pain in the intestines)], *a.* (*Anat.*) Of or belonging to the smaller intestines; pertaining to the *ilium* or hip-bone. ***iliac passion:** Pains due to obstruction of the bowels. **iliac region:** The part of the abdomen between the ribs and the hips. **ilio-**, *comb. form.* Pertaining to or situated near the *ilium*.

Iliad (il' i ăd) [L. *Ilias -adis*, Gr. *Ilias*, adj., of Ilium or Troy], *n.* An epic poem, usually ascribed to Homer, consisting of twenty-four books, describing the incidents of the tenth and last year of the siege of Troy; (*fig.*) a long narrative or series of events, esp. of a mournful kind.

ilium (il' i ŭm) [L., a part of the abdomen (cp. ILEUM)], *n.* (*pl.* *ia*) (*Anat.*) The upper part of the hip-bone.

ilk (ilk) [A.-S. *ilca* (pron. stem *i-*, *-lic*, LIKE)], *a.* The same. **of that ilk:** Of the same name (used when the surname of a person is the same as the name of his estate). **that ilk:** (*colloq.* and *erron.*) That family or kind.

ilka (il' kă) [*ælc*, EACH, A], *a.* (*Sc.*) Each, every.

ill (il) [M.E., from Icel. *illr*], *a.* Unwell, sick, diseased; bad morally, evil; malevolent, hostile, adverse; tending towards evil, noxious, mischievous, harmful; unfortunate, unfavourable, unlucky; not right, faulty, inferior, incorrect, improper; unskilful; awkward, cross (in temper); *unwholesome. *adv.* Not well, badly; not rightly; not easily; imperfectly, scarcely; unfavourably, in bad part or humour. *n.* Evil; injury, harm; wickedness; (*pl.*) misfortunes. **ill at ease:** Uncomfortable, anxious. **to be taken ill:** To fall sick. **to speak ill:** To speak (of or about) unfavourably. **to take ill** or **in ill part:** To take offence at. **ill-advised,** *a.* Imprudent; injudicious. **ill-advisedly,** *adv.* **ill-affected,** *a.* Not friendly disposed; disaffected, *affected with bad impressions. **ill blood:** Resentment, displeasure, enmity. ***ill-boding,** *a.* Inauspicious. **ill-bred,** *a.* Brought up badly; rude unmannered, offensive. **ill breeding:** Want of good breeding; rudeness. **ill-conditioned,** *a.* Having a bad temper or disposition; in a bad physical condition. **ill-disposed,** *a.* Wickedly or maliciously inclined; unfavourably inclined (towards). **ill-famed,** *n.* Disrepute. **ill-fated,** *a.* Unfortunate, unlucky. **ill-faurd** (*Sc.*), **ill-favoured,** *a.* Ugly, deformed; forbidding, repulsive; unattractive, objectionable. ***ill-favouredly,** *adv.* **ill-favouredness,** *n.* **ill-got, ill-gotten,** *a.* Obtained in an improper way. **ill humour:** Bad temper. **ill-humoured,** *a.* **ill-judged,** *a.* Not well-judged; injudicious, unwise. **ill luck:** Bad luck, misfortune. **ill-manned,** *a.* (*Naut.*) Having an insufficient crew. **ill-mannered,** *a.* Rude, boorish. **ill-matched,** *a.* Not well-matched or suited. **ill-mated,** *a.* Badly joined or mated. **ill nature:** Evil disposition; lack of kindness or good feeling. **ill-natured,** *a.* Of a churlish disposition, bad-tempered; expressive of or indicating ill nature; *not yielding to culture, intractable. **ill-naturedly,** *adv.* **ill-naturedness,** *n.* **ill-omened,** *a.* Unlucky, inauspicious, of evil augury. **ill-starred,** *a.* Born under the influence of an unlucky planet, hence unlucky. **ill-tempered,** *a.* Having a bad temper, sour, peevish. **ill-timed,** *a.* Done, said, or attempted, at an unsuitable time. **ill-treat** [ILL USE]. **ill turn:** An ill-natured act or treatment; *an attack of illness. **ill usage:** Unkind treatment. **ill use:** To treat badly. **ill will:** Malevolence, enmity.

***illapse** (i lăps') [L. *illapsus*, p.p. of *illābī* (IL- (1), LAPSE)], *n.* A gliding of one thing into another; influx, inspiration. *v.i.* To fall, to glide (into).

***illaqueate** (i lăk' wē āt) [L. *illaqueātus*, p.p. of *illaqueāre* (IL- (1), *laqueāre*, from *laqueus*, noose, snare)], *v.t.* To ensnare, to entrap. ***illaqueation** (-ā' shŭn), *n.*

illation (i lā' shŭn) [F., from late L. *illatiōnem*, nom. *-tio* (IL- (1), *lāt-*, p.p. stem of *ferre*, to bear)], *n.* Deduction; a deduction, an inference. **illative** (il' ă tiv), *a.* Denoting, expressing, or of the nature of an inference. *n.* That which denotes inference, as an illative particle. **illatively,** *adv.*

Illawarra Shorthorn (il ă wo' ră shôrt hôrn) [Illawarra, N.S.W.], *n.* A noted breed of Australian dairy cattle.

illegal (i lē' găl) [med. L. *illegālis* (IL- (2), LEGAL)], *a.* Not according to law; contrary to law, unlawful. **illegality** (-găl' i ti), *n.* **illegalize** (i lē' gă līz), *v.t.* To render illegal. **illegally,** *adv.*

illegible (i lej' ibl), *a.* That cannot be read or deciphered. **illegibility** (-bil' i ti), *n.* **illegibly,** *adv.*

illegitimate (il ė jit' i măt), *a.* Not lawfully begotten; born out of wedlock; contrary to law or recognized usage; irregular, improper; illogical, contrary to logical rules, unsound. *n.* An illegitimate child, a bastard; one of illegitimate status. *v.t.* (-māt) To render or declare illegitimate. **illegitimacy,** *n.* The state of being illegitimate. **illegitimately,** *adv.* **illegitimation** (-mā' shŭn), *n.* **illegitimatize,** *v.t.* To illegitimate.

illiberal (i lib' ėr ăl) [F. *illibéral*], *a.* Not generous, petty, sordid; narrow-minded, niggardly, stingy; not catholic; rude, vulgar, not characterized by wide views or by culture. **illiberality** (-ăl' i ti), *n.* **illiberalize,** *v.t.* To render illiberal. **illiberally,** *adv.*

illicit (i lis' it) [F. *illicite*, L. *illicitus*], *a.* Not allowed or permitted; unlawful. **illicitly,** *adv.*

illimitable (i lim' it ăbl), *a.* Boundless, limitless. **illimitability** (-bil' i ti), **illimitableness,** *n.* **illimitably,** *adv.* ***illimitation** (-tā' shŭn), *n.* Absence of or freedom from limitation. ***illimited,** *a.* Unlimited, infinite. **illimitedly,** *adv.* **illimitedness,** *n.*

illinium (il in' i ŭm), *n.* A metallic element of the rare-earth series.

illiquid (i lik' wid) [IL- (2), LIQUID], *a.* (*Law*) Not clearly proved or manifest.

***illision** (i lizh' ŭn) [L. *illīsio -ōnem*, from *illīdere* (IL- (1), *lædere*, to strike)], *n.* A striking or dashing against.

illiterate (i lit' ėr ăt) [L. *illīterātus*], *a.* Unlearned, ignorant of letters; unable to read or write; rude, uncultivated. *n.* An ignorant or uneducated person, esp. one unable to read. **illiterately,** *adv.* **illiteracy, illiterateness,** *n.*

illness (il' nės), *n.* The state of being ill, sickness, physical indisposition; *unfavourableness, depravity; *badness (of the weather).

illogical (i loj' i kăl), *a.* Ignorant or careless of the rules of logic; contrary to reason. **illogically,** *adv.* ***illogicalness, illogicality** (-kăl' i ti), *n.*

illude (i lood') [L. *illūdere* (IL- (1), *lūdere*, to play)], *v.t.* To deceive, to cheat; to mock.

illume (i lūm', -loom') [shortened form of ILLUMINE], *v.t.* To illuminate, to lighten or brighten up; (*fig.*) to enlighten.

illuminate (i loo' mi nāt) [L. *illūminātus*, p.p. *illūmināre* (IL- (1), *lūmināre*, from *lūmen -inis*, light)], *v.t.* To throw light upon; to light up; to adorn (buildings, streets, etc.) with festal lamps; to adorn (a manuscript etc.) with coloured pictures, letters, etc.; (*fig.*) to enlighten mentally or spiritually; to make illustrious. *v.i.* To adorn manuscripts etc. with coloured pictures, letters, etc. **illuminable,** *a.* **illuminant,** *a.* Illuminating. *n.* That which illuminates. **illumination** (-nā' shŭn), **illuminative** (i lū'-, -loo' mi nă tiv), *a.* **illuminator** (i lū'-, -loo' mi nā tôr), *n.*

illuminati (i lū mi nā' tī, i loo mi na' tē) [L., pl. of *illūminātus*, or It., pl. of *illuminato*, as prec.], *n.pl.* A name given to several sects and secret societies professing to have superior enlightenment, esp. a German society of deists and republicans founded by Adam Weishaupt in 1776; hence any persons who affect to possess extraordinary knowledge or gifts. **illuminee** (-nē'), *n.* One of the *Illuminati.* **illuminism,** *n.* The principles or doctrines of the *Illuminati.* **illuminist,** *n.* ***illuminize,** *v.t.* To initiate into or instruct in the doctrines of the *Illuminati.* *v.i.* To become an illuminist.

illumine (i lū'-, -loo' min) [F. *illuminer*, to ILLUMINATE], *v.t.* To illuminate; to enlighten; to brighten.

illusion (i lū' zhůn) [F., from L. *illūsiōnem*, nom. *-sio*, from *illūdere*, to ILLUDE], *n.* The act of deceiving; that which deceives; a false show, a delusion; a conjuring trick; an unreal image presented to the vision; esp. a deceptive sensuous impression; (*Psych.*) a wrong interpretation of what is perceived through the senses. **illusionism,** *n.* A theory that regards the external world as a mere illusion of the senses. **illusionist,** *n.* One given to illusions, a visionary; one who produces illusions, as a conjurer; a believer in illusionism. **illusive** (-loo' siv), **illusory,** *a.* Delusive, deceptive. **illusively, illusorily,** *adv.* **illusiveness, illusoriness,** *n.*

illustrate (il' ůs-, i lůs' trāt) [L. *illustrātus*, p.p. of *illustrāre* (IL- (1), *lustrāre*, as foll.)], *v.t.* To make clear, to explain or elucidate by means of examples, figures, etc.; to embellish or elucidate by pictures etc.; *to illuminate; *(*fig.*) to make celebrated, to glorify. **a.* (i lůs' tråt) Illustrious, glorified.

illustration (il ůs trā' shůn), *n.* The act of illustrating; the state of being illustrated; that which illustrates, an example, a typical instance; an engraving or drawing illustrating a book or article in a periodical; an embellishment. **illustrative** (i lůs' trå tiv), ***illustratory,** *a.* **illustratively,** *adv.* **illustrator** (il' ůs trā tòr), *n.*

illustrious (i lůs' tri ůs) [L. *illustris* (IL- (1), *-lustris*, from stem of *lux*, light, *lūcidus*, bright), -OUS], *a.* Distinguished, famous; conferring lustre, renown, or glory; brilliant. **illustriously,** *adv.* **illustriousness,** *n.*

im- (1) [IN- (1)], *pref.* (before *b, m, p*), as in *imbibe, imbrue.*

im- (2) [IN- (2)], *pref.* (before *b, m, p*), as in *immaculate, impossible.*

image (im' åj) [F., from L. *imāginem*, nom. *imāgo*, prob. from *im-*, root of IMITATE], *n.* The visible representation or similitude of a person or thing; a likeness, an effigy, a statue, esp. one intended for worship, an idol; a copy, a counterpart; an idea, a conception; a mental picture; a persistent mental conception; (*Rhet.*) an expanded metaphor or simile; a lively description; (*Opt.*) the figure of an object formed (through the medium of a mirror, lens, etc.) by rays of light; (*Psych.*) a mental representation of a sense impression. *v.t.* To make an image of; to mirror; to portray; to represent mentally; to conceive in the mind; to typify, to symbolize. **image-worship,** *n.* Idolatry. **imageable,** *a.* **imageless,** *a.* **imagery,** *n.* An image; (*collect.*) images, statues; appearance, imitation; figures evoked by the fancy; rhetorical figures, figurative description. **imagist,** *n.* A follower of a poetical school that seeks to express itself through precise images of nature etc.

imaginable, etc. [IMAGINE].

imaginal (i măj' i nål) [L. *imāgo -ginis*, IMAGE, -AL], *a.* (*Ent.*) Pertaining to the imago or perfect form of an insect.

imaginary (i măj' in å ri), *a.* Existing only in imagination or fancy; not real, esp. a mathematical quantity or value assumed as real for the purposes of an equation etc. **imaginarily,** *adv.*

imagination (i măj i nā' shůn), *n.* The act or process of imagining; the power of imagining; the mental faculty that forms ideal images or combinations of images from the impressions left by sensuous experience; fancy, fantasy; the constructive or creative faculty of the mind; a mental image; a fanciful opinion, a fancy; *a contrivance, a plot.

imaginative (i măj' in å tiv), *a.* Endowed with imagination; creative, constructive; produced or characterized by imagination; *imaginary; **n.* Imagination. **imaginatively,** *adv.* **imaginativeness,** *n.*

imagine (i măj' in) [F. *imaginer*, L. *imāgināri*, as prec.], *v.t.* To form an image of in the mind, to conceive, to form an idea of; (*colloq.*) to suppose, to think; to conjecture, to guess; to plot, to devise. *v.i.* To form images or ideas in the mind. **imaginable,** *a.* That can be imagined. **imaginably,** *adv.* **imaginer,** *n.* **imagining,** *n.* Imagination; a conception, an idea. ***imaginist,** *n.* **imaginal,** *a.*

imago (i mā' gō) [L., IMAGE], *n.* (*pl.* **-gines,** i mā' ji nēz) (*Ent.*) The adult, fully-developed insect after its metamorphoses.

imam (i mam') [Arab. *imām*, from *amma*, to precede], *n.* A Mohammedan priest charged with the ceremonies of public worship; a Mohammedan title. **imamate, imamship,** *n.*

imbalance (im bal' ans), *n.* A lack of balance.

imbalm, imbank, imbar, imbargo, imbark imbathe [EMBALM, etc.].

imbecile (im' bė sēl, im' bė sil) [F. *imbécille* (now *imbécile*), L. *imbecillum*, nom. *-lus*, etym. doubtful], *a.* Mentally weak, half-witted; stupid, fatuous physically weak. *n.* One mentally weak; one who though mentally deficient, shows signs of rudimentary intelligence. **imbecilely,** *adv.* ***imbecilitate** (im bė sil' i tāt), *v.t.* To render feeble or weak. **imbecility,** *n.*

imbed, imbellish [EMBED, etc.].

imbibe (im bīb) [through F. *imbiber* or directly from L. *imbibere* (IM- (1), *bibere*, to drink, to BIB)], *v.t.* To drink in; to draw in, to absorb; (*fig.*) to receive into the mind. **imbiber,** *n.* **imbibition** (-bi bishůn), *n.* Absorption; drinking in; (*facet.*) drinking. **water of imbibition:** (*Geol.*) The quantity of water absorbed by rocks and remaining present above the level of saturation.

imbitter, imblaze, imbody, imbolden [EMBITTER, etc.].

***imbosk** (im bosk') [It. *imboscare* (IM- (1), *bosco* wood, BUSH)], *v.t.* To hide (oneself) as in an ambush. *v.i.* To lie concealed.

imbosom, imbound, imbow, imbrangle [EMBOSOM, etc.].

imbricate (im' bri kāt) [L. *imbricātus*, p.p. of *imbricāre*, from *imbrex -bricis*, a tile, from *imber -bris* shower], *v.t.* To lap (leaves, scales on fish, etc.) the one over the other like tiles. *v.i.* To be arranged in this position. *a.* (-kåt) Arranged in this fashion. **imbrication** (-kā' shůn), *n.* **imbricative** (im bri kā tiv), *a.*

imbroglio (im brō' li ō) [It. (IM- (1), *broglio* BROIL)], *n.* (*pl.* **-os**) A complicated plot, as of a play or novel; a perplexing or confused state of affairs; a disorderly heap; a misunderstanding.

imbrown [EMBROWN].

imbrue (im broo') [O.F. *embruer*, *-breuver*, *-beuvrer* causal of *bevre* (F. *boire*), L. *bibere*, to drink], *v.t.* To steep, to soak or moisten (in or with blood carnage, etc.); to stain, to dye (in or with); *to pour out. ***imbruement,** *n.*

imbrute (im broot') [IM- (1), BRUTE], *v.t.* To brutalize. *v.i.* To become brutalized.

imbue (im' bū') [L. *imbuere* (IM- (1), *buere*, rel. to *bibere*, to drink)], *v.t.* To cause to drink in, to saturate (with); to dye (with); to tinge strongly (with); (*fig.*) to inspire, to impregnate (with). ***imbuement,** *n.*

imburse (im bĕrs') [late L. *imbursāre* (IM- (1), *bursa* PURSE)], *v.t.* To furnish with money; to stow away. ***imbursement,** *n.*

imide (im' id, i mid') [altered from AMIDE, see AMIC], *n.* (*Chem.*) A compound derived from ammonia by the replacement of two atoms of hydrogen by a metal or organic radical.

imido-, *comb. form*, from prec. **imidogen** (i mī' dō jĕn) [-GEN], *n.* The hypothetical radical representing ammonia deprived of two atoms of hydrogen as explained above.

imitate (im' i tāt) [L. *imitātus*, p.p. of *imitārī*], *v.t.* To produce a likeness of in form, colour, or appearance; to follow the example of; to mimic, to ape. **imitable,** *a.* **imitability** (-bil' i ti), *n.* **imitation** (-tā' shŭn), *n.* The act of imitating; a copy or likeness; (*Mus.*) the repetition of a phrase or subject by another part or key. **imitative** (im' i tā tiv), *a.* Given to or aiming at imitation; done in imitation (of); counterfeit. **imitatively,** *adv.* **imitativeness,** *n.* **imitator,** *n.* **imitatress,** *n.*

immaculate (i măk' ū lăt) [L. *immaculātus* (IM- (2), *macula*, spot)], *a.* Spotless, pure; free from blemish; absolutely faultless; (*Biol.*) not spotted. **Immaculate Conception:** The R.C. doctrine (made an article of faith in 1854) that the Virgin Mary was conceived and born free from original sin. **immaculacy, immaculateness,** *n.* **immaculately,** *adv.*

immalleable (i măl' ē ăbl) [IM- (2), MALLEABLE], *a.* Not malleable.

***immanation** (im ă nā' shŭn) [IM- (1), L. *mānāre*, to flow (on anal. of EMANATION)], *n.* A flowing in.

***immane** (i mān') [L. *immānis* (IM- (2), *mānus*, hand)], *a.* Monstrous, prodigious, immense; savage, cruel. ***immanely,** *adv.* ***immanity,** *n.*

immanent (im' ă nĕnt) [late L. *immanens -ntem*, pres.p. of *immanēre* (IM- (1), *manēre*, to dwell)], *a.* Remaining within, inherent, not transient; indwelling; (*Theol.*) present throughout the universe as an essential sustaining spirit. **immanence, -manency,** *n.*

immantle (i măntl') [IM- (1), MANTLE], *v.t.* To wrap in or as in a mantle.

immarginate (i mar' ji năt) [IM- (2), MARGINATE], *a.* (*Bot.*) Not having a rim or edge.

immaterial (im ă tēr' i ăl) [M.F. *immatériel*, from med. L. *immateriālis* (IM- (2), MATERIAL)], *a.* Not consisting of matter; incorporeal; spiritual; irrelevant, unimportant. **immaterialism,** *n.* (*Phil.*) The doctrine that there is no material substance, and that all being may be reduced to mind and ideas in mind; the doctrine that affirms the existence of spirit independently of matter, spiritism. **immaterialist,** *n.* **immateriality** (-ăl' i ti), *n.* The quality of being immaterial. **immaterialize,** *v.t.* To make immaterial. **immaterially,** *adv.*

immature (im' ă tūr) [L. *immātūrus* (IM- (2), MATURE)], *a.* Not mature, not ripe, imperfect; *premature. **immaturely,** *adv.* **immaturity** (-tūr' i ti), *n.*

immeasurable (i mezh' ŭr ăbl) [IM- (2), MEASURABLE], *a.* That cannot be measured; immense. **immeasurability** (-bil' i ti). **immeasurableness,** *n.* **immeasurably,** *adv.* ***immeasured,** *a.* Unmeasured; immeasurable.

immediate (i mē' di ăt) [M.F. *immédiat*, med. L. *immediātus* (IM- (2), MEDIATE)], *a.* Situated in the closest relation; not separated by any space etc.; acting or acted upon by direct agency, direct; proximate, next, present; done or occurring at once, without delay, instant. ***immediacy,** *n.* **immediately,** *adv.* **immediateness,** *n.* **immediatism,** *n.* (*U.S.A. Hist.*) The docrine of the abolitionists who advocated immediate emancipation of slaves. **immediatist,** *n.*

***immedicable** (i med' i kăbl) [F., from L. *immedicābilis*], *a.* That cannot be healed; incurable.

***immemorable** (i mem' ŏr ăbl) [L. *immemorābilis*], *a.* Not memorable, not worthy of remembrance.

immemorial (im ē mōr' i ăl) [M.F. *immémorial*, med. L. *immemorālis*], *a.* Beyond memory or record; extending or existing beyond the reach of record or tradition. **immemorially,** *adv.*

immense (i mens') [F., from L. *immensus* (IM- (2), *mensus*, p.p. of *metīrī*, to measure, to METE)], *a.* Huge, vast, immeasurable; (*colloq.*) very great, very large; (*slang*) very good, excellent. *n.* Boundless space or expanse. **immensely,** *adv.* **immensity,** *n.*

***immensurable** (i men' sūr ăbl) [late L. *immensūrābilis*], *a.* Immeasurable.

***immerge** (i mĕrj') [L. *immergere* (IM- (1), *mergere*, to plunge, to sink)], *v.t.* To immerse. *v.i.* (*Astron.*) To disappear in the shadow of or behind another heavenly body, opp. to emerge.

immerse (i mĕrs') [L. *immersus*, p.p. of *immergere*, to IMMERGE], *v.t.* To plunge, to dip (into or under water or other fluid); to baptize in this manner; (*fig.*) to involve or absorb deeply (in difficulty, debt, study, etc.). **immersible,** *a.*

immersion (i mĕr' shŭn), *n.* The act of immersing; the state of being immersed; baptism by plunging completely under water; (*fig.*) the state of being deeply involved (in thought etc.); (*Astron.*) the disappearance of a celestial body behind or into the shadow of another. **immersion heater,** *n.* An electrical appliance that is immersed in a tank, etc. to heat the water contained therein. **immersion lens,** *n.* The object-glass of a high-powered microscope that carries a drop of cedar-wood oil between it and the cover-glass. **immersionist,** *n.* One who believes in baptism by immersion.

***immesh** [ENMESH].

***immethodical** (im ē thod' i kăl), *a.* Not methodical; confused. ***immethodically,** *adv.*

***immew** (i mū'), *v.t.* To mew up or confine.

immigrate (im' i grāt) [L. *immigrātus*, p.p. of *immigrāre* (IM- (1), *migrāre*, to MIGRATE)], *v.i.* To come into a foreign country for settlement there. *v.t.* To bring into a foreign country for settlement. **immigrant** (im' i grănt), *n.* One who immigrates. **immigration** (-grā' shŭn), *n.*

imminent (im' i nĕnt) [L. *imminens -ntem*, pres.p. of *imminēre* (IM- (1), *minere*, cp. EMINENT)], *a.* Impending; close at hand; overhanging; *intent (upon). **imminence,** *n.* **imminently,** *adv.*

***immingle** (i mingl'), *v.t.* To intermingle, to mix together.

immiscible (i mis' ibl) [IM- (2), MISCIBLE], *a.* Not capable of being mixed. **immiscibility** (-bil' i ti), *n.* **immiscibly,** *adv.*

***immit** (i mit') [L. *immittere* (IM- (1), *mittere*, to send)], *v.t.* To send or put in; to inject. ***immission** (i mish' ŭn), *n.*

immitigable (i mit' i găbl) [L. *immītigābilis*], *a.* Incapable of mitigation or softening down. **immitigably,** *adv.*

***immix** (i miks') [obs. p.p. *immixt*, L. *immixtus*, from *immiscēre* (IM- (1), *miscēre*, to mix)], *v.t.* To mix or mingle together; to blend (with); to involve (with). ***immixable,** *a.* **immixture,** *n.*

immobile (i mō' bil) [F., from L. *immōbilis*], *a.* Not mobile, immovable; impassible; (*colloq.*) not moving. **immobility** (-bil' i ti), *n.* **immobilize** (i mō' bi līz), *v.t.* To render immovable; to withdraw (specie) from circulation; (*Mil.*) to render (troops) incapable of being moved. **immobilization** (-zā' shun), *n.*

immoderate (i mod' ĕr ăt) [L. *immoderātus*], *a.* Excessive; unreasonable. **immoderately,** *adv.* **immoderation** (-ā' shŭn), *n.*

immodest (i mod' ĕst) [F. *immodeste*, L. *immodestus*], *a.* Not modest, forward, pretentious; unchaste, indelicate, indecent. **immodestly,** *adv.* **immodesty,** *n.*

immolate (im' ō lāt) [L. *immolātus*, p.p. of *immolāre* (IM- (1), *molāre*, to sprinkle with meal, to sacrifice, from *mola*, meal)], *v.t.* To kill in sacrifice, to offer up; to sacrifice (to). **immolation** (-lā' shŭn), *n.* **immolator** (im' ō lā tŏr), *n.*

immoral (i mor′ ăl), *a.* Not moral; inconsistent with or contrary to morality (esp. sexual); licentious, vicious. **immorality** (im ŏ răl′ i ti), *n.* **immorally,** *adv.*

immortal (i môr′ tăl) [L. *immortālis*], *a.* Not mortal, not subject to death; imperishable; relating to immortality; eternally famous; (*colloq.*) not changing, constant, *excessive, grievous. *n.* One who is immortal, esp. one of the ancient gods; (*pl.*) the royal bodyguard in ancient Persia; the forty members of the French Academy. **immortality** (-tăl′ i ti), *n.* The state of being immortal; exemption from annihilation or oblivion. **immortalize,** *v.t.* To make immortal; to perpetuate the memory of. **v.i.* To become immortal. **immortalization** (-zā′ shŭn), *n.* **immortally,** *adv.* With endless existence; (*colloq.*) extremely, excessively.

immortelle (im ôr tel′) [F., fem. of *immortel,* IMMORTAL], *n.* A plant with flowers that keep their shape and colour for a long period after being gathered, an 'everlasting,' esp. *Helichrysum Orientale.*

immovable (i moo′ văbl), *a.* That cannot be moved; firmly fixed; steadfast; unchanging, unalterable; unfeeling; (*Law*) not liable to be removed. **immovability** (-bil′ i ti), **immovableness,** *n.* **immovably,** *adv.* In an immovable manner.

immune (i mūn′) [L. *immūnis* (IM- (2), *mūnis,* serving, rel. to *mūnus,* service, duty)], *a.* Free or exempt (from infection, etc.). *n.* One who is not liable to infection. **immunist,** *n.*

immunity (i mūn′ i ti), *n.* Freedom or exemption from any obligation, duty, or office; (*Law*) exemption from a penalty, taxation, etc.; (*Hyg.*) freedom from liability to infection. **immunize** (im′ ū-, mū′ nīz), *v.t.* **immunization,** *n.* (*Med.*) The conferring of immunity to a disease by artificial means.

immure (i mūr′) [F. *emmurer,* med. L. *immūrāre* (IM- (1), *mūrāre,* from *mūrus,* wall)], *v.t.* To shut in or up; to surround, as with a wall; to confine. **n.* A wall. **immurement,** *n.*

immutable (i mū′ tăbl) [F., from *immūtābilis*], *a.* Unchangeable, not susceptible to change or variation, invariable. **immutability** (-bil′ i ti), *n.* **immutably,** *adv.*

imp (imp) [A.-S. *impa,* shoot, graft, *impian,* to graft, prob. from Gr. *emphuein,* to implant], *n.* A young or little devil; a little malignant spirit; a mischievous child; (*prov.*) an addition to lengthen or repair; *a graft; *an offspring; *a child. *v.t.* To supply (esp. the wing of a falcon) with new feathers; *to strengthen, to eke out; *to graft.

***impacable** (im pā′ kăbl) [IM- (2), L. *pācāre,* to pacify, from *pax pācem,* PEACE], *a.* That cannot be appeased.

impact (im′ păkt) [L. *impactus,* p.p. of *impingere,* to IMPINGE], *n.* A forcible striking (upon or against), a collision; effect, influence. *v.t.* (im păkt′) To press or drive firmly together, to pack firmly in. **impaction** (im păk′ shŭn), *n.*

impair (1) (im pâr′) [O.F. *empeirer,* late L. *impēiōrāre* (IM- (1), *pejor,* worse)], *v.t.* To diminish in excellence, value, strength, etc.; to damage, to injure. **v.i.* To become worse, to be lessened. *n.* Diminution, deterioration, disgrace. **impairment,** *n.*

***impair** (2) (im pâr′) [F. (IM- (2), *pair,* L. PAR)], *a.* Unsuitable; odd, unequal. *n.* An odd number, thing, person, etc.

impale (im pāl′) [F. *empaler* (IM- (1), *pal,* L. *pālus,* a stake)], *v.t.* To transfix, esp. to put to death by transfixing with a sharp stake; (*Her.*) to arrange two coats of arms on one shield, divided by a vertical line; (*fig.*) to render helpless, as though by impaling; *to fence, to enclose. **impalement,** *n.*

impalpable (im păl′ păbl) [F., from L. *impalpābilis*], *a.* Not perceptible to the touch; not coarse; not to be readily apprehended by the mind, intangible. **impalpability** (-bil′ i ti), *n.* **impalpably,** *adv.*

impaludism (im păl′ ū dizm) [IM- (1), L. *palus palūdis,* marsh], *n.* (*Path.*) The morbid condition disposing to intermittent fever and enlarged spleen to which those living in marshy regions are liable.

impanate (im pā′ năt, im′ pă năt) [med L. *impānātus,* p.p. of *impānāre* (IM- (1), *pānis,* bread)], *a.* (*Eccles.*) Embodied in bread. *v.t.* (-nāt) To embody in bread. **impanation** (-nā′ shŭn), *n.* The doctrine of the local union of the body of Christ with the consecrated elements in the Eucharist.

impanel [EMPANEL].

imparadise (im păr′ ă dīs), *v.t.* To put in a place or state of perfect happiness; to make perfectly happy.

***imparasite** (im păr′ ă sīt), *n.* (*Ent.*) An insect that is not a parasite (applied to those whose larvæ feed upon dead insects).

imparipinnate (im păr i pin′ ăt) [L. *impar,* see foll., PINNATE], *a.* (*Bot.*) Pinnate with an odd terminal leaflet.

imparisyllabic (im păr i si lăb′ ik) [L. *impar* (IM- (2), PAR-, SYLLABIC)], *a.* Not having the same number of syllables. *n.* A noun not having the same number of syllables in all its cases.

***imparity** (im păr′ i ti) [late L. *imparitas*], *n.* Disparity, inequality, disproportion; difference in degree, rank, power, etc.; oddness, indivisibility into equal parts.

impark (im park′)[A.-F. *emparker,* O.F. *emparquer*], *v.t.* To form (land) into a park; to enclose (animals) in a park. **imparkation** (-kā′ shŭn), *n.*

***imparl** (im parl′) [M.F. *emparler* (IM- (1), *parler,* to speak)], *v.i.* To talk together, to consult (with); (*Law*) to have delay for the adjustment or compromise of a suit. ***imparlance,** *n.* Conversation, parley; (*Law*) time granted for the compromise of a suit, the continuance of a cause till another day.

impart (im part′) [O.F. *impartir,* L. *impartīre* (IM- (1), *partīre,* to PART)], *v.t.* To grant or bestow a share of; to communicate the knowledge of; to give, to bestow; *to share with. *v.i.* To give a portion. **impartance, impartation** (-tā′ shŭn), **impartment** (im part′ mĕnt), *n.* The act of imparting. **imparter,** *n.* ***impartible** (1), *a.* **impartibility** (1) (-bil′ i ti), *n.*

impartial (im par′ shăl), *a.* Not partial; not favouring one party or one side more than another; equitable, disinterested. **impartiality** (-shi ăl′ i ti), *n.* **impartially,** *adv.*

impartible (2) (im par′ tibl) [late L. *impartībilis*], *a.* Not subject to or capable of partition. **impartibility** (2) (-bil′ i ti), *n.*

impassable (im pas′ ăbl), *a.* That cannot be passed; *unable to pass (as a coin). **impassability** (-bil′ i ti), **impassableness,** *n.* **impassably,** *adv.*

impasse (ăn pas′, im pas′) [F. *passer,* to PASS)], *n.* A blind alley; (*fig.*) an insurmountable obstacle.

impassible (im păs′ ibl) [F., from L. *impassibilis*], *a.* Insensible to pain or suffering; incapable of being injured; not subject to feeling or passion. **impassibility** (-bil′ i ti), **impassibleness,** *n.* **impassibly,** *adv.*

impassion (im păsh′ ŏn) [It. *impassionare* (IM- (1), *passione,* PASSION)], *v.t.* To rouse the deepest feelings of, to stir to ardour or passion. **impassionable,** *a.* ***impassionate** (1) (im păsh′ ŏ năt), *a.* Strongly or deeply affected or moved. *v.t.* (-nāt) To impassion.

impassive (im păs′ iv), *a.* Not affected by pain, feeling, or passion; impassible, apathetic; unmoved, serene (of the expression). **impassively,** *adv.* **impassiveness, impassivity** (-siv′ i ti), *n.*

impaste (im pāst′) [It. *impastare* (IM- (1), *pasta,* PASTE)], *v.t.* To make into paste; (*Paint.*) to lay on colours thickly and boldly. **impastation** (-tā′ shŭn), *n.* (*Ceram.*) The act or process of making into a paste; a combination of materials of different colours or consistencies baked and united by a cement. **impasto** (im păs' tō), *n.* The application of a thick layer or body of pigment, to give relief, etc.

impatient (im pā' shėnt) [F., from L. *impatientem*, nom. *-iens*], *a.* Not able to endure; fretful; not patient or tolerant (of); eager (for or to); *intolerable. **n.* One who is impatient. **impatience, *-ency,** *n.* **impatiently,** *adv.*

impave (im pāv'), *v.t.* (*poet.*) To set in a pavement.

impavid (im păv' id) [L. *impavidus* (IM- (2), *pavidus*, fearful)], *a.* Fearless, dauntless. **impavidly,** *adv.*

impawn (im pawn'), *v.t.* To deposit as security; to pledge.

impayable (im pā' ȧbl, ȧn pā yabl') [F. (IM- (2), *payer*, to PAY)], *a.* Not to be paid, priceless; (*colloq.*) beyond anything.

impeach (im pēch') [O.F. *empescher* (F. *empêcher*), late L. *impedicāre* (IM- (1), *pedica*, fetter, from *pēs pedis*, foot) (Brachet, however, connects the word with a late L. *impactāre*, from *impactus*, p.p. of *impingere*, to impinge)], *v.t.* To charge with a crime or misdemeanour; to bring a charge of maladministration or treason against; to accuse, to charge, to find fault; to call in question; to bring discredit upon. **impeachable,** *a.* **impeacher,** *n.* **impeachment,** *n.* The act of impeaching; the arraignment before a proper tribunal for maladministration or treason; an accusation; a calling in question; *hindrance, obstruction.

impearl (im pĕrl'), *v.t.* To form into pearls or pearl-like drops; to adorn with pearls.

impeccable (im pek' ȧbl) [L. *impeccābilis*], *a.* Not liable to fall into sin; blameless; faultless. **impeccability** (-bil' i ti), *n.* **impeccably,** *adv.* **impeccant,** *a.* Sinless, impeccable. ***impeccance, -ancy,** *n.*

impecunious (im pė kū' ni ŭs), *a.* Destitute of money. **impecuniosity** (-ni os' i ti), *n.*

impedance (im' pe dȧns), *n.* (*Elec.*) Resistance to alternating current, esp. due to inductance or capacitance together with ohmic resistance.

impede (im pēd') [L. *impedīre* (IM- (1), *pēs pedis*, foot), to entangle the feet], *v.t.* To hinder, to obstruct.

impediment (im ped' i mėnt), *n.* That which impedes; hindrance, obstruction. **impediment in the speech:** Indistinct articulation. **impedimental,** *a.*

impedimenta (im ped i men' tȧ) [L. *pl.* of *impedimentum*, an impediment], *n.pl.* Baggage, supplies for an army on the march; things that impede progress.

impel (im pel') [L. *impellere* (IM- (1), *pellere*, to drive)], *v.t.* To drive or push forward; to drive or urge (to an action or to do). **impellent,** *a.* That impels. *n.* One who or that which impels. **impeller,** *n.*

impen (im pen'), *v.t.* To shut or enclose in or as in a pen.

impend (im pend') [L. *impendēre* (IM- (1), *pendēre*, to hang)], *v.i.* To hang (over), to be suspended (over); (*fig.*) to threaten, to be imminent. **impendence, -ency,** *n.* **impendent,** *a.*

impenetrable (im pen' ė trȧbl) [F. *impénétrable*, L. *impenetrābilis*], *a.* That cannot be penetrated or pierced; (*fig.*) inscrutable, incomprehensible; not penetrable to ideas, etc., dull, obtuse, stupid; (*Phys.*) preventing any other substance from occupying the same place at the same time. **impenetrability** (-bil' i ti). **impenetrableness,** *n.* **impenetrably,** *adv.*

impenetrate (im pen' ė trāt), *v.t.* To penetrate deeply into.

impenitent (im pen' i tėnt) [L. *impœnitentem*, nom. *-tens*], *a.* Not penitent, not contrite. *n.* A hardened sinner. **impenitence, -tency,** *n.* **impenitently,** *adv.*

impennate (im pen ȧt) [IM- (2), PENNATE], *a.* (*Ornith.*) Wingless; belonging to the *Impennes*, a family of swimming birds having short wings covered with scale-like feathers, containing the auks, penguins, etc. *n.* One of these birds. ***impennuous,** *a.* Wingless.

imperative (im per' ȧ tiv) [late L. *imperātīvus*, from *imperāre*, to command (IM- (1), *parāre*, to make ready)], *a.* (*Gram.*) Expressive of command; authoritative, peremptory; obligatory; urgent. *n.* That mood of a verb which expresses command, entreaty, or exhortation. **categorical imperative** [CATEGORICAL]. **imperatival** (-tī' vȧl), *a.* (*Gram.*) **imperatively,** *adv.* **imperativeness,** *n.*

imperator (im pėr ā' tor) [L., as prec.], *n.* (*Rom. Hist.*) A title originally bestowed upon a victorious leader on the field of battle by his soldiers; afterwards the equivalent of the modern 'emperor.' **imperatorial,** *a.* **imperatorially,** *adv.* ***imperatrix,*** *n.* An empress.

imperceivable (im pėr sē' vȧbl), *a.* Imperceptible.

imperceptible (im pėr sep' tibl), *a.* Not perceptible; not easily apprehended, indistinguishable; insignificant, extremely slight, small, or gradual. **imperceptibility** (-bil' i ti), **imperceptibleness,** *n.* **imperceptibly,** *adv.* **imperceptive,** *a.*

impercipient (im pėr sip' i ėnt), *a.* Not perceiving; not having power to perceive. *n.* An unperceiving person.

imperfect (im pĕr' fėkt) [O.F. *imparfait*, L. *imperfectus* (IM- (2), PERFECT), assim. to L.], *a.* Not perfect, defective; incomplete, not fully made, done, etc.; unfinished; lacking some part or member; (*Gram.*) expressing action as continuous and not completed. *n.* The imperfect tense. **imperfectible** (im pėr fek' tibl), *a.* Incapable of being perfected. **imperfectibility** (-bil' i ti), *n.* **imperfect tense:** A tense expressing or denoting an uncompleted action or state, usu. relating to past time. **imperfection,** *n.* A moral or physical fault; a defect; a deficiency. **imperfective** (-fek' tiv), *a.* **imperfectly,** *adv.* **imperfectness,** *n.*

imperforate (im pĕr' fō rȧt), *a.* Not perforated; not separated by rows of perforations (as stamps); (*Anat.*) having no opening or normal orifice, etc. **imperforable,** *a.* That cannot be perforated. **imperforation** (-rā' shŭn), *n.* Imperforate condition.

imperial (im pēr' i ȧl) [O.F., from L. *imperiālis*, from IMPERIUM], *a.* Of or pertaining to an empire, an emperor, or other supreme ruler; pertaining to the British Empire, as dist. from any particular kingdom, dominion, colony, etc.; suitable to or like an emperor; sovereign, supreme; lordly, majestic. *n.* A baggage-case on a travelling carriage; an outside seat on a diligence or coach; a size of paper about 22 × 30 in.; a tuft of hair on a man's chin (named from Napoleon III); (*G. Hist.*) an adherent of the Emperor's party, one of the Imperialist troops. **Imperial City:** Rome; a city that was an independent member of the Holy Roman Empire. **imperial federation:** A scheme for the consolidation of the British Empire, on the basis of joint control and a share in the cost of imperial defence by the Colonies. **imperial pint, gallon,** etc., **imperial weights and measures:** Those prescribed by statute in the United Kingdom. **imperiality** (-ăl' i ti), *n.* Imperial power or authority. **imperialize,** *v.t.* To render imperial. **imperialization** (-zā' shŭn), *n.* **imperially,** *adv.*

imperialism (im pēr' i ȧl izm), *n.* Government by an emperor; imperial spirit, state, or authority; the policy of imperial federation; the policy of extending the British Empire; the policy of extending the authority of a nation by means of colonies or dependencies. **imperialist,** *n.* A supporter of imperialism; (*Hist.*) an adherent of the Emperor, esp. during the Thirty Years' War; an advocate of imperial rule. **imperialistic** (-lis' tik), *a.*

imperil (im per′ il), *v.t.* To endanger.

imperious (im pēr′ i ůs) [L. *imperiōsus*, from IMPERIUM], *a.* Arbitrary, dictatorial, overbearing; haughty, arrogant; urgent, pressing; *imperial. **imperiously,** *adv.* **imperiousness,** *n.*

imperishable (im per′ ish ȧbl), *a.* Enduring permanently; not subject to decay. **imperishability** (-bil′ i ti), **imperishableness,** *n.* **imperishably,** *adv.*

imperium (im pēr′ i ům) [L., command, supreme authority], *n.* Absolute command, authority, or rule. ***imperium in imperio:*** An independent authority within the dominion of another authority.

impermanent (im pĕr′ mȧ nėnt), *a.* Not permanent. **impermanence,** *n.*

impermeable (im pĕr′ mė ȧbl) [F. *imperméable*, late L. *impermeābilis*], *a.* Not allowing passage, esp. of a fluid, impervious. **impermeability** (-bil′ i ti) ***impermeableness,** *n.* **impermeably,** *adv.*

impermeator (im pĕr′ mė ā tȯr), *n.* (*Steam-eng.*) A contrivance for lubricating the cylinder of an engine by the forcing in of oil.

impermissible (im pėr mis′ ibl), *a.* Not permissible.

imperscriptible (im pėr skrip′ tibl) [IM- (2), L. *perscrībere* (PER-, *scrībere*, to write, p.p. *scriptus*)], *a.* Not derived from written authority.

impersonal (im pĕr′ sȯ nȧl) [late L. *impersōnālis*], *a.* Without personality; not relating to any particular person or thing; (*Gram.*) applied to verbs used only in the third person singular in English with the neuter pronoun *it* as the nominative. *n.* An impersonal verb. **impersonality** (-năl′ i ti), *n.* **impersonally,** *adv.*

impersonate (im pĕr′ sȯn āt), *v.t.* To invest with personality; to personify; to represent in character, to personate. **impersonation** (-nā′ shůn), *n.* **impersonator** (-pĕr′ sȯ nā tȯr), *n.* **impersonify** (im pĕr son′ i fī), *v.t.* To personify.

impertinent (im pĕr′ ti nėnt) [F., from L. *impertinentem*, nom. *-ens*], *a.* Not pertinent, not pertaining to the matter in hand; trifling, frivolous; offensive, impudent, insolent. *n.* An officious or unmannerly person; a meddler, an intruder. **impertinence, *-ency,** *n.* **impertinently,** *adv.*

imperturbable (im pĕr tĕr′ bȧbl) [late L. *imperturbābilis*], *a.* That cannot be easily disturbed or excited; unmoved, calm, cool. **imperturbability** (-bil′ i ti), **imperturbableness, *imperturbation** (bā′ shůn), *n.* **imperturbably,** *adv.*

impervious (im pĕr′ vi ůs) [L. *impervius*], *a.* Not admitting of passage or entrance; (*fig.*) impenetrable (to feeling, argument, etc.). **imperviously,** *adv.* **imperviousness,** *n.*

impeticos (im pet′ i kos) [comic perversion of IMPOCKET, with alln. to PETTICOAT], *v.t.* (*Shak.*) To put in one's pocket.

impetigo (im pė tī′ gō) [L., from *impetere*, to assail (IM- (1), *petĕre*, to seek)], *n.* (*pl.* **-tigines,** tij′ i nēz) A clustered yellow-scaled pustular eruption on the skin. **impetiginous** (tij′ i nůs), *a.*

impetrate (im′ pė trāt) [L. *impetrātus*, p.p. of *impetrāre* (IM- (1) *patrāre*, to bring to pass)], *v.t.* To obtain by petition or entreaty. **impetration** (-trā′-shůn), *n.* The act of obtaining by petition or entreaty; *(*Law*) the obtaining, by petition from the court of Rome, of benefices and Church offices in England, the disposition of which by law belonged to lay patrons. **impetrative, impetratory** (im′ pė trā tiv, -tȯr i), *a.*

impetuous (im pet′ ū ůs) [F. *impetueux -euse*, L. *impetuōsus*, from foll.], *a.* Moving with violence or great speed; acting violently or suddenly, hasty, impulsive, precipitate. **impetuously,** *adv.* **impetuosity** (-os′ i ti), **impetuousness,** *n.*

impetus (im′ pė tůs) [L. (IM- (1), *petere*, to seek)], *n.* The force with which a body moves or is impelled; impulse, driving force.

impeyan (im′ pi ȧn) [Lady *Impey*, wife of Sir Elijah Impey (1732–1809), who tried to introduce it to England], *n.* An East Indian pheasant, *Lophophorus Impeyanus*, with brilliant plumage and crested head.

imphee (im′ fi) [Natal native *imfe*], *n.* The African or Chinese sugar-cane.

impi (im′ pi) [Zulu], *n.* A body of Kafir warriors.

***impicture** (im pik′ chůr) [IM- (1), PICTURE], *v.t.* To stamp or impress with a picture or resemblance of.

impiety (im pī′ ė ti) [F. *impieté*, L. *impietātem*, nom. *-tas*, from *impius*, IMPIOUS], *n.* The quality of being impious; an impious act; want of filial affection or of reverence towards God.

impignorate (im pig′ nȯ rāt) [med. L. *impignorātus*, p.p. of *impignorāre* (IM- (1), *pignus -noris*, a pledge)], *v.t.* (*Sc.*) To pawn or pledge; to mortgage. **impignoration** (-rā′ shůn), *n.*

impinge (im pinj′) [L. *impingere* (IM- (1), *pangere*, to drive, fasten)], *v.i.* To come into collision, to strike (on, against, etc.). **impingement,** *n.* ***impingent,** *a.*

impious (im′ pi ůs) [L. *impius*], *a.* Wanting in piety or reverence towards the Supreme Being; irreverent, profane. ***impiously,** *adv.* **impiousness,** *n.* Impiety.

impish (im′ pish), *a.* Having the characteristics of an imp. **impishly,** *adv.*

impiteous (im pit′ ė ůs), *a.* (*poet.*) Pitiless, ruthless.

implacable (im plăk′ ȧbl, -plā′ kȧbl) [F., from L. *implācābilis*], *a.* Not to be appeased; inexorable, unrelenting. **implacability** (-bil′ i ti), ***implacableness,** *n.* **implacably,** *adv.*

implacental (im plȧ sen′ tȧl), *a.* (*Zool.*) Without a placenta (used of marsupials and monotremes).

implant (im plant′) [F. *implanter*, late L. *implantāre*], *v.t.* To plant for the purpose of growth; to set or fix (in); (*fig.*) to inculcate, to instil. ***implantation** (-tā′ shůn), *n.*

implausible (im plaw′ zibl), *a.* Not having an appearance of truth and credibility. **implausibility** (-bil′ i ti), ***implausibleness,** *n.* **implausibly,** *adv.*

***implead** (im plēd′) [M.E. *enpleden*, A.-F. *enpleder*, O.F. *empleidier*], *v.t.* To bring an action against; to accuse, to impeach. *v.i.* To bring an action. ***impleader,** *n.*

impledge (im plej′), *v.t.* To pledge, to pawn.

implement (im′ plė mėnt) [L. *implēmentum*, a filling up or accomplishing, from *implēre* (IM- (1), *plēre*, to fill)], *n.* A tool, a utensil; an instrument used in labour; (*fig.*) an instrument, an agent; (*pl.*) things that serve for equipment, furniture, use, etc.; (*Sc. Law*) fulfilment, complete performance. *v.t.* To fulfil; to carry into effect; to complete, to supplement. **implemental** (-men′ tȧl), *a.* **implementation,** *n.* **implementiferous** (-tif′ ėr ůs) [-FEROUS], *a.* (*Palæont.*) Containing stone implements (of strata).

implete (im plēt′) [L. *implētus*, p.p. of *implēre* (IM- (1), *plēre*, to fill)], *v.t.* (*Am.*) To fill up. **impletion** (im plē′ shůn), *n.* The act of filling; fulness.

***implex** (im′ pleks) [L. *implexus*, p.p. of *implectere* (IM- (1), *plectere*, to plait)], *a.* Involved, complicated. ***implexion** (im plek′ shůn), *n.* **implexous,** *a.* (*Bot.*) Folded or plaited.

implicate (im′ pli kāt) [L. *implicātus*, p.p. of *implicāre* (IM- (1), *plicāre*, to fold)], *v.t.* To enfold, to entangle, to entwine; to involve, to bring into connexion with. *n.* (-kȧt) That which is involved or implied. **implication** (-kā′ shůn), *n.* The act of implicating; the state of being implicated; entanglement; an inference. **implicative,** *a.*

implicit (im plis′ it) [L. *implicitus*, var. of *implicātus*, see prec.], *a.* Implied; understood or inferable; tacitly contained but not expressed; depending upon complete belief or trust in another;

hence, unquestioning, unreserved. **implicitly,** *adv.* **implicitness,** *n.*

implied, etc. [IMPLY].

implode (im plōd′) [L. *plodere,* to clap], *v.t. and i.* To burst inwards. **implosion,** *n.* **implosive,** *a.*

implore (im plôr′) [F. *implorer,* L. *implorāre* (IM- (1), *plorāre,* to weep)], *v.t.* To call upon in earnest supplication; to ask for earnestly. *v.i.* To entreat, to beg, to supplicate. **n.* An act of imploring. **imploration** (-ā′ shŭn), *n.* ***implorator,** *n.* One who implores. ***imploratory** (im plor′ ȧ tôr i), *a.* Earnestly imploring. **implorer,** *n.* One who implores; a suppliant. **imploringly,** *adv.* **imploringness,** *n.*

implosion [IMPLODE].

impluvium (im ploo′ vi ŭm) [L., from *impluere* (IM- (1), *pluere,* to rain)], *n.* (*Rom. Ant.*) A cistern or basin for receiving the rain-water in the open central part of the court or atrium of a Roman house.

imply (im plī′) [O.F. *emplier,* L. *implicāre,* see IMPLICATE], *v.t.* To involve or contain by implication; to signify; to import; to mean indirectly, to hint; *to enfold, to entangle. **implied,** *a.* Contained in substance or essence, though not actually expressed. **impliedly** (-plī′ ėd li), *adv.*

impolarizable (im pō′ lȧ rīz′ ȧ bėl), *a.* (*Elec.*) Incapable of polarization (as some voltaic batteries).

impolicy (im pol′ i si), *n.* The quality of being impolitic or inexpedient.

impolite (im pȯ līt′) [L. *impolītus*], *a.* Not polite, ill-mannered. **impolitely,** *adv.* **impoliteness,** *n.*

impolitic (im pol′ i tik), *a.* Not politic; injudicious, inexpedient. **impolitically,** *adv.*

imponderabilia (im pon der ȧ bil′ i ȧ), *n.pl.* Imponderables.

imponderable (im pon′ dėr ȧbl), *a.* Not having sensible weight; very light; (*fig.*) incalculable. *n.* A body or agent without sensible weight (as light, heat, electricity); a matter that cannot be weighed by judgement or argument. **imponderability** (-bil′ i ti), **imponderableness,** *n.* ***imponderous,** *a.* ***imponderousness,** *n.*

***impone** (im pōn′) [L. *impōnere* (IM- (1), *pōnere,* to place)], *v.t.* To impose; to stake, to wager. **imponent,** *a.* That imposes. *n.* One who imposes.

imporous (im pôr′ ŭs) [IM- (2), POROUS], *a.* Destitute of pores; close and compact in texture. **imporosity** (-pȯ ros′ i ti), *n.*

import (im pōrt′) [F. *importer,* L. *importāre* (IM- (1), *portāre,* to bring)], *v.t.* To bring (goods) from a foreign country (into); to introduce; to imply, to signify, to mean; to concern, to be of interest to. *v.i.* To be important, to matter. *n.* (im′ pôrt) That which is imported from abroad (*usu. in pl.*); importation; that which is signified or implied; importance, moment, consequence. **importable,** *a.* That may be imported; *intolerable. **importability** (-bil′ i ti), *n.* **importation,** *n.* The act or practice of importing; that which is imported. **importer** (im pôr′ tėr), *n.* One who imports goods. ***importless** (im′ pôrt lės), *a.* Without import; insignificant.

importance (im pôr′ tȧns), *n.* The quality of being important; weight, authority, consequence; personal consideration, self-esteem, pretentiousness; *pressing solicitation. ***importancy,** *n.* Importance; an important matter.

important (im pôr′ tȧnt), *a.* Of great moment or consequence, weighty; of great personal consequence, pretentious; *urgent. **importantly,** *adv.*

importunate (im pôr′ tū nȧt) [L. *importūnus,* unfit, unsuitable, rel. to *portus,* PORT (1)], *a.* Unreasonably and pertinaciously solicitous or urgent; insupportable, troublesome. **v.t.* (-nāt) To importune. **importunately,** *adv.* **importunacy,** ***importunateness,** **importunity** (-tū′ ni ti), *n.*

importune (im′ pȯr tūn, im pôr′ tūn) [as prec.], *a.* Untimely; importunate; violent, grievous; pertinacious, irksome. *v.t.* To solicit pertinaciously or urgently; to press with solicitation; *to mean, to signify. **v.i.* To be importunate. ***importunely,** *adv.* Inopportunely; importunately. **importuner,** *n.*

importunity [IMPORTUNATE].

impose (im pōz′) [F. *imposer,* L. *impōnere* (cp. COMPOSE)], *v.t.* *To lay or place upon; to set, to attach; to lay (as a burden, tax, toll, etc.) upon; to force (views, etc.) upon; to palm off (upon); (*Print.*) to arrange (pages of type) in a forme for printing. *v.i.* To impress oneself (upon); to practise trickery or deception (upon). **n.* A command, charge, or injunction. **to impose on** or **upon:** To cheat, to deceive; to take advantage of. **imposer,** *n.* **imposing,** *a.* Commanding; impressive, majestic. **imposing-stone:** (*Print.*) A slab of stone or metal on which type is made up into formes. **imposingly,** *adv.* **imposingness,** *n.*

imposition (im pō zish′ ŭn), *n.* The act of imposing or placing upon; that which is laid or placed upon; an exercise enjoined as a punishment in schools etc.; a duty, a tax, an impost; a deceit, an imposture, a fraud; (*Print.*) the process of assembling pages in type on the stone and then locking them into a chase, the whole then becoming a forme. **imposition of hands:** (*Eccles.*) The laying on of hands in the ordination ceremony, etc.

impossible (im pos′ ibl) [F., from L. *impossibilis*], *a.* Not possible; (*colloq.*) impracticable, not feasible; that cannot be done, thought, endured, etc.; outrageous, monstrous; (*Math.*) imaginary. **n.* An impossibility. **impossibility** (-bil′ i ti), *n.* **impossibly,** *adv.*

impost (1) (im′ pōst) [O.F. (F. *impôt*), late L. *impostum,* L. *impositum,* nom. *-tus,* p.p. of *impōnere,* to IMPOSE], *n.* That which is imposed or levied as a tax, a tribute, a duty (esp. on imported goods); (*Racing*) a weight carried by a horse in a handicap.

impost (2) (im′ pōst) [F. *imposte,* It. *imposta,* as prec.], *n.* (*Arch.*) The upper member of a pillar or entablature on which an arch rests.

impostor (im pos′ tȯr) [F. *imposteur,* late L. *impostor,* from *impōnere,* to IMPOSE; assim. to L.], *n.* One who falsely assumes a character; a deceiver by false pretences. **impostorship,** *n.* **impostrous,** *a.* **imposture,** *n.* Deception by the assumption of a false character, imposition; a fraud, a swindle.

***impostume, *-thume** (im pos′ tūm) [O.F. *empostume, apostume,* L. and Gr. *apostēma* (APO-, *sta-,* base of *istanai,* to stand)], *n.* A collection of purulent matter in any part of the body; an abscess. *v.i.* To impostumate. **impostumate,** *v.i.* To form an abscess, to gather. *v.t.* To affect with an abscess. **impostumation** (-mā′ shŭn), *n.*

impotent (im′ pȯ tėnt) [F., from L. *impotentem,* nom. *-tens*], *a.* Wanting in physical, intellectual, or moral power; lacking the power of sexual intercourse (said of the male). *n.* One who is sexually impotent. **impotence, -tency,** *n.* **impotently,** *adv.*

impound (im pound′), *v.t.* To shut up (cattle) in a pound; to confine; to collect and confine or retain (water) in a reservoir, mill-pond, etc.; to take possession of or confiscate (a document, etc.). **impoundage,** *n.* The act of impounding.

impoverish (im pov′ ėr ish) [O.F. *empoveriss-,* part. stem of *empoverir* (IM- (1), *povre, pauvre,* POOR)], *v.t.* To make poor; to exhaust the strength, fertility, or resources of. **impoverisher,** *n.* **impoverishment,** *n.*

impracticable (im prăk′ ti kȧbl), *a.* Not possible to be effected by the means at command; not feasible; intractable, stubborn. **impracticability** (-bil′ i ti), **impracticableness,** *n.* **impracticably,** *adv.*

imprecate (im′ prė kāt) [L. *imprecātus,* p.p. of *imprecārī* (IM- (1), *precārī,* to PRAY)], *v.t.* To invoke (as an evil on); to invoke a curse (on). **imprecation** (-kā′ shŭn), *n.* The act of imprecating;

a prayer for evil to fall on any one; a curse. **imprecatory** (im' prė kă tȯr i), *a.* Involving a curse.

***impregn** (im prēn') [abbr. of IMPREGNATE], *v.t.* To impregnate.

impregnable (im preg' nȧbl) [O.F. *imprenable* (IM- (2), *prendre*, L. *prehendre*, to seize), -*g*- as in REIGN, SOVEREIGN, etc.], *a.* That cannot be stormed or taken by assault; (*fig.*) able to resist all attacks, invincible. **impregnability,** *n.* **impregnably,** *adv.*

impregnate (im preg' nāt) [late L. *imprægnātus*, p.p. of *imprægnāre* (IM- (1), *prægnāre*, to be PREGNANT)], *v.t.* To make pregnant; to fertilize, to fecundate; to render fruitful or fertile; to infuse the particles or qualities of any other substance into; to saturate (with); (*fig.*) to imbue, to inspire (with). **a.* (-nȧt) Impregnated, pregnant; (*fig.*) imbued, inspired (with). **impregnation** (-nā' shŭn), *n.*

impresario (im prė za' ri ō) [It. *impresa*, IMPRESE], *n.* One who organizes or manages a concert, an opera company, etc.

imprescriptible (im prė skrip' tibl) [F. (IM- (2), PRESCRIPTIBLE)], *a.* That cannot be lost or impaired by usage or claims founded on prescription. **imprescriptibility** (-bil' i ti), *n.*

***imprese** (im prēs'), **impress** (1) (im' pres) [It. *impresa*, undertaking, device, fem. of *impreso*, undertaken, cp. EMPRISE], *n.* An heraldic device; a motto.

impress (2) (im pres') [L. *impressāre*, freq. of *imprimere* (IM- (1), *premere*, to PRESS)], *v.t.* To press or stamp (a mark, etc., in or upon); to produce (a mark or figure) by pressure; to fix deeply (in or on the mind); to affect strongly. *n.* (im' pres) The act of marking by pressure; a mark or stamp made by pressure; a stamp, an impression; a characteristic mark. **impressible,** *a.* Capable of being impressed; yielding to pressure; susceptible. ***impressibly,** *adv.*

impress (3) (impres'), *v.t.* To compel (seamen) to enter the public service; to seize or set apart (goods, property, etc.) for the public service. **impressment,** *n.*

impression (im presh' ŭn), *n.* The act of impressing; the mark made by impressing; a copy taken from type, an engraved plate, etc.; the visible or tangible effect of an action, etc.; (*collect.*) copies constituting a single issue of a book, engraving, etc., esp. a reprint from standing type, as dist. from an edition; (*fig.*) effect produced upon the senses, feelings, etc.; an indistinct notion, a slight recollection, belief, etc.; (*Psych.*) a mental effect of a previous experience. **impressionable,** *a.* Easily impressed, impressible. **impressionability** (-bil' i ti), *n.* **impressionism,** *n.* (*Art*) A movement that began in France acting on the principle that the hand should paint what the eye sees, thus ruling out all conventions of lighting and composition. **impressionist,** *a.* Pertaining to impressionism. **impressionary, impressionistic** (-nis' tik), *a.*

impressive (im pres' iv), *a.* Adapted to make an impression on the mind; *impressible. **impressively,** *adv.* **impressiveness,** *n.*

imprest (im' prest) [IM- (1), PREST, prob. after obs. *in prest*, in ready money], *n.* A loan, an advance, esp. for carrying on any of the public services. **bill of imprest** or **imprest bill:** An order entitling the bearer to have money paid in advance. **imprest office:** A former department of the Admiralty which advanced money to paymasters and other officers.

imprimatur (im pri ma' tŭr) [L., let it be printed, from *imprimere*, to IMPRESS (2)], *n.* A licence to print a book, granted by the authorities (esp. of the R.-C. Ch.) where there is a censor of the press; (*fig.*) a mark of sanction or approval.

imprimis (im prī' mis) [L. (IM- (1), *primis*), among the first things], *adv.* First in order.

imprint (im print') [O.F. *empreinter*, *empreindre*, L. *imprimere*, to IMPRESS (2)], *v.t.* To impress, to stamp; to print; (*fig.*) to impress (on or in the mind). *n.* (im' print) A mark, stamp, or impression, esp. the name of the printer or publisher of a book, periodical, etc., with the place and usu. the date of publication (on the title-page or at the end of a book).

imprison (im priz' ȯn) [O.F. *emprisoner*], *v.t.* To put into prison; (*fig.*) to confine, to hold in custody or captivity. **imprisonment,** *n.*

improbable (im prob' ȧbl) [L. *improbābilis*], *a.* Not likely to be true; not likely to happen. **improbability** (-bil' i ti), *n.* **improbably,** *adv.*

improbation (im prȯ bā' shŭn) [L. *improbātio*, from *improbāre*, to disapprove, from *improbus*, wicked (IM- (2), *probus*, good, see PROBITY)], *n.* (*Sc. Law*) The proving of falsehood or forgery; an action to set aside a deed on account of falsity or forgery. **improbative, improbatory** (im prob' ȧ tiv, -tȯr i), *a.* Tending to disprove.

improbity (im prŏb' i ti) [L. *improbitās*, from *improbus*, see prec.], *n.* Want of probity; dishonesty.

impromptu (im promp' tū) [L. *in promptū*, in readiness (*promptū*, abl. of -*tus*, from *prōmere*, to PROMPT)], *adv.* Off-hand, without previous study. *a.* Done or said off-hand, extempore. *n.* (*pl.* **-tus**) An extemporaneous composition, performance, act, etc. **impromptuary,** *a.* **impromptuist,** *n.* An improvisator.

improper (im prop' ėr) [F. *impropre*], *a.* Not proper; unsuitable, unfit; unbecoming, indecent; not accurate, erroneous. **improper fraction:** A fraction the numerator of which is equal to or greater than the denominator. **improperly,** *adv.*

impropriate (im prō' pri āt) [IM- (1), L. *propriāre*, to appropriate, from *proprius*, one's own], *v.t.* To convert (esp. ecclesiastical property) to one's own or to private use; to place the revenues, profits, etc., of in the hands of a layman. *a.* (-ȧt) Vested in a layman. **impropriation** (-ā' shŭn), *n.* **impropriator** (im prō' pri ā tȯr), *n.* One, esp. a layman, to whom church lands or an ecclesiastical benefice are impropriated.

impropriety (im prō prī' ė ti) [L. *improprietās*], *n.* The quality of being improper; an unbecoming act, expression, etc.; indecency.

improve (im proov') [M.E. *emprowen*, A.-F. *emprouwer*, from O.F. *prou*, profit, perh. from L. *prōd-* (*prōdesse*, to be useful or profitable to)], *v.t.* To make better; to increase the value, goodness, or power of; to turn to profitable account; to take advantage of, to utilize. *v.i.* To grow or become better; to recover from illness, to regain health or strength; to increase in value, to rise, to be enhanced. **to improve on** or **upon:** To make something better than; to make use of for edification; to draw a moral from. **improvable** (im proo' vȧbl), *a.* Admitting of improvement or amelioration; capable of being used to advantage. **improvability** (-bil' i ti), ***improvableness,** *n.* **improving,** *a.* Tending to improve. **improving lease:** (*Sc. Law*) A lease granted for a longer period to encourage a tenant to make improvements. **improvingly,** *adv.*

improvement (im proov' mėnt), *n.* The act of improving; advancement in value, goodness, knowledge, etc.; profitable use or employment; progress, growth, increase; that which is added or done to anything in order to improve it; a beneficial or valuable addition; the practical application of a discourse.

improver (im proov' ėr), *n.* One who or that which improves; a worker who accepts low wages in order to learn a trade, esp. an apprentice in millinery or dressmaking.

improvident (im prov' i dėnt), *a.* Not provident; neglecting to make provision for future exigencies; thriftless; careless, heedless. ***improvided,** *a.* Unforeseen, unexpected. **improvidence,** *n.* Want of foresight or thrift. **improvidently,** *adv.*

improvise (im' prȯ vīz) [F. *improviser*, It. *improvvisare*, from *improvviso*, L. *imprōvīsus* (IM- (2), *prōvīsus*, p.p. of *prōvidēre*, to PROVIDE)], *v.t.* To compose and recite or sing off-hand; to extemporize; to do, produce, or prepare on the spur of the moment. **improvisate** (im prov′ i zāt), *v.t.* To improvise. ***a.* (-zȧt) Improvised, impromptu. **improvisation** (-zā′ shŭn), *n.* **improvisator** (im prov′ i zā tôr), *n.* **improvisatore** (im prō vē za tôr′ ā) [It.], *n.* (*pl.* **-ori**, -ôr′ ē) One who improvises; a versifier who can compose verses extemporaneously on any given subject. **improvisatorial** (-tôr′ i ȧl), **improvisatory** (-viz′ ȧ tòr i), *a.* Pertaining to improvisation. **improvisatrice** (im prō vē za trē′ chā), *n.* (*pl.* **-ci**, -chē) A female improvisatore. ***improviso** (-vī′ zō), *a.* Impromptu, extemporaneous.

imprudent (im proo′ dėnt) [L. *imprūdens -ntem*], *a.* Wanting in foresight or discretion; rash, incautious, indiscreet. **imprudence**, *n.* **imprudently**, *adv.*

impuberal (im pū′ bėr ȧl) [L. *impūbes -erem* (IM- (2), *pūbes -berem*, of ripe age)], *a.* Not yet arrived at the age of puberty. **impuberty**, *n.* **impubescent** (-bes′ ėnt), *a.*

impudent (im′ pū dėnt) [F., from L. *impudentem*, nom. *-dens* (IM- (2), *pudens*, pres.p. of *pudēre*, to feel shame)], *a.* Wanting in shame or modesty; impertinent, insolent. **impudence**, ***-pudency**, *n.* **impudently**, *adv.* **impudicity** (im pū dis′ i ti), *n.* Immodesty, shamelessness.

impugn (im pūn′) [F. *impugner*, L. *impugnāre* (IM- (1), *pugnāre*, to fight)], *v.t.* To call in question, to contradict, to gainsay; *to oppose. **impugnable** (im pū′ nȧbl), *a.* **impugner**, *n.* **impugnment**, *n.*

impuissant (im pū′ i sȧnt) [F.], *a.* Powerless, impotent. **impuissance**, *n.*

impulse (im′ pŭls) [L. *impulsus*, from *impellere*, to IMPEL], *n.* The application or effect of an impelling force; influence acting suddenly on the mind tending to produce action; a sudden tendency to action; (*Dynam.*) a large force acting for an extremely short time, the momentum due to such a force; *attack, onset. **impulsion** (im pŭl′ shŭn), *n.* The act of impelling; the state of being impelled; impetus; instigation, incitement. **impulsive**, *a.* Communicating impulse, urging forward; liable to be actuated by impulse rather than reflection. **impulsively**, *adv.* **impulsiveness**, *n.*

impunity (im pū′ ni ti) [F. *impunité*, L. *impūnitātem*, nom. *-tās* (IM- (2), *pœna*, Gr. *poinē*, penalty)], *n.* Exemption from punishment, penalty, injury, damage or loss.

impure (im pūr′) [L. *impūrus*], *a.* Not pure; mixed with foreign matter, adulterated; defiled, unclean, unchaste; not grammatically correct; (*Phys.*) mixed with other colours. **impurely**, *adv.* ***impureness**, *n.* **impurity**, *n.*

***impurple** [EMPURPLE].

impute (im pūt′) [F. *imputer*, L. *impūtāre* (IM- (1), *putāre*, to reckon)], *v.t.* To ascribe, to attribute; to set to the account or charge of; (*Theol.*) to ascribe (righteousness, guilt, etc.) on account of another; *to charge. **imputable**, *a.* **imputability** (-bil′ i ti), *n.* **imputation** (-tā′ shŭn), *n.* The act of imputing; that which is imputed as a charge or fault; reproach, censure; (*Theol.*) the attributing of righteousness or personal guilt and its consequences to a person or persons, on account of another. **imputative**, *a.* Coming by imputation. **imputatively**, *adv.* **imputer**, *n.*

in (in) [A.-S., Dut., G., Goth., cogn. with L. *in*, Gr. *en*], *prep.* Within, inside of, contained or existing within; denoting presence or situation within the limits of time, place, circumstance, reason, tendency, ratio, relation, etc. *adv.* Within or inside some place; indoors, at home; in office; into the bargain, over and above; (*Cricket*) at the wicket. *a.* Internal, living inside (as a hospital). *n.pl.* The political party in office. **v.t.* To take in, to harvest. **in-and-in**, **n.* A game played by three persons with four dice. *adv.* (*Zool.*) From animals of the same breed. **in-and-out**, *adv.* and *a.* Alternately in and out (as in running); now in, now out. **in any case**: Whatever happens. **in cash**: (*colloq.*) Supplied with money. **in itself**: By itself, apart from other things or considerations, absolutely. **inpass**, *n.* (*Rugby football*) A pass from back to the centre. **in-patient**, *n.* A person residing inside a hospital and receiving regular treatment. **in-phase**, *a.* (*Elec.*) (of two currents) Alternating simultaneously. **in-player**, *n.* (*Rackets*) The server. **in-shoot**, *n.* (*Baseball*) The act of moving the ball swiftly inwards; a ball so moved. **in so** (or **as**) **far as**: In such measure as. **not in it**: (*slang*) Not in the running, standing no chance of success. **in that**: Seeing that; since. **in the air**: Floating, current (as a rumour, etc.). **in the name of**: Under the authority of. **to be in for**: To be committed to or involved in; to be entered for (a race, etc.). **to be in for it**: To be certainly heading for trouble. **to be in with**: To be on intimate terms with. **to keep the fire in**: To keep the fire burning.

in- (1) [A.-S. *in-*, or O.F. *in-*, *en-*, or directly from L. *in-*], *pref.* In; into; within; on; against, towards; as in *indicate*, *induce*.

in- (2) [L., not], *pref.* Un-, not, without, as in *incomprehensible*.

-in [INE], *suf.* (*Chem.*) Denoting neutral compounds, and usu. dist. from alkaloids and basic compounds in -INE, as *albumin*, *casein*.

-ina (1) [L. *-īna*, fem. of *-īnus*], *suf.* Denoting the feminine, as *Tsarina*, and proper names, as *Thomasina*.

-ina (2) [L. *-īna*, neut. pl. of *-īnus*], *suf.* (*Zool.*) Forming names of groups of animals, usu. from the name of a genus, as *globigerina*.

inability (in ȧ bil′ i ti), *n.* The state of being unable (to do, understand, etc.); lack of power or means.

***inabstinence** (in ăb′ sti nėns) [IN- (2), ABSTINENCE], *n.* Lack of abstinence.

inaccessible (in ȧk ses′ ibl) [F., from late L. *inaccessibilis*], *a.* Not accessible; that cannot be reached, attained, or approached; not affable, not encouraging advances. **inaccessibility** (-bil′ i ti), **inaccessibleness**, *n.* **inaccessibly**, *adv.*

inaccurate (in ăk′ ū rȧt), *a.* Not accurate. **inaccuracy**, *n.* Want of accuracy; an inaccurate statement, an error. **inaccurately**, *adv.*

inaction (in ăk′ shŭn), *n.* Inactivity, idleness, sloth; sluggishness, supineness. **inactive**, *a.* **inactively**, *adv.* **inactivity** (-tiv′ i ti), *n.*

inadaptable (in ȧ dăp′ tȧbl), *a.* Not adaptable. **inadaptability** (-bil′ i ti), *n.* **inadaptation** (-tā shŭn), *n.*

inadequate (in ăd′ ė kwȧt), *a.* Not adequate; insufficient, unequal. **inadequately**, *adv.* **inadequacy**, **inadequateness**, *n.*

inadherent (in ȧd hēr′ ėnt), *a.* (*Bot.*) Not adherent, free.

inadhesive (in ȧd hē′ siv), *a.* Not adhesive.

inadmissible (in ȧd mis′ ibl), *a.* That cannot be admitted, allowed, or received. **inadmissibility** (-bil′ i ti), *n.*

inadvertent (in ȧd vĕr′ tėnt), *a.* Not paying attention; heedless, careless, negligent; unintentional, accidental (of actions). **inadvertence**, **-ency**, *n.* **inadvertently**, *adv.*

inadvisable [UNADVISABLE].

***inaidable** (in ā′ dȧbl), *a.* That cannot be aided, helpless.

inalienable (in ā′ li ė nȧbl), *a.* That cannot be alienated or transferred. **inalienability** (-bil′ i ti), *n.* **inalienably**, *adv.*

inalterable (in awl′ tėr ȧbl), *a.* Incapable of alteration. **inalterability** (-bil′ i ti), *n.* **inalterably**, *adv.*

inamorato (i năm ȯ ra′ tō) [It. *innamorato*, p.p. of *innamorare* (IN- (1), *amore*, L. *amor -em*, love)], *n.* (*fem.* **-ata**) A lover.

inane (i nān′) [L. *inānis*, empty, etym. doubtful], *a.* Empty, void; purposeless, senseless; silly, fatuous. *n.* Infinite void space. **inanely,** *adv.* **inanity** (i năn′ i ti), *n.*

inanga (ē ning′ gȧ) [Maori], *n.* The N. Zealand whitebait.

inanimate (i năn′ i mȧt) [L. *inanimātus*], *a.* Not animate, not living; not endowed with animal life; (*fig.*) void of animation, dull, lifeless. ***inanimated,** *a.* Lifeless. **inanimately,** *adv.* **inanimateness, inanimation** (-mā′ shŭn), *n.*

inanition (in ȧ nish′ ŭn) [F., from L. *inānītiōnem*, nom. *-tio*, from *inānīre*, to make empty, from *inānis*, INANE], *n.* Emptiness, voidness; exhaustion from want of food or nourishment. **inanitiate** (-āt), *v.t.*

inanity [INANE].

inappeasable (in ȧ pē′ zȧbl), *a.* Not to be appeased,

inappellable (in ȧ pel′ ȧbl), *a.* Beyond appeal. absolute, final. **inappellability** (-bil′ i ti), *n.*

inappetence (in ăp′ ė tėns), *n.* Lack of appetence or appetite. **inappetent,** *a.*

inapplicable (in ăp′ li kȧbl), *a.* Not applicable; irrelevant. **inapplicability** (-bil′ i ti), ***inapplicableness,** *n.* **inapplicably,** *adv.* ***inapplication** (kā′ shŭn), *n.* Want of application, energy, or assiduity.

inapposite (in ăp′ ŏ zit), *a.* Not apposite; not pertinent. **inappositely,** *adv.*

inappreciable (in ȧ prē′ shȧbl), *a.* Not appreciable, not perceptible; too insignificant to be considered. **inappreciably,** *adv.* **inappreciation** (-shi ā′ shŭn), *n.* Want of appreciation; inability to appreciate properly. **inappreciative** (-prē′ shȧ tiv), *a.*

inapprehensible (in ap rė hen′ sibl), *a.* Unintelligible, not to be apprehended or understood. **inapprehension,** *n.* Want of apprehension. **inapprehensive,** *a.* Not apprehensive; regardless (of danger, etc.). **inapprehensiveness,** *n.*

inapproachable (in ȧ prō′ chȧbl), *a.* Inaccessible; unrivalled. **inapproachably,** *adv.*

inappropriate (in ȧ prō′ pri ȧt), *a.* Not appropriate, unsuitable. **inappropriately,** *adv.* **inappropriateness,** *n.*

inapt (in ăpt′), *a.* Not apt; unsuitable. **inaptitude, inaptness,** *n.* **inaptly,** *adv.*

***inarable** (in ăr′ ȧbl), *a.* Not fit for tillage.

inarch (in arch′) [IN- (1), ARCH (1)], *v.t.* To graft by inserting a scion, without separating it from the parent tree, into a stock growing near.

inarm (in arm′), *v.t.* To encircle with the arms, to embrace.

inarticulate (in ar tik′ ū lȧt) [L. *inarticulātus*], *a.* Not articulated, not jointed; belonging to the *Inarticulata*, a division of brachiopoda having non-articulated valves; not uttered with distinct articulation, indistinct, dumb, speechless. **inarticulately,** *adv.* **inarticulateness,** *n.* ***inarticulation,** *n.* Indistinctness of sounds in speaking.

inartificial (in ar ti fish′ ȧl) [L. *inartificiālis*], *a.* Not artistic; devoid of art, unaffected, artless, simple, natural. **inartificially,** *adv.*

inartistic (in ar tis′ tik), *a.* Not designed, done, etc., according to the principles of art; not having artistic taste or ability. **inartistically,** *adv.*

inasmuch (in ȧz mŭch′) [IN, AS, MUCH], *adv.* Seeing that, since (followed by *as*).

inattention (in ȧ ten′ shŭn) *n.* Want of attention; heedlessness, negligence; disregard of courtesy. **inattentive,** *a.* **inattentively,** *adv.* **inattentiveness,** *n.*

inaudible (in aw′ dibl) [L. *inaudībilis*], *a.* Not audible, so low as not to be heard. **inaudibility** (-bil′ i ti), *n.* **inaudibly,** *adv.*

inaugurate (in aw′ gū rāt) [L. *inaugurātus*, p.p. of *inaugurāre* (IN- (1), *augurāre*, to take omens, from AUGUR)], *v.t.* To install or induct into an office solemnly or with appropriate ceremonies; to commence, introduce, or celebrate the opening of with some degree of formality, solemnity, pomp, or dignity. **inaugural** (in aw′ gūr ȧl), *a.* Pertaining to or performed at an inauguration. *n.* (*Am.*) An inaugural address. **inauguration** (-rā′ shŭn), *n.* The act of inaugurating; a formal or solemn commencement. **inaugurator** (in aw′ gū rā tŏr), *n.* **inauguratory,** *a.*

***inaurate** (in aw′ rȧt) [L. *inaurātus*, p.p. of *inaurāre* (IN- (1), *aurāre*, from *aurum*, gold)], *a.* Covered with gold, gilt.

inauspicious (in aw spish′ ŭs), *a.* Unlucky, unfortunate, ill-omened, unfavourable. **inauspiciously,** *adv.* **inauspiciousness,** *n.*

inbeing (in′ bē ing) [IN- (1), BEING], *n.* Inherence; inherent existence; essence, essential nature.

inboard (in′ bôrd), *adv.* (*Naut.*) Within the sides or towards the middle of a ship. *a.* Situated thus. *prep.* Inside, within (a vessel).

inbond (in′ bond), *a.* (*Build.*) A term applied to a stone or brick laid lengthwise across a wall, also called a header, opp. to outbond.

inborn (in′ bôrn), *a.* Innate, naturally inherent.

inbreak (in′ brāk), *n.* The act of breaking **in**; an inroad, an incursion. ***inbreaking,** *n.* and *a.*

***inbreathe** (in brēth′), *v.t.* To breathe into, to draw in (breath); (*fig.*) to inspire.

inbred (in bred′), *a.* Innate, inborn, natural; bred in-and-in.

inbreed (in brēd′), *v.t.* To breed or produce within; (in′ brēd) to breed in-and-in, to breed from animals nearly related.

in-by, -bye (in bī), *adv.* (*Sc.*) Towards the inside, towards the middle of a house, mine, etc.

Inca (ing′ kȧ) [Peruv.], *n.* The title given to the sovereigns of Peru up to the conquest under Pizarro, A.D. 1531; one of the royal race formerly dominant in Peru.

***incage** [ENCAGE].

incalculable (in kăl′ kū lȧbl), *a.* Not calculable, not to be reckoned or estimated in advance; not to be reckoned upon, uncertain. **incalculability** (-bil′ i ti), **incalculableness,** *n.* **incalculably,** *adv.*

***incalescent** (in kȧ les′ ėnt) [L. *incalescens -ntem* pres.p. of *incalescere* (IN- (1), *calescere*, freq. of *calere*, to be hot)], *a.* Becoming warm; increasing in heat. ***incalescence,** *n.*

incandesce (in kăn des′) [L. *incandescere* (IN- (1), *candescere*, incept. of *candēre*, to be white)], *v.i.* To glow with heat. *v.t.* To cause to glow with heat. **incandescence,** *n.* **incandescent,** *a.* Glowing with heat; intensely luminous with heat. **incandescent lamp:** An electric or other lamp in which a filament or mantle is made intensely luminous by heat.

incantation (in kăn tā′ shun) [F., from L. *incantātiōnem*, nom. *-tio*, from *incantāre*, see ENCHANT], *n.* A formula, said or sung, supposed to add force to magical ceremonies, a charm. ***incantator** (in′ kăn tā tŏr), *n.* ***incantatory** (in kăn′ tȧ tŏr i), *a.*

incapable (in kā′ pȧbl) [F., from med. L. *incapabilis*], *a.* Not physically, intellectually, or morally capable (of); wanting in power, ability, or fitness (of doing, committing, etc.); not susceptible (of); legally incapacitated; unable to take care of oneself. *n.* One who is incapable. ***incapability** (-bil′ i ti), ***incapableness,** *n.* **incapably,** *adv.*

***incapacious** (in kȧ pā′ shŭs) [L. *incapax*], *a.* Not capacious; not roomy. ***incapaciousness,** *n.*

incapacitate (in kȧ păs′ i tāt) [from foll.], *v.t.* To render incapable, to disable; to render unfit, to disqualify (for, from, etc.). **incapacitation** (-tā′ shŭn), *n.*

incapacity (in kă păs' i ti) [F. *incapacité*], *n.* Want of capacity; inability, incompetency; legal disqualification.

incarcerate (in kar' sėr āt) [med. L. *incaecerātus*, p.p. of *incarcerāre* (IN- (1), *carcer*, prison)], *v.t.* To imprison; (*fig.*) to shut up or confine. **a.* (-ăt) Imprisoned, shut up; confined. **incarceration** (-rā' shŭn), *n.* **incarcerator** (in kar' sėr ā tŏr), *n.*

incardinate (in kar' di nāt) [med. L. *incardinātus*, p.p. of *incardināre* (IN- (1), *cardo -dinis*, hinge, see CARDINAL)], *v.t.* (*R.-C. Ch.*) To institute as principal priest, deacon, etc., of a particular church, diocese, etc.; to raise to the rank of cardinal.

***incarnadine** (in kar' nå dīn, -din) [F. *incarnadin*, It. *incarnadino*, *-tino*, from *incarnato*, INCARNATE], *a.* Of a flesh or carnation colour. **v.t.* To dye this colour; to tinge with red.

incarnate (in kar' nåt) [L. *incarnātus*, p.p. of *incarnāre* (IN- (1), *caro carnis*, flesh)], *a.* Invested or clothed with flesh, embodied in flesh, esp. in human form; flesh-coloured, pink (*esp. in Bot.*). *v.t.* (in' kar nāt) To clothe with flesh; to embody in flesh; to embody (an idea) in a living form; to be the embodiment of. **incarnant,** *a.* (*Surg.*) Promoting the formation of flesh (over a wound, etc.). *n.* An agent promoting this. **incarnation** (in kar nā' shŭn), *n.* The act of assuming flesh; embodiment, esp. in human form; Christ's assumption of human nature; a vivid exemplification or personification; carnation, flesh-colour; (*Surg.*) the process of healing wounds, and filling or covering the part with new flesh.

incase [ENCASE].

***incatenation** (in kăt ė nā' shŭn) [med. L. *incatēnātio*, from *incatēnāre* (IN- (1), *catēna*, a CHAIN)], *n.* A linking together.

incautious (in kaw' shŭs), *a.* Wanting in caution; rash, unwary. ***incaution,** *n.* Lack of caution. **incautiously,** *adv.* **incautiousness,** *n.*

incavate (in kā' vāt) [L. *incavātus*, p.p. of *incavāre* (IN- (1), *cavāre*, to hollow, from *cavus*, CAVE)], *v.t.* To hollow, to make hollow. *a.* (-vȧt) Hollowed, bent inwards. **incavation** (-kȧ vā' shŭn), *n.*

incavo (in cā' vō) [It.], *n.* The incised portion of an intaglio.

***incede** (in sēd') [L. *incēdere* (IN- (1), *cēdere*, to go)], *v.i.* To move in a majestic way. **incedingly,** *adv.*

incendiary (in sen' di ȧr i) [L. *incendiārius*, from *incendium*, a conflagration, from *incendere*, see foll.], *a.* Pertaining to the malicious burning of property; (*fig.*) exciting or tending to excite factions, seditions, or quarrels; inflammatory. *n.* One who maliciously sets fire to a dwelling-house or other building; (*fig.*) one who excites factions, seditions, etc. **incendiary bomb,** *n.* (*Mil.*) Bomb containing violently incendiary materials that are scattered in flames on detonation. **incendiarism,** *n.* ***incendious,** *a.* ***incendiously,** *adv.*

incense (1) (in' sens) [M.E. and O.F. *encens*, L. *incensum*, that which is burnt, neut. p.p. of *incendere*, to burn (IN- (1), *-candere*, to burn, rel. to *candēre*, to glow)], *n.* A mixture of fragrant gums, spices, etc., used for producing perfumes when burnt, esp. in religious rites; the smoke of this; (*fig.*) flattery; an agreeable perfume; any offering to a superior being; the resin or gum of olibanum. *v.t.* To perfume with or as with incense; to offer incense to. **incense-boat:** A small boat-shaped vessel for holding incense. **incense-breathing,** *a.* Exhaling sweet odours. **incense-tree,** *n.* One of various trees producing incense. **incense wood:** The wood of *Icica heptaphylla*, a South American tree. **incensation** (-sā' shŭn), *n.* The offering of incense as an act of divine worship, or as a ceremonial adjunct. **incenser** (in' sen sėr), **incensory** (in' sen sŏr i), *n.* A censer.

incense (2) (in sens') [from O.F. *incenser*, or directly L. *incensus*, p.p. of *incendre*, see prec.], *v.t.* To inflame, to exasperate, to provoke, to enrage. ***incensement,** *n.* **incension,** *n.* The act of setting on fire; the state of being on fire.

incentive (in sen' tiv) [L. *incentīvus*, setting a tune, from *incinere* (IN- (1), *canere*, to sing)], *a.* Inciting, urging. *n.* That which acts as a motive, incitement, or spur.

incept (in sept') [L. *inceptus*, p.p. of *incipere*, to begin (IN- (1), *capere*, to take)], *v.i.* (*Camb. Univ.*) To be finally admitted to the degree of Master or Doctor. *v.t.* (*Biol.*) To receive, to take in.

inception (in sep' shŭn), *n.* A commencement; (*Camb. Univ.*) the act or ceremony of incepting. **inceptive,** *a.* Beginning, commencing; (*Gram.*) denoting the beginning of an action. *n.* (*Gram.*) A verb that denotes the beginning of an action.

inceptor (in sep' tŏr), *n.* One at the point of taking his degree in Arts at Camb. Univ.

***incertain** [UNCERTAIN].

incertitude (in sėr' ti tūd) [F. (IN- (2), late L. *certitūdo*, from *certus*, CERTAIN)], *n.* Uncertainty.

incessant (in ses' ȧnt) [late L. *incessans -ntem* (IN- (2), *cessans -ntem*, pres.p. of *cessāre*, to CEASE)], *a.* Unceasing, unintermittent, perpetual. **incessantly,** *adv.* ***incessably,** *adv.* Unceasingly, continually. **incessancy, *incessantness,** *n.*

incest (in' sest) [F. *inceste*, L. *incestus*, from *incestus -tum*, adj. (IN- (2), *castus*, CHASTE)], *n.* Sexual intercourse between persons related within the prohibited degrees of matrimony. **incestuous** (in ses' tū ŭs), *a.* Guilty of or involving incest. **incestuously,** *adv.* ***incestuousness,** *n.*

inch (1) (inch) [A.-S. *ynce*, L. *uncia*], *n.* The twelfth part of a linear foot; (*fig.*) the least quantity or degree; (*Meteor.*) the unit of measurement of the rainfall, the quantity that would cover the surface of the ground to the depth of one inch; (*Phys.*) the pressure, atmospheric or other, equivalent to the weight of a column of mercury one inch high in a barometer; (*pl.*) stature. *v.t.* To drive by inches or small degrees. *v.i.* To move thus. **by inches, inch by inch:** Bit by bit; gradually, by very small degrees. **every inch:** Entirely, from head to foot. **inchmeal, by inchmeal:** By inches, bit by bit. **inch-measure, -rule, -tape,** *n.* A measure divided into inches. **inch-stuff,** *n.* (*Carp.*) Deal in planks one inch thick. **incher,** *n.* (*usu. in comb.*, as *six-incher*).

inch (2) (inch) [Gael. *innis* (cp. Ir. *inis*, W. *ynys*, also L. *insula*)], *n.* An island.

***inchase** [ENCHASE]. **inchmeal** [INCH (1)].

inchoate (in' kō āt) [L. *inchoātus*, *incohātus*, p.p. of *incohāre*, to begin], *a.* Only begun, commenced; existing only in elements, incomplete, undeveloped. *v.t.* To begin, to originate. **inchoately,** *adv.* **inchoateness,** *n.* **inchoation** (-ā' shŭn), *n.* An inception, a beginning. **inchoative** (in kō' ȧ tiv), *a.*

***inch-pin** (inch' pin) [etym. doubtful], *n.* The sweetbread of a deer.

incidence (in' si dėns) [F., as foll.], *n.* The act or state of falling on or upon; (*Phys.*) the direction in which a body, or a ray of light, heat, etc., falls upon any surface; (*fig.*) scope, bearing, range; frequency of occurrence; *an incident. ***incidency,** *n.* An incident; incidence. **angle of incidence:** An angle formed by the line of incidence of a ray of light, heat, etc., moving to strike a plane and the perpendicular to that plane. **line of incidence:** The line in which a ray of light, heat, etc., moves to strike a plane.

incident (in' si dėnt) [F., from *incidentem*, nom. *dens*, pres.p. of *incidere* (IN- (1), *cadere*, to fall)], *a.* Falling or striking (on or upon); likely to happen; naturally; appertaining or belonging (to); occasional, fortuitous. *n.* That which falls out or happens; a fortuitous event; a concomitant or subsidiary event; an occurrence, esp. one of a picturesque or striking nature; (*Law*) a privilege, burden, etc., legally attaching to property, etc.; all circumstances attendant upon the fall of a bomb in an air-raid.

incidental (in si den′ tȧl), *a.* Casual, accidental, contingent; undesigned, fortuitous, not essential; concomitant, naturally connected with or related (to). *n.* Something that is incidental; (*pl.*) casual expenses. **incidentally,** *adv.* ***incidentalness,** *n.*

incinerate (in sin′ ėr āt) [med. L. *incinerātus*, p.p. of *incinerāre* (IN- (1), L. *cinis cineris*, ashes)], *v.t.* To reduce to ashes. **incineration** (-ā′ shŭn), *n.* **incinerator** (in sin′ ėr ā tȯr), *n.* A receptacle in which refuse, etc. is burned.

incipient (in sip′ i ėnt) [L. *incipiens -ntem*, pres.p. of *incipere*, to INCEPT], *a.* Beginning, in the first stages. **incipiently,** *adv.* **incipience, -iency,** *n.*

incipit (in′ si pit) [L., as prec.], *phr.* Here begins (a book, manuscript, etc.).

incircle [ENCIRCLE].

incise (in siz′) [F. *inciser*, from L. *incīsus*, p.p. of *incīdere* (IN- (1), *cædere*, to cut)], *v.t.* To cut into, to engrave, to carve (with inscription, pattern, etc.). **incision** (in sizh′ ŭn), *n.* The art of incising; a cut, a gash; separation of the parts of any substance by a sharp instrument; *sharpness, trenchancy, decision. **incisive** (in sī′ siv), *a.* Having the quality of cutting into; (*fig.*) sharp, penetrating; trenchant, acute. **incisively,** *adv.* **incisiveness,** *n.*

incisor (in sī′ zȯr), *n.* A tooth adapted for cutting or dividing the food, one of those between the canines. ***incisory,** *a.* Incisive. ***incisure** (in sī′ zhŭr), *n.* An incision, a notch.

incite (in sīt′) [F. *inciter*, L. *incitāre* (IN- (1), CITE)], *v.t.* To stir up, to urge; to stimulate, to prompt, to encourage (to action, to do, etc.). **incitant** (in′ si-, in sī′ tȧnt), *a.* Exciting, stimulating. *n.* A stimulant. **incitation** (in si tā′ shŭn), *n.* The act of inciting; that which incites; an incitement. **incitement,** *n.* A stimulus, an incentive, a motive. **inciter,** *n.* **incitingly,** *adv.* **incito-,** *comb. form.*

***incivil** (in siv′ il) [F., from L. *incivīlis*], *a.* Rude, unpolished. **incivility** (-vil′ i ti), *n.* Want of civilization; rudeness, impoliteness; an act of rudeness. **incivilization** (in siv i lī zā′ shŭn), *n.* Lack of civilization; barbarism. **incivism** (in′ si vizm), *n.* Want of good citizenship or of patriotism, esp. as interpreted on the principles of the French Revolution.

inclasp [ENCLASP]. **inclave** [ENCLAVE].

in-clearing (in′ klēr ing), *n.* (*Clearing House*) The amount received in cheques, etc., payable by a particular bank. **in-clearer,** *n.*

inclement (in klem′ ėnt) [F., from L. *inclemens -ntem*], *a.* Without clemency, merciless; rough, severe; boisterous, stormy. **inclemently,** *adv.* **inclemency,** *n.*

incline (in klīn′) [F. *incliner*, L. *inclināre* (IN- (1), *clināre*, to bend)], *v.i.* To deviate from any direction that is regarded as the normal one; to lean, to bend down or forward; (*fig.*) to be disposed; to have a propensity, proneness, or inclination. *v.t.* To cause to deviate from a line or direction; to give an inclination or leaning to; to direct; to cause to bend (the head or body) down, to bow or stoop; (*fig.*) to dispose, to turn. *n.* (in′ klīn) An inclination; an inclined plane, a slope, a gradient. **inclinable,** *a.* Having a tendency; inclined, disposed, willing (to). **inclinableness,** *n.* ***inclinatory** (in klī′ nȧ tȯr i), *a.* Having the quality of leaning or inclining. **inclined plane:** One of the mechanical powers, consisting of a plane set at an acute angle to the horizon. **incliner,** *n.* One who or that which inclines.

inclination (in kli nā′ shŭn), *n.* The act of inclining or bending; a deviation from any direction regarded as the normal one; (*fig.*) leaning or bent of the mind or will; disposition, proclivity, propensity (to, for, etc.); liking, affection (for); (*Geom.*) the mutual approach or tendency of two bodies, lines, or planes towards each other, esp. as measured by the angle between them. **inclinational,** *a.*

inclinatorium (in klī nȧ tôr′ i ŭm), *n.* A dipping-compass.

inclinograph (in klī′ nō grăf), *n.* An instrument for recording the declinations of a compass.

inclinometer (in klī nom′ ė tėr), *n.* An instrument for detecting the vertical intensity of the magnetic force, a dipping-compass; a clinometer.

inclose [ENCLOSE].

include (in klood′) [L. *inclūdere* (IN- (1), *claudere*, to shut), p.p. *inclūsus*], *v.t.* To contain, to hold, to comprise, to comprehend as a component part, member, etc.; to enclose, to confine within; *to conclude, to terminate. **included,** *a.* Enclosed; contained, comprehended; (*Bot.*) not projecting beyond the mouth of the corolla (of the style and stamens).

inclusion (in kloo′ zhȯn), *n.* The act of including.

inclusive (in kloo′ ziv), *a.* Including, containing, comprehending (usu. with *of*); comprehending in the total sum or number. **inclusive terms:** Terms including all subsidiary charges (at an hotel, etc.) (called in U.S.A. 'American plan'). **inclusively,** *adv.*

incogitable (in koj′ i tȧbl) [late L. *incōgitābilis*], *a.* Not cogitable, not thinkable. ***incogitability** (-bil′ i ti), *n.* ***incogitant** (in koj′ i tȧnt), *a.* Thoughtless; not thinking. ***incogitative,** *a.*

incognito (in kog′ ni tō) [It., from L. *incognitus* (IN- (2), *cognitus*, p.p. of *cognōscere*, see COGNITION)], *a.* (*pl.* **-ti,** *fem.* **-ta,** *pl.* **-tæ**) Living or going under an assumed name or character. *n.* A person who is unknown or under an assumed name or character; the state of being unknown or in disguise. *adv.* With one's real name, etc., unknown or disguised.

incognizable (in kog′ ni-, -kon′ i zȧbl), *a.* Not cognizable, not capable of being perceived or apprehended. **incognizant** (in kog′-, in kon′-), *a.* **incognizance,** *n.* **incognoscible** (in kog nos′ ibl) [IN- (2), COGNOSCIBLE], *a.* Not cognoscible, beyond cognition. **incognoscibility** (-bil′ i ti), *n.*

incoherent (in kō hēr′ ėnt), *a.* Wanting cohesion of parts; loose, disconnected, inconsistent. **incoherence, -ency, incohesion** (-hē′ zhŭn), *n.* **incoherently,** *adv.* **incohesive** (-hē′ siv), *a.*

incombustible (in kȯm bŭs′ tibl) [F., from med. L. *incombustibilis*], *a.* Incapable of being burnt or consumed by fire. *n.* An incombustible thing, substance, etc. **incombustibility** (-bil′ i ti), *n.* **incombustibly,** *adv.*

income (in′ kŭm) [IN- (1), COME], *n.* The amount of money (usu. annual) accruing as payment, profit, interest, etc., from labour, business, profession, or property; *advent, arrival; (*Sc.*) a tumour or similar bodily affection, an ailment that comes on with no apparent cause. **income-tax:** A tax exacted for State purposes upon incomes above a certain amount.

incomer (in′ kŭm ėr), *n.* One who comes in, an immigrant; an intruder; one who succeeds another as a tenant, esp. a stranger by birth, etc. **incoming,** *a.* Coming in or entering into possession; accruing. *n.* An entrance or arrival; income, gain, revenue (*usu. in pl.*).

incommensurable (in kȯ men′ shŭr ȧbl) [F., from late L. *incommensūrābilis*], *a.* Having no common measure (with another integral or fractional number or quantity); not fit or worthy to be measured (with). *n.* One or two (or more) quantities that have no common measure. **incommensurability** (-bil′ i ti), *n.* **incommensurably,** *adv.* **incommensurate,** *a.* Not commensurate; incommensurable, inadequate (to or with). **incommensurately,** *adv.* **incommensurateness,** *n.*

***incommiscible** (in kȯ mis′ ibl) [L. *incommiscibilis*], *a.* That cannot be mixed together.

incommode (in kȯ mōd′) [F. *incommoder*, L. *incommodāre* (IN- (2), *commodāre*, from *commodus*, COMMODIOUS)], *v.t.* To cause trouble or inconvenience to; to disquiet, to embarrass, to disturb, to hinder. ***incommodation** (-dā′ shŭn), *n.* **incommodious** (-mō′ di ŭs), *a.* Not commodious; inconvenient. **incommodiously,** *adv.* **incom-**

modiousness, *n.* **incommodity** (-mod′ i ti), *n.* Inconvenience, incommodiousness; anything that causes this.

incommunicable (in kŏ mū′ ni kȧbl), *a.* That cannot be communicated to, or shared with another. **incommunicability** (-bil′ i ti), **incommunicableness,** *n.* **incommunicably,** *adv.* **incommunicative,** *a.* Not communicative; not disposed to intercourse, communion, or fellowship with others, reserved. ***incommunicatively,** *adv.* **incommunicativeness,** *n.*

incommunicado (in kom ū ni ka′ dō) [Sp.], *a.* With no means of communication with the outside world; in solitary confinement.

incommutable (in kŏ mū′ tȧbl) [F., from L. *incommūtābilis*], *a.* Not commutable; that cannot be exchanged with another; that cannot be changed. **incommutability** (-bil′ i ti), *n.* **incommutably,** *adv.*

incompact (in kŏm păkt′), *a.* Not compact; (*fig.*) loosely organized, combined, etc.; incoherent. **incompactly,** *adv.* **incompactness,** *n.*

incomparable (in kom′ pȧr ȧbl) [F., from L. *incomparābilis*], *a.* Not to be compared (to or with); unequalled, peerless. **incomparableness,** *n.* **incomparably,** *adv.* ***incompared,** *a.* Unmatched, matchless.

incompatible (in kŏm păt′ ibl) [F., from L. *incompatibilis*], *a.* Inconsistent with something else; incapable of subsisting with something else; incongruous. *n.* An incompatible person or thing. **incompatible terms:** (*Log.*) Terms which cannot both be affirmed of the same subject. **incompatibility** (-bil′ i ti), ***incompatibleness,** *n.* **incompatibly,** *adv.*

incompetent (in kom′ pė tėnt) [F. *incompétent*, L. *incompetentem*, nom. *-ens*], *a.* Lacking adequate power, means, capacity, or qualifications (to do); wanting legal fitness or qualification. **incompetence, incompetency,** *n.* **incompetently,** *adv.* Lacking competence; (*colloq.*) inefficiently.

incomplete (in kŏm plēt′) [L. *incomplētus*], *a.* Not complete, not perfect. **incomplete flower:** One destitute of calyx, corolla, or of both. **incompletely,** *adv.* **incompleteness, incompletion,** *n.*

***incompliant** (in kŏm plī′ ȧnt), *a.* Indisposed to yield to solicitation or request. ***incompliance,** *n.* ***incompliantly,** *adv.*

incomposite (in kom′ pŏ zĭt) [L. *incompositus*], *a.* Not composite; not properly composed.

incomprehensible (in kom prė hen′ sibl) [F., from L. *incomprehensibilis*], *a.* That cannot be comprehended, conceived, or understood, inconceivable; *(*Athanasian Creed*) unlimited, boundless. **incomprehensibility** (-bil′ i ti), **incomprehensibleness,** *n.* **incomprehensibly,** *adv.* **incomprehension,** *n.* Want of comprehension; failure to understand. ***incomprehensive,** *a.* Not comprehensive or inclusive; not understanding. ***incomprehensively,** *adv.* ***incomprehensiveness,** *n.*

incompressible (in kŏm pres′ ibl), *a.* Not compressible; strongly resisting compression. **incompressibility** (-bil′ i ti), *n.*

incomputable (in kŏm pū′ tȧbl), *a.* Not computable; incalculable.

inconceivable (in kŏn sē′ vȧbl), *a.* Not conceivable, incomprehensible; hence, incredible, most extraordinary. **inconceivability** (-bil′ i ti), **inconceivableness,** *n.* **inconceivably,** *adv.*

inconclusive (in kŏn kloo′ siv), *a.* Not conclusive; not cogent or decisive (of evidence, etc.). **inconclusively,** *adv.* **inconclusiveness,** *n.*

incondensable (in kŏn den′ sȧbl), *a.* Not condensable, not reducible from the liquid to a solid condition.

incondite (in kon′ dit) [L. *inconditus* (IN- (2), *conditus*, p.p. of *condere*, to put together)], *a.* Irregular, ill-composed, unfinished, crude.

inconformity (in kŏn fôr′ mi ti), *n.* Lack of conformity, correspondence, or similarity (to or with); non-conformity.

incongruous (in kong′ groo ŭs) [L. *incongruus*], *a.* Not congruous, not agreeing or harmonizing; unsuitable, inconsistent; not fitting, improper, out of place. ***incongruent,** *a.* **incongruity** (-groo′ i ti), **incongruousness,** ***incongruence,** *n.* **incongruously,** *adv.*

inconscient (in kon′ shi ėnt), *a.* Unconscious. ***inconscious,** etc. [UNCONSCIOUS].

inconsecutive (in kŏn sek′ ū tiv), *a.* Not consecutive, not in regular order. **inconsecutively,** *adv.* **inconsecutiveness,** *n.*

inconsequent (in kon′ sė kwėnt) [L. *inconsequens -ntem*], *a.* Not following regularly from the premises, irrelevant; illogical; disconnected. **inconsequence,** *n.* **inconsequential,** *a.* Not consequential, inconsequent; of no consequence. **inconsequentiality** (-shi ăl′ i ti), *n.* **inconsequentially,** *adv.* **inconsequently,** *adv.*

inconsiderable (in kŏn sid′ ėr ȧbl) [F. *inconsidérable* (IN- (2), CONSIDERABLE)], *a.* Not deserving consideration or notice; insignificant, unimportant, trivial. **inconsiderableness,** *n.* **inconsiderably,** *adv.*

inconsiderate (in kŏn sid′ ėr ȧt) [L. *inconsiderātus*], *a.* Not considerate; hasty, incautious; having no consideration for the feelings of others. **inconsiderately,** *adv.* **inconsiderateness, inconsideration** (-ā′ shŭn), *n.*

inconsistent (in kŏn sis tėnt), *a.* Discordant, incongruous; not suitable, incompatible (with); self-contradictory, not agreeing with itself or oneself; not uniform, changeable, unsteady. **inconsistency, *-tence,** *n.* **inconsistently,** *adv.*

inconsolable (in kŏn sō′ lȧbl) [F., from L. *inconsōlābilis*], *a.* Not to be consoled (of a person, grief, etc.). **inconsolably,** *adv.*

inconsonant (in kon′ sŏ nȧnt) [F.], *a.* Not consonant, discordant (with). **inconsonance,** *n.* ***inconsonantly,** *adv.*

inconspicuous (in kŏn spik′ ū ŭs) [L. *inconspicuus*], *a.* Not conspicuous; not readily discernible by the sight; (*Bot.*) small in size, obscure in colour, etc. **inconspicuously,** *adv.* **inconspicuousness,** *n.*

inconstant (in kon′ stȧnt) [F., from L. *inconstāntem*, nom. *-tāns*], *a.* Not constant, changeable, fickle; variable, unsteady, irregular. **inconstancy,** *n.* **inconstantly,** *adv.*

inconsumable (in kŏn sū′ mȧbl), *a.* Not consumable; indestructible; (*Polit. Econ.*) not intended for consumption. **inconsumably,** *adv.*

incontestable (in kŏn tes′ tȧbl), *a.* Indisputable, undeniable, unquestionable. **incontestability** (-bil′ i ti), *n.* **incontestably,** *adv.* ***incontested,** *a.* Uncontested, undisputed.

***incontiguous** (in kŏn tig′ ū ŭs) [late L. *incontiguus*], *a.* Not contiguous. ***incontiguously,** *adv.* ***incontiguousness,** *n.*

incontinent (in kon′ ti nėnt) [F., from L. *incontinentem*, nom. *-ens*], *a.* Not restraining the passions or appetites, esp. the sexual; licentious, unchaste; (*Med.*) not able to restrain natural evacuations. **adv.* Incontinently. **n.* An unchaste person. **incontinence, *-tinency,** *n.* **incontinently,** *adv.* Unchastely; at once, straightway, immediately.

incontrollable (in kŏn trō′ lȧbl), *a.* Not controllable. **incontrollably,** *adv.*

incontrovertible (in kon trŏ vĕr′ tibl), *a.* That cannot be controverted; incontestable, indisputable. **incontrovertibility** (-bil′ i ti), **incontrovertibleness,** *n.* **incontrovertibility,** *adv.*

inconvenience (in kon vē′ ni ėns), *n.* The quality or state of being inconvenient; that which inconveniences. a cause of difficulty. *v.t.* To put to inconvenience; to incommode, to embarrass.

inconvenient (in kȯn vē′ ni ėnt) [F. *inconvénient*, L. *inconvenientem*, nom. *-ens* (IN- (2), CONVENIENT)], *a.* Not convenient, incommodious; causing or tending to cause trouble, uneasiness, or difficulty; inopportune, awkward. **inconveniently,** *adv.*

***inconversable** (in kȯn vĕr′ sȧbl), *a.* Not conversable; reserved, taciturn.

***inconversant** (in kon′ vėr sȧnt), *a.* Not conversant (with).

inconvertible (in kȯn vĕr′ tibl), *a.* Incapable of being converted into or exchanged for something else, esp. money. **inconvertibility** (-bil′ i ti), ***inconvertibleness,** *n.* **inconvertibly,** *adv.*

inconvincible (in kȯn vin′ sibl), *a.* Not to be convinced. **inconvincibility** (-bil′ i ti), *n.*

inco-ordinate (in kō ôr′ di nȧt), *a.* Not co-ordinate. **inco-ordination** (-nā′ shŭn), *n.*

incoronate (in kor′ ȯ nȧt) [med. L. *incorōnātus*], *a.* Crowned. **incoronation** (-nā′ shŭn), *n.*

***incorporal** [INCORPOREAL].

incorporate (1) (in kôr′ pȯ rȧt) [late L. *incorporātus*, p.p. of *incorporāre* (IN- (1), *corpus -poris*, body)], *a.* Combined into one body or corporation, closely united; made into a corporation (of a society, company, etc.); *closely combined or associated (with); *embodied.

incorporate (2) (in kôr′ pȯ rāt), *v.t.* To unite, combine, or mingle into one mass or body (with); to combine into one body (with); to form into a legal corporation; to receive into a corporation; to embody; (*Am.*) to form a limited company. *v.i.* To become united or incorporated (with another substance, society, etc.) so as to form one body. **incorporation** (-rā′ shŭn), *n.* The act of incorporating; the state of being incorporated; embodiment; formation of or reception into a corporate body; a corporate body, a corporation. **Incorporated,** *a.* (*Am. Comm.*) Limited (of a joint stock company; **Inc.** corresponds to Eng. "Ltd.") **incorporative,** *a.* Incorporating or tending to incorporate; (*Philol.*) applied to languages such as the Basque and those of the North American Indians, which run a whole phrase into one long word. **incorporator** (in kôr′ pȯ rā tȯr), *n.*

***incorporate** (3) (in kôr′ pȯ rȧt) [IN- (2), CORPORATE], *a.* Incorporeal, not embodied in matter.

incorporeal (in kȯr pôr′ ė ȧl) [L. *incorporeus* (IN- (2), *corpus -poris*, body, see CORPOREAL)], *a.* Not corporeal; immaterial; (*Law*) not material, intangible (as a right in corporeal property). ***incorporal** (in kôr′ pȯ rȧl), *a.* ***incorporeality** (-ăl′ i ti), **incorporeity** (-rē′ i ti), *n.* Immateriality. **incorporeally,** *adv.*

incorrect (in kȯ rekt′) [L. *incorrectus*], *a.* Not in accordance with truth, propriety, etc.; faulty, wrong, inaccurate, inexact; improper, unbecoming; not corrected. **incorrectly,** *adv.* **incorrectness,** *n.*

incorrigible (in kor′ i jibl) [F., from L. *incorrigibilis*], *a.* Incapable of being amended or improved; bad beyond hope of amendment. *n.* One who is incorrigible. **incorrigibility** (-bil′ i ti), ***incorrigibleness,** *n.* **incorrigibly,** *adv.*

incorrodible (in kȯ rō′ dibl), *a.* That cannot be corroded. **incorrosive** (-rō′ siv), *a.*

incorrupt (in kȯ rŭpt′) [L. *incorruptus*], *a.* Not corrupt; not decayed, marred, or impaired; pure, untainted; not depraved; above the influence of bribery. ***incorrupted,** *a.* **incorruptible,** *a.* Incapable of corruption, decay, or dissolution; eternal; not to be bribed; high-principled. **incorruptibility** (-bil′ i ti), *n.* **incorruptibly,** *adv.* **incorruption** (-rŭp′ shŭn), *n.* Freedom from corruption. ***incorruptive,** *a.* **incorruptly,** *adv.* **incorruptness,** *n.*

incrassate (in krăs′ ȧt) [L. *incrassātus*, p.p of *incrassāre* (IN- (1), *crassāre*, to make thick, from *crassus*, CRASS)], *a.* (*Nat. Hist.*) Thick, thickened (in form). **v.t.* (-āt) To make thick or thicker; to thicken (as fluids) by mixture or evaporation. **v.i.* To become thick or thicker. **incrassation** (-sā′ shŭn), *n.* **incrassative** (in krăs′ ȧ tiv), *a.*

increase (1) (in krēs′) [A.-F. *encress-*, O.F. *encreis-*, stem of *encreistre* (cp. F. *croître*), L. *increscere* (IN- (1), *crescere*, to grow)], *v.i.* To grow; to become greater in bulk, quantity, number, value, degree, etc.; to multiply by the production of young. *v.t.* To make greater in number, bulk, quantity, etc.; to add to, to extend, to enlarge, to intensify. **increasable,** *a.* ***increaseful,** *a.* Prolific, fruitful. **increasingly,** *adv.*

increase (2) (in′ krēs), *n.* The act, state, or process of increasing; growth, multiplication; that which is added; increment; produce, crops; progeny; profit.

incredible (in kred′ ibl) [F., from L. *incrēdibilis*], *a.* Not credible; passing belief; (*colloq.*) extraordinarily great, astounding. **incredibility** (-bil′ i ti), ***incredibleness,** *n.* **incredibly,** *adv.*

incredulous (in kred′ ū lŭs) [L. *incrēdulus*], *a.* Indisposed to believe, sceptical (of); unbelieving; *incredible. **incredulity** (in krė dū′ li ti), ***incredulousness,** *n.* **incredulously,** *adv.*

increment (in′ krė mėnt) [L. *incrēmentum*, from *increscere*, to INCREASE], *n.* The act or process of increasing; an addition, an increase; the amount of increase; (*Math.*) the finite increase of a variable. **unearned increment:** (*Polit. Econ.*) An increase of value or wealth accruing without labour or effort, as by the increase in the value of land near a populous place. **incremental,** *a.*

increscent (in kres′ ėnt) [L. *increscens -entem*, pres.p. of *increscere*, to INCREASE], *a.* Increasing, growing; (*Her.*) waxing (of the moon when represented with the horns towards the dexter side). *n.* (*Her.*) The moon represented thus.

incriminate (in krim′ i nāt) [med. L. *incrimīnātus*, p.p. of *incrimināre* (IN- (1), CRIMINATE)], *v.i.* To charge with a crime, to criminate; to involve (a person) in a charge. **incriminatory,** *a.*

incroach [ENCROACH]. **incrust** [ENCRUST].

incrustation (in krŭs tā′ shŭn) [late L. *incrustātio*, from *incrustāre*, to ENCRUST], *n.* The act or process of encrusting; a crust or hard coating on a surface, etc.; a facing or lining of foreign material, as marble, stone, etc., on masonry, etc.

incubate (in′ kū bāt) [L. *incubātus*, p.p. of *incubāre* (IN- (1), *cubāre*, to lie)], *v.t.* To sit on (eggs) in order to hatch; to hatch by sitting on or by artificial means; (*fig.*) to evolve (a plan, etc.) by meditation. *v.i.* To sit on eggs for hatching, to brood. **incubation** (-bā′ shŭn), *n.* The act or process of incubating or hatching; brooding, as of a hen upon eggs; (*fig.*) the brooding of the Holy Spirit over chaos at the Creation; meditation on a scheme, etc.; (*Path.*) the maturation of morbific matter in the system; (*Gr. Ant.*) the act of sleeping for oracular dreams. **incubative, incubatory** (in′ kū bā tiv, -tȯr i), *a.* **incubator** (in′ kū bā tȯr), *n.* An apparatus for hatching eggs by artificial heat, for developing bacteria, etc., or rearing a child prematurely born.

incubous (in′ kū bŭs), *a.* (*Bot.*) Having the tip of one leaf lying over the base of the leaf above it.

incubus (in′ kū bŭs) [late L., nightmare, as prec.], *n.* (*pl.* **-bi, -buses**) A demon supposed (esp. in the Middle Ages) to lie with men or women at night, credited with the power of producing supernatural births; a nightmare; (*fig.*) any person, thing, or influence that oppresses, harasses, or restrains, such as a nightmare.

inculcate (in′ kŭl kāt) [L. *inculcātus*, p.p. of *inculcāre* (IN- (1), *calcāre*, to tread, from *calx calcis*, heel)], *v.t.* To impress (upon the mind) by emphasis or frequent repetition; to enforce, to instil. **inculcation** (-kā′ shŭn), *n.* **inculcator** (in′ kŭl kā tȯr), *n.*

inculpate (in′ kŭl pāt) [late L. *inculpātus*, p.p. of *inculpāre* (IN- (1), *culpa*, fault)], *v.t.* To charge with participation in a crime, to incriminate. ***inculp-**

able, *a.* ***inculpably,** *adv.* **inculpation** (-pā′ shŭn), *n.* **inculpatory** (in kŭl′ pȧ tȯr i), *a.*

incumbent (in kŭm′ bėnt) [L. *incumbens -ntem*, pres.p. of *incumbere* (IN- (1), *cumbere*, to lie)], *a.* Lying or resting (on); pressing or weighing (upon); (*fig.*) imposed (upon) as a duty or obligation; (*Bot.*) used of anthers when they lie against the inner side of the filament; (*Ent.*) of the wings of insects when they fold along the body. *n.* A person in possession of an office, etc., esp. a clergyman holding a benefice. **incumbency,** *n.* The act, state, sphere, or period of holding a benefice as incumbent.

***incumber** [ENCUMBER].

incunabula (in kū năb′ ū lȧ) [L., swaddling clothes (IN- (1), *cūnābula*, dim. of *cūnæ*, cradle)], *n.pl.* (*sing.* ***-lum***) The beginning (of a race, art, development, etc.); examples of books, etc., printed during the early period of the art, esp. before A.D. 1500. **incunabular,** *a.*

incur (in kĕr′) [L. *incurrere* (IN- (1), *currere*, to run)], *v.t.* (*past* **incurred**) To render oneself liable to (risk, injury, punishment, etc.); (*Law*) to bring upon oneself.

incurable (in kūr′ ȧbl) [O.F., from L. *incūrābilis*], *a.* That cannot be cured or healed; irremediable, hopeless, irreparable. *n.* One suffering from an incurable disease. **incurability** (-bil′ i ti), **incurableness,** *n.* **incurably,** *adv.*

incurious (in kūr′ i ŭs) [L. *incūriōsus*], *a.* Not curious or inquisitive; indifferent, heedless. **incuriosity** (-i os′ i ti), **incuriousness,** *n.* **incuriously,** *adv.*

incursion (in kĕr′ shŭn) [F., from L. *incursiōnem*, nom. *-sio*, from *incurrere*, see INCUR], *n.* A sudden inroad, a raid; an irruption. **incursive** (in kĕr′ siv), *a.*

incurve (in kĕrv′) [L. *incurvāre*], *v.t.* To cause to curve inwards; to make crooked. **incurvate** (in kĕr′ vāt), *v.t.* To cause to turn or bend from a straight course or line, esp. to bend inwards. *a.* (-vȧt) Curved inward. **incurvation** (-vā′ shŭn), *n.* ***incurvity,** *n.*

incus (in′ kŭs) [L., anvil], *n.* (*pl.* ***-cudes***) One of the small bones of the middle ear or tympanum which receives vibrations, as an anvil, from the *malleus.*

incuse (in kūz′) [L. *incūsus*, p.p. of *incūdere*, to forge, from prec.], *v.t.* To impress (a device, etc.) by stamping; to stamp with a device, etc. *a.* Stamped or impressed (on a coin, etc.). *n.* An impression made by stamping (on a coin, etc.).

indaba (in da′ ba) [Zulu, news], *n.* (*S. Afr.*) A council; a conference.

***indagate** (in′ dȧ gāt) [L. *indāgātus*, p.p. of *indāgāre*, to trace out], *v.t.* To seek or search out, to investigate. **indagation** (-gā′ shŭn), *n.* **indagator** (in′ dȧ gā tȯr), *n.*

indebted (in det′ ėd) [M.E. *endetted*, O.F. *endetté*, p.p. of *endetter* (EN-, *dette*, DEBT)], *a.* Being under a debt or obligation (to or for), esp. owing money (to). **indebtedness,** *n.*

indecent (in dē′ sėnt) [F. *indécent*, L. *indecentem*, nom. *-cens* (IN- (2), DECENT)], *a.* Unbecoming, unseemly; offensive to modesty or propriety; immodest, grossly indelicate, obscene. **indecency,** *n.* **indecently,** *adv.*

indeciduous (in dė sid′ ū ŭs), *a.* Not deciduous (used of leaves, petals, etc.).

indecipherable (in dė sī′ fėr ȧbl), *a.* Not decipherable, illegible.

indecision (in dė sizh′ ŭn) [F. *indécision*], *n.* Want of decision; wavering of the mind, irresolution. **indecisive** (in dė sī′ siv), *a.* Not decisive, final, or conclusive; irresolute, vacillating, hesitating. **indecisively,** *adv.* **indecisiveness,** *n.*

indeclinable (in dė klī′ nȧbl) [F. *indéclinable*, L. *indēclīnābilis*], *a.* (*Gram.*) Not varied by terminations, having no inflexions. *n.* An indeclinable word. **indeclinably,** *adv.*

indecomposable (in dē kŏm pō′ zȧbl), *a.* That cannot be decomposed.

indecorous (in dė kôr′ ŭs, -dek′ ȯ rŭs) [L. *indecōrus*], *a.* Violating propriety, decorum, or good manners. **indecorously,** *adv.* **indecorousness,** *n.* **indecorum** (in dė kôr′ ŭm), *n.* Violation of decorum or propriety; an indecorous act.

indeed (in dēd′), *adv.* In reality, in truth, of a truth (expressing emphasis, interrogation, concession, etc.). *int.* Expressing surprise, irony, interrogation, etc.

indefatigable (in dė făt′ i gȧbl) [obs. F. *indéfatigable*, L. *indēfatigābilis* (IN- (2), *defatigāre*, to wear out, from *fatigāre*, to FATIGUE)], *a.* Not yielding to fatigue or exertion; unwearied, unremitting. **indefatigability** (-bil′ i ti), **indefatigableness,** *n.* **indefatigably,** *adv.*

indefeasible (in dė fē′ zibl), *a.* Not defeasible, incapable of being annulled or forfeited. **indefeasibility** (-bil′ i ti), *n.* **indefeasibly,** *adv.*

indefectible (in dė fek′ tibl) [F. *indéfectible*], *a,* Not liable to defect, decay, or failure; faultless, flawless. **indefectibility** (-bil′ i ti), *n.* ***indefective,** *a.* Free from defect.

indefensible (in dė fen′ sibl), *a.* Incapable of being defended. **indefensibly,** *adv.* **indefensibility** (-bil′ i ti), *n.* ***indefensive,** *a.* Defenceless.

indefinable (in dė fī′ nȧbl), *a.* That cannot be defined. **indefinably,** *adv.*

indefinite (in def′ i nit) [L. *indēfīnītus*], *a.* Not limited or defined, not determinate; vague, uncertain, large beyond the comprehension of man; infinite, without limit; (*Gram.*) not defining or determining the persons, things, etc., to which they apply (of certain adjectives, adverbs, and pronouns); also applied to tenses like the Greek aorist and English past by which an action is expressed but not when it is continuous or complete; (*Bot.*) not constant in number (of stamens, usually more than 20); (*Math.*) without definite or conceivable limits. **indefinitely,** *adv.* **indefiniteness, -finitude** (-fin′-), *n.*

indehiscent (in dė his′ ėnt), *a.* (*Bot.*) Not splitting open to set free the seeds (of seed-capsules, etc.).

indelible (in del′ ibl) [earlier *indeleble*, L. *indēlēbilis* (IN- (2), *dēlēbilis*, from *dēlēre*, to DELETE)], *a.* That cannot be blotted out or effaced. **indelible pencil,** *n.* A pencil that makes ineffaceable marks. **indelibility** (-bil′ i ti), ***indelibleness,** *n.* **indelibly,** *adv.*

indelicate (in del′ i kȧt), *a.* Wanting in delicacy; coarse, unrefined; offensive to modesty or propriety. **indelicacy,** *n.* **indelicately,** *adv.*

indemnify (in dem′ ni fī) [L. *indemnis* (IN- (2), *damnum*, loss), -FY], *v.t.* To secure from or compensate for damage, loss, penalty, or responsibility. **indemnification** (-kā′ shŭn), *n.*

indemnity (in dem′ ni ti), *n.* Security against damage, loss, or penalty; indemnification or compensation for damage, loss, or penalties incurred; a sum paid as such compensation, esp. by a defeated State to the conqueror as a condition of peace.

indemonstrable (in dė mon′ strȧbl), *a.* That cannot be demonstrated; assumed as self-evident, axiomatic. **indemonstrability** (-bil′ i ti), *n.*

indent (1) (in dent′) [acc. to Skeat from low L. *indentāre*, to notch or cut into like teeth (IN- (1), *dens dentis*, tooth)], *v.t.* To notch or cut into as with teeth; (*Print*) to set in farther from the margin than the rest of the paragraph; (*Law*) to indenture; to order by an indent. *v.i.* To make an indent or order (upon); *to wind in and out, to run zigzag; to requisition. *n.* A notch in the margin of anything; an indentation or recess; an official order for stores from the commissariat; an order for goods, esp. one from abroad; (*Am.*) *an indented certificate for the principal or interest of the public debt. **indentation** (-tā′ shŭn), *n.* The act of indenting; a notch, dent, or incision, esp. in a margin;

a deep recess, esp. in a coast-line; a zigzag moulding. **indented,** *a.* Notched, serrated, zigzag, winding; bound by an indenture. **indentation,** *n.* (*Print.*) The setting in of a line of print farther from the margin; indentation.

indent (2) (in dent′), *v.t.* To dent; to make a dent in; to mark with a dent. *n.* A dent.

indenture (in den′ tyůr), *n.* (*Law*) An agreement or contract under seal, especially one binding an apprentice to a master (so called because the two documents had their edges cut or indented exactly alike so as to correspond with each other); an official voucher, certificate, register, etc.; an indentation. *v.t.* To bind (esp. an apprentice) by an indenture. **v.i.* To run in and out in a zigzag course.

independence (in dė pen′ dėns), *n.* The quality or state of being independent; income sufficient to make one independent of others, a competency. **Independence Day:** *n.* 4 July, the day on which the American colonies declared their independence in 1776. **independency,** *n.* Independence; the principles of the Independents or Congregationalists; *an independent State.

independent (in dė pen′ dėnt), *a.* Not dependent upon or subject to the control, power, or authority of another, not subordinate; free to manage one's own affairs without the interference of others; not depending on anything for its value, cogency, etc.; affording the means of independence; self-asserting, self-reliant; free from bias or prejudice; pertaining to the Independents or Congregationalists. *n.* One who exercises his judgment and choice of action without dependence on any person, party, etc.; a Congregationalist. **independently,** *adv.*

indescribable (in dė skrī′ båbl), *a.* Not describable, too fine or too bad for description, passing description; (*slang, pl.*) trousers. **indescribability** (-bil′ i ti), *n.* **indescribably,** *adv.* ***indescriptive,** *a.* Not furnishing proper description (of).

indesignate (in dez′ ig nåt), *a.* Indefinite in quantity; not qualified.

indestructible (in dė strŭk′ tibl), *a.* Incapable of being destroyed. **indestructibility** (-bil′ i ti), *n.* **indestructibly,** *adv.*

indeterminable (in dė tĕr′ mi nåbl) [L. *indēterminābilis*], *a.* That cannot be determined or defined; that cannot be terminated (as a dispute). **indeterminably,** *adv.*

indeterminate (in dė tĕr′ mi nåt) [L. *indēterminātus*], *a.* Not determinate; indefinite, undefined, not precise; (*Math.*) having no fixed value. **indeterminate vowel,** *n.* (*Phon.*) A vowel with an obscure or slurred sound, as the *a* in *advice*. It is indicated in this dictionary by a dot over it. **indeterminately,** *adv.* ***indeterminacy, indeterminateness,** *n.*

indetermination (in dė tĕr mi nā′ shůn), *n.* Lack of determination, vacillation. **indetermined,** *a.* Not determined; indefinite.

indeterminism (in dė tĕr′ mi nizm), *n.* (*Ethics*) The theory that conduct is not solely determined by motives, esp. that the will is able to choose between motives. **indeterminist,** *n.*

index (in′ deks) [L. *index -dicis*, a forefinger, an informer (*indicāre*, to INDICATE)], *n.* (*pl.* **indexes,** *Math.* **indices**) That which serves to point out or indicate; the forefinger; a hand (as of a watch, etc.), an arm, or a pointer, that directs to anything; a table of the contents of a book in alphabetical order with page-references; (*fig.*) anything that indicates or denotes (an inner meaning, character, etc.); (*Alg.*) the exponent of a power; (*Anthropometry*) the decimal number expressing the ratio between the length and breadth of a skull; (*slang*) the face. *v.t.* To provide with an index; to enter in an index. **the Index:** [INDEX EXPURGATORIUS, LIBRORUM, etc.]. **index of a globe:** A little style on the north, serving to point to certain divisions of the hour-circle when the globe is turned. **index of a logarithm:** (*Math.*) The integral part of the logarithm. **index of refraction:** (*Opt.*) The ratio of the sines of the angles of incidence and refraction. **index expurgatorius:** (*R.-C. Ch.*) A list of passages from current literature condemned to be expunged as heretical. **index-finger,** *n.* The forefinger, from its being used in pointing. ***index-learning,** *n.* Superficial knowledge. **index librorum expurgandorum:** (*R.-C. Ch.*) A list of books to be read only in expurgated editions. **index librorum prohibitorum:** (*R.-C. Ch.*) A list of books forbidden to be read by Roman Catholics on pain of excommunication. **indexer,** *n.* One who makes an index. **indexical,** *a.* Pertaining to or of the form of an index. **indexless,** *a.*

India (in′ di å) [L. and Gr., from *Indos*, the Indus, Pers. *hind*, Sansk. *sindhu*, river], *n.* A great peninsula in the south of Asia. **Republic of India:** (*Pol.*) The non-Moslem portion of India (including the princely states) declared independent in the political partition of 1947. **East India Company:** A chartered company (1600–1858) established for trading with India and later armed with territorial powers. **Further India:** The region between India and China. **India ink** [INDIAN INK]. **Indiaman,** *n.* (*pl.* **-men**) A large ship employed in the Indian trade. **india-matting,** *n.* Matting made from *Papyrus corymbosus*. **India Office:** The department of the British Government formerly dealing with affairs of India. **India paper:** A fine paper, imported from China, used by engravers for taking proofs. **Oxford India paper:** A very thin, tough, and opaque paper made by the Oxford University Press. **India proof:** A proof on India paper. **india-rubber,** *n.* A soft, elastic substance obtained from the coagulated juice of certain tropical plants, usu. called rubber. **india-rubbery,** *a.* **Indian,** *a.* Belonging to the East or West Indies, to the natives of India, or to the aborigines of America. *n.* A native of India; one of the aborigines of America or the West Indies. **Red Indian:** One of the aborigines of North America. **Indian berry:** *Cocculus Indicus*, or the climbing shrub *Anamirta cocculus* which bears this. **Indian club:** A bottle-shaped club used in gymnastic exercises. **Indian corn:** Maize. **Indian cress:** A Peruvian climbing plant of the genus *Tropæolum*, the best known being *T. major*, the nasturtium. **Indian date:** The tamarind. **Indian file:** Single file. **Indian fire:** A brilliant white signal light, composed of sulphur, realgar, and nitre. **Indian ink:** A black pigment, composed of lamp-black and animal glue, manufactured in China and Japan, there used for writing, etc., and employed in Europe in water-colour painting. **Indian meal:** Meal made from maize (*Am.* cornmeal). **Indian National Congress:** Indian political organization founded in 1885 and reformed in 1916, to work for the political progress and final independence of India. **Indian-rubber** [INDIA-RUBBER]. **Indian summer:** Summer-like weather, occurring late in autumn. **Indic,** *a.*

indican (in′ di kån) [L. *indicum*, INDIGO, -AN], *n.* (*Chem.*) The natural glucoside contained in the indigo-plant and other plants, by the decomposition of which indigo is yielded; a normal constituent of urine. **indicanein** (in′ di kå nīn), *n.*

indicant (in′ di kånt), *a.* Indicating or pointing out, *esp.* (*Med.*) suggesting a specific disease or remedy. *n.* (*Med.*) That which indicates a disease or its remedy.

indicate (in′ di kāt) [L. *indicātus*, p.p. of *indicāre* (IN- (1), *dicāre*, to point out)], *v.t.* To show, to point out; to be a sign or token of; (*Med.*) to point out or suggest (as a remedy).

indication (in di kā′ shůn), *n.* The act of indicating; that which indicates; intimation; (*Med.*) a symptom suggesting certain treatment.

indicative (in dik′ å tiv), *a.* (*Gram.*) Applied to that mood of a verb which affirms, denies, or asks questions; (*sometimes pron.* in′ di kā tiv) indicating; denoting something not visible or obvious. *n.* The indicative mood. **indicatively,** *adv.*

indicator (in′ di kā tôr), *n.* One who or that which indicates; (*Chem.*) a reagent used to indicate, by change of colour, the presence of an acid, alkali, etc.; (*Mech.*) an instrument attached to apparatus, machinery, a vehicle, etc., to indicate or record pressure, speed, number, etc.; (*Rail.*) a device for indicating the times of departure, etc., of trains. **indicatory,** *a.*

indices [INDEX].

indicium (in dish′ i ŭm) [L., from *indic-*, INDEX], *n.* (*pl.* ***-cia***) An indicating sign or mark; a symptom.

indict (in dīt′) [O.F. *enditer*, INDITE], *v.t.* To charge with a crime or misdemeanour, esp. by means of an indictment. **indictable,** *a.* Liable to be indicted (of a person); forming a ground of indictment (of an offence). **indictably,** *adv.* ***indictee** (in dī tē′), *n.* A person indicted. **indicter** (-dī′ tėr), *n.*

indiction (in dik′ shŭn) [through F. or directly from L. *indictio -ōnem*, from *indīcere*, to appoint (IN- (1), *dīcere*, to say)], *n.* A period of fifteen years arbitrarily fixed by Constantine the Great as a fiscal arrangement, beginning 1 Sept. 312, adopted by the Popes as part of their chronological system; a land-tax imposed by the Roman emperors at the beginning of each of these periods; a particular year in one of these cycles reckoned from the beginning; *a proclamation. **indictive,** *a.* Proclaimed, declared publicly.

indictment (in dīt′ mėnt), *n.* The act of indicting; a formal accusation of a crime or misdemeanour, presented upon oath by the grand jury to a court; the document embodying this; (*Sc. Law*) a process by which a criminal is brought to trial at the instance of the Lord Advocate.

Indies (in′ diz) [pl. of *Indie*, INDIA], *n.pl.* India and the neighbouring regions, also called the East Indies; the West Indies.

indifferent (in dif′ ėr ėnt) [F., from L. *indifferentem*, nom. *-ens*], *a.* Impartial, unbiased, neutral; having no inclination or disinclination (to); unconcerned, apathetic; neither good nor bad; of no importance, of little moment (to); of a barely passable quality, not good; (*Chem.*, *Elec.*, *etc.*) neutral, not active. *n.* A neutral person.

indifference (in dif′ ė rėns), *n.* The quality or state of being indifferent; impartiality, neutrality, absence of inclination or disinclination; lack of interest or attention (to or towards); unconcern, inattention; mediocrity; unimportance, insignificance. **indifferential** (-en′ shăl), *a.* **indifferentiated** (-shi ā′ tėd), *a.* **indifferentism,** *n.* Systematic indifference, esp. with regard to religious belief. **indifferentist,** *n.* **indifferently,** *adv.*

indigenous (in dij′ ė nŭs) [L. *indigenus* (*indi-*, *indu*, IN- (1), *gen-*, root of *gignere*, to produce)], *a.* Native, not exotic; natural, innate (to). **indigene** (in′ di jēn), *n.* **indigenously,** *adv.*

indigent (in′ di jėnt) [F., from L. *indigentem*, nom. *-gens* (*indi-*, as prec., *egēre*, to be in want)], *a.* In want, poor, needy, necessitous; in need (of); destitute (of). **indigence,** ***-digency,** *n.* **indigently,** *adv.*

indigest (in di jest′) [L. *indīgestus* (IN- (2), *dīgestus*, p.p. of *dīgerere*, to DIGEST)], *a.* Undigested. **n.* A shapeless, undigested mass. *v.t.* To fail to digest. **indigested,** *a* Not digested; not reduced to order, not methodized; crude; shapeless; not digested (in the stomach).

indigestible (in di jes′ ti bėl), *a.* Not easily digested; not acceptable. *n.* An indigestible substance or thing. **indigestibility,** *n.* **indigestibly,** *adv.*

indigestion (in di jes′ chŭn), *n.* Difficulty of digestion, dyspepsia; want of proper digestive power; the state of being undigested, unorganized, or immature. **indigestive,** *a.*

indignant (in dig′ nănt) [L. *indignans -ntem*, pres.p. of *indignārī*, as prec.], *a.* Inflamed with or expressive of wrath and disdain, esp. at meanness, injustice, etc., or with a person acting meanly, etc. ***indignance,** *n.* **indignantly,** *adv.*

indignation (in dig nā′ shŭn), *n.* A mingled feeling of anger and disdain; the feeling excited by that which is unworthy, mean, base, or unjust. **indignation-meeting,** *n.* A public meeting to protest against some abuse.

indignity (in dig′ ni ti), *n.* Undeserved contemptuous conduct; an act of incivility, a slight, an insult.

indigo (in′ di gō) [formerly *indico*, Sp., from L. *indicum*, Gr. *indikon*, Indian], *n.* A beautiful and very durable blue dye obtained from the indigo-plant, largely used in calico printing, etc.; a deep-blue colour. *a.* Of a deep-blue colour. **indigo-bird,** *n.* A North American finch, *Cyanospiza cyanea.* **indigo-blue,** *n.* The colour or the colouring-matter of indigo. **indigo-plant,** *n.* A plant of the genus *Indigofera*, esp. *I. tinctoria.* **indigo-white,** *n.* (*Chem.*) A colourless crystalline powder obtained by the reduction or deoxidation of indigo. **native indigo:** (*Austral.*) The poisonous Darling pea. **indigotic** (-got′ ik), *a.*

indirect (in di rekt′) [F., from L. *indīrectus*], *a.* Not direct, deviating from a direct line; not straight or rectilinear; not resulting directly or immediately from a cause; (*Polit. Econ.*) not paid directly to the Government, but in the form of increased prices, etc. (of taxes); (*Gram.*) in oblique oration or reported speech; not fair, not honest, not open or straightforward. **indirect evidence or testimony:** Evidence deduced from collateral circumstances. **indirect object:** (*Gram.*) The person or thing indirectly affected by an action though not the direct object of the verb. ***indirection,** *n.* Dishonest or indirect means. **indirectly,** *adv.* **indirectness,** *n.*

indiretin (in di rē′ tin) [*indi-*, *Indus*, root of INDIGO, *rhetinē*, RESIN], *n.* (*Chem.*) A resinous compound obtained by the decomposition of indican. **indirubin** (in di roo′ bin) [L. *ruber*, red], *n.* A brownish-red amorphous compound obtained by the decomposition of indican.

indiscernible (in di zėr′ nibl), *a.* Not discernible, not distinguishable, not visible. *n.* An indiscernible thing. **indiscernibleness,** *n.* **indiscernibly,** *adv.*

indiscerptible (in di sėrp′ tibl), *a.* Not to be destroyed by dissolution of parts. **indiscerptibility** (-bil′ i ti), *n.*

indiscipline (in dis′ i plin), *n.* Want of discipline. **indisciplinable,** *a.* Incapable of being disciplined or improved by discipline.

indiscoverable (in dis kŭv′ ėr ăbl), *a.* Not discoverable.

indiscreet (in dis krēt′) [L. *indiscrētus*], *a.* Wanting in discretion; injudicious, incautious; foolish, rash. **indiscreetly,** *adv.* **indiscreetness,** *n.* Indiscretion.

indiscrete (in dis′ krēt), *a.* Not discrete or separated.

indiscretion (in dis kresh′ ŭn), *n.* Want of discretion; imprudence, rashness; an indiscreet act, indiscreet conduct.

indiscriminate (in dis krim′ i nȧt), *a.* Wanting in discrimination; making no distinction; confused, promiscuous. **indiscriminately,** *adv.* **indiscriminating, indiscriminative,** *a.* **indiscriminateness, indiscrimination** (-nā′ shŭn), *n.*

indispensable (in dis pen′ săbl) [med. L. *indispensābilis*], *a.* That cannot be dispensed with; absolutely necessary or requisite; *not admitting dispensation; (*pl. slang*) trousers. **indispensability** (-bil′ i ti), **indispensableness,** *n.* **indispensably,** *adv.*

indispose (in dis pōz′), *v.t.* To make disinclined or unfavourable; to render unfit or unable (for or to); to make slightly ill. **indisposed,** *a.* Disinclined, unwilling, unfavourable; slightly ill. ***indisposedness, indisposition** (-pŏ zish′ ŭn), *n.* Disinclination, aversion, unsuitableness; a slight illness.

indisputable (in dis′ pŭ tȧbl), *a.* Not disputable; too clear to admit of question or dispute. **indisputability** (-bil′ i ti), **indisputableness,** *n.* **indisputably,** *adv.* ***indisputed,** *a.*

indissociable (in di sō′ shȧbl), *a.* Not to be separated or disassociated.

indissoluble (in di sol′ ūbl) [F., from L. *indissolūbilis*], *a.* Not dissoluble; not to be dissolved or disintegrated; stable, binding, subsisting and binding for ever. **indissolubility** (-bil′-), **indissolubleness,** *n.* **indissolubly,** *adv.*

indistinct (in dis tingkt′) [F., from L. *indistinctus*], *a.* Not distinct, obscure; not readily distinguishable; confused, faint. ***indistinction,** *n.* Want of distinction or distinctness; inability to distinguish. **indistinctive,** *a.* Not distinctive. **indistinctively,** *adv.* **indistinctly,** *adv.* **indistinctness,** *n.*

indistinguishable (in dis ting′ gwish ȧbl), *a.* Not distinguishable. **indistinguishably,** *adv.* ***indistinguished,** *a.* Indistinct, confused.

indistributable (in dis trib′ ū tȧbl), *a.* That cannot be distributed.

indite (in dīt′) [O.F. *enditer*, late L. *indictāre* (IN- (1), *dictāre*, to DICTATE)], *v.t.* To put in words, to compose; to set down, to write; *to indict; *to dictate; *to invite. ***inditement,** *n.* The act of inditing; an indictment. **inditer,** *n.*

indium (in′ di ŭm) [L. *ind-icum*, see INDIGO, -IUM], *n.* (*Chem.*) A soft, silver-white metallic element occurring in minute quantities in zinc ores.

indivertible (in di vĕr′ tibl), *a.* That cannot be turned aside. **indivertibly,** *adv.*

***individable** (in di vī′ dȧbl), *a.* Incapable of division.

individual (in di vid′ ū ȧl) [med. L. *indīviduālis*, from *indīviduus*, indivisible (IN- (2), *dīvidere*, to DIVIDE)], *a.* Subsisting as a single indivisible entity; single, particular as opp. to general; characteristic of a particular person or thing, distinctive; *indivisible. *n.* A single person, animal, or thing, esp. a single human being; a single member of a species, class, etc.; (*vulg.*) a person; (*Biol.*) the result of the development of a single ovum; an organism that has attained separate existence. **individual psychology,** *n.* (*Psych.*) A system founded by the Viennese psychologist Adler which considers the main factor of neurosis to be fear, and the desire for power to be the driving force behind every motive. **individualism,** *n.* Individuality; conduct or feeling centred in self, egoism, self-interest, selfishness; idiosyncrasy, personal peculiarity; an attitude, tendency or system in which each individual works for his own ends; independent action as opposed to co-operation, or as opp. to collectivism or Socialism. **individualist,** *n.* **individualistic,** *a.* **individuality** (-ăl′ i ti), *n.* Separate or distinct existence; distinctive character, strongly-marked personality. **individualize,** *v.t.* To mark out or distinguish from other individuals; to connect with one particular individual. **individualization** (-zā′ shŭn), *n.* **individually,** *adv.* Separately, in an individual capacity.

individuate (in di vid′ ū āt), *v.t.* To give the character of individuality to; to make an individual or a distinct entity. **individuation** (-ā′ shŭn), *n.* **principle of individuation:** (*Scholastic Phil.*) The principle individuating an *ens* from all other *entia.*

indivisible (in di viz′ ibl) [F., from L. *indīvīsibilis*], *a.* Not divisible; (*Math.*) that cannot be exactly divided. *n.* That which is indivisible, an infinitely small quantity or particle. **indivisibility** (-bil′ i ti), *n.* **indivisibly,** *adv.* ***indivision,** *n.* The state of being undivided.

Indo- [INDIA], *comb. form.* Indian; derived from, belonging to, or connected with India. **Indo-Aryan** (in′ dō âr′ i ȧn), *a.* Pertaining to the Indian division of the Aryan family of races. **Indo-Chinese,** *a.* Pertaining to the south-eastern peninsula of Asia or Further India, its people, or their languages. **Indo-European, -Germanic,** *a.* Of or pertaining to the family of languages spoken over most of Europe and over Asia as far as northern India.

indocile (in dō′ sīl, -dos′ il) [F., from L. *indocilis*], *a.* Not docile; not capable of being instructed. ***indocible,** *a.* **indocility** (-sil′ i ti), *n.*

indoctrinate (in dok′ tri nāt), *v.t.* To instruct in any body of doctrine; to imbue with the distinctive principles of any system. **indoctrination** (-nā′ shŭn), *n.*

indolent (in′ dŏ lĕnt) [late L. *indolens -ntem* (IN- (2), DOLENT)], *a.* Habitually idle or lazy; (*Path.*) causing no pain. **indolent tumour:** A tumour causing no pain. **indolence, *-lency,** *n.* **indolently,** *adv.*

indomitable (in dom′ i tȧbl) [late L. *indomitābilis* (IN- (2), *domitāre*, to tame)], *a.* Untameable, unconquerable; indefatigable. **indomitably,** *adv.*

Indonesian (in dō nē′ zi ȧn) [Gr. *nesos*, an island], *a.* Pertaining to the East Indian islands forming the Republic of Indonesia. *n.* An inhabitant of Indonesia; the language.

indoor (in′ dôr), *a.* Being or done within doors. **indoor relief:** Relief granted to paupers domiciled in a workhouse. **indoors** (in dôrz′), *adv.* Within a house or building.

indorsation (in dôr sā′ shŭn), *n.* The act or process of endorsing.

indorse [ENDORSE].

indraught (in′ draft), *n.* An inward flow, draught or current.

indrawn (in′ drawn), *a.* Drawn in.

indri (in′ dri) [Malagasy *indry*, lo! look! (mistaken for the name)], *n.* The babacoote, a Madagascan lemur.

indubitable (in dū′ bi tȧbl) [F., from L. *indubitābilis*], *a.* Not doubtful, unquestionable; too evident to admit of doubt. **indubitableness,** *n.* **indubitably,** *adv.* ***indubitate,** *a.*

induce (in dūs′) [L. *indūcere* (IN- (1), *dūcere*, to lead), p.p. *inductus*], *v.t.* To lead by persuasion or reasoning, to prevail on; to bring about, to cause; (*Elec.*) to produce by induction; (*Log.*) to derive as a deduction, opp. to deduce. **inducement,** *n.* The act of inducing; that which induces; a motive, a reason, an incitement; (*Law*) a preamble or statement of facts introducing other material facts. **inducer,** *n.* **inducible,** *a.*

induct (in dŭkt′) [L. *inductus*, see prec.], *v.t.* To introduce (as into a benefice or office); to put in actual possession of an ecclesiastical benefice or of any office, with the customary forms and ceremonies.

inductance [INDUCTION].

inductile (in dŭk′ til, -tīl), *a.* Not ductile. **inductility** (-til′ i ti), *n.*

induction (in dŭk′ shŭn) [F., from L. *inductiōnem*, *-tio*], *a.* The process of adducing facts to prove a general statement; (*Log.*) the process of inferring a law or general principle from particular instances, dist. from deduction; a general statement or conclusion attained by this kind of reasoning; (*Math.*) the proving of the universal truth of a theorem by showing it to be true of any case in a series or of a particular case; (*Phys.*) the production of an electric or magnetic state by the proximity or movement of an electric or magnetized body; instalment in an office or benefice; an introduction, a prologue, a prelude; *a beginning, a preliminary measure. **induction coil:** (*Elec.*) An apparatus for producing currents by electro-magnetic induction. **inductional,** *a.* **inductance** (in dŭk′ tȧns), *n.* (*Elec.*) The tendency of an electric circuit to oppose any change in the current passing through it.

inductive (in dŭk′ tiv), *a.* (*Log.*) Proceeding or characterized by induction; (*Elec.*) pertaining to, producing, or susceptible of induction; leading or drawing on, inductive; *introductory. **inductive method:** (*Log.*) The process of reasoning from particular instances to general principles. **inductive sciences:** Sciences based on induction from positive fact. **inductively,** *adv.* **inductivity** (-tiv′ i ti), *n.*

inductor (in dŭk′ tôr), *n.* One who inducts a clergyman into office; (*Elec.*) any part of an electrical apparatus acting inductively. **inductorium** (in dŭk tôr′ i ŭm), *n.* (*pl.* **inductoria**) (*Elec.*) An induction coil. **inductory,** *a.* **inductric,** *a.* (*Elec.*).

indue [ENDUE].

indulge (in dŭlj′) [L. *indulgēre*], *v.t.* To yield, esp. unduly, to the desires, humours, or wishes of, to humour (in or with); to gratify (one's desires, weakness, etc.); to harbour, to entertain, to foster. *v.i.* To yield to one's desires (in); *to yield or grant compliance (to), **indulgent,** *a.* Indulging or disposed to indulge the wishes, humours, or caprices of others; forbearing restraint or control. ***indulgential,** *a.* Relating to indulgences. **indulgently,** *adv.* **indulger,** *n.* One who indulges (in).

indulgence (in dŭl′ jens), *n.* The act or practice of indulging, yielding, or complying to desires, etc.; an indulgent act, a favour or privilege granted; liberality, tolerance, leniency; (*R.-C. Ch.*) a remission of the punishment still due to sin after sacramental absolution. **Declaration of Indulgence:** (*Eng. Hist.*) A proclamation granting religious liberty, esp. that of Charles II in 1672 suspending the penal laws against Nonconformists and recusants, and that of James II in 1687 in favour of Roman Catholics. **indulgenced,** *a.* (*R.-C. Ch.*) Bestowing an indulgence (of certain prayers, objects, etc.). ***indulgency,** *n.*

induline (in′ dū lin) [*ind-icum*, see INDIGO, *-ul-* dim. suf., -INE], *a.* One of a series of blue, blue-black, and grey dye-stuffs related to aniline.

indult (in dŭlt′) [F., from L. *indultum*, p.p. of *indulgēre*, to INDULGE], *n.* (*R.-C. Ch.*) An indulgence or privilege granted by the Pope, exempting from some canonical duty or authorizing something not normally permitted.

indumentum (in dū men′ tŭm) [L., from *induere*, to ENDUE], *n.* (*pl.* **-ta**) A covering, as of hair, feathers, etc. ***indument** (in′ dū ment), *n.*

induna (in dū′ nȧ) [Zulu], *n.* A leader or general of an impi.

induplicate (in dū′ pli kȧt), *a.* (*Bot.*) Having the edges folded in (of leaves and flowers in æstivation).

indurate (in′ dū rāt) [L. *indūrātus*, p.p. of *indūrāre* (IN- (1), *dūrāre*, to make hard)], *v.t.* To make hard, to harden; to render obdurate or unfeeling. *v.i.* To become hard; to become fixed or inveterate (as a custom). **a.* (-rȧt) Hardened; obstinate, callous. **induration** (-rā′ shŭn), *n.* Insensibility. **indurative** (in′ dū rā tiv), *a.*

indusium (in dū′ zi ŭm) [L., from *induere*, to ENDUE], *n.* (*pl.* **-ia**) (*Bot.*) A hairy cup enclosing a stigma; a shield or scale covering the fruit-cluster in some ferns; (*Ent.*) the larval case of an insect. **indusial** (in dū′ shi ȧl), *a.* (*Geol.*) Consisting in large measure of the fossil larva-cases of the caddis-worm (of limestone in Auvergne). **indusiate,** *a.* (*Bot.*) Having an indusium. **indusiform, indusioid,** *a.* (*Bot.*)

industrial (in dŭs′ tri ȧl), *a.* Pertaining to industry, to productive occupations, or to produce. *n.* A person engaged in an industrial occupation; (*pl.*) shares or securities relating to industrial enterprises. **industrial estate,** *n.* An industrial area specially planned to provide employment in factories of different kinds. **industrial exhibition:** An exhibition of industrial products, machinery, appliances, etc. **industrial relations:** A general term covering the relationships between employer and employees. **Industrial Revolution,** *n.* The changes brought about in the way of life by the extensive introduction of machinery in the early part of the 19th cent. **industrial school:** A school for teaching trades to neglected or convicted children. **industrialism,** *n.* A state of society in which the object of statesmanship is the success of industrial pursuits, the opposite to militarism; the modern industrial system. **industrialist,** *n.* **industrialize,** *v.t.* **industrially,** *adv.*

industrious (in dŭs′ tri ŭs) [L. *industriōsus*, as foll.], *a.* Characterized by industry; diligent and assiduous in business or study. **industriously,** *adv.* **industriousness,** *n.*

industry (in′ dŭs tri) [F. *industrie*, L. *industria* (prob. *indu*, in, in, *struere*, see CONSTRUCT)], *n.* Diligence, assiduity, steady application to any business or pursuit; useful work, esp. mechanical and manufacturing pursuits as dist. from agriculture and commerce; any branch of these; (*Polit. Econ.*) the employment of labour in production.

induviæ (in dū′ vi ē) [L., clothing, from *induere*, to ENDUE], *n.pl.* (*Bot.*) The withered remains of leaves which remain and decay on the stem of some plants. **induviate,** *a.*

indwell (in dwel′), *v.t.* (*past & p.p.* **indwelt**) To abide in; to inhabit (*usu. fig.*). *v.i.* To dwell (in the soul, etc.). **indweller,** *n.*

-ine [L. *-īnus*, *īnus*; or from F. *-ine*, L. *īna*], *suf.* Pertaining to, of the nature of; forming adjectives, as *crystalline*, *divine*, *equine*, *hyacinthine*, *marine*; forming feminine nouns, as *heroine*, *landgravine*; abstract nouns, as *discipline*, *medicine*; (*Chem.*) names of alkaloids and basic substances, as *cocaine*, *morphine*.

inebriate (in ē′ bri āt), *v.t.* To make drunk; to intoxicate. *a.* (-ȧt) Intoxicated, drunk (*lit.* or *fig.*). *n.* An habitual drunkard. **inebriant,** *a.* Intoxicating. *n.* Anything which intoxicates. **inebriation** (-ā′ shŭn), *n.* **inebriety** (in ė brī′ ė ti), *n.* Intoxication; habitual drinking.

ineconomy (in ė kon′ ȯ mi), *n.* Lack of economy. **ineconomical** (-nom′ i kȧl), *a.*

inedible (in ed′ ibl), *a.* Not edible. **inedibility** (-bil′ i ti), *n.*

inedited (in ed′ i tėd), *a.* Not edited or revised, not published.

ineffable (in ef′ ȧbl) [F., from L. *ineffābilis* (IN- (2), *effāri*, EF-, *fāri*, to speak)], *a.* Unspeakable, unutterable, beyond expression. **ineffableness,** *n.* **ineffably,** *adv.*

ineffaceable (in ė fā′ sȧbl), *a.* That cannot be rubbed out. **ineffaceably,** *adv.*

ineffective (in ė fek′ tiv), *a.* Not producing any or the desired effect; inefficient; not having artistic effect. **ineffectively,** *adv.* **ineffectiveness,** *n.*

ineffectual (in ė fek′ tū ȧl), *a.* Not producing any effect; powerless, vain. ***ineffectuality** (-ăl′ i ti), **ineffectualness,** *n.* **ineffectually,** *adv.*

inefficacious (in ef i kā′ shŭs), *a.* Not efficacious; producing no result or effect. **inefficacy** (in ef′ i kȧ si), *n.*

inefficient (in ė fish′ ėnt), *a.* Not efficient; wanting in ability or capacity. **inefficiently,** *adv.* **inefficiency,** *n.*

inelastic (in ė lăs′ tik), *a.* Wanting in elasticity. **inelasticity** (-lăs tis′ i ti), *n.*

inelegant (in el′ ė gȧnt) [F. *inélégant*, L. *inēlĕgantem*, nom. *-gans*], *a.* Not elegant; wanting in grace, polish, refinement, etc. **inelegance, *-gancy,** *n.* **inelegantly,** *adv.*

ineligible (in el′ i jibl), *a.* Not eligible; not capable of being selected or preferred. **ineligibility** (-bil′ i ti), *n.* **ineligibly,** *adv.*

ineluctable (in ė lŭk′ tȧbl) [L. *inēluctābilis* (IN- (2), *ēluctāri*, E-, *luctāri*, to struggle)], *a.* Not to be escaped; not to be overcome by struggling.

***inenarrable** (in ė năr′ ȧbl) [F. *inénarrable*, L. *inēnarrābilis* (IN- (2), *ēnarrāre*, to narrate)], *a.* That cannot be told; unspeakable, indescribable.

inept (in ept′) [L. *ineptus* (IN- (2), *aptus*, APT)], *a.* Not apt, fit, or suitable; silly, absurd. **ineptitude, ineptness,** *n.* **ineptly,** *adv.*

inequality (in ė kwol′ i ti) [O.F. *inéqualité* (F. *inégalité*), L. *inæquālitas*], *n.* Want of equality; difference, diversity, irregularity, variability, unevenness (of dimensions, position, intensity, etc.); disparity; inadequacy, incompetency; unfairness, partiality; (*Astron.*) deviation from uniformity of motion in a heavenly body.

inequilateral (in ē kwi lăt′ ėr ȧl), *a.* Not equilateral; having unequal sides.

inequitable (in ek′ wi tȧbl), *a.* Not equitable, not fair or just. **inequitably,** *adv.* **inequity,** *n.* A want of equity; injustice, unfairness.

ineradicable (in ė răd′ i kȧbl), *a.* That cannot be eradicated. **ineradicably,** *adv.*

inerrable (in er′ ȧbl) [L. *inerrābilis* (IN- (2), *errāre*, to ERR)], *a.* Exempt from error; infallible. **inerrability** (-bil′ i ti), **inerrancy,** *n.* **inerrably,** *adv.* **inerrant,** *a.* **inerratic** (-răt′ ik), *a.* Not wandering; fixed (as a star).

inert (in ĕrt′) [L. *iners -rtem* (IN- (2), *ars*, ART)], *a.* Destitute of inherent power of motion or of active resistance to motive power applied; motionless, slow, sluggish; indisposed to move or act; (*Chem.*) destitute of active chemical powers, neutral.

inertia (in ĕr′ shȧ), *n.* Inertness; (*Phys.*) that property of a body by which it persists in an existing state of rest or of uniform motion in a straight line, unless an external force changes that state. **inertial navigation:** A system of gyroscopic guidance for aircraft, missiles, etc., that dispenses with magnetic compass or ground-based radio direction. **vis inertiæ:** The resistance of matter to a force operating to move it. **inertly,** *adv.* **inertness,** *n.*

inescapable (in ės kā′ pȧbl), *a.* Inevitable, not to be escaped.

inescutcheon (in ės kŭch′ ȯn), *n.* (*Her.*) A small escutcheon borne within a shield.

inessential (in ė sen′ shȧl), *a.* Unessential; not indispensable.

inestimable (in es′ ti mȧbl) [F., from L. *inæstimābilis*], *a.* That cannot be estimated; too valuable or excellent to be valued or rated. **inestimably,** *adv.*

ineunt (in′ ė ŭnt) [L. *ineuntem*, nom. *iniens*, pres.p). of *inīre* (IN- (1), *īre*, to go)], *a.* Entering. *n.* (*Math.*) A point of a curve.

inevitable (in ev′ i tȧbl) [L. *inēvītābilis* (IN- (2), *ēvītāre*, to avoid)], *a.* That cannot be avoided or prevented; (*colloq.*) customary, wonted. **inevitability** (-bil′ i ti), **inevitableness,** *n.* **inevitably,** *adv.*

inexact (in ėg zăkt), *a.* Not exact, not precisely accurate. **inexactitude, inexactness,** *n.* **inexactly,** *adv.*

inexcusable (in ėks kū′ zȧbl) [F., from L. *inexcūsābilis*], *a.* Not to be excused or justified. **inexcusability** (-bil′ i ti), *n.* **inexcusably,** *adv.*

inexecutable (in ėk sek′ ū tȧbl), *a.* Incapable of being performed. **inexecution** (in ek sė kū′ shŭn), *n.* Neglect of execution.

inexertion (in ėg′ zĕr′ shŭn), *n.* Want of exertion or effort.

inexhausted (in ėg zaw′ stėd), *a.* Not exhausted. **inexhaustible,** *a.* That cannot be exhausted; unfailing, unceasing. **inexhaustibility** (-bil′ i ti), **inexhaustibleness,** *n.* **inexhaustibly,** *adv.* **inexhaustive,** *a.* Inexhaustible; not exhausting (the subject, etc.). **inexhaustively,** *adv.*

inexistent (1) (in ėg zis′ tėnt), *a.* Not existing. **inexistence** (1), *n.*

inexistent (2) (in ėg zis′ tėnt), *a.* Existent in or within. **inexistence** (2), *n.*

inexorable (in ek′ sȯr ȧbl) [F., from L. *inexōrābilis* (IN- (2), EX-, *ōrāre*, to pray)], *a.* Incapable of being persuaded or moved by entreaty or prayer; unbending, inflexible, relentless. **inexorability** (-bil′ i ti), *n.* **inexorably,** *adv.*

inexpansible (in ėk spăn′ sibl), *a.* Not capable of being expanded. **inexpansive,** *a.*

inexpectant (in ėk spek′ tȧnt), *a.* Not expectant.

inexpedient (in ėk spē′ di ėnt), *a.* Not expedient; unadvisable, disadvantageous, unprofitable. **inexpedience, -diency,** *n.* **inexpediently,** *adv.*

inexpensive (in ėk spen′ siv), *a.* Not expensive; cheap. **inexpensively,** *adv.* **inexpensiveness,** *n.*

inexperience (in ėk spēr′ i ėns) [F. *inexpérience*, L. *inexperientia*], *n.* Want of knowledge gained by experience. **inexperienced,** *a.*

inexpert (in ėk spĕrt′) [O.F., from L. *inexpertus*], *a.* Not expert, unskilful. **inexpertly,** *adv.*

inexpiable (in ek′ spi ȧbl) [L. *inexpiābilis*], *a.* That cannot be expiated or atoned for; implacable. **inexpiably,** *adv.*

inexplicable (in ek′ spli kȧbl) [F., from L. *inexplicābilis*], *a.* Not capable of being made plain or intelligible; not to be explained. *n.pl.* (*slang*) Trousers. **inexplicability** (-bil′ i ti), ***inexplicableness,** *n.* **inexplicably,** *adv.*

inexplicit (in ėk splis′ it), *a.* Not definitely or clearly stated. **inexplicitly,** *adv.* **inexplicitness,** *n.*

***inexplorable** (in ėk splôr′ ȧbl), *a.* Not capable of being explored, inscrutable.

inexplosive (in ėk splō′ siv), *a.* Not explosive.

inexpressible (in ėk spres′ ibl), *a.* Not expressible; incapable of being expressed or described; unutterable, unspeakable. *n.pl.* (*slang*) Trousers. **inexpressibly,** *adv.* **inexpressive,** *a.* **inexpressively,** *adv.* **inexpressiveness,** *n.*

inexpugnable (in ėk spŭg′ nȧbl) [F., from L. *inexpugnābilis*], *a.* Not expugnable, impregnable. **inexpugnably,** *adv.*

inextensible (in ėk sten′ sibl), *a.* Not extensible.

inextinguishable (in ėk sting′ gwish ȧbl), *a.* Incapable of being extinguished. **inextinguishably,** *adv.*

inextricable (in ek′ stri kȧbl) [F., from L. *inextricābilis*], *a.* That cannot be disentangled or solved; inescapable. **inextricably,** *adv.*

infall (in′ fawl), *n.* A hostile descent, an inroad; the place where the water enters a reservoir, etc., an inlet.

infallible (in făl′ ibl) [F., from med L. *infallibilis*], *a.* Exempt from liability to error or to failure. **infallibility** (-bil′ i ti), ***infallibleness,** *n.* **papal infallibility:** The dogma that the Roman Pontiff, when he defines a doctrine regarding faith or morals to be held by the universal Church, is infallible. **infallibilism** (in făl′ i bil izm), *n.* **infallibilist,** *a.* and *n.* **infallibly,** *adv.*

infamous (in′ fȧ mŭs) [O.F. *infameux*, med. L. *infamōsus*, L. *infāmis*], *a.* Having a reputation of an ill kind; notoriously vile; detestable, scandalous; (*Law*) branded with infamy by conviction for a crime. ***infame** (in fām′), **infamize** (in′ fȧ mīz), *(*Shak.*) **infamonize,** *v.t.* To make infamous; to defame. **infamously,** *adv.* **infamy,** *n.* Total loss of reputation or character; public reproach; extreme baseness; (*Law*) loss of character or position attaching to a convict.

infant (in′ fȧnt) [O.F. *enfant*, L. *infantem*, nom. *-fans* (IN- (2), *fans*, pres.p. of *fārī*, to speak)], *n.* A child during the earliest years of its life (*usu.* a babe, *also*, a child less than seven years old); (*Law*) a person under the age of twenty-one years, a minor; *the child of a king or prince. *a.* Young, tender; pertaining to or designed for infants. **v.t.* To bear or bring forth (as a child); to produce. **infancy,** *n.*

infanta (in fan′ tȧ) [Sp. and Port., as prec.], *n.* (In Spain and Portugal) any royal princess (usu. the eldest) except an heiress-apparent. ***infante*** (-tā), *n.* Any son of the king except the heir-apparent.

infanticide (in făn′ ti sīd) [late L. *infanticīdium*], *n.* Murder of a new-born infant; the practice of killing new-born children prevalent among savages and among the ancients; the murderer of an infant. **infanticidal** (-sī′ dȧl), *a.*

infantile (in′ fan tīl, -til) [late L. *infantilis*, from *infāns -tis*, INFANT], *a.* Pertaining to infants or infancy; characteristic of infancy, childish. **infantine,** *a.*

infantry (in′ făn tri) [F. *infanterie*, Ital. *infanteria*, from *infante*, a youth, a foot-soldier, as INFANT], *n.* (*collect.*) Foot-soldiers, usu. armed with small arms or rifle and bayonet; (*facet.*) children. **light infantry:** Infantry formerly equipped and trained for rapid evolutions. **mounted infantry:** Infantry mounted for rapid transportation, but fighting on foot. **infantryman:** A soldier in an infantry regiment.

infatuate (in făt′ ū āt) [L. *infatuātus*, p.p. of *infatuāre* (IN-, *fatuus*, FATUOUS)], *v.t.* To deprive of judgment, to affect with folly or extravagance; to inspire with an extravagant passion. **a.* (-ȧt) Affected with folly or infatuation. **infatuatedly,** *adv.* **infatuation** (-ā′ shŭn), *n.*

infect (in fekt′) [L. *infectus*, p.p. of *inficere*, to taint (IN- (1), *facere*, to make)], *v.t.* To act upon by contagion or infection; to taint with the germs of disease; (*fig.*) to corrupt, to affect (with depravity, etc.); to imbue (with noxious opinions, etc.); (*Law*) to taint with crime or illegality. **a.* Infected. **infectedly,** *adv.*

infection (in fek′ shŭn), *n.* The act or process of infecting, esp. the communication of disease by means of water, the atmosphere, etc., as distinct from contagion; that which infects, infectious matter; (*fig.*) moral contamination; the act of diffusing or instilling (esp. evil qualities) by means of example, etc.

infectious (in fek′ shŭs), *a.* Infecting or capable of infecting; likely to communicate disease; liable to be communicated by the atmosphere, water, etc.; (*fig.*) apt to spread, catching (of feelings, etc.). **infectiously,** *adv.* **infectiousness,** *n.* **infective,** *a.* Infectious. **infectiveness, infectivity** (-tiv′ i ti), *n.*

***infecund** (in fek′ ŭnd) [L. *infēcundus* (IN- (2), FECUND)], *a.* Not fecund; barren. ***infecundity,** *n.*

infeft (in feft′) [Sc. var. of ENFEOFF], *v.t.* To enfeoff. **infeftment,** *n.* (*Sc. Law*) The act of giving symbolical possession of heritable property.

infelicitous (in fė lis′ i tŭs) [IN- (2), FELICITOUS], *a.* Not felicitous; unfortunate; inappropriate, inept. **infelicity,** *n.* Unhappiness, misery; misfortune; inappropriateness, ineptness.

infelt (in′ felt) [IN, FELT (2)], *a.* Felt within, felt in one's heart.

infer (in fĕr′) [L. *inferre* (IN- (1), *ferre*, to bear, to bring)], *v.t.* To deduce as a fact, consequence, or result; to conclude; to prove, to imply; *to bring in, to adduce. *v.i.* To draw inferences. **inferable** (in fĕr′-, in′ fėr abl), *a.* **inference** (in′ fėr ėns), *n.* The act of inferring; that which is inferred from premises, a conclusion or deduction. **inferential** (in fėr en′ shȧl), *a.* **inferentially,** *adv.*

inferior (in fēr′ i ŏr) [L., comp. of *inferus*, low, nether], *a.* Lower in place, rank, value, quality, degree, etc.; subordinate; (*Astron.*) within the earth's orbit; below the horizon; (*Bot.*) growing below another organ, as the calyx or the ovary; (*Print.*) set below ordinary letters or below the line, as the figures in H_2SO_4. *n.* A person who is inferior to another in station, etc.; a subordinate. **inferiority** (-ŏr′ i ti), *n.* **inferiority complex,** *n.* (*Psych.*) A suppressed sense of inferiority which produces as compensation some abnormal reaction such as megalomania, assertiveness or the like. **inferiorly,** *adv.*

infernal (in fĕr′ nȧl) [F., from L. *infernālis*, from *infernus*, *inferus*, lower], *a.* Pertaining to hell or the lower regions; worthy of hell, hellish; detestable, diabolical; (*colloq.*) abominable, confounded. **infernal machine:** An explosive machine employed for the purposes of assassination or wilful damage. **infernally,** *adv.* **inferno** [It.], *n.* Hell (esp. as conceived by Dante); any place supposed to resemble hell.

inferrable [INFERABLE].

infertile (in fĕr′ tīl, -til) [F., from late L. *infertilis*] *a.* Not fertile; unfruitful. **infertility** (-til′ i ti), *n.*

infest (in fest′) [F. *infester*, L. *infestāre*, from *infestus*, hostile], *v.t.* To overrun, to swarm over or about, to haunt, so as to harass, annoy, or injure; *to attack, to harass, to plague; *to infect. **infestation** (-tā′ shŭn), *n.* **infester,** *n.*

infeudation (in fū dā′ shŭn) [med. L. *infeudātio*, from *infeudāre* (IN- (1), *feudum*, FEUD (2)], *n.* The granting of or putting one in possession of an estate in fee; the granting of tithes to laymen.

infibulate (in fib′ ū lāt) [L. *infībulātus*, p.p. of *infībulāre* (IN- (1), *fībula*, a clasp)], *v.t.* To fasten with or as with a clasp. ***infibulation** (-lā′ shŭn), *n.* The act of confining or fastening the sexual organs with a clasp or buckle to prevent copulation.

infidel (in′ fi dėl) [O.F. *infidele*, from L. *infidēlis* (IN- (2), *fidēlis*)], *a.* Disbelieving in a given form of faith (that of the person using the epithet), esp. rejecting the Christian religion; rejecting revelation, agnostic, sceptical; also non-Jewish or non-Mohammedan. *n.* One who disbelieves in a given form of faith; (*Hist.*) a Turk, a pagan, a Jew; one who rejects revelation, an agnostic, a sceptic; a non-Mohammedan, a non-Jew. **infidelity** (-del′ i ti), *n.* Disbelief in Christianity; breach of trust, disloyalty, deceit, esp. unfaithfulness to the marriage vow. **infidelize** (in′ fi dė līz), *v.t.*

infield (in′ fēld), *n.* Land near home or the base, dist. from outfield; (*Sc.*) land under tillage; (*Baseball*) the ground within the base lines. *v.t.* (in fēld′) To enclose, to make into a field. **infielder** (in′-) *n.* (*Baseball*) One of the players in the infield.

infighting (in′ fī ting), *n.* (*Pugil.*) Fighting or boxing at close quarters, so that blows from the shoulder are impossible.

infill (in fil′), *v.t.* To fill in; to fill up.

infilter (in fil′ tėr), **infiltrate** (-trāt), *v.t.* To cause to enter by penetrating the pores or interstices of; to enter or permeate in this way. *v.i.* To pass or percolate (into) thus. **infiltration** (-trā′ shŭn), *n.*

infinitate (in fin′ i tāt) [med. L. *infīnītātus*, p.p. of *infīnītāre*, from *infīnītus*, see foll.], *v.t.* (*Log.*) To render infinite, to make (a proposition) infinite in extent by prefixing a negative. **infinitant,** *a.* **infinitation** (-tā′ shŭn), *n.*

infinite (in′ fi nit) [L. *infīnītus*], *a.* Having no bounds or limits, endless; indefinitely great or numerous; (*Gram.*) not limited by person, mood, etc.; (*Mus.*) a term applied to certain forms of the canon in which the ending leads back to the beginning; (*Math.*) greater than any assignable quantity. *n.* Infinite space, infinity; (*fig.*) a vast or infinite amount; (*Math.*) an infinite quantity. **the Infinite:** The infinite Being, God. **the infinite:** Infinite space. **infinitely,** *adv.* **infiniteness,** *n.* **infinitesimal** (-tes′ i-, -tē′ si mȧl), *a.* Infinitely small; (*colloq.*) insignificant; negligible; (*Math.*) less than any assignable quantity. *n.* A quantity less than any assignable quantity. **infinitesimally,** *adv.*

infinitive (in fin′ i tiv) [L. *infīnītīvus*, as prec.], *a.* (*Gram.*) Unlimited; applied to that mood of a verb which expresses the action without regard to any person, etc. *n.* The infinitive mood. **infinitival** (-tī′ vȧl), *a.*

infinitude (in fin′ i tūd), **infinity** (in fin′ i ti), *n.* Boundlessness; an infinite quantity or distance; a boundless expanse, vastness, immensity.

infirm (in fĕrm′) [L. *infirmus* (IN- (2), FIRM (1))], *a.* Lacking bodily strength or health, esp. through age or disease; weak-minded, irresolute; uncertain, unstable. **v.t.* To weaken, to enfeeble. **infirmity,** *n.* **infirmly,** *adv.*

infirmary (in fĕr′ mȧ ri), *n.* A hospital or establishment in which the sick or injured are lodged and nursed. **infirmarian** (-mâr′ i ȧn), *n.* One in charge of an infirmary or of the sick, esp. in connexion with a religious order in the Middle Ages.

infix (in fiks′) [IN, FIX], *v.t.* To fasten or fix in; to implant firmly; (*Gram.*) to insert (an infix) in a word. *n.* (in′ fiks) (*Gram.*) A modifying element in the body of a word, in certain languages.

inflame (in flām′) [O.F. *enflamber*, L. *inflammāre* (IN- (1), *flammāre*, from *flamma*, FLAME)], *v.t.* To cause to blaze, to kindle; to cause inflammation in, to render morbidly hot by exciting excessive action in the blood-vessels and tissues; to excite, to stir up passion, etc.; to intensify, to aggravate. *v.i.* To burst into a blaze; to become inflamed; to become excited.

inflammable (in flăm′ ȧ bėl), *a.* That may be easily set on fire; readily enkindled, excited or morbidly inflamed. ***inflammable air:** Hydrogen. **inflammability** (-bil′ i ti), **inflammableness,** *n.* ***inflammably,** *adv.*

inflammation (in flȧ mā′ shŭn) [INFLAME], *n,* (*Path.*) A morbid condition characterized by heat, redness, swelling, pain and loss of function in the part affected. **inflammatory** (in flăm′ ȧ tȯr i), *a.* Tending to inflame; exciting or arousing (political) passions.

inflate (in flāt′) [L. *inflātus*, p.p. of *inflāre* (IN- (1), *flāre*, to blow)], *v.t.* To distend with air or wind; to puff out; (*fig.*) to puff up, to elate; to expand or raise (prices, reputation, etc.) artificially. **a.* Inflated. **inflatable,** *a.* **inflatant,** *n.* That which inflates (a balloon, etc.). **inflated,** *a.* Distended with air; (*fig.*) tumid, bombastic, turgid; expanded or raised artificially; (*Bot.*) hollow and distended.

inflation (in flā′ shŭn), *n.* The state of being inflated; (*Fin.*) an increase in price above the real value; an expansion of credit. **inflationist,** *n.* (*U.S.A.*) One who favours an increased issue of paper money.

inflatus (in flā′ tŭs), *n.* A breathing into; (*fig.*) inspiration.

inflect (in flekt′) [L. *inflectere* (IN- (1), *flectere*, to bend), p.p. *inflexus*], *v.t.* To bend, to curve; to turn from a straight or direct course; to modulate (as the voice); (*Gram.*) to change the terminations of (words) for purposes of declension or conjugation. **inflectedness,** *n.* **inflective,** *a.* Capable of bending; (*Gram.*) inflexional. **inflector,** *n.* **inflexed** (in flekst′), *a.* Bent, curved; (*Bot.*) bent inwards.

inflexible (in flek′ si bėl), *a.* Incapable of being bent or curved; that will not yield to prayers or entreaties; (*fig.*) firm of will or purpose. **inflexibility** (-bil′ i ti), *n.* **inflexibly,** *adv.*

inflexion (in flek′ shŭn), *n.* The act of inflecting; the state of being inflected; modulation of the voice; (*Gram.*) the variation of the termination of nouns, etc., in declension, and of verbs in conjugation; (*Opt.*) diffraction; (*Geom.*) change from concave to convex in a curve. **inflexional,** *a.* Pertaining to or having grammatical inflexions. **inflexionless,** *n.* ***inflexure,** *n.* A bend, a curve, a bow.

inflict (in flikt′) [L. *inflictus*, p.p. of *inflīgere* (IN- (1,) *flīgere*, to dash)], *v.t.* To impose upon as a penalty or punishment; to cause to feel or experience (something of an unpleasant nature); *to afflict. **inflictable,** *a.* **inflicter,** *n.* **infliction** (-flik′ shŭn), *n.* The act of inflicting; a punishment inflicted; (*colloq.*) a trouble, an annoyance. **inflictive,** *a.*

inflorescence (in flȯ res′ ėns) [F., from L. *inflōrescens -tem*, pres.p. of *inflōrēscere*], *n.* (*Bot.*) The act or process of flowering; the arrangement of flowers upon a branch or stem; the collective flower or flowers of a plant.

inflow (in′ flō), *n.* Flowing in; influx; (*Aviat.*) the increase in air velocity in front of an air-screw produced by its rotation. *v.i.* (in flō′) To flow in.

influence (in′ flu̇ ėns) [O.F., from late L. *influentia* (IN- (1), *fluere*, to flow)], *n.* Agency or power (upon) serving or tending to affect, modify, or control; power to move, direct, or control, ascendency (over); (*Astrol.*) an ethereal fluid supposed to flow from the stars and to affect character and control human destinies; (*Phys.*) energy affecting other bodies, as electric and magnetic induction; (*fig.*) a person, thing, feeling, etc., exercising moral power (over). *v.t.* To exercise influence upon; to modify (motives, etc.) to any end or purpose; to bias, to sway. **influencer,** *n.* **influential** (-en′ shȧl), *a.* **influentially,** *adv.*

influent (in′ flu̇ ėnt) [as prec.], *a.* Flowing in; influential. *n.* A tributary, an affluent.

influenza (in flu̇ en′ zȧ) [It., as INFLUENCE], *n.* A catarrhal inflammation of the mucous membranes of the air-passages, attended by fever and nervous prostration, contagious and infective; (*fig.*) an epidemic.

influx (in′ flŭks) [late *influxus*, p.p. of *influere*, see INFLUENCE], *n.* A flowing of or as of water (into); the point of inflow (of a stream); an introduction in abundance, an infusion; *influence. **influxion** (in flŭk′ shŭn), *n.* **influxive,** *a.*

infold [ENFOLD].

in-folio (in fō′ li ō) [F. (L. *in folio*, see FOLIO)], *n.* A folio volume.

inforce [ENFORCE].

inform (1) (in fôrm′) [O.F. *enformer*, L. *informāre* (IN- (1), *formāre*, from *forma*, FORM)], *v.t.* To animate, to imbue (with feeling, vitality, etc.); to communicate knowledge to, to tell; to give form or shape to. *v.i.* To take form or shape; to disclose facts, to bring a charge (against). **to inform against:** To lay an information against. **informant,** *n.* **informed,** *a.* Having information; apprized of the facts; educated, enlightened; *formed, shaped.

***inform** (2) (in fôrm′) [L. *informis* (IN- (2), *forma*, FORM)], *a.* Without regular form; shapeless.

informal (in fôr′ mȧl) [IN- (2), FORMAL], *a.* Not in accordance with official, proper, or customary forms; without formality. **informality** (-măl′ i ti) *n.* **informally,** *adv.*

information (in fôr mā′ shŭn), *n.* The act of informing or communicating knowledge, etc.; intelligence communicated; notice, knowledge acquired; (*Law*) a complaint or accusation presented to a court or magistrate as a preliminary to criminal proceedings. **informational,** *a.*

informative (in fôr′ mȧ tiv), *a.* Conveying information or instruction; *having power to animate or give vitality. **informatory,** *a.* Affording knowledge or information.

informer (in for′ mer), *n.* One who informs, esp. one who lays an information against a person offending against the law or any penal statute. **common informer:** One who makes a business of detecting offenders and laying information against them, usu. for the sake of reward.

infra (in′ frȧ) [L.], *adv.* Below, further on (of a passage in a book, etc.).

infra- [L., as prec.], *pref.* Below, beneath. **infracostal** (in frȧ kos′ tȧl) [COSTAL], *a.* (*Anat.*) Situated below the ribs.

infraction (in frăk′ shŭn) [F., from L. *infractiōnem*, nom. *-tio*, from *infringere*, to INFRINGE], *n.* The act of breaking or violating; violation, infringement. **infract** (in frăkt′), *v.t.* (*Am.*) To infringe. ***infractor,** *n.* **infractous,** *a.* (*Bot.*).

infra dig (in′ frȧ dig′) [short for L. *infrā dignitātem*, beneath the dignity (of)], *phr.* Beneath one's dignity, undignified.

infragrant (in frā′ grȧnt) [IN- (2), FRAGRANT], *a.* Not fragrant; malodorous.

infrahuman (in frȧ hū′ mȧn) [INFRA-, HUMAN], *a.* Having qualities or characteristics inferior to human.

infralapsarian (in frȧ lăp sâr′ i ȧn) [INFRA-, L. *lapsus*, fall, see LAPSE, -ARIAN], *n.* One of a branch of Calvinists who held that God, having permitted the Fall, then decreed the salvation of the elect [see also SUBLAPSARIAN, SUPRALAPSARIAN]. *a.* Belonging to the infralapsarians or their doctrine. **infralapsarianism,** *n.*

inframaxillary (in frȧ măk′ si lȧr i) [INFRA-, MAXILLARY], *a.* (*Anat.*) Situated under the jaw; pertaining to the lower jaw-bone. *n.* The lower jaw-bone.

***inframundane** (in frȧ mŭn′ dān) [INFRA-, MUNDANE], *a.* Lying beneath the world.

infranchise [ENFRANCHISE].

infrangible (in frăn′ jibl), *a.* That cannot be broken, that cannot be infringed or violated. **infrangibility** (-bil′ i ti), *n.* **infrangibly,** *adv.*

infra-orbital (in frȧ ôr′ bi tȧl), *a.* (*Anat.*) Situated below the orbit of the eye. **infra-red rays,** *n.pl.* (*Phys.*) Invisible radiations beyond the limit of the visible spectrum at the red end. They are employed in actinotherapy. **infrarenal** (-rē′ nȧl) [RENAL], *a.* Situated below the kidneys. **infrascapular** (-skăp′ ū lȧr) [SCAPULAR], *a.* Situated below the shoulder-blade. **infrasternal** (-stĕr′ nȧl) [STERNAL], *a.* Situated below the breastbone. **infra-structure,** *n.* (*Mil.*) The system of communications and public services that forms a basis for the defence of Europe.

infrequent (in frē′ kwėnt) [L. *infrequens -ntem*]; *a.* Rare, uncommon, unusual. **infrequency, *-quence,** *n.* ***infrequently,** *adv.*

infringe (in frinj′) [L. *infringere* (IN- (1), *frangere*, to break)], *v.t.* To break (a law, compact, contract, etc.); to violate, to neglect to obey, to transgress; *to destroy; *to hinder, to obstruct. *v.i.* To encroach, to intrude (upon). **infringement,** *n.* **infringer,** *n.*

infructuous (in frŭk′ tū ŭs), ***-tuose** (in frŭk tū ōs′) [L. *infructuōsus*], *a.* Not fruitful; (*fig.*) fruitless, unprofitable. **infructuosity** (-os′ i ti), *n.* **infructuously,** *adv.*

infula (in′ fū lȧ) [L.], *n.* (*Rom. Ant.*) A fillet worn by priests and victims; (*Ecclesiol.*) one of the ribbons hanging from a bishop's mitre.

infundibulum (in fŭn dib′ ū lŭm) [L., a funnel, from *infundere* (IN- (1), *fundere*, to pour)], *n.* (*pl.* **dibula**) (*Anat.*) Any funnel-shaped part; (*Zool.*) the siphon or funnel of a cephalopod, the gastric cavity in the ctenophora. **infundibular, -ulate, infundibuliform,** *a.* Funnel-shaped.

infuriate (in fū′ ri āt) [late L. *infuriātus*, p.p. of *infuriāre* (IN- (1), *furia*, FURY)], *v.t.* To provoke to madness or fury. *a.* (-ȧt) Infuriated, enraged, mad.

***infuscate** (in fŭs′ kāt) [L. *infuscātus*, p.p. of *infuscāre* (IN- (1), *fuscus*, dark-brown)], *v.t.* To make black or dusky; to darken, to obscure. *a.* (-kȧt) Darkened, clouded. ***infuscation** (-kā′ shŭn), *n.*

infuse (in fūz′) [F. *infuser*, L. *infūsus*, p.p. of *infundere* (IN- (1), *fundere*, to pour)], *v.t.* To pour (into); (*fig.*) to inculcate, to implant; to steep in liquid so as to obtain an extract or infusion. **infusive** (in fū′ siv), *a.* Having the power of infusing. **n.* An infusion. **infuser,** *n.*

infusible (in fū′ zibl), *a.* That cannot be fused or melted. **infusibility** (-bil′ i ti), *n.*

infusion (in fū′ zhŏn), *n.* The act of infusing; (*fig.*) instillation; inculcation; the act or process of steeping; the liquid extract obtained by steeping any substance; that which is instilled or implanted, an admixture, a tincture; *immersion. **infusionism,** *n.* (*Theol.*) The doctrine that the human soul is an emanation from or an influx of the divine substance. **infusionist,** *n.*

infusoria (in fū zôr′ i ȧ) [mod. L., pl. of *infūsōrium*, from *infūsus*, see INFUSE], *n.pl.* (*Zool.*) The name first given by Otto Frederick Müller to the protozoa developed in infusions of decaying organic matter. **infusorial,** *a.* (*Zool.*) Pertaining to the infusoria; (*Geol.*) containing or composed of infusoria. **infusorian, infusory** (-fū′ zŏr i), *a.* and *n.*

-ing [A.-S. (1) *-ung*, *-ing*, ending of verbal nouns; (2) *-ende*, part. ending, later *-inde*, confused with *-ing*, -ING (1); (3) *-ing*, *-ung*, forming nouns with sense of belonging to, of the kind of, the son of, etc.], *suf.* Forming verbal nouns, as *cleansing, hunting*; denoting occupations, as *bricklaying, lumbering, soldiering*; denoting the results, material used, etc., as *painting, roofing, scaffolding, washing*; [A.-S. *-ende*], used as a gerund, as *in coming, my having written, to begin writing*, etc.; as participial adjectives, as *charming, fleeting, horrifying*; forming diminutives, as *farthing, lording, shilling*; patronymics, etc., as *atheling, gelding, whiting*.

ingate (in′ gāt), *n.* Entrance, way in; (*Metal.*) the aperture in a mould at which the metal enters.

ingathering (in găth′ ėr ing), *n.* The act of gathering or collecting, esp. of getting in the harvest.

ingeminate (in jėm′ i nāt) [L. *ingeminātus*, p.p. of *ingemināre*], *v.t.* To redouble, to repeat, to reiterate. **ingemination** (-nā′ shŭn), *n.*

ingender [ENGENDER].

***ingenerate** (in jen′ ėr āt) [L. *ingenerātus*, p.p. of *ingenerāre* (IN- (1), GENERATE)], *v.t.* To generate or produce within; to engender. *a.* (-ȧt) Inborn, innate. ***ingenerable** (2), *a.* That can be ingenerated.

ingenious (in jē′ ni ŭs) [L. *ingeniōsus*, from *ingenium*, genius], *a.* Possessed of natural capacity or talent; skilful, clever, esp. in inventing or contriving; curious in design or contrivance; *ingenuous. **ingeniously,** *adv.* **ingeniousness, ingenuity** (in jė nū′ i ti), *n.*

ingénue (an zhė nu) [F., as INGENUOUS], *n.* An ingenuous or naïve girl, esp. such a character on the stage.

ingenuous (in jen′ ū ŭs) [L. *ingenuus*, free-born, frank (IN- (1), *gen-*, base of *gignere*, to produce, to beget)], *a.* Open, candid, frank, sincere; of honourable or noble extraction. **ingenuously,** *adv.* **ingenuousness,** *n.*

ingest (in jest′) [L. *ingestus*, p.p. of *ingerere* (IN- (1), *gerere*, to carry)], *v.t.* To take (food) into the stomach. **ingesta,** *n.pl.* (*Physiol.*) Food; that which is taken into the body. **ingestion** (in jes′ chŭn), *n.* **ingestive,** *a.*

ingle (1) (ing′ gėl) [Sc., etym doubtful, perh. from Gael. *aingeal*, fire], *n.* A fire on the hearth; (*erron.*) a fireplace. **ingle-cheek,** *n.* The jamb of a fireplace. **ingle-nook,** *n.* A chimney-corner. **ingleside,** *n.*

***ingle** (2) (ing gėl) [etym. doubtful, perh. rel. to M.Dut. *ingel*, *engel*, ANGEL (Skeat)], *n.* A male favourite or paramour. *v.t.* To coax, to wheedle.

inglobate (in glō′ bȧt), *a.* Formed into a globe (as by gravitation).

inglorious (in glôr′ i ŭs) [L. *inglōriōsus*], *a.* Not glorious; shameful, ignominious. **ingloriously,** *adv.* **ingloriousness,** *n.*

ingluvies (in gloo′ vi ēz) [L., maw, craw, prob. rel. to *glutīre*, to swallow], *n.* (*Anat.*) The crop of birds; the stomach of ruminants. **ingluvial,** *a.*

ingoing (in′ gō ing), *a.* Going in, entering. *n.* Entrance.

ingot (ing′ gŏt) [prob. from A.-S. IN, *goten*, p.p. of *gēotan*, to pour, to fuse (Skeat)], *n.* A mass of cast metal, esp. steel, gold, or silver; a bar of gold or silver for assaying; *a mould.

ingraft, etc. [ENGRAFT]. **ingrail** [ENGRAIL].

ingrain (1) (in′ grān, predicately in grān′) [*orig. in grain*, F. *en graine*, see GRAIN (1)], *a.* Dyed in the grain or yarn before manufacture; (*fig.*) thoroughly imbued, inherent, inveterate. *n.* A yarn or fabric dyed with fast colours before manufacture. **ingrain carpet:** A carpet manufactured from wool dyed in the grain, the pattern showing through the fabric.

ingrain (2) [ENGRAIN].

ingrate (in grāt′) [L. *ingrātus* (IN- (2), *grātus*, pleasing)], *a.* Unpleasant to the senses; ungrateful; unpleasant. *n.* An ungrateful person. ***ingrateful,** *a.*

ingratiate (in grā′ shi āt) [It. *ingratiāre* (L. *in grātiam*, into favour, see GRACE)], *v.t.* To insinuate (oneself) into goodwill or favour (with) another. **ingratiatingly,** *adv.*

ingratitude (in grăt′ i tūd) [F., from late L. *ingrātitūdo*, from *ingrātus*, INGRATE], *n.* Want of gratitude.

ingravescent (in grȧ ves′ ėnt) [L. *ingravescens -ntem*, pres.p. of *ingravescere* (IN- (1), *gravis*, heavy)], *a.* (*Med.*) Increasing in severity (of an illness). **ingravescence,** *n.*

ingredient (in grē′ di ėnt) [F., from L. *ingredientem*, nom. *-ens*, pres.p. of *ingredī* (IN- (1), *gradī*, to walk), *p.p. ingressus*], *n.* That which enters into a compound as an element, a component part. **a.* Forming a component part.

ingress (in′ gres) [L. *ingressus*, see prec.], *n.* The act of entering, entrance; power or liberty of entrance. **ingression** (in gresh′ ůn), *n.* **ingressive,** *a.*

ingroove [ENGROOVE]. ***ingross** [ENGROSS].

ingrowing (in′ grō ing), *a.* Growing inwards. **ingrown,** *a.* **ingrowth,** *n.*

inguinal (ing′ gwi nȧl) [L. *inguinālis*, from *inguen -inis*, the groin], *n.* (*Anat.*) Of, pertaining to, or situated near the groin. **inguino-,** *comb. form.*

ingulf [ENGULF].

ingurgitate (in gĕr′ ji tāt) [L. *ingurgitātus*, p.p. of *ingurgitāre* (IN- (1), *gurges gurgitis*, a whirlpool)], *v.t.* To swallow down greedily; (*fig.*) to engulf. *v.i.* To eat greedily, to gorge. **ingurgitation** (-tā′ shůn), *n.*

inhabit (in hăb′ it) [M.E. *enhabiten*, O.F. *enhabiter*, L. *inhabitāre* (IN- (1), *habitāre*, to dwell, see HABIT)], *v.t.* To live or dwell in; to occupy as a place of settled residence. **v.i.* To live, to dwell, to reside. **inhabitable** (1), *a.* Fit for habitation. **inhabitancy, *-itance,** *n.* Domiciliation or residence for a considerable period, esp. such as confers the rights of an inhabitant; *a habitation. **inhabitant,** *n.* **inhabitation** (-tā′ shůn), *n.* The act of inhabiting; the state of being inhabited; a dwelling; *population. **inhabitativeness, inhabitiveness,** *n.* **inhabiter,** *n.* **inhabitress,** *n.* A female inhabitant.

***inhabitable** (2) (in hăb′ i tȧbl) [F., from L. *inhabitābilis*], *a.* Not habitable, uninhabitable.

inhale (in hāl′) [L. *inhālāre* (IN- (1), *hālāre*, to breathe)], *v.t.* To breathe in, to draw into the lungs; to inspire, as dist. from exhale. **inhalant,** *a.* and *n.* **inhalation** (-lā′ shůn), *n.* **inhaler,** *n.* One who inhales; a respirator; (*Med.*) an instrument for enabling the inhalation of medicated vapours, etc.

inharmonious (in har mō′ ni ůs), *a.* Not harmonious; unmusical. **inharmonic, al** (-mon′ ik, -ȧl), *a.* **inharmoniously,** *adv.* ***inharmony,** *n.*

inhaust (in hawst′) [IN- (1), L. *haustus*, p.p. of *haurire*, to draw (cp. EXHAUST)], *v.t.* To draw or drink in.

inhere (in hēr′) [L. *inhærēre* (IN- (1), *hærēre*, to stick)], *v.i.* To belong or exist (in) as an attribute or quality; to be an essential or necessary part (in); to be vested (in). **inherence, -ency,** *n.*

inherent (in hē′ rėnt), *a.* Permanently belonging (in or to); not to be removed, inseparable; naturally conjoined or attached (to); innate, inborn. **inherently,** *adv.*

inherit (in her′ it) [O.F. *enheriter* (IN- (2), late L. *hērēditāre*, from *hēres -ēdis*, HEIR)], *v.t.* To receive by legal succession as the representative of a former possessor; to derive from one's ancestors as part of one's nature; to receive as one's proper portion; *to put in possession. *v.i.* To take or come into possession as an heir. **inheritable,** *a.* Capable of inheriting or of being inherited. **inheritability** (-bil′ i ti), *n.* **inheritably,** *adv.* **inheritance,** *n.* The act of inheriting; that which is inherited; a possession acquired as one's proper portion; *acquisition, ownership. **inheritor, inheritress, -trix,** *n.*

inhesion (in hē′ zhůn) [late L. *inhæsio*, from *inhærēre*, to INHERE], *n.* Inherence.

inhibit (in hib′ it) [L. *inhibitus*, p.p. of *inhibēre* (IN- (1), *habēre*, to have, to hold)], *v.t.* To restrain, to hinder, to put a stop to (an action, nervous process, etc.); to prohibit, to forbid, to interdict; (*Eccles.*) to prohibit (a priest) from exercising his office. **inhibiter,** *n.*

inhibition (in hi bish′ ůn), *n.* The act of inhibiting; the state of being inhibited; (*Law*) *a writ to inhibit a judge from proceeding further in a cause, now called prohibition; an order forbidding a priest to exercise his functions; (*Sc. Law*) a writ to prevent a person from burdening his heritable property to the prejudice of a creditor; (*Psych.*) habitual shrinking from some action which is instinctively thought of as a thing forbidden. **inhibitory,** *a.*

inhospitable (in hos′ pi tȧbl), *a.* Not inclined to show hospitality to strangers; (*fig.*) affording no shelter, desolate. **inhospitableness,** *n.* **inhospitably,** *adv.*

inhuman (in hū′ mȧn) [F. *inhumain*, L. *inhūmānus*], *a.* Destitute of a feeling of kindness towards one's fellow-creatures; brutal, savage, unfeeling. **inhumanity** (-măn′ i ti), *n.* **inhumanly,** *adv.*

inhume (in hūm′) [F. *inhumer*, L. *inhumāre* (IN- (1), *humus*, the ground)], *v.t.* To bury, to inter. ***inhumate** (in′ hū māt), *v.t.* **inhumation** (-mā′ shůn), *n.*

inimical (i nim′ i kȧl) [late L. *inimīcālis*, from *inimīcus* (IN- (2), *amīcus*, friend)], *a.* Having the temper or disposition of an enemy; adverse, unfavourable (to). **inimically,** *adv.*

inimitable (i nim′ i tȧbl) [F., from L. *inimitābilis*], *a.* That cannot be imitated. **inimitability** (-bil′ i ti), **inimitableness,** *n.* **inimitably,** *adv.*

inion (in′ i ȯn) [Gr.], *n.* (*Anat.*) The ridge of the occiput.

iniquity (i nik′ wi ti) [O.F. *iniquité*, L. *inīquitātem*, nom. *-tas*, from *inīquus* (IN- (2), *æquus*, just)], *n.* Want of equity, gross injustice; unrighteousness, wickedness, crime; the name of one of the comic characters, the Vice, in the old Moralities. **iniquitous,** *a.* **iniquitously,** *adv.*

inisle [ENISLE].

initial (i nish′ ȧl) [L. *initiālis*, from *initium*, beginning (IN- (1), *īre*, to go)], *a.* Beginning; incipient; placed at or pertaining to the beginning. *n.* The first letter of a word; (*pl.*) the first letters of a Christian name and surname. *v.t.* (*past & p.p.* **initialled**) To mark with one's initials, as a guarantee of correctness, a sign of ownership, etc. **initially,** *adv.* At the beginning.

initiate (i nish′ i āt), *v.t.* To begin or originate; to set afoot, to start; to instruct in the rudiments or principles; to admit (into a society or association or mysteries or secret science), usu. with ceremonial rites. *v.i.* To do the first act; to perform the first rite. *a.* Initiated; *unpractised, new. *n.* One who is newly initiated, a novice.

initiation (i nish i ā′ shŭn), *n.* A beginning; the making one acquainted with new principles, rites, etc.; admission into a new society or association; the ceremony by which one is so admitted.

initiative (i nish′ i ȧ tiv), *a.* Serving to begin or initiate; initiatory; *n.* The first step or action in any business; power or right to take the lead or originate (esp. legislation). **initiator** (i nish′ i ā tôr), **initiatrix,** One who initiates. **initiatory,** *a.* and *n.*

inject (in jekt′) [L. *injectus*, p.p. of *injicere* (IN- (1), *jacere*, to throw)], *v.t.* To throw or force (into); to introduce (as a liquid) by mechanical means; to charge (with a liquid) by injection; to interject.

injection (in jek′ shŭn), *n.* The act of injecting; that which is injected; the introduction of colouring substance or a therapeutic agent into the body; the spraying of oil fuel into the cylinder of a compression ignition engine; the forcing of cold water into the condenser of a steam-engine. **injection-cock, -pipe,** *n.* The cock or pipe through which water is injected into a condenser. **injection engine:** A steam-engine with a condenser in which steam is condensed by this means.

injector (in jek′ tôr), *n.* One who, or that which injects; an apparatus for supplying the boiler of a steam-engine with water; an injection nozzle.

injelly (in jel′ i), *v.i.* To imbed in jelly.

injoin [ENJOIN].

***injoint** (in joint′), *v.i.* To join (with).

injudicious (in jŭ dish′ ŭs), *a.* Not judicious; void of judgment, rash, hasty; done without judgment, unwise. **injudiciously,** *adv.* **injudicial,** *a.* Not judicial. **injudiciousness,** *n.*

injunction (in jŭngk′ shŭn) [late L. *injunctio*, from *injungere*, to ENJOIN], *n.* The act of enjoining; that which is enjoined; (*Law*) a writ or process whereby a party is required to do or (more usually) to refrain from doing certain acts; an admonition, direction, or order. **injunct** (in jŭngkt′), *v.t.* (*colloq.*) To restrain by a legal injunction.

injure (in′ jŭr) [from INJURY], *v.t.* To do wrong or harm to; to hurt, to damage; to slander, to depreciate; to impair or diminish. **injurer,** *n.* **injurious** (in joo′ ri ŭs), *a.* That injures or tends to injure; wrongful, hurtful, pernicious, detrimental; insulting, abusive. **injuriously,** *adv.* **injuriousness,** *n.*

injury (in′ jŭ ri) [A.-F. *injurie*, L. *injūria* (IN- (2), *jūs jūris*, justice, right)], *n.* A wrong; that which occasions loss, detriment, or mischief; damage, hurt, harm; *an insult, an affront.

injustice (in jŭs′ tis) [F., from L. *injustitia*], *n.* The quality of being unjust, lack of right or equity, unfairness; violation of justice, a wrong.

ink (ingk) [O.F. *enque* (F. *encre*), late L. *encaustum*, purple ink used by the Roman emperors, from Gr. *enkaustos*, burnt in, see ENCAUSTIC], *n.* A coloured, usually black, liquid or viscous material used in writing or printing; the dark fluid exuded by a cuttle-fish to cover its escape. *v.t.* To blacken, daub, or cover with ink (as type, etc.); to mark (in or over) with ink. **printer's ink:** Viscous material used by printers. **ink-bag,** *n.* The ink-bladder of a cuttle-fish and other cephalopods. **ink-bottle, -holder, inkpot,** *n.* A bottle, etc., for holding ink. **ink-eraser,** *n.* Indiarubber treated with fine sand, used for rubbing out ink-marks. ***ink-fish,** *n.* The cuttle-fish. ***inkhorn,** *n.* A small vessel, formerly made of horn, to hold ink; a portable writing-case. ***inkhorn mate** or **varlet:** A pedantic fellow, a scribbler. **inkhorn terms:** Pedantic, high-sounding terms. **ink-pencil,** *n.* A copying-pencil. **ink-slinger,** *n.* A writer, esp. a newspaper editor or reporter. **inkstand,** *n.* A stand for one or more inkpots, usu. with a place for pens. **inking-roller,** *n.* (*Print.*) A roller receiving the ink from the inking-table and transferring it to the type. **inking-table,** *n.* A slab on which printing-ink is spread to be taken up by the inking-roller. **inker,** *n.* (*Print.*) An inking-roller; (*Teleg.*) a device for recording telegraphic messages in ink. **inkless,** *a.* **inky,** *a.* Of the nature of or resembling ink; discoloured with ink; black as ink; *black, gloomy, miserable. **inkies,** *n.pl.* (*Cinema.*) Studio slang for incandescent lights. **inkiness,** *n.*

***inkle** (1) (ing′ kėl) [etym. doubtful], *n.* A broad linen tape; (*Shak.*) prob. a kind of crewel or worsted.

inkling (ingk′ ling), *n.* A hint, a whisper, an intimation; a mere suspicion (of); (*prov.*) a desire, an inclination.

***inlace** [ENLACE], **inlaid** [INLAY].

inland (in′ lȧnd), *a.* Remote from the sea; situated in the interior of a country; carried on within a country, domestic, not foreign; *refined, civilized. *adv.* In or towards the interior of a country. *n.* The interior of a country; (*Sc.*) the mainland as dist. from outer islands; *demesne land. **inland revenue:** Taxes and duties levied on home trade, etc., not foreign; excise. **inlander,** *n.* **inlandish,** *a.*

in-laws (in lawz′), *n.pl.* (*colloq.*) Relatives by marriage.

inlay (in lā′), *v.t.* (*past & p.p.* **-laid**) To lay or insert in; to decorate by inserting different materials into a groundwork, leaving the surfaces even; to fasten a print, picture, etc., evenly (into a page or sheet). *n.* (in′ lā) Material inlaid or prepared for inlaying. **inlayer,** *n.* **inlaying,** *n.* The business of an inlayer; inlaid work.

inlet (in′ lėt), *n.* A means of entrance, admission, entrance; a small arm of the sea; a creek. *a.* Let in.

inlier (in′ lī ėr), *n.* (*Geol.*) An isolated portion of an underlying bed, which has become surrounded by a later formation.

inly (in′ li) [A.-S. *inlīce* (IN, -LY)], *adv.* Inwardly, internally; closely, deeply. *a.* *Inward, internal, secret.

inlying (in′ lī ing), *a.* Lying inside.

inmate (in′ māt), *n.* One who dwells in the same house as another; a resident or occupant (of). **a.* Dwelling or resident under the same roof (with).

inmost (in′ mōst) [A.-S. *innemest*], *a.* Remotest from the surface; most inward; (*fig.*) deepest, most heartfelt, most secret.

inn (in) [A.-S., cogn. with IN], *n.* A public house of lodging and entertainment for travellers; *lodging, abode; *a place of residence or hostel for students. **v.i.* To stay at an inn. **v.t.* To lodge and entertain. **Inns of Chancery:** Colleges in which young students formerly began their law studies, now occupied as chambers by lawyers, etc.; the societies formerly occupying these buildings. **Inns of Court:** Four corporate societies in London (*Inner Temple, Middle Temple, Lincoln's Inn, Gray's Inn*), which have the exclusive right of admitting persons to practise at the bar; the buildings belonging to such societies. **innkeeper, *innholder,** *n.*

innate (i nāt′) [L. *innātus* (IN- (1), *nātus*, p.p. of *nascī*, to be born)], *a.* Inborn, natural; native, not acquired. **innate ideas:** (*Phil.*) General notions which (according to the Stoics and other philosophers) are inborn or developed by intuition in all men, opp. to acquired ideas. **innately,** *adv.* **innateness,** *n.*

innavigable (i năv′ i gȧbl) [F., from L. *innāvigābilis*], *a.* Not navigable. **innavigably,** *adv.*

inner (in′ ėr) [A.-S. *innera*, comp. of IN], *a.* Interior; farther inward or nearer the centre; internal; spiritual; dark, hidden, esoteric. *n.* That part of a target immediately outside the bull's eye; a shot striking that part. **inner man:** The inner or spiritual part of man; (*colloq.*) the stomach, the appetite for food. **innerly,** *a.* (*Sc.*) Intimate, familiar; kindly. **adv.* Inwardly. **innerliness,** *n.* **innermost,** *a.*

innervate (i nĕr′ vāt), *v.t.* (*Physiol.*) To give a nerve impulse to; to supply with nerves or nerve filaments. **innervation** (-vā′ shŭn), *n.* **innerve,** *v.t.* To give nerve to, to invigorate, to strengthen.

inning (in′ ing), *n.* *The gathering in of crops, harvest; (*pl.*) (*Cricket*) the time or turn for batting of a player or a side; (*fig.*) the time during which a party or person is in possession, in power, etc.; *lands recovered from the sea.

innkeeper [INN].

innocent (in′ ȯ sẽnt) [F., from L. *innocentem*, nom. *-cens* (IN- (2), *nocens*, pres.p. of *nocēre*, to hurt)], *a.* Free from moral guilt; guiltless (of); blameless, sinless; pure, unspotted, guileless; (*colloq.*) without; (*prov.*) weak in intellect. **n.* An innocent person, esp. a child; (*prov.*) an imbecile, an idiot. **Massacre of the Innocents:** Innocents' Day; (*Parl. slang*) the abandonment of Government Bills not sufficiently advanced to be passed during the session. **Innocents' Day:** The festival (28 Dec.) commemorating the massacre of the children of Bethlehem by Herod (Matt. ii. 16). **innocence, *-cy,** *n.* **innocently,** *adv.*

innocuous (in ok′ ū ŭs) [L. *innocuus*], *a.* Having no injurious qualities, harmless; (*Zool.*) belonging to the *Innocua* or harmless serpents. **innocuously,** *adv.* **innocuousness,** *n.*

innominate (i nom′ i nȧt) [late L. *innōminātus* (IN- (2), *nōminātus*, p.p. of *nōmināre*, to NOMINATE)], *a.* Not named; nameless. **innominate artery:** (*Anat.*) A large but short artery given off from the arch of the aorta. **innominate bone:** (*Anat.*) The hip-bone.

innovate (in′ ȯ vāt) [L. *innovātus*, p.p. of *innovāre* (IN- (1), *novāre*, to make new, from *novus*, new)], *v.i.* To introduce alterations (in anything); to put forward novelties. *v.t.* To alter or change, by the introduction of something new. **innovation** (-vā′ shŭn), *n.* **innovative, -tory** (in′ ȯ vā tiv, -tȯr i), *a.* **innovator,** *n.*

innoxious (i nok′ shŭs) [L. *innoxius*], *a.* Harmless, innocuous. **innoxiously,** *adv.* **innoxiousness,** *n.*

innuendo (in ū en′ dō) [L. *innuendō*, by way of intimation, abl. gerund of *innuere* (IN- (1), *nuere*, to nod)], *n.* (*pl.* **-oes**) An indirect or oblique hint or intimation; an insinuation. *v.t.* To insinuate. *v.i.* To make innuendoes.

innumerable (i nū′ mẽr ȧbl) [F., from L. *innumerābilis*], *a.* Countless, numberless; indefinitely numerous. ***innumerableness,** *n.* **innumerably,** *adv.* ***innumerous,** *a.*

innutrition (in ū trish′ ŭn), *n.* Want or failure of nutrition. **innutritious, innutritive** (i nū′ tri tiv), *a.*

inobservant (in ȯb zẽr′ vȧnt) [L. *inobservans -ntem*], *a.* Not observant; heedless. **inobservance,** *n.* Want of observance (of a law, etc.). ***inobservation** (in ob zẽr vā′ shŭn), *n.*

inobtrusive [UNOBTRUSIVE].

inocular (in ok′ ū lȧr), *a.* (*Ent.*) Inserted in the inner margin of the eye, as the antennæ of some insects.

inoculate (in ok′ ū lāt) [L. *inoculātus*, p.p. of *inoculāre*, to engraft (IN- (1), *oculus*, eye)], *v.t.* To communicate a disease to (man or the lower animals) by the introduction of infectious matter, in order to induce a mild form of the disease and render the subject immune against further attack; (*fig.*) to impregnate, to infect, to imbue (with); (*Hort.*) to graft on by the insertion of buds. *v.i.* To graft trees by budding; to practise inoculation. **inoculable,** *a.* **inoculation** (-lā′ shŭn), *n.* **inoculative** (in ok′ ū lā tiv, -lȧ tiv), *a.* **inoculator,** *n.*

inodorous (in ō′ dȯr ŭs) [L. *inodōrus*], *a.* Odourless.

inoffensive (in ȯ fen′ siv), *a.* Giving no offence; unobjectionable, harmless. **inoffensively,** *adv.* **inoffensiveness,** *n.*

***inofficial** [UNOFFICIAL].

inofficious (in ȯ fish′ ŭs) [L. *inofficiōsus*], *a.* Without office, inoperative; (*Law*) regardless of natural obligation and duty.

inoperable (in op′ ẽr ȧbl), *a.* (*Med.*) That cannot be operated on.

inoperative (in op′ ėr ȧ tiv), *a.* Producing no result.

inoperculate (in ȯ pẽr′ kū lȧt), *a.* (*Conch. and Bot.*) Without an operculum or lid. **inopercular,** *a.*

inopportune (in op′ ȯr tūn) [F., from late L. *inopportūnus*], *a.* Not opportune; unseasonable. **inopportunely,** *adv.* **inopportuneness, inopportunity** (-tū′ ni ti), *n.*

***inoppressive** [UNOPPRESSIVE].

inorb (in ôrb′), *v.t.* To place in or as in an orb, to ensphere.

inordinate (in ôr′ di nȧt) [L. *inordinātus* (IN- (2), *ordinātus*, p.p. of *ordināre*, from *ordo -inis*, ORDER)], *a.* Irregular, disorderly; excessive, immoderate, passing all bounds. **inordinately,** *adv.* **inordinateness,** *n.* ***inordination** (-nā′ shŭn), *n.*

inorganic (in ôr găn′ ik), *a.* Not organic, not having the organs or instruments of life; not having organic structure, *e.g.* rocks, metals, etc. **inorganic chemistry** [CHEMISTRY]. **inorganically,** *adv.* Without organization. **inorganizable** (-nī′ zȧbl), *a.* **inorganization** (-zā′ shŭn), *n.* ***inorganized,** *a.*

inornate (in ôr′ nȧt) [L. *inornātus*], *a.* Not ornate.

inosculate (in os′ kū lāt) [IN- (1), L. *osculātus*, furnished with a mouth, from *osculum*, dim. of *os*, mouth], *v.i.* To become united (with, as two vessels) by the mouth of one fitting into the mouth of the other, or by a duct; to anastomose. *v.t.* To cause to unite (as two vessels) in an animal body; to blend. **inosculation** (-lā′ shŭn), *n.*

inoxidize (in ok′ si dīz), *v.t.* To render incapable of or not liable to oxidizing. **inoxidable, inoxidizable,** *a.* **inoxidized,** *a.*

in-patient [IN].

inpouring (in′ pôr ing), *n.* A pouring in. *a.* That pours in.

input (in′ put), *n.* The amount put into (a machine, the body, etc.); (*Sc.*) a contribution.

inquest (in′ kwest) [O.F. *enqueste*, med. L. *inquesta*, orig. fem. of *inquistus*, L. *inquīsītus*, p.p. of *inquīrere*, to INQUIRE], *n.* A judicial inquiry or investigation into a matter, usu. an inquiry before a jury, esp. a coroner's inquest; the jury itself; an inquiry, an investigation. **coroner's inquest:** A judicial inquiry before a coroner and a jury into death occurring suddenly, from violence, an unknown cause, or in a prison; also into cases of treasure trove. **grand inquest:** A grand jury; (*fig.*) the House of Commons. **great inquest:** The Last Judgment.

inquiet (in kwī′ ėt) [L. *inquiētus*], *a.* Unquiet. **v.t.* To disquiet, to disturb. **inquietude,** *n.* Restlessness, uneasiness (bodily or mental).

inquiline (in′ kwi līn) [L. *inquilīnus*, a sojourner, for *incolīnus*, from *incolere* (IN- (1), *colere*, to dwell)], *n.* (*Zool.*) An animal living in the abode of another, as certain beetles in ants' nests, or certain insects in the galls of other insects. **inquilinous** (-lī′ nŭs), *a.*

inquire (in kwīr′) [M.E. *enquere*, O.F. *enquerre*, L. *inquīrere* (IN- (1), *quærere*, to seek)], *v.i.* To ask questions (of); to seek information by asking questions (about or after); to investigate (into); *to seek or search (out). *v.t.* To ask information about; to search out, to find out; to ask (what, whether, how, etc.); *to ask, to interrogate; *to call. ***inquirable,** *a.* That may be inquired into. ***inquiration** (-rā′ shŭn), *n.* (*prov.*). ***inquirendo*** (in kwī ren′ dō) [L., by inquiring, abl. gerund of *inquīrere*], *n.* (*Law*) An authority given in general to some person or persons to inquire into something for the benefit of the Crown. ***de lunatico inquirendo*:** A writ to inquire into the sanity of a person said to be incapable of managing his estate. **inquirer,** *n.* **inquiring,** *a.* Given to inquiry; inquisitive. **inquiringly,** *adv.*

inquiry (in kwī' ri), *n.* The act of inquiring; a question, an interrogation; a searching for truth, information, or knowledge; examination of facts or principles; a judicial investigation. **court of inquiry:** A court appointed to make a legal investigation into charges against soldiers, usu. before proceedings are instituted before a court-martial.

inquisition (in kwi zish' ůn) [O.F., from L. *inquīsītiōnem*, nom. *-tio*, from *inquīrere*, to INQUIRE], *n.* Inquiry, search, investigation; a judicial inquiry, an inquest; the verdict of a jury under a writ of inquiry; (*Eccles.*) a tribunal in the R.-C. Church for inquiring into offences against the canon law, aimed especially at the suppression of heresy, also called the Holy Office. **inquisitional,** *a.*

inquisitive (in kwiz' i tiv), *a.* Unduly given to asking questions; prying, curious. *n.* An inquisitive person. **inquisitively,** *adv.* **inquisitiveness,** *n.*

inquisitor (in kwiz' i tŏr), *n.* One who inquires; one who makes inquisition officially; a functionary of the Inquisition. **Grand Inquisitor:** The president of a court of the Inquisition. **Inquisitor-General,** *n.* The head of the Inquisition in Spain. **inquisitorial** (-tôr' i ǎl), ***inquisitorious,** *a.* Pertaining to or like the Inquisition; prying, searching. **inquisitorially,** *adv.* **inquisitress** (-kwiz' i trės), *n.* ***inquisiturient** (-tūr' i ėnt), *a.* (*Milton*) Desirous of playing the inquisitor.

inroad (in' rōd), *n.* A hostile incursion; a sudden or desultory invasion; (*fig.*) an encroachment.

inroll [ENROL].

inrush (in' rŭsh), *n.* An irruption; an inpouring.

insalivate (in săl' i vāt), *v.t.* To mix (food) with saliva during eating. **insalivation** (-vā' shůn), *n.*

insalubrious (in sǎl ū' bri ůs) [L. *insalūbris*], *a.* Not salubrious, unhealthy. **insalubrity,** *n.*

***insalutary** (in săl' ū tǎr i) [late L. *insalūtāris*], *a.* Not salutary; not favourable to health; unwholesome.

insane (in sān') [L. *insanus*], *a.* Deranged in mind, mad; (*fig.*) exceedingly rash or foolish; *causing insanity. ***insane root:** (*Shak.*) Hemlock. **insanely,** *adv.* **insanity** (in săn' i ti), **insaneness,** ***insanie,** *n.* Madness, mental derangement.

insanitary (in săn' i tǎr i), *a.* Not sanitary. **insanitation** (-tā' shůn), *n.*

insatiable (in sā' shǎbl) [F., from *insatiābilis*], *a.* That cannot be satisfied or appeased; immoderately greedy (of). **insatiability** (-bil' i ti). **insatiableness,** *n.* **insatiably,** *adv.* **insatiate,** *a.* Never satisfied; insatiable. ***insatiately,** *adv.* ***insatiety** (-tī' ė ti), *n.*

insconce [ENSCONCE].

inscribe (in skrīb') [L. *inscrībere* (IN- (1) *scrībere*, to write), p.p. *inscriptus*], *v.t.* To write, carve, or engrave (in or upon a stone, paper, or other surface); to mark (a stone etc. with writing or letters); to address, to dedicate (as a book to a friend); to enter in or on a book, list, etc., esp. to register the names of shareholders; to issue (loans) with the names of holders so registered; (*Geom.*) to delineate (a figure) within another so that it touches the boundary surfaces of the latter. **inscribable,** *a.* **inscriber,** *n.*

inscription (in skrip' shůn,) *n.* The art or act of inscribing; that which is inscribed, as a dedicatory address, the words on the reverse of some coins and medals, or the titular line or lines of an illustration. **inscriptional, inscriptive,** *a.*

***inscroll** (in skrōl'), *v.t.* To inscribe on a scroll.

inscrutable (in skroo' tǎbl) [F., from late L. *inscrūtābilis* (IN- (2), *scrūtābilis*, from *scrūtārī*, to search)], *a.* Incapable of being penetrated or understood; unfathomable, mysterious. **inscrutability** (-bil' i ti), **inscrutableness,** *n.* **inscrutably,** *adv.*

***insculp** (in skŭlp') [L. *insculpere* (IN- (1), *sculpere*, to carve)], *v.t.* To insculpture; to carve. ***insculpture,** *n.* An engraving, an inscription. *v.t.* To engrave, to inscribe, to carve (upon).

insect (in' sekt) [F. *insecte*, L. *insectum*, neut. p.p. of *insecāre* (IN- (1), *secāre*, to cut)], *n.* One of the *Insecta*, a class of articulate, usually winged, animals, with three pairs of legs, and divided into three distinct segments, the head, thorax, and abdomen (termed in *Am.* 'bug'); used incorrectly of other articulated animals resembling these, as a spider or centipede; (*fig.*) a small or contemptible person or creature. **insect-net,** *n.* A net for catching insects. **insect-powder,** *n.* A powder for destroying insects such as fleas, bugs, etc. **insectarium** (-târ' i ům), **insectary** (in' sėk tǎr i), *n.* A place for keeping or breeding insects. ***insected,** *a.* Segmented like an insect. **insecticide** (in sek' ti sīd) [-CIDE], *n.* A preparation for killing insects. **insecticidal** (-sī' dǎl), *a.* **insectifuge** (in sek' ti fūj) [-FUGE], *n.* A substance for keeping insects away. **insectile** (in sek' til, -tīl), *a.* Of the nature of insects. *n.* An insect. ***Insectivora*** (-tiv' ŏ rǎ) [from L. *insectivorus*, insect-eating, see -VOROUS], *n.pl.* (*Zool.*) An order of mammals containing the moles, shrews, hedgehogs, etc. that feeds on insects. **insectivore** (in sek' ti vôr), *n.* A member of the *Insectivora*. **insectivorous** (-tiv' ŏ růs), *a.* Feeding on insects; belonging to the *Insectivora*. **insectology** (-tol' ŏ ji) [-LOGY], *n.* Entomology, esp. in its economic relations. **insectologist,** *n.*

insection (in sek' shůn), *n.* A cutting in; an incision.

insecure (in sė kūr') [L. *insēcūrus*], *a.* Not secure, not safe; apprehensive of danger; not effectually guarded. **insecurely,** *adv.* **insecurity,** *n.*

inseminate (in sem' i nāt) [L. *insēmināre*, p.p. of *insēmināre* (IN- (1), *sēmināre*, to sow, from *sēmen -minis*, seed)], *v.t.* To sow (in the soil); (*fig.*) to implant (in the mind, etc.). **insemination** (-nā' shůn), *n.* **artificial insemination,** *n.* The introduction into the uterus by artificial means of semen from a selected male [ARTIFICIAL].

insensate (in sen' sāt) [late L. *insensātus*], *a.* Destitute of sense, inanimate or unconscious; wanting in sensibility, unfeeling; (*fig.*) besotted, foolish, mad. **insensately,** *adv.*

insensible (in sen' sibl) [F., from L. *insensibilis*], *a.* That cannot be perceived or felt; imperceptible, inappreciable; destitute of the power of feeling or perceiving, unconscious; unaware; indifferent, heedless (of, how, etc.); not susceptible of feeling, emotion, or passion, callous, apathetic. **insensibility** (-bil' i ti), *n.* Lack of feeling, emotion, or passion; unconsciousness; insusceptibility or indifference (to). **insensibilize,** *v.t.* **insensibilization** (-zā' shůn), *n.* **insensibly,** *adv.* Imperceptibly, gradually.

insensitive (in sen' si tiv), *a.* Not sensitive (to). **insensitiveness,** *n.* **insensuous** (in sen' sū ůs) [IN- (2), SENSUOUS], *a.* Not sensuous.

insentient (in sen' shi ėnt), *a.* Not sentient, inanimate.

inseparable (in sep' ǎr ǎbl) [F., from L. *insēparābilis*], *a.* Incapable of being separated; (*Gram.*) incapable of being employed separately (as the prefixes DIS-, RE-). *n.* (*usu. pl.*) Things which cannot be separated; persons who are constantly together. **inseparable accident:** (*Log.*) An attribute inseparable from its subject. **inseparability** (-bil' i ti), ***inseparableness,** *n.* **inseparably,** *adv.* **inseparate,** *a.* Not separated or disjoined, united; inseparable.

insert (in sĕrt') [L. *insertus*, p.p. of *inserere* (IN- (1), *serere*, to join)], *v.t.* To set or place (in, amongst, etc.); to introduce (in or into). **inserted,** *a.* Placed or set in or upon; (*Bot.*) growing from or upon a part.

insertion (in ser' shun), *n.* The act of inserting; that which is inserted, an intercalation, a passage, etc. introduced (in or into); a band of lace or embroidery inserted in a dress, handkerchief, fancy work, etc.;

(*Anat.*, *Bot.*, *etc.*) the manner in which one part is inserted into or adheres to another.

Insessores (in sė sôr′ ēz) [mod. L., pl. of *insessor*, from *insidēre* (IN- (1), *sedēre*, to sit)], *n.pl.* (*Ornith.*) An order of birds with feet adapted for perching and walking, more generally called *Passeres*. **insessorial,** *a.*

inset (in set′), *v.t.* (*past & p.p.* **inset**) To set or fix (in), to insert (in). *n.* (in′ set) That which is set or fixed in; an insertion, as a piece let into a dress etc., a small map or diagram set within a larger one, a page or number of pages inserted in a book, newspaper, etc.

inseverable (in sev′ ėr ȧbl), *a.* That cannot be severed. **inseverably,** *adv.*

inshore (in shôr′), *a.* or *adv.* On, near, or towards the shore.

inside (in′ sīd), *a.* Situated within; interior, internal, inner. *adv.* (in sīd′) In or into the interior, within. *prep.* (in sīd′) Within, on the inner side of, into. *n.* (in′ sīd) The inner or interior part; the inner side, surface, part, etc. (of); (*Print.*) the side of a sheet containing the second page; the middle part (of); (in sīd′) the contents; the bowels; a passenger travelling inside. **inside of a mile, an hour,** etc.: (*colloq.*) Within or in less than a mile, an hour, etc. **inside information:** Confidential knowledge not generally accessible. **inside out:** Having the inner side turned out and vice versa. **insider** (in sī′ dėr), *n.* One inside; one who belongs to a society, clique, etc.; one who has inside information.

insidious (in sid′ i ŭs) [L. *insidiōsus*, from *insidia*, an ambush, a snare, from *insidēre* (IN- (1), *sedēre*, to sit)], *a.* Lying in wait; treacherous, sly; working secretly or deceptively; intended to deceive or betray. **insidiously,** *adv.* **insidiousness,** *n.*

insight (in′ sīt), *n.* Power of observation or discernment of the real character of things; penetration.

insignia (in sig′ ni ȧ) [L., pl. of *insigne*, remarkable (IN- (1), *signum*, SIGN)], *n.pl.* Badges of office or honour; distinguishing marks or signs (of).

insignificant (in sig nif′ i kȧnt), *a.* Unimportant, trivial; contemptible; without meaning. **insignificance, -cy,** *n.* **insignificantly,** *adv.* ***insignificative,** *a.* Not expressing by external signs.

insincere (in sin sēr′) [L. *insincērus*], *a.* Not sincere; false, dissembling; hypocritical, deceitful. **insincerely,** *adv.* **insincerity** (in sin ser′ i ti), *n.*

***insinew** (in sin′ ū) [IN- (1), SINEW], *v.t.* To strengthen, to invigorate. ***insinewed,** *a.* (*Shak.*) Joined together, allied (?).

insinuate (in sin′ ū āt) [L. *insinuātus*, p.p. of *insinuāre* (IN- (1), *sinuāre*, to wind, from *sinus*, a curve)], *v.t.* To introduce (into favour, office, etc.) by gradual and artful means; to indicate indirectly or obliquely; to hint or suggest by remote allusion. *v.i.* To make way (into) by indirect means; to work into one's affections by artful means. **insinuatingly,** *adv.* **insinuation** (-ā′ shŭn), *n.* The art or power of insinuating; a hint, an indirect suggestion. **insinuative** (in sin′ ū ā tiv, -ȧ tiv), *a.* **insinuator,** *n.*

insipid (in sip′ id) [F. *insipide*, late L. *insipidus* (IN- (2), *sapidus*, well-tasting)], *a.* Tasteless, savourless; wanting in life or animation, dull, vapid. **insipidity** (-pid′ i ti), **insipidness,** *n.* **insipidly,** *adv.*

insist (in sist′) [F. *insister*, L. *insistere* (IN- (1), *sistere*, to set, causal of *stāre*, to stand)], *v.i.* To dwell, to dilate (on); to be emphatic, positive, urgent, or persistent (on or upon). **to insist on:** To demand emphatically; to assert positively. **insistence, -ency,** *n.* **insistent,** *a.* **insistently,** *adv.* ***insisture,** *n.* (*Shak.*) Persistency, constancy, or fixity (?).

insnare [ENSNARE].

insobriety (in sō brī′ ė ti), *n.* Want of sobriety; intemperance (usu. in drinking).

***insolate** (in′ so lāt) [L. *insolātus*, p.p. of *insolāre* (IN- (1), *sol*, sun)], *v.t.* To expose to the sun's rays (for bleaching, etc., or as a form of medical treatment). ***insolation,** *n.* Exposed to the sun; sunstroke.

insole (in′ sōl), *n.* The inner sole of a boot or shoe; a strip of waterproof or other material placed inside a shoe.

insolent (in′ sȯ lėnt) [F., from L. *insolentum*, nom. *-lens* (IN- (2), *solens*, pres.p. of *solēre*, to be wont)], *a.* Showing overbearing contempt; impudent, offensive, insulting. **insolence,** *n.* **insolently,** *adv.*

***insolidity** (in sȯ lid′ i ti), *n.* Want of solidity; flimsiness, weakness.

insoluble (in sol′ ūbl) [F., from L. *insolūbilis*], *a.* That cannot be dissolved; that cannot be solved; inexplicable. **insolubility** (-bil′ i ti), **insolubleness,** *n.* **insolubly,** *adv.*

insolvable (in sol′ vȧbl), *a.* That cannot be solved or explained, insoluble; that cannot be dissolved; that cannot be paid, discharged, or cashed.

insolvent (in sol′ vėnt), *a.* Not able to discharge all debts or liabilities; pertaining to insolvents. *n.* A debtor unable to pay his debts. **insolvency,** *n.*

insomnia (in som′ ni ȧ) [L., from *insomnis*, sleepless (IN- (2), *somnis*, sleep)], *n.* Sleeplessness ***insomnious,** *a.* ***insomnolence, -ency,** *n.*

insomuch (in sȯ mŭch′), *adv.* So, to such a degree, in such wise (that).

insouciant (in soo′ si ȧnt, an su syan) [F. (IN- (2), *souciant*, caring, from *soucier*, L. *sollicitāre*, to make anxious)], *a.* Careless, unconcerned. **insouciance,** *n.*

inspan (in spăn′) [Dut. *inspannen* (IN, SPAN (1))], *v.t.* (*S. Afr.*) To yoke (horses, oxen, etc.) to a wagon, etc.; to harness draught animals to (a wagon). *v.i.* To harness or yoke up draught animals.

inspect (in spekt′) [L. *inspectāre*, freq. of *inspicere* (IN- (1), *specere*, to look)], *v.t.* To look closely into, to view and examine officially. **v.i.* To inquire (into or among). **inspectingly,** *adv.*

inspection (in spek′ shŭn), *n.* The act of inspecting; a careful, narrow, or critical examination or survey; an official examination. ***inspective,** *a.*

inspector (in spek′ tȯr), *n.* One who inspects; an overseer, a superintendent; a police officer usu. ranking next below a superintendent. **inspectoral, inspectorial** (-tôr′ i ȧl), *a.* **inspectorate, inspectorship,** *n.* **inspectress,** *n.*

inspiration (in spi rā′ shŭn). The act of drawing air into the lungs; act of inspiring, breathing in, or infusing feelings, ideas, etc.; (*Theol.*) supernatural influence, esp. that exerted by the Holy Spirit on certain teachers and writers so as to impart a certain divine element to their utterances; the feeling, ideas, or other influences imparted by or as by divine agency; an inspiring idea. **inspirational,** *a.* **inspirationist,** *n.* One who holds that every word of the Bible is inspired. **inspirationism,** *n.*

inspirator (in′ spī rā tȯr), *n.* A device or apparatus for drawing in air, steam, etc., a variety of injector for steam-boilers; a kind of respirator. **inspiratory** (in spīr′ ȧ tȯr i), *a.* Pertaining to inspiration; aiding in the process of inspiration.

inspire (in spīr′) [O.F. *enspirer*, L. *inspirāre* (IN- (1), *spirāre*, to breathe)], *v.t.* To breathe or take (air) into the lungs, to breathe into; to instil or infuse (ideas, feelings, etc.) into, esp. by or as by supernatural agency; to imbue or animate (with); to infuse or instil (as emotion in or into); to convey privately suggestions or material for (an article on Government affairs, etc.). *v.i.* To take air into the lungs. **inspirable,** *a.* **inspired,** *a.* Inhaled; infused; imparted, actuated or produced by or as by supernatural agency. **inspirer,** *n.* **inspiringly,** *adv.*

inspirit (in spir′ it), *v.t.* To infuse spirit, life, or animation into; to inspire, to encourage (to action or to do). **inspiriting,** *a.*

inspissate (in spis'-, in' spi sāt) [late L. *inspissātus,* p.p. of *inspissāre* (IN- (1), *spissus,* thick)], *v.t.* To thicken, to render more dense, to bring to a greater consistence by boiling or evaporation. *a.* (-sât) Thickened, rendered more dense. **inspissation** (-sā' shŭn), *n.*

instability (in stȧ bil' i ti) [F. *instabilité,* L. *instābilitātem,* nom. *-tas*], *n.* Want of stability or firmness; inconstancy, inconsistency of purpose; (*Aviat.*) the tendency of an aeroplane to depart involuntarily from the set line of flight.

***instable** [UNSTABLE].

install (in stawl') [F. *installer,* low L. *installāre* (IN- (1), *stallum,* STALL)], *v.t.* To induct or invest by placing (in an office, charge, or dignity) with customary ceremonies; to set or establish in an office, etc.; to put (apparatus, etc.) in position for use. **installation** (in stȧ lā' shŭn), ***instalment** (1) (-stawl' mênt), *n.* The act of installing; a complete plant or set of apparatus, machinery, etc.

instalment (2) (in stawl' mênt) [perh. from an obs. verb *install,* to arrange or fix, as a payment, -MENT (O.E.D.)], *n.* A part of a debt or sum due paid at successive periods; a part (of anything) supplied at different times; part of a serial story, etc. **instalment plan:** (*Am.*) The hire-purchase system.

instance (in' stȧns) [F., from L. *instantia,* as foll.], *n.* An example, illustrative case, or precedent; solicitation or asking; suggestion, prompting; (*Law*) a process or suit; *a cause, a motive; *a proof; *presence, present time. *v.t.* To bring forward as an instance or example. **at the instance of:** At the suggestion or desire of. **for instance:** For example. **in the first instance:** At the first stage, in the first place. **instancy,** *n.* Urgency.

instant (in' stȧnt) [F., from L. *instantem,* nom. *-stans* (IN- (1), *stāre,* to stand)], *a.* Pressing, urgent, importunate, immediate; present, current, still going on, of the current month. *n.* A particular point of time; a moment, a very brief space of time; *instance; *a pressing application. *adv.* (*poet.*) Quickly, without delay. **instantly,** *adv.* Immediately; without delay.

instantaneous (in stȧn tā' ni ŭs), *a.* Happening or done in an instant; (*Dynam.*) relating to a particular instant. **instantaneously,** *adv.* **instantaneity** (in stăn tȧ nē' i ti), **instantaneousness,** *n.*

instanter (in stăn' tėr), L. *adv.* At once, immediately.

instar (1) (in' star) [L., resemblance, form], *n.* (*Zool.*) A stage in development; the form of an insect or other arthropod after each successive stage.

instate (in stāt'), *v.t.* To put in a certain place, office, condition, etc., to install; *to invest.

***instauration** (in staw rā' shŭn) [L. *instaurātio,* from *instaurāre* (IN- (1), *-staurāre,* see RESTORE)], *n.* Renewal, restoration. **instaurator** (in' staw rā tôr), *n.*

instead (in sted'), *adv.* In the place, stead, or room of; as an alternative or substitute.

instep (in' step) [IN, STEP, or perh. STOOP, bend], *n.* The arched upper side of the human foot, near the ankle; the part of a shoe, stocking, etc., corresponding to this; the front part of the hind leg of a horse reaching from the ham to the pastern-joint; (*fig.*) anything shaped like a human instep.

instigate (in' sti gāt) [L. *instigātus,* p.p. of *instigāre* (IN- (1), *stig-,* cp. Gr. *stig-,* root of *stizein,* to prick)], *v.t.* To incite, to urge on (to an action or to do); to provoke or bring about (an action, esp. of an evil kind). **instigation** (-gā' shŭn), *n.* **instigator** (in' sti gā tôr), *n.*

instil (in stil') [F. *instiller,* L. *instillāre* (IN- (1), *stillāre,* to drop)], *v.t.* To pour by drops (into); (*fig.*) to infuse slowly and gradually (into the mind of a person). **instillation** (-lā' shŭn), **instilment,** *n.* **instillator** (in' sti lā tôr), *n.*

instinct (in' stingkt) [through F. *instinct* or directly from L. *instinctus,* from *instinguere,* as INSTIGATE], *n.* A natural impulse, esp. in the lower animals, leading them without reasoning or conscious design to perform certain actions tending to the welfare of the individual or the perpetuation of the species; an innate or intuitive impulse, tendency, or aptitude; intuition, unreasoning perception of rightness, beauty, etc. *a.* (in stingkt') Animated or impelled from within; moved or imbued (with). **instinctive,** *a.* Prompted by instinct; spontaneous, impulsive. **instinctively,** *adv.*

instipulate (in stip' ū lȧt), *a.* (*Bot.*) Destitute of stipules.

institor (in' sti tôr) [L., from *insistere,* to INSIST], *n.* (*Law, esp. Sc.*) An agent, a factor. **institorial** (-tôr i ȧl), *a.*

institute (in' sti tūt) [L. *institūtus,* p.p. of *instituere* (IN- (1), *statuere,* to place, from *status,* see STATUS)], *v.t.* To set up, to establish, to originate, to set in operation, to start, to begin; to nominate, to appoint (to or into), esp. to invest with the spiritual part of a benefice. *n.* A society established for the promotion or furtherance of some particular object (usu. literary or scientific); the building in which such a society meets; an established law, precept, or principle; (*pl.*) a book of elements or principles, esp. of jurisprudence or medicine.

institution (in sti tū' shŭn), *n.* The act of instituting; that which is instituted; an established order, law, regulation, or custom; a society or association for the promotion of some particular object; the building in which such a society meets; building for the recipients of indoor public relief, workhouse, orphanage, etc.; the act or ceremony of investing a clergyman with the spiritual part of a benefice; (*colloq.*) a familiar custom, person, etc. **institutional,** *a.* Pertaining to an institution; (*Relig.*) organized churches, etc., finding expression in this. **institutionalism,** *n.* **institutionalist,** *n.* **institutional religion,** *n.* The form of religion that expresses itself through ritual and church services. **institutionalize,** *v.t.* To make an institution of; to confine to an institution.

instreaming (in' strē ming), *n.* A streaming or flowing in, an influx.

instruct (in strŭkt') [L. *instructus,* p.p. of *instruere* (IN- (1), *struere,* to pile up)], *v.t.* To teach, to educate (in a subject); to inform; to furnish with orders or directions; to supply (a solicitor, counsel, etc.) with information relating to a cause. ***instructible,** *a.* **instruction** (in strŭk' shŭn), *n.* The act of instructing; teaching, education; (*pl.*) directions, orders, injunctions; (*Law*) directions to a solicitor, counsel, etc. **instructional,** *a.* **instructive,** *a.* Conveying instruction. **instructively,** *adv.* **instructiveness,** *n.* **instructor, instructress,** *n.*

instrument (in' strŭ mênt) [F., from L. *instrūmentum,* from *instruere,* see prec.], *n.* That by means of which work is done or any object or purpose effected; a tool, a mechanical implement, esp. one for scientific and other delicate operations; a mechanical contrivance for producing musical sound; (*Law*) a document giving formal expression to an act; (*fig.*) an agent, a person used as a means by another. *v.t.* (*Mus.*) To arrange (music) for instruments. **stringed instrument:** A musical instrument in which sounds are generated by the vibration of strings. **wind instrument:** One in which the agency is a column of air vibrating in a tube.

instrumental (in strŭ men' tȧl), *a.* Serving as instrument or means (to some end or in some act); pertaining or due to the instrument used (of errors, etc.); (*Mus.*) pertaining to or produced by musical instruments; (*Gram.*) denoting the means or instrument as certain cases in Sanskrit, etc. **instrumentalist,** *n.* (*Mus.*) One who plays an instrument. **instrumentality** (-tăl′ i ti), *n.* **instrumentally,** *adv.*

instrumentation (in strū men tā′ shŭn), *n.* The arrangement of music for several instruments in combination; the art or manner of using an instrument or instruments; instrumentality.

insubordinate (in sŭ bôr′ di nȧt), *a* Not submissive to authority; disobedient, disorderly. **insubordination** (-nā′ shŭn), *n.*

insubstantial (in sŭb stăn′ shȧl) [late L. *insubstantiālis*], *a.* Unsubstantial, unreal. **insubstantiality** (-shi ăl′ i ti), *n.* **insubstantiate,** *v.t.* **insubstantiation** (-ā′ shŭn), *n.*

insufferable (in sŭf′ ėr ȧbl), *a.* Not to be borne or endured; detestable, intolerable. **insufferably,** *adv.*

insufficient (in sŭ fish′ ėnt) [O.F., from L. *insufficientem*, nom. *-ens*], *a.* Not sufficient; deficient, inadequate. **insufficiency, *-cience,** *n.* **insufficiently,** *adv.*

insufflate (in′ sŭ flāt) [L. *insufflātus*, p.p. of *insufflāre* (IN- (1), SUF-, *flāre*, to blow)], *v.t.* (*Med.*) To blow or breathe (air, vapour, powder, etc.) into an opening, cavity, etc.; to treat (a person, organ, etc.) by insufflation. **insufflator,** *n.* An instrument used for this purpose. **insufflation** (-flā′ shŭn), *n.* The act of blowing or breathing upon or into; (*Med.*) blowing or breathing (therapeutic vapour, etc.) into the lungs, etc.; (*Eccles.*) a symbolic breathing upon a person.

insular (in′ sū lȧr) [L. *insulāris*, from *insula*, island], *a.* Pertaining to or of the nature of an island; pertaining to or like the inhabitants of an island; narrow, contracted (in outlook). **insularism, insularity** (-lăr′ i ti), *n.* **insularly,** *adv.*

insulate (in′ sū lāt) [L. *insulātus*, made like an island, as prec.], *v.t.* To make into an island; to place in a detached situation or position; to isolate; (*Phys.*) to separate from other bodies by a non-conductor, so as to prevent the passage of electricity or heat. **insulation** (-lā′ shŭn), *n.* **insulator** (in′ sū lā tŏr), *n.*

insulin (in′ sū lin) [L. *insula*, an island], *n.* (*Med.*) An extract obtained from the pancreas of sheep which regulates the metabolism of sugar and fat and is employed in the treatment of diabetes.

insult (in sŭlt′) [F. *insulter*, L. *insultāre*, freq. of *insilīre* (IN- (1), *salīre*, to leap)], *v.t.* To treat with gross indignity, insolence, or contempt; to affront; *to assail. *v.i.* To use insults; to glory, to triumph (over); *to make an attack (upon). *n.* (in′-) An affront, an indignity; an insulting act or speech; *an attack, an assault. **insultable** (in sŭl′ tȧbl), *a.* ***insultant,** *a.* **insulter,** *n.* **insultingly,** *adv.* ***insultment,** *n.*

insuperable (in sū′ pėr ȧbl) [F., from L. *superābilis*], *a.* Insurmountable, invincible; *unsurpassable. **insuperability** (-bil′ i ti), *n.* **insuperably,** *adv.*

insupportable (in sŭ pôr′ tȧbl), *a.* Insufferable, intolerable; *irresistible. ***insupportableness,** *n.* **insupportably,** *adv.*

insuppressible (in sŭ pres′ ibl), *a.* That cannot be suppressed. ***insuppressive,** *a.*

insurance (in shoor′ ȧns), *n.* The act of insuring against damage or loss; a contract by which a company, in consideration of a sum of money, becomes bound to indemnify the insured against loss by fire, shipwreck, etc.; the sum so insured; the premium so paid. **insurance company:** A company which insures persons against loss or damage. **insurance policy** [POLICY (2)].

insure (1) (in shoor′) [var. of ENSURE], *v.t.* To secure compensation, whole or partial, for loss or injury of (property, life, etc.) by paying a periodical premium; to secure the payment of (a specified sum) in the event of loss, injury, etc. (said of the owner or the insurance company). *v.i.* To take out an insurance policy. **the insured:** The person to whom compensation for fire, etc. will be paid; the person whose life is insured. **insurable,** *a.*

insure (2) [ENSURE].

insurgent (in sėr′ jėnt) [L. *insurgens*, *-ntem*, pres.p. of *insurgere* (IN- (1), *surgere*, to rise)], *a.* Rising up against the constituted government, rebellious; (of waves) surging or rushing in. *n.* One who rises up against established government or authority; a rebel. **insurgence, -gency,** *n.*

insurmountable (in sŭr moun′ tȧbl), *a.* That cannot be surmounted, passed over, or overcome. **insurmountability,** *n.* **insurmountably,** *adv.*

insurrection (in sŭ rek′ shŭn) [F., from L. *insurrectiōnem*, nom. *-tio*, from *insurgere*, see INSURGENT], *n.* The act of rising in open opposition to established authority; uprising, rebellion in the initial stage. **insurrectional, -tionary,** *a.* **insurrectionist,** *n.*

insusceptible (in sŭ sep′ tibl), *a.* Not susceptible (of); incapable of being moved by any feeling or impression. **insusceptibility** (in sŭ sep ti bil′ i ti), *n.* ***insusceptive,** *a.*

intact (in tăkt′) [L. *intactus* (IN- (2), *tactus*, p.p. of *tangere*, to touch)], *a.* Untouched; unimpaired, uninjured; entire. **intactness,** *n.*

intaglio (in ta′ lyo) [It., from *intagliare*, to cut, to engrave, late L. *intaleāre*, to cut, from *talea*, a twig], *n.* (*pl.* **-lios**) A figure cut or engraved in a hard substance; a gem with a figure cut or engraved into it; (*Am.*) a rotogravure. *v.t.* To cut or engrave in this manner. **intagliated,** *a.* Carved or engraved on a hard surface.

intail [ENTAIL].

intake (in′ tāk), *n.* That which is taken in; the point where a tube or woven article narrows; a place where water is taken in, an inlet; an air-shaft in a mine; land enclosed, esp. a tract taken in from a moorland and cultivated.

intangible (in tăn′ jibl) [med. L. *intangibilis*], *a.* Not tangible; imperceptible to the touch, impalpable; (*fig.*) not to be grasped mentally; unfounded. **intangibility** (-bil′ i ti), *n.* **intangibly,** *adv.*

integer (in′ tė jėr) [L. (IN- (2), *tag-*, root of *tangere*, to touch)], *n.* The whole of anything; a whole number as distinguished from a fraction.

integrable (in tė grȧbl), *a.* Capable of being integrated.

integral (in′ tė grȧl) [INTEGER], *a.* Whole, entire, complete; necessary to completeness, an essential part of a whole; (*Math.*) pertaining to or constituting an integer; pertaining to or produced by integration. *n.* (*Math.*) The limit of the sum of a series of values of a differential $f(x)\,dx$ when x varies by indefinitely small increments from one given value to another [cp. DIFFERENTIAL]; a whole, a total, an integer; *an integral part. **integral calculus:** A method of summing up differential quantities. **integrality** (-grăl′ i ti), *n.* **integrally,** *adv.*

integrand (in′ te grănd), *n.* (*Math.*) An expression to be integrated.

integrant (in′ te grȧnt), *a.* Making part of a whole; necessary to constitute an entire entity. **integrant parts:** Parts into which a body may be reduced, each remaining of the same nature as the whole.

integrate (in′ tė grāt) [INTEGER], *v.t.* To make into a whole, to complete by addition of the parts; to combine into a whole; to indicate the whole or mean value of; (*Math.*) to find the integral of. *a.* (-grȧt) Made up of integrant parts; whole, entire, complete.

integration (in te grā′ shŭn), *n.* The making into a whole; the unification of all elements in a society, esp. of white and coloured in U.S.A.

integrator (in′ te grā tŏr), *n.* One who or that which integrates; a device or instrument for determining the value of an integral, as an area, rate of speed etc.

integrity (in teg′ ri ti) [F. *integrité*, from L. *integritātem*, wholeness, nom. *-tas*, from prec.], *n*

Entireness, completeness; soundness; genuine, unadulterated state; probity, rectitude, high principle.

integument (in teg′ ū ment) [L. *integumentum*, from *integere* (IN- (1), *tegere*, to cover)], *n.* A covering, esp. a natural one; the skin; (*Bot.*) the outer covering of a seed, the husk, rind, etc. **integumentary** (-men′ tȧr i), *a.*

intellect (in′ tė lekt) [L. *intellectus*, as INTELLIGENT], The faculty of the human mind by which it receives and comprehends, as distinguished from the faculty of feeling and willing; the understanding; (*fig.*) the philosophic mind; intellectual people collectively; *(*pl.*) wits, senses; *meaning, purport. **intellection** (-lek′ shŭn), *n.* The act or process of understanding or comprehending, esp. as dist. from sensation or imagination. **intellective,** *a.* Pertaining to or produced by the intellect; having power to understand. ***intellectively,** *adv.*

intellectual (in te lek′ tū ȧl), *a.* Possessing intellect in a high degree; pertaining to or performed by the intellect; appealing to or perceived by the intellect. *n.* An intellectual person; (*pl.*) the most enlightened people (in a country, etc.). **intellectualism,** *n.* The cultivation of the intellect; the doctrine that knowledge is exclusively or principally derived from pure reason. **intellectualist,** *n.* **intellectuality** (-ăl′ i ti), *n.* **intellectualize** *v.t.* To make intellectual; to treat intellectually; to give an intellectual character or significance to. *v.i.* To become intellectual; to employ the intellect. **intellectualization** (-lī zā′ shŭn), *n.* **intellectually,** *adv.*

intelligence (in tel′ i jėns) [F., from L. *intelligentia*, as foll.], *n.* The exercise of the understanding; intellectual power; capacity for the higher functions of the intellect; acquired knowledge; quickness or sharpness of intellect; news, information, notice, notification; an intelligent being, esp. an incorporeal or spiritual being regarded as pure intellect. **intelligence department:** (*Mil.*) A department for supplying an officer in command with all necessary intelligence, signalling, etc. **intelligence office:** An office where information may be obtained, esp. (*Am.*) with reference to servants. **intelligence quotient** (I.Q.): A number denoting a person's intelligence by dividing his mental age by his age in years. **intelligence test:** A psychological test to determine a person's relative mental capacity. **intelligential** (-jen′ shȧl), *a.* **intelligencer** (in tel′ i jėn sėr), *n.* One who conveys intelligence; a messenger, a spy.

intelligent (in tel′ i jėnt) [L. *intelligens -ntem*, pres. p. of *intelligere*, to understand (INTER-, *legere*, to gather, to choose)], *a.* Endowed with understanding; sagacious, sensible, clever, quick. **intelligently,** *adv.* **intelligential** [INTELLIGENCE]. **intelligentzia** (in tel i jen′ si ȧ), *n.* (*usu. iron.*) People who claim or assume special enlightenment or culture.

intelligible (in tel′ i jibl) [F., from L. *intelligibilis*, as prec.], *a.* Capable of being understood, comprehensible; plain, clear; (*Metaph.*) apprehensible only by the intellect, dist. from sensible. **intelligibility** (-bil′ i ti), ***intelligibleness,** *n.* **intelligibly,** *adv.*

intemperate (in tem′ pėr ȧt) [L. *intemperātus*], *a.* Not exercising due moderation or self-restraint; indulging any appetite or passion in excess; addicted to excessive indulgence in alcoholic liquors; immoderate, excessive, exceeding proper bounds; violent, inclement. **intemperance,** *n.* Want of moderation or self-restraint, esp. excessive indulgence in alcoholic liquors. **intemperately,** *adv.* ***intemperateness,** *n.*

***intempestive** (in tem pes′ tiv) [L. *intempestīvus* (IN- (2), *tempestīvus*, from *tempus*, time, season)], *a.* Unseasonable.

intend (in tend′) [F. *entendre*, L. *intendere*, to stretch to, to direct (IN- (1), *tendere*, to stretch, see TEND (1))], *v.t.* To design, to purpose; to signify, to mean; to design (for); to destine (for); to mean, to have a certain intention; *to extend; *to bend, to direct (one's course etc.); *to intensify; to look after, to superintend. *v.i.* *To direct one's course, to proceed (towards, for, etc.); *to start (for, etc.); *to attend. **intendant,** *n.* A superintendent or manager. **intendancy,** *n.* **intended,** *n.* (*colloq.*) An affianced lover. **intendedly,** *adv.* ***intender,** *n.* ***intendiment,** *n.* Attention, consideration; intendment, knowledge, skill. **intendment,** *n.* (*Law*) True intent or meaning as determined by the law; *intention, purpose.

***intenerate** (in ten′ ėr āt) [IN- (1), L. *tener*, tender, -ATE], *v.t.* To make tender, to soften.

***intenible** (in ten′ ibl), *a.* (*Shak.*) Incapable of holding or containing.

intense (in tens′) [F., from L. *intensus*, p.p. of *intendere*, to INTEND], *a.* Raised to a high pitch; strained, forced; violent, vehement; extreme in degree; severe, immoderate, excessive; ardent, eager, fervent; strongly or deeply emotional. ***intensate,** *v.t.* To intensify. **intensative** [INTENSIVE], **intensely,** *adv.* **intenseness,** *n.*

intensify (in ten′ si fī), *v.t.* To render more intense; (*Phot.*) to increase the density of (a negative) so as to produce stronger contrasts. *v.i.* To become more intense. **intensifier,** *n.*

intension (in ten′ shŭn), *n.* The act of straining or stretching; the state of being strained or stretched; tension; intense exertion or concentration (of will etc.); intensity, high degree (of a quality), as dist. from extension; (*Log.*) the content of a notion. **intensity** (-ten′ si ti), *n.*

intensive (in ten′ siv), *a.* Admitting of intension; concentrated, thorough, as opp. to extensive; (*Econ.*) conducive to high productiveness within a narrow area; (*Path.*) pertaining to methods (of inoculation etc.) in which injections, doses, etc., are successively increased; (*Gram.*) serving to intensify, or to add force or emphasis. *n.* An intensive particle, word, or phrase. **intensive cultivation,** *n.* (*Agric.*) The system whereby land is kept under cultivation by a rotation of crops and manuring. **intensively,** *adv.*

intent (1) (in tent′) [L. *intentus*, p.p. of *intendere*, to INTEND], *a.* Having the mind bent or strained on an object; sedulously applied (on); fixed, resolved, earnest.

intent (2) (in tent′) [O.F. *entent*, *entente*, intention, meaning, L. *intentus*, a stretching out, late L., intention, from *intendere*, to INTEND], *n.* Design, purpose, intention; meaning, drift. **to all intents and purposes:** Practically, really, in reality. **to the intent that:** In order that.

intention (in ten′ shŭn), *n.* Determination to act in some particular manner; purpose, design, intent; (*pl.*, *colloq.*) designs with regard to marriage; (*Log.*) a general concept; (*R.-C. Ch.*) special purpose to perform any act of devotion with a particular object in view; ultimate aim or object; (*Med.*) a process of healing wounds. **first intentions:** (*Log.*) Primary conceptions formed by the application of the mind to the objects themselves. **second intentions:** Secondary conceptions formed by the action of the mind upon first intentions and their inter-relations. **to heal by first intention:** (*Med.*) To cicatrize without suppuration. **to heal by second intention:** To unite by granulation after suppuration. **intentional,** *a.* Done with design or purpose. **intentionally,** *adv.* **intentioned,** *a.* (*chiefly in comb.*, as *well-intentioned*). ***intentive,** *a.* Attentive; intent. ***intentively,** *adv.* ***intentiveness,** *n.* **intently,** *adv.* **intentness,** *n.*

inter (in tėr′) [O.F. *interrer*, late L. *interrāre* (IN- (1), *terra*, earth)], *v.t.* (*past & p.p.* **interred**) To bury; to place in a grave or tomb; (*fig.*) to put out of sight. **interment,** *n.*

inter- [L.], *pref.* Between, among; with, into or upon each other; as *intercede*, *intercostal*, *international*, *interstellar*, *intertexture*, *interwoven*.

interact (1) (in tėr ăkt'), *v.i.* To act reciprocally; to act on each other. **interaction,** *n.* **interactionism,** *n.* The theory that mind and body interact, opp. to automatism and phenomenal parallelism. **interactionist,** *n.* **interactive,** *a.*

interact (2) (in' tėr ăkt), *n.* (*Theat.*) The interval between two acts of a play; an interlude.

interbed (in tėr bed'), *v.t.* (*Geol.*) To interstratify.

interblend (in tėr blend'), *v.t.* To mingle with one another; *v.i.* To blend together.

interbreed (in tėr brēd'), *v.t.* To breed by crossing different sub-varieties or species of animals or plants. *v.i.* To breed together.

intercalary, intercalar (in tĕr' kȧ lȧr i, -lȧr) [L. *intercalārius*, from *intercalāre* (INTER-, *calāre*, to proclaim), p.p. *intercalātus*], *a.* Inserted between or amongst others, as a day inserted in the calendar to make this correspond with the solar year; containing such an addition (of a year); inserted, interpolated. **intercalate,** *v.t.* To insert between or amongst others (esp. a day, etc. into a calendar); to interpolate, to insert anything in an unusual or irregular way. **intercalation** (-lā' shŭn), *n.* **intercalative,** *a.*

intercede (in tėr sēd') [F. *intercéder*, L. *intercēdere* (INTER-, *cēdere*, to go), p.p. *intercessus*], *v.i.* To plead (with someone) in favour of another; to mediate; *to intervene. ***intercedent,** *a.* **interceder,** *n.*

intercellular (in tėr sel' ū lȧr), *a.* (*Biol., etc.*) Situated between or among cells.

intercensal (in tėr sen' sȧl), *a.* Pertaining to the interval between two censuses.

intercept (in tėr sept') [L. *interceptus*, p.p. of *intercipere* (INTER-, *capere*, to take)], *v.t.* To stop, take, or seize by the way or in passage; to obstruct, to stop, to shut off; (*Math.*) to mark off or include between two points etc. **interception** (-sep' shŭn), *n.* **interceptive,** *a.* **interceptor,** *n.* Person or thing that intercepts; (*Aviat.*) a swift aeroplane for purposes of pursuit.

intercerebral (in tėr ser' ė brȧl), *a.* (*Anat.*) Connecting two parts of the brain.

intercession (in tėr sesh' ŭn) [L. *intercessio*, see INTERCEDE], *n.* The act of interceding; a prayer offered for others. **intercessional,** *a.*

intercessor (in ter ses' ŏr), *n.* One who intercedes; a mediator; (*Eccles.*) one who administered a bishopric during the vacancy of a see. ***intercessorial** (-sôr' i ȧl), **intercessory** (-ses' ŏ ri), *a.*

interchange (in tėr chānj') [O.F. *entre-changier* (INTER-, *changier*, to CHANGE)], *v.t.* To exchange with each other, to give and take; to put each (of two things) in the place of the other, to cause to alternate. *v.i.* To alternate. *n.* Reciprocal exchange; alternate succession, alternation. **interchangeable,** *a.* **interchangeability** (-bil' i ti), **interchangeableness,** *n.* **interchangeably,** *adv.* ***interchangement,** *n.* **interchanger,** *n.*

intercilium (in tėr sil' i ŭm) [INTER-, L. *cilium*, eyelid], *n.* (*Anat.*) The part between the eyebrows.

intercipient (in tėr sip' i ėnt) [L. *intercipiens -ntem*, pres.p. of *intercipere*, to INTERCEPT], *a.* Intercepting. **n.* One who or that which intercepts.

intercitizenship (in tėr cit' i zėn ship), *n.* (*U.S.A.*) The right to citizenship in any State. **intercity,** *a.* Existing or carried on between different cities.

interclavicle (in tėr klăv' ikl), *n.* (*Anat.*) A median bony plate attached to the clavicles, in many reptiles. **interclavicular** (-klȧ vik' ū lȧr), *a.*

intercollegiate (in tėr kȯ lē' ji ȧt), *a.* Existing or carried on between colleges.

intercolline (in tėr kol' īn) [INTER-, L. *collīnus*, from *collis*, hill], *a.* (*Geol.*) Lying between hills formed of volcanic matter.

intercolonial (in tėr kȯ lō' ni ȧl), *a.* Existing or carried on between colonies.

intercolumnar (in tėr kȯ lŭm' nȧr), *a.* (*Arch.*) Placed between columns; (*Anat.*) situated between the columns of the external abdominal ring. **intercolumniation** (-ȧ' shŭn), *n.* (*Arch.*) The spacing of columns in a building; the interval between two columns.

intercom (in' tĕr com), *n.* System of intercommunication in aircraft, etc.

***intercommune** (in tėr kȯ mūn'), *v.i.* To have mutual intercourse or communion (with); *(*Sc. Hist.*) to have intercourse with rebels. **letters of intercommuning:** (*Sc. Hist.*) Writs issued by the Scottish Privy Council forbidding anyone to harbour or communicate with persons therein denounced. **intercommunion,** *n.* (*Eccles.*) The partaking of communion in common between members of different Churches or sects.

intercommunicate (in tėr kȯ mū' ni kāt), *v.i.* To hold or enjoy mutual communication; to have free passage to and from each other. *v.t.* To give or communicate mutually. **intercommunicable,** *a.* **intercommunication** (-kā' shŭn), *n.* **intercommunion** [INTERCOMMUNE].

intercommunity (in tėr kȯ mū' ni ti), *n.* The quality of being common to various persons or of holding things in common.

intercomparison (in tėr kŏm păr' i sŏn), *n.* Mutual comparison.

interconnect (in tėr kȯ nekt'), *v.i.* To connect (with) by links or parts acting reciprocally.

intercontinental (in tėr kon ti nen' tȧl), *a.* Existing between or connecting different continents or persons belonging thereto.

interconvertible (in tėr kŏn vĕr' tibl), *a.* Convertible into each other.

intercostal (in tėr kos' tȧl), *a.* (*Anat.*) Situated between the ribs; (*Shipbuilding*) between the framework of the keel. *n.pl.* (*Anat.*) The intercostal muscles; (*Shipbuilding*) the parts between the frames.

intercourse (in' tėr kôrs) [O.F. *entrecours*, late L. *intercursus*, commerce, L., intervention (INTER-, COURSE)], *n.* Reciprocal dealings, association, communication, etc., between persons, nations, etc.; spiritual communion; copulation.

intercrop (in' tėr krop), *n.* A crop raised between the rows of another crop; a quickly-maturing crop between crops grown in a regular series. *v.t.* To raise (a crop) in this way. *v.i.* To plant intercrops.

intercross (in' tėr kros), *v.t.* To cross each other; to cause to interbreed. *v.i.* To interbreed. *n.* An instance of cross-breeding.

intercurrent (in tėr kŭr' ėnt) [L. *intercurrens -ntem*, pres.p. of *intercurrere* (INTER-, *currere*, to run)], *a.* Occurring between or among; intervening; (*Path.*) occurring during the progress of another disease, occurring at different seasons. **intercurrence,** *n.*

interdeal (in tėr dēl') [INTER-, DEAL (1)], *v.i.* (*past & p.p.* **interdealt**) To have reciprocal dealings (with). **n.* Mutual dealing, traffic.

interdenominational (in tėr dė nom i nā' shȧ nȧl) [INTER-, DENOMINATIONAL], *a.* Existing or carried on between different denominations.

interdental (in tėr den' tȧl) [INTER-, DENTAL], *a.* Situated between teeth (of an animal or a machine); (*Phon.*) sounded between the teeth.

interdepend (in tėr dė pend') [INTER-, DEPEND], *v.i.* To depend upon each other. **interdependent,** *a.* **interdependence,** *n.* **interdependently,** *adv.*

interdict (in' tėr dikt) [L. *interdictum*, a decree, from *interdictus*, p.p. of *interdīcere*, to interpose, to forbid by a decree (INTER-, *dīcere*, to say)], *n.* A prohibitory decree; (*Rom. Law*) a decree of the prætor pronounced between two litigants, sometimes enjoining, but more frequently forbidding something to be done; (*Sc. Law*) an order of the Court of Session equivalent to an injunction; (*R.-C. Ch.*) a sentence by which places or persons are debarred from ecclesiastical functions and privileges. *v.t.* (in tėr dikt') To forbid, to prohibit;

to restrain (from); (*R.-C. Ch.*) to lay under an interdict. **interdiction,** *n.* **interdictory,** *a.*

interdigital (in tėr dij' i tȧl) [L. *interdigitālis* (INTER-, *digitus*, finger, see DIGIT)], *a.* (*Anat. and Zool.*) Situated between the fingers. **interdigitate** (-tāt), *v.t.* (*Anat.*) To insert between the fingers; to interlock. *v.i.* To interlock, as when the fingers of one hand are inserted between those of the other.

interest (1) (in' tėr ėst) [earlier *interess*, altered after O.F. *interest* (F. *intérêt*), L. *interesse*, to concern (INTER-, *esse*, to be)], *n.* Lively, sympathetic, or curious attention; personal concern, sympathy; participation in advantages, benefits, or profits; (*pl.*) benefit, advantage, behoof; proprietary right or concern, a share, a portion or stake (in); (*collect.*) those having a concern in a particular business etc.; influence with or over others; payment for the use of borrowed money or on a debt. **compound interest** [COMPOUND]. **simple interest** [SIMPLE]. **to make interest with:** To bring personal influence to bear upon (for the sake of another). **to take an interest in:** To pay sympathetic or curious attention to.

interest (2) (in' tėr ėst) [earlier *interess* (influ. by prec. or formed from the p.p. *interess'd*), as prec.], *v.t.* To arouse or hold the attention or curiosity of; to concern; to cause to participate or take a share (in). **interested** (in' tėr ės tėd), *a.* Having the interest excited; concerned (in); having an interest, concern, or share in; liable to be biased through personal interest, not disinterested. **interestedly,** *adv.* **interesting,** *a.* Arousing interest, attention, or curiosity. **to be in an interesting condition:** To be pregnant. **interestingly,** *adv.*

interface (in' tėr fās) [INTER-, FACE], *n.* (*Geom. and Cryst.*) A surface lying between two spaces. **interfacial** (-fā' shȧl), *a.* Included between two faces of a crystal etc.

interfemoral (in tėr fem' ŏr ȧl), *a.* (*Anat.*) Situated or extending between the thighs.

interfere (in tėr fēr') [O.F. *entreferir* (INTER-, *ferir*, L. *ferīre*, to strike), to exchange blows], *v.i.* To come into collision, to clash (with); to intermeddle (with); to interpose, to intervene (in); (*Phys.*) to act reciprocally, to modify each other; to strike the hoof against the opposite fetlock (of a horse). **interference,** *n.* The act of interfering; meddling; hindrance; (*Radio.*) the spoiling of reception by atmospherics or by other signals; (*U.S.A.*) an appeal against a patent by the holder of a prior patent. **interferer,** *n.* **interfering,** *a.* Inclined to interfere; officious. *n.* Interference. **interferingly,** *adv.* **interferometer** (in tĕr fēr om' et ėr), *n.* (*Phys.*) An optical instrument for the accurate measuring of the wavelength of light.

interferon (in tėr fēr' on), *n.* (*Biol.*) An antiviral substance produced in living cells in man and other creatures in response to infection from various viruses.

interfluent (in tĕr' flu ėnt) [L. *interfluens -ntem*, pres.p. of *interfluere* (INTER-, *fluere*, to flow)], *a.* Flowing between; flowing together or into each other. ***interfluous,** *a.*

interfoliaceous (in tėr fō li ā' shŭs), *a.* (*Bot.*) Situated between opposite leaves.

interfrontal (in tėr fron' tȧl), *a.* (*Anat.*) Situated between the two frontal bones.

interfuse (in tėr fūz') [L. *interfūsus*, p.p. of *interfundere* (INTER-, *fundere*, to pour)], *v.t.* To cause to flow into each other; to commix or intersperse; to blend together. *v.i.* To blend into each other. **interfusion** (-fū' zhŭn), *n.*

interglacial (in tėr glā' shi ȧl), *a.* (*Geol.*) Occurring or formed between two of the glacial periods.

interglandular (in tėr glăn' dū lȧr), *a.* (*Anat.*) Situated between glands.

intergrade (in' tėr grād), *n.* An intermediate grade. *v.i.* To pass into or mingle gradually with another form. **intergradation** (-grȧ dā' shŭn), *n.*

intergrow (in tėr grō'), *v.i.* To grow together or into each other. **intergrowth** (in' tėr grōth), *n.*

interhæmal (in tėr hē' mȧl), *a.* (*Ichthyol.*) Situated between the hæmal spines or arches. *n.* A hæmal spine or bone.

interim (in' tėr im) [L., in the meantime (INTER-, *-im*, adv. suf.)], *n.* The meantime; the intervening time or period. *a.* Temporary, provisional.

interior (in tēr' i ŏr) [L., compar. of *inter*, see INTER-], *a.* Internal, inner; inland; remote from the coast, frontier, or exterior; domestic, as dist. from foreign; pertaining to the inner consciousness, the soul, or spiritual matters. *n.* The internal part of anything, the inside; the central or inland part of a country; the inside of a building or room, esp. as portrayed in a picture, photograph, etc.; the domestic affairs of a country; the Government department dealing with these; the inward nature, the soul. **interiorly,** *adv.*

interjacent (in tėr jā' sėnt) [L. *interjacens -ntem*, pres.p. of *interjacēre* (INTER-, *jacēre*, to lie)], *a.* Lying between or among; intervening. ***interjacency,** *n.*

interjaculate (in tėr jăk' ū lāt), *v.t.* To interject, to ejaculate in the midst of a conversation.

interject (in tėr jekt') [L. *interjectus*, p.p. of *interjicere* (INTER-, *jacere*, to throw)], *v.t.* To throw or cast between (as a parenthetic remark); to insert, to interpose. **interjection** (-jek' shŭn), *n.* The act of interjecting; an exclamation, a word thrown in to express feeling, differentiated as a separate part of speech. **interjectional, interjectory, interjectural,** *a.* **interjectionally,** *adv.*

***interjoin** (in tėr join'), *v.t.* To join with one another. **interjointal,** *a.* (*Geol.*) Occurring between the joint planes in rocks.

interlace (in tėr lās') [M.E. *entrelace*, F. *entrelacer* (INTER-, *lacer*, to LACE)], *v.t.* To lace or weave together; to interweave; to entangle together; (*fig.*) to intermix. *v.i.* To be interwoven (with each other); to intersect in a complicated fashion. *v.t.* To intersect. **interlaced arches:** (*Arch.*) Arches (usu. semicircular) which intersect each other. **interlacement,** *n.*

interlard (in tėr lard') [F. *entrelarder* (INTER-, *larder*, to LARD)], *v.t.* *To mix with alternate layers of fat; (*fig.*) to diversify (a conversation, passage in a book, etc., with unusual phrases, etc.).

interleaf (in' tėr lēf), *n.* A leaf (usu. blank) inserted among others for purposes of illustration, etc. **interleave** (in tėr lēv'), *v.t.* To insert (a blank leaf or leaves) between the leaves of.

interline (in tėr līn') [prob. from late L. *interlineāre* (after MF. *entreligner*)], *v.t.* To write or print (between the lines of); to insert between lines; to write or print in alternate lines; to insert a lining between the outer cloth and the lining (of a garment). **interlineal** (-lin' ė ȧl), **interlinear,** ***interlineary,** *a.* **interlineation** (-lin ė ā' shŭn), *n.* **interlining,** *n.*

Interlingua (in tėr ling' gwȧ) [INTER-, L. *lingua*, tongue], *n.* An artificial language based on Latin roots.

interlink (in tėr lingk'), *v.t.* To connect (together or with) by links. *n.* An intermediate link.

interlobate (in tėr lō' bȧt), *a.* (*Geol.*) Formed or lying between loops or lobes (usu. the terminal lobes of a moraine).

interlobular (in tėr lob' ū lȧr), *a.* (*Anat. and Path.*) Situated or occurring between the lobes of a gland or other organ.

interlocation (intėr lō kā' shŭn), *n.* The act of placing between, intercalating, or interposing.

interlock (in tėr lok'), *v.t.* To connect firmly together by reciprocal engagement of parts; to link or lock together. *v.i.* To engage with each other by reciprocal connections. **interlocking system:** (*Railway*) A method of connecting points and signals by interlocking mechanism so as to keep the signal at danger until each movement has been completed and to prevent the movement of two points at once.

interlocution (in tėr lō kū′ shŭn) [L. *interlocūtio* (INTER-, *loquī*, to speak)], *n.* Conversation, dialogue, discussion; *(*Law*) an intermediate decree. **interlocutor** (in tėr lok′ ū tŏr), *n.* One who takes part in a conversation; the compère of a minstrel show; (*Sc. Law*) an interlocutory or interim decree in a case. **interlocutory,** *a.* Consisting of dialogue; (*Law*) intermediate, not final. **interlocutress, -trice, -trix,** *n.* A female interlocutor.

interloper (in′ tėr lō pėr) [from INTERLOPE], *n.* One who interlopes or thrusts himself into a place, office, affairs, etc., without a right; an intruder; one who trades without a licence or infringes upon another's business. ***interlope,** *v.i.* To run between parties and intercept the advantage that one would gain from the other; to traffic without a proper licence; to forestall others.

interlude (in′ tėr lood) [med. L. *interlūdium* (INTER-*lūdus*, play)], *n.* A pause or a short entertainment between the acts of a play, or between a play and the after-piece; (*Mus.*) a piece of instrumental music played between the acts of a drama, between the verses of a hymn, portions of a church service, etc.; (*fig.*) an incident, esp. an amusing one, coming between graver events; (*Hist.*) a dramatic representation, usu. farcical, intervening between the acts of the mystery-plays and moralities.

interlunar, *-nary (in tėr loo′ năr), *a.* Pertaining to the time when the moon, about to change from old to new, is invisible.

intermarriage (in tėr măr′ ĭj), *n.* Marriage between persons of different families, tribes, castes, or nations; marriage between persons closely akin. **intermarry,** *v.i.* To become connected by marriage (of different families, tribes, etc.); (*Law*) to marry.

intermaxillary (in tėr măk′ si lăr i, -măk sil′ a ri), *a.* (*Anat.*) Situated between the *maxillæ* or jawbones. *n.* The intermaxillary bone.

intermeddle (in tėr medl′) [A.-F. *entremedler*, O.F. *entremesler*], *v.i.* To interfere improperly or officiously (with). **v.t.* To intermix, to intermingle. **intermeddler,** *n.*

intermediary (in tėr mē′ di ăr i) [F. *intermédiaire*, from L. *intermedius* (INTER-, *medius*, middle)], *a.* Being, coming, or acting between; intermediate; mediatory. *n.* An intermediate agent, a go-between; intermediation. **intermediate, *intermedial,** *a.* Coming or being between; intervening, interposing. *n.* An intermediate thing. *v.i.* To act as intermediary; to mediate (between). **intermediately,** *adv.* ***intermediacy, intermediateness, intermediation,** *n.*

intermedium (in tėr mē′ di ŭm), *n.* (*pl.* **intermedia**) An intermediate agent or agency; (*Anat.*) an intermediate bone of the wrist or ankle.

intermembral (in tėr mem′ brăl), *a.* (*Biol.*) Subsisting between members.

interment [INTER].

intermezzo (in tėr med′ zō) [It., pop. var. of *intermedio*, L. *intermedius*, INTERMEDIARY], *n.* A short dramatic or other entertainment between the acts of a play; (*Mus.*) a short movement connecting the main divisions of a large musical composition.

intermigration (in tėr mī grā′ shŭn), *n.* Reciprocal migration.

interminable (in tĕr′ mi năbl) [late L. *interminābilis* (IN- (2), *termināre*, to TERMINATE)], *a.* Endless; tediously protracted. **interminableness,** *n.* **interminably,** *adv.* ***interminate,** *a.* Having no limits; (*Alg.*) interminable (as a recurring decimal).

intermingle (in tėr ming′ gėl), *v.t.* To mingle together, to intermix. *v.i.* To be mingled (with).

intermit (in tėr mit′) [L. *intermittere* (INTER-, *mittere*, to send), p.p. *-missus*], *v.t.* To cause to cease for a time; to suspend. *v.i.* To cease or relax at intervals (as a fever, pain, etc.). **intermittence, intermission** (-mish′ ŭn), *n.* The act or state of intermitting; temporary cessation of a paroxysm; a pause; an interlude; (*Am.*) interval between acts of a play, etc.; (*Am.*) school break; *disuse; *interference. ***intermissive, intermittent,** *a.* Ceasing or relaxing at intervals. *n.* An intermittent fever. **intermittently,** *adv.*

intermix (in tėr miks′), *v.t.* To mix together, to intermingle. *v.i.* To be intermingled. **intermixture,** *n.*

intermobility (in tėr mō bil′ i ti), *n.* Capacity (of atoms, etc.) to move about among themselves.

intermundane (in tėr mŭn′ dān), *a.* Being or existing between worlds.

intermural (in tėr mū′ răl) [L. *intermūrālis*], *a.* Situated between walls.

intermuscular (in tėr mŭs′ kū lăr), *a.* (*Anat.*) Lying between the muscles.

intermutation (in tėr mū tā′ shŭn), *n.* Interchange of elements.

intern (in tĕrn′) [F. *interner*, from L. *internus*, INTERNAL], *v.t.* To send to or confine in the interior of a country; to keep under restraint; to confine aliens (in time of war), political opponents, prisoners of war, etc. **internee,** *n.* One who is interned. **internment,** *n.* **internment camp,** *n.* Camp for the internment of aliens in time of war, or of prisoners of war.

internal (in tĕr′ năl) [med. L. *internālis*, from *internus*, inward (*in*, IN)], *a.* Situated in the inside; of or pertaining to the inside, inherent, intrinsic; domestic as opp. to foreign; pertaining to the inner being, inward. *n.pl.* The internal organs, the entrails; intrinsic or essential qualities. **internal-combustion engine:** An engine in which mechanical energy is produced by the combustion or explosion of a mixture of air and gas, oil-vapour, etc., in its cylinder. **internal evidence,** *n.* Evidence derived from what the thing itself contains. **internality** (-năl′ i ti), *n.* **internally,** *adv.*

international (in tėr năsh′ ō năl) [INTER-, NATIONAL], *a.* Pertaining to, subsisting or carried on between, or mutually affecting different nations; pertaining to the International. *n.* A society (called in full the International Working Men's Association) for promoting the joint political action of the working classes throughout the world. The First International (1862–73) was Marxist in principle; the Second (1889–) was French socialist; the Third (1918–1943), also known as the Comintern, was Russian communist; a member of this; a person belonging to different nations, as a native or a citizen; a person taking part in an international sporting or other contest. **International Court of Justice:** The principal judicial organ of the United Nations, inaugurated in 1946. **International Labour Organization,** *n.* An independent body established at Geneva at the same time as the League of Nations, with the object of raising the level of the standard of labour conditions throughout the world. **international law:** An accepted system of laws or jurisprudence regulating intercourse between nations. **internationalism,** *n.* The promotion of community of interests between nations; the principles or objects advocated by the Internationalists. **internationalist,** *n.* An advocate of internationalism; a member of the International; one versed in international law. **internationality** (-năl′ i ti), *n.* **internationalize** (-năsh′ ŭ nă līz), *v.t.* To make international; to bring under the joint protection or control of different nations. **internationalization** (-zā′ shŭn), *n.* **internationally,** *adv.* **Internationale,** *n.* The French socialist hymn adopted by the International.

interne (in′ tĕrn), *n.* (*Am.*) A last-year student or a graduate who resides in a hospital and acts as an assistant surgeon.

internecine (in tėr nē′ sīn) [L. *internecīnus* (INTER-, *necāre*, to kill)], *a.* Deadly, destructive; mutually destructive. ***internecive**, *a.*

internee [INTERN].

interneural (in tėr nū′ rǎl), *a.* (*Anat.*) Situated between two nerves or neural processes; (*Ichthyol.*) applied to the spines supporting the rays of the dorsal fin.

internment [INTERN].

internode (in′ tėr nōd), *n.* (*Anat.*) A part between two nodes or joints; (*Bot.*) a part of a stem between two nodes or leaf-knots. **internodal** (-nō′ dǎl), *a.*

internuncio (in tėr nŭn′ shi ō) [It. *internunzio*, L. *internuntius* (INTER-, *nuntius*, see NUNCIO)], *n.* A messenger between two parties; an ambassador of the Pope sent to a court when there is no nuncio present or to minor States; an envoy or minister representing a government. **internuncial**, *a.* Pertaining to an internuncio or his functions; (*Physiol.*) communicating between different parts (as nerves).

interoceanic (in tėr ō shi ăn′ ik), *a.* Situated between or connecting two oceans.

interocular (in tėr ok′ ū lǎr), *a.* (*Anat.*) Situated between the eyes.

interorbital (in tėr ôr′ bi tǎl), *a.* (*Anat.*) Situated between the orbits of the eyes.

interosseal, -seous (in tėr os′ ė ǎl, -ŭs), *a.* (*Anat.*) Situated between bones.

interpage (in tėr pāj′), *v.t.* To insert pages between other pages (in a book); to insert on intermediate pages.

interparietal (in tėr pǎ rī′ ė tǎl), *a.* (*Anat.*) Situated between the parietal bones of the skull. *n.* An interparietal bone, esp. in fishes.

interpellate (in tėr pel′ āt, in tĕr′ pel āt) [L. *interpellātus* (INTER-, *pellāre*, var. of *pellere*, to drive)], *v.t.* To interrogate, esp. to interrupt discussion etc. in order to demand a statement or explanation from (a minister). **interpellant**, *a.* and *n.* **interpellation** (-lā′ shŭn), **interpellator**, *n.*

interpenetrate (in tėr pen′ ė trāt), *v.t.* To penetrate thoroughly, to permeate; to penetrate (each other). *v.i.* To penetrate each other. **interpenetration** (-trā′ shŭn), *n.* **interpenetrative** (-pen′ ė trā tiv), *a.*

interpetiolar (in tėr pet′ i ȯ lǎr), *a.* (*Bot.*) Situated between petioles.

interpilaster (in tėr pi lăs′ tėr), *n.* (*Arch.*) The space between two pilasters.

interplanetary (in tėr plăn′ ė tǎr i), *a.* Pertaining to the regions between the planets.

interplay (in′ tėr plā), *n.* Reciprocal action between parts or things.

interplead (in tėr plēd′) [A.-F. *enterpleder*], *v.i.* (*Law*) To take legal proceedings in order to discuss and determine an incidental issue. **interpleader**, *n.* (*Law*) A suit by which the claims of two parties to money or property are determined, in order that a third party, on whom the claim is made, may know to which party payment is due.

***interpledge** (in tėr plej′), *v.t.* To pledge mutually.

interpleural (in tėr ploo′ rǎl), *a.* (*Anat.*) Situated between the pleuræ of the right and left lungs.

Interpol (in′ tĕr pol), *n.* The International Police Commission that ensures co-operation between police forces in the suppression and detection of crime.

interpolar (in tėr pō′ lǎr), *a.* Situated between the poles (of a galvanic battery, etc.).

interpolate (in tĕr′ pȯ lāt) [L. *interpolātus*, p.p. of *interpolāre* (INTER-, *polāre*, rel. to *polīre*, to POLISH)], *v.t.* To insert (esp. a spurious word or passage) in (a book or document); to insert or intercalate; to alter or corrupt; (*Math.*) to introduce (intermediate terms) in a series. *v.i.* To make interpolations. **interpolator**, *n.* **interpolation** (-lā′ shŭn), *n.* The act of interpolating; that which is interpolated; (*Math.*) the operation of finding terms (conformable to the law of the series) between any two consecutive terms of a series.

interpose (in tėr pōz′) [F. *interposer*], *v.t.* To place between or among; to put forward (as an objection, veto, obstruction, etc.) by way of intervention or interference. *v.i.* To intervene, to intercede, to mediate between; to remark by way of interruption, to interrupt. **interposer**, *n.* **interposal**, *n.*

interposition (in tėr pȯ zish′ ŭn) [F., from L. *interpositiōnem*, nom. *-tio*], *n.* The act of interposing; intervention, mediation; that which is interposed.

interpret (in tĕr′ prėt) [F. *interpréter*, L. *interpretāri*, from *interpres -pretis* (INTER-, *-pret-*, cogn. with Sansk. *prath-*, to spread abroad)], *v.t.* To explain the meaning of; to translate from one language into another; to expound, to make intelligible; to find out the meaning of, to construe or understand (in a particular way); to represent the meaning of or one's idea of artistically. *v.i.* To act as an interpreter. **interpretable**, *a.* **interpretation** (-tā′ shŭn), *n.* **interpretative** (in tĕr′ prė tā tiv), *a.* **interpretatively**, *adv.* **interpreter**, *n.* One who interprets, esp. one employed to translate orally to persons speaking a foreign language. **interpretership**, *n.* **interpretress**, *n.*

interprovincial (in tėr prȯ vin′ shǎl), *a.* Existing, carried on, etc., between different provinces.

interpubic (in tėr pū′ bik), *a.* (*Anat.*) Situated between the right and left pubic bones.

interpunctuate (in tėr pŭngk′ tū āt), *v.t.* To insert the punctuation marks in or between. **interpunctuation** (-ā′ shŭn), ***interpunction**, *n.*

interracial (in tėr rā′ shi ǎl, -shǎl), *a.* Between different races.

interradial (in tėr rā′ di ǎl), *a.* (*Zool.*) Situated between the radii or rays. *n.* An interradial part (in a crinoid). **interradially**, *adv.* ***interradius***, *n.* (*pl.* ***-dii***) An interradial part (as in an echinoderm).

interradiate (in tėr rā′ di āt), *v.i.* To radiate into each other. **interradiation** (-ā′ shŭn), *n.*

interramal (in tėr rā′ mǎl), *a.* (*Ornith.*) Situated between two rami or branches as of the lower jaw.

interregnum (in tėr reg′ nŭm) [L. (INTER-, *regnum*, REIGN)], *n.* (*pl.* **-nums**) The period between two reigns, ministries, or governments; (*fig.*) a suspension or interruption of normal authority, succession, etc.; an interval, a pause. ***interregnal**, *a.* ***intereign** (in′ tėr rān), *n.* **interrex** (in′ tėr reks) [L. *rex*, king], *n.* (*pl.* **-reges**) One who governs during an interregnum; a regent.

interrelation (in tėr rė lā′ shŭn), *n.* Mutual relation. **interrelationship**, *n.*

interrex [INTERREGNUM].

interrogate (in tĕr′ ȯ gāt) [L. *interrogātus*, p.p. of *interrogāre* (INTER-, *rogāre*, to ask)], *v.t.* To put questions to; to examine in a formal manner. *v.i.* To ask questions. **interrogable**, *a.* ***interrogant**, *n.* An interrogator. **interrogation** (-gā′ shŭn), *n.* The act of interrogating; a question put; (*Gram.*) the sign (?) marking a question. **interrogational**, *a.* **interrogative** (in tėr rog′ ǎ tiv), *a.* Denoting a question; expressed in the form or having the character of a question. *n.* (*Gram.*) A word used in asking questions. **interrogatively**, *adv.* **interrogator** (-tĕr′ ȯ gā tŏr), *n.* **interrogatory** (-rog′-), *a.* Interrogative. *n.* A question; an inquiry; (*Law*) a question or set of questions put formally to a defendant, etc.

interrupt (in tėr rŭpt′) [L. *interruptus*, p.p. of *interrumpere* (INTER-, *rumpere*, to break)], *v.t.* To stop or obstruct by breaking in upon; to break the continuity of; to cause a break or gap in; to obstruct (a view, etc.); (*colloq.*) to disturb. *v.i.* To make interruption. **a.* Interrupted. **n.* A gap, a chasm. **interruptedly**, *adv.* **interrupter**, *n.* **interruption** (-rŭp′ shŭn), *n.* **interruptive, -tory**, *a.* **interruptively**, *adv.*

interscapular (in tėr skăp′ ū lăr), *a.* (*Anat.*) Situated between the shoulder blades. *n.* An interscapular feather.

intersecant (in tėr sek′ ȧnt), *a.* Intersecting. *n.pl.* Intersecting lines.

intersect (in tėr sekt′) [L. *intersectus*, p.p. of *intersecāre* (INTER-, *secāre*, to cut)], *v.t.* To pass or cut across; to divide by cutting or passing across. *v.i.* To cut or cross each other. **intersection** (-sek′ shůn), *n.* The act or state of intersecting; (*Geom.*) the point or line in which two lines or planes cut each other. **intersectional,** *a.*

intersegmental (in tėr seg men′ tȧl), *a.* (*Zool.*) Situated between two segments.

interseptal (in tėr sep′ tȧl) [L. *intersæptum*, a partition, the diaphragm, -AL], *a.* (*Anat. and Zool.*) Situated between or pertaining to septa or partitions.

intersidereal (in tėr sī dēr′ ė ȧl), *a.* Interstellar.

interspace (in′ tėr spās), *n.* Intervening space; an interval between two things or occurrences. *v.t.* (in tėr spās′) To put a space or spaces between; to fill the intervals between. **interspatial,** *a.* **interspatially,** *adv.*

interspecific (in tėr spė sĭf′ ik), *a.* (*Biol.*) Subsisting between different species.

intersperse (in tėr spěrs′) [L. *interspersus*, p.p. of *interspergere* (INTER-, *spargere*, to scatter)], *v.t.* To scatter here and there (among etc.); *to diversify or variegate (with scattered objects, colours, etc.). **interspersion,** *n.*

interspinal, -spinous (in tėr spī′ nȧl, -nůs), *a.* (*Anat. and Zool.*) Situated between spines or spinal processes.

interstate (in′ tėr stāt), *a.* (*U.S.A.*) Subsisting, maintained, or carried on between States.

interstellar, -lary (in tėr stel′ ȧr, -ȧr i), *a.* Situated between or passing through the regions between the stars.

interstice (in těr′ stis, in′ tėr stis) [M.F., from L. *interstitium*, from *intersistere* (INTER-, *sistere*, to place, causal from *stāre*, to stand)], *n.* A space, opening, crevice, etc., between things near together or between the component parts of a body. **interstitial** (-stish′ ȧl), *a.* Of, pertaining to, occupying, or forming interstices.

interstratify (in tėr străt′ i fī), *v.t.* (*Geol.*) To stratify between or among other strata (*usu. in p.p.*). **interstratification** (-kā′ shůn), *n.*

intertangle (in tėr tăng′ gėl), *v.t.* To entangle together. **intertanglement,** *n.*

intertarsal (in tėr tar′ sȧl), *a.* (*Anat. and Zool.*) Situated between the bones of the ankle.

intertergal (in tėr těr′ gȧl), *a.* (*Zool.*) Situated between the *terga* or *tergites* of an arthropod.

intertie (in′ tėr tī), *n.* (*Build.*) A horizontal timber framed between two posts to tie them together; a binding joist.

intertransverse (in tėr trănz′ věrs), *a.* (*Anat.*) Situated between the transverse processes of the vertebræ.

intertribal (in tėr trī′ bȧl), *a.* Occurring or carried on between different tribes.

intertrigo (in tėr trī′ gō) [L. *interterīgo* (INTER-, *terere*, to rub)], *n.* (*Path.*) Inflammation of the skin through the rubbing of two parts together.

intertropical (in tėr trop′ i kȧl), *a.* Situated within or between the tropics. **intertropics,** *n.pl.*

interwine (in tėr twīn′), *v.t.* To entwine or twist together. *v.i.* To be twisted together. *n.* An intertwinement. **interwinement,** *n.* An intertwining. **intertwiningly,** *adv.*

intertwist (in tėr twist′), *v.t.* To twist together. **intertwistingly,** *adv.*

interunion (in tėr ū′ nyȯn), *n.* Reciprocal union.

interurban (in tėr ěr′ bȧn), *a.* Between cities.

interval (in′ tėr vȧl) [O.F. *intervalle*, *entreval*, L. *intervallum*, the space between palisades or ramparts (INTER-, *vallum*, rampart)], *n.* Intermediate space, distance, or time; a break, a gap; the extent of difference between two things, persons, etc.; (*Mus.*) the difference of pitch between two sounds; (*Theat., etc.*) the break between scenes or acts (*Am.* intermission); (*Am.*) an intervale. *v.t.* To separate or interrupt at intervals. **intervallic** (-văl′ ik), *a.* ***intervallum,** *n.* (*pl.* **-la**) An interval. **at intervals:** From time to time.

intervale (in′ tėr vāl) [var. of prec., assim. to VALE], *a.* (*Am.*) A tract of low or plain ground between hills or along the banks of rivers.

interveined (in tėr vānd′), *a.* Intersected as with veins.

intervene (in tėr vēn′) [L. *intervenīre* (INTER-, *venīre*, to come), p.p. *interventus*], *v.i.* To come in as an extraneous feature or thing; to come or be situated (between); to occur between points of time or events; to happen or break in so as to interrupt or disturb, to interfere, to interpose. **intervener,** *n.* One who intervenes, esp. in a law-suit. **intervenient,** *a.* **intervention** (-ven′ shůn), *n.* The act of intervening; (*Pol.*) violating a sovereign state's independence by interfering in its domestic or external affairs.

interventricular (in tėr ven trik′ ū lȧr) [INTER-, VENTRICULAR], *a.* (*Anat.*) Situated between the ventricles (of the heart or the brain).

intervertebral (in tėr věr′ tė brȧl), *a.* (*Anat.*) Situated between vertebræ.

interview (in′ tėr vū) [O.F. *entrevue*, from *entrevoir* (INTER-, *voir*, L. *vidēre*, to see)], *n.* A meeting between two persons face to face; a conference; a formal meeting between some person and a press representative employed to obtain information or opinions for publication; the article describing this or recording the result. *v.t.* To have an interview with, esp. in order to obtain matter for publication. **interviewer,** *n.*

intervisible (in tėr viz′ ibl), *a.* Said of two surveying stations, each of which is visible from the other.

intervital (in tėr vī′ tȧl), *a.* Existing between lives, esp. between death and resurrection.

intervocal (in tėr vō′ kȧl), *a.* Occurring between vowels. **intervocalic** (-kăl′ ik), *a.*

intervolve (in tėr volv′) [INTER-, L. *volvere*, to roll], *v.t.* To involve or wind one (thing) within another.

interweave (in tėr wēv′), *v.t.* (*p.p.* **-woven**) To weave together; to blend or mingle closely together.

interwind (in tėr wīnd′), *v.t.* To wind together.

interwork (in tėr wěrk′), *v.t.* (*past & p.p.* **-wrought, -worked**) To work things together or into each other. *v.i.* To work reciprocally, to interact.

interzonal (in těr zōn′ ȧl), *a.* (*Pol.*) Between zones in occupied territory.

intestacy (in tes′ tȧ si), *n.* Lack of a will or testament.

intestate (in tes′ tȧt) [L. *intestātus* (IN-, *testātus*, p.p. of *testārī*, to witness, to make a will)], *a.* Dying without having made a will; not disposed of by will. *n.* An intestate person. ***intestable,** *a.* Legally incompetent to make a will or benefit by one.

intestine (in tes′ tin) [L. *intestīnus*, from *intus*, within], *a.* Internal, domestic, not foreign; civil, *innate. *n.* (*usu. pl.*) The long membranous tube from the stomach to the anus; the bowels, the guts. **intestinal,** *a.* Pertaining to the intestines.

inthral, etc. [ENTHRAL].

intil (in′ til) [Sc.], *prep.* Into.

intimate (1) (in′ ti māt) [late L. *intimātus*, p.p. of *intimāre*, from *intimus*, within], *v.t.* To make known, to announce; to signify, to indicate, to hint. **intimation** (-mā′ shůn), *n.*

intimate (2) (in′ tim ȧt) [as prec.], *a.* Close in friendship or fellowship; familiar, confidential;

pertaining to one's inner being; adhering closely; internal, inward; having illicit sexual relations. *n. A familar friend or associate. **intimately,** *adv.* **intimacy,** *n.*

intimidate (in tim′ i dāt) [med. L. *intimidātus*, p.p. of *intimidāre* (IN-, *timidus*, TIMID)], *v.t.* To frighten, to make fearful, to dishearten, to cow; to deter (from an action or doing). **intimidation** (-dā′ shŭn), *n.* **intimidator** (in tim′ i dā tŏr), *n.* **intimidatory,** *a.*

intimity (in tim′ i ti) [F. *intimité*, from *intime*, L. *intimus*, inmost], *n.* The quality of being intimate; inwardness; privacy.

intinction (in tingk′ shŭn) [late L. *intinctio*, from *intingere* (IN- (1), *tinguere*, to moisten)], *n.* (*Eastern Ch.*) The method of administering the Eucharist in both kinds by dipping the bread in the wine.

intituled (in tī′ tūld) [F. *intitulé*, L. *intitulāre*, to ENTITLE], *a.* Having a specified name or title, entitled (chiefly of Acts of Parliament).

into (in′ too) [A.-S. *in to* (IN, adv., TO)], *prep.* Expressing motion or direction towards the interior, or change from one state to another; entrance; penetration; insertion; inclusion or comprehension.

intoed (in′ tōd), *a.* Having the toes turned inwards.

intolerable (in tol′ ėr ȧbl) [F., from L. *intolerābilis*], *a.* Not tolerable, unendurable; *enormous, monstrous, extreme. **intolerableness,** *n.* **intolerably,** *adv.*

intolerant (in tol′ ėr ȧnt) [F., from L. *intolerantem*, nom. *-ans*], *a.* Not tolerant (of); not enduring or allowing difference of opinion, teaching, or worship; bigoted. *n.* One who is intolerant, a bigot. **intolerance, intoleration** (-ā′ shŭn), *n.* **intolerantly,** *adv.*

***intomb** [ENTOMB].

intonation (in tō nā′ shŭn), *n.* Modulation of the voice, accent; intoning; the opening phrase of a plain-song melody, usu. sung by a priest or chorister; the mode of producing sound from a voice or an instrument, esp. as regards correctness of pitch.

intone (in tōn′) [med. L. *intonāre* (*in tonum*, in tone (*tonus*, TONE))], *v.i.* To recite or chant prayers, etc. in a monotone; to give a musical tone to one's delivery. *v.t.* To recite or chant in a monotone. **intonate,** *v.i.* To sound the notes of the musical scale; to intone. *v.t.* To intone. **intonation.**

intort (in tôrt′) [L. *intortus*, p.p. of *intorquere* (IN- (1), *torquere*, to twist)], *v.t.* To twist, to twine, to involve. **intorsion, -tion** (in tôr′ shŭn), *n.* A winding, bending, or twisting; (*Bot.*) the twisting of any part of a plant upon itself.

intoxicate (in tok′ si kāt) [med. L. *intoxicātus*, p.p. of *intoxicāre*, to smear with poison (IN- (1), *toxicāre*, from *toxicum*, Gr. *toxikon*, from *toxa*, arrows)], *v.t.* To make drunk; (*fig.*) to excite to enthusiasm; to make delirious, as with joy; (*Med.*) to poison. **n.* Intoxicated, delirious. **intoxicant,** *a.* and *n.* ***intoxicatedly,** *adv.* **intoxicating,** *a.* Tending to intoxicate. **intoxicatingly,** *adv.* **intoxication** (-kā′ shŭn), *n.* The act of intoxicating; the state of being intoxicated; (*fig.*) excitement, elation.

intra- [L. *intrā*, within], *pref.* Within, on the inside. **intra-abdominal** (in trȧ ăb dom′ i nȧl) [ABDOMINAL], *a.* Situated inside the abdomen. **intra-arterial** (-ar tēr′ i ȧl) [ARTERIAL], *a.* Occurring within an artery. **intra-capsular** (-kăp′ sū lȧr) [CAPSULAR], *a.* Situated or occurring inside a capsule. **intra-cardiac, -cardial** (-kar′ di ăk, -ȧl) [CARDIAC, -IAL], *a.* Situated or occurring inside the heart. **intracellular** (-sel′ ū lȧr) [CELLULAR], *a.* Situated or occurring in a cell.

intractable (in trăk′ tȧbl) [F., from L. *intractābilis* (IN-, TRACTABLE)], *a.* Unmanageable, indocile, refractory. **intractability** (-bil′ i ti), **intractableness,** *n.* **intractably,** *adv.*

intrados (in trā′ dos) [F. (INTRA-, *dos*, the back)], *n.* (*Arch.*) The under surface or curve of an arch [cp. EXTRADOS].

intramundane (in trȧ mŭn′ dān), *a.* Existing within this world or the material world.

intramural (in trȧ mū′ rȧl), *a.* Situated or happening within the walls or boundaries, as of a city, town, etc.; (*Anat., etc.*) situated or occurring within the walls of an organ etc.

intransigent (in trăn′ si jėnt) [F. *intransigeant*, Sp. *intransigente* (IN- (2), L. *transigens -ntem*, pres.p. of *transigere*, to come to an understanding, to TRANSACT)], *n.* Irreconcilable, uncompromising, esp. in political opinions. *n.* An irreconcilable; an uncompromising adherent of any creed (political, artistic, etc.). **intransigentism,** *n.* **intransigentist,** *n.*

intransitive (in trăn′ si tiv) [L. *intransitīvus* (IN- (2), TRANSITIVE)], *a.* Not passing on or over; (*Gram.*) denoting action confined to the agent. *n.* An intransitive verb. **intransitively,** *adv.*

intransmissible (in trănz mis′ ibl), *a.* Not transmissible.

***intransmutable** (in trȧnz mū′ tȧbl), *a.* Not transmutable. **intransmutability** (-bil′ i ti), *n.*

intrant (in′ trȧnt) [L. *intrans -ntem*, pres.p. of *intrāre*, to ENTER], *n.* One who enters on a duty, property, etc., esp. one who enters a college, society, etc.

intranuclear (in trȧ nū′ kli ȧr), *a.* (*Biol.*) Situated within the nucleus of a cell.

intraparietal (in trȧ pȧ rī′ e tȧl), *a.* Situated or occurring within walls, private; (*Anat.*) situated within the walls of an organ, esp. within the parietal lobe of the brain.

intraspecific (in trȧ spe sif′ ik), *a.* (*Biol.*) Relating to the internal development of a species.

intratelluric (in trȧ te lū′ rik), *a.* (*Geol.*) Occurring, existing, or formed in the interior of the earth.

intratropical (in trȧ trop′ i kȧl), *a.* Situated or happening within the tropics.

intra-urban (in trȧ ĕr′ bȧn), *a.* Existing or carried on within a city.

intravascular (in trȧ văs′ kū lȧr), *a.* (*Path.*) Situated or occurring within a vessel, esp. a blood-vessel.

intravenous (in trȧ vēn′ ŭs), *a.* (*Med.*) Into a vein or veins.

intrepid (in trep′ id) [L. *intrepidus* (IN- (2), TREPID)], *a.* Fearless, brave, bold. **intrepidity** (in trė pid′ i ti), *n.* **intrepidly,** *adv.*

intricate (in′ tri kȧt) [L. *intrīcātus*, p.p. of *intricāre* (IN- (1), *tricæ*, hindrances, wiles)], *a.* Entangled, involved, complicated; obscure. **v.t.* (-kāt) To involve, to perplex, to make obscure. **intricacy,** *n.* **intricately,** *adv.*

intrigant, *fem.* **intrigante** (in′ tri gȧnt, an trē gant) [F. *intriguant, -nte*, pres.p. of *intriguer*, see foll.], *n.* An intriguer.

intrigue (in trēg′) [F. *intriguer*, It. *intrigare*, L. *intricāre*, see INTRICATE], *v.i.* To carry on a plot or scheme to effect some object by underhand means; to carry on illicit love. *v.t.* To perplex; *to render intricate. *n.* The act of intriguing; a plot to effect some object by underhand means; secret love; a liaison. **intriguer,** *n.* ***intriguery,** *n.* **intriguingly,** *adv.*

***intrince, *intrinse** (in trins′) [prob. from INTRINSICATE], *a.* (*Shak.*) Intricate.

intrinsic, *-al (in trin′ sik, -ȧl) [F. *intrinsèque*, L. *intrinsecus* (INTRA-, *secus*, following, rel. to *secundus*, SECOND, *sequī*, to follow)], *a.* Inward, inherent; belonging to the nature of a thing; essential; genuine, real; *intimate, familiar. **intrinsically,** *adv.*

***intrinsicate, *-secate** (in trin′ si kȧt) [perh. from It. *intrinsecato*, familiar, confused with *intricato*, INTRICATE], *a.* (*Shak.*) Entangled, perplexed.

intro- [L. *intrō*, to the inside, rel. to *intrā*, in], *pref.* In, into; inward. **intro-active** (in trō ăk' tiv) [ACTIVE], *a.* Acting internally; acting upon itself.

introcession (in trō sesh' ŭn) [CESSION (after L. *intrōcēdere*, to go in, from *cēdere*, to go)], *n.* (*Path.*) A going inwards or shrinking of parts.

introduce (in trŏ dūs') [L. *intrōdūcere* (INTRO-, *dūcere*, to lead), p.p. *introductus*], *v.t.* To bring or lead in; to usher in; to insert; to bring into use or notice; to bring (to a person's notice); to make known, esp. (a person) in a formal way (to another); to bring before the public; to bring out into society; to bring before Parliament; *to occasion; to induce. **introducer,** *n.*

introduction (in trō dŭk' shŭn), *n.* The act of introducing; formal presentation of a person to another; a preface or preliminary discourse; an elementary treatise. **letter of introduction:** A letter introducing a friend to a third person. **introductive, introductory,** *a.* **introductively, introductorily,** *adv.*

introflexed (in trō flekst'), *a.* (*Bot.*) Bent inwards.

***introgression** (in trō gresh' ŭn) [L. *intrōgressus*, p.p. of *intrōgredī* (INTRO-, *gradī*, to walk)], *n.* Entrance.

introit (in trō' it) [F. *introït*, L. *introitus*, from *introīre*, to enter (INTRO-, *īre*, to go)], *n.* A psalm or antiphon sung or recited as the priest approaches the altar to begin the Mass.

intromit (in trŏ mit') [L. *intrōmittere* (INTRO-, *mittere*, to send, p.p. *intrōmissus*)], *v.t.* To send in; to admit, to allow to enter; to insert. *v.i.* (*Sc. Law*) To intermeddle (with another's property). **intromission** (-mish' ŭn), *n.* **intromittent,** *a.*

introrse (in trôrs') [L. *introrsus*, adv., from *introversus* (INTRO-, *versus*, towards)], *a.* (*Bot.*) Turned towards the axis.

introspect (in trŏ spekt') [L. *intrōspectus*, p.p. of *intrōspicere* (INTRO-, *specere*, to look)], *v.t.* To look into or within; to examine one's own mind and its working. **introspection** (in trŏ spek' shŭn), *n.* **introspectionist,** *n.* One who introspects; one who employs introspection as a psychological instrument. **introspective,** *a.* **introspectively,** *adv.* **introspectiveness,** *n.*

introsusception (in trō sŭ sep' shŭn) [L. *susceptio*, from *suscipere* (SUS-, *capere*, to take)], *n.* The act of taking or receiving in or within, *intussusception.

introvert (in trŏ vĕrt') [L. *intrōvertere* (INTRO-, *vertere*, to turn)], *v.t.* To turn inward; to turn (the mind or thoughts) inward; (*Zool.*) to turn (an organ or a part) in upon itself; (*Pros., etc.*) to invert (verses, etc.). *n.* (*Zool.*) A part or organ that is introverted or introversible; (*Psych.*) a person who is interested chiefly in his own mental processes and his standing with other people, this making him shy and unsociable. **introversible,** *a.* **introversion,** *n.* **introversive, -tive,** *a.*

intrude (in trood') [L. *intrūdere* (IN- (1), *trūdere*, to thrust)], *v.t.* To thrust or force (into); (*Geol.*) to force in (volcanic rock, etc.) into sedimentary strata; *to invade. *v.i.* To thrust oneself or force one's way (into); to force oneself (upon others); to enter without invitation; *to encroach. **intruder,** *n.*

intrusion (in trū' zhŏn), *n.* The act of intruding; an encroachment; (*Geol.*) the penetration of volcanic rocks into sedimentary strata; (*Law*) unlawful entry by a stranger upon lands or tenements, invasion, usurpation; (*Sc. Ch.*) the settlement of a minister in opposition to the wishes of the congregation. ***intrusionist,** *n.* (*Sc. Ch.*) One who favoured settlement of a minister in a church or congregation without the consent of the congregation.

intrusive (in trū' ziv), *a.* Tending to intrude; entering without invitation or welcome. **intrusive rocks:** (*Geol.*) Igneous rocks which have forced their way into sedimentary strata. **intrusively,** *adv.* **intrusiveness,** *n.*

intrust [ENTRUST].

intubate (in' tū bāt) [IN- (1), L. *tuba*, TUBE, -ATE], *v.t.* (*Surg.*) To insert a tube into (the larynx), as in a case of diphtheria. **intubation** (-bā' shŭn), *n.* **intubator** (in' tū bā tŏr), *n.* An instrument for inserting a tube thus.

intuition (in tū ish' ŭn) [F., from med. L. *intuitiōnem*, nom. *-tio*, from *intuērī* (IN- (1), *tuērī*, to look)], *n.* Immediate perception by the mind without reasoning; instinctive knowledge; a truth so perceived; *the action of looking upon, a sight. **intuit** (in tū' it), *v.t.* To know by intuition. *v.i.* To acquire knowledge by means of intuition. **intuitional,** *a.* **intuitionalism,** *n.* (*Phil.*) The doctrine that the perception of truth, or of certain truths, is by intuition. **intuitionalist,** *n.* **intuitionism,** *n.* (*Phil.*) Intuitionalism; an extreme form of this held by Reid and other Scottish philosophers, that the objects of sense-perception are known intuitively as real. **intuitionist,** *n.* **intuitive** (in tū' i tiv), *a.* Perceived by intuition; perceiving by intuition; seeing immediately and clearly. **intuitively,** *adv.* **intuitiveness,** *n.* **intuitivism,** *n.* (*Ethics*) The doctrine that ideas of right and wrong are intuitive.

intumesce (in tū mes') [L. *intumescere* (IN- (1), *tumescere*, incept. of *tumēre*, to become tumid)], *v.i.* To swell up, to become tumid; to enlarge or expand by heat. **intumescent,** *a.* **intumescence,** *n.*

inturn (in' tĕrn), *n.* An inward turn, bend, step, etc. **inturned** (in tĕrnd'), *a.*

intussuscept (in tŭ sŭ sept') [L. *intus*, within, *susceptus*, p.p. of *suscipere* (SUS-, *capere*, to take)], *v.t.* (*Path.*) To receive within itself or another part; to invaginate. **intussusception** (-sep' shŭn), *n.* Reception within; the taking in of anything (as of ideas into the mind); (*Physiol.*) the reception of foreign matter (as food) by an organism and its conversion into living tissue; (*Path.*) the accidental insertion or protrusion of an upper segment of the bowels into a lower. **intussusceptive,** *a.*

intwine [ENTWINE]. **intwist** [ENTWIST].

inuendo [INNUENDO].

inula (in' ū lă) [L., elecampane], *n.* (*Bot.*) A genus of *Compositæ* comprising the elecampane. **inulinaceous** (-nā' shŭs), *a.*

inulin (in' ū lin), *n.* (*Chem.*) A soluble, white starchy powder, obtained from the roots of elecampane and other *Compositæ*.

inunction (in ŭngk' shŭn) [L. *inunctio*, from *inunguere* (IN- (1), *unguere*, to ANOINT)], *n.* Anointing or smearing with ointment, oil, etc.

inundate (in' ŭn dāt) [L. *inundātus*, p.p. of *inundāre* (IN- (1), *unda*, a wave)], *v.t.* To overflow, to flood; to submerge, to deluge. ***inundant,** *a.* Overflowing. **inundation** (-dā' shŭn), *n.* A flood, a deluge.

inurbane (in ŭr bān') [L. *inurbānus*], *a.* Discourteous, rude, unpolished. **inurbanely,** *adv.* ***inurbanity** (-băn' i ti), *n.*

inure (i nūr'), *v.t.* To use or practise habitually; to accustom, to habituate, to harden (to); *to exercise; to practise. *v.i.* (*Law*) To come into operation; to take or have effect. **inurement,** *n.* Practice, use, habit.

inurn (in ĕrn'), *v.t.* To place in a cinerary urn; to bury.

***inusitate** (in ū' zi tāt) [L. *inūsitātus* (IN- (2), *ūsitātus*, p.p. of *ūsitārī*, freq. of *ūtī*, to USE)], *a.* Unusual; out of use. ***inusitation** (in ū zi tā' shŭn), *n.* Disuse.

inutile (in ū' til) [L. *inūtilis* (IN- (2), *ūtilis*, useful)], *a.* Useless. **inutility** (in ū til' i ti), *n.*

inutterable [UNUTTERABLE].

invade (in vād') [F. *invader*, L. *invādere* (IN- (1), *vādere*, to go)], *v.t.* To enter (a country) as an enemy; to enter by force; to assail; to encroach on, to violate. *v.i.* To make an invasion. **invader,** *n.*

invaginate (in văj' i nāt) [IN- (1), L. *vagīna*, a

sheathe, -ATE], *v.t.* To put into or as into a sheath; to introvert or turn (a tubular sheath) upon itself. **invaginable,** *a.* **invagination** (-nā′ shŭn), *n.*

invalid (1) (in văl′ id) [L. *invalidus*], *a.* Of no force, weight, or cogency; null. **invalidate,** *v.t.* To weaken or destroy the validity of, to render not valid; to overthrow. **invalidation** (-dā′ shŭn), *n.* **invalidator** (in văl′ i dā tŏr), *n.* **invalidity** (-lid′ i ti), ***invalidness,** *n.* **invalidly,** *adv.*

invalid (2) (in′ vȧl ēd) [as prec.], *a.* Infirm or disabled through ill-health or injury. *n.* An infirm or disabled person. *v.t.* To disable by illness or injury; to register as unfit for military or naval duty on account of illness, etc. *v.i.* To become an invalid; to be enrolled as such. **invalidism** (in′ vȧ lēd izm), *n.* Chronic ill health, esp. neurotic.

invaluable (in văl′ ū ȧbl) [IN- (2), VALUABLE], *a.* Precious above estimation; priceless. **invaluably,** *adv.*

invar (in′ var), *n.* (*Metal.*) Proprietary name of a nickel-steel alloy with small coefficient of expansion.

invariable (in vâr′ i ȧbl) [F.], *a.* Not variable, uniform; not liable to change; (*Math.*) fixed, constant. *n.* (*Math.*) A constant quantity. **invariability** (-bil′ i ti), **invariableness,** *n.* **invariably,** *adv.* **invariant,** *a.* Not varying or subject to variation. *n.* (*Math.*) That which remains fixed and unchanged though its constituents may vary. ***invaried,** *a.* Unvaried; invariable.

invasion (in vā′ zhŭn) [F., from L. *invāsiōnem*, nom. *-sio*, from *invādere*, to INVADE], *n.* The act of invading; a hostile attack upon or entrance into the territory of others; infringement, violation; the approach or assault of anything dangerous or pernicious. **invasive** (-siv), *a.*

invecked, invected (in vekt′, -vek′ tėd) [L. *invectus*, as foll.], *a.* (*Her.*) Bordered by a line of convex arcs or scallops; curved in this way (of a border-line), opp. to engrailed.

invective (in vek′ tiv) [F., from late L. *invectīva*, fem. adj. from *invectus*, p.p. of *invehere*, see foll.], *n.* A violent expression of censure or abuse; vituperation. *a.* Abusive. **invectively,** *adv.*

inveigh (in vā′) [L. *invehī*, to attack, to abuse, refl. of *invehere* (IN- (1), *vehere*, to carry)], *v.t.* To utter or make use of invectives; to declaim censoriously and abusively (against). **inveigher,** *n.*

inveigle (in vēgl′, -vāgl′) [prob. from F. *aveugler* (altered to *enveoglir*), to blind, from *aveugle*, low L. *aboculum*, nom. *-lus* (AB-, *oculus*, eye)], *v.t.* To seduce, to wheedle, to entrap (into an action, fault, etc.). **inveiglement,** *n.* **inveigler,** *n.*

invent (in vent′) [F. *inventer*, L. *inventus*, p.p. of *invenīre*, to find, to invent (IN- (1), *venīre*, to come)], *v.t.* To devise or contrive (a new means, instrument, etc.); to concoct, to fabricate; *to meet with; *to discover. ***inventful,** *a.* ***inventible,** *a.* **invention** (in ven′ shŭn), *n.* The act of inventing; the production of something new; the faculty or power of inventing, inventiveness; that which is invented, a contrivance; a fabrication, a fiction, a scheme; a discovery, a finding. **Invention of the Cross:** The finding of the true Cross by Helena, the mother of Constantine the Great, A.D. 326; the festival (3 May) commemorating this. **inventive,** *a.* Quick at contrivance; able to invent; ready at expedients, ingenious; imaginative. **inventively,** *adv.* **inventiveness,** *n.* **inventor, inventress,** *n.*

inventory (in′ vėn tŏr i) [med. L. *inventōrium*, from *inventus*, as prec.], *n.* A detailed list or catalogue of goods and chattels; the articles enumerated in such a list; the material in a nuclear reactor. *v.t.* To enter in an inventory; to make a list, catalogue, or schedule of. **inventorial** (-tôr′ i ȧl), *a.* **inventorially,** *adv.*

inveracity (in vė răs′ i ti), *n.* Untruthfulness.

Inverness (in vėr nes′) [town in Scotland], *n.* A kind of sleeveless cloak with a cape hanging loosely over the shoulders, usu. **Inverness cape.**

inverse (in vĕrs′, in′ vĕrs) [F. *inverse*, L. *inversus*, as INVERT], *a.* Opposite in order or relation; contrary, inverted. *n.* That which is inverted; the direct opposite of; (*Math.*) the result of inversion. **inverse proportion** or **ratio:** (*Math.*) The ratio of the reciprocals of two quantities. **inversely,** *adv.*

inversion (in vĕr′ shŭn), *n.* The act of inverting; reversal of order, place, or relation; (*Gram.*) reversal of the natural order of words in a sentence; the rearrangement of molecular structure taking place when starch, dextrin, or sugar is boiled with a dilute acid; (*Geol.*) the overturning of strata by igneous agency; (*Math.*) the operation of changing the order of the terms, so that the antecedent takes the place of the consequent and the reverse in both ratios; (*Psych.*) the assumption of the characteristics of the other sex; (*Mil.*) a movement by which the order of companies in line is inverted. **inversive,** *a.*

invert (1) (in vĕrt′) [L. *invertere* (IN- (1), *vertere*, to turn)], *v.t.* To turn upside down; to place in a contrary position or order; to reverse; (*Mus.*) to transpose (a chord, interval, part for a voice, etc.); *to divert.

invert (2) (in′ vĕrt), *n.* An inverted arch, esp. such as forms the bottom of a sewer, etc.; (*Psych.*) one with inverted sexual instincts, a homosexual. **invert sugar:** A mixture of laevulose and dextrose. **invertend** (in′ vėr tend), *n.* (*Log.*) A proposition from which another is derived by inversion. **invertible,** *a.* **invertedly,** *adv.*

invertebrate (in vĕr′ tė brȧt) [IN- (2), VERTEBRATE], *a.* Destitute of a backbone or vertebral column; (*fig.*) lacking strength or firmness. *n.* An invertebrate animal; (*fig.*) an irresolute person. ***invertebral,** ***invertebrated,** *a.* **Invertebrata** (in vĕr tė brā′ tȧ), *n.pl.* (*Zool.*) A former subdivision of the animal kingdom, containing animals without a vertebral column.

invest (in vest′) [F. *investir*, L. *investīre* (IN- (1), *vestīre*, to clothe)], *v.t.* To clothe (with or in); to cover (with or as with a garment); to clothe or endue (with office, authority, dignity, etc.); to surround, beleaguer, besiege; to employ (money in remunerative property, business, stocks, etc.); *to give, to bestow. *v.i.* To make an investment; (*colloq.*) to spend money (as in a small purchase). **investable,** *a.* **investive,** *a.* **investor,** *n.*

investigate (in ves′ ti gāt) [L. *investigātus*, p.p. of *investīgāre* (IN- (1), *vestigāre*, to track, see VESTIGE)], *v.t.* To search or trace out; to examine or inquire into closely. ***investigable,** *a.* **investigation** (-gā′ shŭn), *n.* **investigative** (in ves′ ti gā tiv), **investigatory,** *a.* **investigator,** *n.*

investiture (in ves′ ti tūr) [F., from med. L. *investītūra*, from *investīre*, to INVEST], *n.* The act of investing, esp. the ceremonial of investing (with office, rank, etc.); the state of being invested; that with which one is invested or endued; (*Feudal Law*) the open delivery of possession. **investive** [INVEST].

investment (in vest′ mėnt), *n.* The act of laying out money; money invested; that in which money is invested; the act of surrounding or besieging; investiture; *clothing, covering. **investor** [INVEST].

inveterate (in vet′ ėr ȧt) [L. *inveterātus*, p.p. of *inveterāre* (IN- (1), *vetus*, *veteris*, old)], *a.* Long-established; firmly established by long continuance, deeply-rooted, obstinate, confirmed by long use; *malignant, virulent. **v.t.* (-āt) To establish firmly by long continuance. **inveteracy, inveterateness,** *n.* **inveterately,** *adv.* ***inveteration** (-ā′ shŭn), *n.*

invexed (in vekst′) [late L. *invexus*, L. *invectus*, p.p. of *invehere* (IN- (1), *vehere*, to carry)], *a.* (*Her.*) Arched or concave.

invidious (in vid′ i ŭs) [L. *invidiōsus*, from *invidia*, ENVY], *a.* Tending to incur or provoke envy or ill-will; likely to give offence; offending through real or apparent unfairness or injustice; *envious; *enviable. **invidiously,** *adv.* **invidiousness,** *n.*

invigilate (in vij′ i lāt) [L. *invigilātus*, p.p. of *invigilāre* (IN- (1), *vigilāre*, to watch, see VIGIL)], *v.i.* To keep a watch over students during an examination. **invigilation** (-lā′ shůn), *n.* **invigilator** (in vij′ i lā tòr), *n.*

invigorate (in vig′ ò rāt) [L. *vigor*], *v.t.* To give vigour or strength to; (*fig.*) to animate, to encourage. **invigorant,** *a.* **invigoration** (-ā′ shůn), *n.* **invigorative** (in vig′ òr ȧ tiv), *a.* **invigorator** (-ā tòr), *n.*

invincible (in vin′ sibl) [F., from L. *invincibilis*], *a.* Not to be conquered. **invincibility** (-bil′ i ti), **invincibleness,** *n.* **invincibly,** *adv.*

inviolable (in vī′ ò lȧbl) [F., from L. *inviolābilis*], *a.* Not to be violated, profaned, or dishonoured; not to be broken or disturbed. **inviolability** (-bil′ i ti), ***inviolableness,** *n.* **inviolably,** *adv.* **inviolate, *-lated** (in vī′ ò lȧt, -lā tėd), *a.* Not violated or profaned; unbroken. **inviolacy, inviolateness,** *n.* **inviolately,** *adv.*

invisible (in viz′ ibl) [F., from L. *invīsibilis*], *a.* Not visible; imperceptible to the eye; too small, distant, misty, etc. to be seen; (*colloq.*) not in sight, away, not at home. **the invisible:** The invisible world; the supreme Being. **invisible ink:** Ink that does not show until heated or otherwise treated. **invisibly,** *adv.* ***invised,** *a.* Unseen; invisible. **invisibility** (-bil′ i ti), **invisibleness,** *n.*

invitatory (in vī′ tȧ tò ri), *a.* Containing or using invitation. *n.* An invitatory psalm, antiphon, etc., esp. the psalm *Venite exultemus Domino.*

invite (1) (in vīt′) [F. *inviter*, L. *invītāre*, to bid, rel. to *-vītus*, willing (in *invītus*, unwilling)], *v.t.* To solicit the company of (to or in); to request courteously (to do something); to solicit; to allure, to attract; to tempt; to draw upon one, esp. unintentionally. *v.i.* To give invitation; to allure, to tempt. **invitation** (in vi tā′ shůn), *n.* The act of inviting; words, written or oral, with which one is invited; allurement; attraction. **invitee** (in vi tē′), *n.* One invited. **inviter,** *n.* **inviting,** *a.* That invites; seductive; physically attractive. **invitingly,** *adv.* **invitingness,** *n.*

invite (2) (in′ vīt), *n.* (*colloq.*) An invitation.

invocation (in vò kā′ shůn) [F., from L. *invocātiōnem*, nom. *-tio*, from *invocāre*, to INVOKE], *n.* The act of invoking; a supplication or call, esp. to God; a petition addressed to a muse, saint, etc., for help or inspiration; *(*Law*) a judicial call, demand, or order. ***invocable** (in′ vò kȧbl), *a.* ***invocate** (in′ vò kāt), *v.t.* To invoke, to call upon; to address in prayer. **invocatory** (in vok′ ȧ-, in vò kā′ tò ri), *a.*

invoice (in′ vois) [prob. from earlier *invoyes*, pl. from F. *envoi*, see ENVOY (1)], *n.* A list of goods dispatched, with particulars of quantity and price, sent to a consignee. *v.t.* To enter (goods) in an invoice.

invoke (in vōk′) [F. *invoquer*, L. *invocāre* (IN- (1), *vocāre*, to call)], *v.t.* To address in prayer; to solicit earnestly for assistance and protection; to call upon solemnly; to call on as a witness, to appeal to as an authority; to summon by magical means; *to call for judicially.

involucre (in vò lū′ kėr) [F., from L. *involūcrum*, from *involvere* (IN- (1), *volvere*, to roll)], *n.* (*Bot.*) A whorl of bracts surrounding the flowers of certain *Compositæ* and other plants; the indusium of ferns; (*Anat.*) a membranous envelope or cover of certain parts and organs. **involucel** (in vol′ ū sel), **involucellum** (in vol ū sel′ ům), *n.* A secondary involucre. **involucellate** (-sel′ ȧt), **involucral** (in′ vò lū krȧl), **involucrate** (in vò lū′ krȧt), *a.* **involucret,** *n.*

involuntary (in vol′ ůn tȧr i) [L. *involuntārius*], *a.* Done unintentionally, not from choice, not spontaneous; independent of will or volition; *unwilling. **involuntarily,** *adv.* **involuntariness,** *n.*

involute (in′ vò lūt) [L. *involūtus*, p.p. of *involvere*, to INVOLVE], *a.* Rolled up, folded; (*Bot.*) rolled inward at the margin (as certain leaves, petals, etc.), complicated, involved. *n.* (*Math.*) A curve traced by the end of a string unwinding itself from another curve, which is called the evolute. **involuted, involutive,** *a.*

involution (in vò lū′ shòn), *n.* The act of involving; the state of being involved; complication, entanglement, intricacy; a rolling up or curling of parts; anything folding up or enveloping; a complicated grammatical construction; (*Math.*) the act or process of raising a quantity to any power.

involve (in volv′) [F. *involver*, from L. *involvere* (IN- (1), *volvere*, to roll)], *v.t.* To enwrap, to enfold, or envelop (in); to entangle (in); to implicate (in); to include (in); to comprise as a logical or necessary consequence; to imply, to entail; to complicate, to make intricate; (*Math.*) to raise to any power. **involvement,** *n.* The act of involving; the state of being involved, esp. financially. **involvedness,** *n.*

invulnerable (in vŭl′ nėr ȧbl) [F., from L. *invulnerābilis*], *a.* Incapable of being wounded or injured. **invulnerably,** *adv.* **invulnerability** (-bil′ i ti), ***invulnerableness,** *n.*

***invultuation** (in vŭl tū ā′ shůn) [low L. *invultuātiōnem*, nom. *-tio*, from *invultuāre* (IN- (1), *vultus*, face)], *n.* The practice of pricking or stabbing the wax or clay image of an enemy, in the belief that his death would thereby be magically brought about.

inward (in′ wȧrd) [A.-S. *innan-weard*], *a.* Internal; situated or being within; towards the interior, connected with the mind or soul; *intimate; *domestic; *confidential. *adv.* (*also* **inwards**) Towards the interior, internal parts, or centre; in the mind or soul. *n.pl.* The viscera; *intellectual parts; (*sing.*) *an intimate associate. **inwardly,** *adv.* Internally, within; towards the centre; in one's thoughts and feelings, mentally, secretly; *intimately. **inwardness,** *n.* The inner quality or essence (of); the quality of being inward; the mental and spiritual nature; *familiarity, intimacy.

inweave (in wēv′), *v.t.* To weave in or together; to interlace (with).

inwick (in′ wik), *n.* (*Curling*) A stroke in which the stone strikes the inside of another and glances off it to the tee. *v.i.* To make an inwick; (of the stone) to glance off another stone and reach the tee.

inworn (in wôrn′), *a.* Worn or pressed in; inveterate.

inwrap [ENWRAP]. **inwreathe** [ENWREATHE].

inwrought (in′ rawt, in rawt′), *a.* Wrought or worked in among other things (of a pattern, etc.); adorned with work or figures (of a fabric).

inyala (in ya′ la), *n.* (*Zool.*) The S. African antelope.

iodal (ī′ ō dăl), *n.* An oily liquid obtained by treating iodine with alcohol and nitric acid, analogous to chloral.

iodate (ī′ ō dāt), *n.* A salt of iodic acid.

iodic (ī od′ ik), *a.* Belonging to, or containing, iodine.

iodide (i′ ō dīd), *n.* A compound of iodine with an element or radical.

iodine (ī′ ō dēn, ī′ ō din, ī′ ō dīn) [F. *iode*, Gr. *iōdēs*, *ioeidēs* (*ion*, a violet, *eidos*, appearance), -INE], *n.* (*Chem.*) A non-metallic bluish-black element, yielding violet fumes when heated, and resembling bromine and chlorine in chemical properties, used in photography. It is largely used in medicine for its antiseptic and disinfectant qualities.

iodism (ī′ ō dizm), *n.* (*Path.*) The morbid effects of overdoses of iodine or iodic preparations.

iodize (ī′ ō dīz), *v.t.* To place under the influence of iodine; to prepare with iodine.

iodo-, *comb. form.*

iodoform (ī ō′ dō fôrm), *n.* An iodine compound resembling chloroform in its antiseptic effects. **iodoformin,** *n.*

iodol (ī' ō dol), *n.* An antiseptic compound of iodine.

iolite (ī' ō līt) [Gr. *ion*, as prec., -LITE], *n.* (*Min.*) A blue orthorhombic transparent or translucent silicate of aluminium, iron, and magnesium.

ion (ī' ŏn) [Gr. *ion*, neut. pres.p. of *ienai*, to go], *n.* (*Phys.*) An electrically charged atom or group of atoms formed, for example, by the solution of a salt in water, esp. an atom become positively charged by the loss of one or more electrons. **ionic,** *a.* **ionize,** *v.t.* To convert into an ion or ions. **ionization,** *n.*

-ion [F. *-ion*, L. *iōnem*, nom. *-io* (cp. -ATION, -ITION, -SION, -TION)], *suf.*

Ionian (ī ō' ni ȧn) [L. *Iōnius*, Gr. *Iōnios* (*Ionia*, -AN)], *a.* Pertaining to Ionia, a district of Asia Minor, or to the Ionians. *n.* A member of the division of the Hellenic race which settled in Attica and the northern coast of the Peloponnesus and founded colonies on the shores of the Mediterranean and Euxine and esp. in Asia Minor. **Ionian mode:** (*Mus.*) One of the ancient Greek modes, characterized as soft and effeminate; the last of the ecclesiastical modes, commencing on C, corresponding in tonality with the major diatonic scale in modern music. **Ionic** (ī on' ik), *a.* Ionian. **Ionic dialect:** The Greek dialect spoken in Ionia. **Ionic foot:** (*Pros.*) A metrical foot of four syllables (either *ionic a majore*, two long and two short, or *ionic a minore*, two short and two long). **Ionic metre:** Metre consisting of Ionic feet. **Ionic order:** (*Arch.*) One of the five orders of architecture, the distinguishing characteristic of which is the volute on both sides of the capital. **Ionic sect or school:** (*Phil.*) The first school of Greek philosophy, founded by Thales of Miletus, the distinctive characteristic of which was its inquiry into the material and formative constitution of the universe. **ionicism,** *n.* **ionicist,** *n.* **ionicize,** *v.t.* **ionicization** (-zā' shŭn), *n.*

ionic, ionize, etc. [ION] [IONIAN].

ionization [ION].

ionosphere (ī on' ō sfēr), *n.* The region surrounding the earth at a height of from 6 miles to about 250 miles in which ionized layers of gas occur.

-ior [(1) L. *-ior*, compar. suf. of adjectives; (2) var. of -IOUR], *suf.* As in *junior, superior, warrior.*

iota (ī ō' tȧ) [Gr.], *n.* The Greek letter *ι*, which, being frequently indicated by a dot under other letters (as ῳ), known as **iota subscript,** has come to mean a jot, a tittle, a very small quantity. **iotacism** (ī ō' tȧ sizm), *n.* The pronunciation of the other Greek vowels like the classical *i* or modern *ē* as in modern Greek; excessive employment of the letter *i*. **iotacist,** *n.*

I.O.U. (ī ō ū) [I, OWE, YOU], *n.* A formal acknowledgment of debt, bearing these letters, the sum involved, and the debtor's signature.

-iour [O.F. *-ur*, *-or* (F. *-eur*), L. *-ātōrem*, nom. *-ātor*], *suf.* As in *behaviour, saviour.*

-ious [L. *-iōsus* (cp. F. *-ieux*), *-i-*, -OUS], *suf.* Characterized by, full of; forming adjectives, as *ambitious, cautious, suspicious.*

ipecacuanha (ip ė kăk ū ăn' ȧ) [Port., from Guarani *ipe-kaa-guaña*], *n.* The dried root of *Cephaelis ipecacuanha*, a cinchonaceous plant from Brazil, used in medicine as emetic and purgative. **ipecac** (ip' ė kăk), **ipecacuanhic,** *a.*

***ipocras** [HIPPOCRAS].

Ipomœa (ip ō mē' ȧ) [Gr. *ip-*, stem of *ips*, worm, *omoios*, like], *n.* (*Bot.*) A genus of *Convolvulaceæ*, with many species.

ipse dixit (ip' si diks' it) [L., he himself has said it], *n.* A mere assertion; a dogmatic statement. ***ipsissima verba*** (ip sis' i ma vĕr' ba) [L.], *n.pl.* The identical words. ***ipso facto*** (ip' sō făk' tō) [L.], *adv.* By the fact itself.

ir- (1) [See IN- (1)], *pref.* (*before r*) As in *irradiate.*

ir- (2) [See IN- (2)], *pref.* (*before r*) As in *irrelevant, irreligion.*

***iracund** (īr' ȧ kŭnd) [L. *īracundus*, from *īra*, IRE], *a.* Angry, passionate.

irade (i ra' di) [Turk., from Arab. *irādah*, desire], *n.* A written decree of the Porte.

Iran (ē ran') [Pers.], *n.* The land of Persia. **Iranian,** *a.* Of or belonging to Persia. *n.* A member of the Iranian race; a native of Iran. **Iranian languages:** The Asiatic family of languages comprising Zend, Old Persian, and those derived from them; *Aryan or Indo-European.

Iraq (ē rak'), *n.* The Arab republic which contains Mesopotamia. **Iraqui** (ē ra' ki), *a.*

irascible (i-, ī răs' i bėl) [F., from L. *īrascibilis*, from *īrasci*, to be angry, from *īra*, IRE], *a.* Easily excited to anger; passionate, irritable. **irascibly,** *adv.* **irascibility** (-bil' i ti), **irascibleness,** *n.* **irate** (ī rāt'), *a.* Angry, enraged.

ire (ī' ėr) [O.F., from L. *īra*], *n.* Anger, passion. **ireful,** *a.* **irefully,** *adv.* ***irefulness,** *n.*

***irenic, *-al** (ī rē' nik, -ren' ik, -ȧl) [Gr. *eirēnikos*, from *eirēnē*, peace], *a.* Pacific; promoting peace. **irenicon** [EIRENICON].

Iricism [IRISHISM, see IRISH].

iridescent (ir i des' ėnt) [Gr. *īris īridos*, IRIS, -ESCENT], *a.* Exhibiting changing colours like those of the rainbow. **iridescence,** *n.*

iridium (ī rid' i ŭm) [as prec., -IUM], *n.* A shining white metallic element belonging to the platinum group. **iridize** (ī' ri dīz), *v.t.* To tip (a pen) with iridium.

irido- [Gr. *īris īridos*, IRIS], *comb. form.* Of or pertaining to the iris of the eye.

iridosmine (ir id oz' mīn), *n.* A native alloy of iridium and osmium, used for the points of gold pens.

iridotomy (i ri dot' ō mi), *n.* (*Surg.*) Incision of the iris to relieve occlusion of the pupil, etc. **iridotome,** *n.* A knife used for this.

iris (ī' ris) [Gr. *īris īridos*], *n.* (*Gr. Myth.*) The rainbow personified as a goddess, the messenger of the gods; (pl. **-ses**) the rainbow; an appearance resembling the rainbow, an iridescence; (*Anat.*) the circular coloured membrane or curtain surrounding the pupil of the eye; (*Bot.*) a genus of plants of the family *Iridaceæ*, with tuberous roots, sword-shaped leaves, and large variously-coloured flowers, the commonest British species being *I. pseudacorus*, the yellow flag; a flower of this genus, a fleur-de-lis or flower-de-luce; (*Min.*) a rock-crystal with iridescent properties. **irisated,** *a.* Exhibiting prismatic colours. **irisation** (-sā' shŭn), *n.* **iriscope,** *n.* An instrument for exhibiting the prismatic colours. **irised,** *a.* Containing colours like the rainbow.

Irish (ī' rish) [A.-S. *Iras*, pl.], *a.* Of or pertaining to Ireland or its inhabitants; like an Irishman. *n.* A native of Ireland; the Irish language; (*Am. slang*) temper, contentiousness. **Irishman, -woman,** *n.* A native of Ireland; one of Irish race. **Irish moss** [CARRAGEEN]. **Irish stew:** A kind of hash, consisting of vegetables and meat boiled together. **Irishism,** *n.* A mode of expression or idiom peculiar to the Irish, esp. a 'bull.' **Irishize,** *v.t.* ***Irishry,** *n.* The people of Ireland as opposed to English settlers.

iritis (ī rī' tis) [IRIS, -ITIS], *n.* (*Path.*) Inflammation of the iris of the eye.

irk (ĕrk) [M.G. *irken*, etym. doubtful], *v.t.* To tire, to bore; to annoy, to disgust. *v.i.* To become tired or worried. **irksome,** *a.* Wearisome, tedious, tiring; *tired. **irksomely,** *adv.* **irksomeness,** *n.*

iron (ī' ėrn) [A.-S. *īren*, *īsen*, *īsern* (cp. Dut. *ijzer*, Icel. *jārn*, *isarn*, G. *eisen*)], *n.* A malleable tenacious metallic element used for tools, etc., the commonest and most useful of all the metals; an article, tool, utensil, etc., made of iron; an iron implement for smoothing clothes; (*Golf*) a metal-headed club used for lofting; (*pl.*) fetters. *a.* Made or composed of iron; like iron, robust, strong, inflexible, or unyielding, merciless. *v.t.* To furnish or cover with iron; to fetter with irons; to smooth with a smoothing-iron. **curling-, driving-, grappling-iron:** Various implements, tools, etc., made of iron. **in irons:** In fetters. **to have (too) many irons in the fire:** To be attempting or dealing with (too) many projects at the some time; to have several expedients. **flat-iron, smoothing-iron,** *n.* An iron implement that is heated for smoothing cloth. **iron age:** The late prehistoric age when weapons and many implements began to be made of iron; (*Gr. Myth.*) the last of the four ages of the world, described by Hesiod, Ovid, etc., in which oppression and vice prevailed. **iron-bark,** *n.* An Australian eucalyptus with a hard, firm bark. **iron-bound,** *a.* Bound with iron; surrounded with rocks (of a coast); (*fig.*) unyielding, hard and fast. **ironclad,** *n.* A war-vessel having the parts above water plated with iron. *a.* Covered or protected with iron. **Iron Cross,** *n.* A Prussian war-medal first struck in 1813 and revived in 1870. **Iron Curtain,** *n.* The imperceptible barrier to communication between U.S.S.R. with its satellites and the rest of Europe. **Iron Duke,** *n.* The first Duke of Wellington. **iron-filings:** Fine particles of iron made by filing. **iron-fisted,** *a.* Close-fisted, covetous. ***iron-flint,** *n.* Ferruginous quartz. **iron-founder,** *n.* One who makes iron castings. **iron-foundry,** *n.* **iron-gang,** *n.* (*Austral. hist.*) A gang of convicts in chains. **iron-grey,** *n.* A grey hue like that of iron freshly broken; a horse of this colour. *a.* Of an iron-grey hue. **ironheart,** *n.* A hard-wood New Zealand tree. **iron-hearted,** *a.* Hard-hearted, cruel. **iron-heater,** *n.* The piece of metal heated in the fire for a laundress's box-iron. **iron horse,** *n.* (*old colloq.*) A railway locomotive. **iron-liquor,** *n.* Acetate of iron, used by dyers as a mordant. **iron lung,** *n.* A mechanical device employed for maintaining or assisting respiration. **iron man,** *n.* A self-acting spinning mule; (*Am. slang*) a dollar. **iron-master,** *n.* A manufacturer of iron. **ironmonger,** *n.* One who deals in ironware or hardware (*Am.* hardware dealer). **ironmongery,** *n.* **iron-mould,** *n.* A spot on cloth, etc. caused by ink or rust. *v.t.* To stain (as cloth) with ink or rust. *v.i.* To be stained in this way. **iron rations,** *n.pl.* (*Mil.*) Complete emergency rations packed in a sealed case. **iron-sand,** *n.* (*Geol.*) Sand full of particles of iron, usu. magnetite. ***iron-sick,** *a.* (*Naut.*) Applied to a ship with bolts and nails so corroded with rust as to cause her to leak. **iron-smith,** *n.* A worker in iron. **iron-stone,** *n.* An iron-ore containing oxygen and silica. **ironware,** *n.* Goods made of iron, hardware. **iron-wood,** *n.* The popular name given to several very hard and heavy woods. **ironwork,** *n.* Any thing made of iron; (*pl., usu. as sing.*) an establishment where iron is manufactured, wrought or cast. ***iron-witted,** *a.* Unfeeling, insensible. **ironer,** *n.* One who irons or smooths (linen, etc.) with a flat-iron; a machine for ironing. **ironing,** *n.* **ironing-board,** *n.* **irony** (1) (ī′ ėr ni), *a.* Consisting of, containing, or resembling iron.

ironic, ironical [IRONY].

Ironside, Ironsides (ī′ ėrn sīd, -sīdz), *n.* One of Cromwell's troopers; a hardy veteran.

irony (2) (ī′ rȯ ni) [F. *ironie*, L. *īronīa*, Gr. *eirōneia*, from *eirōn*, a dissembler], *n.* An expression intended to convey the opposite to the literal meaning; language having a meaning or implication for those who understand different from the ostensible one, or different from that of which the speaker is conscious; subtle sarcasm in which apparent praise really conveys disapprobation. **irony of fate or circumstances:** The apparent malice or perversity of events not under human control. **Socratic irony:** Simulation of ignorance in order to lead on and eventually to confute an opponent. **ironic, -al** (ī ron′ ik, ȧl), *a.* **ironically,** *adv.* **ironist** (ī′ rȯ nist), *n.*

irradiate (i rā′ di āt) [L. *irradiātus*, p.p. of *irradiāre* (IR- (1), *radius*, RAY)], *v.t.* To shed light upon; to make bright or brilliant; (*fig.*) to light up (a subject, etc.); to brighten up (a face, expression, etc.); to subject to sunlight or ultra-violet rays. **v.i.* To shine. **a.* Made brilliant or bright. **irradiant,** *a.* **irradiance, *-diancy, irradiation** (-ā′ shŭn), *n.* **irradiative** (i rā′ di ȧ tiv), *a.*

irradicate (i răd′ i kāt) [IR- (1), L. *rādīcātus*, p.p. of *rādīcāre*, to take root, from *rādix rādīcem*, root], *v.t.* To fix firmly, to enroot.

irrational (i răsh′ ȯ nȧl) [L. *irrātiōnālis*], *a.* Not rational; without reason or understanding; illogical, contrary to reason, absurd; (*Math.*) not expressible by a whole number or common fraction, not commensurable with a finite number. *n.* An irrational number; absurd. **irrationality** (-năl′ i ti), *n.* **irrationalize,** *v.t.* **irrationally,** *adv.*

irreceptive [UNRECEPTIVE].

irreciprocal (ir ė sip′ rȯ kȧl), *a.* Not reciprocal.

irreclaimable (ir ė klā′ mȧbl), *a.* Incapable of being reclaimed; obstinate, inveterate. **irreclaimably,** *adv.*

irrecognizable (i rek ŏg nī′ zȧbl), *a.* Unrecognizable. **irrecognizability** (-bil′ i ti), *n.* **irrecognizably,** *adv.* **irrecognizant** (ir ė kog′ ni zȧnt), *a.* **irrecognition** (-nish′ ŭn), *n.*

irreconcilable (i rek ŏn sī′ lȧbl), *a.* Incapable of being reconciled; implacably hostile; incompatible, inconsistent, incongruous; (*Math.*) independent, never coinciding within given limits. *n.* One who cannot be reconciled, appeased, or satisfied, an intransigent. **irreconcilability** (-bil′ i ti), **irreconcilableness,** *n.* **irreconcilably,** *adv.* ***irreconciled,** *a.* **irreconcilement,** *n.*

irrecoverable (ir ė kŭv′ ėr ȧbl), *a.* That cannot be recovered; irreparable. **irrecoverableness,** *n.* **irrecoverably,** *adv.*

irrecusable (ir ė kū′ zȧbl) [F., from late L. *irrecūsābilis* (IR- (2), *recūsāre*, to refuse)], *a.* Not to be refused or rejected.

irredeemable (ir ė dē′ mȧbl), *a.* Not redeemable; not terminable by payment of the principal (as an annuity); not convertible into cash (as a banknote); irreclaimable. **irredeemably,** *adv.* **irredeemability** (-bil′ i ti), **irredeemableness,** *n.*

irredentist (ir ė den′ tist) [It. *irredentista*, from *Italia irredenta*, unredeemed Italy], *n.* One of a party formed about 1878 to bring about the inclusion of all Italian-speaking districts in the kingdom of Italy. **irredentism,** *n.*

irreducible (ir ė dū′ sibl), *a.* Not reducible; not to be lessened; not to be brought to a required condition etc.; (*Surg.*) not giving way to treatment; (*Math.*) not to be simplified. **irreducibility** (-bil′ i ti), **irreducibleness,** *n.* ***irreduction** (-dŭk′ shŭn), *n.*

irreformable (ir ė fôr′ mȧbl), *a.* Unalterable; incapable of being reformed.

irrefragable (i ref′ rȧ gȧbl) [late L. *irrefrāgābilis*], *a.* Incapable of being refuted; undeniable, unanswerable. **irrefragably,** *adv.* **irrefragability** (-bil′ i ti), ***irrefragableness,** *n.*

irrefrangible (ir ė frăn′ jibl), *a.* Not to be broken, inviolable; (*Opt.*) not susceptible of refraction.

irrefutable (ir ė fū′-, i ref′ ū tȧbl) [F., from L. *irrefutābilis*], *a.* Incapable of being refuted. **irrefutability** (-bil′ i ti), *n.* **irrefutably,** *adv.*

irregular (i reg′ ū lȧr) [O.F. *irreguler*, late L. *irrēgulāris*], *a.* Not regular, not according to rule or established principles or custom; departing from rules, not in conformity with law, duty, etc., lawless, disorderly; not according to type, abnormal, asymmetrical; not straight, not direct, not uniform; (*Gram.*) deviating from the common form in inflexion; (*Mil.*) not belonging to the regular army. *n.* One who does not conform to established rule, discipline, authority, etc.; (*pl.*) irregular troops. **irregularity** (-lăr′ i ti), *n.* **irregularly,** *adv.* ***irregulous,** *a.* Lawless, licentious.

irrelative (i rel' å tiv), *a.* Not relative, unconnected; (*Metaph.*) having no relations, absolute. *n.* That which is without relations. **irrelated** (ir ė lā' tėd), *a.* **irrelation,** *n.* **irrelatively** (i rel'-), adv.

irrelevant (i rel' ė vånt), *a.* Not applicable or pertinent, not to the point; having no application (to the matter in hand). **irrelevance, -vancy,** *n.* **irrelevantly,** *adv.*

irreligion (ir ė lij' ȯn) [F. *irréligion*, L. *irreligiōnem*, nom. *-gio*], *n.* Indifference or hostility to religion. **irreligionist,** *n.* **irreligious,** *a.* **irreligiously,** *adv.* **irreligiousness,** *n.*

irremediable (ir ė mē' di åbl) [M.F. *irrémédiable*, L. *irremediābilis*], *a.* Incurable, irreparable; incapable of being remedied or corrected. **irremediableness,** *n.* **irremediably,** *adv.*

irremissible (ir ė mis' ibl) [F. *irrémissible*, L. *irremissibilis*], *a.* That cannot be remitted or pardoned. **irremissibility** (-bil' i ti), *n.* **irremissibly,** *adv.* ***irremissive,** *a.* Unremitting.

irremovable (ir ė moo' våbl), *a.* That cannot be removed or displaced, permanent, immovable; *inflexible, determined. **irremovability** (-bil' i ti), *n.* **irremovably,** *adv.*

irreparable (i rep' å råbl) [F., from L. *irreparābilis*], *a.* Incapable of being repaired, remedied, or restored. ***irreparability** (-bil' i ti), **irreparableness,** *n.* **irreparably,** *adv.*

irrepealable (ir ė pē' låbl), *a.* Incapable of being repealed, irrevocable. **irrepealability** (-bil' i ti), *n.* **irrepealably,** *adv.*

irreplaceable (ir ė plā' såbl), *a.* Not to be made good in case of loss.

irreprehensible (i rep rė hen' sibl) [late L. *irreprehensibilis*], *a.* Free from blame. **irreprehensibly,** *adv.*

irrepressible (ir ė pres' ibl), *a.* Not to be repressed. **irrepressibly,** *adv.*

irreproachable (ir ė prō' chåbl) [F. *irreprochable*], *a.* Blameless, faultless. **irreproachability** (-bil' i ti), **irreproachableness,** *n.* **irreproachably,** *adv.*

irresistible (ir ė zis' tibl) [late L. *irresistibilis*], *a.* That cannot be resisted; not to be withstood. ***irresistance,** *n.* **irresistibility** (-bil' i ti), **irresistibleness,** *n.* **irresistibly,** *adv.*

***irresoluble** (i rez' ȯ lūbl) *a.* Incapable of being resolved into its elements; indissoluble; insoluble in water.

irresolute (i rez' ȯ lūt) [L. *irresolūtus*], *a.* Not resolute; undecided, hesitating. **irresolutely,** *adv.* **irresoluteness, irresolution** (-lū' shůn), *n.*

irresolvable (ir ė zol' våbl), *a.* Incapable of being resolved, insoluble; not to be analysed or separated into elements. **irresolvability** (-bil' i ti), *n.*

irrespective (ir ė spek' tiv), *a.* Not respective, regardless of, without reference to; irrespectively; *disrespectful. **irrespectively,** *adv.* Without regard to circumstances or conditions.

irrespirable (i res' pir åbl, ir ės pīr' åbl), *a.* Not fit to be breathed.

irresponsible (ir ė spon' sibl), *a.* Not responsible; not trustworthy; performed or acting without a proper sense of responsibility. **irresponsibility** (-bil' i ti), *n.* **irresponsibly,** *adv.*

irresponsive (ir ė spon' siv), *a.* Not responsive (to). **irresponsiveness,** *n.*

irretentive (ir ė ten' tiv), *a.* Not retentive. **irretention** (-ten' shůn), **irretentiveness,** *n.*

irretrievable (ir ė trē' våbl), *a.* Not to be retrieved; irreparable. **irretrievability** (-bil' i ti), *n.* **irretrievably,** *adv.*

irreverent (i rev' ėr ėnt) [F. *irrévérent*, L. *irreverentem*, nom. *-ens*], *a.* Lacking in reverence; disrespectful; proceeding from irreverence. **irreverence,** *n.* **irreverential** (-en' shål), *a.* **irreverently,** *adv.*

irreversible (ir ė vėr' sibl), *a.* Not reversible; irrevocable. **irreversibility** (-bil' i ti), ***irreversibleness,** *n.* **irreversibly,** *adv.*

irrevocable (i rev' ȯ kåbl) [F., from L. *irrevocābilis*], *a.* Incapable of being revoked or altered, unalterable. **irrevocability** (-bil' i ti), **irrevocableness,** *n.* **irrevocably,** *adv.*

irrigate (ir' i gāt) [L. *irrigātus*, p.p. of *irrigāre* (IR- (1), *rigāre*, to moisten)], *v.t.* To water (land) by causing a stream to flow over it; to supply (land) with water (of streams); (*Med.*) to moisten (a wound, etc.) with a continuous jet or stream of antiseptic fluid; (*fig.*) to refresh or fertilize the mind as with a stream. **irrigable,** *a.* **irrigant,** *a.* Irrigating. *n.* A ditch for irrigation. **irrigative,** *a.* **irrigation** (ir i gā' shůn), *n.* **irrigator** (ir' i gā tȯr), *n.* ***irriguous** (i rig' ū ůs), *a.*

***irrision** (i rizh' ůn) [L. *irrīsio -ōnem*, from *irrīdēre* (IR- (1), *rīdēre*, to laugh)], *n.* Mockery, derision.

irritate (1) (ir' i tāt) [L. *irrītātus*, p.p. of *irrītāre*, prob. freq. of *irrīre*, *hirrīre*, to snarl], *v.t.* To excite impatience or ill-temper; to fret, to annoy, to exasperate; to stir up, to excite; to cause an uneasy sensation in (the skin, an organ, etc.); to stimulate (an organ) artificially. **irritable** (ir' i tåbl), *a.* Easily provoked, fretful; easily inflamed or made painful, highly sensitive; responsive to artificial stimulation (of nerves, muscles, etc.). **irritability** (-bil' i ti), ***irritableness,** *n.* **irritably,** *adv.* **irritant,** *a.* and *n.* **irritancy** (1), *n.* **irritation** (-tā' shůn), *n.* **irritative** (ir' i tā tiv), ***irritatory,** *a.*

irritate (2) (ir' i tāt) [L. *irritātus*, p.p. of *irritāre*, from *irritus*, invalid (IR- (2), *ratus*, established)], *v.t.* (*Sc. Law*) To render null and void. **irritancy** (2), *n.* Nullification, invalidity.

irruption (i rŭp' shůn) [F., from L. *irruptiōnem*, nom. *-tio*, from *irrumpere* (IR- (1), *rumpere*, to break), p.p. *irruptus*], *n.* A bursting in; a sudden invasion or incursion. **irruptive,** *a.*

Irvingite (ėr' ving īt) [Edward *Irving* (1792–1834), minister of the Church of Scotland], *n.* A member of a religious body known as the Catholic Apostolic Church, of which Irving was an early leader. **Irvingism,** *n.*

is (iz) *3rd. pers. sing. pres. ind.* [see AM, BE].

Isabel (iz' å bel), **Isabella** (iz å bel' å) [female name], *a.* and *n.* Greyish yellow, light buff, or straw colour. **Isabelline,** *a.*

isagogic (ī så goj' ik) [L. *īsagōgicus*, Gr. *eisagōgikos*, from *eisagōgē*, introduction (*eis*, into, *agōgē*, from *agein*, to lead)], *a.* Introductory. *n.pl.* Preliminary investigation regarding the Scriptures, the department of biblical study concerned with literary history, authorship, etc.

isandrous (ī săn' drůs) [Gr. *isos*, equal, *anēr andros*, a male], *a.* (*Bot.*) Having the stamens all similar and equal in number to the petals. **isantherous** (ī săn' thėr ůs) [ANTHER, -OUS], *a.* (*Bot.*) Having equal anthers. **isanthous** (ī săn' thůs) [Gr. *anthos*, flower], *a.* (*Bot.*) Having regular flowers.

isatin (ī' så tin) [L. and Gr. *isatis*, -IN], *n.* (*Chem.*) A compound obtained by oxidizing indigo, crystallizing in yellowish-red prisms. **Isatis,** *n.* (*Bot.*) A genus of cruciferous herbs, comprising *I. tinctoria*, the woad, cultivated for dyeing.

ischiatic (is ki ăt' ik) [med. L. *ischiaticus*, *ischiadicus*, Gr. *ischiadikos*, from *ischias -ados*, pain in the hip, from *ischion*, hip], *n.* Pertaining to the hip or to sciatica. **ischial** (is' ki ål), *a.* **ischialgia** (is ki ăl' ji å) [Gr. *-algia*, *algos*, pain], *n.* (*Path.*) Pain in the hip-joint, sciatica.

ischuria (is kū' ri å) [L. *ischūria*, Gr. *ischouiar* (*ischein*, to hold, *ouria*, URINE)], *n.* (*Path.*) Retention or suppression of the urine. **ischuretic** (is kū ret' ik), *a.* Relieving ischuria. *n.* An ischuretic medicine.

-ise [O.F. *-ise*, L. *-ītia*, *-itia*, *-icia*, *-itium*, *-icium* (cp. -ICE)], *suf.* Forming abstract nouns, as *franchise*, *merchandise.*

isenergic (ī sė nėr' jik) [Gr. *isos*, equal, ENERGIC], *a.* (*Phys.*) Of or indicating equal energy.

-ish (1) [A.-S. *-isc* (cp. Dut. and G. *-isch*, Icel. *-iskr*, also Gr. *iskos*)], *suf.* Of the nature of, pertaining to; rather, somewhat; as in *childish, English, outlandish, reddish, yellowish.*

-ish (2) [F. *-iss-*, in pres.p. etc. of verbs in *-ir*, L. incept. suf. *-isc-*], *suf.* Forming verb, as *cherish, finish, punish.*

Ishmael (ish' mā ėl) [son of Abraham and Hagar], *n.* (*fig.*) An outcast (Gen. xvi. 12); one whose hand is against every man. **Ishmaelite,** *n.* A descendant of Ishmael; one at war against society. **Ishmaelitish,** *a.*

Isiac (ī' si ăk) [L. *īsiacus*, Gr. *isiakos*, from ISIS], *a.* Of or pertaining to Isis. *n.* A priest or worshipper of Isis, the principal Egyptian goddess.

isidium (ī sid' i ům) [mod. L., from *Isis -idis*], *n.* (*pl.* **-dia**) (*Bot.*) A coral-like growth on the thallus of lichens acting as soredia.

Isidorian (ī si dôr' i ȧn), *a.* Of or pertaining to St. Isidore (560–636), Archbishop of Seville, or to his collection of canons and decretals (applied to the interpolated collection later recognized as the pseudo-Isidorian or false decretals).

isinglass (ī' zing glas) [said to be a corr. of M.Dut. *huyzenblas* (cp. G. *hausenblase*), sturgeon's bladder], *n.* A gelatinous substance prepared from the swimming-bladders of the sturgeon, cod, and other fish, used for making jellies, glue, etc.

Islam (iz' lȧm, iz lam') [Arab. *islām*, submission, from *salama*, he was resigned, whence SALAAM], *n.* Mohammedanism; (*collect.*) the believers in Mohammedanism or the peoples under Mohammedan rule. **Islamic** (iz lăm' ik), **Islamitic** (-mit' ik), *a.* **Islamism** (iz' lȧ mizm), **Islamite,** *n.*

island (ī' lȧnd) [M.E. *iland*, A.-S. *īgland* (*īg, īeg*, -LAND), cp. Icel. *eyland*, Dut. *eiland* (*s* introd. by conf. with foll.)], *n.* A piece of land surrounded by water; anything isolated or resembling an island; an area in the middle of a highway which divides the traffic and affords a refuge for the pedestrian; (*Am.*) wood surrounded by prairie; (*Anat.*) a cluster of cells, mass of tissue, etc., different in formation from those surrounding it. ***v.t.* To form into an island; to isolate; to dot as with islands. **Islands of the Blest:** (*Gr. Mythol.*) Imaginary islands situated in the western ocean, supposed to be the abode of good men after death. **islander,** *n.*

isle (īl) [M.E. *ile*, O.F. *ile, isle*, L. *insula*], *n.* An island, esp. a small island. ***v.t.* To form into an island; to isolate. **islesman,** *n.* An islander, esp. belonging to the Hebrides, Orkneys, or Shetlands. **islet,** *n.* A little island.

ism (izm) [as foll.], *n.* A doctrine or system of a distinctive kind (*usu. disparagingly*). **ismatic, -al** (iz măt' ik, -ȧl), *a.* **ismaticalness,** *n.*

-ism [F. *-isme*, L. *-ismus*, Gr. *-ismos* or *-isma*, from verbal ending *-izein*], *suf.* Forming abstract nouns denoting doctrine, theory, principle, system, etc., as *altruism, Conservatism, Socialism, spiritualism, Gallicism, scoundrelism.*

iso- [Gr. *isos*], *comb. form.* Equal; having the same number of parts.

isobar (ī' sō bar) [Gr. *baros*, weight], *n.* A line on a map connecting places having the same mean barometric pressure, or the same pressure at a given time. **isobaric, isobarometric,** *a.* Of equal barometric pressure; pertaining to isobars. **isobathytherm** (ī sō băth' i thĕrm), *n.* A line connecting points having the same temperature in a vertical section of a part of the sea. **isobathythermal,** *a.* **isobront** (ī' sō bront), *n.* A line connecting points at which a peal of thunder is heard simultaneously.

isochasm (ī' sō kăzm), *n.* A line connecting points having an equal frequency of auroras. **isochasmic,** *a.* **isocheim** (ī' sȯ kīm) [Gr. *cheima*, winter (cp. L. *heims*)], *n.* A line connecting places having the same mean winter temperature. **isocheimal** (-kī' mȧl), **isochimenal,** *a.* Marking equal winters. *n.* An isochimenal line. **isochor** (ī' sȯ kôr) [Gr. *chōra*, space], *n.* A line (on a diagram representing relations between pressure and temperature) connecting the points denoting equal volumes. **isochoric** (-kor' ik), *a.* **isochromatic** (ī sȯ krȯ măt' ik) [CHROMATIC], *a.* Of the same colour.

isochronal, isochronous, isochronic (ī sō krō' nȧl, -nůs, ī sō kron' ik), *a.* Denoting or occupying equal spaces of time, esp. performing their beats in the same time (of two or more pendulums). **isochronism,** *n.* The occupying of an equal space of time; regular periodicity (as the swinging of a pendulum). **isochronously,** *adv.* **isochroous** (ī sok' rȯ ůs) [Gr. *chroa*, colour], *a.* Having a uniform colour throughout.

isoclinal, isoclinic (ī sō klī' nȧl, -nik), *a.* Having the same inclination or dip; (*Geog.*) having the same magnetic inclination; (*Geol.*) having the same angle or dip. **isocrymal** (ī sȯ krī' mȧl) [Gr. *krumos*, cold], *a.* Connecting points having the same temperature at the coldest season. *n.* An isocrymal line. **isocryme** (ī' sȯ krīm), *n.*

isodiametric (ī sō dī ȧ met' rik), *a.* (*Bot. & Cryst.*) Equal in diameter. **isodimorphic** (ī sō dī môr' fik), *a.* Characterized by isodimorphism. **isodimorphism,** *n.* (*Cryst.*) Isomorphism between substances that are dimorphous. **isodomon, -omum** (ī sod' ȯ mȯn, -mům) [Gr. *isodomon* (L. *-domum*), from *domos*, a layer or course], *n.* (*Arch.*) A method of building practised by the ancient Greeks, with blocks of equal length, the vertical joints being above the middle of the blocks immediately below. **isodomous,** *a.* **isodynamic** (ī sȯ di năm' ik) [DYNAMIC], *a.* Having equal force, esp. of terrestrial magnetism. **isodont** (ī' sȯ dont) [Gr. *odous odontos*, tooth], *a.* (*Anat.*) Having the teeth all alike. **isodontous** (-don' tůs), *a.*

isogamy (ī sog' ȧ mi) [Gr. *gamia*, marriage], *n.* (*Biol.*) The conjugation of two cells or protoplasmic masses not differentiated into male or female. **isogamous,** *a.* **isogeny** (ī soj' ė ni) [-GENY], *n.* (*Biol.*) General similarity of origin; general correspondence or homology. **isogenous,** *a.*

isogeotherm (ī sō jē' ō thĕrm), *n.* A line connecting places having the same mean temperature below the surface. **isogeothermal, isogeothermic,** *a.*

isognathous (ī sog' nȧ thus) [Gr. *gnathos*, jaw], *a.* (*Zool.*) Having the jaws projecting equally.

isogon (ī' sō gon), *n.* (*Geom.*) A figure having the angles all equal. **isogonal** (ī sog' ȯ nȧl), *a.* Equiangular; isogonic. **isogonic** (1) (ī sȯ gon' ik), *a.* Connecting points (on the earth's surface) having the same magnetic declination or variation from true north. *n.* An isogonic line. **isogonism** (ī sog' ȯ nizm) [Gr. *gonos, gonē*, offspring, -ISM], *n.* The production of like sexual individuals from different stocks, as in certain hydrozoa. **isogonic** (2) (-gon' ik), *a.*

isolate (ī' sȯ lāt) [F. *isoler*, It. *isolare*, L. *insulāre*, to INSULATE], *v.t.* To place in a detached situation; (*Elec.*) to insulate; (*Chem.*) to obtain in an uncombined form; to subject to quarantine. **isolation** (-lā' shůn), *n.* **isolationist,** *n.* (*U.S.A. polit.*) One who believes in the policy of holding aloof from all political entanglements with other countries. **isolator** (ī' sȯ lā tȯr), *n.*

isomeric, -al (ī sȯ mer' ik, -ȧl) [Gr. *isomerēs* (ISO-, *meros*, share)], *a.* (*Chem.*) Having identical elements, molecular weight, and proportions, with difference in physical characteristics or chemical properties owing to different grouping. **isomerism** (ī som' ėr izm), *n.* **isomerous,** *a.* (*Chem.*) Isomeric; (*Bot., Zool., etc.*) having the parts or segments equal in number.

isometric, isometrical (ī sō met' rik, -ȧl), *a.* Of equal measure. **isometric projection:** (*Eng.*) A drawing in approximate perspective from which lengths can be scaled. **isomorphism** (ī sȯ môr' fizm) [Gr. *morphē*, form, -ISM], *n.* (*Cryst.*) The property of crystallizing in identical or nearly identical forms; (*Math.*) identity of form and construction between two or more groups. **isomorphic, -phous,** *a.*

-ison [F. *-aison, -eison, -ison,* L. *-ātiōnem, -etiōnem, -itiōnem*], *suf.* As in *comparison, orison.*

isonomy (ī son′ ŏ mi) [Gr. *isonomia* (ISO-, *nomos,* law)], *n.* Equality of political or legal rights.

isopathy (ī sop′ ȧ thi) [ISO-, -PATHY], *n.* (*Med.*) The theory that disease may be cured by a product of the same disease. **isopathic** (-păth′ ik), *a.* **isoperimetrical** (īs ō per i met′ ri kȧl) [PERIMETRICAL], *a.* (*Geom.*) Having equal perimeters. **isoperimetry** (-im′ ĕ tri), *n.* The science of perimetrical figures.

isopod (ī′ sō pod) [Gr. *pous, podos,* a foot], *n.* (*Zool.*) One of the *Isopoda* or sessile-eyed crustaceans characterized by seven pairs of thoracic legs almost of the same length. *a.* Isopodous. **isopodan** (ī sop′ ŏ dȧn), *a.n.* **isopodous,** *a.* **isopolity** (ī sŏ pol′ i ti) [POLITY], *n.* Equality or reciprocity of civil rights between different states. **isopterous** (ī sop′ tėr ŭs) [Gr. *pteron,* wing, -OUS], *a.* (*Ent.*) Having the wings equal. **isorhythmic** (ī sŏ *rith′ mik*) [RHYTHMIC], *a.* (*Pros.*) Having the same number of time units in the thesis and arsis as a dactyl and an anapæst; composed in the same rhythm, structure, etc.

isosceles (ī sos′ ĕ lēz) [late L. *īsoscelēs,* Gr. *isoskelēs,* lit. equal-legged (ISO-, *skelos,* leg)], *a.* (*Geom.*) Having two sides equal (of a triangle).

isoseismal (ī sŏ sīz′ mȧl) [ISO-, SEISMAL], *a.* (*Geol.*) Connecting points at which an earthquake has been of the same intensity. *n.* An isoseismal line. **isoseismic,** *a.* **isosmotic** (ī sŏz mot′ ik) [OSMOTIC], *a.* Equal in osmotic pressure. **isostatic** (ī sŏ stăt′ ik) [STATIC], *a.* (*Geol.*) In equilibrium owing to equality of pressure on every side, as that normally prevailing in the crust of the earth. **isostasy** (ī sos′ tȧ si), *n.* **isotheral** (ī sŏ ther′ ȧl, -thēr′ ȧl) [Gr. *theros,* summer], *a.* Connecting points having the same mean summer temperature. *n.* An isotheral line.

isotherm (ī′ sō thĕrm), *n.* A line on a globe or map passing over places having the same mean temperature. **isothermal** (-thĕr′ mȧl), *a.* and *n.* **isotonic** (ī sŏ ton′ ik) [Gr. *isotonos* (ISO-, TONE)], *a.* (*Mus.*) Having equal tones; (*Physiol.*) having equal tension or tonicity (of muscles); isosmotic (of the corpuscles of the blood).

isotopes (ī′ sō tōps) [Gr. *topos,* place], *n.pl.* Varieties of an element, identical in properties but differing in atomic weight. **isotropic** (ī sŏ trop′ ik) [Gr. *isotropos* (*tropos,* way, from *trepein,* to turn)], *a.* Manifesting the same physical properties in every direction. **isotropous** (ī sot′ trŏ pŭs), *a.* **isotropism, isotropy,** *n.*

I-spy [HY-SPY].

Israel (iz′ rā ĕl) [L. and Gr. *Isrāēl,* Heb. *yisrāēl,* striver with God], *n.* (*collect.*) The Israelites, the Jewish people; (*Pol.*) an autonomous country founded in Palestine in 1948. **Israeli** (iz-rā′ li) *n.a.* An inhabitant of, or pertaining to the State of Israel. **Israelite,** *n.* A descendant of Israel, a Jew. **Israelitic** (-lit′ ik), **Israelitish** (-lī′ tish), *a.* **British Israelite:** One who imagines that the British are of the Lost Tribes of Israel.

Issei (ē′ sā) [Jap.], *n.* Japanese immigrant in U.S.A. not eligible for citizenship.

issue (ish′ ū, is′ ū) [O.F., from pop. L. *exūtus,* L. *exitus,* from *exīre* (EX-, *īre,* to go)], *n.* The act of passing or flowing out; egress, outgoing, outflow; a discharge, as of blood; way or means of exit or escape, outlet; the mouth of a river; progeny, offspring; the produce of the earth; profits from land or other property; result, consequence; the point in debate; (*Law*) the point between contending parties; the act of sending or giving out; publication; that which is published at a particular time; the whole quantity or number sent out at one time. *v.i.* To pass or flow out; to be published; to emerge (from); to be descended; to proceed, to be derived (from); to end or result (in). *v.t.* To send out; to publish; to put into circulation. **at issue:** In dispute; at variance. **to join** or **take issue:** To take opposite sides upon a point in dispute; (*Law*) to submit an issue jointly for decision. **issuable,** *a.* **issuance,** *n.* The act of issuing. **issuant,** *a.* (*Her.*) Emerging or issuing (from a chief). **issueless,** *a.* **issuer,** *n.*

-ist [F. *-iste,* L. *-ista,* Gr. *-istēs*], *suf.* Denoting an agent, adherent, follower, etc., as *Baptist, botanist, Calvinist, fatalist, monogamist, Socialist.*

-ister [O.F. *-istre,* var. of prec.], *suf.* Denoting an agent etc., as *chorister, sophister.*

isthmus (is′-, ist′ mŭs) [L., from Gr. *isthmos*], *n.* (*pl.* **-uses**) A neck of land connecting two larger portions of land; (*Anat., etc.*) a narrow passage or part between two larger cavities or parts. **Isthmian,** *a.* Pertaining to an isthmus, esp. to the Isthmus of Corinth in Greece. **Isthmian games:** Games celebrated in ancient times at Corinth in the first and third years of each Olympiad, forming one of the four great Panhellenic festivals. **isthmitis** (is mī′ tis), *n.* (*Path.*) Inflammation of the fauces.

istle (ist′ li) [Mex. *ixtli*], *n.* A species of Mexican agave, or the tough wiry fibre of its leaves, used for cordage, etc.

it (1) (it) [A.-S. *hit,* neut. of *hē,* HE (cp. Dut. *het,* Icel. *hit*)], *3rd pers. neut. pron.* (*poss.* **its,** *pl.* **they,** *poss.* **their,** *obj.* **them**). The thing spoken about (ref. to noun mentioned or understood); the person understood (esp. in questions and replies, also as subject of a verb the actual subject of which follows, usu. in apposition or introduced by 'that'); the grammatical subject of an impersonal verb; the indefinite object of an intr. or tr. verb (as *to rough it, to fight it out*). *n.* (*facet.*) Sex appeal.

it (2) (it), *n.* (*colloq.*) Italian vermouth.

itacism (ē′ tȧ sizm) [Gr. *ēta,* η (cp. IOTACISM)], *n.* Pronunciation of the Greek η as ē [cp. ETACISM].

itacolumite (ī tȧ kol′ ū mīt) [*Itacolumi,* mountain in Brazil, -ITE], *n.* (*Min.*) A granular quartzose slate which in thin slabs is sometimes flexible.

Italian (i tăl′ yȧn) [L. *Italiānus,* from *Italia,* Italy], *a.* Pertaining to Italy. *n.* A native of Italy; the Italian language. **Italian handwriting:** The cursive writing adopted from Italy, opp. to Gothic. **Italian iron:** A laundress's cylindrical iron for fluting frills, etc. **Italian warehouse:** A shop for the sale of oils, macaroni, dried fruits, etc. ***Italianate,** *v.t.* To render Italian. *a.* Italianized. **Italianism,** *n.* **Italianize,** *v.i.* and *t.*

italic (i tăl′ ik) [L. *Italicus,* Gr. *Italikos,* as prec.], *a.* Applied to a sloping type (*thus*), introduced by the Venetian printer Aldus Manutius, *c.* 1500; pertaining to ancient Italy or the Italian races or their languages, esp. as distinguished from Roman. *n.pl.* Italic letters or type. **italicize** (-sīz), *v.t.* To print in italics; (*fig.*) to emphasize. **italicism, italicization** (-zā′ shŭn), *n.*

Italiot (i tăl′ i ŏt) [Gr. *Italiōtēs,* from *Italia,* Italy], *a.* Pertaining to the Greek colonies in Italy. *n.* A native or inhabitant of these.

itch (ich) [A.-S. *giccan* (cp. Dut. *jeuken,* G. *jucken*)], *v.i.* To have a sensation of uneasiness in the skin exciting a desire to scratch the part; (*fig.*) to feel a constant teasing desire (for, etc.). *n.* A sensation of uneasiness in the skin causing a desire to scratch; (*fig.*) an uneasy desire or craving (for, etc.); (*Path.*) a contagious skin-disease produced by the itch-mite *Sarcoptes scabiei.* **itchy,** *a.* **itchiness,** *n.*

-ite [F. *-ite,* L. *-ita,* Gr. *-itēs*], *suf.* Belonging to, a follower of, as *Browningite, Pre-Raphaelite, Spinozite*; denoting fossils, minerals, chemical substances, explosives, etc., as *belemnite, ichnite, dolomite, quartzite.*

item (1) (ī′ tĕm) [L., in like manner, cp. *ita,* so, from *is,* he, with adv. suf. *-tem*], *n.* A separate article or particular in an enumeration; an individual entry in an account, schedule, etc.; a paragraph or detail of news in a newspaper; *a maxim, a saying. ***item*** (2), *adv.* Likewise, also. **v.t.* To make a note or memorandum of. **itemize,** *v.t.* To set forth in detail.

iterate (it′ ėr āt) [L. *iterātus*, p.p. of *iterāre*, from *iterum*, again], *v.t.* To repeat, to say, make, or do over and over again. **iterant,** *a.* Repeating, iterating. **iteration** (-ā′ shŭn), *n.* **iterative,** *a.*

Ithuriel's spear (i thūr′ i ėlz spēr) [angel in *Paradise Lost*], *n.* Test of genuineness.

ithyphallic (ith i făl′ ik) [L. *ithyphallicus*, Gr. *ithuphallikos* (*ithus*, straight, *phallikos*, from PHALLUS)], *a.* Of or pertaining to the erect phallus carried in Bacchic processions; in the metre of Bacchic verse; (*fig.*) grossly indecent. *n.* A poem in this metre or style.

itinerant (ī-, i tin′ ėr ănt) [L. *itinerans -ntem*, pres.p. of *itinerārī*, from *iter itineris*, a journey], *a.* Passing or moving from place to place; travelling on a circuit. *n.* One who journeys from place to place; a travelling preacher, a strolling player, etc. **itineracy, itinerancy,** *n.* ***itinerantly,** *adv.*

itinerary (ī tin′ ėr ă ri), *n.* An account of places and their distances on a road, a guide-book; a route taken or to be taken; an account of travels; *(*R.-C. Ch.*) a form of prayer for clerics when travelling. *a.* Pertaining to roads or to travel. **itinerate,** *v.i.* To journey from place to place; to preach on circuit. **itineration** (-ā′ shŭn), *n.*

-ition [F. *-ition*, L. *-itiōnem*, -ION], *suf.*

-itious [(1) L. *-icius* or *-īcius*; (2) L. *-ōsus*, -OUS, added to stems in *-it-*], *suf.* As in *adventitious, factitious, ambitious, nutritious.*

-itis [mod. L. *-ītis*, Gr. *-itis*, orig. fem. of adjectives in *-itēs* (qualifying *nosos*, disease)], *suf.* (*Path.*) Denoting inflammation, as *gastritis, peritonitis.*

-itous [F. *-iteux*, L. *-itōsus* (*-it-*, OUS)], *suf.*

its, *poss.* [IT]. **it's** [abbrev. IT IS].

itself (it self′), *pron.* Used emphatically (*usu. in apposition*); used reflexively. **by itself:** Alone, separately. **in itself:** Independently of other things; in its essential qualities.

ittria, etc. [YTTRIA].

-ity [F. *-ité*, L. *-itātem*, nom. *-itas*, see -TY], *suf.*

-ium [L.], *suf.* (*Chem.*) Used chiefly to form names of metals, as *aluminium, lithium, sodium.*

-ive [F. *-if*, fem. *-ive*, L. *-ivus*], *suf.* Disposed, serving, or tending to; of the nature or quality of; as *active, massive, pensive, restive, talkative.*

ivied [IVY].

ivory (ī′ vŏr i) [A.-F. *ivorie*, O.F. *yvoire* (F. *ivoire*), L. *eboreus*, made of ivory, from *ebur eboris*, ivory], *n.* The hard white substance composing the tusks of the elephant, the narwhal, etc.; the colour of ivory; (*slang, pl.*) teeth, billiard-balls, dice, keys of a piano, etc. *a.* Consisting, made of, or resembling ivory; **black ivory,** *n.* African negro slaves. **vegetable ivory:** The hard albumen of ivory-nuts. **ivory-black,** *n.* A kind of bone-black made of calcined ivory. **ivory-nut,** *n.* The seed of a tropical American palm, *Phytelephas macrocarpa.* **ivory tower,** *n.* (*fig.*) A shelter from realities. **ivory turner:** A worker in ivory.

ivy (ī′ vi) [A.-S. *ifig*], *n.* (*pl.* **ivies**) An evergreen climbing plant, *Hedera helix*, usu. having five-angled leaves, and adhering by aerial rootlets. **ivy-bush,** *n.* A large bunch of ivy formerly hung in front of a tavern; a painted sign representing this. **ivy-geranium,** *n.* The ivy-leaved pelargonium. **ivy-mantled,** *a.* Overgrown with ivy. **ivied,** *a.*

iwis (i wis′) [A.-S. *gewis*, certain (cp. Dut. *gewis*, G. *gewiss*)], *adv.* Certainly (often spelt erron. *I wis*).

ixia (ik′ si ă) [Gr.], *n.* (*Bot.*) A genus of South African bulbous flowering plants of the iris family.

Ixion's wheel (ik′ si onz wēl), *n.* (*Gr. Myth.*) Wheel on which Ixion was condemned to revolve forever in Hades.

ixolite (ik′ sŏ līt) [G. *ixolyt* (Gr. *ixos*, mistletoe, birdlime, -LITE)], *n.* (*Min.*) An amorphous mineral resin found in bituminous coal, of greasy lustre and hyacinth-red colour.

izard (iz′ ărd) [F. *isard*, etym. doubtful], *n.* A kind of antelope related to the chamois, inhabiting the Pyrenees.

-ize [F. *-iser*, late L. *-izāre*, Gr. *-izein*], *suf.* Forming verbs denoting to speak or act as; to follow or practise; to come to resemble, to come into such a state; (*transitively*) to cause to follow, resemble, or come into such a state; as *Anglicize, Christianize, evangelize, Hellenize.*

Izod Test (ī′ zod test), *n.* A test to determine particular characteristics of structural materials.

Izvestia (iz vest′ i ă) [Rus., news], *n.* The official organ of the legislature of the U.S.S.R.

***izzard** (iz′ ărd) [formerly *ezod*, F. *ézed*, Gr. *zēta*], *n.* The letter *z.*

J

J, j, the tenth letter in the English alphabet (*pl.* **jay's, Js, J's**), has the sound of a voiced explosive consonant, that of *g* in *gem.*

jaal-goat (jā′ al gōt) [Afr.], *n.* A type of ibex or goat found in Abyssinia and Upper Egypt.

jab (jăb) [prob. imit. (cp. JOB (2))], *v.t.* To poke violently; to stab; to thrust (something) roughly (into). *n.* A sharp poke, a stab, a thrust.

jabber (jăb′ ėr) [prob. onomat., cp. GABBLE], *v.i.* To talk volubly and incoherently; to chatter; to utter nonsensical or unintelligible sounds. *v.t.* To utter rapidly and indistinctly. *n.* Rapid, indistinct, or nonsensical talk; gabble. **jabberer,** *n.* ***jabberment,** *n.*

jabbernowl [JOBBERNOWL].

jabble (jăbl) [Sc., prob. onomat. (cp. DABBLE)], *v.i.* To splash, to dash in wavelets. *n.* A splashing; an agitation.

jabiru (jăb′ i roo) [Tupi-Guarani], *n.* A bird of the genus *Mycteria*, S. American stork-like wading-birds.

jaborandi (jăb ŏr ăn′ di) [Tupi-Guarani], *n.* The dried leaflets of certain species of *Pilocarpus*, tropical American shrubs, used as sudorific and diuretic drugs.

jabot (zha bō′) [F., etym. unknown], *n.* A lace frill worn at the neck of a woman's bodice; *a ruffle on a shirt front.

jacamar (jăk′ ă mar) [F., from Tupi-Guarani], *n.* Any bird of the tropical American genus *Galbula*, resembling the kingfisher.

jacana (jăk′ ă nă) [Port., *jaçanã*, Tupi-Guarani *jasanã*], *n.* Any bird of the grallatorial genus *Parra*, from the warmer parts of N. and S. America.

jacaranda (jăk ă răn′ dă) [Tupi-Guarani], *n.* A genus of tropical American trees of the order *Bignoniaceæ*, yielding fragrant and ornamental wood.

Jacchus (jak′ ŭs) [Gr. Iakkos, Bacchus], *n.* A small squirrel-like South-American monkey.

***jacent** (jā′ sėnt) [L. *jācens -ntem*, pres.p. of *jacēre*, to lie], *a.* Recumbent, lying at length.

jacinth (jăs′ inth) [O.F. *jacinthe*, HYACINTH], *n.* (*Min.*) A variety of zircon; *a hyacinth.

jack (1) (jăk) [prob. dim. of *John* (E. W. B. Nicholson traced it (1892) to *Jackin, Jankin, John*), but perh. conn. with F. *Jacques*, James, L. *Jacōbus*, Gr. *Jakōbos*, Jacob], *n.* Familiar or diminutive for John; hence, a fellow, one of the common people; a labourer, an odd-job man; a sailor; a pike, esp. a young or small one; the knave of cards; a contrivance for turning a spit; a contrivance for lifting heavy weights; a device for lifting a carriage-wheel, etc.; a lever or other part in various machines; a wooden frame on which wood or timber is sawn; (*Mining*) a gad, a wooden wedge; (*Naut.*) a small flag [cp. UNION-JACK]. *v.t.* To lift, hoist, or move with a jack; (*slang*) to resign, to give (up). **before one can say Jack Robinson:** Quite suddenly and unexpectedly. **every man jack:** Every individual. **cheap-jack** [CHEAP]. **steeple-jack** [STEEPLE]. **yellow jack:** Yellow fever. **jack-a-dandy,** *n.* A little foppish fellow. ***Jack-a-Lent,** *n.* A puppet thrown at in Lenten games; (*fig.*) a simple fellow. **jack-bean,** *n.* A climbing plant of the *Camavali* genus. **jack-block,** *n.* (*Naut.*) A block for raising and lowering the top-gallant mast. **jack-boot,** *n.* A large overall boot reaching to the thigh, worn by fishermen; *a large boot with a front piece coming above the knee; (*fig.*) unintelligent and inhuman behaviour in dictatorial rule (from the high boots worn by German soldiers). **jack-by-the-hedge:** Hedge garlic, *Sisymbrium alliaria.* **jack-chain,** *n.* (*Forestry*) An endless spiked chain which carries logs from one point to another. **jack-flag,** *n.* (*Naut.*) A flag hoisted at the spritsail top-mast head. **Jack Frost:** Frost personified. **jack-high,** *a.* and *adv.* (*Bowls*) The distance up the green to the jack. **Jack-in-office,** *n.* One who assumes authority on account of holding a petty office. **jack-in-the-box:** A grotesque figure that springs out of a box when the lid is raised; a kind of firework; a large wooden male screw turning in a nut. **Jack-in-the-green,** *n.* A chimney-sweep enclosed in a framework covered with leaves, in old-fashioned May-day festivities. **Jack of all trades:** One who can turn his hand to any business. **jack o' lantern:** An ignis fatuus. **Jack Ketch:** The public hangman. **jack-knife,** *n.* A large clasp-knife, esp. one with a horn handle, carried by seamen. **jack-plane,** *n.* The first and coarsest of the joiner's bench-planes. **jack-pot,** *n.* The money pool in card games and competitions; a fund of prize-money. **jack-pudding,** *n.* A merry-andrew. **jack-screw,** *n.* A lifting implement worked by a screw. ***jack-smith,** *n.* One who makes roasting jacks. **jack-snipe,** *n.* A small European species of snipe. **jack-staff,** *n.* (*Naut.*) A flagstaff on the bowsprit cap for flying the jack. **jack-stay,** *n.* (*Naut.*) A rib or plate with holes, or a rod running through eye-bolts, passing along the upper side of a yard, to which the sail is bent. **jack-straw,** *n.* *A scarecrow; a person of no weight or substance. **jack-tar** [TAR (2)]. **jack-towel,** *n.* A long round towel on a roller. **Jacky,** *n.* (*Austral. colloq.*) An Aboriginal man.

***jack** (2) (jăk) [O.F. *jaque*, perh. ident. with *jaques*], *n.* A jacket, usu. of leather, formerly worn by foot-soldiers; a coat of mail; a vessel for liquor, usu. of leather.

jack (3) (jăk) [Port. *jaca*, Malayalam *chukka*], *n.* An East Indian fruit, like a coarser bread-fruit. **jack-tree,** *n.*

jackal (jăk' awl) [Turk. *chakāl*, Pers. *shaghāl*], *n.* A gregarious animal, *Canis aureus*, closely allied to the dog; one who does dirty work or drudgery for another (from the belief that the jackal hunts up prey for the lion).

jackanapes (jăk' ȧ nāps) [*Jack Napes*, nickname of William de la Pole, Duke of Suffolk (*d.* 1450), whose badge was a clog and chain such as was commonly used for a tame ape], *n.* A pert fellow; a coxcomb; *an ape.

jackaroo (jăk ȧ roo') [*Jack*; *kangaroo*], *n.* (*Austral. slang*) A new-comer, a novice.

jackass (jăk' ăs), *n.* A male ass; (*fig.*) a stupid ignorant fellow. **jackass fish,** *n.* The edible 'morwong' of Australia and N. Zealand. **jackass rabbit,** *n.* A male rabbit. **laughing jackass,** *n.* The Australian giant kingfisher, so called from its discordant cry.

jackdaw (jăk' daw), *n.* The smallest of the British crows, *Corvus monedula.*

jacket (jăk' ėt) [O.F. *jaquette*, dim of *jaque*, JACK (2)], *n.* A short coat or sleeved outer garment for men or women; (*fig.*) the coat of an animal; a wrapper, a cover; an outer covering of paper put on a book bound in cloth or leather; (*colloq.*) the skin of a potato; a covering round a boiler, steam-pipe, cylinder of an internal-combustion engine, etc., to prevent radiation of heat. *v.t.* To envelop in a jacket; (*colloq.*) to thrash. **to dust one's jacket** [DUST]. **jacketed,** *a.* Wearing a jacket. **jacketing,** *n.* (*colloq.*) A thrashing.

jack-flag, etc. [JACK (1)].

jacko [JOCKO].

jack o' lantern, etc. [JACK (1)].

Jacobean (jăk ō bē' ȧn) [late L. *Jacōbæus*, from *Jacōbus*, Jacob, whence also *James*], *a.* Belonging to the reign of James I; pertaining to the Apostle St. James the Less.

Jacobin (jăk' ō bin) [F., from low L. *Jacōbinus*, as prec.], *n.* A Dominican friar; a member of a revolutionary republican club, that met in the hall of the Jacobin friars, in the Rue St. Jacques, Paris, 1789–94; an extreme revolutionist, a violent republican; a variety of hooded pigeon. **Jacobinic, *-al** (-bin' ik, -ȧl), *a.* **Jacobinism** (jăk' ō bin izm), *n.* **Jacobinize,** *v.t.*

Jacobite (jăk' ō bīt) [L. *Jacōbus*, James, -ITE], *n.* A partisan of James II after his abdication, or of the Stuart pretenders to the throne. *a.* Pertaining to or holding the opinions of the Jacobites. **Jacobitic, -al** (-bit' ik, -ȧl), *a.* **Jacobitism,** *n.*

Jacob's ladder (jā' kobz lăd' ėr) [with alln. to the patriarch Jacob's dream (Gen. xxviii. 12)], *n.* A garden plant, *Polemonium cœruleum*, with closely pinnate leaves; (*Naut.*) a rope ladder with wooden rounds.

Jacob's staff (jā' kobz staf) [with alln. to St. James the Less, whose emblem was a pilgrim's staff and a scallop], *n.* *A pilgrim's staff; *a staff containing a concealed dagger; a cross-staff, an intrument for measuring distances and heights.

Jacobus (jȧ kō' bŭs) [L., see JACOBITE], *n.* A gold coin, struck in the reign of James I, value 20–25s.

jaconet (jăk' ō net) [corr. from Hind. *Jagganāthī*, whence JUGGERNAUT], *n.* A fine, close, white cotton cloth, rather heavier than cambric.

Jacquard loom (jăk' ard, jȧ kard' loom) [inventor J. M. Jacquard, 1752–1834], *n.* A loom for weaving figured fabrics.

jacquerie (zhȧ kė rē') [F., from *Jacques*, a peasant], *n.* A revolt of the peasants against the nobles in France, in 1357–8; any peasant revolt.

jactation (jăk tā' shŭn) [L. *jactātio*, from *jactāre*, to throw, freq. of *jacere*, see foll.], *n.* The act of throwing; agitation of the body in exercise, as in riding; jactitation; *boasting, bragging. **jactitation** (jăk ti tā' shŭn), *n.* (*Path.*) Restlessness, a tossing or twitching of the body or limbs; (*Law*) a false pretension to marriage.

***jaculate** (jăk' ū lāt) [L. *jaculātus*, p.p. of *jaculārī*, from *jaculum*, javelin, from *jacere*, to throw], *v.t.* To throw, dart, or hurl. ***jaculation** (-lā' shŭn), *n.* **jaculator,** *n.* One who throws or darts; the archer-fish. ***jaculatory,** *a.* Throwing or darting out suddenly; ejaculatory.

jade (1) (jād) [etym. doubtful], *n.* A broken-down, worthless horse; (*playfully or in contempt*) an old woman, a wench, a young woman. *v.t.* *To over-drive; (*usu. in p.p.*) to tire out. **v.i.* To become weary. **jadedly,** *adv.* **jadedness,** *n.* ***jadery,** *n.* **jadish,** *a.*

jade (2) (jād) [F., from Sp. *piedra di ijada* (stone of the side), L. ILIA, ILIUM (because supposed to cure colic)], *n.* A green, massive, sometimes cryptocrystalline, silicate of lime and magnesia, used for ornamental purposes; applied to other minerals of a similar appearance.

jaeger (yā' gĕr) [G. from *jagen*, hunt], *n.* A huntsman; (*Mil.*) a sharpshooter; an attendant waiting on a person of quality; trade mark of a woven material.

jag (jăg) [prob. imit.], *n.* A notch; a ragged piece, tooth, or point; a stab, a prick; (*Am. slang*) a drinking debauch. *v.t.* To cut or tear raggedly; to cut into notches, to form denticulations in. **jagged** (jăg′ ed), *a.* Having notches; ragged, sharply uneven; (*Bot.*) cut coarsely. **jaggedly,** *adv.* **jaggedness,** *n.* **jagger,** *n.* One who or that which jags; a toothed chisel. **jaggy,** *a.*

***jaggery** (jăg′ ėr i) [Port. *jágara*, Canarese *sharkare*, Hind. *shakkar*, Sansk. *çarkarā*, SUGAR], *n.* A coarse dark-brown kind of sugar made in India from the juice of certain palms.

jaguar (jăg′ wȧr, -ū ȧr) [Tupi-Guarani *yagouara*], *n.* A South American feline animal, *Felis onca*, resembling the leopard.

Jah (ja) [Heb. *Yah*, shortened form of *Yahiveh*, JEHOVAH], *n.* Jehovah. **Jahveh,** *n.* (*form adopted by Bibl. critics*). **Jahvism, Jahvist** (ya′ vizm, -vist), *n.*

jahad [JIHAD].

jail, gaol (jāl) [A.-F. *gaole*, O.F. *jaiole* (F. *geôle*), late L. *gabiola*, dim. of *gabia*, L. *cavea*, CAGE], *n.* A prison, a public place of confinement for persons charged with or convicted of crime. **jail-bird,** *n.* One who has been to prison; an inveterate criminal. **jail-delivery,** *n.* (*Law*) A commission empowering judges to try the prisoners in a place, and so clear the jail. **jail-fever,** *n.* An old name for typhus formerly endemic in jails. **jailer, gaoler,** *n.* The keeper of a prison. **jaileress, gaoleress,** *n.*

Jain, Jaina (jān, jā′ nȧ) [Hindi, from Sansk. *jaina*, pertaining to a Buddha or Saint, *jina*], *n.* A professor of Jainism. *a.* Of or belonging to the Jains or Jainism. **Jainism,** *n.* An Indian non-Brahminical religion akin to Buddhism. **Jainist,** *n.*

jake (jāk) [?], *a.* Honest; correct; very good.

***jakes** (jāks) [etym. doubtful], *n.* A privy; excrement.

jalap (jăl′ ȧp) [F., from Sp. *jalapa*, *Xalapa*, Aztec *Xalapan*, place in Mexico], *n.* The dried tubercles of *Exogonium purga*, used as a purgative. **jalapin,** *n.* (*Chem.*) An amorphous glucoside existing in jalap root.

jalopy (jȧ lop′ i) [etym. unknown], *n.* (*Am. colloq.*) A much-worn automobile.

jalouse (jȧ looz′) [Sc. from F. *jalouser*, from *jaloux*, JEALOUS], *v.t.* To suspect; to surmise.

jalousie (zhăl′ u zi) [F., JEALOUSY], *n.* A louvre blind, a Venetian shutter. **jalousied,** *a.*

jam (1) (jăm) [prob. imit., cp. CHAMP], *v.t.* (*past & p.p.* **jammed**) To wedge or squeeze (in or into); to squeeze, to compress between two surfaces; to squeeze together; to block up by crowding into; to make (a machine, etc.) immovable or unworkable by forcible handling; (*Radio.*) to prevent clear radio reception of a signal by transmitting an interfering signal on the same wavelength. *v.i.* To become immovable or unworkable by rough handling (of a machine etc.). *n.* A crush, a squeeze; a stoppage in a machine due to jamming; a crowd, a press. **to be in a jam:** To be in a predicament.

jam (2) (jăm) [prob. from prec.], *n.* A conserve of fruit made by boiling with sugar. **jam-pot,** *n.*

Jamaica pepper (ja mā′ kȧ pep′ ėr) [*Jamaica*, West Indian island], *n.* Allspice; pimento.

jamb (jăm) [F. *jambe*, leg, late L. *gamba*, a hoof, prob. from Celt. (cp. W. *cam*, crooked)], *n.* One of the upright sides of a doorway, window, or fireplace; *a piece of armour for the leg; (*Her.*) a leg.

***jambeaux, giambeaux** (jăm′ bō) [A.-F., from prec.], *n.pl.* Leg or shin-pieces of armour; leggings.

***jambee** (jăm′ bė) [*Jambi*, in Sumatra], *n.* A walking-stick or cane from the Jambi district.

jambok [SJAMBOK].

jamboree (jăm bȯ rē′), *n.* A rally of Boy Scouts; a frolic.

jampan (jăm′ păn) [Bengali *jhāmpān*, Hind. *jhappān*], *n.* A sedan-chair borne on two bamboo poles by four men. **jampanee** (jăm pȧ nē′), *n.* One of the bearers of a jampan.

jane (jān) [name], *n.* (*Am. & Austral. slang*) A woman.

jangle (jăng′ gėl) [O.F. *jangler*, prob. onomat.], *v.i.* To sound harshly or discordantly; to wrangle, to bicker; *to chatter. *v.t.* To cause to sound discordantly; to utter harshly. *n.* Wrangling, bickering; discordant sound, as of bells out of tune; noisy chatter. **jangler,** *n.* A wrangler.

janitor (jăn′ i tȯr) [L. from *jānua*, door], *n.* A doorkeeper; (*Am.*) caretaker, porter. **janitorial** (-tôr′ i ȧl), *a.* **janitorship,** *n.* **janitress, -trix,** *n.*

janizary (jăn′-, yăn′ i zȧr i) [Turk. *yeni-tsheri* (*yeni*, new, *tscheri*, soldiery)], *n.* A soldier of the old Turkish infantry forming the Sultan's bodyguard (originally young prisoners trained to arms), disbanded in 1826. ***janizarian** (-zâr′ i ȧn), *a.*

jannock (1) (jăn′ ȯk) [North., chiefly Lancs.], *n.* Oaten bread, an oaten loaf.

jannock (2) (jăn′ ȯk) [North. dial.], *a.* and *adv.* Fair, straightforward.

Jansenist (jăn′ sė nist), *n.* A follower of Cornelius Jansenius, bishop of Ypres, Flanders (*d.* 1638), who founded a party in the R.-C. Church that denied the freedom of the human will and that Christ died for all mankind. *a.* Pertaining to or characteristic of Jansenism. **Jansenism,** *n.* **Jansenistic** (-nis′ tik), *a.*

Janty, jantily, etc. [JAUNTY].

January (jăn′ ū ȧr i) [L. *jānuārius*, from foll.], *n.* The name given to the first month of the year.

janus (jā′ nŭs) [L.], *n.* An ancient Italian deity presiding over doors and gates, and usually represented with two heads looking in opposite directions. **Janus-cloth,** *n.* A fabric with different colours on opposite sides.

Jap [short for JAPANESE], *a.n.* (*colloq.*) **Jap silk,** *n.* (*Textiles*) A pure silk fabric plainly woven from net silk yarns.

japan (jȧ păn′) [island empire lying east of China], *n.* An intensely hard varnish, or varnishing liquid, made from linseed oil, resin, shellac, etc.; orig. a hard, black varnish obtained from *Stagmaria verniciflua*; work varnished and figured in the Japanese style. *v.t.* (*past & p.p.* **japanned**) To cover with or as with japan. **Japan earth:** Catechu. **Japanese,** *a.* Pertaining to Japan or its inhabitants. *n.* A native or inhabitant of Japan; the language of Japan. **Japanize** (jăp′ ȧ nīz), *v.t.* **Japanization** (-zā′ shŭn), *n.* **japanner** (jȧ păn′ ėr), *n.* One whose business is to japan goods; *a shoeblack.

jape (jāp) [etym. doubtful], *v.i.* To jest, to play tricks. **v.t.* To mock, to deride, to cheat. *n.* A jest, a trick, a joke. ***japer,** *n.*

Japhetic (jȧ fet′ ik), *a.* Of, pertaining to, or descended from Japheth, the third son of Noah.

Japonic (jȧ pon′ ik) [F. *Japon*], *a.* Japanese. **japonica** [L.], *n.* The Japanese quince, *Pyrus Japonica*, a common garden shrub. **japonically,** *adv.* **japonicize,** *v.t.*

jar (1) (jar) [prob. onomat.], *v.i.* (*past & p.p.* **jarred**) To emit a harsh or discordant sound; to vibrate harshly; to be discordant, disagreeable, or offensive; to disagree, to clash, to be inconsistent (with). *v.t.* To cause to shake or tremble; to give a shock to; *to offend, to displease. *n.* A harsh vibration as from a shock; a harsh discordant sound; a shock; a disagreement, a conflict of opinions or interests. **jarringly,** *adv.*

jar (2) (jar) [F. *jarre*, prob. through Sp. *jarra*, from Arab. *jarrah*], *n.* A vessel of glass or earthenware of various shapes and sizes, used for various domestic purposes. **jarful,** *n.*

jar (3) (jar) [CHAR (2)], *n.* A word found only in the phrase 'on the jar', partly closed, ajar [cp. AJAR (1)].

jardinière (zhar di nyâr') [F., fem. of *jardinier*, gardener], *n.* An ornamental pot or stand for growing flowers in a room etc.

jargon (1) (jar' gòn) [O.F. *jargon, gargon*, etym. doubtful], *n.* Unintelligible talk; gibberish, gabble; debased or illiterate speech or language; any professional, technical, or specialized language. *v.i.* To talk unintelligibly; (of birds) to twitter. **jargoner,** *n.* **jargonesque** (-gò nesk'), **jargonic** (-gon' ik), *a.* **jargonist,** *n.* **jargonize,** *v.i.* **jargonization** (-zā' shùn), *n.*

jargon (2) (jar' gòn) [F., from It. *giargone*, ZIRCON], *n.* A transparent, colourless or smoky variety of zircon found in Ceylon.

jargonelle (jar gò nel') [F.], *n.* A kind of early pear.

jarl (yarl) [Icel., EARL], *n.* A Norse or Dutch nobleman or chieftain, an earl or count.

jarrah (jăr' à) [Austral. abor. *jerryh*], *n.* The W. Australian mahogany gum-tree, *Eucalyptus marginata.*

jarringly [JAR (1)].

jarvey (jar' vi) [pers. name *Jarvis*], *n.* The driver of a hackney-coach or Irish jaunting-car; *a hackney-coach.

jasey (jā' zi) [said to be a corr. of *Jersey*, as being made of Jersey yarn], *n.* A familiar name for a worsted wig.

jasmine (jăs' min) [F. *jasmin, jassemin, jessemin*, Arab. *yāsmīn, yāsamīn*], *n.* Any plant of the genus *Jasminum*, many of which are climbers with sweet-scented white or yellow flowers, esp. the common white *Jasminum officinale.*

jaspé (jăs' pā) [F. *jasper*, to marble], *a.* (*Ceram.*) Having an appearance like jasper; of mottled appearance.

jasper (jăs' pėr) [O.F. *jaspre, jaspe*, L. and Gr. *iaspis*, Oriental in origin (cp. Arab. *yasb*, Pers. *yashp*, Heb. *yāshpeh*)], *n.* An impure variety of quartz, of many colours and shades, opaque even in thin splinters; a greenish marble, with small red spots; (*Am. slang*) a fellow, a man. ***jasperated,** *a.* Mixed with jasper. **jasperite,** *n.* A red variety of jasper found near Lake Superior. **jasperize,** *v.t.* ***jaspery, *jaspidean, -eous,** *a.* Like jasper; of the nature of or containing jasper. ***jaspoid,** *a.* Resembling jasper. **jasperous,** *a.* ***jasponyx,** *n.* Jasper marked like the human nail.

***jaunce** (jawns) [prob. from an O.F. *jancer*], *v.i.* To make a horse prance.

jaunder (jawn' dėr) [Sc., etym. unknown], *v.i.* To gossip, to chat. *n.* Idle talk.

jaundice (jan' dis, jawn' dis) [M.E. *jaunys*, F. *jaunisse*, from *jaune*, L. *galbinus*, from *galbus*, yellow], *n.* A morbid affection due to obstruction of the bile or absorption of the colouring matter into the blood, characterized by yellowness of the skin, diarrhœa, and general debility; (*fig.*) a mental attitude or condition, such as that caused by jealousy, prejudice, etc., which warps the vision. *v.t.* To affect with or as with jaundice; (*fig.*) to poison the mind with jealousy, prejudice, etc.

jaunt (jawnt) [perh. conn. with JAUNCE], *v.i.* To ramble or rove about; to take a short excursion. *n.* A ramble, an excursion, a short journey, a trip. **jaunting-car,** *n.* An Irish vehicle having two seats, back to back, over the wheels, and a seat for the driver in front.

jaunty (jawn' ti) [earlier *janty*, F. *gentil*, see GENTEEL], *n.* (*Naut.*) The head of a ship's police. *a.* Sprightly, airy, self-satisfied, perky. **jauntily,** *adv.* **jauntiness,** *n.*

Javanese (jăv à nēz'), *a.* Of or pertaining to Java. *n.* A native of Java; the language of Java.

***javel** (jăv' ėl) [etym. unknown], *n.* A low fellow, a tramp.

javelin (jăv' ė lin) [F. *javeline*, It. *giavelina*, prob. from Celt. (cp. Ir. *gabhla*, spear, Gael. *gobhal*, a fork)], *n.* A light spear thrown by the hand, used in ancient warfare. *v.t.* To wound or pierce with or as with a javelin. **javelin-men,** *n.pl.* A sheriff's retinue, now the escort of a judge at assizes.

jaw (1) (jaw) [etym. doubtful, perh. rel. to CHEW], *n.* One of two bones or bony structures in which the teeth are fixed, forming the framework of the mouth; (*pl.*) the mouth; (*fig., pl.*) the narrow opening of a gorge, narrow valley, etc.; (*Mach.*) one of two opposing members of a vice or similar implement or machine; (*Naut., pl.*) the concave or forked end of a boom or gaff; (*slang*) abuse, wrangling, long-winded talk. *v.i.* (*colloq.*) To talk lengthily; *to rail. *v.t.* To abuse; to lecture. **hold your jaw:** (*slang*) Shut up. **jaw-bone,** *n.* One of the pair of bones forming the lower jaw. **jaw-breaker,** *n.* (*colloq.*) An unpronounceable word. **jawed,** *a.* Having jaws (*usu. in comb.*, as *heavy-jawed*). **jaw-lever,** *n.* An instrument for opening the mouths of cattle for the administration of medicine. **jaw-tooth,** *n.* A molar.

jaw (2) (jaw) [Sc., etym. unknown], *n.* A wave, a billow; a quantity of water poured out. *v.i.* To dash, to plunge, to surge. *v.t.* To cause to surge; to pour out. **jaw-box, -hole, -tub,** *n.* A sink.

jay (jā) [O.F. *jay* (F. *geai*), etym. doubtful], *n.* A chattering bird, *Garrulus glandarius*, of brilliant plumage; a bird of several allied genera; (*fig.*) an impudent chatterer; a loud, coarse woman. **jay-walker** (jā' waw kėr), *n.* (*colloq.*) A pedestrian who crosses the street heedless of the traffic.

***jazerant** (jăz' ėr ânt) [O.F. *jaserant, -ant*, prob. from Sp. *jazarino*, Algerian, from Arab. *al-jazīrah*, Algiers], *n.* A light coat of armour composed of small plates of metal, usu. fastened to a flexible lining.

jazz (jăz) [Creole *jazz*, to speed up, prob. Af. origin], *n.* Syncopated music of Negro origin; the form of dancing that goes to this music. *v.i.* To dance jazz.

jealous (jel' ùs) [M.E. and O.F. *gelos*, late L. *zēlōsus*, from *zēlus*, ZEAL], *a.* Suspicious or apprehensive of being supplanted in the love or favour (of a wife, husband, lover, or friend); suspicious or apprehensive (of a rival); solicitous or anxiously watchful (of one's honour, rights, etc.); envious (of another or another's advantages, etc.); (*Bibl.*) requiring exclusive devotion (of God). **jealously,** *adv.* ***jealousness, jealousy,** *n.*

Jeames (jēms) [after Thackeray's *Jeames* (James) de la Pluche], *n.* A footman, a flunkey.

jean (jēn, jān) [M.E. *Gene*, It. *Genova*, Genoa], *n.* A twilled undressed cloth with cotton warp; (*pl.*) a garment or garments made of this.

jeep (jēp) [G.P., initials of General Purposes], *n.* (*U.S.A. mil.*) A fast, light car; a utility motor-van.

jeer (1) (jēr) [etym. doubtful], *v.i.* To scoff, to mock (at). *v.t.* To scoff at, to make a mock of, to deride. *n.* A scoff, a gibe, a taunt, mockery. **jeerer,** *n.* **jeeringly,** *adv.*

jeer (2) (jēr) [etym. doubtful], *n.* (*Naut.*) Tackle for hoisting, swaying, and lowering lower yards (*usu. in pl.*).

jeffersonite (jef' ėr sòn īt) [Thomas *Jefferson* (1743–1826), U.S. President], *n.* (*Min.*) A greenish-black variety of pyroxene.

Jehovah (jė hō' vâ) [Heb. *Yahōvāh*], *n.* The most sacred name given in the Old Testament to God, esp. regarded as the God of the Jewish people. **Jehovist,** *n.* The presumed author, or one of the authors, of the Jehovistic portions of the Pentateuch. **Jehovistic,** *a.* (*Bibl.*) A term used regarding portions of the Pentateuch in which the name of Jehovah is habitually employed (cp. ELOHIST). **Jehovah's Witnesses,** *n.* A millenarian sect, the International Bible Students' Association, founded by the American Pastor C. T. Russell (1852–1916).

Jehu (jē' hū) [see 2 Kings ix. 20], *n.* A coachman, a driver, esp. one who drives fast or furiously.

jejune (jė joon') [L. *jējūnus*, fasting, etym. doubtful], *a.* Bare, meagre, scanty; wanting in substance; (*fig.*) devoid of interest or life. **jejunely,** *adv.* **jejuneness,** *n.*

jejunum (je jū' nŭm), *n.* (*Anat.*) The second portion of the small intestine between the duodenum and the ileum. **jejuno-,** *comb. form.* Pertaining to the jejunum.

jelly (jel' i) [F. *gelée*, frost, L. *gelāta*, fem., p.p. of *gelāre*, to freeze], *n.* Any gelatinous substance, esp. that obtained by decoction from animal matter; a conserve made of the inspissated juice of fruit boiled with sugar. *v.i.* To turn into jelly. *v.t.* To convert into jelly. **jelly-bag, -cloth,** *n.* A bag or cloth used for straining jelly. **jelly-fish,** *n.* The popular name of the medusas and other cœlenterates. **jell,** *v.i.* (*colloq.*) To jelly. **jellify,** *v.t.* and *i.* **jellygraph** (jĕl' i grăf), *n.* An apparatus, whose essential parts are a sheet of jelly and a special kind of ink, used for multiplying copies of writing.

jemadar (jem' a dar) [Hind.], *n.* An officer in the Indian army.

jemimas (je mi' mȧs), *n.pl.* (*colloq.*) Elastic-sided boots; long galoshes for boots.

jeminy [GEMINI].

jemmy (1) (jem' i) [dim. of *James*], *n.* A short, stout crowbar, used by burglars; a baked sheep's head; a great-coat.

jemmy (2) (jem' i) [cp. JIMP], *a.* (*prov.*) Spruce, neat. **jemminess,** *n.*

jennet (jen' ėt) [F. *genet*, Sp. *ginete*, orig. light-armed horseman, perh. from Arab. *Zenāta*, Barbary tribe famous for horsemanship], *n.* A small Spanish horse.

jenneting (jen' ė ting) [prob. from F. *jeanneton*, from *Jeannet*, *Jean* (cp. *pomme de St. Jean*, St. John's apple)], *n.* An early kind of apple.

jenny (jen' i) [familiar form of *Jane* or *Janet*], *n.* A popular name for a female ass, animal, bird, etc.; a spinning-jenny; a travelling crane; (*Billiards*) a stroke pocketing the ball from an awkward position. **jenny-ass,** *n.* A female ass. **jenny-wren,** *n.* A wren.

***jeofail** (jė fāl') [A.-F. *jeo fail*, O.F. *je faille*, I fail], *n.* (*Law*) An error or oversight in pleading or other proceeding.

jeopardy (jep' ȧr di) [O.F. *jeu parti*, divided or even game (*jeu*, L. *jocus*, game, *parti*, L. *partītus*, p.p. of *partīrī*, to PART (2))], *n.* Exposure to danger, loss, or injury; risk, hazard, danger, peril. ***jeopard, jeopardize,** *v.t.* To put in jeopardy; to risk. ***jeopardous,** *a.* ***jeopardously,** *adv.*

jequirity (jė kwir' i ti) [Tupi-Guarani, *jekiriti*] *n.* A tropical twining shrub, *Abrus precatorius* or Indian liquorice, with parti-coloured seeds or beans which are used for ornaments and for medicinal purposes. **jequirity-beans,** *n.pl.*

jerboa (jĕr' bō ȧ, jĕr bō' ȧ) [Arab. *yarbū'*, the flesh of the loins, from the powerful muscles of its hind leg], *n.* A small mouse-like rodent, *Dipus Ægyptius*, with long hind legs adapted for leaping.

jereed, -id (jė rēd') [Arab. *jarīd*, orig. a stripped palm-branch], *n.* A javelin, used in Persia and Turkey, esp. in games; a game with this.

jeremiad (jer ė mī' ȧd) [F. *jérémiade*], *n.* A lamentation, esp. over modern degeneracy, in the style of the prophet Jeremiah.

jerfalcon [GERFALCON].

jerk (1) (jĕrk) [prob. onomat.], *v.t.* To pull, push, or thrust sharply; to throw with a sharp, suddenly arrested action. *v.i.* To move with jerks. *n.* A sharp, sudden push or tug; a twitch, a spasmodic movement due to involuntary contraction of a muscle; (*pl.*) violent twitches or spasmodic movements of the face or members, often due to religious excitement. **jerker,** *n.* **jerky,** *a.* **jerkily,** *adv.* **jerkiness,** *n.*

jerk (2) (jĕrk) [corr. from Am. Sp. *cha quear*, from CHARQUI], *v.t.* To cut (beef) into long pieces and dry in the sun. **jerked beef,** *n.* Charqui.

jerk (3) [JERQUE].

jerkin (1) (jĕr' kin) [etym. unknown], *n.* A short coat or jacket, formerly often made of leather; a close waistcoat. ***jerkinet,** *n.* A woman's jacket or blouse.

***jerkin** (2) [GERFALCON].

jerkin-head (jĕr' kin hed) [etym. doubtful], *n.* (*Arch.*) A combination of truncated gable and hipped roof.

Jeroboam (jer ō bō' ȧm) [in alln. to 1 Kings ix. 28], *n.* A drinking-bowl or beaker of great size; a wine-bottle holding 10–12 quarts.

jerque (jĕrk) [etym. doubtful], *v.t.* To search (a vessel or her papers) for unentered goods. **jerquer,** *n.* A custom-house searcher.

Jerry (1) (jer' i) [perh. from GERMAN], *n.* (*slang*) A German soldier.

jerry (2) (jer' i) [prob. fam. form of *Jeremiah*], *a.* Cheaply and badly built, flimsy, *n.* (*slang*) A chamber-pot. **jerry-builder,** *n.* A speculative builder of cheap and inferior houses. **jerry-building,** *n.* **jerry-built,** *a.* **jerry-shop,** *n.* A beerhouse.

jerrymander [GERRYMANDER].

jersey (jĕr' zi) [the island of *Jersey*], *n.* A close-fitting woollen knitted tunic worn in athletic exercises; a similar close-fitting garment worn as a jacket or pull-over by women and children; fine wool yarn or combed wool, as that produced in Jersey.

jerupigia [GEROPIGIA].

Jerusalem artichoke, pony [ARTICHOKE, PONY].

jess (jes) [O.F. *ges*, obj. *gel*, L. *jactus -tum*, a cast, from *jacere*, to throw], *n.* (*Falconry*) A short leather strap or silk ribbon which was tied round each leg of a hawk, and to which the leash was usually attached. **jessed,** *a.* Having jesses on (said of a hawk); (*Her.*) with jesses of a specified tincture.

jessamine [JASMINE].

jessamy (jes' ȧ mi) [corr. of prec.], *n.* Jasmine; a fop, a dandy.

jessant (jes' ȧnt) [O.F. *iessant*, pres.p. of *issir*, to ISSUE], *a.* (*Her.*) Issuing or springing (from).

Jesse (jes' i) [the father of David (Is. xi. 1)], *n.* A genealogical tree representing the genealogy of Christ, esp. in the form of a large brass candlestick with many branches. **Jesse-window,** *n.* A window of which the tracery and glazing represent a genealogical tree of Jesse.

jesserant [JAZERANT].

jest (jest) [O.F. *geste*, orig. an exploit, L. *gesta*, neut. pl. p.p. of *gerere*, to do], *n.* A joke, something ludicrous said or done to provoke mirth; a jeer, a taunt; a laughing-stock; a prank, a frolic; *a masque, a masquerade. *v.i.* To joke; to utter jests; to provoke mirth by ludicrous actions or words; to make game, to jeer (at). **in jest:** As a jest or joke; not seriously or in earnest. **jest-book,** *n.* A collection of jokes or jocular tales or sayings. **jester,** *n.* One who jests or jokes, a buffoon, esp. one formerly retained by persons of high rank to make sport. ***jestful,** *a.* ***jesting-stock,** *n.* A laughing-stock. **jestingly,** *adv.*

Jesuit (jez' ū it), *n.* A member of the Society of Jesus, a R.-C. order founded in 1534 by Ignatius Loyola; (*fig.*) a crafty, insidious person, a subtle casuist or prevaricator. **Jesuits' bark:** Cinchona bark. ***Jesuitess,** *n.* A member of an order of nuns, abolished by Pope Urban VIII. in 1630. **Jesuitic, -al** (jez ū it' ik, -ȧl), *a.* Crafty, cunning, designing. **Jesuitically,** *adv.* **Jesuitism, Jesuitry,** *n.* **Jesuitize,** *v.t.* and *i.*

Jesus (jē′ zůs) [L., from Gr. *Iēsous*, Heb. *yēshūa*, Joshua], *n.* The Saviour. **Company or Society of Jesus:** The Jesuits.

jet (1) (jet) [O.F. *jaiet*, L. *gagātem*, nom. *-tēs*, Gr. *gagatēs*, from *Gagai*, in Lycia], *n.* A black compact variety of lignite susceptible of a brilliant polish, formerly much used for articles of personal ornament. *a.* The colour of jet. **jet-black,** *a.* **jetty** (2), *a.*

jet (2) (jet) [O.F. *jetter* (F. *jeter*), L. *jactāre*, freq. of *jacere*, to throw] *v.i.* (*past & p.p.* **jetted**) To spurt or shoot out, to come out in a jet or jets; *to shoot forward, to jut out; (*Shak.*) to encroach (upon); *to strut, to swagger. *v.t.* To send out in a jet or jets. *n.* A sudden spurt or shooting out of water or flame, esp. from a small orifice; a spout or nozzle for the discharge of water, etc.; (*Foundry*) a channel for passing molten metal into a mould; also the piece of metal remaining in the aperture after the metal is cold, the spruce; (*colloq.*) a jet-propelled plane. **jet-propelled,** *a.* (*Mech.*) Descriptive of an aircraft or vehicle propelled by heating and expanding air which is directed in a jet from the rear of the plane.

jetsam (jet′ såm) [var. of foll.], *n.* Goods, cargo, etc., thrown overboard in order to lighten a ship in distress and subsequently washed ashore.

jettison (jet′ i sŏn) [A.-F. *getteson*, O.F. *getaison*, L. *jactātiōnem*, nom. *-tio*, from *jactāre*, freq. of *jacere*, to throw], *n.* The casting of goods overboard to lighten a vessel in distress. *v.t.* To throw goods overboard in order to lighten a vessel.

jetty (1) (jet′ i) [O.F. *getee* (F. *jetée*), p.p. of *jeter*, to throw, see JET (2)], *n.* A structure of stone or timber projecting into water and serving as a mole, pier, or wharf; a landing pier; (*Arch.*) a part of a building which juts beyond the ground-plan.

jetty (2) [JET (1)].

jeu, (zhėr) [F., from L. *jocus*, see JOKE], *n.* (*pl.* ***jeux***) A game, a play, a jest. ***jeu de mots*** (dė mō), *n.* A pun. ***jeu d'esprit*** (dė sprē′), *n.* A witticism, a play of wit, a witty sally.

Jew (joo) [A.-F. *Jeu*, *Geu*, O.F. *giu* (F. *juif*), L. *Iūdæum*, nom. *-us*, Gr. *Ioudaios*, Heb. *y'hūdāh*, Judah, son of Jacob], *n.* Originally a member of the kingdom of Judah, but later used for all adherents of the Mosaic Law, frequently also called 'Israelite' or 'Hebrew'; now applied to professing members of the synagogue and, loosely, to racial descendants of the Hebrew tribe; incorr. a citizen of the State of Israel; (*fig.*) a usurer, an extortionate tradesman, moneylender, etc. *v.t.* (*colloq.*) To get the better of in a bargain, to overreach. **jew's-ear,** *n.* A tough edible fungus, *Hirneola auricula Judæ*, growing on elder and elm-trees. **jew's harp:** A musical instrument held between the teeth, the sound produced by the vibrations of a metal tongue set in motion by the forefinger. **jew's-mallow,** *n.* A plant, *Corchorus capsularis*, used in the East as a potherb. **Jewess,** *n.* **Jewish,** *a.* **Jewish Agency,** *n.* An organization that links the state of Israel with Jews throughout the world.

jewel (joo′ ėl) [A.-F. *juel*, O.F. *joiel*, *joel*, etym. doubtful; perh. from late L. *jocāle*, from L. *jocāre*, to play (whence *juer*, *jouer*), or dim. of *joie*, L. *gaudium*, joy], *n.* A precious stone, a gem; a personal ornament containing a precious stone or stones; (*fig.*) a person or thing of very great value or excellence (frequently a term of endearment). *v.t.* To adorn with or as with jewels; to fit (a watch) with jewels in the pivot-holes. **jewel-block,** *n.* (*Naut.*) A block at the yard-arm of a ship, for the halyard of a studding-sail yard to pass through. **jewel-case,** *n.* ***Jewel-house, *-office,** *n.* The place (in the Tower of London) where the Crown jewels are deposited. **jewel-like,** *a.* **jeweller,** *n.* A maker of or dealer in jewels. **jewellery, jewelry** (joo′ ėl ri), *n.* (*collect.*) Jewels in general; the art or trade of a jeweller.

jewfish (joo′ fish), *n.* The name given to several large edible fish caught in Australian waters; the kingfish of S. Australia and Victoria.

jewing (joo′ ing) [JEW, -ING], *n.* The wattles at the base of the beak in some domestic pigeons (supposed to have some resemblance to a hooked nose).

Jewry (joo′ ri) [O.F. *juierie*, JEW, -ERY], *n.* (*collect.*) The Jews or the land where they dwell or dwelt; (*Hist.*) Judæa; the Jews' quarter in a town or country.

jewstone (jū′ stōn) [W. *ddu*, black], *n.* A local name for a black basalt found in the Clee Hills, Shropshire; the fossil spine of a sea-urchin or echinus, formerly used as a medicine.

Jezebel (jez′ ė bėl) [wife of Ahab, king of Israel, 1 Kings, xvi. 31], *n.* A wicked, bold, or vicious woman, esp. a woman who paints her face.

jib (1) (jib) [etym. doubtful; perh. abbr. of GIBBET, or from JIB (2)], *n.* A large triangular sail set on a stay between the fore-topmast-head and bowsprit or jib-boom in large vessels, and between the masthead and the bowsprit in smaller ones; the extended arm of a crane or derrick. **the cut of his jib:** (*orig. Naut. slang*) One's physical appearance. **jib-boom,** *n.* A movable spar running out beyond the bowsprit. **jib-door,** *n.* A door flush with the wall on both sides, and usu. papered or painted over so as to be concealed.

jib (2) (jib) [cp. Dan. *gibbe*, Dut. *gijpen*], *v.t.* (*past & p.p.* **jibbed**) To shift (a boom, yard, or sail) from one side of a vessel to the other. *v.i.* To swing round (of a sail, etc.). Cp. GYBE.

jib (3) (jib) [etym. doubtful], *v.i.* To move restively sideways or backwards, as a horse; (*fig.*) to make difficulties (at some task, course, person, etc.). **jibber** (1), *n.* A horse that jibs.

jibbah (ji′ bå) [Ar.] *n.* Long, loose coat worn by Mohammedans; a loose overall or pinafore.

jibber (2) [GIBBER].

jibe [GIBE]. **jiblet** [GIBLET].

jiff, jiffy (jif′, -i [etym. unknown], *n.* (*colloq.*) A moment, an instant, an extremely short time.

jig (jig) [etym. doubtful], *n.* A lively dance for one or more performers; the music for such a dance; a fish-hook with a weighted shank, used for snatching at fish; a device for holding an object and guiding a cutting-tool in a machine for the manufacture of standard parts. *v.i.* (*past & p.p.* **jigged**) To dance a jig; to skip about. *v.t.* To sing or play in jig time; to jerk up and down rapidly; to separate finer and coarser qualities of (ore, etc.) by treatment in a jigger; (*fig.*) to cheat, to hoax. **jig-saw,** *n.* A vertically-reciprocating saw moved by a vibrating lever or crank-rod, used for cutting scrolls, fret-work, etc. **jigsaw puzzle,** *n.* A puzzle to put together a picture cut into irregularly shaped pieces. **jigging,** *n.* **jigging-machine,** *n.* (*Mining*) An apparatus for sifting ore in water, a jigger. ***jiggish,** *a.* Resembling or fitted for a jig; playful, frisky.

jigger (1) (jig′ ėr), *n.* One who or that which jigs; (*Mining*) a sieve shaken vertically in water to separate the contained ore; the man using such sieve; (*Naut.*) small tackle used for holding on to the cable as it is heaved in, and similar work; a small sail, usu. set on a jigger-mast; a small smack carrying this; (*Mach.*) a potter's wheel on which earthen vessels are shaped; a throwing-wheel; (*slang*) a rest for a billiard-cue; (*colloq.*) any kind of mechanical contrivance, implement, etc.; (*Golf*) an iron club coming between a mid-iron and a mashie; (*Textiles*) a machine for dyeing cloth. **jigger-mast,** *n.* A small mast at the stem of a yawl, a small mizen-mast.

jigger (2) [CHIGOE].

jigger (3) (jig′ er) [etym. doubtful], (*in p.p.*) **I'm jiggered:** I'm blessed (a mild oath).

jiggery-pokery (jig′ ėr i pō′ kėr i) [onomat.], *n.* Underhand goings-on.

jiggle (jig′ ėl) [freq. of JIG], *v.t.* To jerk or rock lightly to and fro.

jig-jog (jig′ jog), *n.* A jogging, jolting motion.

jigot [GIGOT].

jihad, jehad (jē had′) [Arab. *jihād*], *n.* A holy war proclaimed by Mussulmans against unbelievers or the enemies of Islam; (*fig.*) a war or crusade on behalf of a principle, etc.

Jill [GILL (3)]. **jilliflower** [GILLY-FLOWER].

jilt (jilt) [prob. from a dim. (**-et**) of JILL], *n.* A woman who capriciously or wantonly gives her lover encouragement and then throws him over. *v.t.* To throw over (one's lover). *v.i.* To play the jilt.

jimcrack [GIMCRACK]. **jimmy** [JEMMY (1)]. **Jimmy Woodser,** *n.* (*Austral. colloq.*) A drink one pays for oneself; a drink taken alone.

Jim Crow (jim krō′), *n.* (*U.S.A.*) A Negro (from the refrain of a negro-minstrel song); (*Mach.*) an implement for bending or straightening rails; a planing-machine with a cutting-tool adapted for turning about and cutting both ways; (*Mining*) a crowbar with an iron claw like a burglar's jemmy.

jim-jams (jim′ jăms), *n.pl.* (*slang*) Fluster, jumpiness; delirium tremens.

jimp (jimp) [Sc. and North., etym. unknown], *a.* Neat, spruce, comely; slender, scant; short in measure or weight. *adv.* Scarcely. *n.* A witty jest; a quirk. **jimply,** *adv.*

jingal [GINGAL]. **jingko** [GINGKO].

jingle (jing′ gėl) [imit.], *v.i.* To make a clinking or tinkling sound like that of small bells, bits of metal, etc.; to correspond in sound, rhyme, etc.; also, to rhyme, alliterate, etc. (both in a depreciative sense). *v.t.* To cause to make such a clinking or tinkling sound. *n.* A tinkling metallic sound; a correspondence or repetition of sounds in words, esp. of a catchy inartistic kind; doggerel; a covered two-wheeled Irish or Australian car. **jingle-jangle,** *n.* **jingling-match,** *n.* An obsolete game in which a player carrying a bell is chased by others blindfolded.

Jingo (jing′ gō) [prob. conjurer's nonsense], *n.* (*pl.* **-goes**) A word used as a mild oath; one of a party advocating a spirited foreign policy, esp. those who championed the cause of the Turks during and after the Russo-Turkish war of 1877–8 (in this sense derived directly from the refrain of a song then popular). *a.* Pertaining to the Jingoes. **jingoish,** *a.* **Jingoism,** *n.* **jingoist,** *n.* **jingoistic** (-is′ tik), *a.*

jink (jingk) [Sc., prob. onomat.], *v.i.* To move nimbly; to dance, to fling; to dodge. *v.t.* To dodge; to cheat, to take in; (*Football*) to trick an opponent. *n.* A slip, an evasion, a dodging turn, a dodge. **high jinks:** Pranks, frolics.

jinker (jing′ kėr), *n.* (*Austral.*) A sort of two-wheeled bogey for transporting heavy logs and timber.

jinnee (ji nē′) [Arab. *jinnī*], *n.* (*pl.* **jinn,** often taken for sing.) One of a race of spirits or demons in Mohammedan mythology supposed to have the power of assuming human or animal forms [cp. GENIE].

jinricksha (jin rik′ sha) [Jap. *jen-riki-sha* (*jin,* man, *riki,* strength, *sha,* vehicle)], *n.* A light two-wheeled Japanese carriage with a hood, drawn by one or two men.

jinx (jingkz), *n.* (*Am. slang*) A person or thing that brings ill luck.

jitney (jit′ ni), *n.* (*Am. slang*) A motor-car.

jitters (jit′ ėrz), *n.pl.* (*slang*) Nervous apprehension. **jitter-bug,** *n.* A person who spreads alarm; (*Dancing*) a dancer who greatly exaggerates swing dancing. **jittery,** *a.*

jiu-jitsu [JU-JITSU].

jive (jīv) [etym. uncer.], *v.t.* To dance to swing or hot music.

jo (jō) [Sc., JOY], *n.* One's sweetheart; one's delight.

Job (jōb) [the Patriarch, subject of the *Book of Job* in the O.T.], *n.* (*fig.*) An uncomplaining sufferer or victim. **Job's comforter:** A false friend who lacerates one's feelings whilst pretending to sympathize. **Job's news:** Ill tidings. **Job's post:** A bearer of ill tidings. ***jobe** (jōb), *v.t.* To reprove, to reprimand. **jobation** (jō bā′ shŭn), *n.* A long-winded reproof, a lecture.

job (1) (job) [etym. unknown], *n.* A piece of work, esp. one done for a stated price; a piece of work or business yielding unfair profit or advantage, esp. one in which public interests are sacrificed to personal gain; (*colloq.*) a situation, a berth. *a.* Applied to collections of things sold together; let on hire. *v.t.* (*past & p.p.* **jobbed**) To let out (as work) by the job; to let out thus for hire; to hire thus; to buy up in miscellaneous lots and retail; to deal in (stocks); to deal with in an underhand way for one's private benefit. *v.i.* To buy and sell as a broker; to do job-work; to let or hire by the job; to make profit corruptly out of a position of trust, esp. at the public expense. **a bad** or **good job:** (*colloq.*) A sad, an unfortunate, or a satisfactory turn of affairs. **job lot:** A miscellaneous lot of goods bought cheap in the expectation of random profit. **to job out:** To sublet a piece of work. **to do the job for one:** To ruin or kill one. **jobmaster,** *n.* One who lets out carriages or horses. **job-printer,** *n.* [see JOBBING HOUSE]. **job-work,** *n.* Work done or paid for by the job. **jobber,** *n.* One who does small jobs; a jobmaster; one who deals in stocks and shares on the Stock Exchange; one who uses a position of trust, esp. a public office, commission, etc., to private advantage; one who does dishonourable work. **jobber's turn,** *n.* (*Stock Exch.*) A term denoting the middle price between which a jobber is prepared to buy or sell. **jobbery,** *n.* **jobbing house:** A printing-office where miscellaneous work (as distinct from newspapers or books) is done.

job (2) (job) [prob. onomat. (cp. JAB)], *v.t.* To stab, poke, or prod with a sharp instrument; to drive (a sharp instrument) in. *v.i.* To stab or thrust (at). *n.* A sudden stab, poke, or prod.

jobber [JOB (1)].

jobbernowl (job′ ėr nōl) [F. *jobard,* a fool, from *jobe,* silly, NOLL], *n.* A blockhead.

Jock (jok) [pers. name], *n.* (*colloq.*) A soldier of a Scottish regiment.

jockey (jok′ i) [North. form of *Jackey,* dim of JACK (1)], *n.* A professional rider in horse-races (*contemp.*) a groom, a lad, an under-strapper; *a horse-dealer; one given to sharp practice, prob from the bad reputation of horse-dealers, a cheat *v.t.* To deceive in a bargain; to employ sharp practices against; to outwit, out-manœuvre, etc. to cheat; (*Horse-racing*) to jostle by riding against *v.i.* To be tricky; to play a tricky game. **to jockey for position:** To try by skill to get an advantageous position; to gain an unfair advantage. **jockey pulley,** *n.* (*Motor.*) A pulley that rotates on a spring-loaded mounting. used to keep a belt taut on two fixed pulleys. **jockeydom, jockeyism jockeyship,** *n.* **disk-jockey** [DISK].

jocko (jok′ ō) [F., formed by Buffon from W. Afr *engeco* or *nchenko*], *n.* A chimpanzee.

jockteleg (jok′ tė leg) [Sc., said by Lord Hailes to be a corr. of *Jacques de Liège,* name of cutler], *n.* A large clasp-knife.

jocose (jō kōs′) [L. *jocōsus,* from *jocus,* JOKE], *a.* Humorous, facetious; given to jokes or jesting containing jokes, amusing. **jocosely,** *adv.* **jocoseness, jocosity** (jo kos′ i ti), *n.* ***jocoserious,** *a.* Partaking of mirth and sadness.

jocular (jok′ ū lȧr), *a.* Addicted to jesting; merry facetious, amusing; embodying a joke. **jocularity** (-lăr′ i ti), *n.* **jocularly,** *adv.* ***joculator** (jok′ lā tȯr), *n.* A professional jester. ***joculatory,** *a.*

jocund (jō′ kŭnd, jok′ ŭnd) [O.F. *jocond,* L. *jūcundus,* from *juvāre,* to help, to delight],

Sportive, gay; inspiring mirth. **jocundity,** *n.* **jocundly,** *adv.*

odel [YODEL].

odhpurs (jod poorz') [place in India], *n. pl.* Long riding-breeches fitting closely from the knee to the ankle.

oe (1), **joey** (1) (jō, jō' i) [Joseph Hume, M.P. 1836], *n.* (*old slang*) A fourpenny or threepenny bit.

Joe (2) (jō), **Joe Miller** (mil' ėr) [*Joseph Miller* (1684–1738), comedian, whose name was attached to a jest-book (1739)], *n.* An old joke, a chestnut. **Joe-Millerism,** *n.*

oey (2) (jō' i) [Austral. abor. *joè*], *n.* A young kangaroo.

og (jog) [prob. onomat. (cp. F. *choquer*)], *v.t.* (*past & p.p.* **jogged**) To push or jerk lightly, usually with the hand or elbow; to nudge, esp. to excite attention; (*fig.*) to stimulate (one's memory or attention). *v.i.* To move with an up-and-down leisurely pace; to walk or trudge idly, heavily, or slowly (on, along, etc.); to go, to depart, to be off. *n.* A light push or nudge to arouse attention; a leisurely trotting or jogging motion. **to be jogging:** To take one's departure. **to jog on:** To get along (somehow or in some specified manner). **jog-trot,** *n.* A slow, easy, monotonous trot; humdrum progress; slow routine. *a.* (*fig.*) Monotonous. ***jogger,** *n.*

oggle (jog' ėl) [prob. freq. of prec.], *v.t.* To shake, push, nudge, or jerk slightly; (*Build.*, perh. from JAG) to unite by means of joggles, to prevent sliding. *v.i.* To shake slightly, to totter. *n.* A joint in stone or other material to prevent sliding of one piece over another; a notch, projection, dowel, etc., used to form such joints.

***Johannes** (jò hăn' ēz) [L. *Joannes*, JOHN], *n.* An old Portuguese coin (of Joannes V), worth about 36s.

Johannine (jò hăn' īn) [as prec., -INE], *a.* Of or pertaining to the Apostle John, or (rarely) to John the Baptist. **Johannean,** *a.*

Johannisberger (yò hăn' is bĕr gėr) [G., from *Johannisberg*, a vineyard near Wiesbaden], *n.* A fine white Rhenish wine.

John (jon) [O.F. *Jehan* (F. *jean*), late L. *Johannes*, L. *Joannes*, Gr. *Jōannēs*, Heb. *Yōchānāni*, Jah is gracious], *n.* A masculine Christian name. **John-a-Dreams:** (*Shak.*) A dreamy fellow. **John-a-Nokes** and **John-a-Stiles:** John at the oak and John at the stile, two fictitious parties to an imaginary action at law. **John Barleycorn** [BARLEY (1)]. **John Bull** [BULL (1)]. **John Chinaman,** *n.* A Chinaman. **John Company** [after Dut. *Jan Kompanie*]: A familiar name for the East India Company. **John Doe:** (*Law*) The fictitious plaintiff in an (obsolete) action for ejectment, the defendant being called Richard Roe. **John Dory** [DORY].

Johnian (jō' ni ăn), *a.* Of or pertaining to St. John's College, Cambridge. *n.* A member or student of this.

Johnny (jon' i), *n.* (*slang*) A fellow, a chap; a toff, a swell, a young man about town. **Johnny cake,** *n.* (*Am.*) A maize cake baked on the hearth; (*Austral.*) a similar wheat-meal cake. **Johnny Crapaud** (kra pō'): A Frenchman. **Johnny Raw,** *n.* A raw beginner, a novice.

Johnsonian (jon sō' ni ăn), *a.* Pertaining to Dr. Samuel Johnson or his style; pompous, inflated, abounding in words of classical origin. **Johnsonism** (jon' sò nizm), *n.* **Johnsonese** (-nēz'), *n.*

join (join) [O.F. *joign-*, stem of *joindre*, L. *jungere* (p.p. *junctus*), cp. Gr. *zeugnunai*, to YOKE], *v.t.* To connect, to fasten together, to unite; to couple, to associate; to unite (two persons, or a person or persons with or to) in marriage, etc.; to begin, to engage in (battle, etc.). *v.i.* To be contiguous or in contact; to become associated or combined (with, etc.) in views, partnership, action, etc.; to become a member of (a society, etc.); *to begin battle. *n.* A joint; a point, line, or mark of junction. ***join-, joining-hand,** *n.* Writing in which the letters are joined, cursive writing. **to join hands:** To clasp hands (with); (*fig.*) to come to an understanding or combine (with). **to join issue** [ISSUE]. **to join up:** (*colloq.*) To enlist. **joinant,** *a.* (*Her.*) Conjoined. **joinder,** *n.* *The act of joining; conjunction; (*Law*) the coupling of two things in one suit or action, or two or more parties as defendants in a suit; the acceptance by a party in an action of the challenge in his adversary's demurrer or last pleading. **joiner,** *n.* One who joins; a carpenter who makes articles of furniture, finishes woodwork, etc.; (*Am.*) a carpenter. **joinery,** *n.*

joint (joint) [O.F., p.p. of *joindre*, see prec.], *n.* A junction or mode of joining parts together; the place where two things are joined together; (*Anat.*) the union of two bones in an animal body; an analogous point or mechanical device connecting parts of any structure, whether fixed or movable; one of the pieces into which a butcher cuts up a carcass; this piece as served at table (*Am.* a roast); (*Bot.*) a node; an internode; (*Geol.*) a natural fissure or line of parting traversing rocks in a straight and well-determined line; (*Am. slang*) an eating-house; a low and usu. illicit opium or gambling den. *a.* Of, belonging to, performed or produced by different persons in conjunction; sharing or participating (with others). *v.t.* To form with joints or articulations; to connect by joints; to plane and prepare (boards, etc.) for joining; to point (masonry); to divide or cut (meat) into joints, to disjoint. **out of joint:** Dislocated; out of order. **to put someone's nose out of joint:** To upset, disconcert, or supplant a person. **joint-action,** *n.* (*Law*) The joining of several actions in one. **joint-heir,** *n.* An heir having a joint interest with another. **joint stock:** Stock or capital divided into shares and held jointly by several persons, hence **joint-stock company, firm,** etc. **joint-stool,** *n.* A stool made with parts jointed (orig. *joined*) together. **joint-tenancy,** *n.* (*Law*) Tenure of an estate by unity of interest, title, time, and possession. **joint-tenant,** *n.* **jointweed,** *n.* The mare's-tail or Equisetum; (*Am.*) a herb, *Polygonella articulatum*, of the buckwheat family. **jointed,** *a.* Having joints, esp. of a specified kind. **jointedly,** *adv.* **jointer,** *n.* One who or that which joints; (*Carp.*) a long plane used to true the edges of boards to be joined; (*Build.*) a pointing tool used by masons and bricklayers. **jointing-plane,** *n.* **jointing-rule,** *n.* (*Build.*) A straight rule used in marking the joints of brickwork. **jointless,** *a.* **jointly,** *adv.* Together or in conjunction with others. **jointress, *jointuress,** *n.* A woman who has a jointure. **jointure,** *n.* (*Law*) An estate in lands or tenements, settled upon a woman in consideration of marriage, which she is to enjoy after her husband's decease. *v.t.* To settle a jointure upon.

joist (joist) [M.E. and O.F. *giste* (F. *gîte*), a bed, a place to lie in, from *gesir*, L. *jacēre*, to lie], *n.* One of a series of parallel horizontal timbers to which floor-boards or the laths of a ceiling are nailed. *v.t.* To furnish with joists.

joke (jōk) [L. *jocus*], *n.* Something said or done to excite laughter or merriment; a jest; a ridiculous incident, circumstance, etc. *v.i.* To make jokes, to jest. *v.t.* To crack jokes upon; to rally, to banter. **practical joke,** *n.* A trick played on a person to raise a laugh at his expense. **jokee** (jò kē'), *n.* One on whom a joke is played. **jokeless,** *a.* **jokelet,** *n.* **joker,** *n.* One who jokes, a jester; (*slang*) a fellow; (*Cards*) an extra card (often printed with a comic device) used with various values in some games. **jokesman, jokesmith, jokester, jokist,** *n.* **jokesome,** *a.* **jokingly,** *adv.* **joky,** *a.*

jokul (yō' kul) [Icel. *jökull*, icicle, glacier, dim. of *jaki*, piece of ice (cp. ICICLE)], *n.* A glacier or snow mountain in Iceland.

***jole, joll** [JOWL].

jolly (jol' i) [O.F. *jolif*, *joli*, gay, fine, etym. doubtful], *a.* Merry, mirthful, gay, jovial, festive;

inspiring or expressing mirth; (*colloq.*) pleasant, agreeable, charming; remarkable, extraordinary; (*iron.*) nice, precious; (*slang*) slightly drunk; *gallant; *wanton, amorous; *fine in appearance; *plump, buxom. *adv.* (*colloq.*) Very, exceedingly. *v.i.* To be jolly, to make merry. *v.t.* (*slang*) To banter, to joke, to rally; to treat agreeably so as to keep in good humour or secure a favour (usu. with *along*). **jolly Roger:** A pirate's flag with skull and cross-bones. **jollify,** *v.i.* To make merry; to tipple. *v.t.* To make (a person) merry, esp. with drink. **jollification** (-kā' shůn), *n.* Merry-making, a jolly party. **jollily,** *adv.* ***jolliment, jolliness, jollity,** *n.*

jolly-boat (jol' i bōt) [cp. Dan. *jolle*, Dut. *jol*, YAWL], *n.* A small boat for the general work of a ship.

jolt (jōlt) [etym. doubtful, perh. conn. with JOWL], *v.t.* To shake with sharp, sudden jerks, as in a carriage along a rough road. *v.i.* To move thus. *n.* A sudden shock or jerk. **jolter-, *jolt-head,** *n.* A blockhead, a dolt. **jolter,** *n.* **joltingly,** *adv.*

Jonathan (jon' å thån) [prob. from *Jonathan* Trumbull (1710–85), Governor of Connecticut, to whom Washington frequently referred for advice], *n.* The American people; a typical American; a kind of late-ripening red apple.

jongleur (zhon' glĕr) [F., from O.F. *jogleor*, JUGGLER], *n.* An itinerant minstrel or reciter of the Middle Ages, esp. in N. France.

jonquil (jong'-, jŭng' kwil) [F. *jonquille*, Sp. *junquillo*, dim. of *junco*, L. *juncus*, rush], *n.* The rush-leaved narcissus, *Narcissus jonquilla*, with 2 to 6 flowers on a stem.

jordan (jôr' dån) [doubtfully conjectured to mean orig. a Jordan-vessel, *i.e.*, one in which pilgrims brought water from the river Jordan for baptismal purposes], *n.* A chamber-pot.

jorum (jôr' ům) [etym. doubtful], *n.* A large bowl or drinking-vessel; its contents.

Joseph (jō' zėf) [the patriarch *Joseph* (alln. to Gen. xxxvii. 3)], *n.* A man of invincible chastity (alln. to Gen. xxxix. 12); an eighteenth-century caped riding-dress for ladies, having buttons down to the skirts.

josh (josh) [etym. uncertain], *v.t.* (*Am. slang*) To make fun of, to ridicule. *n.* A friendly joke.

joskin (jos' kin), *n.* (*slang*) A bumpkin, a yokel.

joss (jos) [corr. of Port. *deos*, L. *deus*, God], *n.* A Chinese idol. **joss-house,** *n.* A Chinese temple. **joss-stick,** *n.* A stick of perfumed material burnt before idols in China.

jostle (jos' ėl) [formerly *justle*, freq. of *just*, JOUST], *v.t.* To push against, to hustle; to elbow. *v.i.* To push (against, along, etc.); to hustle, to crowd. *n.* A hustling; a collision, a conflict.

jot (jot) [L. and Gr. *iōta*, the letter *i*], *n.* A tittle, an iota. *v.t.* To write (down a brief note or memorandum of). **jotting,** *n.* A note or memorandum.

jougs (jugz) [Sc., prob. from F. *joug*, L. *jugum*, YOKE], *n.pl.* An iron collar attached by a chain to a post, corresponding to the English pillory.

***jouisance** (zhoo' i såns) [F. *jouissance*, from *jouir*, to enjoy], *n.* Jollity, mirth.

jouk (jook) [Sc., etym. doubtful], *v.i.* To dodge, to duck; to skulk, to hide. *v.t.* To dodge, to evade. *n.* A dodge, a quick movement; the slip. **joukery, joukery-cookery, joukery-pawkery,** *n.*

joul [JOWL].

joule (jool) [Dr. J. P. *Joule* (1818–89), physicist], *n.* (*Elec.*) The unit of electrical energy, the work done in one second by a current of one ampere against a resistance of one ohm. **joulemeter,** *n.*

jounce (jouns) [etym. doubtful], *v.t.* and *i.* To jolt or shake. *n.* A jolt, a shake.

journal (jĕr' nål) [O.F., from L. *diurnālis*, DIURNAL], *n.* An account of daily transactions; (*Book-keeping*) the book from which daily entries are posted up in the ledger; a daily record of events, a diary; a record of events or news, properly one published daily, but now extended to any newspaper or other periodical published at regular intervals; the transactions of a learned society, etc.; (*Naut.*) a log-book or daily register of the ship's course and distance, etc.; (*Mach.*) the part of a shaft that rests on the bearings. **journal-box,** *n.* The metal case in which the journal moves.

journalese (jĕr nå lēz'), *n.* The style of writing characteristic of the cheaper types of newspapers.

journalist (jĕr' nå list), *n.* An editor of or contributor to a newspaper or other journal; one who keeps a diary. **journalism,** *n.* **journalistic,** *a.*

journalize (jĕr' nå līz), *v.t.* (*Book-keeping*) To enter in a journal; to enter in a diary. *v.i.* To follow the profession of a journalist; to keep a journal or diary.

journey (jĕr' ni) [O.F. *jornée*, late L. *jornāta*, *diurnāta*, a day's work as prec.], *n.* Passage or travel from one place to another, esp. by land as dist. from a voyage; the distance travelled in a given time; *a day's work or travel; (*prov.*) a round of work, a turn, a spell. *v.i.* To travel; to make a journey. ***journeybated,** *a.* Worn out with a journey.

journeyman (jĕr' ni mån), *n.* A mechanic or artisan who has served his apprenticeship and works for an employer; a mere drudge, hack, or hireling. **journey-work,** *n.* Work performed for hire (*lit. and fig.*). ***journeyer,** *n.*

joust (joost), **just** (2) (jŭst) [O.F. *jouster* (F. *jouter*), from low L. *juxtāre*, to approach, from *juxtā*, near], *v.i.* To tilt, to encounter on horseback with lances. *n.* A tilting-match; a combat between knights or men-at-arms on horseback.

Jove (jōv) [L. *Jovem*, acc. of O.L. *Jovis*, JUPITER], *n.* Jupiter, the chief of the Roman divinities. **Jovian,** *a.* Pertaining to or like Jupiter; pertaining to the planet Jupiter.

jovial (jō' vi ål) [O.F., from L. *joviālis*, of Jupiter, as prec.], *a.* Mirthful, merry, joyous; *(*Astrol.*) under the influence of the planet Jupiter; *propitious. **joviality** (-ăl' i ti), **jovialness,** *n.* Good humour. **jovially,** *adv.*

jow (jou) [Sc., perh. var. of foll.], *v.t.* To knock, to strike. *v.i.* To rock, to swing. *n.* A stroke, esp. of a bell.

jowl (joul) [M.E. *chowl*, *chavel*, A.-S. *cēafl*, jaw blended obscurely with M.E. *cholle*, A.-S. *ceolur* throat], *n.* The jaw; the cheek; the throat or neck esp. of a double-chinned person; the dewlap; the crop or wattle of a fowl; the head and shoulders of fish. ***v.t.** To bump, to dash (together, against etc.). **cheek by jowl:** With the cheeks close together; close together. **jowler,** *n.* A dog with heavy jowls.

joy (joi) [O.F. *joie*, L. *gaudia*, orig. pl. of *gaudium*], *n.* The emotion produced by gratified desire success, happy fortune, exultation, etc.; gladness happiness, delight; a cause of joy or happiness *mirth, gaiety. *v.i.* To rejoice. *v.t.* To gladden; to congratulate; to enjoy. **joy-bells,** *n.pl.* Peals rung on festive occasions. **joy-ride,** *n.* (*colloq.*) A ride in a car for pleasure, especially when unauthorized. **joy-stick,** *n.* (*Aviat.*) The control-lever of an aeroplane. ***joyance,** *n.* **joyful,** *a.* **joyfully,** *adv.* **joyfulness,** *n.* **joyless,** *a.* **joylessly,** *adv.* **joylessness,** *n.* **joyous,** *a.* Joyful; causing joy. **joyously,** *adv.* **joyousness,** *n.*

juba (1) (joo' bå) [L.], *n.* A mane, as of a horse (*Bot.*) a loose beard or tuft of awns (as on certain grasses, maize, etc.). **jubate,** *a.* (*Zool.*) Maned fringed with or as with a mane.

juba (2) (joo' bå), *n.* A characteristic Negro dance

jube (joo' bi) [F. *jubé*, L. *jubē*, imper. of *jubēre*, to command, from the formula, *jubē*, *domine*, *bene dīcere*], *n.* (*Arch.*) A rood-loft or gallery dividing the choir from the nave.

jubilate (1) (joo' bi lāt) [L. *jūbilātus*, p.p. of *jūbilāre*, from *jūbilum*, a shout of joy], *v.i.* To exult; to express intense joy. **jubilance, jubilation** (-lā' shŭn), *n.* **jubilant,** *a.* **jubilantly,** *adv.*

jubilate (2) (joo-, yoo bi la' ti) [L., shout ye for joy, as prec.], *n.* The 100th Psalm used as canticle in the evening service of the English Church, from its Latin commencing words *Jubilate Deo*; (*fig.*) a shout of joy or exultation.

jubilee (joo' bi lē) [O.F. *jubilé*, late L. *jūbilæus* (assim. to *jūbilum*, see JUBILATE (1)), Gr. *iōbēlaios*, pertaining to the jubilee, from *iōbēlos*, Heb. *yōbēl*, orig., ram, ram's-horn trumpet], *n.* The most important festival among the Jews, proclaimed by the sound of a trumpet, and celebrated every 50th year to commemorate their deliverance from Egyptian slavery; the 50th anniversary of an event of public interest; (*fig.*) a season of great public rejoicing or festivity; an outburst of joy; (*R.-C. Ch.*) a year of special indulgence or remission of the guilt of sin, formerly periodical now occasional. **diamond jubilee:** A sixtieth anniversary. **golden jubilee:** A jubilee, a fiftieth anniversary. **silver jubilee:** A twenty-fifth anniversary, esp. of a marriage.

Judæo- [Gr. *Ioudaios*, as foll.], *comb. form.* Of or relating to the Jews or Judaism. **Judæophobe** (jŭ dē' ŏ fōb) [-PHOBE], *n.* One who fears or dislikes the Jews. **Judæophobia,** *n.*

Judaic, -al (joo dā' ik, -ăl) [L. *Judāicus*, Gr. *Ioudaïkos*, from *Ioudais*, JEW], *a.* Pertaining to the Jews, Jewish. **Judaically,** *adv.* **Judaism** (joo' dā izm), *n.* The religious doctrines and rites of the Jews, according to the law of Moses; conformity to such doctrines and rites. **Judaist,** *n.* **Judaize,** *v.t.* and *i.* **Judaization** (-zā' shŭn), *n.* **Judaizer,** *n.*

Judas (joo' dås) [L. *Jūdas*, Gr. *Ioudas*, Heb. *y'hūdāh*, Judah], *n.* The name of several persons mentioned in the New Testament, esp. the disciple who betrayed Christ; (*fig.*) a traitor. **Judas-coloured,** *a.* Red, reddish (from a tradition that Judas had red hair). ***Judas-hole,** *n.* A small hole cut in a door, etc. to enable a person to pry into a room. **Judas-tree,** *n.* The leguminous tree, *Cercis siliquastrum*, which flowers before the leaves appear (traditionally the tree on which Judas hanged himself).

judder (jŭd' ėr) [?], *v.i.* To wobble; in singing to make rapid changes in intensity during the emission of a note. *n.* A wobble; (*Aviat.*) the vibration of an aircraft.

judge (jŭj) [M.E. and O.F. *juge*, L. *jūdicem*, nom. *jūdex* (*jūs*, law, *dic-*, root of *dicāre*, to point out, cp. INDICATE)], *n.* A civil officer invested with power to hear and determine causes in a court of justice; one authorized to decide a dispute or contest; (*Am.*) any person who sits in judgment, from a Supreme Court judge to a local magistrate; one skilled in deciding on relative merits, a connoisseur; (*Jewish Hist.*) a chief civil and military magistrate among the Jews, from the death of Joshua to the Kings. *v.t.* To decide (a question); to hear or try (a cause); to pass sentence upon; to examine and form an opinion upon (an exhibition, etc.); to criticize; (*colloq.*) to consider, to estimate, to decide; (*Jewish Hist.*) to act as chief magistrate over, to rule. *v.i.* To hear and determine a case; to give sentence; to form or give an opinion; to come to a conclusion; to criticize, to be censorious; to sit in judgment. **judger,** *n.* **judgeship,** *n.* **judgingly,** *adv.* **judgmatic, -al** (jŭj măt' ik, -ăl), *a.*, **-ally,** *adv.*

judgment, judgement (jŭj' mėnt), *n.* The act of judging; a judicial decision, a sentence of a court of justice; discernment, discrimination; the capacity for arriving at reasonable conclusions leading to well-adapted behaviour, especially as indicated by conduct in the practical affairs of life; criticism; the critical faculty; opinion, estimate; (*fig.*) a misfortune regarded as sent by God. **Last Judgment:** The judgment of mankind by God at the end of the world. **Judgment Day:** The day of this. **judgment debt:** (*Law*) A debt secured by a judge's order, under which an execution can be levied at any time. **judgment seat:** The seat or bench on which judges sit; (*fig.*) a court, a tribunal.

***Judica** (joo' di kȧ) [words of the introit, *Judica me*, judge me], *n.* Passion Sunday.

judicature (joo' di kȧ tūr) [F., from med. L. *jūdicātūra*, from *judicāre*, to JUDGE], *n.* The administration of justice by trial and judgment; the authority of a judge; a court of justice; the jurisdiction of a court. **Supreme Court of Judicature in England:** The court established by Acts in 1873 and 1875, combining the functions of the former Courts of Chancery, King's Bench, Common Pleas, Exchequer, Admiralty, etc. ***judicable,** *a.* ***judicative,** *a.* ***judicatory,** *a.* Pertaining to the administration of justice. *n.* A court of justice; the administration of justice.

judicial (joo dish' ăl) [L. *jūdiciālis*, from *jūdicium*, a trial, a judgment, from *jūdex*, JUDGE], *a.* Pertaining or proper to courts of law or the administration of justice; proceeding from a court of justice; showing judgment; critical, discriminating; impartial. **judicial factor:** (*Sc. Law*) An administrator appointed by the Court of Session to manage estates. **judicial murder:** Capital punishment inflicted as the result of a legal but unjust sentence. **judicial separation:** Separation of married persons by order of the Divorce Court. **judicially,** *adv.* **judiciary,** *a.* Judicial; passing judgment. *n.* The judicature.

judicious (joo dish' ŭs) [F. *judicieux*, as prec.], *a.* Sagacious, clear-headed, discerning; wise, prudent; done with reason or judgment. ***judicial, judiciously,** *adv.* **judiciousness,** *n.*

Judo (joo' dō) [Jap.], *n.* A form of ju-jitsu.

Judy (joo' di) [short for *Judith*], *n.* The name of Punch's wife in the Punch and Judy show; (*contemp.*) a woman, a wench, a sweetheart.

jug (1) (jŭg) [etym. doubtful], *n.* A vessel, usually with a swelling body, narrow neck, and handle, for holding liquors; (*slang*) a prison, a lock-up. *v.t.* (*usu. in p.p.*) To stew (a hare) in a jug or jar; (*slang*) to imprison. **jugful,** *n.*

jug (2) (jŭg) [imit.], *v.i.* To make a sound like 'jug' (of the nightingale, etc.). **jug-jug,** *n.*

jugal (joo' găl) [L. *jugālis*, from *jugum*, yoke], *a.* (*Anat.*) Pertaining to the cheek-bone.

jugate (joo' gȧt) [L. *jugātus*, p.p. of *jugāre*, to couple, as prec.], *a.* (*Bot.*) Having leaflets in pairs.

juggernaut (jŭg' ėr nawt) [Hindi, *Jagganāth*, Sansk. *Jagganātha*, lord of the world (*jagat*, world, *nātha*, lord)], *n.* Vishnu in his eighth avatar; his idol at Krishna or Puri in Orissa, which is annually dragged in a procession on a huge car, under the wheels of which fanatics are said to have thrown themselves; (*fig.*) a belief, institution, etc., to which one is ruthlessly sacrificed or by which one is ruthlessly destroyed.

juggins (jŭg' inz), *n.* (*slang*) A blockhead, a dolt.

juggle (jŭg' ėl) [from O.F. *jogleor*, juggler, late L. *joculātōrem*, nom. *-tor*, from *joculāre*, L. *joculārī*, to jest, from *joculus*, dim. of *jocus*, JOKE], *v.i.* To play tricks by sleight of hand, to conjure; to practise artifice or imposture (with). *v.t.* To deceive by trickery; to obtain, convey, etc. (away, out of, etc.) by trickery. *n.* A trick by sleight of hand; an imposture. **juggler,** *n.* **jugglery,** *n.*

juglans (joo' glăns) [L., the walnut (*Jovis glans*, Jove's acorn)], *n.* (*Bot.*) A genus of trees containing the walnuts. **juglandaceous** (-dā' shŭs), *a.*

Jugo-Slav [YUGOSLAV].

jugular (jŭ' gū lȧr) [L. *jugŭlum*, the collarbone, -AR], *a.* (*Anat.*) Belonging to the neck or throat; (*Ichthyol.*) having the ventral fins anterior to the pectoral. *n.* A jugular vein. **jugular veins:** The veins of the neck which return the blood from the head.

jugulate (jŭ' gū lāt) [L. *jugulātus*, p.p. of *jugulāre*, to cut the throat of, as prec.], *v.t.* To kill; (*Med.*) to put an end to (a disease, etc.) by drastic measures.

juice (joos) [O.F. *jus*, L. *jūs*, soup, sauce], *n.* The watery part of vegetable or the fluid part of animal bodies; (*colloq.*) electricity, electric current, petrol; (*fig.*) the essence or characteristic element of anything. **juiceless,** *a.* **juicy,** *a.* Abounding in juice, succulent. **juiciness,** *n.*

ju-ju (joo' joo) [W. Afr., perh. from F. *joujou*, a toy], *n.* A fetish, an idol credited with supernatural powers; the ban or taboo worked by this.

jujube (joo' joob) [F., from late L. *jujuba*, L. *zizyphum*, Gr. *zizuphon*], *n.* The berry-like fruit of *Zizyphus vulgaris* or *Z. jujuba*, spiny shrubs of the buckthorn family, dried as a sweetmeat; a lozenge of sweetened gum-arabic or gelatine flavoured with or imitating this.

ju-jitsu (joo jit' soo) [Jap.], *n.* The Japanese art of wrestling, based on the principle of making one's opponent exert his strength to his own disadvantage.

juke-box (jook' boks) [unkn.], *n.* A mechanical musical box operated by the insertion of a coin.

julep (joo' lėp) [F., from Sp. *julepe*, Arab. *julāb*, Pers. *gulāb* (*gul*, rose, *āb*, water)], *n.* A sweet drink, esp. a preparation with some liquid used as a vehicle for medicine, a stimulant composed of spirit, usu. flavoured with mint.

Julian (joo' li ȧn), *a.* Pertaining to or originated by Julius Cæsar. **Julian calendar:** The calendar instituted by him in 46 B.C. **Julian year:** The year of this, containing 365¼ days.

julienne (zhu li en') [F., from *Jules* or *Julien*], *n.* A clear soup from meat with chopped or shredded vegetables; a variety of pear.

July (ju lī') [A.-F. *Julie*, L. *Jūlius*, after *Jūlius* Cæsar], *n.* The seventh month of the year.

jumble (jŭm' bėl) [prob. onomat.], *v.t.* To mix confusedly; to throw or put together without order. **v.i.* To be mixed in a confused way; to move (about, along, etc.) confusedly. *n.* A confused mixture; a muddle, disorder, confusion. **jumble-sale,** *n.* A sale of miscellaneous articles at a bazaar. **jumbleshop,** *n.* ***jumblement,** *n.* **jumbly,** *a.*

jumbo (jŭm' bō) [etym. doubtful], *n.* A huge, unwieldy person, animal, or thing, used as the proper name of a famous elephant (sold from the Zoological Gardens, London, to Barnum and killed by accident in 1885); an over-sized object. **jumbo-esque** (-esk'), *a.* **jumboism,** *n.*

jumbuck (jŭm' bŭk) [Austral. abor. pidgin English], *n.* A sheep.

jumelle (zhu mel') [F., from L. *gemellus*, GIMMAL], *a.* Twin, paired. *n.* (*Her.*) A gimmal; a pair of opera-glasses; (*pl.*) the side-pieces of a loom carrying the cylinders.

jump (1) (jŭmp) [prob. onomat. (cp. G. dial. *gumpen*, Dan. *gumpe*, Swed. dial. *gumpa*)], *v.i.* To throw oneself from the ground by a sudden movement of the muscles of the legs and feet; to spring, to leap, to bound; to move suddenly (along, up, out) with such springs or bounds; to start or rise (up) abruptly; (*fig.*) to agree, to tally (with or together). *v.t.* To pass over or cross by leaping; to cause to leap over; to skip (a chapter, pages, etc.). **adv.* Exactly. *n.* The act of jumping; a leap, a spring, a bound; a start, an involuntary nervous movement, esp. (*pl.*) convulsive twitching as in delirium tremens; a sudden rise (in price, value, etc.); a break, a gap; (*Geol.*) a fault; *risk, hazard. **to jump a claim:** To seize upon a mining claim by force or fraud. **to jump at:** To accept eagerly; to reach hastily (as a conclusion). **to jump down one's throat:** To answer or interrupt violently. **to jump one's bail, country, town,** etc. To abscond. **to jump the queue:** To get ahead of one's turn. **to jump on** or **upon:** To reprimand, abuse, or assail violently; to pounce upon. **jump-seat,** *n.* (*Am.*) A movable seat; an open buggy with a shifting seat or seats. **jumped-up,** *a.* (*colloq.*) Up-start. **jumpable,** *a.* **jumper** (1), *n.* One who or that which jumps or leaps; (*pl.*) certain Welsh Methodists in the eighteenth cent. and other religious sects who danced or jumped during worship; a hopper, a jumping insect; (*Mech.*) a tool or implement worked with a jumping motion; a quarryman's boring-tool. **jumping bean** or **seed:** The seed of various plants belonging to the *Euphorbiaceæ*, which jump about through the movements of larvæ inside them. **jumping-deer,** *n.* The black-tailed deer found west of the Mississippi. **jumping-rope,** *n.* (*Am.*) A skipping-rope. **jumpy,** *a.* **jumpiness,** *n.*

jumper (2) (jŭm' pėr), *n.* A loose, coarse outer jacket worn by sailors, labourers, etc.; a woman's knitted or crocheted woollen upper garment. **jumper suit:** A woman's jacket and skirt made of a stockingette material.

juncaceous (jŭng kā' shŭs) [L. *juncus*, rush, -ACEOUS], *a.* (*Bot.*) Of or resembling rushes; belonging to the order *Juncaceæ*. **juncal** (jŭng' kȧl), *a.*

junco (jŭng' kō) [Sp., from L. *juncus*, rush], *n.* The snow-bird, a genus of North American finches.

junction (jŭnk' shŭn) [L. *junctio*, from *jungere*, to JOIN], *n.* The act of joining or the state of being joined, a combination; a joint, a point or place of union, esp. the point where lines of railway meet.

juncture (jŭnk' tyŭr, -chŭr) [L. *junctūra*, as prec.], *n.* A junction, a union; the place, line, or point at which two things are joined, a joint, an articulation; a point of time marked by the concurrence of critical events or circumstances.

June (joon) [L. *Jūnius*], *n.* The sixth month of the year. **June-bug,** *n.* An insect or beetle that appears about June, chiefly in the U.S.A.

jungle (jŭng' gėl) [Hind. *jangal*, from Sansk. *jangala*, desert], *n.* Land covered with forest trees or dense, matted vegetation, esp. in India. **jungle-bear,** *n.* The Indian sloth-bear, *Prochylus labiatus.* **jungle-cat,** *n.* The marsh lynx, *Felis chaus.* **jungle-fever,** *n.* A remittent tropical fever. **jungle-fowl,** *n.* An East Indian bird, *Gallus sonnerati*, and others of the same genus; the Australian mound-bird, *Megapodius tumulus.* **jungle-cock, -hen,** *n.* **jungled, jungly,** *a.* **jungli, jungly,** *a.* Inhabiting the jungle, uncouth, unrefined.

junior (joo' ni ŏr, joo' nyŏr) [L. *jūnior*, comp. of *juvenis*, young], *a.* The younger (esp. as distinguishing a son from his father of the same name or two of the same surname); lower in standing. *n.* One younger or of lower standing than another; (*Am.*) a son. **juniorate,** *n.* (*Society of Jesus*) A two years' course of higher studies for juniors before they enter the priesthood. **juniorship,** *n.*

juniper (joo' ni pėr) [L. *jūniperus*, etym. doubtful], *n.* A genus of prickly evergreen shrubs, comprising *Juniperus communis*, the berries of which are used to flavour gin.

junk (1) (jŭngk) [Port. and Sp. *junco*, Jav. *jong*], *n.* A flat-bottomed vessel with lug-sails, used in the Chinese seas.

junk (2) (jŭngk) [prob. corr. of CHUNK], *n.* A lump or chunk of anything. **junk-bottle,** *n.* (*Am.*) A stout bottle of green or black glass.

junk (3) (jŭngk) [etym. doubtful], *n.* Pieces of old cable and rope cut into lengths for making mats, swabs, gaskets, fenders, oakum, etc.; rubbish, valueless odds and ends; salt beef supplied to ships bound on long voyages, from its being as tough as old rope. **junk-dealer,** *n.* A marine-store dealer. **junk-ring,** *n.* A steam-tight packing round a piston. **junk-shop,** *n.* A shop where second-hand goods of all kinds are sold. **junk-wad,** *n.* An oakum wad for a muzzle-loading gun, placed between the charge and the ball.

junker (yung' kėr) [G. (*jung*, YOUNG, HERR)], *n.* A young German noble; a member of the German reactionary aristocratic party. **junkerdom, junkerism,** *n.*

junket (jŭng′ kĕt) [M.F. *juncade* (cp. Norm. patois *jonquette*), Prov. *joncada*, It. *giuncata*, p.p. of *giuncare*, from *giunco*, L. *juncus*, rush], *n.* A dish of curds sweetened and flavoured, and served with cream; a sweetmeat, a delicacy, a confection; a feast, a banquet, an entertainment. *v.i.* To feast, to picnic, to make good cheer. *v.t.* To regale at a feast. **junketer,** *n.* ***junketing,** *n*

Juno (joo′ nō) [L.], *n.* The wife of Jupiter, identified with the Greek Hera; (*fig.*) a beautiful queenly woman; (*Astron.*) the 3rd asteroid.

junta (jŭn′ ta) [Sp., from L. *juncta*, fem. p.p. of *jungere*, to JOIN], *n.* A legislative or administrative council, esp. in Spain, Italy, and South America.

junto (jŭn′ tō) [erron. from prec.], *n.* A secret political or other council; a cabal, a clique, a faction.

jupati-palm (joo pȧ tē′ pam) [S. Am. native *jupati*, PALM], *n.* The South American palm yielding raffia fibre.

jupe (joop) [F., from O.F. *juppe*, Arab. *jubbah*], *n.* A woman's skirt; *a loose jacket or tunic; *(*Sc.*) a woman's long jacket.

Jupiter (joo′ pi tėr) [L. (*Jovis*, JOVE, *pater*, father)], *n.* The supreme Roman deity, identified with the Greek Zeus; (*Astron.*) the largest planet of the solar system. **Jupiter Pluvius:** Jupiter as the god of rain.

jupon (joo′ pŏn, joo pon′) [F., from JUPE], *n.* A skirt or petticoat; *a sleeveless surcoat worn outside armour; earlier a tunic worn underneath the armour.

jural (joor′ ȧl) [L. *jūs jūris*, law, -AL], *a.* Of or relating to law or jurisprudence, esp. with regard to rights and obligations.

Jurassic (joo răs′ ik) [F. *Jurassique*, from *Jura* (cp. LIASSIC)], *a.* (*Geol.*) Belonging to the oolitic limestone formation well developed in the Jura mountains; belonging to the second period of the Mesozoic era. *n.* The Jurassic system or period, coming between the Triassic and the Cretaceous.

jurat (joor′ ăt, zhu′ ra) [F., from med. L. *jurātus*, one who is sworn, orig. p.p. of L. *jurāre*, to swear], *n.* A person under oath; a member of a corporation corresponding to an alderman, esp. of the Cinque Ports; a magistrate in the Channel Islands. **jurant,** *a.* Taking an oath. *n.* One who takes an oath. **juratory,** *a.* Containing an oath.

juridical (joo rid′ i kȧl) [L. *jūridicus* (*jūs jūris*, law, *dic-*, stem of *dicāre*, to proclaim)], *a.* Pertaining to the administration of justice, to courts of justice, or to jurisprudence. **juridically,** *adv.*

jurisconsult (joor ris kŏn sŭlt′) [L. *jūrisconsultus* (*jūris*, as prec., *consultus*, see CONSULT)], *n.* One learned in law, esp. civil or international law; a jurist.

jurisdiction (joo ris dik′ shŭn) [F., from L. *jūrisdictiōnem*, nom. *-tio* (*jūris*, see JURIDICAL, *dictio*, DICTION)], *n.* The legal power or right of administering justice, making and enforcing laws, or exercising other authority; the district or extent within which such power may be exercised. **jurisdictional,** *a.* **jurisdictive,** *a.* Having jurisdiction.

jurisprudence (joo ris proo′ dĕns) [L. *jūrisprudentia*], *n.* The science or philosophy of law; the science of the laws, constitutions, and rights of men; the legal system of a particular country. **jurisprudent** *a.* and *n.* **jurisprudential,** *a.*

jurist (joo′ rist) [F. *juriste*, med. L. *jūrista*, from *jūs jūris*, law], *n.* One learned in the law; a writer on legal subjects; a student of law. **juristic, -al** (jů ris′ tik, -ȧl), *a.* **juristically,** *adv.*

juror (joor′ ŏr) [A.-F. *jurour*, O.F. *jureor*, L. *jūrātōrem*, nom. *-tor*, from *jūrāre*, to swear], *n.* One who serves on a jury; one who takes an oath.

jury (joor′ i) [A.-F. *juree*, O.F. *jurée*, an oath, an inquest, a body of sworn men, p.p. of *jurer*, L. *jūrāre*, to swear], *n.* A body of persons selected according to law and sworn to try, and give a true verdict upon, questions put before them; a body of persons selected to award prizes at public shows, exhibitions, etc. **common, petty, transverse,** or **trial jury:** A jury usu. of twelve persons who (by a unanimous verdict) determine the question of fact in a trial. **grand jury:** A jury (usu. of twelve to twenty-three) who decide by a majority whether there is prima facie ground for an indictment before it goes to trial. **special jury:** A jury composed of persons of a certain class or station. **jury of matrons:** Married women who have borne children, empanelled in cases where pregnancy is pleaded in stay of execution. **jury-box,** *n.* The enclosure in a court where the jury sit. **juryman,** *n.*

jury-mast (joor′ i mast) [etym. doubtful (Skeat proposes *ajúry-mast*, from O.F. *ajuirie*, aid, succour, from L. *adjūtāre*, to AID)], *n.* A temporary mast erected in place of one carried away. **jury-rudder,** *n.*

jussive (jŭs′ iv) [L. *juss-us*, p.p. of *jubēre*, to command], *a.* (*Gram.*) Expressing command. *n.* A form or construction expressing command.

just (1) (jŭst) [F. *juste*, L. *justus*, from *jūs*, right], *a.* Acting according to what is right and fair; fair, equitable, impartial, upright, honest; exact, accurate, precise; fit, proper, suitable; merited, deserved; righteous. *adv.* Exactly, precisely; barely, only, with nothing to spare; precisely at the moment; only a moment ago, a very little time ago; (*colloq.*) perfectly, quite. **just now:** A very little time since, but a moment ago; at this instant. **justly,** *adv.* **justness,** *n.*

just (2) (JOUST).

justice (jŭs′ tis) [O.F., from L. *justitia*, from *justus*, just], *n.* The quality of being just; fairness in dealing with others; uprightness, rectitude, honesty; just requital of deserts; the authoritative administration or maintenance of law and right: a person legally commissioned to hold courts, hear causes, and administer justice between individuals; a magistrate; a judge, esp. of the Supreme Court of Judicature in England. **Justice of the Peace:** A local magistrate commissioned under the Great Seal to keep the peace and try cases of felony and other misdemeanours. **Lord Chief Justice:** A judge combining the former functions of President of the King's Bench and of the Court of Common Pleas. **to do justice to:** To treat fairly; to treat appreciatively. **to do oneself justice:** To acquit oneself worthily of one's ability. **Justice-Clerk,** *n.* (*Sc. Law*) The President of the Outer House or Second Division of The Court of Session, and Vice-President of the High Court of Justiciary. **Justice-General,** *n.* The highest judge in Scotland, Lord President of the Court of Session. ***justicer,** *n.* A justiciary. **justiceship,** *n.* **justiciable** (jŭs tish′ i ȧbl), *a.* Liable to be tried in a court of justice. *n.* One subject to (another's) jurisdiction. **justiciar,** *n.* A chief officer or deputy of the Crown (under the Norman and Plantagenet kings) who exercised both judicial and administrative powers. **justiciary,** *n.* An administrator of justice, a justiciar. *a.* Pertaining to the administration of justice. **High Court of Justiciary:** The supreme court of Scotland in criminal causes.

justify (jŭs′ ti fī) [F. *justifier*, L. *justificāre* (*jūs*, JUSTICE, *facere*, to make)], *v.t.* To prove or show to be just or right; to vindicate, to make good, to show grounds for; to exonerate; (*Theol.*) to declare free from the penalty of sin; (*Print.*) to adjust and make (lines or type) even in length. *v.i.* (*Print.*) To coincide or range uniformly (of lines of type). **justifiable,** *a.* **justifiability** (-bil′ i ti), **justifiableness,** *n.* **justifiably,** *adv.* **justification** (-kā′ shŭn), *n.* **justificative** (jŭs′ ti fi kā tiv), **justificatory,** *a.* ***justificator, justifier,** *n.*

justle [JOSTLE].

justly, justness [JUST (1)].

jut (jŭt) [var. of JET (2)], *v.i.* To project, to protrude; to stick (out). *n.* A projection; a protruding point or part. **jut-window,** *n.* A projecting window.

jute (joot) [Bengali, *jhōto* (pop. *jhūto*), Sansk. *jūta*, *jatā*, a braid of hair], *n.* The fibre from the inner bark of two plants, *Corchorus capsularis* and *C. olitorius*, from which fabrics, paper, and cordage are prepared.

***juvenal** (joo′ vė nȧl) [L. *juvenālis*, from *juvenis*, young], *n.* A youth, a juvenile.

juvenescent (joo vė nes′ ėnt) [L. *juvenescere*, as prec.], *a.* Growing or being young. **juvenescence,** *n.*

juvenile (joo′ vė nīl) [L. *juvenīlis*, from *juvenis*, JUVENAL], *a.* Young, youthful; befitting or characteristic of youth. *n.* A young person; a book for children. **juvenile offender,** *n.* A criminal under 16 years of age. **juvenileness,** *n.* **juvenilely,** *adv.* **juvenility** (-nil′ i ti), *n.* **juvenilia** (joo ven il′ yȧ), *n.pl.* Writings, etc., produced in youth.

juxtapose (jŭk stȧ pōz′) [F. *juxtaposer* (L. *juxtā*, next, F. *poser*, to put)]. *v.t.* To place (a thing) next to or (things) side by side. **juxtaposition** (-pȯ zish′ ůn), *n.*

K

K, k (kā), the eleventh letter and eighth consonant of the English alphabet, is a voiceless guttural mute (*pl.* **Ks, K's, Kays**).

Kaaba [CAABA].

kaama (ka′ mȧ) [S. Afr. native], *n.* The hartebeest.

kaava [KAVA]. **kabbala** [CABBALA].

Kabyle (kȧ bil′) [F., from Arab. *Qabāil*, pl. of *qabīla*, tribe], *n.* One of the agricultural branch of the Berber race inhabiting the highlands of Algeria; the Berber dialect spoken by the Kabyles.

kaddish (kăd′ ish) [Aram. *qaddīsh*, holy], *n.* A form of thanksgiving and prayer used by the Jews, esp. in mourning.

kadi [CADI].

kae (kā) [Sc., cp. Dut. *ka*, Dan. *kaa*, Norw. *kaae*], *n.* A jackdaw.

Kafir (kăf′ ir) [Arab. *kāfir*, infidel], *n.* One of a South African Bantu race, esp. the Xosa tribe; their language; a native of Kafiristan in northern Afghanistan; (*pl., Stock Exc.*) South African mining shares. *a.* Of or pertaining to the Kafirs.

kaftan [CAFTAN].

kago (ka′ gō) [Jap. *kango*], *n.* A Japanese basketwork palanquin slung on a pole and carried by men.

kahawai (kā ha′ wi) [Maori], *n.* The N. Zealand salmon.

kahikatea (kā hik ȧ tē′ ȧ) [Maori], *n.* The white pine of N. Zealands.

kai (kī) [Maori], *n.* A general word for 'food' in N. Zealand and the South Sea Islands.

kaikomoko (kī kō mō′ kō) [Maori], *n.* The N. Zealand ribbonwood tree.

kaiak [KAYAK, CAÏQUE].

kail [KALE].

kaim [KAME]. **kaiman** [CAYMAN]. **kain** [CAIN (2)].

kainga (kā ing′ gȧ) [Maori], *n.* A Maori settlement, village.

kainite (kī′ nīt) [G. *kainit* (Gr. *kainos*, new, -ITE)], *n.* Hydrous chlorosulphate of magnesium and potassium, used as a fertilizer.

Kaiser (kī′ zėr) [G., from L. *Cæsar*], *n.* An emperor; the Emperor of Germany or Austria; (*Hist.*) the head of the Holy Roman Empire. **Kaisership,** *n.*

kaitaka (kī ta′ kȧ) [Maori], *n.* A mat used as a cloak.

kajawah (kȧ ja′ wȧ) [Hind. and Pers.], *n.* A pannier carried in pairs on a camel, horse, or mule, used by women and children.

kajeput [CAJUPUT].

kaka (ka′ kȧ) [Maori], *n.* A New Zealand parrot belonging to the genus *Nestor*. **kakapo** (ka′ kȧ pō), *n.* The ground- or owl-parrot of New Zealand. **kakariki** (ka ka rē′ ki), *n.* A small green parrot; a green lizard.

kakemono (kăk ė mō′ nō) [Jap.], *n.* A Japanese wall-picture mounted on rollers for putting away.

kaki (ka′ ki) [Jap.], *n.* The Chinese date-plum or Japanese persimmon.

kakistocracy (kăk i stok′ rȧ′ si) [Gr. *kakistos*, superl. of *kakos*, bad, -CRACY], *n.* Government by the worst citizens. **kakistocrat** (kȧ kis′ tȯ krăt), *n.*

kakodyl [CACODYL].

kala-azar (ka′ la a′ zar) [Hind.], *n.* (*Path.*) A chronic tropical disease with a high mortality, also known as Black Fever.

kale (kāl) [Sc. and North., var. of COLE], *n.* Cabbage, esp. that with crinkled leaves, borecole; (*Sc.*) cabbage soup. **Scotch kale:** Kale with purplish leaves. **kale-yard,** (*Sc.*) **kail-yaird,** *n.* A kitchen-garden. **kale-yard school:** A group of novelists and writers depicting the homely life of Scottish lowlanders, with liberal use of broad dialect.

kaleidophone (kȧ lī dȯ fōn) [Gr. *kalos*, beautiful, *eidos*, appearance, -PHONE], *n.* An instrument for exhibiting the character of sound-waves by means of a vibrating bar or plate armed with a reflector.

kaleidoscope (kȧ lī′ dȯ skōp), *n.* An instrument showing, by means of bits of coloured glass and a series of reflecting surfaces, an endless variety of symmetrical forms. **kaleidoscopic** (-skop′ ik), *a.*

kalendar, etc. [CALENDAR].

kali (kăl′ i, kā′ li) [Arab. *qalī*, see ALKALI], *n.* The salt-wort, *Salsola kali*, from which soda-ash was obtained. **kaligenous** (kȧ lij′ ė nůs), *a.* **kalinite,** *n.* (*Min.*) Native potash alum.

kalian (kal yan′) [Arab. *qalyan*], *n.* A Persian form of hookah.

kalif [CALIPH].

kalmia (kăl′ mi ȧ) [Peter *Kalm* (1715–79), Swed. naturalist, professor at Abo], *n.* (*Bot.*) A genus of smooth, evergreen North American flowering shrubs.

Kalmuck (kăl′ mŭk) [Rus. *Kalmuikŭ*], *n.* One of a race of Mongols living in a region extending from W. China to the Volga; a coarse shaggy cloth like bearskin; a coarse, coloured cotton made in Persia.

kalology (kȧ lol′ ȯ ji) [Gr. *kalos*, beautiful, -LOGY], *n.* The science or theory of beauty.

kalong (ka′ long) [Malay], *n.* The Malay fox-bat, *Pteropus edulis.*

kalpa (kăl′ pȧ) [Sansk.], *n.* A day of Brahma, or a period of 4,320,000 years, constituting the age or cycle of a world.

***kam** (kăm) [cp. W., Gael., and Manx *cam*], *a.* Crooked. *adv.* Awry, askew. **clean kam:** Quite away from the purpose.

Kama (ka′ mȧ) [Sansk.], *n.* The god of love in the puranas; impure or sensual desire.

kamala (kăm′ ȧ lȧ) [Sansk.], *n.* An orange dye obtained from the down on the fruit capsules of the East Indian tree, *Rottlera tinctoria*, belonging to the *Euphorbiaceæ* or spurge family.

kamaraband [CUMMERBUND].

kame, kaim (kām) [Sc. and North., var. of COMB], *n.* (*Geol.*) A long mound of glacial detritus, an eskar.

kami (ka′ mi) [Jap.], *n.* A Japanese title, equivalent to lord, given to nobles, ministers, governors, etc.; (*Shintoism*) a divinity, a god.

kamichi (ka′ mi shi) [F., from Brazil], *n.* A S. American bird, the horned screamer.

kampong (kăm pong') [Malay], *n.* A Malay village.

kamptulicon (kămp tū' li kŏn) [Gr. *kampt-os*, flexible, *oul-os*, thick, *-ikon*, neut. adj. suf.], *n.* A floor-covering of india-rubber, gutta-percha, and cork, pressed into sheets.

Kanaka (kȧ năk' ȧ, kăn' ȧ kȧ) [Hawaiian, a man], *n.* A Sandwich islander; a South Sea islander; (*Austral.*) one of these employed as an indentured labourer on the Queensland sugar-plantations.

kang (kang) [Chin.], *n.* A brick structure in Chinese houses for sleeping on, warmed by a fire inside in cold weather; a large Chinese water-jar.

kangaroo (kăng gȧ roo') [prob. from abor. name], *n.* A name for several marsupial quadrupeds peculiar to Australia, Tasmania, New Guinea, and adjacent islands, distinguished by their large hind limbs, used for leaping, and short fore limbs, almost useless for walking; (*pl., Stock Exc.*) Australian mining shares; dealers in these. **kangaroo-apple,** *n.* An Australian shrub with fruit like an apple. **kangaroo-bicycle,** *n.* An obsolete form of bicycle with sloping backbone, a forerunner of the modern safety. **kangaroo-dog,** *n.* A kind of greyhound used in Australia for hunting. **kangaroo-grass,** *n.* An Australian fodder-grass. **kangaroo-rat,** *n.* A small Australian marsupial, an American pouched burrowing-mouse.

kanoon (kȧ noon) [Pers. and Arab. *qānūn*], *n.* A kind of dulcimer or zither with fifty or sixty strings.

Kantian (kăn' ti ȧn) [Immanuel *Kant* (1724–1804), -IAN], *a.* Pertaining to the philosophy of Kant. *n.* A Kantist. **Kantianism, *Kantism,** *n.* **Kantist,** *n.*

kantikoy (kăn' ti koi) [Algonkin], *n.* A North American Indian ceremonial dance; a meeting for dancing, a dancing match.

kaolin (kā'-, ka' ȯ lin) [F., from Chin. *kaoling*, name of a mountain whence orig. obtained (*kao*, high, *ling*, ridge or hill)], *n.* A porcelain clay (also used medicinally as a poultice or internally) derived principally from the decomposition of feldspar, China clay. **kaolinic** (-lin' ik), *a.* **kaolinize** (kā' ȯ li nīz), *v.t.* **kaolinization** (-zā' shŭn), *n.*

kapellmeister (kȧ pel' mī' stėr) [G. (*kapelle*, med. L. *capella*, CHAPEL, *meister*, MASTER)], *n.* The musical director of a choir, band, or orchestra.

kapnography (kăp nog' rȧ fi) [Gr. *kapnos*, smoke, -GRAPHY], *n.* Drawing or writing on a smoked surface with a pointed instrument, shading with further films of carbon from a flame, and varnishing. **kapnographic** (-grăf' ik), *a.*

kapok (kā' pok) [Malay *kāpoq*], *n.* A fine woolly or silky fibre enveloping the seeds of a tropical silk-cotton tree, used for stuffing cushions, etc.

kaput (ka put') [G. slang], *adv.* Finished, done for, smashed up.

Karaite (kâr' ȧ īt) [Heb. *q'rāīm*, readers, -ITE], *n.* A member of a Jewish sect who hold by the literal inspiration of the Scriptures, rejecting rabbinical tradition. **Karaism,** *n.*

karri (ka' rē) [Austral abor.], *n.* A W. Australian timber tree.

Karrikot (kă' ri kot), *n.* Protected trade name of an infant's portable cot.

karma (kar' mȧ) [Sansk.], *n.* (*Buddhism*) The results of action, ethical causation as determining future existence, esp. the cumulative consequence of a person's acts in one stage of existence as controlling his destiny in the next.

Karmathian (kar mā' thi ȧn) [*Karmat*, the founder], *n.* One of a Mohammedan rationalistic sect, with pantheistic and socialistic tenets, founded in the ninth century.

karoo, karroo (kȧ roo') [Hottentot in orig.], *n.* One of the waterless South African tablelands, esp. the Great Karoo in the middle of Cape Colony.

kaross (kȧ ros') [S. Afr. native *karos*], *n.* A South African native mantle or jacket made of skins with the hair left on.

kartel (kar' tėl) [S. Afr. Dut., said to be from Port. *catel*, Tamil *kattil*, bedstead], *n.* A kind of wooden hammock swung in a South African ox-wagon.

karyo- [CARYO-], *comb. form.* (*Biol.*) Relating to the changes which occur in the structure of an animal or vegetable cell. **karyokinesis** (kăr i ȯ kī nē' sis) [Gr. *kinēsis*, motion, from *kinein*, to move], *n.* The series of changes that take place in indirect or mitotic cell-division. **karyokinetic** (-ki net' ik), *a.*

katabolism (kȧ tăb' ȯ lizm) [Gr. *katabolē*, from *kataballein* (CAT-, CATA-, *ballein*, to throw)], *n.* The process of change by which complex organic compounds break down into simpler compounds, destructive metabolism.

katalysis, katalytic, etc. [CATALYTIC].

kata-thermometer (kăt' ȧ thĕr mom' ė tėr) [CATA-, THERMOMETER] *n.* An instrument for indicating the evaporating and cooling power of the air.

kation [CATION].

katipo (ka tē' pō) [Maori], *n.* A venomous spider found in New Zealand and Australia.

katydid (kā' ti did) [imit. of its stridulating cry], *n.* A large green orthopterous insect, *Curtophyllum concavum*, common in North America.

kauri (kou' ri) [Maori], *n.* A New Zealand coniferous forest-tree, *Dammaris Australis*. **kauri-gum,** *n.* A resinous gum from the kauri. **kauri-pine,** *n.*

kava (ka' vȧ) [Polynesian native], *n.* A beverage prepared from the chewed or pounded roots of a Polynesian shrub. **kava-ring,** *n.* A gathering for the ceremonial drinking of kava.

kavass (kȧ văs') [Turk. *gawwās*, bow-maker, from Arab. *qaws*, a bow], *n.* A Turkish armed constable, courier, or attendant.

kayak (kī' ăk) [Eskimo], *n.* The Eskimo and Alaskan canoe, made of sealskins stretched upon a light wooden framework.

kea (kā' ȧ) [Maori, imit. of cry], *n.* A green and blue mountain parrot, *Nestor notabilis*, of New Zealand, feeding on carrion and attacking living sheep for their kidney-fat.

keb (keb) [Sc. and North., etym. doubtful], *v.i.* To cast a lamb prematurely or dead. *n.* A ewe that has kebbed.

kebbie (keb' i) [Sc. and North.], *n.* A cudgel.

kebbuck (keb' ŭk) [Sc., etym. doubtful], *n.* A cheese.

keck (1) (kek) [imit.], *v.i.* To retch, to heave; to make a retching sound.

keck (2), ***kecksy, *kecky** [KEX, KEXY].

keckle (kek' ė) [Sc., var. of CACKLE], *v.i.* To cackle; to giggle, to chuckle. *v.t.* To utter with a keckle. *n.* A short, chuckling laugh.

kedge (kej) [cp. CADGE], *n.* (*Naut.*) A small portable anchor, used in warping. *v.t.* To move (a ship) by a light cable attached to a kedge. *v.i.* To move in this way (of a ship). **kedger,** *n.* A kedge.

kedgeree (kej' ėr ē) [Hind. *khichrī*, Sansk. *k'rsara*], *n.* A stew of rice, pulse, onions, etc., a common dish in India; a dish of fish, rice, etc., eaten by Europeans.

***keech** (kēch) [etym. doubtful], *n.* The fat of an ox or cow, rolled in a lump; a term of contempt.

keek (kēk) [Sc. and North., M.E. *kyken* (cp. Dut. *kijken*, L.G. *kiken*)], *v.i.* To peep, to pry. *n.* A peep. **keek-hole,** *n.* **keeker,** *n.* (*Coal-min.*) An inspector or overlooker. **keeking-glass,** *n.* A looking-glass.

keel (1) (kēl) [prob. from Icel. *kjölr*], *n.* The principal timber of a ship, extending from bow to stern and supporting the whole structure; the structure corresponding to this in an iron vessel; (*fig.*) a ship; (*Bot.*) the two lower petals of a papilionaceous corolla; (*Anat., Zool., etc.*) a projecting ridge or longitudinal process. *v.i.* To roll on her keel (of a vessel); to turn (over), to careen. *v.t.* To turn up the keel of, to turn over or keel upwards. **false keel:** A supplementary keel fastened below the true keel to protect this and promote stability. **keelboat,** *n.* (*U.S.A.*) A large covered river-boat without sails. **keelhaul,** *v.t.* To punish by dragging under water on one side of the ship and up again on the other. ***keelage,** *n.* A toll paid by vessels entering a harbour. **keeled,** *a.* Having a keel; (*Bot., etc.*) carinate. **keelless,** *a.*

keel (2) (kēl) [prob. from M.Dut. *kiel* (cp. A.-S. *cēol*, ship)], *n.* A lighter or flat-bottomed barge, esp. one of those used for loading colliers in the Tyne. **keeler, keelman,** *n.*

***keel** (3) (kēl) [A.-S. *cēlan*, cogn. with *cōl*, COOL], *v.t.* To cool; to keep from boiling over by scumming; (*fig.*) to mitigate, to lessen.

keel (4) (kēl) [Sc., etym. unknown], *n.* Ruddle. *v.t.* To mark with this.

keelhaul [KEEL (1)].

keelie (kē′ li), *n.* (*Sc.*) City-bred hooligan, rough.

keeling (kē′ ling) [Sc., etym. doubtful], *n.* A cod, esp. a kind of small cod.

keelivine (kē′ li vīn) [Sc. and North., etym. unknown], *n.* A lead-pencil.

keelson [KELSON].

keen (1) (kēn) [A.-S. *cēne* (cp. Dut. *koen*, Icel. *kœnn*, *kœnn*, G. *kühn*, bold, daring)], *a.* Having a sharp edge or point; sharp (of an edge); sensitive, acute, penetrating; biting, piercing, intense (of cold, etc.); bitter, acrimonious; eager, ardent (on); *fierce, bold. **keen-set,** *a.* Eager; hungry. **keen-witted,** *a.* **keenly,** *adv.* **keenness,** *n.*

keen (2) (kēn) [Ir. *caoine*, from *caoinim*, to weep], *n.* Lamentation over the body of a deceased person. *v.i.* To raise the keen. *v.t.* To mourn with the keen; to utter with keening.

keep (1) (kēp) [A.-S. *cēpan*, etym. doubtful], *v.t.* (*past* and *p.p.* **kept**) To hold, to retain; to have in charge; to guard, preserve, protect; to maintain; to observe, to pay proper regard to; to fulfil, to celebrate; to supply with the necessaries of life; to protect; to tend, to look after; to remain in; to have in pay; to make business entries in; to have regularly on sale; to restrain (from); to detain (in custody, etc.); to reserve (for). *v.i.* To continue or retain one's place (in, on, etc.); to remain; to continue to be (in a specified condition, etc.); to remain unspoiled, untainted, etc.; to adhere (to); to restrict oneself (to); to lodge, to reside. **to keep a term:** To reside in college, etc. during a term. **to keep back:** To restrain, to hold back; to reserve; to keep secret. **to keep cave:** (*School slang*) To keep a look-out. **to keep company with** [COMPANY]. **to keep down:** To repress, to subdue; to keep (expenses, etc.) low. **to keep from:** To abstain or refrain from. **to keep house:** To manage a household. **to keep in:** To repress, to restrain; to confine, esp. after school-hours; to maintain (a fire); to remain indoors. **to keep in with:** To remain on friendly terms with. **to keep in touch with:** To maintain connexion with. **to keep off:** To hinder from approach; to avert; to remain at a distance. **to keep on:** To continue to employ, etc.; to continue (doing, etc.), to persist. **to keep one's feet** [FOOT]. **keep your hair on** [HAIR]. **to keep one's hand in:** To keep oneself in practice. **to keep on foot:** To maintain, to support (as a standing army). **to keep out:** To hinder from entering or taking possession (of). **to keep school, shop, etc.:** To conduct a school, shop, etc., on one's own account. **to keep to:** To adhere strictly to. **to keep together:** To remain or cause to remain together. **to keep the pot boiling:** (*colloq.*) To go on (doing); to keep the game alive. **to keep under:** To hold down. **to keep up:** To maintain; to keep in repair or good condition; to prevent from falling or diminishing; to carry on; to cause to stay up at night; to bear up; to go on at the same pace (with). **to keep up with the Joneses:** (*colloq.*) To keep on the same social level as one's friends and neighbours.

keep (2) (kēp) [from prec.], *n.* Subsistence, maintenance; food required for subsistence; a donjon, the main tower or stronghold of a mediæval castle; *care, heed.

keeper (kē′ pėr), *n.* One who or that which keeps; one who retains others (esp. lunatics) in custody or charge; one who has the charge, care or superintendence of anything, esp. of a park; a game-keeper; a ring worn to protect another, esp. a wedding-ring; the bar of soft iron used to prevent permanent magnets from losing magnetism. **Keeper of the Great Seal:** The officer of State who holds the Great Seal; the Lord Chancellor. **keepership,** *n.*

keeping (kē′ ping), *n.* The action of holding, guarding, preserving, etc.; charge, custody, guardianship; harmony, accord; consistency, congruity. *a.* That can be kept (as fruit). **in** or **out of keeping:** In or not in harmony (with), esp. in painting.

keepsake (kēp′ sāk), *n.* Anything kept or given to be kept for the sake of the giver; an illustrated or decorated gift-book, usu. containing extracts in verse and prose of a sentimental character, in fashion early in the nineteenth cent.

keeve (kēv) [A.-S. *cyf*], *n.* A large tub or vat, esp. a mash-tub. *v.t.* To put in a keeve; (*prov.*) to tilt up (as a cart).

kef, keif [KIEF].

keffiyeh (kef ē′ ya) [Arab. *kaffiyah*], *n.* A Bedouin Arab's kerchief headdress.

kefir (kef′ ėr) [Caucasian], *n.* A species of koumiss produced by fermenting milk, used medicinally esp. as a food for invalids.

keg (keg) [formerly *cag* (cp. Icel. *kaggi*, Swed. *kagge*)], *n.* A small cask or barrel.

keir (kēr) [cp. Icel. *ker*, Swed. and Dan. *kar*], *n.* A vat for bleaching-liquor, in cloth-, paper-making, etc.

***kell** (kel) [North. var. of M.E. *calle*, CAUL], *n.* A woman's hair-net or cap; a film, a web, a cocoon; a caul.

kelp (kelp) [M.E. *culp*, etym. unknown], *n.* The calcined ashes of seaweed, from which carbonate of soda was obtained for glass- and soap-making, now chiefly used for obtaining iodine; the large, coarse seaweed from which kelp is produced.

kelpie (kel′ pi) [etym. doubtful (Skeat suggests Gael. *calpach*, a heifer, a colt)], *n.* A water-spirit usu. in the form of a horse, supposed to haunt fords, and to rejoice in the drowning of wayfarers; (*Austral.*) a smooth-haired variety of sheep-dog.

kelson (kel′ sȯn) [KEEL (1), *-son*, etym. doubtful (cp. Swed. *kölsvin*, Dut. *kolzwijn*, G. *kielschwein*)], *n.* A longitudinal piece placed along the floor-timbers of a ship binding them to the keel.

kelt (1) (kelt) [Sc., etym. unknown], *n.* A spent salmon or sea-trout.

kelt (2) (kelt) [Sc., etym. doubtful (cp. Ir. and Gael. *cealt*)], *n.* Cloth of native black wool.

Kelt (3) **Keltic,** etc. [CELT (1)].

***kelty** (kel′ ti) [Sc., prob. from *Keltie*, pers. name], *n.* A bumper imposed as a fine; the draining off of a glass or bumper.

kelvin (kel′ vin) [Lord *Kelvin* (1824–1907)], *n.* (*Elec.*) The kilowatt hour—the accepted regulation unit of electric energy; the scale of absolute temperature.

Kemalist (kė mal′ ist), *n.* An adherent of Kemal Atatürk (1882–1938), first president of the Turkish republic.

***kemb** [COMB].

kemp (kemp) [prob. from Icel. *kampr*, beard, whisker], *n.* The coarse rough hairs of wool; (*pl.*) knotty hairs that will not felt. **kempy,** *a.*

ken (1) (ken) [immediate source doubtful (cp. A.-S. *cennan*, to make known, to declare, Goth. *kannjan*

Dut. and G. *kennen*, Icel. *kenna*, to know)], *v.t.* (*past & p.p.* **kenned**) (*chiefly Sc.*) To be acquainted with; to understand; to know; to see at or from a distance; to descry; *to teach. **v.i.* To look round. *n.* View, sight; range of sight or knowledge, apprehension.

ken (2) (ken) [*slang*], *n.* A low tavern or lodging-house.

Kendal green (ken' dȧl grēn) [*Kendal*, Westmorland], *n.* Green cloth, orig. made at Kendal for foresters.

kennel (1) (ken' ėl) [O.North.F. *kenil*, O.F. *chenil*, low L. *canīle*, from L. *canis*, dog], *n.* A house or shelter for a dog or hounds; (*fig.*) a hovel, a wretched haunt or den; a pack of hounds; *the hole of a fox or other animal. *v.i.* To lie or lodge in or as in a kennel. *v.t.* To confine in or as in a kennel.

kennel (2) (ken' ėl) [M.E. and O.F. *canel*, CHANNEL], *n.* A gutter, the watercourse at the side of a street; a puddle. ***kennel-raker**, *n.* A scavenger.

kennel-coal [CANNEL].

kenosis (kė nō' sis) [Gr. *kenōsis*, from *kenoein*, to empty], *n.* (*Theol.*) Christ's relinquishment of the divine nature at the incarnation. **kenotic** (kė not' ik), *a.* **kenoticist** (kė not'-), **kenotist** (ken'-), *n.*

kenotron (kĕn' ō trŏn) [as prec.], *n.* (*Elec.*) A thermionic valve which is exhausted to a high vacuum and has an incandescent filament as cathode and a molybdenum or tungsten anode acting as a rectifier.

kent (1) (kent) [etym. doubtful], *n.* A staff, a pole, esp. a long leaping-staff or a punting-pole. *v.t.* and *i.* To punt.

kent (2) [KEN], *a.* (*Sc.*) Known, recognized.

Kentish (ken' tish) [A.-S. *Centisc* (*Cent*, Kent, -ISH)], *a.* Pertaining to the county of Kent. **Kentish man**, *n.* A native of Kent born west of the Medway. **Man of Kent**, *n.* A native of Kent born east of the Medway. **Kentish rag:** A calcareous rock belonging to the lower Greensand.

kentledge (kent' lėj) [etym. unknown], *n.* Pigs of iron used for permanent ballast, laid over the kelson-plates.

kep (kep) [Sc. var. of KEEP], *v.t.* To catch; to intercept, to stop. *n.* A catch.

kephalic [CEPHALIC].

képi (kep' i) [F., from G. Swiss *käppi*, dim. of *kappe*, CAP], *n.* A French flat-topped military hat with a horizontal peak.

Kepler's laws (kep' lĕrz lawz), *n.pl.* Laws formulated by Johann *Kepler* (1571–1630) concerning the revolution of planets round the sun.

kept, *past* and *p.p.* [KEEP].

keramic [CERAMIC].

keratin (ker' ȧ tin) [Gr. *keras keratos*, horn, -IN], *n.* (*Chem.*) A nitrogenous substance, the chief constituent of hair, feathers, claws, and horns. **keratinize**, *v.i.*

keratitis (ke rȧ tī' tis), *n.* (*Path.*) Inflammation of the cornea of the eye.

keratose (ke' rȧ tōz), *n.* The substance of the skeleton of horny sponges. *a.* Horny.

kerb (kĕrb) [var. of CURB (1)], *n.* A row of stones set as edging to a pavement, etc. **kerb-stone**, *n.* **kerb-stone broker:** A stockbroker who is not a member of the Stock Exchange.

kerchief (kĕr' chif) [M.E. *curchef*, *coverchef*, O.F. *couvrechief* (*couvrir*, to COVER, *chief*, L. *caput*, head)], *n.* A cloth to cover the head; a handkerchief, a napkin. **kerchiefed**, *a.*

kerf (kĕrf) [A.-S. *cyrf*, cogn. with CARVE], *n.* The slit, notch, or channel made by a saw or axe in cutting; the spot where something has been cut or lopped off; a cutting or lopping; a quantity of hay, straw, etc., cut for thatching, etc.; a heap of clay, ashes, etc., exposed to the weather until suitable for use in brick-making.

kerion (kē' i ŏn) [Gr., honeycomb], *n.* (*Path.*) An inflammation of the hair-follicles of the scalp, causing baldness.

kerite (kēr' īt) [Gr. *kēros*, wax, -ITE], *n.* Artificial caoutchouc used as an insulating material in telegraphy.

kermes (kĕr' mēz) [F. *kermès*, Arab. and Pers. *qirmiz*, CRIMSON], *n.* The dried bodies of the females of an insect, *Coccus ilicis*, yielding a red or scarlet dye.

kermis (kĕr' mis) [Dut. *kirk*, CHURCH, *mis*, MASS (1)], *n.* (*Holland*) A fair or outdoor festival or merrymaking, orig. a church festival.

kern (1), **kerne** (kĕrn) [Ir. *ceatharn* (kā' ėrn)], *n.* A light-armed Irish foot-soldier; a country lout; *a vagabond.

kern (2) (kĕrn) [F. *carne*, L. *cardinem*, nom. *cardo*, hinge], *n.* (*Print.*) The projecting part of a type. **kerned**, *a.*

kernel (kĕr' nėl) [A.-S. *cyrnel*, dim. of CORN], *n.* The substance, usu. edible, contained in the shell of a nut or the stone of a fruit; that which is enclosed in a shell, husk, integument, etc.; (*fig.*) the nucleus, core, gist or essence. *v.i.* To ripen or harden into kernels. **kernelled**, *a.* Having a kernel. **kernelly**, *a.*

kerosene (ker' ō sēn) [Gr. *kēros*, wax], *n.* An oil distilled from petroleum, coal, or bituminous shale, chiefly used for burning in lamps.

Kerry blue (ke' ri bloo) [Ir. place], *n.* A large, grey-blue, longhaired breed of terrier.

kersey (kĕr' zi) [place in Suffolk], *n.* A coarse woollen cloth, usu. ribbed. *a.* Made of kersey; (*fig.*) homely, plain.

kerseymere [CASSIMERE].

kestrel (kes' trėl) [prob. from O.F. *cresserelle*, etym. doubtful], *n.* A small species of hawk, *Falco tinnunculus*.

***ket** (ket) [Sc. and North. (cp. mod. Icel. *ket*, flesh)], *n.* Carrion; (*fig.*) filth, trash.

ketch (kech) [formerly CATCH], *n.* A fore-and-aft rigged two-masted vessel.

ketchup (kech' ŭp) [Malay *kēchap*, perh. from Chin. *kôe-chiap*, fish-brine], *n.* A sauce, usu. prepared from mushrooms, tomatoes, etc.; (*Am.*) tomato sauce.

ketone (kē' tōn) [G. *keton*, ACETONE], *n.* (*Chem.*) One of a class of organic compounds, usu. formed by oxidation of a secondary alcohol.

kettle (ket' ėl) [A.-S. *cetel* or Icel. *ketill* (cp. Dut. *ketel*, G. *kessel*)], *n.* A metallic vessel for heating water or other liquid. **a pretty kettle of fish:** A pretty mess, a muddle, a troublesome state of affairs. **kettleholder**, *n.* A thick piece of cloth for protecting the hand in holding a hot kettle.

kettledrum (ketl' drŭm), *n.* A drum made of a thin hemispherical shell of copper or brass, with a parchment head; *an afternoon tea party. **kettle-drummer**, *n.*

keuper (koi' pėr) [G., mining term], *n.* (*Geol.*) The upper portion of the Triassic, consisting chiefly of marls and sandstones.

kevel (kev' ėl) [O.North.F. *keville* (F. *cheville*), L. *clāvicula*, dim. of *clāvis*, key], *n.* (*Naut.*) A belaying-cleat, usu. fixed in pairs.

kex (keks) [etym. unknown], *n.* The dry hollow stem of umbelliferous plants, as the hemlock, the cow-parsnip, or the angelica. **kexy**, *a.*

key (1) (kē) [A.-S. *cæg*, etym. doubtful], *n.* A portable instrument, usu. of metal, for working the bolt of a lock to and fro; a tool or instrument by which something is screwed up or turned; (*fig.*) that which gives access to or opportunity for something; a place whose military occupation gives control over a region of land or sea; that which explains anything difficult; a solution, an explanation; a translation; a series of solutions of problems, etc.; (*Carp.*) a piece of wood or metal let transversely into the back of a board to prevent warping; a keystone; (*Plastering*) the first coat of plaster on a wall or ceiling which goes between the laths and binds the whole together; a small lever actuated by the fingers in operating certain instruments, machines, etc.; (*Mus.*) one of several systems of notes having definite tonic relations among themselves and to one fundamental note called the key-note; (*fig.*) the general tone or style (of a picture, literary composition, speech, etc.). *v.t.* To fasten (on, in, etc.) with a key, bolt, wedge, etc.; (*Mus.*) to tune, to regulate; (*fig.*) to stir (up) to an action etc. **to have the key of the street,** *v.i.* To be homeless. **House of Keys:** The representative branch of the legislature in the Isle of Man. **power of the keys:** The supreme ecclesiastical authority claimed by the Pope (Matt. xvi. 19). **St. Peter's keys:** The cross-keys on the Papal arms symbolizing this. **keyboard,** *n.* The range of keys on a piano, organ, etc. **key-bugle,** *n.* A keyed bugle. **key-cold,** *a.* Cold as a key; lifeless. **key colour,** *n.* The leading colour of a picture. **key fruit,** *n.* (*Bot.*) A winged fruit, like that of the sycamore, which hangs like bunches of keys. **keyhole,** *n.* The hole in a lock, door, cover, etc., by which a key is inserted. **key industry,** *n.* An industry upon which the other interests and the economic welfare of a country depend. **key-man,** *n.* An indispensable worker. **key-money,** *n.* A premium demanded, in addition to rent, for the granting or renewal of a tenancy. **key-note,** *n.* (*Mus.*) The fundamental note of a key; (*fig.*) the general tone or spirit (of a picture, poem, etc.). **key-ring,** *n.* A ring for carrying keys upon. **key-seat,** *n.* (*Mach.*) A groove to receive a key for preventing a wheel or other part from sliding. **keystone,** *n.* The central stone of an arch locking the others together; (*fig.*) the fundamental element, principle, etc. **to key-up,** *v.t.* To brace up, to incite, to encourage. **keyed,** *a.* **keyless,** *a.* Not having a key; wound without a key (as a clock or watch).

key (2) [var. of CAY], *n.* A low island, esp. of coral, on the coast of Florida.

keystone [KEY (1)].

khaddar (kad' ar) [Hind.], *n.* Hand-woven cloth.

khaki (ka' ki) [Hind., dusty, from *khāk*, dust], *a.* Dust-coloured, dull-yellow. *n.* Cloth or cotton material of this colour, used for army uniforms.

khalif [CALIPH].

khamsin (kăm' sin) [Arab., fifty], *n.* A hot southerly wind blowing in Egypt for some fifty days in Mar.–May.

khan (1) (kăn, kan) [Turk. *khān*, perh. orig. *khāqan*], *n.* Orig. a prince, a lord, a chief; now a title (in India, Central Asia, etc.) equivalent to 'esquire'; *a king or emperor, esp. the chief rulers of Tatar, Turkish, and Mongol tribes. **khanate,** *n.*

khan (2) (kăn, kan) [Arab. *khān*], *n.* A caravanserai.

kheda (kā' da) [Hind.], *n.* Enclosure used in Bengal and other parts of India for catching elephants.

Khedive (kė dēv') [F. *khédive*, Turk. (Pers.) *khedīv*], *n.* The official title of the Governor of Egypt, conferred upon Ismail Pasha in 1867 by the Porte. **Khediva** (kė dē' vȧ), **Khediviah,** *n.* The wife of the Khedive. **khedival, khedivial,** *a.* **khedivate,** *n.*

khud (kŭd) [Hind.], *n.* A deep ravine or chasm; a steep descent.

kiak [KAYAK].

kiang (kyăng) [Tibetan], *n.* Tibetan wild ass.

kia ora (kē ȧ ō' rȧ) [Maori], *int.* Your health!

kiaugh (ki a*ch*') [Sc., etym. doubtful], *n.* Care, trouble.

kibble (1) (kib' ėl) [cp. G. *kübel*], *n.* (*Mining*) A strong iron (formerly wooden) bucket for raising ore from a mine. **kibble-chain,** *n.* A chain for drawing this up.

kibble (2) (kib' ėl) [etym. unknown], *v.t.* To grind (grain, beans, etc.) coarsely.

kibbutz (kē boots') [Heb.], *n.* A communal agricultural settlement in Israel.

kibe (kīb) [perh. from W. *cibi* (*cib*, a cup, a husk)], *n.* A chap occasioned by cold; an ulcerated chilblain. **to tread on** or **gall one's kibes:** To irritate one's feelings. **kibed, kiby,** *a.* Affected with kibes.

kibitka (ki bit' kȧ) [Rus.], *n.* A Tatar circular tent, usu. made of lattice-work and felt; a Russian wheeled vehicle with a tent-like covering, used as a sledge in snowy weather.

kibitzer (kib' it sėr) [Yiddish, fr. G., a looker-on], *n.* (*Am. colloq.*) An interfering looker-on, a meddler; a spectator.

Kiblah (kib' lȧ) [Arab. *qiblah*], *n.* The direction of the Caaba at Mecca, to which Mohammedans turn during prayer.

kibosh (kī bosh', ki' bosh) [Slang], *n.* Bosh, humbug. **to put the kibosh on:** To checkmate, to do for.

kick (1) (kik) [M.E. *kiken*, etym. doubtful], *v.t.* To strike with the foot; to push, move, or drive, by kicking; to strike in recoil. *v.i.* To strike out with the foot or feet; to recoil (as a gun); (*fig.*) to show opposition, dislike, etc. (against, at, etc.). *n.* The act of kicking; a blow with the foot; a recoil (of a gun); (*Archery*) the erratic course of an arrow owing to wrong handling of the bow; (*Elec.*) a transient high-voltage discharge in an inductive electric current; (*fig.*) a stimulating reaction to alcohol or pungent seasoning; a sudden thrill of excitement. **kick-off,** *n.* (*Football*) The first kick in the game. **to kick off:** To throw off by kicking; (*Football*) to give the ball the first kick. **to kick one's heels:** To stand idly waiting. **to kick out:** To eject or dismiss contumeliously or with violence. **to kick up a dust, fuss, rumpus,** etc. [DUST]. **kicker,** *n.* One who or that which kicks; a horse given to kicking.

kick (2) (kik) [perh. from prec.], *n.* The pushed-in base of a glass bottle.

kickshaw (kik' shaw) [corr. of F. *quelque chose*, something], *n.* Something fantastical, a trifle; a light, unsubstantial dish.

***kicksywicksy** (kik' si wik' si)) [perh. conn. with prec.], *a.* Fanciful, erratic, uncertain. *n.* (*Shak., contemp.*) A wife.

kid (1) (kid) [M.E. *kid*, *kide* (cp. Norw., Swed., and Dan. *kid*, Icel. *kith*, G. *kitze*)], *n.* The young of the goat; leather from the skin of this; (*pl.*) gloves of this leather; (*slang*) a child. *v.i.* (*past & p.p.* **kidded**) To bring forth a kid or kids. ***kid-fox,** *n.* A young fox. **kid glove:** A glove made of kid; (*fig.*) too fastidious for common tasks, etc. **kiddy,** *n.* A little child. **kidling,** *n.*

kid (2) (kid) [prob. var. of KIT (1)], *n.* A small wooden tub, esp. one used at mess by sailors.

kid (3) (kid) [etym. doubtful], *n.* A faggot, a bundle.

kid (4) (kid) [Slang, perh. from KID (1)], *v.t.* (*past & p.p.* **kidded**) To humbug, to hoax. *n.* A deception, a fraud. **kidder** (1), *n.*

***kidder** (2) (kid' ėr) [etym. unknown], *n.* A dealer in corn, esp. an engrosser of corn to enhance its price.

Kidderminster (kid' ėr min stėr) [town in Worcestershire], *a.* Of or pertaining to Kidderminster. *n.* Two-ply ingrain carpet orig. made there.

kiddle (kid' ėl) [A.-S. *kidel*, O.F. *quidel*, later *quideau*, etym. doubtful], *n.* A weir or dam in a river with traps or nets for catching fish; a set of stake-nets for the same purpose on a beach.

kidnap (kid' năp) [KID (1), *nap*, NAB], *v.t.* To steal (a child); to carry off by force or illegally, to abduct. **kidnapper,** *n.*

kidney (kid′ ni) [etym. obscure], *n.* An oblong flattened glandular organ embedded in fatty tissue in the lumbar region on each side of the spine, and serving to secrete urine and remove nitrogenous matter from the blood; anything resembling a kidney; (*fig.*) temperament, kind, fashion; *(*slang*) a waiter. **kidney bean:** The name of two species of *Phaseolus*, the dwarf French bean and the scarlet runner. **kidney-form, -shaped,** *a.* **kidney-potato,** *n.* An oval-shaped potato. **kidney-vetch,** *n.* A leguminous plant, *Anthyllis vulneraria*, or lady's fingers. **kidney-wort,** *n.* The navelwort, *Cotyledon umbilicus*; the star saxifrage, *Saxifraga stellaris.*

kief (kēf) [Arab. *kaif*], *n.* The drowsy, dreamy, trance-like condition produced by the use of bhang, etc.; (*fig.*) dreamy repose, happy idleness; Indian hemp, smoked in Morocco and Algeria to produce this condition.

kiekie (kē′ kē) [Maori], *n.* A New Zealand climber, *Freycinetia Banksii*, the berries of which are eaten and the leaves used for baskets, etc.

Kikuyu (kē koo′ ū) [Bantu], *n.* A Negro tribe of Kenya, E. Africa; a member of the tribe; its language.

kilderkin (kil′ dėr kin) [corr. of M.Dut. *kindeken*, dim. of *kintal*, O.F. QUINTAL], *n.* A small barrel, usu. of 18 gals.; a liquid measure of this capacity.

kilerg (kī′ lĕrg) [*kil-*, KILO-, ERG], *n.* (*Phys.*) A unit of measurement of work, one thousand ergs.

kiley [KYLIE].

kill (kil) [etym. doubtful, prob. not rel. to QUELL], *v.t.* To deprive of life; to put to death, to slay; to put an end to, to destroy, to quell; (*fig.*) to deaden, to still (pain, etc.); to neutralize (effects of colour, etc.); to pass or consume (time) idly; to discard, to cancel; (*Printing*) to mark a paragraph or article not to be used; to order type to be distributed; (*colloq.*) to overwhelm with admiration, astonishment, personal charms, etc.; (*Lawn Tennis*) to strike (the ball) so forcibly that it cannot be returned. *v.i.* To put to death; to slaughter, esp. in sport; (*slang*) to fascinate, to do execution. *n.* The act of killing; an animal or number of animals killed, esp. in sport; an animal used as a bait in hunting wild beasts; (*Lawn Tennis and Rackets*) the hitting of a ball in such a manner that it cannot be returned. **to kill off:** To get rid of by killing. ***to kill up:** To exterminate. **kill-devil,** *n.* An artificial spinning bait used in angling. **kill-joy,** *n.* A person who sheds a general depression on company, a wet blanket. **to kill the sea:** (*Naut.*) To make the sea become calmer. **to kill the skin:** (*Leather manuf.*) To remove the natural grease from the skin. **to kill the wind:** (*Naut.*) To check wind-velocity. **kill-time,** *n.* An amusement for whiling away time. **killer,** *n.* **killing,** *ger.* The number of animals killed by sportsmen; (*Metal.*) the precaution against the evolution of gas in steel during the process of manufacture; (*Bridge*) a heavy defeat of a contract. *a.* That kills; fascinating, irresistibly charming; (*colloq.*) excruciatingly funny. **killingly,** *adv.*

killas (kil′ ȧs) [Cornish], *n.* (*Mining*) Clay-slate.

killdee (kil′ dē), **killdeer** (-dēr) [imit. of the cry], *n.* A North American ring-plover, *Ægialites vocifera.*

killick (kil′ ik) [etym. unknown], *n.* (*Naut.*) A stone or small anchor used for mooring a fishing-boat.

killogie (ki lō′ gi) [Sc. (KILN, *logie*, the space by the fire)], *n.* The sheltered space in front of the fire-place in a kiln.

kiln (kiln, kil) [A.-S. *cyln, cyline*, L. *culīna*, kitchen], *n.* A furnace, oven, or stove for calcining, drying, hardening, etc., esp. a lime-kiln. *v.t.* To dry or bake in a kiln. **brick-kiln,** *n.* A kiln for baking bricks. **lime-kiln,** *n.* A kiln for calcining lime. **kiln-dry,** *v.t.* To dry in a kiln. **kiln-hole,** *n.* The mouth of a kiln.

kilo- [F., from Gr. *chilioi*, a thousand], *comb. form.* **kilocalorie** (kil′ ȯ kăl′ ȯ ri), *n.* (*Phys.*) 1,000 units of heat. (See CALORIE.) **kilocurie** (kil ō kūr′ i), *n.* The unit of radioactivity equal to 1,000 curies. **kilocycle,** *n.* (*Elec.*) 1,000 cycles per second; a unit for measuring the frequency of alternating current. **kilodyne,** *n.* A unit of force equivalent to 1,000 dynes. **kilo-electron-volt,** *n.* The energy of an electron accelerated through 1,000 volts. **kilogramme** (kil′ ȯ grăm), *n.* A French measure of weight, 1,000 grammes or 2·2046 lb. av. **kilogrammetre** (kil ȯ grăm′ ė tėr) [F. *kilogrammètre* (prec., METRE)], *n.* A unit of measurement of work, the energy expended in raising one kilogramme to the height of one metre. **kilojoule,** *n.* A unit equal to 1,000 joules. **kilolitre** (kil′ ȯ lē tėr) [LITRE], *n.* A French liquid measure, 1,000 litres. **kilometre** (kil′ ȯ mē tėr) [METRE], *n.* A French measure of distance, 1,000 metres or ·621 mile. **kilometrical** (-met′ ri kȧl), *a.* **kilovolt,** *n.* (*Elec.*) A unit of electromotive force equivalent to 1,000 volts. **kilowatt** (kil′ ȯ wot) [WATT], *n.* (*Elec.*) A unit of measurement of electrical energy, 1,000 watts. **kilowatt hour,** *n.* (*Elec.*) A unit of energy or work equivalent to that performed by one kilowatt acting for one hour.

kilt (kilt) [prob. from Scand. (cp. Dan. *kilte*, Icel. *kilting*, a skirt)], *v.t.* To tuck up (the skirts of a dress); to gather together (the material of a dress) into vertical pleats. *n.* A kind of short skirt usu. of tartan cloth gathered in vertical pleats, worn as a male dress by the Highlanders of Scotland. **kiltie,** *n.* (*colloq.*) A soldier of a kilted regiment.

kilter (kil′ tėr) [etym. unknown], *n.* (*colloq.*) Good condition, fitness, form.

kimberlite (kim′ bĕr līt) [*Kimberley*, S. Afr.], *n.* A diamond-bearing clay-like substance, called by miners 'blue earth' or 'blue ground,' found in South Africa.

kimbo [AKIMBO].

Kimmeridge clay (kim′ ėr ij klā′), *n.* (*Geol.*) A thick bed of Upper Oolitic clay or bituminous shale, occurring near Kimmeridge, on the Dorset coast. **Kimmeridgian** (-ij′ i ȧn), *a.*

kimono (ki mō′ nō) [Jap.], *n.* A loose robe fastened with a sash, the principal outer garment of Japanese costume.

kin (kin) [A.-S. *cynn* (cp. Dut. *kunne*, Icel. *kyn*), cogn. with L. *genus*, Gr. *genos*], *n.* Stock, family; relations or connexions collectively, kindred; a relation, a connexion. *a.* Of the same family, nature, or kind; akin. **near of kin:** Closely related. **next of kin:** The nearest blood relation. **kinless,** *a.*

-kin [cog. with M.Dut. *-kijn*, O.H.G. *-chîn*, G. *-chen*], *dim. suf.* As in *bumpkin, buskin, cannikin, catkin.*

kinæsthesis (kī nės thē′ sis) [Gr. *kinein*, to move, Gr. *æsthesis*, perception], *n.* The muscular sense, the perception of muscular movement, also called **kinæsthesia** (-thē′ si ȧ). **kinæsthetic** (-thet′ ik), *a.*

kinchin (kin′ chin) [*slang*, perh. from G. *kindchen* or M.L.G. *kindekin*, little child], *n.* A little child. **kinchin-cove,** *n.* A little man; a raw thief. **kinchin-lay,** *n.* Stealing money from children. **kinchin-mort,** *n.* A baby girl.

kincob (king′ kob) [Hind. *kimkhāb*], *n.* A rich East Indian stuff interwoven with gold or silver thread.

kind (kīnd) [A.-S. *cynd, gecynd*, cogn. with KIN], *n.* Race, genus, species, natural group; sort, class, variety; manner, fashion, way; *nature; *natural way, natural propensity or inclination; *parentage, descent. *a.* Disposed to do good to others; sympathetic, benevolent, tender; proceeding from or characterized by goodness of heart; *affectionate. **v.t.* To beget. **a kind of:** A sort of; roughly or approximately of the description or class expressed. **in kind:** In produce or commodities (of payment, wages, etc.); in the same way or manner. **to differ in kind:** To differ in nature, not merely in degree. **kind-hearted,** *a.* ***kind-less,** *a.* Unnatural; unparalleled. **kindness,** *n.*

kindergarten (kin′ dėr gar tėn) [G., children's garden], *n.* A school for infants and young children, in which knowledge is imparted chiefly by simple object-lessons, by toys, games, singing, and work. **kindergartenism,** *n.* **kindergartener,** *n.*

kindle (1) (kin′ dėl) [prob. from Icel. *kynda*, -LE], *v.t.* To set fire to; to light; (*fig.*) to inflame, to inspire (the passions, etc.); to excite, to stir up (to action or feeling); to light up or illumine. *v.i.* To take fire, to begin to burn or flame; (*fig.*) to become inflamed or excited, to become illumined. **kindler,** *n.* **kindling,** *n.* The act of setting on fire; wood, shavings, etc., for lighting fires, firewood.

***kindle** (2) (kin′ dėl) [from KIND], *n.* A brood, a litter. *v.t.* To bring forth, to bear. *v.i.* To bring forth young.

kindly (kīnd′ li) [*cyndlic, gecyndlic* (KIND, -LY)], *a.* Kind, good-natured, benevolent, genial, beneficial; favourable, auspicious; *native, akin, natural. **kindlily,** *adv.* **kindliness,** *n.*

kindred (kin′ drėd) [KIN, *-red*, A.-S. *-ræden*, condition], *n.* Relationship by blood or marriage; (*fig.*) affinity or likeness of character; (*collect.*) relatives, kin; *family, race, descent. *a.* Related by blood; (*fig.*) congenial, sympathetic; of like nature or qualities.

kine, *n.pl.* [COW (1)].

kinema, cinema (kī-, si nē′ mȧ) [short for KINEMATOGRAPH], *n.* A building used for cinematographic exhibitions.

kinematic (kī nė măt′ ik) [Gr. *kinēma -matos*, movement, from *kinein*, to move], *a.* Pertaining to movement or to kinematics. *n.pl.* The science of pure motion, admitting conceptions of time and velocity but excluding that of force. **kinematical,** *a.*

kinematograph [CINEMATOGRAPH].

kinesi- [Gr. *kinēsis*, motion, from *kinein*, to move], *comb. form.* **kinesipathy** (kī nė sip′ ȧ thi) [-PATHY], *n.* The treatment of disease by muscular movements; cure by gymnastic exercises. **kinesipath** (kī nē′ si păth), **kinesipathist** (-sip′ ȧ thist), *n.* **kinesitherapy** (-ther′ ȧ pi), *n.* Kinesipathy.

kinetic (kī net′ ik) [Gr. *kinētikos*, as prec.], *a.* Of or producing motion; due to or depending upon motion. *n.pl.* That branch of dynamics which treats of forces imparting motion to or influencing motion already imparted to bodies. **kinetic energy,** *n.* The energy possessed by a body by virtue of its motion. **kinetic pressure,** *n.* (*Phys.*) The increase in pressure when a stream of fluid meets an obstruction. **kinetic theory,** *n.* (*Phys.*) A theory which accounts for the behaviour of gases, vapours, liquids, etc. in terms of the motions of molecules or atoms comprising them.

kineto-, *comb. form.*

kinetogenesis (kī net ō jen′ ė sis), *n.* (*Biol.*) The theory that animal structures originated and were developed through movements.

kinetograph (kī net′ ō grăf), *n.* A camera for obtaining photographs of objects in motion. **kinetographer,** *n.* **kinetographic,** *a.* **kinetography,** *n.*

kinetoscope (kī net′ ō skōp), *n.* A device for exhibiting pictures taken by the kinetograph, an early form of cinematograph; an instrument for combining arcs of different radii into continuous curves.

king (king) [A.-S. *cyning* (*cyn*, KIN, -ING), cp. Dut. *koning*, Icel. *konungr*, G. *könig*], *n.* The male sovereign of a nation, esp. an hereditary sovereign of an independent State; (*fig.*) one who or that which is pre-eminent in any sphere; (*Cards*) a card bearing a representation of a king, usu. ranking next to the ace and before the queen; (*Chess*) a piece which has to be protected from checkmate; (*Draughts*) a piece which has been crowned and is entitled to move in any direction. *v.i.* To act as king, to govern; to play the king. *v.t.* To make a king of; to raise to a throne. **King Charles's spaniel** [SPANIEL]. **king-of-arms,** *n.* A senic herald. **king-bird,** *n.* An American tyrant fly catcher, *Tyrannus Carolinensis*; a king bird (Paradise, *Paradisea regia.* **king-bolt,** *n.* A main c central pin, bolt, or pivot. **king-crab,** *n.* A larg crustacean with a carapace shaped like a horsesho of the genus *Limulus.* **king-craft,** *n.* The art c governing; kingly statesmanship. **king-cup,** The bulbous buttercup, *Ranunculus bulbosus*, th marsh marigold, *Caltha palustris*, and some allie species. **kingfisher,** *n.* Any bird of the genu *Alcedo*, esp. *A. ispida*, a small British bird wi brilliant blue and green plumage, subsisting o fish. **king-maker,** *n.* One who sets up kings, es Richard Neville, Earl of Warwick, who supporte the Houses of York and Lancaster alternately in th Wars of the Roses. **King of Kings:** God, the tit of various Oriental monarchs. **king penguin:** Th largest of the penguins, *Aptenodytes longirostris* *A. Patagonica*, also called the emperor pengui **king-pin,** *n.* The centre pin in ninepins; (*colloq* a most important person. **kingpost,** *n.* (*Arch.*) Th middle post of a roof, reaching from the ridge the tie-beam; (*Aviat.*) a strut to which an aer plane's bracing wires are fixed. **King's Benc** [BENCH]. **king's** or **queen's evidence** [EVIDENCE **king's evil:** Scrofula, formerly believed to cured by the royal touch. **king's spear:** The whi asphodel, *Asphodelus albus.* **king's yellow:** Orp ment or yellow arsenic used as a pigment. **kin hood,** *n.* **kingless,** *a.* **kinglet,** *n.* A petty kin the golden-crested wren, *Regulus cristatus.* **kin like,** *a.* ***kingling,** *n.* **kingly,** *a.* and *adv.* **king ness, kinglihood,** *n.* **kingship,** *n.*

kingdom (king′ dŏm), *n.* The territory under ru of a king; the position or attributes of a kin sovereign power or authority; a domain, a ter tory; the highest and most comprehensive of th divisions into which natural objects are arrange **kingdom come:** (*slang*) The world to com **United Kingdom:** Great Britain and Northe Ireland. **kingdomed,** *a.* In the condition of kingdom; *furnished with a kingdom.

kingwood (king′ wud), *n.* A fine, hard wood fro Brazil, used for turning and cabinet work.

kink (kingk) [prob. from Dut. *kink* (cp. Dan., Swe Norse, and G. *kink*)], *n.* A twist or abrupt bend a rope, thread, wire, etc.; (*fig.*) a prejudice, crotchet, a whim. *v.i.* To twist or run into kin *v.t.* To cause to kink. **kinkle,** *n.* A slight twi (*Brickmaking*) an arrangement of bricks in an ov or for drying, courses being laid at opposite ang in alternate courses. **kinky,** *a.*

kinkajou (king′ kȧ joo) [F. *quincajou*, from N.A Ind.], *n.* An arboreal carnivorous quadrupe *Cercoleptes caudivolvulus*, of S. and Cent America, allied to the racoon, with long body a prehensile tail.

kinless [KIN].

kinnikinic (kin′ i ki nik′) [Algonkin], *n.* The lea of the sumach or the bark of willow or corn dried and prepared for smoking; one of vario plants used for this purpose.

kino (kē′ nō) [prob. W. Afr.], *n.* An astringent g used for tanning or dyeing and in medici obtained from certain Indian, African, a Australian trees.

kinsfolk (kinz′ fōk) [KIN, FOLK], *n.* (*collect.*) Fam relations, kindred. **kinsman, -woman,** *n.*

kiosk (kē osk′) [F. *kiosque*, Turk. *kiushk*, Pe *kūshk*, palace, villa], *n.* An open pavilion summerhouse; a light ornamental structure for sale of newspapers, etc.; a public telephone boo band-stand.

kip (1) (kip) [etym. doubtful], *n.* The hide of a c or of small cattle, used for leather; leather ma from such skins. **kip-leather, kip-skin,** *n.*

kip (2) (kip) [Slang, cp. Dan. *kippe*], *n.* A comm lodging-house; a bed; a brothel. *v.i.* (*past & p* **kipped**) To lie down to sleep. **kip-house, -sh** *n.*

kip (3) (kip) [Austral.], *n.* A wooden bat for tossing coins in the game of two-up.

kipe (kīp) [A.-S. *cype*], *n.* An osier basket for catching fish.

kippage (kip′ āj) [Sc., corr. of EQUIPAGE], *n.* A state of excitement or rage, a tantrum.

kipper (kip′ ėr) [etym. doubtful; identity with A.-S. *cypera*, a kind of salmon, uncertain], *n.* A male salmon during the spawning season; a salmon or herring split open, salted, and smoke-dried. *v.t.* To cure and preserve (salmon, herrings, etc.) by rubbing with salt, pepper, etc., and drying or smoking.

kirk (kĕrk) [Sc. and North. var. of CHURCH], *n.* A church; the Established Church of Scotland, esp. in contradistinction to the Church of England or the Scottish Episcopal Church. **at kirk and market:** (*Sc. colloq.*) On all occasions. **Auld Kirk:** The Established Church of Scotland. **Free Kirk:** The Free Church of Scotland. **kirkman,** *n.* **kirk-session,** *n.* The lowest court in the Kirk of Scotland and other Presbyterian Churches consisting of the minister and elders.

kirn (1) (kĕrn) [Sc., etym. doubtful], *n.* A harvest home; the last sheaf of the harvest. **to win** or **get the kirn:** To cut the last armful of corn; to finish the harvest. **kirn-baby,** *n.* An image dressed up with corn, carried before reapers to the harvest home.

kirn (2) [CHURN].

kirsch, kirschwasser (kĕrsh, kĕrsh′ va sėr) [G. (*kirsche*, cherry, *wasser*, water)], *n.* An alcoholic liqueur distilled from the fermented juice of the black cherry.

kirtle (kir′ tėl) [A.-S. *cyrtel* (cp. Icel. *kyrtill*, Dan. and Swed. *kjortel*), perh. from L. *curtus*], *n.* An upper garment of various kinds; a woman's gown or petticoat; a man's short jacket, tunic, or coat. *v.t.* To dress in a kirtle.

kismet (kis′ mėt) [Turk. *qismet*, Pers. *qismat*, Arab. *qisma(t)*, from *qasama*, to divide], *n.* Fate, destiny.

kiss (kis) [A.-S. *coss*, whence the v. *cyssan* (cp. Dut. *kus* and *kussen*, Icel. *koss* and *kyssa*, G. *kuss* and *küssen*)], *n.* A caress or salute with the lips; (*Billiards*) a mere touch of the moving balls; a confection of sugar, white of eggs, etc. *v.t.* To salute or caress by pressing or touching with the lips; (*Billiards*) to touch or graze in passing (of a ball or balls). *v.i.* To join lips in affection or respect; (*Billiards*) to come in contact (of moving balls). **to kiss away:** To wipe away by kissing. **to kiss the book:** To touch the Bible with the lips in taking an oath. **to kiss the dust:** To be conquered, to yield; to die, to be slain. **to kiss the ground** or **earth:** To bow down, to prostrate oneself; (*fig.*) to be conquered. **to kiss the rod:** To submit tamely to punishment. **kiss-curl,** *n.* A curl hanging over the forehead, in front of the ear, or at the nape of the neck. **kiss in the ring:** A game for a number of young people in which the player chases and kisses one of the opposite sex. **kiss-me-quick,** *n.* The wild pansy or heartsease, *Viola tricolor*; a small old-fashioned bonnet. **kisser,** *n.* One who kisses; (*slang*) the mouth. ***kissing-comfits,** *n.pl.* Perfumed sugar-plums. **kissing-crust,** *n.* The soft portion of the crust of a loaf where it touched another loaf in baking. **kissing-gate,** *n.* A gate hung in a U- or V-shaped enclosure. **kissing kind:** On affectionate terms. **kissable,** *a.*

kist [CIST].

kistvaen (kist′ vīn) [W. *cist faen* (*cist*, chest, *faen*, *maen*, stone)], *n.* (*Archæol.*) A cist, a tomb formed of stone slabs.

kit (1) (kit) [M.Dut. *kitte*, a wooden bowl or tub], *n.* A wooden tub, a milk-pail, a tub for pickled fish, butter, etc.; a chest, a box; that which contains the necessaries, tools, etc., of a workman; hence, an outfit, esp. the equipment of a soldier; the bag or valise containing these; (*colloq.*) the whole lot.

kit (2) (kit) [etym. doubtful], *n.* A small violin used by dancing-masters.

kit (3) [short for KITTEN], *n.* A kitten. **kit-cat** (1), *n.* The game of tip-cat.

kit-cat (2) [*Kit* (or Christopher) *Cat* or *Catling*], *n.* A portrait of a particular size, rather less than half-length; a size of canvas 28 by 36 in., used for portraits, that size being adopted by Kneller for the portraits he painted of the Kit-cat Club; a member of this club. **Kit-cat Club:** A club founded in 1688 by Whig politicians, meeting at a pie-house near Temple Bar kept by Christopher Cat or Catling.

kitchen (kich′ ėn) [A.-S. *cycene*, late L. *cucīna*, L. *coquīna*, from *coquere*, to cook], *n.* The room in a house, etc. where food is cooked. ***v.t.** To regale or feed in a kitchen. **kitchen-dresser** [DRESSER (2)]. **Kitchen Dutch,** *n.* A mixture of Dutch or Kaffir with English. **kitchen-garden,** *n.* A garden in which fruit and vegetables are cultivated for the table. **kitchen-knave,** *n.* A scullion. **kitchen-maid,** *n.* A female servant whose business it is to assist the cook. **kitchen-midden** [Dan. *kjökken-mödding*], *n.* A prehistoric refuse-heap, or shell-mound, first noticed on the coast of Denmark, and since found in the British Isles, etc. **kitchen-range,** *n.* A kitchen grate with oven, boiler, etc., for cooking. **kitchen sideboard:** (*Am.*) a dresser. **kitchen-stuff,** *n.* Fat collected from dripping-pans; materials for cooking, esp. vegetables. **kitchen-wench,** *n.* **kitchener,** *n.* A close cooking-range; one employed in a kitchen, esp. that of a monastery. **kitchenette** (kich in et′), *n.* A miniature kitchen and scullery.

kite (kīt) [A.-S. *cȳta*], *n.* A medium-sized bird of the raptorial genus *Milvus*, esp. *M. ictinus*, the common or European kite or glede; (*fig.*) a greedy or rapacious person, a sharper; a device consisting of a light frame of wood and paper constructed to fly in the air by means of a string; (*Comm. slang*) an accommodation note or bill; (*pl.*) light sails, set only in very light winds, above the other sails. *v.i.* To fly like a kite; (*slang*) to fly a kite. *v.t.* (*slang*) To issue or convert into an accommodation bill. **to fly a kite:** (*fig.*) To try how the wind blows; (*Comm. slang*) to raise money on an accommodation bill. **kite-balloon,** *n.* An observation-balloon moored to the ground. **kite-flyer,** *n.* **kite-flying,** *n.* **kite-mark** (kīt′ mark), *n.* A kite-shaped mark indicating that goods conform in all particulars with the specifications of the British Standards Institution.

kith (kith) [A.-S. *cythth*, knowledge, native country, from *cūth*, known (*cunnan*, to know)], *n.* Kindred. **kith and kin:** Close friends and relations; relatives only.

kithe [KYTHE].

kitling (kit′ ling) [prob. from Icel. *ketlingr*, dim. of *köttr*, cat], *n.* (*prov.*) A kitten. **kittle** (1) (kitl), *v.i.* (*Sc.*) To kitten.

kitmutgar (kit′ mŭt gar) [Hind.], *n.* A male servant.

kitten (kit′ ėn) [M.E. *kitoun*, O.F. *chitoun* (F. *chaton*), from *chat*, cat], *n.* The young of the cat; (*fig.*) a playful girl. *v.i.* To bring forth young (as a cat). **kittenish,** *a.* **kitty,** *n.* A pet-name for a kitten.

kittiwake (kit′ i wāk) [imit. of its cry], *n.* A sea-gull of the genus *Rissa*, esp. *R. tridactyla*, common on the British coasts.

kittle (1) [KITLING].

kittle (2) (kit′ ėl) [etym. doubtful, perh. from a non-extant A.-S. *citelian*, or from Scand. (cp. Icel. *kitla*, Swed. *kittla*)], *v.t.* (*now chiefly Sc.*) To tickle; (*fig.*) to excite a pleasant sensation in, to rouse. *a.* Ticklish, awkward to deal with, intractable. **kittly,** *a.*

kitty, *n.* (*Cards*) Pool into which each player puts a stake in poker, and other games.

kiwi (kē′ wi) [Maori], *n.* The New Zealand apteryx or wingless bird; (*colloq.*) a New Zealander.

kleisto- [CLEISTO-].

Klepht (kleft) [mod. Gr. *klephtēs*, Gr. *kleptēs*, thief], *n.* One of the Greeks who refused to submit to the Turks after the conquest (15th cent.), and carried on a predatory existence in the mountains.

klepsydra [CLEPSYDRA].

kleptomania (klep tō mā′ ni ȧ) [Gr. *kleptēs*, as KLEPHT, -MANIA], *n.* A form of insanity or mental aberration displaying itself in an irresistible propensity to steal. **kleptomaniac,** *n.*

klipdas (klip′ das) [S. Afr. Dut.], *n.* The Cape hyrax, *Hyrax Capensis.*

klipspringer (klip′ spring ėr) [S. Afr. Dut. (*klip*, rock, SPRINGER)], *n.* A small South African antelope, *Oreotragus saltator.*

kloof (kloof) [Dut., cleft], *n.* (*S. Afr.*) A ravine, gully, or mountain gorge.

knack (năk) [prob. onomat.], *n.* A trick or adroit way of doing a thing; dexterity, adroitness; (*fig.*) a habit, a mannerism; *a toy, a knick-knack. ***knacker** (1), *n.* A maker of knick-knacks; (*pl.*) two pieces of wood used as castanets. **knackish, knacky,** *a.* **knackiness,** *n.*

knacker (2) (năk′ ėr) [perh. from prec., a dealer in KNACKS], *n.* A dealer in worn-out horses; a horse-slaughterer; a dealer in second-hand goods, houses, ships, etc. **knackery,** *n.*

knag (năg) [cp. G. *knagge*, Norw. and Swed. *knagg*], *n.* A knot in wood; a knob, a peg; the shoot of a deer's horn; the rough or rugged top of a hill or rock. **knagged, knaggy,** *a.*

knap (1) (năp) [A.-S. *cnæpp*, prob. cogn. with Icel. *knappr*, Dan. *knap*, a KNOB], *n.* A protuberance, a knob; a hill-crest, rising ground.

knap (2) (năp) [imit., cp. Dut. *knappen*], *v.t.* (*past & p.p.* **knapped**) To break into pieces, esp. with a sharp snapping noise; to break, flake, or chip flint; to strike smartly. *v.i.* To make a sharp, cracking noise. **knapper, flint-knapper,** *n.* One who breaks flints; one who shapes gun-flints, flint implements, etc. ***knap-bottle,** *n.* The bladder-campion, *Silene inflata.* ***knapple,** *v.i.* To break off with a sharp, cracking noise.

knapsack (năp′ săk) [cp. Dut. *knapzak* (*knappen*, to snap, to bite, to eat, *zak*, SACK)], *n.* A case or bag for clothes, etc., carried on the back during a march by soldiers or tourists. **knapsackwise,** *adv.*

knapweed (năp′ wēd) [formerly *knopweed* (KNOP, WEED)], *n.* A composite plant with purple globular flowers, of the genus *Centaurea*, esp. *C. nigra*, the black knapweed, and *C. scabiosa*, the great knapweed.

***knar** (nar) [M.E. *knarre* (cp. L.G. *knarre*, Dut. *knar*)], *n.* A knot in wood; a protuberance on the trunk or branch of a tree; (*fig.*) a tough, thickset, rough fellow.

***knarled** [GNARL (2)].

knave (nāv) [A.-S. *cnafa*, a boy (cp. Dut. *knaap*, Icel. *knapi*, G. *knabe*)], *n.* A deceitful tricky fellow, a rogue; (*Cards*) a court-card with a representation of a soldier or servant, the jack; *a boy; *a servant. **knave-bairn, -child,** *n.* A male child. **knaveship,** *n.* The quality of being a knave; (*Sc.*) a portion of corn or meal paid to a miller's servant as his due. **knavery,** *n.* **knavish,** *a.* **knavishly,** *adv.* **knavishness,** *n.*

knead (nēd) [A.-S. *cnedan* (cp. Dut. *kneden*, G. *kneten*)], *v.t.* To work up (flour, clay, etc.) with the hands into a plastic mass; to work or incorporate into dough: to shape, fashion, mingle, or blend by this method; to work thus on (the muscles, etc.) in massage. **kneadable,** *a.* **kneader,** *n.* **kneading-trough,** *n.* A trough in which dough is worked up.

knee (nē) [A.-S. *cnēo*, *cnēow* (cp. Dut. and G. *knie*, Icel. *knē*, also L. *genu*, Gr. *gonu*)], *n.* The joint of the thigh or femur with the leg; a joint roughly corresponding to this in animals; the part of a garment covering the knee; (*Shipbuilding, Carp., etc.*) a piece of timber or metal cut or cast with an angle like that of the knee to connect beams, etc.; (*fig.*) anything resembling a knee in shape or function; *a genuflexion; *a courtesy. *v.t.* To touch or strike with the knee; (*Shipbuilding, Carp., etc.*) to fasten or strengthen with knees; (*colloq.*) to cause (trousers) to bag at the knees. **to bring to his knees:** To reduce to submission. **to give a knee to:** (*Pugil.*) To support on one's knee during a pause in a fight or contest; to act as second to. **on the knees of the gods:** As yet undetermined. **knee-breeches,** *n.pl.* Breeches reaching just below the knee. **knee-cap,** *n.* A padded cover for the knee; the heart-shaped sesamoid bone in front of the knee-joint. ***knee-crooking,** *a.* Prone to bend the knee; cringing. **knee-deep,** *a.* **knee-high,** *a.* **knee-hole,** *n.* The hole between the pedestals of a writing-table or desk. **knee-hole table,** *n.* **knee-holly, -holm,** *n.* Butcher's broom, *Ruscus aculeatus.* **knee-joint,** *n.* The articulation of the femur with the tibia; a joint between two pieces hinged together (in carpentry, shipbuilding, etc.). **knee-jointed,** *a.* (*Bot.*) Forming an obtuse angle like the knee. **knee-pan,** *n.* The knee-cap or socket of the knee. **knee-swell,** *n.* (*Am. Organ, etc.*) A lever for working the swell operated by the knee. **knee-tribute,** *n.* Reverence shown by kneeling. **kneed,** *a.* (*usu. in comb.*, as *loose-kneed*).

kneel (nēl) [A.-S. *cnēowlian*, from *cnēow*, KNEE], *v.i.* (*past & p.p.* **knelt**) To bend or incline the knees; to fall on the knees; to support the body on the knees. **kneeler,** *n.* One who kneels; a stool or cushion for kneeling on; (*Eccles. Hist.*) a name given to certain catechumens and penitents allowed to be present at certain parts of the liturgy, and to receive the benediction.

knell (nel) [A.-S. *cnyllan*, from Teut. *knel-* (cp. Dut. and G. *knallen*, Swed. *knalla*), imit. in orig.], *v.i.* To ring, to toll, as a funeral bell; to sound in a mournful or ominous manner. *v.t.* To proclaim or summon by or as by a knell. *n.* The sound of a bell when struck, esp. at a death or funeral; (*fig.*) an evil omen, a death-blow.

knelt, *past & p.p.* [KNEEL].

Knesset (knes′ et) [Heb., assembly], *n.* (*Pol.*) The single-chamber parliament of the state of Israel.

knew, *past* [KNOW].

Knickerbocker (nik′ ėr bok ėr) [imag. author of Washington Irving's 'History of New York'], *n.* A New Yorker of original Dutch descent; (*pl.*) loose breeches gathered in below the knee. **knickers:** A woman's undergarment covering the upper part of the legs up to the waist.

knick-knack (nik′ năk) [redupl. of KNACK], *n.* Any little ornamental article; a showy trifle. **knickery-knackery,** *n.*

knife (nīf) [A.-S. *cnīf* (cp. Dut. *knijf*, Icel. *knīfr*, *hnīfr*, G. *kneif*)], *n.* (*pl.* **knives** (nīvz)) A blade with one edge sharpened, usu. set in a handle; a cutting-blade forming part of a machine; *a sword or dagger. *v.t.* To cut out (shoe-maker's work, etc.); to prune, to cut back; (*slang*) to stab or cut with a knife. **the knife:** Surgical operations. **war to the knife:** Mortal combat. **knife-bayonet,** *n.* (*Mil.*) A bayonet with a broad blade that enables it to be used as a dagger. **knife-board,** *n.* A board covered with leather or composition to clean knives on; (*colloq.*) a long seat for passengers on the roof of an omnibus, etc. **knife-boy,** *n.* A boy employed to clean table-knives. **knife-edge,** *n.* The edge of a knife; a hard steel edge used as fulcrum for a balance, pendulum, etc. **knife-grass,** *n.* (*Bot.*) A tropical American sedge with knife-like edges. **knife-grinder,** *n.* One who grinds or sharpens knives, esp. an itinerant knife-sharpener. **knife-machine,** *n.* A machine for cleaning knives. **knife money,** *n.* Knife-shaped bronze money current in China about 300 B.C. **knife-rest,** *n.* A support for a carving knife or fork at table. **knife switch,** *n.* (*Elec.*) A switch consisting of knife-like pieces hinged at one end, and having contact at the other with springs. **knife tool,** *n.* A small wheel used in seal engraving.

knight (nīt) [A.-S. *cniht*, a boy, a servant (cp. Dut. and G. *knecht*, Swed. *knekt*, soldier)], *n.* (*Hist.*) A man of gentle birth, usu. one who had served as page and esquire, admitted to an honourable degree of military rank, with peculiar ceremonies or religious rites; one who holds a corresponding non-hereditary dignity conferred by the sovereign or his representative, and entitling the possessor to the title of 'Sir' prefixed to his name; (*Rom. Ant.*) one of the class of *Equites*; (*Gr. Ant.*) an Athenian citizen of the middle class, as constituted by Solon; (*Chess*) a piece shaped like a horse's head entitled to move two squares straight and one at right-angles; (*fig.*) a chivalrous or quixotic person; one acting as chevalier to a lady. *v.t.* To create or dub (a person) a knight. **knight-bachelor** [BACHELOR]. **knight-banneret,** *n.* A knight holding the rank of banneret. **knight-errant,** *n.* A mediæval knight who wandered about in quest of adventures to show his prowess and generosity. **knight-errantry,** *n.* **knight-head** [the tops were formerly ornamented with figures resembling human heads], *n.* (*Naut.*) One of a pair of vertical posts supporting the bowsprit. ***knight-marshal,** *n.* An official in the household of the British sovereign having cognizance of offences committed within the royal verge. ***knight of the post:** A rogue, one well acquainted with the whipping-post; one who gave false evidence for hire. **knight of the road:** A footpad, a highwayman. **knight of the shire:** (*Hist.*) A representative of an English county in Parliament. **knight service,** *n.* (*Feud. Law*) Tenure of land on condition of military service. **knight's fee:** (*Feud. Law*) The amount of land for which the services of a knight were accorded. **knightage,** *n.* **knighthood,** *n.* **knightlike,** *a.* **knightly,** *a.* and *adv.* **knightliness,** *n.*

knit (nit) [A.-S. *cnyttan* (cp. M.Dut. *knutten*, Icel. *knytja*, G. *knüten*), rel. to KNOT], *v.t.* (*past & p.p.* **knit, knitted**) To form into a fabric or form (a fabric, garment, etc.) by looping or knotting a continuous yarn or thread; (*fig.*) to join closely together, to unite; to make close or compact; to contract into folds or wrinkles; *to compound, to mix. *v.i.* To make a textile fabric by interweaving yarn or thread; (*fig.*) to grow together; to become closely united. **n.* Style of knitting; texture. **a.* Allied, connected. **to knit up:** To repair by knitting; (*fig.*) to conclude, to wind up (a speech, argument, etc.). **knitter,** *n.* One who knits; a knitting machine. **knitting,** *n.* **knitting-machine,** *n.* An apparatus for mechanically knitting jerseys, stockings, etc. **knitting-needle, -pin,** *n.* A long eyeless needle of metal, bone, wood, etc., used in knitting.

knitch (nich) [etym. doubtful], *n.* (*prov.*) A bundle, a faggot.

knittle (nitl), *n.* (*Naut.*) A small line such as is used for slinging a hammock.

knives, *pl.* [KNIFE].

knob (nob) [cogn. with KNOP (cp. G. *knobbe*, Dut. *knobbel*)], *n.* A rounded protuberance, usu. at the end of something; a rounded handle of a door, lock, drawer, etc.; (*Am.*) a rounded hill, a knoll; an ornamental terminal boss; a small lump (of coal, sugar, etc.). *v.t.* To furnish with a knob or knobs. *v.i.* To become knobby; to bulge or bunch (out). **knobbed, knobby,** *a.* **knobbiness,** *n.*

knobkerrie (nob′ ke ri) [S. Afr. Dut. *knopkirie*], *n.* The round-headed club used as weapon by S. African natives.

knobstick (nob′ stik), *n.* A knobbed stick used as a weapon; (*slang*) a workman who refuses to join a strike.

knock (nok) [A.-S. *cnocian*, *cnucian* (cp. Icel. *knoka*), prob. imit.], *v.t.* To strike, to hit, to give a hard blow to; to drive or force by striking; to cause to strike together. *v.i.* To strike hard or smartly (at, against, together, etc.). *n.* A blow; a rap, esp. on a door for admission. **to knock about:** To strike with repeated blows; to handle violently; (*colloq.*) to wander about; to lead an irregular life. **to knock down:** To fell with a blow; (*fig.*) to prostrate (with astonishment, etc.); to sell (with a blow of the hammer) to a bidder at an auction; (*colloq.*) to call upon (for a song); to lower in price, quality, etc. **to knock off:** To strike off; to dispatch, to do or finish quickly; to cease work; to leave off (work); to deduct. **to knock one's head against:** (*fig.*) To come into collision with (awkward facts, etc.). **to knock on the head:** To stun or kill with a blow on the head; (*fig.*) to frustrate, to spoil, to defeat. **to knock out:** To force or dash out with a blow; (*Pugil.*) to disable by a particular blow. **to knock out of time:** (*Pugil.*) To disable (an opponent) so that he is unable to respond when 'time' is called. **to knock together:** To put hastily or roughly into shape. **to knock the bottom out of:** To refute (an argument). **to knock under:** To acknowledge oneself beaten. **to knock up:** To strike or force upwards; to arouse by knocking; to fatigue, to wear out, to exhaust; to put together or make up hastily; to make (a score of runs) at cricket. **knock-about,** *a.* Noisy, rough, violent; suitable for rough usage (as clothes); irregular, bohemian. *n.* A noisy, boisterous performance or performer (at a music-hall, etc.); (*Naut.*) a light, partly-decked yacht or sailing-boat. **knock-down,** *a.* Overwhelming (of a blow); reserve or minimum (of a price at auction). *n.* A knock-down blow; a free fight. **knock-knees,** *n.pl.* Knees bent inwards in walking. **knock-kneed,** *a.* **knock-out,** *a.* Disabling (of a blow). *n.* A knock-out blow; (*vulg.*) a marvel, wonder; (*slang*) one of a gang who combine to keep bidding low at auctions and afterwards sell the purchases among themselves, dividing the profits; the sale at which the goods so obtained are resold; an auction at which this practice is carried on. **knocker,** *n.* One who knocks; a hammer-like attachment to an outer door to give notice that some one desires admittance; (*Folklore*) a gnome or goblin who indicates the presence of hidden ore by knocking. **knocking,** *n.* (*Motor.*) Explosions in the cylinder due to over-compression of the mixture of air and petrol vapour before sparking.

knoll (1) (nōl) [A.-S. *cnoll* (cp. Dut. *knol*, a turnip, Swed. *knöl*, G. *knollen*)], *n.* A rounded hill; a mound, a hillock. **knolly,** *a.*

knoll (2) (nōl) [var. of KNELL], *v.t.* To ring; to toll or sound out (hours); to proclaim or summon by ringing; to ring a bell or knell for. *v.i.* To sound (as a bell). **knoller,** *n.*

knop (nop) [perh. rel. to KNAP (cp. Dut. and Dan. *knop*, G. *knopf*)], *n.* A knob, a button; (*Arch.*) a bunch of leaves, flowers, or similar ornaments; *a bud. **knopped,** *a.* Adorned with knops.

***knosp** (nosp) [prob. from G. *knospe*], *n.* A knob, a boss; (*Arch.*) an ornamental flower-bud or boss.

knot (1) (not) [A.-S. *cnotta* (cp. Dut. *knot*, G. *knoten*)], *n.* The interlacement or intertwining of a rope or ropes, cords, etc., so as to fasten one part to another part of the rope, etc. or to another object; an ornamental bow or interlacement of a ribbon, etc. on a dress; a kind of double shoulder-pad, with a loop passing round the forehead, used by London market-porters for carrying burdens, usu. called a shoulder-knot; (*fig.*) a difficulty, a perplexity, a problem; something not easily solved; the gist or kernel of a matter; anything resembling a knot; an irregular or twisted portion in a tree caused by branches, buds, etc.; a node or joint in a stem; a protuberance or excrescence; a flower-bud; a hard cross-grained part in a piece of wood, caused by interlacing fibres; a hard lump in the body of an animal; (*fig.*) a group, a cluster; (*Naut.*) a division of the log-line marked off by knots, used as a unit for measuring speed, (loosely) a nautical mile per hour. *v.t.* (*past & p.p.* **knotted**) To tie in a knot or knots; to fasten with a knot; to intertwine; to make (fringe) by means of knots; to knit (the brows); to join together closely or intricately; to entangle, to perplex. *v.i.* To form knots (of plants); to make knots for fringe. **knot-grass,** *n.* A prostrate plant, *Polygonum aviculare*, with internodes and white, pink, crimson, or green inconspicuous flowers. **knot-work,** *n.* Ornamental fringe made by knotting cords together; representation of this in painting or carving; a kind of ornamental needlework. **knotless,** *a.* **knotted,** *a.* **knotting,** *n.* Fancy knotted work; the removal of knots from textile fabrics. **knotty,** *a.* Full of knots; (*fig.*) rugged, rough; intricate; perplexing, difficult of solution. **knottiness,** *n.* ***knottypated,** *a.* Blockheaded.

knot (2) (not) [etym. unknown], *n.* A small wading-bird, *Tringa canutus*, of the snipe family, visiting Britain in the late summer and autumn.

knout (nout) [F., from Rus. *knutu*], *n.* A whip or scourge formerly used as an instrument of punishment in Russia. *v.t.* To punish with the knout.

know (nō) [A.-S. *cnāwan* (cp. Icel. *knā*, O.H.G. *chnāan*, cogn. with L. *gnōscere*, Gr. *gignōskein*, Sansk. *jnā-*)], *v.t.* (*past* **knew** (nū), *p.p.* **known**) To have a clear and certain perception of; to recognize from memory or description, to identify; to be convinced of the truth or reality of; to be acquainted with; to have personal experience of; to be familiar with; to be on intimate terms with; to be aware of; to understand from learning or study; *to have sexual intercourse with; to be informed of. *v.i.* To have knowledge; to be assured (of); *to be acquainted. *n.* Knowledge, knowing. **in the know:** In the secret; acquainted with what is going on. **to know better:** To be well informed (to believe, etc.). **know-how** (nō' hou), *n.* (*colloq.*) Specialized skill. **to know of:** To be informed of; *to ask, to inquire. **to know the ropes:** (*colloq.*) To be acquainted with the particular conditions of any affair or proceeding. **to know what's what:** To be wideawake; to know the ways of the world; to appreciate a good thing. **know-nothing,** *n.* An ignorant person; an agnostic. **knowable,** *a.* **knowability** (-bil' i ti), **knowableness,** *n.* **knower,** *n.* **knowing,** *a.* Intelligent; conscious; skilful, experienced; sharp, cunning, wideawake; (*colloq.*) smart, stylish. **knowingly,** *adv.* **knowingness,** *n.*

knowledge (nol' ėj) [M.E. *knowledge* (KNOW, *-lege*, etym. doubtful)], *n.* The result of knowing; that which is known; certain or clear apprehension of truth or fact; cognition, the process of knowing; familiarity gained by actual experience; learning; erudition, science, the sum of what is known; information, notice; range or scope of information; *sexual intercourse. **knowledgeable,** *a.* (*colloq.*) Sharp, intelligent.

known, *p.p.* [KNOW].

knub (nŭb) [var. of KNOB], *n.* A lump, a knob; (*usu.* in *pl.*) the waste silk produced in winding off from the cocoon, the innermost wrapping of the chrysalis.

knuckle (nŭk' ėl) [M.E. *knokil* (cp. M.Dut. *knökkel*, L.G. *knukkel*, G. *knochel*, rel. to G. *knochen*, bone)], *n.* One of the joints of a finger, esp. at the base; the middle or tarsal joint of a quadruped; a joint of meat comprising this and adjoining parts; a knuckle-shaped joint or part in a structure, machinery, etc.; *a joint in a plant stem. *v.t.* To hit with the knuckles. *v.i.* To submit, to yield (with *down* or *under*). **near the knuckle:** Verging on the indecent. **knuckle-bone,** *n.* A bone forming the knuckle of a sheep or other animal; (*pl.*) a game played with such bones. **knuckle-duster,** *n.* An iron instrument to protect the knuckles, and to add force to a blow. **knuckle-joint,** *n.* A joint in which a projection on one part lies between two projections in the other, and is held in place by a screw or pin.

knur (nĕr) [M.E. *knor* (cp. Dut. *knor*, Dan. *knort*, G. *knorren*)], *n.* A hard swelling on the trunk of a tree; a knot; a hard concretion; the hard ball used in knur and spell. **knur and spell,** *n.* A northern ball-game, in some respects resembling trap-ball and in others somewhat like golf.

knurl (nĕrl) [prob. from prec.], *n.* A knot, a lump, an excrescence; a bead or ridge produced on a metal surface as a kind of ornamentation; a hunch-backed dwarf; a surly, obstinate fellow. *v.t.* To make knurls, beadings, or ridges. **knurled,** *a.* Milled. **knurled work:** Woodwork shaped on the lathe into a series of knots or knurls. **knurly,** *a.*

koa (kō' ȧ) [Hawaiian], *n.* An acacia used for cabinet-work and building, from the Sandwich Isles.

kob (kob) [native name], *n.* An African water-antelope of the genus *Kobus*.

kobold (kō' bȯld) [G., etym. unknown], *n.* A German house-spirit, corresponding to the English Robin Goodfellow, and the Scottish brownie; a gnome or goblin haunting mines and hidden lodes.

kodak (kō' dăk) [trade name of Eastman *Kodak* Co.], *n.* Protected trade name of a portable camera with a continuous roll of sensitized film manufactured by this company; (*colloq.*) a hand-camera. *v.t.* To photograph with this; (*fig.*) to take a quick vivid impression of; to describe vividly. **kodaker, kodakist,** *n.*

koel (kō' ėl) [Hind. *kōil*, from Sansk. *kokila*], *n.* An East Indian or Australasian cuckoo of the genus *Eudynamis*.

koff (kof) [Dut.], *n.* (*Naut.*) A two-masted Dutch fishing-vessel, with a sprit-sail on each mast.

koh-i-noor (kō' i noor) [Pers. *kōh-i-nūr*, mountain of light], *n.* A famous Indian diamond which became one of the British Crown jewels on the annexation of the Punjab in 1849; (*fig.*) anything splendid or unexampled in its own kind.

kohl (kōl) [Arab. *kuḥ'l, koḥ'l*], *n.* Fine powder of antimony used in Oriental countries to darken the eyelids.

kohlrabi (kōl ra' bi) [G., from It. *cavoli rapa*, cole-rape], *n.* The turnip-stemmed cabbage, *Brassica oleracea caulorapa*.

kokra (kok' rȧ) [Hind.], *n.* The wood of an East Indian tree, *Aporosa dioica*, used for flutes, etc.

kola [COLA].

Komsomol (kom' sō mol) [Rus.], *n.* Young Communist League of U.S.S.R.; a member of this.

koniscope (kon' i skōp) [Gr. *konis*, dust, -SCOPE], *n.* An instrument for indicating the amount of dust in the atmosphere.

koodoo (koo' doo) [native name], *n.* A South African antelope, *Strepsiceros kudu*, with white stripes.

kookaburra (koo kȧ bur' ra) [Austral. aboriginal], *n.* The laughing jackass; Australian kingfisher.

koolah (koo' lȧ) [abor. name], *n.* A small tailless Australian marsupial, *Phascolarctos cinereus*.

koomis [KUMISS].

kopek [COPECK].

kopje, koppie (kop' i) [Dut., dim. of *kop*, head (cp. COP (1))], *n.* A small hill.

Koran (kȯ ran') [Arab. *qurān*, from *qara'a*, to read], *n.* The Mohammedan sacred scriptures consisting of the revelations delivered orally by Mohammed and collected after his death. **Koranic,** *a.*

kosher (kō' shėr) [Heb. *kāshēr*, right], *a.* Permitted, right, good (of food or a shop where it is sold, fulfilling the requirements of the Jewish law). *n.* A kosher shop or food. *v.t.* To make kosher.

kosmos [COSMOS].

kotow (kō tou', kou tou') [Chin. *k'o-t'ou* (*k'o*, knock, *t'ou*, the head)], *n.* The ancient Chinese method of obeisance by kneeling or prostrating oneself, and touching the ground with the forehead. *v.i.* To perform the kotow; to act obsequiously.

koumiss [KUMISS].

kourbash (koor' băsh) [Arab.], *n.* A hide whip used as an instrument of punishment in Turkey and Egypt.

kow-tow [KOTOW].

kraal (kral) [S. Afr. Dut., from Port. CORRAL], *n.* A

South African village or group of huts enclosed by a palisade; a hut; an enclosure for cattle or sheep.

krait (krāt) [Hind.], *n.* (*Zool.*) A poisonous rock snake.

kraken (kra'-, krā' kėn) [Norw.], *a.* A fabulous sea-monster, said to have been seen at different times off the coast of Norway.

krantz, kranz (krănts) [S. Afr. Dut., from Dut. *krans*, coronet, chaplet (cp. G. *kranz*)], *n.* A precipitous acclivity, esp. of crags walling in a valley.

krasis [CRASIS]. **kreatin** [CREATINE].

Kremlin (krem' lin) [F., from Rus. *kreml*, citadel], *n.* The citadel of a Russian town, esp. that of Moscow enclosing the old imperial palace, now government buildings, etc.; (*Pol.*) the Russian Government.

kreng (kreng) [Dut.], *n.* The carcass of a whale after the blubber has been removed.

kreuzer (kroit' sėr) [G., from *kreuz*, cross], *n.* A copper coin (earlier silver), formerly current in Germany (value about ⅓d.) and Austria (value about ½d.).

kris [CREESE].

Krishnaism (krish' nȧ izm) [*Krishna*, a Hindu hero or divinity, an avatar of Vishnu], *n.* The worship of Krishna. **Krishnaist, Krishnaite,** *n.*

kromesky (krō mes' ki) [Rus.], *n.* Chicken minced and rolled in bacon, then fried.

krone (krō' nė) [G., crown], *n.* A silver coin of Denmark, Norway, and Sweden, worth 1s. 1½d.; a German gold coin; an Austrian silver coin.

Kroo (kroo) [W. Afr. native], *n.* One of a Negro race on the coast of Liberia, famous for their skill as seamen. *a.* Of or pertaining to the Kroos.

krummhorn (krum' hôrn) [G. (*krumm*, crooked, HORN)], *n.* *A wind instrument with a curved tube, and a tone like that of a clarinet; an organ stop consisting of reed pipes, with a similar tone.

kryo- [CRYO-], *comb. form.* **kryometer** (krī om' ė tėr) [-METER], *n.* A thermometer for measuring low temperatures, esp. below freezing-point.

krypton (krip' tŏn) [Gr. *krupton*, neut. of *kruptos*, concealed (cp. CRYPT)], *n.* (*Chem.*) An inert gaseous element discovered by Ramsay in 1898 as a constituent of the atmosphere.

kudos (kū' dos) [Gr.], *n.* (*colloq.*) Glory, fame, credit.

kudu [KOODOO].

ku-klux-klan (kū' klŭks klăn') [Gr. *kuklos*, circle, CLAN], *n.* A secret society formed in the Southern States after the American Civil War of 1861–65 to keep down the Negro population. Suppressed by the U.S. government in 1871 but revived since then.

kukri (kuk' ri) [Hind.], *n.* A curved knife broadening at the end, used by the Gurkhas.

kulak (koo' lak) [Rus.], *n.* A prosperous Russian peasant.

kumiss (koo' mis) [Tartar *kumiz*], *n.* A spirituous liquor made by Tartars from fermented mare's milk.

kummel (kim' ėl) [G.], *n.* A liqueur flavoured with caraway-seeds made in Germany and Russia.

kummerbund [CUMMERBUND].

Kuomintang (kwō' min tăng), *n.* (*Pol.*) The Chinese Nationalist party founded by Sun Yat Sen in 1891 and replaced by the Communist Party in 1948.

Kurd (koord) [Arab.], *n.* A native of Kurdistan.

kursaal (koor' sal) [G. (*kur*, CURE, *saal*, room)], *n.* A public room for the use of visitors, esp. at German health resorts.

kvass (kvas) [Rus.], *n.* Beer made from rye.

kyanite [CYANITE].

kyanize (kī' ȧ nīz) [J. H. *Kyan* (1774–1830), inventor], *v.t.* To impregnate (wood) with a solution of mercuric chloride (corrosive sublimate) to prevent dry-rot.

kyat (kyat), *n.* The unit of currency in Burma, worth about 1s. 6d.

***kye, kyen** [KINE, COW (1)].

kylie (kī' li) [W. Austral. native], *n.* A boomerang.

kyloe (kī' lō) [Sc., etym. doubtful], *n.* One of a small Highland breed of cattle.

Kymric [CYMRIC].

kymograph (kī' mȯ grăf) [Gr. *kuma*, a wave, -GRAPH], *n.* An instrument for recording wave-like oscillations, as of the pulsation of the blood in a living body. **kymographic** (-grăf' ik), *a.*

Kyrie (kī' ri ē, kī ri), **Kyrie eleison** (e lā' i sŏn) [Gr. *Kurie eleēson*, Lord have mercy], *n.* This phrase used as a short petition in the liturgies of the Eastern and Western Churches, at the beginning of the Mass; a musical setting of this.

kyte (kīt) [Sc. and North., etym. doubtful], *n.* The belly, the paunch, the stomach.

kythe (kīth) [Sc. and North., from A.-S. *cӯthan*, rel. to *cūth*, COUTH, see CAN (2)], *v.t.* To make known. *v.i.* To show oneself, to appear.

L

L, l (el), the twelfth letter of the English alphabet (*pl.* **Els, Ls, L's**), commonly described as a semi-vowel or liquid, but more accurately as a voiced or sonorous consonant, having the value of an unstressed vowel in such words as *cattle, trouble*; an L-shaped thing, part, or building; a rectangular joint; (*Roman numeral*) 50.

***la (1)** (la) [A.-S. *lā*], *int.* Lo! see! behold! (*derisively, etc.*) really!

la (2) (la) [It., orig. first syl. of L. *labii*, one of the words of the gamut], *n.* (*Mus.*) The name for the sixth note of the scale in solmization.

laager (la' gėr) [S. Afr. Dut. *lager* (cp. G. *lager*, Dut. *leger*, LEAGUER)], *n.* A defensive encampment, esp. one formed with wagons, etc. *v.t.* To form into a laager; to encamp (a body of people) in a laager. *v.i.* To encamp.

lab [short for LABORATORY].

labarum (lăb' ȧ rŭm) [L., from Gr. *labaron*, etym. unknown], *n.* The imperial standard of Constantine the Great (bearing the cross and a monogram of the Greek name of Christ), adopted by him after his conversion to Christianity.

labdacism [LAMBDACISM].

labdanum [LADANUM].

labefaction (lăb ė făk' shŭn) [more correctly *labefactation*, L. *labefactātio*, from *labefactāre* (*labāre*, to totter, *facere*, to make)], *n.* A weakening; decay; downfall, ruin.

label (lā' bel) [O.F., a ribbon, a fillet (etym. doubtful)], *n.* A narrow strip of paper, parchment, or other material, attached to an object to indicate contents, destination, ownership, or other particulars; (*fig.*) a descriptive phrase associated with a person, etc.; a slip of paper, parchment, etc., attached to a document to carry the appended seal; an addition to a document, as a codicil; an adhesive stamp; (*Arch.*) a moulding over a doorway or window, a dripstone; (*Her.*) a fillet, with pendants or points, used as marks of cadency; (*Surv.*) a brass rule with sights, formerly used to take altitudes. *v.t.* (*past & p.p.* **labelled**) To affix a label to; (*fig.*) to describe, to set down (as).

labellum (lȧ bel' ŭm) [L., dim. of LABRUM], *n.* The lower part of the corolla in an orchidaceous flower.

L

labial (lā′ bi ål) [late L. *labiālis*, from L. LABIUM], *a.* Of or pertaining to the lips; (*Zool.*, *Bot.*, *etc.*) of or pertaining to the *labium*, serving as or resembling a lip; (*Organ*) having lips or lip-like edges (as a flue-pipe); (*Phon.*) formed or modified in sound by the lips. *n.* A sound or letter representing a sound formed with the lips, as *b*, *f*, *v*, *p*, *m*, or *w*. **labialism,** *n.* **labialize,** *v.t.* **labialization** (-zā′ shŭn), *n.* **labially,** *adv.* By means of the lips.

labiate (lā′ bi åt) [LABIUM], *a.* (*Bot.*) Having lips or parts like lips, esp. having a corolla with an upper and lower part like a pair of lips; belonging to the natural order *Labiatæ*, the mint family.

labile (lăb′ il, lā′ bil) [L. *lābilis*, from *lābī*, to fall], *a.* (*Chem.*, *Phys.*, *etc.*) Unstable, liable to chemical or other change.

labio- [LABIUM], *comb. form.* **labiodental** (lā bi ō den′ tål) [DENTAL], *a.* (*Phon.*) Produced by the agency of lips and teeth. *n.* A letter or sound so produced, as *f* or *v*.

labium (lā′ bi ŭm) [L., lip], *n.* (*pl.* **-ia**) (*Anat.*) A lip or lip-like part, as of the female genitals; (*Zool.*) the lower surface of the mouth in insects, crustaceans, etc.; (*Conch.*) the inner lip of a univalve shell; (*Bot.*) the lower lip of a labiate corolla.

laboratory (lăb′ ŏr å tŏr i) [med. L. *labōrātōrium*, from *labōrāre*, to LABOUR], *n.* A room or building in which chemical or other scientific experiments are conducted; a manufactory of chemical articles, explosives, fireworks, etc.; (*fig.*) a place where anything is prepared for use, or where natural changes go on. **laboratorial** (-tôr′ i ål), *a.*

laborious (lå bôr′ i ŭs) [L. *labōriōsus*, from foll.], *a.* Working hard or perseveringly; industrious, assiduous; betraying marks of labour, laboured; toilsome, difficult, hard, arduous, fatiguing. **laboriously,** *adv.* **laboriousness,** *n.*

labour (lā′ bŏr) [O.F., from L. *labōrem*, acc. of *labor*, whence *labōrāre*, F. *labourer*, to labour], *n.* Physical or mental exertion, esp. in obtaining the means of subsistence; the performance of work, toil; work to be done, a task, esp. a task requiring great effort; travail, the pains of childbirth; (*Polit. Econ.*) the element contributed by toil to production, esp. in opp. to capital; (*collect.*) members of the Labour Party. *v.i.* To work hard; to exert oneself; to move or proceed with difficulty; to be burdened or oppressed with difficulties; (*Naut.*) to move heavily and slowly or to pitch or roll heavily; to be in travail or the pains of childbirth. *v.t.* To fabricate, to work out laboriously; to elaborate, to deal with in much detail or at great length; *to till; *to belabour. **Labour Exchange,** *n.* An office established by the State for the registration of unemployed workmen and assistance in procuring them employment. **labour exchange:** An institution for the exchange or sale of the products of labour; an early form of co-operative supply association; a building where labour organizations meet. **labour market:** The supply of unemployed labour in relation to the demand. **Labour Party,** *n.* A British political party claiming to represent 'workers by hand or brain', composed of the chief socialist organizations and supported by the Trade Unions. Formed in 1900, it received its name in 1906 and first came into power in 1924. **labour-saving,** *a.* **labourer,** *n.* One who labours; esp. one who performs work requiring manual labour but little skill, also **labouring man.** ***labourless,** *a.* ***laboursome,** *a.*

labradorite (lăb′ rå dôr īt) [*Labrador*, -ITE], *n.* (*Min.*) A feldspar from Labrador and other places, exhibiting a brilliant display of colour.

labret (lā′ brėt) [LABRUM], *n.* A plug of stone, shell, etc., inserted into the lip as an ornament, as among the natives of Alaska.

labrum (lā′ brŭm) [L. cogn. with LABIUM], *n.* (*pl.* **-bra**) A lip or lip-like part, as in insects, crustaceans, etc. **labrose** (lā′ brōs), *a.* Having thick lips.

laburnum (lå bĕr′ nŭm) [L.], *n.* A tree or shrub, *Cytisus laburnum*, with racemes of yellow flowers.

labyrinth (lăb′ i rinth) [F. *labyrinthe*, L. *labyrinthus*, Gr. *laburinthos*, etym. doubtful], *n.* A structure similar to that constructed by Dædalus, in Crete, composed of intricate winding passages, rendering it difficult to penetrate to the interior and equally difficult to return, a maze; (*fig.*) a complication, an intricate combination, arrangement, etc.; (*Anat.*) the internal portion of the ear; (*Mining*, *etc.*) a sinuous channel in which the ground ore (slime) and water are conducted, in order that the metallic portions may be deposited. *v.t.* To enclose in or as in a labyrinth. ***labyrinthian** (-rin′ thi ån), ***labyrinthic, -ical, labyrinthiform, labyrinthine,** *a.* **labyrinthodon** (lăb i rin′ thō don) [Gr. *odous odontos*, tooth], *n.* (*Palæont.*) A genus of fossil amphibians, so called from the labyrinthine structure seen in a cross-section of a tooth. **labyrinthodont,** *a.* and *n.*

lac (1) (lăk) [Hind. *lākh*, from Sansk. *lākshā*], *n.* A resinous incrustation caused, chiefly on the banyan-tree, by the parasitic insect *Coccus lacca*; a similar exudation or resin otherwise produced; ware coated with lac or lacquer. **lac-dye, lac-lake,** *n.* Colouring matters obtained from lac, and used in dyeing scarlet or purple. **laccic** (lăk′ sik), *a.* **laccin,** *n.* (*Chem.*) The colouring principle in lac.

lac (2) (lăk) [Hind. *lākh*, Sansk. *lakshā*], *n.* One hundred thousand (usu. of rupees).

laccolite (lăk′ ō līt) [Gr. *lakkos*, reservoir, -LITE], *n.* (*Geol.*) An intrusive mass of lava penetrating between strata and raising the surface into domes, also called **laccolith.**

lace (lās) [O.F. *las* (L. *laqueus*, nom. *-us*, a noose), whence O.F. *lacier* (F. *lacer*), to ensnare], *n.* A cord or string used to bind or fasten, esp. by interweaving, as a stay-lace, etc.; a kind of ornamental network of threads of linen, cotton, gold or silver wire, or other suitable material, forming a fabric of open texture; an ornamental braid or edging for uniforms, etc.; *a snare, a noose, a gin. *v.t.* To fasten by means of a lace or string through eyelet-holes, etc.; to compress the waist by tightening stay-laces; to intertwist or interweave (with thread, etc.); to trim or adorn with lace; to embellish with or as with stripes; to flavour or fortify by adding spirits to; (*colloq.*) to beat, to thrash; to trap, to ensnare; to embroil in. *v.i.* To compress one's waist by tightening the corsets; to wear tight corsets; to fasten with laces (of boots, etc.); (*colloq.*) to lash (into). **Algerian lace,** *n.* A richly-designed lace of gold and silver threads. **antique lace,** *n.* Hand-made pillow-lace in a broad, open pattern. **baby lace,** *n.* A simple, narrow-width bobbin lace. **balloon-net lace,** *n.* A design of woven lace with the freeing threads twisted about the warps. **Battenberg lace,** *n.* A linen-thread lace with connecting bars worked with buttonhole-stitch and picots. **Bourdon lace,** *n.* A machine-made silk-and-cotton lace. **Bretonne lace,** *n.* A narrow pillow-lace. **Cluny lace,** *n.* Square-net lace with inwrought patterns. **torchon lace,** *n.* Peasants' bobbin-lace of loose texture. **lace-bark,** *n.* The inner bark of a West Indian shrub, *Lagetta lintearia*, which resembles coarse lace; (*Austral.*) the ribbon-wood tree. **lace-boot,** *n.* A boot fastened by a lace. **lace-frame,** *n.* A machine used in lace-making. **lace-glass,** *n.* Venetian glass decorated with lace-like patterns. **lace-maker,** *n.* **lace-man,** *n.* One dealing in lace. **lace-pillow,** *n.* A cushion on which various kinds of lace are made. **lace-wing, lace-wing fly,** *n.* **lace-winged,** *a.* **lacing,** *n.* **lacy,** *a.*

lacerate (lăs′ ėr āt) [L. *lacerātus*, p.p. of *lacerāre*, from lacer, torn (cp. Gr. *lakeros*)], *v.t.* To tear, to mangle; (*fig.*) to rend, to harrow, to wound. **lacerable,** *a.* **lacerate** (-åt), *a.* Torn, mangled; (*Bot.*) having the edge in irregular segments, as if torn. **laceration** (-ā′ shŭn), *n.* **lacerative** (lăs′ ėr å tiv), *a.*

Lacerta (lå sĕr′ tå) [L., lizard], *n.* (*Zool.*) The typical genus of the *Lacertilia*, an order of reptiles containing the lizards, iguanas, etc. **lacertian** (lå sĕr′ ti ȧn, -sĕr′ shȧn), *a.* and *n.* **lacertine** (lȧ sĕr′ tīn), **lacertoid,** *a.*

lacet (lȧ set′), *n.* Work with braid or tape made into designs with crochet or lace-stitches. *a.* Of or pertaining to this.

laches (lăch′ ĕz) [O.F. *laschesse*, from *lasche*, L. *laxus*, LAX (with transposition of *cs* (*x*) to *sc*)], *n.* Negligence, neglect to do; (*Law*) culpable negligence or remissness.

Lachesis (lăk′ ė sis) [Gr., one of the three Fates], *n.* (*Zool.*) A genus of venomous rattlesnakes, with the rudiments of a rattle, from Surinam and Brazil.

Lachryma Christi (lăk′ ri mȧ kris′ tī) [L., Christ's tears], *n.* A sweet white wine from S. Italy.

lachrymal (lăk′ ri mȧl) [med. L. *lacrymālis*, from L. *lacryma*, tear (cp. Gr. *dakru*)], *a.* Pertaining to tears; (*Anat.*) secreting or conveying tears (of glands, ducts, etc.). *n.* A lachrymal bone; a lachrymatory. ***lachrymary,** *a.* **lachrymation** (-mā′ shŭn), *n.* **lachrymatory,** *a.* Of, pertaining to, or causing tears. *n.* A small glass vessel found in ancient tombs, said to be intended for holding tears, but prob. for perfumes or ointments. **lachrymose,** *a.* Shedding or ready to shed tears; sad, mournful. **lachrymosely,** *adv.*

lacing (lā′ sing), *n.* A fastening by a cord passing through holes, etc.; a lace or cord for fastening; various interlacing structures of timber, iron, etc., in mining, shipbuilding, etc.; a dose of spirit added to a liquor to strengthen or flavour it; (*colloq.*) a thrashing.

lacinia (lȧ sin′ i ȧ) [L., lappet], *n.* (*pl.* ***-niæ***) (*Bot.*) An incision or slash in a leaf or petal; a slender lobe like the result of slashing or cutting; (*Ent.*) the blade of a maxilla. **laciniate, -iated** (lȧ sin′ i ȧt, -ā tėd), *a.*

lack (lăk) [cp. Dut. and L.G. *lak*], *n.* Deficiency, want, need (of); that which is needed; *blame, reproach. *v.t.* To be in need of, to be deficient in; to be without; to feel the want of. *v.i.* To be deficient (in); to be wanting; *to be absent. ***lackland,** *a.* Having no property or estate. ***lack-linen,** *a.* Destitute of a shirt. **lack-lustre,** *a.* Wanting brightness or lustre. **lack-all,** *n.* One perfectly destitute. ***lack-beard,** *n.* ***lack-brain,** *n.*

lackadaisical (lăk ȧ dā′ zi kȧl) [obs. *lackadaisy*], *a.* Affectedly pensive, languishing, or sentimental; listless, absent-minded. **lackadaisically,** *adv.* **lackadaisicalness,** *n.* **lack-a-day.**

***lacker** [LAQUER].

lackey (lăk′ i) [F. *laquais*, etym. doubtful], *n.* A footman, a menial attendant; (*fig.*) a servile follower. *v.t.* To follow or attend as a servant; to attend servilely. *v.i.* To act as a lackey; to act servilely.

lacmus [LITMUS].

laconic (lȧ kon′ ik) [L. *Lacōnicus*, Gr. *Lakōnikos*, from *Lakōn*, Spartan], *a.* Pertaining to Laconia or Sparta, or its inhabitants; hence (*fig.*) brief, sententious, pithy, concise. **laconically,** *adv.* **laconicism, laconism,** *n.* A concise, pithy, or sententious style; a laconic saying.

lacquer (lăk′ ėr) [M.F. *lacre*, Port. *lacre*, var. of *lacca*, from LAC], *n.* A varnish composed of shellac dissolved in alcohol and coloured with gold, gamboge, saffron, etc., used to coat articles of metal or wood; a hard varnish capable of taking a high polish; woodwork coated with such a varnish, usu. decorated with inlaid figures. *v.t.* To cover with lacquer. **lacquerer,** *n.*

lacrosse (la kros′) [F., the CROSSE], *n.* A Canadian ball-game resembling hockey, but played with a crosse or stringed bat.

lacrymal [LACHRYMAL].

lactarene (lăk′ tȧ rēn) [as foll.], *n.* A preparation of the casein of milk, used by calico printers.

lactate (lăk′ tāt), *n.* (*Chem.*) A salt of lactic acid.

lactation (lăk tā′ shŭn) [L. *lactātio*, from *lactāre*, to suckle, from *lac lactis*, milk], *n.* The act or process of giving suck to an infant; (*Physiol.*) the secretion and excretion of milk.

lacteal (lăk′ tė ȧl) [L. *lacteus*, from *lac lactis*, milk], *a.* Pertaining to milk; milky; (*Physiol.*) conveying chyle. *n.pl.* The vessels which convey chyle from the alimentary canal. **lacteous,** *a.* Milky; lacteal. **lactescent** (lăk tes′ ėnt), *a.* Turning to milk; having a milky appearance or consistence; (*Bot.*) yielding milky juice. **lactescence,** *n.* **lactiferous, lactific,** *a.*

lactic (lăk′ tik), *a.* Pertaining to milk; (*Chem.*) contained in or derived from sour milk. **lactic acid,** *n.* (*Chem.*) A colourless liquid acid present in human perspiration and also formed during the souring of milk.

lacto-, *comb. form.*

lactobutyrometer, lactocrite (lăk tō bū ti rom′ ė tėr, lăk′ tō krīt), *n.* An apparatus for estimating the amount of butter in a given sample of milk.

lactoid (lăk′ toid), *n.* A plastic material prepared from casein.

lactometer (lăk tom′ ė tėr), *n.* A kind of hydrometer for showing the specific gravity and consequent value of different samples of milk.

lactoscope (lăk′ tō skōp), *n.* An instrument for determining the quality of milk by ascertaining its relative opacity.

lactose (lăk′ tōs), *n.* (*Chem.*) Milk-sugar, the form in which sugar occurs in milk.

Lactuca (lăk tū′ kȧ) [L.], *n.* (*Bot.*) A genus of plants containing the lettuce. **lactucic** (-tū′ sik), *a.*

lacuna (lȧ kū′ nȧ) [L., from *lacus*, LAKE (I)], *n.* (*pl.* **-næ**) A gap, an hiatus; a vacancy; a cavity, a small pit or depression. **lacunal, lacunose,** *a.* Pertaining to or containing lacunæ. **lacunar,** *a.* Lacunal. *n.* (*Arch.*) A ceiling having sunk or hollowed compartments; (*pl.*) the panels or compartments of this.

lacustrine (lȧ kŭs′ trin) [from L. *lacus*, LAKE, onomat. of *palustrine*, from *palus*], *a.* Of or pertaining to or living on or in a lake. **lacustrine age:** That of the lake dwellings. **lacustral,** *a.* **lacustrian,** *a.* and *n.*

lacy [LACE].

lad (lăd) [M.E. *ladde*, perh. rel. to *lad*, *led*, p.p. of *leden*, to LEAD], *n.* A boy, a youth, a stripling; (*colloq.*) a fellow, a companion, a mate. **laddie,** *n.* Familiar or affectionate term. **lad's love:** (*prov.*) The southern-wood.

ladanum (lăd′ ȧ nŭm) [L. *lādanum*, Gr. *ladanon*, *lēdanon*, from *lēdon*, mastic], *n.* An odorous, resinous substance, which exudes from the leaves and twigs of various kinds of cistus; *laudanum.

ladder (lăd ėr) [A.-S. *hlæder* (cp. Dut. *ladder*, G. *leiter*), cogn. with Gr. *klimax*, CLIMAX], *n.* A device of wood, iron, rope, etc., usu. portable, and consisting of two long uprights, connected by rungs or cross-pieces, which form steps by which one may ascend; (*Am.*) a step-ladder; a vertical rent in a stocking; (*fig.*) anything serving as a means of ascent physically, economically, or morally. *v.i.* (Of stockings and knitted fabrics) to form a rent through the snapping of a longitudinal thread. *n.* **ladder-proof,** *a.* Descriptive of a type of knitted fabrics that are unlikely to ladder. **ladder-dredge,** *n.* A dredging-machine with a series of buckets carried round on a ladder-like chain. **ladder-stitch,** *n.* A cross-bar stitch in embroidery and fancy-work.

laddie [LAD].

lade (lād) [A.-S. *hladan* (cp. Dut. and G. *laden*, Icel. *hlather*)], *v.t.* (*p.p.* **laden**) To put a load or burden on; to put a cargo or freight on board; to ship (goods) as cargo; to load, to weigh down (*esp. in p.p.*); to lift or throw out or in (as water) with a ladle, bowl, etc. **lading,** *n.* Cargo. **bill of lading** [BILL (3)].

la-di-da (la' di da') [Slang, imit. of affected speech], *a.* Affectedly genteel, swaggering, pretentious, foppish. *n.* Such a person.

ladify [LADY].

Ladin (lȧ dēn') [as foll.], *n.* The Rhæto-Romanic language spoken in the Engadine and part of Tyrol; one who speaks this.

lading [LADE].

Ladino (lȧ dē' nō) [Sp. and It., from L. *Latinus*, LATIN], *n.* The old Castilian language; a Spanish-Portuguese dialect spoken by Turkish Jews; a Central American white and Indian half-breed.

ladle (lā' dėl) [A.-S. *hlædel*, from *hladan*, to LADE], *n.* A large spoon with which liquids are lifted out or served from a vessel; a pan or bowl with a long handle to hold molten metal; the float-board of a mill-wheel. *v.t.* To serve out or transfer with a ladle. **ladleful,** *n.*

ladrone (lȧ drōn') [Sp., from L. *latrōnem*, nom. *latro*, robber], *n.* A thief, a highwayman, a brigand; (*Sc.*, lăd' rŏn) a rascal, a rogue, a vagabond.

lady (lā' di) [A.-S. *hlǣfdīge* (*hlāf*, LOAF, *-dīge*, prob. kneader, cp. DOUGH)], *n.* (*pl.* **ladies**) A gentlewoman; a woman of good breeding or social standing; one's mistress or love; a wife (usu. restricted in use to the husband); a sweetheart; the mistress of a house or family; a title prefixed to the surname or territorial title of the wife of a knight or any superior to him in rank, or the Christian name of the daughter of an earl, marquess, or duke, or to the Christian name of the husband if a son of marquess or duke; also in such titles as lady mayoress. **my lady:** A form of address for those holding the title (usu. restricted to servants, etc.). **Our Lady:** The Virgin Mary. **painted lady** [PAINT]. **lady-altar,** *n.* The altar of a chapel (usu. in a cathedral or large church) dedicated to the Virgin Mary. **lady-bird,** *n.* A small red coleopterous insect, of the genus *Coccinella*, with black spots. **lady-chair,** *n.* A seat made by interlacing two people's arms for carrying an injured person. **Lady chapel:** A chapel dedicated to the Virgin Mary (usually in a cathedral or large church). **lady-clerk, -doctor,** etc., A woman clerk, doctor, etc. **lady-cook, -help,** etc., *n.* A cook, domestic help, etc., who claims to be treated as one of the family. **lady-cow** [LADY-BIRD]. **Lady Day:** The Feast of the Annunciation of the Virgin Mary, 25th March. **lady-fern,** *n.* A tall slender fern, *Asplenium filix-fœmina.* **lady-killer,** *n.* (*facet.*) One who devotes himself to conquests of women; one who is irresistibly fascinating to women. **Lady of the Lamp,** *n.* Name given to Florence Nightingale in the Crimean War by wounded soldiers whom she used to visit in the wards at night, carrying a lantern. **lady-love,** *n.* A female sweetheart, a mistress. **lady-in-waiting, lady of the bedchamber:** A lady attending on the sovereign. **lady of pleasure:** (*colloq.*) A prostitute. **lady's bedstraw:** The herb bedstraw. **lady's cushion:** The thrift or sea-pink; mossy saxifrage. **lady's finger:** The kidney vetch. **Ladies' Gallery,** *n.* A gallery in the House of Commons, formerly screened off by a grille and the only place where women were admitted. **lady's maid:** A female attendant on a lady, esp. at the toilet. **lady's mantle:** The rosaceous herb, *Alchemilla vulgaris.* **lady's slipper,** *n.* An orchid of the genus *Cypripedium.* **lady's-smock, lady-smock,** *n.* The cuckoo flower, *Cardamine pratensis.* **lady's-tresses,** *n.pl.* Orchidaceous plants of the genus *Spiranthes*; grasses of the genus *Briza.* **ladify,** *v.t.* To make a lady of; to treat as a lady. **ladified,** *a.* Affecting the manners and air of a fine lady. **ladyhood, ladyism,** *n.* **ladykin,** *n.* **ladylike,** *a.* **ladyship,** *n.* The quality of being a lady; used with 'her' or 'your' as title in addressing or in reference to a lady of title.

Lætare (lē târ' ē) [L., to rejoice], *n.* The fourth Sunday in Lent, so called from the first word of the introit of the Mass on that day.

lævo- [L. *lævus*, left], *comb. form.* Left, as opposed to right; noting the turning of a ray of polarized light to the left, as opp. to DEXTRO-. **lævo-glucose** (lē vȯ gloo kōs) [GLUCOSE], **lævulose** (lē vū lōs), *n.* (*Chem.*) A sugar or glucose distinguished from dextrose by its turning the plane of polarization to the left. **lævo-gyrate, -gyrous** (lē vȯ jī' rȧt, -rŭs) [GYRATE], **lævo-rotatory** (lē vȯ rō' tȧ tȯr i) [ROTATORY], *a.* Turning the plane of polarization to the left. **lævo-rotation** (-tā shŭn), *n.*

lag (1) (lăg) [etym. doubtful, perh. from LAST or LACK], *a.* Last; long-delayed; *slow, sluggish, tardy. *v.i.* (*past & p.p.* **lagged**) To loiter, to move slowly; to fall behind. *n.* Retardation of current or movement; delay in response; one who or that which lags behind or comes last, the last comer; *the lag-end; the grey lag. **lag of the tide:** The interval by which the tide lags behind the mean time during the first and third quarters of the moon. ***lag-end,** *n.* The hinder part; the fag-end; the dregs. **laggard,** *a.* Slow, sluggish, backward; wanting in energy. *n.* A slow, sluggish fellow; a loiterer. **lagger,** *n.* **lagging** (1), *a.* and *n.* **laggingly,** *adv.*

lag (2) (lăg) [Slang, etym. doubtful], *v.t.* To arrest; to send to penal servitude. *n.* A convict; a long-term prisoner, a gaol-bird; *a sentence of transportation.

lag (3) (lăg) [Icel. *lögg*, the end of a cask], *n.* A stave, lath, or strip of wood, felt, etc.; (*steam-eng.*) one of the pieces of the non-conducting jacket of a boiler or cylinder. *v.t.* To cover or encase with lags or lagging, esp. to preserve against freezing. **lagging** (2), *n.*

lagan (lăg' ȧn) [A.-F. (cp. Icel. *lögn*, pl. *lagnir*, nets laid in the sea, cogn. with LIE (2))], *n.* (*Law*) Wreckage or goods lying at the bottom of the sea, usu. marked by a float or buoy.

lagena (lȧ jē' nȧ) [L., an amphora], *n.* (*pl.* ***-næ***) (*Rom. Ant.*) An amphora; (*Zool.*) the termination of the cochlea in birds and reptiles. **lageniform,** *a.*

lager, lager beer (la' gėr bēr') [G. *lager-bier* (*lager*, a store)], *n.* A light beer, the ordinary beer of Germany.

laggard, etc. [LAG (1)].

laggin (lăg' in) [Sc., var. of LAGGING (2)], *n.* The angle between the side and bottom of a wooden dish; *the projecting rim of staves at the end of a cask, etc.

lagging [LAG (3)].

lagomys (lăg' ȯ mis) [Gr. *lagōs*, hare, *mus*, mouse], *n.* (*Zool.*) A genus of small rodents, containing the calling hares.

lagoon (lȧ goon') [F. *lagune*, It. and Sp. *laguna*, L. LACUNA], *n.* A shallow lake near a river or the sea, due to the infiltration or overflow of water from the larger body; the water enclosed by an atoll or coral island. **lagoon-island, -reef,** *n.* An atoll.

lagophthalmia (lăg of thăl' mi ȧ) [Gr. *lagōphthalmos*, hare-eyed (*lagōs*, hare, *ophthalmos*, eye)], *n.* (*Path.*) A disease of the eyes in which they remain open during sleep. **lagophthalmic,** *a.*

lagopus (lȧ gō' pŭs) [L., from Gr. *lagōpous* (*lagōs*, hare, *pous*, foot)], *n.* (*Zool.*) A genus of game-birds, containing the ptarmigan. **lagopodous** (lȧ gop' ȯ dŭs), *a.*

lagostoma (lȧ gos' tō mă) [Gr. *stoma*, mouth], *n.* (*Path.*) Hare-lip.

lagotic (lȧ got' ik), *a.* Having ears like a hare's.

lagrimoso (la grē mō' sō) [It., as LACHRYMOSE], *adv.* (*Mus.*) Solemnly, plaintively.

laic (lā' ik) [late L. *lāicus*, Gr. *laikos*, from *laos*, the people], *a.* Lay, not clerical, secular. *n.* A layman. **laical,** *a.* **laically,** *adv.* **laicize** (lā' i sīz), *v.t.* To render lay or secular; to throw open or hand over to laymen. **laicization** (-zā' shŭn), *n.*

laid (lād) [p.p. of LAY (1)], *a.* **laid paper:** Paper made with a ribbed surface, marked by the wires on which the pulp is laid, opp. to wove paper.

***laidly** (lād′ li) [Sc. and North., var. of LOATHLY], *a.* Loathsome, hideous, repulsive.

lain, *past & p.p.* [LIE (2)].

lair (1) (lâr) [A.-S. *leger*, a bed (cp. Dut. *leger*, G. *lager*, LAAGER), cogn. with LIE (2)], *n.* The den or retreat of a wild beast; a pen or shed for cattle on the way to slaughter or the market; *a resting-place; *a tomb; *a litter. *v.i.* To go to or lie in a lair; to make one's lair (in). *v.t.* To place in a lair. **lairage,** *n.*

***lair** (2) (lâr) [Icel. *leir*], *n.* Mire, mud; soil, earth; (*Sc.*) a quagmire. *v.i.* To sink or stick in a quagmire.

lair (3) (lâr), *n.* (*Austral. colloq.*) An over-dressed man. **all laired up:** Dressed in a flashy manner.

laird (lârd) [Sc., var. of LORD], *n.* The owner of a landed estate; a landlord. **lairdship,** *n.*

laissez-aller (lā sā ăl′ ā) [F., let (them or things) go (*laissez*, imper. of *laisser*, to let, *aller*, to go)], *n.* Unrestraint; absence of conventionality. ***laissez-faire*** (lā sā fâr′) [F. *faire*, to do], *n.* The principle of non-interference, esp. by the Government in industrial and commercial affairs.

laity (lā′ i ti) [A.-F. *laité*, from O.F. *lai*, LAY (2)], *n.* (*collect.*) The people, as distinct from the clergy, laymen; those not belonging to a particular profession; *the state of being a layman.

lake (1) (lāk) [O.F. *lac*, L. *lacum*, nom. *lacus*], *n.* A large sheet of water entirely surrounded by land. **lake-country, Lake District, lakeland,** *n.* The mountainous district occupied by the English lakes in Cumberland, Westmorland, and Lancashire. **lake-dwellers,** *n.pl.* (*Archæol.*) The prehistoric inhabitants of dwellings built on piles on the shallow edges of lakes. **lake-dwellings,** *n.pl.* **Lake Poets, Lake School:** Coleridge, Southey, and Wordsworth, grouped as a school by the *Edinburgh Review* because they happened to live in the Lake District. **lake-settlement,** *n.* **lake trout, great lake trout:** A fish of the salmon family living in lakes, esp. *Salmo ferox.* **Laker, Lakist,** *n.* One of the Lake Poets. **lakeless,** *a.* **lake-like,** *a.* **lakelet,** *n.* **laky,** *a.*

lake (2) (lāk) [var. of LAC (1)], *n.* A crimson pigment, usu. prepared by precipitating coloured tinctures upon alumina and other earths.

lakh [LAC (2)].

laky [LAKE (1)].

Lallan, Lallans (lăl′ ản, lăl′ ảnz) [Sc.], *n.* The Lowlands of Scotland; the broad Scots dialect.

lallation (lả lā′ shŭn) [F., from L. *lallāre*, to sing (a lullaby)], *n.* Pronunciation of *r* as *l*.

lalling (lăl′ ing), *n.* The continuous repetition of a single sound, as in infants. **lalopathy** (lả lop′ ả thi), *n.* Any speech disorder.

lam (lăm) [cp. Icel. *lemja*, A.-S. *lemian*, to LAME], *v.t.* (*slang*) To thrash, to wallop. **to lam it into:** To thrash.

lama (1) (la′ mả) [Tibetan *blama* (*b* silent)], *n.* A Tibetan or Mongolian Buddhist priest or monk. **Dalai** or **Grand Lama:** The chief lama of Tibet. **Teshu Lama:** That of Mongolia. **lamaism,** *n.* **lamaist,** *n.* **lamaserie** (la′ ma sėr i), *n.* A lamaist monastery.

lama (2) [LLAMA].

lamantin (lả măn′ tin) [F.], *n.* The manatee.

Lamarckian (lả mar′ ki ản) [*Lamarck* (1744–1829), French naturalist, -IAN], *a.* Of or pertaining to Lamarck. *n.* An adherent of the theory of Lamarck that all the evolution of organisms and the development of species have been due to inheritable modifications caused by habits, efforts at adaptation to environment, etc. **Lamarckianism, Lamarckism,** *n.* **Lamarckite,** *n.*

lamaserie [LAMA (1)].

lamb (lăm) [A.-S. (cp. Dut. *lam*, Icel. *lamb*, G. *lamm*)], *n.* The young of the sheep; the flesh of this used for food; (*fig.*) one as innocent and gentle as a lamb; a member of a church flock; a term of endearment; *(*ironically*) a cruel, merciless person, esp. one of gangs of roughs formerly employed to terrorize voters at elections; *a dupe. *v.i.* To bring forth lambs. **the Lamb:** Christ. **lamb-ale,** *n.* A rural festivity at sheep-shearing. **lambskin,** *n.* The skin of a lamb dressed as a leather with the fleece on. **lamb's tails:** Catkins of hazel and filbert. **lamb's-wool,** *n.* Wool from lambs used for hosiery; ale mixed with sugar, nutmeg, and the pulp of roasted apples. *a.* Made of lamb's wool. **lambhood** (lăm hud), **lambkin,** *n.* **lamb-like,** *a.* **lamb down:** (*Austral. colloq.*) To spend money on a spree; to throw money about lavishly.

lambaste, lambast (lam bāst′), *v.t.* (*slang*) To beat, to give a thrashing.

lambative [LAMBITIVE].

lambdacism (lăm′ dả sizm) [L. *lambdacimus*, Gr. *labdakismos*, from *lambda*, the letter λ or *l*], *n.* The too frequent repetition or improper pronunciation of the letter *l*; lallation. **lambdoid** (lăm′ doid), **lambdoidal** (-doi dảl), *a.* (*Anat.*) Resembling the Greek letter lambda (λ) in form, as the suture between the parietal and the occipital bones of the skull.

lambent (lăm′ bėnt) [L. *lambens -entis*, pres.p. of *lambere*, to lick], *a.* Playing or moving about, touching slightly without burning (as flame or light); softly radiant. **lambency,** *n.* **lambently,** *a.* ***lambitive** (lăm′ bi tiv), *a.* (*Med.*) To be taken by licking. *n.* A medicine to be taken thus.

lambert (lam′ bĕrt), *n.* (*Phys.*) Measure of brightness of surface radiating 1 lumen for every square centimetre.

Lambeth (lăm′ beth), *n.* The palace of the Archbishop of Canterbury; (*fig.*) the chief hierarchy of the Church of England. **Lambeth degree,** *n.* An honorary degree conferred by the Archbishop of Canterbury.

lambrequin (lăm′ brė kin) [F., etym. doubtful], *n.* A strip of cloth or other material worn as covering over a helmet for protection from heat; (*Her.*) the floating wreath of a helmet; (*Am.*) an ornamental strip of drapery over a door, window, mantelshelf, etc.

lame (lām) [A.-S. *lama* (cp. Dut. *lam*, Icel. *lami*, G. *lahm*)], *a.* Disabled in one or more of the limbs, esp. the foot or leg; limping, halting; (*fig.*) not running smoothly or evenly; unsatisfactory; imperfect. *v.t.* To make lame; to cripple, to disable. **lame duck:** (*slang*) A defaulter on the Stock Exchange. **lamely,** *a.* **lameness,** *n.* **lamish,** *a.*

lamella (lả mel′ ả) [L., dim. of LAMINA], *n.* (*pl.* **-læ**) A thin plate, layer, or scale. **lamellar, lamellate** (-ảt), **-ated** (lăm′ ė lā tėd), **lamellose** (lả mel′ ōs), *a.* **lamellarly,** *adv.*

lamelli-, *comb. form.*

lamellibranch (lả mel′ i brăngk) [Gr. *branchia*, gills], *n.* (*Zool.*) One of the *Lamellibranchiata*, a class of molluscs breathing by two pairs of gills. **lamellibranchiate,** *a.* Pertaining to the *Lamellibranchiata.* *n.* Any individual of the *Lamellibranchiata.*

lamellicorn (lả mel′ i kôrn) [L. *cornu*, a horn], *a.* (*Zool.*) Pertaining to the *Lamellicornia*, a group of beetles having short antennæ terminated by a short lamellated club. *n.* A lamellicorn beetle. **lamellicornate, -cornous,** *a.* **lamelliferous** (-lif′ ėr ŭs), **lamelliform** (lả mel′ i fôrm), *a.*

lamellirostral (lả mel i ros′ trảl), *a.* (*Zool.*) Pertaining to the *Lamellirostres*, a group of birds (acc. to Cuvier) having lamellose bills, containing the ducks, geese, etc.

lament (lả ment′) [F. *lamenter*, L. *lāmentāri*, from *lāmentum*, a wail], *v.i.* To mourn, to wail; to feel or express sorrow. *v.t.* To bewail, to mourn over; to deplore, to grieve for. *n.* Sorrow expressed in cries or complaints; an elegy, a dirge; a mournful song or melody. **lamentable** (lăm′ ėn tảbl), *a.* To be lamented; mournful, sad; very unfortunate, deplorable. **lamentably,** *adv.* **lamentation** (-tā' shŭn), *n.* The act of lamenting; an audible expression of grief; a wail; (*pl.*) the book of the Old Testament containing the lamentations of Jeremiah. **lamented** (lȧ men' tėd), *a.* Mourned for; deceased, late. ***lamentedly,** *adv.* **lamenter,** *n.* **lamentingly,** *adv.*

lameter (lā' mė tėr) [LAME (*-eter*, etym. doubtful)], *n.* (*chiefly Sc.*) A lame person, a cripple.

lametta (lȧ met' ȧ) [It., dim. of *lama*, L. LAMINA], *n.* Gold, silver, or brass foil or wire.

lamia (lā' mi ȧ) [L., from Gr.], *n.* A lascivious evil spirit in the form of a serpent with a woman's head; a sorceress, a witch.

lamina (lăm' i nȧ) [L.], *n.* (*pl.* **-næ**) A thin plate, layer, coat, flake, stratum, etc. **laminable,** *a.* **laminal, -nar, -nary,** *a.* **laminarian,** *a.* Pertaining to the genus *Laminaria*, a genus of algæ with a flat ribless expansion in place of leaves, or to the sea-depths where these occur. **laminiferous** (-nif' ėr ŭs), **laminose** (lăm' i nōs), *a.* **lamini-,** *comb. form.*

laminate (lăm' in āt), *v.t.* To beat, press, or roll into thin plates; to cut or split into thin layers or sheets. *v.i.* To split into thin plates. *a.* (-nȧt) Consisting of laminæ. **laminated core,** *n.* (*Wire.*) An iron core consisting of laminations, used in chokes, transformers, etc. **lamination** (-nā' shŭn), *n.*

lamish [LAME]. **lamm** [LAM].

Lammas (lăm' ȧs) [A.-S. *hlāfmæsse* (LOAF, MASS (1))], *n.* The 1st August, the day on which first-fruits were offered in Anglo-Saxon times. **latter Lammas:** A day that will never arrive. **Lammas-day, -tide,** *n.* **Lammas land,** *n.* Land cultivated by individual occupiers but thrown open for common pasturage after harvest or Lammas Day.

lammergeyer (lăm' ėr gī ėr) [G. *lämmergeier* (*lämmer*, lambs, *geier*, vulture)], *n.* The great bearded vulture, *Gypaëtus barbatus*, an inhabitant of lofty mountains of S. Europe, Asia, and N. Africa.

lamp (1) (lămp) [O.F. *lampe*, L. and Gr. *lampas*, from *lampein*, to shine], *n.* A vessel for the production of artificial light, esp. by the combustion of oil with a wick; any vessel enclosing a gas-jet, incandescent wire, or other source of artificial light; (*fig.*) any source of light, as the sun, moon, etc.; a source of intellectual or spiritual light; (*slang, pl.*) the eyes. *v.i.* To shine; to give light. *v.t.* To supply with lamps; to light, to illuminate. **to smell of the lamp:** To show signs of laborious preparation (as a sermon, speech, etc.). **lamp-black,** *n.* Amorphous carbon, obtained by the imperfect combustion of oil or resin. **lamp-chimney, -glass,** *n.* The upright chimney for a lamp. **lamp-light,** *n.* The light from a lamp or lamps. **lamp-lighter,** *n.* One employed to light the public lamps. **lamp-post,** *n.* A pillar supporting a street lamp. ***lamping,** *a.* Shining, sparkling. **lampless,** *a.*

lamp (2) (lămp) [Sc., etym. doubtful], *v.i.* To go rapidly or jauntily; to go with long strides.

lampad (lăm' pȧd) [Gr. *lampas -pados*, LAMP (1)], *n.* A lamp, a torch. **lampadary,** *n.* (*Gr. Ch.*) An officer who attended to the lighting of the church and carried a lighted taper before the patriarch. **lampadedromy** (lăm pȧ ded' rȯ mi) [Gr. *lampadēdromia* (*-dromia*, from *dramein*, to run)], *n.* (*Gr. Ant.*) A torch-race; a race in which a lighted torch was passed from hand to hand. **lampadomancy** (lăm păd' ȯ măn si) [-MANCY], *n.* Divination by the flame of a torch or lamp.

lampas (1) (lăm' pȧs) [F., etym. doubtful], *n.* A swelling of the roof of the mouth in horses.

lampas (2) (lăm' pȧs) [F., etym. doubtful], *n.* A flowered silk or woollen cloth used in upholstery.

lampern (lăm' pėrn) [O.F. *lamproyon*, dim. of *lampreie*], *n.* The river lamprey, *Petromyzon fluviatilis*.

lampion (lăm' pi ŏn) [F., from It. *lampione*, from *lampa*, LAMP (1)], *n.* A small coloured globe or cup with wick, etc., used in illuminations.

lampoon (lăm poon') [F. *lampon*, from *lampons*, let us drink (*lamper*, to booze, perh. a var. of *lapper*, to lap up)], *n.* A sarcastic personal satire. *v.t.* To write lampoons upon; to abuse with personal satire. **lampooner, lampoonist,** *n.* ***lampoonry,** *n.*

lamprey (lăm' pri) [O.F. *lampreie* (F. *lamproie*), It. *lampreda*, late L. *lampetra* (*lambere*, to lick, *petra*, rock)], *n.* An eel-like fish with a suctorial mouth, belonging to the genus *Petromyzon*.

lana (lā' nȧ) [native name], *n.* The close-grained, tough wood of a S. American tree, *Genipa Americana*. **lana dye:** A pigment obtained from the fruit of this.

lanate (lā' nāt) [L. *lānātus*, from *lāna*, wool], *a.* (*Bot. and Ent.*) Woolly, covered with curly hairs. ***lanary,** *n.* A wool-store.

Lancasterian (lăng kȧs tēr' i ȧn) [Joseph *Lancaster* (1778–1838)], *a.* Of or pertaining to Joseph Lancaster or his monitorial system of education.

Lancastrian (lăng kăs' tri ȧn), *a.* Pertaining to the family descended from John of Gaunt, Duke of Lancaster. *n.* An adherent of this, one of the Red Rose party in the Wars of the Roses; a native of Lancashire.

lance (lans) [F., from L. *lancea*], *n.* A thrusting weapon consisting of a long shaft with a sharp point, formerly the peculiar weapon of knights, later used by some regiments of cavalry; a similar weapon used for killing a harpooned whale, for spearing fish, etc.; a lancer. *v.t.* To pierce with or as with a lance; (*Surg.*) to open with a lancet; *to hurl or fling (a lance). **lance-corporal,** *n.* (*Mil.*) A private who performs the duties and holds the rank of a corporal. **lance-sergeant,** *n.* An acting sergeant. **lance-snake,** *n.* A venomous American snake, the fer-de-lance, of the genus *Bothrops*, allied to the rattlesnake. **lance-wood,** *n.* The tough, elastic wood of *Duguetia quitarensis*, other S. American and W. Indian trees, much used by coach-builders. **lancer,** *n.* A cavalry soldier armed with a lance; (*pl.*) a particular set of quadrilles; the music for this.

***lancegay** (lans' gā) [O.F. *lancegaye*, corr. of *lancezagaye* (LANCE (1), *zagaye*, ASSAGAI)], *n.* A kind of spear.

lancelet (lans' lėt), *n.* A small transparent iridescent fish, *Amphioxus lanceolatus*, of very low organization.

lanceolate (lan' sė ȯ lȧt) [L. *lanceolātus*, from *lanceola*, dim. of *lancea*, LANCE], *a.* Tapering to a point at each end.

lancet (lan' sėt) [O.F. *lancette*, dim. of LANCE], *n.* A sharp surgical instrument, used in bleeding, cutting of abscesses, tumours, etc.; (*Arch.*) a lancet-window. **lanceted,** *a.* (*Arch.*) **lancet-arch,** *n.* (*Arch.*) An arch with a sharply pointed top. **lancet-light, -window,** *n.* (*Arch.*) A high narrow window with a sharply pointed arch.

lancinate (lan' si nāt) [L. *lancinātus*, p.p. of *lancināre*, to rend], *v.t.* To tear, to lacerate. **lancinating,** *a.* Piercing, cutting, keen (applied to a pain). **lancination** (-nā' shŭn), *n.*

land (lănd) [A.-S. (cp. Dut., Icel., G., etc., *land*)], *n.* The solid portion of the earth, esp. of the earth's surface, as distinct from the oceans and seas; the ground, the soil, a tract of country; a country, a district, a region; a nation, a people; landed property, real estate; (*pl.*) estates; (*local*) a strip of land divided off by deep furrows; (*Eng.*) a small flat surface; (*Artill.*) the raised portion of a fire-arm's rifling. *v.t.* To set or place on shore; to bring to shore; to set down from a vehicle; to bring to or place in a certain position; to deal (a blow); to bring (fish) to land; (*slang*) to win (a prize). *v.i.* To come or go ashore; to disembark; to find oneself in a certain position; to alight. **land of promise:** Canaan. **land of the leal:** The land of the faithful or blessed; heaven. **land of the living:** The present life. **to make land, to make the land:** (*Naut.*) To come in sight of land as the ship approaches it from the sea. **land-agent,** *n.* One employed to manage land for the proprietor, a steward; an agent for the sale of land. **land-agency,** *n.* **Land Army,** *n.* A national organization of volunteer farm-workers. **land-bank,** *n.* A bank lending money on the security of land. **land-breeze,** *n.* A wind blowing seawards off the land. **land-carriage,** *n.* Transportation by land. **land-crab,** *n.* A crab of the family *Gecarcinidæ*, which lives mainly on land, visiting the sea chiefly for breeding. **land-fish,** *n.* One who is as much out of his element as a fish out of water. **land-flood,** *n.* An overflow of water on land. **land-force,** *n.* A military force employed on land. ***land-gavel,** *n.* (*Hist.*) A tax, tribute, or rent on land. **land-girl,** *n.* A girl or woman employed in the Land Army. **land-grabber** [GRAB]. **land-grabbing,** *a.* and *n.* **landholder,** *n.* One who owns or (usu.) rents land. **land-hungry,** *a.* Eager to acquire land. **land-hunger,** *n.* **land-jobber,** *n.* One who speculates in land. **Land League:** An association formed in Ireland in 1879 to agitate for a settlement of the land question, by reducing rents, introducing peasant proprietorship, etc., suppressed in 1881. **Land Leaguer:** A member of this. **landlock,** *v.t.* (*usu. in p.p.*) To enclose with land. **land-loper, *-louper** [Dut. *landlooper* (*loopen*, to run, cp. LEAP)], *n.* (*Sc.*) A vagabond, a vagrant; a landsman, a land-lubber. **land-lubber,** *n.* (*Naut.*) A landsman, one unused to the sea or ships. ***landman,** *n.* One who lives on the land, a countryman, a peasant; one belonging to a specified country. **land-measuring,** *n.* **land-mine,** *n.* (*Mil.*) A mine set in the ground to explode under advancing troops, etc. **land-office,** *n.* An office in which the sale or letting of new land is registered. **landowner,** *n.* **landowning,** *a.* **land-rail,** *n.* The corn-crake. ***land-raker,** *n.* A vagabond. **land-rat,** *n.* A rat living on land; hence, a thief, a robber. ***land-reeve,** *n.* An assistant to a land-steward. **land reform,** *n.* (*Pol.*) A redistribution of land, or adjustment of land-rent. **land-roller, *-roll,** *n.* A roller for crushing clods. **land-shark,** *n.* (*Naut. slang*) A person who preys on seamen ashore. **land-scrip,** *n.* (*U.S.A.*) A certificate entitling the holder to become the owner of a specified amount of public land. **land-sick,** *a.* (*Naut.*) Moving slowly and warily, as a ship nearing land. **land-side,** *n.* The flat side of a plough away from the furrow. **landslide,** *n.* A landslip; a political debacle. **landslip,** *n.* The sliding down of a considerable portion of ground from a higher to a lower level; the ground thus slipping. **land-steward,** *n.* One who manages a landed estate. **land-surveyor,** *n.* One who measures and draws plans of estates, etc. **land-surveying,** *n.* **land-swell,** *n.* The roll of the sea inshore. **land-tax,** *n.* A tax assessed upon land and property. **land-tie,** *n.* A rod, beam, or piece of masonry anchoring a wall, etc., to the ground. **land-waiter,** *n.* A custom-house officer who watches the landing of dutiable goods. **land-wind,** *n.* A wind blowing off the land. **landed,** *a.* Having an estate in land; consisting of real estate. **lander,** *n.* One who lands or disembarks; (*Mining*) one who attends at the mouth of the pit to receive the buckets of ore. **landless,** *a.* **landocracy** (lăn dok′ ră si) [-CRACY], *n.* The landed classes. **landocrat** (lăn′ dŏ krăt), *n.* **landward,** *a.* and *adv.* **landwards,** *adv.*

landamman (lan′ dăm ăn) [Swiss G.], *n.* The chief magistrate in some of the Swiss cantons.

landau (lăn′ dō) [*Landau*, Germany, where orig. made], *n.* A four-wheeled carriage with a folding top that may be opened and thrown back. **landaulet** (lăn dŏ let′), *n.* ***landaulette,*** *n.* A motor-car with a covering or hood, fixed in front, movable behind.

landdrost (lănd′ rŏst) [S. Afr. Dut.], *n.* A district magistrate, civil commissioner, fiscal agent, etc., in S. Africa.

lande (land) [F., see LAWN (1)], *n.* A heathy and sandy plain; a moor.

landfall (lănd′ fawl), *n.* (*Naut.*) Approach to land after a voyage; the first land descried after a voyage; a sudden transference of property in land by the death of a rich man; a landslip. **to make a good, or bad landfall:** To reach land according to, or not according to, calculation.

landgrave (lănd′ grāv) [M.H.G. *lantgrave* (G. *landgraf*), cp. Dut. *landgraaf* (LAND, GRAVE (4))], *n.* A German title, dating from the twelfth century, orig. used to distinguish a governor of a province from inferior counts. **landgraviate** (-grā′ vi ăt), **landgraveship** (lănd′ grāv ship), *n.* **landgravine** (-gră vēn), *n.* The wife of a landgrave.

landing (lăn′ ding), *n.* The act of going or setting on land, esp. from a vessel; a pier, wharf, or jetty; (*U.S.A.*) the platform of a railway-station; a level space at the top of a flight of stairs. **landing beam,** *n.* (*Aviat.*) A radio beam that guides an aircraft to ground. **landing-net,** *n.* A small bag-net used to take fish from the water when hooked. **landing-place, landing-stage,** *n.* A platform, fixed or floating, on which passengers and goods are disembarked. **landing-surveyor,** *n.* An officer who superintends the land-waiters. **landing-waiter,** *n.* A land-waiter.

landlady (lănd′ lā di), *n.* A woman who keeps an inn or lodging-house; a woman who lets houses, lodgings, etc.

landlord (lănd′ lôrd), *n.* One who has tenants holding under him; the master of an inn or of a lodging-house. **landlordism,** *n.* The proceedings of land-owners as a body, esp. with regard to their tenantry; the system under which land is owned by individuals to whom tenants pay a fixed rent.

landmark (lănd′ mark), *n.* Anything set up to mark the boundaries of land; a prominent object on land serving as a guide for sailors; (*fig.*) a conspicuous object in a place or district.

Landsborough grass (lăndz′ bŏ rŏ), *n.* (*Austral.*) The rich fodder grass of Queensland.

landscape, *-skip (lănd′ skăp, -skip) [Dut. *landschap* (LAND, SHIP)], *n.* A picture representing country scenery; a view, esp. a picturesque view of country scenery. **landscape-gardening,** *n.* The art of laying out grounds so as to develop their natural beauties. **landscape-gardener,** *n.* **landscape-marble,** *n.* A variety of marble with dendriform markings. **landscape-painter,** *n.* A painter of landscapes. **landscapist,** *n.* A landscape-painter.

landsman (lăndz′ măn), *n.* One who lives on land; (*Naut.*) one unused to the sea and its ways. **land-spring,** *n.* A spring of water appearing only after a heavy rain.

lane (1) (lān) [A.-S. (cp. O.Fris. *lana*, Dut. *laan*)], *n.* A narrow road, way, or passage, esp. between hedges; a narrow street; a passage between persons standing on each side; a prescribed route, as for ocean steamers; (*Motor.*) a division of a road for a single stream of traffic. **red lane:** (*colloq.*) The throat.

lane (2) [LONE].

lang [Sc., var. of LONG (1)].

***langrage** (lăng′ răj) [etym. unknown], *n.* Canister or case-shot loaded with bolts, nails, and pieces of iron, formerly used against rigging.

***langspiel** (lăng′ spēl) [Norw. *langspil*], *n.* A kind of harp formerly used in the Shetland Isles.

langsyne (lăng sīn′) [Sc. (LANG, SYNE)], *adv.* Long since, long ago. *n.* Time long ago.

language (lăng′ gwăj) [F. *langage*, from *langue*, L. *lingua*, tongue], *n.* Human speech; the communication of ideas by articulate sounds or words; the vocabulary peculiar to a nation, tribe, or people; the vocabulary appropriate to a particular science, profession, etc.; the phrases and manner of expression peculiar to an individual; literary style;

the phraseology or wording (of a book, passage, speech, etc.); any method of communicating ideas by symbols, etc.; *a nation. **to speak the same language:** (*fig.*) To have a similar background or upbringing; to have the same habits of mind. **language-master, -teacher,** *n.* **languaged,** *a.* (*usu. in comb.* as *well-languaged*). **languageless,** *a.*

langue (lang) [F., see prec.], *n.* A language, ***langue d'oc*** (dok), *n.* The Provençal language, so called from the use of the word *oc*, yes, instead of *oïl* or *oui*. ***langue d'oïl, d'oui*** (dwē), *n.* Northern French, that spoken north of the Loire in the Middle Ages, the original of modern French.

languet (lăng' gwĕt) [F. *languette*, dim. of *langue*, as prec.], *n.* A tongue-shaped part; a small metal tongue on a sword-hilt fitting over the scabbard; the tongue of an organ flue-pipe or the reed of a harmonium; the tongue of a balance; (*Zool.*) one of a row of tongue-like appendages along the dorsal edge of the bronchial sac of ascidians.

languid (lăng' gwid) [L. *languidus*, as foll.], *a.* Faint, relaxed, lacking energy; indisposed to exertion; spiritless, lacking animation, listless, dull; sluggish, slow. **languidly,** *adv.* **languidness,** *n.*

languish (lăng' gwish) [F. *languiss-*, stem. of *languir*, L. *languēre*, rel. to *laxus*, LAX], *v.i.* To become weak, feeble, or sluggish; to lose vitality, energy, or animation; to fall off, to fade, to grow slack; to droop, to pine (for); to put on a languid expression, to affect a tender, wistful, or sentimental air. *n.* Languishment; the act of languishing; a soft, tender look. **languisher,** *n.* **languishingly,** *adv.* **languishment,** *n.*

languor (lăng' gŏr) [O.F., from L. *languor -ōrem*, as prec.], *n.* Languidness, lassitude, faintness, laxity, inertness; (*Path.*) debility, nervous prostration; softness, tenderness of mood or expression; oppressive stillness (of the air, etc.). **languorous,** *a.* **languorousness,** *n.*

laniard [LANYARD].

laniary (lăn' i ăr i) [L. *laniārius*, pertaining to a butcher, *lanius*, from *laniāre*, to tear], *a.* Adapted for tearing. *n.* A canine tooth in the carnivora; *a slaughter-house, a shambles. ***laniate,** *v.t.*

laniferous (lă nif' ĕr ŭs) [L. *lāna*, wool, -FEROUS], **lanigerous** (lă nij' ĕr ŭs) [-GEROUS], *a.* Bearing wool.

lank (lăngk) [A.-S. *hlanc*], *a.* Lean, long and thin, shrunken-looking; long and straight (of the hair); *languid, drooping. *v.i.* To be or become lank; to shrink or fall away. **lankly,** *adv.* **lankness,** *n.* **lanky,** *a.*

lanner (lăn' ĕr) [O.F. *lanier*, prob. ident. with *lanier*, cowardly], *n.* The female of a falcon, *Falco lanarius*. **lannaret,** *n.* The male *Falco lanarius*, which is smaller than the female.

lanolin (lăn' ō lin) [L. *lāna*, wool, *oleum*, oil], *n.* An unctuous substance forming the basis of ointments, etc., extracted from wool.

lansquenet (lans' kĕ net) [F., from G. *landsknecht* (LAND, *knetcht*, servant, cp. KNIGHT)], *n.* A mercenary foot-soldier of Germany and France (15th to 17th cent.); a game at cards of German origin, consisting largely of betting.

lantern (lăn' tĕrn) [F. *lanterne*, L. *lanterna*, prob. from Gr. *lamptēr*, from *lampein*, to shine (see LAMP (1))], *n.* A case with transparent sides or panes for holding and protecting a light; the upper chamber of a lighthouse containing the light; a glazed structure on the top of a dome or roof, for the admission of light and air; a magic lantern. *v.t.* To furnish or provide with a lantern; to put to death by hanging from a lamp-post. **Chinese lantern** [CHINA]. **dark lantern** [DARK]. **magic lantern:** An apparatus with a lens through which a magnified image from a glass slide is cast on a screen by a powerful light. **lantern-fly,** *n.* An insect of the tropical genus *Fulgora*, formerly believed to produce light. **lantern-jawed,** *a.* Having a long, thin face. **lantern-jaws,** *n.pl.* **lantern-wheel,** *n.* A form of cog-wheel acting as a pinion to a spur-wheel.

lanthanum (lăn' thă nŭm) [from Gr. *lanthanein*, to lurk, to escape detection (from the lateness of its discovery)], *n.* (*Chem.*) A metallic divalent element discovered in 1839, usu. occurring with didymium and cerium in cerite.

***lanthorn** [LANTERN].

***lanuginous, *-ginose** (lă nū' ji nŭs, -nōs) [L. *lānūginōsus*, from *lānūgo -ginis*, down, from *lāna*, wool], *a.* Downy, covered with soft downy hair. **lanugo** (lăn ū' gō), *n.* (*Biol.*) Pre-natal hair.

lanx (lăngks) [L.], *n.* (*Rom. Ant.*) A large dish or platter for serving meat.

lanyard (lăn' yărd) [earlier *lannier*, F. *lanière* (assim. to YARD (1))], *n.* (*Naut.*) A short cord, line, or gasket for seizing or lashing; (*Artill.*) cord for firing a gun; (*Mil.*) cord to which a whistle or knife is attached.

Laodicean (lā ō di sē' ăn), *a.* Pertaining to Laodicea, a city of Phrygia; (*fig.*) lukewarm in religion, politics, etc. (with alln. to Rev. iii. 15, 16). *n.* A native or citizen of Laodicea; (*fig.*) a person of this character.

Laotian (lou' shăn), *a.* Pertaining to the state of Laos, Indo-China.

lap (1) (lăp) [A.-S. *læppa* (cp. Dut. and Dan. *lap*, G. *lappen*)], *n.* A loose hanging part of a garment or other object; that part of the dress which hangs over the knees when a person sits down; the part of the person from the waist to the knees in sitting, esp. as a place for holding a child, etc.; (*fig.*) a place where anything rests or lies securely. **lap-dog,** *n.* A small pet dog. **lapstone,** *n.* A stone held in the lap by a shoemaker for hammering leather on. **lapful,** *n.*

lap (2) (lăp) [prob. from prec.], *v.t.* (*past & p.p.* **lapped**) To wrap, to twist, to roll (round, about, etc.); to lay (one thing) partly over another; to fold, to bend over; to enfold, to enwrap, to surround, to involve; to cause to overlap; to tie, to bind; (*Racing*) to get ahead of by a lap or laps; to polish with a lap. *v.i.* To be turned over; to lie partly over something else, to overlap. *n.* That part of anything that extends over something else, the overlap; the amount of overlap; a continuous band of cotton-fibre, etc., ready for carding; the length of rope, cord, thread, etc., making one turn round a wheel, roller, etc.; one round of a race-course; a wheel, disk, or piece of leather made to rotate, for polishing gems, metal articles, etc. **the last lap:** (*fig.*) The beginning of the end, closing stages. **lap-joint,** *n.* A joint in which one part laps over the other. **lap-jointed,** *a.* **lap-robe,** *n.* (*Am.*) A carriage rug. **lap-streak,** *a.* Clinker-built. *n.* A clinker-built boat. **lap-work,** *n.* Work constructed with lap-joints; work polished by lapping. **lapper,** *n.*

lap (3) (lăp) [A.-S. *lapian* (cp. Icel. *lepja*, O.H.G. *laffan*, L. *lambere*, Gr. *laptein*)], *v.i.* To take up liquid with the tongue; to drink by lifting with the tongue; (*fig.*) to beat (as waves on the shore) with a sound as of lapping. *v.t.* To lick or take up with the tongue; to drink or consume by lapping. *n.* The act of lapping; a lick; the amount taken up by this; food or drink that can be lapped up, esp. liquid food for animals; (*slang*) a weak kind of drink [cp. CAT-LAP]; the sound of water beating softly on a beach.

laparo- [Gr. *lapara*, the flank, from *laparos*, soft], *comb. form* (*Anat., etc.*). **laparectomy** (lăp ă rek' tō mi) [Gr. *ektomē*, a cutting-out (*ek-*, out, *temnein*, to cut)], *n.* (*Surg.*) Excision of a part of the intestine at the side. **laparotomy** (-rot' ō' mi) [-TOMY], *n.* Incision into the cavity of the abdomen to form an artificial anus. **laparotomist,** *n.* **laparotomize,** *v.t.*

lapel (lă pel') [LAP (1), -EL], *n.* That part of a garment made to lap or fold over, esp. the fold on the front of a coat below the collar. **lapelled,** *a.*

lapidary (lăp′ i dȧr i) [L. *lapidārius*, from *lapis* -*idis*, stone], *n.* One who cuts, polishes, or engraves gems; a dealer in or connoisseur of gems. *a.* Pertaining to the art of cutting, engraving, or polishing gems; inscribed on or suitable for inscription on stones; hence, formal or monumental (of style); *pertaining to stones. **lapidary-bee,** *n.* *Bombus lapidarius*, which nests in or among stones. ***lapidarian** (-dâr′ i ȧn), *a.*

lapidate (lăp′ i dāt) [L. *lapidātus*, p.p. of *lapidāre*, as prec.], *v.t.* To stone, esp. to kill by stoning. **lapidation** (-dā′ shŭn), *n.* ***lapidescent** (-des′ ėnt), *a.* Turning into stone, having the quality of converting into stone. *n.* A liquid converting substances into stone. **lapidescence,** *n.*

lapidify (lȧ pid′ i fī) [F. *lapidifier*, med. L. *lapidificāre* (*lapis* -*idis*, *ficāre*, *facere*, to make)], *v.t.* To form or convert into stone. *v.i.* To become petrified. ***lapidific, -al** (lăp i dif′ ik′, -ȧl), *a.* ***lapidification** (-kā′ shŭn), *n.* ***lapidist** (lăp′ i dist), *n.* A lapidary. **lapidose,** *a.* Stony; (*Bot.*) growing in stony soil.

lapilli (lȧ pil′ ī) [L., pl. of *lapillus*, dim. of *lapis*, stone], *n.pl.* Volcanic ashes, consisting of small, angular, stony or slaggy fragments. **lapilliform,** *a.*

lapis lazuli (lăp′ is lăz′ ū lī) [med. L., stone of azure (*lapis* stone, *lazulum*, azure)], *n.* A rich blue silicate of alumina, lime, and soda; a pigment made from this; its colour.

lapje, lappie (lăp′ i) [S. African], *n.* A small rag, a patch.

Laplander (lăp′ lȧn dėr) [Swed. *Lappland* (*Lapp*, cp. M.H.G. *lappe*, a simpleton)], *n.* An inhabitant of Lapland. **Laplandish,** *a.* **Lapp,** *n.* One of a dwarfish nomadic Mongoloid race inhabiting northern Scandinavia. **Lappish, Lapponian** (lȧ pō′ ni ȧn), *a.* and *n.*

lappel [LAPEL]. **lapper** [LAP (2)].

lappet (lăp′ ėt), *n.* A little lap, fold, or loose part of a dress, esp. a part of a lady's head-dress hanging loose; a flap; a loose, fleshy process, a lobe, a wattle; (*Textiles*) a cloth, usually of the muslin type, on which is woven a small pattern. **lappeted,** *a.*

lapse (lăps) [L. *lapsāre*, freq. of *lābī* (p.p. *lapsus*), to glide], *v.i.* To slide, to glide, to pass insensibly or by degrees; to pass away, to fall back or away; to fall into disuse, decay, or ruin; to make a slip or fault, to fail in duty; to pass from one proprietor to another by omission, negligence or failure of a patron, legatee, etc.; to become void. **v.t.* To allow to slide or slip away; to catch, to seize. *n.* The act of lapsing, gliding, slipping, or gradually falling (away, from, etc.); easy, smooth, and almost imperceptible movement, gentle flow, etc.; the imperceptible passage of time; a mistake, a slip, an error, a fault, deviation from what is right; a falling into disuse, neglect, decay, or ruin; termination of a right or privilege through desuetude. **lapsable,** *a.* ***lapsus*** (lăp′ sŭs) [L.], *n.* (*pl.* ***lapsus*** -sūs) A lapse, a slip. ***lapsus calami*** (kăl ȧ mī): A slip of the pen. ***lapsus linguæ*** (ling′ gwē): A slip of the tongue.

Laputan (lȧ pū′ tȧn), *a.* Pertaining to Laputa the flying island in 'Gulliver's Travels'; (*fig.*) visionary, chimerical. *n.* An inhabitant of Laputa; a visionary.

lapwing [A.-S. *hlēapewince* (*hlēapan*, to LEAP), WING], *n.* A bird of the genus *Vanellus*, of the plover family, esp. *V. cristatus*, a British bird, the peewit.

lar (lar) [L.], *n.* (*pl.* ***lares*** lâr′ ēz) A tutelary Roman divinity, usu. a deified ancestor or hero; the white-handed gibbon (*pl.* ***lars***). **lares and penates:** The home; household gods.

larach (lăr′ ȧch) [Gael.], *n.* The site, esp. the abandoned site, of a building, village, etc.

larboard (lar′ bôrd, -bȯrd) [M.E. *ladeborde* (etym. doubtful), assim. to STARBOARD], *n.* The port or left side of a vessel to a person standing on deck and facing the bow. *a.* Pertaining to the left side of a vessel.

larceny (lar′ sė ni) [A.-F. *larcin*, O.F. *larrecin*, L. *latrōcinium*, from *latro*, a robber], *n.* The unlawful taking away of another's personal goods with intent to convert them for one's own use, theft. **petty larceny:** Theft of anything under a value fixed by statute, in England formerly twelve pence. **larcener,** *n.* **larcenous,** *a.* **larcenously,** *adv.*

larch (larch) [G. *lärche*, L. *laricem*, nom. *larix*], *n.* A tree of the coniferous genus *Larix*, having deciduous bright-green foliage, and tough, durable timber, and yielding Venetian turpentine.

lard (lard) [O.F., from L. *lardum*, rel. to Gr. *laros*, pleasant to the taste, *larinos*, fat], *n.* The fat of hogs melted and separated from the flesh; *the flesh of swine, pork, bacon. *v.t.* To fatten; to cover or smear with lard; to insert strips of bacon in (a fowl, etc.) before roasting; (*fig.*) to intermix or garnish (writing, talk, etc.) with foreign phrases, flowers of speech, etc.; *to make rich or fertile. **v.i.* To grow fat. **lardaceous** (lar dā′ shŭs), *a.* (*chiefly Path.*) Of the nature or consisting of lard. **lardon,** *n.* A strip of bacon for larding fowls, etc. **lardy,** *a.*

larder (lar′ dėr) [A.-F., from O.F. *lardier*, med. L. *lardārium*, as prec.], *n.* A room where meat and other provisions are kept, (*Am.* a pantry). ***larderer,** *n.*

lares, *n.pl.* [LAR (1)].

large (larj) [F., from L. *larga*, fem. of largus], *a.* Great in size, number, quantity, extent, or capacity; big, bulky; wide, extensive; abundant, ample, copious; liberal, generous, lavish, prodigal; wide in range or comprehension, comprehensive, far-seeing; *free, unrestrained, licentious. **at large:** At liberty, free; freely, without restraint; diffusely, with ample detail. **by and large:** [BY]. **to go** or **sail large:** (*Naut.*) To have the wind abaft the beam or on the quarter. **large-handed,** *a.* Profuse; *rapacious, greedy. **large-hearted,** *a.* Having a liberal heart or disposition. **large-heartedness,** *n.* **large-minded,** *a.* **large-mindedness,** *n.* **large-paper,** *a.* Applied to books, prints, etc., having wider margins than the ordinary. **largely,** *adv.* To a large extent. **largen,** *v.t.* and *i.* (*poet.*). **largeness,** *n.* **largish,** *a.*

largess (lar′ jes) [F. *largesse*, as prec.], *n.* A present, a reward, a generous bounty (usually from a superior to inferiors); liberality, esp. in giving. ***largition** (lar jish′ ŭn), *n.* The bestowing of largess.

largo (lar′ gō) [It., from L. *largus*, LARGE], *adv.* (*Mus.*) Slowly, broadly, in an ample, dignified style. ***larghetto*** (lar get′ ō), *adv.* Somewhat slow. ***larghissimo*** (lar gis′ i mō), *adv.* Very slowly.

lariat (lăr′ i ȧt) [Sp. *la reata*, the rope or tie (see REATA)], *n.* A rope for picketing horses in camp; a lasso. *v.t.* To secure or catch with a lariat.

lark (1) (lark) [A.-S. *laferce*, *lāwerce* (cp. Dut. *leeuwerik*, G. *lerche*, Icel. *laeverki*, Swed. *lärka*)], *n.* Any bird of the genus *Alauda*, with five British species, esp. the skylark, *A. arvensis*. **lark-, lark's-heel,** *n.* The larkspur; the nasturtium or Indian cress, *Tropæolum majus*. **larkspur,** *n.* A plant with spur-shaped calyx belonging to the genus *Delphinium*, esp. *D. Ajacis*.

lark (2) (lark) [etym. doubtful], *n.* (*slang*) A prank, a frolic, a spree. *v.i.* To sport, to frolic. **larkish, larky,** *a.*

larrikin (lăr′ i kin) [Austral., perh. dim. of pers. name *Larry*], *n.* A rowdy youngster, a young hooligan. **larrikinism,** *n.*

larrup (lăr′ ŭp) [dial., etym. unknown], *v.t.* To thrash, to flog, to lash. **larruping,** *n.*

larry (lăr′ i) [dial., etym. unknown], *n.* Excitement, distraction.

larus (lâr′ ŭs) [late L., from Gr. *laros*], *n.* (*Ornith.*) A genus of swimming-birds, containing the seagulls.

larva (lar′ vȧ) [L., a ghost, a mask], *n.* (*pl.* **-væ**) The first condition of an insect on its issuing from the egg, when it is usually in the form of a grub, caterpillar, or maggot; sometimes used of the half-developed state of other invertebrates that undergo metamorphosis. **larval,** *a.* **larvate, *-vated,** *a.* Wearing a mask. ***larve,** *n.* A larva; *a mask. **larvicide** [-CIDE], *a.* Killing larvæ. *n.* A preparation for this purpose. **larviform,** *a.* **larvigerous** (lar vij′ ėr ůs) [-GEROUS], **larviparous** (-vip′ ȧ růs) [L. *parere*, to bring forth], *a.* Producing larvæ.

larynx (lăr′ ingks) [Gr. *larunx -ngos*], *n.* (*pl.* **larynges,** lȧ rin′ jēz) The vocal organ, consisting of the upper part of the windpipe, containing the vocal cords. **laryngeal** (lȧ rin′ jė ȧl), **laryngic,** *a.* Pertaining to the larynx. **laryngismus** (lăr in jiz′ můs), *n.* (*Path.*) A spasmodic affection of the glottis, croup. **laryngitis** (-jī′ tis) [-ITIS], *n.* (*Path.*) Inflammation of the larynx. **laryngitic** (-jit′ ik), *a.* **laryngology** (-gol′ ȯ ji) [-LOGY], *n.* The branch of medical science dealing with the windpipe and its diseases. **laryngological** (-gȯ loj′ i kȧl), *a.* **laryngologist** (-gol′ ȯ jist), *n.* **laryngophony** (-gof′ ȯ ni) [Gr. *-phonia*, sounding, from *phonein*, to speak], *n.* (*Med.*) The sound of the voice as heard through the stethoscope over the larynx. **laryngoscope** (lȧ rin′ gȯ skōp) [-SCOPE], *n.* An instrument with a reflecting mirror for obtaining a view of the larynx. **laryngoscopic** (-skop′ ik), *a.* **laryngoscopist** (-gos′ kȯ pist), *n.* **laryngoscopy,** *n.* **laryngotomy** (-got ȯ mi) [-TOMY], *n.* (*Surg.*) The operation of making an incision into the larynx in order to provide an artificial channel for breathing. **laryngotracheotomy** (lȧ ring gō trăk ė ot′ ȯ mi) [TRACHEOTOMY], *n.* (*Surg.*) The operation of cutting into the windpipe through the cricoid cartilage, trachea, etc.

lascar (lăs′ kȧr, lȧs kar′) [prob. from Pers. *lashkarī*, a soldier, from *lashkar*, army], *n.* An East Indian sailor employed on European vessels.

lascivious (lȧ siv′ i ůs) [late L. *lascīviōsus*, from L. *lascīvia*, from *lascīvus*, sportive, lustful], *a.* Lewd, wanton, lustful; exciting or provoking lust. **lasciviously,** *adv.* **lasciviousness,** *n.*

lash (lăsh) [etym. obscure, perh. from O.F. *lache*, whence *lachier*, var. of *lacier*, to LACE, or imit. in orig. through the verb], *n.* The thong or flexible part of a whip; a whip, a scourge; a stroke with a whip; flogging; an eyelash; a stroke of satire; sarcasm, satire, vituperation; *a leash, a snare. *v.t.* To strike or flog with anything pliant and tough; to whip; to drive with or as with a whip; to beat or dash against; to throw or dash out suddenly or with a jerk; to fasten or bind with a rope or cord; (*fig.*) to assail fiercely with satire. *v.i.* To use a whip; to strike, fling, or kick violently (at, out, etc.); (*fig.*) to fling out satire or sarcasm. **to lash out:** To kick out (as a horse); to be unruly; (*fig.*) to be extravagant. **lasher,** *n.* One who lashes or flogs; the water rushing over a weir; the water below a weir; (*Naut.*) a lashing. **lashing,** *n.* (*Naut.*) A rope or gasket by which anything is secured; a whipping, a flogging; (*pl.*) abundance, a plentiful supply. **lashless,** *a.*

lasket (lăs′ kėt) [perh. from F. *lacet*, LATCHET], *n.* (*Naut.*) A loop of line at the foot of a sail by which the bonnet is attached.

laspring (lă′ spring) [A.-S. *leax*, a salmon], *n.* Young salmon of the first year.

lasque (lăsk), *n.* A thin, flat diamond; an ill-formed or veiny diamond.

lass (lăs) [M.E. *lasce*, cogn. with Icel. *löskr*, weak (cp. Swed. *lösk kona*, a spinster, an unoccupied woman)], *n.* A young woman, a girl; a sweetheart; a servant-maid. **lassie,** *n.*

lassitude (lăs′ i tūd) [F., from L. *lassitūdo*, from *lassus*, weary], *n.* Weariness, lack of energy or animation; languor.

lasso (lăs oo′, lăs′ ō) [O.Sp. *laso* (Sp. *lazo*)], *n.* A rope of untanned hide with a running noose, used in Spanish America and Texas for catching cattle, etc. *v.t.* To catch with a lasso.

last (1) (last) [A.-S. *latost*, *lætest*, superl. of *læt*, LATE], *a.* Coming after all others or at the end; closing, final; pertaining to the end, esp. of life or of the world; conclusive, definitive; utmost, extreme; lowest, meanest; only remaining; furthest from the thoughts; least likely, etc.; next before the present, most recent. *n.* The end, the conclusion; the last moment, hour, day, etc.; death; (*ellipt.*) the last thing done, mentioned, etc., or the last doing, mention, etc. *adv.* On the last time or occasion; for the last time; after all others; *lately. **at last:** In the end, ultimately. **at long last:** In the end, after long delay. **on one's last legs:** In an extreme stage of exhaustion; on the verge of ruin. **to the last:** To the end; till death. **last day:** The Day of Judgment. **last post,** *n.* (*Mil.*) The bugle-call signalling the time of turning-in; a bugle-salute at military funerals. **lastly,** *adv.* At last; finally.

last (2) (last) [A.-S. *lāst*, foot-track, *læste*, fem., shoemaker's last (cp. Dut. *leest*, Icel. *leistr*, G. *leisten*)], *n.* A shaped wooden block on which boots and shoes are fashioned.

last (3) (last) [A.-S. *hlæst*, rel. to *hladan*, to LADE (cp. Dut., G., Swed., and Dan. *last*)], *n.* A certain weight or quantity, varying in different commodities; *a unit in measuring the cargo or burden of a ship; *a load, a burden. **lastage,** *n.* A cargo, a load; ballast; tonnage; *a payment for the right of loading (a vessel) with goods.

last (4) (last) [A.-S. *lǣstan*, from *lāst*, see LAST (2)], *v.i.* To continue in existence, to go on; to hold out, to continue unexhausted or unimpaired, to endure; *to reach, to extend. **n.* Continuance; endurance. **lasting,** *a.* Continuing in existence; enduring, permanent, durable. *n.* *Endurance, continuance, permanence; a durable woollen fabric used in making women's shoes. **lastingly,** *adv.* **lastingness,** *n.*

Latakia (lăt ȧ kē′ ȧ) [a port in Syria], *n.* A superior kind of Turkish tobacco.

latch (lăch) [M.E. *lacche*, from *lacchen*, A.-S. *læccan*, to catch (prob. blended with O.F. *lache*, LACE)], *n.* A fastening for a door, gate, etc., consisting of a bolt and catch; a spring-lock fastening with the shutting of a door and opened with a key. *v.t.* To fasten with a latch; *to catch, to seize. **on the latch:** Fastened by the latch only, not locked. **latch-key,** *n.* Key of latch on front door; (*colloq.*) right to enter or leave a house without accounting for one's movements.

latchet (lăch′ ėt) [O.F. *lachet*, *lacet*], *n.* A string for a shoe or sandal.

late (lāt) [A.-S. *læt* (cp. Dut. *laat*, Icel. *latr*, G. *lass*, cogn. with L. *lassus*, weary)], *a.* Coming after the proper or usual time; slow, tardy, backward, long delayed; far on towards the close or end; far on in any period; far advanced, far on in development; existing at a previous time but now gone or ceased; deceased, departed; lately or recently alive, in office, etc.; recent in date. *adv.* After the proper or usual time; at or till a late hour, season, stage, etc.; (*poet.*) a short time ago, lately, recently; *formerly, of old. **late fee:** Extra postage on letters, etc., posted after the usual time for collection. **of late:** A short time ago, lately, recently; latterly, formerly. **the late:** The recently deceased, resigned, etc.; the recent. **lately,** *adv.* **laten,** *v.t.* and *i.* **lateness,** *n.* **latish,** *a.* and *adv.*

latebra (lăt′ ė brȧ) [L., hiding-place, from *latēre*, to lie hid], *n.* (*Biol.*) The cavity in the food-yolk of a mesoblastic ovum, as a hen's egg.

lateen (lȧ tēn′) [F. *latine*, fem. of *atin*, LATIN], *a.* A term applied to a triangular sail, inclined at an angle of about 45°, used principally in the Mediterranean. *n.* A vessel so rigged.

latent (lā′ tėnt) [L. *latens -ntem*, pres.p. of *latēre*, to lie hid], *a.* Lying hid or concealed; not seen, not apparent; dormant, not active, potential. **latent heat** [HEAT]. **latency, *-ence,** *n.* **latently,** *adv.*

-later [see -LATRY], *comb form*, as *idolater*, etc.

lateral (lăt′ ėr ȧl) [L. *laterālis*, from *latus lateris*, side], *a.* Of, pertaining to, at, from, or towards the side. *n.* A part, member, process, shoot, etc., situated or developing at the side. **laterality** (lăt ėr ăl′ i ti), *n.* Physical one-sidedness. **lateral axis,** *n.* (*Aviat.*) The cross-wise axis of an aircraft. **laterally,** *adv.* **lateri-, latero-,** *comb. form.*

Lateran (lăt′ ėr ȧn) [after the Roman *familia* of the Plautii *Laterani*, on the site of whose palace the church is built], *n.* A cathedral church at Rome, dedicated to St. John the Baptist. **Lateran Council:** Name given to five general councils held in the church of St. John Lateran. **Lateran Treaty:** A treaty concluded between the Italian State and the Papacy (1929) creating the sovereign state of the Vatican City.

laterite (lăt′ ėr īt) [L. *later*, brick, -ITE], *n.* (*Min.*) A red porous rock, composed of silicate of alumina and oxide of iron, found in extensive beds in India and S.-W. Asia. **lateritic** (-it′ ik), *a.*

latescent (lā tes′ ėnt) [L. *latescens -ntem*, pres.p. of *latescere*, incept. of *latēre*, to lie hid], *a.* Becoming latent or obscure. **latescence,** *n.*

latex (lā′ tėks) [L., liquid, fluid], *n.* (*Bot.*) The juice of milky plants. **laticiferous** (lăt i sif′ ėr ŭs), *a.* (*Bot.*) Conveying or producing latex.

lath (lath) [cp. A.-S. *læth*, Dut. *lat*, G. *latte*], *n.* (*pl.* lat*h*z) A thin strip of wood, esp. such as one nailed to rafters to support tiles, or to the studs of partitions to support plastering. *v.t.* To cover or line with laths. **lathing,** *n.* **lath-and-plaster,** *a.* **lath-render, -splitter,** *n.* **lath-work,** *n.* A lining of laths to receive plaster. **lathy,** *a.* Thin as a lath; made of lath or laths.

lathe (1) (lā*th*) [cp. Dan. *lad* in *dreie-lad*, turning wheel (perh. however from A.-S. *hlæd-wheōgl*, lade-wheel, a wheel for drawing water)], *n.* A machine for turning and polishing wood, ivory, metal, etc.; a potter's wheel; the swing-frame or batten of a loom. **lathe-bearer, -carrier, -dog,** *n.* A contrivance for holding the object rotated in a lathe. **lathe-bed,** *n.* The part of the framework of a lathe with a longitudinal slot for moving the head or heads to and fro.

lathe (2) (lā*th*) [A.-S. *læth*, cp. Icel. *lāth*], *n.* A division of a county, comprising several hundreds (the term survives only in Kent).

lather (lă*th*′ ėr la*th*′ ėr) [A.-S. *lēathor* (cp. Icel. *lauthr*, *lōthr*, also Gr. *loutron*, bath, L. *lavare*, to wash)], *n.* Froth or foam made by soap moistened with water, or caused by profuse sweating. *v.i.* To form a lather, as with soap and water; to form lather (of soap); to become covered with lather (of a horse). *v.t.* To cover with lather; (*colloq.*) to thrash, to flog. **lathering,** *n.* A beating. **lathery,** *a.*

lathi (la′ thi) [Hind.], *n.* A long, heavy stick, usu. of bamboo, bound with iron.

laticiferous [LATEX].

laticlave (lă′ ti klāv) [late L. *lāticlāvium*, *lāticlāvus*, (*lātus*, broad, *clāvus*, stripe)], *n.* (*Rom. Ant.*) A broad purple stripe worn on the front of the tunic, as a mark of senatorial rank.

laticostate (lă ti kos′ tȧt) [L. *lātus*, as prec., COSTATE], *a.* (*Zool.*) Having broad ribs. **latidentate** (-den′ tȧt) [DENTATE], *a.* Having broad teeth. **latifoliate, -lious** (-fō′ li ȧt, -ŭs) [FOLIATE], *a.* Broad-leaved.

Latin (lăt′ in) [F., from L. *Latīnus*, from *Latium*, a region in Italy], *a.* Of or pertaining to ancient Latium or ancient Rome, the inhabitants, or their language; of, pertaining to, or expressed in the language of the ancient Romans; pertaining to one or any of the languages derived from this, Romance. *n.* The Latin language, the language of ancient Latium and Rome. **classical Latin:** That of the golden age of Latin literature (*c.* 75 B.C. to A.D. 175). **dog Latin:** Latin of a barbarous or illiterate kind. **late Latin:** That of the period *c.* A.D. 175–600. **low Latin:** Mediæval Latin, esp. of a debased or semi-popular kind. **mediæval Latin:** That of the Middle Ages (*c.* A.D. 600–1500). **modern Latin:** That of later periods. **thieves' Latin:** Cant or jargon employed as a secret language by thieves. **Latin-American,** *n.* and *a.* A citizen of, or pertaining to, those American states where languages sprung from Latin are spoken. **Latin Church:** The Church of the West, the Roman Catholic Church. **Latin cross** [CROSS]. **Latin peoples or races:** Those whose language is of Latin origin, the French, Spanish, Portuguese, and Italians. **Latin Union,** *n.* A monetary alliance established in 1865 between France, Belgium, Italy and Switzerland with a view to maintaining a similar standard of currency. ***Latine*** (lȧ tī′ nē), *adv.* In Latin, as in Latin. **Latinism,** *n.* **Latinist,** *n.* **latinity** (lȧ tin′ i ti), *n.* Quality of Latin style or idiom, or of Latin scholarship. **latinize,** *v.t.* To give a Latin form to (a word, phrase, etc.); to translate into Latin; to bring into conformity with the ideas, customs, forms, etc., of the Romans, the Latin peoples, or the R.-C. Church. *v.i.* To use Latin words, idioms, or phrases. **latinization** (-zā′ shŭn), *n.* **latinizer,** *n.* **Latinless,** *a.*

latipennate (lā ti pen′ ȧt) [L. *lātus*, broad, -PENNATE], *a.* Broad-winged. **latirostral, -trate, -trous** (-ros′-) [ROSTRATE], *a.* Having a wide or broad beak.

latish [LATE].

latissimus (lȧ tis′ i mŭs) [L., superl. of *lātus*, wide], *n.* (*Anat.*) A broad muscle extending from the lower back to the humerus, acting on the arm.

latitude (lăt′ i tūd) [F., from L. *lātitūdo*, from *lātus*, broad], *n.* Breadth, width; extent, scope, comprehensiveness; looseness of application or meaning; absence of strictness, laxity, freedom from rule, restraint, or limits; extent of deviation from a standard or rule; (*Astron.*) the angular distance of a heavenly body from the ecliptic; (*Geog.*) angular distance on a meridian, angular distance of a place north or south of the equator; (*pl.*) regions, climates, esp. with reference to distance from the equator or the tropics. **latitudinal,** *a.* **latitudinary, latitudinous,** *a.* **latitudinarian** (lăt i tū di nâr′ i ȧn), *n.* One who does not attach great importance to dogmas; one of a party in the Church of England (middle of the 17th cent.) who aimed at a comprehensive system which should embrace those points on which Christians are agreed. *a.* Wide in range or scope; not confined within narrow limits; free from prejudice, attaching little importance to speculative opinions; lax; libertine. **latitudinarianism,** *n.*

latria (lăt′ ri ȧ) [late L., see -LATRY], *n.* (*R.-C. Ch.*) That supreme worship which can lawfully be offered to God alone [cp. DULIA, HYPERDULIA].

latrine (lȧ trēn′) [F., from L. *lātrīna* (*lavātrīna*), from *lavāre*, to wash], *n.* A privy, a water-closet, esp. in the army, hospitals, and prisons.

-latry [Gr. *-latreia*, worship (*-later*, Gr. *-latrēs*, worshipper)], *comb. form.* As in *bibliolatry*, *idolatry*, *zoolatry*.

latten (lăt′ ėn) [O.F. *laton* (F. *laiton*), prob. cogn. with *latte*, LATH, from Teut.], *n.* A finer kind of brass, of which the incised plates for sepulchral monuments, crosses, etc., were made; metal in sheets. *a.* Made of latten.

latter (lăt′ ėr) [A.-S. *lætra*, compar. of *læt*, LATE], *a.* Coming or happening after something else; last-mentioned; late, modern, present; lately done or past; later, second, second-mentioned; pertaining to the end of a period, life, the world, etc. ***latter-born,** *a.* Last-born, youngest. **latter-day:** Modern. **Latter-day Saints:** The Fifth Monarchy Men; the Mormons. **latter-end:** Death. **latterly,** *adv.* **latter grass, *lattermath,** *n.* Aftermath.

lattice (lăt′ is) [M.E. *latis*, O.F. *lattis*, from *latte*, see LATTEN], *n.* A structure of laths or strips of metal crossing and forming open work. *a.* Consisting of or furnished with lattice-work. *v.t.* To furnish with a lattice or lattice-work; to intertwine. **lattice bridge:** One built of lattice girders. **lattice bar, beam, frame,** or **girder:** A beam or girder consisting of bars connected together by iron lattice-work. **lattice-window,** *n.* A window consisting of small (usu. diamond-shaped) panes set in strips of lead. **latticed,** *a.* **latticing,** *n.* **lattice-work,** *n.* The arrangement of laths, etc., forming a lattice.

laud (lawd) [L. *laudāre*, from *laus laudis*, praise], *v.t.* To praise, to celebrate, to extol. *n.* Praise; thankful adoration; worship consisting of praise; a song of praise, a hymn; (*pl.*) the psalms immediately following matins. **laudable,** *a.* Praiseworthy, commendable; (*Med.*) healthful, wholesome (of pus or bodily secretions). **laudability** (-bil′ i ti), *n.* **laudably,** *adv.* **laudation** (-dā′ shŭn), *n.* The act of praising; praise. **laudator** (law dā′ tŏr), *n.* **laudative** (law′ dȧ tiv), **laudatory,** *a.* and **n.*

laudanum (lod′ nŭm) [prob. var. of LADANUM or LABDANUM], *n.* Opium prepared in alcohol, tincture of opium; *ladanum.

laugh (laf) [A.-S. *hlehhan* (cp. Dut. and G. *lachen*, Icel. *hlæja*), prob. from an Aryan imit. base *klak-* (cp. Gr. *klōssein*, to cluck)], *v.i.* To express amusement, scorn, or exultation by inarticulate sounds and the convulsive movements of the face and body which are the involuntary effects of such emotions; to deride, jeer, or scoff (at); to be or appear gay, sparkling, or sportive (as natural scenery). *v.t.* To express by laughing; to utter with laughter; to move or influence by ridicule or laughter. *n.* The action of laughing; an act or explosion of laughter; manner of laughing. **to laugh at:** To mock, to deride, to ridicule. **to laugh away:** To dismiss with a laugh; to pass (time) away in jesting. **to laugh down:** To suppress or silence with derisive laughter. **to laugh in one's sleeve:** To be inwardly amused while one's expression remains serious or demure. **to laugh off:** To treat as of trifling moment. **to laugh on the other side** or **corner of the mouth,** or **on the wrong side of one's mouth** or **face:** To be made to feel vexation or disappointment after mirth or satisfaction; to cry. **to laugh out of court:** To treat as not worth considering or listening to. **to laugh over:** To talk about or recall to mind with amusement. **to laugh to scorn:** To treat with the utmost contempt. **laughable,** *a.* Exciting laughter; comical, ridiculous. **laughableness,** *n.* **laughably,** *adv.* **no laughing matter:** Something serious, not a proper subject for levity. **laughing-gas,** *n.* Nitrous oxide, used as an anæsthetic (so-called because when inhaled it produces violent exhilaration). **laughing hyena** [HYENA]. **laughing jackass** [JACKASS, *see* JACK (1)]. **laughing-stock,** *n.* An object of ridicule; a butt. **laughingly,** *adv.* **laughter,** *n.* ***laughterless,** *a.*

launce (1) (lans) [perh. var. of LANCE (1) (cp. LANCELET)], *n.* A sand-eel.

***launce** (2) (lans) [L., LANX], *n.* A balance.

launch (1) (lawnch, lanch) [O.North.F. *lanchier*, var. of *lancier* (F. *lancer*), to LANCE (1)], *v.t.* To throw, to hurl, to propel; to cause (a vessel) to glide into the water; to start or set (a person, etc.) going; to fulminate; *to lance. *v.i.* To be launched (of a ship); to put to sea; to put forth, to enter on a new sphere; to expatiate, to burst (out); *to dart or dash forwards. *n.* The act of launching a boat or ship; the gliding of a vessel into the water; the apparatus for launching a ship.

launch (2) (lawnch, lanch) [Sp. and Port. *lancha*, perh. from Malay *lanchār*, swift], *n.* The largest boat belonging to a man-of-war, usu. sloop-rigged; a large open pleasure-boat propelled by steam, electricity, or internal-combustion engine.

***launa** (lawnd) [LAWN (1)], *n.* An open space in a wood or forest, a glade.

launderette (lawn dė ret′) [as foll.], *n.* An establishment containing washing-machines, etc., for public use at fixed charges.

laundress (lawn′ drės) [(M.E. *lavender*, a launder, O.F. *lavandier*, fem. *-diere*, late L. *lavandārius*, from *lavanda*, things to be washed, from *lavāre*, to wash), -ESS], *n.* A washerwoman, a woman who washes and gets up linen clothing; a woman who looks after chambers in the Inns of Court. **launder,** *n.* (*Mining*) a wooden trough or gutter. *v.t.* To wash and get up (linen). ***launderer,** *n.* **laundry** (lawn′ dri), *n.* A room or establishment where clothes are washed and dressed; the batch of clothes sent to or received from a laundry. ***a** laundress. **laundry-maid,** *n.*

laura (law′ rȧ) [Gr., passage, alley], *n.* (*Eccles. Hist.*) An aggregation of separate cells tenanted by monks, esp. in the desert.

laureate (law′ rė ȧt) [L. *laureātus*, from *laurea*, a laurel-wreath, fem. of *laureus*, adj., from *laurus*], *a.* Crowned or decked with laurel; worthy of laurels, eminent, distinguished, esp. as a poet; consisting or made of laurels. *n.* One crowned with laurel; a Poet Laureate. **v.t.* (-āt) To crown with laurel; to confer a degree on, together with a wreath of laurel. **laureateship,** *n.* ***laureation** (-ā′ shŭn), *n.*

laurel (lor′ ėl, law′ rėl) [M.E. *laurer*, F. *laurier*, prob. through a L. *laurārius*, from *laurus*], *n.* A glossy-leaved evergreen shrub, *Laurus nobilis*, also called bay-tree; (*sing. or pl.*) the foliage of this, esp in the form of a wreath, conferred as a distinction on victorious competitors in the ancient classical games, on heroes, poets, etc.; any other species of the genus *Laurus*; the common laurel or cherry laurel, *Cerasus laurocerasus*. **to look to one's laurels:** To guard against rivalry, to take care not to lose one's pre-eminence. **to reap** or **win laurels:** To acquire distinction or glory. **to rest on one's laurels:** To retire from active life, or to cease from one's efforts. **laurel-bottle,** *n.* A bottle filled with crushed laurel leaves, used by entomologists for killing insects. **laurel water:** (*Med.*) Water distilled from the leaves of the *Cerasus laurocerasus*, used as a sedative or narcotic. **laurelled,** *a.* Crowned with laurel. **laurin,** *n.* (*Chem.*) A crystalline substance contained in the leaves and berries of the laurel or bay-tree.

Laurentian (law ren′ shi ȧn), *a.* (*Geol.*) A term designating a vast series of rocks north of the St Lawrence River, older than the Cambrian.

Laurus (law′ rŭs) [L.], *n.* A genus of plants containing the laurels, bay-tree, etc.

laurustinus (law rŭs tī′ nŭs), **laurestine** (law′ rė tīn) [L. *laurus*, laurel, *tīnus*, a plant, prob. laurus tinus], *n.* An ornamental evergreen shrub, *Viburnum tinus*, with pinkish-white winter flowers and dark-blue berries.

lauwine (law′ in, law′ vin) [G.], *n.* An avalanche.

lava (la′ vȧ) [It., from *lavare*, to wash, see LAVE], *n.* Molten matter flowing in streams from volcanic vents, or solidified by cooling. **lava-cone,** *n.* A volcanic cone formed by successive outflows of lava. **lava-flow, -stream,** *n.* **lava-like,** *a.* and *adv.*

lavabo (lȧ va′ bō) [L., I will wash (*lavāre*, LAVE)], *n.* (*Eccles.*) The washing of the celebrant's hands, in the R.-C. and other churches, after the offertory and before the Eucharist; the towel used in this ceremony, also the basin; a washing-trough or basin, often with running water, in monasteries.

lavation (lȧ vā′ shŭn), *n.* The act of washing.

lavatory (lăv′ ȧ tŏr i) [L. *lavātōrium*, from *lavāre* see foll.], *n.* A room or place for washing; a retiring place in a large house, hotel, or public building with appliances for washing, water-closets, etc., toilet; (*Eccles.*) a piscina, a vessel for washing; (*Mining*) where gold is obtained by washing. *a* Cleansing by washing.

lave (1) (lāv) [prob. from A.-S. *lafian* (cp. Dut. *laven*, G. *laben*), coalescing with foll., or from F. *laver*, L. *lavāre* (cp. Gr. *louein*)], *v.t.* To wash or flow against, as the sea, streams, etc.; to ladle, scoop, or bale (out, up, etc.). *v.i.* To wash oneself, to bathe. **lavement,** *n.*

lave (2) (lāv) [A.-S. *lāf*, remains, remainder], *n.* (*now Sc.*) What is left over, the residue, the rest (of things or of persons).

lavender (lăv′ ėn dėr) [A.-F. *lavendre* (F. *lavande*), med. L. *lavendula*, perh. from L. *lividus*, LIVID (cp. var. *livendula*)], *n.* A sweet-scented flowering shrub, *Lavandula vera*, cultivated for its oil which is used in perfumery; the flower and stalks or the oil used for perfuming linen, etc.; the colour of the flowers, a pale lilac. *v.t.* To perfume, sprinkle, or lay up with lavender. **lavender-cotton,** *n.* Santolin or ground-cypress. **lavender-water,** *n.* A liquid perfume, consisting of essential oil of lavender, ambergris, and spirits of wine.

laver (1) (lā′ vėr) [O.F. *lavur, laveoir*, L. *lavātōrium*, LAVATORY], *n.* *A vessel in which to wash, a piscina; (*Bibl.*) a brazen vessel, containing water for the Jewish priests to wash when they offered sacrifices; a font; (*fig.*) baptism.

laver (2) (lā′ vėr) [L.], *n.* A name given to various marine algæ, esp. *Porphyra laciniata, P. vulgaris*, and other edible species.

laverock (lăv′ ėr ŏk, lā′ vėr ŏk) [var. of LARK (1)].

lavish (lăv′ ish) [orig. a noun, lavishness, from O.F. *lavache, lavasse*, a deluge of words, from *laver*, L. *lavāre*, see LAVE (1)], *a.* Spending or giving with profusion; prodigal, spendthrift, unrestrained; existing or produced in profusion; excessive, superabundant. *v.t.* To expend or bestow profusely; to be excessively free or liberal with, to squander. **lavisher,** *n.* **lavishly,** *adv.* ***lavishment, lavishness,** *n.*

***lavolta** (là vol′ tà) [It. *la*, the, *volta*, turn], *n.* An old Italian dance for two persons, with much high leaping, popular in the sixteenth century.

law (1) (law) [A.-S. *lagu*, from old Icel., cogn. with LAID, LAY (1)], *n.* A rule of conduct imposed by authority or accepted by the community as binding; a system of such rules regulating the intercourse of mankind, of individuals within a State, or of States with one another; the controlling influence of this; the condition of order and stability it secures; the practical application of these rules, esp. by trial in courts of justice, litigation, judicial process; the interpretation or the science of legal principles and enactments, jurisprudence; legal knowledge; the legal profession; rules governing the conduct of a profession, art, association, sport, game, or other activity or department of life; the orderly recurrence of natural phenomena as the uniform results of corresponding conditions; a generalized statement of such conditions and their consequences; (*Theol.*) the will of God as set forth in the Pentateuch, esp. in the Commandments; (*Ethics*) a principle of conduct emanating from the conscience; (*Sport*) a start or an allowance of time given in a hunt or race; (*fig.*) grace, respite. *v.t.* and *i.* (*colloq.*) To go to law, to take legal proceedings. **canon, civil, common, international, martial law** [CANON, CIVIL, COMMON, INTERNATIONAL, MARTIAL]. **to go to law:** To take legal proceedings. **to have the law of:** To take legal proceedings against. **to lay down the law:** To talk or direct in a dictatorial manner. **to take the law into one's own hands:** To try to secure satisfaction or retaliation by force. **law-Latin,** *n.* The debased Latin used in legal documents. **laws of honour:** The rules of conduct in polite society. **laws of motion** [MOTION]. **law-abiding,** *a.* Obedient to the law. **law-abidingness,** *n.* **law-book,** *n.* A treatise on law. **law-binding,** *a.* A binding in plain sheep or calf used largely for law-books. **law-breaker,** *n.* One who violates the law. **law-calf** [LAW-BINDING]. ***law-day,** *n.* A day on which a court sat, esp. a leet or sheriff's court. **law-French,** *n.* Anglo-Norman terms and phrases used in law. **lawgiver,** *n.* One who makes or enacts laws, a legislator. ***lawgiving,** *a.* **law-hand,** *n.* Handwriting used in legal documents. **law-lord,** *n.* A member of the House of Lords qualified to deal with the judicial business of the House. **law-maker,** *n.* A legislator. **law-making,** *n.* **law merchant,** *n.* Mercantile law. **law-monger,** *n.* A pettifogging lawyer. **law officer:** A public legal functionary, esp. the Attorney-General and Solicitor-General. **law stationer,** *n.* One who deals in stationery used in legal work and takes in documents to be copied and engrossed. **law-sheep** [LAW-BINDING]. **lawsuit,** *n.* An action in a court of law. **law-term,** *n.* A word or phrase used in law; one of the periods appointed for the sitting of the Law Courts. **law-writer,** *n.* One who writes on law; one who copies or engrosses legal documents. **lawful,** *a.* Conformable to law; allowed by law; legitimate; valid, rightful; *law-abiding; loyal, faithful. **lawfully,** *adv.* **lawfulness,** *n.* ***lawing,** *n.* Litigation; (*Sc.*) a tavern reckoning. **lawless,** *a.* Regardless of or unrestrained by the law, unbridled, licentious; not subject to or governed by law; illegal; anomalous, irregular; *outlawed. **lawlessly,** *adv.* **lawlessness,** *n.*

***law** (2) (law) [A.-S. *hlǣw*], *n.* (*Sc. and North.*) A hill, esp. a rounded or conical hill of moderate size.

lawine [LAUWINE].

lawk, lawks (lawk, lawks) [corr. of ALACK or LORD], *int.* (*vulg.*) An old exclamation of surprise or wonder. **lawk-a-mussy:** Lord have mercy!

lawn (1) (lawn) [M.E. *laund*, O.F. *launde*, from Celt. (cp. Bret. *lann*, W. *llan*)], *n.* *An open space between woods, a glade in a forest; a grassy space kept smooth and closely mown in a garden or pleasure-ground. **lawn-mower,** *n.* A machine for mowing a lawn. **lawn-sprinkler,** *n.* A machine with a perforated revolving collar for watering lawns. **lawn-tennis,** *n.* A game somewhat resembling tennis, orig. played on a lawn but now frequently on a hard court. **lawny** (1), *a.*

lawn (2) (lawn) [O.F. *Lan*, now *Laon*, a town N.-W. of Rheims], *n.* A cotton or linen fabric, finer than cambric, used for the sleeves of an Anglican bishop's rochet; (*fig.*) the dignity of a bishop. **lawny** (2), *a.*

lawsuit [LAW (1)].

lawyer (law′ yėr), *n.* One who practises law, esp. an attorney or solicitor; one versed in the law; (*N.T.*) a professional expounder of the Mosaic law; (*Am.*) the black-necked stilt, *Himantopus nigricollis*; the turbot, also the mud-fish. **lawyer-like, lawyerly,** *a.* **lawyership,** *n.*

lax (lăks) [L. *laxus*, cogn. with *languēre*, to LANGUISH], *a.* Slack, loose, not tight, firm, or compact; porous; (*fig.*) not exact, not strict; negligent, careless; equivocal, ambiguous, vague; relaxed in the bowels. ***laxation** (lăk sā′ shŭn), *n.* ***laxist,** *n.* One of a school of R.-C. theologians, who held that merely probable opinions might be followed in cases of doubt, esp. in ethical matters. **laxity, laxness,** *n.* **laxly,** *adv.*

laxative (lăks′ à tĭv), *a.* Opening or loosening the bowels. *n.* A laxative medicine.

lay (1) (lā) [A.-S. *lecgan* (cp. Dut. *leggen*, Icel. *leggja*, G. *legen*), casual of LIE (2)], *v.t.* (*past & p.p.* **laid**) To cause to lie; to place in a prostrate or recumbent position; to bury; to drop (as eggs); to put down, to place, to deposit; to stake, to wager; to set, to apply; to dispose regularly, to put in proper position; to spread on a surface; to beat down, to prostrate; to overthrow; to cause to settle (as dust); to cause to be still, to allay, to calm; to exorcize; to put or bring into a certain state or position; to put forward, to present; *to charge, to impute; to impose, to enjoin, to inflict; to bring down (a weapon, blows, etc., on); to think out, to devise, to plan, to prepare; (*Mil.*) to point (a gun); (*Hort.*) to propagate by layers; (*Lit.*) to locate (a scene, story, etc.). *v.i.* To drop or deposit eggs; (*vulg. and Naut.*) to lie; to make a bet. *n.* The way, direction, or position in which a region or object is situated; (*Naut.*) the direction the strands of a rope are twisted; (*slang*) particular business, occupation, job, etc. **in lay:** (Of hens) laying eggs. **to lay a cable:** To bury or sink an electric cable; to twist the strands of a cable. **to lay about one:** To hit out on all sides; to fight vigorously. ***to lay apart:** To put away. **to lay aside:** To reject, to abandon, to put away. **to lay bare:** To reveal; to strip. **to lay before:** To exhibit to; to bring to the notice of.

lay-by, *n.* A widening of a road to enable vehicles to stop without holding up traffic. **to lay by:** To save; to reserve for a future occasion. **to lay by the heels** [HEEL (1)]. **to lay down:** To put down; to resign; to draft, to delineate (as the lines of a ship); to declare, to affirm, to assert; to formulate, to deposit; to pay; to wager; to sacrifice; to put down the main structural parts of; to store (wine, etc.); to stipulate. **to lay down the law** [LAW (1)]. **to lay fast:** To seize and keep fast, to prevent from escaping. **to lay for:** (*colloq.*) To lie in wait for. **to lay hands on** [HAND (1)]. **to lay heads together:** To deliberate, to confer. **to lay hold of** or **on:** To seize, to catch; to grasp; (*fig.*) to utilize, to make a pretext of. **to lay in:** To store, to stock oneself with. **to lay into:** (*slang*) To belabour. **to lay off:** To suspend from employment for a period on account of slack work, etc. **to lay it on thick:** (*slang*) To speak or flatter extravagantly; to charge exorbitantly. **to lay on:** To impose, to inflict; to deal (blows, etc.); to supply (as water or gas); to prepare or put into the machine (as paper) for printing. **to lay open:** To cut so as to expose the interior of; to expose, to reveal; to explain. **lay-out,** *n.* The make-up of newspaper advertisement, etc. **to lay out:** To arrange according to plan; to spread out; to expound, to explain; to expend; to dress in grave-clothes and dispose for burial; (*slang*) to kill; to render unconscious; to busy or exert (oneself) to do something. **to lay over:** To spread over, to overlay. **to lay siege to:** To besiege; to importune. **to lay the land:** (*Naut.*) To cause the land to sink below the horizon by sailing away from it. **to lay to:** To apply vigorously; (*Naut.*) to check the motion of (a ship). **to lay together:** To place side by side; to add together. **to lay to heart:** To feel strongly or deeply; to take into serious consideration. **to lay to sleep** or **rest:** To bury. **to lay under:** To subject to. **to lay up:** To store, to treasure, to save; to confine to one's bed or room (of illness); to dismantle and place in dock. **to lay waste:** To ravage, to devastate. **lay-days,** *n.pl.* (*Comm.*) A certain number of days allowed to a charter-party for loading or unloading. **laying,** *n.* The act or period of setting, placing, or depositing; the act or period of depositing eggs; the eggs laid; the twisting of yarns into a strand or of strands into a rope. **laying on of hands:** Sacramental imposition of hands for healing or other purposes.

lay (2) (lā) [F. *lai*, L. *lāicus*, Gr. *laikos*, from *laos*, the people], *a.* Pertaining to the people as distinct from the clergy; non-professional, esp. with reference to the legal or the medical profession; (*Cards*) other than trumps. **lay brother** or **sister:** A brother or sister in a monastery, under vows and wearing the habit of the order, engaged chiefly in manual labour and exempt from other duties. **lay clerk:** A singing man in a cathedral or collegiate church who leads the responses; a parish clerk. **lay communion:** Communicating of the laity at the Eucharist; membership of the church as a layman. **lay deacon:** One in deacon's orders engaged in secular employment. **lay elder:** A ruling elder in the Presbyterian Church. **lay lord:** A member of the House of Lords not a law-lord. **layman,** *n.* One of the people, as distinguished from the clergy; a non-professional, one not an expert, esp. in reference to law and medicine. **lay reader:** A layman authorized to conduct certain religious services. **lay sister** [LAY BROTHER].

lay (3) (lā) [O.F. *lai*, prob. from O.H.G. *leth*, *leich* (not rel. to G. *lied*)], *n.* A lyric song or ballad; a short narrative poem for singing or recitation; (*fig.*) song, singing (of birds, etc.).

lay (4), *past* [LIE (2)].

lay (5) [LEY].

layer (lā' ėr), *n.* One who or that which lays; a thickness of anything spread out (usu. one of several), a stratum, a bed; a shoot laid a part of its length on or beneath the surface of the ground in order that it may take root; an artificial oyster-bed; a tanning-pit. *v.t.* To propagate by layers. *v.i.* To be laid flat by weather, weak growth, etc. (of growing corn). **layer-on,** *n.* One who feeds down sheets into a printing-machine. **layer-out,** *n.* One who lays out a corpse; one who expends money; a steward. **layer-stool,** *n.* The stock from which a layer is rooted. **layered,** *a.* **layered map:** A map in which the areas between contours are marked by distinctive colouring. **layering,** *n.* (*Agric.*) A method of propagation in which shoots and stems are pegged to the ground and left until they root, when they can be separated.

layette (lā et') [F., dim. of O.F. *laye* (cp. O.H.G. *lada*)], *n.* The outfit for a new-born infant.

lay figure (lā' fig' ůr) [*lay*, from obs. *layman*, Dut. *leeman*, joint-man (*lid*, joint, *lith*, limb, MAN), FIGURE], *n.* A jointed figure of the human body (usu. of wood), used by artists for hanging drapery on, etc.; (*fig.*) a puppet, a nonentity; an unreal character in a story, etc.

laying [LAY (1)].

layman [LAY (2)].

laystall (lā' stawl), *n.* A heap of dung or refuse; a place where dung or refuse is kept; a place where milch cows are kept.

lazar (lăz' ȧr) [F. *lazare*, from name *Lazarus* (Luke xvi. 20)], *n.* A poor person infected with a loathsome disease, esp. a leper. **lazar-house,** *n.* A lazaretto. **Lazarists, Lazarites,** *n.pl.* The popular name for the Congregation of Priests of the Mission, founded by St. Vincent de Paul in 1624. **Lazarus,** *n.* A lazar. **lazarus-house,** *n.*

lazaretto, lazaret (lăz ȧ ret ō, -ret') [F. *lazaret*, It. *lazzaretto*, as prec.], *n.* A hospital (chiefly abroad) for persons suffering from some contagious disease; a ship or other place of quarantine; a store-room for provisions in large merchant-vessels.

lazarone [LAZZARONE].

laze (lāz), *v.i.* To be lazy; to live in idleness. *v.t.* To waste or spend in idleness. *n.* Idleness; a time or spell of idleness.

lazuli [LAPIS LAZULI].

lazulite (lăz' ū līt) [med. L. *lazulum*, LAPIS LAZULI, -ITE], *n.* (*Min.*) An azure-blue to pale greenish-blue mineral, composed of phosphate of aluminium and magnesium.

lazy (lā' zi) (etym. doubtful), *a.* Idle, indolent, slothful, disinclined for labour or exertion; disposing to idleness or sloth. **lazy-bed,** *n.* A bed in which seed potatoes are placed on the surface of the ground and covered with soil from trenches dug on each side. **lazy-bones,** *n.* A lazy fellow, an idler. **lazy daisy,** *n.* A type of embroidery stitch. **lazy-pinion,** *n.* A pinion transmitting motion in the manner of an idle-wheel. **lazy-tongs,** *n.pl.* Tongs consisting of levers, in pairs, crossing one another, and turning on a pin like scissors, for picking up distant objects. **lazily,** *adv.* **laziness,** *n.*

lazzarone (lăts ȧ rō' nā) [It., from *lazzaro*, LAZAR], *n.* (*pl.* ***-ni***, -nē) One of the poorer class of Neapolitans, who idle about, depending for their living upon begging.

-le [M.E. *-el*, *-ele*, *-le*, A.-S. *-el*, *-ela* (in nouns), *-ol*, *-ul*, *-el* (in adjectives)], *suf.* Forming diminutives of nouns, as *bramble*, *kittle*; frequentatives or diminutives of verbs, as *crumple*, *dabble*, *drizzle*, *dwindle*, *grapple*, *nestle*, *nibble*, *waddle*; nouns denoting an instrument or agent, as *beadle*, *bridle*, *girdle*, *needle*; adjectives, as *brittle*, *idle*, *mickle*.

lea (1) (lē) [A.-S. *lēah* (cp. O.H.G. *lôh*, also L. *lūcus*, grove, glade)], *n.* A meadow; grassland; open country.

lea (2) (lē, lā) [A.-S. *lǽge* in *lǽghrycg*, lea-rig (*lǽg-*, *liegan*, to LIE (2))], *n.* Land left untilled, fallow land, grass-land. *a.* Fallow, unploughed.

lea (3) (lē) [perh. from F. *lier*, L. *ligāre*, to tie], *n.* A measure of yarn (varying from 80 to 300 yds. in different localities).

leach (1) (lēch) [prob. from A.-S. *leccan*, to water], *v.t.* To wash or wet by letting liquid percolate through; to strain or drain (liquid) from some material (*usu.* out or away). *v.i.* To drain out (of liquid in any material). *n.* A tub, vat, or other vessel in which ashes are leached; a quantity of wood-ashes through which water passes, thus imbibing the alkali; the solution obtained by leaching; (*Tanning*) a pot for mixing tan-liquor in. **leachy,** *a.* **leach-tub,** *n.*

leach (2) [LEECH (1)].

lead (1) (led) [A.-S. *lēad* (cp. Dut. *lood,* Dan. *lod,* G. *lot*)], *n.* A soft malleable and ductile, bluish-grey, heavy metal; (*Print.*) a thin plate of type-metal used to separate lines; blacklead, plumbago, or graphite, used in lead-pencils; (*pl.*) strips of lead used for covering a roof; a roof, esp. a flat roof, or part of a roof, covered with lead; (*Naut.*) a plummet, usu. consisting of a mass of lead, used for sounding. *a.* Pertaining to or containing lead; consisting more or less of lead; the metal strips or cames holding the glass in diamond-paned windows. *v.t.* To cover, fasten, weight, frame, or fit with lead; (*Print.*) to space out (as lines of type) by inserting leads. **to swing the lead:** (*colloq.*) To malinger. **lead-arming,** *n.* (*Naut.*) A piece of tallow pressed into the lower part of the sounding-lead, to ascertain the nature of the sea-bottom. **lead-comb,** *n.* A comb made of lead for darkening the hair. **lead-glance,** *n.* Galena or lead-ore. **lead-line,** *n.* (*Naut.*) A sounding-line. **lead-mill,** *n.* A mill for grinding white lead; a circular disk of lead used with an abrading powder by lapidaries for roughing and grinding. **lead-pencil,** *n.* A pencil consisting of a slip of graphite or blacklead enclosed in wood. **lead-poisoning,** *n.* (*Path.*) A morbid condition caused by the prolonged absorption of lead into the system. **leadsman,** *n.* (*Naut.*) The sailor who heaves the lead in sounding. **lead-work,** *n.* Plumber's or glazier's work. **lead-works,** *n.* A place for smelting lead. **blacklead** [BLACK]. **red lead:** Red oxide of lead, used chiefly as a pigment and as a cement in plumbing, minium. **white lead:** A pigment made of lead carbonate and lead oxide, ceruse. **leaded,** *a.* Set in or fitted with lead; separated by leads, as lines of printing. **leaden,** *a.* Made of lead; of the colour of lead, dark; heavy as lead; (*fig.*) heavy, slow, burdensome; inert, indisposed to action or exertion. ***leaden-hearted,** *a.* Destitute of feeling. ***leaden-heeled, *-paced, *-stepping,** *a.* Moving slowly; slow, tardy. **leady,** *a.*

lead (2) (lēd) [A.-S. *lǣdant,* causal of *līthan,* to go (cp. Dut. *leiden,* G. *leitan,* to lead, O.H.G. *līdan,* to go)], *v.t.* (*past & p.p.* led). To conduct, to guide by the hand or by showing the way; to direct the movements of; to be in command of; to direct or induce by persuasion, instruction, or advice; to keep in front of, to take the first place among; to be at the head of, to direct by example; to point out, to indicate, esp. by going in advance; to pass or spend (time, etc.); to cause to spend or pass; to draw or drag after one; (*Cards*) to begin a round at cards with; to transport (as hay, etc.) in a cart. *v.i.* To act as conductor or guide; to go in advance; to be the commander, head, or foremost person in any undertaking, etc.; (*Cards*) to be the first player, to play in a specified way; to go towards, to extend, to reach (to); to tend (to) as a result. *n.* Guidance, direction, esp. by going in front; the first place, precedence, command, leadership; the leading rôle; an example; a way, passage, channel, esp. through ice; an artificial water-course, esp. a mill-race; a cord for leading a dog; (*Elec.*) a principal conductor for distribution of current in an electrical installation; (*Cards*) the first play or the right to this; (*Naut.*) the direction in which a rope runs. **to lead astray:** To lead into error. **to lead away:** To cause to follow unthinkingly. **to lead captive:** To take captive. **to lead off:** To make a start. **lead-in,** *n.* (*Radio.*) The wire or other type of conductor which links a portion of an apparatus outside with a portion inside. **to lead on:** To entice, to draw further towards some end. **to lead the way:** To go first so as to point the way; to take the precedence. **to lead up to:** To conduct conversation towards (some particular subject); to conduct towards; to pave the way for; (*Cards*) to play so as to induce an opponent to play (a certain card). **leadable,** *a.* **led captain:** A hanger-on, a parasite, a toady. **led horse:** A spare horse led by a groom; a sumpter-horse or pack-horse.

leaden [LEAD (1)].

leader (lē' dėr), *n.* One who or that which leads; a guide, a conductor; a chief, a commander; the leading counsel in a case; the senior counsel of a circuit; a chief editorial article (usu. in large type) in a newspaper; the foremost horse, or one of the foremost horses abreast, in a team; (*Print.*) a row of dots to lead the eye across a page or column; (*Mining*) a small vein of ore, usually leading to a lode; the terminal bud or shoot at the apex of a stem or branch. **leaderette,** *n.* A short editorial article. **leaderless,** *a.* **leadership,** *n.*

leading (le' ding), *a.* Guiding, conducting; alluring, enticing; chief, principal. *n.* The action of the verb TO LEAD; guidance, influence. **leading article:** A leader in a newspaper; an article sold at a low price to attract customers. **leading business:** The chief rôle, in a play, etc. **leading case:** (*Law*) A case that forms a precedent for the decision of others. **leading edge,** *n.* (*Aviat.*) The foremost edge of the wing. **leading lady, man,** etc.: Persons taking the chief rôle in a play. **leading motive** [LEIT-MOTIV]. **leading question:** A question (esp. in cross-examination) that suggests a certain answer. **leading-rein,** *n.* A rein for leading a horse by. **leading-staff,** *n.* A staff for leading a bull by the ring in his nose; a commander's truncheon. **leading-strings,** *n.pl.* Strings by which children were formerly supported when learning to walk. **to be in leading-strings:** To be in a state of dependence on others. ***leadingly,** *adv.*

leaf (lēf) [A.-S. *lēaf* (cp. Dut., *loof* Icel. *lauf,* G. *laub*)], *n.* (*pl.* **leaves**) One of the expanded (usually lateral) organs of plants which aid in the functions of assimilation of food-materials, transpiration, and absorption of carbonic-acid gas from the atmosphere; (*fig.*) anything resembling this; a folded sheet of paper in a book or manuscript, usu. comprising two pages; a thin sheet of metal or other material; a valved or hinged member of a bridge, table, door, shutter, screen, etc.; a tooth of a gear-pinion; (*incorr.*) a petal. *v.i.* To shoot out or produce leaves or foliage. **to take a leaf out of one's book:** To follow the example of, to imitate. **to turn over a new leaf:** To change one's mode of life or conduct for the better. **leaf-brass,** *n.* Dutch metal. **leaf-bridge,** *n.* A bridge with a rising leaf or leaves swinging vertically on hinges. **leaf-bud,** *n.* A bud developing into a leaf. **leaf-crowned,** *a.* **leaf-fat, leaf-lard,** *n.* Fat lying in layers round the kidneys of a pig or other animal. **leaf-louse,** *n.* An aphis. **leaf-metal,** *n.* Metal, esp. silver or gold, beaten into thin sheets, and used for decoration, etc. **leaf-mould,** *n.* Decayed leaves reduced to mould and used as compost. **leaf-roll,** *n.* A form of potato virus. **leaf-spring,** *n.* A spring consisting of several broad, flat pieces of metal, used for springing vehicles. **leaf-stalk,** *n.* A petiole supporting a leaf. **leaf-work,** *n.* Decorative work embodying designs from leaves. **leafage,** *n.* **leafed,** *a.* (*usu. in comb.,* as *thick-leafed*). **leafless,** *a.* **leaflessness,** *n.* **leaflet,** *n.* A small leaf of paper, etc.; a one-page handbill, circular, etc.; (*Bot.*) one of the primary divisions of a compound leaf. **leafy,** *a.* **leafiness,** *n.*

league (1) (lēg) [F. *ligue,* It. *liga,* L. *ligāre,* to tie, to bind], *n.* A combination or union for mutual help or protection or the pursuit of common interests; a treaty or compact of alliance or confederation. *v.i.* To join in a league, to confederate. *v.t.* To combine together (with). **Football League:** A union of Association clubs for playing matches against each other. **league match,** *n.* (*Football*) A match between clubs of the same league. **League of Nations,** *n.* An international organization formed in 1920 pledged to co-operate in securing peace and the rigorous observance of treaties by its member states. It came to an end in 1946 when the United Nations Organization was founded. **League of Nations Union,** *n.* Organized association of supporters of the League of Nations. **leaguer** (1), *n.* A party to a league.

league (2) (lēg) [perh. through Prov. *legua*, from late L. *leuga*, prob. from Gaulish], *n.* A measure of length, varying in different countries. The English land league is usu. 3 statute miles, and the nautical league 3 nautical or nearly 3½ statute miles.

***leaguer** (2) (lē′ gėr) [Dut. *leger*, cp. LAIR (1), LAAGER], *n.* A siege; the camp of a besieging army. *v.t.* To beleaguer.

leak (lēk) [cp. Icel. *leka*, Dut. *lekken*, G. *lecken*, also A.-S. *leccan*, to wet], *v.i.* To let liquid, gas, etc., pass in or out through a hole, crevice, or fissure; to ooze, as water, through a hole or fissure; *to urinate. *n.* A crevice or hole which admits water or other fluid; the oozing of water or other fluid through such crevice. **a.* Leaky. **to leak out:** To become gradually known or public, esp. in an underhand manner. **to spring a leak:** (*Naut.*) To open or crack so as to admit water. **leakage,** *n.* A leak; the quantity that escapes by a leak; (*Comm.*) an allowance at a certain rate per cent. for loss by leaking, etc.; the divulgence of confidential information. **leaky,** *a.* **leakiness,** *n.*

leal (lēl) [A.-F., from O.F. *leel*, as LOYAL], *a.* (*Sc.*) Loyal, true.

***leam** (lēm) [A.-S. *lēoma* (cp. Icel. *liome*, also L. *lūmen*), cogn. with *lēoht*, LIGHT], *n.* A gleam, a light, a glow; brightness. *v.i.* To shine.

lean (1) (lēn) [A.-S. *hlinian*, *hleonian*, whence *hlǣnan*, to cause to lean (cogn. with L. *inclīnāre*, Gr. *klinein*)], *v.i.* (*past & p.p.* **leaned** or **leant,** lent) To incline one's body from an erect attitude; to incline one's body so as to rest (against or upon); to deviate from a straight or perpendicular line or direction; (*fig.*) to depend (upon) as for support; to have a tendency or propensity (to or towards). *v.t.* To cause to incline; to support, to rest (upon or against). *n.* A leaning, inclination, slope, or deviation. **lean-to,** *a.* Leaning against or supported by a wall. *n.* A building the rafters of which are supported by another building, a penthouse. **leaning,** *n.* Inclination, partiality, propensity (towards or to).

lean (2) (lēn) [A.-S. *hlǣne*, etym. doubtful], *a.* Thin, lank; not fat, consisting of muscular tissue (of meat); wanting in plumpness; (*fig.*) meagre, poor; unproductive, sterile; unprofitable, unremunerative. *n.* The part of meat that consists of muscular tissue without fat; (*Print.*) work or copy unremunerative to the compositor. **lean-face,** *a.* (*Print.*) Applied to type with unusually thin face-lines. ***lean-witted,** *a.* Silly, stupid, foolish. **leanly,** *adv.* **leanness,** *n.* ***leany,** *a.*

leap (lēp) [A.-S. *hlēapan* (cp. Dut. *loopen*, Icel. *hlaupa*, G. *laufen*, to run)], *v.i.* (*past & p.p.* **leapt** (lept), **leaped** (lēpd) To jump, to spring upward or forward; to rush, to fly, to dart; (*fig.*) to pass over an interval, esp. in music. *v.t.* To jump or spring over or across; to cause to jump or spring; (*Mus.*) to pass from one note to another by an interval which is greater than a degree of the scale; *to copulate with (of male animals). *n.* The act of leaping; a jump, a spring, a bound; the space passed over by leaping; a collection of leopards; *copulation (of the lower mammals); (*fig.*) a sudden transition. **a leap in the dark:** A hazardous step or action, one whose consequences cannot be foreseen. **by leaps and bounds** [BOUND (1)]. **leap-day,** *n.* The 29th February. **leap-frog,** *n.* (*Mil.*) The deploying of units in advance of each other in turns; a game in which one stoops down and another vaults over him. *v.t.* and *i.* To vault in this way. **leap year:** An intercalary year of 366 days, which adds one day to February, after which every fixed festival leaps over, as it were, one week-day more than an ordinary year (leap year is every year the number of which is a multiple of four, except those divisible by 100 and not by 400). **leaper,** *n.* **leaping-fish,** *n.* A small East Indian fish, *Salarias tridactylus*, which goes on land and moves along by leaps. **leapingly,** *adv.*

learn (lĕrn) [A.-S. *leornian* (cp. G. *lernen*), cogn. with LORE, cp. A.-S. *lǣran*, to teach, to LERE], *v.t.* (*past & p.p.* **learnt** (lĕrnt), **learned** (lĕrnd)) To acquire knowledge of or skill in by study, experience, or instruction; to fix in the memory; to find out, to be informed of, to ascertain; *to teach, to tell. *v.i.* To acquire knowledge; to receive instruction. **learnable,** *a.* **learned** (2) (lĕr′ ned), *a.* Having acquired learning by study; skilled, skilful (in); erudite; characterized by great learning or scholarship; (of words, etc.) introduced or chiefly used by learned people. **learnedly,** *adv.* **learnedness,** *n.* **learner,** *n.* ***learner-like,** *a.* **learning,** *n.* The act of learning; knowledge (esp. of literature, philology, and history) acquired by study; erudition; scholarship.

lease (1) (lēs) [A.-F. *lesser* (F. *laisser*), L. *laxāre*, to loose, from *laxus*, LAX], *v.t* To grant or to take or hold (land or tenements) on lease, (*Am.* to let). *n.* A letting of lands or tenements, usu. for a fixed rent, for a specified period; the written contract for or the term of such letting. **a new lease of life:** An anticipated spell of life or enjoyment after recovery from illness or release from trouble. **lease and release,** *n.* (*Law*) Obsolete legal device for the transfer of real estate. **leasehold,** *n.* Tenure by lease; property held by lease. *a.* Held thus. **leaseholder,** *n.* **leasable,** *a.*

***lease** (2) (lēz) [A.-S. *lesan*, to gather], *v.i.* To glean.

lease (3) (lēs) [var. of foll.], *n.* (*Weaving*) The leash, or the crossing of the warp-threads in the loom.

leash (lēsh) [O.F. *lesse* (F. *laisse*), late L. *laxa*, orig. fem. of *laxus*, LAX], *n.* A thong by which a hound or a hawk is held; (*Sport*) a brace and a half, three; a band with which anything is tied; (*Weaving*) one of the eyed cords for the loom-thread, stretched between the parallel laths forming the heddle. *v.t.* To bind, hold, or fasten by a leash.

***leasing** (lē′ zing) [A.-S. *lēasung*, from *lēasian*, to lie, from *lēas*, false, destitute of, -LESS], *n.* A lie; falsehood.

leasow (lē′ sō) [A.-S. *lǣswe*, oblique case of *lǣs*], *n.* (*now chiefly Sc.*) Pasture, meadowland. *v.t.* and *i.* To pasture.

least (lēst) [A.-S. *lǣst*, *lǣsast*, superl. of *lǣs*, LESS], *a.* Smallest; less than all others in size, amount, degree, quantity, value, importance, etc. *adv.* In the smallest or slightest degree. *n.* The smallest amount, degree, etc. **at least, at the least:** At or in the lowest degree; at any rate. **in the least:** In the slightest degree, at all. **leastways** (*vulg. or prov.*), ***leastwise,** *adv.* At least; or rather.

leat (lēt) [A.-S. *gelǣt*, cross-roads, *wæter-gelǣt*, water-conduit, from *lǣtan*, see LET (1)], *n.* A water-course conveying water to a mill, etc.

leather (le*th*′ ėr) [A.-S. *lether* (cp. Dut. and G. *leder*, Icel. *lethr*)], *n.* The tanned or dressed skin or hide of an animal; dressed hides collectively; an article or part made of leather (*often in comb.*, as *stirrup-leather*); (*pl.*) a pair of breeches or leggings; (*slang*) a cricket- or foot-ball; (*facet.*) one's skin; (*fig.*) power of resistance, impenetrability to ideas, sympathy, etc. *v.t.* To cover or furnish with leather; to thrash, as with a thong of leather. **fair leather:** Leather with its natural colour. **leather and prunella:** Anything worthless, a matter of no account (from a misinterpretation of Pope's *Essay on Man*, iv. 204). **patent** or **japanned leather:** Leather with a polished enamel surface. **leather-back,** *n.* A leathery, soft-shelled turtle. **leather-backed,** *a.* (*Bookbinding*) Having the back covered with leather extending only far enough on each side to cover the hinges. **leather-carp,** *n.* A variety of the common carp in which almost all trace of scales is lost. **leather-cloth,** *n.* A fabric covered with a waterproof composition to resemble leather. **leather-coat,** *n.* An apple with a tough skin, esp. the golden russet. **leather-dresser,** *n.* One whose occupation is to dress leather or hides. **leather-head,** *n.* A blockhead. **leather-jacket,** *n.* An Australian tree, *Eucalyptus resinifera*; the larva of a crane-fly; one of various fishes. **leather-neck,** *n.* (*Austral.*) A handy man. **leather-wood,** *n.* A North American shrub, *Dirca palustris*, the tough bark of which was used by the Indians for thongs. **leatherette** (leth ėr et'), *n.* A kind of imitation leather. **leathern,** *a.* **leathery,** *a.*

leave (1) (lēv) [A.-S. *lēaf*, cogn. with *lēof*, pleasing, LIEF], *n.* Liberty or permission; permission to be absent from duty; the period of this; the act of departing, a formal parting from friends, hence a farewell, an adieu. **on leave:** Absent from duty by permission. **to take leave:** To say good-bye; to depart. **leave-taking,** *n.* A parting; a farewell.

leave (2) (lēv) [A.-S. *lǣfan* (cp. Icel. *leifa*, Goth. *-laibjan*), cogn. with *lāf*, LAVE (2)], *v.t.* (*past & p.p.* **left** (2)) To allow to remain, to go without taking; to bequeath, to part from at death; to refrain from removing, consuming, or interfering with; to depart from, to quit; to withdraw from, to forsake, to abandon; to cease to live or work at or belong to; to desist from, to cease, to discontinue; to commit, to entrust, to refer for consideration, approval, etc. *v.i.* To depart, to go away; to cease, to discontinue. **french leave** [FRENCH]. **to leave alone:** Not to interfere with; to have no dealings with. **to leave behind:** To go away without; to outstrip; to leave as a record, mark, consequence, etc. **to leave off:** To desist from, to discontinue; to cease to wear. **to leave out:** To omit. **to leave over:** To leave for future consideration, etc. **leaving,** *n.* The act of departing; (*pl.*) residue, remnant, refuse, offal. **leaving-shop,** *n.* (*slang*) An unlicensed pawn-shop.

leave (3) (lēv) [LEAF], *v.i.* To come into leaf. **leaved,** *a.* Leafed (*usu. in comb.*, as *thick-leaved*).

leaven (lev' ėn) [F. *levain*, L. *levāmen*, from *levāre*, to live], *n.* Fermenting dough for mixing with other dough in order to cause fermentation and make it lighter; any substance used for this purpose; (*fig.*) any influence tending to cause a general change (esp. for the worse). *v.t.* To raise and make light with leaven; (*fig.*) to imbue, to taint, to corrupt. **leavening,** *n.* Leaven. ***leavenous,** *a.*

leaves [LEAF], ***leavy** [LEAFY].

Lebanese (leb à nēz'), *a.* Pertaining to the independent Mediterranean state of Lebanon.

lebensraum (lā' bėns roum) [G., living-space], *n.* Space necessary for the existence of a country's expanding population.

lecher (lech' ėr) [O.F. *lecheor*, from *lechier*, to lick, to live in gluttony, O.H.G. *leccôn*, to LICK], *n.* A man addicted to lewdness, a fornicator. **v.i.* To practise lewdness. **lecherous,** *a.* **lecherously,** *adv.* ***lecherousness, lechery,** *n.*

lecithin (les' i thin) [Gr. *lekithos*, yolk of an egg], *n.* (*Chem.*) A nitrogenous fatty substance contained in the cellular tissue of animal and vegetable bodies.

Leclanché Cell (le klăn' shā sel), *n.* (*Elec.*) A primary cell consisting of a carbon cathode covered with manganese dioxide, all in a porous pot, and a zinc anode dipping into ammonium chloride solution.

lectern (lek' tĕrn) [O.F. *letrun*, late L. *lectrum*, from *lect-*, p.p. stem of *legere*, to read], *n.* A reading-desk from which parts of divine service, esp. the lessons, are said or sung; (*Sc.*) the precentor's desk.

lection (lek' shŭn) [O.F., from L. *lectiōnem*, nom. as prec.], *n.* A reading or variation in a text; a portion of Scripture to be read in divine service, a lesson. **lectionary,** *n.* A collection of passages of Scripture to be read in public service. **lector,** *n.* A cleric in minor orders whose duty it was to read the lessons; a reader, esp. in a German University.

lectual (lek' tū ăl) [late L. *lectuālis*, from *lectus*, bed], *a.* (*Path.*) That confines to bed.

lecture (lek' chŭr) [F., from late Latin *lectūra*, from *lectus*, p.p. of *legere*, to read], *n.* A formal expository or instructive discourse on any subject, before an audience or a class; (*fig.*) a reproof, a reprimand. *v.i.* To deliver a lecture or lectures; to give instruction by means of lectures. *v.t.* To instruct by lectures; (*fig.*) to reprimand. **to read one a lecture:** To reprimand one. **lecturer,** *n.* **lectureship,** *n.*

lecythus (les' i thŭs) [late L. *lēcythus*, Gr. *lēkuthos*], *n.* (*pl.* **-thi,** -thī) (*Gr. Ant.*) A narrow-necked vase or flask for oil, unguents, etc.

led [LEAD (2)].

ledge (lej) [prob. from M.E. *leggen*, to LAY (1)], *n.* A shelf or shelf-like projection; a shelf-like ridge or outcrop of rock; (*Mining*) a metal-bearing stratum of rock. **ledged,** *a.* **ledgeless,** *a.* **ledgy,** *a.*

ledger (lej' ėr) [prob. from M.E. *leggen*, as prec., after M.Dut. *ligger* (Dut. *legger*), that which lies in a place], *n.* The principal book in a set of account-books, in which is entered a record of all trade transactions, so as to show on one side all the debits and on the other all the credits; (*Arch.*) a large flat stone as for an altar-table or grave; (*Build.*) a horizontal pole parallel to the walls in scaffolding, to support the putlogs; (*Angling*) a ledger-line or tackle; *a resident ambassador. **a.* Resident (as an ambassador). *v.i.* To fish with a ledger-tackle. **ledger-bait,** *n.* (*Angling*) A bait fixed or made to remain in one place; hence **ledger-hook, -line, -tackle.** **ledger-blade,** *n.* The stationary blade on a cloth-shearing machine, against which a spiral blade revolves.

Ledum (lē'dŭm) [mod. L., from Gr. *lēdon*, mastic], *n.* (*Bot.*) A genus of low shrubs of the heath family.

lee (1) (lē) [A.-S. *hlēo*, *hlēow*, a covering, shelter (cp. Icel. *hlē*, lee, *hly*, warmth, shelter)], *n.* The side or quarter opposite to that against which the wind blows, opp. to windward or weather side; the sheltered side; shelter, protection. *a.* Pertaining to the side or quarter away from the wind. **under the lee of:** On the sheltered side of; protected from the wind by. **lee-board,** *n.* (*Naut.*) A board let down on the lee-side of a flat-bottomed vessel to prevent the vessel drifting to leeward. **lee-gage,** *n.* (*Naut.*) Position to leeward of another ship. **lee-shore,** *n.* (*Naut.*) The shore under the lee of a vessel; the shore towards which the wind blows. **lee-side,** *n.* (*Naut.*) The lee of a vessel. **lee-tide,** *n.* (*Naut.*) A tide running in the same direction as the wind blows. **lee-way,** *n.* (*Naut.*) The drift of a vessel to leeward of her course; (*fig.*) arrears of work; lost time.

lee (2) [LEES].

leech (1) (lēch) [A.-S. *lǣce*, rel. to *lācnian* to heal (cp. Icel. *lǣknir*, Dan. *læge*, a physician)], *n.* *A physician, a healer; an aquatic annelid of the suctorial order *Hirudinea*, largely employed for the local extraction of blood; (*fig.*) one who abstracts or absorbs the gains of others. *v.t.* To apply leeches to; *to heal, to treat medically. *v.i.* To apply leeches. **leechcraft,** *n.* The art of healing; medicine.

leech (2) (lēch) [cp. Icel. *līk*, Dut. *ijk*, G. *liek*], *n.* (*Naut.*) The perpendicular ledge of a square sail; the after edge of a fore-and-aft sail.

leek (lēk) [A.-S. *lēac* (cp. Dut. *look*, Icel. *laukr*, G. *lauch*)], *n.* A culinary vegetable, *Allium porrum*, allied to the onion, with a cylindrical bulb, the national emblem of Wales. **to eat the leek:** To be compelled to retract (offensive) statements; to be forced to accept an affront.

leer (1) (lēr) [A.-S. *hlēor*, the cheek, the face, the look], *n.* An oblique, sly, or arch look; a look expressive of a feeling of malice, amorousness, or triumph; *the face, the countenance, hue, complexion. *v.i.* To look with a leer; to sneak away. *v.t.* To glance (the eye) with a leer; *to allure with sly or arch looks. **leeringly,** *adv.*

leer (2) (lēr) [etym. unknown], *n.* An annealing-furnace.

leery (lēr′ i) [slang, LEER (1)], *a.* Knowing, sly, wide-awake.

lees (lēz) [formerly *lee*, O.F. *lie*, Gaulish L. *lia*, perh. from Celt.], *n.pl.* (*often used as sing.*) Dregs, the grosser parts of liquor which settle to the bottom; (*fig.*) the grosser part, the refuse.

***leese** (lēz) [A.-S. *lēosan* (in *belēosan, forlēosan*), cp. LEASING], *v.t.* (*past* **lore,** *p.p.* **loren lorn**) To lose.

***leet** (1) (let) [prob. from A.-F. *lete*, A.-S. *lǣth*, LATHE (2)], *n.* A court leet; the jurisdiction of a court leet; a day on which a court leet is held. **leet-ale,** *n.* A merrymaking at the time of a leet.

***leet** (2) (lēt) [perh. from ÉLITE], *n.* (*now chiefly Sc.*) A list of candidates for any office. **short leet:** The final select list of such candidates.

leeward (loo′ ȧrd), *a.* Pertaining to the part away from that against which the wind blows. *adv.* Towards the lee side. *n.* The lee side or direction. **leewardly,** *a.* **leewardmost,** *a.* **leeway** [LEE (1)].

leeze (lēz)[Sc., LIEF IS], *v.impers.* It pleases. **leeze me:** It pleases me.

left (1) (left) [A.-S. *left, lyft*, weak, worthless], *a.* Of, pertaining to, or situated on the side that is to the east when one faces south, opp. to right; correspondingly situated in relation to the front or the direction of anything. *adv.* On or towards the left. *n.* The side opposite to the right; the left hand; the left wing of an army; the party which sits on the left of the president in a legislative assembly, the opposition; the advanced or socialist party, school, or sect. **left hand:** Situated on or pertaining to the left side; the left side, direction, or region. **left-handed,** *a.* Using the left hand more readily than the right; moving from right to left; delivered with the left hand (of a blow); (*fig.*) awkward, clumsy, stupid; insincere, malicious, sinister; ambiguous, equivocal; morganatic, fictitious (of marriages). **left-handedly,** *adv.* **left-handedness,** *n.* **left-hander,** *n.* A left-handed person or a left-handed blow. **leftward,** *adv.* and *a.* **leftwards,** *adv.* **left-wing,** *n.* and *a.* The advanced or socialistic attitude towards politics, pertaining thereto.

left (2) [p.p. of LEAVE (1)]. **left-luggage,** *n.* Luggage deposited temporarily at a railway-station, etc. **left-luggage office,** *n.* **left-off,** *a.* Discarded as no longer serviceable, laid aside.

left (3) [*past & p.p.* LEAVE].

leftism (lef′ tizm), *n.* (*Pol.*) A tendency towards the left, or socialist side; left-wing.

leg (leg) [Icel. *leggr*], *n.* One of the limbs by which man and the lower animals walk, esp. the part from the knee to the ankle; the part of a garment that covers the leg; anything resembling a leg in form or function; one of a set of posts or rods supporting a table, bedstead, chair, machine, etc.; a limb of a pair of dividers, etc.; (*Naut.*) the course run by a vessel on one tack; (*Aviat.*) a stage in a long-distance flight. (*Cricket*) that part of the field to the rear and left of a batsman; a fielder in such part; (*slang*) a swindler, a blackleg; (*Sport*, etc.) the first event won when a second is necessary to decide the contest. **leg-and-leg:** (*slang*) Equal (in a race, card-game, etc.). **leg before wicket** (L.B.W.): (*Cricket*) Stoppage by the batsman's leg of a ball when it would have hit the wicket. **to be on one's last legs:** To be in an extreme stage of exhaustion; to be on the verge of ruin. **to feel** or **find one's legs:** To acquire the power of standing or walking (of an infant); to attain ease or mastery. **to get on one's legs:** To stand up, esp. to make a speech. **to make a leg:** To make a bow or curtsy. **to pull one's leg:** (*colloq.*) To hoax, to make a fool of. **to shake a leg:** (*colloq.*) To dance. **to show a leg:** (*colloq.*) To get out of bed. **to stand on one's own legs:** To depend on oneself. **leg-bail,** *n.* Escape from custody. **to give leg-bail:** To decamp. **leg-break,** *n.* (*Cricket*) A ball which breaks from the leg side. **leg-bye,** *n.* (*Cricket*) A run scored for a ball that touches the batsman. **leg-guard,** *n.* (*Cricket and Baseball*) A pad to protect the leg from knee to ankle. **leg-iron,** *n.* A fetter for the leg. **leg-of-mutton,** *a.* Shaped like a leg of mutton. **leg-rest,** *n.* A support for an injured leg. **leg show,** *n.* (*Theat.*) A low-down entertainment involving the exhibition of women's legs. **a leg up:** (*colloq.*) Assistance. **legged,** *a.* (*usu. in comb.*, as *four-legged*). **legless,** *a.* **leggy,** *a.* **legginess,** *n.*

legacy (leg′ ȧ si) [O.F. *legacie*, legateship, med. L. *lēgātia*, L. *lēgātus*, LEGATE], *n.* A bequest; property bequeathed by will; (*fig.*) anything left or handed on by a predecessor; *a legateship. **legacy-duty,** *n.* A tax on legacies, usu. at graduated rates, increasing in proportion as relationship diminishes. **legacy-hunter,** *n.* One who pays court to another in the hope of receiving a legacy.

legal (lē′ gȧl) [F. *légal*, L. *lēgālis*, from *lex lēgis*], *a.* Of, pertaining to, or according to law; lawful, legitimate; recognized or sanctioned by the law; appointed or laid down by the law; concerned with the law, characteristic of lawyers; (*Theol.*) belonging or conformable to the Mosaic law, or the principle of salvation by works, not by grace. **legal tender:** Money which a creditor is bound to accept in discharge of a debt. **legalism,** *n.* Strict adherence to law and formulas; (*Theol.*) the doctrine of justification by works; respect for the letter rather than the spirit of religious or ethical laws. **legalist,** *n.* **legality** (lė găl′ i ti), *n.* **legalize,** *v.t.* **legalization** (-zā′ shŭn), *n.* **legally,** *adv.*

legate (1) (leg′ ȧt) [O.F. *legat*, L. *lēgātus*, orig. p.p. of *lēgāre*, to appoint, to commission], *n.* An ecclesiastic sent by the Pope to a foreign prince or State; an ambassador, an envoy; (*Rom. Hist.*) a lieutenant or deputy attached to a general or governor; the governor of a province under the Empire. **legateship,** *n.* **legatine,** *a.*

legate (2) (lė gāt′) [L. *lēgātus*, as prec.], *v.t.* To bequeath. **legatee** (leg ȧ tē′), *n.* One to whom a legacy is bequeathed. **legator** (lė gā′ tȯr), *n.*

legation (lė gā′ shŭn) [L. *lēgātio*, from *lēgāre*, see LEGATE (1)], *n.* The act of sending one as legate or deputy, a diplomatic mission; a diplomatic representative and his suite (usu. when the former does not rank as an ambassador); the official residence of a diplomatic representative; a legateship.

legato (lė ga′ tō) [It., bound, p.p. of *legare*, L. *ligāre*, see LIGATE], *adv.* (*Mus.*) In an even gliding manner without a break. ***legatissimo*** (leg ȧ tis′ i mō), *adv.* As smoothly as possible.

legend (lej′ ėnd) [O.F. *legende*, med. L. *legenda*, that which is to be read, from L. *legere*, to read], *n.* *A chronicle, biography, or series of selections from the lives of saints or sacred history, formerly read in the refectories of religious houses, and as lessons at matins; a traditional story, esp. one popularly accepted as true; a myth, a fable; traditional or non-historical story-telling or literature; an inscription on a coat of arms, round the field of a medal or coin, beneath an illustration, etc. **legendary,** *a.* **legendry,** *n.* **legendist,** *n.*

leger (1) (lej′ ėr) [F. *léger*, ult. from L. *levis*], *a.* Light. **leger-line,** *n.* (*Mus.*) A short line added above or below the stave to express ascending or descending notes.

leger (2) (*Angling*) [LEDGER].

legerdemain (lej ėr dė mān′) [O.F. *legier de main* (F. *léger*), light of hand], *n.* Sleight of hand, a trick in which the eye is deceived by the quickness of the hand, conjuring; (*fig.*) jugglery, sophistry.

***legerity** (lė jer' i ti) [F. *légèrité*, from *léger*, light], *n.* Lightness, nimbleness.

legging (leg' ing), *n.* (*usu. in pl.*) A covering of leather, canvas, etc., for the leg, gaiters.

leggy [LEG].

leghorn (lė gôrn') [*Leghorn* (*Livorno*), Italy], *n.* A plait of the straw of bearded wheat cut green and bleached, used for bonnets and hats (orig. imported from Leghorn); a bonnet or hat made of this plait; a breed of domestic fowl.

legible (lej' ibl) [O.F., from late L. *legibilis*, from *legere*, to choose, to read], *a.* That may be read; easily decipherable; clear, plain, evident. **legibility** (-bil' i ti), *n.* **legibly,** *adv.*

legion (lē' jȯn) [O.F., from L. *legiōnem*, nom. *legio*, from *legere*, to choose], *n.* A division of the ancient Roman army, varying, at different periods, from 3,000 to 6,000 men; a military force, esp. in France and other foreign countries; (*fig.*) a host, a vast army or multitude. **British Legion,** *n.* An association of ex-Service men formed after the war of 1914–1918. **Foreign Legion,** *n.* Corps of foreign volunteers in the French army, serving in French colonies. **Legion of Honour:** A French order of merit founded by Napoleon I as a reward for services or merit, civil or military. **legionary,** *a.* Pertaining to a legion or legions; consisting of one or more legions. *n.* A soldier of a legion; a member of the Legion of Honour. **legioned,** *a.* (*poet.*) Formed or drawn up in legions.

legislate (lej' is lāt) [from LEGISLATOR, or LEGISLATION], *v.i.* To make or enact a law or laws; to issue instructions; to make allowance for. **legislation** (lej is lā' shŭn) [late L. *lēgis-lātio*, see LEGISLATOR], *n.* The act of making laws. **legislative,** *a.* Enacting laws; having power to legislate; enacted by or pertaining to legislation. *n.* The legislative power or function; the legislature. **legislatively,** *adv.* **legislator** (lej' is lā tŏr) [L. *lēgis-lātor* (*lēgis*, gen. of *lex*, law, *-lātor*, one who bears, agent-noun of *ferre*, to bear)], *n.* A lawgiver, a member of a legislative assembly. **legislatorial** (-tôr' i ăl), *a.* ***legislatorship,** *n.* **legislatress, *-trix,** *n.* **legislature,** *n.* The body of men in a State in which is vested the power or right to enact, alter, repeal, or suspend laws.

legist (lej' ist) [O.F. *legiste*, med. L. *lēgista*, from *lex lēgis*, law], *n.* One learned in the law.

legitim, legitime (lej' i tim), *n.* (*Sc. Law*) The portion of a person's property that must be inherited by the children. *a.* Legitimate.

legitimate (lė jit' i măt) [med. L. *lēgitimātus*, p.p. of *lēgitimāre*, from L. *lēgitimus*, as prec.], *a.* Lawful; legal, properly authorized; lawfully begotten, born in wedlock, legally descended; derived from strict hereditary right (of a title to sovereignty); proper, regular, natural; conformable to accepted usage; following by logical sequence. *n.* One who is legitimate; (*slang*) the legitimate drama. *v.t.* (-māt) To make lawful; to render legitimate; to invest with the rights of one legitimately born; to justify, to serve as justification for. **legitimate drama:** (*Theat.*) The body of plays of recognized merit; plays written and produced according to the recognized canons of dramatic art. **legitimacy, legitimateness,** *n.* **legitimately,** *adv.* **legitimatize, legitimize,** *v.t.* To render legitimate. **legitimation** (-mā' shŭn), **legitimization** (-zā' shŭn), *n.* **legitimism,** *n.* The doctrine of hereditary monarchical government and divine right; support of the claims of a pretender to a crown on the ground of direct descent, esp. in France or Spain. **legitimist,** *n.*

legume (leg' ūm), **legumen** (lė gū' mėn) [F. *légume*, L. *legūmen*, pulse, from *legere*, to gather], *n.* The fruit or pod of a leguminous plant; (*Bot.*) a two-valved fruit, usually dehiscent along its face and back, and bearing its seeds on either margin of the ventral suture (as the pod of the pea). **legumin,** *n.* (*Chem.*) A protein resembling casein, contained in leguminous and other seeds. **leguminous,** *a.* Producing legumes; (*Bot.*) pertaining to the *Leguminosæ*, an order of herbs, shrubs, and trees bearing legumes.

Leibnitzian (līb nit' si ăn) [Gottfried Wilhelm *Leibnitz* (1646–1716), German philosopher, -IAN], *a.* Pertaining to Leibnitz or his philosophy, esp. his doctrine of pre-established harmony and the optimism based on this. *n.* A follower of Leibnitz or his philosophy. **Leibnitzianism,** *n.*

leiotrichi (lī ot' ri kī) [Gr. *leios*, smooth, *trich-*, stem of *thrix*, hair], *n.* (*Ethn.*) A primary division of mankind comprising the races characterized by having smooth hair. **leiotrichous,** *a.*

leipoa (lī pō' ȧ) [abor. name], *n.* A genus of mound-birds, containing the native pheasant of Australia, *Leipoa ocellata.*

leister (lēs' tėr) [Icel. *liôstr*, from *liôsta*, to strike], *n.* (*Sc.*) A pronged fishing-spear. *v.t.* To spear with a leister.

leisure (lezh' ŭr) [O.F. *leisir*, orig. inf. verb, L. *licēre*, to be allowed], *n.* Freedom from business, occupation, or hurry; time at one's own disposal, unoccupied time; opportunity, convenience. *a.* Unoccupied, free, idle. **at leisure:** At one's ease or convenience; without hurry; deliberately. **leisured,** *a.* **leisureless,** *a.* **leisurely,** *a.* and *adv.* **leisureliness,** *n.*

leitmotiv (līt mȯ tēf') [G. (*leit*, leading, MOTIVE)], *n.* The leading or representative theme in a composition, orig. a musical theme invariably associated with a certain person, situation, or idea throughout an opera, etc.

***leman** (lē'măn) [M.E. *lemman*, *leofman* (A.-S. *lēof*, dear, see LIEF- MAN)], *n.* A sweetheart of either sex; a gallant, a mistress; a concubine, a paramour.

lemma (1) (lem' ȧ) [L. and Gr. *lēmma*, from *lambanein*, to take], *n.* (*pl.* **-mas**) (*Math.*) An auxiliary proposition, demonstrated on account of its immediate application to some other proposition; (*Log.*) a proposition serving as a subsidiary proposition, esp. in another science; a theme, a subject, esp. when prefixed as a heading.

lemma (2) (lem' ȧ) [Gr., from *lepein*, to peel], *n.* (*pl.* **-ata**) (*Bot.*) The husk of a fruit.

lemming (lem' ing) [Norw.], *n.* A small rodent of northern Europe, *Myodes lemmus*, allied to the mouse and rat, remarkable for migrating at certain periods in immense multitudes.

Lemnian (lem' ni ăn), *a.* Of or pertaining to Lemnos, an island in the Ægean Sea. *n.* An inhabitant of Lemnos. **Lemnian earth:** A medicinal earth obtained from Lemnos. **Lemnian reddle:** A reddish ochre found with this and used as a pigment.

lemniscate (lem nis' kăt) [L. *lēmniscātus*, from *lēmniscus*, Gr. *lēmniskos*, ribbon], *n.* (*Geom.*) A curve of the general form of a figure 8 (∞). **lemniscate function:** (*Math.*) An elliptic function used in formulæ expressing the properties of such curves.

lemniscus (lem nis' kŭs) [see prec.], *n.* (*pl.* **-ci** -nis' ī) (*Rom. Ant.*) A fillet or ribbon; the character ÷ employed by ancient textual critics; (*Anat.* and *Zool.*) a bundle of fibres or ribbon-like appendages.

lemon (lem' ȯn) [F. *limon*, med. L. *limōnem*, nom. *limo*, Oriental in orig. (cp. Arab. *laimūn*, Pers. *līmū*)], *n.* The pointed oval acid fruit of *Citrus limonum*; the tree bearing this; the colour of a lemon. *a.* Pertaining to the lemon; of the colour of a lemon, pale-yellowish. **salt of lemon:** Acid oxalate of potassium. **lemon-dab** [LEMON-SOLE]. **lemon-drop,** *n.* A sugar-plum flavoured with lemon. **lemon-kali,** *n.* An effervescing drink made of lemon-juice or tartaric acid with bicarbonate of potash in water. **lemon-peel,** *n.* The peel or rind of the lemon, dried, preserved, and candied, used as a flavouring material. **lemon-plant, -verbena,** *n.* A South American shrub cultivated for its lemon-scented foliage. **lemon-sole** [prob. from F. *limande*, a mud-fish], *n.* A flat-fish of inferior quality resembling sole. **lemon-squash,** *n.* A beverage composed of soda-water and lemon-juice. **lemon-squeezer,** *n.* **lemonade** (lem ȯ nād'), *n.* Lemon-juice mixed with water and sweetened; aerated water flavoured with essence of lemons, etc. **lemon-wood,** *n.* A small N. Zealand tree, the Maori tarata.

lemur (lē' mŭr, lem' ŭr) [L., foll.], *n.* A genus of nocturnal animals allied to the monkeys. **lemurid** (lem' ū rid), *n.* **lemuroid** (lem' ū roid), *a.* and *n.*

lemures (lem' ū rēz) [L., pl. of *lemur*, a ghost], *n.pl.* A term applied by the Romans to spectres or spirits of the dead.

lend (lend) [M.E. *lenen*, A.-S. *lǣnan* (cp. Dut. *leenen*, Icel. *lāna*, G. *lehnen*)], *v.t.* (*past & p.p.* **lent**) To grant for temporary use; to grant the use of on condition of repayment or compensation; to let out (money) at interest; to furnish, to contribute, esp. for temporary service; to accommodate (oneself); *to devote. *v.i.* To make loans. **to lend an ear:** To listen. **to lend a hand** [HAND (1)]. **Lend-Lease,** *n.* Act signed by Pres. Roosevelt in March, 1941, enabling military and other equipment to be lent or leased by the U.S.A. to the governments of the democracies of the world. **lendable,** *a.* **lender,** *n.* One who lends, esp. money upon interest. **lending-library,** *n.* A library from which books are lent out on hire or for a subscription.

length (length) [A.-S. *lengthu*, from *lang*, LONG (1) (cp. Dut. *lengte*, Icel. *lengd*)], *n.* Measure or extent from end to end, as distinguished from breadth or thickness; the longest line that can be drawn from one extremity of anything material to the other; a definite portion of the linear extent of anything; the state of being long; extent of time, duration, long continuance; the distance anything extends; extent or degree of action, etc.; (*Pros.*) the quantity of a vowel or syllable; (*Cricket*) the distance traversed by a ball before striking the ground; (*Racing*) the linear measure of the body of a horse, boat, etc.; (*Theat.*) forty-two lines of an actor's part. **arm's length** [ARM (1)]. **at length:** To the full extent, in full detail; at last. **to go to any length:** To stop at no obstacle; to be restrained by no scruples. **lengthen,** *v.t.* To make long or longer; to draw out, to extend; to protract. *v.i.* To grow longer. ***lengthful,** *a.* **lengthways,** *adv.* **lengthwise,** *adv.* and *a.* **lengthy,** *a.* Long and tedious; prolix. **lengthily,** *adv.* **lengthiness,** *n.*

lenient (lē' ni ėnt) [L. *lēniens*, -*ntem*, pres.p. of *lēnīre*, to soothe, from *lēnis*, soft, gentle], *a.* Mild, gentle; merciful, clement; *soothing, emollient, mitigating. **n.* An emollient preparation or application. **lenience, leniency,** *n.* **leniently,** *adv.*

Leninite (len' in īt) [*Lenin*, *alias* of Vladimir Ilitch Ulianoff (1870–1924)], *n.* A follower of Lenin, a Bolshevist. **Leninism,** *n.*

lenitive (len' i tiv), *a.* Having the power or quality of softening or mitigating; mitigating, palliative; *n.* (*Med.*) A lenitive medicine or application. **lenity,** *n.*

leno (lē' nō) [perh. corr. of F. *linon*], *n.* An open cotton fabric, thinner than book-muslin.

lenocinium (len ō sin' i ŭm) [L. the trade of a pander], *n.* (*Sc. Law*) A husband's connivance at his wife's adultery.

lens (lenz) [L. *lens*, *lentis*, seed of lentil], *n.* (*pl.* **lenses**) A piece of a transparent substance, usually glass, or a combination of such, with the surface or both surfaces curved so as to change the direction of rays of light, and diminish or increase the apparent size of objects viewed through it; (*Anat.*) the crystalline body through which rays of light are focussed on the retina. **lensed,** *a.* **lensless,** *a.*

Lent (1) (lent) [M.E. *lenten*, A.-S. *lencten*, spring (cp. Dut. *lente*, G. *lenz*, prob. cogn. with LONG (1), because the days lengthen in spring)], *n.* A fast of forty days (excluding Sundays) from Ash Wednesday to Easter Eve; a season of penitence and fasting in commemoration of Christ's fasting in the wilderness; (*pl.*) the Lent boat-races at Cambridge. **Lent-lily,** *n.* The daffodil. **Lent term:** The school and University term in which Lent falls. **lenten,** *a.* Of, pertaining to, or used in Lent; sparing, meagre. **lenten colour:** Mourning or sombre colour.

lent (2), *past & p.p.* [LEND].

-lent [L. -*lentus*], *suf.* Full, as in *corpulent*, *opulent*, *violent*.

lentamente (len tȧ men' tā) [It., from LENTO], *adv.* (*Mus.*) Slowly; in slow time. ***lentando*** (len tan' dō), *adv.* (*Mus.*) With increasing slowness.

lenten [LENT (1)].

lenticel (len' ti sel) [F. *lenticelle*, dim. from L. *lentēm*, nom. *lens*], *n.* (*Bot.*) A lens-shaped mass of cells in the bark of a plant, through which respiration takes place. **lenticellate** (-sel' ȧt), *a.*

lenticular (len tik' ū lȧr) [late L. *lenticulāris*, from *lenticula*, dim. of *lens lentis*, LENS], *a.* Resembling in shape a lentil or lens doubly convex; of or pertaining to the lens of the eye. ***lenticula,*** *n.* A lenticel; a small lens; a freckle. **lentiform, lentoid, lentigerous** (-tij' ėr ŭs), *a.* **lenticularly,** *adv.*

lentigo (len tī' gō) [L., from *lens lentis*, LENS], *n.* (*Path.*) A freckle, freckly eruption. **lentigenous** (-tij' i nŭs), *a.*

lentil (len' til) [O.F. *lentille*, L. *lenticula*], *n.* A small branching leguminous plant, *Ervum lens*; (*pl.*) the seeds of this plant, largely used for food.

lentisk (len' tisk) [F. *lentisque*, L. *lentiscum*, nom. -*cus*], *n.* The mastic tree, *Pistacia lentiscus*.

lentitude (len' ti tūd) [F., from L. *lentitūdo*, from *lentus*, slow], *n.* Slowness. **lento** (len' tō) [It.], *adv.* (*Mus.*) Slowly.

lentoid [LENTICULAR].

lentor (len' tŏr) [F. *lenteur*, or directly from L. *lentor*, as LENTITUDE], *n.* (*Physiol.*) Slowness, sluggishness (of temperament, vital functions, etc.); viscidity, tenacity (of blood, etc.). ***lentous,** *a.*

l'envoy, *lenvoy [ENVOY (1)].

Leo (lē' ō) [L. *leo leōnis*], *n.* One of the twelve zodiacal constellations; the fifth sign of the zodiac.

leonid (lē' ō nid), *n.* (*Astron.*) One of the meteors that appear in numbers about 14 November in some years, radiating from the constellation Leo.

leonine (lē' ȯ nīn) [L. *leōnīnus*, as prec.], *a.* Pertaining to or like a lion; (*fig.*) majestic, undaunted.

Leonine (lē' ȯ nīn) [as prec.], *a.* Of, pertaining to, or made by Leo; (*Pros.*) an epithet used to describe pentameter or hexameter verse the last word of which rhymes with that preceding the cæsura; pertaining to one of the popes Leo. *n.* A Leonine verse. **Leonine City:** The portion of Rome comprising the Vatican which was walled by Leo IV.

leopard (lep' ȧrd) [O.F., from late L. *leopardus*, late Gr. *leopardos* (LION, PARD (1))], *n.* A large, fierce mammal, *Felis pardus*, of the cat tribe, of Africa and S. Asia, with pale fawn to rufous-buff coat, having dark spots, the panther (pop. applied to large leopards); a leopard-like animal, as the **American leopard** or jaguar, the **hunting leopard** or cheetah, and the **snow leopard** or ounce; (*Her.*) a lion passant guardant, as in the English royal arms. **leopard's bane:** A plant of the composite genus *Doronicum*; other composite plants, also herb Paris. **leopardess,** *n.*

leper (lep' ėr) [O.F. *lepre*, leprosy, L. and Gr. *lepra*, fem. of *lepros*, from *lepos*, scale], *n.* One affected with leprosy. **a.* Leprous.

***lepid** (lep' id) [L. *lepidus*], *a.* Pleasant, merry; jocose, facetious.

lepido- [Gr. *lepis lepidos*, a scale], *comb. form.* Having scales; resembling scales.

lepidodendron (lep i dō den′ dron) [Gr. *dendron*, tree], *n.* (*Palæont.*) A genus of fossil plants abounding in the coal-measures, so named from the scars on the stems where the leaves were attached. **lepidodendroid,** *a.*

Lepidoptera (lep i dop′ tėr å) [LEPIDO-, Gr. *pteron*, wing], *n.pl.* (*Ent.*) An order of insects, characterized by having four wings clothed with minute powder-like scales, containing the butterflies and moths. **lepidopteral, -an,** *a.* and *n.* **lepidopterous,** *a.* **lepidopterist,** *n.*

lepidosaurian (lep i dō saw′ ri ån) [LEPIDO-, SAURIAN], *a.* (*Zool.*) Pertaining to the *Lepidosauria*, a sub-class of reptiles having a scaly integument. *n.* A member of this sub-class.

lepidosiren (lep i dō sī′ rėn) [LEPIDO-, SIREN], *n.* A genus of dipnoan fishes with one species, *L. paradoxa*, the South American mud-fish, from the river Amazon.

leporide (lep′ ō rid) [F. *léporide*, as foll.], *n.* An animal supposed to be a hybrid between a hare and a rabbit.

leporine (lep′ ō rīn) [L. *leporīnus*, from *lepus leporis*, hare], *a.* Of or pertaining to hares, having the nature or form of a hare. *n.* A leporide.

leprechaun (lep rė *ch*awn′) [Ir.], *n.* (*Folklore*) A brownie or dwarfish sprite who performs domestic offices, mends shoes, and always carries a purse.

leprosy (lep′ rō si) [O.F. *leprosie*, from L. *leprōsus*, from *lepra*, see LEPER], *n.* A chronic disease, usually characterized by shining tubercles of various sizes, thickening of the skin, loss of feeling, and ulceration and necrosis of parts. **leprous,** *a.* ***leprously,** *adv.* ***leprousness,** *n.*

lepto- [Gr. *leptos*], *comb. form.* Fine, small, thin, delicate; narrow, slender.

leptocardian (lep tō kar′ di ån) [Gr. *kardia*, heart], *a.* (*Zool.*) Belonging to the *Leptocardii*, the lowest division of vertebrates, typified by the lancelet. *n.* An individual of this class.

leptocephalic (lep tō se făl′ ik) [CEPHALIC], *a.* Having a long and narrow skull. **leptocephalid** (lep tō sef′ å lid), *n.* (*Ichthyol.*) One of a family of eel-like fishes, the *Leptocephalidæ*. **leptocephaloid,** *a.* and *n.* **leptocephalous,** *a.* **leptocephaly,** *n.*

leptodactyl (lep tō dăk′ til) [Gr. *daktulos*, digit], *a.* (*Ornith.*) Having long, slender toes. *n.* A bird having such toes. **leptodactylous,** *a.*

lepton (lep′ tŏn) [Gr., neut. of *leptos*, LEPTO-], *n.* (*pl.* **lepta**) A small Greek coin, worth anciently about one-fourth of a farthing—the mite of the N.T. parable—now worth one-hundredth of a drachma.

leptorrhine (lep′ tō rin) [LEPTO-, Gr. *rhis rhinos*, nose], *a.* (*Ethn.*) Having a long, narrow nose. **leptorrhinian, -rhinic,** *a.*

leptosome (lep′ tō sōm) [LEPTO-; Gr. *soma*, body], *a.* Slender; (*fig.*) slick, crafty.

leptosperm (lep′ tō spĕrm), *n.* (*Bot.*) A plant of the Australian genus *Leptospermum*, of myrtaceous shrubs and trees.

***lere** (lēr) [A.-S. *lǣran* (cp. LEARN and LORE)], *v.t.* To teach; to learn.

lerp (lĕrp) [Austral. abor., sweet], *n.* An edible saccharine substance secreted by a desert insect.

Lesbianism (lez′ bi ån izm) [Gr. island of Lesbos], *n.* Homosexuality in women, Sapphism. **Lesbian,** *n.* A woman addicted to this form of perversion; a native of the island of Lesbos.

lese-majesty (lēz măj′ ė sti) [F. *lèse-majesté*, L. *læsa mājestās* (*læsa*, hurt, violated, fem. p.p. of *lædere*, see foll.)], *n.* An offence against the sovereign power or its representative, high treason.

lesion (lē′ zhŭn) [F. *lésion*, L. *læsiōnem*, nom. *-sio*, from *lædere*, to injure], *n.* A hurt, an injury; (*Path.*) morbid change in a tissue or organ.

less (les) [A.-S. *læssa*, a., *lǣs*, adv.], *a.* Smaller; of smaller size, extent, number, amount, degree, importance, rank, etc. *prep.* Minus, with deduction of. *adv.* In a smaller or lower degree; not so much. *n.* A smaller part, quantity, or number; the smaller, the inferior, the junior, etc., of things compared. *conj.* Unless. **nothing less:** Anything else (than), anything rather; (*colloq.*) nothing of a smaller or milder kind. **lesser** [double comp.], *a.* Less, smaller; inferior.

-less [A.-S. *lēas*, loose, free from, cogn. with LOOSE], *suf.* Devoid of, free from; as in *fearless, godless, sinless, tireless.*

lessee (lė sē′) [A.-F., from O.F. *lessé*, p.p. of *lesser*, to LEASE (1)], *n.* One to whom a lease is granted. **lesseeship,** *n.*

lessen (les′ ėn), *v.t.* To make less or diminish in size, extent, number, quantity, or degree; to reduce, to depreciate, to degrade. *v.i.* To become less in size, extent, number, degree, or quantity; to decrease, to shrink.

lesser [LESS].

lesson (les′ ŏn) [O.F. *lecon*, L. *lectiōnem*, nom. *-tio*, from *legere*, to read, p.p *lectus*], *n.* Any exercise done, or portion of a book learnt, read, or recited by a pupil to a teacher; the amount of instruction given to a pupil at one time; (*pl.*) a course of instruction (in any subject); (*Eccles.*) one of two portions of Scripture read during divine service; (*fig.*) a reprimand, admonition, or lecture; an occurrence or example taken as a warning or caution. *v.t.* To teach, to instruct; to discipline; to admonish, to lecture.

lessor (les′ ŏr) [A.-F., from *lesser*, to LEASE (1)], *n.* One who grants a lease.

lest (lest) [M.E. *leste lesthe*, from A.-S. *thȳ lǣs the*, the (instrumental) less that], *conj.* For fear that; in order that not; (after words expressing alarm, anxiety, etc.) that.

let (1) (let) [A.-S. *lǣtan* (cp. Dut. *laten*, Icel. *lāta*, G. *lassen*), cogn. with LATE], *v.t.* (*past & p.p.* **let**) To permit, to allow, to suffer (to be or do); to give leave to; to cause to; to grant the use, occupation, or possession of for a stipulated sum, to lease; to give out on contract. *aux.v.* Used in the imperative mood, with the force of prayer, exhortation, assumption, permission, or command. *v.i.* To be let or leased (*Am.* for rent). *n.* A letting. **let alone:** (*colloq.*) Not to mention; much less. **to let alone:** To leave without interference; not to do or deal with; not to mention. **to let be:** Not to interfere with; to suffer to be as at present (sometimes absolutely). **to let blood:** To open a vein and allow the blood to flow. **to let down:** To allow to sink or fall; to humiliate; to fail (someone). **to let drive** [DRIVE]. **to let fall:** To drop; (*fig.*) to mention by or as if by accident; (*Geom.*) to draw (a perpendicular) upon a line. **to let fly** [FLY (2)]. **to let go:** To release; to relinquish hold of; to cease to retain; to dismiss from the mind; (*Naut.*) to drop anchor; to cease to hold a rope. **to let oneself go:** To give way to any impulse. **to let in:** To allow to enter; to insert; (*slang*) to cheat, to defraud. **to let into:** To admit to; to insert; to admit to knowledge of; to assail; to abuse. **to let loose:** To free from restraint, to release. **to let off:** To suffer to go free; to refrain from punishing or to punish lightly; to pardon, to excuse; to discharge, to fire off (an arrow, gun, etc.). **to let on:** (*slang*) To divulge, to let out. **to let out:** To open the door for; to suffer to escape; to divulge; to enlarge (as a dress); to lease or let on hire; (*colloq.*) to strike or lash out, to let fly. **to let slip:** To allow to escape; to lose, to miss. **to let up:** To become less, to abate. **let-up,** *n.* A cessation, an alleviation.

let (2) (let) [A.-S. *lettan* (cp. Dut. *letten*, Icel. *letja*), rel. to LATE], ***v.t.** (*past & p.p.* **let**) To hinder, to impede, to obstruct, to prevent. ***v.i.** To cause obstruction. *n.* *A hindrance, an obstacle; (*Rackets, Tennis, etc.*) a stoppage, hindrance, etc., requiring the ball to be served again.

-let [O.F. *-let, -lete, -et* (L. *-ellus, -ella, -ellum,* -ET)], *suf.* Diminutive, as in *bracelet, cutlet, tartlet.*

letch (1) (lech) [LEACH (1)], *n.* (*Sc.*) A stream running through boggy ground.

letch (2) (lech) [LECHER], *n.* A strong desire, a craving.

lethal (lē′ thȧl) [F., from L. *lēthālis, lētālis,* from *lētum,* death], *a.* Deadly, fatal, mortal. **lethal chamber,** *n.* Chamber for killing painlessly by gas. **lethality** (lė thăl′ i ti), *n.* **lethalize** (lē′-), *v.t.* **lethiferal, -ferous** (lė thif′ ėr ȧl, -ŭs) [-FEROUS], *a.*

lethargy (leth′ ȧr ji) [L. and Gr. *lēthargia,* from *lēthargos,* forgetting, from foll.], *n.* Morbid drowsiness; unnatural sleepiness; a state of torpor, apathy, dullness, or inactivity. **v.t.* To affect with lethargy. **lethargic, -al** (lė thar′ jik, -ȧl), *a.* **lethargically,** *adv.* ***lethargicalness,** *n.* **lethargize** (leth′ ȧr jīz), *v.t.* **lethargus** (lė thar′ gŭs), *n.* (*Path.*) Sleeping-sickness.

Lethe (1) (lē′ thē) [L., from Gr. *lēthē,* forgetfulness, *lēth-, lath-,* root of *lanthanesthai,* to forget], *n.* (*Gr. Ant.*) A river of Hades whose waters produced forgetfulness in those who drank them; (*fig.*) forgetfulness, oblivion. **Lethean** (lė thē′ ȧn), *a.*

***lethe** (2) (lē′ thē) [Shak., from prec. or L. *lētum, death*], *n.* Death.

letheon (lē′ thi ŏn), *n.* (Med.) An anæsthetic, esp. sulphuric ether.

lethiferal, lethiferous [LETHAL].

Lett (let) [G. *Lette,* native *Latvi*], *n.* A member of one of the three divisions of the Lithuanians inhabiting Livonia and adjoining districts; Lettish. **Lettic,** *a.* Lettish; of the group of peoples or languages comprising Lettish, Lithuanian, and Old Prussian. *n.* Lettish; the Lettic group of languages. **Lettish,** *a.* Of or pertaining to the Letts. *n.* The language of the Letts.

letter (let′ ėr) [O.F. *lettre,* L. *littera*], *n.* A mark or character employed to represent a sound in speech; one of the characters in the alphabet; a written message or communication; the literal or precise meaning of a term or terms, distinguished from the spirit; a character used in printing, type, fount of type; (*pl.*) literature, literary culture; learning, erudition; *an inscription, lettering. *v.t.* To impress or stamp with letters. **commonwealth** or **republic of letters:** The world of literature, authors taken collectively. **letter of advice:** A letter notifying dispatch of goods, drawing of bill of exchange, etc. **letter of attorney** [ATTORNEY]. **letter of marque** or **marque and reprisal:** A commission to a private person to undertake reprisals against a foreign State or its subjects. **letters of administration:** A document issued by a court authorizing a person to administer an intestate estate. **letters patent:** A document under the Great Seal authorizing a person to do some act or enjoy some right. **man of letters:** An author. **letter-balance,** *n.* A pair of scales for weighing letters for the post. **letter-board,** *n.* (*Print.*) A board on which type for distribution is placed; (*Naut.*) a name-board. **letter-book,** *n.* A book in which copies of letters are kept. **letter-box,** *n.* A box for the reception of letters. **letter-card,** *n.* A folded card with gummed edges for sending by post as a letter. ***letter-carrier,** *n.* A postman. **letter-case,** *n.* A portable writing-case; a pocket-book for holding letters. **letter-founder,** *n.* A type-founder. **letter-paper,** *n.* Paper for writing letters upon, esp. paper of quarto size. **letter-perfect,** *a.* Having learnt one's part thoroughly (of actors). **letterpress,** *n.* Matter printed by types; printed matter other than illustrations. **letter-weight,** *n.* A weight for holding loose papers down; a letter-balance. **letter-writer,** *n.* One who writes letters, esp. for hire; a book professing to teach letter-writing. **lettered,** *a.* Marked or impressed with letters; learned, erudite; pertaining to or suited for literature or learning. **lettering,** *n.* The act of impressing letters; an inscription, a title. **letterless,** *a.* Having received no letters; (*fig.*) illiterate, ignorant.

Lettic, Lettish [LETT].

lettre de cachet [CACHET].

lettuce (let′ ŭs) [M.E. *letuce,* ult. from L. *lactūca,* cogn. with *lac lactis,* milk], *n.* A crisp-leaved garden plant of the genus *Lactuca,* esp. *L. sativa,* much used for salad.

leuc-, leuco- [Gr. *leukos*], *comb. form.* White, pale.

leuchæmia (lū kē′ mi ȧ), *n.* (*Path.*) Leucocythæmia.

leucin (lū′ sin), *n.* (*Chem.*) A white crystalline substance obtained from the decomposition of animal fibre. **leucic, leucinic,** *a.*

leucite (lū′ sīt), *n.* (*Min.*) A dull, glassy silicate of aluminium and potassium, occurring at Mt. Vesuvius and Monte Somma. **leucitic,** *a.*

leucocyte (lū′ kō sīt), *n.* (*Phys.*) A colourless corpuscle, either a white blood-corpuscle, or one of the free cells in glands, marrow, tissue, etc. **leucocytic** (-sit′ ik), *a.* **leucocythæmia** (lū kō sī thē′ mi ȧ) [LEUCOCYTE, Gr. *-haima,* blood], *n.* (*Path.*) A disease characterized by hypertrophy of the spleen, loss of the red and increase of the white corpuscles of the blood. **leucocytogenesis** (lū kō sī tō jen′ ė sis) [GENESIS], *n.* The production of leucocytes. **leucocytolysis** (-tol′ i sis), *n.* Extermination of leucocytes by the agency of leucocytotoxins. **leucocytosis** (-tō′ sis), *n.* (*Path.*) A condition characterized by an increase in the number of white corpuscles in the blood. **leucocytotoxin** (-tok′ sin) [TOXIN], *n.* An agent that destroys leucocytes.

leucol, leucoline (lū′ kol, lū′ ko lin), *n.* (*Chem.*) An organic compound distilled from coal-tar, isomeric with quinoline. **leucolinic,** *a.*

leucoma (lū kō′ mȧ) [Gr. *leukōma,* from *leukos,* see prec.], *n.* (*Path.*) A white opaque spot in the cornea, due to a wound, inflammation, etc.

leucomaine (lū′ kō mān) [as prec.], *n.* (*Chem.*) An alkaloid found in living animal tissue, as distinguished from ptomaine found in decaying tissue. **leucomatus** (lū kom′ ȧ tŭs), *a.*

leucopathy (lū kop′ ȧ thi) [LEUCO-, -PATHY], *n.* Albinism. **leucorrhœa** (lū kō rē′ ȧ) [Gr. *rhoia,* a flow], *n.* (*Path.*) A mucous discharge from the vagina, commonly called whites. **leucorrhœal, -rhœic,** *a.*

leucosis (lū kō′ sis) [Gr. *leukōsis,* from *leukoun,* to make white, from leukos, white], *n.* (*Path.*) Pallor, whiteness; the morbid condition resulting in albinism. **leucism,** *n.* **leucous,** *a.*

leucotomy [LOBOTOMY].

Levant (1) (le vănt′) [F., from It. *levante,* L. *levantem,* nom. *-vans,* pres.p. of *levāre,* to raise], *n.* The eastern part of the Mediterranean with the adjoining countries; a levanter or easterly wind in the Mediterranean; levant morocco [MOROCCO]. **levanter** (1), *n.* An inhabitant of the Levant; an easterly wind in the Mediterranean. **Levantine** (lė văn′ tīn, -tin), *a.* Pertaining to the Levant. *n.* A native inhabitant or trader of the Levant; a stout, twilled, reversible kind of silk cloth.

levant (2) (lė vănt′) [Sp. *levantar,* to break up (camp, house, etc.), from *levar,* to raise, as prec.], *v.i.* To abscond, to run away, esp. with gambling liabilities undischarged. **levanter** (2), *n.*

levator (lė vā′ tȯr) [late L., from *levāre,* to raise], *n.* (*Anat.*) A muscle that raises some part; (*Surg.*) a lever for raising a depressed portion of bone.

levee (1) (lev′ i) [F. *levé* or *lever,* rising, as prec.], *n.* *The action of rising; a morning reception held by a sovereign or personage of high rank; a reception in the early afternoon by the British sovereign or his representative at which only men are received; a general reception or assembly of visitors.

levee (2) (lev′ i) [F. *levée,* p.p. of *lever,* to raise], *n.* The natural bank of a river formed by the deposition of silt; an artificial bank to prevent overflow and flooding. *v.t.* To raise a levee or levees along (a river) or in (a district).

level (lev′ ėl) [O.F. *livel* (F. *niveau*), L. *lībella*, dim. of *lībra*, balance, a level], *n.* A horizontal line or plane or plane surface; a line or plane at all points at right angles to the vertical; an instrument for determining whether a surface or a series of objects are horizonal; the altitude of any point or surface; level country; (*fig.*) the mean standard of elevation in a community as regards morality, culture, etc.; (*Mining*) a horizontal gallery or passage. *a.* Horizontal, even, not higher or lower at any part, flat; equal in rank or degree; (*fig.*) equable, uniform, well-balanced. *v.t.* (*past & p.p.* **levelled**) To make horizontal; to reduce to a horizontal plane; to bring (up or down) to the same level; to make smooth or even; to point (a gun) in taking aim; to aim, to direct (an attack, satire, etc.); to raze, to overthrow, to make level (with the ground, etc.), to knock down; to bring to an equality of state, rank, condition, or degree. **v.i.* To aim or point a gun; (*fig.*) to conjecture, to guess. **to do one's level best:** To put forth all one's exertions. **on the level:** Honestly. **level crossing:** A place for crossing a railway on the level; the intersection of railway lines on the same level, (*Am.* a grade-crossing). **level-headed,** *a.* (*colloq.*) Sensible, shrewd, common-sense. **leveller,** *n.* One who or that which levels; one who wishes to destroy all social distinctions. **levelling-instrument,** *n.* (*Surv.*) An instrument with a telescope for taking levels. **levelling-pole, -rod, -staff,** *n.* (*Surv.*) **levelling-screw,** *n.* A screw for adjusting the parts of a machine to an exact level. **levelly,** *adv.* **levelness,** *n.*

lever (lē′ vėr) [O.F. *leveor*, from *lever*, to raise], *n.* A bar of wood, metal, or other rigid substance, having a fixed point (or fulcrum), used to overcome a certain resistance (or weight) at some part of the bar by means of a force (or power) applied at another part (of three kinds or orders, the first, those with the fulcrum, the second, those with the weight, the third, those with the power, between the other two); a part of a machine, instrument, etc., acting on the same principle; the part by which the breech of a rifle, etc., is opened; a lever watch; (*fig.*) anything that brings power or influence to bear. *v.t.* To move or lift with or as with a lever. *v.i.* To use a lever. **lever escapement:** An escapement in which two levers connect the pallet and balance. **lever watch:** A watch with a lever escapement. **leverage,** *n.* The action of a lever; the mechanical power or advantage gained by the use of a lever; an arrangement of levers; (*fig.*) means of accomplishing, influencing, etc.

leveret (lev′ ėr ėt) [A.-F., from O.F. *levrete*, dim. of *levre* (F. *lièvre*), L. *leporem*, nom. *lepus*, hare], *n.* A hare in its first year.

leviable [LEVY].

leviathan (lė vī′ à thȧn) [late L., from Heb. *livyāthān*, etym. doubtful], *n.* A huge aquatic monster (perh. the Nilotic crocodile) described in *Job*, etc.; anything huge or monstrous, esp. a huge ship or a whale.

levigate (lev′ i gāt) [L. *lēvigātus*, p.p. of *lēvigāre*, from *lēvis*, smooth], *v.t.* To make smooth; to grind or rub down to an impalpable powder. *a.* (-gȧt) Smooth as if polished. **levigable,** *a.* **levigation** (-gā′ shŭn), *n*

***levin** (lev′ in) [M.E. *levene*, etym. doubtful], *n.* Lightning; a flash of lightning. ***levin-brand,** *n.* A thunderbolt.

levir (lē′ vir) [L., brother-in-law (cp. Sansk. *dēvar*, Gr. *daēr*)], *n.* (*Anthropology*) One on whom devolves the obligation of marrying the widow of, and thus begetting issue to, a deceased brother or person to whom he was next of kin. **levirate** (lē′ vir ȧt), *n.* The law prevalent among the Jews and other nations binding the brother or next of kin of a man dying without issue to marry the widow. *a.* **Leviratical. leviratic, -al** (-ăt′ ik, -ȧl), *a.*

levitate (lev′ i tāt) [L. *levis*, light, after GRAVITATE], *v.t.* To make lighter; to free (a vehicle, railway, etc.) from the retarding influence of gravity; (*Spiritualism*) to rise or move about in the air by annulling the effects of gravity. **levitation** (-tā′ shŭn), *n.*

Levite (lē′ vīt) [L. *Levīta*, Gr. *Leuitēs*, from *Leui*, Heb. *Lēvī*, son of Jacob], *n.* One of the tribe or family of Levi, esp. one of those who acted as assistants to the priests in the Jewish temple; (*fig.*) a priest, a parson. **Levitical** (lė vit′ i kȧl), *a.* Pertaining to the Levites; pertaining to the book of Leviticus or the laws contained in it; *priestly. **Levitical degrees:** Degrees of relationship which according to the Levitical law precluded marriage. **Levitically,** *adv.* **Leviticus,** *n.* The third book of the Pentateuch, containing the Levitical law and ritual. **levitism** (lē′ vī tizm), *n.*

levity (lev′ i ti) [O.F. *levité*, L. *levitātem*, nom. *-tas*, from *levis*, light], *n.* (*rare*) Lightness of weight; (*fig.*) lightness of disposition, conduct, or manner; want of seriousness or earnestness, thoughtlessness, frivolity.

levo- [LÆVO-]. **levulose** [LÆVULOSE].

levy (lev′ i) [F. *levée*, fem. p.p. of *lever*, L. *levāre*, to raise], *n.* The act of raising or collecting for public service; that which is so raised or collected; a body of troops called out for military service; *a duty, tax, or impost. *v.t.* To raise, to collect together (as an army); to call out, to enlist (soldiers or an army); to impose and collect (as a tax or forced contribution); (*Law*) to raise (a sum) by a tax on property; to seize (property) by a judicial writ, etc. **capital levy,** *n.* A tax on capital. **levy in mass:** A levy of all the able-bodied men of a country for military service. **to levy a fine:** To commence and carry on a suit for assuring the title to lands or tenements. **to levy war:** To assemble forces, collect arms and munitions in commencement of hostilities (upon or against). **leviable,** *a.*

lewd (lūd) [A.-S. *lǣwede*, lay, belonging to the laity], *a.* Lascivious, unchaste, indecent; depraved, wicked, worthless. **lewdly,** *adv.* **lewdness,** *n.* ***lewdster,** *n.* A lecher.

lewis (loo′ is) [perh. from the inventor], *n.* A contrivance for attaching a chain, etc., for lifting heavy blocks of stone, consisting of two dovetail tenons, expanded by a key in a dovetail mortise; the son of a Freemason.

Lewis-gun (loo′ is gŭn) [name of inventor], *n.* A rapid-firing rifle, mounted on two legs for use as a portable machine-gun.

lewisite (loo′ is īt), *n.* (*Mil.*) Liquid used in chemical warfare obtained from arsenic and acetylene.

lexicon (lek′ si kȯn) [Gr. *lexikon*, orig. neut. of *lexikos*, pertaining to words, from *lexis*, a saying, a word, from *legein*, to speak], *n.* A dictionary (usu. applied to Greek, Hebrew, Arabic, or Syriac). **lexical,** *a.* Pertaining to the words of a language, as opp. to grammar; pertaining to a lexicon or lexicography. **lexically,** *adv.* **lexicography** (lek si kog′ rȧ fi) [-GRAPHY], *n.* The art or process of compiling lexicons or dictionaries. **lexicographer,** *n.* **lexicographic, -ical** (-grăf′ ik, -ȧl), *a.* **lexicology** (-kol′ ȯ ji) [-LOGY], *n.* That branch of learning which treats of the derivation, signification, and application of words. ***lexigraphy** (lek sig′ rȧ fi), *n.* A system of writing in which each word is represented by a distinct character. **lexigraphic** (-grăf′ ik), *a.*

ley (lā) [LEA (2)], *n.* (*Agric.*) Pasture land; fallow land. *a.* Cultivated for pasture; fallow.

Leyden (lī′ dėn) [city of Holland], *a.* **Leyden battery:** A battery composed of Leyden jars. **Leyden jar** or ***phial:** A glass bottle or jar coated inside and out with tinfoil used to accumulate electricity (invented at Leyden in 1745).

leze-majesty [LESE-MAJESTY].

lherzolite (lėr′ zȯ līt) [Lake *Lherz*, in the Pyrenees, -ITE], *n.* (*Min.*) A greenish-grey igneous rock composed of pyroxene, chrysolite, diallage, and picotite.

li (lē) [Chin.], *n.* A Chinese measure of weight, the thousandth part of a liang; a Chinese measure of distance, rather more than one-third of a mile.

liable (lī′ ȧbl) [perh. from non-extant A.-F. *liable*, or med. L. *ligābilis* (F. *lier*, L. *ligāre*, to bind)], *a.* Bound or obliged in law or equity; responsible (for); subject or amenable (to); exposed or open (to); tending, apt, or likely (to).

liability (lī ȧ bil′ i ti), *n.* The state of being liable; that for which one is liable; (*pl.*) debts, pecuniary obligations. **limited liability:** Responsibility for debts of a company only to a specified amount, in proportion to the amount of stock held; hence, **limited liability company** or **limited company.**

liaison (li ā′ zȯn) [F., from L. *ligātiōnem*, nom. *-tio*, from *ligāre*, to bind], *n.* An illicit initimacy between a man and woman; (*Cookery*) a thickening, usu. made of yolk of egg; (*Phon.*) the carrying on of the sound of a final consonant to a succeeding word beginning with a vowel or *h* mute; (*Mil.*) connexion, touch. **liaison officer,** *n.* An officer acting as go-between for allied forces or bodies of men under different commands. **liaize** (li āz), *v.i.* To make liaison.

liana (li a′ nȧ), **liane** (li an′) [F. *liane*, prob. from *lier*, L. *ligāre*, to bind], *n.* A general name for the climbing and twining plants abounding in the forests of tropical America.

liang (lyăng) [Chin.], *n.* A Chinese weight, equal to about one and a third oz. av.; this weight of silver as money of account.

liangle (lē′ ăng gėl) [Austral. abor.], *n.* A type of wooden club.

liar (lī′ ȧr) [A.-S. *lēogere*, from *lēogan*, to LIE (I)], *n.* One who knowingly utters falsehoods, esp. one addicted to lying.

***liard** (lyar) [F., perh. from *liard*, grey, LYART], *n.* A former French coin worth a quarter of a sou.

lias (lī′ ȧs) [F. *liais*, etym. doubtful], *n.* (*Geol.*) A blue limestone underlying the Oolite; the series of strata characterized by this, forming the lowest portion of the Jurassic system. **liassic** (lī ăs′ ik), *a.*

***lib** (lib) [cp. E.Fris. *lübben*, M.Dut. *lubben*], *v.t.* To castrate, to geld.

libation (lī-, li bā′ shun) [L. *lībātio*, from *lībāre*, to sip, to pour out (cp. Gr. *leibein*)], *n.* A sacrifice, by a drink-offering or by pouring oil or wine on the ground; (*fig.*) a drinking, a potation. **libate** (lī bāt′), *v.t.* and *i.* **libatory** (lī′ bȧ tȯr i), *a.*

***libbard** [LEOPARD].

libeccio (li bech′ ō) [It., from L. *Libs*, Gr. *Lips*], *n.* The south-west wind.

libel (lī′ bėl) [O.F., from L. *libellum*, nom. *-lus*, dim. of *liber*, book], *n.* A defamatory writing, print, picture, or publication of any kind, containing any malicious statements or representations tending to bring any person into ridicule, contempt, or disrepute; the act or crime of publishing a libel; (*Law*) the written statement commencing a suit, containing the plaintiff's allegations; a lampoon, satire, or defamatory statement. *v.t.* (*past & p.p.* **libelled**) To publish a libel upon; to defame or lampoon; (*Law*) to bring a suit against by means of a libel; to bring a suit against (a ship) in admiralty. *v.i.* To spread libels or defamatory statements. ***libellant,** *n.* (*Law*) One who exhibits a charge in an ecclesiastical or admiralty court. **libellee** (lī bė lē′), *n.* **libeller, libellist,** *n.* One who libels; a lampooner. **libellous,** *a.* **libellously,** *adv.*

liber (lī′ bėr) [L., bark], *n.* (*Bot.*) The bast or inner bark of exogens.

liberal (lib′ ėr ȧl) [O.F., from L. *līberālis*, from *līber*, free], *a.* Generous, open-handed, bountiful, munificent; ample, abundant, profuse; free, open, candid; favourable to liberty and progress; not too strict, narrow, or literal; broad-minded, unprejudiced; (*Polit.*) favourable to freedom and democratic government, opposed to aristocratic privileges; befitting a gentleman, not technical, tending to free mental development (esp. of education). *n.* One who advocates progress and reform, especially in the direction of conferring greater power upon the people. **Liberal Conservative:** A Conservative willing to accept certain reforms; a Tory Democrat. **Liberal Party:** One of the principal political parties in Britain, being the successor of the Whig Party and largely identified with the doctrine of Free Trade. **Liberal Unionist:** A member of the Liberal Party who seceded in 1886 on the adoption of the Home Rule Bill. **liberalism,** *n.* **liberalist,** *n.* **liberalistic** (-lis′ tik), *a.* **liberality** (-ăl′ i ti), *n.* The quality of being liberal; bounty, munificence, generosity; largeness or breadth of views, catholicity; freedom from prejudice; a donation, a gratuity. **liberalize,** *v.t.* **liberalization** (-zā′ shun), *n.* **liberally,** *adv.*

liberate (lib′ ėr āt) [L. *līberātus*, from *līberāre*, as prec.], *v.t.* To set at liberty; to release from restraint or confinement; (*Army slang*) to steal; (*Chem.*) to set free from chemical combination. **liberation** (-ā′ shun), *n.* **Liberation Society:** An association advocating the disestablishment of the Church of England; hence, **liberationism,** *n.* **liberator,** *n.*

libertarian (lib ėr târ′ i ȧn), *a.* Pertaining to liberty, inculcating the doctrine of free will as opposed to necessitarianism. *n.* An advocate of the doctrine of free will; advocate of liberty. **libertarianism,** *n.*

liberticide (li bĕr′ ti sīd), *n.* Destruction of liberty; one who destroys liberty. *a.* Destroying liberty.

libertine (lib′ ėr tin) [L. *lībertīnus*, a freed-man, from *lībertus* (*līber*, free)], *n.* A free-thinker in religious matters; one free in moral practice; a debauchee, a profligate; one free from restraint; *a freeman; *a freedman, a manumitted slave. *a.* Latitudinarian, antinomian; loose, licentious, dissolute; free from restraint. **libertinage, libertinism,** *n.*

liberty (lib′ ėr ti) [F. *liberté*, L. *lībertātem*, nom. *-tas*, from *līber*, free], *n.* The quality or state of being free from captivity, bondage, subjection, or despotic control; the right of self-government, in politics, or religion; the right or power to act as one pleases, or to do a particular thing; permission granted to do any act; (*pl.*) rights, privileges, or exemptions, enjoyed by grant or prescription; a place or district within which certain privileges or immunities are enjoyed; a slight of decorum or courtesy; (*Phil.*) the power to do or to leave undone any particular action, according to the determination of one's mind or judgment without external restraint, freedom of the will; *a district beyond a debtors' prison where prisoners were sometimes allowed to reside. **at liberty:** Free; having the right (to do, etc.); disengaged, not occupied. **cap of liberty:** A cap of Phrygian shape worn as a symbol of liberty in ancient times by manumitted slaves; a red cap worn by the French revolutionaries. **civil liberty:** A state of natural liberty, abridged only by the laws established in the interests of the nation, State, or society. **liberty of the press:** The right to publish whatever one pleases, subject only to penalty for publishing anything mischievous, hurtful, or libellous to the public or to individuals. **natural liberty:** The power to act or do as one pleases, subject only to the laws of nature. **political liberty:** The freedom of a nation from any unjust abridgment of its rights and independence. **religious liberty:** The free right to hold what opinions one pleases in religious matters. **to set at liberty:** To free from confinement or restraint. **to take liberties:** To be unduly familiar; to act with disregard of rules or usages. **to take the liberty:** To venture; to do something without permission. **liberty hall,** *n.* A place where one may do as one pleases. **liberty man:** (*Naut.*) A sailor having permission to go ashore.

liberty ship, *n.* (*Naut.*) A prefabricated, mass-produced cargo ship produced during World War II.

libidinous (li bid' i nŭs) [L. *libīdinōsus*, from *libīdo -dinis*, lust], *a.* Characterized by lewdness or lust, lustful; lascivious. **libidinously,** *adv.* **libidinousness,** *n.*

libido (li bī' dō) [L., desire], *n.* (*Psych.*) The will to live, life force; urge of sex.

Libra (lī' brȧ) [L.], *n.* (*pl.* **-ræ**) The Balance, the seventh sign of the zodiac; one of the twelve ancient zodiacal constellations; (*Rom. Ant.*) a Roman pound; hence, a pound weight (*lb.*), a pound sterling (£).

librarian (lī brâr' i ȧn) [L. *librārius*, as foll.], *n.* One who has charge of a library. **librarianship,** *n.*

library (lī' brȧr i) [F. *librarie*, L. *librārius*, pertaining to books, from *liber*, book, orig. bark], *n.* A collection of books, esp. classified, or otherwise organized, and catalogued, to facilitate use either by the public or by private persons; a building, room, or series of rooms containing such a collection; an institution established for the formation or maintenance of such a collection; a series of books similar in subject, literary form, etc., issued (usu. in similar format) by a publisher. **circulating library** [CIRCULATE]. **free library** [PUBLIC LIBRARY]. **lending-library** [LENDING]. **public library:** A library open free to any member of the public, usu. supported by rates. **reference library:** A library the books in which may be consulted but are not usually lent out.

librate (lī brāt') [L. *librātus*, p.p. of *librāre*, to poise, from *lībra*, balance], *v.t.* To balance, to hold in equipoise. *v.i.* To be in equipoise; to move as a balance, to oscillate, to swing or sway. **libration** (lī brā' shŭn), *n.* **libration of the moon:** (*Astron.*) A real or apparent oscillation by which parts near the edges of the moon's disk are alternately visible and invisible. **libratory** (lī' brȧ tŏr i), *a.*

libretto (li bret' ō) [It., dim. of *libro*, L. *liber*, book], *n.* (*pl.* **-ti**) The words of an opera, oratorio, etc.; a book containing such words. **librettist,** *n.* One who writes a libretto.

Libyan (lib' i ȧn), *a.* Of or pertaining to ancient Libya; (*Philol.*) denoting a group of Hamitic languages comprising Berber, etc. *n.* A native or inhabitant of ancient Libya; a Libyan language.

lice, *pl.* [LOUSE].

licence (lī' sĕns) [F., from L. *licentia*, from *licēre*, to be allowed or lawful], *n.* Authority, leave, permission; consent or permission granted by a constituted authority (to marry, to publish a book, produce a play, carry on a business, etc.); a document containing such permission; a certificate of competence issued by a University or other examining body; unrestrained liberty of action, disregard of law or propriety; abuse of freedom, licentiousness; in literature or art, deviation from the ordinary rules or mode of treatment. **special licence,** *n.* A licence authorizing a marriage without banns.

license (lī' sĕns), *v.t.* To authorize by a legal grant or permission; to allow, to permit, esp. to allow entire freedom of action, comment, etc. **licensable,** *a.* **licensed victualler:** One who holds a licence to sell spirits, wines, beer, etc. **licensee** (lī sĕn sē'), *n.* One holding a licence (esp. a licensed victualler). **licenser,** *n.* **licenser of plays** or **of the press:** An officer appointed by the Crown to license performance or publication after ascertaining that certain regulations or observances have not been infringed. ***licensure,** *n.* The act of licensing, esp. to preach. **licentiate** (lī sen' shi ȧt), *n.* One holding a certificate of competence in some profession from a University or other collegiate body: (*Presbyterian Ch.*) one who has a licence to preach, and is eligible for a charge.† *v.t.* (-āt) To give a licence to. ***licentiation** (-ā' shŭn), *n.*

licentious (lī sen' shŭs) [med. L. *licentiōsus*, from L. *licentia*, LICENCE], *a.* Lascivious, dissolute, profligate, loose; unrestrained by rule or accepted laws of style, etc. **licentiously,** *adv.* **licentiousness,** *n.*

lich (lich) [A.-S. *līc*, body, orig. form (cp. Dut. *lijk*, Icel. *līk*, G. *leiche*)], *n.* A dead body, a corpse. **lich-gate,** *n.* A churchyard gate with a roof, under which a coffin may be placed while the introductory portion of the burial service is read. **lich-house,** *n.* A mortuary. **lich-owl,** *n.* The screech-owl, supposed to foretell death. **lich-stone,** *n.* A stone at the lich-gate, on which the coffin is placed. ***lich-wake** [LYKE-WAKE].

lichen (lī' kĕn) [L. *līchēn*, Gr. *leichēn*, prob. rel. to *leichein*, to lick], *n.* A cryptogamic thallophytic plant of the order *Lichenaceæ*, parasitic fungi on algal cells covering rocks, tree-trunks, etc., with variously coloured crusts; (*Path.*) a popular inflammatory eruption of the skin. **lichened,** *a.* **lichenic, licheniform** (lī ken' ik, -i fôrm), **lichenous** (lī kė nŭs), *a.* **lichenist,** *n.* **lichenography** (-nog' rȧ fi) [-GRAPHY], *n.* A description of or treatise on lichens. **lichenographer,** *n.* **lichenology** (-nol' ŏ ji) [-LOGY], *n.* That branch of botany which deals with lichens. **lichenologist,** *n.*

lichenin (lī' ke nin), *n.* (*Chem.*) A kind of starch occurring in Iceland moss and other lichens.

licit (lis' it) [L. *licitus*, p.p. of *licēre*, to be allowed], *a.* Lawful, allowed. **licitly,** *adv.*

lick (lik) [A.-S. *liccian* (cp. Dut. *likken*, G. *lecken*, also Gr. *leichein*, L. *lingere*)], *v.t.* To draw or pass the tongue over; to take in or lap (up) with the tongue; to stroke or pass lightly over (of flame, etc.); (*slang*) to flog, to chastise, to beat, to overcome, to surpass. *v.i.* To make a licking motion (of flames, etc.); (*slang*) to beat, to win. *n.* The act of licking; a slight smear or coat (as of paint); (*Am.*) a salt-lick; (*colloq.*) a smart blow or slap; (*Am. slang, usu. pl.*) great exertion, effort, or pace. **salt lick** [SALT]. **to lick into shape:** To give form or method to (from the once popular notion that young bears are born shapeless, and are licked into shape by their dam). **to lick someone's shoes:** To be servile towards. **to lick the dust:** To be beaten, to be killed; *to act in a servile manner. **to lick up:** To consume, to devour. **to take a licking:** To take a beating. **lickspittle,** *n.* An abject parasite or toady. **licker,** *n.*

lickerish (lik' ėr ish) [North. var. of O.F. *lecheros*, LECHEROUS], *a.* Nice in the choice of food; dainty, greedy of good fare; pleasing to the taste; lecherous. **lickerishly,** *adv.* **lickerishness,** *n.* ***lickerous,** *a.*

***licorice** [LIQUORICE]. **licorous** [LICKERISH].

lictor (lik' tŏr) [L., rel. to *ligāre*, to bind], *n.* (*Rom. Ant.*) A civil officer who attended the chief magistrates, and bore the fasces as a sign of authority.

lid (lid) [A.-S. *hlid* (cp. Dut. *lid*, Icel. *hlith*, G. *-lid*, in *augenlid*)], *n.* A hinged or detachable cover or cap, usu. for shutting a vessel, box, or aperture; an eyelid; (*Bot.*) an operculum; (*slang*) a hat. **lidded,** *a.* (*usu. in comb.*, as *azure-lidded*). **lidless,** *a.* Uncovered, bare; (*fig.*) sleepless, vigilant.

lido (lē' dō) [Resort near Venice], *n.* A bathing-beach, an out-door bathing-pool.

lie (1) (lī) [A.-S. *lēogan* (cp. Dut. *liegen*, G. *lügen*), whence *lyge*, a lie, *lēogere*, LIAR], *v.i.* (*pres.p.* **lying,** *past & p.p.* **lied**). To say or write anything with the deliberate intention of deceiving; to convey a false impression, to deceive. *v.t.* To take (away) or get (oneself into or out of) by lying. *n.* An intentional violation of the truth; a false statement deliberately made for the purpose of deception; (*fig.*) a deception, an imposture. **to give one the lie:** To accuse of deliberate falsehood. **to give the lie to:** To show to be false; to belie. **white lie:** A pardonable fiction or misstatement. **lie-detector,** *n.* A mechanical device which is alleged to record the emotional reactions of the person under scrutiny in terms of accompanying electrical changes in his body.

lie (2) (lī) [A.-S. *licgan* (cp. Dut. *liggen*, Icel. *liggja*, G. *liegen*, cogn. with Gr. *lechos*, L. *lectus*, bed)], *v.i.* (*pres.p.* **lying,** *past* **lay,** *p.p.* **lain, *lien** (2), lī' ėn). To rest or place oneself in a reclining or horizontal posture; to be situated or fixed in a specified condition or direction; to sleep, to lodge, to encamp (usu. at a specified place); to rest, to remain, to abide; to exist, to be, to reside, in a specified state, position, relation, etc.; (*Law*) to be sustainable (of an action, objection, etc.). *n.* Position, arrangement, direction, manner of lying; the retiring-place or lair (of an animal). **lie of the land:** (*fig.*) The posture of affairs. **to lie at one's heart:** To be a source of anxiety, care, or desire. **to lie by:** To be or stay near; to be put aside; to rest; to be quiet; to remain unused. **to lie down:** To go to rest; *to sink into the grave; (*in pres.p.*) to submit tamely. **to lie hard** or **heavy on:** To oppress, to be a weight upon. **to lie in:** To be in childbed. **to lie in one:** To be in one's power or capacity. **to lie in the way:** To be an obstacle or impediment. **to lie in wait:** To wait in ambush or concealment. **to lie low:** (*slang*) To remain in hiding; to conceal one's knowledge or intentions in order to outwit, forestall, etc. **to lie off:** (*Naut.*) To stay at a distance from the shore or another ship (of a vessel). **to lie on** or **upon:** To be incumbent upon; to depend or be dependent upon. **to lie on one's hands:** To remain unsold or undisposed of; to hang heavy (of time). **to lie on the head of:** To be imputable or chargeable to. **to lie over:** To remain unpaid; to be deferred. **to lie to:** (*Naut.*) To be checked or stopped in her course (as a ship by backing the yards or taking in sail). **to lie under:** To be subject to or oppressed by. **to lie up:** To rest, to stay in bed or in one's room to recuperate; (*Naut.*) to go into dock. **to lie with:** To lodge or sleep with; to have sexual intercourse with; to belong to, to depend on. **lie-a-bed,** *n.* A late riser.

Lied (lēd) [G.], *n.* (*pl.* ***Lieder***) A German song or ballad.

lief (lēf) [A.-S. *lēof* (cp. Dut. *lief*, G. *lieb*), cogn. with LOVE], *adv.* Willingly, gladly, freely. **a.* Dear, beloved; willing, ready, blessed. **n.* A sweetheart, a dear friend.

liege (lēj) [O.F. *lige*, prob. from O.H.G. *ledig*, free], *n.* Bound by some feudal tenure, either as a vassal or as a lord; pertaining to such tenure. *n.* A vassal bound to do service to his lord; a lord, a superior, a sovereign; a law-abiding citizen, a subject. **liegedom,** *n.* **liegeless,** *a.* **liegeman,** *n.* A liege vassal.

lien (lē' ėn, lēn, lī' ėn) [F., from L. *ligāmen*, a band, from *ligāre*, to bind], *n.* (*Law*) A right to detain the goods of another until some claim has been satisfied; (*colloq.*) an option.

lientery (lī' ėn tėr i) [F. *lienterie*, Gr. *leienteria* (*leios*, smooth, *entera*, bowels)], *n.* (*Path.*) Diarrhœa in which the food passes rapidly through the bowels undigested. **lienteric** (-ter' ik), *a.*

***lier** (lī' ėr) [LIE (2), -ER], *n.* One who lies (usu. in adv. phrases, as **lier in wait**).

lierne (li ĕrn') [F., etym. doubtful], *n.* (*Arch.*) A cross-rib connecting the main ribs in Gothic vaulting, introduced about the middle of the fourteenth century.

lieu (lū) [F., from L. *locum*, nom. *locus*, place], *n.* Place, stead, room. **in lieu of:** Instead of.

lieutenant (lėf ten' ȧnt, Am. loo-) [F. (LIEU, TENANT), cp. LOCUM TENENS], *n.* An officer acting as deputy or substitute to a superior; (*Mil.*) an officer ranking next below a captain; (*Nav.*) (lė ten' ȧnt) an officer ranking next below a lieutenant-commander. **Deputy-Lieutenant,** *n.* An officer appointed by the Lord-Lieutenant of a county to act, in certain cases, as his deputy. **Lord-Lieutenant** [LORD]. **second-lieutenant,** *n.* (*Mil.*) The lowest commissioned rank in the British army. **lieutenant-colonel,** *n.* (*Mil.*) An officer next in rank below a colonel, in actual command of a battalion. **lieutenant-commander,** *n.* (*Nav.*) An officer ranking between a lieutenant and a commander. **lieutenant-general,** *n.* (*Mil.*) An officer next in rank below a general and above a major-general. **lieutenant-governor,** *n.* A deputy governor, usu. the acting governor in subordination to a governor-general. **lieutenancy, *-antry, *lieutenantship,** *n.*

***liever** [comp. of LIEF].

life (līf) [A.-S. *līf* (cp. Icel. *līf*, O.Fris. *līf*, Dut. *lijf*, G. *leib*, cogn. with LIVE, LEAVE (2), from Aryan root *leip-*), cp. Gr. *aleiphein*, to anoint, *liparēs*, persistent], *n.* (*pl.* **lives**) The state or condition of being alive; the state of an organism in which it is capable of performing its animal or vegetable functions; animate existence; the period of such existence, any specified portion of a person's existence; the average period which a person of a given age may expect to live; a person considered as object of a policy of assurance; the living form; (*collect.*) animated existence, living things; mode, manner, or course of living; the vehicle or source of life; (*fig.*) the animating principle, the essential or inspiring idea (of a movement, etc.); animation, vivacity, spirit; one who or that which imparts spirit or animation; the active side of existence; human affairs; a narrative of one's existence, a biography; (*Theol.*) a state of spiritual regeneration, as opp. to worldly or material state of mind; existence after death; (*Games*) one of the points or chances to which each player is entitled that are lost in certain contingencies. **for one's life, for dear life:** In order to escape death. **for the life of me, upon my life:** As if my life depended upon it (in asseveration). **to bring to life:** To restore (an unconscious or apparently lifeless person). **to come to life:** To revive from such a state. **to the life:** As if the original stood before one (of a portrait, etc.). **good, bad life,** *n.* (*Insurance*) A person likely, or unlikely, to reach the expectation of life age. **high life,** *n.* Social custom of the fashionable class. **life-annuity,** *n.* A sum of money paid yearly during the portion of a person's life from a specified age to death. **life-assurance,** *n.* An assurance on a person's life. **life-belt,** *n.* A belt of buoyant or inflated material for supporting a person in the water. **life-blood,** *n.* The blood necessary to life; (*fig.*) that which is essential to existence, success, or strength. **life-boat,** *n.* A boat specially constructed for saving life in storms and heavy seas. **lifebuoy** [BUOY]. **life-estate,** *n.* A property that is held only until one's death, and then reverts to a specified heir. **life-giving,** *a.* Inspiriting, invigorating, animating. **life-guard,** *n.* A guard appointed to protect the person of some one, esp. a sovereign; an attendant on a bathing beach who renders aid to swimmers in difficulties. **Life Guards:** A regiment of cavalry forming part of the body-guard of the British sovereign, hence **Life Guardsman. life-insurance** [LIFE-ASSURANCE]. **life-interest,** *n.* An interest or estate terminating with the life of a person. **life-jacket,** *n.* A sleeveless jacket used as a life-belt. **life-line,** *n.* A rope used for saving life; a rope used as an additional safeguard; a vital line of communication. **lifelong, livelong,** *a.* Lasting throughout life. **life-office,** *n.* A life-assurance company or its office. **life-peer,** *n.* **life-peerage,** *n.* A peerage lapsing with the death of the holder. **life-preserver,** *n.* An apparatus for preserving life from drowning or fire; a loaded stick or cane for defending one's life. **liferent,** *n.* (*Sc. Law*) A rent to which one is entitled for one's life. **liferenter,** *n.* **life-spring,** *n.* A spring or source of life. **life-string,** *n.* One's hold on life. **life-table,** *n.* A table of statistics showing the average expectation of life at different ages. **lifetime,** *n.* The duration of one's life. **life-weary,** *a.* **life-work,** *n.* The work to which one devotes the best part of one's life. ***lifeful,** *a.* **lifeless,** *a.* Destitute or deprived of life; dead, inanimate, inorganic, inert; deprived of physical energy; (*fig.*) dull, heavy, spiritless, vapid. **lifelessly,** *adv.* **lifelessness,** *n.* **lifelike,** *a.* Like a living being; like the original (of a portrait). **lifelikeness,** *n.* **lifer,** *n.* (*slang*) One sentenced to imprisonment for life; a sentence of this.

lift (1) (lift) [Icel. *lypta* (pron. lif′ tȧ), rel. to *lopt*, the air, and foll.], *v.t.* To raise to a higher position, to elevate; to hold or support on high; to raise or take up from the ground, to pick up; (*colloq.*) to carry off, to steal, to appropriate, to plagiarize; to dig up (potatoes); to raise or remove (a weight, anxiety, etc.); (*fig.*) to exalt, to elate; *to bear, to support. *v.i.* To perform or attempt to perform the act of raising something; to rise (as a ship on the waves, or a sail in the wind); to rise and disperse (as a mist). *n.* The act of lifting; the degree of elevation; a rise; a hoisting-machine, an elevator for persons, goods, or material; assistance in lifting; a helping hand; that which is or has to be raised; a rise in condition; *a thing stolen. **dead lift** [DEAD]. **to lift one's elbow** [ELBOW]. **to lift the hand:** To strike a blow (at). **to lift up the eyes:** To look, to gaze; to direct prayers (to). **to lift up one's head:** To recover from illness or prostration. ***to lift up the voice:** To cry aloud in joy or sorrow. **lift-lock,** *n.* A canal lock. **lift-pump,** *n.* A pump that lifts to its own level, distinguished from a force-pump.

***lift** (2) (lift) [A.-S. *lyft*, cogn. with prec. and with LOFT], *n.* The sky, the upper regions of the air.

ligament (lig′ ȧ mėnt) [F., from L. *ligāmentum*, from *ligāre*, see foll.], *n.* Anything which binds; a bond, a tie; (*Anat.*) a short band of fibrous tissue by which bones are bound together; any tough bands or tissues holding parts together. **ligamental, -tary, -tous** (lig ȧ men′ tȧl, -tȧr i, -tŭs), *a.*

ligate (lī′ gāt) [L. *ligātus*, p.p. of *ligāre* to tie], *v.t.* To tie with a ligature. **ligation** (-gā′ shŭn), *n.*

ligature (lig′ ȧ chŭr) [as prec.], *n.* That which binds, esp. a thread or cord to tie arteries or veins or a wire used in removing tumours; anything that unites, a bond; (*Print.*) two or more letters cast on one shank, as *ff*, *ffi*; (*Mus.*) a tie connecting notes, a slur. *v.t.* To bind with a ligature.

liger (lī′ gėr), *n.* (*Zool.*) A cross between a lion and a tigress.

light (1) (līt) [A.-S. *lēoht* (cp. Dut. and G. *licht*, Icel. *ljos*, *logi*, L. *lux*, Gr. *leukos*, white)], *n.* The natural agent which, by acting on the retina, stimulates the sense of sight; the sensation produced by the stimulation of the visual organs; the state or condition in which things are visible, opp. to darkness; the amount of illumination in a place or required by a person; (*fig.*) one's fair opportunities, one's chances; a source of light, a lamp, a candle, the sun, a beacon, a lighthouse, a ship's lamp, etc.; daylight; that by which light is admitted into a place, a window, a division of a window, esp. a perpendicular division in a mullioned window, a pane or glazed compartment in a greenhouse; (*fig.*) exposure, publicity, general knowledge; point of view, aspect; mental illumination, elucidation, enlightenment; (*fig.*) one who enlightens, a model, an example; (*pl.*) one's intellectual powers or capacity; (*slang*, *pl.*) eyes, optics; (*Law*) the right to have the light falling on windows unobstructed; (*Paint.*) the manner in which the light falls on a picture; the illuminated part of a picture. *a.* Having light, bright, clear, not dark; pale-coloured, fair. *v.t.* (*p.* & *p.p.* **lit, lighted**) To kindle, to set fire to; to give light to; to fill (up) with light; to conduct with a light; to brighten. *v.i.* To take fire, to begin to burn; to be illuminated; to brighten (up). (*colloq.*) To decamp, to make tracks, to hurry away. **ancient lights** [ANCIENT (1)]. **between the lights:** In the twilight. **men of light and leading:** Men of enlightenment and influence. **the light of one's countenance:** One's favour, approval, sanction. **to bring to light:** To discover, to detect, to disclose. **to come to light:** To become known. **to see light, to see the light:** To come into existence, to be born; to come into view; to be published; to be enlightened. **to shed** or **throw light upon:** To elucidate, to explain. **to stand in one's own light:** To frustrate one's own purposes or wishes. **light-due, -duty,** *n.* A toll on ships for the maintenance of lighthouses, etc. **light-year,** *n.* (*Astron.*) The distance (about 6,000,000,000,000 miles) travelled by light in one year. **lit-up,** *adv.* (*colloq.*) Slightly drunk. **lightish** (1), *a.* **lightless,** *a.*

light (2) (līt) [A.-S. *lēoht* (cp. Icel. *lēttr*, G. *leicht*, Sansk. *laghu*, Gr. *elachus*)], *a.* Of small weight, not heavy; easy to be lifted, carried, moved, handled, etc.; not burdensome, easily borne; easy to be performed; not cumbersome, adapted for small loads; lightly armed and equipped (of troops); nimble, active, quick; of low specific gravity; short in weight, below the standard weight; not heavily laden; adapted for rapid movement; employed in or adapted for easy work; not massive, not heavy in construction or appearance; graceful, elegant; thin, delicate (of fabrics); loose or sandy (as soil); not dense (of bread); not strong (of wine, beer, etc.); not forcible or violent, gentle, slight; not intense or emphatic; of little consequence, unimportant, trivial; thoughtless, flighty, frivolous; volatile, fickle; wanton, unchaste; cheerful, merry, gay, airy; dizzy, giddy, deranged, delirious. **to make light of:** To disregard, to slight; to treat as pardonable or excusable. **light-armed,** *a.* ***light-brain,** *n.* An empty-headed person. **light-bread,** *n.* (*Am.*) Bread made of wheat-flour, opp. to that made from corn-meal. **light engine:** An engine running light, that is, with no train attached. **light-fingered,** *a.* Dexterous in stealing; given to thieving. **light-foot,** *a.* Nimble, active. **n.* A name for the hare, also for the deer. **light-footed,** *a.* **light-handed,** *a.* Light of touch, light in handling; (*Naut.*) short of the proper complement of men. **light-handedly,** *adv.* **light-handedness,** *n.* **light-headed,** *a.* Delirious; *unsteady, loose, thoughtless. **light-headedness,** *n.* **light-hearted,** *a.* Free from care or anxiety; gay, merry, cheerful. **light-heartedly,** *adv.* **light-heartedness,** *n.* **light-heeled,** *a.* Nimble, quick-moving, light-footed. **light-legged,** *a.* Swift of foot, active. **light literature:** Books intended for entertainment; sometimes applied to belles-lettres as a class. **light marching order:** (*Mil.*) Marching order in which each man's burden is restricted to his arms and a supply of ammunition. **light-minded,** *a.* Fickle, unsteady, volatile. **light-mindedly,** *adv.* **light-mindedness,** *n.* **light o' love:** An inconstant woman; a harlot; *an old dance-tune. **light-porter:** A porter carrying light loads. **light railway:** A railway, usu. less than the standard gauge, adapted for light traffic. **light-skirts,** *n.* A woman of light character; a strumpet. **light-spirited,** *a.* Cheerful, merry, gay. **light-weight,** *n.* A horse or man below the average weight; a boxer of 135 lb. or under. **light-winged,** *a.* Having swift wings; (*fig.*) volatile. **lightish** (2), *a.* **lightly,** *adv.* In a light manner. **lightness,** *n.*

light (3) (līt) [*lihtan*, orig. to lighten or relieve of a burden, as prec.], *v.i.* To descend as from flight, to settle (of a bird); to alight, to dismount; to come down, to chance (upon). *v.t.* (*Naut.*) To lift or help to move (along, etc.). **to light up:** (*Naut.*) To slacken.

lighten (1) (lī′ tėn) [A.-S. *lēohtan*], *v.i.* To become light, to brighten; to emit lightning, to flash; to shine out. *v.t.* To illuminate, to enlighten.

lighten (2) (lī′ tėn) [LIGHT (2), -EN], *v.t.* To reduce in weight; to reduce the weight or load of; to relieve, to mitigate, to alleviate; to cheer. *v.i.* To be lightened, to grow lighter; to become less burdensome.

lighter (1) (lī′ tėr), *n.* A pocket appliance for lighting cigarettes, pipe, etc.

lighter (2) (lī′ tėr) [perh. from Dut. *lichter* or LIGHT (2), -ER], *n.* A large, open, usu. flat-bottom boat, used in loading and unloading ships; a heavy barge for carrying railway trains, etc. *v.t.* To carry or remove in a lighter. **lighterage,** *n.* **lighterman,** *n.*

lighthouse (līt′ hows), *n.* A tower or other structure supporting a powerful light for the warning and guidance of mariners.

lightning (līt′ ning), *n.* The dazzling flash caused by the discharge of electricity between clouds or from a cloud to the earth; (*poet.*) lightening, brightening. **lightning-arrester,** *n.* A contrivance for deflecting the electrical discharge in thunderstorms and protecting electrical instruments **lightning-bug,** *n.* (*Am.*) A fire-fly. **lightning-conductor, -rod,** *n.* A wire or rod for carrying the electrical discharge to earth and protecting a building, mast, etc., against damage. **lightning strike,** *n.* Workers' strike without notice being given.

lights (līts), *n.pl.* The lungs of animals, esp. as food for cats, etc.

lightship (līt′ ship), *n.* A moored vessel carrying a light to give warning or guidance to mariners.

lightsome (1) (līt′ sŏm), *a.* Light-hearted, playful, gay; airy, graceful, nimble. **lightsomely,** *adv.* **lightsomeness,** *n.*

***lightsome** (2) (līt′ sŏm), *a.* Luminous, light-giving; bright, lighted up.

lightwood (līt′ wud), *n.* Applied to various American trees having resinous wood, easily kindled; the Australian *Acacia melonoxylon* and other trees yielding light timber.

lign-aloes (līn ăl′ ōz) [late L. *lignum aloēs*, trans. of Gr. *xulaloē*, wood of the aloe], *n.* The bitter drug aloe; a fragrant Mexican wood.

ligneous (lig′ nė ŭs) [L. *ligneus*, from *lignum*, wood], *a.* Made or consisting of wood; resembling wood; woody. **lignescent** (lig nes′ ėnt), *a.* **ligniferous** (lig nif′ ėr ŭs) [-FEROUS], *a.* **ligniform** (lig′ ni fôrm) [-FORM], *a.* **lignify,** *v.t.* and *i.* **lignification** (-kā′ shŭn), *n.* **lignin,** *n.* (*Chem.*) The essential substance of woody fibre, xylogen. **ligniperdous** (lig ni per′ dŭs) [L. *perdere*, to destroy], *a.* Destructive of wood (as certain insects). **lignite** (lig′ nīt) [-ITE], *n.* A partially carbonized coal showing fibrous woody structure, usually of Cretaceous or Tertiary age. **lignitic** (-nit′ ik), *a.* **lignivorous** (-niv′ ŏr ŭs), *a.*

ligno-, *comb. form.* Pertaining to wood.

lignose (lig′ nōs), *n.* One of the constituents of lignin, a powerful explosive.

lignum (lig′ nŭm), *n.* (*Bot.*) The dense, fibrous, durable substance of exogenous plants, wood, etc. **lignum vitæ:** The very hard and heavy wood of *Guaiacum officinale* used for rollers, presses, blocks, skittle-balls, etc.

ligula (lig′ ū lȧ) [L., dim. of *lingua*, tongue], *n.* (*pl.* **-læ**) A tongue-like organ or part; (*Bot.*) a membranous process at the top of the sheath beneath the blade of a grass; one of the rays of a composite plant. **ligular, liguliform** (li gū′ li fôrm), *a.* **ligulate** (lig′ ū lȧt), **-lated** -(lā′ tėd), *a.* (*Bot.*) Strap-shaped; having a ligula. **ligule,** *n.* A ligula.

ligurite (lig′ ū rīt) [*Liguria*, in northern Italy], *n.* (*Min.*) An apple-green variety of titanite, ranking as a gem, found in the Apennines.

like (1) (līk) [A.-S. *līc* in *gelīc* (cp. Dut. *gelijk*, Icel. *līkr*, *glīkr*, G. *gleich*, also LICH)], *a.* Resembling, similar; such as; almost the same as; equal or nearly equal in quantity, quality, or degree; characteristic of; disposed towards, inclined to; *probable, likely. *adv.* *In the same manner as; (*colloq.*, *used ellipt. as prep. or conj.*) as, in the manner of, to the same extent or degree as; (*vulg.*) as it were, so to speak; *likely, probably. *n.* A counterpart; a similar or equal thing, person, or event; (*Golf*) a stroke that brings the number of strokes on that side up to an equality with the other. **had like:** (*now colloq.*) Came near to; was or were nearly; had a narrow escape of. **something like:** In some way or nearly resembling; first-rate, highly satisfactory (*with emphasis on* like). **the likes of:** (*colloq.*) People like you or me (*usu. deprecatingly*). **to feel like:** To feel as if one resembled; to feel as if one were the same as; (*colloq.*) to feel disposed or inclined to. **to look like:** To resemble in appearance; to have the appearance of; to seem likely. **like-minded,** *a.* Having similar disposition, opinions, purpose, etc.

like (2) (līk) [A.-S. *līcian* (cp. Dut. *lijken*, Icel. *līka*), as prec.], *v.t.* To be pleased with; to be inclined towards or attracted by; to enjoy; to be fond of. *to be pleasing to, to suit (*usu. impers.*). *v.i.* To be pleased; to choose; *to thrive. *n.* Liking; a longing desire; predilection (*usu. in pl.*). **likeable,** *a.* **likeableness,** *n.*

-like [LIKE (1)], *suf.* Forming adjectives; as in *childlike, saintlike, warlike*; forming adverbs, as in *childlike she replied.*

likely (līk′ li) [Icel. *līkligr*], *a.* (**-lier, -liest**) Probable, credible, plausible; liable, to be expected (to); promising, suitable, well-adapted. *adv.* Probably. **likelihood, likeliness,** *n.*

liken (lī′ kėn), *v.t.* To compare, to represent as similar (to); *to make like.

likeness (līk′ nės), *n.* Similarity, resemblance; a picture or other representation of a person or thing; form, appearance, guise.

likewise (līk′ wīz), *adv.* or *conj.* In like manner; also, moreover, too.

liking (lī′ king) [A.-S. *līcung*], *n.* The state of being pleased; inclination, fondness, regard, fancy; *state of the body. **to one's liking:** To one's taste.

lilac (lī′ lȧk) [F. and Sp., from Arab. and Pers. *līlăk*, var. of *nīlak*, dim. of *nīl*, blue, indigo], *n.* A shrub of the genus *Syringa*, esp. *S. vulgaris*, with very fragrant pale violet or purple flowers, white in cultivated varieties. *a.* Of the colour of lilac.

liliaceous (lil i ā′ shŭs) [L. *līliaceus*, from *līlium*, LILY], *a.* Pertaining to lilies, or the *Liliaceæ*, an order of endogens. **lilied** [LILY].

lilli-pilli (li lē′ pi lē′) [Austral. abor.], *n.* A large timber tree with edible fruit.

Lilliputian (lil i pū′ shȧn), *a.* Of or pertaining to Lilliput, an imaginary country in Swift's 'Gulliver's Travels,' the inhabitants of which were pigmies; pigmy, diminutive. *n.* A native of Lilliput; a pigmy.

lills (lilz) [unknown], *n.pl.* Very small pins.

lilt (lilt) [M.E. *lulte*, etym. doubtful], *v.i.* To sing in cheerful, lively style; (*prov.*) to jerk, to spring. *v.t.* To sing in a lively style. *n.* A lively tune; the melody, rhythm, or cadence of a song.

lily (lil′ i) [A.-S. *lilie*, L. *līlium*, Gr. *leirion*], *n.* A flower or plant of the bulbous genus *Lilium*, producing white or coloured flowers of great beauty, esp. the Madonna lily, *L. candidum*; applied to various plants having resemblances, as the Lent-lily or daffodil, the water-lily, etc.; (*Her.*) the fleur-de-lis; hence (*pl.*) the royal arms of France; (*fig.*) a person or thing of unsullied whiteness or purity; a fair complexion. *a.* Pure white; pure, unsullied. **to paint the lily:** To try to improve what is already perfect. **lilied,** *a.* Lilylike in complexion; *full of or covered with lilies. **lily of the valley:** A fragrant spring-flowering plant of the genus *Convallaria*, with a scape of white hanging cuplike flowers. **lily-handed,** *a.* Having delicate hands. **lily-iron,** *n.* The detachable barbed head of a harpoon. **lily-livered,** *a.* Cowardly, dastardly. **lily-pad,** *n.* The broad floating leaf of the water-lily. **lily-white,** *a.* Pure white.

Lima (lē′ mȧ) [capital of Peru], *n.* **Lima bean:** An edible climbing bean, *Phaseolus lunatus.*

limaceous (lī mā′ shŭs) [L. *līmax -ācis*, slug or snail, -ACEOUS], *a.* (*Zool.*) Pertaining to the genus *Limax* or the family *Limacidæ* which contains the slugs. **limaciform** (lī măs′ i fôrm), *a.* **limacoid** (lī′ mȧ koid), *a.* and *n.*

limaçon (lē ma son) [F., snail, as prec.], *n.* (*Math.*) A particular curve based on the union of two ovals.

***limation** (lī mā′ shŭn) [L. *līmātio -ōnem*, from *līmāre*, to file], *n.* The act of filing or polishing. ***limature** (lī′ mȧ tūr), *n.* Filing, particles filed off.

limb (1) (lim) [A.-S. *lim* (cp. Icel. *limr*)], *n.* One of the articulated extremities of an animal, an arm, leg, or wing; a main branch of a tree; (*fig.*) a member, branch, or arm; (*colloq.*) an impish child or urchin. *v.t.* To tear the limbs from, to dismember. **limb of the law:** A lawyer; a policeman. ***limb-meal,** *adv.* Limb from limb. **limbed,** *a.* Having limbs (*usu. in comb.* as *large-limbed*). **limbless,** *a.* **on a limb:** (*Amer. colloq.*) In a predicament.

limb (2) (lim) [L. *limbus*, border, edging], *n.* An edge or border; (*Astron.*) the outermost edge of the sun, moon, or other heavenly body; the graduated arc of a sextant, etc.; (*Bot.*) the expanded portion of a gamosepalous corolla, petal, etc. **limbation** (-bā′ shůn), *n.* **limbic, limbiferous** (-bif′ ėr ůs), **limbous,** *a.*

limbate (lim′ bāt) [L. *limbus*, a border], *a.* Bordered, having a differently-coloured border.

limber (1) (lim′ bėr) [formerly *limmer*, *lymor*, perh. from F. *limonière*, from *limon*, shaft], *n.* The detachable part of a gun-carriage consisting of two wheels and ammunition-box. *v.t.* To attach the limber to the gun (usu. with *up*). *v.i.* To fasten (up) the limber and gun.

limber (2) (lim′ bėr) [perh. a corr. of F. *lumière*, light, hole], *n.* (*Naut.*) A gutter on each side of the kelson for draining; (*pl.*) the gutters and holes in the floor-timbers. **limber-passage,** *n.*

limber (3) (lim′ bėr) [etym. doubtful], *a.* Flexible, lithe. **limberness,** *n.*

limbo (lim′ bō) [L., abl. of *limbus*, see LIMB (2)], *n.* The edge or uttermost limit of hell, the abode of souls to whom the benefits of redemption could not be applied, through no fault of their own; prison, confinement; (*fig.*) a place to which things of no value or importance may be relegated.

limbus (lim′ bůs), *n.* A limb (2); limbo.

lime (1) (līm) [A.-S. *līm* (cp. Dut. *lijm*, Icel. *līm*, G. *leim*, also L. *līmus*, mud, LOAM)], *n.* Calcium oxide, a calcareous earth obtained by burning limestone, used for making mortar, for manure, etc.; bird-lime. *v.t.* To smear with bird-lime; (*fig.*) to ensnare; to manure with lime; to spread lime over (land); to dress (hides) in lime and water. **quicklime,** *n.* Anhydrous calcium oxide. **slaked lime:** This after combination with water, hydrate of lime. **lime-burner,** *n.* One who burns limestone to make lime. **lime-cast,** *n.* A covering of lime in the form of mortar. *a.* Covered with this (of a building). **lime-kiln,** *n.* A kiln in which limestone is calcined and reduced to lime. **limelight,** *n.* A light produced by projecting a jet of ignited hydrogen and oxygen upon a ball of lime, making it incandescent; (*fig.*) the glare of publicity. **lime-pit,** *n.* (*Tanning*) A pit for liming hides. **limestone,** *n.* Any rock the basis of which is carbonate of lime, esp. mountain limestone, the principal rock of the Carboniferous series. **lime-twig,** *n.* A twig smeared with bird-lime to catch birds. **limewash,** *n.* Whitewash. *v.t.* To whitewash. **lime-water,** *n.* A solution of lime in water used medicinally and for refining sugar. **limewort,** *n.* The brook-lime. **limy,** *a.* Viscous, tenacious; of the nature of, resembling, or containing lime. **liminess,** *n.*

lime (2) (līm) [perh. var. of A.-S. *lind*, LINDEN], *n.* The linden-tree. **lime-tree,** *n.*

lime (3) (līm) [F., from Sp. *lima*, Arab. *līmah* (cp. LEMON)], *n.* The fruit of a West Indian tree, *Citrus medica*, var. *acida*, smaller and more acid than the lemon, or of *C. medica*, var. *limetta*, the sweet lime. **lime-juice,** n. The juice of the lime used as a beverage. **limey,** *n.* (*U.S.A. slang*) A British sailor.

lime-hound [LYAM-HOUND].

Limehouse (līm hous) [*Limehouse*, a district in East London], *n.* Passionate political orations in the vein of Lloyd George at Limehouse in 1909.

limelight [LIME (1)].

limen (lī′ mėn) [L., threshold], *n.* (*Psych.*) The stage of consciousness at which a given stimulus begins to produce sensation and below which it is imperceptible. **liminal, liminary** (im′ i nål, -når i), *a.*

Limerick (lim′ ėr ik) [said to be from the chorus 'Will you come up to *Limerick*?' sung at the end of impromptu verses at convivial parties in Ireland], *n.* A nonsense verse, usu. of five lines, the first, second, and fifth, and the third and fourth of which rhyme together respectively.

limit (lim′ it) [F. *limite*, L. *līmitem*, nom. *līmes*, rel. to LIMEN], *n.* A boundary, a line, point, or edge marking termination or utmost extent; a restraint, a check; that which has bounds, a district, a period, etc.; (*slang*) a person, demand, opinion, or the like, of an exaggerated kind. *v.t.* To set a limit or bound to; to confine within certain bounds; to restrict (to); to serve as boundary or restriction to. **limit man,** *n.* (*Running, etc.*) The person having the longest start. ***limitable,** *a.* **limitarian** (lim i târ′ i ån), *a.* (*Theol.*) Tending to limit. *n.* One who believes in limited redemption. **limitary** (lim′ i tår i), *a.* Stationed at the limits (of a guard); limited, circumscribed; limiting, confining. **limitation** (-tā′ shůn), *n.* The act of limiting; the state of being limited; that which limits; a restriction; (*Law*) the period within which an action must be brought and beyond which it may not lie. **statute of limitation:** A statute fixing such periods. **limitative** (lim′ i tā tiv), *a.* **limited liability** [LIABLE]. **limited monarchy:** A monarchy in which the power of the sovereign is limited by a constitution. **limited redemption:** (*Theol.*) The doctrine that only a portion of the human race can be saved. **limitedly,** *adv.* **limitedness,** *n.* **limiter,** ***limitour** (lim′ i tėr), *n.* One who or that which limits; *a friar licensed to beg or exercise his functions within certain limits. **limitless,** *a.*

limitrophe (lim′ i trōf) [F., from late L. *līmi trophus*, L. *līmes līmitis*, LIMIT, Gr. *-trophos*, feeding, from trephein, to feed], *a.* On the border, adjacent (to).

limma (lim′ å) [late L., from Gr. *leimma*, remnant, from *leipein*, to leave], *n.* (*Mus.*) The semitone in the Pythagorean scale; (*Gr. Pros.*) a time or pause unexpressed by a syllable, indicated by the mark ʌ.

limmer (lim′ ėr) [Sc., etym. doubtful], *n.* A jade, a huzzy; a strumpet; a rogue, a scoundrel.

limn (lim) [M.E. *limnen*, contr. from *luminen*, O.F. *luminer*, to LUMINE], *v.t.* To paint or draw, to depict, to portray; *to paint in water-colour, *to illuminate (a book, manuscript, etc.). **limner** (lim′ nėr), *n.*

limnology (lim nol′ ǒ ji) [*limnē*, lake, -LOGY], *n.* The study of lakes, esp. of their physical phenomena; the study of pond life. **limnobiology** [BIOLOGY], *n.* The study of living organisms found in fresh water.

limonite (lī′ mǒ nīt) [Gr. *leimōn*, meadow], *n.* (*Min.*) A hydrated sesquioxide of iron, orig. bog iron-ore.

limousine (li moo zēn′) [F., orig. a coarse cape or cloak of wool or goat's hair], *n.* A motor-car having a closed body like a coupé with a roof projecting over the driver's seat.

limp (1) (limp) [etym. obscure, cogn. with M.H.G. *limphin*], *v.i.* To walk lamely; to halt; to be irregular (of verse, logic, etc.). *n.* The act of limping; a limping step or walk. **limpingly,** *adv.*

limp (2) (limp) [etym. doubtful], *a.* Wanting in stiffness, flaccid, flexible, pliable; (*fig.*) lacking in firmness. **limply,** *adv.* **limpness,** *n.*

limpet (lim′ pėt) [M.E. *lempet*, A.-S. *lempedu*, late L. *lampēdra*, limpet, LAMPREY], *n.* Any individual of the genus of gasteropods *Patella*, having an open conical shell, found adhering firmly to rocks.

limpid (lim′ pid) [F. *limpide*, L. *limpidus*, rel. to *lympha*, LYMPH], *a.* Clear, pellucid, transparent; (*fig.*) lucid, perspicuous. **limpidly,** *adv.* **limpidity** (-pid′ i ti), **limpidness,** *n.*

limp-wort [LIME-WORT, see LIME (1)].

limy [LIME (1)].

lin [LINN].

linage (lī′ nȧj), *n.* Amount of printed matter reckoned by lines; payment by the line.

linch (linch) [A.-S. *hlinc*, cp. LINKS], *n.* A ledge; a linchet; a steep bank or ridge; an unploughed strip between fields. **linchet,** *n.* An unploughed strip serving as a boundary; a cultivation terrace on the side of a steep hill.

linch-pin (linch′ pin) [A.-S. *lynis*, an axle-tree (cp. Dut. *luns*, G. *lünse*), PIN], *n.* A pin serving to hold a wheel on the axle.

Lincoln green (ling′ kȯn grēn′), *n.* Bright green cloth formerly made at Lincoln, worn by archers.

lincrusta (ling krŭs′ tȧ) [L. *linum*, thread, *crusta*, skin, crust], *n.* A canvas-backed material with designs in bold relief, used for decorating walls and ceilings.

linctus (lingk′ tŭs) [L., a licking, from *lingere*, to lick], *n.* (*pl.* **-uses**) A medicine taken by licking, also called **lincture.**

linden (lin′ dėn) [A.-S. *lind* (cp. Dut. and G. *linde*, Gr. *elatē*, fir)], *n.* A tree of the genus *Tilia*, esp. *T. Europæa*, with soft timber, heart-shaped leaves, and small clusters of delicately-scented flowers, the lime-tree.

line (1) (līn) [ult. from L. *līnea*, fem. of *līneus*, flaxen. from *līnum*, flax, through A.-S. *line*, and in later senses F. *ligne*], *n.* A thread or string; (*Naut.*) a rope, a piece of rope used for sounding or other purposes; a cord, string, wire, etc., used for specific purposes, as with hooks for fishing, with a plumb for testing verticality; a clothes-line; a cord for measuring, etc.; a wire or cable for telegraph or telephone; the route traversed by this; (*fig.*) a rule or direction; (*pl.*) one's lot in life; a thread-like mark; such a mark drawn by a pencil, pen, graver, or other instrument; a streak, narrow band, seam, furrow, wrinkle, etc., resembling this; (*Math.*) that which has length without breadth or thickness, the boundary of a surface, the track of a moving point, the curve connecting a series of points; (*Elec.*) the electro-magnetic unit of magnetic force or flux; (*Naut.*) the equator; shape of contour, outline, lineament; (*pl.*) the plan or outlines shown in the sections of a ship; (*fig.*) a scheme, a plan, design; a limit, a boundary; a row or continuous series of letters, words, men, or other objects; (*colloq.*) a short letter, a note; a single verse of poetry; (*pl.*) a piece of poetry, a specified quantity of verse or prose for a schoolboy to copy out as an imposition; (*pl.*) a certificate of marriage; (*Mil.*, *pl.*) a series of trenches, ramparts, etc.; also a double row of men ranged as in order of battle; the aggregate of troops in the army apart from the Guards, engineers, artillery, supply corps, etc., and usu. cavalry; (*Nav.*) a row of ships drawn up in order; a series of persons related in direct descent or succession, family, lineage; a series of ships or public conveyances plying between certain places or under one management; a railway track; a railway system under one management; (*Comm.*) a certain branch of business, a certain class of goods, a stock of these, an order for these; (*fig.*) field of activity, province; particular interest; the twelfth part of an inch (U.S.A., $\frac{1}{1000}$th). *v.t.* To draw lines upon, to cover with lines; to mark (in, off, etc.) with lines; to spread out, extend, or post (troops, etc.) in line. *v.i.* To come or extend into line; to form a line beside or along (of troops). **hard lines** [HARD]. **to line through:** To cross out. **to line up:** To arrange, to array; to take the side of. **line-up:** (*Cinema*) To get the camera into position and focus before taking a scene. **line-of-battle ship** or **ship of the line:** A ship powerful enough to fight in the line of battle. **one's line of country:** One's special field of interest. **line of distance** [DISTANCE]. **to give one line enough:** To give a person his fling so as to catch or defeat him at last. **to read between the lines:** To detect the hidden or unexpressed meaning of a letter, speech, etc. **line block:** (*Print.*) A metal plate on which the black and white parts only of a subject are reproduced by photography and etched into relief on the metal. **line-drawing,** *n.* A drawing with pen or pencil. **line-engraving,** *n.* An engraving with incised lines. **line frequency:** (*Television*) The frequency with which the lines in a scanned image are repeated. **line scanning:** (*Television*) That system of scanning in which the field of the image is repeatedly traversed by the scanning spot in straight lines. **lineman,** *n.* A man employed in the maintenance and repair of a line of railway, telegraph, etc.; (*Surveying*) a man who carries the line or chain. **linesman,** *n.* A soldier in a regiment of the line; a lineman; (*Lawn Tennis and Football*) a person who has to note when and where a ball crosses a line.

line (2) (līn) [A.-S. *līn*, flax (cp. Dut. *lijn*, O.H.G. *lin*, Icel. *līn*), perh. from or cogn. with L. *līnum*, see prec.], *n.* The fine long fibre of flax separated from the tow.

line (3) (līn) [from prec.], *v.t.* To put a covering of different material on the inside of (a garment, box, etc.); to serve as such a covering for; (*fig.*) to fill the inside of. **liner** (1), *n.* One who makes or fits linings; (*Mach.*) a lining of a cylinder; one cylinder lining another; a strip of metal put between parts to adjust them; (*Motor.*) the friction substance of a brake. **lining,** *n.* The covering of the inside of anything; that which is within, contents.

line (4) (līn) [F. *ligner*, cp. LINE (1)]. *v.t.* To cover, to impregnate (a bitch).

lineage (lin′ ė ȧj) [O.F. *lignage* (LINE (1), -AGE)], *n.* Descendants in a direct line from a common progenitor, ancestry, pedigree.

lineal (lin′ ė ȧl) [F. *linéal*, late L. *līneālis*, from *līnea*, LINE (1)], *a.* Ascending or descending in the direct line of ancestry, opp. to collateral; linear. **lineality** (-ăl′ i ti), *n.* **lineally,** *adv.*

lineament (lin′ ė ȧ mėnt) [F. *linéament*, L. *līneāmentum*, from *lineāre*, from *līnea*, LINE (1)], *n.* (*usu. in pl.*) Characteristic lines or features; outline, contour.

linear (lin′ ė ȧr) [L. *līneāris*, as prec.], *a.* Composed of or having the form of lines; having a straight or lengthwise direction; (*Math.*) involving magnitudes one degree or dimension only; (*Bot. and Zool.*) narrow, slender. **linear accelerator,** *n.* (*Phys.*) An apparatus for accelerating changed particles to high energies. **linear perspective:** Perspective dealing with the apparent positions, magnitudes, and forms of objects, opp. to aerial perspective. **linearly,** *adv.* **lineate** (lin′ ė ȧt), *a.* (*Bot.*) Marked with lines, esp. long straight lines (of leaves). **lineation** (-ā′ shŭn), *n.* **lineolate** (lin′ ė ō lăt), *a.* (*Bot.*) Marked with minute lines.

lineman [LINE (1)].

linen (lin′ ėn) [A.-S. *līnen*, adj. (*līn*, LINE (2), -EN)], *n.* A cloth made of flax; (*collect.*) articles chiefly made of linen, esp. underclothing, sheets, tablecloths, etc. *a.* Made of flax; (*fig.*) white, blanched. **linen-draper,** *n.*

liner (2) (lī′ nėr), *n.* (*Naut.*) One of a regular line of passenger ships; colouring material for pencilling the eyebrows; a slab of metal on which pieces of marble, etc., are fastened for polishing; see also LINE (3).

linesman [LINE (1)].

ling (1) (ling) [cp. E.Fris. and Dut. *leng*, G. *länge*, Icel. *langa*, cogn. with LONG], *n.* A long slender food-fish, *Molva vulgaris*, of the northern seas.

ling (2) (ling) [Icel. *lyng*], *n.* Heather or heath, *Calluna vulgaris*.

-ling (1) [A.-S. and O.H.G. *-ling* (-EL or -LE, -ING)], *suf.* Forming nouns (now only with a diminutive force), as *darling*, *gosling*, *lordling*, *youngling*.

-ling (2) [A.-S. *-linga*, *-lunga*, adverbial suffix], *suf.* Forming adverbs, as *darkling*.

lingam (ling′ gȧm) [Sansk. a mark, a penis], *n.* The phallus representative of the god Siva, in Hindu mythology.

lingel (ling′ gėl) [O.F. *ligneul*, ult. from L. *linea*, LINE (1)], *n.* (*now Sc.*) A cobbler's waxed thread.

linger (ling′ gėr) [M.E. *lengen*, A.-S. *lengan*, to protract (cp. Icel. *lengja*, G. *längen*), from *lang*, LONG], *v.i.* To delay going, to tarry, to loiter; to be long in going or coming, to hesitate; to be protracted. *v.t.* To spend or pass (time) wearily or in delays. **lingerer,** *n.* **lingeringly,** *adv.*

lingerie (lan zhri) [F., from *linge*, linen], *n.* (*collect.*) Linen articles, esp. of attire; underwear.

lingo (ling′ gō) [prob. corr. of *lingua*, see LINGUA FRANCA], *n.* (*slang*) A foreign language, peculiar dialect, or technical phraseology.

***lingot** (ling′ got) [F., from INGOT], *n.* An ingot.

lingua franca (ling′ gwȧ frăng′ kȧ) [It., Frankish tongue], *n.* A mixture of Italian with French, Greek, Arabic etc., used in the Levant; any language serving as a medium of communication between different peoples.

lingual (ling′ gwȧl) [med. L. *linguālis*, from *lingua*, tongue], *a.* (*Anat.*) Pertaining to the tongue; (*Phon.*) formed by the tongue. *n.* A letter or sound, produced by the tongue, as *t, d, n, l, r.* **linguadental** (-den′ tȧl) [DENTILINGUAL]. **lingualize,** *v.t.* **lingually,** *adv.* **linguiform,** *a.* Having the form of a tongue.

linguist (ling′ gwist), *n.* One skilled in languages. **linguistic,** *a.* Of or pertaining to linguistics. *n.pl.* The science of languages; comparative grammar. **linguistically,** *adv.*

lingula (ling′ gū lȧ) [L., dim. of *lingua*, see prec.], *n.* (*pl.* **-læ**) (*Anat.*) A tongue-shaped part; (*Zool.*) a genus of brachiopods, largely fossil. **lingula flags:** (*Geol.*) A series of flagstones and slates in North Wales containing immense numbers of fossil lingulæ. **lingular,** *a.* **lingulate** (-lȧt), *a.* Tongue-shaped.

linhay (lin′ i) [etym. doubtful], *n.* A shed, usu. a lean-to, open at the sides for cattle or carts.

liniment (lin′ i mėnt) [F., from L. *linīmentum*, from *linīre*, to anoint], *n.* A liquid preparation, usu. with oil, for rubbing on bruised or inflamed parts, embrocation.

lining [LINE (3)].

link (1) (lingk) [Icel. *hlekkr* (O.Icel. *hlenkr*), cp. Swed. *länk*, A.-S. *hlence* (cogn. with G. *gelenk*, joint)], *n.* A ring or loop of a chain; a connecting part in machinery, etc., or in a series, sequence, argument, etc.; (*Surveying*) a measure of 7·92 inches. *v.t.* To connect or attach (to, together, up, etc.) by or as by a link or links. *v.i.* To be connected. **missing link,** *n.* As yet undiscovered link of relationship between man and the anthropoid ape. **link-motion,** *n.* (*Mach.*) Gear by which the valve is operated in locomotives and similar engines. **linkage,** *n.*

link (2) (lingk) [etym. doubtful, perh. a use of prec.], *n.* A torch made of tow and pitch, used formerly for lighting persons in the streets. **link-boy, -man,** *n.* A boy or man carrying a link.

link (3) (lingk) [Sc. and North., cp. Norw. *linka*], *v.i.* To walk or trip along quickly.

links (lingks) [Sc., from A.-S. *hlinc*, LINCH], *n.pl.* Flattish or undulating sandy ground near the seashore, covered with coarse grass, etc.; ground on which golf is played.

linn (lin) [A.-S. *hlynn*, torrent, confused with Gael. *linne*, Ir. *linn*, W. *llyn*, a pool], *n.* A waterfall, a torrent; a pool, esp. one below a fall; a precipice or precipitous ravine.

Linnæan (li nē′ ȧn) [*Linnæus*, Latinized name of *Linné* (1707–78), the celebrated Swedish naturalist, -AN], *a.* Of or pertaining to Linnæus or his artificial system of classification. *n.* A follower of Linnæus.

linnet (lin′ ėt) [O.F. *linette* (F. *linotte*), from *lin*, flax (see LINEN), on which it feeds], *n.* A common song-bird, *Linota cannabina*, of the family *Fringillidæ*.

lino (lī′ nō) [LINOLEUM].

linocut (lī′ nō kŭt), *n.* An engraving on linoleum in the manner of a woodcut.

linoleum (li nō′ lė ŭm) [L. *līnum*, flax, *oleum*, OIL], *n.* A preparation of oxidized linseed-oil mixed with ground cork and laid upon canvas, used for floor-cloth.

linotype (lī′ nȯ tīp) [LINE (1), OF, TYPE], *n.* **Pro**tected name of a typesetting machine for producing castings or slugs of whole lines of words.

linsang (lin′ săng) [Javanese], *n.* A kind of civet cat common in Borneo and Java; a related African species.

linseed (lin′ sēd) [M.E. *lin-seed* (A.-S. *līn*, LINE (2), SEED)], *n.* The seed of the flax-plant. **linseed-cake,** *n.* The solid mass left after the oil has been pressed out of flax-seed. **linseed-meal,** *n.* Ground linseed used for poultices. **linseed-oil,** *n.* The oil expressed from linseed. **linseed-poultice,** *n.*

linsey-woolsey (lin′ zi wul′ zi) [prob. formed from LINE (2) and WOOL, with a jingling suf., or perh. from a place-name as *Lindsey*], *n.* A coarse fabric of linen or cotton warp with wool filling; (*fig.*) a motley composition, a jargon.

***linstock** (lin′ stok) [formerly *lintstock*, Dut. *lontstok* (*lont*, match, *stok*, stick)], *n.* A forked staff to hold a lighted match for firing a gun.

lint (lint) [rel. to LINE (2), perh. through F. *linette* or *lin*, linen], *n.* The down of linen cloth scraped on one side, used for dressing wounds, etc.

lintel (lin′ tėl) [O.F., from med. L. *lintellus*, prob. for *līmitellus*, dim. of *līmes*, LIMIT], *n.* The horizontal beam or stone over a door or window **lintelled,** *a.*

lintie, lintwhite (lin′ ti, lint whīt) [A.-S. *līnetwige*], *n.* (*Sc.*) A linnet.

liny (lī′ ni) [LINE (1), -Y], *a.* Full of lines; streaky, wrinkled. **lininess,** *a.*

lion (lī′ ȯn) [A.-F. *liun* (O.F. *leon*), L. *leōnem*, nom. *leo*, Gr. *leōn leontos*], *n.* A large and powerful carnivorous quadruped, *Felis leo*, usu. brown or tawny, with tufted tail and (in the adult male) a long mane, inhabiting southern Asia and Africa; the sign of the zodiac and constellation Leo; the British national emblem; (*fig.*, *pl.*) sights to be seen by visitors (from the lions formerly kept at the Tower of London); (*fig.*) an eminent celebrity, an object of general attention. **a lion in the path or way:** A danger or obstacle, esp. imaginary. **the lion's share:** The largest part or the whole. **to twist the lion's tail:** To insult or provoke the British people or Government (said of foreign journalists, etc.). **lion-heart,** *n.* **lion-hearted,** *a.* Having great courage. **lion-hunter,** *n.* One who courts celebrities, esp. a host or hostess who shows off lions. ***lion-sick,** *a.* Sick of a proud heart. **lion's-provider,** *n.* The jackal [see JACKAL]; (*fig.*) a tool, a sycophant. **lioncel,** *n.* (*Her.*) A small lion, esp. one of several borne on the same coat of arms. **lionesque** (lī ȯ nesk′), **lion-like,** *a.* **lioness,** *n.* **lionet,** *n.* A young lion. **lionhood, -ship,** *n.* **lionize** (lī′ ȯ nīz), *v.t.* To treat as an object of interest or curiosity; to visit or show off (a place or sights) to visitors. *v.i.* To visit the objects of interest or curiosity in a place.

lios [LIS (1)]. **liotrichi** [LEIOTRICHI].

lip (lip) [A.-S. *lippa* (cp. Dut. *lip*, Dan. *læbe*, G. *lippe*, also L. *labium*, *labrum*)], *n.* One of the two fleshy parts enclosing the opening of the mouth; the edge or margin of an orifice, chasm, etc.; (*pl.*) the projecting lobes of a bilabiate corolla; (*pl.*) the mouth, as organ of speech; (*slang*) impudence, cheek. *v.t.* (*past & p.p.* **lipped**) To touch with the lips; to kiss; (of water) to lap against; to breathe, whisper, murmur. *v.i.* To lap (of water). **to bite one's lips:** To express vexation, to repress anger, laughter, or other emotion. **to carry (or wear) a**

stiff upper lip: (*colloq.*) To be self-reliant, inflexible, unflinching. **to hang on one's lips:** To listen eagerly for every word spoken. ***to make a lip:** To pout the lips in sullenness or contempt. **lip-deep,** *a.* In up to the lips; only from the lips, superficial, insincere. ***lip-devotion, -homage, -worship,** etc., *n.* Worship, etc., with the lips only, not sincere. ***lip-good,** *a.* Hypocritical. ***lip-labour,** *n.* Words without corresponding deeds. **lip-reading,** etc., *n.* The practice of following what is said by observing the movements of the speaker's lips. **lipsalve,** *n.* Ointment for the lips; (*fig.*) compliments, flattery. **lip service:** Flattery, servile agreement. **lipstick,** *n.* Stick of cosmetic for colouring the lips. ***lip-wisdom,** *n.* Theory dissociated from practice. **lipless,** *a.* **lipped,** *a.* (*usu. in comb.*, as *thick-lipped*).

liparocele (lip′ ȧ rō sēl) [Gr. *liparos*, oily, -CELE], *n.* (*Path.*) A fatty tumour of the scrotum.

lipase (lip′ ās), *n.* (*Chem.*) An enzyme or ferment which decomposes fats, producing fatty acids and glycerine.

lipo-, lip- [Gr. *lipos*, fat], *comb. form.* **lipogenesis** (lip ō jen′ ė sis), *n.* The formation of fat. **lipogenic,** *a.*

lipogram (lip′ ȯ grăm) [Gr. *lipogrammatos*, wanting a letter (*leipein*, to leave, *gramma -atos*, letter)], *n.* A writing in which a particular letter is omitted. **lipogrammatic** (-măt′ ik), *a.* **lipogrammatism,** *n.* **lipogrammatist,** *n.* **lipography** (li pog′ rȧ fi), *n.*

lipohæmia (lip ō hē′ mi ȧ), *n.* (*Path.*) Prevalence of fatty matter in the blood.

lipoma (li pō′ mȧ) [as prec.], *n.* (*pl.* **-mata**) (*Path.*) A fatty tumour. **lipomatosis** (-tō′ sis), *n.* Excessive growth of fatty tissue. **lipomatous** (-pō′ mȧ′ tůs), *a.*

lippen (lip′ ėn) [Sc., etym. doubtful], *v.i.* To confide, to rely, to depend (on, to, etc.). *v.t.* To entrust.

lipper (lip′ ėr) [perh. rel. to LAP (3)], *n.* (*Naut.*) A superficial rippling or ruffling of the sea.

***lippitude** (lip′ i tūd) [L. *lippitūdo*, from *lippus*, blear-eyed], *n.* (*Path.* Blearedness; soreness of the eyes; chronic ophthalmia.

lippy (lip′ i) [Sc., dim. of obs. *leap*, A.-S. *lēap* (cp. Icel. *laupr*)], *n.* *A basket; an old dry-measure equal to a quarter of a peck.

liquate (li kwāt′) [L. *liquātus*, p.p. of *liquāre*, to melt, cogn. with LIQUOR], *v.t.* To melt; to liquefy (metals) in order to purify. **v.i.* To melt, to liquefy. ***liquable,** *a.* **liquation** (li kwā′ shůn), *n.*

liquefy (lik′ wė fī) [F. *liquéfier*, L. *liquefacere* (*liquāre*, to become fluid, *facere*, to make)], *v.t.* To melt, to dissolve; to convert from a solid (or gaseous) to a liquid form. *v.i.* To become liquid. **liquefacient** (-fā′ shi ėnt), *n.* That which liquefies. *a.* Serving to liquefy. **liquefaction** (-făk′ shůn), *n.* **liquefactive** (lik′-), *a.* **liquefiable,** *a.* **liquefier,** *n.* **liquescent** (li kwes′ ėnt), *a.* **liquescence, *-ency,** *n.*

liqueur (li kūr′) [F., LIQUOR], *n.* An alcoholic cordial flavoured with aromatic substance and drunk in small quantities; a sweetened wine or alcoholic syrup for flavouring champagne. *v.t.* To treat or flavour (champagne) with this. **liqueur brandy:** Brandy of special quality drunk as a liqueur. **liqueur-glass,** *n.* A small glass for drinking liqueurs.

liquid (lik′ wid) [O.F. *liquide*, L. *liquidus*, from *liquēre*, cp. LIQUEFY, LIQUATE], *a.* Fluid; flowing or capable of flowing, being a liquid; (*fig.*) transparent, limpid, clear; (of vowels) not guttural, fluent, smooth, easily pronounced; (of assets) readily convertible into cash; (of principles, etc.) unstable, changeable. *n.* A substance whose particles are incompressible and inelastic and move freely among themselves, as water or oil in a fluid, but not a gaseous state; a letter pronounced with a slight contact of the organs of articulation, as *l*, *r*, and sometimes *m*, *n*. **liquid assets,** *n.pl.* Assets easily convertible into cash. **liquidity** (li kwid′ i ti), **liquidness,** *n.* **liquidize,** *v.t.* **liquidly,** *adv.*

liquidambar (lik wid ăm′ bȧr) [LIQUID, med. L. *ambar*, AMBER], *n.* A genus of tropical trees, several species of which yield a fragrant resin or balsam called storax; the resin so produced.

liquidate (lik′ wi dāt), *v.t.* To pay off (a debt, etc.); to wind up (a bankrupt estate, etc.); to suppress; to assassinate. *v.i.* To have its debts, liabilities, and assets liquidated (of a company). **liquidation,** *n.* **liquidator,** *n.* The person officially appointed to effect a liquidation.

liquidity, etc. [LIQUID].

liquor (lik′ ȯr) [A.-F. *licur* (F. LIQUEUR), L. *liquor*, from *liquēre*, see LIQUID], *n.* A liquid or fluid substance, esp. the liquid part of anything as of a solution, a secretion, food, etc.; a solution or dilution; an alcoholic beverage, usu. not including wine or beer; (*Pharmacy*, lī′ kwôr) an aqueous solution of a drug, as **liquor sodæ,** solution of soda. *v.t.* To moisten, to wet, to steep; to grease, to dress (leather, etc.). **liquor laws:** (*Am.*) Licensing laws. **liquor store:** (*Am.*) A wine-merchant's business. **hard liquor:** (*Am.*) Spirits. **malt liquor:** Ale, porter, etc. **spiritous liquor:** Spirits. **in liquor, the worse for liquor:** Intoxicated. **liquor-up,** *n.* (*slang*) A drink. *v.i.* To take a lot of drink.

liquorice (lik′ ȯr is) [A.-F. *lycorys* (F. *liquerice*), late L. *liquiritia*, Gr. *glukurrhiza* (*glukus*, sweet, *rhiza*, root)], *n.* The rhizome of a bean-like plant of the genus *Glycyrrhiza*; a sweetmeat or drug prepared from the rhizome of *G. glabra*.

liquorish (1) (lik′ ȯr ish) [from LIQUOR, after LICKERISH], *a.* Fond of liquor. **liquorishly,** *adv.* **liquorishness,** *n.* **liquorish** (2) [LICKERISH].

lira (lēr′ ȧ) [It., from L. LIBRA], *n.* (*pl.* **lire,** lēr′ ā, **liras**) An Italian silver coin serving as the unit of value.

liriodendron (lī ri ȯ den′ drȯn) [Gr. *leirion*, LILY, *dendron*, tree], *n.* A genus of North American trees belonging to the *Magnoliaceæ* and containing the tulip tree.

***liripoop** (lir′ i poop) [med. L. *liripipium*, etym. doubtful], *n.* A graduate's hood or the scarf attached thereto; the string to a jester's cap. (*fig.*) acuteness; a smart trick; a silly person.

lirk (lĕrk) [Sc. and North.], *n.* A fold, crease, or wrinkle. *v.i.* To fold, to crease.

lis (1) (lis) [O.Ir. *liss* (Ir. *lios*), cp. W. *llys*], *n.* (*Ir. Ant.*) A circular earthwork, usu. a fort.

lis (2) [FLEUR-DE-LIS].

Lisle thread (līl thred) [town in France, now *Lille*], *n.* A fine, hard thread orig. made at Lille.

lisp (lisp) [A.-S. *wlispian*, extant only in *āwlispian*, from *wlisp*, lisping (cp. Dut. *lispen*, Teut. *læspe*, G. *lispeln*)], *v.i.* To pronounce *s* and *z* with the sound of *th* or *dh*; to speak affectedly or imperfectly as a child. *v.t.* To pronounce with a lisp. *n.* The act or habit of lisping; (*fig.*) a whispering or rustling sound. **lisper,** *n.* **lispingly,** *adv.*

lisse (lēs) [F. *lisse*, *lice*, LEASE (3)], *n.* (*Tapestry weaving*) The warp-threads taken together.

lissencephalous (lis ėn sef′ ȧ lůs) [Gr. *lissos*, smooth, *enkephalos*, brain], *n.* Smooth-brained, pertaining to the *Lissencephala* or smooth-brained mammals, in Owen's classification.

lissom (lis′ ȯm) [var. of LITHESOME], *a.* Lithe, supple, nimble. **lissomness,** *n.*

lissotrichous [LEIOTRICHOUS].

list (1) (list) [A.-S. *līste* (cp. Dut. *lijst*, G. *leiste*, O.H.G. *lista*, whence It. *lista*, F. *liste*, whence the sense of roll or catalogue)], *n.* The border, edge, or selvedge of cloth; a strip of this used as material; a boundary, a limit; (*pl.*) the palisades enclosing a piece of ground for a tournament, the ground so enclosed; (*fig.*) a scene of contest, an area; a roll, a catalogue or schedule of persons or things. *v.t.*

To enter in a list; to cover or line with list (as the edge of a door); to sew together so as to form a border; (*Am.*) to prepare (land) for corn or cotton by making alternate beds and furrows. *v.i.* (*vulg.*) To enlist, to go as a soldier.

list (2) (list) [A.-S. *lystan* (cp. Dut. *lusten*, Icel. *lysta*, G. *lüsten*), from *lust*, see LUST]. *v.t.* (3rd *sing.* **list, listeth,** *past* **list, listed**) To please, to be pleasing to. *v.i.* To please, to choose, to be disposed. *n.* Desire, pleasure, inclination.

list (3) (list) [perh. from prec. n.], *n.* A leaning over (of a ship, building, etc.). *v.i.* To lean over, to careen. *v.t.* To careen or heel (a ship) over.

***list** (4) (list) [A.-S. *hlystan*, from *hlyst*, hearing (cp. Icel. *hlust*, ear), cogn. with L. *cluere*, Gr. *kluein*], *v.i.* To listen. *v.t.* To listen to.

listel (lis′ tėl) [F., from It. *listella*, dim. of *lista*, LIST (1)], *n.* (*Arch.*) A small list, reglet, or fillet.

listen (lis′ ėn) [O. Northum. *lysna* (cp. A.-S. *hlosnian*), cogn. with LIST (4)], *v.i.* To give ear or attention (to), to hearken; (*fig.*) to heed, to obey, to follow. **to listen in:** To listen to radio; to tap a telephone message. **v.t.* To hearken to. **listener,** *n.* One who listens, esp. to broadcasting. **listening post,** *n.* (*Mil.*) A position where men are posted to overhear what the enemy is saying or planning.

lister (1) (lis′ tėr), *n.* One who makes out lists; (*U.S.A.*) an assessor of taxes.

lister (2) (lis′ tėr) [as prec., from sense of throwing up ridges], *n.* (*Am.*) A plough specially designed for throwing up ridges.

Listerian (lis tēr′ i ȧn) [Lord *Lister* (1827–1912), introducer of antiseptic surgery], *a.* Pertaining to Lister or his antiseptic methods in surgery. **Listerize,** *v.t.* To treat by Listerian methods. **Listerism,** *n.*

listless (list′ lės), *a.* Careless, heedless; indifferent to what is going on; inattentive, languid. **listlessly,** *adv.* **listlessness,** *n.*

lit, *past.* & *p.p.* [LIGHT (1 and 3)].

litany (lit′ ȧ ni) [M.E. and O.F. *letanie* (F. *litanie*), med. L. *litania*, Gr. *litaneia*, from *litaneuein*, to pray, from *litanos*, a suppliant, from *litē*, prayer], *n.* A solemn form of supplicatory prayer, used in public worship, esp. a series of short prayers with responses in the Prayer Book. **lesser litany:** The Kyrie eleison, or the response 'Lord have mercy upon us.' **litany-desk, -stool,** *n.* The desk or stool at which the clergyman reciting the litany kneels.

litchi (lē chē) [Chin. *li-chi*], *n.* The tree, *Nephelium litchi*, bearing a famous Chinese fruit; this fruit.

-lite [F., from Gr. *lithos*, stone], *suf.* Forming names of minerals, as *aerolite, coprolite, radiolite.*

liter [LITRE].

literacy [LITERATE].

literal (lit′ ėr ȧl) [O.F., from L. *litterālis*, from *littera*, LETTER], *a.* According to the primitive or verbal meaning; not figurative or metaphorical; following the exact words (as a translation); consisting of or expressed by letters; (*fig.*) unimaginative, prosaic, matter-of-fact (of persons). *n.* (*Print.*) A misprint. **literalism,** *n.* **literalist,** *n.* **literality** (-ăl′ i ti), **literalness,** *n.* **literalize,** *v.t.* To interpret, understand, or put in practice in a literal sense. **literally,** *adv.*

literary (lit′ ėr ȧr i) [L. *litterārius*, as prec.], *a.* Of or pertaining to literature or polite learning; derived from, versed or engaged in literature; consisting of written or printed compositions. **literary man:** An author; a man of letters.

literate (lit′ ėr ȧt) [L. *litterātus*, as LITERARY], *a.* Instructed in letters or literature, esp. able to read and write; *literary. *n.* One able to read and write; a person of liberal education; (*Ang. Ch.*) a candidate for Holy orders who is not a graduate. **literacy,** *n.* ***literati*** (lit ėr ā′ tī) [L.], *n.pl.* The learned; men of letters. ***literatim*** (-ā′ tim) [L.], *adv.* Letter for letter, literally. **literation** (-ā′ shŭn), *n.* Representation (of a language, etc.) by means of letters. **literator** (lit′ ėr ā tôr), *n.* A literary man, a *littérateur*; an elementary teacher; a sciolist, a pretender to learning. **literose,** *a.* Affecting literary tastes. **literosity** (-os′ i ti), *n.*

literature (lit′ ėr ȧ tūr, -tyŭr) [F., from L. *litterātūra*, as prec.], *n.* (*collect.*) The written or printed productions of a country or period or pertaining to a particular subject; (*colloq.*) printed matter; the class of writings distinguished for beauty of form or expression, as distinguished from works dealing with positive knowledge; the production of literary works; the literary profession; literary culture.

lith (lith) [A.-S.], *n.* A joint, a limb; a division.

lith-, litho- [Gr. *lithos*, a stone], *comb. form.* Pertaining to, resembling, or executed in or on stone.

-lith [as prec., cp. -LITE], *suf.*, as in *monolith.*

lithæmia (li thē′ mi ȧ) [LITH-, Gr. *haima*, blood], *n.* (*Path.*) Excess of lithic or uric acid in the blood. **lithæmic,** *a.*

lithagogue (lith′ ȧ gog) [LITH-, Gr. *agōgos*, drawing forth, from *agein*, to draw], *n.* (*Surg.*) Expelling or tending to expel stone from the kidneys or bladder.

lithanthrax (lith ăn′ thrăks) [LITH-, *anthrax*, charcoal], *n.* Mineral coal, as dist. from charcoal.

litharge (li tharj′) [O.F. *litarge*, L. *lithargyrus*, Gr. *litharguros* (LITH-, *arguros*, silver)], *n.* Protoxide of lead.

lithe (līth) [A.-S. *līthe*, cogn. with L. *lentus*], *a.* Flexible, limber, supple. **lithely,** *adv.* **litheness,** *n.* **lithesome,** *a.* **lithsomeness,** *n.*

***lither** (lith′ ėr) [A.-S. *lythre* (cp. G. *liederlich*)], *a.* Depraved, dissolute; lazy; yielding, pliant; supple, nimble. ***litherly,** *a.* and *adv.*

lithia (lith′ i ȧ) [formerly *lithion*, Gr. *litheion*, neut. adj. stony, from *lithos*, stone], *n.* Oxide of lithium. **lithia-water,** *n.* A mineral water containing lithia used for gout.

lithiasis (li thī′ ȧ sis) [Gr., from *lithiān*, from *lithos*, stone], *n.* (*Path.*) The formation of stone or gravel in the bladder and urinary passages. **lithic** (1) (lith′ ik), *a.* Pertaining to stone in the bladder.

lithium (lith′ i ŭm) [*lithia*, -IUM], *n.* (*Chem.*) A metallic element belonging to the alkaline group. **lithic** (2), *a.*

litho- [LITH-].

lithocarp (lith′ ō karp) [Gr. *karpos*, fruit], *n.* A fossil fruit.

lithochromatics (lith ō krō măt′ iks), *n.pl.* The art of painting in oil upon stone and taking impressions therefrom. **lithochromatic,** *a.*

lithoclast (lith ō klăst), *n.* (*Surg.*) An instrument for breaking up stone in the bladder.

lithodome (lith′ ō dōm), [Gr.], *n.* (*Zool.*) Any member of the genus *Lithodomus*, small molluscs which excavate and live in rocks, shells, etc.

lithogenous (lith oj′ ėn ŭs), *a.* Stone-producing; forming coral.

lithoglyph (lith′ ō glif) [Gr. *gluphein*, to carve], *n.* A carving on stone, esp. a gem. **lithoglyphic,** *a.*

lithoglyphite (lith og′ li fīt), *n.* A fossil substance resembling carving.

lithograph (lith′ ȯ grăf), *v.t.* To engrave or draw on stone and transfer to paper, etc., by printing; to print by lithography. *n.* An impression from a drawing on stone. **lithographer** (li thog′ rȧ fėr), *n.* **lithographic, -al** (-grăf′ ik, -ȧl), *a.* **lithographic lime-stone:** A slaty limestone from the upper bed of the Jurassic formation, used in lithography. **lithographically,** *adv.* **lithography** (li thog′ rȧ fi), *n.* The art or process of making a lithograph.

lithoid (lith′ oid), **lithoidal** (li thoi′ dȧl), *a.* Resembling a stone in nature or structure.

litholabe (lith′ ō lăb) [Gr.], *n.* (*Surg.*) An instrument for grasping a stone in lithotomy.

lithology (li thol′ ȯ ji), *n.* The science of the composition, structure, and classification of rocks, petrology; (*Med.*) the branch of medical science dealing with calculus. **lithologic -al** (-loj′ ik, -ål), *a.* **lithologist** (-thol′ ȯ jist), *n.*

lithomancy (lith′ ȯ măn si), *n.* Divination by means of stones.

lithomarge (lith′ ō marj), *n.* (*Geol.*) A hydrated silicate of alumina related to or identical with kaolin.

lithontriptic (lith ȯn trip′ tik) [F. *lithontriptique*, Gr. *lithōn, thruptika* (*lithōn*, gen. pl. of *lithos*, stone, *thruptikos*, from *thruptein*, to crush)], *a.* (*Med.*) Breaking up stone in the bladder. *n.* A medicine that does this.

lithophagous (li thof′ å gůs) [LITHO-, -PHAGOUS], *a.* Eating or perforating stones (as some molluscs).

lithophane (lith′ ō fān), *n.* Ornamental porcelain suitable for lamps, windows, and other transparencies.

lithophotography [PHOTOLITHOGRAPHY].

lithophyl (lith′ ȯ fil) [LITHO-, Gr. *phullon*, leaf], *n.* (*Palæont.*) A fossil leaf or impression of a leaf.

lithophyte (lith′ ō fīt), *n.* (*Zool.*) A calcareous polyp, as some corals; (*Bot.*) a plant that grows on stone.

lithosis (lith ō′ sis) [Gr. *lithosis*, turning into stone], *n.* A disease of the lungs caused by tiny particles of stone; grinders' or stone-masons' disease.

lithosphere (lith′ ō sfēr), *n.* (*Geol.*) The outer, rocky shell of the earth, the crust of the earth.

lithotint (lith′ ō tint), *n.* A process of drawing and printing coloured pictures on lithographic stone; such a drawing.

lithotome (lith′ ȯ tōm) [Gr. *lithotomos*, stone-cutting (LITHO-, *tomos*, cutting, from *temnein*, to cut)], *n.* (*Min.*) A natural stone so formed as to appear to have been cut artificially; (*Surg.*) an instrument used for cutting the bladder in lithotomy. **lithotomy** (li thot′ ȯ mi) [late L. and Gr. *lithotomia* (LITHO-, -TOMY)], *n.* (*Surg.*) The operation of cutting for stone in the bladder. **lithotomic** (-tom′ ik), *a.* **lithotomist** (li thot′ ȯ mist), *n.*

lithotripsy (lith′ ȯ trip si) [LITHO-, Gr. *tripsis*, rubbing, from *tribein*, to rub], *n.* Lithotrity. **lithotriptic** (-trip′ tik), *a.* **lithotriptist**, *n.* **lithotriptor**, *n.*

lithotrity (li thŏt′ ri ti) [from LITHONTRIPTIC (L. *trit-*, part. stem of *tĕrere*, to rub, substituted for Gr. *tribein*, to rub, adopted erroneously for *thruptein*, to crush)], *n.* (*Surg.*) The operation of crushing stones in the bladder to small fragments by means of instruments. **lithotrite** (lith′ ȯ trīt), **lithotritor**, *n.* An instrument so used. **lithotritic** (-trit′ ik), *a.* **lithotritist** (li thot′ ri tist), *n.* **lithotritize**, *v.t.*

lithotype (lith′ ȯ tīp) [LITHO-, TYPE], *n.* A stereotype made with shellac, sand, tar, and linseed-oil, pressed hot on a plaster mould taken from type; an etched stone surface for printing; a machine for preparing a lithographic transfer-sheet. *v.t.* To prepare for printing by lithotypes. **lithotypy** (li thot′ i pi), *n.*

Lithuanian (lith ū ā′ ni ån) [*Lithuania*, -AN], *a.* Pertaining to Lithuania. *n.* A native of Lithuania; the language of Lithuania.

litigate (lit′ i gāt) [L. *lītigātus*, p.p. of *lītigāre*, from *līs, lītis*, lawsuit], *v.t.* To contest in a court of law. *v.i.* To go to law; to carry on a lawsuit. **litigable**, *a.* **litigant**, *a.* and *n.* **litigation** (-gā′ shůn), *n.*

litigious (li tij′ ůs) [F. *litigieux*, L. *lītigiōsus*, as prec.], *a.* Fond of litigation; (*fig.*) quarrelsome, contentious; subject or open to legal dispute; pertaining to litigation. **litigiously**, *adv.* **litigiosity** (-i os′ iti), **litigiousness**, *n.*

litmus (lit′ můs) [M.Dut. *leecmos*, or Dut. *lakmoes* (LAC, *moes*, pulp), *lac*, assim. to obs. *lit*, to dye], *n.* A blue dye obtained from *Roccella tinctoria* or other lichens, turned red by acids or restored to its original colour by alkalis. **litmus-paper**, *n.* Unsized paper stained with litmus, used to test the acidity or the alkaline nature of a solution.

litotes (lī′ tȯ tēz) [Gr., from *lītos*, smooth, meagre], *a.* (*Rhet.*) A figure by which an affirmative is expressed by negation of its contrary, or a weaker expression used to suggest a stronger one, as, 'Something has happened to him,' meaning 'He is dead.'

litrameter (li trăm′ ė tėr) [Gr. *litra*, a pound, -METER], *n.* An instrument for ascertaining the specific gravity of liquids.

litre (lē′ tėr) [F., late L. *lītra*, as prec.], *n.* The unit of capacity in the metric system, equal to a cubic decimetre [see DECI-], or about 1¾ pints.

litter (lit′ ėr) [A.-F. *littere*, O.F. *litiere*, med. L. *lectāria*, from *lectus*, bed], *n.* A stretcher with shafts supporting a couch in which a person may be carried by animals or on men's shoulders, now chiefly used for transporting the sick or wounded; straw, hay, or other soft material used as a bed for horses, cattle, etc., or as a covering for plants; refuse, rubbish, odds and ends scattered about; hence, a state of disorder or untidiness; the young brought forth by a sow, bitch, cat, etc., at one birth. *v.t.* To supply (beasts) with litter; to spread bedding for; to scatter (things) about carelessly; to make (a place) untidy with articles scattered about; to bring forth (said esp. of the sow, dog, cat, etc., applied in contempt to human beings); *to carry in a litter. *v.i.* To bring forth a litter of young. **littery**, *a.*

littérateur (lit ėr å tĕr) [F., from L. *litterātōrem*, nom. *-tor*, from *littera*, LETTER], *n.* A literary man.

little (lit′ ėl) [A.-S. *lȳtel, lytel*, cogn. with *lūtan*, to LOUT], *a.* (*comp.* **less**, ***lesser**, *colloq.* **littler**, *superl.* **least**, *colloq.* **littlest**) Small, not great or big in size, extent, amount, or quantity; short in duration; short in distance; of small dignity, weight, or importance; slight, inconsiderable, insignificant, petty; narrow, mean, contemptible, paltry; smaller than normal, diminutive, short in stature; young like a child, weak; (*colloq.*) entitled to indulgence or forbearance, calling for amusement. *adv.* In a small degree; not much, slightly; not at all. *n.* A small amount, quantity, space, distance, time, etc.; only a trifle. **by little and little, little by little**: By small degrees. **in little**: In miniature. **little or nothing**: Scarcely anything. **not a little**: A great deal; extremely. **little-ease**, *n.* Bodily discomfort; (*fig.*) a form of punishment, as the pillory, the stocks or a cell too small for the inmate. **little-endian**, *n.* One of the political faction in *Gulliver's Travels* who maintained that eggs should be broken at the small end; (*fig.*) one who disputes about trifles. **littleness**, *n.* **little-Englander**, *n.* One who advocates the reduction or restriction of British world responsibilities, opp. to Imperialist. **little-Englandism**, *n.* **Little-go** [GO (2)]. **little Mary**, *n.* (*colloq.*) Stomach. **Little Masters**: Certain 16th-century German engravers, followers of Dürer, noted for the small size of their prints. **little people**: The fairies.

littoral (lit′ ȯr ål) [L. *littorālis, lītorālis*, from *lītus -toris*, shore], *a.* Pertaining to the shore, esp. the zone between high- and low-water marks. *n.* A coastal region.

liturgy (lit′ ůr ji) [through F. *liturgie* or directly from med. L. *lītūrgia*, Gr. *leitourgia*, a public service, from *leitourgos* (*leitos*, public, *ergon*, work)], *n.* A form of public worship, the entire ritual for public worship, or the set of formularies in which this is set forth; (*R.-C. and Gr. Ch.*) the Mass, the formulary of the Eucharist; (*Gr. Ant.*) a public duty discharged at his own cost by a wealthy Athenian citizen in rotation, such as the building of a warship, production of a play, etc. **liturgic** (li tĕr jik), *a.* Liturgical, pertaining to a liturgy or liturgies; *n.pl.* The study or doctrine of liturgies. **liturgical**, *a.* **liturgically**, *adv.* **liturgiology** (li tĕr ji ol′ ȯ ji) [-LOGY], *n.* **liturgiologist**, *n.* **liturgist** (lit′ ůr jist), *n.*

live (1) (līv) [ALIVE], *a.* Alive, living; burning, ignited; ready for use; charged with electricity (as a wire); unexploded (as a shell); effective, unexhausted (as steam); moving or transmitting motion (of machinery); (*fig.*) full of energy, of present interest, etc.; (*colloq.*) real, not a picture, toy, etc.; (*Radio.*) of a broadcast transmitted at the actual time of speaking, not a recording. **live axle,** *n.* (*Motor.*) Driving shafts in back axle. **live-bait,** *n.* Live fish, worms, etc., used as bait in fishing. *v.t.* To fish with this. **live-box,** *n.* A case in which living microscopic objects are confined for observation. **live-cartridge,** *n.* One containing a bullet. **live feathers, hair,** etc.: Feathers, hair, etc., plucked from a living fowl or animal. **live-oak,** *n.* A North American evergreen tree, esp. *Quercus virens*, valuable for shipbuilding. **live rail,** *n.* (*Rail.*) A rail charged with an electric current. **live-stock:** Animals kept for farming or domestic purposes. **live wire,** *n.* (*Elec.*) A wire through which an electric current is flowing; (*colloq.*) a pushing, energetic fellow.

live (2) (liv) [A.-S. *lifian, libban* (cp. Dut. *leven*, Icel. *lifa*, G. *leben*), cogn. with LIFE], *v.i.* To have life; to be alive; to exist in such a way as to be capable of performing the animal or vegetable functions; to continue in life or as in life; (*fig.*) to remain in operation or as an active principle; to reside, to dwell (at, in, etc.); to be nourished, to subsist (upon); to depend for subsistence (upon); to receive or gain a livelihood (by); to pass or conduct one's life in a particular condition, manner, etc.; to live strenuously, to enjoy life intensely; to continue alive, to survive. *v.t.* To pass, to spend (a specified kind of life); to remain alive through; to survive; to manifest, express, or effect, by living. **live and let live:** To wink at the deficiencies of others in return for indulgence of one's own. **to live close:** To live stingily. **to live down:** To falsify or efface the recollection of (scandal, etc.) by one's conduct. **to live in** or **out:** To reside or not on the premises (of shop-assistants). **liveable,** *a.* Worth living (of life); fit to live in; fit to live with. **liveableness,** *n.* **lived,** *a.* (*in comb.* as *long-lived*).

livelihood (līv' li hud) [A.-S. *līflād* (LIFE, *lād*, course, cogn. with LOAD and LODE)], *n.* Means of subsistence.

livelong (līv' long) [orig. *lief-long* (LIEF, LONG (1))], *a.* Long-lasting; the whole, entire, the whole length of.

lively (līv' li) [A.-S. *liflīc*], *a.* Life-like, actual, vivid; full of life, brisk, active, vigorous; animated, vivacious, gay, bright; (*colloq.*) striking, forcible, exciting. **livelily,** *adv.* **liveliness,** *n.*

liven (lī' vėn), *v.t.* To make lively, to enliven. *v.i.* To cheer (up).

liver (1) (liv' er), *n.* One who lives; a resident, a dweller; one who spends his life in a specified way (as a *good liver*).

liver (2) (liv' ėr) [A.-S. *lifer* (cp. Dut. *lever*, Icel. *lifr*, G. *leber*)], *n.* A glandular organ in the abdominal cavity of vertebrates which secretes the bile and purifies the blood; the flesh of this from a sheep, calf, etc., used as food; (*colloq.*) a distorted liver; (*Chem.*) applied to certain liver-coloured sulphides or other compounds of specified elements. *a.* Liver-coloured. **liver-colour,** *n.* The colour of the liver; a reddish-brown. **liver-coloured,** *a.* **liver-complaint,** *n.* A disordered state of the liver. **liver-fluke,** *n.* A parasitic worm causing disease in the human liver. **liver-grown,** *a.* Having an enlarged liver. **liver-leaf,** *n.* (*Am.*) One of the hepaticæ or anemones. **liver-vein,** *n.* (*Shak.*) The way of a man in love. **liver-wing,** *n.* The right wing of a cooked fowl; (*facet.*) the right arm. **livered,** *a.* (*in comb.*, as *white-livered*, cowardly). **liverish,** *a.* Having a disordered liver.

liver (3) (lī' vėr) [from *Liverpool*], *n.* A fabulous bird, supposed to have given its name to Liverpool, and still commemorated in the arms of that town.

liverish, liver-leaf, etc. [LIVER (2)].

Liverpudlian (liv ėr pŭd' li ȧn) [*Liverpool* (with PUDDLE, for POOL), -IAN], *n.* A native or inhabitant of Liverpool.

liverstone (liv' ėr stōn), *n.* (*Geol.*) Hepatite.

liverwort (liv' ėr wĕrt), *n.* (*Bot.*) Any plant of the genus Hepaticæ, cryptogamic plants.

livery (liv' ėr i) [A.-F. *liveré*, O.F. *livrée*, fem. p.p. of *livrer*, late L. *līberāre*, to give, to DELIVER], *n.* A distinctive dress worn by the servants of a particular person or the members of a city company, orig. a ration or allowance of clothing, food, etc., to retainers of a baron or knight; (*fig.*) any distinctive dress, guise, or outward appearance; the privileges of a city company or guild; (*Law*) delivery of property; a writ granting possession; *allowance for keeping and feeding a horse. **v.t.* To dress or clothe in or as in livery. **at livery:** Kept at a stable for the owner at a fixed charge. **livery company:** One of the guilds or companies of the City of London that formerly had a distinctive costume. **liveryman,** *n.* One who wears a livery (as a footman, etc.); a freeman of the City of London, who is entitled to wear the livery of the company to which he belongs, and to vote in the election of Lord Mayor, sheriffs, chamberlain, etc. **livery-servant,** *n.* A servant wearing a livery. **livery-stable,** *n.* A stable where horses are kept for owners at livery or let out on hire. **liveried,** *a.*

livid (liv' id) [L. *līvidus*], *a.* Of a leaden colour; black and blue, discoloured (as by a bruise). **lividity** (li vid' i ti), ***lividness,** *n.* **lividly,** *adv.*

living (liv' ing) [LIVE (2), -ING], *a.* Alive, having life; flowing, running; in a state of combustion; vivifying, quickening; operative, active, efficient; alive now, existing, contemporary; true to life, exact (of a portrait). *n.* The state of being alive, existence; livelihood, the power of continuing life; the benefice of a clergyman; manner of life, esp. feeding. **living rock:** Rock in its native state or location (prob. from the obs. idea that rock grows). **living-room,** *n.* A family sitting-room. **living wage:** The lowest wage on which it is possible to maintain oneself and family. ***livingly,** *adv.*

livre (lēvr) [F., from L. LIBRA], *n.* An old French money of account worth about 10d.

lixiviate (lik siv' i āt) [from mod. L. *lixīviāre*, from *lixīvium*, neut. adj., from *lix*, ashes, lye], *v.t.* To leach, to dissolve out by lixiviation; to impregnate with salts by lixiviation. ***lixivial, -ious,** *a.* ***lixiviate** (-ȧt), *a.* and *n.* **lixiviation** (-ā' shŭn), *n.* The process of separating a soluble from an insoluble material by a washing or filtering action; leaching. **lixivium,** *n.* Water impregnated with alkaline salts from wood-ash.

lizard (liz' ȧrd) [O.F. *lesard*, L. *lacerta, -tus*], *n.* Any member of the reptilian order *Lacertilia*, esp. of the typical genus *Lacerta*, having a long, scaly body and tail, and four limbs, each with five toes of unequal length; a fancy variety of canary. **lizard-stone,** *n.* A variety of serpentine found in the Lizard peninsula in Cornwall.

llama (1) (la' mȧ, lya' ma) [Sp., from Peruvian], *n.* A domesticated Peruvian wool-bearing animal, *Auchenia lama*, resembling a camel, but humpless and smaller, used as a beast of burden; its wool, material made from this. **llama** (2) [LAMA (1)].

llano (la' nō, lya' nō) [Sp., from L. *plānum*, PLAIN (1)], *n.* A level, treeless steppe or plain in the northern part of South America. **llanero** (lya nâr' ō), *n.* One who lives on the llanos of South America.

Lloyd's (loidz) [Edward *Lloyd*, who kept a coffee-house frequented by shippers in the 17th cent.], *n.* A corporation, having offices at the Royal Exchange, dealing with marine insurance, the classification and registration of vessels, etc. **Lloyd's List:** A newspaper, orig. started by Edward Lloyd in 1696 as **Lloyd's News,** devoted to maritime intelligence. **Lloyd's Register:** An annual alphabetical list of shipping belonging to all nations, classified according to seaworthiness.

lo (lō) [A.-S. *lā*, perh. blended with M.E. *lo*, short for loke, A.-S. *lōca*, LOOK], *int.* See! Behold! Observe!

loach (lōch) [F. *loche*, etym. unknown], *n.* A popular name for any of the *Cobitidæ*, a group of the carp family, esp. *Nemachilus barbatulus*, a small British river-fish.

load (lōd) [A.-S. *lād*, way, course, cogn. with LEAD (2) and LODE], *n.* A burden; that which is laid on or put in anything for conveyance; as much as can be carried at a time; hence, a measure of weight varying according to the material carried; that which is borne with difficulty; that which presses upon, obstructs, or resists; the downward pressure of a superstructure; the resistance to an engine or motor apart from friction; (*Elec.*) the amount of electrical energy required from a source; (*Eng.*) what a process calls for in fuel or energy output; (*fig.*) any mental burden; (*colloq.*, *pl.*) heaps, lots, any amount. *v.t.* To put a load upon or in; to put (a load or cargo) on or in a ship, vehicle, etc.; to add weight to, to make heavy or heavier, to weight; to weigh down, to encumber, to oppress; to charge (a gun, etc.); to fill to overflowing; to cover, to heap or overwhelm (with abuse, honours, etc.); to adulterate, esp. with something to increase strength or weight; (*Stock Exch.*) to buy heavily (cp. UNLOAD). *v.i.* To take in a load or cargo (usu. with *up*); to charge a firearm. **load-displacement, -draught, -line,** *n.* A ship's displacement when full loaded, or the line to which she sinks. **loading-gauge,** *n.* A gauge indicating the height to which railway-trucks can be loaded so that they can pass bridges and tunnels safely. **loadstone** [LODESTONE]. **load-water-line** [LOAD-LINE]. **loaded,** *a.* Biased, weighted in a certain direction; likely to cause argument. **loaded dice,** *n.pl.* Dice so weighted that they fall with a required face up. **loader,** *n.* One who or that which loads; a person employed to load a sportsman's gun; a loading-machine; in comb., as *breech-* or *muzzle-loader.* **loading,** *n.* A load, a burden; also in comb., as *breech-loading.* **loading-coil,** *n.* (*Radio.*) An extra coil inserted in an aerial circuit to increase the wave-length.

loadstar [LODESTAR].

loaf (1) (lōf) [A.-S. *hlāf* (cp. Icel. *hleifr*, G. *leib*)], *n.* (*pl.* **loaves**) A shaped mass of bread, esp. of a standard size or weight; a moulded mass of any material, esp. a conical mass of refined sugar; the head of a cabbage or lettuce. **loaf-sugar,** *n.* **sugar-loaf,** *n.* **loaves and fishes:** Personal gains, material benefits, as an inducement in religious profession or public service.

loaf (2) (lōf) [etym. doubtful], *v.i.* To lounge or idle about. *v.t.* To spend or pass (time away) idly. *n.* A saunter, an idle time, a loafing. **loafer,** *n.*

loam (lōm) [A.-S. *lām* (cp. Dut. *leem*, G. *lehm*) cogn. with *līm*, LIME], *n.* Soil consisting of sand and clay loosely coherent, with admixture of organic matter or humus; a mixture of sand and clay with chopped straw, used for making moulds, in brick-making, etc. *v.t.* To cover with loam. **loamy,** *a.* **loaminess,** *n.*

loan (lōn) [A.-S. *lān* (cp. Dut. *leen*, Icel. *lān*, G. *lehn*), cogn. with *leōn*, to lend, also with Gr. *leipein*, L. *linquere*, to leave], *n.* The act of lending; the state of being lent; that which is lent, esp. a sum of money lent at interest; permission to make use of; (*fig.*) a word, myth, custom, etc., adopted from another people. *v.t.* To grant the loan of. **loan-collection,** *n.* A set of pictures, etc., lent by the owners for public exhibition. **loan-office,** *n.* An office where loans are negotiated; an office for receiving subscriptions to a public loan; a pawnshop. **loan-society,** *n.* A society lending money to members who repay by instalments. **loan-word,** *n.* A word borrowed from another language. **loanable,** *a.* **loanee** (lō nē'), *n.* **loaner,** *n.*

loath (lōth) [A.-S. *lāth* (cp. Dut. *leed*, Icel. *leithr*), cogn. with G. *leid*, sorrow], *a.* Unwilling, averse, reluctant. **nothing loath:** Quite willing; willingly. **loathness,** *n.* Unwillingness, reluctance.

loathe (lōth) [A.-S. *lathian*, from prec.], *v.t.* To feel disgust at; to abhor, to detest. *v.i.* To feel disgust (at). **loather,** *n.* ***loathful,** *a.* Full of loathing, disgusting; (*Sc.*) reluctant, bashful. ***loathfully,** *adv.* **loathfulness,** *n.* **loathing,** *a.* Abhorring. *n.* Disgust, aversion, abhorrence. **loathingly,** *adv.* ***loathly,** *a.* Creating loathing, loathsome. **adv.* Unwillingly. ***loathliness,** *n.* **loathsome,** *a.* Causing loathing or disgust; odious, detestable. **loathsomely,** *adv.* **loathsomeness,** *n.*

loave (lōv) [LOAF], *v.i.* To expand into a head (of cabbages, etc.).

lob (lob) [etym. doubtful, perh. onomat.], *n.* A heavy, dull, stupid fellow; anything thick and heavy; (*Cricket*) a slow underhand ball; (*Lawn-tennis*) a ball pitched high into the air. *v.t.* (*past & p.p.* **lobbed**) *To hang or allow to droop heavily; (*Cricket or Lawn-tennis*) to bowl a lob. *v.i.* To make a lob.

lobate, lobated (lō' bāt, -ĕd) [from L. *lobus*, LOBE], *a.* Having, characterized by, or consisting of lobes. **lobation** (-lob ā' shŭn), *n.*

lobby (lob' i) [low L. *lobia*, LODGE], *n.* A passage, corridor or vestibule, usu. opening into several apartments; a small hall or ante-room; that part of a hall of a legislative assembly to which the public are admitted; also one of two corridors to which members go to vote; an enclosed space for cattle. *v.i.* To solicit the votes of members. *v.t.* To influence or solicit (members); to secure the passage of (a Bill) by lobbying. **lobby-member,** *n.* A person who frequents the lobbies of a legislative assembly to solicit the votes of members. **lobbyist,** *n.*

lobe (lōb) [F., from late L. *lobus*, Gr. *lobos*, lobe or pod, cogn. with L. *legūmen*, LEGUME, cp. *legula*, lobe of ear], *n.* Any rounded and projecting or hanging part; the soft lower part of the ear; (*Bot.*) a rounded division of a leaf. **lobed,** *a.* **lobeless,** *a.* **lobelet,** *n.*

lobelia (lō bē' li å) [Matthias de *Lobel* (1538–1616), botanist to James I], *n.* A genus of herbaceous and brilliant flowering plants, including the Indian tobacco, *L. inflata*, used in medicine, and the cardinal-flower, *L. cardinalis.*

loblolly (lob lol' i) [etym. doubtful], *n.* Water gruel; spoon-meat. **loblolly man** or **boy:** (*Naut.*) A man or boy who attends on the ship's surgeon.

lobotomy (lō bot' ŏ mi), *n.* (*Surg.*) Operation in which the fibres connecting the frontal lobes of the brain to the rest of the brain are cut; used in the treatment of severe depression.

lobscouse (lob' skous) [G. *labskaus*], *n.* (*Naut.*) A hash of meat with vegetables of various kinds and ship's biscuit.

lob-sided [LOP-SIDED, see LOP (2)].

lobster (lob' stĕr) [A.-S. *loppestre*, corr. of L. *locusta*, LOCUST], *n.* A large marine long-tailed and stalk-eyed decapod crustacean of the genus *Homarus*, esteemed for food; (*contemp.*) a British soldier, orig. one of a regiment of Cromwell's cuirassiers. **lobster-pot,** *n.* A wickerwork trap for lobsters.

lobule (lob' ūl), *n.* A small lobe. **lobular,** *a.*

lobworm (lob' wĕrm), *n.* A large earthworm, used as bait by anglers; a lugworm.

local (lō' kål) [F., from L. *locālis*, from *locus*, place], *a.* Of or pertaining to a place; pertaining to, existing in, or peculiar to a particular place or places; pertaining to a part, not the whole (as a disease, etc.); (*Math.*) of or pertaining to a *locus.* *n.* An inhabitant of a particular place; a professional man practising there; a train serving a suburban district; an examination held in a provincial centre; a postage-stamp valid in certain districts; (*colloq.*) an item of local news; (*colloq.*) a public-house; (*pronun.* lō kal') the scene or locality of an event, etc. **local colour:** Features characteristic of a place or district emphasized in a literary work in order to promote actuality; (*Painting*) the colour of individual objects considered apart from the general colour-scheme. **local examination,** *n.* A university examination held at a local centre. **local government:** Administration of towns, districts, etc., by elective councils; decentralization, opp. to centralization. **Local Government Board:** A State department in the U.K. formerly supervising and controlling local government. **local option** or **veto:** The regulation or prohibition of the liquor traffic by the inhabitants of a district. **local taxes:** (*U.S.A.*) Rates. **local time:** Time calculated on the noon of the meridian of a place, as against standard time. **locale** (lò kal′) [LOCAL]. **localism,** *n.* The state of being local; affection for a place; limitations due to confinement to a place, provincialism; a local idiom, custom, etc. **locally,** *adv.*

locality (lō kăl′ i ti), *n.* Particular place or region, site, geographical position; existence in a certain portion of space; limitation to a place.

localize (lō′ kà līz), *v.t.* To make local; to ascertain or indicate the exact place or locality of; to identify with a place; to restrict to a particular place; to decentralize; to concentrate (attention) upon. **localizable,** *a.* **localization,** *n.* **locally,** *adv.*

Locarno Pact (lō kar′ nō păkt) [*Locarno*, in Switzerland, PACT], *n.* The comprehensive name given to the series of treaties negotiated at Locarno, in October, 1925, between Germany and Belgium, France, Great Britain, Italy, Poland, and Czechoslovakia.

locate (lō kāt′), *v.t.* To set or place in a particular locality; (*in p.p.*) to situate; to discover or determine the site of; (*Am.*) to survey and settle the future situation or course of (a railway, etc.); (*Am. colloq.*) to settle, to take up residence. **location** (-kā′ shŭn), *n.* Situation or position; (*Am.*) a tract of land marked out, a place of settlement or residence; (*Cinema.*) a site outside the studio grounds where a scene is shot.

locative (lok′ à tiv), *a.* (*Gram.*) Denoting place. *n.* A case denoting place.

loch (lo*ch*) [Gael.], *n.* A lake, a narrow or land-locked arm of the sea in Scotland. **lochan,** *n.* A small lake, a tarn; a pond.

lochia (lok′ i à) [Gr., from *lochos*, a childbed], *n.pl.* (*Path.*) The uterine evacuations which follow childbirth. **lochial,** *a.*

lock (1) (lok) [A.-S. *loc* (cp. Icel. *loka*, lock, *lok*, lid, G. *loch*)], *n.* A device for fastening doors, etc., usu. having a bolt moved by a key of a particular shape; a mechanical device for checking or preventing movement, as of a carriage-wheel; the firing-apparatus of a gun; an enclosure in a canal, between gates, for raising and lowering vessels by the introduction or liberation of water; an air-tight antechamber to a caisson or tunnel; the oblique position of a fore-axle to a rear-axle in turning; (*fig.*) a fastening together or interlocking; a block, a jam; a hug or grapple in wrestling. *v.t.* To fasten with a lock; to shut (up a house, box, contents of these, etc.) thus; to prevent passage (in, out, etc.) by fastening doors, etc. with locks; to shut (in), enclose or hem (in); to bind or fix together, to fasten by means of mechanism or parts that engage together; (*in p.p.*) to embrace, to tangle together; to furnish with locks (as a canal); to seize the sword-arm of and disarm (an antagonist) in fencing. *v.i.* To become fastened by or as by a lock; to intertwine. **lock, stock and barrel:** The whole lot. **to lock up:** To close, fasten, or secure with lock and key; to invest (money) so that it cannot be readily realized. **to lock up a form:** To fasten the types in a chase ready for the press. **lock-chain,** *n.* One for locking the wheels of a vehicle. **lock-fast,** *a.* Secured by a lock. **lock-gate,** *n.* The gate of a canal-lock. **Lock hospital:** A hospital for the treatment of venereal diseases. **lock-jaw,** *n.* A variety of tetanus in which the muscles of the jaw are violently contracted and its motion suspended. **lock-keeper,** *n.* One who attends to a canal-lock. **lockman,** *n.* (*Isle of Man*) An officer corresponding to sheriff. **lock-nut,** *n.* A check-nut screwed over another. **lock-out,** *n.* The temporary discharge of workmen by employers to bring them to terms. *v.t.* To try to coerce workers by closing a works or factory. **lock-paddle,** *n.* A sluice for filling and emptying a lock-chamber. **lock-sill,** *n.* A piece of timber at the bottom of a canal-lock, against which the gates shut. **locksman,** *n.* A lock-keeper. **locksmith,** *n.* A maker and repairer of locks. **lock-spring,** *n.* A spring for closing a watch-case. **lock-stitch,** *n.* A sewing-machine stitch which locks two threads together. **lock-up,** *n.* A place where prisoners are temporarily confined; time for locking up; the investing of capital in such a way that it cannot be realized; the amount so invested. *a.* That may be locked. **lock-up shop,** *n.* Shop having access only from the street, with no connection with the rest of the building. **lockless,** *a.*

lock (2) (lok) [A.-S. *locc* (cp. Dut. *lok*, Icel. *lokkr*, G. *locke*), cogn. with Gr. *lugos*, a withy, and *lugizein*, to bend], *n.* A tuft of hair, wool, or similar substance; a tress, a ringlet; a love-lock.

lockage (lok′ àj), *n.* The works of a canal-lock; the rise and fall in a canal through the working of locks; a toll for passing through locks.

locker (lok′ ėr), *n.* One who or that which locks; a cupboard, chest, or other closed receptacle, with lock and key; (*Naut.*) a chest or compartment for locking up stores, etc. **not a shot in one's locker:** (Having) no money in one's pocket.

locket (lok′ ėt) [F. *loquet*, dim. of O.F. *loc*, latch, from Teut. (cp. Icel. *loka*, LOCK (1))], *n.* A small gold or silver case, worn as an ornament, and adapted to contain hair, a miniature, etc.; a plate or band on a scabbard to which the hook is fastened.

lockfast [LOCK (1)].

Lockian (lok′ i àn) [John *Locke* (1632–1704), English philosopher], *a.* Characteristic of the teaching of Locke or his followers. **Lockist,** *n.*

***lockram** (lok′ ràm) [F. *locrenan*, from *Locronan*, Brittany, where orig. made], *n.* A coarse linen cloth.

loco (1) (lō′ kō) [short for LOCOMOTIVE], *n.* (*colloq.*) A locomotive works; a locomotive.

loco (2) (lō′ kō) [Sp., insane], *a.* (*U.S.A. slang*) Insane, mad.

loco-foco (lō′ kō fō′ kō) [Am., a coined word], *n.* A lucifer-match; a name given to the Radicals or Equal Rights faction by the Democratic party in the U.S.A., because at a meeting in Tammany Hall, New York, in 1835, when the lights were extinguished to break up the turbulent assembly, they relighted the lamps with their matches.

locomobile (lō kò mō′ bil) [L. *locō*, see foll., MOBILE], *a.* Able to change place. *n.* A road locomotive. **locomobility** (-bil′ i ti), *n.*

locomotion (lō kò mō′ shŭn) [L. *locō*, abl. of *locus*, place, MOTION], *n.* The act or power of moving from place to place; moving about, travel, travelling. **locomote** (lō′ kò mōt), *v.i.* (*Biol.*) To move from one place to another. **locomotility** (-til′ i ti), *n.* **locomotive** (lō kō mō′ tiv), *a.* Of or pertaining to locomotion; moving from place to place, not stationary; having the power of locomotion, or causing locomotion; pertaining to travel. *n.* A self-propelling machine, esp. a railway engine; an animal capable of locomotion. **locomotively,** *adv.* **locomotivity** (-tiv′ i ti), **locomotiveness,** *n.* **locomotor** (lō kō mō′ tŏr), *a.* Of or pertaining to locomotion. *n.* One who or that which is capable of locomotion. **locomotor ataxy** [ATAXY]. **locomotory,** *a.*

loculus (lok′ ū lŭs) [L., dim. of LOCUS], *n.* (*pl.* **-li,** -lī) A small cavity, a cell; (*Ant.*) a separate chamber or cell in a large tomb; (*Biol. etc.*) one of numerous cavities in various organisms. **loculament,** *n.* (*Bot.*) One of the cells of a seed-vessel. **locular, loculose, -lous,** *a.*

locum-tenens (lō′ kŭm tē′ nĕns) [L., holding place (see foll.)], *n.* (*pl.* **-tenentes,** -tĕ nen′ tēz) A deputy or substitute, esp. one acting in the place of a doctor or clergyman. **locum-tenency,** *n.*

locus (lō′ kŭs) [L.], *n.* (*pl.* ***-ci,*** -sī) The exact place, the locality (of); (*Math.*) the line generated by a point, or the surface generated by a line, moving according to specified conditions. ***locus citatus:*** The passage quoted. ***locus classicus:*** The best or most authoritative passage quoted as an instance or illustration. ***locus in quo:*** The scene of some event. ***locus pœnitentiæ:*** (*Law*) An opportunity for withdrawing at an early stage. ***locus standi:*** Recognized place or position authorizing intervention, application to a court, etc.

locust (lō′ kŭst) [L. *locusta*, lobster, locust], *n.* An East European, African, and Arabian winged insect of various species allied to the grasshopper, which migrates in vast swarms and is very destructive to vegetation; applied to certain American and Australian grasshoppers; a locust-tree. **locust-bean,** *n.* The sweet pod of the carob. **locust-bird, -eater,** *n.* One of various species of birds that feed on locusts. **locust-tree,** *n.* The carob; the North American acacia, *Robinia pseudacacia*; applied to various West Indian trees.

locution (lō kū′ shŭn) [L. *locūtio*, from *loquī*, to speak], *n.* Style of speech, mode of delivery; a phrase or expression considered with regard to style or idiom. **locutor,** *n.* A spokesman.

locutory (lok′ ū tŏr i) [med. L. *locūtōrium*, from L. *locūtor*, see prec.], *n.* A conversation-room or parlour in a monastery; a grille at which inmates and visitors might converse.

lode (lōd) [A.-S. *lād*, see LOAD], *n.* An open ditch or watercourse for draining; a reach of water in a canal; a vein bearing metal. **lodestar,** *n.* A guiding star or one that is steered by, usu. the pole-star; (*fig.*) one's aim, ambition, or guiding principle.

lodestone (lōd′ stōn), *n.* Magnetic oxide of iron, a natural magnet.

lodge (loj) [O.F. *loge*, low L. *lobia*, LOBBY, from Teut. (cp. O.H.G. *louba*, G. *laube*, cogn. with *laub*, LEAF)], *n.* A temporary residence; a cottage, a hut, a cabin, a small house in a park; a gate-keeper's or gardener's cottage; a small house attached or pertaining to a larger; a room or apartment for a porter in a college, chambers, etc.; (*Freemasonry, etc.*) a local branch or its place of meeting; a beaver's or otter's lair; a N. Am. Indian wigwam, the family that lives in it. *v.t.* To supply with temporary quarters, esp. for sleeping; to receive as an inmate, usu. for a fixed charge; to entertain as a guest; to establish in temporary or permanent quarters; to accommodate with rooms, etc.; to deposit, to leave for security (in, with, etc.); to deposit in court or with a prosecuting officer (as a complaint); to implant, to fix; to beat down (crops, of wind). *v.i.* To reside temporarily, esp. to have sleeping quarters; to reside as an inmate at a fixed charge; to stay or become fixed (in); (of crops) to be laid flat. **Grand Lodge:** The principal or governing lodge of the Freemasons, Good Templars, etc. **lodger,** *n.* One who rents and occupies furnished rooms (*Am.* a roomer). **lodging,** *n.* A temporary residence; a room or rooms hired in another's house (*usu. in pl.*). **lodging-house,** *n.* **lodgement,** *n.* The act of lodging; the state of being lodged; an accumulation of matter that remains at rest, a deposit; (*Mil.*) an entrenchment hastily constructed to defend a captured work; (*fig.*) a position, advantage, or foothold secured.

loess (lō′ es, lŭs) [G.], *n.* (*Geol.*) A post-Tertiary deposit of clay, loam, sand, etc., in the Rhine, Mississippi, and other river-valleys.

loft (loft) [Icel. *lopt* (pronun. loft), orig. the sky (cp. LIFT (1))], *n.* The room or air space under a roof; an elevated gallery in a church or hall; a room over a barn or stable; a pigeon-house, hence, a flock of pigeons; (*Golf*) a backward inclination of the face of a club, a lofting stroke. *v.t.* To strike (the ball) so that it rises high in the air; to provide (pigeons) with a loft. **lofter,** *n.* (*Golf*) A club for lofting.

lofty (lof′ ti) [prec., -Y], *a.* Very high, towering, of imposing height; (*fig.*) elevated in character, sentiment, style, etc., sublime; high-flown, grandiose; haughty, arrogant. **loftily,** *adv.* **loftiness,** *n.*

log (1) (log) [M.E. *logge*, etym. doubtful], *n.* A bulky piece of unhewn timber; a block; (*Naut.*) a piece of wood with a line attached used as a float for ascertaining the rate of a ship's motion; a log-book; (*fig.*) a dolt, a blockhead. *v.t.* (*past & p.p.* **logged**) To cut into logs; (*Naut.*) to enter in the log-book; to make (a specified distance) by the log (of a ship). **log-board,** *n.* (*Naut.*) A hinged pair of boards on which memoranda of time, wind, rate, etc., are noted for transcription into the log-book. **log-book,** *n.* (*Naut.*) A book, in which an official diary of events occurring in a ship's voyage is kept, together with a record of observations with the log. **log-cabin, -house, -hut,** *n.* One built of logs. **log-canoe,** *n.* A dug-out. **log-line,** *n.* (*Naut.*) A knotted line, usu. 150 fathoms in length, fastened to the log for finding the speed of the vessel. **log-man,** *n.* One employed to carry logs. **log-reel,** *n.* The reel on which the log-line is wound. **log-roll,** *v.i.* **log-roller,** *n.* **log-rolling,** *n.* Mutual assistance in collecting logs for burning; (*U.S.A.*) mutual assistance in carrying legislative measures; (*colloq.*) mutual puffing of each other's literary work by authors. **logwood,** *n.* The wood of *Hæmatoxylon Campeachianum*, used as a dark-red dye-stuff. **logger,** *n.* A lumberman. **logging,** *n.*

***log** (2) (log) [Heb.], *n.* A Hebrew liquid measure, variously estimated at $\frac{3}{4}$ and $\frac{5}{6}$ of a pint.

log (3) [abbrev. LOGARITHM].

loganberry (lō′ găn bĕr i) [J. H. *Logan* of California (d. 1928), originator], *n.* A permanent hybrid obtained by crossing the raspberry and a species of blackberry; the fruit of this.

logan-stone (log′ ăn stōn) [obs. *logging*, pres.p. of *log* (prob. onomat.), to rock, STONE], *n.* A rocking-stone.

logaœdic (log ă ē′ dik) [late L. *logaœdicus*, Gr. *logaoidikos* (*log-os*, speech, *aoidē*, song)], *a.* (*Pros.*) Applied to lines consisting of a mixture of dactyls and trochees. *n.* A line of this character.

logarithm (log′ ă rithm) [Gr. *log-os*, word, ratio, *arithmos*, number], *n.* The exponent of the power to which a fixed number, called the base, must be raised to produce a given number (tabulated and used as a means of simplifying arithmetical processes by enabling addition and subtraction to be substituted for multiplication and division). **logarithmic** (-rith′ mik), *a.* **logarithmic scale,** *n.* A scale of measurement in which an increase of one unit represents a tenfold increase in the quantity measured. **logarithmically,** *adv.*

-loger [-LOG-Y, -ER], *suf.* As in *astrologer* (usu. superseded by -LOGIST).

***loggat** (log′ ăt) [perh. a dim. of LOG (1)], *n.* A pole, a stake; a kind of truncheon or heavy peg; (*pl.*) a game in which pieces of wood were thrown at a fixed stake, the nearest winning.

loggerhead (log′ ĕr hed) [dial. *logger*, from LOG (1), HEAD], *n.* A stupid fellow, a dolt; a round mass of iron with a long handle, used to melt tar; a large turtle, *Thalassochelys olivacea*; the shrike; (*prov.*) the chub, also the miller's thumb; (*Naut.*) a post built into a whale-boat for turning a rope round and taking a heavy strain. **at loggerheads:** Disagreeing, quarrelling. ***loggerheaded,** *a.* Doltish, stupid.

loggia (loj′ i ă) [It., LODGE], *n.* An open corridor, gallery, or arcade along the front of a large building; an open balcony in a theatre or concert hall.

logia, *pl.* [LOGION].

logic (loj′ ik) [O.F. *logique*, L. *logica*, Gr. *logikē* (*technē*), the art of reasoning (*logikos*, pertaining to reasoning, from LOGOS)], *n.* The science of reasoning, correct thinking, proving and deducing; a treatise on this; a particular mode or system of reasoning; reasoning, argument, etc., considered with regard to correctness or incorrectness; force of argument; (*fig.*) force of circumstances, situation, etc. **logical,** *a.* Pertaining to, used in, or according to the rules of logic, consistent or accurate in reasoning; reasonable; versed or skilled in accurate reasoning. **logicality** (-kăl′ i ti), **logicalness,** *n.* **logically,** *adv.* **logician** (lŏ jish′ ăn), *n.* One skilled in logic. ***logicize,** *v.i.*

-logic, -logical [Gr. *logikos* (-LOGY, -IC, -AL)], *suf.*

logie (lō′ gi) [said to be from D. *Logie*, the inventor], *n.* (*Theat.*) A cheap ornament or imitation jewel made of zinc.

logion (log′ i ŏn) [Gr., oracle, dim. of LOGOS], *n.* (*pl.* **-gia**) A traditional saying, revelation, or truth, esp. one of those ascribed to Christ but not recorded in the Gospels.

-logist [-LOGY, -IST], *suf.* As in *anthropologist.*

logistics (lŏ jis′ tiks), *n.pl.* The art of arithmetical calculation; a system of arithmetic in which the logarithms of sexagesimal numbers are employed; (*Mil.*) the branch of strategy concerned with the moving and quartering of troops. **logistic** (lŏ jis′ tik), *a.* (*Math.*) Pertaining to proportion; applied to logarithms of sexagesimal numbers or fractions; pertaining to logistics. **logistic curve, line,** or **spiral:** A logarithmic curve, etc.

logo- [LOGOS], *comb. form.* Pertaining to words; wordy. **logogram** (log′ ŏ grăm), *n.* A sign representing a word, esp. in shorthand; a puzzle in verse containing words synonymous with others formed from the transposition of the letters of an original word to be found out. **logograph** (log′ ŏ grăf), *n.* A logogram; a logotype. **logographer** (lŏ gog′ ră fėr), *n.* (*Gr. Ant.*) A prose-writer, esp. one of the historians preceding Herodotus, also a professional speech-writer. **logography,** *n.* A method of printing in which a type represents a word instead of a letter. **logographic, -al** (-grăf′ ik, -ăl), *a.* **logogryph** (log′ ŏ grif) [F. *logogriphe*, Gr. *griphos*, basket, riddle], *n.* A word-puzzle, a logogram. **logomachy** (lŏ gom′ ă ki) [Gr. *logomachia* (*-machia*, battle, from *machesthai*, to fight)], *n.* Contention about words, controversy hingeing on verbal matters. **logomachist,** *n.* **logomachize,** *v.i.* **logomania** (log ŏ mā′ ni ă) [-MANIA], *n.* (*Path.*) A form of insanity or organic disease of the nervous system characterized by uncontrollable loquacity.

logometer (lo gom′ ė tėr), *n.* (*Chem.*) A scale for measuring chemical equivalents.

logorrhea (log ō rē′ ă), *n.* (*Path.*) An abnormal volubility which is a symptom of certain forms of insanity.

logos (log′ ŏs) [Gr., word, speech, reason, cogn. with *legein*, to speak], *n.* (*Theol.*) The Divine Word, the Son of God, the Second Person of the Trinity.

logotype (log′ ŏ tīp) [LOGO-, TYPE], *n.* (*Print.*) A type having two or more letters cast in one piece, but not as a ligature, as *are, was,* etc.

-logue [Gr. *-logos -on*, see LOGOS], *suf.* As in *epilogue, prologue.*

logwood [LOG (1)].

-logy [Gr. *-logia*, *-logos*, see LOGOS (older examples through F. *-logie*, med. L. *-logia*)], *suf.* Forming names of sciences and departments of knowledge, and nouns denoting modes of speaking; as *astrology, eulogy, tautology.*

***loimic** (loi′ mik) [Gr. *loimikos*, from *loimos*, plague], *a.* Pertaining to the plague or to contagious diseases.

loin (loin) [O.F. *loigne*, ult. from L. *lumbus*, cogn. with A.-S. *lendenu*, and Dut. *lende*], *n.* The part of the body of a man or quadruped lying between the false ribs and the hip-joint; (*pl.*) this part as representing strength and generative power; a joint of meat from this part. **to gird up the loins:** To prepare oneself for a great effort. **loincloth,** *n.* A cloth worn round the waist as an elementary kind of garment.

loir (loir) [F., from L. *glīrem*, nom. *glīs*], *n.* The fat dormouse, *Myoxus glis.*

loiter (loi′ tėr) [perh. from M.Dut. *loteren* (Dut. *leuteren*), cp. W.Flem. *lutteren*, Norw. *lutra*], *v.i.* To linger, to dawdle; to move or travel with frequent halts; to spend time idly; to be dilatory. *v.t.* To waste or consume (time) in trifles; to idle (time) away. **loiterer,** *n.* **loiteringly,** *adv.*

Loligo (lŏ lī′ gō) [L.], *n.* (*Zool.*) A genus of cephalopods containing the calamaries or squids.

loll (lol) [prob. imit. (cp. M.Dut. *lollen*, Icel. *lolla*, also LULL)], *v.i.* To hang from the mouth (of the tongue); to stand, sit, or lie in a lazy attitude, to lounge. *v.t.* To allow (the tongue) to hang from the mouth; to let (one's head or limbs) hang or recline lazily (on or against). **loller,** *n.* **lollingly,** *adv.*

Lollard (lol′ ărd) [M.Dut. *lollaerd*, from *lollen*, to hum (conf. with LOLLER)], *n.* One of a sect of reformers in the 14th and 15th centuries, followers of John Wyclif. **Lollardism, Lollardy,** *n.*

lollipop (lol′ i pop) [etym. doubtful], *n.* A sweetmeat, a sugar-plum.

lollop (lol′ ŏp) [from LOLL], *v.i.* To loll about; to roll or flop about heavily; to go or do in a lounging or idle way.

lolly (lol′ i), *n.* A lollipop, a sweet on a stick; (*slang*) money.

Lombard (1) (lŭm′-, lom′ bărd) [F., from It. *Lombardo*, late L. *Longo-*, *Langobardus* (Teut. *lang-*, LONG, *Bardi*, L. name of the people)], *n.* One of the Teutonic Longobardi who conquered Italy in the 6th cent.; a native of Lombardy; *a money-lender or banker (a profession exercised in London during the Tudor period by Italians from Lombardy); *a bank, a money-lender's office, or a pawnshop. *a.* Of or pertaining to the Lombards or to Lombardy. **Lombard Street:** A street in the City of London formerly occupied by Lombard merchants and money-lenders; (*fig.*) the money-market; (*collect.*) financiers. **Lombardic** (lom bar′ dik), *a.* Lombard, applied esp. to a style of architecture flourishing in Italy, 7th–13th cent., a school of Italian painters of the 15th and 16th cent., and a style of handwriting used in mediæval manuscripts.

***lombard** (2) (lom′ bărd) [Sp. *lombarda*], *n.* A mediæval species of artillery.

loment (lō′ mėnt) [L. *lōmentum*, bean-meal, used as a cosmetic, from *lavāre* (*p.p.* *lōtum*), to wash], *n.* (*Bot.*) An indehiscent legume, separating by a transverse articulation between each seed. **lomentum** (lŏ men′ tŭm) [L.], *n.* (*pl.* **-ta**). **lomentaceous** (-tā′ shŭs), *a.*

London (lŭn′ dŏn) [L. *Londinium*, perh. of Celt. orig.], *n.* The capital of England. **London-clay,** *n.* (*Geol.*) A formation of lower Eocene age in south-east England. **London particular,** *n.* (*old colloq.*) Dense yellow fog. **London pride:** An Irish saxifrage, *Saxifraga umbrosa*, cultivated in gardens. **Londoner,** *n.* A native, inhabitant, or citizen of London. **Londonism,** *n.* **Londonize,** *v.t.* and *i.*

lone (lōn), *a.* (*chiefly poet. or rhet.*) Solitary, retired, uninhabited, lonely, deserted; without company or a comrade; (of a woman) unmarried, widowed. **lone hand:** (*Cards*) One played without help from one's partner's cards. ***loneness,** *n.*

lonely (lōn′ li), *a.* Solitary, unfrequented, sequestered; companionless, lone; addicted to solitude or seclusion. **loneliness,** *n.* **lonesome,** *a.* Lonely, unfrequented; adapted for solitude. ***lonesomely,** *adv.* **lonesomeness,** *n.*

long (1) (long) [A.-S. *lang* (cp. Dut., G., and Dan. *lang*, Icel. *langr*, also L. *longus*)], *a.* Of considerable or relatively great linear extent; of great extent in time; of a specified linear extent or duration in time; protracted in sound, not short; stressed (of vowels or syllables); delayed in coming, dilatory; far-reaching; lengthy, verbose, tedious. *adv.* To a great extent in distance or time; for a long time; by a long time; throughout a specified period. *n.* Anything that is long, esp. a period, interval, etc.;

(*Pros.*) a long syllable; (*Mus.*) a note equal in common time to two breves; (*Univ.*) the Long Vacation. **before long:** Soon, shortly. **a long chalk** [CHALK]. **in the long run:** In the end, eventually. **to make a long nose:** To cock a snook. **the long and the short of it:** The whole matter in a few words. **long-bill,** *n.* The snipe, woodcock, or other long-billed birds. **long-boat,** *n.* (*Naut.*) The largest boat of a sailing-ship. **long-bow,** *n.* A long powerful bow drawn by hand, formerly the national English weapon. **to draw the long bow** [BOW (1)]. **long-breathed,** *a.* Able to retain the breath for a long time. **long-clay:** A churchwarden pipe. **long cloth,** *n.* A kind of fine, soft, cotton cloth. **long date:** A distant date. **long-dated,** *a.* **long-distance,** *a.* From or at long range. **long-distance call:** (*Am.*) A trunk telephone call. **long dozen:** Thirteen. **long face:** A gloomy or dejected expression. **long firm** [FIRM (2)]. **longhand,** *n.* Ordinary writing, opp. to shorthand. **long hop:** (*Cricket*) A short-pitched ball making a long bounce. **long-headed,** *a.* Shrewd, sensible, far-sighted; dolichocephalic. **long-headedness,** *n.* **long hundred:** One hundred and twenty. **long-lived,** *a.* Enjoying long life. **long-liver,** *n.* **long-measure,** *n.* Measure of length. **long metre,** *n.* Hymn stanza consisting of four 8-syllable lines. **long odds:** Unequal or unfavourable odds (in betting). **long off** or **on:** (*Cricket*) The fielder to the left or right rear of the bowler. **long-playing,** *a.* (*Gramophone*) Of a fine-grooved record that plays a long time. **long primer:** A size of printing type between small pica and bourgeois. **long pull:** The over-measure sometimes given by publicans. **long robe:** Legal attire; hence, **gentlemen of the long robe:** Lawyers. **longshanks,** *n.* A person with long legs; the long-legged plover or stilt. **long-shot,** *n.* (*Cinema*) A shot with the camera at sufficient distance to take in all the principal characters in a film; a random guess. **long-sighted,** *a.* Able to see to a great distance; (*fig.*) shrewd, far-sighted. **long-sight, -sightedness,** *n.* **long-sleever,** *n.* (*Austral. colloq.*) A long drink; the glass for this. **long-staple,** *n.* A superior kind of long-fibred cotton. **long-stop,** *n.* (*Cricket*) A fielder placed behind the wicket-keeper to stop balls which pass him. *v.i.* To act as long-stop. **long-suffering,** *a.* Forbearing, patient. *n.* Forbearance to punish. ***long-sufferance,** *n.* **long-tail,** *n.* An animal, esp. *a dog, having an uncut tail (the dogs of persons not qualified to hunt had their tails cut); *a native of Kent. *a.* Having the tail uncut. **long-term,** *a.* Of a policy that looks to the future rather than the immediate present. **long-tongued,** *a.* Talkative, chattering. **Long Vacation:** (*Univ. and Law*) The vacation between Trinity and Michaelmas terms. **long wave,** *a.* (*Radio*) Having a wave-length of 800 metres or more. **long-winded,** *a.* Long-breathed, wearisome from prolixity. **long-windedness,** *n.* **longish,** *a.* ***longly,** *adv.* For a long time; at great length, wearisomely. **longways, -wise,** *adv.*

long (2) (long) [A.-S. *longian*, perh. rel. to prec.], *v.i.* To have an earnest desire (for); to yearn (to or for). **longing,** *a.* **longingly,** *adv.*

***long** (3) (long) [shortened form of M.E. *ilong*, A.-S. *gelang*, ALONG], *a.* ***long of:** On account or because of.

-long [LONG (1), largely substituted for -LING], *suf.* Forming adverbs, as *endlong*, *sidelong*.

longanimity (long gă nim′ i ti) [late L. *longanimitās*, from *long animus* (*longus*, LONG (1), ANIMUS)], *n.* Long-suffering, forbearance. **longanimous** (long găn′ i mŭs), *a.*

longe [LUNGE (2)].

longeron (lon′ jĕr on) [F., girder], *n.* (*Aviat.*) Longitudinal spar of an aeroplane's fuselage.

longeval (lŏn jē′ văl) [L. *longævus* (*longus*, LONG (1), *ævum*, age)], *a.* Long-lived. **longevity** (-jev′ i ti), *n.* ***longevous** (-jē′ vŭs), *a.*

longi- [L. *longus*, LONG (1)], *comb. form.*

longicaudal, longicaudate (lon ji kaw′ dăl, lon ji kaw′ dăt), *a.* Long-tailed.

longicorn (lon′ ji kôrn), *a.* Pertaining to the *Longicornes*, a division of beetles with large filiform antennæ. *n.* A beetle of this division.

longimanous (lon ji mā′ nŭs), *a.* Having long hands.

longipennate (lon ji pen′ ăt), *a.* Having long wings.

longiroster (lon ji ros′ tĕr), *n.* (*Zool.*) Any individual of the *Longirostres*, a family of wading-birds having a long, slender bill. **longirostral,** *a.*

longitude (lon′ ji tūd) [F., from L. *longitūdinem*, nom. *-tūdo*, from *longus*, LONG (1)], *n.* *Length; (*Geog.*) angular distance of a place east or west of a given meridian, usu. that of Greenwich; (*Astron.*) distance in degrees on the ecliptic from the vernal equinox to the foot of a perpendicular from, or circle of latitude of, a heavenly body. **longitudinal,** *a.* Pertaining to longitude or length; running lengthwise. **longitudinally,** *adv.* **longitudinal axis,** *n.* A straight line right through the centre of gravity of an aircraft and in the plane of symmetry. **longitudinal divergence,** *n.* The deflection from stability in aircraft which causes a nose-dive or stall. **longitudinal force,** *n.* The component of the resultant force on an aircraft along a longitudinal axis. **longitudinal stability,** *n.* The stability of rise, fall, and pitching in the plane of symmetry.

Longobard [LOMBARD (1)].

long-shore (long′ shôr) [shortened from ALONG SHORE], *a.* Of or belonging to, existing or working on the shore. **longshoreman,** *n.* A landsman working on the shore; a man who works in or about boats along the shore; a stevedore; one employed in fishing from the shore; (*Am.*) a docker, labourer.

longways, -wise [LONG (1)].

loo (loo) [short from obs. *lanterloo*, F. *lanturelu*, orig. nonsense, the refrain of a 17th-cent. song], *n.* A round game at cards; the pool in this game into which penalties are paid; the penalty. *v.t.* To cause to pay this penalty, to beat at loo. **loo-table,** *n.* A table for loo; a round table.

looby (loo′ bi) [rel. to LUBBER], *n.* An awkward, clumsy fellow; a lubber. ***loobily,** *a.*

loof (1) (loof) [Sc. and North., from Icel. *lōfe* (cp. O.H.G. *laffa*, oar-blade, O.Slav. *lapa*, paw)], *n.* The palm of the hand. **loof** (2) [LUFF].

loofah (loo′ fâ) [Egyptian Arab. *lūfa*, plant], *n.* The fibre of the sponge-gourd, *Luffa Ægyptiaca*, used as a flesh-brush.

look (luk) [A.-S. *lōcian* (cp. G. dial. *lugen*)], *v.i.* To direct the eye (towards, at, etc.) in order to see an object; to exercise the sight; to gaze, to stare; to stare in astonishment, wonder, etc.; to direct the mind or understanding, to give consideration; to face, to front, to be turned or have a particular direction (towards, to, into, etc.); to suggest, to have a particular tendency; to seem, to appear; to watch; to take care; *to expect, to anticipate. *v.t.* To express or show by the looks; to view, to inspect, to examine; *to search for. *n.* The act of looking or seeing, a glance; (*usu. in pl.*) appearance, esp. of the face, aspect, mien; expression of the eye and countenance; general appearance. **look alive** [ALIVE]. **look before you leap:** Be cautious before acting. **look here:** (*imper.*) Give heed, pay attention! **look lively:** (*colloq.*) Make haste. **look out:** Be careful. **look sharp:** (*imper.*) Bestir yourself, be quick! **to look about:** To turn the eyes on all sides; to be on the watch or in search (of or for). **to look about one:** To be watchful or observant; to examine one's surroundings, circumstances, prospects, etc. **to look after:** To search, to seek, to attend to; to take care of. **to look down upon:** To despise; to assume superiority over. **to look for:** To seek; to hope for; to expect, anticipate, be on the watch for. **to look in:** To call, to pay a brief visit; to watch television. **to look into:** To inspect carefully, to investigate; to examine the inside of.

to look on: To be a mere spectator; to regard, to consider (as, with, etc.). **to look out:** To be on the watch, to be prepared (for); to put one's head out of window, etc.; to choose by selection. **to look over:** To examine; to overlook or excuse. **to look through:** To see or direct the eyes through; to penetrate with one's sight or insight; to examine the contents of. **to look to** or **unto:** To take heed, to attend; to keep a watch over; to rely upon (for). **to look in the face** [FACE]. **to look up:** To search for; to pay a visit to; to raise one's eyes to in respect; to improve, to become more prosperous. **to look upon:** To regard (as or with). **look in:** A call, a short visit; (*slang*) a chance, as of winning in a game. **look out:** A watch; a person engaged in watching or looking out; a place from which watch or observation is kept; a view, a prospect; (*fig.*) future prospect; one's personal affair or concern. **look-see,** *n.* (*colloq.*) An inspection. **on the look out:** On the watch. **looker,** *n.* **looker-on,** *n.* A mere spectator. ***looking-for,** *n.* Expectation. **looking-glass,** *n.* A mirror.

loom (1) (loom) [A.-S. *gelōma*, orig. a tool or implement (cp. *andlōma*)], *n.* A machine in which yarn or thread is woven into a fabric; (*Naut.*) the handle or inboard part of an oar.

loom (2) (loom) [cp. E.Fris. *lōmen*, Swed. dial. *loma*, to move slowly, O.H.G., *luomen*, to be weary], *v.i.* To appear indistinctly or faintly in the distance; to appear larger than the real size, as in a mist; *to appear to the mind faintly or obscurely; *to shine. *n.* The first indistinct appearance, as of land at sea.

loom (3) (loom) [Icel. *lōmr*], *n.* A guillemot.

loon (1) (loon) [Sc. and North., etym. doubtful], *n.* A rogue, a scamp, a worthless person.

loon (2) (loon) [corr. of LOOM (3)], *n.* The great northern diver, *Colymbus glacialis*; the grebe; the guillemot.

loony (loo′ ni) [short for LUNATIC], *n.* (*vulg.*) A lunatic, a foolish fellow. **loony-bin,** *n.* (*vulg.*) Lunatic asylum.

loop (1) (loop) [prob. from Celt. (cp. Gael. and Ir. *lub*)], *n.* A folding or doubling of a string, rope, etc., across itself to form a curve or eye; a noose, a bight; anything resembling this; a ring, eye, or curved piece by which anything is hung up, fastened, held, etc.; a stitch in crochet or knitting; a hinge of a door; a loop-line; a circuit in a nearly vertical plane on a centrifugal railway by which passengers are carried head-downwards; (*Skating*) a curve performed on one edge and crossing itself. *v.t.* To form into a loop or loops; to fasten or secure with loops. *v.i.* To make a loop; (*Aviat.*) a complete revolution in flight in a vertical plane, the upper surface of the aircraft being on the inside of the circle. **to loop the loop:** To travel round a loop on a centrifugal railway; (*fig.*) to perform a similar evolution in an aeroplane, etc. **loop-line,** *n.* A railway, telegraph-line, etc., diverging from the main line and joining it again. **loop-work,** *n.* Fancy-work with loose stitches. **looped,** *a.*

***loop** (2) (loop) [prob. rel. to M.Dut. *lūpen* (Dut. *luipen*), to watch, to peer (cp. Dut. *gluip*, a narrow opening)], *n.* A loop-hole.

looper (loo′ pėr), *n.* One who or that which loops; the larva of the geometer moth, which moves by drawing up the hinder part of its body to the head, forming a loop; a part in a sewing-machine for making loops; an instrument for looping pieces together in making rag-carpets.

loop-hole (loop′ hōl), *n.* An aperture in a wall for shooting or looking through or for admission of light; (*fig.*) an outlet, a means of evasion or escape. *v.t.* To make loop-holes in.

***loord** (loord) [F. *lourd*, heavy], *n.* A stupid good-for-nothing fellow.

loose (loos) [Icel. *lauss* (cogn. with A.-S. *lēas*, G. *los*), cp. Gr. *leuin*], *a.* Not tied, fastened, or confined; unfastened, freed, detachable, hanging partly free; not fixed or tight; not crowded together, not compact or dense; relaxed, slack; careless, slovenly, straggling, rambling; not strict; vague, indefinite, incorrect; ungrammatical; dissolute, wanton; lax in the bowels, opp. to costive. *v.t.* To undo, to untie, to unfasten; to release, to set at liberty, to unbind; to dissolve; to relax; to free from obligation or burden; to discharge; *to forgive, to absolve. **v.i.* To set sail. *n.* Release, discharge, vent; *the issue or conclusion. **at a loose end:** With nothing to do. **on the loose:** (*slang*) On the spree. **to give a loose to:** To give free vent to (one's tongue, feelings, etc.). **to let loose** [LET (1)], **to set loose:** To set at liberty. **loose bowels:** Laxity of the bowels, tendency to diarrhœa. **loose box** [BOX (2)]. **loose-leaf,** *n.* A system of binding books in which the leaves are held together by some device which can be easily unlocked to allow of leaves being removed or added. **loose pulley:** (*Mach.*) A pulley mounted freely on a shaft. **loosely,** *adv.* **loosen,** *v.t.* and *i.* **loosener,** *n.* **looseness,** *n.* **loosish,** *a.*

loosestrife (loos′ strīf) [(LOOSE, STRIFE), erron. translation of late L. *lysimachia*, Gr. *lusimachion*, from *Lusimachos*, a pers. name (*lusi-*, from *luein*, to loose, *machē*, strife)], *n.* The golden or yellow loosestrife, *Lysimachia vulgaris*, or the red or purple loosestrife, *Lythrum salicaria*, two tall summer-flowering plants growing by the water-side.

loot (loot) [Hind. *lut*], *n.* Booty, plunder, esp. from a conquered city; (*fig.*) illicit gains, esp. by a public servant. *v.t.* To plunder, to pillage, esp. a city; to carry off as plunder. *v.i.* To plunder. **looter,** *n.* One who loots, a pillager.

lop (1) (lop) [etym. doubtful, perh. *n.* from *v.*], *v.t.* (*past & p.p.* **lopped**) To cut off the top or extremities of; to trim (trees, shrubs, etc.) by cutting; to cut off (as a person's head); to omit a part of. *v.i.* To cut (at) as if to lop. *n.* (*usu. in pl.*) That which is lopped. **lop and top:** Trimmings of trees. **lopper,** *n.*

lop (2) (lop) [prob. onomat.], *v.i.* To hang down limply; to flop, to droop; (*fig.*) to hang or idle (about). *v.t.* To allow to hang down; to let fall. *n.* A lop-eared rabbit. **lop-ear,** *n.* A lop. **lop-eared,** *a.* Having hanging ears. **lop-sided,** *a.* Heavier on one side than the other; not symmetrical; ill-balanced. **lop-sidedly,** *adv.* **lop-sidedness,** *n.*

lop (3) (lop) [onomat. (cp. LAP (3))], *v.i.* (*Naut.*) To break in short lumpy waves. *n.* A sea with such waves.

lope (lōp) [var. of LOUP (1)], *v.i.* To gallop, swing, or move (along) with long strides or leaps. *n.* Motion of this kind. **loper,** *n.*

lopho- [Gr. *lophos*, crest], *comb. form.* Having a crest; crested. **lophobranchiate** (lō fō brăng′ ki ăt) [BRANCHIATE]. (*Ichthyol.*) Belonging to or like the *Lophobranchiata*, a division of teleosteous fishes having the gills arranged in tufts. *n.* A fish in this division. **lophodont** (lō′ fō dont) [Gr. *odous odontos*, tooth], *a.* (*Zool.*) Having ridges on the crowns of the molar teeth. *n.* An animal with such teeth.

lop-sided, etc. [LOP (2)].

loquacious (lō kwā′ shŭs) [L. *loquax -ācis*, from *loquī*, to talk, -ACIOUS], *a.* Talkative, garrulous, chattering; apt to disclose secrets. **loquaciously,** *adv.* **loquaciousness, loquacity** (lō kwăs′ i ti), *n.*

loquat (lō′ kwot) [Chin. *luh kwat*, lit. rush orange]. *n.* A Chinese and Japanese fruit-tree, *Eriobotrya Japonica*, cultivated in the southern U.S.A., southern Europe, Australia, etc.; its fruit.

loral, lorate [LORE (2)].

lorcha (lôr′ chȧ) [Port., etym. doubtful], *n.* A light Chinese coaster, of European build, rigged like a junk.

lord (lôrd) [A.-S. *hlāford* (*hlāf*, LOAF (1), WARD)], *n.* A ruler, a master; one possessing supreme power, a sovereign; the Supreme Being; a feudal superior, the holder of a manor, hence (*poet.*) an owner; (*fig.*) a magnate or controlling capitalist in a trade; (*poet. and facet.*) one's husband; a nobleman, a peer of the realm; a courtesy-title given to the son of a duke or marquis, or the son of an earl holding a barony; a title of honour conferred on certain official personages as Lord Chief Justice, Lord Commissioner, Lord Mayor, Lord Rector, etc.; (*pl.*) the peers, the members of the House of Lords. *v.i.* To play the lord (over). *v.t.* To raise to the peerage. **House of Lords:** The upper legislative chamber in the United Kingdom comprising the lords spiritual and temporal. **Lords Commissioners:** Members of boards performing the duties of various offices of State put in commission. ***lord of misrule:** One who superintended the games and revels at Christmas. **Lord-Lieutenant,** *n.* An official representing the sovereign, and the chief executive authority and head of the magistracy in a county. **Lord Mayor:** The chief magistrate of London, York, and certain other large towns. **Lord Rector:** The head officer of certain Scottish Universities, elected annually. **Lord's day:** Sunday. **Lord's supper:** The Eucharist. **lords spiritual:** The archbishops and bishops having seats in the House of Lords. **lords temporal:** Lay peers having seats in the House of Lords. **Lord's table:** The altar in a Christian church; the Eucharist. **my lord:** A formula for addressing a nobleman (not a duke), bishop, lord mayor, or judge of the Supreme Court. ***lording,** *n.* A lord used as a respectful mode of address. **lordless,** *a.* **lordlet, lordling,** *n.* **lord-like,** *a.* and *adv.* **lordly,** *a.* Becoming or befitting a lord; noble, grand, magnificent; superb, lofty, proud, haughty, insolent. *adv.* Proudly; imperiously; arrogantly. **lordliness,** *n.* **lordolatry,** *n.* **lordship,** *n.* **your or his lordship:** A formula used in speaking deferentially to or of a lord. **Lord's Cricket Ground:** The headquarters of Marylebone Cricket Club and of cricket generally. **lords and ladies:** (*pop.*) The wild arum lily, *Arum maculatum.*

lordosis (lôr dō′ sis) [Gr., from *lordos,* bent backwards], *n.* (*Path.*) Curvature of a bone, esp. of the spine forward.

lore (1) (lôr) [A.-S. *lār* (cogn. with LEARN)], *n.* That which may be learned; (*collect.*) the traditions and facts relating to a given subject; *erudition, scholarship; *admonition, instruction.

lore (2) (lôr) [F., from L. *lōrum,* a strap], *n.* (*Nat. Hist.*) A strap-like part, the surface between the eye and the beak in birds, the corresponding part in snakes. **loral,** *a.* Pertaining to the lore. **lorate,** *a.* (*Bot.*) Strap-shaped.

lorette (lȯ ret′) [Church of Notre Dame de *Lorette* (*Loretto*), Paris, near which they lived], *n.* A courtesan of a more pretentious class than the grisette.

lorgnette (lôr nyet′) [F., from *lorgner,* squint], *n.* A pair of eye-glasses with a long handle; an opera-glass.

lorica (lȯ rī′ kȧ) [L. *lōrica,* from *lōrium,* strap], *n.* (*Rom. Ant.*) A cuirass; (*Zool.*) the carapace of a crustacean, the sheath of certain infusorians and rotifers.

loricata (lo ri ka′ tȧ), *n.* (*Zool.*) An order of reptiles including such large amphibious creatures as crocodiles, alligators, caimans, etc.

loricate (lo′ ri kȧt), *a.* Covered with defensive plates, scales, or other natural armour. *v.t.* (lo′ ri kāt). To plate or coat over; to encrust. **lorication,** *n.*

lorikeet (lor′ i kēt) [dim. of LORY (*-keet,* as PARRAKEET)], *n.* A genus of brightly-coloured parrots belonging to the Malay Archipelago.

***lorimer** (lor′ i mėr), ***loriner** (lor′ i nėr) [O.F. *loremier, lorenier* (F. *lorimer*), from *lorain,* med. L. *loranum,* a bridle, from L. *lōrum,* thong], *n.* A maker of bits and spurs, a spurrier; applied also to makers of small ironwork.

loriot (lôr′ i ȯt) [F., from O.F. *l'oriot,* the ORIOLE], *n.* The golden oriole.

loris (lôr′ is) [F., prob. from M.Dut. *loeris,* a clown], *n.* An Asiatic lemur, usu. called the slender loris; also the slow lemur or East Indian loris.

***lorn** (lôrn) [p.p. of obs. *leese* (A.-S. *loren,* p.p. of *lēosan,* to LOSE (1))], *a.* Lost, abandoned, forlorn.

lorry (lor′ i) [etym. doubtful], *n.* A low, flat, four-wheeled wagon without sides; a motor-wagon for heavy loads; a truck used on railways and tramways, esp. in mines.

lory (lôr′ i) [Malay *lūri*], *n.* A brilliantly coloured parrot-like bird of various genera of *Loriinæ,* found in S.E. Asia, the Malay Archipelago, and Australia.

lose (1) (looz) [A.-S. *losian,* to escape (from), becoming transitive by gradually superseding the obs. *leese,* A.-S. *lēosan*], *v.t.* (*past & p.p.* **lost**) To be deprived of; to part with accidentally or as a forfeit, penalty, etc.; to be freed from; to miss, to stray from, to be unable to find; to fail to gain, win, hear, obtain, or enjoy; to fail to keep possession of, to fail to hold or grasp; to spend uselessly, to waste; (*in p.p.*) to cause to disappear, to die, or to perish; to cause one the loss of; to make (oneself or itself) disappear; *to dislodge. *v.i.* To fail to be successful, to be beaten; to suffer loss; to be worse off (by). **losing game:** A hopeless game or contest. **lost soul:** One who is damned or beyond redemption. **to be lost in:** To be engrossed in; to merge or be obscured in. **to lose ground** [GROUND (1)]. **to lose oneself:** To lose one's way; to be bewildered. **losable,** *a.* **loser,** *n.* One who loses; a person, horse, boat, etc., failing to win a race; (*Billiards*) a losing hazard, (*pl.*) the beaten party in a game, battle, etc. **losingly,** *adv.*

***lose** (2) (lōz) [O.F. *los,* L. *laudēs,* pl. of *laus,* praise], *n.* Praise, fame, renown.

***losel** (lō′ zėl) [rel. to A.-S. *-lēosan,* see LOSE (1)], *n.* A worthless fellow; a scamp, a ne'er-do-well; a lazy vagabond. *a.* Worthless, lazy.

losh (losh) [Sc., distortion of LORD], *int.* Indicating surprise.

loss (los, laws) [A.-S. *los,* dissolution, rout, dispersion, from *-lēosan,* see LOSE (1) (cp. Icel. *los*)], *n.* The act or state of losing or being lost; failure to win or gain; that which is lost or the amount of this; detriment, disadvantage; wasted expenditure, effort, etc. **to bear a loss:** To sustain a loss without giving way; to make good a loss. **to be at a loss:** To be embarrassed or puzzled, to be at fault.

loss [LOESS]. **lost,** *past & p.p.* [LOSE (1)].

lot (lot) [A.-S. *hlot* (cp. Dut. *lot,* Icel. *hluti,* G. *loos*)], *n.* Anything, such as a die, paper, or other object, used in determining chances; choice or decision by chance drawing of these; the chance, share, or fortune falling to anyone; one's fortune, destiny, or condition in life; a distinct portion, collection, or parcel of things offered for sale, esp. at auction; a parcel of land; a number or quantity of things or persons; (*colloq.*) a considerable quantity or amount, a great deal (*often in pl.*); one's proportion of a tax, a due; *a lottery prize; (*Cinema*) a plot of land in the vicinity of the studio on which special exterior sets are built. *v.t.* To divide into lots; to apportion. **the lot,** *n.* (*colloq.*) The whole quantity. **a bad lot, a nice lot:** (*slang*) A person of bad or doubtful character. **to cast lots:** To determine by the throw of a die or other contrivance. **to draw lots:** To determine by drawing one name, etc., from a number.

***lote** [LOTUS]. **loth** [LOATH].

Lothario (lȯ thâr′ i ō) [character in Rowe's 'Fair Penitent'], *n.* A libertine, a gay deceiver.

lotion (lō′ shŭn) [L. *lōtio,* from *lavāre* (p.p. *lōtus*), to wash], *n.* A liquid application for a wound, diseased part, etc.; a cosmetic; *the act of washing.

lottery (lot′ ėr i) [It. *lotteria,* from foll.], *n.* A method of allotting valuable prizes by chance or lot among purchasers of tickets; the drawing of lots; a mere hazard. **lottery bonds,** *n.pl.* (*Stock Exch.*) Bonds issued by foreign governments, a bonus in the form of cash prizes being offered to subscribers. **lottery-wheel,** *n.* A drum-like wheel used for shuffling lottery-tickets.

lotto (lot′ ō) [It., from Teut. (cp. O.H.G. *hlōz*, LOT)], *n.* A game of chance, played with disks placed on cards divided into squares numbered from 1 to 90.

lotus (lō′ tŭs) [L., from Gr. *lōtos*], *n.* (*pl.* **lotuses**) (*Gr. Ant.*) A name for several plants the fruit of which was said to induce a dreamy languor in those who ate it; the Egyptian water-lily; (*Arch.*) a conventional representation of this; (*Bot.*) a genus of leguminous plants containing the bird's-foot trefoil. **lotus-eater,** *n.* One of the Lotophagi, mentioned in Homer's *Odyssey,* who lived on the fruit of the lotus; (*fig.*) one who gives himself up to dreamy ease. **lotus-eating,** *a.* and *n.* **lotus-land,** *n.*

loud (loud) [A.-S. *hlūd* (cp. Dut. *luid*, G. *laut*), cogn. with Gr. *kluein*, to hear, L. *cluēre*], *a.* Powerful in sound, sonorous; noisy, clamorous; (*fig.*) conspicuous, ostentatious, flashy (of attire, manners, etc.). *adv.* Loudly. **loudish,** *a.* **loudly,** *adv.* **loudness,** *n.* **loud speaker,** *n.* (*Radio*) An electrical reproducing mechanism in which a cone diaphragm vibrates with the aid of either a moving iron armature or a moving coil.

lough (lo*ch*) [Ir. *loch* or Northum. *luh*], *n.* (*Ang.-Ir.*) A lake, an arm of the sea.

louis (loo′ i), **louis d'or** (loo′ i dôr) [F. *Louis*, name of many French kings, *d'or*, of gold], *n.* (*unchanged in pl.*) An old French gold coin issued from Louis XIII to Louis XVI, worth at different times 20 or 23 francs (16s. 5¾d. or 18s. 11¾d.), superseded by the 20-franc piece. **Louis Treize, Quatorze, Quinze** or **Seize:** Louis XIII, XIV, XV, or XVI (used to denote styles of furniture fashionable in those reigns).

lounder (loon′ dĕr) [Sc., prob. onomat.], *n.* A heavy blow. *v.t.* To beat, to thrash.

lounge (lounj) [acc. to Skeat, from obs. *lungis*, F. *longis*, an idle fellow, L. name *Longinus* (punningly connected with *longus*, LONG (1))], *v.i.* To idle about, to saunter; to move lazily; to loll or recline. *v.t.* To idle (time) away. *n.* The act of lounging; a saunter; a place for lounging; the sitting-room in a house; a sofa with a back and one raised end. **lounge suit,** *n.* A man's suit for daily wear. **lounge-lizard,** *n.* (*contempt.*) A professional dance partner, a gigolo; a hanger-on. **lounger,** *n.* **loungingly,** *adv.*

loup (1) (loup) [Sc., from Icel. *hlaupa*, to LEAP], *v.t.* and *i.* To leap. **loup-the-dike,** *a.* Runaway, skittish, giddy.

***loup** (2) [LOOP (1)].

lour, lower (3) (lour) [M.E. *louren* (cp. L.G. *lūren*, M.Dut. *loeren*, G. *lauern*, to lie in wait)], *v.i.* To appear dark or gloomy; to frown, to scowl; to look threatening (of clouds, weather, etc.). *n.* A scowl; sullenness; gloominess (of weather, etc.). **louring, loury,** *a.* **louringly,** *adv.*

louse (lous) [A.-S. *lūs* (cp. Dut. *luis*, Icel. *lūs*, G. *laus*)], *n.* (*pl.* **lice,** līs) An insect of the genus *Pediculus*, three species of which are parasitic on man; applied to various parasites infesting animals, birds, fish, and plants. *v.t.* (louz) To clean from lice. **lousy** (lou′ zi), *a.* Infested with lice; (*fig.*) low, mean, or obscene; (*slang*) bad, inferior. **lousily,** *adv.* **lousiness,** *n.*

lout (lout) [A.-S. *lūtan* (cp. Icel. *lūta*)], *v.i.* To bend, to bow, to stoop. **v.t.* To treat as a lout; to make a fool of. *n.* An awkward fellow; a clown, a bumpkin. **loutish,** *a.* **loutishly,** *adv.* **loutishness,** *n.*

louver (loo′ vĕr) [M.E. and O.F. *lover*, med. L. *lōdium*, etym. doubtful], *n.* A turret on the roof of a mediæval hall with openings for the escape of smoke; an opening in a chimney pot, etc., to let out smoke; (*pl.*) louvre-boards. **louvre-boards, *luffer-boards,** *n.pl.* Sloping overlapping boards across a window to exclude rain but allow the passage of air. **louvre-window,** *n.* A window partially closed by louvre-boards. **louvred,** *a.*

lovable (lŭv′ ȧ bĕl), *a.* Worthy of love; amiable. **lovably,** *adv.* **lovableness,** *n.*

lovage (lŭv′ ăj) [M.E. *loveache*, O.F. *levesche*, ult. from L. *ligusticum*, Ligurian], *n.* A name applied to various umbelliferous herbs, esp. *Levisticum officinale*; (*Bot.*) the genus *Levisticum.*

love (lŭv) [A.-S. *lufu*, whence *lufigan*, *lufian*, to love (cp. Dut. *lieven*, G. *lieben*), rel. to LIEF], *n.* A feeling of deep regard, fondness, and devotion (for, towards, etc.); deep affection, usu. accompanied by yearning or desire for; affection between persons of the opposite sex, more or less founded on or combined with desire or passion; a personification of this or of Cupid, usu. in the form of a naked winged boy; a beloved one, a sweetheart (as a term of endearment); (*colloq.*) a delightful person, a charming thing; (*Games*) no points scored, nil; *traveller's joy, *Clematis vitalba.* *v.t.* To have strong affection for, to be fond of, to be in love with; to like greatly, to delight in, to have a strong partiality or predilection for. *v.i.* To be in love. **for love or money:** By some means or other. **for the love of:** For the sake of (esp. in adjuration). **labour of love:** Work done for its own sake, for love of some other person, or from devotion to a cause. **love all:** (*In games*) Nothing scored on either side. **there's no love lost between them:** They have anything but love for each other. **to give** or **send one's love:** To give or send an affectionate message. **to fall in love:** To become enamoured. **to make love to:** To woo, to pay court or attentions to. **to play for love:** To play without stakes. **love-affair,** *n.* An amour. ***love-apple,** *n.* The tomato. **love-begotten,** *a.* Illegitimate. **love-bird,** *n.* A short-tailed parrot of the African genus *Agapornis* or the American *Psittacus*, from the attachment they show to their mates. ***love-broker,** *n.* A go-between for lovers; a procurer. **love-child,** *n.* An illegitimate child. ***love-drink,** *n.* A philtre. **love-feast,** *n.* A religious meeting like the agape held by Methodists, etc. **love game:** A game in which the loser has not scored. **love-god,** *n.* Cupid. **love-in-a-mist,** *n.* The fennel-flower, *Nigella damascena.* **love-in-idleness,** *n.* The pansy or heartsease, *Viola tricolor.* ***love-juice,** *n.* A lotion supposed to produce love. **love-knot,** *n.* An intricate bow or knot (a token of love). **love-letter,** *n.* A letter between lovers or professing love. **love-lies-bleeding,** *n.* A species of amaranth, esp. *Amaranthus caudatus.* ***love-line,** *n.* A love-letter. **love-lock,** *n.* A curl or tress hanging at the ear or on the forehead. **love-lorn,** *a.* Forsaken by one's love; pining away for love. **love-making,** *n.* Courtship, amorous attentions. **love-match,** *n.* A marriage for love, not other considerations. **love-monger,** *n.* A love-broker. ***love-prate,** *n.* Idle talk about love. **love-shaft,** *n.* A shaft of love, esp. Cupid's arrow. **lovesick,** *a.* Languishing with love; expressive of languishing love. **love-sickness,** *n.* **love-song,** *n.* A song expressing love. **love-spring,** *n.* The beginnings of love. ***love-suit,** *n.* Courtship. **love-story,** *n.* A story dealing mainly with the history of an amour or wooing. **love-token,** *n.* A present in token of love. **loveless,** *a.* Destitute of love; not loving; not loved. **lovelessly,** *adv.* **lovelessness,** *n.* **lovely,** *a.* Beautiful and attractive, inspiring admiration and affection, winsome, tempting, delightful; *affectionate, loving. *adv.* So as to excite love or admiration. *n.* A beautiful woman. **lovelily,** *adv.* **loveliness,** *n.* **lover,** *n.* One who loves, one in love (used only of the man); a suitor or woman's sweetheart; a paramour, a gallant; (*pl.*) a pair of sweethearts; one fond of anything. ***lovered,** *a.* Having a lover. **loverless,** *a.* **loverlike,** *a.* and *adv.* **loverly,** *a.* and *adv.* ***lovesome,** *a.* Lovely. **loving-cup,** *n.* A large two- or three-handled drinking-vessel passed round with wine at a banquet. **lovingly,** *adv.* **lovingness,** *n.*

Lovelace (lŭv′ lās) [character in Richardson's 'Clarissa Harlowe'], *n.* A fascinating or accomplished libertine.

lovely, lover [LOVE].

low (1) (lō) [late A.-S. *lāh*, Icel. *lāgr* (cp. Dut. *laag*), cogn. with LIE (1)], *a.* (*comp.* **lower** (1), *superl.* **lowest**) Not reaching or situated far up; not high or tall, below the usual or normal height; below or little above a given surface or level; not elevated; near the horizon (of the sun, moon, etc.); near the equator; below the common standard in rank, condition, quality, character, etc.; humble, mean, degraded; base, dishonourable; not sublime, not exalted; coarse, vulgar; not advanced in civilization; not high in organization; lacking in vigour, weak, feeble; badly nourished; affording poor nourishment; (of sounds) not raised in pitch, deep, produced by slow vibrations, not loud or intense, soft; not large in amount, scanty, nearly exhausted; moderate, cheap; (*Ch. of Eng.*) inclined to evangelical doctrine, not favouring sacerdotal pretensions, not characterized by elaborate ritual. *adv.* Not on high; in or to a low position; deeply; at a low price; in a humble rank or position; of humble birth; with a subdued voice, in low tones; softly, quietly; on a poor diet; of or in times approaching our own. **at lowest:** To mention or judge by the least possible amount, etc. **to bring low:** To reduce in wealth, position, health, etc. **to lay low:** To overthrow; to kill. **to lie low:** To crouch; to be prostrate or abased; to be dead; (*colloq.*) to keep quiet, to do nothing for the moment, to await one's opportunity. **low birth:** Humble parentage. **low born,** *a.* **low-bred,** *a.* Vulgar in manners, ill-bred. **low-brow,** *n.* (*colloq.*) A person making no claims to intellectuality. *a.* Unintellectual; assuming no airs of intellectual superiority. **low-browed,** *a.* Having a low brow or forehead; beetling; having a low entrance, etc. **Low Church:** The evangelical party in the Church of England. **Low-Churchman,** *n.* **low comedy:** Comedy bordering on farce, hence **low comedian. Low Countries,** *n.pl.* A collective name for Belgium, Luxemburg, and the Netherlands. **low-down,** *a.* Degraded, mean, abject. *adv.* Meanly, ungenerously, contemptibly. **low-down,** *n.* (*colloq.*) The inner history, real facts. **low dress:** A dress cut low at the neck, exposing part of the shoulders and breast. **Low Dutch** [DUTCH]. **lower boy:** A boy in the lower school. **lower case:** (*Print.*) The case which contains the small letters; the small letters. **Lower Chamber** or **House:** The second of two legislative chambers, as the House of Commons. **lower deck:** (*Naut.*) The deck just above the hold; petty officers and men of the Royal Navy. **lower Empire:** The later Roman or the Byzantine Empire. **lower school:** The forms below the fifth in a public school. **lower world:** The earth. **low frequency,** *n.* (*Radio*) Term denoting frequencies of below 10,000. **Low German** [GERMAN]. **lowland,** *n.* Low-lying or level country. *a.* Pertaining to a lowland or the Lowlands. **Low Latin** [LATIN]. **low latitudes,** *n.pl.* Latitudes near the Equator. **low life:** A mean or low state of life; persons of a low position in life. **low-lived,** *a.* **low Mass:** Mass said without music, and without deacon and subdeacon. **low-minded,** *a.* **low-neck, -necked,** *a.* Cut low at the neck (said of a woman's dress). **low pitch:** (*Mus.*) A low tone or key; (*Arch.*) low angular elevation in a roof. **low-pitched,** *a.* **low pressure:** (*Steam, etc.*) A small degree of expansive force. *a.* Having only a small degree of expansive force (of steam and steam-engines). **low-rated,** *a.* Despised. **low relief:** Bas-relief. **low side window:** (*Arch.*) A small window lower than the others, usu. on the south side of the chancel, in old churches erron. supposed to have been used by lepers. **low-spirited,** *a.* Dejected in spirit. **low-studded,** *a.* (*Am.*) Built with short studs (of a house). **Low Sunday** or **Week:** The Sunday or week next after Easter. **low tension,** *n.* (*Radio*) Term indicating low potential difference or voltage. **low-tension battery:** (*Radio*) A battery for supplying current to the filament, or heater, of a valve. **low tide:** The lowest point of the ebb tide; the level of the sea at ebb tide. **low-velocity,** *a.* (*Artill.*) Applied to projectiles propelled at a comparatively low velocity and having a high trajectory. **low-voiced,** *a.* Having a soft, gentle voice. **low voltage:** (*Elec.*) Any voltage not exceeding 250 volts. **low water:** Low tide; hence **low-water mark. in low water:** (*fig.*) Impecunious; in low circumstances or health. **low wine:** A liquor produced by the first distillation of alcohol. **lower** (2), *v.t.* To bring down in height, force, intensity, amount, price, estimation, etc.; to haul or let down; to reduce the condition of. *v.i.* To become lower or less; to sink, to fall. **lowermost,** *a.* **lowish,** *a.* **lowly,** *a.* Humble, modest, unpretentious; low in size, rank, or condition; low, mean, inferior. *adv.* Humbly, modestly; *in a low or inferior way. **lowlily,** *adv.* **lowliness, *lowlihead, -hood,** *n.* **lowness,** *n.*

low (2) (lō) [A.-S. *hlōwan* (cp. Dut. *lōeien*, O.H.G. *hlōjan*), cogn. with L. *clāmāre*, Gr. *kalein*, to call], *v.i.* To utter the moo of a cow. *v.t.* To utter with such a sound. *n.* The moo of a cow. **lowing,** *n.*

low (3) (lō) [Sc. and North., from Icel. *loge* (cp. O.Fris. *loga*, G. *lohe*), cogn. with L. *lux*, LIGHT (1)], *n.* Flame; a blaze. *v.i.* To flame, to blaze (up).

low (4) (lō) [A.-S. *hlāw*, *hlǣw*, LAW (2)], *n.* A rounded hill; *a barrow or tumulus.

lower (1 and 2) [LOW (1)].

lower (3) [LOUR].

Lowlands (lō' lȧndz), *n.pl.* The eastern and southern or less mountainous parts of Scotland. **Lowlander,** *n.*

lown (loun) [Sc. and North., prob. from Icel.], *a.* Quiet, tranquil, serene; gentle, calm. *n.* Quietness, tranquillity; shelter. *v.i.* To become calm.

loxodromic (lok sȯ drom' ik) [Gr. *loxos*, oblique, *dromos*, course, from *dramein*, to run], *a.* Pertaining to oblique sailing. *n.* A loxodromic line or table. *n.pl.* The art of oblique sailing by the rhumb-line. **loxodromic curve, line,** or **spiral:** A rhumb-line.

loxotomy (lok sot' ȯ mi) [as prec., -TOMY], *n.* (*Surg.*) Amputation by an oblique cut.

loyal (loi' ȧl) [F., from L. *lēgālis*, LEGAL], *a.* Faithful, true, constant, in a trust or obligation (to); faithful to one's sovereign, government, or country. **n.* A loyal subject, esp. in a time of disaffection. **loyalism,** *n.* **loyalist,** *n.* **loyalize,** *v.t.* **loyally,** *adv.* **loyalty,** *n.*

lozenge (loz' ėnj) [O.F. *losenge*, Prov. *lauza*, tombstone, prob. from L. *lapidem*, nom. *lapis*, stone], *n.* A rhombus or oblique-angled parallelogram; (*Her.*) a diamond-shaped bearing, appropriated to the arms of spinsters and widows; a rhomb-shaped facet in a cut gem; a small rhomb-shaped pane of glass; a confection, a sweetmeat, etc., in a tablet of this shape. **lozenge moulding:** (*Arch.*) An ornament enclosing diamond-shaped panels. **lozenge-shaped,** *a.* **lozenged,** *a.* Shaped like a rhomb or diamond; arranged in series of lozenges in alternate colours; having diamond panes. **lozengewise,** *adv.* **lozengy,** *a.* (*Her.*) Divided lozengewise.

lubber (lŭb' ėr) [prob. rel. to LOB], *n.* A lazy, clumsy fellow; an awkward lout; a bad seaman. **lubber's hole,** *n.* (*Naut.*) A hole in the top through which sailors can reach the masthead without climbing the futtock-shrouds. **lubber's line,** *n.* The mark inside a compass-case which shows the direction of the ship's head. **lubberlike,** *a.* **lubberly,** *a.* Like a lubber. *adv.* Clumsily. **lubberliness,** *n.*

lubra (loo' brȧ) [aboriginal Austral.], *n.* An Aboriginal woman.

lubricate (loo'-, lū' bri kāt) [L. *lūbricātus*, p.p. of *lūbricāre*, from *lūbricus*, slippery, cogn. with SLIP], *v.t.* To make smooth or slippery by means of grease, oil, or similar substance, in order to reduce friction; (*fig.*) to make (anything) work easily; (*slang*) to drink. **a.* (-kȧt) Slippery, smooth; oily. ***lubric, *-brical,** *a.* Smooth and slippery; changeable, deceitful; lascivious. **lubricant,** *a.* and *n.* **lubrication** (-kā' shŭn), *n.* **lubricator** (loo' bri kā tȯr), *n.* One who or that which lubricates.

*lubricous (loo' bri kŭs), *a.* **lubrify,** *v.t.* To lubricate. ***lubrifaction, *lubrification,** *n.*

lubricity (lù bris' i ti), *n.* Smoothness; slipperiness; (*fig.*) shiftiness, instability; lewdness, lasciviousness. **lubricious,** *a.*

Lucan (loo'-, lū' kȧn) [L. *Lūcas*, Luke, -AN], *a.* Pertaining to the evangelist St. Luke.

lucarne (lù-, lū karn') [F., etym. doubtful], *n.* A dormer or garret window, a light in a spire.

luce (loos, lūs) [O.F. *lus*, L. *lūcius*], *n.* (*Zool.*) A pike, esp. when full-grown; (*Her.*) a figure of a pike used as an armorial bearing.

lucent (loo'-, lū' sėnt) [L. *lūcens -ntis*, pres.p. of *lūcēre*, to shine (*lux lūcis*, light, cogn. with Gr. *leukos*, white)], *a.* Shining, bright, luminous, resplendent. **luceny,** *n.*

lucernal (lù-, lū sĕr' nȧl) [L. *lucerna*, lamp, from the root *luc-*, see prec.], *a.* Pertaining to a lamp.

lucerne (lù-, lū sĕrn') [F. *luzerne*, etym. unknown], *n.* Purple medick, *Medicago sativa*, a fodder-plant.

Lucianic (loo-, lū si ăn' ik) [L. *Lūciānus*, Gr. *Loukianos*, -IC], *a.* Of, pertaining to, or in the style or manner of Lucian of Samosata (*c.* A.D. 125–*c.* 210), writer of witty, scoffing Greek dialogues.

lucid (loo'-, lū' sid) [L. *lūcidus*, from *lūcēre*, see LUCENT], *a.* (*poet.*) Bright, shining, radiant; clear, transparent, perspicuous, easily understood. **lucidity** (lù sid' i ti), ***lucidness,** *n.* **lucidly,** *adv.*

Lucifer (loo'-, lū' si fėr) [L., light-bringing (*lūci-*, see LUCENT, *-fer*, from *ferre*, to bring)], *n.* The morning star; Satan, the chief of the rebel angels; a match tipped with combustible substance and ignited by friction. **lucifer-match,** *n.* **Luciferian** (-fēr' i ȧn), *a.* ***luciferous** (lù sif' ėr ŭs) [-FEROUS], *a.* Bearing or giving light; making plain or clear; Satanic, devilish. ***lucific,** *a.* ***luciform** (loo'-, lū' si fôrm), *a.*

lucifugous (lū sif' ū gŭs), *a.* Shunning the light (of certain animals).

lucigen (lū' si jėn), *n.* A lamp in which a spray of oil is mixed with air.

lucimeter (lū' si mē tėr), *n.* A photometer.

luck (lŭk) [Dut. *luk*, *geluk* (cp. G. *glück*), etym. doubtful], *n.* Chance, accident, as bringer of fortune, whether good or bad; what happens to one, fortune, hap; the supposed good or evil tendency of fortuitous events as regards a person; good fortune, success. **luck-money, -penny,** *n.* A small sum returned to the buyer 'for luck' by the person who receives money on a sale or contract. **luckless,** *a.* Unfortunate. **lucklessly,** *adv.*

lucky (lŭk' i), *a.* Characterized or usually attended by good-luck; favoured by fortune; successful, esp. by a fluke or more than is deserved; bringing luck, auspicious; (*Sc.*) full to the brim, abundant. **lucky-bag,** *n.* (*Bazaars, etc.*) A bag containing miscellaneous articles in which one may dip on paying a small sum; (*Naut.*) a receptacle for lost property on a warship. **lucky dip,** *n.* Receptacle containing an assortment of articles, for one of which one dips blindly (*Am.* a grab-bag). **luckily,** *adv.* Fortunately (for). **luckiness,** *n.* **lucky-bone,** *n.* A bone from a sheep's head supposed to bring luck.

lucrative (loo'-, lū' krȧ tiv) [*lucrātīvus*, from *lucrārī*, to gain, see foll.], *a.* Producing gain, profitable, bringing in money; *greedy of gain. **lucratively,** *adv.*

lucre (loo'-, lū' kėr) [F., from L. *lucrum* (cp. Gr. *leia*, booty, *apolauein*, to enjoy, G. *lohn*, reward)], *n.* Pecuniary gain or advantage, usu. as an object of greed.

lucubrate (loo'-, lū' kū brāt) [L. *lūcubrātus*, p.p. of *lūcubrāre*, from *lux lūcis*, light], *v.i.* To study by lamplight; to produce lucubrations. *v.t.* To compose or elaborate, as by night study. **lucubration** (-brā' shŭn), *n.* Night work, night study; that which is composed at night; composition of a learned or too elaborate and pedantic character.

luculent (loo'-, lū' kū lėnt) [L. *lūculentus*, from *lux lūcis*, light], *a.* Clear, lucid, plain, manifest. **luculently,** *adv.*

lucumo (lū' kū mō) [L.], *n.* One of the Etruscan nobles who were at once priests and princes.

Luddites (lŭd' īts) [perh. from Captain *Ludd* or King *Lud*, a nickname of the ringleaders], *n.* A number of bands of mechanics who organized riots (1811–16) for the destruction of machinery. **Luddism,** *n.*

ludicrous (loo'-, lū' di krŭs) [L. *lūdicrus*, from *lūdi-*, stem of *lūdus*, play], *a.* Adapted to excite laughter, or derision; comical, ridiculous. **ludicrously,** *adv.* **ludicrousness,** *n.* **ludicro-,** *comb. form.*

ludo (loo' dō) [L. *ludo*, I play], *n.* A parlour game played with counters on a specially-chequered board.

lues (loo'-, lū' ēz) [L.]. Plague, contagious disease, infection, contagion. ***lues venerea:*** Syphilis. **luetic** (lù et' ik), *a.*

luff (lŭf) [etym. doubtful, conn. by Skeat with LOOF (1), palm of the hand, oar-blade, whence perh. Dut. *loef*, weather-gauge, and *loeven*, to luff (O.E.D. favours derivation from F. *lof*, something used for altering the course of a ship)], *n.* (*Naut.*) That part of a ship's bows where the timbers begin to curve in towards the stem; the weather-edge of a fore-and-aft sail; the weather-gauge, or part of a ship toward the wind; the act of sailing close to the wind. *v.i.* To bring a ship's head or to steer nearer the wind. *v.t.* To bring (a ship's head) or the head of (ship) nearer the wind; to turn (the helm) so as to do this. **luffing-match,** *n.* (*Yacht-racing*) A struggle to secure the windward position. **luff-tackle,** *n.* A large tackle composed of a double and single block.

luffa [LOOFAH]. ***luffer** [LOUVER].

Luftwaffe (looft' vaf ė), *n.* The German Air Force.

lug (1) (lŭg) [cp. LOG (1)], *n.* A large marine worm, *Arenicola marina*, burrowing in the sand, used for bait. **lugworm,** *n.*

lug (2) [LUG-SAIL].

lug (3) (lŭg) [prob. from Scand. (cp. Swed. and Norw. *lugga*, to pull by the hair, *lugg*, the forelock)], *v.t.* (*past & p.p.* **lugged**) To drag, to pull, esp. roughly or with exertion; to tug, to haul; (*fig.*) to drag in, to insert unnecessarily. *v.i.* To drag; to move heavily or slowly. *n.* A drag or tug.

lug (4) (lŭg) [etym. doubtful], *n.* A projecting part; (*Mach.*) a projecting part made to hold or grip another part; the lobe of the ear; the ear; a pliable rod or twig; a measure of land, usu. about a pole or perch; unlooped handle of a pot. **lug-mark,** *n.* A mark cut in the ear of a sow, sheep, etc., for identification.

luge (loozh) [F.], *n.* A small raised toboggan used in Switzerland. *v.t.* To toboggan in one of these.

luggage (lŭg' ȧj) [LUG (3), -AGE], *n.* Anything heavy and cumbersome to be carried; the baggage of an army; a traveller's trunks, etc. **luggage-train,** *n.* A goods train.

lugger (lŭg' ėr) [prob. from LUG-SAIL], *n.* A small vessel with two or three masts, a running bowsprit, and lug-sails.

lug-sail (lŭgsl) [etym. doubtful, perh. from LUG (3)], *n.* (*Naut.*) A four-cornered sail bent to a yard lashed obliquely to the mast.

lugubrious (loo-, lū gū' bri ŭs) [L. *lūgubris*, from *lūgēre*, to mourn], *a.* Mournful, dismal, funereal. **lugubriously,** *adv.* **lugubriousness,** *n.*

lukewarm (look' wôrm) [M.E. *luke*, tepid, prob. cogn. with A.-S. *hleow*, LEE (1), WARM], *a.* Moderately warm; tepid; (*fig.*) indifferent, cool. *n.* A person who is indifferent or unenthusiastic. **lukewarmly,** *adv.* **lukewarmness,** *n.*

lull (lŭl) [imit. (cp. Swed. *lulla*, M.Dut. *lullen*, G. *lallen*, Gr. *lalein*)], *v.t.* To sooth to sleep, to calm, to quiet. *v.i.* To subside, to become quiet. *n.* A

temporary calm; an intermission or abatement.
lullaby (lŭl' ȧ bī), *n.* A refrain or song for lulling a child to sleep. *v.t.* To sing to sleep. **lullingly,** *adv.*

lum (lŭm) [Sc.], *n.* A chimney. **lum-hat,** *n.* A top-hat.

lumbago (lŭm bā' gō) [L. *lumbus*, loin], *n.* Rheumatism in the region of the loins.

lumbar, lumbal (lŭm' bȧr, -bȧl), *a.* Pertaining to the loins. *n.* A lumbar nerve, vertebra, artery, etc. **lumbar puncture,** *n.* The insertion of a needle between two lumbar vertebræ to withdraw cerebrospinal fluid. **lumbar region,** *n.* The portion of the body between the false ribs and the upper part of the haunch bone.

lumber (1) (lŭm' bėr) [etym. doubtful, perh. imit. (cp. Swed. dial. *lomra*, to roar, Icel. *hljōmr*, a sound), or freq. of LAME], *v.i.* To move heavily, cumbrously, or clumsily; to make a heavy rumbling noise. **lumbering,** *a.* **lumberingly,** *adv.* **lumbersome,** *a.*

lumber (2) (lŭm' bėr) [perh. var. of LOMBARD (1), the room where the Lombard bankers stored their unredeemed pledges, or from prec.], *n.* Discarded articles of furniture and other rubbish taking up room; useless and cumbersome things; rubbish, refuse; superfluous bulk or fat, esp. in horses. *v.t.* To fill with lumber; to encumber, to obstruct; to heap up in a disorderly way. **lumber-room,** *n.* A room for the storage of lumber, trunks, etc.

lumber (3) (lŭm' bėr), *n.* Timber sawn into marketable shape. *v.t.* To cut and prepare timber for the market. **lumber camp,** *n.* A lumberman's camp. **lumber-dealer,** *n.* A timber merchant. **lumberjack, lumberman,** *n.* One who is employed in lumbering. **lumber-jacket,** *n.* A man's loose-fitting jacket that fastens up to the neck; a woman's cardigan similarly fastened.

lumbo- [L. *lumbus*. LOIN], *comb. form.* **lumbo-abdominal** (lŭm' bō ăb dom' i nȧl) [ABDOMINAL], *a.* Pertaining to the lumbar region and the abdomen.

lumbrical (lŭm' bri kȧl) [L. *lumbrīcus*, worm, -AL], *a.* (*Zool.*) Pertaining to, or resembling, a worm; (*Anat.*) applied to certain muscles. *n.pl.* Four vermiform muscles, two of the foot and two of the hand, which help to flex the digits. **lumbriciform** (lŭm bris' i fôrm), *a.* Resembling a worm, vermiform.

lumen (loo' men) [L., light], *n.* (*Phys.*) Unit of light, being the quantity of light falling in 1 sq. ft. of the inner surface of a sphere of 1 ft. radius at the centre of which 1 international candle is placed.

luminary (loo'-, lū' mi nȧr i) [O.F. *luminarie*, med. L. *lūminārium*, L. *lūmināre*, from *lūmen -inis*, light], *n.* Any body yielding light, esp. a heavenly body; (*fig.*) one who enlightens mankind or is a brilliant exponent of a subject. **luminant,** *a.* and *n.* ***lumine,** *v.i.* To illumine. **luminescent** (-nes' ėnt), *a.* (*Phys.*) Emitting light otherwise than from the heat producing incandescence. **luminesce,** *v.i.* **luminescence,** *n.* **luminiferous** (-nif' ėr ŭs) [-FEROUS], *a.* **luminist** (loo'-, lū' mi nist), *n.* A painter who makes a special study of light-effects. **luminous** (loo'-, lū' mi nŭs), *a.* Emitting light; shining brightly, brilliant; lucid, perspicuous, shedding light (on a subject, etc.). **luminosity** (-nos' i ti), **luminousness,** *n.* **luminously,** *adv.*

lump (1) (lŭmp) [prob. from Scand. (cp. Swed. dial. and Norw. *lump*, block, stump, Dan. *lumpe*)], *n.* A small mass of matter of no definite shape; a mass, a quantity, a heap, a lot; a swelling, a protuberance; a heavy, stupid person. *v.t.* To put together in a lump, to form into a mass; hence, to take collectively, to treat as all alike; (*Turf*) to lay the whole of (a sum) on one horse, etc. *v.i.* To form or collect into lumps; to move (about) heavily or clumsily; (*Turf*) to stake heavily, to plunge. **in the lump:** The whole taken together; altogether, in gross. **lump-sugar,** *n.* Loaf sugar broken into small lumps (in *Am.* cube-sugar). **lump sum:** The whole amount, all items taken together, as opp. to instalments. **lumper,** *n.* One who lumps things together; a labourer who loads or unloads ships; (*slang*) a militiaman, a small contractor or sweater who takes work in the lump and puts it out. **lumping,** *a.* Large, heavy; big, bulky, plentiful. **lumpish,** *a.* Like a lump; gross; lazy, inert; stupid. **lumpishly,** *adv.* **lumpishness,** *n.* **lumpy,** *a.* Full of lumps; (*Naut.*) running in short waves that do not break. **lumpily,** *adv.* **lumpiness,** *n.*

lump (2) (lŭmp) [prob. imit.], *v.t.* (*slang*) To dislike, to put up with.

lump (3) (lŭmp) [cp. M.Dut. *lompe*, G. *lump*, F. *lompe*], *n.* A suctorial fish, *Cyclopterus lumpus*, of northern seas.

lunacy (loo'-, lū' nȧ si) [see LUNATIC], *n.* Unsoundness of mind, insanity, formerly supposed to be caused by the moon; gross folly, senseless conduct. **master in lunacy:** A person appointed to inspect lunatic asylums or investigate cases of alleged insanity.

lunar (loo'-, lū' nȧr) [L. *lūnārus*, from *lūna*, the moon], *a.* Of, pertaining to, caused or influenced by the moon; resembling the moon. *n.* A lunar distance or observation. **lunar caustic:** (*Chem.*) Nitrate of silver fused at a low heat. **lunar cycle** [CYCLE]. **lunar distance:** The angular distance of the moon from the sun, a planet, or a star, used at sea in finding longitude. **lunar month:** The period of a complete revolution of the moon, 29½ days, (*pop.*) 4 weeks. **lunar observation:** Observation of the moon's distance from the sun or a star to find the longitude. **lunar year:** A period of twelve lunar months. **lunarian** (-nâr' i ȧn), *n.* An inhabitant of the moon; one using the lunar method of finding longitude; a lunarist. **lunarist** (loo'-, lū' nȧr ist), *n.* An investigator of the moon; one who believes that the weather is largely affected by the moon. **lunary,** *a.* Lunar. *n.* The moonwort. **lunate, *-nated, luniform,** *a.* Crescent-shaped. **lunation** (-nā' shŭn), *n.* The period between two returns of the moon, a lunar month.

lunatic (loo'-, lū' nȧ tik) [F. *lunatique*, late L. *lūnāticus*, as prec.], *a.* Insane; (*fig.*) mad, frantic, crazy, extremely foolish. *n.* An insane person. **lunatic asylum,** *n.* A hospital for the care and treatment of lunatics.

lunation [LUNAR].

lunch (lŭnch) [prob. a var. of LUMP (1), a lump or slice, as of bread], *n.* A light repast between breakfast and dinner; a midday meal; (*Am.*) a snack. *v.i.* To take lunch. *v.t.* To provide lunch for. **luncheon** (lŭn' chŏn), *n.* Lunch (in more formal usage).

lune (1) (loon, lūn) [F., from *lūna*, moon], *n.* (*Geom.*) A figure enclosed by two intersecting arcs; anything in the shape of a half-moon; *(*pl.*) fits of lunacy, crotchets, freaks.

***lune** (2) (loon, lūn) [prob. var. of M.E. and O.F. *loigne*, med. L. *longia*, from *longus*, LONG (1)], *n.* A leash for a hawk.

lunette (loo'-, lū net') [F.], *n.* A semicircular aperture in a concave ceiling; a crescent-shaped or semicircular space or panel for a picture or decorative painting; a horseshoe lacking the branches; (*Fort.*) an advanced work of two faces and two flanks; a flattened watch-glass; a blinder for a draught horse; the hole for the neck in a guillotine.

lung (lŭng) [A.-S. *lungen* (cp. Dut. *long*, Icel. *lunga*, G. *lunge*), cogn. with LIGHT (2), *cp.* LIGHTS], *n.* One of the two organs of respiration in vertebrates, situated on each side of the chest; an analogous organ in invertebrates; (*fig.*) an open space in or near a city. **lung-fish,** *n.* A dipnoan, having lungs as well as gills. **lung-grown,** *a.* (*Path.*) Having the lungs adhering to the pleura. **lung-power,** *n.* Strength of voice. **lunged,** *a.* **lungless,** *a.*

lunge (1) (lŭnj) [earlier *allonge*, see ALLONGE], *n.* A sudden thrust with a sword, etc.; a sudden forward movement, a plunge. *v.i.* To make a lunge;

(*Boxing*) to strike out from the shoulder; to plunge or rush forward suddenly.

lunge (2) (lŭnj), **longe** (lonj) [F. *longe*, var. of *loigne*, LUNE (2)], *n.* A long rope or rein used in training horses. *v.t.* To drive a horse round in a circle at the end of a lunge.

lungi (loon′ gē) [Hind.], *n.* A long cloth used as a loincloth or sash, sometimes as a turban.

lungwort (lŭng′ wĕrt), *n.* (*Bot.*) A lichen, *Sticta pulmonacea*, growing on the trunks of trees; the genus *Pulmonaria*, of the borage family, formerly held to be good for pulmonary diseases.

luniform [LUNAR].

Lunik (loo′ nik), *n.* The first projectile to reach the moon from the earth, fired by Russians 13 Sept., 1959.

lunisolar (loo-, lū ni sō′ lȧr) [L. *lūna*, moon, *sōl*, sun], *a.* Pertaining to, or compounded of the revolutions of, the sun and the moon. **lunisolar period** or **year:** A period of 532 years found by multiplying the cycle of the sun by that of the moon.

lunkah (lŭng′ kȧ) [Hind. *lanka*, name of parts of the delta of the Godavery where the tobacco is grown], *n.* A strong variety of cheroot.

lunt (lŭnt) [Dut. *lont* (see LINSTOCK)], *n.* A match-cord for firing cannon; flame, smoke. *v.i.* To flame, to emit smoke.

lunula (loo′-, lū′ nū lȧ) [L., dim. of *lūna*, moon], *n.* (*Nat. Hist.*) A crescent-shaped mark, spot, or part. **lunular, lunulate, -nulated,** *a.* **lunule,** *n.* **lunulet,** *n.* (*Ent.*) A small semicircular spot, of different colour from the other parts, on some insects.

Lupercal (lū′ pėr kăl) [L., pertaining to *Lupercus*, a deity identified with Pan], *n.* (*pl.* **-*calia***, -kā′ li ȧ) A Roman festival in honour of Lupercus. ***Lupercal, Lupercalian** (-kā′ li ȧn), *a.*

lupine (1) (loo′-, lū′ pin) [L. *lupīnus*], *n.* A leguminous plant of the genus *Lupinus*, with spikes of white or coloured flowers, grown in flower-gardens and for fodder. **lupinin,** *n.* (*Chem.*) A bitter glucoside obtained from *L. albus* and *L. luteus*.

lupine (2) (loo′-, lū pīn) [L. *lupīnus*, from *lupus*, wolf], *a.* Pertaining to wolves; like a wolf.

lupoid, lupous [LUPUS].

lupulin (lū′ pū lin) [mod. L. *lupulus*, hop, -IN], *n.* (*Chem.*) The bitter principle of hops; a yellow granular aromatic powder containing that principle. **lupulite,** *n.* Lupulin.

lupus (loo′-, lū′ pŭs) [L., wolf], *n.* (*Path.*) A spreading tuberculous or ulcerous inflammation of the skin, usually of the face. **lupoid, lupous,** *a.*

lurch (1) (lĕrch) [F. *lourche*, a 16th-century game like backgammon, etym. doubtful], *n.* A losing position in the game of cribbage and some other games; *a swindle. **to leave in the lurch:** To leave in difficulties.

lurch (2) (lĕrch) [etym. doubtful], *v.i.* To roll suddenly to one side (of a ship); to stagger. *n.* A sudden roll sideways, as of a ship; a stagger.

lurch (3) (lĕrch) [var. of LURK], *v.i.* To lie in wait; to steal, to rob; to play tricks. *v.t.* To overreach, to cheat, to rob; to take or gain privily; to filch, to steal. **lurcher,** *n.* One who lurks about to steal or entrap; a dog supposed to be a cross between a collie and a greyhound; *a glutton.

lurdan (lĕr′ dȧn) [O.F. *lourdin*, from *lourd*, heavy], *a.* Stupid, lazy, useless. *n.* A blockhead.

lure (1) (lūr) [O.F. *leurre*, prob. from Teut. (cp. G. *luder*, bait)], *n.* (*Falconry*) An object resembling a fowl, used to recall a hawk; hence, an enticement, an allurement. *v.t.* To attract or bring back by a lure; (*fig.*) to entice. *v.i.* To call or tempt an animal, esp. a hawk.

lure (2) (lūr) [Icel. *lūthr*], *n.* A trumpet with long, curved tube, used in Scandinavia for calling cattle home.

lurid (lū′-, loo′ rid) [L. *lūridus*, perh. cogn. with Gr. *chlōros*, green], *a.* Of a pale yellow colour, wan, gloomy; ghastly, unearthly; (*fig.*) sensational (of a story, etc.); (*Bot.*) of a dirty brown colour. **luridly,** *adv.* **luridness,** *n.*

lurk (lĕrk) [perh. cogn. with LOUR (cp. Norw. and Swed. dial. *lurka*, G. *lauern*)], *v.i.* To lie hid; to lie in wait; to be latent, to exist unperceived; *to move about furtively. **lurker,** *n.* **lurking-hole, -place,** *n.*

lurry [LORRY]. **lury** [LORY].

luscious (lŭsh′ ŭs) [etym. doubtful], *a.* Very sweet, delicious; sweet to excess; (*fig.*) cloying, fulsome, over-rich in imagery, sensuousness, etc. (of music, poetry, etc.); *lascivious, voluptuous. **lusciously,** *adv.* **lusciousness,** *n.*

lush (1) (lŭsh) [var. of obs. *lash*, O.F. *lasche* (F. *lâche*), L. *laxus*, LAX], *a.* Luxuriant in growth; succulent, juicy. **lushness,** *n.*

lush (2) (lŭsh) [Slang, etym. doubtful], *n.* Drink, liquor. *v.i.* To drink. *v.t.* To ply with liquor. **lushy,** *a.* Drunk.

lusk, luskish (lŭsk, lŭsk′ ish) [etym. doubtful], *a.* Sluggish, indolent. **luskishness,** *n.*

lust (lŭst) [A.-S. (cp. Dut., Swed., and G. *lust*), cogn. with LIST (2)], *n.* Animal desire of sexual pleasure, concupiscence, lasciviousness; sensual appetite; (*fig.*) passionate desire for; *vigour. *v.i.* To have powerful or inordinate desire (for or after). ***luster,** *n.* **lustful,** *a.* **lustfully,** *adv.* **lustfulness,** *n.* ***lustick,** *a.* **lustless,** *a.* Listless; joyless; free from lust.

lustral (lŭs′ trȧl) [L. *lustrālis*, from LUSTRUM], *a.* Pertaining to or used in purification; pertaining to a lustrum. **lustrate,** *v.t.* To purify. **v.i.* To go about inspecting for cleansing purposes. **lustration** (-trā′ shŭn), *n.* Cleansing, esp. ceremonial cleansing.

lustre (1) (lŭs′ tėr) [F., from L. *lūstrāre*, to lighten, illumine (cogn. with *lux lūcis*, light)], *n.* Brightness, splendour, luminousness, gloss, sheen, bright light; the reflection of a light; a chandelier ornamented with pendants of cut glass; a cotton, woollen, or other fabric with a glossy surface; a glossy enamel on pottery, etc.; (*fig.*) illustriousness, radiant beauty. **lustreless,** *a.* **lustrous,** *a.* **lustrously,** *adv.*

lustre (2) [LUSTRUM].

lustrine, lustring (lŭs′ trin, -tring) [F. *lustrine*, from LUSTRE (1)], *n.* A glossy silk fabric.

lustrous [LUSTRE (1)].

lustrum (lŭs′ trŭm) [L., a purification; an expiatory offering made by the Roman censors every five years, prob. from *luere*, to wash (cogn. with *lavāre*, to wash, see LAVE (1))], *n.* A period of five years.

lustwort (lŭst′ wĕrt) [LUST, WORT], *n.* The *Drosera* or sundew.

lusty (lŭs′ ti), *a.* Full of health and vigour. ***lustihead, *-hood, -ness,** *n.* **lustily,** *adv.*

***lutanist** [LUTE (1)]. ***lutation** [LUTE (2)].

lute (1) (loot, lūt) [F. *lut* (now *luth*), Prov. *laut*, Sp. *laud*, Arab. *al-‘ūd*, the lute, orig. wood], *n.* A stringed instrument somewhat resembling the guitar. *v.t.* To play on or as on the lute. *v.i.* To sound sweetly, like a lute. **lute-string,** *n.* A string of a lute; a noctuid moth with string-like markings on its wings. ***lutanist, *luter, lutist,** *n.* A lute-player.

lute (2) (loot, lūt) [O.F. *lut*, from L. *lutum*, mud], *n.* A composition of clay or cement used to secure the joints of vessels and tubes, or as a covering to protect retorts, etc., from fire; an india-rubber washer. *v.t.* To seal up or coat with lute. ***lutation** (-tā′ shŭn), *n.* The act or process of luting. ***lutose,** *a.* Muddy, covered with clay or mud; (*Ent.*) covered with a powder resembling this.

lutecium (loo tē′ si ŭm) [L. *Lutetia*, Paris], *n.* An extremely rare metallic element, grey in colour, discovered in 1907.

luteo- [L. *luteus*, LUTEOUS], *comb. form.* Yellow, orange-colour. **luteo-fulvous** (loo-, lū tė ȯ fŭl′ vŭs) [FULVOUS], *a.* (*Bot.*) Tawny.

luteolin (lū′-, loo′ tė ȯ lin) [F. *lutéolin*, L. *luteolus*], *n.* (*Chem.*) A crystalline body obtained by boiling weld.

luteous (lū′-, loo′ tė ŭs) [L. *luteus*, from *lutum*, mud], *a.* Of a brownish-yellow colour. **luteolus,** *a.* Yellowish.

lute-string [LUTE (1)].

lutestring [corr. of LUSTRING].

Lutetian (loo-, lū tē′ shi ȧn) [L. *Lutetia Parisiorum* Paris], *a.* Parisian.

Lutheran (loo′-, lū′ thėr ȧn) [Martin *Luther* (1483–1546), German Protestant reformer], *a.* Of or belonging to Luther or his followers. *n.* A follower of Luther; a member of the Church based on the principles of the Augsburg confession. **Lutheranism, -therism,** *n.* **Lutheranize,** *v.t.* and *i.*

lutist [LUTE (1)]. **lutose** [LUTE (2)].

luxate (lŭk′ sāt) [L. *luxātus*, p.p. of *luxāre*, to put out of joint, from *luxus*, Gr. *loxos*, oblique], *v.t.* To put out of joint, to dislocate. **a.* Out of joint. **luxation** (-sā′ shŭn), *n.*

luxe (luks) [F., from L. *luxus*], *n.* Luxury, sumptuousness, superfine elegance. **edition de luxe** (ā dis i *on* dė luks): A limited large-paper edition of a book sumptuously produced. **train de luxe:** A railway train furnished with special comforts, etc.

luxuriant (lŭk sūr′-, lŭg zūr′ i ȧnt) [L. *luxurians -ntem*, pres.p. of *luxuriāre*, from *luxuria*, *luxus*, extravagance, sumptuousness], *a.* Abundant in growth; plentiful, copious, profuse, exuberant; fertile, prolific, rank; (*fig.*) ornate, florid, extravagant, sumptuous. **luxuriance, -iancy,** *n.* **luxuriantly,** *adv.* **luxuriate,** *v.i.* To feed or live luxuriously; to revel, to indulge oneself to excess. ***luxuriation** (-ā′ shŭn), *n.* **luxurious,** *a.* **luxuriously,** *adv.* **luxuriousness,** *n.* ***luxurist** (lŭk′ sŭ rist), *n.*

luxury (lŭk′ sŭ ri, lŭk′ shė ri), *n.* Habitual indulgence in dainty and expensive pleasures; luxurious living; that which is delightful, esp. to the appetite; luxuriousness; *luxuriance, exuberance.

luzerne [LUCERNE].

-ly [A.-S. *-*līc*, a., LIKE (1); *līce*, adv.], *suf.* Forming adjectives, as *ghastly*, *godly*, *manly*, or adverbs, as *badly*, *heavily*, *mightily*.

lyam (lī′ ȧm) [O.F. *liem* (F. *lien*), see LIEN (1)], *n.* A leash for holding hounds. **lyam-hound,** *n.* A blood-hound.

***lyard, *lyart** (lī′ ȧrd, -ȧrt) [O.F. *liart*, etym. doubtful], *a.* Roan, dappled; grey; grey-headed. *n.* A dapple-grey horse.

lycanthrope (lī′ kȧn thrōp) [Gr. *lukanthrōpos* (*lukos*, wolf, *anthrōpos*, man)], *n.* A werwolf, one suffering from lycanthropy. **lycanthropic** (-throp′ ik), *a.* **lycanthropist** (lī kăn′ thrȯ pist), *n.* **lycanthropy,** *n.* Insanity in which the patient believes himself a wolf or some other animal, whose instincts and habits he assumes; belief in a form of witchcraft by which men or women transform themselves into wolves.

lycée (lē′ sā) [F.], *n.* A French State secondary school.

lyceum (lī sē′ ŭm) [L. *lycēum*, Gr. *Lukeion*, nom. *-os*, pertaining to Apollo, whose temple was adjoining], *n.* The garden at Athens in which Aristotle taught; hence, the Aristotelean philosophy or philosophic school; a place devoted to instruction; an institution for literary instruction or mutual improvement by means of lectures, libraries, etc.; a lycée.

***lych, lych-gate,** etc. [LICH].

lychnis (lik′ nis) [L., from Gr. *luchnis*, from *luchnos*, lamp], *n.* A genus of plants belonging to the *Silenaceæ*, comprising the campions.

lychnoscope (lik′ nȯ skōp) [Gr. *luchnos*, lamp, -SCOPE], *n.* (*Arch.*) A low side window in a church, thus called on the now-obsolete theory that it was used by lepers to see the altar lights. **lychnoscopic** (-skop′ ik), *a.*

lycopod (lī′ kȯ pod) [mod. L. *lycopodium* (Gr. *lukos*, wolf, *pous podos*, foot, from the claw-like shape of root)], *n.* A club-moss, a member of the genus *Lycopodium*, or the order *Lycopodiaceæ*. **lycopodiaceous** (-ā′ shŭs), *a.* **lycopodium** (lī kȯ pō′ di ŭm), *n.* (*Bot.*) A genus of perennial plants comprising the club-mosses; an inflammable yellow powder in the spore-cases of some species, used for stage-lighting and as an absorbent in surgery.

lyddite (lid′ īt) [*Lydd*, in Kent], *n.* A powerful explosive composed mainly of picric acid, used in shells.

Lydian (lid′ i ȧn), *a.* Pertaining to Lydia, in Asia Minor, whose inhabitants were noted for effeminacy and voluptuousness; hence, effeminate, soft, voluptuous; (*Mus.*) applied to one of the modes in Greek music, and the third ecclesiastical mode. *n.* An inhabitant or the language of Lydia. **Lydian-stone,** *n.* (*Min.*) Basanite.

lye (lī) [A.-S. *lēag* (cp. Dut. *loog*, G. *lauge*), prob. cogn. with LAVE (1) and LATHER], *n.* An alkaline solution leached from vegetable ashes or other alkaline substance; a lixivium, a detergent.

lyencephalous (lī ėn sef′ ȧ lŭs) [Gr. *lu-ein*, to loose, ENCEPHALOUS], *a.* (*Zool.*) Of or characteristic of the *Lyencephala*, a division of mammals in Owen's classification comprising the monotremes and the marsupials.

lying (1) (lī′ ing), *n.* The act or habit of telling lies; a lie. *a.* Telling lies; false, deceitful. **lyingly,** *adv.*

lying (2) (lī′ ing), *n.* The act or state of being recumbent; a place to lie in. **low-lying,** *a.* Situated at a low level. **lying-in,** *n.* Child-bed; lying in child-birth; hence **lying-in hospital.**

***lyke** [LICH].

lyke-wake (lik′ wāk) [LICH, WAKE (2)], *n.* A night watch over a dead body.

lyme-grass (līm′ gras) [perh. from LIME (1)], *n.* A coarse grass of the genus *Elymus*, planted in sand in order to bind it.

lymph (limf) [L. *lympha*, prob. cogn. with *limpidus*, LIMPID], *n.* (*poet.*) Water or any clear transparent fluid; (*Physiol.*) the comparatively transparent, colourless, alkaline fluid in the tissues and organs of the body, bearing a strong resemblance to blood without the red corpuscles; (*Path.*) the morbid exudation from the blood-vessels in inflammation; matter containing the virus of a disease, obtained from a diseased body or by culture, and used in vaccination. **lymphæ-duct** (lim′ fi dŭkt), *n.* A vessel conveying lymph. **lymphatic** (lim făt′ ik), *a.* Pertaining to, containing, secreting, or conveying lymph; phlegmatic, sluggish, flabby-tissued (of temperament, etc., formerly supposed to be so affected by excess of lymph). *n.* *A madman, an enthusiast; (*Physiol.*, *pl.*) vessels conveying lymph. **lymphoid, lymphous, *lymphy,** *a.* Containing or resembling lymph.

***lymphad** (lim′ făd) [Sc., corr. of Gael. *longfhada*], *n.* A one-masted galley; (*Her.*) this as a charge.

lyncean (lin sē′ ȧn) [L. *lyncēus*, Gr. *lunkeios*, from *lunx*, LYNX], *a.* Pertaining to the lynx; lynx-eyed, sharp-sighted.

lynch (linch) [Charles *Lynch* (1736–96) a Virginian farmer who inflicted summary punishment on lawless persons during the Revolutionary War], *v.t.* To judge and punish, esp. to execute, by lynch law. **Judge Lynch:** Lynch law personified. **lynch law:** Summary punishment without trial or upon trial by a self-appointed court.

lynx (lingks) [L., from Gr. *lunx*, rel. to *lussein*, to see (cp. with G. *luchs*, A.-S. *lox*)], *n.* One of several species of animals of the cat tribe, characterized by tufted ear-tips, short tail, and extremely sharp sight. **lynx-eyed,** *n.* Having sharp sight.

Lyon (lī' ŏn) [LION], *n.* The chief of the Scottish heralds, also called **Lyon King of Arms.**

Lyra (līr' ȧ) [L.], *n.* A northern constellation. **Lyraid** (-ȧ id), **Lyrid,** *n.* One of the meteors radiating from Lyra about 20 April.

lyre (lī' ėr) [F., from L. *lyra*, Gr. *lura*], *n.* A stringed musical instrument of the harp kind, anciently used as an accompaniment to the voice; the constellation Lyra. **lyre-bird,** *n.* An insectivorous Australian bird, *Menura superba*, having the 16 tail-feathers of the male disposed in the form of a lyre. **lyrate, -rated,** *a.* Shaped like a lyre.

lyric (lir' ik) [L. *lyricus*, Gr. *lurikos*, as prec.], *a.* Relating to or suited for the lyre; intended to be sung or fitted for expression in song; (of a poem) expressing the individual emotions of the poet; writing poetry of this kind. *n.* A lyric poem; the words of a song; (*pl.*) verses used in lyric poetry. **lyrical,** *a.* **lyrically,** *adv.* **lyricism,** *n.* **lyrico-,** *comb. form.* **lyrist,** *n.*

lysimeter (lī sim' ė tėr) [Gr. *lusis*, as foll., -METER], *n.* An instrument for measuring the rate of percolation of rain through soil.

lysis (lī' sis) [L., from Gr. *lusis*, a loosening, from *luein*, to loose], *n.* (*Anc. Arch.*) A plinth above the cornice of the podium surrounding a stylobate; (*Path.*) a gradual cooling down in fever, etc., opp. to crisis.

lythe (līth) [Sc.], *n.* (*Sc. and Ir.*) The pollack.

M

M, m, the thirteenth letter and tenth consonant (*pl.* **Ems, M's, Ms),** has but one sound, that of a labial nasal, as in *man*, *time*; (*Print.*) an em; (*Roman numeral*) 1000. **M roof:** A roof formed by the junction of two parallel ridges with a cross section like a broad M. **M & B 693** [initials of makers May & Baker], (*Med.*) A proprietary drug of the sulphanilamide group termed 2-sulphanilyl aminopyridine, used in the treatment of lobar pneumonia, etc.

ma (ma) [childish shortening of MAMMA (1)].

ma'am (măm, mam, m'm) [MADAM], *n.* (*colloq.*) Madam (used by servants, etc., and at Courts in addressing the queen or a royal princess).

macabre (mȧ ka' br') [F., etym. doubtful], *a.* Gruesome. ***dance macabre*:** Dance of death. ***macaberesque*** (mȧ ka bėr esk'), *a.*

macaco (1) (mȧ kā' kō) [Port., monkey], *n.* Orig. a S. African monkey, now any monkey of the genus *Macacus.*

macaco (2) (mȧ kā' kō) [F., etym. doubtful], *n.* Applied to various kinds of lemur.

macadam (mȧ kăd' ȧm). [J. L. *McAdam* (1756–1836), road-engineer], *n.* Broken stone for macadamizing; a road made by macadamizing. *v.t.* To macadamize. **macadamize,** *v.t.* To make, cover, or pave (a road) with layers of broken stone so as to form a smooth hard surface. **macadamizer,** *n.* **macadamization** (-zā' shŭn), *n.* **tar macadam** [TAR].

macarize (măk' ȧ rīz) [Gr. *makarizein*, from *makar*, blessed], *v.t.* To bless, to make or to pronounce happy. **macarism,** *n.*

macaroni (măk ȧ rō' ni) [It. *maccaroni* (now *maccheroni*, pl., see foll.) perh. from earlier *maccare*, L. *mācerāre*, to MACERATE], *n.* An Italian paste made of fine wheaten flour formed into long slender tubes; (*pl.* **-nies**) a medley; a crested variety of penguin; *an exquisite, a fop, a dandy. **a.* Foppish, fashionable, affected. **macaronic** (-ron' ik), *a.* *Of, pertaining to, or like macaroni; *of, pertaining to, or like a macaroni or exquisite; consisting of a jumble of incongruous words, as of different languages, or of modern words Latinized or Latin words modernized, in burlesque poetry. *n.* A confused medley or jumble; (*pl.*) macaronic verse.

macaroon (măk ȧ roon') [F. *macaron*, It. *maccarone*, sing. of *maccaroni*, as prec.], *n.* A small sweet cake or biscuit made of flour, almonds, sugar, etc.

macartney (mȧ kart' ni) [George, 1st Earl *Macartney* (1737–1806), introducer], *n.* The fireback pheasant, *Euplocamus ignitus.*

macassar (mȧ kăs' ȧr) [name of district], *n.* An oil for the hair, orig. brought from Macassar, in the island of Celebes, also called **macassar oil.**

macaw (mȧ kaw') [Port. *macao*, prob. from Tupi-Guarani], *n.* A S. American parrot, of various species distinguished by their large size and beautiful plumage.

macaw-tree (mȧ kaw' trē) [prob. Carib., TREE], *n.* A palm of the genus *Acrocomia*, esp. *A. fusiformis* or *A. lasiospatha.*

Maccabean (măk ȧ bē' ȧn), *a.* Pertaining to the Maccabees, a patriotic Jewish family who successfully resisted the attempts of Antiochus Epiphanes (175–164 B.C.) to substitute Hellenism for Judaism in Judæa.

maccoboy (măk' ō boi), *n.* A rose-scented snuff, orig. grown at Macouba, in Martinique.

mace (1) (mās) [O.F. (F. *masse*), from a L. *matea*, known from its dim. *mateola*, a mallet], *n.* A mediæval weapon shaped like a club with a heavy metal head, usu. spiked; an ornamented staff of office of analogous shape; a mace-bearer; a flat-headed stick formerly used in billiards; a similar stick used in bagatelle. **mace-bearer,** *n.* A person who carries the mace before a judge, etc. ***mace-proof,** *a.* Secure against arrest. **macer,** *n.* A mace-bearer; (*Sc.*) an officer who keeps order in courts of law.

mace (2) (mās) [F. *macis*, etym. doubtful], *n.* A spice made from the dried covering of the nutmeg. ***mace-ale,** *n.* Ale spiced with mace.

macedoine (ma sā dwan) [F., etym. unknown], *n.* A dish of mixed vegetables; (*fig.*) a medley.

macerate (măs' ė rāt) [L. *mācerātus*, p.p. of *mācerāre*, perh. cogn. with Gr. *massein*, to knead], *v.t.* To soften by steeping; to separate the parts of by a digestive process; to make lean, to cause to waste away; *to harass. *v.i.* To undergo maceration. **maceration** (-ā' shŭn), *n.*

machairodus (mȧ kīr' ō dŭs) [Gr. *machaira*, sabre, *odous*, tooth], *n.* (*Palæont.*) The sabre-toothed lion or tiger, an extinct genus.

machan (mȧ chan') [Hind.], *n.* An elevated platform for tiger-shooting.

machete [MATCHET].

Machiavel (măk i ȧ vel) [Niccolo *Machiavelli* (1469–1527), Florentine statesman and author of *Il Principe*, an exposition of unscrupulous statecraft], *n.* An unscrupulous intriguer; an intriguing and unscrupulous statesman or politician. **Machiavellian,** *a.* and *n.* **Machiavellianism** (-vel' i ȧ nizm), **Machiavellism** (măk' i ȧ vel izm), *n.*

machicolate (mȧ chik' ō lāt) [low L. *machicolātus*, p.p. of *machicolāre*, perh. from O.F. *machecoller*, cogn. with *mâchicoulis*, see foll.], *v.t.* To furnish with machicolations. **machicolation** (-lā' shŭn), *n.* An aperture between the corbels supporting a projecting parapet, through which missiles were hurled upon assailants; a parapet or gallery with a series of such apertures. **machicoulis** (ma shi koo' li), *n.* A machicolation.

machinate (măk' i nāt) [L. *māchinātus*, p.p. of *māchinārī*, to contrive, see foll.], *v.i.* To contrive, to plot, to intrigue. **machination** (-nā' shŭn), *n.* **machinator** (măk' i nā tŏr), *n.*

machine (mȧ shēn') [F., from L. *māchina*, Gr. *mēchanē*, from *mēchos*, means, contrivance, cogn. with MAY (1)], *n.* A mechanical apparatus by which motive power is applied; (*Mech.*) any mechanism, simple (as a lever or tool) or compound, for applying or directing force; (*fig.*) a person who acts mechanically and without intelligence; any organization of a complex character designed to apply power of any kind; a bicycle or tricycle; (*Sc.*) a light vehicle; (*Gr. Ant.*) a theatrical contrivance for effecting change of scenery or introducing a supernatural being; hence, supernatural agency in a poem etc. *v.t.* To effect by means of machinery; to print by machinery; to sew with a sewing-machine. *v.i.* To be employed in or upon machinery. **machine-gun,** *n.* A light piece of ordnance loaded and fired automatically. **machine head,** *n.* (*Mus.*) A simple worm and tooth-wheel mechanism fitted to the head of a bass viol or other instrument for stretching the strings to the required pitch. **machine-made,** *a.* Made by machinery, opp. to hand-made. **machine-ruler,** *n.* A machine for ruling paper. **machine-shop,** *n.* A large workshop where machines are made or repaired. **machine-tool,** *n.* A machine for doing work with a tool, such as a chisel, plane, drill, etc. **machine-work,** *n.*

machinery (mȧ shēn′ ė ri), *n.* (*collect.*) Machines; the parts or mechanism of a machine; mechanical combination; (*fig.*) any combination to keep anything in action or to effect a purpose; the means and combinations, esp. supernatural, employed to develop a plot in a poem, etc.

machinist (mȧ shēn′ ist), *n.* One who constructs machines; one versed in the principles of machinery; one who works or tends a machine, esp. a sewing-machine. **machinize,** v.t. To convert to machinery.

macintosh, mackintosh (măk′ in tosh) [Charles *Mackintosh* (1766–1843), inventor], *n.* A waterproof material made of rubber and cloth; a coat or cloak made of this, a raincoat.

mack, mac (*Abbr.*) [MACKINTOSH], *n.*

mackerel (măk′ ėr ėl) [O.F. *makerel* (F. *maquereou*), etym. unknown], *n.* A well-known sea-fish, *Scomber scomber*, moving in shoals in the N. Atlantic and coming inshore in summer to spawn, valuable as a food-fish. **mackerel-breeze, -gale,** *n.* A strong fresh breeze good for mackerel-fishing. **mackerel-shark,** *n.* The porbeagle. **mackerel-sky,** *n.* A sky with small roundish masses of cirro-cumulus, frequent in summer.

mackinaw (măk′ in aw) [Michilli-mackinac, isl. in Lake Michigan where they were first distributed to Indians], *n.* (*Am.*) A heavy woollen blanket.

mackle (măk′ ėl) [MACULE], *n.* (*Print.*) A blurred impression, causing printed matter to appear double. *v.t.* To spot, stain, blur.

macle (măk′ ėl) [F., from MACULA], *n.* (*Cryst.*) A twin crystal; (*Her.*) a mascle. **macled,** *a.* (*Cryst.*) Hemitropic; (*Her.*) mascled.

macrame (mȧ kra′ mā) [Turk. *maqrama*], *n.* A fringe or trimming of knotted thread or cord; knotted work.

macro- [Gr. *makros*, long], *comb. form.* Great, large (as opp. to small).

macrobiote (măk rō bī′ ōt), *n.* One who lives long.

macrocephalic (măk rō se făl′ ik), *a.* Large-headed, macrocephalous. **macrocephalism,** *n.* **macrocephalous,** *a.*

macrocosm (măk′ rō kozm), *n.* The great world, the universe, opp. to microcosm; the great whole of any body, etc., esp. as imagined on a small scale by a part. **macrocosmic,** *a.*

macrocrystalline (măk rō kris′ tȧ līn), *a.* Having crystals visible to the naked eye.

macrocyte (măk′ rō sīt), *n.* A large, red blood-corpuscle.

macrodactylic, macrodactylous (măk rō dăk til′ ik, -ůs). *a.* Having long fingers or toes.

macrodiagonal (măk rō dī ăg′ ȯ nȧl), *n.* The longer diagonal of a rhombic prism.

macrometer (mȧ krom′ e tėr), *n.* An instrument with two telescopes used by surveyors for measuring distant objects.

macron (măk′ ròn) [Gr. neut. adj. of *makros*, see prec.], *n.* A short horizontal line (ē) put over a vowel to show that it is pronounced with a long sound.

macropod (măk′ rȯ pod) [MACRO-, Gr. *pous podos*, foot]. *a.* Long-footed. *n.* A long-footed animal, esp. a spider-crab. **macropodal, -dous** (-krop′ ȯ dȧl, -důs), *a.* (*Bot.*) Large-footed, as an embryo with the radicle large relatively to the cotyledon, or a leaf with a long foot-stalk.

macropterous (mȧ krop′ tėr ůs) [Gr. *pteron*, a wing], *a.* Long-winged.

macroscopic (măk rō skop′ ik), *a.* Visible with the naked eye, opp. to microscopic. **macroscopical,** *a.* **macroscopically,** *adv.*

macrospore (măk′ rō spôr), *n.* (*Bot.*) A relatively large spore, as in the club-mosses, etc.; (*Zool.*) one of the spore-like parts resulting from the division of a monad.

macrosporange, macrosporangium (măk rō spȯ rănj′, -i um) *n.* (*Bot.*) A sporangium or capsule containing macrospores.

macrurus (mȧ kroor′ ůs) [MACRO-, Gr. *oura*, tail], *a.* Long-tailed; (*Zool.*) of or belonging to the *Macrura*, a division of decapod crustaceans comprising the lobsters and shrimps.

macula (măk′ ū lȧ) [L.], *n.* (*pl.* **-læ**) A spot, as on the skin, the surface of the sun, etc. **macular,** *a.* **maculate** (măk′ ū lāt), *v.t.* To spot, to stain. *a.* (-lȧt) Spotted, stained, impure. **maculation** (lā′ shůn), *n.* **macule,** *n.* A spot, a stain; a mackle.

mad (măd) [A.-S. *gemǣdd*, *gemæded*, p.p. of *gemædan* (cp. Icel. *meiddr*, O.H.G. *gameit*, cogn. with L. *mūtāre*, to change)], *a.* (*comp.* **madder** (1), *superl.* **maddest**) Disordered in mind, lunatic, insane, crazy; furious, frantic, wildly excited; rabid (of animals); extravagant, infatuated, inflamed, wild, frolicsome; exceedingly foolish, very unwise; (*colloq.*) enraged, annoyed, vexed. *v.i.* To be or go mad; to act madly. *v.t.* To make mad. **like mad:** (*colloq.*) Violently, wildly, excitedly. **mad-brain, madbrained,** *a.* Hot-headed, eccentric. **madcap,** *a.* Mad, eccentric. *n.* A person of wild and eccentric habits. **mad-doctor,** *n.* (*colloq.*) A doctor attending lunatics. **mad-headed,** *a.* **mad-house,** *n.* A lunatic-asylum. ***madly,** *adv.* **mad-man, -woman,** *n.* **madness,** *n.* **madden,** *v.t.* and *i.* **maddeningly,** *adv.* ***madding,** *a.* Furious, raging, acting madly.

madam (măd′ ȧm) [O.F. *ma dame*, my lady (see DAME)], *n.* A polite title, usu. given to married or elderly ladies; the formal opening of a letter to a lady; (*colloq.*) a brothel keeper.

Madame (mȧ dam′, măd′ ȧm) [F., as prec.], *n.* The French title for married ladies and mode of address to a lady; *the title of a French princess, esp. the eldest daughter of the king or the dauphin.

madarosis (măd ȧ rō′ sis) [Gr. (*madaros*, bald, -OSIS)], *n.* (*Path.*) Loss of the hair, esp. of the eyebrows.

madder (1) [MAD].

madder (2) (măd′ ėr) [A.-S. *mædere* (cp. Icel *mathra*, Swed. *madra*)], *n.* A shrubby climbing-plant of the genus *Rubia*, esp. *R. tinctoria*, the root of which is used in dyeing; the dye obtained thence. **madder-bleach** (măd′ ėr blēch), *n.* A style of bleaching cotton. **madder-print,** *n.* Cloth or cotton treated by madder-printing.

made (mād) [p.p. of MAKE (2)], *a.* **made dish:** A dish made up of various ingredients. **made ground** or **earth:** Ground that has been formed artificially. **made up:** Artificial (of complexion, etc.); invented, coined (as a story). **made to measure:** Clothes, footwear, etc., made according to the customer's measurements (*Am.* custom made).

Madeira (mȧ dēr′ ȧ) [Port., wood, timber (the island being well wooded), L. *matēria*, MATTER], *n.* A white wine made in Madeira. **madeira cake:** A light, spongy cake without fruit.

Mademoiselle (măd ė mô zel′) [F. (*ma*, MY, *demoiselle*, see DAMSEL) (cp. MADAME)], *n.* (*pl.* **mesdemoiselles,** mā-) A title given to an unmarried Frenchwoman.

madge (măj) [fam. form of *Margaret*], *n.* The barn-owl; the magpie.

madhouse [MAD].

madia (mā′ di ȧ) [Chilian *madi*], *n.* A plant, *Madia sativa*, allied to the sunflowers, cultivated for the oil it yields.

***madid** (măd′ id) [L. *madidus*, from *madēre*, to be wet], *a.* Wet, moist.

madman [MAD].

Madonna (mȧ don′ ȧ) [It. (*ma*, *mia*, MY, *donna*, L. *domina*, lady)], *n.* The Virgin Mary; a picture or statue of the Virgin Mary. **Madonna lily:** The white lily, *Lilium candidum*.

Madras (mȧ dras′) [city in India], *n.* A large bright-coloured handkerchief worn on the head by West Indian Negroes, formerly exported from Madras.

madrepore (măd′ rė pôr) [F. *madrépore*, It. *madrepora* (*madre*, matter, *poro*, L. *porus*, PORE (1), or late L. *pōrus*, Gr. *pōros*, calcareous stone)], *n.* A perforated coral or the animal producing such. **madreporic** (-por′ ik), **madreporiform** (-pôr′ i fôrm), *a.* **madreporid** (-pôr′ id), *a.* and *n.* **madreporigenous** (ij′ ė nŭs), *a.* **madreporite,** *n.* A fossil madrepore; a calcareous rock of columnar structure; (*Zool.*) the madreporic tubercle in echinoderms.

madrigal (măd′ ri gȧl) [It. *madrigale*, perh. from *mandria*, herd, flock, fold, L. and Gr. *mandra*, fold, etc.], *n.* A short amorous poem; an unaccompanied vocal composition in five or six parts; loosely, a part-song, a glee.

madroño (ma drō′ nyō) [Sp.], *n.* A large evergreen tree, *Arbutus Menziesii*, of N. California, with hard wood, and berries eaten by the Indians.

madwort (măd′ wĕrt) [MAD, WORT, perh. translating Gr. *alusson* (A-, priv., *lussa*, rabies)], *n.* Alyssum; also the catchweed, *Asperugo procumbens*.

Mæcenas (mē sē′ nȧs) [a Roman knight (*c.* 37–8 B.C.), patron of Horace and Virgil], *n.* A munificent patron of literature or art.

maelstrom (māl′ strom) [Dut. (now *maalstroom* (*malen*, to grind, to whirl, *stroom*, stream))], *n.* A dangerous whirlpool off the coast of Norway; (*fig.*) a turmoil, an overwhelming situation.

mænad (mē′ năd) [L. *Mænas -adis*, Gr. *Mainas -ados*, from *mainesthai*, to rave], *n.* (*pl.* **-nads**) A woman who took part in the orgies of Bacchus, a bacchante; (*fig.*) a frenzied woman.

maestoso (ma es tō′ zō) [It., MAJESTIC], *adv.* (*Mus.*) With dignity, grandeur, and strength.

maestro (ma es′ trō) [It.], *n.* (*pl.* ***-tri***, -trē) A master in any art, esp. in music; a great composer or conductor.

mae west (mā west), *n.* (*Aviat.*) An airman's life-jacket (from name of actress).

maffick (măf′ ik) [from *Mafeking*, in S. Africa, besieged by the Boers and relieved 16 May 1900, which event was celebrated with wild rejoicings], *v.i.* (*colloq.*) To celebrate an event uproariously. **mafficker,** *n.* **mafficking,** *n.*

maffled (măf′ ėld) [p.p. of obs. *maffle*, to stammer (cp. Dut. *maffelen*)], *a.* Confused, muddled. **maffling,** *n.* A simpleton.

Mafia (ma fē′ ȧ) [Sicilian], *n.* Active hostility to the law and its agents, widespread especially among the population of Sicily, where it frequently leads to violent crimes; the persons implicated in this.

mag (1) (măg) [Slang, etym. doubtful], *n.* A half-penny. **magflying,** *n.* Pitch-and-toss.

mag (2) (măg) [short for *Margaret*], *n.* The magpie; (*Shooting*) a magpie; the long-tailed titmouse; *a chatterbox. *v.i.* To chatter.

magazine (măg ȧ zēn′) [F. *magasin*, It. *magazzino*, Arab. *makhāzin*, pl. of *makhzan*, storehouse, from *khazn*, a laying up], *n.* A place for storage, a depot, a warehouse; a building or apartment for military stores, esp. ammunition; a storeroom for explosives, etc., aboard ship; the chamber holding cartridges in a magazine-gun; (*Phot.*) a light-tight receptacle or enclosure for holding exposed or unexposed films or plates; a periodical publication containing miscellaneous articles by different writers. **magazine-gun,** *n.* A rifle or other gun fed with cartridges from a magazine.

magdalen (măg′ dȧ lėn) [Mary *Magdalene*, or of *Magdala* (Luke viii. 2), identified with the woman mentioned in Luke vii. 37–50], *n.* A reformed prostitute; an asylum for such women. **Magdalen** (Oxford), **Magdalene** (Cambridge) **College,** *both pron.* mawd′ lin.

Magdalenian (măg dȧ lē′ ni ȧn) [rock-shelter of *La Madeleine*, Dordogne, France], *a.* (*Anthrop.*) Of or pertaining to the period of Upper Palæolithic culture, succeeding the Solutrian period, typified by the implements and weapons of bone, horn, ivory and stone, and carvings and engravings found at this station.

mage (māj) [L. MAGUS], *n.* A magician.

magenta (mȧ jen′ tȧ) [after a city of Italy near which the Austrians were defeated in a bloody battle by the French and Sardinians in 1859], *n.* An aniline dye of a brilliant crimson colour.

maggot (măg′ ȯt) [perh. corr. of M.E. *maddock*, *mathek* (cp. Icel. *mathkr*, A.-S. *mathu*)], *n.* A grub, a worm, esp. the larva of the cheese- or flesh-fly; (*fig.*) a whim, a crochet; *a whimsical person. ***maggot-pie,** *n.* The magpie. **maggoty,** *a.* **maggotiness,** *n.*

magi, magian, etc. [MAGUS].

magic (măj′ ik) [F. *magique*, L. *magicus*, Gr. *magikos*, from *magos*, MAGUS], *n.* The pretended art of employing supernatural power to influence or control events; sorcery, witchcraft; (*fig.*) any agency, power or action that has astonishing results. *a.* Pertaining to or used in magic; using magic; exercising supernatural powers; produced by magic. **black magic** [BLACK]. **white magic** [WHITE]. **magic circle:** A circle possessing properties analogous to those of the magic square. **magic lantern** [LANTERN]. **magic square:** A series of numbers so disposed in a square that the totals, taken perpendicularly, horizontally, or diagonally, are equal. **magical,** *a.* **magically,** *adv.* **magician** (mȧ jish′ ȧn), *n.*

magisterial (măj is tēr′ i ȧl) [med. L. *magisteriālis*, L. *magisterius*, from *magister*, MASTER], *a.* Pertaining to or befitting a master or magistrate; authoritative, commanding; dictatorial, domineering; oracular. **magisterially,** *adv.* **magisterium,** *n.* (*R.-C. Ch.*) The teaching authority of the Church; *magistery. ***magistery** (măj′ is tėr i), *n.* Mastership, authority; (*Alch.*) a master-principle of nature, esp. the principle of transmuting substances or a substance, such as the philosopher's stone, possessing this.

magistral (mȧ jis′ trȧl) [L. *magistrālis*, as prec.], *a.* Of or like a master, magisterial; (*Med.*) specially prescribed or devised, not in the ordinary pharmacopœia; *acting as a sovereign remedy. **n.* A magistral preparation; a sovereign remedy.

magistrand (măj′ is trănd) [from med. L. *magistrandus*, ger.p. of *magistrārī*, to become an M.A. (see MASTER)], *n.* (*Sc. Univ.*) An Arts student in the fourth year.

magistrate (măj′ is trāt) [F. *magistrat*, L. *magistrātus*, as MASTER], *n.* A public officer, commissioned to administer the law, a Justice of the Peace. **magistracy, magistrateship, magistrature,** *n.* ***magistratic, -al** (-trăt′ ik, -ȧl), *a.*

magma (măg′ mȧ) [L., from Gr., from *massein*, to knead], *n.* (*pl.* **-mata**) A crude mixture of mineral or organic matter in a thin paste; (*Pharmacy*) a confection, a thick residuum, etc.; (*Geol.*) the molten semi-fluid matter below the earth's crust.

Magna Carta (măg′ nȧ kar′ tȧ) [med. L., great CHARTER], *n.* The Great Charter of English liberties sealed by King John on 15 June 1215; any fundamental constitution guaranteeing rights and privileges.

magnalium (măg nā′ li ŭm) [*Metal.*], *n.* Alloy of magnesium and aluminium.

magnanerie (ma nya′ nė rē) [F., from *magnan*, silkworm], *n.* Silkworm culture; a silkworm house.

magnanimous (măg năn′ i mŭs) [L. *magnanimus* (*magnus*, great, *animus*, soul)], *a.* Great minded, elevated in soul or sentiment; brave, generous. **magnanimity** (-nim′ i ti), *n.* **magnanimously,** *adv.*

magnate (măg′ nāt) [late L. *magnas -nātem*, from *magnus*, great], *n.* A person of rank or distinction.

***magnes** (măg′ nēz) [L., MAGNET], *n.* A magnet.

magnesia (măg nē′ shȧ) [med. L., from Gr., fem. of *Magnēsios*, of or pertaining to Magnesia in Thessaly (applied to two minerals, the lodestone and a silver-like stone, perh. talc)], *n.* Oxide of magnesium, a white alkaline antacid earth; (*pop.*) hydrated carbonate of magnesia, used as an antacid and laxative. **magnesian,** *a.*

magnesium (măg nē′ zi ŭm), *n.* (*Chem.*) A divalent metallic element, the base of magnesia. **magnesium-ribbon, -wire,** *n.* Magnesium prepared for burning as an illuminant.

magnet (măg′ nėt) [O.F. *magnete*, L. *magnēta*, nom. *-nēs*, Gr. *magnēs -nētos*, (stone) of magnetite, see prec.], *n.* The loadstone; a body, usu. of iron or steel, to which the properties of the loadstone, of attracting iron and pointing to the poles, have been imparted; (*fig.*) a thing or person exercising a powerful attractive influence.

magnetic (măg net′ ik), *a.* Pertaining to the magnet or magnetism; having the properties of a magnet; (*fig.*) attractive; mesmeric. *n.* Any metal capable of receiving the properties of the loadstone; (*pl.*) the science or principles of magnetism. **compound magnet** or **magnetic battery:** A combination of magnets with their poles similarly arranged. **magnetic dip,** *n.* The angle between the earth's magnetic field and the horizontal. **magnetic equator:** A line round the globe where the magnetic needle has no dip. ***magnetic fluid:** A fluid formerly supposed to account for magnetism. **magnetic friction,** *n.* The reaction of a strong magnetic field on an electric discharge. **magnetic iron:** Magnetite. **magnetic mine,** *n.* A submarine mine detonated by the passing over it of a metal ship. **magnetic needle:** A slender poised bar of magnetized steel, as in the mariner's compass, pointing north and south. **magnetic north, south,** or **poles:** Two nearly opposite points of the earth's surface where the magnetic needle dips vertically. **magnetic screen:** A screen of soft iron cutting off a magnetic needle from the influence of a magnet. **magnetic storm:** A disturbance of the earth's magnetism setting up an oscillation of the magnetic needle. **magnetic tape,** *n.* A tape covered with a magnetic powder used for the recording and reproduction of sound and television pictures. **magnetical,** *a.* **magnetically,** *adv.*

magnetism (măg′ ne tizm), *n.* The property whereby certain bodies, esp. iron and its compounds, attract or repel each other according to certain laws; the science treating of this property, its conditions or laws; the attractive power itself; (*fig.*) personal attractiveness, charm. **animal magnetism:** Mesmerism. **magnetist,** *n.* One skilled in the science of magnetism or in animal magnetism.

magnetite (măg ne tīt), *n.* Magnetic oxide of iron.

magnetize (măg′ ne tīz), *v.t.* To communicate magnetic properties to; to attract as with a magnet; to mesmerize. *v.i.* To become magnetic. **magnetization** (-zā′ shŭn), *n.* **magnetizer,** *n.*

magneto (măg nē′ tō) [MAGNET], *n.* (*pl.* **-os**) A magneto-electric machine (esp. the igniting apparatus of an internal combustion engine). **magneto-electricity:** Electricity generated by the inductive action of magnets; the science treating of such electricity. **magneto-electric-telegraph,** *n.* A system of telegraphy in which magneto-electric machines, not voltaic batteries, produce the current. **magneto-ignition,** *n.* Ignition by a magneto-generated spark in a petrol engine. **magneto-pointer,** *n.* The index of a magneto-electric dial telegraph. **magneto-printer,** *n.* A printing-telegraph worked by a magneto-electric machine.

magnetograph (măg net′ ō grăf), *n.* An instrument for measuring magnetic forces, esp. terrestrial magnetism.

magneton (măg′ nė tȯn), *n.* The unit of magnetic moment.

magnetophone (măg net′ ō fōn), *n.* An instrument on the principle of the telephone for producing loud musical tones. **magneto-phonograph,** *n.* A phonograph which records speech magnetically.

magnetoscope (măg net′ ō skōp), *n.* An instrument which shows the presence of magnetic force-lines.

magnetron (măg′ ne tron), *n.* (*Phys.*) A thermionic tube for generating very high frequency oscillations.

***magnific, -al** (măg nif′ ik, -ȧl) [F. *magnifique*, L. *magnificus* (*magnus*, -FIC)], *a.* Magnificent, grand, sublime. ***magnifically,** *adv.*

Magnificat (măg nif′ i kăt) [L., 3rd sing. pres. of *magnificāre*, to MAGNIFY], *n.* The song of the Virgin Mary (Luke i. 46–55), so called from the first word in the Latin version; a setting of the same to music.

magnification [MAGNIFY].

magnificent (măg nif′ i sėnt), [O.F. from L. *magnificent-*, stem of *magnificentior*, compar. of *magnificus*, MAGNIFIC], *a.* Grand in appearance, majestic, splendid; characterized by sumptuousness, luxury, splendour, or generous profusion; (*colloq.*) first-rate, excellent. **magnificence,** *n.* **magnificently,** *adv.*

magnifico (măg nif′ i kō) [It.], *n.* A grandee, orig. of Venice.

magnify (măg′ ni fī) [F. *magnifier*, L. *magnificāre* (*magnus*, great, *-ficāre*, *facere*, to make)], *v.t.* To increase the apparent size of (an object) as with an optical instrument; to make greater, to increase; (*fig.*) to extol, to glorify; to exaggerate. *v.i.* To increase the apparent size of objects. **magnification** (-kā′ shŭn), *n.* **magnifier,** *n.*

magniloquent (măg nil′ ȯ kwėnt) [L. *magniloquus* (*magnus*, great, *-loquus*, assim. to *loquens -ntem*, pres.p. of *loquī*, to speak)], *a.* Using high-flown, pompous, or bombastic language. **magniloquence,** *n.* **magniloquently,** *adv.*

magnitude (măg′ ni tūd) [L. *magnitūdo*, from *magnus*, great, -TUDE], *n.* Size, bulk, extent, quantity, amount; anything that can be measured; importance; (*Astron.*) the order of brilliance of a star.

magnolia (măg nō′ li ȧ) [P. *Magnol* (1638–1715), F. botanist], *n.* A genus of beautiful flowering trees or shrubs, chiefly N. American.

magnum (măg′ nŭm) [L., orig., neut. sing. of *magnus*, great], *n.* A bottle containing two quarts; two quarts.

magnum bonum (măg′ nŭm bō′ nŭm) [neut. sing. of *magnus*, great, and *bonus*, good], *n.* The name applied to large kinds of plums and potatoes.

magot (măg′ ôt, ma gō) [F.], *n.* The tailless Barbary ape, *Macacus inuus* of Gibraltar and N. Africa.

magpie (măg′ pī) [MAG (2), PIE (1)], *n.* A well-known chattering bird, *Pica caudata*, with black and white plumage; (*fig.*) a chatterer; a variety of domestic pigeon resembling a magpie; (*Austral.*) the black and white crow-shrike. (*Rifle-shooting*) a shot that hits the outermost division but one of the target. **magpie lark,** *n.* The Austral. peewee.

magra (măg′ rȧ) [Austral. abor.], *n.* An Aboriginal woman's sling for carrying a child.

Magus (mā′ gŭs) [L., from Gr. *magos*, O.Pers. *magus*], *n.* (*pl.* **-gi,** -jī) A member of the priestly caste among the Medes and Persians; a magician. **the Magi:** The three holy men of the East who brought presents to the infant Saviour. **magian** (mā′ ji ȧn), *a.* and *n.* **magianism,** *n.*

Magyar (mod′ yȧr, măg′ yar) [native name], *n.* One of the Mongoloid race (entering Europe in 884), dominant in Hungary; a Magyar blouse or bodice. *a.* (*Dressmaking*) Pertaining to a type of blouse in which the sleeves and the rest of the garment are all one piece. **Magyarism,** *n.* **Magyarize,** *v.t.*

Maharajah (ma ha ra′ jȧ) [Sansk. *mahā-rājā* (*mahā*, great, RAJAH)], *n.* A title assumed by some Indian princes. **Maharani** (ma ha ra′ nē), *n.* A princess; the wife of a Maharajah.

Mahatma (mȧ hăt′ mȧ) [Sansk. *mahātman* (*mahā*, great, *ātman*, soul)], *n.* (*Esoteric Buddhism*) An adept of the highest order.

Mahdi (ma′ di) [Arab. *mahdīy*, he who is divinely guided], *n.* The Mohammedan messiah, a title often assumed by leaders of insurrection in the Sudan. **Mahdism,** *n.*

mahjong, mahjongg (ma′ jǒng) [Chin. sparrow], *n.* A Chinese table game played with 144 pieces called tiles.

mahlstick [MAULSTICK].

mahoe (mȧ hō′ ē) [Maori], *n.* The N. Zealand white-wood tree.

mahogany (mȧ hog′ ȧ ni) [prob. native Amer.], *n.* The hard, fine-grained wood of *Swietenia mahagoni*, a tree of tropical America, largely used in making furniture; the tree itself; applied also to other trees yielding similar wood; (*fig.*) a dining-table; the colour of mahogany, reddish-brown.

Mahomedan, -etan, etc. [MOHAMMEDAN].

***Mahound** (mȧ hoond′) [M.E. and O.F. *Mahun*, Mahomet], *n.* The prophet Mohammed; the following definitions arise from the erroneous mediæval belief that Mohammed was worshipped as a god: an evil spirit; a false god; the devil.

mahout (mȧ hout′) [Hind. *mahāwat*], *n.* An elephant-driver or keeper.

mahwa (ma′ wȧ), *n.* An East Indian tree.

maid (mād) [shortened from MAIDEN], *n.* A girl, a young unmarried woman, a virgin; a female servant; *a man who has not known woman. **maid of all work:** A general servant. **maid of honour:** An unmarried lady attending upon a royal personage; a variety of cheese-cake. **old maid:** An elderly spinster. ***maid-child,** *n.* **maidhood** [MAIDENHEAD]. **maid-servant,** *n.* **maid's sickness** [GREEN SICKNESS].

maidan (mī dan′) [Pers.], *n.* A parade ground.

maiden (mā′ dėn) [A.-S. *mægden*, dim. of *mægth* (cp. Dut. *maagd*, G. *magd*) cogn. with MAY (1)], *n.* A girl; a spinster; an apparatus for washing linen; *a machine used in Scotland for beheading, not so efficient as the guillotine. *a.* Of or pertaining to a maid; unmarried; uncoupled (of female animals); first, new, unused, untried; never captured (of a city or fortress); never having won a prize (of a horse); open to such horses (of a race). **maiden assize:** An assize at which there are no cases. **maiden name:** The surname of a woman before marriage. **maiden over,** *n.* (*Cricket*) An over in which no runs are scored. **maiden speech:** The first speech made by a member of Parliament in the House. ***maiden-tongued,** *a.* Speaking in a gentle and insinuating manner. **maidenhead, maidenhood,** *n.* The state of being a maid or virgin, virginity; the virginal membrane; *newness, freshness. **maidenish,** *a.* **maidenlike,** *a.* **maidenly,** *a.* and *adv.* **maidenliness,** *n.*

maidenhair (mā′ dėn hâr), *n.* (*Bot.*) A fern with delicate fronds, esp. *Asplenium trichomanes* or *Adiantum capillus-Veneris.*

maieutic (mā ū′ tik) [Gr. *maieutikos*, from *maieuesthai*, to act as a midwife, from *maia*, midwife], *a.* Helping to bring forth or evolve (applied to the system pursued by Socrates, in which he endeavoured to bring out latent ideas by persistent questioning).

maigre (mā′ gėr) [F.], *a.* Suitable for fast days, not made from meat nor containing gravy (of food, esp. soup); applied to fast days. *n.* A large Mediterranean fish, *Sciæna aquila.*

mail (1) (māl) [O.F. *maille*, L. *macula*, spot, mesh], *n.* Defensive armour for the body, formed of rings, chains, or scales; (*fig.*) any defensive covering. *v.t.* To invest in or as in mail. **mailed fist,** *n.* The application of physical force.

mail (2) (māl) [O.F. *male* (F. *malle*), from Teut. (cp. Dut. *maal*, O.H.G. *malha*)], *n.* A bag for the conveyance of letters, etc.; the letters, etc., conveyed by the post; the system of conveying letters, etc., the post, esp. for abroad; a mail-train or ship. *v.t.* To send by mail, to post. **mail-cart,** *n.* A cart for carrying the mail; a light vehicle for carrying children. **mail-coach,** *n.* **mail-train,** *n.* **mailable,** *a.*

***mail** (3) (māl) [late A.-S. and Icel. *māl* (cp. A.-S. *mæl*, speech)], *n.* Rent, tribute, tax [cp. BLACKMAIL].

maim (mām) [M.E. *mahaym*, from O.F. *mahaignier*, etym. doubtful], *n.* A serious, esp. a disabling mutilation or injury; an essential defect. *v.t.* To deprive of the use of a limb; to cripple, to mutilate. **maimedness,** *n.*

main (1) (mān) [from Icel. *megn*, strong, or foll., or from both], *a.* Concentrated or fully exerted (of force); principal, chief, most important; *mighty, powerful. **main-boom,** *n.* (*Naut.*) The lower spar of a small vessel on which the mainsail is extended. **main-brace,** *n.* (*Naut.*) A brace attached to the mainyard. **to splice the main-brace** [BRACE]. **main chance** [CHANCE]. ***main-course,** *n.* The mainsail of a square-rigged ship. **main-deck,** *n.* (*Naut.*) The deck below the spar-deck in a man-of-war; the portion of the upper deck between poop and forecastle on a merchantman. **mainland,** *n.* The principal body of land as opposed to islands, etc. **mainlander,** *n.* The Tasmanian term for a resident on the Australian continent. **mainmast,** *n.* The principal mast of a ship. **mainsail** (mān′ sāl, mānsl), *n.* A sail bent to the main-yard of a square-rigged ship; the sail set on the after part of the mainmast of a fore-and-aft rigged vessel. **main-sheet,** *n.* The rope that extends and fastens the mainsail. **mainspring,** *n.* The chief spring of a watch, etc. **mainstay,** *n.* (*Naut.*) The stay from the main-top to the foot of the foremast; (*fig.*) the chief support. **main-top,** *n.* (*Naut.*) A platform above the head of the lower mainmast. **main-yard,** *n.* (*Naut.*) The yard on which the mainsail is extended. **mainly,** *adv.* Principally, chiefly; in the main; greatly, strongly.

main (2) (mān) [A.-S. *mægen*, cogn. with MAY (1)], *n.* Strength, force, violent effort; the main or high sea, the ocean; a chief sewer, conduit, conductor, electric cable, etc. **in the main:** For the most part. **Spanish Main:** (*Hist.*) The N.E. coast of S. America and the adjacent part of the Caribbean Sea. **with might and main:** With all one's strength.

***main** (3) (mān) [etym. doubtful], *n.* A throw at dice, or a number (5–9) called by the caster before throwing; a match at cock-fighting; a match in various sports.

mainland, mainly, etc. [MAIN (1)].

***mainour** (mā′ nǒr) [A.-F. *meinoure*, O.F. *maneuvre*, MANŒUVRE], *n.* (*Law*) Stolen property found in the hands of the thief.

***mainprize** (mān′ prīz) [A.-F. and O.F. *mainprise*, from *mainprendre* (*main*, hand, *prendre*, to take)], *n.* (*Law*) Releasing a prisoner by becoming surety for his appearance; a writ commanding bail to be accepted.

mains (mānz) [Sc., from DOMAIN], *n.pl.* A home-farm.

mainsail, mainstay, etc. [MAIN (1)].

maintain (mȧn-, mān tān′) [F. *maintenir*, L. *manū tenēre* (*manū*, with the hand, abl. of *manus*, *tenēre*, to hold)], *v.t.* To hold, preserve, or carry on in any state; to sustain, to keep up; to support, to provide with the means of living; to keep in order, proper condition, or repair; to assert, to affirm, to support by reasoning, argument, etc.; *to represent. **maintainable,** *a.* **maintainer,** *n.* **maintenance** (mān′ tė nȧns), *n.* The act of maintaining; means of support; (*Law*) an officious intermeddling in a suit in which the person has no interest. **cap of maintenance** [CAP (1)]. **maintenance man,** *n.* Workman employed to keep machines, etc., in working order.

maiolica, majolica (1) (mȧ yol′ i kȧ) [MAJOLICA (2)], *n.* (*Ceramics*) Staffordshire name for ware decorated with coloured lead glazes.

maire (mī′ rē) [Maori], *n.* A close-grained N. Zealand tree the wood of which is used for many purposes.

maisonette, maisonnette (mā zon et′), [Fr. *maison*, house], *n.* Part of a house let separately.

***maister, maistery,** etc. [MASTER].

maize (māz) [Sp. *maiz*, Cuban, *mahiz*], *n.* Indian corn, *Zea mays* (*Am.* corn). **maizena** (mā zē′ nȧ), *n.* Maize-starch prepared for food.

majesty (măj′ ė sti) [F. *majesté*, L. *majestātem*, nom. *-tas*, cogn. with MAJOR], *n.* The quality of inspiring awe or reverence; impressive dignity, grandeur, stateliness; sovereign power and dignity, esp. (*with poss. pron.*); a title of kings, queens, and emperors; (*Religious Art*) a representation of the Father or the Son in glory. **majestic *-al** (mȧ jĕs′ tik, -ȧl), *a.* **majestically,** *adv.* ***majesticalness,** *n.*

majolica (2) (mȧ yol′ i kȧ) [It. *maiolica*, prob. *Majorca*], *n.* A fine enamelled Italian pottery, said to have come orig. from Majorca, or an imitation of this.

major (mā′ jǒr) [L., comp. of *magnus*, great], *a.* Greater in number, quantity, or extent; more important; (*Mus.*) standard, normal, applied to a third consisting of four semitones; of full age (21 years). *n.* The first premise of a regular syllogism containing the major term; (*Law*) a person of full age; (*Mil.*) an officer next above captain and below lieutenant-colonel; (*Am.*) a graduate. **major axis:** (*Math.*) The axis passing through the foci (in a conic section). **majordomo,** *n.* The chief officer of a royal or princely household (*chiefly It. and Sp.*); one who takes charge of a household, a steward. **major-general,** *n.* An officer commanding a division, ranking next below lieutenant-general. **major interval:** (*Mus.*) An interval greater by a semitone than the minor interval of the same denomination. **major mode:** (*Mus.*) The mode in which the third and sixth tones of the scale form major intervals with the key-note. **major premise:** (*Log.*) The premise containing the major term. **major term:** (*Log.*) That term which forms the predicate of the conclusion. ***majorat*** (ma′ zhôr a) [F.], *n.* (*Continental Law*) The right of primogeniture. **majorate** (mā′ jǒr ȧt), *n.* The rank or office of a major. **majority** (mȧ jor′ i ti), *n.* The greater number; the greater part, more than half; the amount of the difference between the greater and the less number, esp. of votes in an election; full age; majorate; *superiority; *ancestry. **the majority:** The dead. **to join the majority:** To die.

majuscule (măj′ ŭs kūl) [F., from L. *mājuscula*, fem. of *-ulus*, dim of *mājor*, see prec.], *n.* (*Palæont.*) A capital or large letter, as in Latin MSS. before the introduction of minuscules.

***make** (1) (māk) [A.-S. *gemaca* (*gemæc*, equal, well-matched, cp. Dut. *gemac*, G. *gemach*, O.H.G. *gimah*)], *n.* One's equal, like, or match; a mate, a husband or wife. ***makeless,** *a.* Matchless, unequalled.

make (2) (māk) [A.-S. *macian* (cp. Dut. *maken*, G. *machen*), cogn. with MATCH (1)], *v.t.* (*past & p.p.* **made,** **2nd and 3rd sing.* **makest, maketh**) To frame, construct, produce; to bring into existence, to create; to give rise to, to effect, to bring about; to execute, to perform, to accomplish (with nouns expressing action); to result in, to cause to be or become; to compose (as a book, verses, etc.; to prepare for use; to establish, to enact; to **raise** to a rank or dignity; to constitute, to form, to become, to turn out to be; to gain, to acquire; to move or proceed (towards, etc.); (*Cards*) to win (a trick) or cause (a card) to win, to shuffle; to score; to cause, to compel (to do); to cause to appear, to represent to be; to reckon, to calculate or decide to be; to conclude, to think; to reach the end of; to amount to, to serve for; to travel over (a distance, etc.); to fetch, as a price; (*Naut.*) to come near; to arrive at; to infuse tea. *v.i.* To go, move, tend, or lie (in a specified direction); to contribute, to have effect (for or to); to rise, to flow (of the tide); to do, to act in a specified way (usu. with adj. as *make bold*). *n.* Form, shape; arrangement of parts; making; style; disposition, mental or moral constitution; (*Elec.*) making of contact, completion of a circuit. **on the make:** (*colloq.*) Intent on personal profit, after the main chance. **to make account of:** To esteem; to consider. **to make against:** To be unfavourable to, to tend to injure. **to make as if:** To pretend, to feint. **to make at:** To attack. **to make away:** To hurry away. **to make away with:** To get rid of, to kill; to waste, to squander. **to make believe** [BELIEVE]. **to make bold** [BOLD]. **to make for:** To conduce to; to corroborate; to move toward; to attack. **to make free:** To venture (to). **to make free with:** To treat without ceremony. **to make good** [GOOD]. **to make hay of** [HAY (1)]. **to make headway:** To advance. **to make it:** (*colloq.*) To reach an objective; to succeed. **to make light of** [LIGHT (2)]. **to make love** [LOVE]. **to make merry:** To feast, to be jovial. **to make much of:** To treat with fondness or favour; to treat as of great importance. **to make no doubt:** To be sure. **to make off:** To run away; to abscond. **to make out:** To understand, to decipher; to prove, to establish; to draw up. **to make over:** To transfer. **to make place or room:** To move so as to leave space (for). **to make sail:** (*Naut.*) To set more sails; to set sail. **to make sure of:** To consider as certain. **to make tea:** To infuse tea. **to make up:** To compose; to compound; to collect together; to complete; to supply (what is wanting); to compensate; to settle, to adjust; to repair; to dress up, to prepare the face to represent a character (of an actor); to fabricate, to concoct; to arrange (as type) in columns or pages. **to make up one's mind:** To decide, to resolve. **to make up to:** To make advances. **to make water:** To void urine; (*Naut.*) to leak. **to make way:** To make room, to open a passage; to progress. **to make words:** To multiply words; to raise a quarrel. ***makebate,** *n.* A breeder of quarrels. **make-believe,** *n.* A pretending, a pretence, a sham. *a.* Unreal; counterfeit. **makeshift,** *n.* A temporary expedient; *a thief, a rogue. *a.* Used as a makeshift. **make-up,** *n.* (*Print.*) The arrangement of type into columns or pages; the manner in which an actor's face is made to represent a character; the material used for this; a made-up story, a fiction; cosmetics for use on the face. **make-weight,** *n.* That which is thrown into a scale to make weight; a stop-gap; anything that counterbalances, a counterpoise. **maker,** *n.* One who makes. **making,** *n.* The act of constructing, producing, causing, etc.; possibility or opportunity of success or full development; (*pl.*) composition, essential qualities; (*pl.*) profits, earnings. **making-up,** *n.* Balancing of accounts.

mako (ma' kō) [Maori], *n.* A small N. Zealand tree; a kind of shark.

mal- [F., from L. *male*, badly], *pref.* Bad, badly, as in *malodorous, maltreat.*

Malacca (mȧ lăk' ȧ) [town and district in Malay peninsula], *n.* A palm-stem used as a walking-stick.

malachite (măl' ȧ kīt) [O.F. *melochite* (Gr. *malache*, mallow, -ITE)], *n.* (*Min.*) A bright green monoclinic carbonate of copper.

malaco- [Gr. *malakos*], *comb. form.* Soft.

malacoderm (măl' ȧ kȯ dĕrm), *n.* (*Zool.*) A soft-skinned animal, esp. one of the *Malacodermata* or sea-anemones.

malacolite (măl' ȧ kō līt), *n.* (*Min.*) A greenish calcium-magnesium variety of pyroxene.

malacology (măl ȧ kol' ō ji), *n.* (*Zool.*) The natural history of the mollusca. **malacologist,** *n.*

malacopterygian (măl ȧ kop tėr ij' i ȧn) [Gr. *pteryx*, a wing], *a.* (*Zool.*) Belonging to the *Malacopterygii*, a group of soft-finned fishes. *n.* Any individual of this group. **malacopterygious,** *a.*

malacostomous (măl ȧ kos' tō mŭs), *a.* (*Zool.*) Having soft jaws without teeth (as some fish).

malacostracan (măl ȧ kos' trȧ kȧn) [Gr. *ostrakon*, a shell], *a.* (*Zool.*) Of or belonging to the *Malacostraca*, a division of crustaceans containing crabs, lobsters, etc. *n.* A member of this division. **malacostracous,** *a.* **malacostracology** (-kol' ȯ ji), *n.* Crustaceology. **malacostrological** (-loj' i kȧl), *a.* **malacostrocologist** (-kol' ȯ jist), *n.*

malacozoic (măl ȧ kō zō' ik), *a.* (*Zool.*) Of or belonging to the *Malacozoa*, or soft-bodied animals, *i.e.* the mollusca.

maladaptation (măl ăd ăp tā' shŭn), *n.* Defective adaptation.

maladjustment (măl ȧ jŭst' mėnt), *n.* Defective adjustment; (*Psych.*) the condition of being unable to adjust oneself to physical or social environment.

maladministration (măl ăd min is trā' shŭn), *n.* Defective or vicious management, esp. of public affairs.

maladroit (măl ȧ droit'), *a.* Awkward, clumsy. **maladroitly,** *adv.*

malady (măl' ȧ di) [F. *maladie*, from *malade*, sick, late L. *male habitus* (*male*, see MAL-, *habitus*, p.p. of *habēre*, to have, hold, keep)], *n.* A disease, an ailment, esp. a lingering or deep-seated disorder; (*fig.*) a moral defect or disorder.

malaga (măl' ȧ gȧ) [seaport and province in S. Spain], *n.* White wine imported from Malaga.

Malagasy (măl ȧ găs' i) [now native, but said to be of foreign origin], *n.* Of or pertaining to Madagascar or its inhabitants or language. *n.* A native or the natives of Madagascar; their language.

malaise (mȧ lāz') [F. (O.F. *mal*, as MAL-, *aise*, EASE)], *n.* A feeling of uneasiness, esp. as premonition of a serious malady.

malander (măl' ȧn dėr) [F. *malandre*], *n.* (*now always pl.*) A scaly eruption at the back of the knee in horses.

***malapert** (măl' ȧ pĕrt) [O.F. *mal appert* (MAL-, *espert*, EXPERT)], *a.* Pert, impudent, saucy, forward. *n.* A pert, saucy person. ***malapertly,** *adv.* ***malapertness,** *n.*

malaprop (măl' ȧ prop) [Mrs. *Malaprop* in Sheridan's 'Rivals,' see foll.], **malapropism,** *n.* Grotesque misapplication of words; a word so misapplied. **malapropian** (-prop' i-, -prō' pi ȧn), *a.*

malapropos (măl' a prȯ pō, -ăp rȯ pō') [F. *mal à propos* (MAL-, APROPOS)], *adv.* Unseasonably, unsuitably, out of place. *a.* Unseasonable etc. *n.* An unseasonable or inopportune thing, remark, event, etc.

malar (mā' lȧr) [L. *māla* (prob. rel. to MAXILLA), cheek, -AR], *a.* (*Anat.*) Pertaining to the cheek or cheek-bone. *n.* The bone which forms the prominence of the cheek.

malaria (mȧ lâr' i ȧ) [It. *mal'aria* (MAL-, AIR)], *n.* The noxious exhalations of marshy districts, formerly believed to produce fevers etc.; applied to various kinds of fever of an intermittent and remittent nature now known to be due to a parasite introduced by the bite of mosquitoes. **malarial, -ian, -ious,** *a.*

malassimilation (măl ȧ sim i lā' shŭn) [MAL-, ASSIMILATION], *n.* Imperfect assimilation, esp. of nutriment.

Malay (mȧ lā') [native *Malayu*], *a.* Of or pertaining to the predominant race in Malaya and the Eastern Archipelago. *n.* A member of this race; their language. **Malayan,** *a.* and *n.*

Malayalam (măl ȧ ya' lȧm) [native], *n.* The language of Malabar, a Dravidian dialect akin to Tamil. **Malayalim,** *n.pl.* The Dravidians of Malabar speaking this.

malconformation (măl kon fȯr mā' shŭn) [MAL-, CONFORMATION], *n.* Imperfect conformation, disproportion of parts.

malcontent (măl' kȯn tent) [O.F. (MAL-, CONTENT)], *a.* Discontented, esp. with the Government or its administration. *n.* One who is discontented with the Government. **malcontented,** *a.* **malcontentedly, malcontently,** *adv.* **malcontentedness,** *n.*

male (māl) [O.F., from L. *masculum*, nom. *-lus*, from *mās*, male] *a.* Pertaining to the sex that begets young or has organs for impregnating ova; adapted for fertilization (of organs); (*Bot.*) having stamens but no pistil (of flowers); consisting of or pertaining to individuals of this sex; (*Mech.*) designed for entering a correlative female part; (*fig.*) masculine, virile. *n.* One of the male sex; a plant, or part of a plant, that bears the fecundating organs. **male fern:** A fern, *Nephrodium filix-mas*, with the fronds clustered in a crown. **male screw:** A screw whose threads enter the grooves of a corresponding screw.

male- [L. *male*, ill, badly], *pref.* Ill, as in *malefactor, malevolent.*

malediction (măl ė dik' shŭn) [F., from L. *maledictiōnem*, nom. *-tio*, from *maledīcere* (*dīcere*, to speak)], *n.* A curse, an imprecation. **maledictory,** *a.*

malefactor (măl' ė făk tȯr) [L. *factor*, from *facere*, to do)], *n.* An evil-doer, a criminal. ***malefaction,** *n.* **maleficent** (mȧ lef' i sėnt), *a.* Hurtful, mischievous, causing evil (to.) **maleficence,** *n.*

malefic (mȧ lef' ik) [L. *maleficus*], *a.* Mischief-making, harmful, hateful.

maleic (mȧ lē' ik) [F. *maléique*, from *malique*, MALIC], *a.* (*Chem.*) Applied to an acid obtained by the dry distillation of malic acid.

malevolent (mȧ lev' ȯ lėnt) [L. *malevolens -ntem* (*volens*, pres.p. of *velle*, to wish)], *a.* Wishing evil or injury to others; ill-disposed, envious, malicious, spiteful. **malevolence,** *n.* **malevolently,** *adv.*

malfeasance (măl fē' zȧns) [from O.F. *mafaisant* (*faisant*, pres.p. of *faire*, to do)], *n.* Evil-doing, esp. illegal conduct by a public official.

malformation (măl fȯr mā' shŭn), *n.* Faulty formation; a faulty structure or irregularity of form. **malformed** (măl fŏrmed'), *a.*

malgré [MAUGRE].

malic (mā' lik) [F. *malique*, from L. *mālum*, apple], *a.* (*Chem.*) Derived from fruit (of malic acid).

malice (măl' is) [F., from L. *malitia*, from *malus*, bad], *n.* A disposition to injure others, active malevolence; (*Law*) a premeditated design to do evil or injure another. *v.t. To bear malice towards. **malicious** (mȧ lish′ ůs), *a.* **maliciously,** *adv.* ***maliciousness,** *n.*

malign (mȧ līn′) [O.F. *maligne*, L. *malignus* (*mali-*, MALE-, *genus*, cp. BENIGN)], *a.* Unfavourable, pernicious, malignant, hurtful; *malevolent. *v.t.* To speak evil of, to slander. **v.i.* To be malicious. **maligner,** *n.* **malignly,** *adv.*

malignant (mȧ lig′ nȧnt), *a.* Actuated by extreme enmity or malice; exercising a pernicious influence, virulent; (*Path.*) applied to fever etc., when threatening to life. *n.* A malevolent person, esp. applied by the Puritans to a Royalist in the time of the Civil War. **malignancy,** *n.* **malignantly,** *adv.* **malignity,** *n.*

malinger (mȧ ling′ gėr) [F. *malingre*, sickly, etym. doubtful], *v.i.* To pretend illness in order to shirk duty. **malingerer,** *n.*

malism (mā′ lizm) [L. *malus*, bad], *n.* The doctrine that on the whole this is a bad world.

***malison** (măl′ i sŏn) [O.F. *maleison*, MALEDICTION], *n.* A curse, a malediction.

***malkin** (maw′ kin) [dim. of *Matilda* or *Maud*], *n.* A kitchen-wench; a slattern; a mop; a scarecrow, esp. one representing a woman.

mall (măl, mawl) [MAUL], *n.* A public walk, orig. a place where pall-mall was played; *the game of pall-mall; *the mallet used in this.

mallard (măl′ ȧrd) [O.F. *malart*, perh. from O.H.G. proper name *Madehart*], *n.* A wild drake; a wild duck; the flesh of this.

malleable (măl′ ė ȧ bėl) [O.F., prob. from a L. *malleābilis*, from *malleāre*, from *malleus*, hammer], *a.* Capable of being rolled out or shaped by hammering without being broken; (*fig.*) pliant. **malleability** (-bil′ i ti), ***malleableness,** *n.* ***malleate,** *v.t.* ***malleation** (-ā′ shůn), *n.*

mallecho [MICHING MALICHO].

mallee (măl′ i) [Austral. abor.], *n.* One of various dwarf species of eucalyptus growing in the deserts of Victoria and S. Australia. **mallee-bird, -fowl, -hen,** *n.* A mound-bird. **mallee-scrub,** *n.*

malleiform [MALLEUS].

mallemuck (măl′ ė mŭk) [Dut. *mallemok* (*mal*, foolish, *mok*, gull)], *n.* The fulmar.

mallender [MALANDER].

malleolus (mȧ lē′ ŏ lůs) [L., dim. of MALLEUS], *n.* (*Anat.*) One of two bony processes extending either side of the ankle. **malleolar** (mȧ lē′-, măl′ ė ŏ lȧr), *a.*

mallet (măl′ ėt) [F. *maillet*, dim. of *mail*, MAUL], *n.* A light hammer, usu. of wood; a long-handled wooden one for striking the ball in croquet or polo.

malleus (măl′ ė ůs) [L., hammer], *n.* (*Anat.*) One of the small bones of the tympanum. **malleiform,** *a.*

mallow, -lows (măl′ ō, -ōz) [A.-S. *mealwe*, L. *malva* (cp. Gr. *malachē*, perh. rel. to *malakos*, soft)], *n.* A plant of various species belonging to the genus *Malva*, usu. with pink or mauve flowers and hairy stems and foliage, and having emollient properties whence perhaps its name.

malm (mawm) [A.-S. *mealm* (cp. Icel. *mālmr*, Goth. *malma*, from Teut. *mal-*, to grind)], *n.* A soft, friable chalky rock or loam, used with clay and sand for brick-making. *v.t.* To mix (clay, chalk, etc.) to make malm for bricks; to cover brick-earth with this.

Malmaison (măl mā′ zŏn) [house near Paris of the Empress Josephine], *n.* A variety of blush-rose; a variety of carnation like this in colour.

malmsey (mam′ zi) [ult. from med. L. *malmasia*, corr of Gr. *Monembasia*, Napoli di Monemvasia, town in Morea (cp. *malvoisie*)], *n.* A strong sweet white wine now chiefly made in the Canaries and Spain.

malnutrition (măl nū trish′ ůn), *n.* Insufficient or defective nutrition.

malodorous (mȧ lō′ dŏr ůs), *a.* Having an unpleasant smell. **malodour,** *n.* An offensive odour.

Malpighian (măl pig′ i ȧn) [Marcello *Malpighi* (1628–94) It. anatomist], *a.* (*Anat.*) Applied to certain corpuscles, layers, and other structures, in the spleen and kidneys.

malpractice (măl prăk′ tis), *n.* An evil practice; illegal or immoral conduct, esp. improper treatment of a case by a physician or surgeon.

malpresentation (măl pre zen tā′ shůn), *n.* (*Med.*) An abnormal position of the fœtus at birth.

malt (mawlt) [A.-S. *mealt* (cp. Dut. *mout*, Icel. *malt*, G. *malz*), cogn with O.H.G. *malz*, soft, and MELT], *n.* Grain, usually barley, steeped in water and fermented, dried in a kiln, and used for brewing and distilling; malt-liquor. *a.* Pertaining to, containing, or made of malt. *v.t.* To convert into malt; to treat with malt. *v.i.* To be converted into malt; (*facet.*) to drink malt-liquor. **malt-floor,** *n.* The floor in a malt-house on which the grain is spread to germinate. **malt-horse,** *n.* A horse employed in grinding malt; a dull, stupid fellow. **malt-house, maltings,** *n.* Building where malt is prepared and stored. **malt-liquor,** *n.* Liquor made from malt by fermentation, beer, stout, etc. ***malt-worm,** *n.* A tippler. **maltster,** *n.* A man whose occupation is to make malt. **malty,** *a.*

Malta (mawl′ tȧ) [island in the Mediterranean], *n.* **Malta fever:** A fever common in Malta and other places in the Mediterranean, said to be conveyed by goat's milk. **Maltese** (mawl tēz′), *a.* Pertaining to Malta or its inhabitants. *n.* A native of Malta; the Maltese language or the people; a Maltese dog. **Maltese cross** [CROSS (1)]. **Maltese dog:** A small variety of spaniel with long silky hair.

maltha (măl′ thȧ) [L., from Gr.], *n.* A bituminous cement used by the ancients; applied to various kinds of mineral pitch.

Malthusian (măl thū′ zi ȧn) [T. R. *Malthus* (1766–1834), political economist and advocate of restraint in the propagation of children, -IAN], *a.* Pertaining to or supporting the teachings of Malthus. *n.* A follower of Malthus; one who holds that some check is necessary to prevent over-population. **Malthusianism,** *n.*

maltose (mawl′ tōs) [F. (MALT, -OSE)], *n.* (*Chem.*) A sugar obtained by the action of malt or diastase on starch paste.

maltreat (măl trēt′) [F. *maltraiter*, L. *male tractāre* (MAL-, TREAT)], *v.t.* To ill-treat; to abuse. **maltreatment,** *n.*

maltster, malty [MALT].

malvaceous (măl vā′ shůs) [late L. *malvaceus*, from *malva*, MALLOW], *a.* Belonging to or resembling the genus *Malva* or the family *Malvaceæ*, comprising the mallows.

malversation (măl vėr sā′ shůn) [F. *malverser* (L. *male*, badly, *versārī*, to behave, freq. of *vertere*, to turn), -ATION], *n.* Fraudulent conduct or corruption in a position of trust, esp. corrupt administration of public funds.

mambo (măm′ bō), *n.* A West Indian syncopated dance or dance tune, like the rumba.

mamelon (măm′ ė lŏn) [F., a teat, from *mamelle*, L. MAMILLA], *n.* A small rounded hill or mound, from its resemblance to a woman's breast.

mameluke (măm′ ė look) [Arab. *mamlūk*, slave, from *malaka*, to possess], *n.* One of the mounted soldiers of Egypt (orig. Circassian slaves) who formed the ruling class in that country, destroyed by Mehemet Ali in 1811.

mamilla (mȧ mil′ ȧ) [L., dim. of MAMMA (2)], *n.* A nipple or teat; a nipple-shaped organ or part. **mamillary, mamillate, mamillated** (măm′ i lȧr i, -lȧt, -lā tėd), **mamilliform** (-mil′ i fôrm), *a.*

mamma (1) (mȧ ma′) [reduplication of instinctive sound made by infants], *n.* Mother (used chiefly by young children). **mammy,** *n.* (*Childish*). Mother; a Negro nurse.

mamma (2) (măm′ ȧ) [L.], *n.* (*pl.* ***-mæ***) The milk-secreting organ in mammals. **mammary,** *a.* **mammifer,** *n.* **mammiferous** (-mif′ ėr ŭs) [-FEROUS], *a.* (*Zool.*) Mammalian; (*Anat.*) bearing the breasts (of a part of the body). **mammiform** (măm′ i fôrm), *a.* In shape like a breast.

mammal (măm′ ȧl) [sing. from mod. L. *mammālia*, neut. pl. of late L. *mammālis*, from L. MAMMA (2)], *n.* (*Zool.*) Any individual of the Mammalia. **Mammalia** (mȧ mā′ li ȧ), *n.pl.* The class of animals having milk-secreting organs for suckling their young, the highest division of vertebrates. **mammalian,** *a.* **mammaliferous** (-lif′ ėr ŭs) [-FEROUS], *a.* (*Geol.*) Containing mammalian remains. **mammalogy** (-măl′ ŏ ji) [-LOGY], *n.* **mammalogist,** *n.*

mammee (mȧ mē′) [through F. *mammée* or Sp. *mamey*, from Haitian], *n.* A tropical American tree, *Mammea Americana*, bearing edible pulpy fruit.

***mammer** (măm′ ėr) [imit. with freq. suf. -ER], *v.i.* To hesitate, to stand muttering.

mammifer [MAMMA (2)], **mammillary** [MAMILLA].

***mammock** (măm′ ŏk) [etym. unknown], *n.* A shapeless piece. *v.t.* To tear in or into pieces.

mammon (măm′ ŏn) [L. *mammōna*, Gr. *mamōnas*, Aram. *māmōnā*, riches], *n.* Riches personified as an idol or an evil influence. **mammonish,** *a.* **mammonism,** *n.* **mammonist, -ite,** *n.* **mammonize,** *v.t.*

mammoth (măm′ ŏth) [Russ. *mammat* (now *mamant*)], *n.* A large extinct species of elephant, *Elephas primigenius*. *a.* Gigantic, huge.

mammy [MAMMA (1)].

man (măn) [A.-S. *mann* (cp. Dut. and Swed. *man*, G. *mann*)], *n.* (*pl.* **men**) A human being, a person; (*collect.*) mankind, the human race; an adult male of the human race; an individual, one; one with manly qualities; manhood; a husband; a manservant, a valet, a workman; a person under one's control; *a vassal, a tenant; (*pl.*) soldiers, esp. privates; (*pl.*) pieces used in playing chess or draughts; (*in comb.*) a ship (as *man-of-war*, *merchantman*, etc.). *v.t.* (*past & p.p.* **manned**) To furnish with a man or men, esp. for defence or other military service; (*fig.*) to fortify the courage of (esp. oneself); *to tame. **best man,** *n.* A groomsman. **inner man** [INNER]. **man about town:** A fashionable idler. **man and boy:** From boyhood upwards. **man-at-arms,** *n.* A heavily-armed mounted soldier, esp. in the Middle Ages. **man-child,** *n.* A male child. **man-eater,** *n.* A cannibal; a tiger, shark, etc., that devours human beings; a horse that bites. **man-eating,** *a.* **man Friday,** *n.* A personal servant, factotum. **man for man:** (Reckoning) as mere individual male persons. **man-handle,** *v.t.* To move by manpower alone; (*colloq.*) to handle roughly, to maltreat. **man-hater,** *n.* One (usu. a woman) who hates men. **man-hole,** *n.* A hole in a floor, drain, or parts of machinery, etc., to allow entrance for cleansing and repairs. **man-hour,** *n.* The amount of work done by one man in one hour. **man in the street,** *n.* Ordinary person. **man of the world,** *n.* Experienced person, tolerant and urbane. **man-midwife,** *n.* **man-milliner,** *n.* A man who makes or sells millinery; (*fig.*) one who busies himself with trifles. **man of straw:** A man of no substance, a male puppet. **man-of-war,** *n.* A warship belonging to a navy. **man-power:** Amount of men available for any purpose. **man-rope,** *n.* (*Naut.*) A rope at the side of a gangway etc. **manservant,** *n.* **man-slayer,** *n.* One who kills a human being or commits manslaughter. **man-tiger,** *n.* (*Anthrop.*) A lycanthrope or werewolf assuming the form of a tiger. **man to man:** With complete frankness. **man-trap,** *n.* **manful,** *a.* Brave, courageous; resolute, manly. **manfully,** *adv.* **manfulness,** *n.* **manhood,** *n.* The state of being a man; the state of being a male person of full age; manliness, courage, resolution. **manhood suffrage:** The right of voting granted to every citizen of full age not disqualified by crime etc. **mankind** (măn kīnd′), *n.* The human species; (măn′ kīnd) men collectively as dist. from humanity. **manlike,** *a.* **manly,** *a.* Having the finer qualities characteristic of a man, courageous, resolute, magnanimous; befitting a man; mannish. **manliness,** *n.* **mannish,** *a.* Masculine, characteristic of a man, unwomanly. **mannishly,** *adv.* **mannishness,** *n.* **manward,** *a.* and *adv.*

Mana (ma′ nȧ) [Polynesian native], *n.* Spiritual power exerted through man or inanimate objects; power, authority.

manacle (măn′ ȧ kėl) [O.F. *manicle*, L. *manicula*, dim. of *manus*, hand], *n.* A handcuff, a fetter (*usu. in pl.*). *v.t.* To put manacles on; to fetter.

manage (măn′ ȧj) [It. *maneggiare*, from L. *manus*, hand], *v.t.* To conduct, to direct, to carry on, to control; to conduct the affairs of; to handle, to wield; to bring or keep under control; to lead or guide by flattery etc.; to break in, to train (as a horse); to deal with, to make use of; *to husband, to use cautiously. *v.i.* To direct affairs; to contrive (to do etc.); to get on (with or without); to succeed (with). *n.* Management; a *manège*. **manageable,** *a.* **manageability** (-bil′ i ti), **manageableness,** *n.* **manageably,** *adv.* **management,** *n.* The act of managing; conduct, administration; those who manage, a board of directors etc.; skilful employment of means; *skill, ingenuity. **manager,** *n.* One who manages, esp. a business, institution, etc.; (*Law*) one appointed to administer a business in chancery etc.; one skilled in economical management (*usu. with* good, bad, *etc.*); (*pl.*) a committee appointed by either House of Parliament to perform a duty concerning both Houses. **manageress,** *n.* **managerial** (-jēr′ i ȧl), *a.* **managership,** *n.* **managing,** *a.* Having the management or control of a business, department, etc.; careful, economical.

mañana (ma nya′ na) [Sp., from L. *māne*], *n.* Tomorrow, presently, later on; procrastination.

manatee (măn ȧ tē′) [Sp. *manati*, Carib. *manatoui*], *n.* The sea-cow, a large herbivorous sirenian.

manche (mansh) [F., from L. *manica*, from *manus*, hand], *n.* A sleeve, with long hanging ends.; (*Her.*) a bearing representing such a sleeve; (*Mus.*) the neck of a violin, etc.

Manchester (măn′ ches tėr) [City in Lancashire], **Manchester goods,** *n.pl.* Cotton textiles. **Manchesterism,** *n.* (*Pol.*) The doctrines of the school of thought of Cobden and Bright advocating Free Trade and the principle of *laissez-faire*.

***manchet** (măn′ chėt) [etym. doubtful], *n.* A small loaf of fine wheaten bread. *a.* Fine and white (of bread).

manchette (man′ shet) [F., dim. of MANCHE], *n.* An ornamental cuff or trimming for a sleeve.

manchineel (măn chi nēl′) [F. *mancenille*, Sp. *manzanilla*, dim. of *manzana*, L. *matiāna*, a certain kind of apple, from *Matius*, name of a Roman gens], *n.* A West Indian tree, *Hippomane mancinella*, with a poisonous sap and apple-like fruit; its timber used for cabinet-work.

mancipate (măn′ si pāt) [L. *mancipātus*, p.p. of *mancipāre*, as foll], *v.t.* (*Rom. Law*) To hand over, to deliver possession, by the formal method of mancipation. **mancipable,** *a.* **mancipant,** *n.* **mancipation** (-pā′ shŭn), *n.* The formal method of transferring property required by Roman law. **mancipative, -atory,** *a.*

manciple (măn′ si pėl) [O.F. *manciple*, *mancipe*, L. *mancipium*, from *manceps*, a buyer, a manager (*manus*, hand, *capere*, to take)], *n.* A steward, a purveyor of stores, esp. for a college, inn of court, etc.

Mancunian (măng kū′ ni ȧn) [mod. Lat. *Mancunium*, Manchester], *n.* A native or citizen of

Manchester; a pupil at the Manchester Grammar School.

-mancy [Gr. *manteia*, divination, from *manteuesthai*, to prophesy, from *mantis*, prophet], *suf.* Divination by, as in *necromancy, pyromancy.*

mandamus (măn dā′ mŭs) [L., we command (cp. MANDATE)], *n.* (*Law*) A writ issued from the King's Bench Division of the High Court of Justice directed to a person, corporation, or inferior court, requiring them to do some particular thing therein specified which appertains to their office or duty.

mandarin (măn′ dȧ rin) [Port. *mandarim*, from Malay and Hindi *mantrī*, Sansk, *mantrin*, counsellor, from *man*, to think, cogn. with MIND], *n.* A Chinese official; a grotesque toy figure in Chinese costume; a mandarin orange; a dye the colour of this; a mandarin duck; a liqueur flavoured with juice of the mandarin orange. **mandarin duck:** A brightly-coloured Asiatic duck, *Aix galericulata.* **mandarin orange:** A small flattish sweet Chinese orange, *Citrus nobilis*, of a dark-yellow colour. **mandarinate,** *n.*

mandate (măn′ dāt) [L. *mandātum*, neut. p.p. of *mandāre*, to command (*manus*, hand, *dare*, to give)], *n.* An authoritative charge, order, or command; (*Law*) a judicial command to an officer or a subordinate court; a contract of bailment by which the mandatary undertakes to perform gratuitously a duty regarding property committed to him; a rescript of the Pope; (*Polit.*) a direction from electors to a representative or a representative body to undertake certain legislation etc.; the authority given (esp. by the League of Nations) to a larger power to govern a backward country in trust for its native inhabitants. **mandatary** (măn′ dȧ tȧr i), *n.* **mandator,** *n.* **mandatory,** *a.* Containing, or of the nature of a mandate; bestowing a mandate; (*Am.*) obligatory, compulsory.

mandible (măn′ di bėl) [L. *mandibula*, from *mandere*, to chew], *n.* (*Anat.*) The jaw, the under jaw in vertebrates, the upper or lower in birds, and the pair in insects. **mandibular, -late, -lated** (măn dib′ ū lȧr, -lȧt, -lā tėd), *a.*

mandolin (măn′ dȯ lin) [F. *mandoline*, It. *mandolino*, dim. of *mandola*, *mandora*, var. of PANDORA (cp. BANDORE)], *n.* A musical instrument with a deep almond-shaped body and two or three pairs of metal strings.

mandragora (măn drăg′ ȯr ȧ) [A.-S. and late L., from Gr. *mandragoras*], *n.* *The mandrake; (*Bot.*) a genus of thick, fleshy-rooted plants yielding a narcotic poison; (*fig.*) a narcotic.

mandrake (măn′ drāk) [M.E. *mandrage*, from prec. (cp. Dut. *mandrage*)], *n.* The plant mandragora, the root of which was anciently believed to be like the human form and to shriek when pulled up.

mandrel (măn′ drėl) [perh. corr. of F. *mandrin*], *n.* An arbor or axis on which work is fixed for turning; the revolving spindle of a circular saw; a cylindrical rod or core round which metal or other material is forged or shaped; (*prov.*) a miner's pick.

mandrill (măn′ dril) [MAN, DRILL (4)], *n.* A ferocious W. African baboon, *Cynocephalus maimon.*

manducate (măn′ dū kāt) [L. *mandūcātus*, p.p. of *mandūcāre*, to chew], *v.t.* To chew, to eat. **manducable,** *a.* **manducation** (-kā′ shŭn), *n.* **manducatory,** *a.*

mane (mān) [A.-S. *manu* (cp. Dut. *mane*, Icel. *mön*, pl. *manar*, G. *mähne*), cogn. with Sansk. *manyā*, nape of the neck, L. *monīle*, necklace], *n.* The long hair on the neck of some animals, as the horse. **mane-sheet,** *n.* A covering for the upper part of a horse's head. **maned,** *a.* (*usu. in comb.* as *thick-maned*). **maneless,** *a.*

manège (ma nāzh′) [F.], *n.* A school for training horses or teaching horsemanship; the training of horses; horsemanship. *v.t.* To manage; to break in and train (a horse).

manes (mā′ nēz) [L.], *n.pl.* The spirits of the dead, esp. of ancestors worshipped as tutelary divinities; the shade of a deceased person regarded as an object of reverence.

manful, etc. [MAN].

manga (mang′ gȧ) [Sp., from L. *manica*, sleeve], *n.* (*Mexico*) A flowing robe like a poncho; (*Eccles.*) a case or covering for a processional cross.

mangabey (măng′ gȧ bā) [part of Madagascar], *n.* An African monkey of the genus *Cercocebus.*

manganese (măng′ gȧ nēz, -nēs) [F. *manganèse*, corr. of MAGNESIA], *n.* A metallic element of a greyish-white colour; the oxide of this occurring as a black mineral, used in glass-making. **manganate,** *n.* (*Chem.*) A salt of manganic acid. **manganesian, manganesic** (-nē′ zi ȧn, -sik), **manganic** (-găn′ ik), *a.* **manganiferous** (nif′ ėr ŭs) [-FEROUS], *a.* **manganite** (măng′ gȧ nīt), *n.* Grey manganese ore.

mangaroo (măng gȧ roo′) [Austral. abor.], *n.* A small flying phalanger.

mange (mānj) [M.E. *manjewe*, O.F. *manjue*, from *manjuer* (F. *manger*, to eat), L. *mandūcāre*, to MANDUCATE], *n.* A skin disease, resembling the itch, occurring in cattle, dogs, etc. **mangy,** *a.* Infected with the mange; (*fig.*) mean, squalid. **manginess,** *n.*

mangel-wurzel (măng′ gėl wĕr′ zėl) [G. *mangold-wurzel* (*mangold*, beet, *wurzel*, root)], *n.* A large-rooted variety of the common beet, *Beta vulgaris*, cultivated as fodder for cattle.

manger (mān′ jėr) [O.F. *mangeure*, from *manger*, to eat, see MANGE], *n.* A trough for horses or cattle to eat out of.

mangle (1) (măng′ gėl) [A.-F. *mangler*, *mahangler*, freq. of O.F. *mahaigner*, to MAIM], *v.t.* To lacerate, to mutilate; to disfigure by hacking; (*fig.*) to mar, to ruin, to destroy the symmetry or completeness of, by blundering etc.

mangle (2) (măng′ gėl) [Dut. *mangel* (whence *mangelen*, to mangle), late L. *manganum*, Gr. *manganon*, see MANGONEL], *n.* A rolling-machine for pressing and smoothing damp linen. *v.t.* To press and smooth with a mangle; to calender. **mangler,** *n.*

mango (măng′ gō) [Port. *manga*, Malay *mañggā*, Tamil *mānkāy* (*mān*, mango-tree, *kay*, fruit)], *n.* (*pl.* **-goes**) An East Indian tree, *Mangifera Indica*, or its fruit; (*Am.*) a green musk-melon pickled. **mango-fish,** *n.* An East Indian food-fish, *Polynemus paradiseus*, of a beautiful yellow colour. **mango-trick,** *n.* An Indian juggler's trick of making a mango-tree appear to spring up and bear fruit.

mangonel (măng′ gȯ nel) [O.F., from late L. *mangona*, *mango -ōnem*, Gr. *manganon*], *n.* A mediæval engine for throwing missiles.

mangosteen (măng′ gȯ stēn) [Malay *manggustan*], *n.* An East Indian tree, *Garcinia mangostana*, or its orange-like fruit, with a sweet, juicy pulp.

mangrove (măng′ grōv) [etym. doubtful], *n.* A tropical tree of the genus *Rhizophora*, esp. *R. mangle*, growing in muddy places by the coast, the bark of which is used for medicine and in tanning.

mangy, etc. [MANGE].

man-handle, manhood [MAN].

mania (mā′ ni ȧ) [L. and Gr., cogn. with *mainesthai*, to be mad], *n.* A form of mental derangement characterized by hallucination, emotional excitement, and violence; (*fig.*) an infatuation, a craze. **maniac,** *a.* Affected with mania, insane, raving. *n.* A madman, a raving lunatic. **maniacal** (mă nī′ ȧ kȧl), *a.* **maniacally,** *adv.* **manic** (măn′ ik) *a.* Of or affected by mania.

-mania [as prec.], *suf.* Denoting special kinds of derangement, hallucination, infatuation, or excessive enthusiasm, as *erotomania, kleptomania, megalomania, monomania.* **-maniac,** *pers. suf.*

Manichæan (măn i kē′ ȧn) [L. *Manichæus*, late Gr. *Manichaios*, from name of founder], *a.* Pertaining to Manichæism. *n.* A believer in Manichæism. **Manichæism** (măn′ i kē izm), *n.* A religious doctrine widely prevailing in the 3rd–5th century, that the universe is controlled by two antagonistic powers, light or goodness, identified with God, and darkness, chaos or evil. **Manichee** (măn i kē′), *n.*

manicure (măn′ i kūr) [F. (L. *manus*, hand, *cura*, care)], *n.* One who undertakes the treatment of the hands and finger-nails as a business; the care of the hands, nails, etc. *v.t.* To treat the hands and finger-nails.

manifest (măn′ i fest) [through F. *manifeste* or directly from L. *manifestus* (prob. *mani-*, *manu*, *manus*, hand, *festus*, struck, cogn. with DEFEND)], *a.* Not concealed; plainly apparent, clear, obvious; *detected. *v.t.* To make manifest, to show clearly; to display, to exhibit, to evince; to be evidence of; to reveal or exhibit (itself); to record in a ship's manifest. *v.i.* To make a public demonstration of opinion; (*Spiritualism*) to reveal its presence (of a spirit). *n.* A list of a ship's cargo for the use of the custom-house officers; *a manifesto. **manifestable**, *a.* **manifestation** (-tā′ shŭn), *n.* **manifestative** (-fes′ tȧ tiv), *a.* **manifester**, *n.* **manifestly**, *adv.* **manifestness**, *n.*

manifesto (măn i fes′ tō) [It.], *n.* (*pl.* **-tos**) A public declaration, esp. by a government, sovereign, or other authoritative body, of opinions, motives, or intentions. **v.i.* To issue a manifesto.

manifold (măn′ i fōld) [A.-S. *manigfeald*], *a.* Of various forms or kinds; many and various, abundant; shown, applied, or acting in various ways. *n.* That which is manifold; (*Phil.*) a sum or aggregate of sense-impressions, etc.; (*Math.*) manifoldness; a copy made by a manifold writer; (*Mach. etc.*) a tube or system of tubes for conveying steam, gas, etc., in an engine, motor, etc. *v.t.* To multiply, esp. by a manifold writer. **manifold writer:** An apparatus for making several copies of a document at once. **manifolder**, *n.* **manifoldly**, *adv.* **manifoldness**, *n.* The state of being manifold; (*Math.*) a conception of space or magnitude comprehending several particular concepts.

manikin (măn′ i kin) [Dut. *manneken*, dim. of *man* (cp. F. *mannequin*)], *n.* A little man, a dwarf; an anatomical model exhibiting the parts, organs, and structure of the human body; a lay figure; a small tropical American passerine bird.

Manila, Manilla (1) (mȧ nil′ ȧ) [capital of Philippine Islands], *n.* A kind of cheroot made at Manila; Manila hemp; a rope of this. **Manilla hemp:** Hemp made from the fibre of *Musa textilis*, used for making rope. **Manila man**, *n.* (*Austral. colloq.*) A native of the East Indies. **Manilla paper:** A strong brown paper.

manilla (2) (mȧ nil′ ȧ) [Sp., from It. *maniglia* (perh. dim. of L. *manus*, hand, or from *monīlia*, pl. of *monīle*, necklace)], *n.* A metal ring worn by Africans on the legs or arms; a piece of metal shaped like a ring horseshoe used as a medium of exchange among the natives of the West African coast.

manille (mȧ nil′) [corr. of Sp. *malilla*, dim. of *mala*, L. *malus*, bad], *n.* In ombre or quadrille, the highest but one trump or honour.

manioc (măn′ i ok) [Port., from Tupi-Guarani], *n.* The cassava, *Manihot utilissima*; meal made from the root of this.

maniple (măn′ i pėl) [O.F., from L. *manipulus*, handful (*mani-*, *manus*, *-pulus*, form of root *plē-*, to fill, as in *plēnus*, full)], *n.* (*Eccles.*) A strip worn as a eucharistic vestment on the left arm; (*Rom. Ant.*) a subdivision of the Roman legion consisting of 60 or 120 men with their officers; *a handful. **manipular** (1) (mȧ nip′ ū lȧr), *a.*

maniplies [MANYPLIES].

manipulate (mȧ nip′ ū lāt) [prob. from MANIPULATION, from F. *manipuler*, from L. *manipulus*, see MANIPLE], *v.t.* To operate on with or as with the hands, to handle, to treat, esp. skilfully or dexterously; to manage, influence, or tamper with by artful means. *v.i.* To use the hands skilfully, as in scientific experiments etc. **manipular** (2), *a.* **manipulation** (-lā′ shŭn), *n.* **manipulative, -tory** (mȧ nip′ ū lȧ tiv, -tȯr i), *a.* **manipulator**, *n.*

manis (mā′ nis) [mod. L., prob. from MANES], *n.* (*Zool.*) A genus of edentate mammals, containing the scaly ant-eaters.

manitou (măn′ i too) [Algonkin *manitu*], *n.* Among certain American Indians a spirit or being endowed with supernatural power; an amulet, a fetish.

mankind, manlike, etc. [MAN].

manna (măn′ ȧ) [late L. and Gr., from Heb. *mān* (said to be from Heb. *mān hu*, what is this?; but more prob. the same as Arab. *mann*, applied to Hebrew or Persian manna)], *n.* The food miraculously supplied to the Israelites in the wilderness; (*fig.*) divine food, spiritual nourishment, as the Eucharist; a sweetish exudation, of a slightly laxative nature, from certain species of ash, chiefly *Fraxinus ornus*. **Hebrew, Jews', or Persian manna, or manna of Mount Sinai:** An exudation from an Arabian variety of tamarisk, *Tamarix Gallica*. **manna-croup**, *n.* Underground granular wheat-meal, separated by bolting. **manniferous** (mȧ nif′ ėr ŭs) [-FEROUS], *a.* **manna gum**, *n.* (*Austral.*) Dried sap of the Eucalyptus, lerp.

mannequin (măn′ ė kin) [Fr., a lay figure], *n.* A woman employed to wear and display clothes.

manner (măn′ ėr) [O.F. *maniere*, from L. *manuārius*, pertaining to the hand, from *manus*, hand], *n.* The mode in which anything is done or happens; method, style, mannerism; practice, habit, use, custom; demeanour, bearing, address; sort, kind; (*pl.*) conduct in social intercourse, behaviour, deportment; politeness, habits showing good breeding; general modes of life, social conditions. **in a manner:** In a certain way, somewhat, so to speak. **to the manner born:** (*Shak.*) Born to follow a certain practice or custom; accustomed to something from birth. **what manner of:** What kind of. **mannered**, *a.* Having manners (*usu. in comb.*, as *ill-mannered*); having or betraying mannerism, affected. **mannerism**, *n.* Excessive adherence to the same manner or peculiarity; peculiarity of style. **mannerist**, *n.* **manneristic, -al** (-is′ tik, -ȧl), *a.* **mannerless**, *a.* Devoid of manners or breeding. **mannerly**, *a.* **adv.* **mannerliness**, *n.*

mannikin [MANIKIN]. **mannish**, *etc.* [MAN].

mannite (măn′ īt), *n.* (*Chem.*) A sweetish substance obtained from manna. **mannitose** (-i tōs), *n.*

manoao (mȧ nō′ ō) [Maori], *n.* The yellow pine of N. Zealand.

manœuvre (mȧ noo′ vėr) [F., from late L. *manopera*, from *manoperāre*, L. *manū operārī* (*manū*, abl. of *manus*, hand, *operārī*, to work)], *n.* A tactical movement or change of position by troops or warships; (*pl.*) tactical exercises in imitation of war; (*fig.*) skilful or artful management; a trick, a stratagem. *v.i.* To perform manœuvres; to manage with skill; to employ stratagem. *v.t.* To cause (troops) to perform manœuvres; to move, drive, or effect by means of strategy or skilful management; to manipulate. **manœuvrer**, *n.*

manometer (mȧ nom′ ė tėr) [F. *manomètre* (Gr. *manos*, thin, rare, -METER)], *n.* An instrument for measuring the pressure of a gas. **manometric** (-met′ rik), *a.*

manor (măn′ ȯr) [O.F. *manoir*, mansion, from L. *manēre*, to remain, dwell], *n.* A landed estate consisting of a demesne and certain rights over lands held by freehold tenants etc., orig. a barony held by a lord and subject to the jurisdiction of his court-baron; (*Am.*) a tract of land occupied in perpetuity or for long terms by tenants who pay a fee-farm rent to the proprietor; (*slang*) a police district. **lord of the manor:** A person or corporation holding the rights of a manor. **manor-house**, *n.* **manorial** (mȧ nôr′ i ȧl), *a.* Pertaining to a manor.

mansard roof (măn′ sȧrd roof) [F. *mansarde* after F. *Mansard* (1598–1666), French architect], *n.* A roof with two sets of rafters on each side, the lower nearly vertical, the upper much inclined, giving space for attics.

manse (măns) [med. L. *mansa*, a house, a farm, from *manēre*, to dwell, p.p. *mansus*], *n.* The residence of a clergyman, esp. a Presbyterian minister.

mansion (măn' shŭn) [O.F., from L. *mansiōnem*, nom. *-sio*, as prec.], *n.* A residence of considerable size and pretensions; a manor-house; (*pl.*) a large building or set of buildings divided into residential flats; (*poet.*) an abiding-place, a place of abode. **mansion-house,** *n.* A manor-house; an official residence, esp. of the Lord Mayors in London and Dublin. ***mansionry,** *n.*

manslaughter (măn' slaw tėr), *n.* The killing of a human being or beings; (*Law*) the unlawful killing of a person but without malice.

***mansuete** (măn' swēt, măn swēt') [L. *mansuētus*, p.p. of *mansuescere*, to tame (*manus*, hand, *suescere*, to accustom)], *a.* Tame, gentle. ***mansuetude** (măn' swė tūd), *n.*

mantel (măn' tėl) [var. of MANTLE], *n.* The ornamental facing around a fire-place with the shelf above it. **mantel-board,** *n.* A mantelshelf or a shelf resting on it, formerly draped. **mantelpiece,** *n.* A mantel; a mantel-tree. **mantelshelf,** *n.* The shelf above a fire-place. ***mantel-tree,** *n.* The beam forming the lintel of a fire-place.

mantelet (măn' tlet) [O.F., dim. of prec.], *n.* A short mantle; a bullet-proof shield, enclosure, or shelter.

mantic (măn' tik) [Gr. *mantikos*, from *mantis*, prophet], *a.* Pertaining to prophecy or divination.

manticore (măn' ti kôr) [L. *manticora*, Gr. *mantivhōras*, *mantichoras*, prob. from O.Pers.], *n.* A fabulous monster with a human head, a lion's body, and the tail of a scorpion.

mantilla (măn til' ȧ) [Sp., dim. of *manta*, MANTLE], *n.* A woman's light cloak or cape, esp. a veil for the head and shoulders, worn in Spain and Italy.

mantis (măn' tis) [Gr., prophet], *n.* A genus of carnivorous orthopterous insects, which hold their forelegs as if in prayer whilst lying in wait for other insects as prey.

mantissa (măn tis' ȧ) [L., make-weight], *n.* (*Math.*) The decimal or fractional part of a logarithm.

mantle (1) (măn' tel) [O.F. *mantel* (F. *manteau*), L. *mantellum*, whence also A.-S. *mentel*], *n.* A sleeveless cloak or loose outer garment; (*fig.*) a covering; a conical or tubular network coated with refractory earth placed round a gas-jet to give an incandescent light; (*Anat. and Zool.*) a covering or concealing skin, part, or organ, as the fold enclosing the viscera in the mollusca.

mantle (2) (măn' tel), *v.t.* To clothe in or as in a mantle; to cover, to envelop, to conceal; to suffuse. *v.i.* To be overspread or suffused (as with a blush); to suffuse the cheeks (of a blush); to become covered or coated (of liquids); to stretch the wings (as a hawk on its perch). **mantling,** *a.* Foaming, creamy, suffusing. *n.* Material for mantles; (*Her.*) drapery or scroll-work round an achievement. **mantlet** [MANTELET].

Manton (măn' tŏn) [Joseph *Manton* (*c.* 1766–1835), gunsmith], *n.* A fowling-piece made by Manton.

mantra (măn' trȧ) [Sansk., from *man*, to think], *n.* A Hindu formula or charm; a Vedic hymn of praise.

***mantua** (măn' tū ȧ) [corr. of F. *manteau*, MANTLE, confused with *Mantua* in Italy], *n.* A woman's loose gown worn in the 17th and 18th centuries. **mantua-maker,** *n.* A dressmaker.

manual (1) (măn' ū ăl) [F. *manuel*, L. *manuālis*, from *manus*, hand], *a.* Pertaining to or performed with the hands. **sign manual** [SIGN]. **manual alphabet** [FINGER ALPHABET]. **manual exercise:** (*Mil.*) The drill by which soldiers are taught to handle their rifles etc. properly. **manually,** *adv.*

manual (2) (măn' ū ăl), *n.* A small book or handy compendium, a handbook; a fire-engine worked by hands; a service book, esp. that used by priests in the mediæval Church; an organ keyboard played by the hands. **manual engine:** A fire-engine worked by hand.

manubrium (mȧ nū' bri ŭm) [L., a haft, from *manus*, hand], *n.* (*pl.* **-bria, -briums**) (*Anat. and Zool.*) A handle-like part or process, as the presternum in mammals, the peduncle hanging from the umbrella in medusæ; the handle of an organ-stop.

manucode (măn' ū cōd), *n.* The Australian rifle-bird or bird of paradise.

manufacture (măn ū făk' tyŭr, -chŭr) [F., from L. *manū*, by hand, abl of *manus*, hand, *factūra*, from *facere*, to make], *n.* The making of articles by means of labour or machinery, esp. on a large scale; industrial production; any particular branch of this; (*pl.*) the products of industry or any particular industry. *v.t.* To make or work up into suitable forms for use; to produce or fashion by labour or machinery, esp. on a large scale; (*fig.*) to produce (pictures, literature, etc.) in a mechanical way; to fabricate, to invent (a story, evidence, etc.). *v.i.* To be occupied in manufacture. **manufactory** (măn ū făk' tŏr i), *n.* ***manufactural,** *a.* **manufacturer,** *n.*

manuka (măn' ū kȧ) [Maori], *n.* The N. Zealand tea-tree.

manumit (măn ū mit') [L. *manūmittere* (*manū*, abl. of *manus*, hand, *mittere*, to send)], *v.t.* (*past & p.p.* **manumitted**) To release from slavery. **manumission,** *n.*

manumotor (măn ū mō' tŏr) [L. *manū*, as prec.], *n.* A wheeled carriage worked by the hands of the rider. **manumotive,** *a.*

manure (mȧ nūr') [corr. of MANŒUVRE], *v.t.* To enrich (a soil) with fertilizing substances. *n.* Any substance, as dung, compost, or chemical preparations, used to fertilize land. ***manurance,** *n.* Manuring; cultivation or tillage; (*Law*) tenure or occupation. **manurer,** *n.* **manurial,** *a.*

manuscript (măn' ū skript) [med. L. *manuscriptus* (*manū*, abl. of *manus*, hand, *scriptus*, p.p. of *scrībere*, to write)], *a.* Written by hand. *n.* A book or document written by hand, opp. to printed.

manward [MAN].

Manx (măngks) [earlier *Maniske*, Icel. *manskr*], *a.* Pertaining to the Isle of Man or its inhabitants. *n.* The Celtic language spoken by natives of Man; the people of the Isle of Man. **Manx cat:** A tailless variety of domestic cat. **Manxman, -woman,** *n.*

many (men' i) [A.-S. *manig* (cp. Dut. *menig*, Dan. *mange*, G. *manch*)], *a.* Numerous; comprising a great number. *n.* A multitude; a great number. **the many:** The majority; the multitude, the common crowd. **too many:** Superfluous, not wanted, in the way; (*colloq.*) too clever, too able or skilful (*for*). **many-headed,** *a.* (*fig.*) Fickle (of the populace). **many-headedness,** *n.* **many-sided,** *a.* Having many sides, aspects, etc.; (*fig.*) widely sympathetic, versatile, liberal. **many-sidedness,** *n.*

manyplies (men' i plīz) [MANY, *plies*, pl. of PLY (1)], *n.* The third stomach of a ruminant, the omasum.

Manzanilla (măn zȧ nil' ȧ) [Sp., camomile], *n.* A dry brown sherry with a bitter flavour.

Maori (mour' i) [native word], *n.* One of the Polynesian original inhabitants of New Zealand; their language. *a.* Pertaining to them. **Maori chief,** *n.* A N. Zealand flat fish. **Maori hen,** *n.* The flightless wood hen of N. Zealand. **Maoriland,** *n.* New Zealand. **Maorilander,** *n.* A white person native of New Zealand.

map (măp) [L. *mappa*, orig. napkin], *n.* A representation of a portion of the earth's surface, or the heavens, upon a plane; (*fig.*) any delineation. *v.t.* (*past & p.p.* **mapped**) To represent or se down in a map; to plan (out) in exact detail. **off the map,** *adv.* (*colloq.*) Of no account, not worth consideration, remote; out-of-the-way. ***mapless,** *a.* **maplike,** *a.* **mapper, mappist,** *n.* ***mappery,** *n.*

maple (mā′ pėl) [A.-S. in *mapulder* and *mapeltrēow*], *n.* A tree or shrub of the genus *Acer*; the wood of this. **maple-sugar,** *n.* A coarse sugar obtained from *Acer saccharinum* and other maples.

maqui (mȧ kē′) [Chilian Sp.], *n.* A Chilian evergreen shrub, the berries of which produce a wine used in adulteration.

maquis (ma′ kē) [Fr.], *n.* Scrub or bush in Corsica; (*fig.*) the name taken by those surreptitiously resisting the German invaders of France etc., in 1940–45.

mar (mar) [A.-S. *merran* (cp. M.Dut. *merren,* to hinder, Dut. *marren,* to tarry)], *v.t.* To spoil, to ruin; to disfigure. *n.* A blemish, a drawback.

marabou (măr′ ȧ boo) [from foll.], *n.* A West African stork, *Leptoptilus marabou,* the downy feathers from under the wings and tail of which are used for trimming hats etc.; the adjutant-bird.

marabout (măr′ ȧ boot) [F., from Port. *marabuto,* Arab. *murābit*], *n.* A Mohammedan hermit or saint, esp. one of a priestly caste in N. Africa; the tomb or dwelling of such a saint.

maranatha [ANATHEMA].

maraschino (măr ȧ skē′ nō) [It., adj. from *marasca, amarasca,* a sharp black cherry, from *amaro,* L. *amārus,* bitter], *n.* A cordial or liqueur distilled from bitter cherries grown in Dalmatia.

marasmus (mȧ răz′ mŭs) [Gr. *marasmos,* from *marainein,* to wither away], *n.* (*Path.*) Wasting away of the body. **marasmic,** *a.*

Marathon (mă′ rȧ thon) [*Marathon,* in Greece], *n.* A long foot-race in the Olympic Games; a contest requiring great endurance.

maraud (mȧ rawd′) [F. *marauder,* from *maraud,* rogue, etym. doubtful], *v.i.* To rove in quest of plunder; to make a raid (on). *v.t.* To plunder. ****n.*** A raid, a foray. **marauder,** *n.*

***maravedi** (măr ȧ vā′ di) [Sp., from Arab. *Murābitīn,* pl. of *murābit,* MARABOUT, the name of a Moorish dynasty at Cordova (1087–1147)], *n.* A Spanish copper coin worth less than a farthing; a Spanish gold coin worth about 14s.

marble (mar′ bėl) [O.F. *marbre,* L. *marmor,* cogn. with Gr. *marmaros,* sparkling *marmairein,* to sparkle, to glisten], *n.* A fine-grained or crystalline limestone capable of taking a fine polish; a piece of sculpture in this material (*usu. in pl.*); (*fig.*) a type of smoothness, hardness, or inflexibility; a small ball of marble, glass, or other hard substance used as a toy. *v.t.* To stain or vein (end-papers of books etc.) to look like marble. *a.* Composed of marble; veined like marble; (*fig.*) hard, unfeeling; *pure, pellucid. **marble-edged,** *a.* Marbled. **marble-hearted,** *a.* Hard-hearted. **marbleize,** *v.t.* (*Am.*) **marbler,** *n.* **marbly,** *a.*

marc (mark) [F. *marcher,* to tread], *n.* The compressed residue of grapes left after pressing, in the making of wine or oil; liqueur-brandy made from this.

***marcantant** [corr. of It. *mercatante,* MERCHANT], *n.* (*Shak.*) A merchant.

marcasite (mar′ kȧ sīt) [med. L. *marcasīta,* etym. doubtful], *n.* Pyrites, esp. a white orthorhombic form of iron pyrites, used for making ornaments.

marcel (mar sĕl′) [*Marcel,* a French hairdresser], *n.* A style of permanent wave hairdressing. **marcel wave,** *n.* A permanent wave.

marcescent (mar ses′ ėnt) [L. *marcescēns -ntem,* pres.p. of *marcescere,* freq. of *marcēre,* to wither], *a.* (*Bot.*) Withering without falling (of blooms, leaves, etc.). **marcescence,** *n.* ***marcescible,** *a.*

march (1) (march) [F. *marche,* MARK (1)], *n.* (*pl.* **-ches)** The frontier or boundary of a territory; a borderland or debatable land between two countries (*often in pl.,* as the border country of England and Wales). *v.i.* To border (upon) or have a common frontier (with). **marcher,** *n.* An officer or warden having jurisdiction over marches; an inhabitant of a march. **Lord Marcher:** (*pl.* **Lords Marchers)** Lords holding jurisdiction and privileges on the Welsh border. **marchman,** *n.*

march (2) (march) [F. *marcher,* etym. doubtful], *v.i.* To move with regular steps as soldiers; to walk in a grave deliberate manner. *v.t.* To cause to move (on, off, etc.) in military order. *n.* The act of marching; a stately, deliberate, or measured movement, esp. of soldiers; the distance marched in a day; (*fig.*) progress, advance; (*Mus.*) a composition for accompanying a march. **march past:** A marching of troops in a review past a superior officer etc.

March (3) (march) [A.-F. *marche* (F. *mars*), from L. *Martium,* nom. *-tius,* pertaining to Mars], *n.* The third month of the year. **March chick:** A precocious young person.

Marchantia (mar kăn′ ti ȧ) [Nicholas *Marchant* (*fl.* 17th cent.), French botanist], *n.pl.* (*Bot.*) A genus of *Hepaticæ* or liverworts.

marchioness (mar′ shŏ nės) [low L. *marchiōnissa,* from *marchio -ōnem,* MARQUESS], *n.* The wife or widow of a marquess, or a woman holding this rank in her own right.

marchpane (march′ pān), **marzipan** (mar′ zi păn) [F. *marcepain* (now *massepain*), etym. doubtful, cp. It. *marciapane,* G. *marzipan*], *n.* A confection of almonds, sugar, and white of egg.

***marcid** (mar′ sid) [L. *marcidus*], *a.* Wasted, withered; causing wasting (as fever). ***marcidity** (-sid′ i ti), *n.*

marconigram (mar kō′ ni grăm) [Guglielmo *Marconi* (1874–1937), inventor, -GRAM], *n.* A message sent by the Marconi system of wireless telegraphy.

mare (mâr) [A.-S. *mere* (cp. Dut. *merrie,* Icel. *merr,* G. *mähre*)], *n.* The female of the horse or other equine animal. **mare's-nest,** *n.* A discovery that turns out a hoax or a delusion. **mare's-tail,** *n.* An aquatic plant, *Hippuris vulgaris*; long fibrous cirrus-clouds, supposed to prognosticate rain. **Shanks's mare,** *n.* One's own legs.

maremma (mȧ rem′ ȧ) [It.], *n.* (*pl.* **-me,** -mā) A marshy and usu. malarious region by the sea-shore.

***mareschal** [MARSHAL].

margaric (mar găr′ ik) [Gr. *margar,* in *margaritēs,* pearl, -IC], *a.* (*Chem.*) Pertaining to pearl, pearly. **margarate** (mar′ gȧ rȧt), *n.* A salt of margaric acid. **margarin,** *n.* Margarate of glyceryl.

margarine (mar′ gȧ rin, mar′ gȧ rēn, mar′ jȧ rin, mar′ jȧ rēn) [Fr. *margarin*], *n.* An emulsion of edible oils and fat with water or skimmed milk or other substances with or without the addition of colouring matter, capable of being used for the same purposes as butter.

margarite (mar′ gȧ rīt) [O.F., from L. *margarīta,* as MARGARIC], *n.* *A pearl; (*Min.*) pearl mica, a hydrous silicate. **margaritiferous** (tif′ ėr ŭs), *a.*

margay (mar′ gā) [F., from Tupi *mbaracaīa*], *n.* A Brazilian tiger-cat, *Felis tigrina.*

marge (1) [MARGIN].

marge (2) (marj) [abbr. MARGARINE].

margin (mar′ jin) [L. *margo -ginis*], *n.* An edge, a border, a brink; the blank space round the printed matter on a page; (*fig.*) the space of time or the range of conditions within which a thing is just possible; an allowance of time, money, space, etc., for contingencies, growth, etc.; (*Comm.*) the difference between cost and selling price; a sum deposited with a broker to protect him against loss; (*Polit. Econ.*) the lowest amount of profit allowing an industry etc. to continue. *v.t.* To furnish with a margin; to enter on the margin. *v.i.* To deposit margin on stock. **marginal,** *a.* Of, pertaining to, or at the margin; written or printed on the margin; near the limit; (*Agric.*) difficult to cultivate. **marginal constituency,** *n.* (*Pol.*) A parliamentary constituency where there are less than 3,000 votes between the two leading candidates. **marginalia** (-nā' li à), *n.pl.* Marginal notes. **marginally,** *adv.* **marginate, -ated** (mar' ji nȧt, -nā tėd), *a.* Having a margin; edged. *v.t.* (-nāt) To furnish with a margin. **margination** (-nā' shŭn), *n.*

margrave (mar' grāv) [Dut. *markgrave* (now *markgraaf*) (MARK (1), GRAVE (4))], *n.* Orig. a lord or governor of a march or border province, now a German title of nobility. **margravate** (mar' grȧ vȧt), **margraviate** (mar grā' vi ȧt), *n.* **margravine** (mar' grȧ vēn), *n.* The wife of a margrave.

marguerite (mar' gėr ēt) [F., from L. *margarīta*, Gr. *margaritēs*, from *margaron*, pearl], *n.* The ox-eye daisy and other wild or cultivated varieties of chrysanthemum.

Marian (mâr' i ȧn) [L. *Marīa*, -AN], *a.* Pertaining to the Virgin Mary, to Mary I of England, or Mary Queen of Scots. *n.* An adherent or defender of either of the two last. **Marian year,** *n.* The year as reckoned from beginning on March 25th, the Feast of the Annunciation.

marigold (măr' i gōld) [*Mary*, the Virgin Mary, GOLD], *n.* A plant bearing a bright yellow flower, *Calendula officinalis*; applied to other composite yellow-flowered plants. **marsh marigold** [MARSH].

marijuana (mă ri hwa' nȧ) [Sp.], *n.* Dried leaves of Indian hemp, used to make narcotic cigarettes called reefers.

marimba (mȧ rim' bȧ), *n.* A musical instrument of the nature of a xylophone.

marinade, marinate (măr i nād', -āt) [F., from Sp. *marinada*, from *marinar*, to pickle in brine, from *marino*, as foll.], *n.* A pickle of vinegar flavoured with wine and spices; fish or meat pickled in this. *v.t.* To pickle in marinade.

marine (mȧ rēn') [F. *marin*, fem. *-ine*, L. *marīnus*, from *mare*, the sea], *a.* Pertaining to, found in, or produced by the sea; used at sea or in navigation, nautical, naval; serving on shipboard. *n.* The shipping, fleet, or navy of a country; (*pl.*) troops for service on board warships; (*Mil.*) a member of the Royal Marines; a specialist in commando and amphibious operations. **horse-marine** [HORSE]. **mercantile marine:** (*collect.*) The merchant shipping of a country. **tell it to the marines:** An expression of incredulity and derision (from the sailor's contempt for landsmen). **marine glue:** A glue made of rubber, shellac and oil which resists the action of water. **marine store:** A place where old ship's stores are bought and sold; (*pl.*) old ship's materials as articles of merchandise. **mariner** (măr' i nėr), *n.* A seaman, a sailor. **master mariner:** The captain of a merchant ship.

Marinism (mȧ rē' nizm) [Giambattista *Marini* (1569–1625), Italian poet, -ISM], *n.* Excessive literary ornateness and affectation. **Marinist,** *n.*

Mariolatry (mâr i ol' ȧ tri) [Gr. *Maria*, Mary, -LATRY], *n.* Idolatrous worship of the Virgin Mary.

marionette (măr i ȯ net') [F. *marionnette*, dim of *Marion*, dim. of *Marie*, Mary], *n.* A puppet moved by strings on a mimic stage.

mariput (măr' i pŭt) [native name], *n.* The African zoril, *Zorilla Capensis*.

***marish** (măr' ish) [O.F. *mareis*, *maresche*, med. L. *mariscus*, MARSH], *n.* A marsh. *a.* Marshy.

Marist (mâr' ist), *n.* A member of the R.-C. congregation of Mary for teaching and foreign missions. *a.* Pertaining or devoted to this or to the Virgin Mary.

marital (măr' i tȧl) [F., from L. *marītālis*, from *marītus*, husband], *a.* Pertaining to a husband or to wedded life. **maritally,** *adv.*

maritime (măr' i tīm) [F., from L. *maritimus* (*mare*, the sea, *-timus*, cp. *ultimus*)], *a.* Pertaining to, connected with, or bordering on the sea; having a navy or commerce by sea (of countries, cities, etc.).

marjoram (mar' jȯ rȧm) [O.F. *marjorane*, med. L. *majorāna*, etym. doubtful], *n.* A herb of the genus *Origanum* of the mint family, esp. *O. vulgare*, the wild marjoram, and *O. majorana*, sweet marjoram, a fragrant plant used as a pot-herb.

mark (1) (mark) [A.-S. *mearc* (cp. Dut. *mark*, neut. *merk*, Icel. *mark*, G. *mark*, neut. *marke*, O.Teut. *markā*), whence *mearcian*, to mark], *n.* A visible sign or impression, as a stroke, cut, dot, etc.; an indication, symbol, character, brand, device, or token; a target, an object to aim at; the point to be reached; a limit, a standard; a distinguishing sign, a seal, etc.; a character made by one who cannot write; a number or sign indicating merit in an examination; a distinguishing feature, a characteristic, a symptom; (*Boxing*) the pit of the stomach; (*Rugby*) an indentation made by the heel of a player who has secured a fair catch; *a tract of land held in common by the ancient Teutonic community; a boundary, frontier, or limit. *v.t.* To make a mark on; to distinguish or designate or indicate, by a mark or marks; to select, to single out; to pay heed to; to indicate or serve as a mark to; to characterize, to be a feature of; to express or produce by marks; to record (points in games); to award (merit in examination); (*Football*) to keep close to an opponent so as to be ready to tackle him. *v.i.* To observe something critically, to take note. **below the** or **not up to the mark:** Not equal to a desired standard. **beside** or **wide of the mark:** Not hitting the object: (*fig.*) not to the point, irrelevant. **man of mark:** A distinguished or famous man. **mark down, up,** *v.t.* To lower or raise the price. **save the mark:** An exclamation of irony, deprecation, or contempt, perh. orig. used in archery. **to mark out:** (*Build.*) To set out boundaries and levels for a proposed building; (*Eng.*) to set out lines and marks on material as a guide for cutting, drilling or other operations. **to mark time:** To move the feet alternately as in marching, without changing position. **to toe the mark:** To touch a chalk line with the toes so as to be in rank abreast with others; (*fig.*) to do one's duty, to perform one's obligations. **markedly,** *adv.* **markedness,** *n.* **marker,** *n.* One who marks; a counter used in card-playing; one who notes the score at billiards; a book-mark.

mark (2) (mark) [A.-S. *marc* (Icel. *mörk*, Dan., Swed., Dut., and G. *mark*)], *n.* The name of several coins of various values, that of Germany about 1s. 8d.; (*Hist.*) English money of account valued at 13s. 4d.; a unit of weight (about ½ or ⅔ lb.) formerly used for gold and silver, still used abroad but gradually becoming superseded by the metric system.

market (mar' kėt) [late A.-S. and O.North.F. (F. *marché*), from L. *mercātum*, nom. *-tus*, p.p. of *mercārī*, to trade (cp. MERCANTILE)], *n.* A meeting for buying and selling; the place for this; an open space or large building in which cattle, provisions, or other commodities are offered for sale; a county or locality regarded as a place for buying and selling commodities in general or a particular form of merchandise; (*fig.*) demand for a commodity, value as determined by this. *v.i.* To buy or sell in a market. *v.t.* To sell in a market. **to come into** or **put on the market:** To be offered or to offer for sale. ***market-bell,** *n.* A bell rung at the beginning of a market. **market-cross,** *n.* A cross set up in a market-place. **market-day,** *n.* **market-garden,** *n.* A garden in which vegetables and fruit are raised for market. **market-gardener,** *n.* **market overt:** Open market. **market-place,** *n.* **market-price, -rate,** *n.* **market town,** *n.* A town having the privilege of holding a public market. **marketable,** *a.* **marketability** (-bil' i ti). **marketableness,** *n.* **marketably,** *adv.* **marketer,** *n.*

markhor (mar' kôr) [Pers. *mārkhōr*, serpent-eater], *n.* A wild mountain goat, *Capra Falconeri*, inhabiting the border-land of India, Persia, and Tibet.

marking (mar' king), *a.* Producing a mark. *n.* Marks or colouring, esp. on natural objects. **marking-ink,** *n.* An indelible ink for marking linen etc. **marking-nut,** *n.* The nut of *Semecarpus anacardium,* the juice of which produces an indelible ink.

marksman, *markman (marks'-, mark' mȧn), *n.* One skilled in aiming at a mark; one who shoots well. **marksmanship,** *n.*

marl (marl) [O.F. *marle,* late L. *margila,* dim. of *marga,* perh. from Gaulish], *n.* Clay containing much calcareous matter, much used as a fertilizer; (*poet.*) earth. *v.t.* To manure with marl. **marl-pit,** *n.* **marlstone,** *n.* (*Geol.*) Sandy, calcareous and ferruginous strata dividing the upper from the lower Lias clays. **marlaceous** (mar lā' shŭs), **marly,** *a.* **marlite** (mar' līt), *n.* (*Min.*) A variety of marl that remains solid after exposure to the air. **marlitic** (-lit' ik), *a.*

marline (mar' lin) [Dut. *marlijn* (*marren,* to tie, LINE (1))], *n.* (*Naut.*) A small two-stranded line, used for lashing, etc. **marline-spike,** *n.* A pointed iron pin for opening the strands of rope in splicing.

marmalade (mar' mȧ lād) [F. *marmelade,* Port. *marmelada* (*marmelo,* quince, L. *melimēlum,* Gr. *melimēlon,* from *meli,* honey, and *mēlon,* apple)], *n.* A jam or preserve prepared from fruit, esp. oranges or lemons, boiled with the sliced rind.

marmarize, etc. [MARMOREAL].

marmolite (mar mō līt) [from Gr. *marmairein,* to shine, -LITE], *n.* (*Min.*) A laminated variety of serpentine of a pearly green colour.

marmoreal, -ean (mar môr' ē ȧl, -ȧn) [L. *marmoreus,* from *marmor,* MARBLE], *a.* Like marble, esp. cold, smooth or polished, pure white; made of marble. **marmoraceous** (mō rā' shŭs), *a.* ***marmorate, *-rated** (mar' mō rȧt, -rā tėd), *a.* **marmarize,** *v.t.* (*Geol.*) To convert (limestone) into marble by metamorphism. **marmarosis** (-rō' sis), *n.* This process.

marmose (mar mōs) [F., ult. from foll.], *n.* One of various S. American pouchless opossums, as *Didelphys dorsigera* or *D. murina.*

marmoset (mar' mō zet) [O.F., a grotesque image (etym. doubtful, prob. conn. with *marmot,* a little child)], *n.* A small tropical American monkey of various species belonging to the *Hapalidæ,* called squirrel-monkeys from their bushy tails.

marmot (mar' mȯt) [F. *marmotte,* Romansch *murmont* (L. *mūrem,* nom. *mūs,* MOUSE, *montis,* gen. of *mons,* MOUNTAIN)], *n.* A squirrel-like rodent about the size of a rabbit, esp. *Arctomys marmotta,* the Alpine marmot.

marocain (ma' ro kān) [F. *maroquin,* fr. *Maroc,* Morocco], *n.* (*Textiles*) A cloth similar in structure to crêpe de Chine, but made from coarser yarns.

Maronite (măr' ō nīt) [late L. *Marōnīta,* from *Marōn,* a Syrian monk (5th cent.) the founder, or the patriarch of the same name (7th cent.)], *n.* A member of a Christian sect whose home is the Lebanon region.

maroon (1) (mȧ roon') [F. *marron,* It. *marrone,* chestnut, etym. unknown], *a.* Of a brownish-crimson colour. *n.* This colour; a detonating firework.

maroon (2) (mȧ roon') [F. *marron,* fugitive, corr. of Sp. *cimarron,* savage, etym. doubtful (perh. from *cima,* mountain-top, L. *cȳma,* Gr. *kūma,* wave)], *n.* One of a class of Negroes in the West Indies and Guiana, orig. fugitive slaves and their descendants; one who has been marooned. *v.t.* To put ashore and abandon on a desolate island. *v.i.* (*Am.*) To picnic or camp out; to loaf, to hang about. **marooner,** *n.*

maroquin (măr' ō kin) [F., adj., from *Maroc,* Morocco], *n.* Morocco leather.

marplot (mar' plot), *n.* One who by officious interference spoils a plot or undertaking.

marque (mark) [O.F., from Prov. *marca,* from *marcar,* to seize, perh. rel. to MARK (1)], *n.* **letter of marque** [LETTER].

marquee (mar kē') [from MARQUISE, regarded as pl.], *n.* A large field-tent.

marquetry (mar' kėt ri) [F. *marqueterie* from *marqueter,* to inlay, to spot, from *marquer,* to MARK (1)], *n.* Work inlaid with different pieces of fine wood, ivory, plates of metal, steel, etc.

marquis, marquess (mar' kwis, -kwės) [O.F. *marchis* (F. *marquis*), low L. *marchensis,* warden or prefect of the marches, from *marcha,* MARCH (1), MARK (1)], *n.* A title or rank of nobility in England, ranking next below a duke and above an earl. **marquessate, marquisate,** *n.* ***marquise*** (mar kēz') [F.], *n.* A marchioness; a marquise-ring; *a large tent, a marquee. **marquise-ring,** *n.* A finger-ring set with gems in a pointed oval cluster.

Marquoi's scale (mar' kwoiz skāl') [prob. from F. *marquoir,* a marker], *n.* An instrument for drawing equidistant parallel lines.

marram (mă' rȧm) [O.N. *marr,* sea; *halmr,* haulm], *n.* Bent-grass.

marriage (măr' ȧj) [F. *mariage,* low L. *marītāticum,* from *maritus,* husband, see MARITAL], *n.* The legal union of a man and woman, wedlock; the act or ceremony of marrying, a wedding, a nuptial celebration; (*fig.*) sexual union; close conjunction or union; (*Cards*) the declaration of a king and queen of the same suit. **civil marriage:** A marriage carried out by civil contract before a public officer, without religious ceremony. **communal marriage:** (*Anthrop.*) A system by which the women of a tribe are married to all the men. **companionate marriage,** *n.* Trial marriage without marriage ceremony. **Gretna Green marriage:** A marriage at Gretna Green, a border village in Dumfriesshire where eloping couples were formerly married; a runaway marriage. **marriage articles** or **contract:** A contract embodying the marriage settlement made before marriage. **marriage favour** [WEDDING-FAVOUR]. **marriage licence:** A licence for the solemnization of a marriage without the proclamation of banns. **marriage lines:** (*colloq.*) A marriage certificate. **marriage settlement:** An arrangement made before marriage securing a provision for the wife and sometimes for future children. **marriageable,** *a.* Fit or of age for marriage; (*Bot., etc.*), suitable for close union.

married (măr' id), *a.* United in marriage; pertaining to married persons, conjugal.

marrow (1) (măr' ō) [A.-S. *mearg* (cp. Dut. *merg,* Icel. *mergr,* G. *mark*)], *n.* A fatty substance contained in the cavities of bones; (*fig.*) the essence, the pith; the pulpy interior of a fruit etc.; a vegetable marrow. **marrow-bone,** *n.* A bone containing marrow; (*pl.*) the knees. **marrowfat,** *n.* A large variety of pea. **marrowless,** *a.* **marrowy,** *a.*

***marrow** (2) (măr' ō) [etym. doubtful], *n.* (*chiefly Sc.*) A match, a mate, a partner; a husband or wife; one's equal or peer; one of a pair.

marry (1) (măr' i) [F. *marier,* L. *marītāre,* from L. *marītus,* husband, see MARITAL], *v.t.* To unite as man and wife; to give in marriage; to take for one's husband or wife; (*fig.*) to join closely together, to unite intimately. *v.i.* To enter into the state of wedlock.

***marry** (2) (măr' i) [corr. of *Mary,* the Virgin], *int.* Indeed, forsooth.

Mars (marz) [L.], *n.* The Roman god of war; (*fig.*) war; (*Astron.*) the fourth planet in order of distance from the sun.

Marsala (mar sa' lȧ), *n.* A white wine somewhat like sherry, made at Marsala in Sicily.

Marseillaise (mar sė lāz', mar sā lyā) [F.], *n.* The national hymn of the French Republic, composed by Rouget de l'Isle and introduced into Paris by the Marseillaise contingent in 1792.

Marseilles (mar sālz′) [seaport in France], *n.* A stiff and heavy cotton fabric quilted in the loom.

marsh (marsh) [A.-S. *mersc*, *merisc*, from Teut. *mari-* MERE (1) (cp. MARISH)], *n.* A tract of low land covered wholly or partially with water. **marsh-fire, -light,** *n.* A will-o'-the-wisp. **marsh-gas,** *n.* Carburetted hydrogen evolved from stagnant water. **marsh harrier:** A hawk, *Circus æruginosus.* **marsh-mallow,** *n.* A shrubby herb, *Althæa officinalis*, growing near salt marshes; a confection made from its root. **marsh marigold:** A ranunculaceous plant, *Caltha palustris*, with bright yellow flowers, growing in marshy places. **marshy,** *a.* **marshiness,** *n.*

marshal (mar′ shȧl) [O.F. *mareschal*, O.H.G. *marahscalh*, *marah*, horse, cogn. with MARE, *scalh*, cogn. with A.-S. *sceale*, servant], *n.* An officer regulating ceremonies and directing processions; an officer of state with functions varying by country and period; an earl-marshal; a provost-marshal; (*Foreign*) a military officer of the highest rank; a field-marshal; (*U.S.A.*) a civil officer corresponding to an English sheriff. *v.t.* (*past & p.p.* **marshalled**) To arrange or rank in order; to conduct in a ceremonious manner; (*Her.*) to dispose in order, as the coats in a shield. *v.i.* To assemble, to take up a position (of armies, processions, etc.). **Marshal of the Air,** *n.* (*Aviat.*) The highest rank in the R.A.F., corresponding in rank to Field-Marshal in the Army. ***knight marshal** [KNIGHT]. **marshaller,** *n.* **marshalling yard,** *n.* (*Rail.*) A place where goods trucks are sorted according to their destination, and goods trains made up. ***marshalsea,** [-CY], *n.* A former court and a prison in Southwark controlled by the knight marshal. **marshalship,** *n.*

Marshall aid (mar′ shȧl) [G. C. *Marshall* (1881–1959), U.S. statesman], *n.* Economic aid for war-stricken countries in Europe given by U.S.A. according to a plan initiated by Marshall in 1947.

marsipobranch (mar′ si pō brănk) [Gr. *marsipos*, see foll., *branchia*, gills], *n.* One of the *Marsipobranchii*, vertebrates with sacciform gills, as the lampreys and shags. **marsipobranchiate** (-brăng′ ki ȧt), *a.* and *n.*

marsupial (mar sū′ pi ȧl) [L. *marsūpium*, Gr. *marsupion*, dim. of *marsipos*, purse, bag, -AL], *a.* Of or resembling a pouch; belonging to the *Marsupialia*, carrying the young in a pouch, as the kangaroos and opossums. *n.* Any individual of the *Marsupialia.* ***marsupium,*** *n.* A pouch for carrying the imperfectly developed young of marsupial animals; a pouch-like part or organ in other animals.

mart (mart) [prob. from Dut. *markt*, MARKET], *n.* A market, a market-place; an auction-room; (*fig.*) traffic, purchase and sale.

martagon (mar′ tȧ gȯn) [F., from Turk. *martagān*, a kind of turban], *n.* The Turk's-cap lily, *Lilium martagon.*

***martel** (mar′ tėl) [O.F. (F. *marteau*), from pop. L. (cp. L. *martulus*)], *n.* A hammer. *v.t.* To strike, to hammer.

martello (mar tel′ ō) [corr. of *Mortella*, from a tower at Cape Mortella in Corsica captured by the British in 1793–94], *n.* A martello tower. **martello tower:** A circular, isolated tower of masonry, erected on the coast to oppose the landing of invaders.

marten (mar′ tėn) [M.E. *martren*, O.F. *matrine*, marten's fur, fem. of *matrin*, adj., from *martre*, from O.Teut. *marthuz* (cp. Dut. *marter*, G. *marder*, A.-S. *mearth*)], *n.* A small carnivorous mammal, *Mustela martes*, allied to the weasel, with a valuable fur.

***martext** (mar′ tekst) [MAR, TEXT], *n.* A blundering or ignorant preacher.

martial (mar′ shȧl) [F., from L. *Martiālis*, from MARS], *a.* Pertaining to or suited for war; military; warlike, courageous, bellicose; (*Astrol.* and *Astron.*) under the influence of the planet Mars. **martial law:** Military law abrogating ordinary law for the time being, proclaimed only in time of war, insurrection, or like emergency. **martialism,** *n.* **martialist,** *n.* **martialize,** *v.t.* **martially,** *adv.*

Martian (mar′ shȧn) [L. *Martius*, as prec.], *n.* An inhabitant of the planet Mars.

martin (mar′ tin) [F., St. *Martin*, Bishop of Tours (4th cent.)], *n.* A bird allied to the swallow, *Chelidon urbica.*

martinet (mar ti net′) [Gen. *Martinet*, a very strict officer under Louis XIV], *n.* A strict disciplinarian.

martingale (mar′ ting gāl) [F., etym. doubtful], *n.* A strap fastened to a horse's girth to keep the head down; (*Naut.*) a lower stay for the jib-boom or flying jib-boom; the system of doubling stakes after every loss in gambling.

martini (mar tēn′ i) [name of It. firm], *n.* Italian vermouth; a cocktail based on this.

Martinmas (mar′ tin mȧs), *n.* The feast of St. Martin, 11th Nov. ***Martlemass,** *n.*

martlet (mart′ lėt) [F. *martelet*, prob. corr. of *martinet*, dim. of MARTIN], *n.* A swift, *Cypselus apus*; (*Her.*) a fanciful bird without legs.

martyr (mar′ tėr) [A.-S. and L., from Gr. *martur*, *martus*, a witness], *n.* One who suffers death or persecution in defence of his faith or principles, esp. one of the early Christians who suffered death for their religion. *v.t.* To put to death for adherence to one's religion or principles; to persecute, to torture. **a martyr to:** A continual sufferer from. **martyrdom,** *n.* ***martyrium*** (mar tir′ i ŭm), **martyry** (mar′ tėr i), *n.* A chapel or shrine built in honour of a martyr. **martyrize,** *v.t.* **martyrolatry** (mar tėr ol′ ȧ tri) [-LATRY], *n.* Worship of martyrs. **martyrology** (ol′ ō ji) [-LOGY], *n.* A list or history of martyrs. **martyrological** (-loj′ i kȧl), *a.* **martyrologist,** *n.*

marvel (mar′ vėl) [O.F. *merveille*, L. *mīrābilia*, pl. of *mīrābilis*, wonderful, from *mīrārī*, to wonder, from *mīrus*, wonderful], *n.* A wonderful or astonishing thing; a prodigy; *wonder, astonishment. *v.i.* (*past & p.p.* **marvelled**) To be astonished (at or that); to be curious to know (why etc.). **marvellous,** *a.* and **adv.* **marvellously,** *adv.* **marvellousness,** *n.*

Marxian (mark′ si ȧn) [Karl *Marx* (1818–83), G. Socialist], *a.* Of, or pertaining to Marx. **Marxism** or **Marxianism,** *n.* The theory that human and political motives are at root economic, and that the class struggle explains the events of history; State Socialism as taught by Marx.

Masai (ma sī′) [native name], *n.pl.* A dark Hamito-Negroid people inhabiting British and the former German E. Africa.

mascara (măs car′ ȧ) [Sp., mask], *n.* A cosmetic for eyelashes etc.

marzipan [MARCHPANE].

mascle (măs′ kėl) [F., etym. doubtful, perh. corr. of MACLE], *n.* A lozenge-shaped plate or scale used in 13th-cent. armour; (*Her.*) a lozenge perforated. **mascled, masculy,** *a.*

mascot (măs′ kȯt) [F. prov. *mascotte*, perh. rel. to Prov. *masco*, witch], *n.* An object or person that acts as a talisman and brings luck.

masculine (măs′ kū lin) [F. *masculin*, L. *masculīnus*, see MALE], *a.* Belonging to or having the characteristic qualities of the male sex; strong, robust, vigorous; manly, spirited; mannish, forward, coarse; (*Gram.*) denoting the male gender. *n.* The masculine gender; a masculine word. **masculine rhyme:** (*F. Pros.*) A rhyme on a word ending with a stressed syllable not in *e* mute. **masculinely,** *adv.* **masculineness, masculinity** (-lin′ i ti), *n.*

mash (1) (măsh) [A.-S. *masc-*, *max-*, in *maxwyrt*, mash-wort (cp. Dan. and Swed. dial. *mask*, G. *meisch*), prob. cogn. with MIX], *n.* A mass of ingredients crushed and mixed into a pulp; a mixture of bran and hot water for horses; crushed or ground grain or malt steeped in hot water to form wort; *a confused mixture, a mess. *v.t.* To crush into a pulpy mass; to make an infusion of (malt) in hot water; to infuse (tea). *v.i.* To be in process of infusion (of tea). **mash-tub, -vat,** *n.* A brewer's tub or vat in which malt is mashed. ***mashy** (1), *a.*

mash (2) (măsh) [Slang, etym. doubtful], *v.t.* To ogle, to flirt with. *n.* The object of such attention. **to be mashed on:** To be in love with. **masher,** *n.* A vulgar fop or lady-killer.

mashie, mashy (2) (măsh' i) [perh. corr. of F. *massue,* a club], *n.* (*Golf*) An iron club with a deep short blade, lofted.

masjid (mŭs' jid) [Arab.], *n.* A mosque.

mask (1) (mask) [F. *masque,* from Sp. *máscara* (see MASQUERADE) or med. L. *mascus, masca,* etym. doubtful], *n.* A covering for the face, for protection or to conceal one's identity; a face-guard; an impression of a face in plastic material: (*Arch.*) a reproduction of a face used as a gargoyle or part of a moulding; a disguise, a pretence, a subterfuge; a masque; (*Phot.*) an opaque screen for framing the image in lantern slides, a silhouette used in printing to cover part of the plate; (*Hunting*) the head of a fox. *v.t.* To cover with a mask; (*in p.p.*) to disguise with a mask; (*Mil.*) to hide (a battery or force) behind natural or artificial covering; to watch (a hostile force) so as to hinder its effective action. *v.i.* To go in disguise. **masker,** *n.* A masquer.

mask (2) (mask) [Sc. and North., var. of MASH (1)], *v.t.* To infuse (tea).

maskinonge (măs' ki nonj, măs ki nonj') [Algonkin], *n.* A large pike inhabiting the Great Lakes of North America.

maslin (măz' lin) [acc. to O.E.D., from O.F. *mesteillon,* late L. *mistiliōnem,* nom. *-lio,* from L. *mistus,* p.p. of *miscēre,* to MIX]. *n.* (*dial.*) A mixture of grain, esp. wheat and rye. *a.* Made of this; (*fig.*) mingled, mixed.

masochism (măz' ŏ kizm) [L. von Sacher-*Masoch* (1836–1895), Austrian novelist, who described it], *n.* A variety of sexual perversion in which a person takes delight in being dominated or cruelly maltreated by another.

mason (mā' sŏn) [O.F. *maçon,* med. L. *maciōnem,* nom. *-cio*], *n.* A mechanic who works in stone; a Freemason. *v.t.* To build with masonry. **masonic** (mȧ son' ik), *a.* Pertaining to Freemasonry. **masonry** (mā' sŏn ri), *n.* The art or occupation of a mason; mason's work, stonework; Freemasonry.

Masorah (mȧ sôr' ȧ) [Heb. *māsōreth*], *n.* A mass of traditional criticism and illustrative matter on the text of the Hebrew Bible, compiled before the 10th century. **Masorete** (măs' ŏ rēt). *n.* One of the scholars who contributed to this. **Masoretic** (-ret' ik), *a.*

masque (mask) [F., see MASK (1)], *n.* A play or dramatic entertainment, usu. presented by amateurs at court or in noblemen's houses, the performers wearing masks, orig. in dumb show, later with dialogue and poetical accompaniments. **masquer,** *n.*

masquerade (mas-, măs kėr ād') [Sp. *mascarada,* from *máscara* perh. from Arab. *maskhara,* a buffoon], *n.* A ball or assembly at which people wear masks; disguise, pretence. *v.i.* To wear a mask or disguise, to pass oneself off in a false guise. **masquerader,** *n.*

Mass (1) (măs) [A.-S. *mæsse,* eccles. L. *missa,* fem. p.p. of *mittere,* to send], *n.* The celebration of the Eucharist as a sacrifice in which the body and blood of Christ are really and truly offered to God under the species of bread and wine (also applied by some to the Anglican communion service); the office for this; a setting of certain portions of this to music. **black mass** [BLACK]. **High Mass** [HIGH (1)]. **Low Mass** [LOW (1)]. **mass-bell,** *n.* The sanctus bell. **mass-book,** *n.* A missal.

mass (2) (măs) [F. *masse,* L. *massa,* prob. from Gr. *maza,* a barley-cake, rel. to *massein,* to knead], *n.* A body of matter collected, concreted, or formed into a coherent whole of indefinite shape; a compact aggregation of things; a great quantity or amount; the greater proportion, the principal part, or the majority (of); volume, bulk, magnitude; (*Phys.*) the quantity of matter which a body contains. *v.t.* To form or gather into a mass; to concentrate (as troops). *v.i.* To gather into a mass. **in the mass:** In the aggregate. **the great mass:** The great majority; the bulk. **the masses:** The ordinary people; the populace. **mass meeting,** *n.* A large meeting for some specific purpose. **mass observation,** *n.* Method of obtaining public opinion by observing and interviewing people of various modes of life. **mass production,** *n.* The production of standardized articles in large quantities in which the processes are reduced to simple, usually mechanical, operations performed often along a conveyor belt. **massive,** *a.* Heavy, weighty, ponderous; bulky; (*fig.*) substantial, solid; (*Psych.*) applied to sensations of large magnitude; (*Min.*) without definite crystalline form. **massively,** *adv.* **massiveness,** *n.* **massy,** *a.* **massiness,** *n.*

massacre (măs' ȧ kėr) [F., from O.F. *maçacre,* etym. doubtful], *n.* Indiscriminate slaughter; carnage, wholesale murder. *v.t.* To kill or slaughter indiscriminately.

massage (mȧ sazh', măs' aj) [F., from *masser,* to apply massage, perh. from Port. *amassar,* to knead, from *massa,* dough, MASS (2)], *n.* (*Therap.*) Treatment by rubbing or kneading the muscles and body, usu. with the hands. *v.t.* To subject to this treatment. **massagist** (măs' ȧ jist), **masseur** (ma sėr') (*fem.* **masseuse,** -sėrz'), *n.* One skilled in massage.

massé (ma sā, măs' ā) [F., p.p. of *masser,* to make such a stroke, from *masse,* MACE (1)], *n.* (*Billiards*) A stroke with the cue held vertically.

masseter (mă sē' tėr) [Gr. *masētēr,* from *masāsthai,* to chew], *n.* (*Anat.*) The muscle which raises the lower jaw.

masseur, etc. [MASSAGE].

massicot (măs' i kot) [F., etym. doubtful], *n.* Yellow protoxide of lead, used as a pigment.

massif (măs' if) [F.], *n.* The main or central mass of a mountain or range.

massive, etc. [MASS (2)].

Massorah, etc. [MASORAH].

mast (1) (mast) [A.-S. *mæst* (cp. Dut., Swed., Dan., and G. *mast*)], *n.* A long pole of timber, or iron or steel tube, placed upright in a ship to support the yards, sails, etc. **mast-head,** *n.* The top of a mast, usu. of the lower-mast as a place for a look-out etc., or of the topmast. *v.t.* To send to the masthead as a punishment. **masted,** *a.* Furnished with a mast or masts. **mastless,** *a.*

mast (2) (mast) [A.-S. *mæst* (cp. G. *mast*), prob. cogn. with Sansk. *mēda,* fat], *n.* The fruit of the oak and beech or other forest trees.

mastaba (măs' tȧ bȧ) [Arab.], *n.* (*Egypt. Ant.*) An ancient tomb or chapel covering a sepulchral pit, used for the deposit of offerings.

mastectomy (măs tek' tō mi) [Gr. *mastos,* breast; *ektome,* a cutting-out], *n.* (*Surg.*) Surgical removal of the breast.

master (mas' tėr) [M.E. *meister,* through A.-S. *mægester* or O.F. *maistre, meistre* (or both), from L. *magister* (cogn. with *magis,* more, Gr. *megas,* great)], *n.* A man who has control or authority over others; an employer; the head of a household; the owner of a slave, dog, horse, etc.; one who has secured the control or upper hand; one thoroughly acquainted with or skilled in an art, craft, etc., a great artist; a schoolmaster, a teacher, a tutor, an expert, a proficient; the highest degree in arts and surgery; a title given to the head of certain colleges, corporations, etc.; a title of certain judicial officers; a title prefixed to the names of young gentlemen; (*Sc.*) the courtesy title of a viscount's or baron's eldest son; (*Naut.*) the captain of a merchant vessel; an officer who navigates a ship of war under the direction of the captain; *a respectful form of address. *a.* Having control or authority; employing workmen; in charge of work or of workmen. *v.t.* To become the master of; to overpower, to defeat; to subdue, to bring under control; to become thoroughly conversant with or skilled in using; to be the master of, to rule as a master. **Little Masters** [LITTLE]. **Old Masters:** The great painters of the 13th–17th centuries; their pictures. **master-at-arms:** (*Naut.*) A first-class petty officer acting as head of the ship's police. **master-builder,** *n.* A builder who employs workmen; (*fig.*) the chief builder, the architect. **master-carpenter,** *n.* One who works on his own account; one employing other carpenters; a skilled carpenter. **master-hand,** *n.* An expert; the hand or skill of an expert. **master-key,** *n.* A key which opens all the locks of a set, opened each by a separate key. **master-mason,** *n.* A Freemason who has attained the third degree. **master-mind,** *n.* The ruling mind or intellect. **Master of Arts** [ART (2)]. **master of ceremonies** [CEREMONY]. **master of foxhounds, harriers,** etc.: One elected to control a hunt. **master of the horse:** An officer of the royal household, formerly in charge of the horses; (*Rom. Ant.*) an officer appointed by a dictator to command the cavalry. **master of the revels:** A court official who had charge of entertainments etc. **master-spring,** *n.* The spring which sets in motion or regulates the whole. **masterdom, masterhood,** *n.* **masterful,** *a.* Expressing mastery; domineering, self-willed. **masterfully,** *adv.* **masterfulness,** *n.* **masterless,** *a.* **masterly,** *a.* and *adv.* With the skill of a master. **masterliness,** *n.* ***masterous,** *a.* **mastership,** *n.* **mastery,** *n.*

masterpiece (ma′ stėr pēs), *n.* A performance superior to anything of the same kind; an achievement showing surpassing skill.

masterwort (ma′ stėr wĕrt), *n.* (*Bot.*) A herb of the parsley family, esp. *Peucedanum ostruthium,* formerly cultivated as a pot-herb, now used as a stimulant.

mastic (măs′ tik) [F., from late L. *mastichum,* earlier *masticha,* Gr. *mastichē,* etym. doubtful], *n.* A resin exuding from a Mediterranean evergreen tree, *Pistacia lentiscus,* chiefly used for varnish; a putty-like preparation used for bedding window-frames etc. in buildings; a liquor flavoured with gum mastic used in Greece and the Levant. **masticic** (-tis′ ik), *a.* (*Chem.*) **masticin** (măs′ ti sin), *n.* (*Chem.*) That portion of mastic insoluble in alcohol.

masticate (măs′ ti kāt) [late L. *masticātus,* p.p. of *masticāre,* perh. as prec. or rel. to Gr. *mastax -akos,* the jaw], *v.t.* To grind and crush with the teeth. **masticable,** *a.* **masticability** (-bil′ i ti), *n.* **mastication** (-kā- shŭn), *n.* **masticator** (măs′ ti kā tŏr), *n.* **masticatory,** *a.*

mastiff (măs′ tif) [A.-F. and O.F. *mastin* (F. *mâtin*), through a late L. *mansuētīnus,* from *mansuētus,* MANSUETE], *n.* A large dog of great strength and courage, characterized by drooping ears, used as a watch-dog.

mastitis (măs tī′ tis) [Gr. *mastos,* breast, rel. to *madaein* and L. *madēre,* to be moist, -ITIS], *n.* (*Path.*) Inflammation of the breast in women.

mastodon (măs′ tŏ dŏn) [Gr. *odous odontos,* tooth], *n.* (*Palæont.*) An extinct mammal closely allied to the elephant, with nipple-shaped crests on the molar teeth. **mastodontik** (-don′ tik), *a.*

mastodynia (măs tō din′ i ȧ) [Gr. *odunē,* pain], *n.* (*Path.*) Neuralgia in the breast.

mastoid process, *n.* (*Anat.*) A process of bone behind the ear.

masturbate (măs′ tŭr bāt) [L. *masturbātus,* p.p. of *masturbārī,* etym. doubtful], *v.i.* To excite artificially the genital organs, to practise onanism or self-abuse. **masturbation** (-bā′ shŭn), *n.* **masturbator,** *n.*

mat (1) (măt) [A.-S. *meatte, matte,* late L. *matta,* perh. from Semitic (cp. Heb. *mattāh,* a bed, a thing spread out)], *n.* A coarse fabric of fibre, rushes, hemp, wire, etc., or of perforated rubber etc., used as a carpet, to wipe shoes on, for packing, etc.; (*Naut.*) a mass of old rope, etc., to prevent chafing; (*fig.*) a tangled mass of anything. *v.t.* (*past & p.p.* **matted**) To cover or lay with mats; to twist or twine together. *v.i.* To become twisted into a mat (of hair etc.).

mat (2) (măt) [F., prob. from O.F. *mat,* mated at chess, see CHECKMATE], *a.* Dull, lustreless, not glossy. *n.* A dull, lustreless surface, groundwork, border, etc., esp. in metal roughened or frosted. *v.t.* To dull; to give a wet surface or appearance to.

matador (măt′ ȧ dôr) [Sp.] *n.* In Spanish bull-fights the man who has to kill the bull; one of the three principal cards at ombre and quadrille; a game played with dominoes.

match (1) (măch) [A.-S. *mæcca* (cp. Icel. *maki,* a mate, *makr,* suitable), cogn. with MAKE (2)], *n.* A person or thing, equal, like, or corresponding to another; a counterpart, a facsimile; one able to cope with another; a contest of skill, strength, etc., (*Am.* a football game etc.,); a pairing or alliance by marriage; one eligible for marrying; *a bargain, an agreement. *v.t.* To be a match for; to compare as equal; to oppose as equal; to oppose (against or with) as a rival, opponent, etc.; to be the equal of, to correspond, to join. *v.i.* To agree, to be equal, to tally (of different things or persons); *to be married. **matchboard,** *n.* A board having a tongue along one edge and a corresponding groove on the other for fitting into similar boards. **matchmaker,** *n.* One fond of planning and bringing about marriages. **matchmaking,** *a.* and *n.* **matchable,** *a.* **matcher,** *n.* **matchless,** *a.* Without equal, incomparable. **matchlessly,** *adv.* **matchlessness,** *n.*

match (2) (măch) [O.F. *mesche* (F. *mèche*), wick, etym. doubtful], *n.* A small strip of wood or taper tipped with combustible material for producing or communicating fire; a fuse burning at a uniform rate for firing charges. **match-box,** *n.* A box for holding matches. **match-lock,** *n.* The lock of an obsolete musket fired by means of a lighted match; a musket so fired. **matchwood,** *n.* Wood suitable for making matches; (*fig.*) wood reduced to small splinters.

matchet (măch′ ėt) [Sp. *machete*], *n.* A broad knife or cutlass used in tropical America as a weapon, to cut down sugar-canes etc.

mate (1) (māt) [from CHECKMATE], *v.t.* To checkmate; to confound, to paralyse. *a.* Confounded, paralysed. *n.* A checkmate. **fool's mate:** (*Chess*) A game in which a player suffers checkmate at his opponent's second move. **smothered mate:** (*Chess*) A game in which the king is surrounded by his own pieces so that he cannot move.

mate (2) (māt) [prob. M.L.G. (cp. L.G. *maat,* M.Dut. *maet*), cogn. with MEAT], *n.* A companion, a comrade, a fellow-worker, an equal, a match; a suitable partner, esp. in marriage; one of a pair of the lower animals, esp. birds, associated for breeding; (*Naut.*) an officer in a merchant ship ranking below the captain; an assistant to the surgeon, cook, etc. *v.t.* To match, to couple; to join together in marriage; to pair (birds); to vie with. *v.i.* To pair. **mateless,** *a.*

maté (măt′ ā) [Sp. *mate,* from Quicha *mati*], *n.* Paraguay-tea, an infusion of the leaves of *Ilex Paraguayensis,* a Brazilian holly; this shrub; the vessel in which the tea is made.

matelassé (ma tė la′ sā) [F., from *matelas,* MATTRESS], *a.* Having a raised pattern as in quilting. *n.* A variety of silk and wool dress-goods with such a pattern.

matelote (ma′ tė lōt) [F., from *matelot,* sailor, etym. unknown], *n.* A dish of fish with wine, seasoning, etc.

mater (mā′ tėr) [L.], *n.* (*pl.* ***-tres,*** -trēz) A mother [cp. DURA MATER, PIA MATER].

material (mȧ tēr′ i ȧl) [O.F. *materiel,* late L. *matēriālis,* from *matēria,* MATTER], *a.* Pertaining to or consisting of matter; corporeal, substantial; pertaining to or concerning the physical nature or the appetites of man; sensual, unspiritual, pertaining to the matter or essence of a thing, not to the form; important, momentous, essential. *n.* The substance or matter from which anything is made; stuff, fabric; elements or component parts (of); notes, ideas, etc., for a written or oral composition. **raw material:** [RAW]. **materially,** *adv.* **materialism** (mȧ tēr' ȧl i izm), *n.* The theory that there is nothing in the universe but matter, that mind is a phenomenon of matter, and that there is no ground for assuming a spiritual First Cause; regard for secular to the neglect of spiritual interests. **dialectical materialism** [DIALECTICAL]. **materialist,** *n.* **materialistic** (-lis' tik), *a.* **materialistically,** *adv.* **materiality** (-ăl' i ti), *n.* **materialize** (mȧ tēr' i ȧl īz), *v.t.* To make material, to invest with matter or corporeity; to cause (a spirit) to become material or to appear; to make materialistic. *v.i.* To appear (of a spirit); to become actual fact. **materialization** (-zā shŭn), *n.*

materia medica (mȧ tēr' i ȧ med' i kȧ) [L.], *n.* (*Med.*) A general term for the different substances employed in medicine; a list or description of such substances.

materiel (ma târ i el') [F., as prec.], *n.* The material, supplies, machinery, or instruments, as distinguished from the personnel or persons, employed in an art, business, military or naval activity, etc.

maternal (mȧ tĕr' nȧl) [F. *maternel*, late L. *māternālis*, L. *māternus*, from MATER], *a.* Motherly; pertaining to a mother or to maternity; connected or related on the mother's side. **maternally,** *adv.* **maternity,** *n.* Motherhood; motherliness.

***math** (math) [A.-S. *mæth*], *n.* A mowing.

mathematical (măth e măt' i kȧl) [O.F. *mathematique*, L. *mathēmaticus*, Gr. *mathēmatikos*, from *mathē-*, stem of *manthanein*, see foll], *a.* Pertaining to mathematics; rigidly precise or accurate. **mathematically,** *adv.* **mathematician** (-mȧ tish' ȧn), *n.*

mathematics (măth ė măt' iks), *n.* The science of quantity, magnitude as expressed by numbers. **pure mathematics:** The abstract science of magnitudes etc. **mixed** or **applied mathematics:** The application of this to branches of physical research, as mechanics, astronomy, etc.

mathesis (mȧ thē' sis) [Gr., cogn. with *manthanein*, to learn], *n.* Learning, esp. knowledge of mathematics. **mathetic** (-thet' ik), *a.*

maths (măths) [abbrev. MATHEMATICS], *n.* (*colloq.*) The study of mathematics.

matico (mȧ tē' kō) [Sp. *yerba Matico* (*yerba*, herb, *Matico*, dim. of *Mateo*, Matthew)], *n.* A Peruvian shrub, *Piper angustifolium*, the leaves of which are a powerful styptic.

matilda (mȧ til' dȧ), *n.* (*Austral. colloq.*) A swag, a bag of belongings. **waltzing matilda:** Carrying the swag.

matinal (măt' i nȧl), *a.* Of, pertaining to, or occurring in the afternoon.

matinée (măt' i nā), *n.* (*Theat.*) An afternoon performance. **matinée jacket,** *n.* An infant's top garment of wool or material.

matins (măt' inz) [F. *matines*, fem. pl., eccles. L. *mātūtinas*, acc. fem. pl. of *mātūtinus*, of the morning], *n.pl.* One of the canonical hours of the R.-C. breviary, properly recited at midnight but also at daybreak; the daily office of morning prayer in the Anglican Church; (*fig.*) a morning song as of birds; *morning, dawn.

***matrass** (măt' rȧs) [F. *matras*, etym. doubtful], *n.* A round or oval glass vessel with a long neck, used for distilling.

matriarch (mā' tri ark) [L. *mātri-*, stem of MATER, *-arch*, as in PATRIARCH], *n.* A woman in a primitive tribe who is regarded as at once ruler and mother; a venerable or patriarchal lady. **matriarchy,** *n.* A social system in which the mother is head of the family, or in which descent is reckoned through the female line. **matriarchal** (-ar' kȧl), *a.* **matriarchate,** *n.* **matriarchalism,** *n.* **matriarchalist,** *n.*

matricide (mā' tri sīd) [F., from L. *mātricīda* (*mātri-*, MATER, -CIDE)], *n.* One who murders his mother; the murder of a mother. **matricidal,** *a.*

matriculate (mȧ trik' ū lāt) [med. L. *mātriculātus*, p.p. of *mātriculāre*, from *mātricula*, register dim. of MATRIX], *v.t.* To enter in a register, to admit to membership of a body or society, esp. a college or University. *v.i.* To be admitted as a member or student; to pass the examination formerly required to ensure such admission. *a.* Matriculated. *n.* One who has matriculated. **matricular,** *a.* and *n.* **matriculation** (-lā' shŭn), *n.* The examination that must be passed to matriculate; the act of matriculating.

matrilinear (măt ri lin' ė ȧr) [MATER; LINEAR], *adv.* By succession through the mother.

matrimony (măt' ri mȯ ni) [O.F. *matrimonie*, L. *mātrimōnium*, from *māter mātris*, mother], *n.* The act of marrying; the state of being married, marriage, wedlock; a card-game; the combination of king and queen of one suit in this and other games; slices of cake and bread-and-butter eaten together; *a partner in marriage. **matrimonial, *-nious** (-mō' ni ȧl, -ŭs), *a.* **matrimonially,** *adv.*

matrix (mā' triks) [L., from *mātri-*, stem of *māter*, mother], *n.* The womb; a place where anything is generated or developed; (*Biol.*) the formative part from which a structure is produced, intercellular substance; (*Type-founding etc.*) a mould in which anything, esp. type or a die, is cast or shaped; the concave bed into which a stamp or die fits; (*Geol.*) a mass of rock in which a mineral or fossil is embedded, also the impression left by a fossil, crystal, etc., after its removal from the rock; (*Maths.*) an array of numbers or symbols with special mathematical properties.

matron (mā' trȯn) [F. *matrone*, L. *mātrōna*, as prec.], *n.* A married woman, esp. an elderly one; the head of the nursing staff in a hospital; the female superintendent of an institution. **matronlike,** *a.* **matronage,** *n.* **matronal,** *a.* **matronhood, matronship,** *n.* **matronize,** *v.t.* To render matronlike; to chaperon; (*facet.*) to patronize. **matronly,** *a.* and *adv.* **matronymic** (măt ron im' ic), *n.* A name derived from the mother or ancestress.

matt [MAT (2)].

mattamore (măt ȧ mōr') [F. *matamore*, Arab. *maṭmūrah*, from *ṭamara*, to store up], *n.* An underground storage-place for grain.

matte (măt) [F., from G., MAT (1)], *n.* (*Metal.*) An impure metallic product containing sulphur, from the smelting of ore, esp. copper.

matter (măt' ėr) [M.E. and O.F. *matere*, F. *matière*, L. *māteria*, stuff, esp. for building], *n.* That which constitutes the substance of physical things; that which has weight or mass, occupies space, and is perceptible by the senses; physical substance as distinguished from thought, mind, spirit, etc.; meaning, sense, or substance (of a book, discourse, etc.); (*Log.*) content as opposed to form; a subject for thought or feeling; an object of or for attention; an affair, a business; the cause or occasion of or for difficulty, regret, etc.; importance, moment; an indefinite amount, quantity, or portion; (*Print.*) type set up; (*Law*) fact or fact forming the ground of an action etc.; (*Path.*) purulent substance in an abscess, pus. *v.i.* To be of moment, to signify; *to form pus. **for that matter:** So far as that is concerned. **in the matter of:** As regards. **matter of course:** What may be expected in the natural course of events. **matter of fact:** A reality, a fact. **matter-of-fact,** *a.* Treating of or adhering to facts or realities; not fanciful or imaginary; commonplace, prosaic, plain, ordinary. ***matterful,** *a.* ***matterless,** *a.* Unimportant. **mattery,** *a.* Full of matter or pus, purulent.

matting (măt′ ing), *n.* Matwork; mats; material for mats; the making of mats; a coarse fabric of rushes, bast, hemp, etc., esp. for packing and covering.

mattock (măt′ ŏk) [A.-S. *mattuc*, etym. doubtful], *n.* A kind of pick with one broad adze-edged end, for loosening ground, severing roots, etc.

mattoid (măt′ oid) [It. (*matto*, foolish)], *a.* Semi-insane. *n.* A stupid or foolish person regarded by Lombroso, the Italian criminologist and alienist, as semi-insane.

mattress (măt′ rės) [O.F. *materas* (F. *matelas*), It. *materasso*, Arab. *maṭraḥ*, a place where anything is thrown, from *ṭaraḥa*, to throw], *n.* A case of coarse material stuffed with hair, wool, etc., used for the bottom of a bed; a similar appliance called a spring, box, or interior sprung mattress.

maturate (măt′ ū rāt) [L. *mātūrātus*, p.p. of *mātūrāre*, to MATURE], *v.t.* To mature; (*Med.*) to promote suppuration in. *v.i.* To ripen, to suppurate perfectly. **maturation** (1) (-rā′ shŭn), *n.* **maturative** (mȧ tūr′ ȧ tiv), *a.* and *n.*

mature (mȧ tūr′) [L. *mātūrus*, ripe, whence *mātūrāre*, to ripen], *a.* Ripe, ripened; completely developed; fully elaborated, considered, etc.; become payable (as a bill); (*Path.*) in a state of perfect suppuration. *v.t.* To bring to a state of ripeness or complete development; (*Path.*) to bring to a state of suppuration. *v.i.* To become ripened or fully developed; to become payable (of a bill). **maturation** (2) (mă tūr ā′ shŏn), *n.* (*Biol.*) The attainment of maturity, the completion of growth. **maturely,** *adv.* **matureness, maturity,** *n.* ***maturescent** (-măt ū res′ ėnt), *a.* **maturescence,** *n.*

matutinal (măt ū tī′ nal), **matutine** (măt′ ū tin) [L. *mātūtīnālis*, from *mātūtīnus*, pertaining to *Mātūta*, goddess of dawn (rel. to *mātūrus*, early)], *a.* Pertaining to the morning; early.

maud (mawd) [Sc., etym. unknown], *n.* A grey-striped plaid worn by shepherds etc., or used as a travelling rug.

maudlin (mawd′ lin) [O.F. *mawdeleine*, L. *Magdalēnē*, MAGDALEN], *a.* Muddled with drink; characterized by sickly sentimentality, mawkish; *weeping, tearful. *n.* Mawkish sentimentality.

***maugre** (maw′ gėr) [O.F. *maugré*, *malgré* (*mal*, L. *malum*, nom. *-us*, bad, *gré*, L. *gratum*, nom. *-tus*, pleasing)], *prep.* In spite of.

maul (mawl) [M.E. *malle*, O.F. *mail*, L. *malleum*, nom. *-leus*, hammer], *n.* A heavy wooden hammer, a beetle. *v.t.* To beat, to bruise (as with a maul); to handle roughly; to damage.

Mau Mau (mou mou), *n.* A terrorist organization of the Kikuyu tribe in Kenya; a member of this.

maulstick (mawl′ stik) [Dut. *maalstok* (*malen*, to paint, STICK)], *n.* A light stick with a round pad at the end used as a rest for the right hand by painters.

maund (mawnd) [Hind. *man*], *n.* An Asiatic measure of weight varying from place to place—in India 83 lb.

maunder (mawn′ dėr) [perh. imit.], *v.i.* To grumble, to mutter; to talk incoherently, to ramble; to act or move about aimlessly. *v.t.* To utter in a grumbling or incoherent manner. **maunderer,** *n.*

maundy (mawn′ di) [O.F. *mandé*, L. *mandātum*, MANDATE], *n.* The ceremony of washing the feet of poor people on Holy Thursday, in commemoration of Christ's performing this office for His disciples; a distribution of alms following this. **Maundy money, penny:** Silver money specially struck and distributed on Maundy Thursday. **Maundy Thursday:** The day before Good Friday, when the royal alms or maundy money is distributed by the royal almoner.

mauresque [MORESQUE].

Mauser (mow′ zėr) [Paul *Mauser*, G. inventor], *n.* A variety of military magazine rifle. **Mauser pistol,** *n.*

mausoleum (maw sȯ lē′ ŭm) [L., from Gr. *Mausōleion*, from *Mausōlos*], *n.* (*pl.* **-lea, -leums**) The stately tomb of Mausolus, king of Caria, erected by his widow Artemisia, and reckoned one of the seven wonders of the world; a sepulchral monument of considerable size or architectural pretensions. ***mausolean,** *a.*

mauve (mōv) [F., from L. *malva*, MALLOW], *n.* A purple- or lilac-coloured aniline dye; the colour of this. *a.* Of this colour.

maverick (măv′ ėr ik) [Samuel *Maverick*, Texan cattle-raiser, who refrained from branding his stock (*c.* 1840)], *n.* (*Am.*) An unbranded beast; (*fig.*) anything got hold of dishonestly; an irresponsible person. *v.t.* To brand (a stray beast); hence, to seize or appropriate illegally.

mavis (mā′ vis) [F. *mauvis* (cp. Sp. *malvis*), etym. doubtful], *n.* The song-thrush.

mavourneen (mȧ voor′ nēn) [Ir. *mo mhurnín*], *n.* My dear one.

maw (maw) [A.-S. *maga* (cp. Dut. *maag*, Icel. *mage*, G. *magen*)], *n.* The stomach of lower animals, esp. the fourth stomach of ruminants; the crop of birds; (*facet.*) the human stomach; (*slang*) the mouth. **mawworm,** *n.* An intestinal worm.

***mawk** (mawk) [Icel. *mathkr* (cp. A.-S *mathu*, *matha*)], *n.* A maggot.

mawkin [MALKIN].

mawkish (maw′ kish), *a.* Apt to cause satiety or loathing; sickly, insipid; (*fig.*) falsely or feebly sentimental. **mawkishly,** *adv.* **mawkishness,** *n.*

maxilla (măk sil′ ȧ) [L.], *n.* (*pl.* **-læ**, -lē) One of the jaw-bones, esp. the upper in mammals. **maxillary,** *a.* and *n.* **maxilliferous** (-lif′ ėr ŭs), *a.* **maxilliform** (-sil′ i fôrm), *a.* **maxilliped,** *n.* A foot-jaw or limb modified into a maxillary organ, in crustacea. **maxillo-,** *comb. form.*

maxim (1) (măk′ sim) [F. *maxime*, L. *maxima*, fem. superl. of *magnus*, great], *n.* A general principle of a practical kind; a rule derived from experience; (*Law*) an established or accepted principle. **maximist, maxim-monger,** *n.* **maximistic** (-mis′ tik), *a.*

Maxim (2) (măk′ sim) [Sir Hiram S. *Maxim* (1840–1916), inventor], *n.* An automatic single-barrelled quick-firing machine-gun.

Maximalist (măk′ sim ȧl ist) [MAXIMUM], *n.* (*Pol.*) An adherent of the extremist section of the former Social Revolutionary Party in Russia.

maximum (măk′ si mŭm) [L., neut. superl. of *magnus*, great], *n.* (*pl* **-ma**) The greatest quantity or degree attainable in any given case. *a.* Greatest; at the greatest or highest degree. **maxima and minima:** (*Math.*) The greatest and least values of a variable quantity. **maximum thermometer:** A thermometer automatically recording the highest temperature reached during a given period. **maximize,** *v.t.* To raise to a maximum; to increase to the utmost extent; (*Theol.*) to hold rigorous opinions. *v.i.* (*Theol.*) To interpret doctrines in the most rigorous way.

maxwell (măks′ wėl) [J. C. *Maxwell* (1831–1879)], *n.* (*Phys.*) A unit of magnetic flux.

may (1) (mā) [A.-S. *mæg*, 1st sing. of *mugan*, to be able, past *mihte*, *meahte* (cp. Dut. *mag*, *mocht*, *mogen*, Icel. *mā*, *megom*, *mātte*, G. *mag*, *mochte*, *mögen*)], *aux.v.* (*2nd sing.* **mayest, *mayst,** *past* **might**) Expressing possibility, ability, permission, desire, obligation, contingency, or uncertainty. **maybe,** *adv.* Perhaps, possibly. ***mayhap,** *conj.* Peradventure.

May (2) (mā) [F. *mai*, L. *Māius*, perh. pertaining to *Māia*], *n.* The fifth month of the year; the spring-time of life, youth; hawthorn blossom from its appearing in May; May-day festivities; (*Camb. Univ. pl.*) the Easter term examinations, the boat-races held in May Week. **v.i.* To engage in the festivities of May-day. **Queen of the May** [MAY-QUEEN]. **May-blossom,** *n.* Hawthorn bloom. **May-bug,** *n.* The cockchafer. **May-day:** The first of May. **mayduke,** *n.* A variety of cherry said to have been introduced from Médoc. **mayflower,** *n.* A flower blooming in May, as the cowslip, lady's smock, or hawthorn; (*Am.*) the trailing arbutus, *Epigæa repens.* **May-fly,** *n.* An ephemeral insect, esp. *Ephemera vulgata* or *E. dania*; an angler's fly made in imitation of this; the caddis-fly. **May-games,** *n.pl.* Games held on May Day. ***May-lady** [MAY-QUEEN]. **May-lily,** *n.* The lily of the valley. ***May-morn,** *n.* Freshness, vigour. **maypole,** *n.* A pole decorated with garlands etc., round which people dance on May Day. **May-queen,** *n.* A young girl chosen to act as queen of the games on May-Day. **Mays Week:** (*Camb. Univ.*) The boat-race week held late in May or early in June. **mayer,** *n.*

***may** (3) (mā) [A.-S. *mæg*, kinswoman (see MAIDEN)], *n.* A maiden, a girl.

maya (1) (mā' yȧ) [Sansk.], *n.* (*Theosophy*) Illusion, deceptive appearance.

Maya (2) (ma' yȧ), *n.* An Indian of the native tribes of Yucatan, Honduras, etc.; the language of these tribes.

maybe [MAY (1)].

mayflower [MAY (2)].

***mayhem** (mā' hem), *n.* (*Old Law*) The offence of maiming a person.

mayonnaise (mā' ō nāz) [F., etym. doubtful], *n.* A thick sauce or salad-dressing made of egg-yolk, vinegar, etc.; a dish with this as a dressing.

mayor (mâr, mā' ȯr) [F. *maire*, L. MAJOR], *n.* The chief officer of a city or borough. **Lord Mayor** [LORD]. **mayoral,** *a.* **mayoralty,** *n.* **mayoress,** *n.*

maypole [MAY (2)].

mayst [MAY (1)].

mayweed (mā' wēd) [obs. *maythe*, A.-S. *magothe*, -WEED], *n.* The stinking camomile, *Anthemis cotula*; other composite plants, esp. the feverfew.

mazard (măz' ȧrd) [etym. doubtful, perh. var. of MAZER], *n.* *The head, the skull; *the face; a small kind of black cherry.

mazarine (măz ȧ rēn') [etym. doubtful], *n.* and *a.* A deep rich blue.

maze (māz) [etym. doubtful, perh. from a non-extant A.-S. v. *masian*, see AMAZE], *n.* A labyrinth, a confusing network of winding and turning passages; a state of bewilderment, uncertainty, perplexity. *v.t.* To bewilder, to confuse. **v.i.* To be bewildered; to wind about perplexedly. **mazeful,** *a.* **mazy,** *a.* Involved, winding, perplexing, intricate; giddy, dizzy. **the mazy:** (*facet.*) The dance, dancing. **mazily,** *adv.* **maziness,** *n.*

***mazer** (mā' zėr) [O.F. *masere*, prob. from O.H.G. *masar*, a knot in wood, maple-wood (cp. G. *maser*, Icel. *mösurr*)], *n.* A large cup or drinking-vessel, orig. made of maple-wood.

mazurka (mȧ zėr' kȧ) [Pol., a woman of the province Mazovia (cp. POLONAISE)], *n.* A lively Polish dance like the polka; the music for this.

mazy [MAZE].

McCarthyism (mȧ kar' thi izm) [J. *McCarthy* (1909–57) U.S. politician], *n.* Intolerance of liberalism; the hunting down of suspected Communists and their dismissal from public employment.

McNaghten rules (măk naw' tȯn) [defendant in a lawsuit of 1843], *n.* (*Law*) Rules governing the degree of responsibility of a mentally abnormal criminal defendant.

me (mē, mė) [A.-S. *mē*, *mec*, acc. (cp. Dut. *mij*, Swed. and Dan. *mig*, G. *mich*, dat. *mir*, L. *mē*, dat. *mihi*, Gr. *me*, *eme*, *moi*, *emoi*)] *pers. pron.* The dative and objective of the first personal pronoun.

mead (1) (mēd) [A.-S. *medu* (cp. Dut. *mede*, Dan. *miöd*, G. *met*, also Sansk. *madhu*, honey, Gr. *methu*, wine)], *n.* A fermented liquor made from honey, water, and spices.

mead (2) (mēd) [A.-S. *mǣd*], *m.* A meadow.

meadow (med' ō) [A.-S. *mǣdwe*, dat. of *mǣd*, cogn. with MOW (3)], *n.* A tract of land under grass, esp. if grown for hay; low, rich, moist ground, esp. near a river. **meadow-lark,** *n.* An American song-bird, *Sturnella magna.* **meadow-saffron,** *n.* A plant of the genus *Colchicum*, esp. *C. autumnale.* **meadow-sweet,** *n.* A rosaceous plant, *Spiræa ulmaria*, with white plumy fragrant flowers. **meadowy,** *a.*

meagre (mē' gėr) [M.E. and O.F. *megre*, *maigre*, L. *macrum*, nom. *macer*, cogn. with Gr. *makros*, long], *a.* Lean, thin, wanting flesh; destitute of richness, fertility, or productiveness; (*fig.*) poor, scanty. **v.t.* To make meagre. **meagrely,** *adv.* **meagreness,** *n.*

meal (1) (mēl) [A.-S. *mæl* (cp. Dut. *maal*, Icel. *māl*, G. *mal*, time, *mahl*, meal), cogn. with METE], *n.* Food taken at one of the customary times of eating, a repast; the occasion or usual time of this; (*prov.*) the yield of milk from a cow at one milking. *v.i.* To have a meal. **meal-time, *-tide,** *n.*

meal (2) (mēl) [A.-S. *melu* (cp. Dut. and Dan. *meel*, G. *mehl*), cogn. with L. *molere*, to grind], *n.* The edible portion of grain or pulse ground into flour. **meal-ark,** *n.* (*Sc.*) A receptacle for meal. **meal-man, meal-monger,** *n.* One who deals in meal. **meal-worm,** *n.* The larva of a beetle that infests meal. **mealy,** *a.* Of, containing, or resembling meal; powdery, friable, floury; farinaceous; besprinkled with or as with meal, spotty; pale (of the complexion); mealy-mouthed. **mealy bug:** An insect infesting vines and hothouse plants. **mealy-mouthed,** *a.* Soft-spoken, hypocritical. **mealiness,** *n.*

mealie (mē' li) [S. Afric. Dut. *milje*, Port. *milho*, MILLET], *n.* (*usu. pl.*) Maize.

mean (1) (mēn) [A.-S. *mǣnan* (*cp.* Dut. *meenen*, Dan. *mene*, G. *meinen*)], *v.t.* (*past & p.p.* **meant,** ment) To have in the mind; to purpose, to intend; to design, to destine (for); to denote, to signify; to intend to convey or to indicate. *v.i.* To have a specified intention or disposition. **to mean well to or by:** To be well disposed towards. **meaning,** *n.* That which is meant, significance, import. *a.* Significant, expressive. **meaningless,** *a.* **meaningly,** *adv.*

mean (2) (mēn) [O.F. *meien*, *moien* (F. *moyen*), late L. *mediānus*, L. *medius*, middle], *a.* Occupying a middle position; equidistant from two extremes; not extreme, moderate, not excessive; intervening; (*Math.*) intermediate in value between two extremes, average. *n.* The middle point, state, course, quality, or degree between two extremes; (*Math.*) a quantity intermediate between two extremes, an average. **means** (*n.pl.*) That by which anything is done or a result attained; available resources, income, wealth. **means-test,** *n.* The official investigation into the means of a person applying for pension, dole, etc. **by all means:** Certainly, undoubtedly. **by any means:** In any way possible, somehow; at all. **by means of:** By the agency or instrumentality of. **by no means:** Certainly not, on no account whatever. **meantime, -while,** *adv.* In the intervening time. *n.* The interval between two given times.

mean (3) (mēn) [A.-S. *mǣne*, *gemǣne* (cp. Dut. *gemeen*, Icel. *meinn*, G. *gemein*), cogn. with L. *commūnis*, COMMON], *a.* Low in quality, capacity, value, rank, etc.; inferior, poor, inefficient, shabby; low-minded, petty, stingy; shabby, contemptible, miserly; ignoble, of no account, disreputable; despicable. **mean-born,** *a.* Of humble birth. **mean-spirited,** *a.* **mean-spiritedly,** *adv.* **meanly,** *adv.* **meanness,** *n.*

meander (mė ăn' dėr) [L. *Meander*, Gr. *Maiandros*, a winding river in Phrygia], *n.* A tortuous or intricate course or bend (*usu. in pl.*); a winding, a circuitous path or movement, a deviation (*usu. in pl.*); a decorative pattern, fretwork, etc., composed of intricately interlacing lines; *a maze, a labyrinth. *v.i.* To wander, wind, or flow in a tortuous course. **meandering, *meandrian, meandriform,** *a.* **meandrine,** *a.* Meandering; (*Zool.*) belonging to the *Meandrina*, a genus of tropical corals, in appearance somewhat resembling the convolutions of the brain.

means [MEAN (2)].

meant, *past & p.p.* [MEAN (1)].

measles (mē′ zėls) [M.E. *maseles* (cp. Dut. *maselen*), from O.Teut. *mas- mæs*, whence MAZER], *n.pl.* An infectious disease, indicated by a red papular rash, usu. attacking children; applied to the effects of a cystic worm in swine and oxen. **German measles** [GERMAN]. **measled,** *a.* **measly,** *a.* Infected with measles; (*slang*) worthless, paltry, meagre.

measure (mezh′ ůr) [O.F. *mesure*, L. *mensūra*, from *mens-*, pres.p. stem of *mētīrī*, to measure], *n.* The extent or dimensions of a thing as determined by measuring; the measurements necessary to make an article of dress; a standard of measurement; a definite unit of capacity or extent; an instrument for measuring, as a rod, tape, etc., or a vessel of standard capacity; a system of measuring; the act of measuring, measurement; a quantity measured out taken as a rule or standard; prescribed or allotted extent, length, or quantity; limit, moderation, just degree or amount; metre, poetical rhythm; means to an end; a law, a statute, an Act of Parliament: (*Geol.*) (*pl.*) a series of beds, strata; (*Mus.*) time, pace, the contents of a bar; *a slow and stately dance. *v.t.* To determine the extent or quantity of by comparison with a definite unit or standard; to take the dimensions of; to weigh, to judge, to value or estimate by comparison with a rule or standard; to serve as the measure of; to allot or apportion by measure; (*fig.*) to travel over, to cover; to survey, to look up and down; to bring into competition (with); *to regulate, to keep within bounds; *to set to metre. *v.i.* To take measurements; to be in extent, to show by measurement. **beyond measure:** Exceedingly, excessively. **in a measure:** To some extent, in a certain degree. **to take measures:** To adopt means, to take steps (to). **to measure one's length:** To fall prostrate. **to measure swords:** To see whether the swords are of the same length (of duellists); (*fig.*) to try one's strength with or against. **to measure up to:** To be adequate for. **to take one's measure:** To measure a person for clothes; (*fig.*) to find out what kind of a person one is. **without measure:** Immoderately. **measurable,** *a.* **measurably,** *adv.* **measured,** *a.* Of definite measure; deliberate and uniform; rhythmical; well-considered, carefully weighed. **measureless,** *a.* **measurement,** *n* **measurer,** *n.*

meat (mēt) [A.-S. *mete* (cp. Icel. *matr*, Swed. *mat*, O.H.G. *maz*)], *n.* The flesh of animals, usu. excluding fish and fowl, used as food; solid food of any kind; the partaking of food, a meal; the edible part of a nut, egg, shell-fish, etc. **after** or **before meat:** Immediately after or before a meal. **to sit at meat:** To sit at table. **meat-biscuit,** *n.* Dried meat mixed with meal and baked. **meat-safe,** *n.* A cupboard, usu. of wire gauze or perforated zinc, for storing meat. **meat-salesman,** *n.* One who receives carcases and sells them to butchers. **meaty,** *a.* **meatiness,** *n.*

meatus (mė ā′ tůs) [L., from *meāre*, to flow], *n.* (*pl.* ***-tus,*** -tus) (*Anat.*) A passage, channel, or tubular canal. **auditory meatus:** The passage of the ear.

Mecca (mek′ ȧ) [city in Arabia, birthplace of Mohammed], *n.* (*fig.*) A holy place; the object of one's aspirations.

Meccano (me ka′ nō), *n.* Protected trade name of a set of toy engineering parts that can be built up into various mechanical models.

mechanic (mė kăn′ ik) [L. *mēchanicus*, Gr. *mēchanikos*, from *mēchanē*, MACHINE], *n.* A handicraftsman, an artisan; a skilled workman; one who is employed or skilled in any craft or mechanical occupation; (*pl.*) the branch of physics treating of the motion and equilibrium of material bodies; also the science of machinery. *a.* Mechanical; industrial; pertaining to or of the nature of machinery, machine-like; *vulgar, low.

mechanical (mė kăn′ ik ȧl), *a.* Pertaining to mechanics; in accordance with physical laws; acting or affected by physical power without chemical change; pertaining to or acting as machinery or mechanism; produced by machinery; of or pertaining to handicraft; working with tools or machinery; machine-like, automatic, done from force of habit; slavish, unoriginal; *vulgar, rude, base. ****n.*** A mechanic. **mechanical engineering:** The branch of engineering concerned with the design and production of mechanical contrivances and appliances. **mechanical powers:** The simple machines, the wedge, the inclined plane, the screw, the lever, the wheel and axle, and the pulley. **mechanical rectifier,** *n.* (*Radio.*) A rectifier operating through the medium of a commutator. **mechanical transport,** *n.* Road transportation by motor vehicles. **mechanicalism,** *n.* **mechanicalist, mechanist** (mek′ ȧ nist), *n.* A mechanician; a supporter of the mechanical philosophy. **mechanically,** *adv.* **mechanicalness,** *n.* **mechanician** (-nish′ ȧn), *n.* **mechanico-,** *comb form.*

mechanism (mek′ ȧ nizm), *n.* The structure or correlation of parts of a machine; machinery; a system of correlated parts working reciprocally together, as a machine; (*Art*) mechanical execution as dist. from style etc., technique.

mechanize (mek′ ȧ nīz), *v.t.* To make mechanical; (*Mil.*) to equip with mechanical transport. **mechanization,** *n.*

mechanography (mek ȧ nog′ rȧ fi), *n.* Reproduction of a work of art, a writing, etc. by mechanical means. **mechanograph,** *n.*

mechanotherapy (me kăn ō thēr′ ȧ pi), *n.* The treatment of disease through the agency of mechanical appliances.

mechanotropism (me kăn ō trōp′ izm), *n.* (*Bot.*) The bending of tendrils or other plant organs through reaction to contact or other mechanical stimulus.

Mechlin (mek′ lin) [*Mechlin* (Malines), near Brussels], *n.* A light lace made at Mechlin.

meconic (mė kon′ ik) [Gr. *mēkōn*, poppy], *a.* (*Chem.*) Contained in or derived from the poppy. **meconin** (mē′ kȯ nin), *n.* (*Chem.*) A neutral substance existing in opium. **meconium** (mē kō′ ni ům), *n.* Inspissated poppy juice; the first fæces of infants consisting of excretions from the liver, etc. **Meconopsis** (mē kȯ nop′ sis), *n.* A genus of beautiful flowering-plants related to and resembling the poppy.

medal (med′ ȧl) [F. *médaille*, It. *medaglia*, pop. L. *metallea*, L. *metallum*, METAL], *n.* A piece of metal, often in the form of a coin, stamped with a figure and inscription to commemorate some illustrious person or event. **medalled,** *a.* ***medalet,** *n.* A small medal. **medallic** (mė dăl′ ik), *a.* **medallion,** *n.* A large medal; (*Arch.*) a tablet or panel, usually round or oval, containing painted or sculptured figures, decorations, etc. **medallist** (med′ ȧ list), *n.* One who designs or engraves medals; a collector of or dealer in medals; one who has gained a medal. ***medallurgy** (med′ ȧ lĕr ji), *n.* The art of engraving or stamping medals.

meddle (med′ ȧl) [A.-F. *medler*, O.F. *mesler* (F. *mêler*), med. L. *misculāre*, L. *miscēre*, to mix], *v.i.* To interfere (in) officiously; to concern or busy oneself (with) unnecessarily; *to mix. **meddler,** *n.* **meddlesome,** *a.* **meddlesomeness,** *n.*

media (mē′ di ȧ) [L., fem. of *medius*, middle], *n.* (*pl.* ***-iæ***) (*Anat.*) The middle coat or tunic of a vessel; (Phon.) a voiced mute, g, *d*, or *h*, regarded as intermediate between smooth and rough or aspirate.

mediacy [MEDIATE]. **mediaeval** [MEDIEVAL].

medial (mē' di ăl) [late L. *mediālis*, as prec.], *a.* Pertaining to or situated in the middle, intermediate; mean or average. *n.* A medial letter; (*Phon.*) a *media*.

median (mē' di ăn), *a.* (*Anat.*) Situated in the middle, esp. in the median plane, dividing the body longitudinally into two equal halves; (*Geol.*) intermediate, as a line or zone between the extreme limits of winds, calm belts, etc. **medianly,** *adv.*

mediant (mē' di ănt) [It. *mediante*, late L. *medians -ntem*, pres.p. of *mediāre*, to MEDIATE], *n.* (*Mus.*) The third tone of any scale.

mediastinum (mē di ăs tī' nŭm) [L., neut. of *mediastīnus*, orig. a common servant, a drudge, as prec.], *n.* (*pl.* ***-na***) (*Anat.*) A membranous septum or cavity between the two main parts of an organ etc., esp. the folds of the pleura between the right and left lung.

mediate (mē' di ăt) [late L. *mediātus*, p.p. of *mediāre*, from *medius*, middle], *a.* Situated in the middle or between two extremes; intervening, indirect, secondary; serving or acting as an intervening or indirect means or agency; effected or connected by such means. *v.t.* (-āt) To interpose between (parties) in order to reconcile them; to effect by means of intervention. *v.i.* To interpose (between) in order to reconcile parties etc.; to serve as connecting link or medium (between). **mediacy** (mē di ă si), *n.* **mediateness,** *n.* **mediately,** *adv.* **mediation** (-ā' shŭn), *n.* **mediator** (mē' di ā tŏr), *n.* **mediatorial** (-tōr' i ăl), *a.* **mediatory** (mē di ā' tŏr i), *a.* **mediatorially,** *adv.* **mediatorship,** *n.* **mediatrix, *mediatress,** *n.*

mediatize (mē' di ă tīz) [F. *médiatiser*, from *médiat*, MEDIATE], *v.t.* To render dependent; to disestablish politically and subject to a larger State, leaving the ruler a nominal sovereignty. **mediatization** (-zā' shŭn), *n.*

medical (med' i kăl) [F. *médical*, late L. *medicālis*, from *medicus*, a physician, cognate with *medērē*, to heal], *a.* Pertaining to, connected with, or employed in medicine; curative, healing, medicinal; pertaining to medicine as opposed to surgery etc. *n.* (*colloq.*) A medical student. **medical benefit,** *n.* Benefit under the National Health Insurance scheme, comprising medical attendance, medicine, and appliances. **medical jurisprudence** [FORENSIC MEDICINE]. **medically,** *adv.* **medicament** (med' i kă-, mė dik' ă mĕnt), *n.* A healing substance or application. **medicamental** (-men' tăl), *a.* **medicamentally,** *adv.* **medicaster** (med' i kăs tėr), *n.* A quack. **medicate** (med' i kāt), *v.t.* To impregnate with anything medicinal; to treat medically. **medicable,** *a.* **medication** (-kā' shŭn), *n.* **medicative** (med' i kă tiv), *a.*

Medicean (med i sē' ăn), *a.* Of or pertaining to the Medici, a wealthy family who were rulers of Florence in the 15th and 16th centuries.

medicine (med' sin) [O.F. *medecine*, L. *medicīna*, from *medicus*, see MEDICAL], *n.* A substance, usu. taken internally, used for the alleviation or removal of disease; the art or science of preserving health and curing or alleviating disease, esp. as distinguished from surgery and obstetrics; a term applied by the N. American Indians to anything supposed to possess supernatural powers or influence, a charm, a fetish. *v.t.* To treat or cure with or as with medicine. **medicine-man,** *n.* A witch-doctor, a magician. **medicinable** (mė dis' i năbl), *a.* **medicinal,** *a.* **medicinally,** *adv.* **medico** (med' i kō), *n.* (*facet.*) A physician; a medical student. **medico-,** *comb. form.* **medico-chirurgical,** *a.* **medico-legal, -judicial,** *a.*

medick (med' ik) [L. *mēdica*, Gr. *Mēdikē*, fem. of *-kos*, (grass) of Media], *n.* A plant of the genus *Medicago*, allied to the clover, esp. *M. sativa*, lucerne.

medieval, mediæval (med i ē' văl) [L. *medius*, middle; *ævum*, age], *a.* Of, or pertaining to, or characteristic of the Middle Ages (*c.* A.D. 400–1400). *n.* One who lived in the Middle Ages. **medievalism,** *n.* **medievalist,** *n.* **medievalize,** *v.t.* **medievally,** *adv.*

medio- [L. *medius*, middle], *comb. form.* Situated in or pertaining to the middle.

mediocre (mē' di ō kėr) [F. *médiocre*, L. *mediocrem*, nom. *-cris*, from *medius*, as prec.], *a.* Of middling quality; indifferently good or bad, average, commonplace. **mediocrity** (-ok' ri ti), *n.*

meditate (med' i tāt) [L. *meditātus*, p.p. of *meditārī*, cogn. with Gr. *medesthai*, to think about], *v.i.* To ponder, to engage in thought (upon); to muse, to cogitate. *v.t.* To dwell upon mentally; to plan, to design, to intend. **meditation** (-tā' shŭn), *n.* **meditative** (med' i tă tiv), *a.* **meditatively,** *adv.* **meditativeness,** *n.* **meditator,** *n.*

Mediterranean (med i tėr ā' nė ăn) [L. *mediterrāneus* (*medi-*, MEDIO, *terra*, land)], *a.* Inland; surrounded by or lying between lands; pertaining to the Mediterranean Sea. *n.* The sea between Europe and Africa.

medium (mē' di ŭm) [L., neut. of *medius*, middle], *n.* (*pl.* **-diums**) Anything serving as an intermediary, agent, or instrument; instrumentality, agency; an intervening substance or element, such as the air or ether, through which forces act, impressions are conveyed, etc.; a substance in which germs are developed; an instrument of exchange, as money; a middle or intermediate object, quality, degree, etc.; a size of paper, $23\frac{1}{2} \times 18\frac{1}{2}$ in., between demy and royal; (*Painting*) a liquid vehicle for dry pigments; (*Log.*) the middle term of a syllogism; (*Spiritualism*) a person claiming to receive communications from the spirit world. *a.* Intermediate in quantity, quality, or degree; average, moderate; middling, mediocre. **medium waves,** *n.* (*Radio.*) Waves of between 200 and 1,000 metres in accordance with the Hague definition. **mediumism, mediumship,** *n.* **mediumistic** (-mis' tik), *a.* Of the nature of, or pertaining to, a spiritualistic medium. **mediumize,** *v.t.* (*Spiritualism*) To act as a medium.

Medjidie (mė jē' di ė) [Turk. *mejīdie*], *n.* A Turkish order of knighthood established by the Sultan Abdul-Medjid in 1851; a Turkish coin worth about 3s. 8d. first minted by the Sultan Abdul-Medjid.

medlar (med' lăr) [A.-F. *medler*, O.F. *meslier*, L. *mespila*, Gr. *mespilē*], *n.* A rosaceous tree, *Pyrus Germanica*, the fruit of which is eaten when beginning to decay.

medley (med' li) [A.-F. *medlee*, O.F. *meslee* (F. *mêlée*), as MEDDLE], *n.* A mixed or confused mass, esp. of incongruous objects, persons, materials, etc.; a literary miscellany. *a.* Mixed, multifarious, motley. *v.t.* To make a medley of.

Médoc (mā dok') [*Médoc*, a district in Gironde, S.W. France], *n.* A red wine from Médoc.

medulla (mė dŭl' ă) [L., prob. rel. to *medius*, middle], *n.* (*Anat.*) The marrow of bones, esp. that of the spine; the spinal cord; the inner part of certain organs, as the kidneys; the pith of hair; (*Bot.*) the internal tissue or pith of plants. ***medulla oblongata:*** The elongated medulla or continuation of the spinal cord forming the hindmost segment of the brain. **medullary** (mė dŭl' ă ri), ***medullar.** **medullated, medullose,** *a.* **medullin,** *n.* (*Chem.*) Cellulose or lignin from the pith of certain plants.

medusa (mė dū' să) [L., from Gr. *Medousa*, one of the three Gorgons whose head (which turned beholders to stone) was cut off by Perseus and placed by Athene on her ægis], *n.* (*Zool.*) (*pl.* **-sæ**) A jelly-fish. **medusal, medusiform,** *a.* **medusan, -oid,** *a.* and *n.*

meed (mēd) [A.-S. *mēd* (cp. G. *miete*, also Gr. *misthos*, Sansk. *mīdha*, reward)], *n.* Reward, recompense, esp. for merit; *merit, worth. **meedless,** *a.*

meek (mēk) [M.G. *meoc*, Icel. *mjūkr* (cp. Swed. *mjūk*, Dan. *myg*)], *a.* Mild, submissive, humble, tame, gentle, forbearing. ***meeken**, *v.t.* **meekly**, *adv.* **meekness**, *n.*

meerschaum (mēr′ shawm, -shŭm) [G., sea-foam (*meer*, sea, *schaum*, foam)], *n.* A white compact hydrous silicate of magnesia, used for tobacco-pipes; a pipe made of this.

meet (1) (mēt) [M.G. *mēte*, A.-S. *gemæte*, fitting well, cogn. with METE], *a.* Fit, proper, suitable. **meetly**, *adv.* **meetness**, *n.*

meet (2) (mēt) [A.-S. *mētan* (cp. Dut. *moeten*, Icel. *mæta*, Swed. *möta*), cogn. with *mōt*, *gemōt*, MOOT], *v.t.* (*past & p.p.* **met**) To come face to face with; to go to a place so as to join or receive; to reach and touch or unite with (of a road, railway, etc.); to encounter, to confront, to oppose; to refute; to answer, to satisfy; to pay, to discharge. *v.i.* To come together; to assemble; to come into contact; to be united. *n.* A meeting of persons and hounds for hunting, or of cyclists etc.; the persons assembled or the place appointed for a meet; (*Austral.*) an appointment. **meeting**, *n.* A coming together, an assembly; the persons assembled; a duel; a race-meeting; a conflux. **meeting-house**, *n.* A dissenting place of worship, esp. of Quakers. **to meet the eye** or **ear:** To be seen or heard. **to meet with:** To come across; to experience; to encounter, to engage. ***well met:** Welcome (a greeting).

mega-, megalo- [Gr., *megas*, fem. *megalē*, great], *comb. form.* Great, large.

megacephalic, megacephalous (meg å se făl′ ik, meg å sef′ å lŭs), *a.* Large-headed.

megacycle per second (meg′ å sī kel), *n.* A frequency of a million cycles per second, usu. applied to electric waves.

megadyne (meg′ å dīn), *n.* (*Phys.*) One million dynes.

megafog (meg′ å fog), *n.* A fog-signal equipped with several megaphones.

megalichthys (meg å lik′ this), *n.* (*Palæont.*) A genus of fossil ganoid fishes, from the coal-measures.

megalith (meg′ å lith), *n.* A great stone; a megalithic monument as a cromlech, stone circle, etc. **megalithic**, *a.*

megalomania (meg å lō mā′ ni å), *n.* A form of insanity characterized by self-exaltation; a craze for exaggeration, over-statement, etc. **megalomaniac**, *a.* and *n.*

megalosaurus (meg å lō saw′ rŭs), *n.* (*Palæont.*) An extinct genus of gigantic carnivorous lizards from the Oolite.

megaparsec (meg å par′ sek), *n.* (*Astron.*) One million parsecs.

megaphone (meg′ å fōn), *n.* An apparatus for enabling persons to converse at a long distance; a large speaking-trumpet.

megapod (meg′ å pod), *n.* (*Ornith.*) An Australian or Malaysian mound-bird.

megascope (meg′ å skōp), *n.* A form of solar microscope for throwing enlarged images on a screen; (*Phot.*) an enlarging camera. **megascopic**, *a.*

megass (meg′ ås) [etym. unknown], *n.* Fibrous residue after sugar has been extracted from the cane.

megatherium (meg å thēr′ i ŭm), *n.* A genus of extinct gigantic sloth-like edentates from South America. **megatherial**, *a.*

megavolt (meg′ å vōlt), *n.* (*Elect.*) One million volts. **megawatt**, *n.* One million watts.

megerg (meg′ ĕrg), *n.* A million ergs.

megger (meg′ ĕr), *n.* Protected trade name of an instrument for measuring high resistances.

megilp (mė gilp′) [etym. doubtful], *n.* A vehicle for colours, consisting of a compound of linseed-oil and mastic varnish.

megohm (meg′ ōm), *n.* A million ohms.

megrim (mē′ grim) [corr. of *migrane*, F. *migraine*, L. *hēmicrania*, Gr. *hēmikrania* (HEMI-, *kranion*, skull)], *n.* A severe headache, esp. on one side of the head only; a sudden attack due to congestion of the brain causing a horse at work to reel or fall, staggers; (*pl.*) low spirits, depression; (*fig.*) a whim, a fad; bilious headache.

***meinie** (mā′ ni) [O.F. *meyné*, *mesnie*, ult. from L. *mansiōnem*, nom. *-sio*, MANSION], *n.* A household; a body of household attendants; a retinue.

meiosis (mī ō′ sis) [Gr., from *meioun*, to lessen, from *meiōn*, less], *n.* (*Rhet.*) Litotes, depreciative hyperbole; (*Path.*) the stage of a malady when the symptoms tend to abate; (*Biol.*) the diminution of the number of chromosomes in the nuclei.

meistersinger (mī′ stėr sing′ ėr) [G., master-singer], *n.* A German burgher poet and musician of the 14th–16th cent., one of the successors of the minnesingers.

melampod (mel′ åm pod) [L. *melampodium*, Gr. *melampodion* (*melas -anos*, black, *pous podos*, foot)], *n.* Black hellebore.

melampyre (mel′ åm pīr) [Gr. *melampūron* (*melan-melas*, black, *pūros*, wheat)], *n.* The cow-wheat, *Melampyrum boreale*, an herbaceous scrophulareous woodland plant.

melanæmia (mel å nē′ mi å) [Gr. *melas melanos*, black, *haima*, blood], *n.* (*Path.*) A morbid condition in which the blood contains an excessive proportion of black colouring-matter. **melanæmic**, *a.*

melancholia (mel ån kō′ li å) [MELANCHOLY], *n.* A mental disorder, often preceding mania, characterized by lowness of spirits, frequently with suicidal tendencies (formerly supposed to be due to excess of black bile).

melancholy (mel′ ån kŏl i) [O.F. *melancolie*, L. and Gr. *melancholia* (*melas melanos*, black, *cholos*, bile)], *n.* A gloomy, dejected state of mind; sadness, gloom, depression, despondency; (*poet.*) pensive contemplation; (*Path.*) melancholia. *a.* Sad, gloomy, depressed in spirits; mournful, saddening; pensive; afflicted with melancholia. **melancholic** (-kol′ ik), *a.*

Melanesian (mel å nē′ zhån) [Gr. *melas*, black; *nesos*, an island], *a.* Of or pertaining to Melanesia, the group of islands in the Pacific ocean lying to the east of New Guinea. *n.* A native of Melanesia.

mélange (mā lanzh) [F., from *méler*, to mix, see MEDDLE], *n.* A mixture, medley, or miscellany; (*Text.*) a mixed worsted yarn.

melanic (mė lăn′ ik) [Gr. *melan- melas*, black, -IC], *a.* (*Ethn.*) Black, negroid, dark-complexioned; (*Path.*) applied to the black pigment characteristic of melanosis. **melanin** (mel′ ån in), *n.* (*Chem.*) A black or dark brown pigment occurring in the hair and skin of dark-skinned races. **melanism** (mel′ å nizm), *n.* Excess of colouring matter in the skin, hair, and tissues; (*Bot.*) a disease producing blackness in plants. **melanistic** (-nis′ tik), *a.* **melanochroi** (mel å nok′ rō ī) [pl. of Gr. *melanochroos* (*chroa*, skin, or *ōchros*, pale)], *n.pl.* (*Ethn.*) A subdivision of the leiotrichi, comprising the races with dark hair and pale complexion. **melanochroic** (-krō′ ik), **melanochrous** (-nok′ rŭs), *a.* **melanoid** (mel′ å noid), *a.* (*Path.*) **melanosis** (mel å nō′ sis), *n.* (*Path.*) An organic affection, characterized by a deposit of black pigment in the tissues; black cancer. **melanotic** (-not′ ik), *a.* **melanous** (mel′ å nŭs), *a.* (*Ethn.*) Dark or sallow-complexioned. **melanuria** (mel å nūr i å) [Gr. *ouron*, urine], *n.* (*Path.*) A disorder characterized by blackness of the urine. **melanuric**, *a.*

melanism [MELANIC].

melanite (mel′ å nīt), *n.* (*Min.*) A black variety of garnet.

melasma (mė lăz′ må) [Gr., from *melas melanos*, black], *n.* (*Path.*) A skin disease characterized by excess of black pigment.

meld (meld) [G. *melden*, to announce], *v.t.* and *i.* (*Cards*) To declare for a score.

mêlée (mel' ā) [F.], *n.* A confused hand-to-hand fight, an affray.

Melibœan (mel i bē' ȧn) [*Melibœus*, shepherd in Virgil's first Eclogue], *a.* Alternately responding.

melic (mel' ik) [Gr. *melikos*, from *melos*, song], *a.* For singing, applied to certain Greek lyric poetry.

melilot (mel' i lot) [O.F., from late L. and Gr. *melilōtos* (*meli*, honey, LOTUS)], *n.* A plant of the leguminous genus *Melilotus*.

melinite (mel' i nīt) [F. *mélinite* (Gr. *mēlinos*, from *mēlon*, apple)], *n.* A French explosive containing picric acid; (*Min.*) a soft unctuous clay like yellow ochre.

meliorate (mē' li ȯ rāt) [late L. *meliōrātus*, p.p. of *meliōrāre*, from L. *melior*, better], *v.t.* To make better. *v.i.* To grow better. **melioration** (-rā' shŭn), *n.* **meliorism,** *n.* The doctrine that society etc., may be improved by persistent practical effort. **meliorist,** *n.*

meliphagous (mė lif' ȧ gŭs) [Gr. *meli*, honey, *-phagos*, eating, from *phagein*, to eat], *a.* (*Ornith.*) Belonging to the *Meliphagidæ* or honey-eaters.

melisma (mel is' mȧ) [Gr., a song tune], *n.* (*Mus.*) A melodic embellishment; a group of notes sung to a single syllable.

***mell** (mel) [O.F. *meller*, var. of *mesler*, to MEDDLE], *v.t.* To mix, to mingle. *v.i.* To meddle, to concern oneself (with); to mingle, esp. in combat; to mix or associate (with).

melliferous (mė lif' ėr ŭs) [L. *mellifer* (*mel mellis*, honey, -FEROUS)], *a.* Producing or yielding honey. ***mellific** (mė lif' ik), *a.* **mellification** (-kā' shŭn), *n.* ***melligenous** (-lij'-), *a.* **mellivorous** (-liv' ȯ rŭs), *a.*

mellifluous (mė lif' lu ŭs) [L. *mellifluus* (*mel mellis*, honey, *fluere*, to flow)], *a.* Flowing smoothly and sweetly. **mellifluent,** *a.* **mellifluence,** *n.*

mellite (mel' īt) [L. *mel mellis*, honey, -ITE], *n.* (*Min.*) Native mellitate of aluminium, honey-stone. **mellitic** (mė lit' ik), *a.* (*Chem.*) Applied to an acid found in mellite in combination with aluminium. **mellitate, mellate** (mel'-), *n.* A salt of mellitic acid.

mellow (mel' ō) [perh. from A.-S. *melo*, MEAL (2), perh. conf. with *mearu*, tender], *a.* Fully ripe, pulpy, sweet; rich, friable, soft and rich (of tones and colours); loamy (of soil); ripened or softened by age and experience; genial, kindly; (*colloq.*) jolly, half tipsy. *v.t.* To ripen, mature, soften. *v.i.* To become ripe, mature, or softened, by age etc. **mellowly,** *adv.* **mellowness,** *n.* **mellowy,** *a.*

melodeon, -dion (mė lō' dė ȯn) [earlier *melodium*, Latinized from MELODY], *n.* A wind-instrument with a row of reeds and a keyboard, an early type of American organ.

melodic, melodious, etc. [MELODY].

melodrama (mel' ȯ dra mȧ, mel ȯ dra' mȧ) [earlier *melodrame*, F. *mélodrame* (Gr. *melos*, song, DRAMA)], *n.* A sensational play with a plot characterized by startling situations; (*fig.*) a novel of a similar kind; orig. a dramatic composition with songs intermixed. **melodramatic** (-măt' ik), *a.* **melodramatically,** *adv.* **melodramatist** (-drăm' ȧ tist), *n.* **melodramatize,** *v.t.* **melo-tragedy,** *n.* Operatic tragedy.

melody (mel' ȯ di) [O.F. *melodie*, late L. and Gr. *melōdia*, from *melōdos*, singing, musical (*melos*, song, *ōdē*, see ODE)], *n.* An agreeable succession of sounds, esp. of simple tones in the same key, an air or tune; a simple setting of words to music; the chief part in harmonic music, the air; music. **melodic** (mė lod' ik), **melodious** (mė lō' di ŭs), *a.* Of, characterized by, or producing melody; musical, sounding sweetly. **melodiously,** *adv.* **melodiousness,** *n.* **melodist** (mel' ȯ dist), *n.* **melodize,** *v.t.* and *i.*

melon (mel' ȯn) [O.F., from late L. *mēlōnem*, nom. *mēlo*, for *mēlopepo*, Gr. *mēlopepōn* (*mēlon*, apple, fruit, *pepōn*, a kind of gourd)], *n.* A kind of gourd, esp. *Cucumis melo*, the musk-melon, and *Citrullus vulgaris*, the water-melon. **melon-cactus, -thistle,** *n.* A tropical American cactaceous plant.

Melpomene (mel pom' ė nē) [the Muse of tragedy], *n.* (*Astron.*) One of the minor planets.

melt (melt) [A.-S. *meltan*, intr., and *mieltan*, tr. (cp. Icel. *melta*), cogn. with Gr. *meldein*, to melt, and L. *mollis*, soft], *v.i.* (*p.p.* **melted, molten,** mōl' tėn) To pass from a solid to a liquid state by heat; to dissolve; (*fig.*) to be dissipated, to disappear, to vanish (away); to be softened to kindly influences, to give way; to dissolve in tears; to dissolve or blend (into). *v.t.* To make liquid by heat; to dissolve; to soften to tenderness; to dissipate. **melting-pot,** *n.* A crucible. **in the melting-pot:** (*fig.*) With an undecided future. **melter,** *n.* **meltingly,** *adv.* **meltingness,** *n.*

melton (mel' tȯn) [*Melton* Mowbray, in Leicestershire], *n.* A jacket worn in hunting; a stout make of cloth without nap, used largely for overcoats.

member (mem' bėr) [F. *membre*, L. *membrum*], *n.* A limb, a part or organ of the body; a component part or element of an organism or complex whole; one belonging to a society or body; a branch or division of a society or organization; a set of figures or symbols forming part of a mathematical expression. **unruly member,** *n.* (*fig.*) The tongue. **Member of Parliament:** One representing a constituency in the House of Commons. **memberless,** *a.* **membership,** *n.* **membral,** *a.* (*Anat.* and *Zool.*).

membrane (mem' brān) [L. *membrāna*, as prec.], *n.* A thin sheet of tissue lining or covering parts of an organism; a morbid tissue produced in certain diseases; a skin of parchment or vellum. **membranaceous** (mem brȧ nā' shŭs), **membraneous** (-brā' nė ŭs), **membraniform, membranous** (mem' brȧ nŭs), *a.*

memento (mė men' tō) [L., imper. of *meminisse*, to remember], *n.* (*pl.* **-oes**) A memorial, a souvenir, a reminder. ***memento mori*** [L., remember you must die]: An emblem of mortality, esp. a skull.

memoir (mem' war) [F. *mémoire*, L. *memoria*, MEMORY], *n.* (*usu. in pl.*) An account of events or transactions in which the narrator took part; an autobiography or a biography; a communication to some learned society on a special subject. **memoirist,** *n.*

memorabilia (mem ȯr ȧ bil' i ȧ) [L. memorable things, as foll.], *n.pl.* Things worthy to be remembered.

memorable (mem' ȯr ȧbl) [L. *memorābilis*, from *memorāre*, to call to remembrance, from *memor*, see MEMORY], *a.* Worthy to be remembered; notable, remarkable. ***memorableness, memorability** (-bil' i ti), *n.* **memorably,** *adv.*

memorandum (mem ȯ răn' dŭm) [L., neut. ger. of *memorāre*, see prec.], *n.* (*pl.* **-da**) A note to help the memory; a brief record or note; a short informal letter, usu. unsigned, with the sender's name etc., printed at the head; (*Law*) a summary, outline, or draft of an agreement, etc. ***memorative,** *a.*

memorial (mė mô' i ȧl) [O.F., L. *memoriālis*], *a.* Preservative of memory; commemorative; preserved in memory. *n.* That which preserves the memory of something; a monument, festival, etc., commemorating a person, event, etc.; a written statement of facts, esp. of the nature of a petition, remonstrance, etc.; an informal diplomatic paper; (*usu. in pl.*) a chronicle or record. **Memorial Day** [DECORATION DAY]. **memorialist,** *n.* **memorialize,** *v.t.*

memorize (mem' ȯ rīz), *v.t.* To commit to memory; to learn by heart.

memory (mem' ȯ ri) [A.-F. *memorie*, O.F. *memoire*, L. *memoria*, from *memor*, mindful, redupl. of *mer-*, to remember (cp. Gr. *merimna*, care, thought)], *n.* The mental faculty that retains and recalls previous ideas and impressions; the exercise of this faculty.

remembrance, recollection; the state of being remembered; posthumous reputation; the period during which anything is remembered; *a memorial, a memento.

mem sahib (mem′ sa ib), *n.* A term formerly applied to European married women living in India.

men, *pl.* [MAN].

menace (men′ ȧs) [O.F., from L. *minācia*, from *minax -ācis*, threatening, from *minæ*, threats], *n.* A threat. *v.t.* To threaten. **menacer,** *n.* **menacingly,** *adv.*

ménage (mā nazh′) [O.F., earlier *mesnage, maisnage*, pop. L. *mansiōnāticum*, from *mansio*, MANSION], *n.* A household; house-keeping, household management.

menagerie (mė năj′ ėr i) [F. *ménagerie*, as prec.], *n.* A collection of wild animals; a place or enclosure where wild animals are kept.

menagogue (men′ ȧ gog) [F. *ménagogue* (Gr. *mēn*, month, *agōgos*, leading)], *n.* A medicine that promotes the flow of the menses.

mend (mend) [from AMEND], *v.t.* To repair, to restore, to make good; to improve, to make better; to correct, to amend. *v.i.* To grow better, to improve; to amend, to recover health. *n.* The act or process of mending; improvement; a repaired part (in a garment etc.). **mendable,** *a.* **mender,** *n.*

mendacious (men dā′ shŭs) [L. *mendax -dācis*, lying, cogn. with *mentīrī*, to lie, -OUS], *a.* Given to lying, untruthful. **mendaciously,** *adv.* **mendacity** (-dăs′ i ti), *n.*

Mendelism (men′ dėl izm) [G. J. *Mendel* (1822–84)], *n.* A theory of heredity based on researches and generalizations by Mendel showing that the characters of the parents of cross-bred offspring reappear by certain proportions in successive generations according to definite laws. **Mendelian** (-dē li ȧn), *a.* **Mendelize,** *v.t.*

mendicant (men′ di kȧnt) [L. *mendīcans -ntem*, pres.p. of *mendīcāre*, from *mendīcus*, beggar], *a.* Begging; reduced to beggary. *n.* A beggar; a member of a mendicant order. **mendicant orders:** Monastic orders subsisting on alms. **mendicancy,** *n.* **mendicity** (men dis′ i ti), *n.*

menhaden (men hā′ dėn) [Am. Ind. *munnawhattsang*], *n.* A North American sea-fish allied to the herring.

menhir (men′ hēr) [Bret. *men*, stone, *hir*, long], *n.* A prehistoric monument consisting of a tall upright stone.

menial (mē′ ni ȧl) [A.-F., as MEINIE], *a.* Pertaining to or suitable for servants; servile, low, mean. *n.* A domestic servant; one doing servile work. **menially,** *adv.*

meninx (mē′ ningks) [Gr.], *n.* (*pl.* **meninges,** mė nin′ jēz) One of the three membranes enclosing the brain and spinal cord, comprising the *dura mater*, arachnoid, and *pia mater*. **meningeal** (mė nin′ jė ȧl), *a.* **meningitis** (-jī′ tis) [-ITIS], *n.* (*Path.*) Inflammation of the meninges. **meningocele** (mė nin′ jō sēl) [-CELE], *n.* Protrusion of the meninges through the skull.

meniscus (mė nis′ kŭs) [Gr. *mēniskos*, a crescent, dim. of *mēnē*, moon], *n.* (*Opt.*) A lens convex on one side and concave on the other; (*Phys.*) the top of a liquid column made convex or concave by capillarity (as mercury in a barometer). **meniscal,** *a.*

menisperm (men′ i spĕrm) [Gr. *mēnē*, as prec., SPERM], *n.* (*Bot.*) A plant of the *Menispermaceæ*, containing the cocculus indicus.

menology (mė nol′ ō ji) [late Gr. *mēnologion* (*mēn mēnos*, month, -LOGY)], *n.* A calendar of months, esp. the martyrology of the Greek Church.

menopause (men′ ō pawz) [Gr. *mēn mēnos*, month, PAUSE], *n.* (*Path.*) Final cessation of the menses, change of life. **menorrhagia** (men ō rā′ ji ȧ) [Gr. *-ragia*, from *rhēgnunai*, to break forth], *n.* Excessive flow of the menses. **menorrhœa** (-rē′ ȧ) [Gr. *rhoia*, flow], *n.* Ordinary flow of the menses.

mensal (1) (men′ sȧl) [L. *mensa*, table], *a.* Of, pertaining to, or used at the table.

mensal (2) (men′ sȧl) [as foll.], *a.* Monthly.

menses (men′ sēz) [L., pl. of *mensis*, month], *n.pl.* The periodic flow of blood from the uterus of women, usu. occurring once every lunar month. **menstrual, menstruous,** *a.* Monthly; pertaining to the menses. **menstruant,** *a.* **menstruation** (-*a*′ shŭn), *n.*

Menshevik (men′ she vik) [Rus., the minority], *n.* The moderate party in the Russian Revolution.

menstruum (men′ stru ŭm) [L., neut. of *menstruus*, monthly, from *mensis*, month (from the alchemistic analogy with the menstrual flow)], *n.* (*pl.* **-trua**) Any fluid that dissolves a solid, a solvent.

mensurable (men′ shoor ȧbl) [late L. *mensūrābilis*, from *mensūrāre*, to measure, from *mensūra*, MEASURE], *a.* Measurable; (*Mus.*) having rhythm and measure. **mensurability** (-bil′ i ti), *n.* **mensural,** *a.*

mensuration (men sū rā′ shŭn) [late L. *mensūrātio*, as prec.], *n.* The act or practice of measuring; (*Math.*) the branch of mathematics concerned with the determination of lengths, areas, and volumes.

-ment [O.F., from L. *-mentum*], *suf.* Forming nouns denoting result, state, action, etc., as in *agreement, impediment, ornament.*

mental (1) (men′ tȧl) [F., from late L. *mentālis*, from *mens mentis*, mind], *a.* Pertaining to the mind, intellectual; due to or done by the mind; (*fig.*) slightly deranged in mind. **mentality** (-tăl′ i ti), *n.* **mentalize,** *v.t.* **mentalization** (-zā′ shŭn), *n.* **mentally,** *adv.* **mentation** (-tā′ shŭn), *n.* Mental action; cerebration. **menticulture** [CULTURE], *n.* **menticultural** (-kŭl′ tūr ȧl), *a.*

mental (2) (men′ tȧl) [F., from L. *mentum*, chin], *a.* (*Anat.*) Of or pertaining to the chin.

menthol (men′ thōl) [G. (L. *mentha*, MINT (2), -OL)], *n.* A waxy crystalline substance obtained from oil of peppermint, used as a local anæsthetic for neuralgia etc.

mention (men′ shŭn) [F., from L. *mentiōnem*, nom. *-tio*, rel. to *mens mentis*, see MENTAL (1)], *n.* A concise notice, allusion to (or of); a naming. *v.t.* To refer to, to allude to; to indicate by naming without describing. **honourable mention:** A distinction sometimes awarded to a competitor who has just failed to win a prize. **mention in dispatches:** (*Mil.*) Reference by name (in official dispatches) to an officer who has done well in battle. **mentionable,** *a.*

mentor (men′ tôr) [F., from Gr. *Mentōr*, counsellor to Telemachus], *n.* A faithful monitor, a wise counsellor. ***mentorial** (-tôr′-), *a.* **mentorship,** *n.*

menu (men′ oo, men′ ū) [F., orig. small, L. *minūtus*, MINUTE (1)], *n.* A bill of fare.

Mephistopheles (mef is tof′ ė lēz) [the spirit in ancient legend to whom Faust sells his soul, etym. doubtful], *n.* (*fig.*) A tempter; a diabolical person. **Mephistophelian** (-fē′ li ȧn), *a.* Sardonical, cynically sceptical, scoffing.

mephitis (mė fī′ tis) [L.], *n.* A foul, offensive, or pestilential exhalation; (*Zool.*) a genus of American carnivora containing the skunks. **mephitism** (mef′ i tizm), *n.* **mephitic, -al** (mė fit′ ik, -ȧl), *a.*

mercantile (mĕr′ kȧn tīl) [F., from It. *mercantile*, from *mercante*, MERCHANT], *a.* Commercial, pertaining to buying and selling; mercenary. **mercantile marine** [MERCHANT SERVICE]. **mercantilism,** *n.* **mercantilist,** *n.*

***mercatante** [MARCANTANT (*Shak.*)].

Mercator's projection [PROJECTION].

mercenary (mĕr′ sė nȧr i) [L. *mercēnārius*, from *merces -cēdis*, reward, from *merx -cis*, see foll.], *a.* Hired or serving for money; done from or actuated by motives of gain; venal. *n.* One who is hired, esp. a soldier hired in foreign service. **mercenarily,** *adv.* **mercenariness,** *n.*

mercer (mĕr′ sėr) [F. *mercier*, through pop. L. *merciarius*, from L. *merx mercis*, MERCHANDISE], *n.* One who deals in silk, cotton, woollen, and linen goods. **mercery,** *n.*

mercerize (mėr′ sėr īz) [J. *Mercer* (1791–1866), patentee of process], *v.t.* To treat cotton fabrics with an alkaline solution in preparation for dyeing. **mercerization** (-zā′ shŭn), *n.*

merchandise (mĕr′ chȧn dīz) [F. *marchandise*, as foll.], *n.* Articles of commerce; commodities for purchase; *trade, commerce. *v.t.* and *i.* To trade, to barter.

merchant (mĕr′ chȧnt) [O.F. *marchand, marchant*, from L. *mercantem*, nom. *-cans*, pres.p. of *mercārī*, to trade, from *merx mercis*, MERCHANDISE], *n.* One who carries on trade on a large scale, esp. with foreign countries; (*Am. and Sc.*) a shopkeeper, a tradesman; *a merchant vessel; *a fellow; (*colloq.*) one given to, *e.g. speed merchant.* *a.* Mercantile, commercial. **merchantman,** *n.* A merchant ship. **merchant navy:** Collective name for sea-going vessels other than those of the Royal Navy. **merchant prince:** A wealthy merchant. **merchant service:** Personnel etc. of shipping employed in commerce. **merchant ship:** Ship for conveying merchandise. ***merchantable,** *a.* **merchantlike,** *a.*

merciful, etc [MERCY].

mercurial (mĕr kū′ ri ȧl), *a.* Pertaining to the god Mercury; flighty, volatile, fickle; pertaining to, consisting of, or caused by mercury. *n.* A preparation containing mercury, used as a drug. **mercurialism,** *n.* (*Path.*) A morbid condition due to excessive use of mercurial drugs. ***mercurialist,** *n.* **mercuriality** (-ăl′ i ti), *n.* **mercurialize,** *v.t.* **mercurially,** *adv.* **mercuric.**

Mercury (mĕr′ kū ri) [A.-F. *Mercurie*, O.F. *Mercure*, L. *Mercurius*, prob. from *merx mercis*, MERCHANDISE], *n.* The Roman god of commerce, identified with the Greek Hermes, the messenger of the gods; the planet nearest the sun; (*fig.*) a messenger; a title for a newspaper, formerly a newspaper; a liquid metallic element often called quicksilver. **mercurous** (-kūr′ ŭs), *a.* ***mercurify,** *v.t.* To obtain mercury from (metallic minerals); to mercurialize. ***mercurification** (-kā′ shŭn), *n.*

mercy (mĕr′ si) [F. *merci*, L. *mercēdem*, nom. *-ces*, reward, late L., pity, from *merx -cis*, MERCHANDISE], *n.* A disposition to temper justice with mildness; forbearance, clemency, compassion; an act of clemency, pity, or compassion; pardon, forgiveness; control, discretion, liberty to punish or spare; (*colloq.*) something to be thankful for. **at the mercy of:** Wholly in the power of. **for mercy's sake:** An exclamation or appeal for mercy, or of expostulation. **sister of mercy** [SISTER]. **mercy-seat,** *n.* (*Bibl.*) The covering of the ark of the Covenant; (*fig.*) the throne of God as dispenser of mercy. **merciful, *merciable,** *a.* **mercifully,** *adv.* **mercifulness,** *n.* ***mercify,** *v.t.* **merciless,** *a.* **mercilessly,** *adv.* **mercilessness,** *n.*

merdivorous (mĕr div′ ŏr ŭs) [L. *merda*, dung; *vorare*, devour], *a.* Feeding upon dung.

mere (1) (mēr) [A.-S. (cp. Dut. and G. *meer*, Icel. *marr*, and L. *mare*, sea)], *n.* A lake, a pool.

mere (2) (mēr) [L. *merus*, pure, unadulterated], *a.* Such and no more; absolute, unqualified. **merely,** *adv.* Purely, only, solely.

mere (3) (mēr) [A.-S. *mære, gemære* (cp. M.Dut. *mere, meer*, Icel. *landa-mæri*, also L. *mūrus*, **moiros*, wall)], *n.* A boundary; a boundary-stone; a landmark. **v.t.* To limit, to mark off. ***merestone,** *n.*

meretricious (mer ė trish′ ŭs) [L. *meretrīcius*, from *meretrix -trīcis*, harlot, from *merērī*, to earn, see MERIT], *a.* Pertaining to or befitting a harlot; alluring by false or empty show; unreal, tawdry. **meretriciously,** *adv.* **meretriciousness,** *n.*

merganser (mėr găn′ sėr) [L. *mergus*, a diving-bird, *anser*, goose], *n.* The goosander and other diving or fish-eating ducks belonging to the genus *Mergus.*

merge (mĕrj) [L. *mergere*, to dip (partly through low F. *merger*)], *v.t.* To cause to be swallowed up or absorbed, to sink (in a larger estate, title, etc.). *v.i.* To be absorbed or swallowed up; to lose individuality or identity (in). **merger,** *n.* The merging of an estate, limited company, etc., into another; extinction, absorption.

meri, mere (mē′ rē) [Maori], *n.* A war-club; a greenstone trinket shaped like this.

mericarp (mer′ i karp) [F. *méricarpe* (Gr. *meros*, part, *karpos*, fruit)], *n.* (*Bot.*) One of the two carpels forming the fruit of umbelliferous plants.

meridian (mė rid′ i ȧn) [O.F. *meridien*, L. *merīdiānus*, from *merīdiēs*, midday (*medius*, middle, *diēs*, day)], *a.* Pertaining to midday or to a geographical or astronomical meridian, or to the point or period of highest splendour or vigour. *n.* (*Astron.*) A great circle drawn through the poles and the zenith of any given place on the earth's surface; (*Geog.*) the line in which the plane of this circle intersects the earth's surface; the time when the sun or other heavenly body crosses this; midday, noon; (*fig.*) culmination, zenith, point of highest splendour or vigour. **first** or **prime meridian:** A meridian from which longitude is reckoned, usu. that of Greenwich. **meridional,** *a.* Pertaining to a meridian; highest, culminating; pertaining to the south, esp. of Europe; running north and south (as a mountain range). *n.* An inhabitant of the south, usu. of the south of France. **meridionality** (-năl′ i ti), *n.* **meridionally,** *adv.*

meringue (mė răng′) [F., etym. doubtful], *n.* A confection of white of eggs, sugar, etc., used as icing; a cake made of this.

merino (mė rē′ nō) [Sp., prob. from L. *majōrīnus* (perh. overseer or major-domo), from *mājor*, greater], *n.* A breed of sheep introduced from Spain, valuable for their fine wool; a fine woollen dress-fabric, orig. of this wool; a fine woollen yarn used for hosiery. *a.* Pertaining to this breed of sheep; made of merino. **pure merino:** (*Austral. colloq.*) Descendant of an early settler with no convict connexion.

meristem (mer′ i stem) [from Gr. *meristos*, from *merizein*, to divide (ending assim. to PHLOEM, XYLEM)], *n.* (*Bot.*) Vegetable tissue or cells in process of growth. **meristematic** (-măt′ ik), *a.*

merit (mer′ it) [O.F. *merite*, L. *meritum*, neut. *p.p.* of *merērī*, to earn, perh. cogn. with Gr. *meros*, a share, whence *meireisthai*, to receive a portion], *n.* The quality of deserving, desert; excellence deserving honour or reward; worth, worthiness; a reward or recompense, a mark or award of merit; (*pl.*) the essential rights and wrongs of a case. *v.t.* To deserve, to earn; to be entitled to receive as a reward; to have a just title to. *v.i.* To acquire merit. **merited,** *a.* **meritorious** (-tôr′ i ŭs), *a.* Deserving reward; praiseworthy. **meritoriously,** *adv.* **meritoriousness,** *n.*

***merk** (mĕrk) [MARK (2)], *n.* An old Scottish silver coin, value 13⅓d. sterling, or 13s. 4d. Scots.

merle (mĕrl) [O.F., from L. *merula*], *n.* (*poet.*) The blackbird.

merlin (mĕr′ lin) [A.-F. *merilun*, O.F. *esmerillon*, prob. from Teut.], *n.* The smallest of the European falcons, *Falco æsalon*, and other falcons of the subdivision *Æsalon.*

***merling** (mĕr′ ling) [O.F. *merlanke* (F. *merlan*), from MERLE], *n.* The whiting.

merlon (mĕr′ lŏn) [F., from It. *merlone*, from *merlo*, *merla*, battlement, prob. from *mergola*, dim. of L. *mergæ*, pl., a pitchfork], *n.* The part of an embattled parapet between two embrasures.

mermaid (mĕr′ mād) [MERE (1), MAID (cp. A.-S. *mere-wif*, mere-woman)], *n.* A fabulous marine creature, having the upper half like a woman and the lower like a fish. **mermaiden,** *n.* (*poet.*) **merman,** *n.*

mero- [Gr. *meros*, part, portion], *comb. form.* Partly.

meroblast (mer′ ō blăst), *n.* (*Biol.*) An ovum only a portion of which is directly germinal. **meroblastic,** *a.*

merogony (me rog′ ō ni), *n.* (*Biol.*) The growth of an organism from a portion of the ovum not containing a nucleus. **merogonic,** *a.*

merohedral (me rō hē′ drȧl), *a.* (*Cryst.*) Having less than the number of faces belonging to the type.

meroistic (me rō is′ tik), *a.* (*Ent.*) Secreting vitilligenous cells as well as ova (of the ovaries of certain insects).

meropidan (mė rop′ i dȧn) [mod. L. *Meropidæ*, from Gr. *merops*, bee-eater, -AN], *a.* Of or pertaining to the *Meropidæ*, a family of birds containing the bee-eater. *n.* A bird of this family.

merosome (mer′ ȯ sōm) [MERO-, Gr. *sōma*, body], *n.* (*Zool.*) A segment of the body of a segmented animal, as the ring of a worm. **merosomal** (-sō′ mȧl), *a.*

Merovingian (mer ȯ vin′ ji ȧn) [F. *Merovingien*, med. L. *Merovingī*, from Teut.], *a.* A term applied to the Frankish dynasty reigning in Gaul and Germany, founded by Clovis in A.D. 486. *n.* A sovereign of this dynasty.

merriment, etc. [MERRY (2)].

merry (1) (mer′ i) [F. *merise*, taken as pl.], *n.* The wild black cherry.

merry (2) (mer′ i) [A.-S. *myrige*, whence MIRTH, prob. from O.Teut. *murgjo-*, lasting a short time, cogn. with Gr. *brachus*, short], *a.* Joyous, gay, jovial, mirthful; causing merriment; (*colloq.*) slightly tipsy; *sarcastic. **to make merry** [MAKE (2)]. **to make merry over:** To make a laughing matter of. **merry-andrew,** *n.* A buffoon, a jester, esp. one assisting a mountebank or quack. **merry-dancers,** *n.pl.* The aurora borealis. **merry-go-round,** *n.* A revolving frame with seats or wooden horses on which persons ride at fairs etc.; (*colloq.*) a traffic roundabout. **merry-make,** *v.i.* To make merry. *n.* A merry-making. **merry-making,** *a.* Making merry, jovial. *n.* Merriment; a festivity. ***merry-man,** *n.* A merry-andrew. **merry-thought,** *n.* The furcula or forked bone in the breast of a bird. **merrily,** *adv.* **merriment, merriness,** *n.*

merulidan (mė roo′ li dȧn) [mod. L. *Merulidæ*, from L. *merula*, MERLE], *a.* Of or pertaining to the *Turdidæ* or *Merulidæ*, a family of birds comprising the thrush and blackbird. *n.* A bird of this family.

merycism (mer′ i sizm) [Gr. *mērukismos*, from *mērukizein*, to ruminate], *n.* (*Path.*) A disorder in which food is brought back from the stomach and chewed again.

mesa (mā′ zȧ) [Sp., table], *n.* (*U.S.A.*) A table-land; a plateau with steep sides.

mesail (mes′ āl) [F. *mésail*, prob. from O.F. *muçaille*, from *mucier*, to hide], *n.* (*Ant.*) The visor of a helmet, esp. if made in two parts.

mésalliance (mā zăl′ i ȧns) [F. (*més-*, MIS-, ALLIANCE)], *n.* Marriage with one of inferior social position.

mesaraic (mes ȧ rā′ ik) [med. L. *mesaraïcus*, Gr. *mesaraïkos*, from *mesaraion* (*meson*, middle, *araia*, the belly)], *a.* (*Anat.*) Mesenteric.

Mesdemoiselles, *pl.* [MADEMOISELLE].

***meseems** (mė sēmz′) [ME, dat., SEEM], *v. impers.* It seems to me.

mesembrianthemum (mė sem bri ăn′ thė mŭm) [Gr. *mesēmbria*, noon, *anthemon*, flower], *n.* (*Bot.*) A genus of very succulent plants, with thick, fleshy leaves and brilliant flowers, containing the ice-plant or fig-marigold.

mesencephalon (mes ėn sef′ ȧ lȯn) [Gr. *mesos*, middle, ENCEPHALON], *n.* (*Anat.*) The mid-brain. **mesencephalic** (-făl′ ik), *a.*

mesentery (mes′ ėn tėr i) [med. L. *mesenterium*, Gr. *mesenterion* (*mesos*, middle, *enteron*, entrail)], *n.* (*Anat.*) A fold of the peritoneum investing the small intestines and connecting them with the wall of the abdomen. **mesenteric** (-ter′ ik), *a.* **mesenteritis** (-ī′ tis), *n.* (*Path.*) Inflammation of the mesentery.

mesh (mesh) [perh. from A.-S. *max* (cp. Dut. *maas*, G. *masche*), or from M.Dut. *maesche*], *n.* The space or interstice between the threads of a net; (*pl.*) network; (*fig.*) a trap, a snare; (*Mach. etc.*) the engagement of gear-teeth etc.; interlacing structure. *v.t.* To catch in a net, to ensnare; (*Mach.*) to engage (of gear-teeth etc.). **in mesh:** (of cogs) Engaged. **mesh-work,** *n.* **meshy,** *a.*

mesial (mē′ si ȧl) [Gr. *mesos*, middle, -IAL], *a.* Pertaining to, situated or directed towards the middle, esp. the middle line of the body; median. **mesially,** *adv.*

mesmerism (mez′ mėr izm) [F. A. *Mesmer* (1733–1815), Swiss-German physician, -ISM], *n.* The art or power of inducing an abnormal state of the nervous system, in which the will of the patient is controlled by that of the agent; the hypnotic state so induced. **mesmeric** (-mer′ ik), *a.* **mesmerist,** *n.* **mesmerize,** *v.t.* **mesmerizee** (-zē′), *n.* **mesmerizer** (mez′ mėr ī zėr), *n.* **mesmerization** (-zā′ shŭn), *n.*

mesne (mēn) [F., legal var. of A.-F. *meen*, MEAN (1)], *a.* Middle, intermediate. **mesne lord:** (*Feud. Law*) One holding of a superior lord. **mesne profits:** (*Law*) The profits of an estate received by a person wrongfully in possession.

meso-, mes- [Gr. *mesos*, middle], *comb. form.* Intermediate, in the middle; pertaining to the middle. **mesoblast** (mes′ ȯ blăst) [-BLAST], *n.* The intermediate layer of the blastoderm of the embryo. **mesoblastic** (-blăs′ tik), *a.* **mesocarp** (mes′ ȯ karp) [Gr. *karpos*, fruit], *n.* (*Bot.*) The middle layer of a pericarp. **mesocephalic** (-sė făl′ ik) [CEPHALIC], *a.* (*Craniometry*) Intermediate between dolichocephalic and brachycephalic (of skulls). **mesocephalous** (-sef′ ȧ lŭs), *a.* **mesocephalism, mesocephaly,** *n.* **mesoderm** (mes′ ȯ dĕrm) [DERM], *n.* (*Biol.*) The mesoblast; (*Bot.*) the middle layer of the bark, of the wall of a spore-case, etc. **mesodermal, -dermic** (-dĕr′ mȧl, -mik), *a.* **mesode** (mes′ ōd) [Gr. *mesōdos* (MESO-, ODE)], *n.* (*Gr. Pros.*) A passage between the strophe and antistrophe in a choral ode. **mesodic** (mė sod′ ik), *a.* **mesogaster** (mes ȯ găs′ tėr) [Gr. *gastēr*, stomach], *n.* (*Anat.*) A membrane attaching the stomach to the dorsal wall of the abdomen. **mesogastric,** *a.* **mesolithic** (mes ȯ lith′ ik) [LITHIC], *a.* (*Archæol.*) Intervening between the neolithic and palæolithic divisions of the stone age. **meson** (mes′ on), *n.* (*Phys.*) A particle intermediate in mass between a proton and an electron. **mesophlœum** (-flē′ ŭm) [Gr. *phloios*, bark], *n.* (*Bot.*) The middle or green layer of bark in exogens. **mesophyll** (mes′ ȯ fil) [Gr. *phullon*, leaf], *n.* (*Bot.*) The inner parenchymatous tissue of a leaf. **mesoplast,** *n.* The nucleus of a cell. **mesothorax** (mes ȯ thôr′ ăks) [THORAX], *n.* (*Ent.*) The middle segment of the thorax bearing the anterior legs and the middle wings. **mesozoic** (mes ȯ zō′ ik) [ZOIC], *a.* (*Geol.*) Belonging to the second great geological epoch, secondary.

mesquit (mes kēt′, mes′ kit) [Mex., Sp. *mezquite*], *n.* Either of two leguminous shrubs or trees growing in the S.-W. United States and as far south as Peru, the larger yielding the sweetish screw-pod used for fodder. **mesquit-bean,** *n.* **mesquit-grass,** *n.*

mess (mes) [O.F. *mes*, late L. *missum*, neut. p.p. of *mittere*, to send], *n.* A dish or a portion of food sent to table at one time; liquid or semi-liquid food, esp.

for animals; a quantity of such food; a number of persons who sit down to table together (used esp. of soldiers and sailors); a meal taken thus; officers' living quarters; a state of dirt and disorder; a muddle, a difficulty; *a set or party of four, orig. one of the parties into which a company were divided at a banquet etc. *v.i.* To take a meal or meals in company, esp. of soldiers etc.; (*fig.*) to muddle or potter (about). *v.t.* To mix together, to muddle, to jumble; to dirty, to soil. **to mess about:** (*colloq.*) To tumble about; to treat roughly; to potter about. **messmate,** *n.* A member of the same mess; an associate; (*Biol.*) a parasite which does not actually feed on the body of its host, a commensal. **messy,** *a.* Dirty, muddled. **messiness,** *n.* A state of dirt or disorder.

message (mes' ȧj) [F., from pop. L. *missāticum*, as prec.], *n.* A communication, oral or written, from one person to another; (*fig.*) the truths, ideas, or opinions of a writer or inspired person; *a messenger; (*Naut.*) A rope from the capstan to the cable for lifting the anchor.

messan (mes' ȧn) [Sc., prob. from Gael. *measàn*], *n.* A lap-dog. **messan-cur, -dog, -tyke,** *n.*

messenger [MESSAGE] [F. *messager*], *n.* One who carries a message or goes on an errand. **queen's, king's messenger,** *n.* Official bearer of Foreign Office despatches to foreign countries.

Messiah (mė sī' ȧ), **Messias** (-ȧs) [F. *Messie*, L. and Gr. *Messīās*, Heb. *māshīah*, from *māshah*, to anoint], *n.* The Anointed One, Christ, as the promised deliverer of the Jews; an expected saviour or deliverer. **messiahship,** *n.* **messianic** (mes i ăn' ik), *a.* Of the, or inspired by the hope of, a Messiah.

messieurs (mes' yůrz) [see MONSIEUR], *n.pl.* Sirs; gentlemen (pl. of Mr., usu. abbr. to Messrs. (mes' ėrz)).

messmate [MESS].

messuage (mes' wȧj) [A.-F. *mesuage*, perh. scriptorial corr. of *mesnage*, but acc. to Skeat from O.F. *masuage*, med. L. *mansuāgium*, from *mansa*, see MANSE], *n.* (*Law*) A dwelling-house with the adjacent buildings and curtilage for the use of the household.

mestee (mes tē') [Sp. *mestizo*, mongrel], *n.* (W. Ind.) The offspring of a white and a quadroon, an octaroon.

mestizo (mes tē' zō) [Sp., from pop. L. *mixtīcius*, *mixtus*, p.p. of *miscēre*, to mix], *n.* One of mixed Spanish or Portuguese and Indian blood; applied also to one of mixed Chinese and Philippine blood.

met, *past & p.p.* [MEET (2)].

meta-, met-, meth- [Gr., on, with, among or between, after (implying change or transposition)], *comb. form.*

metabasis (me tăb' ȧ sis) [Gr.], *n.* (*Rhet.*) Transition from one subject to another; (*Med.*) change or remedies.

Metabola (me tăb' ō lȧ) [as foll.], *n.* (*Ent.*) A division of insects containing those undergoing complete metamorphosis. **metabolian,** *n.* One of the *metabola*.

metabolism (me tăb' ō lizm) [Gr. *metabolē*, change, rel. to *metaballein*, to change (META-, *ballein*, to throw), -ISM], *n.* (*Biol.*) The continuous chemical change going on in living matter, either constructive, by which nutritive material is built up into complex and unstable living matter, or destructive, by which protoplasm is broken down into simpler and more stable substances. **metabolic** (-bol' ik), *a.* **metabolize** (mė tăb' ō liz), *v.t.*

metacarpus (met ȧ kar' pŭs) [META-, CARPUS], *n.* (*Anat.*) The part of the hand between the wrist and the fingers. **metacarpal,** *a.*

metacentre (met ȧ sen' tėr), *n.* The point in a floating body slightly out of equilibrium where the vertical drawn through the centre of gravity when it is in equilibrium intersects the vertical passing through the centre of buoyancy.

metachrosis (met ȧ krō' sis), *n.* Change of colour, as in certain lizards.

metagalaxy (met ȧ găl' ȧk si), *n.* (*Astron.*) The universe beyond our galaxy.

metage (mē' tȧj) [METE, -AGE], *n.* Official measurement, esp. of coal; toll charged for measuring.

metagenesis (met ȧ jen' ė sis) [META-, GENESIS], *n.* (*Biol.*) Alternation of like and unlike generations. **metagenetic** (-je net' ik), **metagenic** (-jen' ik), *a.*

metal (met' ȧl) [O.F., from L. *metallum*, Gr. *metallon*, mine, mineral, perh. rel. to *metallan*, to search after], *n.* One of a class of elementary substances which usu. present in various degrees certain physical characters, as lustre, malleability, and ductility, possessed by the six metals known to the ancients, viz., gold, silver, copper, iron, lead, and tin; a compound of the elementary metals, an alloy; broken stone for road-making etc.; molten glass ready for blowing or casting; the effective power of the guns of a warship; (*pl.*) rails of a railway etc.; (*fig.*) mettle, essential quality. *v.t.* (*past & p.p.* **metalled**) To furnish or fit with metal; to cover or repair (a road) with metal. **metallic** (mė tăl' ik), *a.* **metallic currency:** Money composed of gold, silver, etc., as opp. to paper. **metalliferous** (-lif' ėr ŭs), *a.* **metalliform** (-tăl' i fôrm), *a.* **metalline** (met' ȧ līn), *a.* **metalling,** *n.* Broken stones etc., used in making or mending roads. ***metallist,** *n.* **metallize,** *v.t.* To form into a metal; to give metallic properties to; to vulcanize. **metallization** (-zā' shŭn), *n.* **metallo-,** *comb. form.* **metallography** (-log' rȧ fi), *n.* The science of metals, esp. the microscopic study of their internal structure. **metalloid** (met' ȧ loid), *a.* and *n.* **metalloidal** (-loi' dȧl), *a.* **metallophone,** *n.* A piano with metal bars instead of wires; a musical instrument like the xylophone with metal bars.

metalepsis (met ȧ lep' sis) [L. and Gr. *metalēpsis*, from *metalambanein*, to substitute (META-, *lambanein*, to take)], *n.* (*Rhet.*) The substitution of one word for another that is itself figurative, or the union of two or more tropes of a different kind in one word. **metaleptic, -al** (-lep' tik, -ȧl), *a.* **metaleptically,** *adv.*

metallurgy (met' ȧ lėr ji) [Gr. *metallourgos* (METALLO-, *-ergos*, working)], *n.* The science of metals; the art of separating metals from ores; the art of working in metal. **metallurgic, -al** (-lėr' jik, -ȧl), *a.* **metallurgist** (met'-), *n.*

metamere (met' ȧ mēr) [META-, Gr. *meros*, part], *n.* (*Zool.*) One of a series of similar parts of a body. **metameric** (met ȧ mer' ik), *a.* (*Zool.*) Of, pertaining to, or of the nature of a metamere; (*Chem.*) having the same composition and molecular weight, isomeric but different in chemical properties. **metamerism** (mė tăm' ėr izm), *n.*

metamorphic (met ȧ môr' fik) [META-, Gr. *morphē*, form, -IC], *a.* Causing or showing the results of metamorphosis; transforming or transformed. **metamorphism,** *n.* **metamorphology** (-fol' ȯ ji), *n.* The science of the metamorphoses of organisms.

metamorphose (met ȧ môr' fōz) [F. *métamorphoser*, from L. and Gr. *metamorphōsis*, transformation from *metamorphoun* (META-, *morphē*, form)], *v.t.* To change into a different form; to transmute. **metamorphosis** (met ȧ môr' fō sis), *n.* A change of form; the result of such a change; (*Biol.*) transformation, as of a chrysalis into a winged insect; (*fig.*) a complete change of character, purpose, etc.

metaphor (met' ȧ fôr) [F. *métaphore*, L. and Gr. *metaphora* (META-, *pherein*, to bear)], *n.* A figure of speech by which a word is transferred from one object to another, so as to imply comparison. **metaphoric, -al** (-for' ik, -ȧl), *a.* **metaphorically,** *adv.* ***metaphorist** (met' ȧ fôr ist), *n.*

metaphrase (met' ȧ frāz), **metaphrasis** (mė tăf' rȧ sis) [Gr. *metaphrasis* (META-, *phrazein*, to speak)], *n.* A literal translation. **metaphrist,** *n.* **metaphrastic** (-frăs′ tik), *a.*

metaphysics (met à fiz′ iks) [formerly *metaphysic,* med. L. *metaphysica,* Gr. *metaphusica* (*meta ta phusika,* after physics, or coming next after the study of natural science)], *n.pl.* (*usu. in sing.*) The philosophy of being and knowing; the theoretical principles forming the basis of any particular science; the philosophy of mind. **metaphysical,** *a.* Of or pertaining to metaphysics; transcendental, dealing with abstractions; abstruse, over-subtle; imaginary, fantastic. **metaphysically,** *adv.* **metaphysician** (-zish′ ăn), *n.* **metaphysicize** (-fiz′ i sīz), *v.t.* and *i.*

metaphyte (met′ à fīt), *n.* (*Bot.*) A multicellular plant, opp. to protophyte.

metaplasia (met à plā′ zi à) [Gr.], *n.* (*Physiol.*) Change of one form of tissue into another.

metaplasm (met′ à plăzm), *n.* (*Biol.*) The formative material of protoplasm; (*Gram.*) change in a word by alteration of a letter or syllable. **metaplastic,** *a.*

metapolitics (met à pol′ it iks), *n.pl.* Abstract political theories of an impractical nature.

metapophysis (met à pof′ i sis) [Gr.], *n.* (*Anat.*) A tubercular prominence on the vertebræ.

metastasis (me tăs′ tà sis), *n.* (*Biol.*) Metabolism; (*Path.*) a change in the seat of a disease from one organ to another. **metastatic,** *a.*

metatarsus (met à tar′ sŭs), *n.* (*Anat.*) That part of the foot between the tarsus and the toes, in man consisting of five long bones. **metatarsal,** *a.*

metathesis (met à thē′ sis), *n.* The transposition of sounds or letters in a word; (*Surg.*) the removal of a morbific agent etc., from one place to another; (*Chem.*) interchange of radicals or groups of atoms in a compound with others. **metathetic,** *a.*

metathorax (met à thôr′ ăks), *n.* (*Ent.*) The posterior segment of the thorax in an insect.

metatome (met′ à tōm), *n.* (*Arch.*) The space between two dentils.

metayer (mė tā′ ėr) [F., from med. L. *medietārius,* from *medietas,* MOIETY], *n.* A cultivator paying a certain proportion of the produce to the landlord, who provides seed, stock, etc. **metayage,** *n.*

Metazoa (met à zō′ à) [META-, Gr. *zōa,* pl. of *zōon,* animal], *n.pl.* (*Zool.*) A primary division of the animal kingdom including all animals in which the germs are differentiated into a mass of cells which may or may not be developed into more complex tissues. **metazoan,** *a.* Pertaining to the Metazoa. *n.* Any individual of the Metazoa. **metazoic,** *a.*

mete (1) (mēt) [A.-S. *metan* (cp. Dut. *meten,* G. *messen*)], *v.t.* To measure; to allot, to apportion (out); to appraise; to be the measure of. ***v.i.** To measure; to aim. ***metewand, *meteyard,** *n.* A measuring-rod.

mete (2) (mēt) [O.F., from L. *meta,* a goal], *n.* A limit, a boundary.

metempiric (met em pir′ ik), *n.* The science of things lying beyond the bounds of experience; one who believes in this. **metempirical,** *a.* **metempiricism,** *n.* **metempiricist,** *n.*

metempsychosis (mė temp′ si kō′ sis) [late L., from Gr. *metempsuchōsis*], *n.* The passage of the soul after death from one animal body to another.

metensomatosis (met en sō mà tō′ sis) [Gr.], *n.* The transference of the elements of one body into another body as by decomposition and assimilation.

meteor (mē′ tė ŏr) [Gr. *meteōron,* n. from adj. *meteōros,* raised (META-, *eōra,* var. of *aiōra,* from *aeirein,* to raise)], *n.* A luminous body appearing for a few moments in the sky and then disappearing, a shooting-star; any atmospheric phenomenon, as rain, hail, etc.; (*fig.*) anything which transiently dazzles or strikes with wonder. **meteoric** (-or′ ik), *a.* Pertaining to or consisting of meteors; resembling a meteor; (*fig.*) brilliant but fading quickly, dazzling; of or pertaining to the atmosphere or its phenomena. **meteorite** (mē′-), *n.* A fallen meteor; stone, metal, or a compound of earth and metal, that has fallen upon the earth from space. **meteorolite,** *n.* **meteorograph,** *n.* An instrument for recording meteorological phenomena. **meteorography** (-og′ rà fi), *n.* **meteoroid,** *n.* **meteroidal** (-oi′ dăl), *a.*

meteorology (-ol′ ŏ ji), *n.* The science of the atmosphere and its phenomena, esp. for the purpose of forecasting the weather; the general character of the weather in a particular place. **meteorologic, -al** (-loj′ ik, -ăl), *a.* **meteorologically,** *adv.* **meteorologist** (-ol′ ŏ jist), *n.*

meter (1) (mē′ tėr), *n.* One who or that which measures, esp. instruments for registering the quantity of gas, water, electric energy, etc., supplied. **meterage,** *n.*

-meter [Gr. *metron,* measure], *suf.* A measuring instrument; as *barometer, thermometer.*

meteward, meteyard [METE (1)].

meth- [META-, before aspirates].

methane (meth′ ān) [METH, -YL, -ANE], *n.* (*Chem.*) A light, colourless gas, methyl hydride or carburetted hydrogen, produced by the decomposition or dry distillation of vegetable matter, one of the chief constituents of coal-gas, and also of fire-damp and marsh-gas. **methanometer** (-nom′ ė tėr), *n.*

***metheglin** (mē theg′ lin) [W. *meddyglyn* (*meddyg,* L. *medicus,* healing, *llyn,* liquor)], *n.* A variety of mead, orig. Welsh.

methinks (mė thinks′), *v.impers.* (*past* **-thought,** -thawt) It seems to me; I think.

method (meth′ ŏd) [F. *méthode,* L. *methodus,* Gr. *methodos* (METH-, *hodos,* way)], *n.* Mode of procedure, way or order of doing; an orderly, systematic, or logical arrangement; orderliness, system; a system or the basis of a system of classification. **method acting,** *n.* (*Theat.*) An actor's identification of himself with the part rather than giving just a technical performance. **methodic, -al** (mė thod′ ik, -ăl), *a.* **methodically,** *adv.*

Methodism (meth′ ŏ dizm) [prec., -ISM], *n.* The doctrines, practices, or Church system of the Methodists. **Methodist,** *n.* A strict observer of method in philosophical inquiry or medical practice; a member of any of the religious bodies that have grown out of the evangelical movement begun in the middle of the 18th cent. by John Wesley (1703–91), his brother Charles, and George Whitefield (1714–70). **methodistic, -al** (-dis′ tik, -ăl), *a.* **methodistically,** *adv.*

methodize (meth′ ŏ dīz), *v.t.* To reduce to order; to arrange systematically. **methodizer,** *n.* **methodology** (-dol′ ŏ ji) [-LOGY], *n.* (*Log.*) The branch of logic dealing with the methods of accurate thinking.

methomania (meth ŏ mā′ ni à) [Gr. *methē,* drink, drunkenness, -MANIA], *n.* (*Path.*) Morbid craving for intoxicating drink.

methought [METHINKS].

methyl (meth′ il) [F. *méthyle,* from *methylène* (Gr. *methu,* wine, *hulē,* wood)], *n.* (*Chem.*) The hypothetical radical of wood spirit, formic acid, and many other organic compounds. **methylate** (meth′ i lāt), *v.t.* To mix or saturate with methyl alcohol. **methylated spirit:** Spirit of wine, mixed with 10 per cent. of methyl alcohol so as to be rendered unfit to drink and accordingly duty-free.

methylene (meth′ i lēn), *n.* A hypothetical organic radical in which two atoms of hydrogen are in chemical combination with one atom of carbon, occurring in numerous compounds. **methylic** (-thil′ ik), *a.*

metic (mĕt′ ic) [Gr. *metoikos,* resident alien], *n.* An immigrant, a resident alien.

meticulous (mė tik′ ū lùs) [L. *meticulōsus*, from *metus*, fear], *a.* Cautious or over-scrupulous about trivial details, finical; very careful; *cautious, timid. **meticulously,** *adv.* **meticulousness,** *n.*

métier (met′ yā) [F., earlier *mestier*, pop. L. *misterium*, L. *ministerium*, MINISTRY], *n.* Trade, profession, one's particular 'line'.

métis (mā′ tēs, mā tēs′) [F. *métis*, MESTIZO], *n.* One of mixed blood, esp. (in Canada) the offspring of a European and an American Indian.

metonic (mė ton′ ik), *a.* Pertaining to Meton, Athenian astronomer, applied to the cycle of 19 Julian years at the end of which the new and full moons recur on the same dates.

metonymy (mė ton′ i mi) [late L. *metōnymia*, Gr. *metōnumia* (META-, *onoma*, Æolic *onuma*, name)], *n.* A figure in which one word is used for another, as the effect for the cause, the material for the thing made, etc., *e.g.* 'bench' for 'magistrates'. **metonymic, -al** (-nim′ ik, -ȧl), *a.* **metonymically,** *adv.*

metope (1) (met′ ȯ pi) [Gr. *metopē* (MET-, *opē*, hole for a beam)], *n.* (*Arch.*) The space between the triglyphs in a Doric frieze.

metope (2) (met′ ōp) [Gr. *metōpon*, forehead], *n.* (*Zool.*) The face or front (of a crab). **metopic** (-top′ ik), *a.* Frontal. **metopism** (met′ ȯ pizm), *n.* Persistence of the frontal suture. **metoposcopy** (met ȯ pos′ kȯ pi), *n.* The study of physiognomy. **metoposcopic** (-skop′ ik), *a.* **metoposcopist,** *n.*

metre (1) (mē′ tėr) [O.F., from L. *metrum*, Gr. *metron*, measure], *n.* The rhythmical arrangement of syllables in verse; verse; any particular form of poetic rhythm. **metric** (1), *a.* Metrical. *n.* (*usu. in pl.*) The science or art of metre, prosody. **metrical,** *a.* Of, pertaining to, or composed in metre; of or pertaining to measurement. **metrically,** *adv.* **metrician** (mė trish′ ȧn), **metrist** (met′ rist), *n.* One skilled in metres; a versifier. **metrify** (met′ ri fī), *v.t.*

metre (2) (mē′ tėr) [F. *mètre*, as prec.], *n.* The French standard measure of length, the ten-millionth part of the quadrant of a meridian, 39·37 in. **metre-ampere,** *n.* (*Radio.*) A measure of the power which a transmitter radiates. **metre-bridge,** *n.* (*Elec.*) Wheat-stone bridge of slide-wire pattern with one-metre length wire. **metric** (2), *a.* **metric system:** A system of weights and measures in which ascending units carry Greek prefixes and descending units Latin prefixes. Units are multiples of ten times the basic unit.

metro- [Gr. *metron*, measure], *comb. form.* **metrograph** (met′ rȯ grăf) [-GRAPH], *n.* A contrivance on a locomotive recording the speed achieved with the number and duration of the stoppages.

***metromania** (met rȯ mā′ ni ȧ) [METRO-, -MANIA], *n.* A passion for writing verses.

metronome (met′ rȯ nōm) [F. *métronome* (Gr. *nomos*, law, rule)], *n.* An instrument for indicating and marking time in music by means of a pendulum. **metronomic** (-nom′ ik), *a.* **metronomically,** *adv.* **metronomy** (mė tron′ ȯ mi), *n.*

metronymic (mē trȯ nim′ ik) [Gr. *mētrōnumikos* (*mētēr -tros*, mother, *onoma*, *onuma*, name)], *a.* Derived from the name of a mother or maternal ancestor (of names). *n.* A name so derived. **metronymy** (-tron′ i mi), *n.*

metropolis (mė trop′ ȯ lis) [L. and Gr. *mētropolis*, mother-state (*mētēr -tros*, mother, *polis*, city)], *n.* The chief town or capital of a country; the seat or see of a metropolitan bishop; (*fig.*) a centre or focus of activity etc.

metropolitan (met rō pol′ i tȧn), *a.* Pertaining to a capital city or to an archbishopric. *n.* A bishop having authority over other bishops in a province, in the Western Church an archbishop, in the ancient and in the modern Greek Church ranking above an archbishop and next to a patriarch; forming part of a sovereign state as distinct from its colonies. **metropolitanate,** *n.* ***metropolite** (mė trop′ ȯ līt), *n.* ***metropolitical** (-pȯ lit′ i kȧl), **metropolitic** (-pol′ i tic), *a.*

-metry [Gr. *metria*, measurement, from *metrēs*, measurer, see -METER], *suf.* Science of measuring; as *geometry*, *trigonometry*.

mettle (met′ ȧl) [var. of METAL], *n.* Quality of temperament or disposition; constitutional ardour; spirit, courage; *stuff, material one is made of. **mettled, mettlesome,** *a.* High-spirited, fiery, ardent. **mettlesomeness,** *n.*

***meuse** (mūs, mūz) [O.F. *muce*, from *musser*, *muchier*, to hide (cp. MICHE, MOUCH)], *n.* A gap in a fence etc., through which a hare runs; (*fig.*) a way of escape, a loophole.

mew (1) (mū) [A.-S. *mæw* (cp. Dut. *meeuw*, Icel. *mar*, G. *möwe*)], *n.* A kind of sea-gull, esp. *Larus canus*.

mew (2) (mū) [imit.], *v.i.* To cry 'mew' as a cat. *n.* This cry of the cat.

mew (3) (mū) [O.F. *mue*, from *muer*, L. *mūtāre*, to change], *n.* A cage for hawks, esp. whilst moulting; a place of confinement; a den; (*pl.*) royal stables in London (built on the spot where the royal hawks were formerly mewed); (*pl.*) stables for carriage-horses etc. (*pl. Am.*) a back alley. *v.t.* *To moult, to shed (the feathers); to put (a hawk) in a mew or cage; (*fig.*) to shut (up), to confine. **v.i.* To shed the feathers.

mewl (mūl), *v.i.* To cry, whine, or whimper, as a child; to mew (as a cat). **mewler,** *n.*

Mexican (mek′ si kȧn), *a.* Of or pertaining to Mexico. *n.* A native or inhabitant of Mexico.

mezereon (mė zēr′ i ȯn) [med. L., from Arab. *māzaryūn*], *n.* A small ornamental shrub, *Daphne mezereum*.

mezzanine (mez′ ȧ nēn, -nin) [F., from It. *mezzanino*, dim. of *mezzano*, L. *mediānus*, MEDIAN], *n.* A low storey between two higher ones (usu. between the ground and first floors); a window in such a storey; (*Theat.*) a floor beneath the stage from which the traps etc. are worked. **mezzanine-floor, -window,** *n.*

mezzo (med′ zō) [It., from L. *medius*, middle], *a.* Half or medium. **mezzo-soprano,** *n.* A voice lower than a soprano and higher than a contralto; a singer with such a voice. **mezzo-rilievo** (med′ zō rė lyā′ vō), *n.* (*pl.* -os) Half-relief, sculpture in which the figures stand out from the background to a half of their proportions.

mezzotint, *mezzotinto (med′ zō tint, -tin′ tō) [It. *mezzotinto*], *n.* A process of engraving in which a copper plate is uniformly roughened so as to print a deep black, lights and half-lights being then produced by scraping away the burr; a print from this. *v.t.* To engrave in mezzotint.

mho (mō) [*ohm* reversed], *n.* (*Elec.*) Unit of conductivity.

mi (mē) [It., orig. first syl. of L. *mīra*, see GAMUT], *n.* The third note of the diatonic scale.

miaow (mi ou′), *n.* The cry of a cat. *v.t.* To cry 'miaow' (of a cat).

miasma (mī ăz′ mȧ) [Gr., from *miainein*, to pollute], *n.* (*pl.* -mata) Poisonous or infectious exhalation, malaria. ***miasm** (mī′ ăzm), *n.* **miasmal** (mī ăz′ mȧl), **miasmatic, -al** (mī ăz măt′ ik, -ȧl), **miasmatous, miasmic, miasmous** (mī ăz′ mȧ tùs, -mik, -mùs), *a.* **miasmology** (-mol′ ȯ ji), *n.*

miaul (mi awl′), *v.t.* To cry 'miaow' (of a cat). *v.t.* To sing or utter with the voice of a cat. **miauler,** *n.* A cat.

mica (mī′ kȧ) [L., a crumb], *n.* (*Min.*) A name for a group of silicates having a perfect basal cleavage into thin, tough, and shining plates, formerly used instead of glass. **mica-schist, -slate,** *n.* **micaceous** (mī kā′ shùs), *a.*

mice, *pl.* [MOUSE]. **mich** [MICHE].

Michaelmas (mik′ ėl mȧs) [L. *Michael*, Heb. *Mīkhāēl*, who is like God, MASS (1)], *n.* The feast of St. Michael the Archangel, 29 Sept.; (*colloq.*) autumn. **Michaelmas-daisy,** *n.* The wild aster, *Aster tripolium*; also various perennial cultivated asters. (*Am.*) Aster.

miche (mich) [prob. from O.North.F. *muchier*, O.F. *mucier* (F. *musser*), from Teut. (cp. O.H.G. *mūhhōn*, to hide, G. dial. *maucheln*, to hide, to cheat)], *v.i.* To hide, to skulk, to play truant. **micher,** *n.*

miching malicho (mich′ ing măl′ i kō) [Shak. (MICHE, -ING, *malicho*, of uncertain meaning)]: Sneaking or stealthy mischief.

mickle (mik′ ėl) [A.-S. *micel*, *mycel*], *a.* (*now chiefly Sc.*). Much, great. *n.* A large amount.

micky (mik′ i) [fam. form of *Michael*, see MICHAELMAS], *n.* (*Austral. slang*) A young wild bull; (*Am. slang*) an Irish lad. **to take the micky out of:** (*slang*) To debunk; to tease. **Mickey Finn,** *n.* (*Am.*) A doped drink.

micr-, micro- [Gr. *mikros*, small], *comb. form.* Noting smallness; pertaining to small things (as opposed to large ones). **micracoustic** (mī krȧ kou′ stik) [F. *micracoustique* (ACOUSTIC)], *a.* Serving to increase small or indistinct sounds. *n.* An instrument for augmenting sounds for the partially deaf.

microbe (mī′ krōb) [F. (MICRO-, Gr. *bios*, life)], *n.* Any minute organism, esp. a bacterium or microzyme causing disease or fermentation. **microbial, -ian, -bic** (mī krō′ bi ȧl, -bi ȧn, -bik), *a.* **microbiology** (-bī ol ȯ ji), *n.* **microbiologist,** *n.*

microcephalic (mī krȯ sė făl′ ik) [MICRO-, CEPHALIC], *a.* (*Craniometry*) Having an unusually small skull. **microcephalous** (-sef ȧ lȯs), *a.*

microchronometer (mī krō krō nom′ ė tėr), *n.* A chronometer for measuring minute intervals of time.

micrococcus (mī krō kok′ ȯs), *n.* (*pl.* **micrococci**) One of a genus of minute spherical bacteria, usu. regarded as fission-fungi.

microcosm (mī′ krȯ kozm) [F. *microcosme*, med. L. *microcosmus*, Gr. *mikrokosmos* (MICRO-, COSMOS)], *n.* The universe on a small scale; man as an epitome of the macrocosm or universe; a little community; a representation (of) in little. **microcosmic** (-koz′ mik), *a.* **microcosmography** (-mog′ rȧ fi), *n.* **microcosmology** (-mol′ ȯ ji), *n.*

microcrith (mī′ krȯ krith) [MICRO-, Gr. *krithē*, barley-corn], *n.* (*Chem.*) The weight of an atom of hydrogen. **microcyte** (mī′ krȯ sīt) [-CYTE], *n.* (*Path.*) A small red blood-corpuscle, such as appear in cases of anæmia. **microcythæmia** (-thē′ mi ȧ), **microcytosis** (-tō′ sis), *n.* **microdont** (mī′ krȯ dont) [Gr. *odous odontos*, tooth], *n.* Having abnormally small teeth.

microfarad (mī krō făr′ ȧd), *n.* (*Elec.*) A unit of electrical capacitance, one-millionth of a farad.

microfilm (mī′ krō film), *n.* A strip of cinematograph film on which successive pages of a document or book are photographed for purposes of record. **microgeology** (mī krȯ jė ol′ ȯ ji) [GEOLOGY], *n.* The department of geology dealing with microscopic structures. **micrograph** (mī′ krȯ grăf) [-GRAPH], *n.* A kind of pantograph for extremely minute engraving; a very small picture, photograph, etc. **micrography** (-krog′ rȧ fi), *n.* A description of microscopic objects. **micrographer,** *n.* **micrographic** (-grăf′ ik), *a.* **microgroove,** *n.* The groove of a long-playing gramophone record.

microhm (mī′ krōm), *n.* (*Elec.*) A unit of electrical measurement, one-millionth of an ohm.

microlite (mī′ krȯ līt) [-LITE], *n.* (*Min.*) A native salt of calcium found in small crystals; microlith.

microlith (mī′ krō lith), *n.* (*Min.*) One of the microscopic bodies found in vitreous feldspar, hornblende, etc. **microlithic** (mī krȯ lith′ ik) [LITHIC], *a.* (*Archæol.*) Applied to a particular style of funeral monuments, in which extremely small stones are used.

micrology (mī krol′ ō ji), *n.* The branch of science dealing with microscopic objects, excessive concern with petty matters, over-minuteness, hair-splitting. **micrological** (-loj′ i kȧl), *a.* **micrologically,** *adv.* **micrologist** (-krol′ ȯ jist), *n.*

micrometer (mī krom′ ė tėr), *n.* An instrument to measure small distances or objects. **micrometric, -al** (-met′ rik, -ȧl), *a.* **micron** (mī′ crȯn), *n.* The millionth of a metre, the unit of length in microscopic research.

microphone (mī′ krō fōn), *n.* An instrument for converting sound into electrical waves; (*Radio.*) the mouthpiece for broadcasting. **microphonic** (-fon′ ik), *a.* Pertaining to the microphone; behaving in a manner similar to a microphone. *n.pl.* The branch of acoustics dealing with the magnifying of weak sounds.

microphotography (mī krō fō tog′ rȧ fi), *n.* The photography of objects on a minute scale; the photography of microscopic objects. **microphotograph,** *n.* **microphylline** (mī krȯ fil′ īn) [Gr. *phullon*, leaf, -INE], *a.* (*Bot.*) Composed of or having minute leaflets or scales. **microphyllous,** *a.* Having small leaves. **microphyte** (mī′ krȯ fīt) [-PHYTE], *n.* A microscopic vegetable organism, esp. a bacterium. **micropodal** (mī krop′ ȯ dȧl) [Gr. *pous podos*, foot, -AL], *a.* Having abnormally small feet. **micropsia** (mī krop′ si ȧ) [Gr. *-opsia*, vision], *n.* (*Path.*) A state of vision in which objects appear unnaturally small. **micropterous** (mī krop′ tėr ȯs) [Gr. *pteron*, wing], *n.* (*Zool.*) Having small wings or fins.

micropyle (mī′ krō pīl), *n.* (*Zool.*) A minute opening in the external membrane of the ova by which spermatozoa may enter; (*Bot.*) the foramen in an ovule by which the pollen reaches the apex of the nucleus; the aperture representing this in the ripe seed.

microscope (mī′ krȯ skōp) [MICRO-, -SCOPE], *n.* An optical instrument by which objects are so magnified that details invisible to the naked eye are clearly seen. **microscopic** (-skop′ ik), *a.* Pertaining to the microscope; too small to be visible except by the aid of a microscope. **microscopically,** *adv.* **microscopy** (-kros′ kȯ pi), *n.* **microscopist,** *n.*

microseism (mī′ krȯ sizm) [MICRO-, Gr. *seismos*, earthquake], *n.* A slight tremor or vibration of the earth's crust. **microseismic** (-sīz′ mik), *a.* **microseismograph** (-sīz′ mȯ grăf), *n.* An instrument for recording microseisms. **microseismology** (-mol′ ȯ ji), *n.* **microseismometry** (-mom′ ė tri), *n.*

microsoma (mī krō sō′ mȧ), *n.* (*pl.* **microsomata**) (*Biol.*) One of the minute granules in the endoplasm of protoplasmic cells. **microsome** (mī′ krȯ sōm), *n.* **microsomatous** (-sō′ mȧ tȯs), *a.* **microspectroscope** (mī krȯ spek′ trȯ skōp) [SPECTROSCOPE], *n.* A combination of microscope and spectroscope for examining minute traces of substances. **microsporangium** (mī krȯ spȯ răn′ ji ȯm) [SPORANGIUM], *n.* (*Bot.*) A sporangium containing microspores.

microspore (mī′ krō spôr), *n.* (*Bot.*) A small spore, sexual in function, as in the *Selaginellæ*; (*Path. etc.*) a parasitic fungus with small spores; (*Zool.*) a spore-like body in certain protozoa. **microsporous** (-spôr′ ȯs), *a.*

microtome (mī′ krō tōm), *n.* An instrument for cutting thin sections for microscopic examination. **microtomic, -al** (-tom′ ik, -ȧl), *a.* **microtomist** (-krot′ ȯ mist), *n.* **microtomy,** *n.*

microzoa (mī krō zō′ ȧ), *n.pl.* (*Zool.*) Microscopic animals. **microzoic, microzoal,** *a.* **microzoan,** *n.* **microzoid,** *n.a.*

microzyme (mī′ krō zīm), *n.* Any of the minute organisms floating in the air, probably the germs of certain infectious diseases.

micturition (mik tū rish′ ŭn) [L. *micturīre*, desiderative of *mingere*, to make water, -ITION], *n.* A morbid desire to urinate; (*incorr.*) the act of making water.

mid (mid) [A.-S. *mid*, *midd* (cp. Dut., Swed. and Dan. *mid-*, O.H.G. *mitti*, L. *medius*, Gr. *mesos*)], *a.* (*superl.* **midmost**) Middle (*usu. in comb.*). ***n.** The middle. *prep.* (*poet.*) Amid. ***mid-age,** *n.* Middle age. **midday,** *n.* Noon. *a.* Pertaining to noon. **mid-heaven,** *n.* **mid-iron,** *n* (*Golf*) An iron club with a moderate amount of loft. **mid-off,** *n.* (*Cricket*) The fieldsman to the left of the bowler. **mid-on,** *n.* The fieldsman to the right of the bowler. (These definitions apply only when the batsman is right-handed.)

Midas (mī′ dăs) [legendary king of Phrygia to whom Dionysus granted the power of turning all he touched into gold], *n.* (*fig.*) A fabulously rich man.

midden (mid′ ėn) [M.E. *midding*, from Scand. (cp. Dan. *mödding*, cogn. with MUCK, *dynge*, heap)], *n.* A dunghill. **kitchen-midden** [KITCHEN].

middle (mid′ ėl) [A.-S. *middel*, from *midd*, MID (cp. Dut. *middle*, G. *mittel*)], *a.* (*superl.* **middlemost**) Placed equally distant from the extremes; intervening; intermediate; (*Gram.*) between active and passive, reflexive. *n.* The point equally distant from the extremes; the waist; the midst, the centre. *v.t.* To place in the middle; (*Naut.*) to fold or double in the middle; (*Football*) to pass or return the ball to mid-field from one of the wings. **in the middle of:** During, while. **middle age:** The period of life between youth and old age, or about the middle of the ordinary human life (35–55). **middle-aged,** *a.* **Middle Ages:** The period from the 5th to the 15th cent. inclusive. **middle class:** The class between the leisured class and artisans, the bourgeoisie. **middle-class,** *a.* **middle-distance** [DISTANCE]. **Middle English** [ENGLISH]. **middle finger:** The second finger (third from the little finger inclusive). **Middle Kingdom:** China. **middleman,** *n.* An agent, an intermediary; one through whose hands a commodity passes between the producer and the consumer. **middle term:** (*Log.*) The term of a syllogism that appears in both major and minor premise. **middling,** *a.* Of middle size, quality, or condition; mediocre; moderately good, second-rate. *adv.* Moderately, tolerably. **middlingly,** *adv.* **middlings,** *n.pl.* The coarser part of flour; the middling grade of other commodities.

middy (1) [MIDSHIPMAN].

middy (2) (mid′ i), *n.* (*Austral. colloq.*) A glass of beer; a 10 oz. pot or container.

midge (mij) [A.-S. *mycg* (cp. Dut. *mug*, G. *mücke*, Dan. *myg*)], *n.* A gnat or other minute fly; (*fig.*) a tiny person. **midget,** *n.* A very small person. *a.* Very small.

midland (mid′ lȧnd), *a.* Situated in the middle or interior of a country; surrounded by land. *n.* The interior of a country; (*pl.*) the midland counties of England.

midnight (mid′ nīt), *n.* The middle of the night, twelve o'clock; intense darkness. *a.* Pertaining to or occurring in the middle of the night; very dark.

mid-off, -on [MID].

midrib (mid′ rib), *n.* (*Bot.*) The continuation of the petiole to the apex of a leaf.

midriff (mid′ rif) [A.-S. *midrif*, *-hrif* (*mid*, *hrif*, belly)], *n.* The diaphragm.

midship (mid′ ship), *n.* The middle part of a ship or boat. *a.* Situated in or belonging to this. **midshipman,** *n.* Formerly an officer ranking between a cadet and a sub-lieutenant, a young officer under instruction on shipboard. **midshipmite,** *n.* (*facet.*) A very young or small midshipman. **midships** [AMIDSHIPS].

midst (midst) [earlier *middest* (A.-S. *middes*, gen. of MID used adverbially, prob. confused or blended with superl. of MID)], *n.* The middle. *prep.* In the middle of, amidst. ******adv.* In the middle. **in the midst of:** Among, surrounded by or involved in.

midsummer (mid′ sŭm ėr), *n.* The middle of summer, esp. the period of the summer solstice, about 21 June. **midsummer day:** 24 June.

midway (mid′ wā), *a.* Situated in the middle or the middle of the way. *adv.* In the middle; half-way.

midwife (mid′ wīf) [A.-S. *mid*, with (cp. G. *mit*, also Gr. *meta*), WIFE], *n.* (*pl.* **-wives**) A woman who assists at childbirth; (*fig.*) any person who helps to bring something forth. *v.i.* To perform the office of a midwife. *v.t.* To assist in childbirth. **midwifery** (mid′ wif ri), *n.*

midwinter (mid′ win tėr), *n.* The middle of winter, esp. the winter solstice, 21 Dec.

mien (mēn) [F. *mine* or shortened from DEMEAN], *n.* Air or manner; appearance, deportment, demeanour, bearing, carriage.

miff (mif) [prob. imit. of instinctive expression of annoyance], *n.* A petty quarrel; a huff. *v.i.* To be vexed (with or at). *v.t.* To vex, to annoy slightly.

might (1) (mīt) [A.-S. *miht*, cogn. with *megan*, MAY (1) (cp. G. *macht*, Dan. *magt*)], *n.* Strength, force; power, esp. to enforce will or arbitrary authority. **with might and main:** With all one's strength. ***mightful,** *a.* **mighty,** *a.* Strong, powerful; very great, huge, immense; (*colloq.*) great, considerable. *adv.* (*colloq.*) Exceedingly, very. **mightily,** *adv.* **mightiness,** *n.*

might (2), *past* [MAY (1)].

mignon (mēn′ yōn) [F.], *a.* Delicate and small, dainty.

mignonette (min yō net′) [F., dim. of prec.], *n.* An annual plant, *Reseda odorata*, with fragrant greenish flowers.

migraine (mē′ grān) [F. *migranie*, see MEGRIM], *n.* Megrim.

migrate (mī grāt′, mī′ grāt) [L. *migrātus*, p.p. of *migrāre*, to wander], *v.i.* To remove from one country, place, or habitation to another; to pass from one region to another according to the season (of birds, fishes, etc.). **migrant** (mī′ grȧnt), *a.* and *n.* **migration** (-grā′ shŭn), *n.* **migrator** (mī grā′ tȯr), *n.* **migratory** (mī′ grȧ tȯr i), *a.*

mihanere (mē hā nē′ rē) [Maori], *n.* A convert to Christianity.

mikado (mi ka′ dō) [Jap. (*mi*, august, *kado*, gate, door)], *n.* The Emperor of Japan.

mike (mīk) *abbr.* MICROPHONE.

mil (mil) [L. *mille*, a thousand], *n.* A unit of length, the 1000th part of an inch, in measuring wire; basis of suggested British decimal coinage.

miladi, milady (mi lā′ di), *n.* (*Continental*) My lady (used as address or appellation).

milage [MILEAGE, *see* MILE].

milch (milch) [A.-S. *meolc*, *melc*, cogn. with MILK], *a.* Giving milk. **milch-cow,** *n.* A cow kept for milk; (*fig.*) a person from whom money is easily obtained.

mild (mīld) [A.-S. *milde* (cp. Dut., G., Dan., and Swed. *mild*, Icel. *mildr*), cogn. with Gr. *malthakos*], *a.* Gentle in manners or disposition; tender, pacific, clement, placid, bland, pleasant; soft, not harsh, sharp, or strong (of fruit, liquor, etc.); not bitter, not strongly flavoured with hops (of beer); moderate, not extreme, tame; moderate in degree; demulcent, lenitive; operating gently (of medicines). **draw it mild:** (*colloq.*) Do not exaggerate. **milden,** *v.t.* and *i.* **mildly,** *adv.* **mildness,** *n.*

mildew (mil′ dū) [A.-S. *meledēaw*, honeydew, cp. O.H.G. *militou* (*milith*, cp. Gr. *meli*, honey, DEW)], *n.* A deleterious fungoid growth on plants, cloth, paper, food, etc., after exposure to damp. *v.t.* To taint with mildew. *v.i.* To be tainted with mildew. **mildewy,** *a.*

mile (mīl) [A.-S. *mīl*, L. *mīlia*, pl. of *mille*, a thousand (paces)], *n.* A measure of length or distance,

1760 yards; orig. a Roman measure of 1000 paces, about 1620 yards. **geographical** or **nautical mile:** One-sixtieth of a degree, acc. to the British Admiralty 6080 feet, or 2026⅔ yards. **milepost, milestone,** *n.* A post or stone marking the miles on a road. **mileage,** *n.* The number of miles concerned. **miler,** *n.* A person, animal, or thing qualified to run or travel a mile, or (*in comb.*) a specified number of miles (as *ten-miler*).

Milesian (mī lē′ shi ȧn) [*Milesius*, legendary king of Spain, whose sons are said to have conquered Ireland about 1300 B.C., -AN], *a.* Irish. *n.* An Irishman.

milfoil (mil′ foil) [O.F., from L. *millefolium* (*mille*, thousand, *folium*, leaf)], *n.* The yarrow, *Achillea millefolium*, named because the leaves are thrice pinnatifid; the genus *Achillea*; applied to some other plants.

miliary (mil′ i ȧr i) [L. *miliārius*, from *milium*, MILLET], *a.* Like millet seed; (*Path.*) attended with an eruption like millet seeds.

militant (mil′ i tȧnt) [L. *mīlitans -ntem*, pres.p. of *mīlitāre*, to MILITATE], *a.* Fighting; combative, warlike, military. **Church militant:** The body of Christians on earth. **militant suffragette:** (*Hist.*) One of the female advocates of woman suffrage (1905–1918) who undertook violent means to gain a hearing. **militancy,** *n.* **militantly,** *adv.*

military (mil′ i tȧr i) [F. *militaire*, L. *mīlitāris*, from *mīles mīlitis*, soldier], *a.* Pertaining to soldiers, arms, or warfare; soldierly, warlike, martial; engaged in war. *n.* (*collect.*) Soldiers generally; the army; troops. **Military Cross (Medal):** A British army decoration awarded for conspicuous courage under fire. **military fever:** Enteric or typhus. **military service:** Service (usu. compulsory) in the armed forces; the service due in time of war from a vassal to his superior. **military tenure:** Tenure by this. **militarism** (mil′ i tȧr izm), *n.* Military spirit; military or warlike policy; domination by the military or the spirit of aggression. **militarist,** *n.* **militarize,** *v.t.* **militarization** (-zā′ shŭn), *n.*

militate (mil′ i tāt) [L. *mīlitātus*, p.p. of *mīlitāre*, from *mīles mīlitis*, soldier], *v.i.* To be or stand opposed; to have weight or influence, to tell (against).

militia (mi lish′ ȧ) [L., as prec.], *n.* A military force consisting of the body of citizens not enrolled in the regular army; the former constitutional force of England, consisting usu. of volunteers enrolled and disciplined, but called out only in case of emergency, superseded by the Territorial Army in 1907. **militiaman,** *n.*

milk (milk) [A.-S. *meolc* (cp. Dut. and Dan. *melk*, G. *milch*, Icel. *mjōlk*), cogn. with Gr. *amelgein*, L. *mulgēre*, to milk], *n.* The whitish fluid secreted by female mammals for the nourishment of their young, esp. that of the cow; the white juice of certain plants; an emulsion made from herbs, drugs, etc. *v.t.* To draw milk from; (*fig.*) to plunder (creditors); to exploit or get money out of (a person) in an underhand or disreputable way; (*slang*) to tap (a telegraph wire or message); *to give milk to; *to suck. *v.i.* To yield milk. **milk-and-water,** *n.* Milk diluted with water; (*fig.*) namby-pamby or mawkish talk, sentiment, etc. *a.* Namby-pamby, weak, twaddling. **milk-fever,** *n.* A fever attacking women when milk is first secreted after childbirth. ***milk-livered,** *a.* Cowardly. **milkmaid,** *n.* A woman employed in dairywork. **milkman,** *n.* A man who sells milk; a dairy worker. **milk-punch,** *n.* Spirits mixed with milk and sweetened. **milk-shake,** *n.* An iced drink of sweetened milk and carbonated water, shaken up in a machine. **milk-sickness,** *n.* A fatal spasmodic cattle disease, sometimes communicated to man, peculiar to the Western States of the U.S.A. **milksop,** *n.* An effeminate person. **milk-sugar,** *n.* (*Chem.*) Lactose. **milk-thistle,** *n.* A thistle-like herb of the aster family, *Silbyum marianum.* **milk-tooth,** *n.* One of the temporary teeth in young mammals; the foretooth of a foal. **milk-vetch,** *n.* A plant of the leguminous genus *Astragalus*, supposed to increase milk-bearing in goats. **milker,** *n.* **milky,** *a.* Consisting of, mixed with, or resembling milk; mild, effeminate; white, opaque, clouded (of liquids); yielding milk (of cattle); timid. **Milky Way:** A luminous zone, composed of innumerable stars, stretching across the heavens; the Galaxy. **milkily,** *adv.* **milkiness,** *n.*

milkweed (milk′ wēd), *n.* A plant, of various species, with milky juice.

milkwort (milk′ wĕrt), *n.* (*Bot.*) A plant of the genus *Polygala*, formerly believed to promote the secretion of milk, *esp. P. vulgaris*, a small plant with blue, white, or pink flowers.

mill (1) (mil) [A.-S. *myln*, from late L. *mulīna*, *molīna*, L. *mola*, a mill (*molere*, to grind)], *n.* A machine for grinding corn to a fine powder; a building with machinery for this purpose; a machine for reducing solid substances of any kind to a finer consistency; a building fitted up with machinery for any industrial purpose, a factory; (*slang*) a fight with fists. *v.t.* To grind (as corn); to produce (flour) by grinding; to serrate the edge of (a coin); to full (cloth); (*slang*) to thrash, to pummel. *v.i.* (*Am.*) To move slowly round and round (of a mass of cattle). **millboard,** *n.* Thick pasteboard used by bookbinders for book-covers. **mill-cog,** *n.* A cog of a mill-wheel. **mill-dam,** *n.* A wall or dam built across a stream to divert it to a mill; a mill-pond. **mill-hand,** *n.* Factory worker. **mill-pond,** *n.* **mill-race,** *n.* The canal or the current of water for driving a mill-wheel. **mill-rind,** *n.* An iron fitting for fixing an upper millstone to the spindle. **millstone,** *n.* One of a pair of circular stones for grinding corn. **to see far into a millstone:** To be remarkably acute. **millstone grit:** A coarse quartzose sandstone used for making millstones. **mill-tail,** *n.* The stream flowing from a mill-wheel. **mill-tooth,** *n.* A molar tooth. **mill-wheel,** *n.* A large wheel moved by water, flowing over or under it, for driving the machinery in a mill. **millwright,** *n.* One who constructs or repairs the machinery of mills. **milled,** *a.* Passed through a mill; having the edges serrated (of coin); fulled (of cloth).

mill (2) (mil) [short for L. *millēsimum*, thousandth, from *mille*, a thousand], *n.* A money of account in the U.S.A., the 1000th part of a dollar or 10th of a cent.

millennium (mi len′ i ŭm) [L. *mille*, thousand, *annus*, year], *n.* A period of 1000 years, esp. that when Satan shall be bound and Christ reign on earth (in alln. to Rev. xx. 1–5). **millenarian** (mil ė nâr′ i ȧn), *a.* Consisting of 1000 years; pertaining to the millennium. *n.* One who believes in this. **millenarianism,** *n.* **millenary** (mil′ ė nȧr i), *a.* and *n.* **millenial,** *a.* Pertaining to the millennium. *n.* A thousandth anniversary. **millenialist,** *n.*

millipede (mil′ ė pēd) [L. *millipeda*, wood-louse (*mille*, thousand, *pes pedis*, foot)], *n.* A segmented myriapod, esp. of the genus *Iulus*; any articulate animal with numerous feet.

***millepore** (mil′ ė pôr) [L. *mille*, thousand, *porus*, PORE], *n.* (*Zool.*) Any coral of the genus *Millepora*, the surface of which is full of minute pores. **milleporite,** *n.* A fossil millepore.

miller (mil′ ėr), *n.* One who keeps or works in a flour mill; one who works any mill; applied to various moths and other insects with white or powdery wings, etc. **miller's thumb:** The bullhead, *Cottus gobio*.

millesimal (mi les′ i mȧl) [L. *millēsimus*, thousandth, from *mille*, thousand], *a.* Consisting of one-thousandth parts. *n.* A thousandth.

millet (mil′ ėt) [F., dim. of *mil*, L. *milium* (cp. Gr. *meline*)], *n.* *Panicum miliaceum* of East Indian origin, or its nutritive seeds; applied to some other species of grasses bearing edible seeds. **millet-grass,** *n.* A tall North American grass, *Milium effusum*.

milliard (mil' i ărd) [F., from L. *mille*, a thousand], *n.* A thousand millions.

***milliary** (mil' i ăr i) [L. *milliārius*, from *mille*, a thousand (paces)], *a.* Pertaining to or denoting a mile, esp. a Roman mile; pertaining to a millennium. *n.* A milestone.

millibar (mil' i bar) [L. *mille*, a thousand; BAR (3)], *n.* (*Meteor.*) One-thousandth of a bar, equivalent to the pressure exerted by a column of mercury about 0·03 in. high. **millicurie,** *n.* A thousandth of a curie. **milligramme,** *n.* The 1000th part of a gramme, 0·0154 of an English grain. **millilitre,** *n.* The 1000th part of a litre, 0·06103 cubic in. **millimetre,** *n.* The 1000th part of a metre, or 0·03937 in.

milliner (mil' i nėr) [prob. *Milaner*, a dealer in Milan wares], *n.* One, usu. a woman, who makes and sells hats, bonnets, etc., for women; *a haberdasher. **millinery,** *n.*

milling (mil' ing), *n.* The act or process of working a mill or mills; the serrated edging of a coin.

million (mil' yŏn) [F., from It. *millione*, from L. *mille*, thousand], *n.* A thousand thousand, esp. of pounds, francs, or dollars; (*fig.*) an indefinitely great number. **the million:** The multitude, the masses. **millionaire** (mil yŏ nâr'), *n.* A man having a million pounds, francs, or dollars; one immensely rich. **millionary** (mil' yŏ năr i), *a.* Pertaining to or consisting of millions. *n.* A millionaire. **millionfold,** *a.* and *adv.* **millionocracy** (-nok' ră si), *n.* Government by millionaires. **millionth,** *a.* and *n.*

millocrat (mil' ŏ krăt), *n.* A wealthy mill-owner; one of the mill-owning class. **millocracy** (-lok' ră si), **millocratism,** *n.*

Mills-bomb [from name of inventor, Sir W. *Mills* (1856–1932)], *n.* A type of hand grenade.

millwright [MILL].

milord (mi lôr), *n.* (*Continental*) My lord (applied to rich Englishmen).

milreis (mil' rās) [Port. (*mil*, thousand, REIS)], *n.* A Portuguese coin worth about 4s. 5½d.

milt (milt) [A.-S. *milte* (cp. Dut. and Dan. *milt*, G. *milz*), prob. cogn. with MELT], *n.* The spleen; the spermatic organ of a male fish; the soft roe of fishes. *v.t.* To impregnate with milt (as fish ova). **milter,** *n.*

Miltonic, Miltonian (mil ton' ik, -tō' ni ăn), *a.* Of or resembling the style of the poet John Milton (1608–74); elevated, stately and sonorous, sublime. **Miltonism** (mil' tŏ nizm), *n.*

milvine (mil' vīn) [L. *milvus*, kite, -INE], *a.* (*Ornith.*) Of or belonging to the *Milvinæ* or kites. *n.* A bird of this family.

mim (mim) [Sc., prob. imit.], *a.* Prim, demure, quiet, precise.

mime (mīm) [L. *mīmus*, Gr. *mīmos*], *n.* A simple kind of farce characterized by mimicry and gesture, popular among the ancient Greeks and Romans; an actor in a mime; a mimic, a clown or buffoon. *v.i.* To act in mime; to play the mime. *v.t.* To mimic.

mimeograph (mim' ė ŏ grăf) [Gr. *mīmeisthai*, to imitate, -GRAPH], *n.* A duplicating apparatus in which a paraffin-coated sheet is used as a stencil for reproducing written or typewritten matter. *v.t.* To reproduce by means of this.

mimesis (mī mē' sis) [Gr., from *mīmos*, MIME], *n.* Mimicry; imitation of or close natural resemblance to the appearance of another animal or of a natural object. **mimetic** (mi met' ik), *a.* **mimetically,** *adv.*

mimetite (mī' mė tīt) [G. *mimetit*, Gr. *mīmētēs*, imitator, as prec., -ITE], *n.* (*Min.*) A native arsenate of lead.

mimic (mim' ik) [L. *mīmicus*, Gr. *mīmikos*, from *mīmos*, MIME], *a.* Given to imitation; imitative; imitating, counterfeit. *n.* One who mimics; *an actor, a mime. *v.t.* (*past & p.p.* **mimicked**) To imitate, esp. in order to ridicule; to ape, to copy; to resemble closely (of animals, plants, etc.). **mimicry,** *n.*

miminy-piminy (mim' i ni pim' i ni) [imit., cp. MIM], *a.* Too fastidious, finical; affectedly nice or delicate. *n.* Writing or diction of this character.

mimosa (mi-, mī mō' să) [L. *mīmus*, MIME, *-ōsa*, -OSE], *n.* A genus of leguminous shrubs, including the sensitive plant, *Mimosa pudica.*

mimulus (mim' ū lŭs) [dim. of L. *mīmus*, MIME], *n.* A genus of plants with a mask-like corolla, comprising the monkey-flower.

mina (1) (mī' nă) [L., from Gr. *mina*, prob. Eastern in orig.], *n.* A Greek weight of 100 drachmæ, or about 1 lb. avoirdupois; a coin worth 100 drachmæ.

mina (2) (mī' nă) [Hind. *maina*], *n.* One of various Eastern and Australian passerine birds. **mina-bird,** *n.* Also **myna, mynah.**

minacious (mi nā' shŭs) [L. *minax -ācis*, -OUS], *a.* Threatening. **minaciously,** *adv.* **minacity** (mi năs' i ti), *n.*

minaret (min' ăr ėt) [F. *minaret* or Sp. *minarete*, from Arab. *manārat*, rel. to *nār*, fire], *n.* A lofty slender turret on a mosque, from which the muezzin summons the people to prayers.

minatory (min' ă tŏr i) [late L. *minātōrius*, from *minārī*, to threaten], *a.* Threatening, menacing.

minauderie (mi nō' dėr i) [F., from *minauder*, to put on airs, from *mine*, MIEN], *n.* Affectation, coquettish airs.

mince (mins) [O.F. *mincier*, pop. L. *minūtiāre*, from MINUTIA], *v.t.* To cut or chop into very small pieces; to utter or pronounce with affected delicacy; to minimize, to palliate, to gloss over; to restrain (one's words) for politeness' sake. *v.i.* To talk with affected elegance; to walk in a prim and affected manner. *n.* Minced meat; mincemeat. **not to mince matters:** To speak plainly. **mincemeat,** *n.* A filling for pies etc., composed of suet, raisins, currants, candied-peel, etc., chopped fine; (*fig.*) very fine or small pieces or fragments. **to make mincemeat of:** To crush or destroy completely. **mince-pie,** *n.* **mincing,** *a.* Affectedly elegant. **mincingly,** *adv.*

mind (mīnd) [A.-S. *gemynd*, cogn. with *munan*, to think, to remember (cp. O.H.G. *gimunt*, Goth. *gamunds*, memory, from root *men-*, *mun-*, cp. L. *mens*, mind, Gr. *menos*, rage)], *n.* The intellectual powers in man; the understanding, the intellect; the soul; intellectual capacity; recollection, memory; one's candid opinion; disposition, liking, way of feeling or thinking; intention, purpose; desire, inclination. *v.t.* To heed, to regard; to pay attention to, to apply oneself to; (*colloq.*) to object to; (*colloq.*) to look after; *to remember, to bear in mind. *v.i.* To take care, to be on the watch. **absence** or **presence of mind** [ABSENT, PRESENCE]. **to bring** or **call to mind** [CALL (1)]. **to have a mind:** To be inclined (to). **to make up one's mind** [MAKE (2)]. **to put in mind:** To remind (of). **to speak one's mind:** To express one's candid opinion (of or about). **minded,** *a.* (*usu. in comb.*, as *evil-minded*). **mindful,** *a.* Attentive, heedful. **mindfully,** *adv.* **mindfulness,** *n.* **mindless,** *a.*

mine (1) (mīn) [A.-S. *mīn* (cp. Dut. *mijn*, G. *mein*)], *poss. pron.* Belonging to me. **a.* My (used bef. vowels and sometimes *h*).

mine (2) (mīn) [F. *miner* (cp. It. *minare*, Sp. *minar*), etym doubtful], *v.t.* To dig into or burrow in; to obtain by excavating in the earth; to make by digging; to undermine, to sap; to set with mines. *v.i.* To dig a mine, to engage in digging for ore etc.; (*fig.*) to burrow; to practise secret methods of inquiry. *n.* An excavation in the earth for the purpose of obtaining minerals; a rich deposit of minerals suitable for mining; crude ironstone; an excavation under an enemy's works for blowing them up, formerly to form a means of entering or to cause a collapse of the wall, etc.; (*Nav.* and *Mil.*) a receptacle filled with explosive, floating in the sea or buried in the ground, which is exploded by contact; (*fig.*) a rich source of wealth, or of information, etc. **mine-captain,** *n.* The overseer of a mine. **mine-crater,** *n.* (*Mil.*) A crater formed by the explosion of a mine. **mine-layer,** *n.* (*Nav.*) A ship employed to lay mines. **mine-sweeper,** *n.* (*Nav.*) A trawler or other vessel employed to clear mines laid by the enemy. **magnetic mine,** *n.* A mine detonated by the effect on a magnet of the metal parts of a ship passing over it. **miner,** *n.* One who digs for minerals; one who works in mines; a soldier employed to lay mines; (*Austral.*) a variety of honey-eater bird.

mineral (min' ėr ȧl) [F. *minéral*, med. L. *minerāle*, neut. of *minerālis*, from *minera*, from prec.], *n.* An inorganic body, homogeneous in structure, with a definite chemical composition, found in the earth; any inorganic substance found in the ground; (*pl.*) mineral waters; *a mine. *a.* Pertaining to or consisting of minerals; impregnated with mineral matter. **mineral caoutchouc:** Elaterite. **mineral green:** Arsenite of copper. **mineral jelly,** *n.* A soft, soap-like substance obtained from the residue of petroleum. **mineral kingdom:** The inorganic kingdom of Nature. **mineral oil:** (*Am.*) liquid paraffin. **mineral salt:** (*Chem.*) The salt of a mineral acid; native salt. **mineral waters:** Waters naturally impregnated with mineral matter; artificial imitations of these. ***mineralist,** *n.* **mineralize,** *v.t.* To convert into a mineral; to give mineral qualities to; to impregnate with mineral matter. *v.i.* To become mineralized; to study mineralogy. **mineralization** (-zā' shun), *n.* **mineralizer,** *n.*

mineralogy (min ėr ăl' ȯ ji), *n.* The science of minerals, their nature and properties. **mineralogical** (-loj' i kȧl), *a.* **mineralogically,** *adv.* **mineralogist** (-ăl' ȯ jist), *n.*

mingle (ming' gėl) [freq. of M.E. *mengen*, A.-S. *mengan* (cp. Dut. *mengelen*, *mengen*, Icel. *menga*)], *v.t.* To mix up together; to blend (with); *to associate; *to debase by mixture. *v.i.* To be mixed, blended, or united (with). **n.* A mixture; a medley. **mingler,** *n.* **minglingly,** *adv.*

mingy (min' ji) [onomat.], *a.* (*slang*) Mean, stingy.

miniate (min' i āt) [L. *miniātus*, p.p. of *miniāre*, from *minium*, cinnabar, native red lead], *v.t.* To paint with vermilion; to illuminate.

miniature (min' i ȧ tūr, min' ȧ chur) [med. L. *miniātūra*, as prec.], *n.* A small-sized painting, esp. a portrait on ivory, vellum, etc., orig. a small picture in an illuminated manuscript; the art of painting on a small scale; an image on a greatly reduced scale; a reproduction on a small scale. *a.* Represented on a very small scale. *v.t.* To portray in miniature. **miniature camera:** (*Phot.*) A camera using film negative material usu. of 35 m.m. **miniaturist,** *n.*

minify (min' i fī) [MINOR, -FY], *v.t.* To make little or less; to represent (a thing) as of less size or importance than it is.

minikin (min' i kin) [Dut. *minnekyn*, a cupid, dim. of *minne*, love, see -KIN], *n.* A little darling; a pet; a diminutive thing; a small sort of pin. *a.* Tiny, delicate; affected, mincing.

minim (min' im) [O.F. *minime*, L. *minimum*, nom. *-mus*, very small], *n.* (*Mus.*) A note of the value of two crotchets or half a semi-breve; an apothecaries' fluid-measure, one drop, or the sixtieth of a drachm; a down-stroke in writing; an insignificant person, a dwarf, a pigmy; a member of an order of hermits founded by St. Francis of Paula (1416–1507).

minimal (min' i mȧl), *a.* Pertaining to or being a minimum; least possible; smallest, very small. **minimalist,** *n.* A person ready to accept the minimum.

minimize (min' i mīz), *v.t.* To reduce to smallest possible amount or degree; to belittle. **minimization,** *n.*

minimum (min' i mum), *n.* (*pl.* **-ma**) The smallest amount or degree possible or usual. *a.* Least possible. **minimum thermometer:** A thermometer automatically recording the lowest temperature reached in a given period. **minimum wage,** *n.* The rate of wages established by law or collective bargaining below which workers cannot be employed. **minimus,** *n.* A being of the smallest size. *a.* Applied to the youngest of several boys of the same name in a school.

minion (min' yȯn) [F. *mignon*, etym. doubtful], *n.* A darling, a favourite; a servile dependant; (*Print.*) a size of type between nonpareil and brevier. **minions of the moon:** Highwaymen, footpads.

***minish** (min' ish) [O.F. *menuisier*, pop. L. *minūtiāre*, from MINUTIA], *v.t.* To diminish; to reduce in power, etc. *v.i.* To diminish.

minister (min' is tėr) [F. *minister*, L. *minister*, from *minus*, less (cp. *magister*, from *magis*)], *n.* One charged with the performance of a duty, or the execution of a will, etc.; a person entrusted with the direction of a State department; a person representing his Government with another State, an ambassador; the pastor of a church, esp. a Nonconformist; one who acts under the authority of another, a subordinate, an instrument; a servant. *v.i.* To render aid, service, or attendance; to contribute, to be conducive (to); to serve as minister. **v.t.* To furnish, to supply. **ministerial** (-tēr' i ȧl), *a.* Pertaining to a minister of State or of religion; pertaining to the Ministry, esp. in contradistinction to the Opposition; subsidiary, instrumental; pertaining to the execution of a legal mandate etc. **ministerialist,** *n.* **ministerially,** *adv.* **ministrant,** *a.* and *n.* **ministration** (-trā' shun), *n.* **ministrative** (min' is trā tiv), *a.* **ministress,** *n.* **ministry,** *n.* The act of ministering; administration; the ministers of State or of religion collectively.

***minium** (min' i um) [L.], *n.* Red oxide of lead vermilion.

miniver (min' i vėr) [A.-F. *meniver*, F. *menu vair* (*menu*, little, small, *vair*, a kind of fur, from L. *varius*, VARIOUS)], *n.* A kind of fur used for ceremonial robes; applied to the Siberian squirrel and its fur.

mink (mingk) [cp. L.G. *mink*, Swed. *menk*], *n.* A name for several species of *Putorius*, amphibious stoat-like animals esteemed for their fur.

minnesinger (min' ė sing ėr) [G. (*minne*, love, SINGER)], *n.* One of a body of German lyric poets and singers (1138–1347) whose chief theme was love.

minnow (min' ō) [cp. O.H.G. *minewa* and A.-S. *myne*], *n.* A small fish common all over Europe, *Leuciscus phoxinus*; loosely applied to any tiny fishes.

Minoan (mi nō' ȧn) [*Minos*, king of Crete, -AN], *a.* Pertaining to ancient Crete or its people. *n.* An inhabitant of ancient Crete; their language. **Minoan period:** The bronze age of Crete, loosely 2500–1200 B.C.

minor (mī' nȯr) [L.], *a.* Less, smaller (not with *than*); petty, comparatively unimportant; (*Mus.*) less by a semitone; *under age. *n.* A person under age; (*Log.*) a minor term or premise; a minor key or a composition or strain in this; a Minorite. **minor canon:** A clergyman, not a member of the chapter, assisting in the daily service at a cathedral. **minor key:** (*Mus.*) A key in which the scale has a minor third. **minor premise:** (*Log.*) That which contains the minor term. **minor term:** (*Log.*) The subject of the conclusion of a categorical syllogism. **Minorite,** *n.* A Franciscan friar. **minority** (mī nor' i ti), *n.* The smaller number, esp. the smaller of a group or party voting together in an election, on a Bill, etc.; the state of being under age; the period of this.

Minorca (mi nôr' kȧ) [one of the Balearic Isles], *n.* A black variety of domestic fowl from Spain, also **Minorca fowl.**

Minotaur (min′ ô tawr) [Gr. *Minōtauros* (*Minōs*, the king of Crete, husband of Pasiphäe, *tauros*, bull)], *n.* (*Gr. Myth.*) A monster having the head of a bull and the rest of the body human, devouring human flesh.

minster (min′ stėr) [A.-S. *mynster*, L. *monastērium*, MONASTERY], *n.* The church of a monastery; a cathedral or other large and important church.

minstrel (min′ strėl) [O.F. *menestral*, late L. *ministeriālem*, nom. *-lis*, MINISTERIAL], *n.* One of a class of men in the Middle Ages who lived by singing and reciting; a travelling gleeman, musician, performer, or entertainer; (*fig.*) a poet; a musician. **minstrelsy,** *n.* The art or occupation of minstrels; a body of minstrels; minstrels collectively; a collection of ballad poetry; *musical instruments.

mint (1) (mint) [A.-S. *mynet*, L. *monēta*, MONEY], *n.* A place where money is coined, usu. under State authority; (*fig.*) a source of invention or fabrication; a great quantity, supply, or amount. *v.t.* To coin, to stamp (money); (*fig.*) to invent, to coin (a phrase etc.). *a.* (Of a book, coin, etc.) in its unused state; as new. **in mint condition:** (*fig.*) As perfect as when first produced. **mintman,** *n.* A man versed in coins or coining. **mint-mark,** *n.* A mark distinguishing the coins struck at a particular mint; (*fig.*) a distinctive mark of origin. ***mint-master,** *n.* **mintage,** *n.* **minter,** *n.*

mint (2) (mint) [A.-S. *minte* (L. *menta, mentha*, Gr. *mintha*)], *n.* Any plant of the aromatic genus *Mentha*, esp. *M. viridis*, the garden mint, from which an essential oil is distilled. **mint-julep,** *n.* Spirits, sugar, and pounded ice flavoured with mint. **mint-sauce,** *n.* Mint chopped up with vinegar and sugar, used as a sauce with roast lamb.

minuend (min′ ū end) [L. *minuendus*, ger. of *minuere*, to DIMINISH], *n.* (*Arith.*) The quantity from which another is to be subtracted.

minuet (min ū et′) [F. *menuet*, dim. of *menu*, MINUTE], *n.* A slow stately dance in triple measure; music for this or in the same measure.

minus (mī′ nus) [L., neut. of MINOR], *prep.* or *a.* Less by, with the deduction of; (*colloq.*) short of, lacking; negative. *n.* The sign of subtraction (−).

minuscule (mi nŭs′ kūl) [F., from L. *minuscula*, fem. dim. of MINOR], *a.* Small; miniature (esp. applied to mediæval script). *n.* A minute kind of letter in cursive script of the 7th–9th cent.; a small or lower-case letter; anything very small.

minute (1) (mi-, mī nūt′) [L. *minūtus*, p.p. of *minuere*, to DIMINISH], *a.* Very small; petty, trifling; particular, exact, precise. **minutely** (1) (mī nūt′ li), *adv.* **minuteness,** *n.*

minute (2) (min′ it) [F., from late L. *minūta*, as prec.], *n.* The 60th part of an hour; a very small portion of time, an instant; an exact point of time; the 60th part of a degree; a memorandum; an official memorandum of a court or other authority; (*pl.*) official records of proceedings of a committee, etc. *v.t.* To write minutes of; to take a note of; to time to the exact minute. **minute-book,** *n.* A book in which the minutes of meetings are recorded. **minute-glass,** *n.* A sand-glass running sixty seconds. **minute-gun,** *n.* A gun fired at intervals of one minute as a signal of distress or mourning. **minute-hand,** *n.* The hand pointing to minutes in a clock or watch. **minute-man,** *n.* (*U.S.A.*) Enrolled militiaman of Revolutionary period who held himself ready for service at a minute's notice. **minute-watch,** *n.* A watch on which the minutes are marked. ***minute-while,** *n.* A minute's time. **minutely** (2) (min′ it li), *a.* and *adv.* Every minute.

minutia (mi nū′ shi ȧ) [L., smallness, as MINUTE (1)], *n.* (*usu. in pl.* **-iæ**) Small and precise or trivial particulars.

minx (mingks) [perh. corr. of L.G. *minsk*, a man, a pert female (cp. G. *mensch*)], *n.* A pert girl, a jade, a hussy.

miocene (mī′ ô sēn) [Gr. *meiōn*, less, *kainos*, new], *a.* (*Geol.*) A term applied to the middle division of the Tertiary strata or period.

miosis [MEIOSIS].

miracle (mir′ ȧ kėl) [O.F., from L. *mīrāculum*, as prec.], *n.* A wonder, a marvel, a prodigy; a marvellous event or act due to supernatural agency; an extraordinary occurrence; an extraordinary example (of cleverness etc.); a miracle play. **v.i.* (*Shak.*) To render or seem miraculous. ***miracle-monger,** *n.* **miracle play:** A mediæval dramatic representation, usu. dealing with historical or traditional events in the life of Christ or of the Saints. **miraculous** (mi răk′ ū lŭs), *a.* **miraculously,** *adv.* **miraculousness,** *n.*

mirador (mir ȧ dôr′) [Sp., from *mirar*, to look, L. *mīrārī*, as foll.], *n.* A belvedere turret, or gallery, commanding an extensive view.

mirage (mi razh′) [F., from *se mirer*, to see oneself in a mirror, L. *mīrārī*, to wonder at, to gaze], *n.* An optical illusion by which images of distant objects are seen as if inverted, esp. in a desert where the inverted sky appears as a sheet of water.

mire (mī′ ėr) [M.E., from Icel. *mȳrr* (cp. Swed. *myra* and A.-S. *mēos*, MOSS)], *n.* Wet, clayey soil, swampy ground, bog; mud, dirt. *v.t.* To plunge in mire; to soil with mire; (*fig.*) to involve in difficulties. *v.i.* To sink in mire. **miry,** *a.* **miriness,** *n.* **mire-crow,** *n.* The laughing gull, *Larus ridibundus.*

mirific (mir if′ ik) [L. *mirificus*, wonder-working], *a.* Wonderful, marvellous; wonder-working.

mirk, etc. [MURK].

miro (mē′ rō) [Maori], *n.* The N. Zealand robin.

mirror (mir′ ôr) [O.F. *mirour* (F. *miroir*), prob. through a non-extant pop. L. *mīrātōrium*, from *mīrārī*, see MIRAGE], *n.* An appliance with a polished surface for reflecting images; a looking-glass; (*fig.*) anything that reflects objects; an exemplar, a pattern, a model. *v.t.* To reflect in or as in a mirror. **mirror writing,** *n.* Handwriting from right to left.

mirth (mĕrth) [A.-S. *myrgth*, cogn. with MERRY (2)], *n.* Merriment, jollity, gaiety, hilarity. **mirthful,** *a.* **mirthfully,** *adv.* **mirthfulness,** *n.* **mirthless,** *a.* **mirthlessness,** *n.*

miry [MIRE].

mirza (mĕr′ za) [Pers.], *n.* A Persian title of honour, prince; doctor.

mis- [two prefixes have coalesced; A.-S. *mis-*, wrongly, amiss (cp. Dut., Dan., and Icel. *mis-*, G. *miss-*); O.F. *mes-*, L. *minus*, less], *pref.* Wrongly, badly, amiss, unfavourably. **misadventure** (mis ȧd ven′ chŭr) [O.F. *mesaventure*], *n.* Bad luck; ill fortune; an unlucky chance or accident. ***misadventured, -turous,** *a.* **misadvise** (mis ȧd vīz), *v.t.* To advise wrongly; to give bad advice to. **misadvice,** *n.* **misadvised,** *a.* Ill-advised, ill-directed. ***misadvisedly,** *adv.* **misadvisedness,** *n.* ***misaim** (mis ām′), *v.t.* To aim amiss. **misalliance** (mis ȧ lī′ ȧns), *n.* An improper alliance, esp. by marriage. **misallied,** *a.* ***misallotment** (mis ȧ lot′ mėnt), *n.* A wrong allotment.

misanthrope (mis′ ȧn thrōp) [Gr. *misanthrōpos* (*misein*, to hate, *anthrōpos*, man)], *n.* A hater of mankind; one who has a morbid dislike of his fellow-men. **misanthropic, -al** (-throp′ ik, -ȧl), *a.* **misanthropist** (mis ăn′ thrô pist), *n.* **misanthropize,** *v.i.* **misanthropy,** *n.*

misapply (mis ȧ plī′), *v.t.* To apply wrongly. **misapplication** (-kā′ shŭn), *n.* **misappreciate** (mis ȧ prē′ shi āt), *v.t.* To fail to appreciate rightly or fully. **misappreciation** (-ā′ shŭn), *n.* **misappreciative** (-prē′ shi ȧ tiv), *a.* **misapprehend** (mis ăp rė hend′), *v.t.* To misunderstand. **misapprehension,** *n.* **misapprehensive,** *a.* **misapprehensively,** *adv.* **misappropriate** (mis ȧ prō′ pri āt), *v.t.* To apply to a wrong use or purpose (esp. funds to one's own use). **misappropriation** (-ā′ shŭn), *n.* **misarrange** (mis ȧ rānj′), *v.t.* To arrange wrongly. **misarrangement,** *n.* **misarray,** *v.t.* **misbecome** (mis bė kŭm'), *v.t.* To be improper or unseemly to, to ill become. **misbecomingly,** *adv.* ***misbecomingness,** *n.* **misbegotten** (mis bė got' ėn), ***misbegot,** *a.* Begotten unlawfully, illegitimate, bastard; (*fig.*) hideous, despicable. **misbehave** (mis bė hāv'), *v.i.* To behave (*usu.* oneself) ill or improperly. **misbehaved,** *a.* Guilty of misbehaviour, ill-mannered. **misbehaviour,** *n.* **misbelief** (mis bė lēf'), *n.* False or erroneous belief. **misbelieve,** *v.t.* **misbeliever,** *n.* **misbeseem** (mis bė sēm'), *v.t.* To misbecome. **misborn** (mis bôrn'), *a.* Base-born; born to evil or misfortune. **misbirth,** *n.* **miscalculate** (mis kăl' kū lāt), *v.t.* To calculate wrongly. **miscalculation** (-lā' shŭn), *n.* **miscall** (mis kawl'), *v.t.* To misname; (*prov.*) to abuse, to call (a person) names. **miscarry** (mis kăr' i), *v.i.* To be carried to the wrong place; to fail, to be unsuccessful; to be delivered of a child prematurely. **miscarriage,** *n.* **miscarriage of justice:** A mistake or wrong committed by a court of justice. **miscast** (mis kast'), *v.t.* To cast or add up wrongly; (*Theat.*) to cast a play inappropriately.

miscegenation (mis ė jė nā' shŭn) [L. *miscēre,* to mix, *genus,* race, -ATION], *n.* Mixture of races, esp. of whites and Negroes.

miscellaneous (mis ė lā' nė ŭs) [L. *miscellāneus,* from *miscellus,* mixed, from *miscēre,* to mix], *a.* Consisting of several kinds; mixed, multifarious, diversified; various, many-sided. **miscellanea,** *n.pl.* A collection of miscellaneous literary compositions. **miscellaneously,** *adv.* **miscellaneousness,** *n.* **miscellany** (mi sel' å ni), *n.* A mixture of various kinds, a medley, a number of compositions on various subjects in one volume. **miscellanist,** *n.*

mischance (mis chans') [O.F. *meschance*], *n.* Misfortune, ill-luck. ***v.i.** To happen unfortunately. **mischancy,** *a.* (*Sc.*) ***mischarge** (mis charj'), *v.t.* To charge wrongly. *n.* A wrong charge.

mischief (mis' chif) [O.F. *meschief* (MIS-, CHIEF, aim, result)], *n.* Harm, injury, damage; vexatious action or conduct, esp. a vexatious prank; (*euphem.*) the devil. ***v.t.** (also ***mischieve**) To hurt, to harm. **mischief-maker,** *n.* One who stirs up ill-will. **mischief-making,** *a.* and *n.* **mischievous,** *a.* Making mischief; naughty; (of a child) full of pranks, continually in mischief; arch, roguish; vexatious. **mischievously,** *adv.* **mischievousness,** *n.*

misch metal (mish' met ål) [G. *mischen,* to mix], *n.* An alloy of cerium with other rare earth metals, used for automatic-lighter flints.

miscible (mis' ibl) [F., from L. *miscēre,* to mix, -BLE], *a.* That may be mixed (with). **miscibility** (-bil' i ti), *n.*

miscolour (mis kŭl' ŏr), *v.t.* To misrepresent. **miscoloration** (-ā' shŭn), *n.* Discoloration. **miscomprehend** (mis kom prė hend'), *v.t.* To comprehend wrongly, to misunderstand. **miscomprehension,** *n.* **miscompute** (mis kŏm pūt'), *v.t.* To compute wrongly. ***n.** A miscalculation. **miscomputation** (-tā' shŭn), *n.* **misconceive** (mis kŏn sēv'), *v.t.* To have a wrong idea of, to misapprehend. **misconception** (-sep' shŭn), *n.* **misconduct** (mis kon' dŭkt), *n.* Improper conduct, esp. adultery; mismanagement. *v.t.* (-kŏn dŭkt') To mismanage. *v.i.* To misbehave. **misconstrue** (mis kŏn stroo'), *v.t.* To mistake the meaning of; to put a wrong interpretation or construction upon. **misconstruction,** *n.* **miscopy** (mis kop' i), *v.t.* To copy incorrectly. **miscounsel** (mis koun' sėl), *v.t.* To advise wrongly. **miscount** (mis kount'), *v.t.* To count wrongly; to estimate or regard wrongly. *v.i.* To make a false account. *n.* A mistake in counting, esp. of votes. **miscreant** (mis' krė ånt) [O.F. *mescreant* (*creant,* L. *crēdentem,* nom. *-dens,* pres.p. of *crēdere,* to believe)], *n.* *An unbeliever, infidel, or heretic; a vile wretch, a scoundrel. *a.* *Infidel; abandoned, vile. ***miscreance,** ***miscreancy,** *n.* ***miscreated** (mis krė ā' tėd), ***miscreate,** *a.* Deformed, shapeless. **miscreation** (-ā' shŭn), *n.* **miscreative,** *a.* **miscreed** (mis krēd'), *n.* A false or mistaken creed.

miscue (mis kū'), *n.* (*Billiards*) Failure to strike a ball properly with the cue. *v.i.* To make a miscue.

misdate (mis dāt'), *v.t.* To date wrongly. *n.* A wrong date. **misdeal** (mis dēl), *v.t.* To deal wrongly (as cards). *v.i.* To make a misdeal. *n.* A wrong or false deal. **misdecision** (mis dė sizh' ŭn), *n.* A wrong decision. **misdeed** (mis dēd') [A.-S. *misdǣd*], *n.* An evil deed, a crime. **misdeem** (mis dēm'), *v.t.* To judge wrongly; to have wrong views about; to mistake (for some one or something else). *v.i.* To have a wrong idea or judgment (of). **misdemean** (mis dė mēn'), *v.t.* To misconduct (oneself). **misdemeanant,** *n.* **misdemeanour,** *n.* Misbehaviour, misconduct; (*Law*) an indictable offence of less gravity than a felony. **misdescribe** (mis dė skrīb'), *v.t.* To describe wrongly. ***misdesert** (mis dė zĕrt'), *n.* Ill-desert. ***misdevotion** (mis dė vō' shŭn), *n.* Misdirected devotion. **misdirect** (mis di rekt'), *v.t.* To direct wrongly. **misdirection,** *n.* ***misdistinguish** (mis di sting' gwish), *v.i.* To make erroneous distinctions (concerning). **misdivision** (mis di vizh' ŭn), *n.* Wrong or erroneous division. **misdo** (mis doo'), *v.t.* To do wrongly. *v.i.* To commit a crime. **misdoer,** *n.* ***misdoubt** (mis dout'), *v.t.* To have doubts or misgiving as to the truth or fact of; to suspect, surmise, or apprehend. *v.i.* To have suspicions or misgivings. *n.* Doubt, hesitation; suspicion.

mise** (mēz, mīz) [O.F., frm. p.p. of *mettre,* to put, L. *mittere,* to send], *n.* A treaty, esp. a settlement by arbitration or compromise; (*Law*) the issue in a writ of right; cost, expense (*usu. in pl.*). ***mise en scène (mēz an sān): The scenery and general setting of a play; (*fig.*) the visible surroundings of an event.

miseducate (mis ed' ū kāt), *v.t.* To educate wrongly. **miseducation** (-kā' shŭn), *n.* **misemploy** (mis ėm ploi'), *v.t.* To misapply, to misuse. **misemployment,** *n.* **misentry** (mis en' tri), *n.* An erroneous entry.

miser (1) (mī' zėr) [L., wretched], *n.* One who denies himself the comforts of life for the sake of hoarding; an avaricious person; a wretched person. **miserly,** *a.* **miserliness,** *n.*

miser (2) (mī' zėr) [etym. unknown], *n.* A large auger for well-boring.

miserable (miz' ėr åbl) [F. *misérable,* L. *miserābilis,* from *miserārī,* to pity, from *miser,* wretched], *a.* Very wretched or unhappy, distressed; causing misery, distressing; sorry, despicable, worthless; very poor or mean. *n.* A miserable person, a wretch. ***miserableness,** *n.* **miserably,** *adv.*

misère (mi zâr') [F.], *n.* (*Cards*) A declaration in solo-whist etc., by which a player undertakes not to take a single trick.

miserere (miz ėr ēr' i) [L., have mercy, imper. of *miserērī,* see prec.], *n.* The 51st Psalm, beginning with this word in the Vulgate; a musical setting of this psalm; a prayer or cry for mercy; a misericord.

misericord (miz' ėr i kôrd) [O.F., from L. *misericordia,* from *misericors -cordis* (*miseri-,* stem of *miserērī,* see MISERABLE, *cor cordis,* heart)], *n.* An apartment in a monastery for monks to whom special indulgences were granted; a bracketed projection on the underside of the seat of a choir-stall, to afford rest to a person standing; a small, straight dagger for giving the *coup de grâce*; *mercy.

miserly [MISER (1)].

misery (miz' ėr i) [O.F., from L. *miseria,* from *miser,* wretched], *n.* Great unhappiness or wretchedness of mind or body; affliction, poverty; misère; *miserliness, avarice.

***misesteem** (mis ė stēm'), *v.t.* To esteem wrongly. *n.* Want of esteem, disrespect; disregard. **misestimate,** *v.t.* and *n.* **misexpress** (mis ėk spres'), *v.t.* To express (oneself) wrongly. **misexpression,** *n.* ***misfall** (mis fawl'), *v.t.* To befall unluckily.

***misfare** (mis fâr′) [A.-S. *misfaran*], *v.i.* To fare ill. *n.* Misfortune, mishap. **misfeasance** (mis fē′ zȧns) [O.F. *mesfaisance*, from *mesfaire* (*faire*, L. *facere*, to do)], *n.* (*Law*) A trespass, a wrong, esp. negligent or improper performance of a lawful act.

misfire (mis fīr′), *n.* Failure to go off or explode (of a gun, charge, etc.). *v.i.* To fail to go off.

misfit (mis fit′), *n.* A bad fit; a garment that does not fit properly; (*fig.*) an awkward person. *v.t.* and *i.* To fail to fit. **misform** (mis fôrm′), *v.t.* To form badly or amiss. **misformation** (-mā′ shŭn), *n.* **misfortune** (mis fôr′ tyŭn), *n.* Ill luck, calamity; a mishap, a disaster. ***misfortuned,** *a.* **misgive** (mis giv′), *v.t.* (*impers.*) To fill (one's mind) with doubt or suspicion. **misgiving,** *n.* **misgo** (mis gō′) [GO (1)], *v.i.* To go wrong. **misgovern** (mis gŭv′ ėrn), *v.t.* To govern ill; to administer unfaithfully. ***misgovernance, misgovernment,** *n.* **misgoverned,** *a.* Badly governed, rude. **misguide** (mis gīd′), *v.t.* To guide wrongly; to lead astray. **misguidance,** *n.* **misguided,** *a.* Foolish. **misguidedly,** *adv.* **mishandle** (mis hăndl′), *v.t.* To handle roughly; to ill-treat.

mishanter (mi shan′ tėr) [Sc., earlier *misaunter*, MISADVENTURE], *n.* Misadventure, mischance.

mishap (mis hăp′), *n.* A mischance; ill luck. ***mishappen,** *v.i.*

mishmash (mish′ măsh) [redupl. of MASH (1)], *n.* A hotchpotch, a jumble.

Mishmee, Mishmi (mish′ mē), [mountains, east of Assam], *n.* The dried root of *Coptes Teeta*, a bitter tonic. **mishmee-bitter,** *n.*

Mishna (mish′ nȧ) [Heb. *mishnah*, a repetition, instruction, from *shānāh*, to repeat], *n.* The second or oral law, the collection of traditions etc. forming the text of the Talmud. **Mishnic,** *a.*

misinform (mis in fôrm′), *v.t.* To give erroneous information to. **misinformant, misinformer,** *n.* **misinformation** (-mā′ shŭn), *n.* **misintelligence** (mis in tel′ i jėns) [F. *mésintelligence*], *n.* False information; lack of intelligence. **misinterpret** (mis in tĕr′ prėt), *v.t.* To interpret wrongly; to draw a wrong conclusion from. **misinterpretation** (-tā′ shŭn), *n.* **misinterpreter,** *n.* **misjoin** (mis join′), *v.t.* To join or connect badly or improperly. **misjoinder,** *n.* (*Law*) The improper uniting of parties or things in a suit or action. **misjudge** (mis jŭj′), *v.t.* To judge erroneously; to form an erroneous opinion of. **misjudgment,** *n.* **misken** (mis ken′) [Sc. (KEN (1))], *v.t.* To fail to recognize; to pretend not to know. **misknow** (mis nō′), *v.t.* To misunderstand; to know imperfectly. **misknowledge** (-nol′ ėj), *n.* **mislay** (mis lā′), *v.t.* (*past & p.p.* **-laid**) To lay in a wrong place or in a place that cannot be remembered; to lose.

misle [MIZZLE].

mislead (mis lēd′), *v.t.* (*past & p.p.* **misled**) To lead astray; to cause to go wrong, esp. in conduct; to deceive, to delude. **misleader,** *n.*

mislike (mis līk′) [A.-S. *mislīcian*], *v.t.* To dislike. *v.i.* To feel dislike or aversion. *n.* Dislike, aversion. **mislippen** (mis lipn′) [Sc. and North. (LIPPEN)], *v.t.* To deceive; to neglect, not to attend to; to suspect. **mismanage** (mis măn′ ȧj), *v.t.* and *i.* To manage ill. **mismanagement,** *n.* **mismanager,** *n.* **mismarriage** (mis măr′ ȧj), *n.* An unsuitable, incongruous, or unfortunate marriage. **mismatch** (mis măch′), *v.t.* To match unsuitably. ***mismatchment,** *n.* **mismate** (mis māt′), *v.t.* (*in p.p.*) To mate or match unsuitably. **mismeasure** (mis mezh′ ŭr), *v.t.* To measure wrongly; to form an erroneous measurement of. **mismeasurement,** *n.* **misname** (mis nām)′, *v.t.* To call by a wrong name. **misnomer** (mis nō′ mėr) [O.F. *mesnommer* (*nommer*, L. *nōmināre*, to name)], *n.* A mistaken or misapplied name or designation; an incorrect term.

misogamy (mi-, mī sog′ ȧ mi) [Gr. *miso-*, from *misein*, to hate, *-gamia*, from *gamos*, marriage], *n.* Hatred of marriage. **misogamist,** *n.* **misogyny** (mi-, mī soj′ i ni) [Gr. *mīsogunēs* (*gunē*, woman)], *n.* Hatred of women. **misogynic** (-jin′ ik), *a.* **misogynist** (-soj′ i nist), *n.* **misology** (mi-, mī sol′ ȯ ji) [Gr. *mīsologia* (-LOGY)], *n.* Hatred of reason or knowledge. **misoneism** (mi-, mī sȯ nē′ izm) [It. *misoneismo* (Gr. *neos*, new, -ISM)], *n.* Hatred of what is new. **misoneist,** *n.* **misotheism** (mi-, mī sȯ thē′ izm) [Gr. *mīsotheos*, *theos*, god (see THEISM)], *n.* Hatred of God. **misotheist,** *n.*

misplace (mis plās′), *v.t.* To mislay; to set on or devote to an undeserving object. *v.i.* To misapply terms. **misplacement,** *n.* **misplay** (mis plā′), *n.* Wrong or foul play. ***misplead** (mis plēd′) [PLEAD], *v.t.* and *i.* To plead wrongly. **mispleading,** *n.* An error in pleading. ***mispoint** (mis point′) [POINT], *v.t.* To punctuate improperly. **misprint** (mis print′), *v.t.* To print incorrectly. (mis′ print), *n.* A mistake in printing.

misprision (1) (mis prizh′ ȯn) [O.F. *mesprision* (MIS-, L. *prensio -ōnem*, see PRISON)], *n.* (*Law*) An offence under the degree of capital but bordering thereon, esp. one of neglect or concealment; *mistake, misconception. **misprision of treason or felony:** Concealment of treason or felony without actual participation.

***misprision** (2) (mis prizh′ ȯn) [from MISPRIZE (2)], *n.* Scorn, contempt; undervaluing, failure to appreciate.

misprize (1) (mis prīz′) [O.F. *mespriser*], *v.t.* To undervalue, to slight, to despise. **n.* Neglect; contempt. ***misprize** (2) (mis prīz′) [O.F. *mesprise* (F. *méprise*), from *mesprendre* (L. *prendere*, to take)], *n.* A mistake. **mispronounce** (mis prȯ nouns′), *v.t.* To pronounce wrongly. **mispronunciation** (-nŭn si ā′ shŭn), *n.* **misproportion** (mis prȯ pôr′ shŭn), *v.t.* To proportion wrongly. ***misproud** (mis proud′) [PROUD], *a.* Viciously proud. **mispunctuate** (mis pŭnk′ tū āt), *v.t.* and *i.* To punctuate wrongly. **misquote** (mis kwōt′), *v.t.* To quote erroneously. **misquotation** (-tā′ shŭn), *n.* **misread** (mis rēd′), *v.t.* (*past & p.p.* **-read,** -red) To read incorrectly; to misinterpret. ***misreckon** (mis rek′ ȯn), *v.t.* To miscalculate. ***misreckoning,** *n.* **misrelate** (mis rė lāt′), *v.t.* To relate inaccurately. **misrelation,** *n.* **misremember** (mis rė mem′ bėr), *v.t.* To remember imperfectly; (*prov.*) to forget. **misremembrance,** *n.* **misreport** (mis rė pôrt), *v.t.* To report wrongly; *to slander. *n.* A false report. **misrepresent** (mis rep rė zent′), *v.t.* To represent falsely or incorrectly. **misrepresentation** (-tā′ shŭn), *n.* **misrepresentative** (-zen′ tȧ tiv), *a.* and *n.* **misrepresenter,** *n.* **misrule** (mis rool′), *n.* Bad government; disorder, confusion, tumult, riot. **lord of misrule** [LORD].

miss (1) (mis) [contr. of MISTRESS], *n.* (*pl.* **misses**) A title of address for an unmarried woman or girl; (*colloq.*) a girl; *a kept mistress. **missish,** *a.* Like a self-conscious young girl; prim, affected. **missishness,** *n.*

miss (2) (mis) [A.-S. *missan* (cp. Dut. and G. *missen*, Icel. *missa*), cogn. with A.-S. *mis-*, see MIS-], *v.t.* To fail to reach, hit, meet, perceive, find, or obtain; to fall short of, to let slip, to overlook; to fail to understand; to omit; to escape, to dispense with; to feel or perceive the want of. *v.i.* To fail to hit the mark; to be unsuccessful; *to go astray, to err. *n.* A failure to hit, reach, obtain, etc.; *loss, want, feeling of loss; *error, mistake. **a miss is as good as a mile:** Escape or failure, no matter how narrow the margin, is the point of importance. **to give a miss:** (*Billiards*) To avoid hitting the object ball in order to leave one's own in a safe position. **to miss fire:** To fail to go off (of a gun, explosive, etc.). **to miss stays:** (*Naut.*) To fail in trying to go on another tack (of a sailing-vessel). **missing,** *a.* That misses; lost, wanting; absent, not in its place. **missing link:** (*fig.*) Something required to complete a series; (*Zool.*) a hypothetical form connecting types that are probably related, as man and the anthropoid apes. ***missingly,** *adv.*

missal (mis′ ȧl) [late L. *missāle*, orig. neut. adj. from *missa*, MASS (1)], *n.* The book containing the service of the Mass for the whole year; a mediæval illuminated manuscript.

missel-thrush [MISTLE].

misshape (mis shāp), *v.t.* (*p.p.* **misshapen**) To shape ill; to deform. *n.* Deformity.

missile (mis′ il, -īl) [L. *missilis*, from *miss-*, p.p. stem of *mittere*, to send], *a.* That may be thrown or discharged. *n.* A weapon or other object projected or propelled through the air.

mission (mish′ ȯn) [L. *missio -ōnem*, as prec.], *n.* A sending or being sent; the commission, charge, or office of a messenger, agent, etc.; a person's appointed or chosen end, a vocation; a body of persons sent on a diplomatic errand, an embassy or legation; a body of missionaries established in a district at home or sent to a foreign country to spread religious teaching; their field of work; a missionary station; (*R.-C. Ch.*) a religious organization ranking below that of a regular parish; a series of special services for rousing spiritual interest.

missionary (mish′ ȯn ȧ ri), *a.* Pertaining to missions, esp. those of a religious nature; pertaining to the propagation of religion or other moral, social, or political influence. *n.* One sent to carry on such work. **missionary box:** A box for contributions to missionary work. **missioner,** *n.* A missionary; one in charge of a parochial mission.

missis, missus (mis′ is, -ůs) [corr. of MISTRESS], *n.* (*colloq.*) The mistress of a household; (*vulg.*) a wife.

missish [MISS (1)].

missive (mis′ iv) [F., from med. L. *missīvus*, as MISSILE], *a.* Sent or for sending. *n.* A message, a letter; *a messenger. **letter** or **letters missive:** A letter or letters sent by an authority, esp. from the sovereign to a dean and chapter nominating a person for the office of bishop; (*Sc. Law*) a document given by the parties to a contract etc.

***misspeak** (mis spēk′), *v.i.* To speak wrongly; to speak evil. *v.t.* To speak or pronounce incorrectly. **misspell** (mis spel′), *v.t.* To spell incorrectly. **misspelling,** *n.* **misspend** (mis spend′), *v.t.* (*past & p.p.* **-spent**) To spend ill; to waste. **misstate** (mis stāt′), *v.t.* To state wrongly. **misstatement,** *n.* ***misstep** (mis step′), *n.* A false step. **missuit** (mis sūt′), *v.t.* To suit ill.

missy (mis′ i) [MISS (1), -Y], *n.* (*fam. or playfully*) Miss. **a.* Missish.

mist (mist) [A.-S., cp. Icel. *mistr*, Swed. and Dut. *mist*, cogn. with Gr. *omichlē*], *n.* Visible watery vapour in the atmosphere at or near the surface of the earth; a watery condensation dimming a surface; a watery film before the eyes; (*fig.*) anything which dims, obscures, or darkens. *v.t.* To cover as with mist. *v.i.* To be misty. **mistful,** *a.* **mistlike,** *a.* and *adv.* **misty,** *a.* Characterized by or overspread with mist; vague, dim, indistinct, obscure. **mistily,** *adv.* **mistiness,** *n.*

mistake (mis tāk′) [Icel. *mistaka*], *v.t.* (*past* **-took,** *p.p.* **-taken**) To take or understand wrongly; to take in a wrong sense; to take one person or thing for another. *v.i.* To be in error; to err in judgment or opinion; *to transgress. *n.* An error of judgment or opinion; a misunderstanding, a blunder. **mistakable,** *a.* **mistakably,** *adv.* **mistakenly,** *adv.* **mistakenness,** *n.* **mistaker,** *n.*

Mister (1) (mis′ tėr) [var. of MASTER], *n.* The common form of address prefixed to men's names or certain official titles (abbrev. in writing, MR.). *v.t.* To speak of or address (a person) as 'Mister'.

***mister** (2) (mis′ tėr) [O.F. *mestier* (F. *métier*), L. *ministerium*, MINISTRY], *n.* A trade, craft; manner, kind; (*Sc.*) need, necessity. **v.t.* To occasion loss to. *v.i.* To be needed; to require.

misterm (mis tĕrm′), *v.t.* To misname; to apply a wrong term to.

misthink (mis think′), *v.i.* To think wrongly. *v.t.* To misjudge, to think ill of. ***misthought,** *n.*

mistic, mistico (mis′ tik, -ti kō) [Sp. *mistico*, prob. from Arab. *misṭeḥ*, from *sataha*, to flatten], *n.* A small coasting-vessel used in the Mediterranean.

mistime (mis tīm′), *v.t.* To say or do inappropriately or not suitably to the time or occasion.

mistitle (mis tītl′), *v.t.* To call by a wrong title.

mistle, mistle-thrush (mis′ ėl thrŭsh) [A.-S. *mistel*, basil, mistletoe (cp. G. *mistel-drossel*)], *n.* The largest of the European thrushes, *Turdus viscivorus*, feeding largely on mistletoe-berries.

mistletoe (mis′ ėl tō) [A.-S. *misteltān* (prec., *tān*, twig)], *n.* A plant, *Viscum album*, parasitic on the apple and other trees, bearing white glutinous berries used in making bird-lime.

mistral (mis′ trȧl) [F. and Prov., from L. *magistrālis*, MAGISTRAL], *n.* A cold dry N.W. wind in the Gulf of the Lion and the contiguous provinces of S. France.

mistranslate (mis trȧn slāt), *v.t.* To translate wrongly. **mistranslation** (-slā′ shůn), *n.* **mistreat** (mis trēt′), *v.t.* To ill-treat.

mistress (mis′ trės) [M.E. and O.F. *maistresse* (MASTER, -ESS)], *n.* A woman who has authority or control; the female head of a family, school, etc.; a woman having the control or disposal (of); a woman who has mastery (of a subject etc.); a female teacher; a woman beloved and courted, a sweetheart; a woman who, without marriage, takes the place of wife; a title of address to a married woman (abbrev. in writing to MRS., mis′ is); *a patroness. **Mistress of the Robes:** A lady of the royal household nominally in charge of the Queen's wardrobe. **mistress-ship,** *n.*

mistrial (mis trī′ ȧl), *n.* An abortive or inconclusive trial. **mistrust** (mis trŭst′), *v.t.* To regard with doubt or suspicion. *n.* Distrust, suspicion. **mistrustful,** *a.* **mistrustfully,** *adv.* **mistrustfulness,** *n.* **mistrustingly,** *adv.* **mistrustless,** *a.* **mistryst** (mis trīst′), *v.t.* To fail to keep an engagement with; to trouble, embarrass, or perplex. **mistune** (mis tūn′), *v.t.* To tune wrongly; to make discordant.

misunderstand (mis ŭn dėr stand′), *v.t.* (*past & p.p.* **-stood**) To misconceive, to misapprehend, to mistake the meaning or sense of. **misunderstanding,** *n.*

misuse (mis ūz′), *v.t.* To use or treat improperly; to apply to a wrong purpose; to ill-treat. *n.* (mis ūs′) Improper use; abuse. **misusage,** *n.* **misventure** (mis ven′ tyůr), *n.* A misadventure. **misventurous,** *a.* **miswend** (mis wend′), *v.i.* (*p.p.* **miswent**) To go astray; (*fig.*) to go wrong, to go to ruin. **misword** (mis wĕrd′), *v.t.* To word incorrectly. **miswrite** (mis rīt′), *v.t.* To write incorrectly. ***miswrought** (mis rawt′), *a.* Badly wrought.

mite (1) (mīt) [A.-S. (cp. L.G. *mite*, Dut. *mijt*, O.H.G. *mīza*, gnat)], *n.* A very small coin, orig. Flemish; (*pop.*) a half or smaller portion of a farthing; (*fig.*) a small contribution; a minute amount, a tiny thing, esp. a child. **the widow's mite:** A small contribution but the best that one can do. (Matt. xii. 42).

mite (2) (mīt) [O.F. *mite*, prob. cogn. with prec.], *n.* A name common to the minute arachnids of the order *Acarida*, esp. those infesting cheese. **mity,** *a.*

Mithra, Mithras (mith′ rȧ, -răs) [L. and Gr. *Mithrās*, O.Pers. *Mithra*], *n.* The Persian god of light or sun-god. **Mithraic** (-rā′ ik), *a.* **Mithraism** (mith′ rȧ izm), *n.* **Mithraist,** *n.*

mithridate (mith′ ri dāt) [*Mithridates* VI, king of Pontus, said to have made himself poison-proof], *n.* An antidote against poison. **mithridatic** (-dăt′ ik), *a.* **mithridatism** (mith′ ri dȧ tizm), *n.* **mithridatize** (mi thrid′ ȧ tiz), *v.t.* To render immune against poison by taking larger and larger doses of it.

mitigate (mit′ i gāt) [L. *mītigātus*, p.p. of *mītigāre*, from *mītis*, gentle], *v.t.* To make less rigorous or harsh; to relax (severity); to alleviate (pain, violence, etc.); to soften, to diminish, to moderate. *v.i.* To become assuaged, relaxed, or moderated.

***mitigable,** *a.* ***mitigant,** *a.* and *n.* **mitigation** (-gā' shùn), *n.* **mitigative** (mit' i gā tiv), **mitigatory,** *a.* **mitigator,** *n.*

mitokinetic (mit ō ki net' ik) [MITOSIS, KINETIC], *a.* (*Biol.*) Productive of mitosis.

mitosis (mī tō' sis) [Gr. *mitos*, a thread, -OSIS], *n.* (*pl.* **-oses**) (*Biol.*) Indirect cell-division; the appearance of the nucleus during karyokinesis. **mitotic** (-tot' ik), *a.*

mitrailleuse (mē tra yĕrz') [F., from *mitrailler*, to fire small missiles, from *mitraille*, from MITE (2)], *n.* A breech-loading machine-gun consisting of several barrels united, for firing simultaneously or in succession. ***mitraille*** (mē trā', mi trāl'), *n.* Small shot from this. ***mitrailleur*** (mē tra yĕr'), *n.*

mitral (mī' tràl), *a.* Of or resembling a mitre. **mitral valve,** *n.* (*Anat.*) The valve between the left auricle and ventricle of the heart, which prevents the blood flowing back into the auricle.

mitre (mī' tėr) [O.F. *mitre*, L. and Gr. *mitra*], *n.* A tall ornamental cap shaped like a cleft cone rising into two peaks, worn as symbol of office by bishops; (*fig.*) the dignity of a bishop; (*Carp.*) a joint at an angle (usu. of 90°), as the corner of a picture-frame, each jointing surface being cut at an angle to the piece on which it is formed; hence, an angle of 45°. *v.t.* To confer a mitre upon; to join with a mitre; to shape off at an angle of 45°. **mitre-block, -box,** *n.* A block or box used to guide the saw in cutting mitres. **mitre-joint,** *n.* **mitre-wheel,** *n.* A bevelled cog-wheel engaged with another at an angle of 45°. **mitred,** *a.* Wearing a mitre, of episcopal rank; (*Carp.*) joined or cut at an angle of 45°. **mitriform,** *a.* (*Bot.*).

mitt (mit) [shortened from foll.], *n.* A kind of glove or covering, usu. of lace or knitting, for the wrist and palm; (*slang*) a hand. **frozen mitt:** (*slang*) A snub.

mitten (mit' ėn) [O.F. *mitaine*, etym. doubtful], *n.* A glove with a thumb but no fingers; (*slang*) a boxing-glove. **to give or get the mitten:** To reject (a lover) or dismiss (from office etc.) or to be rejected or dismissed.

mittimus (mit' i mùs) [L., we send, from *mittere*, see MISSION], *n.* (*Law*) A warrant of commitment to prison; *a writ to remove records from one court to another; (*colloq.*) dismissal.

mity [MITE (2)].

mix (miks) [back-formation from obs. *mixt*, F. *mixte*, L. *mixtus*, p.p. of *miscēre*, to mix], *v.t.* To put together or blend into one mass or compound; to mingle or incorporate (several substances, quantities, or groups) so that the particles of each are indiscriminately associated; to compound by mingling various ingredients; to cross (breeds); to join. *v.i.* To become united; to be mingled (with or together); to be associated or have intercourse (with); to copulate; *to join (in battle etc.). **to mix up:** To mix thoroughly; (*fig.*) to confuse, to bewilder. **mixable,** *a.*

mixed (mikzd), *a.* Consisting of various kinds or constituents; promiscuous, not select (of company); (*colloq.*) confused, bewildered, muddled. **mixed bathing:** Bathing of both sexes together. **mixed doubles:** (*Tennis*) Matches with a man and woman player as partners on each side. **mixed marriage:** One in which the contracting parties are of different creeds. **mixed mathematics** [MATHEMATICS]. **mixed train,** *n.* (*Rail.*) A train composed of both passenger and goods wagons. **mixedly,** *adv.*

mixen (mik' sėn) [A.-S., from *meox*, dung], *n.* A dunghill.

mixer (mik' zėr), *n.* A person or thing that causes mixing, that mixes; (*colloq.*) a person with social tact; one who gets on well with all sorts of people.

mixture (miks' chùr), *n.* That which is mixed; a mixing, compound; gas or vaporized oil mixed with air to form the explosive charge in an internal-combustion engine.

mizen (miz' ėn) [F. *misaine*, It. *mezzana*, fem. of *mezzano*, see MEZZANINE], *n.* A fore-and-aft sail set on the mizen-mast, also called the **mizen-sail. mizen-mast,** *n.* The aftermost mast of a three-masted ship. **mizen-rigging, -top, -yard,** *n.*

mizzle (1) (miz' ėl) [cp. Dut. dial. *miezelen*], *v.i.* To rain in very fine drops, to drizzle. *n.* Very fine rain. **mizzly,** *a.*

mizzle (2) (miz' ėl) [etym. doubtful], *v.i.* (*slang*) To decamp.

mnemonic (nė mon' ik) [Gr. *mnēmonikos*, from *mnēmōn*, mindful (*mnāsthai*, to remember)], *a.* Pertaining to or aiding the memory. *n.pl.* The art of or a system for aiding or strengthening memory. **mnemonist** (nē' mō nist), *n.* **mnemotechny** (-tek' ni), *n.* The art of developing the memory. **mnemotechnic,** *a.* and *n.pl.*

***mo** (mō) [A.-S. *mā*, MORE], *a.*, *adv.*, and *n.* More.

moa (mō' à) [Maori], *n.* An extinct, flightless bird of the genus *dinornis*.

moan (mōn) [cogn. with A.-S. *mǣnan*, to moan], *n.* A low prolonged sound expressing pain or sorrow; (*fig.*) a complaint; *grief, woe. *v.i.* To utter a moan or moans. *v.t.* To lament, to deplore; to mourn; to utter moaningly. **moanful,** *a.* **moanfully, moaningly,** *adv.*

moat (mōt) [O.F. *mote*, a dike, a mound (cp. F. *motte*, a mound, a clod), prob. from Teut.], *n.* A ditch round a castle, fort, etc., usu. filled with water. *v.t.* To surround with or as with a moat.

mob (1) (mob) [contr. from L. *mōbile* (*vulgus*), the fickle (crowd)], *n.* A disorderly or riotous crowd, a rabble; the masses, the lower orders. *v.t.* (*past & p.p.* **mobbed**) To attack in a mob; to crowd roughly round and annoy. *v.i.* To gather together in a mob. **mob law:** The rule of the mob; lynch law. **swell mob:** A class of thieves who dress stylishly. **mobbish,** *a.* **mobbism,** *n.* **mobocracy** (mob ok' rà si), *n.* Rule by mob or by the lower orders. **mobsman,** *n.*

***mob** (2) (mob) [cp. Dut. *mopmuts*, woman's night-cap], *n.* A mob-cap. **v.t.* To muffle up (the head). **mob-cap,** *n.* A plain indoor cap or head-dress for women, usu. tied under the chin. ***moble** (mōbl), *v.t.* To wrap in a hood.

mobbee, mobie (mob' i) [Carib. *mabi*, batata], *n.* Spirituous liquor distilled from the batata; (*Am.*) the juice of apples or peaches distilled to make apple or peach brandy.

mobile (mō' bil, mō' bīl) [L. *mōbilis*, from *movēre*, to MOVE], *a.* Movable, free to move; easily moved; easily changing (as expression); that may be moved from place to place (as troops); *fickle, excitable. *n.* That which moves or causes motion; an artistic concoction of dangling wires etc. **mobility** (-bil' i ti), *n.* **mobilize,** *v.t.* To make mobile; to put into circulation; to put (troops, a fleet, etc.) in a state of readiness for active service. **mobilizable,** *a.* **mobilization** (-zā' shùn), *n.*

moble [MOB (2)]. **mobocracy** [MOB (1)].

moccasin (mok' à sin) [Powhatan *mockasin*], *n.* A foot-covering, usu. of deer-skin or soft leather in one piece, worn by N. American Indians; a bedroom slipper of soft leather made of one piece.

Mocha (1) (mō' kà) [fortified seaport in S.W. Arabia], *n.* A choice quality of coffee, orig. from Mocha.

mocha (2) (mō' kà) [prob. as prec.], *n.* A dendritic variety of chalcedony.

mock (mok) [O.F. *mocquer* (F. *moquer*), perh. from pop. L. *muccāre*, to wipe the nose, L. *muccus*, see MUCUS], *v.t.* To deride, to laugh at; to mimic, esp. in derision; to defy contemptuously; to delude, to take in. *v.i.* To express ridicule, derision, or contempt. *a.* Sham, false, counterfeit; imitating reality. **n.* A derision, a sneer; that which is derided; an imitation. **mock-heroic,** *a.* Burlesquing the heroic style. *n.* A burlesque of the heroic style. **mock-orange,** *n.* The common syringa, *Philadelphus coronarius*, the flowers of which smell like orange-blossoms. **mock-sun,** *n.* A parhelion. **mock-turtle soup:** A soup prepared from calf's head, veal, etc., to imitate turtle soup. **mock-up,** *n.* A full-size dummy model; an unprinted model of a book. **mock-velvet,** *n.* An imitation of velvet. **mockable,** *a.* **mocker,** *n.* **mockery,** *n.* The act of mocking; ridicule, derision; a subject of ridicule; a delusive imitation; a futile effort. **mocking-bird,** *n.* An American song-bird, *Mimus polyglottus*, with great powers of mimicry; the lyre-bird of Australia; a small N. Zealand bird that imitates voices etc. **mockingly,** *adv.*

mod (mod) [Gael. *mòd*, cogn. with MOOT], *n.* A Highland gathering analogous to a Welsh eisteddfod.

modal (mō' dȧl) [med. L. *modālis*, from L. *modus*, MODE], *a.* Pertaining to mode, form, or manner, as opp. to substance; (*Gram.*) pertaining to mood or denoting manner. *n.* A modal proposition. **modal proposition:** (*Log.*) A proposition that affirms or denies with some qualification. **modalism,** *n.* (*Theol.*) The doctrine that the three Persons of the Trinity are merely different modes of being. **modalist,** *n.* **modality** (-dăl' i ti), *n.* **modally,** *adv.*

mode (mōd) [F., from L. *modum*, nom. *-us*, rel. to Gr. *mēdos*, plan, and Eng. METE], *n.* Manner, method, way of doing, existing, etc.; common fashion, prevailing custom; (*Mus.*) one of the systems of dividing the octave, the form of the scale; (*Log.*) the character of the connexion in or the modality of a proposition; an open-work filling in lace; *(*Gram.*) mood; a kind of silk, alamode.

model (mod' ėl) [O.F. *modelle*, It. *modello*, dim. of *modo*, as prec.], *n.* A representation or pattern in miniature, in three dimensions, of something to be made on a larger scale; a figure in clay, plaster, etc., for execution in durable material; a thing or person to be represented by a sculptor or painter; one employed to pose as subject to an artist; a person employed in a shop to wear clothes to display their effect; a standard, an example regarded as a canon of artistic execution. *a.* Serving as a model or example; worthy of imitation, perfect. *v.t.* (*past & p.p.* **modelled**) To shape, mould, or fashion in clay etc.; to form after or upon a model; to give a plan or shape to (a document, book, etc.). *v.i.* To make a model or models; to act as a mannequin. **modeller,** *n.*

modena (mod' ė nȧ) [Italian city of *Modena*], *n.* A deep crimson or purple.

moderate (mod' ėr ȧt) [L. *moderātus*, p.p. of *moderārī*, from *moder-*, stem. of *modestus*, MODEST, cogn. with *modus*, MODE], *a.* Keeping within bounds; temperate, reasonable, mild; not extreme or excessive; of medium quantity or quality. *n.* One of moderate views in politics, religion, etc. *v.t.* (-āt) To reduce to a calmer, less violent, energetic, or intense condition; to restrain from excess; to temper, to mitigate. *v.i.* To become less violent; to quiet or settle down; to preside as a moderator. **moderant,** *n.* A moderate; something that moderates. **moderately,** *adv.* With moderation; not excessively. **moderateness,** *n.* **moderation** (-ā' shŭn), *n.* The act of moderating; the quality or state of being moderate; temperance; self-restraint; (*pl.*) the first public examination for a degree at Oxford. **moderatism** (mod' ėr ȧ tizm), *n.* ***moderato*** (mod ėr a' tō) [It.], *adv.* (*Mus.*) In moderate time. **moderator** (mod' ė rā tŏr), *n.* One who or that which moderates; one who presides at a meeting, esp. the presiding officer at a court of the Presbyterian Church; (*Oxf. and Camb. Univ.*) one who superintends certain examinations for degrees and honours; *an umpire, an arbitrator. **moderatorship,** *n.* **moderatrix,** *n.*

modern (mod' ėrn) [F. *moderne*, late L. *modernus*, from *modo*, just now], *a.* Pertaining to the present or recent time; late, recent; not ancient, old-fashioned, or obsolete; *commonplace, trite. *n.* A person of modern times; an exponent of modernism (as artist, writer, etc.). **modern side,** *n.* The division of school in which subjects other than classics are taught. **modernism,** *n.* A modern mode of expression or thought; a modern term or idiom; (*R.-C. Ch.*) a tendency towards freedom of thought and the acceptance of the results of modern criticism and research in religious matters. **modernist,** *n.* **modernity** (mŏ dĕr' ni ti), **modernness** (mod' ėrn nės), *n.* **modernize,** *v.t.* and *i.* **modernization** (-zā' shŭn), *n.* **modernizer,** *n.* **modernly,** *adv.*

modest (mod' ėst) [F. *modeste*, L. *modestus*, as MODERATE], *a.* Humble, unassuming or diffident in regard to one's merits or importance; not presumptuous, forward, or arrogant; bashful, retiring; restrained by a sense of propriety; decorous, chaste; moderate, not extreme or excessive. **modestly,** *adv.* **modesty,** *n.* The quality of being modest; a sense of propriety; delicacy; chastity. **modesty vest,** *n.* A narrow piece of lace worn over the bosom with an open dress.

modicum (mod' i kŭm) [L., neut. of *modicus*, moderate, as prec.], *n.* A little; a small amount, a scanty allowance.

modify (mod' i fī) [F. *modifier*, L. *modificāre* (*modus*, MODE, -FY)], *v.t.* To alter, to make different; to change to a moderate extent the form, character, or other qualities of; to reduce in degree or extent; to moderate, to tone down; (*Gram.*) to qualify the sense of, to alter (a vowel) by umlaut. **modifiable,** *a.* **modifiability** (-bil' i ti), *n.* **modification** (-kā' shŭn), *n.* ***modificative** (mod' i fi kā tiv), *a.* and *n.* ***modificator,** *n.* **modificatory,** *a.* **modifier,** *n.*

modillion (mŏ dil' yŏn) [It. *modiglione*, etym. doubtful], *n.* (*Arch.*) An ornamental bracket beneath the cornice of a Corinthian or other order.

modiolus (mŏ dī' ŏ lŭs) [L., bucket on waterwheel, dim. of *modius*, a corn-measure], *n.* (*Anat.*) The central column round which the cochlea of the ear winds. **modiolar,** *a.*

modish (mō' dish) [MODE, -ISH], *a.* Fashionable; stylish. **modishly,** *adv.* **modishness,** *n.* **modist,** *n.* A follower of the fashion. ***modiste*** (mŏ dēst') [F.], *n.* A milliner or dressmaker.

modulate (mod' ū lāt) [L. *modulātus*, p.p. of *modulārī*, to measure, from MODULUS], *v.t.* To adjust, to regulate; to vary or inflect the sound or tone of; (*Mus.*) to change the key of. *v.i.* (*Mus.*) To pass from one key to another. **modulation,** *n.* The act of modulating or being modulated; (*Radio.*) alterations in the amplitude or frequency of an electrical wave at a different frequency, usually at a lower. **modulative** (mod' ū lā tiv), *a.* **modulator,** *n.* One who or that which modulates; (*Mus.*) a chart of the modulations in the tonic sol-fa system; (*Radio.*) a transmitter valve which superinduces microphone signals on the high-frequency carrier.

module (mod' ūl) [F., as foll.], *n.* A measure or unit of proportion, esp. (*Arch.*) the semidiameter or other unit taken as a standard for regulating the proportions of a column; *(*fig.*) an image or counterfeit.

modulus (mod' ū lŭs) [L., dim. of foll.], *n.* (*pl.* **-li,** -lī) (*Math. etc.*) A constant number or coefficient expressing a force, effect, function, etc.; a constant multiplier in a function of a variable; the numerical value of quantity.

modus (mō' dŭs) [L., MODE], *n.* (*pl.* ***di,*** -dī) Mode, manner, way; money compensation in lieu of tithe. ***modus operandi:*** The way any one does something; the way a thing works. ***modus vivendi:*** Way of living; a compromise or temporary arrangement pending a final settlement of matters in dispute.

mofette (mŏ fet') [F., from It. *mofetta*], *n.* An exhalation of noxious gas from the earth; a fissure giving vent to such gas.

moff (mof) [etym. doubtful], *n.* A Circassian silk stuff.

Mogul (mò gŭl′) [Pers. *mugul*, Mongol], *n.* A Mongolian; a follower of Baber, descendant of Tamerlane, or of Jenghis Khan. **Great Mogul:** The emperor of Delhi (1526–1857), formerly sovereign of the greater part of Hindustan.

mohair (mō′ hâr) [Arab. *mukhayyar* (assim. to HAIR)], *n.* The hair of the angora goat; a fabric made from it; an imitation of this fabric in cotton and wool.

Mohammedan (mò hăm′ ė dȧn) [Arab. *Muḥammad*, praiseworthy, from *ḥamada*, to praise], *a.* Pertaining to Mohammed or Mohammedanism. *n.* A follower of Mohammed; an adherent of Mohammedanism. **Mohammedanism, *-medism,** *n.* The Moslem religion founded by Mohammed (*c.* 570–632). **Mohammedanize, *-medize,** *v.t.*

Moharram (mò hŭr′ ŭm) [Arab. *muḥarram*, sacred)], *n.* The first month (thirty days) of the Mohammedan year; the first ten days of this observed as a fast in memory of the martyrdom of Husain, the son of Ali.

Mohawk (mō′ hawk) [from the native name], *n.* The name of a tribe of North-American Indians; their language; (*Skating*) a stroke from either edge to the same edge on the other foot, but in the opposite direction. **Mohock** (mō′ hok) [corr. of this], *n.* A name given to a set of aristocratic ruffians who infested the streets of London at night early in the 18th cent.

mohr (môr) [Arab.], *n.* A West African gazelle, *Gazella mohr.*

moider (moi′ der) [perh. conn. with MUDDLE], *v.t.* (*prov.*) To confuse, to muddle; to weary; to labour (one's life etc.) away. *v.i.* To ramble, to talk incoherently.

moidore (moi′ dôr) [Port. *moeda d'ouro* (*moeda*, L. *monēta*, MONEY, *de*, of, *ouro*, L. *aurum*, gold)], *n.* A Portuguese gold coin.

moiety (moi′ ė ti) [O.F. *moitié*, L. *medietātem*, nom. *-tas*, middle point, half, from *medius*, see MEDIUM], *n.* A half; a part or share.

moil (moil) [O.F. *moiller* (F. *mouiller*), to wet, to paddle through mud, from L. *mollis*, soft], *v.i.* To toil, to drudge, to work hard. *v.t.* To weary, to fatigue; *to moisten, to bedaub, to defile.

moineau (moi′ nō, mwa′ nō) [F., sparrow], *n.* (*Fort.*) A small flat bastion.

moire (mwar) [F., prob. a form of MOHAIR], *n.* Watered silk; a watered appearance on textile fabrics or metals. **moire antique:** A heavy, watered silk. ***moiré*** (mwa′ rā) [F., p.p. of *moirer*], *v.t.* To give a watered appearance to. *a.* Watered (of silk, surfaces of metal, etc.). *n.* A surface or finish like watered silk.

moist (moist) [O.F. *moiste* (F. *moite*), perh. from late L. *muccidus*, L. *mūcidus*, MUCID], *a.* Moderately wet, damp, humid; rainy; (*Path.*) discharging pus etc.; *fresh, new. **moisten** (moisn), *v.t.* and *i.* **moistener,** *n.* ***moistful,** *a.* **moistify,** *v.t.* **moistness,** **moisture,** *n.* **moistureless,** *a.* **moisty,** *a.*

moke (mōk) [slang, etym. unknown], *n.* A donkey; (*Austral.*) an inferior horse.

moki (mō′ kē) [Maori], *n.* A variety of N. Zealand fish.

moko (mō′ kō) [Maori], *n.* Tattooing; the Maori method of doing this.

molar (1) (mō′ lȧr) [L. *molāris*, from *mola*, mill], *a.* Having power to grind; grinding. *n.* One of the back or grinding teeth. **molary,** *a.*

molar (2) (mō′ lȧr) [MOLE (2), -AR], *a.* Of or pertaining to mass; acted on or exerted by a large mass or masses.

molasses (mò lăs′ ėz) [Port. *melaço*, late L. *mellāceum*, must, from *mel*, honey], *n.pl.* (*usu. as sing.*) The viscid, dark-brown uncrystallizable syrup drained from sugar during the refining process; treacle.

mold [MOULD].

mole (1) (mōl) [A.-S. *māl*], *n.* A spot on the human skin, usu. dark-coloured and sometimes covered with hair.

mole (2) (mōl) [F. *môle*, L. *mōles*, mass, etym. doubtful], *n.* A pile of masonry, such as a breakwater, pier, or jetty before a port; a port, a harbour.

mole (3) (mōl) [cp. M.Dut. and L.G. *mol*], *n.* A small soft-furred burrowing mammal of the genus *Talpa*, esp. *T. Europœa.* *v.t.* To burrow or ferret (something out). **mole-cricket,** *n.* A burrowing cricket of the genus *Gryllotalpa*, esp. *G. vulgaris.* **mole-eyed,** *a.* Having very small eyes or imperfect vision. **mole-hill,** *n.* A hillock thrown up by a mole burrowing underground. **mole-rat,** *n.* A mouse-like burrowing rodent, *Spalax typhlus.* **moleskin,** *n.* The skin of the mole used as fur; a kind of fustian, dyed after the surface has been shaved; (*pl.*) clothes, esp. trousers, of this material.

molecule (mol′ ė-, mō′ lė kūl) [F. *molécule*, dim. from L. *mōles*, see MOLE (2)], *n.* One of the structural units of which matter is built up; the smallest quantity of substance capable of separate existence without losing its chemical identity with that substance; a particle. **molecular,** *a.* **molecular weight:** The weight of a molecule of any substance in terms of one-sixteenth the molecular weight of oxygen. **molecularity** (-lăr′ i ti), *n.*

molendinaceous (mò len di nā′ shŭs) [med. L. *molendīnum*, a mill, from *molere*, to grind], *a.* (*Bot.*) Resembling the sails of a windmill (applied to the wings of certain seeds). ***molendinar** (mò len′ di nȧr), *a.* Of or pertaining to a mill. *n.* A molar. ***molendinary,** *a.*

moleskin [MOLE (3)].

molest (mò lest′) [O.F. *molester*, L. *molestāre*, from *molestus*, troublesome], *v.t.* To trouble, to disturb, to harm, to interfere with. **molestation** (mol ės-, mō lės tā′ shŭn), *n.* **molester,** *n.* ***molestful,** *a.*

molimen (mò lī′ mėn) [L., effort, from *mōlīrī*, to make an effort], *n.* (*pl.* ***-mina***) (*Physiol.*) An effort, esp. a periodical effort of the system as in the catamenial discharge.

moline (mò līn′) [cp. F. *moulin*, late L. *molīna*, MILL (1)], *a.* (*Her.*) Shaped like a mill-rind (of the arms of a cross). *n.* A moline cross.

Molinism (1) (mol′ i nizm), *n.* The doctrine taught by the Spanish Jesuit Luis Molina (1535–1600) that the efficacy of divine grace depends on free acceptance by the will. **Molinist** (1), *n.*

Molinism (2) (mol′ i nizm) [Miguel de *Molinos* (1640–97), the Quietist], *n.* Quietism. **Molinist** (2), *n.*

moll (mol) [fam. form of *Mary*], *n.* (*slang*) A wench, a prostitute.

Mollah [MULLAH].

mollify (mol′ i fī) [F. *mollifier*, L. *mollificāre* (*mollis*, soft, *-ficāre*, from *facere*, to make)], *v.t.* To soften, to assuage; to pacify, to appease. ***mollient,** *a.* **mollifiable,** *a.* **mollification** (-kā′ shŭn), *n.* **mollifier,** *n.*

mollusc (mol′ ŭsk) [L. *molluscus*, softish, from *mollis*, soft], *n.* Any animal of the Mollusca. **Mollusca** (mò lŭs′ kȧ), *n.pl.* (*Zool.*) A division of invertebrates comprising those with soft bodies, as snails, mussels, cuttlefishes, etc. **molluscan, molluscoid,** *a.* and *n.* **Molluscoidea** (mol ŭs koi′ dė ȧ), *n.pl.* A group of invertebrates, containing the brachiopoda and polyzoa. **molluscous** (mò lŭs′ kŭs), *a.*

molly (1) (mol′ i) [form of *Mary*], *n.* An effeminate fellow, one who likes to be coddled, a milksop; (*slang*) a wench, a prostitute. **molly-coddle,** *n.* A milksop. *v.t.* To coddle.

molly (2) (mol′ i) [corr. of MALLEMUCK], *n.* The fulmar: a convivial meeting on board one of a company of whalers.

Moloch (mō′ lok) [Heb. *molek*], *n.* An idol of the Phœnicians to which human sacrifices were offered; (*fig.*) a devouring influence such as overbearing wealth, tyranny, etc.; an Australian spiny lizard, *Moloch horridus*.

molossus (mo los′ ŭs) [Gr.], *n.* (*pl.* **molossi**) (*Pros.*) A foot composed of three long syllables, or a spondee and a half.

molten (mōl′ tėn) [p.p. of MELT], *a.* Made of melted metal. **moltenly,** *adv.*

molto (mol′ tō) [It.], *adv.* (*Mus.*) Much, very.

moly (mō′ li) [L., from Gr. *mōlu*], *n.* A fabulous herb with white flower and black root, given to Ulysses to counteract the spells of Circe; **wild** garlic.

molybdenum (mol ib dē′ nům), ***molybdena** [L. *molybdæna*, Gr. *molubdaina*, from *molubdos*, lead], *n.* (*Chem.*) A rare metallic element, found in combination as molybdenite. **molybdate** (mo lib′ dåt), *n.* **molybdenite,** *n.* A sulphide or native disulphide of molybdenum. **molybdenous,** *a.* **molybdic, -dous** (mo lib′ dik, -důs), *a.* **molybdo-,** *comb. form.*

***mome** (mōm) [etym. doubtful], *n.* A block-head.

moment (mō′ mėnt) [F., from L. MOMENTUM], *n.* A minute portion of time, an instant; importance, consequence; (*Mech.*) the measure of a force by its power to cause rotation; ***momentum.** **at the moment:** At the present, just now. **moment of a force** (*Mech.*) The product of a force and the perpendicular from the point of application to the point of action. **the moment:** The right time for anything, the opportunity. **this moment:** At once. **momentary,** *a.* Lasting only for a moment; done or past in a moment; transient, ephemeral. **momentarily,** *adv.* **momentariness,** *n.* **momently,** *adv.* From moment to moment; at any moment, for a moment. **momentous** (mo men′-), *a.* Weighty, important. **momentously,** *adv.* **momentousness,** *n.*

momentum (mo men′ tům) [L., for *movimentum* (*movēre*, to MOVE, -MENT)], *n.* (*pl.* **-ta**) Impetus, power of overcoming resistance to motion; (*Mech.*) the quantity of motion in a body, the product of the mass and the velocity.

Momus (mō′ můs) [Gr. *Mōmos*], *n.* A Greek divinity, the son of Night, the god of blame and ridicule; a fault-finding or querulous person.

mon- [MONO-].

monachal (mon′ å kål) [med. L. *monachālis*, from *monachus*, MONK], *a.* Monastic. **monachism,** *n.* Monasticism; monkery, monkishness. **monachist,** *n.* **monachize,** *v.t.* and *i.*

monacid (mo năs′ id), *a.* (*Chem.*) Capable of saturating one molecule of a monobasic acid. **monactinal** (mo năk′ ti nål) [Gr. *aktis aktinos*, ray], *n.* Single-rayed, rod-shaped (of a sponge-spicule). **monactine,** *a.* **monactinellid** (-nel′ id), *a.* Of or pertaining to the *Monactinellida*, a Palæozoic order of sponges. *n.* A sponge of this order.

monad (mon′ åd) [late L. and Gr. *monad-*, nom. *monas*, from *monos*, sole], *n.* A simple, indivisible unit; one of the primary elements of being, esp. according to the philosophy of Leibnitz; (*Chem.*) a univalent atom, radical, or element; (*Biol.*) an elementary, single-celled organism. **monadic, -al** (mo năd′ ik, -ål), *a.* **monadism** (mon′ å dizm), *n.* (*Phil.*) **monadology** (-dol′ ŏ ji), *n.*

monadelphous (mon å del′ fůs) [MON-, Gr. *adelphos*, brother], *a.* (*Bot.*) Having the stamens united by their filaments; having the filaments united (of stamens).

Monagasque (mon′ å găsk) [Fr.], *a.* Pertaining to the principality of Monaco. *n.* An inhabitant of Monaco.

monandry (mo năn′ dri), *n.* That form of marriage in which one woman has only one husband at a time; (*Bot.*) the quality of being monandrous. **monandrous** (mo năn′ drůs) [Gr. *anēr andros*, male], *a.* (*Bot.*) Having but one stamen.

monanthous (mo năn′ thůs), *a.* (*Bot.*) Bearing but one flower (on each stalk).

monarch (mon′ årk) [F. *monarque*, L. *monarche*, Gr. *monarchēs* (MON-, *archein*, to rule)], *n.* A sole ruler; an hereditary sovereign, as emperor, empress, king, or queen; the chief of its class; a large red and black butterfly, *Danais archippus*. **monarchic, -al** (mo nar′ kik, -ål), **monarchal,** *a.* **monarchically,** ***monarchally,** *adv.* **monarchism** (mon′ år kizm), *n.* **monarchist,** *n.* **monarchize,** *v.t.* ***Monarcho,** *n.* A crack-brained Italian who thought himself emperor of the world; (*fig.*) a pretender. **monarchy,** *n.* Government in which the supreme power is vested in a monarch; a state under this system, a kingdom; supreme control.

monastery (mon′ å stėr i) [med. L. *monastērium*, Gr. *monastērion*, from *monazein*, to live alone, from *monos*, see MONAD], *n.* A residence for a community, esp. of monks, living under religious vows of seclusion. ***monasterial** (-stēr′ i ål), *a.* **monastic** (mo năs′ tik), *a.* Monasterial; (*Bookbinding*) applied to an antique style of tooling without gold. **monastical,** *a.* **monastically,** *adv.* **monasticism** (-sizm), *n.* The theory and system of the monastic life. **monasticize,** *v.t.* **monasticon,** *n.* A book treating of monasteries.

monaural (mon awr′ ål) [MON-, L. *auris*, an ear], *a.* Having or using one ear; (*Gramophone*) not stereophonic.

Monday (mŭn′ dā, -di) [A.-S. *Mōnandæg* (*Mōnan*, gen. of *Mōna*, moon, DAY)], *n.* The second day of the week. **Mondayish,** *a.* Reluctant to start the week's work.

monde (mond) [F., from L. *mundum*, nom. *-us*, the world], *n.* Society; one's circle or set.

Monera (mo nēr′ å) [Gr. *monērēs*, single, from *monos*, sole], *n.pl.* A class of amœbiform protozoa of the most elementary organization. **moneral, -ic, -an,** *a.*

monergism (mon′ ėr jizm) [MON-, Gr. *ergon*, work, -ISM], *n.* (*Theol.*) The Lutheran doctrine that regeneration is entirely the work of the Holy Spirit, opp. to synergism.

monetary (mŭn′-, mon′ ė tår i) [L. *monētārius*, from *monēta*, see foll.], *a.* Of or pertaining to money or the coinage. **monetize,** *v.t.* To give a standard value to (a metal) as currency; to form into coin. **monetization** (-zā′ shůn), *n.*

money (mŭn′ i) [M.E. and O.F. *moneie* (F. *monnaie*), L. *monēta*, mint, money, orig. name of Juno in whose temple money was coined], *n.* (*pl.* **moneys,** incorr. **monies**) Coin or other material used as medium of exchange; bank-notes, bills, notes of hand, and other documents representing coin; wealth, property, regarded as convertible into coin; (*with pl.*) coins of a particular country or denomination; (*pl.*) sums of money, receipts, or payments. **money of account:** A denomination (as of the guinea), not actually coined, but used for convenience in keeping accounts. **ready money:** Cash; money paid or ready to be paid for a purchase etc. **money-bag,** *n.* A bag for money; (*pl.*) wealth; (*as sing.*) a rich or miserly person. **money-box,** *n.* A box with a slit through which savings or contributions are put in. **money-changer,** *n.* One who changes foreign money at a fixed rate. **money-grubber,** *n.* A person who saves or amasses money in sordid ways. **money-lender,** *n.* A person whose business is to lend money at interest. **money-making,** *a.* and *n.* Highly profitable (business). **money-market,** *n.* The field of operation of dealers in stocks etc., the financial world. **money-matter,** *n.* An affair involving money. **money-order,** *n.* An order for money, granted at one post-office and payable at another. **money-spider, -spinner,** *n.* A small spider, *Aranea scenica*, supposed to bring good luck; (*fig.*) one who makes great profits. **money-wort,** *n.* A trailing plant, *Lysimachia nummularia*, with round glossy leaves. **money's-worth, *moneyworth,** *n.* Full value, an equivalent for money paid. **moneyed,** *a.* Rich; consisting of money. **moneyer,** *n.* A banker; an authorized coiner of money. **moneyless,** *a.*

monger (mŭng′ gėr) [A.-S. *mangere*, from *mangian*, to traffic, from L. *mango*, a dealer], *n.* A trader, a dealer (now only in comb., as *ironmonger*, *scandal-monger*).

Mongol (mong′ gŏl) [native name], *n.* One of an Asiatic race now inhabiting Mongolia. *a.* Of or pertaining to the Mongols. **Mongolian** (mong gō′ li ȧn), *a.* (*Ethn.*) Pertaining to the straight-haired yellow peoples of Asia; (*Path.*) denoting a type of idiot resembling the Mongolians in physiognomy. *n.* A Mongol; one belonging to the Mongolian races; the language of the Mongols or of the Mongolian stock. **Mongoloid,** *a.* and *n.*

mongoose [MUNGOOSE].

mongrel (mŭng′ grėl) [prob. cogn. with A.-S. *mang*, a mixture], *a.* Of mixed breed, arising from the crossing of two varieties; of mixed nature or character. *n.* Anything, esp. a dog, of mixed breed. **mongrelism,** *n.* **mongrelize,** *v.t.* **mongrelly,** *adv.*

monial (mō′ ni ȧl) [O.F., etym. unknown], *n.* (*Ant.*) A mullion.

moniker (mon′ ik ĕr) [etym. unknown], *n.* (*slang*) Name.

moniliform (mŏ nil′ i fôrm) [L. *monīle*, necklace, -FORM], *a.* Shaped like a necklace or string of beads.

***moniment** [MONUMENT].

moniplies [MANYPLIES].

monism (mon′ izm) [Gr. *monos*, one, -ISM], *n.* The doctrine that all existing things and activities are forms of manifestations of one ultimate principle or substance; any philosophic theory such as idealism, pantheism, or materialism, opposed to dualism. **monist,** *n.* **monistic** (mŏ nis′ tik), *a.*

monition (mŏ nish′ ŭn) [F., from L. *monitiōnem*, nom. *-tio*, from *monēre*, to warn], *n.* A warning; an intimation or notice; (*Civil Law*) a summons or citation; (*Eccles. Law*) a formal letter from a bishop or court warning a clergyman to abstain from certain practices. **monitive** (mon′-), *a.*

monitor (mon′ i tŏr), *n.* One who warns or admonishes; a senior pupil appointed to keep order in a school or to look after junior classes; (*Radio.*) one whose duty it is to listen to foreign or other broadcasts; a detector for radio-activity; an iron-clad of low draught having revolving turrets; a genus of large tropical lizards found in Asia, Africa, and Australia. **monitorial** (-tôr′ i ȧl), *a.* **monitorially,** *adv.* **monitorship** (mon′ i tŏr ship), *n.* **monitory,** *a.* Giving warning or admonition. *n.* A warning or admonition from a bishop, pope, etc. **monitress,** *n.*

monk (mŭngk) [A.-S. *munec*, *munuc*, L. and Gr. *monachos*, from *monos*, alone], *n.* A member of a religious community of men, living apart under vows of poverty, chastity, and obedience; (*Print.*) a patch of print with too much ink. **monk's-hood,** *n.* A plant of the genus *Aconitum*, esp. *A. napellus* (from its hooded sepals). **monkery,** *n.* (*opprobriously*) Monasticism; monkish practices; monks collectively. **monkdom, monkhood, monkship,** *n.* **monkish,** *a.* **monkishness,** *n.*

monkey (mŭng′ ki) [prob. from L.G.], *n.* A quadrumanous mammal of various species and families ranging from the anthropoid apes to the lemurs; (*colloq.*) a rogue, an imp; an ape, a mimic; a pile-driving machine; a monkey-jar; a mixture of hydrochloric acid and zinc used in soldering; (*slang*) a sum of £500 or $500. *v.t.* To mimic, to ape; to meddle with, to interfere with. *v.i.* To play foolish or mischievous tricks. **to get** or **put one's monkey up:** (*colloq.*) To be angry or to enrage. **monkey-block,** *n.* (*Naut.*) A single block strapped to a swivel. **monkey-bread,** *n.* The fruit of the baobab tree, *Adansonia digitata*. **monkey-engine,** *n.* A pile-driving machine. **monkey-flower,** *n.* A plant of the genus *Mimulus*. **monkey-jacket,** *n.* A pea-jacket worn by sailors etc. **monkey-jar,** *n.* A globular earthenware vessel used in tropical countries for cooling water. **monkey-puzzle,** *n.* The Chilean pine, *Araucaria imbricata*, having spiny leaves and branches. **monkey-rail,** *n.* (*Naut.*) A light rail running above the quarter-rail. **monkey-wrench,** *n.* A spanner with a movable jaw. **monkeyish,** *a.* **monkeyishness,** *n.* **monkeyism,** *n.*

monkish, etc. [MONK].

mono-, mon- [Gr. *monos*], *comb. form.* Alone, single; as in *monograph*, *monosyllable*.

monobasic (mon ŏ bā′ sik) [MONO-, BASIC], *a.* (*Chem.*) With one base or replaceable atom. **monoblastic** (-blăs′ tik) [Gr. *blastos*, sprout], *a.* (*Biol.*) Having a single germ-layer. **monoblepsis** (-blep′ sis) [Gr. *blepsis*, vision], *n.* (*Path.*) A defective state of vision in which objects can be seen clearly only when one eye is used.

monobloc (mon′ ō blok), *n.* Denoting a type of internal-combustion engine having all its cylinders cast in one piece. **monocardian** (-kar′ di ȧn) [Gr. *kardia*, heart], *a.* (*Zool.*) Having a single heart. **monocarp** (mon′ ŏ karp), *n.* (*Bot.*) A monocarpous plant. **monocarpic, -ous** (-kar′ pik, -pŭs), *a.* Bearing fruit but once, and dying after fructification. **monocentric** (-sen′ trik), *a.* (*Biol.*) Having a single centre; (*Anat.*) unipolar. **monocephalous** (-sef′ ȧ lŭs), *a.* Having one head; (*Bot.*) having a single head of flowers.

monoceros (mŏ nos′ ė rŏs) [Gr. *keras*, a horn], *n.* A one-horned creature, the unicorn; *a sea-unicorn, a sword-fish or narwhal, the constellation unicorn. **monocerous,** *a.* **monochlamydeous** (mon ŏ klȧ mid′ ė ŭs) [CHLAMYD-, -EOUS], *a.* (*Bot.*) Having a single floral envelope, as a calyx, but no corolla.

monochord (mon′ ō kôrd), *n.* A musical instrument with one string; an apparatus for determining the ratios of musical intervals.

monochromatic (mon ō krō măt′ ik), *a.* Presenting rays of one colour only (of light); painted, etc., in monochrome. **monochromator,** *n.* (*Phys.*) A spectroscope capable of segregating for use a narrow portion of spectrum. **monochrome** (mon′ ŏ krōm), *n.* A painting in tints of one colour only; any representation in one colour. *a.* Monochromic. **monochromic** (-krō′ mik), *a.* Executed in one colour. **monochromy** (mon′ ŏ krō mi), *n.*

monocle (mon′ ŏkl), *n.* An eye-glass for one eye. **monocleid, monocleide,** *n.* A cabinet in which all the drawers are shut simultaneously by one key. **monoclinal** (mon ŏ klī′ nȧl) [Gr. *klinein*, to bend], *a.* (*Geol.*) Dipping continuously in one direction (of strata). **monocline** (mon′-), *n.* A monoclinal fold, a hogback. **monoclinic** (-klin′ ik), **-clinate** (-klī′ nȧt), *a.* (*Cryst.*) Having two oblique axes and a third at right angles to these. **monoclinous** (-klī′ nŭs) [Gr. *klīnē*, couch], *a.* (*Bot.*) Hermaphrodite; (*Geol.*) monoclinal. **monocoque,** *n.* (*Aviat.*) A form of stream-lined fuselage shaped like an elongated egg; an aeroplane with such a fuselage.

monocotyledon (mon ō kot i lē′ dŏn), *n.* (*Bot.*) A plant having a single cotyledon. **monocotyledonous,** *a.* **monocracy** (mŏ nok′ rȧ si), *n.* Government by a single person. **monocrat** (mon′ ŏ krăt), *n.*

monocular (mŏ nok′ ū lȧr) [late L. *monoculus*, see MONOCLE], *a.* One-eyed; for use with one eye only. **monocularity** (-lăr′ i ti), *n.* **monocule** [MONOCULUS]. **monoculist** (mŏ nok′ ū list), *n.* **monoculous,** *a.* **monoculus,** *n.* A one-eyed creature, a cyclops; (*Surg.*) a bandage for one eye; (*Zool.*) a Linnæan genus containing the water-fleas.

monocycle (mon′ ō sīkl), *n.* A one-wheeled velocipede. **monocyte** (mon′ o sit), *n.* (*Biol.*) The largest white blood cell in vertebrate blood. **monodactylous** (mon ŏ dăk′ ti lŭs) [Gr. *monodaktulos* (*daktulos*, finger)], *a.* Having but one finger, toe, or claw. **monodelph** (mon′ ŏ delf) [F. *monodelphe*, mod. L. *Monodelphia* (Gr. *delphus*, womb)], *n.* A mammal belonging to the *Monodelphia*, a division of Mammalia in which the uterus and vagina are single. **monodelphian** (-del′ fi ȧn), *a.* and *n.* **monodelphic, -phous,** *a.* **monodon** (mon′ ȯ don) [Gr. *monodous -dontos* (*odous odontos*, tooth)], *n.* A genus of cetacea containing only the narwhal. **monodrama** (mon′ ȯ dra mȧ, mon ȯ dra′ mȧ) [DRAMA], *n.* A dramatic piece for one performer only. **monodramatic** (-drȧ măt′ ik), *a.*

monody (mon′ ō di), *n.* An ode, usu. of a mournful character, for a single actor; a song for one voice, or a musical composition in which one voice predominates; a mournful or plaintive song or poetical composition, a threnody. **monodic** (mȯ nod′ ik), *a.* **monodist** (mon′ ȯ dist), *n.* **Monœcia** (mȯ nē′ shi ȧ) [mod. L. (Gr. *oikos*, house)], *n.pl.* (*Bot.*) A Linnæan class, comprising plants in which the stamens and pistils are in distinct flowers. **monœcious,** *a.* (*Bot.*) Belonging to the Monœcia; having separate male and female flowers on the same plant; (*Zool.*) hermaphrodite. **monofil** (mon′ ō fil), *n.* A single strand of synthetic fibre.

monogamy (mȯ nog′ ȧ mi) [F. *monogamie*, L. and Gr. *monogamia* (Gr. *gamos*, marriage)], *n.* Marriage to one wife or husband only; (*rare*) the practice of marrying only once; (*Zool.*) the habit of pairing with a single mate. **monogamous** (-nog′ ȧ mŭs), **monogamic** (-găm′ ik), *a.* **monogamist** (mȯ nog′ ȧ mist), *n.*

monogenesis (mon ȯ jen′ ė sis), *n.* (*Biol.*) Generation from one parent, asexual reproduction; development of an organism from a parent resembling itself. **monogenetic** (-net′ ik), **monogenic** (-jen′ ik), **monogenous** (-noj′ ė nŭs), *a.* **monogenism, -eny** (mȯ noj′ ė nizm, -ni), *n.* The doctrine that all men are descended from a single pair. **monogenist,** *n.* **monoglot** (mon′ ȯ glot) [Gr. *monoglōttos* (*glōtta*, tongue)], *a.* Speaking only one language. *n.* A monoglot person. **monogony** (mȯ nog′ ȯ ni) [Gr. *-gonia*, begetting, from *gon-*, *gen-*, to beget], *n.* Asexual propagation. **monogonic** (-gon′ ik), *a.*

monogram (mon′ ȯ grăm) [late L. *monogramma*, Gr. *monogrammon* (MONO-, -GRAM)], *n.* A character composed of two or more letters interwoven; a single character representing a word etc. **monogrammatic** (-măt′ ik), *a.*

monograph (mon′ ȯ grăf), *n.* A treatise on a single thing or class of things. *v.t.* To treat of in a monograph. **monographer, -phist** (-nog′ rȧ fėr, -fist), *n.* **monographic, -al** (-grăf′ ik, -ȧl), *a.* **monographically,** *adv.*

Monogynia (mon ȯ jin′ i ȧ) [mod. L., from *monogynus* (Gr. *gunē*, woman)], *n.pl.* (*Bot.*) A Linnæan order containing plants having flowers with one pistil. **monogyn** (mon′ ȯ jin), *n.* A plant of this kind. **monogynian** (-jin′ i ȧn), **-gynous** (-noj′ i nŭs), *a.* **monogyny,** *n.* The practice of mating with only one female.

monoïdeism (mon ȯ ī dē′ izm), *n.* Fixation of the mind upon one idea, esp. in monomania or hypnotic condition. **monolatry** (mȯ nol′ ȧ tri), *n.* Worship of one god, esp. among many. **monolater, -trist,** *n.* **monolatrous,** *a.*

monolith (mon′ ō lith) [from F. *monolithe* or L. *monolithus*, Gr. *monolithos*, made of a single stone], *n.* A monument or other structure formed of a single stone. **monolithic** (-lith′ ik), *a.*

monologue (mon′ ȯ log) [F., one who likes to hear himself talk, Gr. *monologos*], *n.* A dramatic scene in which a person speaks by himself; a dramatic piece for one actor; a soliloquy; a long speech in conversation. **monological** (-loj′ i kȧl), *a.* **monologist, -guist** (mȯ nol′ ȯ jist, -gist), *n.* **monologize, -guise** (-jīz, -gīz), *v.i.* ***monology,** *n.*

***monomachy** (mȯ nom′ ȧ ki) [F. *monomachie*, L. and Gr. *monomachia*, from *monomachos*, one fighting alone (*machesthai*, to fight)], *n.* A single combat, a duel. **monomachist,** *n.*

monomania (mon ȯ mā′ ni ȧ), *n.* Mental derangement on one subject only. **monomaniac,** *n.* and *a.* **monomaniacal** (-nī′ ȧ kȧl), *a.* **monomark,** *n.* One of a system of registered combinations of numbers, serving to identify property or manufactured goods. (Protected trade name.) **monomerous** (mȯ nom′ ėr ŭs) [Gr. *monomerēs* (*meros*, part)], *a.* (*Bot.*) Having one member in each whorl (of flowers); (*Ent.*) single-jointed (of tarsi), having the tarsi single-jointed. **monometallism** (mon ȯ met′ ȧ lizm), *n.* A one-metal standard of value for coinage. **monometallic** (-tăl′ ik), *a.* **monometallist** (-met′ ȧ list), *n.* **monometer** (mȯ nom′ ė tėr) [L., from Gr. *monometros*], *n.* (*Pros.*) A verse consisting of one foot; metre of this kind. **monometric** (-met′ rik), *a.* (*Pros.*) In this metre; (*Cryst.*) having the axes equal or similar, isometric.

monomial (mȯ nō′ mi ȧl), *n.* (*Alg.*) An expression consisting of a single term. *a.* Consisting of a single term. **monomorphic, -phous** (mon ȯ môr′ fik, -fŭs) [Gr. *morphē*, form, -IC, -OUS], *a.* Having the same structure or morphological character, esp. throughout successive stages of development. **monomorphism,** *n.* **monomyary** (mon ȯ mī′ ȧ ri) [Gr. *mus*, muscle], *a.* Belonging to the *Monomyaria*, a section of bivalves in which there is only one abductor muscle, as in the oyster. *n.* A bivalve of this section. **monomyarian** (-âr′ i ȧn), *a.* and *n.* **mononym** (mon′ ȯ nim) [Gr. *onoma*, Æolic *onuma*, name], *n.* A name consisting of a single word. **mononymic** (-nim′ ik), *a.* **mononymy** (mȯ non′ i mi), *n.* **mononymize,** *v.t.* **mononymization** (-zā′ shŭn), *n.*

monoousious (mon ȯ oo′ zi ŭs) [late Gr. *monoousios* (MONO-, *ousia*, essence)], *a.* (*Theol.*) Having the same substance (of the Son and the Father).

monopathy (mȯ nop′ ȧ thi), *n.* (*Path.*) Disease affecting only one organ or function; *solitary suffering or sensibility. **monopathic** (-păth′ ik), *a.* **monopetalous** (mon ȯ pet′ ȧ lŭs), *a.* (*Bot.*) Having the petals coherent in a single corolla. **monophobia,** *n.* Morbid dread of being alone. **monophone** (mon′ ȯ fōn), *n.* A monophonous sound; a homophone. **monophonic** (-fon′ ik), *a.* Homophonic. **monophonous** (mȯ nof′ ȯ nŭs), *a.* Homophonous; (*Mus.*) producing only one tone at a time. **monophthong** (mȯ nof′ thong) [Gr. *monophthongos* (*phthongos*, sound)], *n.* A simple or single vowel sound; two written vowels pronounced as one. **monophthongal** (-thong′ gȧl), *a.* **monophyletic** (mon ȯ fī let′ ik) [Gr. *phuletikos*, from *phulē*, tribe], *a.* Pertaining to a single family or race or descended from one parental form. **monophyllous** (mon ȯ fil′ ŭs) [Gr. *phullon*, leaf], *a.* (*Bot.*) Having or formed of one leaf. **monophyodont** (-fi-′ ȯ dont) [Gr. *phu-ein*, to generate, *odous odontos*, tooth], *a.* (*Zool.*) Having only one set of teeth, as the cetacea. *n.* A monophyodont animal. **monophysite** (mȯ nof′ i sīt) [eccles. L. *Monophysīta*, eccles. Gr. *Monophysītēs* (*phusis*, nature, from *phuein*, see prec., -ITE)], *n.* (*Eccles. Hist.*) One of an Eastern 5th-cent. sect affirming that there is only one nature in the person of Christ. **monophysitic, -al** (-sit′ ik, -ȧl), *a.* **monophysitism** (mȯ nof′ i sī tizm), *n.*

monoplane (mon′ ō plān), *n.* (*Aviat.*) An aeroplane with one supporting plane. **monoplast** (mon′ ȯ plăst) [Gr. *plastos*, moulded, from *plassein*, to mould], *n.* (*Biol.*) A structure or organism consisting of a single cell. **monoplastic** (-plăs′ tik), *a.* **monoplegia** (-plē′ ji ȧ) [Gr. *plēgē*, stroke], *n.* (*Path.*) Paralysis of a single part or limb. **monopode** (mon′ ȯ pōd) [Gr. *pous podos*, foot], *n.* An animal having one foot; one of a fabulous race of men having one foot with which they shaded themselves against the heat of the sun. **monopodous** (-nop′ ȯ dŭs), *a.*

monopoly (mȯ nop′ ȯ li) [late L. *monopōlium*, Gr. *monopōlion* (*pōlein*, to sell)], *n.* An exclusive trading right in a certain commodity or class of commerce or business, usu. conferred by Government; a company or combination enjoying this; the subject of such a right; exclusive possession, control, or enjoyment (of). **monopolism,** *n.* **monopolist, -lizer,** *n.* **monopolistic** (-lis′ tik), *a.* **monopolize,** *v.t.* To obtain or possess a monopoly of; to engross the whole of (attention, conversation, etc.). **monopolization** (-zā′ shŭn), *n.*

monopolylogue (mon ŏ pol′ i log), *n.* A dramatic entertainment in which one performer takes many parts. **monopolylogist** (-lil′ ŏ jist), *n.* **monopteros** (mŏ nop′ tėr ŏs) [late L. *monopteros* (Gr. *pteron*, wing)], *n.* A circular temple composed of columns supporting a roof. **monopteral,** *a.* and *n.* **monopterous,** *a.* (*Bot.*) One-winged (of seeds). **monoptote** (mŏ nop′ tōt) [late L. *monoptōtus*, Gr. *monoptōtos* (*ptōtos*, falling, rel. to *piptein*, to fall)], *n.* (*Gram.*) A word having a single case-form. **monoptotic** (-tot′ ik), *a.*

monorail (mon′ ō rāl), *n.* A railway with a track consisting of a single rail; *a.* Consisting of one rail. **monorailway** (-rāl′ wā), *n.* **monorchid** (mŏ nôr′ kid) [Gr. *monorchis* (*orchis*, testicle)], *n.* A person or animal having only one testicle. **monorchidism, monorchism,** *n.* **monorganic** (mon ŏr găn′ ik), *a.* (*Path.*) Affecting one organ or set of organs. **monorhine** (mon′ ŏ rīn) [Gr. *rhis rhīnos*, nose], *a.* (*Zool.*) Having a single nasal passage. *n.* One of the *Monorhina*, a section of monorhine vertebrates comprising the lampreys and hags. **monorhyme** (mon′ ŏ rīm) [F. *monorime*], *n.* A composition in which all the lines end in the same rhyme. *a.* Having but one rhyme.

monosepalous (mon ō sep′ ȧ lŭs), *a.* (*Bot.*) Having one sepal. **monospermous** (-spĕr′ mŭs) [Gr. *sperma*, seed, -OUS], *a.* (*Bot.*) Having but one seed. **monospermal, -matous, -mic,** *a.* **monospherical** (-sfer′ i kȧl), *a.* Consisting of a single sphere. **monosporous** (-spôr′ ŭs) [SPORE, -OUS], *a.* (*Bot.*) Having but one spore. **monostich** (mon′ ŏ stik) [late L. *monostichum*, Gr. *monostichon* (*stichos*, row)], *n.* (*Pros.*) A single metrical line forming a complete composition, as an epigram. *a.* Consisting of a single metrical line. **monostichous** (-nos′ ti kŭs), *a.* (*Bot., Zool., etc.*) Having, arranged in, or consisting of a single row or layer. **monostrophic** (-strof′ ik) [Gr. *monostrophikos*], *a.* Having only one form of strophe. **monostyle (1)** (mon′ ŏ stīl) [Gr. *stulos*, pillar], *a.* (*Arch.*) Of a single shaft. **monostyle (2)** [STYLE (1)], *a.* Built in the same style throughout. **monostylar** (stī′ lȧr), *a.*

monosyllable (mon′ ō sil ȧ bėl), *n.* A word of one syllable. **monosyllabic** (-lăb′ ik), *a.* **monosyllabism** (-sil′ ȧ bizm), *n.* **monosyllabize,** *v.t.* **monosymmetric** (mon ŏ si met′ rik), *a.* (*Cryst.*) Monoclinic. **monosymmetrical,** *a.* (*Bot.*) Divisible into symmetrical halves in only one plane. **monosymmetry** (-sim′ ė tri), *n.* **monotelephone,** *n.* A telephone which carries sounds of one pitch only. **monotessaron** (mon ŏ tes′ ȧ rŏn) [med. L., Gr. *tessares*, four, after DIATESSARON], *a.* A continuous narrative embodying the stories in the four Gospels. **monothalamous** (mon ŏ thăl′ ȧ mŭs), *a.* Possessing a single chamber, as some shells. **monothalamic** (-thȧ lăm′ ik), *a.* Monothalamous; (*Bot.*) developed from a single pistil (of certain fruits).

monotheism (mon′ ŏ thē izm) [Gr. *theos*, God, -ISM], *n.* The doctrine that there is only one God. **monotheist,** *n.* **monotheistic** (-is′ tik), *a.* **monotheistically,** *adv.*

monothelete, -lite (mŏ noth′ ė lēt, -līt) [med. L. *monothelīta*, late Gr. *monothelētēs* (*thelein*, to will)], *n.* One of a sect arising in the 7th cent. who maintained that Christ has but one will, opp. to dyothelete. **monothelism, -theletism,** *n.* **monotheletic, -litic** (-let′-, -lit′ ik), *a.* **monotint** (mon′ ŏ tint) [TINT], *n.* A picture or other representation in one colour.

monotone (mon′ ŏ tōn) [late Gr. *monotonos*, monotonous], *n.* Continuance of or repetition in the same tone; a succession of sounds of the same pitch; intoning of words on a single note; monotony; monotint. *a.* Monotonous. *v.t.* and *i.* To chant, recite, or speak in the same tone or note. **monotonic** (-ton′ ik), *a.* **monotonize** (mŏ not′ ŏ nīz), *v.t.* **monotonous** (-not′ ŏ nŭs), *a.* Wearisome through sameness, tedious. **monotonously,** *adv.* **monotonousness, monotony,** *n.*

monotremata (mon ŏ trē′ mȧ tȧ) [Gr. *trēma -tos*, perforation, hole)], *n.pl.* (*Zool.*) A sub-class of mammals having only one aperture or vent for the genital organs and the excretions. **monotrematous,** *a.* **monotreme** (mon′ ŏ trēm), *n.* and *a.*

Monotype (mon′ o tīp), *n.* (*Print.*) Protected trade name of a type-setting machine that casts and sets single printing-types.

monoxide (mon oks′ īd), *n.* (*Chem.*) An oxide containing one atom of oxygen in combination with a radical. **monoxy-, monox-,** *comb. form.*

Monroe Doctrine (mŭn rō′ dok′ trin) [James *Monroe* (1758–1831), Pres. U.S.A. (1816–25)], *n.* The principle that non-American powers should not intervene in affairs in either of the American continents, formulated by Monroe in 1823.

Monseigneur (mon sā′ nyĕr) [F. *mon*, my, SEIGNEUR], *n.* (*pl.* **Messeigneurs,** mā sā′ nyĕr) A French title of honour given to high dignitaries, esp. in the Church.

Monsieur (mo syėr′) [F. *mon*, my, *sieur*, as prec.], *n.* (*pl.* **Messieurs)** The French title of address, Mr. or Sir; a Frenchman; *the title of a French king's second son or next younger brother.

Monsignor (mon sē′ nyôr, mon sē nyôr′) [It.], *n.* (*pl.* **Monsignori,** mon sē nyôr′ ee) A title given to prelates, officers of the Pope's court, and others.

monsoon (mon soon′) [M.Dut. *monssoen*, Port. *monção*, Arab. *mausim*, time, season], *n.* A wind in S.W. Asia and the Indian Ocean, blowing from the south-west from April to October, and from the north-east the rest of the year; applied to other periodical winds.

monster (mon′ stėr) [O.F. *monstre*, L. *monstrum*, a portent or omen, from *monēre*, to warn], *n.* Something misshapen, abnormal, out of the ordinary course of nature; an abortion, a deformed creature; an imaginary animal, usually compounded of incongruous parts, such as a centaur, griffin, mermaid, gorgon, etc.; an abominably cruel or depraved person; a person, animal, or thing of extraordinary size; *a prodigy, a marvel, a portent. *a.* Of extraordinary size, huge. **v.t.* To make monstrous. ***monsterful,** *a.*

monstrance (mon′ strȧns) [O.F., from med. L. *monstrantia*, from *monstrāre*, to show], *n.* (*R.-C. Ch.*) An open or transparent vessel in which the Host is carried in procession or exposed for adoration.

monstrous (mon′ strŭs) [O.F. *monstreux*, late L. *monstrōsus*, from *monstrum*, MONSTER], *a.* Unnatural in form; out of the ordinary course of nature; enormous, huge; shocking, atrocious, outrageous; absurd, incredible; *full of monsters. **adv.* Extraordinarily, very, exceedingly. ***monstriferous** (-strif′ ėr ŭs), *a.* **monstrosity** (-stros′ i ti), *n.* The quality of being monstrous; a monster, an abortion; a deformity, a distortion. **monstrously,** *adv.* **monstrousness,** *n.*

montage (mon′ tij), *n.* (*Cinema*) Cutting and assembling of shots taken when making a film picture.

montagnard (mon tan′ yar) [F., from *montagne*, MOUNTAIN], *n.* A mountaineer, an inhabitant of mountain country; (*Fr. Hist.*) a member of the 'Mountain' or extreme democratic wing in the Revolutionary Legislative Assembly (1791–2).

montane (mon′ tān) [L. *montānus*, from *mons montis*, MOUNT], *a.* (*Nat. Hist.*) Of or pertaining to mountainous regions.

Montanism (mon′ tȧ nizm) [*Montānus*, -ISM], *n.* The doctrine of a religious sect founded in the 2nd cent. by Montanus of Phrygia, who claimed the gift of prophecy, and taught asceticism. **Montanist,** *n.*

***montant** (mon′ tȧnt) [F., p.p. of *monter*, to MOUNT], *n.* An upright cut or thrust in fencing; (*Carp.*) an upright part in framing. *a.* Rising; (*Her.*) ascending.

montbretia (mont brē′ shi ȧ) [A. F. E. Coquebert de *Montbret* (1780–1801), French botanist], *n.* A genus of bulbous-rooted flowering plants of the iridaceous genus *Tritonia.*

monte (mon′ ti) [Sp., mountain, as MOUNT], *n.* A Spanish game of chance with 45 cards, resembling faro; (*Sp. Am.*) a tract of wooded country. **three-card monte:** A Mexican game of sleight-of-hand with three cards.

montem (mon′ tėm) [L. *ad montem*, to the hill], *n.* A custom formerly observed at Eton College of collecting money, called 'salt money,' at a mound called Salt Hill, to defray the expenses of the senior scholar at King's College, Cambridge.

montero (mon târ′ ō) [Sp., a huntsman, a mountaineer, from *monte*, MOUNT], *n.* A Spanish huntsman's cap with flaps and a round crown.

Montessori method (mon tes ôr′ i) [Dr. Maria *Montessori* (1870–1952)], *n.* A system of teaching the very young, in which physical activity, individual tuition and early attention to writing are main features.

Montgolfier (mont gol′ fi ėr) [J. M. and J. E. *Montgolfier*, Frenchmen, the inventors (1783)], *n.* A balloon inflated and raised by heated air, called fully **Montgolfier balloon.**

month (mŭnth) [A.-S. *mōnath* (cp. Dut. *maand*, G. *monat*, Icel. *mānuthr*, also L. *mensis*), cogn. with MOON], *n.* One of the twelve parts into which the year is divided, orig. the period of one revolution of the moon round the earth; (*loosely*) four weeks. **calendar month:** One of the twelve months of the year according to the calendar, varying from 28 to 31 days. **lunar month:** A month measured by a revolution of the moon; (*loosely*) four weeks or 28 days. **month of Sundays:** An indefinitely long period. ***month's mind:** Mass said for a deceased person a month after death; a desire, a liking, an inclination. ***monthling,** *n.* That which lasts for a month, esp. a child a month old. **monthly,** *a.* Done in or continuing for a month; happening or payable once a month. *adv.* Once a month. *n.* A periodical published every month; (*pl.*) the menses. **monthly nurse:** A nurse attending women during the month after confinement. **monthly rose:** The Indian or China rose, erroneously supposed to flower monthly.

monticle, -ticule (mon′ ti kėl, -ti kūl) [F. *monticule*, late L. *monticulus*, dim. of *montĕm*, nom. *mons*, MOUNT], *n.* A little hill, a mound, a hillock, esp. a small volcanic cone. ***monticulate, *-lous,** *a.* Having little knobs or projections.

***montoir** (mon′ twar) [F., from *monter*, to MOUNT], *n.* A horse-block; a stone or step used in mounting a horse.

monton (mon′ tȯn) [Sp., from *monte*, MOUNT], *n.* (*Mining*) A heap of ore, a batch under process of amalgamation; a Mexican unit of weight for ore, varying from 1800 to 3200 Spanish pounds.

montre (montr) [F., from *montrer*, L. *monstrāre*, to show], *n.* (*Organ-building*) A flue-stop the pipes of which are visible in the external case.

monture (mon′ tyůr) [F., from *monter*, to MOUNT], *n.* A setting or frame; the way (a gem etc.) is set.

monument (mon′ ū mėnt) [L. *monumentum*, from *monēre*, to remind], *n.* Anything by which the memory of persons or things is preserved, esp. a building or permanent structure; anything that serves as a memorial of a person, event, or of past times; a document, a record; a distinctive mark; (*U.S.A. Surv.*) a natural or artificial landmark; *a tomb; *a statue, an effigy; *a portent. **the Monument:** Column in London commemorating the Great Fire of 1666. **monumental** (-men′ tȧl), *a.* Serving as a monument; stupendous (as of ignorance). **monumental mason,** *n.* A stone mason who engraves and erects tombstones etc. **monumentalize,** *v.t.* **monumentally,** *adv.*

-mony [L. *-monium, -monia*], *suf.* Forming nouns, as *ceremony, matrimony, parsimony.*

monyplies [MANYPLIES].

moo (moo) [imit.], *v.i.* To make a noise like a cow. *n.* The sound 'moo.'

mood (1) (mood) [var. of MODE, assim. to foll.], *n.* (*Gram.*) A verb-form expressing the manner in which the act, event, or fact is conceived, whether as actual, contingent, possible, desirable, etc.; (*Log.*) the nature of the connexion between antecedent and consequent in a proposition, modality; the form of a syllogism with regard to the quantity and quality of the propositions; (*Mus.*) mode.

mood (2) (mood) [A.-S. *mōd* (cp. Dut. *moed*, Icel. *mōthr*, Dan. and Swed. *mod*, G. *mut*)], *n.* Temper of mind, disposition, humour; a morbid state of mind. **in the mood:** Inclined (to or for). **moody,** *a.* Indulging in moods or humours; peevish, sullen, out of temper. ***moody-mad,** *a.* Mad with passion. **moodily,** *adv.* **moodiness,** *n.*

mool [Sc. var. of MOULD (1)].

moon (moon) [A.-S. *mōna* (cp. Dut. *maan*, Icel. *māni*, Goth. *mēna*, G. *mond*), cogn. with Gr. *mēnē*, L. *mensis*, MONTH], *n.* The earth's satellite revolving round it monthly; the satellite of any planet; a lunar month; anything shaped like a moon or crescent. *v.i.* To wander (about) or stare in a listless manner. *v.t.* To pass (time) in this way. **blue moon** [BLUE]. **cycle of the moon** [CYCLE]. **full moon:** The moon with its face fully illuminated. **new moon:** The moon at the beginning of its course with its face invisible or partially illuminated. **moonbeam,** *n.* **moon-blind,** *a.* Suffering from moon-eye; blind from sleeping under the moon's rays. **moon-blindness,** *a.* **moon-calf,** *n.* A blockhead; a born fool; *a creature deformed in the womb; a monstrosity; a false conception. **moon-daisy, -flower,** *n.* The ox-eye daisy. **moon-eye,** *n.* An affection of the eyes in horses; an eye affected with this; applied to two N. American freshwater fish. **moon-eyed,** *a.* Purblind, dim-eyed; round-eyed. **moon-glade,** *n.* The track of moonlight on water. **moonlight,** *n.* and *a.* **moonlight flitting:** A removal of household furniture after dark to escape paying rent. **moonlighter,** *n.* A member of gangs of ruffians who committed violent nocturnal outrages on tenants in Ireland who had transgressed the mandates of the Land League. **moonlit,** *a.* **moonseed,** *n.* A plant of the genus *Menispermum.* **moon-trefoil,** *n.* Medick, *Medicago arborea.* **moon-raker,** *n.* A foolish person (from the Wiltshire legend that some stupid rustics mistook the reflection of the moon in the water for a cheese). **moonrise,** *n.* The rising of the moon; the time of this. **moonshine,** *n.* Moonlight; (*fig.*) unreality, visionary ideas, nonsense; smuggled or illicitly-distilled spirits; *a month. **moonshiner,** *n.* An illicit distiller; a smuggler, esp. of spirits. **moonshiny,** *a.* **moonstruck, -stricken,** *a.* Affected by the moon; deranged, lunatic; fanciful, sentimental. **mooned,** *a.* Shaped like the moon, crescent-shaped; moonlit. ***moonish,** *a.* Fickle, changeable, capricious. **moonless,** *a.* **moony,** *a.* Like the moon; crescent-shaped; like moonlight; moon-struck, listless, dreamy, silly; (*slang*) tipsy. **moonily,** *adv.* **mooniness,** *n.*

moonshee [MUNSHI].

moonstone (moon′ stōn), *n.* (*Min.*) A variety of feldspar with whitish or opalescent reflections.

moonwort (moon′ wĕrt), *n.* (*Bot.*) A fern, *Botrychium lunaria*; honesty, *Lunaria biennis*; applied to other plants.

moor (1) (moor) [prob. from a non-extant A.-S. *mārian* (cp. *mærels*, mooring-rope, and M.Dut. *maren*, to tie)], *v.t.* To secure (a ship, boat, etc.) with chains, ropes, or cable and anchor. *v.i.* To secure a ship in this way, to anchor; to lie at anchor or secured by cables, etc. **moorage,** *n.* **mooring,** *n.* (*usu. in pl.*) The place where a ship is moored; anchors, chains, etc., by which a ship is moored.

moor (2) (moor) [A.-S. *mōr* (cp. Dut. *moer*, G. *moor*)], *n.* A tract of wild open land, esp. if overgrown with heather. **moor-cock, -fowl,** *n.* The male of the red grouse, *Lagopus Scoticus.* **moor-hen,** *n.* The red female of this; the water-hen. **moor game:** Red grouse. **moorland,** *n.* and *a.* **moorman, moorsman,** *n.*

Moor (3) (moor) [F. *More*, L. and Gr. *Maurus*, etym. doubtful], *n.* A member of a mixed Berber and Arab race inhabiting Morocco and the adjoining parts of N.W. Africa. **Moorish,** *a.*

moorstone (moor′ stōn), *n.* A kind of granite, chiefly from Cornwall.

moose (moos) [Algonkin *musu*], *n.* A large animal, *Alces Americana*, allied to the **elk**, inhabiting the colder parts of North America.

moot (moot) [A.-S. *mōtian*, rel. to *gemōt*, an assembly (cp. Dut. *genoet*)], *v.t.* To raise for discussion; *to debate. *v.i.* To argue or plead on a supposed case. *n.* (*Hist.*) An assembly of freemen in a township, tithing, etc.; (*Law*) a students' debate on a supposed case. *a.* Open to discussion or argument. **moot case,** or **point:** A debatable case or point; an open question. **moot court:** A meeting in an inn of court for discussing points of law. ***moot hall:** A hall of meeting; a town-hall; a judgment-hall. ***mootable,** *a.* **mooter,** *n.*

mop (1) (mop) [15th cent. *mappe*, L. *mappa*, see NAPKIN], *n.* A bundle of rags, coarse yarn, etc., fastened to a long handle, and used for cleaning floors etc.; applied to various similar implements; a thick mass (as of hair); *a fair at which servants are hired. *v.t.* (*past & p.p.* **mopped**) To wipe, clean, or dry with or as with a mop. **to mop the floor with:** (*slang*) To worst an opponent completely in a contest, argument, etc. **to mop up:** To wipe up with or as with a mop; (*Mil.*) to clear (a place) of enemy; (*slang*) to seize, to appropriate, to get hold of; to worst, to despatch. **mop-board,** *n.* (*Am.*) A narrow skirting round a room. **mop-fair,** *n.* (*prov.*) An annual fair at which servants are hired. **mop-head,** *n.* A thick head of hair; a person with such a head. **mopstick,** *n.* The handle of a mop; (*Pianoforte*) a rod working the damper in an old-fashioned movement.

***mop** (2) (mop) [prob. imit. of pouting], *v.i.* To make wry faces or grimaces. *n.* A grimace, a wry face. **mops and mows:** Grimaces.

mope (mōp) [etym. doubtful], *v.i.* To be dull or dispirited. *v.t.* To make dull or dispirited (*usu. refl., p.p.*). *n.* One who mopes; (*pl.*) ennui, the blues. **mope-eyed,** *a.* Purblind, short-sighted. **moper,** *n.* **mopish,** *a.* **mopishly,** *adv.* **mopishness,** *n.*

moped (mō′ ped), *n.* A motorized pedal cycle.

mopoke (mō′ pōk), **morepork** (môr′ pôrk) [imit. of cry], *n.* (*Austral. and Tasmania*) A night-jar, *Podargus Cuvieri*; applied to other birds; (*New Zealand*) a small owl.

moppet (mop′ ėt) [perh. dim. of MOP (2)], *n.* A pet, a darling (applied to children, young girls, etc.); a variety of lap-dog; *a rag doll; *an effeminate man. **mops,** *n.* A pug-dog. ***mopsy,** *n.* A pet, a dear; a slatternly woman.

mopus (mō′ pus) [*slang*], *n.* (*pl.* **-uses**) A small coin; (*pl.*) money.

moquette (mō ket′) [F., etym. doubtful], *n.* A woven fabric of wool and hemp or linen with a velvety pile, used for carpets.

mora (1) (mor′ å) [L.], *n.* (*Sc. Law*) Delay, esp. if due to negligence; (*Pros. with pl.* ***moræ***) a unit of time equal to a short syllable.

mora (2) (mor′ å) [It.], *n.* An Italian game in which one has to guess the number of fingers held up by another player, popular also in China and other countries.

mora (3) (môr′ å) [Tupi-Guarani *moiratinga*, white-tree], *n.* A tall S. American tree, *Mora excelsa*, the timber of which is used for shipbuilding.

moraine (mo rān′) [F.], *n.* The debris of rocks brought down by glaciers. **morainic,** *a.*

moral (1) (mor′ ål) [F., from L. *mōrālis*, from *mōr-*, *mōs*, custom], *a.* Pertaining to character and conduct as regards the distinction between right and wrong; conforming to or regulated by right, good, virtuous, esp. in sexual relations; subject to the rules of morality, distinguishing between right and wrong; based on morality; concerned with or treating of conduct or morality; conveying a moral; probable, virtual; *moralizing. *n.* The moral lesson taught by a story, incident, etc.; (*pl.*) moral habits, conduct, behaviour, esp. in sexual relations; (*pl.*) ethics, moral science; (*vulg.*) counterpart, likeness, double (prob. corr. of MODEL). **v.i.* To moralize. **moral certainty:** Probability that leaves little doubt. **moral courage:** Fortitude in matters of life and conduct, esp. in resisting unjust or iniquitous opposition, odium, and abuse, as opp. to physical courage. **moral defeat** [MORAL VICTORY]. **moral faculty,** *n.* The capacity to distinguish between right and wrong. **moral judgment,** *n.* Judgment as to the rightness or wrongness of an act. **moral philosophy** or **science:** Ethics. **Moral Rearmament:** [BUCHMANISM]. **moral victory:** An indecisive result or a partial success the moral effects of which are equivalent to victory. **moralism** (mor′ å lizm), *n.* Morality distinguished from religion or divested of religious teaching; *a moral maxim. **moralist,** *n.* **moralistic** (-lis′ tik), *a.* **morally,** *adv.* According to morality; practically, virtually.

morale (mo ral′), *n.* Mental or moral condition; courage and endurance in supporting fatigue and danger, esp. of troops in war.

morality (mo răl′ i ti), *n.* The doctrine, principles, or practice of moral duties; moral science, ethics; morals, moral conduct, esp. in sexual relations; moralizing; a kind of drama (popular in the 16th cent.) in which the characters represented virtues, vices, etc.

moralize (mo′ rå līz), *v.t.* To interpret or apply in a moral sense; to provide with moral lessons; to render moral. *v.i.* To make moral reflections (on). **moralization** (zā′ shůn), *n.* **moralizer,** *n.*

morass (mo răs′) [Dut. *moeras*, earlier *moerasch*, O.F. *maresche*, MARISH], *n.* A swamp, a bog. **morass ore:** Bog iron-ore. ***morassy,** *a.*

***morat** (môr′ åt) [med. L. *mōrātum*, from *mōrus*, mulberry], *n.* A kind of mead flavoured with mulberries.

moratorium (mor å tôr′ i ům) [L., from *morārī*, to delay, from MORA (1)], *n.* (*Law*) An act authorizing a debtor or bank to defer or suspend payment for a time.

Moravian (mo rā′ vi ån) [*Moravia*, -AN], *a.* Pertaining to Moravia or the Moravians. *n.* A native of Moravia; (*pl.*) a Protestant sect founded in Saxony in the 18th cent. by emigrants from Moravia adhering to the doctrines taught by John Hus (1369–1415).

morbid (môr′ bid) [L. *morbidus*, from *morbus*, disease], *a.* Sickly, unhealthy, diseased; pathological. **morbidity** (-bid′ i ti), *n.* Unhealthiness, prevalence of morbid conditions; morbidness. **morbidly** (môr′ bid li), *adv.* **morbidness,** *n.* **morbiferal, -ferous** (môr bif′ ėr ål, -ůs), *a.* Causing disease. **morbific** (-bif′ ik), *a.* Producing disease. **morbilliform, morbillous** (môr bil′ i fôrm, -ůs), *a.* Like *Morbilli* or measles. **morbose** (môr′ bōs), *a.* **morbosity** (-bos′ i ti), *n.*

morbidezza (môr bi det′ så) [It.], *n.* (*Painting*) The delicate quality in the rendering of flesh-tints that gives the effect of life.

morceau (môr′ sō) [F.], *n.* (*pl.* ***-eaux***) A small piece, a short literary or musical composition.

morcellement (môr′ sel man) [F.], *n.* Division of property, esp. land, into small portions.

mordant (môr′ dånt) [F., pres.p. of *mordre*, L. *mordēre*, to bite], *a.* Biting, caustic, pungent; causing pain or smarting; serving to fix colours etc. *n.* A substance for fixing colouring-matter in dyeing; an adhesive substance used in applying gold-leaf; acid or other corrosive used by etchers. **mordacious** (-dā′ shŭs), *a.* Biting, acrid; sarcastic. **mordaciously,** *adv.* **mordacity** (-dăs′ i ti), **mordancy** (môr′ dȧn si), *n.* **mordantly,** *adv.* ***mordicant,** *a.* Biting, sharp, acrid. *n.* A mordant. ***mordicancy,** *n.* ***mordication** (-kā′ shŭn), *n.*

mordent (môr′ dėnt) [G., from It. *mordente*, as prec.], *n.* (*Mus.*) A rapid alternation of a note with the one immediately below it, a kind of trill; the character indicating this.

more (1) (môr) [A.-S. *māra* (cp. M.Dut. *mêre*, Icel. *meire*, Goth. *maiza*), from an adverbial form *maiz*, whence MO], *a.* (*superl.* **most**) Greater in quantity, extent, degree, number, importance, etc.; additional, extra. *adv.* In or to a greater degree, extent, or quantity (used to form compar. of most adjectives and adverbs of more than one syllable); further, besides, again. *n.* A greater quantity, amount, number, or degree; an additional quantity. **more and more:** With continual increase. **more by token:** As further proof. **more or less:** To a greater or less extent; about; thereabouts. **no more:** Nothing in addition; no longer existing, dead.

***more** (2) (môr) [A.-S. *more, moru* (cp. G. *möhre*, carrot)], *n.* A root, a tree-stock; a plant.

moreen (mȯ rēn′) [etym. doubtful], *n.* A stout woollen or wool and cotton stuff for hangings etc.

morel (1) (mȯ rel′) [F. *morille*, prob. from Teut., cogn. with MORE (2)], *n.* An edible fungus, *Morchella esculenta*, and other species of *Morchella.*

morel (2) (mȯ rel′) [O.F. *morele*, It. *morello*, perh. from L. *mōrum*, mulberry], *n.* The black nightshade, *Solanum nigrum*, and other species of nightshade.

morello (mȯ rel′ ō) [etym. doubtful], *n.* A bitter dark-red cherry.

moreover (môr ō′ vėr) Besides, in addition, further.

morepork [MOPOKE].

moresque (môr esk′) [F., from It. *Moresco*], *a.* Moorish in style and decoration. *n.* Moorish decoration, as the profusely ornamented work in the Alhambra.

Morgana [FATA MORGANA].

morganatic (môr gȧ năt′ ik) [low L. *morganātica*, M.H.G. *morgengâbe*, morning-gift], *a.* Applied to a marriage between a man of high rank and a woman of inferior station, by virtue of which she does not acquire the husband's rank and neither she nor the children of the marriage are entitled to inherit his title or possessions.

morgen (môr′ gen) [G., morning], *n.* A unit of land measurement based on area that can be ploughed by one team in one morning. In S. Africa, Holland and parts of U.S.A. it is slightly over 2 acres.

morgue (môrg) [F., etym. unknown], *n.* A building or room where the bodies of unknown persons found dead are exposed for identification.

***Morian** (môr′ i ȧn) [O.F. *Morien*, from late L. *Mauritānus* or *-tānius*, country of the *Mauri* or Moors], *a.* Moorish. *n.* A Moor.

moribund (mor′ i bŭnd) [L. *moribundus*, from *morī*, to die], *a.* In a dying state. **n.* A dying person.

***morion** (mor′ i ȯn) [F., from Sp. *morrion*, perh. from *morra*, crown of the head], *n.* A helmet having no beaver or visor.

Moriori (mor ē ôr′ ē) [Maori], *n.pl.* The original inhabitants of N. Zealand before the arrival of the Maoris.

***Morisco** (mȯ ris′ kō), ***Morisk** [Sp. *morisco*, from *Moro*, MOOR (3)], *a.* Moorish. *n.* A Moor, esp. one of the Moors remaining in Spain after the conquest of Granada; the language of the Moors; a morris dance; *a morris dancer; Moresque ornament or architecture.

***morkin** (môr′ kin) [M.E. *mortkyn*, A.-F. *mortekine*, O.F. *mortecine*, L. *morticīna*, carrion, from *mors mortis*, death], *n.* An animal that has died from disease or accident. ***morling, *mortling,** *n.* A sheep that has died of disease; wool from such sheep.

morlop (môr′ lop) [etym. doubtful], *n.* (*Min.*) A jasper pebble found in New South Wales.

mormaor (môr mā′ ȯr) [Gael. *mormaer* (*mor*, great, *maor*, steward)], *n.* (*Sc. Hist.*) A high steward, usu. hereditary, of a province, before the introduction of feudalism.

***mormo** (môr′ mō) [Gr.], *n.* A bugbear.

Mormon (môr′ mȯn) [from a mythic personage, author of the *Book of Mormon*, containing the alleged divine revelations on which their creed was based], *n.* A member of an American religious body, founded by Joseph Smith in 1830, now calling themselves the Latter-day Saints, who claim continuous divine revelation through their priesthood, and formerly practised polygamy; a polygamist. **Mormonism,** *n.*

morn (môrn) [A.-S. *morgen* (cp. Dut., Dan., and G. *morgen*, Icel. *morginn*, perh. from root *mergh-*, to blink or twinkle)], *n.* (*poet.*) Morning. **the morn:** (*Sc.*) To-morrow.

***morne** (1) (môrn) [F., from *morner*, to blunt, from foll.], *n.* The blunted head of a tilting lance. **morné** (môr′ nā), *a.* (*Her.*) Applied to a lion rampant without teeth or claws. **morned,** *a.* Blunted (of a spear).

morne (2) (môrn) [F., prob. cogn. with MOURN], *a.* Dreary, doleful.

morning (môr′ ning), [M.E. *morwening*, dawning (*morwen*, MORN, -ING)], *n.* The first part of the day, beginning at twelve o'clock at night and extending to twelve noon, or from dawn to midday; (*fig.*) the early part of a period or epoch; (*socially*) the part of the day before the dinner-hour, hence including the afternoon; (*poet.*) dawn. *a.* Pertaining to or meant to be taken or worn in the morning. **good morning:** A salutation. **morning call:** A social visit usu. paid in the afternoon. **morning coat,** *n.* A tail-coat with cutaway front. **morning dress:** Clothes usu. worn before the dinner-hour, dist. from evening dress. **morning-glory,** *n.* Various climbing or twining plants, species of *Ipomœa* and *Pharbitis.* **morning gown,** *n.* A woman's dress worn in paying morning calls; a dressing-gown. **morning prayer:** (*Ang. Ch.*) Matins. **morning room,** *n.* A sitting-room used in the morning. **morning sickness,** *n.* (*Path.*) Nausea and vomiting frequently accompanying pregnancy. **morning star:** The planet Venus when visible in the east at dawn; *a weapon consisting of a ball with spikes, united by a chain to a staff. **morning watch:** (*Naut.*) The watch from 4 to 8 a.m.

morocco (mȯ rok′ ō) [It. *Marocco*, ult. from native *Marrākesh*], *n.* A fancy leather from goat- or sheep-skin, tanned with sumach and dyed (formerly made in Morocco). **French morocco:** An inferior small-grained kind of Levant morocco. **Levant morocco:** A high grade of morocco with large grain, properly made from the skin of the Angora goat. **Persian morocco:** An inferior kind finished on one side of the skin only.

moron (mor′ on) [Gr. *moros*, stupid], *n.* A feeble-minded person; an adult with the mentality of the average child aged between eight and twelve. **moronic** (mo ron′ ik), *a.*

morone [MAROON (1)].

morose (mȯ rōs′) [L. *mōrōsus*, from *mōs mōris*, manner, self-will], *a.* Peevish, sullen; gloomy, churlish; given to morbid brooding. **morosely,** *adv.* **moroseness,** *n.*

Morpheus (môr′ fūs, -fė ŭs) [L., prob. from Gr. *morphē*, form], *n.* (*Ovid*) The god of dreams. **in the arms of Morpheus:** Asleep.

morphia, -phine (môr′ fi ȧ, -fin) [G. *morphin*, as prec.], *n.* The alkaloid constituting the narcotic principle of opium, used in medicine as a sedative.

morphinism, *n.* Addiction to the abuse of morphine. **morphinist,** *n.* **morphinize,** *v.t.* **morphinomania, morphiomania** (-mā' ni ȧ), *n.* A craving for morphia and its sedative effect. **morphino-, morphomaniac,** *n.*

morphic (môr' fik) [Gr. *morphē*, form, -IC], *a.* Morphological. **morphogenesis** (-jen' ė sis) [GENESIS], **morphogeny** (-foj' ė ni), *n.* The evolution of morphological characters. **morphogenetic** (-jė net' ik), *a.* **morphography** (-fog' rȧ fi), *n.* Descriptive morphology. **morphographer,** *n.*

morphology (môr fol' ȯ ji) [Gr. *morphē*, form, -LOGY], *n.* The branch of biology dealing with the form of organisms; (*Philol.*) the science of the forms of words. **morphologic, -al** (loj' ik, -ȧl), *a.* **morphologically,** *adv.* **morphologist** (-fol' ȯ jist), *n.* **morphosis** (môr fō' sis), *n.* The mode or order of development of an organ or organism. **morphotic** (-fot' ik), *a.*

morris (mor' is) [var. of MORISCO, Moorish], *n.* A grotesque dance; a rustic dance in which the performers formerly represented characters from the Robin Hood legend; any similar dancing performance. *v.i.* (*slang*) To decamp. ***morris-pike,** *n.* A pike supposed to be of Moorish origin.

Morrison shelter (mor' is ȯn shel' tėr) [H. *Morrison*, minister responsible for its introduction in 1941], *n.* An indoor air-raid shelter in the form of a steel table.

Morris tube (mor' is tūb) [Richard *Morris*, inventor (1881)], *n.* A small-bore barrel for fixing on a large-bore rifle or gun for practice at close range at a miniature target.

morrow (mor' ō) [M.E. *morwe*, *morwen*, MORNING], *n.* The day next after the present, the following day; (*fig.*) the succeeding period; *morning, morn. **to-morrow:** The morrow; on the morrow.

morse (1) (môrs) [Lapp. *morsa* or Finn. *mursu*], *n.* The walrus.

morse (2) (môrs) [O.F. *mors*, from L. *morsus*, bite, from *mordēre*, to bite], *n.* The clasp of a cope.

Morse (3) (môrs) [G. F. B. *Morse* (1791–1872), Am. inventor], *n.* (*ellipt.*) The Morse telegraph; (*colloq.*) a message sent by the Morse code. **Morse alphabet** or **code:** A system of expressing messages by the recording telegraph invented by Morse in combinations of dots and dashes. **Morse finger** or **Morse key paralysis:** Forms of a nervous disease, also called telegraphist's cramp, due to the reaction of prolonged muscular strain upon the controlling mechanism in the brain.

morsel (môr' sėl) [O.F., dim. of *mors*, MORSE (2)], *n.* A mouthful, a bite; a small piece of food; a small quantity, a piece. ***morsure,** *n.* Biting.

***morsing** (môr' sing) [Sc., from obs. *mors*, F. *amorcer*, to prime], *n.* The act of priming a gun. **morsing-hole,** *n.* The touch-hole of a gun. **morsing-horn, -powder,** *n.* The powder-horn and powder used for this.

mort (1) (môrt) [F., from L. *mortem*, nom. *mors*, death], *n.* A note sounded on the horn at the death of the deer.

mort (2) (môrt) [etym. unknown], *n.* A salmon in the third year.

mort (3) (môrt) [etym. unknown], *n.* A woman or girl; a harlot.

mortal (môr' tȧl) [O.F., from L. *mortālis*, from *mors mortis*, death], *a.* Subject to death, causing death, deadly, fatal; inveterate, implacable; involving physical or spiritual death (as a sin or crime); pertaining to death; liable to death, hence human; (*slang*) extreme, excessive; long and tedious. *n.* A being subject to death; a human being; (*facet.*) a person. *adv.* (*colloq.*) Exceedingly, extremely. **mortality** (-tăl' i ti), *n.* The quality of being mortal; human nature; (*collect.*) human beings; loss of life, esp. on a large scale; the number of deaths in a given period, the death-rate. ***mortalize,** *v.t.* **mortally,** *adv.*

mortar (môr' tȧr) [A.-S. *mortere*, or F. *mortier*, L. *mortārium*, etym. doubtful], *n.* A vessel in which substances are pounded with a pestle; a short piece of ordnance used for throwing shells at a high angle; a device for firing pyrotechnic shells; a cement, made of lime, sand, and water, for joining bricks, etc., in building. *v.t.* To join, plaster, or close up with mortar. **mortar-board,** *n.* A square board for holding mortar; a square-topped college cap. **mortarless,** *a.* **mortary,** *a.*

mortgage (môr' gāj) [O.F. (*mort*, L. *mortuus*, dead, from *mors mortis*, death, GAGE (1))], *n.* The grant of an estate or other immovable property in fee as security for the payment of money, to be voided on the discharge of the debt or loan. *v.t.* To grant or make over property on mortgage; (*fig.*) to pledge, to plight (oneself, etc., to or for). **mortgagee** (môr gȧ jē'), *n.* The one who accepts a mortgage. **mortgagor** (môr gȧ jôr'), *n.* The one who mortgages his property.

mortice [MORTISE].

mortician (môr tish' ȧn) [L. *mors*, *mortis*, death], *n.* (*Am.*) An undertaker.

mortier (môr tyā) [F., as MORTAR], *n.* A cap of state formerly worn by legal and other functionaries in France.

mortify (môr' ti fī) [F. *mortifier*, L. *mortificāre* (*mors mortis*, death, *-ficāre*, *facere*, to make)], *v.t.* To subdue (the passions etc.) by abstinence or self-discipline; to humiliate, to chagrin, to wound. *v.i.* To lose vitality, to decay, to gangrene. ***mortiferous** (môr tif' ėr ŭs), *a.* Bringing or producing death; fatal, mortal, deadly. **mortification** (-kā' shŭn), *n.* ***mortifiedness,** *n.* **mortifier,** *n.* **mortifyingly,** *adv.*

mortise (môr' tis) [F. *mortaise*, etym. unknown], *n.* A hole cut in timber or other material to receive a tenon. *v.t.* To cut a mortise in; to join by means of mortise and tenon. **mortise-chisel,** *n.* A chisel with a stout blade for cutting mortises.

mortling [MORLING].

mortmain (mŏrt' mān) [A.-F. *morte mayn*, O.F. *mortemain*, med. L. *mortua manus*, dead hand], *n.* Possession or tenure of lands or tenements by an ecclesiastical or other corporation who cannot alienate. **in mortmain:** In unalienable possession.

mortuary (môr' tū ȧr i) [A.-F. *mortuarie*, L. *mortuārius*, from *mortuus*, dead], *a.* Pertaining to death or the burial of the dead. *n.* A building for the temporary reception of the dead; *a fee paid to a parson of a parish on the death of a parishioner; *a burial-ground.

morula (mor' ū lȧ) [mod. L., dim. of *mōrum*, mulberry], *n.* (*Biol.*) The stage of development in which an ovum has become completely segmented; an ovum at this stage; (*Path.*) applied to various kinds of tuberculous affections of the skin.

Morus (môr' ŭs) [L., from Gr. *moron*], *n.* (*Bot.*) A genus of trees, containing the mulberry.

morwong (môr' wong) [Austral. abor.], *n.* An edible fish found off the coasts of Australia and N. Zealand.

mosaic (1) (mō zā' ik) [F. *mosaïque*, med. L. *mōsāicus*, *mūsāicus*, as from a late Gr. *mousaikos*, *mouseios*, pertaining to the Muses], *a.* A term applied to any work in which a pattern or representation is produced by the junction of small pieces of differently-coloured marble, glass, or stone; tesselated, inlaid. *n.* A pattern, picture, etc., produced in this style. *v.t.* To decorate with mosaic; to combine into or as into a mosaic. **mosaically,** *adv.* **mosaicist, mosaist** (1), *n.*

Mosaic (2) (mō zā' ik) [*Moses*, -IC], *a.* Pertaining to Moses or to the law given through him. **Mosaism** (mō' zā izm), **Mosaist** (2), *n.*

mosasaurus (mō sȧ saw' rŭs) [L. *Mosa*, Meuse or Maas, Gr. *sauros*, lizard], *n.* (*Palæont.*) A large fossil marine reptile of the Cretaceous period, first found near Maestricht on the Meuse.

moschate (mos′ kāt) [med. L. *moschus*, musk, -ATE], *a.* Having a musky smell. **moschatous, moschiferous** (-kif′ ėr ůs), *a.*

moschatel (mos kȧ tel′) [F. *moscatelle*, It. *moscatella*, dim. of *moscato*, MUSK], *n.* A small perennial herb, *Adoxa moschatellina*, with yellowish-green flowers and a musky scent.

Moscow (mos′ kō), *n.* (*Austral. colloq.*) A pawnshop. **gone to Moscow:** Pawned.

moselle (mȯ zel′) [F., name of river], *n.* A white wine made in the Moselle district.

Moslem (moz′ lėm) [Arab. *muslim*, pres.p. of *aslama*, to be safe or at rest, whence ISLAM], *n.* A Mohammedan. *a.* Of or pertaining to the Mohammedans. **Moslem Brotherhood,** *n.* A religious movement founded in 1929 for the purpose of influencing social and political action by a return to strict Islamic faith. **Moslemism,** *n.* **Moslemize,** *v.t.*

moslings (moz′ lingz) [prob. corr. from MORSEL], *n.pl.* Thin shreds of leather shaved off by the currier in dressing skins.

mosque (mosk) [F. *mosquée* (later *mosque*), It. *moschea*, Arab. *masgid*, MASJID], *n.* A Mohammedan place of worship.

mosquito (mos kē′ tō) (*pl.* **-oes**) [Sp., dim. of *mosca*, L. *musca*, fly], *n.* An insect of the genus *Culex* or allied genera, with a proboscis for piercing the skin of animals and sucking their blood; (*Aviat.*) a type of fast aeroplane. **mosquito-curtain, -net,** *n.* A netting round a bed, over windows, etc., to ward off mosquitoes.

moss (mos) [A.-S. *mos*, bog (cp. Dut. *mos*, Icel. *mosi*, G. *moos*, also A.-S. *mēos*, moss, G. *mies*, lichen)], *n.* A bog, a peat-bog, wet, spongy land; a low, tufted, herbaceous plant of the cryptogamous class *Musci*, usually growing on damp soil or the surface of stones, trees, etc. *v.t.* To cover with moss. **mossbunker,** *n.* The menhaden. **moss-clad,** *a.* **moss-grown,** *a.* **moss-hag,** *n.* A pit or cutting in a moss from which peat has been taken; a mass of firm heathery ground in a peat-moss. **moss-rose,** *n.* A variety of *Rosa centifolia*, with moss-like calyx. **moss-trooper,** *n.* A common name for the marauders who formerly infested the borders of England and Scotland. **mossy,** *a.* **mossiness,** *n.*

most (mōst) [A.-S. *mǣst* (cp. Dut. *meest*, Icel. *mestr*, G. *meist*), cogn. with MORE (1)], *a.* Greatest in amount, number, extent, quality, degree, etc. *adv.* In the greatest or highest degree (forming the superl. of most adjectives and adverbs of more than one syllable). *n.* The greatest number, quantity, amount, etc.; the best, the worst, etc.; the majority. **at most:** At the utmost extent; not more than. **for the most part:** In the main; usually. **mostly,** *adv.*

-most [A.-S. *-mest*, double superl. suf. (*-ma*, O.Teut. *-mo-*, -EST, O.Teut. *-isto*), conj. with prec.], *suf.* Forming superlatives of adjectives and adverbs denoting position, order, etc., as in *hindmost*, *inmost*, *utmost*.

mot (1) (mō) [F., a word, It. *motto*, L. *muttum*, from *muttīre*, to murmur], *n.* A witty or pithy saying; *a motto.

***mot** (2) (mot) [as prec.], *n.* A note on a bugle.

motatorious (mō tȧ tôr′ i ůs) [L. *mōtātor*, from *mōtāre*, freq. of *movēre*, to MOVE, -OUS], *a.* (*Ent.*) In continual motion, vibratile (of the legs of insects). **motatory** (mō′ tȧ tȯr i), *a.*

mote (1) (mōt) [A.-S. *mot* (cp. Dut. *mot*, sawdust, dirt, L.G. *mut*, dust)], *n.* A particle of dust, a speck, a spot; anything proverbially small. **moted, motty,** *a.* (*Sc.*).

***mote** (2) (mōt) [M.E. and O.F. *mote* (F. *motte*), clod, mound, castle, prob. identical with MOAT], *n.* A mound, an embankment; a tumulus.

***mote** (3) [MAY (1), MUST (3)].

motel (mō tel′), *n.* A roadside hotel or furnished cabins where motorists may put up for the night.

motet (mȯ tet′) [F., dim. of MOT (1)], *n.* (*Mus.*) A vocal composition in harmony, of a sacred character.

moth (moth) [A.-S. *moththe* (cp. Dut. *mot*, Icel. *motti*, G. *motte*)], *n.* One of a group of nocturnal or crepuscular Lepidoptera, distinguished from butterflies by not having knotted antennæ, comprising a small insect breeding in cloths, furs, etc., on which the larvæ feed; (*fig.*) that which gradually eats, consumes, or wears away anything. **moth-ball,** *n.* A ball of naphthalene or similar substance that keeps away clothes-moths. *v.t.* To lay up in moth-balls; to spray with a plastic for laying-up and preserving. **moth-eaten,** *a.* Eaten into holes by moths; ragged. **mothy,** *a.* Full of moths; moth-eaten.

mother (1) (mŭ*th*′ ėr) [A.-S. *mōder*, *mōdor* (cp. Dut. *moeder*, Icel. *mōthur*, G. *mutter*), cogn. with L. *māter*, Gr. *mētēr*], *n.* A female parent; the source or origin of anything; a motherly woman; the head of a religious community; a contrivance for rearing chickens artificially; *hysteria. *v.t.* To act as mother towards; to adopt as a son or daughter; (*lit. or fig.*) to profess oneself to be mother of; to give birth to. *a.* Holding the place of a mother; giving birth or origin; native, natural, inborn, vernacular. **Mother Carey's chicken** [CHICKEN]. **mother-cell,** *n.* (*Biol.*) One that produces other cells by division. **Mother Church:** The Church regarded as having the status and authority of a parent. **Mother-Church,** *n.* One from which others have sprung. **mother complex,** *n.* (*Psych.*) The Œdipus complex. **mother country:** One's native country; a country in relation to its colonies. **mothercraft,** *n.* Application of scientific methods in rearing children. **mother earth:** The earth regarded as parent of all that lives on her surface; (*facet.*) the ground. **Mother Hubbard:** The old woman in a nursery rhyme; a woman's flowing gown or cloak. **Mothering Sunday,** *n.* The mid-Lent Sunday. **mother language** [MOTHER TONGUE]. **mother-in-law,** *n.* (*pl.* **mothers-in-law**) The mother of one's wife or husband. **motherland,** *n.* One's native country. **mother-liquor, -water,** *n.* The portion of a mixed solution which remains after the less soluble salts or other bodies have crystallized out. **mother-of-pearl,** *n.* The iridescent nacreous or pearly substance forming the internal layer of many shells. *a.* Made of this (*usu. in comb.*). **Mother's Day,** *n.* (U.S.A. and Canada) The 2nd Sunday in May, set apart for the remembrance of one's mother. **mother's son:** (*colloq.*) A man. **every mother's son:** All without exception. **mother tongue:** One's native language; a language from which others have sprung. **mother wit:** Natural sagacity, common sense. **motherhood,** *n.* **motherless,** *a.* **motherlike,** *a.* and *adv.* **motherly,** *a.* and *adv.* **motherliness,** *n.*

mother (2) (mŭ*th*′ ėr) [prob. same as prec. (cp. M.Dut. *moeder*, Dut. *maer*, G. *mutter*)], *n.* A thick slimy substance forming in vinegar during fermentation. *v.i.* To become mothery (as vinegar). **mothery,** *a.*

motherwort (mŭ*th*′ ėr wẽrt), *n.* (*Bot.*) A plant, *Leonurus cardiaca*, supposed to be of efficacy for diseases of the womb; the mugwort, *Artemisia vulgaris*.

mothy [MOTH].

motif (mō tēf′) [F., MOTIVE], *n.* The dominant feature or idea in a literary, musical, or other artistic composition; (*Mus.*) a theme; (*Dressmaking*) an ornamental piece of lace etc. sewn on a dress.

motile (mō′ til) [L. *mōt-*, stem, *movēre*, to move, -ILE], *a.* Capable of motion. **motility** (-til′ i ti), *n.*

motion (mō′ shůn) [F., from L. *mōtiōnem*, nom. *-tio*, as prec.], *n.* The act, process, or state of moving; passage of a body from place to place; change of posture; a gesture; an evacuation of the bowels; a combination of moving parts in a machine etc.; a proposal, esp. in a deliberative assembly; (*Law*) an application to a court for a rule or order; (*fig.*) impulse, instigation. *v.t.* To direct by a gesture; *to propose. *v.i.* To make significant gestures; *to make proposals. **angular**

motion: Motion of a body as measured by the increase of the angle made with some standard direction by a line drawn from the body to a fixed point. **in motion:** Moving; not at rest. **to put in motion:** To set going or in operation. **laws of motion:** Three axioms laid down by Sir Isaac Newton: (1) Every body remains in a state of rest or of uniform motion in the same direction, unless it is compelled to change that state; (2) change of motion is proportional to the force applied, and takes place in the direction of the straight line in which the force acts; (3) to every action there is always an equal and contrary reaction. **motion picture,** *n.* A cinematograph film. **motion study,** *n.* The study of repetitive movement in industrial work with a view to the elimination of unnecessary movement. **motional,** *a.* ***motioner, -ist,** *n.* **motionless,** *a.*

motive (mō′ tiv) [O.F. *motif*, med. L. *mōtīvum*, nom. *-vus*, from *mot*, stem of *movēre*, to MOVE], *a.* Causing or initiating motion; tending to cause motion; pertaining to movement; *pertaining to a motive or motives. *n.* That which incites to action, or determines the will; cause, ground, incentive; (*Art*) the predominant idea, feeling, etc., motif. *v.t.* (*usu. in p.p.*) To furnish with an adequate motive (as a story, play, etc.). **motivate,** *v.t.* To motive; to instigate; to provide an incentive. **motivation** (-vā′ shŭn), *n.* **motive power:** The power by which mechanical motion is imparted; (*fig.*) any impelling force; the act of motivating; a method of employing posters, loud-speakers, etc., in factories to induce workers to speed up output. **motiveless,** *a.* **motivelessness,** *n.* **motivity** (mȯ tiv′ i ti), *n.*

motley (mot′ li) [etym. doubtful, perh. rel. to MOTE (1 or 2)], *a.* Variegated in colour; dressed in particoloured clothes; heterogeneous. *n.* The particoloured dress of fools or jesters; a fool, a jester; a heterogeneous mixture. **man of motley:** A jester. **to wear motley:** To play the fool. **motley-minded,** *a.* Having the fickle and inconstant mind of a fool or jester.

motmot (mot′ mot) [imit.], *n.* A South American and Mexican bird allied to the kingfishers, a sawbill.

motograph (mō′ tȯ graf′) [L. *mōt-*, *mōtus*, p.p. of *movēre*, to MOVE, -GRAPH], *n.* A device invented by Edison in which friction is reduced periodically between two conductors, used as a receiver for an electric telegraph or telephone. **motographic** (-grăf′ ik), *a.* **motophone** (mō′ tȯ fōn) [-PHONE], *n.* A sound-engine actuated by aerial waves, invented by Edison.

motor (mō′ tȯr) [L., from *movēre*, to MOVE], *n.* That which imparts motive power, esp. a machine imparting motion to a vehicle or vessel (usu. excluding steam-engines); (*colloq.*) a motor-car; (*Anat.*) a muscle for moving some part of the body; a nerve exciting muscular action. *a.* Causing or imparting motion. *v.i.* To drive or ride in a motor-car. *v.t.* To convey in a motor-car. **motor-boat,** *n.* A boat propelled by a motor carried by itself. **motor-bicycle, -bus, -cab, -car, -coach, -cycle, -truck,** etc.: Various kinds of vehicle propelled by their own motor. **motor bandit,** *n.* A highwayman using a motor-car for raids etc. **motorcade** (mō′ tor kăd), *n.* A procession of motor-cars. **motordrome,** *n.* An enclosure or track where motor-vehicles compete or are tested. **motor launch,** *n.* A motor-driven small boat, for plying between vessels and the shore. **motor-man,** *n.* A man in charge of a motor, esp. of an electric tram or train. **motor nerve:** An efferent nerve that excites muscular activity. **motorway,** *n.* A road for fast motor traffic, usu. with no speed limit. **motorial** (-tôr′ i ăl), **motory** (mō′ tȯr i), *a.* **motorist,** *n.* **motorize,** *v.t.* (*Mil.*) To equip with petrol-driven vehicles.

mottle (mot′ ėl) [prob. from MOTLEY], *v.t.* To blotch, to variegate with spots of different colours or shades of colour. *n.* A blotch or patch of colour; a spotted, blotched, or variegated appearance on a surface.

motto (mot′ ō) [It., as MOT (1)], *n.* (*pl.* **-oes**) A short pithy sentence or phrase expressing a sentiment or maxim; a principle or maxim adopted as a rule of conduct; (*Her.*) a word or sentence used with a crest or coat of arms. ***mottoed,** *a.*

motty [MOTE (1)].

mouch (mooch) [prob. from O.North.F. *muchier*, as MICHE], *v.i.* To play truant; to skulk, to sneak about; to loaf, to slouch (along or about). *n.* The act of mouching. **moucher,** *n.*

mouchoir (moo′ shwar) [F., from *moucher*, to wipe the nose], *n.* A handkerchief.

mouflon, moufflon (moo′ flon) [F., from late L. *mufron*], *n.* A wild sheep, *Ovis musimon*, of Sardinia and Corsica.

moujik [MUZHIK].

moulage (moo′ laj) [Fr., cast from a mould], *n.* (*U.S.A.*) Section of police force that specializes in taking plaster casts of footprints etc.

mould (1) (mōld) [A.-S. *molde* (cp. Dut. *moude*, Icel. *mold*, Dan. *muld*), cogn. with L. *molere*, to grind, Eng. MEAL (1)], *n.* Fine soft earth, easily pulverized, suitable for tillage; the earth, the ground; (*fig.*) the grave. **mould-board,** *n.* The curved plate in a plough which turns the furrow-slice over. **mould-warp,** *n.* The mole.

mould (2) (mōld) [O.North.F. *molde*, O.F. *modle*, L. MODULUS], *n.* A hollow shape into which molten metal or other substance is poured in a fluid state to cool into a permanent shape; a templet used by plasterers for shaping cornices, etc.; various analogous appliances used in trades and manufactures; a tin, wooden, or earthenware vessel for shaping puddings, etc.; (*Arch.*) a moulding or group of mouldings; (*fig.*) physical form, shape, build; character, nature. *v.t.* To form into a particular shape; to fashion, to make, to produce; to shape (bread) into loaves. **mould candle:** Candle made in a mould. **mould-loft,** *n.* A large room in a dockyard, in which the several parts of a ship are laid off on full-size drawings. **mouldable,** *a.* That may be moulded. **moulder** (1), *n.*

mould (3) (mōld) [prob. from *mould*, *mouled*, p.p. of M.E. *moulen*, to become mouldy (cp. Swed. *mögla*, Dan. *muggeh*, also Eng. MUGGY)], *n.* A minute fungoid growth forming a woolly or furry coating on matter left in the damp. **mouldy,** *a.* **mouldiness,** *n.*

moulder (1) [MOULD (2)].

moulder (2) (mōl′ dėr) [prob. from MOULD (1)], *v.i.* To turn to dust by natural decay; to crumble; (*fig.*) to waste away gradually.

moulding (mōl′ ding), *n.* The act or process of shaping anything in or as in a mould; anything formed in or as in a mould; an ornamental part of a cornice, capital, arch, woodwork, etc., usu. in the form of continuous grooves and projections, showing in profile a complex series of curves.

mouldy [MOULD (3)].

moulin (moo′ lăn) [F., a mill], *n.* A vertical pit in a glacier engulfing water from the surface.

moulinet (moo li net′), *n.* A machine for turning the drum of a hoisting-machine; a kind of turnstile; *a machine for bending a crossbow.

moult (mōlt) [M.E. *mouten*, A.-S. *bemūtian*, L. *mūtāre*, to change], *v.i.* To cast the feathers, hair, skin, horns, etc. (of certain birds and animals). *v.t.* To shed or cast. *n.* The act of moulting.

mound (1) (mound) [etym. doubtful, acc. to Skeat from A.-F. *mund*, var. of *munt*, O.F. *mont*, MOUNT], *n.* An artificial elevation of earth, stones, etc.; a hillock, a knoll; a barrow, a tumulus. *v.t.* To heap up in a mound or mounds; to furnish, enclose, or protect with a mound. **mound-bird,** *n.* A bird of Australia and the Pacific islands laying large eggs in mounds to hatch by themselves.

mound (2) (mound) [F. *monde*, L. *mundus*, the world], *n.* A ball or globe representing the earth, usu. of gold and surmounted by a cross, used as part of regalia.

mount (mount) [A.-S. *munt*, L. *mons montis*], *n.* A high hill; a mountain (in poetry, or as first part of a proper name); (*Palmistry*) one of the fleshy protuberances on the palm of the hand; (*Her.*) a figure of a green hill occupying the base of a shield; that upon which anything is mounted; the margin round a picture; a cardboard etc. upon which a drawing is placed; the parts by which various objects are prepared for use, strengthened, or ornamented; a horse with the appurtenances necessary for riding; a horse-block or other means of mounting on horseback. *v.i.* To rise, to ascend; to soar; to get on horseback; to rise in amount. *v.t.* To ascend, to climb; to ascend upon, to get on; to form a path up; to copulate with; to raise; to prepare for use; to put into working order; to put (a picture) on a mount; to stage (a play); to put (a person) on a horse; to furnish with a horse or horses. **mount!** Get on horseback. **to mount guard:** To go on duty as sentry. **mountable,** *a.* **mounter,** *n.* **mounting,** *n.*

mountain (moun' tȧn) [O.F. *montaigne* (F. *montagne*), pop. L. *montānea*, L. *montāna*, pertaining to a mountain, from *mons montis*, mountain], *n.* A natural elevation of the earth's surface rising high above the surrounding land; a large heap or pile; something of very great bulk. **the Mountain:** The extreme democratic party in the first French Revolution, from their occupying the highest seats in the National Convention. **mountain ash:** The rowan, *Pyrus aucuparia*; (*Austral.*) various kinds of Eucalyptus. **mountain cork, leather, paper, wood:** Varieties of asbestos, sufficiently light to float in water. **mountain-chain,** *n.* A range or series of mountains. **mountain dew:** Scotch whisky, in former times often secretly distilled in the mountains. **mountain flour:** Bergmehl. **mountain-high,** *a.* and *adv.* (*fig.*) As high as mountains (of waves). **mountain limestone:** Carboniferous limestone. **mountains high** (MOUNTAIN-HIGH]. **mountain sickness:** A feeling of indisposition, varying in different people, brought on by ascending into rarefied mountain air. **mountain soap:** A soft, earthy, brownish-black mineral, used in crayon painting. **mountaineer** (-nēr'), *n.* One who dwells among mountains; one who climbs mountains for amusement or scientific purposes. **mountaineering,** *n.* ***mountainet** (-net'), *n.* **mountainous,** *a.* Full of mountains; exceedingly large; *inhabiting mountains. **mountainously,** *adv.* **mountainousness,** *n.* **mountainy,** *a.* (*Ang.-Ir.*)

***mountant** (1) (moun' tȧnt) [F.], *a.* Mounting; lifted up.

mountant (2) (moun' tȧnt), *n.* An adhesive substance for mounting photographs etc.

mountebank (moun' tė bănk) [It. *montambanco* (*monta in banco*, to mount on a bench)], *n.* A quack doctor, orig. one who proclaimed his nostrums from a platform; a boastful pretender, a charlatan. *v.t.* To cheat by false boasts or pretences. **mountebankery, -ism,** *n.*

moup (moop) [Sc., etym. unknown], *v.t.* To nibble; to mumble. *v.i.* To associate (with).

mourn (môrn, moorn) [A.-S. *murnan* (cp. Icel. *morna*, O.H.G. *mornēn*), cogn. with Gr. *merimna*, sorrow], *v.i.* To express or feel sorrow or grief; to wear mourning. *v.t.* To grieve or sorrow for; to deplore; to utter mournfully. **mourner,** *n.* **mournful,** *a.* **mournfully,** *adv.* **mournfulness,** *n.* **mourning,** *a.* Grieving, sorrowing; expressive of grief or sorrow. *n.* Grief, sorrow, lamentation; the customary dress, usu. black, worn by mourners. **in mourning:** Wearing mourning garments. **mourning-brooch,** *n.* A jet brooch. **mourning-coach,** *n.* A black coach, drawn by black horses, used at funerals. **mourning-dove,** *n.* The Carolina turtle dove, *Columba Carolinensis*, so called from its plaintive note. **mourning-paper,** *n.* Note-paper edged with black, used during a period of mourning. **mourning-ring,** *n.* A black ring worn as memorial of a deceased person. **mourningly,** *adv.*

mouse (mous) [A.-S. *mūs* (cp. Dut. *muis*, Icel. *mūs*, pl. *mȳss*, G. *maus*, L. and Gr. *mūs*)], *n.* (*pl.* **mice,** mīs) A small rodent quadruped of various species belonging to the genus *Mus*, esp. *M. musculus*, the common house mouse; applied to similar animals, as the shrews, voles, etc.; (*slang*), a black eye. *v.i.* (mouz) To hunt for or catch mice; to hunt, to watch craftily, to prowl (about). *v.t.* To hunt for persistently; to rend or pull about as a cat does a mouse. **mouse-colour,** *n.* Darkish grey with a tinge of brown. **mouse-ear,** *n.* A popular name for several plants, from the shape and velvety surface of their leaves (usu. attrib. as *mouse-ear chickweed, mouse-ear hawkweed*). ***mousefall,** *n.* A mouse-trap. **mouse-trap,** *n.* **mouser** (mou' zėr), *n.* A cat good at catching mice. **mousy,** *a.* **mousiness,** *n.*

mousetail (mous' tāl), *n.* (*Bot.*) A plant of the ranunculaceous genus, *Myosurus*.

mousquetaire [MUSKETEER].

mousse (moos) [Fr., froth], *n.* A dish of flavoured cream whipped and frozen.

mousseline (moos lēn') [F., as MUSLIN], *n.* Fine French muslin. ***mousseline-de-laine*** (-lān), *n.* An untwilled woollen dress-fabric resembling muslin. ***mousseline-de-soie*** (-dė swa), *n.* A thin silk fabric resembling muslin in texture, usu. figured.

moustache (mŭs tash') [F., from It. *mostaccio*, Gr. *mustax -takos*], *n.* The hair on the upper lip of men; applied to growths of hair on various animals, esp. round the mouth. **moustache-cup,** *n.* A drinking-cup with a guard to keep liquid from wetting the moustache.

mouth (mouth) [A.-S. *mūth* (cp. Dut. *mond*, G. *mund*, Icel. *munnr*), cogn. with L. *mentum*, chin], *n.* The opening at which food is taken into the body with the cavity behind containing the organs of mastication, insalivation, and speech; (*fig.*) any thing analogous to a mouth; the opening of a vessel, pit, cave, or the like; the outfall of a river; *a cry, a voice. *v.t.* (*mouth*) To utter pompously or in an elaborate or constrained manner, to declaim; to take up or seize with the mouth; to chew or roll with the mouth; to train (a horse) to the use of the bit; *to insult. *v.i.* To talk pompously or affectedly; to make grimaces; *to bill and coo. **down in the mouth** [DOWN (3)]. **to give mouth:** To bark or bay (of a dog). **to laugh on the wrong side of the mouth** [LAUGH]. **to make mouths** or **to make a wry mouth:** To make grimaces. **to stop the mouth of:** To put to silence. **mouth-filling,** *a.* Filling the mouth; (*fig.*) inflated; sonorous. **mouth-organ,** *n.* A small musical instrument, played by blowing on metallic reeds. **mouthpiece,** *n.* A tube by which a cigar or cigarette is held in the mouth; that part of a musical instrument put between the lips; (*fig.*) a spokesman for others. **mouthable** (mou' *th*ȧbl), *a.* **mouthed,** *a.* (*usu. in comb.*, as *big-mouthed*). ***mouther,** *n.* **mouthful** (mouth' ful), *n.* **mouthless,** *a.* **mouthy** (mou' *th*i), *a.* Talkative; ranting, bombastic.

move (moov) [O.F. *movoir* (F. *mouvoir*), L. *movēre*], *v.t.* To cause to change position or posture; to carry, lift, draw, or push from one place to another; to put in motion, to stir; to cause (the bowels) to act; to incite, to incline, to prompt, to rouse (to action); to excite, to provoke (laughter, etc.); to prevail upon; to affect with feelings usu. of tenderness, to touch; to propose, to submit for discussion; *to apply to. *v.i.* To change place or posture; to go from one place to another; to advance, to progress; to change one's place of residence; to change the position of a piece at chess, etc.; to make an application, appeal, etc.; to begin to act; to take action, to proceed; to be moved, to have an evacuation (of the bowels); to live, to exercise one's activities (in or among); (*colloq.*) to bow. *n.* The act of moving; the right to move (in chess, etc.); proceeding, action, line of conduct; a step, a device to obtain an object; a change of abode. **move on:** A policeman's order to a person not to stand in one place. **on the move:** Stirring; moving from place to place, travelling about. **to make a move:** To go, to leave the table, etc.; to start; to begin to go; to move a piece at chess etc. **to move heaven and earth:** To make every effort, to leave no stone unturned (to secure an object). **mover,** *n.* One who or that which moves; a cause or source of motive power; a proposer (of a resolution etc.); one who originates or instigates.

movable (moov' ȧbl), *a.* Capable of being moved; occurring at varying times (as a festival); *changeable, inconstant. *n.* Anything that can be moved or removed, esp. a movable or portable piece of furniture etc. that is not a fixture; (*pl.*) goods, furniture, chattels, etc., as distinct from houses and lands, personal as opp. to real property; (*Sc. Law*) not heritable as distinguished from heritable property. **movability** (-bil' i ti), **movableness,** *n.* **movable feast:** A festival the date of which varies; (*facet.*) a meal taken at irregular times. ***movably,** *adv.*

movement (moov' mėnt), *n.* The act or process of changing position, place, or posture; a military evolution; change in temper, disposition, feeling, etc.; manner or style of moving; action, incident, or process of development in a story etc.; the working mechanism of a watch, clock, machine, etc., or a connected group of parts of this; a connected series of impulses, efforts, and actions, directed to a special end; activity in a market, esp. change of value; (*Mus.*) the mode or rate of a piece of music, also a section of a large work having the same general measure or time. **Brownian movement** [John *Brown*, Sc. botanist, discoverer (1757–1831), -IAN]: The rapid movement or oscillation of small particles suspended in liquid.

movies (moo' viz), *n.pl.* (*colloq.*) A cinematograph entertainment, the pictures.

Movietone (moov' i tōn), *n.* (*Cinema.*) The registered name of a system of producing sound films.

moving (mov' ing), *a.* Causing motion; in motion; impelling, persuading; pathetic, affecting. **moving-coil microphone,** *n.* (*Radio.*) A type of microphone in which currents at audio-frequencies are generated by the moving of a coil of wire hanging in a magnetic field. **moving staircase,** *n.* An escalator. **movingly,** *adv.*

mow (1) (mou) [A.-S. *mūga* (cp. Icel. *mūge*, a swathe, Swed. and Norw. *muga*)], *n.* A heap or pile of hay, corn, or other field produce; a stack. **v.t.* To put in a mow or mows.

***mow** (2) (mō, mou) [O.F. *moué*, *moe*, mouth, pout, perh. from M.Dut. *mouwe*, etym. doubtful], *n.* A wry face, a grimace. *v.i.* To make grimaces. **mops and mows** [MOP (2)].

mow (3) (mō) [A.-S. *māwan* (cp. Dut. *maaien*, G. *mahen*, also Gr. *amân* and L. *mētere*, to reap)], *v.t.* To cut down (grass, corn, etc.) with a scythe, mowing-machine, etc.; to cut the grass off (a lawn etc.); (*fig.*) to destroy indiscriminately; to cut (down) in great numbers. *v.i.* To cut grass by mowing. **mower,** *n.* **mowing,** *n.* The act of cutting with a scythe or mowing-machine; land from which grass is cut. *a.* Intended to be mown (of land, crops, etc.).

moxa (mok' sȧ) [Jap. *mokusa* (*moe kusa*, burning herb)], *n.* A downy material obtained from the dried leaves of *Artemisia*, esp. *A. moxa* and *A. Chinensis*, burnt on the skin as a cautery or counter-irritant for gout etc. **moxibustion** (-bŭs' tyȯn), *n.* Cauterization by means of moxa.

moya (moi' ȧ) [prob. S.Am.Sp.], *n.* Mud ejected from volcanoes.

Mozarab (mŏ zăr' ȧb) [Sp. *Mozárabe*, Arab. *musta 'rib*, desiderative from *arab*, ARAB], *n.* One of those Christians in Spain after the Moorish conquest who were allowed the exercise of their religion in return for allegiance to the Moors. **Mozarabic,** *n.*

mozetta (mȯ zet' ȧ, mot set' ȧ) [It. *mozzetta*, dim. of *mozza*, see AMICE], *n.* (*R.-C. Ch.*) A short cape with a small hood worn by cardinals, bishops, abbots, etc.

mpret (mpret) [Alban. corrupt. of L. *imperator*], *n.* An Albanian ruler.

Mr. [MISTER (1)].

Mrs. [MISTRESS].

mucedinous (mū sē' di nŭs) [L. *mūcēdo -dinis*, from *mūcēre*, to be mouldy, from MUCUS], *a.* Mouldy, mildewy; of or like mould or mildew.

much (mŭch) [M.E. *moche*, *miche*, *michel*, A.-S. *micel*, MICKLE], *a.* Great in quantity or amount; long in duration; *numerous, many. *adv.* In or to a great degree or extent; almost, nearly, about. *n.* A great quantity, a great deal; something uncommon. **as much:** An equal quantity. **not much:** (*slang*) Certainly not, not likely. **to make much of** [MAKE (2)]. **too much:** More than enough. **muchness,** *n.* **much of a muchness:** Practically the same, very nearly alike.

mucic (mū' sik) [F. *mucique*, from L. MUCUS], *a.* (*Chem.*) Applied to an acid formed by the oxidation of milk, sugar, and various gums.

mucid (mū' sid) [L. *mūcidus*, from *mūcēre*, to be mouldy, as prec.], *a.* Mouldy, musty. ***mucidness,** *n.* **mucidous, muciferous** (-sif' ėr ŭs), **mucific,** *a.*

mucilage (mū' si lȧj) [F., from L. *mūcilāgo -ginis*, as prec.], *n.* A gummy or viscous substance from the seeds, bark, or roots of various plants; gum prepared for use; a viscous lubricating secretion in animal bodies. **mucilaginous** (-lăj' i nŭs), *a.*

muciparous, etc. [MUCUS].

mucivorus (mū siv' ȯ rŭs), *a.* (*Ent.*) Feeding on the juices of plants (of some insects).

muck (mŭk) [prob. from Scand. (cp. Icel. *myki*, dung, Norw. *myk*, Dan. *mög*], *n.* Dung or manure; refuse, filth; (*fig.*) anything filthy, disgusting or nasty; (*colloq.*) untidiness; (*contemp.*) money. *v.t.* To make dirty; (*slang*) to bungle, to make a mess of. **muck-heap, -hill,** *n.* **muck-rake,** *n.* (*fig.*) A person who has dirty dealings, esp. in politics. **muckworm,** *n.* A worm found in dung-heaps; (*fig.*) a miser. **mucker,** *n.* (*slang*) A bad fall, esp. in the mud. **to come a mucker:** To have a bad fall; to come to grief. **to go a mucker:** To plunge; to be extravagant. **mucky,** *a.* **muckiness,** *n.*

muckle (*Sc.*) [MICKLE].

muco-, mucoso-, *comb. form* [MUCUS].

mucosaccharine [SACCHARINE].

mucor (mu' kor), *n.* (*Bot.*) A genus of fungi comprising the moulds, growing on substances in a state of decay; animal mucus.

mucous (mu' kus), *a.* Pertaining to, like, or covered with mucus; secreting mucus; slimy, viscid. **mucous membrane:** The membranous lining of the cavities and canals of the body.

mucro (mū' krō) [L.], *n.* (*pl.* **mucrones, -krō' nēz**) (*Zool.* and *Bot.*) A sharp point, process, or organ. **mucronate, -cronated,** *a.* Terminating abruptly in a point. **mucronately,** *adv.*

mucus (mū' kŭs) [L. *mūcus*, *muccus*, cogn. with Gr. *mussessthai*, L. *ēmungere*, to blow the nose], *n.* The viscid secretion of the mucous membrane; applied to other slimy secretions in animals and fishes; (*Bot.*) gummy matter found in all plants, soluble in water but not in alcohol. **muciparous** (-sip' ȧ rŭs), *a.* Secreting mucus. **mucoid,** *a.* **mucosity,** *n.* **muculent,** *a.*

mud (mŭd) [cp. L.G. *mudde*, *mōde*, Dut. *modder*, G. dial. *mott*], *n.* Moist, soft earth, or earthy matter; mire; (*fig.*) anything that is worthless or defiling. **v.t.* To bury in or bedaub with mud; to make turbid or foul. **to throw mud:** To make disgraceful imputations. **mud-bath,** *n.* A bath of mineral water and mud in which patients are immersed for medicinal purposes. **mudcart,** *n.* **mudfish,** *n.* A New Zealand fish that burrows in the mud at a distance from water. **mudguard,** *n.* A board or strip of metal fastened over a wheel of a carriage or cycle to protect persons riding from mud. **mud-hole,** *n.* A place full of mud; an opening in a boiler for discharging sediment. **mudlark,** *n.* One who cleans out sewers, or fishes up pieces of coal, metal, etc., from the mud of tidal rivers; a street arab; (*Austral.*) the pee-wee. **mud pie:** A heap of mud shaped by a child to resemble a pie. **mud-scow,** *n.* (*Am.*) A heavy boat for carrying mud, esp. that from dredging. **mud slinger:** (*fig.*) One who throws mud, a slanderer. **mud-valve** [MUD-HOLE]. **muddy,** *a.* Covered or foul with mud; of the colour of mud; resembling mud; turbid, cloudy; (*fig.*) confused, muddled, obscure. *v.t.* To make muddy or foul; *to muddle, to confuse. ***muddy-brained, *-headed,** *a.* ***muddy-mettled,** *a.* Dull-spirited. **muddily,** *adv.* **muddiness,** *n.*

muddle (mŭ′ dėl) [freq., from prec.], *v.t.* To confuse, to bewilder, to stupefy; to make half drunk; to mix (up), to jumble (together) confusedly; to make a mess of, to bungle, to waste, to squander; *to make muddy or turbid. *v.i.* To act or proceed in a confused or bungling way; *to become muddy; to become confused. *n.* A mess; a state of confusion or bewilderment. **to muddle on** or **along:** To get along somehow. **to muddle through:** To attain a desired result without knowing how. **muddle-headed,** *a.* **muddle-headedly,** *adv.* **muddle-headedness,** *n.* **muddler,** *n.*

mudir (mood dẽr′) [Turk. and Arab., from *adāra,* to administer], *n.* (*Turkey*) A governor of a village or canton; (*Egypt*) a governor of a province. ***mudirate, mudirieh*** (moo dẽr′ ȧt, -i ā), *n.*

muezzin (moo ez′ in) [Arab. *mu 'azzin, mu 'aththin,* from *azana, athana,* to call, to proclaim], *n.* A Mohammedan crier of the hour of prayer.

muff (1) (mŭf) [prob. from Dut. *mof,* F. *moufle,* to MUFFLE], *n.* A covering, usu. cylindrical, of fur or other material, carried by women, in which the hands are placed to keep them warm. **muffatee** (-tē′), *n.* A small muff or woollen cuff worn on the wrist; *a muffler for the neck.

muff (2) (mŭf) [etym. doubtful], *n.* An awkward or stupid fellow; a bungling action, esp. failure to catch the ball at cricket. *v.t.* To miss (a catch) or to fail to catch (the ball) at cricket; to bungle or fail in. *v.i.* To fail, to bungle badly.

muffin (mŭf′ in) [perh. rel. to O.F. *moufflet,* soft bread], *n.* A plain, light, spongy, round cake, usu. toasted and eaten hot with butter. **muffin-bell,** *n.* A bell rung by a street muffin-man. **muffin-man,** *n.* One who sells muffins. **muffineer** (-nēr′), *n.* A castor for sprinkling salt or sugar on muffins etc.

muffle (1) (mŭf′ ėl) [perh. from O.F. *mofle, moufle,* med. L. *muffula,* a winter glove, a mitten, etym. unknown], *v.t.* To wrap or cover (up) closely and warmly; to wrap up the head of so as to silence; to wrap up (oars, bells, etc.) so as to deaden the sound; to dull, to deaden. *n.* A muffler, a boxing-glove; a large mitten; anything employed to deaden sound; an oven or receptacle placed in a furnace used in operations in which the pottery etc. is not in direct contact with the products of combustion. **muffler,** *n.* A wrapper or scarf for the throat; a boxing-glove; a mitten, a thick stuffed glove, a pad or other contrivance for deadening sound, as in a piano; (*Am.*) the silencer on a motor vehicle; a bandage for blindfolding.

muffle (2) (mŭf′ el) [F. *mufle,* etym. doubtful], *n.* The thick, naked upper lip and nose of ruminants and rodents.

mufti (mŭf′ ti) [Arab. *muftī*], *n.* An official interpreter or expounder of the Koran and Mohammedan law; civilian dress worn by service men off duty, ordinary dress as distinguished from that worn on state or ceremonial occasions.

mug (1) (mŭg) [cp. L.G. *mokke, mukke,* Norw. *mugga, mugge,* Swed. *mugg*], *n.* A drinking-cup, usu. cylindrical without a lip; the contents of this; a cooling drink; (*slang*) the face or mouth. *v.i.* To make faces, to grimace.

mug (2) (mŭg) [slang], *n.* A simple-minded or silly person.

mug (3) (mŭg) [slang], *v.i.* To study hard, to grind. *v.t.* To work or get up (a subject). *n.* One who works hard for examinations, esp. one who neglects outdoor sports.

mugger (mŭg′ ėr) [Hind. *magar*], *n.* An East Indian crocodile, *Crocodilus palustris,* with a broad snout.

muggins (mŭg′ inz) [etym. doubtful, perh. from the surname *Muggins*], *n.* A children's card-game; a game of dominoes; (*slang*) a fool, a simpleton.

Muggletonian (mŭgl tō′ ni ȧn), *n.* One of a sect founded in 1657 who believed the statements of Lodowicke Muggleton (1609–98) and his coadjutor Reeve that they were the two witnesses mentioned in Rev. xi. 3–6.

muggy (mŭg′ i) [cp. Icel. *mugga,* Norw. *mugg,* drizzle], *a.* Damp and close, sultry; moist, damp, mouldy (of hay etc.). **mugginess,** *n.*

mugwort (mŭg′ wẽrt) [*mucg-wyrt* (cp. L.G. *mugge,* Dut. *mug,* MIDGE, WORT)], *n.* A herb of the genus *Artemisia,* esp. *A. vulgaris,* the motherwort.

mugwump (mŭg′ wŭmp) [Algonkin *mugquomp,* a chief], *n.* (*U.S.A.*) An independent member of the Republican party; one who abstains from voting or otherwise declines to be led by party politics; a consequential person; *a person of importance, a leader. *v.i.* To act like a mugwump; to assert one's independence.

mulatto (mū lăt′ ō) [Sp. *mulato,* from *mulo,* MULE], *n.* The offspring of a white and a Negro. *a.* Of this colour, tawny, esp. when intermediate in colour between the parents.

mulberry (mŭl′ bėr i) [prob. from O.H.G. *mūlberi, mūrberi* (*mūr,* L. MORUS, *beri,* BERRY), cp. G. *maulbeere,* and A.-S. *mōrbēam*], *n.* Any tree of the genus *Morus,* bearing a collective fruit like a large blackberry; its fruit; the colour of this; (*Mil.*) the code name for the pre-fabricated port towed across to France for the invasion of 1944.

mulch (mŭlch) [prob. from the obs. a. *mulch,* soft (cp. A.-S *melse* and G. dial. *molsch*)], *n.* A surface layer of dead vegetable matter, manure, etc., to keep the ground or the roots of plants moist. *v.t.* To cover with mulch.

mulct (mŭlkt) [L. *mulcta,* a fine, whence *mulctāre,* to fine], *n.* A fine, esp. for an offence or misdemeanour. *v.t.* To punish with a fine or forfeiture; to deprive (a person of). ***mulctuary,** *a.*

mule (mūl) [A.-S. *mūl,* or O.F. *mul, mule,* L. *mūlus*], *n.* The offspring of a male ass and a mare; also a hinny; (*fig.*) a stupidly stubborn or obstinate person; a hybrid between different animals or plants; an instrument for cotton-spinning. **mule-bird, -canary,** *n.* A cross between a canary and a goldfinch. **mule-deer,** *n.* The N. American black-tail, *Cariacus macrotis.* **mule-spinner,** *n.* **mule-twist,** *n.* Yarn spun on a mule. **mulewort,** *n.* A fern of the genus *Hemionitis.* **muleteer** (mū lė tēr′), *n.* A mule-driver. **mulish,** *a.* Like a mule; obstinate, sullen. **mulishly,** *adv.* **mulishness,** *n.*

muley (mū′ li) [var. of Sc. and Ang.-Ir. *moiley,* from *moil,* Ir. *maol* (cp. W. *moll,* bald)], *n.* (*Am.*) A hornless cow; any cow. *a.* Hornless.

mulga (mŭl′ ga) [Austral. abor.], *n.* An Australian acacia, used as fodder. **mulga grass:** A fodder grass.

***muliebrity** (mū li ē′ bri ti) [L. *muliebritas,* from *muliebris,* pertaining to women, from *mulier,* woman], *n.* Womanhood; effeminacy. ***mulierosity** (-os′ i ti), *n.* Excessive fondness for women.

mulish, etc. [MULE].

mull (1) (mŭl) [etym. doubtful], *v.t.* To warm (wine, beer, etc.), sweeten, and flavour with spices. **muller** (1), *n.*

mull (2) (mŭl) [etym. doubtful], *v.t.* To miss, to fail in (a catch etc. in a game). *n.* A failure, a miss; a mess, a muddle.

mull (3) (mŭl) [earlier *mulmull*, Hindi *malmal*], *n.* A thin soft muslin.

mull (4) (mŭl) [Sc. var. of MILL (1)], *n.* A snuff-box made of horn; a snuff-box.

Mullah (mŭl′ ȧ) [Arab. *maulā*, a judge (in Pers., Turk., and Hind. *mullā*)], *n.* An honorary title in Mohammedan countries for persons learned in theology and sacred law, and for ecclesiastical and civil dignitaries.

mullein (mŭl′ in) [A.-F. *moleyne* (F. *molène*), perh. from *mol*, L. *mollis*, soft], *n.* An herbaceous plant with woolly leaves and tall spikes of yellow flowers, sometimes called Aaron's rod; other plants of the genus *Verbascum*.

muller (1) [MULL (1)].

muller (2) (mŭl′ ėr) [perh. from *moloir*, grinding, from O.F. *moldre* (F. *moudre*), L. *molere*, to grind], *n.* A stone with a flat surface, used to grind and mix pigment etc. on a slab.

mullet (1) (mŭl′ ėt) [M.E. and O.F. *mulet*, dim. of L. *mullus* (cp. Gr. *mullos*)], *n.* A fish living near coasts and ascending rivers, belonging either to the genus *Mullus* and family *Mullidæ* or the genus *Mugil* and the family *Mugilidæ*, the former distinguished as red and the latter as grey mullet.

mullet (2) (mŭl′ ėt) [O.F. *molette*, rowel, etym. doubtful], *n.* (*Her.*) The figure of a five-pointed star, supposed to resemble the rowel of a spur; the mark of cadency indicating a third son.

mulligatawny (mŭl i gȧ taw′ ni) [Tamil *milagutannīr*, pepper-water], *n.* An East Indian highly-flavoured curry-soup.

mulligrubs (mŭl′ i grŭbz) [facetious coinage], *n.pl.* Depression, the blues; a pain in the stomach, colic.

mullion (mŭl′ i ŏn) [formerly *muniall*, prob. var. of MONIAL], *n.* A vertical bar separating the compartments of a window. *v.t.* To divide by mullions.

mullock (mŭl′ ŏk) [from obs. or dial. *mull*, dust, powder, from the root *mul*, to grind, cogn. with MEAL (2)], *n.* (*Austral.*) Rock containing no gold; mining refuse from which the gold has been extracted; (*prov.*) rubbish; a muddle.

***mulse** (mŭls) [L. *mulsum*, neut. p.p. of *mulcere*, to sweeten], *n.* Wine heated and sweetened with honey.

mult- [MULTI-], *comb. form.* **multangular** (mŭl tăng′ gū lȧr) [ANGULAR], *a.* Having many angles. **multangularly**, *adv.* **multanimous** (mŭl tăn′ i mŭs) [L. *animus*, mind], *a.* Many-sided mentally. **multarticulate** (mŭl tar tik′ ū lȧt) [ARTICULATE], *a.* Many-jointed.

multeity (mŭl tē′ i ti) [as foll.], *n.* The quality or state of being manifold; a manifold thing.

multi, mult- [L. *multus*, many, much], *pref.* **multiarticulate** [MULTARTICULATE], **multiaxial** (-ăk′ si ȧl) [AXIAL], *a.* Having many axes or lines of growth. **multicamerate** (-kăm′ ėr ȧt) [CAMERA, -ATE], *a.* Having many chambers or cells. **multicapitate** (-kăp′ i tȧt) [CAPITATE], *a.* Many-headed. **multicapsular** (-kăp′ sū lȧr) [CAPSULAR], *a.* (*Bot.*) Having many capsules. **multicarinate** (-kăr′ i nȧt) [CARINATE], *a.* (*Conch.*) Having many ridges. **multicauline** (-kaw′ lin) [CAULINE], *a.* (*Bot.*) Having many stems. ***multicavous** (-kā′ vŭs) [L. *multicavus* (*cavus*, CAVI (1))], *a.* Full of holes or cavities. **multicellular** (-sel′ ū lȧr) [CELLULAR], *a.* Many-celled. **multicentral** (-sen′ trȧl) [CENTRAL], *a.* Having many centres (of development etc.). **multicharge** (mŭl′ ti charj) [CHARGE], *a.* Having or firing several charges in rapid succession (of a gun). **multicipital** (-sip′ i tȧl) [as BICIPITAL, see BICEPS], *a.* (*Bot.*) Having many heads. **multicolour, -ed** (-kŭl′ ŏr, -ŏrd) [COLOUR], *a.* Of or in many colours; many-coloured. **multicostate** (-kos′ tȧt) [COSTATE, see COSTA], *a.* Having many ribs. **multicuspid, -ate** (-kŭs′ pid, -pi dȧt) [see CUSP], *a.* Having more than two cusps (of teeth). **multicycle** (mŭl′ ti sīkl) [CYCLE], *n.* A velocipede having four or more wheels, usu. for carrying a number of men for military purposes. **multicylinder** (-sil′ in dėr) [CYLINDER], *a.* Having a number of cylinders (of steam-engines). **multidentate** (-den′ tȧt) [DENTATE, see DENTAL], *a.* Having many teeth, or tooth-like processes. **multidenticulate** (-tik′ ū lȧt), *a.* Having many denticulations or a finely indented margin. **multidigitate** (-dij′ i tȧt) [DIGITATE], *a.* Having many fingers or finger-like processes. **multidimensional** (-di men′ shŏ nȧl) [DIMENSION, -AL], *a.* Having more than three dimensions. **multifaced,** *a.* Having many faces (of some crystals).

multifarious (mŭl ti fâr′ i ŭs) [L. *multifārius* (MULTI-, *-fārius*, perh. rel. to *fārī*, to speak), cp. *multifāriam*, adv.], *a.* Having great multiplicity, variety, or diversity. **multifariously,** *adv.* **multifariousness,** *n.*

multifid (mŭl′ ti fid), **multifidous** (mŭl tif′ i dŭs) [MULTI, *fid-*, stem of *findere*, to cleave], *a.* (*Bot., Zool., etc.*) Having many divisions; cleft into parts, lobes, segments, etc. **multifil** (mŭl′ ti fil), *n.* A multiple strand of synthetic fibre. **multiflagellate** (mŭl ti flăj′ ė lȧt), *a.* Having many flagella. **multiflorous** (mŭl ti flôr′ ŭs) [late L. *multiflōrus* (L. *flos flōris*, flower)], *a.* (*Bot.*) Having many flowers. **multiflue** (mŭl′ ti floo), *a.* Having many flues. **multifoil** (mŭl′ ti foil), *a.* (*Arch.*) Having more than five foils. *n.* An ornament having more than five foils. **multifold,** *a.* Manifold; many times doubled. **multiform** (mŭl′ ti fôrm) [-FORM], *a.* Having many forms. **multiformity,** *n.* **multiganglionate** (-găng′ gli ŏ nȧt), *a.* (*Physiol.*) Having many ganglia. **multigenerate** (-jen′ ėr ȧt) [GENERATE], *a.* (*Math. etc.*) Generated in many different ways. **multigenerous** [L. *multigenerus* (see GENUS)], *a.* Having many kinds. **multigranulate** (-grăn′ ū lȧt), *a.* Containing or consisting of many grains. **multigyrate** (-jīr′ ȧt), *a.* Having many gyri or convolutions. **multijugous** (-joo′ gŭs) [L. *jugum*, yoke, pair], *a.* (*Bot.*) Having many pairs of leaflets.

multilateral (mŭl ti lăt′ ėr ȧl), *a.* Many-sided; (*Pol.*) of an agreement or treaty in which more than two states participate. **multilineal, multilinear** (mŭl ti lin′ i ȧl, -ar), *a.* Having many lines. **multilingual** (mŭl ti ling′ gwȧl), *a.* In many languages. **multilobate, -lobular** (-lō′ bȧt, -bū lȧr), *a.* Many-lobed. **multilocular, -late** (-lok′ ū lȧr, -lȧt), *a.* Divided into many chambers. **multiloquent, -quous** (mŭl til′ ŏ kwėnt -kwŭs) [cp. MAGNILOQUENT], *a.* Talkative, loquacious. **multiloquence,** *n.* **multi-millionaire** (-mil yŏ nâr′), *n.* One who possesses several millions. **multimodal** (-mō′ dȧl) [MODAL], *a.* (*Biol.*) Having more than one maximum (of statistical curves exhibiting the relative frequency of certain characters in organisms). **multimodalism,** *n.* **multinodal, -date** (-nō′ dȧl, -dȧt), *a.* Having many knots or nodes.

multinomial (mŭl ti nōm′ i ȧl), *a.* (*Alg.*) Having many terms. *n.* A quantity of more than two terms, connected by the signs plus or minus. **multinominal, *-ous** (-nom′ i nȧl, -nŭs), *a.* Having many names. **multinucleate, -ated** (-nū klė ȧt, -ā tėd), *a.* (*Biol.*) Having several nuclei (of cells). **multinucleolate,** *a.* **multiovulate** (-ō′ vū lȧt), *a.* (*Bot.*) Having many ovules. **multiovulation** (-lā′ shŭn), *n.* **multiparous** (-tip′ ȧ rŭs) [L. *multiparus* (-PAROUS)], *a.* Bringing forth many at a birth; bearing or having borne more than one child. **multipara** (mŭl tip′ ȧ rȧ), *n.* (*Obstetrics*) A woman who has borne more than one child. **multiparity** (-păr′ i ti), *n.* **multipartite** (-par′ tīt), *a.* Divided into many parts; having several parts or divisions. **multiped** (mŭl′ ti ped) [L. *multipēs -pedis* (*pēs pedis*, foot)], *a.* Having many feet. *n.* An animal having many feet. **multiplane** (mŭl′ ti plān) [PLANE (3)], *n.* An aeroplane having more than one plane.

multiple (mŭl′ ti pėl) [F., from late L. *multiplus* (MULTI-, *-plus*, see DUPLE)], *a.* Manifold; numerous and multifarious; having many parts, components, or relations. *n.* A quantity that contains another a number of times without a remainder. **common multiple:** Any number containing two or more numbers an exact number of times without a remainder. **multiple mark:** The sign × indicating multiplication. **multiple personality:** (*Psych.*) A condition occasioned by the splitting of the normal organization of mental life into a number of distinct parts, each of which is comparable with an individual personality. **multiple-poinding,** *n.* (*Sc. Law*) An action in which several claimants to a fund or property are compelled to come into court and settle their claims together. **multiplicity** (-plis′ i ti), *n.* The quality of being many or manifold; many of the same kind.

multiplex (mŭl′ ti pleks), *a.* Manifold; multiple.

multiply (mŭl′ ti plī) [O.F. *multiplier*, L. *multiplicāre* (MULTI- *plicāre*, to fold)], *v.t.* To add (a quantity called the multiplicand) to itself a certain number of times (called the multiplier) so as to produce a quantity called the product; to make more numerous, to increase in number or quantity. *v.i.* To increase in number or extent; to increase by propagation. **multiplicable, *multipliable** (-plik′-, -plī′ ȧbl), *a.* **multiplicand** (mŭl ti pli kănd′), *n.* The quantity to be multiplied. ***multiplicate** (mŭl′ ti pli kȧt, mŭl tip′ li kȧt), *a.* **multiplication** (-kā′ shŭn), *n.* **multiplication table:** A table exhibiting the products of quantities taken in pairs, usually to 12 times 12. **multiplicative** (mŭl′ ti pli kā tiv), *a.* **multiplier, *multiplicator,** *n.* One who or that which multiplies or increases; (*Math.*) the number by which the multiplicand is multiplied; (*Elec.*) an instrument for intensifying an electric current. **multiplying glass** or **lens:** A lens with a number of facets giving many reflections of an object.

multipolar (mŭl ti pō′ lȧr) [MULTI-, POLAR], *a.* (*Physiol. and Elec.*) Having more than two poles. *n.* A machine having several magnetic poles.

multiradial (mŭl ti rā′ di ȧl), *a.* Having many radii. **multiradiate** (-rā′ di ȧt), *a.* Having many rays. **multiradicate** (-răd′ i kȧt), *a.* Having many roots. **multiradicular** (-rȧ dik′ ū lȧr), *a.* **multiramified** (-răm′ i fīd), *a.* Having many ramifications or branches. **multiramose, *-ramous** (-rā′-), *a.* **multisaccate** (-săk′ ȧt), *a.* Having many sacs. **multisect** (mŭl′ ti sekt) [L. *sectus*, p.p. of *secāre*, to cut], *a.* Divided into many parts or segments. **multisection** (-sek′ shŭn), *n.* **multiseptate** (mŭl ti sep′ tȧt) [SEPTATE], *a.* (*Bot. etc.*) Having many septa or divisions. **multiserial, *-ate** (-sēr′ i ȧl, -ȧt), *a.* Having many series or rows. **multisiliquose, -quous** (-sil′ i kwōs, -kwŭs) [SILIQUOUS], *a.* (*Bot.*) Having many pods or seed-vessels. **multisonous** (mŭl tis′ ŏ nŭs) [L. *multisonus* (*sonous*, see SONANT)], *a.* Having many sounds; sounding much. **multisonant,** *a.* **multispiral** (mŭl ti spīr′ ȧl) [SPIRAL], *a.* (*Conch.*) Having many spirals or convolutions (said of an operculum). **multistaminate** (-stăm′ i nȧt), *a.* (*Bot.*) Having many stamens. **multistriate** (-strī′ ȧt), *a.* Marked with numerous striæ or streaks. **multisulcate** (-sŭl′ kȧt), *a.* Many-furrowed. **multisyllable** (-sil′ ȧbl), *n.* A polysyllable. **multisyllabic** (-lăb′ ik), *a.* **multitentaculate** (-ten tăk′ ū lȧt), *a.* Having many tentacles. **multititular** (-tit′ ū lȧr), *a.* Having many titles. **multituberculate** (-tū bĕr′ kū lȧt), *a.* Having many tubercles (as teeth). **multitubular** (-tū′ bū lȧr), *a.* Having many tubes.

multitude (mŭl′ ti tūd) [F., from L. *multitūdinem*, nom. *-tūdo* (MULTI-, -TUDE)], *n.* The state of being numerous; a great number; a very large crowd or throng of people; the common people. **multitudinous,** *a.* Very numerous; *pertaining to or composing a multitude. **multitudinously,** *adv.* **multitudinousness,** *n.* **multitudinism** (-tū′ di nizm), *n.* The doctrine that the welfare of the many is of higher importance than that of the individual. **multitudinist,** *n.*

***multivagant** (mŭl tiv′ ȧ gȧnt) [L. *multivagus* (MULTI-, *vagus*, wandering, from *vagārī*, to wander)], *a.* Much-wandering. ***multivagous,** *a.*

multivalent (mŭl tiv′ ȧ lėnt) [L. *valens -ntem*, pres.p. of *valēre*, to be worth], *a.* Having several degrees of valency; (*Chem.*) having a valency greater than unity. **multivalence, -valency** (-văl′ ėn si), *n.*

multivalve (mŭl′ ti vălv) [MULTI-, VALVE], *a.* Having many valves. *n.* An animal having a shell of many valves or pieces; a multivalve shell. **multivalvular** (-văl′ vū lȧr), *a.* ***multiversant** (-vĕr′ sȧnt) [L. *versans -ntem*, pres.p. of *vertere*, to turn], *a.* Assuming many shapes, protean. **multivious** (-tiv′ i ŭs) [L. *via*, way, -OUS], *a.* Having many ways: pointing in several directions. **multivocal** (mŭl tiv′ ŏ kȧl) [cp. EQUIVOCAL], *a.* Susceptible of several interpretations; ambiguous. *n.* An ambiguous word. ***multocular** (mŭl tok′ ū lȧr) [OCULAR], *a.* Having many eyes.

multungulate (mŭl tŭng′ gū lȧt), *a.* Having more than two functional hoofs. *n.* A multungulate mammal, as an elephant or tapir.

multure (mŭl′ tyŭr) [O.F. *moulture* (F. *mouture*), med. L. *molitūra*, from *molere*, to grind], *n.* (*Sc.*) The toll or percentage paid for grinding grain at a mill; the percentage of ore paid to the owner of a pulverizing-mill for grinding. **multurer,** *n.* (*Sc.*) One who has corn ground at a certain mill to which he pays multure, usu. on the terms of his lease.

mum (1) (mŭm) [onomat. (cp. G. *mumm*, Dut. *mommen*, to mum)], *a.* Silent. *int.* Silence, hush! *v.i.* To act in dumb-show; to play as a mummer. ***mumbudget,** *n.* An expression impressing silence and secrecy. ***mumchance,** *n.* A game of hazard with cards or dice; a silent, tongue-tied person. *a.* Silent.

mum (2) (mŭm) [G. *mumme*], *n.* A strong, sweet beer, orig. made in Brunswick.

mum (3) (*vulg.*) [MA′AM] [(*fam.*) MAMA].

mumble (mŭm′ bėl) [M.E. *momelen*, from MUM (1)], *v.i.* To speak indistinctly; to mutter; to speak with the lips closed. *v.t.* To mutter indistinctly or inarticulately; to chew or mouth gently. *n.* Indistinct utterance; a mutter. ***mumble-news,** *n.* A tale-bearer. **mumblement,** *n.* **mumbler,** *n.* **mumblingly,** *adv.*

mumbo-jumbo (mŭm′ bō jŭm′ bō) [etym. doubtful], *n.* A West African idol, deity, or malignant spirit; an absurd object of popular veneration.

mummer (mŭm′ ėr) [O.F. *momeur*, from *momer*, to mum, perh. from Teut. (cp. MUM (1))], *n.* An actor in dumb-show, esp. one of a number of persons who formerly went from house to house at Christmas in fantastic disguises performing a kind of play; (*contemp.*) an actor. **mummery,** *n.* The act or performance of mumming; (*contemp.*) tomfoolery, hypocritical parade of ritual, etc.

mummy (1) (mŭm′ i) [F. *momie*, med. L. *mumia*, Arab. *mūmiyā*, from *mūm*, wax used in embalming], *n.* A body of a person or animal preserved from decay by embalming, esp. after the manner of the ancient Egyptians; (*Hort.*) a kind of wax used in grafting; (*Paint.*) a bituminous pigment giving a rich brown tint; dried flesh, like that of a mummy; (*fig.*) a dried-up person or body. *v.t.* To mummify. **mummy-case,** *a.* A wooden or papier-mâché case, usu. semi-human in shape, and decorated with hieroglyphics, in which Egyptian mummies were preserved. **mummify,** *v.t.* **mummification** (-kā′ shŭn), *n.* **mummiform,** *a.*

mummy (2) (mŭm′ i) [MAMA].

mump (1) (mŭmp) [perh. from Dut. *mompen*, to cheat], *v.i.* To beg in a whining tone. *v.t.* To obtain by begging; to overreach. **mumper,** *n.* A beggar.

mump (2) (mŭmp) [etym. doubtful, perh. imit. (identified with prec. by Skeat)], *v.i.* To sulk, to mope; (*prov.*) to mumble, to munch; *to grimace. *v.t.* (*prov.*) To munch. *n.pl.* (*as sing.*) The sulks; a contagious disease characterized by a swelling and inflammation in the parotid and salivary glands. **mumpish,** *a.* ***mumpishly,** *adv.*

***mumpsimus** (mŭmp′ si mŭs) [from the blunder of an illiterate priest who said this for L. SUMPSIMUS in the Mass], *n.* A blunder, prejudice, or obsolete custom persistently adhered to; *an old fogy.

munch (mŭnch) [prob. onomat.], *v.t.* To chew audibly; to eat with much movement of the jaws. *v.i.* To chew audibly or with much movement of the jaws; to work the jaws up and down (as an aged person in talking). **muncher,** *n.*

mundane (mŭn′ dān) [F. *mondain*, L. *mundānus*, from *mundus*, the world], *a.* Belonging to this world, earthly, worldly; matter-of-fact; (*Astrol.*) pertaining to the horizon. **mundanely,** *adv.* **mundaneness, *mundanity** (-dăn′ i ti), *n.*

***mundify** (mŭn′ di fī) [F. *mondifier*, L. *mundificāre* (*mundus*, clean, *-ficāre*, from *facere*, to make)], *v.t.* To cleanse, to purify. ***mundificant, *mundificative,** *a.* and *n.* ***mundification** (-kā shŭn), *n.* ***mundatory,** *a.* Cleansing. *n.* That which cleanses or purifies.

***mundungus** (mŭn dŭng′ gŭs) [Sp. *mondongo*, tripe, black-pudding], *n.* Ill-smelling tobacco.

mungo (mŭng′ gō) [etym. doubtful], *n.* Woollen cloth made of second-hand material (of rather higher grade than shoddy).

mungoose (mŭng′ goos) [Marathi *mangūs*, Telegu *mangīsu*], *n.* (*pl.* **-gooses**) An East Indian ichneumon, *Herpestes griseus*, preying on venomous snakes.

Munich (mū′ nik), *n.* (*Pol.*) An act of appeasement, so called from the attempt to buy peace from Hitler at Munich in 1938.

municipal (mū nis′ i păl) [F., from L. *mūnicipālis*, from *mūniceps -cipis*, a citizen of a town having the rights of Roman citizenship (*mūnia*, civic offices, pl. of *mūnus*, duty, *capere*, to take)], *a.* Pertaining to the government of a town or city, or to local self-government in general; *pertaining to the internal government of a State, kingdom, or nation. **municipalism,** *n.* **municipalist,** *n.* **municipalize,** *v.t.* **municipality** (-păl′ i ti), *n.* A town, city, or district having a charter of incorporation or enjoying local self-government. **municipally,** *adv.*

munificent (mū nif′ i sĕnt) [L. *mūnificus* (*mūnus*, duty, -FIC), after MAGNIFICENT], *a.* Liberal, generous, bountiful; characterized by splendid liberality. **munificence,** *n.* **munificently,** *adv.*

muniment (mū′ ni mĕnt) [O.F., from L. *mūnīmentum*, from *mūnīre*, to fortify], *n.* A title-deed, charter, or record kept as evidence or defence of a title; *a fortification, a stronghold; help, support, defence. **muniment-room, -house,** *n.* A strong-room or building in which muniments are preserved.

munition (mū nish′ ŭn) [F., from L. *mūnītiōnem*, nom. *-tio*, as prec.], *n.* (*usu. in pl.*) Military stores of all kinds; anything required for an undertaking; *a stronghold. *v.t.* To furnish with munitions.

munnion [MULLION].

munshi (moon′ shi) [Hind.], *n.* A native secretary, teacher of languages, or interpreter, in India.

muntjak (mŭnt′ jăk) [Sunda *minchek*], *n.* A small Asiatic deer, *Cervulus muntjac*.

muræna (mū rē′ nă) [L., from Gr. *muraina*, fem. of *mūros smūros*, sea-eel], *n.* A genus of marine eels.

murage (mūr′ āj) [O.F., from *mur*, L. *mūrum*, nom. *-us*, wall], *n.* A toll formerly paid for the repair or maintenance of the walls of a town.

mural (mūr′ ăl) [F., from L. *mūrālis*, as prec.], *a.* Pertaining to, on, or like a wall. **mural arc, circle, quadrant:** A graduated arc, circle, or quadrant, formerly fixed to a wall in the plane of the meridian, for determining altitudes and zenith distances. **mural crown:** A crown, indented and embattled, given to the Roman soldier who first mounted a breach in storming a town.

Muratorian (mūr ă tôr′ i ăn), *a.* Of or pertaining to the Italian scholar L. A. Muratori (1672–1750). **Muratorian fragment** or **canon:** The oldest Western canon of the New Testament writings (compiled *c.* 170 A.D., and edited by Muratori).

murder (mĕr′ dĕr) [A.-S. *morthor* (cp. Goth. *maurthr*, Dut. *moord*, Icel. *morth*, L. *mors -tis*, death), whence *myrthrian*, to murder (cp. Goth. *maurthrjan*)], *n.* Homicide with malice aforethought. *v.t.* To kill (a human being) with malice aforethought; to slay barbarously; (*fig.*) to spoil, to mar, by blundering or clumsiness; to mangle, to ruin. **capital murder** [CAPITAL]. **murder will out:** A hidden matter will certainly come to light. **murderer,** *n.* **murderess,** *n.* **murderous,** *a.* **murderously,** *adv.*

mure (mūr) [F. *murer*, L. *mūrāre*, from *mūrus*, wall], *v.t.* To immure, to shut up; to wall in. **n.* A wall.

murex (mūr′ eks) [L. prob. cogn. with Gr. *muax*], *n.* (*pl.* **murices,** mūr′ i sēz) A genus of molluscs, one species of which yields a purple dye.

murgeon (mĕr′ jŏn) [Sc., etym. doubtful], *n.* (*pl.*) Grimaces, smirks, antics. *v.t.* To make grimaces at.

muriate (mūr′ i ăt) [F., from *muriatique*, L. *muriāticus*, pickled in brine, from *muria*, brine], *n.* Chloride (now used only commercially). **muriate of soda:** Common salt. **muriated,** *a.* Impregnated with chloride (of mineral waters). **muriatic** (-ăt′ ik), *a.* Derived from sea-water or brine; hydrochloric. **muriatiferous** (-tif′ ĕr ŭs), *a.*

muricate (mūr′ i kāt) [L. *mūricātus*, shaped like the *mūrex*, see MUREX], *a.* (*Bot.*) Armed with sharp points or prickles.

muriform (mūr′ i fôrm) [L. *mūrus*, wall], *a.* (*Bot.*) Arranged like bricks in a wall.

murk (mĕrk) [A.-S. *mirce* (cp. Icel. *myrkr*, Dan. and Swed. *mörk*)], *n.* Darkness. **a.* Murky; thick, obscure. **murky, murksome,** *a.* **murkily,** *adv.* **murkiness,** *n.*

murmur (mĕr′ mŭr) [F. *murmure*, L. *murmur*, whence *murmurāre* (cp. Gr. *mormurein*, to boil up (as waves))], *n.* A low, confused, continuous or repeated sound, as of running water; a half-suppressed protest or complaint, a grumble; a subdued speech; (*Path.*) an abnormal sound heard on auscultation of the heart, lungs or arteries. *v.i.* To make a low continued noise, like that of running water; to mutter in discontent; to find fault. *v.t.* To utter in a low voice. **murmurer,** *n.* A grumbler, a complainer. **murmuringly,** *adv.* **murmurous,** *a.*

murrain (mŭr′ ăn) [O.F. *morine*, perh. rel. to L. *morī*, to die], *n.* An infectious disease among cattle. *a.* Affected with murrain.

Murray cod (mŭr′ i kod) [Murray river, Australia], *n.* A freshwater fish found in that river.

murrey (mŭr′ i) [O.F. *moré*, *morée*, L. *mōrātus*, *-ta*, from *mōrum*, mulberry], *a.* Of a dark-red colour.

murrhine (mŭr′ in, -īn) [L. *murrhinus*, from *murra*, late Gr. *morria*, a material of which costly vases were made], *a.* A term applied to a delicate kind of Eastern ware made of fluorspar.

murrnong (mĕr′ nong) [Austral. abor.], *n.* A sweet tuberous root found in S. Australia furnishing food for the Aborigines.

Murrumbidgee oyster (mu rŭm′ bi jē oi′ stĕr) [Austral. river], *n.* A raw egg taken with vinegar. **Murrumbidgee whaler,** *n.* A tramp, a hobo.

***murther** [MURDER].

Musca (mŭs′ kă) [L.], *n.* (*pl.* **-cæ**) (*Ent.*) A genus of dipterous insects containing the house-flies. ***muscæ volitantes:*** (*Path.*) Black specks or motes apparently moving before the eyes.

muscadel (mŭs kă del′) [O.F., from M.It. *moscadello*, *-tello*, dim. of *moscato*, from *musco*, MUSK], *n.* A kind of rich wine made from muscadine grapes; the grapes from which such wine is made; a sweet fragrant pear. **muscadine** (mŭs′ kă dīn, -din), *n.* One of several varieties of grape with a musky flavour or odour; *the wine muscadel.

muscardine (mŭs′ kăr din) [F. *muscardine*, *muscadin*, It. *moscardino*, nutmeg, musk-lozenge, as prec.], *n.* A disease fatal to silkworms, caused by a fungoid or parasitic growth.

***muscat, *muscatel** [MUSCADEL].

Muschelkalk (mush′ ėl kălk) [G. (*muschel*, mussel, *kalk*, lime)], *n.* (*Geol.*) A series of German shelly limestone beds of Middle Triassic age, absent in Britain.

Musci (mŭs′ i) [L.], *n.pl.* (*Bot.*) The true mosses. **musciform,** *a.*

muscle (mŭs′ ėl) [F., from L. *musculum*, nom. *-us*, dim. of *mus*, MOUSE], *n.* An organ consisting of a band or bundle of contractile fibrous tissue serving to effect movement of some part of the animal body; the tissue of which this is composed; (*fig.*) muscular strength. **muscled,** *a.* (*usu. in comb.*, as *brawny-muscled*). **muscleless,** *a.*

muscoid (mŭs′ koid) [L. *musc-*, see MUSCI, -OID], *a.* (*Bot.*) Resembling moss. *n.* A moss-like plant. **muscology** (-kol′ ȯ ji) [-LOGY], *n.* The science of mosses, bryology. **muscologist,** *n.* **muscose,** *a.* ***muscosity** (-kos′ i ti), *n.*

muscovado (mŭs kȯ va′ dō) [Sp. *mascabado*, unrefined], *n.* Moist, dark-coloured, unrefined sugar left after evaporation from cane-juice and draining off from the molasses.

Muscovite (mŭs′ kȯ vīt) [from F. *Muscovie*, Russ. *Moskova*, Moscow], *n.* A native of Muscovy (an old name for Russia); common mica, formerly called Muscovy glass. **Muscovy duck:** The musk-duck, *Cairina moschata.*

muscular (mŭs′ kū lȧr) [L. *musculus*, MUSCLE], *a.* Pertaining to, consisting of, or performed by the muscles; having well-developed muscles; strong, brawny. **muscular Christianity:** The combination of full physical, moral, and religious development inculcated by Charles Kingsley, Thomas Hughes, etc. **muscularity** (-lăr′ i ti), *n.* **muscularly,** *adv.* **musculature** (mŭs′ kū lȧ tyȯr), *n.* The arrangement or disposition of the muscles in the body or an organ. **musculo-,** *comb. form.* ***musculous,** *a.*

Muse (I) (mūz) [F., from L. *Mūsa*, Gr. *Mousa*], *n.* (*Gr. Myth.*) One of nine goddesses, daughters of Zeus and Mnemosyne, who presided over the liberal arts; Clio was the muse of history; Euterpe, of lyric poetry; Thalia, of comedy and idyllic poetry; Melpomene, of tragedy; Terpsichore, of music and dancing; Erato, of amatory poetry; Calliope, of epic poetry; Urania, of astronomy; and Polyhymnia, of singing and harmony; the inspiring power of poetry, poetical genius; *a poet. ***museless,** *a.*

muse (2) (mūz) [F. *muser*, prob. from O.F. *muse*, mouth, snout, whence *musel*, *museau*, MUZZLE], *v.i.* To ponder, to meditate (upon); to study or reflect (upon) in silence; to dream, to engage in reverie; *to wonder. *v.t.* To meditate on. *n.* Abstraction of mind; reverie; *wonder, surprise. ***museful,** *a.* ***musefully,** *adv.* **muser,** *n.* **musingly,** *adv.*

***muset** (mū zet′) [O.F. *mucette*, *mussette*, dim. of *muce*, *musse*, MEUSE], *n.* A gap in a hedge, a meuse.

musette (mū zet′) [F., dim. of O.F. *muse*, bagpipe], *n.* A small bagpipe formerly used in France; a soft pastoral melody imitating the sound of the bagpipe; a reed-stop on the organ; *a rustic dance.

museum (mū zē′ ŭm) [L., from Gr. *mouseion*, a temple of the Muses (see MUSE (I))], *n.* A room or building for the preservation or exhibition of objects illustrating antiquities, art, natural science, etc. **museography** (-og′ rȧ fi), *n.* The art of describing or cataloguing museums. **museographer,** *n.* **museology** (-ol′ ȯ ji), *n.* The science of organizing and managing museums. **museologist,** *n.*

mush (mŭsh) [prob. var. of MASH (I)], *n.* A mash; a soft pulp, pulpy mass; (*Am.*) porridge made of maize-meal boiled; (*slang*) sentimental nonsense. **mushy,** *a.*

mushroom (mŭsh′ rum) [F. *mousseron*, prob. from O.F. *mousse*, moss], *n.* A quick-growing edible fungus, esp. *Agaricus campestris*, the common or meadow mushroom; (*fig.*) an upstart. *a.* Pertaining to or made from mushrooms; (*fig.*) ephemeral, upstart. *v.i.* To gather mushrooms; to expand and flatten out (of bullets).

music (mū′ zik) [F. *musique*, L. *mūsica*, Gr. *mousikē technē*, the art of the Muses (see MUSE (I))], *n.* The art of combining vocal and instrumental tones in a rhythmic form for the expression of emotion under the laws of beauty; such an artistic combination of tones; any pleasant combination of sounds; melody, harmony; musical taste; a musical score; *a band, an orchestra. **set to music:** Furnished with music to which it can be sung (of a poem or other composition). **to face the music** [FACE]. **music-book,** *n.* **music-case, -folio, -holder,** *n.* A cover for sheet-music. **music-hall,** *n.* A theatre devoted to variety entertainments, (*Am.* vaudeville theater). **music-master, -mistress,** *n.* One who teaches music. **music-stand,** *n.* A light frame for supporting a sheet of music. **music-stool,** *n.* A stool with a revolving adjustable seat. **musical,** *a.* Of or pertaining to music; fond of or skilled in music; harmonious, melodious. **musical-box,** *n.* A box with barrel-organ mechanism for playing different tunes. **musical chairs,** *n.* A parlour game. **musical-clock,** *n.* A clock that plays tunes at the hours. **musical-glasses,** *n.pl.* A musical instrument consisting of a series of glass vessels or tubes of varying pitch. **musicality** (-kăl′ i ti), **musicalness,** *n.* **musically,** *adv.* **musician** (mū zish′ ȧn), *n.* **musicology,** *n.* The science of musical lore and history. **musicologist,** *n.* A writer on this.

musk (mŭsk) [F. *musc*, late L. *muscum*, nom. *-cus*, late Gr. *moschos*, Pers. *musk*, perh. from Sansk. *muska*, testicle], *n.* An odoriferous, resinous substance obtained from a sac in the male musk-deer; the odour of this; similar perfumes; the musk-plant, *Mimulus moschatus*; the musk-cranesbill, *Erodium moschatum*; applied to other plants. **musk-bag,** *n.* The bag or sac containing musk in various animals, esp. the musk-deer. **musk-beaver,** *n.* The musk-rat. ***musk-cat,** *n.* A civet; (*fig.*) a dandy. **musk-deer,** *n.* A small hornless deer, *Moschus moschiferus*, of Central Asia, from which musk is obtained. **musk-duck,** *n.* A tropical American duck, *Cairina moschata*, erroneously called the Muscovy or Barbary duck; an Australian duck, *Biziura lobata.* **musk melon:** The melon, *Cucumis melo.* **musk-ox,** *n.* An Arctic-American bovine ruminant, *Ovibos moschatus.* **musk-pear,** *n.* A pear with a musky smell. **musk-rat,** *n.* A name for several rodents emitting a musky odour, esp. the musquash, *Fiber zibethicus*; applied also to Indian shrews, *Crocidura cærulea* and *C. murina.* **musk-rose,** *n.* A rambling rose with large white flowers and a musky odour. **musk-tree, -wood,** *n.* A Jamaica tree, *Moschoxylum Swartzii*, and various Oceanic and Australian trees and shrubs with musky odour. **musky,** *a.* **muskiness,** *n.*

musket (mŭs′ kėt) [F. *mousquet*, It. *mosquetto*, orig. a sparrowhawk, perh. from L. MUSCA], *n.* The old fire-arm of the infantry now superseded by the rifle; any old-fashioned smooth-bore gun; *the male of the sparrow-hawk. **musket-proof,** *a.* **musket-shot,** *n.* The distance a musket will carry; a ball or shot from a musket. **musketeer** (-tēr′), *n.* A soldier armed with a musket. ***musketoon** (-toon′), *n.* A short musket or carbine with a large bore; a soldier armed with this. **musketry,** *n.* Muskets collectively; the art of using the musket; fire from small-arms.

Muslim [MOSLEM].

muslin (mŭz′ lin) [F. *mousseline*, It. *mussolina*, *-ino*, dim. of *Mussolo*, Mosul in Mesopotamia where it was formerly made], *n.* A fine, thin, cotton fabric used for dresses, curtains, etc.; a dress made of this; (*Am.*) calico. *a.* Made of muslin. **a bit of muslin** [BIT (I)], **muslin-de-laine** [MOUSSELINE-DE-LAINE]. **muslined,** *a.* **muslinet** (-net′), *n.* A coarse kind of muslin.

musmon (mŭs′ mon) [L. *mūsimon*, late Gr. *mousmōn*], *n.* The *mouflon.*

musquash (mŭs′ kwosh) [Algonkin *musk-wessu*], *n.* A North American aquatic rodent, *Fiber zibethicus*, yielding a valuable fur and secreting a musky substance in a large gland, also called the musk-rat.

muss (mŭs) [var. of MESS], *n.* A state of confusion or disorder, a mess. *v.t.* To disarrange, to throw into disorder. **mussy,** *a.* Untidy; disordered. **mussiness,** *n.*

mussel (mŭs′ ėl) [A.-S. *mūscelle, muxle*, late L. *muscula*, as MUSCLE], *n.* Any mollusc of the bivalve genus *Mytilus*, esp. the edible *M. edulis.*

mussitation (mŭs i tā′ shŭn) [late L. *mussitātio*, from L. *mussitāre*, freq. of *mussāre*, to mutter], *n.* A muttering or mumbling; a movement of the lips as in mumbling.

Mussulman (mŭs′ ŭl mȧn) [Pers. *musulmān*, that is a true believer, from Arab. *muslim*, MOSLEM], *n.* (*pl.* **-mans**) A Mohammedan, a Moslem.

mussy, etc. [MUSS (1)].

must (1) (mŭst) [A.-S. from L. *mustum*, neut. of *mustus*, fresh, new], *n.* New wine, the expressed juice of the grape before fermentation; mustiness, mould. *v.t.* To make mouldy. *v.i.* To grow mouldy.

must (2) (mŭst) [prob. from MUSTY (Skeat identifies with prec.)], *n.* Mustiness, mould.

must (3) (mŭst) [A.-S. *mōste*, past of *mōt*, may, be free to (infin. *mōtan*, not found)], *aux. v.* To be obliged to, to be under a necessity to; to be requisite, to be virtually or logically necessary to; to be certain to; (used also with p.p. as a kind of historic present). *n.* A thing that must not be missed.

must (4) (must) [Hind. and Pers. *mast*, primarily, intoxicated], *a.* In a dangerous state of frenzy (of male elephants and camels). *n.* This state which recurs irregularly.

***mustache, -chio** [MOUSTACHE].

mustang (mŭs′ tăng) [Sp. *mestengo* (now *mesteño*), prob. from *mesta* (rel. to L. *mixta*, see MIX), a company of graziers, conf. with *mostrenco*, astray, rel. to L. *monstrāre*, to show, to point out], *n.* The wild horse of the American prairies. **mustang grape:** A small red Texan grape, *Vitis candicans.* **mustanger,** *n.* One who lassoes mustangs for the market.

mustard (mŭs′ tȧrd) [O.F. *mostarde* (F. *moutarde*), from Rom. *mosto*, MUST (1)], *n.* The seeds of *Sinapis alba* and *nigra* ground and used as a condiment and as a rubefacient; any plant of the Linnæan cruciferous genus *Sinapis*, now included in *Brassica.* **French mustard:** Mustard mixed with vinegar, etc. **mustard and cress:** White mustard, *S. alba*, and cress, *Lepidium sativum*, used in the seed-leaf as salad herbs. **mustard gas,** *n.* An irritant poison gas. **mustard-oil,** *n.* Oil expressed from black mustard. **mustard-pot,** *n.* A pot or cruet for holding mustard at table. **mustard-tree,** *n.* (*Bibl.*) The white mustard, *Sinapis alba* or some shrub or small tree.

mustee (mŭs tē′) [Sp. MESTIZO], *n.* The offspring of a white person and a quadroon.

mustela (mŭs tē′ lȧ) [L., weasel, from *mūs*, MOUSE], *n.* A genus of small carnivora containing the weasels or martens. **musteline** (mŭs′ tė lin), *a.* and *n.* **mustelinous,** *a.* **musteloid,** *a.* and *n.*

muster (mŭs′ tėr) [O.F. *mostre*, It. *mostra*, a show, a display, from L. *monstrāre*, to show (see MONSTER)], *n.* The assembling of troops for parade or review; a register of forces mustered; a collection, a gathering; a collection of peacocks; *a pattern, a show. *v.t.* To collect or assemble for review, checking of rolls, etc.; to bring together; to summon (up strength, courage, etc.). *v.i.* To meet in one place. **to pass muster:** To pass inspection without censure; to be accepted as satisfactory. **muster-book,** *n.* A book in which military forces are registered. ***muster-master,** *n.* One who takes account of troops and their equipment. **muster-roll,** *n.* A roll or register of troops, a ship's company, etc.

musty (mŭs′ ti) [etym. doubtful, see MUST (2)], *a.* Mouldy; sour, stale; (*fig.*) vapid, antiquated, spiritless. **mustily,** *adv.* **mustiness,** *n.*

mutable (mū′ tȧ bėl) [L. *mūtabilis*, from *mūtāre*, to change], *a.* Liable to change; inconstant, fickle, unstable. **mutability** (-bil′ i ti), ***mutableness,** *n.* **mutably,** *adv.*

mutage (mū′ tȧj) [F., from *muter*, from L. *mūtus*, dumb], *n.* The process of checking fermentation of must (1).

mutate (mū tāt′), *v.i.* To change; to be transmuted; (*Biol.*) to sport. *v.t.* (*Gram.*) To change or modify (as by umlaut). *a.* (mū′-) (*Bot.*) Changed. *n.* (*Gram.*) A form having a mutated vowel. **mutation** (-tā′ shŭn), *n.* The act or process of changing; (*Gram.*) umlaut; the change of an initial consonant in Welsh; (*Biol.*) a permanent variation in organisms giving rise to a new species; a species so produced. **mutative, mutatory** (mū′ tȧ tiv, -tȯr i), *a.*

mutch (mŭch) [M.Dut. *mutse* (Dut. *muts*), prob. from *amutse* or *almutse*, cp. AMICE (2) and MOZETTA], *n.* (*Sc.*) A woman's cap or coif.

mutchkin (mŭch′ kin) [M.Dut. *mudseken*, dim. of *mudde*, *mud*, L. *modius*, a corn-measure], *n.* A Scotch measure, about ¾ of a pint.

mute (1) (mūt) [M.E. and O.F. *muet*, pop. L. *mūtettus*, dim. of *mūtus*, assim. later to L.], *a.* Silent, uttering no sound, speechless; not having the power of speech, dumb; not giving tongue (of hounds); not spoken; (*Philol.*) not sounded, unpronounced; produced by complete closure of the organs of the mouth or interruption of the pasage of breath (as *h, p, ph, d, t, th, k*, and *g*). *n.* One who is silent or speechless; a dumb person; a hired attendant at a funeral; a dumb porter or janitor in Eastern countries; an actor in dumb show or whose part is speechless; a contrivance for deadening sound (as in a piano); (*Philol.*) a letter which is not pronounced; a consonant that stops the sound entirely. *v.t.* To deaden or muffle the sound of. **to stand mute:** To refuse or be unable to speak; (*Law*) to refuse to plead (usu. from malice). **mutely,** *adv.* **muteness,** *n.* **mutism,** *n.* Muteness; silence; inability to hear, dumbness.

mute (2) (mūt) [O.F. *mutir, muetir, esmeutir, esmaltir*, perh. from Teut. (cp. SMELT (1))], *v.i.* To dung (said of birds). *v.t.* To void (as excrement). *n.* Muting.

mutilate (mū′ ti lāt) [L. *mutilātus*, p.p. of *mutilāre*, from *mutilus*, maimed (perh. rel. to Gr. *mutilos*, *mutulos*, hornless)], *v.t.* To cut off a limb or an essential part of; to maim, to mangle; to disfigure; to injure (literary and other work) by excision. **mutilation** (-lā′ shŭn), *n.* **mutilator** (mū′ ti lā tȯr), *n.*

mutineer (mū ti nēr′) [F. *mutinier*, from *mutin*, mutinous, pop. L. *movita*, a movement, commotion, from L. *movēre*, to MOVE], *n.* One who mutinies. *v.t.* To mutiny. ***mutine** (mū′ tin), *n.* A mutineer. *v.i.* To mutiny. **mutinous,** *a.* **mutinously,** *adv.* ***mutinousness,** *n.* **mutiny** (mū′ ti ni), *n.* Open resistance to or revolt against constituted authority, esp. by sailors or soldiers against their officers. *v.i.* To rise or rebel against authority (esp. in the army or navy). **Mutiny Act:** An act formerly passed every year for the maintenance of discipline in the army and navy, now embodied in the annual Army Act of 1881.

mutism [MUTE (1)].

mutograph (mū′ tȯ grăf) [*muto-* from L. *mūtāre*, to change, -GRAPH], *n.* A variety of kinetograph for photographing moving objects. *v.t.* To photograph with this. **mutoscope,** *n.* An apparatus for displaying such photographic pictures by means of rapidly revolving wheels. **mutoscopic** (-skop′ ik), *a.*

mutt (mŭt) [etym. doubtful], *n.* (*Slang*) A fool, a silly ass.

mutter (mŭt′ ėr) [prob. imit.], *v.i.* To speak, in a low voice or with compressed lips; to grumble, to murmur (at or against); to make a low, rumbling noise. *v.t.* To utter in a low or indistinct voice; to say in secret. *n.* A low or indistinct utterance; a low rumbling sound; a murmur, a grumble. **mutterer,** *n.* **mutteringly,** *adv.*

mutton (mŭt′ ȯn) [O.F. *moton* (F. *mouton*), med. L. *multōnem*, nom. *-to*, prob. from Celt. (cp. O.Ir. *molt*, Gael. *mult*, W. *mollt*)], *n.* The flesh of sheep used as food; (*facet.*) a sheep; (*slang*) a loose woman. **mutton-chop,** *n.* A rib or other small piece of mutton for broiling; a side whisker of this shape. **mutton-fist,** *n.* (*slang*) A large, coarse, red hand. **mutton-ham,** *n.* A leg of mutton salted and cured. **mutton-head,** *n.* A stupid person. **mutton-headed,** *a.* **muttony,** *a.*

mutual (mū′ tū ȧl) [F. *mutuel*, L. *mūtuus*, reciprocal, from *mūtāre*, to change], *a.* Reciprocal, reciprocally given and received; possessed, done, felt, etc., by each of two persons, parties, etc., to or towards the other; (*incorr.*) shared by or common to two or more persons (as *mutual friend*). **mutual accounts:** Accounts in which each of two parties submit charges against the other. **mutual conductance,** *n.* (*Radio.*) A measure of a valve's efficiency. **mutual inductance,** *n.* (*Elec.*) The coupling of two circuits in such a way that an alteration of current in one effects an electromotive force in the other. **mutual insurance:** A system of insurance in which parties agree to indemnify each other for specified losses; insurance under a company granting a certain share of the profits to policy-holders. **mutualism,** *n.* The doctrine that true welfare is based on mutual dependence; (*Biol.*) symbiosis in which organisms are associated without detriment to either. **mutualist,** *n.* **mutuality** (-ăl′ i ti), *n.* **mutualize,** *v.t.* and *i.* **mutually,** *adv.*

mutule (mū′ tūl) [F., from L. *mūtulus*], *n.* A modillion, or one of the projecting blocks under the corona of a Doric cornice.

***mutuum** (mū′ tū ŭm) [L., neut. of *mūtuus*, borrowed], *n.* (*Comm. Law*) A contract under which goods are lent for consumption, to be repaid in property of the same kind and quantity.

muzhik (moo′ zhik) [Rus.], *n.* A Russian peasant; a serf.

muzzle (mŭz′ ėl) [O.F. *musel* (F. *museau*), prob. from med. L. *mūsellum*, dim. of *mūsum*, nom. *-us*, etym. doubtful], *n.* The projecting mouth and nose of an animal, as of a horse, dog, etc.; the snout; the mouth of a gun or cannon; a guard put over an animal's muzzle to prevent biting. *v.t.* To put a muzzle on; (*fig.*) to silence. **muzzle-loader,** *n.* A gun loaded at the muzzle.

muzzy (mŭz′ i) [etym. doubtful], *a.* Muddled, dazed; dull; fuddled, tipsy. **muzzily,** *adv.* **muzziness,** *n.*

my (mī, mi) [M.E. *mī*, *mīn*, MINE], *poss. a.* (*absol.* **mine**) Belonging to me; used as a vocative in some forms of address (as *my boy, my dear*). *int.* A mild ejaculation of surprise.

Mya (mī′ ȧ) [mod. L., prob. from Gr. *mūs*, MUSSEL], *n.* (*pl.* **Myæ, Myas**) (*Zool.*) A genus of bivalves containing the soft clams. **Myaria** (mī âr′ i ȧ), *n.pl.* An old name for the family comprising these, now called *Myidæ*. **myarian,** *a.* and *n.*

myalgia (mī ăl′ ji ȧ) [Gr. *mūs*, MUSCLE, *-algia*, *algos*, pain], *n.* (*Path.*) A morbid state of the muscles characterized by pain and cramp. **myalgic,** *a.*

myalism (mī′ ȧ lizm) [*myal*, prob. from native W. African, -ISM], *n.* A species of witchcraft practised in the West Indies.

myall (mī′ ȧl) [Austral. abor. *maiāl*], *n.* One of two Australian acacias, *A. pendula* and *A. homalophylla*, yielding scented wood used in making tobacco-pipes. **myall-tree, myall-wood,** *n.*

mycelium (mī sē′ li ŭm) [Gr. *mukēs*, mushroom, *-l-*, -IUM], *n.* (*pl.* **-ia**) The vegetative parts of fungi, mushroom spawn. **mycelial,** *a.*

Mycenæan (mī sē nē′ ȧn), *a.* Pertaining to Mycenæ, an ancient city of Argolis, Greece.

mycetes (mī sē′ tēz) [Gr. *mukētes*, pl. of *mukēs*, mushroom], *n.pl.* (*Biol.*) Microbes. **myceto-, myco-,** *comb. form.* **mycetology** [MYCOLOGY]. **mycetoma** (-tō′ mȧ), *n.* (*Path.*) A fungoid disease affecting the bones of the feet or hand. **mycetomatous,** *a.* **Mycetozoa** (-zō′ ȧ), *n.pl.* A group of fungoid organisms now usu. regarded as protophytes and included in the division. Myxomycetes.

myco- [MYCETO-], *comb. form.* **mycoderma** (mī kō dĕr′ mȧ) [DERM], *n.* A genus of fermentation-fungi including those that form the mother of vinegar. **mycology** (mī kol′ ȯ ji) [-LOGY], *n.* The science of fungi; a treatise on fungi. **mycological** (-loj′ ik ȧl), *a.* **mycologically,** *adv.* **mycologist** (-kol′ ȯ jist), *n.* **mycophagy** (-kof′ ȧ ji) [-PHAGY], *n.* Eating of fungi. **mycophagous** (-gŭs), *a.* **mycophagist** (-jist), *n.* **mycose** (mī′ kōs), *n.* (*Chem.*) A kind of sugar obtained from certain lichens and fungi. **mycorrhiza** (mī cō rī′ zȧ) [Gr. *rhiza*, a root], *n.* A fungoid growth supplying the roots of a plant with material from humus. **mycosis** (mī kō′ sis) [-OSIS], *n.* (*Path.*) The presence of parasitic fungi in the body. **mycotic** (-kot′ ik), *a.*

mydriasis (mī dri ā′ sis) [late L., from Gr. *mudriāsis*], *n.* (*Path.*) A normal dilatation of the pupil of the eye. **mydriatic** (-ăt′ ik), *a.*

myelitis (mī ė lī′ tis) [Gr. *muelon*, var. of *muelos*, marrow, -ITIS], *n.* (*Path.*) Inflammation of the spinal cord. **myelitic** (-lit′ ik), *a.* **myelasthenia** (-lăs thē′ ni ȧ), *n.* Spinal debility. **myelatrophia** (-lȧ trof′ i ȧ), *n.* Atrophy of the spinal cord. **myelo-,** *comb. form.* **myelomalacia** (-mȧ lā′ shi ȧ), *n.* Softening of the spinal marrow. **myelomeningitis** (-men in jī′ tis), *n.* Spinal meningitis. **myelon,** *n.* (*Anat.*) The spinal cord. **myelonal** (-el′ ȯ nȧl), *a.* **myelonic** (-lon′ ik), *a.*

mygale (mig′ ȧ lē) [Gr., field-mouse], *n.* (*Zool.*) A genus of large hairy South American spiders.

mylodon (mī′ lȯ don) [Gr. *mulē*, mill, *odous odontos*, tooth], *n.* (*Palæont.*) A genus of gigantic fossil sloth-like edentates. **mylodont,** *a.* and *n.*

mylohyoid (mī lȯ hī′ oid) [as prec., HYOID], *a.* (*Anat.*) Of or pertaining to the molar teeth and the hyoid bone. **mylohyoidean** (-oi′ dė ȧn), *a.* and *n.*

myna, mynah [MINA (2)].

mynheer (mīn hēr′, -hâr′) [Dut. *mijnheer*, Mr., Sir (*mijn*, my, *heer*, lord, master, cp. HERR)], *n.* A Dutchman.

myo- [Gr. *mūs muos*, muscle], *comb. form.* Pertaining to muscles. **myocarditis** (mī ȯ kar dī′ tis) [CARDITIS, see CARDIAC], *n.* (*Path.*) Inflammation of the myocardium. **myocardium** (-kar′ di ŭm), *n.* The muscular substance of the heart. **myodynamics** (-dī năm′ iks) [DYNAMICS], *n.* The science of muscular contraction. **myography** (-og′ rȧ fi) [-GRAPHY], *n.* A description of the muscles. **myographic, -al** (grăf′ ik, -ȧl), *a.* **myographist** (-og′ rȧ fist), *n.* **myology** (mī ol′ ȯ ji) [-LOGY], *n.* The science dealing with the muscles; a treatise on the muscles. **myologic, -al** (-loj′ ik, -ȧl), *a.* **myologist** (-ol′ ȯ jist), *n.*

myomancy (mī′ ȯ măn si) [Gr. *mūs*, MOUSE, -MANCY], *n.* Divination by the movements of mice. **myomantic** (-măn′ tik), *a.*

myope (mī′ ōp) [F., from late L. *myōps myōpis*, Gr. *muōps muōpos* (*muein*, to shut, *ōps*, *eye*)], *n.* A short-sighted person. **myopia** (-ō′ pi ȧ), **myopy** (mī′ ȯ pi), *n.* Short-sightedness. **myopic** (-op′ ik), *a.*

myosin (mī′ ȯ sin) [Gr. *mūs*, muscle, -IN], *n.* (*Chem.*) An albuminous compound in the contractile muscular tissue.

myosis (mī ōs′ is) [Gr. *muein*, shut], *n.* (*Path.*) Contraction of the eye-pupil.

myositis (mī ō sī′ tis), *n.* (*Path.*) Inflammation of a muscle.

myosotis (mī ō sō′ tis) [L., from Gr. *muosōtis* (*mūs muos*, MOUSE, *ous ōtos*, ear)], *n.* A genus of hardy plants comprising the forget-me-not. **myosote** (mī′ ō sōt), *n.* The forget-me-not.

myotomy (mī ot′ ō mi) [Gr. *mūs mous*, muscle, -TOMY], *n.* Dissection of muscles.

myriad (mir′ i ȧd) [med. L. *myrias -adis*, Gr. *mūrias -ados* (from *mūrios*, countless, *mūrioi*, ten thousand)], *a.* Innumerable, countless. *n.* Ten thousand; a very great number. **myriapod** (mir′ i ȧ pod) [Gr. *pous podos*, foot], *a.* Having numerous legs. *n.* One of the *Myriapoda*. **Myriapoda** (-ăp′ ō dȧ), *n.pl.* (*Zool.*) A class of Arthropoda, comprising the centipedes and millipedes, characterized by a very large indeterminate number of jointed feet.

Myrica (mi rī′ kȧ) [L., from Gr. *murikē*], *n.* The tamarisk; (*Bot.*) a Linnæan genus of plants comprising the bog-myrtle or sweet-gale. **myricin** (mi rī′-, mir′ i sin), *n.* (*Chem.*) The part of beeswax insoluble in boiling alcohol.

myriophyllous (mir i of′ i lŭs) [Gr. *mūrios*, see MYRIAD, *phullon*, leaf], *a.* (*Bot.*) Having many leaves.

myriorama (mir i ō răm′ ȧ, -ra′ mȧ) [as prec., Gr. *horama*, view], *n.* A kind of landscape kaleidoscope in which separate sections of views are combined in various ways.

myrioscope (mir′ i ō skōp), *n.* A variety of kaleidoscope giving multiple reflections, esp. a form used to show by means of a small piece how a whole carpet would look on a floor.

myristic (mī-, mi ris′ tik) [med. L. *myristica*, nutmeg, from Gr. *murizein*, to anoint], *a.* (*Chem.*) Applied to a fatty acid obtained from nutmeg oil and other vegetable and animal sources. **myristicin** (-ti sin), *n.* A colourless crystalline compound contained in oil of nutmeg.

Myrmidon (mĕr′ mi dŏn) [L., from Gr. *Murmidones*], *n.* One of a warlike people of Thessaly, ruled over by Achilles, and led by him to the siege of Troy; a faithful follower, esp. an unscrupulous underling. ***Myrmidonian** (-dō′ ni ȧn), *a.*

myrobalan (mī rob′ ȧ lăn) [F., from L. *myrobalanum*, Gr. *murobalanos* (*muron*, unguent, *balanos*, acorn)], *n.* The dried plum-like fruit of species of *Terminalia*, used in the East in calico-printing, and in England for dyeing and tanning; a variety of plum-tree largely used as a stock for budding.

myrrh (1) (mĕr) [A.-S. *myrre* or O.F. *mirre*, L. *myrrha*, Gr. *murra*, from Semitic (cp. Arab. *murr*, Heb. *mōr*)], *n.* A gum resin from *Balsamodendron myrrha* or other trees growing in Arabia and Abyssinia, used in the manufacture of incense, perfumes, etc. **myrrhic** (mĕr′-, mir′ ik), **myrrhy** (mĕr′ i), *a.*

myrrh (2) (mĕr) [late L. *myrrhis*, Gr. *murris*], *n.* An umbelliferous plant, *Myrrhis odorata*, also called sweet cicely.

myrrhine [MURRHINE].

myrtle (mĕr′ tėl) [O.F. *myrtille*, L. *myrtus*, Gr. *murtos*], *n.* A tree or shrub of the genus *Myrtus*, esp. *M. communis*, a tall shrub with glossy evergreen leaves and sweet-scented white or rose-coloured flowers, anciently sacred to Venus. **myrtle-berry**, *n.* **myrtle-wax**, *n.* A vegetable wax, from *Myrica cerifera*, also called bay-berry tallow. **myrtaceous** (-tā′ shŭs), *a.*

myself (mī-, mi self′), *pron.* Used in the nominative after 'I,' to express emphasis; in the objective reflexively.

mysophobia (mī sō fō′ bya) [Gr. *musos*, uncleanness; *phobos*, fear of, flight from], *n.* Fear of contamination; mania for cleanness.

mystagogue (mis′ tȧ gog) [L. *mystagōgus*, Gr. *mustagōgos* (*mustēs*, from *muein*, to close the eyes or lips, *agein*, to lead)], *n.* One who interprets or initiates into divine mysteries, esp. an initiator into the Eleusinian and other ancient Greek mysteries.

mystagogic, -al (-goj′ ik, -ȧl), *a.* **mystagogy** (mis′ tȧ goj i), *n.*

mystery (1) (mis′ tėr i) [prob. through an A.-F. *misterie*, O.F. *mistere* (F. *mystère*), L. *mystērium*, Gr. *mustērion*, as prec.], *n.* Something beyond human comprehension; a secret or obscure matter; secrecy, obscurity; a form of mediæval drama the characters and events of which were drawn from sacred history, a miracle-play; a divine truth partially revealed; (*pl.*) secret rites and ceremonies known to and practised only by the initiated; the esoteric rites practised by the ancient Greeks, Romans, etc.; the Eucharist. ***mysterial** (mis tēr′ i ȧl), *a.* ***mysteriarch**, *n.* One presiding over mysteries. **mysterious**, *a.* Not plain to the understanding; obscure, mystic, occult; fond of mystery. **mysteriously**, *adv.* **mysteriousness**, *n.*

***mystery** (2) (mis′ tėr i) [M.E. *mistere*, med. L. *misterium*, *ministerium*, MINISTRY], *n.* A handicraft, trade, or occupation.

mystic (mis′ tik) [O.F. *mystique*, L. *mysticus*, Gr. *mustikos*, as MYSTERY (1)], *a.* Pertaining to or involving mystery or mysticism; occult, esoteric; allegorical, emblematical. *n.* One addicted to mysticism; a supporter of the doctrine of mysticism. **mystical**, *a.* **mystically**, *adv.* ***mysticalness**, *n.*

mysticism (mis′ ti sizm), *n.* The doctrine that man may by self-surrender and spiritual apprehension attain to direct communion with and absorption in God, or that truth may be apprehended directly by the soul without the intervention of the senses and intellect. **mysticize**, *v.t.*

mystify (mis′ ti fī) [F. *mystifier* (as prec., -FY)], *v.t.* To involve in mystery; to bewilder, to puzzle, to hoax. **mystification** (-kā′ shŭn), *n.*

mystique (mis tēk′) [MYSTIC], *n.* Professional skill or technique that impresses the layman; the mystery surrounding some creeds, professions, etc.

mytacism (mī′ ti sizm) [med. L. *mytacismus*, Gr. *mutakismos* (*mû*, *μ*, m, -ISM)], *n.* The wrong use or too frequent repetition of the letter *m*, esp. in Latin composition before words beginning with a vowel.

myth (mith) [Gr. *muthos*, fable], *n.* A fictitious legend or tradition, accepted as historical, usu. embodying the beliefs of a people on the creation, the gods, the universe, etc.; a parable, an allegorical story; a fictitious event, person, thing, etc. **mythic, -al**, *a.* **mythically**, *adv.* **mythicism**, *n.* **mythicist**, *n.* **mythicize**, *v.t.* **mythicizer**, *n.* **mythico-**, **mytho-**, *comb. form.* **mythogenesis** (-jen′ ė sis), *n.* The creation or production of myths. **mythogony** (mi thog′ ō ni), *n.* The study of the origin of myths. **mythographer, -phist**, *n.* One who writes or narrates myths, fables, etc. **mythography**, *n.*

mythology (mī-, mi thol′ ō ji) [F. *mythologie*, late L. *mythologia*, Gr. *mūthologia* (MYTHO-, -LOGY)], *n.* A system of myths in which are embodied the beliefs of a people concerning their origin, deities, heroes, etc.; the science of myths, a treatise on myths. **mythologer, -gist** (-thol′ ō jėr, -jist), *n.* **mythologic, -al** (-loj′ ik, -ȧl), *a.* **mythologically**, *adv.* **mythologize** (mi thol′ ō jīz), *v.t.* and *i.* **mythometer** (-thom′ ė tėr), *n.* A standard for judging myths by. ***mythoplasm** (mith′ ō plăzm), *n.* A fabulous narration. **mythopœic** (-pē′ ik), **mythopoetic** (-pō et′ ik) [Gr. *mūthopoios* (*poiein*, to make)], *a.* Myth-making; pertaining to a stage of culture when myths were developed. **mythus** (mī′ thŭs) [MYTH].

mytilus (mī′ ti lŭs) [L.], *n.* A genus of bivalves containing the marine mussels. **mytilite**, *n.* (*Geol.*) A fossil mussel. **mytiloid**, *a.* and *n.*

myxo- [Gr. *muxa*, slime, mucus], *comb. form.* Pertaining to or living in slime; pertaining to or consisting of mucus.

myxoedema (mik si dē′ mȧ), *n.* (*Path.*) A cretinous disease characterized by atrophy of the thyroid gland and conversion of the connective tissue throughout the body into gelatinous matter. **myxoedematous**, *a.*

myxoma (mik sō′ mȧ), *n.* (*pl.* **myxomata**) (*Path.*) A tumour composed of mucous tissue.

myxomatosis (mik sō mȧ tō′ sis), *n.* A contagious and fatal virus disease in rabbits.

Myxomycetes (mik sō mī sē′ tēz), *n.pl.* The slime moulds or fungi, a group of organisms by some regarded as belonging to the *Mycetozoa*, by others as related to the fungi.

myxopod (miks′ ō pod), *n.* A protozoan having pseudopodia.

myxosarcoma (mik sō sar kō′ mȧ), *n.* (*Path.*) A tumour consisting of myxomatous and sarcomatous tissue.

Myzontes (mī zon′ tēz) [Gr. *muzontes*, pl. pres.p. of *muzein*, to suck], *n.pl.* (*Zool.*) A class of vertebrates characterized by an incomplete cartilaginous skull, no lower jaw, and pouch-like gills, comprising the lampreys and hags.

N

N, n (en), the fourteenth letter and eleventh consonant (*pl.* **Ns, N's, Ens**) is a dentilingual nasal, and its ordinary sound is heard in *not*, *ton*, but before *g* or *k* it often has a sound almost equivalent to *ng*, as in *sink*, *link*; (*Print.*) *n*, *en*, a unit of measurement; (*Math.*) an indefinite number.

na (na) (*Sc.*) [NO (1)].

Naafi (nă′ fi) [initials of the Navy, Army, and Air Force Institutes], *n.* An organization for supplying the Services with canteens.

nab (1) (năb) [cp. Norw. and Swed. *nappa*, Dan. *nappe*], *v.t.* (*slang*) (*past & p.p.* **nabbed**) To catch, to seize, to apprehend.

nab (2) (nab) [Icel. *nabbr*, *nabbi*, Norw. *dial. nabb*, *nabbe*, Swed. *nabb*], *n.* (*chiefly North. and Sc.*) A rocky or projecting hill or part of a hill; a projection on the bolt of a lock or the keeper into which the bolt catches.

nabob (nā′ bob) [NAWAB], *n.* A deputy-governor or prince under the Mogul empire in India; (*fig.*) a very rich man, esp. one who amassed wealth in India.

nacarat (năk′ ȧ răt) [F., from Sp. and Port. *nacarado*, from *nacar*, NACRE], *n.* A pale-red colour tinged with orange; a fine linen or crape dyed this colour.

nacelle (na sel′) [F., from late L. *nāvicella*, dim. of *nāvis*, ship], *n.* The basket suspended from a balloon; a small, streamlined body on an aircraft, distinct from the fuselage, housing engines, crew, etc.

nache [NATCH].

nacket (năk′ ėt) [Sc. and North., var. of *nocket*, etym. doubtful], *n.* A snack, a light luncheon; a small cake.

nacre (nā′ kėr) [F., from Sp. and Port. *nacar* (cp. Arab. *naqrah*, a cavity)], *n.* The pinna, sea-pen, or other fish yielding mother-of-pearl; mother-of-pearl. **nacreous, nacrous,** *a.* **nacrite,** *n.* (*Min.*) A pearly variety of mica.

nadir (nā′ dir) [Arab., opposite to (the zenith)], *n.* The point of the heavens directly opposite to the zenith or directly under our feet; (*fig.*) the lowest point or stage (of decline, degradation, etc.).

nævus (nē′ vůs) [L.], *n.* (*pl.* **-vi**) (*Path.*) A congenital discoloration of the skin, a mother's mark, a birth-mark. ***næve,** *n.* **nævoid, nævose, nævous,** *a.*

nag (1) (năg) [etym. doubtful], *n.* A small horse or pony for riding; (*colloq.*) a horse.

nag (2) (năg) [perh. from Scand. (cp. Norw. and Swed. *nagga*, Dan. *nage*, Icel. *gnaga*, to gnaw)], *v.i.* (*past & p.p.* **nagged**) To be continually finding fault; to scold (at). *v.t.* To find fault with or scold continually; to be continually pestering with complaints or fault-finding. **nagger,** *n.* **naggish, naggy,** *a.*

Nagari [DEVANAGARI].

nagor (nā′ gȯr) [arbitrary name, by Buffon], *n.* A small brown antelope from Senegal.

naiad (nā′ ăd, nī′ ăd) [L. and Gr. *naiad-*, nom. *naias*, from *naiein*, to flow], *n.* (*pl.* **-ads**) A water-nymph. **naiades** (nā′-, nī′ ȧ dēz) [L. and Gr., pl.], *n.pl.* Water-nymphs; (*Bot.*) an order of aquatic plants; (*Zool.*) a family of freshwater shell-fish.

naiant (nā′ ȧnt) [prob. through an A.-F. *naiant* (O.F. *noiant*, pres.p. of *noier*), L. *natāre*, to swim], *a.* (*Her.*) Swimming, natant.

naif [NAÏVE].

nail (nāl) [A.-S. *nægel* (cp. Dut. and G. *nagel*, Icel. *nagl*), cogn. with L. *unguis*, Gr. *onux*], *n.* The horny substance at the tip of the human fingers and toes; a claw, a talon; a horny plate on the soft bill of certain birds; a measure of 2¼ inches; a pointed spike, usu. of metal, with a head, for hammering into wood or other material to fasten things together, or for use as a peg etc. *v.t.* To fasten or secure with nails; to stud with nails; (*fig.*) to hold, to fix; to seize, to catch; to engage (attention); to clinch (a bargain); (*slang*) to nab, to steal; *to spike (a gun). **hard as nails:** (*colloq.*) In a hard state of training. **on the nail:** On the spot; at once. **right as nails:** (*colloq.*) Perfectly right. **to hit the nail on the head:** To hit upon the true facts of a case; to do exactly the right thing. **to nail to the counter** or **barn-door:** To expose, to brand as spurious. **to nail up:** To close or fasten up by nailing; to fix at a height with nails. **nailed,** *a.* (*usu. in comb.*, as *long-nailed*, *nailed-on*). **nail-brush,** *n.* A small brush for cleaning the finger-nails. **nail-head,** *n.* (*Arch.*) An ornament on late Norman and Early English mouldings, shaped like the head of a nail. **nail-headed,** *a.* **nailrod,** *n.* (*Austral.*) A coarse tobacco. **nailer,** *n.* A maker of nails; (*slang*) a fine specimen, one who is first-rate (at). **nailery,** *n.* **nailing,** *a.* (*slang*) First-rate.

nain (nān) [Sc., corr. of MINE OWN], *a.* One's own. **nainsell,** *n.* One's own self.

nainsook (nān′ suk) [Hind. *nainsukh* (*nain*, eye, *sukh*, pleasure)], *n.* A thick muslin or jaconet, formerly made in India.

naissant (nā′ sȧnt) [F., pres.p. of *naître*, ult. from L. *nascī*, to be born], *a.* (*Her.*) Rising or coming forth, as from a fesse or other ordinary.

naïve (na ēv′) [F., fem. of *naïf*, L. *nātīvus*, NATIVE], *a.* Artless, ingenuous, simple, unaffected. **naïvely,** *adv.* **naïveté** (-tā), *n.*

naja (nā′ jȧ, -yȧ) [mod. L. from Hind. *nāg*], *n.* A genus of venomous snakes comprising the Indian and the African cobra.

naked (nā′ kėd) [A.-S. *nacod* (cp. Dut. *naakt*, G. *nackt*, Swed. *naken*, Dan. *nögen*), cogn. with L. *nūdus*], *a.* Destitute of clothing, uncovered, nude; without natural covering, as leaves, hair, shell, etc.; not sheathed; exposed, unsheltered, defenceless, unarmed, stripped, destitute, devoid (of); unfurnished; not ornamented; bare, plain, undisguised; unsupported, uncorroborated, unconfirmed; unassisted, as without a telescope (of the eye). ***naked-bed,** *n.* A bed the occupant of which is naked. **naked eye:** The eye unassisted by any optical instrument. **naked lady:** The meadow saffron, *Colchicum autumnale*. **nakedly,** *adv.* **nakedness,** *n.*

***naker** (nā′ kėr) [O.F. *nacre*, *nacaire*, Arab. *naqārah*], *n.* A kind of kettle-drum.

***namable** [NAMEABLE, see NAME].

namby-pamby (năm′ bi păm′ bi) [from *Ambrose* Philips (1671–1749), a sentimental, pastoral poet], *a.* Weakly and insipidly sentimental; affectedly pretty or simple. *n.* Namby-pamby talk or writing. **namby-pambyism,** *n.*

name (nām) [A.-S. *nama* (cp. Dut. *naam*, G. *name*, Icel. *nafn*, Sansk. *nāman*, L. *nōmen*, Gr. *onoma*), whence A.-S. *genamian*, *nemnan*], *n.* A word denoting any object of thought, esp. that by which a person, animal, place, or thing is known, spoken of, or addressed; a mere term as distinct from substance, sound, or appearance, as opp. to reality; (*fig.*) reputation, honourable character, fame, glory; authority, countenance; *a race, a family; *a noun. *v.t.* To give a name to, to call, to style; to call by name; to nominate, to appoint; to mention, to specify, to cite. **by name:** Called. **give it a name:** Mention what you will have (to drink, as a present, etc.). **in the name of:** By the authority of; in reliance upon (esp. as an invocation); under the designation of. **to call names** [CALL (1)]. **to name the day:** (*colloq.*) To fix the date for her wedding (of a woman). **to take a name in vain:** To use it profanely. **name-child,** *n.* A child or person named after one. **name-day,** *n.* The day sacred to a saint after whom one is named. **name-sake,** *n.* A person or thing having the same name as or named after another. **nameable,** *a.* **name-less,** *a.* Having no name; anonymous; illegitimate, unknown, obscure, inglorious; inexpressible, indefinable; unfit to be named, abominable, detestable. **namelessly,** *adv.* **namely,** *adv.* That is to say. **namer,** *n.*

namma hole (năm' ȧ hōl) [Austral. abor.], *n.* A native well.

nancy (năn' si) [etym. doubtful], *n.* An effeminate young man; a homosexual.

nandine (năn' din) [prob. native name], *n.* A small West African paradoxure.

nanism (nā' nizm) [F. *nanisme* (L. *nānus*, Gr. *nānos*, dwarf)], *n.* Dwarfishness; being stunted. **naniza-tion** (-zā' shŭn), *n.*

nankeen (năn kēn') [*Nankin*, capital of province of Kiangsu, China], *n.* A cotton fabric, usu. of a buff or yellow colour, exported from Nankin; a fabric made in imitation of this; (*pl.*) clothes, esp. trousers, made of this.

nanny (năn' i) [dim. of Anne], *n.* A children's nurse.

nannygai (năn' i gī) [Austral. abor.], *n.* An edible red fish found in Australian rivers.

nanny-goat (năn' i gōt) [*Nanny*, fem. name], *n.* A she-goat.

nap (1) (năp) [A.-S. *hnæppian* (cp. O.H.G. *hnaffezan*)], *v.i.* To sleep lightly or briefly, to doze; (*fig.*) to be careless or unprepared. *n.* A short sleep, a doze, esp. in the day-time. **to catch napping:** To take unawares; to catch unprepared or at a disadvantage.

nap (2) (năp) [prob. from M.Dut. or M.L.G. *noppe* (cp. Dut. *nop*, Dan. *noppe*, Norw. *napp*)], *n.* The smooth and even surface produced on cloth or other fabric by cutting and smoothing the fibre or pile; a smooth, woolly, downy, or hairy growth on a surface. *v.t.* To put a nap on. **napless,** *a.*

nap (3) (năp) [short for NAPOLEON], *n.* A card-game in which five cards are dealt to each player, the one engaging to take the highest number of tricks playing against the others; (*Racing*) a tip claimed to be a certainty. **to go nap:** To offer to take all five tricks.

***nap** (4) [NAB (1)].

napalm (năp' am), *n.* A highly inflammable petroleum jelly produced from naphthalene and coconut palm oil, largely used for bombs.

nape (nāp) [etym. doubtful], *n.* The back of the neck.

napery (nā' pėr i) [O.F. *naperie*, *napperie*, from *nape*, *nappe*, L. *mappa*, NAPKIN], *n.* Linen, esp. table-linen; *linen underclothing. ***naperer,** *n.*

naphtha (năf' thȧ) [L. and Gr.], *n.* An inflammable oil produced by dry distillation of organic substances, as bituminous shale or coal. **naph-thalic** (năf thăl' ik), *a.* (*Chem.*) **naphthaline** (năf' thȧ lin), *n.* A white crystalline product of the dry distillation of coal-tar, used as a disinfectant and in the manufacture of dyes and explosives. **naphthalize,** *v.t.* **naphthene,** *n.* A liquid hydrocarbon obtained from Caucasian naphtha. **naph-thol,** *n.* (*Chem.*) Either of two phenols derived from naphthaline. **naphthylamine** [AMINE], *n.*

Napier's bones (nā pērz', nā' pērz bōnz) [John *Napier* of Merchiston (1550–1617)], *n.pl.* A contrivance invented by Napier for facilitating the multiplication and division of high numbers by means of slips of bone or other material divided into compartments. **Naperian** (nā pēr' i ȧn), *a.*

napiform (nā' pi fôrm) [L. *nāpus*, turnip, -FORM], *a.* (*Bot.*) Turnip-shaped.

napkin (năp' kin) [M.E. *nappekyn* (F. *nappe*, see NAPERY)], *n.* A small cloth usu. of linen, esp. one used at table to wipe the hands etc., protect the clothes, or serve fish, etc., on; a serviette; a small towel; a handkerchief. **table-napkin,** *n.* **napkin-ring,** *n.* A ring used to enclose a table-napkin and indicate the owner.

napless [NAP (2)].

Naples yellow (nā' pėlz yel' ō) [*Naples*, city in S. Italy], *n.* A yellow pigment made from antimony; the colour of this.

napoleon (nȧ pō' lė ȯn), *n.* A French gold coin of 20 francs issued by Napoleon I; a variety of top-boot; a card-game [see NAP (3)].

Napoleonic (nȧ pō lė on' ik), *a.* Resembling Napoleon I; dominating, masterful; spectacular. **Napoleonically,** *adv.* **Napoleonism,** *n.* Belief in the hereditary claims of the Napoleonic dynasty; belief in autocracy. **Napoleonist,** *n.* **Napoleon-ize,** *v.t.*

nappy (1) [NAP.].

nappy (2) (năp' i) [prob. from NAP (1)], *a.* Foaming, strong, heady (of ale or beer). *n.* Ale, liquor.

nappy (3) (năp' i) [NAPKIN], *n.* A square of towelling used hygienically for small babies, (*Am.* a diaper).

narceine (nar' sė in, -īn) [F. *narcéine*, Gr. *narkē*, numbness, torpor, -INE], *n.* (*Chem.*) A bitter crystalline alkaloid contained in opium after the extraction of morphine, also called **narceia** (nar sē' ȧ).

narcissism (nar sis' izm) [Narcissus, in Gr. myth. a beautiful youth who fell in love with his own reflection], *n.* (*Psych.*) A state of self-love present at an early stage of development when one's own body rather than an outside love-object furnishes sensual gratification.

narcissus (nar sis' ŭs) [L., from Gr. *Narkissos*, perh. rel. to prec.], *n.* (*pl.* **-es, -i**) A genus of ornamental bulbous plants, containing the daffodils and jonquils; a plant of this genus, esp. the white *N. poeticus*.

narcolepsy (nar kȯ lep' si) [Gr. *narkē*, torpor, *-lepsy* (see EPILEPSY)], *n.* (*Path.*) A nervous disease characterized by fits of irresistible drowsiness.

narcomania (nar kō măn' i ȧ) [Gr. *narkē*, torpor], *n.* (*Path.*) A morbid craving for, or insanity resulting from, narcotics.

narcosis (nar kō' sis) [Gr., from *narkoun*, to benumb, as prec., -OSIS], *n.* (*Path.*) Narcotic poisoning, the effect of continuous use of narcotics; a state of stupor.

narcotic (nar kot' ik) [as prec.], *a.* Producing torpor or coma; soporific; (*fig.*) causing sleep or dullness. *n.* (*Med.*) A substance that allays pain by inducing sleep or torpor. **narcotically,** *adv.* **narcoticism,** **narcotism,** *n.* **narcotist,** *n.* **narcotize,** *v.t.* **narcotization,** *n.* **narco-therapy,** *n.* The treatment of mental disorder by drug-induced sleep.

nard (nard) [F., from L. *nardus*, Gr. *nardos*, of Oriental orig. (cp. Heb. *nērd*, Sansk. *narada*, *nalada*)], *n.* An unguent or balsam used by the

N

ancients, prepared from an aromatic plant, spikenard. ***nardine,** *a.*

nardoo (nar doo′) [abor. Austral.], *n.* (*Bot.*) An Australian plant, *Marsilea Drummondii*, the spore-case of which is pounded and eaten by the Aborigines.

nares (nâr′ ēz) [L.], *n.pl.* The nostrils.

narghile (nar′ gi lā) [Pers. *nārgīleh*, from *nārgīl*, coco-nut], *n.* A hookah or tobacco-pipe in which the smoke is drawn through water.

nark (nark) [Romany *nak*, nose], *n.* (*slang*) A police spy, a decoy.

narrate (nȧ rāt′) [L. *narrātus*, p.p. of *narrāre* (prob. cogn. with *gnārus*, aware, and Eng. KNOW)], *v.t.* To tell, to relate, to give an account of the successive particulars of in speech or writing. **narration** (-rā′ shŭn), *n.* **narrative** (năr′ ȧ tiv), *a.* In the form of narration; relating to an event or story. *n.* A recital of a series of events; a tale, a story. **narratively,** *adv.* **narrator** (nȧ rā′ tŏr), *n.* **narratress,** *n.*

narrow (năr′ ō) [A.-S. *nearu* (cp. Dut. *naar*, dismal)], *a.* Of little breadth or extent from side to side; constricted, limited, restricted, of limited scope; illiberal in views or sentiments; prejudiced, bigoted; selfish, niggardly; straitened, impoverished; close, near, within a small distance, with little margin; precise, accurate. *v.t.* To make narrow or narrower; to contract in range, views, or sentiments; to confine, to limit, to restrict. *v.i.* To become narrow or narrower; to take too little ground (said of a horse). *n.* (*usu. pl.*) A strait; a narrow mountain-pass; the contracted part of an ocean current. **narrow circumstances:** Poverty. **narrow cloth:** Cloth, esp. woollen, under 52 inches in width. **narrow gauge:** A railway gauge of less than 4 ft. 8½ in. **narrow goods:** Braid, ribbons. **narrow-minded,** *a.* Illiberal, bigoted. **narrow-mindedness,** *n.* **narrowly,** *adv.* **narrowness,** *n.*

narthex (nar′ theks) [Gr. *narthēx*, a plant], *n.* (*Arch.*) A vestibule or porch across the west end in early Christian churches, to which catechumens, women, and penitents were admitted.

narwhal (nar′ wȧl) [Dan. or Swed. *narhval* (cp. Icel. *nāhvalr*)], *n.* An Arctic delphinoid cetacean, *Monodon monoceros*, with a long tusk (or tusks) developed from one (or both) of its teeth.

nasal (nā′ zȧl) [F., from med. L. *nāsālis* (*nāsus*, nose)], *a.* Of or pertaining to the nose; sounded or produced with the nasal passage open; pronounced through or as if through the nose. *n.* A letter or sound produced with the nasal passage open; a nose-guard. **nasality** (nȧ zăl′ i ti), *n.* **nasalize** (nā′ zȧ līz), *v.t.* **nasalization** (-zā′ shŭn), *n.* **nasally,** *adv.* **nasicorn** (nā′ zi kôrn), *a.* Having a horn or horns on the nose (as the rhinoceros). **nasiform,** *a.* **naso-** (*Anat. and Path.*), *comb. form.* **naso-bronchial** (nā zō brong′ ki ȧl) [BRONCHIAL], *a.* Pertaining to or involving the nasal and the bronchial tubes. **naso-frontal** (-frŭn′ tȧl), *a.* **naso-labial** (-lā′ bi ȧl) [LABIAL], *a.* **naso-lachrymal** (-lăk′ ri mȧl) [LACHRYMAL], *a.* **nasorbital** (nā zôr′ bi tȧl), *a.* Of or pertaining to the nose and the ocular orbit.

Nasalis (nȧ sā′ lis) [NASAL], *n.* (*Zool.*) The genus comprising *Semnopithecus nasalis*, the proboscis monkey.

nascent (năs′ ȇnt) [L. *nascens -ntis*, pres.p. of *nascī*, to be born], *a.* Coming into being; beginning to develop; immature. **nascency,** *n.*

naseberry (nāz′ ber i) [Sp. or Port. *nespera*, L. *mespila*, Gr. *mespilē*, MEDLAR], *n.* The sapodilla.

naso- [NASAL].

nasturtium (nȧ stĕr′ shŭm) [L. (*nās-us*, *tort-*, stem of *torquēre*, to TORMENT)], *n.* (*pl.* **-ums**) A genus of *Cruciferæ* containing the watercress; a trailing plant of the genus *Tropæolum* with vivid orange flowers, also called Indian cress.

nasty (nas′ ti) [cp. Dut. *nestig*, Swed. dial. *naskug*], *a.* Dirty, foul, filthy to a repulsive degree; indecent, obscene; repellent to taste, smell, etc., nauseous; objectionable, annoying, vexatious; spiteful, odious, vicious, unpleasant, awkward, trying. **nastily,** *adv.* **nastiness,** *n.*

natal (1) (nā tȧl) [F., from L. *nātālis*, from *nātus*, p.p. of *nascī*, to be born], *a.* Of, from, or pertaining to one's birth. ***natalitial** (-lish′ i ȧl), *a.* **natality** (-tăl′ i ti), *n.*

natal (2) (nā′ tȧl) [NATES], *a.* (*Anat.*) Pertaining to the buttocks.

natant (nā′ tȧnt) [L. *natans -ntem*, pres.p. of *natāre*, freq. of *nāre*, to swim], *a.* Swimming; (*Bot.*) floating; (*Her.*) applied to fish represented as swimming. ***natantly,** *adv.* **natation** (nȧ tā′ shŭn), *n.* **natatores** (nā tȧ tôr′ ēz), *n.pl.* (*Zool.*) An order of birds containing the gulls, divers, ducks, etc. **natatorial** (-tôr′ i ȧl), **natatory** (nā′-), *a.*

natch (năch) [var. of *nache*, see AITCHBONE], *n.* The part of an ox between the loins, the rump.

nates (nā′ tēz) [L.], *n.pl.* (*Anat.*) The buttocks; the anterior pair of lobes in the brain, connected with the optic tracts. **natiform,** *a.* Having the form of buttocks.

***natheless, *nathless** [NEVERTHELESS].

nation (nā′ shŭn) [F., from L. *nātiōnem*, nom. *-tio*, from *nāt-*, see NATAL (1)], *n.* A people under the same government and inhabiting the same country; a people belonging to the same ethnological family and speaking the same language; (*Aberdeen, Glasgow, and mediæv. Univ.*) a body of students from the same country or district; *a family; *a kingdom or country. **national** (năsh′ ŏ nȧl), *a.* Of or pertaining to the nation, esp. to the whole nation; public, general, as opp. to local; peculiar to a nation; attached to one's country. *n.* A member or subject of a particular nation; one's fellow-countryman. **national anthem:** A hymn or song embodying the patriotic sentiments of a nation, as the Eng. 'God Save the King,' the French 'Marseillaise,' etc. **National Assembly** [CONSTITUENT ASSEMBLY]. **National Defence Contribution,** *n.* (*Fin.*) A tax introduced in 1937 to help to finance the cost of rearmament. **national service:** Compulsory service in the armed forces. **National Socialism,** *n.* The political doctrine of the National Socialist German Workers Party, which came into power in Germany under Adolf Hitler in 1933. Prominent among its teachings were the superiority of the German race, hatred of Jews, and a need for world-expansion. **nationalism,** *n.* Devotion to the nation, esp. the whole nation as opp. to sectionalism; nationalization of industry; the policy of national independence, esp. in Ireland; patriotic effort, sentiment, etc. **nationality** (-năl′ i ti), ***nationalness,** *n.* **nationalize,** *v.t.* **nationalization** (-zā′ shŭn), *n.* **nationally,** *adv.* **nationhood** (nā′-), *n.*

native (nā′ tiv) [L. *nātīvus*, as prec.], *a.* Pertaining to a place or country by birth, indigenous not exotic; belonging to a person, animal, or thing, by nature; inborn, innate, natural not acquired; pertaining to the time or place of one's birth; *rightful, hereditary; natural (to); plain, simple, unaffected; occurring in a pure or uncombined state (of metals); raised in British waters (of oysters); of or pertaining to the natives of a place or region. *n.* One born in a place; a produce of a place or country; a plant or animal indigenous to a district or country; (*Austral.*) a white born in Australia; (freq.) a coloured person; an oyster raised in British waters, esp. in an artificial bed; *natural source. **natively,** *adv.* **nativeness,** *n.* **nativism,** *n.* (*U.S.A.*) Advocacy of the rights of natives as opp. to naturalized Americans; (*Phil.*) the doctrine of innate ideas.

nativity (nȧ tiv′ i ti) [as prec.], *n.* Birth, esp. that of Jesus Christ, the Virgin, or St. John the Baptist; a festival in commemoration of this; a picture of the birth of Christ; a horoscope.

NATO (nā′ tō) [acronym North Atlantic Treaty

Organization] *n.* (*Pol.*) A treaty for mutual defence, dating from 1949, adhered to by Belgium, Britain, Canada, Denmark, France, Holland, Iceland, Italy, Luxemburg, Norway, Portugal, U.S.A. and later by Greece, Turkey, and Western Germany.

natron (nā′ trŏn, năt′ rŏn) [F. and Sp., from Arab. *natrūn, nitrūn,* Gr. *nitron,* NITRE], *n.* Native sesquicarbonate of soda. ***natrium,** *n.* Sodium. **natrolite,** *n.* (*Min.*) A hydrated silicate of aluminium containing much soda.

natter (năt′ ėr) [etym. doubtful], *v.i.* (*prov.*) To find fault, to be peevish; to chatter idly. **nattered,** *a.* **natteredness,** *n.*

natterjack (năt′ ėr jăk) [etym. doubtful], *n.* A European toad, *Bufo calamita,* with a yellow stripe down the back.

natty (năt′ i) [etym. doubtful], *a.* Neat, tidy, spruce. **nattily,** *adv.* **nattiness,** *n.*

natural (năt′ yŭr ăl, năch′ ŭr ăl) [L. *nātūrālis* (NATURE, -AL)], *a.* Of, pertaining to, produced, or constituted by nature; innate, inherent, uncultivated, not artificial; inborn, instinctive; in conformity with the ordinary course of nature, normal, not irregular, exceptional, or supernatural; pertaining to physical things, animal, not spiritual; true to life; unaffected, not forced or exaggerated; undisguised; ordinary, to be expected, not surprising; coming by nature, easy (to); related by nature only, illegitimate; concerned with nature; concerned with animal life; (*Mus.*) applied to the diatonic scale of C; (*Theol.*) unregenerate. *adv.* Naturally. *n.* An idiot; (*Mus.*) a sign cancelling the effect of a preceding sharp or flat; a certainty, something by its very nature certain. **natural history:** The science or study of animal life, zoology; the study or description of the earth and its productions, loosely applied to botany, zoology, geology, and mineralogy. **natural law:** The sense of right and wrong implanted by nature; a law governing the operations of physical life etc. **natural order:** (*Bot.*) An order of plants in a system of classification based on the nature of their sexual organs or their natural affinities. **natural philosophy:** Physics. **natural religion,** *n.* Religion not depending upon revelation. **natural scale:** (*Mus.*) A scale without sharps or flats. **natural science:** The science of physical things as distinguished from mental and moral science; natural history. **natural selection:** The process by which plants and animals best fitted for the conditions in which they are placed survive, while the less fitted die out. **natural theology:** Theology based on principles established by reason, not derived from revelation. **naturalness,** *n.*

naturalism (năt′ ū ră lizm, năch′ ū ră lizm) [as prec.], *n.* A mere state of nature; condition or action based on natural instincts; a philosophical or theological system that explains the universe as produced and governed entirely by physical laws; strict adherence to nature in literature and art, realism.

naturalist (năt′ ū ră list, năch′ ū ra list), *n.* One versed in natural history; (*Phil., etc.*) a believer in naturalism; a realist as distinct from an idealist. **naturalistic** (-lis′ tik), *a.* In accordance with nature; realistic, not conventional or ideal; of or pertaining to natural history. **naturalistically,** *adv.*

naturalize (năt′ ū ră līz, năch′ ū ră līz), *v.t.* To make natural; to adopt; to acclimatize; to confer the rights and privileges of a natural-born subject on; to explain by natural laws, to free from the miraculous. *v.i.* To become naturalized; to explain phenomena by naturalistic reasoning; to study natural history. **naturalization** (-zā′ shŭn), *n.*

naturally (năt′ ū ră li, năch′ ū ră li), *adv.* According to nature; spontaneously; as might be expected, of course.

nature (nā′ tyŭr, -chŭr) [F., from L. *nātūra,* from *nāt-,* p.p. stem of *nasci,* to be born], *n.* The essential qualities of anything; the physical or psychical constitution of a person or animal; natural character or disposition; kind, sort, class; the inherent energy or impulse determining these; vital or animal force; the whole sum of things, forces, activities, and laws constituting the physical universe; the physical power that produces the phenomena of the material world; this personified; the sum of physical things and forces regarded as distinct from man; the material universe regarded as distinct from the supernatural or from a creator; the natural condition of man preceding social organization; the undomesticated condition of animals or plants; unregenerate condition as opp. to a state of grace; nakedness; fidelity to nature in art. **by nature:** Innately. **from nature:** Directly from the living model or natural landscape. **in nature:** In actual existence; anywhere, at all; in the sphere of possibility. **state of nature,** *n.* Nudity. **nature-myth,** *n.* A myth symbolizing some natural phenomenon. **nature-printing,** *n.* A process by which impressions are produced from natural objects such as leaves, feathers, etc. on a metal plate from which prints may then be made. **nature-worship,** *n.* Worship of natural objects or phenomena or of the powers of nature. **natured,** *a.* (*usu. in comb.* as *ill-natured.*) **naturism,** *n.* Nature-worship; naturalism in religion; nudism; (*Med.*) belief in the sanative work of nature. **naturist,** *n.* **naturistic** (-is′ tik), *a.* ***naturize,** *v.t.*

naught (nawt) [A.-S. *nāwiht* (*nā,* NO, *wiht,* WHIT)], *n.* Nothing; a cipher. *a.* Worthless; *bad, wicked; *lost, ruined. *adv.* In no degree. **to set at naught:** To disregard.

naughty (naw′ ti) [prec.], *a.* Perverse, mischievous; disobedient, ill-behaved; disagreeable; *worthless; *wicked. **naughtily,** *adv.* **naughtiness,** *n.*

naumachia (naw măk′ i ȧ), **naumachy** (naw′ mȧ ki) [L. and Gr. *naumachia* (*naus,* ship, *machē,* a battle)], *n.* A naval combat, esp. a mock battle shown as a spectacle; an artificial basin for the production of this.

nauplius (naw′ pli ŭs) [L., from Gr. *Nauplios,* son of Poseidon], *n.* (*pl.* **-plii**) (*Zool.*) A larval stage of development in certain of the lower crustaceans. **nauplial, naupliiform, nauplioid,** *a.*

nausea (naw′ shi ȧ, -si ȧ) [L., from Gr. *naus,* ship], *n.* A feeling of sickness, with a propensity to vomit; loathing; sea-sickness. ***nauseant,** *a.* and *n.* **nauseate,** *v.i.* To feel nausea; to turn away in disgust (at). *v.t.* To cause to feel nausea; to reject with loathing. **nauseating,** *a.* Causing nausea. **nauseation** (-ā′ shŭn), *n.* **nauseous,** *a.* **nauseously,** *adv.* **nauseousness,** *n.*

nautch (nawch) [Hind. *nach*], *n.* An East Indian exhibition of dancing by girls. **nautch-girl,** *n.*

nautical (naw′ ti kăl) [L. *nauticus,* Gr. *nautikos,* from *nautēs,* sailor, from *naus,* ship], *a.* Pertaining to ships, navigation, or sailors; naval. **nautically,** *adv.* **Nautical Almanac,** *n.* An astronomical ephemeris published in advance, for use by navigators and astronomers. **nautical mile** [MILE].

nautilus (naw′ ti lŭs) [L., from Gr. *nautilos,* a seaman, as prec.], *n.* (*pl.* **-li**) A genus of cephalopods comprising the pearly nautilus, with a many-chambered shell (the outermost and last-formed of which is occupied by the living animal), and the paper nautilus or argonaut; a diving-bell requiring no suspension. **nautilite,** *n.* (*Geol.*) **nautiloid,** *a.* and *n.*

naval (nā′ văl) [F., from L. *nāvālis,* from *nāvis,* a ship], *a.* Consisting of or pertaining to ships or a navy; fought or won by war-ships or navies. **navally,** *a.*

nave (1) (nāv) [A.-S. *nafu* (cp. Dut. *naaf,* G. *nabe,* Icel. *nöf,* Dan. *nav,* Swed. *naf*), cp. NAVEL], *n.* The central block of a wheel in which the axle and spokes are inserted, the hub; *the navel.

nave (2) (nāv) [L. *nāvis,* ship (cp. Gr. *naus*)], *n.* The body of a church, extending from the main doorway to the choir or chancel, distinct, and usually separated by pillars, from the aisles.

navel (nā′ vėl) [A.-S. *nafela* (cp. Dut. *navel*, G. *nabel*, Icel. *nafli*, Dan. *navle*), cogn. with NAVE (1), cp. Sansk. *nābhīla*, Gr. *omphalos*, L. *umbilicus*], *n.* The cicatrix of the umbilical cord, forming a depression on the surface of the abdomen. **navel-string,** *n.* The umbilical cord. **navelwort,** *n.* Applied to the marsh pennywort, *Cotyledon umbilicus*, and other plants.

navew (nā′ vū) [M.F. *naveau*, L. *nāpellum*, *-lus*, dim. of *nāpus*, turnip], *n.* The wild turnip or rape, *Brassica campestris*.

navicert (nā′ vi sěrt), *n.* A certificate authorizing the passage in war-time of approved seaborne merchandise to neutral ports.

navicular (nȧ vik′ ū lȧr) [late L. *nāviculāris*, from *nāvicula*, dim. of *nāvis*, ship], *a.* Pertaining to small ships or boats; (*Bot.*, *Anat.*, *etc.*) shaped like a boat; (*Anat.*) pertaining to the navicular bone. *n.* The navicular bone; inflammation of the navicular bone in horses. **navicular bone:** The scaphoid bone of the foot or (rarely) the hand. **naviculoid,** *a.*

navigate (năv′ i gāt) [L. *nāvigātus*, p.p. of *nāvigāre* (*nāvis*, ship, *agere*, to drive)], *v.i.* To sail, to pass from place to place by water or air; to manage a ship. *v.t.* To pass over or up or down, in a ship etc.; to manage, to conduct (a ship, flying-machine, etc.). **navigable,** *a.* **navigability** (-bil′ i ti), *n.* **navigableness,** *n.* **navigably,** *adv.* **navigation** (-gā′ shŭn), *n.* The act, art, or science of navigating; (*prov.*) a canal or waterway. **navigator** (năv′ i gā tȯr), *n.* One who navigates; one skilled in navigation; an explorer by sea; a navvy.

navvy (năv′ i) [short for NAVIGATOR], *n.* (*pl.* **-vies**) Orig. a labourer employed on making canals; now a labourer in any kind of excavating work, as the construction of railways etc. **steam navvy,** *n.* A mechanical excavator.

navy (nā′ vi) [O.F. *navie*, L. *nāvis*, ship], *n.* (*poet.*) A fleet; the shipping of a country; the warships of a nation; their officers, men, dockyards, etc. **navy blue:** The dark-blue colour used for naval uniforms. **navy-blue,** *a.* **Navy List:** An official list of naval officers. **navy-yard,** *n.* A naval dockyard.

nawab (nȧ wawb′) [Hind. *nawwāb*], *n.* An Indian governor or nobleman; a nabob.

nay (nā) [Icel. *nei* (*ne*, not, *ei*, AYE (1)), cp. Swed. and Dan. *nei*], *adv.* *No; a word expressing negation or refusal; not only so, not this alone, more than that, and even. *n.* The word 'nay'; a denial, a refusal. *v.t.* To deny, to refuse. *v.i.* To make refusal or denial. ***nayward,** *adv.* ***nayword,** *n.* A byword; a watchword; a refusal.

Nazarene (năz ȧ rēn′) [L. *Nazarēnus*, Gr. *Nazarēnos*, from *Nazaret*, Nazareth], *n.* A native of Nazareth; a name applied in reproach to Christ and the early Christians; an early Judaizing sect of Christians. *a.* Of or belonging to this sect; of or pertaining to Nazareth.

Nazarite (năz′ ȧ rīt) [Heb. *nāzar*, to separate oneself, -ITE], *n.* A Hebrew who had taken certain vows of abstinence set forth in Numbers vi. **Nazaritism,** *n.*

naze (nāz) [A.-S. *næs*, NESS], *n.* A promontory, a headland.

Nazi (năt′ zi) [abbr. of G. *National Sozialist*], *n.* A member of the German National-Socialist Party. *a.* Pertaining to that party.

nazir (na′ zir) [Hind.], *n.* A native official formerly employed in Anglo-Indian courts; a title of various Mohammedan officials.

***ne** (nē) [A.-S., cp. O.H.G. *ni*, Icel. *nē*, L. and Gr. *nē*], *adv.* Not; never. *conj.* Nor.

nealogy (nė ăl′ ȯ ji) [Gr. *neos*, new, -LOGY], *n.* The study or description of the early adolescent stages in the development of an animal.

Neanderthaloid (nė ăn dėr tal′ oid) [*Neanderthal*, a valley in the North Rhineland district of Prussia, -OID], *a.* (*Ethn.*) Resembling the prehistoric skulls found in a limestone cave in the Neanderthal in 1857; characterized by the same low type of skull.

neap (nēp) [A.-S. *nēp*, in *nēp flōd*, etym. doubtful], *a.* Low or lowest (applied to the tides which happen in the middle of the second and fourth quarters of the moon, when the rise and fall are least). *n.* A neap tide. *v.i.* To diminish towards the neap (of the tides); to reach the flood (of a neap tide); to be left aground by a neap tide (of a vessel).

Neapolitan (nē ȧ pol′ i tȧn) [L. *Neāpolitānus*, from *Neāpolītēs*, from L. and Gr. *Neāpolis*, Naples], *a.* Pertaining to or distinctive of Naples or its inhabitants. *n.* An inhabitant of Naples. **Neapolitan ice:** Ice-cream made of two different ices in distinct layers; a sweetmeat resembling this. **Neapolitan violet:** A double, sweet-scented viola.

near (nēr) [A.-S. *nēar* (compar. of *nēah*, NIGH), blended with Icel. *nær* (compar. of *nā*, nigh, also used as positive)], *adv.* At or to a short distance, at hand, nigh; not far off, not remote in place, time, or degree; nearly, almost; closely; carefully, sparingly, parsimoniously. *prep.* Close to in place, time, condition, etc. *a.* Nigh, close at hand, not distant in place, time, or degree; closely resembling, almost; closely related; familiar, intimate; literal, not free or loose (of a likeness, translation, etc.); close, narrow; direct, short, straight (of roads etc.); on the left (of horses, parts or sides of vehicles, etc.); parsimonious, niggardly. *v.t.* To approach, to draw nigh to. *v.i.* To draw nigh. **near beer,** *n.* Comprehensive term for all the malt liquors permitted in U.S.A. in the era of Prohibition. **near-sighted,** *a.* Short-sighted. **near-sightedness,** *n.* **nearish,** *a.* **nearly,** *adv.* Almost; intimately; in a parsimonious manner. **nearness,** *n.*

Nearctic (nē ark′ tik) [Gr. *neos*, new], *a.* (*Zool.*) Of or pertaining to the northern (Arctic and temperate) part of North America.

neat (1) (nēt) [A.-S. *nēat* (cp. Icel. *naut*, Swed. *nöt*, Dan. *nōd*), cogn. with *nēotan*, to use, to enjoy], *n.* Cattle of the bovine kind; an animal of this kind. *a.* Pertaining to animals of this kind. **neat-herd,** *n.* A cowherd. **neat-house,** *n.* **neat's-foot-oil,** *n.*

neat (2) (nēt) [A.-F. *neit*, F. *net*, L. *nitidum*, nom. *-dus*, from *nitēre*, to shine], *a.* Tidy, trim; simply but becomingly ordered; nicely proportioned, well made; elegantly and concisely phrased; adroit, dexterous, clever; undiluted, pure; *net. **neat-handed,** *a.* Clever, dexterous, deft. **neatly,** *adv.* **neatness,** *n.*

'neath (nēth) [BENEATH], *prep.* (*poet.*) Beneath.

neb (neb) [A.-S. *nebb*, cp. Dut. *nebbe*, *neb*, Icel. *nef*, Dan. *næb*], *n.* A beak or bill; a nose or snout; the tip or point of anything; a spout; a nib; (*Sc.*) the face, the mouth.

nebbuk (neb′ ŭk) [Arab. *nebq*], *n.* A thorny Eastern shrub, *Zizyphus spina-Christi*, supposed to have furnished the thorns for Christ's crown.

nebula (neb′ ū lȧ) [L., mist (cp. Gr. *nephelē*, G. *nebel*, Dut. *nevel*, Icel. *nifl*)], *n.* (*pl.* **-læ**) A cloudy patch of light in the heavens produced by groups of stars or by a mass of gaseous or stellar matter; (*Path.*) a speck on the cornea causing defective vision. **nebular,** *a.* Of or pertaining to nebulæ. **nebular hypothesis:** That the bodies composing the solar and stellar systems once existed in the form of nebulæ. ***nebule,** *n.* A cloud, a mist; a nebula. **nebulé** [NEBULY]. **nebulous** (neb′ ū lŭs), *a.* Cloudy; turbid; hazy, vague, indistinct, obscure, uncertain; muddled, bewildered; (*Astron.*) belonging to or resembling a nebula. **nebulosity** (-los′ i ti), **nebulousness,** *n.*

nebulium (ne bū′ li ŭm), *n.* (*Chem.*) A hypothetical element which was thought to give the lines in the spectra of gaseous nebulæ now known to be due to ionized oxygen.

nebuly (neb′ ū li) [F. *nebulé*, med. L. *nebulātus*, p.p. of *nebulāre*, to cloud, as prec.], *a.* (*Her.*) Represented by, shaped in, or ornamented with wavy lines; (*Arch.*) undulating (of mouldings).

necessary (nes′ ė sȧr i) [L. *necessārius*, from *necesse*, unavoidable], *a.* Needful, requisite, indispensable, requiring to be done; such as cannot be avoided, inevitable; happening or existing by necessity; resulting from external causes or determinism; determined by natural laws; not voluntary, not of free will, compulsory; resulting from the constitution of the mind, intuitive, conclusive. *n.* That which is indispensably requisite; (*pl.*) things that are essentially requisite, esp. to life; that which must be as opposed to the contingent; (*slang*) money; *a privy. **necessarian,** etc. [NECESSITARIAN]. **necessarily,** *adv.* Of necessity; inevitably. ***necessariness,** *n.*

Necessitarian (nė ses i târ′ i ȧn), *n.* One believing in the doctrine that man's will is not free, but that actions and volitions are determined by antecedent causes. **necessitarianism,** *n.*

necessitate (nė ses′ i tāt) [med. L. *necessitātus*, p.p. of *necessitāre*, as foll.], *v.t.* To make necessary or unavoidable; to constrain, to compel; to entail as an unavoidable condition, result, etc. **necessitation** (-tā′ shŭn), *n.*

necessity (nė ses′ i ti) [O.F. *necessité*, L. *necessitātem*, nom. *-tas*, from *necesse*, unavoidable], *n.* The quality of being necessary; inevitableness; absolute need, indispensability; constraint, compulsion; the compelling force of circumstances, the external conditions that compel one to act in a certain way; that which is necessary, an essential requisite (*often in pl.*); want, poverty. ***necessitied,** *a.* **necessitous,** *a.* Needy, destitute, in poverty. ***necessitously,** *adv.*

neck (nek) [A.-S. *hnecca* (cp. Dut. *nek*, G. *nacken*, Icel. *nakki*)], *n.* The narrow portion of the body connecting the trunk with the head; this part of an animal used for food; anything resembling this, as an isthmus, a narrow passage or strait; the slender part of a bottle near the mouth; (*Arch.*) the lower part of a capital; the part of a garment that is close to the neck. *v.t.* (*slang*) To hug, to fondle. **a stiff neck:** Obstinacy, esp. in sin. **neck and crop** [CROP]. **neck and neck:** Equal, very close (in a race). **neck or nothing:** At all risks; desperately. **to get it in the neck:** To be hard hit. ***to harden the neck:** To grow obstinate. **neck-band,** *n.* A part of a garment fitting round the neck. **necked,** *a.* (*in comb.*, as *stiff-necked*). **neck-cloth,** *n.* A cravat or neck-tie. **neck-mould, -moulding,** *n.* A moulding surrounding a column at the junction of the shaft and capital. **neck-tie,** *n.* A strip of silk or other material encircling or worn as if encircling the neck and collar and tied in front. ***neck-verse,** *n.* A Latin verse printed in black-letter placed before a prisoner claiming benefit of clergy, by reading which he might save his neck. **necking,** *n.* (*Arch.*) The hollow part of a column between the shaft and the capital; (*Am. slang*) fondling, cuddling.

neckerchief (nek′ ĕr chēf), *n.* A kerchief worn round the neck.

necklace (nek′ lȧs), *n.* A string of beads or gems worn round the neck. **necklaced,** *a.*

necklet (nek′ let), *n.* A small fur boa for the neck; an ornament for the neck.

necro- [Gr. *nekros*, a dead body], *comb. form.* Pertaining to dead bodies or the dead.

necrobiosis (nek rō bī ō′ sis) [Gr. *bios*, life], *n.* Decay of living tissue, as in old age. **necrobiotic,** *a.*

necrogenic (nek rō jen′ ik), *a.* Of or derived from contact with dead bodies.

necrolatry (ne krol′ ȧ tri), *n.* Worship of the dead, esp. ancestors.

necrology (nek rol′ ō ji), *n.* A register of deaths, a death-roll; an account of the dead. **necrological,** *a.* **necrologist,** *n.*

necromancy (nek′ rō măn si) [M.E. and O.F. *nigromancie*, med. L. *nigromantia*, L. *necromantia*, Gr. *nekromanteia*, -MANCY], *n.* The art of revealing future events by communication with the dead; enchantment, magic. **necromancer,** *n.* **necromantic** (-măn′ tik), *a.* ***necromantically,** *adv.*

necron (nek′ ron), *n.* (*Bot.*) Dead plant material not yet rotted into humus.

necronite (nek′ rō nīt), *n.* (*Min.*) A variety of orthoclase emitting a fetid odour when struck.

necrophagous (nek rof′ ȧ gŭs), *a.* Eating or feeding on carrion.

necrophobia (nek rō fō′ bi ȧ), *n.* Revulsion from or fear of anything to do with the dead.

necropolis (ne krop′ ō lis) [Gr.], *n.* A cemetery, esp. one on a large scale.

necropsy (ne krop′ si) [Gr. *opsis*, sight], *n.* An examination of a dead body, an autopsy; a post-mortem examination. **necroscopy,** *n.* Necropsy. **necroscopic,** *a.*

necrosis (nė krō′ sis), *n.* (*Path.*) The mortification of part of the body, esp. of bone. **necrotic** (-krot′ ik), *a.* **necrotize** (nek′ rō tīz), *v.i.*

nectar (nek′ tȧr) [L., from Gr. *nektar*, etym. doubtful], *n.* The drink of the gods; (*fig.*) any delicious drink; the honey or sweet fluid secretion of plants. **nectarean, *-eal, nectareous** (nek târ′ ė ȧn, -ȧl, -ŭs), **nectarous,** *a.* **nectared,** *a.* Imbued or filled with nectar. **nectarial,** *a.* Of the nature of a nectary. **nectariferous** (nek tȧ rif′ ĕr ŭs), *a.* **nectarine** (nek′ tȧ rin), *a.* Nectarean. *n.* A smooth-skinned and firm variety of the peach. **nectary,** *n.* The organ or part of a plant or flower secreting honey.

nectocalyx (nek tō kā′ liks) [Gr. *nēktos*, swimming, from *nēchein*, to swim], *n.* (*pl.* **-lyces**) (*Zool.*) The bell-shaped swimming-organ in the hydrozoa. **nectocalycine** (-kā′ li sīn), *a.*

Neddy (ned′ i) [fam. form of *Edward*], *n.* A donkey.

née (nā) [F., fem. p.p. of *naître*, to be born], *a.* Born (used with the maiden name of a married woman).

need (nēd) [A.-S. *nied*, *nēad*, *nēod* (cp. Dut. *nood*, G. *noth*, Icel. *nauth*), whence *nēadian*, to need], *n.* A state of urgently requiring something; lack of something; a state requiring relief, urgent want; indigence, destitution; a difficult, critical, or perilous situation; emergency; that which is wanted, requirement. *v.i.* (*3rd sing.* **need** or **needs**) To be wanting or necessary, to require, to be bound, to be under necessity or obligation to; to be in want. *v.t.* To be in want of, to require. **needfire,** *n.* A fire produced by friction, from dry wood; a signal-fire. ***needer,** *n.* **needful,** *a.* **the needful:** (*colloq.*) What is required, esp. money. **needfully,** *adv.* **needfulness,** *n.* **needless,** *a.* Unnecessary, not required; useless, superfluous; *not in want. **needlessly,** *adv.* **needlessness,** *n.* ***needly** (1), *adv.* **needs,** *adv.* Of necessity, necessarily, indispensably (*usu. with* must). **needy,** *a.* In need; necessitous, indigent; *needful. **needily,** *adv.* ***neediness,** *n.*

needle (nē′ dėl) [A.-S. *nædl* (cp. Dut. *neald*, G. *nadel*, Icel. *nāl*, Dan. *naal*), prob. cogn. with Gr. *neein*, L. *nēre*, to spin], *n.* A small, thin, rod-shaped, pointed steel instrument with an eye for carrying a thread, used in sewing; analogous instruments of metal, bone, wood, etc., used in knitting, crocheting, etc.; a piece of magnetized steel used as indicator in a mariner's compass, a telegraphic receiver, etc.; applied to pointed instruments used in surgery, assaying, etching, etc., and in machinery, fire-arms, etc.; a beam, esp. one used as a temporary support in underpinning, etc.; a pointed peak or pinnacle of rock; an obelisk; a needle-like leaf of a pine-tree; a needle-shaped crystal; a pointed piece of metal, fibre, etc., used to receive or transmit the vibrations in the groove of a revolving gramophone record. *v.t.* To make or sew with the needle; to work upon with the needle; to penetrate; to thread (one's way) through or between; to shore up or underpin with needle-beams. *v.i.* To form needle-like crystals; to thread one's way; to work with the needle; (*colloq.*) to irritate; to force into action. **needle-bath,** *n.* A variety of shower-bath in which the water is emitted in thin needle-like jets. **needle-beam,** *n.* A cross-beam in the flooring of a bridge etc. **needle-book, -case,** *n.* A case, usu. with flannel leaves, for sticking needles in. **needle-fish,** *n.* A long, slender fish of the family *Belonidæ.* **needle-gun,** *n.* A breech-loading gun in which a cartridge is exploded by the prick of a needle. **needle-lace,** *n.* Lace made with needles, not with bobbins. **needle-point,** *n.* Any fine sharp point; point-lace. **needle-woman,** *n.* A seamstress. **needlework,** *n.* **needleful,** *n.* **needly** (2), *a.*

needless, etc. [NEED].

ne'er (nâr) [contr. of NEVER], *adv.* (*poet.*) Never. **n'er-do-well,** *a.* Good for nothing. *n.* A good-for-nothing.

***neeze** (nēz) [prob. from Icel. *hnōjsa* (cp. Dan. *nyse,* Dut. *niezen,* G. *niesen*)], *v.i.* To sneeze. *n.* A sneeze.

nef (nef, nāf) [F., ship], *n.* An ornamental piece of plate shaped like a boat or ship formerly used for holding the salt-cellars, table-napkins, etc., of persons of great distinction; an incense-boat; a sanctuary lamp in the shape of a ship; *the nave of a church.

nefandous (nė făn' dụs) [L. *nefandus* (*ne,* not, *fandus,* ger. of *fārī,* to speak)], *a.* Unspeakable, atrocious.

nefarious (nė fâr' i ụs) [L. *nefārius,* from *nefas* (*ne,* not, *fas,* right, divine justice)], *a.* Wicked, abominable, infamous. **nefariously,** *adv.* **nefariousness,** *n.*

negate (nė gāt') [as foll.], *v.t.* To render negative, to nullify; to be the negation of; to deny, to affirm the non-existence of.

negation (nė gā' shụn) [F. from L. *negātiōnem,* nom. *-tio,* from *negāre,* to deny], *n.* Denial; a declaration of falsity; refusal, contradiction; the absence or the opposite of certain qualities, nullity, voidness; (*Log.*) negative statement, affirmation of absence or exclusion. **negationist,** *n.* One who denies, esp. one who holds merely negative views in religion. **negatory,** *a.*

negative (neg' ȧ tiv) [late L. *negātīvus,* as prec.], *a.* Containing, declaring, or implying negation; denying, contradicting, prohibiting, refusing; (*Log.*) denoting difference or discrepancy; (*Alg.*) denoting the opposite to positive, denoting that which is to be subtracted (expressed by the minus sign −); (*Elec.*) denoting the kind of electricity produced by friction on resin, opp. to positive, produced on glass; (*Phot.*) showing the lights dark and the shadows light. *n.* A proposition, reply, word, etc., expressing negation; the right of veto; a veto; the side of a question that denies; a negative quality, lack or absence of something; (*Phot.*) an image or plate bearing an image in which the lights and shades of the object are reversed; (*Elec.*) negative electricity, or the negative plates in a voltaic cell; (*Alg.*) a negative or minus sign or quantity. *v.t.* To veto, to reject, to refuse to accept, sanction, or enact; to reprove; to contradict; to reverse (a positive statement or sentence); to neutralize. **negative feed-back,** *n.* (*Elec.*) Interconnexion of input and output terminals of an amplifier in such a manner that the output opposes the input. This decreases the gain but increases the stability and the fidelity of the amplifier. **negative pole:** (*Elec.*) The pole of a freely-swinging magnet that swings to the south. **negative quantity:** A minus quantity, nothing. **negatively,** *adv.* **negativeness, negativity** (-tiv' i ti), *n.* **negativism,** *n.* The doctrine of a negationist. **negativist,** *n.*

neglect (nėg lekt') [L. *neglectus,* p.p. of *negligere* (*neg-,* not, *legere,* to pick up)], *v.t.* To treat carelessly; to slight, to disregard; to pass over; to leave undone; to omit (to do or doing). *n.* Disregard (of); omission to do anything that should be done; carelessness, negligence; the state of being neglected. ***neglectable** [NEGLIGIBLE]. ***neglectedness,** *n.* **neglecter, -or,** *n.* **neglectful,** *a.* **neglectfully,** *adv.* **neglectfulness,** *n.* ***neglectingly,** *adv.* **neglection,** *n.*

negligé (neg' li zhā) [F.], *n.* A state of undress or free-and-easy attire. **negligée** (neg' li zhē), *n.* A lady's loose gown worn in the 18th century; a long necklace of irregular beads or coral.

negligence, negligency (neg' li jėnt, neg' li jėn si), *n.* Disregard of appearances, conventions, etc., in conduct, literature, etc.; (*Law*) failure to exercise proper care and precaution. **negligent,** *a.* Careless, neglectful. **negligently,** *adv.*

negligible (neg' li ji bėl), *a.* That can be ignored, not worth notice.

negotiate (nė gō' shi āt) [L. *negōtiātus,* p.p. of *negōtiārī,* from *negōtium,* business (*neg-,* not, *ōtium,* leisure)], *v.i.* To treat (with another) in order to make a bargain, agreement, compromise, etc.; to traffic. *v.t.* To arrange, bring about, or procure by negotiating; to carry on negotiations concerning; to transfer (a bill, note, etc.) for value received; to obtain or give value for; (*colloq.*) to accomplish, to get over successfully. **negotiable,** *a.* **negotiability** (-bil' i ti), *n.* **negotiant,** *n.* A negotiator; *a merchant, a trader. **negotiation** (-ā' shụn), *n.* **negotiator** (nė gō' shi ā tȯr), *n.* **negotiatory,** *a.* **negotiatress, -trix,** *n.*

negress (nē' grės) [NEGRO].

negrilo (nė gril' ō) [Sp., dim. of NEGRO], *n.* A dwarfish Negro; one of a dwarfish Negro race in Central and South Africa. **negrito** (nė grē' tō), *n.* One of a dwarfish negroid race in some islands of the Malay archipelago, etc. **negriloid** (nė gril' oid), *a.*

Negro (nē' grō) [Sp. from L. *nigrum,* nom. *niger,* black], *n.* (*pl.* **-oes,** *fem.* **Negress**) One of the woolly-haired black or dark-brown, flat-nosed and thick-lipped African race. *a.* Of or pertaining to this race; black or dark-skinned. **negro-corn,** *n.* Indian millet. **Negro-head,** *n.* Strong, black, plug tobacco soaked in molasses. **Negroland,** *n.* The portion of Africa inhabited by Negroes. **negroid** (nē' groid), **negroidal** (nė groi' dȧl), *a.* **negroism,** *n.* An idiomatic peculiarity of Negro speech. **negrophil,** *n.* A friend of the Negroes. **negrophilism** (-grof' i lizm), *n.* **negrophobia** (-fō' bi ȧ), *n.* Hatred or dislike of Negroes.

negus (1) (nē' gụs) [Colonel Francis *Negus* (*d.* 1732), its inventor], *n.* A beverage of wine, hot water, sugar, and spices.

negus (2) (nē' gụs) [Ethiopian], *n.* The sovereign of Abyssinia.

neigh (nā) [A.-S. *hnægan* (cp. L.G. *neigen,* M.H.G. *nêgen*), imit. in orig.], *v.i.* To utter the cry of a horse; to whinny. *n.* The cry of a horse.

neighbour (nā' bȯr) [A.-S. *nēahgebūr* (NIGH, BOOR)], *n.* One who lives near, one in the same street, village, community, etc.; a person or thing standing or happening to be next or near another; one having the claims of a fellow-man, etc.; (*fig.*) an inhabitant of an adjoining town, district, or country; *a confidant. *a.* Near, adjoining, neighbouring. *v.t.* To adjoin; to lie near to; *to associate with familiarly. *v.i.* To border (upon). **neighbourhood,** *n.* The state of being neighbours; neighbourliness; the locality round or near; the vicinity; nearness; (*collect.*) those who live near, neighbours. **neighbouring,** *a.* Situated or living near. **neighbourly,** *a.* and *adv.* **neighbourliness,** *n.* **neighbourless,** *a.* **neighbourship,** *n.*

neinei (nē' nē) [Maori], *n.* An ornamental shrub found in N. Zealand.

neither (nī'-, nē' thėr) [A.-S. *nawther, nāhwæther* (*nā,* not, WHETHER), assim. to EITHER], *a.* Not either. *pron.* Not the one nor the other. *conj.* Not either, not on the one hand (usu. preceding one of two alternatives and correlative with *nor* preceding the other); nor, nor yet. *adv.* (*colloq., at end of sentence*) Either, any more than another person or thing.

nekton (nek′ tŏn) [Gr. *nēchein*, to swim], *n.* (*Biol.*) Term for all forms of organic life found in various depths of salt and fresh water.

nelli (nel′ i) [prob. *Nelly*, fam. form of *Ellen*], *n.* A large petrel, *Ossifraga gigantea.*

Nelumbo, Nelumbium (nė lŭm′ bō, -bi ŭm) [Cingalese *nelumbu*], *n.* A genus of water-beans belonging to the family *Nymphæaceæ*, comprising *N. speciosum*, the sacred lotus.

nemalite (nem′ ȧ līt) [Gr. *nema*, a thread; *lithos*, a stone], *n.* The fibrous variety of brucite, or native hydrate of magnesium.

nemathecium (nem ȧ thē′ shi ŭm) [mod. L. (Gr. *nēma*, thread, *thēkē*, box)], *n.* (*Bot.*) A wart-like elevation on the thallus of certain algæ containing tetraspores or other generative bodies. **nemathecial,** *a.*

nemathelminth (nem ȧ thel′ minth) [*nēma matos*, as foll., *helmins -nthos*, worm], *n.* (*Zool.*) A thread-worm or nematode. **nemathelminthic** (-min′ thik), *a.*

nemato- [Gr. *nēma nēmatos*, thread], *comb. form.* Thread-like; filamentous. **nematocerous** (nem ȧ tos′ ėr ŭs) [Gr. *keras*, horn], *a.* (*Ent.*) Having filiform antennæ. **nematocide** (nem′ ȧ tō sīd) [-CIDE], *a.* (*Med.*) A substance that destroys nematodes. **nematocyst** (nem′ ȧ tō sist) [CYST], *n.* (*Zool.*) A thread-cell in jelly-fish and other cœlenterates from which the stinging thread is projected.

nematode (nem′ ȧ tōd), **nematoid** (-toid), *a.* Thread-like; pertaining to the *Nematoidea*, a class of worms comprising the parasitic round-worm, thread-worm, etc. *n.* A nematode worm.

Nemean (nē mē′ ȧn, nē′ mė ȧn) [L. *Nemeæus*, *Nemæus*, *Neneus*, Gr. *Nemeæos*, *Nemeios*, *Nemeos*, from *Nemea*, in Argolis], *a.* Of or pertaining to Nemea. **Nemean games:** One of the great Hellenic festivals held at Nemea in the second and fourth of each Olympiad.

nemertean, -tine (nė mĕr′ tė ȧn, -tīn) [Gr. *Nēmertēs*, a sea-nymph], *a.* Belonging to the *Nemertea*, a division of flat- or ribbon-worms, chiefly marine. *n.* A worm of this class.

Nemesis (nem′ ė sis) [Gr., from *nemein*, to allot], *n.* The Greek goddess of retribution; retributive justice.

nemocerous (nė mos′ ėr ŭs) [Gr. *nēma*, thread, *keras*, horn], *a.* (*Ent.*) Belonging to the *Nemocera*, a family of dipterous insects, with filamentous antennæ. **nemoceran,** *a.* and *n.*

***nemoral** (nem′ ō rȧl) [L. *nemorālis*, from *nemus*, grove], *a.* Pertaining to a wood. ***nemorous,** *a.*

nenuphar (nen′ ū far) [F., from Pers. *nīnūfar*, Sansk. *nīlōtpala* (*nīla*, blue, *utpala*, lotus)], *n.* The white water-lily, *Nymphæa alba.*

neo- [Gr. *neos*], *comb. form.* New, recent, modern, later, fresh. **neo-Catholic** (nē ō kăth′ ō lik), *a.* Of or pertaining to the Puseyite school in the Church of England, or to the school of Liberal Catholicism headed by Lamennais and Lacordaire in the Church of France. **neo-Christian,** *a.* Of or pertaining to neo-Christianity or rationalism. **neo-Classic** (-klăs′ ik), *a.* Belonging to the 18th-century revival of classicism. **neo-classicism,** *n.* **neo-classicist,** *n.* **neo-Darwinism,** *n.* Darwinism as modified by later investigators, esp. those who accept the theory of natural selection but not that of the inheritance of acquired characters. **neo-Darwinian,** *a.* and *n.* ***neogamist** (nė og′ ȧ mist) [Gr. *neogamos*, from *gamos*, marriage], *n.* A person recently married. **neo-Gothic** (-goth′ ik), *n.* and *a.* (*Archit.*) The Gothic revival of the mid-19th century, or pertaining to this. **neo-Hellenism** (-hel′ ė nizm), *n.* The revival of Greek ideals in art and literature, as in the Italian Renaissance. **neo-Kantian** (-kăn′ ti ȧn), *a.* Pertaining to the teaching of Kant as modified by recent interpreters. *n.* An adherent of neo-Kantianism. **neo-Kantianism,** *n.* **neo-Lamarckian** (-lȧ mar′ ki ȧn), *a.* The teaching of Lamarck on organic evolution as revived in a modified form by those who believe in the inheritance of acquired characters. **neo-paganism,** *n.* A revived form of paganism. **neo-pagan,** *n.* and *a.* **neo-paganize,** *v.t.*

Neocomian (nē ō kō′ mi ȧn) [F. *Néocomien*, from *Neocomium* (NEO-, Gr. *kōmē*, village), latinized from *Neuchâtel*], *a.* Of or pertaining to the lower division of the Cretaceous strata typically exhibited near Neuchâtel in Switzerland.

neocosmic (nē ō koz′ mik) [NEO-, COSMIC], *a.* Pertaining to the later or existing stage of development of the universe; pertaining to mankind in the historical period.

neocracy (nē ok′ rȧ si), *n.* Government by new or upstart persons.

neodox (nē′ ō doks), *a.* Holding new views. **neodoxy,** *n.*

neodymium (nē ō dim′ i ŭm) [Gr. *neos*, new, *didymos*, twins], *n.* A metallic element, of the cerium group of rare earth elements.

neogrammarian (nē ō grȧ mâr′ i ȧn), *n.* One of a modern school of grammarians who insist upon the invariability of the laws governing phonetic change. **neogrammatical,** *a.*

neolite (nē′ ō līt), *n.* A dark-green hydrous silicate of aluminium and magnesium.

neolithic (nē ō lith′ ik) [Gr. *lithos*, stone], *a.* Pertaining to the later Stone Age characterized by ground and polished implements. **neolith,** *n.* A weapon, implement, or person belonging to this period.

neology (nė ol′ ō ji) [F. *néologie*], *n.* The introduction or use of new words; a neologism; the adoption of or the tendency towards rationalistic views in theology. **neologian** (-lō′ ji ȧn), *a.* and *n.* **neological** (-loj′ i kȧl), *a.* **neologically,** *adv.* **neologism** (-ol′ ō jizm), *n.* A new word or phrase, or a new sense for an old one; the use of new words; neology. **neologist,** *n.* **neologistic** (-jis′ tik), *a.* **neologize,** *v.i.*

neon (nē′ ŏn) [neut. of Gr. *neos*, new], *n.* (*Chem.*) A gaseous element existing in minute quantities in the air, isolated from argon in 1898. **neon lamp,** *n.* (*Elect.*) A lamp possessing two electrodes and containing an atmosphere of rarefied neon gas.

neonomous (nė on′ ō mŭs) [NEO-, *nomos*, law], *a.* (*Biol.*) Modified in accordance with recent conditions of environment.

neomycin (nē ō mī′ sin) [Gr. *mykes*, fungus], *n.* An antibiotic effective against some infections that resist ordinary antibiotics.

neontology (nē on tol′ ō ji) [ONTOLOGY], *n.* The study of living as distinguished from extinct species.

neophron (nē′ ō fron) [Gr.], *n.* The white Egyptian vulture.

neophyte (nē′ ō fīt) [late L. *neophytus*, Gr. *neophutos* (*phutos*, grown, from *phuein*, to plant)], *n.* One newly converted or newly baptized; one newly admitted to a monastery or to the priesthood; a beginner, a novice, a tyro. *a.* Newly entered. **neophytic** (-fit′ ik), *a.* **neophytism** (nē′ ō fī tizm), *n.*

neoplasm (nē′ ō plăzm) [Gr. *plasma*, from *plassein*, to form], *n.* (*Path.*) A morbid growth of new tissue in some part of the body.

neoplasty (nē′ ō plăs ti), *n.* (*Surg.*) Restoration of a part by granulation, adhesive inflammation, etc. **neoplastic,** *a.*

Neoplatonism (nē ō plăt′ ŏn izm), *n.* A system of philosophy combining the Platonic ideas with the theosophy of the East, originating in Alexandria in the 3rd century. **Neoplatonic,** *a.* **Neoplatonist,** *n.*

neoteric (nē ō ter′ ik) [Gr. *neoteros*, newer], *a.* New; of recent origin. *n.* One of modern times. **neoterically,** *adv.* **neoterism** (nē ot′ ĕr izm), *n.* **neoterist,** *n.* **neoterize,** *v.t.i.*

neotropical (nē ō trop′ i kăl), *a.* (*Zool.*) Of, pertaining to, or characteristic of tropical and South America.

neozoic (nē ō zō′ ik), *a.* (*Geol.*) Belonging to the later or post-Palæozoic period, including both Mesozoic and Cainozoic, or corresponding to Cainozoic.

nep (nep) [?], *n.* A bunch or knot in cotton-fibre.

nepenthe, -thes (nė pen′ thi, -thēz) [L. and Gr. *nēpenthes* (*nē-*, not, *penthos*, grief)], *n.* A drug or potion that drives away sorrow or grief; (*Med.*) a drug that relieves pain; (*Bot.*) a genus of plants containing the pitcher plant.

nephalism (nef′ ȧ lizm) [late Gr. *nēphalismos*, from *nēphalios*, sober], *n.* Total abstinence from intoxicants, teetotalism.

nepheline, -lite (nef′ ė lin, -līt) [F. *néphéline*, as foll.], *n.* (*Min.*) A vitreous silicate of aluminium and sodium found in volcanic rocks.

nephelo- [Gr. *nephelē*, cloud], *comb. form.* **nepheloid** (nef′ ė loid), *a.* Clouded, turbid. **nephelology** (nef ė lol′ ȯ ji) [-LOGY], *n.* The scientific study of clouds. **nephelosphere** (nef′ ė lȯ sfēr), *n.* An atmosphere of cloud enveloping a planet or other heavenly body.

nephew (nev′ ū) [O.F. *neveu*, L. *nepōtem*, nom. *-pos*, grandson, nephew (cp. A.-S. *nefa*, Dut. *neef*, G. *neffe*)], *n.* The son of a brother or sister; extended to the son of a brother- or sister-in-law, also to a grandnephew; (*euphem.*) an illegitimate son; *a descendant, a cousin.

nephoscope (nef′ ō skōp) [Gr. *nephos*, cloud, -SCOPE], *n.* (*Meteor.*) An instrument for observing the elevation, direction and velocity of clouds.

nephralgia (nė frăl′ ji ȧ) [*nephr-*, NEPHRO-, Gr. *-algia*, from *algos*, pain], *n.* (*Path.*) Pain or disease in the kidneys. **nephrectomy** (nef rek′ tō mi), *n.* (*Surg.*) Removal of a kidney by surgical means. **nephric** (nef′ rik), *a.* Pertaining to the kidney.

nephrite (nef′ rīt) [Gr. *nephrit*], *n.* (*Min.*) Jade, formerly believed to cure kidney-disease.

nephritis (nė frī′ tis) [late L. and Gr., as prec.], *n.* (*Path.*) **nephritic, *-al** (nė frit′ ik, -ăl), *a.* Pertaining to the kidneys; suffering from kidney disease; relieving disorders of the kidney. *n.* A medicine for relieving kidney diseases.

nephro- [Gr. *nephros*, kidney], *comb. form.* Pertaining to the kidneys. **nephrocele** (nef′ rȯ sēl) [-CELE], *n.* (*Path.*) Hernia of the kidneys. **nephrography** (nė frog′ rȧ fi) [-GRAPHY], *n.* **nephroid** (nef′ roid) [-OID], *a.* **nephrology** (nė frol′ ȯ ji) [-LOGY], *n.* **nephrotomy** (-frot′ ȯ mi) [-TOMY], *n.* (*Surg.*) Incision of the kidney, esp. for the extraction of a stone.

nepotism (nep′ ȯ-, nē′ pȯ tizm) [It. *nepotismo* (*nepote*, see NEPHEW, -ISM)], *n.* Favouritism (as in bestowing patronage) towards one's relations (orig. applied to the patronage of a Pope's illegitimate sons, euphem. called 'nephews'). **nepotal** (nep′-), *a.* **nepotic** (nė pot′ ik), *a.* **nepotist** (nē′-, nep′-), *n.*

Neptune (nep′ tūn) [L. *Neptūnus*], *n.* The Roman god of the sea; (*fig.*) the sea; one of the sun's planets. **Neptunian** (-tū′ ni ăn), *a.* Pertaining to Neptune or the sea; (*Geol.*) deposited by the sea or produced by the agency of water. *n.* A Neptunist. **Neptunist** (nep′ tū nist), *n.* (*Geol.*) One asserting the aqueous origin of certain rocks. **Neptunium,** *n.* (*Phys.*) A radio-active element obtained by the bombardment of uranium with neutrons.

nereid (nēr′ ė id) [L. and Gr. Nēreid-, stem of *Nēreis*, daughter of Nereus, a sea-god], *n.* (*pl.* **-ids**) A sea-nymph; (*Zool.*) a sea-worm or marine centipede of the genus *Nereis.* **nereidian** (-id′ i ăn), *a.* and *n.* (*Zool.*). **nereidous** (nė rē′ i dŭs), *a.*

nerite (nēr′ īt) [L. *nērita*, from Gr. *nēritēs, nēreitēs*, sea-mussel], *n.* (*Zool.*) A gasteropod mollusc of the genus *Nerita.* **neritine** (nēr′ i tin), *a.*

neroli (nēr′ ȯ li) [name of Italian princess said to have discovered it], *n.* An essential oil distilled from the flowers of the bitter or Seville orange, used as a perfume.

Neronian (nė rō′ ni ăn) [L. *Nerōniānus*, from C. Claudius *Nero*, Roman emperor], *a.* Of, pertaining to, or like the emperor Nero; cruel, tyrannical, debauched.

nerve (nĕrv) [L. *nervus* (cp. Gr. *neuron*)], *n.* One of the fibres or bundles of fibres conveying sensations and impulses to and from the brain or other organ; (*poet.*) a tendon or sinew; (*fig.*) strength, coolness, resolution, pluck; (*Bot.*) one of the ribs or fibro-vascular bundles in a leaf; (*pl.*) the nervous system, esp. as regards its state of health or the state of interaction between it and the other parts of the organism; also, an excited or disordered condition of the nerves, nervousness; (*Comm.*) a non-porous kind of cork; (*colloq.*) impudence, cheek, audacity. *v.t.* To give strength or firmness to. **nervate,** *a.* (*Bot.*) Having nerves or ribs. **nervation** (-vā′ shŭn), *n.* **nerved** (nĕrvd), *a.* (*usu. in comb.*, as *strong-nerved*). **nerveless,** *a.* Destitute of strength, energy, or vigour; (*Anat. etc.*) without nerves; (*Bot. etc.*) without nervures; (*fig.*) feeble, flabby. **nervelessly,** *adv.* **nervelessness,** *n.* **nervelet,** *n.* **nervi-, nervo-,** *comb. form.* **nervine** (nĕr′ vīn), *a.* (*Med.*) Capable of acting upon the nerves. *n.* A medicine that acts on the nerves. **nervose,** *a.* (*Bot.*) Nerved; (*Ent.*) having nervures.

nervous (nĕr′ vŭs) [as prec.], *a.* Pertaining to or composed of nerves; abounding in nervous energy; having weak or sensitive nerves, excitable, highly-strung, timid; sinewy, muscular; vigorous in sentiment or style. **nervously,** *adv.* **nervousness,** *n.*

nervule (nĕr′ vūl), *n.* A small nerve or nervure. **nervular, nervulose,** *a.*

nervure (nĕr′ vūr), *n.* (*Bot.*) The principal vein of a leaf; (*Ent.*) the ribs supporting the membranous wings of insects. **nervuration,** *n.*

nervy (nĕr′ vi), *a.* Nervous, jerky, jumpy; strong, muscular, sinewy; full of nerve, cool, confident.

nescient (nesh′ i ėnt) [L. *nesciens -ntem*, pres.p of *nescīre* (*ne-*, not, *scīre*, to know)], *a.* Ignorant, having no knowledge (of); agnostic. *n.* An agnostic. **nescience** (nesh′ i ens), *n.*

nesh (nesh) [A.-S. *hnesce* (cp. Dut. *nesch, nisch*, Goth. *hnasqus*), etym. unknown], *a.* Soft, friable; tender, succulent; delicate, poor-spirited. **neshen,** *v.t.* (*prov.*). **neshness,** *n.*

nesiote (nes′ i ōt) [Gr. *nesiotes*, an islander], *a.* Insular, inhabiting an island.

ness (nes) [A.-S. *næs* (cp. Icel. *nes*), rel. to *nasu*, NOSE], *n.* A promontory, a cape.

-ness [A-S. *-nes, -ness, -nis, -niss* (cp. Dut. *-nis*, G. *-niss*, O.H.G. *-nessi, -nassi, -nissi*, Goth. *-nassus*, orig. *-assus*)], *suf.* Forming abstract nouns denoting state or quality, as *goodness, holiness, wilderness.*

nest (nest) [A.-S. (cp. Dut. and G. *nest*, and O.Ir. *net*, W. *nyth*, also L. *nīdus*, from *ni-*, down, and the root *sed-*, to sit)], *n.* The bed or shelter constructed or prepared by a bird for laying its eggs and rearing its young; any place used by animals or insects for similar purposes; a snug place of abode, shelter, or retreat; a haunt (as of robbers); a series or set, esp. a number of boxes each inside the next larger. *v.t.* To put, lodge, or establish in or as in a nest; to pack one inside another. *v.i.* To build and occupy a nest; to hunt for or take birds' nests. **nest-egg,** *n.* A real or artificial egg left in a nest to prevent a hen from forsaking it; (*fig.*) something laid by, as a sum of money, as a nucleus for saving or a reserve. **nestful,** *n.* **nestlike,** *a.* **nestling,** *n.* A bird too young to leave the nest; (*fig.*) a young child; *a little nest.

nestitherapy (nĕs ti ther′ ȧ pi) [Gr. *nestis*, fasting, *therapeutikos*, cure], *n.* Hunger cure, treatment by fasting.

nestle (nes′ ėl) [A.-S. *nestlian*, from prec.], *v.i.* To nest; to be close or snug; to settle oneself (down, in, or among); to press closely (up to). *v.t.* To put or shelter in or as in a nest; to settle down snugly; to cuddle, to cherish. **nestler,** *n.*

nestling [NEST].

Nestor (nes′ tŏr) [Gr. *Nestŏr*, king of Pylus, character in Homer], *n.* A wise counsellor; a sage; a venerable senior.

Nestorian (nes tōr′ i ȧn) [L. *Nestoriānus* (*Nestorius*, -AN)], *a.* Pertaining to Nestorius or his doctrines. *n.* A follower of Nestorius, patriarch of Constantinople (5th cent.), who held that there were two distinct persons and two natures, divine and human, in Christ. **Nestorianism,** *n.*

net (1) (net) [A.-S. (cp. Dut., Icel., and Dan. *net*, G. *netz*), cogn. with L. *nassa*, creel], *n.* A fabric of twine, cord, etc., knotted into meshes, for catching fish, birds, or other animals, or for covering, protecting, carrying, etc.; (*fig.*) a snare; network. *v.t.* (*past & p.p.* **netted**) To make into a net or netting; to make or form in a network; to make network of, to reticulate; to cover, hold, or confine with a net; to catch in a net; to fish with nets or set nets in (a stream, pond, etc.); to catch as in a net, to ensnare. *v.i.* To make netting or network; to make nets; to fish with a net or nets. **net-ball,** *n.* A game in which a ball has to be thrown into a suspended net. **net-veined,** *a.* Having a reticulated series of veins or nervules (as the wings of insects, leaves, etc.). **net-winged,** *a.* Having net-veined wings. **network,** *n.* An open-work fabric, netting; a system of intersecting lines, a reticulation, a ramification; (*Radio.*) a system of stations for simultaneous broadcasting; (*fig.*) any system of lines, roads, etc., resembling this. **netted,** *a.* Reticulated. **netting,** *n.* **netting-needle,** *n.* ***netty,** *a.*

net (2) (net) [F., NEAT (2)], *a.* Free from all deductions; obtained or left after all deductions; not subject to discount; unadulterated, pure; *clean, spotless. *v.t.* To yield or realize as clear profit.

Ne Temere (nē tem′ ė ri) [L. *ne*, not, *temere*, rashly], *n.* (*Eccles.*) A papal decree declaring that marriage between Roman Catholics and members of other faiths is not valid unless the ceremony is performed by a Roman Catholic bishop or a priest deputed by him.

nether (ne*th*′ ėr) [A.-S. *neothera* (cp. Dut. *neder*, G. *nieder*, Icel. *nethri*)], *a.* Lower; belonging to the region below the heavens or the earth. **nether garments:** Trousers. **nether regions** or **world:** Hell; (*rare*) the earth. ***netherstock,** *n.* A stocking. ***nethermore,** *a.* Lower. **nethermost,** *a.* ***netherward, -wards,** *adv.*

Netherlander (ne*th* ėr lȧn dėr) [Dut. *Nederlander*, from *Nederland*, Netherlands], *n.* An inhabitant of the Netherlands, a Hollander; *a native of Flanders or Belgium. **Netherlandish,** *a.*

netsuke (net′ su kā) [Jap.], *n.* A small piece of carved wood or ivory worn or attached to various articles, as a toggle or button, by the Japanese.

nett (NET (2)]. **netting** [NET (1)].

nettle (net′ ėl) [A.-S. *netele* (cp. Dut. *netel*, G. *nessel*, Dan. *nelde*, Swed. *nässla*)], *n.* A plant of the genus *Urtica*, with two European species, the great or common and the small nettle, with inconspicuous flowers and minute stinging hairs; applied to various plants bearing some resemblance to these. *v.t.* To sting; (*fig.*) to irritate, to provoke; to sting with nettles. **dead-nettle** [DEAD]. **nettle-rash,** *n.* An eruption on the skin resembling the sting of a nettle. ***nettler,** *n.*

nettling (net′ ling) [*nettle*, var. of *knittle*, from KNIT, -ING], *n.* (*Naut.*) The joining of two ropes by twisting the loosened ends together; the tying of yarns together in pairs to prevent entangling.

neume (nūm) [F., from med. L. *neuma*, Gr. *pneuma*, breath], *n.* (*Mus.*) A sequence of notes to be sung to one syllable in plain-song.

neur- [NEURO-].

neural (nūr′ ȧl) [Gr. *neuron*, NERVE, -AL], *a.* Of or pertaining to the nerves or the nervous system.

neuralgia (nū răl′ jȧ) [Gr. *algos*, pain], *n.* (*Path.*) An acute pain in a nerve or series of nerves, esp. in the head or face. **neuralgic,** *a.*

neurasthenia (nūr ȧs thē′ ni ȧ), *n.* Weakness of the nervous system, nervous debility. **neurasthenic,** *a.*

neuration (nū rā′ shŭn) [NEUR-, -ATION], *n.* The arrangement of the nervures, as in insects' wings.

neurectomy (nūr′ ek tom i) [Gr. *neuron*, a nerve, *ektome*, excision], *n.* (*Surg.*) Excision of a nerve, or part of it.

neuric (nū′ rik), *a.* Of or pertaining to the nerves. **neuricity,** *n.*

neurilemma (nū ri lem′ ȧ) [Gr. *eilema*, covering], *n.* (*Anat.*) The membranous sheath encasing a nerve.

neurility (nū ril′ i ti), *n.* The power of a nerve to convey stimuli.

neurin (nūr′ in), *n.* Nerve-energy, the force or stimulus produced in or conveyed to neurons.

neurine (nūr′ ĭn), *n.* The matter of which nerves are composed, nerve-fibre or tissue; a poisonous ptomaine derived from putrefying organic matter.

neuritis (nū rī′ tis), *n.* (*Path.*) Inflammation of a nerve.

neuro- [Gr. *neuron*, a nerve], *comb. form.*

neurohypnology (nū rō hip nol′ ō ji), *n.* (*Med.*) The study of sleep and its hygiene; the study of hypnotism. **neurohypnologist,** *n.* **neurohypnotism** (nū rō hip′ nȯ tizm), *n.* Nervous sleep induced by hypnotic means. **neurohypnotic,** *a.*

neurology (nū rol′ ō ji), *n.* The scientific study of the anatomy, physiology, and pathology of nerves. **neurological,** *a.* **neurologist,** *n.*

neuroma (nū rō′ mȧ), *n.pl.* **neuromata,** *n.* (*Path.*) A nerve-tumour.

neuron (nū′ ron), *n.* (*Physiol.*) A nerve-cell with its processes and ramifications, one of the structural units of the nervous system; *the cerebro-spinal axis comprising the spinal cord and brain.

neuropath (nū′ rō păth), *n.* A person suffering from a nervous disorder or having abnormal nervous sensibility; a physician who regards nervous conditions as the main factor in pathology. **neuropathic** (-păth′ ik), *a.* Relating to or suffering from a nervous disease. **neuropathology** (-pȧ thol′ ȯ ji), *n.* The pathology of the nervous system. **neuropathy** (nū rop′ ȧ thi), *n.* Any nervous disease. **neuropathist,** *n.*

neurophysiology (nū rō fiz i ol′ ō ji), *n.* The physiology of the nervous system.

neuropsychic (nū rō sī′ kik), *a.* Relating to the nervous and psychic functions and phenomena.

neuropsychology (nū rō sī kol′ ō ji), *n.* Psychology based upon the study of the nervous system.

neuroptera (nū rop′ tėr ȧ) [NEURO-, Gr. *pteron*, wing], *n.pl.* (*Ent.*) An order of insects with four reticulated membranous wings. **neuropteral, -oid, -ous,** *a.* **neuropteran,** *a.* and *n.*

neuroradiology (nū rō rā di ol′ ō ji), *n.* (*Med.*) A method of diagnosis of such conditions as cerebral tumours, aneurysms, etc., by X-ray examination.

neurose (nū′ rōs), *a.* (*Ent.*) Having numerous nervures; (*Path.*) neurotic.

neurosis (nū rō′ sis), *n.* (*Path.*) Functional disorder of the nervous system; (*Physiol.*) the change in the nerve-cells or neurons, or the discharge of nerve-energy, forming the physical basis of psychic activity.

neurotic (nū rot′ ik), *a.* (*Med.*) Pertaining to or situated in the nerves; acting on the nerves; suffering from neurosis. *n.* A substance acting upon the nerves; a person suffering from neurosis; a person of abnormal nervous excitability.

neuropnology [NEUROHYPNOLOGY].

neuropod (nū′ rō pod), *n.* (*Zool.*) An annulose or invertebrate animal whose limbs are in the neural aspect of its body.

neurotomy (nū rot′ ō mi), *n.* (*Surg.*) Dissection of the nerves; an incision in a nerve, usu. to produce sensory paralysis. **neurotomical,** *a.* **neurotomist,** *a.*

neurotonic (nū rō ton′ ik), *a.* (*Med.*) Strengthening the nervous system. *n.* A medicine for this purpose.

neuter (nū′ tėr) [L., neither (*ne-*, not, *uter*, either)], *a.* (*Gram.*) Neither masculine, nor feminine; (of verbs) intransitive; (*Bot.*) neither male nor female, without pistil or stamen; (*Ent.*) undeveloped sexually, sterile; *neutral, taking neither side. *n.* A neuter noun, adjective, or verb; the neuter gender; (*Bot.*) a flower having neither stamens nor pistils; (*Zool.*) a sterile female insect, as a working bee; a castrated animal; a neutral.

neutral (nū′ trål) [L. *neutrālis*, as prec.], *a.* Taking no part with either side, esp. not assisting either of two belligerents; belonging to a State that takes no part in hostilities; indifferent, impartial; having no distinct or determinate character, colour, etc.; neither good nor bad, indefinite, indeterminate; (*Eng.*) the position of parts in gear mechanism when no power is transmitted; (*Chem.*) neither acid nor alkaline; (*Elec.*) neither positive nor negative; (*Bot., Ent., etc.*) neuter, asexual. *n.* A State or person that stands aloof from a contest; a subject of a neutral State. **neutral-tinted,** *a.* **neutrality** (-trăl′ i ti), *n.* **neutralize,** *v.t.* To render neutral; to render inoperative or ineffective, to counteract; to declare (a State or territory) neutral either permanently or during hostilities. **neutralization** (-zā′ shůn), *n.* **neutralizer,** *n.* **neutrally,** *adv.*

neutrino (nū trī′ nō), *n.* A sub-atomic particle with almost zero mass, zero charge but specified spin.

neutrodyne (nū′ trō dīn) [L. *neuter*, neither, Gr. *dunamos*, power], *n.* (*Radio.*) The protected trade name of an apparatus for neutralizing capacity between plate and grid in a valve.

neutron (nū′ tron), *n.* (*Phys.*) A particle that is neutral electrically with approximately the same mass as a proton.

névé (nev′ ā, nā vā) [F. ult. from L. *nivem*, nom. *nix*, snow], *n.* Consolidated snow above the glaciers, in process of being converted into ice.

never (nev′ ėr) [A.-S. *nǣfre* (*ne*, not, *ǣfre*, ever)], *adv.* Not ever, at no time; on no occasion; not at all; none; (*ellipt. in exclamations*) surely not. **never a one:** Not a single person, etc., none. **never-ending, -failing,** *a.* **nevermore,** *adv.* At no future time; never again. **The Never-never:** Term applied to areas in North and West Queensland. **never-never system:** (*colloq.*) The hire-purchase system. **never so:** (*vulg.* **ever so**) To an unlimited extent; exceedingly. **nevertheless,** *conj.* But for all that; notwithstanding; all the same.

new (nū) [A.-S. *nīwe* (cp. Dut. *nieuw*, G. *neu*, Icel. *nӯr*, Gr. *neos*, L. *novus*)], *a.* Not formerly in existence; lately made, invented, or introduced; not before known; recently entered upon or begun; never before used, not worn or exhausted; fresh, unfamiliar, unaccustomed; (of bread) newly baked; fresh (from), not yet accustomed (to). *adv.* Newly, recently (*in comb.*, as *new-blown, new-born*); anew, fresh. **New Australian:** A non-British immigrant to Australia. **new-blown,** *a.* Having just come into bloom. **new-born,** *a.* Just born; regenerate. **new chum,** *n.* (*Austral. colloq.*) An immigrant. **new-come,** *a.* Modern, new-fangled; beginning afresh, recurring; changed, different, another. **new-comer,** *n.* **new-create,** *v.t.* **New Deal,** *n.* Economic and social measures introduced by Pres. Roosevelt in U.S.A. in 1933, after the economic crisis of 1929. ***newfangle** [M.E. *fangel*, from A.-S. *fang-*, p.p. *fōn*, to take (see FANG)], *v.t.* To change by introducing novelties. **newfangled,** *a.* New-fashioned; different from the accepted fashion; fond of novelties, inconstant. **newfangledly,** *adv.* **newfangledness,** *n.* **new-fashioned,** *a.* **new-fledged,** *a.* **new learning,** *n.* The Renaissance. **new look:** An up-to-date appearance. **new-made,** *a.* **new-model,** *v.t.* To give a fresh form to. **New Order,** *n.* A scheme for the organization and government of Europe devised by Adolf Hitler, its principal basis being the hegemony of the German nation. ***New Red Sandstone:** (*Geol.*) The sandstone strata between the Carboniferous and the Jurassic systems. **new woman:** A term formerly applied to a woman of advanced ideas, esp. one who claimed equality with men in the social, economic, and political spheres. **the New World:** the Western Hemisphere. **New Year's day:** The first day of the year. **newish,** *a.* **newly,** *adv.* Recently (*usu. in comb.*). **newness,** *n.*

newel (nū′ ėl) [O.F. *nuel* (F. *noyau*), kernel, from late L. *nucāle*, from *nux nucis*, nut], *n.* The central column from which the steps of a winding stair radiate; the hollow or well of a winding stair; an upright post at the top or bottom of a stair supporting the hand-rail.

newfangled [NEW].

Newfoundland (nū found′ lånd) [island in Gulf of St. Lawrence], *n.* A large breed of dog, famous for swimming powers, orig. from Newfoundland.

Newgate (nū′ gåt) [from the new gate of the City of London near which it was built in 1218], *n.* A London prison, demolished in 1902. **Newgate Calendar:** A list of prisoners in Newgate with accounts of their careers and crimes. **Newgate frill** or **fringe:** A beard under the chin and jaw (with alln. to the hangman's noose). **Newgate knocker:** A lock of hair twisted over the ear.

Newmarket (nū′ mar kėt) [town in Cambridgeshire], *n.* A Newmarket coat; a card game. **Newmarket coat:** A close-fitting overcoat, orig. for riding, worn by men or women.

news (nūz) [pl. of NEW (cp. F. *nouvelles*, L. *nova*, pl. of *novus*, new)], *n.pl.* (*usu. as sing.*) Recent or fresh information, tidings; *a newspaper. **news-agency,** *n.* An organization for supplying telegraphic information to newspapers etc. **news-agent,** *n.* A dealer in newspapers and other periodicals. **news-boy, -man,** *n.* One who delivers or sells newspapers in the street. **news-caster** (nūz′ kas tėr), *n.* (*Radio.*) A news broadcaster. **news editor,** *n.* (*Print.*) A newspaper editor specially engaged with the editing and display of news. **news-letter,** *n.* A weekly letter in the 17th cent. circulating news. **news-room,** *n.* A room for the reading of newspapers etc.; room where news is edited. **news-sheet,** *n.* A printed sheet of news, an early form of newspaper. **news stand:** A newspaper kiosk. **news-vendor,** *n.* A seller of newspapers. ***news-writer,** *n.* **newsless,** *a.* **newsy,** *a.* **newsiness,** *n.*

newsmonger (nūz′ mŭng gėr), *n.* One who makes it his business to spread news, usu. false; a busybody in news.

newspaper (nūz′ pā pėr), *n.* A printed publication, usu. issued daily or weekly, containing news usu. with leaders expressing opinions on questions of the hour, articles on special topics, advertisements, and often reviews of literature, plays, etc.

newsprint (nūz′ print), *n.* The cheap-quality paper upon which newspapers are printed.

newsreel (nūz′ rēl), *n.* (*Cinema.*) A film giving the day's news.

newt (nūt) [M.E. *ewte* (*a newt*, from *an ewt*), A.S. *efeta*, EFT], *n.* A small tailed amphibian like the salamander, an eft.

newton (nū′ tǒn), *n.* A unit of force equal to 100,000 dynes.

Newtonian (nū tō′ ni ȧn) [Sir Isaac *Newton* (1642–1727), -IAN], *a.* Of or pertaining to Newton or his theories; discovered or invented by Newton. *n.* A follower of Newton; a Newtonian telescope.

next (nekst) [A.-S. *nēahst* (NIGH, -EST)], *a.* Nearest in place, time or degree; nearest in order or succession, immediately following. *adv.* Nearest or immediately after; in the next place or degree. *prep.* Nearest to. *n.* The next person or thing. **next but one:** The one next to that immediately preceding or following. **next best:** Second best. **next door to:** In or at the house adjoining. **next, please:** Let the next person come; what else do you want? **what next:** (*int.*) Can anything exceed or surpass this? **next to:** Almost; all but. **next to nothing:** Scarcely anything.

nexus (nek′ sŭs) [L., from *nec-*, stem of *nectere*, to bind], *n.* (*pl.* **nexus,** -sūs) A link, a connexion.

ngaio (nī′ ō) [Maori], *n.* A N. Zealand tree noted for its fine white wood.

***nias** [EYAS].

nib (nib) [prob. var. of NEB], *n.* The point of a pen; a pen-point for insertion in a pen-holder; the point of a tool etc.; the beak of a bird; one of the handles projecting from the shaft of a scythe; (*pl.*) crushed cocoa-seeds. *v.t.* (*past & p.p.* **nibbed**) To put a nib into (a pen); to sharpen the nib of (a quill-pen). **his nibs:** (*slang*) A burlesque title.

nibble (nib′ ėl) [etym. doubtful, cp. L.G. *nibbelen*, Dut. *knibbelen*], *v.t.* To bite little by little; to bite little bits off; to bite at cautiously (as a fish at a bait); (*slang*) to nab, to catch. *v.i.* To take small bites or bite cautiously (at); (*fig.*) to criticize carpingly, to cavil. *n.* The act of nibbling; a little bite; a bit nibbled off. **nibbler,** *n.* **nibblingly,** *adv.*

niblick (nib′ lik) [etym. doubtful], *n.* (*Golf*) A club with a small cup-shaped iron head.

niccolite (nik′ ȯ līt), *n.* (*Min.*) Native arsenide of nickel.

nice (nīs) [O.F., from L. *nescium*, nom. *-us*, ignorant (see NESCIENT)], *a.* Fastidious, over-particular, hard to please, dainty, punctilious, scrupulous; acute, discerning, discriminating, sensitive to minute differences; requiring delicate discrimination or tact, delicate, subtle, minute; (*colloq.*) pleasing or agreeable, toothsome, well-flavoured; satisfactory; delightful, attractive, friendly, kind; *trivial; *ignorant, silly, foolish. **nicely,** *adv.* **niceness,** *n.* **niceish,** *adv.* Rather nice, rather pleasant.

Nicene (nī sēn′, nī′ sēn) [late L. *Nicēnus*, from *Nīcæa*, Gr. *Nikaia*, a town in Asia Minor], *a.* Of or pertaining to Nicæa. **Nicene councils:** Two councils held at Nicæa (the first in A.D. 325 to settle the Arian controversy, the second in 787 on the question of images and the iconoclasts). **Nicene creed:** A statement of Christian belief formulated by the first council of Nicæa.

nicety (nī′ si ti), *n.* Exactness, precision; a minute point, a delicate distinction; a small detail; *a delicacy, a dainty. **to a nicety:** Exactly, with precision.

niche (nich) [F., from It. *nicchia*, etym. doubtful], *n.* A recess in a wall for a statue, vase, etc.; (*fig.*) one's proper place or natural position. *v.t.* To put in a niche; to settle (oneself) in a comfortable place.

nick (1) (nik) [etym. doubtful], *n.* A small notch, cut, or dent, esp. used as a guide, a tally, or score for keeping account; the critical moment; a winning throw at dice; the exact point or moment; (*slang*) prison, police cell. *v.t.* To cut or make a nick or nicks in; to snip, to cut; to hit upon, to hit luckily or at the lucky moment; to catch at the exact moment; to make (a lucky throw), as at dice; *to cheat; (*slang*) to steal. *v.i.* To fit in exactly; (*Stock-breeding*) to mingle well, to produce offspring of good quality; to make a lucky throw, as at dice; to cut (in), to make a short cut (in, at, or past), as in a race. **in the nick of time:** Only just in time. **to nick a horse or a horse's tail:** To make an incision at the root of the tail, in order to make him carry it higher. **nick-eared,** *a.* Crop-eared.

Nick (2) (nik) [short for *Nicholas*], *n.* The devil, also Old Nick.

nickel (nik′ ėl) [Swed., abbrev. from G. *kupfernickel* (*kupfer*, copper, *nickel*, a demon, cp. A.-S. *nicol*), so called from disgust at its not yielding copper], *n.* A lustrous silvery-white ductile metallic element, usu. found in association with cobalt, used in the manufacture of German silver and in other alloys; a U.S. five-cent piece (formerly a one-cent piece). *v.t.* To coat with nickel. **nickel-plate,** *v.t.* To cover with nickel. **nickel-plating,** *n.* **nickel-silver,** *n.* An alloy like German silver but containing more nickel. **nickel-steel,** *n.* An alloy of nickel and steel. **nickelage** (nik′ ė lȧj), *n.* The process of nickeling. **nickelic,** *a.* **nickeliferous** (nik ė lif′ ėr ŭs), *a.* **nickeline, -lite,** *n.* Niccolite. **nickelize,** *v.t.*

nicker (1) (nik′ ėr) [Sc. and North., imit.], *v.i.* To neigh; (*fig.*) to guffaw. *n.* A neigh; a guffaw.

nicker (2) (nik′ ėr), *n.* (*slang*) A pound (money), £1.

nicknack [KNICK-KNACK].

nickname (nik′ nām) [M.E. *nekename*, corr. of *ekename*, from *an ekename* (EKE (1), NAME)], *n.* A name given in derision or familiarity. *v.t.* To give a nickname to; to call by a nickname.

nicotine (nik′ ȯ tēn) [F. Jean *Nicot*, 1530–1600, who introduced tobacco into France], *n.* An acrid, poisonous alkaloid contained in tobacco. **nicotinism** (nik′ ȯ ti nizm), *n.* (*Path.*) A morbid condition caused by over-indulgence in tobacco. **nicotinize,** *v.t.* **nicotian** (ni kō′ shi ȧn) *a.* Of or pertaining to tobacco. *n.* One who uses tobacco;* tobacco. **nicotianin,** *n.* (*Chem.*) A camphorous oil obtained from tobacco.

nictate, nictitate (nik′ tāt, -ti tāt) [L. *nictātus*, p.p. of *nictāre*, to wink (freq. *nictitāre*)], *v.i.* To wink, esp. to open and shut the eyes rapidly. **nictation, nictitation** (-tā′ shŭn), *n.* **nictitating membrane:** A third or inner eyelid possessed by birds, fishes, and many animals.

nidamental (nī dȧ men′ tȧl) [L. *nīdōmentum*, from *nīdus*, nest], *a.* Serving as a receptacle or protection for ova, eggs or young.

niddle-noddle (nidl nodl), *v.i.* To wag the head. *v.t.* To wag (the head). *a.* Vacillating.

nide (nīd) [L. nidus, a nest], *n.* A nest, esp. of young pheasants; a collection of pheasants.

nidge (nij) [from NICK], *v.t.* To dress the face of stone with a pointed hammer.

nidificate, nidify (nid′ i fi kāt, -i fī) [L. *nīdificātus*, p.p. of *nīdificāre* (*nīdus*, *-ficāre*, *facere*, to make)], *v.i.* To build a nest or nests. **nidification** (-kā′ shŭn), *n.* ***nidulation,** etc. [NIDUS], *n.*

nid-nod (nid nod) [redupl. from NOD], *v.i.* To keep nodding, as if sleepy.

***nidorose** (nī dȯ rōs′), **nidorous** (nī′ dȯ rŭs), *a.* ***nidor** (nī′ dȯr) [L.], *n.* The smell of cooked meat; any strong odour.

nidus (nī′ dŭs) [L.], *n.* (*pl.* **-di**) A nest, a place for the deposit of eggs by birds, insects, etc.; (*Bot.*) a place in which spores develop; (*Physiol. and Path.*) a place in an organism where germs develop, a centre of infection; (*Biol.*) a group of eggs, tubercles, etc.; (*fig.*) a source or origin, a place of development. ***nidulate,** *v.i.* To build a nest. ***nidulation** (-lā′ shŭn), *n.* Nidification.

niece (nēs) [O.F. *niece*, pop. L. *neptia*, L. *neptis*, rel. to *nepos*, NEPHEW], *n.* The daughter of one's brother or sister, or one's brother-in-law or sister-in-law; orig. a granddaughter.

niello (ni el′ ō) [It., from L. *nigellum*, neut. of *nigellus*, dim. of *niger*, black], *n.* (*pl.* **-li,** -lē) A black alloy used to fill the lines of incised designs on metal plates; an example of this work. **niellist,** *n.*

Niersteiner (nēr′ stī-, -shtī nėr) [*Nierstein*, near Hesse, Germany], *n.* A white Rhenish hock.

***nieve** (nēv) [M.E. *neve*, Icel. *hnefi* (cp. Swed. *näfre*, Dan. *næve*)], *n.* A fist. **nieveful,** *n.* (*Sc.*) A handful.

nifer (nif′ ėr) [Sc. and North., etym. doubtful (perh. rel. to prec.)], *v.t.* To exchange, to barter. *n.* An exchange.

nifty (nif′ ty) [slang], *a.* Smart, stylish.

Nigella (nī jel′ ȧ) [L., fem. of *nīgellus*, dim. of *niger*, black], *n.* (*Bot.*) A genus of ranunculaceous plants comprising love-in-a-mist.

niggard (nig′ ȧrd) [etym. obscure (Skeat compares Icel. *hnöggr*, Swed. *nugg*, Swed. dial. *nugger*, also A.-S. *hnēaw*, sparing)], *n.* A stingy person, a miser; one who is grudging (of). *a.* Miserly, mean, parsimonious. **v.t.* To begrudge, to stint. **v.i.* To be stingy. ***niggardish,** *a.* **niggardly,** *a.* and *adv.* **niggardliness,** *n.*

nigger (nig′ ėr) [F. *nègre*, Sp. NEGRO], *n.* A Negro (*used in contempt*); one of any dark-skinned race; a person of colour; the black caterpillar of the turnip saw-fly. **nigger in the woodpile:** A person or thing that spoils something good. **nigger brown:** A very dark shade of brown.

niggle (nig′ ėl) [cp. Norw. *nigla*], *v.i.* To busy oneself with petty details; to fiddle, to trifle. **v.t.* To trick. *n.* Small, cramped handwriting. **niggler,** *n.* **niggling,** *a.* and *n.*

nigh (nī) [A.-S. *nēah* (cp. Dut. *na*, G. *nah*, Icel. *na-*), cp. NEAR, NEXT], *adv.* Near; almost. *a.* Near; closely related. *prep.* Near, close to. **v.t.* and *i.* To approach. ***nighly,** *adv.* ***nighness,** *n.*

night (nīt) [A.-S. *niht* (cp. Dut. and G. *nacht*, Icel. *nātt*, *nōtt*, L. *nox*, Gr. *nux*, Sansk. *nekta*)], *n.* The time of darkness from sunset to sunrise; the darkness of this period; the end of daylight, nightfall; a period or state of darkness; (*fig.*) ignorance; intellectual and moral darkness; death; old age; a period of grief or mourning. **a night out:** An evening spent in festivity; the evening on which a servant is allowed out. **to make a night of it:** To spend an evening in festivity. **night-bell,** *n.* A bell for use at night, as a physician's. ***night-bird,** *n.* The owl or nightingale; (*fig.*) a disreputable character who goes about at night. **night-blindness,** *n.* Nyctalopia. **nightcap,** *n.* A cap worn in bed; (*fig.*) an alcoholic drink taken at bed-time. **night-cart,** *n.* A cart for removing night-soil. **night-chair** [NIGHT-STOOL]. **night-clothes,** *n.* Clothes worn in bed. **night-club,** *n.* A club open late at night and in the early hours of the morning. ***night-crow,** *n.* A bird croaking at night, and supposed to be of ill omen. **night-dog,** *n.* A watch-dog. **night-dress, -gown,** *n.* A woman's or child's night attire. **night-effect,** *n.* (*Radio.*) Transmission phenomena which are produced after sunset. **night-fall,** *n.* The beginning of night, the coming of darkness; dusk. **night-faring,** *a.* Travelling by night. **night-gear** [NIGHT-CLOTHES]. **night-fire,** *n.* A fire burning at night; an ignis fatuus. **night-fly,** *n.* A moth or other insect that flies by night; an angler's artificial fly for use after dark. **night-flower,** *n.* A flower that opens at night and shuts in the day. **night-foundered,** *a.* Wrecked by night. **night-glass,** *n.* A telescope enabling one to see objects at night. **night-gown** [NIGHT-DRESS]. ***night-hag,** *n.* A witch riding the air at night; a nightmare. **night-hawk,** *n.* The night-jar; an American bird, *Chordeiles Virginianus*. **night-jar,** *n.* The goatsucker. **night-light,** *n.* A short, thick candle for keeping alight at night; the light of the moon or stars. **night-line,** *n.* A line with baited hooks left in the water at night to catch fish. **night-long,** *a.* Lasting through a night. *adv.* All night. **nightman,** *n.* One who removes night-soil. **nightmare,** *n.* A terrifying dream often accompanied with pressure on the chest and a feeling of powerlessness; orig. a monster supposed to sit upon a sleeper, an incubus; (*fig.*) a haunting sense of dread or anything inspiring such a feeling. **nightmarish,** *a.* **night-piece,** *n.* A picture or description representing a night scene; a picture best seen by artificial light. **night-raven,** *n.* A bird of ill-omen supposed to cry at night. **night-school,** *n.* An evening school for those at work during the day. **night-season,** *n.* Night-time. **night-shirt,** *n.* A long shirt worn in bed by men or boys. **night-soil,** *n.* The contents of privies and cesspools removed at night. **night-stick:** (*Am.*) A truncheon. **night-stool, -chair,** *n.* A bedroom commode. **night-time,** *n.* **night-terrors:** (*Path.*) A nightmare of childhood, *pavor nocturnus*. ***night-waking,** *n.* **night-walker,** *n.* A somnambulist; one who prowls about at night for evil purposes, esp. a prostitute. **night-walking,** *n.* **night-wanderer,** *n.* ***night-wandering,** *a.* ***night-warbling,** *a.* Singing at night. **night-watch,** *n.* A watch or guard on duty at night; one of the periods into which the Jews and Romans divided the night. **night-watcher,** *n.* **night-work,** *n.* ***nighted,** *a.* Darkened; benighted. **nightless,** *a.* **nightly,** *a.* **nightward,** *a.* and *adv.* **nightwards,** *adv.* **nighty,** *a.* (*colloq.*) A night-gown.

nightingale (1) (nī′ ting gāl) [A.-S. *nihtegale* (NIGHT, *galan*, to sing)], *n.* A small migratory bird, *Daulias luscinia*, singing at night as well as by day.

nightingale (2) (nī′ ting gāl) [Florence *Nightingale* (1820–1910), philanthropist and hospital reformer], *n.* A jacket or wrap worn by invalids sitting up in bed.

nightmare [NIGHT].

nightshade (nīt′ shād), *n.* One of several plants of the genus *Solanum*, esp. the black nightshade, *S. nigrum*, with white flowers and poisonous black berries, and the woody nightshade, *S. dulcamara*, a trailing plant with purple flowers and brilliant red berries; also the deadly nightshade, *Atropa belladonna*.

nigrescent (nī-, ni gres′ ėnt) [L. *nigrescens -ntem*, pres.p. of *nigrescere*, incept. of *nigrēre*, to grow black, from *niger*, black], *adj.* Growing black; blackish. **nigrescence,** *n.* **nigrify** (nī′ gri fī), *v.t.* To blacken. **nigrification** (-kā′ shŭn), *n.* **nigrine** (nig′ rīn), *n.* (*Min.*) A ferriferous variety of rutile. **nigritude** (nī′ gri-, nig′ ri tūd), *n.* **nigro-,** *comb. form.* (*Bot. and Ent.*). **nigrosine** (nig′ rō sin), *n.* (*Chem.*) A blue-black dye-stuff obtained from aniline hydrochlorates.

nihil (nī′ hil) [L.], *n.* Nothing; *(*Law*) a return of no effects to a writ of distraint. **nihilism** (nī′ il izm), *n.* Any theological, philosophical, or political doctrine of a negative kind; (*Phil.*) denial of all existence, or of the knowledge of all existence; (*Polit.*) a Russian form of anarchism aiming at subversion of all existing institutions. **nihilist,** *n.* **nihilistic** (-lis′ tik), *a.* **nihility** (nī hil′ i ti), *n.* The state of being nothing, nothingness; (*fig.*) a mere nothing. **nil** (nil) [L., contr. of NIHIL], *n.* Nothing.

nikau (nē′ kou) [Maori], *n.* The New Zealand palm.

nilghau [NYLGHAU].

nill (nil) [A.-S. *nyllan* (NE, WILL)], *v.i.* To be unwilling (now only in 3rd sing. in phrase *will he, nill he* or *willing, nilling* or *willy-nilly*).

Nilometer (nī lom′ ė tėr), *n.* An instrument for measuring the rise of the Nile during its floods. **Nilotic** (nī lot′ ik), *a.* Pertaining to the Nile, etc.

nim (1) (nim) [?], *n.* An ancient game for two players in which a number of counters are used.

***nim** (2) (nim) [A.-S. *niman* (cp. M.Dut. *nemen*, O.H.G. *neman*, Icel. *nema*), prob. cogn. with Gr. *nemein*, to deal out], *v.t.* To steal, to filch. *v.i.* To steal, to pilfer.

nimble (nim′ bėl) [A.-S. *numol* (root of prec., -LE)], *a.* Light and quick in motion; agile, swift, dexterous; alert, clever, brisk, lively, versatile. **nimble-fingered,** *a.* **nimble-footed,** *a.* ***nimble-witted,** *a.* **nimbleness,** *n.* **nimbly,** *adv.*

nimbus (nim′ bŭs) [L., cloud], *n.* (*pl.* **-buses**) A halo or glory surrounding the heads of divine or sacred personages in paintings, etc.; (*Meteor.*) a rain-cloud, a dark mass of cloud, usu. with ragged edges, from which rain is falling or likely to fall. **nimbused,** *a.* ***nimbiferous** (-bif′ ėr ůs), *a.* Bringing storms. ***nimbose,** *a.* Stormy.

***nimiety** (ni mī′ ė ti) [late L. *nimietas*, from *nimis*], *n.* Excess, redundancy.

niminy-piminy (nim′ i ni pim′ i ni) [imit. of affected pronun.], *a.* Affecting niceness or delicacy; mincing.

Nimrod (nim′ rod) [the mighty hunter of Gen. x. 8–9], *n.* (*fig.*) A great hunter.

nincompoop (nin′ kŏm poop) [etym. unknown], *n.* A noodle, a blockhead, a fool.

nine (nīn) [A.-S. *nigon* (cp. Dut. *negen*, G. *neun*, Icel. *nīu*, L. *novem*, Gr. *ennea*, Sansk. *navan*)], *a.* Containing eight and one. *n.* The number composed of eight and one, 9, ix; a card of nine pips. **nine days' wonder:** An event, person, or thing that is a novelty for the moment but is soon forgotten. **nine times out of ten:** Usually, generally. **to the nines:** To perfection, elaborately. **the Nine:** The Muses. **nine-pins,** *n.* A game with nine skittles set up to be bowled at, (*Am.* ten-pins). **nine-tenths,** *n.* (*colloq.*) Nearly all. **ninefold,** *a.* Nine times repeated. **nineteen,** *a.* Containing one more than eighteen. *n.* The number representing this quantity, 19, xix. **nineteen to the dozen:** Volubly. **nineteenth,** *a.* **nineteenth hole:** (*colloq. Golf*) The clubhouse bar. **ninety,** *a.* Containing nine times ten. *n.* The number containing nine times ten, 90, xc; (*pl.*) the years between 89 and 100 in a century or a person's life. **ninetieth,** *a.*

ninny (nin′ i) [perh. imit., cp. Sp. *niño*, It. *ninno*, child], *n.* A fool, a simpleton.

ninon (nē′ non) [F.], *n.* (*Textiles*) A semi-diaphanous light silk material.

ninth (nīnth) [NINE, -TH], *a.* Next after the eighth. *n.* One of nine equal parts; (*Mus.*) an interval of an octave and a second. **ninthly,** *adv.*

niobium (nī ō′ bi ům) [*Niobe*, daughter of Tantalus, -IUM], *n.* (*Chem.*) A metallic element occurring in tantalite etc. **niobic** (ni ō′ bik), *a.* **niobite** (nī′ ŏ bīt), *n.* A niobic salt; (*Min.*) a variety of tantalite.

nip (1) (nip) [cp. Dut. *nijpen*, G. *kneifen*], *v.t.* (*past & p.p.* **nipped**) To pinch, to squeeze or compress sharply; to cut or pinch off the end or point of; (*fig.*) to bite; to sting, to pain; to check the growth of; to blast, to wither; to benumb; *to slander. *v.i.* To cause pain; (*slang*) to move, go, or step quickly (in, out, etc.). *n.* A pinch, a sharp squeeze or compression; a bite; (*fig.*) a check to vegetation, esp. by frost; a sharp saying, a sarcasm. **nip-cheese,** *n.* (*Naut. slang*) A purser. **nipper,** *n.* One who or that which nips; a device for seizing and holding; a horse's fore-tooth or incisor; a chela or great claw of a crab or other crustacean; a fish of various kinds; (*slang*) a boy, a lad; (*pl.*) a pair of pincers, forceps, or pliers; a pair of pince-nez. **nippingly,** *adv.* Keenly. **nippy,** *a.* Cold; active, agile; sharp in temper; quick, alert.

nip (2) (nip) [etym. doubtful], *n.* A small drink, esp. of spirits. *v.i.* To take a nip or nips. *v.t.* To take a nip of. **nipperkin** (nip′ ėr kin), *n.* (*now chiefly Sc.*) A small cup or the quantity held in this; orig. a measure of capacity less than half a pint.

nipa (nī′-, nē′ pȧ) [Malay *nīpah*], *n.* A palm tree of tropical S.-E. Asia and the islands of the Indian Ocean, with feathery leaves used in thatching, basket-weaving, etc., and packing bunches of fruit; an intoxicating beverage made from the sap of this.

nipper, etc. [NIP (1)].

nipple (nip′ ėl) [etym. doubtful], *n.* The small prominence in the breast of female mammals, esp. women, by which milk is sucked or drawn, a teat; a similar contrivance attached to a nursing-bottle; a nipple-shield; a nipple-shaped perforated projection, as on a gun-breach for holding a percussion-cap; a nipple-shaped prominence on the surface of metal or glass; a pap-shaped elevation on a mountain etc. **nipple-shield,** *n.* A protection worn over the nipple by nursing women. **nipplewort,** *n.* A slender weed, *Lapsana communis*, with small yellow flowers.

nippy [NIP (1)].

Nirvana (něr va′ nȧ) [Sansk., from *nirvā*, to blow], *n.* Absorption of individuality into the divine spirit with extinction of personal desires and passions, the Buddhist state of beatitude.

nis (1) (nis) [from Dan. or Swed. *nisse*], *n.* (*Scand. folklore*) A brownie or hobgoblin.

***nis** (2) (nis) [NE, IS], *v.i.* Is not.

Nisei (nē′ sā) [Jap.], *n.* A person of Japanese descent born in U.S.A. and loyal to that country.

nisi (nī′ sī) [L.], *conj.* (*Law*) Unless, if not. **decree, order,** or **rule nisi:** One that takes effect, or is made absolute, after a certain period, unless cause is shown for rescinding it. ***nisi prius*:** Orig. a writ commanding a sheriff to empanel a jury; an authority to judges of assize to try causes; applied to the trial of civil causes before judges of assize.

nissen (nis′ en), *n.* (*Mil.*) A long hut of corrugated iron with semicircular roof.

nisus (nī′ sůs) [L., from *nītī*, to endeavour], *n.* An effort, a conatus.

nit (nit) [A.-S. *hnitu* (cp. Dut. *neet*, G. *niss*, Icel. *nitr*)], *n.* The egg of a louse or other small, esp. parasitic, insect. **nitter,** *n.* A fly that deposits nits on horses; the bot-fly. **nitty,** *a.*

***nither** (nith′ ėr) [A.-S. *nitherian*, from *nither*, NETHER], *v.t.* To bring low; to humiliate, to abase.

nitid (nit′ id) [L. *nitidus*, from *nitēre*, to shine], *a.* Shining; bright, gay.

niton (nī′ tŏn) [L. *nitere*, to shine], *n.* Gaseous radioactive element.

nitrate (nī′ trȧt), *a.* A salt of nitric acid; (*ellipt.*) sodium or potassium nitrate. *v.t.* (-trāt) To treat or combine with nitric acid. **nitration** (nī trā′ shůn), *n.*

nitre (nī′ tėr) [F., from L. *nitrum*, Gr. *nitron*, perh. of Oriental orig. (cp. Heb. *nether*)], *n.* Saltpetre, potassium nitrate, occurring as an orthorhombic mineral. **nitriferous** (nī trif′ ėr ůs), *a.* **nitrify** (nī′ tri fī), *v.t.* To turn into nitre; to make nitrous. *v.i.* To become nitrous. **nitrification** (-kā′ shůn), *n.* **nitrite,** *n.*

nitric (nī′ trik), *a.* Pertaining to nitre. **nitric acid,** *n.* A colourless, corrosive acid liquid based on the ingredients of nitre, aqua fortis.

nitride (nī′ trīd), *n.* A compound of nitrogen with phosphorus, boron, silicon, etc.

nitro-, *comb. form.* **nitro-benzene, nitro-benzol,** *n.* An oily compound of benzene with nitric acid, having an odour of oil of bitter almonds, used for flavouring perfumes and confectionery. **nitro-calcite,** *n.* (*Min.*). **nitro-compound,** *n.* A compound obtained by treatment with nitric acid. **nitro-explosive,** *n.* One of a class of explosives prepared by treatment with nitric acid. **nitro-glucose,** *n.* A compound obtained from powdered cane-sugar treated with nitro-sulphuric acid. **nitro-glycerine,** *n.* A highly explosive colourless oil, obtained by adding glycerine to a mixture of nitric and sulphuric acids. **nitroleum** (nī trō′ lė ům), *n.* Nitro-glycerine. **nitro-magnesite,** *n.* (*Min.*) A white, bitter magnesium nitrate found as an efflorescent mineral in limestone caves. **nitrometer** (nī trom′ ė tėr), *n.* An instrument for determining nitrogen in some of its combinations. **nitro-muriatic,** *a.* Nitro-hydrochloric. **nitro-naphthalene,** *n.* A substance obtained by mixing naphthalene with nitric acid. **nitro-powder,** *n.* An explosive prepared from an organic compound by treatment with nitric acid.

nitrogen (nī′ trŏ jėn) [F. *nitrogène*], *n.* A colourless, tasteless, gaseous element forming four-fifths of the atmosphere, the basis of nitre and nitric acid. **nitrogenize** (nī troj′ ė nīz), *v.t.* **nitrogenic** (nī trŏ jen′ ik), **nitrogenous** (-troj′ ė nůs), *a.*

nitrous (nī′ trůs), *a.* (*Chem.*) Obtained from, impregnated with, or resembling nitre. **nitrous oxide:** Nitrogen monoxide used as an anæsthetic, laughing-gas.

nitroxyl (nī trok′ sil), *n.* A radical composed of one atom of nitrogen in chemical combination with two of oxygen.

nitter, nitty [NIT].

nitwit (nit′ wit), *n.* (*slang*) An ass, blockhead.

***nival** (nī′ vål) [L. *nivālis*, from *nivem*, nom. *nix*, snow], *a.* Growing in or under snow; niveous. **nivation,** *n.* Erosion due to the action of snow. **niveous** (niv′ ė ůs), *a.* Resembling snow; snowy. **nivosity** (ni vos′ i ti), *n.*

nix (1) (niks) [G., colloq. for *nichts*], *n.* (*slang*) Nothing, nobody.

nix (2) (niks) [Slang], *int.* Look out! **keeping nix:** Keeping watch.

nix (3), **nixie** (niks, nik′ si) [G. *nix*, fem. *nixe* (cogn. with A.-S. *nicor*, Icel. *nykr*, prob. rel. to Gr. *nizein, niptein*, to wash)], *n.* A water-sprite.

nizam (ni zam′) [Hind. from Arab. *nidhām*, order, government], *n.* (*pl. unaltered*) A man in the Turkish regular army; the title of the ruler of Hyderabad.

no (1) (nō) [A.-S. *nā* (NE, ever)], *adv.* A word of denial or refusal, the categorical negative; not; (*with comp.*) not at all, by no amount. *n.* (*pl.* **noes**) The word 'no'; a negative reply, a denial, a refusal; (*pl.*) voters against a motion. **no less:** As much, as much as. **no more:** Not any more; nothing further; no longer; dead, gone; never again; just as little as.

no (2) (nō) [NONE], *a.* Not any; not one, not a; quite other, quite opposite or the reverse; not the least; hardly any; absent, lacking; expressing opposition, objection, or rejection (as *no popery*). *adv.* Not (usu. at end of sentence with *or*). **no ball:** (*Cricket*) A ball not delivered according to the rules, counting for one to the other side. **no-ball,** *v.t.* To declare (a ball) to be no-ball; to declare (a bowler) to have bowled this. **no go** [GO (2)]. **nohow,** *adv.* In no way, not by any means. **no man:** No one, no person, nobody. **no-man's-land:** Waste or unclaimed land; (*Mil.*) the contested land between two opposing forces. **no one:** Nobody, no person. **no thoroughfare:** A notice that a road, path, etc., is closed or has no exit or through way. **noway, *noways, nowise,** *adv.* In no way, not at all. **nowhence,** *adv.* **nowhither,** *adv.* **no whit:** Not at all, not in the least.

Noachian, Noachic (nō ā′ ki ån, -kik). *a.* Pertaining to Noah or his times. **Noah's ark** [ARK].

nob (1) (nob) [prob. var. of KNOB], *n.* (*slang*) The head; (*Cribbage*) a point scored for holding the knave of the same suit as the turn-up. *v.t.* (*Boxing*) To hit on the head.

nob (2) (nob) [Slang, etym. doubtful], *n.* A person of rank or distinction; a swell. **nobby,** *a.* Smart, elegant.

nobble (nob′ ėl) [Slang, etym. doubtful], *v.t.* To dose, lame, or otherwise tamper with (a horse) to prevent its winning a race; to circumvent, to overreach; to get round, to square; to get hold of dishonestly; to catch, to nab; to nob, to hit on the head; to buttonhole (a person). **nobbler,** *n.*

Nobel Prizes (nō bel′ prī′ zėz) [Alfred *Nobel* (1833–1896)], *n. pl.* Prizes awarded by the will of Nobel for excellence in various branches of learning and the furtherance of universal peace.

nobility (nȯ bil′ i ti) [F. *nobilité*, L. *nōbilitātem*, nom. *-tas*, as foll.], *n.* The quality of being noble; magnanimity, greatness, dignity; nobleness of birth or family; (*collect.*) the nobles, the peerage. **nobiliary,** *a.* ***nobilitate,** *v.t.* ***nobilitation** (-tā′ shůn), *n.*

noble (nō′ bėl) [F., from L. *nōbilis*, from base of *noscere*, to KNOW], *a.* Lofty or illustrious in character, worth, or dignity; magnanimous, high-minded, morally elevated; of high rank, of ancient or illustrious lineage; belonging to the nobility; magnificent, grand, stately, splendid, imposing; excellent, fine, admirable; valuable, pure (of metals). *n.* A nobleman, a peer; an obsolete gold coin worth usu. 6s. 8d. **nobleman,** *n.* A peer. **noble metals,** *n.pl.* Metals such as gold, silver, platinum, which are not affected by air or water, and not easily by acids. **noble-minded,** *a.* **noble-mindedness,** *n.* **noble-woman,** *n.* **nobleness,** *n.* ***noblesse*** (nȯ bles′), *n.* The nobility (of a foreign country); *noblemen, nobility. ***noblesse oblige:*** Rank imposes obligations. **nobly,** *adv.*

nobody (nō′ bȯ di), *n.* No one, no person; (*fig.*) a person of no importance.

***nocent** (nō′ sėnt) [L. *nocens -ntem*, pres.p. of *nocēre*, to injure], *a.* Hurtful, mischievous; criminal, guilty. *n.* A guilty person.

nock (nok) [M.E. *nokke*, prob. from Dut. or L.G. *nokk*], *n.* A notched tip of horn etc. at the butt-end of an arrow; the notch in this; *the notched tip at each end of a bow; (*Naut.*) the upper fore corner of a sail. *v.t.* To fit (an arrow) to the bowstring.

noct-, nocti- [L. *nox, noctis*, night], *comb. form.* Nocturnal, by night.

noctambulant (nok tăm′ bū lånt) [L. *ambulare*, to walk], *a.* Night-walking. **noctambulation,** *n.* Somnambulism. **noctambulism,** *n.* **noctambulist,** *n.* **noctambulous,** *a.*

noctiflorus (nok ti flôr′ ůs), *a.* (*Bot.*) Night-flowering.

noctilionine (nok til′ i ȯn īn), *a.* Belonging to the genus of bats *Noctilio*.

noctiluca (nok ti loo′ kå), *n.* A phosphorescent marine animalcule.

noctilucent (nok ti loo′ sėnt), *a.* Shining by night.

noctivagant (nok tiv′ å gånt), *a.* Wandering by night. **noctivagation,** *n.* **noctivagous,** *a.*

noctograph (nok′ tō grăf), *n.* A writing-frame for the blind; a nocturnograph; a noctuary.

Noctua (nok′ tū å) [L. night-owl], *n.* (*Ent.*) A genus of moths typical of the *Noctuidæ*, the largest family of Lepidoptera. **noctuid,** *a.* and *n.*

noctuary (nok′ tū å ri), *n.* An account of nightly events, experiences, etc.

noctule (nok′ tūl), *n.* The great bat *Vesperugo noctula.*

nocturn (nok′ tĕrn), *n.* (*R.-C. Church*) One of the divisions of matins.

Nocturnæ (nok tĕrn′ e), *n.pl.* (*Zool.*) The owls.

nocturnal (nok tĕrn′ ål), *a.* Relating to, or occurring, performed, or active by, night. **nocturnally,** *adv.*

nocturne (nok′ tĕrn), *n.* A painting or drawing of a night scene; a dreamy piece of music suited to the night or evening.

nocturnograph (nok tĕrn′ ō grăf), *n.* An instrument for recording work done at night in factories, mines, etc.

nocuous (nok′ ū ůs) [L. *nocuus*, from *nocēre*, to injure], *a.* Hurtful, noxious; poisonous, venomous. **nocuously,** *adv.*

nod (nod) [etym. doubtful], *v.i.* (*past & p.p.* **nodded**) To incline the head with a slight, quick motion in token of assent, command, indication, or salutation; to incline, to totter (of a building); to let the head fall forward; (*fig.*) to be drowsy, to sleep; to make a careless mistake. *v.t.* To bend or incline (the head etc.); to signify by a nod. *n.* A quick bend of the head; a bending downwards; (*fig.*) command. **Land of Nod:** Sleep. **nodder,** *n.*

nodal [NODE].

noddle (1) (nodl) [etym. doubtful], *n.* (*contemp.*) The head.

noddle (2) (nodl), *v.t.* and *i.* To nod frequently, to wag.

noddy (nod' i) [prob. rel. to NOD], *n.* A simpleton, a fool; a tropical sea-bird, *Anous stolida*, from its being easily caught; *a light two-wheeled hackney-vehicle; an inverted pendulum used to indicate vibration.

node (nōd) [L. *nodus*, a knot], *n.* A knot, a knob; (*Bot.*) the point of a stem from which leaves arise; (*Path.*) a tumour on a bone, tendon, etc.; an induration or concretion due to gout, rheumatism, etc.; (*Astron.*) the point at which the orbit of a planet intersects the ecliptic, or in which two great circles of the celestial sphere intersect; (*Math.*) the point at which a curve crosses itself and at which more than one tangent can be drawn; a similar point on a surface; (*Phys.*) a point of rest in a vibrating body; (*fig.*) the plot of a story, play, or poem. **nodal,** *a.* **nodal lines:** Lines on the surface of an elastic body which remain at rest when the body is made to vibrate. **nodal points:** The points in a string extended between two fixed objects which remain at rest when the string is made to vibrate. **nodical,** *a.* (*Astron.*) Relating to the nodes. **nodose** (nò dōs', nō' dōs), *a.* Knotty; having nodes. **nodosity** (nò dos' i ti), *n.* **nodule** (nod' ūl), *n.* A small knot, node or lump; (*Geol.*) a rounded lump or mass of irregularly-rounded shape; (*Bot.*) a small node; (*Path.*) a small knot or tumour. **nodular, nodulated, noduled, nodulose** (nod ū lōs'), **nodulous** (nod' ū lūs), *a.* **nodulation** (-lā' shŭn), *n.* **nodus** (nō' dŭs), *n.* A knotty point, a complication, a difficulty; a node.

Noel (nō ĕl') [F.], *n.* Christmas.

Noetian (nò ē' shăn), *n.* A follower of Noetus of Smyrna (2nd cent. A.D.), who taught that there was only one person in the Godhead, and that Christ was a mode of manifestation of the Father. *a.* Of or pertaining to Noetus or Noetianism. **Noetianism,** *n.*

noetic, -al (nò et' ik, -ăl) [Gr. *noētokos*, from *noēsis*, mental perception, from *noein*, to perceive (*noos*, mind, thought)], *a.* Relating to the intellect; performed by or originating in the intellect. ***noematic, -al** (-măt' ik, -ăl), *a.* **noesis** (nò ē' sis), *n.* Pure thought; an intellectual view of the world.

***nog** (1) (nog) [etym. doubtful], *n.* A strong ale, brewed in East Anglia.

nog (2) (nog) [etym. doubtful], *n.* A pin, tree-nail, or peg; a wooden block shaped like a brick, built into a wall to take nails; a snag or stump. *v.t.* To fix or secure with a nog or nogs; to build with nogging.

noggin (nog' in) [etym. doubtful], *n.* A small mug; a measure, usu. a gill; the contents of such a measure.

nogging (nog' ing) [NOG (2), -ING], *n.* A wall of scantling filled with bricks.

nohow [NO (2)].

noil (noil) [etym. doubtful], *n.* (*often in pl.*) Tangles and knots of wool removed by the comb.

noise (noiz) [F., etym. doubtful], *n.* A sound of any kind, esp. a loud, discordant, harsh, or disagreeable one; clamour, din, loud or continuous talk; evil report, scandal; *rumour; a band of musicians. **v.i.* To make a noise. *v.t.* To make public, to spread (about or abroad). **big noise,** *n.* (*colloq.*) A person of importance. ***noiseful,** *a.* **noiseless,** *a.* **noiselessly,** *adv.* **noiselessness,** *n.* **noisy,** *a.* Causing noise; making much noise; (*fig.*) glaring, violent, loud (of colours, dress, style, etc.). **noisily,** *adv.* **noisiness,** *n.*

noisette (1) (nwa zet') [Philippe *Noisette*, of Charleston, S. Carolina, grower], *n.* A variety of rose, a cross between the China rose and the musk-rose.

noisette (2) (nwa zet') [F., hazel nut, dim. of *noix*], *n.* (*pl.*) Small pieces of mutton, veal, etc., cooked for the table in a special way.

noisome (noi' sŏm) [M.E. *noy*, ANNOY, SOME], *a.* Hurtful, noxious; unwholesome, offensive, disgusting (esp. of smells). **noisomely,** *adv.* **noisomeness,** *n.*

nolens volens (nō' lĕnz vō' lĕnz) [*nōlens*, pres.p. of *nolle*, to be unwilling, *volens*, pres.p. of *velle*, to be willing], *adv.* Willing or unwilling, willy-nilly, perforce.

noli-me-tangere (nō' lī mē tăn' jĕr ē) [L., touch me not], *n.* A plant of the genus *Impatiens*, esp. *I. noli-me-tangere*, the yellow balsam; an ulcerous disease of the skin, lupus.

noll (nōl) [A.-S. *hnol* (cp. O.H.G. *hnol*, top)], *n.* The head.

nomad (nom' ăd, nō' măd) [L. and Gr. *nomad-*, nom. *nomas*, from *nemein*, to allot, to pasture], *n.* One of a tribe that wanders about seeking pasture for their flocks, a wanderer. *a.* Wandering. **nomadic** (nò măd' ik), *a.* **nomadically,** *adv.* **nomadism** (nom' ă dizm), *n.* **nomadize,** *v.i.*

no-man's-land [NO (2)].

nomarch (nom' ark) [Gr. *nomarchēs* or *nomarchos* (*nomos*, NOME, *archein*, to govern)], *n.* A ruler or governor of an Egyptian nome or Greek nomarchy. **nomarchy,** *n.* A province of modern Greece.

nombril (nom' bril) [F., the navel], *n.* (*Her.*) The point of an escutcheon between the fesse-point and the base-point.

nom de guerre (non dė gâr') [F., war-name], *n.* An assumed name, a pseudonym. ***nom de plume*** (ploom) [incorrect F.], *n.* A pen-name.

nome (nōm) [Gr. *nomos*, from *nemein*, to divide], *n.* A province of a country, esp. in modern Greece and Egypt.

nomenclator (nō' mĕn klā tŏr) [L. (*nōmen*, name, *calāre*, to call)], *n.* One who gives names to things, esp. in classification of natural history etc.; (*Rom. Ant.*) a servant or attendant, esp. on a candidate for office, whose duty it was to name or introduce persons met; an officer who assigned places at banquets. **nomenclative, *nomenclatory** (nò men' klă tŏr i), *a.* **nomenclatress** (nō' mĕn klā trĕs), *n.* **nomenclature** (nō' mĕn klā tyŭr, nō men' klă chŭr), *n.* A system of names for the objects of study in any branch of science; a system of terminology; a vocabulary, a glossary; *a name. **nomenclatural** (nō men klā' tyŭ răl), *a.*

***nomial** (nō' mi ăl) [from BINOMIAL], *n.* (*Alg.*) A single term or name.

nomic (nom' ik) [Gr. *nomikos*, from *nomos*, law], *a.* Ordinary, customary (of spelling). *n.* The usual spelling.

nominal (nom' i năl) [L. *nōminālis*, from *nōmen -inis*, name], *a.* Existing in name only; opp. to real; (*fig.*) trivial, inconsiderable; of, pertaining to, or consisting of a name or names; containing names; of or pertaining to a noun, substantival. **nominalism,** *n.* The doctrine that general or abstract concepts have no existence but as names or words [cp. REALISM]. **nominalist,** *n.* **nominalistic** (-lis' tik), *a.* **nominally,** *adv.* In name only.

nominate (nom' i nāt) [L. *nōminātus*, p.p. of *nōmināre*, as prec.], *v.t.* To name, to designate; to mention by name; to appoint to an office or duty; to propose as a candidate; to call, to denominate. ***nominately,** *adv.* **nomination** (-nā' shŭn), *n.* **nominator,** *n.* **nominee** (nom i nē'), *n.* A person named or appointed by name. **nomineeism,** *n.*

nominative (nom' i nă tiv) [L. *nōminātīvus*, as prec.], *a.* (*Gram.*) Applied to the case of the subject. *n.* The case of the subject; the subject of the verb. **nominatival** (-tī' văl), *a.*

nomistic (nò mis' tik) [Gr. *nomos*, law, -IST, -IC], *a.* Of or based upon law. **nomocracy** (nō mok' ră si), *n.* A system of government according to a code of laws. **nomogeny** (nō moj' ĕn i), *n.* Origination of life according to natural law, not by miracle. **nomogram** (nō' mō grăm), *n.* (*Math.*) A chart with scales of quantities arranged side by side, which can be used to carry out rapid calculations. **nomography** (nò mog' ră fi) [-GRAPHY], *n.*

The art of drafting laws or a treatise on this. **nomographer,** *n.* **nomology** (nŏ mol′ ŏ ji) [-LOGY], *n.* The science of law. **nomologist,** *n.* **nomothetical** (nom ŏ thet′ i kăl) [Gr. *nomothetikos*, from *nomothetēs*, lawgiver (*tithenai*, to put or set)], *a.* Legislative.

non- [L., not], *pref.* Freely prefixed to indicate a negative, only a selection of such words is given below. **non-ability** (non ă bil′ i ti), *n.* A want of ability. **non-abstainer,** *n.* One who is not a total abstainer from intoxicating liquors. **non-acceptance** (non ăk sep′ tăns), *n.* **non-access** (-ăk′ ses), *n.* (*Law*) Absence of opportunity for sexual intercourse, a plea in questions of paternity. **non-acquaintance,** *n.* Lack of acquaintance (with). **non-acquiescence,** *n.* Refusal of acquiescence. **non-aggression pact,** *n.* (*Pol.*) An agreement between two states to settle differences by negotiation rather than by force. **non-appearance,** *n.* Default of appearance, esp. in court. **non-attendance,** *n.* **non-belligerent,** *n.* (*Pol.*) A neutral; a country that remains neutral in name only, supporting a belligerent country with everything save armed force. **non-claim,** *n.* (*Law*) Failure to make a claim within the legal time. **non-collegiate,** *a.* Not belonging to a college (of a student); not having colleges (of a University). **non-combatant,** *a.* Not in the fighting line. *n.* A civilian, esp. a surgeon, chaplain, etc., attached to troops. **non-com.,** *n.* (*slang*) A non-commissioned officer. **non-commissioned,** *a.* Not holding a commission, applied to military officers below the rank of 2nd lieutenant. **non-committal,** *n.* Refusal to commit or pledge oneself; the state of not being committed to either side. *a.* Not committing one, impartial. **non-communicant,** *n.* One who fails to attend Holy Communion. **non-compliance,** *n.* (*Law*) Failure to comply. **non-complying,** *a.* **non-concurrence,** *n.* **non-conducting,** *a.* Not conducting heat or electricity. **non-conductor,** *n.* A substance or medium that offers resistance to heat or electricity. **non-conductibility,** *n.* **non-contagious,** *a.* Not contagious. **non-content,** *n.* (*House of Lords*) One who votes in the negative. **non-co-operation,** *n.* Refusal to co-operate; inactive opposition; refusal, by non-payment of taxes, to co-operate with the government of a country. **non-delivery,** *n.* **non-development.** *n.* **non-discovery,** *n.* **non-effective,** *a.* (*Mil. and Nav.*) Not qualified for active service. **non-ego** [L., not I], *n.* (*Phil.*) The external or objective in perception or thought. **non-egoistical,** *a.* **non-elect,** *a.* Not elected. *n.* One not elected; one not predestined for salvation. **non-election,** *n.* ***non-electric,** *a.* Not electric; conducting electricity. *n.* A non-electric substance. **non-emphatic,** *a.* Without emphasis. **non-episcopal,** *a.* Not belonging to the Episcopalian Church. **non-episcopalian,** *n.* **non-essential,** *a.* and *n.* **non-execution,** *n.* **non-existence,** *n.* **non-existent,** *a.* **non-exportation,** *n.* **non-feasance,** *n.* (*Law*) Failure to perform an act that is legally incumbent on one. **non-ferrous,** *a.* (*Metal.*) Containing no iron. **non-forfeiting,** *a.* (*Insurance*) Applied to policies which are not forfeited upon non-payment of premiums. **non-fulfilment,** *n.* **non-human,** *a.* Not belonging to the human race. **non-importation,** *n.* **non-importing,** *a.* **non-interference, non-intervention,** *n.* The principle or policy of keeping aloof from the disputes of other nations. **non-intrusion,** *n.* (*Sc. Ch.*) The principle that a patron should not impose an unacceptable minister on a congregation. **non-intrusionist,** *n.* **non-joinder,** *n.* (*Law*) Failure to join with another as party to a suit. **non-juring,** *a.* Not swearing allegiance; pertaining to the non-jurors. **non-juror,** *n.* One who would not swear allegiance to William and Mary in 1689. **non-jury,** *a.* Tried without jury. **non-manufacturing,** *a.* **non-member,** *n.* One who is not a member. **non-membership,** *n.* **non-metal,** *n.* An element that is not a metal. **non-metallic,** *a.* **non-moral,** *a.* Not involving ethical considerations. **non-natural,** *a.* Not natural; *(*Med.*) not part of the nature of man but essential to his existence, as air, food, sleep, etc. **non-obedience,** *n.* **non-observance,** *n.* **non-party,** *a.* Not concerned with questions of party. **non-payment,** *n.* **non-performance,** *n.* **non-placental,** *a.* Not having a placenta. **non-ponderous,** *a.* Having no weight. **non-production,** *n.* **non-professional,** *a.* Not professional, amateur; unskilled. **non-proficient,** *a.* and *n.* **non-provided,** *a.* Denoting schools which are not provided by the Education Authority, *e.g.* Church Schools. **non-regardance,** *n.* Want of due regard. **non-residence,** *n.* The state of not residing in a place, on one's estate, at one's office, etc. **non-resident,** *a.* and *n.* **non-resistance,** *n.* Passive obedience or submission even to power unjustly exercised. ***non-resistant,** *a.* and *n.* **non-resisting,** *a.* **non-sexual,** *a.* Asexual, sexless. **non-skid,** *n.* and *a.* A tyre designed to prevent skidding. **non-society** [NON-UNION]. **non-solvent,** *a.* Insolvent. *n.* An insolvent. **non-solvency,** *n.* **non-stop,** *a.* Without a pause; (*Rail.*) not stopping at certain stations. **non-submissive,** *a.* **non-union,** *a.* Not connected with a society or trade union. **non-unionist,** *n.* **non-user,** *n.* (*Law*) Neglect to use a right by which it may become void.

nonage (nō′ năj, non′ ăj) [O.F. (NON-, AGE)], *n.* The state of being under age; minority; a period of immaturity.

nonagenarian (non ă jĕ nâr′ i ăn) [L. *nōnāgēnārius*, from *nōnāgēnī*, ninety each], *a.* Ninety years old. *n.* A person 90 years old, or between 90 and 100.

nonagesimal (non ă jes′ i măl) [L. *nōnāgēsimus*, from *nōnāginta*, ninety], *a.* Pertaining to 90 or to a nonagesimal. *n.* (*Astron.*) The point of the ecliptic highest above the horizon.

nonagon (non′ ă gŏn) [from L. *nōnus*, ninth, after DECAGON, etc.], *n.* A figure having nine sides and nine angles.

nonary (nō′ nă ri) [L. *nōnārius*, from *nōnus*, ninth], *a.* Based on the number nine (of a scale of notation). *n.* A group of nine; *(*Path.*) a tertian fever recurring on the ninth day.

nonce (nons) [*for then once*, read as *for the nonce* (ONCE)], *n.* The present time, occasion, purpose, etc. **nonce-word,** *n.* A word coined for the occasion.

nonchalant (non′ shă lănt) [F., pres.p. of O.F. *nonchaloir* (L. *calere*, to glow)], *a.* Careless, cool, unmoved, indifferent. **nonchalance,** *n.* **nonchalantly,** *adv.*

nonconformist (non kŏn fôr′ mist), *n.* One who does not conform, esp. a member of a Protestant Church or sect dissenting from the Church of England. **nonconforming,** *a.* **nonconformity,** *n.*

nondescript (non′ dĕ skript) [L. *descriptus*, p.p. of *descrībere*, to DESCRIBE], *a.* Not easily described or classified; neither one thing nor another; hybrid. *n.* Such a person or thing that is odd or abnormal.

none (1) (nŭn) [A.-S. *nān* (NE, ONE)], *pron.* No one, no person; (*colloq.*) no persons; not any, not any portion (of). *a.* No, not any. *adv.* In no respect; by no amount; not at all. **none-so-pretty,** *n.* The London pride, *Saxifraga umbrosa.* ***none-sparing,** *a.* All-destroying.

none (2) (nōn) [NONES].

nonentity (non en′ ti ti) [NON-, ENTITY], *n.* Non-existence; a thing not existing, a mere figment, an imaginary thing; (*fig.*) an unimportant person or thing.

nones (nōnz) [F., from L. *nōnas*, nom. *nōnæ*, fem. pl. of *nōnus*, ninth (or pl. of obs. *none*, L. *nōna*, NOON)], *n.pl.* (*Rom. Ant.*) The ninth day before the ides; (*R.-C. Ch.*) the office for the ninth hour after sunrise, or 3 p.m.

nonesuch (nŭn′ sŭch), *n.* One who or that which is without an equal, a paragon, a nonpareil; black medick; *the scarlet lychnis; a variety of apple.

nonet (no net′) [It. *nonetto*, ninth], *n.* (*Mus.*) Musical composition for nine players or singers.

non-feasance, etc. [NON-].

nonillion (nō nil' yȯn) [from L. *nōnus*, ninth, after BILLION], *n.* A million raised to the ninth power, denoted by a unit with 54 ciphers annexed; (*F. and Am.*) the tenth power of a thousand, denoted by a unit with 30 ciphers. **nonillionth,** *a.* and *n.*

nonius (nō' ni ŭs) [mod. L., from Pedro *Nuñez* (1492–1577), Port. mathematician], *n.* A contrivance for the graduation of mathematical instruments, now superseded by the vernier.

non-juror, etc. [NON-].

non-natural, etc. [NON-].

***nonny** (non' i) [meaningless sound], *n.* A refrain in old ballads etc., often covering indecent allusions; also **hey nonny, nonny-no, nonny-nonny.**

nonpareil (non på rel') [F. *pareil*, med. L. *pariculus*, dim. of *par*, equal], *a.* Having no equal; peerless, unrivalled, unique. *n.* A paragon, a thing of unequalled excellence; a variety of apple, bird, wheat, etc.; (*Print.*) (non' på rĕl) a size of type [as this].

non placet (non plā' set) [L., it does not please], *n.* The formula used in university and ecclesiastical assemblies in giving a negative vote. **non-possumus** (non pos' ū mŭs) [L., we cannot], *n.* A plea of inability. **non sequitur** (non sek' wi tĕr) [L., it does not follow], *n.* An inference not warrantable from the premises.

nonplus (non' plŭs) [L. *nōn plūs*, no more], *n.* A state of perplexity; a puzzle, a quandary. *v.t.* (*past* **nonplussed**) To puzzle, to confound, to bewilder.

non-residence, etc. [NON-].

nonsense (non' sĕns), *n.* Unmeaning words, ideas, etc.; foolish or extravagant talk, conduct, etc.; foolery, absurdity; rubbish, worthless stuff, trifles. **nonsense book:** A book containing amusing absurdities. **nonsense name:** A name or term arbitrarily made up for mnemonic or other purposes. **nonsense verses:** Verses having no meaning, used for mnemonic purposes; verses intentionally absurd written to amuse. **nonsensical** (non sens' i kål), *a.* **nonsensicality** (-kăl' i ti), **nonsensicalness,** *n.* **nonsensically,** *adv.*

nonsuch [NONESUCH].

nonsuit (non' sūt), *n.* (*Law*) The stoppage of a suit during trial through insufficient evidence or non-appearance of the plaintiff. *v.t.* To subject to a nonsuit. **non-union,** etc. [NON-].

noodle (1) (noo' del) [etym. doubtful], *n.* A simpleton, a fool. **noodledom, noodleism,** *n.*

noodle (2) (noo' del) [G. *nudel*, etym. doubtful], *n.* A strip or ball of dried dough made of wheat-flour and eggs, served with soup etc.

nook (nuk) [M.E. *nōk*, etym. doubtful], *n.* A corner; a cozy place, as in an angle; a secluded retreat.

noology (nō ol' i ji) [Gr. *noos*, mind], *n.* The science of the understanding. **noological** (nō ō loj' i kål), *a.* **noologist** (-ol' ŏ jist), *n.*

noon (noon) [A.-S. *nōn* (in *nōn-tīd*), from L. *nōna hōra*, ninth hour], *n.* The middle of the day, twelve o'clock; (*fig.*) the culmination or height. *a.* Pertaining to noon. **noonday,** *n.* and *a.* **noontide,** *n.* **noontide prick:** (*Shak.*) The point of noon. ***nooning,** *n.* A rest or a meal at noon.

noose (noos) [perh. from O.F. or Prov. *nous*, L. NODUS], *n.* A loop with a running knot binding the closer the more it is pulled, as in a snare, a hangman's halter, etc.; (*fig.*) a tie, a bond, a snare. *v.t.* To catch in a noose; to entrap; to tie a noose on; to tie in a noose.

nopal (nō' pål) [Sp. or Port., from Mex. *nopalli*], *n.* An American genus of cacti resembling *Opuntia*, grown for the support of the cochineal insect. **nopalry,** *n.* A plantation of these.

nor (nôr) [prob. short for M.E. *nother*, A.-S. *nāwæther* (*nā*, NO (2), WHETHER)], *conj.* And not (a word marking the second or subsequent part of a negative proposition); occasionally used without the correlative. ******adv.* Neither.

noraghe (nō ra' gā) [It.], *n.* (*pl.* **noraghi**) A prehistoric stone structure common in Sardinia.

nor' [NORTH].

Nordenfelt (nôr' dėn felt) [I. V. *Nordenfeld* (*b.* 1842), Swedish inventor], *n.* A machine-gun invented by Nordenfeld.

Nordic (nôr' dik) [Scand. *nord*, north], *n.* (*Ethn.*) A tall, blond dolichocephalic racial type inhabiting Scandinavia, parts of Scotland and other parts of N. Europe.

Norfolk (nôr' fȯk) [English county], *n.* (*colloq.*) A Norfolk jacket. **Norfolk dumpling:** A dumpling made in Norfolk; (*fig.*) a native or inhabitant of Norfolk. **Norfolk jacket:** A man's loose jacket with vertical pleats in the back and front and a waist-band.

noria (nôr' i å) [Sp., from Arab. *nā' ūrah*], *n.* A rude contrivance used in Spain, Palestine, etc., for raising water by means of buckets etc.

norland (*Sc.*) [NORTHLAND].

norm (nôrm) [L. *norma*, carpenter's square], *n.* A standard, a model, pattern, or type; (*Biol.*) a typical structure etc.

normal (nôr' mål) [as prec.], *a.* According to rule, standard, or established law; regular, typical, usual; (*Geom.*) perpendicular. *n.* The usual state, quality, quantity, etc.; (*Geom.*) a perpendicular line; (*Phys.*) the average or mean value of observed quantities; (*Meteor.*) the mean temperature, volume, etc. **Normal school:** A school where teachers are trained. **normality** (nôr măl' i ti), *n.* **normalize,** *v.t.* **normalization** (-zā' shŭn), *n.* **normally,** *adv.*

Norman (1) (nôr' mån) [O.F. *Normans*, pl. of *Normant* (F. *Normand*), from Teut. NORTHMAN], *n.* A native or inhabitant of Normandy; a member of a mixed race of Northmen and Franks established there. *a.* Of or pertaining to Normandy or the Normans. **Norman-English,** *n.* English mixed with Norman-French forms as spoken in England after the Norman Conquest. **Norman-French,** *n.* French as spoken by the Normans; the form of this that continued in use in the English law-courts. **Normanesque** (-nesk'), *a.* **Normanism,** *n.* **Normanize,** *v.t.* **Normanization** (-zā' shŭn), *n.*

norman (2) (nôr' mån) [perh. ident. with prec. (cp. Dut. *noorman*, G. *normann*, Dan. *normand*)], *n.* (*Naut.*) A bar inserted in a capstan or bitt for fastening the cable.

Norn, Norna (nôrn, nôr' nå) [Icel.], *n.* One of the Norse Fates.

Norroy (nor' oi) [A.-F. *nor*, NORTH, *roy*, king], *n.* The third King-of-Arms, having jurisdiction north of the Trent.

Norse (nôrs) [prob. from Dut. *noorsch, noordsch* (*noord*, NORTH, -ISH)], *a.* Pertaining to Norway or its inhabitants, Norwegian. *n.* The Norwegian language; the language of Norway and its colonies (till the 14th cent.); (*loosely*) the Scandinavian languages, including early Swedish and Danish. **Norseman,** *n.*

north (nôrth), **nor'** (nôr) [A.-S. (cp. Dut. *noord*, G., Dan., and Swed. *nord*, Icel. *northr*)], *n.* One of the four cardinal points, that to the right of a person facing the setting sun at the equinox; a region or part north of any given point; the northern part (of any country); the portion of the United States to the north of the former slave-holding States; the north wind. *a.* Situated in or towards the north; belonging or pertaining to the north, northern. *adv.* Towards or in the north. *v.i.* To change or veer towards the north. *v.t.* To steer to the north of (a place). **north and south:** Along a line running to and from north and south. **North Britain:** Scotland. **North Briton:** A Scot. **north by east:** One point east of north. **north of:**

Further north than. **north-cock,** *n.* (*Sc.*) The snow-bunting. **north country:** The part of a country to the north, esp. northern England or the northern part of Great Britain; of, pertaining to, or characteristic of this. **north-countryman,** *n.* **north-east, -west,** *n.* The point midway between the north and east, or north and west, a region lying in this quarter. *a.* Pertaining to or proceeding from the north-east etc. **north-easter,** *n.* A north-east wind. **north-easterly,** *a.* Towards or from the north-east. **north-eastern,** *a.* In or towards this. **north-eastward,** *a.* **north-eastwardly,** *a.* and *adv.* **northland,** *n.* (*poet.*) Countries in the north; the northern part of a country. **north latitude:** Latitude north of the equator. **north-light** [NORTHERN LIGHTS]. **northman,** *n.* An inhabitant of the north of Europe, esp. of Scandinavia. **north pole** [POLE]. **north-star,** *n.* The pole-star. **north-west, -wester, -westerly, -western, -westward, -westwardly** [NORTH-EAST]. **northerly** (nôr′ *th*ėr li), *a.* and *adv.* **northerliness,** *n.* **northern** (nôr′ *th*ėrn), *a.* Pertaining to, situated or living in, or proceeding from the north; (*U.S.A.*) of the Northern States; towards the north. *n.* A northerner. **northern lights:** The aurora borealis. **northerner,** *n.* A native or inhabitant of the north. **northernmost, *northmost,** *a.* **northing** (nôr′ thing), *n.* The distance or progress in a northward direction. **northward,** *a., adv.* and *n.* **northwardly,** *a.* and *adv.* **northwards,** *adv.* and *n.* **nor'-wester,** *n.* A wind from the north-west; a glass of strong liquor; a sou'-wester hat.

Northumbrian (nôr thŭm′ bri ȧn) [A.-S. *Northhymbre* (NORTH, *Humber*)], *n.* A native or inhabitant of ancient Northumbria (England north of the Humber) or of Northumberland; the old English dialect of Northumbria. *a.* Of or pertaining to one of these districts.

northward, etc. [NORTH].

Norwegian (nôr wē′ jȧn) [med. L. *Norvegia*], *a.* Pertaining to Norway or its inhabitants. *n.* A native of Norway; the language of the Norwegians.

nose (nōz) [A.-S. *nosu* (cp. Dut. *neus*, Icel. *nōs*)], *n.* The projecting part of the face between the forehead and mouth, containing the nostrils and the organ of smell; the power of smelling; odour, scent; (*fig.*) sagacity; a part or thing resembling a nose, as the nozzle of a pipe, tube, bellows, etc., a beak, point, prow, etc. *v.t.* To perceive, trace, or detect by smelling; (*fig.*) to find out; to rub or push with the nose; to push (one's way). *v.i.* To smell, to sniff (about, after, at, etc.); (*fig.*) to search, to pry; to push one's way, to push ahead. **nose of wax:** One who or that which is easily influenced or moulded. **to count** or **tell noses:** To reckon the number of persons present; to count votes, supporters, etc. **to follow one's nose:** To go straight ahead. **to lead by the nose:** To cause to follow blindly. **to pay through the nose:** To be charged an exorbitant price. **to put one's nose out of joint** [JOINT]. **to thrust** or **put one's nose into:** To meddle officiously. **to turn up the nose:** To show contempt (at). **under one's nose:** In one's actual presence or sight. **nose-bag,** *n.* A bag containing provender for hanging over a horse's head; (*slang*) a bag of provisions. **nose-band,** *n.* The part of a bridle passing over the nose and attached to the cheek-straps. **nose-dive,** *n.* (*Aviat.*) A sudden plunge towards the earth. *v.t.* To make this plunge. **nose-leaf,** *n.* A membranous process on the nose of certain bats, constituting an organ of touch. **nose-piece,** *n.* A nozzle; a nose-band; the end-piece of a microscope to which the object-glass is fastened. **nose-pipe,** *n.* A piece of pipe used as a nozzle. **nose-rag,** *n.* (*slang*) A handkerchief. **nose-ring,** *n.* A ring worn in the nose as ornament; a leading-ring for a bull etc. **nosed,** *a.* (*usu. in comb.*, as *red-nosed*). **noseless,** *a.* **noser,** *n.* (*colloq.*) A wind in one's face, a head wind; a fall on the nose. **nosy,** *a.* Having a large or prominent nose; strong- or evil-smelling; fragrant; sensitive to bad odours; (*colloq.*) very inquisitive.

nosegay (nōz′ gā), *n.* A bunch of flowers, esp. fragrant flowers.

nosing (nō′ zing), *n.* The prominent edge of a moulding, step, etc.

noso- [Gr. *nosos*, disease], *comb. form.* Pertaining to diseases.

nosocomial (nos ō kō′ mi ȧl) [Gr. *nosokomeion*, a hospital], *a.* Pertaining to hospitals.

nosography (no sog′ rȧ fi), *n.* The scientific description of diseases.

nosology (no sol′ ō ji), *n.* A systematic classification of diseases; the branch of medical science treating of such a classification. **nosological,** *a.* **nosologist,** *n.*

nosonomy (nō son′ ō mi), *n.* The nomenclature of diseases.

nosophobia (nos ō fō′ bi ȧ), *n.* Morbid fear of disease.

nostalgia (nos tăl′ ji ȧ) [Gr. *nostos*, return, *-algia* from *algos*, pain], *n.* (*Path.*) Morbid longing for home; home-sickness; a yearning for the past. **nostalgic,** *a.*

nostoc (nos′ tok) [G. *nostoch*, a term invented by Paracelsus], *n.* A genus of gelatinous freshwater algæ, also called star-jelly or witches' butter.

nostology (nos tol′ ō ji) [Gr. *nostos*, return, -LOGY], *n.* The scientific study of senility and second childhood.

nostomania (nos tō mā′ ni ȧ), *n.* An abnormal anxiety to go back to a familiar place.

nostophobia (nos tō fō′ bi ȧ), *n.* An abnormal fear of going back thus.

Nostradamus (nos trȧ dā′ mŭs) [Michel de *Nostredame* (1503–66), French physician, astrologer, and professional prophet], *n.* One who predicts or professes to predict.

nostril (nos′ tril) [A.-S. *nosthyrl* (NOSE, *thyrel*, hole, cogn. with THRILL)], *n.* One of the apertures of the nose.

nostrum (nos′ trŭm) [L., neut. of *noster*, our], *n.* (*pl.* **-ums**) A medicine based on a secret formula; a quack remedy; (*fig.*) a political or other scheme of a charlatanic kind.

nosy [NOSE].

not (1) (not) [NAUGHT], *adv.* (*enclitically* **n't**) A particle expressing negation, denial, prohibition, or refusal. **not that:** It is not meant however that. **not but what,** or **not but that:** Nevertheless. **not a few** [FEW]. **not in it:** (*colloq.*) Not aware of (a secret); not participating in (an advantage); not in the running. **not in the running:** Standing no chance, not worth considering. **not once or twice:** Many times, often. **not well, not too well:** Feeling rather unwell.

notable (nō′ tȧbl) [F., from L. *notābilis*, from *notāre*, to note], *a.* Worthy of note; remarkable, memorable, distinguished; notorious; eminent, conspicuous; excellent, capable. *n.* A person or thing of note or distinction; (*Fr. Hist., pl.*) persons summoned by the king to a council of State or temporary parliament, at times of emergency, in France prior to 1789. ***notabilia*** (-bil′ i ȧ) [L.], *n.pl.* Notable things. **notability,** *n.* ***notableness,** *n.* **notably,** *adv.*

notalgia (nȯ tăl′ ji ȧ) [Gr. *notos*, back, *-algia*, *algos*, pain], *n.* (*Path.*) Pain in the back. **notalgic,** *a.*

notandum (nȯ tăn′ dŭm) [L., ger. of *notāre*, to NOTE], *n.* (*pl.* ***-da***) Something to be noted, a memorandum.

notary (nō′ tȧr i) [A.-F. *notarie* (F. *notaire*), L. *notārium*, nom. *-us*, from *notāre*, to NOTE], *n.* A public official (chiefly in foreign countries) appointed to attest deeds, contracts, etc., administer oaths etc., frequently called a **notary public. notarial** (nȯ târ′ i ȧl), *a.* **notarially,** *adv.*

notation (nȯ tā′ shŭn) [L. *notātio*, as prec.], *n.* The act or process of representing by signs, figures, etc.;

a system of signs, figures, etc., employed in any science or art. **notate** (nō′ tȧt), *a.* (*Bot.*) Marked with spots, etc., of a different colour.

notch (noch) [F. *oche* (now *hoche*) through *an oche* (cp. NEWT)], *n.* A nick, a cut, a V-shaped indentation; a tally-point; *(*Cricket*) a run scored; (*Am.*) an opening, narrow pass, or short defile. *v.t.* To cut a notch or notches in; to score by notches; to get (a number of runs); to fix (stairs etc.) by means of notches. **notch-wing,** *n.* Applied to various moths. **notched, notchy,** *a.*

note (nōt) [O.F., from L. *nota*, a mark (whence *notāre*, to mark, O.F. *noter*)], *n.* A sign, mark, or token; a distinctive feature, a characteristic, a mark of identity, genuineness, quality, etc.; a mark of interrogation, exclamation, etc.; a stigma; a brief record, a memorandum, a short or informal letter; a diplomatic communication; a bank-note or piece of paper money; a written promise to pay a certain sum of money; note-paper; an annotation, a comment, explanation, or gloss, appended to a passage in a book etc.; (*fig.*) notice, attention, observation; distinction, repute, importance; a sign representing the pitch and duration of a sound; a musical sound; (*fig.*) a significant sound, tone, or mode of expression; a key in a musical instrument; *notice, information. *v.t.* To observe, to take notice of; to show respect to; to pay attention to; to make a memorandum of; to set down or record as worth remembering; to annotate; (*in p.p.*) to celebrate. **note of hand:** A promissory note. **of note:** Distinguished. **to compare notes** [COMPARE]. **notebook,** *n.* A book for entering memoranda in. **note-case,** *n.* A pocket wallet for holding paper money. **note-paper,** *n.* A small size of paper for letters, esp. private correspondence. **noted,** *a.* Eminent, remarkable. ***notedly,** *adv.* **noteless,** *a.* Not noteworthy; unmusical, discordant. **noter,** *n.* **noteworthy,** *a.* Outstanding, famous; worth attention.

nothing (nŭth′ ing), *n.* No thing that exists; not anything, naught; (*Arith.*) no amount, a cipher, a naught; nothingness, non-existence; an insignificant or unimportant thing, a trifle. *adv.* In no degree, in no way, not at all. **mere nothings:** Trifling, unimportant things, events, etc. **next to nothing:** Almost nothing. **nothing doing:** (*colloq.*) Nothing happening; a refusal to do something. **nothing else than** or **but:** Merely, only, no more than (this or that). **nothing for it but:** No alternative but. **nothing to you:** Not your business. **to come to nothing:** To turn out a failure; to result in no amount or naught. **to make nothing of:** To fail to understand or deal with. ***nothing-gift,** *n.* A worthless gift. **nothingarian** (-âr′ i ȧn), *a.* Believing nothing; having no creed, purpose, etc. **nothingarianism,** *n.* **nothingism,** *n.* Nihilism. **nothingness,** *n.*

notice (nō′ tis) [F., from L. *nōtitia*, from *nōtus*, p.p. of *noscere*, to know], *n.* Intelligence, information, warning; a written or printed paper giving information or directions; an intimation or instruction; intimation of the termination of an agreement etc., at a specified date; an account of something in a newspaper etc., esp. a review of a book, play, etc.; observation, regard, attention; the act of noting. *v.t.* To take notice of, to perceive; to remark upon; to pay respect to; to serve a notice upon; to give notice to. **notice board,** *n.* A board exposed to public view on which notices are posted (*Am.* bulletin-board). **noticeable,** *a.* **noticeably,** *adv.*

notify (nō′ ti fī) [F. *notifier*, L. *nōtificāre* (*nōtus* known, *-ficāre*, *facere*, to make)], *v.t.* To make known, to announce, to declare, to publish; to give notice to, to inform (of or that). **notifiable** (nō ti fī′ ȧbl), *a.* To be notified (esp. of cases of disease that must be reported to the sanitary authorities). **notification** (-kā′ shŭn), *n.*

notion (nō′ shŭn) [F., from L. *nōtiōnem*, nom. *-tio*, as prec.], *n.* An idea, a conception; an opinion, a view; a theory, a scheme, a device; (*colloq.*) an inclination, desire, intention, or whim; (*Am.*) a small ingenious device or useful article; (*pl. Am.*) fancy goods, haberdashery, novelties, etc.; a knick-knack; (*Phil.*) a general concept or idea. **notional,** *a.* Pertaining to notions or concepts; abstract, imaginary, speculative, ideal; given to notions or whims, fanciful. **notionist,** *n.* **notionally,** *adv.*

notitia (nȯ tish′ i ȧ) [L.], *n.* A list, register, or catalogue.

noto- [Gr. *notos*, back], *comb. form.*

notobranchiate (nō tō brăng′ ki ȧt), *a.* (*Ichthyol.*) Having dorsal branchiæ or gills.

notochord (nō′ tō kôrd), *n.* The elastic cartilaginous band constituting a rudimentary form of the spinal column in the embryo and some primitive fishes.

Notogæa (nō tȯ jē′ ȧ) [Gr. *notos*, south, *gaia*, land], *n.* (*Zool.*) A zoological division of the earth embracing Australia, New Zealand, and the neotropical regions.

notonecta (nō tȯ nek′ tȧ) [Gr. *nēktēs*, swimmer], *n.* A boat-fly or back-swimmer, a species of water-beetle. **notonectal, -toid,** *a.*

notopodium (nō tȯ pod′ i ŭm) [Gr. *podion*, dim. of *pous podos*, foot], *n.* (*Biol.*) The dorsal or upper part of the parapodium of an annelid. **notopodial,** *a.*

notorious (nȯ tôr′ i ŭs) [med. L. *nōtōrius*, from *nōtus*, known], *a.* Widely or publicly or commonly known (now used only in a bad sense); manifest, evident, patent; *notable. **notoriety** (-rī′ ė ti), **notoriousness,** *n.* **notoriously,** *adv.*

notornis (nȯ tôr′ nis) [Gr. *ornis*, bird], *n.* (*Ornith.*) A gigantic New Zealand coot, *Notornis Mantelli*, now extinct or very rare.

nototherium (nō tō thēr′ i ŭm) [Gr. *thērion*, beast], *n.* (*Palæont.*) An extinct Australian family of gigantic marsupials.

notum (nō′ tŭm) [mod. L., from Gr. *noton*, *notos*, back], *n.* (*pl.* ***-ta***) (*Ent.*) The back of the thorax in insects.

Notus (nō′ tŭs) [L., from Gr. *Notos*], *n.* The south wind.

notwithstanding (not with stăn′ ding), *prep.* In spite of, despite. *adv.* Nevertheless; in spite of this. **conj.* Although; in spite of the fact (that).

nougat (noo′ ga) [F., from Sp. *nogado*, from L. *nucem*, nom. *nux*], *n.* A confection of almonds or other nuts and sugar.

nought [NAUGHT].

noumenon (nou′ mė non) [Gr. *nooumenon*, neut. pres.p. of *noein*, to apprehend], *n.* (*pl.* **-mena**) (*Phil., esp. Kantian*) The substance underlying a phenomenon; an object or the conception of an object as it is in itself, or as it appears to pure thought. **noumenal,** *a.* **noumenally,** *adv.*

noun (noun) [A.-F., from O.F. *nun*, *num*, L. *nōmen*, NAME, rel. to *noscere*, to KNOW], *n.* (*Gram.*) A word used as the name of anything, a substantive; *the name of a thing or of an attribute, called noun substantive or noun adjective. ***nounal,** *a.*

nourish (nŭr′ ish) [O.F. *noris-*, stem of *norir* (F. *nourrir*), from L. *nutrīre*], *v.t.* To feed, to sustain, to support; (*fig.*) to maintain, to educate; to foster, to cherish, to nurse. *v.i.* To promote growth. ***nourice** [NURSE, *n*]. ***nourishable,** *a.* **nourisher,** *n.* **nourishment,** *n.* The act of nourishing; the state of being nourished; that which nourishes, food, sustenance. **nouriture** (nŭr′ i chŭr), *n.* Nourishment, sustenance; nurture, education.

nous (nous) [Gr.], *n.* Mind, intellect; (*colloq.*) sense, wit, intelligence.

nova (nō′ va) [L. *novus*, new], *n.* (*Astron.*) A star; a star that flares up to great brightness and subsides after a time.

novachord (nō′ vȧ kôrd) [L. *novus*, new, CHORD], *n.* (*Mus.*) An electrically-operated musical instrument with keys and pedals, the sound being produced by the oscillation of radio valves and the power obtained from low-frequency alternating current.

The sound effects are percussive, as of a piano, and sustained, as of an organ.

novaculite (nŏ văk′ ū līt) [L. *novacula*, razor, -ITE], *n.* (*Geol.*) A fine-grained slate used for hones; a hone, a whetstone.

novalia (nŏ vā′ li ȧ) [L., pl. of *novāle*, neut. sing., from *novus*, new], *n.pl.* (*Sc. Law*) Waste lands newly brought into cultivation.

Novatian (nŏ vā′ shi ȧn), *n.* A follower of Novatianus (3rd cent.), who taught that the Church had no power to absolve the lapsed or to admit them to the Eucharist. *a.* Of or pertaining to Novatianus or the Novatians. **Novatianism,** *n.* **Novatianist,** *n.*

novation (nŏ vā′ shŭn) [L. *novātio*, from *novāre*, to make new, from *novus*, new], *n.* (*Law*) The substitution of a new obligation or debt for an old one. **novate** (nŏ vāt′), *v.t.* (*Law*) To replace by a new obligation, debt, etc.

novel (nov′ ėl) [O.F. *novelle* (F. *nouvelle*) or It. *novella*, L. *novella*, neut. pl. of *novellus*, dim of *novus*, new], *a.* New, recent, fresh; unusual, strange. *n.* A fictitious narrative in prose, usu. of sufficient length to fill a volume, portraying characters and actions from real life; this type of literature; (*Law*) a new or supplementary decree or constitution; *(*pl.*) news. **novelese** (nov ė lēz′), *n.* The language or style considered appropriate for novels. **novelette** (nov ė let′), *n.* A short novel, usu. of a sentimental nature; (*Mus.*) a kind of romance dealing freely with several themes. **novelettish,** *a.* Cheaply sentimental. **novelish** (nov′ ė lish), *a.* **novelism,** *n.* **novelist,** *n.* A writer of novels. **novelistic** (-lis′ tik), *a.* **novelize,** *v.t.* To make (a play, facts, etc.) into a novel. **novelization** (-zā′ shŭn), *n.* **novelty,** *n.* Newness, freshness; something new.

November (nŏ vem′ bėr) [L., from *novem*, nine (cp. DECEMBER)], *n.* The eleventh month of the year, the ninth of the Roman year.

novena (nŏ vē′ nȧ) [med. L., from *novem*, nine], *n.* (*R.-C. Ch.*) A devotion consisting of a prayer or service repeated on nine successive days.

novenary (nov′ ė nȧr i) [L. *novēnārius*, as prec.], *n.* Nine collectively; a group or set of nine; a novena. **a.* Pertaining to or consisting of the number nine. ***novene** (nov′ ēn), *a.* Proceeding by nines. **novennial** (nŏ ven′ i ȧl), *a.* Happening every ninth year.

novercal (nŏ vĕr′ kȧl) [L. *novercālis*, from *noverca*, stepmother], *a.* Pertaining or suitable to a stepmother.

Novial (nō′ vi al), *n.* An artificial language invented by Otto Jespersen.

novice (nov′ is) [O.F., from L. *novīcius*, from *novus*, new], *n.* One entering a religious house on probation before taking the vows; a new convert; one who is new to any business, an inexperienced person, a beginner. **a.* Inexperienced.

novilunar (nov′ i loo nȧr) [late L. *novilūnium* (*novus*, new, LUNAR)], *a.* Pertaining to the new moon.

novitiate (nŏ vish′ i ȧt), *n.* The term of probation passed by a novice; the part of a religious house allotted to novices; (*fig.*) a period of probation or apprenticeship.

novocaine (nō′ vō kān) [L. *novus*, new; COCAINE], *n.* (*Med.*) Protected trade name of a synthetic product derived from coal tar, used as a local anæsthetic.

***novum** (nō′ vŭm) [prob. L., neut. sing. of *novus*, new], *n.* An old game with dice, the principal throws at which were five and nine.

now (nou) [A.-S. *nu* (cp. Dut. *nu*, G. *nun*, Icel. *nū*, Dan. and Swed. *nu*, Gr. *nūn*, L. *nunc*, Sansk. *nu*)], *adv.* At the present time; at once, forthwith, immediately; very recently; at this point or time, then (in narrative); in these circumstances; used as an expletive in explaining, remonstrating, conciliating, threatening, etc. *conj.* Since, seeing that, this being the case (that). *n.* The present time. *a.* (*colloq.*) Present, existing. **just now:** A little time or a moment ago. **now and then** or **again:** From time to time; occasionally. **now or never:** At this moment or the chance is gone for ever. **nowaday,** *a.* Of the present time. **nowadays,** *adv.* At the present time; in these days. *n.* The present time.

noway, -ways [NO (1)].

nowel (nō′ el, nō el′) [O.F. *noel*, Prov. *nadal*, L. *nātalem*, nom. *-lis*, NATAL], *int.* A shout of joy in Christmas carols.

nowhere (nō′ wâr), *adv.* Not in, at, or to any place or state. **nowhere near:** Not at all near. **to be** or **come in nowhere:** (*colloq.*) To be badly defeated (esp. in a race or other contest). **nowhither, nowise** [NO (2)].

nowt (nout) [Sc., from Icel. *naut* (cp. A.-S. *nēat*, NEAT (2))], *n.* Cattle, a bovine animal; (*fig.*) a coarse, stupid, or ungainly man.

nowy (nou′ i) [O.F. *noé* (F. *noué*), p.p. of *noer*, L. *nōdāre*, to tie, from *nōdus*, knot], *a.* (*Her.*) Having a convex projection in the middle (of a line etc., on a shield).

noxious (nok′ shŭs) [L. *noxius*, from *noxa*, harm, rel. to *nocēre*, to injure], *a.* Hurtful, harmful, unwholesome; pernicious, destructive. **noxiously,** *adv.* **noxiousness,** *n.*

noyade (nwa yad′) [F., from *noyer*, to drown, L. *necāre*, to kill], *n.* A mode of executing political prisoners by drowning, esp. wholesale, as during the Reign of Terror in France in 1794.

noyau (nwa yō′) [F., from L. *nucāle*, from *nucem*, nom. *nux*, nut], *n.* Brandy cordial flavoured with bitter almonds etc.

***noyous** (noi′ ŭs) [earlier *anoyous*, from ANNOY], *a.* Vexatious, troublesome.

nozzle (noz′ ėl) [NOSE], *n.* A spout, projecting mouthpiece, or end of pipe or hose.

nuance (nū′ ans) [F., from *nuer*, to shade, from *nue*, L. *nūbes*, cloud], *n.* A delicate gradation in colour or tone; (*fig.*) a nice distinction between things, feelings, opinions, etc.

nub (nŭb) [var. of KNOB], *n.* A small lump, as of coal; a tangle, a knot, a snarl; the pith or gist (of). **nubble,** *n.* A nub. **nubbly** (*prov.*), **nubby,** *adv.*

nubecula (nū bē′ kū lȧ) [L., dim. of *nūbes*, cloud], *n.* (*pl.* **-læ**) (*Path.*) A cloudy appearance in the urine; a film on the eye; (*Astron.*) one of the two southern nebulæ called the Magellanic clouds.

nubiferous (nū bif′ ėr ŭs) [L. *nūbifer* (*nūbes*, see prec., -FEROUS)], *a.* Producing or bringing clouds. ***nubigenous** (-bij′ ė nŭs), *a.* ***nubilose** (nū bi lōs), ***nubilous** (nū′ bi lŭs), *a.* Cloudy.

nubile (nū′ bil) [L. *nūbilis*, from *nūbere*, to marry], *a.* Marriageable (usu. of women). **nubility** (-bil′ i ti), *n.*

nucellus (nū sel′ ŭs) [mod. L. dim. of NUCLEUS], *n.* (*Bot.*) The nucleus of an ovule.

nuchal (nū′ kȧl) [med. L. *nucha*, Arab. *nukhā′*, spinal cord, -AL], *a.* (*Anat.*) Pertaining to the nape of the neck.

nuciferous (nū sif′ ėr ŭs) [L. *nuci-*, *nux*, nut, -FEROUS], *a.* Bearing nuts. **nuciform** (nū′ si fôrm), *a.* Nut-shaped. **nucifrage** (nū′ si frāj), *n.* (*Ornith.*) The nut-cracker. **nucifragous** (nū sif′ rȧ gŭs), **nucivorous** (nū siv′ ō rŭs), *a.* Eating or feeding on nuts.

nuclear (nū′ kli ȧr) [NUCLEUS], *a.* Relating to atomic nuclei. **nuclear charge,** *n.* The positive electric charge in the nucleus of an atom. **nuclear energy:** Energy released from an atomic nucleus at the expense of its mass. **nuclear fission,** *n.* The breaking up of a heavy atom, as of uranium, into atoms of smaller mass, thus causing a great release of energy. **nuclear fuel,** *n.* Uranium, plutonium, and other metals consumed to produce atomic energy. **nuclear physics:** The study of atomic nuclei. **nuclear reaction:** Reaction in which the nuclei of atoms are transformed into isotopes of the element itself, or atoms of a different element. **nuclear reactor:** A structure of fissile material such as uranium, with a moderator such as carbon or heavy water, so arranged that nuclear energy is continuously released under control. Also called an atomic pile. **nuclear warfare:** The use of atomic or hydrogen bombs in warfare.

nucleate (nū' kli āt) [NUCLEUS], *v.t.* To form into a nucleus; *v.i.* To form a nucleus. (nū' kli ȧt), *a.* Having a nucleus, nucleated. **nucleation,** *n.* **nucleiform,** *a.* **nucleic acids,** *n.pl.* Complex organic acids forming part of nucleo proteins. **nuclein** (nū' kli in), *n.* The protein forming the chief constituent of cell-nuclei. **nucleolus** (nū klē' ō lŭs), *n.* (*pl.* **-li**) A nucleus of or within another nucleus. **nucleolar, nucleolated** (nū' klė ō lā tėd), *a.* **nucleo-,** *comb. form.* **nucleobranch** (nū' klė ō brăngk) [Gr. *branchia*, gills], *a.* (*Zool.*) Belonging to the *Nucleobranchiata*, a family of molluscs having the gills in a tuft. *n.* One of the *Nucleobranchiata*, a heteropod.

nucleus (nū' klė ŭs) [L., from *nucula*, dim. of *nux nucis*, nut], *n* (*pl.* **-clei**) A central part about which aggregation, accretion, or growth goes on; a kernel; the charged centre of an atom consisting of protons and neutrons; (*Biol.*) the central body in an ovule, seed, cell, etc., constituting the organ of vitality, growth, or other functions; (*fig.*) a centre of growth, development, activity, etc.; (*Astron.*) the brightest part of the head of a comet. **nucleal, nuclear, nucleary,** *a.* **nucleonics,** *n.* The science of the nucleus of the atom.

nucule (nū' kūl) [F., from L. *nucula*, see prec.], *n.* (*Bot.*) A small nut or nut-like fruit or seed; the female productive organ in the cryptogamic genus *Chara.*

nude (nūd) [L. *nūdus*], *a.* Bare, naked, uncovered, unclothed, undraped; (*Law*) made without any consideration and consequently void. *n.* An undraped figure in painting or sculpture. **the nude:** The undraped human figure or the state of being undraped. **nudely,** *adv.* **nudeness, nudity,** *n.* **nudism,** *n.* The cult of the nude; belief in the physical and spiritual benefit of being nude. **nudist,** *n.* A member of the cult of the nude. **nudist colony,** *n.* An open-air camp inhabited by nudists.

nudge (nŭj) [etym. doubtful], *v.t.* To push gently, as with the elbow; to draw attention or give a hint with, or as with such a push. *n.* Such a push.

nudi- [L. *nudus*, nude], *comb. form.*

nudibranch (nū' di brăngk) [Gr. *branchia*, gills], *n.* (*Zool.*) A mollusc of the order *Nudibranchiata* characterized by naked gills or the absence of a shell. **nudibranchial, nudibranchian,** *a.* **nudibranchiate,** *a.* and *n.*

nudifolious (nū di fō' li ŭs), *a.* (*Bot.*) Having smooth or bare leaves.

nudirostrate (nū di ros' trȧt), *a.* (*Zool.*) Having a naked beak.

nudism, nudist, nudity [NUDE].

nugæ (nū' gē, nū' jē) [L.], *n.pl.* Trifles, esp. literary compositions of a trifling and fugitive kind. **nugatory** (nū' gȧ tŏr i), *a.* Trifling, insignificant; futile, ineffective, inoperative.

nugger (nŭg' ėr) [Egyptian native], *n.* A broad, strongly-built boat about 30 ft. long used on the upper Nile.

nugget (nŭg' ėt) [etym. doubtful], *n.* A lump of native metal, esp. of gold.

nuisance (nū' sȧns) [O.F., from *nuire*, L. *nocēre*, to injure], *n.* Anything that annoys, irritates, or troubles; an offensive or disagreeable person, action, experience, etc.; (*Law*) anything causing annoyance, inconvenience, or injury to another. ***nuisances,** *n.*

null (nŭl) [O.F. *nul*, *nulle*, L. *nullum*, nom. *-lus* (*ne*, not, *ullus*, any)], *a.* Void, having no legal force or validity; (*fig.*) without character, expression, or individuality; (*Math.* and *Log.*) amounting to nothing, equal to zero, nil. ****v.t.*** To nullify.

nullah (nŭl' ȧ) [Hind. *nālā*], *n.* A ravine, gully, or water-course.

nulla-nulla (nŭl' ȧ nŭl' ȧ) [Austral. abor.], *n.* A club-shaped weapon of hard wood used by the Australian aborigines.

nullifidian (nŭl i fid' i ȧn) [L. *nulli-*, NULLUS, *fidēs*, faith], *a.* Of no religion. *n.* An unbeliever.

nullify (nŭl i fī) [late L. *nullificāre* (L. *nulli-*, *nullus*, *-ficāre*, *facere*, to make)], *v.t.* To make void; to cancel, to annul, to invalidate; to efface, to destroy. **nullification** (-kā' shŭn), *n.* **nullifier** (nŭl' i fī ėr), *n.* **nullity,** *n.* Invalidity; an invalid act, instrument, etc.; nothingness, non-existence; a non-entity, a mere cipher. **nullipara** (nŭ lip' ȧ rȧ) [*parĕre*, to bring forth], *n.* A woman who has never given birth to a child. **nulliparous,** *a.* **nullipore** (nŭl' i pōr) [NULLUS, PORE (1)], *n.* A seaweed with calcareous fronds, a coralline.

numb (nŭm) [earlier, *num*, A.-S. *numen*, p.p. of *niman*, to take (*b* excrescent, cp. NIMBLE)], *a.* Deprived of sensation and motion; torpid, stupefied, dulled; *causing numbness. *v.t.* To benumb, to paralyse. **numb-fish,** *n.* The electric ray or torpedo. **numb-hand,** *n.* A clumsy person. **numbly** (nŭm' li), *adv.* **numbness,** *n.*

number (nŭm' bėr) [O.F. *nombre*, *numbre*, L. *numerum*, nom. *-rus*, cogn. with Gr. *nemein*, to distribute], *n.* A measure of discrete quantity; a name or symbol representing any such quantity, a numeral; a sum or aggregate of persons, things, or abstract units; one of a numbered series; a single issue of a periodical, one of the parts of a literary or other work so issued, a division of an opera, etc.; numerical reckoning, arithmetic; poetical measure, verse, rhythm (*often in pl.*); plurality, multitude, numerical preponderance (*usu. in pl.*); (*Gram.*) the distinctive form of a word according as it denotes unity or plurality. *v.t.* To count, to reckon; to ascertain the number of; to amount to; to assign a number to, to distinguish with a number; to include, to comprise (among etc.); to have lived (a specified amount of years). **Numbers,** *n.* The fourth book of the Old Testament, giving an account of the two censuses of the Israelites. **his number is up:** He is going to die. **number one:** (*colloq.*) Oneself. **without number:** Innumerable. **numberer,** *n.* **numberless,** *a.*

numbles (nŭm' bėlz) [O.F. *nombles*, prob. var. of *lombles*, L. *lumbulus*, dim. of *lumbus*, loin], *n.pl.* Certain inward parts of a deer used as food [cp. UMBLE].

numeral (nū' mėr ȧl) [late L. *numerālis*, from *numerus*, NUMBER], *a.* Pertaining to, consisting of, or denoting number. *n.* A word, symbol or group of symbols denoting number; (*Print.*) Roman figures, *e.g.* I, III, V, X, C. **numerable,** *a.* **numerableness,** *n.* **numerally,** *adv.* **numerary,** *a.* **numerical,** *a.* **numerically,** *adv.*

numerate (nū' mėr āt), *v.t.* To reckon, to number. **numeration,** *n.*

numerator (nū' mė rā tŏr), *n.* One who numbers; the part of a vulgar fraction written above the line indicating how many fractional parts are taken.

numeric (nū mer' ik), *n.* (*Math.*) The numerical part of an expression.

numérotage (nū mâr' ō tazh) [F., from *numéroter*, to number, from It. *numero*, NUMBER], *n.* The numbering of yarns so as to denote their fineness.

numerous (nū' mėr ŭs), *a.* Many in number; consisting of a great number of individuals; rhythmical, musical, harmonious; *thronged. **numerously,** *adv.* **numerousness,** *n.* **numerology** (nū mėr ol' ōj i), *n.* The study of the alleged significance of numbers.

numinous (nū' mi nŭs) [L. *numen*, divinity], *a.* Pertaining to divinity; feeling awe of the divine.

numismatic (nū miz măt′ ik) [F. *numismatique*, L. *numismat-*, stem of *numisma*, Gr. *nomisma*, from *nomizein*, to practise, to have in current use], *a.* Pertaining to coins or coinage. **numismatically,** *adv.* **numismatics, numismatology** (-tol′ ŏ ji), *n.* The science or study of coins and medals. **numismatist** (-miz′ mȧ tist), **numismatologist,** *n.*

nummary (nŭm′ ȧr i) [L. *nummārius*, from *nummus*, coin], *a.* Of or pertaining to money. **nummular, -lary,** *a.* Pertaining to or resembling coins. **nummulated,** *a.* Coin-shaped.

nummulation (nŭm ū lā′ shŭn), *n.* (*Microsc.*) The arrangement of the blood-corpuscles like piles of coins.

nummulite (nŭm′ ū līt), *n.* (*Geol.*) A fossil foraminifer resembling a coin. **nummuline, nummulitic,** *a.*

numskull (nŭm′ skŭl), *n.* A blockhead, a dunce; the head of a doll, a thick head. **numskulled,** *a.*

nun (nŭn) [A.-S. *nunne*, late L. *nonna*, fem. of *nonnus*, monk, orig. a title of address to old people], *n.* A woman devoted to a religious life and living in a convent under certain vows, usu. of poverty, chastity, and obedience; a variety of pigeon; the smew; the blue titmouse. **nun's cloth:** A variety of bunting used as material for dresses etc. **nun's thread:** Fine thread used in lace-making. **nun's veiling:** A soft, thin, woollen dress-stuff. **nunhood, nunship,** *n.* **nunlike,** *a.* and *adv.* **nunnery,** *n.* A religious home for women. **nunnish,** *a.*

nunatak (nŭn′ ȧ tăk) [Eskimo], *n.* (*Geol.*) A mountain peak which projects through an ice sheet.

nun-buoy (nŭn′ boi) [obsolete *nun* (perh. from prec.), a spinning-top, BUOY], *n.* A buoy shaped like two cones united at the base.

Nunc dimittis (nŭngk di mit′ is) [L., now lettest thou depart], *n.* The canticle 'Lord, now lettest thou thy servant depart in peace' (Luke ii, 29); (*fig.*) a peaceful death.

***nuncheon** (nŭn′ shŭn) [M.E. *noneschenh* (*none*, L. *nōna*, NOON, *schench*, A.-S. *scenc*, cup, draught)], *n.* Luncheon.

nuncio (nŭn′s hi ō) [It., from L. *nuncius*, messenger], *n.* (*pl.* **-ios**) A papal envoy to a foreign Catholic power. **nunciature,** *n.*

***nuncle** (nŭng′ kėl) [UNCLE (through *mine uncle*, cp. NEWT, NONCE)], *n.* Uncle.

nuncupate (nŭn′ kū pāt) [L. *nuncupātus*, p.p. of *nuncupāre* (*nōmen*, name, *capere*, to take)], *v.t.* To declare (a will, vow, etc.) orally, as dist. from in writing. **nuncupation** (-pā′ shŭn), *n.* **nuncupative, *-tory** (nŭn′ kū pā tiv, -tŏr i), *a.* Oral, not written; designative, nominal. **nuncupative will** or **legacy:** A will or legacy made orally.

nundinal (nŭn′ di nȧl) [L. *nundinālis*, from *nundinæ*, pl., a market-day (*novem*, nine, *dies*, day)], *a.* Relating to fairs or markets. ***nundinary,** *a.*

nunhood, nunnery, etc. [NUN].

nunnation (nŭ nā′ shŭn) [Arab. *nun*, the letter *n*, -ATION], *n.* The addition of final *n* to words, in the declension of Arabic nouns etc. **nunnated,** *a.*

nuphar (nū′ fȧr) [NENUPHAR], *n.* The yellow water-lily.

nuptial (nŭp′ shȧl) [F., from L. *nuptiālis*, from *nuptiæ*, wedding, from *nubere* (p.p. *nuptus*), to marry], *a.* Pertaining to, done at, or constituting a wedding. *n.pl.* A wedding. **nuptial flight:** The flight of a virgin queen-bee, during which she is impregnated.

nurl [KNURL]. ***nurr** [KNUR].

nurse (nĕrs) [M.E. and O.F. *norice*, late L. *nūtrīcia*, fem. of *nūtrīcius*, from *nūtrix -īcis*, from *nūtrīre*, to nourish], *n.* A woman employed to suckle the child of another, usu. called a wet-nurse, or to have the care of young children, also called a dry-nurse; one who tends the sick, wounded, or infirm; one who or that which fosters or promotes; the condition of being nursed; (*Forestry*) a tree planted to protect another or others during growth; (*Ent.*) a sexually imperfect bee, ant, etc., which tends the young brood; (*Zool.*) an individual in a sexual stage of metagenesis; one of various sharks or dogfish. *v.t.* To suckle; to give suck to or feed (an infant); to hold or clasp, esp. on one's knees or lap; to rear, to nurture; to foster, to tend, to promote growth in; to tend in sickness; to manage with care; to cherish, to brood over; to economize, to husband; (*Billiards*) to keep (the balls) in a good position for cannons. *v.i.* To act as nurse; to suckle a baby. **wet nurse:** A woman able to breast-feed a baby as well as, or in place of, her own. **nurser,** *n.* **nursling,** *n.* An infant, esp. in relation to the one who nurses it.

nursery (nĕrs′ ri), *n.* A room set apart for young children; a place or garden for rearing plants; the place, sphere, or condition in which persons, qualities, etc., are bred or fostered; an establishment for rearing fish; a place where animal life is developed; a handicap or race for two-year-old horses. **nursemaid,** *n.* A woman or girl in charge of young children. **nursery-maid,** *n.* A servant who looks after a children's nursery. **nurseryman,** *n.* One who raises plants in a nursery. **nursery-governess,** *n.* A woman or girl in charge of young children, usu. combining the duties of a nurse and a teacher.

nurture (nĕr′ tyŭr) [A.-F., from O.F. *nourture*, *nourriture*, L. *nūtrītūra*, from *nūtrīre*, to NOURISH], *n.* The act of bringing up, training, fostering; nourishment; education, breeding. *v.t.* To nourish, to rear, to train, to educate.

nut (nŭt) [A.-S. *hnutu* (cp. Dut. *noot*, G. *nuss*, Icel. *hnot*)], *n.* The indehiscent fruit of certain trees, containing a kernel in a hard shell; a metal block with a hole for screwing on and securing a bolt, screw, etc.; a projection on a spindle engaging with a cog-wheel; various parts of machinery, usu. in which a screw works; (*Naut.*) a projection on the shank of an anchor; (*slang*) the head; (*slang*) a harum-scarum fellow; a masher, a dude, a swell; (*pl.*) small lumps of coal; (*fig.*) a person, thing or problem that is hard to deal with. *v.i.* (*past & p.p.* **nutted**) To gather nuts. **can't do it for nuts:** (*slang*) Can't succeed in doing it even in the most favourable circumstances. **a hard nut to crack:** A difficult problem to solve. **off his nut:** (*slang*) Mad; drunk. **to be nuts** or **dead nuts on:** (*slang*) To delight in; to be very fond of; to be skilled at. **nut-brown,** *a.* Brown as a hazel-nut long kept. **nut-butter,** *n.* A substitute for butter, extracted from the oil of nuts. **nut-cake,** *n.* (*Am.*) A dough-nut. **nutcracker,** *n.* (*usu. pl.*) An instrument for cracking nuts; (*fig.*) a nose and chin that tend to meet; a European bird of the genus *Nucifraga.* **nut-gall,** *n.* An oak-gall. **nut-hatch,** *n.* A small bird of the genus *Sitta*, allied to the woodpecker, esp. *S. Europæa.* **nut-hook,** *n.* A hooked stick to pull down boughs in nutting; *a bailiff. **nut-oil,** *n.* Oil expressed from hazel-nuts or walnuts, used in paints and varnishes. **nut-palm,** *n.* An Australian tree bearing edible nuts. **nut-pine,** *n.* One of various pines bearing nut-like edible seeds. **nut-shell,** *n.* The hard shell enclosing the kernel of a nut; (*fig.*) something holding, containing, or sheltering in a very small compass. **to be** or **lie in a nut-shell:** To be contained or expressed in a very concise statement. **nut-tree,** *n.* A tree bearing nuts, esp. the hazel. **nut-weevil,** *n.* A beetle infesting nuts, esp. one laying eggs in green hazel-nuts etc. **nut-wrench,** *n.* A spanner. **nuts:** (*slang*) Crazy. **nutlet,** *n.* **nutty,** *a.* Abounding in nuts; tasting like nuts; (*slang*) sweet (on); spicy; smart.

nutate (nū′ tāt) (L. *nūtātus*, p.p. of *nūtāre*, freq. of *nuere* (in *abnuere*), to nod], *v.i.* (*Bot.*) To nod, to bend forward, to droop. **nutant,** *a.* (*Bot.*) Drooping, hanging with the apex downwards. **nutation** (-tā′ shŭn), *n.* A nodding or oscillation; (*Bot.*) a movement of the tips of growing plants, usu. towards the sun; (*Astron.*) a periodical oscillation of the earth's axis due to the attractive influence of the sun and moon on the greater mass round the equator; (*Path.*) morbid oscillation of the head.

nutmeg (nŭt' meg) [M.E. *notemuge* (NUT, O.F. *muge, mugue*, in *noix mugue* or *muguede*, med. L. *nux muscāta*, musk-like nut)], *n.* The hard aromatic seed of the fruit of species of *Myristica*, esp. *M. fragrans*, the nutmeg-tree, used for flavouring and in medicine. **nutmeg-apple,** *n.* The pear-shaped drupaceous fruit of the nutmeg tree. **nutmeg-liver,** *n.* A diseased condition of the liver, due to excessive drinking. **nutmeggy,** *a.*

nutria (nū' tri ȧ) [Sp., from L. *lutra*, otter], *n.* A S. American beaver, *Myopotamus coypus*; its skin, formerly much used in hat-making [COYPU].

nutrient (nū' tri ėnt) [L. *nūtriens -ntem*, pres.p. of *nūtrīre*, to nourish], *a.* Nourishing; serving as or conveying nourishment. *n.* A nutritious substance. **nutriment,** *n.* That which nourishes or promotes growth, esp. food. **nutrimental,** *a.* **nutrition** (nū trish' ŭn), *n.* The function or process of promoting the growth of organic bodies; nourishment, food. **nutritional,** *a.* **nutritious,** *a.* Affording nourishment, efficient as food. **nutritiously,** *adv.* **nutritiousness,** *n.* **nutritive** (nū' tri tiv), *a.* and *n.* **nutritively,** *adv.* **nutritiveness,** *n.*

nutshell, nutty [NUT].

nux vomica (nŭks vom' i kȧ) [med. L. *nux*, nut, *vomere*, to VOMIT], *n.* The seed of an East Indian tree, *Strychnos nux-vomica*, which yields strychnine.

nuzzle (1) (nŭz' el) [NOSE, -LE], *v.t.* To rub or press the nose against; to fondle; to root up with the nose. *v.i.* To burrow or root about with the nose; to nestle, to hide the head, as a child in its mother's bosom.

***nuzzle** (2) (nŭz' el) [etym. doubtful], *v.t.* To bring (up), to nurse, to nourish, to nurture; (*fig.*) to cherish, to foster.

nyctalopia (nik tȧ lō' pi ȧ), **nyctalopy** (nik' tȧ lō pi) [late L. *nyctalōpia*, from Gr. *nuktalōps* (*nukti-*, *nux*, night, *alaos*, blind, *ōps*, eye)], *n.* (*Path.*) A disease of the eyes in which vision is better in shade or twilight than in daylight, day-blindness; *night-blindness. ***nyctalops,*** *n.* A person affected with this.

nyctitropic (nik ti trop' ik) [Gr. *nukti-*, *nux*, night, *tropos*, turn, -IC], *a.* (*Bot.*) Changing position or direction at night (of leaves). **nyctitropism** (nik tit' rŏ pizm), *n.*

nyctophobia (nik tō fō' bi ȧ), *n.* (*Path.*) A morbid fear of darkness.

nycturia (nik tūr' i ȧ), *n.* (*Path.*) Nocturnal incontinence of urine, bed-wetting.

nylghau (nil' gaw) [Pers. *nīlgāw*, blue ox], *n.* A large, short-horned Indian antelope, the male of which is slate-coloured.

nylon (nī' lon), *n.* (*Plastics*) Name applied to a group of thermoplastics, used largely for hosiery, shirts, dress fabrics, imitation furs, ropes, brushes, etc.

nymph (nimf) [F. *nymphe*, L. *nympha*, Gr. *numphē*, bride], *n.* (*Class. Myth.*) One of a class of youthful female divinities inhabiting groves, springs, mountains, the sea, etc.; (*fig.*) a beautiful or attractive young woman; a nympha. **nymphean** (nim fē' ȧn), ***nymphal** (nim' fȧl), *a.* ***nymphical, nymphish,** *a.* **nymphlike,** *a.* ***nymphly,** *adv.*

nympha (nim' fȧ) [as prec.], *n.* (*pl.* **-phæ**) A pupa or chrysalis. **nymphiparous** (-fip' ȧ rŭs), *a.* Producing nymphæ or pupæ.

nymphæa (nim fē' ȧ) [Gr. *numphaia*, fem. of *numphaios* (see NYMPH), sacred to the nymphs], *n.* (*Bot.*) A genus of aquatic plants, containing the white water-lily.

nympholepsy (nim' fō lep si) [NYMPH], *n.* A state of ecstasy or frenzy supposed to befall one who has gazed on a nymph; (*fig.*) a wild desire for the unattainable. **nympholept,** *n.* **nympholeptic,** *a.*

nymphomania (nim fō mā' ni ȧ), *n.* (*Path.*) Morbid sexual desire, erotic insanity in women. **nymphomaniac,** *n.* **nymphomaniacal,** *a.*

nystagmus (nis tăg' mŭs) [Gr. *nustagmos*, a nodding, from *nustazein*, to nod, to be sleepy], *n.* (*Path.*) A spasmodic movement of the eyeballs, affecting miners and others working in a dim light.

O

O, o (ō), the fifteenth letter, and the fourth vowel (*pl.* **Os, O's, Oes**), has three distinct sounds: (1) as in *pot* (unaccented in this dictionary); (2) this lengthened by a following *r* as in *or* (marked ô); (3) as in *go* (marked ō); there is also the indeterminate sound marked ŏ. *n.* An O-shaped mark; a circle, oval, or any round or nearly round shape; (*colloq.*) a naught or cipher.

O, oh (ō) [prob. from L.], *int.* An exclamation of earnest or solemn address, entreaty, invocation, surprise, etc.

O' (ō) [Ir. *ó*, *ua*, descendant], *pref.* Descendant of, used with Irish patronymic surnames.

oaf (ōf) [var. of obs. *auf*, Icel. *ālfr*, ELF], *n.* (*pl.* **oafs**) Orig. a silly child left by fairies in place of one taken by them; a deformed child; a silly, stupid person, a lout. **oafish,** *a.*

oak (ōk) [A.-S. *āc* (cp. Dut. and Icel. *eik*, G. *eiche*)], *n.* Any tree or shrub of the genus *Quercus*, esp. *Q. robur*, a forest tree much valued for its timber; the wood of this; any tree of the Australian genus *Casuarina*; applied to various trees and plants bearing a real or fancied resemblance to the oak; one of various species of moth; (*Univ.*) a door, esp. the outer door of a set of rooms. **oak-apple, -ball, -berry, -button, -fig, -gall, -plum, -potato, -spangle, -wort,** *n.* A gall or excrescence of various kinds produced on oaks by various gall-flies. **oak-fern,** *n.* A slender, three-branched polypody, *P. dryopteris.* **oak-leather,** *n.* A tough fungus growing on old oak; oak-tanned leather. **Oak-apple Day:** The 29th May, anniversary of the escape of Charles II at Boscobel in 1651. **royal oak:** The tree in which he concealed himself. **the Oaks** [name of estate]: A race at Epsom for three-year-old fillies. **to sport one's oak:** (*Univ.*) To shut the outer door of one's rooms to exclude visitors. **oaken,** *a.* **oaklet, oakling,** *n.*

oakum (ō' kŭm) [A.-S. *ācumba*, tow, lit. combings (*ā-*, *æ-*, off, *cemban*, to comb)], *n.* Old rope, untwisted and pulled into loose fibres, used for caulking seams, stopping leaks, etc.

oamauru stone (ō mar' oo stōn) [place name], *n.* A N. Zealand building stone.

oar (ôr) [A.-S. *ār* (cp. Icel. *-ār*, Dan. *aare*), perh. rel. to Gr. *eretēs*, rower], *n.* A long pole with a flattened blade, for rowing, sculling, or steering a boat; (*fig.*) an oarsman; anything resembling an oar in form or function, as a fin, wing, or arm used in swimming, etc. *v.i.* To row. *v.t.* To propel by or as by rowing. **chained to the oar,** *adv.* Forced to work hard. **to lie or rest on the oars:** To cease rowing without shipping the oars; (*fig.*) to stop for rest. **to pull a good oar:** To be a practised oarsman. **to put in one's oar:** To intrude into conversation; to interfere, esp. with unasked-for advice. **to ship or unship oars:** To place them in or take them out of the rowlocks. **oarage,** *n.* (*poet.*). **oared,** *a.* (*usu. in comb.*). **oarless,** *a.* **oarsman, -woman,** *n.* A rower. **oarsmanship,** *n.* **oarlock,** *n.* (*Am.*) A rowlock. **oary,** *a.* (*poet.*).

oarium (ō âr' i ŭm) [mod. L., from Gr. *ōarion*, dim. of *ōion*, egg], *n.* (*pl.* **-ria**) An ovary.

oasis (ō ā' sis) [L. and Gr., prob. from Egyptian (cp. Copt. *ouahe*, from *ouih*, to dwell)], *n.* (*pl.* **oases** (ō a' sēz)) A fertile spot in a waste or desert.

oast (ōst) [A.-S. *āst* (cp. Dut. *eest*), rel. to L. *æstus*, heat, *ædes*, house, Gr. *aithos*, heat], *n.* A kiln for drying hops. **oast-house,** *n.*

oat (ōt) [A.-S. *āte*, etym. doubtful], *n.* (*usu. in pl.*) A cereal plant of the genus *Avena*, esp. *A. sativa*; (*pl.*) the grain of this, used for food; a musical pipe made from an oat-stem; hence, pastoral or bucolic poetry. **wild oats:** A tall grass of the same genus as the oat-plant; (*fig.*) youthful dissipation. **oatcake,** *n.* **oatmeal,** *n.* Oats ground into meal, used chiefly for making porridge or oatcake. **oaten,** *n.* **boiled oatmeal:** (*Am.*) Porridge.

oath (ōth) [A.-S. *āth* (cp. Dut. *eed*, G. *eid*, Icel. *eithr*, O.H.G. *eit*)], *n.* (*pl.* **oaths,** ōthz) A solemn appeal to God or some holy or dreaded person or thing in witness of the truth of a statement or of the binding nature of a promise, esp. an attestation made according to prescribed forms in a court of law; a frivolous use of the name of God, a profane imprecation or expletive, a curse. **Oath of Supremacy:** An oath acknowledging the supremacy of the British sovereign over any power, spiritual or temporal, in the realm. **oath-breaking,** *n.* ***oathable,** *n.*

oatmeal [OAT].

ob- [L., in the way of, against], *pref.* Toward, to, meeting, in, facing; against, opposing, hindering, resisting, hostile; reversely, obversely, contrary to the normal; as in *object, objurgate, oblique, obovate.*

obang (ō′ băng) [Jap. *-ôban*, great sheet], *n.* An oblong gold coin formerly current in Japan.

obbligato (ob li ga′ tō) [It., from L. *obligātus*, p.p. of *obligāre*, to OBLIGE], *a.* (*Mus.*) Inseparable, indispensably attached. *n.* An instrumental part or accompaniment that forms an integral part of the composition.

obconical (ob kon′ i kȧl), *a.* (*Nat. Hist.*) Inversely conical.

obdurate (ob′ dū rȧt, ob dūr′ ȧt) [L., *obdūrātus*, p.p. of *obdūrāre* (OB-, *dūrāre*, to harden, from *dūrus*, hard)], *a.* Hardened in heart, esp. against moral influence; stubborn; impenitent. *v.t.* To make obdurate. **obduracy, *obdurateness,** *n.* **obdurately,** *adv.* ***obdure,** *v.t.* To obdurate. **obduration** (-rā′ shŭn), *n.*

obeah (ō′ bė ȧ) [W. African native], *n.* A system of sorcery prevalent among Negroes in Africa and the W. Indies.

obedience (ȯ bē′ di ėns) [O.F., from L. *obēdientia*, from *obēdīre*, to OBEY], *n.* The act or practice of obeying; dutiful submission to authority; compliance with law, command, or direction; the act of being obeyed, authority; (*R.-C. Ch.*) a written command or instruction; a body of persons, a monastery, or other sphere subject to obedience. **passive obedience:** Submission to the authority of a person or body without participation, unquestioning submission to laws or commands whatever their nature. **obedient,** *a.* **your obedient servant:** A formula used as a polite or ironical phrase in taking leave or subscribing a letter. ***obediential** (-en′ shȧl), *a.* **obedientiary,** *n.* A member of, esp. a holder of office in, a monastery or convent, subject to obedience to the superior. **obediently,** *adv.*

obeisance (ȯ bā′ sȧns) [F. *obéissance*, orig. obedience], *n.* A bow, a curtsy, or any gesture signifying deference, submission, respect, or salutation; homage; *obedience. **obeisant,** *a.*

obelion (ȯ bē′ li ȯn) [mod. L., dim. from Gr. *obelos*, see foll.], *n.* (*Anat.*) The part of the skull between the two parietal foramina where the sagittal suture becomes simple.

obelisk (ob′ ė lisk) [L. *obeliscus*, Gr. *obeliskos*, dim. of *obelos*, a spit], *n.* A quadrangular stone shaft, usually monolithic and tapering, with a pyramidal apex; the dagger (†) used in printing etc., as a reference-mark. **double obelisk:** The mark (‡). **obeliscal** (-lis′ kȧl), *a.*

obelus (ob′ ė lŭs) [L., from Gr. *obelos*, a spit], *n.* (*pl.* **-li**) A mark (—, ÷, or †), used to mark spurious or doubtful passages in ancient MSS. **obelize** (ob′ ė līz), *v.t.*

obese (ȯ bēs′) [L. *obēsus*, p.p. of *obedere* (OB-, *edere*, to eat)], *a.* Fat, fleshy, corpulent. **obeseness, obesity** (ȯ bēs′ i ti), *n.*

obex (ō′ beks) [L., cogn. with *obicere* (OB-, *jacere*, to cast)], *n.* (*Anat.*) A band of white matter in the *medulla oblongata*; *an obstacle, an impediment.

obey (ȯ bā′) [F. *obéir*, L. *obēdīre* (OB-, *audīre*, to hear)], *v.t.* To perform or carry out (a command, instruction, or direction); to be obedient to; to yield to the direction or control of, to act according to. *v.i.* To do what one is directed or commanded. **obeyer,** *n.* **obeyingly,** *adv.*

obfuscate (ob fŭs′- ob′ fŭs kāt) [L. *obfuscātus*, p.p. of *obfuscāre* (OB-, *fuscāre* from *fuscus*, dark)], *v.t.* To darken, to obscure; to bewilder, to confuse. **obfuscation** (kā′ shŭn), *n.*

obi (ō′ bi) [Jap.], *n.* A coloured sash worn by Japanese children and women.

obit (ob′ it, ō′ bit) [O.F., from L. *obitus*, p.p. of *obīre*, to set, to die], *n.* Death, decease; a notice or the date of a person's death; a service, esp. a Mass, for the soul of a deceased person on the anniversary of his death; a funeral ceremony. **obitual,** *a.* and *n.*

obituary (ȯ bit′ ū ȧ ri) [as prec.], *a.* Relating to or recording a death or deaths. *n.* A notice or account of a person or persons deceased, usu. in the form of a short biography; (*R.-C. Church*) a register or list of deceased persons, with their anniversaries. **obituarily,** *adv.* **obituarist,** *n.*

object (1) (ȯb jekt′) [L. *objectāre*, freq. of *objicere* (OB-, *jacere*, to throw)], *v.t.* To oppose; to offer or adduce in opposition, to allege (a fact, usu. with *that*) in criticism, disapproval, or condemnation; *to propose. *v.i.* To make objections; to dislike, to disapprove.

object (2) (ob′ jekt) [as prec.], *n.* Anything presented to the senses or the mind, esp. anything visible or tangible; a material thing; that to which an action or feeling is directed; aim, end, ultimate purpose; (*fig.*) a person or thing of pitiable or ridiculous appearance; (*Gram.*) a noun, or word, phrase, or sentence equivalent to a noun, governed by a transitive verb or preposition; (*Phil.*) a thing or idea regarded as brought before consciousness, the correlative to the subjective, an external as distinct from the ego. **object-ball,** *n.* (*Billiards*) The ball at which a player aims. **object-finder,** *n.* An eye-piece on a microscope for enabling one to locate the object on a slide; an analogous instrument on a large telescope. **object-glass, -lens,** *n.* The lens at the end of a microscope or telescope nearest the object. **object-lesson,** *n.* A lesson in which the actual object described or a representation of it is used for illustration; (*fig.*) a practical illustration. **object-soul,** *n.* A soul attributed to material objects by certain savages to account for their appearing in dreams. **object-staff,** *n.* An engineer's or surveyor's levelling-staff. **object-teaching, objectless,** *a.*

objectify (ob jekt′ i fī), *v.t.* To render objective; to present to the mind as a concrete or sensible reality. **objectification,** *n.*

objection (ob jek′ shŭn) [OBJECT (1)], *n.* The act of objecting; an adverse argument, reason, or statement; disapproval, dislike, or the expression of this. **objectionable,** *a.* Liable to objection, reprehensible; offensive, unpleasant. **objectionably,** *adv.*

objective (ob jekt′ iv) [OBJECT (2)], *a.* Proceeding from the object of knowledge or thought as dist. from the perceiving or thinking subject; external, actual, real, self-existent, substantive; pertaining to or concerned with outward things as dist. from thoughts or feelings; (*Gram.*) denoting the case of the object of a transitive verb or preposition. *n.* An objective point; (*Mil.*) the point towards which troops are to advance; the objective case; an object-glass. **objective case:** The case governed in English by a transitive verb or a preposition. **objectively,** *adv.* **objectiveness, objectivity** (tiv′ i ti), *n.*

objectivism (ob jekt′ i vizm), *n.* The tendency to

or practice of treating subjects objectively, or apart from one's own personality, esp. in painting or literature; (*Phil.*) the doctrine that the knowledge of objects is anterior and superior to that of the ego. **objectivist,** *n.* **objectivize,** *v.t.* and *i.*

objector (ob jekt' or) [OBJECT (1)], *n.* One who objects for whim or principle. **conscientious objector,** *n.* One who pleads conscientious scruples against taking part in war; an objector to inoculation.

objet d'art (ob zhā da) [F.], *n.* Object of art.

***objure** (ob joor') [L. *objūrāre* (OB-, *jūrāre*, to swear)], *v.i.* To swear. **objuration** (-rā' shŭn), *n.*

objurgate (ob' jŭr gāt) [L. *objurgātus*, p.p. of *objurgare* (OB-, *jurgāre*, to chide)], *v.t.* To chide, to reprove. **objurgation** (-gā' shŭn), *n.* **objurgatory** (ob' jŭr gă tor i), *a.*

oblanceolate (ob lăn' sē ŏ lāt), *a.* (*Bot.*) Inversely lanceolate.

oblate (1) (ob lāt') [L. *oblātus* (OB-, *lātus*, p.p. of *ferre*, to carry)], *a.* Flattened at the poles, opp. to prolate. **oblate spheroid:** Such a sphere as is produced by the revolution of an ellipse about its shorter axis. **oblately,** *adv.* **oblateness,** *n.*

oblate (2) (ob' lāt) [as prec.], *n.* One not under vows but dedicated to monastic or religious life or work, esp. one of a congregation of secular priests or sisters who live in community.

oblation (ob lā' shŭn) [F., from L. *oblātiōnem*, nom. *-tio*, as prec.], *n.* The act of offering or anything offered in worship; the presentation of the elements in the Eucharist; anything offered to God as a sacrifice; a sacrificial victim; a gift or donation to the Church. **oblational, oblatory** (ob' lă tŏr i), *a.*

obligation (ob li gā' shŭn) [O.F., from L. *obligātiōnem*, nom. *-tio*, from *obligāre*, to oblige], *n.* The binding power of a promise, contract, vow, duty, law, etc.; one's duty towards one's fellow-men; indebtedness for some benefit, favour, or kindness; (*Law*) a binding agreement, esp. one with a penal condition annexed. **obligate** (ob' li gāt), *v.t.* To place under an obligation, legal or moral; to compel. *a.* (*Bot., Zool.*) Compelled, without a choice of a mode of life. ***obligable,** *a.* **obligant,** *a.* and *n.* **obligatory** (ob li gă' tŏr i, ob lig' ă tŏr i), *a.* (*Am.* mandatory).

obligato [OBBLIGATO].

oblige (ŏ blīj') [O.F. *obliger*, L. *obligāre* (OB-, *ligāre*, to bind)], *v.t.* To bind or constrain by legal, moral, or physical force; to be binding on; to place under a debt of gratitude by a favour or kindness; to do a favour to, to gratify; (*in p.p.*) to put under an obligation (for). *v.i.* To be obliging. **obligee** (ob li jē'), *n.* (*Law*) One to whom a bond is given. ***obligement,** *n.* (*Law*). **obliger,** *n.* **obliging,** *a.* Kind, complaisant; imposing obligation. **obligingly,** *adv.* **obligingness,** *n.* **obligor** (ob' li gor), *n.* (*Law*) One bound by a bond.

oblique (ob lēk') [F., from L. *oblīquus* (OB-, *-līquus*, *-līcus*, cp. *licinus*, bent)], *a.* Slanting, deviating from the vertical or horizontal; deviating from the straight or direct line, indirect, roundabout; (*fig.*) evasive, not to the point; (*Geom.*) inclined at an angle other than a right angle; differing from a right angle, acute or obtuse; (*Anat.*) slanting, neither parallel nor vertical to the longer axis of the body or limb (of muscles etc.); (*Bot.*) unequal-sided (of leaves); (*Gram.*) of or pertaining to other cases than the nominative or vocative. *v.i.* (*Mil.*) To move forwards obliquely . ***obliquation** (ob li kwā' shŭn), *n.* **oblique angle:** An angle greater or less than a right angle. **oblique case,** *n.* (*Gram.*) Case other than the nominative or vocative. **oblique narration** or **oration:** (*Gram.*) Words or statements put into reported form, as in a narrative by another, with the consequent changes of person, tense, etc., indirect discourse. **obliquely,** *adv.* **obliqueness,** *n.* **obliquity** (ob lik' wi ti), *n.* Obliqueness; deviation from the moral code.

obliterate (ŏb lit' ĕr āt) [L. *obliterātus*, p.p. of *obliterāre* (OB-, *litera*, LETTER)], *v.t.* To efface, to erase; to wear out, to destroy by time or other means; to reduce to an almost imperceptible state. **obliteration** (-ā' shŭn), *n.*

oblivion (ŏb liv' i ŏn) [O.F., from L. *oblīviōnem*, nom. *-vio*, from *oblīvīscī* (OB-, *līvīscī*, to forget, perh. rel. to *līvēre*, to be livid or black and blue)], *n.* Forgetfulness, disregard; the state of being forgotten. **Act of Oblivion:** A general amnesty. **oblivious,** *a.* Forgetful, regardless (of); lost in thought or abstraction; causing forgetfulness. **obliviously,** *adv.* **obliviousness, obliviscence** (-vis' ĕns), *n.*

oblong (ob' long) [L. *oblongus* (OB-, *longus*, LONG (1))], *a.* Longer than broad, esp. if rectangular; of greater breadth than height (of books, postage-stamps, etc.); (*Math.*) having one axis longer than the other or others; rectangular with adjoining sides unequal; (*Bot.*) elliptical (of leaves). *n.* An oblong figure or thing. ***oblongish,** *a.* ***oblongly,** *adv.* **oblongness,** *n.* **oblongo-,** *comb. form.*

obloquy (ob' lŏ kwi) [late L. *obloquium*, from *obloquī*, to speak against (OB-, *loquī*, to speak)], *n.* Abusive or reproachful language; detraction, disgrace, infamy.

obmutescence (ob mū tes' ĕns) [L. *obmūtescere* (*mūtescere*, incept., from *mūtus*, MUTE)], *n.* Loss of speech; obstinate silence or taciturnity. **obmutescent,** *a.*

obnoxious (ob nok' shŭs) [L. *obnoxius* (*noxa*, harm)], *a.* Liable or exposed (to injury, attack, criticism, etc.); offensive, objectionable, hateful, odious. **obnoxiously,** *adv.* **obnoxiousness,** *n.*

***obnubilate** (ob nū' bi lāt) [L. *obnūbilātus*, p.p. of *obnūbilāre* (*nūbilus*, cloudy)], *v.t.* To cloud, to obscure. **obnubilation** (-lā' shŭn), *n.*

oboe (ō' bō) [It., from F. *hautbois*, HAUTBOY], *n.* A wind-instrument of wood played through a double reed, usu. of soprano pitch; a reed organ-stop of similar tone.

obolus (ob' ŏ lŭs), **obol** (ob' ŏl) [L., from Gr. *obolos*], *n.* (*pl.* **-li,** -lī) A small coin of ancient Greece worth ⅙ of a drachma. **obole** (ob' ōl), *n.* A small French coin (10th–15th cent.) worth half a denier; *an apothecaries' weight of 10 grains.

obovate (ob ō' vāt), *a.* (*Nat. Hist.*) Inversely ovate. **obovato-,** *comb. form.* **obovoid,** *a.*

obreption (ob rep' shŭn) [F., from L. *obreptiōnem*, nom. *-tio* (*repere*, to creep)], *n.* (*Sc. Law*) Acquisition of gifts etc., by falsehood or craft. **obreptitious** (-tish' ŭs), *a.*

obscene (ŏb sēn') [L. *obscēnus* (*scēnus*, etym. doubtful)], *a.* Vile, repulsive, disgusting, loathsome; indecent, lewd, unchaste; ill-omened. **obscenely,** *adv.* ***obsceneness, obscenity** (ob sen' i ti), *n.*

obscurant (ob skūr' ănt), *n.* An opponent of intellectual progress. **obscurantism,** *n.* **obscurantist,** *a.* and *n.*

obscure (ŏb skūr') [O.F. *obscur*, L. *obscurus* (*scurus*, from *scu-*, Sansk. *sku-*, to cover, cp. *scūtum*, shield)], *a.* Dark, dim; not clear, indefinite, indistinct; abstruse; difficult to understand; unexplained, doubtful; hidden, secluded, remote from public observation; unknown, lowly, humble; dull, dingy; *gloomy, murky. *v.t.* To make dark, to cloud; to make less intelligible, visible, or legible; to dim, to throw into the shade, to outshine; to conceal; *to degrade, to disparage. *n.* Obscurity; indistinctness. **obscuration** (ob skū rā' shŭn), *n.* **obscurely,** *adv.* ***obscurement, *obscureness, obscurity,** *n.* ***obscurer,** *n.*

obsecration (ob sē krā' shŭn) [L. *obsecrātio*, from *obsecrāre*, to beseech (*sacrāre*, to make sacred, from *sacer*, SACRED)], *n.* The act of imploring, entreaty; a clause in the Litany beginning with 'by.' ***obsecrate** (ob' sē krāt), *v.t.*

obsequent (ob' sē kwent) [L. *sequi*, to follow], *a.* Of a stream which flows in the opposite direction to the original slope of the land.

obsequies (ob′ sė kwiz) [pl. of obs. *obsequy*, A.-F. *obsequie* (O.F. *obsèque*), med. L. *obsequiæ* (L. *exsequiæ*, acc. to O.E.D. conf. with *obsequium*, see foll.)], *n.pl.* Funeral rites. **obsequial** (-sē′ kwi ȧl), *a.*

obsequious (ob sē′ kwi ůs) [L. *obsequiōsus*, from *obsequium*, from *obsèquī*, to comply (*sequī*, to follow)], *a.* Servile, cringing, fawning, over ready to comply with the desires of others; *obedient, submissive, yielding. **obsequiously,** *adv.* **obsequiousness,** *n.*

observe (ȯb zerv′) [O.F. *observer*, L. *observāre* (*servāre*, to keep, to heed)], *v.t.* To regard attentively, to note, to take notice of, to perceive; to watch, to scrutinize; to examine and note scientifically; to follow attentively, to heed; to perform duly; to comply with; to celebrate; to remark, to express as an opinion. *v.i.* To make a remark or remarks (upon); *to take notice. **observable,** *a.* **observably,** *adv.* **observer,** *n.* One who observes, a looker-on; (*Aviat.*) the member of an aircraft's crew employed on reconnaissance. **observingly,** *adv.* **observatorial** (ob zěr vȧ tôr′ i ȧl), *a.* **observedly,** *adv.*

observance (ob zěr′ vȧns), *n.* The act of observing, complying with, keeping, following, performing, etc.; a customary rite, form, or ceremony; a rule or practice, esp. in a religious order; *observation, heed; *respectful attention, compliance, or submission, deference. ***observancy,** *n.*

observanda (ob zěr văn′ dȧ), *n.pl.* Things to be observed or taken notice of.

observant (ob zěr′ vȧnt), *a.* Watchful, attentive; quick or strict in observing, esp. rules etc.; *obedient. *n.* An Observantine; *one who observes carefully; an obsequious attendant. **Observantine** (ob zěr′ vȧn tin), *n.* One of a branch of the Franciscan order observing the stricter rule, also called Observant Friars. **observantly,** *adv.*

observation (ob zěr vā′ shůn), *n.* The act, habit, or faculty of observing; scientific watching and noting of phenomena as they occur, as dist. from experiment; the result of such a scrutiny, a fact scientifically noted; experience and knowledge gained by systematic observing; a remark, an incidental comment or expression of opinion or reflection; *observance. **observation-balloon,** *n.* (*Mil.*) A captive balloon used for observing the enemy's movement. **observation-post,** *n.* (*Mil.*) Post from which an observer can watch the effect of artillery fire.

observatory (ob zěr′ vȧ tȯr i), *n.* A building, room, etc., for observation of astronomical phenomena.

obsess (ob ses′) [L. *obsessus*, p.p. of *obsidēre*, to besiege (*sedēre*, to sit)], *v.t.* To haunt, to beset, to trouble (as an evil spirit); to preoccupy the mind of (as a fixed idea). **obsession** (-sesh′ ůn), *n.*

obsidian (ob sid′ i ȧn) [L. *Obsidiānus*, from *Obsidius*, erron. for *Obsius*, personal name], *n.* A black or dark-coloured vitreous lava, used by primitive peoples for making weapons, implements, etc.

obsidional (ob sid′ yȯ nȧl) [L. *obsidiōnālis*, from *obsidio -ōnis*, siege], *a.* Pertaining to a siege.

***obsignate** (ob sig′ nāt) [L. *obsignātus*, p.p. of *obsignāre* (*signāre*, to SIGN)], *v.t.* To seal, to ratify. ***obsignation** (-nā′ shůn), *n.*

obsolescent (ob sȯ les′ ėnt) [L. *obsolescens -ntem*, pres.p. of *obsolescere*, incept. of *obsolēre* (*solēre*, to be accustomed)], *a.* Becoming obsolete; (*Biol.*) gradually disappearing, not fully developed. **obsolescence,** *n.* **obsolete** (ob′ sȯ lēt), *a.* Passed out of use, no longer practised, current, or accepted; discarded, bygone, out-of-date; (*Biol.*) imperfectly developed, atrophied, suppressed, indistinct (of markings, organs, etc.). **obsoleteness, *obsoletion, obsoletism,** *n.*

obstacle (ob′ stȧ kėl) [O.F., from L. *obstāculum* (*stāre*, to stand)], *n.* An impediment, an obstruction. **a.* Obstinate. **obstacle-race,** *n.* A race in which the competitors have to surmount a series of natural or artificial obstacles.

obstetric, -al (ob stet′ rik, -ȧl) [L. *obstetrīcius*, from *obstetrix*, midwife (*stāre*, as prec.)], *a.* Of or pertaining to midwifery or childbirth; (*pl.*) midwifery, the branch of medical science dealing with gestation, parturition, etc. **obstetrician** (-trish′ ȧn), *n.* **obstetrix,** *n.*

obstinate (ob′ sti nȧt) [L. *obstinātus*, p.p. of *obstināre* (*stanāre*, from *stāre*, to stand)], *a.* Pertinaciously adhering to one's opinion or purpose, stubborn, refractory; (*Med.*) not yielding easily to remedies. **obstinacy, obstinateness,** *n.* **obstinately,** *adv.*

obstipation (ob sti pā′ shůn) [L. *stīpāre*, to cram, to pack], *n.* (*Path.*) Extreme costiveness.

obstreperous (ob strep′ ėr ůs) [L. *obstreperus* (*strepere*, to make a noise)], *a.* Noisy, clamorous; boisterous, unruly. **obstreperously,** *adv.* **obstreperousness,** *n.*

***obstriction** (ob strik′ shůn) [med. L. *obstrictio*, from *stringere*, to tie], *n.* The state of being legally constrained; obligation.

obstruct (ob strŭkt′) [L. *obstructus*, p.p. of *obstruere* (*struere*, to build)], *v.t.* To block up, to close by means of obstacles; to hinder, to impede; to hamper, to check, to retard, to stop. *v.i.* To practise obstruction, esp. in Parliament. **obstructer,** *n.* **obstruction,** *n.* **obstructionism,** *n.* **obstructionist,** *n.* **obstructive,** *a.* Causing or tending to cause obstruction; intended to retard progress, esp. of parliamentary business. *n.* One who causes obstruction, esp. in Parliament. **obstruent** (ob′ strụ ėnt), *a.* and *n.* (*Med.*)

obtain (ȯb tān′) [F. *obtenir*, L. *obtinēre* (*tenēre*, to hold)], *v.t.* To gain, to acquire, to secure; to procure, to get; to attain, to reach. *v.i.* To be prevalent or in vogue; to be in common use. **obtainable,** *a.* **obtainer,** *n.* **obtainment,** *n.*

obtected (ob tek′ tėd) [L. *obtectus*, p.p. of *obtegere* (*tegere*, to cover)], *a.* (*Ent.*) Protected, encased by a chitinous covering (of the pupæ of some insects).

obtemper (ob tem′ pėr) [F. *obtempérer*, L. *obtemperāre* (*temperāre*, to qualify, to TEMPER)], *v.t.* (*Sc. Law*) To obey, to comply with (the judgment of a court).

obtest (ob test′) [L. *obtestārī* (*testārī*, to bear witness)], *v.t.* To beseech, to supplicate, to adjure; to beg for. *v.i.* To protest. **obtestation** (-tā′ shůn), *n.*

obtrude (ȯb trood′) [L. *obtrūdere* (*trūdere*, to thrust, p.p. *trūsus*)], *v.t.* To thrust in or upon; to introduce without warrant or invitation. *v.i.* To enter without right. **obtruder,** *n.* **obtrusion,** *n.* **obtrusive,** *a.* **obtrusively,** *adv.* **obtrusiveness,** *n.* A thrusting forward, a desire to be noticed.

***obtruncate** (ob trŭng′ kāt) [L. *obtruncātus*, p.p. of *obtruncāre* (*truncāre*, to cut off)], *v.t.* To lop, to cut the head off, to decapitate.

obtund (ob tŭnd′) [L. *obtundere* (OB-, *tundere*, to beat)], *v.t.* To blunt, to deaden. **obtundent,** *n.* (*Med.*). **obtundity,** *n.*

obturate (ob′ tū rāt) [L. *obturātus*, p.p. of *obturāre*, to close], *v.t.* To stop up or close, esp. the breech of a gun. **obturation** (-rā′ shůn), *n.* **obturator** (ob′ tū rā tȯr), *n.* (*Anat.*) That which closes a cavity or the like, as a membrane closing the thyroid foramen; one of two muscles of the gluteal region; (*Surg.*) a plate for closing an aperture, such as a cleft palate; (*Gunnery*) a device for closing the aperture of the breech and preventing the escape of gas.

obturbinate (ob těr′ bi nȧt), *a.* (*Nat. Hist.*) Inversely turbinate.

obtuse (ob tūs′) [L. *obtūsus*, p.p. of *obtundere*, to OBTUND], *a.* Blunt or rounded, not pointed or acute; (*Geom.*) denoting an angle larger than a right angle; (*fig.*) dull, stupid, slow of apprehension. **obtuse-angular, obtuse-angled,** *a.* **obtusely,** *adv.* **obtuseness,** *n.* **obtusion,** *n.* (*Path.*) A blunting of normal sensation. **obtusi-,** *comb. form.*

***obumbrate** (ob ŭm′ brāt) [L. *obumbrātus*, p.p. of

obumbrāre (*umbrāre*, to shade)], *v.t.* To overshadow, to darken. *a.* (-brȧt) (*Ent.*) Overhung or concealed by a projecting part, as the abdomen of spiders.

obvallate (ob văl' ȧt) [L. *obvallātus*, p.p. of *obvallāre* (*vallāre*, to palisade, from *vallus*, a stake)], *a.* (*Nat. Hist.*) Walled up.

obverse (ob' vĕrs) [L. *obversus*, p.p. of *obvertere* (*vertere*, to turn)], *a.* Turned towards one (said of the side of a coin or medal bearing the head or main device); (*Nat. Hist.*) having the base narrower than the apex (of leaves, organs, etc.). *n.* The face or front; the side of a coin or medal bearing the main device; the other or complementary side or aspect of a statement, fact, etc. **obversely** (ob vĕrs' li), *adv.*

obvert (ob vĕrt') [see prec.], *v.t.* To turn the front towards one; (*Log.*) to alter a proposition by obversion. **obversion**, *n.* (*Log.*) A method of immediate inference by reversing the predicate and changing the quality of a proposition. **obvertend**, *n.* (*Log.*).

obviate (ob' vi āt) [L. *obviātus*, p.p. of *obviāre* (*via*, way)], *v.t.* To clear away, to remove, to overcome, counteract, or neutralize (as dangers, difficulties, etc.); to anticipate, to forestall. **obviation** (-ā' shŭn), *n.*

obvious (ob' vi ŭs) [L. *obvius* (*ob viam*, in the way)], *a.* Plain to the eye, perfectly manifest, immediately evident; *standing or situated in the way. *n.* What is obvious, needing no explanation. **obviously**, *adv.* **obviousness**, *n.*

obvolute (ob' vŏ lūt) [L. *obvolūtus*, p.p. of *obvolvere* (*volvere*, to roll)], *a.* (*Bot.*) Folded together so that the alternate margins are respectively exposed or covered (by the other or the next leaf). **obvolution** (-lū' shŭn), *n.* **obvolvent, obvolving** (ob vol' vėnt, -ving), *a.*

oc- [OB-, before c], *pref.*

ocarina (ok ȧ rē' nȧ) [It. *oca*, goose], *n.* A musical instrument of terracotta with finger-notes and mouthpiece, giving a mellow whistling sound.

Occamism (ok' ȧ mizm) [William of *Occam* (*c.* 1270–*c.* 1349), English scholastic philosopher and teacher of nominalism], *n.* The doctrines of William of Occam. **Occamist, -ite**, *n.* **Occamistic** (-mis' tik), *a.*

***occamy** (ok' ȧ mi) [corr. of ALCHEMY], *n.* An alloy imitating silver.

occasion (ŏ kā' zhŭn) [F., from L. *occāsiōnem*, nom. *-sio*, from *occidere* (*cadere*, to fall)], *n.* An event, circumstance, or position of affairs, giving an opportunity, reason, or motive for doing something; motive, ground, reason, need; an incidental or subsidiary cause; the immediate cause or condition as dist. from the primary cause; a time or occurrence having special interest; an occurrence or time of importance; (*pl.*) needs, affairs; *(*Sc.*) a communion service. *v.t.* To cause directly or indirectly; to be the occasion or incidental cause of; to induce, to influence. **on occasion:** Now and then. **as occasion arises:** When needful, when circumstances demand. **to rise to the occasion:** To be equal to an emergency.

occasional (o kā' zhŏn ȧl), *a.* Happening, made, or done as opportunity arises; irregular, frequent but not at fixed intervals; incidental, casual; made for special occasions. **occasionally**, *adv.* **occasionality**, *n.*

occasionalism (o kā' zhŏn ȧl izm), *n.* The doctrine of certain Cartesians that body and mind form a dualism of heterogeneous entities, and that there is no real interaction, the corresponding phenomena of sensation and volition being due to the simultaneous action of God; sometimes applied to the modern doctrine of psycho-physical parallelism. **occasionalist**, *n.*

Occident (ok' si dėnt) [F., from L. *occidentem*, nom. *-dens*, pres.p. of *occidere* (OC-, *cadere*, to fall)], *n.* The west; western Europe, Europe and America; the western quarter of the sky as the region of sunset; (*fig.*) western civilization, culture, thought, etc., as opp. to Oriental. **Occidental**, *a.* Western; inferior in excellence (applied to gems, the best of which are supposed to come from the East). **occidentalism**, *n.* **occidentalist**, *n.* **occidentalize**, *v.t.* **occidentally**, *adv.*

occiput (ok' si pŭt) [L. *occiput* (OC-, *caput*, head)], *n.* (*Anat.*) The back part of the head. **occipital** (-sip' i tȧl), *a.* **occipito-, occipito-axial** (*comb. form.* ăk' si ȧl), *a.* Of or pertaining to the occipital bone and the axis or second cervical vertebra. **occipito-frontal** (-frŭn'-, -fron' tȧl), *a.* Of or pertaining to the occipital bone and the frontal region or forehead. **occipito-temporal** (-tem' pŏr ȧl), *a.* Of or pertaining to the occipital and temporal lobes of the cerebellum, or to the occipital and temporal bones.

occlude (ŏ klood') [L. *occlūdere* (OC-, *claudere*, to shut), p.p. *occlūsus*], *v.t.* To shut or stop up; (*Chem. of metals*) to absorb (a gas). **occlusion** (-kloo' zhŭn), *n.* A shutting or stopping up; (*Meteor.*) the closing of a cold front upon a warm one, which is narrowed and raised up. **occlusor** (-kloo' zŏr), *n.*

occult (1) (ŏ kŭlt') [L. *occultus*, p.p. of *occulere* (OC-, -*celere*, rel. to *celāre*, to hide, cp. HELE)], *a.* Concealed, kept secret, esoteric; mysterious, recondite, beyond the range of ordinary knowledge or perception; (*Spiritualism*) perceptible only by clairvoyance; involving supernatural agency. **occultism**, *n.* **occultist**, *n.* **occultly**, *adv.* **occultness**, *n.*

occult (2) (ŏ kŭlt') [L. *occultāre*, freq. of *occulere*, see prec.], *v.t.* To hide, to conceal, to cover or cut off from view (esp. of a heavenly body passing before one of apparently smaller size). **occultation** (-tā' shŭn), *n.* **occulting apparatus:** A contrivance for cutting off the light in a lighthouse at regular intervals, also **occulting light.**

occupant (ok' ū pȧnt) [OCCUPY], *n.* One who occupies; one who resides or is in a place; a tenant in possession as dist. from an owner; one who establishes a claim by taking possession. **occupancy**, *n.*

occupation (ok ū pā' shŭn), *n.* The act of occupying or taking possession; the state of being occupied; occupancy, tenure; the state of being employed or engaged in some way; pursuit, employment, business, calling. **occupational**, *a.* Caused by employment. **occupational disease**, *n.* A disease resulting directly from an occupation. **occupational therapy**, *n.* (*Med.*) Treatment of various diseases, notably mental, by providing instruction in an occupation or hobby. ***occupative**, *a.* **occupier**, *n.* An occupant of a house etc.

occupy (ok' ū pī) [F. *occuper*, L. *occupāre* (OC-, *capere*, to take)], *v.t.* To take possession of; to hold in possession, to be the tenant of; to reside in, to be in; to take up, to fill; to give occupation to; to employ, to engage (oneself, or in p.p.); *to use in business, to employ for profit (as capital); *to have and enjoy, to cohabit with; *to follow (as a business). **v.i.* To be an occupant; to carry on traffic or business.

occur (ŏ kĕr') [M.F. *occurrer*, L. *occurrere* (OC-, *currere*, to run)], *v.i.* (*past & p.p.* **occurred**) To happen, to take place; to be met with, to be found; to present itself to the mind. **occurrence** (ŏ kŭr' ėns), *n.* An event, an incident; the happening or taking place of anything. ***occurrent**, *a.* and *n.*

ocean (ō' shȧn) [O.F., from L. *ōceanum*, nom. *-us*, Gr. *ōkeanos*], *n.* The vast body of water covering about two-thirds of the surface of the globe; any one of its principal divisions, the Antarctic, Atlantic, Arctic, Indian, and Pacific Oceans; the sea; (*fig.*) an immense expanse; (*often in pl.*) an immense quantity. *a.* Pertaining to the ocean. **ocean-basin**, *n.* The depression of the earth's surface containing an ocean. **ocean-greyhound**, *n.* A fast ocean-steamer. **ocean-lane**, *n.* A route prescribed for ocean-steamers. **ocean-palace**, *n.* A luxuriously-appointed ocean-steamer. **ocean-tramp**, *n.* An ocean-steamer carrying cargo but having no regular schedule. **oceanarium** (ō shŏn âr′ i ŭm), *n.* An aquarium for specimens of deep-sea animal life. **Oceania** (ō shė-, -sė ā′ ni a), *n.* The island-region of the Pacific and adjoining seas. **Oceanian,** *a.* and *n.* **oceanic** (ō shė-, -sė ăn′ ik), *a.* Of, pertaining to, occurring in, or like the ocean; pertaining to Oceania. **Oceanid** (ȯ sē′ å nid), *n.* (*pl.* **-ids, -anides,** -ăn′ i dēz) (*Gr. Myth.*) An ocean-nymph, a daughter of Oceanus, the god of the great stream which the ancients imagined encircled the earth; (*pl.* **-anides**) marine as dist. from freshwater mollusca. **oceano-,** *comb. form.* **oceanography** (ō shå nog′ rå fi), *n.* **oceanographer,** *n.* **oceanographic, -al** (-grăf′ ik, -ål), *a.* **oceanology** (-nol′ ȯ ji), *n.* **oceanward, -wards,** *adv.*

ocellus (ȯ sel′ ŭs) [L., dim. of *oculus*, eye], *n.* (*pl.* **-li,** -li) A simple as opposed to the compound eye of insects; a part or facet of a compound eye; an eyespot or spot of colour surrounded by a ring or rings of other colour, as on feathers, wings, etc. **ocellate, -lated,** *a.* **ocelli-,** *comb. form.*

ocelot (ō′ sė lot) [F., from Mex. *ocelotl*], *n.* A small American feline animal, *Felis pardalis*, the tiger-cat or leopard-cat.

och (o*ch*) [Ir. and Gael.], *int.* Oh! ah!

ochlesis (ok lē′ sis) [Gr., from *ochlein*, to disturb, as foll.], *n.* (*Path.*) An unhealthy condition produced by overcrowding.

ochlocracy (ok lok′ rå si) [F. *ochlocratie*, Gr. *ochlokratia* (*ochlos*, crowd, -CRACY)], *n.* Government by the mob. **ochlocrat** (ok′ lȯ krăt), *n.* **ochlocratic, -al** (-krăt′ ik, -ål), *a.* **ochlocratically,** *adv.*

ochlophobia (ok lō fō′ bi ā), *n.* A morbid fear of crowds.

ochone [OHONE].

ochre (ō′ kėr) [O.F. *ocre*, L. and Gr. *ōchra*, from *ōchros*, yellow], *n.* A native earth consisting of hydrated peroxide of iron with clay in various proportions, used as a pigment (applied to many metallic oxides occurring in an earthy form); a yellow colour; (*slang*) money (from the yellow colour of gold). **ochraceous** (ō krā′ shŭs), **ochreous** (ō′ krė ŭs), **ochroid, ochrous, ochreish** (ō′ kėr ish), **ochry,** *a.* **ochreo-,** *comb. form.*

o'clock [CLOCK (1)].

ocrea (ok′ rė å) [L., a legging, a greave], *n.* (*pl.* **-eæ**) (*Bot.*) A sheath formed by the union of two stipules round a stem; (*Zool.*) a sheath round the foot or leg of a bird. **ocreaceous** (-ā′ shŭs), **ocreate** (ok′ rė ăt), *a.*

oct-, octa, octo- [Gr. *oktō*, eight], *comb. form.* Having eight; consisting of eight.

octachord (ok′ tå kôrd), *n.* A musical instrument with eight strings; a system of eight sounds, as the diatonic scale.

octad (ok′ tăd), *n.* A group or series of eight; (*Chem.*) an element or radical with a valency power of eight; (*Math.*) the eight points of intersection of three quadratic surfaces.

octagon (ok′ tå gŏn) [L. *octă-*, *octōgōnos*, Gr. *oktagōnos*, *gōnia*, corner], *n.* A plane figure of eight sides and angles; any object or building of this shape; (*Fort.*) a work having eight bastions. **octagonal** (-tăg′ ȯ nål), *a.* **octagonally,** *adv.*

octahedron (ok tå hed′ rŏn, -hē′ drŏn) [Gr. *hedra*, seat, base], *n.* (*pl.* **-dra**) A solid figure contained by eight plane faces, usu. by triangles. **regular octahedron:** One contained by eight equal equilateral triangles. **octahedral,** *a.* **octahedrite,** *n.* (*Min.*) Native titanic dioxide.

octamerous (ok tăm′ ėr ŭs), *a.* (*Bot. and Zool.*) Having the parts eight-fold or in series of eight. **octameral,** *a.*

octameter (ok tăm′ e tėr), *n.* (*Pros.*) A line of eight metrical feet. *a.* Having eight metrical feet.

octandria (ok tăn′ dri å) [Gr. *andros*, male], *n.pl.* (*Bot.*) A Linnæan class of plants having flowers with eight stamens. **octandrian, octandrous,** *a.*

octane (ok′ tān), *n.* A hydrocarbon of the paraffin series. **high octane:** Of internal-combustion engine fuels that do not ignite readily during the compression stroke as a result of compression only; having a high octane number.

octangular (ok tăng′ gū lår), *a.* Having eight angles.

octant (ok′ tånt) [late L. *octans -ntem*, from *octo*, eight, see OCTO-], *n.* An arc comprising the 8th part of a circle; an eighth of a circular area contained within two radii and the arc subtending them; one of the eight parts into which space is divided by three planes (usu. at right angles) intersecting at one point; (*Astron.*) the position of a heavenly body when it is 45° distant from another or from a particular point; (*Naut.*) an instrument like a sextant for measuring angles, having a graduated arc of 45°.

octapodic (ok tå pod′ ik) [Gr., *pous podos*, foot)], *a.* (*Pros.*) Containing eight metrical feet. **octapody** (-tăp′ ȯ di), *n.*

octarchy (ok′ tar ki) [Gr. *archein*, to rule], *n.* A group of eight petty kingdoms, a country under eight rulers or kings.

octaroon [OCTOROON].

octastich (ok′ tå stik) [Gr. *stichos*, a row], *n.* A strophe, stanza, or series of eight lines of verse. **ocastichous,** *a.*

octastrophic (ok tå strof′ ik), *a.* Consisting of eight strophes.

octastyle (ok′ tå stīl), *n.* A building having eight columns in front.

octateuch (ok′ tå tūk) [Gr. *teuchos*, book], *n.* The first eight books of the Old Testament.

octave (ok′ tåv) [F., from L. *octava*, fem. of *octavus*, eighth, from *octo*, eight], *n.* The 8th day after a church festival, the festival itself being counted; (*Mus.*) the interval between any note and that produced by twice or half as many vibrations per second; a note at this interval above or below a given note; two notes separated by this interval sounded together; the scale of notes filling this interval; (*fig.*) any group of eight, as the first eight lines of a sonnet or a stanza of eight lines; a measure equal to one-eighth of a pipe of wine or 13⅛ gallons, a cask of this volume; (*Fencing*) a low thrust towards the right side of the opponent. **octave-coupler,** *n.* (*Organ*) A contrivance attached to a keyboard for connecting each note with its octave.

octavo (ok tā′ vō) [L. *in* OCTAVO (cp. INFOLIO)], *n.* (*pl.* **-vos**) A book in which a sheet is folded into 8 leaves or 16 pages; the size of such book or paper (written 8vo). *a.* Of this size.

octennial (ok ten′ i ål) [L. *octennium* (OCT-, *annus*, year), -AL], *a.* Recurring every 8th year; lasting 8 years. **octennially,** *adv.* **octet** (ok tet′) [after DUET], *n.* A musical composition of eight parts or for eight instruments or singers; a group of eight, as the octave of a sonnet.

octile (ok′ tīl), *n.* An eighth part.

octillion (ok til′ yŏn), *n.* The number produced by raising a million to the 8th power of a thousand, represented by 1 followed by 48 ciphers; (*Am.* and *Fr.*) the 8th power of a thousand, 1 followed by 27 ciphers. **octillienth,** *a.* and *n.*

octingentenary (ok tin jen tē′ nå ri), *n.* The 800th anniversary.

octo- [OCT-].

October (ok tō′ bėr) [L., from prec.], *n.* The 10th month of the modern, the 8th of the Roman year; *ale or cider brewed in October, hence, good ale. **Octobrists,** *n.pl.* Name of a moderate reforming party in Tsarist Russia.

octobrachiate (ok tō brăk′ i ăt), *a.* (*Zool.*) Having eight limbs, arms, or rays.

octocentenary (ok tȯ sen tē′ nå ri, -sen′ tė nå ri), *n.* The eight-hundredth anniversary. **octocentennial,** *n.*

octoceratous (-ser′ å tŭs) [Gr. *keras*, horn], *a.*

Eight horned. **octocerous** (ok tos' ėr ůs), *a.* Having eight horns or rays.

octodecimo (ok tȯ des' i mō) [L. *octodecimus* eighteenth (*decimus*, tenth), after OCTAVO], *n.* (*pl.* **-mos**) A book having 18 leaves to the sheet; the size of such book (written 18mo); having 18 leaves to the sheet.

octodentate (ok tȯ den' tāt), *a.* Having eight teeth.

octofid (ok' tō fid), *a.* (*Bot.*) Having eight segments.

octogenarian (ok tȯ jė nâr' i ȧn) [L. *octogēnārius* (*octōgēni*, eighty each)], *n.* One who is 80 years old or between 80 and 90. *a.* Eighty years old, or pertaining to this age. **octogenary** (ok toj' ė nȧ ri), *a.*

octogynous (ok toj' i nůs) [Gr. *gunē*, woman], *a.* (*Bot.*) Having eight pistils.

octohedron [OCTAHEDRON].

octolateral (ok tō lăt' ėr ȧl), *a.* Eight-sided.

octonal (ok' tȯ nȧl) [L. *octōnī*, eight each], *a.* Computing or proceeding by eight (of coins, numbers, etc.). **octonarian** (-nâr' i ȧn), *a.* (*Pros.*) Consisting of eight metrical feet. *n.* A verse of eight metrical feet. **octonary** (ok' tȯ nȧr i), *a.* **octonal,** *n.* A group of eight, a stanza or group of eight lines. ***octonocular** (ok tȯ nok' ū lȧr) [OCULAR], *a.* Having eight eyes.

octoped (ok' tȯ ped) [L. *pes pedis*, foot], *n.* An eight-footed animal. **octopetalous** (-pet' ȧ lůs), *a.* Having eight petals.

octopod (ok' tȯ pod) [Gr. *oktōpod-*, stem of *oktōpous*, see foll.], *a.* Having eight feet. *n.* An animal with eight feet.

octopus (ok' tȯ-, ok tō' půs) [Gr. *oktōpous* (*pous podos*, foot)], *n.* (*pl.* **octopuses**) One of a genus of cephalopods, having 8 arms furnished with suckers, a cuttlefish; (*fig.*) an organization or influence having far-extending powers for harm.

octoradiate (ok tȯ rā' di ȧt), *a.* Having eight rays.

octoroon (ok tȯ roon'), *n.* The offspring of a quadroon and a white.

octosepalous (ok tō sep' ȧ lůs), *a.* (*Bot.*) Having eight sepals.

octospermous (ok tō spėr' můs), *a.* (*Bot.*) Containing eight seeds.

octosporous (ok tō spôr' ůs), *a.* (*Bot.*) Eight-spored.

octosyllabic (ok tō si lăb' ik), *a.* Having eight syllables. **octosyllable,** *n.* A word of eight syllables.

octroi (ok' trwa) [F., from *octroyer*, from late L. *auctorizāre*, to AUTHORISE], *n.* A tax levied at the gates of some Continental, esp. French, towns on goods brought in; the barrier or place where this is levied; the body of officials collecting it.

octuple (ok' tūpl) [L. *octuplus*], *a.* Eightfold. *n.* The product of multiplication by eight. *v.t.* To multiply by eight.

octyl (ok' til), *n.* (*Chem.*) The hypothetical organic radical of a hydrocarbon series. **octylene** (ok' ti lēn), *n.* An oily hydrocarbon obtained by heating octylic alcohol with sulphuric acid. **octylic,** *a.*

ocular (ok' ū lȧr) [L. *oculāris*, from *oculus*, eye], *a.* Of, pertaining to, by or with the eye or eyes, visual; known from actual sight. **ocularist,** *n.* A maker of artificial eyes. **ocularly,** *adv.* **oculate,** *a.* (*Nat. Hist.*) Having eye-like spots; *having eyes or sight. **oculauditory** (ok ūl aw' di tȯr i) [AUDITORY], *a.* Combining the functions of eye and ear, as the sense-organs of some hydrozoa. **oculiferous** (-lif' ėr ůs), **oculigerous** (-lij' ėr ůs), *a.* Bearing an eye or eyes. **oculiform** (ok' ū li fôrm), *a.* **oculist,** *n.* One skilled in the treatment of diseases of the eye. **oculistic** (-lis' tik), *a.* **oculo-,** *comb. form.* **oculomotor** (ok ū lȯ mō' tȯr) [-MOTOR], *a.* Of or pertaining to the movement of the eye; serving to move the eyes.

od (od) [arbitrary], *n.* A natural force supposed by von Reichenbach (1788–1869) to pervade nature and to produce the phenomena of magnetism, crystallization, mesmerism, etc. **odic** (1) (od' ik), *a.* **odism,** *n.* **odize,** *v.t.*

***'od** (od), *int.* A minced form of 'God' used as an expletive or asseveration. ***od's bodikins** [BODIKIN]. ***od's life:** God's life.

odal (ō' dȧl) [Icel. *ōthal* (cp. O.H.G. *uodal*, a homestead, A.-S. *æthele*, noble)], *n.* Freehold tenure based on uninterrupted possession as in N. Europe before feudalism and in Orkney and Shetland at the present day.

odalisque (ō' dȧ lisk) [F., from Turk. *ōdalīq*, chambermaid, from *ōdah*, chamber], *n.* An Oriental female slave or concubine, esp. in the Sultan's seraglio.

odd (od) [Icel. *odda-* (in *oddamathr*, odd man, *oddalala*, odd number), cogn. with A.-S. *ord*, point, tip], *a.* Remaining after a number or quantity has been divided into pairs; not even; not divisible by two; bearing such a number; wanting a match or pair; singular, strange, eccentric, queer; occasional, casual; indefinite, incalculable; (*ellipt.*) and more, with others thrown in (added to a round number in enumeration as *two hundred odd*); *at variance. *n.* (*Golf*) A handicap entitling the weaker player to deduct a stroke for each hole from his total. **odd-come-short,** *n.* An odd bit or remnant of anything. **Odd Fellow:** A member of a friendly society known as the Order of Odd Fellows. **odd-looking** *a.* **oddish,** *a.* **oddity,** *n.* Oddness; a peculiar feature or trait; an odd person or thing. **oddly,** *adv.* **odd man out:** One who is left when a number pair off. **oddments,** *n.pl.* Odds and ends. **oddness,** *n.* **odds,** *n.pl.* (*usu. as sing.*) Inequality, difference; balance of superiority, advantage; the chances in favour of a given event; an allowance to the weaker of two competitors; the ratio by which the amount staked by one party to a bet exceeds that by the other; variance, strife, dispute. **at odds:** At variance. **odds and ends:** Miscellaneous trifles, scraps, etc.

ode (ōd) [F., from late L. *ōda*, Gr. *ōde*, *aoidē*, from *aeidein*, to sing], *n.* (*Classical*) A lyric poem meant to be sung; (*Modern*) a lyric of lofty style, rhymed or unrhymed, of varied and often irregular metre, usu. in the form of an address or invocation. **odic** (2) (ō' dik), *a.* ***odist,** *n.*

-ode [Gr. *-ōdēs* (*-o-*, *eidēs*, like, cogn. with *eidos*, form)], *suf.* Denoting a thing resembling or of the nature of, as *geode*, *sarcode* (cp. *anode* and *cathode*, which are formed from Gr. *hodos*, way).

odeon, odeum (o' dė ȯn, ȯ dē' ům) [Gr. *odeion*, as ODE], *n.* A theatre among the ancient Greeks and Romans in which poets and musicians contended for prizes; hence, a concert-hall, a theatre used for musical performances; a picture-palace, cinematograph hall.

odious (ō' di ůs) [L. *odiōsus*, from *odium*, hatred, cogn. with *ōdī*, I hate], *a.* Hateful, repulsive; unpopular. **odiously,** *adv.* **odiousness,** *n.* **odium,** *n.* Contumely; general dislike, reprobation.

odometer [HODOMETER].

odont-, odonto- [Gr. *odous odontos*, tooth], *comb. form.* Having teeth or processes resembling teeth.

odontalgia, odontalgy (o don tăl' ji ȧ, -i) [Gr. *algos*, pain], *n.* Toothache. **odontalgic,** *a.* and *n.*

odontiasis (o don tī' ȧ sis), *n.* Cutting of teeth; dentition.

odontic (o don' tik), *a.* Dental.

odontoblast (o don' tō blast), *n.* A cell producing a denture.

odontocete (o don' tō sēt), *n.* (*Zool.*) Belonging to the *Odontoceti* or toothed whales.

odontogeny (o don toj' e ni), *n.* The origin and development of teeth. **odontogenic,** *a.*

odontoglossum (o don tō glos' ům) [Gr. *glossa*, a tongue], *n.* (*Bot.*) A genus of tropical American epiphytal orchids with finely coloured flowers.

odontography (o don tog′ ra fi), *n.* The description of teeth.

odontoid (o don′ toid), *a.* (*Anat.*) Toothlike. *n.* An odontoid bone or process; a toothlike projection from the axis or second cervical vertebra in certain mammals and birds.

odontology (o don tol′ ō ji), *n.* The science dealing with the structure and development of teeth; a treatise on the teeth. **odontologic, odontological,** *a.* **odontologist,** *n.*

odontotoxia (o don tō toks′ i ȧ), *n.* Unevenness of the teeth.

odontoma (o don tō′ mȧ), *n.* A small tumour or excrescence composed of dentine. **odontomous,** *a.*

odontophore (o don′ tō fôr), *n.* A ribbon-like organ covered with teeth used for mastication by certain mollusca. **odontophoran,** *a.* and *n.* **odontophorous,** *a.*

odontorhyncus (o don tō ring′ kůs), *a.* Having toothlike serrations in the bill or beak.

odontotherapia (o don tō thēr ȧ pī′ ȧ), *n.* The treatment and care of the teeth, dental hygiene or therapeutics.

odontotrypy (o don tot′ ri pi), *n.* The operation of perforating a tooth to draw off pus from an abscess in the internal cavity.

odour (ō′ dǒr) [O.F. *odor*, L. *odōrem*, nom. *odor*], *n.* A smell, whether pleasant or unpleasant; scent, fragrance; (*fig.*) repute, esteem; *(*usu. in pl.*) substances exhaling fragrance, perfumes. **in bad odour:** In bad repute; out of favour. **odour of sanctity,** *n.* A reputation for holiness. **odorant, odoriferous** (-if′ ėr ůs), *a.* Diffusing fragrance; (*facet.*) smelly. **odoriferously,** *adv.* **odoriferousness,** *n.* ***odorine** (ō′ dȯ rin), *n.* (*Chem.*) A volatile base obtained from bone-oil. **odorize,** *v.t.* **odorizer,** *n.* **odorous,** *a.* Having a sweet scent, fragrant. **odorously,** *adv.* **odorousness,** *n.* **odourless,** *a.*

Odyssey (od′ i si) [L. *Odyssēa*, Gr. *Odusseia*, from *Odusseus*, Ulysses], *n.* An epic poem attributed to Homer, describing the wanderings of Ulysses after the fall of Troy; (*fig.*) a series of adventures and vicissitudes. **Odyssean** (-sē′ ȧn), *a.*

œcology [ECOLOGY].

œcumenical (ē kū men′ i kȧl) [L. *œcūmenicus*, Gr. *oikoumenikos*, from *oikoumenē(gē)*, the inhabited (earth), from *oikein*, to inhabit], *a.* General, universal, world-wide, catholic; used of certain councils composed of representatives from the whole of Christendom. **œcumenicity** (-nis′ i ti), *n.*

œdema (ē dē′ mȧ) [Gr. *oidēma -matos*, from *oideein*, to swell], *n.* (*Path.*) Swelling due to accumulation of serous fluid in the cellular tissue, local, as distinguished from general, dropsy. **œdematic** (-măt′ ik), **œdematose, -tous** (-dē′ mȧ tōs, -tůs), *a.* **œdematously,** *adv.*

Œdipus complex (ēd′ i pùs kom′ pleks) [Œdipus, king of Thebes, COMPLEX], *n.* (*Psych.*) A complex in a boy entailing excessive love of his mother with bias against his father. See ELECTRA COMPLEX.

œnanthic (ē năn′ thik) [L. *œnanthē*, Gr. *oinanthē* (*oinē*, vine, *anthē*, bloom), -IC], *a.* (*Chem.*) Possessing a vinous odour (said of an oily liquid, œnanthic ether, which gives the characteristic odour to wine).

œnology (ē nol′ ō ji) [as prec.], *n.* The science or study of wines. **œnological** (-loj′ i kȧl), *a.* **œnologist** (-nol′ ȯ jist), *n.* **œnomancy** (ē′ nȯ măn si), *n.* Divination from the appearance of wine poured out in libations. **œnomania** (-mā′ ni ȧ), *n.* Dipsomania; mania due to intoxication. **œnomaniac,** *n.* **œnometer** (-nom′ ė tėr), *n.* An instrument for testing the alcoholic strength of wines. **œnophilist** (nof′ i list), *n.* A lover of wine.

œnomel (ē′ nȯ mel) [L. *œnomeli*, Gr. *oinomeli* (*oinos*, wine, *meli*, honey)], *n.* Wine mingled with honey, a beverage used by the ancient Greeks.

Œnothera (ē nȯ thēr′ ȧ) [L., from Gr. *oinothēras* (*oinos*, wine, *-thēras*, catcher, from *thēran*, to hunt)], *n.* (*Bot.*) A genus of plants containing the evening-primroses.

o'er (*poet.*) [OVER].

oersted (ō ėr′ sted) [H. C. *Oersted* (1777–1851)], *n.* (*Elec.*) The unit of magnetic field or magnetizing force.

œsophagus (ē sof′ ȧ gůs) [late L., from Gr. *oisophagos*, etym. unknown], *n.* (*pl.* **-gi,** -jī) (*Anat.*) The gullet, the canal by which food passes to the stomach. **œsophagalgia** (-găl′ ji ȧ), *n.* Pain, esp. neuralgia, in the œsophagus. **œsophageal** (-jē′ ȧl), *a.* **œsophagectomy** (-jek′ tȯ mi), *n.* Excision of part of the œsophagus. **œsophagitis** (jī′ tis), *n.* Inflammation of the œsophagus. **œsophago-,** *comb. form.* **œsophagocele** (ē sof′ ȧ gȯ sēl), *n.* Hernia of the mucous membrane of the œsophagus. **œsophagopathy** (-gop′ ȧ thi), *n.* Disease of the œsophagus. **œsophagoplegia** (-plē′ ji ȧ), *n.* Paralysis of the œsophagus. **œsophagorrhagia** (-rā′ ji ȧ), *n.* Hæmorrhage of the œsophagus. **œsophagospasmus** (-spăz′ mùs), *n.* Spasm of the œsophagus. **œsophagotome** (ē sof′ ȧ gȯ tōm), *n.* A cutting-instrument for use in œsophagotomy. **œsophagotomy** (-got′ ȯ mi), *n.* The operation of opening the œsophagus.

œstrogen (ēs′ trō jen) [L. *œstrus*, gadfly; -GEN], *n.* (*Biol.*) Any one of the female sex hormones.

œstrum, -trus (ēs′ trům, -trůs) [L. *œstrus*, Gr. *oistros*], *n.* A gadfly; (*fig.*) a violent impulse, a raging desire or passion, esp. the sexual impulse in animals. **œstrous,** *a.* **œstruate,** *v.i.* (of an animal) To be on heat. **œstruation** (-ā′ shůn), *n.*

of (ov, ȯv) [A.-S. (cp. Dut. *af*, G. *ab*, Icel., Swed., and Dan. *af*, L. *ab*, Gr. *apo*)], *prep.* Denoting connexion with or relation to, in situation, point of departure, separation, origin, motive or cause, agency, substance or material, possession, inclusion, partition, equivalence or identity, reference, respect, direction, distance, quality, condition, objectivity; *during; *among; *from.

of- [OB-, before *f*], *pref.* As in offence.

off (awf, of) [stressed form of OF], *adv.* Away, at a distance or to a distance in space or time (expressing removal, separation, suspension, discontinuance, or termination); to the end, utterly, completely; (*Naut.*) away from the wind. *prep.* From (denoting deviation, separation, distance, disjunction, removal, etc.). *a.* More distant, farther, opp. to near; right, opp. to left; removed or aside from the main street, etc., divergent, subsidiary; contingent, possible; not occupied, disengaged (as an off day); (*Cricket*) applied to that part of the field to the left side of the bowler when the batsman is right-handed. *n.* (*Cricket*) The off side. *v.i.* (*colloq.*) To go off, to put off, to withdraw; (*Naut.*) to go away from the land. *int.* Away, begone. **off and on:** Intermittently, now and again. **to be off:** To break or cancel an engagement or undertaking. **to be off one's head:** To lose one's reason. **to come off** [COME]. **to go off** [GO (1)]. **to take off:** To divest oneself of; to mimic; (*Aviat.*) (of a plane) To leave the ground. **well** or **badly off:** In good or bad circumstances. **off-chance:** A bare possibility. **off colour** [COLOUR]. **off day,** *n.* (*colloq.*) Day when one is disengaged or is in bad form. **off-drive,** *v.t.* (*Cricket*) To drive (the ball) off. **off hand** [HAND]. **off-hand, off-handed,** *a.* **off-handedly,** *adv.* **off-handedness,** *n.* **off-licence,** *n.* A publican's licence to sell intoxicating liquors to be consumed off the premises. **off-print,** *n.* A reprint of an article or separate part of a periodical etc. **off-reckoning,** *n.* (*usu. in pl.*) A deduction formerly made from soldiers' pay to meet various expenses. **off-shore,** *a.* Blowing off the land; situated a short way from the land. **offside,** *n.* (*Foot.*) The field between the ball and the opponents' goal. **to be offside:** For a player to be in a position to kick a goal when no defender is between him and the goal-keeper. **offsider:** (*Austral. colloq.*) A friend, a partner. **off-white,** *a.* Not quite white.

offal (of′ ȧl) [OFF, FALL], *n.* Refuse, waste; parts of the carcass of an animal cut off when cutting up a carcass for food, including the head, tail, kidneys, heart, liver, etc.; inferior fish as dist. from prime; carrion; rubbish, garbage.

offence (ŏ fens´) [O.F. *offens*, L. *offensus*, annoyance, blended with O.F. *offense*, L. *offensa*, an offence, orig. fem. of *offensus*, p.p. of *offendere*, to OFFEND], *n.* The act of offending, an aggressive act; an affront, an insult; the state or a sense of being hurt, annoyed, or affronted, umbrage; a breach of rule or custom, a transgression, a trespass, a misdeed; an illegal action; a cause of stumbling. **to take offence:** To be offended, to feel a grievance. **offenceless,** *a.*

offend (ŏ fend´) [O.F. *offendre*, L. *offendere* (OF-, *fendere*, to strike), p.p. *offensus*], *v.t.* To wound the feelings of, to hurt; to make angry, to cause displeasure or disgust in, to outrage, to annoy, to molest; to transgress; *to tempt to go astray; *to attack, to assail. *v.i.* To transgress or violate any human or divine law; to give offence, to scandalize. **offendedly,** *adv.* **offender,** *n.* ***offendress,** *n.*

offensive (ŏ fen´ siv) [med. L. *offensīvus*, as prec.], *a.* Pertaining to or used for attack, aggressive; causing or meant to cause offence; irritating, vexing, annoying; disgusting, disagreeable, repulsive. *n.* The attitude, method, or act of attacking; (*Mil.*) a strategic attack. **offensively,** *adv.* **offensiveness,** *n.*

offer (of´ ėr) [A.-S. *offrian*, to bring an offering, to sacrifice; in later senses from F. *offrir*; both from L. *offerre* (OF-, *ferre*, to bring)], *v.t.* To present as an act of worship; to sacrifice, to immolate; to present, to put forward, to tender for acceptance or refusal; to propose (oneself etc.) in marriage; to bid (as a price); to evince readiness (to do something); to essay, to attempt; to proffer, to show; to show an intention (to); to show for sale. *v.i.* To present or show itself, to appear, to occur; to make an attempt (at). *n.* An act or offering; an expression of willingness or readiness (to); a tender, proffer, or proposal, to be accepted or refused; a price or sum bid; a proposal, esp. of marriage; an attempt, an essay. ***offerable,** *a.* **offerer,** *n.* **offering,** *n.* **offertory,** *n.* That part of the Mass or liturgical service during which offerings or oblations are made; an anthem sung or the sentences from Scripture repeated in the Church of England while these are being made; the offering of these oblations; the gifts offered; any collection made at a religious service. ***offertorial** (-tôr´ i ăl), *a.*

office (of´ is) [O.F., from L. *officium* (OF-, *facere*, to make or do)], *n.* Duty, charge, function, the task or service attaching to a particular post or station; a post of service, trust, or authority, esp. under a public body; a particular task, service, or duty; an act of worship of prescribed form, as the Mass, the services of the Breviary, or those of the Prayer Book; an act of help, kindness, or duty; a service (*often in pl.*); a room, building, or other place where business is carried on, esp. where clerks work, a counting-house; (*collect.*) persons charged with such business, the official staff, or the official organization as a whole; (*pl.*) the rooms or places in which the domestic duties of a house are discharged; (*colloq.*) a privy; (*slang*) a hint, a private signal. **Holy Office,** *n.* (*Eccles.*) The Inquisition. **to give** or **take the office:** To give a hint or information, or to accept and make use of this. **last offices,** *n.pl.* Rites due to the dead. **office-bearer,** *n.* One who holds office.

officer (of´ i sėr) [as prec.], *n.* One holding an office under a public or semi-public authority, esp. a Government functionary or minister, or one elected to perform certain duties by a society, committee, etc.; one appointed to a post of authority in the armed services by warrant, commission, etc.; (*colloq.*) a police-constable, sergeant, etc.; a bailiff. *v.t.* To furnish with officers; to act as commander of.

official (o fish´ ăl), *a.* Of or pertaining to an office or public duty; holding an office, employed in public duties; derived from or executed under proper authority; duly authorized; characteristic of persons in office; (*Med.*) authorized by the pharmacopœia, officinal. *n.* One who holds a public office; a judge or presiding officer in an ecclesiastical court. **official assignees,** *n.pl.* (*Fin.*) Two or more members of the Stock Exchange who manage a defaulter's estate during the liquidation of his affairs. **official principal,** *n.* (*Law*) Presiding official at an archbishop's or archdeacon's court. **official receiver,** *n.* (*Law*) A person appointed by a receiving order granted on petition to administer a debtor's estate. **officialese,** *n.* Official jargon. **officialdom, -ism,** *n.* ***officiality** (-i ăl´ i ti), *n.* **officialize** (ŏ fish´ ȧ līz), *v.t.* ***officialty** [OFFICIALITY]. **officially,** *adv.* **officiate,** *v.i.* To perform official duties, to act in an official capacity; to perform a prescribed function or duty; to conduct public worship. **officiant,** *n.* **officiation** (-ā´ shŭn), *n.*

officinal (ŏ fis´ i năl) [med. L. *officīnālis*, from L. *officīna*, contr. from *opificīna*, from *opifex*, workman (*opus*, work, -*fic*, cogn. with *facere*, to do)], *a.* (*Med.*) Prepared and kept on hand at druggists; authorized by the pharmacopœia (now usu. OFFICIAL); employed in the arts or in medicine (of herbs etc.); *used in or pertaining to a shop. **officinally,** *adv.*

officious (ŏ fish´ ŭs) [L. *officiōsus*, from *officium*, OFFICE], *a.* Forward in doing or offering kindness, meddling, intrusive; (*Diplomacy*) informally related to official concerns or objects, friendly without official authority; *official; *observant, attentive, obliging. **officiously,** *adv.* **officiousness,** *n.*

offing (of´ ing), *n.* That portion of the sea beyond the half-way line between the coast and the horizon.

offish (of´ ish), *a.* Inclined to be distant, reserved, or stiff in manner. **offishness,** *n.*

off-print [OFF].

off-scouring (of´ skour ing), *n.* (*usu. in pl.*) That which is scoured off; refuse, rubbish, dregs. **off-scum,** *n.*

off-set (of´ set), *n.* A lateral shoot or branch that takes root or is caused to take root and is used for propagation, an off-shoot, a scion; a spur or branch of a mountain range; anything allowed as a counterbalance, equivalent, or compensation; an amount set off (against); (*Surv.*) a short course measured perpendicularly to the main line; (*Build.*) a part where the thickness of a wall is diminished, usu. towards the top; a bend or fitting bringing a pipe past an obstacle; **(offset)** a method of printing from a rubber substance which has received an inked impression from plates of the matter to be printed. *v.t.* To balance by an equivalent; to counterbalance, to compensate.

offshoot (of´ shoot), *n.* A branch or shoot from a main stem; (*fig.*) a side-issue.

offshore [OFF]. **offside** [OFF]. **offward** [OFF].

offspring (of´ spring) [A.-S. *of-spring*], *n.* Issue, progeny; (*collect.*) children, descendants; a child; a production or result of any kind; *origin, descent.

oft (oft, awft) [A.-S., cp. Icel. and G. *oft*, Dan. *ofte*, Swed. *ofta*], *adv.* Often (*now poet. exc. in comb.*). **a.* Frequent. **oft-times,** *adv.* Often. **oft-recurring,** *a.* Frequently recurring.

often (ofn, awfn) [lengthened form of prec.], *adv.* Frequently, many times; in many instances. **a.* Frequent, repeated. ***oftenness,** *n.* ***oftentimes,** *adv.*

ogee (ō jē´) [prob. from F. OGIVE, this moulding being commonly used for ribs in groining], *n.* (*Arch.*) A wave-like moulding having an inner and outer curve like the letter S; a pointed arch each side of which is formed of a concave and a convex curve. *a.* Having such a double curve (or arches, windows, etc.).

ogham (og´ ăm) [O.Ir. *ogam*, *ogum*, said to be from the inventor *Ogam*], *n.* A kind of writing used by the ancient Irish and other Celts, consisting of twenty characters derived from the runes; any character in this; an inscription in this. **oghamic,** *a.*

ogive (ō′ jīv, ō jīv′) [F., earlier *augive*, perh. from Sp. *auge*, Arab. *āwf*, the summit, vertex, highest point], *n.* A diagonal rib of a vault; a pointed or Gothic arch. **ogival** (ō jī′ vål), *a.*

ogle (ō′ gėl) [cp. L.G. *äegeln*, G. *hugeln*, freq. of *augen*, to look, from *auge*, eye], *v.t.* To look at coquettishly or amorously. *v.i.* To cast amorous or coquettish glances. *n.* A coquettish or amorous glance. **ogler,** *n.*

Ogpu (og′ poo, ō gā pā oo) [initials of Rus. *Obedinyonnoye Gosudarstvennoye Polititsheksoye Upravleniye*, United State Political Administration], *n.* The organization for fighting counter-revolutionary activities in Soviet Russia between 1922 and 1934.

ogre (ō′ gėr) [F., first used by Perrault in his *Contes* (1697)], *n.* A giant living on human flesh; (*fig.*) a monster, a barbarously cruel person. **ogreish,** *a.* **ogress,** *n.*

Ogygian (og ij′ i ån) [L. *Ogygius*, Gr. *Ōgugios*, from *Ōgugos* or *Ōēsgug*], *a.* Pertaining to Ogyges, a legendary king of Attica or Bœotia; (*fig.*) of great or obscure antiquity, primeval.

oh [o (2)].

ohm (ōm) [Georg S. *Ohm* (1787–1854), German electrician], *n.* (*Elec.*) The unit of electrical resistance, roughly equal to that of 1000 ft. of $\frac{1}{10}$ in. dia. copper wire. **ohmage,** *n.* **ohmic,** *a.* **ohmmeter,** *n.*

oho (ȯ hō′) [o (2), HO], *int.* Expressing surprise, irony, or exultation. **ohone** (ȯ hōn′) [Gael. and Ir. *ochōin*], *int.* and *n.* A Scottish and Irish cry of lamentation. **oh yes** [OYEZ].

-oid [mod. L. *-oīdes*, Gr. *-oeidēs* (*-eidēs*, like, rel. to *eidos*, form)], *comb. form.* Denoting resemblance, as in *colloid, cycloid, rhomboid.*

Oidium (ȯ id′ i ŭm) [mod. L., from Gr. *ōon*, egg, *-idion*, dim. suf.], *n.* (*Bot.*) A former genus of fungi containing the mildews etc.

oil (oil) [M.E. and O.F. *oile* (F. *huile*), L. *oleum*, from *olea*, olive], *n.* An unctuous liquid, insoluble in water, soluble in ether and usually in alcohol, obtained from various animal and vegetable substances; (*pl.*) oil-colours. *v.t.* To smear, anoint, rub, soak, treat, or impregnate with oil; to lubricate with or as with oil. *v.i.* To turn into oil; to take oil aboard as fuel; to become oily. **essential** or **volatile oils:** Distillable oils, chiefly the volatile principles of plants, used in medicine or perfumery. **mineral oils:** Oils distilled from peat, shale, etc., used as illuminants. **fatty** or **fixed oils:** Greasy, non-distillable oils, of animal or vegetable origin, glycerides of stearic, palmitic, or oleic acids. **to burn the midnight oil:** To study or work far into the night. **to oil a man's palm:** (*colloq.*) To bribe him. **to strike oil** [STRIKE]. **oil-bag,** *n.* An oil-gland or cyst in animals. **oilcake,** *n.* The refuse after oil is pressed from linseed etc. **oil-can,** *n.* A can for holding oil, esp. one used for oiling machinery. **oil-coat,** *n.* A coat or layer of oil; an oilskin. **oil-colour,** *n.* A paint made by grinding a pigment in oil. **oil-cooler,** *n.* An apparatus for cooling lubricating oil. **oil-cup,** *n.* A cup with a supply of lubricating oil for a journal. **oil-derrick,** *n.* A frame used in boring for oil. **oil-engine,** *n.* An internal-combustion engine which burns vaporized oil as an explosive mixture. **oil-gas,** *n.* Gas obtained from oil by distillation in closed retorts. **oil-field,** *n.* A region where mineral oil is obtained. **oil-gauge,** *n.* An instrument for determining the specific gravity of oil; a gauge for showing the level of oil in a tank etc. **oil-gland,** *n.* A gland secreting oil. **oil-hole,** *n.* A hole through which lubricating oil is applied to parts of machinery. **oilman,** *n.* **oil-mill,** *n.* An oil-press; a factory where oil is expressed. **oil-meal,** *n.* Oilcake ground into meal. **oil-nut,** *n.* The butternut. **oil of vitriol:** Sulphuric acid. **oil-paint,** *n.* Oil-colour. **oil-painting,** *n.* The art of painting in oil-colours; a painting in oil-colours. **oil-paper,** *n.* Paper rendered waterproof or transparent by soaking in oil. **oil-press,** *n.* A machine for pressing the oil from seeds, nuts, etc. **oil-rectifier,** *n.* A plant for adapting used oil for other purposes. **oil-shark,** *n.* (*Zool.*) A species of shark that yields oil. **oil-spring** [OIL-WELL]. **oil-stock,** *n.* (*Eccles.*) A vessel for holding Holy Oil. **oil-stone,** *n.* A fine-grained hone-stone used with oil. **oil-test,** *n.* An apparatus for discovering the burning-point, flash-point and lubricating efficiency of oils. **oil-tree,** *n.* Term applied to any bush or tree which yields oil, *e.g.* the castor-oil plant. **oil-well,** *n.* A boring made for petroleum. **oiler,** *n.* One who or that which oils; an oil-can for lubricating machinery, etc. **oilless,** *a.* **oily,** *a.* Consisting of, containing, covered with, or like oil; (*fig.*) unctuous, smooth, insinuating. **oiliness,** *n.*

oilcloth (oil′ kloth), *n.* A fabric coated with white lead ground in oil, used as a covering for floors, tables, etc.; an oilskin.

oilskin (oil′ skin), *n.* Cloth rendered waterproof by treatment with oil; (*pl.*) a suit of such garments.

ointment (oint′ mėnt) [M.E. *oinement*, O.F. *oignement*, L. *unguentum*, UNGUENT], *n.* A soft unctuous preparation for dressing diseased or injured parts or for use as a cosmetic, an unguent.

oireachtas (âr ėch dės) [Ir.], *n.* The national parliament of Eire.

O.K. (ō kā) [said to be short for *orl korrect*], *a.* (*colloq.*) Quite correct, all right.

okapi (ȯ ka′ pi) [W. African native], *n.* A deer-like animal akin to and partially marked like a giraffe, discovered in the Belgian Congo by Sir Harry Johnston in 1900.

okra (ō′ krå) [W. Indian native], *n.* An African herb cultivated in the E. and W. Indies and the U.S. for its green pods used in soups, etc.

Okrana (ō kra′ na) [Rus., guard, police], *n.* The Russian secret police in Tsarist days.

-ol [L. *ol-eum*, OIL], *suf.* (*Chem.*) Denoting an alcohol, or (loosely) an oil, as *benzol, menthol, phenol.*

old (ōld) [A.-S. *eald, ald* (cp. Dut. *oud*, G. *alt*, L. *ultus*, in *adultus*), from the root *al-*, to nourish, as in L. *alere*, to feed], *a.* (**older, oldest,** cp. ELDER (1), -EST) Advanced in years or existence; not young, fresh, or recent; like an old person, experienced, thoughtful; crafty, cunning, practised (at), confirmed (in); decayed by process of time, worn, dilapidated; stale, trite with keeping; customary, wonted; obsolete, effete, out-of-date, antiquated, matured; of any specified duration; belonging to a former period, made or established long ago, ancient, bygone, long cultivated or worked; early, previous, former, quondam; (*colloq.*) expressing familiarity or endearment. **of old:** In or from ancient times; long ago. **of old standing:** Long established. **old age:** The latter part of life. **old age pension,** *n.* A weekly payment by the State to a person over 70 years of age; contributory pension for an insured person over 65 (spinster aged 60). **old bachelor:** A man confirmed in living singly. **old bird:** A parent bird; (*fig.*) one grown old in experience, craft, wickedness, etc. **old boy, chap,** or **fellow:** An intimate friend. **Old English** [ENGLISH]. **old-fashioned,** *a.* Long out of fashion; quaint. **Old Glory:** (*Am.*) The U.S. flag. **old gold** [GOLD]. **old hand:** One who is skilled or practised at a trade, craft, or practice of any kind; (*Austral. hist.*) one of the early convicts. **old identity,** *n.* (*Austral. colloq.*) An old and respected resident. **Old Lady of Threadneedle Street,** *n.* (*facet.*) The Bank of England. **old maid:** An unmarried woman somewhat advanced in years; a card game; (*fig.*) a precise, prudish, fidgety person of either sex. **old-maidish,** *a.* **old man:** (*colloq.*) One's husband; friend (a familiar mode of address); (*Austral.*) a full-grown kangaroo. **old man's beard,** *n.* A kind of moss; wild clematis. **old master,** *n.* Painter or painting of some century previous to the 19th (more particularly of the Renaissance). **Old Nick,** *n.* (*colloq.*) The devil. **Old One:** (*slang*) The devil. **Old Red Sandstone:** The strata belonging to the Devonian formation underlying the Carboniferous. **old-style** [STYLE]. **Old Testament** [TESTAMENT]. **old-time,** *a.* Old, ancient. **Old Tom:** A strong variety of gin. **the Old 'un** [OLD ONE]. **old woman:** (*colloq.*) One's wife: a timid, fidgety, or fussy man. **old-womanish, old-womanly,** *adj.* **old-womanishness, old-womanliness,** *n.* **Old World:** The eastern hemisphere; belonging to this, not American; old-fashioned. **old year:** The year just ended or on the point of ending. **olden,** *a.* Old, ancient, bygone. *v.i.* To grow old, to age. *v.t.* To render old, to age. **oldish,** *a.* **oldness,** *n.* **oldster,** *n.* An old or oldish person.

oleaginous (ō lē ăj' i nŭs) [through F. *oléagineux* or directly from L. *oleāginus*, from *olea*, olive], *a.* Oily, greasy, unctuous; (*fig.*) fawning, insinuating. **oleaginousness,** *n.*

oleander (ō lė ăn' dėr) [med. L., perh. var. of *lōrandrum*, corr. of *rhododendrum*, RHODODENDRON, or *lauridendrum* (L. *laurus*, LAUREL, Gr. *dendron*, tree)], *n.* A poisonous evergreen shrub of the genus *Nerium*, esp. *N. oleander* and *N. odorosum*, with lanceolate leaves and pink or white flowers.

oleaster (ō lė ăs' tėr) [L. (*olea*, olive, -ASTER)], *n.* Any shrub or tree of the genus *Elæagnus*, called the wild olive; the true wild olive, *Olea oleaster*.

oleic (ō lē' ik, ō' lė ik) [L. *oleum*, OIL], *a.* (*Chem.*) Pertaining to or derived from oil. **oleiferous** (ō lif' ėr ŭs), *a.* **oleate** (ō' lė āt), *n.* ***olefiant** (ō lė fī' ănt, ō lē' fi ănt), *a.* **olefine** (ō' lė fin), *n.* Any one of a group of hydrocarbons containing two atoms of hydrogen to one of carbon. **olein,** *n.* An oily compound, chief constituent of fatty oils; the liquid portion of oil or fat.

olent (ō' lėnt) [L. *olens -ntem*, pres.p. of *olēre*, to smell], *a.* (*Browning*) Smelling, yielding fragrance.

oleo (ō' li ō), *n.* (*Am.*) Margarine.

oleo- [L. *oleum*, oil], *comb. form.*

oleograph (ō' lė ō grăf), *n.* A lithographic picture printed in oil-colours. **oleography,** *n.*

oleomargarine (ō le ō mar' jȧ rēn, -mar' gȧ rėn), *n.* An artificial butter made from animal fat and milk, or vegetable oils.

oleometer (ō le om' ė tĕr), *n.* An instrument for determining the relative densities of oil.

oleon (ō' le on), *n.* An oily liquid obtained by the dry distillation of oleic acid with lime.

oleoresin (ō le ō rez' in), *n.* A mixture of an essential oil and a resin.

oleraceous (ol ėr ā' shŭs) [L. *oleraceus* (*olus oleris*, pot-herb, -ACEOUS)], *a.* (*Bot.*) Of the nature of a pot-herb; edible, esculent. **olericulture** (ol' ėr i kŭl tyŭr), *n.* The culture of esculent plants, esp. pot-herbs.

olfaction (ol făk' shŭn) [L. *olfacere* (*olēre*, to smell, *facere*, to make), -TION], *n.* The sense or process of smelling. **olfactive,** *a.* **olfactory,** *a.* Pertaining to or used in smelling. *n.* (*usu. in pl.*) An organ of smell. **olfactometer,** *n.* An instrument for calculating the keenness of the sense of smell.

olibanum (ŏ lib' a nŭm), ***oliban** (ol' i băn) [med. L., from late L. and Gr. *libanos*, incense], *n.* A gum-resin from an Abyssinian species of *Boswellia*, formerly used in medicine, now as incense.

olid (ol' id) [L. *olidus*, from *olēre*, to smell], *a.* Rank, stinking.

oligarch (ol' i gark) [Gr. *oligarchēs* (OLIGO-, *archein*, to govern)], *n.* A member of an oligarchy. **oligarchic -al** (-gar' kik, -ăl), *a.* **oligarchically,** *adv.* **oligarchist,** *n.* **oligarchy** (ol' i gar ki), *n.* A form of government in which supreme power is vested in the hands of a small exclusive class; the members of such a class; a State so governed.

oligo- [Gr. *oligos*, small, *oligoi*, few], *comb. form.*

oligocarpus (ol i gō kar' pŭs), *a.* (*Bot.*) Having few fruits.

oligocene (ol' i gō sēn), *a.* (*Geol.*) Tertiary, of the age or strata between the Eocene and Miocene.

oligochrome (ol' i gō krōm), *a.* Painted or decorated in few colours.

oligoclase (ol' i gō klās), *n.* (*Min.*) A soda-lime feldspar resembling albite.

oligopod (o lig' ō pod), *a.* (*Zool.*) Having few legs or feet.

olio (ō' li ō) [Sp. *olla*, stew, L., a pot], *n.* A mixed dish; (*fig.*) a mixture, a medley.

***oliphant** (ol' i fănt) [ELEPHANT], *n.* A horn or trumpet of ivory.

***olitory** (ol' i tŏr i) [L. *olitōrius*, from *olitor*, kitchen-gardener, from *olus oleris*, pot-herb], *a.* Pertaining to a kitchen-garden. *n.* A kitchen-garden.

olive (ol' iv) [F., from L. *olīva*], *n.* An evergreen tree, *Olea Europæa*, with narrow leathery leaves and clusters of oval drupes yielding oil when ripe and eaten unripe as a relish; the fruit of this tree; its wood; the colour of the unripe olive, a dull, yellowish green or brown; an oval bar or button fitting into a loop, for fastening a garment; (*pl.*) slices of beef or veal rolled with onions etc., stewed; like an olive, esp. in colour. **olive-branch,** *n.* A branch of the olive-tree as an emblem of peace; (*pl., facet.*) children. **olive-crown,** *n.* A garland of olive-leaves as a symbol of victory. **olive-oil,** *n.* **olive-yard,** *n.* A piece of ground on which olives are cultivated. **olivaceous** (ol i vā' shŭs), *a.* (*Nat. Hist.*). **olivary,** *a.* (*Anat.*) Olive-shaped, oval.

oliver (ol' i vėr) [etym. doubtful, prob. from the proper name], *n.* A small trip-hammer worked by the foot, used in making nails etc.

Oliverian (ol i vēr' i ăn) [*Oliver* Cromwell (1599–1658)], *a.* Of or pertaining to the Protector Cromwell. *n.* A partisan or adherent of Cromwell.

olivet (ol' i vėt) [F. *olivette*, dim. of OLIVE], *n.* An olive or button; a kind of mock pearl, used as a bead.

olivine (ol' i vīn, -vin) [L. *olīva*], *n.* (*Min.*) A variety of chrysolite.

olla (ol' ȧ) [Sp.] *n.* An olio; an olla podrida. **olla podrida** (ol ȧ po drē' dȧ): A favourite Spanish dish, consisting of meat chopped fine, stewed with vegetables; (*fig.*) a multifarious or incongruous mixture.

ollamh (ol' ăv) [Ir.], *n.* A learned man, a doctor, a scholar, among the ancient Irish.

ology (ol' ŏ ji), *n.* (*facet.*) A science; one of the sciences whose names end thus; (*pl.*) learning, theory.

olympiad (ŏ lim' pi ăd) [F. *olympiade*, L. *olympias -adis*, Gr. *olumpias -ados*, from *Olumpios*, pertaining to *Olumpos*], *n.* (*Gr. Ant.*) A period of four years, being the interval between the celebrations of the Olympic games, a method of reckoning employed from 776 B.C. to A.D. 394. **Olympian,** *a.* Pertaining to Mount Olympus, the home of the gods, celestial; magnificent, lofty, superb; *Olympic. *n.* A dweller in Olympus; one of the Greek gods; *one who contended at the Olympic games. **Olympianism,** *n.* **Olympianly, Olympianwise,** *adv.* **Olympic,** *a.* Pertaining to Olympia or the Olympic games; *Olympian. **Olympic games:** The greatest of the Greek national games, held every four years at Olympia, in Elis, so called in honour of Zeus; festival revived in 1896 as an international four-yearly sports meeting.

-oma (ō' mȧ) [Gr. *oma*, tumour], *suff.* To denote a tumour or growth.

omadhaun (om' ȧ dawn) [Ir. *amedan*], *n.* A fool, a simpleton.

omasum (ŏ mā' sŭm) [L.], *n.* The third stomach of a ruminant.

ombre (om' bėr) [Sp. *hombre*, L. *hominem*, nom. *homo*, man], *n.* A game of cards, for two, three, or five players, popular in the 17th and 18th cents.

ombrology (om brol′ ŏ ji) [Gr. *ombros*, rain, -LOGY], *n.* The branch of meteorology concerned with the rainfall. **ombrometer** (om brom′ ė tėr), *n.* A rain-gauge.

omega (ō′ mė gȧ) [Gr. *ō mega*, the great *o*], *n.* The last letter of the Greek alphabet, *Ω*, *ω*, *ō*; (*fig.*) the last of a series; the conclusion, the end, the last stage or phase.

omelet (om′ lėt, om′ ė lėt) [F. *omelette*, earlier *amelette*, corr. of *alemette*, var. of *alemelle*, a thin plate, acc. to Littré prob. from L. LAMELLA], *n.* A kind of pancake made with beaten eggs and milk, eaten plain or with jam, or seasoned and cooked with herbs, cheese, meat, etc.

omen (ō′ mėn) [L., earlier *osmen*, perh. for *ausmen* (cogn. with *audīre*, to hear)], *n.* An incident, object, or appearance taken as indicating a good or evil event, issue, fortune, etc.; a prognostic; prognostication or prophetic signification. *v.t.* To prognosticate, to portend.

omentum (ŏ men′ tŭm) [L.], *n.* (*pl.* **-ta**) A fold of the peritoneum connecting the viscera with each other. **omental,** *a.*

***omer** (ō′ mėr) [Heb.], *n.* A Hebrew measure of capacity, the tenth part of an ephah or $5\frac{1}{10}$ pints.

omicron (ō mī′ krŏn) [Gr. *o mikron*, the small *o*], *n.* The short o of the Greek alphabet.

ominous (om′ i nŭs) [L. *ōminōsus* (OMEN, -OUS)], *a.* Portending evil; of evil omen, inauspicious. **ominously,** *adv.* **ominousness,** *n.*

omit (ŏ mit′) [L. *omittere* (*o*-, OB-, *mittere*, to send), p.p. *omissus*], *v.t.* To leave out; not to include, insert, or mention; to neglect; to leave undone. **omissible,** *a.* **omission** (ŏ mish′ ŭn), *n.* ***omissive,** *a.* ***omittance,** *n.* **omitter,** *n.*

omni- [L. *omnis*, all], *comb. form.* Universally, in all ways, of all things.

omnibus (om′ ni bŭs) [L., dat. pl. of *omnis* (see prec.), for all], *n.* A public passenger-vehicle for conveying passengers along a particular route at stated times; a bus; a similar vehicle employed by an hotel, railway company, etc., for conveying persons, often with luggage; a volume containing reprints of a number of works, usually by the same author. *a.* Inclusive, embracing several or various items, objects, etc. **omnibus Bill, clause,** or **resolution:** One dealing with several subjects.

omnifarious (om ni fâr′ i ŭs) [L. *omnifarius*], *a.* Of all kinds.

omnipotent (om nip′ ō tėnt), *a.* Almighty; having unlimited power. **The Omnipotent,** *n.* God. **omnipotence,** *n.* **omnipotently,** *adv.*

omnipresent (om ni prez′ ėnt), *a.* Present in every place at the same time. **omnipresence,** *n.*

omniscience (om nish′ ėns), *n.* Infinite knowledge. **omniscient,** *a.* **omnisciently,** *adv.*

omnivorous (om niv′ ŏr ŭs), *a.* All-devouring; feeding on anything available; (*fig.*) reading anything and everything. **omnivorously,** *adv.*

omnium (om′ ni ŭm) [L., of all (things, kinds, etc.), as prec.], *n.* (*Stock Exch.*) A term used to express the aggregate value of the different stocks in which a loan is funded. **omnium gatherum:** A miscellaneous collection or assemblage, a medley.

omo- [Gr. *omos*, shoulder], *comb. form.* (*Anat.*) **omo-hyoid** (ō mŏ hī′ oid) [HYOID], *a.* Of or pertaining to the shoulder-blade and the hyoid bone. **omo-hyoidean, -deous,** *a.* **omoplate** (ō′ mŏ plāt), *n.* The shoulder-blade. **omosternum** (-stĕr′ nŭm), *n.* An ossified process at the anterior extremity of the sternum, in certain animals.

omophagic (ō mŏ făj′ ik), **omophagous** (ō mof′ ȧ gŭs) [Gr. *ōmophagos* (*ōmos*, raw, *-phagein*, to eat)], *a.* Eating raw flesh. **omophagist** (-jist), *n.*

omphacite (om′ fȧ sīt) [G. *omphazit* (Gr. *omphax*, unripe, -ITE)], *n.* (*Min.*) A green variety of pyroxene.

omphalic (om făl′ ik) [Gr. *omphalos*, navel, -IC], *a.* Pertaining to the navel. **omphalitis** (-lī′ tis) [-ITIS], *n.* (*Path.*). **omphalocele** (om′ fȧ lŏ sēl) [-CELE], *n.* Umbilical hernia. **omphaloid,** *a.* **omphalotomy** (-lot′ ŏ mi) [-TOMY], *n.* The operation of cutting the umbilical cord. **omphalos** (om′ fȧ los), *n.* (*Gr. Ant.*) The boss of a shield; a stone in the temple of Apollo at Delphi, believed to be the middle point or navel of the earth; a central point, a hub.

on (on) [A.-S. *on*, *an*, cp. Dut. *aan*, G. *an*, Icel. *ā*, Dan. *an*, Gr. *ana*], *prep.* In or as in contact with, esp. as supported by, covering, environing, or suspended from, the upper surface of; into contact with the upper surface of, or in contact with from above; in the direction of, tending toward, arrived at, against; exactly at, next in order to, immediately after; about, concerning, in the act of, in the making, performance, support, interest, etc., of. *adv.* So as to be in contact with and supported by, covering, environing, suspended from or adhering to something; in advance, forward, in operation, action, movement, progress, or continuance of action or movement. *a.* (*Cricket*) Denoting the side of the field to the left of the batsman. *n.* (*Cricket*) The on side. **on licence:** A licence to sell intoxicating liquor for consumption on the premises. **on high:** To heaven. **on time:** Punctually. **on to, onto,** *prep.* (*colloq.*) To and upon, to a position on or upon. **to be a little bit on:** (*slang*) To be slightly the worse for drink. **to have a little bit on:** (*slang*) To have a small bet. **to get on** [GET].

on- [prec.], *pref.* **oncome,** *n.* (*Sc.*) Something that comes on one, as a disease; a fall of rain or snow. **on-coming,** *n.* The coming on, advance, or approach (of). **onfall,** *n.* An attack, an onset; (*Sc.*) a fall of rain or snow. **onflow,** *n.* Onward flow. **ongoing,** *n.* Procedure, progress; (*pl.*) goings-on. **onlooker,** *n.* A spectator, one who looks on. **onrush,** *n.* A rushing on, an attack, an onset.

onager (on′ ȧ jėr) [L., from Gr. *onagros* (*onos*, ass, *agrios*, wild)], *n.* The wild ass, esp. the *Equus onager* of the Asiatic deserts.

onanism (ō′ nȧ nizm) [*Onan* (Gen. xxxviii. 9), -ISM], *n.* Masturbation. **onanist,** *n.* **onanistic** (-nis′ tik), *a.*

once (wŭns) [A.-S. *ānes*, gen. of *ān*, ONE], *adv.* One time; one time only; at one time, formerly, at some past time; at any time, ever, at all; as soon as; at some future time, some time or other. *conj.* As soon as. *n.* One time. **all at once:** All together, simultaneously, suddenly. **at once:** Immediately, without delay; simultaneously. **for once:** For one time or occasion only. **once for all:** Finally; definitively. **once in a way** or **while:** Very seldom. **once-over,** *n.* (*slang*) Look of appraisal. **once upon a time:** At some past date or period.

onco- [Gr. *onkos*, mass], *comb. form.*

oncograph (ong′ kō grăf), *n.* (*Surg.*) An instrument for recording variations in the size of organs and other parts of the body.

oncology (ong kol′ ō ji), *n.* (*Med.*) The study of new growths (tumours) of body tissue.

oncometer (ong kom′ e tėr), *n.* An instrument for measuring variations in the size of an organ.

oncosis (ong kō′ sis), *n.* A swelling intumescence.

oncost (on′ kost) *n.* (*Sc.*) Supplementary or additional expenses, esp. (*Mining*) expenses of maintenance of roads, shafts, etc., work on which is usu. paid for by time-wages. **oncost men** or **oncosts:** Men employed on time-wages.

oncotomy (ong kot′ ō mi), *n.* The opening of an abscess or the excision of a tumour.

onding (on′ ding), *n.* (*Sc.*) A sudden fall of rain or snow.

on dit (*on* dē) [F., they say], *n.* Hearsay, gossip; a bit of gossip.

one (wŭn) [A.-S. *ān* (cp. Dut. *een*, G. *ein*, Icel. *einn*), cogn. with L. *ūnus*, Gr. *oinē*, ace], *a.* Single, undivided; being a unit and integral; a or an; single in kind, the only, the same; this, some, any, a certain. *pron.* A person or thing of the kind implied, some one or something, anyone or anything; a person unspecified; (*colloq.*) any person, esp. the speaker; (*incorrectly*) I. *n.* A single unit, unity; the number 1, a thing or person so numbered; a single thing or person. **v.t.* To make one. **all in one:** Combined. **all one** [ALL]. **at one:** In accord or agreement. **to be one up on:** To gain an advantage over someone else. **one and all:** Jointly and severally. **one and only:** Unique. **one by one:** Singly, individually, successively. **one too many:** Too difficult or too hard (*for*). **one with another:** On the average, in general. **one-eyed,** *a.* **one-fold,** *a.* Having only one member or constituent; single; (*fig.*) single-minded, simple in character. **one-handed,** *a.* Single-handed, done with one hand; having only one hand. **one-horse,** *a.* Drawn by a single horse; (*slang*) of meagre capacity, resources, or efficiency; insignificant, petty. **one-ideaed,** *a.* Moved or controlled by one idea; narrow-minded. **one-legged** (-legd, leg ėd), *a.* **one-man,** *a.* Employing, worked by, or consisting of one man. **one-pair,** *a.* Applied to rooms on the first floor or up one flight of stairs. **one-shot,** *n.* (*Motor.*) A system of lubricating a chassis. **one-step,** *n.* and *v.i.* Form of American dance. **one-track,** *a.* (*Rail.*) Single-track; (*colloq.*) capable of only one idea at a time. **one-way,** *a.* (*Agric.*) Applied to a plough which turns the furrows in one direction; denoting a system of traffic control by which vehicles are allowed to go in one direction only through certain streets. **oner** (wŭn′ ėr), *n.* (*slang*) A striking, extraordinary, or pre-eminent person or thing; an expert, an adept; a heavy blow; (*Cricket*) a hit for one run. **oneself,** *pron.* The reflexive form of one. **onefold,** *a.* **one-sided,** *a.* Having or happening on one side only; partial, unfair. **one-sidedly,** *adv.* **one-sidedness,** *n.* **one-way ticket:** (*Am.*) A single ticket, a single fare.

-one [Gr. *ōnē*, fem. patronymic], *suf.* (*Chem.*) Denoting certain compounds, esp. hydrocarbons, as in *acetone, ketone, ozone.*

oneiro- [Gr. *oneiros*, dream], *comb. form.*

oneirodynia (o nīr ō din′ i ȧ) [Gr. *odune*, pain], *n.* Nightmare, disturbed sleep.

oneirology (o nī rol′ ō ji), *n.* The science of dreams. **oneirologist,** *n.*

oneiromancy (o nī′ rō măn si), *n.* Divination by dreams. **oneiromancer,** *n.* **oneiromantist,** *n.*

oneness (wŭn′ nės), *n.* Singleness; singularity, uniqueness; unity, union, agreement, harmony; sameness. **oner** [ONE].

onerous (on′ ėr ŭs) [O.F. *onereus*, L. *onerōsus*, from *onus oneris*, burden], *a.* Burdensome, heavy, weighty, troublesome. **onerously,** *adv.* **onerousness,** *n.*

oneself [ONE].

onfall, onflow, on-going, etc. [ON-].

onion (ŭn′ yŏn) [F. *oignon*, L. *ūniōnem*, nom. *ūnio*, a large pearl, a kind of onion], *n.* A plant, *Allium cepa*, with an underground bulb of several coats and a pungent smell and flavour much used in cookery; other species of the genus *Allium.* *v.t.* To season or treat with onions; to rub (the eyes) so as to produce tears. **onion-eyed,** *a.* Ready to weep. **oniony,** *a.*

onkus (ong′ kŭs) [?], *a.* (*Austral. slang*) Bad, no good.

onlooker [ON-].

only (ōn′ li) [A.-S. *ānlīc* (ONE, -LY)], *a.* Solitary, single or alone in its or their kind; the single, the sole; *mere. *adv.* Solely, merely, exclusively, alone; with no other, singly; wholly. *conj.* Except that; but; were it not (that). **only-begotten,** *a.* Begotten as the sole issue. **onliness,** *n.*

onomancy (on′ ō măn si), ***onomatomancy** (ō nom′ ȧ tō măn si) [med. L. *onomantia, onomatomantia* (Gr. *onoma -matos*, name)], *n.* Divination by the letters of a name. **onomantic, -al** (-măn′ tik, -ăl), *a.*

onomastic (on ō măs′ tik), *a.* Pertaining to a name. **onomasticon,** *n.* A dictionary, lexicon, a vocabulary.

onomatology (on ō mȧ tol′ ō ji), *n.* The science of names or nomenclatures.

onomatopœia (ō nom ȧ tō pē′ ȧ, -yȧ) [L., from Gr. *onomatopoiia* (as prec., *-poios*, making, from *poiein*, to make)], *n.* The formation of words in imitation of the sounds associated with or suggested by the things signified; a word so formed. **onomatopœic** (-pē′ ik), **onomatopoetic** (-pō et′ ik), *a.* **onomatopœically, -poetically,** *adv.* **onomatopoesis** (-pō ē′ sis), **-poesy** (-pō′ ė si), *n.*

onrush [ON-].

onset (on′ set), *n.* An attack, an assault, an onslaught. **onsetting,** *n.*

onslaught (on′ slawt) [etym. doubtful, perh. from Dut. *aanslag*, G. *anschlag* (ON-, *slag*, cp. A-S. *sleaht*, a blow)], *n.* A furious attack or onset.

onstead (on′ sted), *n.* (*Sc.*) A farmstead; the farm-buildings apart from the house.

onto- [Gr. *on, ontos*, being] *comb. form.*

ontogenesis (on tō jen′ e sis), *n.* (*Biol.*) The origin and development of the individual organism. **ontogenetic,** *a.* **ontogenetically,** *adv.*

ontogeny (on toj′ ė ni), *n.* Ontogenesis; the history or science of this, embryology.

ontology (on tol′ ō ji), *n.* (*Phil.*) The branch of metaphysics dealing with the theory of pure being or reality.

onus (ō′ nŭs) [L.], *n.* A burden; a duty, obligation, or responsibility.

onward (on′ wȧrd) [ON, -WARD], *adv.* Toward the front or a point in advance, forward, on. *a.* Moving, tending, or directed forward; advancing, progressive. **onwards,** *adv.*

onychia (ō nik′ i ȧ) [mod. L., from Gr. *onux onuchos*, nail], *n.* (*Path.*) Inflammation of or near the nail, a whitlow. **onychitis** (-kī′ tis), *n.*

onym (on′ im) [Gr. *onoma* (Æolic *onuma*)], *n.* A technical term. **onymal, onymatic** (-măt′ ik), *a.* **onymally,** *adv.* **onymize,** *v.i.* **onymy,** *n.* **onymous** (on′ i mŭs), *a.* Having or bearing a name or signature, opp. to anonymous.

onyx (on′ iks, ō′ niks) [Gr. *onux*, a nail, onyx], *n.* A variety of quartz resembling agate, with variously-coloured layers.

oo- [Gr. *ōon*, egg], *comb. form.* Pertaining to ova.

oœcium (ō ē′ shi ŭm) [Gr. *oikion*, dim. of *oikos*, house], *n.* A sac-like receptacle in which ova are received and fertilized, as in certain polyzoa. **oœcial,** *a.* **oocyte** (ō′ ō sīt), *n.* The unfertilized ovum or egg cell.

oodles (oo′ dlz) (*colloq.*) *n.* A great quantity, superabundance.

oof (oof) [said to be short for Yiddish *oof-tish*, G. *auf tische* or *auf dem tische*, on the table], *n.* (*slang*) Money; gain, pelf, lucre. **oof-bird,** *n.* A personification of money; a provider of funds or source of profit. **oofy,** *a.*

oogamous (ō og′ ȧ mŭs) [oo-, Gr. *gamos*, marriage], *a.* (*Biol.*) Reproducing by the union of male and female cells. **oogamete,** *n.* One of such cells. **oogamy,** *n.*

oogeny (ō oj′ e ni), *n.* The origin and development of an ovum. **oogenetic,** *a.*

oolite (ō′ ō līt) [F. *oölithe*], *n.* A limestone composed of grains or particles of sand like the roe of a fish; the upper portion of the Jurassic strata in England, composed in great part of oolitic limestone. **oolitic** (-lit′ ik), *a.*

oology (ō ol′ ȯ ji), *n.* The study of or a treatise on birds' eggs. **oological** (-loj′ i kȧl), *a.* **oologically,** *adv.* **oologist** (ō ol′ ȯ jist), *n.* **oometer** (ō om′ ė tėr) [-METER], *n.* A device for measuring eggs. **oometry,** *n.*

oolong (oo long′) [Chin. *wu*, black; *lung*, dragon], *n.* A kind of China tea.

oom (oom) [Dut.), *n.* (*S. Afr.*) Uncle.

oomiak (oo′ mi ăk) [Eskimo], *n.* An Eskimo boat, adopted by Arctic and Antarctic explorers, consisting of a framework covered with skins.

oopak (oo′ păk) [Chin. *u-pak*, *Hu-peh*, province in central China], *n.* A variety of black tea.

oosperm (ō′ ō spĕrm), *n.* (*Biol.*) A fertilized egg. **oospore,** *n.* (*Zool.*) A fertilized ovum.

ooss (oos) [Sc.], *n.* Fluff.

ooze (ooz) [A.-S. *wāse*, mud (cp. Icel. and Norw. *veisa*), blended with A.-S. *wōs*, juice (cp. Icel. *vās*)], *n.* Wet mud, slime; a slimy deposit consisting of foraminiferal remains found on ocean-beds; the liquor of a tan-vat, consisting of an infusion of bark etc.; a gentle, sluggish flow, an exudation; *sea-weed. *v.i.* To flow or pass gently; to percolate (through the pores of a body etc.); (*fig.*) to escape, to be divulged, to leak (out). *v.t.* To emit or exude. **oozy,** *a.* **oozily,** *adv.* **ooziness,** *n.*

op- [OB-, before *p*], *pref.* As in *oppose.*

opacity, *opacous [OPAQUE].

opah (ō′ pȧ) [W. African native], *n.* A rare Atlantic fish, *Lampris guttatus*, of the mackerel family, famous for its brilliant colours.

opal (ō′ pȧl) [F. *opale*, L. *opalus*, Sansk. *upala*], *n.* An amorphous, transparent, vitreous form of hydrous silica, several kinds of which are characterized by a play of iridescent colours. **opalesce** (ō pȧ les′), *v.i.* To give a play of colours like an opal. **opalescence,** *n.* **opalescent,** *a.* **opalesque** (-lesk′), *a.* **opaline** (ō′ pȧ lin, -līn), *a.* Pertaining to or like opal. *n.* A translucent variety of glass; a yellow chalcedony. **opalize,** *v.t.* **opaloid,** *a.*

opaque (ȯ pāk′) [F., from L. *opācum*, nom. *-cus*, shady], *a.* Impervious to rays of light; not transparent or translucent; impenetrable to sight; (*fig.*) obscure, unintelligible; *dark. *n.* Opacity; darkness. **opaquely,** *adv.* **opaqueness, opacity** (ȯ păs′ i ti), *n.* ***opacous** (ȯ pā′ kŭs), *a.*

ope [OPEN], *a.* (*poet.*) Open. *v.t.* and *i.* To open.

opeidoscope (ȯ pī′ dȯ skōp) [Gr. *ōps*, voice, *eidos*, form, -SCOPE], *n.* An instrument for exhibiting sound-vibrations by means of reflections of light.

open (ō′ pėn) [A.-S. (cp. Dut. *open*, G. *offen*, Icel. *opinn*), rel. to UP], *a.* Not closed, obstructed, or enclosed; affording entrance, passage, access, or view; unclosed, unshut, having any barrier, gate, cover, etc., removed, withdrawn, or unfastened; uncovered, bare, unsheltered, exposed; unconcealed, undisguised, manifest; unrestricted, not exclusive or limited; ready to admit, receive or be affected; liable, subject (to); unoccupied, vacant; disengaged, free; unobstructed, clear, affording wide views; (*fig.*) free, generous, liberal; frank, candid; not closed or decided, debatable, moot; (of weather) not frosty; (*Mus.*) not stopped, or produced from an unstopped pipe, string, etc.; (*Phon.*) enunciated with the vocal organs comparatively unclosed; (of a vowel or syllable) not ended by a consonant. *n.* Unenclosed space or ground; (*fig.*) public view. *v.t.* To make open; to unclose; to unfasten, to unlock; to remove the covering from; to unfold, to spread out, to expand; to free from obstruction or restriction, to make free of access; (*fig.*) to reveal, to make manifest or public; to widen, to enlarge, to develop; to make a start in, to begin; to set a-going; (*Law*) to state a case before calling evidence. *v.i.* To become unclosed or unfastened; to crack, to fissure, to gape; to unfold, to expand; (*fig.*) to develop; to make a start, to begin; (*Hunting*) to give tongue on view or scent of the game. **to open fire:** To begin firing. **to open out:** To unfold; to develop; to reveal; to become communicative; (*Naut.*) to bring into full view. **to open the ball** [BALL (2)]. **to open a person's eyes:** To undeceive. **to open up:** To make accessible; to reveal; to discover, to explore. **open air,** *n.*, *a.* Outdoors, open-air. **open-armed,** *a.* Ready to receive with cordiality or frankness. **open-bill,** *n.* (*Zool.*) A bird of the *Anastomus* family, akin to the stork, indigenous to Africa and Asia. **open book,** *n.* (*fig.*) Perfectly plain. **open-cast:** Of coal found on the surface. **open circuit,** *n.* (*Elec.*) A circuit that has been broken so that no current can flow; (*Radio.*) the ordinary television system for general and not restricted viewing. **open-eared,** *a.* Eagerly attentive. **open-eyed,** *a.* Watchful, vigilant; astonished, surprised. **open door,** *n.* (*fig.*) Free admission or access; (*Polit.*) admission to a country on equal terms, especially for commerce. **open field,** *n.* (*Agric.*) Undivided arable land; common land of a village before it was wrested from the villagers by Enclosure Acts. **open-handed,** *a.* Generous, liberal. **open-handedly,** *adv.* **open-handedness,** *n.* **open-hearted,** *a.* Frank, ingenuous, sincere, candid, unsuspicious. **open-heartedly,** *adv.* **open-heartedness,** *n.* **open letter,** *n.* A letter addressed to an individual but published in a newspaper. **open-minded,** *a.* Accessible to ideas, unprejudiced, candid, unreserved. **open-mindedly,** *adv.* **open-mindedness,** *n.* **open-mouthed** (-mou*th*d), *a.* Gaping with voracity, surprise, stupidity, etc.; greedy, ravenous; clamorous. **open order,** *n.* (*Mil.*) Interval between infantrymen in attack; space between ranks for inspection; (*Naval*) interval between warships. **open sesame** [SESAME]. **open shop:** A works, factory, etc., which does not recognize or deal with a trade union; an establishment where union membership is not a condition of employment. **open verdict,** *n.* (*Law*) A verdict which names no criminal. **open-work,** *n.* Ornamental work showing openings through its substance. **openable,** *a.* **opener,** *n.* **opening,** *a.* That opens; beginning, first in order, initial. *n.* The act of making or becoming open; a gap, a breach, an aperture; a beginning, a commencement, the first part or stage, a prelude; (*Law*) a counsel's statement of a case before evidence is called; (*Chess, etc.*) a series of moves beginning a game; (*fig.*) a vacancy, an opportunity. **openly,** *adv.* **openness,** *n.*

opera (op′ ėr ȧ) [It., from L., work], *n.* A dramatic entertainment in which music forms an essential part; a composition comprising words and music for this; a drama wholly sung; this form of dramatic art. **opera-bouffe** (-boof), *n.* A farcical variety of opera. **opera-cloak, -hood,** *n.* A cloak or hood for women at the opera or in going to evening parties. **opera-dancer,** *n.* **opera-glass,** *n.* (*often in pl.*) A small binocular for use in theatres. **opera-hat,** *n.* A collapsible tall hat for men. **opera-house,** *n.* **operatic** (-ăt′ ik), *a.* **operatically,** *adv.* **operatize,** *v.t.* To put into operatic form.

operate (op′ ėr āt) [L. *operātus*, p.p. of *operārī*, from *opus*, work], *v.i.* To work, to act; to produce effect; to exert power, force, strength, influence, etc.; (*Med.*) to produce a certain effect on the human system; (*Surg.*) to perform an operation on a body; (*Mil.*) to carry out strategic movements; (*Comm.*) to deal in stocks, esp. with a deliberate design to affect prices etc. *v.t.* To work or conduct the working of. ***operant** (op′ ėr ȧnt), *a.* and *n.* **operating costs:** (*Am.*) Working expenses. **operating theatre,** *n.* (*Surg.*) A specially-fitted room in a hospital where operations are performed.

operameter (op ĕr ăm′ ė tĕr), *n.* An apparatus for registering revolutions, strokes, etc., made by machinery.

operation (op ĕr ā′ shŭn), *n.* The act or process of operating; working, action, mode of working; activity, performance of function; effect; a series of military or naval movements; (*Surg.*) an act performed with or without instruments upon the body, to remove diseased parts, extract foreign matter, remedy deformities, etc.; (*Math.*) the act of altering the value or form of a number or quantity by such a process as multiplication or division. **operational** (op e rā' shŏn ăl), *a.* Ready for action.

operative (op' ėr ȧ tiv), *a.* Acting; producing the proper result; efficacious, effective; practical, as distinguished from theoretical or contemplative; *n.* A workman, an artisan, a mechanic. **operatively,** *adv.* **operator,** *n.*

operculum (ȯ pĕr' kū lŭm) [L., from *operīre*, to cover, rel. to *aperīre*, see APERIENT], *n.* (*pl.* **-la**) A lid or cover as of the pitcher in nepenthes, or of the spore-vessel in mosses; the gill-cover in fishes; the plate closing the mouth of many univalve shells. **opercular, -late, -lated,** *a.* **operculiferous** (-lif' ėr ŭs), *a.* **operculiform** (ȯ pĕr kū' li fôrm), *a.* **operculigenous** (-lij' ė nŭs), *a.*

operetta (op ėr et' ȧ) [It., dim. of OPERA], *n.* A short opera of a light character.

***operose** (op' ėr ōs) [L. *operōsus*, from *opus operis*, work], *a.* Done with or requiring much labour, laborious, wearisome. ***operosely,** *adv.* **operoseness,** *n.*

ophicleide (of' i klīd) [F. *ophicléide* (Gr. *ophis*, serpent, *kleis kleidos*, key)], *n.* (*Mus.*) A musical wind-instrument, consisting of a wide conical tube with usu. eleven finger-levers and a bass or alto pitch; a powerful reed-stop in an organ, now usu. called tuba.

ophidian (ȯ fid' i ăn) [mod. L. *ophidia*, pl., from Gr. *ophis*, snake, -AN], *a.* Pertaining to the *Ophidia*; snake-like. *n.* Any individual of the *Ophidia*. **ophidiarium** (of i di âr' i ŭm), *n.* A place where snakes are kept. **ophidious,** *a.*

ophio- [Gr. *ophis*, serpent], *comb. form.*

ophiography (of i og' rȧ fi), *n.* A treatise on serpents.

ophiolatry (of i ol' ȧ tri), *n.* Serpent worship.

ophiophagous (of i of' ȧ gŭs), *a.* Feeding on serpents.

ophite (1) (of' īt), *n.* Serpentine, serpentine marble. **ophitic,** *a.*

ophite (2) (of' īt) [late L. *Ophitæ*, Gr. *Ophītai*, from *ophis*, serpent], *n.* (*Ch. Hist.*) A member of a gnostic sect who regarded the serpent as an embodiment of divine wisdom.

ophiuran (of i ūr' ăn) [mod. L. *Ophiura* (Gr. *ophis*, serpent, *oura*, tail)], *a.* Belonging to the genus *Ophiura* or the class *Ophiuroidea* of echinoderms comprising the sand-stars. *n.* A starfish of this genus. **ophiuroid,** *a.* and *n.*

ophthalmia (of thăl' mi ȧ) [Gr. *ophthalmos*, eye], *n.* Inflammation of the eye. **ophthalmic,** *a.*

ophthalmitis (of thăl mī' tis), *n.* Ophthalmia, esp. inflammation involving all the structures of the eye.

ophthalmology (of thăl mol' ō ji), *n.* The science of the eye, its structure, functions and diseases. **ophthalmologist,** *n.*

ophthalmoscope (of thăl' mō skōp), *n.* An instrument for examining the inner structure of the eye. **ophthalmoscopy,** *n.*

ophthalmotomy (of thăl mot' ō mi). Dissection of the eye.

opiate (ō' pi ăt) [med. L. *opiātus*, from L. OPIUM], *n.* A medicine compounded with opium; a narcotic; (*fig.*) anything serving to dull sensation or relieve uneasiness. **a.* Soporific, narcotic, soothing. *v.t.* To mix with opium; to dull the sensibility of.

***opificer** (ȯ pif' i sėr) [L. *opifex -ficis* (*opus*, work, *facere*, to do)], *n.* A workman, an artificer.

opine (ȯ pīn') [L. *opīnārī*], *v.i.* To think, to suppose; to express an opinion. *v.t.* To think, to suppose. ***opinative,** *a.*

opinion (ȯ pin' yŏn) [F., from L. *opīniōnem*, nom. *-nio*, as prec.], *n.* A judgment, conviction, or belief falling short of positive knowledge; a view regarded as probable; views, sentiments, esp. those generally prevailing; one's judgment, belief, or conviction with regard to a particular subject; the formal statement of a judge, counsel, physician, or other expert on a question submitted to him; estimation, reputation; *opinionativeness. **opinionated** (ȯ pin' yȯ nā tėd), **opinionative,** *a.* Stiff or obstinate in one's opinions; dogmatic, stubborn. **opinionatively,** *adv.* **opinionatedness, opinionativeness,** *n.* ***opinionist,** *n.* **opinionless,** *a.*

opisometer (op i som' ė tėr) [Gr. *opisō*, backwards, -METER], *n.* An instrument for measuring curved lines, as on a map.

opistho- [Gr. *opisthen*, behind], *comb. form.* (*Comp. Anat. and Zool.*). **opisthobranchiate** (ȯ pis thȯ brăng' ki ăt) [Gr. *branchia*, gills], *a.* Belonging to the *Opisthobranchiata*, an order of gasteropods having the gills behind the heart. *n.* A gasteropod of this order. **opisthobranchism** (ȯ pis' thȯ brăng kizm), *n.* **opisthocœlian** (-sē' li ăn) [Gr. *koilos*, hollow], *a.* Hollow behind (of vertebræ). *n.* An opisthocœlian animal. **opisthocœlous,** *a.* **opisthodomos** (-thod' ȯ mos) [Gr. *domos*, house], *n.* (*Gr. Ant.*) A chamber at the back of an ancient Greek temple. **opisthodont** (ȯ pis' thȯ dont) [Gr. *odous odontos*, tooth], *a.* Having back teeth only. **opisthogastric** (-găs' trik) [GASTRIC], *a.* (*Anat.*) Situated behind the stomach. **opisthognathous** (-nā' thŭs), *a.* Having retreating jaws or teeth. **opisthograph** (ȯ pis' thȯ grăf) [-GRAPH], *n.* (*Class. Ant.*) A manuscript having writing on the back as well as the front. **opisthographic** (-grăf' ik), *a.*

opium (ō' pi ŭm) [L., from Gr. *opion*, dim. of *opos*, juice, sap], *n.* A narcotic drug prepared from the dried exudation of the unripe capsules of the poppy, esp. the dried juice obtained from *Papaver somniferum*. **opium-den,** (*Am.*) **-joint,** *n.* A haunt of opium-smokers. **opium-eater,** *n.* One who habitually eats opium as a stimulant or narcotic. **opiumism,** *n.* **opiumize,** *v.t.*

opobalsam (op ȯ bawl' săm), **opobalsamum** (-să mŭm) [L. *opobalsamum*, Gr. *opobalsamon* (*opos*, juice, BALSAM)], *n.* Balm of Gilead.

opodeldoc (op ȯ del' dok) [said to be coined by Paracelsus, prob. from *opos*, see prec.], *n.* A liniment prepared by dissolving soap and camphor in alcohol, soap-liniment.

opoponax (ȯ pop' ȯ năks) [L. and Gr. (*opos*, juice, *panax*, all-heal, cp. PANACEA)], *n.* The resinous juice from the root of *Opoponax chironium*, formerly used as a stimulant and in medicine; a gum-resin used in perfumery.

opossum (ȯ pos' ŭm) [N. Am. Ind.], *n.* An American marsupial quadruped with a prehensile tail and a thumb on the hind-foot, most species of which are arboreal and one aquatic; applied to small marsupials of Australia and Tasmania.

opotherapy (op ō ther' ȧ pi) [Gr. *opokos*, juice; *therapeia*, medical treatment], *n.* (*Med.*) The treatment of diseases with prepared extracts of glands or organs.

oppidan (op' i dăn) [L. *oppidānus*, from *oppīdus*, town], *n.* (*Eton College*) A student not on the foundation who boards in the town; *a townsman.

oppilate (op' i lāt) [L. *oppīlātus*, p.p. of *oppīlāre* (OP-, *pīlāre*, to ram, from *pīlum*, pestle)], *v.t.* (*Med.*) To block up, to obstruct. **oppilation** (-lā' shŭn), *n.*

opponent (ȯ pō' nėnt) [L. *oppōnens -ntem*, pres.p. of *oppōnere* (OP-, *pōnere*, to put)], *a.* Opposing, opposed, antagonistic, adverse, *n.* One who opposes, esp. in debate or argument; an adversary, an antagonist. **opponency,** *n.*

opportune (op' ȯr tūn, op ȯr tūn') [F. *opportun*, L. *opportūnus* (OP-, *-portunus*, from *portus*, harbour, PORT (1))], *a.* Situated, occurring, done, etc., at a favourable moment, seasonable, timely, well-timed; fit, suitable. **opportunely** (op'-), *adv.* **opportuneness.**

opportunism (op ȯr tūn' izm), *n.* Utilizing circumstances or opportunities to gain one's ends, esp. the act or practice of shaping policy according to the needs or circumstances of the moment; acceptance of what may be realized as a partial advance towards an ideal; adaptation to circumstances, compromise; sacrifice of principle to expediency; political time-serving. **opportunist,** *n.*

opportunity (op ȯr tūn′ i ti), *n.* An opportune or convenient time or occasion; a chance, an opening; a favourable circumstance.

oppose (ȯ pōz′) [F. *opposer* (OP-, *poser*, to POSE (1))], *v.t.* To set against, to place or bring forward as an obstacle, adverse force, counterpoise, contrast, or refutation (to); to set oneself against or act against, to resist, withstand, obstruct; to object to, to dispute; (*in p.p.*) opposite, contrasted. *v.i.* To offer resistance or objection. **opposable,** *a.* **opposability** (-bil′ i ti), *n.* **opposeless,** *a.* (*poet.*) **opposer,** *n.*

opposite (op′ o zit), *a.* Situated in front of or contrary in position (to); fronting, facing; antagonistic, adverse, contrary, diametrically different (to or from); (*Bot.*) placed in pairs on contrary sides on the same horizontal plane (of leaves on a stem). *n.* One who or that which is opposite; an opponent, an adversary; a contrary thing or term; (*Log.*) a contradictory; (*colloq.*) a person facing one. *adv.* In an opposite place or direction. *prep.* Opposite to. **opposite prompter:** (*Theat.*) The left-hand side of the stage facing the audience (usually abbr. O.P.). **oppositely,** *adv.* **oppositeness,** *n.* **oppositi-,** *comb. form.*

opposition (op o zish′ un), *n.* The act or state of opposing; antagonism, resistance, hostility; the state of being opposite; antithesis, contrast, contrariety; an obstacle, a hindrance; the chief parliamentary party opposed to the party in office; (*Astron.*) the situation of two heavenly bodies when their longitudes differ by 180°; (*Log.*) difference of quantity or quality, or of both, in propositions having the same subject and predicate. **oppositional,** *a.* **oppositionist,** *a.* and *n.*

oppress (ȯ pres′) [O.F. *oppresser*, med. L. *oppressāre* (OP-, *pressāre*, to PRESS (1))], *v.t.* To overburden; to lie heavy on; to weigh down (*lit. or fig.*); to inflict hardships, cruelties, or exactions upon, to govern cruelly or unjustly; to tyrannize over; *to ravish. **oppression,** *n.* **oppressive,** *a.* Overbearing, exacting, tyrannous; (of the weather) close, muggy, sultry. **oppressively,** *adv.* **oppressiveness,** *n.* **oppressor,** *n.*

opprobrious (ȯ prō′bri ůs) [through O.F. *opprobrieux* or directly from late L. *opprobriōsus*, from *opprobrium* (OP-, *probrum*, infamous act)], *a.* Abusive, vituperative, contumelious. **opprobriously,** *adv.* **opprobriousness,**

opprobrium (o prō′ bri ům) [as prec.], *n.* Disgrace, infamy, ignominy, obloquy.

oppugn (ȯ pūn′) [F. *oppugner*, L. *oppugnāre* (OP-, *pugnāre*, to fight)], *v.t.* To oppose, to controvert, to call in question; *to fight against, to oppose, to resist. ***oppugnant** (ȯ pŭg′ nånt), *a.* ***oppugnancy, *oppugnation** (ȯ pŭg nā′ shůn), *n.* ***oppugner** (ȯ pū′ nėr), *n.*

***opsimath** (op′ si măth) [Gr. *opsimathēs* (*opse*, late, *manthanein*, to learn)], *n.* One who gets education late in life. **opsimathy** (-sim′ å thi), *n.*

opsomania (op sō mā′ ni å) [Gr. *opson*, food; MANIA], *n.* (*Path.*) An abnormal craving for some special kind of food; morbid daintiness of the appetite.

opsonin (op′ sō nin), *n.* A substance in the blood which reacts in such a manner on germs that the white corpuscles annihilate them. **opsonic index,** *n.* (*Med.*) A standard for calculating the power of resistance to disease.

opt (opt) [OPTION], *v.i.* To choose, to make a choice between.

optative (op′ tå tiv, op tā′ tiv) [F. *optatif*, *-tive*, late L. *optātīvus*, from *optāre*, to choose, to opt], *a.* (*Gram.*) Expressing a wish or desire. *n.* (*Gram.*) The optative mood; a verbal form expressing this. **optatively,** *adv.*

optic (op′ tik) [F. *optique*, med. L. *opticus*, Gr. *optikos*, from *optos*, seen, from *op-*, stem of *opsomai*, I shall see], *a.* Pertaining to vision or the eye. *n.* (*now facet.*) An eye; a glass device fixed to the neck of a bottle to measure out spirits, etc. **optic disc,** *n.* The blind spot. **optic glass** or **lens:** A lens for an optical instrument. **optic nerve:** A nerve of sight connecting the retina with the brain. **optical,** *a.* **optically,** *adv.* **optician** (-tish′ ån), *n.* One who makes or deals in optical instruments; *one versed in optics.

optics (op′ tiks), *n.* The science of the properties of light and vision.

optimates (op ti mā′ tēz) [L., from *optimus*, best], *n.pl.* The Roman patricians; any aristocracy or nobility.

optime (op′ ti mi) [L., very well, as prec.], *n.* (*Camb. Univ.*) One of those who are ranked in the mathematical tripos immediately below the wranglers (the **senior optimes** in the second, and the **junior** in the third class).

optimism (op′ ti mizm) [F. *optimisme* (L. *optimus*, best)], *n.* The view that the existing state of things is the best possible, orig. set forth by Leibnitz from the postulate of the omnipotence of God; the view that the universe is tending towards a better state and that good must ultimately prevail; (*fig.*) a sanguine temperament, disposition to take a hopeful view of things. **optimist,** *n.* **optimistic** (-mis′ tik), *a.* **optimistically,** *adv.* **optimize** (op′ ti mīz), *v.i.* **optimum** (op′ tim ům), *n.* The most favourable condition.

option (op′ shůn) [F., from L. *optiōnem*, nom. *-tio*, rel. to *optāre* to choose], *n.* The right, power, or liberty of choosing; choice, preference; the thing chosen or preferred; (*Comm.*) the purchased right to deliver or call for the delivery of securities, land, commodities, etc., at a specified rate within a specified time. **local option** [LOCAL]. **optional,** *a.* **optionally,** *adv.*

opto- [Gr. *optos*, seen], *comb. form.* Pertaining to sight or optics.

optometer (op tom′ ė tėr), *n.* An instrument for ascertaining the range of vision and other powers of the eye. **optometry,** *n.*

optophone (op′ tō fōn), *n.* A device for enabling the blind to read by sound.

opulent (op′ ū lėnt) [L. *opulentus*, from *opem*, pl. *opes*, power, wealth], *a.* Rich, wealthy, affluent; abounding (in); abundant, profuse, copious. **opulence, *-cy,** *n.* **opulently,** *adv.*

opuntia (ȯ pŭn′ shi å) [L., from *Opus*, a city of Locris], *n.* A genus of cactaceous plants comprising the prickly pear or Indian fig.

opus (op′ ůs, ō′ půs) [L.], *n.* (*pl.* ***opera***) A work, esp. a musical composition (*usu.* written **op.,** *pl.* **opp.**). **opuscule, *opusculum*** (ȯ pŭs′ kūl, -kū lům), *n.* (*pl.* **-cules,** -kūlz, ***-cula***) A minor literary or musical work.

or (1) (ôr) [contr. of obs. *other*, prob. from A.-S. *oththe*, or], *conj.* A disjunctive particle introducing an alternative; used also to connect synonyms, words explaining, correcting, etc.

***or** (2) (ôr) [A.-S. *ǣr*, early, with sense of the compar. *aer*, ERE], *adv.* Ere, before; sooner than.

or (3) (ôr) [F., from L. *aurum*], *n.* (*Her.*) Gold.

or [(1) through O.F. *-or*, *-ur*, or F. *-eur*, or directly from L. *-or*, *-ōrem*, denoting agency; (2) through O.F. *-eor*, *-eur*, from L. *-ātor*, *-ētor*, *-itor*, or *-ītor*, denoting agency; (3) A.-F. *-our*, O.F. *-or*, *-ur* (F. *-eur*), L. *-or*, *-ōrem*, denoting nouns of conditions (in Eng. usu. *-our*, Am. always *-or*)], *suf.*, as in *actor*, *author*, *creator*, *equator*, *favour*, *vigour*.

orache (or′ åch) [previously *arache*, F. *arroche*, L. *atriplicem*, nom. *atriplex*, Gr. *atraphaxus*], *n.* The mountain spinach, *Atriplex hortensis*, formerly used as a pot-herb.

oracle (or′ å kėl) [F., from L. *ōrāculum*, from *ōrāre*, to speak, to pray], *n.* The answer of a god or inspired priest to a request for advice or prophecy; the agency or medium giving such responses; the seat of the worship of a deity where these were sought; the sanctuary or holy of holies in the Jewish Temple; a person of profound wisdom, knowledge, or infallible judgment; an utterance regarded as profoundly wise, authoritative, or infallible; a mysterious, ambiguous, or obscure utterance; a divine messenger, a prophet. *v.i.* To speak as an oracle. **v.t.* To utter as an oracle. **to work the oracle:** To secure a desired answer from the mouthpiece of an oracle by craft; (*fig.*) to obtain some object by secret influence; to gain one's point by stratagem. **oracular, *-lous** (ȯ răk′ ū lȧr, -lůs), *a.* **oracularly,** *adv.* **oracularity** (-lăr′ i ti), *n.*

oral (ôr′ ȧl) [L. *ōs ōris*, mouth, -AL], *a.* Spoken, not written, by word of mouth; (*Anat.*) of, at, or near the mouth. *n.* An oral examination. **orally,** *adv.* **orale** (ȯ rā li, ȯ ra′ lā), *n.* (*R.-C. Ch.*) A silk veil covering the face and breast, worn by the Pope on certain solemn occasions.

orange (1) (or′ ȧnj) [M.E. and O.F. *orenge, orange*, It. *narancia* (now *arancia*), Arab. *nāranj*], *n.* The large roundish cellular pulpy fruit of *Citrus aurantium*; the evergreen tree, *C. aurantium*; the colour of the fruit, reddish-yellow. *a.* Of the colour of an orange. **Blenheim orange:** A variety of apple. **mock orange:** The shrub syringa, bearing white flowers like orange-blossom. **orange-blossom,** *n.* The blossom of the orange-tree (commonly worn in wreaths by brides). **orange-lily,** *n.* *Lilium croceum* or *L. bulbiferum*, var. *aurantium*, with large reddish or orange flowers. **orange-marmalade,** *n.* Marmalade made from oranges. **orange-peel,** *n.* **orange-stick,** *n.* A thin piece of orange-tree wood used for manicure purposes. **orange-tawny,** *a.* **orange-tip,** *n.* A variety of butterfly. **orange-wife,** *n.* A woman who sells oranges. **orangeade** (or ȧn jād′), *n.* A drink made from orange-juice. **oranges and lemons,** *n.* A children's game. **orangery,** *n.*

Orange (2) (or ȧnj) [town in department of Vaucluse, France, formerly seat of a principality, whence the Princes of Orange, including William III, King of England, took their title], *a.* Pertaining to the Irish extreme-Protestant party or to the Society of Orangemen formed 1795 to uphold the Protestant ascendancy in Ireland (prob. named after the Orange lodge of Freemasons in Belfast who prob. took their title from William III). **Orangeism,** *n.* **Orangeman,** *n.*

orang-utan, -outang (ȯ răng′ ů tăn′, -tăng′) [Malay *ōrang ūtan*, wild man of the woods], *n.* A large, red-haired, arboreal anthropoid ape, *Simia satyrus*, of Borneo and Sumatra.

orarium (ȯ râr′ i ům) [L., from *ōs ōris*, mouth, face], *n.* (*Eccles.*) A linen napkin or neck-cloth, a stole; a scarf sometimes twined round the handle of the mediæval crozier. ***orarion,*** *n.* (*Gr. Ch.*) A deacon's stole, wider than the *orarium.*

orate (o rāt′), *v.i.* (*colloq.*) To make an oration; to talk at length.

oration (ȯ rā′ shůn) [L. *ōrātio*, from *ōrāre*, to speak], *n.* A formal speech, treating of some important subject in elevated language; (*Gram.*) language, discourse. **oblique oration** [OBLIQUE]. **orator** (or′ ȧ tȯr), *n.* One who delivers an oration; an eloquent speaker; an officer at a University who acts as public speaker on ceremonial occasions; *(*Law*) a petitioner or complainant. ***oratorial** (-tôr′ i ȧl), *a.* Oratorical; pertaining to an oratorio. **oratorian** [ORATORY (2)]. **oratorical** (-tor′ i kȧl), *a.* **oratorically,** *adv.* **oratorize** (or′ ȧ tȯr īz), *v.i.* **oratress,** *n.* **oratory** (1) (or′ ȧ tȯr i), *n.* The art of public speaking, rhetoric; eloquence; rhetorical language.

oratorio (or ȧ tôr′ i ō) [It., from L. *ōrātōrium*, ORATORY (2)], *n.* (*pl.* **-ios**) A musical composition for voices and instruments, usually semi-dramatic in character, and treating of a scriptural theme.

oratory (2) (or′ ȧ tȯr i) [L. *ōrātōrium*, neut. of *ōrātōrius*, from *ōrāre*, to pray], *n.* A small chapel, esp. one for private devotions; one of several congregations of Roman Catholic priests living in community without vows, the first of which was established at Rome by St. Philip Neri in 1564 to preach and hold services among the people. **Oratorian** (-tôr′ i ȧn), *a.* Belonging to any congregation of the Oratory. *n.* A member of any congregation of the Oratory.

orb (ôrb) [L. *orbis*, ring], *n.* A sphere, a globe; a heavenly body; (*poet.*) an eye or eyeball; a circle, ring, or orbit; anything circular; the globe forming part of the regalia; (*fig.*) a round or complete whole. *v.t.* To form into a circle; to surround, encircle, or enclose in an orb. *v.i.* To become round or like an orb. **orbicular** (ôr bik′ ū lȧr), *a.* **orbicularity** (-lăr′ i ti), *n.* **orbicularly** (ôr bik′ ū lȧr li), *adv.* **orbiculate,** *a.* ***orbiculation,** *n.* ***orby,** *a.* **orbless,** *a.* **orblet,** *n.*

orbit (ôr′ bit) [L. *orbita*, a track, as prec.], *n.* (*Anat.*, *Zool.*, etc.) The bony cavity of the eye; the ring or border round the eye in insects, birds, etc.; (*Astron.*) the path of a heavenly body; (*fig.*) a course or sphere of action, a career. **orbital, orbitar, orbitary,** *a.*

orc (ôrk) [F. *orque*, L. *orca*], *n.* A cetacean of the genus *Orca*, esp. *O. gladiator*, a grampus; a marine animal, a sea-monster, an ogre.

Orcadian (ôr kā′ di ȧn) [L. *Orcades*, Orkney Islands], *a.* Pertaining to the Orkney Islands. *n.* A native of these.

orcein (ôr′ sė in), *n.* The colouring principle of archil and cudbear.

orchard (ôr′ chȧrd) [A.-S. *orceard*, *ortgeard* (L. *hortus*, garden)], *n.* An enclosure containing fruit trees, or a plantation of these. **orchard-house,** *n.* A glass-house for fruit trees. **orchardman, orchardist,** *n.* **orcharding,** *n.*

orchesis (ôr kē′ sis) [Gr., from *orcheesthai*, to dance], *n.* The art of dancing, esp. in the Greek choral performances. **orchestic** (-kes′-, -kēs′ tik), *a.* **orchestics,** *n.* Orchesis.

orchestra (ôr′ kės trȧ) [L. and Gr. *orchēstra*, as prec.], *n.* (*Gr. Ant.*) The semi-circular space between the stage and the seats for the spectators, where the chorus danced and sang; the place for the band, or band and chorus, in modern concert-rooms, theatres, etc.; the body of musicians in a theatre or concert-room; the music performed by them. **orchestra seats:** (*Am.*) Stalls. **orchestral** (ôr kes′ trȧl), *a.* **orchestrate** (ôr′ kės trāt), *v.t.* To compose or arrange (music) for an orchestra. **orchestration** (-trā′ shůn), *n.* **orchestrina** (-trē′ nȧ), **orchestrion** (-kes′ tri ȯn), **orchestrionette** (-net′), *n.* A mechanical musical instrument designed on the principle of the barrel-organ to give the effect of an orchestra.

orchid (ôr′ kid) [coined by Lindley from L. and Gr. *orchis -ios*, testicle, an orchis, from the shape of the tubers], *n.* One of a large order of monocotyledonous plants, the *Orchidaceæ*, of which the genus *Orchis* is the type, characterized by tuberous roots and flowers usually of a fantastic shape and brilliant colours in which the pistils and stamens are united with the floral axis. **orchidaceous** (-dā′ shůs), **orchidean, orchideous** (-kid′ ė ȧn, -ůs), *a.* **orchidist** (ôr′ ki dist), *n.* **orchido-,** *comb. form.* **orchidology** (-dol′ ȯ ji), *n.* **orchidomania** (-mā′ ni ȧ), *n.* **orchis** (ôr′ kis), *n.* The typical genus of the *Orchidaceæ*, comprising those belonging to temperate regions; a plant of this genus; (*loosely*) an orchid.

orchil (ôr′ chil), **orchilla** (ôr chil′ ȧ) [O.F. *orchel*, etym. doubtful (cp. ARCHIL)], *n.* A violet, purple, or red colouring-matter obtained from various lichens, esp. *Roccella tinctoria*; this and other species of lichen yielding such colouring-matter.

orchis [ORCHID].

orchitis (ôr kī' is) [Gr. *orchis*, a testicle; -ITIS], *n.* (*Path.*) Inflammation of the testicles.

orcin (ôr' sin) [as prec.], *n.* (*Chem.*) A colourless crystalline compound obtained from several species of *Roccella*, yielding colours used for dyeing on treatment with various reagents.

ordain (ôr dān') [O.F. *ordener* (F. *ordonner*), L. *ordinăre*, from *ordo -dinis*, ORDER], *v.t.* To set apart for an office or duty, to appoint and consecrate, to confer Holy Orders on; to decree, to establish, to destine. **ordainable,** *a.* **ordainer,** *n.* **ordainment,** *n.* **ordinand,** *n.* One preparing for Holy Orders.

ordeal (ôr' dēl, -dė ȧl) [A.-S. *ordēl, ordāl* (cp. Dut. *oordeel*, G. *urteil*), rel. to *dælan*, to DEAL (1), *adælan*, to divide, to allot, to judge], *n.* The ancient Teutonic practice of referring disputed questions of criminality to supernatural decision, by subjecting a suspected person to physical tests by fire, boiling water, battle, etc.; (*fig.*) an experience testing endurance, patience, courage, etc.

order (ôr' dėr) [M.E. and O.F. *ordre*, L. *ordinem*, nom. *ordo*], *n.* Regular or methodical disposition or arrangement; sequence, succession, esp. as regulated by a system or principle; normal, proper, or right condition; a state of efficiency, a condition suitable for working; tidiness, absence of confusion or disturbance; established state of things, general constitution of the world; customary mode of procedure, esp. the rules and regulations governing an assembly or meeting; a rule, regulation; a mandate, an injunction, an authoritative direction; (*Comm.*) a direction to supply specified commodities or to carry out specified work; a signed document instructing a person or persons to pay money or deliver property; a tier; a social class, rank, or degree; kind, sort, quality; a class or body of persons united by some common purpose; a fraternity of monks or friars, or formerly of knights, bound by the same rule of life; a grade of the Christian ministry; (*pl.*) the clerical office or status; a body usually instituted by a sovereign, organized in grades like the mediæval orders of knights, to which distinguished persons are admitted as an honour; the insignia worn by members of this; any of the nine grades of angels and archangels; (*Arch.*) a system of parts, ornaments, and proportions of columns, etc., distinguishing styles of architecture, esp. Classical, as the Doric, Ionic, Corinthian, Tuscan, and Composite; (*R.-C. Ch.*) a sacrament bestowing grace for the performance of sacred duties conferred on those entering any of the seven grades or orders of priestly office; (*Math.*) degree of complexity; (*Nat. Hist.*) a division below that of class and above that of family and genus. *v.t.* To put in order; to regulate; to manage; to ordain; to direct, to command; to arrange beforehand; to instruct (a person, firm, etc.) to supply goods or perform work; to direct the supplying, doing, or making of. *v.i.* To give orders. **by order:** According to direction by the proper authority. **Holy Orders:** The different ranks of clergy in an episcopal church; the clerical office. **in order:** Properly or systematically arranged; in due sequence. **in order to:** To the end that; so as to. **order of battle:** The disposition of troops for attack or defence. **Order in Council:** (*Pol.*) An order issued by the sovereign on the advice of the Privy Council. **order of the day:** Business arranged beforehand, esp. the programme of business in a legislative assembly; (*fig.*) the prevailing state of things. **out of order:** Disarranged; untidy; not consecutive; not systematically arranged; not fit for working or using. **to order about:** To send from one place to another; (*fig.*) to domineer over. **to order arms:** (*Mil.*) To bring rifles vertically against the right side with the butts resting on the ground. **to take orders:** To be ordained. **order-book,** *n.* A book, usu. with counterfoils and detachable leaves, on which orders for goods, work, etc., are written; (*House of Commons*) a book in which motions to be submitted must be entered. **order-clerk,** *n.* One appointed to enter orders. **order-form,** *n.* A printed paper with blanks for a customer to enter goods to be supplied. **order-paper,** *n.* (*House of Commons*) A paper on which the order of the day is written or printed. **orderer,** *n.* **ordering,** *n.* Arrangement, disposition; ordination of priests, etc. ***orderless,** *a.* **orderly** (1), *a.* In order; methodical, regular; keeping or disposed to keep order, free from disorder or confusion; (*Mil.*) pertaining to orders and their execution. *adv.* Duly, regularly. **orderly-bin,** *n.* A box for street-refuse. **orderliness,** *n.*

orderly (2), *n.* A soldier who attends on an officer to carry orders, messages, etc. **orderly book,** *n.* A book for regimental orders. **orderly officer,** *n.* The officer of the day. **orderly-room,** *n.* A room in barracks used as the office for company or regimental business.

ordinaire (ôr di nâr') [F., ordinary], *n.* Wine of ordinary grade, *vin ordinaire.*

ordinal (ôr' di nȧl) [late L. *ordinālis*, as prec.], *a.* Denoting order or position in a series. *n.* A number denoting this, *e.g.* first, second; a book containing orders, rules, rubrics, etc., esp. (*Ang. Ch.*) forms for ordination.

ordinance (ôr' di nȧns) [O.F. *ordenance* (F. *ordonnance*), med. L. *ordinantia*, from *ordināre*, to ORDAIN], *n.* An order, decree, or regulation laid down by a constituted authority; an established rule, rite, or ceremony, etc. **ordinant,** *a.* Ordaining, regulating, directing. *n.* One who confers orders.

ordinand [ORDAIN].

ordinary (ôr' di nȧr i) [L. *ordinārius*, from *ordo -dinis*, ORDER], *a.* Usual, habitual, customary, regular, normal, not exceptional or unusual; commonplace; mediocre; having immediate or ex officio jurisdiction; (*colloq.*) ill-looking, plain. *n.* A rule or order, as of the Mass; a tavern or inn meal prepared at a fixed rate for all comers; hence, an eating-house; (*Her.*) one of the simplest and commonest charges, esp. the chief, pale, fesse, bend, bar, chevron, cross, and saltire; (*Sc. Law*) a judge of the Court of Session; (*Eccles. Law*) a bishop or his deputy, esp. sitting as ecclesiastical judge; (*fig.*) the ordinary run of humanity, course of life, procedure, etc. **in ordinary:** In actual and constant service. **ordinary seaman:** A sailor not fully qualified as able seaman. **ordinarily,** *adv.* **ordinariness,** *n.* **ordinaryship,** *n.*

ordinate (ôr' di nȧt) [L. *ordinātus*, p.p. of *ordināre*, to ORDAIN], *a.* (*Ent.*) Arranged in a row of rows; ordinary, regular, proper. *n.* (*Geom.*) A line drawn from a point parallel to one of a pair of reference lines, called the co-ordinate axes, and meeting the other.

ordination (ôr di nā' shŭn), *n.* The act of ordaining; the state of being ordained or appointed; arrangement in order, classification; appointment, ordainment. ***ordinative** (ôr' di nā tiv), *a.* ***ordinator,** *n.* **ordinee** (ôr di nē'), *n.* One newly ordained.

ordnance (ôrd' nȧns) [var. of ORDINANCE], *n.* (*collect.*) Heavy guns, cannon, artillery; the department of the public service dealing with military stores and equipment, except those pertaining to the quartermaster's department. **Ordnance datum:** The level taken as the basis for the Ordnance Survey, since 1921 the mean sea level at Newlyn, Cornwall. **Ordnance Survey:** The Goverment survey of Great Britain and Northern Ireland.

Ordovician (ôr dō vish' yȧn) [*Ordovices*, ancient British tribe], *n.* (*Geol.*) The middle period of the lower Palæozoic era, which followed the Cambrian period.

ordure (ôr' dyŭr) [F., from O.F. *ord*, foul, L. *horridus*, see HORRID], *n.* Excrement, dung, filth.

ore (ôr) [A.-S. *ār*, brass (cp. Icel. *eir*, Goth. *aiz*, L.

æs æris), confused with *ōra*, unwrought metal (cp. Dut. *oer*)], *n.* A natural substance from which metal may be profitably extracted; (*poet.*) precious metal.

Oread (ôr′ ė ăd) [L. *orēkas -ados*, Gr. *oreias*, from *oros*, mountain], *n.* A mountain nymph.

orectic (ŏ rek′ tĭk) [Gr. *orektikos*, from *orektos*, stretched out, from *oregein*, to stretch out, to grasp after, to desire], *a.* Of or pertaining to appetite or desire; appetitive. **orexis,** *n.*

orfe (ôrf) [Gr. *orphos*, a sea-perch], *n.* (*Zool.*) A kind of gold-fish.

organ (ôr′ gȧn) [M.E. and O.F. *organe* (F. *orgue*), L. *organa*, pl. treated as sing. of *organum*, Gr. *organon*, rel. to *ergon*, work], *n.* A musical wind-instrument composed of an assemblage of pipes sounded by means of a bellows and played by keys; a wind-instrument having some resemblance to this, played by keys or other mechanism; an instrument; a medium or agent of communication, etc., as a newspaper or other periodical; a mental faculty regarded as an instrument; the human voice with regard to its musical quality, power, etc.; a part of an animal or vegetable body performing some definite vital function. **American organ,** *n.* (*Mus.*) A harmonium. **great organ:** The principal organ of a large composite organ, comprising the main flue-work and having a separate keyboard. **mouth-organ** [MOUTH]. **organ-blower,** *n.* **organ-builder,** *n.* **organ-grinder,** *n.* A player on a barrel-organ. **organ-loft,** *n.* **organ-piano,** *n.* A piano with a series of small hammers for striking the strings repeatedly and giving a sustained organ-like sound. **organ-pipe,** *n.* One of the sounding-pipes of a pipe-organ. **organ-screen,** *n.* A screen or partition, usu. between the nave and the choir, on which the organ is placed in a large church. **organ-stop,** *n.* The handle by which a set of pipes in an organ is put in or out of action; the set of pipes or reeds of a certain quality controlled by this. **organless,** *a.* ***organry,** *n.*

organdie (ôr′ gȧn di) [F. *organdi*, etym. doubtful], *n.* A stiff light transparent muslin.

organic (ôr găn′ ik) [L. *organicus*, Gr. *organikos* (ORGAN, -IC)], *a.* (*Physiol.*) Of or pertaining to a bodily organ or organs; of, pertaining to, or of the nature of organisms or plants or animals; (*Path.*) pertaining to or affecting an organ or organs (of diseases, etc.); (*Chem.*) existing as parts of or derived from organisms; hence, of hydrocarbons and their derivatives whether of natural or artificial origin; of or pertaining to an organized system; organized, systematic, co-ordinated; structural, fundamental, inherent, not accidental; vital, not mechanical. **organic chemistry,** *n.* (*Chem.*) The study of the compounds of carbon. **organic compounds:** Chemical compounds containing carbon combined with oxygen and other elements. ***organical,** *a.* Organic; instrumental; performed on an organ (of music). **organically,** *adv.* ***organicalness,** *n.* **organicism,** *n.* (*Biol.*) The theory that all things in nature have an organic basis. **organify,** *v.t.* (*Phot.*) To treat or coat with organic matter. **organifier,** *n.*

organism (ôr′ gȧ nizm), *n.* An organized body consisting of mutually dependent parts fulfilling functions necessary to the life of the whole; an animal, a plant; organic structure; (*fig.*) a whole having mutually related parts analogous to those of a living body.

organist (ôr′ gȧ nist), *n.* One who plays a church or other organ.

organize (ôr′ gȧ nīz), *v.t.* To form or furnish with organs; to make organic, to make into an organism, to make into a living part, structure, or being; to correlate the parts of and make into an organic whole; to put into proper working order; to arrange or dispose things or a body of people in order to carry out some purpose effectively; (*Mus.*) to render or sing in parts. *v.i.* To become organic; to unite into an organic whole. **organizable,** *a.* **organization** (-zā′ shŭn), *n.* The act of organizing; the state of being organized; an organized system, body, or society. **organizational,** *a.* **organizer** (ôr′ gȧ nī zėr), *n.*

organo-, *comb. form.*

organogenesis, organogeny (ôr gȧ nō jen′ e sis, ôr gȧ noj′ e ni) *n.* (*Biol.*) The development of organs in animals and plants.

organography (ôr gȧ nog′ rȧ fi), *n.* A description of the organs of plants and animals. **organographist,** *n.*

organology (ôr gȧ nol′ ō ji), *n.* The branch of biology or physiology treating of the organs of the body. **organological,** *a.* **organologist,** *n.*

organonomy (ôr gȧ non′ ō mi), *n.* The science of the laws of organic life.

organoplastic (ôr gȧ nō plăs′ tik), *a.* Producing or evolving organic tissues. **organoplasty,** *n.*

organon (ôr′ gȧ non), *n.* A system of principles and rules of investigation, deduction, and demonstration regarded as an instrument of knowledge.

organotherapy (ôr gȧ nō thĕr′ ȧ pi), *n.* (*Med.*) The treatment of disease by the administration of one or more hormones in which the body is deficient.

organum, etc. [ORGANON].

organzine (ôr′ gȧn zēn) [F. *organsin*, It. *organzino*, etym. unknown], *n.* Silk thread made of several threads twisted together in a direction contrary to that of the strands, thrown silk; a fabric made therefrom.

orgasm (ôr′ găzm) [Gr. *orgaein*, to swell (for *-sm* cp. SPASM)], *n.* Immoderate excitement; a paroxysm of excitement or passion; (*Physiol.*) violent excitation and turgescence of an organ, as in sexual coition; the culminating excitement in the sexual act. **orgastic** (-găs′ tik), *a.*

orgeat (ôr′ jė ȧt, ôr zha) [F., from *orge*, L. *hordeum*, barley], *n.* A liquor made from barley or sweet almonds and orange-flower water.

orgies, etc. [ORGY].

***orgulous** (ôr′ gū lŭs) [O.F. *orguillus* (F. *orgueilleux*), from *orgueil*, pride, prob. from Teut.], *a.* Proud, haughty.

orgy (ôr′ ji) [orig. in pl. only, F. *orgeis*, L. and Gr. *orgia*], *n.* (*Gr. and Rom. Ant., usu. in pl.* **-gies**) Secret and licentious rites, the worship of Dionysus or Bacchus, etc.; a wild revel, a drunken carouse; (*pl.*) revelry, debauchery. **orgiastic** (-ăs′ tik), ***orgiastical,** *a.*

oriel (ôr′ i ėl) [O.F. *oriol*, etym. doubtful], *n.* A projecting polygonal recess with a window or windows, usu. built out from an upper story and supported on corbels or a pier. **oriel window:** The window of such a structure.

orient (ôr′ i ėnt) [F., from L. *orientem*, nom. *-ens*, pres.p. of *orīrī*, to rise], *n.* The East, the countries east of S. Europe and the Mediterranean; (*poet.*) the eastern sky; the peculiar lustre of a pearl of the finest quality; an orient pearl. *a.* (*poet.*) Rising, ascending, as the sun; (*poet.*) eastern, Oriental; bright, shining; lustrous, perfect, without a flaw (of pearls). *v.t.* (ôr′ i ėnt, ôr i ent′) To define the position of in respect to the east; to orientate. **oriency,** *n.* **Oriental** (ôr-, or i en′ tȧl), *a.* Situated in or pertaining to the East or the (esp. Asiatic) countries east of S. Europe and the Mediterranean; derived from or characteristic of the civilization, etc., of the East; (*poet.*) easterly, orient; excellent, precious (of pearls). *n.* A native or inhabitant of the East. **Orientalism,** *n.* An idiom or custom peculiar to the East; knowledge of Oriental languages and literature. **Orientalist,** *n.* **Orientality** (-tăl′ i ti), *n.* **orientalize,** *v.t.* and *i.* **orientalization** (-zā′ shŭn), *n.* **Orientally,** *adv.*

orientate (ôr i en′ tāt, ôr i ėn tāt′), *v.t.* To place (a church) so that the chancel points due east; to bury (a body) with feet towards the east; to determine the position of, with reference to the east and accordingly to all points of the compass; to find the bearings of; (*fig.*) to find or correct one's mental relations and principles. *v.i.* To turn or face towards the east. **orientation** (-tā′ shŭn), *n.* The act of orientating oneself; the determination of one's position, mental or physical, with regard to the surroundings. **orientator** (ōr′ i ėn tā tȯr), *n.* (*Surv.*) An instrument for orientating.

orifice (or′ i fis) [F., from late L. *orificium* (*ōs ōris*, mouth, *-facere*, to make)], *n.* An opening or aperture, as of a tube, etc.; a perforation, a mouth, a vent.

oriflamme (or′ i flăm) [F. (*or*, L. *aurum*, gold *flamme*, FLAME)], *n.* The ancient royal banner of France, orig. the red silk banderole of the Abbey of St. Denis handed to the early kings in setting out for war; (*fig.*) a symbol of lofty endeavour; a bright or glorious object.

origan (or′ i gȧn), **origanum** (ȯ rig′ ȧ nŭm) [F. *origan*, L. *origanum*, Gr. *origanon* (*oros*, mountain, *ganos*, brightness)], *n.* A plant of the genus *Origanum*, a genus of aromatic labiate herbs and shrubs comprising the wild marjoram.

origin (or′ i jin) [F. *origine*, L. *orīginem*, nom. *orīgo*, rel. to *orīrī*, to rise], *n.* Beginning, commencement, or rise (of anything); derivation, source; extraction, ancestry; ground, foundation, occasion. **originable**, *a.* **original** (ȯ rij′ i nȧl), *a.* Of or pertaining to the origin, beginning, or first stage; first, primary, primitive; initial, innate; not copied, not imitated, not produced by translation; fresh, novel; able to devise, produce, think, or act for oneself; inventive, creative. *n.* The pattern, the archetype, the first copy; that from which a work is copied or translated; the language in which a work is written; an eccentric person; *origin, derivation, cause, primitive stock, ancestry. **original sin:** The sin of Adam in eating the forbidden fruit; the innate depravity of man. **originality** (-năl′ i ti), *n.* **originally** (ȯ rij′ i nȧl i), *adv.* **originate**, *v.t.* To be the origin of; to cause to begin, to bring into existence. *v.i.* To rise, to begin; to have origin (in, from, or with). **origination** (-nā′ shŭn), *n.* **originative** (ȯ rij′ i nȧ tiv), *a.* **originator** (ȯ rij′ i nā tȯr), *n.* **originist**, *n.* One who holds definite views about the origin of the varieties of living things.

orinasal (ōr i nā′ zȧl) [L. *ōri-*, *ōs*, mouth, NASAL], *a.* Of or pertaining to or sounded by the mouth and nose. *n.* A vowel sounded both by mouth and nose, as the nasal vowels in French.

oriole (ōr′ i ōl) [med. L. *oriolus*, L. *aureolus*, from *aureus*, golden, from *aurum*, gold], *n.* A bird of the European genus *Oriolus*, esp. *O. galbula*, with bright-yellow and black plumage; a bird of the American genus *Icterus*, a hangbird.

Orion (ȯ rī′ ȯn) [L. and Gr., a giant in Gr. myth.], *n.* One of the best-known constellations, a group of stars representing a hunter with belt and sword. **Orion's belt:** A row of three bright stars across the middle of this constellation. **Orion's hound:** The star Sirius. **Orionid**, *n.* One of a system of meteors the radiant point of which is in Orion.

orismology (or iz mol′ ȯ ji) [Gr. *horismos*, definition, from *horizein*, to define, from *horos*, boundary], *n.* The branch of science concerned with definitions and the explanation of technical terms. **orismologic, -al** (ȯ riz mȯ loj′ ik, -ȧl), *a.*

orison (or′ i zȯn) [O.F. (F. *oraison*), from L. *ōrātiōnem*, nom. *-tio*, from *ōrāre*, to pray], *n.* A prayer, a supplication.

orle (ōrl) [F., from med. L. *orla*, dim. of *ora*, border], *n.* (*Her.*) A bearing in the form of a narrow band round the edge of a shield; *(*Arch.*) a fillet under the ovolo of a capital.

Orleans (ōr′ lė ȧnz) [city in France], *n.* A cloth of cotton and wool used for women's dresses; a kind of plum. **Orleanist**, *n.* (*Fr. Hist.*) An adherent of the branch of the French royal family descended from the Duke of Orleans, younger brother of Louis XIV, one of whom, Louis Philippe, reigned as King of the French (1830–48). *a.* Of or pertaining to this house. **Orleanism**, *n.* **Orleanistic** (-nis′ tik), *a.*

orlop (ōr′ lŏp) [Dut. *overloop*, a covering, rel. to *overloopen* (OVER, *loopen*, to run, see LEAP)], *n.* The lowest deck of a vessel having three or more decks.

ormer (ōr′ mėr) [Channel Is. var. of F. *ormier* (*oreille-de-mer*, sea-ear)], *n.* A sea-ear, esp. *Haliotis tuberculata*, an edible univalve.

ormolu (ōr′ mȯ loo) [F. *ormoulu* (*or*, gold, *moulu*, p.p. of *moudre*, to grind)], *n.* Orig. leaf-gold ground and used as a pigment for decorating furniture, etc.; a gold-coloured alloy of copper, zinc, and tin, used for cheap jewellery; (*collect.*) metallic ware, furniture, etc., decorated with this.

Ormuzd (ōr′ mŭzd) [Pers. *Ahura-mazdah*, the wise lord], *n.* The good principle in the Zoroastrian religious dualism, opp. to Ahriman.

ornament (ōr′ nȧ mėnt) [O.F. *ornement*, L. *ornāmentum*, from *ornāre*, to equip], *n.* A thing or part that adorns; an embellishment, a decoration; ornamentation; (*fig.*) a person, possession, or quality that reflects honour or credit; a mark of distinction, a badge; *furniture or accessories, esp. such as pertain to a church or worship. *v.t.* To adorn, to decorate, to embellish. **ornaments rubric:** The short rubric respecting the ornaments to be used in church immediately preceding the order for Morning and Evening Prayer in the Prayer Book. **ornamental** (-men′ tȧl), *a.* **ornamentalism**, *n.* **ornamentalist**, *n.* **ornamentally**, *adv.* **ornamentation** (-tā′ shŭn), *n.* **ornamenter**, *n.*

ornate (ōr nāt′) [L. *ornātus*, p.p. of *ornāre*, see prec.], *a.* Adorned, ornamented, richly embellished; florid, elaborately finished (of literary style, etc.). **ornately**, *adv.* **ornateness**, *n.*

ornery (ōr′ nėr i) [corr. of ORDINARY], *a.* (*Am. prov.*) Mean, low.

Ornithodelphia (ōr nith ō del′ fi a) [Gr. *delphus*, womb], *n.pl.* (*Zool.*) A sub-class of oviparous mammals comprising the *Monotremata*. **ornithodelphian, ornithodelphic, ornithodelphid, ornithodelphous**, *a.*

ornithology (ōr ni thol′ ō ji), *n.* The branch of zoology dealing with birds. **ornithological**, *a.* **ornithologist**, *n.*

ornithopter (ōr ni thop′ tėr), *n.* (*Aviat.*) An aeroplane driven by power supplied by the aviator and not by an engine.

ornithorhyncus (ōr nith ō ring′ kŭs) [Gr. *rhunchos*, a bill], *n.* (*Zool.*) A genus of monotremes containing the duck-billed platypus; the duck-billed platypus, an Australian aquatic oviparous mammal.

ornithoscopy (ōr ni thos′ kō pi), *n.* Observation of birds for purposes of divination.

orogenesis (o rō jen′ e sis) [Gr. *oros*, a mountain], *n.* The process of forming mountains.

orography (o rog′ rȧ fi), *n.* The branch of physical geography treating of mountains and mountain systems. **orographic**, *a.*

orohippus (o rō hip′ ŭs) [Gr. *hippos*, a horse], *n.* (*Palæont.*) Fossil quadruped considered to be the ancestor of the horse.

oroide (ōr′ oid) [F. *or*, L. *aurum*, gold, -OID], *n.* An alloy of copper and zinc, resembling gold in appearance, used for cheap jewellery.

orometer (o′ ro me tėr), *n.* An instrument for measuring the height of mountains.

oropesa float (or o pē′ zȧ flōt), *n.* (*Naut.*) A float used in mine-sweeping to support the sweeping wire between two trawlers.

orotund (or′ ȯ tŭnd) [L. *ore rotundo*, lit. with round mouth], *a.* Characterized by fullness and resonance; rich and musical (said of the voice and utterance); pompous, magniloquent, inflated. *n.* Orotund quality of voice.

orphan (ōr fȧn) [late L. *orphanus*, Gr. *orphanos*, destitute, bereaved, from *orphus* (cp. L. *orbus*)], *n.*

A child bereft of one parent, or of both. *a.* Bereft of one parent, or of both. **orphanage,** *n.* Orphan condition; an institution for bringing up orphans. **orphaned,** *a.* **orphanhood, orphanism,** *n.* **orphanize,** *v.t.*

Orphean (ôr fē′ ȧn) [L. *Orphēus*, Gr. *Orpheios*], *a.* Pertaining to Orpheus, a celebrated mythical musician of Thrace, or his music; melodious, enchanting. **Orphic** (ôr′ fik), *a.* Pertaining to Orpheus or the mysteries supposed to be founded by him; oracular, mysterious. **Orphism,** *n.*

orphrey (ôr′ frā, -fri) [M.E. and O.F. *orfreis*, med. L. *aurifrisium*, L. *auriphrygium* (*aurum*, gold, *Phrygium*, Phrygian)], *n.* A band of gold and silver embroidery decorating an ecclesiastical vestment.

orpiment (ôr′ pi mėnt) [O.F., from L. *auripigmentum* (*aurum*, gold, PIGMENT)], *n.* (*Min.*) Native yellow trisulphide of arsenic, used as a pigment and a dye-stuff.

orpine (ôr′ pin) [F. *orpin*, corr. of prec.], *n.* A fleshy-leaved plant, *Sedum telephium*, of the stonecrop family, with purple flowers; orpiment.

Orpington (ôr′ ping tȯn) [village in W. Kent], *n.* A variety of domestic fowl.

orra (or′ ȧ) [Sc., etym. unknown], *a.* Odd, extra, left over; incidental; disreputable, low.

orrery (or′ ėr i) [4th Earl of *Orrery* (1676–1731), for whom one of the first was made], *n.* A contrivance for illustrating the motions, magnitudes, and positions of the planetary system.

orris (1) (or′ is) [prob. corr. of IRIS], *n.* A kind of iris. **orris-root,** *n.* The root of one of three species of iris, used as a perfume and in medicine. **orris-powder,** *n.*

orris (2) (or′ is) [contr. of ORPHREY], *n.* Varieties of gold and silver lace.

ort (ôrt) [late M.E. *ortes*, pl., cp. Dut. *oor-aete* (*oor-*, not, *etan*, to eat, cogn. with A.-S. *æt*, food)], *n.* (*usu. in pl.*) Refuse, fragments, odds and ends, leavings.

ortho- [Gr. *orthos*, straight], *comb. form.*

orthocephalic (ôr thō se făl′ ik), *a.* (*Craniology*) Having a breadth of skull from 70 to 75 per cent of the length, between brachycephalic and dolichocephalic.

orthochromatic (ôr thō krō măt′ ik), *a.* (*Phot.*) Giving the correct values of colours in relations of light and shade.

orthoclase (ôr′ thō klās) [Gr. *klasis*, cleavage], *n.* (*Min.*) Common or potash feldspar having a rectangular cleavage.

orthodiagraph (ôr thō dī′ ȧ grăf), *n.* (*Med.*) An instrument which procures an exact outline of an internal organ, or of foreign matter in the body, by means of X-rays. **orthodontia,** *n.* (*Med.*) The correct alinement of irregular teeth.

orthodox (ôr′ thȯ doks) [F. *orthodoxe*, late L. *orthodoxus*, Gr. *orthodoxos* (ORTHO-, *doxa*, opinion)], *n.* Holding right or accepted views, esp. in matters of faith and religious doctrine; in accordance with sound or accepted doctrine; approved, accepted, conventional, not heretical, heterodox, or original. **Orthodox Church:** The Eastern or Greek Church, officially styled, the Holy Orthodox Catholic Apostolic Oriental Church. ***orthodoxal, *orthodoxical,** *a.* **orthodoxly, *orthodoxically,** *adv.* **orthodoxy, *orthodoxness,** *n.*

orthodromic (ôr thȯ drom′ ik) [Gr. *dromos*, course], *a.* Pertaining to orthodromics. **orthodromics, orthodromy** (-thod′ rȯ mi), *n.* The art of sailing in the arc of some great circle the shortest distance between any two points on the surface of the globe.

orthoepy (ôr thō ĕ′ pi, ôr thō′ ė pi) [Gr. *epos*, a word], *n.* The branch of grammar dealing with pronunciation, phonology; correct speech or pronunciation. **orthoepic, -al,** *a.* **orthoepically,** *adv.* **orthoepist,** *n.*

orthogamy (ôr thog′ ȧ mi), *n.* (*Bot.*) Direct or immediate fertilization.

orthogenesis (ôr thō jen′ e sis), *n.* (*Biol.*) A theory of evolution that postulates that variation is determined by the action of environment.

orthognathous (ôr thog′ nȧ thŭs), *a.* (*Craniology*) Straight-jawed, having little forward projection of the jaws. **orthognathic,** *a.* **orthognathism,** *n.*

orthogon (ôr′ thō gon) [Gr. *gonia*, corner, angle], *n.* A rectangular figure; a right-angled triangle. **orthogonal,** *a.* **orthogonally,** *adv.*

orthography (ôr thog′ rȧ fi) [O.F. *ortographie*, L. and Gr. *orthographia* (ORTHO-, -GRAPHY)], *n.* Correct spelling that part of grammar which deals with letters and spelling; mode of spelling as regards correctness and incorrectness; the art of drawing plans, elevations, etc., in accurate projection, as if the object were seen from an infinite distance. **orthographer, -phist** (ôr thog′ rȧ fėr, -fist), *n.* **orthographic, -al** (-grăf′ ik, -ȧl), *a.* **orthographically,** *adv.* **orthology** (ôr thol′ ō ji), *n.* The right use of symbols; the normative science of language. **orthological,** *a.*

orthometry (ôr thom′ e tri), *n.* The art of correct versification. **orthometric,** *a.*

orthopædy (ôr′ thȯ pē di) [F. *orthopédie* (Gr. *paideia*, rearing of children, from *pais paidos*, child)], *n.* (*Surg.*) The act or art of curing deformities, esp. in children. **orthopædic** (-pē′ dik), *a.* **orthopædics,** *n.* Orthopædy. **orthopædist,** *n.*

orthopnœa (ôr thop nē′ ȧ) [L., from Gr. *orthopnoia* (*pnoē*, breathing)], *n.* (*Path.*) Difficulty of breathing except in an upright posture, a form of asthma. **orthopnoic** (-nō′ ik), *a.*

orthopraxy (ôr′ thō prăk si) [Gr. *praxis*, doing], *n.* Orthodox procedure or behaviour, correct practice.

Orthoptera (ôr thop′ tėr ȧ) [Gr. *pteron*, wing], *n.pl.* (*Ent.*) An order of insects with two pairs of wings, the hind wings membranous and those in front coriaceous and usually straight. **orthopteral, -ous,** *a.* **orthopteran,** *a.* and *n.*

orthoptic (ôr thop′ tik), *a.* Relating to correct vision with both eyes; (*Math.*) referring to tangents that intersect at right angles. *n.* A perforated disk on the backsight of a fire-arm used in aiming.

orthorhombic (ôr thȯ rom′ bik), *a.* (*Cryst.*) Having three planes of dissimilar symmetry at right angles to each other.

orthoscope (ôr′ thō skōp), *n.* An instrument for examining the interior of the eye, the refraction of the cornea being corrected by a body of water. **orthoscopic** (ôr thō skop′ ik), *a.* Having correct vision, seeing correctly.

orthotone (ôr′ thō tōn), *a.* (*Gr. grammar*) Having its own accent, independently accented. *n.* An orthotone word. **orthotonic,** *a.*

orthotropal, orthotropous (ôr thot′ rop al, or thot′ rop us) [Gr. *tropos*, turning], *a.* (*Bot.*) Turned or growing straight (of ovules, embryos, etc.). **orthotropic,** *a.* Growing vertically upwards or downwards. **orthotropism,** *n.*

orthotypous (ôr thot′ i pus), *a.* (*Min.*) Having a perpendicular cleavage.

ortolan (ôr′ tȯ lȧn) [F., from It. *ortolano*, earlier *hortolano*, gardener, L. *hortulānus*, from *hortulus*, dim. of *hortus*, garden], *n.* A small bunting, *Emberiza hortulana*, the garden bunting or ortolan bunting, esteemed as a delicacy; applied to several W. Indian and American birds.

***Orvietan** (ôr vi ē′ tȧn) [*Orvieto* in Italy, -AN], *n.* A compound of treacle formerly used as an antidote to poison.

-ory (1) [A.F. *-orie*, L. *-ōrium*, *-ōria*, from adjectives in *-ōrius*], *suf.* Denoting place where or instrument, as in *dormitory*, *lavatory*, *refectory*. (2) [O. North.F. *-ori*, *-orie*, L. *-ōrius*, *-ōria*, *-ōrium*]. Forming adjectives, as *amatory*, *admonitory*, *illusory*.

***oryctics** (ŏ rik′ tiks) [Gr. *oruktikos*, pertaining to digging, from *oruktos*, dug up], *n.pl.* The branch of geology concerned with fossils. **orycto-**, *comb. form.* ***oryctography** (-tog′ ră fi) [-GRAPHY], *n.* Descriptive mineralogy. ***oryctology** (-tol′ ŏ ji) [-LOGY], *n.* The science of fossils, now divided into geology, petrology, mineralogy, and palæontology. **oryctozoology** (-zō ol′ ŏ ji) [ZOOLOGY], *n.* The science dealing with fossil animal remains.

oryx (or′ iks) [L., from Gr. *orux*], *n.* A genus of straight-horned African antelopes.

oryza (o rī za) [Gr. *oruza*, rice], *n.* (*Bot.*) A tropical genus of grasses comprising *Oryza sativa*, rice.

os (os) [L.], *n.* (*pl. ossa*) (*Anat.*) A bone.

Oscan (os′ kăn) [L. *Oscī*, -AN], *n.* One of an ancient Italian people; their language. *a.* Pertaining to this people or their language.

Oscar (os′ kar) [?], *n.* (*Cinema.*) A gold-plated statuette awarded by the American Academy of Motion Picture Arts & Sciences to the actor, director, film-writer, etc., whose work is adjudged the best of the year; (*Austral. slang*) money.

oscillate (os′ i lāt) [L. *oscillātus*, p.p. of *oscillāre*, from *oscillum*, a swing, orig. a little mask of Bacchus suspended from a tree, dim. of *osculum*, dim. of *ōs*, mouth], *v.i.* To swing, to move like a pendulum; to vibrate; to fluctuate, to vacillate, to vary. **oscillation** (-lā′ shŭn), *n.* The movement of oscillation; (*Radio.*) the generating of alternating currents in a resonant circuit, *e.g.* by thermionic valves. **oscillation valve,** *n.* Anything that acts as an electrical valve and produces continuous oscillations. **oscillative, -tory** (os′ i lā tiv, -tŏr i), *a.* **oscillator,** *n.* **local oscillator,** *n.* (*Radio.*) An oscillator which generates oscillations in a receiver for heterodyne reception. **oscillograph** (os′ i lŏ grăf), *n.* (*Elec.*) A device for giving a visible representation of the oscillations of an electric current. **oscillogram,** *n.* **oscillometer** (-lom′ ĕ tĕr), *n.* An instrument for measuring the roll of a ship at sea. **oscilloscope** (o sil′ ō skōp), *n.* (*Elec.*) An instrument which records the oscillations of an alternating current; an instrument to facilitate the detection of vibrations and other faults in machinery.

***oscitant** (os′ i tănt) [L. *oscitans -ntem*, pres.p. of *oscitāre*, to gape (*ōs*, mouth, *citāre*, to move)], *a.* Yawning, sleepy; dull, negligent. ***oscitancy,** *n.* ***oscitantly,** *adv.* ***oscitate,** *v.i.* ***oscitation** (-tā shŭn), *n.*

osculate (os′ kū lāt) [L. *osculātus*, p.p. of *osculārī*, to kiss, from *osculum*, dim. of *ōs*, mouth], *v.t.* ***To** kiss; (*Geom.*) to touch by osculation. *v.i.* To kiss; (*Geom.*) to touch each other by osculation; (*Nat. Hist.*) to come into contact with through having characters in common or through an intermediate species, etc. **osculant,** *a.* **osculation** (-lā′ shŭn), *n.* **osculatory** (os′-), *a.* Kissing; (*Geom.*) osculating. *n.* A tablet or board on which a sacred picture is painted, to be kissed by the priest and people during Mass.

oscule (os′ kūl) [L., OSCULUM, dim. of *ōs*, mouth], *n.* A small mouth or bilabiate opening. **osculum,** *n.* (*pl.* **-la**).

-ose (1) [L. *-ōsus*], *suf.* Denoting fulness, abundance, as in *gradiose, jocose, verbose*; (2) [after GLUCOSE], (*Chem.*) denoting the carbohydrates and isomeric compounds.

osier (ō′ zhi ĕr, -zĕr) [F., from L. *ausāria, ōsāria*, willow-bed], *n.* A species of willow, *Salix viminalis*, the pliable shoots of which are used for basket-making. **osier-bed, -holt,** *n.* ***osiered,** *a.*

-osis [Gr. *-ōsis*, suf. forming nouns from verbs in *-oein*], *suf.* Denoting condition, esp. morbid states, as *chlorosis, necrosis.*

-osity [F. *-osité*, L. *-ōsitātem*, nom. *-ōsitas* (-OSE, -OUS, -TY)], *suf.* Forming nouns from adjectives in -OSE or -OUS, as *grandiosity, luminosity.*

Osmanli (os măn′ li) [Turk. *osmānli*, from *Osman* or Othman I, founder of the Turkish empire], *a* and *n.* Ottoman.

osmazome (os′ mā zōm) [Gr. *osme*, a smell; *zomos* broth], *n.* (*Chem.*) The portion of the aqueou product of meat in which are found those con stituents of the flesh which decide its taste an smell.

osmium (os′-, oz′ mi ŭm) [Gr. *osmē*, smell (fron the disagreeable smell of the oxide), -IUM], *n* (*Chem.*) A metallic element, usu. found in associa tion with platinum. **osmic, -mious,** *a.* **osmit** (-mīt), *n.* **osmo-,** *comb. form.*

osmose (os′-, oz′ mōs), **osmosis** (-mō′ sis) [Gr *ōsmos*, push, thrust, from *ōthein*, to push], *n.* Th diffusion of a solvent through a semi-permeabl membrane into a more concentrated solution **osmograph, osmometer** (-mom′ ĕ tĕr), *n.* A instrument for measuring osmotic pressures **osmotic** (-mot′ ik), *a.* **osmotically,** *adv.*

osmund (oz′-, os′ mŭnd) [A.F. *osmunde*, O.F *osmonde*, etym. unknown], *n.* The flowering ferr *Osmunda regalis*, also called the royal fern or th king fern.

osnaburg (oz′ na bĕrg) [Osnaburg, in Germany], *n* A coarse kind of linen.

osprey (os′ prā) [ult. from L. *ossifraga* (*os ossi* bone, *frag-*, stem of *frangere*, to break)], *n.* A large bird, *Pandion haliaëtus*, preying on fish, als known as the sea-eagle or sea-hawk; an egret plum used for trimming hats and bonnets (a term use erroneously by milliners).

ossein (os′ ĕn) [as foll.], *n.* The gelatinous tissu left when mineral matter is eliminated from a bon

osselet (os′ e let), *n.* An ossicle; the cuttle-bone c cephalopods.

osseous (os′ ĕ ŭs) [L. *osseus*, from *os ossis*, bone], Of the nature of or like bone, bony; consisting bone, ossified; containing or abounding in foss bones. **ossa** [OS]. **ossein,** *n.* (*Chem.*) Th gelatinous tissue left when mineral matter is elim inated from bone.

Ossianic (os i ăn′ ik) [*Ossian*, Gael. *Oisin*, -IC], Pertaining or relating to Ossian, the legendar Celtic poet.

ossicle (os′ i kĕl), *n.* (*Anat.*) A small bone; a bon calcareous, or chitonous part or process in variou animals.

ossiferous (o sif′ ĕr ŭs), *a.* Containing or yieldin bones (of cave deposits, etc.).

ossifrage [OSPREY].

ossify (os′ i fī), *v.t.i.* To turn into bone, to becom bone.

ossuary (os′ ū ă ri), *n.* A charnel-house; a bon urn; a deposit of bones (as in a cave).

osteal (os′ tĕ ăl) [Gr. *oste-on*, bone], *a.* Osseou bony, sounding like bone (of sounds produced b percussion of bones). **ostealgia** (os tē ăl′ jă), (*Path.*) Pain in a bone. **ostein,** *n.* Ossein. **osteit** (os tĕ ī′ tis) [-ITIS], *n.* (*Path.*) Inflammation bone. **osteitic, ostitic** (-it′-, -tit′ ik), *a.* **oste logy** (os tē ol′ ō ji), *n.* (*Anat.*) The study of bone

ostensible (os ten′ sibl) [F., from L. *ostens-*, p. stem of *ostendere*, to show (*os-*, OB-, *tendere*, stretch)], *a.* Put forward for show or to hide t reality; professed, pretended, seeming. **ostensib** *adv.* **ostension,** *n.* (*R.-C. Ch.*) The uplifting holding forth of the Host for public adoratio **ostensive,** *a.* Exhibiting, showing; ostensib (*Log.*) setting forth a general principle obviou including the proposition to be proved. **oste sively,** *adv.* **ostensory** (os ten′ sŏ ri), *n.* (*R.- Ch.*) A monstrance. ***ostent** (os tent′), *n.* Sho manifestation, appearance; a portent, a prodig **ostentation** (-tā′ shŭn), *n.* Pretentious or an bitious display; parade, pomp; *a show, a pagear **ostentatious,** *a.* **ostentatiously,** *adv.* **ostent tiousness,** *n.*

osteo- [Gr. *osteon*, bone], *comb. form.*

osteoblast (os′ ti ō blast) [Gr. *blastos*, bud], *n.* (*Biol.*) A cell concerned in the development of bone.

osteoclasis (os ti ō klā′ sis), *n.* (*Surg.*) The operation of breaking a bone to remedy a deformity, etc. **osteoclast**, *n.*

osteocolla (os ti ō kol′ ȧ) [Gr. *kolla*, glue], *n.* An incrustation of carbonate of lime on the roots and stems of plants growing in sandy ground; an inferior kind of glue obtained from bones.

osteoid (os′ ti oid), *a.* Like bone.

osteology (os ti ol′ ō ji), *n.* The branch of anatomy treating of bones, osseous tissue, etc.; the bony structure of an animal. **osteologic**, *a.* **osteologist**, *n.*

osteomalacia (os ti ō mȧ lā′ shi a) [Gr. *malakia*, softness], *n.* (*Path.*) Softening of the bones.

osteomyelitis (os ti ō mī ė lī′ tis), *n.* Inflammation of the marrow of the bones.

osteopathy (os ti op′ ȧ thi), *n.* (*Med.*) A method of treating diseases by eliminating structural derangement by manipulation, mainly of the spinal column. **osteopath** (os′ ti o path), *n.* A practitioner of oestopathy.

osteophone (os′ ti ō fōn), *n.* An audiphone.

osteoplasty (os′ ti ō plăs ti), *n.* (*Surg.*) Transplantation of bone with its periosteum. **osteoplastic**, *a.*

osteosarcoma (os ti ō sar kō mȧ), *n.* (*Path.*) A disease of the bones due to the growth of medullary or cartilaginous matter within them.

osteotome (os′ ti ō tōm), *n.* (*Surg.*) An instrument used in the dissection of bones. **osteotomy**, *n.*

ostitis [OSTEITIS].

ostium (os′ ti ŭm) [L.], *n.* (*Anat.*) The mouth or opening of a passage. **ostiole**, *n.* (*Bot.*) A small opening in the perithecia of fungi, etc. **ostiolar** (-tī′ ō lar), **ostiolate** (os′ ti ō lāt), *a.*

ostler (os′ lėr) [orig. *hostler* (HOSTEL, -ER)], *n.* A man who looks after horses at an inn, a stableman; *an inn-keeper.

ostracean (os trā′ sė ȧn) [Gr. *ostrakeos*, from *ostrakon*, tile, potsherd, oyster-shell], *n.* Any mollusc of the family *Ostracea*, a family of bivalves containing the oysters. *a.* Pertaining to the *Ostracea*. **ostraceous** (-trā′ shŭs), *a.* **ostracite** (os′ trȧ sīt), *n.* (*Palæont.*) A fossil shell of a species related to the oyster.

ostracize (os′ trȧ sīz) [Gr. *ostrakizein*, as prec.]. *v.t.* (*Gr. Ant.*) To banish by a popular vote recorded on a potsherd or shell; to exclude from society, to ban, to send to Coventry. **ostracism**, *n.*

ostraco- [Gr. *ostracon*, see foll.], *comb. form.*

ostreo- [L. *ostrea*, *ostreum*, Gr. *ostreon*, oyster], *comb. form.* **ostreiculture** (os′ trė i kŭl tūr), *n.* The artificial breeding of oysters. **ostreophagous** (-of′ ȧ gŭs), *a.* Eating or feeding on oysters.

ostrich (os′ trich) [M.E. *ostrice*, O.F. *ostruce*, pop. L. *avis strūthio* (*avis*, bird, late L. *strūthio*, Gr. *strouthiōn*, from *strouthos*)], *n.* A large African and Arabian bird, *Struthio camelus*, having rudimentary wings, but capable of running with great speed, and greatly valued for its feathers, which are used as plumes. **ostrich-farm**, *n.* **ostrich policy**, *n.* (*fig.*) A shutting of one's eyes to facts. **ostrich-tip**, *n.* The end of an ostrich-feather.

Ostrogoth (os′ trō goth) [late L. *Ostrogothī*, pl. (cp. O.S. *ōstar*, eastward, GOTH)], *n.* An eastern Goth, one of the division of the Gothic race who conquered Italy in the 5th cent. **ostrogothic** (-goth′ ik), *a.*

ot-, oto- [Gr. *ous ōtos*, ear]. ***otacoustic** (ō tȧ kou′ stik, -koo′ stik) [ACOUSTIC], *a.* Assisting the sense of hearing. *n.* An instrument to assist the hearing. ***otacousticon**, *n.* **otalgia** (ō tăl′ ji ȧ) [Gr. *algos*, pain], *n.* (*Path.*) Ear-ache.

otarian (ō târ′ i ȧn) [Gr. *otaros*, large-eared], *a.* Of or pertaining to the *Otariidæ*, a genus of pinipeds with external ears, including the fur-seals and sealions. **otariid**, *n.* **otaroid, otarine.**

other (ŭth′ ėr) [A.-S. *ōther* (cp. Dut. and G. *ander*, Icel. *annarr*, Swed. *andra*, Sansk. *antaras*, L. *alter*)], *a.* Not the same as one specified or implied; different, distinct in kind; alternative, additional, extra; second, only remaining (of two alternatives); opposite, contrary. *n.* and *pron.* An or the other person, thing, example, instance, etc. *adv.* Otherwise. **every other** [EVERY]. **the other day** [DAY]. ***othergates, otherguess**, *adv.* Otherwise. *a.* Of another kind. ***otherguise**, *a.* Other. *adv.* Otherwise. **otherness**, *n.* **otherwhence**, *adv.* From elsewhere. **otherwhere, -wheres**, *adv.* (*poet.*) Elsewhere. **other-while, -whiles**, *adv.* **otherwise**, *adv.* In a different way or manner; in other respects; by or from other causes; in quite a different state. **conj.* Else, or; but for this. **other world:** The future life; (*Myth.*) a world existing outside of or in a different mode from this; fairy-land. **otherworld**, *a.* Interested or concerned only with the future life. **otherworldly**, *a.* **otherworldliness**, *n.*

otic (ō′ tik) [Gr. *ōtikos*, from *ous ōtos*, ear], *a.* (*Anat.*) Pertaining to the ear.

-otic [Gr. *ōtikos*, formed on the same stems as -OSIS], *suf.* Forming adjectives corresponding to nouns in -OSIS, as *neurotic*, *osmotic*.

otiose (ō′ shi ōs) [L. *ōtiōsus*, from *ōtium*, leisure], *a.* Not wanted, useless, superfluous; futile, sterile; *at leisure, unemployed, lazy. **otiosely**, *adv.* **otioseness**, *n.*

otitis (ō tī′ tis), *n.* (*Path.*) Inflammation of the ear.

otolith (ō′ tō lith), *n.* An ear-stone or calcareous concretion found in the inner ear of vertebrates and some invertebrates.

otology (ō tol′ ō ji), *n.* The science of the ear or of diseases of the ear; anatomy of the ear; a treatise on the ear. **otologist**, *n.*

otorrhoea (ō tō rē′ ȧ), *n.* Purulent discharge from the ear.

otoscope (ō′ tō skōp), *n.* An instrument for inspecting the ear and ear-drum.

ottava rima (ō tȧ′ vȧ rē′ mȧ) [It., octave rhyme], *n.* (*Pros.*) A form of versification consisting of stanzas of eight lines, of which the first six rhyme alternately, and the last two form a couplet (as in Byron's *Don Juan*).

otter (ot′ ėr) [A.-S. *oter ottor* (cp. Dut. and G. *otter*, Icel. *otr*), cogn. with Gr. *hudra*, water-snake, *hudōr*, water], *n.* A furred, web-footed aquatic mammal of the genus *Lutra*, esp. *L. vulgaris*, a European animal feeding exclusively on fish; the fur of this; the sea-otter; a device for catching fish consisting usu. of a float armed with hooks. **otter-dog, -hound**, *n.* A variety of dog used for hunting otters.

otto [ATTAR].

Ottoman (1) (ot′ ō mȧn) [F., ult. from Arab. *Othmān*, Turk. *Osmān*, see OSMANLI], *a.* Of or pertaining to the dynasty of Othman or Osman I; pertaining to the Turks. *n.* A Turk. ***Ottomite**, *n.*

ottoman (2) (ot′ ō mȧn) [F. *ottomane*, as prec.], *n.* A cushioned seat or sofa without back or arms, introduced from Turkey.

oubit (oo′ bit), **woobut** (woo′ bŭt) [perh. from A.-S. *wibba*, beetle, or *wull*, WOOL], *n.* A hairy caterpillar.

oubliette (oo bli et′) [F., from *oublier*, to forget], *n.* An underground dungeon in which persons condemned to perpetual imprisonment or secret death were confined.

***ouch** (ouch) [O.F. *nouche* (cp. ADDER, APRON), late L. *nusca*, O.H.G. *nusche*, prob. of Celtic orig.], *n.* A clasp or buckle; a clasped necklace, etc., the setting of a gem.

ought (1) (awt) [A.-S. *āhte*, past of *āgan*, to possess, to OWE], *v.aux.* To be found in duty or rightness, to be necessary, fit, or proper; to behove. *n.* Duty, obligation. **oughtness**, *n.* (*rare*).

ought (2) (awt) (*vulg.*) [NAUGHT].

ouija (wē′ ja) [F. *oui*, yes; G. *ja*, yes], *n.* A board incribed with the letters of the alphabet, used for receiving messages, etc., in spiritualistic manifestations.

ouistiti [WISTITI].

ounce (1) (ouns) [O.F. *unce* (F. *once*), L. *uncia* (cp. INCH)], *n.* A unit of weight; the twelfth part of a pound troy, and sixteenth part of a pound avoirdupois; (*fig.*) a small quantity.

ounce (2) (ouns) [O.F. *once* (*l'once*), *lonce*, It. *lonza*, L. *lyncea*, LYNX (cp. ADDER, APRON)], *n.* A lynx or other leopard-like animal; (*Zool.*) the mountain-panther, *Felis uncia*, of S. and Central Asia, also called the snow leopard.

our (our) [A.-S. *ūre*, orig. gen. pl. of *ūs*, US (cp. G. *unser*, Goth. *unsar*)], *a.* Of, pertaining to or belonging to us; used instead of 'my' by royalty, editors, reviewers, etc. **ours** (ourz), *pred.a.* Belonging to us. *n.* That or those belonging to **us**; our regiment or corps. **of ours:** Belonging to our regiment.

-our [-OR], *suf.* Forming nouns, as *amour*, *ardour*, *clamour* (Am. usage drops the **u**).

ourang-outang [ORANG-OUTANG].

ouranography, etc. [URANO-].

ourie (our′ i, oor′ i) [Sc., cp. Icel. *ūrig*, from *ūr*, drizzle], *a.* Shivering, chilly; dreary, depressed, dejected.

ourology, etc. [URINO-]. **ours** [OUR].

ourself (our self′), *pron.* (*pl.* **-selves,** or **-self** when a sovereign) Myself (used in regal or formal style); (*pl.*) we, not others, we alone (usu. in apposition with *we*); (*reflex.*) the persons previously alluded to as we.

ous [O.F. *-ous*, *-os*, *-us* (F. *-eux*), L. *-ōsus* (cp. -OSE)], *suf.* Full of, abounding in; (*Chem.*) denoting a compound having more of the element indicated in the stem than those whose names end in -IC; as *dubious*, *glorious*, *nitrous*, *sulphurous*.

ousel [OUZEL].

oust (oust) [O.F. *oster* (*F. ôter*), to take away, etym. doubtful], *v.t.* To eject, to expel, to turn out (from); to dispossess, to deprive (of); *to take away, to deprive. **ouster,** *n.* (*Law*) Ejectment, dispossession; one who ousts.

out (out) [A.-S. *ūt*, whence *ūte*, away, abroad, *ūtan*, from outside (cp. Dut. *uit*, Icel. *ūt*, G. *aus*)], *adv.* From the inside or within; not in, not within; from among; forth or away; not at home, not in office; not engaged or employed; on strike; (*Cricket*) not batting; dismissed from the wicket; (*Boxing*) denoting defeat through inability to rise within the ten seconds allowed after being knocked down; not in fashion; not in practice; in error, wrong; at a loss; at odds, not in agreement; not to be thought of; so as to be visible, audible, revealed, published, etc.; introduced to society; to end or conclusion, completely, thoroughly. *prep.* (*colloq.*) From inside of. *n.* (*usu. in pl.*) Those out of office, the opposition; an outing; (*Print.*) an omission, matter omitted. *a.* External; outlying, remote, distant; played away from the home ground (of a cricket match). *int.* (*ellipt.*). Begone! away! an expression of impatience, anger, or abhorrence. *v.t.* *To turn out, to expel; to knock out, to disable. **all out:** Striving to the uttermost. **from out:** (*poet.*) Out of. **murder will out:** The guilt will be disclosed; the secret is bound to be revealed. **out and about:** Able to get up and go outside. **out and away** [AWAY]. **out and out:** Completely, unreservedly. **out-and-outer,** *n.* (*slang*) A thorough-going person. **out at elbows** [ELBOW]. **outback,** *n.*, *a.* and *adv.* (*Austral.*) The Australian back settlements or hinterland, and pertaining thereto. **out-breeding,** *ger.* Breeding from parents not related by kinship ties. **out for:** Striving for. **out of:** From the inside of; from among; beyond the reach of; without; denoting deprivation or want. **out of date** [DATE (1)]. **out-of-door:** Outdoor. **out of hand** [HAND]. **out of it:** Not included, neglected; at a loss; in error, mistaken. **out of one's head:** Delirious. **out of one's time:** Having served one's apprenticeship. **out of print:** Not on sale by the publisher (of books). **out of sorts:** Indisposed, unwell. **out of temper:** Irritated, vexed. **out of the way:** Unusual; remote. **out of trim:** Not in good order. **outness,** *n.* Externality, objectivity, separateness from the perceiving mind.

out- [prec.], *pref.* Out, towards the outside, external; from within, forth; separate, detached, at a distance; denoting issue or result; expressing excess, exaggeration, superiority, surpassing, defeating, enduring, getting through or beyond. **outact** (out ăkt′), *v.t.* To exceed in action, to excel, to outdo. **outask** (out ask′), *v.t.* (*prov.*) To publish the banns of for the last time. **outback,** *n.* (*Austral.*) The hinterland, the bush, the interior. **outbalance** (out băl′ ȧns), *v.t.* To outweigh, to exceed. **outbargain** (out bar′ gȧn), *v.t.* To get the better of in a bargain. **outbid** (out bid′), *v.t.* (*past* **-bad, -bade,** *p.p.* **-bidden**) To bid more than; to outdo by offering more. **outbluster** (out blŭs′ tėr), *v.t.* To silence, worst, or get the better of by blustering. **outboard** (out′ bôrd), *a.* (*Naut.*) Situated on or directed towards the outside of a ship; (*Naut.*) having an engine and propeller outside the boat. *adv.* Out from a ship's side or away from the centre. **outbound** (out bound′), *v.t.* To leap farther than, to overleap. **out-bound** (out′ bound), *a.* Outward bound. ***out-bounds** (out′ boundz), *n.pl.* The outer bounds (the utmost limits). **outbrag** (out brăg′), *v.t.* To outdo in bragging; *to excel, to surpass. **outbrave** (out brāv′), *v.t.* To surpass in bravery, beauty, splendour, etc.; to stand up against defiantly. **outbreak** (out′ brāk), **-breaking,** *n.* A sudden bursting forth, an eruption; a riot or insurrection. **outbreaker,** *n.* A breaker far from the shore. **out-breathe** (out brēth′), *v.t.* To breathe out; to exhaust, to wear out; *v.i.* To be exhaled. **outbudding** (out′ bŭd ing), *n.* A budding out, a bursting forth. **out-building** (out′ bil ding), *n.* A detached building, an outhouse. **outburn** (out bĕrn′), *v.i.* To burn out, to be consumed; *v.t.* To burn longer than. **outburst** (out′ bĕrst), *n.* An outbreak, an explosion; an outcry. **outby, -bye** (out bī′), *adv.* (*Sc.*) Outside, abroad; to the outside. **outcast** (out′ kast), *a.* Rejected, cast out; exiled; *n.* A castaway, a vagabond; an exile. **outclass** (out klas′), *v.t.* (*colloq.*) To be of a superior class, kind or qualifications than; to surpass as a competitor. **out-clearing** (out′ klēr ing), *n.* (*Banking*) The sending out of cheques, bills, etc., drawn on other banks to the Clearing House; the total amount thus standing to the account of a bank. **outcome** (out′ kŭm), *n.* Issue, result, consequence, effect. **outcraft** (out kraft′), *v.t.* To excel in cunning. **outcrop** (out′ krop), *n.* (*Geol.*) The exposure of a stratum at the surface; *v.i.* (out krop′) To crop out at the surface. **outcry** (out′ krī), *n.* A vehement or loud cry; noise, clamour; *a public auction; *v.t.* (out′ krī′) To cry louder than. **outdare** (out dâr′), *v.t.* To exceed in daring; to defy. **outdistance** (out dis′ tȧns), *v.t.* To outstrip. **outdo** (out doo′), *v.t.* To excel, to surpass. **outdoor** (out′ dôr), *a.* Living, existing, being, happening, etc., out of doors or in the open air. **outdoors** (out dôrz′), *adv.* In the open air, out of the house. ***outdwell** (out dwel′), *v.t.* To stay beyond one's time. **outdweller,** *n.* One who lives outside of or beyond certain limits.

outed (ou′ tėd), *a.* Driven out.

outer (ou′ tėr), *a.* Being on the exterior side, external; farther from the centre or the inside, objective, material, not subjective or psychical. *n.* (*Rifle-shooting*) The part of a target outside the rings round the bull's-eye. **outer man:** External appearance, attire. **outer space:** The vast, immeasurable region beyond the earth. **outer world:** The world beyond one's familiar sphere, people in general. **outermost,** *a.* **on the outer:** (*Austral. colloq.*) Penniless.

outface (out fās'), *v.t.* To brave; to confront boldly; to stare down. **outfall** (out' fawl), *n.* The point of discharge of a river, drain, etc.; an outlet; *a sortie; *a falling out. ***outfang-thief** (out' făng thēf) [*A.-S. ūtfangenne thēof* (OUT, *fangen*, p.p. of *fōn*, to seize, THIEF)], *n.* (*A.-S. Law*) The right of a lord to try a thief who was his own man in his own court. **outfield** (out' fēld), *n.* (*Sc.*) The outlying land of a farm formerly cropped but not manured; (*Cricket and Baseball*) the part of the field at a distance from the batsman; *the players occupying this. **outfielder,** *n.* **outfit** (out' fit), *n.* The act of equipping for a journey, expedition, etc.; the tools and equipment required for a trade, profession, etc.; (*fig.*) mental equipment; (*Am.*) workmen engaged on a task; *v.t.* To fit out, to provide with an outfit. **outfitter,** *n.* One who deals in outfits for journeys, athletic sports, ceremonies, schools, etc. **outflank** (out flănk'), *v.t.* To extend beyond or turn the flank of; (*fig.*) to get the better of. **outflow** (out' flō), *n.* The process of flowing out; that which flows out; a place of flowing out, an outlet. **outfly** (out flī'), *v.t.* To fly faster than; to outstrip. **outfoot** (out fut'), *v.t.* To outstrip, to outrun, outpace, etc. **outfrown** (out froun'), *v.t.* To frown down. ***outgate** (out' gāt) [GATE (2)], *n.* A passage out; an outlet. **outgeneral** (out jen' ėr ȧl), *v.t.* To surpass in generalship; to manœuvre so as to get the better of. **outgive** (out giv'), *v.t.* To give more than; to surpass in giving; *v.i.* (*poet.*) To give out, to come to an end. **outgo** (out' gō), *n.* That which goes out; expenditure, outlay, cost, outflow, issue; *v.t.* (out gō') To surpass, to go beyond, to excel. **outgoer,** *n.* **outgoing,** *a.* Leaving; *n.* A going out, departure, termination; outlay, expenditure (*usu. in pl.*). **outgrow** (out grō'), *v.t.* To surpass in growth; to grow too much or too great for; to grow out of. **outgrowth,** *n.* **outguard** (out' gard), *n.* A guard at a distance from the main body; an outpost. **out-Herod** (out her' ȯd) [*Herod*, Tetrarch of Galilee, represented in the old miracle-plays as a swaggering tyrant], *v.t.* To outdo, to exaggerate, to overact; to surpass any kind of excess. **outhouse** (out' hous), *n.* A smaller building away from the main building.

outing (out' ing), *n.* An excursion, a pleasure-trip, an airing.

outjest (out jest'), *v.t.* To jest or laugh away. **outjet** (out' jet), *n.* A projection. **outjut, outjutting,** *n.* **outland** (out' lȧnd), *n.* A foreign land; *the outlying part of an estate; land beyond the domain lands, let to tenants; *a.* Foreign, alien; outlying. **outlander,** *n.* A foreigner, a stranger; an alien settler. **outlandish** (out lăn' dish), *a.* Foreign-looking, strange, extraordinary; foreign, alien. **outlast** (out last') [LAST (4)], *v.t.* To last longer than; to surpass in duration, endurance, etc. **outlaw** (out' law), *n.* One deprived of the protection of the law; a lawless person; *an exile, a fugitive; (*Austral.*) an untamable horse; *v.t.* To deprive of the protection of the law. **outlawry,** *n.* **outlay** (out' lā), *n.* Expenditure; *v.t.* (out lā') To expend, to lay out; *to display. **outleap** (out lēp'), *v.t.* To surpass in leaping, to leap farther than; *n.* (out' lēp) A leaping out. **outlet** (out' lėt), *n.* A passage outwards; a vent; a means of egress. **outlier** (out' lī ėr), *n.* One who lodges or resides away from his office or business; (*Geol.*) a portion of a bed detached from the main mass by denudation of the intervening parts. **outline** (out' līn), *n.* The line or lines enclosing and defining a figure; a drawing of such lines without shading; the first general sketch, rough draft, or summary; (*pl.*) general features, facts, principles, etc.; *v.t.* To draw the outline of; to sketch. **outlive** (out liv'), *v.t.* To survive; to outlast; *v.i.* To survive. **outliver,** *n.* **outlook** (out luk'), *v.t.* To stare down; *to look out, to select; *n.* (out' luk) Prospect, general appearance of things, esp. as regards the future; a view, a prospect; looking out, watch, vigilance. ***outlustre** (out lŭs' tėr), *v.t.* To shine more brightly than. **outlying** (out' lī ing), *a.* Situate at a distance, or on the exterior frontier. **outmanœuvre** (out mȧ noo' vėr), *v.t.* To get the better of by manœuvring. **outmarch** (out march'), *v.t.* To march faster than or to outstrip by marching. **outmoded** (out mō' ded), *a.* Out of fashion.

outmost [OUTERMOST, see OUTER]. **outness** [OUT].

outnumber (out nŭm' bėr), *v.t.* To exceed in number. **out-of-date** [DATE]. **outpace** (out pās'), *v.t.* To walk faster than. **out-paramour** (out păr' ȧ moor), *v.t.* To surpass in number of mistresses. **out-part** (out' part), *n.* An outer or exterior part. **out-patient** (out' pā shėnt), *n.* A patient receiving treatment at a hospital without being an inmate. ***outpeer** (out pēr'), *v.t.* To outmatch, to excel. **out-pensioner** (out' pen shȯ nėr), *n.* A non-resident pensioner. **outport** (out' pôrt), *n.* A seaport outside a chief town or chief seat of trade. **outpost** (out' pōst) [POST (3)], *n.* A post or station at a distance from the main body. **outpour** (out pôr'), *v.t.* (*poet.*) To pour out, to discharge; *v.i.* To flow forth; *n.* A pouring out; an overflow. **outpouring,** *n.* ***outpray** (out prā'), *v.t.* To exceed in entreaty. ***outprise** (out prīz'), *v.t.* To exceed in value. **output** (out' put) [PUT (1)], *n.* The produce of a factory, mine, etc.; the aggregate amount produced; the waste produce expelled from the body. ***outquench** (out kwench'), *v.t.* To extinguish.

outrage (out' rāj) [O.F. *ultrage, oultrage* (L. *ultrā*, beyond, -AGE)], *n.* Wanton injury to or violation of the rights of others; a gross offence against order or decency; a flagrant insult; *violence, excess, extravagance; *a furious outbreak. *v.t.* To commit an outrage on; to injure or insult in a flagrant manner; to violate, to commit a rape upon; to transgress, flagrantly. **v.i.* To act outrageously. **outrageous** (out rā' jŭs), *a.* Flagrant, heinous, atrocious, extravagant; excessive, shocking; violent, furious; grossly offensive or abusive. **outrageously,** *adv.* **outrageousness,** *n.*

outrance, à outrance (oo trans) [Fr.]. To the bitter end.

outrange (out rānj), *v.t.* (*Gunnery*) To have a longer range than. **outrank** (out rănk'), *v.t.* To excel in rank.

outré (oo trā) [F., p.p. of *outrer* (from L. *ultrā*, beyond)], *a.* (*fem.* ***-trée***) Extravagant, exaggerated, eccentric; outraging convention or decorum.

outreach (out rēch'), *v.t.* To exceed in reach, to surpass; to overreach, to reach out. *v.i.* (*poet.*) To extend. **outredden** (out redn'), *v.t.* (*poet.*) To grow redder than. **outreign** (out rān'), *v.t.* To reign longer than; to reign throughout (a long period). **out-relief** (out' rė lēf) [OUT-, RELIEF], *n.* Aid given out of the rates to the poor who are not inmates of an institution. **outride** (out rīd'), *v.t.* To ride faster than. **outrider** (out' rī dėr), *n.* A mounted servant who rides ahead of or beside a carriage. **outrigger** (out' rig ėr), *n.* A projecting spar, boom, beam, or framework extended from the sides of a ship for various purposes; a bracket carrying a rowlock projecting from the sides of a boat to give increased leverage in rowing; a boat with these; a projecting beam or framework used in building, etc.; a projection from the shafts for attaching an extra horse to a vehicle; the horse so attached. **outrigged,** *a.* **outright** (out rīt'), *adv.* Completely, entirely; at once, once for all; openly; *a.* (out' rīt) Downright, positive; unrestrained, thorough. **outrightness,** *n.* **outrival** (out rī' vȧl), *v.t.* To surpass as a rival. ***outroad** (out' rōd), *n.* An excursion, a foray. **outroar** (out rôr'), *v.t.* To roar louder than. **outrun** (out rŭn'), *v.t.* To run faster or farther than, to outstrip; to escape by running; *n.* (*Austral.*) a distant sheep-run. **outrunner** (out'-), *n.* **outscold** (out skōld'), *v.t.* To scold louder than. **outscorn** (out skôrn'), *v.t.* To bear down with contempt. **outscouring** (out skour' ing), *n.* (*usu. in pl.*) Anything scoured or washed out, refuse. **outsell** (out sel'), *v.t.* To exceed in price or value; to sell more or faster than. **outset** (out' set), *n.* Commencement, beginning, start. **outshine** (out shīn'), *v.i.* (*poet.*) To shine forth; *v.t.* To excel in lustre; to surpass in splendour.

outside (out sīd', out' sīd), *n.* The external part or surface, the exterior; external appearance, superficial aspect; that which is without; external space, region, position, etc.; the utmost limit, the extreme; (*colloq.*) an outside passenger on a coach, etc.; (*pl.*) outer sheets of a ream of paper. *a.* Pertaining to, situated on, near, or nearer to the outside, outer; external, superficial; highest or greatest possible, extreme; remote, most unlikely. *adv.* To or on the outside; without, not within. *prep.* At, on, to, or of the exterior of; without, out from, forth from; beyond the limits of. **outside in:** Having the outer side turned in, and vice versa. **outside of:** (*prep.*) Outside. **outside broker:** A broker not belonging to the Stock Exchange. **outside edge:** (*Skating*) A stroke on the outer edge of the skate. **outside-left, -right,** *n.* (*Football, Hockey*) A member of a team who plays on the extreme left or right of the forward line. **outside porter:** One not employed by the railway company, who carries luggage, etc. **outside seat:** One at the end of a row. **outsider,** *n.* One who is not a member of a profession, party, circle, coterie, etc.; one not acquainted with or interested in something that is going on; one not admissible to decent society; (*Racing, etc.*) a horse or competitor not included among the favourites.

outsight (out' sīt), *n.* Perception of external things, observation; *outlook, prospect; (*Sc., pl.*) movable goods, also called **outsight plenishing. outsit** (out sit'), *v.t.* To sit beyond the time of; to sit longer than. **outsize,** *n.* A person or thing abnormally large; a ready-made garment larger than the standard size. *a.* **outskirt** (out' skėrt), *n.* (*usu. in pl.*) The outer border; **v.t.* To be the outskirt of; to pass along the outskirts of. **outsleep** (out slēp'), *v.t.* To sleep beyond (a particular time); to sleep longer than. **outsoar** (out sôr'), *v.t.* To soar beyond or higher than. **out-sole** (out' sōl), *n.* The outside or lower sole, which comes in contact with the ground. **outspan** (out' spăn) [Dut. *uitspannen* (SPAN)], *v.t.* (*S. Afr.*) To unyoke or unharness; *v.i.* To unyoke or unharness animals; *n.* The act or the place of this. **outspeak** (out spēk'), *v.t.* To express more than; *v.i.* To speak out or aloud. **outspoken,** *a.* Open, candid, frank. **outspokenly,** *adv.* **outspokenness,** *n.* **outsport** (out spôrt'), *v.t.* To outdo in sport. **outspread** (out spred'), *v.t.* To spread out; *a.* (out' spred) Spread out. **outstand** (out stand'), *v.t.* To stand out against, to withstand; *to outstay. **outstanding,** *a.* Remaining unpaid; projecting outward; salient, conspicuous, prominent. ***outstare** (out stâr'), *v.t.* To outface, to abash by staring. **out-station,** *n.* (*Austral.*) A distant station. **outstay** (out stā'), *v.t.* To stay longer than (a specified time or another person). **outstep** (out step'), *v.t.* To overstep. **outstretch** (out strech'), *v.t.* To extend, to expand; to stretch out; to stretch or strain to the utmost. **outstrike** (out strīk'), *v.t.* To strike faster or heavier blows than. **outstrip** (out strip') [STRIP, in obs. sense to run fast], *v.t.* To outrun, to leave behind; to escape by running; to surpass in progress. **outswear** (out swâr'), *v.t.* To bear down by swearing. ***outsweeten** (out swētn'), *v.t.* To exceed in sweetness. ***outswell** (out swel'), *v.t.* To exceed in swelling, to swell more than. **out-talk** (out tawk'), *v.t.* To outdo in talking; to talk down. ***out-throw** (out thrō'), *v.t.* To cast out. **outthrust** (out' thrŭst), *n.* Outward thrust or pressure; *a.* (out thrŭst') Thrust or projected forward; *v.t.* To thrust forth or forward. ***out-tongue** (out tŭng'), *v.t.* To out-talk. ***outvalue** (out văl' ū), *v.t.* To exceed in value. ***outvenom** (out ven' ŏm), *v.t.* To exceed in venom. ***outvie** (out vī'), *v.t.* To exceed, to surpass, in rivalry, emulation, etc. ***outvillain** (out vil' ăn), *v.t.* To surpass in villainy. ***outvoice** (out vois'), *v.t.* To sound louder than. **outvote** (out vōt'), *v.t.* To outnumber in voting; to cast more votes than. **outvoter,** *n.* A voter who does not reside in the constituency. **outwalk** (out wawk'), *v.t.* To outdo or outstrip in walking. ***outwall** (out' wawl), *n.* The outside, the exterior; (*fig.*) the body.

outward (out' wărd) [A.-S. *ūteweard* (OUT, -WARD)], *a.* Exterior, outer; tending or directed toward the outside; external, visible, apparent, superficial; material, worldly, corporeal, not spiritual; extraneous, extrinsic; *foreign. *adv.* Outwards. *n.* Outward or external appearance; (*pl.*) externals. **to outward seeming:** Apparently. **outward bound,** *a.* Going away from home. **outward form:** Appearance. **outward man:** The carnal man as opp. to the spiritual or the soul. **outward things:** Visible or sensible things; things of this world. **outwardly,** *adv.* **outwardness,** *n.* **outwards,** *adv.*

outwatch (out woch'), *v.t.* To watch longer than; to watch throughout (a specified time). **outwear** (out wâr'), *v.t.* To wear out; to exhaust, to weary out; to last longer than. ***outweed** (out wēd'), *v.t.* To root out. **outweigh** (out wā'), *v.t.* To weigh more than; to be too heavy for; to be of more value, importance, etc., than. **outwell** (out wel'), *v.i.* To pour or flow forth; **v.t.* To pour out. **outwick** (out' wik) [etym. unknown], *n.* (*Curling*) A shot striking another stone so as to drive it nearer the tee. ***outwin** (out win'), *v.t.* To get out of. ***outwind** (out wīnd'), *v.t.* To disentangle. ***outwing** (out wing'), *v.t.* To outstrip in flying; (*Mil.*) to outflank. **outwit** (out wit'), *v.t.* To defeat by superior ingenuity or cunning; to overreach, to cheat. **outwork** (out' wĕrk), *n.* A work included in the defence of a place, but outside the parapet; *v.t.* (out wĕrk') (*poet.*) To work out, to complete; to work faster than. **outworker** (out' wŏr kėr), *n.* One who works outside (a factory, shop, etc.). **outworn** (-wôrn'), *a.* Worn out; obsolete. **outworth,** *v.t.* To exceed in value. ***outwrest,** *v.t.* To extort.

ouzel (oo' zėl) [A.-S. *ōsle* (cp. G. *amsel*, O.H.G. *amsala*)], *n.* One of various thrush-like birds, including the dipper or water-ouzel. **ouzel-cock,** *n.* (*Shak.*) The blackbird.

ova [OVUM].

oval (ō' văl) [perhaps through F. (L. OVUM, -AL)], *a.* Egg-shaped, roughly elliptical. *n.* A closed convex curve with one axis longer than the other; an egg-shaped figure or thing. **ovally,** *adv.* **ovalness,** *n.*

ovary (ō' văr i) [OVUM, -ARY], *n.* One of the organs (two in number in the higher vertebrates) in a female animal in which the ova are produced; (*Bot.*) the portion of the pistil in which the ovules are contained. **ovarian** (ȯ vâr' i ăn), *a.* **ovario-,** *comb. form.* **ovariotomy** (-ot' ȯ mi) [-TOMY], *n.* (*Surg.*) The removal of the ovary by excision, or of a tumour from the ovary. **ovariotomist,** *n.* **ovaritis** (-rī' tis) [-ITIS], *n.* (*Path.*). **ovate,** *a.* Egg-shaped. **ovato-,** *comb. form.* **ovato-oblong** (ȯ vā' tō ob' long), *a.* Longer than oval.

ovation (ō vā' shŭn) [L. *ovātio*, from *ovāre*, to rejoice], *n.* (*Rome. Ant.*) A Roman minor triumph; (*fig.*) an enthusiastic display of popular favour.

oven (ŭv' ėn) [A.-S. *ofn* (cp. Dut. *oven*, G. *ofen*, Icel. *ofn*), cogn. with Gr. *ipnos*], *n.* A close chamber in which substances are baked, etc.; a furnace or kiln for assaying, annealing, etc. **Dutch oven** [DUTCH]. **oven-bird, -builder,** *n.* The long-tailed titmouse and other birds making oven-shaped nests. **ovenette** (ŭv ėn et'), *n.* A small oven.

over (ō' vėr) (*poet.*), **o'er** (ŏr) [A.-S. *ofer* (cp. Dut. *over*, G. *über*, *ober*, Icel. *yfir*, *ofr*), cogn. with Gr. *huper*, Sansk. *upari*], *prep.* Above, in a higher position than, above or superior to in excellence, dignity, or value; more than, in excess of; in charge of, concerned or engaged with; across from side to side of; through the extent or duration of. *adv.* So as to pass from side to side or across some space, barrier, etc.; in width, in distance across; on the opposite side; from one side to another; so as to be turned down or upside down from an erect position; so as to be across or down from a brink, brim, etc.; so as to traverse a space, etc.; from end to end, throughout; at an end; in excess, in addition;

excessively, with repetition, again. *a.* Upper, outer, covering, excessive. *n.* (*Cricket*) The interval between the times when the umpire calls 'over'; the number of balls (6 or 8) delivered by one bowler during this. **all over** [ALL]. **over again:** Afresh, anew. **over against:** Opposite; in front of; in contrast with. **over and above** [ABOVE]. **over and over:** So as to turn completely round several times; repeatedly. **over head and ears** [HEAD]. **over one's head:** Beyond one's comprehension. **oversea,** *a.* Denoting dominions, etc., across the sea. **over seas:** In foreign parts. **to give over** [GIVE]. **to turn over** [TURN].

over- [prec.], *pref.* Above; across; outer, upper; as a covering; past, beyond; extra; excessively, too much, too great. **overabound** (ō vėr ȧ bound'), *v.i.* To be superabundant; to abound too much (with or on). **overact** (ō vėr ăkt'), *v.t.* To overdo; to act (a part) in an exaggerated way; *v.i.* To act more than is necessary. **overall:** From end to end, total. **overalls** (ō' vėr awlz), *n.pl.* Trousers or other garments worn over others as a protection against dirt, etc.; trousers worn by cavalry in riding, a cavalryman's trousers. ***overall,** *adv.* Everywhere, in all parts or directions. **overarch** (ō vėr arch'), *v.t.* To form an arch over; *v.i.* To form an arch overhead. **overawe** (ō vėr aw'), *v.t.* To keep in awe; to control or restrain by awe. **overbalance** (ō vėr băl' ȧns), *v.t.* To outweigh; to destroy the equilibrium of; to upset; *v.i.* To lose one's equilibrium; to topple over; *n.* (ō' vėr băl ȧns) Excess of value or amount; that which exceeds an equivalent. **overbear** (ō vėr bâr'), *v.t.* To bear down, to overpower. **overbearing,** *a.* Arrogant, haughty, imperious. **overbearingly,** *adv.* **overbid** (ō vėr bid'), *v.t.* To outbid. **overblow** (ō vėr blô'), *v.i.* and *t.* To blow over. **overblown** (1), *a.* Blown over; inflated. **overblown** (2) (ō' vėr blōn'), *a.* More than full blown. **overboard** (ō' vėr bôrd), *adv.* Over the side of a ship; out of a ship. **over-bold** (ō vėr bōld'), *a.* Bold to excess. **overboldly,** *adv.* **overboldness,** *n.* **overbuild** (ō vėr bild'), *v.t.* To build more than is required; to build too much upon (land, etc.). ***overbulk** (-bŭlk'), *v.t.* To surpass in bulk; to overtop. **overburden** (-bėr' dėn), *v.t.* To overload, to overweigh. **overbuy** (ō vėr bī'), *v.i.* To buy more than is required; *v.t.* To pay too much for.

over-by (ō' vėr bī), *adv.* (*Sc.*) A little way across; over the way.

overcanopy (ō vėr kăn' ȯ pi), *v.t.* To cover with or as with a canopy. **over-capitalize** (ō vėr kăp' i tȧ līz), *v.t.* To rate or fix the nominal value of the capital of (a company, etc.) at too high a figure. **overcareful** (ō vėr kâr' fŭl), *a.* Careful to excess. **overcast** (ō vėr kast'), *v.t.* To darken, to cloud; to render gloomy or depressed; to sew (an edge, etc.) with long stitches to prevent unravelling, etc., or as embroidering; to cast off (an illness, etc.); *to rate too high; *a.* (ō vėr kast') Clouded all over (of the sky); sewn or embroidered by overcasting; in excess of the proper amount; *n.* Something thrown over; a cloud covering the sky; overcast needlework. **overcasting,** *n.* ***overcatch** (ō vėr kăch'), *v.t.* To overtake; to outwit. **over-caution** (ō vėr kaw' shŭn), *n.* Excess of caution. **over-cautious,** *a.* **over-cautiously,** *adv.* **overcharge** (ō vėr charj'), *v.t.* To charge with more than is properly due; to overburden, to overload; to load (a fire-arm) with an excessive charge; to saturate; to exaggerate; *n.* (ō' vėr charj) An excessive charge, load, or burden. **overcloud** (ō vėr kloud'), *v.t.* To cloud over; to depress, to deject; *v.i.* To become overcast (of the sky). **overcloy** (ō vėr kloi'), *v.t.* To surfeit, to satiate. **overcoat** (ō' vėr kōt), *n.* A great-coat, a top-coat. **overcoated,** *a.* **overcoating,** *n.* Material for overcoats. **overcome** (ō vėr kŭm'), *v.t.* To overpower, to vanquish, to conquer. **overcomer,** *n.* **over-confidence** (ō vėr kon' fi dėns), *n.* Excessive confidence. **over-confident,** *a.* **over-confidently,** *adv.* ***overcount** (ō vėr kount') *v.t.* To rate above the true value. ***over-cover** (ō vėr kŭv' ėr), *v.t.* To cover completely over. **over-credulous** (ō vėr kred' ū lŭs), *a.* Too credulous. **over-credulously,** *adv.* **over-credulity** (-dū' li ti), *n.* **overcrop** (ō vėr krop'), *v.t.* To crop (land) to excess; to exhaust by continual cropping. **overcrow** (ō vėr krō'), *v.t.* To crow or triumph over. **overcrowd** (ō vėr kroud), *v.t.* and *i.* To crowd to excess. **overcrust** (ō vėr krŭst'), *v.t.* To cover with a crust. **over-cunning** (ō vėr kŭn' ing), *a.* Too cunning. **over-curious** (ō vėr kū' ri ŭs), *a.* Too curious. **over-develop** (ō vėr dė vel' ȯp), *v.t.* (*Phot.*) To develop a plate too much so that the image is too dense. ***overdight** (ō vėr dīt'), *a.* Overspread; decked all over. **overdo** (ō vėr doo') [DO (1)], *v.t.* (*past* **-did,** *p.p.* **-done**) To do to excess; to exaggerate; to overact; to excel; to cook to excess; to fatigue, to wear out. **overdose** (ō' vėr dōs), *n.* An excessive dose; *v.t.* (ō vėr dōs') To give too large a dose to. **overdraft** (ō' vėr draft), *n.* A draft on a bank in excess of the amount to one's credit. **overdraw** (ō vėr draw'), *v.t.* (*past* **-drew,** *p.p.* **-drawn**) To exaggerate; to draw upon for a larger sum than stands to one's credit. **overdrive** (ō vėr drīv'), *v.t.* (*past* **-drove,** *p.p.* **-driven**) To drive (a horse) too far or too hard. **overdue** (ō vėr dū') [DUE (1)], *a.* Remaining unpaid after the date on which it is due; not arrived at the time it was due; *n.* A debt or account that is overdue. ***overdye** (ō vėr dī'), *v.t.* To dye too deeply or with a second colour. **over-earnest** (ō vėr ĕr' nėst), *a.* Too earnest. **over-eat** (ō vėr ēt'), *v.i.* To eat to excess; (*reflex.*) to injure (oneself) by eating to excess; *v.t.* To eat or nibble all over. **over-estimate** (ō vėr es' ti māt), *v.t.* To give too high a value to. **over-expose** (ō vėr ėk spōz'), *v.t.* (*Phot.*) To expose (a plate) to light too long so as to make the negative defective. **over-exposure,** *n.* ***over-exquisite** (ō vėr eks' kwi zit), *a.* Too nice or exact. **overfall** (ō vėr fawl), *n.* (*Naut.*) A turbulent race or current with choppy waves caused by shoals, the meeting of cross-currents, etc.; a structure for the overflow of water from a canal, etc. **overfeed** (ō vėr fēd'), *v.t.* To surfeit with food; *v.i.* To eat to excess. ***overflourish** (ō vėr flŭr' ish), *v.t.* To adorn superficially; to cover with flowers and verdure. **overflow** (ō vėr flō'), *v.t.* To flow over, to flood, to inundate; to cover as with a liquid; *v.i.* To run over; to abound; to overflow the banks (of a stream); *n.* (ō' vėr flō) A flood, an inundation; (*fig.*) a superabundance, a profusion. **overflowing,** *a.* **overflowingly,** *adv.* **overfold** (ō' vėr fōld), *n.* (*Geol.*) A fold of strata in which the lower part has been pushed over the upper; a reflexed or inverted fold; *v.t.* (ō vėr fōld') To push or fold (strata) over in this manner (*usu. in p.p.*). **over-fond** (ō vėr fond'), *a.* Too fond; doting. **over-fondly,** *adv.* ***overfraught** (ō vėr frawt'), *a.* Overladen. ***over-freight,** *v.t.* To overload, to freight too heavily. **overfull** (ō vėr ful'), *a.* Too full; surfeited. ***overgive** (ō vėr giv'), *v.t.* To give over, to surrender. ***overglance** (ō vėr glans'), *v.t.* To glance over. ***overgo** (ō vėr gō'), *v.t.* To go beyond; to pass over; to overcome; *v.i.* To go by; to pass away. ***overgorge** (ō vėr gôrj'), *v.i.* To gorge to excess. ***overgrassed** (ō vėr grast'), *a.* Overgrown with grass. **over-greedy** (ō vėr grē' di), *a.* Excessively greedy. ***overgreen** (ō vėr grēn'), *v.t.* To cover with green, to embellish.

overground (ō' vėr ground), *a.* Situated or running above ground, opp. to underground. **overgrow** (ō vėr grō'), *v.t.* (*past* **-grew,** *p.p.* **-grown**) To cover with vegetation; to outgrow (one's strength, etc.); *v.i.* To grow too large. **overgrowth,** *n.* **overhand** (ō' vėr hănd), *a.* Thrown or done with the hand raised above the level of the shoulder or elbow (of a ball, bowling, etc.); *adv.* (ō vėr hănd') In this manner. **overhanded** (ō' vėr hăn dėd), *a.* With the hand over the object grasped; (ō vėr hăn' dėd) Having too many hands or workers employed. ***over-handle** (ō vėr hăndl'), *v.t.* To handle or mention too much. **overhang** (ō vėr hăng'), *v.i.* (*past & p.p.* **-hung**) To hang over, to jut out; *v.t.* To hang or impend over; (*fig.*) to threaten; *n.* The act of overhanging; the part or thing that overhangs. **over-happy** (ō vėr hăp' i), *a.* Too happy. **overhaul** (ō vėr hawl'), *v.t.* To turn over thoroughly for examination; to examine thoroughly; (*Naut.*) to overtake, to gain upon; *n.* (ō′ vėr hawl) Inspection, thorough examination.

overhead (ō vėr hed′), *adv.* Above the head, aloft; in the zenith, ceiling, roof, etc.; *a.* Situated overhead; (*Mach.*) working from above downwards; (*fig.*) all round, average, general. **overheads,** *n.pl.* (*Comm.*) Expenses of administration, etc. **overhear** (ō vėr hēr′), *v.t.* To hear (words not meant for one) by accident or stratagem; *to hear over again. ***overhent** (ō vėr hent′), *v.t.* To overtake. ***overhold** (ō vėr hōld′) [HOLD (1)], *v.t.* To value too highly. **over-indulge** (ō vėr in dŭlj′), *v.t.* To indulge to excess (*often reflex.*). **over-indulgence,** *n.* **over-indulgent,** *a.* **over-indulgently,** *adv.* **over-issue** (ō vėr ish′-, -is′ ū), *v.t.* To issue in excess (as bank-notes, etc.); *n.* An issue in excess. **overjoy** (ō vėr joi′), *v.t.* To transport with joy. **overjump** (ō vėr jŭmp′), *v.t.* To jump over; to jump beyond; to injure (oneself) by too great a jump. **over-knee** (ō vėr nē′), *a.* Reaching above the knee. **over-labour** (ō vėr lā′ bŏr), *v.t.* To harass with labour; to work upon excessively, to elaborate too much. ***overlade** (ō vėr lād′), *v.t.* (*p.p.* **-laden**) To overburden. **overlaid** [OVERLAY]. **overland** (ō′ vėr lănd), *a.* Lying, going, made, or performed by land; *adv.* Across the land; *v.t.* (*Austral.*) to take stock across country. **Overland Route,** *n.* The route from England to India by way of France and Italy to Brindisi and thence by steamer through the Suez Canal. **overlander,** *n.* (*Austral.*) One who takes his stock a great distance for sale or to a new station. **overlap** (ō vėr lăp′), *v.t.* To lap or fold over; to extend so as to lie or rest upon; *n.* An act, case, or the extent of overlapping; the part that overlaps something else. **over-lavish** (ō vėr lăv′ ish), *a.* Lavish to excess. **overlay** (ō vėr lā′), *v.t.* (*past & p.p.* **-laid**) To cover or spread over the surface of; to cover with a layer; to overcast, to cloud; (*Print.*) to put overlays on; *to weigh down; *n.* (ō′ vėr lā) Something laid over (as a covering, layer, etc.); (*Print.*) paper pasted on the tympan to produce a heavier impression. **overlaying,** *n.* A covering. **overleaf** (ō vėr lēf′), *adv.* On the other side of the leaf (of a book, etc.). **overleap** (ō vėr lēp′), *v.t.* To leap over; to leap beyond; to leap too far; (*fig.*) to omit. **to overleap oneself:** To miss one's aim by leaping too far or too high. ***overleather** (ō′ vėr le*th* ėr), *n.* The upper leather of a boot or shoe. **overlie** (ō vėr lī′), *v.t.* (*past* **-lay**) To lie above or upon; to smother by lying on. ***over-light** (ō vėr līt′), *a.* Too light. **overlighted,** *a.*

overload (ō vėr lōd′), *v.t.* To load too heavily, to overcharge; *n.* (ō′ vėr lōd) An excessive load. **overlook** (ō vėr luk′), *v.t.* To view from a high place; to be situated so as to command a view of from above; to superintend, to oversee; to inspect or peruse, esp. in a cursory way; to look over, to pass over with indulgence, to disregard, to slight; to bewitch, to look at with an evil eye. **overlooker,** *n.* **overlord** (ō′ vėr lôrd), *n.* A superior lord, one who is lord over other lords; one who is supreme over another or others; *v.t.* To lord it over; to rule as an overlord. **overlordship,** *n.* ***overlusty** (ō vėr lŭs′ ti), *a.* Too lusty or merry. **overman** (ō′ vėr măn), *n.* A superman; an overseer or foreman. **over-man** (-măn′), *v.t.* To furnish with too many men. **overmantel** (ō′ vėr măntl), *n.* Ornamental woodwork placed over a mantelpiece. **over-many** (ō vėr men′ i), *a.* Too many. ***overmaster** (ō vėr mas′ tėr), *v.t.* To overcome, to subdue. **overmasteringly,** *adv.* **overmasterful,** *a.* **overmasterfulness,** *n.* **overmatch** (ō vėr măch′), *v.t.* To be more than a match for; *n.* (ō′ vėr măch) A person or thing that is superior in power, skill, etc. ***over-measure** (ō vėr mezh′ ŭr), *v.t.* To estimate too largely; *n.* Measure above what is sufficient or due. ***overmount** (ō vėr mount′), *v.t.* To rise above; *v.i.* To mount too high; *n.* A mount for a picture, etc. **overmuch** (ō′ vėr mŭch′, ō vėr mŭch′), *a.* Too much, more than is sufficient or necessary; *adv.* In or to too great a degree; *n.* More than enough. ***overmultitude** (ō vėr mŭl′ ti tūd), *v.t.* To outnumber. ***overname** (ō vėr nām′), *v.t.* To name in order. **over-nice** (ō vėr nīs′), *a.* Too nice, scrupulous, or fastidious. **over-nicely,** *adv.* **over-niceness, -nicety,** *n.* **overnight** (ō vėr nīt′), *a.* Done or happening the night before; *adv.* In the course of the night or evening; in or on the evening before; during or through the night; *n.* (*Am.*) The preceding evening. ***over-office** (ō vėr of′ is), *v.t.* To lord over in virtue of one's office. **over-officious** (-ŏ fish′ ŭs), *a.* Too officious. **over-officiously,** *adv.* **over-officiousness,** *n.* **overpass** (ō vėr pas′), *v.t.* (*past & p.p.* **-passed, -past**) To pass or go over; to overlook; to pass or go beyond. **overpay** (ō vėr pā′), *v.t.* and *i.* To pay more than is sufficient; to pay in excess. **overpayment,** *n.* **overpeer** (ō vėr pēr′), *v.t.* To look or peer over; to rise above, to overcrow. **overpeople** (ō vėr pēpl′), *v.t.* To overstock with people. **over-persuade** (ō vėr pėr swād′), *v.t.* To persuade against one's inclination or judgment. **overpicture** (ō vėr pik′ tyŭr), *v.t.* To represent in an exaggerated manner.

overplus (ō vėr plŭs), *n.* Surplus, excess; an amount left over. **overply** (ō vėr plī′), *v.t.* To ply or exercise to excess. ***overpoise** (ō vėr′ poiz′), *v.t.* To outweigh; to cause to outweigh; *n.* (ō′ vėr poiz) Preponderant weight. ***overpost** (ō vėr pōst′) [POST (2)], *v.t.* To get over quickly and easily. **overpower** (ō vėr pou′ ėr), *v.t.* To be too strong or powerful for; to overcome, conquer, vanquish; to overcome the feelings or judgment of, to overwhelm. **overpoweringly,** *adv.* **overpraise** (ō vėr prāz′), *v.t.* To praise too highly. **over-praising,** *n.* Excessive eulogy. **overpress** (ō vėr pres′), *v.t.* To overwhelm, to crush, to overpower. **overprize** (ō vėr prīz′), *v.t.* To overvalue; to exceed in value. **over-production** (ō vėr prŏ dŭk′ shŭn), *n.* Production in excess of demand. **over-produce** (ō vėr prŏ dūs′), *v.t.* and *i.* **overproof** (ō′ vėr proof), *a.* Above proof, containing a larger proportion of alcohol than is contained in proof-spirit. **over-proud** (ō vėr proud′), *a.* Excessively proud. ***overrake** (ō vėr rāk′), *v.t.* (*Naut.*) To sweep over or through (of shot or waves). **overrate** (ō vėr rāt′), *v.t.* To rate too highly. **overreach** (ō vėr rēch′), *v.t.* To reach or extend beyond; to get the better of, to outwit, to cheat; *to overtake; *v.i.* To bring the hind feet too far forwards so as to strike the fore foot (of horses). **over-read** (ō vėr rēd′), *v.t.* To injure (oneself) by too much reading; *to peruse. **over-red** (ō vėr red′), *v.t.* (*Shak.*) To cover with red. **over-refine** (ō vėr rė fīn′), *v.t.* To refine too much, to be over-subtle. **over-refinement,** *n.* **override** (ō vėr rīd′), *v.t.* (*past* **-rode,** *p.p.* **-ridden**) To ride over; (*fig.*) to trample as if underfoot, to disregard, to set aside, to supersede; to fatigue or exhaust by excessive riding; to outride, to overtake; (*Surg.*) to slide over (as one end of a fractured bone over the other). **over-ripe** (ō vėr rīp′), *a.* Ripe to excess. **over-ripen,** *v.i.* and *t.* **over-roast** (ō vėr rōst′), *v.t.* To roast too much. **overrule** (ō vėr rool′), *v.t.* To control by superior power or authority; to set aside; to reject, to disallow; *v.i.* *To bear sway.

overrun (ō vėr rŭn′), *v.t.* To run or spread over; to grow over; to invade or harass by hostile incursions; to extend over; to run beyond, to outrun; (*Print.*) to carry over and change the arrangement of (type set up); *v.i.* To overflow; to extend beyond the proper limits. **overruner,** *n.* ***overscutched** (*Shak.*), *a.* Prob. worn out in service. **oversea** (ō vėr sē′), *a.* Beyond the sea, foreign; *adv.* From beyond sea. **over-seas,** *adv.* **oversee** (ō vėr sē′), *v.t.* To overlook, to superintend; to overlook, to disregard, to neglect. **overseer,** *n.* A superintendent, an inspector; a parish officer charged with the care of the poor. **overseership,** *n.* **oversell** (ō vėr sel′), *v.t.* To sell more than; to sell more of (stocks, etc.) than one can deliver. **overset** (ōvėr set′), *v.t.* To upset; to overthrow; (*Print.*) to set up too much type for (a page, etc.); *v.i.* To upset, to be turned over. **oversew** (ō vėr sō'), *v.t.* To sew (two pieces or edges) together by passing the needle through from one side only so that the thread between the stitches lies over the edges. **overshade** (ō vėr shād'), *v.t.* To cover with shade. **overshadow** (ō vėr shăd' ō), *v.t.* To throw a shadow over, to shade over, to obscure with or as with cloud; (*fig.*) to shelter, to protect; to tower high above, to cast in the shade. **overshine** (ō vėr shīn'), *v.t.* To shine upon. **overshoe** (ō' vėr shoo), *n.* A shoe worn over another.

overshoot (ō vėr shoot'), *v.t.* To shoot over or beyond; to go beyond, to overstep, to exceed; to shoot more game than is good for (a moor, covert, etc.); *v.i.* To go beyond the mark. **to overshoot oneself:** To go too far, to overreach oneself; to make assertions not to be substantiated. **overshot** (ō' vėr shot), *a.* Driven by water sent over the top; projecting, overlapping. **overshot wheel:** A water-wheel driven by water flowing over the top. **overside** (ō vėr sīd'), *adv.* Over the side (as of a ship); *a.* (ō' vėr' sīd). Discharging, unloaded, or effected over the side. **oversight** (ō' vėr sīt), *n.* Superintendence, supervision, care; a mistake, an inadvertence, an unintentional error or omission. **oversize** (1) (ō vėr sīz'), *v.t.* To surpass in bulk; *n.* (ō' vėr sīz') A size above the ordinary. **oversize** (2) (ō vėr sīz'), *v.t.* To cover or treat with too much size; to size too much. **overslaugh** (ō' vėr slaw) [Dut. *overslaan* (*slaan*, to strike)], *v.t.* *(*Mil.*) To pass over, to skip (a turn of duty, etc.); (*Am.*) to set aside, to supersede; (*Am.*) to obstruct; to override. **oversleep** (-slēp'), *v.i.* and *t.* To sleep too long (*often reflex.*). **oversman** (*Sc.*) [OVER-MAN]. ***oversnow** (ō vėr snō'), *v.t.* To cover with or as with snow. **oversoul** (ō' vėr sōl), *n.* (*Emerson*) The spiritual being or absolute unity animating the universe, in which all things subsist and subject and object are one. **overspend** (ō vėr spend'), *v.t.* (*past and p.p.* **-spent**) To spend too much of (income, etc.); to wear out, to exhaust; *v.i.* To spend beyond one's means (*often reflex.*). **overspread** (ō vėr spred'), *v.t.* To spread over; to cover (with); to be spread over. **overspring** (ō vėr spring'), *v.t.* To leap over; to surmount. **overstand** (ō vėr stand'), *v.t.* To insist too strictly on the conditions of. **overstare** (ō vėr stâr'), *v.t.* To outstare. **overstate** (ō vėr stāt'), *v.t.* To state too strongly, to exaggerate. **overstatement,** *n.* **overstay** (ō vėr stā'), *v.t.* To stay longer than or beyond the limits of. **overstep** (ō vėr step'), *v.t.* To exceed, to transgress. **overstock** (ō' vėr stok), *n.* Superabundance, excess; *v.t.* (ō vėr stok') To stock to excess; to fill too full. **overstrain** (ō vėr strān'), *v.i.* To strain or exert too much; *n.* (ō' vėr strān) Excessive strain or exertion. **overstrike** (ō vėr strīk'), *v.t.* To strike beyond. **overstrung** (ō vėr strŭng') [*strung*, p.p. of STRING], *a.* Too highly strung. **oversubtle** (ō vėr sŭtl'), *a.* Too subtle. **over-subtlety,** *n.* **oversure** (ō vėr shoor'), *a.* Too confident. **oversway** (ō vėr swā'), *v.t.* To overrule; to surpass. **overswell** (ō vėr swel'), *v.t.* and *i.* To overflow. **overswift** (ō vėr swift'), *a.* Too swift.

overt (ō vėrt) [O.F., p.p. of *ovrir* (F. *ouvrir*), L. *operire*, to open], *a.* Open, plain, public, apparent; (*Her.*) spread open (of wings). **overtly,** *adv.*

overtake (ō vėr tāk'), *v.t.* (*past* **-took,** *p.p.* **-taken**) To come up with, to catch; to reach, to attain to; to take by surprise, to come upon suddenly. **overtask** (ō vėr task'), *v.t.* To burden with too heavy a task. **overtax** (ō vėr tăks'), *v.t.* To tax too heavily; (*fig.*) to overburden. **over-tedious** (ō vėr tē' di ŭs), *a.* Too tedious.

overthrow (ō vėr thrō') [OVER-, THROW], *v.t.* (*past* **overthrew,** *p.p.* **overthrown**) To overturn, throw down, demolish; to overcome, conquer, subvert. *n.* (ō' vėr thrō) Defeat, discomfiture; ruin, destruction; (*Cricket*) a ball returned to but missed by the wicket-keeper, allowing further runs to be made. **overthrust** (ō' vėr thrŭst), *n.* (*Geol.*) The thrust of strata over those on the other side of a fault; the amount of this; *a.* Thrust over (of strata). ***overthwart** (ō vėr thwôrt'), *adv.* Across, over from side to side; *prep.* From side to side of; across, athwart. **overtime** (ō' vėr tīme), *n.* Time during which one works beyond the regular hours.

overtly [OVERT].

overtone (ō' vėr tōn), *n.* (*Acoustics*) An harmonic. *v.t.* (ō vėr tōn') To drown (a tone) with a more powerful one; (*Phot.*) to tone too much. **overtop** (ō vėr top'), *v.t.* To tower over, to surmount, to surpass; to override. **overtrade** (ō vėr trād'), *v.i.* To trade beyond one's capital. ***overtrip** (ō vėr trip'), *v.t.* To trip or skip over. ***overtrust** (ō vėr trŭst'), *v.i.* To be too trusting.

overture (ō' vėr tyůr) [O.F. (OVERT, -URE)], *n.* A preliminary proposal, an offer to negotiate or of suggested terms (*usu. in pl.*); an exordium of a poem, etc.; (*Mus.*) an introductory piece for instruments, a prelude; (*Presbyterian Ch.*) a preliminary proposition or the sending of this from the presbyteries to the General Assembly or vice versa. *v.t.* To bring forward, introduce, or transmit as an overture.

overturn (ō' vėr tĕrn'), *v.t.* To turn over, to upset. *v.i.* To be upset or turned over. *n.* The act of overturning; the state of being overturned. **overturner,** *n.* **overvalue** (ō' vėr văl' ū), *v.t.* To value too highly. **overvaluation** (-ā' shŭn), *n.* ***overveil** (ō vėr vāl'), *v.t.* To veil, to shroud. ***overview** (ō' vėr vū), *n.* An inspection, a survey. **overweather** (ō vėr weth' ėr), *v.t.* To damage by violence of weather. **overween** (ō vėr wēn'), *v.i.* To think too highly (of). **overweening,** *a.* Arrogant, conceited, presumptuous; *n.* Excessive conceit. **overweeningly,** *adv.* **overweigh** (ō vėr wā'), *v.t.* To exceed in weight; to weigh down. **overweight** (ō' vėr wāt), *n.* Excess of weight; preponderance. **overwhelm** (-welm'), *v.t.* To cover completely, to submerge; to crush, to engulf; to destroy utterly; to overcome, to bear down, to overpower. **overwhelmingly,** *adv.* **overwind** (ō vėr wīnd'), *v.t.* (*past and p.p.* **-wound**) To wind too much or too tight. **overwise** (ō vėr wīz'), *a.* Too wise; wise to affectation. **overwork** (ō vėr wĕrk'), *v.t.* (*past and p.p.* **-worked, -wrought**) To impose too much work upon; to exhaust with work; to work up into a morbid state of excitement; *v.i.* To work to excess; *n.* Work beyond what is required or regular. **overworn** (ō vėr wôrn'), *a.* Worn out; wearied; trite, commonplace. ***overwrestle** (ō vėr resl'), *v.t.* To vanquish in wrestling. **overwrought** [OVERWORK].

ovi- (1), **ovo-** [OVUM], *comb. form.*

ovi- (2) [L. *ovis*, sheep], *comb. form.*

ovibovine (ō vi bō' vīn) [OVI- (2)], *a.* Belonging to the *Ovibovinæ*, a sub-family of the *Bovinæ* having characters intermediate between those of sheep and oxen. *n.* An animal of this sub-family, a musk-ox.

Ovidian (o vid' i an), *a.* Of or in the manner of the Roman poet Ovid.

oviduct (ō' vi dŭkt) [OVI- (1)], *n.* A passage through which ova pass from the ovary, esp. in oviparous animals. **oviducal, oviductal,** *a.*

oviferous (ō vif' ėr ŭs) [OVI- (1)], *a.* Egg-bearing; applied to the receptacle for ova in certain crustaceans.

oviform (ō' vi fôrm) *a.* Egg-shaped.

ovigerous (ō vij' ėr ŭs) [OVI- (1)], *a.* Egg-bearing, carrying eggs.

ovine (ō' vīn) [OVI- (2)], *a.* Of, pertaining to, or like sheep.

oviparous (ō vip' ȧ rŭs) [OVI- (1)], *a.* Producing young by means of eggs that are expelled and hatched outside the body. **oviparity,** *n.* **oviparously,** *adv.* **oviparousness,** *n.*

oviposit (ō vi poz' it) [OVI- (1)], *v.i.* To deposit eggs, esp. with an ovipositor. **oviposition,** *n.* **ovipositor,** *n.* A tubular organ in many insects serving to deposit the eggs.

ovisac (ō' vi săk) [OVI- (1)], *n.* A closed receptacle in the ovary in which ova are developed.

ovoid (ō′ void) [OVI- (1)], *a.* Egg-shaped, oval with one end larger than the other; ovate. *n.* An ovoid body or figure. **ovoidal,** *a.*

ovolo (ō′ vȯ lō) [It. (now *uovolo*), dim. of *ovo*, egg, L. *ōvum*], *n.* (*pl.* **-li,** -lē) (*Arch.*) A convex moulding, in Roman architecture a quarter-circle in outline, in Greek, elliptical with the greatest curve at the top.

ovology (ō vol′ ō ji) [OVI- (1)], *n.* The study of ova.

ovoviviparous (ō vō vī vip′ ȧ rŭs) [(OVO- (1)], *a.* Producing young by ova hatched within the body of the parent.

Ovra (ov′ ra) [initials of It. *Organizazione per Vigilanza e Ripressione di Antifascismo*], *n.* Political police of the government of Fascist Italy, the equivalent of the Gestapo in Germany.

ovule (ō′ vūl) [F., from mod. L. *ōvulum*, dim. of foll.], *n.* (*Bot.*) The rudimentary seed; the body in the ovary which develops into the seed after fertilization; (*Zool.*) the ovum or germ-cell in an animal, esp. before fertilization. **ovular,** *a.* **ovulate,** *v.i.* **ovulation** (-lā′ shŭn), *n.* The periodical discharge of the ovum or egg-cell from the ovary. **ovulite** (ō′ vū līt) [-LITE], *n.* (*Palæont.*) A fossil egg.

ovum (ō′ vŭm) [L., egg], *n.* (*pl.* **ova**) The female germ in animals, produced within the ovary and capable, usu. after fertilization by the male, of developing into a new individual; applied to the eggs of oviparous animals when small; (*Bot.*) an ovule; (*Arch.*) an egg-shaped ornament.

owe (ō) [A.-S. *āgan* (cp. Icel. *eiga*, Dan. *eie*, O.H.G. *aigan*)], *v.t.* To be indebted to for a specified amount; to be under obligation to pay or repay (a specified amount); to be obliged or indebted for; to have to thank for (a service, a grudge, etc.). *v.i.* To be indebted or in debt. **owing,** *a.* Due as a debt; attributable, ascribable, resulting from, on account of.

Owenism (ō′ ĕn izm) [Robert *Owen* (1771–1858), pioneer Socialist, -ISM], *n.* The principles of humanitarian and communistic co-operation taught by Owen. ***Owenian** (ō ē′ ni ȧn), **Owenist, -ite** (ō′ĕn ist, īt), *n.*

ower, owercome, etc. [Sc., OVER, OVER-].

owl (oul)) [A.-S. *ūle* (cp. Dut. *uil*, G. *eule*, Icel. *ugla*), cp. L. *ulula*, owl, *ululāre*, Gr. *ololuzein*, to HOWL], *n.* A nocturnal raptorial bird with large head, short neck, and short hooked beak, of various species belonging to the family *Strigidæ*, akin to the night-jars; a fancy breed of domestic pigeons; (*fig.*) a solemn-looking blockhead. **owl-light,** *n.* Imperfect light, dusk, twilight. **owl-like,** *a.* and *adv.* **owlery,** *n.* **owlet,** *n.* **owlish,** *a.* **owlishly,** *adv.*

own (1) (ōn) [A.-S. *āgen*, p.p. of *āgan*, OWE], *a.* Belonging or proper to, particular, individual, not anyone else's (usu. appended as an intensive to the poss. pronoun, adjective, etc.); (*ellipt.*) in the closest degree, by both parents (of a brother or sister). **on one's own:** (*colloq.*) Without aid from other people, independently. **to get one's own back:** To be even with. **to hold one's own** [HOLD].

own (2) (ōn) [A.-S. *āgnian*, from *āgen*, OWN (1)], *v.t.* To possess; to have as property by right; to acknowledge as one's own; to recognize the authorship, paternity, etc., of; to admit, to concede as true or existent. *v.i.* To confess (to). **to own up:** To confess, to make a clean breast (of). **owner,** *n.* A lawful proprietor; (*Naut. slang*) the captain. **ownerless,** *a.* **ownership,** *n.*

ox (oks) [A.-S. *oxa* (cp. Dut. *os*, G. *ochse*, Icel. *uxe*, *oxe*, Sansk. *ukshan*, pl.)], *n.* (*pl.* **oxen**) The castrated male of the domesticated *Bos taurus*; any bovine animal, esp. of domesticated species of the taurine group, large cloven-hoofed ruminants, usu. horned. **ox-bot, -fly,** *n.* A bot-fly, *Œstrus bovis*, or its larva. **ox-bow,** *n.* The bow-shaped piece of wood in an ox-yoke; a bend in a river. **ox-eye,** *n.* The great titmouse; applied to other birds; the moon-daisy, *Chrysanthemum leucanthemum*, and other composite plants. **ox-eyed,** *a.* Having large, full eyes. **ox-fly** [OX-BOT]. **ox-gall,** *n.* The gall of the ox, used as a cleansing agent in water-colour drawing. **ox-head,** *n.* A dolt, a blockhead. **ox-hide,** *n.* The skin of an ox; ox-skin. **oxlip,** *n.* A cross between the cowslip and primrose. **ox-tail,** *n.* The tail of an ox, esp. when used for making soup. **ox-tongue,** *n.* The alkanet and other plants with tongue-like leaves.

oxacid [OXYACID, see OXY-].

oxalic (ŏk săl′ ik) [F. *oxalique*, from L. OXALIS], *a.* Belonging to or derived from oxalis. **oxalic acid:** A sour, highly-poisonous acid found in numerous plants. **oxalate** (ok′ sȧ lȧt), *n.* **oxalo-,** *comb. form.*

Oxalis (ok′ sȧ lis) [L. and Gr., from *oxus*, sour], *n.* (*Bot.*) A genus of plants containing the wood-sorrel.

Oxford (oks′ fŏrd) [University city in England], *a.* Of, pertaining to, or derived from Oxford. **Oxford accent,** *n.* (*colloq.*) An affected, mincing enunciation. **Oxford bags,** *n.pl.* (*colloq.*) Trousers very wide at the ankles. **Oxford blue,** *n.* A dark shade of blue. **Oxford clay,** *n.* (*Geol.*) A stiff blue clay underlying the coral rag in the midland counties, the most characteristic bed of the Middle Oolite series. **Oxford corner,** *n.* (*Printing and Binding*) A plain border rule extending in each outward direction in such a manner as to make a square outside each corner. **Oxford grey,** *n.* A very dark grey. **Oxford Group,** *n.* The religious sect of BUCHMANITES. It has no connection with Oxford. **Oxford mixture,** *n.* A dark-grey cloth. **Oxford Movement,** *n.* A movement in the Church of England against a tendency toward liberalism, rationalism and Erastianism, originating in the University of Oxford (1833–41) under the leadership of J. H. Newman. **Oxford ochre,** *n.* A yellow ochre found near Oxford. **Oxford ragwort,** *n.* (*Bot.*) A kind of ragwort, *Senecio squalidus*. **Oxford School,** *n.* The school of thought represented by the Oxford Movement. **Oxford shoe,** *n.* A low shoe laced over the instep.

oxide (ok′ sīd) [OXYGEN, -IDE)], *n.* A binary compound of oxygen with another element or an organic radical. ***oxidate** [OXIDIZE]. ***oxidability** (-bil′ i ti), *n.* ***oxidable** [OXIDIZABLE], *a.* **oxidation** [OXIDIZATION]. **oxidize,** *v.t.* To combine with oxygen; to cover with a coating of oxide, to make rusty. *v.i.* To enter into chemical combination with oxygen; to rust. **oxidized silver:** Silver coated with sulphide of silver. **oxidizable,** *a.* **oxidization** (-zā′ shŭn), *n.* **oxidizer,** *n.*

oxlip, etc. [OX].

Oxonian (ok sō′ ni ȧn) [mod. L. *Oxonia*, Oxford, -AN], *n.* A member or graduate of Oxford University, *a.* Belonging to Oxford.

oxter (ok′ stėr) [A.-S. *ōxta*, cogn. with *ōxn*, cogn. with L. *axilla*], *n.* (*Sc.*) The armpit.

oxy- [Gr. *oxus*, sharp, biting, acid], *comb. form.* Sharp, keen; (*Chem.*) denoting the presence of oxygen or its acids or of an atom of hydroxyl substituted for one of hydrogen.

oxyacetylene (ok si ȧ set′ i lēn), *a.* (*Chem.*) Yielding a very hot blowpipe flame from the combustion of oxygen and acetylene, used for welding metals, etc.

oxyacid (ok si ăs′ id), *n.* An acid containing oxygen as distinguished from one formed with hydrogen; (*pl.*) one of the groups of acids derived from the fatty or aromatic series by the substitution of an atom of hydroxyl for one of hydrogen.

oxycarpous (ok si kar′ pŭs) [Gr. *karpos*, fruit], *a.* (*Bot.*) Having pointed fruit.

oxychloride (ok si klôr′ īd), *n.* (*Chem.*) A chemical compound formed by the union of oxygen and chlorine with another element.

oxygen (ok′ si jėn) [F. *oxygène* (OXY-, -GEN), from the belief that it was the essential element in all acids], *n.* A colourless, tasteless, odourless divalent element existing in a free state in the atmosphere, combined with hydrogen in water, and with other elements in most mineral and organic substances. **oxygen mask:** An apparatus for supplying oxygen in rarefied atmospheres to aviators, etc. **oxygen tent:** An oxygen-filled tent placed over a patient to assist breathing. **oxygenate** (ok′ si jė nāt, ok sij′ ė nāt), *v.t.* To treat or impregnate with oxygen; to oxidize. ***oxygenant,** *n.* **oxygenation** (-nā′ shŭn), *n.* **oxygenous,** *a.* **oxygenize,** *v.t.*

oxyhydrogen (ok si hi′ drŏ jėn) [OXY-, HYDROGEN], *n.* Consisting of a mixture of oxygen and hydrogen.

oxymoron (ok si môr′ ŏn) [Gr. *oxumōron* (OXY-, *mōros*, stupid)], *n.* (*Rhet.*) A rhetorical figure in which an epithet of a quite contrary signification is added to a word for the sake of point or emphasis, *e.g.* a clever fool, a cheerful pessimist.

oxytone (ok′ si tōn) [Gr. *oxutonos* (OXY-, *tonos*, TONE)], *a.* (*Gr. Gram.*) Having an acute accent on the last syllable. *n.* An oxytone word.

oyer (oi′ ėr) [A.-F., in *oyer et terminer*, hear and determine (L. *audīre*, to hear, *termināre*, to TERMINATE)], *n.* (*Law*) A hearing or trial of causes under writ of oyer and terminer. **oyer and terminer:** A commission formerly issued to two or more of the judges of assize, empowering them to hear and determine specified offences.

oyez (ō′ yės) [O.F., hear ye, imper. of *oir* (F. *ouïr*), L. *audīre*, to hear], *int.* Thrice repeated as introduction to any proclamation made by an officer of a court of law or public crier.

oyster (oi′ stėr) [O.F. *oistre* (F. *huître*), L. *ostrea*, Gr. *ostreon*], *n.* An edible bivalve mollusc of the genus *Ostrea*, found in salt or brackish water, eaten as food; an oyster-shaped morsel of meat in the hollow on either side of a fowl's back. **oyster-bank, -bed,** *n.* A part of a shallow sea-bottom forming a breeding-place for oysters. **oyster-bar,** *n.* Tavern where oysters are served. **oyster-catcher,** *n.* A wading-bird, *Hæmatopus ostralegus*, the sea-pie; also the American *H. palliatus*. **oyster-farm, -field, -park,** *n.* A part of the sea-bottom used for breeding oysters. **oyster-knife,** *n.* Knife specially shaped for opening oysters. **oyster-patty,** *n.*

ozocerite, ozokerite (ŏ zos′-, ŏ zok′ ėr īt, ōz ŏ sēr′-, -kēr′ īt) [G. *ozokerit* (Gr. *ozō*, I smell, *kēr-os*, wax, -ITE)], *n.* A fossil resin like spermaceti in appearance, used for making candles, insulators, etc.

ozone (ō zōn′) [F. (Gr. *oz-ein*, to smell, -ONE)], *n.* An allotropic form of oxygen, having three atoms to the molecule, with a slightly pungent odour and a stimulating and exhilarating influence on the human system, found in the atmosphere, probably as the result of electrical action. **ozonic** (-zon′ ik), **ozoniferous** (-nif′ ėr ŭs) [-FEROUS], *a.* **ozonize** (ō′ zŏ nīz), *v.t.* To charge with ozone. **ozonizer,** *n.* **ozonometer** (-nom′ ė tėr) [-METER], *n.* An instrument for ascertaining the amount of ozone in the atmosphere.

P

P, p, the sixteenth letter, and the twelfth consonant (*pl.* **Pees, P's Ps**), is a voiceless labial mute, having the sound heard in *pull*, *cap*, except when in combination with *h* it forms the digraph *ph*, sounded as *f*. **to mind one's Ps and Qs:** To be careful over details, esp. in behaviour.

pa (pa) [short for PAPA], *n.* A child's name for father.

pabulum (păb′ ū lŭm) [L. *pābulum*, cogn. with *pascere*, to feed], *n.* Food; nourishment; (*fig.*) nutriment of a physical, mental, or spiritual kind. **pabular,** *a.*

paca (păk′ ȧ) [Tupi-Guarani], *n.* A large Central and South American semi-nocturnal rodent, *Cœlogenys paca*, and others of the same genus.

pacable (pā′ kȧbl) [L. *pācābilis*, from *pācāre*, to appease, from *pax pācis*, PEACE], *a.* Able to be pacified or appeased, placable. ***pacation** (pȧ kā′ shŭn), *n.*

pace (1) (pās) [M.E. and O.F. *pas*, L. *passum*, nom. *-sus*, p.p. of *pandere*, to stretch], *n.* A step, the space between the feet in stepping (about 30 in.); (*Rom. Ant.*) the space between the point where the heel left the ground to that where the same heel descended in the next stride (about 60 in.); gait, manner of going, either in walking or running; the carriage and action of a horse, etc.; an amble, rate of speed or progress. *v.i.* To walk with slow or regular steps; to walk with even strides or in a slow, deliberate manner; to amble. *v.t.* To measure by carefully regulated steps; to traverse in slow and measured steps; to set the pace for. **to be put through one's paces:** To be examined closely, to be tested. **to go the pace:** To go very fast; (*fig.*) to run a course of dissipation or recklessness. **to keep pace with:** To go or progress at equal rate with. **to set** or **make the pace:** To fix the rate of going in a race. **pace-maker,** *n.* A rider or runner who sets the pace in a race. **paced,** *a.* Having a particular pace or gait (*in comb.*, as *thorough-paced*). **pacer,** *n.* One who paces; a horse trained in pacing.

pace (2) (pā′ si) [L., abl. of PAX], *prep.* With the permission of.

pacha, etc. [PASHA]. **pachak** [PUTCHUK].

pachisi (pȧ chē′ si) [Hindi, lit. 25], *n.* (*Ang.-Ind.*) A game played on a board with cowries for dice, named after the highest throw.

pachy- [Gr. *pachus*, thick, large], *comb. form.* Denoting thickness. **pachydactyl** (păk i dăk′ til) [DACTYL], *n.* An animal having thick toes. **pachyderm** (păk′ i dĕrm) [DERM], *n.* Any individual of the *Pachydermata*, an order of mammals containing hoofed non-ruminant animals with thick integuments; (*fig.*) a thick-skinned person. **pachydermatoid, -tous** (-dĕr′ mȧ toid, -tŭs), **pachydermoid,** *a.* **pachydermia,** *n.* (*Path*). Thickening of the skin. **pachyhæmia** (-hē′ mi ȧ) [Gr. *haima*, blood], *n.* Thickness of the blood. **pachymeter** (pȧ kim′ ė tėr) [-METER], *n.* An instrument for determining the thickness of glass, paper, etc.

pacific (pȧ sif′ ik) [F. *pacifique*, L. *pacificus* (*pax pācis*, *-ficāre*, *facere*, to make)], *a.* Inclined or tending to peace, conciliatory; tranquil, quiet, peaceful. **the Pacific:** The ocean between America and Asia, so named by Magellan. ***pacifical,** *a.* **pacifically,** *adv.* **pacification, pacifist,** etc. [PACIFY].

pacifism (păs′ i fizm), *n.* The doctrine of non-resistance to hostilities and of total non-co-operation with any form of warfare. Positively, it holds that all disputes should be settled by negotiation. **pacifist,** *n.* One who practises pacifism.

pacify (păs′ i fī) [F. *pacifier*, L. *pācificāre*, as PACIFIC], *v.t.* To appease, to calm, to quiet; to restore peace to. **pacification** (-kā′ shŭn), *n.* **pacificator** (pȧ sif′ i kā tŏr), *n.* **pacificatory,** *a.* **pacifier,** *n.*

pack (1) (păk) [cp. Dut. *pak*, Icel. *pakki*, G. *pack*], *n.* A bundle of things tied or wrapped together for carrying; a parcel, a burden, a load; a quantity going in such a bundle or parcel taken as a measure, varying with different commodities; a set, a crew, a gang; a set of playing-cards; a number of dogs kept together; a number of wolves or other beasts or birds, esp. grouse, going together; a quantity of broken ice floating in the sea; a quantity of fish packed for the market. *v.t.* To put together into a pack or packs; to stow into a bundle, box, barrel, bag, tin, etc., for keeping, carrying, etc.; to crowd closely together, to compress; to fill completely;

to cram (with); to wrap tightly, to cover or surround with some material to prevent leakage, loss of heat, etc.; to load with a pack; to arrange (cards) in a pack; to manipulate (cards) so as to win unfairly; to select or bring together (a jury, etc.) so as to obtain some unfair advantage; to send off or dismiss without ceremony. *v.i.* To put things in a pack, bag, trunk, etc., for sending away, carrying, or keeping; to crowd together, to form a pack (of animals); to leave with one's belongings; to depart hurriedly. **to pack on all sail:** (*Naut.*) To put all sail on. **to send one packing:** To dismiss summarily. **packdrill,** *n.* (*Mil.*) Form of punishment consisting of high-speed drill in full kit. **pack-horse,** *n.* A horse employed in carrying goods. **pack-ice,** *n.* Large piece of ice floating in the polar seas. **packman,** *n.* A pedlar. **packsaddle,** *n.* One for supporting packs. **packstaff,** *n.* A pedlar's staff for slinging his pack on. **packthread,** *n.* Strong thread for sewing or tying up parcels. **packer,** *n.* One who packs, esp. one employed to pack meat, fish, fruit, etc. for the market; a machine for doing this. **wet-pack,** *n.* (*Med.*) A wet sheet in which a patient is wrapped.

pack (2) (păk) [Sc., etym. doubtful], *a.* Intimate, closely confederate, confidential.

package (păk' ij), *n.* A parcel, a bundle; the packing of goods, the manner in which they are packed.

packet (păk' et) [PACK (1)], *n.* A small package; a packet-boat. *v.t.* To make up in a packet. **packet-boat,** *n.* A vessel conveying mails, goods, and passengers at regular intervals.

packing (păk' ing), *n.* That which is used for packing; (*Radio.*) trouble arising in a loose-contact carbon microphone owing to granules settling in a mass; (*Mach.*) material closing a joint or helping to lubricate a journal. **packing-case,** *n.* Large box made of unplaned wood. **packing-needle,** *n.* A long curved needle, used for sewing up bales, etc. **packing-ring,** *n.* (*Mach.*) The piston-ring in an internal-combustion engine. **packing-sheet,** *n.* A large sheet for packing; a wet sheet for wrapping a patient, in hydropathic treatment.

paco (păk' ō) [Sp. and Quichua], *n.* The alpaca; (*Min.*) a native brown, earthy, iron oxide.

pact (păkt) [O.F., from L. *pactum*, agreement, orig. neut. p.p. of *paciscere*, cogn. with PAX], *n.* An agreement, a compact.

pad (1) (păd) [Dut., PATH], *n.* (*orig. slang, now prov.*) The road, the way; a footpad; highway robbery; an easy-paced horse. *v.i.* To travel on foot; to trudge. *v.t.* To tramp or travel over; to tread. **knight or squire of the pad:** A knight of the road, a highwayman. **to pad the hoof:** To tramp on foot. **pad-groom,** *n.* A groom of light weight who rides a second horse for his master when hunting. ***pad-nag,** *n.* An ambling nag.

pad (2) (păd) [etym. doubtful], *n.* A soft cushion; a bundle or mass of soft stuff of the nature of a cushion; a soft saddle without a tree; a cushion-like package, cap, guard, etc., for stuffing, filling out, protecting parts of the body, etc.; a quantity of blotting-paper or soft material for writing on; a number of sheets of paper fastened together at the edge for writing upon and then detaching; (*Mil.*) a rocket-launching platform; the cushion-like sole of the foot, or the soft cushion-like paw of certain animals. *v.t.* (*past & p.p.* **padded**) To stuff or line with padding; to furnish with a pad or padding; to fill out (a sentence, article, etc.) with unnecessary words; (*Dyeing*) to impregnate with a mordant. **padded cell** or **room:** A room with padded walls in a lunatic asylum for confining violent patients. **padding,** *n.* Material used for stuffing a saddle, cushion, etc.; (*fig.*) matter inserted to fill out an article, magazine, or book.

paddle (1) (păd' ėl) [etym. doubtful], *n.* A broad short oar used without a rowlock; the blade of this or of an oar; a paddle-board; a paddle-wheel; a spell of paddling; (*prov.*) a spade-like implement used for cleaning a plough-share of earth, digging up weeds, etc.; a similar implement used in washing clothes. *v.t.* To propel by means of paddles. *v.i.* To ply a paddle; to move along by means of a paddle; to row gently; to swim with short, downward strokes. **paddle-board,** *n.* One of the floats or blades of a paddle-wheel. **paddle-box,** *n.* The casing over the upper part of a paddle-wheel. **paddle-wheel,** *n.* A wheel with floats or boards projecting from the periphery for pressing against the water and propelling a vessel.

paddle (2) (păd' ėl) [etym. doubtful], *v.i.* To dabble in the water with the hands or, more usually, the feet; to move the fingers in a fondling way (in, upon, or about); to toddle.

paddock (1) (păd' ȯk) [prob. corr. of A.-S. *pearruc*, cp. PARK], *n.* A small field or enclosure, usu. under pasture and near a stable; a turfed enclosure attached to a stud-farm; (*Austral.*) any pasture land enclosed by a fence; a turfed enclosure adjoining a racecourse where horses are kept before racing.

paddock (2) (păd' ȯk) [M.E. *padde* (cp. Icel. *padda*, Dut. *padde*), -OCK], *n.* (*Sc.*) a frog; *a toad; *(*fig.*) a repulsive person. ***paddock-stool,** *n.* A toadstool.

Paddy (1) (păd' i) [short for *Padraig*, St. *Patrick*, the patron of Ireland], *n.* (*nickname*) An Irishman. **Paddy's lucerne,** *n.* (*Austral.*) A Queensland weed.

paddy (2) (păd' i) [Malay *paddi*], *n.* Rice in the straw or in the husk.

paddy (3) (păd' i), *n.* (*colloq.*) A rage, temper.

paddymelon (păd' i mel ȯn) [corr. of abor. name], *n.* (*Austral.*) A small bush kangaroo or wallaby.

padella (pȧ del' ȧ) [It., from L. PATELLA], *n.* A shallow vessel containing oil, etc. in which a wick is set, used esp. in Italy for illuminations.

padishah (pa' di sha) [Turk., from Pers. *pādshāh* (Sansk. *pati*, master, lord, SHAH)], *n.* The title of the Shah of Persia, also formerly in India of the British sovereign and of the Great Mogul.

padkos (păd' kos) [S. African], *n.* Food for a journey.

padlock (păd' lok) [*pad*, etym. doubtful, LOCK (1)], *n.* A detachable lock with a bow or loop for fastening to a staple, etc. *v.t.* To fasten with this.

padre (pa' drā) [Port., Span., and It., father or priest], *n.* Used in addressing a priest in Italy, Spain, and Spanish America; (*Mil. and Nav. slang*) a chaplain.

padrone (pȧ drō' nā) [It., from med. L. *patrōnem*, nom. *patro*, L. *patrōnus*, PATRON], *n.* A master, an Italian employer or house-owner; the proprietor of an inn in Italy; the master of a small trading-vessel in the Mediterranean.

paduasoy (păd' ū ȧ soi) [F. *pou-de-soie*, corr. by association with *Padua*, a city in Italy], *n.* A kind of silk stuff, much worn in the 18th cent.; a garment of this.

pæan (pē' ȧn) [L., from Gr. *Paian*, a name of Apollo], *n.* A choral song addressed to Apollo or some other deity; a song of triumph or rejoicing.

pædagogy, etc. [PEDAGOGY].

pæderast [PEDERAST].

pædeutics (pē dū' tiks) [Gr. *paideutikos*, from *paideuein*, to bring up a child, from *pais paidos*, a child], *n.* The science of education.

pædo- [Gr. *pais paidos*, boy, child], *comb. form.* Relating to children. **Pædobaptism** (pē dȯ băp' tizm) [BAPTISM], *n.* Infant as opposed to adult baptism. **Pædobaptist,** *n.*

pæon (pē' ȯn) [L., from Gr. *paiōn*, Attic form of *paian*, PÆAN], *n.* (*Pros.*) A metrical foot of four syllables, one long the others short in different order.

pæony [PEONY].

pagan (pā' gȧn) [L. *pāgānus* (from *pāgus*, the country), a countryman, hence a non-militant (opp. to *miles Christi*, a soldier of Christ)], *n.* A heathen; (*fig.*) a barbarous or unenlightened person; a person who has no religion or disregards Christian beliefs. *a.* Heathen, heathenish; unenlightened; irreligious. **pagandom, paganism,** *n.* **paganish,** *a.* **paganize,** *v.t.* and *i.*

page (1) (pāj) [O.F., etym. doubtful], *n.* A young male attendant on persons of rank; hence, a title of various functionaries attached to the royal household; a boy in livery employed to go on errands, attend to the door, etc., (*Am.*) a bell-hop. *a youth in training for knighthood attached to a knight's retinue. **v.t.* (1) To attend on as a page; to summon a person (in a hotel, etc.) by calling his name aloud. **pagehood, pageship,** *n.*

page (2) (pāj) [F., from L. *pāgina*, from *pāg-*, stem of *pangere*, to fasten], *n.* One side of a leaf of a book; (*fig.*) a record, a book; an episode. *v.t.* (2) To put numbers on the pages of (a book). **paginal,** ***paginary** (pāj'-), *a.* **paginate,** *v.t.* **pagination** (-nā' shŭn), *n.* **paging,** *n.*

pageant (păj' ent, pā' jent) [perh. as prec.], *n.* A brilliant display or spectacle, esp. a parade or procession of an elaborate kind; a theatrical exhibition, usu. representing well-known historical events, and illustrating costumes, buildings, manners, etc.; a tableau or allegorical design usu. mounted on a car in a procession; empty and specious show. **v.t.* To exhibit in a show. **pageantry,** *n.*

paginate, pagination [PAGE (2)].

pagoda (pă gō' dă) [Port. *pagode*, corr. of Indian name], *n.* A sacred temple, usu. in the form of a pyramidal tower in many receding stories, all elaborately decorated, in India, China, and other Eastern countries; a building imitating this; a gold coin formerly current in India. **pagoda-tree,** *n.* The name of several kinds of Indian and Chinese trees shaped more or less like pagodas. **to shake the pagoda-tree:** (*facet.*) To shake it and bring down pagodas (coins), hence to make money fast. **pagodite** (păg' ŏ dīt), *n.* A soft limestone which the Chinese carve into figures.

pagurian, paguroid (pă gūr' i ăn, -oid) [L. *pagūrus*, Gr. *pagouros*], *a.* Of or pertaining to the *Paguridæ* or decapod crustaceans. *n.* A member of this family, a hermit crab.

pah (1) (pa) [instinctive sound], *int.* An exclamation of disgust, etc.

pah (2), **pa** (pa) [Maori], *n.* A native settlement.

Pahlavi (pa' lă vi) [Pers., from *Pahlav*, a district in Persia], *n.* The character used for the sacred writings of the Persians; the literary language of Persia under the Sassanian kings, old Persian.

paid [PAY (1)]. **paideutics** [PÆDEUTICS].

paigle (pā' gĕl) [etym. doubtful], *n.* (*prov.*) The cowslip; applied to the oxslip, buttercup, and other flowers.

paik (pāk) [Sc., etym. unknown], *v.t.* To hit, to beat. *n.* A hard blow, a beating.

pail (pāl) [cp. A.-S. *pægel*, Dut. and G. *pegel*, a small measure of liquid; also O.F. *paelle, paielle*, dim. of L. PATELLA], *n.* An open vessel, usu. round, of metal or wood, for carrying liquids; a pailful. **pailful,** *n.* (*pl.* **pailfuls**).

paillette (păl yet') [F., dim. of *paille*, L. *palea*, straw, chaff], *n.* A small piece of metal or foil used in enamel-painting; a spangle. **paillon** (pa yon, păl' yŏn), *n.* A bright metal backing for enamel or painting in translucent colours.

pain (pān) [O.F. *peine*, L. *pæna*, Gr. *poinē*, penalty], *n.* Bodily or mental suffering; a disagreeable sensation in animal bodies; (*pl.*) labour, trouble; *punishment, penalty. *v.t.* To inflict pain upon, to afflict or distress bodily or mentally; *to torture, to punish. **to take pains:** To take trouble, to labour hard or be exceedingly careful. **on pain of, under pain of:** Subject to the penalty of. **painful,** *a.* Attended with or causing mental or physical pain; laborious, toilsome, difficult. **painfully,** *adv.* **painfulness,** *n.* **painless,** *a.* **painlessly,** *adv.* **painlessness,** *n.* **painstaker,** *n.* One who takes pains, a laborious worker. **painstaking,** *a.* and *n.*

paint (pānt) [O.F. *peint*, p.p. of *peindre*, L. *pingere*], *v.t.* To cover or coat with paint; to give a specified colour to with paint; to tinge; to portray or represent in colours; to adorn with painting; (*fig.*) to depict or image vividly in words. *v.i.* To practise painting; to rouge. *n.* A solid colouring-substance or pigment, usu. dissolved in a liquid vehicle, used to give a coloured coating to surfaces; colouring-matter used as a cosmetic, rouge. **paint-box,** *n.* A box in which oil- or water-colours are kept in compartments. **paint-brush,** *n.* **to paint out:** To efface by painting over. **to paint the town red:** (*slang*) To make a disturbance by a noisy spree. **painted lady:** An orange-red butterfly spotted with black and white; the sweet pea. **painty,** *a.*

painter (1) (pān' tėr), *n.* One whose occupation is to colour walls, woodwork, etc. with paint; an artist who paints pictures. **painter's colic,** *n.* A kind of lead-poisoning to which painters are subject.

painter (2) (pān' tėr) [perh. from O.F. *pentoir*, med. L. *penditōrium*, from *pendēre*, to hang; or from A.-F. *panter* (F. *pantière*), a snare], *n.* A bow-rope for fastening a boat to a ring, stake, etc. **to cut the painter:** To cast (oneself) adrift.

painting (pān' ting), *n.* The act, art, or occupation of laying on colours or producing representations in colours; a picture.

pair (1) (pâr) [F. *paire*, L. *paria*, neut. pl. of *par*, equal], *n.* Two things of a kind, similar in form, or applied to the same purpose or use; a set of two, a couple, usu. corresponding to each other; an implement or article having two corresponding and mutually dependent parts, as scissors, spectacles; an engaged or married couple; a flight (of stairs); (*Parl.*) two members of opposite views abstaining from voting by mutual agreement. *v.t.* To make or arrange in pairs or couples; to cause to mate. *v.i.* To be arranged in pairs; to mate; to unite in love; (*colloq.*) to marry; (*Parl.*) to make a pair (with). **to pair off:** To separate into couples; to go off in pairs; (*Parl.*) to make a pair (with). **pair-horse,** *a.* For a pair of horses (of harness, etc.). **pair-oar,** *n.* A boat rowed by two men each with one oar. ***pair royal:** Three cards of the same denomination in certain games. **pairing-time,** *n.* The time when birds mate. **one-pair, two-pair front (back),** *n.* Front (back) room on the first or second floor.

***pair** (2) (pâr) [from obs. *appair empeirer*, IMPAIR], *v.t.* To impair.

pake (pa' kē) [Maori], *n.* A Maori mat or cloak.

pakeha (pa kē' ha) [Maori], *n.* A white man. **Pakeha Maori,** *n.* A European who lives as a Maori with them.

Pakistani (pa ki stan' ē), *n.a.* A native of, or pertaining to Pakistan.

paktong (păk' tong) [Cantonese for Chin. *peh t'ung* (*peh*, white, *t'ung*, copper)], *n.* A Chinese alloy of zinc, nickel, and copper, like silver.

pal (păl) [Gipsy], *n.* (*slang*) A friend, chum, or mate. *v.i.* **to pal up with:** To become friendly with.

palace (păl' ăs, păl' is) [O.F. *palais*, L. *palātium*, orig. a house built by Augustus on the Palatine Hill at Rome], *n.* The official residence of an emperor, king, bishop, or other distinguished personage; a splendid mansion; a large building for entertainments, a music-hall, cinema-theatre, showy drinking-saloon, etc. **gin palace** [GIN (1)]. **palace-car,** *n.* A luxuriously-appointed railway car.

paladin (păl' ă din) [F., from L. *palātīnus*, PALATINE (2)], *n.* One of Charlemagne's twelve Peers; a knight-errant.

palæ-, palæo- [Gr. *palaios*, old, ancient], *comb. form.* Pertaining to or existing in the earliest times. **palæarctic** (păl ē ark' tik) [ARCTIC], *a.* Pertaining to the northern parts of the Old World, including Europe, N. Africa, and Asia north of the Himalayas, esp. as a zoogeographical region. **palæichthyology** (-ik thi ol' ŏ ji) [ICHTHYOLOGY].

n. The branch of palæontology concerned with extinct fishes. **palæobotany** (-bot′ ȧ ni) [BOTANY], *n.* The botany of extinct or fossil plants. **palæobotanical** (-tăn′ i kȧl), *a.* **palæobotanist** (-bot′ ȧ nist), *n.* **palæogean** (-jē′ ȧn) [Gr. *gaia*, *gē*, the earth], *a.* Pertaining to the early conditions of the earth's surface; pertaining to the Old World as a zoogeographical region.

palæography (păl i og′ rȧ fi), *n.* The art or science of deciphering ancient inscriptions or manuscripts; ancient manuscripts collectively. **palæograph,** *n.* **palæographer,** *n.* **palæographic,** *a.*

palæolithic (păl i ō lith′ ik) [Gr. *lithos*, a stone], *n.* Pertaining to the earlier Stone Age. **palæolith,** *n.* A stone implement of this period.

palæology (păl i ol′ ō ji), *n.* The science of antiquities, archæology. **palæologist,** *n.*

palæontology (păl ė on tol′ ȯ ji) [PALÆ- ONTO-, -LOGY], *n.* The science or the branch of biology or geology dealing with fossil animals and plants. **palæontological** (-loj′ i kȧl), *a.* **palæontologist** (-tol′ ȯ jist), *n.* **palæothere,** ***palæotherium*** (păl ė ȯ thēr′, -i ŭm) [Gr. *therion*, beast], *n.* (*Palæont.*) An extinct genus of pachydermatous mammals chiefly from the Eocene strata. **palæozoic** (păl ė ȯ zō′ ik) [-ZOIC], *a.* (*Geol.*) Denoting the lowest fossiliferous strata and the earliest forms of life.

palæstra (pȧ lē′ strȧ) [Gr. *palaistra*, from *palaiein*, to wrestle], *n.* (*Gr. Ant.*) A place where athletic exercises were taught and practised; a gymnasium or wrestling-school. **palæstral, -tric,** *a.*

palafitte (păl′ ȧ fit) [F., from It. *palafitta* (*palo*, PALE (1), *fitto*, fixed)], *n.* A prehistoric house built on piles, a lake-dwelling.

palama (păl′ ȧ mȧ) [Gr., *palame*, palm of the hand], *n.* (*Zool.*) The webbing of the feet in aquatic birds.

palampore (păl′ ȧm pôr) [etym. doubtful], *n.* (*Ang.-Ind.*) A decorated chintz counterpane, formerly made in India.

palankeen (păl ȧn kēn′), **palanquin** [Port. *palanquim*, Hindi *pālakī* or *palang*, Sansk. *palyaṅka*, *paryaṅka*, couch, bed], *n.* A couch or litter borne by four or six men on their shoulders.

palatable (păl′ ȧ tȧ bėl) [PALATE, -ABLE], *a.* Pleasing to the taste; (*fig.*) agreeable, acceptable. **palatableness,** *n.* **palatably,** *adv.*

palate (păl′ ȧt) [L. *palātum*], *n.* The roof of the mouth; (*fig.*) the sense of taste; liking, fancy. *v.t.* To try with the taste; (*fig.*) to relish. **hard** or **bony palate:** The anterior or bony part of the palate. **soft palate:** The posterior part consisting of muscular tissue and mucous membrane terminating in the uvula. **palatal,** *a.* Pertaining to or uttered by the aid of the palate. *n.* A sound produced with the palate, esp. the hard palate, as *k, g, ch, y, s, n.* **palatalize, palatize,** *v.t.* **palatic** (pȧ lăt′ ik), *a.* **palatine** (1) (păl′ ȧ tīn, -tin), *a.* (*Anat.*) Of or pertaining to the palate. *n.pl.* The two bones forming the hard palate, also called palatine bones.

palatial (pȧ lā′ shȧl) [L. *palātium*, PALACE, -AL], *a.* Pertaining to or befitting a palace; magnificent, splendid.

palatine (1) [PALATE].

palatine (2) (păl′ ȧ tīn, -tin) [F. *palatin*, *-tine*, L. *palātīnus*, from *palātium*, PALACE], *a.* Pertaining to or connected with a palace, orig. the palace of the Cæsars, later of the German Emperors; palatial; possessing or exercising royal privileges (as the counties of Chester, Durham, and Lancaster); of or pertaining to a count palatine. *n.* One invested with royal privileges; a count or earl palatine; a woman's fur tippet worn over the shoulders. **The Palatine:** The territory of the Count Palatine of the Rhine, an elector of the Holy Roman Empire. **palatinate** (pȧ lăt′ i nāt), *n.*

palaver (pȧ la′ vėr) [Port. (Sp. *palabra*), from L. *parabola*, PARABLE], *n.* A discussion, a conference, a parley, esp. between African or other natives and traders; talk, chatter; cajolery, flattery. *v.t.* To talk over, to flatter. *v.i.* To confer; to talk idly and profusely. **palaverer,** *n.*

palay (pȧ lā′) [Tamil], *n.* A small Indian tree with hard, close-grained wood used for turnery.

palberry (păl′ be ri) [Austral. abor., *palbri*], *n.* A type of currant.

pale (1) (pāl) [F. *pal*, L. *pālus*], *n.* A pointed stake; a narrow board used in fencing; a limit or boundary; a region, a district, a territory, a sphere; (*Her.*) a vertical band down the middle of a shield. *v.t.* To enclose with or as with pales. **the Pale:** (*Hist.*) The part of Ireland in which English authority was recognized. ***paled,** *a.* Fenced in; *striped.

pale (2) (pāl) [O.F. *pale*, *palle*, L. *pallidus*, from *pallēre*, to be pale], *a.* Whitish, ashen, wanting in colour, not ruddy; dim, faint (of colours or light). *v.t.* To make pale. *v.i.* To turn pale; (*fig.*) to be pale, dim, or poor in comparison. **pale ale:** Light-coloured ale. **pale-eyed,** *a.* **pale-face,** *n.* A name supposed to be given by North American Indians to white persons. **pale-faced,** *a.* ***pale-hearted,** *a.* Fearful, timid. **pale-visaged,** *a.* **palely,** *adv.* **paleness,** *n.* **paiish, paly** (2), *a.*

palea (pā′ lė ȧ) [L., chaff], *n.* (*Bot.*) A bract or scale resembling chaff, at the base of the florets in composite flowers, enclosing the stamens and pistil in grass-flowers, or on the stems of ferns. **paleaceous** (-ā′ shŭs), *a.*

paleo- [PALÆO-].

paletot (păl′ tō) [F., etym. doubtful (perh. *palle*, L. *palla*, cloak, TOQUE)], *n.* A loose overcoat for men or women.

Palestinian (păl ės tin′ i ȧn), *a.* Of or pertaining to Palestine, a country of S.W. Syria, the Holy Land. **palestra** [PALÆSTRA].

palette (păl′ ėt) [F., dim. of *pale*, L. *pāla*, shovel], *n.* A flat board used by artists for mixing colours on; the colours or arrangement of colours used for a particular picture or by a particular artist. **palette-knife,** *n.* A thin, flexible knife for mixing and sometimes for putting on colours.

palfrey (pawl′-, păl′ fri) [O.F. *palefrei* (F. *palefroi*), low L. *palafrēdus*, *paraverēdus* (PARA-, *verēdus*, post-horse, prob. of Celt. orig.)], *n.* A small saddle-horse, esp. for a lady.

Pali (pa′ li) [Hind., line (of letters), canon], *n.* The canonical language of Buddhist literature, akin to Sanskrit.

***palification** (pā li fi kā′ shŭn) [med. L. *pālificātio*, from *pālificāre* (*pālus*, PALE (1), *-ficāre*, *facere*, to make)], *n.* The driving of piles for a foundation, etc. **paliform** (pā′ li fôrm), *a.* Having the form of a palus.

palimpsest (păl′ imp sest) [L. *palimpsēstus*, Gr. *palimpsēstos* (*palin*, again, *psēstos*, scraped, from *psaein*, Ionic *pseen*, to scrape or rub)], *n.* A manuscript on parchment or other material from which the original writing has been erased to make room for another record. *a.* Treated in this manner. *v.t.* To write on (parchment, etc.) from which a previous record has been erased.

palin- [Gr. *palin*, again, back], *comb. form.* **palinal** (păl′ i nȧl), *a.* Moving backward. **palindrome** (păl′ in drōm) [Gr. *palindromos* (*dromos*, from *dromein*, to run)], *n.* A word, verse, or sentence that reads the same backwards or forwards. *e.g.* "Madam I'm Adam" (Adam's alleged self-introduction to Eve). **palindromic** (-drom′ ik), *a.* **palindromist** (pȧ lin′ drȯ mist), *n.*

paling (pā′ ling), *n.* A fence made with pales.

palingenesia (păl in jė nē′ si ȧ), **palingenesy** (păl in jen′ ė si) [Gr. *palingenesia*, as foll.], *n.* A new birth, a regeneration.

palingenesis (păl in jen′ ė sis) [PALIN-, GENESIS], *n.* Palingenesy; (*Biol.*) the form of ontogeny in which the development of the ancestors is exactly reproduced; the repetition of historical events in the same order in an infinite number of cycles, or the theory of such repetition. **palingenetic** (-jė net′ ik), *a.* **palingenetically,** *adv.*

palinode (păl′ i nōd) [from L. and Gr. *palinōdia*], *n.* A poem in which a previous poem, usu. satirical, is retracted; a recantation. *v.t.* To retract. **palinodial, -dic** (-nō′ di ăl, -nō′ dik), *a.* **palinodist,** *n.* ***palinody** (păl′ i nō di), *n.*

palisade (păl i sād′) [F. *palissade*, from *palisser*, to enclose with poles, from *palis*, PALE (1)], *n.* A fence or fortification of stakes, timbers, or iron railings. *v.t.* To enclose or to fortify with stakes. ***palisado** (-sā′ dō), *n.* and *v.t.*

palish [PALE (2)].

pall (1) (pawl) [A.-S. *pæll*, L. *pallium*, cloak], *n.* A large cloth (usu. of black, purple, or white cloth, velvet, etc.) thrown over a coffin, hearse, or tomb; a pallium; (*fig.*) a cloak, a mantle. **v.t.* To cover with or as with a pall, to shroud. **pall-bearer, *-holder,** *n.* One who attends the coffin at a funeral, or who holds up the funeral pall.

pall (2) (pawl) [prob. from APPAL], *v.i.* To become vapid or insipid. *v.t.* To make vapid, insipid, or spiritless; to cloy, to dull.

Palladian (1) (pă lā′ di ăn), *a.* Of or according to the Italian architect Andrea Palladio (1518–80) or his school of architecture; pertaining to the free and ornate classical style modelled on the teaching of Vitruvius. **Palladianism,** *n.* **Palladianize,** *v.t.*

palladium (1) (pă lā′ di ŭm) [L., from Gr. *palladion*], *n.* A statue of Pallas on the preservation of which, according to tradition, the safety of Troy depended; (*fig.*) a defence, a safeguard. **palladian** (2), *a.*

palladium (2) (pă lā′ di ŭm) [Gr. *Pallas -ados*, Greek goddess of wisdom, the 2nd asteroid], *n.* (*Metall.*) A greyish-white metallic element of the platinum group, used as an alloy with gold and other metals.

pallescent (pă les′ ent) [L. *pallescens -ntem*, pres.p. of *pallescere*, incept. of *pallēre*, to pale], *a.* (*rare*) Growing pale. **pallescence,** *n.*

pallet (1) (păl′ ėt) [PALETTE], *n.* A palette; a tool, usu. consisting of a flat blade and handle, used for mixing and shaping clay in pottery-making, or for taking up gold-leaf and for gilding or lettering in bookbinding; a pawl or projection on a part of a machine, for converting reciprocating into rotary motion or vice versa; a valve regulating the admission of air from the wind-chest to an organ-pipe.

pallet (2) (păl′ ėt) [M.E. and prov. F. *paillet*, from *paille*, L. *pălea*, straw], *n.* A small rude bed; a straw mattress.

pallial (păl′ i ăl), *a.* (*Zool.*) Pertaining to the pallium or mantle of molluscs. ***palliament** (păl i ă ment′) [med. L. *palliāmentum*], *n.* A robe.

palliasse (păl′ i ăs) [F. *paillasse*, from *paille*, L. *pălea*, straw], *n.* A mattress or under-bed of straw or other material.

palliate (păl′ i āt) [L. *palliātus*, p.p. of *palliāre*, to cloak, from PALLIUM], *v.t.* To cover with excuses; to extenuate; to mitigate, to alleviate (a disease, etc.) without entirely curing. **palliation** (-ā′ shŭn), *n.* **palliative** (păl′ i ă tiv), *a.* and *n.* **palliatively,** *adv.* ***palliatory,** *a.*

pallid (păl′ id) [L. *pallidus*], *a.* Pale, wan. **pallidly,** *adv.* **pallidness,** *n.*

pallium (păl′ i ŭm) [L.], *n.* (*pl.* **-lia**) A man's square woollen cloak, worn esp. by the ancient Greeks; (*Eccles.*) a scarf-like vestment of white wool with red crosses, worn by the Pope and certain metropolitans and archbishops; (*Zool.*) the mantle of a bivalve.

pall-mall (pel mel, păl măl) [M.F. *pallemaille*, It. *pallamaglio* (*palla*, ball, *maglio*, L. *malleus*, MAUL (1))], *n.* An old game in which a ball was driven with a mallet through an iron ring; an alley or long space in which this was played, whence the name of the London thoroughfare Pall Mall.

pallone (pal lō′ nā) [It., from *palla*, ball], *n.* An Italian game like tennis, in which the ball is struck with the arm protected by a wooden guard.

pallor (păl′ ŏr) [L., from *pallēre*, to be pale], *n.* Paleness, want of healthy colour.

palm (1) (pam) [A.-S., from L. *palma*, cp. Gr. *palamē*], *n.* A tree or shrub belonging to the *Palmaceæ*, a family of tropical or subtropical endogens, usu. with a tall branched stem and head of large fan-shaped leaves; a palm-branch or leaf as a symbol of victory or triumph; victory, triumph, the prize, the pre-eminence; applied to the sallow and other trees, or their branches carried instead of palms in northern countries on Palm Sunday. **to bear the palm:** To have the pre-eminence. **palm-cabbage,** *n.* The edible terminal bud of some palms. **palm-house,** *n.* A glass-house for palms and other tropical plants. **palm-oil,** *n.* An oil obtained from the fruit of certain kinds of palm; (*colloq.*) a tip, a bribe. **Palm Sunday:** The Sunday immediately preceding Easter, commemorating the triumphal entry of Christ into Jerusalem. **palmaceous** (-mā′ shŭs), *a.* **palmary** (păl′ mă ri), *a.* Bearing or worthy of the palm; pre-eminent, chief, noblest.

palm (2) (pam) [M.E. and F. *paume*, L. *palma*], *n.* The inner part of the hand; the part of a glove, etc., covering this; a measure of breadth (3–4 ins.) or of length (8–8½ ins.); the under part of the foot; the broad flat part of an oar, tie, strut, antler, etc.; the fluke of an anchor. *v.t.* To conceal (dice, etc.) in the palm; hence, to pass (off) fraudulently; to touch with the palm, to handle; (*slang*) to bribe. **to palm off:** To foist. **palmar** (păl′ măr), *a.* Of, pertaining to, in, or connected with the palm. *n.* A palmar muscle or nerve; a brachial plate or joint in crinoids. **palmate, palmated,** *a.* (*Bot.* *and Zool.*) Resembling a hand with the fingers spread out; webbed (of the foot of a bird). **palmately,** *adv.* **palmati-,** *comb. form.* **palmatifid** (păl măt′ i fid), *a.* (*Bot.*) Palmately cleft or divided. **palmatiform,** *a.* (*Bot.*) **palmed** (pamd), *a.* Having a palm or palms (*usu. in comb.*, as *full-palmed*).

palmary [PALM (1)].

palmer (pa′ mėr) [A.-F. *palmer*, O.F. *palmier*, med. L. *palmārius*, PALMARY], *n.* A pilgrim who carried a palm-branch in token of his having been to the Holy Land; a pilgrim, devotee, itinerant monk, etc.; a palmer-worm; an angler's imitation of this. **palmer-worm,** *n.* A hairy caterpillar.

palmette (păl met′) [F., dim. of *palme*, PALM (1)], *n.* (*Archæol.*) A carved or painted ornament in the form of a palm-leaf.

palmetto (păl met′ ō) [Sp. *palmito*, dim. of *palma*, PALM (1)], *n.* A small variety of palm, esp. *Sabal palmetto*, a fan-palm of the Southern United States; the dwarf fan-palm and other species of *Chamærops*.

palmi- [L. *palma*, PALM (1 and 2)], *comb. form.* ***palmiferous** (păl mif′ ėr ŭs) [-FEROUS], *a.* Producing or carrying palms. **palmification** (-kā′ shŭn) [cp. CAPRIFICATION], *n.* A method, employed by the Babylonians, of artificially fecundating the female flowers of the date palm by suspending clusters of male flowers of the wild date above them. **palmigrade** [PLANTIGRADE]. **palmiped** (păl′ mi ped) [L. *palmipēs* (*pes pedis*, foot)], *a.* (*Ornith.*) Having palmate or webbed feet. *n.* A web-footed bird.

palmistry (pa′ mis tri) [M.E. *pawmestry*], *n.* Fortune-telling by the lines and marks on the palm of the hand. **palmist, *palmister,** *n.*

palmitic (păl mit′ ik) [F. *palmitique* (*palmite*, palm-pith, from L. *palma*], *a.* (*Chem.*) Of or derived from palm-oil. **palmitin** (păl′ mi tin), *n.* A natural fatty compound contained in palm-oil, etc.

palmy (pa′ mi), *a.* Abounding in palms; victorious, flourishing.

palmyra (păl mī′ ră) [Port *palmeira*, as PALMARY, assim. to *Palmyra*, city of Syria], *n.* An East

Indian palm, *Borassus flabelliformis*, with fan-shaped leaves used for mat-making.

palp (pălp), **palpus** (păl′ pŭs) [L. *palpus*], *n.* (*usu. in pl.* **palps, palpi,** -pī) Jointed sense-organs developed from the lower jaws of insects, etc., feelers. **palpal, palped,** *a.*

palpable (păl′ pȧ bėl) [late L. *palpābilis*, from L. *palpāre*, to feel, as prec.], *a.* Perceptible to the touch; easily perceived, plain, obvious. ***palpableness** (păl′-), **palpability** (-bil′ i ti), *n.* **palpably,** *adv.* **palpate,** *v.t.* To feel, to handle, to examine by feeling. **palpation** (-pā′ shŭn), *n.*

palpebral (păl′ pė brȧl) [F. *palpébral*, L. *palpebrālis*, from *palpebra*, eyelid], *a.* Pertaining to the eyelid. ***palpebrate,** *a.*

palpi [PALP].

palpifer (păl′ pi fėr) [L. *pilpi-*, PALPUS, *-fer*, bearing], *n.* (*Ent.*) The feeler-bearer, or the sclerite bearing the maxillary palpi. **palpiform** (păl′ pi fôrm), *a.* **palpiferous** (-pif′ ėr ŭs), *a.* Bearing palpi, esp. maxillary palpi. **palpiger** (păl′ pi jėr), *n.* The part of the labium bearing the labial palpi. **palpigerous** (-pij′ ėr ŭs), *a.*

palpitate (păl′ pi tāt) [L. *palpitātus*, p.p. of *palpitāre*, freq. of *palpāre*, to PALPATE], *v.i.* To throb, to pulsate; to flutter; to beat rapidly (of the heart). **palpitation** (-tā′ shŭn), *n.* **palpus** [PALP].

palsgrave (pawlz′ grāv) [Dut. *paltsgrave* (now *paltsgraaf*), cp. G. *pfalzgraf*, O.H.G. *pfalenzgrâvo* (*pfalenza*, PALACE, *grâvo*, GRAVE (4))], *n.* A count palatine, orig. one who had the superintendence of a prince's palace. **palsgravine,** *n.* His wife.

palstave (pawl′ stāv) [Dan. *paalstav*, from Icel. *pālstafr* (*pāll*, hoe, STAVE)], *n.* A bronze celt shaped like an axe-head, made to fit into a handle instead of being socketed.

palsy (pawl′ zi) [M.E. *palesy*, O.F. *paralisie*, PARALYSIS], *n.* Paralysis; (*fig.*) infirmity, inefficiency, helplessness. ****v.t.*** To paralyse. **palsied,** *a.*

palter (pawl′ tėr) [etym. unknown], *v.i.* To equivocate, to shuffle, to act trickily (with); to haggle; to trifle; *to chatter. ***palterer,** *n.*

paltry (pawl′ tri) [cp. dial. *paltry*, rubbish, trash, M.E. *palter*, pl., rags (cp. Swed. *paltor*, Dan. *pjalter*, rags, L.G. *palte*, M.Dut. and Fris. *palt*)], *a.* Mean, petty, despicable. **paltrily,** *adv.* **paltriness,** *n.*

paludal (pȧ lū′-, păl′ ū dȧl), **paludic** (pȧ lū′ dik), **paludine** (păl′ ū din, -dīn), **paludinal, -ous** (pȧ lū′ di nȧl, -nŭs) [L. *palus*, *palūdis*, marsh], *a.* Pertaining to marshes or fens, marshy; malarial. **paludism** (păl′ ū dizm), *n.* The morbid conditions produced by living among marshes. **paludous** (pȧ lū′ dŭs), **paludose** (păl ū dōs′), *a.* Growing in or among or produced by marshes.

paludament (pȧ lū′ dȧ mėnt) [L. *palūdāmentum*], *n.* (*Rom. Ant.*) A cloak or mantle worn by a Roman general and his chief officers.

paludrine (păl′ ū drīn), *n.* A synthetic quinine substitute for the treatment of malaria.

palus (pā′ lŭs) [L., PALE (1)], *n.* (*pl.* **-li,** -lī) (*Biol.*) One of the upright calcareous laminæ or septa in corals.

paly (1) (pā′ li) [PALE (1), -Y], *a.* (*Her.*) Divided into several equal parts by perpendicular lines. **paly** (2) [PALE (2)].

palynology (păl i nol′ ō ji) [Gr. *palynein*, to sprinkle], *n.* (*Biol.*) The study of pollen grains and other spores.

pam (păm) [F. *pamphile*, prob. from L. *Pamphilus*, Gr. *Pamphilos*, personal name, beloved of all], *n.* The knave of clubs, esp. in five-card loo, where this is the highest trump; a nick-name of Lord Palmerston.

pampas (păm′ pȧz, -pȧs) [Sp., pl. of *pampa*, Peruv. *bamba*, a plain, a steppe], *n.pl.* (*sing.* **pampa**) The open, far-extending, treeless plains in South America, south of the Amazon. **pampas-grass,** *n.* A lofty grass, *Gynerium argenteum*, originally from the pampas.

pamper (păm′ pėr) [prob. freq. of obs. *pamp*. L.G. *pampen*, to cram, to gorge oneself], *v.t.* To feed (a person, oneself, etc.) luxuriously; to gratify (tastes, etc.) to excess. **pamperedness,** *n.* **pamperer,** *n.*

pampero (păm pâr′ ō) [Sp.], *n.* A violent westerly or south-westerly wind blowing over the pampas.

pamphlet (păm′ flėt) [O.F. *Pamphilet*, fem. form of *Pamphile*, L. *Pamphilus*, title of a Latin erotic poem of the 12th cent.], *n.* A small book of a few sheets, stitched, but not bound, usu. on some subject of temporary interest. **pamphleteer** (păm flė tēr′), *n.* and *v.i.*

pamphysical (păm fiz′ i kȧl) [Gr. *pam-*, PAN-, PHYSICAL], *a.* (*Phil.*) Of or pertaining to material nature regarded as originating and embracing all things.

pampiniform (păm pin′ i fôrm) [L. *pampinus*, vine-shoot, -FORM], *a.* (*Anat.*) Curling like a vine-tendril. **pampiniform plexus:** A convoluted plexus of veins carrying blood from the genital gland.

pamplegia (păm plē′ ji ȧ) [Gr. *pam-*, as prec., *plēgē*, stroke, blow], *n.* (*Path.*) General paralysis.

pan (1) (păn) [A.-S. *panne* (cp. Dut. *pan*, G. *pfanne*, Icel. *panna*)], *n.* A broad shallow vessel of metal or earthenware, usu. for domestic uses; a vessel for boiling, evaporating, etc., used in manufacturing, etc.; a hollow in the ground for evaporating brine in salt-making; a sheet-iron dish used for separating gold from gravel, etc., by shaking in water; the part of a flint-lock that holds the priming; hard pan; *the skull, the brain-pan. *v.t.* (*past & p.p.* **panned**) To wash (gold-bearing earth or gravel) in a pan (usu. with *out*). *v.t.i.* (*Cinema., Radio.*) To move the camera while taking the picture of a moving object. **to pan out:** To yield gold; (*fig.*) to yield a specified result (esp. well or badly). **pancake,** *n.* A thin flat cake of batter fried in a frying-pan. *v.i.* (*Aviat.*) To alight from a low altitude at a large angle of incidence, remaining on an even keel. **panful,** *n.*

Pan (2) (păn) [Gr.], *n.* The chief rural divinity of the Greeks, represented as horned and with the hindquarters of a goat. **Pan-pipe,** *n.* A musical instrument made of a number of pipes or reeds, a mouth-organ.

pan- [Gr. *pas pantos*, all], *comb. form.* **panacea** (păn ȧ sē′ ȧ) [L., from Gr. *panakeia* (*ak-*, root of *akeomai*, I heal)], *n.* A universal remedy, *a plant of healing virtue. **panaceist,** *n.*

panache (pȧ nash′) [F., from It. *pennacchio*, from PENNA], *n.* A tuft or plume, esp. on a head-dress or helmet; (*fig.*) show, swagger, bounce; airs.

panada (pȧ na′ dȧ), ***panade** (pȧ nad′) [Sp. *panada* (F. *panade*), ult. from L. *pānis*, bread], *n.* Bread boiled to a pulp, sweetened and flavoured.

panæsthesia (pan ēs thē′ si ȧ) [Gr. *panaisthēsia* (PAN-, *æsthesis*, perception, *asthanesthei*, to perceive)], *n.* The whole sum of perceptions by an individual at any given time. **panæsthetic** (-thet′ ik), *a.* **Pan-African** (păn ăf′ ri kȧn) [AFRICAN], *a.* Of, pertaining to, or for all Africans. **Pan-Africander.**

Panama-hat (păn′ ȧ ma hăt) [*Panama*, town in Isthmus of Panama], *n.* A hat made from the undeveloped leaves of the S. American screw-pine, *Carludovica palmata*.

Pan-American (păn ȧ mer′ i kȧn) [PAN-, AMERICAN], *a.* Of or pertaining to the whole of both N. and S. America. **Pan-Americanism,** *n.* **Pan-Anglican** (păn ăng′ gli kȧn) [ANGLICAN], *a.* Of, including, or representing all members of the Anglican and allied Churches. **Panathenæa** (păn ăth ė nē′ ȧ) [Gr. *panathēnaia*], *n.pl.* The chief annual festival of the Athenians, celebrating with games and processions the union of Attica under Theseus. **Pan-Christian,** *a.* Pertaining to all

Christians. **Pan-German** (păn jĕr′ mȧn) [GERMAN (2)], *a.* Relating to Germans collectively or to Pan-Germanism. **Pan-Germanism,** *n.* The movement to unite all Teutonic peoples into one nation. **Pan-Hellenic,** *a.* Of, characteristic of, or representing all Greeks. **Panhellenism,** *n.* **Panislam** (păn iz′ lȧm), *n.* The whole of Islam; a union of the Mohammedan peoples. **Panislamic** (-lăm′ ik), *a.* **Panislamism** (-iz′ lȧm izm), *n.* **Pan-Presbyterian** (păn prez bi tēr′ i ȧn), *a.* Of or pertaining to all Presbyterians. **Panslavism,** *n.* A movement for the union of all the Slavic races. **Panslavic** (păn slăv′ ik) [SLAVIC], *a.* **Panslavist,** *n.* **Panslavistic** (-vis′ tik), *a.* ***Panslavonian, -ic** (-slȧ vō′ ni ȧn, -nik), *a.*

panarthritis (păn ar thrī′ tis), *n.* (*Path.*) Inflammation involving the whole structure of a joint.

pancake [PAN (1)]. ***panch** [PAUNCH].

pancheon (păn′ chȯn), *n.* A large earthenware pan, used for standing milk in, etc.

panchromatic (păn krō măt′ ik) [PAN-, CHROMATIC], *a.* (*Phot.*) Uniformly sensitive to all colours.

panclastite (păn klăs′ tīt) [Gr. *klastos*, broken, from *klaiein*, to break], *n.* An explosive produced by mixing together nitrogen tetroxide and certain carbon preparations.

pancratium (păn krā′ shi ŭm) [L., from Gr. *pankration* (PAN-, *kratos*, strength)], *n.* (*Gr. Ant.*) An athletic contest including both boxing and wrestling. **pancratiast, pancratist** (păn′ krȧ tist), *n.* **pancratic** (-krăt′ ik), *a.* Pertaining to the pancratium; excellent in athletic exercises; (*Opt.*) capable of adjustment to many degrees of power (of lenses).

pancreas (păn′ krė ȧs) [L. and Gr. (PAN-, *kreas*, *-atos*, flesh)], *n.* A gland near the stomach secreting a fluid that aids digestive action, the sweetbread. **pancreatic** (-ăt′ ik), *a.* **pancreatin** (păn′ krė ȧ tin), *n.* (*Chem.*) A proteid compound found in the pancreas and the pancreatic juice. **pancreatitis** (-tī′ tis), *n.* (*Path.*) Inflammation of the pancreas.

pand (pănd) [Sc., prob. from O.F. *pandre*, L. *pendēre*, to hang], *n.* (*Sc.*) A narrow bed-curtain, a valance.

panda (păn′ dȧ) [native name], *n.* A small racoon-like animal, *Ælurus fulgens*, from the S.E. Himalayas and Tibet. **giant panda,** *n.* The *Ailuropus melanoleucus*, linking the panda with the bears.

Pandanus (păn dā′ nŭs) [mod. L., from Malay *pandan*], *n.* (*Bot.*) A genus of trees or bushes containing the screw-pines.

Pandean (păn dē′ ȧn), *a.* Pertaining to the god Pan. **Pandean pipes:** Pan-pipes.

pandect (păn′ dekt) [F. *pandecte*, L. *pandecta*, Gr. *pandektēs* (PAN-, *dechomai*, to receive)], *n.* (*usu. pl.*) The digest of the Roman civil law made by direction of the emperor Justinian in the 6th cent.; any complete system or body of laws; *a comprehensive treatise or digest.

pandemic (păn′ dem′ ik) [Gr. *pandēm-os* (PAN-, *dēmos*, people), -IC], *a.* Widely epidemic, affecting a whole country or the whole world.

pandemonium (păn dė mō′ ni ŭm) [coined by Milton (PAN-, DEMON)], *n.* (*pl.* **-iums**) The abode of all demons or evil spirits; a place or state of lawlessness, confusion, or uproar; (*fig.*) confusion, uproar.

pander (păn′ dėr) [*Pandare* (L. *Pandarus*), who procured for Troilus the favour of Criseyde, in Chaucer's 'Troilus and Criseyde'], *n.* A procurer, a pimp, a go-between in an amorous intrigue; (*fig.*) one who ministers to base or evil passions, prejudices, etc. *v.t.* To act as pander to; to minister to the gratification of. *v.i.* To act as an agent (to) for the gratification of evil passions, desires, lusts, etc. **panderess,** *n.* **panderism,** ***panderage,** *n.*

pandiculation (păn dik ū lā′ shŭn) [L. *pandiculāri*, to stretch oneself, from *pandere*, to stretch, -TION], *n.* A stretching of the body and limbs in drowsiness or in certain nervous disorders; yawning.

Pandora (1) (păn dôr′ ȧ) [Gr. (PAN-, *dōra*, pl. of *dōron*, gift)], *n.* (*Gr. Myth.*) According to Hesiod, the first woman. **Pandora's box:** A box containing all human ills and blessings, which Pandora brought with her from heaven; on its being opened by her husband Epimetheus, all escaped except Hope.

pandora (2) (păn dôr′ ȧ), **pandore** (-dôr′) [It. *pandora*, *pandura* (F. *pandore*), L. *pandūra*, Gr. *pandoura*, etym. unknown], *n.* A lute-like musical instrument, a bandore.

pandour, -door (păn′ door) [F. *Pandour*, Serbo-Croatian *pàndūr*, *bàndūr*, med. L. *banderius*, from *bandum*, see BANNER], *n.* One of a body of foot-soldiers, noted for their ferocity, raised by Baron von der Trenck in 1741, and subsequently enrolled in the Austrian army; hence, a rapacious and brutal soldier.

panduriform (păn dūr′ i fôrm) [L. *pandūra*, PANDORA (2), -FORM], *a.* Fiddle-shaped.

pandy (păn′ di) [Sc., said to be from L. *pande*, stretch out], *n.* A stroke on the palm with a cane, ferule, etc. *v.t.* To strike on the palm.

pane (pān) [F. *pan*, L. *pannum*, nom. *-nus*, piece of cloth], *n.* A sheet of glass in a window, etc.; one square of the pattern in a plaid, etc.; *a piece, part, or division; *a side, face, or surface. *v.t.* To make up (a garment, etc.) with panes or strips of different colours; to put panes in (a window). **paned,** *a.* **paneless,** *a.*

panegyric (păn ė jir′ ik) [F. *panégyrique*, L. *panēgyricus*, Gr. *panēgurikos* (PAN-, AGORA)], *n.* A eulogy written or spoken in praise of some person, act, or thing; an elaborate encomium. **a.* Panegyrical. **panegyrical,** *a.* **panegyrist,** *n.* **panegyrically,** *adv.* **panegyrism** (păn′ ė ji rizm), *n.* **panegyrize,** *v.t.* and *i.*

panel (păn′ ėl) [O.F., from med. L. *pannellus*, dim. of *pannus*, PANE], *n.* A rectangular piece (orig. of cloth); a rectangular piece of wood or other material inserted in or as in a frame, forming a compartment of a door, wainscot, etc.; a thin board on which a picture is painted; a picture, photograph, etc., the height of which is much greater than the width; a piece of stuff of a different colour let in lengthwise in a woman's dress; a cloth placed under a saddle to prevent chafing; a kind of saddle; (*Law*) a list of persons summoned by the sheriff as jurors; a jury; the team in a quiz game, brains trust, etc.; an official list of persons; persons receiving medical treatment under the Insurance Act; (*Sc. Law*) a prisoner or the prisoners at the bar. *v.t.* (*past & p.p.* **panelled**) To fit or furnish (a door, wall, etc.) with panels; to decorate (a dress) with panels; to put a panel on (a horse, etc.). **panel-doctor,** *n.* A doctor on the official list of those undertaking duty in connexion with the National Insurance Acts. **panel-game,** *n.* A quiz game in which a panel of experts, etc., answer questions from an audience. ***panel-house,** *n.* A house of ill-fame into which persons were enticed and robbed by means of panels in the walls. **panel-plane, -saw,** *n.* A plane or saw used in panel-making. **panel-strip,** *n.* A strip of wood for covering the joint between a panel and a post or between two panels. **panel-work, panelling,** *n.*

paneless [PANE]. **panful** [PAN (1)].

pang (1) (păng) [etym. doubtful], *n.* A sudden paroxysm of extreme pain; a throe, agony. **v.t.* To torture; to torment. **pangless,** *a.*

pang (2) (păng) [Sc. and North., etym. doubtful], *v.i.* To cram, to stuff.

pangenesis (păn jen′ ė sis), *n.* (*Biol.*) Reproduction from every unit of the organism, a theory of heredity provisionally suggested by Darwin. **pangenetic** (-net′ ik), *a.*

pangolin (păng gō′ lin) [Malay *pang-gōling*, a roller (from its habit of rolling itself up)], *n.* A scaly ant-eater, of various species belonging to the genus *Manis*.

panhandle (păn' hăndl) [PAN (1), HANDLE], *n.* (*Am.*) A strip of territory belonging to one political division extending between two others.

panharmonic (păn har mon' ik) [PAN-, HARMONIC], *a.* Universally harmonic. **panharmonicon,** *n.* A mechanical musical instrument.

panic (1) (păn' ik) [F. *panique*, Gr. *panikos*, from PAN (2)], *n.* Sudden, over-powering, unreasoning fear, esp. when many persons are affected; a general alarm about financial concerns causing ill-considered action. *a.* Sudden, extreme, unreasoning; caused by fear. *v.t.i.* (**panicked**) To affect or be affected with panic. **panic-monger,** *n.* **panic-stricken, -struck,** *a.* Struck with sudden fear. **panicky,** *a.*

panic (2) (păn' ik) [L. *pānicum*], *n.* A common name for several species of the genus *Panicum*, esp. the Italian millet. **panic-grass,** *n.*

panicky [PANIC (1)].

panicle (păn' i kėl) [L. *pānicula*, dim. of *pānus*, a swelling, ear of millet], *n.* (*Bot.*) A loose and irregular compound flower-cluster. **panicled, paniculate** (pȧ nik' ū lȧt), *a.* **paniculately,** *adv.*

Panicum (păn' i kŭm) [L., PANIC (2)], *n.* A genus of grasses with numerous species, some (as the millet) valuable for food.

panification (păn i fi kā' shŭn) [F., from *panifier*, to make into bread, from L. *pānis*, bread], *n.* (*Chem.*) The process of making or converting into bread.

panjandrum (păn jăn' drŭm) [humorous coinage by Samuel Foote], *n.* A mock title for a self-important or arrogant person; a high and mighty functionary or pompous pretender.

panlogism (păn' lȯ jizm) [PAN-, Gr. *logos*, word, reason, -ISM], *n.* (*Phil.*) The doctrine that the universe is the outward manifestation of the inward idea or logos.

panmixia (păn miks' i ȧ) [Gr. *-mixia*, *mixis*, mixing, from *mignunai*, to MIX], *n.* (*Biol.*) Fortuitous mingling of hereditary characters due to the cessation of the influence of natural selection in regard to organs that have become useless.

•**pannade** (pȧ năd') [obs. F., from *panader*, to strut, to curvet], *n.* The curvet of a horse.

pannage (păn' ȧj) [A.-F. *panage*, O.F. *pasnage*, late L. *pastionāticum*, from *pastio*, grazing, from *pascere*, to feed], *n.* The feeding or the right of feeding swine in a forest, or the payment for this; mast picked up by swine in a forest.

panne (pan) [F.], *n.* (*Text.*) A soft, long-napped fabric.

pannier (1) (păn' i ėr) [M.E. and F. *panier*, L. *pānārium*, bread-basket, from *pānis*, bread], *n.* A large basket, esp. one of a pair slung over the back of a beast of burden; a covered basket for drugs and surgical instruments for a military ambulance; a framework, usu. of whalebone, formerly used for distending a woman's skirt at the hips; (*Arch.*) a sculptured basket, a corbel. **panniered,** *a.*

pannier (2) (păn' i ėr) [etym. doubtful], *n.* One of the robed waiters in the dining-hall at Inns of Court.

pannikin (păn' i kin) [PAN (1), -KIN], *n.* A small drinking-cup of metal; that contained in it; (*Am.*) a dipper, a small saucepan. **pannikin boss,** *n.* (*Austral.*) A sub-overseer on a station.

pannus (păn' ŭs) [prob. L. *pannus*, cloth, see PANE], *n.* (*Path.*) An opaque vascular state of the cornea; a tent for a wound; a birthmark. **pannose** (pȧ nōs') *a.* (*Bot.*) Like cloth in texture. **pannous** (păn' ŭs), *a.* (*Path.*) Of the nature of *pannus*.

panoistic (păn ȯ is' tik) [PAN-, Gr. *ōon*, egg, -IST, -IC], *a.* (*Ent.*) Producing ova only, opp. to meroistic.

panophobia (păn ō fō' bi ȧ) [PAN-, PHOBIA], *n.* (*Path.*) Excessive fear (literally of everything).

panoply (păn' ȯ pli) [Gr. *panoplia* (PAN-, *hopla*, arms, pl. of *hoplon*, tool, implement)], *n.* A complete suit of armour; (*fig.*) complete defence. **panoplied,** *a.*

panopticon (păn op' ti kȯn) [PAN-, Gr. *optikon*, neut. of *-kos*, of sight, OPTIC], *n.* A prison constructed on a circular plan with a central well for the warders so that the prisoners would be always under observation; an exhibition-room for novelties, etc.

panorama (păn ȯ ra' mȧ, -răm' ȧ) [PAN-, Gr. *horama*, view, from *horaein*, to see], *n.* A continuous picture of a complete scene on a sheet unrolled before the spectator or on the inside of a large cylindrical surface viewed from the centre; complete view in all directions; a general survey. **panoramic** (-răm' ik), *a.* **panoramically,** *adv.*

panotitis (păn ȯ tī' tis) [PAN-, Gr. *ous ōtos*, ear, -ITIS], *n.* (*Path.*) Inflammation of both the middle and internal ear.

panotrope (pan' o trop) [PAN-, Gr. *tropos*, a turn], *n.* (*Acous.*) An electrical reproducer of disk gramophone records operating one or more loudspeakers.

Pan-pipe [PAN (2)].

pansclerosis (păn skle rō' sis), *n.* (*Path.*) Complete induration of the interstitial tissue of a part.

pansophy (păn' sȯ fi) [Gr. *sophia*, wisdom], *n.* Universal knowledge; a scheme of universal knowledge; pretence of universal wisdom. **pansophic, -al** (-sof' ik, -ȧl), *a.* **pansophically,** *adv.*

panspermia (păn spĕr' mi ȧ) [Gr. *sperma*, seed], **panspermatism, panspermism, panspermy,** *n.* The theory that the atmosphere is pervaded by invisible germs which develop on finding a suitable environment. **panspermatist,** *n.* **panspermic,** *a.*

pansy (păn' zi) [F. *pensée*, thought, orig. fem. p.p. of *penser*, to think, L. *pensāre*, freq. of *pendere*, to weigh], *n.* A species of viola, with large flowers of various colours in the cultivated varieties, the heartsease; (*colloq.*) an effeminate fellow. **pansied,** *a.*

pant (pănt) [cp. A.-F. *pantoiser*, O.F. *pantaisier* (F. *panteler*), pop. L. *phantasiāre*, to dream, to have nightmare, L. *phantasiārī*, see PHANTASM], *v.i.* To breathe quickly; to gasp for breath; to throb, to palpitate; (*fig.*) to long, to yearn (after, for, etc.). *v.t.* To utter gaspingly or convulsively. *n.* A gasp; a throb, a palpitation. **panting,** *ger.* (*Shipbuilding*) The bulging in and out of the plating of a ship under the stress of heavy seas.

pant- [PANTO-], *comb. form.*

pantagamy (păn tăg' ȧ mi) [*panta-*, irreg. for PANTO-, *-gamia*, *gamos*, marriage], *n.* A system of communistic marriage in which all the men are married to all the women, as practised in the Oneida Community in Idaho, from 1838 onwards.

pantagogue (păn' tȧ gog) [Gr. *agogos*, leading, driving out], *n.* A medicine supposed to be capable of expelling all morbid matter.

pantagraph [PANTOGRAPH].

Pantagruelism (păn tȧ groo' ėl izm) [*Pantagruel*, character in Rabelais], *n.* Coarse and boisterous burlesque and buffoonery, esp. with a serious purpose, like that of Pantagruel. **Pantagruelian** (el' i ȧn), *a.* **Pantagruelist** (-groo' ė list), *n.*

pantalets, pantalettes (păn tȧ lets'), *n.pl.* Loose drawers for children, extending below the skirts with frills at the bottom; detachable frilled legs for these; drawers, cycling knickerbockers, etc., for women.

pantaloon (păn tȧ loon') [F. *pantalon*, It. *pantalone* (Venetian character on the Italian stage, prob. from San *Pantaleone*, a popular saint in Venice)], *n.* A character in pantomime, the butt of the clowns' jokes; (*pl.*) tight trousers fastened below the shoe, as worn in the Regency period; (*Am.*) trousers.

pantechnicon (păn tek′ ni kŏn) [PAN-, Gr. *technikon* (*technē*, art), -IC], *n.* A storehouse for furniture; a place where all sorts of manufactured articles are exposed for sale; a pantechnicon van. **pantechnicon van:** A large van for removing furniture.

pantheism (păn′ thė izm) [PAN-, Gr. *theos*, god, -IZM], *n.* The doctrine that God and the universe are identical; the heathen worship of all the gods. **pantheist,** *n.* **pantheistic, -ical** (-is′ tik, -ăl), *a.*

Pantheon (păn thē′-, păn′ thė ŏn) [L., from Gr. *pantheion* (PAN-, *theios*, divine, from *theos*, god)], *n.* A famous temple with a circular dome at Rome, built about 27 B.C., and dedicated to all the gods; (*collect.*) the divinities of a nation; a treatise on all the gods; a building dedicated to the illustrious dead, esp. a building at Paris, orig. a church, so dedicated in 1791; applied to buildings for public entertainment, after the one opened in London in 1772.

panther (păn′ thėr) [M.E. and O.F. *pantere*, L. *panthēra*, Gr. *panthēr*], *n.* The leopard.

panties (păn′ tiz), *n.pl.* Women's short knickers.

pantile (păn′ tīl), *n.* A tile curved transversely to an ogee shape.

pantisocracy (păn ti sok′ rȧ si) [PANT-, Gr. *isokratia*], *n.* A Utopian scheme of communism in which all are equal in rank, and all are ruled by all. **pantisocrat** (-tī′ sȯ krăt), *n.* **pantisocratic** (tī′ sȯ krăt′ ik), *a.*

***pantler** (pănt′ lėr) [corr. of M.E. *paneter*, O.F. *panetier*, med. L. *pānetārius*, from *pānis*, bread], *n.* The officer who has charge of the bread or the pantry in large establishments.

panto- [Gr. *pas pantos*, all], *comb. form.* ***pantochronometer** (păn tȯ krȯ nom′ ė tėr) [CHRONOMETER], *n.* A combination of compass, sun-dial, and universal sun-dial.

***pantofle** (păn′ tȯfl, păn tofl′, -tufl′) [F. *pantoufle*, It. *pantofola*, etym. unknown], *n.* A slipper.

pantograph (păn′ tȯ grăf), *n.* An instrument used to enlarge, copy, or reduce plans, etc. **pantographic, -al** (-grăf′ ik, -ăl), *a.*

pantography (păn tog′ rȧ fi), *n.* A general description.

pantology (păn tol′ ō ji), *n.* Universal knowledge; a work of universal information. **pantologic, -al,** *a.*

pantometer (păn tom′ ė tėr), *n.* An instrument for measuring angles and determining elevations, distances, etc.

pantomime (păn′ tȯ mīm) [L. *pantomīmus*, Gr. *pantomimos*], *n.* (*Rom. Ant.*) One who performed in dumb show; representation in dumb show; a theatrical entertainment, usu. produced at Christmas-time, consisting largely of farce and burlesque. *v.t.* To express or represent by dumb show. *v.i.* To express oneself by dumb show. **pantomimic, -al** (-mim′ ik, -ăl), *a.* **pantomimist** (-mī′ mist), *n.*

pantomorphic (păn tȯ môr′ fik) [PANTO-, Gr. *morphē*, form, -IC], *a.* Assuming all or any shapes.

panton (păn′ tŏn) [Sc., etym. doubtful, prob. rel. to PANTOFLE], *n.* A slipper; a kind of horseshoe.

pantophagist (păn tof′ ȧ jist) [Gr. *pantophagos* (PANTO-, *phagein*, to eat)], *n.* A man or beast that eats all kinds of food. **pantophagous** (-gŭs), *a.* **pantophagy** (-ji), *n.*

pantoscope (păn′ tȯ skōp), *n.* A panoramic camera; a lens with a very wide angle. **pantoscopic** (-skop′ ik), *a.* Having great breadth of vision.

pantry (păn′ tri) [O.F. *paneterie*, med. L. *pānetāria*, a place where bread is made, etc., from L. *pānis*, bread], *n.* A room or closet in which bread and other provisions are kept. **pantryman,** *n.* A butler or his assistant.

pants (pănts) [short for PANTALOONS], *n.pl.* Drawers for men and boys; (*Am.*) men's trousers, women's knickers.

panurgic (păn ĕr′ jik) [late Gr. *panourgikos*, from *panourgos* (PAN-, *ergon*, work)], *a.* Able to do any kind of work.

panzer (păn′ tser) [G., armour, armour-plating], *a.* Term applied to armoured bodies, esp. an armoured division, in the German army.

panzoism (păn zō′ izm) [PAN-, Fr. *zoē*, life, -ISM], *n.* (*Herbert Spencer*) The sum of the elements making up vital force.

pap (păp) [prob. imit.], *n.* Soft or semi-liquid food for infants, etc.; pulp; (*fig.*) weak mental nutriment. **pappy,** *a.* **pap** (2) (păp) [imit., cp. prec.], *n.* A teat, a nipple; a conical hill or small peak.

papa (1) (pȧ pa′) [F., from L. *pāpa*, imit. in orig. (cp. Gr. *pappas*)], *n.* (*Childish*) Father.

papa (2) (pa′ pȧ) [med. L., from Gr. *pappas*, see prec.], *n.* The Pope; (*Gr. Ch.*) a parish priest or one of the inferior clergy.

papa (3) (pa′ pa) [Maori], *n.* A blue clay found in N. Zealand.

papacy (pā′ pȧ si) [med. L. *pāpātia*, from prec.], *n.* The office, dignity, or tenure of office of the Pope; the papal system or government; the Popes collectively. **papal,** *a.* Pertaining to the Pope or his office, or to the R.-C. Church. **papalism,** *n.* ***papalist,** *n.* ***papalize,** *v.t.* and *i.* **papalization** (-zā′ shŭn), *n.* **papally** (pā′ pȧ li), *adv.* ***papaphobia** (-fō′ bi ȧ) [-PHOBIA], *n.* **paparchy** (pā′ par ki) [-ARCHY], *n.*

papain (pȧ pā′ in) [Sp. *papaya*, PAPAW, -IN], *n.* (*Chem.*) A protein compound found in the milky juice of the papaw.

papaverous (pȧ pā′ vėr ŭs) [L. *papāver*, poppy, -OUS], *a.* Resembling or allied to the poppy. **papaveraceous** (-ā′ shŭs), *a.*

papaw (pȧ paw′) [Sp. *papaya*, Carib. *abábai*], *n.* A tropical American palm-like tree, *Carica papaya*, the milky juice of which, obtained from the stem, leaves, or fruit, makes meat tender; its fruit.

paper (pā′ pėr) [O.F. *papier*, L. PAPYRUS], *n.* A thin flexible substance made of rags, wood-fibre, grass, or similar materials, used for writing and printing on, wrapping, etc.; a piece, sheet, or leaf of this; a written or printed document; an essay, a dissertation; a newspaper; a set of questions for an examination; negotiable instruments, as bills of exchange; paper money; paper-hangings; (*slang*) free passes, also persons admitted to a theatre, etc., by such passes; (*pl.*) documents establishing identity, etc., a ship's documents. *a.* Made of paper; like paper; stated only on paper, having no real existence. *v.t.* To cover with or decorate with paper; to wrap or fold up in paper; to rub with sandpaper; to furnish with paper; (*slang*) to admit a large number to (a theatre, etc.) by free passes. **to commit to paper:** To write down; to record. **to send in one's papers:** To resign. **paper-chase,** *n.* A game in which one or more persons called the hares drop pieces of paper as scent for pursuers called the hounds, to track them by. **paper credit:** Credit allowed on the score of bills, promissory notes, etc., showing that money is due to the person borrowing. **paper-currency** [PAPER MONEY], *n.* **paper-cutter, -knife,** *n.* A flat piece of wood, ivory, etc., for cutting open the pages of a book, etc. **paper-hangings,** *n.pl.* Paper ornamented or prepared for covering the walls of rooms, etc. **paper-hanger,** *n.* **paper-making,** *n.* **paper-mill,** *n.* A mill in which paper is manufactured. **paper-money:** Bank-notes or bills used as currency, opp. to coin. **paper-profits:** Hypothetical profits shown on a company's prospectus, etc. **paper-stainer,** *n.* A manufacturer of paper-hangings. **paper-weight,** *n.* A weight for keeping loose papers from being displaced. ***paper-white,** *a.* **papery,** *a.* **paperiness,** *n.*

papeterie (pȧ pė tri′) [F., from *papetier*, a paper-manufactory, paper-maker, med. L. *papeterius*, as prec.], *n.* An ornamental case for writing materials.

Paphian (pā′ fi ăn), *a.* Pertaining to Paphos, a city of Cyprus sacred to Venus; pertaining to Venus or her worship. *n.* A native of Paphos; (*fig.*) a courtesan.

papier mâché (păp yā măsh′ ā) [F., chewed paper], *n.* A material made from pulped paper, moulded into trays, boxes, etc., and usu. japanned.

papilionaceous (pȧ pil i ȯ nā′ shůs) [L. *papilio -ōnis*, butterfly, -ACEOUS], *a.* (*Bot.*) Resembling a butterfly; used of plants with butterfly-shaped flowers, as the pea.

papilla (pȧ pil′ ȧ) [L., dim. of PAPULA], *n.* (*pl.* **-læ**) A small pap, nipple, or similar process; a small protuberance on an organ or part of the body or on plants. **papillary, -late, -lose, *-lous** (păp′-), *a.* **papilliferous** (-lif′ ĕr ůs), **papilliform** (-pil′ i fôrm), *a.* **papillitis** (-lī′ tis) [-ITIS], *n.* (*Path.*) Inflammation of the optic papilla. **papilloma** (păp i lō′ mȧ), *n.* A tumour formed by the growth of a papilla or group of papillæ, as a wart, corn, etc. **papillomatous,** *a.* **papilloso-,** *comb. form.*

***papillote** (păp′ i lōt) [F., perh. from *papillon*, L. *papilio -ōnis*, butterfly], *n.* A curl-paper.

papist (pā′ pist) [F. *papiste* (PAPA (2), -IST)], *n.* A Roman Catholic. **papism, papistry,** *n.* **papistic, -al** (-pis′ tik, -ȧl), *a.*

papoose (pȧ poos′) [N. Am. Ind.], *n.* A young child.

pappus (păp′ ůs) [mod. L., from Gr. *pappos*], *n.* (*Bot.*) The calyx of composite plants, consisting of a tuft of down or fine hairs or similar agent for dispersing the seed; (*Anat.*) the first hair of the chin. **pappous** (păp′ ůs), **-pose** (pȧ pōs′), *a.* Downy.

paprika (păp′ ri kȧ) [Hung.], *n.* Red pepper.

pappy [PAP (1)].

Papuan (păp′ ū ȧn), *a.* Of or pertaining to Papua or New Guinea. *n.* One of the dark, frizzly-haired, dolichocephalic race inhabiting the Melanesian archipelago.

papula (păp′ ū lȧ) [L., a pustule, dim. from *pap-*, to swell], *n.* (*pl.* **-læ**) A pimple; a small fleshy projection on a plant. **papular** (păp′ ū lȧr), **-lose** (păp ū lōs′), **-lous** (păp′ ū lůs), *a.* **papulation** (-lā′ shůn), *n.* **papule** (păp′ ūl), *n.* **papuliferous** (-lif′ ėr ůs), *a.*

papyrus (pȧ pī′ rŭs) [L., from Gr. *papuros*, of Egyptian orig.], *n.* (*pl.* **-ri**) A rush-like plant of the genus *Cypereæ*, common formerly on the Nile and still found in Abyssinia, Syria, etc.; a writing-material made from this by the Egyptians and other ancient peoples; a manuscript written on this material. **papyraceous** (-rā′ shůs), *a.* Made of or of the nature of papyrus; of the consistence of paper, papery. **papyral** (-pī′ rȧl), **papyrian** (-pir′ i ȧn), **papyriferous** (-rif′ ėr ůs), **papyrine** (-pī′ rin), *a.* **papyro-,** *comb. form.* **papyrograph** (pȧ pir′ ȯ-, -pī rȯ graf) [-GRAPH], *n.* An apparatus for multiplying copies of a document, esp. by the use of a paper stencil. **papyrographic** (-grăf′ ik), *a.* **papyrography** (-rog′ rȧ fi), *n.* Printing or copying by means of a papyrograph; papyrotype. **papyrotype** (pȧ pir′ ȯ-, -pī rȯ tīp) [TYPE], *n.* A form of photo-lithography in which the writing or drawing is executed on paper before transfer to the zinc plate for printing.

par (1) (par) [L., equal, equally], *n.* State of equality, parity; equal value, esp. equality between the selling value and the nominal value expressed on share certificates and other scrip; average or normal condition, rate, etc.; (*Golf*) less than bogey. **above par:** At a price above the face value, at a premium. **below par:** At a discount; out of sorts. **on a par with:** Of equal value, degree, etc., to.

par (2) (*colloq.*) [PARAGRAPH]. **par** (3) [PARR].

para- [Gr. *para*, by the side of, beyond], *comb. form.* Denoting closeness of position, correspondence of parts, situation on the other side, wrongness, irregularity, alteration, etc. **parabaptism** (păr ȧ băp′ tizm) [late Gr. *parabaptisma* (BAPTISM)], *n.* Irregular or uncanonical baptism. **parabasis** (pȧ răb′ ȧ sis) [Gr., from *parabainein* (*bainein*, to go)], *n.* (*pl.* **-ases,** -ȧ sēz) A choral part in ancient Greek comedy in which the chorus addressed the audience, in the name of the poet, on personal or public topics. **parablast** (păr′ ȧ blăst) [Gr. *blastos*, sprout], *n.* (*Biol.*) The peripheral nutritive yolk of an ovum, or a germ-layer supposed to be developed from this and to produce the blood, etc. **parablastic** (-blăs′ tik), *a.*

parable (păr′ ȧ bėl) [O.F. *parabole*, as foll.], *n.* An allegorical narrative of real or fictitious events from which a moral is drawn; an allegory, esp. of a religious kind; a cryptic or oracular saying. ****v.t.*** To represent in a parable.

parabola (pȧ răb′ ȯ lȧ) [L., from Gr. *parabolē* (PARA-, *ballein*, to throw)], *n.* A plane curve formed by the intersection of the surface of a cone with a plane parallel to one of its sides. ***parabole** (pȧ răb′ ȯ li), *n.* A parable; comparison, similitude. **parabolic, -al** (-bol′ ik, -ȧl), *a.* Pertaining to or of the form of a parabola; pertaining to or of the nature of a parable; allegorical, figurative. **parabolically,** *adv.* **paraboliform,** *a.* **parabolist** (pȧ răb′ ȯ list), *n.* **parabolize,** *v.t.* **paraboloid,** *n.* A solid of which all the plane sections parallel to a certain line are parabolas, esp. that generated by the revolution of a parabola about its axis.

Paracelsian (păr ȧ sel′ si ȧn), *a.* Pertaining to or characteristic of the philosophical teaching of medical practice of Swiss physician and philosopher Paracelsus (1493–1541). *n.* A follower of Paracelsus, esp. as opp. to Galenist.

paracentesis (păr ȧ sen tē′ sis) [L., from Gr. *parakentēsis* (PARA-, *kentein*, to pierce)], *n.* (*Surg.*) The operation of perforating a cavity of the body, or tapping, for the removal of fluid, etc. **paracentral** (-sen′ trȧl), *a.* Situated beside or near the centre. **parachordal** (-kôr′ dȧl) [CHORDAL], *a.* (*Embryol.*) Situated near the notochord. *n.* Parachordal cartilage. **parachromatism** (-krō′ mȧ tizm) [CHROMATISM], *n.* (*Path.*) Colour-blindness. **parachronism** (pȧ răk′ rȯ nizm) [Gr. *chronos*, time, -ISM], *n.* An error in chronology, esp. post-dating of an event.

parachute (păr′ ȧ shoot) [F. (It. *para*, imper. of *parare*, to ward off, F. *chute*, fall)], *n.* An umbrella-shaped contrivance by which a descent is made from a height, esp. from an aircraft; (*Nat. Hist.*) a part of an animal or an appendage to a fruit or seed serving for descent or dispersion by the wind. **parachute flare,** *n.* A pyrotechnic flare which can be dropped from an aeroplane to illuminate the ground below. **parachute troops, paratroops,** *n.pl.* (*Mil.*) Troops borne in aeroplanes and gliders and dropped by parachute, with full equipment, usually behind the enemy lines. **parachutism,** *n.* **parachutist,** *n.*

paraclete (păr′ ȧ klēt) [F. *paraclet*, L. *paraclētus*, Gr. *paraklētos* (PARA- *kalein*, to call)], *n.* An advocate, esp. as a title of the Holy Ghost, the Comforter.

paracme (pȧ răk′ mē) [Gr. (PARA-, ACME)], *n.* (*Biol.*) A point past the acme or highest development; (*Path.*) a point past the crisis (of a fever, etc.). **paracolpitis** (păr ȧ kol pī′ tis) [Gr. *kolpos*, womb, -ITIS], *n.* (*Path.*) Inflammation of the external coat of the vagina. **paracorolla** (-kȯ rol′ ȧ) [COROLLA], *n.* (*Bot.*) A crown or appendage of a corolla, esp. one forming a nectary. **paracrostic** (-kros′ tik), *n.* A poetical composition in which the first verse contains, in order, all the letters which commence the remaining verses. **paracyanogen** (păr ȧ sī ăn′ ȯ jėn) [CYANOGEN], *n.* (*Chem.*) A porous brown substance obtained from cyanide of mercury when heated. **paracyesis** (-sī ē′ sis) [Gr. *kuēsis*, conception], *n.* (*Path.*) Extra-uterine pregnancy. **paradactyl** (-dăk′ til) [see DACTYL], *n.* (*Ornith.*) The side of a digit or toe.

parade (pȧ rād′) [F., from Sp. *parada*, It. *parata*, from L. *parāre*, to get ready], *n.* Show, ostentatious display; a muster of troops for inspection, etc.; ground where soldiers are paraded, drill, etc.; a public promenade. *v.t.* To make display of; to assemble and marshal (troops) in military order for or as for review. *v.i.* To be marshalled in military order for display or review; to show oneself or walk about ostentatiously.

paradigm (păr′ å dīm) [F. *paradigme*, L. *paradigma*, Gr. *paradeigma* (PARA-, *deiknunai*, to show)], *n.* An example, a pattern; an example of a word in its grammatical inflections. **paradigmatic** (-dig măt′ ik), *a.* ***paradigmatically,** *adv.*

paradise (păr′ å dīs) [F. *paradis*, L. *paradīsus*, Gr. *paradeisos*, O.Pers. *paradaeza* (*pairi*, PERI-, *diz*, to mould)], *n.* The garden of Eden; a place or state of bliss; heaven; (*fig.*) a place or condition of perfect bliss; a park or pleasure-ground, esp. one in which animals are kept, a preserve. **paradise-fish,** *n.* An East Indian fish, *Macropodus viridiauratus*, sometimes kept in aquariums for its brilliant colouring. **paradisaic, -al** (-sā′ ik, -ål), ***paradisiac, *-al** (-dis′ i ăk, -ål), **paradisial, -ian, paradisic, -al,** *a.*

parados (păr′ å dos) [F.], *n.* (*Mil.*) Rampart or earthwork to protect against fire from the rear.

paradox (păr′ å doks) [F. *paradoxe*, L. *paradoxum*, Gr. *paradoxon* (PARA-, *doxa*, opinion)], *n.* A statement, view, or doctrine contrary to received opinion; an assertion seemingly absurd but really correct; a self-contradictory or essentially false and absurd statement; (*fig.*) a person, thing, or phenomenon at variance with normal ideas of what is probable, natural, or possible. **paradoxer, paradoxist,** *n.* **paradoxical,** *a.* **paradoxically,** *adv.* **paradoxicality** (-kăl′ i ti), **paradoxicalness, paradoxy** (păr′-), *n.*

paradoxure (păr å dok′ sūr) [PARADOX, Gr. *oura*, tail], *n.* A civet-like animal with a long, curving tail, the palm-cat of S. Asia and Malaysia. **paradoxurine,** *a.* and *n.*

parænetic, -al (păr ė net′ ik, -ål) [med. L. *paræneticus*, Gr. *parainetikos*, from *parainein* (PARA-, *ainein*, to speak of, to praise)], *a.* Exhorting, persuasive, advisory. **parænesis** (pá rē′ nė sis), *n.*

paræsthesia (păr ēs-, -es thē′ si å) [PARA-, Gr. *aisthesis*, perception], *n.* (*Path.*) Disordered perception or hallucination.

paraffins (păr′ å finz) [F. *paraffine*, from L. *parum*, little, *affinis*, akin, so called from the small affinity with other bodies], *n.pl.* Hydrocarbons which may be gaseous, liquid or solid depending on the number of atoms per molecule (*e.g.* methane, butane, octane). **paraffin oil, paraffin,** *n.* A mixture of liquid paraffins used as a lubricant or fuel; kerosene. **paraffin wax,** *n.* A colourless, tasteless, odourless, fatty substance consisting primarily of a mixture of paraffins, and obtained from distillation of coal, bituminous shale, petroleum, peat, etc., used for making candles, waterproofing, etc.; (*Am.*) white wax. **liquid paraffin,** *n.* An intestinal lubricant and laxative.

paragastric (păr å găs′ trik), *a.* (*Zool.*) Situated near the gastric cavity; pertaining to the gastric cavity of a sponge.

***parage** (păr′ åj) [F., from med. L. *parāticum*, from PAR (1)], *n.* Lineage, descent; (*Feud. Law*) equality of condition, as among brothers holding part of a fief as co-heirs.

paragenesis (păr å jen′ ė sis), *n.* (*Biol.*) The production in an organism of characteristics of two different species; hybridism in which the individuals of one generation are sterile among themselves but those of the next fertile. **paragenetic** (-net′ ik), **paragenic** (-jen′ ik), *a.* **paraglobulin** (-glob′ ū lin) [GLOBULIN], *n.* (*Chem.*) The globulin of blood-serum. **paraglossa** (-glos′ å) [Gr. *glōssa*, tongue], *n.* (*pl.* **-sæ**) (*Ent.*) Either of the two appendages of the ligula in insects.

paragoge (pă rå go′ ji) [Gr., leading past], *n.* (*Gram.*) The addition of a letter or syllable to a word.

paragon (păr′ å gọn) [F., from It. *paragone*, etym. doubtful], *n.* A pattern of perfection; a model, an exemplar; a person or thing of supreme excellence; a diamond of 100 carats or more; *a match, an equal, a companion; emulation, rivalry; (*Print.*) a size of type, now usu. called two-line long primer. *v.t.* To compare; to rival, to equal.

***paragram** (păr′ å grăm) [PARA-, -GRAM], *n.* A play upon words; a pun. ***paragrammatist** (-grăm′ å tist), *n.*

paragraph (păr′ å graf) [F. *paragraphe*, late L. *paragraphus*, Gr. *paragraphos* (PARA-, -GRAPH)], *n.* A distinct portion of a discourse or writing marked by a break in the lines; a reference mark [¶]; a mark used to denote a division in the text; an item of news in a newspaper, etc. *v.t.* To form into paragraphs; to mention or write about in a paragraph. **paragrapher, paragraphist,** *n.* **paragraphic, -al** (-grăf′ ik, -ål), *a.* **paragraphy** (păr′ å grăf i), *n.*

Paraguay (păr′ å gwī) [S. American republic named after a river], *n.* An infusion of the leaves of *Ilex Paraguayensis*, maté. **Paraguay Reservations:** A Jesuit colony that existed in Paraguay 1608–1750.

paraheliotropic (păr å hē li ō trop′ ik), *a.* (*Bot.*) Turning so that the surfaces are parallel to the rays of sunlight (of leaves). **paraheliotropism** (-ot′ rō pizm), *n.*

parakeet (păr′ a kēt) [O.F. *paroquet* (F. *perroquet*), perh. from It. *parrochetto*, dim. of *parroco*, a parson, or of *parrucca*, PERUKE], *n.* A popular name for any of the smaller long-tailed parrots.

parakite (păr å kīt) [from KITE, after PARACHUTE], *n.* A series of kites connected together for the purpose of raising a man; a tailless kite used for scientific purposes.

paraldehyde (pa răl′ di hīd) [PARA-, ALDEHYDE], *n.* (*Med.*) A hypnotic used in asthma, respiratory and cardiac diseases, also for children.

paralipsis (păr å lip′ sis) [Gr. *paraleipsis* (PARA-, *leipein*, to leave)], *n.* A rhetorical figure by which a speaker pretends to omit mention of what at the same time he really calls attention to. **paralipomena** (păr å lī pom′ ė nå) [L., from Gr. *paraleipomena*], *n.pl.* Things omitted in a work; *(*Bibl.* **paralipomenon,** *gen. sing.*) the Books of Chronicles as giving particulars omitted in the Books of Kings.

parallax (păr′ å lăks) [F. *parallaxe*, Gr. *parallaxis*, alternation, change (PARA-, *allassein*, to change)], *n.* Apparent change in the position of an object due to change in the position of the observer; (*Astron.*) angular measurement of the difference between the position of a heavenly body as viewed from different places on the earth's surface or from the earth at different positions in its orbit round the sun. **parallactic** (-lăk′ tic), *a.*

parallel (păr′ å lel) [M.E. *parallele*, L. *parallēlus*, Gr. *parallēlos* (PARA-, *allēlos*, one another)], *a.* Having the same direction and everywhere equidistant (of lines, etc.); having the same tendency, similar, running on all fours, corresponding. *n.* A line which throughout its whole length is everywhere equidistant from another; any one of the parallel circles on a map or globe marking degrees of latitude on the earth's surface; direction parallel to that of another line; (*Mil.*) a trench parallel to the front of a place that is being attacked; a comparison; a person or thing corresponding to or analogous with another, a counterpart; (*Print.*) a reference mark (‖) calling attention to a note, etc. *v.t.* (*past & p.p.* **paralleled)** To be parallel to, to match, to rival, to equal; to put in comparison with; to find a match for; to compare. **parallel connexion,** *n.* (*Elec.*) The arrangement of pieces of apparatus across a common voltage supply. **parallel rule:** A draughtsman's instrument consisting of two rulers movable about hinged joints, but always remaining parallel. **parallelism,** *n.* The state of being parallel, correspondence, esp. of successive paragraphs, as in Hebrew poetry, a comparison, a parallel. **phenomenal parallelism:** The theory that the relation between physical and psychical activity is one of parallel variation and not of cause and effect.

parallelepiped (păr ȧ lel ep′ i ped, -ė pī′ pėd), **-pipedon** (-pip′ ė dȯn) [Gr. *parallēlepipedon* (PARALLEL, *epipedon*, a level, a plane, from *epi*, upon, and *pedon*, the ground)], *n.* A regular solid bounded by six parallelograms, the opposite pairs of which are parallel.

parallelogram (păr ȧ lel′ ȯ grăm) [F. *parallèlogramme*, L. *parallēlogrammum*, Gr. *parallēlogrammon* (PARALLEL, *grammē*, line)], *n.* A four-sided rectilineal figure whose opposite sides are parallel; (*pop.*) any quadrilateral figure of greater length than breadth. **parallelogrammatic, -al** (-măt′ ik, -ȧl), **parallelogrammic, -al** (-grăm′ ik, -ȧl), *a.*

paralogism (pȧ răl′ ȯ jizm) [F. *paralogisme*, L. *paralogismus*, Gr. *paralogismos*, from *paralogizesthai* (PARA-, *logizesthai*, to reason, from *logos*, reason)], *n.* A fallacious argument, esp. one of which the reasoner is unconscious. ***paralogize,** *v.i.* ***paralogy,** *n.*

paralyse (păr′ ȧ līz) [F. *paralyser*, as foll.], *v.t.* To affect with paralysis; (*fig.*) to render powerless or ineffective. **paralysation** (-zā′ shŭn), *n.*

paralysis (pȧ răl′ i sis) [L., from Gr. *paralusis* (PARA-, *lusis*, from *luein*, to loosen)], *n.* Total or partial loss of the power of muscular contraction or of sensation in the whole or part of the body; palsy; (*fig.*) complete helplessness or inability to act. **paralytic** (-lit′ ik), *a.* and *n.* **paralytically,** *adv.*

paramagnetic (păr ȧ măg net′ ik) [PARA-, MAGNETIC], *a.* Having the property of being attracted by the poles of a magnet, magnetic, distinguished from diamagnetic. **paramagnetism** (-măg′ nė tizm), *n.* **paramastoid** (păr ȧ măs′ toid) [MASTOID], *a.* (*Anat.*) Situated near the mastoid process of the temporal bone. *n.* A paramastoid process. **paramecium** (păr ȧ mē′ si ŭm) [mod. L., from Gr. *paramēkēs* (*mēkos*, length)], *n.* (*pl.* **-cia**) A genus of infusoria; a slipper-animalcule. **paramenia** (-mē′ ni ȧ) [Gr. *mēnes*, MENSES], *n.pl.* Disordered menses. **paramere** (păr′ ȧ mēr) [Gr. *meros*, part], *n.* (*Biol.*) One of a series of radiating parts, as in starfish; either of the symmetrical halves of a bilateral animal or somite. **parameric** (-mer′ ik), *a.* **parameter** (pȧ răm′ ė tėr) [Gr. *metron*, measure], *n.* (*Math.*) A quantity remaining constant for a particular case, esp. a constant quantity entering into the equation of a curve, etc.

paramorph (păr′ ȧ môrf) [PARA-, Gr. *morphē*, form], *n.* (*Min.*) A pseudomorph having the same chemical composition but differing in molecular structure. **paramorphic, -phous** (-môr′ fik, -fŭs), *a.* **paramorphism, -morphosis** (-fō′ sis), *n.*

paramount (păr′ ȧ mount) [A.-F. *paramount*, O.F. *par amont*, at the top (*par*, by, AMOUNT)], *a.* Supreme above all others, pre-eminent; superior (to). *n.* The highest in rank or authority; a lord paramount. **paramountcy,** *n.* **paramountly,** *adv.*

paramour (păr′ ȧ moor) [O.F. *par amour*, L. *per amōrem*, by love], *n.* An illicit mistress; *a sweetheart, a lover.

parang (pȧ răng′) [Malay], *n.* A heavy sheath-knife.

paranoia (păr ȧ noi′ ȧ), **paranœa** (-nē′ ȧ) [Gr. *paranoia* (PARA-, *nous*, mind)], *n.* Mental derangement, esp. in a chronic form characterized by delusions, etc. **paranoiac, -nœac,** *a.* and *n.* **paranoic** (-nō′ ik), **-nœic** (-nē′ ik), *a.* ***paranomasia** [PARONOMASIA]. **paranthelion** (păr ăn thē′ li ȯn) [Gr. *anth′*, ANTI-, *helios*, sun], *n.* A diffuse image of the sun at the same altitude and at an angular distance of 120° due to reflection from ice-spicules in the air. **paranucleus** (păr ȧ nū′ klė ŭs) [NUCLEUS], *n.* (*pl.* **-ei**) A subsidiary nucleus in some protozoa. **paranuclear, -cleate,** *a.* **paranucleolus** (-klē′ ȯ lŭs), *n.* A mass of substance extruded from the mother-cell in pollen-grains and spores. **paranymph** (păr′ ȧ nimf) [L. *paranymphus*, Gr. *paranumphos* (*numphē*, bride)], *n.* (*Gr. Ant.*) A friend of the bridegroom who went with the bridegroom to fetch the bride, or the maiden who conducted the bride to the bridegroom; a 'best man,' a bridesman, or a bridesmaid; *(*fig.*) an advocate or spokesman for another.

parapet (păr′ ȧ pėt) [F., from It. *parapetto* (*para*, to depend, *petto*, L. *pectus*, breast)], *n.* A low or breast-high wall at the edge of a roof, bridge, etc.; (*Fort.*) a breast-high wall or rampart for covering troops from observation and attack. **parapetted,** *a.*

paraph (păr′ ȧf) [F. *paraphe*, med. L. *paraphus*, *paragraphus*, PARAGRAPH], *n.* A flourish after a signature, orig. intended as a protection against forgery. *v.t.* To sign; to initial.

paraphernalia (păr ȧ fėr nā′ li ȧ) [neut. pl. of L. *paraphernālis*, from Gr. *parapherna*, neut. pl. (PARA-, Gr. *phernē*, a dowry, from *pherein*, to bring)], *n.pl.* (*Law*) Personal property allowed to a wife over and above her dower, including her personal apparel, ornaments, etc.; miscellaneous belongings, ornaments, trappings, equipments. **paraphernal** (-fėr′ nȧl), *a.*

paraphimosis (păr ȧ fī mōs′ sis) [PARA-, PHIMOSIS], *n.* (*Path.*) Permanent retraction of the prepuce.

paraphrase (păr′ ȧ frāz) [F., from L. and Gr. *paraphrasis* (PARA-, *phrazein*, to tell)], *n.* A free translation or rendering of a passage; a restatement of a passage in different terms; any one of a series of hymns, used in the Church of Scotland, etc., consisting of poetical versions of passages of Scripture. *v.t.* To express or interpret in other words. *v.i.* To make a paraphrase. **paraphrast,** *n.* One who paraphrases. **paraphrastic, *-al** (-frăs′ tik, -ȧl), *a.* **paraphrastically,** *adv.*

paraphyllum (păr ȧ fil′ ŭm) [PARA-, Gr. *phullon*, leaf], *n.* (*pl.* **-la**) (*Bot.*) A small foliaceous or hair-like organ in certain mosses; a stipule. **paraphysis** (pȧ răf′ i sis) [Gr. *phusis*, growth], *n.* (*pl.* **-physes**) A sterile filament accompanying sexual organs in some cryptogams. **paraplegia** (păr ȧ plē′ ji ȧ) [Gr. *paraplēgia* (*plēssein*, to strike)], *n.* (*Path.*) Paralysis of the lower limbs and the lower part of the body. **paraplegic** (-plē′ jik, -plej′ ik), *a.* **parapleurum** (păr ȧ ploor′ ŭm) [Gr. *pleuron*, rib], *n.* (*Ent.*) One of the sternal side-pieces in a beetle. **parapleuritis** (-ī′ tis) [-ITIS], *n.* (*Path.*) Pleurodynia, or a mild form of pleuritis. **parapodium** (păr ȧ pō′ di ŭm) [Gr. *pous podos*, foot], *n.* (*Zool.*) One of the jointless lateral locomotory organs of an annelid. **parapophysis** (păr ȧ pof′ i sis) [Gr. *apophusis*, an off-shoot (APO-, *phusis*, growth)], *n.* (*Anat.*) A process on the side of a vertebra, usu. serving as the point of articulation of a rib. **paraphrenia** (păr ȧ frē′ nyȧ), *n.* (*Psych.*) A type of schizophrenia characterized by ideas of persecution, grandeur, etc. **parapsychical** (păr ȧ sī′ kik ȧl), *a.* (*Psych.*) Denoting phenomena such as hypnotism or telepathy which appear to be beyond explanation by the ascertained laws of science.

***paraquet** [PARAKEET].

parasang (păr′ ȧ săng) [L. *parasanga*, Gr. *parasangēs*, from Pers.], *n.* An ancient Persian measure of length, about $3\frac{1}{4}$ miles.

parasceve (păr′ ȧ sēv, păr ȧ sē′ vē) [L. *parascēvē*, Gr. *paraskeuē* (PARA-, *skeuē*, outfit)], *n.* The day of preparation for the Jewish Sabbath.

paraselene (păr ȧ sė lē′ nē) [PARA-, Gr. *selēnē*, moon], *n.* (*pl.* **-næ**) A mock moon appearing in a lunar halo. **paraselenic** (-len′ ik), *a.*

parasite (păr′ ȧ sīt) [L. *parasītus*, Gr. *parasitos* (PARA-, *sitos*, food)], *n.* One who frequents the tables of the rich, earning his welcome by flattery; a hanger-on, a sponger; (*Nat. Hist.*) an animal or plant subsisting at the expense of another organism; (*loosely*) a plant that lives on another without deriving its nutriment from it, a commensal; (*pop.*) a plant that climbs about another. **parasitic, -al** (-sit′ ik, -ȧl), *a.* **parasitically,** *adv.* ***parasiticalness, parasiticide** (-sit′ i sīd) [-CIDE], *n.* A preparation for destroying parasites. **parasitism**

(păr′ ȧ sī tizm), *n.* **parasitize** (păr′ ȧ sī tīz), *v.t.* **parasitology** (-tol′ ȯ ji), *n.* **parasitologist,** *n.*

parasol (păr ȧ sol′, păr′ ȧ sol) [F., from It. *parasole* (*para*, imper. of *parare*, to ward off, *sole*, L. *sol*, sun)], *n.* A small umbrella used by women to shelter themselves from the sun; a sunshade. **parasolette** (-let′), *n.*

parasynthesis (păr ȧ sin′ thė sis) [PARA-, SYNTHESIS], *n.* (*Philol.*) The principle or process of forming derivatives from compounds. **parasynthetic** (-thet′ ik), *a.* **parasyntheton** (-sin′ thė ton), *n.* (*pl.* -ta) A word so formed. **parataxis** (păr ȧ tăk′ sis) [Gr. *parataxis* (*tassein*, to arrange)], *n.* (*Gram.*) An arrangement of clauses, sentences, etc., without connectives indicating subordination, etc. **paratactic** (-tăk′ tik), *a.* **paratactically,** *adv.* **parathesis** (pȧ răth′ ė sis) [Gr. *tithenai*, to place], *n.* (*Philol.*) Juxtaposition of primary elements, etc. equivalent in relation or meaning, as the monosyllabic roots in Chinese; (*Gram.*) apposition; (*Rhet.*) a parenthetical notice; matter contained between brackets. **parathyroid** (pă rȧ thī′ roid), *n.* (*Anat.*) A small endocrine gland, one of which is situated on each side of the thyroid. **paratonic** (păr ȧ ton′ ik) [TONIC], *a.* (*Bot.*) Due to external stimuli (of plant-movements, etc.); retarding growth (of the effect of light in certain cases); (*Path.*) pertaining to overstrain. **paratonically,** *adv.* **paratroops** [PARACHUTE TROOPS]. **paratyphoid** (pă rȧ tī′ foid), *n.* (*Path.*) An infectious fever of the enteric group, similar in symptoms to typhoid but of milder character.

paravane (păr′ ȧ vān) [PARA-, VANE], *n.* (*Nav.*) A mine-sweeping appliance for severing the moorings of submerged mines.

***paravant, *-vaunt** [O.F. *paravant* (*par*, by, *avant*, before)], *adv.* and *prep.* Before, in front.

parboil (par′ boil) [O.F. *parboillir*, from late L. *perbullīre*, to boil thoroughly (PER-, *bullīre*, to BOIL), conf. with PART], *v.t.* To boil partially; *to boil thoroughly. **parbake,** *v.t.* To bake partially.

***parbreak** (par brāk′) [F. *par-*, as prec., BREAK (1)], *v.t.* and *i.* To vomit. *n.* Vomit, spewing.

parbuckle (par′ bŭk ėl) [etym. unknown], *n.* A double sling usu. made by passing the two ends of a rope through a bight for hoisting or lowering a cask or gun. *v.t.* To hoist or lower by a parbuckle.

Parcæ (par′ sē) [L.], *n.pl.* (*Rom. Myth.*) The Fates.

parcel (par′ sėl) [F. *parcelle*, late L. *particella*, dim. of *particula*, PARTICLE], *n.* *A portion or part, an item; a number or quantity of things dealt with as a separate lot; a distinct portion, as of land; a quantity of things wrapped up together; a bundle, a package; (*Am.*) a package. **adv.* Partly. *v.t.* (*past & p.p.* **parcelled**) To divide (*usu.* out) into parts or lots; (*Naut.*) to wrap (a rope) with strips of canvas, or cover (a seam) with strips of canvas and pitch; to make into a parcel; *to detail, to enumerate, to specify. ***parcel-bearded, -blind, -drunk, -gilt,** *a.* Partly bearded, blind, drunk, or gilt. **parcel-office,** *n.* An office for the receipt or dispatch of parcels. **parcel-post,** *n.* A branch of the postal service for the delivery of parcels. **parcelling,** *n.* (*Naut.*) A wrapping of tarred canvas to prevent chafing of a rope, etc.

parcenary (par′ sė nȧr i) [A.-F. *parcenarie*, O.F. *parçonerie*, from *parçonier*, *parcener*, med. L. *partiōnārius*, *partitiōnārius* (PARTITION, -ER)], *n.* Coheirship, coparcenary. **parcener,** *n.*

parch (parch) [etym. unknown], *v.t.* To scorch or roast partially dry, to dry up. *v.i.* To become hot or dry. ***parchedly,** *adv.* ***parchedness,** *n.*

parchment (parch′ mėnt) [F. *parchemin*, L. *pergamēna*, orig. fem. of *Pergamēnus*, pertaining to *Pergamum*, city of Mysia], *n.* The skin of calves, sheep, goats, etc., prepared for writing upon, painting, etc.; a manuscript on this, esp. a deed; a tough skin, as the husk of the coffee-berry. *a.* Made of or resembling parchment. **parchmenty,** *a.*

parcimony [PARSIMONY].

parclose (par′ klōz) [M.E. and O.F. *parclos*, *-close*, p.p. of *parclore* (PER-, *claudere*, to CLOSE)], *n.* (*Eccles.*) A screen or railing enclosing an altar, tomb, etc., in a church.

***pard** (1) (pard), ***pardal** (par′ dȧl) [O.F. *pard*, L. *pardus*, Gr. *pardos*, earlier *pardalis*, of Eastern orig. (cp. Pers. *pārs*, *pārsh*)], *n.* A panther, a leopard.

pard (2) (pard) [colloq. abbr. of PARTNER], *n.* (*Am. slang*) A partner.

pardie, *parde (par dē′) [O.F. *par dé* (F. *par dieu*), by God], *int.* or *adv.* Certainly, assuredly; of a truth.

pardon (par′ dȯn) [O.F. *pardoner*, *perduner*, late L. *perdōnāre* (PER-, *dōnāre*, to give, from *dōnum*, gift)], *v.t.* To forgive, to absolve from; to remit the penalty of; to refrain from exacting; to excuse, to make allowance for. *n.* The act of pardoning; (*Law*) a complete or partial remission of the legal consequences of crime; an official warrant of a penalty remitted; a papal indulgence; a religious festival when this is granted; courteous forbearance; *permission. **I beg your pardon** or **pardon me:** Excuse me, a polite apology for an action, contradiction, or failure to hear or understand what is said. **pardonable,** *a.* **pardonableness,** *n.* **pardonably,** *adv.* **pardoner,** *n.* One who pardons; a person licensed to sell papal pardons or indulgences.

pare (pâr) [F. *parer*, L. *parāre*, to prepare], *v.t.* To cut or shave (away or off); to cut away or remove the rind, etc., of (fruit, etc.); to trim by cutting the edges or irregularities of; (*fig.*) to diminish by degrees. **parer,** *n.*

***paregal** (par e găl′) [O.F. *parigal* (PER-, EQUAL)], *a.* Equal, fully equal. *n.* An equal or peer.

paregoric (păr ė gor′ ik) [late L. *parēgoricus*, Gr. *parēgorikos*, soothing, from *parēgoros*, addressing, *exhorting* (PARA-, AGORA, assembly)], *a.* Assuaging or soothing pain. *n.* A camphorated tincture of opium for assuaging pain.

pareira (pȧ rȃr′ ȧ) [Port. *parreira*], *n.* A drug used in urinary disorders, obtained from the root of *Chondrodendron tomentosum* or *Cissampelos pareira*, a Brazilian climbing plant.

parella (pȧ rel′ ȧ) [mod. L., from F. *parelle*, med. L. *paratella*], *n.* A crustaceous lichen, *Leocanora parella*, from which litmus and orchil are obtained. **parellic,** *a.*

parembole (pȧ rem′ bȯ lē) [Gr. (PARA-, *embolē*, insertion)], *n.* (*Rhet.*) An insertion, usu. more intimately related to the subject of the sentence than a parenthesis.

parenchyma (pȧ reng′ ki mȧ) [Gr. *parenchuma* (PARA-, *enchuma*, infusion, from *encheein*, to pour in)], *n.* (*Anat.*) The soft cellular tissue of glands and other organs, distinguished from connective tissue, etc.; (*Bot.*) thin cellular tissue in the softer part of plants, as pith, fruit pulp, etc. **parenchymal, parenchymatous** (-kī′ mȧl, -mȧ tŭs), **parenchymous** (-eng′ ki mŭs), *a.*

parent (pâr′ ėnt) [F., from L. *parentem*, nom. *-ens*, from *parēre*, to produce, to beget], *n.* A father or mother; a forefather; an organism from which others are produced; (*fig.*) a source, origin, cause, or occasion. **parentage,** *n.* Birth, extraction, lineage, origin; *a parent or parents collectively. **parental** (pȧ ren′ tȧl), *a.* **parentally,** *adv.* **parenthood** (pâr′ ėnt hud), *n.* **parenticide** (pȧ ren′ ti sīd) [-CIDE], *n.* One who kills a parent; the killing of parents. **parentless,** *a.*

parenthesis (pȧ ren′ thė sis) [med. L. and Gr., from *parentithenai* (PARA-, EN-, *tithenai*, to put)], *n.* (*pl.* **-theses**) A word, phrase, or sentence inserted in a sentence that is grammatically complete without it, usu. marked off by brackets, dashes, or commas; (*pl.*) round brackets () to include such words; (*fig.*) an interval, interlude, incident, etc. **parenthesize,** v.t. To insert as a parenthesis;

to place (a clause, etc.) between parentheses. **parenthetic, -al** (-thet′ ik, -ȧl), **parenthetically,** *adv.*

parergon (pȧ rĕr′ gȯn) [L. and Gr. (PARA-, *ergon,* work)], *n.* (*pl.* **-ga**) A subsidiary work, a by-work.

paresis (păr′ ė sis) [Gr., from *parienai* (PARA-, *hienai,* to let go)], *n.* (*Path.*) Incomplete paralysis, affecting muscular movement but not sensation. **paretic** (pȧ ret′ ik), *a.*

par excellence (par eks′ el *ons*) [Fr.], *adv.* Above all others, pre-eminently.

***parfilage** (par fē lazh′) [F., from *parfiler,* to unravel (*par,* by, *filer,* from *fil,* thread)], *n.* The unravelling of woven fabrics, or of gold and silver thread from laces, an amusement among women in the 18th cent.

parfleche (par flesh′) [Canadian Fr., from N. Am. Ind.], *n.* A hide, usu. of buffalo, stripped of hair and dried on a stretcher; a tent, wallet, or other article made of this.

pargasite (par′ gȧ sīt) [G. *pargasit,* from *Pargas,* Finland], *n.* (*Min.*) A greenish variety of hornblende.

parget (par′ jėt) [O.F. *pargeter, porgeter,* L. *prōjectāre* (PRO-, *jactāre,* freq. of *jacere,* to throw)], *v.t.* To plaster over; to paint (the face, etc.). *n.* Plaster; *pargeting; *paint, esp. for the face. ***pargework,** *n.* **pargeter,** *n.* **pargeting,** *n.* Plasterwork, esp. decorative plaster-work.

parhelion (par hē′ li ȯn) [L. and Gr. (PARA-, *hēlios,* sun)], *n.* (*pl.* **-lia**) A mock-sun or bright spot in a solar halo, due to ice-crystals in the atmosphere. **parheliacal** (-lī′ ȧ kȧl), **parhelic** (-hē′ lik, hel′ ik), *a.*

pariah (pâr′ i ȧ, pa′ ri ȧ [Tamil *paṛaiyar,* pl. of *paṛaiyan,* a drummer, from *parai,* drum], *n.* One of a people of very low caste in S. India and Burma; one of low caste or without caste; (*fig.*) a social outcast. **pariah-dog,** *n.* A vagabond mongrel dog, esp. in India.

Parian (pâr′ i ȧn), *a.* Pertaining to the island of Paros, celebrated for its white marble. *n.* A white variety of porcelain, used for statuettes, etc.

paridigitate (păr i dij′ i tȧt) [L. *pari-, par,* equal, DIGITATE], *a.* (*Zool.*) Having an even number of toes or digits on each foot.

parietal (pȧ rī′ ė tȧl) [F. *pariétal,* L. *parietālis,* from *paries -etis,* wall], *a.* Pertaining to a wall or walls, esp. those of the body and its cavities; (*Bot.*) pertaining to or attached to the wall of a structure, esp. of placentæ or ovaries; (*Am.*) pertaining to residence within the walls of a college. **parieto-,** *comb. form.* (*Anat.*)

paring (pâr′ ing), *n.* The act of cutting off, pruning, or trimming; that which is pared off; a shaving, rind, etc.

pari mutuel (pa′ ri mū′ tū el) [F.], *n.* A system of betting in which the winners divide the losers' stakes less a percentage for management. **pari passu** (pâr′ i păs′ ū) [L.], *adv.* With equal pace, in a similar degree, equally.

paripinnate (păr i pin′ ȧt) [L. *pari-, par,* equal, PINNATE], *a.* (*Bot.*) Equally pinnate, without a terminal leaflet.

Paris (păr′ is) [capital of France], *a.* Used attributively of things derived from Paris. **plaster of Paris** [PLASTER]. **paris blue:** A bright Prussian blue; a bright-blue colouring-matter obtained from aniline. **paris doll:** A lay-figure used by dressmakers as a model. **paris green:** A light-green pigment obtained from arsenite of copper. **paris white:** A fine grade of whiting used for polishing.

parish (păr′ ish) [A.-F. *parosse, paroche* (F. *paroisse*), late L. *parochia,* Gr. *paroikia* (PARA-, *oikos,* dwelling)], *n.* An ecclesiastical district with its own church and clergyman; a subdivision of a county; a civil district for purposes of local government, etc. *a.* Pertaining to or maintained by a parish. **to go on the parish:** To become chargeable to the parish for whole or partial maintenance by the poor-rate. **parish clerk,** *n.* A subordinate lay official in the church, formerly leading the congregation in the responses. **parish council:** A local administrative body elected by the parishioners in rural districts. **parish register:** A register of christenings, marriages, burials, etc., kept at a parish church. **parishioner** (pȧ rish′ ȯ nėr), *n.* One who belongs to a parish.

parisyllabic (păr i si lăb′ ik), *a.* Having the same number of syllables, esp. in all the cases (of Greek and Latin nouns).

parity (păr′ i ti) [F. *parité,* L. *paritātem,* nom. *-tas,* from *pār,* equal], *n.* Equality of rank, condition, value, etc., esp. of rank among ministers as in a non-prelatical church; parallelism, analogy.

park (park) [O.F. *parc* (cp. Dut. *perk,* Swed. and Dan. *park,* G. *pferch*), from Teut., cp. A.-S. *pearruc,* PADDOCK (1)], *n.* A piece of land, usu. for ornament, pleasure, or recreation, with trees, pasture, etc., surrounding or adjoining a mansion; a piece of ground, ornamentally laid out, enclosed for public recreation; a large tract or region, usu. with interesting physical features, preserved in its natural state for public enjoyment; (*Mil.*) a space occupied by the artillery, stores, etc., in an encampment; the train of artillery, with stores and equipment, pertaining to a field army. *v.t.* To enclose in or as in a park; to mass (artillery) in a park; (*Motor. and colloq.*) to leave in a place allotted for the purpose; to leave temporarily. **parking lot:** (*Am.*) A car-park. **parking-meter,** *n.* A coin-operated appliance on a kerb that charges for the time cars are parked there. **park-keeper,** *n.* **parkish,** *a.*

parkin (par′ kin) [etym. unknown], *n.* (*North.*) A cake made of gingerbread or oatmeal and treacle.

parky (par′ ki) [etym. doubtful], *a.* (*colloq.*) Chilly, uncomfortable.

parlance (par′ lȧns) [O.F., as foll.], *n.* Way of speaking, idiom; *conversation, a conference, a parley. ***parle,** *n.* and *v.i.*

parley (par′ li) [F. *parler* or O.F. *parlee,* fem. p.p. of *parler,* pop. L. *parabolāre,* from *parabola,* PARABLE], *v.i.* To confer with an enemy with pacific intentions; to talk, to dispute. *v.t.* To converse in, to speak (esp. a foreign language). *n.* A conference for discussing terms, esp. between enemies.

parleyvoo (par li voo′) [F. *parlez-vous français,* do you speak French?], *n.* (*old slang*) French; a Frenchman. *v.i.* To speak French.

Parliament (par′ lȧ mėnt) [M.E. and O.F. *parlement* (PARLEY, -MENT)], *n.* A deliberative assembly; a legislative body, esp. the British legislature, consisting of the Houses of Lords and Commons, together with the sovereign. **parliament-cake,** *n.* A thin crisp gingerbread cake. **Parliamentarian** (-târ′ i ȧn), *n.* One versed in parliamentary rules and usages or in parliamentary debate; (*Hist.*) one who supported the Parliament against Charles I in the time of the Great Civil War. *a.* Parliamentary. **parliamentary** (-li men′ tȧr i), *a.* Of, pertaining to, or enacted by Parliament, according to the rules of or admissible in Parliament (esp. of language); (*colloq.*) civil. **parliamentary agent:** A person employed by a private person or persons to draft Bills or manage the business of private legislation. **parliamentary train:** (*Hist.*) A train carrying passengers at a rate not exceeding 1d. per mile which by Act of Parliament (repealed 1883) every railway was obliged to run daily each way over its system.

parlour (par′ lȯr) [O.F. *parleor,* med. L. *parlātōrium,* from *parlāre, parabolāre,* to speak, see PARLEY], *n.* Orig. a room in a convent for conversation; the family sitting-room in a private house. **parlour-boarder,** *n.* A pupil at a boarding-school living with the principal's family. **parlour-car,** *n.* (*Am.*) A luxuriously fitted railway-carriage, a drawing-room car. **parlour-maid,** *n.* A maid-servant waiting at table.

parlous (par′ lŭs), *a.* Perilous, awkward, trying; shrewd, clever, venturesome. *adv.* Extremely.

Parmesan (par mė zăn′), *n.* A kind of cheese made at Parma and elsewhere in N. Italy.

Parnassus (par năs′ ŭs) [mountain in Greece, anciently famous as the favourite resort of the Muses], *n.* (*fig.*) Poetry, literature.

Parnellism (par′ nė lizm) [C. S. *Parnell* (1846–91), leader of the Irish Home Rule party (1880–91)], *n.* The political views and tactics of Parnell, who aimed to force Parliament to grant Home Rule, by persistent obstruction, etc. **Parnellite,** *n.*

parochial (pȧ rō′ ki ȧl) [O.F., from Late L. *parochiālis*, from *parochia*, PARISH], *a.* Relating to a parish; (*fig.*) petty, narrow. **parochialism, parochiality** (-ăl′ i ti), *n.* **parochialize,** *v.t.* **parochially,** *adv.*

parody (păr′ ŏ di) [L. and Gr. *parōdia* (PARA-, ODE)], *n.* A literary composition imitating an author's work for the purpose of ridicule; (*fig.*) a poor imitation, a mere travesty. *v.t.* To turn into a parody, to burlesque. ***parodic, *-al** [pȧ rod′ ik, -ȧl), *a.* **parodist.**

parole (pȧ rōl′) [F., from late L. *parabola*, PARABLE], *n.* A word of honour, esp. a promise by, *e.g.*, a prisoner of war that he will not attempt to escape, that he will return to custody on a certain day if released, or will not take up arms against his captors unless exchanged; (*Mil.*) the daily password used by officers, etc., as distinguished from the countersign. *v.t.* To put or release on parole. **on parole:** On the understanding stated above (of the release of a prisoner).

paronomasia (păr ŏ nŏ mā′ zi ȧ, -si ȧ) [L. and Gr. (PARA-, *anomazein*, to name, from *onoma*, name)], *n.* A play upon words, a pun. **paronomasial, -ian, paronomastic, -al** (-măs′ tik, -ȧl), *a.* ***paronomasy,** *n.*

paronym (păr′ ŏ nim) [Gr. *parōnumos*, *paronymous* (PARA-, *onoma*, name)], *n.* A paronymous word. **paronymous** (pȧr on′ i mŭs), *a.* Having the same root, cognate; alike in sound, but differing in origin, spelling, and meaning. **paronymy,** *n.*

parotid (pȧ rot′ id) [F. *parotide*, from L. and Gr. *parōtis -tidos* (PARA-, *ous ōtos*, ear)], *a.* Situated near the ear. *n.* A *parotis*; *a parotid tumour. **parotid duct:** A duct from the parotid gland by which saliva is conveyed to the mouth. **parotid gland** [PAROTIS]. **parotic, parotideal, -dean** (-dē′ ȧl, -ȧn), *a.* **parotiditis, parotitis** (-dī′ tis, -tī tis) [-ITIS], *n.* (*Path.*) Inflammation of the parotid gland, mumps. ***parotis,*** *n.* One of a pair of salivary glands situated on either side of the cheek in front of the ear, with a duct to the mouth; *a tumour on one of these glands.

-parous [L. *-parus*, from *parere*, to bring forth], *suf.* Producing, bringing forth.

parousia (par ooz′ i ȧ) [Gr. presence], *n.* (*Theol.*) Christ's second coming, to judge the world.

paroxysm (păr′ ŏk sizm) [F. *paroxysme*, L. *paroxysmus*, Gr. *paroxusmos* (PARA-, *oxunein*, to sharpen, from *oxus*, sharp)], *n.* A sudden and violent fit; the exacerbation of a disease at periodic times; (*fig.*) a fit of laughter or other emotion. **paroxysmal, -mic** (-siz′ mȧl, -mik), *a.* **paroxysmally,** *adv.*

paroxytone (pȧ rok′ si tōn) [Gr. *paroxutonos* (PARA-, OXYTONE)], *a.* (*Gr. Gram.*) Applied to a word having an acute accent on the penultimate syllable. *n.* A word having such an accent. **paroxytonic** (-ton′ ik), *a.*

parpen (par′ pėn) [O.F. *parpain* (F. *parpaing*), etym. doubtful], *n.* A bonding-stone.

parquet (par′ ki, par ket′) [F., a floor, orig. a compartment, dim. of *parc*, PARK], *n.* A flooring of parquetry; (*Am.*) the part of the floor of a theatre between the orchestra and the row immediately under the front of the gallery. *v.t.* To floor a room with parquetry. **parquetry** (par′ kė tri), *n.* Inlaid woodwork for floors.

parr (par) [etym. doubtful], *n.* A young salmon.

parrakeet [PARAKEET].

parramata (păr ȧ măt′ ȧ), *n.* A light twilled dress-fabric of merino wool and cotton, orig. from Parramatta in New South Wales.

parrhesia (pȧ rē′ zi ȧ, -si ȧ) [late L. and Gr. (PARA-, *rhēsis*, speech)], *n.* Freedom or boldness in speaking.

parricide (păr′ i sīd) [F., from L. *parricīda* or *parricīdium*], *n.* One who murders or the murder of a parent or a revered person; (*fig.*) treason or one guilty of treason against his country. **parricidal** (-sī′ dȧl), *a.*

parrot (păr′ ŏt) [etym. doubtful, perh. from *periquito*, dim. of *perico*, cp. PARAKEET], *n.* One of a group of tropical birds with brilliant plumage, esp. the genus *Psittacus*, remarkable for their faculty of imitating the human voice; (*fig.*) one who repeats words or imitates actions mechanically or unintelligently; a chatterbox. *v.i.* To repeat mechanically or by rote. *v.t.* To repeat words or to chatter as a parrot. **parrot-fish,** *n.* A fish of the genus *Scarus*, or some allied genera, from their brilliant coloration, and the beak-like projection of the jaws. **parroter,** *n.* **parrotism,** *n.* **parrotry,** *n.*

parry (păr′ i) [F. *parer*, to parry, L. *parāre*, see PARADE], *v.t.* To ward off (a blow or thrust); to evade; to shirk. *n.* A defensive movement in fencing, the warding off of a blow, etc.

parse (parz) [L. *pars*, PART], *n.* To describe or classify a word grammatically, its inflexional forms, relations in the sentence, etc.; to analyse a sentence and describe its component words and their relations grammatically; to be conformable to grammatical rules (of a word or sentence).

parsec (par′ sek) [PAR in PARALLAX, SEC in SECOND], *n.* (*Astron.*) A unit of length in calculating the distance of the stars, being 19×10^{12} miles or 3·3 light years.

Parsee (par sē′) [Pers. *Pārsī*, Persian from *Pārs*, Persia], *n.* A Zoroastrian, a descendant of the Persians who fled to India from the Mohammedan persecution in the 7th and 8th centuries; the language of the Persians under the Sassanian kings, before it was corrupted by Arabic. **Parseeism,** *n.* The Parsee religion, Zoroastrianism.

parsimonious (par si mō′ ni ŭs) [L. *parsi-*, *parcimōnia*, from *parcere*, to spare], *a.* Sparing in the expenditure of money; frugal, niggardly, penurious, miserly, stingy. **parsimoniously,** *adv.* **parsimoniousness, parsimony** (par′ si mŏ ni), *n.*

parsley (pars′ li) [M.E. *percil*, O.F. *peresil* (F. *persil*), late L. *petrosillum*, L. *petroselīnum*, Gr. *petroselinon* (*petro-*, *petros*, stone, *selinon*)], *n.* An umbelliferous herb, *Petroselinum sativum*, cultivated for its aromatic leaves used for seasoning and garnishing dishes.

parsnip (par′ snip) [M.E. *pasnep*, O.F. *pastenaque*, L. *pastināca*, from *pastinum*, a fork for digging], *n.* An umbelliferous plant, *Pastinaca sativa*, with an edible root used as a culinary vegetable.

parson (par′ sŏn) [M.E. *persone*, PERSON], *n.* A rector, vicar, or other clergyman holding a benefice: (*colloq.*) a clergyman. **parson's nose:** The rump of a fowl. **parsonage,** *n.* The dwelling-house of a parson; the benefice of a parish. **parsonic** (-son′ ik), **parsonish** (par′ sŏ nish), *a.* **parson-bird,** *n.* The poe-bird.

part (part) [A.-S., from L. *partem*, nom. *pars*, whence *partīre*, F. *partir*, to divide], *n.* A portion, piece, or amount of a thing or number of things; a portion separate from the rest or considered as separate; a member, an organ; a proportional quantity; one of several equal portions, quantities, or numbers into which a thing is divided, or of which it is composed; a section of a book, periodical, etc., as issued at one time; a share, a lot; interest, concern; share of work, etc., act, duty; side, party; the rôle, character, words, etc., allotted to an actor; a copy of the words so allotted; (*pl.*) qualities, accomplishments, talents; quarters; (*pl.*) region, district; (*Mus.*) one of the constituent melodies of a harmony; a melody allotted to a particular voice or instrument. *v.t.* To divide into portions, shares, pieces, etc.; to separate; to brush the hair with a division along the head. *v.i.* To divide; to separate (from); to resign; (*Naut.*) to give way (of a cable, etc.). *adv.* Partly. **for my part:** So far as I am concerned. **for the most part:** [MOST]. **in good part:** With good temper, without offence. **in ill part** [ILL]. **in part:** Partly. **on the part of:** Done by or proceeding from. **part and parcel:** An essential part or element. **part of speech,** *n.* A grammatical class of words of a particular character, comprising noun, pronoun, adjective, verb, adverb, preposition, conjunction, interjection. **to play a part:** To act deceitfully. **to take part:** To assist; to participate. **to take the part of:** To back up or support the cause of. **to part with:** To relinquish, to give up. **part-owner,** *n.* One who has a share in property with others. **part-song,** *n.* A composition for at least three voices in harmony, usu. without accompaniment. **part time:** Less than full time.

partake (par tāk'), *v.t.* To take or have a part or share in common with others, *to distribute; *to share with. *v.i.* To take or have a part or share (of or in, with another or others); to have something of the nature (of); (*colloq.*) to eat and drink (of). **partaker,** *n.*

partan (par' tȧn) [Sc., prob. from Gael.], *n.* A crab, esp. the edible sea-crab.

parterre (par' târ') [F. *par terre*, on the ground], *n.* An ornamental arrangement of flower-beds, with intervening walks; the ground-floor of a theatre or the part of this behind the orchestra; (*Am.*) the part under the galleries.

parthenogenesis (par thė nō jen' ė sis) [Gr. *parthenos*, virgin, GENESIS], *n.* (*Biol.*) Generation without sexual union. **parthenogenetic** (-net' ik), *a.* **parthenogenetically,** *adv.*

Parthenon (par' thė nȯn), *n.* The temple of Athene Parthenos on the Acropolis at Athens.

Parthian (par' thi ȧn), *a.* Of or pertaining to Parthia, an ancient kingdom in W. Asia. **Parthian arrow, glance, shaft** or **shot:** A look, word, etc., delivered as a parting blow, like the arrows shot by the Parthians in the act of fleeing.

parti (par' tē) [Fr.], *n.* A person regarded as eligible matrimonially. **parti pris** (par tē prē'), *n.* Preconceived view, bias, prejudice.

partial (par' shȧl) [F., from L. *partiālis*, from *pars partis*, PART], *a.* Affecting a part only, incomplete; biased in favour of one side or party, unfair; having a preference for. **partiality** (-i ăl' i ti), *n.* ***partialize,** *v.t.* and *i.* **partially,** *adv.*

***partible** (par' ti bėl) [L. *partibilis*, from *partīrī*, to divide, as prec.], *a.* Divisible; separable. **partibility** (-bil' i ti), *n.*

participate (par tis' i pāt) [L. *participātus*, p.p. of *participāre* (PART, *capere*, to take)], *v.i.* To have or enjoy a share, to partake (in); to have something (of the nature of). *v.t.* To have a part or share in (with). **participating policy,** *n.* (*Insur.*) A policy entitling the holder to a share in the surplus profits of the business. **participating stock,** *n.* (*Fin.*) A type of preferred capital stock which in addition to dividends at a fixed rate is entitled to share in any surplus earnings. **participable,** *a.* **participant,** *a.* **participation** (-pā' shůn), *n.* **participative** (par tis' i pă tiv), *a.* **participator,** *n.*

participle (par' ti si pėl) [O.F. (F. *participe*), L. *participium*, as prec.], *n.* A word partaking of the nature of a verb and of an adjective, a verbal adjective qualifying a substantive. **participial** (-sip' i ȧl), *a.* **participially,** *adv.*

particle (par' ti kėl) [L. *particula*, dim. of *pars*, PART], *n.* A minute part or portion; an atom; (*Gram.*) a word not inflected, or one not used except in combination. **particulate** (par tik' ū lȧt), *a.*

***parti-coated** (par' ti kō tėd), *a.* Having a parti-coloured coat; dressed in motley. **parti-coloured** (par' ti kŭl ȯrd), *a.* Partly of one colour, partly of another; variegated.

particular (pȧr tik' ū lȧr) [M.E. and O.F. *particuler*, L. *particulāris*, from *particula*, PARTICLE], *a.* Pertaining to a single person or thing as distinguished from others; special, peculiar, characteristic; private, personal; single, separate, individual; minute, circumstantial; fastidious, exact, precise; remarkable, noteworthy; *intimate, specially attentive. *n.* An item, a detail, an instance; (*pl.*) a detailed account; *personal interest or concern; *personal character, idiosyncrasy. **Particular Baptists:** A sect holding the doctrines of particular election and redemption [see PARTICULARISM]. **in particular:** Particularly. **particularism,** *n.* Devotion to private interests or those of a party, sect, etc.; the policy of allowing political independence to the separate states of an empire, confederation, etc.; (*Theol.*) the doctrine of the election or redemption of particular individuals of the human race. **particularist,** *n.* **particularity** (-lăr' i ti), *n.* The quality of being particular; circumstantiality; *a minute point or instance; *a peculiarity; *a particular or private interest. **particularistic** (-is' tik) *a.* **particularize,** *v.t.* To mention individually; to specify; to give the particulars of. *v.i.* To be attentive to particulars or details. **particularization** (-zā' shůn), *n.* **particularly,** *adv.* **particularness,** *n.* **particulate** [PARTICLE].

partim (par' tim) [L., from *pars partis*, PART], *adv.* Partly.

parting (par' ting), *a.* Serving to part; departing; given or bestowed on departure or separation. *n.* Separation, division; a point of separation or departure; a dividing-line; a departure; leave-taking; a dividing of the hair.

partisan (1) (par ti zăn', par' ti zȧn) [It. *partigiano*], *n.* An adherent of a party, faction, cause, etc., esp. one showing unreasoning devotion; one of a body of irregular troops carrying out special enterprises, such as raids. *a.* Pertaining or attached to a party. **partisanship,** *n.*

partisan (2) (par' ti zȧn) [F. *partizane* (now *pertuisane*), It. *partesana*, *partegiana*, perh. rel. to prec., or from Teut. (cp. O.H.G. *parta*, halberd)], *n.* A pike or long-handled spear like a halberd; a quarter-staff, a truncheon or baton.

partite (par' tīt) [L. *partītus*], *a.* (*Bot.*, *Ent.*, *etc.*). Divided nearly to the base.

partition (par tish' ůn) [F., from L. *partītiōnem*, nom. *-tio*, from L. *partīrī*, to PART], *n.* Division into parts, distribution; a separate part; that which separates into parts, esp. a wall or other barrier; (*Law*) division of property among joint-owners, etc.; *v.t.* To separate (off); to divide into parts or shares. **partitioned,** *a.* **partitive** (par' ti tive), *a.* Denoting a part. *n.* A word denoting partition, as *some*, *any*, etc. **partitively,** *adv.*

***partlet** (1) (part' let) [M.E. *patelet*, O.F. *patelette*, perh. dim. of *patte*, paw], *n.* A neck-covering worn by women; a ruff. ***partlet** (2) (part' let) [O.F. *Pertelote*, a female name], *n.* A hen; a woman.

partly (part' li), *adv.* In part; to some extent; not wholly.

partner (part' nėr) [var. of PARCENER], *n.* One who shares with another, esp. one associated with others in business; an associate; one of two persons who dance together; one of two playing on the same side in a game; a husband or a wife; (*Naut.*, *pl.*) timber framing round a mast, pump, etc., relieving the strain on the deck-timbers. *v.t.* To join in partnership, to be a partner (of). **partnerless,** *a.* **partnership,** *n.*

partridge (par' trij) [M.E. *pertriche*, O.F. *perdiz*, *pertuz*, L. *perdīcem*, nom. *perdix*, Gr. *perdix -dīka*], *n.* A gallinaceous bird of the genus *Perdix*, esp. *P. cinerea*, preserved for game.

part-song [PART]. ***parture** [DEPARTURE].

parturient (par tūr′ i ėnt) [L. *parturiens -ntem*, pres.p. of *parturīre*, to be in labour, from *parere*, to produce], *a.* About to bring forth young; (*fig.*) learned, fertile (of the mind, etc.). **parturition** (-rish′ ŭn), *n.* The act of bringing forth. ***parturitive** (-tūr′ i tiv), *a.*

party (1) (par′ ti) [F. *partie*, L. *partīta*, fem. p.p. of *partīrī*, to divide, from *pars partis*, PART], *n.* A number of persons united together for a particular purpose; the principle or practice of taking sides on questions of public policy; a number of persons gathered together for some purpose, esp. of persons invited to a house for social entertainment; each of the actual or fictitious personages on either side in a legal action, contract, etc.; an accessory, one concerned in any affair; (*colloq.*) a person; *a game, a match. ***party-coated, -coloured** [PARTI-COATED]. **party line:** (*Tel.*) A telephone exchange line used by a number of subscribers; (*Pol.*) the policy laid down by a party. **party-spirit,** *n.* Zeal for a party. **party-spirited,** *a.* **party-verdict,** *n.* A joint verdict. **party-wall,** *n.* A wall separating two buildings, etc., the joint-property of the respective owners. ***partyism,** *n.*

party (2) (par′ ti) [F. *parti*, as prec.], *a.* (*Her.*) Divided into compartments distinguished by different tinctures (of a shield).

parure (pa rur′) [F., from *parer*, L. *parāre*, to adorn], *n.* A set of jewels or other personal ornaments.

parvanimity (par vȧ nim′ i ti) [L. *parvus*, petty, *animus*, mind, after MAGNANIMITY], *n.* Littleness of mind; mean-spiritedness.

parvenu (par′ vė nū) [F., past p. of *parvenir*, L. *pervenīre*, to arrive (PER, *venīre*, to come)], *n.* (*fem.* **-nue**) An upstart.

parvis (par′ vis) [F., from L. *paradīsus*, PARADISE], *n.* The name given in the Middle Ages to the vacant space before a church where the mysteries were performed.

pas (pa) [F. step, from L. *passus*, PACE], *n.* Precedence. **to have the *pas*:** To take precedence (of).

paschal (păs′ kȧl) [F. *pascal*, L. *paschālis*, from L. and Gr. *pascha*, Heb. *pasakh*, the Passover, from *pāskh*, be passed over], *a.* Pertaining to the Passover or to Easter. ***pasch** (păsk), *n.* The Passover; Easter. **pasch-egg,** *n.* An Easter-egg.

***pash** (1) (păsh) [etym. doubtful], *n.* The face, the head.

***pash** (2) (păsh) [prob. onomat.], *v.t.* To strike violently, esp. so as to smash. *v.i.* To beat (o waves, etc.). *n.* A blow; (*colloq.*) [PASSION] a violent fancy.

pasha (pa′ shȧ, păsh′ ȧ) [Turk.], *n.* A Turkish title of honour, usu. conferred on officers of high rank, governors, etc. **pashalic** (pa′ shȧ lik, pȧ sha′ lik), *n.* The jurisdiction of a pasha.

pasigraphy (pȧ sig′ rȧ fi) [Gr. *pasi*, for all, pl. dat. of *pan*, PAN-, -GRAPHY], *n.* A universal system of writing, by means of signs representing ideas not words. **pasigraphic, -al** (-grăf′ ik, -ȧl), *a.*

pasque-flower (păsk′ flou ėr) [formerly *passe-flower*, F. *passefleur* (*pasque*, Easter, FLOWER), assim. to PASCH], *n.* A species of anemone, *Anemone pulsatilla*, with bell-shaped purple flowers.

pasquinade (păs kwi nād′) [*Pasquino*, or *Pasquillo*, popular name of a piece of ancient statuary at Rome on which in the 15th cent. Latin verses were displayed, said to be so named after a satirical cobbler], *n.* A lampoon, a satire. *v.t.* To lampoon, to satirize. ***pasquin, *pasquil,** *n.* and *v.t.* ***pasquillant, *-ler,** *n.*

pass (pas) [F. *passer*, from L. *passus*, PACE], *v.i.* To move from one place to another, to proceed, to go (along, on, swiftly, etc.); to circulate, to be current; to be changed from one state to another; to change gradually; to change hands; to be transferred; to disappear, to vanish; to die; to go by, to elapse; to go through, to be accepted without censure or challenge; to be enacted (as a Bill before Parliament); to receive current recognition; to be approved by examining; to take place, to happen, to occur; (*Cards*) to give up one's option of playing, making trumps, etc.; (*Fencing*) to lunge or thrust; (*Law*) to be transferred or handed on; *to exceed all bounds; *to give heed, to care for; *to be tolerably well off. *v.t.* To go by, beyond, over, or through; to transfer, to hand round, to circulate, to give currency to, to spend (time, etc.); to endure; to admit, to approve, to enact; to satisfy the requirements of (examiners, etc.); to outstrip, to surpass; to move, to cause to move; to cause to go by; to allow to go through (as a Bill, a candidate, etc.) after examination; to pledge (one's word, etc.); to pronounce, to utter; to void, to discharge; to overlook, to disregard, to reject; (*Am.*) to omit; *to make (a thrust). *n.* The art of passing; a passage, avenue, or opening, esp. a narrow or difficult way; a narrow passage through mountains, a defile; a navigable passage, as at the mouth of a river; a written or printed permission to pass; a ticket authorizing one to travel (on a railway, steamer, etc.) or to be admitted (to a theatre, etc.) free; a critical state or condition of things; the act of passing an examination, esp. without special merit or honours; a thrust; a sexual advance; a passing of hands over anything (as in mesmerism); a juggling trick; the act of passing a ball in various games. **to bring to pass** [BRING]. **to come to pass** [COME]. **to pass away:** To die, to come to an end. **to pass by:** To omit, to disregard. **to pass for:** To be taken for. **to pass off:** To proceed (without a hitch, etc.); to disappear gradually; to circulate as genuine, to palm off. **to pass out:** (*colloq.*) To faint. **to pass over:** To go across; to allow to go by without notice, to overlook; to omit; (*fig.*) to die. **to pass the time of day:** To exchange greetings. **to pass through:** To undergo, to experience. **to pass up:** To renounce. **pass-book,** *n.* A book that passes between a tradesman and his customer, in which purchases on credit are entered; a bank-book. **pass-key,** *n.* A master-key; a key for passing in when a gate, etc., is locked. **passman,** *n.* A candidate in an examination obtaining only a pass not honours. **passable,** *a.* That may be passed; acceptable, allowable, tolerable, fairly good. **passably,** *adv.*

***passade** (pȧ sād′) [F., from Prov. *passada* or It. *passata*, p.p. of *passare*, to PASS], *n.* A turn or course of a horse backwards or forwards on the same spot; a passado. ***passado** (pȧ sa′ dō), *n.* A thrust in fencing.

passage (păs′ ȧj) [F., from *passer*, to PASS], *n.* The act of passing; movement from one place to another, transit, migration; transition from one state to another; a journey, a voyage, a crossing; a way by which one passes, a way of entrance or exit; a corridor or gallery giving admission to different rooms in a building; right or liberty of passing; a separate portion of a discourse, etc., esp. in a book; the passing of a Bill, etc., into law; (*pl.*) events, etc., that pass between persons, incidents, episodes; reception, currency. **bird of passage** [BIRD]. **North-West Passage,** *n.* Ship route from the Atlantic to the Pacific round the north of America. **passage of** or **at arms:** A fight; a contest or encounter. **to work one's passage:** To work as a sailor, etc., receiving a free passage in lieu of wages; (*fig.*) to work one's way without help from influence, etc.

passant (păs′ ȧnt) [F., pres.p. of *passer*, to PASS], *a.* (*Her.*) Walking and looking towards the dexter side with the dexter fore-paw raised.

passé (păs′ ā) [F., p.p. of *passer*, to PASS], *a.* (*fem.* **-sée**) Past the prime, faded; old-fashioned, behind the times.

***passemeasure** (păs ė mezh′ ŭr) [corr. of It. *passemezzo* (prob. *passo e mezzo*, a step and a half)], *n.* An Italian variety of pavan.

passementerie (pas man′ tri) [F., from *passement*, gold or silver lace], *n.* Trimming for dresses, esp. gold and silver lace.

passenger (păs′ ėn jėr) [M.E. and O.F. *passager*], *n.*

One who travels on a public conveyance; *a traveller, a wayfarer. **passenger-pigeon,** *n.* The wild pigeon of S. America, having extraordinary powers of flight.

passepartout (pas par too') [F., pass everywhere], *n.* A paper frame for a picture, photograph, etc.; a master-key; *a safe-conduct.

passer (pa' sėr), *n.* One who passes. **passer-by,** *n.* One who passes by or near, esp. casually.

passerine (păs' ėr īn) [L. *passer*, sparrow], *a.* Pertaining to the order *Passeres* or perchers, which contains the great mass of the smaller birds; like a sparrow, esp. in size. *n.* A passerine bird.

passible (păs' i bėl) [O.F., from late L. *passibilis*, from *patī*, to suffer], *a.* Capable of feeling or suffering; susceptible to impressions from external agents. **passibility** (-bil' i ti), ***passibleness,** *n.*

Passiflora (păs i flôr' á) [L. *passi-*, *passio*, PASSION, *-florus*, flowering], *n.* (*Bot.*) A genus of plants containing the passion-flower.

passim (păs' im) [L., from *passus*, p.p. of *pandere*, to scatter], *adv.* Here and there, throughout (of words, allusions, etc.).

passimeter (păs' i mē ter), *n.* An automatic ticket-issuing machine.

passing (pa' sing), *a.* Going by, occurring; incidental, casual, cursory; transient, fleeting; *surpassing, egregious, notable. **adv.* Surpassingly; exceedingly. *n.* Passage, transit, lapse. **passing-bell,** *n.* A bell tolled at the hour of a person's death to invite prayers on his behalf. **passing-note,** *n.* (*Mus.*) A note forming a transition between two others, but not an essential part of the harmony.

passion (păsh' ón) [O.F., from L. *passiōnem*, nom. *-sio*, from *patī*, to suffer], *n.* Intense emotion, a deep and overpowering affection of the mind, as grief, anger, hatred, etc.; violent anger; sexual love; zeal, ardent enthusiasm (for); the last agonies of Christ; an artistic representation of this; a musical setting of the Gospel narrative of the Passion. *v.i.* (*poet.*) To be affected with passion. **passion-flower,** *n.* A plant of the genus *Passiflora*, chiefly consisting of climbers, with flowers bearing a fancied resemblance to the instruments of the Passion. **passion-play,** *n.* A mystery-play representing the Passion. **Passion Sunday:** The fifth Sunday in Lent. **Passion Week:** The week following Passion Sunday; (*erron.*) Holy Week. **passional, passionary,** *n.* A book describing the sufferings of saints and martyrs. **passionate** (păsh' ó nát), *a.* Easily moved to strong feeling, esp. anger; excited, vehement, warm, intense; *sorrowful; compassionate; **passionately,** *adv.* **passionateness,** *n.* **passioned,** *a.* Impassioned. **Passionist,** *n.* A religious order in the Roman Catholic Church devoted to the commemoration of Christ's passion. **passionless,** *a.* **passionlessly,** *adv.* **passionlessness,** *n.*

passive (păs' iv) [L. *passīvus*, as prec.], *a.* Suffering, acted upon, not acting; capable of receiving impressions; inactive, inert, submissive, not opposing. *n.* The passive voice. **passive resistance:** Inert resistance, without active opposition. **passive voice:** The form of a transitive verb representing the subject as the object of the action. **passively,** *adv.* **passiveness, passivity** (pá siv' i ti), *n*

passman [PASS].

Passover (pas' ō vėr), *n.* A feast of the Jews, on the 14th day of the month Nisan, commemorating the destruction of the first-born of the Egyptians and the 'passing over' of the Israelites by the destroying angel (Exod. xii); (*fig.*) Christ, the paschal lamb.

passport (pas' pōrt) [F. *passe-port*], *n.* An official document authorizing a person to travel in a foreign country and entitling him or her to legal protection; (*fig.*) anything ensuring admission (to society, etc.).

password (pas' wĕrd), *n.* A word by which to distinguish friends from strangers, a watchword.

past (past) [p.p. of PASS], *a.* Gone by, neither present nor future; just elapsed; (*Gram.*) denoting action or state belonging to the past. *n.* Past times; one's past career or the history of this, esp. a disreputable one. *adv.* So as to go by. *prep.* Beyond in time or place; after, beyond the influence or range of; more than. **past-master,** *n.* One who has been master of a Freemasons' lodge, a guild etc.; (*fig.*) a thorough master (of a subject, etc.).

paste (pāst) [O.F. (F. *pâte*), Prov., It., and Sp. *pasta*, perh. from Gr. *pastē*, fem. of *pastos*, sprinkled], *n.* A mixture of flour and water, usu. with butter, lard, etc., kneaded and used for making pastry, etc.; sweetmeats of similar consistency; a relish of pounded meat or fish; an adhesive compound of flour, water, starch, etc., boiled; any doughy or plastic mixture, esp. of solid substances with liquid; a vitreous composition used for making imitations of gems. *v.t.* To fasten or stick with paste; to stick (up) with paste; (*slang*) to thrash. **paste and scissors:** Extracts, padding. **pasteboard,** *n.* A board made of sheets of paper pasted together or of compressed paper pulp; (*Am.*) cardboard; (*slang*) a card, as a visiting-card, railway-ticket, or playing-card; a board on which dough is rolled. *a.* Made of pasteboard; (*fig.*) thin, flimsy, sham.

pastel (păs' tėl) [F., from It. *pastello*, dim. of *pasta*, PASTE], *n.* Woad; a dry paste composed of a pigment mixed with gum-water; a coloured crayon made from this; a picture drawn with such crayons; the art of drawing with these. **pastellist,** *n.*

pastern (păs' tėrn) [O.F. *pasturon* (F. *paturon*), from *pasture*, a shackle, prob. ident. with PASTURE], *n.* The part of a horse's leg between the fetlock and the hoof. **pastern-joint,** *n.*

Pasteurism (pas' tėr izm) [Louis *Pasteur* (1822–1895), French chemist and biologist], *n.* A method of preventing or curing certain diseases, esp. hydrophobia, by progressive inoculation. **pasteurize,** *v.t.* **pasteurized milk,** *n.* Milk subjected to treatment by heat in order to destroy the organisms which may be present. **pasteurization** (-zā' shŭn), *n.*

pasticcio (păs tich' ō), **pastiche** (păs tēsh') [F. *pastiche*, It. *pasticcio*, from *pasta*, PASTE], *n.* A medley, a musical work, painting, etc., composed of elements drawn from other works.

pastille (pás tēl') [F., from L. *pastillum*, nom. *-lus*, etym. doubtful], *n.* A roll, cone, or pellet of aromatic paste for burning as a fumigator or disinfectant; an aromatic lozenge.

pastime (pas' tīm) [PASS, TIME], *n.* That which serves to make time pass agreeably; a game, a recreation; sport, diversion.

pastor (pas' tór) [M.E. and O.F. *pastour*, O.F. *pastor*, L. *pastōrem*, nom. *-or*, from *pascere*, to feed], *n.* *A shepherd; a minister having charge of a church and congregation; one acting as a spiritual guide; the crested starling. **pastorate** (pas' tór āt), *n.* **pastorless,** *a.* ***pastorly,** *a.* **pastorship,** *n.*

pastoral (pas' tó rál), *a.* Pertaining to shepherds; used for pasture (of land); treating of country life (of romances, etc.); rural, rustic; relating to the cure of souls or the duties of a pastor; befitting a pastor. *n.* A poem, romance, play, picture, etc., descriptive of the life and manners of shepherds or rustics; a letter or address from a pastor, esp. from a bishop to his diocese; a pastorale. **pastorale** (pas tó ra' li) [It.], *n.* A simple rustic melody; a cantata on a pastoral theme; a symphony dealing with a pastoral subject. **pastoralism,** *n.* **pastoralist,** *n.* (*Austral.*) A sheep- or cattle-raiser as distinct from an agriculturist. **pastorality,** *n.* **pastorally,** *adv.*

pastry (pās' tri), *n.* Articles of food made with a crust of baked flour-paste. **pastry-cook,** *n.*

pasture (pas' chŭr) [F. *pâture*, from late L. *pastūra*, as PASTOR], *n.* Ground fit for the grazing of cattle;

grass for grazing. *v.t.* To put (cattle, etc.) on land to graze; (of sheep) to eat down (grass-land), to feed by grazing. *v.i.* To graze. **pasturable,** *a.* **pasturage,** *n.* **pastureless,** *a.*

pasty (1) (pās′ ti), *a.* Of or like paste. **pasty-faced,** *a.* Having a pale, dull complexion. **pastiness,** *n.*

pasty (2) (pa′ sti) [M.E. and O.F. *pastee* (F. *pâté*), from *pasta*, PASTE], *n.* A small pie, usu. of meat, baked without a dish.

pat (1) (păt) [prob. onomat.], *n.* A light quick blow with the hand; a tap, a stroke; a small mass or lump (of butter, etc.) moulded by patting; the sound of a light blow with something flat. *v.t.* (*past & p.p.* **patted**) To strike gently and quickly with something flat, esp. the fingers or hand; to tap, to stroke gently. *v.i.* To strike gently; to run with light steps. *a.* Exactly suitable or fitting; opportune, apposite, apt. *adv.* Aptly, opportunely. **patly,** *adv.* **patness,** *n.*

Pat (2) (păt) [short for *Patrick*], *n.* An Irishman. **on one's Pat:** (*Austral.*) On one's own, all alone.

patagium (păt ā gī′ ŭm, pȧ tā′ ji ŭm) [L., from Gr. *patageion*, a gold border], *n.* (*pl.* **-gia**) The wing-membrane of a bat, flying-lemur, etc.

patch (păch) [etym. doubtful], *n.* A piece of cloth, metal or other material put on to mend anything; anything similar; a piece put on to strengthen a fabric, etc.; a piece of cloth worn over an injured eye; a piece of court-plaster, etc., covering a wound, etc.; a small piece of black silk or court-plaster worn (esp. in the 17th and 18th cents.) to conceal a blemish or to set off the complexion; a differently coloured part of a surface; a small piece of ground, a plot; a scrap, a shred; *a clown, a fool. *v.t.* To put a patch or patches on; to mend with a patch or patches (usu. up); to mend clumsily; to make (up) of or as of shreds or patches; to put together or arrange hastily; to serve as a patch for; to show as a patch or patches on. **to patch up:** To mend. **to patch up a quarrel:** To be reconciled temporarily. **not a patch on:** (*slang*) Not to be compared with. **patchwork,** *n.* Work composed of pieces of different colours, sizes, etc., sewn together; clumsy work. **patcher,** *n.* **patchery,** *n.* **patchy,** *a.* **patchily,** *adv.* **patchiness,** *n.*

patchouli (pȧ choo′ li, păch′ ŭ li) [F., from Ind. native name], *n.* An Indian plant, *Pogostemon patchouli*, yielding a fragrant oil; a perfume prepared from this.

pate (pāt) [etym. doubtful], *n.* The head, esp. the top of the head. **pated,** *a.* (*usu. in comb.*)

pâté (păt′ ā) [F.], *n.* A pie, a patty. **pâté de foie gras** (dė fwa gra): A patty made of fatted goose liver.

***patefaction** (păt ė făk′ shŭn) [L. *patefactio*, from *patefacere* (*patēre*, to be open, *facere*, to make)], *n.* Disclosure; open manifestation.

patella (pȧ tel′ ȧ) [L., dim. of *patina*, PATEN], *n.* (*Anat.*) The knee-cap; *a small dish or pan; (*Zool.*) a genus of molluscs containing the limpets. **patellar, patellate** (păt′ ė lȧt), **patelliform** (pȧ tel′ i fôrm), *a.* **patellite** (păt′ ė līt), *n.* (*Palæont.*) A fossil limpet.

paten (păt′ ėn) [O.F. *patene*, L. *patena*, *patina*], *n.* A plate or shallow dish for receiving the eucharistic bread; *a circular metal plate.

patent (pā′ tėnt, păt′ ėnt) [O.F., from L. *patentem*, nom. *-tens*, pres.p. of *patēre*, to lie open], *a.* Open to the perusal of all; protected or conferred by letters patent; plain, obvious, manifest; (*Bot., etc.*) expanded, spreading. *n.* A grant from the Crown by letters patent of a title of nobility, or of the exclusive right to make or sell a new invention; an invention so protected; (*fig.*) anything serving as a sign or certificate (of quality, etc.). *v.t.* To secure by patent. **patent-leather,** *n.* A leather with a japanned or varnished surface. **patent medicine,** *n.* A medicine sold under a licence with a registered name and trade mark. **patent rolls:** The rolls or register of patents granted by the Crown since 1201. **patency,** *n.* **letters patent:** An open document from the sovereign or an officer of the Crown conferring a title, right, privilege, etc., esp. the exclusive right to make or sell a new invention. **patentable,** *a.* **patentee** (-tē′), *n.* **patently,** *adv.*

pater (păt′ ėr) [L., father], *n.* A paternoster; (*colloq.*, pā′ tėr) father. **paterfamilias** (pā tėr-, păt ėr fȧ mil′ i ȧs), *n.* The head or father of a family or household.

patera (păt′ ėr ȧ) [L., from *patēre*, to be open], *n.* (*pl.* **-ræ**) (*Rom. Ant.*) A round dish used for libations; (*Arch.*) a flat round ornament on a frieze or in bas-reliefs.

paternal (pȧ tĕr′ nȧl) [F. *paternel*, late L. *paternālis*, from *paternus*, fatherly, from PATER], *a.* Of or pertaining to a father; fatherly; connected or related through the father. **paternally,** *adv.* **paternalism,** *n.* **paternalistic** (-lis′ tik), *a.* **paternity,** *n.* Fatherhood; ancestry or origin on the male side, descent from a father; (*fig.*) authorship, source.

paternoster (păt ėr nos′ tėr) [L., our Father], *n.* The Lord's Prayer, esp. in Latin; every eleventh bead of a rosary, indicating that the Lord's Prayer is to be repeated; hence, a rosary; (*Angling*) a fishing-line with a weight at the end and short lines with hooks extending at intervals.

path (path) [A.-S. *pæth* (cp. Dut. *pad*, G. *pfad*)], *n.* A footway, esp. one beaten only by feet; a course or track; (*fig.*) course of life, action, etc. **v.t.* To walk on. **v.i.* To go, as in a path. **cinder path** [CINDER]. **pathfinder,** *n.* An explorer or pioneer. **pathless,** *a.* **pathway,** *n.*

Pathan (pȧ tan′, pā′ thȧn) [prob. Afghan, rel. to *Pushtu*, *Pukhtu*, the Afghan language, cp. Gr. *Paktues* (Herodotus)], *n.* An Afghan belonging to independent tribes on the N.W. frontier of India.

pathetic (pȧ thet′ ik) [late L. *pathēticus*, Gr. *pathētikos*, from PATHOS], *a.* Affecting or moving the feelings, esp. those of pity and sorrow; *passionate. *n.* That which is pathetic; (*pl.*) the display of pathos or sentiment; (*pl.*) the study of pathetic emotions. ***pathetical,** *a.* **pathetically,** *adv.* ***patheticalness,** *n.*

pathfinder, pathless [PATH].

pathic (păth′ ik) [Gr. *pathikos*, passive], *n.* A catamite.

patho- [Gr. *pathos*, suffering], *comb. form.*

pathogen (păth′ ō jen), *n.* (*Med.*) Any disease-producing substance or micro-organism.

pathogenesis (păth ō jen′ e sis), *n.* The origin and development of disease. **pathogenetic, pathogenic, pathogenous,** *a.* **pathogeny,** *n.*

pathognomy (pȧ thog′ nō mi), *n.* Expression of the passions; the science of their signs. **pathognomic,** *a.*

pathology (pȧ thol′ ō ji), *n.* The science of diseases, esp. of the human body. **pathologic, -al,** *a.* **pathologically,** *adv.* **pathologist,** *n.*

pathophobia (păth ō fō′ bi ȧ), *n.* A morbid fear of disease.

pathos (pā′ thos) [Gr., suffering, from *path-*, root of *paschein*, to suffer], *n.* A quality or element in events or expression that excites emotion, esp. pity or sorrow.

pathway [PATH].

-pathy [Gr. *-patheia*, PATHOS, suffering], *suf.* Suffering, feeling; disease, treatment of this, as in *homœopathy*, *sympathy*.

***patibulary** (pȧ tib′ ū lȧ ri) [L. *patibulum*, gibbet, from *patēre*, to lie open, -ARY], *a.* (*usu. facet.*) Belonging to or shaped like a gallows.

patience (pā′ shėns) [O.F., from L. *patientia*, from *patī*, to suffer], *n.* The quality of being patient; calm endurance of pain, provocation, or other evils, fortitude; a card-game, usu. played by one person. **out of patience with:** Unable to endure or put

---

n: caboshon. ng: sing. sh: *sh*awl. zh: measure. th: *th*in. *th*: brea*th*e. *See page* xi.

up with. **to have no patience with:** To be unable to stand or put up with; to be irritated by.

patient (pā shėnt), *a.* Capable of bearing pain, suffering, etc., without fretfulness; not easily provoked, indulgent; persevering, diligent. *n.* One who suffers; a person under medical treatment. **v.t.* To compose, to calm. **patiently,** *adv.*

patiki (pȧ tē′ kē) [Maori], *n.* The N. Zealand sole or flounder.

patina (păt′ i nȧ) [L. *patina, patena,* a shallow dish, or F. *patine,* perh. from this], *n.* The green incrustation that covers ancient bronzes; *a Roman dish or pan, a paten. **patinated, patinous** (pat′ i nā tėd, -nŭs), *a.* Covered with patina. **patination** (-nā′ shŭn), *n.*

patio (pa′ ti ō) [Sp.], *n.* The open inner court of a Spanish or Spanish-American residence.

patisserie (păt is′ ėr ē) [Fr.], *n.* A pastry-cook's shop.

patois (păt′ wa) [F., etym. doubtful], *n.* A dialect spoken by the illiterate people of a district; broken language.

patonce (pȧ tons′) [etym. doubtful, cp. POTENCE], *a.* (*Her.*) Applied to a cross the four arms of which expand in curves from the centre and have floriated ends.

***patrial** (pā′ tri ȧl) [L. *patri-, pater,* father, -AL], *a.* Of or pertaining to one's native land; (*Gram.*) derived from the name of a country. *n.* (*Gram.*) A patrial noun.

patriarch (pā′ tri ark) [O.F. *patriarche,* L. *patriarcha,* Gr. *patriarchēs* (*patria,* family, from *patēr,* father, *archein,* to rule)], *n.* The head of a family or tribe, ruling by paternal right; (*Bibl.*) applied to Abraham, Isaac, and Jacob, their forefathers, and the sons of Jacob; (*R.-C. Ch.*) the highest grade in the hierarchy; (*Eastern and early Churches*) a bishop, esp. of Alexandria, Antioch, Constantinople, Jerusalem, and some other sees; (*fig.*) the founder of a religion, science, etc.; a venerable old man, the oldest living person (in an assembly, order, etc.). **patriarchal** (-ar′ kȧl), ***patriarchical,** *a.* **patriarchate** (pā′ tri ar kȧt), *n.* **patriarchism, patriarchy,** *n.* A patriarchal system of government or social organization, esp. as distinguished from matriarchy.

patrician (pȧ trish′ ȧn) [L. *patricius,* from *pater,* father, *patres,* senators, nobles], *a.* (*Rom. Ant.*) Senatorial, not plebeian; noble, aristocratic. *n.* A member of the Roman aristocracy; a member of ancient or later orders established by the Western and the Byzantine Emperors, esp. a chief magistrate of a Roman province in Italy or Africa; a noble, an aristocrat, a member of the highest class of society. **patricianship,** *n.* **patriciate,** *n.* ***patricide** [PARRICIDE].

patrilineal (păt ri lin′ i ȧl) [L. *pater, patri,* LINEAL], *a.* By descent through the father.

patrimony (păt′ ri mȯ ni) [F. *patrimoine,* L. *patrimōnium,* as prec.], *n.* An estate or right inherited from one's father or ancestors; a church estate or endowment; (*fig.*) a heritage. **patrimonial** (-mō′ ni ȧl), *a.* **patrimonially,** *adv.*

patriot (pā′ tri ȯt, păt′ ri ȯt) [F. *patriote,* late L. *patriōta,* Gr. *patriōtēs,* from *patrios,* of one's fathers, from *patēr -tros,* father], *n.* One who loves his country and is devoted to its interests, esp. its freedom and independence. **patriotic** (-ot′ ik), *a.* **patriotically,** *adv.* **patriotism** (pā′ tri-, păt′ ri ȯt izm), *n.*

patristic, -al (pȧ tris′ tik, -ȧl) [F. *patristique* (L. *patri-, pater,* father)], *a.* Pertaining to the ancient Fathers of the Church or their writings. *n.pl.* The study of patristic writings.

patrol (pȧ trōl′) [F. *patrouiller, patouiller,* to dabble in the mud (cp. O.F. *patouil,* a pool)], *v.i.* (*past & p.p.* **patrolled**) To go the rounds of a camp, garrison, town, etc. *v.t.* To go round. *n.* The perambulation of a camp, etc., esp. at night, for the maintenance of order and for security; the detachment of soldiers, police, firemen, etc., or the soldier, constable, etc., doing this; a detachment of troops, sent out to reconnoitre; (*Aviat.*) a routine operational flight. **patrolman,** *n.* (*Am.*) A police constable. **patrol wagon,** *n.* (*Am.*) A black Maria.

patron (pā′ trȯn, păt′ rȯn) [O.F., from L. *patrōnum,* nom. *-us,* from *pater patris,* father], *n.* One who supports, fosters, or protects a person, cause, art, etc.; a tutelary saint; one who holds the gift of a benefice; (*colloq.*) a regular customer (at a shop); (*Rom. Ant.*) the former owner of a manumitted slave; a guardian or protector of a client; an advocate or defender in a court of law. **patronal** (păt′ rȯ nȧl), *a.* **patroness,** *n.*

patronage (păt′ rȯ nij), *n.* Support, fostering encouragement, or protection; the right of presentation to a benefice or office; the act of patronizing; (*colloq.*) support by customers (of a shop, etc.).

patronize (păt′ rȯ nīz), *v.t.* To act as a patron towards; to assume the air of a patron towards, to treat in a condescending way; to frequent as a customer. **patronizer,** *n.* **patronizingly,** *adv.* **patronless,** *a.*

patronymic (păt rȯ nim′ ik) [L. *patrōnymicus,* Gr. *patrōnumikos,* from *patrōnumos* (*patēr patros,* father, *onoma,* Æolic *onuma,* name)], *a.* Derived (as a name) from a father or ancestor. *n.* A name so derived; a family name. ***patronymical,** *a.* **patronymically,** *adv.*

patroon (pȧ troon′) [var. of PATRON], *n.* (*Am.*) A proprietor of land with manorial privileges and right of entail under a Dutch grant, esp. in New York and New Jersey (abolished 1850).

patten (păt′ ėn) [F. *patin,* perh. from O.F. *patte,* paw], *n.* A clog or overshoe mounted on an iron ring, etc., for keeping the shoes out of the mud or wet; (*Arch.*) a sole for the foundation of a wall; the base-ring of a column.

patter (1) (păt′ ėr) [freq. of PAT (1)], *v.i.* To strike, as rain, with a quick succession of light, sharp sounds; to move with short, quick steps. *v.t.* To cause (water, etc.) to patter. *n.* A quick succession of sharp, light sounds or taps.

patter (2) (păt′ ėr) [M.E. *pateren,* from PATERNOSTER], *v.t.* To say (one's prayers) in a mechanical, singsong way. *v.i.* To pray in this manner; to talk glibly. *n.* The patois or slangy lingo of a particular class; glib talk, chattering, gossip; rapid speech introduced impromptu into a song, comedy, etc.

pattern (păt′ ėrn) [M.E. *patron,* as PATRON], *n.* A model or original to be copied or serving as a guide in making something; a model, an exemplar; a sample or specimen (of cloth, etc.); a decorative design for a carpet, wall-paper, frieze, etc.; hence type, style; the marks made by shot on a target. *v.t.* To copy, to model (after, from, or upon); to decorate with a pattern; *to match, to equal. **pattern-box,** *n.* (*Weaving*) A box at either side of the loom from which a shuttle is sent along as required for the pattern. **pattern-maker,** *n.* A maker of patterns for the moulders in a foundry. **pattern-shop,** *n.* A room or shop in a foundry, etc., where patterns are made.

pattle (pătl), *n.* An implement used for cleaning the earth from a ploughshare.

patty (păt′ i) [F. PÂTÉ], *n.* A little pie.

patulous (păt′ ū lŭs) [L. *patulus,* cogn. with *patēre,* to be open], *a.* Open, having a wide aperture; spreading, expanding (of boughs, etc.). **patulously,** *adv.* **patulousness,** *n.*

paua (pou′ ȧ) [Maori], *n.* The N. Zealand mutton-fish; a handsome iridescent shell; a fish-hook.

paucity (paw′ si ti) [F. *paucité,* L. *paucitātem,* nom. *-tas,* from *pāucus,* few], *n.* Fewness.

***paul** [PAWL]. ***pauldron** [POULDRON].

Pauline (paw′ līn), *a.* Of or pertaining to St. Paul or his writings. *n.* A scholar of St. Paul's School, London. **Paulinism,** *n.* The theological doctrine taught by or ascribed to the apostle Paul.

paulo-post-future (paw′ lō pōst fū′ tūr) [L. *paulo*

post futurum, future after a little], *n.* (*Gr. Gram.*) The future-perfect tense.

paunch (pawnch, panch) [O.North.F. *panch*, L. *panticem*, nom. *pantex*], *n.* The belly, the abdomen; the first and largest stomach in ruminants; (*Naut.*) a thick mat or wooden shield fastened on a mast, etc., to prevent chafing. *v.t.* To rip open the belly of, to disembowel; to stab in the belly; to stuff with food. **paunchy**, *a.*

pauper (paw' pėr) [L., poor], *n.* One without means of support, a destitute person, a beggar; one entitled to public assistance; one permitted to sue *in forma pauperis*. ***in forma pauperis:*** (*Law*) Allowed on account of poverty to sue without paying costs. **pauperdom, pauperism,** *n.* **pauperize,** *v.t.* **pauperization** (-zā' shŭn), *n.*

pause (pawz) [F., from L. *pausa*, Gr. *pausis*, from *pauein*, to cease], *n.* A cessation or intermission of action, speaking, etc.; a break in reading, speaking, music, etc., for the sake of emphasis; a mark to denote a break or pause; (*Mus.*) a mark 𝄐 or ◡ over a note, etc., indicating that it is to be prolonged. *v.i.* To make a pause or short stop; to wait; to linger (upon or over). **v.t.* To repose oneself. ***pausingly,** *adv.*

pavan (păv' an) [F. *pavane*, It. or Sp. *pavana*, etym. doubtful], *n.* A slow and stately dance, usu. in elaborate dress, in vogue in the 16th and 17th centuries.

pave (pāv) [O.F. *paver*, L. *pavīre*, to ram], *v.t.* To make a hard, level surface upon, with stone, bricks, etc.; to cover with or as with a pavement. **to pave a way for** or **to:** To prepare for. ***pavage,** *n.* **pavé** (păv' ā), *n.* Pavement; a stone-paved road in France. **pavement** (pāv' mėnt), *n.* That with which anything is paved; a hard level covering of stones, bricks, tiles, wood-blocks, etc.; a paved footway at the side of a street or road; (*Zool., etc.*) a close, level structure or formation (as of teeth) resembling a pavement. **pavement-artist,** *n.* A person drawing figures, etc., on a pavement in order to obtain money from passers-by. **paver, paviour,** *n.* One who lays pavements; a rammer for driving paving-stones. **paving,** *n.* **paving-stone,** *n.*

***pavid** (păv' id) [L. *pavidus*], *a.* Timid.

pavilion (pȧ vil' yȯn) [F. *pavillon*, L. *pāpiliōnem*, nom. *-lio*, butterfly], *n.* A tent, esp. a large one, of conical shape; a temporary or movable structure for entertainment, shelter, etc.; an ornamental building, usu. of light construction, for amusements, etc., esp. one for spectators and players on a cricket-ground, etc.; a belvedere, projecting turret, or other portion of a building, usu. of ornamental design; *a flag; (*Her.*) a bearing in the form of a tent. **v.t.* To furnish with or shelter in a pavilion.

paving, paviour [PAVE].

***pavis,** ***pavise** (păv' is) [O.F. *pavais* (F. *pavois*), It. *pavese*, prob. from *Pavia*, town in Italy], *n.* A convex shield for the whole body. *v.t.* To shelter or defend with this.

pavonazzo (pa vō năt' sō) [It., from L. *pāvōnāceum*, as foll.], *a.* Brilliantly coloured like a peacock. *n.* A variety of marble with brilliant markings like the colours of a peacock.

pavonine (păv' ȯ nīn) [L. *pāvōnīnus*, from *pāvo -ōnis*, peacock], *a.* Pertaining to or resembling a peacock; resembling the tail of a peacock; iridescent. *n.* A pavonine lustre or tarnish on certain ores and metals. ***pavone** (pȧ vōn'), *n.* A peacock. **pavonian** (pȧ vō' ni ȧn), *a.*

paw (paw) [O.F. *powe*, prob. from Frankish (cp. Dut. *poot*, G. *pfote*)], *n.* The foot of a quadruped having claws, as dist. from a hoof; (*slang*) the hand or handwriting. *v.t.* To scrape or strike with the forefoot; to strike the ground with the hoofs (of a horse); (*colloq.*) to handle roughly, familiarly or clumsily. ***pawed,** *a.*

pawky (paw' ki) [Sc. and North. (obs. *pawk*, a trick, -Y)], *a.* Sly, shrewd; humorous, arch. **pawkily,** *adv.* **pawkiness,** *n.*

pawl (pawl) [prob. from O.F. *paul* (F. *pal*), L. *pālum*, nom. *-lus*, stake, PALE (1)], *n.* A hinged piece of metal or lever engaging with the teeth of a wheel, etc., to prevent it from running back, etc.; (*Naut.*) a bar for preventing the recoil of a windlass, etc. *v.t.* To stop from recoiling with this.

pawn (1) (pawn) [M.E. and A.-F. *poun*, O.F. *paon*, *peon* (F. *pion*), med. L. *pedōnem*, nom. *pedo*, foot-soldier, from *pes pedis*, foot], *n.* A piece of the lowest value in chess. **pawn in the game:** (*fig.*) An insignificant person used in the plans of a cleverer one.

pawn (2) (pawn) [O.F. *pan*, prob. from Teut. (cp. O.Fris. and Dut. *pand*, G. *pfand*)], *n.* Something deposited as security for a debt or loan, a pledge; the state of being held as a pledge. *v.t.* To deliver or deposit as a pledge for the repayment of a debt or loan, or the performance of a promise; (*fig.*) to stake, to wager, to risk. **in pawn** or **at pawn:** Deposited as a pledge or security. **pawnbroker,** *n.* One who lends money on the security of goods pawned. **pawnbroking,** *n.* **pawnshop,** *n.* The place where this is carried on. **pawnee** (paw nē'), *n.* **pawner,** *n.*

pax (păks) [L., PEACE], *n.* A tablet or plaque bearing a representation of the Crucifixion or other sacred subject which was formerly kissed by the priest and congregation at Mass, an osculatory. **Pax Romana,** *n.* Peace imposed by the Roman Empire.

paxwax (păks' wăks) [formerly *faxwax* (A.-S. *feax*, hair, *weaxan*, to grow, to WAX (2))], *n.* A strong, stiff tendon from the dorsal vertebræ to the occiput in many mammals and, in a modified form, in man.

pay (1) (pā) [O.F. *paier* (F. *payer*), L. *pācāre*, to appease, from *pax pācem*, peace], *v.t.* (*past & p.p.* **paid**) To hand over what is due in discharge of a debt or for services or goods; to discharge (a bill, claim, obligation, etc.); to deliver as due; to deliver the amount, defray the cost or expense of; to expend (away); to compensate, to recompense, to requite; to bestow, to render (a compliment, visit, etc.). *v.i.* To make payment; to discharge a debt; to make an adequate return (to); to be remunerative. *n.* Payment, compensation, recompense; wages, salary. **pay as you earn (P.A.Y.E.):** A method of collecting Income Tax by deducting it before payment of the earnings. **to pay away:** To hand out (money, a fund, etc.) in wages, etc.; (*Naut.*) to let a rope run out by slackening it. **to pay off:** To pay the full amount of, to pay in full and discharge; (*Naut.*) to fall to leeward. **to pay one's way:** To keep out of debt. **to pay out:** To punish; to disburse; (*Naut.*) to cause (a rope) to run out. **to pay the piper:** To bear the cost. **to pay through the nose:** To pay an exorbitant price. **pay-bill,** *n.* A bill stating the amounts due as wages to workmen, soldiers, etc. **pay-day,** *n.* (*Stock Exch.*) The day on which transfers of stock are to be paid for. **paying guest,** *n.* A lodger who lives with the family. **pay-dirt,** *n.* (*Mining*) A deposit containing enough gold to make mining worth while. **paymaster,** *n.* One who pays, esp. one who regularly pays wages, etc.; (*Mil. and Nav.*) an officer whose duty it is to pay the officers and men. **Paymaster-General,** *n.* The officer at the head of the treasury department concerned with the payment of civil salaries and other expenses. **pay-office,** *n.* A place where payment is made of wages, debts, etc. **pay-roll,** *n.* List of employees. **payable,** *a.* **payee** (pā ē'), *n.* Person to whom money is paid. **payer,** *n.* **payment,** *n.*

pay (2) (pā) [O.North.F. *peier*, L. *picāre*, from *pix picis*, PITCH (1)], *v.t.* (*past & p.p.* **payed**) (*Naut.*) To coat, cover, or fill with hot pitch for water-proofing.

***paynim** (pā' nim) [A.-F. *paienime*, late L. *pāgānismus*], *n.* A pagan, a heathen; a Mohammedan.

paynize (pā' nīz) [*Payne*, inventor], *v.t.* To inject calcium or barium sulphide, followed by calcium sulphate, into wood in order to preserve it.

***paysage** (pā zazh') [F., from *pays*, country], *n.* A rural scene or landscape.

pea (1) (pē) [from PEASE, taken as *pl.*], *n.* A leguminous plant, *Pisum sativum*, the seeds of which are used as food. **pea-cod** [PEASE-COD]: The seed of this. **pea-crab,** *n.* A small crab living in the shell of a mollusc. **pea-flour,** *n.* Pease-meal. **pea-green,** *a.* and *n.* A colour like that of fresh green peas. **pea-maggot,** *n.* A caterpillar infesting peas. **pea-nut,** *n.* A plant of the bean family with pods ripening underground which are edible and are used for their oil; a monkey-nut. **pea-pod,** *n.* The pericarp of the pea. **pea-rigger,** *n.* (*slang*) A thimble-rigger. **pea-shooter,** *n.* A tube through which dried peas are shot, usu. from the mouth. **peasoup,** *n.* Soup made with peas, esp. dried and split peas. **peasouper,** *n.* (*colloq.*) A dense yellowish fog. **peasoupy,** *a.* **peastone,** *n.* Pisolite.

pea (2) [PEACOCK, PEAFOWL].

peace (pēs) [M.E. and O.F. *pais*, L. *pācem*, nom. *pax*], *n.* A state of quiet or tranquillity; absence of civil disturbance or agitation; freedom from or cessation of war or hostilities; a treaty reconciling two hostile nations; a state of friendliness; calmness of mind. **Justice of the Peace** [JUSTICE]. **king's** or **queen's peace:** The state of tranquillity, order, and absence of strife throughout the realm, for which the sovereign is responsible. **peace be with you:** A solemn formula of leave-taking. **to hold one's peace:** To be silent. **to keep the peace:** To abstain from strife; to prevent a conflict. **to make peace:** To reconcile or be reconciled (with); to bring about a treaty of peace. **peace-breaker,** *n.* **peacemaker,** *n.* One who reconciles. **peace-offering,** *n.* An offering to God as a token of thanksgiving, etc.; a gift to procure peace or reconciliation. **peace-officer,** *n.* A civil officer whose duty it is to preserve the public peace. **peaceable,** *a.* Peaceful, quiet; disposed to peace. **peaceableness,** *n.* **peaceably,** *adv.* **peaceful,** *a.* In a state of peace; free from noise or disturbance; quiet, pacific, mild. **peacefully,** *adv.* **peacefulness,** *n.* **peaceless,** *a.*

peach (1) (pēch) [O.F. *pesche*, L. *persicum*, Persian (*apple*)], *n.* The fleshy, downy fruit of *Amygdalus persica*, or the tree; (*colloq.*) a pretty girl, anything superlatively good or pretty. **peach-bloom,** *n.* The delicate powder on a ripe peach; (*fig.*) a soft, pink colour on the cheeks. **peach-blossom,** *n.* Peach-flower; a delicate purplish pink; a moth with spots of rosy white on its wings. **peach-blow,** *n.* A light purple or pink glaze on porcelain. **peach-brandy,** *n.* A spirit distilled from peach-juice. **peach-colour,** *n.* **peach-coloured,** *a.* Of the colour of peach-blossom. **peach-yellows,** *n.* A disease attacking peach-trees in the Eastern U.S. **peachwort,** *n.* Persicaria.

peach (2) (pēch) [M.E. *apechen*, as IMPEACH], *v.i.* To turn informer against an accomplice; to inform (against or upon). ******v.t.* To impeach or inform against.

peacock (pē' kok) [A.-S. *pēa*, *pāwe*, L. *pāvo*, COCK (1)], *n.* Any individual, esp. the male, of the genus *Pavo* or peafowl, esp. *Pavo cristatus*, a bird with gorgeous plumage and long tail capable of expanding like a fan; (*fig.*) a vainglorious person. *v.t.* To display or plume (oneself). *v.i.* To strut about ostentatiously. **peacock-butterfly,** *n.* One of various butterflies with ocellated wings. **peacock-fish,** *n.* A brilliantly variegated fish, *Crenilabrus pavo*. **pea-chick,** *n.* **peacockery,** *n.* **peacockish,** **peacocklike,** *a.* **peafowl,** *n.* **peahen,** *n.*

pea-jacket (pē' jăk ėt) [prob. after Dut. *pij-jakker* (*pij*, pea-jacket)], *n.* A coarse, thick, loose overcoat worn by seamen, etc.

peak (1) (pēk) [var. of PIKE (1)], *n.* A sharp point or top, esp. of a mountain; the projecting brim in front of a cap; (*Naut.*) the upper after-corner of a sail extended by a gaff; the upper end of a gaff; (*Elec.*) the culminating point of a load curve during a specified period, and the maximum load of electricity required. **peak value, peak voltage,** *n.* (*Elec.*) The highest value of an alternating quantity. **peaked, peaky** (1), *a.*

peak (2) (pēk) [etym. doubtful], *v.i.* To look sickly; to pine away; (*in p.p.*) to look sharp-featured or emaciated. **peaky** (2), *a.*

peak (3) (pēk) [from APEAK], *v.t.* (*Naut.*) To raise (a gaff or yard) more nearly vertical; to raise the oars apeak. *v.i.* (*Aviat.*) To dive vertically so as to raise the tail into the air.

peal (1) (pēl) [prob. from APPEAL], *n.* A loud, esp. a prolonged or repercussive sound, as of thunder, bells, etc.; a set of bells tuned to each other; a series of changes rung on these. *v.i.* To sound a peal; to resound. *v.t.* To cause to give out loud and solemn sounds; to utter or give forth sonorously; *to celebrate; *to assail with noise.

peal (2) (pēl) [etym. unknown], *n.* (*local*) A grilse or young salmon, usu. under 2 lb.; a sea-trout.

pean (pēn) [etym. doubtful], *n.* (*Her.*) An heraldic fur, represented by sable with or (golden) spots.

pear (pâr) [A.-S. *pere*, late L. *pira*, L. *pirum*], *n.* The fleshy obovoid fruit of *Pyrus communis*; the fruit of the pear-tree. **pear-shaped,** *a.* **pear-tree,** *n.*

pearl (1) (pĕrl) [F. *perle*, etym. doubtful], *n.* A smooth, white or bluish-grey lustrous and iridescent calcareous concretion, found in several bivalves, the best in the pearl-oyster, prized as a gem; mother-of-pearl; something round and clear and resembling a pearl, as a dewdrop, tooth, etc.; pearl-eye; (*fig.*) anything exceedingly valuable, or the finest specimen of its kind; (*Print.*) a small size of type [as this]. *a.* Pertaining to, containing, or made of pearls. *v.t.* To set or embroider with pearls; to sprinkle with pearly drops; to rub and strip barley into pearly grains. *v.i.* To form pearly drops or fragments; to fish for pearls. **pearl-ash,** *n.* Crude carbonate of potash. **pearl-barley** [BARLEY]. **pearl-button,** *n.* A button made of mother-of-pearl. **pearl-diver,** *n.* One who dives for pearl-oysters. **pearl-eye,** *n.* A pearl-coloured film or speck on the eye, causing cataract. **pearl-eyed,** *a.* **pearl-fisher,** *n.* One who fishes for pearls. **pearl-fishing,** *n.* **pearl-oyster,** *n.* **pearl-powder** [PEARL-WHITE]. **pearl-shell,** *n.* Mother-of-pearl in its natural state. **pearl-sinter,** *n.* Fiorite. **pearl-spar,** *n.* A variety of dolomite. **pearl-stone,** *n.* Perlite. **pearl-studded,** *a.* **pearl-white,** *n.* Oxychloride of bismuth, used as a cosmetic for whitening the skin. **pearlaceous** [PERLACEOUS]. **pearled** (1), **pearly,** *a.* **pearlies,** *n.pl.* Costermonger's festal dress covered with pearl buttons. **pearliness,** *n.* **pearling** (1), *n.* The process of removing the outer coat of barley, etc.

pearl (2) (pĕrl) [prob. var. of PURL (1)], *n.* A fine loop, a row of which forms an ornamental edging on various fabrics. *v.t.* To knit this. **pearled** (2), *a.* **pearl-edge,** *n.* A border or edging made of this. **pearling** (2), *n.*

pearmain (pâr' mān) [Fr. *permain*], *n.* A kind of apple.

peasant (pez' ȧnt) [O.F. *paisant* (F. *paysan*), L. *pāgensem*, nom. *-sis*, of or pertaining to a *pāgus* or village], *n.* A countryman; a rustic labourer. *a.* Rustic, rural; *base. **peasantlike,** *a.* **peasantry** (pez' ȧn tri), *n.*

pease (pēz) [A.-S. *pise*, pea, pl. *pisan*, late L. *pisa*, L. *pisum*, Gr. *pison* (cp. PEA (1))], *n.* (*pl. or collect. sing.*) Peas. **peasecod,** *n.* A pea-pod. **peasecod-bellied,** *a.* Applied to a 16th-cent. doublet with the lower part padded and quilted. **peascod-doublet,** *n.* ***peasecod-time,** *n.* The season for peas. **pease-meal,** *n.* Meal obtained by grinding peas. **pease-porridge, -pudding,** *n.* Porridge or pudding made of peas.

peat (pēt) [M.E. *pete*, etym. doubtful], *n.* Decayed and partly carbonized vegetable-matter found in boggy places and used as fuel. **peat-bog, -moss,** *n.* A bog containing peat. **peat-hag** [MOSS-HAG]. **peat-reek,** *n.* Smoke from a peat-fire; (*slang*) whisky distilled over this, whisky illicitly distilled, mountain-dew. **peatery,** *n.* A place where peat is cut and prepared for use. **peaty,** *a.*

pebble (peb' ėl) [A.-S. *papol-stān*, pebble-stone, etym. doubtful], *n.* A small stone rounded by the action of water; an agate; a transparent rock-crystal, used for spectacles, etc.; a lens made of this. *v.t.* To pelt with pebbles; to pave with pebbles; to impart a rough indented surface or grain to (leather). **pebble-crystal,** *n.* A crystal in the rough state in the form of a pebble. **pebble-stone,** *n.* **pebble-ware,** *n.* A variety of Wedgwood ware having different coloured clays worked into the paste. **pebbled, pebbly,** *a.*

pebrine (pė brēn', peb' rin) [F., from Port. *pebrino*, from *pebre*, PEPPER], *n.* An epidemic disease characterized by black spots, attacking silkworms.

pecan (pė kăn') [F. *pacane*, Sp. *pacana*, from native name], *n.* A N. American hickory, *Carya olivæformis*, or its fruit or nut.

peccable (pek' ȧ bėl) [med. L. *peccābilis*, from *peccāre*, to sin], *a.* Liable to sin. **peccability** (-bil' i ti), *n.*

peccadillo (pek ȧ dil' ō) [Sp., dim. of *pecado*, L. *peccātum*, sin, as prec.], *n.* (*pl.* **-oes**) A slight fault or offence.

peccant (pek' ȧnt) [F., from L. *peccantem*, nom. *-cans*, pres.p. of *peccāre*, to sin], *a.* Sinful; guilty; informal, wrong; (*Path.*) morbid, inducing or indicating disease. ***n.** An offender. **peccancy,** *n.*

peccary (pek' ȧ ri) [Carib. *pakira*], *n.* One of two small American species of hog-like mammals, *Dicotyles torquatus* and *D. labiatus*.

peccavi (pė kā' vī) [L., I have sinned], *phr.* Expressing contrition or error. *n.* A confession of error.

pech (pā*ch*) [Sc. and North., perh. onomat.], *v.i.* To breathe hard, to pant. *n.* A pant, a puff.

peck (1) (pek) [A.-F. and O.F. *pek*, etym. doubtful], *n.* A measure of capacity for dry goods, two gallons; the fourth part of a bushel; a vessel used for measuring this; (*fig.*) a large quantity.

peck (2) (pek) [var. of PICK (1)], *v.t.* To strike with a beak or a pointed instrument; to pick up with or as with the beak; to break, open, eat, etc., thus; to break (up or down) with a pointed implement; (*colloq.*) to eat. *v.i.* To strike or aim with a beak or pointed implement. *n.* A sharp stroke with or as with a beak; a mark made by this; a sharp kiss. **pecker,** *n.* One who or that which pecks; a woodpecker; a kind of hoe; (*slang*) the mouth, the appetite; spirits, courage. **keep your pecker up:** Keep cheerful. **peckish,** *a.* (*slang*) Hungry.

Pecksniff (pek' snif) [character in Dickens's 'Martin Chuzzlewit'], *n.* An unctuous, canting hypocrite.

pecten (pek' tėn) [L. *pecten -tinis*, comb, from *pectere*, to comb (cp. Gr. *pektein*)], *n.* (*Anat. and Zool.*) A comb-like process forming a membrane in the eyes of birds and some reptiles, an appendage behind the posterior legs in scorpions, and various other parts or organs; a genus of *Ostreidæ* containing the scallops.

pectic (pek' tik) [Gr. *pēktos*, from *pēg-*, stem of *pēgnuein*, to make firm or solid, -IC], *a.* (*Chem.*) Derived from or containing pectin.

pectin (pek' tin), *n.* A white, amorphous compound found in fruits and certain fleshy roots, formed from pectose by the process of ripening.

pectinate, pectinated (pek' tin ȧt, pek' tin ā ted), *a.* Having projections like the teeth of a comb. **pectination,** *n.*

pectinato-, pectini-, *comb. form.* Comb-like.

pectoral (pek' tȯ rȧl) [F., from L. *pectorālis*, from *pectus -toris*, breast], *a.* Pertaining to or for the breast; (*Med.*) good for diseases of the breast. *n.* An ornament worn on the breast, esp. the breast-plate of the Jewish high priest; (*Zool.*) a pectoral fin; (*Med.*) a medicine to relieve chest complaints.

pectoriloquism, -quy (il' ȯ kwizm, -kwi), *n.* The transmission of the sound of the voice through the walls of the chest, as heard with the stethoscope, a symptom of certain chest disorders.

pectose (pek' tōz), *n.* An insoluble compound allied to cellulose found in unripe fruits and other vegetable tissue.

peculate (pek' ū lāt) [L. *peculātus*, p.p. of *peculāri*, as foll.], *v.t.* To appropriate to one's own use money or goods entrusted to one's care. **peculation** (-lā' shŭn), *n.* **peculator** (pek' ū lā tȯr), *n.*

peculiar (pė kū' li ȧr) [L. *peculiāris*, from *peculium*, private property, from *pecu*, cattle], *a.* Belonging particularly and exclusively (to); one's own, private, not general; pertaining to the individual; particular, special; singular, strange, odd. *n.* Exclusive property, right, or privilege; a parish or church exempt from diocesan jurisdiction; one of the Peculiar People. **Peculiar People:** A Christian sect, founded 1838, having no ministry or regular organization and believing in the cure of diseases by prayer. **peculiarity** (-ăr' i ti), *n.* The quality of being peculiar; a characteristic; an idiosyncrasy. **peculiarize,** *v.t.* **peculiarly,** *adv.*

pecuniary (pė kū' ni ȧ ri) [L. *pecūniārius*, from *pecūnia*, as prec.], *a.* Relating to or consisting of money. **pecuniarily,** *adv.* ***pecunious,** *a.* Having plenty of money.

pedagogue (ped' ȧ gog) [M.F., from L. *pædagōgus*, Gr. *paidagōgos* (*pais paidos*, boy, *agein*, to lead)], *n.* A teacher of young children, a schoolmaster (usu. in contempt, implying conceit or pedantry). ***v.t.** To teach; to instruct superciliously. **pedagogic, -al** (-goj' ik, -ȧl), *a.* **pedagogics,** *n.* The science of teaching. **pedagogism, -goguism** (ped' ȧ gog izm), *n.* The occupation, manners, or character of a pedagogue. **pedagogy** (ped' ȧ goj i), *n.* Pedagogics; pedagogism.

pedal (ped' ȧl) [prob. through F. *pedale*, It. *pedale*, L. *pedālem*, nom. *-lis*, from *pes pedis*, foot], *n.* A lever acted on by the foot; (*Organ*) a wooden key moved by the feet, or a foot-lever for working several stops at once, for opening and shutting the swell-box, etc.; (*Piano*) a foot-lever for lifting the damper, for muffing the notes, and other purposes; (*Mus.*) a sustained note, usu. in the bass. *v.t.* (*past & p.p.* **pedalled**) To work (a bicycle, sewing-machine, etc.) by pedals; to play on (an organ) by pedals. *v.i.* To play an organ or work a bicycle, etc., by pedals. *a.* (*Anat.*) Of or pertaining to a foot or foot-like part (esp. of mollusca). **pedal-note,** *n.* (*Mus.*) A tonic or dominant note sustained through various harmonics. **pedal-pipe,** *n.* An organ pipe acted on by a pedal. **pedalist** (ped' ȧ list), *n.* One expert in the use of pedals; a cyclist.

pedant (ped' ȧnt) [F. *pédant*, It. *pedante*, a schoolmaster, prob. cogn. with PEDAGOGUE], *n.* One who makes a pretentious show of book-learning, or lays undue stress on rules and formulas; one with more book-learning than practical experience or common sense; *a schoolmaster. **pedantic, *-al** (pė dăn' tik, -ȧl), *a.* **pedantically,** *adv.* ***pedantize** (ped' ȧn tīz), *v.i.* **pedantocracy** (-tok' rȧ si), *n.* **pedantry** (ped' ȧn tri), *n.*

pedate (ped' ȧt) [L. *pedātus*, from *pes pedis*, foot], *a.* (*Zool.*) Having feet; (*Bot.*) palmately divided with the two lateral lobes divided into smaller segments like digits or toes. **pedately,** *adv.*

peddle (ped' ėl) [etym. doubtful; in first sense prob. from PEDLAR], *v.i.* To travel about the country selling small wares; to busy oneself about trifles. *v.t.* To hawk; to sell in small quantities, to retail. **peddler,** etc. [PEDLAR]. **peddling,** *a.* Trifling, insignificant.

pederast (ped' ėr ăst) [Gr. *paiderastēs* (*paiss paidos*, boy, *eraein*, to love)], *n.* A sodomite. **pederastic** (-ăs' tik), *a.* **pederasty** (ped' ėr ăs ti), *n.*

pedestal (ped' ės tȧl) [G. *pedestal* or F. *piédestal*, It. *piedestallo* (*piè*, L. *pes pedis*, foot, *di*, of, *stallo*, STALL (1))], *n.* An insulated base for a column, statue, etc.; either of the supports of a knee-hole desk; a base, foundation, or support; movable cupboard for a chamber-pot; the china pan of a water-closet. *v.t.* To set on a pedestal; to serve as a pedestal for. **to set on a pedestal:** (*fig.*) To look up to.

pedestrian (pė des′ tri ȧn) [L. *pedester -tris*, from *pes pedis*, foot, -IAN], *a.* Going or performed on foot; pertaining to walking; (*fig.*) prosaic, dull, commonplace. *n.* One who journeys on foot; an expert walker; one who races on foot. **pedestrial,** *a.* **pedestrianism,** *n.* **pedestrianize,** *v.i.*

pediatric (pe di ăt′ rik) [PÆDO-], *a.* Relating to the medical treatment of children. **pediatrics,** *n.* **pediatrician** (pe di ȧ trish′ ȧn), *n.* A specialist in children's diseases.

pedicel (ped′ i sėl) [mod. L. *pedicellus*, dim. of *pedĭculus*, dim. of *pes pedis*, foot], *n.* (*Bot. and Zool.*) The stalk supporting a single flower, etc.; any small foot-stalk or stalk-like structure. **pedicellate,** *a.* **pedicle** (ped′ ikl), *n.* A pedicel or peduncle. **pediculate** (pė dik′ ū lȧt), *a.*

pedicular, -lous (pė dik′ ū lȧr, -lůs) [L. *pedĭculāris*, *-lōsus*, from *pediculus*, louse], *a.* Lousy. ***pedicularis*** (-lâr′ is), *n.* (*Bot.*) A genus of *Scrophulariaceæ* containing the betony. ***pediculation** (-lā′ shůn), **pediculosis** (-lō′ sis), *n.* (*Path.*) Lousiness, phthiriasis.

pedicure (ped′ i kūr) [F. *pédicure* (L. *pes pedis*, foot, *curāre*, to CURE)], *n.* The surgical treatment of the feet; a chiropodist.

pediferous (pė dif′ ėr ůs), **pedigerous** (pė dij′ ėr ůs) [L. *pes pedis*, foot, -FEROUS, -GEROUS], *a.* Having feet or foot-like parts.

pedigree (ped′ i grē) [formerly *pedegru*, O.F. *pee de grue*, F. *pié de grue* (L. *pes pedis*, foot, *de*, of, *grue*, L. *gruem*, nom. *grus*, crane)], *n.* Genealogy, lineage, esp. ancient lineage, a genealogical table or tree; derivation, etymology. *a.* Pure-bred, having a known ancestry (of cattle, dogs, etc.). **pedigreed,** *a.*

pedimanous (pė dim′ ȧ nůs) [L. *pes pedis*, foot, *manus*, hand], *a.* Having the feet shaped like hands (of lemurs, opossums, etc.). **pedimane** (ped′ i mān), *n.*

pediment (ped′ i mėnt) [formerly *periment*, perh. corr. of L. *operīmentum*, from *operīre*, to cover, or of PYRAMID], *n.* The triangular part surmounting a portico, in buildings in the Grecian style; a similar member crowning doorways, windows, etc., in buildings in classical Renaissance styles. **pedimental** (-men′ tȧl), *a.* **pedimented** (ped′ i mėn tėd), *a.*

pedipalp (ped′ i pălp) [L. *pes pedis*, foot, *palpus*, PALP], *n.* (*Zool.*) An arachnid of the order *Pedipalpi*, characterized by pincer-like feelers, comprising the true scorpions. **pedipalpal, -pous** (-păl′ pȧl, -půs), *a.*

pedlar (ped′ lȧr) [etym. doubtful, prob. cogn. with obs. *ped*, basket], *n.* A travelling (on foot) hawker of small wares, usu. carried in a pack; (*fig.*) one who retails (gossip, etc.). **pedlar's pony, horse,** or **pad:** (*slang*) A walking-stick. **pedlary,** *n.*

pedology (ped ol′ ō ji) [Gr. *pedon*, ground], *n.* The science of soils. **pedologist,** *n.*

pedometer (pė dom′ ė tėr) [F. *pédomètre* (L. *pes pedis*, foot, -METER)], *n.* An instrument for measuring the distance covered on foot by registering the number of the steps taken. **pedomotive** (ped′ ȯ mō tiv), *a.* Moved or propelled by the feet. *n.* A velocipede. **pedomotor,** *n.* A contrivance for using the feet as motive power; a vehicle so propelled, a velocipede.

pedrail (ped′ rāl), *n.* A contrivance for enabling a traction-engine to move over rough ground; the traction-engine so equipped.

peduncle (pė dŭng′ kėl) [L. *pes pedis*, foot, -UNCLE], *n.* (*Bot.*) A flower-stalk, esp. of a solitary flower or one bearing the subsidiary stalks of a cluster; (*Zool.*) a stalk-like process for the attachment of an organ or an organism. **peduncular, pedunculate, -lated,** *a.*

peek (pēk) [etym. doubtful], *v.i.* To peer, to peep, to pry. *n.* A peep.

peel (1) (pēl) [var. of PILL (2), perh. influ. by F. *peler*, to peel], *v.t.* To strip the skin, bark, or rind off; to strip (rind, etc., off); to pillage, to plunder. *v.i.* To lose the skin or rind, to become bare; (*slang*) to undress. *n.* Skin or rind. **peeler** (1), *n.*

peel (2) (pēl) [O.F. *pele* (F. *pelle*), L. *pāla*], *n.* A wooden shovel used by bakers; (*Naut.*) the blade of an oar.

peel (3) **pele** (pēl) [M.E. and O.F. *pel*, a palisade, L. *pālum*, nom. *-lus*, stake, PALE (1)], *n.* A square fortified tower, esp. those built about the 16th cent. in the border counties of Scotland and England for defence against raids.

peeler (2) (pē′ lėr), *n.* (*slang*) A policeman, orig. a constable in the police organized by Sir Robert Peel in 1828.

Peelite (pēl′ īt) [as prec.], *n.* An adherent of Sir Robert Peel (1788–1850), esp. a Conservative supporting his measure for the repeal of the Corn Laws.

peen (pēn) [etym. doubtful], *n.* (*prov. and Am.*) The point of a mason's hammer, opposite to the face. *v.t.* To hammer.

peep (1) (pēp) [perh. from O.F. *pipier*, L. *pīpāre*, of imit. orig., or var. of PIPE (1)], *v.i.* To cry, chirp, or squeak, as a young bird, a mouse, etc. *n.* A chirp, squeak, etc. **peeper** (1), *n.* A chicken just out of the shell.

peep (2) (pēp) [perh. rel. to PEEK], *v.i.* To look through a crevice or narrow opening; to look slyly or furtively; to show oneself or appear partially or cautiously, to come (out) gradually into view. *n.* A furtive look, a hasty glance, a glimpse; the first appearance. **peep-hole,** *n.* **Peep-o'-day boys:** A secret society of Protestants in Ireland, founded in 1784, from their early visits to the houses of Roman Catholics in search of arms. **peep-show,** *n.* An exhibition of pictures, etc., shown through a small aperture containing a lens. **peep-sight,** *n.* A movable disk on the breech of a fire-arm pierced with a small hole through which aim can be taken with accuracy. **peeper** (2), *n.* One who peeps; (*slang*) an eye. **peeping Tom:** One guilty of prurient curiosity.

peer (1) (pēr) [O.F. *per*, L. *parem*, nom. *par*, equal], *n.* One of the same rank; an equal in any respect; a noble, esp. a member of a hereditary legislative body; (*United Kingdom*) a member of one of the degrees of nobility, comprising dukes, marquesses, earls, viscounts, and barons. *v.t.* To equal, to rank with; to make a peer. *v.i.* To be equal. **peers of the United Kingdom** or **of the realm:** Those British peers all of whom are entitled to sit in the House of Lords; **peers of Ireland:** Twenty-eight representatives of whom are elected for life; **peers of Scotland:** Sixteen representatives of whom are elected to each Parliament. **peerage,** *n.* The rank of a peer; the body of peers; the nobility, the aristocracy; a book containing particulars of the nobility. **peeress,** *n.* **peerless,** *a.* Without an equal. **peerlessly,** *adv.* **peerlessness,** *n.*

peer (2) (pēr) [etym. doubtful], *v.i.* To peep, to pry (at, into, etc.); to peep out; to appear, to come into sight.

peerless [PEER].

peesweep (pēz′ wēp) [Sc., imit. of the bird's cry], *n.* The pewit.

peevers (pē′ vĕrz), *n.* (*Sc.*) The game of hopscotch.

peevish (pē′ vish) [etym. doubtful], *a.* Fretful, irritable, petulant; expressing discontent; *childish. **peevishly,** *adv.* **peevishness,** *n.* **peeved,** *a.* (*slang*) Irritated, annoyed.

peewit [PEWIT].

peg (peg) [M.E. *pegge* (cp. Dut. dial. *peg*, Swed. dial *pegg*)], *n.* A pin or bolt, usu. of wood, for holding parts of a structure or fastening articles together, hanging things on, supporting, holding, marking, etc.; (*fig.*) a step, a degree; an occasion, pretext, excuse, or topic for discourse, etc.; (*colloq.*) a drink. *v.t.* (*past & p.p.* **pegged**) To fix or fasten (down, in, out, etc.) with a peg or pegs; to mark (a score) with pegs on a cribbage-board; to mark (out) boundaries; (*Comm. slang*) to prevent (the price of stocks) from falling or rising by buying or selling freely at a given price. **to peg away:** To work at or struggle persistently. **to peg down:** To fasten down with pegs; (*fig.*) to restrict (to rules, etc.). **to peg out:** (*Croquet*) To go out by hitting the final peg; (*Cribbage*) to win by attaining the final hole in the cribbage-board; to mark out a claim; (*slang*) to die; to fail, to be done for. **to take** (one) **down a peg:** To humiliate, to degrade. **off the peg:** Ready-made. **peg-top,** *n.* A spinning-top with a metal peg, usually spun by means of string which unwinds rapidly when the top is thrown from the hand; (*pl.*) trousers very wide at the top and narrowing towards the ankles.

Pegamoid (peg′ ȧm oid), *n.* Protected trade name of an imitation leather used in upholstery, etc.

Pegasus (peg′ ȧ sŭs) [L., from Gr. *Pēgasos*, from *pēgē*, fountain], *n.* (*Gr. Myth.*) A winged steed that sprang from the blood of Medusa and with a blow of its hoofs produced the fountain Hippocrene or Helicon, whence poets were fabled to draw their inspiration; (*fig.*) poetic inspiration or genius; a genus of fishes with broad pectoral fins, typical of the family *Pegasidæ*.

pegmatite (peg′ mȧ tīt) [L. and Gr. *pēgma*, from *pēgnuein*, to fasten, -ITE], *n.* A coarse-grained variety of granite, with a little mica. **pegmatitic** (-tit′ ik), *a.*

Pehlevi [PAHLAVI].

peignoir (pā′ nwar) [F., from *peigner*, to comb], *n.* A loose robe or dressing-gown worn by women during the toilet.

peirameter (pī răm′ ė tėr) [Gr. *peiran*, to try, -METER], *n.* An instrument for measuring the resistance of road surfaces to traction.

***peise** (pāz, pēz) [A.-F. *peiser*, O.F. *peser*, L. *pensāre*, freq. of *pendere*, to weigh], *v.t.* To weigh, to balance; to poise; to weight, to burden. *v.i.* To press down. *n.* Heaviness, weight; a weight; a heavy impact, a blow.

peishwa [PESHWA].

pejorative (pē′ jȯ rā-, pė jor′ ȧ tiv) [L. *pējōrātus*, p.p. of *pējōrāre*, to make worse, from *pējor*, worse, -ATIVE], *a.* Depreciatory. *n.* (*Gram.*) A word or form expressing depreciation, as the suffix -ASTER. **pejorate** (pē′ jȯ rāt), *v.t.* **pejoration** (-rā shŭn), *n.*

pekan (pek′ ȧn) [Canadian F., from Algonkin *pékané*], *n.* A N. American carnivorous animal, *Mustela Pennanti*, of the weasel family, prized for its fur.

pekin (pē kin′, -king′) [F. *pékin*, Chin. *Pe-king*, lit. northern capital], *n.* A fabric of silk or satin, usu. with stripes running the way of the warp; a civilian (orig. used by the soldiers of Napoleon I). **Pekinese** (-ēz′), *a.* Of or pertaining to Pekin. **Peke** (pēk), **Pekinese,** *n.* A rough-coated variety of Chinese pug.

pekoe (pek′ ō) [Chin. *pek-ho* (*pek*, white, *ho*, down)], *n.* A fine black tea.

pelage (pel′ ȧj) [F., from O.F. *pel*, ult. from L. *pilus*, hair], *n.* The coat or hair of an animal, esp. of fur.

Pelagian (1) (pė lā′ ji ȧn), *n.* A follower of Pelagius, a British monk of the 5th cent., who denied the doctrine of original sin. *a.* Of or pertaining to Pelagius or his doctrines. **Pelagianism,** *n.*

pelagian (2) (pe lā′ ji ȧn), **pelagic** (pė lăj′ ik) [L. *pelagius*, Gr. *pelagios*, from *pelagos*, sea], *a.* Of or inhabiting the deep sea. *n.* A pelagian animal.

pelargonium (pel ȧr gō′ ni ŭm) [Gr. *pelargos*, stork], *n.* A large genus of ornamental plants of the family *Geraniaceæ*, popularly called geraniums.

Pelasgic (pė lăz′ jik, -gik), *a.* Of or pertaining to the Pelasgi, a widely-diffused prehistoric race inhabiting the coasts and islands of the eastern Mediterranean and the Ægean.

Pele [PEEL (3)].

pelecoid (pel′ e koid) [Gr. *pelekoeides*, axe-like], *n.* (*Geom.*) A figure enclosed by a semicircle and two concave quadrants meeting in a point.

pelerine (pel′ ėr in, -ēn) [F. *pèlerine*, fem. of *pèlerin*, L. *peregrinus*, PILGRIM], *n.* A lady's long narrow fur cape.

pelf (pelf) [M.E. *pelfe*, O.F. *pelfre*, etym. doubtful], *n.* Money, wealth, gain (in contempt).

pelican (pel′ i kȧn) [F., from late L. *pelicānus*, Gr. *pelekan*, prob. rel. to *pelekus*, axe], *n.* A large piscivorous water-fowl of the genus *Pelecanus onocrotalus*, with an enormous pouch beneath the mandibles for storing fish when caught.

pelisse (pė lēs′) [F., from L. *pellicia*, fem. of *pellicius*, of skin, from *pellis*, skin], *n.* A woman's long cloak or mantle; a garment worn over other clothes by a child.

***pell** (pel) [O.F. *pel* (F. *peau*), L. *pellem*, nom. *-lis*, skin], *n.* A skin, a hide; a roll of parchment. ***pellage,** *n.*

pellagra (pė lăg′ rȧ, -lā′ grȧ) [prob. from It. *pelle agra*, rough skin], *n.* A virulent endemic disease attacking the skin and causing nervous disorders and mania, common in Italy and caused by deficiency of Vitamins B.

pellet (pel′ ėt) [O.F. *pelote*, med. L. *pelōta*, dim. of L. *pila*, ball], *n.* A little ball, esp. of bread, paper, or something easily moulded; a small pill; a small shot, a rounded boss or prominence. *v.t.* To form into pellets; to hit with pellets.

pellicle (pel′ i kėl) [F. *pellicule*, from L. *pellicula*, dim. of *pellis*, skin], *n.* A thin skin; a membrane or film. **pellicular** (-lik′ ū lȧr), *a.*

pellitory (pel′ i tȯr i) [obs. *pelleter*, A.-F. *peletre*, L. *piretārum*, Gr. *purethron*, feverfew, coalescing with obs. *parietary*, A.-F. *paritarie*, L. *parietāria*, from *paries parietis*, wall], *n.* A herb of the genus *Parietaria*, esp. the wall-pellitory, *P. officinalis*; also applied to a herb of the aster family, *Anacyclus purethrum*, or pellitory of Spain.

pell-mell (pel mel) [F. *pêle-mêle*, prob. a redup. of *mêle*, from *mêler*, late L. *misculāre*, L. *miscēre*, to mix], *adv.* In a confused or disorderly manner, promiscuously, anyhow. *a.* Confused, disorderly, promiscuous. *n.* Disorder, confusion; a medley.

pellucid (pė lū′ sid) [F. *pellucide*, L. *pellūcidus*, from *pel-*, *perlūcēre* (PER-, *lūcēre*, to shine)], *a.* Clear, limpid, transparent; clear in thought, expression, or style. **pellucidly,** *adv.* **pellucidity** (-sid′ i ti), **pellucidness,** *n.*

pelmet (pel′ mėt), *n.* (*Build.*) A canopy, built-in or detachable, which conceals the fittings from which curtains hang; a vallance.

peloria (pė lôr′ i ȧ) [mod. L., from Gr. *pelōros*, monstrous, from *pelōr*, prodigy], *n.* (*Bot.*) Symmetry or regularity in flowers that are normally irregular.

pelorus (pe lôr′ ŭs), *n.* (*Naut.*) A sighting device on a ship's compass.

pelota (pė lō′ tȧ) [Sp., from *pella*, L. *pila*, ball], *n.* A game somewhat like tennis played with a ball and a curved racket fitting upon the hand, popular in Spain and the Basque country.

pelotherapy (pe lō ther′ ȧ pi) [Gr. *pelos*, mud, *therapeuein*, to heal], *n.* (*Med.*) Treatment of disease by the application of mud.

pelt (1) (pelt) [M.E. rel. to PELL], *n.* A hide or skin with the hair on, esp. of a sheep or goat; an undressed fur-skin; a raw skin stripped of hair or wool; (*facet.*) the human skin. **pelt-monger,** *n.* **pelt-wool,** *n.* Wool from a dead sheep or lamb. **peltry,** *n.*

pelt (2) (pelt) [etym. doubtful], *v.t.* To strike or assail by throwing missiles. *v.i.* To throw missiles; to keep on throwing, firing, etc. (at); to beat heavily (of rain, etc.); (*slang*) to hurry (along). *n.* A blow from something thrown. **full pelt:** At full speed, with violent impetus. **pelter,** *n.* **pelting** (1), *a.*

pelta (pel' tȧ) [L., from Gr. *peltē*, perh. rel. to *pella*, hide], *n.* (*Class. Ant.*) A small light shield or target used by the ancient Greeks and Romans; (*Bot.*) a structure or part like a shield in form or function. **peltate, -tated,** *a.* (*Bot.*) Shield-shaped and fixed to the stalk at the centre (of leaves, etc.). **peltation** (-tā' shŭn), *n.* **peltati-, peltato-,** *comb. form.* (*Bot.*).

***pelting** (2) (pel' ting) [prob. rel. to PALTRY], *a.* Petty, mean, paltry, contemptible. ***peltingly,** *adv.*

pelvis (pel' vis) [L., basin], *n.* (*Anat.*) The lower portion of the great abdominal cavity; the bony walls of this cavity; the interior cavity of the kidney. **pelvic, pelviform,** *a.* **pelvimeter** (-vim' ė tėr), *n.* An instrument for measuring the diameter of the pelvis. **pelvimetry,** *n.*

pemmican (pem' i kȧn) [Cree *pimikan*], *n.* Dried meat, pounded, mixed with a large proportion of melted fat and pressed into cakes; a similar preparation of beef with currants; (*fig.*) digested or condensed information.

pemphigus (pem' fig ŭs) [Gr. *pemphix*, a bubble], *n.* (*Path.*) A condition characterized by the eruption of watery vesicles on the skin.

pen (1) (pen) [A.-S. *penn*, whence prob. *pennian* (found only in *onpennad*, unpenned)], *n.* A small enclosure for cattle, sheep, poultry, etc.; (*W. Indies*) a country-house, a farm, etc.; (*Am. slang*) prison. *v.t.* (*past & p.p.* **penned**) To enclose, to confine; to shut or coop (up or in); to confine (water) with a dam, etc.

pen (2) (pen) [M.E. and O.F. *penne*, L. *penna*, a feather], *n.* A quill; an instrument for writing with ink; writing, style of writing; a writer; a penman; *a feather, a wing; a female swan. *v.t.* (*past & p.p.* **penned**) To write, to compose and write. **pen and ink:** Instruments for writing; writing. **pen-and-ink,** *a.* Written or drawn with these. **pen-case,** *n.* **pencraft,** *n.* Penmanship, authorship. **pen-feather,** *n.* A quill feather; a pin-feather. **pen-feathered,** *a.* Half-fledged. **penholder,** *n.* A rod of wood or other material forming a handle for a pen. **pen-fish,** *n.* A squid or calamary. **pen-friend,** *n.* A person unknown except by correspondence. **penknife,** *n.* A small knife (orig. for cutting quill pens), usu. carried in the pocket. **penman,** *n.* **penmanship,** *n.* The art of writing; style of writing. **pen-name,** *n.* A *nom-de-guerre*, a literary pseudonym. **pen-point,** *n.* (*Am.*) A nib. **penwiper,** *n.* **penwoman,** *n.* **penful,** *n.*

penal (pē' nȧl) [F. *pénal*, L. *pēnālis*, from *pœna*, penalty, Gr. *poinē*, fine], *a.* Enacting, inflicting, or pertaining to punishment; of the nature of punishment; punishable, esp. by law. **penal servitude:** Imprisonment with hard labour. **penalize,** *v.t.* To make or declare penal; (*Sport*) to subject to a penalty or handicap; (*fig.*) to put under an unfair disadvantage. **penally,** *adv.*

penalty (pen' ȧl ti) [F. *pénalité*, med. L. *pœnālitas*, as prec.], *n.* Legal punishment for a crime, offence, or misdemeanour; a sum of money to be forfeited for non-performance or breach of conditions; a fine, a forfeit; (*Sport*) a handicap imposed for a breach of rules or on the winner in a previous contest. **penalty kick,** *n.* (*Football*) Kick allowed to the opposite side when a penalty has been incurred. A goal thus scored is a **penalty goal.**

penance (pen' ȧns) [O.F. *penance*, *peneance*, L. *pœnitentia*, PENITENCE], *n.* Sorrow for sin evinced by acts of self-mortification, etc.; (*R.-C. and Gr. Ch.*) a sacrament consisting of contrition, confession, and satisfaction, with absolution by the priest; an act of self-mortification undertaken as a satisfaction for sin, esp. one imposed by a priest before giving absolution. *v.t.* To inflict penance on.

penannular (pē năn' ū lȧr) [L. *pæne*, nearly], *a.* Nearly annular, almost a complete ring.

Penates (pė nā' tēz) [L., rel. to *penes*, within], *n.pl.* (*Rom. Myth.*) The Roman household gods, orig. of the store-room and kitchen.

pence, *n.pl.* [PENNY].

penchant (pen' chȧnt, pa*n* sha*n*') [F., orig. pres.p. of *pencher*, to lean, ult. from L. *pendēre*, to hang], *n.* A strong inclination or liking; a bias.

pencil (pen' sil) [O.F. *pincel* (F. *pinceau*), L. *pēnicillum*, *-lus*, dim. of *pēniculus*, brush, dim. of PENIS], *n.* A cylinder or slip of graphite, crayon, etc., usu. enclosed in a casing of wood; a small brush used by painters and by Chinese writers; (*fig.*) skill or style in painting, the art of painting; (*Opt.*) a system of rays diverging from or converging to a point; (*Math.*) the figure formed by a series of straight lines meeting at a point; applied to various appliances in the form of a small stick. *v.t.* (*past & p.p.* **pencilled**) To paint, draw, write, or mark with or as with a pencil; to jot (down); to mark or shade in delicate lines; (*Racing*) to enter (a horse's name) in a betting-book. **pencil-case,** *n.* A case for holding pencils; a holder or hollow handle for a pencil. **pencilled,** *a.* Painted, drawn, or marked with or as with a pencil; radiating; (*Bot.*) marked with fine lines. **pencilling,** *n.*

pencraft [PEN (2)].

pendant (pen' dȧnt) [F., orig. pres.p. of *pendre*, L. *pendēre*, to hang], *n.* Anything hanging down or suspended by way of ornament, etc., as an ear-ring, a locket, a tassel, etc.; a pendant chandelier, gaselier, or electrolier; a boss hanging from a ceiling or roof; the shank and ring of a watch-case; (*Naut.*) a short rope hanging from a mast-head, etc., a tapering flag or pennant; (*sometimes pron.* pan' dan) a companionpiece, a counterpart, a match.

pendent (pen' dent) [as PENDANT], *a.* Hanging; overhanging; (*fig.*) pending, undetermined; (*Gram.*) incomplete in construction, having the sense suspended. **pendency,** *n.* **pendentive,** *n.* (*Arch.*) One of the triangular pieces of vaulting resting on piers or arches and forming segments of a dome. **pendently,** *adv.* **pending** (pen' ding), *a.* Depending, awaiting settlement, undecided. *prep.* During; until.

pendulous (pen' dū lŭs) [L. *pendulus*, hanging, from *pendēre*, to hang], *a.* Hanging, suspended; swinging, oscillating. **pendulate,** *v.i.* To swing as a pendulum; (*fig.*) to waver, to hesitate. **penduline,** *a.* Hanging (as a nest); building a hanging nest (of birds). **pendulously,** *adv.* **pendulousness,** *n.*

pendulum (pen' dū lŭm) [L., neut. of *pendulus*, prec.], *n.* (*pl.* **-ums**) A body suspended from a fixed point and oscillating freely by the force of gravity, as the weighted rod regulating the movement of the works in a clock. **the swing of the pendulum:** The alternation of the weight of political opinion or of the power of a party.

Penelope (pė nel' ō pē) [Gr. *Pēnelopē*, wife of Ulysses], *n.* A chaste wife. **penelopize,** *v.t.* To undo a piece of work, as Penelope, who undid at night the work she had done by day as a check to the importunity of her suitors.

penetralia (pen ė trā' li ȧ) [L., pl. of *penetrāle*, as foll.], *n.pl.* The inner part of a house, palace, temple, or shrine; (*fig.*) secrets, mysteries.

penetrate (pen' ė trāt) [L. *penetrātus*, p.p. of *penetrāre*, rel. to *penitus*, within], *v.t.* To enter, to pass into or through; to pierce; to permeate; to saturate or imbue (with); to move or affect the feelings of; (*fig.*) to reach or discern by the senses or intellect. *v.i.* To make way, to pass (into, through, to, etc.). ***penetrance, *-trancy, penetrativeness,** *n.* **penetrant, penetrative,** *a.* **penetratively,** *adv.* **penetrability** (-bil' i ti), *n.* **penetrable** (pen' ė trȧbl), *a.* Capable of being penetrated; (*fig.*) impressible, susceptible. **penetrating,** *a.* Sharp, piercing; subtle, discerning. **penetratingly,** *adv.* **penetration** (-trā′ shŭn), *n.*

penfold [PINFOLD]. **penful,** etc. [PEN (2)].

penguin (pen′ gwin) [etym. doubtful], *n.* A bird of the family *Sphæniscidæ,* belonging to the southern hemisphere, consisting of swimming-birds with rudimentary wings or paddles and scale-like feathers, a great auk. **penguinery,** *n.*

penholder [PEN (2)]. **penial** (pē′ ni ȧl) [PENIS].

penicil (pen′ i sil) [L. *pēnicillus,* PENCIL], *n.* (*Nat. Hist.*) A small tuft of hairs, like a hair-pencil; (*Surg.*) a tent or pledget. **penicillate,** *a.* (*Nat. Hist.*) Furnished with, forming, or consisting of a bundle of short close hairs or fibres; having delicate markings, pencilled. **penicillately,** *adv.* **penicillation** (-lā′ shŭn), *n.* **penicilliform** (-sil′ i fôrm), *a.*

penicillin (pen i sil′ in), *n.* (*Chem.*) An ether-soluble substance produced from the mould *Penicillium* and having an intense growth-inhibiting action against various bacteria, especially in wounds, etc.

peninsula (pė nin′ sū lȧ) [L. *pæninsula* (*pæne,* almost, *insula,* island)], *n.* A piece of land almost surrounded by water, usu. connected with the mainland by an isthmus. **the Peninsula:** Spain and Portugal. **peninsular,** *a.* Of, pertaining to, or resembling a peninsula. *n.* An inhabitant of a peninsula; a soldier in the Peninsular War. **Peninsular War:** The war in Spain and Portugal (1808–14) between the British (in support of the native insurrection) and the French. **peninsularity** (-lăr′ i ti), *n.* **peninsulate,** *v.t.* To form or convert into a peninsula.

penis (pē′ nis) [L., tail], *n.* The copulatory and urethral organ of a male mammal. **penial,** *a.*

penitent (pen′ i tėnt) [O.F., from L. *pænitentem,* nom. *-tens,* pres.p. of *pænitēre,* rel. to *punīre,* to PUNISH], *a.* Contrite, repentant, sorry; *doing penance. *n.* One who is penitent; a contrite sinner; one submitting to penance under the direction of a confessor; one belonging to any of various R.-C. orders devoted to the practice of penance and mutual discipline. **penitence,** *n.* **penitential** (-ten′ shȧl), *a.* Pertaining to or expressing penitence; relating to or of the nature of penance. *n.* A book containing rules relating to penitence. **penitentially, penitently** (pen′ i tėnt li), *adv.* **penitentiary** (pen i ten′ shȧ ri), *a.* Penitential; pertaining to the reformatory treatment of criminals, etc. *n.* A reformatory prison, a house of correction, (*Am.*) a prison; an asylum for prostitutes seeking reformation; (*R.-C. Ch.*) a papal court granting dispensations and dealing with matters relating to confessions. **Grand Penitentiary:** The president of this court.

penknife, penman, etc. [PEN (2)].

pennant (pen′ ȧnt) [conf. of PENNON and PENDANT], *n.* A pennon; (*Naut.*) a long narrow streamer borne at the mast-head of a ship of war, a pendant.

pennate, -nated [PINNATE].

***penner** (pen′ ėr) [med. L. *pennārium,* from *penna,* PEN (2)], *n.* A pen-case, formerly carried at the girdle.

penniform (pen′ i fôrm) [L. *penna,* feather, -FORM], *a.* (*Nat. Hist.*) Having the form of a feather. **penniferous** (-nif′ ėr ŭs), **pennigerous** (-nij′ ėr ŭs), *a.*

penniless (pen′ i lės), *a.* Without money; destitute. **pennilessness,** *n.*

pennill (pen′ il) [W., from *pen,* head], *n.* (*pl.* **pennillion,** pė nil′ yŏn) A short stanza of improvised verse sung to the harp at Eisteddfods, etc.

pennon (pen′ ŏn) [M.E. and O.F. *penon,* prob. from L. *penna,* feather, see PEN (2)], *n.* A small pointed or swallow-tailed flag, formerly borne on the spears of knights and later as the ensign of a regiment of lancers; a long streamer carried by a ship. **pennoned,** *a.*

penny (pen′ i) [A.-S. *pening* (cp. Dut., Dan. and Swed. *penning,* G. *pfennig*)], *n.* (*pl.* **pennies,** denoting the number of coins; **pence,** denoting the amount) A bronze coin, the 12th part of a shilling; (*Am.*) a one-cent piece; (*Bibl.*) a denarius; *(*fig.*) money, a small sum of money. **a pretty penny:** A good round sum; considerable cost or expense. **Peter's pence** [PETER (1)]. **to turn an honest penny:** To earn money by honest work. **penny-a-line,** *a.* (*fig.*) Cheap, shoddy, superficial. **penny-a-liner,** *n.* One who writes for newspapers at the rate of 1d. per line; a hack writer. **penny-in-the-slot,** *a.* Applied to automatic machines for giving out small articles, tickets, etc., in return for a coin inserted in a slot. **penny dreadful,** *n.* Cheap crime-story, shocker. **penny post:** (*Hist.*) A post for conveying letters at the ordinary rate of 1d. **penny-wedding,** *n.* (*Sc.*) A wedding where the guests contribute towards the expenses. **penny-wise,** *a.* Saving small sums at the risk of larger ones. **pennyworth** (pen′ i wĕrth, pen′ ŏrth), *n.* As much as can be bought for a penny; anything bought or sold; (*fig.*) a good (or bad) bargain; a small amount, a trifle.

pennyroyal (pen i roi′ ȧl) [prob. a corr. of *puliol ryale* (O.F. *puliol, poliol,* prob. from a dim. of *pūlēgium,* thyme, ROYAL)], *n.* A kind of mint, *Mentha pulegium,* formerly and still popularly used for medicinal purposes.

pennyweight (pen′ i wāt), *n.* Twenty-four grains or one-twentieth of an ounce troy.

pennywort (pen′ i wĕrt), *n.* (*Bot.*) One of several plants with round peltate leaves.

penology (pė nol′ ȯ ji) [Gr. *poinē,* fine, PENALTY, -LOGY], *n.* The science of punishment and prison management. **penological** (-loj′ i kȧl), *a.* **penologist** (-nol′ ȯ jist), *n.*

pensile (pen′ sil, -sīl) [L. *pensilis,* from *pensus,* p.p. of *pendēre,* to hang], *a.* Hanging, suspended, pendulous; constructing a pendent nest (of birds). ***pensileness,** *n.*

pension (1) (pen′ shŭn) [F., from L. *pensiōnem,* nom. *-sio,* payment, from *pendere,* to pay], *n.* A periodical allowance for past services paid by the Government or employers; a similar allowance to a person for good will, to secure services when required, etc., or to literary men, scientists, etc., to enable them to carry on their work; money paid to a clergyman in lieu of tithes; a consultative assembly of the members of Gray's Inn. *v.t.* To grant a pension to; to pay a pension to for the retention of services. **old-age pension:** A weekly allowance paid by the Government to persons who have attained a certain age. **pensionable,** *a.* **pensionary,** *a.* and *n.*

pension (2) (pon′ si on) [Fr.], *n.* A boarding-house; a boarding-school. **en pension** (an pon syon′): As a boarder.

pensioner (pen′ shŭn ėr), *n.* One in receipt of a pension; a dependant; a hireling; a Cambridge undergraduate who is not a scholar on the foundation or a sizar. **Grand Pensioner:** The President of the States-General of Holland and Zealand (1618–1794).

pensive (pen′ siv) [F. *pensif, -sive,* from *penser,* to think, L. *pensāre,* freq. of *pendere,* to weigh], *a.* Thoughtful; serious, anxious, melancholy; expressing sad thoughtfulness. **v.t.* To make pensive. **pensively,** *adv.* **pensiveness,** *n.*

penstemon [PENTSTEMON].

penstock (pen′ stok) [PEN (1), STOCK], *n.* A conduit, usu. in the form of a wooden trough, conveying water to a water-wheel; a flood-gate.

pent (pent) [for *penned,* p.p. of PEN (1)], *a.* Penned in or confined; shut (up or in).

pent-, penta- [Gr. *pente,* five], *comb. form.* **pentacapsular** (pen tȧ kăp′ sū lȧr) [CAPSULAR], *a.* (*Bot.*) Having five seed-vessels. **pentachord** (pen′ tȧ kôrd) [Gr. *chordē,* CHORD], *n.* A scale of five notes; a musical instrument with five strings.

pentacle (pen′ tȧ kėl) [med. L. *pentaculum* (prob. PENTA-, -CULE)], *n.* A figure like a star with five points formed by producing the sides of a pentagon in both directions to their points of intersection; a pentagram, used as a symbol by the mystics and astrologers of the Middle Ages.

pentacoccous (pen tȧ kok′ ŭs) [PENTA-, Gr. *kokkos*, grain], *a.* (*Bot.*) Having five seeds, or five cells with a seed in each. **pentacrostic** (-kros′ tik) [ACROSTIC], *a.* Containing five acrostics on the same name.

pentad (pen′ tȧd) [Gr. *pentas -ados*, from *pente*, five], *n.* The number five; a group of five; (*Chem.*) an element or radical having a valency of five.

pentadactyl (pen tȧ dăk′ til) [PENTA-, Gr. *daktulos*, toe], *a.* (*Anat.*) Having five fingers or toes. *n.* A person or animal having five digits on each limb. **pentadactylic** (-til′ ik), *a.* **pentadactylism** (-dăk′ til izm), *n.* **pentadelphous** (-del′ fŭs) [Gr. *adelphos*, brother], *a.* (*Bot.*) Having the stamens united in five sets. **pentaglot** (pen′ tȧ glot) [Gr. *glōtta*, tongue], *a.* In five languages. *n.* A work in five languages.

pentagon (pen′ tȧ gŏn) [L. *pentagōnus*, Gr. *pentagōnos* (PENTA-, *gōnia*, angle)], *n.* A plane (usu. rectilineal) figure having five sides and five angles. **pentagonal** (-tăg′ ŏ nȧl), *a.* **The Pentagon,** *n.* The War Office of the U.S.A. in Washington, D.C.

pentagram (pen′ tȧ grăm) [Gr. *pentegrammon*], *n.* A pentacle. **pentagraph** [PANTOGRAPH]. ***pentagynia*** (pen tȧ jin′ i ȧ) [Gr. *gunē*, woman, female], *n.pl.* (*Bot.*) A Linnæan order containing plants with five pistils. **pentagynian** (-jin′ i ȧn), **pentagynous** (-tăj′ i nŭs), *a.* **pentahedron** (pen tȧ hē′ drŏn) [Gr. *hedra*, base], *n.* A figure having five sides, esp. equal sides. **pentahedral,** *a.* **pentahexahedral** (hek sȧ hē′ drȧl) [HEXAHEDRAL], *a.* Having five ranges of faces, one above another, each with six faces. **pentahexahedron,** *n.* **pentalpha** (-tăl′ fȧ) [Gr. ALPHA, the letter *a*], *n.* A pentagram or pentacle. **pentamerous** (pen tăm′ ėr ŭs) [Gr. *meros*, part], *a.* (*Bot.*) Composed of five parts (of a flower-whorl); (*Zool.*) five-jointed. **pentameter** (pen tăm′ ė tėr) [L., from Gr. *pentametros* (*metron*, METRE)], *n.* A verse of five feet; (*Gr. and L. Pros.*) a dactylic verse consisting of two halves each containing two feet (dactyls or spondees in the first half, dactyls in the second, and one long syllable), used principally with alternate hexameters in elegiacs; (*Eng. Pros.*) the iambic verse of ten syllables. ***pentandria*** (pen tăn dri ȧ) [Gr. *anēr andros*, man, male], *n.pl.* (*Bot.*) A Linnæan class containing plants with five stamens. **pentandrian, pentandrous,** *a.*

pentane (pen′ tān), *n.* (*Chem.*) A volatile fluid paraffin hydrocarbon contained in petroleum, etc.

pentapetalous (pen tȧ pet′ ȧ lŭs) [PENTA-, PETALOUS], *a.* (*Bot.*) Having five petals. **pentaphyllous** (pen tăf′ i lŭs) [Gr. *phullon*, leaf], *a.* (*Bot.*) Having five leaves. **pentapody** (pen tăp′ ŏ di) [Gr. *pentapous* (*pous podos*, foot)], *n.* (*Pros.*) A verse or sequence of five natural feet.

pentapolis (pen tăp′ ŏ lis) [Gr. PENTA-, *polis*, city], *n.* A group or confederacy of five towns. **pentapolitan** (-pol i tȧn), *a.* Of or pertaining to a pentapolis, esp. that of Cyrenaica. **pentarchy** (pen′ tar ki) [Gr. *archia*, from *archein*, to rule], *n.* Government by five rulers; a group of five kingdoms. **pentasepalous** (pen tȧ sep′ ȧ lŭs) [SEPAL, -OUS], *a.* (*Bot.*) Having five sepals. **pentaspermous** (-spĕr mŭs) [Gr. *sperma*, seed], *a.* (*Bot.*) Having five seeds. **pentastich** (pen′ tȧ stik) [Gr. *pentastichos* (*stichos*, row)], *n.* A stanza or group of five lines of verse. **pentastichous** (-tăs′ ti kŭs), *a.* **pentastyle** (pen′ tȧ stīl) [Gr. *stulos*, pillar], *a.* (*Arch.*) Having five columns at the front or end. *n.* A pentastyle building or portico.

Pentateuch (pen′ tȧ tūk) [L. *Pentateuchus*, Gr. *Pentateuchos* (PENTA-, *teuchos*, tool, book)], *n.* The first five books of the Old Testament, usu. ascribed to Moses.

pentathlon (pen tăth′ lŏn) [Gr. (PENT- *athlon*, contest)], *n.* (*Gr. Ant.*) An athletic contest comprising leaping, running, wrestling, throwing the discus, and hurling the spear. **pentathlete,** *n.*

pentatomic (pen tȧ tom′ ik), *a.* (*Chem.*) Containing five atoms in the molecule, esp. five replaceable atoms of hydrogen. **pentatonic** (-ton′ ik), *a.* (*Mus.*) Consisting of five tones. **pentavalent** (pen tăv′ ȧ lėnt), *a.* (*Chem.*) Having a valency of five.

Pentecost (pen′ tė kost) [L. *pentēcostē*, Gr. *pentēkostē*, fiftieth (day), from *pentēkonta*, fifty], *n.* A solemn Jewish festival at the close of harvest, held on the fiftieth day from the second day of the Passover; *Whit-sunday. **pentecostal** (-kos′ tȧl), *a.*

penthemimer (pen thė mim′ ėr) [Gr. *penthēmimerēs* (PENT-, *hēmimerēs*, halved)], *n.* (*Gr. Pros.*) A group of two and a half metrical feet, as a half of a pentameter. **penthemimeral,** *a.*

penthouse (pent′ hous), ***pentice** (pen′ tis) [M.E. *pentice, pentis*, prob. from O.F. *apentis*, late L. *appendicium*, from *appendere*, to APPEND], *n.* A roof or shed standing aslope against a main wall or building; a shed-like structure against a wall, a canopy, a protection over a window or door, etc.; (*Am.*) a subsidiary roof construction, a small dwelling-house built on the roof of a larger block of flats, offices, etc. *v.t.* To furnish with or as with a penthouse. *a.* Overhanging.

pentode (pen′ tōd) [PENT-], *n.* (*Elec.*) A five-electrode thermionic valve.

pent-roof (pent′ roof) [PENTHOUSE], *n.* A lean-to roof.

pentstemon (pent stē′ mŏn) [PENT-, *stēmōn*, erron. for STAMEN], *n.* A genus of scrophulariaceous plants with showy tubular flowers.

penult, *penultima (pė nŭlt′, -i mȧ) [L. *pænultima*, fem. adj. (*pæne*, almost, *ultimus*, last)], *n.* The last syllable but one of a word. **penultimate,** *a.* and *n.* The last but one.

penumbra (pė nŭm′ brȧ) [L. *pæne*, almost, *umbra*, shadow], *n.* (*pl.* **-bras**) The partly-shaded zone around the total shadow caused by an opaque body intercepting the light from a luminous body, esp. round that of the earth or moon in an eclipse; the lighter fringe of a sun-spot; the blending or boundary of light and shade in a painting, etc.

penury (pen′ ū ri) [F. *pénurie*, L. *pēnūria*, cogn. with Gr. *peina*, hunger, *penia*, poverty], *n.* Extreme poverty, destitution; lack or scarcity (of). **penurious** (pė nūr′ i ŭs), *a.* Niggardly, stingy; poor, scanty. **penuriously,** *adv.* **penuriousness,** *n.*

peon (pē′ ŏn) [Sp., from L. *pedōnem*, nom. *pedo*, foot-soldier, see PAWN (I)], *n.* (*India*) A foot-soldier; a native constable, an attendant; (*Mexico*) a labourer, formerly a bondman serving his creditor in order to work off a debt; (*Sp. Am.*) a day-labourer, etc. **peonage,** *n.*

peony (pē′ ŏ ni) [A.-S. *peonie*, L. *pæōnia*, Gr. *paiōnia* from *Paiōn*, god of healing], *n.* A plant of the genus *Pæonia*, with large globular terminal flowers, usu. double in cultivation.

people (pē′ pŭl) [A.-F. *people, poeple*, O.F. *pople* (F. *peuple*), L. *populum*, nom. *populus*], *n.* The persons composing a nation, community, or race (*collect. sing. with pl.* **peoples**); any body of persons, as those belonging to a place, a class, a congregation or company of any sort, etc.; persons generally or indefinitely; one's family, kindred, or tribe; followers, retinue, servants, workpeople, etc. *v.t.* To stock with inhabitants, to populate; to occupy, to inhabit. **the people:** The commonalty, the populace, as dist. from the self-styled higher orders.

pep (pep) [PEPPER], *n.* (*colloq.*) Vigour, spirit, energy.

peperino (pep ėr ē′ nō) [It., from *pepere*, PEPPER], *n.* (Geol.) A porous volcanic tuff, composed of sand, cinders, etc., cemented together.

peplum, peplus (pep′ lŭm, -lŭs) [L. *peplum*, Gr. *peplos*], *n.* (*pl.* **-lums, -la**) An outer robe or gown worn by women in ancient Greece; an over-skirt supposed to resemble the ancient peplum.

pepper (pep′ ėr) [A.-S. *pipor*, L. *piper*, Gr. *peperi*, of Oriental orig. (cp. Sansk. *pippalī*)], *n.* A pungent aromatic condiment made from the dried berries of *Piper nigrum* or other species of *Piper* used whole or ground into powder; the pepper-plant, *P. nigrum*, or other species; applied also to plants of the genus *Capsicum*; (*fig.*) rough treatment, pungent criticism or sarcasm, etc. *v.t.* To sprinkle or season with pepper; to besprinkle; (*fig.*) to season with pungent remarks; to pelt with missiles; to beat severely. **black pepper:** *Piper nigrum*, the common pepper. **Cayenne pepper** [CAYENNE]. **white pepper:** Pepper made by removing the skin by rubbing, etc., before grinding. **pepper-and-salt,** *n.* A cloth of grey and black or black and white closely intermingled and having a speckled appearance. **pepper-box,** *n.* A small round box with a perforated top for sprinkling pepper on food. **pepper-cake,** *n.* A kind of gingerbread or spiced cake. **pepper-caster, -castor** [PEPPER-BOX]. **pepper-corn,** *n.* The dried fruit of the pepper-tree; (*fig.*) anything of little value. **pepper-corn rent:** A nominal rent. **pepper-gingerbread,** *n.* Hot-spiced gingerbread. **pepper-grass,** *n.* The pillwort, *Pilularia globulifera*; a garden herb, *Lepidum sativum*, with a pungent taste. **pepper-pot,** *n.* A pepper-box; a W. Indian dish of meat or fish with okra, chillies, etc., flavoured with cassareep. **pepper tree,** *n.* (*Austral.*) A shrub with leaves and bark having a biting taste like pepper. ***pepperwater,** *n.* A liquor prepared from powdered black pepper, used in microscopical observations. **pepper-wort,** *n.* The dittany, *Lepidium latifolium.* **peppery,** *a.* Having the qualities of pepper; pungent; (*fig.*) choleric, hot-tempered; irascible, hasty.

peppermint (pep′ ėr mint), *n.* A pungent aromatic herb, *Mentha piperita*; an essential oil distilled from this plant; a lozenge flavoured with this. **peppermint tree,** *n.* (*Austral.*) A Eucalyptus with fragrant leaves.

pepsin (pep′ sin) [F. *pepsine* (Gr. *pepsis*, digestion, cogn. with *peptein*, to cook, -IN)], *n.* A ferment contained in gastric juice, the chief agent in digestion.

peptic (pep′ tik), *n.* Promoting digestion; pertaining to digestion; having good digestive powers. *n.* A medicine that promotes digestion; (*pl.*, *facet.*) the digestive organs. **pepticity** (-tis′ i ti), *n.*

peptogen (pep′ to jen), *n.* (*Chem.*) A substance promoting the formation of pepsin. **peptogenic,** *a.*

peptone (pep′ ton), *n.* Any of the soluble protein compounds into which the albuminous substances in food are converted by the action of pepsin. **peptonize,** *v.t.* **peptonization** (-zā′ shŭn), *n.* **peptonoid,** *n.*

per (pĕr) [L.], *prep.* By; through, by means of. **per annum:** Yearly; by the year. **per capita:** By the head, for each person. **per cent, per centum** [CENT]: By the hundred.

per- [prec.], *pref.* Through, completely; very, exceedingly, to the extreme; (*Chem.*) denoting the highest degree of combination or of valence in similar compounds. **per-acute** (pĕr ȧ kūt′) [ACUTE], *a.* (*Path.*) Very acute or violent.

peradventure (pĕr ăd ven′ chŭr) [M.E. *peraventure*, O.F. *par aventure*], *adv.* Perhaps, perchance. *n.* Uncertainty; doubt, conjecture.

perambulate (pėr ăm′ bū lāt) [L. *perambulātus*, p.p. of *perambulāre* (PER-, *ambulāre*, to walk)], *v.t.* To walk over or through, esp. for the purpose of surveying or inspecting; to walk along the boundaries of (a parish, etc.) in order to survey or preserve them. **perambulation** (-lā′ shŭn), *n.* **perambulatory** (pėr ăm′ bū lā tȯr i), *a.*

perambulator, pram (pė răm′ bū lā tȯr, prăm), *n.* A child's carriage propelled from behind, (*Am.* a baby carriage); an instrument for measuring distances travelled, an hodometer, a pedometer.

percale (pėr kāl′, -kal′) [F., etym. doubtful], *n.* A closely woven cotton cambric. **percaline** (pĕr kȧ lēn′, pĕr′ kȧ lēn), *n.* A glossy cotton cloth.

***perceant** (pĕr′ sȧnt) [F. *perçant*, pres.p. of *percer*, to PIERCE], *a.* Piercing, sharp, penetrating.

perceive (pėr sēv′) [O.F. *perceiv-*, stem of *perceivre*, *perçoivre* (F. *percevoir*), L. *percipere* (PER-, *capere*, to take)], *v.t.* To apprehend with the mind; to discern, to understand; to have cognizance of by the senses. **perceivable,** *a.* **perceiver,** *n.*

percentage (pėr sen′ tȧj), *n.* Rate or proportion for each hundred; allowance, commission, duty.

percept (pĕr′ sept) [L. *perceptum*, neut. p.p. of *percipere*, to PERCEIVE], *n.* (*Phil.*) That which is perceived, the mental product of perception. **perceptible** (pėr sep′ tibl), *a.* That may be perceived by the senses or intellect. **perceptibility** (-bil′ i ti), *n.* **perceptibly,** *adv.* **perceptive,** *a.* Having the faculty of perceiving. **perceptively,** *adv.* **perceptiveness, perceptivity** (-tiv′ i ti), *n.*

perception (per sep′ shŭn), *n.* The act, process, or faculty of perceiving; the mental action of knowing external things through the medium of sense presentations; intuitive apprehension, insight, or discernment; (*Law*) collection or receipt of rents.

perch (1) (pĕrch) [F. *perche*, L. *perca*, Gr. *perkē*], *n.* A striped spiny-finned freshwater fish, *Perca fluviatilis*, also *P. flavescens*, the yellow perch of the U.S.A. **percoid,** *a.* and *n.*

perch (2) (pĕrch) [M.E. and O.F. *perche*, L. *pertica*, pole], *n.* A pole or bar used as a rest or roost for birds; anything serving this purpose; (*fig.*) an elevated seat or position; the centre-pole connecting the front and back gear of a spring-carriage; a land measure of 5½ yards. *v.i.* To alight or rest as a bird; to alight or settle on or as on a perch. *v.t.* To set or place on or as on a perch. **percher,** *n.* One who or that which perches; one of the *Insessores* or perching-birds.

***perchance** (pėr chans′) [M.E. and O.F. *par chance* (*par*, by, CHANCE)], *adv.* Perhaps, by chance.

percheron (pĕr′ shė ron) [F.], *n.* One of a breed of swift and powerful horses from the district of le Perche.

perchlorate (pĕr klôr′ ȧt), *n.* (*Chem.*) A salt of perchloric acid. **perchloric,** *a.* Pertaining to or containing chlorine and oxygen. **perchloride,** *n.*

percipient (pėr sip′ i ėnt) [L. *percipiens -ntem*, pres.p. of *percipere*, to PERCEIVE], *a.* Perceiving, apprehending, conscious. *n.* One who or that which perceives, esp. one receiving a supposed telepathic message. **percipience, *-ency,** *n.*

percoct (pėr kokt′) [L. *percoctus*, p.p. of *percoquere* (PER-, *coquere*, to COOK)], *a.* (*fig.*) Overdone, hackneyed.

percoid [PERCH (1)].

percolate (pĕr′ kȯ lāt) [L. *percōlātus*, p.p. of *percōlāre* (PER-, *cōlum*, strainer)], *v.i.* To pass through small interstices, to filter (through). *v.t.* To ooze through, to permeate; *to strain, to filter. **percolation** (-lā′ shŭn), *n.* **percolator** (pĕr′ kȯ lā tȯr), *n.* One who or that which strains or filters; a filter; a coffee-pot in which the boiling water filters through the coffee.

***percurrent** (pėr kŭr′ ėnt) [L. *percurrens -ntem*, pres.p. of *percurrere* (PER-, *currere*, to run)], *a.* (*Bot.*) Going through the entire length (as the midrib of a leaf). ***percursory** (-kĕr′ sȯ ri), *a.* Cursory, slight; running swiftly.

percuss (pėr kŭs′) [L. *percussus*, p.p. of *percutere* (PER-, *quatere*, to shake)], *v.t.* To strike quickly or tap forcibly, esp. to test or diagnose by percussion. **percussant,** *a.* (*Her.*) Beating or lashing (of the tail of a lion, etc.).

percussion (pėr kŭsh′ ȯn) [L. *percussio*, as prec.], *n.* Forcible striking or collision; the shock of such collision; the effect of the sound of a collision on the ear; (*Med.*) physical examination by gently striking some part of the body with the fingers or an instrument; (*Mus.*) the production of sound by striking on an instrument. **percussion-cap,** *n.* A small copper cap containing fulminating powder, used in a percussion-lock. **percussion-lock,** *n.* A gunlock in which the hammer strikes a cap to explode the charge in a fire-arm. **percussive, *percutient** (pėr kū′ shi ėnt), *a.*

percutaneous (pĕr kū tā′ nė ůs), *a.* (*Med.*) Acting or done through the skin.

***perdie** [PARDIE]. ***peregal** [PAREGAL].

perdition (pėr dish′ ůn) [M.E. and O.F. *perdiciun*, L. *perditiōnem*, nom. *-tio*, from *perdere*, to destroy (PER-, *dare*, to give)], *n.* Utter destruction, entire ruin; the loss of the soul or of happiness in a future state, damnation.

perdu (pėr dū′, pĕr′ dū) [F., p.p. of *perdre*, to lose, as prec.], *a.* (*fem.* ***perdue***) Hidden, concealed; (*Mil.*) forlorn, exposed, desperate, in ambush. *n.* One in ambush; one of a forlorn hope; one employed in a desperate enterprise or in a hopeless case. **to lie perdue:** To lie in ambush; to be hidden or out of sight; to be in a hazardous situation.

perdurable (pėr dūr′ ȧbl) [O.F., from late L. *perdūrābilis*], *a.* Very lasting or durable; permanent, everlasting. **perdurability** (-bil′ i ti), *n.* **perdurably** (-dūr′ ȧ bli), *adv.* ***perdurance, *perduration** (pėr dū rā′ shůn), *n.*

peregrination (per ė gri nā′ shůn) [F. *pérégrination*, L. *peregrīnātiōnem*, nom. *-tio*, from *peregrīnārī*, from *peregrīnus*, foreign, as foll.], *n.* A travelling about; a sojourning in foreign countries. ***peregrinate** (per′ ė gri nāt), *v.i.* **peregrinator,** *n.*

peregrine (per′ ė grin) [L. *peregrīnus*, from *peregre*, abroad (PER, *ager*, field)], *a.* *Foreign, outlandish; migratory, travelling abroad. *n.* A peregrine falcon. **peregrine falcon:** A widely-distributed species of falcon, *Falco peregrinus*, used for hawking.

pereion (pė rī′ ǒn) [Gr. *peraiōn*, pres.p. of *peraioun*, to transport (in mistake for *periienai*, to walk about)], *n.* (*Zool.*) The thorax in crustacea.

peremptory (per′ emp-, pėr emp′ tȯr i) [A.-F. *peremptorie*, L. *peremptōrius*, destructive, from *perimere* (PER-, *emere*, to take, to buy)], *a.* Precluding question or hesitation; absolute, positive, decisive, determined; imperious, dogmatic, dictatorial; (*Law*) final, determinate. **peremptorily,** *adv.* **peremptoriness,** *n.*

perennial (pė ren′ i ȧl) [L. *perennis* (PER-, *annus*, year)], *a.* Lasting throughout the year; unfailing, unceasing, lasting long, never ceasing; (of plants) living for more than two years. *n.* A perennial plant. **perenniality** (-ăl′ i ti), *n.* **perennially,** *adv.*

perennibranchiate (pėr en i brăng′ ki ȧt) [as prec., BRANCHIATE], *a.* (*Zool.*) Belonging to the *Perennibranchiata*, a division of amphibians retaining their gills through life. *n.* An animal of this division.

perfect (pĕr′ fėkt) [M.E. and O.F. *perfit*, L. *perfectus* (PER-, *factus*, p.p. of *facere*, to make)], *a.* Complete in all its parts, qualities, etc., without defect or fault; finished, thoroughly versed, trained, skilled, etc.; thoroughly learned (of a lesson); of the best, highest, and most complete kind; entire, complete, unqualified; (*Bot.*) having all the essential parts (of a flower); (*Gram.*) expressing action completed. *v.t.* (pĕr fekt′) To finish or complete, to bring to perfection; to render thoroughly versed or skilled (in). **future perfect** [FUTURE]. **perfecter,** *n.* **perfectible,** *a.* **perfectibilian, -bilist** (-bil′ i ȧn, -tib′ i list), *n.* One believing that it is possible for humanity to attain moral and social perfection, a perfectionist. **perfectibility** (-bil′ i ti), *n.* **perfection** (pėr fek′ shůn), *n.* The act of making or the state of being perfect; supreme excellence; complete development; faultlessness; (*fig.*) a perfect person or thing; the highest degree, the extreme (of); an excellent quality or acquirement. **to perfection:** Completely, perfectly. **Perfectionist,** *n.* One believing in the possibility of attaining moral or religious perfection; a member of a communistic community founded by J. H. Noyes in 1838 at Oneida Creek, in Madison County, N.Y. ***perfectionism,** *n.* ***perfectionment,** *n.* ***perfective** (pėr fek′ tiv), *a.* Tending to make perfect; (*Gram.*) expressing completed action. **perfectly** (pĕr′ fėkt li), *adv.* **perfectness,** *n.*

perfervid (pėr fĕr′ vid), *a.* Very fervid. **perfervidness, perfervor,** *n.*

***perficient** (pėr fish′ ėnt) [L. *perficiens -ntem*, pres.p. of *perficere* (PER-, *facere*, to make)], *a.* Effectual, efficient; actual. *n.* One who perfects.

perfidy (pĕr′ fi di) [F. *perfidie*, L. *perfidia*, from *perfidus*, treacherous (PER-, *fides*, faith)], *n.* Violation of faith, allegiance, or confidence. **perfidious** (-fid′ i ůs), *a.* Treacherous, faithless, deceitful, false. **perfidiously,** *adv.* **perfidiousness,** *n.*

perfoliate (pėr fō′ li ȧt) [PER-, *folium*, leaf, -ATE], *a.* (*Bot.*) Applied to leaves so surrounding the stem as to appear as if perforated by it.

perforate (pĕr′ fȯ rāt) [L. *perforātus*, p.p. of *perforāre* (PER-, *forāre*, to bore)], *v.t.* To bore through, to pierce; to make a hole or holes through by boring; to pass or reach through. *v.i.* To penetrate (into or through). *a.* (-rȧt) Perforated; (*Bot.*) pierced with small holes or having small transparent dots like holes. **perforation** (-rā′ shůn), *n.* **perforative** (pĕr′ fȯ rȧ tiv), *a.* **perforator,** *n.*

perforce (pėr fôrs′) [earlier *parforce*, O.F. *par force*, by FORCE], *adv.* Of necessity; compulsorily.

perform (pėr fôrm′) [M.E. *perfourmer*, prob. var. (assim. to FORM) of M.E. and O.F. *perfournir* (*par-*, PER-, *fournir*, to FURNISH)], *v.t.* To carry through, to execute, to accomplish; to discharge, to fulfil; to represent, as on the stage; to play, to render (music, etc.). *v.i.* To act a part; to play a musical instrument, etc. **performable,** *a.* **performance,** *n.* Execution, carrying out, completion; a thing done, an action; a feat, a notable deed; a literary work; the performing of a play, display of feats, etc.; an entertainment. **performer,** *n.* One who performs, esp. an actor, musician, gymnast, etc. **performing,** *a.*

perfume (pėr fūm′) [F. *parfumer* (*par-*, PER-, L. *fūmāre*, to smoke, from *fūmus*, smoke)], *v.t.* To fill or impregnate with a scent or sweet odour; to scent. *n.* (pĕr′ fūm) A substance emitting a sweet odour; fragrance, scent; fumes of something burning, cooking, etc. **perfumatory** (-fū′ mȧ tȯ ri), *a.* **perfumeless,** *a.* **perfumer** (pėr fū′ mėr), *n.* One who or that which perfumes; one who makes or sells perfumes. **perfumery,** *n.*

perfunctory (pėr fŭngk′ tȯ ri) [late L. *perfunctōrius*, from *perfunctus*, p.p. of *perfungī* (PER-, *fungī*, to perform)], *a.* Done merely for the sake of having done with, done in a half-hearted or careless manner; careless, negligent, superficial, mechanical. **perfunctorily,** *adv.* **perfunctoriness,** *n.*

perfuse (pėr fūz′) [L. *perfūsus*, p.p. of *perfundere* (PER-, *fundere*, to pour)], *v.t.* To besprinkle; to spread over, to suffuse (with), to pour (water, etc.) over or through. **perfusion** (-fū′ zhůn), *n.* **perfusive** (-fū′ ziv), *a.*

pergameneous (pĕr gȧ mē′ nė ůs) [from L. *Pergamēna*, PARCHMENT], *a.* Of the texture of parchment (of skin, etc.). **pergamentaceous** (-tā′ shůs), *a.*

pergola (pĕr′ gȯ lȧ) [It., from L. *pergula*, projecting roof, balcony, etc., from *pergere*, to proceed], *n.* A covered walk or arbour with climbing plants trained over posts, trellis-work, etc.

perhaps (pėr hăps′, prăps) [PER, HAP], *adv.* It may be, by chance, possibly, (*Am.* maybe).

peri (pĕr′ i) [Pers. *parī*], *n.* A being represented as a descendant of fallen angels, excluded from paradise until some penance is accomplished; a beautiful being, a fairy.

peri- [Gr., around, about], *pref.* **perianth** (per′ i ănth) [Gr. *anthos*, flower], *n.* (*Bot.*) A floral envelope. **periapt** (per′ i ăpt) [F. *périapte*, Gr. *periapton* (*haptein*, to fasten)], *n.* Something worn about the person as an amulet or charm. **periaxial** (per i ăk′ si ål) [AXIAL], *a.* Surrounding an axis. **periblast** (per′ i blăst) [PERI-, -BLAST], *n.* (*Biol.*) The protoplasm around a cell-nucleus. **periblastic** (-blăs′ tik), *a.*

pericardium (pe ri kar′ di ŭm) [Gr. *perikardion* (*kardia*, heart)], *n.* (*Anat.*) The membrane enveloping the heart. **pericardiac, -dial, -dic,** *a.* **pericarditis** (-dī′ tis) [-ITIS], *n.* (*Path.*) Inflammation of the pericardium.

pericarp (per′ i karp) [Gr. *perikarpion* (PERI-, *karpos*, fruit)], *n.* (*Bot.*) The seed-vessel or wall of the developed ovary of a plant. **pericarpial** (-kar′ pi ål), *a.* **pericentre** (per i sen′ tėr) [CENTRE], *n.* The point in the orbit of a body where it passes nearest to the centre. **pericentral, -tric,** *a.* **perichondrium** (per i kon′ dri ŭm) [Gr. *chondros*, cartilage], *n.* (*Anat.*) The membrane investing the cartilages except at joints.

periclase (per′ i klās) [Gr. PERI-, very, *klasis*, fracture], *n.* (*Min.*) A greenish mineral composed of magnesia and protoxide of iron, from Vesuvius.

periclinal (per i klī′ nål) [Gr. *periklin-ēs* (PERI-, *klinein*, to lean), -AL], *a.* (*Geol.*) Sloping from a common centre (of strata).

pericope (pė rik′ ŏ pē) [late L., from Gr. *perikopē* (PERI-, *kopein*, to cut)], *n.* An extract, a quotation, esp. a selection from the Gospels or Epistles read in public worship.

pericranium (per i krā′ ni ŭm) [CRANIUM], *n.* (*Anat.*) The membrane investing the skull; (*facet.*) the skull, the brain. **pericranial,** *a.* **pericranially,** *adv.*

pericystic (pe ri sis′ tik) [Gr. *kustis*, bladder], *a.* (*Anat.*) Around the bladder. **pericystitis** (pe ri sis tī′ tis), *n.* (*Path.*) Inflammation of the tissue around the bladder.

periderm (per′ i dĕrm) [PERI-, DERM], *n.* (*Zool.*) The hard integument of certain hydrozoa; (*Bot.*) the outer bark; the whole of the tissues comprising this and the cork-cambium. **peridesmium** (per i des′ mi ŭm) [Gr. *desmos*, band], *n.* (*Anat.*) The sheath of a ligament.

peridium (pė rid′ i ŭm) [Gr. *pēridion*, dim. of *pēra*, bag, wallet], *n.* (*pl.* **-dia**) (*Bot.*) The outer envelope of certain fungi enclosing the spores. **peridial,** *a.* **peridiole** (pė rid′ i ōl), **peridiolum** (per i dī′ ŏ lŭm), *n.* A secondary or inner peridium.

peridot (per′ i dot) [F. *péridot*, etym. doubtful], *n.* A yellowish-green chrysolite; olivine. **peridotic** (-dot′ ik), *a.* **peridotite** (per′ i dŏ tīt), *n.* A mineral composed chiefly of olivine.

peridrome (per′ i drōm) [Gr. *peridromos* (PERI-, *dromos*, course)], *n.* (*Arch.*) The open space between the columns and the wall in ancient temples, etc. **periegesis** (per i ė jē′ sis) [Gr. *periegēsis* (*agein*, to lead)], *n.* A travelling round, a perambulation; a description of this. **perienteron** (per i en′ tėr on) [Gr. *enteron*, intestine], *a.* (*Anat.*) The primitive perivisceral cavity. **perienteric** (-ter′ ik), *a.* **perifibrum** (-fī′ brŭm), *n.* (*Zool.*) The membranous envelope surrounding the fibres, etc., of sponges. **perifibral,** *a.* **periganglionic** (-găng gli on′ ik), *a.* (*Anat.*) Surrounding a ganglion. **perigastric** (-găs′ trik), *a.* Surrounding the alimentary canal.

perigee (per′ i jē) [F. *périgée*, late L. *perigēum*, *perigæum*, Gr. *perigeion* (PERI-, *gē*, earth)], *n.* (*Astron.*) The nearest point to the earth in the orbit of the moon or one of the planets. **perigeal, -an** (-jē′ ål, -ån), *a.*

perigenesis (per i jen′ ė sis) [PERI-, GENESIS], *n.* (*Biol.*) Reproduction through rhythmic vibrations of protoplasmic molecules. **periglottis** (per i glot′ is) [Gr. *glōtta*, tongue], *n.* (*Anat.*) The epithelium or skin of the tongue. **periglottic,** *a.* **perigone** (per′ i gōn) [F. *périgone* (Gr. *gonos*, offspring, seed)], *n.* (*Bot.*) The perianth; (*Zool.*) the walls of a spore-sac in a hydroid. **perigonial** (-gō′ ni ål), *a.* (*Bot.*) **perigynous** (pė rij′ i nŭs) [Gr. *gunē*, female], *a.* (*Bot.*) Growing upon some part surrounding the ovary (of stamens). **perigynium** (-jin′ i ŭm), *n.*

perihelion (per i hē′ li ŏn) [PERI-, Gr. *hēlion*, sun], *n.* (*Astron.*) The part of the orbit of a planet, comet, etc., nearest the sun. **perihepatic** (per i hė păt′ ik) [Gr. *hēpas hēpatos*, liver, -IC], *a.* (*Anat.*) Surrounding the liver.

peril (per′ il) [O.F. *péril*, L. *periclum*, *periculum*, rel. to *perīrī*, to try], *n.* Danger, risk, hazard, jeopardy; exposure to injury, loss, or destruction. *v.t.* (*past & p.p.* **perilled**) To risk, to endanger. ***v.i.** To be in danger. **perilous,** *a.* **perilously,** *adv.* **perilousness,** *n.*

perilymph (per′ i limf) [PERI-, LYMPH], *n.* (*Anat.*) The clear fluid surrounding the membranous labyrinth in the ear. **perimeter** (pė rim′ ė tėr) [L. and Gr. *perimetros* (*metron*, measure)], *n.* The bounding line of a plane figure; the length of this, the circumference; (*Opt.*) an instrument for measuring the field of vision; (*Mil.*) the boundary of a camp. **perimetrical** (-met′ ri kål), *a.* **perimorph** (per′ i môrf) [Gr. *morphē*, form], *n.* (*Min.*) A mineral enclosing another. **perimorphic, -phous** (-môr′ fik, -fŭs), *a.* **perimorphism,** *n.*

perineum (per i nē′ ŭm) [late L. *perinēum* -*næum*, Gr. *peri-*, *pērinaion*, from *pēris* -*inos*, scrotum], *n.* (*Anat.*) The part of the body between the genital organs and the anus. **perineal,** *a.*

period (pēr′ i ŏd) [F. *période*, L. *periodus*, Gr. *periodos* (PERI-, *odos*, way)], *n.* A portion of time marked off by some recurring event, esp. an astronomical phenomenon; the time taken up by the revolution of a planet round the sun; any specified portion of time; a definite or indefinite portion of time, an age, an era, a cycle; length of duration, existence, or performance; a complete sentence, esp. a complex one in which the predicate is not fully stated till the end; a pause; a full stop (.) marking this; (*fig.*) an end, a limit; the menses; (*Math.*) the interval between the recurrences of equal values in a periodic function. *a.* Description of a picture, object, etc.; characteristic of a certain period. ***v.t.** To put an end to. **the period:** The present day. **periodic** (-od′ ik), *a.* Pertaining to a period or periods; performed in a regular revolution; happening or appearing at fixed intervals; constituting a complete sentence. **periodical,** *a.* Periodic; appearing at regular intervals (as a magazine, etc.). *n.* A magazine or other publication published at regular intervals, as monthly, quarterly, etc. ***periodicalist,** *n.* One who writes for a periodical. **periodically,** *adv.* **periodicity** (-dis′ i ti), *n.*

periœci (per i ē′ sī) [Gr. *perioikoi* (PERI-, *oikein*, to dwell)], *n.pl.* The inhabitants of the same latitudes on the opposite sides of the globe; (*Gr. Hist.*) the dwellers in the surrounding country, in relation to a town or city. **periœcian** (-ē′ shi ån), *n.* **periœcic** (-ė sik), *a.* **periorbital** (per i ôr′ bi tål) [ORBITAL], *a.* (*Anat.*) Around the orbit of the eye. **periosteum** (per i os′ tė ŭm) [Gr. *periosteon*, *osteon*, bone], *n.* (*Anat.*) A dense membrane covering the bones. **periosteal, *-teous,** *a.* **periostitis** (-tī′ tis) [-ITIS], *n.* (*Path.*) Inflammation of the periosteum. **periostitic** (-tit′ ik), *a.* **periotic** (-ot′ ik) [Gr. *ous ōtos*, ear], *a.* Surrounding the inner ear. *a.* A periotic bone.

peripatetic (per i pȧ tet′ ik) [F. *péripatétique*, L. *peripatēticus*, Gr. *peripatētikos* (PERI-, *patein*, to walk)], *a.* Walking about, itinerant; pertaining to the philosophy of Aristotle (from his habit of walking about whilst teaching in the Lyceum). *n.* One who walks about; one who cannot afford to ride; a follower of Aristotle. **peripatetically,** *adv.* **peripateticism,** *n.*

peripatus (pė rip′ ȧ tŭs) [mod. L., from Gr. *peripatos*, walking about, as prec.], *n.* (*Zool.*) A genus of worm-like arthropods living in damp places in the southern hemisphere, and believed to represent an ancestral type of both insects and myriapods.

peripeteia (per i pė tī' ȧ) [Gr. (PERI-, *pet-*, stem of *piptein*, to fall)], *n.* A reversal of circumstances or sudden change of fortune in a play or (*fig.*) in life.

periphery (pė rif' ė ri) [M.E. and O.F. *periferie*, late L. *peripheria*, Gr. *periphereia*, circumference (PERI-, *pherein*, to bear)], *n.* The outer surface; the perimeter, or circumference of a figure or surface. **peripheral, peripheric, -al** (-fer' ik, -ȧl), *a.*

periphractic (per i frăk' tik) [Gr. *periphraktos*, fenced round (PERI-, *phrassein*, to fence)], *a.* (*Geom.*) Enclosing round, as the surface of a ring or a globe with an internal cavity.

periphrasis (pė rif' rȧ sis) [L. and Gr. (PERI-, *phrasis*, a speech, a PHRASE)], *n.* Roundabout speaking or expression, circumlocution; a roundabout phrase. ***periphrase** (per' i frāz), *v.t.* To express by circumlocution. *v.i.* To use circumlocution. *n.* Periphrasis. **periphrastic** (-frăs' tik), *a.* **periphrastically,** *adv.*

periplast (per' i plăst) [PERI-, Gr. *plastos*, formed, moulded], *n.* (*Biol.*) The main substance of a cell as distinguished from the external coating of the nucleus; a cell-wall or cell-envelope; *intercellular substance. **periplastic** (-plăs' tik), *a.* ***periplus*** (per' i plůs) [L. *periplūs*, Gr. *periplous* (*-plous*, voyage)], *n.* Circumnavigation. **peripteral** (pė rip' tėr ȧl) [Gr. *peripteron* (*pteron*, wing)], *a.* (*Arch.*) Surrounded by a single row of columns. **peripterous,** *a.* (*Ornith.*) Feathered on all sides; (*Arch.*) peripteral. **periptery,** *n.* (*Arch.*) A peripteral building.

Perique (pė rēk') [etym. doubtful], *n.* A strong, dark-coloured variety of tobacco grown and manufactured in Louisiana, used chiefly in mixtures.

perirhinal (per i rī' nȧl) [PERI-, Gr. *rhis rhinos*, nose], *a.* (*Anat.*) Around the nose.

periscope (per' i skōp) [PERI-, -SCOPE], *n.* An apparatus enabling persons inside a submarine, trench, etc., to look about above the surface of the water, etc.; a look round, a general view. **periscopic, -al** (-skop ik, -ȧl), *a.*

perish (per' ish) [O.F., stem of *perir*, L. *perīre* (PER-, *īre*, to go)], *v.i.* To be destroyed, to come to naught; to die, to lose life or vitality in any way; to decay, to wither; to be lost eternally. **v.t.* To destroy, to ruin. **perishable,** *a.* Liable to perish; subject to rapid decay. *n.pl.* Food-stuff and other things liable to rapid decay or deterioration. **perishability** (-bil' i ti), **perishableness,** *n.* **perishably,** *adv.* **perishing,** *a.* That perishes; deadly, extreme; (*slang*) infernal, damned. **perishingly,** *adv.*

perisperm (per' i spěrm) [F. *périsperme* (PERI-, SPERM)], *n.* The testa of a seed; the mass of albumen outside the embryo-sac in certain seeds. ***perispheric** (per i sfer' ik) [SPHERIC], *a.* Globular.

perispome (per' i spōm), **perispomenon** (per i spō' mė non) [Gr. *perispōmenon*, neut. p.p. of *perispan* (PERI-, *span*, to draw)], *a.* (*Gr. Gram.*) Having a circumflex accent on the last syllable. *n.* A word with this.

perissad (pė ris' ȧd) [Gr. *perissos*, uneven, -AD], *n.* (*Chem.*) An element or radical whose valency is represented by an odd number; (*Zool.*) a perissodactyl.

perissodactyl (pė ris ȯ dăk' til) [Gr. *perissos*, uneven, *daktulos*, digit], *a.* (*Zool.*) Of or belonging to the *Perissodactyla*, a division of *Ungulata* in which all the feet are odd-toed. *n.* Any individual of the *Perissodactyla.*

peristalith (pė ris' tȧ lith) [Gr. *perista-tos* (PERI-, *statos*, standing), -LITH], *n.* (*Archæol.*) A group of stones standing round a burial-mound, etc.

peristalsis (per i stăl' sis) [PERI-, Gr. *stellein*, to send], *n.* (*Physiol.*) The automatic vermicular contractile motion of the alimentary canal and similar organs by which the contents are propelled along. **peristaltic,** *a.* **peristaltically,** *adv.*

peristeronic (per i stė ron' ik) [Gr. *peristerōn*, dovecot, from *peristera*, pigeon, -IC], *a.* Of or pertaining to pigeons. **peristeropod** (pė ris' tėr ȯ pod) [Gr. *pous podos*, foot], *a.* Pigeon-footed. *n.* A member of the *Peristerpodes*, a group of gallinaceous birds with the hind toe on a level with the others.

peristome (per' i stōm) [F. *péristome* (PERI-, Gr. *stoma*, mouth)], *n.* (*Bot.*) The fringe round the mouth of the capsule in mosses; (*Zool.*) the margin of the aperture of a mollusc, the oval opening in insects, crustacea, infusoria, etc. **peristomal, -mial** (-stō' mȧl, -mi ȧl), *a.* **peristyle** (per' i stīl) [F. *péristyle*, L. *peristylum*, Gr. *peristulon* (*stulos*, pillar)], *n.* (*Arch.*) A row of columns about a building, court, etc.; a court, etc., with a colonnade around it. **perisystole** (per i sis' tȯ li) [SYSTOLE], *n.* (*Physiol.*) The interval between the systole and diastole of the heart. **perithoracic** (per i thȯ răs' ik) [THORACIC], *a.* (*Anat.*) Around the thorax. **peritomous** (pė rit' ȯ můs) [Gr. *tomos*, cut], *a.* (*Min.*) Having the faces similar and cleaving in more directions than one parallel to the axis.

peritoneum (per i tȯ nē' ům) [L. *peritonæum*, Gr. *peritonaion* (PERI-, *ton-*, stem of *teinein*, to stretch)], *n.* (*Anat.*) A serous membrane lining the abdominal cavity and enveloping all the abdominal viscera. **peritoneal,** *a.* **peritonitis** (-nī' tis) [-ITIS], *n.* (*Path.*) Inflammation of the peritoneum.

perityphlitis (per i tif lī' tis) [PERI-, *tuphlon*, the cæcum, neut. of *tuphlos*, blind, -ITIS], *n.* (*Path.*) Inflammation of the connective tissue surrounding the cæcum or blind gut. **perivascular** (per i văs' kū lȧr) [VASCULAR], *a.* (*Anat.*) Surrounding a vessel. **perivisceral** (-vis' ėr ȧl), *a.* Surrounding the viscera.

periwig (per' i wig) [earlier *perwigge*, *perwicke*, F. *perruque*, PERUKE], *n.* A peruke, a wig.

periwinkle (1) (per' i wing kėl) [A.-S. *pine-wincle*, *wine-wincle*], *n.* A small univalve mollusc, *Littorina littorea.*

periwinkle (2) (per' i wing kėl) [A.-S. *perwince*, *pervince*, L. *pervinca*], *n.* A plant of the genus *Vinca*, comprising trailing evergreen shrubs with blue or white flowers.

perjink (pėr jingk') [Sc., etym. unknown], *a.* Precise, prim.

perjure (pěr' jůr) [O.F. *parjurer*, L. *perjūrāre* (PER-, *jūrāre*, to swear)], *v.t.* (*reflex.*) To forswear (oneself); *to cause to swear falsely. **v.i.* To swear falsely. **n.* A perjurer. **perjured,** *a.* Forsworn. **perjurer,** *n.* **perjurious** (-joor' i ůs), *a.*

perjury (pěr' ju ri), *n.* The act of swearing falsely, the violating of an oath; the act of wilfully giving false evidence.

perk (1) (pěrk) [etym. doubtful], *v.t.* To make smart or trim; to hold or prick up; to thrust (oneself) forward. *v.i.* To bear oneself saucily or jauntily; to be jaunty, self-assertive, or impudent. *a.* Pert, brisk, smart, trim. **perky,** *a.* **perkily,** *adv.* **perkiness,** *n.*

perk (2) (pěrk) [var. of PERCH (2)], *v.i.* (*prov.*) To perch. *v.t.* (*reflex.*) To perch (oneself) on an elevated spot.

perlaceous (pėr lā' shůs), *a.* Like pearl, pearly, nacreous.

perlite (pěr' līt) [F. *perlite* (*perle*)], *n.* (*Petrol.*) A glassy igneous rock characterized by spheroidal cracks formed by contractile tension in cooling, pearlstone. **perlitic** (-lit' ik), *a.*

perlustration (pěr lůs trā' shůn) [from L. *perlustrāre* (PER-, *lustrāre*, to traverse, to inspect)], *n.* The act of inspecting thoroughly or viewing all over.

perm [abbr. PERMANENT WAVE].

permalloy (pěrm' ȧ loi), *n.* (*Metall.*) An alloy with high magnetic permeability.

permanent (pěr' mȧ nėnt) [F., from L. *perma-*

nentem, nom. *-nens*, pres.p. of *permanēre* (PER-, *manēre*, to remain)], *a*. Lasting, remaining, or intended to remain in the same state, place, or condition. **permanent wave**, *n*. (*Hairdressing*) Artificial wave of hair lasting until it grows out. **permanent way**, *n*. The finished road-bed of a railway. **permanence, -nency**, *n*. **permanently**, *adv*.

permanganate (pĕr măng′ gá nȧt), *n*. (*Chem.*) A salt of permanganic acid. **permanganic** (-găn′ ik), *a*. Of or containing manganese in its highest valency.

permeate (pĕr′ mė āt) [L. *permeātus*, p.p. of *permeāre* (PER-, *meāre*, to run, to pass)], *v.t.* To pass through the pores or interstices of; to penetrate and pass through; to pervade, to saturate. *v.i.* To be diffused (in, through, etc.). **permeable**, *a*. Yielding passage to fluids; penetrable. **permeability** (-bil′ i ti), *n*. **permeably**, *adv*. **permeant**, *a*. **permeance, permeation** (-ā′ shŭn), *n*. **permeative** (pĕr′ mė ā tiv), *a*.

Permian (pĕr′ mė ȧn) [*Perm* in E. Russia], *a*. (*Geol.*) Applied to the uppermost strata of the Palæozoic series, consisting chiefly of red sandstone and magnesian limestone, which rest on the carboniferous strata.

***permiscible** (pėr mis′ ibl) [L. *permiscēre* (PER-, *miscēre*, to MIX), -IBLE], *a*. Capable of being mixed.

permit (pėr mit′) [L. *permittere* (PER-, *mittere*, to send, p.p. *missus*)], *v.t.* (*past & p.p.* **permitted**) To allow by consent, to suffer; to give permission to or for, to authorize; *to resign, to leave. *v.i.* To allow, to admit (of). *n*. (pĕr′ mit) An order to permit, a permission or warrant, esp. a written authority to land or remove dutiable goods. **permissible** (pėr mis′ ibl), *a*. **permissibly**, *adv*. **permission** (-mish′ ŭn), *n*. The act of permitting; leave or licence given. **permissive**, *a*. Permitting, allowing; granting liberty, leave, or permission; not hindering or forbidding. **permissively**, *adv*. **permissiveness**, *n*. ***permittance**, *n*. **permitter**, *n*.

permutation (pĕr mū tā′ shŭn) [M.E. and O.F. *permutacion*, L. *permūtātiōnem*, nom. *-tio*, as foll.], *n*. (*Math.*) Change of the order of a series of quantities; each of the different arrangements, as regards order, that can be made in this; alteration, transmutation; *exchange of one thing for another, exchange, barter. **permutant** (-mū′ tȧnt), *n*. (*Math.*).

permute (pėr mūt′) [L. *permūtāre* (PER-, *mūtāre*, to change)], *v.t.* To change thoroughly; (*Math.*) to subject to permutation; *to interchange, to barter. **permutable**, *a*. Interchangeable. **permutableness**, *n*. **permutably**, *adv*.

pern (pĕrn) [mod. L. *pernis*, erron. from Gr. *pternis*], *n*. A bird of the genus *Pernis*, a honey-buzzard.

pernicious (pėr nish′ ŭs) [F. *pernicieux*, L. *perniciōsus*, from *pernicies*, destruction (PER-, *nex necis*, death)], *a*. Destructive, ruinous, deadly, noxious, hurtful; *malicious, wicked. **perniciously**, *adv*. **perniciousness**, *n*.

pernickety (pėr nik′ ė ti) [Sc., etym. doubtful], *a*. (*colloq.*) Fastidious, fussy, over-particular, awkward to handle, ticklish.

pernoctation (pĕr nok tā′ shŭn) [L. *pernoctātio*, from *pernoctāre* (PER-, *nox noctis*, night)], *n*. A remaining out or watching all night.

perone (per′ ȯ nē) [Gr. *peronē*, pin, the fibula], *n*. (*Anat.*) The fibula or small bone of the leg. **peroneal** (-nē′ ȧl), *a*. **peroneo-**, *comb. form*.

perorate (per′ ȯ rāt) [L. *perōrātus*, p.p. of *perōrāre* (PER-, *ōrāre*, to speak)], *v.i.* To deliver an oration; (*colloq.*) to speechify. *v.t.* To declaim. **peroration** (-rā′ shŭn), *n*. The concluding part or winding up of an oration.

peroxide (pĕr ok′ sīd), *n*. (*Chem.*) The oxide of a given base that contains the greatest quantity of oxygen. **peroxide of hydrogen**, *n*. A bleaching compound, used mainly for lightening the hair and as an antiseptic. **peroxidation** (-dā′ shŭn), *n*. **peroxidize** (-ok′ si dīz), *v.t.* and *i*.

perpend (pėr pend′) [L. *perpendere* (PER-, *pendere*, to weigh)], *v.t.* To consider carefully. *v.i.* To take thought.

perpendicular (pĕr pėn dik′ ū lȧr) [M.E. and O.F. *perpendiculer*, L. *perpendiculāris*, from *perpendiculum*, a plummet, as prec.], *a*. At right angles to the plane of the horizon; perfectly upright or vertical; (*fig.*) nearly vertical, extremely steep (of a hill, road, etc.); (*Geom.*) at right angles to a given line or surface. *n*. A perpendicular line; perpendicular attitude or condition; a plumb-rule, plumb-level, or other instrument for determining the vertical; (*slang*) a meal or entertainment at which the guests stand. **Perpendicular style:** (*Arch.*) The style of pointed architecture in England succeeding the Decorated, characterized by the predominance of vertical, horizontal, and rectangular lines, esp. in window-tracery, flattish arches, and profuse ornamentation. **perpendicularity** (-lăr′ i ti), *n*. **perpendicularly**, *adv*.

perpetrate (pĕr′ pė trāt) [L. *perpetrātus*, p.p. of *perpetrāre* (PER-, *patrāre*, to effect)], *v.t.* To perform, to commit; to be guilty of. **perpetrable**, *a*. **perpetration** (-trā′ shŭn), *n*. **perpetrator** (pĕr′ pė trā tȯr), *n*.

perpetual (pėr pet′ ū ȧl) [F. *perpétuel*, L. *perpetuālis*, from *perpetuus* (PER-, *pet-*, rel. to *petere*, to seek)], *a*. Unending, eternal; always continuing, persistent, continual, constant. **perpetual calendar**, *n*. A calendar adjustable to any year. **perpetual curate:** A clergyman in charge of an ecclesiastical district forming part of an ancient parish (perpetual curates are now called vicars). **perpetually**, *adv*. **perpetuate**, *v.t.* To make perpetual; to preserve from extinction or oblivion. **perpetuable**, *a*. **perpetuance, perpetuation** (-ā′ shŭn), *n*. **perpetuator** (pėr pet′ ū ā tȯr), *n*. **perpetuity** (pėr pė tū′ i ti), *n*. The number of years' purchase to be given for an annuity; a perpetual annuity. **for** or **in perpetuity:** For ever.

perplex (pėr pleks′) [from obs. *perplex*, perplexed, *confused*, L. *perplexus*, p.p. of *perplectere* (PER-, *plectere*, to plait)], *v.t.* To puzzle, to bewilder, to embarrass, to make anxious; to complicate, confuse, or involve; to make difficult to understand or to unravel; to entangle. **perplexedly**, *adv*. **perplexedness**, *n*. **perplexity**, *n*. ***perplexly**, *adv*.

perquisite (pĕr′ kwi zit) [L. *perquīsītum*, neut. p.p. of *perquīrere* (PER-, *quærere*, to seek)], *n*. Gain, profit, or emolument, over and above regular wages or salary; anything to which a servant, etc., has a prescriptive right after it has served its purpose; (*colloq.*) a gratuity, a tip; (*Law*) profit accruing to a lord of a manor over and above the ordinary revenue.

***perquisition** (pėr kwi zish′ ŭn) [F., from L. *perquīsītio*, as prec.], *n*. A thorough search or enquiry.

perradial (pĕr rā′ di ȧl) [PER-, RADIAL], *a*. (*Zool.*) Pertaining to or constituting a primary ray (in hydrozoa, etc.). **perradiate**, *v.t.* To radiate through. **perradius**, *n*. A perradial ray or primary ray (in certain cœlenterates).

perron (per′ ȯn) [F., from It. *petrone*, L. *petra*, stone], *n*. A platform with steps in front of a large building.

perruque, etc. [PERUKE].

perry (per′ i) [O.F. *peré*, from *peire* (O.F. *poire*), PEAR], *n*. A fermented liquor made from the juice of pears.

***perscrutation** (pĕr skrụ tā′ shŭn) [M.F., from L. *perscrūtātiōnem*, nom. *-tio*, from *perscrūtāre* (PER-, *scrūtāre*, to search closely)], *n*. A minute scrutiny.

***perse** (pĕrs) [O.F. *pers, perse*, late L. *persus*, etym. doubtful], *a*. Bluish-grey. *n*. A bluish-grey colour; a kind of cloth of this colour.

persecute (pĕr′ sė kūt) [F. *persécuter*, L. *persecūtus*, p.p. of *persequī* (PER-, *sequī*, to follow)], *v.t.* To pursue in a hostile, envious, or malicious way; to afflict with suffering or loss of life or property, esp. for adherence to a particular opinion or creed; to harass, to worry, to importune. **persecution** (-kū′ shŭn), *n.* ***persecutive** (pĕr′ sė kū tiv). **persecutory,** *a.* **persecutor, persecutrix,** *n.*

Perseus (pĕr′ sūs, -sė ŭs) [Gr., son of Zeus and Danaë, and the slayer of the Gorgon Medusa], *n.* (*Astron.*) One of the northern constellations. **Perseid** (pĕr′ sė id), *n.* One of a group of meteors appearing about 12th Aug. having their radiating point in this constellation.

persevere (pĕr sė vēr′) [F. *persévérer*, L. *persevērāre* (PER-, *sevērus*, SEVERE)], *v.i.* To persist in or with any undertaking, design, or course. **perseverance,** *n.* Persistence in any design or undertaking; sedulous endeavour; (*Theol.*) continuance in a state of grace. **perseverant,** *a.* Persevering. **perseveringly,** *adv.*

Persian (pĕr′ shăn), *a.* Pertaining to Persia, its inhabitants, or language. *n.* A native of Persia; the Persian language; a Persian cat; a kind of thin silk; (*Arch.*) a figure in Persian dress forming a pillar or pilaster supporting an entablature, etc. ***Persian apple:** The peach. **Persian blind** [PERSIENNE]. **Persian carpet:** A carpet made of knotted twine, etc., finely decorated, from Persia. **Persian cat:** A variety of cat with long silky hair. **Persian morocco:** A variety of morocco leather made from the skin of a hairy sheep called the Persian goat. **Persian insect powder:** A preparation from the flowers of *Pyrethrum roseum* used as an insecticide. **Persian wheel:** A wheel with buckets on the rim used for raising water, a noria.

persicaria (pĕr si kâr′ i ȧ) [med. L., from L. *persicum*, peach, neut. of *Persicus*, Persian], *n.* (*Bot.*) A weed, *Polygonum persicaria*, also called peachwort.

persicot (pĕr′ si kō) [F. *persico* (now *persicot*), It. *persico*, L. *persicum*, PEACH (1)], *n.* A cordial made from peaches, nectarines, etc., macerated in spirit and flavoured with their kernels.

persienne (pĕr si en′) [F., Persian], *n.* An Oriental cambric or muslin; (*pl.*) window blinds or shutters like Venetian blinds.

persiflage (pĕr si flazh′) [F., from *persiffler*, to jeer (PER-, *siffler*, L. *sibilāre*, to whistle, to hiss)], *n.* Banter, raillery; frivolous treatment of any subject. ***persifleur*** (-flĕr′), *n.*

persimmon (pėr sim′ ŏn) [corr. of Algonkin name], *n.* The plum-like fruit of *Diospyros Virginiana*, the American date-plum.

persist (pėr sist′) [F. *persister*, L. *persistere* (PER-, *sistere*, causal of *stāre*, to stand)], *v.i.* To continue steadfast in the pursuit of any design; to remain, to continue, to endure. **persistence, -ency,** *n.* **persistence of vision:** The ability of the eye to retain perception for a brief period after the stimulus has been removed, as in the illusion of a continuous picture formed from the number of still pictures in a cinematograph film. **persistent,** *a.* Persisting, persevering; lasting, enduring; (*Bot.*) not falling off (of leaves, etc.). **persistently, -ingly,** *adv.* ***persistive,** *a.*

person (pĕr′ sŏn) [M.E. and O.F. *persone*, L. *persōna*, a mask, a character, a personage, perh. rel. to *personāre* (PER-, *sonāre*, to sound)], *n.* A human being, an individual; a being possessed of personality; a human being as distinguished from one of the lower animals or an inanimate object; the living body of a human being; (*Law*) a human being or body corporate having rights and duties; (*Theol.*) one of the three individualities in the Godhead, Father, Son, or Holy Spirit; (*Gram.*) one of the three relations of the subject or object of a verb, as speaking, spoken to, or spoken of; (*Zool.*) an individual in a compound organism or a hydrozoan colony; (*fig.*) the penis; *a part or character (on the stage); *a parson; a personage. **in person:** By oneself; not by deputy. **personable,** *a.* Handsome, pleasing, attractive. **personage,** *n.* A person of rank, distinction, or importance; a person; a character in a play, story, etc.; *external appearance.

persona grata (pĕr sō′ nȧ gra′ tȧ) [L.], *n.* Acceptable person.

personal (pĕr′ sŏ nȧl), *a.* Pertaining to a person as distinct from a thing; relating to or affecting an individual; individual, private; reflecting on an individual, esp. disparaging, hostile (of remarks, attack, etc.); hence, making or prone to make such remarks; relating to the physical person, bodily, corporeal; transacted or done in person; (*Law*) appertaining to the person (applied to all property except land or heritable interests in land); (*Gram.*) denoting or indicating one of the three persons; *n.* (*Law*) A movable article of property, a chattel. **personal effects:** Articles of property intimately related to the owner. **personal equation** [EQUATION]. **personal estate** or **property:** (*Law*) Personalty, as distinguished from real property. **personally** (pĕr′ sŏ nȧl i), *adv.* In person; particularly, individually; as regards oneself. **personalize,** *v.i.* To personify. *v.t.* To make personal. **personalization** (-zā′ shŭn), *n.*

personality (pĕr sŏ năl′ i ti), *n.* The quality or state of being a person; individual existence or identity; the sum of qualities and characteristics that constitute individuality; a distinctive personal character; a person, a personage; personal application (of remarks, etc.); (*pl.*) disparaging personal remarks; *(*Law*) personalty. **multiple personality,** *n.* (*Psych.*) The existence of more than one personality in one individual. **personality cult:** (*Pol.*) A Russian term to describe the excessive adulation and boosting of individuals.

personalty (pĕr′ sŏn ăl ti), *n.* (*Law*) Personal estate, movable property as distinguished from real property.

personate (pĕr′ sō nāt) [L. *personātus*, p.p. of *personāre*, from *persōna*, mask, see PERSON], *v.t.* To assume the character or to act the part of; to impersonate, esp. for the purpose of voting without being entitled to do so, or for any other fraudulent purpose; *to counterfeit, to feign; *to represent, to describe; *to typify, to symbolize. *a.* (-nȧt) (*Bot.*) Mask-like (applied to a two-lipped corolla in which the mouth is closed by an upward projection of the lower part, as in the snapdragon). **personation** (-nā′ shŭn), *n.* **personator** (pĕr′ sŏ nā tŏr), *n.*

personify (pėr son′ i fī) [F. *personnifier* (PERSON, -FY)], *v.t.* To regard or represent (an abstraction) as possessing the attributes of a living being; to symbolize by a human figure; to embody, to exemplify, to typify, in one's own person. **personification** (-kā′ shŭn), *n.*

personnel (pĕr sŏ nel′) [F., orig. personal], *n.* The body of persons engaged in some service, esp. a public institution, military or naval enterprise, etc.; the staff of a business firm, etc.

perspective (pėr spek′ tiv) [F., from med. L. *perspectīva* (*ars*), perspective (art), from L. *perspectus*, p.p. of *perspicere* (PER-, *specere*, to look)], *n.* The art of representing solid objects on a plane exactly as regards position, shape, and dimensions, as the objects themselves appear to the eye at a particular point; the apparent relation of visible objects as regards position and distance; a representation of objects in perspective; (*fig.*) the relation of facts or other matters as viewed by the mind; a view, a vista, a prospect (*lit. or fig.*). *a.* Of or pertaining to perspective; in perspective; *optical. **in perspective:** According to the laws of perspective. **perspectively,** *adv.* **perspectograph** [-GRAPH], *n.* An instrument for mechanically drawing objects in perspective. **perspectography** (-tog′ rȧ fi), *n.*

perspex (pĕr′ speks), *n.* Protected trade name of a transparent plastic, very tough and of great clarity.

perspicacious (pĕr spi kā′ shŭs) [L. *perspicax -cācis* (PER-, *specere*, to see), -OUS], *a.* Quick-sighted; mentally penetrating or discerning. **per-**

spicaciously, *adv.* **perspicacity** (-kăs′ i ti), **perspicaciousness,** *n.*

perspicuous (pėr spik′ ū ůs) [L. *perspicuus,* as prec.], *a.* Free from obscurity or ambiguity, clearly expressed, lucid. **perspicuity** (-kū′ i ti), **perspicuousness,** *n.* **perspicuously,** *adv.*

perspire (pėr spīr′) [L. *perspīrāre* (PER-, *spīrāre,* to breathe)], *v.i.* To sweat. *v.t.* To give out (the excretions of the body) through the pores of the skin, to sweat; *to breathe or blow gently through. **perspirable,** *a.* That may be perspired or excreted by perspiration; liable to perspire. ***perspirability** (-bil′ i ti), *n.* **perspiration** (-rā′ shůn), *n.* **perspiratory** (-spīr′ a tȯr i), *a.*

perstringe (pėr strinj′) [L. *perstringere* (PER-, *stringere,* to tie, to bind, p.p. *strictus*)], *v.t.* To criticize; *to touch upon. **perstriction** (-strik′ shůn), *n.* ***perstrictive,** *a.*

persuade (pėr swād′) [F. *persuader,* L. *persuādēre* (PER-, *suādēre,* to advise)], *v.t.* To influence or convince by argument, advice, entreaty, or expostulation; to induce; to try to influence, to advise; *to recommend. **persuadable** [PERSUASIBLE]. **persuader,** *n.* One who or that which persuades; (*slang*) a pistol, a fire-arm, a weapon, a burglar's tool. **persuasible,** *a.* Capable of being persuaded. **persuasibility** (-bil′ i ti), ***persuasibleness,** *n.* **persuasion** (-swā′ zhůn), *n.* The act of persuading; power to persuade, persuasiveness; the state of being persuaded, a settled conviction; creed, belief, esp. in religious matters; a religious sect or denomination; (*colloq.*) a sort, a kind. **persuasive** (-swā′ siv), *a.* Able or tending to persuade; winning. *n.* That which persuades, a motive, an inducement. **persuasively,** *adv.* **persuasiveness,** *n.* ***persuasory,** *a.* Persuasive.

persue (1) (pěr′ sū) [prob. from F. *percée,* piercing, n. of action from *percer,* to pierce, conf. with PURSUE], *n.* (*Venery*) The track of a wounded deer, etc. ***persue** (2) [PURSUIT].

persulphate (pěr sŭl′ fāt), *n.* (*Chem.*) A sulphate containing the greatest relative quantity of acid.

pert (pěrt) [corr. of obs. *apert,* O.F., from L. *apertus* (p.p. of *aperīre,* to open), confused with *expertus,* EXPERT], *a.* Sprightly, lively; saucy, forward; *open, evident, plain. **pertly,** *adv.* **pertness,** *n.*

pertain (pėr tān′) [O.F. *partenir,* L. *pertinēre* (PER-, *tenēre,* to hold)], *v.i.* To belong (to) as attribute, appendage, part, etc.; to relate, to apply, to have reference (to).

pertinacious (pėr ti nā′ shůs) [L. *pertinax -ācis* (PER-, *tenax,* TENACIOUS)], *a.* Obstinate; stubborn, persistent; *incessant, constant. **pertinaciously,** *adv.* **pertinaciousness, pertinacity** (-năs i ti), *n.*

pertinent (pěr′ ti nėnt) [F., from L. *pertinentem,* nom. *-ens,* pres.p. of *pertinēre,* to PERTAIN], *a.* Related to the matter in hand; relevant, apposite; fit, suitable. *n.pl.* (*Sc.*) Belongings, appurtenances. **pertinence, -ency,** *n.* **pertinently,** *adv.*

perturb (pėr tėrb′) [L. *perturbāre* (PER-, *turbāre,* to disturb, from *turba,* crowd)], *v.t.* To disturb; to disquiet, to agitate; to throw into confusion or physical disorder. **perturbate** (pěr′ tůr bāt), *v.t.* To perturb. **perturbation** (-bā′ shůn), **perturbment,** *n.* **perturber,** ***perturbator, perturbatrix,** *n.* **perturbative,** *a.*

pertuse, -tused (pėr tūz′, -tūzd′) [L. *pertūsus,* p.p. of *pertundere* (PER-, *tundere,* to beat)], *a.* Punched, pierced with holes (esp. of leaves). ***pertusion** (-tū′ zhůn), *n.*

pertussis (pėr tŭs′ is) [PER-, TUSSIS], *n.* (*Path.*) Whooping-cough. **pertussal,** *a.*

peruke (pė rook′) [F. *perruque,* It. *parrucca* (cp. Sardinian *pilucca*), prob. ult. from L. *pilus,* hair], *n.* A wig, a periwig.

peruse (pė rooz′) [PER-, USE (earlier, to use up)], *v.t.* To read with attention; to read; (*fig.*) to observe or examine carefully. **perusal,** *n.* **peruser,** *n.*

Peruvian (pė roo′ vi ǎn), *a.* Pertaining to Peru. *n.* A native of Peru. **Peruvian balsam:** Balsam obtained from *Myroxylon pereiræ.* **Peruvian bark:** The bark of several species of cinchona, used as a tonic in debility and intermittent fevers. **peruvin** (per′ ů vin), *n.* (*Chem.*) An alcohol distilled from Peruvian balsam.

pervade (pėr vād′) [L. *pervādere* (PER-, *vādere,* to go)], *v.t.* To pass through; to permeate, to saturate; to be diffused throughout. **pervasion** (-vā′ zhůn), *n.* **pervasive** (-vā′ siv), *a.* **pervasively,** *adv.* **pervasiveness,** *n.*

perverse (pėr vėrs′) [F. *pervers,* L. *perversus,* p.p. of *pervertere,* as foll.], *a.* Wilfully or obstinately wrong; turned against what is reasonable or fitting; unreasonable, perverted, untractable; petulant, peevish; *unlucky, unpropitious. **perversely,** *adv.* **perverseness, perversity,** *n.*

perversion (pěr věr′ shůn), *n.* The act of perverting; a misinterpretation, misapplication, or corruption; the act of forsaking one's religion; sexual derangement.

pervert (pėr věrt′) [F. *pervertir,* L. *pervertere* (PER-, *vertere,* to turn)], *v.t.* To turn aside from the proper use; to put to improper use; to misapply, to misinterpret; to lead astray, to mislead, to corrupt. *n.* (pěr′ vėrt) One who has been perverted, esp. one who has forsaken his religion; a sexually-deranged person. **perversive,** *a.* **perverter,** *n.* **pervertible,** *a.*

***perveyaunce** [PURVEYANCE].

pervicacious (pěr vi kā′ shůs) [L. *pervicax -cācis,* -OUS], *a.* Very obstinate, wilfully perverse. ***pervicaciousness, *pervicacity** (-kăs′ i ti), *n.*

pervious (pěr′ vi ůs) [L. *pervius* (PER-, *via,* way)], *a.* Allowing passage (to); permeable; (*fig.*) intelligible; accessible (to facts, ideas, etc.); *pervasive. **perviousness,** *n.*

pesade (pė zād′) [F., earlier *posade,* It. *posata,* from *posare,* to PAUSE], *n.* The motion of a horse when raising his fore-quarters without advancing.

peseta (pė sā′ tă) [Sp., dim. of *pesa,* weight, *cp.* POISE], *n.* A Spanish silver coin worth about 2d.

Peshito (pė shē′ tō) [Syriac *p'shīṭâ, p'shīṭô,* the simple orphan], *n.* The Syriac version of the Holy Scriptures.

peshwa (pēsh′ wa) [Pers., chief], *n.* The hereditary ruler of the Mahrattas; earlier, the chief minister.

pesky (pes′ ki) [etym. doubtful, perh. from PEST], *a.* (*colloq.*) Annoying; plaguy, troublesome. *adv.* Peskily. **peskily,** *adv.*

peso (pā′ sō) [Sp. weight, L. *pensus,* p.p. of *pendere,* to weigh], *n.* A silver coin worth five pesetas, about four shillings, used in the S. American republics, known as the Spanish dollar.

pessary (pes′ ȧ ri) [med. L. *pessārium,* from L. *pessum,* Gr. *pessos,* an oval pebble used in games], *n.* (*Med.*) An instrument introduced into the vagina to prevent or remedy prolapse of the uterus; a medicated plug or suppository introduced into the vagina, usu. contraceptive.

pessimism (pes′ i mizm) [L. *pessimus,* worst, comp. of *pējor,* worse], *n.* The habit of taking a gloomy and despondent view of things; the doctrine that pain and evil predominate enormously over good, or that there is a predominant tendency towards evil throughout the universe. **pessimist,** *n.* and *a.* **pessimistic** (-mis′ tik), *a.* **pessimistically,** *adv.*

pest (pest) [F. *peste,* L. *pestem,* nom. *-tis,* plague], *n.* Anything or anyone extremely destructive, hurtful, or annoying; *plague, pestilence. **pest-house,** *n.* A hospital for contagious diseases.

pester (pes′ tėr) [prob. short for earlier *empester,* F. *empestrer* (now *empêtrer*)], *v.t.* To bother, to worry, to annoy; *to overload, to cram. **pesterer,** *n.*

pestiferous (pes tif′ ėr ůs) [L. *pestifer*], *a.* Pestilential; hurtful or noxious in any way; (*fig.*) bearing social or moral contagion. **pestiferously,** *adv.*

pestilence (pes′ ti lėns) [F., from L. *pestilentia*, from *pestis*, PEST], *n.* Any contagious disease that is epidemic and deadly, esp. bubonic plague, formerly called the Black Death. **pestilent,** *a.* Noxious to health or life, deadly; (*fig.*) fatal to morality or society; vexatious, troublesome, mischievous. **pestilential** (-len′ shål), *a.* **pestilently, pestilentially,** *adv.*

pestle (pes′ el, pes′ tėl) [M.E. and O.F. *pestel*, L. *pistillum*, from *pinsere*, to pound, p.p. *pistus*], *n.* An implement used in braying substances in a mortar; any appliance used for pounding or crushing things. *v.t.* To pound or pulverize with a pestle. *v.i.* To use a pestle.

pestology (pes tol′ ō ji) [PEST], *n.* The study of pests, esp. insects, and methods of dealing with them.

pet (1) (pet) [etym. doubtful], *n.* An animal brought up by hand or kept in the house as a favourite; (*fig.*) a fondling, a darling, a favourite. *a.* Petted, indulged, favourite. *v.t.* (*past & p.p.* **petted**) To make a pet of; to fondle. **pet aversion:** A thing especially disliked.

pet (2) (pet) [etym. doubtful], *n.* A fit of peevishness or ill temper.

petal (pet′ ål) [Gr. *petalon*, a thin plate or leaf (of metal, etc.)], *n.* (*Bot.*) One of the divisions of a corolla consisting of several pieces. **petal-shaped,** *a.* **petaline** (pet′ å līn, -lin). ***petaliform, petalous,** *a.* Having petals. **petalled,** *a.* (*usu. in comb.* as *fine-petalled*). **petaloid,** *a.*

petalite (pet′ å līt), *n.* (*Min.*) A vitreous silicate of lithium and aluminium.

petalon (pet′ å lon), *n.* A leaf of gold worn on the linen mitre of the Jewish high priest.

petard (pė tard′) [F. *pétard*, from *peter*, L. *pēdere*, to break wind], *n.* A conical case or box of iron, etc., formerly used for blowing open gates or barriers; a firework in the form of a bomb or cracker. **hoist with his own petard:** Caught in his own trap.

petasus (pet′ å sůs) [L., from Gr. *petasos*], *n.* A broad-brimmed low-crowned hat worn by the ancient Greeks; the winged cap of Hermes or Mercury.

petaurist (pė taw′ rist) [Gr. *petauristēs*, a performer on the *petauron* or spring-board], *n.* A genus of arboreal marsupials or flying phalangers.

petechiæ (pė tē′ ki ē) [mod. L., from It. *petecchia*, etym. doubtful], *n.pl.* (*Path.*) Spots on the skin formed by extravasated blood, etc., in malignant fevers, etc. **petechial, petechoid,** *a.*

Peter (1) (pē′ tėr) [L., from Gr. *Petros*, a masculine name, orig. a stone], *n.* *A kind of cosmetic; (*slang*) a portmanteau, a cloak-bag. **blue Peter** [BLUE]. **to rob Peter to pay Paul:** To take away from one person in order to give to another; to pay off one debt by incurring a new one. **Peterman,** *n.* A fisherman; (*slang*) a thief who steals peters or portmanteaus. **Peter-penny, Peter's-penny,** *n.* (*pl.* **-pence**) An annual tax of a penny from each householder formerly paid to the Pope; (since 1860) voluntary contributions to the Pope from Roman Catholics. **Peter's fish:** The haddock (from marks supposed to have been made by St. Peter's thumb).

peter (2) (pē′ tėr) [slang, etym. unknown], *v.i.* (of a load or vein in mining) To thin or give (out); to come to an end, to die (out).

petersham (pē′ tėr shåm) [Viscount *Petersham*, one of the 'dandies,' *c.* 1812], *n.* A heavy overcoat, also shooting or riding breeches; a heavy woollen cloth used for these; a thick corded-silk ribbon used for belts, hatbands, etc.

pething-pole (peth′ ing pōl), *n.* (*Austral.*) A sharp-pointed spear for killing cattle by piercing the spinal cord.

petiole (pet′ i ōl) [F. *pétiole*, L. *petiolus*, perh. dim. of *pes pedis*, foot], *n.* (*Bot.*) The leaf-stalk of a plant; a small stalk. **petiolar, petiolate, petiolated,** *a.* **petiolule,** *n.* A small petiole.

petit (pė tē′) [F.], *a.* (*fem.* ***-tite***, -tēt′) Small, petty; inconsiderable, inferior. ***petit-maître,*** *n.* A spruce fellow who affects the society of women; a fop, a coxcomb. ***petit point,*** *n.* Kind of fine embroidery.

petite (pė tēt′) [as prec.], *a.* (Of a woman) slight, dainty, graceful.

petition (pė tish′ ůn) [F. *pétition*, L. *petitiōnem*, nom. *-tio*, from *petere*, to seek], *n.* An entreaty, a request, a supplication, a prayer; a single article in a prayer; a formal written supplication to persons in authority, esp. to the sovereign, Parliament, etc.; the paper containing such supplication; (*Law*) a formal written application to a court, as for a writ of habeas corpus, in bankruptcy, etc. *v.t.* To solicit, to ask humbly (for, etc.); to address a formal supplication to. **Petition of Right:** The declaration of the rights and liberties of the people made by Parliament to Charles I and assented to in 1628. **petitionary,** *a.* **petitioner,** *n.* **petitory** (pet′ i tòr i), *a.* Petitioning, begging, supplicating; (*Law*) claiming title or right of ownership.

***petrean** (pė trē′ ån) [L. *petræus*, Gr. *petraios*, from *petra*, rock], *a.* Of or pertaining to rock or stone; rocky.

petre [SALTPETRE].

petrel (pet′ rėl) [F. *pétre* (prob. dim. of *Pêtre*, PETER)], *n.* Any individual of the genus *Procellaria* or the family *Procellariidæ*, small dusky sea-birds, with long wings and great power of flight. **stormy petrel,** *n.* One variety of petrel; (*fig.*) a fore-runner of trouble, a maker of trouble.

petrify (pet′ ri fī) [F. *pétrifier*, It. *petrificare* (L. *petra*, stone, -FY)], *v.t.* To convert into stone or stony substance; (*fig.*) to stupefy, as with fear, astonishment, etc.; to make hard, callous, benumbed, or stiffened. *v.i.* To be converted into stone or a stony substance; to become stiffened, benumbed, callous, etc. ***petrescent** (pė tres′ ėnt), *a.* Changing into stone; petrifactive. ***petrescence,** *n.* **petrifaction** (-făk′ shůn), *n.* **petrifactive, *petrific** (-trif′ ik), *a.* Having the power to petrify. ***petrification** (-kā′ shůn), *n.* Petrifaction.

Petrine (pē′ trīn), *a.* Of, relating to, or derived from the apostle Peter. **Petrinism** (pē′ tri nizm), *n.* The theological doctrine of or attributed to St. Peter, esp. as distinguished from Paulinism.

petro- [Gr. *petra*, stone, rock], *comb. form.* **petroglyph** (pet′ rō glif) [F. *pétroglyphe* (Gr. *gluphē*, carving)], *n.* A rock carving. **petroglyphic** (-glif′ ik), *a.* **petroglyphy** (pė trog′ li fi), *n.* **petrograph** (pet′ rō grăf) [-GRAPH], *n.* A writing or inscription on rock. **petrography** (pė trog′ rå fi), *n.* Descriptive petrology. **petrographer,** *n.* **petrographic, -al** (-grăf′ ik, -ål), *a.*

petrol (pet′ rōl) [F. *pétrole*, med. L. PETROLEUM], *n.* A refined form of petroleum used in motor-cars, etc., gasoline, (*Am.* gas); (*fig.*) motive power. *v.t.* To supply (a motor, etc.) with petrol. **petrol-lighter,** *n.* A cigarette-lighter with a petrol-soaked wick. **petrolatum** (pet rō lā′ tům), *n.* (*Pharmacy*) A fatty compound of paraffin hydrocarbons obtained by refining the residue from petroleum after distillation, pure petroleum jelly.

petroleum (pė trō′ lė ům) [med. L. *petroleum* (*petr-*, PETRO-, *oleum*, OIL)], *n.* An inflammable oily liquid exuding from rocks or pumped from wells, used for lighting, heating, and the generation of mechanical power. **petroleum jelly,** *n.* A product of petroleum used in pharmacy as a lubricant. ***pétroleur*** (pet rō lěr′) (*fem.* ***-leuse***, -lěrz′), *n.* An incendiary who uses petroleum. **petrolic** (pė trol′ ik), *a.* Of or pertaining to petroleum or petrol. **petroliferous** (-lif′ ėr ůs), *a.* **petrolin** (pet′ rō lin), *n.* A solid mixture of hydrocarbons obtained by distilling Rangoon petroleum. **petrolize,** *v.t.*

petrology (pė trol′ ō ji), *n.* The study of the origin, structure, and mineralogical and chemical composition of rocks. **petrologic, -al** (-loj′ ik, -ȧl), *a.* **petrologically,** *adv.* **petrologist,** *n.*

***petronel** (pet′ rȯ nel) [F. *petrinal,* var. of *poitrinal,* from *poitrine,* L. *pectus, -toris,* breast], *n.* A large horseman's pistol (so-called from being fired with the stock against the breast).

petrosal (pė trō′ sȧl) [L. *petrōsus,* PETROUS, -AL], *a.* (*Anat.*) Of great hardness, like stone. *n.* The petrosal bone, the petrous portion of the temporal bone.

petrosilex (pet rȯ sī′ lėks), *n.* (*Min.*) Felsite. **petrosiliceous** (-si lish′ ůs), *a.*

petrous (pet′ růs) [L. *petrōsus,* from L. and Gr. *petra,* rock], *a.* Like stone, stony; (applied to the hard part of the temporal bone).

pettichaps (pet′ i chăps) [PETTY, CHAP (2)], *n.* The garden warbler, *Sylvia hortensis.*

petticoat (pet′ i kōt) [PETTY, COAT], *n.* A loose under-skirt, depending from the waist; (*fig.*) one who wears this, a woman, a girl; (*pl.*) skirts; (*fig. pl.*) the female sex. *a.* Feminine. **petticoat-government,** *n.* Government by women, esp. in domestic affairs. **petticoated,** *a.* **petticoatless,** *a.*

pettifog (pet′ i fog) [PETTY, *-fog* (perh. from *-fogger*), etym. doubtful], *v.i.* To do legal business in a mean or tricky way, to practise chicanery; to act in a mean, quibbling or shifty way. **pettifogger,** *n.* A petty, second-rate lawyer, esp. one given to sharp practices; a petty, second-rate, or shuffling practitioner in any profession. **pettifoggery,** *n.*

pettily, etc. [PETTY].

pettish (pet′ ish), *a.* Peevish, fretful; inclined to ill-temper. **pettishly,** *adv.* **pettishness,** *n.*

pettitoes (pet′ i tōz) [etym. doubtful, perh. from F. *petite oie,* little goose, giblets], *n.pl.* The feet of a pig as food, pig's trotters.

pettle (pet′ ėl), *v.t.* To pet, to indulge.

petto (pet′ ō) [It., from L. *pectus*], *n.* The breast. ***in petto:*** In secret, in reserve.

petty (pet′ i) [M.E. and F. *petit,* etym. doubtful], *a.* Little, trifling, insignificant; minor, inferior, subordinate, on a small scale; small-minded, mean. **petty bag:** A court formerly attached to the Court of Chancery, dealing with cases involving solicitors and officers of that court. **petty cash:** Minor items of receipt and expenditure. **petty jury:** A jury in criminal cases who try the bills found by the grand jury. **petty larceny** [LARCENY]. **petty officer:** A naval officer corresponding in rank to a non-commissioned officer. **petty sessions,** *n.* (*Law*) Court of two or more justices of the peace for trying minor offences. **pettily,** *adv.* **pettiness,** *n.*

petulant (pet′ ū lȧnt) [F. *pétulant,* L. *petulantem,* nom. *-lans,* prob. from *petere,* to seek, to aim at, through a dim. form *petulāre*], *a.* Given to fits of ill temper; peevish, irritable; *saucy, forward, capricious. *n.* A petulant person. **petulance, -lancy,** *n.* **petulantly,** *adv.*

petunia (pė tū′ ni ȧ) [mod. L. from F. *petun,* Tupi-Guarani *petȳ* (pron. *petun*), tobacco], *n.* A genus of South American plants, allied to the tobacco, cultivated in gardens for their showy funnel-shaped flowers.

petuntse (pė tun′ tsė, -tŭn tsē) [Chin. *pai-tun-tzu*], *n.* A fusible substance of feldspathic nature used for the manufacture of porcelain; China-stone, growan, Cornish-stone.

pew (pū) [M.E. *puwe,* O.F. *puie,* a stage or platform, L. *podia,* pl. of *podium,* Gr. *podion,* pedestal, from *pous podos,* foot], *n.* A box-like enclosed seat in a church for a family, etc.; a long bench with a back, for worshippers in church; (*slang*) a seat, a chair. *v.t.* To furnish with pews; to enclose in a pew. **pew-rent,** *n.* Rent paid for a pew or for sittings in a church. **pewage,** *n.* **pewless,** *a.*

pewit (pē′ wit) [imit. of the cry], *n.* The lapwing; its cry; the pewit-gull or black-headed gull, *Larus ridibundus.*

pewter (pū′ tėr) [O.F. *peutre,* It. *peltro,* etym. doubtful], *n.* An alloy usually of tin and lead, sometimes of tin with other metals; vessels or utensils made of this; a pewter tankard or pot; (*slang*) a prize tankard, prize-money. *a.* Made of pewter. **pewterer,** *n.* **pewtery,** *a.* and *n.*

Pfeiffer's bacillus (pfī′ fėrz bă sil′ ůs), *n.* (*Bacter.*) A rod-shaped bacillus believed to play a part in the causation of influenza.

Pfennig (pfen′ ig) [G. cogn. with PENNY], *n.* (*pl.* ***-ige***) A small copper coin of Germany, worth the hundredth part of a mark.

phænogam, etc. [PHANEROGAM].

phænomenon [PHENOMENON].

phaeton (fā′ ė ton, fā′ tȯn) [F. *phaéton,* L. and Gr. *Phaethōn,* shining, proper name of the son of Helios and Clymene, who, having obtained permission to drive the chariot of the sun for one day, would have set the world on fire had not Jupiter transfixed him with a thunderbolt], *n.* A light four-wheeled open carriage, usually drawn by two horses.

phagocyte (făg′ ȯ sīt) [Gr. *phago-,* as foll., -CYTE], *n.* (*Biol.*) A leucocyte that absorbs microbes, etc., protecting the system against infection. **phagocytal** (sī′ tȧl), **phagocytic** (-sit′ ik), *a.* **phagocytism** (făg′-), *n.* **phagocytosis** (-tō′ sis), *n.* The destruction of microbes, etc., by phagocytes.

-phagous [Gr. *phagos,* eating, devouring, from *phagein,* to eat], *comb. form.* as in *anthropophagous, sarcophagous.*

Phalæna (fȧ lē′ nȧ) [Gr. *phalaina*], *n.* (*Ent.*) A moth. **phalænian, phalænoid,** *a.* and *n.*

phalange [PHALANX].

phalanger (fȧ lăn′ jėr) [F., from Gr. *phalangion,* spider's web], *n.* Any individual of the sub-family *Phalangistinæ,* small Australian woolly-coated arboreal marsupials, comprising the flying squirrel and flying-opossum.

phalangial, etc. [PHALANX].

phalanx (făl′ ȧngks) [L. and Gr. *phalanx -angos*], *n.* (*pl.* **-xes,** *Anat. and Bot.* **-ges,** -jēz) The close order in which the heavy-armed troops of a Greek army were drawn up, esp. a compact body of Macedonian infantry; hence, any compact body of troops or close organization of persons; (*Anat.,* also **phalange**) each of the small bones of the fingers and toes; (*Bot.*) one of the bundles of stamens in polyadelphous flowers. **phalangeal, -gian** (-lăn′ jė ȧl, -ȧn), **phalangiform,** *a.*

phalarope (făl′ ȧ rōp) [F. (Gr. *phalaris,* coot, *pous,* foot)], *n.* A small wading bird of the family *Phalaropodidæ,* related to the snipes.

phallus (făl′ ůs) [Gr. *phallos*], *n.* (*pl.* **-li**) A figure of the male organ of generation, venerated as a symbol of the fertilizing power in nature; (*Bot.*) a genus of fungi containing the stink-horn. **phallic,** *a.* **phallicism, phallism,** *n.* The worship of the phallus.

phanariot (fȧ năr′ i ȯt) [mod. Gr. *phanariōtēs,* from *phanari,* Gr. *phanarion,* lighthouse, dim. of *phanos,* lamp], *n.* A resident in the Greek or Phanar quarter of Constantinople; (*Hist.*) one of the class of Greek officials under Turkey.

phanerogam (făn′ ėr ȯ găm) [F. *phanérogame* (Gr. *phaneros,* visible, *gamos,* marriage)], *n.* (*Bot.*) A plant having pistils and stamens, a flowering plant. **phanerogamic** (-găm′ ik), **phanerogamous** (-og′ ȧ můs), *a.*

phantascope (făn′ tȧ skōp) [Gr. *phantos,* visible, -SCOPE], *n.* An instrument used to illustrate some phenomena of binocular vision; a phenakistoscope.

Phantasiast (făn tā′ zi ăst) [Gr. *Phantasiastēs,* from *phantasia,* FANTASY], *n.* (*Eccles.*) One of those among the *Docetæ,* who believed that Christ's body was not material but mere appearance.

phantasm (făn′ tăzm) [M.E. and O.F. *fantesme* (F. *fantasme*), L. and Gr. *phantasma*, from *phantazein*, to display, from *phan-*, stem of *phainein*, to show], *n.* A phantom; an optical illusion; a deception, a figment, an unreal likeness or presentation (of); an imaginary idea of a fantastic kind; a fancy, a fantasy; (*Psych.*) a mental representation of an object; (*Spiritualism*) a vision or image of an absent or deceased person. **phantasmal, -mic** (făn tăz′ măl, -mik), *a.* **phantasmally,** *adv.*

phantasmagoria (făn tăz mȧ gôr′ i ȧ), **phantasmagory** (făn tăz′ mȧ gôr i) [PHANTASM, Gr. AGORA, assembly], *n.* An exhibition of dissolving views and optical illusions produced by a magic-lantern, produced in London in 1802; (*fig.*) a series of phantasms, fantastic appearances, or illusions appearing to the mind as in nightmare, frenzy, etc. **phantasmagorial, phantasmagoric** (-gor′ ik).

phantasy (făn′ tȧ zi) [FANTASY], *n.* (*Psych.*) A mental state in which thoughts and ideas are associated with desires unobtainable in reality.

phantom (făn′ tȯm) [M.E. and O.F. *fantosme*, as PHANTASM], *n.* An apparition, a ghost, a spectre; a vision, an illusion, an imaginary appearance; an empty show or mere image (of); (*Angling*) an artificial bait that expands in the water and resembles a live fish. *a.* Seeming, apparent; illusory. **phantomatic** (-măt′ ik), **phantomic** (-tom′ ik), *a.* **phantomically,** *adv.*

Pharaoh (fâr′ ō) [L. and Gr., from Egypt. *pr-‘o*, great house], *n.* Any one of the ancient Egyptian kings; (*fig.*) a tyrant, a despotic task-master; *the game of faro. **Pharaoh's serpent:** A chemical toy consisting of sulpho-cyanide of mercury, which fuses into a serpentine shape when lighted. **Pharaonic** (fâr ȧ on′ ik), *a.*

phare (fâr) [F., from L. *pharus*, Gr. PHAROS], *n.* A lighthouse.

Pharisee (făr′ i sē) [O.F., from L. *pharisæus*, *-sēue*, Gr. *pharisaios*, ult. from Heb. *pārūsh*, separated], *n.* One of an ancient Jewish sect who rigidly observed the rites and ceremonies prescribed by the written law, and were marked by their exclusiveness towards the rest of the people; (*fig.*) a self-righteous person, a formalist, an unctuous hypocrite. **pharisaic, -al** (-sā′ ik, -ȧl), *a.* **pharisaically,** *adv.* ***pharisaicalness, pharisaism** (făr′ i sā izm), *n.* The doctrines of the Pharisees as a sect; hypocrisy in religion, self-righteousness.

pharmaceutical (far mȧ sū′-, -kū′ ti kȧl) [L. *pharmaceuticus*, Gr. *pharmakeutikos*, from *pharmakeutēs*, *pharmakeus*, druggist, from *pharmakon*, drug], *a.* Of, pertaining to, or engaged in pharmacy. **pharmaceutically,** *adv.* **pharmaceutics,** *n.* Pharmacy. **pharmaceutist, pharmacist** (far′ mȧ sist), *n.* A druggist legally entitled to sell drugs and poisons.

pharmaco- [Gr. *pharmakon*, drug], *comb. form.* Pertaining to chemistry or to drugs. **pharmacography** (far mȧ kog′ rȧ fi) [-GRAPHY], *n.* A description of drugs and their properties. **pharmacology** (far mȧ kol′ ȯ ji) [-LOGY], *n.* The science of drugs and medicines. **pharmacological** (-loj′ i kȧl), *a.* **pharmacologically,** *adv.* **pharmacologist** (-kol′ ȯ jist), *n.*

pharmacopœia (far mȧ kō pē′ ȧ) [Gr. *pharmakopoiia*, from *pharmakopoios*, a preparer of drugs (*-poios*, from *poiein*, to make)], *n.* A book, esp. an official publication containing a list of drugs, formulas, doses, etc.; a collection of drugs; (*collect.*) the drugs available for use. **pharmacopœial,** *a.* ***pharmacopolist** (far mȧ kop′ ȯ list), *n.* One who sells drugs; an apothecary.

pharmacy (far′ mȧ si) [O.F. *farmacie*, late L. *pharmacīa*, Gr. *pharmakeia*, as prec.], *n.* The art or practice of preparing, compounding, and dispensing drugs, esp. for medicinal purposes; a drug-store, a chemist's shop; a dispensary.

pharos (fâr′ os) [L. and Gr., name of a small island in the bay of Alexandria, on which a beacon was erected], *n.* A lighthouse, a beacon. **pharology** (fâr ol′ ȯ ji) [-LOGY], *n.* The art of directing ships by light-signals from the shore.

pharyngo- [PHARYNX], *comb. form.* **pharyngoglossal** (fȧ ring gȯ glos′ ȧl) [Gr. *glōssa*, tongue], *a.* Of or pertaining to the pharynx and the tongue. **pharyngo-laryngeal** (-lȧ rin′ jė ȧl) [LARYNGEAL], *a.* Of or pertaining to the pharynx and the larynx. **pharyngoscope** (fȧ ring′ gȯ skōp), *n.* An instrument for inspecting the throat. **pharyngoscopy** (-gos′ kȯ pi), *n.* **pharyngotomy** (-got′ ȯ mi) [-TOMY], *n.* The surgical operation of cutting the pharynx. **pharyngotome** (fȧ ring′ gȯ tōm), *n.* An instrument used in this.

pharynx (făr′ ingks) [Gr. *pharunx -ngos*], *n.* (*pl.* **-ringes,** fȧ rin′ jēz) (*Anat.*) The canal or cavity opening from the mouth into the œsophagus and communicating with the air passages of the nose. **pharyngal** (fȧ ring′ gȧl), **pharyngeal** (-rin′ jė ȧl), *a.* **pharyngitis** (-jī′ tis), *n.* (*Path.*) Inflammation of the pharynx. **pharyngitic** (-jit′ ik), *a.*

phase (fāz), ***phasis** [late L. and Gr. *phasis*, from the stem *pha-*, to shine], *n.* (*pl.* **-ses**) A particular aspect or appearance; the form under which anything presents itself to the mind; a stage of change or development; (*Astron.*) a particular aspect of the illuminated surface of the moon or a planet; applied esp. to the successive quarters, etc., of the moon; (*Elect.*) the relationship in time between the peaks of two alternating voltages, etc. *See* SINGLE-PHASE, THREE-PHASE. **phasic** (fā′ sik), *a.* **phaseless** (fāz′ lės), *a.*

phasma (făz′ mȧ) [L. and Gr., a spectre, as prec.], *n.* (*pl.* **phasmata**) (*Zool.*) A genus of orthopterous insects comprising the walking-leaves, etc.

pheasant (fez′ ȧnt) [A.-F. *fesant* (F. *faisan*), L. *phāsiānus*, Gr. *Phasianos*, of or pertaining to the *Phasis*, a river of Colchis], *n.* A game bird, *Phasianus Colchicus*, naturalized in Britain and Europe, noted for its brilliant plumage and its delicate flesh. **pheasantry,** *n.*

***pheeze** (fēz) [A.-S. *fēsian* (cp. Norw. *föysa*, Swed. *fösa*)], *v.t.* To do for; to beat, to drive off. *v.i.* (*Am.*) To fret, to be uneasy. *n.* A state of fretfulness.

phello- [Gr. *phellos*, cork], *comb. form.* **phelloderm** (fel′ ȯ dĕrm) [DERM], *n.* (*Bot.*) A layer of parenchymatous tissue containing chlorophyll, and sometimes formed on the inner side of a layer of phellogen. **phellodermal** (-dĕr′ mȧl), *a.* **phellogen** (fel′ ȯ jen), *n.* The layer of meristematic cells from which the cork-tissue is formed, cork-tissue. **phellogenetic** (-jė net′ ik), **phellogenic** (-jĕn′ ik), *a.* **phelloplastic** (-plăs′ tik), *n.* A figure carved or modelled in cork; (*pl.*) the art of making such figures.

phen- pheno- [Gr. *phainos*, shining, from *phainein*, show], *comb. form.* (*Chem.*) Applied to substances derived from coal-tar, orig. in the production of coal-gas for illuminating.

phenacetin (fė năs′ ė tin), *n.* A white crystalline compound used as an antipyretic.

phenakistoscope (fen ȧ kis′ tȯ skōp) [Gr. *phhenakistēs*, an impostor, from *phenakizein*, to cheat, -SCOPE], *n.* A scientific toy in which a disk bearing figures in successive attitudes of motion is rapidly revolved so as to convey to the observer, by means of a mirror or a series of slits, the impression of continuous movement.

phenobarbitone (fē nō bar′ bi tōn), *n.* A white, crystalline powder used as a sedative or hypnotic drug.

phenol (fē′ nȯl) [PHEN-, -OL], *n.* (*Chem.*) Carbolic acid.

phenology (fė nol′ ȯ ji) [contr. of PHENOMENOLOGY, after G. *phänologisch*], *n.* The study of the times of recurrence of natural phenomena, esp. of the influence of climate on plants and animals. **phenological** (-loj′ i kȧl), *a.*

phenomenon (fė nom′ ė nȯn) [L. *phænomenon*, Gr. *phainomenon*, neut. p.p. of *phainein*, to show], *n.*

(*pl.* **phenomena**) That which appears or is perceived by observation or experiment, esp. a thing or occurrence the law or agency causing which is in question; (*colloq.*) a remarkable or unusual appearance; (*Phil.*) that which is apprehended by the mind, as distinguished from real existence. **phenomenal,** *a.* Of or pertaining to phenomena, esp. as distinguished from underlying realities or causes; of the nature of a phenomenon, perceptible, cognizable by the senses; (*colloq.*) extraordinary, prodigious. **phenomenally,** *adv.* **phenomenalism, -enism,** *n.* The doctrine that phenomena are the sole material of knowledge, and that underlying realities and causes are unknowable. **phenomenalist, -enist,** *n.* **phenomenalistic, -enistic** (-nis' tik), *a.* **phenomenalize,** *v.t.* To treat or conceive as phenomenal. **phenomenize,** *v.t.* To make phenomenal; to phenomenalize. **phenomenology** (-nol' ŏ ji), *n.* The science of phenomena, opp. to ontology; the division of any inductive science treating of the phenomena forming its basis. **phenomenological** (-loj' i kål), *a.* **phenomenologically,** *adv.*

phenyl (fen' il), *n.* (*Chem.*) The organic radical found in benzene, phenol, aniline, etc.

pheon (fē' ŏn) [etym. doubtful], *n.* (*Her.*) The barbed head of a dart, arrow, or javelin, a broad arrow.

phew (fū) [instinctive sound], *int.* Expressing surprise, disgust, impatience, etc.

phial (fī' ål) [M.E. and O.F. *fiole*, L. *phiala*, Gr. *phialē*], *n.* A small glass vessel or bottle, esp. for medicine. *v.t.* To put or keep in or as in a phial.

Phi Beta Kappa (fī bē' tå kăp' å) [initials of Gr. *Philosophia Biou Kubernetes*, Philosophy is the guide of life], *n.* The oldest of the American college fraternities.

phil- [PHILO-], *comb. form.* ***-phil** [-PHILE], *suf.*

philander (fi lăn' dėr) [Gr. *philandros* (PHIL-, *anēr andros*, man, perh. after a character in Beaumont & Fletcher's 'Laws of Candy,' or from a lover in Ariosto's 'Orlando Furioso')], *v.i.* To make love in a trifling or sentimental way; to flirt (with or after). **philanderer,** *n.*

philanthropy (fil ăn' thrŏ pi) [late L. and Gr. *philanthrōpia* (PHIL-, *anthrōpos*, man)], *n.* Love of mankind; active benevolence towards one's fellow-men. **philanthrope** (fil' ån thrōp), *n.* **philanthropic, -al** (fil ån throp' ik, -ål), *a.* **philanthropically,** *adv.* **philanthropist** (-lăn' thrŏ pist), *n.* **philanthropism,** *n.* **philanthropize,** *v.t.* and *i.*

philately (fi lăt' ė li) [F. *philatélie* (PHIL-, Gr. *ateleia*, freedom from toll, from *a*-, not, *telos*, toll, tax)], *n.* The collecting of postage stamps. **philatelic** (-tel' ik), *a.* **philatelist** (-lăt' ė list), *n.* **philatelistic** (-lis' tik), *a.*

-phile [Gr. *philos*, loving, dear, friendly, from *philein*, to love], *suf.* A lover or friend of; loving; as in *bibliophile, gastrophile, Germanophile.*

philharmonic (fil hår mon' ik) [F. *philharmonique*], *a.* Loving music. *n.* A person fond of music; (*ellipt.*) a musical society.

Philhellene (fil' hė lēn), *n.* A friend or lover of the Greeks or a supporter of Greek independence. *a.* Friendly to Greece or supporting Greek independence. **Philhellenic** (-lē' nik, -len' ik), *a.* **Philhellenism** (-hel' ė nizm), *n.* **Philhellenist,** *n.*

philibeg [FILIBEG].

philippic (fi lip' ik) [L. *Philippicus*, Gr. *philippikos*, from *Philippos*, Philip], *n.* One of three orations of Demosthenes against Philip of Macedon; applied also to Cicero's orations against Antony; any speech or declamation full of acrimonious invective. ***philippize** (fil' i pīz), *v.i.* To take the part of Philip of Macedon; hence, to act or speak as if under corrupt influence; (*erron.*) to write or deliver a philippic.

philippina [PHILOPENA].

Philistine (fil' is tin, -tīn) [F. *Philistin*, late L. *Philistīnus*, Gr. *Philistīnoi*, pl., Assyrian *Palastu, Pilistu*], *n.* One of an ancient warlike race in S. Palestine who were hostile to the Jews; (*fig.*) a person of narrow or materialistic views or ideas; one deficient in liberal culture; (after G. *philister*) applied by German students to a non-university man. *a.* Pertaining to the Philistines; (*fig.*) commonplace, uncultured, prosaic. **Philistinism,** *n.*

***phill horse** [THILL].

phillipsite (fil' ip sīt) [J. W. *Phillips* (1800–74), Eng. mineralogist], *n.* (*Min.*) A monoclinic hydrous silicate of aluminium, potassium, and calcium.

philo- [Gr. *philos*, loving, from *philein*, to love, cp. -PHILE], *comb. form.* Fond of, affecting, inhabiting. **philobiblic** (fil ŏ bib' lik) [Gr. *biblos*, book], *a.* Fond of books or literature. **philobiblian,** *a.* **philobiblist,** *n.* **philobiblical,** *a.* Philobiblic; devoted to the study of the Bible. **philogynist** (fi loj' i nist) [Gr. *philogunia*, love of woman (*gunē*, woman)], *n.* One devoted to women. **philogynous,** *a.* **philogyny,** *n.*

philology (fi lol' ŏ ji) [L. and Gr. *philologia* (PHILO-, *logos*, word, discourse)], *n.* The science of language; *love of learning or literature. **philologer, philologian** (-lō' ji ån), **philologist** (-lol' ŏ jist), *n.* **philological** (-loj' i kål), *a.* **philologically,** *adv.* **philologize** (-lol' ŏ jīz), *v.i.* and *t.*

philomath (fil' ŏ măth) [Gr. *philomathēs* (PHILO-, *math-*, stem of *manthanein*, to learn)], *n.* A lover of learning, esp. of mathematics, a scholar. **philomathic, -al** (-măth' ik, -ål), *a.* **philomathy** (-lom' å thi), *n.*

Philomela (fil ŏ mē' lå) [F. *philomèle*, L. and Gr. *Philomēla*, daughter of Pandion, king of Athens, changed by the gods into a nightingale], *n.* (*poet.*) A nightingale. **philomel** (fil' ŏ mel), *n.*

philopena (fil ŏ pē' nå) [corr. of G. *vielliebchen*, dim. of *viellieb* (*viel*, much, *lieb*, dear)], *n.* A game in which two persons at dessert share the double kernel of a nut, esp. an almond, the first being entitled to a forfeit, under certain conditions, on the next meeting with the other sharer; the kernel so shared; the forfeit or present.

philopolemic, -al (fil ŏ pŏ lem' ik, -ål) [Gr. *philopolemos* (PHILO-, *polemos*, war)], *a.* Fond of war or controversy. **philoprogenitive** (-prŏ jen' i tiv) [L. *progenit-*, stem of *progignere*, to beget], *a.* Characterized by love of offspring; prolific. **philoprogenitiveness,** *n.*

philosopher (fi los' ŏ fėr) [F. *philosophre, philosophe*, L. *philosophus*, Gr. *philosophos* (PHILO-, *sophos*, wise)], *n.* A lover of wisdom; one who studies or devotes himself to natural or moral philosophy or to the investigation of the principles of being or of knowledge; one who regulates his conduct and actions by the principles of philosophy; one of philosophic temper. **philosopher's stone:** An imaginary stone, sought for by the alchemists in the belief that it would transmute the baser metals into gold or silver. **philosophe** (fil' ŏ sof), *n.* A philosophist or pretender to philosophy; *a philosopher. **philosophic, -al** (-sof' ik, -ål), *a.* Pertaining or according to philosophy; devoted to or skilled in philosophy; wise, calm, temperate, unimpassioned. **philosophically,** *adv.* **philosophism** (fi los' ŏ fizm), *n.* Affectation of philosophy (applied esp. to the French Encyclopædists); sophistry. **philosophist,** *n.* **philosophistic, *philosophistical** (-fis' tik, -ål), *a.* **philosophize,** *v.t.* and *i.* **philosophizer,** *n.*

philosophy (fi los' ŏ fi), *n.* Love of wisdom; the knowledge or investigation of ultimate reality or of general principles of knowledge or existence; a particular system of philosophic principles; the fundamental principles of a science, etc.; practical wisdom; calmness and coolness of temper; serenity, resignation; *reasoning, argumentation. ***natural philosophy:** The study of natural phenomena, science. **moral philosophy:** Ethics.

philotechnic, *-al (fil ō tek′ nik, -ăl) [Gr. *philotechnos* (PHILO-, *technē*, art)], *a.* Fond of the arts, esp. the industrial arts. **philozoic** (-zō′ ik) [Gr. *zōon*, animal], *a.* Fond of or kind to animals. **philozoist,** *n.*

-philous [Gr. *philos*, loving (PHILE-, -OUS)], *suf.* As in *anemophilous*.

philtre (fil′ tėr) [F., from L. *philtrum*, Gr. *philtron*, from *philein*, to love], *n.* A love-potion, a love-charm. *v.t.* To charm or excite with a love-potion.

phimosis (fī mō′ sis) [Gr., from *phimoein*, to muzzle], *n.* (*Path.*) Constriction of the opening of the prepuce. **phimosed,** *a.*

phiz (fiz) [short for obs. *phisnomy*, PHYSIOGNOMY], *n.* (*slang*) The face, the visage; the expression, the countenance.

phlebitis (flė bī′ tis) [Gr. *phleps phlebos*, vein, -ITIS], *n.* (*Path.*) Inflammation of the inner membrane of a vein. **phlebitic** (-bit′ ik), *a.*

phlebolite, -lith (fleb′ ō līt, -lith) [as prec., -ITE] *n.* A calculus in a vein. **phlebolitic** (-lit′ ik), **-lithic** (-lith′ ik), *a.*

phlebology (flė bol′ ō ji) [as foll., -LOGY], *n.* The department of physiology or anatomy dealing with the veins; a treatise on the veins.

phlebotomy (flė bot′ ō mi) [O.F. *flebothomie* (F. *phlébotomie*), L. and Gr. *phlebotomia* (*phleps phlebos*, vein, -TOMY)], *n.* (*Surg.*) The opening of a vein, blood-letting. **phlebotomist,** *n.* **phlebotomize,** *v.t.* To let blood from. *v.i.* To practise phlebotomy.

phlegm (flem) [M.E. and O.F. *fleume* (F. *phlegme*), L. and G. *phlegma -matos*, from *phlegein*, to burn], *n.* Viscid mucus secreted in the air passages or stomach, esp. as a morbid product and discharged by coughing, etc.; *self-possession; watery matter forming one of the four humours of the body; (*fig.*) coolness, sluggishness, apathy. ***phlegmagogue** (fleg′ mā gog), *n.* (*Med.*) A medicine for expelling phlegm, an expectorant. **phlegmagogic** (-goj′ ik), *a.* and *n.* **phlegmasia** (-mā′ si ȧ, -zi ȧ), *n.* (*Path.*) Inflammation, esp. with fever. **phlegmatic, -al** (fleg măt′ ik, -ăl), *a.* Cool, sluggish, apathetic, unemotional. **phlegmatically,** *adv.* **phlegmy** (flem′ i), *a.* Abounding in or of the nature of phlegm.

phlegmon (fleg′ mȯn) [M.E. *flegmon*, L. *phlegmon -mona*, Gr. *phlegmonē*, as prec.], *n.* (*Path.*) A tumour or inflammation of the cellular tissue. **phlegmonic** (-mon′ ik), **phlegmonous** (fleg′ mȯ nŭs), *a.*

phloem (flō′ ėm) [Gr. *phloos*, bark], *n.* (*Bot.*) The softer cellular portion of fibro-vascular tissue, the bark and the tissues closely connected with it.

phlogiston (flȯ jis′-, -gis′ tȯn) [Gr., neut. of *phlogistos*, burnt up, from *phlogizein*, to set on fire, cogn. with *phlegein*, to burn], *n.* The principle of inflammability formerly supposed to be a necessary constituent of combustible bodies. **phlogistic** (-jis′-, -gis′ tik), *a.* and *n.* **phlogisticate,** *v.t.* ***phlogosis** (-gō′ sis), *n.* (*Path.*) Inflammation.

phlorizin (flȯ rī′ zin, flor′ i zin) [Gr. *phloos*, bark, *rhiza*, root], *n.* (*Chem.*) A bitter substance found in the root-bark of the apple, pear, and other trees.

phlox (floks) [Gr., flame, name of a plant], *n.* A genus of North American plants of the family *Polemoniaceæ*, with clusters of showy flowers.

phlyctæna (flik tē′ nȧ) [Gr. *phluktaina*, from *phluein*, to swell], *n.* (*Path.*) A vesicle, pimple, or blister, esp. on the eye-ball. **phlyctenar, -tenous, -tenoid,** *a.*

-phobe [F., from L. and Gr. *-phobos*, from *phobos*, fear], *suf.* Fearing; as in *Anglophobe*, *Gallophobe*. **-phobia,** *suf.* Fear, morbid dislike; as in *Anglophobia*, *hydrophobia*.

phoca (fō′ kȧ) [L., from Gr. *phokē*, seal], *n.* (*Zool.*) A seal; a genus of pinniped mammals containing the true seals. **phocacean** (fō kā′ sė ȧn), *a.* and *n.* **phocaceous, phocal** (fō′ kăl), **phocine** (fō′ sīn), *a.*

Phœbus (fē′ bŭs) [L., from Gr. *phoibos*, bright, shining], *n.* (*Gr. Myth.*) Apollo as the sun-god; the sun.

Phœnician (fē nish′ ȧn), *a.* Of or pertaining to Phœnicia, an ancient Semitic country on the coast of Syria, or to its colonies, Punic, Carthaginian. *n.* A native or inhabitant of Phœnicia or its colonies.

phœnix (fē′ niks) [L., from Gr. *phoinix*, phœnix, also purple, Carthaginian], *n.* A fabulous Arabian bird, the only one of its kind, said to live for five or six hundred years in the desert and to immolate itself on a funeral pyre, whence it rose again in renewed youth; (*fig.*) a person or thing of extreme rarity or excellence, a paragon.

pholas (fō′ lȧs) [Gr.], *n.* (*pl.* **-lades,** -lȧ dēz). A genus of stone-boring bivalves, a piddock. **pholad,** *n.* **pholadean** (-lăd′ ė ȧn), **pholadid** (fō lȧ did), *n.* **pholadoid,** *a.*

phon (fōn) [Gr. *phonē*, voice], *n.* (*Acous.*) The unit of loudness. **phonmeter,** *n.* Instrument for estimating loudness of sound.

phon-, phono- [Gr. *phōnē*, sound], *comb. form.* Pertaining to sound or sounds. **phonate** (fō′ nāt), *v.i.* To make a vocal sound. *v.t.* To utter vocally. **phonation** (fō nā′ shŭn), *n.* **phonatory** (fō′ nȧ tȯr i), *a.* **phonautograph** (fō naw′ tȯ grăf) [AUTO-, -GRAPH], *n.* An apparatus for recording the vibrations of sounds. **phonautographic** (-grăf′ ik), *a.* **phonautographically,** *adv.*

phone (1) (fōn) [short for TELEPHONE], *v.t.* and *i.* To telephone. *n.* The telephone.

phone (2) (fōn) [Gr. *phōnē*, voice], *n.* An articulate sound, as a simple vowel or consonant sound.

-phone [Gr. *phōnē*, sound, voice], *suf.* As in *dictaphone*, *telephone*.

phoneme (fō′ nēm) [Gr. *phonema*, a sound], *n.* (*phon.*) The smallest distinctive group of phones in a language.

phonendoscope (fō nen′ dȯ skōp) [PHON-, Gr. *endon*, within, -SCOPE], *n.* A variety of stethoscope for enabling small sounds, esp. within the human body, to be distinctly heard.

phonetic (fō net′ ik) [Gr. *phōnētikos*, from *phōnein*, to speak, from *phōnē*, voice, sound], *a.* Pertaining to the voice or vocal sounds; representing sounds, esp. by means of a distinct letter or character for each. *n.pl.* The science of articulate sounds, phonology. **phonetically,** *adv.* **phonetician** (-tish′ ȧn), **phoneticism** (-net′-), *n.* Phonetic writing, phonetic representation of language. **phoneticist,** *n.* **phoneticize,** *v.t.* **phonetist** (fō′ nė tist), *n.* One versed in phonetics, a phonologist; an advocate of phonetic writing, a phoneticist. **phonic** (fō′ nik, fon′ ik), *a.* Pertaining to sounds, acoustic; pertaining to vocal sounds. ***phonics,** *n.* Phonetics; acoustics.

phoney (fō′ ni) [etym. doubtful], *a.* (*colloq.*) Bogus, false.

phono- [PHON-], *comb. form.*

phonogram (fō′ nȯ grăm), *n.* A written character indicating a particular spoken sound, as in Pitman's system of phonography; a sound-record made by a phonograph.

phonograph (fō′ nȯ grăf), *n.* An instrument for automatically recording and reproducing sounds; (*Am.*) a gramophone; *a phonogram; *a phonautograph. *v.t.* To record by means of phonography; to reproduce by means of a phonograph.

phonography (fō nog′ rȧ fi), *n.* A system of shorthand invented by Sir Isaac Pitman (1813–97), in which each sound is represented by a distinct character; automatic recording and reproduction of sounds, as by the phonograph; the art of using the phonograph. **phonographer, phonographist,** *n.* One skilled in phonography. **phonographic** (-grăf′ ik), *a.* **phonographically,** *adv.*

phonolite (fō′ nȯ līt) [PHONO-, -LITE], *n.* (*Min.*) Clinkstone.

phonology (fō nol′ ō ji), *n.* The science of the vocal

sounds; the sounds and combinations of sounds in a particular language. **phonologic, -al** (-loj′ ik, -ȧl), *a.* **phonologist, *-ger** (-nol′ ȯ jist, -jėr), *n.*

phonometer (fō nom′ e tėr), *n.* An instrument for recording the number and intensity of vibrations, esp. of sound-waves.

phonopore (fōn′ ō pôr), *n.* A device attached to a telegraph wire for allowing telephonic messages to be sent over the line at the same time as telegraphic messages, without interference from the current transmitting the latter. **phonoporic,** *a.*

phonoscope (fō′ nō skōp), *n.* An instrument for testing the quality of musical strings; an instrument of various kinds for translating sound vibrations into visible figures; a phenakistoscope representing a person speaking.

phonotype (fō′ nō tīp), *n.* A character used in phonetic printing. **phonotypic, -al,** *a.* **phonotypy,** *n.* Phonetic printing.

-phore [Gr. *phoros*, bearing], *suf.* Bearer; as in *gonophore, gynophore, semaphore.* **-phorous,** *suf.* Bearing, -ferous; as in *electrophorous, galactophorous.*

phosgene (fos′ jēn) [F. *phosgène* (Gr. *phōs*, light, -GEN)], *n.* (*Chem.*) Gaseous carbon oxychloride, used as a poison gas. **phosgenite,** *n.* (*Min.*) A mineral consisting of carbonate and chloride of lead in nearly equal proportions.

phosph- [PHOSPHO-], *comb. form.*

phosphate (fos′ fāt), *n.* (*Chem.*) A salt of phosphoric acid; (*pl.*) phosphates of calcium, iron, and alumina, etc., used as fertilizing agents. **phosphatic** (-făt′ ik), *a.*

phosphene (fos′ fēn) [Gr. *phōs*, light, *phainein*, to show], *n.* A luminous image produced by pressure on the eyeball, caused by irritation of the retina.

phosphide (fos′ fīd) [PHOSPH-, IDE], *n.* (*Chem.*) A combination of phosphorus with another element or radical. **phosphite,** *n.* A salt of phosphorous acid.

phospho- [abbr. of PHOSPHORUS], *comb. form.*

phosphor (fos′ fôr) [L., PHOSPHORUS], *n.* The morning-star, Lucifer; phosphorus. **phosphor-bronze, -copper, -tin,** etc., *n.* A combination of phosphorus with the metal named.

phosphorate (fos′ fȯ rāt), *v.i.* (*Chem.*) To combine or impregnate with phosphorus.

phosphoresce (fos fȯ res′) [as prec., -ESCE], *v.i.* To give out a light unaccompanied by perceptible heat or without combustion. **phosphorescence,** *n.* The emission of or the property of emitting light under such conditions. **phosphorescent,** *a.*

phosphoric (fos for′ ik) [as foll., -IC], *a.* (*Chem.*) Pertaining to phosphorus in its higher valency; phosphorescent. **phosphorism,** *n.* Phosphorus necrosis [see PHOSPHORUS]. **phosphorite** (fos′ fȯ rīt), *n.* (*Min.*) A massive variety of phosphate of lime. **phosphoro-,** *comb. form.* **phosphorogenic** (-jen′ ik), *a.* Causing phosphorescence. **phosphorograph** (fos′ fôr ȯ grăf), *n.* A luminous image produced on a phosphorescent surface. **phosphorographic** (-grăf′ ik), *a.* **phosphorography** (-rog′ rȧ fi), *n.* **phosphoroscope** (fos′ fôr ȯ skōp), *n.* An apparatus for measuring the duration of phosphorescence. **phosphorous,** *a.* Pertaining to, of the nature of, or obtained from phosphorus, esp. in its lower valency.

phosphorus (fos′ fȯ rŭs) [L. the morning star, from Gr. *phosphorus*, bringing light], *n.* A non-metallic element which occurs in two allotropic forms. White phosphorus is waxy, poisonous, spontaneously combustible at room temperature and appears luminous. Red phosphorus is non-poisonous and ignites only when heated. **phosphorus necrosis:** Gangrene of the jaw caused by the fumes of phosphorus, esp. in the manufacture of matches. ***phosphuret** [PHOSPHIDE]. **phosphuretted,** *a.* **phossy jaw:** (*colloq.*) Phosphorus necrosis.

phot (fot, fōt) [Gr. *phos, photos*, light], *n.* The unit of illumination, one lumen per square centimetre.

photism (fō′ tizm) [Gr. *photismos*, from *photizein*, to shine, from *phōs phōtos*, light], *n.* An hallucinatory sensation of colour accompanying some other sensation.

photo (fō′ tō) [short for PHOTOGRAPH], *n.* (*pl.* **-tos**) A photograph. *v.t.* To photograph.

photo-, phot- [Gr. *phōs phōtos*, light], *comb. form.* Pertaining to light or to photography. **photochemical** (fō tȯ kem′ i kȧl), *a.* Of, pertaining to, or produced by the chemical action of light. **photochemically,** *adv.* **photochemistry,** *n.* **photochromatic** (-măt′ ik), *a.* Of, pertaining to, or produced by the chromatic action of light. **photochrome** (fō′ tȯ krōm), *n.* A coloured photograph. **photochromotype** (-krō′ mȯ tīp), *n.* A picture in colours printed from plates prepared by a photo-relief process. *v.t.* To reproduce by this process. **photochromy,** *n.* Colour-photography. **photochronograph** (-krō′ nȯ grăf), *n.* An instrument for taking a series of photographs, as of moving objects, at regular intervals of time; a photograph so taken; an instrument for making a photographic record of an astronomical event. **photochronographic** (-grăf′ ik), *a.* **photochronographically,** *adv.* **photochronography** (-nog′ rȧ fi), *n.* **photo-engraving** (-grā′ ving), *n.* Any process for producing printing-blocks by means of photography. **photo-finish:** A close finish of a race, etc., in which a photograph enables a judge to decide the winner.

photo-electric (fō tō e lek′ trik), *a.* Of or pertaining to photo-electricity, or to the combined action of light and electricity. **photo-electricity** (-tris′ i ti), *n.* Electricity produced or affected by light. **photo-electric cell,** *n.* (*Phys.*) A device for measuring light by a change of electrical resistance when light falls upon a cell, or by the generation of a voltage.

photogen (fō′ tō jen), *n.* (*Chem.*) A light hydrocarbon obtained by distilling coal, shale, peat, etc., used for burning in lamps.

photogenic (fō tō jen′ ik), *a.* Produced by the action of light producing light, phosphorescent; (*Phot.*) descriptive of one who comes out well in photographs or in a cinematograph film.

photoglyph (fō′ tō glif), *n.* A photogravure.

photograph (fō′ tō grăf), *n.* A picture, etc., taken by means of photography. *v.t.* To take a picture of by photography. *v.i.* To practise photography; to appear in a photograph (well or badly). **photographer** (-tog′ rȧ fėr), *n.* **photographic** (-grăf′ ik), *a.* **photographically,** *adv.* **photography** (-tog′ rȧ fi), *n.* The process of producing images or pictures of objects by the chemical action of light on certain sensitive substances. **photogravure** (fō tȯ grȧ vūr′) [F. (GRAVURE)], *n.* The process of producing an intaglio plate for printing by the transfer of a photographic negative to the plate and subsequent etching; a picture so produced. *v.t.* To reproduce by this process. **photolithography** (-li thog′ rȧ fi), *n.* A mode of producing by photography designs upon stones, etc., from which impressions may be taken at a lithographic press. **photolithograph** (fō tȯ lith′ ȯ grăf), *n.*

***photology** (fȯ tol′ ȯ ji) [PHOTO-, -LOGY], *n.* The science of light. **photologic, -al** (-loj′ ik, -ȧl), *a.* **photologist** (-tol′ ȯ jist), *n.*

photomechanical (fō tȯ mė kăn′ i kȧl), *a.* Of or pertaining to a process by which photographic images are reproduced or employed in printing by mechanical means. **photometer** (fȯ tom′ ė tėr), *n.* A contrivance for measuring the relative intensity of light. **photometric, -al** (-met′ rik, -ȧl), *a.* **photometry** (-tom′ ė tri), *n.* **photomicrography** (-krog′ rȧ fi), *n.* The process of making magnified photographs of microscopic objects. **photomicrograph** (-mī krȯ grăf), *n.* **photo-micrographer** (-krog′ rȧ fėr), *n.* **photomicrographic** (-grăf′ ik), *a.*

photon (fō′ ton), *n.* (*Phys.*) Unit of light intensity; quantum of radiant energy.

photophobia (fō tō fō' bi å), *n.* (*Path.*) Morbid shrinking from or intolerance of light. **photophobic** (-fob' ik), *a.* **photophone** (fō' tō fōn) [-PHONE], *n.* An instrument for transmitting sounds by the agency of light. **photoprocess** (-prō' ses), *n.* Any photomechanical process. **photopsia** (fō top' si å), **photopsy** (fō' top si), *n.* (*Path.*) An affection of the eye causing the patient to see lines, flashes of light, etc. **photorelief** (-rē lēf'), *n.* An image in relief produced by a photographic process. *a.* Pertaining to any process of producing such reliefs. **photo-sensitive,** *a.* The property of being sensitive to the action of light. **photosphere** (fō' tō sfēr), *n.* The luminous envelope of the sun or a star. **photospheric** (-sfer' ik), *a.* **photostat** (fō tō stăt), *n.* Protected trade name of a camera to photograph prints, documents, etc.; a photograph so produced. **photosynthesis** (fō tō sin' thē sis) [-SYNTHESIS], *n.* (*Biol.*) The process by which carbohydrates are produced from carbon dioxide and water through the agency of light. **photosynthetic** (-thet' ik), *a.* **photosynthetically,** *adv.* **phototherapy** (fō tō ther' å pi) [-THERAPY], *n.* The treatment of skin-diseases by means of certain kinds of light-rays.

phototype (fō' tō tīp) [PHOTO-, TYPE], *n.* A printing-plate produced by photo-engraving; a print from this. **phototypy,** *n.* **phototypography** (-pog' rå fi), *n.* A photomechanical process of engraving in relief for reproduction with type in an ordinary printing-press. **photoxylography** (-zi log' rå fi), *n.* Engraving on wood from photographs printed on the block. **photozincography** (-zing kog' rå fi), *n.* The process of producing an engraving on zinc by photomechanical means for printing in a manner analogous to photo-lithography. **photozincograph** (-zing' kō grăf), *n.*

phrase (frāz) [F., from L. and Gr. *phrasis*, from *phrazein*, to speak], *n.* An expression denoting a single idea or forming a distinct part of a sentence; a brief or concise expression; mode, manner or style of expression, diction; idiomatic expression; a small group of words equivalent grammatically to a single word, esp. to an adjective, adverb, or noun; (*pl.*) mere words; (*Mus.*) a short, distinct passage forming part of a melody. *v.t.* To express in words or phrases. **phrase-book,** *n.* A handbook of phrases or idioms in a foreign language. **phrasemonger,** *n.* One who uses mere phrases; one addicted to magniloquent phrases. **phrasal,** *a.* ***phraseless,** *a.* Indescribable. **phraseogram, phraseograph,** *n.* A character standing for a whole phrase, as in phonography. **phraseology** (-ē ol' ō ji), *n.* Choice or arrangement of words; manner of expression, diction; *a phrase-book. **phraseological** (-loj' i kål), *a.* **phraseologically,** *adv.* **phraseologist** (-ol' ō jist), *n.* **phraser,** *n.* **phrasing,** *n.*

phratry (frā' tri) [F. *phratrie*, Gr. *phratria*, from *phratēr*, a clansman, cogn. with L. *frāter*, Eng. BROTHER], *n.* (*Gr. Ant.*) A division of the people for political or religious purposes; (*Athens*) one of the three subdivisions of a tribe; any tribal subdivision among primitive races. **phratric,** *a.*

phrenetic (frē net' ik) [M.E. and O.F. *frenetike*, L. *phrenēticus*, Gr. *phrenētikos*, *phrenītikos*, from *phrenītis*, delirium (*phrēn phrenos*, diaphragm, mind, -ITIS)], *a.* Frenzied, frantic, fanatical. *n.* A frantic or frenzied person. **phrenic** (fren' ik), *a.* (*Anat.*) Of or pertaining to the diaphragm. *n.* The phrenic nerve; *(*pl.*) psychology. ***phrenitis*** (frē nī' tis), *n.* (*Path.*) Inflammation of the brain or its membranes, attended with delirium; brain-fever. **phrenitic** (-nit' ik), *a.* **phrenograph** (fren' ō grăf), *n.* An instrument for registering the movements of a diaphragm in breathing; a phrenological chart of a person's mental characteristics. **phrenography** (-nog' rå fi), *n.* The description of phenomena as the first stage in comparative psychology.

phrenology (frē nol' ō ji) [Gr. *phrēn phrenos*, see prec., -LOGY], *n.* The theory that the mental faculties and affections are located in distinct parts of the brain denoted by prominences on the skull. **phrenological** (-loj' i kål), *a.* **phrenologically,** *adv.* **phrenologist** (-nol' ō jist), *n.*

phrontistery (fron' tis tėr i) [Gr. *phrontistērion*, from *phrontizein*, to think, from *phrontis*, thought], *n.* A place for thought or study, a thinking-shop.

Phrygian (frij' i ån), *a.* Pertaining to Phrygia, an ancient country in Asia Minor. *n.* A native or inhabitant of Phrygia. **Phrygian cap:** A conical cap worn by the ancient Phrygians, since adopted as an emblem of liberty. **Phrygian mode:** (*Mus.*) One of the four ancient Greek modes, having a warlike character.

phthalic (thăl' ik) [short for NAPHTHALIC], *a.* (*Chem.*) Of, pertaining to, or derived from naphthalene. **phthalein** (thăl' ē in), *n.* One of a series of organic compounds, largely used for dyeing, produced by the combination of phthalic anhydride with the phenols. **phthalin,** *n.* A colourless crystalline substance obtained from phthalein.

phthiriasis (thī ri ā' sis) [L., from Gr. *phtheiriasis*, from *phtheirian*, to be lousy], *n.* (*Path.*) A morbid condition in which lice multiply on the skin.

***phthisic** (tiz' ik) [M.E. and O.F. *tisike*, L. *phthisicus*, Gr. *phthisikos*, from PHTHISIS], *n.* Phthisis; one suffering from phthisis. **phthisical, phthisicky,** *a.*

phthisis (thī' sis, fthī' sis) [Gr., from *phthiein*, to decay], *n.* A wasting disease, esp. pulmonary consumption. **phthisiology** (tiz i ol' ō ji), *n.*

phut (fŭt) [Hind. *phatna*, to burst]: **to go phut:** To collapse, to stop.

phycology (fī kol' ō ji) [Gr. *phucos*, seaweed, -LOGY], *n.* The botany of seaweeds or algæ. **phycologist,** *n.* **phycography,** *n.* Descriptive phycology.

phylactery (fi lăk' tėr i) [L. *phylactērium*, Gr. *phulaktērion*, from *phulaktēr*, a guard, from *phulassein*, to guard], *n.* A charm, spell, or amulet worn as a preservative against disease or danger; a small leather box in which are enclosed slips of vellum inscribed with passages from the Pentateuch, worn on the head and left arm by Jews during morning prayer, except on the Sabbath. **phylacteried,** *a.* **phylacteric** (-ter' ik), *a.*

phylarch (fī' lark) [L. *phȳlarchus*, Gr. *phularchos* (*phulē*, tribe, *archein*, to rule)], *n.* The chief or commander of a tribe or clan, esp. in ancient Greece. **phylarchic, -al** (-lar' kik, -ål), *a.* **phylarchy** (fī' lar ki), *n.*

phyletic (fī let' ik) [Gr. *phuletikos*, from *phuletēs*, tribesman, as prec.], *a.* (*Biol.*) Pertaining to a phylum, racial.

-phyll [Gr. *phullon*], *suf.* Leaf; as in *chlorophyll*, *xanthophyll*.

phyllite (fil' īt) [Gr. *phullon*, leaf, -ITE], *n.* (*Min.*) An argillaceous schist or slate.

phyllo- [Gr. *phullon*, leaf], *comb. form.* **phyllobranchia** (fil ō brăng' ki å) [Gr. *branchia*, gills], *n.* (*pl.* **-chiæ**) (*Zool.*) A gill of a leaf-like or lamellar structure, as in certain crustaceans.

phyllode (fil' ōd), ***phyllodium*** (fi lō' di ŭm) [F. *phyllode*, mod. L. *phyllōdium*, from Gr. *phyllōdēs* (*phullon*, leaf, -ODE)], *n.* (*pl.* **-odes, -odia**) (*Bot.*) A petiole having the appearance and functions of a leaf. **phylloid,** *a.* **phyllome,** *n.* A leaf or organ analogous to a leaf; foliage. **phyllomic** (-lō' mik), *n.*

phyllomania (fil ō mā' ni å) [PHYLLO-, -MANIA], *n.* (*Bot.*) Abnormal production of leaves. **phyllophagan** (-lof' å gån) [Gr. *phagein*, to eat], *n.* (*Zool.*) An animal feeding on leaves, as a group of lamellicorn beetles including the chafers, or one of the *Phyllophaga*, a group of hymenoptera containing the saw-flies. **phyllophagous,** *a.* **phyllophorous** (-lof' ō rŭs), *a.* Leaf-bearing. **phyllopod** (fil' ō pod) [Gr. *pous podos*, foot], *n.* Any individual of the *Phyllopoda*, a group of entomostracous crustacea with never less than four pairs of leaf-like feet. **phyllopodous** (-lop' ō dŭs), *a.* **phyllo-**

podiform (-pod' i fôrm), *a.* **phyllorhine** (fil' ō rīn) [Gr. *rhis rhīnos*, nose], *a.* Having a leaf-like appendage to the nose. *n.* A leaf-nosed bat. **phyllostome** (fil' ō stōm) [Gr. *stoma -mata*, mouth], *n.* A bat of the genus *Phyllostoma*, characterized by a nose-leaf. **phyllostomatous** (-stom' å tŭs), **phyllostomine, -moid, -mous** (fi los' tō mīn, -moid, -mŭs), *a.* **phyllotaxis** (fil ō tăk' sis) [Gr. *taxis*, from *tassein*, to arrange], *n.* (*Bot.*) The arrangement of the leaves, etc., on the stem or axis of a plant. **phylloxera** (fil ŏk sēr' å) [Gr. *xēros*, dry], *n.* (*Ent.*) An aphid or plant-louse, orig. from America, very destructive to grape-vines.

phylo- [Gr. *phūlon*, *phulē*, tribe], *comb. form.* **phylogeny** (phi loj' ė ni), **phylogenesis** (phī lō jen' ė sis) [GENESIS], *n.* (*Biol.*) The evolution of a group, species, or type of plant or animal life; the history of this. **phylogenetic, -al** (-jė net' ik, -ål), **philogenic** (-jen' ik), *a.* ***phylum*** (fī' lŭm), *n.* (*pl.* ***-la***) (*Biol.*) A primary group consisting of related organisms descended from a common form.

phyma (fī' må) [L., from Gr. *phūma -ata*], *n.* (*pl.* ***-ata***) (*Path.*) An external tubercle or imperfectly suppurating tumour.

Physalia (fī sā' li å) [mod. L., from Gr. *phusaleos*, inflated], *n.* (*Zool.*) A genus of large oceanic hydrozoa comprising the Portuguese man-of-war.

physalite (fī' så līt) [G. *phusalith*, *pyrophusalith*, PYROPHYSALITE], *n.* (*Min.*) A greenish-white variety of topaz.

physeter (fī sē' tėr) [L., from Gr. *phūsētēr*, a blower, a whale, from *phūsan*, to blow], *n.* (*Zool.*) A genus of cetacea, containing the sperm-whales; a filter working by air-pressure.

physi- [PHYSIO-], *comb. form.*

physic (fiz' ik) [M.E. *fisike*, O.F. *fisique*, L. *physica*, Gr. *phusikē*, of nature, from *phusis*, nature, from *phuein*, to produce], *n.* The science or art of healing; the medical profession; medicine, esp. a purge or cathartic; *a physician; (*pl.*) the group of sciences dealing with the phenomena of matter, esp. as affected by energy, and the laws governing these, excluding biology and chemistry. *v.t.* (*past & p.p.* **physicked**) To administer physic to, to dose; to purge. **physical,** *a.* Of or pertaining to matter; obvious to or cognizable by the senses; pertaining to physics, esp. as opposed to chemical; material, bodily, corporeal, as opposed to spiritual; medicinal; *curative; *purgative. **physically,** *adv.* **physicky,** *a.* Resembling or suggestive of physic. **physico-,** *comb. form.* **physico-theology,** *n.* Theology based upon natural philosophy, natural theology.

physician (fi zish' ån), *n.* One versed in or practising the art of healing, including medicine and surgery; a legally qualified practitioner who prescribes remedies for diseases; (*fig.*) a healer; *a physicist.

physicist (fiz' i sist), *n.* One versed in physics; a natural philosopher; (*Biol.*) one who believes in the physical and chemical origin of vital phenomena, opposed to vitalist. **physicism,** *n.*

physio- [Gr. *phusis*, nature], *comb. form.* Pertaining to nature. **physiocracy** (fiz i ok' rå si) [-CRACY], *n.* Government according to a natural order, taught by François Quesnay (1694–1774), founder of the physiocrats, to be inherent in society. **physiocrat** (fiz' i ō krăt), *n.* **physiocratic** (-krăt' ik), *n.* **physiocratism** (-ok' rå tizm), *n.* **physiogeny** (fiz i oj' ė ni) [-GENY], *n.* The genesis or evolution of vital functions; the history of this. **physiogenic** (-jen' ik), *a.*

physiognomy (fiz i on' ō mi, -og' nō mi) [M.E. *fisnomie*, O.F. *phisonomie*, med. L. *phisonomia*, Gr. *phusiognōmonia* (*physio-*, *gnōmōn*, interpreter)], *n.* The art of reading character from features of the face or the form of the body; the face or countenance as an index of character; cast of features; (*colloq.*) the face; the lineaments or external features (of a landscape, etc.); aspect, appearance, look (of a situation, event, etc.). **physiognomic, -al** (-nom' ik, -ål), *a.* **physiognomically,** *adv.* **physiognomist** (-og' nō mist), *n.*

physiography (fiz i og' rå fi) [PHYSIO-, -GRAPHY], *n.* The scientific description of the physical features of the earth, and the causes by which they have been modified; physical geography. **physiographic, -al** (-grăf' ik, -ål), *a.* **physiographer** (-og' rå fėr), *n.*

physiolatry (fiz i ol' å tri), *n.* Nature-worship.

physiology (fiz i ol' ō ji) [L. and G. *physiologia*], *n.* The science of the vital phenomena and the organic functions of animals and plants. **physiologic, -al** (-loj' ik, -ål), *a.* **physiologically,** *adv.* **physiologist** (-ol' ō jist), *n.* One versed in physiology.

physiotherapy (fiz i ō thēr' å pi), *n.* A form of medical treatment in which physical agents such as movement of limbs, massage, electricity, etc., are used in place of drugs or surgery. **physiotherapeutic,** *a.* **physiotherapist,** *n.* A practitioner of this.

physique (fi zēk) [F., as PHYSIC], *n.* Physical structure or constitution of a person.

physitheism (fiz i thē' izm), *n.* Deification of natural forces or phenomena. **physiurgic** (-ĕr' jik) [Gr. *ergon*, work, -IC], *a.* Produced or affected solely by natural causes.

physo- [Gr. *phūsa*, bellows, bladder, cogn. with *phūsan*, to blow], *comb. form.* (*Zool.*) Relating to the bladder. **physoclist** (fī' sō klist) [Gr. *-kleistos*, shut], *n.* Belonging to the *Physioclisti*, a division of teleostean fishes having the air-bladder closed and not connected with the intestine. **physoclistous** (-klis' tŭs), *a* **physograde** (fī' sō grād) [L. *-gradus*, going], *n.* Any individual of the *Physograda*, containing siphonophores with a vesicular organ which renders them buoyant. **physopod** (fiz' ō pod) [Gr. *pous podos*, foot], *n.* A mollusc with suckers on the feet. **physostigma** (fī sō stig' må) [STIGMA], *n.* (*Bot.*) A genus of W. African climbing plants of the bean family containing the highly poisonous Calabar bean; this bean or its extract. **physostigmine,** *n.* A toxic alkaloid constituting the active principle of the Calabar bean. **physostome** (fī' sō stōm) [Gr. *-stoma*, mouth], *a.* Belonging to the *Physostomi*, a division of teleostean fishes having the air-bladder connected by a duct with the intestinal canal. *n.* A fish of this division. **physostomous** (-sos' tō mŭs), *a.*

-phyte [Gr. *phuton*, plant], *suf.* Denoting a vegetable organism; as in *lithophyte*, *zoophyte.*

phyto- [Gr. *phuton*, plant], *comb. form.* **phytobranchiate** (fī tō brăng' ki åt) [BRANCHIATE], *a.* Having leaf-like gills (of certain crustaceans). **phytochemistry** (-kem' is tri), *n.* The chemistry of plants. **phytochemical,** *a.* **phytogenesis** (fī tō jĕn ė sis), **phytogeny** (fī toj' ė ni) [GENESIS, -GENY], *n.* The origin, generation, or evolution of plants. **phytogeography** (-og' rå fi), *n.* The geographical distribution of plants. **phytography** (fī tog' rå fi) [-GRAPHY], *n.* The systematic description and naming of plants. **phytoid,** *a.* Plant-like. *n.* A plant-bud. ***phytology** (fī tol' ō ji) [-LOGY], *n.* Botany. ***phytologist,** *n.* **phytomer** (fī' tō-, fit' ō mĕr) [Gr. *meros*, part], *n.* A phyton. **phyton** (fī' tŏn, fit' ŏn), *n.* A plant-unit. **phytonomy** (fī ton' ō mi) [-NOMY], *n.* The science of plant growth. **phytopathology** (-på thol' ō ji), *n.* The science of the diseases of plants; the pathology of diseases due to vegetable organisms. **phytopathological** (-loj' i kål), *a.* **phytopathologist** (-thol' ō jist), *n.* **phytophagous** (fī tof' å gŭs) [-PHAGOUS], *a.* **phytotomy** (fī tot' ō mi) [-TOMY], *n.* Dissection of plants, vegetable anatomy. **phytozoon** (fī tō zō' ŏn) [Gr *zōon*, animal], *n.* (*pl.* **-zoa**) A plant-like animal, a zoophyte.

pi (1) (pī) [Gr. *pi*], *n.* The Greek letter π, *p*; (*Math.*) the symbol representing the ratio of the circumference of a circle to the diameter, *i.e.* 3·14159265.

pi (2) [PIE (3)].

pia (pē′ ȧ) [Hawaiian], *n.* A Polynesian herb of the genus *Tacca*, esp. *T. pinnatifida*, yielding a variety of arrow-root.

piacular (pī ăk′ ū lȧr) [L. *piāculāris*, from *piāculum*, expiation, from *piāre*, to propitiate], *a.* Expiatory; requiring expiation; atrociously bad.

piaffe (pyăf) [F. *piaffer*, etym. doubtful], *v.i.* To move at a piaffer (of a horse). *n.* An act of piaffing. **piaffer,** *n.* A movement like a trot but slower.

pia mater (pī ȧ mā′ tėr) [med. L. version of Arab. *umm raqīqah*, tender mother], *n.* (*Anat.*) A delicate membrane, the innermost of the three meninges investing the brain and spinal cord; (*fig.*) the brain.

pianette (pē ȧ net′), **pianino** (pē ȧ nē′ nō) [It., dim. of PIANO (2)], *n.* A small piano.

pianissimo (pē ȧ nis′ i mō) [It., superl. of PIANO (1)], *adv.* (*Mus.*) Very softly. *a.* Very soft. *n.* A passage so rendered.

piano (1) (pya′ nō) [It., from L. *plānus*, even, flat, late L., soft, low], *adv.* (*Mus.*) Softly. *a.* Played softly. *n.* A passage so rendered.

piano (2) (pē ăn′ ō), **pianoforte** (pē ăn ȯ fôr′ ti, -ăn′ ȯ fôrt) [It., earlier *piano e forte*, L. *plānus et fortis*, soft and strong], *n.* A musical instrument the sounds of which are produced by blows on the wire strings from hammers acted upon by levers set in motion by keys. **cottage piano:** A small upright piano. **grand piano:** A large horizontal, harp-shaped piano. **upright piano:** A piano with the case standing vertical and the strings usually at right angles to the keyboard. **piano-organ,** *n.* A mechanical organ worked on similar principles to those of the barrel-organ. **piano-player,** *n.* A pianist; a device for playing a piano mechanically. **pianola** (pē ȧn ōl′ ȧ), *n.* Protected trade name of a piano-player. **pianism,** *n.* Piano-playing; the technique of this. **pianist** (pi′ ăn ist, pē′ ȧ nist), *n.* A performer on the pianoforte. **pianiste** (pē′ ȧ nēst) [F.], *n.* A female pianist.

piastre (pi ăs′ tėr) [F., from It. *piastra*, plate or leaf of metal, as PLASTER], *n.* The Spanish dollar or silver peso, worth about 4s. 2d.; a small coin of Turkey and its dependencies with values ranging from about 2d. to 6d.

piazza (pi ăz′ ȧ, -ăt′ sȧ) [It., from pop. L. *plattia*, L. *platea*, Gr. *plateia*, broad, see PLACE], *n.* A square open space, public square, or market-place, esp. in Italian towns; applied to any open space surrounded by buildings or colonnades; improperly applied to a colonnade, or an arcaded or colonnaded walk, and (*Am.*) to a verandah about a house.

pibroch (pē′ bro*ch*) [Gael. *piobaireachd* (*piobair*, piper, from *piob*, from PIPE)], *n.* A series of variations, chiefly martial, played on a bagpipe; (*erron.*) the bagpipe.

pica (1) (pī′ kȧ) [med. L., an ordinal giving rules for movable feasts, perh. ident. with foll.], *n.* A size of type, the standard of measurement in printing.

Pica (2) (pī′ kȧ) [L., magpie], *n.* (*Ornith.*) A genus of *Corvidæ* containing the magpie; (*Path.*) a vitiated appetite causing the person affected to crave for things unfit for food, as coal, chalk, etc.

picador (pik′ ȧ dôr) [Sp., from *picar*, to prick], *n.* In Spanish bull-fights, a horseman with a lance who rouses the bull.

picamar (pik′ ȧ mar) [L. *pix picis*, PITCH (1), AMARUS, bitter], *n.* An oily compound, one of the products of the distillation of wood-tar.

picaroon (pik ȧ roon′) [Sp. *picaron*, from *picaro*, perh. rel. to *picar*, to prick], *n.* A rogue, a vagabond; a cheat; a thief, a robber; a pirate, a corsair; a pirate-ship. **picaresque** (-resk′), *a.* Describing the exploits and adventures of picaroons (applied to a style of fiction emanating from Spain).

picayune (pik ȧ yoon′) [Louisiana, from Prov. *picaioun* (F. *picaillon*), etym. doubtful], *n.* (*Am.*) A small Spanish coin, value 6¼ cents, now obsolete; applied to the five-cent piece and other small coins; hence something of small value.

piccadil, piccadilly (pik′ ȧ dil, -i) [F. *picadille*, *piccadille*, Sp. dim. of *picado*, pricked, slashed, p.p. of *picar*, to prick], *n.* A high collar or ruff, usu. with a laced or perforated edging, worn in the 17th cent.

piccalilli (pik′ ȧ lil i) [etym. doubtful], *n.* A pickle of various chopped vegetables with pungent spices.

piccaninny (pik′ ȧ nin i) [W. Ind., from Sp. *pequeño* or Port. *pequeno*, small, rel. to foll.], *n.* A little child. esp. of Negroes or Australian aborigines. *a.* Tiny, baby.

piccolo (pik′ ȯ lō) [It., small, a small flute], *n.* A small flute, with the notes one octave higher than the ordinary flute.

pice (pīs) [Hindi *paisa*], *n.* An Indian copper coin the quarter of an anna.

piceous (pis′ ė ŭs) [L. *piceus*, from *pix picis*, PITCH (1)], *a.* Pitch-black, brownish or reddish black; inflammable.

pichiciago (pich is i a′ gō, -ā′ gō) [Sp. *pichiciego* (prob. Tupi-Guarani *pichey*, Sp. *ciego*, L. *cæcus*, blind)], *n.* A small S. American armadillo.

pick (1) (pik) [M.E. *pikken*, *piken*, perh. rel. to foll. and to F. *piquer*, to prick], *v.t.* To break, pierce, or indent with a pointed instrument; to make (a hole) or to open thus; to strike at with something pointed; to remove extraneous matter from (the teeth, etc.) thus; to clean by removing that which adheres with the teeth, fingers, etc.; to pluck, to gather; to take up with a beak, etc.; to eat in little bits; to choose, to cull, to select carefully; to find an occasion for (a quarrel, etc.); to steal the contents of; to open (a lock) with an implement other than the key; to pluck, to pull apart; (*Am.*) to twitch the strings of, to play (a banjo); *to strike with the bill, to puncture. *v.i.* To strike at with a pointed implement; to eat in little bits; to make a careful choice; to pilfer. *n.* Choice, selection; the best (of). **to pick and choose:** To make a fastidious selection. **to pick off:** To gather or detach (fruit, etc.) from the tree, etc.; (*fig.*) to shoot with careful aim one by one. **to pick on:** To single out, to select. **to pick out:** To select; to distinguish (with the eye) from surroundings; to relieve or variegate with or as with distinctive colours; to gather (the meaning of a passage, etc.); to gather by ear and play (a tune) on the piano, etc. **to pick to pieces:** To analyse or criticize spitefully. **to pick up:** To take up with the beak, fingers, etc.; to gather or acquire here and there or little by little; to come across, to fall in with; to make acquaintance (with); to regain or recover (health, etc.); to recover one's health. **picklock,** *n.* An instrument for opening a lock without the key; one who picks locks; a thief. **pick-me-up,** *n.* A drink or medicine taken to restore the tone of the system. **pickpocket,** *n.* One who steals from pockets. ***pickpurse,** *n.* and *a.* ***pickthank,** *n.* An officious person; a toady. ***picktooth,** *n.* A toothpick. **pick-up,** *n.* The act of picking up, esp. at cricket; a device holding a needle which follows the track of a gramophone record and converts the resulting mechanical vibrations into acoustic or electrical vibrations. **picked** (1) (pikt), *a.* Gathered, culled; chosen, selected, choice. **picker,** *n.* **picking,** *n.* (*in pl.*) Gleanings, odds-and-ends; pilferings.

pick (2) (pik) [prob. var. of PIKE (1)], *n.* A tool with a long iron head, usu. pointed at one end and pointed or having a chisel-edge at the other, fitted in the middle on a wooden shaft, used for breaking ground, etc.; one of various implements used for picking. **picked** (2) (pik′ ėd), *a.* Having a point or spike, pointed, sharp; *peaked, tapering. ***pickedness,** *n.*

pick-a-back (pik′ a băk) [etym. doubtful], *adv.* On the back or shoulders, like a pack.

pickaxe (pik′ ăks) [M.E. *pikois*, O.F. *picois*, rel. to O.F. *pic*, see PIKE (1)], *n.* An instrument for breaking ground, etc., a pick. *v.t.* To break up with a pickaxe. *v.i.* To use a pickaxe.

pickeer (pi kēr′) [etym. doubtful], *v.i.* To maraud; to skirmish; to reconnoitre.

picker [PICK (1)].

pickerel (pik′ ėr ėl), *n.* A young or small pike.

picket (pik′ ėt) [F. *piquet*, from *piquer*, to prick], *n.* A pointed stake, post, or peg, forming part of a palisade or paling, for tethering a horse to, etc.; a small body of troops posted on the outskirts of a camp, etc., as a guard, sent out to look for the enemy, or kept in camp for immediate service; a guard sent out to bring in men who have exceeded their leave; a man or number of men set by a trade-union to watch a shop, factory, etc., during labour disputes; *a military punishment of making an offender stand with one foot on a pointed stake. *v.t.* To fortify or protect with stakes, etc., to fence in; to tether to a picket; to post as a picket; to set a picket or pickets at the gates of (a factory, etc.). *v.i.* To act as a picket.

pickle (1) (pik′ ėl) [cp. Dut. and L.G. *pekel*, etym. doubtful], *n.* A liquid, as brine, vinegar, etc., for preserving fish, flesh, vegetables, etc.; (*pl.*) vegetable or other food preserved in pickle; dilute acid used for cleaning, etc.; (*fig.*) a disagreeable or embarrassing position; a troublesome child. *v.t.* To preserve in pickle; to treat with pickle; *to rub (a person's back after flogging) with salt and water; *(*fig.*) to imbue thoroughly with any quality. **pickled** (*fig.*), *a.* Drunk. **to have a rod in pickle:** To have a beating or scolding in store (for). ***pickle-herring,** *n.* A pickled herring; a merry-andrew, a buffoon.

pickle (2) (pik′ ėl) [freq. of PICK (1)], *v.t.* (*chiefly Sc.*) To nibble, to eat sparingly; to pilfer. *n.* A small quantity, a little.

picklock, pickpocket, etc. [PICK (1)].

picksome (pik′ sŏm) [PICK (1), -SOME], *a.* Fastidious, select.

Pickwickian (pik wik′ i ȧn) [Mr. *Pickwick*, in Dickens's 'Pickwick Papers'], *a.* Relating to or characteristic of Mr. Pickwick; (*facet.*) merely technical or hypothetical (of the sense of words).

picnic (pik′ nik) [F. *pique-nique*, etym. doubtful], *n.* Originally an entertainment to which each guest contributed his share; an outdoor pleasure-party the members of which carry with them provisions on an excursion into the country, etc.; (*Austral.*) a mess, a confusion; an unpleasant experience or task. *v.i.* (*past & p.p.* **picknicked**) To go on a picnic. **picknicker,** *n.* **picknicky,** *a.*

picot (pi kō′) [F., dim. of *pic*, a peak, see PIKE (1)], *n.* A small loop of thread forming part of an ornamental edging. **picot-edge,** *n.* (*Dressmaking*) Machined stitching for a garment; bisected hem-stitching.

picotee (pik ŏ tē′) [F. *picoté*, p.p. of *picoter*, from *piquer*, to prick, as prec.], *n.* A hardy garden variety of the carnation, with a spotted or dark-coloured margin.

picotite (pik′ o tīt) [*Picot*, Baron de la Peyrouse (1744–1818)], *n.* (*Min.*) A variety of spinel containing chromium oxide.

picra [HIERA PICRA].

picric (pik′ rik) [Gr. *pikr-os*, bitter, -IC], *a.* Having an intensely bitter taste; applied to an acid obtained by the action of nitric acid on phenol, etc., used in dyeing and in certain explosives. **picrate,** *n.* A salt of this. **picrite,** *n.* (*Min.*) A blackish-green rock, composed largely of chrysolite. **picro-,** *comb. form.* **picrotoxin** (pik rŏ tok′ sin), *n.* A bitter crystalline compound constituting the bitter principle of *Cocculus Indicus*.

Pict (pikt) [late L. *Pictī*, perh. from native name, assim. to *pictus*, p.p. of *pingere*, to paint], *n.* One of a race of people who anciently inhabited parts of northern Britain. **Pictish,** *a.*

pictograph (pik′ tŏ grăf) [L. *pictus*, p.p. of *pingere*, to paint, -GRAPH], *n.* A picture standing for an idea, a pictorial character or symbol; a record or primitive writing consisting of these. **pictographic** (-grăf′ ik), *a.* **pictography** (-tog′ rȧ fi), *n.*

pictorial (pik tôr′ i ȧl) [late L. *pictōrius*, from *pictor*, painter, as prec.], *a.* Pertaining to, containing, expressed, or illustrated by pictures. *n.* An illustrated journal, etc. **pictorially,** *adv.*

picture (pik′ chėr) [L. *pictūra*, from *pictus*, p.p. of *pingere*, to paint], *n.* A painting or drawing representing a person, natural scenery, or other objects; a photograph, engraving, or other representation on a plane surface; (*fig.*) an image; a vivid description; a beautiful object; a scene, a subject suitable for pictorial representation. *v.t.* To represent by painting; to depict vividly; to form a mental likeness of, to imagine vividly. **the pictures,** *n.pl.* (*colloq.*) A cinematograph entertainment. **picture-book,** *n.* An illustrated book, esp. one full of illustrations for children. **picture-card,** *n.* (*Cards*) A court card. **picture-gallery,** *n.* A gallery or large room in which pictures are exhibited. **picture-hat,** *n.* A lady's hat with wide drooping brim, like those often seen in Reynolds's and Gainsborough's pictures. **picture-house,** *n.* A cinema. **picture post-card:** A post-card with a picture on the back. **picture-writing,** *n.* A primitive method of recording events, etc., by means of pictorial symbols, as in hieroglyphics, pictography.

picturesque (pik chėr esk′, pik tyů resk′), *a.* Having those qualities that characterize a good picture, natural or artificial; graphic, vivid (of language). *n.* That which is picturesque. **picturesquely,** *adv.* **picturesqueness,** *n.*

piddle (pid′ ėl) [etym. doubtful], *v.i.* To trifle; to work, act, behave, etc., in a trifling way; to urinate. **piddler,** *n.* **piddling,** *a.* Trifling; squeamish.

piddock (pid′ ŏk) [etym. doubtful], *n.* A bivalve mollusc of the burrowing genus *Pholadidae*, of which *P. dactylus* is largely used for bait.

pidgin-English (pij′ in ing′ glish) [Chin. (corr. of BUSINESS, ENGLISH)], *n.* A jargon of English mixed with Chinese, Malay, Portuguese, etc. used in conversation between natives and Europeans in the Far East. **not my pidgin:** (*colloq.*) Not my business, no affair of mine.

pie (1) (pī) [O.F., from L. *pīca*], *n.* A magpie; applied to other pied birds, as the spotted wood-pecker, the oyster-catcher, etc.

pie (2) (pī) [perh. from prec., with alln. to the miscellaneous nature of the contents], *n.* Meat, fruit, etc., baked with a paste over, (*Am.* a tart, *Eng.* 'pie' is known as a **deep pie**).

pie (3) (pī) [perh. from prec. or PIE (1)], *n.* *A set of rules in use before the Reformation relating to the services for movable festivals, etc.; a confused mass of printers' type; (*fig.*) a jumble, disorder, confusion. *v.t.* To mix or confuse (type). ***by cock and pie** [from the appearance of the black-letter type on white paper]: A minced oath—by God and the old Roman Catholic service-book.

pie (4) (pī) [Hindi *pa'i*, prob. cogn. with PICE], *n.* An Indian copper coin one-twelfth of the anna.

piebald (pī′ bawld), *a.* Having patches of two different colours, usu. black and white (of a horse or other animal); parti-coloured, mottled; (*fig.*) motley, mongrel.

piece (pēs) [O.F. *pece* (cp. Prov. *peza, pessa*, It. *pezza, pezzo*, Sp. *pieza*), etym. doubtful], *n.* A distinct part of anything; a detached portion, a fragment (of); a division, a section; a plot or enclosed portion (of land); a definite quantity or portion in which commercial products are made up or sold; a cask (of wine, etc.) of varying capacity; (*fig.*) an example, an instance; an artistic or literary composition or performance, usu. short; a coin; a gun, a fire-arm; a man at chess, draughts, etc.; (*Sc.*) a thick slice of bread with butter, jam, or cheese. *v.t.* To add pieces to, to mend, to patch; to put together so as to form a whole; to join together, to reunite; to fit (on). *v.i.* To come together, to fit (well or ill). **by the piece:** According to the amount of work done (of wages). **in**

pieces: Broken. **of a piece:** Of the same sort, uniform. **to piece on:** To join on, to fit on (to). **to piece out:** To complete by adding one or more pieces to; to eke out. **to piece up:** To patch up. **to go to pieces:** To collapse. **piece goods,** *n.pl.* Textiles woven in standard lengths. **piece-work,** *n.* Work paid for by the piece or job. **pieceless,** *a.* Whole, entire. **piece of eight,** *n.* Old Spanish dollar of eight *reals*, worth about 4s. 6d. **piece-meal,** *adv.* Piece by piece, part at a time; in pieces. *a.* Made up of pieces; done by the piece. **piecer,** *n.*

pied (pīd) [PIE (1), -ED], *a.* Parti-coloured, variegated, spotted. **piedness,** *n.*

pied-à-terre (pē ā da târ) [Fr., foot on the ground], *n.* A footing, a temporary lodging.

***piepowder** (pīʹ pou dėr) [O.F. *pied pouldré* (F. *pied-poudreux*), dusty foot], *n.* A traveller, a wayfarer. **Piepowder Court:** A summary court of record formerly held in fairs and markets by the steward for dealing with disputes arising there.

pier (pēr) [M.E. and A.-F. *pere*, O.F. *piere* (F. *pierre*), L. *petra*, stone], *n.* A mass of masonry supporting an arch, the superstructure of a bridge, or other building; a pillar, a column; a solid portion of masonry between windows, etc.; a buttress; a breakwater, mole, jetty; a structure projecting into the sea, etc., used as a landing-stage, promenade, etc. **pier-glass,** *n.* A looking-glass orig. placed between windows; a large ornamental mirror. **pier-table,** *n.* A low table placed between windows. **pierage,** *n.* Toll for using a pier or jetty.

pierce (pērs) [O.F. *percer*, *percier*, etym. doubtful], *v.t.* To penetrate or transfix with or as with a pointed instrument; to penetrate, to transfix (of the instrument); to prick; to make a hole in; (*fig.*) to move or affect deeply; to force a way into, to explore. *v.i.* To penetrate (into, through, etc.). **pierceable,** *a.* **piercer,** *n.* **piercing,** *a.* Penetrating; (*fig.*) affecting deeply. **piercingly,** *adv.* **piercingness,** *n.*

Pierian (pī ērʹ-, -erʹ i ȧn), *a.* Pertaining to Pieria, in Thessaly, or to the Pierides or Muses.

pierrot (pēʹ ėr ō, pyerʹ ō) [F., dim. of *Pierre*, PETER], *n.* (*fem.* **-rette,** -etʹ) A buffoon or itinerant minstrel, orig. French and usu. dressed in loose white costume and with the face whitened.

piet (pīʹ ėt) [M.E. *piot*, from PIE (1)], *n.* A magpie.

pieta (pyā taʹ) [It., from L. *pietas*, PIETY], *n.* A pictorial or sculptured representation of the Virgin and the dead Christ.

Pietist (pīʹ ė tist), *n.* One who makes a display of strong religious feelings; one of a party of revivalists in the Lutheran Church in the 17th cent., led by P. J. Spener (1635–1705), who professed to cultivate personal godliness to the disregard of dogma and the services of the Church. **Pietism,** *n.* **pietistic, -al** (-tisʹ tik, -ȧl), *a.*

piety (pīʹ ė ti) [F. *piété*, L. *pietas*], *n.* The quality of being pious; reverence towards God; *filial reverence or devotion.

piezochemistry (pī ē zō kemʹ is tri) [Gr. *piezein*, to press], *n.* (*Chem.*) The study of the effect of high pressures on chemical reactions. **piezo-electric effect:** A property possessed by some crystals (*e.g.* those used in gramophone crystal pick-ups) of generating surface electric charges when mechanically strained. They also expand along one axis and contract along another when subjected to an electric field. **piezometer,** *n.* An instrument for determining the compressibility of liquids or other forms of pressure.

piffero (pifʹ ėr ō) [It., from Teut. (cp. FIFE)], *n.* A small flute like an oboe; an organ-stop with a similar tone. ***pifferaro*** (-aʹ rō), *n.* An itinerant player on the *piffero*.

piffle (pifʹ ėl), *v.i.* To talk or act in a feeble, ineffective, or trifling way. *n.* Trash, rubbish, twaddle. **piffler,** *n.*

pig (pig) [M.E. *pigge*, etym. doubtful], *n.* A swine, a hog, esp. when small or young; the flesh of this, pork; (*colloq.*) a greedy, gluttonous, filthy, obstinate, or annoying person; an oblong mass of metal (esp. iron or lead) as run from the furnace. *v.i.* To bring forth pigs; to be huddled together like pigs. *v.t.* (*past & p.p.* **pigged**) To bring forth (pigs). **a pig in a poke:** [POKE (1)]. **pig-eyed,** *a.* Having small sunken eyes. **pigheaded,** *a.* Having a large, ill-shaped head; (*fig.*) stupid; stupidly obstinate or perverse. **pigheadedly,** *adv.* **pigheadedness,** *n.* **pig-fish,** *n.* A fish making a grunting noise. **pig-iron,** *n.* Iron in pigs. **pig-jump,** *v.i.* (*Austral. slang*) To jump with all four legs without bringing them together (of a horse). **pignut,** *n.* An earth-nut. **pigroot,** *v.i.* (*Austral.*) (Of a horse) to kick out with the back legs while the fore legs are firmly planted on the ground. **pigskin,** *n.* The skin of a pig; leather made from this; (*slang*) a saddle; *a.* Made of this leather. ***pigsney** [M.E. *pigges neyge* (*neyge*, var. of EYE, prob. from *a neye*, an eye)], *n.* A term of endearment. **pigsticking,** *n.* The sport of hunting wild boars with a spear; pig-killing. **pigsticker,** *n.* **pigsty,** *n.* A sty or pen for pigs; (*fig.*) a dirty place, a hovel. **pig's wash:** Swill or refuse from kitchens, etc., for feeding pigs. **pigtail,** *n.* The tail of a pig; the hair of the head tied in a long queue like a pig's tail; tobacco prepared in a long twist. **pigtailed,** *a.* **pigwash** [PIG'S WASH]. **pigweed,** *n.* The goosefoot or other herb eaten by pigs. **piggery,** *n.* **piggish,** *a.* **piggishly,** *adv.* **piggishness,** *n.* **piggy,** *n.* A little pig; a dirty child; the game of tipcat. **piggy-wiggy,** *n.* A little pig; a term of endearment applied to children. **piglet, pigling,** *n.* **piglike,** *a.*

pigeon (pijʹ ȯn) [M.E. *pyjon*, O.F. *pijon* (F. *pigeon*), late L. *pīpiōnem*, nom. *pīpio*, from *pīpīre*, to chirp], *n.* A bird of the order *Columbæ*, a dove; (*fig.*) a green horn, a gull, a simpleton. *v.t.* To fleece, to swindle, esp. by tricks in gambling. **pigeon-breast,** *n.* A deformity in which the breast is constricted and the sternum thrust forward. **pigeon-breasted,** *a.* **pigeon-English** [PIDGIN-ENGLISH]. **pigeon-gram,** *n.* A message carried by a pigeon. ***pigeon-hearted,** *a.* Timid, easily frightened. **pigeon-hole,** *n.* A hole in a dove-cot, by which the pigeons pass in or out; a nesting compartment for pigeons; (*fig.*) a compartment in a cabinet, etc., for papers, etc. *v.t.* To put away in this; (*fig.*) to defer for future consideration, to shelve; to give a definite place to in the mind, to label. ***pigeon-livered,** *a.* **pigeon-pea,** *n.* The pea-like seed of an Indian shrub, *Cajanus Indicus*. **pigeon-post,** *n.* The conveyance of letters, etc., by homing pigeons. **pigeon's milk:** A milky substance consisting of half-digested food with which pigeons feed their young; (*fig.*) a sham object for which fools are sent. **pigeon-toed,** *a.* Having the toes turned in. **pigeon-wing,** *n.* The hair at the side of the head dressed like a pigeon's wing, or a wig of this form, fashionable among men in the 18th cent.; (*Am.*) a fancy dance-step, a fancy-figure in skating. **pigeonry,** *n.*

piggery, etc. [PIG].

piggin (pigʹ in) [etym. doubtful], *n.* A small pail or vessel, usu. of wood, with a handle formed by one of the staves, for holding liquids.

piggy-back [PICK-A-BACK].

pightle (pīʹ tel) [?], *n.* A small enclosure of land, a croft.

pigment (pigʹ mėnt) [L. *pigmentum*, cogn. with *pingere*, to paint], *n.* Colouring-matter used as paint or dye; (*Physiol.*) substances giving colour to animal or vegetable tissues. **pigmental** (-menʹ tȧl), **pigmentary** (pigʹ mėn tȧr i), *a.* **pigmentation** (-tāʹ shŭn), *n.*

***pignoration** (pig nȯ rāʹ shŭn) [L. *pignerātio*, from *pignerāre*, from *pignus -noris*, *-neris*, pledge], *n.* The act of pledging or pawning. ***pignorative** (pigʹ nȯ rȧ tiv), *a.*

pignut, pigroot, pigsty, pigtail [PIG].

pike (1) (pīk) [F. *pique*, in first sense, cogn. with *piquer*, to pierce, *pic*, pickaxe, others prob. from cogn. A.-S. *pīc*], *n.* A military weapon, consisting of a narrow, elongated lance-head fixed to a pole; (*prov.*) a pickaxe, a spike; (*Lake District*) a peak, a peaked or pointed hill; (prob. short for *pike-fish*) a large slender voracious freshwater fish of the genus *Esox*, with a long pointed snout. *v.t.* To run through or kill with a pike. **pikeman** (1), *n.* A miner working with a pickaxe; a soldier armed with a pike. **pikestaff,** *n.* The wooden shaft of a pike; a pointed stick carried by pilgrims, etc. **plain as a pikestaff:** [earlier PACKSTAFF] Perfectly clear or obvious. **piked,** *a.* Pointed, peaked.

pike (2) (pīk) [short for TURNPIKE], *n.* A toll-bar; a turnpike road. **pikeman** (2), *n.* A turnpike-man. **piker,** *n.* A tramp; (*Am. slang*) a poor sport; a timid gambler; (*Austral.*) a wild bullock; a trickster, a sharp fellow.

pikelet (pīk′ lĕt) [short for obs. *bara-piklet*, W. *bara-pyglyd*, pitchy bread], *n.* A small round tea-cake or crumpet.

pikeman [PIKE (1 and 2)]. **piker** [PIKE (2)].

pikestaff [PIKE (1)].

pilar (pī′ lȧr) [L. *pil-us*, hair, -AR], *a.* Of or pertaining to hair. **pilary,** *a.*

pilaster (pi lăs′ tėr) [F. *pilastre*, It. *pilastro* (*pila*, L. *pīla*, pillar, -ASTER)], *n.* A rectangular column engaged in a wall or pier. **pilastered,** *a.*

pilau, pilaw (pi lou′) [Pers. *pilāw* (cp. Hind. *pilāo*, *palāo*)], *n.* An Oriental mixed dish consisting of rice boiled with meat, fowl, or fish, together with raisins, spices, etc.

pilch (pilch) [A.-S. *pylce*, med. L. *pellicea*, PELISSE], *n.* A flannel wrapper for an infant; *a garment of fur or skin, a coarse outer garment. ***pilcher,** *n.* (*Shak.*) A scabbard.

pilchard (pil′ chȧrd) [etym. doubtful], *n.* A small sea-fish, *Clupea pilchardus*, allied to the herring, and an important food-fish, caught largely on the coasts of Cornwall and Devon.

pile (1) (pīl) [F., from L. *pīla*, pillar], *n.* A heap, a mass of things heaped together; a funeral pyre, a heap of combustibles for burning a dead body; a very large, massive, or lofty building; an accumulation; (*colloq.*) a great quantity or sum, a fortune; (*Elec.*) a series of plates of different metals arranged alternately so as to produce a current; *the reverse of a coin (from the mark left by the pillar or pile of the minting apparatus). *v.t.* To collect or heap up or together, to accumulate; to load; to stack (rifles) with butts on the ground and muzzles together. **atomic pile:** (*Phys.*) A large mass of graphite in which uranium is decomposed and gives off much heat. **to pile up the agony** [AGONY]. **piler,** *n.*

pile (2) (pīl) [A.-S. *pīl*, L. *pīlum*, javelin], *n.* A sharp stake or post; a heavy timber driven into the ground, esp. under water, to form a foundation. *v.t.* To drive piles into; to furnish or strengthen with piles. **pile-driver, -engine,** *n.* **pile-worm,** *n.* A worm attacking piles.

pile (3) (pīl) [L. *pilus*, hair], *n.* Soft hair, fur, down, wool; the nap of velvet, plush, or other cloth, or of a carpet.

pile (4) (pīl) [L. *pīla*, ball], *n.* (*usu. in pl.*) Small tumours formed by the dilatation of the veins about the anus, hæmorrhoids. **pilewort,** *n.* The lesser celandine or figwort, *Ranunculus ficaria*, supposed to be a remedy for this.

pileate, -eated (pī′ lė ȧt, -ā tėd) [L. *pīleātus*, from PILEUS], *a.* Having a pileus or cap.

pileum (pī′ lė ŭm) [L., var. of foll.], *n.* (*Ornith.*) The top of the head, from the base of the bill to the nape, in a bird.

pileus (pī′ lė ŭs) [L. *pīleus*, *pilleus* (cp. Gr. *pīlos*)], *n.* (*pl.* **-lei**) (*Class. Ant.*) A brimless felt cap; (*Bot.*) the cap of a mushroom; (*Ornith.*) the pileum.

pilfer (pil′ fėr) [O.F. *pelfrer*, from *pelfre*, PELF], *v.t.* To steal in small quantities. **pilferage,** *n.* **pilferer,** *n.* **pilfering,** *n.* **pilferingly,** *adv.*

pilgarlick (pil gar′ lik) [*pilled*, see PILL (2), pealed, *garlick*], *n.* A bald head, one who has lost his hair by disease; a sneaking fellow.

pilgrim (pil′ grim) [M.E. *pelegrim*, prob. through an O.F. *pelegrin* (cp. F. *pélerin*, It. *pellegrino*), L. *peregrīnus*, stranger, see PEREGRINE], *n.* One who travels to a distance to visit some holy place, in performance of a vow, etc.; (*fig.*) a traveller, a wanderer. *v.i.* To go on a pilgrimage; to wander as a pilgrim. **pilgrimage,** *n.* A pilgrim's journey to some holy place; (*fig.*) the journey of human life. *v.i.* To go on a pilgrimage. **pilgrimize,** *v.i.*

piliferous (pī lif′ ėr ŭs) [L. *pilus*, hair, -FEROUS], *a.* (*Bot.*) Bearing hairs. **piliform** (pī′ li fôrm), *a.* **piligerous** (pī lij′ ėr ŭs) [-GEROUS], *a.* Having a covering of hair.

pill (1) (pil) [L. *pilula*, dim. of *pila*, ball], *n.* A little ball of some medicinal substance to be swallowed whole; (*fig.*) something unpleasant which has to be accepted or put up with; (*slang*) a black balloting-ball, (*pl.*) billiard balls. *v.i.* *To dose with pills; (*slang*) to blackball, to reject. **pill-box,** *n.* A small box for holding pills; (*fig.*) a small carriage or building; (*Mil.*) a concrete blockhouse, used as a machine-gun emplacement or for other defensive purposes; (*Mil.*) an old form of headdress. **pill-milliped, -worm,** *n.* A milliped that rolls up into a ball. **pillwort,** *n.* A cryptogamous aquatic plant of the genus *Pillularia.*

***pill** (2) (pil) [F. *piller*, prob. from L. *pilāre*, from *pilus*, hair (cp. PEEL (1))], *v.t.* To pillage, to plunder, to rob; (*prov.*) to peel. *v.i.* (*prov.*) To strip, to peel. **n.* Peel, skin. ***piller,** *n.*

pillage (pil′ ȧj) [F., from *piller*, as prec.], *n.* The act of plundering; plunder, esp. the property of enemies taken in war. *v.t.* To strip of money or goods by open force; to lay waste. *v.i.* To rob, to ravage, to plunder. **pillager,** *n.*

pillar (pil′ ȧr) [M.E. and O.F. *piler*, pop. L. *pīlāre*, from *pīla*], *n.* An upright structure of masonry, iron, timber, etc., of considerable height in proportion to thickness, used for support, ornament, or as a memorial; a column, a post, a pedestal; an upright mass of anything analogous in form or function; a mass of coal, stone, etc., left to support the roof in a mine or quarry; (*fig.*) a person or body of persons acting as chief support of an institution, movement, etc. *v.t.* To support with or as with pillars; to furnish or adorn with pillars. **pillar-box,** *n.* A short hollow pillar in which letters may be placed for collection by the post office. **pillared,** *a.* **pillaret,** *n.*

pillau [PILAU]. ***piller** [PILL (2)].

pillion (pil′ i ŏn) [prob. through Celt. (cp. Gael. *pillean*, *pillin*), from L. *pellis*, skin], *n.* A low light saddle for a woman; a cushion for a person, usu. a woman, to ride on behind a person on horseback or on a motor-cycle.

pillory (pil′ ŏ ri) [M.E. *pillori*, O.F. *pellori* (F. *pilori*), etym. unknown], *n.* A wooden frame supported on a pillar and furnished with holes through which the head and hands of a person were put, so as to expose him to public derision (abolished in 1837). *v.t.* To set in the pillory; (*fig.*) to hold up to ridicule or execration. **pillorize,** *v.t.*

pillow (pil′ ō) [A.-S. *pyle*, *pylu* (cp. Dut. *peluw*, G. *pfühl*), L. *pulvīnus*], *n.* A cushion filled with feathers or other soft material, used as a rest for the head of a person reclining, esp. in bed; (*Mach.*) a block used as a cushion or support; (*Naut.*) the block on which the inner end of the bowsprit rests. *v.t.* To lay or rest on a pillow; to prop up with a pillow or pillows. *v.i.* To rest on a pillow. ***pillow-bere,** *n.* A pillow-case. **pillow-block,** *n.* A metal block or case supporting the end of a revolving shaft, with a movable cover for allowing adjustment of the bearings. **pillow-case, -slip,** *n.* A washable cover of linen, etc., for drawing over a pillow. **pillowy,** *a.*

pill-worm, pillwort [PILL (1)].

pilocarpus (pī lŏ kar′ pŭs) [Gr. *pilos*, wool, *karpos*, fruit], *n.* (*Bot.*) A genus of tropical American shrubs comprising the jaborandi. **pilocarpene** (-pēn), *n.* A volatile oil obtained from this. **pilocarpine** (-pīn), *n.* (*Chem.*) A white crystalline or amorphous alkaloid from the same source.

pilose, -lous (pī' lōs, -lŭs) [L. *pilōsus*, from *pilus*, hair], *a.* Covered with or consisting of hairs. **pilosity** (-los' i ti), *n.*

pilot (pī' lŏt) [F. *pillotte* (now *pilote*), It. *pilota*, perh. corr. of *pedota*, prob. from Gr. *pēdon*, rudder], *n.* A steersman, esp. one qualified to conduct ships into or out of harbour or along particular coasts, channels, etc.; a person directing the course of an aeroplane, airship, etc.; (*fig.*) a guide, a director, esp. in difficult or dangerous circumstances. *v.t.* To act as pilot or to direct the course of (a ship, etc.). **pilot balloon:** (*Meteor.*) A small, free hydrogen-filled balloon sent up to obtain the direction and velocity of the upper winds. **pilot-bird,** *n.* (*Zool.*) A bird found in the vicinity of the Caribbean Islands whose appearance indicates to seamen that they are near land; (*Austral.*) a sweet-toned scrub bird. **pilot-boat,** *n.* A boat in which pilots cruise off the shore to meet incoming ships. **pilot-cloth,** *n.* A heavy blue woollen cloth for seamen's wear. **pilot-engine,** *n.* A locomotive sent in advance to clear the line for a train. **pilot-fish,** *n.* A small sea-fish, *Naucrates ductor*, said to act as guide to sharks. **pilot-jacket,** *n.* A pea-jacket. **pilot-jet,** *n.* (*Motor.*) An auxilliary jet in a carburettor for starting and slow-going. **pilot light:** A small jet of gas kept burning in order to light a cooker, geyser, etc.; (*Radio.*) a small light on the dial of a wireless that goes on when the current is switched on. **pilot officer,** *n.* A junior commissioned rank in the R.A.F. corresponding to second lieutenant in the Army. **pilot scheme:** A scheme on a small scale that helps to develop a larger scheme. **pilotage,** *n.* **pilotism, pilotry,** *n.* **pilotless,** *a.* **pilotless plane,** *n.* (*Aviat.*) A jet-propelled aeroplane, often carrying a charge of high explosive, which travels without a pilot and is kept to a pre-arranged course by gyroscopic devices.

pilous [PILOSE].

pilularia (pil ū lâr' i ȧ) [mod. L., as foll.], *n.* (*Bot.*) A genus of aquatic plants growing near the margins of lakes and pools, the pillworts.

pilule (pil' ūl) [L. *pilula*], *n.* A pill, esp. a small pill. **pilular, pilulous,** *a.*

pilum (pī' lŭm) [L.], *n.* (*pl.* **-la**) The heavy javelin used by the ancient Roman infantry.

pimelode (pim' ė lōd) [Gr. *pīmelōdēs*, from *pīmelē*, fat], *n.* A catfish of the genus *Pimelodus*.

***piment** (pi ment') [O.F., as PIGMENT], *n.* A drink made of wine mixed with spice or honey.

pimento (pi men' tō) [Port. *pimenta* (cp. Sp. *pimienta*), L. *pigmentum*, as prec.], *n.* The dried unripe aromatic berries of a W. Indian tree, allspice; the tree itself.

pimp (pimp) [etym. doubtful, cp. F. *pimpant*, spruce, attractive, seductive], *n.* A procurer, a pander. *v.i.* To pander.

pimpernel (pim' per nėl) [O.F. *pimprenele* (F. *pimprenelle*), med. L. *pipinella*, perh. corr. of *bipinnella*, dim. of *bipennula*, dim. of *bipennis* (BI-, *penna*, feather)], *n.* A plant of the genus *Anagallis* belonging to the family *Primulaceæ*, esp. the common red pimpernel, a small annual found in sandy fields, etc., with scarlet flowers that close in dark or rainy weather.

pimping (pim' ping) [etym. doubtful], *a.* Small, puny; feeble, sickly.

pimple (pim' pėl) [etym. doubtful], *n.* A small tumour, pustule, or inflamed swelling on the skin. **pimpled, -ply,** *a.*

pin (pin) [A.-S. *pinn* (cp. Dut. and G. *pin*, *pinne*, Icel. *pinni*, Norw. and Swed. *pinne*)], *n.* A short, slender, pointed piece of wood, metal, etc., used for fastening parts of clothing, papers, etc., together; a peg or bolt of metal or wood used for various purposes, as the bolt of a lock, a thole, a peg to which the strings of a musical instrument are fastened, a hairpin, a ninepin, etc.; an ornamental device with a pin used as a fastening, etc., or as a decoration for the person; a keg or small cask of 4½ gallons; (*pl.*, *slang.*) legs; (*fig.*) anything of slight value. *v.t.* (*past & p.p.* **pinned**) To fasten (to, on, up, etc.) with or as with a pin; to pierce, to transfix; to seize, to make fast, to secure; to enclose; to bind (down) to a promise or obligation. **don't care a pin:** Don't care in the slightest. **on one's pins:** In good condition. **pins and needles:** A tingling sensation as when a limb has been 'asleep.' **to pin one's faith to** or **on:** To place full reliance upon. **pin-case,** *n.* **pincushion,** *n.* A small cushion for sticking pins into. **pin-dust,** *n.* Small particles of metal rubbed off in pointing pins. **pin-feather,** *n.* An incipient feather. **pin-feathered,** *a.* **pin-fire,** *n.* A mechanism for discharging fire-arms by driving a pin into the fulminate in a cartridge. *a.* Fired or exploded with this. **pin-footed** [FIN-FOOTED]. **pin-head,** *n.* The head of a pin; (*fig.*) a very small object. **pin-hole,** *n.* A very small aperture; a hole into which a pin or peg fits. **pin-maker,** *n.* **pin-money,** *n.* An allowance of money by a husband to his wife for dress or other private expenses. **pin-point,** *n.* The point of a pin; (*fig.*) anything sharp, painful, or critical; *v.t.* To locate accurately and precisely. **pin-prick,** *n.* A prick or minute puncture with or as with a pin; a petty annoyance. *v.t.* To prick with or as with a pin; (*fig.*) to molest with petty insults or annoyances. **pin-table,** *n.* A game in the form of a penny-in-the-slot apparatus in which balls are shot on to a table and must fall back past various pins or holes. **pintail,** *n.* A duck, *Dafila acuta*, with a pointed tail; applied also to some species of grouse. **pintail-duck,** *n.* **pin-up girl:** A girl whose face or figure is so attractive to a soldier, etc., that he pins her photograph on the wall of his quarters. **pin-wheel,** *n.* A wheel with pins set in the face instead of cogs in the rim; a small catherine-wheel. **pin-worm,** *n.* A small threadworm.

piña (pē' nyȧ) [Sp. from L. *pīnea*, pine-cone], *n.* *A pine-apple; pina-cloth. **pina-cloth, -muslin,** *n.* A delicate cloth made in the Philippines from the fibres of the pine-apple leaf.

pinafore (pin' ȧ fôr) [PIN, AFORE], *n.* A sleeveless apron worn by children and women to protect the front of the dress. **pinafored,** *a.*

pinaster (pī năs' tėr) [L., wild pine], *n.* A pine, *Pinus pinaster*, indigenous to the Mediterranean regions of Europe.

pinatype process (pin ȧ tīp prō' ses), *n.* (*Phot.*) A colour process in which prints are made on glass coated with bichromated gelatine.

pince-nez (pa*n*s' nā) [F., pinch-nose, see PINCH], *n.* A pair of eye-glasses held in place by a spring clipping the nose.

pincers (pin' sėrz) [M.E. *pynsors*, *pinsours*], *n.pl.* A tool with two limbs working on a pivot as levers to a pair of jaws, for gripping, crushing, extracting nails, etc.; (*Zool.*) a nipping or grasping organ, as in crustaceans.

pincette (pa*n* set') [F. dim. of *pince*, pincers, see PINCH]. *n.* A pair of tweezers or forceps.

pinch (pinch) [O.North.F. *pinchier* (F. *pincer*), etym. doubtful], *v.t.* To nip or squeeze; to press so as to cause pain or inconvenience; to grip, to bite (of animals); to take off or remove by nipping or squeezing; (*fig.*) to afflict, to distress, esp. with cold, hunger, etc.; to straiten, to stint; to extort, to squeeze (from or out of); (*Racing*) to urge (a horse); (*Naut.*) to steer (a ship) close-hauled; (*colloq.*) to steal, to rob, to arrest, to take into custody. *v.i.* To nip or squeeze anything; (*fig.*) to be niggardly; to be straitened; to cavil. *n.* A sharp nip or squeeze, as with the ends of the fingers; as much as can be taken up between the finger and thumb; (*fig.*) a pain, a pang; distress, straits, a dilemma, stress, pressure. **at a pinch:** In an urgent case; if hard pressed. **pinch-commons, -fist,**

-penny, *n.* A niggard; one who stints his own and other people's allowances. **pincher,** *n.* **pinchers** [PINCERS]. **pinchingly,** *adv.* Sparingly, stingily.

pinchbeck (pinch' bek) [Christopher *Pinchbeck* (*c.* 1670–1732), inventor], *n.* An alloy of copper, zinc, etc., formerly used for cheap jewellery; (*fig.*) anything specious and spurious.

pincushion [PIN].

Pindari (pin da' ri) [Hind.], *n.* A mounted marauder employed as an irregular soldier by native princes in Central India during the 17th and 18th centuries.

Pindaric (pin dăr' ik), *a.* Pertaining to or in the style of Pindar, the Greek lyric poet. *n.* (*usu. pl.*) Applied to odes, metres, etc., of an irregular kind, more or less resembling the style of Pindar. **pindarism** (pin' dă rizm), *n.*

***pinder** (pin' dėr) [obs. *pind*, A.-S. *pyndan*, to shut up (cp. POUND (2)), -ER], *n.* A pound-keeper, an officer appointed by a parish, etc., to impound stray beasts.

pine (1) (pīn) [A.-S. *pīn*, L. *pīnus*], *n.* Any tree of the coniferous genus *Pinus*, consisting of evergreen trees with needle-shaped leaves; timber from various coniferous trees; a pine-apple. **pine-apple,** *n.* The large multiple fruit of the ananas, so-called from its resemblance to a pine-cone. **pinery,** *n.* A hot-house in which pine-apples are grown; a plantation of pine-trees. **pine-barren,** *n.* (*Am.*) A tract of sandy land producing only pines. **pine-beauty, -carpet,** *n.* Moths destructive to Scotch firs. **pine-beetle, -chafer,** *n.* A beetle feeding on pine-leaves. **pine-clad, -covered,** *a.* **pine-marten,** *n.* A European marten, *Mustela martes.* **pine-needle,** *n.* The needle-shaped leaf of the pine. **pine-oil,** *n.* **pinetum** (pī nē' tŭm), *n.* A plantation of pine-trees. **piny,** *a.*

pine (2) (pīn) [A.-S. *pīnian*, to torture, from *pīn*, torment, pain], ****v.t.*** To afflict with suffering; to torment; to spend (time, etc.) in pining. *v.i.* To languish, to waste away; to long or yearn (for, etc.); *to starve, to waste away from hunger. **n.* Pain, suffering; famine, want.

pineal (pin' ė-, pī' nė ăl) [F. *pinéal* (L. *pīnea*, pine-cone, -AL)], *a.* Shaped like a pine-cone. **pineal eye:** A rudimentary eye, perhaps originally connected with the pineal gland, found between the brain and the parietal foramen in many lizards. **pineal gland:** A dark-grey conical structure of unknown function situated behind the third ventricle of the brain, thought by Descartes to be the seat of the soul.

pine-apple, pinery, etc. [PINE (1)].

pin-feather, etc. [PIN].

pinfold (pin' fōld) [A.-S. *punfald* (POUND (2), FOLD (1))], *n.* A pound in which stray cattle are shut up; *(*fig.*) a narrow enclosure. *v.t.* To shut up in a pound.

ping (ping) [imit.], *n.* A sharp ringing sound as of a bullet flying through the air. *v.i.* To make such a sound; to fly with such a sound. **ping-pong,** *n.* An indoor game analogous to lawn-tennis, played with light bats and celluloid balls, usu. over a table.

pingao (ping ga' ō) [Maori], *n.* A N. Zealand plant with a stem like thick cord.

pingle (ping' gėl) [North., etym. doubtful], *v.t.* To worry, to trouble. *v.i.* To dally, to dawdle; to nibble, to eat with feeble appetite.

pinguid (ping' gwid) [L. *pinguis*, fat], *a.* Fat, oily, greasy, unctuous. ***pinguefy,** *v.t.* To make fat. ***pinguescent** (ping gwes' ėnt), *a.* Growing fat. ***pinguescence,** *n.* **Pinguicula** (-gwik' ū lă), (*Bot.*) A genus of bog-plants, the butterworts. **pinguidity** (-gwid' i ti), **pinguitude** (ping' gwi tūd), *n.*

pinguin (ping' gwin) [etym. unknown], *n.* A W. Indian plant of the pine-apple family with a fleshy fruit.

pinion (1) (pin' yŏn) [O.F. *pignon*, L. *penna*, var. *pinna*, feather, wing], *n.* A wing-feather; a wing; the joint of a bird's wing remotest from the body. *v.t.* To cut off the first joint of the wing to prevent flight; to shackle, to fetter the arms of; to bind (the arms, etc.); to bind fast (to).

pinion (2) (pin' yŏn) [F. *pignon*, O.F. *pinon*, *penon*, L. *pinna*, pinnacle, gable, cp. prec.], *n.* The smaller of two cog-wheels in gear with each other; a cogged spindle or arbor engaging with a wheel.

pink (1) (pingk) [etym. doubtful], *n.* A plant or flower of the genus *Dianthus*, largely cultivated in gardens; applied to several allied or similar plants; a pale rose colour or pale red slightly inclining towards purple, from the garden pink; (*fig.*) the supreme excellence, the very height (of); (*Hunting*) a fox-hunter's scarlet coat; (*fig.*) a fox-hunter. *a.* Of the colour of the garden pink, pale red or rose. **in the pink:** In fine condition. **pink-eye,** *n.* A contagious influenza among horses, cattle and sheep, characterized by inflammation of the conjunctiva; a form of ophthalmia in man; the herb *Spigelia Marilandica* and other N. American plants. **pink-wood,** *n.* (*Austral.*) A Tasmanian tree with wood of that colour. **pinking,** *ger.* (*Motor.*) Knocking caused by premature explosion. **pinkiness,** *n.* **pinkish,** *a.* **pinkness,** *n.* **pinky,** *a.*

pink (2) (pingk) [M.E. *pinken* (cp. L.G. *pinken*, also PICK (1) F. *piquer*)], *v.t.* To pierce, to stab; to make small round holes in for ornament; to decorate in this manner. **pinking-iron,** *n.*

***pink** (3) (pingk) [M.Dut. *pinke* (now *pink*), etym. doubtful], *n.* A sailing-ship with a very narrow stern, used chiefly in the Mediterranean.

pink (4) (pingk) [etym. unknown], *n.* A yellow pigment obtained from quercitron bark or other vegetable sources. **Dutch, French,** and **Italian pink:** Various yellow pigments.

***pink** (5) (pingk) [etym. doubtful, cp. Dut. *pink ooghen*, pink eye], *a.* Small; winking, half-shut. ***pink-eyed,** *a.*

pinkie (ping' ki), *n.* (*Sc.*) The little finger.

pinna (pin' ȧ) [L., feather, wing, fin], *n.* (*pl.* **-næ**) (*Bot.*) A leaflet of a pinnate leaf; (*Zool.*) a wing; a fin, or analogous structure; (*Anat.*) the projecting upper part of the external ear.

pinnace (pin' ȧs) [F. *pinasse*, prob. ult. from L. *pīnus*, PINE (1)], *n.* A man-of-war's boat with six or eight oars; *a small schooner-rigged vessel provided with sweeps.

pinnacle (pin' ȧ kėl) [O.F. *pinacle*, late L. *pinnăculum*, dim. of PINNA], *n.* A turret, usu. pointed or tapering, placed as an ornament on the top of a buttress, etc., or as a termination on an angle or gable; (*fig.*) a pointed summit; the apex, the culmination (of). *v.t.* To furnish with pinnacles; to set on or as on a pinnacle; to surmount as a pinnacle.

pinnate, -nated (pin' ăt, -ā tėd) [L. *pinnātus*, from PINNA], *a.* (*Bot.*) Having leaflets arranged featherwise along the stem; divided into leaflets; (*Zool.*) having lateral processes along an axis. **pinnately,** *adv.* **pinnatifid** (pi năt' i fid), *a.* (*Bot.*) Divided into lobes nearly to the midrib. **pinnatiped,** *a.* (*Zool.*) Fin-footed, having the toes bordered by membranes. **pinnatisect,** *a.* (*Bot.*) Having the lobes of a pinnate leaf cleft to the midrib. **pinnato-,** *comb. form.*

pinner (pin' ėr) [PIN, -ER], *n.* One who pins (*usu. in pl.*); a cap or coif with the lappets or laps pinned on; a pin-maker; (*prov.*) a pinafore.

pinnigrade (pin' i grăd) [L. *pinni-* PINNA, *-gradus*, walking], *a.* (*Zool.*) Walking by means of fins or flippers. *n.* A pinnigrade animal. **pinniped** (pin' i pėd) [L. *pes pedis*, foot], *a.* Having feet like fins. *n.* Any individual of the *Pinnipedia*, a group of marine carnivora containing the seals, sea-lions, and walruses.

pinnock (pin' ŏk) [etym. doubtful], *n.* (*prov.*) A hedge-sparrow; a titmouse.

pinnule (pin' ūl) [L. *pinnula*, dim. of PINNA], *n.* (*Bot.*) One of the smaller or ultimate divisions of a pinnate leaf; (*Zool.*) a small fin, fin-ray, wing, barb of a feather, etc. **pinnulate, -lated,** *a.* (*Bot.*) **pinnulet,** *n.*

pinny (*childish*) [PINAFORE].

pinole (pi nō′ lā, pi nōl′) [Am.-Sp., from Aztec *pinolli*], *n.* (*Am.*) Meal made from maize, mesquit-beans, etc., a common article of food in California and Mexico.

pint (pīnt) [F. *pinte*, perh. through Sp. *pinta*, from late L. *pincta, picta*, fem. p.p. of *pingere* to paint], *n.* A measure of capacity, the eighth part of a gallon or 34·659 cub. in.

pintado (pin ta′ dō) [Port. or Sp., p.p. of *pintar*, ult. from L. *pingere* (p.p. *pinctus, pictus*), to PAINT], *n.* A species of petrel; a guinea-fowl; *chintz. **pintado-bird:** The pintado petrel.

pintail [PIN]. **pin-table** [PIN].

pintle (pin′ tėl) [A.-S. *pintel*, penis, etym. doubtful], *n.* A pin or bolt, esp. one used as a pivot; one of the pins on which a rudder swings.

pin-wheel, etc. [PIN]. **piny** [PINE (1)].

pinxit (pingk′ sit) [L.], *v.t.* (He or she) painted it (in the signature to a picture).

piolet (pyō′ lā) [F. Savoy dial., dim. of *pialo*, prob. rel. to *pioche*, from *pic*, see PIKE (1)], *n.* A climber's ice-axe.

***pioned,** *a.* (*Shak.*) Dug, trenched (?).

pioneer (pī ȯ nēr′) [F. *pionnier*, from *pion*, PAWN (1)], *n.* One of a body of soldiers whose duty it is to clear and repair roads, bridges, etc., for troops on the march; (*fig.*) one who goes before to prepare or clear the way; an explorer; an early leader. *v.t.* To prepare the way for; to act as pioneer to; to lead, to conduct.

piopio (pē′ ō pē′ ō) [Maori], *n.* The New Zealand thrush.

pious (pī′ ůs) [L. *pius*, orig. dutiful], *a.* Reverencing God; religious, devout; feeling or exhibiting filial affection; dutiful. **pious fraud:** A deception in the interests of religion or of the person deceived. **pious-minded,** *a.* **piously,** *adv.*

pip (1) (pip) [prob. from M.Dut. *pippe*, ult. from pop. L. *pipita*, corr. of *pītuīta*], *n.* A disease in poultry, etc., consisting in a secretion of thick mucus in the throat; applied facetiously to various human disorders. **to have** or **get the pip:** (*slang*) To be out of sorts or dejected.

pip (2) (pip) [prob. from PIPPIN], *n.* The seed of an apple, orange, etc. **pipless,** *a.*

pip (3) (pip) [formerly *peep*, etym. doubtful], *n.* A spot on a playing-card, domino, die, etc.; one of the segments on the rind of a pine-apple; a small flower in a clustered inflorescence, etc.

pip (4) (pip) [perh. from PIP (2)], *v.t.* (*past & p.p.* **pipped**) (*slang*) To blackball; to beat; to hit with a shot.

pip (5) (pip) [perh. var. of PEEP (1), or imit.], *v.i.* To chirp, as a bird. *v.t.* To break through (the shell) in hatching. *n.* A short, high-pitched sound.

pip (6) (pip), *n.* Signallers' name for letter P. **pip-emma,** *n.* p.m., afternoon.

pipe (pīp) [A.-S. *pipe* (cp. Dut. *pijp*, G. *pfeife*, Icel. *pīpa*), late L. *pīpa*, from L. *pīpāre*, to chirp], *n.* A long hollow tube or line of tubes, esp. for conveying liquids, gas, etc.; a musical wind-instrument formed of a tube; a boatswain's whistle; a signal on this; a tube producing a note of a particular tone in an organ; a tubular organ, vessel, passage, etc., in an animal body; the windpipe; (*fig.*) the voice, esp. in singing; a shrill note or cry of a bird, etc.; a tube with a bowl for smoking tobacco; a pipeful (of tobacco); a large cask for wine; this used as a measure of capacity, usu. 150 gallons; a vein containing ore or extraneous matter penetrating rock; *the pipe-office in the Exchequer; (*pl.*) a bagpipe. *v.t.* To play or execute on a pipe; to whistle; to utter in a shrill tone; to lend or bring (along or to) by playing or whistling on a pipe; to call or direct by a boatswain's pipe or whistle; to furnish with pipes; to propagate (pinks) by slips from the parent stem; to trim or decorate with piping. *v.i.* To play on a pipe; to whistle, to make a shrill high-pitched sound. **to pipe down:** To become subdued. **pipe of peace:** A pipe smoked in token of peace, a calumet. **to pipe one's eye:** (*slang*) To weep. **to pipe up:** To begin to sing; to sing the first notes of. **pipe-clay,** *n.* A fine, white, plastic clay used for making tobacco-pipes, and for cleaning military accoutrements, etc.; (*fig.*) excessive regard for correctness of dress, drill, etc. *v.t.* To whiten with pipe-clay. **pipe-dream,** *n.* A fantastic notion, a castle in the air. **pipe-fish,** *n.* A fish of the family *Syngnathidæ*, from their elongated form. **pipe-light,** *n.* A spill for lighting tobacco-pipes. **pipe-line,** *n.* A long pipe or conduit laid down from an oil-well, or oil region, to convey the petroleum to a port, etc. **pipe-major,** *n.* (*Mil.*) Non-commissioned officer in charge of pipers. ***Pipe-office,** *n.* The office of the Exchequer which dealt with the Pipe-roll. **pipe-rack,** *n.* A stand for tobacco-pipes. **Pipe-roll,** *n.* The great roll of the Exchequer containing the pipes or annual accounts of sheriffs and other officers. **pipe-stone,** *n.* A hard stone used by the N. American Indians for making tobacco-pipes. **pipe-tree,** *n.* The syringa; the lilac. ***pipe-wine,** *n.* Wine from the pipe or cask. **pipeful,** *n.* **pipeless,** *a.* **piper,** *n.* One who plays upon a pipe, esp. a strolling player or a performer on the bagpipes; a broken-winded horse; a dog used to lure birds into a decoy-pipe. **to pay the piper** [PAY (1)]. **pipy,** *a.*

piperaceous (pī pėr ā′ shůs) [L. *piper*, PEPPER, -ACEOUS], *a.* **piperic** (pi per′ ik), *a.* Pertaining to or derived from pepper. **piperine** (pip′ ėr īn), *n.* (*Chem.*) An alkaloid obtained from black pepper.

pipette (pi pet′) [F., dim. of PIPE], *n.* A fine tube for removing small quantities of a fluid, esp. in chemical investigations.

pipi (pī′ pi) [Tupi-Guarani *pipai*], *n.* A tropical American plant, *Cæsalpinia pipai*, with astringent pods used for tanning; the pod, also called **pipi-pod.**

piping (pī′ ping), *n.* The action of one who pipes; a shrill whistling or wailing sound; a fluting; a covered cord for trimming dresses; a cord-like decoration of sugar, etc., on a cake; a quantity, series, or system of pipes. *a.* Playing upon a pipe; shrill, whistling. **piping hot:** Hissing hot; (*fig.*) fresh, newly out. **piping times:** Merry, prosperous times.

pipistrelle (pip′ is trel) [F., from It. *pipistrello*, ult. from L. *vespertilio*, from *vesper*, evening], *n.* A small, reddish-brown bat, *Vesperugo pipistrellus*, the commonest British kind.

pipit (pip′ it) [prob. imit. of the cry], *n.* A lark-like bird belonging to the genus *Anthus*.

pipkin (pip′ kin) [etym. doubtful], *n.* A small earthen pot, pan, or jar.

pippin (pip′ in) [O.F. *pepin*, pip or seed, etym. doubtful], *n.* A name for several varieties of apples.

pippy (1) (pip′ i) [PIP (2 and 1), -Y], *a.* Full of pips; (*slang*) shaky, unsteady (esp. of the prices of stocks).

pippy (2) (pip′ ē) [Maori], *n.* A small N. Zealand shellfish; a sand-worm.

pipy [PIPE].

piquant (pē′ kånt) [F., as foll], *a.* (*fem.* **-ante**) Having an agreeably sharp, pungent taste; (*fig.*) interesting, stimulating, racy, lively, sparkling. **piquancy,** *n.* **piquantly,** *adv.*

pique (1) (pēk) [F. *piquer*, to prick, see PIKE (1)], *v.t.* To irritate; to touch the envy, jealousy, or pride of; to stimulate or excite (curiosity, etc.); to plume or value (oneself on). *n.* Ill-feeling, irritation, resentment.

pique (2) (pēk) [F. *pic*, etym. doubtful], *n.* (*Piquet*) The scoring of 30 points before one's opponent begins to count, entitling one to 30 more points. *v.t.* To score this against. *v.i.* To score a pique.

piqué (pē′ kā) [F., p.p. of *piquer*, see PIQUE (1)], *n.* A heavy cotton fabric with a corded surface, quilting.

piquet (1) (pi ket′, pik′ ėt) [F., etym. doubtful], *n.* A game of cards for two persons, with a pack of cards from which all below the sevens have been withdrawn. ***piquet** (2) [PICKET].

piracy (pī′ rȧ si), *n.* The crime of a pirate; robbery on the high seas; unauthorized publication; infringement of copyright.

piragua (pi răg′ wȧ) [Sp., from Carib., dug-out], *n.* A long narrow boat or canoe made from one or two trunks hollowed out, a dug-out; a pirogue.

pirate (pī′ rȧt) [F., from L. *pīrāta*, Gr. *peiratēs*, from *peiran*, to attempt], *n.* A robber on the high seas; a piratical ship; a marauder; (*fig.*) one who infringes the copyright of another; (*colloq.*) an omnibus that runs on the recognized routes of others or overcharges passengers. *v.i.* To practise piracy. *v.t.* To plunder; to publish (literary or other matter belonging to others) without permission or compensation. **piratic, -al** (pī răt′ ik, -ȧl), *a.* **piratically,** *adv.*

piraya (pi ra′ yȧ) [Tupi-Guarani *piraya*], *n.* A voracious fish, *Serrasalmo piraya*, of tropical S. American rivers.

piriform [PYRIFORM].

pirn (pĕrn) [Sc., etym. doubtful], *n.* A bobbin, reel, or spool; as much as a pirn will take (of yarn, etc.). **pirnie,** *n.* A woollen nightcap, usu. striped.

pirogue (pi rōg′) [F., as PIRAGUA], *n.* A large canoe formed of a hollowed trunk of a tree; a large flat-bottomed boat or barge for shallow water, usu. with two masts rigged fore-and-aft.

pirouette (pir u et′) [F., a whirligig, a top (cp. It. *piruolo*, top)], *n.* A rapid whirling round on the point of one foot, in dancing; a sudden short turn of a horse. *v.i.* To dance or perform a pirouette.

piscatory (pis′ kȧ tȯr i) [L. *piscātōrius*, from *piscātor*, fisher, from foll.], *a.* Pertaining to fishers or fishing. **piscatorial** (pis kȧ tôr′ i ȧl), *a.* Piscatory; fond of or pertaining to angling. **piscary** (pis′ kȧ ri), *n.* (*Law*) Right of fishing. **common of piscary:** The right of fishing in another person's waters, in common with the owner and sometimes with others.

Pisces (pis′ ēz) [L., pl. of *piscis*, fish], *n.pl.* The Fishes, the twelfth sign of the zodiac. **pisciculture** (pis′ i kŭl tyůr) [CULTURE], *n.* The artificial breeding, rearing, and preserving of fish. **piscicultural** (-kŭl′ tyů rȧl), *a.* **pisciculturist,** *n.* **pisciform,** *a.*

piscina (pi sē′-, -sī′ nȧ) [L., as prec.], *n.* (*pl.* **-nas, -næ**) (*Eccles.*) A stone basin with outlet beside the altar in some churches to receive the water used in purifying the chalice, etc.; (*Rom. Ant.*) a fish-pond; a bathing pond. ***piscinal** (pis′ i nȧl), *a.*

piscine (pis′ īn) [as prec.], *a.* Of or pertaining to fish. **piscivorous** (pi siv′ ȯ rŭs) [-VOROUS], *a.* Living on fish.

pisé (pē′ zā) [F. p.p. of *piser*, L. *pīnsāre*, to pound], *n.* A mode of forming walls of rammed clay; rammed clay forming a wall.

pish (pish) [instinctive sound], *int.* An exclamation expressing contempt, disgust, etc., pshaw. *v.i.* To express contempt by saying 'pish.'

pishogue (pi shōg′) [Ir. *píseog*], *n.* Sorcery, witchery or enchantment of a sinister kind.

pisiform (pī′ si-, pīz′ i fŏrm) [L. *pisum*, pea, -FORM], *a.* Pea-shaped.

pisky [PIXY].

pismire (pis′ mīr) [PISS (with alln. to smell of an ant-hill), obs. *mire*, ant (cp. Dut. *mier*, E.Fris. *mīre*)], *n.* An ant, an emmet.

pisolite (piz′ ȯ-, pī′ sȯ līt) [Gr. *pisos*, pea, -LITE], *n.* (*Min.*) A variety of calcite made up of pea-like concretions. **pisolitic** (-lit′ ik), *a.*

piss (pis) [O.F. *pissier* (F. *pisser*), prob. imit.], *n.* Urine. *v.i.* To discharge urine. *v.t.* To discharge in the urine; to wet with urine. **pissabed,** *n.* (*prov.*) The dandelion. **pissed,** *a.* (*vulg.*) Drunk.

pissasphalt (pis′ ȧs fȧlt) [L. *pissasphaltus*, Gr. *pissaphaltos* (*pissa*, pitch, ASPHALT)], *n.* Mineral tar.

pistachio (pis tā′-, -ta′ shi-, -tăch′ ō) [It. *pistacchio* or Sp. *pistacho*, L. *pistācium*, Gr. *pistakion*], *n.* The nut of a W. Asiatic tree, *Pistacia vera*, with a pale greenish kernel; the flavour of this. **pistachio-nut,** *n.*

***pistareen** (pis tȧ rēn′) [from PESETA], *n.* (*Am. and W. Ind.*) A former Spanish silver coin, value 9d. *a.* (*fig.*) Petty, paltry.

pistil (pis′ til) [L. *pistillum*, PESTLE], *n.* (*Bot.*) The female organ in flowering plants, comprising the ovary and stigma, usu. with a style supporting the latter. ***pistillaceous** (-lā′ shůs), **pistillary** (pis′ til ȧr i), **pistillate,** *a.* **pistilliferous** (-lif′ ėr ůs), **pistilline** (pis′ til īn), *a.*

pistol (pis′ tȯl) [F. *pistole*, from *pistolet*, pistol, orig. dagger, It. *pistolese*, dagger, from *Pistoja*, where made], *n.* A small fire-arm for use with one hand. *v.t.* (*past & p.p.* **pistolled**) To shoot with a pistol. **pistol-shot,** *n.* The range of this. **pistoleer, *-ier** (pis tō lēr′), *n.* **pistolet,** *n.* **pistolgraph** [-GRAPH], *n.* A photographic apparatus operated like a pistol, for instantaneous work.

***pistole** (pis tōl′) [F., prob. from *pistolet*, perh. as prec.], *n.* A foreign gold coin formerly current, esp. a 16th- and 17th-cent. Spanish coin worth about 18s.

piston (pis′ tȯn) [F., from It. *pistone*, var. of *pestone*, pestle, cogn. with *pestare*, from late L. *pistāre*, freq. of *pinsere*, to pound, see PESTLE], *n.* A device fitted to occupy the sectional area of a tube and be driven to and fro by alternating pressure on its faces, so as to impart or receive motion, as in a steam-engine or a pump; a valve in a musical wind-instrument; (*Motor.*) a plunger which passes on the working pressure of the burning gases via the connecting rod to the crankshaft. **piston-ring,** *n.* (*Mach.*) A split ring encircling the piston in a groove. **piston-rod,** *n.* A rod attaching a piston to machinery. **piston-slap,** *n.* (*Mach.*) A noise caused by the piston fitting too loosely in the cylinder.

pit (pit) [A.-S. *pytt* (cp. Dut. *put*, G. *pfütze*), L. *puteus*, well], *n.* A natural or artificial hole in the ground, esp. one of considerable depth in proportion to its width; one made in order to obtain minerals or for industrial or agricultural operations; a coal mine; a hole dug and covered over as a trap for wild animals or enemies; an abyss; hell; a hollow or depression in the surface of the ground, of the body, etc.; a hollow scar, esp. one left by smallpox; the ground floor of the auditorium in a theatre, esp. behind the stalls; the part of an audience occupying this; an area for cock-fighting, a cockpit; (*fig.*) a trap, a snare. *v.t.* (*past & p.p.* **pitted**) To put into a pit, esp. for storage; to mark with pits or hollow scars, as with smallpox (*usu. in p.p.*); to match (against) in a pit; (*fig.*) to match, to set in competition (against). **the pit:** The grave; hell; the wheat market at Chicago. **pit-coal,** *n.* Mineral coal. **pitfall,** *n.* A pit slightly covered so that animals may fall in; a trap; (*fig.*) a hidden danger. **pit-hole,** *n.* A pit-like cavity, a pit; (*fig.*) the grave. **pit-man,** *n.* One who works in a pit, a collier. **pit-saw,** *n.* A large saw worked in a sawpit by two men. **pit-sawyer,** *n.* The sawyer who works in the pit, opposed to top-sawyer. **pitting,** *n.* (*Motor.*) The uneven wearing of valve-seatings and other surfaces.

pit-a-pat (pit′ ȧ păt) [imit.], *n.* A tapping, a flutter, a palpitation. *adv.* With this sound, palpitatingly, falteringly.

pitau (pē′ tou) [Maori], *n.* A tree-fern of N. Zealand.

pitch (1) (pich) [A.-S. *pic*, from L. *pix picis* (cp. Dut. *pek*, G. *pech*, Icel. *bik*)], *n.* A dark-brown or black resinous substance obtained from tar, turpentine, and some oils, used for caulking, paving roads, etc. *v.t.* To cover, coat, line, or smear with pitch. **pitch-black,** *a.* Brownish black; as dark as pitch. **pitch-blende,** *n.* Native oxide of uranium, the chief source of radium. **pitch-cap,** *n.* A cap lined with pitch, used as an instrument of torture. **pitch-dark,** *a.* As dark as pitch, very dark. **pitch-darkness,** *n.* **pitch-pine,** *n.* A highly resinous pine, *Abies picea*, much used for woodwork. **pitchstone,** *n.* A brittle vitreous volcanic rock almost identical with obsidian.

pitch (2) (pich) [M.E. *pichen, pykken*, etym. doubtful, perh. rel. to PICK (1)], *v.t.* To fix or plant in the ground; to fix; to set in orderly arrangement, to fix in position; to throw, to fling, esp. with an upward heave or underhand swing; to toss (hay) with a fork; to pave with cobbles or setts; to expose for sale; (*Mus.*) to set to a particular pitch or keynote; (*colloq.*) to put or relate in a particular way; (*Base-ball, etc.*) to deliver or throw (the ball) to the batsman; (*Golf*) to strike (the ball) with a lofted club. *v.i.* To encamp; to light, to settle; to plunge, to fall; to fall headlong; to plunge at the bow or stern, as opposed to rolling. *n.* The act of pitching; mode of pitching; the delivery of the ball in various games; height, degree, intensity; extreme height, extreme point; point or degree of elevation or depression; degree of inclination or steepness; degree of slope in a roof; the place or station taken up by a person for buying and selling, residence, etc.; (*Cricket*) the place in which the wickets are placed or the distance between them; (*Mech.*) the lineal distance between points, etc., arranged in series, as between teeth on the pitch-line of a cog-wheel, etc., between floats on a paddle-wheel, between successive convolutions of the thread of a screw, etc.; (*Mus.*) the degree of acuteness or gravity of a tone. **to queer the pitch:** To spoil a plan, to thwart. ***pitch and pay:** Cash down. **to pitch in:** To begin or set to vigorously. **to pitch into:** (*colloq.*) To assail with blows, abuse, etc.; to attack vigorously. **to pitch upon:** To select, to decide upon. **pitch-and-toss,** *n.* A game in which coins are pitched at a mark, the player getting nearest having the right to toss all the others' coins into the air and take those that come down with heads up. **pitch-circle, -line,** *n.* The circle of contact of a cog-wheel in gear. **pitched battle:** A battle for which both sides have made deliberate preparations. **pitch-farthing** [CHUCK-FARTHING]. **pitch-fork,** *n.* A large fork usu. with two prongs, with a long handle, used for lifting hay, sheaves of corn, etc. *v.t.* To lift or throw with or as with a pitch-fork. **pitch-pipe,** *n.* A small pipe for sounding with the mouth to set the pitch for singing or tuning. **pitch-wheel,** *n.* A gear-wheel.

pitchblende, -cap, etc. [PITCH (1)].

pitcher (1) (pich' ėr), *n.* One who or that which pitches; a player delivering the ball in base-ball and other games; a street performer, costermonger, etc., who pitches a tent or stall in a particular place; a block of stone used for paving.

pitcher (2) (pich' ėr) [M.E. and O.F. *picher*, med. L. *picārium, bicārium*, BEAKER], *n.* A large vessel, usu. of earthenware, with a handle and a spout, for holding liquids; (*Am.*) a jug; (*Bot.*) a pitcher-shaped leaf, usu. closed with an operculum. **pitcher-plant,** *n.* One of various plants with such leaves, esp. the East Indian genus *Nepenthes*, and the N. American genus *Sarracenia*. **pitcherful,** *n.*

pitch-farthing, pitch-fork, etc. [PITCH (2)].

pitchi (pich' i) [Austral. abor.], *n.* A wooden pitcher, a wooden receptacle.

pitch-pine [PITCH (1)].

pitchy (pich' i), *a.* Of the nature of or like pitch; dark, dismal. **pitchiness,** *n.*

piteous (pit' ė ůs), *a.* Exciting or deserving pity; lamentable, sad, mournful; *compassionate; *mean, pitiful. **piteously,** *adv.* **piteousness,** *n.*

pitfall [PIT].

pith (pith) [A.-S. *pitha* (cp. Dut. and Dan. *pit*)], *n.* A cellular spongy substance occupying the middle of a stem or shoot in dicotyledonous plants; the spinal cord; (*fig.*) the essence, the essential part, the main substance; strength, vigour, energy; cogency, point; importance. *v.t.* *To sever the spinal cord of; to kill in this way. **pithless,** *a.* Destitute of strength; weak, feeble.

pithecanthrope (pith ė kăn' thrōp) [Gr. *pithekos*, ape, *anthrōpos*, man], *n.* An ape-man, extinct animal remains of which have been discovered in Java, believed to be a connecting link between the higher apes and man. **pithecanthropic** (-throp' ik), **pithecanthropoid** (-kăn' thrȯ poid), *a.* **pithecoid** (pith' ė koid), *a.* Ape-like.

pithless [PITH].

pithy (pith' i), *a.* Consisting of, like or abounding in pith; (*fig.*) forcible, energetic; condensed, sententious. **pithily,** *adv.* **pithiness,** *n.*

pitiable (pit' i ȧbl), *a.* Deserving or calling for pity; piteous. **pitiableness,** *n.* **pitiably,** *adv.* **pitiful,** *a.* Fully of pity, compassionate; calling for pity; pitiable, contemptible. **pitifully,** *adv.* **pitifulness,** *n.* ***pitikins** [dim. of PITY], *n.* and *int.* Pity, esp. God's pity, used in oaths and imprecations. **pitiless,** *a.* Destitute of pity; merciless, unfeeling, hard-hearted. **pitilessly,** *adv.* **pitilessness,** *n.*

pit-mirk (pit' mĕrk) [PIT, MIRK], *a.* (*Sc.*) As dark as a pit, very dark indeed.

piton (pē' ton) [F., etym. unknown], *n.* A bar, staff, or stanchion used for fixing ropes on precipitous mountain-sides, etc.; a peak, a cone.

pitpan (pit' păn) [etym. doubtful], *n.* A narrow, long, flat-bottomed dug-out canoe, used in Central America.

pitta (pit' a) [Telugu], *n.* The typical genus of *Pittidæ*, including most of the Old World ant-thrushes.

pittacal (pit' ȧ kȧl) [G. (Gr. *pitta*, pitch, *kalos*, beautiful)], *n.* (*Min.*) A blue substance with a bronze-like lustre obtained from wood-tar, used in dyeing.

pittance (pit' ȧns) [O.F. *pitance*, etym. doubtful, perh. from L. *pietas*, PIETY], *n.* Orig. a gift or bequest to a religious house for food, etc.; a dole, an allowance, esp. of a meagre amount.

pitted [PIT]. ***pittikins** [PITIKINS].

pittite (pit' īt), *n.* One who occupies a place in the pit of a theatre.

pituitary (pi tū' i tȧr i) [L. *pītuītārius*, from *pītuīta*, phlegm], *a.* Containing or secreting phlegm, mucus. **pituitary body** or **gland:** A small structure of uncertain function attached by a pedicle to the base of the brain, now supposed to regulate the nutrition of bone and other tissue. ***pituita** (-ī' tȧ), ***pituite** (pit' ū it), *n.* Phlegm, mucus. **pituitrin,** *n.* A compound hormone secreted by the posterior lobe of the pituitary gland. **pituitous** (pi tū' i tůs), *a.*

pituri (pit ū' ri) [Austral. abor.], *n.* A solanaceous genus of shrubs and trees, the Duboisia, the leaves of which are used medicinally and as a narcotic.

pity (pit' i) [O.F. *pitet*, L. *pietātem*, nom. *-tas*, PIETY], *n.* A feeling of grief or tenderness aroused by the sufferings or distress of others, compassion; a subject for pity, a cause of regret, an unfortunate fact. *v.t.* To sympathize with, to commiserate. *v.i.* To be compassionate. **to take pity on:** To be compassionate; to act compassionately towards. **what a pity:** How unfortunate! **pityingly,** *adv.*

pityriasis (pit i rī' ȧ sis) [Gr. *pituriasis*, from *pituron*, bran], *n.* (*Path.*) Squamous inflammation of the skin, dandruff.

piu (pū) [It., from L. *plūs*], *adv.* (*Mus.*) More.

pivot (piv' ȯt) [F., perh. from It. *piva*, L. *pīpa*, PIPE], *n.* A pin, shaft, or bearing on which anything turns or oscillates; (*Mil.*) a soldier at the flank on whom a company wheels; (*fig.*) a thing or event on which an important issue depends. *v.i.* To turn on or as on a pivot; to hinge (upon). **pivotal,** *a.*

piwakawaka (pē wo' kȧ wo' kȧ) [Maori], *n.* The pied fantail pigeon.

pixy (pik' si) [etym. doubtful], *n.* A supernatural being akin to a fairy or elf.

pizzicato (pit si ka' tō) [It., p.p. of *pizzicare*, to twitch, to twang], *a.* (*Mus.*) Played by plucking the strings (of a violin, etc.) with the fingers. *adv.* In this manner. *n.* A passage or work so played.

pizzle (piz' ėl) [cp. Flem. *pēzel*, L.G. *pesel*, Dut. *pees*, sinew], *n.* The penis of some quadrupeds, esp. of a bull, used as a whip for flogging.

placable (plā' kȧ bėl, plăk' kȧ bėl) [F., from L. *plācābilis*, from *plācāre*, to PLACATE], *a.* That may be appeased; ready to forgive, mild, complacent. **placability** (-bil' i ti), *n.* **placableness,** *n.* **placably,** *adv.*

placard (plăk' ȧrd, plȧ kard') [O.F. *placard*, *plaquard*, from *plaquier*, Dut. *plakken*, to paste, to glue], *n.* A written or printed paper or bill posted up in a public place, a poster. *v.t.* To post placards on; to announce or advertise by placards; to display as a placard.

placate (plȧ kāt', plā' kāt, plā kāt') [L. *plācātus*, p.p. of *plācāre*], *v.t.* To appease, to pacify, to conciliate.

place (plās) [F., from L. *platea*, Gr. *plateia*, a broad way, a street, orig. fem. of *platus*, flat, wide], *n.* A particular portion of space; a spot, a locality; a city, a town, a village; a residence, an abode; a building, esp. as devoted to some particular purpose; a residence with its surroundings, esp. in the country; a fortified post; an open space in a town; a passage in a book, etc.; position in a definite order, as of a figure in a relation to others in a series or group; a stage or step in an argument, statement, etc.; stead, lieu; space, room for a person; rank, station in life, official position; situation, employment, appointment, esp. under Government; duty, sphere, province; (*Racing*) a position among the competitors that have been placed. *v.t.* To put or set in a particular place; to put, to set, to fix; to arrange in proper places; to identify; to assign to a class; to put in office, to appoint to a post; to find an appointment, situation, or living for; to put out at interest, to invest, to lend; to dispose of (goods) to a customer; to set or fix (confidence, etc., in or on); to assign a definite date, position, etc., to, to locate; (*Racing*) to indicate the position of (a horse, etc.), usu. among the first three passing the winning-post; (*Football*) to get a goal by a place-kick. **in place:** Suitable, appropriate. **in place of:** Instead of. **out of place:** Unsuitable, inappropriate. **to give place to:** To give precedence, to give way to; to make room for; to be succeeded by. **to take place:** To come to pass, to occur. **to take the place of:** To be substituted for. **place-brick:** A brick imperfectly burnt through being on the windward side of the clamp. **place-hunter,** *n.* One seeking an appointment, esp. under Government. **place-kick,** *n.* (*Football*) A kick after the ball has been placed for the purpose by another player. **placeman,** *n.* One holding an appointment, esp. under Government. **place-name,** *n.* The name of a place, esp. as distinguished from a personal name.

placebo (plȧ sē' bō) [L., I shall please, 1st sing. fut. of *placēre*, to please], *n.* (*pl.* **-bos, -boes**) (*R.-C. Ch.*) The first antiphon in the vespers for the dead, from the opening word; hence, vespers for the dead; (*Med.*) a medicine having no therapeutic action, given to humour the patient or as a control during experiments to test the efficacy of a genuine medicine.

placenta (plȧ sen' tȧ) [L., from Gr. *plakous plakounta*, contr. of *-oenta*, flat cake, from *plax*, flat plate], *n.* (*pl.* **-tas, -tæ**) (*Anat.*) The organ by which the fœtus is nourished in the higher mammals; (*Bot.*) the part of the ovary to which the ovules are attached. **placental,** *a.* and *n.* **placentalian** (-tā' li ȧn), **placentary** (plăs' ėn tȧr i, plȧ sen' tȧr i), *a.* and *n.* **placentate** (plăs' ėn tāt), *a.* **placentiferous** (-tif' ėr ŭs), *a.* **placentation** (-tā' shŭn), *n.* (*Zool. and Bot.*) The formation, arrangement, or mode of attachment of the placenta. **placentitis** (-tī' tis), *n.* (*Path.*) Inflammation of the placenta.

placer (1) (plā' sėr), *n.* One who places or sets; (*Bookbinding*) one who arranges the sheets of a book, etc.; (*Pottery*) one who puts the ware into the kiln for burning.

placer (2) (plā' sėr, plȧ thĕr') [Am. Sp., from *plaza*, PLACE], *n.* (*Mining*) A place where deposits are washed for minerals; an alluvial or other deposit containing valuable minerals; any mineral deposits not classed as veins.

placet (plā' sėt) [L., it pleases, 3rd sing. pres. of *placēre*, to PLEASE], *n.* Permission, assent, sanction.

placid (plăs' id) [F. *placide*, L. *placidus*, as prec.], *a.* Gentle, quiet; calm, peaceful, serene, unruffled. **placidity** (-sid' i ti), **placidness,** *n.* **placidly,** *adv.*

***placitum** (plăs' i tŭm) [L., orig. p.p. of *placēre*, to PLEASE], *n.* A decree, judgment, or decision, esp. in a court of justice or a state assembly. ***placitory,** *a.*

***plack** (plăk) [Sc., prob. from Flem. *placke* (perh. through F. *plaque*), a coin of the Netherlands], *n.* A small copper coin formerly current in Scotland, worth four pennies Scots; (*fig.*) anything of slight value. **plackless,** *a.* Penniless.

placket (plăk' ėt) [var. of PLACARD], *n.* The opening or slit in a petticoat or skirt; a woman's pocket; *(*fig.*) a petticoat, a woman. **placket-hole,** *n.*

placoderm (plăk' ō dĕrm) [as foll., DERM], *a.* (*Palæont.*) Belonging to the *Placodermi*, a Palæozoic division of fishes having the head and pectoral region covered with large bony plates. *n.* A fish of this division.

placoid (plăk' oid) [Gr. *plax plakos*, flat plate, -OID], *a.* (*Ichthyol.*) Plate-shaped (of scales), *n.* One of the *Placoidei*, a group of fish with plate-like scales.

plafond (pla' fon) [F. (*plat*, flat, *fond*, bottom)], *n.* A ceiling, esp. one of a richly decorated kind.

plagal (plā' gȧl) [med. L. *plagālis*, from *plaga*, perh. from med. Gr. *plagios*, orig. oblique, slanting, from Gr. *plagos*, side], *a.* (*Mus.*) Having the principal notes between the dominant and its octave (of Gregorian modes); denoting the cadence formed when a subdominant chord immediately precedes the final tonic chord.

plage (plazh) [F.], *n.* Beach, shore at a seaside resort.

plagiarize (plā' ji ȧ rīz) [PLAGIARY, -IZE], *v.t.* To appropriate and give out as one's own (the writings, inventions, or ideas of another). **plagiarism,** *n.* **plagiarist,** *n.* **plagiary** (plā' ji ȧ ri) [L. *plagiārius*, from *plagiāre*, to kidnap], *n.* One who appropriates the writings or ideas of another and passes them off as his own; literary theft, plagiarism. *a.* Practising literary theft.

plagio- [Gr. *plagios*], *comb. form.* Slanting, oblique. **plagiocephalic** (plăj' ō sė făl' ik) [CEPHALIC], *a.* Having the skull developed more on one side than the other. **plagiocephalous** (-sef' ȧ lŭs), *a.* **plagiocephaly,** *n.* **plagioclastic** (-klăs' tik), *a.* (*Min.*) Having the cleavage oblique, opp. to orthoclastic. **plagioclase** (plăj' i ō klās), *n.* **plagiostome** (-stōm), *n.* (*Ichthyol.*) A fish with the mouth placed transversely beneath the snout, as a shark or ray. **plagiostomatous** (-stom' ȧ tŭs), **plagiostomous** (-os' tō mŭs), *a.* **plagiotropic** (-trop' ik), *a.* (*Bot.*) Obliquely geotropic, the two halves (of plants, organs, etc.) reacting differently to external influences. **plagiotropically,** *adv.* **plagiotropism** (-ot' rō pizm), *n.*

plagium (plā′ ji ŭm) [L., kidnapping, from *plagiāre*, see PLAGIARY], *n.* (*Law*) Kidnapping, man-stealing.

plague (plāg) [O.F. *plage, plague*, L. *plāga*, a stroke, cogn. with *plangere*, to beat (cp. Gr. *plēgē*, blow, *plēssein*, to strike)], *n.* A blow, a calamity, an affliction; a pestilence, an intensely malignant epidemic, esp. an Oriental or bubonic disease; (*fig.*) a nuisance, a trouble. *v.t.* To visit with plague; to afflict with any calamity or evil; to vex, to tease, to annoy. **plague spot,** *n.* A centre of infection. ***plagueful,** *a.* **plagueless,** *a.* **plaguesome,** *a.* (*colloq.*) **plaguer,** *n.* **plaguy** (plā′ gi), *a.* Vexatious, annoying. **plaguily,** *adv.*

plaice (plās) [O.F. *pliïs*, late L. *platessa*, prob. from Gr. *platus*, broad], *n.* A flat-fish, *Pleuronectes platessa*, much used for food.

plaid (plăd, plād) [Gael. *plaide*, cp. Ir. *ploid*], *n.* A long rectangular outer garment of woollen cloth, usu. with a checkered or tartan pattern, worn by Scottish Highlanders; plaiding. *a.* Like a plaid in pattern. **plaided,** *a.* Wearing a plaid; made of plaid cloth. **plaiding,** *n.* Cloth for making plaids.

plain (1) (plān) [O.F., from L. *plānum*, nom. *plānus*, flat], *a.* Clear, evident, manifest; simple, free from difficulties; easily seen, easy to understand; not intricate; devoid of ornament; unvariegated, uncoloured; not luxurious, not seasoned highly; homely, unaffected, unsophisticated; straightforward, sincere, frank; direct, outspoken; (*euphem.*) ugly. *adv.* Plainly. *n.* A tract of level country. **plain-chant** [PLAIN-SONG]. **plain clothes:** Private clothes, as opp. to uniform, mufti. **plain-dealer,** *n.* One who speaks his mind plainly; *a simpleton. **plain-dealing,** *a.* and *n.* **plain-hearted,** *a.* Sincere; free from hypocrisy. **plain sailing** [cp. **plane sailing,** PLANE (3)]: A simple course of action. **plainsman,** *n.* A dweller on a plain. **plain-song,** *n.* A variety of vocal music according to the ecclesiastical modes of the Middle Ages, governed as to time not by metre but by word-accent, and sung in unison. **plain-spoken,** *a.* Speaking or said plainly and without reserve. **plain-wanderer,** *n.* (*Austral.*) The turkey quail. **plain-work,** *n.* Plain needle-work, as dist. from embroidery, etc. **plainly,** *adv.* **plainness,** *n.*

***plain** (2) (plān) [O.F. *plaign-*, stem of *plaindre*, L. *plangere*, to beat (the breast)], *v.i.* To mourn, to lament, to complain; to make a mournful sound.

plaint (plānt) [O.F., from L. *planctus*, lamentation (with which O.F. *plainte*, from L. *plancta*, fem. p.p. of *plangere*, see prec., has been assim.)], *n.* An accusation, a charge; (*poet.*) a lamentation, a mournful song. ***plaintful,** *a.*

plaintiff (plān′ tif), *n.* One who brings a suit against another, a complainant, a prosecutor.

plaintive (plān′ tiv) [O.F. *plaintif, -tive* (as prec., -IVE)], *a.* Expressive of sorrow or grief. **plaintively,** *adv.* ***plaintiveness,** *n.* **plaintless,** *a.*

plaister [PLASTER].

plait (plăt) [O.F. *ploit, pleit*, L. *plicitum*, p.p. of *plicāre*, to fold], *n.* A braid of several strands of hair, straw, twine, etc., esp. a braided tress of hair; a flat fold, a doubling over, as of cloth, a pleat. *v.t.* To braid, to form into a plait or plaits; to fold. **plaiter,** *n.*

plan (plăn) [F., var. of PLAIN (1)], *n.* A delineation of a building, machine, etc., by projection on a plane surface, usu. showing the relative positions of the parts on one floor or level; a map of a town, estate, on a large scale; a scheme; a project, a design; an outline of a discourse, sermon, etc.; method of procedure; habitual method, way, custom; (*Persp.*) one of the ideal planes, perpendicular to the line of vision, passing through the objects in a picture, in which these appear of diminishing size according to the distance. *v.t.* To draw a plan of; to design; to contrive, to scheme, to devise. **planless,** *a.* **planner,** *n.* **planning,** *n.* Organized scheme for reconstruction and redistribution of industries, dwellings, etc.

planarian (plȧ nâr′ i ȧn) [L. *plānārius*, flat], *a.* Belonging to the genus *Planaria* of the suborder *Planarida*, minute, flat, aquatic worms found in salt or fresh water and in moist places. *n.* A flat-worm. **planaridan,** *a.* and *n.* **planariform, planarioid,** *a.*

planch (planch) [F. *planche*, PLANK], *n.* A slab of metal, fire-brick, etc., used in enamelling; *a plank. **v.t.* To plank, to board.

planchet (plan′ chĕt) [dim. of prec.], *n.* A disk of metal for making into a coin.

planchette (plan shet′) [F., dim. of *planche*, PLANK], *n.* A small, usu. heart-shaped, board resting on two castors, and a pencil which makes marks as the board moves under the hands of the person resting upon it, believed by spiritualists to be a mode of communicating with the unseen world.

plane (1) (plān) [F., from L. *platanum*, nom. *-nus*, Gr. *platanos*, from *platus*, broad], *n.* A tree of various species of the genus *Platanus*, consisting of large spreading branches with broad angular leaves palmately lobed. **plane-tree,** *n.*

plane (2) (plān) [F., from late L. *plāna*, as foll., whence *plānāre*, to plane, and F. *planer*], *n.* A tool for smoothing boards and other surfaces. *v.t.* To smooth or dress with a plane; to make flat and even; to remove (away) or pare (down) irregularities. **planer,** *n.* **planing-machine,** *n.* A machine for planing wood or metal.

plane (3) (plān) [L. *plānus*, flat, level (cp. PLAIN (1) in use in this sense till 17th cent.)], *a.* Level, flat, without depressions or elevations; lying or extending in a plane. *n.* A surface such that a straight line joining any two points in it lies wholly within it; such a surface imagined to extend to an indefinite distance, forming the locus for certain points or lines; a level surface; an even surface extending uniformly in some direction; (*Cryst.*) one of the natural faces of a crystal; (*Coal-mining*) a main road in a mine; (*Persp.*) an imaginary surface for determining points in a drawing; (*fig.*) level (of thought, existence, etc.). **plane figure:** A figure all the points in which lie in one plane. **plane geometry:** The geometry of plane figures. **plane sailing:** The art of determining a ship's position on the supposition that she is moving on a plane; (*fig.*) plain sailing, a simple course of action. **plane-table,** *n.* A surveying instrument marked off into degrees from the centre for measuring angles in mapping. *v.t.* To survey with this.

plane (4) (plān). (*abbrev.*) An aeroplane; one of the thin horizontal structures used as wings to sustain an aeroplane in flight.

planet (plăn′ ĕt) [O.F. *planete*, late L. *planēta*, Gr. *planētēs*, from *planan*, to lead astray, *planasthai*, to wander], *n.* A heavenly body revolving round the sun, either as a primary planet in a nearly circular orbit or as a secondary planet or satellite revolving round a primary; (*Ancient Astron.*) one of the major planets, Mercury, Venus, Mars, Jupiter, Saturn, together with the sun and moon, distinguished from other heavenly bodies as having an apparent motion of its own. **planet-gear, -gearing,** *n.* A system of gearing in which planet-wheels are employed. ***planet-struck, -stricken,** *a.* Affected by planetary influence, blasted; panic-stricken, confounded. **planet-wheel,** *n.* A cogged wheel revolving round a wheel with which it engages. **planetarium** (-târ′ i ŭm), *n.* An apparatus for exhibiting the motions of the planets, an orrery; a building in which this is exhibited on a large scale. **planetary** (plăn′ ĕ tȧr i), *a.* Pertaining to the planets or the planetary system. **planetoid** (-toid′), *n.* and *a.* **planetoidal,** *a.* ***planetule,** *n.*

plane-table [PLANE (3)]. **plane-tree** [PLANE (1)].

plangent (plăn′ jĕnt) [L. *plangens -ntem*, pres.p. of *plangere*, see PLAINT], *a.* Sounding noisily; resounding like beating waves. **plangency,** *a.*

plani- [L. *plānus*, PLANE (3)], *comb. form.* Level, flat, smooth. **planigraph** (plăn′ i grăf) [F. *planigraphe* (-GRAPH)], *n.* An instrument for reproducing drawings on a different scale. **planimeter** (plȧ nim′ ė tėr), *n.* An instrument for measuring the area of an irregular plane surface. **planimetric, -al** (-met′ rik, -ål), *a.* **planimetry** (plȧ nim′ ė tri), *n.* The mensuration of plane surfaces. **plani-petalous** (-pet′ ȧ lŭs), *a.* (*Bot.*) Having flat petals.

planish (plăn′ ish) [F. *planiss-*, stem of *planir* (now *aplanir*), from *plan*, level, PLANE (3)], *v.t.* To flatten, smooth, or toughen (metal) by hammering or similar means; to reduce in thickness by rolling; to polish (metal plates, photographs, etc.) by rolling; to polish by hammering. **planisher,** *n.* One who planishes; a planishing tool or machine.

planisphere (plăn′ i sfēr), *n.* A plane projection of a sphere, esp. of part of the celestial sphere. **planispheric** (-sfer′ ik), *a.*

plank (plăngk) [O.North.F. *planke*, late L. *planca*, prob. cogn. with Gr. *plax plakos*, flat plate], *n.* A long piece of sawn timber thicker than a board (usu. from 1½ to 4½ in. thick and 6 to 12 in. wide); (*fig.*) an article or principle of a political programme. *v.t.* To cover or lay with planks; (*slang*) to lay down (money, etc.) as if on a board or table. **to walk the plank:** To be compelled to walk blindfold along a plank thrust over a ship's side (a pirates' mode of putting to death). **plank-bed,** *n.* A bed of boards without a mattress (a form of prison discipline). **planking,** *n.*

plankton (plăngk′ tŏn) [G., from Gr. *plankton*, neut. of *planktos*, wandering, from *plazesthai*, to wander], *n.* (*Biol.*) Pelagic fauna and flora, esp. minute animals and plants or those of low organization, floating at any level. **planktology** (-tol′ ȯ ji), *n.*

planless, planner, planning [PLAN].

plano- [PLANE (3)], *comb. form.* Flat, level. **plano-concave** (plā′ nȯ kon′ kāv), *a.* Plane on one side and concave on the other. **plano-conical,** *a.* **plano-convex,** *a.* **plano-horizontal,** *a.* Having a level horizontal surface or position. **planometer** (plȧ nom′ ė tėr), *n.* A plane plate used as a gauge for plane surfaces. **plano-subulate,** *a.* Smooth and awl-shaped.

plant (1) (plant) [A.-S. *plante*, L. *planta*, a sucker, shoot, or slip (in later senses from foll.)], *n.* Any vegetable organism, usu. one of the smaller plants distinguished from shrubs and trees; (*prov.*) a sapling; *a shoot, a slip, a cutting; (*fig.*) a scion, an offshoot, a descendant; a growth or crop of something planted; the tools, machinery, apparatus, and fixtures used in an industrial concern; (*fig.*) intellectual machinery or equipment; (*slang*) a carefully planned swindle, fraud, theft, dodge, etc.; a detective, a decoy to catch swindlers, etc. **plant-canes,** *n.pl.* The crop of the sugar-cane of the first growth. **plant-louse,** *n.* An insect infesting plants, esp. the aphis. ***plantage,** *n.* **plantlet,** *n.* **plantless,** *a.* **plantlike,** *a.*

plant (2) (plant) [A.-S. *plantian*, L. *plantāre*, as prec.], *v.t.* To set in the ground for growth; to put (young fish, spawn, etc.) into a river, etc.; to furnish or lay out with plants; to fix firmly, to station; to settle, to found, to introduce, to establish; to implant (an idea, etc.); to aim and deliver (a blow, etc.); (*slang*) to conceal (plunder, etc.), to put (ore, etc.) in a supposed mine to deceive investors or purchasers. *v.i.* To sow seed; to perform the act of planting. ***plantable,** *a.*

plantain (1) (plăn′ tȧn) [O.F., from L. *plantāginem*, nom. *-go*, prob. from *planta*, foot-sole, from the prostrate leaves], *n.* Any plant of the genus *Plantago*, esp. *P. major*, a low perennial weed with broad flat leaves and a spike of dull green flowers.

plantain (2) (plăn′ tȧn) [Sp. *plantano*, *platano*, L. *platanus*, PLANE (1)], *n.* A tropical American herbaceous tree, *Musa paradisiaca*, closely akin to the banana, and bearing similar fruit; its fruit.

plantar (plăn′ tȧr) [L. *plantāris*, from *planta*, foot-sole], *a.* (*Anat.*) Pertaining to the sole of the foot.

plantation (plăn tā′ shŭn) [L. *plantātio*, as PLANT (2)], *n.* A large quantity of trees or growing plants that have been planted; a growing wood, a grove; a large estate for the cultivation of sugar, cotton, coffee, etc.; the act of planting; *a colony or settlement, settling of colonists, colonization.

planter (plan′ tėr), *n.* One who plants; an implement or machine for planting; one who owns or works a plantation; a settler in a colony; (*Ireland*) an English or Scottish settler in forfeited lands in the 17th cent.; (*19th cent.*) a person settled in a holding from which another has been evicted; (*slang*) a well-directed blow; (*Austral. slang*) a cattle-stealer. **plantership,** *n.*

plantigrade (plăn′ ti grād) [F. (L. *planta*, sole, *-gradus*, walking)], *a.* Walking on the sole of the foot; of or pertaining to the *Plantigrada*, a section of the carnivora embracing the bears, badgers, etc. *n.* A plantigrade animal.

plantlet, plantlike, etc. [PLANT (1)].

planula (plăn′ ū lȧ) [dim. of L. *plānus*, PLANE (3)], *n.* (*Zool.*) The locomotory embryo of cœlenterates. **planular, planulate, planuliform** (plȧ nū′ li fôrm), **planuloid** (plăn′ ū loid), *a.*

planuria (plȧ nūr′ i ȧ) [Gr. *planos*, wandering, Gr. *ouron*, urine], *n.* (*Path.*) Discharge of urine through an abnormal channel.

planxty (plăngk′ sti) [etym. unknown], *n.* (*Ir.*) A melody of a sportive and animated character for the harp.

plap (plăp) [onomat.], *v.i.* To fall with a flat impact. *n.* The sound of this.

plaque (plak) [F., see PLACK], *n.* A plate, slab, or tablet, of metal, porcelain, ivory, etc., usu. of an artistic or ornamental character; a small plate worn as a badge or personal ornament; (*Path., Zool., etc.*) a patch or spot on the surface of the body. **plaquette** (plȧ ket′), *n.*

plash (1) (plăsh) [A.-S. *plæsc* (cp. Dut. and L.G. *plas*), prob. cogn. with foll.], *n.* A large puddle, a marshy pool, a pond. **plashy** (1), *a.* Marshy, watery.

plash (2) (plăsh) [prob. imit., cp. Dut. *plassen*, G. *platschen*, Swed. *plaska*], *v.t.* To cause (water) to splash; to dabble in; to sprinkle colouring-matter on (walls), in imitation of granite, etc. *v.i.* To dabble in water; to make a splash. *n.* A splash, a plunge; the sound made by this. **plashy** (2), *a.* Marked as if with splashes of colour, etc.

plash (3) (plăsh) [O.F. *plessier*, *plaissier*, to PLEACH], *v.t.* To bend down or cut partly and intertwine the branches of (to form a hedge); to make or repair (a hedge) in this way. *n.* A branch partly cut and interwoven with other branches.

plasm (plăzm) [late L. and Gr. *plasma*, from *plassein*, to mould], *n.* *A mould or matrix, in which anything is cast or formed; (*Biol.*) plasma. **plasma,** *n.* (*Biol.*) The viscous living matter of a cell, protoplasm; (*Physiol.*) the fluid part of the blood in which the red corpuscles float; *a mould or matrix; (*Min.*) a green variety of quartz allied to chalcedony. **plasmatic** (-măt′ ik), **plasmic** (plăz′ mik), *a.* **plasmin,** *n.* (*Chem.*) A protein from the plasma of the blood to which coagulation is due. **plasmo-,** *comb. form.* (*Biol.*) Plasm. **plasmodium** (-mō′ di ŭm), *n.* (*pl.* **-dia**) A mass of mobile, naked protoplasm resulting from the fusion or aggregation of numerous amœboid cells, as in the vegetative stage of *Myxomycetes* and *Mycetozoa*; a genus of protozoa found in the blood in malaria and quartan and tertian ague. **plasmodial, plasmodic** (-mod′ ik), **plasmodiate** (plăz mō′ di ȧt), *a.* **plasmogen** (plăz′ mȯ jėn), *n.* True or formative protoplasm. **plasmogeny, -gony** (plăz moj′ ė ni, -mog′ ȯ ni), *n.* The spontaneous generation of individualized organisms. **plasmology** (-mol′ ȯ ji), *n.* The science of the ultimate corpuscles of living matter. **plasmolysis,** *n.* The contraction of the protoplasm in active cells under the influence of a reagent or of disease. **plasmolyse** (plăz′ mȯ līz), *v.t.* **plasmolytic** (-lit′ ik), *a.*

plaster (plas′ tėr) [A.-S., from L. *emplastrum*, Gr. *emplastron*, *emplaston*, from *emplassein*, to daub on

(EM-, *plassein*, to mould)], *n.* A mixture of lime, sand, etc., for coating walls, etc.; calcined gypsum or sulphate of lime, used, when mixed with water, for coating or for moulding into ornaments, figures, etc.; an adhesive application of some curative substance, usu. spread on linen, muslin or a similar fabric, placed on parts of the body. *v.t.* To cover or overlay with plaster or other adhesive substance; to apply a plaster to (a wound, etc.); to daub, to smear over, to smooth over; to stick (on) as with plaster; to treat (wine) with gypsum to cure acidity. **plaster of Paris:** Gypsum, esp. calcined gypsum used for making casts of statuary, etc. **plaster-stone,** *n.* Raw gypsum. **plasterer,** *n.* **plastering,** *n.* The act of coating or treating with plaster; a covering or coat of plaster. **plastery,** *a.*

plastic (plăs' tik) [L. *plasticus*, Gr. *plastikos*, as prec.], *a.* Having the power of giving form or fashion; capable of being modelled or moulded; pertaining to or produced by modelling or moulding; formative, causing growth; forming living tissue; (*fig.*) fictile, pliant, supple. **plastic art:** The production of art objects by moulding or sculpture. **plastic surgery,** *n.* (*Surg.*) The branch of surgery concerned with the restoration of parts destroyed or deformed as the result of congenital defect, injury, surgical removal, or disease. **plastically,** *adv.* **plasticity** (-tis' i ti), *n.*

Plasticine (plăs' ti sēn), *n.* Proprietary name of a modelling substance for the use of children.

plastics (plăs' tiks), *n.pl.* A group of materials which, though stable in use at ordinary temperatures, are plastic at some stage in their manufacture and can be shaped by the application of heat and pressure. **extruded plastics,** *n.* Plastics materials formed into strips, rods, etc., by extrusion through a die. **moulded plastics,** *n.* Finished articles which have been moulded from plastics materials by heat and pressure; plastics. **plastics,** *a.*

plastin (plăs' tin), *n.* (*Biol.*) A viscous substance found in the nuclei of cells.

plastron (plăs' trŏn) [F., from It. *piastrone*, from *piastria*, breast-plate, see PIASTRE], *n.* A padded leather shield worn by fencers to protect the breast; an ornamental front to a woman's dress; a shirt-front; (*Zool.*) the under part of the buckler of a tortoise or turtle, an analogous part in other animals; *a breast-plate, usu. worn under a coat of mail. **plastral,** *a.*

plat (1) [var. of PLOT], *n.* A small plot, patch, or piece of ground; a small bed (of flowering-plants, etc.); a map, a chart. *v.t.* (*past & p.p.* **platted**) To make a plan of; (*Am.*) to lay out in plats or plots.

plat (2) (plăt) [PLAIT].

platan (plăt' ăn) [L. *platanus*, PLANE (1)], *n.* An Oriental plane-tree. **plataneous** (-tā' nė ŭs), **platanine** (plăt' ȧ nīn), *a.*

platband (plăt' bănd) [F. *plateband* (*plate*, flat, as foll., BAND (2))], *n.* A border or strip (of flowers, turf, etc.); (*Arch.*) a flat, rectangular, slightly-projecting moulding; a fillet between the flutings of pillars; a square lintel; a plain impost.

plate (plāt) [O.F., fem. of *plat*, flat, perh. from Gr. *platus*, broad], *n.* A flat, thin piece of metal, etc., usu. rigid and uniform in thickness; a piece of metal with an inscription for attaching to an object, a piece of metal used for engraving; a print taken from this; a sheet of glass or other material coated with a sensitized film for photography; an electrotype or stereotype cast of a page of type, to be used for printing; the plastic base of a denture, fitting the gums and holding the artificial teeth; a horizontal timber laid on a wall as base for framing; a small shallow vessel, now usu. of crockery, for eating from; a plateful; (collect.) domestic utensils, as spoons, forks, knives, cups, dishes, etc., of gold, silver, or other metal; (*Am.* silverware); a cup or other article of gold or silver offered as a prize in a race, etc.; a race for such a prize; (*slang*) money; *a piece of silver money. *v.t.* To cover or overlay with plates of metal for defence, ornament, etc.; to coat with a layer of metal, esp. gold, silver, or tin; to beat into thin plates; to make an electrotype or stereotype from (type). **half-plate,** *n.* (*Phot.*) A photographic plate $6\frac{1}{2} \times 4\frac{3}{4}$ in. **quarter-plate,** *n.* $4\frac{1}{4} \times 3\frac{1}{4}$ in. **whole-plate,** *n.* $8\frac{1}{2} \times 6\frac{1}{2}$ in. **plate-armour,** *n.* Armour composed of heavy plates of metal with which ships, forts, etc., are covered to protect them against artillery fire; defensive armour formerly worn by knights and men-at-arms, distinguished from chain or mail armour. **plate-basket,** *n.* A receptacle for spoons, forks, etc. **plate-fleet,** *n.* A fleet of vessels carrying bullion, esp. from America to Spain in the 16th cent. **plate-glass,** *n.* A superior kind of glass made in thick sheets, used for mirrors, large windows, etc. **plate-layer,** *n.* One who fixes or repairs railway metals. **plate-paper,** *n.* Fine quality paper for taking engravings, etc. **plate-powder,** *n.* Powder for cleaning domestic plate. **plate-rack,** *n.* A frame for holding plates and dishes. **plate-rail,** *n.* A flat rail formerly used on railways. **plate-ship** [PLATE-FLEET]. **plate-tracery:** (*Arch.*) Tracery, esp. in Early English and Decorated windows, giving the appearance of solid surfaces pierced with ornamental patterns. **plateful,** *n.* **plateless,** *a.* **plating,** *n.* The act, art, or process of covering articles with a coating of metal; a coating of gold, silver, or other metal; (*collect.*) the plates covering a ship, fort, etc.; (*Racing*) competing for plates. **selling-plate,** *n.* (*Racing*) A race the winner of which must be sold at an established price.

plateau (plȧ tō') [F., dim. of *plat*, a platter, a dish, orig. flat, as prec.], *n.* (*pl.* **-eaux**) A table-land, an elevated plain; a large ornamental centre dish; an ornamental plaque; a woman's level-topped hat.

plateful, plateless, etc. [PLATE].

platen (plăt' ėn) [M.E. *plateyne*, O.F. *platine*, from *plat*, flat, as prec.], *n.* The part of a printing-press that presses the paper against the type to give the impression; the roller in a typewriter serving the same purpose.

plater (plā' tėr), *n.* One who plates articles with silver, etc.; one who works upon plates; one who fits plates in shipbuilding; an inferior race-horse that runs chiefly in selling plates.

platform (plăt' fôrm) [F. *plateforme*, a model, a ground plan (*plat*, flat, see PLATE, FORM)], *n.* Any flat or horizontal surface raised above some adjoining level; a stage or raised flooring in a hall, etc., for speaking from, etc.; a landing-stage; a raised pavement, etc., beside the line at a railway station, etc.; a solid bed on which guns are mounted in a fortress, etc.; (*fig.*) platform oratory; a political programme; the principles forming the basis of a party; (*Am.*) a declaration of principles and policy issued by a party before an election. *v.t.* To place on or as on a platform. *v.i.* To speak from a platform.

plating [PLATE].

platinum (plăt' i nŭm) [formerly *platina*, from Sp., dim. of *plata*, silver, PLATE], *n.* A heavy, ductile and malleable metallic element, of a silver colour, fusing only at extremely high temperatures, immune to attack by most chemical reagents. **platinum-black,** *n.* Finely divided platinum in the form of a black powder, obtained by the reduction of platinum salts. **platinum blonde,** *n.* (*colloq.*) A woman with hair so fair as to be almost white. **platinum metals:** The platinoids. **platinic** (-tin' ik), *a.* **platiniferous** (-nif' ėr ŭs), *a.* **platinize** (plăt' i nīz), *v.t.* To coat with platinum. **platinode,** *n.* The cathode or negative pole or plate of a voltaic cell, frequently of platinum, opp. to zincode. **platinoid,** *a.* Like platinum. *n.* A name for certain metals found associated with platinum; an alloy of German silver, etc. **platinotype,** *n.* A photographic printing process in which a deposit of platinum black gives a positive; a print with this. **platinous,** *a.*

platitude (plăt' i tūd) [F., from *plat*, flat, see PLATE], *n.* Flatness, commonplaceness, insipidity, triteness; a trite remark, esp. of a didactic kind. **platitudinize** (-tū′ di nīz), *v.i.* **platitudinous,** *a.* **platitudinously,** *adv.* **platitudinarian** (-nâr′ i ǎn), *n.* and *a.*

Platonic (plȧ ton′ ik), *a.* Of or pertaining to Plato or to his philosophy or school. **Platonic love:** Pure spiritual affection between the sexes. **Platonic period** or **year** [YEAR]. **Platonically,** *adv.* **Platonism** (plā′ tō nizm), *n.* **Platonist,** *n.*

platoon (plȧ toon′) [corr. of F. *peloton*, dim. of *pelote*, PELLET], *n.* A subdivision, usu. half, of a company, formerly a tactical unit under a lieutenant; a volley fired by this; (*fig.*) a body or set of people.

platter (plăt′ ėr) [M.E. and A.-F. *plater*, from *plat*, PLATE], *n.* A large shallow dish or plate, often of wood.

platting (plăt′ ing), *n.* Slips of bark, cane, straw, etc., woven or plaited, for making hats, etc.

platy- [Gr. *platus*, broad], *comb. form.* Broad, flat. **platycephalic** (plăt i sė fǎl′ ik), **-cephalous** (-sef′ ȧ lŭs) [CEPHAL-], *a.* (*Craniol.*) Flat and broad relatively to length (of skulls). **platypus** (plăt′ i pŭs) [Gr. *platupous* (*pous*, foot)], *n.* The ornithorhynchus or duckbill of Australia. **platyrrhine** (plăt′ i rīn) [Gr. *rhis rhinos* nose], *n.* Broad-nosed (of monkeys).

plaudit (plaw′ dit) [L. *plaudite*, plaw′ di tē, imper. of *plaudere*, to applaud (with suppression of final vowel)], *n.* (*usu. in pl.*) An expression of applause; praise or approval. **plauditory,** *a.*

plausible (plaw′ zi bėl) [L. *plausibilis*, from *plaus-*, p.p. stem of *plaudere*, see prec.], *a.* Apparently right, reasonable, or probable, specious; using specious arguments. ***plausibleness, plausibility** (-bil′ i ti), *n.* **plausibly,** *adv.* ***plausive,** *a.* Applauding; plausible; ingratiating.

plaustral (plaw′ strǎl) [L. *plaustr-um*, wagon, -AL], *a.* Of or pertaining to a wagon.

play (plā) [A.-S. *plega* cogn. with *plegian*, *plagian*, *plægian* (cp. Dut. *plegen*, G. *pflegen*, to have the care of, *pflege*, care)], *n.* Free, light, aimless movement or activity; freedom of movement or action; space or scope for this; a state of activity; a series of actions engaged in for pleasure or amusement; sport, exercise, amusement, fun; playing in a game; manner or style of this; style of execution, playing (as on an instrument); exercise in any contest; gaming, gambling; a dramatic composition or performance, a drama; conduct or dealing towards others (esp. as fair or unfair); competitive. *v.i.* To move about in a lively, light, or aimless manner, to dance, frisk, shimmer, etc.; to act or move freely; to have freedom of movement; to perform a regular operation (of instruments, machinery, guns, etc.); to move loosely or irregularly (of a part of a machine, etc.); to sport, to frolic; to do something as an amusement; to toy, to trifle; to take part in a game; to perform on a musical instrument; to take part in a game of chance; to game, to gamble; to behave, to act, to conduct oneself in regard to others; to personate a character; to act a part (esp. on a stage). *v.t.* To put in action or operation; to handle, operate, or wield freely and lightly; to engage in (a game); to employ or make use of as agent or implement in a game; to perform, to execute (a trick, etc.); to perform on (a musical instrument); to perform (a play) on the stage; to pretend to be, to act (a character); to execute on a musical instrument; to manage, to give (a fish) freedom to exhaust itself; to discharge continuously (guns upon); (of hose) to discharge water continuously; to toy or trifle with; *to exercise, to ply. **in play:** Not seriously; actually in the game (of cricket, football, billiards, etc.). **out of play:** Removed (temporarily) from the game. **played out:** Used up, exhausted. **play of words:** Verbiage; trifling with words. **play on words:** Punning, a pun. **play-or-pay bet:** One that holds good whether the horse runs or not. **to play at:** To engage (in a game); to perform or execute in a frivolous or half-hearted way. **to play false:** To betray. **to play fast and loose:** To be fickle; to act recklessly. **to play into the hands of:** To play or act so as to give the advantage to one's partner or opponent. **to play off:** To pass (a thing) off as something else; to oppose (one person) against another, esp. for one's own advantage; to show off. **to play on:** To perform upon; (*Cricket*) to play the ball on to one's own wicket. **to play the game:** To play according to the rules of a game and accept defeat without complaint; (*fig.*) to act honestly and manfully in any undertaking. **to play upon:** To make use of another's (fears, etc.), *to impose upon. **to play up to:** To humour, to draw out. **to play with:** To amuse oneself or sport with; to treat with levity. **play-actor,** *n.* (*contemp.*) An actor. **play-bill,** *n.* A bill or programme announcing or giving the cast of a play. **play-book,** *n.* A book of dramatic compositions; a book of games for children. **play-boy,** *n.* A young man who lives for pleasure, a social parasite. **play-club,** *n.* (*Golf*) A driver. **play-day,** *n.* A holiday; a day on which miners do not work. **play-debt,** *n.* A gambling-debt. **playfellow,** *n.* A companion in play. **playgoer,** *n.* One who frequents theatres. **playgoing,** *a.* **playground,** *n.* A piece of ground used for games, esp. one attached to a school; (*fig.*) a favourite district for tourists, mountain-climbers, etc. **playhouse,** *n.* A theatre. **playmate,** *n* A playfellow. **playpen,** *n.* A portable wooden framework inside which young children can play in safety. **plaything,** *n.* A toy; (*fig.*) a person or article used for one's amusement. **playtime,** *n.* Time allotted for play. **playwright, play-writer,** *n.* A dramatist. **player,** *n.* One who plays; one engaged in a game; a person skilled in a particular game; a professional player (in a game); an actor; a performer on a musical instrument; an automatic device for playing a musical instrument; a gambler; (*Billiards, Croquet, etc.*) the ball coming next into play. **played-out,** *p.p.* Exhausted, finished. **playful,** *a.* Frolicsome, sportive; sprightly, humorous, jocular, amusing. **playfully,** *adv.* **playfulness,** *n.* **playing-cards,** *n.pl.* Cards used for games. ***playsome,** *a.* ***playsomeness,** *n.*

plea (plē) [A.-F. *plee*, O.F. *plai*, *plaid*, L. PLACITUM], *n.* A pleading, an excuse, an apology, an urgent argument; (*Law*) the answer of a defendant to the plaintiff's declaration, a defence; *a suit, an action at law.

pleach (plēch) [M.E. *plechen*, O.F. *plessier*, *plaisser*, late L. *plectiāre* (not extant), L. *plectere*, to PLAIT (cp. PLASH (3))], *v.t.* To interlace, to intertwine, to plash.

plead (plēd) [O.F. *plaidier*, from *plaid*, PLEA], *v.i.* (*past & p.p.* **pleaded**) To speak or argue in support of a claim, or in defence against a claim; to urge arguments for or against; to supplicate earnestly; (*Law*) to put forward a plea or allegation, to address a court on behalf of. *v.t.* To discuss, maintain, or defend by arguments; to allege in pleading or argument; to offer in excuse, to allege in defence. **to plead guilty** or **not guilty:** To admit or deny guilt or liability. **to plead with:** To entreat or supplicate (for, against, etc.). **pleadable,** *a.* **pleader,** *n.* One who pleads in a court of law; one who offers reasons for or against; one who draws up pleas.

pleading (plē′ ding), *n.* The act of making a plea; entreating, imploring; a written statement of a party in a suit at law; the art or practice of drawing up such statements. *a.* Imploring, appealing. **special pleading,** *n.* (*Law*) Argument with marked bias, unfair reasoning. **pleadingly,** *adv.*

***pleasance** (plez′ ǎns) [O.F. *plaisance*, as foll.], *n.* Pleasure, gaiety, pleasantness; a pleasure-ground, esp. a park or garden attached to a mansion.

pleasant (plez′ ǎnt) [M.E. and O.F. *plaisant* (PLEASE, -ANT)], *a.* Pleasing, agreeable, affording gratification to the mind or senses; *cheerful, gay, jocular, merry. **pleasantly,** *adv.* **pleasantness,** *n.*

pleasantry (plez′ ȧn tri), *n.* Jocularity, facetiousness; a jest, a joke, an amusing trick; *pleasure, pleasantness.

please (plēz) [M.E. *plese*, plaise, O.F. *plesir*, *plaisir* (F. *plaire*), L. *placēre*], *v.t.* To afford pleasure to; to be agreeable to; to satisfy; to win approval from. *v.i.* To afford gratification; to like, to think fit, to prefer; (*ellipt.*) may it please you. **if you please:** If it is agreeable to you; with your permission; (*ironically*) expressing sarcasm or protest. **pleasedly** (plē′ zėd li), *adv.* **pleasedness,** *n.* **pleaser,** *n.* **pleasingly,** *adv.* **pleasingness,** *n.*

pleasure (plezh′ ůr) [M.E. and O.F. *plesir*, *plaisir*, to PLEASE, used as noun], *n.* The gratification of the mind or senses; enjoyment, gratification, delight; sensual gratification; a source of gratification; choice, wish, desire. *v.t.* To give pleasure to. *v.i.* To take pleasure (in). **pleasure-boat,** *n.* A boat for pleasure excursions. **pleasure-ground,** *n.* A park or garden (usu. public) used for outdoor entertainments. **pleasure-trip,** *n.* **pleasurable,** *a.* Affording pleasure; pleasant, gratifying, *seeking pleasure. **pleasurableness,** *n.* **pleasurably,** *adv.*

pleat (plēt) [var. of PLAIT], *v.t.* To fold or double over, to crease. *n.* A flattened fold, a crease.

plebeian (plė bē′ ȧn) [F. *plébéien*, L. *plēbēius*, from *plebs*, earlier *plēbes*, the common people], *a.* Pertaining to the ancient Roman *plebs* or commoners; pertaining to the common people; common, vulgar, low. *n.* A commoner in ancient Rome; one of the common people. **plebeianism, plebeianness,** *n.* **plebeianize,** *v.t.* **plebeianly,** *adv.*

plebiscite (pleb′ i sit) [F. *plébiscite*, L. *plēbiscītum* (*plebs plēbis*, *scītum*, decree, p.p. of *sciscere*, to vote, incept. of *scīre*, to know)], *n.* (*Rom. Hist.*) A law enacted by a vote of the commonalty in an assembly presided over by a tribune of the people; a direct vote of the whole body of citizens in a State on a definite question, a referendum; (*fig.*) an expression of opinion by the whole community. **plebiscitary** (plė bis′ i tȧr i), *a.*

plectognath (plek′ tŏg năth) [Gr. *plektos*, plaited, *gnathos*, jaw], *a.* Of the *Plectognathi*, an order of teleostean fishes having the cheek-bones united with the jaws. *n.* A fish of this order. **plectognathic** (-năth′ ik), **plectognathous** (-tog′ nȧ thůs), *a.*

plectrum (plek′ trům) [L., from Gr. *plēktron*, cogn. with *plēssein*, to strike], *n.* (*pl.* **-tra**) A small implement of ivory, etc., with which players pluck the strings of the zither, harp, lyre, etc.

pled (*Sc.*) [p.p. of PLEAD].

pledge (plej) [M.E. and O.F. *plege* (F. *pleige*), prob. rel. to *plevir*, to warrant, to engage, from Teut. (cp. PLIGHT)], *n.* Anything given or handed over by way of guarantee or security for the repayment of money borrowed, or for the performance of some obligation; a thing put in pawn; an earnest, a token; a gage of battle; (*fig.*) one's child; an agreement, promise, or binding engagement; the state of being pledged; a health, a toast; *a person standing surety or bail. *v.t.* To give as a pledge or security; to deposit in pawn; to engage solemnly; to drink a health to. **to take the pledge:** To pledge oneself to abstain from intoxicants. **pledgeable,** *a.* ***pledgee** (plė jē′), *n.* **pledgeless,** *a.* **pledger,** *n.*

pledget (plej′ ėt) [etym. doubtful], *n.* A compress of lint for laying over an ulcer, wound, etc.

Pleiad (plī′ ȧd) [L. *Plēias -adis*, Gr. *Pleias -ados*], *n.* (*pl.* **-ades,** ȧ dēz) (*pl.*) A cluster of small stars in the constellation Taurus, seven of which are discernible by the naked eye; (*fig.*, *sing.*) a cluster of brilliant persons, esp. seven (as the French poets Ronsard, Du Bellay, and their associates, in the 16th cent.).

pleio- [PLIO-]. **pleiocene** [PLIOCENE].

pleistocene (plīs′ tȯ sēn) [Gr. *pleistos*, most, *kainos*, new], *a.* (*Geol.*) Pertaining to the strata or epoch overlying or succeeding the pliocene formation.

plenary (plē′ nȧ ri) [late L. *plēnārius*, from *plēnus*, full], *a.* Full, complete, entire, absolute. **plenary indulgence:** (*R.-C. Ch.*) An indulgence remitting all the temporal penalties due to sin. **plenary inspiration:** Full inspiration, with complete freedom from error. **plenarily,** *adv.* ***plenariness,** *n.*

pleni- [L. *plēnus*], *comb. form.* Full. **plenicorn** (plē′ ni kôrn) [L. *cornu*, horn], *a.* Having solid horns. **plenilune** (plē′ ni-, plen′ i loon) [L. *plēnilūnium* (*lūna*, moon)], *n.* The time of full moon; a full moon. **plenilunal, plenilunar, -nary** (-loo′ nȧl, -nȧr, -nȧ ri), *a.*

plenipotentiary (plen i pȯ ten′ shȧ ri) [med. L. *plēnipotentiārius* (PLENI-, *potentia*)], *a.* Invested with full powers; full, absolute. *n.* An ambassador or envoy to a foreign court, with full powers.

plenish (plen′ ish) [O.F. *pleniss-*, stem of *plenir*, as foll.], *v.t.* (*chiefly Sc.*) To fill up, to replenish, to stock, to furnish (esp. a farm). **plenishing, plenishment,** *n.*

plenist (plē nist) [PLEN-UM, IST], *n.* One who maintains that all space is full of matter.

plenitude (plen′ i tūd) [O.F., from L. *plēnitūdo*, from *plēnus*, full], *n.* Fullness; completeness, abundance; *repletion.

plenty (plen′ ti) [O.F. *plentet*, L. *plēnitātem*, nom. *-tas*, from *plēnus*, full], *n.* Abundance, copiousness; an ample supply; fruitfulness. *a.* (*colloq.*) Plentiful, abundant. *adv.* (*colloq.*) Quite. **horn of plenty:** A cornucopia. **plenteous,** *a.* (*poet.*). **plenteously,** *adv.* **plenteousness,** *n.* **plentiful,** *a.* Existing in abundance; yielding abundance, copious. **plentifully,** *adv.* **plentifulness,** *n.*

plenum (plē′ nům) [L., neut. of *plēnus*, full], *n.* Space, as considered to be full of matter, opposed to vacuum; a condition of fullness, plethora; a full meeting.

pleonasm (plē′ ȯ năzm) [L. *pleonasmus*, Gr. *pleonasmos*, from *pleonazein*, to abound or be redundant, from *pleon*, full], *n.* Redundancy of expression in speaking or writing. **pleonastic** (-năs′ tik), *a.* **pleonastically,** *adv.*

pleroma (plė rō′ mȧ) [Gr. *plērōma*, from *plēroun*, to make full, from *plērēs*, full], *n.* Fullness, abundance; (*Gnosticism*) the divine being filling the universe and including all the æons emanating from it.

plesiomorphous (plē si ȯ môr′ fůs) [Gr. *plēsios*, near, *morphē*, form, -OUS], *a.* (*Cryst.*) Nearly alike in form. **plesiomorphic,** *a.* **plesiomorphism,** *n.*

plesiosaurus (plē si ȯ saw′ růs) [Gr. *plēsios*, near, *sauros*, lizard], *n.* (*Palæont.*) A genus of extinct marine saurians with long necks, small heads, and four paddles.

plethora (pleth′ ȯ rȧ, plė thôr′ ȧ) [med. L., from Gr. *plēthōrē*, fullness, from *plēthein*, to become full], *n.* Superabundance; (*Path.*) excessive fullness of blood. ***plethoretic, -al** (-ret′ ik, -ȧl), **plethoric** (plė thor′ ik, pleth′ ȯ rik), *a.* Of full habit of body; superabundant.

pleura (ploor′ ȧ) [med. L. and Gr., side], *n.* (*pl.* **-ræ**) (*Anat.*) A thin membrane covering the interior of the thorax and investing the lungs; (*Zool.*) a part of the body-wall in arthropods; a part to which the secondary wings are attached in insects; a part on each side of the rachis of the lingual ribbon in molluscs. **pleural,** *a.* **pleurenchyma** (-eng′ ki mȧ) [Gr. *enchuma*, infusion], *n.* (*Bot.*) The woody tissue of plants.

pleurisy (ploo′ ri si), *n.* (*Path.*) Inflammation of the pleura, usu. attended by fever, pain in the chest or side, etc. **pleuritic,** *a.*

pleuro- [Gr. *pleuron*, side, rib], *comb. form.* **pleurocarpous** (ploor ȯ kar′ půs) [Gr. *karpos*, fruit, -OUS], *a.* Bearing the fructification laterally on the branches. **pleuronectid** (-nek′ tid) [Gr. *nēktēs*, swimmer], *n.* (*Ichthyol.*) A fish of the genus

Pleuronectidæ, or the flat-fishes or flounders; a flat-fish. **pleurodynia** (-din' i ȧ), *n.* (*Path.*) Pain in the side due to chronic rheumatism of the walls of the chest. **pleuropneumonia** (-nū mō' ni ȧ), *n.* (*Path.*) Inflammation of the lungs and the pleura, esp. as a contagious disease among cattle.

plexal, plexiform [PLEXUS].

pleximeter (plek sim' ė tėr) [Gr. *plēxis*, stroke, cogn. with *plēssein*, to strike, -METER], *n.* A plate employed in examining the chest by mediate percussion. **pleximetric** (-met' rik), *a.* **pleximetry**, *n.* The art of using the pleximeter. **plexor** (plek' sȯr), *n.* An instrument used as a hammer in this process.

plexus (plek' sŭs) [L., from *plectere*, to PLAIT, p.p. *plexus*], *n.* (*pl.* **plexuses, plexus**) (*Anat.*) A network of veins, fibres, or nerves; a network, a complication. **plexal, plexiform,** *a.*

pliable (plī' ȧ bėl) [F., from *plier*, L. *plicāre*, to bend (see PLY (1))], *a.* Easily bent; flexible, pliant; supple, limber; yielding readily to influence or arguments. **pliableness, pliability** (-bil' i ti), *n.* **pliably,** *adv.* **pliant,** *a.* Pliable, flexible, yielding, compliant. **pliantly,** *adv.* **pliancy, *pliantness,** *n.*

plica (plī' kȧ) [med. L., from *plicāre*, to fold], *n.* (*Anat.* and *Zool.*) A fold of membrane, etc.; (*Path.*) a skin disease, *Plica Polonica*, endemic in Poland, in which the hair becomes matted and filthy; (*Bot.*) undue development of small twigs which form an entangled mass.

plicate, plicated (plī' kȧt, plī' kā-, pli kā' tėd) [L. *plicātus*, p.p. of *plicāre*, to fold], *a.* Plaited; folded like a fan. **plication** (-kā' shŭn), ***plicature** (plik' ȧ tūr), *n.*

pliers (plī' ėrz) [obs. *ply*, F. *plier*, see PLIABLE, -ER], *n.pl.* Small pincers with long jaws for bending wire, etc.

plight (1) (plīt) [A.-S. *plihtan*, from *pliht*, danger (cp. Dut. *plight*, G. *pflicht*, duty, obligation, O.H.G. *plegan*, to engage)], *v.t.* To pledge, to promise, to engage (oneself, one's faith, etc.). *n.* An engagement, a promise.

plight (2) (plīt) [M.E. and A.-F. *plit*, O.F. *ploit*, PLAIT], *n.* Condition, state, case, esp. one of distress or disgrace; *a plait; *attire, dress. **v.t.* To fold, to plait.

plim (plim) [dial., perh. rel. to PLUMP (1)], *v.i.* To fill out, to become plump. *v.t.* To cause to swell or expand.

Plimsoll's mark (plim' sȯl) [Samuel *Plimsoll* (1824–98), promoter of Merchant Shipping Act (1876), MARK (1)], *n.* A line, required to be placed on every British ship, marking the level to which the authorized amount of cargo submerges her. **plimsolls,** *n.pl.* Rubber-soled shoes with fabric uppers.

plinth (plinth) [L. *plinthus*, from Gr. *plinthos*, brick], *n.* A square member forming the lower division of a column, etc.; the plain projecting face at the bottom of a wall.

pliocene (plī' ȯ sēn) [Gr. *pleiōn*, more, *kainos*, new], *a.* (*Geol.*) A name applied to the most modern tertiary deposits.

plisky (plis' ki) [Sc. and North., etym. unknown], *a.* A mischievous prank; an awkward plight.

plod (plod) [prob. onomat.], *v.i.* (*past & p.p.* **plodded**) To walk painfully, slowly, and laboriously; to trudge; (*fig.*) to toil, to drudge; to study with steady diligence. *v.t.* To make (one's way) thus. *n.* A laborious walk, a trudge; a wearisome piece of work. **plodder,** *n.* **plodding,** *a.* **ploddingly,** *adv.*

plonge (plonj), ***plongee** (plon' zhā) [F. *plongée*, p.p. of *plonger*, to PLUNGE], *n.* (*Fort.*) The superior slope of the parapet.

plop (plop) [imit.], *n.* The sound of something falling heavily into water. *adv.* Suddenly; heavily, with the sound 'plop.' *v.i.* (*past & p.p.* **plopped**) To fall thus into water.

plot (1) (plot) [etym. doubtful, cp. PLAT (1)], *n.* A small piece of ground; a plan of a field, farm, estate, etc.; a complicated plan, scheme, or stratagem; a conspiracy; the plan or skeleton of the story in a play, novel, etc. (*Aviat.*) a number of hostile aeroplanes whose position has been plotted by observers. *v.t.* (*past & p.p.* **plotted**) To make a plan, map, or diagram of; to lay out in plots; to mark a position on; to plan, to devise, to contrive secretly. *v.i.* To form schemes or plots against another; to conspire. **plotter,** *n.*

plot (2) (plot) [Sc., etym. doubtful], *v.t.* (*past & p.p.* **plotted**) To scald; to steep in boiling water.

plotty, *n.* A hot drink made of wine, water, spices, etc.

plough (plou) [late A.-S. *plōh* (cp. Dut. *ploeg*, G. *pflug*, Icel. *plōgr*, Swed. *plog*, Dan. *plov*)], *n.* An implement for cutting, furrowing, and turning over land for tillage; (*fig.*) tillage, agriculture; arable land; an implement or machine resembling a plough in form or function, a machine for cutting paper, a grooving-plane, a snow-plough, etc.; a constellation in the northern hemisphere, also called Charles's Wain; (*colloq.*) failure or rejection in an examination. *v.t.* To turn up (ground) with a plough; to make (a furrow) with a plough; to furrow, groove, or scratch, with or as with a plough; (*fig.*) to wrinkle; (*colloq.*) to reject at an examination. *v.i.* To advance laboriously. **to plough back profits:** To reinvest profits. **to plough in:** To bury or cover with earth by ploughing. **to plough out:** To root out or remove by ploughing. **to plough the sands:** To labour uselessly. **to plough up:** To break up by ploughing. **to put one's hand to the plough:** To begin a task or undertaking (Luke ix. 62). ***plough-beam,** *n.* The central beam of a plough-frame. ***plough-bote,** *n.* Timber formerly allowed to a tenant for the repair of instruments of husbandry. **plough-boy,** *n.* A boy leading the horses drawing the plough. **plough-land,** *n.* Land fit for tillage; arable land, a carucate. **ploughman,** *n.* One who ploughs; a husbandman, a rustic. ***Plough Monday:** The Monday after Epiphany. **plough-shoe,** *n.* An appliance attached to a ploughshare in traversing highways, etc., to protect it. **ploughshare,** *n.* The blade of a plough. **plough-staff,** *n.* A spade-shaped appliance for cleaning the coulter, etc., of earth, weeds, etc. **plough-tail,** *n.* The rear part or the handle of the plough; (*fig.*) a ploughman, a farm-labourer. **plough-wright,** *n.* One who makes or repairs ploughs. **ploughable,** *a.* **plougher,** *n.*

plout (plout) [Sc., prob. onomat.], *v.i.* To splash or paddle about. *n.* A heavy fall of rain. **plouter,** *v.i.* To dabble, to paddle, to flounder; to potter (about). *n.* A floundering, a splashing.

plover (plŭv' ėr) [O.F. *pluvier*, prob. from a late L. *pluvārius*, from *pluvia*, rain], *n.* The common English name for several grallatorial birds, esp. the golden, yellow, or green plover, *Charadrius pluvialis.*

plow, etc. [PLOUGH].

ploy (ploi) [Sc. and North., etym. doubtful], *n.* Employment, an undertaking; a game, a pastime; a prank.

pluck (plŭk) [A.-S. *pluccian* (cp. Dut. *plukken*, G. *plücken*, Icel. *plokke*, Dan. *plukke*)], *v.t.* To pull off or out, to pick; to pull at, to twitch; to pull, to drag (away, etc.); to strip by pulling out feathers; (*fig.*) to strip, to swindle; (*colloq.*) to reject (as a candidate for a degree, etc.). *v.i.* To pull, drag, or snatch (at). *n.* The act of plucking; a pull, a twitch; the heart, lights, and liver of an animal; (*fig.*) courage, spirit. **a crow to pluck** [CROW (1)]. **to pluck up heart** or **courage** [HEART]. **plucked,** *a.* (*usu. in comb. as well-plucked*). **plucker,** *n.* **pluckless,** *a.* **plucky,** *a.* Having pluck, spirit, or courage. **pluckily,** *adv.* **pluckiness,** *n.*

pluff (plŭf) [Sc., imit.], *n.* A puff, a burst. *v.t.* To emit in a puff or puffs; to shoot. *v.i.* To become swollen. **pluffy,** *a.*

plug (plŭg) [prob. from M.Dut. *plugge* (Dut. *plug*, cp. G. *pflock*)], *n.* A piece of wood or other substance used to stop a hole; a stopple, a peg, a wedge; anything wedged in or stopping up a pipe, etc.; a cake or stick of compressed tobacco; tobacco sold in this form; (*Mach.*) the sparking-plug of an internal-combustion engine; (*Elec.*) an appliance for connecting and disconnecting a circuit. *v.t.* (*past & p.p.* **plugged**) To stop with a plug; (*slang*) to shoot; (*Am. slang*) to strike with the fist; (*colloq.*) to boom a song or dance tune by getting singers or bands to popularize it. *v.i.* (*colloq.*) To work, trudge, etc. (along) doggedly. **plug-in coil,** *n.* (*Radio.*) An inductance coil equipped with a plug with a view to quick changing. **plug-ugly,** *n.* (*Am. slang*) A hooligan, a rowdy. **plugging,** *n.*

plum (plŭm) [A.-S. *plūme*, late L. *prūna*, L. *prūnum*, late Gr. *prounon*, Gr. *proumnon*], *n.* The fleshy drupaceous fruit of *Prunus domestica* or other trees of the same genus; a tree bearing this; applied to other fruits, esp. to the raisin used in cakes, puddings, etc.; (*fig.*) the best part of anything, the choicest thing of a set, any handsome perquisite, windfall, etc.; (*slang*) £100,000 sterling, a fortune. **plum-cake,** *n.* A cake containing raisins, currants, etc. **plum-duff,** *n.* A plain boiled flour pudding with raisins, etc. **plum-porridge,** *n.* Porridge with raisins or currants. **plum-pudding,** *n.* A pudding containing raisins, currants, etc., esp. a rich one with spices, etc., eaten at Christmas. **plum-pudding dog,** *n.* A Dalmatian dog. **plum-pudding stone:** Pudding-stone, a variety of conglomerate. **plummy,** *a.* Full of or rich in plums; (*fig.*) luscious, inviting.

plumage (ploo' måj) [O.F., from PLUME]. The feathers of a bird. **plumaged,** *a.*

plumassier (ploo må sēr') [F., from *plumasse*, a great plume, as prec.], *n.* One who works or deals in feathers for attire.

plumb (plŭm) [F. *plomb*, L. *plumbum*, lead], *n.* A weight, usu. of lead, attached to a line, used to test perpendicularity; a position parallel to this, the vertical; a sounding-lead, a plummet. *a.* Perpendicular, vertical; downright, sheer, perfect, complete; (*Cricket*) level. *adv.* Vertically; (*fig.*) exactly, correctly, right; completely. *v.t.* To adjust by a plumb-line; to make vertical or perpendicular; to sound with a plummet, to measure the depth of. **out of plumb:** Not exactly vertical. **plumb-bob,** *n.* A conical weight used in a plumb-rule or on a plumb-line. **plumbless,** *a.* Fathomless. **plumb-line,** *n.* The cord by which a plumb is suspended for testing perpendicularity; a vertical line. **plumb-rule,** *n.* A mason's or carpenter's rule with a plumb-line attached.

plumbago (plŭm bā' gō) [L. *plumbāgo -ginis*, from *plumbum*, lead], *n.* A form of carbon used for making pencils, etc., blacklead, graphite; (*Bot.*) a genus of perennial herbs, with blue, rose, or violet flowers. **plumbaginous** (-băj' i nůs), *a.*

plumbean, -beous (plŭm' bė ån, -bė ůs) [L. *plumbeus*, from *plumbum*, lead], *a.* Consisting of or resembling lead; glazed with lead; *(*fig.*) dull, heavy, stupid.

plumber (plŭm' ėr) [O.F. *plummier* (F. *plombier*), L. *plumbārius*, as prec.], *n.* Orig. one who worked in lead; an artisan who fits and repairs cisterns, pipes, drains, etc., in buildings. **plumber-block** [PLUMMER-BLOCK]. **plumbery, plumbing,** *n.* The arrangement of water-pipes, etc.; attention to upkeep of these; (*Am.*) house-drains, etc.

plumbic (plŭm' bik) [L. *plumb-um*, lead, -IC], *a.* (*Chem.*) Pertaining to, derived from, or combined with lead; (*Path.*) due to the presence of lead. **plumbiferous** (-bif' ėr ůs), *a.*

plumbing [PLUMBER]. **plumbless,** etc. [PLUMB].

plume (ploom) [O.F., from L. *plūma*], *n.* A feather, esp. a large or conspicuous feather; a feather-bunch or tuft of feathers, or anything resembling this worn as an ornament; (*Zool.*) a feather-like part or form; (*Bot.*) a feathery appendage to a seed, etc.; *(*fig.*) a token of honour. *v.t.* To trim, dress, or arrange (feathers), to preen; to adorn with or as with feathers, esp. in borrowed plumage; to pride (oneself on); to strip of feathers. **borrowed plumes:** Decorations or honours to which one is not entitled, as the peacock's feathers worn by the jackdaw in the fable. **plumeless,** *a.* **plumelet,** *n.* **plumelike,** *a.* ***plumiform,** *a.* ***plumigerous** (-mij' ėr ůs), *a.* Feathered. ***plumiped** (ploo' mi ped), *a.* Having feathered feet.

plummer-block (plŭm' ėr blok) [etym. doubtful], *n.* A pillow-block.

plummet (plŭm' ėt) [O.F. *plommet*, dim. of *plomb*, PLUMB], *n.* A weight attached to a line used for sounding; a ball of lead for a plumb-line; (*fig.*) a weight, an encumbrance; *a solid lead pencil formerly used to rule paper.

plummy [PLUM].

plumose (plů mōs'), **plumous** (ploo' můs) [L. *plūmōsus*, from *plūma*, PLUME], *a.* Resembling a feather or feathers, feathery. **plumosity** (-mos' i ti), *n.*

plump (1) (plŭmp) [cp. L.G. and E.Fris. *plump*, Dut. *plomp*, rude, blunt, Swed., Dan., and G. *plump*, coarse, rude], *a.* Well-rounded, fat, fleshy, filled out, chubby; well-filled (of a purse, etc.); (*fig.*) rich, abundant. *v.t.* To make plump; to fatten, to distend. *v.i.* To grow plump; to swell (out or up). **plumper** (1), *n.* A dish, ball, or pad carried in the mouth to distend hollow cheeks. **plumply** (1), *adv.* **plumpness,** *n.* **plumpy,** *a.*

plump (2) (plŭmp) [cp. L.G. *plumpen*, Dut. *plompen*], *v.i.* To plunge or fall suddenly and heavily; (*fig.*) to vote for one candidate when more might be voted for; to give all one's votes to a single candidate. *v.t.* To fling or drop suddenly and heavily. *n.* A sudden plunge, a heavy fall; the sound of this. *adv.* Suddenly and heavily; (*fig.*) flatly, bluntly. *a.* Downright, plain, blunt. **plumper** (2), *n.* One who or that which plumps; a vote given to a single candidate when more than one has to be elected; a voter who plumps; (*slang*) a downright lie. **plumply** (2), *adv.* Bluntly, flatly, plainly.

plumpness, plumpy [PLUMP (1)].

Plumularia (ploo mū lâr' i å) [as foll.], *n.pl.* (*Zool.*) A genus of plume-like hydroids. **plumularian,** *a.* and *n.*

plumule (ploo' mūl) [L. *plūmula*, dim. of *plūma*, PLUME], *n.* The rudimentary stem in an embryo; a little feather, one of the down feathers; a downy scale on the wings of butterflies, etc. **plumulaceous** (-lā' shůs), **plumular** (ploo' mū lår), *a.*

plumy (ploo' mi), *a.* Covered with feathers; adorned with plumes; feathery.

plunder (plŭn' dėr) [G. *plündern*, to plunder, orig. household stuff, from *plunder*, bedclothes, etc.], *v.t.* To pillage, to rob, to strip; to take by force, to steal, to embezzle. *n.* Forcible or systematic robbery; spoil, booty; (*slang*) profit, gain; (*Am.*) luggage, personal belongings. **plunderage,** *n.* Pillage, esp. the embezzlement of goods on board ship; the booty so obtained. **plunderer,** *n.*

plunge (plŭnj) [O.F. *plunjer* (F. *plonger*), prob. from late L. *plumbicāre* (not extant), from L. *plumbum*, lead], *v.t.* To force or thrust into water or other fluid; to immerse; to force, to drive (into a condition, action, etc.); to sink (a flower-pot) in the ground. *v.i.* To throw oneself, to dive (into); to rush or enter impetuously (into a place, condition, etc.); to throw the body forward and the hind legs up (of a horse); to pitch (of a ship); (*colloq.*) to gamble or bet recklessly, to spend money or get into debt heavily. *n.* The act of plunging; a dive; a sudden and violent movement; (*fig.*) a risky or critical step. **plunger,** *n.* One who plunges; (*colloq.*) a reckless gambler, speculator, or spendthrift; a cavalry man; (*Mech.*) a part of a machine working with a plunging motion, as the long solid cylinder used as a piston in a force-pump.

pluperfect (ploo pěr' fėkt) [L. *plūs quam perfectum*,

more than perfect], *a.* (*Gram.*) Expressing action or time prior to some other past time. *n.* The pluperfect tense (as of *had* in *it had been*).

plural (ploor′ ȧl) [O.F. *plurel*, L. *plūrālis* from *plūs plūris*, more], *a.* Denoting more than one; consisting of more than one. *n.* The form of a word which expresses more than one, or (in languages having a dual number) more than two. **plural voter,** *n.* (*Polit.*) Elector with a vote in more than one constituency. **pluralism,** *n.* The state of being plural; the holding of more than one office, esp. an ecclesiastical benefice, at the same time; (*Phil.*) the doctrine that there is more than one ultimate principle in the universe, opp. to monism. **pluralist,** *n.* **pluralistic** (-lis′ tik), *a.* **plurality** (-răl′ i ti), *n.* A number consisting of two or more; a majority, or the excess (of votes, etc.) over the next highest number; pluralism; a benefice or other office held by a pluralist. **pluralize,** *v.t.* **pluralization** (-zā′ shŭn), *n.* **plurally,** *adv.*

pluri- [L. *plūs plūris*, more], *comb. form.* **pluriliteral** (ploo ri lit′ ėr ȧl), *a.* (*Heb. Gram.*) Containing more than the usual number of letters, *i.e.* more than three. *n.* A word of more than three letters. **plurilocular** (-lok′ ū lȧr), *a.* Multilocular. **pluriparous** (plu rip′ ȧ rŭs), *a.* Bringing forth more than one at a birth. **pluripara,** *n.* A woman who has borne more than one child. ***pluripresence** (-prez′ ėns), *n.* Presence in more places than one.

plus (plŭs) [L., more], *n.* A character (+) used as the sign of addition; an addition; a positive quantity. *prep.* With the addition of. *a.* Above zero, positive; additional, extra; (*Elec.*) electrified positively. **plus fours,** *n.pl.* Long, baggy knickerbockers.

plush (plŭsh) [F. *pluche*, contr. form of *peluche* (cp. Sp. *peluza*, It. *peluzza*), prob. from a late L. *pilūceus*, hairy, from *pilus*, hair], *n.* A cloth of various materials with a pile or nap longer than that of velvet; (*pl.*) breeches of this, worn by footmen.

plutarchy (ploo′ tar ki) [Gr. *ploutos*, wealth, *archein*, to rule], *n.* Plutocracy.

pluteus (ploo′ tė ŭs) [L.], *n.* (*pl.* ***-tei***) A barrier or light wall closing intervals between columns; (*Zool.*) a free-swimming larva of an echinoid or ophiuroid.

Pluto (ploo′ tō) [L. *Plūtōnius*, Gr. *Ploutōnios*, from *Ploutōn*, god of the infernal regions], *n.* (*Astron.*) The ninth planet in the solar system in order of distance from the sun, from which it is distant 3,666 million miles; (*Eng.*) the operation name in the 2nd World War of a system of pipe lines under the English Channel for carrying petrol from England to the armies in France. **Plutonian** (ploo tō′ nyȧn), *a.* Pertaining to Pluto or the lower regions; infernal, subterranean, dark; (*Geol.*) igneous. *n.* A Plutonist. **Plutonic** (-ton′ ik), *a.* Plutonian; (*Geol.*) igneous, pertaining to the Plutonic theory. **Plutonic rocks:** Igneous rocks, as granite, basalt, etc. **Plutonic theory:** The theory that most geological changes have been caused by igneous agency. **Plutonism,** *n.* **Plutonist,** *n.* An adherent of the Plutonic theory.

plutocracy (plù tok′ rȧ si) [Gr. *ploutokratia* (*ploutos*, wealth, -CRACY)], *n.* The rule of wealth or the rich; a ruling class of rich people; (*colloq.*) the wealthy classes. **plutocrat** (ploo′ tȯ krăt), *n.* **plutocratic** (-krăt′ ik), *a.* **pluto-democracy:** A democracy dominated by wealth. **plutolatry** (-tol′ ȧ tri), *n.* Worship of wealth.

plutonium (ploo tō′ ni ŭm), *n.* A radioactive element formed by the radioactive decay of neptunium.

plutonomy (plù ton′ ȯ mi) [Gr. *ploutos*, wealth, *-nomia*, arrangement, cogn. with *nemein*, to deal out], *n.* Political economy. **plutonomic** (-nom′ ik), *a.*

pluvial (ploo′ vi ȧl) [F., from L. *pluviālis*, from *pluvia*, rain], *a.* Of or pertaining to rain; rainy; humid; (*Geol.*) due to the action of rain. **pluviograph,** *n.* A self-recording rain-gauge. **pluviometer** (-om′ ė tėr), *n.* A rain-gauge. **pluviometrical** (-met′ ri kȧl), *a.* **pluvioscope** (ploo′ vi ȯ skōp) [-SCOPE], *n.* A variety of rain-gauge. **pluvious** (ploo′ vi ŭs), *a.* **pluvius policy:** An insurance policy to cover damage sustained through bad weather.

ply (1) (plī) [F. *pli*, fold, O.F. *ploy*, from *ployer* (F. *plier*), L. *plicāre*, to bend], *n.* A fold, a plait, a twist, a strand (of a rope, twine, etc.); a thickness, a layer; (*fig.*) a bent, a bias. **plywood,** *n.* Board consisting of three or more thin layers of wood glued together in such a manner that the grain of each is at right-angles to that of its neighbour. **two-, three-, four-ply:** (Of) wool, etc., twisted in so many strands.

ply (2) (plī) [from M.E. *applier*, to APPLY], *v.t.* To use or employ vigorously or with diligence; to use (a tool) vigorously or busily; to work at, to employ oneself in; to pursue, to press, to urge; to treat, to supply (with). *v.i.* To go to and fro, to travel or sail regularly; to be busy, to be employed; to stand or wait for custom; (*Naut.*) to work to windward.

plyers [PLIERS].

Plymouth Brethren (plim′ ŭth bre*th*′ ren) [*Plymouth*, town in Devonshire], *n.pl.* An evangelical sect that rose at Plymouth about 1830, having no regular ministry, and formulating no creed. **Plymouthism,** *n.* **Plymouthist, Plymouthite,** *n.* **Plymouth Rock,** *n.* A breed of domestic fowl.

plywood [PLY (1)].

pneuma (nū′ mȧ) [Gr., wind, spirit, see foll.], *n.* Breath, spirit, soul.

pneumatic (nū măt′ ik) [L. *pneumaticus*, Gr. *pneumatikos*, from *pneuma -matos*, wind, cogn. with *pneein*, to breathe], *a.* Pertaining to, consisting of, or actuated by means of air; gaseous; containing or filled with air; *spiritual. *n.* A pneumatic tire; a cycle fitted with such tires; (*pl.*) the science treating of the mechanical properties of air and other gases. **pneumatic brake,** *n.* (*Rail.*) A braking system in which air-pressure is applied simultaneously to brake-cylinders throughout the length of the train. **pneumatic dispatch:** Transmission of parcels, messages, etc., through tubes by means of compression or exhaustion of air. **pneumatic drill,** *n.* (*Eng.*) A rock drill in which compressed air reciprocates a loose piston which hammers a steel bit. **pneumatic railway:** A railway worked by air-pressure. **pneumatic tire:** An india-rubber tube inflated with air under pressure, used as a tire for cycles, motor-cars, etc. **pneumatic trough:** A trough containing mercury or water used for the collection of gases in inverted vessels slightly immersed. **pneumatically,** *adv.* **pneumaticity** (-tis′ i ti), *n.*

pneumato- [PNEUMA], *comb. form.* Air; breath; spirit, soul. **pneumatocyst** (nū′ mȧ tȯ sist) [CYST], *n.* An air-sac or swim-bladder in a bird, hydrozoon, etc. **pneumatology** (-tol′ o ji) [-LOGY], *n.* The science of spiritual existence; (*Theol.*) the doctrine of the Holy Spirit; *psychology. **pneumatological** (-loj′ i kȧl), *a.* **pneumatologist** (-tol′ ȯ jist), *n.* **pneumatometer** (-tom′ ė tėr) [-METER], *n.* An instrument for measuring the air exhaled at one expiration. **pneumatophore** (nū′ mȧ tȯ fôr), *n.* The pneumatocyst or other air-cavity of a compound hydrozoon; (*Bot.*) a respiratory organ in the roots of some tropical trees growing in mud; an apparatus for enabling respiration to be carried on in a mine pervaded by poisonous fumes, as after an explosion of fire-damp.

pneumogastric (nū mȯ găs′ trik) [Gr. *pneumōn -monos*, lung, GASTRIC], *n.* Of or pertaining to the lungs and the stomach.

pneumonia (nū mō′ ni ȧ) [Gr. *pneumōn -monos*, lung], *n.* (*Path.*) Acute inflammation of a lung or the lungs. **pneumonic** (-mon′ ik), *a.* **pneumonitis** (-nī′ tis), *n.* **pneumonitic** (-nit′ ik), *a.*

pneumothorax (nū mŏ thôr′ ăks) [as prec., THORAX], *n.* (*Path.*) Accumulation of air in the pleural cavity, usu. associated with pleurisy.

po [POT].

poa (pō′ ȧ) [Gr., grass], *n.* (*Bot.*) A genus of grasses; meadow grass.

poach (1) (pōch) [O.F. *pochier* (F. *pocher*), from *poche*, pocket, see POKE (1)], *v.t.* To cook (an egg) by dropping it, when divested of its shell, into boiling water. **poacher** (1), *n.* A vessel for poaching eggs in.

poach (2) (pōch) [prob. from O.F. *pocher*, to thrust into, to encroach, prob. rel. to POKE (2)], *v.i.* To encroach or trespass on (another man's lands), esp. to take game, etc.; to take game, fish, etc., by illegal or unsportsmanlike methods; to intrude or take an advantage unfairly, as in a race or game; to become soft, swampy, or miry (of ground); (*Lawn Tennis*) to hit the ball when in the court of one's partner. *v.t.* To take (game, fish, etc.) from another's preserves or by illegitimate methods; to take game from (another's preserves); to trample, to tread into mire; *to thrust, push, or drive (into); *to stab, to spear. **poacher** (2), *n.* One who intrudes on preserves to take game or fish illegally. **poachy,** *a.* Wet and soft; swampy; easily trodden into holes by cattle. **poachiness,** *n.*

poaka (pō a′ kȧ) [Maori], *n.* The N. Zealand white-headed stilt-bird.

pochard (pō′ chȧrd) [etym. doubtful], *n.* A European diving sea-duck, *Æthyia* or *Fuligula ferina*; other ducks of the same genus.

pock (pok) [A.-S. *poc* (cp. Dut. *pok*, G. *pocke*), whence POX], *n.* A pustule in an eruptive disease, as in smallpox. **pock-mark,** *n.* **pock-pitted, *-fretten, pocky,** *a.* **pockiness,** *n.* **pock-pudding** (*Sc.*) [POKE-PUDDING, see POKE (1)].

pocket (pok′ ėt) [M.E. *poket*, Ang.-Norman *pokete*, dim. of O.North.F. *poque*, as F. *poche*, POKE (1)], *n.* A small bag, sack, or pouch, esp. a small bag inserted in the clothing, to contain articles carried about the person; (*fig.*) pecuniary means; a small netted bag at billiards to receive the balls; a measure for hops, wool, ginger, etc.; (*Geol.*) a cavity in rock containing foreign matter; (*Mining*) a cavity containing gold or other ore; an isolated area or patch; (*Aviat.*) a part of the atmosphere, called 'a hole in the air,' where disturbing currents are met with, causing a flying-machine to drop suddenly. *v.t.* To put into a pocket; to keep in or as in the pocket; to hem in (a horse, etc.) in a race; to appropriate, esp. illegitimately; to put up with; to repress or conceal (one's feelings); (*Billiards*) to drive (a ball) into a pocket. **to pocket an affront, insult, wrong,** etc.: To receive or submit to it without showing resentment. **pocket battleship,** *n.* (*Nav.*) Battleship built by Germany in 1929 with a paper tonnage of only 10,000 but actually of 15,000 tons, and as powerful as vessels twice or three times its size. **pocket-book,** *n.* A note-book or book or case for carrying papers, etc., in the pocket; (*Am.*) a hand-bag. **pocket-borough** [BOROUGH]. **pocket-glass,** *n.* A portable looking-glass. **pocket-handkerchief,** *n.* **pocket-knife,** *n.* A knife with blades shutting into the handle, for carrying in the pocket. **pocket-money,** *n.* Money for occasional expenses or amusements. **pocket-piece,** *n.* A coin kept in the pocket as a memento or for luck. **pocket-pistol,** *n.* A small pistol for carrying in the pocket; (*facet.*) a small spirit-flask for the pocket. **pocketable,** *a.* **pocketful,** *n.* **pocketless,** *a.* **pockety,** *a.* (*Mining and Aviat.*) Characterized by pockets.

pocky [POCK]. **pockmanteau** (*Sc.*) [PORTMANTEAU].

pococurante (pō kō koo ran′ tā, -kū răn′ ti) [It., little-caring], *n.* A careless or apathetic person, a trifler. *a.* Indifferent. **pococurantism,** *n.*

poculiform (pŏ kū′ li fôrm) [L. *pōculum*, cup, -FORM], *a.* Cup-shaped.

pod (1) (pod) [etym. unknown], *n.* A long capsule or seed-vessel, esp. of leguminous plants; applied to similar receptacles, as the case enclosing the eggs of a locust, a silk-worm cocoon, a narrow-necked eel-net, etc. *v.i.* (*past & p.p.* **podded**) To produce pods; to swell into pods. *v.t.* To shell (peas, etc.). **podded,** *a.* Bearing pods; pod-bearing, leguminous; (*fig.*) snug, rich.

pod (2) (pod) [etym. doubtful, perh. rel. to PAD (2)], *n.* The socket into which the bit enters in a brace; the channel or groove in an auger, etc.

pod (3) (pod) [etym. doubtful], *n.* A flock, bunch, or small herd, esp. of whales, seals, etc. *v.t.* To drive (seals, etc.) into a pod.

podagra (pod′ ȧ grȧ) [L. and Gr. (*pous podos*, foot, *agra*, catching)], *n.* (*Path.*) Gout, esp. in the foot. **podagral** (pod′ ȧ grȧl), **podagric** (pŏ dăg′ rik), **podagrous** (pod′ ȧ grŭs), *a.*

podal (pō′ dȧl) [Gr. *pous podos*, foot], *n.* (*Zool.*) Of or pertaining to the feet.

poddy (pod′ i), *n.* (*Austral.*) A hand-fed calf or foal. **poddy-dodger,** *n.* A station-hand, a dairyman.

podestà (pŏ des ta′) [It., from L. *potestatem*, nom. *-tas*, power, authority], *n.* A subordinate municipal judge in an Italian city.

podge (poj) [var. of PUDGE], *n.* A short and stout person. **podgy,** *a.*

podium (pō′ di ŭm) [L., from Gr. *podion*, from *pous podos*, foot], *n.* (*pl.* **-dia**) A low projecting wall or basement supporting a building; a platform encircling the arena in an amphitheatre; a continuous structural bench round a hall, etc. **podial,** *a.*

podocarp (pod′ ŏ karp) [Gr. *pous podos*, foot, *karpos*, fruit], *n.* (*Bot.*) A foot-stalk supporting a fruit. **podocarpous** (-kar′ pŭs), *a.* (*Bot.*) Of or pertaining to the genus *Podocarpus*, consisting of evergreen coniferous trees of tropical Asia and New Zealand, the black pines. **podophthalmate** (pod of thăl′ mȧt) [Gr. *ophthalmos*, eye, -ATE], *a.* Stalk-eyed. **podophthalmian,** *n.* A stalk-eyed crustacean. *a.* Belonging to this class. **podophyllum** (-fil′ ŭm) [Gr. *phullon*, leaf], *n.* (*Bot.*) A genus of plants, containing the may-apple. **podophyllic,** *a.* **podophyllin,** *n.* (*Chem.*) A purgative resin extracted from the root of *Podophyllum peltatum*. **podophyllous,** *a.* (*Ent.*) Having the organs of locomotion so compressed as to resemble leaves.

podura (pŏ dūr′ ȧ) [Gr. *pous podos*, foot, *oura*, tail], *n.* A genus of apterous insects comprising the springtails.

poe-bird (pō′ ė bĕrd) [prob. *arbitrary*], *n.* A New Zealand bird, *Prosthemadera Novæ-Zeelandiæ*, larger than a thrush, with dark metallic plumage and a tuft of white feathers on the neck, also called the parson-bird.

poem (pō′ ėm) [F. *poéme*, L. *poēma*, Gr. *poiēma*, from *poiein*, to make], *n.* A metrical composition, esp. of an impassioned and imaginative kind; an artistic and imaginative composition in verse or prose; (*fig.*) any thing, series of actions, events, etc., that gives the impression of a poem.

pœnology [PENOLOGY].

poephagous (pŏ ē′ fȧ gŭs) [Gr. *poēphagos* (*poa*, grass, -PHAGOUS)], *a.* (*Zool.*) Subsisting on grass.

poesy (pō′ ė si) [M.E. and O.F. *poesie*, L. *poēsis*, Gr. *poiēsis*, as prec.], *n.* The art of poetry; (*collect.*) metrical compositions; *a posy.

poet (pō′ ėt) [O.F. *poete*, L. *poēta*, Gr. *poiētes*, maker, poet, as prec.], *n.* A writer of poems or metrical compositions, esp. one possessing high powers of imagination and rhythmical expression; one possessed of high imaginative or creative power. **Poet Laureate:** An officer of the British royal household whose nominal duty is to compose an ode every year for the sovereign's birthday, for any great national victory, etc. **poetaster** (pō ė tăs′ tėr), *n.* An inferior or petty poet; a pitiful versifier. **poetess,** *n.*

poetic, poetical (pō et′ ik, -ăl), *a.* Pertaining to or suitable for poetry; expressed in poetry, written in poetry; having the finer qualities of poetry; fit to be expressed in poetry. **poetic justice:** Ideal justice as conceived by the poets. **poetic licence:** The latitude in grammar, etc., allowed to poets. **poetically,** *adv.* **poeticize,** *v.t.* **poetics,** *n.* The theory or principles of poetry. **poeticule,** *n.* A poetaster. **poetize** (pō′ ė tīz), *v.i.* To compose verses, to write poetry. *v.t.* To poeticize.

poetry (pō′ e tri) [O.F. *poetrie,* late L. *poētria,* from *poēta,* POET], *n.* The art or work of the poet; that one of the fine arts which expresses the imagination and feelings in sensuous and rhythmical language, usu. in metrical forms; imaginative, impassioned, and rhythmical expression whether in verse or prose; imaginative or creative power; a quality in anything that powerfully stirs the imagination; (*collect.*) metrical compositions, verse, poems.

pogrom (pŏ grom′) [Rus., destruction], *n.* An organized attack, usu. with pillage and massacre, upon a class of the population, esp. Jews.

poh (pō) [instinctive sound], *int.* Expressing contempt or disgust.

pohutakawa (pō hu′ tu ka′ wă) [Maori], *n.* The Christmas bush.

poi (1) (poi) [Maori], *n.* An object used by women in a ceremonial dance.

poi (2) (pō′ ē) [Hawaiian], *n.* A paste of fermented taro root.

poignant (poi′ nănt) [O.F., pres.p. of *poindre,* L. *pungere,* to prick], *a.* Sharp; stimulating to the palate, pungent; keen, piercing; bitter, painful. **poignancy,** *n.* **poignantly,** *adv.*

poind (poind) [Sc., from A.-S. *pyndan,* to impound, cogn. with POUND (2), PINFOLD], *v.t.* To distrain upon; to seize and sell (a debtor's goods); to impound. *n.* The act of poinding, distraint.

poinsettia (poin set′ i ă) [J. R. *Poinsett* (1779–1853), American politician, the discoverer], *n.* A genus of S. American and Mexican plants with gorgeous red leaf-like bracts and small greenish-yellow flowerheads.

point (point) [partly through F. *point,* a dot, a point, *pointe,* a sharp end, L. *punctum,* orig. neut. p.p. L. *puncta,* piercing; and *pointer,* to point, med. L. *punctāre,* all from L. *punct-,* p.p. stem of *pungere,* to prick], *n.* A mark made by the end of anything sharp, a dot; a dot used as a mark of punctuation, to indicate vowels, etc.; (*Print.*) a full stop, or decimal mark to separate integral from fractional digits in decimal numbers, etc.; a particular item, a detail; a particular place or position; stage or degree in progress or increase, as in temperature; a particular moment; the precise moment for an event, action, etc., the instant, the verge; a step or stage in an argument, discourse, etc.; a unit in reckoning superiority, etc., in appraising qualities of an exhibit in a show, a racehorse, etc., or in reckoning odds given to an opponent in a game, in betting, or in scoring in games; a salient quality, a trait, a characteristic; the essential matter, the aim, the purpose, the exact object of discussion, the main purport, the gist, the bearing (of a joke, etc.); the sharp end of a tool, weapon, etc., the tip; a cape, a promontory (esp. in place-names); thread-lace made entirely with the needle; a sharp-pointed tool, as an etcher's needle, glass-cutter's diamond, various implements or parts of machinery used in the industrial arts, etc.; a tapering rail moving on a pivot for switching a train from one line to another; hence, a railway switch; a tine of a deer's horn; (*fig.*) pungency, effectiveness, force; (*Geom.*) that which has position but not magnitude; (*Print.*) the unit of measurement for type-bodies; (*Her.*) a position on a shield; (*Cricket*) a fielder or the position of such on the off-side of the batsman; (*Hunting*) a spot to which a straight run is made; (*Mus.*) a passage or subject to which special importance is drawn; (*Mil.*) the leading party of an advanced guard; (*pl.*) the extremities of a horse; (*Stock Exchange*) a unit of increase or decrease in the price of stocks; (*Shooting, etc.*) the act of pointing by a setter, etc.; (*Fencing*) a twist; (*Naut.*) an angular division of the compass; a short cord for reefing sails; (*Horses*) a buckling-strap on harness; *a tagged lace for lacing bodices, doublets, etc.; *a signal on a musical instrument in war or the chase; *the pommel of a saddle. *v.t.* To sharpen; to mark with points, to punctuate; to give force or point to; to fill (the joints of masonry) with mortar or cement pressed in with a trowel; to indicate, to show; to direct (a finger, etc., at); (*fig.*) to give effect or pungency to (a remark, jest, etc.); to indicate the meaning or point of by a gesture; (*Gardening*) to turn in (manure, etc.) with the point of a spade *to prick or pierce. *v.i.* To direct attention to; to draw attention to game by standing and looking at it (of a pointer or setter); to aim (at or towards); to face or be directed (towards); (*Naut.*) to sail close to the wind. **at all points:** In every part or direction; completely, perfectly. ***at point:** In readiness. **at** or **on the point:** On the verge (of). **to carry one's point:** To prevail in an argument or dispute. **to give points to:** To be superior to. **in point:** Apposite, relevant. **in point of fact** [FACT]. **point of distance** [DISTANCE]. **point of honour:** A matter of punctilio, a matter involving personal honour, involving a demand for satisfaction by a duel, etc. **point of no return:** (*Aviat.*) The point in a flight where shortage of fuel makes it necessary to go on as return is impossible. **point of order:** A question of procedure. **point of view:** The position from which a thing is looked at; way of regarding a matter. **point of the compass:** One of the 32 angular divisions of the compass at intervals of 11° 15′. **to make a point:** To score a point; (*fig.*) to establish a point in argument. **to make a point of:** To attach special importance to; to regard as essential. **to point out:** To indicate. **to the point:** Appropriate, apposite, pertinent. **point-blank,** *a.* Fired horizontally; aimed directly at the mark; (*fig.*) direct, flat, plain. *adv.* Horizontally, with direct aim; (*fig.*) directly, flatly, plainly. *n.* A point-blank shot. **point-blank distance:** The distance through which a shot may be fired horizontally. **point-duty,** *n.* The work of a constable stationed at a junction of streets or other point to regulate traffic. **point-lace,** *n.* Lace made with the point of a needle. **pointsman,** *n.* A constable on point-duty; a man in charge of the switches on a railway. **point system:** (*Print.*) A standard system for measuring type bodies, a point being ·0138 in. **point-to-point,** *a.* Denoting a steeplechase or other race in a direct line from one point to another. ***pointal** [POINTEL]. ***point-device,** *a.* Correct, precise, finical, neat. *adv.* Correctly, precisely, to a nicety. **pointing,** *n.* The act of indicating, directing, sharpening, etc.; punctuation; the act of finishing or renewing a mortar-joint in a wall. **pointless,** *a.* Having no point; dull, not apposite. **pointlessly,** *adv.* **pointlessness,** *n.*

pointed (poin′ tĕd), *a.* Having a sharp point; (*fig.*) having point, penetrating, cutting; referring to some particular person or thing; emphasized, made obvious. **pointedly,** *adv.* With special meaning. **pointedness,** *n.*

pointer (poin′ tĕr), *n.* One who or that which points; the index-hand of a clock, etc.; a rod used for pointing on a blackboard, etc.; a dog trained to point at game; (*pl.*) two stars of the Plough a line drawn through which points nearly to the pole-star; (*Austral.*) a trickster, a swindler; (*Austral.*) one of the bullocks next to the pole in a team.

pointillism (pwan′ ti lizm) [F. *pointiller,* draw in points], *n.* (*Art*) Delineation by means of dots of various colours which merge into a whole.

poise (poiz) [M.E. and O.F. *poise,* ind. of *peser,* ult. from L. *pensāre,* freq. of *pendere,* to weigh], *v.t.* To balance, to hold or carry in equilibrium; to counterpoise; (*fig.*) to ponder. *v.i.* To be balanced or in equilibrium; to hang (in the air) over, to hover. *n.* Equipoise, equilibrium, a counterpoise, a state of suspense, indecision, etc.

poison (poi' zȯn) [F. *poison*, as POTION], *n.* A substance that injures or kills an organism into which it is absorbed; (*fig.*) anything noxious or destructive to health or morality; (*slang*) liquor, drink. *v.t.* To put poison in or upon; to infect with poison; to administer poison to; to kill or injure by this means; (*fig.*) to taint, to corrupt, to vitiate, to pervert. **poison gas,** *n.* (*Mil.*) Poisonous or stupefying gas or liquid used in warfare. **poison pen:** A writer of malicious anonymous letters. **poisonable,** *a.* **poisoner,** *n.* **poisonous,** *a.* **poisonously,** *adv.*

*__poitrel__ (poi' trėl) [O.F. *poitral*, L. *pectorāle*, PECTORAL], *n.* Armour for the breast of a horse.

poke (1) (pōk) [cp. O.North.F. *poque*, F. *poche*, Icel. *poki*, perh. rel. to A.-S. *pohha*], *n.* A bag, a sack. **a pig in a poke:** A blind bargain, the purchase of goods, etc., not seen beforehand.

poke (2) (pōk) [cp. Dut. and L.G. *poken*, to thrust, *poke*, dagger, G. *pochen*, also POACH (2)], *v.t.* To thrust, to push (against, into, etc.), esp. with something pointed; to stir, to prod, to incite, to urge; to thrust or butt at with the horns; to thrust (something in, out, through, etc.); to make (a hole, etc.) by poking. *v.i.* (*colloq.*) To pry, to search; to dawdle, to busy oneself without any definite object. *n.* A poking, a push, a thrust, a prod, a nudge; a collar with a drag attached to prevent animals from breaking through fences, etc. **to poke fun at:** To ridicule, to make a laughing-stock. **pokeweed,** *n.* A N. American herb, *Phytolacca decandra.* ***poking-stick, -iron,** *n.* A rod for stiffening the plaits of ruffs. **poky,** *a.* Cramped, confined, stuffy (of a room, etc.); (*colloq.*) shabby; petty, dull.

poke (3) (pōk) [perh. ident. with POKE (1 or 2)], *n.* A projecting front on a woman's hat or bonnet, formerly a detachable rim. **poke-bonnet,** *n.* **poke-bonneted,** *a.*

poker (1) (pō' kėr), *n.* An iron rod used to stir a fire; an instrument employed in poker-work; (*Univ. slang*) one of the bedells carrying a mace before the Vice-Chancellor at Oxford or Cambridge. *v.t.* To adorn with poker-work. *v.i.* To carry out (a design) in this. **red-hot poker,** *n.* Popular name of plant of the genus *Tritoma*, or flame-flower. **poker-work,** *n.* The production of decorative designs on wood by burning or scorching with a heated instrument.

poker (2) (pō' kėr) [etym. doubtful], *n.* A card-game in which the players bet on the value in their hands. **poker-face,** *n.* An expressionless face.

poker (3) (pō' kėr) [Am., cp. Dan. *pokker*, Swed. *pocker*, the devil], *n.* A bugbear, a hobgoblin. **poky** [POKE (2)].

polacca (pȯ lăk' ȧ), **polacre** (pȯ lā' kėr) [F. *polacre*, It. *polacca*, etym. doubtful], *n.* A three-masted vessel used in the Mediterranean.

*__polack__ (pō' lȧk) [Pol. *Polak*], *n.* A Pole.

polar (pō' lȧr) [med. L. *polāris*, from L. *polus*, POLE (2)], *a.* Pertaining to or situated near the poles of the earth or the celestial sphere; coming from the regions near the poles; pertaining to a magnetic pole, having polarity, magnetic; having two opposite elements or tendencies, esp. positive and negative electricity; (*Biol.*) pertaining to the poles of a cell; (*Geom.*) relating to or of the nature of a polar; (*fig.*) remote or opposite as the poles; resembling the polestar, attracting, guiding. *n.* (*Geom.*) A plane curve having a particular relation to another and to a point called the pole; (*Conics*) the line connecting the points of contact of two tangents drawn to a given curve from the pole. **polar angle:** The angles formed by two meridians at a pole. **polar bear:** A white arctic bear, *Ursus maritimus.* **polar caps:** (*Astron.*) Two white regions round the poles of the planet Mars. **polar circles** [CIRCLE]. **polar distance:** The angular distance of a point from the nearest pole. **polarly,** *adv.*

polari- [as prec.], *comb. form.*

polarimetry (pō lȧ rim' i tri), *n.* The disposition in a body to exhibit opposite directions, as attraction and repulsion at the opposite poles of a magnet; the quality (in electricity, etc.) of being attracted to one pole and repelled from the other; the disposition in a body to place its mathematical axis in a particular direction; (*fig.*) possession of antithetic tendencies, principles, etc. **polarimetric,** *a.*

polariscope (pō lă' ri skōp), *n.* (*Optic.*) An instrument for showing the phenomena of polarized light. **polariscopic,** *a.*

polarization (pō lȧ rī zā' shŭn), *n.* (*Elec.*) The collecting of hydrogen on the positive electrode of a battery causing a counter E.M.F.; the act of polarizing; the state of being polarized; (*Opt.*) modification of the rays of light or heat by reflection or transmission so that they exhibit different properties in different planes parallel to the direction of propagation. **polarize,** *v.t.* **polarizable,** *a.* **polarizer,** *n.*

polatouche (pol ȧ tooch') [F., from Rus. *poletuchii*], *n.* A small flying squirrel of Europe and Siberia.

polder (pōl' dėr) [Dut.], *n.* A tract of land below the level of the sea, or a river that has been drained and cultivated.

pole (1) (pōl) [A.-S. *pāl*, L. *pālus*, PALE (1)], *n.* A long slender piece of wood or metal, usu. rounded and tapering, esp. fixed upright in the ground as a flagstaff, support for tent, telegraph wires, etc.; the shaft of a large vehicle; an instrument for measuring; a measure of length, a rod or perch, 5½ yards; (*Naut.*) a mast. *v.t.* To furnish or support with, to convey on or impel by poles. **bare poles:** (*Naut.*) Masts without sails. **up the pole:** (*slang*) Crazy, mad. **poler,** *n.* (*Austral.*) The bullock next to the pole in a team; (*Austral. slang*) a sponger. **poling,** *n.*

pole (2) (pōl) [through O.F. *pole*, or directly from L. *polus*, Gr. *polos*, pivot, axis], *n.* One of the extremities of the axis on which a sphere or spheroid, esp. the earth, revolves; one of the points where the projection of the axis of the earth pierces the celestial sphere and round which the stars appear to revolve; (*Math.*) a point from which a pencil of rays radiates, a fixed point of reference; (*Phys.*) one of the two points in a body where the attractive or repelling force is greatest, as in a magnet; a terminal of an electric cell, battery, etc.; (*Biol.*) the extremity of the axis of a cell nucleus, etc.; (*fig.*) either of the polar regions; (*poet.*) the sky, the firmament. **magnetic pole** [MAGNETIC]. **pole-star,** *n.* A bright star, *Polaris* in *Ursa Minor*, within a degree and a quarter of the northern celestial pole; (*fig.*) a guiding principle, a lodestar. **poleward,** *a.* and *adv.* **polewards,** *adv.* **poles asunder:** As far apart as possible.

Pole (3) (pōl), *n.* A native of Poland or one of Polish race.

poleaxe (pōl' ăks) [M.E. *pollax* (POLL (1), AXE)], *n.* A form of battle-axe consisting of an axe set on a long handle; such a weapon with a hook formerly used by sailors in boarding, etc.; a long-handled butcher's axe with a hammer at the back, used for slaughtering cattle. *v.t.* To strike or kill with a poleaxe.

polecat (pōl' kăt) [M.E. *polcat* (perh. from *poule*, chicken, CAT (1))], *n.* A small carnivorous European weasel-like mammal, *Putorius fœtidus*, with two glands emitting an offensive smell.

polemarch (pol' ė mark) [Gr. *polemarchos* (*polem -os*, war, *archein*, to rule)], *n.* (*Gr. Ant.*) The third archon, orig. a military commander-in-chief; a civil magistrate with varying functions.

polemic (pȯ lem' ik) [Gr. *polemikos*, from *polemos*, war], *a.* Polemical. *n.* A controversy or controversial discussion; a controversialist; (*pl.*) the art or practice of controversial discussion, esp. in theology. **polemical,** *a.* Pertaining to controversy; controversial, disputatious. **polemically,**

adv. **polemize** (pol' ė mīz), *v.t.* **polemicist** (pŏ lem' i sist), *n.*

polemoniaceous (pol ė mō ni ā' shŭs) [mod. L. *Polemoniaceæ*, from Gr. *polemōnion*, Greek valerian], *a.* (*Bot.*) Of or belonging to the *Polemoniaceæ*, a family of plants containing the phloxes, and typified by *Polemonium cæruleum*, the Greek valerian or Jacob's ladder.

polemoscope (pŏ lem' ŏ skŏp) [F. *polémoscope* (Gr. *polem -os*, war, -SCOPE)], *n.* A telescope or other perspective glass with a mirror set at an angle for viewing objects obliquely.

polenta (pŏ len' tȧ) [It.], *n.* A kind of porridge made of maize-meal or chestnut-meal, a common food in Italy; a similar food made of barley-meal.

poley (pō' li) [POLL (2), -Y], *a.* (*prov.*) Hornless (of cattle).

Polianthes (pol i ăn' thēz) [Gr. *polios*, white, *anthos*, flower], *n.* (*Bot.*) A genus of *Amaryllidaceæ*, containing the tuberose.

police (pŏ lēs') [F., from med. L. *polīta*, L. *polītia*, POLICY (1)], *n.* The executive administration concerned in the preservation and enforcement of public order; the Government department responsible for this; a civil force organized for the maintenance of order, the detection of crime, and the apprehension of offenders; (*pl.*) constables, etc., belonging to this force. *v.t.* To control or maintain; (*fig.*) to regulate, to discipline. **police constable** [CONSTABLE]. **police-court:** A court of summary jurisdiction dealing with minor charges, esp. those preferred by the police. **police magistrate:** A magistrate presiding over this. **policeman,** *n.* **police office:** The headquarters of a police force in a town or district. **police officer:** A policeman. **police state:** (*Pol.*) A totalitarian state maintained by the use of political police. **police station:** The headquarters of a local section of the police. **police trap,** *n.* An ambush by police to trap offenders against road regulations. **police woman,** *n.* A female member of a police force.

policlinic (pol i klin' ik) [G. *poliklinik* (Gr. *polis*, city, CLINIC)], *n.* A clinic in a private house instead of a hospital; the dispensary or out-patients' department of a hospital.

policy (1) (pol' i si) [O.F. *policie*, L. *polītia*, Gr. *politeia*, from *polītēs*, citizen, from *polis*, city], *n.* Prudence, foresight, or sagacity in managing or conducting, esp. State affairs; political wisdom, sagacity, artifice, or cunning statecraft; prudent conduct; a course of action or administration recommended or adopted by a party, Government, etc.

policy (2) (pol' i si) [F. *police*, prob. from med. L. *apodissa -dixa*, Gr. *apodeixis*, demonstration, proof, from *apodeiknunai* (APO-, *deiknunai*, to show)], *n.* A document containing a contract of insurance; a warrant, voucher, etc.; (*Am.*) a method of gambling by betting on numbers drawn in a lottery. **policy-shop,** *n.* (*Am.*) An office where drawings take place in connexion with such lotteries.

policy (3) (pol' i si) [Sc., prob. from L. *polītus*, improved, see POLITE, conf. with POLICY (1)], *n.* The pleasure-grounds about a country-house; *the improvement or the improvements and embellishments of an estate.

poligar (pol' i gar) [Marathi *pālegār*], *n.* A subordinate feudal chieftain in S. India; a follower of such a chieftain. **poligar-dog,** *n.* A large hairless variety of dog from S. India. **poligarship,** *n.*

poling [POLE (1)].

poliomyelitis (pol i ō mī e lī' tis), **polio** (pō' li ō) [Gr. *polios*, grey, *meulos*, marrow], *n.* (*Path.*) Inflammation of the grey matter of the spinal cord; infantile paralysis.

polish (1) (pol' ish) [F. *poliss-*, stem of *polir*, L. *polīre*], *v.t.* To make smooth or glossy, usu. by friction; (*fig.*) to refine, to free from rudeness or coarseness. *v.i.* To take a polish. *n.* A smooth glossy surface, esp. produced by friction; friction applied for this purpose; a substance applied to impart a polish; refinement, elegance of manners. **to polish off:** (*colloq.*) To finish speedily and get rid of. **polishable,** *a.* **polisher,** *n.* **polishing-paste, -powder, -slate,** *n.* Substances applied in polishing the surface of various materials. ***polishment,** *n.*

Polish (2) (pō' lish), *a.* Pertaining to Poland or its inhabitants. *n.* The language of the Poles; (*collect.*) the Polish people.

Politburo (pol it bū' rō) [Rus.], *n.* The Political Bureau of the Central Committee of the Communist Party of U.S.S.R.

polite (pŏ līt') [L. *polītus*, p.p. of *polīre*, to POLISH], *a.* Refined in manners; courteous; well-bred; cultivated; elegant, refined (of literature). **politely,** *adv.* **politeness,** *n.* ***politesse*** (pol i tes') [F.], *n.*

politic (pol' i tik) [F. *politique*, L. *polīticus*, Gr. *politikos*, as POLICY (1)], *a.* Prudent and sagacious; prudently devised, judicious, expedient; crafty, scheming, artful; specious; consisting of citizens. *n.pl.* The science or art of civil government; political affairs; political views of a person or persons; (*fig.*) policy, conduct of private affairs. **body politic** [BODY]. **politicize** (-lit'-), *v.t.* To make political. *v.i.* To engage in or discuss politics; to play the politician. **politicly,** *adv.* Artfully, cunningly. **politico-,** *comb. form.* **politics** [POLITIC]. ***politize** (pol' i tīz), *v.i.*

political (pŏ lit' i kȧl), *a.* Relating to civil government and its administration; treating of or relating to politics; having an established system of government. *n.* A civil officer, an administrator, as dist. from a military officer, etc. **political agent, resident,** *n.* Indian government official appointed to advise a native ruler. **political economy** [ECONOMY]. **political geography** [GEOGRAPHY]. **politically,** *adv.* ***politicaster,** *n.*

politician (pol i tish' ȧn), *n.* A person versed in politics, a statesman; one engaged in or devoted to party politics; (*Am.*) one who employs politics for private ends, a spoilsman.

polity (pol' i ti), *n.* The form, system, or constitution of the civil government of a State; the State; an organized community, a body politic; the form of organization of any institution, etc.; *policy.

polka (pōl'-, pol' kȧ) [etym. doubtful, perh. from Pol. *Polka*, fem. of *Polak*, POLACK], *n.* A lively round dance of Bohemian origin; a piece of music for this; a woman's tight-fitting jacket, usu. of knitted wool. **polka dots:** Small dots on cloth material. **polk,** *v.i.* To dance a polka.

poll (1) (pōl) [M.E. and M.Dut. *polle*, head or pate (cp. Dan. *puld*)], *n.* A human head; the part of the head on which the hair grows; a register or enumeration of heads or persons, esp. of persons entitled to vote at elections; the voting at an election, the number of votes polled, or the counting of these; the time or place of election; an attempt to ascertain public opinion by questioning a few individuals; the butt-end of an axe or other tool. *v.t.* To remove the top of (trees, etc.); to crop the hair of; to cut off the horns of; to clip, to shear; to take the votes of; to receive (a specified number of votes); to give (one's vote); *to plunder. *v.i.* To give one's vote. **deed-poll** [DEED]. **to poll a jury:** (*Am.*) To examine each juror as to his concurrence in a verdict. **poll-tax,** *n.* A capitation tax or one levied on every person. **pollable,** *a.*

poll (2) (pōl) [short for dial. *pold*, for *polled*, p.p. of prec.], *a.* Polled; hornless. **poll-beast, -cow, -ox,** *n.* A polled beast, esp. one of a breed of hornless cattle.

poll (3) (pol), **polly** [var. of *Moll*, see MOLL], *n.* A familiar name for a parrot.

poll (4) (pol) [prob. short for POLLOI], *n.* (*slang*) At Cambridge University, the men who take a degree without honours. **poll-man,** *n.*

pollack (pol′ ȧk) [etym. doubtful], *n.* A seafish, *Gadus pollachius*, allied to the cod.

pollan (pol′ ȧn) [rel. to Gael. *pollag* or Ir. *pollôg*, perh. from Gael. *poll*, *phuill*, pool, pit], *n.* A herring-like Irish freshwater fish, *Coregonus pollan*.

pollard (pol′ ȧrd) [POLL (1), -ARD], *n.* A tree with its top cut off so as to have a dense head of young branches; a stag or other animal that has cast its horns; a polled or hornless ox, sheep, or other animal; the chub; a mixture of fine bran with a small quantity of flour, orig. bran sifted from flour. *v.t.* To lop the top of (a tree). **pollarded,** *a.* Lopped, cropped; wanting horns.

pollen (pol′ ėn) [L., fine flour], *n.* The fertilizing powder discharged from the anthers of flowers and causing germination in the ovules. **pollenless,** *a.* **pollinar, pollinarious** (-nâr′ i ůs), **pollinary** (pol′ i nȧr i), **pollinic** (-lin′ ik), *a.* **pollinate, -nize** (pol-′), *v.t.* To sprinkle with pollen so as to cause fertilization. **pollination** (-nā′ shůn), *n.* **polliniferous** (-nif′ ėr ůs), **pollinoid** (pol′ i noid), **pollinose,** *a.*

poller (pō′ lėr), *n.* One who polls trees; one who registers voters; one who votes; *a barber; *a robber, an extortioner.

pollicitation (pȯ lis i tā′ shůn) [L. *pollicitātio*, from *pollicitārī*, to promise], *n.* A voluntary promise or engagement, or a paper containing such engagement; (*Law*) a promise not yet accepted, an offer.

pollinar, pollination, etc. [POLLEN].

polliwog (pol′ i wog) [M.E. *polwygle* (POLL (1), WIGGLE)], *n.* A tadpole.

pollock [POLLACK].

polloi (pol′ oi) [Gr. *hoi polloi*, the many], *n.pl.* The mob, the rabble, the majority.

pollute (pȯ lūt′) [L. *pollūtus*, p.p. of *polluere* (*pol-*, earlier *por-*, *pro-*, forth, *luere*, to wash)], *v.t.* To make foul or unclean; to defile; to corrupt the moral purity of; to dishonour, to ravish; to profane. **a.* Polluted. **pollutedly,** *adv.* **pollutedness,** *n.* **polluter,** *n.* **pollution** (pȯ lū′ shůn), *n.*

polo (pō′ lō) [Tibetan native], *n.* A game of Eastern origin resembling hockey but played on horseback. **polo-jumper,** *n.* (*Dressmaking*) A knitted jumper with a fold-over collar; **polo neck:** A close-fitting, doubled-over collar as in this.

polonaise (pol′ ȯ-, pō′ lȯ nāz) [F., fem. of *polonais*, Polish], *n.* An article of dress for women, consisting of a bodice and short skirt in one piece; a similar garment for men worn early in the 19th cent.; a slow dance of Polish origin; a piece of music for this.

polony (pȯ lō′ ni) [prob. corr. of BOLOGNA], *n.* A sausage of partly-cooked pork.

***polt** (pōlt) [etym. doubtful], *n.* A blow; *a club or pestle. **polt-foot,** *n.* A club-foot.

poltergeist (pol′ tėr gīst) [G., noisy ghost], *n.* An alleged spirit which makes its presence known by noises and violence.

poltroon (pol troon′) [F. *poltron*, It. *poltrone*, from *poltro*, sluggard, orig. bed, perh. cogn. with BOLSTER], *n.* An arrant coward; a dastard. **a.* Cowardly, base, contemptible. **poltroonery,** *n.*

***polverine** (pol′ vėr ēn) [It. *polverino*, from *polvere*, L. *pulverem*, nom. *pulvus*, dust], *n.* The calcined ashes of a plant from the Levant, used in glass-making.

poly- [Gr. *polus*, many], *comb. form.* **polyacoustic** (pol i ȧ kou′ stik), *a.* Capable of multiplying or increasing sound. *n.* An instrument for doing this. **polyact** (pol′ i ăkt), *a.* Having several rays, as a sponge spicule. **polyad,** *n.* (*Chem.*) An element whose valency is greater than two. ***polyadelphia*** (pol i ȧ del′ fi ȧ) [Gr. *adelphos*, brother], *n.pl.* (*Bot.*) A Linnæan class of plants having the stamens in three or more bundles. **polyadelphian, -phous,** *a.* ***polyandria*** (-ăn′ dri ȧ) [Gr. *anēr andros*, man], *n.pl.* (*Bot.*) A Linnæan class of plants having stamens hypogynous and free. **polyandrian, -drous** (-ăn dri ȧn, -drůs), *a.* Having numerous stamens; pertaining to or practising polyandry. **polyandrist,** *n.* A woman having several husbands. **polyandry** (pol′ i ăn dri), *n.* The practice or condition of a woman having more than one husband at once; plurality of husbands.

polyanthus (pol i ăn′ thůs) [Gr. *poluanthos* (POLY-, *anthos*, flower)], *n.* (*pl.* **-uses**) A garden variety of primula, prob. a development from the cowslip or oxlip.

polyarchy (pol′ i ar ki) [POLY-, Gr. *archia*, government, from *archein*, to rule], *n.* Government by many. **polyatomic** (-ȧ tom′ ik), *a.* (*Chem.*) Applied to elements having more than one atom in their molecules, esp. replaceable atoms of hydrogen. ***polyautography** (-aw tog′ rȧ fi), *n.* The process of multiplying copies of handwriting, drawings, etc., an early name for lithography. **polybasic** (-bā′ sik), *a.* (*Chem.*) Having two or more equivalents of a base (of acids, etc.). **polybasite** (pȯ lib′ ȧ sīt), *n.* (*Min.*) An iron-black orthorhombic mineral. **polycarpellary, -carpous** (-kar′ pė lȧr i, -kar′ půs), *a.* (*Bot.*) Composed of several carpels. **polychæte** (pol′ i kēt), *a.* (*Zool.*) Belonging to the *Polychæta*, a class of worms with setæ, mostly marine; *n.* A polychæte worm. **polychætan, -tous** (-kē′ tȧn, -tůs), *a.* **polychord** (pol′ i kôrd), *a.* Having many chords. *n.* (*Mus.*) A ten-stringed musical instrument resembling the double bass without a neck; (*Organ*) an apparatus coupling two octave notes. **polychroite** (pol′ i krō īt), *n.* The yellow colouring-matter of saffron.

polychromatic (pol i krȯ măt′ ik), *a.* Exhibiting many colours or a play of colours. **polychrome** (pol′ i krōm), *n.* A work of art executed in several colours, esp. a statue. *a.* Having or executed in many colours. **polychromic** (-krō′ mik), **polychromous** (pol′ i krō můs), *a.* **polychromy,** *n.* The art of decorating (pottery, statuary, or buildings) in many colours.

polyclinic (pol i klin′ ik), *n.* A clinic dealing with various diseases; a general hospital.

polycotyledon (pol i kot i lē′ dȯn) [POLY-, COTYLEDON], *n.* (*Bot.*) A plant with seeds having more than two cotyledons. **polycotyledonous,** *a.* ***polycracy** [POLYARCHY]. **polydactyl** (pol i dăk′ til), *a.* Having more than the normal number of fingers or toes. *n.* A polydactyl animal. **polydactylism,** *n.* **polydactylous,** *a.* **polydæmonism** (-dē′ mȯ nizm), *n.* Belief in numerous demons or spirits controlling the operations of nature. **polydipsia** (-dip′ si ȧ), *n.* (*Path.*) Insatiable thirst.

polygamia (pol i gā′ mi ȧ) [POLY-, Gr. *gamos*, marriage], *n.pl.* (*Bot.*) A Linnæan class of plants, bearing hermaphrodite and unisexual (male or female) flowers on the same plant. **polygamian,** *a.* and *n.* **polygamic** (-găm′ ik), *a.* Polygamous. **polygamy** (pȯ lig′ ȧ mi), *n.* The practice or condition of having a plurality of wives or husbands at the same time; (*Zool.*) the state of having more than one mate; *(*Bot.*) the state of being polygamian. **polygamist** (pȯ lig′ ȧ mist), *n.* **polygamous,** *a.*

polygastric (pol i găs′ trik), *a.* (*Zool.*) Having many stomachs. **polygastrian,** *a.* and *n.*

polygenesis (pol i jen′ ė sis) [POLY-, GENESIS], *n.* (*Biol.*) The doctrine that living beings originate not in one but in several different cells or embryos. **polygenetic** (-jė net′ ik), *a.* **polygenic** (-jen′ ik), *a.* (*Chem.*) Forming more than one compound with hydrogen; (*Geol.*) polygenous. **polygenism** (pȯ lij′ ė nizm), *n.* (*Ethnol.*) The doctrine that the different races of mankind are descended from different original ancestors, and therefore represent different species. **polygenist,** *n.* **polygenistic** (-nis′- tik), *a.* **polygenous** (pȯ lij′ ė nůs), *a.* (*Geol.*) Consisting of many kinds of material; (*Chem.*) polygenic.

polyglot (pol′ i glot) [Gr. *poluglōttos* (POLY-, *glōtta*, tongue)], *a.* Expressed in or speaking many languages. *n.* A book, esp. the Bible, written or set forth in many languages. **polyglottal, -tic** (-glot′ ȧl, -ik), *a.* **polyglottism** (pol′ i glot izm), *n.*

polygon (pol′ i gȯn) [L. *polygōnum*, Gr. *polugōnon* (POLY-, *gōnia*, corner, angle)], *n.* A figure, usu. rectilinear, of more than four angles or sides. **polygonal, *-nous** (pȯ lig′ ȯ nȧl, -nŭs), *a.* **polygonally,** *adv.*

polygonum (pȯ lig′ ō nŭm) [Gr. *polugōnon* (POLY-*gonu*, knee)], *n.* (*Bot.*) A genus of plants comprising the snakeweed, knot-grass, etc., belonging to the family *Polygonaceæ*.

polygram (pol′ i grăm), *n.* A figure consisting of many lines. **polygraph,** *n.* An apparatus for multiplying copies of writing, drawings, etc.; a writer of multifarious works; a collection of different works. **polygraphic** (-grăf′ ik), *a.* **polygraphy** (pȯ lig′ rȧ fi), *n.*

polygynia (pol i jin′ i ȧ) [POLY-, *gunē*, woman], *n.pl.* (*Bot.*) A Linnæan class of plants containing those having flowers with many pistils. ***polygynian, polygynic** (-jin′ ik), *a.* **polygynous** (pȯ lij′ i nŭs), *a.* Pertaining to or practising polygamy; (*Bot.*) polygynic. **polygyny,** *n.* Plurality of wives.

polyhedron (pol i hē′ drȯn, -hed′ rȯn) [Gr. *poluedron* (POLY-, *hedra*, a base)], *n.* (*pl.* **-dra**) A solid bounded by many (usu. more than four) plane sides. **polyhedral, -hedric** (-hed′ rik), **-hedrous** (-hē′ drŭs), *a.* Having many sides.

polyhistor (pol i his′ tȯr) [Gr. *poluistōr* (POLY-, *histōr*, learned, see HISTORY)], *n.* A person of much and various learning; a great scholar. **polyhybrid** (pol i hī′ brid), *n.* A cross between parents of differing heritable characters. **polymath** (pol′ i măth), *n.* A polyhistor. **polymathic** (-măth′ ik), *a.* **polymathist** (pȯ lim′ ȧ thist), *n.* **polymathy,** *n.* Wide and multifarious learning.

polymerism (pȯ lim′ ėr izm) [Gr. *polumerēs* (POLY-, *meros*, portion), -ISM], *n.* (*Chem.*) The state of having the same percentage composition as another compound of different molecular weights; (*Nat. Hist.*) the state of being polymerous. **polymer,** *n.* The product of this. **polymeric** (-mer′ ik), *a.* **polymerize** (pol′ i mėr īz, pȯ lim′ ėr īz), *v.t.* To render polymerous or polymeric. *v.i.* To become polymeric. **polymerous** (pȯ lim′ ėr ŭs), *a.* (*Nat. Hist.*) Consisting of many parts; (*Chem.*) polymeric.

polymignite (pol i mig′ nīt) [POLY-, Gr. *mignunai*, to mix, -ITE], *n.* (*Min.*) An orthorhombic brilliant black mineral composed of the cerium metals with iron and calcium.

polymorphic, -morphous (pol i môr′ fik, -môr′ fŭs) [POLY-, Gr. *morphē*, form], *a.* Having many forms. **polymorph** (pol′ i môrf), *n.* **polymorphism** (-môr′ fizm), *n.* **polyneme** (pol′ i nēm) [Gr. *nēma*, thread], *n.* (*Ichthyol.*) Any fish belonging to the genus *Polynemus*, consisting of tropical spiny sea-fishes having the pectoral fin divided into free rays.

Polynesia (pol i nē′ shi ȧ, -si ȧ) [POLY-, Gr. *nēsos*, island], *n.* A multitude of islands, the name of the numerous islands in the Pacific, east of Australia. **Polynesian,** *a.* Pertaining to Polynesia. *n.* A native of Polynesia.

polynia (pȯ lin′ i ȧ) [Rus. *poluinya*], *n.* An open place in water that is for the most part frozen over, esp. in the Arctic.

polynomial (pol i nō′ mi ȧl) [POLY-, L. *nōmen*, name], *a.* (*Alg.*) Multinomial. *n.* A multinomial. **polynomialism,** *n.* **polynomialist,** *n.* **polynomic** (-nom′ ik), *a.* **polyonymous** (-on′ i mŭs), *a.* Having many different names. **polyonym** (pol′ i ȯ nim), *n.* **polyonymic** (-nim′ ik), *a.* **polyonymist** (-on′-), *n.* **polyonymy,** *n.* **polyopia** (-ō′ pi ȧ), *n.* (*Path.*) Double or multiple vision. **polyoptrum, -tron** (-op′ trŭm, -trȯn), *n.* A lens giving a number of diminished images of an object. **polyorama** (-ȯ răm′ ȧ, -ȯ ra′ mȧ), *n.* A view of many objects; an optical apparatus presenting many views, a panorama.

polyp (pol′ ip) [F. *polype*, L. POLYPUS], *n.* (*Zool.*) One of various aquatic animals of low organization, as the hydra, the sea-anemone, etc., an individual in a compound organism of various kinds. **polypary** (pol′ i pȧr i), *n.* The calcareous or chitonous structure supporting a colony of polyps.

polypetalous (pol i pet′ ȧ lŭs) [POLY-, PETALOUS], *a.* (*Bot.*) Having many or separate petals. **polyphagous** (pȯ lif′ ȧ gŭs), *a.* (*Zool.*) Feeding on various kinds of food; voracious. **polypharmacy** (pol i far′ mȧ si), *n.* (*Med.*) The prescribing of too many medicines; a prescription composed of many ingredients.

polyphone (pol′ i fōn) [Gr. *poluphōnos* (POLY-, *phōnē*, voice, sound)], *n.* (*Philol.*) A character or sign standing for more than one sound. **polyphonic** (-fon′ ik), *a.* Representing different sounds; (*Mus.*) contrapuntal; having several sounds or voices, many-voiced. **polyphonism, -ony** (pȯ lif′ ȯ nizm, -ȯ ni), *n.* The state of being polyphonic; (*Mus.*) composition in parts, each part having an independent melody of its own, counterpoint. **polyphonist,** *n.* A ventriloquist; (*Mus.*) a contrapuntist. **polyphonous,** *a.* Polyphonic.

polyphyletic (pol i fi let′ ik), *a.* (*Biol.*) Polygenetic. **polyphyllous** (pol i fil′ ŭs), *a.* (*Bot.*) Having many leaves. **polyplastic** (-plăs′ tik), *a.* Having or assuming many forms.

polypidom (pȯ lip′ i dȯm) [POLYPUS, L. *domus*, Gr. *domos*, house], *n.* A polypary. **polypite** (pol′ i pīt), *n.* An individual polyp.

polypod (pol′ i pod) [F. *polypode* (POLY-, Gr. *pous podos*, foot)], *a.* (*Zool.*) Having numerous feet. *n.* A millepede, *e.g.* a wood-louse.

polypody (pol′ i pȯd i) [L. *polypodium*, Gr. *polupodion* (POLY-, *podion*, dim. of *pous podos*, foot)], *n.* (*Bot.*) A fern of the genus *Polypodium*, esp. *P. vulgaris*, the common polypody, growing on rocks, walls, trees, etc. **polypodiaceous** (-ā′ shŭs), *a.*

polypoid (pol′ i poid) [POLYP, -OID], *a.* (*Zool.*) Like a polyp or polypus. **polypose, -pous,** *a.* **polyporous** (pȯ lip′ ȯ rŭs) [POLY-, POROUS], *a.* Having many pores.

Polyporus (pȯ lip′ ȯ rŭs) [Gr. *poluporos*], *n.* (*Bot.*) A genus of hymenomycetous fungi growing on the decaying parts of trees, the spores of which are borne on the inner surface of pores or tubes. **polyporaceous** (-rā′ shŭs), *a.* **polyporoid** (pȯ lip′ ȯ roid), *a*

polypus (pol′ i pŭs) [L., from Gr. *polupous* (POLY-, *pous podos*, foot)], *n.* (*pl.* **-pi**) (*Path.*) A tumour with ramifications growing in a mucous cavity; (*Zool.*) a polyp.

polyrhizous (pol i rī′ zŭs) [POLY-, Gr. *rhiza*, root, -OUS], *a.* Having many roots. **polyscope** (pol′ i skōp) [-SCOPE], *n.* A multiplying-glass; (*Surg.*) an instrument for lighting the cavities of the body for surgical examination. **polysepalous** (pol i sep′ ȧ lŭs), *a.* (*Bot.*) Having the sepals distinct. **polyspermal, -mous** (-spĕr′ mȧl, -mŭs), *a.* (*Bot.*) Having many seeds. **polyspore,** *n.* A compound spore; a spore-case containing many spores. **polysporous** (-spôr′ ŭs), *a.* **polystigmous** (-stig′ mŭs), *a.* Having several carpels each bearing a stigma. **polystome** (pol′ i stōm), *a.* Having many mouths. *n.* An animal with many mouths or suckers. **polystomatous** (-stom′ ȧ tŭs), **polystomous** (-lis′ tȯ mŭs), *a.*

polystyle (pol′ i stīl) [POLY-, Gr. *stulos*, column], *a.* (*Arch.*) Having or supported on many columns. **polystylous** (-stī′ lŭs), *a.*

polysyllabic (pol i si lăb′ ik) [L. *polysyllabus*, Gr. *polusullabos*], *a.* Consisting of many syllables; characterized by polysyllables. **polysyllable,** *n.*

polysyndeton (pol i sin′ dė tȯn) [POLY-, Gr. *sundetos*, from *sundeein* (SYN-, *deein*, to bind)], *n.* A figure in which the conjunction or copulative is repeated several times. **polysynthetic** (-sin thet′ ik), *a.* Compounded of several elements; (*Philol.*) combining several words (as verbs and adverbs, complements, etc.) into one. **polysynthesis** (-sin′ thė sis), *n.* **polysynthetically** (-thet′ i kȧ li), *adv.* **polysyntheticism** (-sizm), **polysynthetism** (-sin′ thė tizm), *n.*

polytechnic (pol i tek′ nik) [F. *polytechnique*, Gr. *polutechnos* (POLY-, *technē*, art), -IC], *a.* Connected with, pertaining to, or giving instruction in many arts. *n.* A polytechnic school or institution. **polytechnic school** or **institution:** A school or educational institution for instruction in arts and science, esp. in their practical application.

polythalamous (pol i thăl′ ȧ mŭs), *a.* (*Nat. Hist.*) Having many cells or chambers.

polytheism (pol′ i thē izm) [F. *polythéisme*, Gr. *polutheos* (POLY-, *theos*, god), -ISM], *n.* The doctrine or worship of a plurality of gods. **polytheist,** *n.* **polytheistic, *-al** (-thė is′ tik, -ȧl), *a.*

polythene (pol′ i thēn), *n.* Name for certain thermoplastics that are polymers of ethylene.

polytocous (pȯ lit′ ȯ kŭs) [Gr. *polutokos* (POLY-, Gr. *tokos*, a bringing forth, cogn. with *tiktein*, to bring forth)], *a.* (*Zool.*) Multiparous, producing several at a birth. **polytomous** (pȯ lit′ ȯ mŭs), *a.* (*Bot.*) Pinnate, the divisions not articulated with a common petiole.

polytype (pol′ i tīp), *a.* A form of stereotype obtained by pressing wood-engravings, etc., into semifluid metal; a print obtained in this way. **polytypage,** *n.* **polytypic** (-tip′ ik), *a.* Having or existing in many forms.

polyzoa (pol i zō′ ȧ) [POLY-, Gr. *zōon*, animal], *n.pl.* (*sing.* **-zoon,** -zō′ on) A class of invertebrate animals, mostly marine, produced by gemmation, sometimes regarded as the lowest members of the mollusca, existing in coral-like or plant-like compound colonies. **polyzoal,** *a.* **polyzoan,** *a.* and *n.* **polyzoary,** *n.* The polypidom of a polyzoic colony. **polyzoarial** (-âr′ i ȧl), *a.* **polyzoic** (-zō′ ik), **polyzooid** (-zō′ oid), *a.*

polyzonal (pol i zō′ nȧl), *a.* Composed of many zones or annular segments (of lighthouse lenses).

pomace (pŭm′ ȧs) [history obscure, from F. *pomme* or L. *pōmum*, apple], *n.* The mashed pulp of apples crushed in a cider-mill, esp. the refuse after the juice has been pressed out. **pomaceous** (pȯ mā′ shŭs), *a.* (*Bot.*) Of the nature of a pome or of trees producing pomes, as the apple, pear, quince, etc.

pomade (pȯ mād′, -mad′) [F. *pommade*, from *pomme*, apple], *n.* Pomatum. *v.t.* To apply this to (the hair, etc.).

pomander (pō′ mȧn-, pom′ ȧn dėr, pȯ man′ dėr) [altered from *pomamber*, O.F. *pomme d'ambre* (*pomme*, apple, *ambre*, AMBER)], *n.* A perfumed ball or powder usu. carried in a box, bag, etc., about the person to prevent infection; the box or hollow ball, usu. of gold or silver and ornamentally designed, in which this was carried.

Pomard (pȯ mar′) [village in Côte d'Or, France], *n.* A red Burgundy wine.

pomatum (pȯ mā′ tŭm) [mod. L., from L. *pōmum*, apple, -ATE], *n.* A perfumed ointment (said to have been prepared partly from apple-pulp) for dressing the hair. *v.t.* To apply pomatum to.

pome (pōm) [O.F. *pome* (F. *pomme*), L. *pōmum*], *n.* (*Bot.*) A compound fleshy fruit, composed of the walls of an adnate inferior calyx enclosing carpels containing the seeds, as the apple, pear, quince, etc.; (*poet.*) an apple; a ball, a globe; (*Eccles.*) a metal ball filled with hot water, with which priests warmed their hands at the altar. ***pomecitron,** *n.* A citron. ***pomeroy, pomeroyal** (-roi′ ȧl), *n.* A variety of apple. **pome-water,** *n.* A large sweet juicy apple.

pomegranate (pom′-, pŭm′ grăn ȧt, pom-, pŭm grăn′ ȧt) [O.F. *pome grenate* (POME, *grenate*, L. *grānāta*, seeded, from *grānum*, seed)], *n.* The fruit of a N. African and W. Asiatic tree, *Punica granatum*, resembling an orange, with a thick, tough rind and acid red pulp enveloping numerous seeds; the tree bearing this fruit.

Pomeranian (pom ėr ā′ ni ȧn), *a.* Of or pertaining to Pomerania. *n.* A native of Pomerania; a Pomeranian dog, esp. a dog about the size of a spaniel, with a fox-like pointed muzzle and long, silky hair.

***pomeroy** [POME].

Pomfret-cake (pom′ frėt kāk) [*Pomfret*, now *Pontefract*, town in Yorkshire, CAKE], *n.* A flat cake of liquorice made in Pomfret.

pomiculture (pō′ mi kŭl tūr) [L. *pōmum*, fruit, CULTURE], *n.* Fruit-growing. **pomiferous** (pȯ mif′ ėr ŭs), *a.* (*Bot.*) Bearing apples or pomes. **pomiform** (pō′ mi fôrm), *a.* Shaped like a pome or apple.

pommel (pŭm′ ėl) [M.E. and O.F. *pomel* (F. *pommeau*), dim. of L. *pōmum*, POME], *n.* A round ball or knob, esp. on the hilt of a sword; the upward projection at the front of a saddle. *v.t.* To beat soundly, as with the handle of a sword or similar instrument; to beat with fists. **pommeling,** *n.*

pomology (pȯ mol′ ȯ ji) [L. *pōmum*, POME, -LOGY], *n.* The art or science of the cultivation of fruit. **pomological** (-loj′ i kȧl), *a.* **pomologist** (pȯ mol′ ȯ jist), *n.*

pommy (pom′ i) [?], *n.* A British immigrant to Australia or New Zealand.

pomp (pomp) [F. *pompe*, L. *pompa*, Gr. *pompē*, sending, procession, cogn. with *pempein*, to send], *n.* A pageant; state, splendour, ostentatious display or parade.

pompadour (pom′ pȧ door) [Marquise de *Pompadour* (1721–64), mistress of Louis XV], *n.* and *a.* Applied to methods of wearing the hair brushed up from the forehead or (in women) turned back in a roll from the forehead, to a style of corsage with low square neck, to a shade of crimson or pink or a fabric of this tint, a pattern on cloth for dresses, a walking-stick with a silver handle, etc.; a Brazilian bird with gorgeous plumage.

pompano (pom′ pȧ nō) [Sp. *pámpano*], *n.* A West Indian food-fish of various species belonging to the genus *Trachinotus*.

Pompeian (pom pē′ ȧn), *a.* Of or pertaining to Pompeii, an Italian town buried by an eruption of Vesuvius in A.D. 78.

pompier (pon pyā, pom′ pyėr) [F., fireman, from *pompe*, PUMP], *n.* A fireman. **pompier ladder:** A fireman's scaling-ladder, consisting of a hooked pole with cross-pieces.

***pompion** (pŭm′ pi ȯn) [M.F. *pompon*, a form of *popon*, L. *pepōnem*, nom. *pepo*, Gr. *pepōn*], *n.* A pumpkin. **pompion-berry,** *n.* (*Am.*) The hackberry, *Celtis occidentalis*.

pom-pom (pom′ pom) [imit.], *n.* An automatic quick-firing gun.

pompon (pom′ pon, pon pon) [F., etym. doubtful], *n.* An ornament in the form of a tuft or ball of feathers, ribbon, etc., worn on women's and children's hats, shoes, etc., on the front of a soldier's shako, on a French sailor's cap, etc.; a small compact chrysanthemum.

pompous (pom′ pŭs) [F. *pompeux*, late L. *pompōsus*], *a.* Displaying pomp; grand, magnificent; ostentatious, pretentious. ***pomposo*** (-pō′ sō), *adv.* (*Mus.*) In a stately or dignified manner. **pompously,** *adv.* **pomposity** (-pos′ i ti), **pompousness,** *n.*

ponce (pons) [perh. from POUNCE (1)], *n.* (*slang*) A prostitute's bully, a fancy man.

poncho (pon′ chō) [S. Am. Sp., from native], *n.* A woollen cloak, worn in S. America, with a slit through which the head passes; a cycling-cape of this pattern.

pond (pond) [prob. var. of POUND (2)], *n.* A body of still water, usu. artificial, smaller than a lake; (*facet.*) the sea, esp. the Atlantic. *v.t.* To dam back; to make into a pond. *v.i.* To form a pool or pond (of water). **pond-lily,** *n.* A water-lily, esp. the yellow *Nuphar lutea*. **pond-weed,** *n.* An aquatic plant growing on stagnant water, esp. species of *Potamogeton*. **pondage,** *n.* **pondlet,** *n.*

ponder (pon' dėr) [O.F. *ponderer*, L. *ponderāre*, from *pondus -deris*, weight], *v.t.* To weigh carefully in the mind; to think over, to consider deeply, to reflect upon; *to examine carefully, to value, to estimate. *v.i.* To think, to deliberate, to muse (on, over, etc.). **n.* Meditation. **ponderer,** *n.* **ponderingly,** *adv.*

ponderable (pon' dėr ȧbl) [late L. *ponderābilis*, as prec.], *a.* Capable of being weighed, having appreciable weight, opp. to imponderable. **ponderability** (-bil' i ti), **ponderableness,** *n.* **ponderal,** *a.* **ponderance,** *n.* Weight; gravity, importance. **ponderation** (-ā' shŭn), *n.* The act of weighing (*lit.* or *fig.*).

ponderous (pon' dėr ŭs) [PONDER, -OUS], *a.* Very heavy or weighty; bulky, unwieldy; (*fig.*) dull, tedious; pompous, self-important. **ponderously,** *adv.* **ponderosity** (-os' i ti), **ponderousness,** *n.*

pone (pōn) [Algonkin], *n.* A kind of bread made by the N. American Indians of maize-meal; similar bread made with eggs, milk, etc.; a loaf of this.

ponent (pō' nėnt) [It. *ponente*, L. *pōnens -ntem*, setting, sunset, orig. p.p. of *pōnere*, to put, to set], *a.* West, western.

pongee (pŭn jē') [perh. from N.Chin. *pun-chī*, own loom], *n.* A soft unbleached kind of Chinese silk.

pongo (pong' gō) [African native], *n.* A large African anthropoid ape; erroneously applied to the orang-outang, etc.; (*Austral. abor.*) the flying-squirrel.

poniard (pon' yȧrd) [F. *poignard*, from *poing*, L. *pugnus*, fist], *n.* A dagger. *v.t.* To stab with a poniard.

pons (ponz) [L. *pons pontis*], *n.* A bridge; (*Anat.*) a connecting part. ***pons asinorum*** [ASS]. **Pons Varolii:** A band of fibres connecting the two hemispheres of the cerebellum. **pontal, pontic** (2), **pontile, pontine,** *a.*

***pontage** (pon' tȧj) [O.F., from med. L. *pontāticum*, from *pons pontis*, bridge], *n.* A toll for the maintenance of a bridge or bridges.

Pontic (1) (pon' tik) [L. *Ponticus*, Gr. *Pontikos*, from *pontos*, sea, esp. the Black Sea], *a.* Pertaining to the Black Sea. **pontic** (2) [PONS].

pontifex (pon' ti feks) [L. (*pons pontis*, bridge, or Oscan-Umbrian *puntis*, sacrifice, *-fex*, *-fic*, from *facere*, to make)], *n.* (*pl.* ***-tifices***) A member of the highest of the ancient Roman colleges of priests. **Pontifex Maximus:** The president of this; the Pope.

pontiff (pon' tif) [F. *pontife*, *pontif*, from prec.], *n.* The Pope; a pontifex, a high priest. **pontifical** (-tif' i kȧl), ***pontific,** *a.* Of, pertaining to, or befitting a pontiff, high priest, or pope; papal, popish; with an assumption of authority. *n.* (*Eccles.*) A book containing the forms for rites and ceremonies to be performed by bishops; (*pl.*) the vestments and insignia of a pontiff or bishop. **pontifically,** *adv.* **pontificate** (-kȧt), *n.* *v.t.* (-kāt) To celebrate (Mass, etc.) as a bishop. *v.i.* To officiate as a pontiff or bishop, esp. at Mass. ***pontifice** (pon' ti fis), *n.* The erection or structure of a bridge. ***pontificial** (-fish' ȧl), ***pontifician,** *a.* **pontify** (pon' ti fī), *v.i.* To act in the style of a pontiff, esp. to pretend to infallibility.

pontil (pon' til) [F., prob. from It. *pontello*, *puntello*, dim. of *punto*, POINT], *n.* (*Glass-making*) An iron rod used for handling, twisting, or carrying glass in process of manufacture.

pontile [PONS].

pont-levis (pon lė vē, pont lev' is) [F. (*pont*, L. *pons pontis*, bridge, O.F. *levеïs*, movable, ult. from L. *levāre*, to raise)], *n.* A draw-bridge; the repeated rearing of a horse on its hind legs.

pontonier (pon tō nēr') [F. *pontonnier* (as foll.)], *n.* A soldier in charge of a pontoon, or who constructs pontoon bridges.

pontoon (pŏn toon') [F. *ponton*, L. *pontōnem*, nom. *-to*, from *pons pontis*, bridge], *n.* A flat-bottomed boat, cylinder, or other buoyant structure supporting a floating bridge; a caisson; a barge or lighter; (*rare*) a pontoon-bridge; a card game of chance. *v.t.* To bridge with pontoons. **pontoon-bridge,** *n.*

pony (pō' ni) [Lowland Sc. *powney*, O.F. *poulenet*, dim. of *poulain*, late L. *pullānus*, L. *pullus*, foal], *n.* A small horse, esp. one of a small breed; (*slang*) twenty-five pounds sterling; (*Am. slang*) a crib used in getting up lessons. **Jerusalem pony:** A donkey. **pony-engine,** *n.* A small locomotive for shunting. **pony-tail:** A woman's hair style in which the hair is gathered at the back and hangs down like a tail.

pooch (pooch), *n.* (*Austral. colloq.*) A greyhound; a small dog.

pood (pood) [Rus. *pudu*, from L.G. or Norse *pund*, POUND], *n.* A Russian weight of about 36 lb. av.

poodle (poo' dėl) [G. *pudel*, *pudelhund*, from *pudeln*, to waddle or to splash (cp. PUDDLE)], *n.* A small variety of pet dog with long silky hair, often clipped in a fanciful style. *v.t.* To clip the hair of (a dog) thus.

pooh (poo, pu) [imit. of instinctive action of blowing away], *int.* An exclamation of contempt or impatience. **pooh-pooh** (poo poo'), *v.t.* To laugh or sneer at; to make light of.

Pooh-bah (poo ba') [character in *The Mikado*], *n.* (*facet.*) A person holding many offices.

pooka (poo' kȧ) [Ir. *púca*], *n.* A hobgoblin, usu. represented in the form of a horse.

pool (1) (pool) [A.-S. *pōl* (cp. Dut. *poel*, G. *pfuhl*)], *n.* A small body of water, still or nearly still; a deep, still part of a stream; a puddle; a pond. *v.t.* (*Quarrying*) To sink (a hole) for a wedge; (*Mining*) to undercut and bring down.

pool (2) (pool) [prob. from F. *poule*, hen], *n.* The receptacle for the stakes in certain games of cards; the collective amount of stakes, forfeits, etc.; a game on a billiard-table in which the players aim to drive different balls into the pockets in a certain order; the collective stakes in a betting arrangement; a combination of persons, companies, etc., for manipulating prices and suppressing competition. *v.t.* To put (funds, risks, etc.) into a common fund or pool. **poolroom,** *n.* (*Am.*) A billiards saloon. **football pool:** A form of gambling by correctly forecasting the results of certain football matches. **petrol pool:** The forced pooling of all petrol as a measure of State economy.

poon (poon) [Cingalese *pūna*], *n.* An Indian tree of the genus *Calophyllum*. **poon-oil,** *n.* A bitter oil obtained from the seeds of this, used in medicine and as an illuminant. **poon-wood,** *n.*

poop (poop) [M.E. and O.F. *pupe* (F. *poupe*), late L. *puppa*, L. *puppis*], *n.* The stern of a ship; a deck over the after part of a spar-deck. *v.t.* (*Naut.*) To break heavily over the poop (of waves); to take (a wave) over the stern (of a ship). **pooped,** *a.* Having a poop (*usu. in comb.*); struck on the poop.

poor (poor) [M.E. and O.F. *povre*, *poure* (F. *pauvre*), L. *pauperem*, nom. PAUPER], *a.* Wanting means of subsistence, needy, indigent; badly supplied, lacking (in); barren, unproductive; scanty, meagre, inadequate in quantity or quality, unsatisfactory; lean, thin, wasted; unhealthy; uncomfortable; inferior, sorry, paltry, miserable, contemptible; insignificant, humble, meek; unfortunate, pitiable, used as a term of slight contempt, pity or endearment. **the poor:** Those who are needy or indigent, esp. those who depend on charity or parochial relief. **poor-box,** *n.* A money-box, esp. in a church for charitable contributions. **poorhouse,** *n.* A workhouse. ***poor-john,** *n.* A coarse kind of fish, salted and dried. **poor-law,** *n.* The body of laws relating to the maintenance of paupers. **poor**

man's weather-glass: The pimpernel. **poor-rate,** *n.* A rate levied for the support of paupers. **poor-spirited,** *a.* Timid, cowardly; mean, base. **poor-spiritedness,** *n.* **poorly,** *adv.* With poor results, with little success; defectively, imperfectly; meanly, despicably; in delicate health; unwell, indisposed. **poorliness,** *n.* **poorness,** *n.* **poortith,** *n.* (*Sc.*) Poverty.

pop (1) (pop) [imit.], *v.i.* (*past & p.p.* **popped**) To make a short, sharp explosive noise as of a light report, snapping, or the drawing of a cork; to enter or issue forth with a quick, sudden motion; to dart; to move quickly; to shoot (at) with a gun, pistol, etc. *v.t.* To push or thrust (in, out, up) suddenly; to put (down, etc.) quickly or hastily; to fire off (a gun, etc.); to cause (a thing) to pop by breaking, etc.; (*slang*) to pawn. *adv.* With a pop; suddenly. *n.* A short, sharp, explosive noise; a dot, spot, or other mark, esp. used in marking sheep, etc.; (*colloq.*) an effervescing drink, esp. ginger-beer or champagne; (*slang*) the art of pawning. **in pop:** (*slang*) In pawn. **to go pop:** To make a popping sound. **to pop corn:** To parch Indian corn until it bursts. **to pop off:** (*colloq.*) To leave hastily; to die. **to pop the question:** (*colloq.*) To propose marriage. **pop-corn,** *n.* Maize suitable for parching, parched maize. **pop-eyed,** *a.* With bulging eyes. **pop-gun,** *n.* A small toy gun used by children, shooting a pellet or cork with air compressed by a piston; (*fig.*) a poor or defective firearm. **pop-shop,** *n.* (*slang*) A pawnshop. **popper,** *n.* Something that pops; (*colloq.*) a kind of dress-fastening. **popping-crease,** *n.* (*Cricket*) A line four feet in front of the stumps parallel with the bowling crease.

pop (2) (pop) [short for POPULAR], *n.* (*colloq.*) A popular concert; a popular song. **Pop,** *n.* Social and debating club at Eton.

pope (pōp) [A.-S. *pāpa*, as PAPA (2)], *n.* The bishop of Rome as the head of the Roman Catholic Church; (*fig.*) a person claiming or credited with infallibility; a priest in the Greek Church, esp. in Russia; a small freshwater fish, *Acerina cernua*, akin to the perch, the ruff. **pope-Joan:** A game at cards named after a legendary female Pope. **pope's eye:** The gland surrounded with fat in the middle of the thigh of an ox or sheep. **pope's head:** A round broom with a long handle; a W. Indian and S. American cactus, *Melocactus communis*. **pope's nose** [PARSON'S NOSE]. **popedom,** *n.* **popeless,** *a.* ***popeling,** *n.* **popery,** *n.* The religion or ecclesiastical system of the Church of Rome (in a hostile sense).

***popinjay** (pop' in jā) [M.E. *popingay*, O.F. *papingay* (cp. It. *papagallo*, med. L. *papagallus*, med. Gr. *papagallos*, *papagas*, Arab. *babaghā*, prob. of imit. orig.)], *n.* A parrot; a mark like a parrot set up on a pole to be shot at by archers, etc.; (*fig.*) a conceited chattering fop; (*prov.*) a woodpecker, esp. the green woodpecker.

popish (pō' pish), *a.* Of or pertaining to the Pope; pertaining to popery, papistical. **popishly,** *adv.*

***popjoy** (pop' joi) [etym. doubtful], *v.i.* To enjoy or amuse oneself.

poplar (pop' lȧr) [O.F. *poplier* (F. *peuplier*), L. *pōpulus*], *n.* A large tree of the genus *Populus*, of rapid growth, and having a soft, light wood.

poplin (pop' lin) [F. *popeline*, earlier *papeline*, It. *papalina*, PAPAL, because made at Avignon], *n.* A silk and worsted fabric with a ribbed surface, now made chiefly in Ireland; (*Am.*) broadcloth.

popliteal, poplitic (pop lit' ė ȧl, -ik) [L. *popliteus*, from *poples poplitem*, ham, hough], *a.* (*Anat.*) Pertaining to the ham or hollow behind the knee-joint.

popper [POP (1)].

poppet (pop' ėt) [early form of PUPPET], *n.* (*Mining*) A framework bearing the hoisting-gear at a pit-head; (*Naut.*) a piece of wood used for various purposes; one of the timbers on which a vessel rests in launching; a puppet, a marionette; a darling, a term of endearment. **poppet-head,** *n.* (*Mining*) A poppet; *(*Mech.*) a lathe-head. **poppet-valve,** *n.*

popping-crease [POP (1)].

popple (pop' ėl) [prob. imit.], *v.i.* To bob up and down, to toss, to heave (of floating bodies or water). *n.* A tossing or rippling; the sound of this.

poppy (pop' i) [A.-S. *popig*, *popæg*, L. *papāver*], *n.* A plant or flower of the genus *Papaver*, containing plants with large showy flowers chiefly of scarlet colour, with a milky juice having narcotic properties; (*Arch.*) a poppy-head. **opium-poppy:** The species, *P. somniferum*, from which opium is collected. **poppy-cock,** *n.* (*slang*) Nonsense, balderdash. **Poppy Day Appeal:** An appeal made annually on November 11 for funds for the British Legion. **poppy-head,** *n.* The seed-capsule of a poppy; (*Arch.*) a finial of foliage or other ornamental top to ecclesiastical wood-work, esp. a bench-end. **poppied,** *a.*

popsy (pop' si) [perh. from *pop*, short for POPPET], *n.* A term of endearment for a child or girl, also **popsy-wopsy.**

populace (pop' ū lȧs) [F., from It. *popolaccio*, *popolazzo*, from *popolo*, L. *populus*, PEOPLE], *n.* The common people; the masses.

popular (pop' ū lȧr) [through O.F. *populeir* (F. *populaire*) or directly from L. *populāris*, as prec.], *a.* Pleasing to or esteemed by the people; pertaining to or carried on by the people; suitable to or easy to be understood by the common people, not expensive, not abstruse, not esoteric; prevailing among the people; *courting the favour of the people; *crowded. **popular front:** (*Polit.*) A coalition of socialist and other parties in a common front against dictatorship. **popularity** (-lăr' i ti), *n.* **popularize,** *v.t.* To make popular; to treat (a subject, etc.) in a popular style; to spread (knowledge, etc.) among the people; to extend (the suffrage, etc.) to the common people. **popularization** (-zā' shŭn), *n.* **popularly,** *adv.*

populate (pop' ū lāt) [late L. *populātus*, p.p. of *populāre*, as prec.], *v.t.* To furnish with inhabitants, to people; to form the population of, to inhabit. *v.i.* To propagate. **population** (-lā' shŭn), *n.* The inhabitants of a country, etc., collectively; the state of a country with respect to the number of its inhabitants.

populin (pop' ū lin) [F. *populine* (L. *pōpul-us*, POPLAR, -INE)], *n.* (*Chem.*) A crystalline substance obtained from the aspen.

populous (pop' ū lŭs) [F. *populeux*, L. *populōsus*, as prec.], *a.* Full of people; thickly populated; *popular; *numerous. **populously,** *adv.* **populousness,** *n.*

poral [PORE (1)].

porbeagle (pôr' bēgl) [Cornish dial., etym. unknown], *n.* A shark of the genus *Lamna*, a mackerel-shark.

porcate, -cated (pôr' kȧt, -kā ted) [L. *porca*, ridge, -ATE], *a.* Formed in ridges.

porcelain (pôr' sė lān, pôr' slȧn) [F. *porcelaine*, It. *porcellana*, the sea-snail, porcelain, dim. of *porco*, L. *porcus*, hog, prob. from the resemblance of the shell to a hog's back], *n.* A fine kind of earthenware, white, thin, and semi-transparent; ware made of this. *a.* Pertaining to or composed of porcelain; (*fig.*) fragile, delicate. **porcelainize,** *v.t.* **porcelainous** (-lā' nŭs), **porcellaneous, porcellanic** (-sė lăn' ik), **porcellanous** (sel' ȧ nŭs), *a.* **porcellanite,** *n.* (*Min.*) A rock composed of hard metamorphosed clay.

porch (pôrch) [F. *porche*, L. *porticum*, nom. *-cus*, PORTICO], *n.* A covered structure before or extending from the entrance to a building; a covered approach to a doorway; (*Am.*) a verandah; *a covered walk or portico. **the Porch:** The school or philosophy of the Stoics (from the painted portico at Athens in which Zeno and his disciples held their discussions). **porched,** *a.* **porchless,** *a.*

porcine (pôr′ sīn) [F. *porcin*, *-cine*, L. *porcīnus*, from *porcus*, hog], *a.* Pertaining to or resembling swine.

porcupine (pôr′ kū pīn) [M.E. *porkepyn*, O.F. *porc espin*, L. *porcus*, hog, *spina*, thorn, SPINE], *n.* Any individual of the genus *Hystrix*, rodent quadrupeds covered with erectile, quill-like spines; one of various appliances or machines armed with pins, knives, teeth, etc. **porcupine ant-eater:** An echidna. **porcupine-fish,** *n.* A tropical fish, *Diodon hystrix*, covered with spines. **porcupine grass,** *n.* A coarse, spiky, tussocky grass, *Triodia*, that covers many areas in Australia, also known as spinifex. **porcupinish, porcupiny,** *a.*

pore (1) (pôr) [F., from L. *porus*, Gr. *poros*, passage], *n.* A minute opening, esp. a hole in the skin for absorption, perspiration, etc.; (*Bot.*) one of the stomata or other apertures in the cuticle of a plant; (*Phys.*) a minute interstice between the molecules of a body. **poral,** *a.* **pory,** *a.* ***poriness,** *n.*

pore (2) (pôr) [M.E. *pouren*, *pūren*, etym. doubtful], *v.i.* To look with steady, continued attention and application (at); to meditate or study patiently and persistently (over, upon, etc.). *v.t.* To fatigue (the eyes) by persistent reading. **porer,** *n.*

porge (pôrj) [prob. var. of PURGE], *v.t.* (*Jewish*) To extract the sinews of (slaughtered animals) in order that they may be ceremonially clean. **porger,** *n.*

porgy (pôr′ ji) [etym. doubtful], *n.* (*Am.*) The name of a number of North American sea-fishes, including various species of *Calemus* and *Sparus*.

Porifera (pŏ rif′ ėr ȧ) [L. *porus*, PORE (1), *-fer*, bearing], *n.pl.* (*Zool.*) The sponges; the Foraminifera. **poriferal,** *a.* **poriferen,** *a.* and *n.*

poriferous (pŏ rif′ ėr ŭs) [as prec., -FEROUS], *a.* Bearing or furnished with pores. **poriform** (pôr′ i fôrm), *a.* ***poriness** [PORE (1)].

porism (pôr′-, por′ izm) [L. and Gr., *porisma*, from *porizein*, to deduce, from *poros*, way], *n.* A proposition dealing with the conditions rendering certain problems indeterminate or capable of innumerable solutions; a corollary. **porismatic** (-măt′ ik), **poristic, -al** (pŏ ris′ tik, -ăl), *a.*

pork (pôrk) [F. *porc*, L. *porcus*, hog], *n.* The flesh of swine, esp. fresh, as food; *(*fig.*) a stupid, obstinate person. **pork-butcher,** *n.* One who kills pigs for sale. ***pork-eater,** *n.* A Christian, as distinguished from a Jew. **pork-pie,** *n.* A pie made of minced pork, usu. round with vertical sides. **pork-pie hat:** A round hat with flat crown and rolled-up brim. **porker, porklet,** *n.* A pig raised for killing, esp. a young fattened pig. **porkling,** *n.* **porky,** *a.* Like pork; (*colloq.*) fat, fleshy.

pornocracy (pôr nok′ rȧ si) [Gr. *pornē*, harlot, -CRACY], *n.* The rule or domination of harlots, as in the papal government during the 10th cent. **pornography** (-nog′ rȧ fi) [-GRAPHY], *n.* Literature dealing with harlots; obscenity or licentiousness in literature. **pornographer,** *n.* **pornographic** (-grăf′ ik), *a.*

poro- [PORE (1)], *comb. form.* **poroplastic** (por ŏ-, pôr ŏ plăs′ tik) [PLASTIC], *a.* (*Surg.*) Both porous and plastic (of a felt used in dressing fractures, etc.). **porotype** (por′-, pôr′ ŏ tīp), *n.* A copy made from an engraving, writing, etc., by subjecting it to a gas that penetrates the paper where it is not protected by the ink.

poroporo (po′ rō po′ rō) [Maori], *n.* A N. Zealand shrub bearing edible fruit like plums.

porose (pôr ōs′), **porous** (pôr′ ŭs) [PORE (1), -OUS], *a.* Having pores or passages for fluids. **porously,** *adv.* **porosity** (-ros′ i ti), **porousness,** *n.*

porphyrogenitism (pôr fi rŏ jen′ i tizm) [med. L. *porphyrogenitus*, late Gr. *porphurogennētos* (*porphuros*, purple, *gennētos*, born, from *gennaein*, to beget)], *n.* Succession to the throne of a younger son born while his father was actually monarch in preference to an older son born before his father's accession. ***porphyrogenite** (-roj′ ėn it), *n.* One born after his father's accession to a throne, one born in the purple; orig. one born of the imperial family of Constantinople. **porphyrogeniture,** *n.*

porphyry (pôr′ fi ri) [through O.F. or L. from Gr. *porphuros*, purple], *n.* An igneous rock consisting of a felsitic or crypto-crystalline ground-mass full of feldspar or quartz crystals; (*Hist.*) a rock quarried in Egypt having a purple ground-mass with enclosed crystals of feldspar. **porphyry-shell,** *n.* A shell of the genus *Murex*, esp. any species yielding a purple dye. **porphyrite,** *n.* Porphyry. **porphyritic, *-al** (pôr fi rit′ ik, -ăl), *a.* **porphyrize,** *v.t.*

porpoise (pôr′ pŭs) [M.E. *porpays*, O.F. *porpeis* (L. *porcum*, nom. *-cus*, hog, *piscem*, nom. *-cis*, fish)], *n.* Any individual of the genus *Phocæna*, esp. *P. communis*, a gregarious delphinine cetacean, about five feet long, with a blunt snout.

porraceous (pŏ rā′ shŭs) [L. *porrāceus*, from *porrum*, leek], *a.* Greenish, leek-green.

porrect (pŏ rekt′) [L. *porrectus*, p.p. of *porrigere* (*por-*, PRO-, *regere*, to stretch, direct)], *v.t.* To stretch forth horizontally (esp. a part of the body, as the palpi of moths); (*Eccles. Law*) to tender or submit. *a.* Stretched forth horizontally.

porret (por′ ĕt) [O.F. *poret*, L. *porrum*, leek], *n.* (*prov.*) A leek or small onion.

porridge (por′ ij) [var. of POTTAGE], *n.* A soft or semi-liquid food made by boiling meal, etc., in water or milk till it thickens; a broth or stew of vegetables or meal; (*Am.* boiled oatmeal).

porrigo (pŏ rī′ gō) [L.], *n.* (*Path.*) A skin-disease affecting the scalp. **porriginous** (-rij′ i nŭs), *a.*

porringer (por′ in jėr) [corr. of earlier *potager*, as PORRIDGE], *n.* A small basin or bowl out of which soup, etc., is eaten by children; *a hat shaped like this.

port (1) (pôrt) [A.-S., from L. *portus*], *n.* A harbour, a sheltered piece of water into which vessels can enter and remain in safety; a town or other place having a harbour, esp. where goods are imported or exported under the customs authorities. **free port** [FREE]. **port of entry:** A port having a custom-house. **port-admiral,** *n.* The admiral commanding at a naval port. **port-bar** (1), *n.* A bar at the mouth of a harbour; a boom across a port to prevent entrance or egress. **port-charges, -dues** [HARBOUR-DUES]. **Port Jackson shark,** *n.* A shark found off the eastern shores of Australia.

port (2) (pôrt) [F. *porte*, L. *porta*], *n.* A gate, an entrance, esp. to a walled town, fortress, etc.; (*Naut.*) a port-hole; (*Mach.*) an opening for the passage of steam, gas, water, etc. **port-bar** (2), *n.* A bar to secure the ports of a ship in a gale. **port-hole,** *n.* (*Naut.*) An aperture in a ship's side for light, air, etc., formerly for discharging guns through; (*Mach.*) a passage for steam, gas, etc., in a cylinder. **port-lanyard, -rope,** *n.* A rope for drawing up a port-lid. **port-lid,** *n.*

port (3) (pôrt) [F. *porter*, L. *portāre*, to carry], *n.* Carriage, mien, deportment; *state. *v.t.* (*Mil.*) To carry or hold (a rifle, etc.) in a slanting position across the body in front. **port-crayon,** *n.* A pencil-case; a handle to hold a crayon.

port (4) (pôrt) [contr. from *Oporto*, in Portugal], *n.* A strong dark-red wine made in Portugal.

port (5) (pôrt) [etym. doubtful, perh. from PORT (1)], *n.* (*Naut.*) The larboard or left-hand side as one looks forward. *a.* Towards or on the larboard. *v.t.* To turn or put (the helm) to the left side of a ship. *v.i.* To turn to port (of a ship).

porta (pôr′ tȧ) [L., gate], *n.* (*Anat.*) The portal or aperture where veins, ducts, etc., enter an organ, esp. the transverse fissure of the liver.

portable (pôr′ tȧ bėl) [F., from L. *portābilis*, from *portāre*, to carry], *a.* Capable of being easily carried, esp. about the person; not bulky or heavy; *endurable. **portability** (-bil′ i ti), ***portableness,** *n.*

portage (1) (pôr' tȧj) [F., from *porter*, PORT (3)], *n.* The act of carrying, carriage; the cost of carriage; a break in a line of water-communication over which boats, goods, etc., have to be carried; transportation of boats, etc., over this. *v.t.* To carry over a portage. *v.i.* To make a portage.

***portage** (2) (pôr' tȧj) [PORT (2), -AGE], *n.* An opening, a port-hole.

portal (1) (pôr' tȧl) [O.F., from med. L. *portāle*, neut. of *portālis*, from L. *porta*, gate, PORT (2)], *n.* A door, a gate, a gateway, an entrance, esp. one of an ornamental or imposing kind.

portal (2) (pôr' tȧl) [med. L. *portālis*, see prec.], *a.* (*Anat.*) Of or connected with the *porta*. **portal vein:** The large vein conveying blood to the liver.

***portance** (pôr' tȧns) [F., from *porter*, to carry, see PORT (3)], *n.* Air, mien, carriage; demeanour.

portative (pôr' tȧ tiv) [F. *portatif*, *-tive*, as prec.], *a.* Pertaining to or capable of carrying or supporting; *portable.

port-crayon [PORT (3)].

portcullis (pôrt kŭl' is) [M.E. *porte-colys*, O.F. *porte coleïce* (*porte*, L. *porta*, door, PORT (2), COULISSE)], *n.* A strong framework of timber or iron resembling a harrow, sliding in vertical grooves over a gateway, and let down to close the passage in case of assault. **portcullised,** *a.*

Porte (pôrt) [F. *Sublime Porte*, sublime gate (see PORT (2)), translation of Turkish name of the chief Government office, the high gate, orig. the gate of the palace where justice was administered], *n.* The old Imperial Turkish Government.

porte-cochère (pôrt ko shâr) [F. (PORT (2), *cochère*, from *coche*, COACH)], *n.* A carriage-entrance. **porte-crayon** [PORT (3)]. **porte-feuille** (pôrt fu' i) [F. *feuille*, L. *folium*, leaf], *n.* A portfolio. **portemonnaie** (pôrt mon ā) [F., *monnaie*, money], *n.* A leathern purse or pocket-book.

portend (pôr tend') [L. *portendere* (*por-*, PRO-, *tendere*, to stretch)], *v.t.* To indicate by previous signs, to presage, to foreshadow; to be an omen of. **portent** (pôr' tėnt), *n.* That which portends; an omen, esp. of evil; a prodigy, a marvel. **portentous** (pôr ten' tŭs), *a.* Ominous; impressive; solemn. **portentously,** *adv.*

porter (1) (pôr' tėr) [M.E. and O.F. *portour* (F. *porteur*), from *porter*, to carry, see PORT (3)], *n.* One who carries parcels, luggage, etc., esp. one employed at a railway station; a dark-brown beer made from charred or chemically-coloured malt, etc. (perh. so called from having been made specially for London porters). **porter-house,** *n.* A tavern at which porter, etc., is sold; an eating-house, a chop-house. **porter-house steak:** (*Am.*) A choice cut of beef-steak next to the sirloin, and including part of the tenderloin. **porterage,** *n.* **porterly,** *a.* **porter's knot:** A pad worn on the shoulders by porters when carrying heavy loads.

porter (2) (pôr' tėr) [O.F. *portier*, L. *portārius*, from *porta*, PORT (2)], *n.* A gatekeeper, a door-keeper; (*Am.*) a janitor.

***porteress** [PORTRESS].

portfire (pôrt' fīr) [F. *porte-feu* (assim. to FIRE)], *n.* A slow match, formerly used for firing guns, now chiefly in mining, etc.

portfolio (pôrt fō' li ō) [It. *portafogli* (*porta*, imper. of *portare*, L. *portāre*, to carry, *fogli*, leaves, from L. *folium*), partly assim. to PORTEFEUILLE], *n.* A portable case for holding papers, drawings, etc.; (*fig.*) the office and duties of a minister of state; a list of investments.

portico (pôr' ti kō) [It., from L. *porticus*, from *porta*, gate], *n.* A colonnade, a roof supported by columns; a porch with columns.

portière (pôr tyâr') [F., from L. *portāria*], *n.* A door-curtain, a portress.

portion (pôr' shŭn) [F., from L. *portiōnem*, nom. *-tio*, cogn. with *pars*, PART], *n.* A part; a share, a part assigned, an allotment; a helping; a wife's fortune, a dowry; the part of an estate descending to an heir; one's lot. *v.t.* To divide, to distribute; to allot, to endow. **portioner,** *n.* One who portions; (*Eccles.*) a portionist. **portionist,** *n.* At Merton College, Oxford, one of the scholars on the foundation; (*Eccles.*) a joint incumbent of a benefice. **portionless,** *a.*

Portland (pôrt' lȧnd) [peninsula in Dorsetshire], *a.* Of or derived from Portland. **Portland cement:** A cement having the colour of Portland stone. **Portland stone:** A yellowish-white freestone, quarried in Portland, much used for building.

portly (pôrt' li) [PORT (3), -LY], *a.* Dignified or stately in mien or appearance; stout, corpulent. **portliness,** *n.*

portmanteau (pôrt măn' tō) [F. *portemanteau*], *n.* (*pl.* **-eaux** (-ōz)) A long leather trunk or case for carrying apparel, etc., in travelling. **portmanteau word:** (*Lewis Carroll*) An artificial word combining two distinct words as *chortle*, from *chuckle* and *snort*.

portrait (pôr' trȧt) [O.F. *pourtraict*, p.p. of *pourtraire*, to portray], *n.* A likeness or representation of a person or animal, esp. from life; a vivid description; (*fig.*) a type, a similitude. **portrait-painter, portraitist,** *n.* One whose occupation is to paint portraits. **portraiture,** *n.* A portrait; portraits collectively; the art of painting portraits; (*fig.*) vivid description. **portray** (pôr trā'), *v.t.* (*fig.*) To describe vividly. **portrayal,** *n.* **portrayer,** *n.*

***portreeve** (pôrt' rēv) [A.-S. *port-gerēfa* (PORT (2), REEVE)], *n.* *The chief magistrate of a town or borough; now, an officer in certain towns subordinate to the mayor, a bailiff.

portress (pôr' trės), *n.* A female doorkeeper.

Portuguese (pôr tū gēz'), *a.* Of or pertaining to Portugal. *n.* A native or inhabitant (*also pl.*) of Portugal; the Portuguese language. **Portuguese man-of-war,** *n.* (*Zool.*) A jelly-fish of the genus *Physalia*.

Portulaca (pôr tū lā' kȧ) [L.], *n.* (*Bot.*) A genus of low succulent herbs with flowers opening only in direct sunshine, comprising the purslane.

posada (pō sa' dȧ) [Sp., from *posar*, to lodge], *n.* A Spanish inn.

posaune (pō zou' nė) [G., a trombone], *n.* (*Organ.*) A rich and powerful reed-stop.

pose (1) (pōz) [F. *poser*, L. *pausāre*, to PAUSE, late L. to rest, to set (conf. with *pōnere*, to put)], *v.t.* To place, to cause to take a certain attitude; to affirm, to lay down. *v.i.* To assume an attitude or character; to appear or set up (as). *n.* A bodily or mental attitude or position, esp. one put on for effect; (*Dominoes*) the first play.

pose (2) (pōz) [short for OPPOSE], *v.t.* To puzzle, to cause to be at a loss. **poser,** *n.* One who or that which puzzles; a puzzling question or proposition. **posingly,** *adv.*

posé (pō' zā) [F., p.p. of *poser*, to POSE (1)], *a.* (*Her.*) Applied to a lion, horse, etc., standing still, with all its feet on the ground.

poseur (pō zĕr') [Fr.], *n.* An affected person (fem. **poseuse**).

posh (posh), *a.* (*colloq.*) Smart, grand, trim, well-dressed, polished.

posit (poz' it) [L. *positus*, p.p. of *pōnere*, to put], *v.t.* To place, to set in position; to lay down as a fact or principle, to assume, to postulate.

position (pȯ zish' ŭn) [L. *positiōnem*, nom. *-tio*, as prec.], *n.* The state of being placed or the manner in which a thing is placed; situation, posture; mental attitude, disposition, way of regarding anything; the place belonging to or assigned to a thing or person; situation relatively to other things or persons; social rank; an office, a post, an appointment; status, rank, condition; a principle laid down, a proposition; the act of positing. *v.t.* To place in position; to locate. **positional,** *a.*

positive (poz' i tiv) [M.E. and F. *positif*, L. *positivus* (POSIT, -IVE)], *a.* Definitely, explicitly, or formally laid down or affirmed; explicit, express, definite; intrinsic, inherent, absolute, not relative; existing, real, actual; authoritatively laid down, prescribed by artificial enactment as distinguished from natural; incontestable, certain, undoubted; confident, cocksure, dogmatic; (*colloq.*) downright, thorough; (*Gram.*) simple, not comparative or superlative; (*Phil.*) practical, positivist; (*Phys.*) denoting the presence of some quality, not negative; (*Elec.*) denoting the kind of electricity generated by glass rubbed with silk, vitreous; (*Magnetism*) denoting the north-seeking pole or the south pole of the earth; (*Math.*) denoting increase or progress, additive, greater than zero; (*Phot.*) exhibiting lights and shades in the same relations as in nature. *n.* That which may be affirmed; (*Gram.*) the positive degree, a positive adjective; (*Math.*) a positive quantity; (*Phot.*) a photograph in which the lights and shades are shown as in nature. **positive organ:** An organ used as a choir organ, orig. not portative, not carried in procession. **positive philosophy:** Positivism. **positive sign:** The sign +, denoting addition. **positively,** *adv.* **positiveness, positivity** (-tiv' i ti), *n.*

positivism (poz' i tiv izm), *n.* The philosophical system of Auguste Comte (1798–1857), which recognizes only observed phenomena and rejects speculation or metaphysics; the religious system based on this, professing to be a synthesis of all human conceptions of the external order of the universe, and to secure the victory of social feeling over self-love. **positivist,** *n.* **positivistic** (-vis' tik), *a.*

positron (poz' i tron), *n.* (*Phys.*) A positive electron.

posnet (pos' nĕt) [O.F. *poçonet*, dim. of *poçon*, pot], *n.* A small basin or pot used for boiling.

posology (pŏ sol' ŏ ji) [F. *posologie* (Gr. *posos*, how much, -LOGY)], *n.* (*Med.*) The art or science treating of doses or the quantities to be administered; (*Math.*) the science of quantity, mathematics. **posological** (-loj' i kăl), *a.*

posse (pos' i) [L., to be able], *n.* A body or force (of persons); a posse comitatus. ***in posse:*** Within possibility, possible. ***posse comitatus:*** A force which the sheriff of a county is empowered to raise in case of riot, etc.

possess (pŏ zes') [O.F. *possesser*, L. *possess-*, p.p. stem of *possidēre* (*port-*, towards, *sedēre*, to sit)], *v.t.* To have the ownership of, to own as property, to have full power over, to control (oneself, one's mind, etc.); to occupy, to dominate; to imbue, to impress (with); to acquire; to gain, to hold; to inhabit; *to attain; to accomplish. **to be possessed of:** To own. **to possess oneself of:** To acquire, to obtain as one's own. **possessed,** *a.* Owned; owning; dominated (by an idea, etc.); controlled (as by a devil), mad.

possession (pŏ zesh' ŭn), *n.* The act or state of possessing; holding or occupancy as owner; (*Law*) the exercise of such control as attaches to ownership, actual detention, or occupancy; that which is possessed; territory, esp. a subject dependency in a foreign country; (*pl.*) property, goods, wealth; (*fig.*) self-possession; the state of being possessed or under physical or supernatural influence; *conviction, certainty. **in possession:** In actual occupancy, possessed (of); holding, possessing; position of a bailiff in a house. **to give possession:** To put another in possession. **to take possession of:** To enter on; to seize. **writ of possession:** An order directing a sheriff to put a person in possession. ***possessionary,** *a.* **possessive,** *a.* Of or pertaining to possession; (*Gram.*) denoting possession. **possessively,** *adv.* **possessiveness,** *n.* **possessor,** *n.* **possessory,** *a.*

posset (pos' ĕt) [M.E. *possyt*, *poshote*, etym. doubtful], *n.* A drink made of hot milk curdled with ale, wine, etc. **v.t.* To curdle.

possible (pos' i bel) [F., from L. *possibilis* (*posse*, to be able, -BLE)], *a.* That may happen, be done, or exist; that may be done, that is not contrary to the nature of things; that may be dealt with or put up with, tolerable, reasonable. *n.* That which is possible; (*Shooting*) the highest score that can be made. **possibilist** (pŏ sib' i list), *n.* A member of a political party, esp. a Spanish constitutional republican or a French Socialist, aiming only at reforms that are actually practicable. **possibility** (-bil' i ti), *n.* **possibly** (pos' i bli), *adv.* By any possible means; perhaps; by a remote chance.

possum (pos' ŭm) [short for OPOSSUM], *n.* (*colloq.*) An opossum. **to play possum:** To feign, to dissemble (in alln. to the opossum's feigning death on the approach of danger).

post (1) (pōst) [A.-S., from L. *postis*, prob. rel. to *pōnere* (p.p. *positus*), to set, to fix], *n.* A piece of timber, metal, etc., set upright, and intended as a support to something; a stake, a stout pole; an upright forming part of various structures, machines, etc.; a pillar or vertical mass of coal or ore left as a support in a mine. *v.t.* To fix (*usu.* up) on a post or in a public place; to fasten bills, etc., upon (a wall, etc.); to advertise, to make known; to enter (a name) in a list posted up of defaulters, etc., esp. of students failing at an examination; to publish (the name of a ship) as overdue or missing.

post (2) (pōst) [F. *poste*, It. and late L. *posta*, from L. *posita*, fem. p.p. of *pōnere*, to set, to place], *n.* A fixed place, position, or station; a military station; the troops at such station; a fort; a place established for trading purposes, esp. among uncivilized natives; a situation, an appointment; an established system of letter-conveyance and delivery; orig. one of a series of men stationed at points along a road whose duty was to ride forward to the next man with letters; a courier, a messenger; a mail-cart; a post-office; a postal letter-box; a dispatch of mails; (*collect.*) the letters, packages, etc., taken from a post-office or letter-box at one time; the letters delivered at a house at one time; a relay of horses; a size of writing-paper, about $18\frac{3}{4}$ in. by $15\frac{1}{4}$; (*Mil.*) a bugle-call announcing the time of retiring for the night, etc. *adv.* In relays of horses; express, with speed. *v.t.* To station, to place in a particular position; to transmit by post; to put into a postal letter-box for transmission; to send by or as by post-horses; to send with speed; to transfer (accounts) to a ledger, to enter in this from a day-book, etc.; *to postpone, to delay. *v.i.* To travel with post-horses; to travel rapidly, to hurry. **first** or **last post:** (*Mil.*) The first or second of two bugle-calls announcing the time for retiring for the night. **to post up:** To complete (a ledger) with entries of accounts from a day-book, etc.; (*fig.*) to supply with full information. **to ride post:** To ride with post-horses; hence, to ride in haste. **post-bag,** *n.* A mail-bag. **post-bill,** *n.* A post-office way-bill of letters, etc., transmitted by mail. **post-boat,** *n.* A boat employed in postal work, a mail-boat, or one conveying passengers, a stage-boat. **post-boy, -rider,** *n.* A boy who carries the post; a boy who rides a post-horse, a postilion. ***post-captain,** *n.* (*Naval*) A full captain, usu. of three years' standing. **post card:** A card for sending by post unenclosed. **post-chaise, *-coach,** *n.* A vehicle for travelling by post. **post-free,** *a.* Carried free of charge for postage. **post haste,** *a.*, *adv.*, and *n.* Great expedition. **post-horn,** *n.* A long straight horn formerly blown to signalize the arrival of a mail-coach, now used on private drags, etc. **post-horse,** *n.* A horse kept as a relay at an inn, etc., for post or for travellers. **post-house,** *n.* A house where post-horses were kept for relays. **postman,** *n.* One who delivers letters brought by post; *a courier or post. **postmark,** *n.* A mark stamped by the post-office officials on letters, etc., usu. stating place, date, and hour of despatch, and serving to deface the postage-stamp. *v.t.* To stamp (an envelope, etc.) with this. **postmaster,** *n.* The superintendent of a post-office; *one who lets out post-horses. **postmastership,** *n.* **postmistress,** *n.* **post-office:** A place for the receipt and delivery of letters, etc.; the public postal department. **post-paid,** *a.* Having the postage prepaid; (*Am.* post-free). **post-rider** [POST-BOY]. **post-road,** *n.* A road on which relays of horses were available for posting. **post-town,** *n.* A town in which a head post-office is established; *a town in which post-horses were kept for travellers.

post- [L. *post*], *pref.* After, behind, since. **post-classical** (pōst klăs′ i kal), *a.* Later than the classical writers, artists, etc., esp. those of Greece and Rome. **post-communion** (-kō mū′ nyon), *n.* That part of the eucharistic service which follows after the act of communion. **post-costal** (-kos′ tal), *a.* (*Anat. and Ent.*) Behind a rib. **post-date** (pōst dāt′), *v.t.* To assign or mark with a date later than the actual one. *n.* (pōst′ dāt) A date later than the actual one. **postdiluvial** (-di loo-, -lū′ vi al), *a.* Being or happening after the Flood. **postdiluvian,** *a.* and *n.* **post-entry** (-en′ tri), *n.* An additional or subsequent entry; a late entry (for a race, etc.). **post-exilian, -exilic** (-eg zil′ i an, -ik), *a.* Later than the Babylonian exile. **post-fix** (pōst fiks′), *v.t.* To append (a letter, etc.) at the end of a word. *n.* (pōst′ fiks) A suffix. **post-glacial** (-glā′ shi al), *a.* Later than the glacial period. **postgraduate** (-grăd′ ū at), *a.* Carried on after graduation. **post-millennial** (-mi len′ i al), *a.* Of or pertaining to a period after the millennium. **post-millennialism,** *n.* The doctrine that the second advent of Christ will follow the millennium. **post-millennialist,** *n.* **post-natal** (-nā′ tal), *a.* Happening after birth. ***post-note,** *n.* (*Am.*) A negotiable note issued by a bank, payable at some future time. **post-nuptial,** *a.* Made or happening after marriage. **post-oral** (-ôr′ al), *a.* (*Anat.*) Behind the mouth. **post-orbital** (-ôr′ bi tal), *a.* (*Anat.*) Behind the orbit of the eye. **post-pliocene** (-plī′ ō sēn), *a.* (*Geol.*) Pertaining to the formation immediately above the pliocene. **postposition** (-pō zish′ un), *n.* The act of placing after; the state of being placed after or behind; (*Gram.*) a word or particle placed after a word, esp. an enclitic. **postpositional,** *a.* **postpositive,** *a.* (*Gram.*) Placed after something else. *n.* A post-positive word or particle. **postprandial** (-prăn′ di al), *a.* After dinner. **post-tertiary** (-tĕr′ sha ri), *a.* Pertaining to formations later than the tertiary.

postage (pōs′ tij), *n.* The fee for conveyance of a letter, etc., by post. **postage-stamp,** *n.* **postal,** *a.* **postal order:** An order for a sum of money (specified on the face of the document) issued to a customer at one post-office for payment at another. **postal union:** A union of governments for the regulation of postal business between the countries they represent.

post-boy, etc. [POST (2)]. **post-date** [POST-].

poster (1) (pōs′ tėr), *n.* A large placard or advertising bill; one who posts this.

***poster** (2) (pōs′ tėr), *n.* One who travels post; a courier, a messenger; a post-horse; one who posts a letter.

poste restante (pōst rės tant′) [F., remaining post], *n.* A department in a post-office where letters are kept until called for.

posterior (pos tēr′ i or) [L., comp. of *posterus*, from *post*, after], *a.* Coming or happening after; later; hinder. *n.* (*usu. in pl.*) The buttocks. **posteriority** (-or′ i ti), *n.* **posteriorly,** *adv.*

posterity (pos ter′ i ti) [F. *postérité*, L. *posteritātem*, nom. *-tas*, as prec.], *n.* Those proceeding in the future from any person, descendants; succeeding generations.

postern (pōs′ tėrn) [O.F. *posterne*, *posterle* (F. *poterne*), late L. *posterula*, dim. of *posterus*, from *post*, after, behind], *n.* A small doorway or gateway at the side or back; a private entrance, esp. to a castle, town, etc.; (*fig.*) a way of escape.

post-haste, etc. [POST (2)].

posthumous (pos′ tū mus) [L. *postumus*, superl. of *post*, after (late L. *posthumus*, as if *post humum*, after the ground)], *a.* Born after the death of the father; happening after one's decease; published after the death of the author. **posthumously,** *adv.*

postiche (pos tēsh′) [F., from It. *posticcio*, from L. *postus*, *positus*, p.p. of *pōnere*, to place], *a.* Artificial, superadded (applied to superfluous ornament). *n.* An imitation, a sham.

posticus (pos tī′ kus) [L. *postīcus*, from *post*, after, behind], *a.* (*Bot.*) On the hinder side; turned away from the axis, extrorse.

***postil** (pos′ til) [M.E. and F. *postille*, med. L. *postilla* (prob. *post illa*, after these)], *n.* A marginal note in a Bible; hence, any explanatory note, esp. one in the margin; a commentary; a homily on the Gospel or Epistle for the day. *v.i.* To write comments. *v.t.* To write marginal notes on. ***postillate,** *v.i.* and *t.* ***postillation** (-lā′ shun), *n.* ***postillator** (pos′ ti lā tor), ***postiller** (pos′ til ėr), *n.*

postilion, postillion (pō stil′ yon) [F. *postillon*, from *posta*, POST (2)], *n.* One who rides on the near horse of the leaders or of a pair drawing a carriage.

post-impressionism (pōst im presh′ ō nizm), *n.* The doctrines and methods of a school of painters, active in the early years of the 20th century, who rejected most of the accepted æsthetic and technical theories and maxims and expressed themselves with primitive freedom and simplicity. **post-impressionist,** *n.*

postliminy (pōst lim′ i ni) [L. *postliminium* (POST-, *limen liminis*, threshold)], *n.* (*Rom. Law*) The right of resumption of former rights and privileges by an exile or captive returning to his own country; (*Inter. Law*) the right of restoration of things taken in war to their former civil status or ownership on their coming back into the power of the nation to which they belonged.

postman, -mark, -master, etc. [POST (2)].

postmeridian (pōst mė rid′ i an) [L. *postmeridiānus*], *a.* Of or belonging to the afternoon; late. ***post meridiem:*** After midday (applied to the hours from noon to midnight, usu. abbrev. *p.m.*). **post-millennium,** etc. [POST-].

post-mortem (pōst môr′ tėm) [L., after death], *adv.* After death. *a.* Made or occurring after death. *n.* An examination of a dead body; a subsequent review, esp. of a game of cards.

post-obit (pōst ob′ it) [L. *post obitum* (*post*, after, *obitus*, decease, from *obīre*, to die)], *a.* Taking effect after death; post-mortem. *n.* A bond securing payment of a sum of money to a lender on the death of a specified person from whose estate the borrower has expectations.

post-office, etc. [POST (2)].

postpone (pōs pōn′) [L. *postpōnere* (POST-, *pōnere*, to put)], *v.t.* To put off, to defer, to delay; to regard as of minor importance to something else. *v.i.* (*Path.*) To be late in recurring. **postponement,** *n.* **postponer,** *n.*

post-position, post-prandial, etc. [POST-].

post-road [POST (2)].

postscenium (pōst sē′ ni um) [L. *postscænium* (POST-, *scæna*, Gr. *skēnē*, stage, SCENE)], *n.* (*Class. Ant.*) The back part of a theatre behind the scenes.

postscript (pōst′ skript) [L. *postscriptum* (POST-, *scriptum*, neut. p.p. of *scrībere*, to write)], *n.* A paragraph added to a letter after the writer's signature; an addition to a book after it is finished. **postscriptal** (-skrip′ tal), *a.*

postulant (pos′ tū lant), *n.* A candidate for entry into a religious order or for an ecclesiastical office; one who demands.

postulate (pos′ tū lat) [L. *postulatum*, neut. p.p. of *postulāre*, to demand], *n.* A position assumed without proof as being self-evident; a fundamental assumption; a necessary condition, an indispensable preliminary; (*Geom.*) a statement of the possibility of a simple operation such as a geometrical construction. *v.t.* (-lāt) To demand, to claim, to assume without proof, to take as self-evident; to stipulate; (*Eccles. Law*) to nominate subject to sanction by superior authority. **postulation** (-lā′ shŭn), *n.* **postulator** (pos′ tū lā tȯr), *n.* ***postulatory,** *a.*

posture (pos′ chūr) [F., from L. *positūra*, from *posit*, p.p. stem of *pōnere*, to put], *n.* Pose, attitude, or arrangement of the parts of the body; situation, condition, state (of affairs, etc.); *situation, location. *v.t.* To arrange the body and limbs of in a particular posture. *v.i.* To assume a posture, to pose. **posture-master,** *n.* One who teaches or practises artificial postures of the body. **postural,** *a.* **posturer,** *n.*

posy (pō′ zi) [contr. of POESY], *n.* A motto or short inscription, esp. in a ring; orig. one in verse; a bunch of flowers, a nosegay.

pot (pot) [A.-S. *pott* (cp. Dut. *pot*, G. *pott*, Icel. *pottr*, F. *pot*), perh. cogn. with L. *pōtus*, drunk, Gr. *potos*, a drinking], *n.* A round vessel of earthenware or metal, usu. deep relatively to breadth, for holding liquids, etc.; a vessel of this kind used for cooking; a large drinking-cup of earthenware, pewter, etc.; the quantity this holds; (*loosely*) a quart; a vessel used for various domestic or industrial purposes; a chamber-pot, a coffee-pot, a flower-pot, a teapot, etc.; a chimney-pot; (*Racing, etc.*) a cup offered as a prize; (*slang*) a large sum; a heavy sum staked on a horse, etc. *v.t.* (*past & p.p.* **potted**) To put into a pot or pots; to plant in pots; to season and preserve in pots, etc.; (*Billiards*) to pocket; (*colloq.*) to bring down, esp. with a pot-shot; to bag, to secure. *v.i.* (*colloq.*) To shoot (at). **big pot** [BIG (1)]. **to go to pot:** (*slang*) To be ruined or done for, to degenerate. **to keep the pot boiling** [KEEP (1)]. **pot-ale,** *n.* Fermented grain as refuse from a distillery. **pot-belly,** *n.* A protuberant belly; a person with this. **pot-bellied,** *a.* **pot-boiler,** *n.* A work of art or literature produced merely for money; one who produces this. **pot-bound,** *a.* Filling the pot with its roots, not having room to grow (of a plant). **pot-boy, -man,** *n.* One employed in a public-house to clean pots, etc. **pot-companion,** *n.* A companion in drinking. **pot-hanger, *-hangle,** *n.* A pot-hook. **pot-herb,** *n.* A culinary herb. **pot-hole,** *n.* A cauldron-shaped cavity in the rocky bed of a stream; a pit-like cavity in mountain limestone, etc., usu. produced by a combination of faulting and water-action; a cavity in a roadway caused by the sloughing of the road metal. **pot-hook,** *n.* An S-shaped hook for suspending a pot or kettle over a fire; (*fig.*) a letter like a pot-hook, esp. in clumsy handwriting. **pot-house,** *n.* A low public house. **pot-hunter,** *n.* One who kills game, fish, etc., for food or profit rather than sport; one who competes for prizes merely for profit. **pot-hunting,** *n.* **pot-lead,** *n.* Blacklead, esp. as used on the hulls of racing yachts to reduce friction. **pot-lid,** *n.* **pot-luck,** *n.* Whatever fare may chance to be provided for dinner, etc. **pot-man** [POT-BOY]. **pot-metal,** *n.* A cheap alloy of copper and lead used for making pots; stained glass coloured throughout while in a state of fusion. **pot-roast,** *n.* A piece of meat stewed in a closed receptacle. **pot-shot,** *n.* A shot at game, etc., that happens to be within easy range; a random shot; a shot for filling the pot, esp. one of an unsportsmanlike kind. **potstone,** *n.* A granular variety of steatite; a large mass of flint found in chalk. **pot-valiant,** *a.* Made courageous by drink. ***pot-walloper** [WALLOP, to boil fast], *n.* A man having a parliamentary vote because he had boiled his pot at his own fireside, a qualification in certain English boroughs previous to 1832. **potful,** *n.* **potted,** *a.* Put in a pot; condensed, abridged; (of music) recorded for reproduction by gramophone, etc.

potable (pō′ tȧbl) [F., from late L. *pōtābilis*, from L. *pōtāre*, to drink], *a.* Drinkable, *n.* (*usu. in pl.*) Anything drinkable. **potableness,** *n.*

potage (pō tazh′) [F., POTAGE], *n.* Soup.

potamic (pȯ tăm′ ik) [Gr. *potamos*, river, -IC], *a.* Of or pertaining to rivers. **potamology** (pot ȧ mol′ ȯ ji) [-LOGY], *n.*

potash (pot′ ăsh), ***potass** (pȯ tăs′, pot′ ăs) [POT, ASH (1) (perh. after Dut. *potasch*)], *n.* A powerful alkali, consisting of potassium carbonate in a crude form, orig. obtained from the ashes of plants. **potash-water,** *n.* An artificial mineral water containing bicarbonate of potash and charged with carbon dioxide.

potassa (pȯ tăs′ ȧ), *n.* (*Chem.*) Potassium monoxide.

potassium (pȯ tăs′ i ŭm), *n.* A bluish or pinkish white metallic element. **potassic,** *a.*

potation (pȯ tā′ shŭn) [M.E. and O.F. *potacion*, L. *pōtātiōnem*, nom. *-tio*, from *pōtāre*, to drink], *n.* The act of drinking; a draught; a beverage; (*usu. pl.*) tippling. ***potator** (pȯ tā′ tȯr), *n.* **potatory** (pō′ tȧ tȯr i), *a.*

potato (pȯ tā′ tō) [Sp. *patata*, Haitian *batata*], *n.* (*pl.* **-toes**) A plant, *Solanum tuberosum*, with edible farinaceous tubers; a tuber of this. **small potatoes:** (*slang*) Something very inferior and contemptible. **the potato:** (*slang*) The best, the tip-top thing; the correct thing. **potato-beetle, -bug,** *n.* The Colorado beetle. **potato-bogle,** *n.* (*Sc.*) A scarecrow. **potato-box, -trap,** *n.* (*slang*) The mouth. **potato chips:** Long slices of potato fried in deep fat (*Am.* french fried). **potato crisps:** Flakes of potato thus fried. **potato fern,** *n.* (*Austral.*) A fern with edible tubers, also called the native potato. **potato-ring,** *n.* A ring or hoop (usu. Irish) formerly used for standing dishes on.

poteen (pȯ tēn′) [Ir. *poitin*, dim. of *poite*, POT], *n.* Irish whisky illicitly distilled.

potence (1) (pō′ tėns) [F., a crutch, as foll.], *n.* (*Her.*) A cross with ends resembling the head of a crutch or a T; (*Eng.*) a T-shaped framework; (*Watch-making*) a stud or support for a bearing, esp. the lower pivot of a verge; *a cross or gibbet. **potent** (1), *n.* *A support, a crutch; (*Her.*) having the arms (of a cross) terminating in cross-pieces or crutch-heads. **potented, potentée,** *a.* (*Her.*).

potent (2) (pō′ tėnt) [L. *potens -ntem*, pres.p. of *posse*, to be able], *a.* Powerful, mighty; having great force or influence; cogent; strong, intoxicating. **n.* A potentate. **potence** (2), **potency,** *n.* **potently,** *adv.* ***potentness,** *n.* **potentiate,** *v.t.* To make potent; to make possible.

potentate (pō′ tėn tāt), *n.* One who possesses great power; a monarch, a ruler.

potential (pȯ ten′ shȧl), *a.* Existing but not in action (of energy), latent; existing in possibility not in actuality; (*Gram.*) expressing possibility; *having force or power, potent. *n.* Anything that may be possible; a possibility; (*Gram.*) the potential mood; (*Phys.*) the voltage of a point above zero or earth. **potential energy:** Energy possessed by a body as a result of its position. **potential function:** (*Math.*) A quantity by the differentiation of which the value of the force at any point in space arising from any system of bodies can be obtained. **potentiality** (-ăl′ i ti), *n.* **potentialize** (pȯ ten′ shȧ līz), *v.t.* To transform into a potential condition. **potentially,** *adv.*

Potentilla (pō tėn til′ ȧ) [med. L., dim. from L. *potens -ntem*, POTENT], *n.* (*Bot.*) A genus of *Rosaceæ*, comprising the cinquefoil, tormentil, etc.

potentiometer (pȯ ten shi om′ ė tėr), *n.* (*Elec.*) An instrument for measuring electromotive force or difference of potential.

pother (poth′, pŭth′ ėr) [etym. doubtful], *n.* Bustle, confusion; *a cloud of dust or smoke. *v.i.* To make a bustle or stir; to make a fuss. *v.t.* To harass, to fluster.

potichomania (pot i shȯ mā′ ni ȧ) [F. *potichomanie* (*potiche*, an Oriental pot or vase, -MANIA)], *n.* A craze for coating glass-ware with varnished paper, etc., to imitate painted ware or china.

potin (pȯ tan) [F., from POT], *n.* A composition of copper, lead, tin, and silver, of which Roman coins were made; pot-metal.

potion (pō′ shŭn) [M.E. and O.F. *pocion*, L. *pōtiōnem*, nom. *-tio*, from *pōtus*, drunk], *n.* A drink, a draught, esp. of medicine, a dose. **v.t.* To drug.

potlatch (pot' lăch) [Chinook], *n.* (*N. Am. Ind.*) A gift; a feast and distribution of largess by one aiming at the headship of a tribe.

potoroo (pot ō roo') [Austral. abor.], *n.* The marsupial kangaroo-rat.

potpourri (pō pu rē') [F., rotten pot], *n.* A mixture of dried flower-petals and spices, usu. kept in a bowl for perfuming a room; (*fig.*) a literary miscellany, a musical medley, etc.

potsherd (pot' shėrd) [POT, SHERD], *n.* A broken piece of earthenware.

pott (pot) [POT], *n.* A size of printing or writing paper, usu. 15½ × 12½ in. **pott-folio, pott-octavo, pott-quarto,** *n.* Sizes of books.

pottage (pot' åj) [F. *potage* (POT, -AGE)], *n.* A kind of soup; porridge.

potter (1) (pot' ėr) [late A.-S. *pottere* (POT, -ER)], *n.* A maker of pottery. **potter's asthma, bronchitis** or **consumption:** An acute form of bronchitis caused by dust in pottery-manufacture. **potter's clay:** A tenacious clay containing kaolin, used for pottery. **potter's field:** A public burying-place for the poor or strangers. **potter's lathe:** A machine for moulding clay. **potter's wheel:** A horizontal wheel used in this.

potter (2) (pot' ėr) [perh. freq. of obs. *pote*, A.-S. *potian*, to prod, to push, etym. doubtful], *v.i.* To work in a trifling, ineffective way (at, in, etc.); to loiter, to idle (about). *v.t.* To waste or pass (time away) in a desultory way.

pottern (pot' ėrn) [from POTTER (1), after LEATHERN], *a.* Pertaining to potters or pottery. **pottern-ore,** *n.* An ore vitrifying with heat, used by potters to glaze their ware.

pottery (pot' ėr i) [F. *poterie*, from POT], *n.* Earthenware; a place where this is manufactured, a potter's workshop; the making of earthenware.

pottle (pot' ėl) [M.E. and O.F. *potel*, dim. of POT], *n.* A liquid measure of four pints; a large tankard; a vessel or basket for holding fruit. ***pottle-deep,** *adv.* To the bottom of the tankard. **pottle-pot,** *n.* A two-quart pot or tankard.

potto (pot' ō) [W. African native], *n.* A W. African lemuroid, *Perodicticus potto.*

potty (pot' i) [?], *a.* Insignificant; crazy, foolish.

pouch (pouch) [M.E. and O.North.F. *pouche*, O.F. *poche*, POKE (1)], *n.* A small bag; a purse, a detachable pocket; a leather bag for holding cartridges, etc.; the bag-like part in which marsupials carry their young; a pouch-like sac in plants. *v.t.* To put into a pouch; to pocket; to cause (a bodice, etc.) to hang like a pouch; to swallow; (*fig.*) to put up with; (*slang*) to supply the pocket of, to tip. *v.i.* To hang like a pouch (of a dress). **pouched, pouchy,** *a.*

***pou-de-soy** [PADUASOY].

poudrette (poo dret') [F., dim of *poudre*, POWDER], *n.* A dry manure made of night-soil with charcoal, gypsum, etc.

pouf (poof) [F.], *n.* A part of a woman's dress gathered into a kind of knot or bunch; a mode of dressing women's hair fashionable in the 18th cent.; a cushion or ottoman.

pouffe (poof) [Fr.], *n.* A large floor-cushion, a humpty.

Poujadist (poo zha' dist) [Pierre *Poujade*, F. politician], *n.a.* Follower of, or on the lines of this champion of the small man and tax reduction.

poulpe (poolp) [F., POLYPUS], *n.* An octopus or cuttle-fish, esp. *Octopus vulgaris.*

poult (pōlt) [var. of PULLET], *n.* A young pullet, partridge, turkey, etc. **poulterer, *poulter,** *n.* One who deals in poultry for the table.

poultice (pōl' tis) [L. *puls pultis*, PULSE (2)], *n.* A soft composition, as of bread, meal, etc., for applying to sores or inflamed parts of the body; a cataplasm. *v.t.* To apply a poultice to.

poultry (pōl' tri) [O.F. *pouletrie* (POULT, -RY)], *n.* Domestic fowls, including barn-door fowls, geese, ducks, turkeys, etc. **poultry-house, poultry-yard,** *n.*

pounamu (pou na' moo) [Maori], *n.* Nephrite, green-stone.

pounce (1) (pouns) [etym. doubtful, perh. rel. to PUNCH, and PUNCHEON (1)], *n.* The claw of a bird of prey; a pouncing, an abrupt swoop, spring, etc. *v.i.* To sweep down or spring upon and seize prey with the claws; to seize (upon), to dart or dash (upon) suddenly; to speak abruptly. **v.t.* To seize in the claws; to perforate. ***pounced,** *a.* (*Her.*) Furnished with claws.

pounce (2) (pouns) [F. *ponce*, L. *pūmicem*, nom. *pūmex*, PUMICE], *n.* A fine powder formerly used to dry up ink on manuscript; a powder used for sprinkling over a perforated pattern in order to transfer the design. *v.t.* To smooth with pounce or pumice; to mark out (a pattern) by means of pounce. **pounce-box,** *n.* A box out of which pounce is sprinkled. ***pouncet-box:** A box with a perforated lid for holding perfumes.

pound (1) (pound) [A.-S. *pund* (cp. Dut. *pond*, G. *pfund*), L. *pondo*, rel. to *pendere*, to weigh, *pendĕre*, to hang], *n.* A measure of weight consisting of 12 oz. troy or 16 oz. avoirdupois; an English money of account consisting of 20s., represented by the gold sovereign. *v.t.* To test the weight of (coins). **pound Australian:** 16s. **pound Scots:** 1s. 8d. **pound-cake,** *n.* A rich sweet cake, from the ingredients being pound for pound of each.

pound (2) (pound) [A.-S. *pund*, enclosure], *n.* An enclosure for confining stray cattle, etc.; an enclosure, a pen; (*fig.*) a trap, a prison; a place whence there is no escape, esp. in hunting; a pond, a part between locks on a canal. *v.t.* To confine in or as in a pound; to shut in, to enclose in front and behind (*usu. in p.p.*). **pound-keeper,** *n.* **pound-net,** *n.* A series of nets, set in shoal water, to form a trap.

pound (3) (pound) [A.-S. *pūnian*], *v.t.* To crush, to pulverize, to comminute; to beat, to strike heavily; to thump, to pommel. *v.i.* To strike heavy blows, to hammer (at, upon, etc.); to fire heavy shot (at); to walk or go heavily along.

poundage (1) (poun' dåj), *n.* An allowance, fee, commission, etc., of so much in the pound; a percentage of the aggregate earnings of an industrial concern paid as or added to wages; a payment or charge per pound weight; the charge on a postal order; (*Eng. Hist.*) a subsidy to the Crown raised by an impost on each pound exported or imported. **v.t.* To impose poundage on.

poundage (2) (poun' dåj), *n.* Confinement in a pound; a charge upon cattle impounded.

pounder (1) (poun' dėr), *n.* (*usu. in comb.*) A piece of ordnance carrying a shot of a specified number of pounds weight; a person worth or possessing a specified sum in pounds sterling; something weighing a pound, or a specified number of pounds, as a fish.

pounder (2) (poun' dėr), *n.* One who or that which pounds, esp. a pestle.

pour (pôr) [M.E. *pouren*, etym. doubtful], *v.t.* To cause (liquids, etc.) to flow; to discharge, to emit copiously; to send (forth or out) in a stream or great numbers; to shed freely; (*fig.*) to utter, to give vent to. *v.i.* To flow in a stream; to fall copiously (of rain); (*fig.*) to rush in great numbers; to come in a constant stream. *n.* A heavy fall, a downpour; (*Foundry*) the amount of molten material poured at one time. **pourer,** *n.*

pourboire (poor bwar') [F., for drinking], *n.* A gratuity, a tip.

pour-parler (poor par' lā) [F., to discuss (*pour*, for, before, *parler*, to speak)], *n.* A preliminary discussion with a view to formal negotiation.

***pour-point** (poor′ point) [O.F., p.p. of *pour-poundre* (*pour-*, *par*, L. PER-, *pungere*, to prick)], *n.* A quilted doublet.

poussette (poo set′) [F., dim. of *pousse*, PUSH], *v.i.* To swing partners with hands joined as in a country dance. *n.* This figure.

pout (1) (pout) [A.-S. *-pūta*, in *æle-pūtan*, eel-pouts (cp. Dut. *puit*, G. *-putte*), cogn. with foll.], *n.* One of various fishes that have a pouting appearance [see EEL-POUT, WHITING-POUT].

pout (2) (pout) [M.E. *pouten* (cp. Swed. *puta*, pad, Dan. *pude*, pillow)], *v.i.* To thrust out the lips in sullenness, displeasure, or contempt; to be protruded or prominent (of lips). *v.t.* To thrust out. *n.* A protrusion of the lips; a fit of sullenness. **in the pouts:** Sullen. **pouter,** *n.* One who pouts; a variety of pigeon, from its way of inflating its crop. **poutingly,** *adv.*

poverty (pov′ ėr ti) [M.E. and O.F. *poverte*, L. *paupertātem*, nom. *-tas*, from PAUPER], *n.* The state of being poor; want, destitution, indigence; scarcity, meagreness, dearth (of); deficiency (in); inferiority. **poverty-stricken,** *a.* Poor; inferior, mean.

powan (pou′ ȧn) [Sc. POLLAN], *n.* A freshwater fish, *Coregonus clupeoides*, found in Loch Lomond, etc.

powder (pou′ dėr) [F. *poudre*, O.F. *poldre*, *polre*, L. *pulver*], *n.* Any dry comminuted substance or fine particles; dust; a cosmetic in the form of fine dust; a medicine in the form of powder; gunpowder. *v.t.* To reduce to powder; to put powder on; to sprinkle or cover with powder; to sprinkle with fine spots or figures for decoration. *v.i.* To become powder or like powder; to powder one's hair. **powder-blue,** *n.* Pulverized smalt, esp. for use in a laundry; the colour of this. *a.* Having the colour of smalt. **powder-box,** *n.* A box for toilet-powder, etc. **powder-cart,** *n.* A cart for conveying ammunition for artillery. **powder-closet,** *n.* A small room where women's hair used to be powdered. **powder-down,** *n.* A peculiar kind of down-feathers disintegrating into fine powder, occurring in definite patches on herons, etc. **powder-flask, -horn,** *n.* A case or horn fitted to hold gunpowder. **powder-magazine,** *n.* A storing-place for gunpowder. **powder-mill,** *n.* Works in which gunpowder is made. **powder-monkey,** *n.* (*Naut.*) A boy formerly employed to bring powder from the magazine to the guns. **powder-puff,** *n.* A soft pad or brush for applying powder to the skin. **powder-room,** *n.* The apartment in a ship where gunpowder is kept; (*colloq.*) a ladies' cloakroom. **powdering-tub,** *n.* A tub in which meat is salted or pickled; (*Shak.*) *a tub in which an infected lecher was sweated. **powdery,** *a.* **powderiness,** *n.*

power (pou′ ėr) [M.E. and O.F. *poër* (F. *pouvoir*), late L. *potēre*, from L. *pot-*, stem of *posse*, to be able], *n.* Ability to do or act so as to effect something; a mental or bodily faculty, or potential capacity; strength, force, energy, esp. as actually exerted; influence, dominion, authority (over); right or ability to control; legal authority or authorization; political ascendancy; a person or body invested with authority; a State having influence on other States; (*vulg.*) a large number or quantity; (*Math.*) the product obtained by multiplication of a quantity or number into itself; (*Math.*) the index showing the number of times a factor is multiplied by itself; (*Mech.*) mechanical energy as distinguished from hand labour; capacity (of a machine, etc.) for performing mechanical work; the rate of doing work, measured in foot-pounds per second, or ergs per second; (*Opt.*) the magnifying capacity of a lens, etc.; *the sixth order of angels; *a naval or military force; *a supernatural being having sway over some part of creation, a deity. **power of attorney** [ATTORNEY]. **power amplifier,** *n.* (*Radio.*) A low-frequency amplifier for powerful loudspeakers. **power component,** *n.* (*Elec.*) That part of an alternating current which is in phase with the voltage. **power factor,** *n.* That fraction which is less than unity by which the product of amperes and volts in an alternating-current circuit has to be multiplied in order to estimate the true power. **power-lathe, -loom,** etc., *n.* A lathe, loom, etc., worked by mechanical power. **power-house,** *n.* A building in which mechanical power is generated for transmission to other parts of a system. **power politics,** *n.* Diplomacy backed by armed force or the threat of it. **power-rail,** *n.* An insulated rail conveying current to the motors on electric railways of certain kinds. **power-station,** *n.* A building for the generation of power, esp. electrical power, for transmission to a railway or other system. **power transmission,** *n.* (*Elec.*) The transmission of power from the generating system to the point of application. **powerful,** *a.* Having great strength or energy; mighty, potent; impressing the mind, forcible, efficacious; producing great effects; (*colloq.*) great, numerous, extreme. **powerfully,** *adv.* **powerfulness,** *n.* **powerless,** *a.* **powerlessly,** *adv.* **powerlessness,** *n.*

powwow (pou′ wou) [N. Am. Ind.], *n.* A N. American Indian medicine-man or wizard; magic rites for the cure of diseases; a dance, feast, or conference. *v.i.* To practise sorcery, esp. for healing the sick; to hold a powwow; (*Am.*) to talk about, to discuss. *v.t.* To treat with sorcery, esp. with a view to healing.

pox (poks) [pl. of POCK], *n.* Pustules or eruptions of any kind, esp. applied to smallpox, chicken-pox, and syphilis; *a mild imprecation.

pozzolana (pot sō la′ nȧ), **pozzuolana** (pot swō la′ nȧ) [It., from *Pozzuoli*, near Naples], *n.* A volcanic ash used in hydraulic cements.

praam [PRAM (1)].

prabble (prăb′ ėl) [var. of BRABBLE], *n.* A squabble, a quarrel. *v.i.* To chatter.

***practic** (prăk′ tik) [O.F. *practique* (F. *pratique*), late L. *practicus*, Gr. *praktikos*, from *prassein*, to do], *a.* Practical; practised, skilful, cunning, treacherous. *n.* Practice; a deed, a doing, a practice (*usu. in pl.*); deceit, a trick, a deception.

practicable (prăk′ ti kȧ bėl) [F. *practicable*, from *practiquer*, to PRACTISE, assim. to foll.], *a.* Capable of being done, traversed, etc., feasible; (*Theat.*) that can be used real, not simulated; (*slang*) easily taken in, gullible. **practicability** (-bil′ i ti), **practicableness,** *n.* **practicably,** *adv.*

practical (prăk′ ti kȧl), *a.* Of, pertaining to, or governed by practice; derived from practice, experienced; capable of being used, available or serving for use; pertaining to action not theory or speculation; such in effect, virtual. **practical joke:** A joke or trick entailing some action. **practically,** *adv.* In a practical manner; virtually, in effect, as regards results. **practicality** (-kăl′ i ti), ***practicalness,** *n.*

practice (prăk′ tis) [prob. from PRACTISE], *n.* Habitual or customary action or procedure; habit, custom; the continued or systematic exercise of any profession, art, craft, etc.; business, professional connexion; actual performance, doing, or execution, as opposed to theory or intention; (*Arith.*) a rule for multiplying quantities of various denominations; (*Law*) legal procedure, the rules governing this; *scheming, artifice, contrivance (*usu. in pl.*); *skill, dexterity acquired by experience. **in practice:** In the sphere of action; in training; in condition for working, acting, playing, etc., effectively. **out of practice:** Out of training. **practician** (prăk tish′ ȧn), *n.* One who works or practises, a practitioner.

practise (prăk′ tis) [O.F. *practiser* (F. *pratiquer*), med. L. *practicāre*, from *practicus*], *v.t.* To do or perform habitually; to carry out; to exercise a profession, etc.; to exercise oneself in or on; to instruct, to exercise, to drill (in a subject, art, etc.); to accustom; *to plot, to scheme. *v.i.* To exercise oneself; to exercise a profession or art; to do a thing or perform an act habitually; *to scheme, to plot, to use stratagems; to use influence, to impose (upon). **practisant,** *n.* An agent, a plotter. **practised,** *a.* **practiser,** *n.*

practitioner (prăk tish′ ŏn ėr), *n.* One who regularly practises any profession, esp. of medicine; *a plotter. **general practitioner:** One practising both medicine and surgery; a physician not a specialist.

prad (prad) [Slang, from Dut. *paard*], *n.* A horse.

præ-, pre- [L. *præ*, before], *pref.* ***præcipe*** (prē′ si pē) [L., imper. of *præcipere*, to enjoin; *capere*, to take], *n.* (*Law*) A writ requiring something to be done, or a reason for its non-performance. **præcocial** (prė kō′ shi ăl) [L. *præcox cocis*, -AL], *a.* (*Ornith.*) Of or belonging to the *Præcoces*, a division of birds the young of which are able to look after and feed themselves as soon as hatched. ***præcognitum*** (prė kog′ ni tŭm) [L. (*cognitum*, p.p. of *cognoscere*, to know)], *n.* (*pl.* ***-nita***) Something known before, esp. a science or branch of knowledge necessary in order to understand something else. ***præcordia*** (prė kôr′ di ȧ) [L. (*cor cordis*, heart)], *n.pl.* (*Anat.*) The chest and the parts it contains, the region about the heart.

præmunire (prē mū nī′ rē) [L., to defend, conf. with *præmonēre*, to forewarn (PRÆ-, *monēre*, to warn)], *n.* (*Law*) A writ or process against a person charged with obeying or maintaining the papal authority in England; an offence against the Statute of Præmunire (1393) on which this is based; the penalty incurred by it.

prænomen [PRENOMEN].

prætexta (prė tek′ stȧ) [L. *toga praetexta*, bordered toga (PRÆ-, *texta*, from p.p. of *texere*, to weave)], *n.* (*Rom. Ant.*) A long white Roman toga or robe with a purple border.

prætor (prē′ tôr) [L., for *præitor*, from *præīre* (PRÆ-, *īre*, to go)], *n.* (*Rom. Hist.*) A Roman magistrate; orig. a consul as leader of the army; later a curule magistrate elected yearly to perform various judicial and consular duties. **prætorial** (-tôr′ i ăl), *a.* **prætorian,** *a.* Of or pertaining to a prætor; pertaining to the body-guard of a Roman general or emperor, esp. the imperial body-guard established by Augustus. *n.* A soldier in this body-guard; a man of prætorian rank. **prætorian gate:** The gate of a Roman camp in front of the general's quarters towards the enemy. **prætorium,** *n.* The general's tent or official quarters in a Roman camp; a Roman governor's official residence or court.

pragmatic (prăg măt′ ik) [F. *pragmatique*, L. *pragmaticus*, Gr. *pragmatikos*, from *pragma pragmatos*, deed, from *prassein*, to do], *a.* Pertaining to the affairs of a State; concerned with the causes and effects and the practical lessons of history; pragmatical. *n.* One busy in affairs; a busybody; a sovereign decree. **pragmatic sanction:** An ordinance made by a sovereign and constituting a fundamental law, esp. that of the Emperor Charles VI settling the succession to the throne of Austria. **pragmatical,** *a.* Busy, diligent, officious, given to interfering in the affairs of others; dogmatic; relating to pragmatism; pragmatic; *pertaining to State affairs. **pragmaticality** (-kăl′ i ti), **pragmaticalness,** *n.* **pragmatically,** *adv.*

pragmatism (prăg′ mȧ tizm), *n.* Pragmaticalness, officiousness; treatment of things, esp. in history, with regard to causes and effects; (*Phil.*) the doctrine that our only test of the truth of human cognitions or philosophical principles is their practical results. **pragmatize,** *v.t.* To represent (an imaginary thing) as real. **pragmatist,** *n.* **pragmatistic** (-tis′ tik), *a.*

prairie (prâr′ i) [F., through a pop. L. *prātāria*, from L. *prātum*, meadow], *n.* An extensive tract of level or rolling grass-land, usu. destitute of trees, esp. in the western United States. **prairie-chicken, -hen,** *n.* A N. American grouse, *Tetrao cupido*. **prairie-dog,** *n.* A small rodent of the genus *Cynomys*, esp. *C. Ludovicianus*, living in large communities on the prairies. **prairie oyster,** *n.* A pick-me-up of egg, Worcester Sauce, etc. **prairie-schooner,** *n.* (*Am.*) An emigrants' name for the covered wagons used in crossing the western plains. **prairie-squirrel,** *n.* A N. American ground-squirrel of the genus *Spermophilus*. **prairie value:** The value of land before labour has been expended on it. **prairie-wolf,** *n.* The coyote, *Canis latrans*.

praise (prāz) [M.E. *preiser*, O.F. *preisier*, late L. *pretiāre*, from L. *pretium*, price, value, cp. PRICE], *v.t.* To express approval and commendation of, to applaud; to extol, to glorify. *n.* Praising, approbation, encomium; glorifying, extolling; an object of praise. **praisable,** *a.* **praiser,** *n.* **praiseful,** *a.* Laudable, commendable. **praisefulness,** *n.* **praiseless,** *a.* **praiseworthy,** *a.* Deserving of praise; laudable, commendable. **praiseworthy,** *adv.* **praiseworthiness,** *n.*

Prakrit (pra′ krit) [Sansk. *prākrta*, natural, vulgar], *n.* A Hindu language or dialect based on the Sanskrit, as many of the northern and central Indian dialects.

praline (pra′ lēn) [F.], *n.* A confection of almond or other nut with a brown coating of sugar.

pram (1) (pram) [Dut.], *n.* A flat-bottomed barge or lighter used in Holland and the Baltic; a similar boat formerly used as a floating battery.

pram (prăm) (2) (*colloq.*) [PERAMBULATOR].

prance (prans) [etym. doubtful, perh. rel. to PRANK (2)], *v.i.* To spring or caper on the hind legs, as a horse in high mettle; to make a horse do this; to walk or strut in a pompous or swaggering style. *n.* The act of prancing. **prancer,** *n.*

prandial (prăn′ di ăl) [L. *prandium*, breakfast], *a.* (*facet.*) Relating to dinner.

prang (prăng) [onomat.], *v.t.* (*Aviat. slang*) To bomb heavily; to strike; to crash. *n.* A bombing raid; a crash landing.

prank (1) (prăngk) [M.E. *pranken*, cp. G. *prangen*, to make a show, Dut. *pronken*, G. *prunken*, to make a show of; also Eng. PRINK], *v.t.* To dress up in a showy fashion; to deck (out); to adorn (with). *v.i.* To make a show.

prank (2) (prăngk) [etym. unknown], *n.* A wild frolic; a trick, a playful act, a practical joke; a gambol, a capricious action. **prankful, prankish, pranky,** *a.* **prankishness,** *n.*

prase (prāz) [F., from L. *prasius*, Gr. *prasios*], *n.* (*Min.*) A dull leek-green translucent quartz. **prasinous, *prasine** (prāz′ in), *a.* Of a light-green colour.

praseodymium (prās ō dim′ i ŭm) [Gr. *prasinos*, leek-green], *n.* A rare metallic element occurring in certain rare-earth minerals.

prate (prāt) [M.E. *praten*, cp. Dut. *praten*, Dan. *prate*, Swed. *prata*], *v.i.* To chatter; to talk much and without purpose or reason; to babble, to cackle. *v.t.* To utter foolishly; to boast idly about. *n.* Idle or silly talk; unmeaning loquacity. **prater,** *n.* **prating,** *a.* and *n.* **pratingly,** *adv.*

pratique (prăt′ ik, prȧ tēk′) [F., PRACTICE], *n.* Licence to a ship to hold communication with a port after quarantine, or upon certification that the vessel has not come from an infected place.

prattle (prăt′ ėl) [freq. of PRATE], *v.i.* To talk in a childish or foolish manner. *v.t.* To utter or divulge thus. *n.* Childish or idle talk; (*fig.*) a babbling sound, as of running water. **prattler,** *n.*

Pravda (prav′ dȧ) [Rus., truth], *n.* The official organ of the Central Committee of the Communist Party in the U.S.S.R.

pravity (prăv′ i ti) [L. *prāvitas*, from *prāvus*, perverse, bad], *n.* Depravity; corruption.

prawn (prawn) [M.E. *prane*, *prayne*, etym. doubtful], *n.* A small crustacean, *Palæmon serratus*, like a large shrimp.

praxis (prăk′ sis) [Gr., rel. to *prassein*, to do], *n.* Use, practice, application as distinguished from theory; (*Gram.*) a collection of examples for practice. **praxinoscope** (prăk′ si nȯ skōp) [F. (-SCOPE)], *n.* An optical toy in which successive positions of moving figures are blended in a rotating cylinder, etc., so as to give reflections in a series of mirrors as of objects in motion.

pray (prā) [O.F. *preier* (F. *prier*), late L. *precāre*, L. *precārī*, from *prex precis*, prayer], *v.t.* To ask for with earnestness or submission; to beseech, to entreat, to supplicate; to petition for, to beg; to address devoutly and earnestly. *v.i.* To address God with adoration or earnest entreaty; to make supplication, to beseech or petition (for). **prayer** (1) (prā′ ėr), *n.* One who prays. **prayingly**, *adv.*

prayer (2) (prâr) [M.E. and O.F. *preiere*, med. L. *precāria*, as PRECARIOUS], *n.* The act of praying; a solemn petition addressed to God or any object of worship; the practice of praying, a formula for praying; a prescribed formula of divine worship; a liturgy; a religious service; an entreaty; a memorial or petition; that part of a petition which specifies the thing desired; (*Parl.*) a petition to the Queen to annul an Order in Council. **prayer-book**, *n.* A book containing prayers and forms of devotion, esp. the Anglican Book of Common Prayer. **prayer-meeting**, *n.* A meeting for divine worship in which prayer is offered by several persons. **prayer-wheel, praying-machine**, *n.* A device for automatic praying, employed by the Tibetans. **prayerful**, *a.* Given to prayer; devotional, devout. **prayerfully**, *adv.* **prayerfulness**, *n.* **prayerless**, *a.* **prayerlessly**, *adv.*

pre- [O.F. and med. L. *pre-*, L. PRÆ-, before], *pref.* ***pre-accusation** (pre ăk ū zā′ shŭn), *n.* A previous accusation.

preach (prēch) [O.F. *prechier*, L. *prædicāre* (PRÆ-, *dicāre*, to proclaim, rel. to *dīcere*, to say)], *v.i.* To deliver a sermon or public discourse on some religious subject; to give earnest religious or moral advice, esp. in an obtrusive or persistent way. *v.t.* To proclaim, to expound in a common or public discourse; to deliver (a sermon); to teach or advocate in this manner. *n.* (*colloq.*) A preaching, a sermon. **to preach down:** To denounce or disparage by preaching; to preach against. **preachable**, *a.* **preacher**, *n.* **preachership**, *n.* **preachify**, *v.i.* To hold forth in a sermon, esp. tediously; to sermonize. **preachification** (-kā′ shŭn), *n.* **preachment**, *n.* A discourse or sermon (*usu. in contempt*). **preachy**, *a.* Fond of preaching or sermonizing, disposed to preach. **preachiness**, *n.*

preacquaint (prē ȧ kwānt′), *v.t.* To acquaint beforehand. **preacquaintance**, *n.* **pre-Adamite** (prē ăd′ ȧ mīt), *n.* An inhabitant of this world before Adam; one who holds that there were persons in existence before Adam. *a.* Existing before Adam; pertaining to the pre-Adamites. **pre-Adamic** (-ȧ dăm′ ik), **pre-Adamitic** (-mit′ ik), *a.* **preadaptation** (prē ăd ăp tā′ shŭn), *n.* Previous adjustment to some end or purpose. **pre-admission** (prē ȧd mish′ ŭn), *n.* Previous admission. **preadmonish** (prē ȧd mon′ ish), *v.t.* **preadmonition** (-ăd mȯ nish′ ŭn), *n.* **preadvise** (prē ȧd vīz), *v.t.*

preamble (prē ăm′ bėl) [O.F. *preambule*, med. L. *præambulum*, from L. *præambulus*, going before (PRÆ-, *ambulāre*, to walk)], *n.* An introductory statement, esp. the introductory portion of a statute setting forth succinctly its reasons and intentions. *v.i.* To make a preamble. **preambulancy**, *a.* **preambulate**, *v.i.* To make a preamble. ***preambulation** (-lā′ shŭn), *n.* **preambulatory** (-ăm′ bū lā tȯr i), *a.*

preannounce (prē ȧ nouns′), *v.t.* To announce beforehand. **preannouncement**, *n.* **preappoint** (prē ȧ point′), *v.t.* **preappointment**, *n.* **preapprehension** (prē ăp rė hen′ shŭn), *n.* A preconceived opinion; a foreboding. **prearrange** (prē ȧ rānj′), *v.t.* **prearrangement**, *n.* **preassurance** (prē ȧ shoor′ ȧns), *n.* **preaudience** (prē aw′ dyėns), *n.* (*Law*) The right of being heard before another, precedence at the bar.

prebend (preb′ ėnd) [O.F. *prebende*, med. L. *præbenda*, payment, pension, orig. neut. pl. ger. of L. *præbēre*, to grant (PRÆ-, *habēre*, to have)], *n.* The stipend or maintenance granted to a canon of a cathedral or collegiate church out of its revenue; the land or tithe yielding this; a prebendary; a prebendaryship. **prebendal**, *a.* **prebendal stall, prebendary stall:** A prebendary's stall in a cathedral or his benefice. **prebendary**, *n.* The holder of a prebend. **prebendaryship**, *n.*

precarious (prė kâr′ i ŭs) [L. *precārius*, obtained by prayer, from *precārī*, to PRAY], *a.* Depending on the will or pleasure of another; held by a doubtful tenure; not well-established, doubtful, dependent on chance, uncertain, hazardous. **precariously**, *adv.* **precariousness**, *n.*

precatory (prek′ ȧ tȯr i) [late L. *precātōrius*, from *precātor -tōris* as prec.], *a.* Begging, suppliant; beseeching; (*Gram.*) expressing entreaty. **precative**, *a.*

precaution (prė kaw′ shŭn) [F. *précaution*, med. L. *præcautiōnem*, nom. *-tio*, from L. *præcavēre* (PRÆ-, *cavēre*, to beware)], *n.* Previous caution, prudent foresight; a measure taken beforehand to guard against or bring about something. *v.t.* To caution or warn beforehand. **precautionary, *-cautional**, *a.* **precautiously**, *adv.*

precede (prė sēd′) [F. *précéder*, L. *præcēdere* (PRÆ-, *cēdere*, to go)], *v.t.* To go before in time, order, rank, or importance; to walk in front of; to exist before; to cause to come before, to preface or prelude. *v.i.* To go or come before; to have precedence. **precedence, *-cy** (prė sē′ dėns, -si), *n.* The act or state of preceding; priority; superiority; the right to a higher position or a place in advance of others at public ceremonies, social functions, etc. **preceding**, *a.*

precedent (1) (pres′ e dėnt), *n.* Something done or said which may serve as an example to be followed in a similar case, esp. a legal decision, usage, etc.; a necessary antecedent. **precedented**, *a.*

precedent (2) (prė sē′ dėnt), *a.* Going before in time, order, rank, etc.; antecedent. **precedently**, *adv.*

precentor (prė sen′ tȯr) [late L. *præcentor* (PRÆ-, *cantor*, from *cantāre*, freq. of *canere*, to sing)], *n.* The leader of a choir in a cathedral; (in pre-Reformation cathedrals) a member of the chapter ranking next below the dean, (in those of new foundation) a minor canon or chaplain, (in Presbyterian churches) the leader of the psalmody. **precent** (prė sent′), *v.i.* To act as precentor. *v.t.* To lead the singing of (psalms, etc.). **precentorship**, *n.* **precentrix**, *n.*

precept (prē′ sept) [O.F. (F. *précepte*), L. *præceptum*, neut. p.p. of *præcipere* (PRÆ-, *capere*, to take)], *n.* A command, a mandate; an injunction respecting conduct; a maxim; a writ, a warrant; a sheriff's order to hold an election; an order for the levying or collection of a rate. **preceptive, *preceptial, preceptual**, *a.* **preceptor**, *n.* A teacher, an instructor; the head of a preceptory among the Knights Templars. ***preceptorial** (-tôr′ i ăl), *a.* **preceptorship**, *n.* **preceptory** (-sep′ tȯr i), *n.* A subordinate house or community of the Knights Templars; the estate, manor, etc., pertaining to this. ******a.* Preceptive. **preceptress**, *n.*

preces (prē′ sēz) [L., pl. of *prex precis*, prayer], *n.pl.* (*Eccles.*) The short petitions said alternately by the minister and the congregation.

precession (prė sesh′ ŭn) [late L. *præcessio*, from *præcēdere*, to PRECEDE], *n.* Precedence in time or order. **precession of the equinoxes:** (*Astron.*) A slow but continual shifting of the equinoctial points from east to west, occasioned by the earth's axis slowly revolving in a small circle about the pole of the ecliptic, causing an earlier occurrence of the equinoxes in successive sidereal years. **precessional**, *a.*

pre-Christian (prē kris′ tyȧn) [PRE-, CHRISTIAN], *a.* Of or pertaining to the times before Christ or before Christianity.

precinct (prē′ singkt) [med. L. *præcinctum*, orig. neut. p.p. of L. *præcingere* (PRÆ-, *cingere*, to gird)], *n.* The space enclosed by the walls or boundaries of a place, esp. a church; a boundary, a limit; a minor territorial division; (*pl.*) the environs or immediate surroundings (of).

precious (presh′ ŭs) [O.F. *precios* (F. *précieux*), L. *pretiōsus*, from *pretium*, PRICE], *a.* Of great price or value; very costly; highly esteemed, dear, beloved; affected, over-refined in manner, style, workmanship, etc.; (*colloq.*) considerable, thorough, out-and-out; (*iron.*) worthless, rascally. **preciosity** (presh i os′ i ti), *n.* Over-fastidiousness or affected delicacy in the use of language, in workmanship, etc. **precious metals:** Gold, silver, and (sometimes) platinum. **precious stone:** A gem. **preciously,** *adv.* **preciousness,** *n.*

precipice (pres′ i pis) [F. *précipice*, L. *præcipitium*, a falling headlong, precipice, from *præceps*, headlong (PRÆ-, *caput*, head)], *n.* A vertical or very steep cliff; *the edge of a cliff, hence a situation of extreme danger.

precipitate (prė sip′ i tāt) [L. *præcipitātus*, p.p. of *præcipitāre*, as prec.], *v.t.* To throw headlong; to urge on with eager haste or violence; to hasten; (*Chem.*) to cause (a substance) to be deposited at the bottom of a vessel, as from a solution; (*Phys.*) to cause (moisture) to condense and be deposited, as from vapour. *v.i.* To fall to the bottom of a vessel (of a substance in solution); to condense and be deposited in drops (of vapour). *a.* (-tȧt) Headlong; flowing or rushing with haste and violence; hasty, rash, inconsiderate; adopted without due deliberation. *n.* A solid substance deposited from a state of solution. ***red precipitate:** (*Chem.*) Red oxide of mercury. **white precipitate:** Ammoniated chloride of mercury. **precipitable,** *a.* Capable of being precipitated, as a substance in solution. **precipitability** (-bil′ i ti), *n.* **precipitant,** *a.* Falling or rushing headlong; headlong, precipitate. *n.* (*Chem.*) Any substance that, being added to a solution, causes precipitation. ***precipitantly, precipitately,** *adv.* **precipitance, -tancy, precipitateness,** *n.* **precipitation** (-tā′ shŭn), *n.* **precipitator** (-sip′ i tā tŏr), *n.*

precipitous (prė sip′ i tŭs) [M.F. *precipiteux*, as PRECIPICE], *a.* Like or of the nature of a precipice, very steep; *headlong, precipitate, hasty, rash. **precipitously,** *adv.* **precipitousness,** *n.*

précis (prā′ sē) [F., as foll.], *n.* An abstract, a summary; the act or practice of drawing up such abstracts.

precise (prė sīs′) [F. *précis, -ise*, L. *præcīsus*, p.p. of *præcīdere* (PRÆ-, *cædere*, to cut)], *a.* Definite, accurate, exact; strictly observant of rule, punctilious, over-nice, over-scrupulous; (*colloq.*) particular, identical. **precisely,** *adv.* In a precise manner; exactly, quite so. **preciseness,** *n.* **precisian** (-sizh′ ȧn), *n.* A punctilious person; one rigidly observant of rules, etc., a formalist, a stickler. *a.* Precise, punctilious; formal. **precisianism, precision** (prė sizh′ ŭn), *n.* **precisionist,** *n.* **precisionize,** *v.t.* **precisive** (prė sī′ siv), *a.*

preclude (prė klood′) [L. *præclūdere* (PRÆ-, *claudere*, to shut), *p.p. præclūsus*], *v.t.* To shut out, to exclude; to hinder, to prevent; to render inoperative; to neutralize. **preclusion** (-kloo′ zhŭn), *n.* **preclusive,** *a.* **preclusively,** *adv.*

precocious (prė kō′ shŭs) [L. *præcox -cōcis*, from *præcoquere* (PRÆ-, *coquere*, to COOK (1))], *a.* Developing or ripe before the normal time; prematurely developed intellectually; characteristic of such development; forward, pert. **precociously,** *adv.* **precociousness, precosity** (-kos′ i ti), *n.*

precogitation (prē koj i tā′ shŭn), *n.* Previous consideration, thought taken beforehand.

precognition (prē kog nish′ ŭn) [late L. *præcognitio*, from *præcognoscere* (PRÆ-, *cognoscere*, to COGNOSCE)], *n.* Previous knowledge; (*Sc. Law*) preliminary examination of witnesses with a view to determining whether there is ground for a prosecution. **precognosce** (prē kog nos′), *v.t.*

precompose (prē kŏm pōz′), *v.t.* To compose beforehand. **preconceive** (prē kŏn sēv′), *v.t.* To conceive or form an opinion of beforehand. **preconceit** (-kŏn sēt′), **preconception** (-sep′ shŭn), *n.* **preconcert** (prē kŏn sĕrt′), *v.t.* To contrive or agree on by previous arrangement. *n.* (prē kon′ sĕrt) An arrangement previously made. **preconcertedly,** *adv.* **preconcertedness,** *n.* **precondemn** (prē kŏn dem′), *v.t.* To condemn in advance. **precondemnation** (-nā′ shŭn), *n.* **precondition** (prē kŏn dish′ ŭn), *n.* A necessary preliminary condition. **preconform** (prē kŏn fôrm′), *v.i.* To conform beforehand. **preconformity,** *n.*

preconize (prē′ kŏ nīz) [med. L. *præcōnīzāre*, from *præco -cōnis*, herald], *v.t.* To proclaim publicly; to cite or summon publicly: (*R.-C. Ch.*, of the Pope) to confirm publicly (an appointment or one nominated). **preconization** (-zā′ shŭn), *n.*

pre-Conquest (prē kon′ kwest), *n.* Before the time of the Norman Conquest (1066).

preconscious (prē kon′ shŭs), *a.* Pertaining to a state antecedent to consciousness. **preconsider** (prē kŏn sid′ ėr), *v.t.* To consider previously. **preconsideration** (-ā′ shŭn), *n.* **precontract** (prē kon′ trăkt), *n.* A previous contract. *v.i.* and *t.* (prē kŏn trăkt′) To contract beforehand. **precordia** [PRÆCORDIA]. **precostal** (prė kos′ tȧl), *a.* (*Anat.*) In front of the ribs. **precourse** (prė kôrs′) [L. *præcursus*, p.p. of *præcurrere* (*currere*, to run)], *v.t.* To run before, to herald. **precritical** (prē krit′ i kȧl), *a.* Preceding the critical treatment of a subject, esp. preceding the critical philosophy of Kant.

precurrent (prē kŭr′ ėnt) [L. *præcurrens -ntens*, pres.p. of *præcurrere* (PRÆ-, *currere*, to run)], *a.* Occurring beforehand, precursory. ***precurrer,** *n.* ***precurse** (prė kĕrs′), *n.* A forerunning, a heralding. **precursive,** *a.* Precursory.

precursor (prē kĕr′ sŏr), *n.* A forerunner, a harbinger; one who or that which precedes the approach of anything, esp. John the Baptist; a predecessor in office, etc. **precursory,** *a.* Preceding and indicating as a forerunner or harbinger; preliminary, introductory.

predaceous (prė dā′ shŭs) [L. *præda-*], *a.* Living by prey, predatory; pertaining to animals living by prey. **predacean,** *n.* **predacity** (-dăs′ i ti), *n.* ***predal,** *a.* Practising plunder; predatory.

pre-Darwinian (prē dar win′ i ȧn), *a.* Preceding the doctrines of evolution, etc., propounded by Charles Darwin in 1859.

predate (prē dāt′), *v.t.* To ante-date.

predatory (pred′ ȧ tŏr i) [L. *prædātōrius*, from *prædātor*, plunderer, from *præda*, booty], *a.* Plundering, pillaging; addicted to pillage; living by preying on others (of animals). **predator** (pred′ ȧ tŏr), *n.* (*Zool.*) A predatory animal.

predecease (prē dė sēs′), *n.* The death of a person before some other. *v.t.* To die before (a particular person).

predecessor (prē′ dė ses ŏr) [F. *prédécesseur*, late L. *prædēcessor* (PRÆ-, *dēcessor*, from *dēcēdere*, to go away, see DECEASE)], *n.* One who precedes another in any position, office, etc.; a thing preceding another thing; a forefather, an ancestor.

***predeclare** (prē dė klâr′), *v.t.* To declare beforehand. **predefine** (prē dė fīn′), *v.t.* To define, limit, or settle beforehand. **predefinition** (-def i nish′ ŭn), *n.* **predelineation** (prē dė lin ė ā′ shŭn), *n.*

predella (prė del′ ȧ) [It., stool, dim. prob. from O.H.G. *pret*, board], *n.* The platform on which an altar stands or the highest of a series of altar-steps; a painting on the face of this; a painting on a step- or shelf-like appendage, usu. at the back of the altar, a gradine.

***predesign** (prē dė zīn′), *v.t.* To design beforehand. **predesignate** (prē dez′ ig nāt), *v.t.* To designate or indicate beforehand; (*Log.*) to designate by a sign or word denoting quantity, as *only, sole, some*; *a.* (-nȧt) (*Log.*) Having such a sign prefixed. **predesignation** (-nā′ shŭn), *n.*

predestinate (prē des′ ti nāt) [L. *prædestinātus*, p.p. of *prædestināre* (PRÆ-, *destināre*, to DESTINE)], **predestine**, *v.t.* To appoint beforehand by irreversible decree; to pre-ordain (to salvation, to do a certain deed, etc.); to predetermine. *a.* (-nȧt) Ordained or appointed beforehand. **predestinarian**, *a.* Pertaining to predestination. *n.* A believer in predestination. **predestination** (-nā′ shŭn), *n.* The act of predestining, esp. (*Theol.*) the act of God in foreordaining some to salvation and some to perdition. **predestinator** (-des′ ti nā tŏr), *n.* ***predestiny**, *n.*

predetermine (prē dė tĕr′ min) [late L. *prædetermināre*], *v.t.* To determine beforehand; to foreordain; to predestine. *v.i.* To determine beforehand. **predeterminable**, *a.* **predeterminate**, *a.* **predetermination** (-nā′ shŭn), *n.*

predial (prē′ di ăl) [F. *prédial*, med. L. *prædiālis*, from L. *prædium*, farm], *a.* Consisting of lands or farms; attached to lands or farms; arising from or produced by land.

predicable (pred′ i kȧ bėl) [F. *prédicable*, L. *prædicābilis*, from *prædicāre*, to PREDICATE], *a.* Capable of being predicated or affirmed of something. *n.* Anything that may be predicated of something; (*Log.*) one of Aristotle's classes of predicates—genus, definition, property, accident. **predicability** (-bil′ i ti), *n.*

predicament (prė dik′ ȧ mėnt) [late L. *prædicāmentum*, as prec.], *n.* That which is predicted, a category; a particular state, condition, or position; esp. a critical or unpleasant one. **predicamental** (-men′ tȧl), *a.*

predicant (pred′ i kȧnt) [L. *prædicans -ntem*, pres.p. of *prædicāre*, see foll.], *n.* A preaching friar, esp. a Dominican; a predikant. *a.* Engaged in preaching.

predicate (pred′ i kāt) [L. *prædicātus*, p.p. of *prædicāre* (PRÆ-, *dicāre*, to proclaim), see PREACH], *v.t.* To affirm, to assert as a property, etc. (of a thing); (*Log.*) to assert about the subject of a proposition; (*Am.*) to found, to base (an argument, etc., on). *v.i.* To make an affirmation. *n.* (-kȧt) (*Log.*) That which is predicated, that which is affirmed or denied of the subject; (*Gram.*) the entire statement made about the subject, including the copula as well as the logical predicate; an inherent quality. **predication** (pred i kā′ shŭn), *n.* **predicative** (-dik′ ȧ tiv), *a.* **predicatively**, *adv.*

predicatory (pred′ i kȧ tŏr i) [late L. *prædicātōrius*, from *prædicātor*, a proclaimer, a preacher, as prec.], *a.* Of or pertaining to a preacher or to preaching.

predict (prė dikt′) [L. *prædictus*, p.p. of *prædīcere* (PRÆ-, *dīcere*, to say)], *v.t.* To tell beforehand; to prophesy. **n.* A prediction. **a.* Predicted. **predictable**, *a.* **predictability** (-bil′ i ti), *n.* **prediction** (-dik′ shŭn), *n.* **predictive**, *a.* **predictively**, *adv.* **predictor**, *n.* One who predicts; (*Aviat.*) a range-finding and radar device for anti-aircraft use.

predigest (prē di-, -dī jest′), *v.t.* To digest beforehand; to digest partially before introducing into the stomach. **predigestion**, *n.*

predikant (pred′ i kȧnt) [Dut., as PREDICANT], *n.* A minister of the Dutch Reformed Church, esp. in S. Africa.

predilection (prē di lek′ shŭn) [F. *prédilection* (PRE-, L. *dīlectio*, from *dīligere*, see DILIGENT)], *n.* A prepossession in favour of something, a preference, a partiality.

predispose (prē dis pōz′) [F. *prédisposer*], *v.t.* To dispose or incline beforehand; to make susceptible or liable to. **predisponent**, *n.* and *a.* **predisposition** (-zish′ ŭn), *n.*

predominate (prē dom′ i nāt) [through F. *prédominer* or a med. L. *prædomināre*], *v.i.* To be superior in strength, influence, or authority; to prevail, to have the ascendancy (over); to have control (over); to preponderate. **v.t.* To dominate over. **predominance, -nancy**, *n.* **predominant**, *a.* Predominating (over); superior, overruling, controlling. **predominantly**, *adv.* **predominatingly**, *adv.* ***predomination** (-nā′ shŭn), *n.*

predoom (prē doom′), *v.t.* To doom beforehand; to foreordain. **predorsal** (prē dôr′ sȧl), *a.* (*Anat.*) Situated in front of the dorsal region.

pree (prē) [Sc., short for *preive*, var. of PROVE], *v.t.* To prove, to try, esp. by tasting.

pre-elect (prē ė lekt′), *v.t.* To elect beforehand. **a.* Chosen beforehand or in preference to others. **pre-election** (-lek′ shŭn), *n.* Previous election. *a.* Occurring or done before an election.

pre-eminent (prē em′ i nėnt) [F. *prééminent*, L. *præēminentem*, nom. *-ens*, pres.p. of *præēminēre* (PRÆ-, *ēminēre*, see EMINENT)], *a.* Eminent beyond others; superior to or surpassing all others. **pre-eminence**, *n.* **pre-eminently**, *adv.*

pre-employ (prē ėm ploi′), *v.t.* To employ previously. **pre-emption** (prē emp′ shŭn), *n.* The act or right of buying before others. **pre-empt**, *v.t.* To purchase thus; (*U.S.A.*) to secure the right of pre-emption to (public land). **pre-emptive**, *a.* **pre-emptor**, *n.*

preen (1) (prēn) [prob. var. of PRUNE, conf. with foll.], *v.t.* To trim (feathers) with the beak (of birds); to trim (oneself).

preen (2) (prēn) [A.-S. *prēon* (cp. L.G. *preen, preem*, Dut. *priem*, G. *pfriem*, Icel. *prjōnn*)], *n.* (*Sc.*) A pin, a brooch; (*fig.*) a trifle. *v.t.* To fasten, to pin.

pre-engage (prē ėn gāj′), *v.t.* To engage by previous contract or pledge; to preoccupy; to engage in conflict beforehand. **pre-engagement**, *n.* **pre-establish** (prē ės tăb′ lish), *v.t.* To establish beforehand. **pre-established harmony** [HARMONY]. ***pre-establishment**, *n.* **pre-estimate** (prē es′ ti māt), *v.t.* To estimate beforehand. *n.* An estimate made beforehand. **pre-examine** (prē ėg zăm′ in), *v.t.* **pre-examination** (-nā′ shŭn), *n.* **pre-exilian** (prē ėk sil′ i ȧn), *a.* Before the period of exile, esp. of the Jewish exile in Babylon. **pre-exilic**, *a.* **pre-exist** (prē ėg zist′), *v.i.* To exist previously, esp. of the soul before its union with the body. **pre-existence**, *n.* **pre-existent**, *a.* **prefabricated**, *a.* (*Build.* and *Eng.*) Of houses, bridges, machinery, etc., the component parts of which are made and finished separately all ready for assembling. **pre-fab** (prē′ făb), *n.* A house thus built.

preface (pref′ ȧs) [O.F., med. L. *præfātia, præfātio*, from *præfārī* (PRÆ-, *fārī*, to speak)], *n.* Something spoken or written as introductory to a discourse or book; an introduction; an exordium, a preamble, a prelude; (*Eccles.*) the thanksgiving, etc., forming the prelude to the consecration of the Eucharist. *v.t.* To furnish with a preface; to introduce (with preliminary remarks, etc.). *v.i.* To make introductory remarks. **prefacer**, *n.* **prefatorial** (-tôr′ i ȧl), **prefatory** (pref′ ȧ tŏr i), *a.* **prefatorily**, *adv.*

prefect (prē′ fekt) [O.F. (F. *préfet*), L. *præfectus*, an overseer, orig. p.p. of *præficere* (PRÆ-, *facere*, to make)], *n.* (*Rom. Ant.*) A commander, a governor, a chief magistrate; in France, the civil governor of a department; in some schools, a monitor or prepositor. **prefectoral** (-fek′ tŏr ȧl), **prefectorial** (-tôr′ i ȧl), *a.* **prefecture** (prē′ fek tūr), *n.* The office, jurisdiction, official residence, or the term of office of a prefect. ***prefectship**, *n.* **prefectural** (-fek′ tū rȧl), *a.*

prefer (prė fĕr′) [F. *préférer*, L. *præferre* (PRÆ-, *ferre*, to bear)], *v.t.* (*past & p.p.* **preferred**) To set before, to hold in higher estimation, to like better; to bring forward, to submit; to promote; to recommend, to favour. **preferred debt:** One having priority of payment. **preferred shares, stock**, etc.: Preference shares, etc. **preferrer**, *n.*

preferable (pref' ėr ȧbl), *a.* **preferability** (-bil' i ti), ***preferableness,** *n.* **preferably,** *adv.* **preference** (pref' ėr ėns), *n.* The act of preferring one thing to another; liking for one thing more than another, predilection; right or liberty of choice; that which is preferred; favour displayed towards a person or country before others, esp. in commercial relations; (*Law*) priority of right to payment, esp. of debts. **preference-bonds,- shares,** or **stock:** Those entitled to a dividend before ordinary shares.

preferential (pref ėr en' shȧl), *a.* Giving, receiving, or constituting preference; favouring certain countries, as in the commercial relations between Great Britain and the rest of the Commonwealth. **preferentialism,** *n.* **preferentialist,** *n.* **preferentially,** *adv.*

preferment (prė fěr' mėnt), *n.* Advancement, promotion; a superior office or dignity, esp. in the Church.

prefigure (prė fig' ůr) [late L. *præfigurāre*], *v.t.* To represent by antecedent figures, types, or similitudes; to picture to oneself beforehand. ***prefigurate,** *v.t.* **prefiguration** (-ā' shůn), ***prefigurement,** *n.* **prefigurative** (-fig' ůr ȧ tiv), *a.*

prefix (prė fiks') [O.F. *prefixer*], *v.t.* To put, place, or set in front of; to attach at the beginning (as an introduction, prefix, etc.); *to determine beforehand, to prearrange. *n.* (prē' fiks) A letter, syllable, or word put at the beginning of a word to modify the meaning; a title prefixed to a name. ***prefixion, prefixture,** *n.*

prefloration (prē flȯ rā' shůn) [F. *préfloraison* (PRE-, PRÆ-, L. *flos flōris*, flower)], *n.* (*Bot.*) Æstivation.

preform (prē fôrm'), *v.t.* To form beforehand. **preformation** (-mā' shůn), *n.* The act of preforming. **theory of preformation:** (*Biol.*) The theory (prevalent in the 18th cent.) that the organism exists in all its parts in the germ and is merely developed. **preformative,** *a.* Forming beforehand. *n.* A formative letter or other element prefixed to a word. **prefrontal** (prē fron' tȧl), *a.* (*Anat.*) Situated in front of the frontal bone or the frontal region of the skull. *n.* A prefrontal bone, esp. in reptiles and fishes. ***prefulgency** (prė fŭl' jėn si), *n.* Superior brightness. **pre-glacial** (prē glā' shi al), *a.* (*Geol.*) Belonging to the period before the glacial epoch.

pregnable (preg' nȧbl) [late M.E. and F. *prenable*, as IMPREGNABLE], *a.* Capable of being taken by force.

pregnant (1) (preg' nȧnt) [L. *prægnans -ntis* (PRÆ-*gna-* root of *gnāscī*, to be born)], *a.* Being with young, gravid; (*fig.*) fruitful, big (with consequences, etc.); full of meaning or suggestion, significant; (*Gram., etc.*) implying more than is expressed. **pregnancy,** ***pregnance,** *n.* **pregnantly,** *adv.*

***pregnant** (2) (preg' nȧnt) [O.F. *preignant*, pres.p. of *preindre*, L. *premere*, to PRESS], *a.* Pressing, urgent, cogent.

prehallux (prė hăl' ůks), *n.* (*Comp. Anat.*) A rudimentary digit or toe found in certain mammals, reptiles, etc.

prehensile (prė hen' sil, -sīl) [F. *préhensile*, from L. *prehens-*, p.p. stem of *prehendere* (PRE-, *hendere*, cogn. with Gr. *chandanein*, to seize)], *a.* Seizing, grasping; adapted to seizing or grasping, as the tails of monkeys. ***prehensible,** *a.* **prehensility** (-sil' i ti), *n.* **prehension** (-hen' shůn), *n.* The act of taking hold of or seizing; apprehension. **prehensive,** ***-sory,** *a.* **prehensor,** *n.*

prehistoric (prē his tor' ik), *a.* Of or pertaining to the time prior to that known to history. **prehistorically,** *adv.* **prehistory** (-his' tȯr i), *n.*

prejudge (prē jŭj') [F. *préjuger*, L. *præjūdicāre*], *v.t.* To judge before a case has been fully heard, to condemn in advance; to form a premature opinion about. **prejudgment, prejudication** (-joo di kā' shůn), *n.* ***prejudicant** (prē joo' di kȧnt), *a.* Prejudging. ***prejudicate** (-kāt), *v.t.* To prejudge; to prejudice. *a.* (-kȧt) Judged beforehand; preconceived; prejudiced.

prejudice (prej' ū dis) [O.F., from L. *præjūdicium* (PRÆ-, *jūdicium*, from *jūdex*, JUDGE)], *n.* Opinion, bias, or judgment formed without due consideration of facts or arguments; mischief, damage, or detriment arising from unfair judgment or action. *v.t.* To prepossess with prejudice, to bias; to affect injuriously, esp. to impair the validity of a right, etc. **without prejudice:** (*Law*) Without impairing any pre-existing right. **prejudiced,** *a.* Prepossessed, biased. **prejudicial** (-dish' ȧl), *a.* Causing prejudice or injury; mischievous, detrimental; *influenced by prejudice, biased. **prejudicially,** *adv.* ***prejudicialness,** *n.*

preknowledge (prē nol' ėj), *n.* Previous knowledge.

prelate (prel' ȧt) [O.F. *prelat*, L. *prælātus* (PRÆ-, *lātus*, p.p. of *ferre*, to bear)], *n.* An ecclesiastical dignitary of the highest order, as an archbishop, bishop, etc., formerly including abbot and prior. **prelacy,** *n.* The office, dignity, or see of a prelate; (*collect.*) prelates; episcopacy (in a hostile sense). **prelateship,** *n.* **prelatess,** *n.* An abbess or prioress; (*facet.*) the wife of a prelate. **prelatic, -al** (prė lăt' ik, -ȧl), *a.* **prelatically,** *adv.* ***prelatish** (prel' ȧ tish), *a.* ***prelatism,** *n.* Prelacy, episcopacy; adherence to or partisanship of this. **prelatist,** *n.* **prelatize,** *v.i.* To support or encourage prelacy. *v.t.* To bring under the influence of prelacy. ***prelature, *-try, *-ty,** *n.* Prelacy.

prelect (prė lekt') [L. *prælectus*, p.p. of *prælegere* (PRÆ-, *legere*, to choose, to read)], *v.i.* To read a lecture or discourse in public. **prelection** (-lek' shůn), *n.* **prelector,** *n.*

prelibation (prē lī bā' shůn) [late L. *prælībātio* (PRÆ-, *lībātio*, from *lībāre*, to taste)], *n.* A foretaste; a libation previous to tasting.

preliminary (prė lim' i nȧ ri) [PRE-, *līmen -minis*, threshold, -ARY], *a.* Introductory; previous to the main business or discourse. *n.* Something introductory; (*pl.*) introductory or preparatory arrangements, etc. **preliminarily,** *adv.* **prelims** (prē' limz), *n.pl.* (*Print.*) Preliminary matter of a book.

prelimit (prē lim' it), *v.t.* To limit beforehand. **prelingual** (prē ling' gwȧl), *a.* Preceding the acquisition or development of language.

prelude (prel' ūd) [F. *prélude*, late L. *prælūdium* (PRÆ-, *lūdere*, to play)], *n.* Something done, happening, etc., introductory or preparatory to that which follows; a harbinger, a precursor; (*Mus.*) a short introductory strain preceding the principal movement, a piece played as introduction to a suite. *v.t.* To perform or serve as a prelude to; to introduce with a prelude; to usher in, to foreshadow. *v.i.* To serve as a prelude (to); to begin with a prelude; (*Mus.*) to play a prelude. ***preluder,** *n.* prelusive (-lū' siv), ***preludial** (-lū' di ȧl), ***-dious,** *a.* **preludize** (prel' ū dīz), *v.i.* **prelusively,** *adv.* **prelusory,** *a.*

premature (prem' ȧ tūr, prē' mȧ tūr) [L. *præmātūrus* (PRÆ-, *mātūrus*, ripe)], *a.* Ripe or mature too soon; happening, arriving, existing, or performed before the proper time. *n.* (*Mil.*) The premature explosion of a shell. **prematurely,** *adv.* **prematureness, prematurity** (-tūr' i ti), *n.*

premaxillary (prē măk' si lȧ ri), *a.* (*Anat.*) Situated in front of the maxilla or upper jaw. *n.* The premaxillary bone.

premeditate (prė med' i tāt) [L. *præmeditātus*, p.p. of *præmeditārī* (PRÆ-, *meditārī*)], *v.t.* To meditate on beforehand; to plan and contrive beforehand. *v.i.* To deliberate previously. **a.* Meditated before-hand; deliberate. **premeditatedly,** *adv.* **premeditation** (-tā' shůn), *n.*

premier (prē' mi ėr, prem' yėr) [F., from L. *prīmārius*, PRIMARY], *a.* (*now vulg.*) First, chief, principal. *n.* The prime minister of Great Britain or of a Commonwealth government; the chief minister of a representative government. **premiership,** *n.*

première (prė myâr′) [F., fem. of *premier*, see prec.], *n.* A first performance of a play or film.

premillennial (prē mi len′ i ȧl), *a.* Previous to the millennium. **premillennarian** (-nâr′ iȧn), *n.* One believing that the Second Advent will precede the millennium. **premillennarianism, premillennialism,** *n.*

premise (prem′ is) [F. *prémisse*, L. *præmissa* (*propositio* or *sententia*), fem. p.p. of *præmittere* (PRÆ-, *mittere*, to send)], *n.* A proposition laid down, assumed, or proved from which another is inferred; (*Log.*) one of the two propositions of a syllogism from which the conclusion is drawn [see MAJOR, MINOR]; (*Law, pl.*) the subject matter of a deed or conveyance previously set forth, esp. the aforesaid houses, lands, etc. *v.t.* (prė mīz′) To put forward as preparatory to what is to follow; to lay down as an antecedent proposition or condition. *v.i.* To lay down antecedent propositions.

premises (prem′ i siz), *n.pl.* Land, buildings, appurtenances, etc.

premiss [PREMISE].

premium (prē′ mi ŭm) [L. *præmium* (PRÆ-, *emere*, to buy, to take)], *n.* A reward, a recompense, a prize; a sum paid in addition to interest, wages, etc., a bonus; a fee for instruction in a craft, profession, etc.; a payment (usu. periodical) made for insurance; the rate at which shares, money, etc., are selling above their nominal value. **at a premium:** Above their nominal value, above par; (*fig.*) in great esteem or demand. **Premium Bonds:** British government bonds bearing no interest but subject to a monthly draw for money prizes.

premolar (prē mō′ lȧr), *n.* One of the teeth situated in front of the molars. *a.* In front of the molars.

premonition (prē mȯ nish′ ŭn) [F., from late L. *præmonitio*, from *præmonēre* (PRÆ-, *monēre*, to warn)], *n.* Previous warning or notice. ***premonish** (prė mon′ ish), *v.t.* **premonitor,** *n.* **premonitory,** *a.*

Premonstratensian (prė mon strȧ ten′ shȧn, -si′ ȧn) [med. L. *Præmonstrātensis*, from *Præmonstrātus*, Prémontré], *n.* A member of an order of regular canons, founded by St. Norbert, at Prémontré, near Laon, France, in 1119, or of the corresponding order of nuns. *a.* Belonging to the Premonstratensians. **Premonstrant** (prė mon′ strȧnt), *n.*

premorse (prė mȯrs′) [L. *præmorsus*, p.p. of *præmordere* (PRÆ-, *mordere*, to bite)], *a.* (*Ent.*) Abruptly truncate as if bitten off.

premotion (prē mō′ shŭn), *n.* Previous motion or impulse to action. **premunire** [PRÆMUNIRE]. ***premunition** (prē mū nish′ ŭn) [late L. *præmūnītio*, from *præmūnīre* (*mūnīre*, to defend)], *n.* The act of guarding beforehand, as against objections.

prenatal (prē nā′ tȧl) [NATAL (1)], *a.* Anterior to birth. **prenatally,** *adv.*

prenomen (prē nō′ men) [PRÆ-, L. *nomen*, name], *n.* (*Rom. Ant.*) A personal name, first name, corresponding to the modern Christian name.

***prenominate** (prē nom′ i nāt) [late L. *prænōminātus*, p.p. of *prænōmināre*], *v.t.* To name or mention beforehand. *a.* (-nȧt) Named beforehand.

***prenotion** (prē nō′ shŭn), *n.* A previous notion or perception; foreknowledge.

prenti (pren′ ti) [Austral. abor.], *n.* The lizard of Central Australia.

***prentice,** etc. [APPRENTICE].

preoccupy (prē ok′ ū pī) [L. *præoccupāre* (PRÆ-, *occupāre*, to OCCUPY)], *v.t.* To take possession of beforehand or before another; to prepossess; to pre-engage, to engross (the mind, etc.). **preoccupancy,** *n.* The act or right of taking possession before others. **preoccupation** (-pā′ shŭn), *n.* Prepossession, prejudice; prior occupation; the state of being preoccupied or engrossed (with); that which preoccupies, as a business affair, etc.; ***preoccupancy. preoccupiedly,** *adv.*

preoption (prē op′ shŭn), *n.* The right of first choice. **pre-oral** (prē ōr′ ȧl) [ORAL], *a.* (*Anat.*) Situated in front of the mouth. **pre-ordain** (prē ōr dān′), *v.t.* To ordain beforehand. **pre-ordainment, pre-ordination** (-nā′ shŭn), *n.* ***preordinance** (-ōr′ di nȧns), *n.* Previous decree or ordinance. ***pre-ordinate,** *a.*

prep (prep) [short for PREPARATION], *n.* (*School slang*) Preparation or private study.

prepaid (prē pād′), *a.* Paid in advance (as postage, etc.).

preparation (prep ȧ rā′ shŭn), *n.* The act of preparing; the state of being prepared; that which is prepared (*usu. in pl.*); anything prepared by a special process, as food, a medicine, a part of a body for anatomical study, etc.; the preparing of lessons or school-work; (*Mus.*) the introduction of a note to be continued in a subsequent discord; *a military or naval force; ceremonious introduction; *accomplishment.

prepare (prė pâr′) [F. *préparer*, L. *præparare* (PRÆ-, *parāre*, to make ready)], *v.t.* To make ready; to bring into a suitable condition, to fit for a certain purpose; to make ready or fit (to do, to receive, etc.); to get (work, a speech, a part, etc.) ready by practice, study, etc.; (*Mus.*) to lead up to (a discord) by sounding the dominant note in a consonance. *v.i.* To get everything ready; to take the measures necessary (for); to make oneself ready. **n.* Preparation. **preparative** (-păr′ ȧ tiv), *a.* Preparatory. *n.* That which tends or serves to prepare; an act of preparation; (*Mil. and Nav.*) a signal to make ready. **preparatively,** *adv.* **preparatory,** *a.* Tending or serving to prepare; introductory (to). **preparatory school:** One preparing pupils for more advanced schools. **preparatorily,** *adv.* **to be prepared:** To be ready; to be willing (to). **preparedly** (-pâr′ ėd li), *adv.* **preparedness,** *n.* **preparer,** *n.*

prepay (prē pā′), *v.t.* To pay beforehand; to pay in advance, esp. by affixing a postage stamp to (a telegram, etc.). **prepayable,** *a.* **prepayment,** *n.*

prepense (prė pens′) [formerly *prepensed*, p.p. of *prepense*, *purpense*, O.F. *purpenser* (*pur-*, *pour-*, L. *prō*, forth, O.F. *penser*, to think)], *a.* Premeditated, deliberate. *v.t.* To premeditate. **malice prepense:** Intentional malice. ***prepensely,** *adv.* ***prepensive,** *a.*

preperception (prē pėr sep′ shŭn), *n.* Previous perception; (*Psychol.*) an impress forming the material of a percept.

***prepollent** (prė pol′ ėnt) [L. *præpollens -ntem*, pres.p. of *præpollēre* (PRÆ, *pollēre*, to be strong)], *a.* Having superior power or influence; predominating. ***prepollence, *-pollency,** *n.*

preponderate (prė pon′ dėr āt) [L. *præponderātus*, p.p. of *præponderāre* (PRÆ-, *ponderāre*, to PONDER)], *v.i.* To be heavier; to be superior or to outweigh in number, power, influence, etc.; to sink (as the scale of a balance). **v.t.* To overweigh, to overpower by superior force or influence. **preponderance, *-ancy,** *n.* **preponderant,** *a.* **preponderantly, preponderatingly,** *adv.* ***preponderation** (-ā′ shŭn), *n.*

preposition (prep ŏ zish′ ŭn) [L. *præpositio*, from *præpōnere* (PRÆ-, *pōnere*, to put, p.p. *positus*)], *n.* A word used to express the relations of a word to another word, which is usually a noun or pronoun. **prepositional,** *a.* **prepositionally,** *adv.*

prepositive (prė poz′ i tiv) [late L. *præpositīvus*, as prec.], *a.* Prefixed, intended to be placed before (a word). *n.* A prepositive word or particle.

prepositor (prė poz′ i tȯr) [L. *præpositor*, as prec.], *n.* A scholar appointed to the charge of others; a prefect, a monitor.

prepossess (prē pȯ zes′), *v.t.* To occupy beforehand; to imbue (with an idea, feeling, etc.); to bias (esp. favourably); to preoccupy (of an idea, etc.). **prepossessing,** *a.* Biasing; tending to win favour, attractive. **prepossessingly,** *adv.* **prepossession,** *n.* **prepostor** [PREPOSITOR].

preposterous (prė pos′ tėr ůs) [L. *præposterus* (*præ*, before, *posterus*, coming after)], *a.* Contrary to nature, reason, or common sense; obviously wrong, foolish, absurd. **preposterously,** *adv.* **preposterousness,** *n.*

prepotent (prė pō′ tėnt) [L. *præpotens -ntem*, pres.p. of *præposse* (PRE-, *posse*, to be able)], *a.* Very powerful; possessing superior force or influence; overbearing; (*Biol.*) possessing superior fertilizing influence. **prepotence, -cy,** *n.* **prepotently,** *adv.* **prepotential** (prē pȯ ten′ shȧl), *a.*

pre-prandial (prē prăn′ di ȧl), *a.* Done, happening, etc., before dinner.

pre-preference (prē pref′ ėr ėns), *a.* (*Fin.*) Ranking before preference shares, etc.

prepuce (prē′ pūs) [L. *præpūtium*], *n.* (*Anat.*) The foreskin, the loose covering of the *glans penis.* **preputial** (-pū′ shi ȧl), *a.*

Pre-Raphaelite (prē răf′ ā ė līt) [PRE-, *Raphael*, -ITE], *n.* An artist who aims at reviving the spirit and technique that characterized painting before the time of Raphael. *a.* Having the characteristics of Pre-Raphaelitism. **Pre-Raphaelite Brotherhood:** A small group of painters formed in London in 1848, including Holman Hunt, Millais, and D. G. Rossetti, to cultivate the spirit and methods of the early Italian painters. **Pre-Raphaelitism,** *n.*

preremote (prē rė mōt′), *a.* Occurring, done, etc., still more remotely in the past. **prerequisite** (prē rek′ wi zit), *a.* Required beforehand. *n.* Something antecedently necessary (for).

prerogative (prė rog′ ȧ tiv) [F. *prérogative*, L. *prærogatīva*, a previous choice, privilege, fem. of *prærogatīvus* (PRE-, *rogātīvus*, rel. to *rogātus*, p.p. of *rogāre*, to ask)], *n.* An exclusive right to privilege vested in a particular person or body of persons, esp. a sovereign, in virtue of his position or relationship; any peculiar right, option, privilege, natural advantage, etc.; *precedence. *a.* Of, pertaining to, or having a prerogative; (*Rom. Hist.*) having the right of voting first; *having precedence. **prerogatived,** *a.*

presage (pres′ ȧj) [F. *présage*, L. *præsāgium* (PRE-, *sāgīre*, to perceive quickly)], *n.* Something that foretells a future event, an omen, a prognostic; foreboding, presentiment. *v.t.* (prė sāj′) To foreshadow, to betoken; to indicate by natural signs, etc.; to forebode, to foretell. **v.i.* To prophesy. **presageful,** *a.* ***presagement,** *n.* ***presager,** *n.*

presbyopia (pres-, prez bi ō′ pi ȧ) [Gr. *presbus*, old man, *ōpia*, from *ōps ōpos*, eye], *n.* (*Path.*) A form of long-sightedness with indistinct vision of near objects, caused by alteration in the refractive power of the eyes with age. **presbyope, *presbyte,** *n.* One affected with this. **presbyopic** (-op′ ik), *a.*

presbyter (pres′-, prez′ bi tėr) [late L., from Gr. *presbuteros*, elder, comp. of *presbus*, see prec.], *n.* (*Eccles. Hist.*) An elder who had authority in the early Church; (*Episcopal Ch.*) a minister of the second order, a priest; (*Presbyterian Ch.*) a minister of a presbytery, an elder. **presbyteral** (-bit′ ėr ȧl), **presbyterial** (-tēr′ i ȧl), *a.* **presbyterate** (-bit′ ėr ȧt), **presbytership,** *n.*

Presbyterian (prez bi tēr′ i ȧn), *n.* Any adherent of Presbyterianism; a member of a Presbyterian Church. *a.* Pertaining to Church government by presbyters; governed by presbyters. **Presbyterian Church:** A Church governed by elders, including ministers, all equal in rank. **United Presbyterian Church:** The Church formed by the union of the United Secession and Relief Churches in 1847, united in 1900 with the Free Church of Scotland. **Presbyterianism,** *n.*

presbytery (prez′ bi tė ri), *n.* A body of elders in the early Church; a court consisting of the pastors and ruling elders of the Presbyterian churches of a given district, ranking above the kirk-session and below the synod; the district represented by a presbytery; (*Arch.*) the eastern portion of a chancel beyond the choir in a cathedral or other large church, the sanctuary; (*R.-C. Ch.*) a priest's residence.

prescient (presh′ i ėnt, prē′ shi ėnt) [F., from L. *præscientem*, nom. *-ens*, pres.p. of *præscīre* (PRÆ-, *scīre*, to know)], *a.* Foreknowing, far-seeing. **prescience,** *n.* **prescientific** (prē sī ėn tif′ ik), *a.* Pertaining to the period before the rise of science or of scientific method; *pertaining to prescience. **presciently,** *adv.*

prescind (prė sind′) [L. *præscindere* (PRÆ-, *scindere*, to cut)], *v.t.* To cut off; to abstract, to consider independently. *v.i.* To separate one's consideration (from).

prescribe (prė skrīb′) [L. *præscrībere* (PRÆ-, *scrībere*, to write), p.p. *præscriptus*], *v.t.* To lay down with authority; to appoint (a rule of conduct, etc.); (*Med.*) to direct to be used as a remedy. *v.i.* To write directions for medical treatment; (*Law*) to assert a prescriptive title (to or for). **prescriber,** *n.* **prescript** (prē′ skript), *n.* A direction, a command, a law; *(*Med.*) a prescription. *a.* Prescribed, directed. ***prescriptible,** *a.*

prescription (pre skrip′ shůn), *n.* The act of prescribing; that which is prescribed, esp. (*Med.*) a written direction for the preparation of remedies, and the manner of using them; (*Law*) long-continued or immemorial use or possession without interruption, as giving right or title; right or title founded on this; (*fig.*) ancient or long-continued custom, esp. when regarded as authoritative; a claim based on long use.

prescriptive (pre skrip′ tiv), *a.* Acquired or authorized by long use; based on long use or prescription; giving precise directions. **prescriptively,** *adv.*

preselective (prē se lek′ tiv), *a.* (*Motor.*) Of gears that can be set in advance.

presence (prez′ ėns) [O.F., from L. *præsentia*, as PRESENT], *n.* The quality or state of being present; situation face to face with a person or persons, the place where a person is; approach to or company with a person of high rank; personal appearance, mien, deportment; an influence as of a being invisibly present; *a presence-chamber. **presence of mind:** A calm, collected state of mind, esp. in danger or emergency. **real presence:** The actual existence of the body and blood of Christ in the Eucharist. **presence-chamber, -room,** *n.* The room in which a great personage receives company.

presensation (prē sen sā′ shůn), *n.* Sensation, feeling, or consciousness of something before it exists. ***presension,** *n.*

present (1) (prez′ ėnt) [O.F., from L. *præsentem*, nom. *-ens*, pres.p. of *præesse* (PRÆ-, *esse*, to be)], *a.* Being in a place referred to; being in view or at hand; being under discussion, consideration, etc.; now existing, occurring, going on, etc.; (*Law*) instant, immediate; (*Gram.*) expressing what is actually going on; ready at hand, assisting in emergency, *attentive, propitious. *n.* The present time; (*Gram.*) the present tense; (*pl.*) these writings, a term used in documents to express the document itself. **by these presents:** (*Law*) By this document. **present tense:** The form of the verb expressing being or action at the present time. **at present:** At the present time, now. **for the present:** For the time being; just now; so far as the time being is concerned.

present (2) (prė zent′) [O.F. *presenter*, L. *præsentāre*, as prec.], *v.t.* To introduce to the acquaintance or presence of, esp. to introduce formally; to introduce to a sovereign at Court; to submit (oneself) as a candidate, applicant, etc.; to offer (a clergyman) to a bishop for institution (to a benefice); to exhibit, to show, to offer to the sight; to hold in position or point (a gun, etc.); to offer or suggest (itself) to the attention; to offer for consideration, to submit; to exhibit (an actor, a play, etc.) on the stage; to offer, to give, to bestow, esp. in a ceremonious way; to invest or endow (with a gift); to tender, to deliver. *n.* (prez′ ėnt) That which is presented, a gift; (*Mil.*) (prė zent′) position for or act of aiming a fire-arm. **to present arms:** To hold a rifle, etc., in a perpendicular position in front of the body to salute a superior officer; this action or position. **presentable,** *a.* Fit to be presented; of suitable appearance for company, etc.; fit to be shown or exhibited; suitable for offering as a gift; suitable for presentation to a living. **presentably,** *adv.* **presentability,** *n.*

presentation (pre zėn tā′ shŭn), *n.* The act of presenting; a formal offering or proffering; a present, a gift; an exhibition, a theatrical representation; an introduction, esp. a formal introduction to a superior personage; a formal introduction to the sovereign at Court; (*Law*) the act or right of presenting to a benefice; (*Obstetrics*) the particular position of the fœtus at birth; (*Psych.*) the process by which an object becomes present to consciousness, or the modification of consciousness involved in the perception of an object. **presentation copy:** A book presented gratis by an author or publisher. **presentational,** *a.* **presentationism,** *n.* The doctrine that the mind has immediate cognition of objects of perception, or of elemental categories such as space, time, etc. **presentationalist, -tionist,** *n.* **presentative** (prė zen′ tȧ tiv), *a.* Pertaining to or of the nature of mental presentation; subserving mental presentation; (of a benefice) admitting of the presentation of an incumbent.

presentee (prez ėn tē′), *n.* One presented to a benefice; one recommended for office; one presented at Court; one receiving a present. **presenter** (prė sen′ tėr), *n.*

presentient (prė zen′ shi ėnt) [L. *præsentiens -ntem,* pres.p. of *præsentīre* (PRÆ-, *sentīre,* to feel)], *a.* Feeling or perceiving beforehand.

presentiment (prė zen′ ti mėnt), *n.* Apprehension or anticipation, more or less vague, of an impending event, esp. of evil, a foreboding.

presentive (prė zen′ tiv), *a.* Presenting an object or conception directly to the mind, opp. to symbolic; presentative. **presentiveness,** *n.*

presently (prez′ ėnt li), *adv.* Soon, shortly; *at once, immediately; (*Am.*) at the present time.

presentment (prė zent′ mėnt) [O.F. *presentement*], *n.* The act of presenting; a theatrical representation, a portrait, a likeness, a semblance; a statement, an account, a description; the act or mode of presentation to the mind; (*Law*) a report by a grand jury respecting an offence, from their own knowledge; formal information by parish authorities respecting a charge to a bishop or archdeacon at his visitation; a formal accusation or indictment.

preserve (prė zĕrv′) [F. *préserver,* late L. *præservāre* (PRÆ-, *servāre,* to keep)], *v.t.* To keep safe, to guard, to protect; to save, to rescue; to maintain in a good or the same condition; to retain, to keep intact; to keep from decay or decomposition by chemical treatment, boiling, pickling, etc.; to keep (a stream, covert, game, etc.) for private use by preventing poaching, etc. *n.* Fruit prepared with sugar or preservative substances; (*Am.*) jam; a place where game is preserved; water where fish are preserved; (*pl.*) goggles worn as a protection against dust, sunlight, etc. **preservable,** *a.* **preservation** (-vā′ shŭn), *n.* **preservative** (prė zĕr′ vȧ tiv), ***-atory,** *a.* Having the power of preserving from injury, decay, or corruption; tending to preserve. *n.* That which preserves, esp. a chemical substance used to prevent decomposition in foodstuffs. **preservatize,** *v.t.* **preserver,** *n.*

preses (prē′ sēz) [L. *præses,* cogn. with foll.], *n.* (*Sc.*) A chairman, a president.

preside (prė zīd′) [F. *présider,* L. *præsidēre* (PRÆ-, *sedēre,* to sit)], *v.i.* To be set in authority over others; to sit at the head of a table; to act as director, controller, chairman, or president; to lead, to superintend; to officiate (at the organ, piano, etc.).

presidency (prez′ i dėn si), *n.* The office, jurisdiction, or term of office of a president; the territory administered by a president, esp. one of the three former great divisions of the East India Company's territory, Bombay, Bengal, Madras.

president (prez′ i dėnt), *n.* One (usu. elected) presiding over a temporary or permanent body of persons; the chief magistrate or elective head of the government in a modern republic; one presiding over the meetings of a society; the chief officer of certain colleges and Universities, esp. in the U.S.; (*Am.*) the permanent chairman and chief executive officer of a railway, banking, or other corporation, board of trustees, Government department, etc. **presidentess,** *n.* **presidential** (-den′ shȧl), *a.* **presidentially,** *adv.* **presidentship,** *n.* **presider** (prė zī′ dėr), *n.*

presidial, -ary (prė sid′ i ȧl, -ȧr i) [F. *présidial,* late L. *præsidiālis,* from *præses -idis,* PRESES], *a.* Pertaining to a garrison; having or serving as a garrison. **presidio** (prė sid′ i ō) [Sp.], *n.* A fort or fortified settlement; a Spanish penal colony.

presignify (prē sig′ ni fī) [M.F. *presignifier,* L. *præsignificare*], *v.t.* To signify or intimate beforehand.

press (1) (pres) [F. *presser,* L. *pressāre,* freq. of *premere*], *v.t.* To act steadily upon with a force or weight; to push (something up, down, against, etc.) with steady force; to put or hold (upon, etc.) with force; to squeeze, to crush, to compress; to clasp, to embrace, to hug; to crowd upon; to urge, to ply hard, to bear heavily on; to weigh down, to distress; to straiten, to constrain; to enforce strictly, to impress; to force (upon); to make smooth by pressure (as cloth or paper). *v.i.* To exert pressure; to bear heavily, or weigh heavily; to be urgent; to throng, to crowd, to encroach, to intrude; to strive eagerly, to hasten, to strain, to push one's way. *n.* The act of pressing, urging, or crowding; a crowd, a throng; urgency, pressure, hurry; an upright case, cupboard, or closet, for storing things, esp. linen; a book-case; cabinet-work made by pressing successive cross-grained veneers together while hot; an instrument or machine for compressing any body or substance, forcing it into a more compact form, shaping, extracting juice, etc.; a machine for printing; a printing-establishment; the process or practice of printing; (*collect.*) printed literature, esp. newspaper and periodical literature. **to go to press:** (Print.) To start printing. **good (bad) press:** Good or bad notices in the newspapers. **freedom of the press:** The right to print and publish statements, opinions, etc., without censorship. **in the press:** Being printed; on the eve of publication. **press of sail:** As much sail as the wind will let a ship carry. **press agent,** *n.* A man who engages to obtain publicity. **press-bed,** *n.* A bed that may be folded and shut up in a case. **press-box** *n.* A shelter for reporters on a cricket-field, etc. **press conference:** A meeting of a statesman, etc., with journalists to announce a policy or answer their questions. **press-cutting,** *n.* A clipping from a newspaper. **press-gallery,** *n.* A gallery set aside for reporters, esp. in the Houses of Parliament. **pressman,** *n.* One who manages a printing-press; a journalist. **press-mark,** *n.* A number, symbol, or other mark indicating the place of a book on the shelves of a library. **press-room,** *n.* The room in a printing-office where the presses are. **press-work,** *n.* The work or management of a printing-press; journalistic work. **presser,** *n.* **pressing,** *a.* Urgent, importunate, insistent. **pressingly,** *adv.* **pression,** *n.* The act of pressing; pressure.

press (2) (pres) [from PREST], *v.t.* To force into naval or military service. *v.i.* To impress soldiers or sailors. *n.* A compulsory enlisting of men into naval or military service; a commission to force men into service. **press-gang,** *n.* A detachment of men employed to impress men, usu. into the navy. **press-money,** *n.* Prest-money.

pressiroster (pres i ros′ tėr) [F. *pressirostre* (L. *pressus,* PRESS (1), *rostrum,* beak)], *n.* (*Ornith.*) Any individual of the Pressirostres, a group of wading birds with a compressed beak. **pressirostral,** *a.*

pressure (presh′ ůr) [O.F., from L. *pressūra*, from PRESS (1)], *n.* The act of pressing; the state of being pressed; a force steadily exerted upon or against a body by another in contact with it; the amount of this, usu. measured in units of weight upon a unit of area; (*fig.*) urgency, rush, hurry, embarrassment, straits, difficulty, trouble, affliction, oppression, onerousness; constraining force, compulsion. **pressure-cabin:** (*Aviat.*) A pressurized cabin in an aircraft. **pressure-cooker:** An apparatus for cooking at a high temperature under high pressure. **pressure group:** (*Pol.*) A group or small party exerting pressure on government for its own ends. **pressure-suit:** (*Aviat.*) An airman's suit that inflates automatically if there is a failure in the pressure-cabin. **pressurize,** *v.t.* To fit an aircraft cabin with a device that maintains normal atmospheric pressure at high altitudes. **high pressure** [HIGH]. **low pressure** [LOW].

***prest** (prest) [O.F. (F. *prêt*), from *prester*, L. *præstāre* (PRÆ-, *stāre*, to come forward, to stand)], *n.* An advance, a loan; earnest-money paid to a sailor or soldier on enlistment. *a.* Ready, prepared. **prest-money,** *n.* Money paid to men who enlist. ***prestation** (-tā′ shůn), *n.* A payment of money as a toll; performance, purveyance.

Prester John (pres′ tėr jon), *n.* A mythical Christian sovereign and priest, supposed in the Middle Ages to rule in Abyssinia or somewhere in the interior of Asia.

pre-sternum (prē stĕr′ nům), *n.* (*Anat.*) The front part of the sternum; (*Ent.*) the prosternum.

prestidigitation (pres ti dij i tā′ shůn) [F. *preste*, It. PRESTO, L. *digitus*, finger, -ATION], *n.* Sleight of hand, conjuring. **prestidigitator** (-dij′ i tā tǒr), *n.*

prestige (pres tēzh′, pres′ tij) [F., from L. *præstigium*, a trick, illusion, glamour, from *præstringere* (PRÆ-, *stringere*, to bind)], *n.* Influence or weight derived from former fame, excellence, achievements, etc.; *an illusion, a trick, an imposture.

presto (1) (pres′ tō) [It., from late L. *præstus*, from L. *præsto* (PRÆ-, *sitū*, abl. of *situs*, SITUATION)], *adv.* (*Mus.*) Quickly. *a.* Quick. *n.* A quick movement. ***prestissimo*** (pres tis′ i mō), *adv.* Very fast indeed. *a.* Very fast. *n.* A very fast movement.

presto (2) (pres′ tō) [from prec.], *adv.* (*Juggling*) Quick, at once. *a.* Quick.

presume (prė zūm′) [O.F. *presumer*, L. *præsūmere* (PRÆ-, *sūmere*, to take)], *v.t.* To venture on without leave; to take for granted or assume without previous inquiry or examination. *v.i.* To venture without previous leave; to form over-confident or arrogant opinions; to behave with assurance or arrogance. **presumable,** *a.* **presumably, presumedly,** *adv.* **presumer,** *n.* **presuming,** *a.* Presumptuous. **presumingly,** *adv.*

presumption (prė zŭmp′ shůn), *n.* The act of presuming; assumption of the truth or existence of something without direct proof; that which is taken for granted; the ground for presuming; over-confidence, arrogance, impudence, effrontery. **presumption of fact:** (*Law*) An inference as to a fact from facts actually known. **presumption of law:** Assumption of the truth of a proposition until the contrary is proved; an inference established by law as universally applicable to particular circumstances.

presumptive (prė zŭmp′ tiv), *a.* Giving grounds for or based on presumption; *presumptuous. **heir presumptive:** An heir whose actual succession may be prevented by the birth of one nearer akin to the present holder of a title, estate, etc. **presumptive evidence:** (*Law*) Evidence derived from circumstances which necessarily or usually attend a fact. **presumptively,** *adv.*

presumptuous (prė zŭmp′ tū ůs) [O.F. *presumptueux*, late L. *præsumptuōsus*, *præsumptiōsus*, as prec.], *a.* Full of presumption; arrogant, forward; rash, venturesome. **presumptuously,** *adv.* **presumptuousness,** *n.*

presuppose (prē sů pōz′) [F. *présupposer*], *v.t.* To assume beforehand; to imply as a necessary antecedent. ***presupposal, presupposition** (-zish′ ůn), *n.* The act of presupposing; a supposition adopted beforehand. ***presurmise** (prē sůr mīz′), *n.* A surmise formed beforehand.

pretend (prė tend′) [F. *prétendre*, L. *prætendere* (PRÆ-, *tendere*, to stretch), p.p. *prætensus*], *v.t.* To assume the appearance of; to feign to be; to simulate, to counterfeit; to allege or put forward falsely; to put forward, to assert, to claim; *to aim at, to aspire to; *to intend to design. *v.i.* To feign, to make believe; to put forward a claim (to); *to aim, to attempt. **pretence** (prė tens′), *n.* A claim (true or false); a false profession; an excuse, a pretext; display, show, ostentation; the act of pretending or feigning; *a purpose, plan, or design. **pretendedly,** *adv.* **pretender,** *n.* One who makes a claim to, esp. a claim that cannot be substantiated; a claimant, esp. a claimant to a throne held by another branch of the same family. **Old Pretender:** James Stuart (1688–1766), son of James II. **Young Pretender:** Charles Edward Stuart (1720–1788) son of Old Pretender. **pretendership,** *n.* **pretendingly,** *adv.*

pretension (prė ten′ shůn), *n.* Assumption of a claim, true or false; a rightful claim; pretentiousness; *a pretence, a deception.

pretentious (prė ten′ shůs), *a.* Full of pretension; making specious claims to excellence, etc.; ostentatious, arrogant, conceited. **pretentiously,** *adv.* **pretentiousness,** *n.*

preter- [L. *præter*, past, beyond, comp. of *præ*, before], *pref.* Beyond; beyond the range of; more than. **pretercanine** (prē tėr kăn′ īn), *a.* More than canine. **preterhuman** (prē tėr hū′ mǎn), *a.* More than human, superhuman. ***preterimperfect** (prē tėr im pĕr′ fėkt), *a.* (*Gram.*) Applied to the imperfect tense as expressing a past action that is described as still going on.

preterist (prē′ tėr ist) [foll.], *n.* One whose chief interest is in the past; (*Theol.*) one who holds that the prophecies in the Apocalypse have already been fulfilled.

preterit, preterite (pret′ ėr it) [O.F., from L. *præteritus*, p.p. of *præterīre* (PRETER-, *īre*, to go)], *a.* (*Gram.*) Denoting completed action or existence in past time; past, gone by. *n.* The preterit tense; *the past. **preteritness** (pret′ er it nės), *n.* **preteritive** (prė ter′ i tiv), *a.* **preteritial** (pret′ ėr ish′ ǎl), *a.* (*Biol.*) Having ceased from activity.

preterition (prē tėr ish′ ůn) [late L. *præteritio*, as prec.], *n.* The act of passing over or omitting; the state of being passed over; (*Rhet.*) the summary mention of a thing while one pretends to pass it over; (*Theol.*) the passing over of the non-elect, opp. to election.

pretermit (prē tėr mit′) [L. *prætermittere* (PRETER-, *mittere*, to send, to let go)], *v.t.* To pass by or over, to neglect, to omit (to mention, to do, etc.); to discontinue. **pretermission** (-mish′ ůn), *n.*

preternatural (prē tėr năt′ ū rǎl), *a.* Beyond what is natural; out of the regular course of nature. **preternaturally,** *adv.* **preternaturalness,** *n.* **preternaturalism,** *n.* The state of being preternatural; a preternatural occurrence, thing, etc.; belief in or doctrine of the preternatural. **preternaturalist,** *n.*

***preterperfect** (prē tėr pĕr′ fėkt), *a.* (*Gram.*) The past perfect tense; more than perfect. ***preterpluperfect.** **pretersensual** (prē tėr sen′ sū ǎl), *a.* Beyond the sphere of the senses.

pretext (prē′ tekst) [F. *prétexte*, L. *prætextus*, p.p. of *prætexere* (PRÆ-, *texere*, to weave)], *n.* An excuse; an ostensible reason or motive. *v.t.* (prė tekst′) To allege as pretext or motive.

pretibial (prė tib′ i ǎl), *a.* (*Anat.*) Situated in front of the tibia. **pretone** (prē′ tōn) [TONE], *n.* (*Phonol.*) The vowel or syllable preceding the accented syllable. **pretonic** (-ton′ ik), *a.*

pretor, *etc.* [PRÆTOR].

pretty (prit′ i) [A.-S. *prætig, prættig*, from *præt, prætt*, trick, trickery (cp. Dut. *part*, Norw. *pretta*)], *a.* Having beauty of a slight or diminutive kind; pleasing in the minor details of form, etc.; pleasing, attractive in form, but lacking in the perfect proportions of beauty; pleasing the ear or the æsthetic sense; nice, fine; brave, bold, stout, strong; *considerable, moderately large, good. *adv.* Tolerably, moderately. **pretty much:** Nearly. **pretty-pretty,** *a.* Affectedly pretty, over-pretty. *n.pl.* Knick-knacks, gewgaws. **prettify,** *v.t.* To make pretty; to put or depict in a pretty way. **pretty-spoken,** *a.* Speaking in a pleasing manner. **prettily,** *adv.* In a pretty manner; daintily, with taste and elegance; pleasingly to the eye, ear, etc. **prettiness,** *n.* **prettyish,** *a.* **prettyism,** *n.*

pretypify (prē tip′ i fī), *v.t.* To prefigure.

pretzel (pret′ sėl) [G.], *n.* A crisp biscuit of wheaten flour flavoured with salt, usu. eaten as a relish with beer.

prevail (prė vāl′) [L. *prævalēre* (PRÆ-, *valēre*, to be strong)], *v.i.* To have the mastery or victory (over, against, etc.); to have or gain influence or effect (upon, with, etc.); to predominate, to be in force, to be current or in vogue. **prevailingly,** *adv.* ***prevailment,** *n.* **prevalence** (prev′ ȧ lėns), ***-lency,** *n.* The act of prevailing; a superiority, predominance; frequency, vogue, currency. **prevalent,** *a.* **prevalently,** *adv.*

prevaricate (prė văr′ i kāt) [L. *prævārīcātus*, p.p. of *prævārīcārī* (PRÆ-, *vārīcus*, straddling, from *vārus*, bent)], *v.i.* To shuffle, to quibble; to act or speak evasively; to equivocate. **prevarication** (-kā′ shŭn), *n.* **prevaricator** (-văr′ i kā tor), *n.*

prevenance, *-ancy (prev′ ė nȧns, -nȧn si) [F. *prévenance*, from *prévenir*, L. *prævenīre*, as foll.], *n.* Anticipation of the wants or wishes of others.

prevenient (prė vē′ ni ėnt) [L. *præveniens -ntem*, pres.p. of *prævenīre*, to precede, to anticipate, to prevent (PRÆ-, *venīre*, to come)], *a.* Going before, preceding, previous; preventive (of). **prevenient grace:** Grace preceding repentance and predisposing to conversion. **prevenience,** *n.*

prevent (prė vent′) [L. *præventus*, p.p. of *prævenīre*, as prec.], *v.t.* To hinder, to thwart, to stop; *to anticipate; to go before, to precede, to be earlier than. **preventable, -ible,** *a.* Capable of prevention. **preventative** [PREVENTIVE]. **preventer,** *n.* One who or that which prevents or hinders; (*Naut.*) a supplementary rope, chain, spar, stay, etc., to support another. **preventingly,** *adv.* **prevention,** *n.* The act of preventing; hindrance, obstruction; *the act of going before, anticipation; *precaution; *prejudice. ***preventional,** *a.* **preventive,** *a.* Tending to hinder or prevent. *n.* That which prevents; a medicine or precaution to ward off disease; a contraceptive; a coastguard. **preventive detention:** A system for dealing with an habitual criminal by detaining him for a definite period after the completion of his sentence for a specific crime. **preventive service:** The coastguard service. **preventively,** *adv.*

prevertebral (prē vĕr′ tė brȧl), *a.* (*Anat.*) Situated in front of the vertebræ.

preview, prevue (prē′ vū′), *n.* (*Cinema.*) The exhibition of a cinema film in advance of its release.

previous (prē′ vi ŭs) [L. *prævius* (PRÆ-, *via*, way)], *a.* Going before, antecedent; prior (to); (*slang*) premature, hasty. *adv.* (*colloq.*) Before, previously (to). **Previous Examination:** (*Camb. Univ.*) The Little-go or first examination for the degree of B.A. **previous question:** (*Parl.*) The question whether a matter under debate shall be put to the vote (in the English Parliament that is moved when it is desired to shelve the main question; a motion to proceed with the next business. **previously,** *adv.* **previousness,** *n.*

previse (prė vīz′) [L. *prævīsus*, p.p. of *prævidēre* (PRÆ-, *vidēre*, to see)], *v.t.* To know beforehand, to foresee; to forewarn. **prevision,** *n.* **previsional,** *a.* **previsionally,** *adv.*

***prewarn** (prē wôrn′), *v.t.* To forewarn.

prey (prā) [O.F., *praie, preia*, L. *præda*, booty], *n.* That which is or may be seized to be devoured by carnivorous animals; booty, spoil, plunder; a victim; (*Bibl.*) that which is brought away safe (from a battle, etc.); *ravage, depredation. *v.i.* To take booty or plunder; to take food by violence. **beast** or **bird of prey:** A carnivorous beast or bird. **to prey on:** To rob, to plunder; to chase and seize as food; (*fig.*) to cause to pine away. **preyer,** *n.* ***preyful,** *a.*

Priapus (prī ā′ pŭs) [L., from Gr. *Priapos*], *n.* (*Class. Myth.*) The god of procreation; a phallus; (*Med.*) the penis. **priapean** (prī ȧ pē′ ȧn), **priapic** (prī ăp′ ik), *a.* **priapism** (prī′ ȧ pizm), *n.* Lasciviousness; (*Path.*) continuous erection of the penis without sexual excitement.

pribble (pri′ bėl) [var. of PRABBLE], *n.* Empty chatter.

price (prīs) [M.E. and O.F. *pris* (F. *prix*), L. *pretium*, cp. PRAISE, PRIZE], *n.* The amount asked for a thing or for which it is sold; the cost of a thing; (*fig.*) that which must be expended, sacrificed, done, etc., to secure a thing; (*betting slang*) the odds; estimation, value, preciousness; *a prize. *v.t.* To fix the price of, to value, to appraise; to ask the price of; *to pay for. **above, beyond,** or **without price:** Priceless. **price-current, price list:** A table of the current prices of merchandise, stocks, etc. **priceless,** *a.* Invaluable, inestimable; *of no value, unsaleable; (*slang*) very funny. **pricelessness,** *n.*

prick (prik) [A.-S. *prica* (cp. Dan. *prik*. Swed. *prick*), cogn. with *prician*, to prick (cp. Dan. *prikke*, Dut. *prikken*)], *n.* The act of pricking; the state or the sensation of being pricked; a puncture; a dot, point, or small mark made by or as by pricking; a pointed instrument, a goad, a spur; (*fig.*) a sharp, stinging pain; (*Naut.*) a small roll (of tobacco). *v.t.* To pierce slightly, to puncture; to make by puncturing; to mark off (names, etc.) with a prick, hence, to select; to cause (the ears) to point upwards; (*fig.*) to goad, to rouse, to incite. *v.i.* To ride rapidly, to spur; to point upward; to feel as if pricked. **to prick off** or **out:** To mark a pattern out with dots; to plant seedlings more widely apart with a view to transplanting later to their permanent quarters. **to prick up the ears:** To raise the ears as if listening (of dogs, etc.); (*fig.*) to become very attentive. **prick-eared,** *a.* Having erect or pointed ears (of dogs, etc.); (*fig.*) priggish (applied to the Roundheads by the Cavaliers). **prick-ears,** *n.pl.* ***pricklouse, *prick-the-louse, *prick-the-clout,** *n.* A tailor. **prick-song,** *n.* Music sung from notes pricked down, written music. **pricker,** *n.* A sharp-pointed instrument, a bradawl; *a light-horseman.

pricket (prik′ ėt) [from prec., in alln. to the straight unbranched horns], *n.* A buck in its second year; a sharp point for sticking a candle on. **pricket's sister:** The female fallow deer in the second year.

prickle (1) (prik′ ėl) [A.-S. *pricel*, cogn. with prec.], *n.* A small, sharp point; (*Bot.*) a thorn-like growth capable of being peeled off with the skin or bark, opp. to thorn or spine; (*loosely*) a small thorn, spine, etc. *v.t.* To prick slightly; to give a pricking or tingling sensation to. *v.i.* To have such a sensation. **prickle-back,** *n.* The stickleback. **prickly,** *a.* Full of or armed with prickles. **prickly heat:** A skin disease characterized by itching and stinging sensations, prevalent in hot countries. **prickly pear:** A cactus of the genus *Opuntia*, bearing pear-shaped fruit, usu. covered with prickles. **prickliness,** *n.*

prickle (2) (prik′ ėl) [etym. unknown], *n.* A variety of wicker basket; a measure of weight of about fifty pounds.

pride (prīd) [A.-S. *prȳto, prȳte*, cogn. with *prūt*, PROUD], *n.* Inordinate self-esteem, unreasonable conceit of one's own superiority; insolence, arrogance; sense of dignity, self-respect, proper self-esteem; generous elation or exultation; a source of such elation; (*fig.*) the acme, the highest point, the best condition; a collection of lions. *v.t.* (*reflex.*) To make proud or exultant. **prideful,** *a.* (*chiefly Sc.*) **pridefully,** *adv.* **pridefulness,** *n.* **prideless,** *a.*

***pridian** (prid′ i ȧn) [L. *prīdiānus*, from *prīdiē*, on the day before (*pri-*, before, *dies*, day)], *a.* Of or pertaining to yesterday.

prie-Dieu (prē dyĕr) [F., pray God], *n.* A kneeling desk for prayers. ***prie-Dieu* chair:** A chair with a tall sloping back, esp. for praying.

prier (prī′ ėr) [PRY, -ER], *n.*

priest (prēst) [A.-S. *prēost*, PRESBYTER], *n.* One who officiates in sacred rites, esp. by offering sacrifice; (*R.-C., Gr., and Ang. Ch.*) a minister of the second order, below a bishop and above a deacon, esp. as having authority to administer the sacraments and pronounce absolution; (*colloq.*) a clergyman, a minister (esp. in a hostile sense); (*Angling*) a small mallet or club for killing fish when caught. **priest-craft,** *n.* Priestly policy based on material interests. **priest-in-the-pulpit** [PRIEST'S HOOD]. **priest-ridden,** *a.* Dominated or swayed by priests. **priest's hole:** A hiding-place for fugitive priests, esp. in Ireland under the penal laws. **priest's hood:** The wild arum. **priest-vicar,** *n.* A minor canon in certain cathedrals. **priestess,** *n.* **priest-hood,** *n.* **priestless,** *a.* **priestlike,** *a.* **priestling,** *n.* **priestly,** *a.* Of, pertaining to, or befitting a priest or the priesthood; sacerdotal. **priestliness,** *n.*

prig (prig) [prob. var. of PRICK], *n.* A conceited, formal, or didactic person; (*slang*) a thief. *v.t.* (*slang*) To filch, to steal. **priggery,** *n.* **priggish,** *a.* Conceited, affectedly precise, formal, didactic. **priggishly,** *adv.* **priggishness,** *n.*

prill (pril) [Cornish dial], *n.* (*Mining*) One of the better portions of copper ore; a button of metal from an assay.

prim (prim) [prob. 17th cent. slang], *a.* Formal, affectedly proper, demure. *v.t.* To put (the lips, mouth, etc.) into a prim expression; to deck with great nicety or preciseness. *v.i.* To make oneself look prim. **primly,** *adv.* **primness,** *n.*

prima (prē′ mȧ) [It., fem. of *primo*, L. *prīmus*, first], *a.* First, chief, principal. ***prima buffa*** (buf′ ȧ): A chief comic singer or actress. ***prima donna*** (don′ ȧ): A chief female singer in an opera. (*pl.* ***prime donne,*** prē′ mā don′ ā).

primacy (prī′ mȧ si) [O.F. *primacie*, med. L. *prīmātia*, L. *prīmātus*, from *prīmus*, PRIME (1)], *n.* The dignity or office of a primate; pre-eminence.

primæval [PRIMEVAL].

prima facie (prī mȧ fā′ shi ē) [L., abl. of *prīma facies*, first face], *adv.* At first sight, on the first impression. **prima facie case:** (*Law*) A case apparently established by the evidence.

primage (prī′ mȧj) [med. L. *primāgium*, etym. doubtful], *n.* A percentage on the freight paid to the owner of a ship for care in loading or unloading cargo.

primal (prī′ mȧl) [L. *prīmālis*, from *prīmus*, PRIME (1)], *a.* Primary, original, primitive; fundamental, chief. **primally** (prī′ mȧ li), *adv.*

primary (prī′ mȧ ri) [L. *prīmārius*, from *prīmus*, PRIME (1)], *a.* First in time, order, or origin; original, radical; primitive, fundamental; first in rank or importance, chief; first or lowest in development, elementary; (*Geol.*) pertaining to the lowest series of strata, Palæozoic; (*Astron.*) revolving round the sun as centre. *n.* That which stands first in order, rank, or importance; (*Astron.*) a primary planet; (*Polit.*) a meeting or assembly for the selection of candidates by a party, esp. in the U.S.A.; (*Ornith.*) one of the large quill-feathers of a bird's wing. **primary assembly** or **meeting:** (*Polit.*) A primary. **primary cell:** (*Elec.*) A battery in which an irreversible chemical action is converted into electrical energy (*cf.* secondary cell). **primary colours** [COLOUR]. **primary education:** Elementary education, esp. for children liable to compulsory attendance, opposed to secondary. **primary feather:** (*Ornith.*) A primary. **primary scholar, school** [PRIMARY EDUCATION]. **primary winding:** (*Elec.*) The winding of a transformer which is on the input side; the input winding on the stator of an induction motor. **primarily,** *adv.* **primariness,** *n.*

primate (prī′ mȧt) [late L. *prīmas -ātis*, from L. *prīmus*, PRIME (1)], *n.* The chief prelate in a national episcopal church, an archbishop. **Primate of all England:** The archbishop of Canterbury. **Primate of England:** The archbishop of York. **primateship,** *n.* **primatial** (prī mā′ shȧl), *a.*

primates (prī mā′ tēz) [pl. of prec.], *n.pl.* (*Zool.*) The highest group of mammals, comprising man, monkeys, and lemurs.

prime (1) (prīm) [F., from L. *prīmus*, first], *a.* First in time, rank, excellence, or importance; chief; first-rate, excellent (esp. of meat and provisions); original, primary, fundamental; in the vigour of maturity, blooming; (*Math.*) divisible by no integral factors except itself and unity (as 2, 3, 5, 7, 11, 13), having no common factor but unity (of two or more numbers). *n.* The period or state of highest perfection; the best part (of anything); the first canonical hour of the day, beginning at 6 A.M. or at sunrise; (*R.-C. Ch.*) the office for this hour; the first stage, the beginning (of anything); (*fig.*) dawn, spring, youth; (*Arith.*) a prime number; (*Fencing*) the first of the eight parries or a thrust in this position; (*Calendar*) the golden number; *eager; *ruttish. **prime cost:** (*Comm.*) The cost of material and labour in the production of an article. **prime-meridian,** *n.* That from which longitude is measured. **prime minister:** The first Minister of State, esp. in Great Britain. **prime mover:** One who or that which originates a movement, esp. the force putting a machine in motion. **prime number:** A number that is divisible by no integral factors except itself and unity. **prime vertical:** A great circle of the heavens passing through the east and west points of the horizon and the zenith. **primely,** *adv.* **primeness,** *n.*

prime (2) (prīm) [etym. doubtful], *v.t.* To prepare (a gun) for firing; to supply (with information); to coach; to fill (with liquor); to pour water to wet the valve of a pump; to lay the first coat of paint, plaster, or oil on. *v.i.* To carry over water with the steam to the cylinder (of a boiler); to come before the mean time (of a tide).

primer (prī′ mėr) [O.F., from med. L. *prīmārius*, PRIMARY], *n.* An elementary reading-book for children; a short introductory book; *a prayer-book or book of religious instruction for the laity, orig. a book for prime; (*Print.*) (prim′ ėr) one of two sizes of type, great primer and long primer.

primero (pri mâr′ ō) [Sp. *primera*, fem. of *primero*, as prec.], *n.* A game of cards fashionable in the 16th and 17th cents., the original of poker.

primeval (prī mē′ vȧl) [L. *primævus* (*prīm-us*, PRIME (1), *ævum*, age)], *a.* Belonging to the earliest ages, ancient, original, primitive. **primevally,** *adv.*

***primigenial, *primigenious** (prī mi jē′ ni ȧl, -ŭs) [L. *prīmigenius* (*prīmi-*, *prīmus*, PRIME (1), *gen-*, stem of *gignere*, to produce)], *a.* First formed or generated; original, primary.

priming (1) (prī′ ming), *n.* The act of preparing a fire-arm for discharge; the powder placed in the pan of a flint gun; a train of powder connecting a blasting-charge with the fuse; water applied to wet the valve of a pump; a first layer of paint, etc.; a mixture used as a preparatory coat; water carried from the boiler into the cylinder of a steam-engine; (*fig.*) hasty instruction, cramming. **priming-iron, -wire,** *n.* A wire for piercing a cartridge when home, or for clearing the vent of a gun, etc.

priming (2) (prī′ ming), *n.* The shortening of the interval between tides (from neap to spring tides), opp. to lagging.

primiparous (prī mip′ ȧ rŭs) [L. *prīmus*, PRIME (1),

-*parous*, from *parere*, to bring forth], *a.* Bringing forth a child for the first time.

primitiæ (prī mish′ i ē) [L., from *prīmus*, PRIME (2)], *n.pl.* First fruits, annates; (*Obstetrics*) the discharge of fluid from the uterus before parturition.

primitive (prim′ i tiv) [F. *primitif*, -*tive*, L. *prīmitīvus*, as prec.], *a.* Pertaining to the beginning or the earliest periods; early, ancient, original, primary, primordial; (*Gram.*) radical, not derivative; rude, simple, plain, old-fashioned; (*Geol.*) belonging to the lowest strata or the earliest period; (*Biol.*) pertaining to an early stage of development; (*Art.*) belonging to the period before the Renaissance. *n.* A painter belonging to the period before the Renaissance; a picture by such a painter; a primitive word; a Primitive Methodist. **primitive colours:** (*pl.*) Primary colours. **Primitive Methodism:** A connexion or sect aiming at a preponderance of lay control in Church government, established in 1810 by secession from the Methodist Church. **Primitive Methodist,** *n.* A member of this connexion. **primitive rocks:** (*pl.*) Primary rocks. **primitively,** *adv.* **primitiveness,** *n.*

primo (prē′ mō) [It., as PRIME (1)], *n.* The first part (in a duet, etc.). ***primo basso:*** The chief bass singer.

***primogenial, -nious** [PRIMIGENIAL].

primogeniture (prī mō jen′ i tūr) [F. *primogéniture*, med. L. *primogenitūra* (L. *prīmō*, PRIME, GENITURE)], *n.* Seniority by birth amongst children of the same parents; (*Law*) the right, system, or rule under which, in cases of intestacy, the eldest son succeeds to the real estate of his father. **primogenital, -ary,** *a.* **primogenitive,** *a.* and *n.* **primogenitor,** *a.* The first father or ancestor; an ancestor. ***primogenitureship,** *n.*

primordial (prī môr′ di ăl) [F., from late L. *prīmordiālis*, from *prīmordium*, origin (*prīmus*, PRIME (1), *ordīrī*, to begin)], *a.* First in order, primary, original, primitive; existing at or from the beginning. *n.* An origin; a first principle or element. **primordiality** (-ăl′ i ti), **primordialism** (prī môr′ di ă lizm), *n.* **primordially,** *adv.*

primp (primp), *v.t.* To make prim; to prink. *v.i.* To prink oneself; to behave primly or put on affected airs.

primrose (prim′ rōz) [M.E. and O.F. *primerose* (med. L. *prīma rōsa*, early rose), corr. of M.E. and O.F. *primerole*, ult. from L. *prīmula*, dim. from *prīmus*, PRIME (1)], *n.* *Primula vulgaris*, a common British wild plant, flowering in early spring; *(*fig.*) the best, the chief, the most excellent. *a.* Like a primrose; of a pale yellow colour; *(*fig.*) gay as with flowers; flowery. **Primrose dame** or **knight:** A member of the Primrose League. **Primrose Day:** The anniversary of the death of Lord Beaconsfield, 19 April (1881), commemorated by the wearing of primroses (said to have been his favourite flower). **Primrose League:** A Conservative league formed in memory of Benjamin Disraeli, Earl of Beaconsfield, having for its objects "the maintenance of religion, of the estates of the realm, and of the imperial ascendancy of the British Empire."

primsie (prim′ zi) [PRIM], *a.* (*Burns*) Prim, demure.

Primula (prim′ ū lă) [L.], *n.* A genus of herbaceous plants belonging to the family Primulaceæ, comprising the primrose, cowslip, etc.

primum mobile (prī′ mŭm mō′ bi lē) [L., first moving thing], *n.* In the Ptolemaic system, an imaginary sphere believed to revolve from east to west in twenty-four hours, carrying the heavenly bodies with it; (*fig.*) the first source of motion, the mainspring of any action.

primus (prī′ mŭs) [L., first], *a.* First, eldest (of the name, among boys in a school). *n.* The presiding bishop in the Scottish Episcopal Church; protected trade name of a stove burning vaporized oil.

prince (prins) [F., from L. *principem*, nom. -*ceps* (*prin-*, *prīm-us*, PRIME (1), *capere*, to take)], *n.* (*now rhet.*) A sovereign, a monarch; the ruler of a principality or small state, usu. feudatory to a king or emperor; a male member of a royal family, esp. the son or grandson of a monarch; a member of a foreign order of nobility usu. ranking next below a duke; (*in Parl. writs*) a duke, marquess, or earl; (*fig.*) a chief, leader, or foremost representative. **prince-bishop,** *n.* A bishop whose see is a principality. **Prince Consort:** A prince who is the husband of a reigning female sovereign. **Prince of Darkness:** The Devil. **prince of the Church:** A cardinal. **Prince Regent:** A prince acting as regent. **Prince of Wales:** The title customarily conferred on the heir-apparent to the British throne. **prince royal,** *n.* The eldest son of a sovereign. **Prince Rupert's drop:** A pear-shaped lump of glass formed by falling in a molten state into water, bursting to dust when the thin end is nipped off. **prince's feather,** *n.* A popular name for several plants, esp. the Mexican *Amaranthus hypochondriacus*. **prince's metal,** *n.* An alloy of copper and zinc. **princedom, *princehood,** *n.* **princekin, princelet, princeling,** *n.* **prince-like,** *a.* **princely,** *a.* Pertaining to or befitting a prince; having the rank of a prince; stately, dignified. *adv.* As becomes a prince. **princeliness,** *n.* **princeship,** *n.* **princess** (prin′ ses, prin ses′), *n.* *A female sovereign; the daughter or granddaughter of a sovereign, the wife of a prince. **Princess Regent:** A princess acting as regent; the wife of a Prince Regent. **princess royal:** Title conferrable for life on the eldest daughter of a reigning sovereign. **princess dress** [PRINCESSE].

princeps (prin′ sĕps) [L., first, chief, see prec.], *a.* (*pl.* **-cipes,** -si pēz) First. *n.* A chief or head man; the title of the Roman emperor as constitutional head of the state. **editio princeps:** (*pl.* **editiones,** ō′ nēz, **principes**) The original edition of a book. **facile princeps:** Easily first, beyond question the chief or most important.

princesse (prin ses′) [F., as PRINCESS], *a.* Having the lengths of skirt and bodice cut in one piece, close-fitting, and undraped (of a woman's dress).

principal (prin′ si păl) [F., from L. *principālis*, from *princeps -cipis*, see PRINCE], *a.* Chief, leading, main; first in rank, authority, importance, influence, or degree; constituting the capital sum invested. *n.* A chief or head; a president, a governor, the head of a college, etc.; a leader or chief actor in any transaction, the chief party; a person employing another as agent; (*Law*) the actual perpetrator of a crime, the principal in the first degree, or one aiding and abetting, principal in the second degree; a capital sum invested or lent, as distinguished from income; a main rafter, esp. one extending to the ridge-pole; the chief metal organ-stop. **principally** (prin′ si păl i), *adv.* Chiefly, mainly, for the most part. ***principalness,** *n.* **principalship,** *n.* **principate,** *n.* (*Rom. Hist.*) The form of government under the early emperors when some republican features were retained; a principality.

principality (prin si păl′ i ti), *n.* The territory or jurisdiction of a prince; the country from which a prince derives his title; *sovereignty, royal state or condition, superiority; (*pl.*) the name given to one order of angels. **the Principality:** Wales.

principia (prin sip′ i ă) [L., pl. of *principium*, see foll.], *n.pl.* Beginnings, origins, elements, first principles. ***principial, *principiant,** *a.*

principle (prin′ si pĕl) [F. *principe*, L. *principium*, beginning, from *princeps -cipis*, see PRINCE], *n.* A source, an origin; a fundamental cause or element; a comprehensive truth or proposition from which others are derived; a general truth forming a basis for reasoning or action; a fundamental doctrine or tenet; a rule of action or conduct deliberately adopted, as distinguished from impulse; a law of nature by virtue of which a given mechanism, etc., brings about certain results; the mechanical contrivance, combination of parts, or mode of operation, forming the basis of a machine, instrument, process, etc.; (*Chem.*) the constituent that gives specific character to a substance; *a beginning. *v.t.* To establish in certain principles.

***princock** (prin′ kok) [etym. doubtful], *n.* A pert young fellow; a coxcomb.

prink (pringk) [rel. to PRANK (2)], *v.i.* To dress for show; to make oneself smart. *v.t.* To prank or dress up. **prinker,** *n.*

print (print) [O.F. *preinte*, from *preint*, p.p. of *preindre*, L. *premere*, to PRESS], *n.* An indentation or other mark made by pressure, an imprint, an impression; an impression from type, an engraved plate, etc.; printed lettering; printed matter; an engraving, a newspaper, etc.; printed cotton cloth; (*Phot.*) a positive image produced from a negative. *v.t.* To impress, to mark by pressure; to take an impression of, to stamp; to impress or make copies of by pressure, as from inked types, plates, or blocks, on paper, cloth, etc.; to cause (a book, etc.) to be so impressed or copied, to issue from the press, to publish; to reproduce a design, writing, etc., by any transfer process; to mark with a design, etc., by stamping; to imprint, to form (letters, etc.), in imitation of printing; (*fig.*) to impress (on the memory, etc.) as if by printing; (*Phot.*) to produce (a positive image) from a negative. *v.i.* To practise the art of printing; to publish books, etc.; to form letters, etc., in imitation of printing. **in print:** In a printed form; on sale (of a printed book, etc.). **out of print:** No longer to be obtained from the publisher. **to rush into print:** To write to a newspaper or publish a book without adequate justification. **print-seller,** *n.* One who deals in engravings. **print-shop,** *n.* **print-works,** *n.* An establishment for printing cotton fabrics. **printable,** *a.* **printless,** *a.* Leaving no impression; bearing no print or impression.

printer (prin′ ter), *n.* One engaged in printing books, pamphlets, newspapers, etc.: a typesetter, a compositor; one who carries on a printing business; one who prints calico, etc.; a machine or instrument for printing copies, designs, etc. **printer's devil,** *n.* A boy of all work in a printing-office. **printer's ink** [PRINTING]. **printer's mark:** An engraved design used as a device or trade-mark by a printer or publisher, an imprint. **printer's pie:** [PIE (3)].

printing (prin′ ting), *n.* The act, process, or practice of impressing letters, characters, or figures on paper, cloth, or other material; the business of a printer; typography. **printing-ink,** *n.* Printer's ink, usually made from linseed-oil and lamp- or ivory-black. **printing-machine,** *n.* A machine for taking impressions from type, etc., esp. one operated by steam, etc., for rapid work. **printing-office,** *n.* An establishment where printing is carried on. **printing-paper,** *n.* Paper suitable for printing. **printing out paper:** (*Phot.*) Sensitized paper for daylight printing. **printing-press,** *n.* A printing-machine; a hand-press for printing.

prior (1) (prī′ ŏr) [L., comp. of obs. *pri*, before], *a.* Former, preceding; earlier, antecedent. *adv.* Previously, antecedently (to). **priority** (prī or′ i ti), *n.*

prior (2) (prī′ ŏr) [late A.-S., as prec.], *n.* A superior of a monastic house or order next in rank below an abbot; (*Hist.*) a chief magistrate in certain Italian republics, a head of a guild at Florence, etc. **claustral prior:** A prior acting as assistant to an abbot. **priorate, priorship,** *n.* **prioress,** *n.* **priority** [PRIOR (1)]. **priory,** *n.* A religious house governed by a prior or prioress.

***prisage** (prī′ zăj) [obs. *prise*, O.F. *prise*, a taking or seizure, from *pris*, *prise*, p.p. of *prendre*, to take, -AGE], *n.* An obsolete customs duty on wine.

prise (prīz) [PRIZE (2)], *n.* Leverage; *a lever. *v.t.* To wrench; to force open with or as with a lever.

prism (prizm) [late L. *prisma*, from Gr. *prisma -matos*, from *prizein*, to saw], *n.* A solid having similar, equal, and parallel plane bases or ends, its sides forming similar parallelograms; a transparent solid of this form, usu. triangular, with two refracting surfaces set at an acute angle to each other, used as an optical instrument; a spectrum produced by refraction through this; any medium acting on light, etc., in a similar manner. **prismal** (priz′ măl), **prismatic, *-al** (priz măt′ ik, -ăl), *a.* Pertaining to or resembling a prism; formed, refracted or distributed by a prism; (*Cryst.*) orthorhombic. **prismatic binoculars:** Binoculars shortened by the insertion of prisms. **prismatic colours** [COLOUR]. **prismatic compass,** *n.* A hand-compass with an attached prism by which the dial can be read while taking the sight. **prismatic powder:** Gunpowder, the grains of which are hexagonal prisms. **prismatically,** *adv.* **prismatoid** (priz′ mă toid), *n.* A solid with parallel polygonal bases connected by triangular faces. **prismatoidal** (-toi′ dăl), *a.* **prismoid,** *n.* **prismoidal** (-moi′ dăl), *a.* **prismy** (priz′ mi), *a.*

prison (priz′ ŏn) [O.F. *prison*, *prisun*, L. *prensiōnem*, nom. *prensio*, *prehensio*, from *prehendere*, to seize], *n.* A place of confinement, esp. a public building for the confinement of criminals, debtors, etc.; confinement, captivity. *v.t.* (*poet.*) To imprison; to confine, to restrain. ***prison-base** [PRISONER'S-BASE]. **prison-bird** [JAIL-BIRD]. **prison-breaker,** *n.* One who escapes from legal imprisonment. **prison-breaking,** *n.* **prison-house,** *n.* (*poet.*) A prison. **prisoner,** *n.* One confined in a prison; one under arrest; a captive. **prisoner's-base, *-bars,** *n.* A game played by two sides occupying opposite goals or bases, the object being to touch and capture a player away from his base. ***prisonment,** *n.* **prisoner at the bar:** A person in custody or on trial upon a criminal charge. **prisoner of State, State prisoner:** A person confined for political reasons. **prisoner of war:** A person captured in war. **to take prisoner:** To capture; to arrest and hold in custody.

pristine (pris′ tīn) [L. *pristinus*, cogn. with *priscus*, see PRISCAN], *a.* Pertaining to an early state or time; ancient, primitive.

***prithee** (pri*th*′ ē) [corr. of PRAY THEE], *int.* Pray, please.

privacy [PRIVATE].

privatdozent (prē vat′ dot sent′) [G., private teacher (as foll., L. *docens -ntem*, pres.p. of *docēre*, to teach)], *n.* (*G. Univ.*) A recognized teacher or lecturer not on the regular staff.

private (prī′ văt) [L. *prīvātus*, p.p. of *prīvāre*, to bereave, to set apart], *a.* Not public; kept or withdrawn from publicity or observation; retired, secluded; secret, confidential; not holding a public position, not official; personal, not pertaining to the community; one's own; secretive, reticent. *n.* A common soldier, a soldier in the ranks; (*pl.*) the private parts; *a private matter; *privacy. **in private:** Privately, confidentially; in private life. **private Act** or **Bill:** One affecting a private person or persons and not the general public. **private judgment:** One's individual judgment, esp. as applied to a religious doctrine or passage of Scripture. **private parts:** The genitals. **private school:** One carried on for private profit. **private view:** Occasion when only those invited to an exhibition are admitted. **privately,** *adv.* **privateness,** *n.* **privacy** (prī′ vă si, priv′ ă si), *n.*

privateer (prī vă tēr′) [prec., -EER], *n.* An armed ship owned and officered by private persons commissioned by Government by letters of marque to engage in war against a hostile nation, esp. to capture merchant shipping; one who engages in privateering; an officer or one of the crew of such a ship. *v.i.* To cruise or engage in hostilities in a privateer. **privateering,** *n.* **privateersman,** *n.*

privation (prī vā′ shŭn) [F., from L. *prīvātiōnem*, nom. *-tio*, from *prīvāre*, see PRIVATE], *n.* Deprivation or lack of what is necessary; want, destitution; absence, loss, negation (of).

privative (prī′ vă tiv), *a.* Causing privation; consisting in the absence of something; expressing privation or absence of a quality, etc., negative. *n.* That which depends on or of which the essence is the absence of something; a prefix or suffix (as *un-* or *-less*) giving a negative meaning to a word. **privatively,** *adv.*

privet (priv' ĕt) [etym. doubtful], *n.* An evergreen, white-flowered shrub of the genus *Ligustrum*, esp. *L. vulgare*, largely used for hedges.

privilege (priv' i lĕj) [O.F., from L. *prīvilēgium* (*prīvi-*, *prīvus*, private, *lex lēgis*, law), whence med. L. *prīvilēgiāre* and F. *privilegier*, to privilege], *n.* A benefit, right, advantage, or immunity pertaining to a person, class, office, etc.; favour, a special advantage; (*Law*) a particular right or power conferred by a special law; an exemption pertaining to an office; a right of priority or precedence in any respect. *v.t.* To invest with a privilege; to license, to authorize (to do); to exempt (from). **bill of privilege:** A peer's petition to be tried by his peers. **breach of privilege:** Infringement of rights belonging to Parliament. **privilege of clergy:** Benefit of clergy. **writ of privilege:** A writ to deliver a privileged person from custody when arrested in a civil suit. **privileged,** *a.* **privileged communication:** (*Law*) A communication which there is no compulsion to disclose in evidence.

privy (priv' i) [F. *privé*, L. *prīvātus*, PRIVATE], *a.* Secluded, hidden, secret, clandestine, private, cognizant of something secret with another, privately knowing (with *to*). *n.* A latrine, a necessary; (*Law*) a person having an interest in any action or thing. **privy chamber:** A private apartment in a royal residence. **Privy Council:** The private council of the British sovereign (the functions of which are now largely exercised by the Cabinet and committees), consisting of the princes of the blood, certain high officers of State, and members appointed by the Crown. **Privy Councillor,** *n.* **privy purse:** An allowance of money for the personal use of the sovereign; the officer in charge of this. **Privy Seal:** The seal appended to grants, etc., which have not to pass the Great Seal. **Lord Privy Seal:** The officer of State entrusted with the Privy Seal. **privily,** *adv.* Secretly, privately. **privity,** *n.* The state of being privy to (certain facts, intentions, etc.); (*Law*) any relationship to another party involving participation in interest, reciprocal liabilities, etc.; *privacy, secrecy.

prize (1) (prīz) [M.E. and O.F. *pris*, PRICE; v. from O.F. *preisier* (F. *priser*), to PRAISE], *n.* That which is offered or won as the reward of merit or superiority in any competition, contest, exhibition, etc.; a sum of money or other object offered for competition in a lottery or other scheme of chance; (*fig.*) a well-paid appointment, a fortune, or other desirable object of perseverance, enterprise, etc. *a.* Offered or gained as a prize; gaining or worthy of a prize, first-class, of superlative merit. *v.t.* To value highly, to esteem. **prize-fellow,** *n.* One who holds a fellowship awarded for pre-eminence in an examination. **prize-fellowship,** *n.* **prize-fight,** *n.* A boxing-match for stakes. **prize-fighter,** *n.* **prize-fighting,** *n.* **prizeman,** *n.* The winner of a prize. **prize-ring,** *n.* The roped space (now usu. square) for a prize-fight; prize-fighting. **prizeless,** *a.* ***prizer,** *n.* A prize-fighter; a valuer, an appraiser.

prize (2) (prīz) [F. *prise*, a taking, a seizure, booty, orig. fem. of *pris*, p.p. of *prendre*, *prehendere*, to take], *n.* That which is taken from an enemy in war, esp. a ship or other property captured at sea. *v.t.* To make a prize of. **to become prize of:** To capture (a ship, cargo, etc.). **prize-court,** *n.* A court adjudicating on cases of prizes captured at sea, in England and U.S. a department of the courts of Admiralty. **prize-money,** *n.* The proceeds of the sale of a captured vessel, etc.

prize (3) [PRISE]. ***prizer** [PRIZE (1)].

pro (1) (prō) [L.], *prep.* For. **pro and con** [L. *pro et contra*]: For and against; on both sides. **pros and cons:** Reasons or arguments for and against. ***pro bono publico:*** For the public good. ***pro forma:*** As a matter of form. ***pro rata:*** In proportion, proportionally; proportional. ***pro tempore*** (tem' pŏ rē): For the time being; temporary.

pro (2) (prō) [short for PROFESSIONAL], *n.* (*colloq.*) A professional football player, cricketer, actor, etc.; (*slang*) a prostitute.

pro- [L. *pro*, before, in front of, in favour of, in the place of, on account of, or Gr. *pro*, before], *pref.*

proa (prō' ȧ) [Malay *prāū*, *prāhū*], *n.* A long, narrow, swift Malayan canoe, usu. equipped with both sails and oars.

probabiliorism (prob ȧ bil' i ŏr izm) [Latin *probābilior*, comp. of *probābilis*, PROBABLE, -ISM], *n.* (*R.-C. Theol.*) The doctrine that in cases of doubt among several courses of conduct it is proper to choose that which appears to have the most likelihood of being right; the teaching that a law is to be obeyed unless a very probable opinion is opposed to it. **probabiliorist,** *n.*

probabilism (prob' ȧ bil izm) [F. *probabilisme*], *n.* (*R.-C. Theol.*) The doctrine that, in matters of conscience about which there is disagreement or doubt, it is lawful to adopt any course, at any rate if this has the support of any recognized authority. **probabilist,** *n.*

probability (prob ȧ bil' i ti) [F. *probabilité*, *probābilitātem*, nom. *-tas*], *n.* The quality of being probable; that which is or appears probable; (*Math.*) likelihood of an event measured by the ratio of the favourable chances to the whole number of chances. **in all probability:** Most likely.

probable (prob' ȧ bĕl) [F., from L. *probābilem*, nom. *-lis* (*probāre*, to PROVE, -ABLE)], *a.* Likely to prove true, having more evidence for than against, likely; *capable of being proved. **probably,** *adv.*

probang (prō' băng) [orig. *provang*, name given by the inventor], *n.* (*Surg.*) A slender whalebone rod with a piece of sponge, a button, or ball at the end, for introducing into or removing obstructions in the throat.

probate (prō' bāt) [L. *probātum*, neut. of *-tus*, p.p. of *probāre*, to PROVE], *n.* The official proving of a will; a certified copy of a proved will; the right or jurisdiction of proving wills. **probate duty:** A tax charged upon the personal property of deceased persons, now merged in estate duty.

probation (prŏ bā' shŭn) [M.E. and O.F. *probacion*, L. *probātiōnem*, nom. *-tio*, as prec.], *n.* A proving or testing of character, ability, etc., esp. of a candidate for a religious ministry, etc., by employment for a fixed period; a moral trial, esp. the discipline undergone in this life as a means to salvation; a method of dealing with criminals by allowing them to go at large under supervision during their good behaviour; the act of proving; evidence, proof. **probation officer:** A police court official whose duty it is to assist offenders, esp. juveniles and children. **probational,** *a.* Serving for or pertaining to probation or trial. **probationary,** *a.* Probational; undergoing probation. *n.* A probationer. **probationer,** *n.* One on probation or trial, esp. a divinity student licensed to preach and eligible for a charge; a nurse in training; an offender under probation. **probationership,** *n.*

probative (prō' bȧ tiv) [L. *probātīvus*], *a.* Proving or tending to prove; serving as proof, evidential; *probational. **probator** (prŏ bā' tŏr), *n.* An examiner; an approver. ***probatory** (prō' bȧ tŏr i), *a.* Probative.

probe (prōb) [late L. *proba*, PROOF], *n.* A surgical instrument, usu. a silver rod with a blunt end, for exploring cavities of the body, wounds, etc. *v.t.* To search or examine (a wound, ulcer, etc.) with a probe; (*fig.*) to scrutinize thoroughly. **probe-scissors,** *n.pl.* Scissors with the points tipped with buttons, used to open wounds.

probity (prob' i ti) [F., *probité*, L. *probitātem*, nom. *-tas*, from *probus*, good], *n.* Tried honesty, sincerity, or integrity; high principle, rectitude.

problem (prob' lĕm) [M.E. and O.F. *probleme*, L.

problēma -atis, Gr. *problēma -atos* (PRO-, *ballein*, to cast)], *n.* A question proposed for solution; a question involving doubt or difficulty; a matter difficult to understand; (*Geom.*) a proposition requiring something to be done; (*Phys., etc.*) an investigation starting from certain conditions for the determination or illustration of a law, etc.; (*Chess.*) an arrangement of pieces on a chess-board from which a certain result has to be attained, usu. in a specified number of moves. **problem play, picture,** *n.* Play or picture dealing with a social problem. **problematic, -al** (-măt′ ik, -ȧl), *a.* Doubtful, questionable, uncertain; (*Log.*) propounding or supporting that which is possible or probable but not necessarily true, contingent. **problematically,** *adv.* **problemist, problematist** (prob′ lėm ȧ tist), *n.* One who studies or composes (chess) problems. ***problematize,** *v.i.*

pro-Boer (prō boor′), *n.* One who favoured the Boers in the S. African war of 1899–1902. *a.* Favouring the Boers.

proboscis (prȯ bos′ is) [L. *proboscis -cidis*, Gr. *proboskis -kidos* (PRO-, *boskein*, to feed)], *n.* (*pl.* **-ides, -i** dēz) The trunk of an elephant or the elongated snout of a tapir, etc.; the elongated mouth of some insects; the suctorial organ of some worms, etc.; (*slang*) the human nose. **proboscis-monkey,** *n.* A monkey of Borneo with a long, flexible nose. **proboscidean** (-sid′ ė ȧn), *a.* Having a proboscis; (*Zool.*) pertaining to the Proboscidea, an order of mammals containing the elephants, the extinct mastodon, etc. *n.* Any individual of the Proboscidea. **proboscidiferous** (-dif′ ėr ůs), *a.*

procacious (prȯ kā′ shůs) [L. *procax -cācis*, OUS], *a.* Forward, pert, petulant.

pro-cathedral (prō kȧ thē′ drȧl), *n.* A church or other building used as a substitute for a cathedral.

procedure (prȯ sē′ dyůr) [F. *procédure*], *n.* The act or manner of proceeding; mode of conducting business, etc.; a course of action. **procedural,** *a.*

proceed (prȯ sēd′) [F. *procéder*, L. *prōcēdere* (PRO-, *cēdere*, to go), p.p. *prōcessus*], *v.i.* To go on; to go forward, to advance, to continue to progress; to carry on a series of actions, to go on (with or in); to take steps; to be carried on; to issue or come forth, to originate; to take a degree; to take or carry on legal proceedings. **proceeder,** *n.* One who proceeds, esp. to a University degree. **proceeding,** *n.* Progress, advancement; an action, a line of conduct, a transaction; (*pl.*) steps in the prosecution of an action at law; (*pl.*) the records of a learned society. **proceeds** (pro′ sēds), *n.pl.* Produce, material results, profits, as the amount realized by the sale of goods.

proceleusmatic (pros ė lūs măt′ ik) [late L. *proceleusmaticus*, Gr. *prokeleusmatikos*, from *prokeleusma*, incitement, from *prokeleuein* (PRO-, *kauleuein*, to urge)], *a.* (*Pros.*) Denoting a metrical foot of four short syllables; *inciting, animating. *n.* Such a foot; (*pl.*) verse in this metre.

procellarian (prō sė lâr′ i ȧn) [mod. L. *Procellāria*, from L. *procella*, storm], *a.* (*Zool.*) Belonging to the genus *Procellaria* or the Procellaridæ, a family of Tubinares containing the petrels. *n.* A bird of this genus.

procephalic (prō sė făl′ ik) [PRO-, Gr. *kephalē*, head)], *a.* Of or pertaining to the anterior part of the head, esp. in invertebrates. **procerebrum** (prȯ ser′ ė brům) [CEREBRUM], *n.* The prosencephalon. **procerebral,** *a.*

***procerity** (prȯ ser′ i ti) [M.F. *procerité*, L. *prōcēritātem*, nom. *-tas*, from *prōcērus*, high, tall], *n.* Tallness, height. ***procerous** (prȯ sēr′ ůs), *a.*

process (1) (prō′ ses, pros′ ės) [O.F. *proces*, L. *prōcessus*, see PROCEED], *n.* A course or method of proceeding or doing, esp. a method of operation in manufacture, scientific research, etc.; a natural series of continuous actions, changes, etc.; a progressive movement or state of activity, progress, course; the course of proceedings in an action at law; a writ or order commencing this; a method of producing a printing surface by photography and mechanical or chemical means; (*Anat., Zool., etc.*) an out-growth, an enlargement, a protuberance of a bone, etc. *v.t.* To proceed against by legal process; to heat (food, etc.) by a preservative or other process; to reproduce by a photo-mechanical process. **process block:** A printing block produced by photo-mechanical means. **process-server,** *n.* A sheriff's officer who serves processes or summonses.

process (2) (prȯ ses′) [from foll.], *v.i.* (*facet.*) To go in procession.

procession (prȯ sesh′ ůn) [F., from L. *prōcessiōnem*, nom. *-sio*, from *prōcēdere*, to PROCEED], *n.* A proceeding of a number of persons, etc., in formal march; a train of persons, etc., so proceeding; the act or state of proceeding or issuing forth, emanation (as of the Holy Ghost from the Father). *v.i.* To go in procession. *v.t.* To go round in procession; to perambulate the bounds of. **processional,** *a.* Pertaining to or used in processions. *n.* A service-book giving the ritual of or the hymns sung in religious processions; a processional hymn. ***processionally,** *adv.* **processionary, processive,** *a.* **processionist,** *n.* One who takes part in a procession. **processionize,** *v.i.*

procès-verbal (prō sā vâr bal′) [F., verbal process], *n.* (*pl.* **-baux,** -bō) (*F. Law*) A written statement of particulars relating to a charge; an official record of proceedings, minutes.

prochain (prō′ shȧn) [F., from *proche*, L. *propius*, comp. of *prope*, near], *a.* (*Law*) Nearest, next. **prochain ami** or **amy** [F. *ami*, friend]: The nearest friend, who is entitled to sue, etc., on behalf of an infant.

prochronism (prō′ krȯ nizm), *n.* An error in chronology dating an event before its actual occurrence.

procidence (prō′ si dėns) [F., from L. *prōcidentia* (PRO-, *cadere*, to fall)], *n.* (*Path.*) A slipping from the normal position, a prolapsus. **procident,** ***prociduous** (-sid′ ū ůs), *a.*

***procinct** (prȯ singkt′) [L. *prōcinctus*, p.p. of *procingere* (PRO-, *cingere*, to gird)], *a.* Prepared, ready. ***in procinct:** Ready, prepared; at hand, close.

proclaim (prȯ klām′) [F. *proclamer*, L. *prōclāmāre* (PRO-, *clāmāre*, to cry out)], *v.t.* To announce publicly, to promulgate; to declare publicly or openly, to publish; to declare (war, etc.); to announce the accession of; to outlaw by public proclamation; (*Ir. Hist.*) to put (a district, etc.) under certain legal restrictions by public proclamation. **proclaimer,** *n.* **proclamation** (prok lȧ mā′ shůn), *n.* **proclamatory** (-klăm′ ȧ tȯr i), *a.*

proclitic (prȯ klit′ ik) [PRO-, after ENCLITIC], *a.* (*Gr. Gram.*) Attached to and depending in accent upon a following word. *n.* A monosyllable attached to a following word and having no separate accent.

proclivity (prȯ kliv′ i ti) [L. *prōclīvitas*, from *prōclīvus* (PRO-, *clīvus*, slope)], *n.* Tendency, bent, propensity. **proclivitous,** *a.* Steep, abrupt. **proclivous** (prȯ klī′ vůs), *a.* Inclined or sloping forward (of teeth).

proconsul (prō kon′ sůl), *n.* A Roman magistrate, usu. an ex-consul, exercising consular power as governor of a province or commander of an army; (*fig.*) a governor or viceroy of a modern dependency, etc. **proconsular** (-sū lȧr), *a.* **proconsulate** (-sū lȧt), **proconsulship,** *n.*

procrastinate (prȯ krăs′ ti nāt) [L. *procrastinātus*, p.p. of *procrastināre* (PRO-, *crastinus*, pertaining to to-morrow)], *v.i.* To put off action; to be dilatory. *v.t.* To put off, to defer. **procrastinatingly,** *adv.* **procrastination** (-nā′ shůn), *n.* **procrastinative, -tory,** *a.* **procrastinator,** *n.*

procreate (prō′ krė āt) [L. *prōcreātus*, p.p. of *prōcreāre* (PRO-, *creāre*, to CREATE)], *v.t.* To generate, to beget. **procreant,** *a.* **procreation**

(-ā′ shŭn), *n.* **procreative,** (prō′ krė ā tiv), *a.* **procreativeness,** *n.* **procreator** (prō′krė ā tŏr), *n.*

Procrustean (prŏ krŭs′ tė ăn) [Gr. *Prokroustēs* (from *prokrouein*, to hammer out), a fabulous robber of Attica, who stretched or mutilated his victims till their length was exactly that of his couch], *a.* Reducing to strict conformity by violent measures.

proctalgia (prok tăl′ ji ȧ) [Gr. *prōktos*, anus, *algos*, pain], *n.* (*Path.*) Pain in the anus. **proctectomy** (-tek′ tŏ mi), *n.* Excision of the rectum or anus. **proctitis** (-tī′ tis), *n.* Inflammation of the anus or rectum.

proctor (prok′ tŏr) [a form of PROCURATOR], *n.* A University official (usu. one of two elected annually) charged with the maintenance of order and discipline; (*Law*) a person employed to manage another's cause, esp. in an ecclesiastical court. **Queen's** or **King's Proctor:** An officer of the Crown who intervenes in probate, divorce, or nullity cases when collusion or other irregularity is alleged. **proctorage,** *n.* Management by a proctor. **proctorial** (-tôr′ i ăl), *a.* **proctorship** (prok′ tŏr ship), *n.* **proctorize,** *v.t.* To deal with (an undergraduate) in the capacity of proctor. **proctorization** (-zā′ shŭn), *n.*

procumbent (prŏ kŭm′ bėnt) [L. *prōcumbens -ntem*, pres.p. of *prōcumbere* (PRO-, *cumbere*, to lie, to lay oneself)], *a.* Lying down on the face, prone; (*Bot.*) lying or trailing along the surface of the ground.

***procuracy** [PROCURATOR].

procuration (prok ū rā′ shŭn) [F., from L. *prōcūrātiōnem*, nom. *-tio*, from *prōcūrāre*, to PROCURE], *n.* The act of procuring or obtaining; action on behalf of another, function of attorney, a proxy; a document authorizing one person to act for another; entertainment formerly provided, or the fee now paid in commutation of this, by the clergy for the bishop, archdeacon, etc., at their visitations; procuring of girls for unlawful purposes.

procurator (prok′ ū rā tŏr) [L., as prec.], *n.* One who manages another's affairs, esp. those of a legal nature, an agent, a proxy, an attorney; a chief magistrate in some Italian cities; (*Mediæval and Sc. Univ.*) an elective officer having financial, electoral, and disciplinary functions, a proctor; (*Rom. Hist.*) a fiscal officer in an imperial province having certain administrative powers. **Procurator-fiscal,** *n.* (*Sc.*) The public prosecutor in a county or district. **procuracy** (prok′ ū rȧ si), **procuratorship,** *n.* **procuratorial** (-tôr′ i ăl), *a.* **procuratory,** *n.* The instrument appointing a procurator; a power of attorney. **procuratrix,** *n.* One of the superiors managing the temporal affairs in a nunnery.

procure (prŏk ūr′) [F. *procurer*, L. *prōcūrāre* (PRO-, *cūrāre*, to see to, from *cūra*, care)], *v.t.* To obtain, to get by some means or effort; to acquire, to gain; to obtain as a pimp; *to bring about. *v.i.* To act as procurer or procuress, to pimp. **procurable,** *a.* **procural, procurance, procurement,** *n.* **procurer,** *n.* One who procures or obtains, esp. one who procures a woman to gratify a person's lust, a pimp, a pander. **procuress,** *n.*

procureur (prok u rêr′) [F., as PROCURATOR], *n.* A procurator. ***procureur général:*** A public prosecutor acting in a court of appeal or of cassation.

Procyon (prō′ si ŏn) [L., from Gr. *Prokuōn* (PRO-, *kuōn*, dog)], *n.* The lesser dog-star; (*Zool.*) a genus of mammals containing the racoons, typical of the Procyonidæ.

prod (prod) [etym. doubtful], *n.* A pointed instrument, a goad, a poke with or as with this. *v.t.* (*past & p.p.* **prodded**) To poke with or as with such an instrument; (*fig.*) to goad, to irritate, to incite.

prod- [PRO-, before vowels], *pref.*

prodelision (prō dė lizh′ ŭn), *n.* (*Pros.*) Elision of the initial vowel (of a word, etc.).

prodigal (prod′ i găl) [F. (now *prodigue*), from L. *prōdigus* (PROD-, *agere*, to drive)], *a.* Given to extravagant expenditure; wasteful, lavish (of). *n.* A prodigal person, a spendthrift. **adv.* Prodigally. **prodigality** (-găl′ i ti), *n.* Extravagance, profusion; lavishness, waste. **prodigalize** (prod′ i gȧ līz), *v.t.* To spend prodigally. **prodigally,** *adv.*

prodigy (prod′ i ji) [L. *prōdigium*, portent (PROD-, *agium*, cp. ADAGE)], *n.* Something wonderful or extraordinary; a wonderful example (of); a person or thing with extraordinary gifts or qualities; something out of the ordinary course of nature, a monstrosity. **prodigious** (prŏ dij′ ŭs), *a.* Wonderful, astounding; enormous in size, quality, extent, etc. **prodigiously,** *adv.* **prodigiousness,** *n.*

prodrome, prodromus (prod′ rŏm, -rŏ mŭs) [Gr. *prodromos* (PRO-, *dromos*, running, from *dramein*, to run)], *n.* (*pl.* **dromes,** -rŏ mēz, **-dromi,** -rŏ mī) An introductory book or treatise; (*Med.*) a symptom of approaching disease. **prodromal, prodromic,** *a.*

produce (1) (prŏ dūs′) [L. *prōdūcere* (PRO-, *dūcere*, to lead)], *v.t.* To bring into view, to bring forward; to publish, to exhibit; to bring into existence, to bring forth; to bear, to yield, to manufacture; to bring about, to cause; (*Geom.*) to extend, to continue (a line) in the same direction.

produce (2) (prod′ ūs), *n.* That which is produced or yielded; the result (of labour, skill, etc.); (*collect.*) natural or agricultural products of a country, etc.; (*Assaying*) the percentage of copper or other metal yielded by a given amount of ore; (*Ordnance*) materials produced from the breaking up of condemned military and naval stores; (*Theat.*) to arrange the technical and acting details of a play, etc., and put it on the stage.

producer (prŏ dūs′ ėr), *n.* One who produces, esp. a cultivator, manufacturer, etc., as distinguished from a consumer; a furnace used for the manufacture of carbon monoxide gas; (*Theat., Cinema., Radio*). One who produces a play, film, features, etc.; (*Am.*) theatrical manager. **producer gas:** Gas produced in a producer. **producible,** *a.* **producibility** (-bil′ i ti), ***producibleness,** *n.*

product (prod′ ŭkt) [L. *prōductus*, p.p. of *prōdūcere*, see prec.], *n.* That which is produced by natural processes, labour, art, or mental application; effect, result; (*Math.*) the quantity obtained by multiplying two or more quantities together; (*Chem.*) a compound not previously existing in a substance but produced by its decomposition [cp. EDUCT]. **productile** (prŏ dŭk′ til), *a.* Capable of being produced or extended. **production** (-dŭk′ shŭn), *n.* The act of producing, esp. as opposed to consumption; a thing produced, a product. **productive,** *a.* Producing or tending to produce; yielding in abundance, fertile; (*Polit. Econ.*) producing commodities having exchangeable value. **productively,** *adv.* **productiveness, productivity** (prō dŭk tiv′ i ti), *n.* Yield in abundance; efficiency of production. **productor,** *n.* **productress,** *n.*

pro-educational (prō ed ū kā′ shŏ năl), *a.* In favour of education.

proem (prō′ ėm) [O.F. *proëme* (F. *proème*), L. *prooemium*, Gr. *prooimion* (PRO-, *oimos*, way, or *oimē*, song)], *n.* A preface, a preamble, an introduction, a prelude. **proemial** (prō ē′ mi ăl), *a.*

proembryo (prō em′ bri ō), *n.* (*Bot.*) A cellular structure of various forms in plants from which the embryo is developed. **proembryonic** (-on′ ik), *a.*

proemptosis (prō emp tō′ sis) [PRO-, Gr. *emptōsis* (EM-, *piptein*, to fall)], *n.* The occurrence of a natural event before the calculated date; hence, the addition of a day to a calendar to correct an error so arising, esp. in connexion with the date of a new moon.

profane (prŏ fān′) [F., from L. *prōfānus* (PRO-, *fānum*, temple, see FANE), whence *prōfānāre*, to profane], *a.* Not sacred, not inspired, not initiated into sacred or esoteric rites or knowledge; secular; irreverent towards holy things; irreverent, impious, blasphemous; heathenish; common, vulgar. *v.t.*

To treat with irreverence; to desecrate, to violate, to pollute. **profanation** (prof å nā' shůn), *n.* **profanely** (prò fān' li), *adv.* **profaneness, profanity** (-făn' i ti), *n.* **profaner,** *n.*

profess (prò fes') [L. *prōfessus,* p.p. of *prōfitērī* (PRO-, *fatērī,* to confess)], *v.t.* To make open or public declaration of, to avow publicly; to affirm one's belief in or allegiance to; to affirm one's skill or proficiency in; to undertake the teaching or practice of (an art, science, etc.); to teach (a subject) as a professor; to lay claim to, to make a show of, to pretend (to be or do). *v.i.* To act as a professor; to make protestations or show of. **professed** (-fest'), *a.* Avowed, declared, acknowledged; pretending to be qualified (as a teacher, practitioner, etc.); (*R.-C. Ch.*) of a religious person who has taken vows. **professedly** (-fes' èd li), *adv.* By profession; avowedly; pretendedly, ostensibly.

profession (prò fesh' òn), *n.* The act of professing; a declaration, an avowal; a protestation, a pretence; an open acknowledgment of sentiments, religious belief, etc.; a vow binding oneself to, or the state of being a member of a religious order; a calling, a vocation, esp. an occupation involving high educational or technical qualifications; the body of persons engaged in such a vocation. **the profession:** (*colloq.*) Actors. **the three professions:** Divinity, law, medicine. **professional,** *a.* Of or pertaining to a profession, esp. as opposed to amateur. *n.* A member of a profession; one who makes his living by some art, sport, etc., as distinguished from one who engages in it for pleasure. **professionalism,** *n.* The qualities, stamp, or spirit of a profession; the employment of professionals, esp. in sports. **professionalize,** *v.t.* **professionally,** *adv.* **professionless,** *a.*

professor (prò fes' òr), *n.* One who makes profession, esp. of a religious faith; a public teacher of the highest rank, esp. in a University. **professoriate** (-sôr' i àt), ***professorate,** *n.* **professoress,** *n.* **professorship** (-fes' òr ship), *n.* **professorial** (-sôr' i àl), *a.* Pertaining to or characteristic of professors. **professorially,** *adv.*

proffer (prof' ėr) [O.F *proffrir* (PRO-, *offrir,* L. *offerre,* to OFFER)], *v.t.* To offer or tender for acceptance; *to attempt. *n.* An offer, a tender; *an attempt. **profferer,** *n.*

proficient (prò fish' ėnt) [L. *proficiens -ntem,* pres.p. of *prōficere,* see PROFIT], *a.* Well versed or skilled in any art, science, etc., expert, competent. *n.* One who is proficient, an adept, an expert. **proficiency, *-cience,** *n.* **proficiently,** *adv.*

profile (prō' fēl, prō' fīl) [It. *profilo* (now *proffilo*), from *profilare,* to draw in outline (PRO-, late L. *fīlāre,* to spin, from *fīlum,* thread)], *n.* An outline, a contour; a side view, esp. of the human face; a drawing, silhouette, or other representation of this; the outline of a vertical section of a building, the contour of architectural detail, etc.; (*Fort.*) a vertical section of a fort, rampart, etc.; hence, the relative thickness of a rampart, etc.; a wooden framework used as a guide in forming an earthwork. *v.t.* To draw in profile or in vertical section; to shape (stone, wood, metal, etc.) to a given profile. **profilist,** *n.* One who draws profiles.

profit (prof' it) [O.F., from L. *prōfectum,* nom. *prōfectus,* p.p. of *prōficere* (PRO-, *facere,* to do)], *n.* Any advantage or benefit resulting from labour or exertion; excess of receipts or returns over outlay, gain (*often in pl.*); (*Polit. Econ.*) the portion of the gains of an industry received by the capitalist or the investors. *v.t.* To benefit, to be of advantage to. *v.i.* To be of advantage (to); to receive benefit or advantage (by or from). **profit and loss:** (*Bookkeeping*) Gains credited and losses debited in an account so as to show the net loss or profit; (*Arith.*) the rule by which such gain or loss is calculated. **profit motive,** *n.* (*Econ.*) The incentive of private profit for the production and distribution of goods. **profit-sharing,** *n.* A system of remuneration by which the workers in an industrial concern are apportioned a percentage of the profits in order to give them an interest in the business. **profitable,** *a.* Yielding or bringing profit or gain, lucrative; advantageous, beneficial, useful. **profitableness,** *n.* **profitably,** *adv.* **profiteer,** *v.i.* To make undue profits at the expense of the public, esp. in a time of national stress. *n.* One guilty of this social crime. **profiteering** (-tēr' ing), *n.* (*Polit. Econ.*) A mercantile or industrial system based solely on the capitalist's or investor's desire of profits. **profitless,** *a.* **profitlessly,** *adv.* **profitlessness,** *n.*

profligate (prof' li gȧt) [L. *prōflīgātus,* p.p. of *prōflīgāre,* to cast down (PRO-, *flīgere,* to strike)], *a.* Abandoned to vice, licentious, dissolute; wildly extravagant. *n.* A profligate person. **profligacy, profligateness,** *n.* **profligately,** *adv.*

***profluent** (prō' flû ėnt) [L. *prōfluens -ntem,* pres.p. of *prōfluere* (PRO-, *fluere,* to flow)], *a.* Flowing forward or forth. ***profluence,** *n.*

profound (prò found') [O.F. *profund* (F. *profond*), L. *profundus* (PRO-, *fundus,* bottom)], *a.* Having great intellectual penetration or insight; having great knowledge; requiring great study or research, abstruse, recondite; deep, intense; reaching to or extending from a great depth; coming from a great depth, deep-drawn; very low (as an obeisance). *n.* A vast depth, an abyss; the deep, the ocean; chaos. **profoundly,** *adv.* **profoundness, profundity** (-fŭn' di ti), *n.*

profunda (prò fŭn' dȧ) [L., fem. of *profundus,* as prec.], *n.* (*Anat.*) One of various deep-seated veins or arteries.

profundity [PROFOUND].

profuse (prò fūs') [L. *profūsus,* p.p. of *prōfundere* (PRO-, *fundere,* to pour)], *a.* Poured forth lavishly, exuberant, copious, super-abundant; liberal to excess, prodigal, extravagant. **profusely,** *adv.* **profuseness, profusion** (-fū' zhůn), *n.*

prog (1) (prog) [etym. doubtful], *v.i.* To poke about (esp. for food); to forage, to beg. *n.* (*slang*) Victuals, provender, food.

prog (2) (prog) [short for PROCTOR], *n.* (*Oxf. and Camb. slang*) A proctor. *v.t.* To proctorize. **proggins,** *n.* A prog.

progenitor (prò jen' i tòr) [M.F. *progeniteur,* L. *prōgenitōrem,* nom. *-tor,* from *prōgignere* (PRO-, *gignere,* to beget)], *n.* An ancestor in the direct line, a forefather, a parent; (*fig.*) a predecessor, an original. ***progenerate,** *v.t.* **progenitorial** (-tôr' i àl), *a.* **progenitress, -trix,** *n.* **progenitorship,** *n.* **progeniture,** *n.* Begetting, generation; offspring.

progeny (proj' ė ni) [O.F. *progenie,* L. *progeniem,* nom. *-ies,* as prec.], *n.* Offspring of human beings, animals, or plants; children, descendants; (*fig.*) issue, results, consequences; *descent, lineage.

progeria (prō jēr' i ȧ) [PRO-, Gr. *geras,* old age], *n.* Premature old age.

proggins [PROG (2)].

proglottis (prò glot' is) [Gr. (PRO-, *glōtta,* tongue)], *n.* (*pl.* **-ides,** -i dēz) A segment of a tape-worm forming a distinct animal with genital organs. **proglottic,** *a.*

prognathic (prog năth' ik), **prognathous** (prog' nȧ thůs) [PRO-, Gr. *gnathos,* jaw], *a.* Having the jaws projecting, as Negroes; projecting (of the jaws). **prognathism** (prog' nȧ thizm), *n.*

prognosis (prog nō' sis) [L. and Gr., from *progignōskein* (PRO-, *gignōskein,* to know)], *n.* (*pl.* **-oses**) An opinion as to the probable result of an illness; a forecast, a prediction.

prognostic (prog nos' tik) [M.E. and O.F. *pronostique,* med. L. *prognōsticon,* Gr. *prognōstikon,* as prec.], *n.* A sign or indication of a future event; an omen, a token; a prediction, a forecast; (*Med.*) a symptom; *a prognosis. *a.* Foreshowing; indicative of something future by signs or symptoms. **prognosticable,** *a.* **prognosticate,** *v.t.* To foreshow by present signs; to foreshadow, to presage, to betoken. **prognostication** (-kā' shůn), *n.* **prognosticative** (-nos′ tik ȧ tiv), *a.* **prognosticator** (-nos′ ti kā tȯr), *n.*

programme (prō′ grăm) [F., from L. and Gr. *programma* (PRO-, *graphein*, to write)], *n.* A list of the successive items of any entertainment, public ceremony, etc.; (*fig.*) a plan or outline of proceedings or actions to be carried out. *v.t.* To arrange a programme for; (*fig.*) to plan, to design (to carry out). **programme music,** *n.* Music intended to suggest a definite series of scenes, incidents, etc.

progress (prō′ grės, prog′ rės) [L. *progressus*, p.p. of *progredī* (PRO-, *gradī*, to walk)], *n.* A moving or going forward; movement onward, advance, growth, development; *a journey of state. *v.i.* (prȯ gres′) To move forward, to advance; to be carried on, to proceed; to advance, to develop; to make improvement. **in progress:** Going on, proceeding. **progression** (-gresh′ ŭn), *n.* Progress, motion onward; (*Mus.*) a regular succession of notes or chords in melody or harmony; (*Math.*) regular or proportional advance by increase or decrease of numbers. **arithmetical progression** [ARITHMETIC]. **geometrical progression** [GEOMETRY]. **progressional,** *a.* **progressionist,** *n.* A believer in or advocate of social and political progress; one who believes in the perfectibility of man and society; one who believes that organisms have advanced from lower to higher forms, an evolutionist. **progressionism,** *n.* **progressist** (prō′ grės ist, prog′ rė sist), *a.* Advocating progress, esp. in politics. *n.* A progressive, a reformer.

progressive (prō gres′ iv), *a.* Moving forward or onward; advancing; improving; in a state of progression, proceeding step by step, successive; continuously increasing; believing in or advocating reform. *n.* A progressive person; an adherent of the Progressive Party. **Progressive Party:** A party advocating progress in municipal administration, esp. in the County of London. **progressive whist** or **bridge:** Whist or bridge played by a number of sets of players at different tables, each winning player moving to another table at the end of each hand or series of hands. **progressively,** *adv.* **progressiveness,** *n.* **progressivism,** *n.* The principles of a progressive or reformer.

progymnasium (prō jim nā′ zi ŭm, -gim na′ zi um) [G.], *n.* (*pl.* **-sia**) A school in Germany preparatory to the gymnasia.

prohibit (prȯ hib′ it) [L. *prōhibitus*, p.p. of *prōhibēre* (PRO-, *habēre*, to have)], *v.t.* To forbid authoritatively, to interdict; to hinder, to prevent. **prohibiter, prohibitor,** *n.* **prohibition** (-bish′ ŭn), *n.* The act of prohibiting; an order or edict prohibiting; the forbidding by law of the manufacture and the sale of intoxicating liquors for consumption as beverages. **prohibitionist,** *n.* One in favour of prohibiting the sale of intoxicating liquors; (*U.S.A.*) one who favours the imposition of prohibitive import duties, a protectionist. **prohibitive, -itory,** *a.* **prohibitively,** *adv.* **prohibitiveness,** *n.*

project (proj′ ėkt) [M.F. (F. *projet*), L. *prōjectum*, neut. p.p. of *prōicere* (PRO-, *jacere*, to throw)], *n.* A plan, a scheme, a design. *v.t.* (prȯ jekt′) To throw or shoot forward; to cause to extend forward or jut out; to throw out (a light, image, etc.); to contrive, to plan; (*fig.*) to make (an idea, etc.) objective; (*Geom.*) to draw straight lines from a given centre through every point of (a figure) so as to form a corresponding figure on a surface; to produce (such a projection); to make a projection of. *v.i.* To jut out, to protrude. **projectment,** *n.* A scheme, a design, a contrivance. **projector,** *n.* One who forms schemes; a promoter, esp. of bubble companies; an intrument or apparatus for projecting rays of light, images, etc. ***projecture,** *n.* A projecting or jutting out; a projection, a prominence.

projectile (prȯ jek′ tīl), *n.* A body projected or thrown forward with force, a missile, esp. one adapted for discharge from a heavy gun. *a.* Impelling forward; adapted to be forcibly projected, esp. from a gun.

projection (prȯ jek′ shŭn), *n.* The act or state of projecting, protruding, throwing, or impelling; a part or thing that projects, a prominence; the act of planning; the process of externalizing an idea or making it objective; a mental image viewed as an external object; the geometrical projecting of a figure; the representation of the terrestrial or celestial sphere, or a part of it, on a plane surface; (*Alch.*) the casting of a substance into a crucible; hence, the transmutation of metals; *a project, a scheme; (*Psych.*) the process whereby one ascribes to others mental factors and attributes really in ourselves. **Mercator's projection:** A projection of the surface of the earth upon a plane so that the lines of latitude are represented by horizontal lines and the meridians by parallel lines at right angles to them.

projective (prȯ jek′ tiv), *a.* Pertaining to or derived by projection; (*Geom.*) such that they may be derived from one another by projection (of two plane figures); externalizing or making objective. **projective property:** A property that remains unchanged after projection. **projectively,** *adv.*

prolapse (prȯ lăps′) [late L. *prōlapsus*, from L. *prōlaps-*, p.p. stem of *prōlābī* (PRO-, *lābī*, to slip)], *n.* (*Path.*) Prolapsus. *v.i.* To fall down or out. **prolapsus,** *n.* A falling down or slipping out of place of an organ or part, as the uterus or rectum.

prolate (prō′ lāt) [L. *prōlātus* (PRO-, *lātus*, p.p. of *-ferre*, to bear)], *a.* Extended in the direction of the longer axis, elongated in the polar diameter, opposed to oblate. **prolately,** *adv.* **prolateness,** *n.* **prolation** (-lā′ shŭn), *n.* (*Mediæval Music*) The time of music as measured by the division of semibreves into minims. **prolative** (prȯ lā′ tiv), *a.* (*Gram.*) Extending or completing the predicate.

proleg (prō′ leg), *n.* (*Ent.*) One of the soft, fleshy appendages or limbs of caterpillars, etc., distinct from the true legs.

prolegomenon (prō lė gom′ ė nȯn) [Gr., neut. p.p. of *prolegein* (PRO-, *legein*, to say)], *n.* (*usu. in pl.* **-ena**) An introductory or preliminary discourse prefixed to a book, etc. **prolegomenary, -enous,** *a.*

prolepsis (prȯ lep′-, -lēp′ sis) [L. and Gr. *prolēpsis* (PRO-, *lambanein*, to take)], *n.* Anticipation; (*Rhet.*) a figure by which objections are anticipated or prevented; (*Gram.*) the anticipatory use of a word as attributive instead of a predicate, as in *their murdered man* for *the man they intended to murder*; a prochronism. **proleptic, -al** (prȯ lep′ tik, -ăl), *a.* **proleptically,** *adv.*

proletaire (prō lė-, prol ė târ′) [F. *prolétaire*], *n.* A proletarian. **proletairism,** *n.*

proletarian (prō lė-, prol ė târ′ i ȧn) [L. *prōlētārius*, one of the lowest class of citizens, one whose only property is his children, from *prōles*, offspring], *a.* Of or pertaining to the common people. *n.* A member of the proletariat. **proletarianism,** *n.* **proletariat,** *n.* The class of the community without property, the wage-earners, the unprivileged classes. **proletary** (prō′ lė tȧr i), *a.* and *n.*

prolicide (prō′ li sīd) [L. *prōles*, offspring, -CIDE], *n.* The crime of killing one's offspring, esp. before or immediately after birth. **prolicidal** (-sī′ dȧl), *a.*

proliferation (prō lif ėr ā′ shŭn) [F. *prolifération*, from *prolifere*, proliferous, med. L. *prōlifer* (*prōles*, *-fer*, bearing)], *n.* Reproduction by budding or multiplication of parts; (*Bot.*) prolification. **proliferate** (-lif′ ėr āt), *v.i.* To grow or reproduce itself by proliferation. *v.t.* To produce by proliferation. **proliferative,** *a.* **proliferous,** *a.* (*Bot.*) Producing buds, shoots, etc., from leaves, flowers, etc.; producing new individuals from buds, parts, etc.; (*Zool. and Path.*) multiplying by proliferation. **proliferously,** *adv.*

prolific (prȯ lif′ ik) [F. *prolifique*, L. *prōlificus* (*prōles*, offspring, -FIC)], *a.* Bearing offspring, esp. abundantly; fruitful, productive, fertile; abounding (in); very productive (of); (*Bot.*) bearing fertile seed. **prolificacy, prolificity** (-fis′ i ti), **prolificness** (prȯ lif′ ik nės), *n.* **prolifically,** *adv.* **prolification** (-kā′ shŭn), *n.* The generation of animals or plants; (*Bot.*) the production of buds from leaves, etc., the development of an abnormal number of parts. **proligerous** (-lij′ ėr ŭs), *a.* Producing offspring, generative; (*Bot.*) proliferous.

prolix (prō′ liks, prȯ liks′) [F. *prolixe*, L. *prōlixus* (PRO-, *-lixus*, p.p. of *liquēre*, to flow)], *a.* Long and wordy; tedious, tiresome, diffuse. ***prolixious,** *a.* **prolixity** (-lik′ si ti), **prolixness,** *n.* **prolixly,** *adv.*

prolocutor (prȯ lok′ ū tȯr, prol′ ȯ-, prō′ lȯ kū tȯr) [L., from *prōloquī* (PRO-, *loquī*, to speak, p.p. *locūtus*)], *n.* A chairman or speaker, esp. of the Lower Houses of Convocation in the Church of England. **prolocutorship,** *n.*

prologue (prō′ log) [F., from L. *prologus*, Gr. *prologos* (PRO-, *logos*, speech)], *n.* An introductory discourse, esp. a poem introducing a play; (*fig.*) an act or event forming an introduction to some proceeding or occurrence; *the speaker of a prologue. ***prologist** (prō′ lȯ jist), *n.* **prologize,** *v.i.*

prolong (prȯ long′) [F. *prolonger*, late L. *prōlongāre* (PRO-, *longāre*, from *longus*, LONG (I))], *v.t.* To extend in duration; to lengthen, to extend in space or distance; to lengthen the pronunciation of. **prolongable,** *a.* ***prolongate** (prȯ long′ gāt), *v.t.* **prolongation** (-gā′ shŭn), *n.* The act of lengthening or extending; a lengthening in time or space; the part by which anything is lengthened; (*slang, pl.*) trousers. **prolonger** (prȯ long′ ėr), *n.*

prolonge (prȯ lonj′) [F., as prec.], *n.* (*Mil.*) A rope in three pieces connected by rings with a hook at one end and a toggle at the other, used for moving a gun, etc.

prolusion (prȯ lū′ zhŭn) [L. *prōlūsio*, from *prōlūdere* (PRO-, *lūdere*, to play)], *n.* A prelude; a preliminary essay, exercise, or attempt. **prolusory** (-loo′ sȯr i), *a.*

prom [PROMENADE CONCERT].

promenade (prom ė nad′, -nād′) [F., from *promener*, to walk, late L. *prōmināre*, to drive (PRO-, *mināre*, to threaten)], *n.* A walk, drive, or ride for pleasure, exercise, or display; a place for promenading, esp. a public walk; (*Am.*) a dance at college, school, unit or association. *v.i.* To take a walk, etc., for pleasure, exercise, or show. *v.t.* To take a promenade along, about, or through; to lead (a person) about, esp. for display. **promenade concert:** A concert at which the floor of the hall is left bare for the audience to stand when there is no room to walk about. **promenader,** *n.*

Promerops (prom′ ėr ops) [PRO-, Gr. *merops*, bee-eater], *n.* A S. African genus of birds, comprising the Cape promerops, *P. cafer*, with a slender, curved bill and a long tail.

Promethean (prȯ mē′ thė ȧn) [Gr. *Promētheus*, son of Iapetus, said to have stolen fire from Olympus, and to have bestowed it on mortals, teaching them the use of it and the arts of civilization], *a.* Of, pertaining to, or like Prometheus. **n.* A small glass tube, containing sulphuric acid, surrounded by an inflammable mixture, which it ignited on being crushed, used before the introduction of matches for getting a light quickly.

prominent (prom′ i nėnt) [F., from L. *prōminentem*, nom. *-ens*, pres.p. of *prōminēre*, to project (PRO-, *minēre*, from *minæ*, projections, threats)], *a.* Standing out, jutting, projecting, protuberant; conspicuous; distinguished. **prominence, -nency,** *n.* **prominently,** *adv.*

promiscuous (prȯ mis′ kū ŭs) [L. *prōmiscuus* (PRO-, *miscēre*, to MIX)], *a.* Mixed together in a disorderly manner; of different kinds mingled confusedly together; indiscriminate, not restricted to a particular person, kind, sex, etc.; (*colloq.*) fortuitous, accidental, casual. **promiscuity** (-kū′ i ti), *n.* Sexual promiscuousness; hetærism or communal marriage. **promiscuously** (-mis′ kū ŭs li), *adv.* **promiscuousness,** *n.*

promise (prom′ is) [L. *prōmissum*, neut. p.p. of *prōmittere* (PRO-, *mittere*, to send)], *n.* A verbal or written engagement to do or forbear from doing some specific act; that which is promised; (*fig.*) ground or basis of expectation. *v.t.* To engage to do or not do; to engage to give or procure; to make a promise of something to; (*fig.*) to give good grounds for expecting. *v.i.* To bind oneself by a promise; to give grounds for favourable expectations; *to become surety (for). **breach of promise** [BREACH]. **land of promise** or **promised land:** The land of Canaan promised to Abraham and his seed; (*fig.*) heaven; any place of expected happiness or prosperity. **to promise oneself:** To expect confidently. **to promise well** or **ill:** To hold out favourable or unfavourable prospects. **promise-breaker,** *n.* One who violates his promises. **promisee** (prom i sē′), *n.* (*Law*) One to whom a promise is made. **promiser** (prom′ i sėr), *n.* **promising,** *a.* Giving grounds for expectation or hope; hopeful, favourable. **promisingly,** *adv.* **promisor,** *n.* (*Law*) One who enters into a covenant. ***promisorily,** *adv.* **promissory,** *a.* Containing or of the nature of a promise, esp. a promise to pay money. **promissory note:** A signed engagement to pay a sum of money to a specified person or the bearer at a stated date or on demand.

promontory (prom′ ȯn tȯr i) [L. *prōmontōrium* (PRO-, *mons montis*, MOUNT)], *n.* A headland; a point of high land projecting into the sea; (*Anat.*) a rounded protuberance. **promontoried,** *a.*

promote (prȯ mōt′) [L. *prōmōtus*, p.p. of *prōmovēre* (PRO-, *movēre*, to MOVE)], *v.t.* To forward, to advance, to contribute to the growth, increase, or advancement of; to support, to foster, to encourage; to raise to a higher rank or position, to exalt, to prefer; to organize and float (a joint-stock company, etc.); (*Chess*) to raise (a pawn) to the rank of queen. **promoter,** *n.* One who or that which promotes or furthers, esp. one who promotes a joint-stock company (usu. in an unfavourable sense); the plaintiff in an ecclesiastical suit. **promoterism,** *n.* The practice of floating joint-stock companies. **promotion** (-mō′ shŭn), *n.* Advancement in position. **on promotion:** Awaiting, expecting, or preparing oneself for promotion; on one's good behaviour. **promotive** (-mō′ tiv), *a.*

prompt (prompt) [F., from L. *promptum*, nom. *-tus*, p.p. of *prōmere* (PRO-, *emere*, to take)], *a.* Acting quickly or ready to act as occasion demands; done, made, or said with alacrity; *inclined, disposed. *n.* Time allowed for payment of a debt as stated in a prompt-note; the act of prompting, or the thing said to prompt an actor, etc. *v.t.* To urge or incite (to action or to do); to instigate; to suggest to the mind, to inspire, to excite (thoughts, feelings, etc.); to assist (a speaker, actor, etc.) when at a loss, by suggesting the words forgotten. **prompt-book,** *n.* A copy of the play for the use of the prompter at a theatre. **prompt-note,** *n.* A note reminding a purchaser of a sum due and the date of payment. **prompt-side,** *n.* The side of a stage on which the prompter stands, usu. to the left of the spectator. **prompter,** *n.* One who prompts, esp. one employed at a theatre to prompt actors. **promptitude, promptness,** *n.* **promptly,** *adv.* ***promptuary,** *n.* A storehouse, a repository; a note-book, a digest. ***prompture,** *n.*

promulgate (prom′ ŭl-, prō′ mŭl gāt) [L. *prōmulgātus*, p.p. of *prōmulgāre*, etym. doubtful, perh. corr. of *prōvulgāre* (PRO-, *vulgus*, the crowd)], *v.t.* To make known to the public; to publish abroad, to disseminate; to announce publicly. **promulgation** (-gā′ shŭn), *n.* **promulgator,** *n.* ***promulge** (prȯ mŭlj′), *v.t.* ***promulger,** *n.*

promuscis (prȯ mŭs′ is) [L., var. of PROBOSCIS], *n.* (*Ent.*) The proboscis of the Hemiptera and some other insects.

pronaos (prȯ nā′ os) [L. and Gr. (PRO-, *naos*, temple)], *n.* (*Gr. and Roman Ant.*) The area immediately before a temple enclosed by the portico; the vestibule.

pronate (prō′ nāt) [late L. *prōnātus*, p.p. of *prōnāre*, from *prōnus*, PRONE], *v.t.* To lay (a hand or fore limb) prone so as to have the palm downwards. **pronation** (-nā′ shŭn), *n.* **pronator,** *n.* (*Anat.*) A muscle of the forearm employed to turn the palm downwards.

prone (prōn) [L. *prōnus*], *a.* Leaning or bent forward or downward; lying with the face downward, opp. to supine; lying flat, prostrate; sloping downwards, descending steeply or vertically; disposed, inclined, apt, propense. **pronely,** *adv.* **proneness,** *n.*

prong (prong) [etym. doubtful], *n.* A forked instrument; one of the spikes of a fork; a sharp-pointed instrument or spike-like projection. *v.t.* To pierce, stab, or prick with a prong. **prongbuck, pronghorn,** or **prong-horned antelope:** A N. American ruminant, *Antilocapra americana.* **prong-hoe,** *n.* A kind of hoe with prongs to break clods. **pronged,** *a.*

pronograde (prō′ nō grād) [L. *prōnus*, PRONE, *gradi*, to walk], *a.* (*Zool.*) Carrying the body horizontally, as quadrupeds.

pronominal (prō nom′ i năl) [late L. *prōnōminālis*, from *prōnōmen*, *-minis*, pronoun], *a.* Pertaining to or of the nature of a pronoun. **pronominally,** *adv.*

prononcé (prō non′ sā) [F., p.p. of *prononcer*, to PRONOUNCE], *a.* (*fem.* ***-cée***) Pronounced, emphatic, obvious.

pronotary [PROTHONOTARY].

pronotum (prō nō′ tŭm) [mod. L. (PRO-, Gr. *nōton*, back)], *n.* (*Ent.*) The dorsal part of the prothorax of an insect.

pronoun (prō′ noun) [PRO-, NOUN, after L. *prōnōmen* or F. *pronom*], *n.* A word used in place of a noun to denote a person or thing already mentioned or implied.

pronounce (prō nouns′) [M.E. *pronunce*, O.F. *pronuncier*, late L. *prōnuntiāre* (PRO-, *nuntiāre*, to announce, from *nuntius*, messenger)], *v.t.* To utter articulately; to utter formally, officially, or rhetorically; to declare, to affirm. *v.i.* To articulate; to declare one's opinion (on, for, against, etc.). **n.* Pronouncement. **pronounceable,** *a.* **pronounced,** *a.* Strongly marked, emphatic, decided; conspicuous, obvious. **pronouncedly** (-sĕd li), *adv.* **pronouncement,** *n.* A statement. **pronouncer,** *n.* **pronouncing,** *a.* Pertaining to, indicating, or teaching pronunciation.

pronunciamento (prō nŭn si ȧ men′ tō) [Sp.], *n.* (*pl.* ***-tos***) A manifesto, a proclamation, esp. one issued by revolutionaries in Spanish-speaking countries.

pronunciation (prō nŭn si ā′ shŭn) [L. *prōnuntiātio*, from *prōnuntiāre*, to PRONOUNCE], *n.* The act or mode of pronouncing words, etc.; (*colloq.*) the correct pronouncing of words, etc.; the art or act of speaking in public with propriety and grace. **pronunciability** (prō nŭn shi ȧ bil′ i ti), *n.* **pronuncial** (-nŭn′ shi ăl), *a.* ***pronunciative, -tory** (prō nŭn′ si-, -shi ȧ tiv, -tŏr i) [L. *prōnuntiātivus*, as prec.], *a.* Declarative, dogmatical.

procemium [PROEM].

proof (proof) [M.E. *preove*, *preve*, O.F. *prueve*, late L. *proba*, from *probāre*, to PROVE], *n.* The act of proving, a test, a trial; testing, assaying, experiment; demonstration; convincing evidence of the truth or falsity of a statement, charge, etc., esp. oral or written evidence submitted in the trial of a cause; (*Sc. Law*) evidence taken before a judge, or a trial before a judge instead of by jury; the state or quality of having been proved or tested; proved impenetrability, esp. of armour; a standard degree of strength in spirit; a trial impression from type for correction; an impression of an engraving taken with special care before the ordinary issue is printed; a first or early impression of a photograph, coin, medal, etc.; rough edges left in a book to show it has not been cut down; *experience. *a.* Proved or tested as to strength, firmness, etc.; impenetrable; able to resist physically or morally (*often in comb.*); used in testing, verifying, etc.; of a certain degree of alcoholic strength. *v.t.* To make proof, esp. waterproof. **armour of proof:** Armour proved impenetrable to ordinary weapons, missiles, etc. **proof before letters:** A proof taken of an engraving, etc., before the inscription is appended. **waterproof** [WATER]. **proof-plane,** *n.* A disk-shaped conductor with insulating handle used in measuring the electrification of a body. **proof-reader,** *n.* A person employed by a printer to correct proofs. **proof-reading,** *n.* **proof-sheet,** *n.* A sheet of printer's proof. **proofless,** *a.*

pro-ostracum (prō os′ trȧ kŭm) [PRO-, Gr. *ostrakon*, potsherd, shell], *n.* (*Palæont.*) The anterior prolongation of the guard or rostrum of a belemnite or other cephalopod. **pro-otic** (prō ō′ tik, -ot′ ik) [OTIC], *a.* In front of the ear. *n.* One of three pro-otic bones usually found in the skulls of lower vertebrates.

prop (1) (prop) [M.E. *proppe*, cp. Dut. *proppe*, etym. doubtful], *n.* A support, esp. a loose or temporary one; a buttress, a pillar, a stay; (*fig.*) a person supporting a cause, etc. *v.t.* (*past & p.p.* **propped**) To support or hold (up) with or as with a prop; to support, to hold up (of a prop).

prop (2) (prop), *n.* (*Theat.*) A stage property.

prop (3) (prop), *abbr.* An aeroplane propeller. **prop-jet engine:** An aircraft engine with a turbine-driven propeller.

prop (4) [Austral. colloq.], *v.i.* (Of a horse) to come to a sudden halt, to pull up sharply.

propædeutic (prō pē dū′ tik) [G. *propaideuein* (PRO-, *paideuein*, to teach, from *pais paidos*, child), -IC], *a.* Pertaining to or of the nature of introductory or preparatory study. *n.pl.* Preliminary learning or instruction introductory to any art or science.

propaganda (prop ȧ găn′ dȧ) [PROPAGATE], *n.* An organization, scheme or other means of propagating tenets, doctrines, systems, etc.; (*Pol.*) statements of facts or policy the real purpose of which differs from their apparent purpose; the twisting or fabrication of news to serve political ends. **Propaganda,** *n.* (*R.-C. Ch.*) A congregation of cardinals charged with all matters connected with foreign missions. **College of the Propaganda:** The college in Rome where missionary priests are trained. **propagandism,** *n.* **propagandist,** *n.* One devoted to or engaged in propaganda. *a.* Propagandistic. **propagandistic** (-dis′ tik), *a.* **propagandize** (-găn′ dīz), *v.t.* and *i.*

propagate (prop′ ȧ gāt) [L. *prōpāgātus*, p.p. of *prōpāgāre*, to propagate by layers (PRO-, *pāg-*, stem of *pangere*, to set, to fix)], *v.t.* To cause to multiply by natural generation or other means; to reproduce; to cause to spread or extend; to diffuse, to disseminate; to impel forward, to transmit, to cause to extend in space. *v.i.* To be reproduced or multiplied by natural generation or other means; to have offspring. **propagable,** *a.* **propagation** (-gā′ shŭn), *n.* The act of propagating; dissemination, diffusing; extension or transmission through space. **propagative** (prop′ ȧ gā tiv), *a.* **propagator,** *n.*

***propale** (prō pāl′) [late L. *prōpalāre*, from *prōpalam* (PRO-, *palam*, openly)], *v.t.* (*chiefly Sc.*) To publish; to reveal, to disclose.

proparoxytone (prō pȧ rok′ si tōn) [Gr. *proparoxutonos*], *a.* (*Gr. Gram.*) Having an acute accent on the antepenultimate syllable. *n.* A proparoxytone word.

propedutic [PROPÆDEUTIC].

propel (prō pel′) [L. *prōpellere* (PRO-, *pellere*, to drive)], *v.t.* (*past & p.p.* **propelled**) To drive forward; to cause to move forward or onward. **propellant,** *a.* That propels. *n.* That which propels, esp. the explosive driving a bullet. **propeller,** *n.* One who or that which propels, esp. a screw-propeller. **screw-propeller:** A rotating device, usu. consisting of two to four blades set at an angle and twisted like the thread of a screw, at the end of a shaft driven by steam, electricity, etc., for propelling a vessel through the water or an aeroplane or air-ship through air. **propelment,** *n.*

***propend** (prŏ pend′) [L. *prōpendēre* (PRO-, *pendēre,* to hang)], *v.t.* To incline, to have a leaning or propensity. ***propendent,** *a.* Hanging forward or outward.

propensity (prŏ pen′ si ti) [L. *prōpensus,* propense, p.p. of *prōpendēre,* as prec., -ITY], *n.* Bent, natural tendency, inclination. ***propense,** *a.* Inclined, disposed. ***propensely,** *adv.* ***propension, *propenseness,** *n.* Propensity.

proper (prop′ ėr) [M.E. and O.F. *propre,* L. *proprium,* nom. *proprius,* one's own], *a.* *Own; belonging or pertaining exclusively or peculiarly (to); (*Gram.*) designating an individual person, animal, place, etc. (of nouns and names); correct, just; suitable, appropriate; fit, becoming; decent, respectable; real, genuine, according to strict definition (*usu. following its noun*); (*colloq.*) well-made, good-looking; (*Her.*) in the natural colours. **proper fraction:** A fraction less than unity. **properly,** *adv.* In a proper manner, fitly, suitably; rightly, justly, correctly, accurately; (*colloq.*) thoroughly, quite. **properness,** *n.*

properispomenon (prŏ per i spō′ mė nŏn, -spom′ ė nŏn) [Gr. *properispōmenon*], *a.* (*Gr. Gram.*) Having the circumflex accent on the penultimate syllable. *n.* A properispomenon word.

properly, etc. [PROPER].

property (prop′ ėr ti) [M.E. *proprete,* O.F. *proprieté,* L. *proprietātem,* nom. *-tas,* from *proprius,* PROPER], *n.* Peculiar or inherent quality; character, nature; that which is owned; a possession, possessions, an estate; exclusive right of possession, ownership; (*pl.*) articles required for the production of a play on the stage. **v.t.* To appropriate; to make a property of, to exploit, to use as one's tool; to endow with properties or qualities. **property-man, -master, -woman,** *n.* The man or woman in charge of theatrical properties. **property qualification:** A qualification for voting, holding an office, etc., derived from the possession of property. **property-tax,** *n.* A direct tax on property. **propertied,** *a.*

prophasis (prof′ ȧ sis) [Gr. (PRO-, *phasis,* PHASE)], *n.* (*Med.*) Prognosis.

prophecy (prof′ ė si) [O.F. *profecie* (F. *prophétie*), late L. *prophētīa,* Gr. *prophēteia,* as foll.], *n.* A prediction, esp. one divinely inspired; the prediction of future events; the gift or faculty of prophesying; (*Bibl.*) a book of prophecies; *the public interpretation of Scripture.

prophesy (prof′ ė sī) [O.F. *profecier, -phecier, -phesier,* as prec.], *v.t.* To predict, to foretell; (*fig.*) to herald. *v.i.* To utter prophecies; *to interpret Scripture, to preach. **prophesier,** *n.*

prophet (prof′ ėt) [M.E. and O.F. *prophete,* L. *prophēta,* Gr. *prophētēs* (PRO-, *phē-,* stem of *phanai,* to speak)], *n.* One who foretells future events, esp. under divine inspiration; a revealer or interpreter of the divine will; a religious leader, a founder of a religion; (*fig.*) a preacher or teacher of a cause, etc.; *an interpreter. **major prophets:** Isaiah, Jeremiah, Ezekiel, Daniel. **minor prophets:** The prophets in the Old Testament from Hosea to Malachi. **the Prophet:** Mohammed. **the prophets:** The prophetic writers of the Old Testament; the books written by them. **prophetess,** *n.* **prophethood, prophetship,** *n.* **prophetic, -al** (-fet′ ik, -ȧl), *a.* Of, pertaining to, or containing prophecy; predictive, anticipative. **prophetically,** *adv.* ***propheticalness,** *n.* **propheticism** (-fet′ i sizm), *n.*

prophylactic (prof i lăk′ tik) [F. *prophylactique,* Gr. *prophulaktikos,* from *prophulassein* (PRO-, *phulassein,* to guard)], *a.* Protecting against disease; preventive. *n.* A preventive medicine. **prophylaxis** (-lăk′ sis), *n.*

***propine** (prŏ pīn′) [L. *propīnāre,* Gr. *propinein* (PRO-, *pinein,* to drink)], *v.t.* To drink (health, fortune, etc.) to; to present, to propose; to reward. *n.* A present, a gift.

propinquity (prŏ ping′ kwi ti) [O.F. *propinquité,* L. *propinquitātem,* nom. *-tas,* from *propinquus,* near, from *prope,* near], *n.* Nearness in time, space, or relationship; similarity. **propinquate,** *v.i.* To approach.

propitiate (prŏ pish′ i āt) [L. *propitiātus,* p.p. of *propitiāre,* from *propitius,* propitious, perh. a term in augury (PRO-, *petere,* to fly)], *v.t.* To appease, to conciliate; to render favourable. **v.i.* To atone. **propitiable,** *a.* **propitiation** (-ā′ shŭn), *n.* The act of propitiating; atonement, esp. that of Christ; *a propitiatory gift. **propitiator** (-pish′ i ā tŏr), *n.* **propitiatory,** *a.* Intended or serving to propitiate. *n.* A propitiation; the mercy-seat, esp. as symbolizing Christ. **propitious,** *a.* Favourable; disposed to be kind or gracious; auspicious, suitable (for, etc.). **propitiously,** *adv.* ***propitiousness,** *n.*

proplasm (prō′ plăzm) [L. and Gr. *proplasma* (PRO-, PLASM)], *n.* A mould, a matrix. ***proplastic** (prŏ plăs′ tik), *n.* The art of making moulds for casting. **propodium** (-pō′ di ŭm) [mod. L. (Gr. *pous podos,* foot)], *n.* (*Zool.*) The anterior of the three lobes of the foot in some molluscs. **propodial,** *a.* **propodite** (prop′ ō dīt), *n.* The penultimate joint of the typical limb of a crustacean. **propoditic** (-dit′ ik), *a.* **propolis** (prop′ ŏ lis) [Gr., a suburb, bee-glue (*polis,* city)], *n.* A resinous substance obtained by bees from buds, etc., and used to cement their combs, stop up crevices, etc., bee-glue.

proponent (prŏ pō′ nėnt) [L. *prōpōnens -ntem,* pres.p. of *prōpōnere,* to PROPOSE], *a.* Proposing. *n.* One who makes a proposal or proposition.

proportion (prŏ pôr′ shŭn) [F., from L. *proportiōnem,* nom. *-tio*) (PRO-, PORTION)], *n.* The comparative relation of one part or thing to another with respect to magnitude, number, or degree; ratio; due relation, suitable adaptation of one part or thing to others; a proportional part, a share; (*pl.*) dimensions; (*Math.*) equality of ratios between pairs of quantities; a series of such quantities; (*Arith.*) the rule by which from three given quantities a fourth may be found bearing the same ratio to the third as the second bears to the first, the rule of three. *v.t.* To adjust in suitable proportion; to make proportionate (to); to apportion. **geometrical, harmonic proportion** [GEOMETRY, HARMONIC]. **in proportion:** In the degree of measure, according as. **out of proportion:** Not in due relation as to magnitude, number, etc. **proportionable,** *a.* *Capable of being made proportional; being in proportion, corresponding, proportional; *well-proportioned, symmetrical. **proportionableness,** *n.* **proportionably,** *adv.* **proportional,** *a.* Having due proportion; pertaining to proportion; (*Math.*) having a constant ratio. *n.* A quantity in proportion with others, one of the terms of a ratio. **proportional representation:** (*Polit.*) A system of dealing with the voting at parliamentary elections by which due representation is afforded to minorities. **proportionalist,** *n.* One who makes designs according to the laws of proportion; an advocate of proportional representation. **proportionalism,** *n.* **proportionality** (-năl′ i ti), *n.* **proportionally** (-pôr′ shŏ nȧ′ li), *adv.* **proportionate,** *a.* In due or a certain proportion (to). *v.t.* (-nāt) To make proportionate or proportional. **proportionately,** *adv.* **proportionateness,** *n.* **proportioned,** *a.* (*usu. in comb.,* as *well-proportioned*). **proportionless,** *a.* Without proportion; unsymmetrical, shapeless. **proportionment,** *n.*

propose (prŏ pōz′) [F. *proposer*], *v.t.* To put forward, to offer, to present, for consideration, etc.; to nominate for election; to put forward as a design, to purpose, to intend. *v.i.* To make an offer, esp. of marriage. **proposal** (prŏ pō′ zȧl), **proposer,** *n.*

proposition (prop ŏ zish′ ŭn) [F., from L. *prōpositiōnem,* nom. *-tio,* as foll.], *n.* That which is propounded; a statement, an assertion; (*Log.*) a sentence in which something is affirmed or denied;

(*Math.*) a formal statement of a theorem or problem, sometimes with the demonstration; (*colloq.*) a proposal, a scheme proposed for consideration or adoption. **propositional,** *a.*

propound (prò pound') [from obs. *propone*, L. *prōpōnere* (PRO-, *pōnere*, to put), p.p. *prōpositus*], *v.t.* To state or set forth for consideration, to propose; (*Law*) to bring forward (a will, etc.) for probate. **propounder,** *n.*

propraetor (prō prē' tòr) [L., orig. *pro praetore*, (acting) for a praetor], *n.* A praetor who at the expiration of his term of office was made governor of a province.

proprietor (prò prī' ė tòr) [formerly *proprietary*, late L. *proprietārius*, from *proprietas*, PROPERTY], *n.* An owner, one who has the exclusive legal right or title to anything, whether in possession or not, a possessor in his own right. **proprietary,** *n.* A body of proprietors collectively; proprietorship; *a proprietor, esp. (*U.S.A.*) a grantee of a proprietary colony, as of Maryland. *a.* Of or pertaining to a proprietor or proprietorship; owned as property. **proprietorial** (-tôr' i ål), *a.* **proprietorially,** *adv.* **proprietorship** (prò prī' ė tòr ship), *n.* **proprietress, -trix,** *n.*

propriety (prò prī' ė ti) [F. *propriété*], *n.* The quality of being conformable to an acknowledged or correct standard or rule; fitness, correctness, rightness; correctness of behaviour, becomingness; *exclusive ownership, property; *individuality, particular nature, particularity, idiosyncrasy.

proprium (prō' pri ŭm) [L., neut. of *proprius*, own], *n.* (*pl.* **-pria**) A distinctive attribute, essential nature; (*Log.*) a property.

pro-proctor (prō prok' tòr), *n.* One acting for or under a proctor.

props (props) [short for PROPERTIES], *n.pl.* (*colloq.*) Theatrical properties; a property-man.

propterygium (prop tėr ij' i ŭm), *n.* (*pl.* **-gia**) (*Ichthyol.*) The anterior basal portion of a pectoral fin. **propterygial,** *a.*

***propugnation** (prō pŭg nā' shŭn) [L. *prōpugnātio*, from *prōpugnāre* (PRO-, *pugnāre*, to fight)], *n.* Defence, vindication. **propugnator** (prō pŭg nā' tòr), **propugner** (prò pū' nėr), *n.* A defender, a champion.

propulsion (prò pŭl' shŭn) [F., from L. *prōpellere*, to PROPEL], *n.* The act of propelling, a driving forward; an impulse. **propulsive, *-sory,** *a.*

propylaeum (prō pi lē' ŭm) [L., from Gr. *propuleion* (PRO-, *pulē*, a gate)], *n.* (*pl.* **-laea**) A gateway or entrance, esp. one of imposing architectural character, to a temple, etc. **the Propylaea:** The entrance to the Athenian Acropolis. **propylon** (prop' i lon), *n.* (*pl.* **-lons, -la**): A propylaeum, esp. before an Egyptian temple.

pro-rate (prō rāt') [L. *pro rata*, for the rate, in proportion], *v.t.* (*Am.*) To distribute proportionally. **pro-rateable,** *a.*

pro-rector (prō rek' tòr), *n.* The deputy of a rector or president, esp. in a German University.

prorogue (prò rōg') [F. *proroger*, L. *prōrogāre*, to extend, to defer (PRO-, *rogāre*, to ask)], *v.t.* To put an end to the meetings of Parliament without dissolving it. *v.i.* To be prorogued. **prorogate** (prō' rò gāt), *v.t.* (*chiefly Sc.*) To prorogue. **prorogation** (-gā' shŭn), *n.*

pros- [Gr., *pros*, prep.], *pref.* To, towards; before, in addition.

prosaic (prō sā' ik) [med. L. *prōsaicus*, from *prōsa*, PROSE], *a.* Pertaining to or resembling prose; unpoetic, unimaginative, dull, commonplace. **prosaically,** *adv.* **prosaicness, prosaism** (prō' sā izm), **prosaicism** (prō sā' i sizm), *n.* **prosaist,** *n.* A writer of prose; a prosaic person.

proscenium (prō sē' ni ŭm) [L., from Gr. *proskēnion* (PRO-, *skēnē*, SCENE)], *n.* (*pl.* **-nia**) The part of a stage between the curtain or drop-scene and the orchestra; (*Ant.*) the space in front of the scenery, the stage.

proscribe (prò skrīb') [L. *prōscrībere* (PRO-, *scrībere*, to write)], *v.t.* To publish the name of, as doomed to death, forfeiture of property, etc., to outlaw; to banish, to exile; to denounce as dangerous; to interdict, to forbid. **proscriber,** *n.* **proscription** (-skrip' shŭn), *n.* **proscriptive,** *a.*

prose (prōz) [F., from L. *prōsa*, from *prōsa* (*prorsa*) *ōrātio*, straightforward discourse, masc. *prorsus* (PRO-, *versus*, p.p. of *vertere*, to turn)], *n.* Ordinary written or spoken language not in metre, opposed to verse; (*fig.*) commonplaceness; a tedious or unimaginative discourse. *a.* Written in or consisting of prose; (*fig.*) dull, commonplace, prosaic. *v.i.* To write or talk in a dull, tedious manner. *v.t.* To write or utter in prose; to turn into prose. **proseman, proser,** *n.* [PROSIFY, PROSY].

prosector (prò sek' tòr) [late L. *prōsector* (PRO-, SECTOR)], *n.* A dissector, esp. one who dissects bodies in preparation for lectures, demonstrations, etc. ***prosect,** *v.t.* and *i.* **prosection,** *n.* **prosectorial** (-tôr' i ål), *a.* **prosectorium,** *n.* (*pl.* **-ria**) A building or laboratory where prosection is performed. **prosectorship,** *n.*

prosecute (pros' ė kūt) [L. *prosecūtus*, p.p. of *prosequī* (PRO-, *sequī*, to follow)], *v.t.* To pursue or follow up with a view to attain or accomplish; to carry on (work, trade, etc.); to take legal proceedings against; to seek to obtain by legal process. *v.i.* To act as a prosecutor. **prosecutable,** *a.* **prosecution** (-kū' shŭn), *n.* The act of prosecuting; the exhibition of a charge against an accused person before a court; the instituting and carrying on of a civil or criminal suit; the prosecutor or prosecutors collectively. **prosecutor** (pros' ė kū tòr), *n.* **public prosecutor:** An officer conducting criminal proceedings on behalf of the public. **prosecutrix,** *n.*

proselyte (pros ė līt) [M.E. and O.F. *proselite*, late L. *proselytus*, Gr. *prosēlutos*, from *prosēluth-*, aorist stem of *proserchesthai* (PROS-, *erchesthai*, to come)], *n.* A new convert to some religion, party or system, esp. a gentile convert to Judaism. **v.t.* To proselytize. **proselytism,** *n.* **proselytize,** *v.t.* and *i.* **proselytizer,** *n.*

prosencephalon (pros ėn sef' å lon), *n.* (*pl.* **-la**) (*Anat.*) The anterior part of the brain comprising the cerebral hemispheres, etc., and sometimes including the olfactory lobes. **prosencephalic** (-făl' ik), *a.*

prosenchyma (prō sen' ki må) [Gr. *enchuma*, infusion, after PARENCHYMA], *n.* (*Bot.*) Tissue composed of elongated thick-walled cells closely interpenetrating, esp. fibro-vascular tissue. **prosenchymatous** (-kim' å tŭs), *a.*

prosify (prō' zi fī), *v.t.* To turn into prose; to render prosaic. *v.i.* To write prose. **prosification** (-kā' shŭn), *n.* **prosifier,** *n.*

prosit (prō' sit) [L., may it be to your good], *int.* May it benefit you, success (used in drinking a health).

pro-slavery (prō slā' vėr i), *a.* Advocating slavery.

prosobranch (pros' ō brăngk) [Gr. *prosō*, forward, *branchia*, gills], *n.* (*Zool.*) A prosobranchiate. *a.* Prosobranchiate. **prosobranchiate** (-brăng' ki åt), *a.* Having the gills anterior to the heart. *n.* One of the Prosobranchiata, an order of aquatic gasteropods with the gills anterior to the heart.

prosody (pros' ō di) [L. and Gr. *prosōdia* (PROS-, ODE)], *n.* The science of versification, formerly a branch of grammar. **prosodiacal** (-dī' å kål), **prosodial** (-sō' di ål), **prosodic** (-sod' ik), *a.* **prosodian** (-sō' di ån), **prosodist** (pros' ō dist), *n.*

prosopopoeia (pros ō pò pē' yå) [L., from Gr. *prosōpopoiia* (*prosōpon*, person, *poiein*, to make)], *n.* A rhetorical figure by which abstract things are represented as persons, or absent persons as speaking.

prospect (pros' pekt) [L. PROSPECTUS], *n.* An

extensive view; the way a house, etc., fronts or looks; mental outlook; expectation, ground of expectation; (*Mining*) an indication of the presence of ore, a sample of ore for testing, the mineral obtained by testing; (*pl.*) expectation of money to come or of an advancement in career; a prospective customer. *v.i.* (prò spekt') To search, to explore, esp. for minerals; to promise well or ill (of a mine). *v.t.* To search or explore (a region) for minerals; to promise (a good or poor yield); *to look over, to survey. ***prospection** (-pek' shùn), *n.*

prospective (prò spek' tiv), *a.* Pertaining to the future; anticipated, expected, probable, characterized by foresight. *n.* Prospect, view, anticipation; *a field-glass, a telescope. ***prospective glass:** A magic crystal in which future events were supposed to be visible; a field-glass, a telescope. **prospectively,** *adv.* **prospectiveness,** *n.* **prospectless** (pros' pekt lès), *a.*

prospector (prò spek' tòr), *n.* One who searches for minerals or mining sites.

prospectus (prò spek' tùs) [L., a look-out, a prospect, from *prōspicere* (PRO-, *specere*, to look)], *n.* A descriptive circular announcing the main objects and plans of a commercial scheme, institution, literary work, etc.

prosper (pros' pėr) [F. *prospérer*, L. *prosperāre*, to cause to succeed, from *prosper*, favourable, fortunate], *v.t.* To make successful or fortunate. *v.i.* To succeed; to thrive. **prosperous,** *a.* Successful, thriving, making progress, or advancement; favourable, fortunate, auspicious. **prosperity** (-per' i ti), ***prosperousness,** *n.* **prosperously,** *adv.*

***prospicience** (pros pish' i èns) [L. *prōspiciens -ntem*, pres.p. of *prōspicere*, see PROSPECT], *n.* The act of looking forward, foresight.

prostate (pros' tāt) [med. L. *prostata*, Gr. *prostatēs*, one who stands before (PRO-, *sta-*, stem of *histanai*, to stand)], *n.* (*Anat.*) The prostate gland. *a.* Situated in front. **prostate gland:** A gland situated before the neck of the bladder in male mammals. **prostatectomy** (prō stă tek' tō mi), *n.* Surgical removal of the prostate gland. **prostatic** (-tăt' ik), *a.* **prostatic body** or **gland:** The prostate. **prostatitis** (-ti' tis), *n.* (*Path.*) Inflammation of the prostate.

prosternum (prò stĕr' nùm) [PRO-, STERNUM], *n.* (*Ent.*) The ventral segment of the thorax of an insect.

prosthesis (pros' thė sis) [L. and Gr. (PROS-, *thesis*, a thing laid down, from *tithenai*, to put)], *n.* (*Gram.*) The addition of one or more letters to the beginning of a word; (*Surg.*) the addition of an artificial part to supply a defect. **prosthetic** (-thet' ik), *a.* **prosthetically,** *adv.*

prostitute (pros' ti tūt) [L. *prostitūtus*, p.p. of *prostituere* (PRO-, *statuere*, to place, to set)], *v.t.* To offer (a woman, oneself, etc.) for lewd purposes; to offer or sell for base or unworthy purposes; to devote to base uses. *a.* Prostituted. *n.* A woman who offers herself for indiscriminate sexual intercourse, esp. for hire; a base hireling. **prostitution** (tū' shùn), *n.* **prostitutor** (pros' ti tū tòr), *n.*

prostrate (pros' trāt) [L. *prostrātus*, p.p. of *prosternere* (PRO-, *sternere*, to lay flat)], *a.* Lying flat or prone; lying in a horizontal position, procumbent, lying in a posture of humility or at mercy; overcome, exhausted. *v.t.* (pròs trāt', pros' trāt) To lay flat; to cast (oneself) down, esp. in reverence or adoration (before); to throw down, to overthrow, to overcome, to demolish; to reduce to physical exhaustion. **prostration** (-trā' shùn), *n.*

prostyle (prō' stīl) [F., from L. *prostylos*, Gr. *prostulos* (PRO-, *stulos*, STYLE (2))], *a.* (*Arch.*) Having a row of columns, usu. four, entirely in front of the building. *n.* A portico supported on columns entirely in front of the building, opp. to those having antæ at the sides.

prosy (prō' zi), *a.* Dull, tedious, tiresome. **prosily,** *adv.* **prosiness,** *n.*

prosyllogism (prò sil' ò jizm) [L. *prosyllogismus*, Gr. *prosyllogismos*], *n.* (*Log.*) A syllogism so connected with another that the conclusion of the first is the major or the minor premise of the second.

prot- [PROTO-], *pref.* **protagon** (prō 'tà gon) [G. (Gr. *agon*, neut. pres.p. of *agein*, to lead)], *n.* (*Chem.*) A fatty nitrogenous compound containing phosphorus, found in brain and nerve tissue.

protagonist (prō tăg' ò nist) [Gr. *prōtagōnistēs* (*agōnistēs*, actor, see AGONISTIC)], *n.* The leading character or actor in a Greek play; a leading character, advocate, champion, etc.

protasis (prot' à sis) [late L. and Gr. (PRO-, *tasis*, from *teinein*, to stretch)], *n.* (*pl.* **-ases**) A clause containing the antecedent, esp. in a conditional sentence; the first part of a classic drama, in which the characters are introduced and the argument explained; *a proposition, a maxim. **protatic** (-tăt' ik), *a.*

protean (prō' tė àn, prò tē' àn) [PROTEUS], *a.* Readily assuming different shapes or aspects; variable, changeable. **proteiform** (prō' tė i fôrm), *a.*

protect (prò tekt') [L. *prōtectus*, p.p. of *prōtegen* (PRO- *tegere*, to cover)], *v.t.* To shield, defend, or keep safe (from or against injury, danger, etc.); (*Polit. Econ.*) to support (industries) against foreign competition by imposing duties on imports; (*Finance*) to provide funds so as to guarantee payment of (bills, etc.). **protectingly,** *adv.* **protection** (prò tek' shùn), *n.* The act of protecting; the state of being protected; that which protects, a covering, shield, or defence; a passport, a safe conduct; (*Am.*) a certificate of citizenship of the U.S. issued to seamen by the customs authorities; *a document granting exemption from arrest in civil suits; (*Polit. Econ.*) the promotion of home industries by bounties or by duties on imports. **protectionism,** *n.* The doctrine or system of protecting home industries against foreign competition. **protectionist,** *n.* and *a.* **protective,** *a.* **protective custody:** (*Law*) Detention before trial in order to ensure an accused's personal safety. **protective detention:** (*Law*) Detention of a criminal to protect Society from his further activities. **protectively,** *adv.* **protectiveness,** *n.*

protector (prò tek' tòr) [M.E. and O.F. *protectour* (F. *protecteur*), L. *prōtectōrem*, nom. *-tor* (PROTECT, -OR)], *n.* One who protects against injury or evil, etc.; one in charge of the kingdom during the minority, incapacity, etc., of the sovereign; title of Oliver Cromwell, Lord Protector of the Commonwealth (1653–58), and his son Richard Cromwell (1658–59). **protectoral, *protectorial** (-tôr' i àl), *a.* **protectorate** (prò tek' tò ràt), *n.* Protection, usu. combined with partial control, of a weak State by a more powerful one; territory under such protection; the office of protector of a kingdom; the period of this, esp. that of Oliver and Richard Cromwell. **protectorless,** *a.* **protectorship,** *n.* **protectory,** *n.* (*R.-C.*) An institution for the care of destitute or vicious children. **protectress, -trix,** *n.*

protégé (prot' ā zhā) [F., p.p. of *protéger*, to PROTECT], *n.* (*fem.* **-gée,** -zhā) One under the protection, care, or patronage of another.

proteid (prō' tė id), *n.* (*Chem.*) A name applied to the amorphous organic substances now usually called proteins.

proteiform [PROTEAN].

protein (prō' tēn) [F. *protéine* or G. *protëin* (Gr. *prōteios*, from *prōtos*, first, -IN)], *n.* (*Chem.*) A complex and unstable organic compound, containing carbon, oxygen, hydrogen, and nitrogen, usu. with some sulphur, found in all organic bodies and forming an essential constituent of animal foods; orig. applied to a nitrogenous compound supposed to form the basic material of all organisms; the essential principle of food, obtained from albumen, fibrin, or casein. **proteinaceous** (-nā' shùs), **proteinic** (-in' ik), **proteinous** (-tē' i nùs), *a.*

***protend** (prȯ tend′) [L. *protendere* (PRO-, *tendere*, to stretch)], *v.t.* To hold out; to stretch forth; to extend. ***protense** (prȯ tens′), ***protension** (-ten′ shŭn), **protensity** (-ten′ si ti), *n.* ***protensive,** *a.*

proteolysis (prō tė ol′ i sis) [PROTE-IN, Gr. *lusis*, loosening, resolving, from *luein*, to loosen], *n.* (*Chem.*) The resolution or splitting up of the proteins by the process of digestion or the application of ferments. **proteolytic** (-lit′ ik), *a.*

proter-, protero- [Gr. *proteros*, comp. of *pro*, before], *comb. form.* Former, anterior. **proterandrous** (prot ėr ăn′ drŭs) [Gr. *anēr andros*, man], *a.* (*Bot.*) Having the stamens mature before the pistil; (*Zool.*) having the male organs or individuals in a zooid colony mature before the female. **proterandrousness, proterandry,** *n.* **proterogynous** (prot ėr oj′ i nŭs) [Gr. *gunē*, woman], *a.* (*Bot.*) Having the pistil mature before the stamens. **proterogyny,** *n.*

protest (prȯ test′) [F. *protester*, L. *prōtestārī* (PRO-, *testārī*, to declare, to witness, from *testis*, witness)], *v.i.* To make a solemn affirmation; to make a formal declaration against some act or proposition. *v.t.* To affirm or declare formally or earnestly; to make a formal declaration, usu. by a notary public, that payment of (a bill) has been demanded and refused; *to appeal to; *to proclaim, to publish. *n.* (prō′ test) The act of protesting; a solemn or formal declaration of opinion, usu. of dissent or remonstrance, a formal declaration by the holder of the non-payment of a bill; a written declaration by the master of a ship, usu. before a magistrate, consul, etc., stating the circumstances attending an injury or loss of a ship or cargo. **protestation** (-tā′ shŭn), *n.* A solemn affirmation or declaration; a solemn declaration of dissent, a protest; a vow or promise; (*Law*) a declaration in pleading. ***protestator, protester,** *n.* **protestingly,** *adv.*

Protestant (prot′ ės tȧnt) [F., pres.p. of *protester*, to PROTEST], *n.* One of the party adhering to Luther at the Reformation, who at the second Diet of Spires (1529) protested against the decree of the majority involving submission to the authority of the Roman Catholic Church; a member of a Church upholding the principles of the Reformation, or (loosely) of any Church not within the Roman communion; (*usu.* prȯ tes′ tȧnt) one who makes a protest. *a.* Pertaining to the Protestants, or to Protestantism; (*usu.* prȯ tes′ tȧnt) making a protest. **Protestantism,** *n.* **Protestantize,** *v.t.* and *i.*

protestation, etc. [PROTEST].

Proteus (prō′ tūs) [L. and Gr., a marine deity, Neptune's herdsman, who had power to change his shape at will], *n.* A changeable, shifty, or fickle person or thing; (*Zool.*) a genus of amphibians, resembling a salamander, found in Austrian caves; a group of bacteria; *an amœba. **proteus animalcule:** An amœba.

protevangelium (prō tev ȧn jėl′ i ŭm) [PROT-, L. *evangelium*, EVANGEL], *n.* The first announcement of the Gospel; an apocryphal gospel attributed to St. James the Less. **protevangelist** (-văn′ jė list), *n.*

prothalamion, -mium (prō thȧ lā′ mi ȯn, -ŭm) [coined by Spenser (PRO-, EPITHALAMIUM)], *n.* A song in honour of the bride and bridegroom before the wedding. **prothallium** (prȯ thăl′ i ŭm) [Gr. *thallion*, dim. of *thallos*, THALLUS], *n.* (*Bot.*) A cellular structure bearing the sexual organs in vascular cryptogams. **prothesis** (proth′ ė sis) [Gr. (*thesis*, a thing laid down, from *tithenai*, to put)], *n* The placing of the elements in readiness for use in the Eucharist; hence, a credence-table, or the part of a church in which this stands; (*Gram.*) prosthesis. **prothetic** (-thet′ ik), *a.*

prothonotary (prȯ thon′ ȯ tȧr i, prō thȯ nō′ tȧr i) [obs. F. *prothonotaire*, late L. *prōtonotārius*, Gr. *prōtonotarios* (PROTO-, L. *notārius*, NOTARY)], *n.* A chief clerk or notary; the chief clerk or registrar of a court, now chiefly in some American and foreign courts, and formerly of the Courts of Chancery, Common Pleas, and King's Bench; a member of the Roman Catholic College of Prothonotaries Apostolic who register the papal acts. **prothonotariat** (-târ′ i ȧt), *n.* **prothonotarial,** *a.* **prothonotaryship** (prȯ thon′ ȯ tȧr i ship), *n.*

prothorax (prȯ thôr′ ăks) [PRO- THORAX], *n.* (*Ent.*) The anterior segment of the thorax in insects. **prothoracic** (-thȯ răs′ ik), *a.*

prothysteron [HYSTERON-PROTERON].

Protista (prȯ tis′ tȧ) [Gr., neut. pl. of *prōtistos*, superl. of *prōtos*, first], *n.pl.* A name proposed by Haeckel, for a kingdom including microscopic organisms whose position (as animals or plants) was doubtful. **protist** (prō′ tist), *n.* Any individual of the Protista.

protium (prō′ ti ŭm) [Gr. *protos*, first], *n.* (*Chem.*) Ordinary hydrogen.

proto- [Gr. *prōtos*, first], *comb. form.* Chief; earliest, original, primitive; (*Chem.*) denoting that chemical compound in a series in which the distinctive element or radical combines in the lowest proportion with another element. **proto-Arabic, -Celtic, Egyptian, -Semitic,** etc., *a.* Denoting the primitive or original tribes, languages, arts, etc., of the Arabs, etc. **Protococcus** (prō tȯ kok′ ŭs) [Gr. *kokkos*, grain, seed], *n.* (*pl.* **-cocci,** -kok′ sī) (*Bot.*) A genus of unicellular algæ such as form the familiar green layers on damp stones, trees, timber, etc.

protocol (prō′ tȯ kol) [O.F. *prothocole* (F. *protocole*), med. L. *prōtocollum*, Gr. *protokollon*, orig. the first leaf glued to a MS. (PROTO-, *kolla*, glue)], *n.* The original draft of an official document or transaction, esp. minutes or a rough draft of a diplomatic instrument or treaty, signed by the parties to a negotiation; the formulary of diplomatic etiquette; the official formulas used in diplomatic instruments, charters, wills, etc. *v.i.* To draft protocols. *v.t.* To reduce to or record in a protocol. **protocolist,** *n.*

protogenic (prō tȯ jen′ ik), **protogenetic** (prō tȯ jė net′ ik) [Gr. *protogenes* (PROTO-, *gen-*, root of *gignesthai*, to be born), -IC], *a.* Primitive, of primitive or earliest origin or production. **protogine** (prō′ tȯ jin), *n.* (*Petrol.*) A variety of granite forming the central mass of Mont Blanc and other mountains in the Alps, having a foliated structure due to dynamic action. **protohippus** (prō tȯ hip′ ŭs) [Gr. *hippos*, horse], *n.* (*Palæont.*) An extinct quadruped about the size of a sheep, from the lower Pliocene in America, probably an ancestor of the horse. **protomartyr** (prō tȯ mar′ tėr) [med. L. (MARTYR)], *n.* A first martyr (applied esp. to St. Stephen); the first who suffers in any cause. **protonotary** [PROTHONOTARY]. **Protophyta** (prō tȯ fī′ tȧ) [Gr. *phuta*, plants, sing. *phuton*], *n.pl.* (*Bot.*) A primary division of the vegetable kingdom comprising plants of the lowest organization, usu. microscopic in size and unicellular. **protophyte** (prō′ tȯ fīt), *n.*

proton (prō′ ton) [Gr. *protos*, first], *n.* (*Elec.*) A particle occurring in atomic nuclei having an electric charge equal and opposite to that of the electron, and a mass 1840 times as great.

protoplasm (prō′ tȯ plăzm) [Gr. *prōtoplasma* (PROTO-, Gr. *plasma*, a moulded thing, from *plassein*, to mould)], *n.* The viscid semifluid substance composed of oxygen, hydrogen, carbon, and nitrogen, constituting the living matter from which all living organisms are developed. **protoplasmatic** (-măt′ ik), **protoplasmic** (-plăz′ mik), *a.*

protoplast (prō′ tȯ plăst) [F. *protoplaste*, late L. *prōtoplastus*, Gr. *protoplastos* (PROTO-, *plastos*, moulded, as prec.)], *n.* The first individual, esp. the first-created man; the original, the archetype, the model; (*Biol.*) a unit of protoplasm, a bioplast, a unicellular organism. **protoplastic** (-plăs′ tik), *a.*

protosalt (prō′ tȯ sawlt) [PROTO-, SALT], *n.* (*Chem.*) A salt corresponding to the protoxide of a metal. **protosulphide** (prō tȯ sŭl fīd) [SULPHIDE], *n.* (*Chem.*) One of a series of sulphides containing the lowest proportion of sulphur. **Prototheria** (prō tô thēr′ i ȧ) [Gr. *thēria*, beasts], *n.pl.* (*Zool.*) Huxley's name for the lowest division of mammals comprising the Monotremata and their ancestors. **protothere** (prō′ tô thēr). **prototherian** (-thēr i ȧn), *a.* and *n.*

prototype (prō′ tô tīp) [F., from Gr. *prototupon*], *n.* An original or primary type or model, an exemplar, an archetype. **prototypal** (-tī′ pȧl), **prototypic, -al** (-tip′ ik, -ȧl), *a.* **protoxide** (prō tok′ sīd) [OXIDE], *n.* (*Chem.*) A compound of oxygen and an element containing the lowest proportion of oxygen. **protoxydize,** *v.t.*

Protozoa (prō tô zō′ ȧ) [PROTO-, Gr. *zōa*, animals, sing. *zōon*], *n.pl.* (*sing.* **-zoon**) (*Zool.*) The lowest division of the animal kingdom, comprising those consisting of a single cell or a group of cells not differentiated into two or more tissues. **protozoal,** *a.* Of or pertaining to the Protozoa; (*Path.*) caused by the agency of Protozoa (of diseases). **protozoan,** *a.* and *n.* **protozoic,** *a.* (*Geol. and Palæont.*) Belonging to the strata in which the earliest traces of life are found; (*Zool.*) protozoal. **protozoology** (-zō ol′ ô ji), *n.* The branch of zoology dealing with the Protozoa.

protract (prô trăkt′) [L. *prōtractus*, p.p. of *prōtrahere* (PRO-, *trahere*, to draw)], *v.t.* To extend in duration, to prolong; (*Surv.*) to draw (a map, plan, etc.) to scale, esp. with a scale and protractor. **protractedly,** *adv.* **protracter,** *n.* **protractile** (-til, -tīl), *a.* Capable of extension (of the organ, etc., of an animal). **protraction** (-trak′ shůn), *n.*

protractor (prô trăk′ tôr), *n.* An instrument, usu. in the form of a graduated arc, for laying down angles on paper, etc.; a muscle that protracts or extends a limb; *(*Surg.*) an instrument for drawing extraneous bodies out of a wound.

protrude (prô trood′) [L. *prōtrūdere* (PRO-, *trūdere*, to thrust, p.p. *trūsus*)], *v.t.* To thrust forward or out; to cause to project or issue; to obtrude. *v.i.* To project, to be thrust forward. **protrudent,** *a.* **protrusible,** *a.* **protrusile** (-sil, -sīl), *a.* **protrusion** (-troo′ zhůn), *n.* **protrusive** (-siv), *a.* **protrusively,** *adv.*

protuberant (prô tū′ bėr ȧnt) [L. *prōtūberans -ntem*, pres.p. of *prōtūberāre* (PRO-, TUBER)], *a.* Swelling, bulging out, prominent. **protuberance,** *n.* A swelling, a prominence, a knob, a bump. **protuberantly,** *adv.* ***protuberate,** *v.i.* ***protuberation** (-ā′ shůn), *n.*

protyle (prō′ tīl), *n.* (*Chem.*) A word introduced by Sir Wm. Crookes (1886) to express the idea of the original primal matter existing before the differentiation of the chemical elements.

proud (proud) [A.-S. *prūt*, perh. from O.F. *prud* (F. *preux*), prob. ult. from L. *prōdesse*, to be of use to (PROD-, *esse*, to be)], *a.* Having high or inordinate self-esteem; haughty, arrogant; having a due sense of dignity; elated, exultant, feeling honoured, pleased, gratified; (*fig.*) of lofty mien, grand, imposing; swollen, in flood (of a stream); inspired by pride (of words, looks, etc.); inspiring pride, noble, grand (of deeds, etc.). **proud flesh:** Swollen flesh growing about a healing wound. **proudish,** *a.* **proudly,** *adv.* ***proudness,** *n.*

prove (proov) [O.F. *prover* (F. *prouver*), L. *probāre*, to test, to approve], *v.t.* (*p.p.* **proved,** proovd, ***proven,** proov′ ėn, prō′ vėn) *To test, to try by experiment, to make trial of; to put to a test, to try by a standard; to have experience of; to take a proof impression from; to establish or demonstrate by argument, reasoning, or testimony; to establish the authenticity or validity of; (*Math.*) to show or ascertain the correctness of, as by a farther calculation. *v.i.* To be found by experience or trial; to turn out to be; to turn out (to be); *to make a trial or attempt. **not proven:** (*Sc. Law*) Not proved (a verdict given when there is not sufficient evidence to convict). **provable,** *a.* **provableness,** *n.* **provably,** *adv.* **prover,** *n.* One who or that which proves or tests; (*Engraving*) one employed in printing proof impressions; (*Law*) an approver.

provection (prô vek′ shůn) [late L. *prōvectio*, from *provehere* (PRO-, *vehere*, to carry)], *n.* (*Philol.*) The mutation of voice consonants to breath consonants, esp. in Celtic languages; the carrying on of a terminal letter to the first syllable of the succeeding word (as in *nickname* from *an eke-name*).

proveditor (prô ved′ i tôr), **provedore** (prov ė dôr′) [It. *proveditore* (now *provveditore*), ult. from L. *prōvidēre*, to PROVIDE], *n.* A commissioner, inspector, governor, or other officer of the Venetian republic; a purveyor, a caterer.

proven [PROVE].

provenance (prov′ ė nȧns) [F., from *provenant*, pres.p. of *provenir*, L. *prōvenīre* (PRO-, *venīre*, to come)], *n.* Origin, source.

Provençal (prov *an* sal′) [F.], *n.* A native of Provence (France); the language of Provence. *a.* Pertaining to Provence, its language, or inhabitants.

***provend** (prov′ ėnd) [O.F. *provende*, corr. of med. L. *præbenda*, PREBEND], *n.* Food, provisions, provender; orig. a prebend, or the allowance of food to each inmate of a monastery.

provender (prov′ ėn dėr) [O.F., var. of prec.], *n.* Dry food for beasts, fodder; (*facet.*) provisions, food; *provend.

provenience [PROVENANCE].

prover [PROVE].

proverb (prov′ ėrb) [F. *proverbe*, L. *prōverbium* (PRO-, *verbum*, word)], *n.* A short, pithy sentence, containing some truth or wise reflection proved by experience or observation; a maxim, a saw, an adage; (*fig.*) a typical example, a byword; a short dramatic composition illustrating some well-known popular saying; (*pl.*) a round game played on well-known sayings. *v.t.* To speak of in a proverb, to make a byword of; to provide with a proverb. **proverbial** (-vĕr′ bi ȧl), *a.* **proverbiality** (-ăl′ i ti), *n.* **proverbialism,** *n.* **proverbialist,** *n.* A writer, composer, or collector of proverbs. **proverbialize,** *v.t.* and *i.* **proverbially,** *adv.*

proviant (prov′ i ȧnt) [G., from It. *provianda*, PROVEND], *n.* Provisions, esp. for an army.

provide (prō vīd′) [L. *prōvidēre* (PRO-, *vidēre*, to see)], *v.t.* To procure or prepare beforehand; to furnish, to supply; to equip (with); to lay down as a preliminary condition, to stipulate; (*Eccles.*) to appoint (to a benefice); (of the Pope) to grant the right to be appointed (to a benefice not yet vacant). *v.i.* To make preparation or provision (for or against); to furnish means of subsistence (for). **provided,** *a.* Supplied, furnished; provided in readiness; laid down, stipulated. *conj.* On the understanding or condition (that). **provided school:** A public elementary school provided by the local authority. **provider,** *n.* **providing,** *n.* The action of supplying, furnishing, or preparing beforehand. *pres.p.* or *conj.* Provided, on the understanding or condition (that).

providence (prov′ i dėns) [F., from L. *prōvidentia*, as prec.], *n.* Foresight, timely care, prevision; frugality, economy, prudence; the beneficent care or control of God over His creatures; God or nature regarded as exercising such care; a manifestation of such care. **provident,** *a.* **providential** (-den′ shȧl), *a.* Due to or effected by divine providence; lucky, fortunate, opportune. **providentially,** *adv.* **providently** (prov′ i dėnt li), *adv.* ***providentness,** *n.*

province (prov′ ins) [F., from L. *prōvincia*, business or duty, province, etym. doubtful], *n.* (*Rom. Hist.*) A country or territory beyond the confines of Italy under a Roman governor; a large administrative division of a kingdom, country, or State; (*Eccles.*) the territory under the authority of an archbishop or metropolitan; (*pl.*) districts at a distance from the metropolis; (*fig.*) proper sphere of action, business, knowledge, etc.

provincial (prô vin′ shȧl), *a.* Pertaining to a province; constituting a province; of, pertaining to, or characteristic of the provinces; narrow, rustic, rude, unpolished. *n.* One who belongs to a province or the provinces; (*Eccles.*) the superior of an order, etc., in a province. **provincialism,** *n.* The quality of being provincial; a mode of speech, thought, behaviour, etc., or a word or expression, peculiar to a province or the provinces; use of such peculiarities as an offence against style, etc. **provincialist,** *n.* **provinciality** (-ăl′ i ti), *n.* **provincialize,** *v.t.* **provincially,** *adv.*

provision (prŏ vizh′ ŭn) [F., from L. *prōvīsiōnem*, from *prōvidēre*, to PROVIDE], *n.* The act of providing; previous preparation, a precautionary measure; a stipulation or condition providing for something; a supply of food, etc.; (*pl.*) victuals, eatables, etc.; *(*Eccles.*) appointment to a benefice not yet vacant. *v.t.* To provide with provisions. **provisional,** *a.* Provided for present need; temporary, not permanent. **provisionality** (-năl′ i ti), **provisionalness,** *n.* **provisionally,** *adv.* ***provisionary,** *a.* **provisionment,** *n.*

proviso (prŏ vī′ zō) [L., being provided that, see PROVIDE], *n.* (*pl.* **-os**) A provisional condition, a stipulation; a clause in a covenant or other document rendering its operation conditional.

provisor (prŏ vī′ zŏr) [M.E. and A.-F. *provisour* (F. *proviseur*), L. *prōvīsōrem*, nom. *-sor*, as prec.], *n.* One appointed, esp. by the Pope, to a benefice before the death of the incumbent; the purveyor, steward, or treasurer of a religious house; a vicar-general. **provisory,** *a.* Conditional; provisional. **provisorily,** *adv.*

provocation [PROVOKE].

provoke (prŏ vōk′) [O.F., *provoker* (F. *provoquer*), L. *prōvocāre* (PRO-, *vocāre*, to call)], *v.t.* To rouse; to incite or stimulate to action, anger, etc.; to irritate, to incense, to exasperate; to instigate, to call forth, to cause. **provocation** (prov ŏ kā′ shŭn), *n.* **provocative** (prŏ vok′ ȧ tiv), *a.* Tending to provoke; irritating, annoying, esp. with the intention to excite anger or rouse to action. *n.* A provocative action, thing, word, etc. **provocatively,** *adv.* **provocativeness,** *n.* ***provokable,** *a.* ***provokement,** *n.* **provoker,** *n.* **provoking,** *a.* Tending to provoke, annoying, exasperating. **provokingly,** *adv.*

provost (prov′ ŏst) [A.-S. *prōfost*, *prāfost*, L. *præpositus*, cp. PRÆPOSITOR], *n.* One appointed to superintend or hold authority; the head of a college; (*Eccles.*) the head of a chapter, a prior, a dignitary in a cathedral corresponding to a dean; in Germany, a Protestant clergyman in charge of the principal church; (*Sc.*) the chief magistrate in a municipal corporation or burgh; (*Hist.*) an officer in charge of a body of men, establishment, etc., a steward, a provost-marshal. **Lord Provost:** The chief magistrate of Edinburgh, Glasgow, Aberdeen, Perth and Dundee. **provost-marshal** (prŏ vō′ mar′ shȧl), *n.* (*Mil.*) A commissioned officer, the head of the military police in a camp or in the field; (*Nav.*) an officer in charge of prisoners awaiting court-martial; (*West Indies*) a chief of police; (*Hist.*) a French semi-military public officer. **provostship, provostry,** *n.*

prow (1) (prou) [F. *proue*, prob. from L. and Gr. *prōra*, rel. to *pro*, before], *n.* The fore part of a vessel, the bow.

***prow** (2) (prou) [O.F. *prou* (F. *preux*), prob. from L. *prōdesse*, see PROUD], *a.* Brave, valiant, worthy.

prowess (prou′ es) [O.F. *prouesse*, from *prou*, see prec.], *n.* Valour, bravery, gallantry.

prowl (proul) [M.E. *prollen*, etym. doubtful], *v.i.* To rove (about) stealthily as if in search of prey. *v.t.* To go through or about in this way. *n.* Prowling. **prowler,** *n.* **prowlingly,** *adv.*

proximal (prok′ si mȧl) [L. *proximus*, superl. of *prope*, near], *a.* (*Anat.*) Nearest the centre of the body or the point of attachment, opposed to distal. **proximally,** *adv.*

proximate (prok′ si mȧt) [late L. *proximātus*, p.p. of *proximāre*, as prec.], *a.* Nearest, next; immediately preceding or following; approximate. **proximate cause:** That which immediately precedes and produces the effect. **proximately,** *adv.* **proximity** (-sim′ i ti), *n.* Immediate nearness in place, time, relation, etc., esp. of kinship. ***proximo*** (prok′ si mō), *a.* In or of the month succeeding the present.

proxy (prok′ si) [contr. from PROCURACY], *n.* The agency of a substitute for a principal; one deputed to act for another, esp. in voting; a document authorizing one person to act or vote for another; a vote given under his authority. *a.* Done, made, etc., by proxy. **proxyship,** *n.*

Prozymite (proz′ i mīt) [Gr. *prozumitēs*, from *prozumion*, leaven (PRO-, *zumē*, leaven)], *n.* (*Eccles. Hist.*) One of those using leavened bread in the Eucharist, opposed to Azymite.

prude (prood) [F., *n.*, and *a.* from O.F. *prude* (fem. of *prou*, *prod*, PROW (2), or from *prudefemme*, cp. *prud'homme*)], *n.* A woman who affects great modesty or propriety. **prudery, prudishness,** *n.* **prudish,** *a.* **prudishly,** *adv.*

prudent (proo′ dėnt) [F., from L. *prūdentem*, nom. *-dens*, *prōvidens*, PROVIDENT], *a.* Cautious, discreet, circumspect, worldly-wise, careful of consequences; *correct, decorous. **prudence,** *n.* **prudential,** *a.* Actuated or characterized by prudence; worldly-wise, mercenary. *n.pl.* Prudential considerations, matters of practical wisdom; prudential maxims or precepts. **prudentialism, prudentiality** (-ăl′ i ti), *n.* **prudentialist,** *n.* **prudentially,** *adv.* **prudently,** *adv.*

prudery [PRUDE].

prud'homme (pru dom′) [F., from O.F. *prodhomme* (PROW (2), *homme*, man)], *n.* (*Hist.*) A trusty man; a member of a French board composed of masters and workmen, for arbitration in trade disputes.

pruinose (proo′ i nōs) [L. *pruīnōsus*, frosty, from *pruīna*, hoar-frost], *a.* (*Nat. Hist.*) Covered with a powdery substance or bloom, frosted. **pruinescence** (-nes′ ėns), *n.* ***pruinous,** *a.*

prune (1) (proon) [F., from L. *prūnum*, Gr. *prounon*], *n.* The dried fruit of various kinds of *Prunus domestica*, the common plum; a plum; the colour of this, dark reddish-purple. **pruniferous** (-nif′ ėr ŭs), *a.*

prune (2) (proon) [O.F. *proignier*, etym. doubtful], *v.t.* To cut or lop off the superfluous branches, etc., from; to cut or lop (off, away, etc.); to free from anything superfluous; *to dress or trim, to preen. **pruner,** *n.* **pruning-hook, -knife, -shears,** *n.* Instruments of various forms for pruning trees, etc.

prunella (1) (prŭ nel′ ȧ) [etym. doubtful (cp. F. *prunelle*, perh. plum-colour, rel. to PRUNE (1))], *n.* A smooth dark woollen stuff, used for making the uppers of shoes and gaiters, and formerly for clergymen's and barristers' gowns.

Prunella (2) (prŭ nel′ ȧ) [var. of med. L. *brunella*, dim. of *brūnus*, brown], *n.* A throat disorder, quinsy, angina; (*Bot.*) a genus of labiate plants, with purplish, bluish, or white flowers, comprising the common self-heal.

prunello (prŭ nel′ ō) [It.], *n.* A superior variety of prune, usu. made from greengages.

pruniferous [PRUNE (1)].

prunt (prŭnt) [perh. dial. var. of PRINT], *n.* A piece of ornamental glass laid on to or impressed on a glass vase or other object; a tool for making prunts.

prurient (proor′ i ėnt) [L. *prūriens -ntem*, pres.p. of *prūrīre*, to itch], *a.* Disposed to or characterized by lewd ideas; characterized by a morbid curiosity. **prurience, -ency,** *n.* **pruriently,** *adv.*

prurigo (proo rī′ gō), *n.* (*Path.*) A papular disease of the skin attended with intolerable itching. **pruriginous,** *a.* **pruritus,** *n.* Itching.

Prussian (prŭsh′ ȧn) [med. L. *Prussiānus* (*Pruzzi*, *Borussi*, -AN)], *a.* Of or pertaining to Prussia; overbearing. *n.* A native or inhabitant of Prussia. **Prussian blue:** A deep-blue pigment obtained from ferrocyanide of iron. **Prussian carp:** A small variety of the common carp. **Prussianism,** *n.* **Prussianize,** *v.t.* **Prussianizer,** *n.* **prussiate,** *n.* (*Chem.*) **prussic,** *a.* Of or derived from Prussian blue. **prussic acid:** Hydrocyanic acid, first obtained from Prussian blue.

pry (1) (prī) [M.E. *prien*, etym. doubtful], *v.i.* To look closely or inquisitively; to peep, to peer; to search or inquire curiously or impertinently (into). *v.t.* To search or find (out) inquisitively or impertinently. *n.* The act of prying. **prying,** *a.* **pryingly,** *adv.*

pry (2), *v.t.* [PRISE (1)]. **pryse** [PRICE, PRIZE (1)].

prytaneum (prit à nē' ùm) [L., from Gr. *prutaneion*, from *prutanis*, president], *n.* (*Gr. Ant.*) The public hall, esp. at Athens, in which the duties of hospitality were exercised towards ambassadors and citizens honoured with special distinction.

psalm (sam) [L. *psalmus*, Gr. *psalmos*, from *psallein*, to twang, to sing to the harp], *n.* A sacred song or hymn. **the Psalms:** A book of the Old Testament consisting of sacred songs, many of which are ascribed to David. **psalmist,** *n.* **the psalmist:** David or other composer of any of the Psalms. **psalmody** (sa'-, săl' mò di), *n.* The act, art, or practice of singing psalms, esp. in divine worship; psalms collectively. **psalmodic** (sa-, săl mod' ik), *a.* **psalmodist** (sa'-, săl' mò dist), *n.* A composer or singer of psalms. **psalmodize,** *v.i.* **psalmographer,** ***psalmographist** (sa-, săl mog' rà fèr, -fist), *n.* A writer of psalms. **psalmography,** *n.* **psalter** (sawl' tèr), *n.* The Book of Psalms; a book containing the Psalms for use in divine service, esp. the version of the Psalms in the Prayer Book or the Latin collection used in the R.-C. Church.

psalterium (sal-, sawl tēr' i ùm) [as foll.], *n.* The third stomach of a ruminant, the manyplies.

psaltery (sawl' tèr i) [O.F. *psalterie*, L. *psaltērium*, Gr. *psaltērion*, cp. prec.], *n.* A mediæval stringed instrument somewhat resembling the dulcimer, but played by plucking the strings. **psalterian** (săl-, sawl tēr' i àn), *a.* **psaltress** (sawl' três), *n.* A female player on the psaltery.

psammite (săm' īt) [F., from Gr. *psammos*, sand], *n.* (*Min.*) Sandstone. **psammitic** (sà mit' ik), *a.*

pschent (pshent) [Gr. *pschent*, Egypt. *p-skhent* (*p*, the, *skhent*, *sekhent*)], *n.* (*Egyptol.*) The double crown of ancient Egypt, combining the white pointed mitre of Upper Egypt and the red crown with square front of Lower Egypt.

psellism (sel' izm) [Gr. *psellismos*, from *psellos*, stammering], *n.* Any defect in speech, such as stammering, lisping, etc. **psellismology** (-mol' ò ji), *n.*

pseud-, pseudo- [Gr., from *pseudēs*, false], *comb. form.* False, counterfeit, spurious; closely resembling. **pseudæsthesia** (sū dēs thē' zi à) [cp. ANÆTHESIA], *n.* Imaginary sense of feeling in organs that have been removed. **Pseudechis** (sū' dè kis) [Gr. *echis*, viper], *n.* A genus of highly venomous snakes. **pseudechic** (-dek' ik), *a.* **pseudepigrapha** (sū dè pig' rà fà) [neut. pl. or Gr. *pseudepigraphos* (*epigraphein*, to inscribe, see EPIGRAPH)], *n.pl.* Spurious writings, esp. uncanonical writings ascribed to Scriptural authors, etc. **pseudepigraphal, pseudepigraphical** (-grăf' i kàl), *a.* **pseudepigraphy** (-è pig' rà fi), *n.* The ascription of false names of authors to books. **pseudoarchaic** (sū dò ar kā' ik) [ARCHAIC], *a.* Artificially or affectedly archaic, archaistic. **pseudoarchaism** (-ar' kā izm), **pseudo-archaist,** *n.* **pseudoblepsia** (sū dò blep' si à) [Gr. *blepsis*, looking], *n.* (*Path.*) Deceptive vision. **pseudocarp** (sū' dò karp) [Gr. *karpos*, fruit], *n.* (*Bot.*) A fruit composed of other parts besides the ovary. **pseudo-Christian,** *a.* Falsely or pretendedly Christian; a pretended Christian. **pseudo-Christianity,** *n.* **pseudo-classic,** *a.* Erroneously supposed to be classic. **pseudo-classicism,** *n.* **pseudo-dipteral** (-dip' tèr àl) [DIPTERAL], *a.* (*Arch.*) Having a single peristyle placed at the same distance from the walls as the outer row of columns in a dipteral temple. **pseudo-Gothic,** *a.* Sham Gothic.

pseudograph (sū' dò grăf) [Gr. *pseudographia* (PSEUDO-, -GRAPH)], *n.* A spurious writing, a literary forgery. **pseudography** (-dog' rà fi), *n.* **pseudologer, -gist** (sū dol' ò jèr, -jist) [-LOGER], *n.* One who makes false statements, a liar. **pseudological** (-loj' i kàl), *a.* **pseudology** (-dol' ò ji), *n.* Untruthful speaking; the art of lying. **pseudomartyr** (sū dò mar' tèr) [G. *pseudomartur*], *n.* A pretended martyr.

pseudomorph (sū' dò môrf) [PSEUDO-, Gr. *morphē*, form], *n.* A mineral having the crystalline form of another. **pseudomorphic, -ous** (-môr' fik, -fùs), *a.* **pseudomorphism,** *n.* **pseudomorphosis** (-fō' sis), *n.*

pseudonym (sū' dò nim) [Gr. *pseudōnumos* (PSEUD-, *onoma*, Æolic, *onuma*, name)], *n.* A fictitious name, esp. a *nom de guerre*. **pseudonymity** (-nim' i ti), *n.* **pseudonymous** (-don' i mùs), *a.* **pseudonymously,** *adv.*

pseudopodium (sū dò pō' di ùm) [PSEUDO-, Gr. *podion*, dim. of *pous podos*, foot], *n.* (*pl.* **-podia**) (*Zool.*) A process formed by the protrusion of the protoplasm of a cell or a unicellular animal, serving for locomotion, ingestion of food, etc.; (*Bot.*) a false pedicel in mosses, etc. **pseudopodial,** *a.* **pseudoscope** (sū' dò skōp) [-SCOPE], *n.* A stereoscopic instrument for producing an apparent reversion of relief, making convex objects appear concave and vice versa. **pseudoscopic** (-skop' ik), *a.* **pseudoscopically,** *adv.* **pseudoscopy** (-dos' kò pi), *n.* **pseudostome** (sū' dò stōm) [Gr. *pseudostoma* (*stoma*, mouth)], *n.* (*Zool.*) The mouth of the larva of an echinoderm; the opening of a secondary canal in a sponge to the exterior. **pseudostomosis** (-mō' sis), *n.* **pseudostomotic** (-mot' ik), **pseudostomous** (-dos' tò mùs), *a.*

pshaw (pshaw) [an instinctive sound], *int.* An exclamation of contempt, impatience, disdain, or dislike. *a.* This exclamation. *v.i.* To say 'pshaw' (at). *v.t.* To express contempt for thus.

psilanthropism (sī lăn' thrò pizm) [Gr. *psilanthrōpos* (*psilos*, bare, mere, *anthrōpos*, man), -ISM], *n.* The doctrine that Christ was a mere man. **psilanthropic** (-throp' ik), *a.* **psilanthropist** (-lăn' thrò pist), *n.*

psilosis (sī' lō sis) [Gr. *psilos*, bare], *n.* (*Path.*) Sprue; shedding of the hair.

psittaceous (si tā' shùs), **psittacine** (sit' à sīn) [L. *psittacus*, parrot, -ACEOUS, -INE], *a.* Belonging or allied to the parrots; parrot-like. **psittacosis** (sit à kō' sis), *n.* (*Path.*) A disease of parrots communicable to man, with a high mortality.

psoas (sò' às) [Gr., acc. pl. of *psoa*, mistaken for the sing.], *n.* (*Anat.*) Either of the two large hip-muscles. **psoatic** (sō ăt' ik), *a.*

psora (sôr' à) [L. and Gr.], *n.* (*Path.*) The itch or an analogous skin-disease. **psoriasis** (sò rī' à sis), *n.* A dry scaly skin-disease. **psoriatic** (-ăt' ik), *a.* **psoriatiform,** *a.* **psoric** (sor' ik), *a.* Pertaining to or suffering from itch. *n.* A remedy for the itch.

psych- [PSYCHO-], *comb. form.*

Psyche (sī' ki) [Gr. *psuchē*, breath, life, soul], *n.* (*Gr. Ant.*) A Greek nymph, the personification of the soul, beloved of Eros or Cupid; the soul, the spirit, the mind; (*Ent.*) a genus of day-flying moths; (*Astron.*) one of the asteroids.

psychiater, psychiatrist (sī kī' à tèr, -trist) [PSYCHE], *n.* One who treats diseases of the mind. **psychiatry,** *n.* The study and treatment of mental diseases. **psychiatric,** *a.*

psychic (sī' kik) [Gr. *psuchikos*], *a.* Pertaining to the human soul, spirit, or mind; of or pertaining to phenomena that appear to be outside the domain of physical law, spiritualistic. *n.* One having psychic powers, a medium; (*pl.*) psychology. **psychic force:** A non-physical force supposed to be the agent in spiritualistic phenomena. **psychi-**

cal, *a.* Psychic. **psychically,** *adv.* **psychicism,** *n.* **psychicist,** *n.*

psycho- [PSYCHE], *comb. form.* Mental; psychical.

psycho-analysis (sī kō ȧ năl′ i sis), *n.* A method devised by Sigmund Freud for exploring the unconscious mind as a form of treatment for functional nervous diseases. **psychoanalytic, -al,** *a.*

psycho-dynamic (sī kō dī năm′ ik), *a.* Of or pertaining to mental action. *n.pl.* The science of the laws of mental action. **psychogenesis** (sī′ kȯ jen′ ė sis) [GENESIS], **psychogony** (sī kog′ ȯ ni), *n.* The genesis or development of the mind or soul. **psychogenetic, -al** (-jė net′ ik, -ȧl), **psychogonical** (-gon′ i kȧl), *a.* **psychogram** (sī′ kȯ grăm) [-GRAM], *n.* A writing supposed to be set down by spiritual agency. **psychograph,** *n.* An instrument used for this purpose. **psychographer** (-kog′ rȧ fėr), *n.* **psychographic** (-grăf′ ik), *a.* **psychography** (-kog′ rȧ fi), *n.*

psychology (sī kol′ ȯ ji) [PSYCHO-, -LOGY], *n.* The science of the human mind or soul; a system or theory of mental laws and phenomena; a treatise on this. **psychological** (-loj′ i kȧl), *a.* Pertaining or relating to psychology. **psychological moment:** The critical moment, the exact time for action, etc. **psychological warfare:** The use of propaganda to reduce enemy morale. **psychologically,** *adv.* **psychologist** (sī kol′ ȯ jist), *n.* **psychologize,** *v.t.* and *i.*

psychomancy (sī′ kȯ măn si) [PSYCHO-, -MANCY], *n.* Divination by means of communication with spirits; *necromancy.

psychometer (sī kom′ ė tėr), *n.* An instrument for measuring times of reactions, etc.; one who measures mental processes. **psychometry** (sī kom′ ė tri) [-METRY], *n.* The measurement of the duration of mental processes; the occult faculty of divining by touching a physical object, the character, surroundings, experiences, etc., of persons who have touched it. **psychometric, -al** (-met′ rik, -ȧl), *a.* **psycho-motor** (sī kȯ mō′ tȯr) [MOTOR], *a.* Inducing movement by the action of the mind or will. **psycho-neurosis,** *n.* (*Path.*) A nervous disorder due to mental conflict. **psychonosology** (sī kȯ nȯ sol′ ȯ ji) [NOSOLOGY], *n.* The science of mental disease.

psychopath (sī′ kō păth), *n.* One suffering from mental derangement. **psychopathic,** *a.* **psychopathist,** *n.* One who studies or treats this. **psychopathology,** *n.*

psychophysics (sī kō fiz′ iks), *n.* The science of the relations between mind and body, or the physical basis of mental phenomena. **psycho-physicist,** *n.*

psychophysiology (sī kō fiz i ol′ ȯ ji), *n.* The branch of physiology treating of mental phenomena.

psychosis (sī kō′ sis), *n.* (*pl.* **psychoses**), *n.* (*Path.*) Mental derangement, esp. one not due to organic lesion or neurosis.

psychosomatic (sī kō sō măt′ ik), *a.* (*Path.*) Denoting a physical disorder caused by or influenced by the patient's emotional condition.

psychotherapeutic (sī kō the rȧ pū′ tik), *a.* Treating disease by psychological methods; *n.pl.* The treatment of disease by psychological or hypnotic means. **psychotherapy** (sī kō ther′ ȧ pi), *n.* (*Med.*) The treatment of mental diseases; the treatment of disease by psychological means.

psychrometer (sī krom ė tėr), *n.* The wet-and-dry bulb hygrometer for measuring the humidity of the atmosphere.

ptarmic (tar′ mik) [L. *ptarmicûs*, Gr. *ptarmikos*, from *ptarmos*, sneeze], *a.* Exciting sneezing. *n.* A ptarmic medicine.

ptarmigan (tar′ mi gȧn) [Gael. *tarmachan*, etym. doubtful], *n.* A bird, *Lagopus mutus*, allied to the grouse, having grey or brown plumage in the summer and white in the winter.

pter-, pteri-, ptero- [Gr. *pteron*, feather, a wing], *comb. form.* Winged; having processes resembling wings. **Pteraspis** (tėr ăs′ pis) [Gr. *aspis*, shield], *n.* (*Palæont.*) A Palæozoic genus of ganoid fishes.

ptere (tēr) [F. *ptere*, as prec.], *n.* A wing-like organ.

pteridology (ter i dol′ ȯ ji) [Gr. *pteris -idos*, fern, from *pteron*, feather, -LOGY], *n.* The science of ferns. **pteridological** (-loj′ i kȧl), *a.* **pteridologist** (-dol′ ȯ jist), *n.*

pterion (ter′ i ȯn) [dim., from Gr. *pteron*, wing], *n.* (*Anat.*) The H-shaped suture where the frontal, parietal, and sphenoid bones meet.

pterodactyl (ter ȯ dăk′ til) [PTERO-, Gr. *daktulos*, finger], *n.* (*Palæont.*) An extinct winged reptile from the Mesozoic strata. **pterography** (tėr og′ rȧ fi) [-GRAPHY], *n.* The science of feathers or plumage. **pterographer,** *n.* **pterographic, -al** (-grăf′ ik, -ȧl), *a.* **pterology** (tėr ol′ ȯ ji), *n.* (*Ent.*) The branch of entomology treating of insects' wings. **pterological** (-loj′ i kȧl), *a.* **Pteromys** (ter′ ȯ mis) [Gr. *mus*, mouse], *n.* (*Zool.*) A genus of rodents, comprising the flying squirrels. **Pteropod** (ter′ ȯ pod) [Gr. *pous podos*, foot], *n.* (*Zool.*) Any individual of the Pteropoda. ***Pteropoda*** (tėr op′ ȯ dȧ), *n.pl.* A sub-class of Mollusca in which the foot is expanded into wing-like lobes or paddles. **pteropus** (ter′ ȯ pŭs), *n.* (*pl.* **-pi**) A genus of tropical and sub-tropical bats comprising the flying-foxes. **pterosaur** (ter′ ȯ sawr) [Gr. *sauros*, lizard], *n.* (*Palæont.*) Any individual of the Pterosauria. **Pterosauria,** *n.pl.* An order of flying reptiles of the Mesozoic age.

pterygium (tėr ij′ i ŭm) [Gr. *pterugion*, dim. as foll.], *n.* (*Path.*) A varicose excrescence of the conjunctiva of the eye. **pterygial,** *a.*

pterygoid (ter′ i goid) [Gr. *pterugoeides* (*pterux -ugos*, wing, -OID)], *a.* (*Anat.*) Wing-shaped; of or connected with the pterygoid processes. *n.* A pterygoid bone or process. **pterygoid process:** Either of the wing-like processes descending from the great wings of the sphenoid bone. **pterygo-,** *comb. form.*

pteryla (ter′ i lȧ) [mod. L., from Gr. *pteron*, feather], *n.* (*pl.* **-læ**) (*Ornith.*) One of the tracts or patches of feathers on the skin of a bird. **pterylography** (-log′ rȧ fi), *n.* The science of or a treatise on pterylosis **pterylographic, -al** (-grăf′ ik, -ȧl), *a.* **pterylographically,** *adv.* **pterylosis** (ter i lō′ sis), *n.* The arrangement of the feather tracts on the skin of birds.

ptisan (tiz′ ȧn, ti zăn′) [F. *tisane*, L. *ptisana*, Gr. *ptisanē*, peeled barley, from *ptissein*, to peel], *n.* Barley-water or other mucilaginous decoction used as a nourshing beverage.

ptochocracy (tō kok′ rȧ si) [Gr. *ptōchos*, poor, -CRACY], *n.* Government by paupers, opposed to plutocracy. **ptochogony** (tō kog′ ȯ ni), *n.* The production of beggars.

Ptolemaic (tol ė mā′ ik), *a.* Pertaining to Ptolemy, Alexandrian astronomer (2nd cent.) who maintained that the earth was a fixed body in the centre of the universe, the sun and moon revolving round it; pertaining to the Ptolemies, kings of Egypt, 323 B.C. to 30 B.C.

ptomaine (tō mān, tȯ mān′) [It. *ptomaina*, from Gr. *ptōma*, corpse, cogn. with *piptein*, to fall], *n.* One of a class of alkaloid bodies possessing highly poisonous qualities derived from decaying animal and vegetable matter. **ptomaic** (tȯ mā′ ik), *a.*

ptosis (tō′ sis) [Gr., falling, as prec.], *n.* A drooping of the upper eyelid from paralysis of the muscle raising it.

ptyalin (tī′ ȧ lin) [Gr. *ptūalon*, spittle, from *ptūein*, to spit], *n.* (*Physiol.*) An enzyme or ferment contained in saliva, which converts starch into dextrin. **ptyalize,** *v.t.* To salivate. **ptyalism,** *n.* Salivation. **ptyalose,** *n.* (*Chem.*) Sugar formed by the action of ptyalin or starch. **ptyalagogue** (tī ăl′ ȧ gog), **ptysmagogue** (tiz′ mȧ gog), *n.* (*Med.*) A medicine inducing a flow of saliva.

pub (pŭb), *n.* (*colloq.*) A public-house.

puberty (pū′ bėr ti) [F. *puberté*, L. *pūbertātem*, nom.

-*tas*, from *pūber*, youth, or *pūbes*, hair], *n.* The period of life at which persons become capable of begetting or bearing children; (*Bot.*) the age at which a plant begins to flower. **age of puberty:** (*Law*) In boys 14, in girls 12. **puberal,** *a.* **puberulent** (pū ber′ ů lėnt), *a.* (*Bot.*) Pubescent, downy.

pubes (pū′ bēz), *n.* The hypogastric region which in the adult becomes covered with hair; the hair of the pubic region; the pubis. **pubescence** (pū bes′ ėns), *n.* The state or age of puberty; *soft, hairy down on plants or parts of animals, esp. insects, downiness, hairiness. **pubescent,** *a.* Arrived at the age of puberty; covered with soft hairy down. **pubic** (pū′ bik), *a.* Of or pertaining to the pubes or pubis. **pubis,** *n.* (*Anat.*) A bone forming the anterior part of the pelvis. **pubo-,** *comb. form.*

public (pŭb′ lik) [F., from L. *pūblicus*, contr. of *populicus*, from *populus*, people], *a.* Pertaining to or affecting the people as a whole, opp. to personal or private; open to the use or enjoyment of all, not restricted to any class; done, existing, or such as may be observed by all, not concealed or clandestine; open, notorious; of or pertaining to the affairs or service of the people. *n.* The people in general; any particular section of the people; (*colloq.*) a public-house. **in public:** Openly, publicly. **public Act** or **Bill:** One involving the interests of the community. **public education:** Education at school, opp. to private education; education at a public school. **public-house,** *n.* A house licensed for the retail of intoxicating liquors, an inn, a tavern. **public law:** International law. **public orator:** The official speaker of a university. **public relations officer (P.R.O.):** An official employed to give the public information about a business, organization, government department, etc. **public school,** *n.* A school under the control of a publicly elected body; a school whose headmaster is a member of the Headmasters' Conference, usu. endowed school providing a liberal education for such as can afford it. **public spirit:** Interest in or devotion to the community. **public-spirited,** *a.* **public-spiritedly,** *adv.* **public-spiritedness,** *n.* **publicness,** *n.* **publicly** (pub′ lik li), *adv.*

publican (pŭb′ li kȧn), *n.* (*Rom. Hist.*) A collector or farmer of the revenues, taxes, etc.; a keeper of a public-house.

publication (pŭb li kā′ shŭn), *n.* The act of making publicly known; the act of publishing a book, periodical, musical composition, etc.; a work printed and published.

publicist (pŭb′ li sist), *n.* A writer or authority on international law; a writer on current social or political topics, esp. a journalist. **publicism,** *n.* **publicistic,** *a.*

publicity (pŭb lis′ i ti), *n.* The quality of being public; the aggregate advertising of a product. **publicity agent,** *n.* A person employed to keep before the public the name of a product, film, etc.

publish (pŭb′ lish) [M.E. *publischen*, F. *publier*, L. *publicāre*, as prec.], *v.t.* To make public, to proclaim abroad, to promulgate, to announce publicly; to ask (the banns of marriage); to issue or print and offer for sale to the public; (*Am.*) to put into circulation; to utter (counterfeit money, etc.). **publishable,** *a.* **publisher,** *n.* One who publishes, esp. books and other literary productions. ***publishment,** *n.*

pubo- [PUBERTY].

puccoon (pů koon′) [N. Am. Ind.], *n.* One of various N. American plants yielding a red or yellow dye.

puce (pūs) [F., from L. *pūlicem*, nom. *pūlex*, flea], *a.* Flea-colour, reddish-brown.

pucelage (pū′ sė lȧj) [F., from *pucelle*, a young girl], *n.* A state of virginity.

Puck (pŭk) [A.-S. *pūca*, cogn. with Icel. *pūki*, Ir. *púca*, POOKA], *n.* A mischievous sprite, elf, or fairy, esp. the fairy celebrated by Shakespeare in *Midsummer Night's Dream*; (*Canada*) a disk of india-rubber used as a ball in hockey. **puckish,** *a.*

pucka, pukka (pŭk′ ȧ) [Hindi, cooked, ripe], *a.* (*Ang.-Ind.*) Of full weight; durable, substantial; genuine; superior.

pucker (pŭk′ ėr) [prob. rel. to POKE (1)], *v.t.* To gather into small folds or wrinkles. *v.i.* To become wrinkled or gathered into small folds, etc. *n.* A fold, a wrinkle, a bulge. **puckery,** *a.*

pud (pŭd) [etym. doubtful, cp. Dut. *poot*], *n.* (*Childish*) A hand; the fore-paw of some animals.

puddening (pud′ ėn ing) [corr. of PUDDING], *n.* (*Naut.*) A pad of rope, etc., used as a fender.

pudding (pud′ ing) [M.E., etym. doubtful], *n.* A mixture of animal or vegetable ingredients, usu. with flour or other farinaceous basis, of a soft or moderately hard consistency, baked or boiled, and eaten either as a main dish or as a sweet; a skin or intestine stuffed with minced meat, etc., a large sausage; (*fig.*) food, victuals, material reward; (*slang*) poisoned liver used by burglars to silence house-dogs; (*Naut.*) a puddening. **pudding-ball,** *n.* (*Austral.*) A fish resembling the mullet. **pudding-face,** *n.* A fat, round, smooth face. **pudding-faced,** *a.* **pudding-head,** *n.* A stupid person. **pudding-heart,** *n.* A spiritless person. **pudding-pie,** *n.* A pudding with meat baked in it; a tart made with pie-crust and custard. **pudding-sleeve,** *n.* A full sleeve as in a clerical gown. **pudding-stone,** *n.* A conglomerate of pebbles in a siliceous matrix. ***pudding-time,** *n.* The time for pudding; (*fig.*) a lucky or favourable time. **puddingy,** *a.*

puddle (pŭ′ dėl) [M.E. *podel*, dim. from A.-S. *pudd*, a ditch], *n.* A small muddy pool; clay and sand worked together to form a watertight lining for a pond, canal, etc.; (*fig.*) a muddle; a bungler, an awkward person. *v.i.* To dabble (in mud, water, etc.); (*fig.*) to mess, to muddle (about). *v.t.* To make dirty or muddy; to work (clay, etc.) into puddle; to line or render watertight with puddle; to stir up (molten iron) in a furnace so as to convert it into wrought-iron. **puddler,** *n.* One who puddles, esp. a workman employed in puddling iron. **puddly,** *a.*

puddock [PADDOCK (2)].

pudency (pū′ dėn si) [late L. *pudentia*, from L. *pudens -ntis*, pres.p. of *pudēre*, to make or be ashamed], *n.* Modesty, shamefacedness. ***pudenda*** (pū den′ dȧ), *n.pl.* The privy parts, the genitals. **pudendal, pudic, *-al** (pū′ dik, -ȧl), *a.* Pertaining to the pudenda. ***pudicity** (pū dis′ i ti), *n.* Modesty, chastity.

pudge (pŭj) [cp. PODGE], *n.* A short, thick, or fat person or figure. **pudgy,** *a.*

pudic [PUDENCY].

pudsy (pŭd′ zi) [etym. doubtful, perh. rel. to PUDGY], *a.* Plump.

pueblo (pweb′ lō) [Sp.], *n.* A village, town, or settlement, esp. of the semi-civilized Indians of New Mexico, etc. **pueblan,** *a.*

puerile (pū′ ėr īl) [L. *puerīlis*, from *puer*, boy], *a.* Boyish, childish, juvenile; suited for children, trivial. **puerilely,** *adv.* ***puerileness, puerility** (-il′ i ti), *n.*

puerperal (pū ĕr′ pėr ȧl) [L. *puerperus* (*puer*, boy, -*parus*, bringing forth, from *parere*, to bring forth)], *a.* Pertaining to or resulting from childbirth. **puerperal fever:** A fever attacking women after childbirth. **puerperalism,** *n.* (*Path.*).

puff (pŭf) [M.E. *puffen*, imit.], *v.i.* To breathe, to blow, to emit or expel air, steam, etc., in short, sudden blasts; to breathe hard; to come (out) in a short, sudden blast; to become inflated or distended. *v.t.* To emit, to blow out, with a short sudden blast or blasts; to blow or drive (away) thus; to utter pantingly; to inflate, to blow (up or out); to blow (away, etc.); (*fig.*) to bid at an auction in order to inflate the price; to cause to be out of breath; (*fig.*) to praise or advertise in an exaggerated or misleading way. *n.* A short, sudden blast of breath, smoke, steam, etc., a whiff, a gust; a small amount of breath, smoke, etc., emitted at one puff; a light, puffy thing or small mass of any material; a cake, tart, etc., of light or spongy consistency; a light wad, pad, or tuft for applying powder to the skin; (*fig.*) an exaggerated or misleading advertisement, review, etc. **to be puffed up:** To be inflated; (*fig.*) to be swollen up with conceit or self-importance. **puff-adder,** *n.* A highly venomous S. African snake, *Clotho arietans,* which inflates part of its body when aroused. **puff-ball,** *n.* A fungus of the genus *Lycoperdon,* the roundish spore-case of which emits dry, dust-like spores. **puff-bird,** *n.* A bird of the family Bucconidæ, so called from their habits of puffing out their plumage. **puff-box,** *n.* A toilet-box for holding powder and puff. **puff-paste,** *n.* Light, flaky paste for tarts, etc. **puffer,** *n.* **puffery,** *n.* Exaggerated or misleading entry, advertisement, etc.; puffs, puffed frilling, etc. **puffily,** *adv.* **puffing,** *a.* and *n.* **puffingly,** *adv.* **puffy,** *a.* Puffing, blowing or breathing in puffs; short-winded; puffed out, swollen, distended; (*fig.*) tumid, turgid, bombastic. **puffiness,** *n.*

puffin (pŭf′ in) [etym. doubtful], *n.* A sea-bird of the genus *Fratercula,* esp. the N. Atlantic *F. arctica.*

puffing, puffy, etc. [PUFF.]

pufftaloonies (pŭf′ tȧ loo niz), *n.pl.* (*Austral.*) Fried cakes eaten hot with jam, honey, syrup, etc.

pug (1) (pŭg) [etym. unknown], *n.* A pug-dog; a proper name for a fox; a pug-engine; (among servants) an upper servant; *an imp, an elf; *a monkey. **pug-dog,** *n.* A dwarf variety of the common dog, like a diminutive bulldog or mastiff. **pug-engine,** *n.* A small locomotive for shunting, etc. **pug-faced,** *a.* **pug-nose,** *n.* A short squat nose. **pug-nosed,** *a.*

pug (2) (pŭg) [etym. doubtful], *n.* Clay and other material mixed and prepared for making into bricks. *v.t.* (*past & p.p.* **pugged**) To grind (clay, etc.) and render plastic for brick-making; to puddle with clay; to pack (a wall, floor, etc.) with sawdust, etc., to deaden sound. **pug-mill,** *n.* A mill in which clay is made into pug. **pugging,** *n.*

pug (3) (pŭg) [Hindi *pag*], *n.* (*Ang.-Ind.*) The footprint or trail of an animal. *v.i.* To track game, etc.

pugaree, puggree (pŭg′ ȧ rē) [Hind. *pagrī*], *n.* An Indian light turban; a long piece of muslin wound round a hat or helmet in hot climates to protect from the sun. **pugareed,** *a.*

pugging [PUG (2)]. ***pugh** [POOH].

pugil (pū′ jil) [L. *pugillus,* a handful, from *pug-,* root of *pugnus,* fist (cp. Gr. *pugmē*)], *n.* A pinch, as much as can be taken up between the thumb and first two fingers.

pugilist (pū′ ji list), *n.* A boxer, a prize-fighter; (*fig.*) a fighter, a pugnacious controversialist, etc. **pugilism** (pū′ ji lizm) [L. *pugil,* boxer, as prec., -ISM], *n.* **pugilistic** (-lis′ tik), *a.*

pugnacious (pŭg nā′ shus) [L. *pugnax -ācis,* from *pugnāre,* to fight, as prec.], *a.* Inclined to fight; quarrelsome. **pugnaciously,** *adv.* **pugnacity** (-năs′ iti), ***pugnaciousness,** *n.*

puisne (pū′ ni) [O.F. *puis,* L. *postea,* from *post,* after, *né,* L. *nātus,* born], *a.* Junior or inferior in rank (applied to judges); (*Law*) later, more recent. *n.* A puisne judge.

puissant (pū′ i sȧnt, pwis′ ȧnt) [F., cp. It. *possente*; both prob. from a low L. *possens -ntem,* pres. p. of L. *posse,* to be able], *a.* Powerful, strong, mighty. **puissance,** *n.* Power, strength; (of a horse) ability to take fences. **puissantly,** *adv.*

puke (1) (pūk) [etym. doubtful], *v.t.* and *i.* (*low*) To vomit. *n.* A vomit; an emetic. ***puker,** *n.*

***puke** (2) (pūk) [prob. from M. Dut. *puyck*], *n.* A kind of woollen cloth; a dark colour formerly used for woollens.

pukka [PUCKA].

puku (poo′ koo) [Zulu *mpuku*], *n.* A red African antelope, *Cobus vardoni.*

***pulchritude** (pŭl′ kri tūd) [L. *pulchritūdo,* from *pulcher,* beautiful], *n.* Beauty.

pule (pūl) [perh. from *F. piaulir* or imit.], *v.i.* To cry plaintively or querulously, to whine, to whimper; to pipe, to chirp. *v.t.* To utter in a querulous, whining tone. **puling,** *a.* and *n.* **pulingly,** *adv.*

Pulex (pū′ lėks) [L., flea], *n.* (*Ent.*) A genus of fleas; the flea.

pulka (pŭl′ kȧ) [Finnish *pulkka*], *n.* A travelling sleigh with a prow like a canoe, used by Laplanders.

pull (pul) [A.-S. *pullian,* etym. doubtful], *v.t.* To draw towards one by force; to drag, to haul, to tug; to draw (up, along, nearer, etc.); to pluck; to row (a boat); to take (a person in a boat) by rowing; (*slang*) to make a raid upon (a gambling-house), to arrest; (*Print.*) to take (an impression) by a hand-press, to take (a proof); (*Cricket*) to strike (a ball) from the off to the on side; (*Golf*) to strike a ball to the left; (*Racing*) to rein in a horse, esp. so as to lose a race. *v.i.* To give a pull; to tug, to haul; to strain against the bit (of a horse); to draw, to suck (at a pipe); to pluck, to tear (at). *n.* The act of pulling, a tug; that which is pulled; a handle by which beer is drawn, a door opened, a bell rung, etc.; a quantity of beer, etc., drawn; a draught, a swig; (*Print.*) an impression from a hand-press, a proof; (*Cricket*) a stroke by which a ball is sent from the off to the on side; (*Golf*) a stroke sending a ball to the left; (*Racing*) the checking of a horse by its rider, esp. to secure defeat; (*Rowing*) a spell of rowing; (*colloq.*) a hold, unfair or illegitimate influence; (*colloq.*) a spell of hard exertion. **to have the pull:** To have the advantage (over). **to pull about:** To pull to and fro, to handle roughly. **to pull apart:** To pull asunder or into pieces; to become separated or severed. **to pull down:** To demolish; to degrade, to humble; to weaken, to cause (prices, etc.) to be reduced. **to pull faces:** To make grimaces. **to pull one's leg:** To tease, to hoax. **to pull one's weight:** To take one's share of work or responsibility. **to pull off:** To separate by pulling; to win (a prize, etc.). **to pull out:** To extract; to row out; to come out (as a train from the station). **to pull to pieces:** To tear (a thing) up; (*fig.*) to criticize, to abuse. **to pull through:** To get oneself or a person through with difficulty; to pass (an examination) with difficulty. **to pull together:** To co-operate. **to pull up:** To drag up forcibly; to pluck up; to cause to stop; to come to a stop. **pull-back,** *n.* A drawback, a restraint, hindrance; a device for holding back and keeping in parts of a woman's skirt. **pullover,** *n.* A jersey which is pulled over the head. **pull-through,** *n.* A cord with a rag attached, used for cleaning the barrel of a firearm. **pulled,** *a.* Plucked, stripped (as fowls, skins, etc.); depressed in health, spirits, etc., dragged (down). **puller,** *n.* One who or that which pulls; an implement, machine, etc., for pulling; a horse that pulls against the bit, a hard-mouthed or high-spirited horse. ***puller-down,** *n.*

pullet (pul′ ėt) [M.E. and O.F. *polete* (F. *poulet*), dim. of *poule,* late L. *pulla,* hen, fem. of L. *pullus,* a young animal, cogn. with FOAL], *n.* A young fowl, esp. a hen before the first moult. ***pullet-sperm,** *n.* The sperm of an egg.

pulley (pul′ i) [O.F. *polie* (F. *poulie*), prob. ult. from a late Gr. *polidion,* dim. of *polos,* POLE (2)], *n.* A wheel with a grooved rim, or a combination of such wheels, mounted in a block for changing the direction or for increasing the effect of a force. *v.t.* To lift or hoist with a pulley; to furnish or fit with pulleys. **fast and loose pulley:** A pair of pulleys on a shaft, one fixed and revolving with the shaft, the other loose, for throwing the shaft into or out of gear by means of a belt running round the one or the other.

pullicat (pul′ i kȧt) [*Pulicat,* on the coast of Madras], *n.* A kind of coloured checked handkerchief, orig. made at Pulicat; the material of which this is made.

Pullman (pul′ mȧn) [George M. *Pullman* (1831–1897), inventor], *n.* A Pullman car. **Pullman car:** A railway saloon or sleeping-car originally built at the Pullman works, Illinois.

pullulate (pul′ ū lāt) [L. *pullulātus*, p.p. of *pullulāre*, to sprout, from *pullulus*, dim. of *pullus*, see PULLET], *v.i.* To shoot, to bud; to germinate, to breed; to swarm; to develop, to spring up. **pullulant,** *a.* **pullulation** (-lā′ shŭn), *n.*

pulmo- [Latin *pulmo -mōnis*, lung], *comb. form.* **pulmobranchiate** (pŭl mȯ brăng′ ki ȧt) [BRANCHIATE], *a.* Having the branchiæ adapted to breathe air, as in some molluscs, etc. **pulmometer** (pŭl mom′ ė tėr) [-METER], *n.* An instrument for measuring the capacity of the lungs. **pulmometry,** *n.*

pulmonary (pŭl′ mȯ nȧ ri), *a.* Pertaining to the lungs. **pulmonary artery,** *n.* The artery carrying blood from the heart to the lungs. **pulmonary disease,** *n.* Lung disease, esp. consumption. **pulmonic** (pŭl mon′ ik), *a.* Pulmonary; affected with or subject to disease of the lungs. *n.* One having diseased lungs; a medicine for lung-diseases.

pulmonate (pŭl′ mȯ nāt), *a.* (*Zool.*) Furnished with lungs. *n.* A pulmonate mollusc.

pulp (pŭlp) [L. *pulpa*], *n.* Any soft, moist, coherent mass; the fleshy or succulent portion of a fruit; the soft tissue of an animal body or in an organ or part, as in the internal cavity of a tooth; the soft mixture of rags, wood, etc., from which paper is made; (*Mining*) pulverized ore mixed with water. *v.t.* To convert into pulp; to extract the pulp from. *v.i.* To become pulpy. **pulper,** *n.* **pulpify,** *v.t.* **pulpless,** *a.* **pulplike,** *a.* **pulpous, pulpy,** *a.* **pulpiness,** *n.*

pulpit (pul′ pit) [L. *pulpitum*], *n.* An elevated enclosed stand from which a preacher delivers his sermon. *a.* Pertaining to the pulpit or to preaching. *v.t.* To provide with a pulpit or pulpits. *v.i.* To preach. **the pulpit:** Preachers generally; preaching. **pulpitarian** (-târ′ i ȧn), *a.* and *n.* **pulpiteer** (pul pi tēr′), *n.* (*contempt.*) A preacher. **pulpiteering,** *n.* **pulpiter** (pul′ pi tėr), *n.*

pulplike, pulpous, pulpy, etc. [PULP].

pulque (pul′ kā) [Mex. Sp.], *n.* A Mexican vinous beverage made by fermenting the sap of species of agave. **pulque brandy:** A liquor distilled from this.

pulsate (pŭl′ sāt) [L. *pulsātus*, p.p. of *pulsāre*, freq. of *pellere*, to drive, p.p. *pulsus*], *v.i.* To move, esp. to expand and contract, with rhythmical alternation, to beat, to throb; (*fig.*) to vibrate, to thrill. *v.t.* To agitate with a pulsator. **pulsatile** (pŭl′ sȧ til, -tīl), *a.* Pulsatory; (*Mus.*) played by beating, percussive.

pulsatilla (pŭl sȧ til′ ȧ) [med. L., dim. of *pulsāta*, beaten, as prec.], *n.* The pasque-flower, *Anemone pulsatilla.*

pulsation (pŭl sā′ shŭn) [as PULSATE, -TION], *n.* The action of pulsating; the movement of the pulse. **pulsatory** (pŭl′ sȧ tȯr i), ***pulsative,** *a.* Of or pertaining to pulsation; actuated by or having the property of pulsation. **pulsator** (pŭl sā′ tȯr), *n.* A machine for separating diamonds from earth, a jigging-machine; part of a milking-machine; a pulsometer.

pulse (1) (pŭls) [M.E. and O.F. *pous*, L. *pulsum*, nom. *-sus*, as prec.], *n.* The rhythmic beating of the arteries caused by the propulsion of blood along them from the heart; a beat of the arteries or the heart; a pulsation, a vibration; a quick, regular stroke or recurrence of strokes (as of oars); (*fig.*) a throb, a thrill. *v.i.* To pulsate. *v.t.* To send (forth, out, etc.) by or as by rhythmic beats. **to feel one's pulse:** To gauge the rate or regularity of one's pulse as a sign of health, etc.; (*fig.*) to sound one's intentions, views, etc. **pulseless,** *a.* **pulselessness,** *n.* ***pulsific** (-sif′ ik), *a.* Causing pulsation; pulsatory.

pulse (2) (pŭls) [M.E. and O.F. *pols*, L. *puls pultis*, pottage of meal, etc.], *n.* Leguminous plants or their seeds.

pulseless, *pulsific, etc. [PULSE (1)].

pulsimeter (pŭl sim′ ė tėr), *n.* An instrument for measuring the rate, force, regularity, etc., of the pulse. **pulsometer** (-som′ ė tėr), *n.* A pumping device operated by the admission and condensation of steam in alternate chambers; a pulsimeter.

***pultaceous** (pŭl tā′ shŭs) [L. *puls pultis*, PULSE (2), -ACEOUS], *a.* Pulplike, macerated, softened.

pulu (poo′ loo) [Hawaiian], *n.* A vegetable silk or wool obtained from certain Hawaiian tree-ferns, used for stuffing mattresses, etc.

pulverize (pŭl′vėr īz) [late L. *pulverizāre*, from L. *pulvus -veris*, dust], *v.t.* To reduce to fine powder or dust; (*fig.*) to demolish, to smash. *v.i.* To be reduced to powder. **pulverate,** *v.t.* **pulverable,** *a.* **pulverizable,** *a.* **pulverization** (-zā′ shŭn), *n.* **pulverizator, pulverizer,** *n.* One who or that which pulverizes; a machine for reducing a liquid to fine spray; (*Agric.*) a machine for pulverizing earth. **pulverous,** *a.* **pulverulent** (pŭl ver′ ū lėnt), *a.* Consisting of fine powder; covered with powder, powdery; liable to disintegrate into fine powder. **pulverulence,** *n.*

***pulvil** (pŭl′ vil) [It. *polviglio*, from *polve*, as prec.], *n.* A scented powder formerly used as a cosmetic. *v.t.* To sprinkle with pulvil.

pulvillus (pŭl vil′ ŭs) [L., contr. for *pulvīnulus*, dim. of *pulvīnus*, a pillow], *n.* (*Ent.*) The pad or cushion of an insect's foot. **pulvillar, pulvilliform,** *a.*

pulvinar (pŭl vī′ nȧr) [L., a couch], *n.* (*Anat.*) A cushion-like prominence at the end of the optic thalamus of the brain. **pulvinate** (pŭl′ vi nȧt), *a.* (*Nat. Hist.*) Cushion-shaped, pad-like. **pulvinated,** *a.* (*Arch.*) Having a convex face (as a frieze).

puma (pū′ mȧ) [Peruv.], *n.* The cougar, *Felis concolor*, a large feline carnivore of N. and S. America.

pumice (pŭm′ is) [O.F. *pomis*, late L. *pumicem*, L. *pūmicem*, nom. *-ex*], *n.* A light, porous or cellular kind of lava, used as a cleansing and polishing material. *v.t.* To rub, polish or clean with this. **pumice-stone,** *n.* Pumice. **pumicate,** *v.t.* **pumiceous** (pū mish′ ŭs), *a.* ***pumiciform** (pū′ mis i fôrm), *a.*

pummace [POMACE]. **pummel** [POMMEL].

pump (1) (pŭmp) [M.E. *pumpe*, Dut. *pomp*, G. *pumpe*, F. *pompe*], *n.* A device or engine usu. in the form of a cylinder and piston, for raising water or other liquid; a machine for exhausting or compressing air, an air-pump; the act of pumping, a stroke of a pump; (*fig.*) an attempt at extracting information from a person; one good at this. *v.t.* To raise or remove with a pump; to free from water or make dry with a pump; to propel, to pour, with or as with a pump; to put out of breath (*usu. in p.p.*); (*fig.*) to elicit information from by artful interrogations. *v.i.* To work a pump; to raise water, etc., with a pump. **to pump up:** To inflate (a pneumatic tire); to inflate the tires of (a cycle, etc.). **pump-brake,** *n.* The handle of a ship's pump. **pump-handle,** *n.* The handle by which a pump is worked; (*colloq.*) the hand or arm. **pump-head,** *n.* The casing at the head of a chain pump for directing the water into the discharge-spout. **pump-room,** *n.* A room where a pump is worked; a room at a spa where the waters from the medicinal spring are dispensed. **pumpage,** *n.* **pumper,** *n.* **pump ship,** *v.i.* (*colloq.*) To urinate.

pump (2) (pŭmp) [etym. doubtful], *n.* A light low-heeled, slipper-like shoe, usu. of patent leather, worn with evening dress and for dancing; (*Am.*) a court shoe.

pumpernickel (pum′ pėr nikl) [G., etym. doubtful], *n.* German whole-meal rye bread.

pumpkin (pŭmp′ kin) [earlier *pumpion*, POMPION], *n.* The large globular fruit of *Cucurbita pepo*; the trailing, annual plant bearing this fruit.

pun (1) (pŭn) [etym. doubtful], *n.* The playful use of a word in two different senses or of words similar in sound but different in meaning. *v.i.* (*past & p.p.* **punned**) To make a pun. **punnage, punning,** *n.* **punningly,** *adv.* **punster,** *n.* One who makes puns; one addicted to pun-making.

pun (2) (pŭn) [dial. form of POUND (3)], *v.t.* To pound, to crush, to consolidate by ramming; to work (up clay, etc.) with a punner.

puna (pū′ nȧ) [Peruv.], *n.* A cold high plateau between the two ranges of the Cordilleras; the cold wind prevalent there; mountain-sickness.

punch (1) (pŭnch) [prob. from PUNCHEON (1)], *n.* A tool, usu. consisting of a short cylindrical piece of steel tapering to a sharp or blunt end, for making holes, indenting, forcing bolts out of holes, etc.; a machine in which a similar tool is used; a tool or machine for stamping a die or impressing a design; a blow with the fist. *v.t.* To stamp or perforate with a punch; to make (a hole or indentation) thus; to drive (out, etc.) with a punch; to strike, esp. with the fist. **punch-card:** A card in which data are represented by perforations, used in automatic computers. **punching-ball,** *n.* An elastic ball punched as a form of exercise. **puncher,** *n.* One who or that which punches; (*Am.*) a cow-puncher, a cowboy.

punch (2) (pŭnch) [perh. from Hindi *panch*, five, from its consisting originally of five ingredients, or from PUNCHEON (2)], *n.* A beverage compounded of wine or spirit, water or milk, lemons, sugar, spice, etc. **punch-bowl,** *n.*

Punch (3) (pŭnch) [short for PUNCHINELLO], *n.* The chief character in the popular puppet-show of Punch and Judy, represented as a grotesque humped-backed man.

punch (4) (pŭnch) [etym. doubtful], *n.* A short, fat fellow; a stout-built cart-horse. **punchy,** *a.*

puncheon (1) (pŭn′ chȯn) [O.North. F. *ponchon*, O.F. *poinçon*, L. *punctiōnem*, nom. *-tio*, a pricking, from *pungere*, to prick, p.p. *punctus*], *n.* A short upright timber, used for supporting the roof in a mine or as an upright in the framework of a roof; *a perforating or stamping tool, a punch.

puncheon (2) (pŭn′ chȯn) [perh. ident. with prec.], *n.* A large cask holding from 72 to 120 gallons.

punchinello (pŭn chi nel′ ō) [It. *polichinello*, *Pulcinello*, a character in Neapolitan low comedy], *n.* A buffoon, a Punch, a grotesque person.

punctate (pŭngk′ tȧt) [L. PUNCT-UM, -ATE], *a.* Covered with points, dots, spots, etc. **punctation** (-tā′ shŭn), *n.* **punctiform** (pŭngk′ ti fôrm), *a.* Like a point or dot; punctate.

punctilio (pŭngk til′ i ō) [Sp. *puntillo*, or It. *puntiglio*, dim. of *punto*, POINT, as prec.], *n.* (*pl.* **-os**) A nice point in conduct, ceremony, or honour; precision in form or etiquette. **punctilious,** *a.* Precise or exacting in punctilio; strictly observant of ceremony or etiquette. **punctiliously,** *adv.* **punctiliousness,** *n.*

punctual (pŭngk′ tū ȧl) [med. L. *punctuālis*, from *punctus*, a POINT], *a.* Observant and exact in matters of time; done, made, or occurring exactly at the proper time; (*Geom.*) of or pertaining to a point; *exact, punctilious. **punctualist,** *n.* One who is very exact in observing forms and ceremonies. **punctuality** (-ăl′ i ti), *n.* **punctually,** *adv.*

punctuate (pŭngk′ tū āt) [med. L. *punctuātus*, p.p. of *punctuāre*, as prec.], *v.t.* To mark with stops, to divide into sentences, clauses, etc., with stops; (*fig.*) to interrupt or intersperse (a speech, etc.) with cheers, remarks, etc.; (*colloq.*) to emphasize, to accentuate; to enforce (with). **punctuation** (-ā′ shŭn), *n.* **punctuative** (pŭngk′ tū ȧ tiv), *a.*

punctum (pŭngk′ tŭm) [L., orig. neut. of *punctus*, POINT], *n.* (*pl.* *-ta*) A point, a speck, a dot, a minute spot of colour, etc. **punctule,** *n.* A minute point, speck, or pit. **punctulate** (pŭngk′ tū lȧt), *a.* **punctulation** (-lā′ shŭn), *n.* A point.

puncture (pŭngk′ tyŭr) [L. *punctūra*, as prec.], *n.* A small hole made with something pointed, a prick; the act of pricking or perforating. *v.t.* To make a puncture in; to pierce or prick with something pointed. *v.i.* To sustain a puncture (of a tire, balloon, etc.).

pundit (pŭn′ dit) [Hindi *paṇḍit*, from Sansk. *paṇḍita*, learned], *n.* A Hindu learned in the Sanskrit language and the science, laws, and religion of India; a learned person; a pretender to learning.

pung (pŭng) [N. Am. Ind. *tom-pung*], *n.* A low sled for one horse; a toboggan.

punga (pŭng′ gȧ) [Maori], *n.* A N. Zealand tree-fern, the pith of which is edible.

pungent (pŭn′ jĕnt) [L. *pungens -ntem*, pres.p. of *pungere*, to prick], *a.* Sharply affecting the senses, esp. those of smell or taste; pricking or stinging to the sense of touch; acrid, keen, caustic, biting; (*fig.*) piquant, stimulating; (*Nat. Hist.*) sharp-pointed, adapted for pricking or piercing. **pungency, *-gence,** *n.* **pungently,** *adv.*

Punic (pū′ nik) [L. *Pūnicus*, *Pœnicus*, from *Pœnus*, Gr. *Phoinix*, Phœnician], *a.* Pertaining to the Carthaginians, Carthaginian; (*fig.*) treacherous, faithless. *n.* The language of the Carthaginians.

puniceous (pū nish′ i ŭs) [L. *pūniceus*, as prec.], *a.* Bright-red, purple.

punier, puniness, etc. [PUNY].

punish (pŭn′ ish) [F. *puniss-*, pres. part. stem of *punir*, L. *pūnīre*, from *pœna*. Gr. *poinē*, fine, PENALTY], *v.t.* To inflict a penalty on for an offence; to visit judicially with pain, loss, confinement, or other penalty, to chastise; to inflict a penalty for (an offence); (*fig.*) to inflict pain or injury on, to handle severely, to maul; to give great trouble to (opponents in a game, race, etc.); (*colloq.*) to consume large quantities of (food, etc.). **punishable,** *a.* **punishability** (-bil′ i ti), **punishableness,** *n.* **punishably,** *adv.* **punisher,** *n.* **punishment,** *n.* **punitive** (pū′ ni tiv), **punitory,** *a.* Awarding or inflicting punishment; retributive.

punk (1) (pŭngk) [etym. doubtful], *n.* (*Am.*) Wood decayed through the growth of a fungus, touch-wood; amadou, a composition for igniting fire-works. *a.* (*Am. slang*) Poor, seedy.

***punk** (2) (pŭngk) [etym. unknown], *n.* A prostitute, a whore.

punkah (pŭng′ kȧ) [Hind. *pankhā*], *n.* A large portable fan; a large screen-like fan suspended from the ceiling and worked by a cord.

punner (pŭn′ ĕr) [PUN (2), -ER], *n.* A tool used for ramming earth, in a hole, etc.

punnet (pŭn′ ĕt) [etym. doubtful], *n.* A small, shallow basket for fruit, flowers, etc.

punster [PUN (1)].

punt (1) (pŭnt) [A.-S., from L. *ponto*, prob. from Gallic], *n.* A shallow, flat-bottomed, square-ended boat, usu. propelled by pushing against the bottom of the stream with a pole. *v.t.* To propel (a punt, etc.) thus; to convey in a punt. *v.i.* To propel about thus; to go (about) in a punt. **punter** (1), **puntist, puntsman,** *n.*

punt (2) (pŭnt) [F. *ponter*, etym. unknown], *v.i.* (*Basset, Faro, Ombre, etc.*) To stake against the bank; (*slang*) to bet on a horse, etc. *n.* (*Faro*) A point in the game; the act of playing basset, faro, etc.; *a punter (2). **punter** (2), *n.* A petty backer of horses; a small gambler on the Stock Exchange.

punt (3) (pŭnt) [etym. doubtful], *v.t.* (*Football*) To kick the ball after dropping it from the hand and before it touches the ground. *n.* Such a kick.

punter, etc. [PUNT (1 and 2)].

punto** (pŭn′ tō) [It. or Sp., as POINT], *n.* A thrust or pass in fencing. ***punto dritto: A direct thrust. ***punto riverso:*** A backhanded thrust.

puntsman [PUNT (1)].

punty (pŭn′ ti) [PONTIL], *n.* A pontil; a round ornamental mark on a glass article, like the hollow left by the end of a pontil.

puny (pū′ ni) [PUISNE], *a.* (*comp.* **punier,** *superl.* **puniest**) Small and feeble, tiny, undersized, weak, poorly developed; petty, trivial; *puisne. *n.* A junior, a freshman. **puniness,** *n.*

pup (pŭp), *n.* A puppy. *v.t.* To bring forth (pups). *v.i.* To bring forth pups, to whelp, to litter. **in pup:** Pregnant. **to sell a pup to:** (*slang*) To swindle.

pupa (pū′ pȧ) [L., a girl, a puppet], *n.* (*pl.* **-pæ**) A chrysalis. **pupal,** *a.* **puparium** (pū pâr′ i ŭm), *n.* A coarctate pupa. **puparial,** *a.* **pupate** (pū′ păt), *v.i.* To become a pupa. **pupation** (pū pā′ shŭn), *n.* **pupigerous** (pū pij′ ėr ŭs), *a.* Forming a puparium. **Pupipara** (pū pip′ ȧ rȧ), *n.pl.* (*Ent.*) A division of Diptera in which the young are developed as pupæ within the body of the mother. **pupiparous,** *a.* **pupivorous,** *a.* Feeding on the pupæ of other insects. **pupoid,** *a.*

pupil (1) (pū′ pil) [F. *pupille,* L. *pūpillum,* nom. *-lus,* dim. of *pūpus,* boy], *n.* A young person of either sex under the care of a teacher, a scholar; (*Law*) a boy or girl under the age of puberty and under the care of a guardian, a ward. **pupil-teacher,** *n.* One in apprenticeship as a teacher and receiving general education at the same time. **pupilage, pupilship,** *n.* **pupilarity** (pū pi lăr′ i ti), *n.* (*Sc. Law*) The period before puberty. **pupilary** (1) (pū′ pi lȧr i), *a.* **pupilize,** *v.t.* To take charge of or teach (pupils). *v.i.* To take pupils.

pupil (2) (pū′ pil) [F. *pupille,* L. *pūpilla,* fem. of *pūpillus,* see prec.], *n.* The circular opening of the iris through which rays of light pass to the retina. **pupilary** (2), *a.* **pupillate, pupilled,** *a.* (*Zool.*) Having a central spot like a pupil (of ocelli). **pupillometer** (-lom′ ė tėr), *n.* An instrument for measuring the pupil of the eye or the distance between the eyes. **pupillometry** (-pi lom′ ė tri) [-METRY], *n.*

Pupipara, etc. [PUPA].

puppet (pŭp′ ėt) [O.F. *poupette,* dim. from L. *puppa, pūpa,* see PUPA], *n.* A small image or doll, representing a human being, moved by cords or wires in a mock drama; (*fig.*) one whose actions are under another's control; a mere tool. **puppet-clack** [PUPPET-VALVE]. **puppet-play, -show,** *n.* A play with puppets as dramatis personæ. **puppet-player,** *n.* One who manages the motion of puppets. **puppet-valve,** *n.* A disk on a stem with vertical motion to and from its seat. **puppetry,** *n.*

puppy (pŭp′ i) [prob. from F. *poupée,* doll, irreg. as prec.], *n.* A young dog; (*fig.*) a silly young fellow, a coxcomb, a fop. **puppy-dog,** *n.* A puppy. **puppy-headed,** *a.* **puppydom, puppyhood,** *n.* The state of being a puppy. **puppyish,** *a.* **puppyism,** *n.*

pur- [A.-F. form of O.F. *por-, pur-* (F. *pour-*), L. *por-,* PRO-], *pref.*

purana (poo ra′ nȧ) [Sansk., from *para,* formerly], *n.* Any of a great division of Sanskrit poems comprising the whole body of Hindu mythology. **puranic,** *a.*

Purbeck (pĕr′ bėk) [Isle of *Purbeck,* a peninsula in Dorset], *n.* Purbeck stone. **Purbeck marble:** One of the finer varieties of Purbeck stone, used for shafts, etc. in architecture. **Purbeck limestone:** A hard limestone from Purbeck.

purblind (pĕr′ blīnd) [orig. totally blind (perh. PURE or PUR-, BLIND)], *a.* Partially blind, near-sighted; dim-sighted. **purblindly,** *adv.* **purblindness,** *n.*

purchase (pĕr′ chȧs) [M.E. *purchasen,* A.-F. *purchacer,* O.F. *pur-, pourchacier,* to procure (PUR-, CHASE (1))], *v.t.* To obtain by payment of an equivalent; to buy; to acquire at the expense of some sacrifice, exertion, danger, etc.; to haul up, hoist, or draw in by means of a pulley, lever, capstan, etc. *n.* The act of purchasing or buying; that which is purchased; annual value, annual return, esp. from land; (*Law*) the acquisition of property by payment of a price or value, any mode of acquiring property other than by inheritance; (*Mech.*) advantage gained by the application of any mechanical power, leverage; an appliance furnishing this, as a rope, pulley, etc.; (*Hist.*) the system of buying commissions in the army, abolished in 1871. **purchase-money,** *n.* The price paid or contracted to be paid for anything purchased. **purchase tax:** A differential tax on certain goods sold to the public. **purchasable,** *a.* **purchaser,** *n.*

purdah (pĕr′ dȧ) [Hind. and Pers. *pardah*], *n.* A curtain, esp. one used to screen women from strangers; the custom in India of secluding women; a cotton cloth for making curtains.

pure (pūr) [O.F. *pur,* fem. *pure,* L. *pūrum,* nom. *-us*], *a.* Unmixed, unadulterated; free from anything foul or polluting, clear, clean; of unmixed descent, free from admixture with any other breed; mere, sheer, absolute; free from moral defilement, innocent, guiltless; unsullied, chaste; (*Mus.*) free from discordance, harshness, etc., perfectly correct in tone-intervals; (*Phon.*) having a single sound or tone, not combined with another; (of sciences) entirely theoretical, not applied. **n.* Purity. **adv.* Purely. **v.t.* To purify, to cleanse. **purely,** *adv.* **pureness,** *n.*

purée (pu rā) [F., etym. doubtful], *n.* A thick soup made by boiling meat or vegetables to a pulp and straining it.

***purfle** (pĕr fėl) [O.F. *porfiler,* as PROFILE], *n.* *To decorate with a wrought or ornamental border, to border; to adorn, to beautify; (*Her.*) to give a border of fur, etc., to; (*Arch.*) to ornament the edge of a canopy, etc., with knobs, crockets, etc. *n.* A border or edging of embroidered work. **purfling,** *n.* Ornamental bordering; the ornamental border on the backs and bellies of stringed instruments.

purgation (pŭr gā′ shŭn) [M.E. and O.F. *purgacion,* L. *purgātiōnem,* nom. *-tio,* from *purgāre,* to PURGE], *n.* The act of purging, purification; cleansing of the bowels by the use of purgatives; (*Hist.*) the act of clearing oneself from an imputed crime by oath or ordeal; (*R.-C. Ch.*) the process of spiritual purification of souls in purgatory. **purgative** (pĕr′ gȧ tiv), *a.* Having the quality of cleansing, esp. evacuating the intestines, aperient. *n.* An aperient or cathartic. **purgatively,** *adv.*

purgatory (pĕr′ gȧ tŏr i) [M.E. and A.-F. *purgatorie* (O.F. *purgatoire*), med. L. *purgātōrium*], *n.* A place or state of spiritual purging, esp. a place or state succeeding the present life in which, according to the R.-C. Church, the souls of the faithful are purified from venial sins by suffering; any place of temporary suffering or tribulation. *a.* Cleansing, purifying. **purgatorial** (-tôr′ i ȧl), ***purgatorious,** *a.* **purgatorian,** *a.* and *n.*

purge (pĕrj) [O.F. *purger,* L. *purgāre*], *v.t.* To cleanse or purify; to free (of or from impurity, sin, etc.); to remove (off or away) by cleansing; to clear (of an accusation, suspicion, etc.); (*Pol.*) to get rid of persons actively in opposition; to atone for, expiate, or annul (guilt, spiritual defilement, etc.); (*Med.*) to cleanse the bowels by cathartic action; *to clear (itself) by defecation (of a liquid). **v.i.* To grow pure by clarification. *n.* A purgative medicine; an act of purging. **purger,** *n.* **purging,** *a.* and *n.*

purification, etc. [PURIFY].

puriform (pūr′ i fôrm) [L. *pūs pūris,* PUS, -FORM], *a.* (*Path.*) In the form of pus; like pus.

purify (pūr′ i fī) [F. *purifier,* late L. *pūrificāre,* (*pūrus,* PURE, *-ficāre, facere,* to make)], *v.t.* To make pure, to cleanse; to free from sin, guilt, pollution, etc.; to make ceremonially clean; to clear of or from foreign elements, corruptions, etc. **purification** (-kā′ shŭn), *n.* The act of physical or spiritual purifying; the act or process of cleansing ceremonially, esp. of women after child-birth. **purificator** (pūr′ if i kā tŏr), *n.* (*Eccles.*) A piece of linen used to wipe the chalice and paten at the Eucharist. **purificatory,** *a.* Having power to purify; tending to purify. **purifier,** *n.*

Purim (pūr′ im) [Heb. *pūrīm*, pl. of *pūr*, prob. lot], *n.* A Jewish festival instituted in commemoration of the deliverance of the Jews from the destruction threatened by Haman's plot (Esther ix. 20–32).

purin (pūr′ in) [G. (PURE, URINE)], *n.* (*Chem.*) A basic compound related to uric acid, of which caffeine, xanthine, etc., are derivatives.

puriri (poo rē′ rē) [Maori], *n.* The N. Zealand oak or teak.

purist (pūr′ ist) [F. *puriste*], *n.* One advocating or affecting purity, esp. in the choice of words; a rigorous critic of literary style. **purism,** *n.* **puristic, -al** (pūr is′ tik, -ål), *a.*

Puritan (pūr′ i tån), *n.* One of a party or school of English Protestants of the 16th and 17th cents., who aimed at purifying religious worship from all ceremonies, etc., not authorized by Scripture, and at the strictest purity of conduct; any person practising or advocating extreme strictness in conduct or religion (usu. applied in a depreciatory sense). *a.* Pertaining to the Puritans; excessively strict in religion or morals. **puritanic, -al** (-tăn′ ik, -ål), *a.* **puritanically,** *adv.* **Puritanism** (pūr′ i tån izm), *n.* **puritanize,** *v.t.* and *i.*

purity (pūr′ i ti) [F. *pureté*], *n.* The state of being pure, cleanness; freedom from pollution, adulteration, or admixture of foreign elements; moral cleanness, innocence, chastity.

purl (1) (pěrl) [perh. from obs. *pirl*, to twist], *n.* An edging or fringe of twisted gold or silver wire; the thread or cord of which this is made; a small loop on the edges of pillow lace; a series of such loops as an ornamental hem or edging; an inversion of the stitches in knitting. *v.t.* To border or decorate with purl or purls; to knit with an inverted stitch.

purl (2) (pěrl) [etym. doubtful], *n.* Beer or ale with an infusion of wormwood; hot spiced gin and beer.

purl (3) (pěrl) [cp. Norw. *purla*, Swed. *porla*, to bubble up], *v.i.* To flow with a soft, bubbling, gurgling, or murmuring sound. *n.* A gentle bubbling, gurgling, or murmuring sound.

purl (4) (pěrl) [prob. from *pirl*, PURL (1)], *v.t.* and *i.* To upset, to overturn. *n.* A heavy fall, an overturn. **purler,** *n.* (*colloq.*) A heavy fall or throw, a cropper, a spill; a knockdown blow.

purlieu (pěr′ lū) [A.-F. *puralé*, O.F. *puralee* (PUR-, *aley*, see ALLEY (1)), assim. to LIEU], *n.* The bounds or limits within which one ranges; (*pl.*) outlying parts, outskirts, environs; (*Hist.*) the borders or outskirts of a forest, esp. a tract of land once included in forest but entirely or partially disafforested.

purlin (pěr′ lin) [etym. doubtful], *n.* A horizontal timber resting on the principal rafters and supporting the common rafters or boards on which the roof is laid.

purloin (pŭr loin′) [A.-F. and O.F. *purloigner* (PUR-, *loign, loin*, L. *longe*, FAR)], *v.t.* To steal, to take by theft; *to rob. *v.i.* To practise theft; to pilfer. **purloiner,** *n.*

purple (pěr′ pėl) [M.E. *purpre*, A.-S. *purpure*, L. PURPURA], *a.* Of the colour of red and blue blended, the former predominating; (*Rom. Ant.*) of the colour obtained from the mollusca, purpura and murex, prob. crimson; dyed with or as with blood; (*fig.*) imperial, regal. *n.* This colour; a purple pigment or dye; a purple dress or robe, esp. of an emperor, king, Roman consul, or a bishop; (*fig.*) imperial or regal power; the cardinalate; (*pl.*) swine fever; *purpura. *v.t.* To make or dye purple *v.i.* To become purple. **born in the purple:** Of high and wealthy, esp. royal or imperial family [see PORPHYROGENITE]. **royal purple:** A deep violet tending to blue. **purple emperor:** A variety of butterfly. **purplish, purply,** *a.*

purport (pŭr pôrt′) [A.-F. and O.F. *purporter* (PUR-, *porter*, L. *portāre*, to carry)], *v.t.* To convey as the meaning, to imply, to signify; to profess, to be meant to appear (to). *n.* (pěr′ pŏrt) Meaning, tenor, import; object, purpose; *pretext, disguise. **purportless,** *a.*

purpose (pěr′ pŏs) [M.E. and O.F. *pourpos*, L. *prōpositum*, p.p. of *prōpōnere*, to propose, see PROPOUND], *n.* End or aim, object, intention, design; meaning, purport; effect, result, consequence. *v.t.* To attend, to design. *v.i.* To have an intention or design; *to be bound (for a place). **purpose-novel** or **novel with a purpose:** A novel written to prove or advocate some social or other view. **on purpose:** Intentionally, designedly, not by accident; in order (that). **to the purpose:** With close relation to the matter in hand, relevantly; usefully. **purposeful,** *a.* **purposefully,** *adv.* **purposefulness,** *n.* **purposeless,** *a.* **purposelessly,** *adv.* **purposelessness,** *n.* **purposelike,** *a.* **purposely,** *adv.* Of set purpose, intentionally, not by accident. **purposive,** *a.* Having, displaying or characterized by purpose; purposeful. **purposiveness,** *n.*

purpresture (pŭr pres′ tyŭr) [O.F. *pourpresture*, from *pourprendre* (PUR-, *prendre*, L. *prendere*, to seize, to take)], *n.* (*Law*) An illegal enclosure or encroachment (now on the property of the public).

Purpura (pěr′ pū rå) [L., from Gr. *porphura*], *n.* A genus of gasteropods, many species of which secrete a fluid from which the ancients obtained their purple dye; (*Path.*) a morbid condition of the blood or blood-vessels characterized by livid spots on the skin. **purpure,** *n.* (*Her.*) Purple, represented in engraving by diagonal lines from left to right. **purpureal** (pŭr pū′ rė ål), *a.* (*Poet.*) Purple. **purpureo-,** *comb. form.* **purpurescent** (-res′ ėnt), *a.* Purplish. **purpuric** (pŭr pūr′ ik), *a.* Of or pertaining to the disease purpura; of or pertaining to a purple colour. **purpurin** (pěr′ pū rin), *n.* A red colouring matter used in dyeing, orig. obtained from madder.

purr (pěr) [imit.], *n.* A soft vibratory murmuring as of a cat when pleased. *v.i.* To make this sound. *v.t.* To signify, express, or utter thus. **purring,** *a.* and *n.* **purringly,** *adv.*

purse (pěrs) [A.-S. *purs*, late L. *bursa*, Gr. *bursa*, hide, leather], *n.* A small bag or pouch for money, usu. carried in the pocket; (*fig.*) money, funds, resources, a treasury; a sum of money subscribed or collected or offered as a gift, prize, etc.; a definite sum (varying in different Eastern countries); (*Nat. Hist.*) a bag-like receptacle, a pouch, a cyst. *v.t.* To wrinkle, to pucker; *to put into one's purse. *v.i.* To become wrinkled or puckered. **a light purse, an empty purse:** Poverty, want of resources. **a long purse, a heavy purse:** Wealth, riches. **privy purse** [PRIVY]. **public purse:** The national treasury. **purse-bearer,** *n.* One who has charge of the purse of another person or of a company, etc., a purser; an officer who carries the Great Seal in a purse before the Lord Chancellor. **purse-net,** *n.* A net the mouth of which can be drawn together with cords like an old-fashioned purse. **purse-proud,** *a.* Proud of one's wealth. **purse-seine,** *n.* A large purse-net for sea-fishing. **purse-strings,** *n.* Strings for drawing together the mouth of an old-fashioned purse; (*fig.*) control of expenditure. ***purse-taking,** *n.* Thieving. **purseful,** *n.* **purseless,** *a.*

purser (pěr′ sėr), *n.* An officer on board ship in charge of the provisions, clothing, pay, and general business. **pursership,** *n.*

purslane (pěr′ slån) [O.F. *porcelaine*, L. *porcilāca*, PORTULACA, assim. to PORCELAIN], *n.* A succulent herb, *Portulaca oleracea*, used as a salad and pot-herb.

pursue (pŭr sū′) [A.-F. *pursuer*, O.F. *porsievre* (F. *poursuivre*), late L. *prōsequere* (PRO-, *sequere, sequī*, to follow)], *v.t.* To follow with intent to seize, kill, etc.; to try persistently to gain or obtain, to seek; to proceed along, to go in accordance with; to follow up, to prosecute, to practise continuously; to attend persistently (of consequences, etc.); *to attend, to accompany. *v.i.* To follow, to seek (after); to go in pursuit; to go on, to proceed, to continue. **pursuable,** *a.* **pursuance,** *n.* **pursuant,** *a.* In accordance, consonant, conformable (to). *adv.* In accordance or conformably (to). **pursuantly,** adv. **pursuer,** *n.* One who pursues; (*Sc. Law*) a plaintiff, a prosecutor.

pursuit (pėr sūt'), *n.* The act of pursuing, a following; a prosecution, an endeavour to attain some end; any employment, occupation, business, or recreation that one follows persistently.

pursuivant (pĕr' swi vȧnt) [O.F. *porsivant* (F. *poursuivant*), pres.p., as prec.], *n.* (*Her.*) An attendant on a herald, an officer of the College of Arms of lower rank than a herald; (*poet.*) a follower, an attendant.

pursy (1) (pĕr' si) [formerly *pursive*, A.-F. *porsif*, O.F. *polsif* (F. *poussif*), from *polser* (F. *pousser*), to breathe with labour, from L. *pulsāre*, to PULSE (1)], *a.* Short-winded, asthmatical; fat, corpulent. **pursiness,** *n.*

pursy (2) (pĕr' si) [PURSE, -Y], *a.* Like a purse, puckered up like a purse-mouth; moneyed, purse-proud.

***purtenance** [APPURTENANCE].

purulent (pūr' ů lėnt) [F., from L. *pūrulentus*, from *pūs pūris*, PUS], *a.* Consisting of or discharging pus or matter. **purulence, -lency,** *n.* **purulently,** *adv.*

purvey (pủr vā') [A.-F. *purveier* (F. *pourvoir*), to PROVIDE], *v.t.* To provide, to supply, esp. provisions; to procure; *to foresee. *v.i.* To make provision; to act as purveyor; to pimp, to pander. **purveyance,** *n.* The purveying or providing of provisions; provisions supplied; (*Hist.*) the old royal prerogative of buying up provisions, impressing horses, etc. **purveyor,** *n.* One who purveys provisions, etc., a caterer, esp. on a large scale; *a procurer, a pimp.

purview (pĕr' vū) [A.-F. *purveu* (F. *pourvu*), p.p. of *purveier*, see prec.], *n.* Extent, range, scope, intention; range of vision, knowledge, etc.; (*Law*) the body of a statute consisting of the enacting clauses.

pus (pŭs) [L.], *n.* The matter secreted from inflamed tissues, the product of suppuration.

Puseyism (pū' zi izm), *n.* The High Church tenets of the Oxford School of which Dr. Pusey (1800–82) was a prominent member, Tractarianism. **Puseyite,** *a.* and *n.*

push (push) [O.F. *pousser*, L. *pulsāre*, to PULSATE], *v.t.* To press against with force, tending to urge forward; to move (a body along, up, down, etc.) thus; to urge forward, to impel, to drive, to carry on vigorously; to make (one's way) vigorously; to cause to shoot out or project; to press hard. *v.i.* To exert pressure (against, upon, etc.); to press forward, to make one's way vigorously, to hasten forward energetically; to thrust or butt (against); (*Billiards*) to make a push-stroke. *n.* The act of pushing, a thrust, a shove; a vigorous effort, an attempt, an onset; pressure; an exigency, a crisis, an extremity; (*colloq.*) persevering energy, self-assertion; (*Mil.*) an offensive; (*Billiards*) a stroke in which the ball is pushed, not struck; (*Austral.*) a gang of larrikins, a clique or party. **to get the push:** (*slang*) To lose one's job. **to push off:** To push against the bank with an oar so as to move a boat off; (*slang*) to go away. **to push on:** To press forward; to hasten; to urge or drive on. **push-cart,** *n.* (*Am.*) A barrow. **push-bike, -bicycle,** *n.* One worked by the rider as distinguished from a motor-bicycle. **push-button,** *n.* (*Elec.*) A device for opening or closing an electric circuit by the pressure of the finger on a button. **push-pin,** *n.* A child's game. **push-stroke,** *n.* (*Billiards*) A push. **pusher,** *n.* **pusher aeroplane,** *n.* (*Aviat.*) An aeroplane with its propeller at the rear. **pushful,** *a.* (*colloq.*) Self-assertive, energetic, vigorous or persistent in advancing oneself. **pushfulness,** *n.* **pushing,** *a.* Enterprising, energetic. **pushingly,** *adv.* **push-pull amplification,** *n.* (*Radio.*) Amplification using, for example, two triodes in parallel in which the grid of one valve is driven negative while the other grid is driven positive, and vice versa. This results in a decrease of distortion.

Pushtoo (pŭsh' too) [Pers. *Pashto*], *n.* The Afghan language.

pusillanimous (pū si lăn' i mủs) [eccles. L. *pusillanimis* (*pusillus*, small, petty, *animus*, soul)], *a.* Destitute of courage, firmness, or strength of mind, fainthearted. **pusillanimity** (-nim' i ti), *n.* **pusillanimousness, pusillanimously,** *adv.*

puss (pus) [cp. Dut. *poes*, L.G. *puus*, Norw. *puse*, Swed. dial. *pus*; prob. imit.], *n.* A pet name for a cat, esp. in calling; a hare; (*colloq.*) a child, a girl. **puss-moth,** *n.* A large Bombycid moth, *Cerura vinula.* **pussy,** *n.* (*Childish*) Puss. **pussy-cat,** *n.* A cat; anything woolly or fuzzy, as a willow catkin. **pussyfoot** [from nickname of W. E. Johnson, 1862–1945], *n.* A fanatic advocate of prohibition. **pussy-willow,** *n.* A small American willow, *Salix discolor.*

pustule (pŭs' tūl) [F., from L. *pustula*, prob. conn. with Gr. *phusalis*, *phuskē*, a bladder, *phusan*, to blow], *n.* A small vesicle containing pus, a pimple; (*Bot., Zool., etc.*) a small excrescence, a wart, a blister. **pustular,** *a.* **pustulate** (pŭs' tū lāt), *v.t.* and *i.* To form into pustules. *a.* (-lȧt) Covered with pustules or excrescences. **pustulation** (-lā' shủn), *n.* **pustulous,** *a.*

put (1) (put) [late A.-S. *putian* (in *putung*), *potian*, to put, *pȳtan*, to put or thrust out], *v.t.* (*past & p.p.* **put**) To move so as to place in some position; to set, lay, place, or deposit; to bring into some particular state or condition; to present, to produce; to express, to state, to render, to translate (into); to apply, to set, to submit, to impose; to stake (money on), to dispose, to inflict; to subject, to commit (to or upon); to advance, to propose (for consideration, etc.); to constrain, to incite, to force, to make (a person do, etc.); to make (one) appear in the right, wrong, etc.; to hurl, to cast, to throw; to thrust, to stab with. *v.i.* (*Naut.*) To go, to proceed, to steer one's course (in a specified direction). *n.* The act of putting; a cast, a throw (of a weight, etc.); an agreement to sell or deliver (stock, goods, etc.) at a stipulated price within a specified time; a thrust; *a game of cards. **to put about:** To inconvenience; (*Naut.*) to go about, to change the course of to the opposite tack; (*colloq.*) to make public, to spread abroad. **to put across:** To effect successfully. **to put away:** To remove; to lay by; to divorce; (*slang*) to consume. **to put back:** To retard, to check the forward motion of; to move the hands of (a clock) back; to replace; (*Naut.*) to return (to land, etc.). **to put by:** To put, set, or lay aside; to evade; to put off with evasion; (*colloq.*) to desist from. **to put down:** To suppress, to crush; to take down, to snub, to degrade; to confute, to silence; to reduce, to diminish; to set down, to enter, to subscribe; to reckon, to consider, to attribute; (*colloq.*) to dispense with, to give up. **to put forth:** To present to notice; to publish, to put into circulation; to extend; to shoot out; to exert; to sprout, to bud. **to put forward:** To set forth, to advance, to propose; to thrust (oneself) into prominence; to move the hands of (a clock) onwards. **to put in:** To introduce, to interject, to interpose; to insert, to enter; to install in office, etc., to present, to submit (in a court of law, etc.); to enter a harbour; (*colloq.*) to spend, to pass (time). **to put in mind:** To remind. **to put it past one:** To consider one incapable of some action. **to put off.** To lay aside, to discard, to take off; to postpone; to disappoint, to evade, to hinder, to dissuade (from); to foist, to palm off (with). **to put on:** To take on; to clothe oneself with; to assume; to add; to bring into play, to exert; to appoint; to move the hands of (a clock) forward. **to put out:** To invest, to place (at interest); to eject; to extinguish; to disconcert; to annoy, to irritate; to inconvenience; to exert; to dislocate. **to put over:** To secure appreciation of. **to put the acid on:** (*Austral. colloq.*) To ask for a loan. **to put to it:** To distress; to press hard. **to put up:** To raise; to offer, to present; to offer (oneself) as a candidate; to present as a candidate; to publish (banns, etc.); to pack up; to place in a safe place; to lay aside; to erect, to build; to lodge and entertain. **to put up with:** To tolerate, to submit to. **to put upon:** To victimize. **to stay put:** To remain, not to move.

***put** (2) (pŭt) [*colloq.*], *n.* A silly fellow, a lout, a bumpkin.

put (3) [PUTT].

putamen (pū tā' mėn) [L., from *putāre*, to prune], *n.* The hard bony stone or endocarp of a drupe; the membrane or skin of an egg; (*Anat.*) the outer zone of the lenticular nucleus of the brain.

putative (pū' tȧ tiv) [F. *putatif*, fem. *-tive*, late L. *putātivus*, from *putāre*, to think], *a.* Reputed, supposed; commonly regarded as. **putatively,** *adv.*

***pute** (pūt) [L. *putus*], *a.* Clean, pure. **pure and pute** or **pure pute:** Pure, mere.

puteal (pū' tė ȧl) [L. *puteāle*, neut. of *puteālis*, from *puteus*, well], *n.* The stone kerb round the opening of a well.

putid (pū' tid) [L. *pūtidus*, from *pūtēre*, to stink], *a.* Foul, mean, low, worthless. **putidness,** *n.*

putlog (pŭt' log) [etym. doubtful], *n.* A short horizontal piece of timber for the floor of a scaffold to rest on.

putrefy (pū' trė fī) [F. *putréfier*, L. *putrefacere* (*putre-*, as in *putrēre*, to be rotten, *facere*, to make)], *v.t.* To make putrid; to cause to rot or decay; to make carious or gangrenous; to corrupt. *v.i.* To become putrid, to rot, to decay; to fester, to suppurate. ***putredinous** (pū tred' i nŭs), *a.* **putrefaction** (-făk' shŭn), *n.* **putrefactive** (pū' trė făk tiv), *a.* **putrescent** (pū tres' ėnt), *a.* **putrescence,** *n.* **putrescible,** *a.* **putrescin** (pū tres' in), *n.* (*Chem.*) A poisonous alkaloid contained in decaying animal matter.

putrid (pū' trid) [L. *putridus*, from *putrēre*, to rot, from *puter*, rotten], *a.* In a state of putrefaction, decomposition, or decay; tainted, foul, noxious; (*fig.*) corrupt. **putrid fever:** Typhus or jail-fever. **putrid sore throat:** A gangrenous form of laryngitis or diphtheria. **putridity** (-trid' i ti), **putridness,** *n.* **putridly,** *adv.*

putsch (puch) [G.], *n.* A rising, revolt.

putt (pŭt) [var. of PUT (1)], *v.i.* (*Golf*) To strike the ball with a putter. *v.t.* To strike (the ball) gently with a putter so as to get it into the hole on the putting-green. *n.* This stroke. **putter** (pŭt' ėr), *n.* A short, stiff golf-club, used for striking the ball on the putting-green. **putting-green,** *n.* The piece of ground on a golf-course, usu. kept rolled, closely mown, and clear of obstacles, round a **putting-hole.**

puttee (pŭt' i) [Hindi *patti*, bandage], *n.* A long strip of cloth wound spirally round the leg, usu. from ankle to knee, as a form of gaiter.

putter, putting-green, etc. [PUTT].

puttier [PUTTY].

***puttock** (pŭt' ŏk) [M.E. *puttocke*, etym. doubtful], *n.* A kite or buzzard.

putty (pŭt' i) [F. *potée*, orig. potful, see POT], *n.* Calcined tin or lead used by jewellers as polishing-powder for glass, metal, etc.; whiting and linseed-oil beaten up into a tenacious cement, used in glazing; fine lime-mortar used by plasterers for filling cracks, etc. *v.t.* To fix, cement, fill up, or cover with putty. **up to putty:** (*Austral. slang*) No good, valueless, of bad quality. **putty-faced,** *a.* Having a smooth, colourless face like putty. **putty-powder,** *n.* Jewellers' putty in the form of powder, used for polishing. **putty-root,** *n.* An American orchid, *Aplectrum hyemale*, the root of which contains glutinous matter used as cement. **puttier,** *n.* A worker with putty, a glazier.

put-up (put ŭp') , *a.* (*colloq.*) Pre-concerted or contrived in an artful way.

puy (pwē) [F., ult. from L. *podium*, elevation, height], *n.* A conical hill of volcanic origin, esp. in Auvergne.

puzzle (pŭz' ėl) [etym. doubtful], *n.* A state of bewilderment or perplexity; a perplexing problem, question, or enigma; a toy, riddle, or other contrivance for exercising ingenuity or patience. *v.t.* To perplex, to embarrass, to mystify; *to make intricate. *v.i.* To be bewildered or perplexed. **to puzzle out:** To discover, or work out by mental labour. **puzzle-headed,** *a.* Having the head full of confused notions. **puzzle-peg,** *n.* A piece of wood fastened under the jaw of a dog so as to keep his nose from the ground. **puzzledom, puzzlement, puzzler,** *n.* **puzzlingly,** *adv.*

puzzolana [POZZOLANA].

pyæmia (pī ē miȧ) [Gr. *puon*, pus, *haima*, blood], *n.* (*Path.*) Blood-poisoning, due to the absorption of putrid matter into the system. **pyæmic,** *a.*

pyalla (pī ăl' ȧ) [Austral. abor.], *v.i.* To shout, to yell.

pycnidium (pik nid' i ŭm) [Gr. *puknos*, thick, *-idion*, dim. suf.], *n.* (*pl.* ***-dia***) (*Bot.*) A receptacle bearing pycnidiospores or stylospores in certain fungi. **pycnid** (pik' nid), *n.* **pycnidiospore** (pik nid' i ō spôr), *n.* A stylospore developed in a *pycnidium.*

pycnite (pik' nīt) [Gr. *pukn-os*, see foll., -ITE], *n.* (*Min.*) A columnar variety of topaz.

pycno- [Gr. *puknos*, thick, dense], *comb. form.* **pycnodont** (pik' nō dont) [Gr. *odous odontos*, tooth], *n.* (*Ichthyol.*) Any individual of the Pycnodontidæ, a family of extinct ganoid fishes. *a.* Pertaining to or having the characteristics of the Pycnodontidæ. **pycnogonid** (pik nog' ō nid) [Gr. *gonu*, knee], *n.* (*Zool.*) A marine arthropod belonging to the group Pycnogonida, comprising the sea-spiders. **pycnogonoid,** *a.* and *n.* **pycnometer** (pik nom' ė tėr) [-METER], *n.* A bottle or flask used in measuring the specific gravity of fluids. **pycnospore** [PYCNIDIOSPORE]. **pycnostyle** (pik' nō stīl) [Gr. *stulos*, column], *a.* (*Arch.*) Having an intercolumniation of one diameter and a half. *n.* A pycnostyle building.

***pye** [PIE (1)]. ***pyebald** [PIEBALD].

pye-dog (pī' dog) [Hind.], *n.* A pariah dog, a cur.

pyelitis (pī ė lī' tis) [mod. L. (Gr. *puelos*, trough, -ITIS)], *n.* (*Path.*) Inflammation of the pelvis of the kidney. **pyelitic** (-lit' ik), *a.* **pyelo-,** *comb. form.* **pyelonephritis** (-nė frī' tis), *n.* Inflammation of the kidney and of the renal pelvis. **pyelonephritic** (-frit' ik), *a.* **pyemia** [PYÆMIA].

pygal (pī' găl) [Gr. *pug-ē*, rump, -AL], *a.* (*Zool.*) Of, pertaining to, or near the rump or hind quarters. *n.* The pygal shield or plate of the carapace of a turtle.

pygarg (pī' garg) [L. *pygargus*, Gr. *pugargus* (*pug-ē*, rump, *argos*, white)], *n.* The osprey; an antelope mentioned by Herodotus and Pliny.

pygmy (pig' mi) [L. *pygmæus*, Gr. *pugmaios*, dwarfish, from *pugmē*, fist, the length from elbow to knuckles], *n.* One of a race of dwarfish people mentioned by Herodotus and other ancient historians as living in Africa and India; one of various dwarfish races living in Malaysia and Central Africa, esp. the Akka, Batwa, and Obongo of equatorial Africa; a dwarf, a small man, anything very diminutive; a pixy, a fairy; (*fig.*) one having a certain faculty or quality in relatively a very small degree; *the chimpanzee. **pygmæan** (-mē' ȧn), *a.*

pygo- [Gr. *pugo-*, *pugē*, rump], *comb. form.* **pygopod** (pī' gō pod) [Gr. *pous podos*, foot], *a.* (*Zool.*) Of or pertaining to the Pygopedes, an order of aquatic birds; of or belonging to the Pygopodidæ, a family of Australian lizards. *n.* One of the Pygopodidæ. **pygostyle** (pī' gō stīl), *n.* (*Ornith.*) The vomer or ploughshare bone forming the end of the vertebral column in most birds. **pygostyled,** *a.*

pyjamas (pi-, pī ja′ maz) [Pers. and Hind. *pāe jāmah* (*pāe*, by, *jāmah*, clothing, garment)], *n.pl.* Loose trousers of silk, cotton, etc., worn by both sexes among Mohammedans in Pakistan; a sleeping-suit consisting of a loose jacket and trousers.

pylon (pī′ lŏn) [Gr. *pulōn*, from *pulē*, gate], *n.* (*Arch.*) A gateway of imposing form or dimensions, esp. the monumental gateway of an Egyptian temple; a stake marking out the course in an aerodrome; a structure, usu. of steel, supporting an electric cable.

pylorus (pī lôr′ ŭs) [late L., from Gr. *pulōros*, gatekeeper (*pulē*, gate, *ouros*, keeper, watcher)], *n.* (*Anat.*) The contracted end of the stomach leading into the small intestine; the adjoining part of the stomach. **pyloric** (-lor′ ik), *a.*

pyo- [Gr. *puon*, pus], *comb. form.* (*Path.*). **pyogenesis** (pī ō jen′ ė sis) [GENESIS], *n.* The formation of pus, suppuration. **pyogenetic** (-nit′ ik), **pyogenic** (-jen′ ik), *a.* **pyoid** (pī′ oid), *a.* Of the nature of pus. **pyonephritis** (pī ō nė frī′ tis) [NEPHRITIS], *n.* Suppurative inflammation of the kidney. **pyonoma** (-nō′ mȧ), *n.* A suppurating sore. **pyopoiesis** [PYOGENESIS]. **pyoptysis** (pī ŏp tī′ sis), *n.* Expectoration of pus, as in consumption. **pyorrhœa** (pī ō rē′ ȧ), *n.* Discharge of pus. **pyosis** (pī ō′ sis), *n.* Suppuration.

pyr- [PYRO-], *comb. form.* **pyracanth** (pīr′ ȧ kănth) [L. *pyracantha*, Gr. *puracantha* (see ACANTHUS)], *n.* An evergreen thorny shrub, *Cratægus pyracantha*, with white flowers and coral-red berries, also called the evergreen thorn, commonly trained against walls as an ornamental climber. **pyrallolite** (pīr ăl′ ō līt) [Gr. *allos*, other, -LITE], *n.* (*Min.*) An altered pyroxene from Finland.

pyramid (pir′ ȧ mid) [L. *pyramis -idis*, Gr. *puramis -idos*, prob. of Egypt. orig.], *n.* A monumental structure of masonry, with a square base and triangular sloping sides meeting at the apex; a similar solid body, with a triangular or polygonal but usu. square base; a pile or heap of this shape; a tree trained in this form; (*Billiards*) a game of pool played with fifteen coloured balls and a cue-ball. **the Pyramids:** The great pyramids of ancient Egypt. **pyramidal** (pi răm′ i dȧl), ***pyramidic, -al** (-mid′ ik, -ȧl), *a.* **pyramidally, pyramidically,** *adv.* **pyramidist** (pir′ ȧ mid ist), *n.* A student or investigator of the origin, structure, etc., of ancient pyramids, esp. those of Egypt. **pyramidalism,** *n.* **pyramidize,** *v.t.* **pyramidoid** (pi răm′ i doid), ***pyramoid** (pir′ ȧ moid), *n.* A solid resembling a pyramid; (*erron.*) a parabolic spindle. **pyramidwise,** *adv.* **pyramidon** (pi răm′ i dŏn) [after ACCORDION], *n.* (*Organ*) A stop having stopped pipes like inverted pyramids, producing very deep tones.

pyrargyrite (pi rar′ ji rīt) [PYR-, Gr. *arguros*, silver, -ITE], *n.* (*Min.*) A native sulphide of silver and antimony.

pyre (pīr) [L. *pyra*, Gr. *pura*, cogn. with *pur*, fire], *n.* A funeral pile for burning a dead body; any pile of combustibles.

pyrene (1) (pī′ rēn) [Gr. *purēn*], *n.* (*Bot.*) The stone of a drupe, a putamen.

pyrene (2) (pī′ rēn) [Gr. *pur*, fire, -ENE], *n.* (*Chem.*) One of the hydrocarbons obtained in the dry distillation of coal.

Pyrethrum (pī rē′ thrŭm, -reth′ rŭm) [L., from Gr. *purethron*, as prec.], *n.* A genus of compositous plants (usu. regarded as a sub-division of *Chrysanthemum*), comprising the feverfew.

pyretic (pī ret′ ik) [Gr. *puretos*, fever, -IC], *a.* Of, relating to, or producing fever; remedial in fever. *n.* A pyretic medicine. **pyretology** (-tol′ ō ji) [-LOGY], *n.* **pyrexia** (pī rek′ si ȧ), *n.* Fever, feverish condition. **pyrexial, -ical,** *a.*

pyrheliometer (pir hē li om′ ė tėr) [PYR-, HELIOMETER], *n.* An instrument for measuring the amount of solar radiation. **pyrheliometric** (-met′ rik), *a.*

pyridine (pir′-, pīr′ i dīn) [PYR-, -ID, -INE], *n.* (*Chem.*) A liquid alkaloid obtained from bone-oil, coal-tar naphtha, etc., used as a remedy for asthma.

pyriform (pīr′-, pir′ i fôrm) [med. L. *pyrum*, L. *pirum*, PEAR, -FORM], *a.* Pear-shaped.

pyrites (pī rī′ tēz) [L., from Gr. *puritēs*, orig. pertaining to fire, from *pur*, fire], *n.* A native sulphide of iron, one of two common sulphides, chalcopyrite, yellow or copper pyrites, or marcasite, usu. called iron pyrites. **pyretaceous** (-tā′ shŭs), **pyritic, -al** (pī-, pi rit′ ik, -ȧl), **pyritous** (pīr′ i tŭs), *a.* **pyritiferous** (-tif′ ėr ŭs), *a.* **pyritize** (pīr′ i tīz), *v.t.* **pyritoid,** *a.* **pyritology** (-tol′ ō ji) [-LOGY], *n.*

pyro (pīr′ ō) [short for PYROGALLIC], *n.* Pyrogallic acid.

pyro- [Gr. *pur puros*, fire], *comb. form.* **pyroacetic** (pīr ō ȧ sē′ tik) [ACETIC], *a.* (*Chem.*) Of or derived from acetic acid by heat. **pyroclastic** (-klăs′ tik) [Gr. *klastos*, broken], *a.* (*Geol.*) Formed from or consisting of the fragments broken up or ejected by volcanic action. **pyro-electric** (pīr′ ō ė lek′ trik), *a.* (*Min.*) Becoming electropolar on heating (of some minerals). **pyro-electricity** (-tris′ i ti), *n.* **pyrogallic** (pīr ō găl′ ik), *a.* Produced from gallic acid by heat. **pyrogallol,** *n.* Pyrogallic acid, used as a developing agent in photography.

pyrogen (pīr′ ō jen) [PYRO-, -GEN], *n.* (*Chem.*) A substance, such as a ptomaine, that produces fever on being introduced into the body; *electricity. **pyrogenetic** (-net′ ik), **pryogenic** (-jen′ ik), *a.* Producing heat; (*Path.*) producing feverishness; (*Geol.*) pyrogenous. **pyrogenous** (pī roj′ ė nŭs), *a.* (*Geol.*) Produced by fire, igneous. **pyrognomic** (pīr ŏg nō′ mik) [GNOMIC], *a.* (*Min.*) Having the property of becoming incandescent when heated. **pyrognostic** (nos′ tik), *a.* Of or pertaining to those properties of a mineral that are determinable by heat. **pyrography** (pī rog′ rȧ fi) [-GRAPHY], *n.* The art of making designs in wood by means of fire, poker-work. **pyrograph** (pīr′ ō grăf), *v.i.* **pyrographer, -phist** (pī rog′ rȧ fėr, -fist), *n.* **pyrographic** (-grăf′ ik), *a.* **pyrogravure** (pīr ō grȧ vūr′), *n.* Pyrography; a picture produced by this means.

Pyrola (pir′ ō lȧ) [dim., from med. L. *pyrus*, L. *pirus*, PEAR], *n.* (*Bot.*) A genus of low evergreen plants of the family Ericaceæ, comprising the winter-greens.

pyrolatry (pī rol′ ȧ tri) [PYRO-, -LATRY], *n.* Fire-worship. **pyroligneous** (pīr ō lig′ nė ŭs) [LIGNEOUS], *a.* Derived from wood by heat. **pyrolignite,** *n.* A salt of pyroligneous acid. **pyrology** (pī rol′ ō ji) [-LOGY], *n.* The science of fire or heat, esp. the branch of chemistry dealing with the application of heat, blow-pipe analysis, etc. **pyrological** (-loj′ i kȧl), *a.* **pyrologist** (-rol′ ō jist), *n.* **pyrolusite** (pīr ō loo′ sīt) [G. *pyrolusit* (Gr. *lousis*, washing, -ITE)], *n.* (*Min.*) Native manganese dioxide, one of the most important of the ores of manganese. **pyromagnetic** (pīr ō măg net′ ik) [MAGNETIC], *a.* Of or pertaining to the alterations of magnetic intensity due to changes in temperature. **pyromagnetic generator:** A dynamo for generating electricity by induction through changes in the temperature of the field-magnets.

***pyromancy** (pīr′ ō măn si) [O.F. *pyromancie*, late L. *pyromantīa*, Gr. *puromanteia* (-MANCY)], *n.* Divination by fire. **pyromania** (pīr ō mā′ ni ȧ) [-MANIA], *n.* Insanity manifested in an irresistible desire to destroy by fire. **pyromaniac,** *n.* **pyromaniacal** (-nī′ ȧ kȧl), *a.* ***pyromantic** (-măn′ tik), *a.* Pertaining to pyromancy.

pyrometer (pī rom′ ė tėr) [PYRO-, -METER], *n.* An instrument for measuring high temperatures; an instrument for measuring the expansion of bodies by heat. **pyrometric, -al** (-met′ rik, -ȧl), *a.* **pyrometrically,** *adv.* **pyrometry** (-rom′ ė tri), *n.* **pyromorphous** (pīr ō môr′ fŭs) [Gr. *morphē*, from, -OUS], *a.* (*Min.*) Crystallizing after fusion by heat. ***pyronomics** (-nom′ iks), *n.* The science of heat.

pyrope (pīr′ ŏp) [O.F. *pirope*, L. *pyrōpus*, Gr. *purō-*

pos (*pur*, fire, *ōps*, face, eye)], *n.* (*Min.*) A deep-red garnet.

pyrophane (pīr′ ō fān) [PYRO-, Gr. *-phanēs*, appearing], *n.* A variety of opal that absorbs melted wax and becomes translucent when heated and opaque again on cooling. **pyrophanous** (pī rof′ ȧ nŭs), *a.* **pyrophone** (pīr′ ō fōn) [-PHONE], *n.* A musical instrument the notes of which are produced in glass tubes each containing two hydrogen flames. ***pyrophorus*** (pī rof′ ō rŭs) [mod. L., from Gr. *purophoros* (*-phoros*, bearing)], *n.* (*pl.* ***-ri***) Any substance taking fire spontaneously on exposure to the air. **pyrophoric** (-for′ ik), **pyrophorous** (-rof′ō rŭs), *a.* **pyrophosphoric** (pīr ō fos for′ ik) [PHOSPHORIC], *a.* (*Chem.*) Derived by heat from phosphoric acid. **pyro-photograph** (pīr ō fō′ tō grăf) [PHOTOGRAPH], *n.* A photographic picture fixed on glass or porcelain by firing. **pyro-photographic** (-grăf′ ik), *a.* **pyro-photography** (-tog′ rȧ fi), *n.* **pyrophysalite** (pīr ō fis′ ȧ līt) [Gr. *phusallis*, bubble], *n.* (*Min.*) A coarse, nearly opaque variety of topaz which swells on being heated. **pyroscope** (pīr′ ō skōp) [-SCOPE], *n.* An instrument for measuring the intensity of radiant heat.

pyrosis (pī rō′ sis) [Gr. *purōsis*, from *puroun*, to set on fire], *n.* (*Path.*) Heartburn, acid dyspepsia, water-brash.

pyrosome (pīr′ ō sōm) [PYRO-, Gr. *sōma*, body], *n.* (*Zool.*) An animal of the genus *Pyrosoma*, consisting of highly phosphorescent compound ascidians united in free-swimming cylindrical colonies, mostly belonging to tropical seas. **pyrotartaric** (pīr ō tar tăr′ ik) [TARTARIC], *a.* (*Chem.*) Obtained by the dry distillation of tartaric acid. **pyrotartrate** (-tar′ trāt), *n.* A salt of pyrotartaric acid.

pyrotechnic (pīr ō tek′ nik) [PYRO-, Gr. *technē*, art, -IC], *a.* Pertaining to fireworks or their manufacture; of the nature of fireworks; (*fig.*) resembling a firework show, brilliant, dazzling. *n.pl.* The art of making fireworks; a display of fireworks. **pyrotechnical**, *a.* **pyrotechnically**, *adv.* **pyrotechnist**, *n.* **pyrotechny** (pīr′ ō tek ni), *n.*

***pyrotic** (pī rot′ ik) [Gr. *purōtikos*, from *puroun*, to burn], *a.* Caustic. *n.* A caustic substance.

pyroxene (pir′ ok sēn, pīr′ ok sēn) [PYRO- Gr. *xenos*, stranger], *n.* (*Min.*) A name used for a group of silicates of lime, magnesium or manganese, of various forms and origin. **pyroxenic** (-sen′ ik), *a.* **pyroxyle** (pī rok′ sil), **pyroxylin** (-si lin) [F. *pyroxyline* (Gr. *xulon*, wood)], *n.* Any explosive, including gun-cotton, obtained by immersing vegetable fibre in nitric or nitro-sulphuric acid, and then drying it. **pyroxylic** (-sil′ ik), *a.* Denoting the crude spirit obtained by the distillation of wood in closed vessels.

pyrrhic (1) (pir′ ik) [L. *pyrrhica*, Gr. *purrhichē*, from *Purrhichos*, the inventor], *n.* A warlike dance among the ancient Greeks; (*Pros.*) a metrical foot of two short syllables. *a.* Of or pertaining to such dance; (*Pros.*) consisting of two short syllables.

Pyrrhic (2) (pir′ ik), *a.* Of or pertaining to Pyrrhus. **Pyrrhic victory:** A victory that is as costly as a defeat, like that of Pyrrhus, king of Epirus, over the Romans at Asculum (279 B.C.).

Pyrrhonism (pir′ ō nizm), *n.* The sceptical philosophy taught by Pyrrho of Ellis, the Greek sceptical philosopher of the 4th cent. B.C.; universal doubt, philosophic nescience. **Pyrrhonian** (pi rō′ ni ȧn), **Pyrrhonic** (-ron′ ik), *a.* **Pyrrhonist** (pir′ ō nist), *n.*

Pyrus (pīr′ ŭs) [med. L., from L. *pirus*, PEAR], *n.* A genus of *Rosaceæ* comprising the apple and pear. **Pyrus Japonica:** A small tree or shrub of this genus bearing bright scarlet flowers.

Pythagorean (pī thăg ō rē′ ȧn), *n.* A follower of Pythagoras of Samos (6th cent. B.C.), philosopher and mathematician. *a.* Pertaining to Pythagoras or his philosophy. **Pythagoreanism, *Pythagorism** (-thăg′ ō rizm), *n.*

Pythian (pith′ i ȧn) [L. *Pythius*, Gr. *Puthios*, from *Puthō*, former name of Delphi], *a.* Pertaining to Delphi, to Apollo, or to his priestess who delivered oracles at Delphi. *n.* Apollo or his priestess at Delphi. **Pythic**, *a.* **Pythian** or **Pythic games:** One of the four great Panhellenic festivals, celebrated once every four years near Delphi.

pythogenic (pith ō jen′ ik) [Gr. *puthein*, to rot, Gr. *-gen*, root of *gennaein*, to produce, -IC], *a.* (*Hygiene*) Produced by filth or putrid matter. **pythogenesis**, *n.* Generation from or through filth.

python (1) (pī′ thōn) [L., from Gr. *Puthōn*. prob. from *Puthō*, see PYTHIAN], *n.* (*Gr. Myth.*) A gigantic serpent slain by Apollo near Delphi; (*Zool.*) a large non-venomous serpent that crushes its prey.

python (2) (pī′ thōn) [late L. *pytho -ōnem*, or late Gr. *puthōn*, prob. rel. to prec. but history obscure], *n.* A familiar spirit or demon; one possessed by this, a soothsayer, a diviner. **pythoness**, *n.* A woman possessed by a familiar spirit or having the gift of prophecy, a witch; applied esp. to the priestess of the temple of Apollo at Delphi who delivered the oracles. **pythonic** (-thon′ ik), *a.* Inspired, oracular, prophetic. **pythonism** (pī′ thō nizm), *n.*

pyuria (pi ū′ ri ȧ) [Gr. *puon*, pus; *ouron*, urine], *n.* (*Path.*) The presence of pus in the urine.

pyx (piks) [L. *pyxis*, Gr. *puxis*, a box, from *puxos*, box-tree], *n.* (*Eccles.*) The covered vessel, usu. of precious metal, in which the host is kept; a box at the Royal Mint in which sample coins are placed for testing at the annual trial by a jury of the Goldsmiths' Company. *v.t.* To test (a coin) by weighing and assaying.

pyxidium (pik sid′ i ŭm) [Gr. *puxidion*, dim. of prec.], *n.* (*pl.* **-dia**) (*Bot.*) A capsule or seed-vessel dehiscing by a transverse suture, as in the pimpernel.

pyxis (pik′ sis) [L., see PYX], *n.* A box, a casket; (*Bot.*) a pyxidium; (*Anat.*) the acetabulum of the hip-bone.

Q

Q, q, the seventeenth letter and the thirteenth consonant (*pl.* **Ques, Q's, Qs**), is always followed by *u*, the combination *qu* having the sound of *kw*. **to mind one's p's and q's** [P]. **Q-boat**, *n.* (*Nav.*) An armed vessel disguised as a merchantman, employed to lure and surprise hostile submarines.

qua (kwā) [L., abl. fem. sing. of *qui*, rel. pron.], *conj.* In the character of, by virtue of being, as.

quack (1) (kwăk) [imit., cp. Dut. *kwakken*, G. *quacken*, Icel. *kvaka*, also L. *coaxāre*, Gr. *koax*, a croak], *v.i.* To make a harsh cry like that of a duck; (*fig.*) to chatter loudly, to brag. *n.* The cry of a duck; a noisy outcry. **quack-quack**, *n.* (*Childish*) A duck.

quack (2) (kwăk) [short for QUACKSALVER], *n.* A mere pretender to knowledge or skill, esp. one in medicine offering pretentious remedies and nostrums; an ignorant practitioner, an empiric, a charlatan. *a.* Pertaining to quacks or quackery. **quackery, quackism**, *n.* **quackish**, *a.*

***quackle** (kwăk′ ėl) [freq. of QUACK (1)], *v.i.* To quack; to choke. *v.t.* To choke.

***quacksalver** (kwăk′ săl vėr) [Dut. *kwakzalver*, earlier *quacksalver*], *n.* One who brags of his medicines or salves; a quack.

quad (1) (kwod) [short for QUADRANGLE], *n.* A quadrangle or court, as of a college, etc.

quad (2) (kwod) [short for QUADRAT], *n.* (*Print.*) A quadrat. *v.i.* To insert quadrats (in a line of type).

quad (3) [QUOD].

quad (4) (kwod) [QUADRUPLET], *n.* (*colloq.*) One child (of quadruplets).

quadr- [QUADRI-], *comb. form.* Four.

Q

quadra (kwod′ rȧ) [L., a square], *n.* (*pl.* **-æ**) (*Arch.*) A socle or plinth of a podium; one of the fillets of an Ionic base.

quadrable [QUADRATE].

quadragenarian (kwod rȧ jė nâr′ i ȧn) [L. *quadrāgēnārius*, from *quadrāgēnī*, distrib. of *quadrāginta*, forty (*quadrus*, cogn. with *quatuor*, four, *-ginta*, prob. for *dekinta*, tenth, from *decem*, ten)], *a.* Forty years old. *n.* One forty years old. ***quadragene** (kwod′ rȧ jēn), *n.* A papal indulgence for forty days.

Quadragesima (kwod rȧ jes′ i mȧ) [med. L., fem. of *quadrāgēsimus*, fortieth, as prec.], *n.* The first Sunday in Lent, also called Quadragesima Sunday; *Lent, so called because it consists of forty days. **quadragesimal,** *a.* Lasting forty days (of a fast); pertaining to or used in Lent, Lenten. *n.pl.* Offerings formerly made to the mother church of a diocese on Mid-Lent Sunday.

quadrangle (kwod′ răng gėl) [F., from L. *quadrangulum*], *n.* A plane figure having four angles and four sides, esp. a square or rectangle; an open square or four-sided court surrounded by buildings; such a court together with the surrounding buildings. **quadrangular,** *a.* **quadrangularly,** *adv.*

quadrant (kwod′ rȧnt) [L. *quadrans -ntis*, as QUADRI-], *n.* The fourth part of the circumference of a circle, an arc of 90°; a plane figure contained by two radii of a circle at right angles to each other and the arc between them; a quarter of a sphere; an instrument shaped like a quarter-circle graduated for taking angular measurements; (*Naut.*) such an instrument formerly used for taking the altitude of the sun, now superseded by the sextant. **quadrantal** (-răn′ tȧl), *a.*

quadrat (kwod′ rȧt) [var. of foll.], *n.* (*Print.*) A block of type-metal lower than the type, used for spacing out lines, etc.; *an instrument formerly used in taking altitudes; (*Bot.*) a square of vegetation taped off for intensive study.

quadrate (kwod′ rȧt) [L. *quadrātus*, p.p. of *quadrāre*, to square, from *quadrus*, square], *a.* Square, rectangular; *(*Math.*) square, raised to the second power. *n.* The quadrate bone; a quadrate muscle; *a square, cubical, or rectangular object; *(*Astron.*) an aspect of the heavenly bodies, in which they are distant from each other 90″; (*Elec.*) the position when there is a phase difference of one quarter of a cycle between two alternating currents. **v.t.* (kwod rāt′, kwod′ rāt) To square; to make conformable. *v.i.* To square, to agree, to match, to correspond. **quadrate bone:** A bone by means of which the jaws are articulated with the skull in birds and reptiles. **quadrate muscle:** A square-shaped muscle in the hip, forearm, etc. **quadrable,** *a.* Capable of quadrature; (*Math.*) capable of being squared or of being represented by a finite number of algebraic terms. **quadratic** (kwod răt′ ik), *a.* (*Math.*) Involving the second and no higher power of the variable or unknown quantity; *square. *n.* A quadratic equation; (*pl.*) the part of algebra dealing with quadratic equations. **quadratrix** (kwod rā′ triks), *n.* (*pl.* **-trices**) A curve by means of which straight lines can be found equal to the circumference of circles or other curves and their several parts. **quadrature** (kwod′ rȧ tyůr), *n.* (*Math.*) The act of squaring or finding a square equal in area to a given curved figure; (*Astron.*) the position of a heavenly body with respect to another 90″ distant.

quadrel (kwod′ rėl) [It. *quadrello*, dim. of *quadro*, square, as QUADRI-], *n.* A square block; a brick or kind of artificial stone, used in Italy, made of chalky earth dried in the sun.

quadrennial (kwod ren′ i ȧl) [L. *quadriennium* (QUADRI-, *annus*, year)], *a.* Comprising or lasting four years; recurring every four years. **quadrennially,** *adv.* **quadrennium,** *n.* A period of four years.

quadri- [L., rel. to *quatuor*, four], *comb. form.* Four. **quadric** (kwod′ rik), *a.* (*Math.*) Of the second degree; quadratic. *n.* A quantic, curve, or surface of the second degree. **quadricapsular** (-kăp′ sū lȧr), *a.* (*Bot.*) Having four capsules. **quadricentennial** (-sen ten′ i ȧl), *n.* The 400th anniversary of an event. *a.* Pertaining to a period of 400 years. **quadriceps** (kwod′ ri seps), *n.* (*Anat.*) A four-headed muscle acting as extensor to the leg. **quadricone** (kwod′ ri kōn), *n.* (*Math.*) A quadric cone. **quadricorn** (kwod′ ri kôrn), *n.* (*Zool.*) Any animal having four horns or antennæ. *a.* Quadricornous. **quadricornous** (-kôr′ nůs), *a.* **quadricycle** (kwod′ ri sīkl), *n.* A cycle having four wheels. **quadridentate** (kwod ri den′ tȧt), *a.* (*Bot.*) Having four indentations or serrations. **quadrifid** (kwod′ ri fid), *a.* (*Bot.*) Cleft into four parts, segments, or lobes. **quadrifoliate** (-fō′ li ȧt), *a.* Four-leaved; having four leaflets. **quadriform** (kwod′ ri fôrm), *a.*

quadriga (kwod rī′ gȧ) [L., orig. in pl. form *quadrīgæ* for *quadrijugæ* (QUADRI-, *jugum*, yoke)], *n.* (*pl.* **-gæ**) An ancient Roman two-wheeled chariot drawn by four horses abreast.

quadrigeminal, -nous (kwod ri jem′ i nȧl, -nůs) [QUADRI-, GEMINOUS, see GEMINI], *n.* (*Anat.*) Pertaining to four medullary tubercles situated at the base of the brain. **quadrigeminate,** *a.* Fourfold; occurring in fours. **quadrigenarious** (kwod ri jė nâr′ i ůs), *a.* Consisting of four hundred. **quadrijugate, -gous** (kwod ri joo′ gȧt, -gůs), *a.* (*Bot.*) Pinnate with four pairs of leaflets.

quadrilateral (kwod ri lăt′ ėr ȧl) [L. *quadrilaterus*], *a.* Having four sides and four angles. *n.* A quadrangular figure or area. **the Quadrilateral:** (*Hist.*) The district in N. Italy defended by the fortresses of Mantua, Verona, Peschiera, and Legnano. **quadrilateralness,** *n.*

quadrilingual (kwod ri ling′ gwȧl) [QUADRI-, LINGUAL], *a.* Speaking or written in four languages. **quadriliteral** (kwod ri lit′ ėr ȧl), *a.* Consisting of four letters. *n.* A quadilateral word, esp. a Semitic root containing four consonants.

quadrille (kwȧ-, kȧ dril′) [F., from Sp. *cuadrillo*, a squadron, a band, dim. of *cuadra*, square, as QUADRI-], *n.* A dance consisting of five figures executed by four sets of couples; a piece of music for such a dance; a game of cards played by four persons with forty cards, fashionable in the 18th cent. *v.i.* To dance a quadrille; to play music for a quadrille.

quadrillion (kwȧ dril′ yȯn) [F. (QUADRI-, MILLION, cp. BILLION)], *n.* The number produced by raising a million to its fourth power, represented by 1 followed by 24 ciphers; (*Am. and F.*) the fifth power of a thousand, 1 followed by 15 ciphers. **quadrillionth,** *a.* and *n.*

quadrilobate (kwod ri lō′ bȧt) [QUADRI-, LOBATE], *a.* (*Bot.*) Having four lobes. **quadrilocular** (-lok′ ū lȧr), *a.* (*Bot.*) Having four cells or chambers. ***quadrimanous** [QUADRUMANOUS]. **quadrinomial** (-nō′ mi ȧl), *a.* (*Math.*) Consisting of four algebraic terms. *n.* A quantity consisting of four terms. **quadripartite** (-par′ tīt), *a.* Divided into or consisting of four parts; affecting or shared by four parties. **quadripartitely,** *adv.* **quadripartition** (-tish′ ůn), *n.* Division by four or into four parts. **quadripennate** (-pen′ ȧt), *a.* (*Ent.*) Having four functional wings. *n.* A quadripennate insect. **quadriphyllous** (-fil′ ůs), *a.* (*Bot.*) Having four leaves. ***quadrireme** (kwod′ ri rēm) [L. *quadrirēmis* (*rēmus*, oar)], *n.* (*Gr. and Rom. Ant.*) A galley having four banks of oars.

quadrisection (kwod ri sek′ shůn) [QUADRI-, SECTION], *n.* Division into four equal parts. **quadrisyllabic** (-si lăb′ ik), *a.* Consisting of four syllables. **quadrisyllable** (-sil′ ȧbl), *n.* **quadrivalent** (-riv′ ȧ lėnt), *a.* (*Chem.*) Having a valency or combining power of four. **quadrivalve** (kwod′ ri vălv), *n.* (*Bot.*) A plant with a quadrivalvular seed-pod; (*Arch.*) a door or shutter in four parts or leaves. *a.* Quadrivalvular. **quadrivalvular** (-văl′ vū lȧr), *a.* (*Bot.*) Opening by four valves.

quadrivium (kwod riv′ i ům) [L. (QUADRI-, *via*,

way)], *n.* In the Middle Ages, an educational course consisting of arithmetic, music, geometry, and astronomy. *****quadrivial,** *a.* Having four ways meeting in a point; pertaining to the quadrivium. *n.pl.* The sciences comprised in this.

quadroon (kwod roon′) [Sp. *cuarteron*, from *cuarto*, fourth, as QUARTO, assim. to QUADRI-], *n.* The offspring of a mulatto and a white; a person of quarter negro and three-quarters white blood; applied to similarly proportioned hybrids in human, animal, and vegetable stocks.

Quadrumana (kwod roo′ mȧ nȧ) [L. *quadru-*, QUADRI-, L. *manus*, hand], *n.pl.* (*Zool.*) An order of mammals in which the hind as well as the fore feet have an opposable digit and are used as hands, containing the monkeys, apes, baboons, and lemurs. **quadrumane** (kwod′ ru̇ mān), *n.* **quadrumanous** (kwod roo′ mȧ nŭs), *a.*

quadruped (kwod′ ru̇ ped) [L. *quadrupes -pedis* (*quadru-*, QUADRI-, *pes pedis*, foot)], *n.* A four-footed animal, esp. a mammal. *a.* Having four legs and feet. **quadrupedal** (-roo′ pė dȧl), *a.*

quadruple (kwod′ ru pėl) [F., from L. *quadruplum*, nom. *-plus* (*quadru-*, QUADRI-, *-plus*, fold)], *a.* Fourfold; consisting of four parts; involving four members, units, etc.; multiplied by four; equal to four times the number or quantity of. *n.* A number or quantity four times as great as another; four times as much or as many. *v.i.* To become fourfold as much; to increase fourfold. *v.t.* To make four times as much; to multiply fourfold. **quadruplet** (kwod′ ru̇ plet), *n.* A compound or combination of four things working together; a bicycle for four; (*pl.*) four children born of the same mother at one birth. **quadruplex,** *a.* Fourfold; used four times over (of a telegraphic wire). *n.* An electrical apparatus by means of which four messages may be sent simultaneously over one telegraphic wire. *v.t.* To arrange (a wire, etc.) for quadruplex working. **quadruplicate** (-roo′ pli kȧt), *a.* Fourfold; four times as many or as much; four times copied. *n.* One of four copies or similar things; quadruplicity. *v.t.* (-kāt) To make fourfold, to quadruple. **quadruplication** (-kā′ shŭn), *n.* **quadruplicity** (-plis′ i ti), *n.* **quadruply,** *adv.*

quære (kwēr′ ē) [L., imp. of *quærere*, to ask, to INQUIRE], *v.t.* Ask, inquire, it is a question. *n.* A question, a query. **quæsitum** (kwē sī′ tŭm), *n.* (*pl.* **-ta**). A query.

quæstor (kwēs′ tŏr) [L., for *quæsitor*, from *quærere*, see prec., p.p. *quæsitus*], *n.* (*Rom. Ant.*) A magistrate having charge of public funds, a public treasurer, paymaster, etc. **quæstorial** (-tôr′ i ȧl), *a.* **quæstorship,** *n.*

*****quæstuary** (kwēs′ tū ȧr i) [L. *quæstuārius*, from *quæstus*, gain, as prec.], *a.* Seeking profit, studious of gain. *n.* One employed to collect profits; a questor.

quaff (kwaf) [etym. doubtful], *v.t.* To drink in large draughts. *v.i.* To drink copiously. *n.* A copious draught. **quaffer,** *n.*

quag (kwăg) [onomat.], *n.* A piece of marshy or boggy ground. **quaggy,** *a.* **quagmire,** *n.* A quaking bog, a marsh, a slough.

quagga (kwăg′ ȧ) [S. African native, prob. imit. of its cry], *n.* A South African quadruped, *Equus quagga*, intermediate between the ass and the zebra, now nearly, if not entirely, extinct; Burchell's zebra, *Equus Burchellii.*

quaggy, quagmire [QUAG].

quahaug (kwȧ hawg′, kwaw′ hog) [N. Amer. Ind., *poquauhock*], *n.* The common round or hard clam, *Venus mercenaria*, of the Atlantic coast of N. America.

quaich (kwăch) [Gael. *cuach*, prob. from L. *caucus*, Gr. *kauka*], *n.* (*Sc.*) A shallow drinking-vessel, usu. of wood.

Quai d'Orsay (kā′ dôr sā′) [F.], *n.* (*Pol.*) Term for the French Foreign Office.

quail (1) (kwāl) [etym. doubtful], *v.i.* To shrink, to be cowed, to lose heart; to give way (before or to); *to wither, to decline, *to slacken. **v.t.* To cast down, to cow, to daunt; to defeat, to conquer.

quail (2) (kwāl) [O.F. *quaille* (F. *caille*), prob. from Teut. (cp. Dut. *kwakkel*, O.H.G. *quatala*), prob. of imit. orig.], *n.* A small migratory bird of the genus *Coturnix*, allied to the partridge, esp. *C. coturnix*; one of various allied gallinaceous birds; *a courtesan. **quail-call,** *n.* **quail-hawk,** *n.* The N. Zealand sparrow-hawk. **quail-pipe,** *n.* A whistle imitating the cry of the quail for enticing them to the net; *(*fig.*) the human throat.

quaint (kwānt) [M.E. and O.F. *cointe*, L. *cognitum*, nom. *-tus*, p.p. of *cognoscere*, to know, to learn], *a.* *Wise, cunning, crafty; old-fashioned and odd, pleasing by virtue of strangeness, oddity or fancifulness; odd, whimsical, singular. **quaintish,** *a.* **quaintly,** *adv.* **quaintness,** *n.*

*****quair** [QUIRE (1)].

quake (kwāk) [A.-S. *cwacian*, prob. of imit. orig., cp. QUAG], *v.i.* To shake, to tremble, to quiver, to rock, to vibrate. **v.t.* To cause to quake. *n.* A tremulous motion, a shudder. **quaking-grass,** *n.* Grass of the genus *Briza*, the spikelets of which have a tremulous motion. **quaky,** *a.* **quakiness,** *n.*

Quaker (kwā′ kėr) [prec., -ER, orig. applied in derision (1650)], *n.* A member of the Society of Friends, founded by George Fox (1624–91). **quaker-bird,** *n.* The sooty albatross. **quaker-gun,** *n.* (*Am.*) A wooden gun mounted to deceive the enemy. **Quakerdom,** *n.* **Quakeress,** *n.* **Quakerish,** *a.* **Quakerism,** *n.*

qualify (kwol′ i fī) [F. *qualifier*, med. L. *quālificāre* (L. *quālis*, such, *-ficāre*, *facere*, to make)], *v.t.* To invest or furnish with the requisite qualities; to make competent, fit, or legally capable (to be, or do, or for any action, place, office, or occupation); to modify, to limit, to narrow the scope, force, etc., of (a statement or opinion); to moderate, to mitigate, to temper; to reduce the strength or flavour of (spirit, etc.) with water, to dilute; to attribute a quality to, to describe or characterize as; *to ease, to soothe. *v.i.* To become qualified or fit; to make oneself competent, suitable, or eligible (for). **qualifiable,** *a.* **qualifier,** *n.* **qualifyingly,** *adv.*

qualification (kwol i fi kā′ shŭn), *n.* The act of qualifying or the state of being qualified; modification, restriction or limitation of meaning, exception or partial negation restricting completeness or absoluteness; any natural or acquired quality fitting a person or thing (for an office, employment, etc.); a condition that must be fulfilled for the exercise of a privilege, etc. **qualificative, -tory** (kwol′ if i kā tiv, -tŏr i), *a.* and *n.* **qualifier,** *n.* **qualifyingly,** *adv.*

qualitative [QUALITY].

quality (kwol′ i ti) [F. *qualité*, L. *quālitātem*, nom. *-tas*, from *quālis*, as prec.], *n.* Relative nature or kind, distinguishing character; a distinctive property or attribute, that which gives individuality; a mental or moral trait or characteristic; particular capacity, value, or function; particular efficacy, degree of excellence, relative goodness; (*Log.*) the affirmative or negative nature of a proposition; (*Mus.*) that which distinguishes sounds of the same pitch and intensity, timbre; *an accomplishment. ***the quality:** Persons of high rank, the upper classes. **qualitative,** *a.* Of or pertaining to quality, opp. to quantitative. **qualitative analysis:** (*Chem.*) The detection of the constituents of a compound body. **qualitatively,** *adv.* **qualitied,** *a.*

qualm (kwawm, kwam) [perh. from A.-S. *cwealm*, pestilence; or rel. to G. *qualm*, vapour, dial. swoon, Dut. *kwalm*, Dan. *kvalm*, Swed. *qvalm*, vapour, closeness], *n.* A sensation of nausea, a feeling of sickness; a sensation of fear or uneasiness; a misgiving, a scruple, compunction. **qualmish,** *a.* **qualmishly,** *adv.* **qualmishness,** *n.*

quamash (kwaw′ măsh, kwȧ măsh′) [N. Am. Ind.], *n.* The bulb of a liliaceous plant, *Camassia esculenta*, eaten by the North American Indians.

quandary (kwon′ dâr i) [etym. doubtful], *n.* A state of difficulty or perplexity; an awkward predicament, a dilemma.

quandong (kwăn′ dong) [Austral. abor.], *n.* A small Australian tree, *Fusanus acuminatus*, with edible drupaceous fruit.

quant (kwont) [perh. from L. *contus*, Gr. *kontos*], *n.* A punting-pole with a flange at the end to prevent its sinking in the mud. *v.t.* To propel with this. *v.i.* To propel a boat with this.

quantic (kwon′ tik) [L. *quantus*, how much], *n.* (*Math.*) A rational integrally homogeneous function of two or more variables.

quantify (kwon′ ti fī) [med. L. *quantificāre* (*quantus*, as prec., *-ficāre*, *facere*, to make)], *v.t.* To determine the quantity of, to measure as to quantity; to express the quantity of; (*Log.*) to define the application of as regards quantity. **quantifiable,** *a.* **quantification** (-kā′ shŭn), *n.*

quantitative (kwon′ ti tā tiv, -tȧ tiv), **quantitive** (kwon′ ti tiv) [QUANTITY], *a.* Pertaining to or concerned with quantity, opp. to qualitative; relating to or based on the quantity of vowels (as accent, verse, etc.). **quantitative analysis:** (*Chem.*) The determination of the amounts and proportions of the constituents of a compound body. **quantitatively,** *adv.* ***quantitive,** *a.* ***quantitively,** *adv.*

quantity (kwon′ ti ti) [O.F. *quantité*, L. *quantitātem*, from *quantus*, as prec.], *n.* That property in virtue of which anything may be measured; extent, measure, size, greatness, volume, amount, or number; a sum, a number; a certain or a large number, amount, or portion; (*pl.*) large quantities, abundance; (*Pros.*) the duration of a syllable; (*Log.*) the extent to which a predicate is asserted of the subject of a proposition; (*Math.*) a thing having such relations, of number or extension, as can be expressed by symbols, a symbol representing this; *a small part, an insignificant thing; *proportion. **quantity-mark,** *n.* A mark placed over a vowel to indicate quantity. **quantity-surveyor,** *n.* One employed to estimate the quantities of materials used in erecting a building.

quantivalence (kwon-, kwăn tiv′ ȧ lĕns) [L. *quanti-*, *quantus*, how much, *-valence*, as in EQUIVALENCE], *n.* (*Chem.*) Valency. **quantivalent,** *a.*

quantum (kwon′ tŭm) [L., neut. of *quantus*, how much, so much], *n.* (*pl.* *-ta*) A quantity, an amount; a portion, a proportion, a share; an amount required, allowed, or sufficient. ***quantum sufficit:*** A sufficient amount (usu. ***quant. suf.*** in prescriptions). **quantum theory,** *n.* (*Phys.*) The theory that energy transferences occur in bursts of a minimum quantity.

quaquaversal (kwā kwȧ vĕr′ sȧl) [late L. *quāquāversus* (*quāquā*, whithersoever, *versus*, towards)], *a.* Pointing in every direction; (*Geol.*) inclined outwards and downwards in all directions (of dip).

quarantine (kwor′ ȧn tēn) [from O.F. *quarantine* (F. *quarantaine*), or from It. *quarantina*, from *quaranta*, L. *quadrāginta*, forty, see QUADRAGENARIAN], *n.* The prescribed period of isolation (usu. 40 days) imposed on persons or ships coming from places infected with contagious disease; the enforced isolation of such persons, ships, goods, etc., or of persons or houses so infected; a place where quarantine is enforced; *any period of forty days, esp. (*Law*) the period of forty days during which a widow is entitled to remain in the mansion-house of her deceased husband. *v.t.* To isolate or put in quarantine.

quarant′ ore (kwa ran tôr′ ā) [It., forty hours], *n.* (*R.-C. Ch.*) Forty hours' exposition of the blessed Sacrament.

quarenden, -der (kwor′ ėn dĕn, -dĕr) [etym. doubtful], *n.* A large red variety of apple, common in Devon and Somerset.

quarl (1) (kwarl) [var. of QUARREL (1)], *n.* A curved segment of fire-clay or fire-brick used to make a support for melting-pots, retort-covers, etc.

quarl (2) (kwarl) [prob. rel. to G. *qualle*, Dut. *kwal*], *n.* A jelly-fish or medusa.

quarrel (1) (kwor′ ėl) [M.E. and O.F. *quarel* (F. *carreau*), It. *quadrello*, dim. of *quadro*, med. L. *quadrus*, square, cp. QUADREL], *n.* A short, heavy bolt or arrow with a square head, formerly used for shooting from cross-bows or arbalests; *a square or diamond-shaped pane of glass used in lattice-windows.

quarrel (2) (kwor′ ėl) [M.E. and O.F. *querele*, L. *querēla*, complaint, from *querī*, to complain], *n.* A falling-out or breach of friendship; a noisy or violent contention or dispute, an altercation, a brawl, a petty fight; a ground or cause of complaint or dispute, a reason for strife or contention. *v.i.* (*past & p.p.* **quarrelled**) To fall out, to break off friendly relations (with); to dispute violently, to wrangle, to squabble; to cavil, to take exception, to find fault (with); (*fig.*) to be at variance, to be discordant or incongruous (of colours or other qualities, etc.). **v.t.* To dispute, to call in question, to find fault with. **quarreller,** *n.* **quarrelling,** *a.* ***quarrellous, quarrelsome,** *a.* Inclined or apt to quarrel, contentious; irascible, choleric, easily provoked. **quarrelsomely,** *adv.* **quarrelsomeness,** *n.*

quarry (1) (kwor′ i) [med. L. *quareia*, *quareria*, *quadrāria*, from L. *quadrāre*, to square, as QUADRATE], *n.* A place whence building-stone, slates, etc., are dug, cut, blasted, etc.; (*fig.*) a source whence information is extracted. *v.t.* To dig or take from or as from a quarry. **quarryman,** *n.* A workman employed in a quarry. **quarrier,** *n.*

quarry (2) (kwor′ i) [M.E. *quirre*, O.F. *cuirée*, from *cuir*, L. *corium*, skin], *n.* *A part of the entrails, etc., of a deer placed on a skin and given to the hounds; any animal pursued by hounds, hunters, a bird of prey, etc.; game, prey; (*fig.*) any object of pursuit. **v.i.* To prey or feed (as a vulture or hawk). **v.t.* To hunt down.

quarry (3) (kwor′ i) [later form of QUARREL (1)], *n.* A square or diamond-shaped pane of glass, a quarrel; a square stone or tile. *v.t.* To glaze with quarries; to pave with quarries.

quart (1) (kwôrt) [F. *quarte*, fem. of *quart*, L. *quarta*, fem. of *quartus*, fourth], *n.* A measure of capacity, the fourth part of a gallon, two pints; a measure, bottle or other vessel, containing such quantity; (*colloq.*) a quart of beer.

quart (2) (kart), *n.* A sequence of four cards in piquet, etc.

quartan (kwôr′ tȧn) [F. *quartaine*, L. *quartāna* (*febris*), fem of *quartānus*, fourth, from *quartus*, see QUART (1)], *a.* Occurring or recurring every fourth day. *n.* A quartan ague or fever. **quartan ague** or **fever:** One recurring every third or, inclusively, every fourth day.

quartation (kwôr tā′ shŭn) [L. *quartus*, fourth], *n.* The addition of silver, usu. in the proportion of three-fourths to one-fourth, in the process of separating gold from its impurities by means of nitric acid.

quarte [CARTE (2)].

quarter (kwôr′ tėr) [O.F., from L. *quartārius*, a fourth part, from *quartus*, fourth], *n.* A fourth part, one of four equal parts; the fourth part of a year, three calendar months; the fourth part of a cwt. (28 lb.); a grain measure of 8 bushels; the fourth of a fathom; (*Am.*) the fourth part of a dollar, 25 cents; one of four parts, each comprising a limb, into which the carcase of an animal or bird may be divided; (*pl.*) the similar parts into which the body of a criminal or traitor was formerly divided after execution; a haunch; (*Her.*) one of the divisions of a shield when this is divided by horizontal and perpendicular lines meeting in the fesse point; (*Naut.*) either side of a ship between the main chains and the stern; the fourth part of a period of the moon; one of the four phases of increase or decrease of the moon's face during a lunation; a point of time fifteen minutes before or after the hour; one of the four chief points of the compass; one of the main divisions of the globe corresponding to this; a particular direction, region, or locality; place of origin or supply, source; a division of a town, esp. one assigned to or occupied by a particular class; (*usu. in pl.*) allotted position, proper place or station, esp. for troops; (*pl.*) place of lodging or abode, esp. a station or encampment occupied by troops; (*Naut. pl.*) appointed stations of a crew at exercise or in action; exemption from death allowed in war to a surrendered enemy; mercy, clemency; *friendship, peace, concord. *v.t.* To divide into four equal parts; to cut the body of (a traitor) into quarters; (*Her.*) to bear or arrange (charges or coats of arms) quarterly on a shield, etc., to add (other arms) to those of one's family, to divide (a shield) into quarters by vertical and horizontal lines; to put into quarters, to assign quarters to, to provide (esp. soldiers) with lodgings and food; to range over (a field) in all directions (of a hound). **v.i.* To be stationed or lodged. **quarter of an hour:** A period of fifteen minutes. **a bad quarter of an hour:** A short disagreeable experience. **quarter-bell,** *n.* A bell sounding the quarter-hours. **quarter-bill,** *n.* (*Nav.*) A list of the stations, posts, and duties of a vessel, with names of officers and men. **quarter-binding,** *n.* Leather or cloth on the back only of a book, with none at the corners. **quarter-bound,** *a.* **quarter-bred,** *a.* Having one-fourth pure blood (of horses or cattle). **quarter-butt,** *n.* (*Billiards*) A long cue, shorter than a half-butt. **quarter-day,** *n.* The day beginning each quarter of the year (Lady Day, 25th March, Midsummer Day, 24th June, Michaelmas Day, 29th Sept., and Christmas Day, 25th Dec.), on which tenancies, etc., begin and end, payments are due, etc. **quarter-deck,** *n.* The upper deck extending from the stern to the mainmast, usu. assigned for the use of officers and cabin passengers. **quarter-hour,** *n.* A quarter of an hour; the point of time 15, 30, or 45 minutes before or after the hour. **quarter-line,** *n.* (*Naut.*) A position of ships such that the bow of one is abaft the beam of the one in front; a line fastened to the lower edge of a seine net to help in hauling it in. **quarter-plate,** *n.* (*Phot.*) A photographic plate measuring $4\frac{1}{4} \times 3\frac{1}{4}$ in.; a picture produced from this. **quarter-round,** *n.* A convex moulding having the contour of a quarter-circle, an ovolo, an echinus. **quarter-sessions,** *n.pl.* A general court of limited criminal and civil jurisdiction held by the Justices of the Peace in every county (and in boroughs where there is a Recorder). **quarter-staff,** *n.* An iron-shod pole about $6\frac{1}{2}$ ft. long, formerly used as a weapon of offence or defence, usu. grasped by one hand in the middle and by the other between the middle and one end. **quarter-tone,** *n.* (*Mus.*) An interval of half a semitone. **quarterage,** *n.* A quarterly payment, wages, allowance, etc. **quartering,** *n.* A dividing into quarters or fourth parts; the assignment of quarters or lodgings; (*Carp.*) a length of square-section timber with side from 2 to 6 inches; (*Her.*) the grouping of several coats of arms on a shield; one of the coats so quartered. **quarterly,** *a.* Containing a quarter; occurring or done every quarter of a year. *adv.* Once in each quarter of the year; (*Her.*) in quarters, arranged in the four quarters of the shield. *n.* A periodical published every quarter. **quarterfoil** [QUATREFOIL].

quartermaster (kwôrt' ėr ma stėr), *n.* (*Mil.*) A regimental officer appointed to provide and assign quarters, lay out camps, and issue rations, clothing, ammunition, etc.; (*Nav.*) a petty officer, having charge of the steering, signals, stowage, etc. **Quartermaster-General,** *n.* A staff-officer in charge of the department dealing with quartering, encamping, moving, or embarking troops. **quartermaster-sergeant,** *n.* A sergeant assisting the quartermaster.

quartern (kwôr' tėrn) [O.F. *quarteron*, from *quarte*, fourth], *n.* A quarter or fourth part of various measures, esp. of a loaf; a pint, peck, or pound. **quartern-loaf,** *n.* A loaf of the weight of 4 lb.

quarteroon [QUADROON].

quartet (kwôr tet') [F. *quartette*, It. *quartetto*, from *quarto*, L. *quartus*, fourth], *n.* A musical composition for four voices or four instruments; a group or set of four similar things.

quartile (kwôr' til) [med. L. *quartīlis*, from L. *quartus*, fourth], *a.* (*Astron.*) Denoting the aspect of two heavenly bodies when distant from each other a quarter of a circle. *n.* A quartile aspect; a quarter of the individuals studied in a statistical survey, whose characteristics lie within stated limits.

quarto (kwôr' tō) [L. *in quarto* (abl. of *quartus*, fourth), in a fourth part], *n.* A size obtained by folding a sheet twice, making four leaves or eight pages (usu. written 4to); a book, pamphlet, etc., having pages of this size. *a.* Having the sheet folded into four leaves.

quartz (kwôrts) [G. *quarz*, etym. unknown], *n.* A mineral consisting of pure silica or silicon dioxide, either massive or crystallizing hexagonally. **quartz clock,** *n.* A synchronous electric clock of high accuracy in which the alternating current frequency is determined by the mechanical resonance of a quartz crystal. The mechanical strain of the crystal is translated into an electrical signal by the piezo-electric effect. **quartziferous** (kwôrt sif' ėr ůs), *a.* **quartzite** (kwôrt' sīt), *n.* A massive or schistose metamorphic rock consisting of sandstone with a deposition of quartz about each grain. **quartzitic** (-sit' ik), *a.* **quartzose** (kwôrt' sōs), **quartzy,** *a.*

quas [KVASS].

quash (kwosh) [O.F. *quasser*, L. *quassāre*], *v.t.* To annul or make void; to put an end to, esp. by legal procedure; to suppress, to extinguish; *to crush, to dash, to quell.

Quashie (kwosh' i) [Ashanti *Kwasi*, boy born on Sunday], *n.* A Negro, a black, esp. from W. Africa (used as a nickname).

quasi (kwā' sī) [L., as if], *conj.* As if. **quasi-,** *pref.* Apparent, seeming, not real; practical, half, not quite. **quasi-crime,** *n.* **quasi-historical, quasi-public, quasi-sovereign,** *a.*

Quasimodo (kwăs i mō' dō) [from first words of the introit for that day. L. *Quasi modo geniti infantes*, as new-born babes], *n.* The first Sunday after Easter.

***quassation** (kwȧ sā' shůn) [L. *quassātio*, from *quassāre*, to QUASH], *n.* The act of shaking; concussion; the state of being shaken. ***quassative** (kwăs' ȧ tiv), *a.*

quassia (kwosh'-, kwăsh' ȧ) [named by Linnæus after *Quassi* (QUASHIE), a Negro who used its bark in fever], *n.* A genus of South American and West Indian (esp. Surinam) trees, the bitter wood, bark, and oil of which yield a tonic. **quassic** (kwăs'-, kwos' ik), *a.* (*Chem.*) **quassin,** *n.* The bitter principle of quassia.

***quat** (kwot) [etym. unknown], *n.* A pustule, a pimple; (*fig.*) a diminutive or insignificant person.

***quatch** (kwoch) [etym. unknown], *a.* (*Shak.*) Squat, flat (?).

quater-centenary (kwăt ėr sen' tē nȧr i) [L. *quater*, four times, CENTENARY], *n.* A four-hundredth anniversary.

quater-cousin [CATER-COUSIN].

quaterfoil [QUATREFOIL].

quaternary (kwȧ tėr' nȧ ri) [L. *quaternārius*, from *quarternī*, four at a time, distrib. of *quater*, four times], *a.* Consisting of four, having four parts, esp. (*Chem.*) composed of four elements or radicals arranged in fours; fourth in order; (*Geol.*) applied to the most recent strata or those above the tertiary. *n.* A set of four; the number four. ***quatern,** *a.* Quaternal, quaternate, fourfold, arranged in or composed of four or fours.

quaternion (kwȧ tėr' ni ǒn), *n.* A set, group, or system of four; a quire of four sheets once folded;

(*Math.*) an operator that changes one vector into another, so called as depending upon four irreducible geometrical elements; (*pl.*) the form of the calculus of vectors employing this. *v.t.* To divide into or arrange in quaternions, files, or companies.

quatorzain (kăt′ ŏr zān) [F. *quatorzaine*, from *quatorze*, L. *quātuordecim* (*quator*, four, *decem*, ten), fourteen], *n.* A poem or stanza of fourteen lines, esp. a sonnet of an irregular form. ***quatorze** (kȧ tôrz′), *n.* (*Piquet*) A set of four aces, kings, queens, knaves, or tens.

quatrain (kwot′ rān) [F., from *quatre*, L. *quātuor*, four], *n.* A stanza of four lines, usu. rhyming alternately.

quatre [CATER (2)].

quatrefoil (kăt′ ėr foil) [O.F. *quatre*, L. *quātuor*, four, FOIL (1)], *n.* An opening, panel, or other figure in ornamental tracery, divided by cusps into four foils; a leaf or flower composed of four divisions or lobes.

Quattrocento (kwa trō chen′ tō) [It., lit. four hundred (L. *quātuor*, four, *centum*, hundred), usu. fourteen hundred], *n.* The fifteenth century regarded as a distinctive period in Italian art and literature. **quattrocentist,** *n.*

quaver (kwā′ vėr) [freq. of obs. *quave*, M.E. *quaven*, rel. to QUAKE], *v.i.* To quiver, to tremble, to vibrate; to sing or play with tremulous modulations or trills. *v.t.* To sing or utter with a tremulous sound. *n.* A shake or rapid vibration of the voice, a trill; a quiver or shakiness in speaking; (*Mus.*) a note equal in duration to half a crotchet or one-eighth of a semibreve. **quaverer,** *n.* **quaveringly,** *adv.* **quavery,** *a.*

quay (1) (kē) [M.E. *key*, A.-F. *kaie*, O.F. *kay* (F. *quai*), prob. Celt. (cp. W. *cae*, Bret. *kaé*, hedge, enclosure)], *n.* A landing-place or wharf, usu. of masonry and stretching along the side of or projecting into a harbour, for loading or unloading ships. *v.t.* To furnish with a quay or quays. **quayage,** *n.*

quean (kwēn) [A.-S. *cwene*, woman (cp. Dut. *kween*, barren cow, O.H.G. *quena*, Gr. *gunē*, woman, Eng. QUEEN)], *n.* A slut, a hussy, a jade, a strumpet; (*Sc.*) a young or unmarried woman, a lass.

queasy (kwē′ zi) [formerly *queisy*, *coisy*, perh. from O.F. *coisié*, p.p. of *coisir*, to hurt], *a.* Sick at the stomach, affected with nausea; causing or tending to cause nausea; unsettling the stomach; easily nauseated; (*fig.*) fastidious, squeamish. **queasiness,** *n.*

quebracho (kė bra′ chō) [Sp., contr. of *quebrahacha* (*quebrar*, to break, *hacha*, axe)], *n.* One of several American trees producing a medicinal bark, used esp. in cases of fever.

queen (kwēn) [A.-S. *cwēn*, cogn. with QUEAN], *n.* The wife of a king; a queen-dowager; a female sovereign of a kingdom; a court-card bearing a conventional figure of a queen; the most powerful piece in chess; a queen-bee; (*fig.*) a woman of majestic presence; one masquerading as a sovereign or presiding at some festivity; a city, nation, or other thing regarded as the supreme example of its class. *v.t.* To make (a woman) queen; (*Chess*) to make (a pawn) into a queen. *v.i.* To act the queen; (*Chess*) to become a queen. **Queen Anne's bounty** [BOUNTY]. **Queen Anne's style:** The architectural style prevalent in the reign of Queen Anne, characterized by plain and unpretentious design with classic details; also applied to a style of decorative art typified by Chippendale furniture. **Queen Anne is dead:** Stale news. **queen-apple,** *n.* A variety of apple. **queen-bee,** *n.* A fully-developed female bee. **queen-cake,** *n.* A small, soft, usu. heart-shaped currant cake. **queen-consort** [CONSORT]. **queen-dowager,** *n.* The widow of a king. **queen-mother,** *n.* A queen-dowager who is also the mother of the reigning sovereign. **queen-post** [POST (1)], *n.* One of two suspending or supporting posts between the tie-beam and rafters in a roof. **Queen's Bench** [BENCH]. **Queen's Counsel** [COUNSEL]. **Queen's flight:** A unit of the R.A.F. reserved for the use of the royal family, established as King's Flight in 1936. **queen's-metal,** *n.* An alloy of tin, antimony, lead, and bismuth. **queen's-ware,** *n.* Glazed Wedgwood earthenware of a creamy colour. **queendom, queenhood, queenship,** *n.* **queening** (kwē′ ning), *n.* A queen-apple. **queenless, queenlike, queenly,** *a.* **queenliness,** *n.*

Queensberry Rules (kwēnz′ bė ri), *n.pl.* Standard rules of boxing drawn up by the 8th Marquess of Queensberry in 1867.

Queensland nut (kwēnz′ lȧnd nŭt), *n.* A proteaceous tree of Queensland and New South Wales; its edible nut. **Queensland sore,** *n.* A festering sore.

queer (kwēr) [prob. from L.G., cp. G. *quer*, crosswise], *a.* Strange, odd; singular, droll; curious, questionable, suspicious; out of sorts; unfavourable; (*colloq.*) in a bad way, in trouble or disgrace; (*colloq., perh. another word*) bad, worthless, counterfeit. *v.t.* (*colloq.*) To spoil, to put out of order. **in Queer Street:** (*colloq.*) In trouble, esp. financial; off colour; under a cloud. **to queer one's pitch:** To spoil one's chances. **queerish,** *a.* **queerly,** *adv.* **queerness,** *n.*

quell (kwel) [A.-S. *cwellan*, to kill (cp. Dut. *kwellen*, G. *kwälen*)], *v.t.* To suppress, to put down, to subdue; to crush; to cause to subside; to calm, to allay, to quiet; *to kill. **v.i.* To be abated. **n.* Slaughter, murder; power or means of quelling or subduing, a weapon. **queller,** *n.*

quench (kwench) [A.-S. *cwencan*, found in *acwencan*, causal of *cwincan*, to go out (cp. Fris. *kwinka*)], *v.t.* To extinguish, to put out, esp. with water; to cool (heat or a heated thing) with water; to allay, to slake; to suppress, to subdue. **v.i.* To be extinguished. **quenchable,** *a.* **quencher,** *n.* One who or that which quenches; (*colloq.*) a draught that allays thirst. **quenchless,** *a.* That cannot be quenched; inextinguishable. **quenchlessly,** *adv.* **quenchlessness,** *n.*

quenelle (kė nel′) [F., etym. doubtful], *n.* A ball of savoury paste made of meat or fish, usu. served as an entrée.

quercitron (kwĕr′ si trŏn) [L. *querci-*, *quercus*, oak, CITRON], *n.* The N. American black or dyer's oak, *Quercus tinctoria*; the bark of this, or a yellow dye made from it. **quercitin,** *n.* (*Chem.*) A yellow crystalline substance obtained from quercitrin, etc. **quercitrin,** *n.* The yellow crystalline colouring-matter contained in the bark of *Quercus tinctoria.*

quercus (kwĕr′ kŭs) [L.], *n.* (*Bot.*) A genus of trees containing the oaks, most of the species valuable for their timber. **quercetum** (kwėr sē′ tŭm), *n.* A collection of living oaks, an arboretum of oak-trees.

***querent** (1) (kwĕr′ ėnt) [L. *quærens -ntem*, pres.p. of *quærere*, see QUÆRE], One who inquires, esp. of an astrologer, etc.

querent (2) (kwēr′ ėnt) [L. *querens -ntem*, pres.p. of *querī*, to complain], *n.* (*Law*) A complainant, a plaintiff. *a.* Complaining.

querimonious (kwer i mō′ ni ŭs) [late L. *querimōniōsus*, from L. *querimōnia*, from *querī*, to complain], *a.* Complaining, querulous, discontented. **querimoniously,** *adv.* **querimoniousness,** *n.*

querist (kwēr′ ist) [L. *quær-ere*, see QUÆRE], *n.* One who asks questions, an inquirer.

querl (kwĕrl), *n.* A twirl, a curl, a twist, a coil. *v.t.* To twirl, to turn or wind round, to coil.

quern (kwĕrn) [A.-S. *cweorn* (cp. Dut. *kweern*, Icel. *kvern*)], *n.* A simple hand-mill for grinding corn, usu. consisting of two stones resting one on the other; a small hand-mill for grinding spices.

querquedule (kwĕr′ kė dūl) [L. *querquedula*], *n.* A pin-tail duck; any species of *Querquedula*, a genus of ducks containing the teals.

querulous (kwer′ ū lŭs) [late L. *querulōsus*, L. *querulus*, from *querī*, to complain], *a.* Complaining; discontented, peevish, fretful; of the nature of complaint; *quarrelsome. **querulously,** *adv.* **querulousness,** *n.*

query (kwēr′ i) [var. of QUÆRE], *n.* A question (often used absolutely as preface to a question); a point or objection to be answered; a mark of interrogation (?). *v.i.* To put a question; to express a doubt or question. *v.t.* To question, to call in question; to express doubt concerning; to mark with a query.

quest (kwest) [O.F. *queste* (F. *quête*), pop. L. *questa*, L. *quæsīta*, p.p. of *quærere*, to seek], *n.* The act of seeking, a search; an expedition or venture in search or pursuit of some object, esp. in the days of chivalry; the object of such an enterprise; an official inquiry; a jury of inquest; *a body of searchers; *a request, a demand. *v.t.* To seek for or after; *to inquire into. *v.i.* To make quest or search; to go (about) in search of something. ***questant, quester,** ***questrist,** *n.* **questful,** *a.*

question (kwes′ tyon) [O.F., from L. *quæstiōnem*, nom. *-tio*, as prec.], *n.* The act of asking or inquiring, interrogation, inquiry; a sentence requiring an answer, an interrogative sentence; a subject for inquiry, a problem requiring solution; a subject under discussion; a proposition or subject to be debated and voted on, esp. in a deliberative assembly; a subject of dispute, a difference, doubt, uncertainty, objection; *examination under torture. *v.t.* To ask a question or questions of, to interrogate, to examine by asking questions; to study (phenomena, etc.) with a view to acquiring information; to call in question, to treat as doubtful or unreliable, to raise objections to. *v.i.* To ask a question or questions; to doubt, to be uncertain. **a burning question:** A subject causing intense interest. **beyond all** or **past question:** Undoubtedly, unquestionably. **indirect** or **oblique question:** One expressed in a dependent clause. **in question:** Referred to, under discussion. **leading question** [LEAD (2)]. **open question:** A question that remains in doubt or unsettled. ***out of question:** Doubtless. **out of the question:** Not worth discussing. **previous question** [PREVIOUS]. **question!** An exclamation recalling a speaker who is wandering from the subject, or expressing incredulity. **to beg the question** [BEG]. **to call in question** [CALL (1)]. **to pop the question** [POP (1)]. **to put the question:** To put to the vote, to divide the meeting or House upon. **question-mark, -stop,** *n.* A mark of interrogation. **questionable,** *a.* Open to doubt or suspicion; disputable; *capable of being questioned. **questionability** (-ȧ bil′ i ti), **questionableness,** *n.* **questionably,** *adv.* **questionary,** *a.* Questioning, inquiring. *n.* A series of questions for the compilation of statistics, etc.; *a questor, an itinerant pedlar of indulgences or relics. **questioner, -ist,** *n.* **questioningly,** *adv.* **questionless,** *adv.* Beyond all question or doubt. ***questionnaire*** [QUESTIONARY].

questor (1) (kwes′ tor) [med. L., as QUÆSTOR], *n.* (*R.-C. Ch.*) A pardoner; a treasurer of the French National Assembly; an Italian commissary of police.

questor (2), etc. [QUÆSTOR]

quetzal (kwet′-, ket′ sȧl) [Sp., from Aztec *quetzalli*], *n.* A brilliant Guatemalan trogon, *Pheromacrus mocinno.*

queue (kū) [F., from L. *cauda*, tail], *n.* A plaited tail hanging at the back of the head, either of the natural hair or a wig, a pigtail; (*fig.*) a file of persons, vehicles, etc., waiting their turn. *v.t.* To dress (the hair, etc.) in a queue. *v.i.* To form into a waiting queue.

quey (kwā) [Sc. and North., from Icel. *kvīga*, prob. cogn. with cow (1)], *n.* A young cow that has not yet had a calf, a heifer.

***quhilk** (*Sc.*) [WHICH]. ***quib** [QUIP].

quibble (kwi′ bel) [prob. freq. of obs. *quip*, L. *quibus*, dat. of *quī*, who, which], *n.* An evasion of the point, an equivocation; a trivial or sophistical argument or distinction, esp. one exploiting a verbal ambiguity; a play upon words; a pun. *v.i.* To evade the point in question; to employ quibbles; to pun. **quibbler,** *n.* **quibblingly,** *adv.*

quick (kwik) [A.-S. *cwic*, *cwicu* (cp. Dut. *kwik*, G. *keck*, Icel. *kvikr*, Swed. *quick*, also L. *vīvus*, lively, Gr. *bios*, life)], *a.* Alive, living; pregnant, with child, esp. when movement is preceptible; lively, vigorous, ready, alert, acutely sensitive or responsive, prompt to feel or act, intelligent; irritable, hasty; rash, precipitate; rapid in movement, acting swiftly, swift, nimble; done or happening in a short time, speedy, expeditious; quickset; *sharp, caustic (of words spoken); *keen, bracing. *adv.* In a short space, at a rapid rate; quickly. *n.* Living persons; living flesh, esp. the sensitive flesh under the nails; (*fig.*) the feelings, the seat of the feelings. *v.t.* and *i.* To quicken. **quick-answered,** *a.* Quick in reply. **quickbeam:** The quicken, *Pyrus aucuparia*, or mountain-ash or rowan. **quick-change,** *a.* Making rapid changes of costume or appearance (of actors, etc.). **quick-eared,** *a.* Having acute hearing; quick to hear. **quick-eyed,** *a.* Having sharp sight. **quick-fence,** *n.* A fence of growing shrubs (as opp. to palings). **quick-firer,** *n.* A gun with a mechanism for firing shots in rapid succession. **quick-firing,** *a.* **quick-freeze:** Very rapid freezing to retain the natural qualities of food; a receptacle in which such food is kept frozen. **quick march:** (*Mil.*) A march in quick time; the music for such a march. **quick-match,** *n.* A quick-burning match for firing cannon, etc., usu. made of cotton wick soaked in a mixture of alcohol, salt-petre, etc. **quick-sighted,** *a.* Having acute sight; quick to see or understand. **quick-sightedness,** *n.* **quick step:** The step used in marching at quick time; (*Dancing*) a fast foxtrot. **quick-tempered,** *a.* Easily irritated, irascible. **quick time:** (*Mil.*) The ordinary rate of marching in the British Army, usu. reckoned at 128 paces of 33 in. to the minute or 4 miles an hour. **the quick and the dead:** The living and the dead. **quick-witted,** *a.* **quick-wittedness,** *n.* **quickly,** *adv.* **quickness,** *n.*

quicken (kwik′ en), *v.t.* To give or restore life or animation to; to stimulate, to rouse, to inspire, to kindle; to cheer, to refresh; to accelerate. *v.i.* To receive life; to come to life; to move with increased rapidity; to be in that state of pregnancy in which the child gives signs of life; to give signs of life in the womb. *n.* The rowan or mountain-ash, the quickbeam; the service tree. **quicken-tree,** *n.* The quickbeam. **quickener,** *n.* **quickening,** *a.*

quicklime (kwik′ līm), *n.* Burned lime not yet slaked.

quicksand (kwik′ sănd), *n.* Loose wet sand easily yielding to pressure and engulfing persons, animals, etc.; a bed of such sand.

quickset (kwik′ set), *a.* Composed of living plants, esp. hawthorn bushes (of a hedge). *n.* Slips of plants, esp. hawthorn, put in the ground to form a quickset hedge; a quickset hedge.

quicksilver (kwik′ sil vėr), *n.* Mercury; (*fig.*) a mobile temperament. *v.t.* To coat the glass of a mirror with an amalgam of quicksilver and tin-foil.

quid (1) (kwid) [var. of CUD], *n.* A piece of tobacco for chewing.

quid (2) (kwid) [etym. doubtful], *n.* (*pl. unchanged*) (*slang*) A sovereign, twenty shillings.

quid (3) (kwid) [L., what, anything, neut. of *quis*, who], *n.* Something. **quid pro quo:** Something in return (for something), an equivalent; *the substitution of one thing for another, or a mistake or blunder consisting in this.

***quidam** (kwi′ dam) [L.], *n.* Somebody; a person unknown.

quiddity (kwid′ i ti) [med. L. *quidditas*, from QUID

(3)], *n.* The essence of a thing; a quibble, a trifling or captious subtlety. **quiddative, quidditative,** *a.*

quiddle (kwidl) [etym. doubtful], *v.i.* (*chiefly Am.*) To waste time in trifling or useless employments. *n.* A quiddle. **quiddler,** *n.*

quidnunc (kwid′ nŭnk) [L., what now?], *n.* One who is curious to know or pretends to know everything that goes on; a newsmonger, a gossip.

quiescent (kwī es′ ėnt) [L. *quiescens -ntem*, pres.p. of *quiescere*, from *quies*, QUIET], *a.* At rest, still, not moving, inert, dormant; tranquil, calm, free from anxiety, agitation, or emotion; (*Phon.*) not sounded. *n.* A silent letter. **quiesce,** *v.i.* **quiescence, -cy,** *n.* **quiescently,** *adv.*

quiet (kwī′ ėt) [L. *quiētus*, p.p. of *quiescere*, to rest, from *quies -ētis*, rest], *a.* In a state of rest, motionless; calm, unruffled, placid, tranquil, peaceful, undisturbed; making no noise, silent, hushed; gentle, mild, peaceable; unobtrusive, not glaring or showy; not overt, private; retired, secluded. *n.* A state of rest or repose; freedom from disturbance, tranquillity; silence, stillness, peace, calmness; peace of mind, calm, patience, placidness. *v.t.* To bring to a state of rest; to soothe, to calm, to appease. *v.i.* To become quiet. **at quiet:** At peace, peaceful. ***quietage,** *n.* **quieten,** *v.t.* and *i.* To quiet. **quieter,** *n.* **quietly,** *adv.* **quietness, quietude,** *n.* ***quietsome,** *a.*

Quietism (kwī′ ė tizm), *n.* A form of religious mysticism based on the doctrine that the essence of religion consists in the withdrawal of the soul from external objects and in fixing it upon the contemplation of God; a state of calmness and placidity. **Quietest,** *a.* Quietistic. *n.* An adherent of Quietism. **quietistic** (-tis′ tik), *a.*

quietus (kwī ē′ tŭs) [med. L. *quiētus est*, he is QUIT], *n.* A final discharge or settlement; (*fig.*) release from life, death.

quiff (kwif) [Fr. *coiffure*, hairdressing], *n.* A curl lying flat on the forehead.

quill (kwil) [etym. doubtful, cp. G. *kiel*], *n.* The hollow stem or barrel of a feather; one of the large strong feathers of a bird's wing or tail; a pen made from such a feather, a pen; also, a plectrum, toothpick, angler's float, etc., made from this; a spine of a porcupine; a tube or hollow stem on which weavers wind their thread, a bobbin, a spool; a musical pipe made from a hollow cane, reed, etc.; a strip of cinnamon or cinchona bark rolled into a tube. *v.t.* To form into rounded folds, flutes, etc., to goffer; to wind on a quill or quills. *v.i.* To wind thread on a quill or quills. **quill-driver,** *n.* (*contemp.*) A writer, an author, a clerk. **quilled,** *a.* (*usu. in comb.*, as *long-quilled*). **quilling,** *n.* Lace, tulle, or ribbon, gathered into small round plaits resembling quills.

quillet (kwil′ ėt) [perh. from obs. *quillity*, var. of QUIDDITY], *n.* A quibble, a quirk.

quillon (ki yon′) [F., from *quille*, ninepin], *n.* One of the arms forming the cross-guard of a sword.

quilt (kwilt) [O.F. *cuilte*, L. *culcita*, cushion], *n.* A bed-cover or coverlet made by stitching one cloth over another with some soft warm material as padding between them, a counterpane. *v.t.* To pad or cover with padded material; to stitch together, esp. with crossing lines of stitching, (two pieces of cloth) with soft material between them; to stitch in crossing lines or ornamental figures, like the stitching in a quilt; to sew up, as in a quilt; *(*fig.*) to put together (literary extracts, etc.) as in a quilt; (*slang*) to beat, to thrash. **quilter,** *n.* **quilting,** *n.* The process of making quilted work; material for making quilts; quilted work.

quin (1) (kwin) [etym. doubtful], *n.* A variety of pecten or scallop.

quin (2) (kwin) [QUINTUPLET], *n.* One child (of quintuplets).

quina [QUINIA].

quinary (kwī′ nȧ ri) [L. *quīnārius*, from *quīnī*, five each, distrib. of *quinque*, five], *a.* Consisting of or arranged in fives. **quinate** (kwī′ nȧt), *a.* (*Bot.*) Composed of five leaflets (of a leaf).

quince (kwins) [orig. pl. of obs. *quine*, M.E. *coine*, O.F. *cooing*, L. *cotōneum*, var. of *cydōnium*, from *Cydōnia*, in Crete], *n.* The hard, acid, yellowish fruit of a shrub or small tree, *Pyrus Cydonia*, used in cookery for flavouring and for preserves, etc.

quincentenary [QUINGENTENARY].

quincunx (kwin′ kŭngks) [L. *quinque*, five, *uncia*, OUNCE], *n.* An arrangement of five things in a square or rectangle, one at each corner and one in the middle, esp. such an arrangement of trees in a plantation. **quincuncial** (kwin kŭn′ shȧl), *a.* **quincuncially,** *adv.*

quindecagon (kwin dek′ ȧ gŏn) [from L. *quindecim*, see foll., after DODECAGON], *n.* A plane figure having fifteen sides and fifteen angles.

quindecemvir (kwin dė sem′ vĕr) [L. *quindecim* (*quinque*, five, *decem*, ten), fifteen, *vir*, man], *n.* (*pl.* **-viri,** -vi rī) (*Rom. Ant.*) One of a body of fifteen men, esp. one of a college of fifteen priests who had the charge of the Sibylline books.

quingentenary (kwin gen′ tė nȧr i) [L. *quingentī*, five hundred], *n.* A five-hundredth anniversary; its celebration.

quinia (kwin′ i ȧ) [Sp. *quina*, from Quichua, *kina*, bark, cp. QUINQUINA], *n.* (*Med.*) Quinine.

quinine (kwi nēn′, -nīn′, kwī′ nin) [F.], *n.* A bitter alkaloid obtained from cinchona barks, used as a febrifuge, tonic, etc.; sulphate of quinine (the form in which it is usually employed as a medicine). **quinic** (kwin′ ik), *a.* (*Chem.*) **quinicine** (kwin′ i sĭn), *n.* A yellow resinous amorphous alkaloid compound obtained from quinidine or quinine. **quinidine,** *n.* An alkaloid, isomeric with quinine, contained in some cinchona barks. **quinize,** *v.t.* **quinism, *quininism,** *n.* **quinology** (-nol′ ŏ ji), *n.* **quinologist,** *n.*

quinnal (kwin′ ȧl) [N. Am. Ind.], *n.* The king-salmon of the Pacific coast of N. America.

quinoa (kē′ nŏ ȧ, ki nō′ ȧ) [Sp., from Quichua, *kinua*], *n.* An annual herb, *Chenopodium quinoa*, the ground farinaceous seeds of which are made into cakes by the Chilians and Peruvians.

quinol (kwin′ ŏl) [QUIN-A, -OL], *n.* Hydroquinone. **quinotic** (-not′ ik), *a.*

quinoline (kwin′ ō līn), *n.* A colourless, pungent, liquid compound, obtained by the dry distillation of bones, coal, and various alkaloids, forming the basis of many dyes and medicinal compounds. **quinology,** etc. [QUININE].

quinone (kwin′ ōn, kwi nōn′) [as prec., -ONE], *n.* (*Chem.*) A yellow crystalline compound, usu. produced by the oxidation of quinic acid; any of a series of similar compounds derived from the benzene hydrocarbons by the substitution of two oxygen atoms for two of hydrogen.

quinquagenarian (kwin kwȧ jė nâr′ i ȧn) [L. *quinquāgēnārius*, from *quinquāgēnī*, fifty each, distrib. of *quinquāginta*, fifty (*quinque*, five, *-ginta*, see QUADRAGENARIAN)], *n.* A person fifty years old. *a.* Fifty years old. **quinquagenary** (-jē′ nȧ ri), *a.* Quinquagenarian. *n.* A quinquagenarian; a fiftieth anniversary.

quinquagesima (kwin kwȧ jes′ i mȧ) [L., fiftieth, as prec.], *n.* Quinquagesima Sunday; *the period from the Sunday before Lent to Easter Sunday, or the first week of this. **Quinquagesima Sunday:** The Sunday next before Lent, about fifty days before Easter.

quinque-, quinqui- [L. *quinque*, five], *comb. form.* **quinquangular** (kwing kwăng′ gū lȧr), *a.* Having five angles. **quinquarticular** (kwing kwar tik′ ū lȧr), *a.* Relating to or consisting of five articles (applied to the controversy between the Arminians and Calvinists). **quinquecostate** (-kos′ tȧt), *a.* Having five ribs. **quinquedentate** (-den′ tȧt), *a.* Having five teeth or indentations. **quinquefarious** (-fâr′ i ŭs), *a.* Arranged in five parts or rows. **quinquefoliate** (-fō′ li ȧt), *a.* (*Bot.*) Having five leaves or leaflets. **quinquelateral** (-lăt′ ėr ȧl), *a.* Having five sides. *n.* A five-sided thing. **quinqueliteral** (-lit′ ėr ȧl), *a.* Consisting of five letters; *n.* A word (esp. a Hebrew root-word) of five letters. **quinquenniad** (-kwen′ i ȧd) [L. *annus*, year, -AD], *n.* A quinquennium. **quinquennium,** *n.* (*pl.* **-nia**) A period of five years. **quinquennial,** *a.* Recurring once in five years; lasting five years. **quinquennially,** *adv.* **quinquepartite** (-par′ tīt), *a.* Divided into five parts. **quinquereme** (kwin′ kwė rēm) [cp. QUADRIREME], *n.* A galley having five banks of rowers. **quinquevalve** (kwin′ kwė vălv), **-valvular** (-văl′ vū lȧr), *a.* (*Bot.*) Opening by five valves, as the pericarp of flax. **quinquifid** (kwing′ kwi fid), *a.* (*Bot.*) Cleft into five divisions. **quinquivalent** (kwin kwiv′ ȧ lėnt), *a.* (*Chem.*) Having a valency or combining power of five. **quinquivalence,** *n.*

quinquina (kin kē′ nȧ, kwin kwī′ nȧ) [Quichua, *kinkina*, redupl. of *kina*, QUINIA], *n.* Peruvian bark, cinchona.

quinsy (kwin′ zi) [O.F. *quinancie*, med. L. *quinancia*, Gr. *kunanche* (*kun-*, *kuōn*, dog, *anchein*, to throttle)], *n.* Inflammatory sore throat, esp. with suppuration of one tonsil or of both. **quinsied,** *a.*

quint (kwint, kint) [F. *quinte*, L. *quinta*, fem. of *quintus*, fifth, from *quinque*, five], *n.* (*Piquet*) A sequence of five cards of the same suit; (*Mus.*) a fifth; (*Organ*) a stop giving tones a fifth above the normal. **quint major:** (*Piquet*) The cards from ten to ace. **quint minor:** Those from seven to knave.

quinta (kwin′ tȧ) [Sp. and Port. (from being orig. let at a fifth of the produce)], *n.* A country-house or villa, in Portugal, Madeira, and Spain.

quintad [PENTAD].

quintain (kwin′ tȧn) [O.F. *quintaine*, perh. from L. *quintāna*, as QUINTAN, the fifth street of a camp], *n.* A post, or a figure or other object set up on a post, in the Middle Ages, to be tilted at, often fitted with a sandbag, sword, or other weapon that swung round and struck a tilter who was too slow; the exercise of tilting at this.

quintal (kwin′ tȧl) [O.F., Sp., and Port., from Arab. *qinṭār*, L. *centum*, hundred], *n.* A weight of 100 or 112 lb.; a hundred kilograms or 220½ lb.

quintan (kwin′ tȧn) [L. *quintāna* (*febris*), fifth-day fever (*quintāna*, fem. of *quintānus*, from *quintus*, fifth, from *quinque*, five)], *a.* Recurring every fourth (or inclusively fifth) day. *n.* An intermittent fever or ague the paroxysms of which return every fourth day.

quinte (kănt) [F., as QUINT], *n.* (*Fencing*) The fifth of the thrusts or parries.

quintessence (kwin tes′ ėns) [F., from L. *quinta essentia*, fifth ESSENCE], *n.* (*Anc. and Med. Phil.*) The fifth, last, or highest essence, apart from the four elements of earth, air, fire, and water, forming the substance of the heavenly bodies and latent in all things; the pure and concentrated essence of any substance, a refined extract; the essential principle or pure embodiment (of a quality, class of things, etc.). **quintessential** (quin tė sen′ shȧl), *a.*

quintet (kwin tet′) [F. *quintette*, It. *quintetto*, from *quinto*, L. *quintus*, fifth], *n.* A musical composition for five voices or instruments; a party, set, or group of five persons or things.

quintic (kwin′ tik) [L. *quint-us*, fifth, -IC], *a.* (*Math.*) Of the fifth degree. *n.* A quantic of the fifth degree.

quintile (kwin′ til), *n.* (*Astrol.*) The aspect of planets when distant from each other one-fifth of a circle or 72°.

quintillion (kwin til′ yȯn) [from L. *quintus*, after BILLION], *n.* The fifth power of a million, represented by 1 followed by 30 ciphers; (*F. and Am.*) the sixth power of a thousand, 1 followed by 18 ciphers.

quintroon (kwin troon′, kwin′ trun) [Sp. *quinteron*, from *quinto*, L. *quintus*, fifth], *n.* One-fifth (inclusively) in descent from a Negro, the offspring of a white and an octoroon.

quintuple (kwin′ tūpl) [F., from L. *quintus*, fifth, after QUADRUPLE], *a.* Fivefold. *n.* A fivefold thing, group, or amount. *v.t.* To multiply fivefold. *v.i.* To increase fivefold. **quintuplet,** *n.* A set of five things; (*pl.*) five children at a birth. **quintuplicate** (-tū′ pli kȧt), *a.* Consisting of five things, parts, etc. *n.* A set of five; one of five similar things. *v.t.* (-kāt) To multiply by five. **quintuplication** (-kā′ shȯn), *n.*

quinzaine (kwin′ zān, kă*n* zā*n*) [F., from foll.], *n.* A poem or stanza of five verses; a fortnightly event, meeting, etc.

quinze (kwinz, kanz) [F., from L. *quindecim* (*quinque*, five, *decem*, ten), fifteen], *n.* A card-game of chance analogous to vingt-et-un, the object being to score nearest to fifteen points without exceeding it.

quip (kwip) [var. of obs. *quippy*, L. *quippe*, forsooth], *n.* A sarcastic jest or sally; a witty retort; a smart saying; a quibble. **v.t.* (*past & p.p.* **quipped**) To utter quips, to sneer at. *v.i.* To make quips, to scoff. **quippish, quipsome,** *a.*

quipu (kē′ pu, kwip′ u) [Peruv., knot], *n.* A contrivance of coloured threads and knots used by the ancient Peruvians in place of writing.

quire (1) (kwīr) [M.E. and O.F. *quaer* (F. *cahier*), L. *quaternī*, four each, a set of four, from *quātuor*, four], *n.* Twenty-four sheets of paper; orig. a set of four sheets of paper or parchment folded into 8 leaves, as in medieval MSS.; *a small book, pamphlet, etc.

***quire** (2) [CHOIR]. ***quirister** [CHORISTER].

Quirites (kwi rī′ tēz) [L., pl. of *Quiris -ītis*, inhabitant of the Sabine town *Cures*], *n.pl.* A name applied to the Roman citizens in their civil capacity. **quiritary** (kwir′ i tȧr i), **quiritarian** (-târ′ i ȧn), *a.* (*Law*) Held in accordance with the Roman or old civil law, legal as distinguished from equitable.

quirk (kwĕrk) [etym. doubtful], *n.* An artful trick, evasion, or subterfuge, a shift; a quibble, a quip, a twist or flourish in drawing or writing; a fantastic turn or flourish in music; (*Arch.*) an acute recess between the moulding proper and the fillet or soffit. **quirk-moulding,** *n.* **quirkish, quirksome,** *a.* **quirky,** *a.* **quirkiness,** *n.*

quirt (kwĕrt) [Sp. *cuerda*, CORD], *n.* (*U.S. and Am. Sp.*) A riding-whip with a short handle and a long, braided leather lash.

quisling (kwiz′ ling) [Vidkun *Quisling* (1887–1945), Norwegian renegade], *n.* A traitor; one who openly allies himself with his nation's enemy.

quit (kwit) [O.F. *quiter* (F. *quitter*), as QUIET], *v.t.* (*past & p.p.* **quitted,** ***quit**) To rid (oneself) of; to give up, to renounce, to abandon; to leave, to depart from; to cease, to desist from; to free, to liberate; *to acquit, to behave, to conduct (one, them, etc., usu. without 'self'); *to acquit; *to remit. *v.i.* To leave, to depart; *to part (with or from). *a.* Clear, absolved; rid (of). ***to quit cost:** To pay or balance the cost. **to quit scores:** To balance or make even. **quitclaim,** *n.* A renunciation of right or claim; *a deed of release. *v.t.* To renounce claim or title (to); *to release, to discharge. **quit-rent,** *n.* A rent (usu. small) paid by a freeholder or copyholder in discharge of other services. **quits,** *a.* and *n.* Even, left on even terms, so that neither has the advantage. **double or quits** [DOUBLE (2)]. **to be** or **cry quits:** To declare things to be even, to agree not to go on with a contest, quarrel, etc., to make it a draw. ***quittal,** *n.* Requital, quittance. **quittance,** *n.* A discharge or release from a debt or obligation; a receipt, an acquittance; *repayment, requital. **v.t.* To repay, to requite. **quitter** (1), *n.* One who quits; a shirker, a coward.

qui tam (kwī tăm) [L., who as well (first words of clause in the statute)], *n.* (*Law*) An action brought by an informer under a penal statute.

quitch (kwich) [A.-S. *cwic*, QUICK], *n.* Couch-grass, *Triticum repens.* **quitch-grass,** *n.*

quite (1) (kwīt) [from foll. a.], *adv.* Completely, entirely, altogether, to the fullest extent, absolutely, perfectly; (*colloq.*) very considerably. **quite so:** Certainly, decidedly (a form of affirmation). **quite the thing:** Quite proper or fashionable.

***quite** (2), *a.* and *v.* [QUIT].

quittance [QUIT].

quitter (2) (kwit′ ėr) [etym. doubtful], *n.* An ulcer or suppurating sore on the quarter of a horse's hoof.

quiver (1) (kwiv′ ėr) [O.F. *cuivre*, prob. from Teut. (cp. A.-S. *cocor*, G. *köcher*)], *n.* A portable case for arrows. **quivered,** *a.* **quiverful,** *n.* **to have one's quiver full:** To have many children.

quiver (2) (kwiv′ ėr) [prob. imit., perh. rel. to QUAVER], *v.i.* To tremble or be agitated with a rapid tremulous motion; to shake, to shiver. *v.t.* To cause (wings, etc.) to quiver. *n.* A quivering motion. **a.* Nimble, active. **quiveringly,** *adv.* **quiverish,** *a.*

qui vive (kē vēv) [F., who lives, who goes there?], *n.* A sentry's challenge. **on the qui vive:** On the look-out, alert, expectant.

quixotic (kwik sot′ ik) [after Don *Quixote*, the hero of Cervantes's romance of that name], *a.* Extravagantly romantic, visionary; aiming at lofty but impracticable ideals. **quixotically,** *adv.* **quixotism, -try** (kwik′ sȯ tizm, -tri), *n.* **quixotize,** *v.t.* and *i.*

quiz (kwiz) [etym. doubtful], *n.* Something designed to puzzle or turn one into ridicule, a hoax; a question; a test of knowledge; a radio game based on this; a quizzer; an odd-looking or eccentric person. *v.t.* (*past & p.p.* **quizzed**) To banter, to chaff, to make fun of, to look at in a mocking or offensively curious way. *v.i.* To behave in a bantering or mocking way. **quizzable,** *a.* **quizzer,** *n.* One given to quizzing. **quizzery, quizzism,** *n.* **quizzical,** *a.* **quizzically,** *adv.* **quizzify,** *v.t.* **quizzing-glass,** *n.* A small eye-glass, a monocle. **quizzingly,** *adv.*

quod (kwod) [etym. doubtful], *n.* (*slang*) Prison, jail.

quodlibet (kwod′ li bėt) [L., what you please], *n.* (*Mus.*) A fantasia, a medley; *a scholastic discussion or argument; a knotty point, a subtlety. ***quodlibetarian** (-târ′ i ȧn), *n.* One fond of quodlibets or subtle arguments. ***quodlibetic, -al** (-bet′ ik, -ȧl), *a.*

quoin (koin) [var. of COIN], *n.* A large stone, brick, etc., at the external angle of a wall, a corner-stone; the external angle of a building; an internal angle, a corner; a wedge-shaped block of wood used by printers, etc., for various purposes, as locking up type in a form, raising the level of a gun, etc. *v.t.* To raise or secure with a quoin or wedge. **quoining,** *n.*

quoit (koit, kwoit) [etym. doubtful], *n.* A flattish circular ring of iron for throwing at a mark; (*pl.*) a game of throwing such rings. **v.t.* To throw or pitch as a quoit.

quokka (kwok′ ȧ) [Austral. abor.], *n.* A variety of bandicoot with short ears.

quondam (kwon′ dăm) [L., formerly], *a.* Having formerly been, sometime, former.

quorum (kwôr′ ŭm) [L., of whom, gen. pl. of *qui*, who], *n.* (*pl.* **-ums**) The minimum number of officers or members of a society, committee, etc., that must be present to transact business.

quota (kwō′ tȧ) [L. *quota* (*pars*), how great (a part), fem. of *quotus*, from *quot*, how many], *n.* A proportional share, part, or contribution.

quote (kwōt) [orig. to mark the number of (chapters, etc.), from med. L. *quotāre*, from QUOTA], *v.t.* To adduce or cite from (an author, book, etc.); to repeat or copy out the words of (a passage in a book, etc.); to name the current price of. *v.i.* To cite or adduce a passage (from). **quotable,** *a.* **quotability** (-bil′ i ti), **quotableness,** *n.* **quotably,** *adv.*

quotation (-tā′ shŭn), *n.* The act of quoting; a passage quoted; a price quoted or current; (*Print.*) a quadrat for filling up blanks, etc. **quotation-marks,** *n.pl.* Punctuation marks (in Eng. usu. double or single inverted commas) at the beginning and end of a passage quoted. **quoter,** *n.*

quoth (kwōth) [past of obs. *quethe*, A.-S. *cwæth*, from *cwethan*, to speak (cp. Icel. *kvetha*, O.H.G. *quedan*)], *v.t.* 1st *and* 3rd *pers.* Said, spoke. ***quotha** [for QUOTH HE], *int.* Forsooth, indeed.

quotidian (kwȯ tid′ i ȧn) [L. *quotīdiānus*, from *quotīdiē*, daily (QUOTA, *dies*, day)], *a.* Daily; (*Path.*) recurring every day; (*fig.*) commonplace, everyday. *n.* A fever or ague of which the paroxysms return every day.

quotient (kwō′ shėnt) [F., irreg. from L. *quotiens*, how many times, as QUOTA], *n.* The result obtained by dividing one quantity by another. **quotiety** (kwȯ tī′ ė ti), *n.* Relative frequency. ***quotity** (kwot′ i ti), *n.* (*Carlyle*) A certain number (of people).

quotum [QUOTA].

quo warranto (kwō wȯr′ ȧn tō) [med. L., by what warrant?], *n.* (*Law*) A writ requiring a person or body to show the authority by which some office or franchise is claimed or exercised.

R

R, r, the eighteenth letter, and the fourteenth consonant of the English alphabet (*pl.* **Ars, R's,** or **Rs**), has two sounds: the first when it precedes a vowel, as in *ran*, *morose*; the second, at the end of syllables and when it is followed by a consonant, as in *her*, *martyr*, *heard*. **the three Rs':** Reading, writing, and arithmetic, the fundamental elements of primary education.

rabat (ra ba′) [F., rel. to *rabattre* (RE-, *abattre*, see ABATE)], *n.* A neck-band with flaps, worn by French ecclesiastics; a turned-down collar; *a stiff collar worn by both sexes in the early 17th cent.; *a similar collar supporting a ruff.

rabbet (răb′ ėt) [O.F. *rabat*, from *rabattre*, to REBATE], *v.t.* To cut a groove or slot along the edge of (a board) so that it may receive the edge of another piece cut to fit it; to unite or fix in this way. *n.* Such a groove or slot made in the edge of a board that it may join with another; a joint so made; a rabbet-plane; a spring-pole. **rabbet-plane,** *n.* A plane for cutting rabbets.

rabbi (răb′ ī) [L., from Gr. *rhabbi*, Heb. *rabbī*, my master (*rabh*, master, *ī*, my)], *n.* (*pl.* **-bis**) A Jewish doctor or teacher of the law, esp. one ordained and having certain juridical and ritual functions. **rabbin,** *n.* A rabbi, esp. one of the great scholars and authorities on Jewish law and doctrine flourishing in the Middle Ages. **rabbinate,** *n.* **rabbinic** (rȧ bin′ ik), *n.* The language or dialect of the rabbins, later Hebrew. *a.* Rabbinical. **rabbinical,** *a.* Pertaining to the rabbins, their opinions, learning, or language. **rabbinically,** *adv.* **rabbinism** (răb′ in izm), *n.* **rabbinist, *-ite,** *n.* **rabbinistic** (-is′ tik), *a.*

rabbit (răb′ it) [perh. from Walloon *robett*, from Flem. *robbe*, etym. unknown], *n.* A burrowing rodent, *Lepus cuniculus*, allied to the hare, killed for its flesh and fur; (*slang*) a bungling player at an outdoor game. **rabbit-hutch,** *n.* A cage for rearing tame rabbits in. ***rabbit-sucker,** *n.* A sucking rabbit. **rabbit-warren, rabbitry,** *n.* A piece of ground where rabbits are allowed to live and breed. **rabbity,** *a.*

rabble (1) (răb′ ėl) [M.E. *rabel*, prob. rel. to Dut. *rabbelen*, to speak in a confused, indistinct way (cp. L.G. *rabbeln*)], *n.* A noisy crowd of people, a mob; the common people, the mob, the lower orders; *a string of meaningless words, a rigmarole. *v.t.* To mob; *to utter in an incoherent manner. **v.i.* To gabble. **rabblement,** *n.*

rabble (2) (răb' ėl) [F. *râble*, ult. from L. *rutābulum*, fire-shovel, from *ruere*, to cast, to rake up], *n.* An iron tool consisting of a bar with the end sharply bent, used for stirring molten metal.

rabdomancy [RHABDOMANCY].

Rabelaisian (răb ė lā' zi ȧn), *a.* Of, pertaining to, or characteristic of the French satirical humorist François Rabelais (1483–1553); extravagant, grotesque, coarsely and boisterously satirical. *n.* A student or admirer of Rabelais. **Rabelaisianism,** *n.*

rabi (răb' i) [Hind., from Arab. *rabī'*, spring], *n.* The grain crop reaped in the spring, the chief of the three Indian crops.

rabic [RABIES].

rabid (răb' id) [L. *rabidus*, from *rabĕre*, to rage], *a.* Mad, raging, furious, violent; fanatical, headstrong, excessively zealous or enthusiastic, unreasoning; (*Path.*) affected with rabies. **rabidity** (rȧ bid' i ti). **rabidness,** *n.* **rabidly,** *adv.*

rabies (rā' bi ēz, răb' i ēz) [L., as prec.], *n.* (*Path.*) Madness arising from the bite of a rabid animal, hydrophobia. **rabic** (răb' ik), **rabietic** (-et' ik), **rabific** (rȧ bif' ik), *a.*

rabot (răb' ot) [F., a plane, from *raboter*, to plane, var. of *rebouter* (RE-, *bouter*, to set, to thrust)], *n.* A block of hard wood used for polishing marble.

raccahout (răk' ȧ hoot) [F., *racahout*, Arab. *rāqaout*], *n.* A starch or meal prepared from the acorns of the Barbary oak, *Quercus ballota.*

raccoon [RACOON].

race (1) (rās) [Icel. *rās* or A.-S. *rǣs*], *n.* A rapid movement, a swift rush; a rapid current of water, esp. in the sea or a tidal river; the channel of a stream, esp. an artificial one; a contest of speed between horses, runners, ships, motor-vehicles, etc.; (*fig.*) any competitive contest depending chiefly on speed; a course or career; (*Mach.*) a channel or groove along which a piece of mechanism, as a shuttle, glides to and fro; (*Austral.*) a fenced passage in a sheep-fold; (*pl.*) a series of racing contests for horses. *v.i.* To run or move swiftly; to go at full speed; to go at a violent pace owing to diminished resistance (as a propeller when lifted out of the water); to contend in speed or in a race (with); to attend races. *v.t.* To cause to contend in a race; to contend against in speed; to cause (a horse) to run in a race; (*fig.*) to get rid of (one's property) on horse-racing. **race-ball,** *n.* A ball held in connexion with a race-meeting. **race-card,** *n.* A programme of a race-meeting with particulars of the horses, prizes, etc. **race-course, -track,** *n.* A piece of ground on which horse-races are run; a mill-race. **race-ground,** *n.* A race-course. **race-horse,** *n.* A blood-horse bred for racing. **race-meeting,** *n.* A meeting for horse-racing. **raceway,** *a.* (*Am.*) A channel or passage for water, as a mill-race; (*Mach.*) a groove for the passage of a shuttle, etc.; (*Elec.*) a conduit or subway for wires or a cable. **racer,** *n.* One who races or contends in a race; a race-horse; a yacht, cycle, motor-car, etc., built for racing.

race (2) (rās) [F. *race*, *rasse*, It. *razza*, etym. unknown], *n.* A group or division of persons, animals, or plants sprung from a common stock; a particular ethnical stock (as the Caucasian, Mongolian, etc.); a subdivision of this, a tribe, nation, or group of peoples, distinguished by less important differences; a clan, a family, a house; (*Bot. and Zool.*) a genus, species, stock, strain, or variety, of plants or animals, persisting through several generations; (*fig.*) lineage, pedigree, descent; a class of persons or animals, differentiated from others by some common characteristic; *a peculiar quality, a strong flavour, as of wine; natural disposition. **race-suicide,** *n.* Term applied to a decrease in population brought about by the excessive practice of birth-control. **racism** (rā' sizm), *n.* Belief in the inherent right of one race to rule over another.

race (3) (rās) [O.F. *raïs*, L. *rādīcem*, nom. *-dix*, root], *n.* A root (of ginger). **race-ginger,** *n.* Ginger in the root, not pulverized.

***race** (4) (rās) [from obs. *arace*, F. *arracher*, L. *eradicāre*, to ERADICATE], *v.t.* To tear or snatch (away) out, etc.

raceme (rȧ sēm') [F. *racème*, L. *racēmus*, bunch of grapes], *n.* (*Bot.*) A centripetal inflorescence in which the flowers are attached separately by nearly equal stalks along a common axis. **racemed,** *a.* **racemic,** *a.* (*Chem.*) Pertaining to or obtained from grape-juice. **racemiferous** (răs ė mif' ėr ŭs), *a.* (*Bot.*). **racemose, *-mous** (răs' ē mōs, -mus), *a.* **racemule,** *n.* A small raceme. **racemulose** (rȧ sē' mū lōs), *a.*

racer, raceway, etc. [RACE (1)].

***rach** (răch) [A.-S. *ræcc*, cp. Icel. *rakki*, dog], *n.* A dog that hunted by scent.

rachel (ra' shel) [Fr. actress Mme *Rachel* (1821–58)], *n.* A type of face powder.

rachi-, rachio- *comb. form.* [Gr. *rachis*, spine.] (*Anat. and Path.*) **rachialgia** (răk i ăl' ji ȧ), *n.* Pain in the spine; *painters'-colic. **rachialgic,** *a.* **rachidial, rachidian** (rȧ kid' i ȧl, -ȧn), *a.* Vertebral, spinal. **rachilla** (rȧ kil' ȧ), *n.* (*Bot.*) The zigzag axis on which the florets are arranged in the spikelets of grasses. **rachiomyelitis** (răk i ȯ mī ė lī' tis), *n.* (*Path.*) Inflammation of the spinal marrow. **rachitis** (rȧ kī' ti), *n.* (*Path.*) Rickets. **rachitic** (-kit' ik), *a.*

rachis (răk' is) [Gr. *rachis*, spine], *n.* (*pl.* **-ides,** -i dēz) (*Bot.*) The axis of an inflorescence; the axis of a pinnate leaf or frond; (*Anat.*) the spinal column; (*Ornith.*) the shaft of a feather, esp. the part bearing the barbs.

rachitome (răk' i tōm), *n.* (*Surg.*) An instrument used for cutting open the vertebral canal.

racial (rā' shȧl) [RACE (2), -IAL], *a.* Of, pertaining, or in regard to race or lineage. **racialism,** *n.* Antagonism between different races; a tendency towards this. **racially,** *adv.*

racily, etc. [RACY].

rack (1) (răk) [prob. from M. Dut. or M.L.G. *recken* (Dut. *rekken*, G. *recken*), cp. Icel. *rekja*, A.-S. *reccan*], *v.t.* To stretch or strain, esp. on the rack; to torture, to cause intense pain or anguish to; to strain, tear, shake violently, or injure; (*fig.*) to strain, to puzzle (one's brains, etc.); to wrest, to exaggerate (a meaning, etc.); to extort or exact (rent) in excess or to the utmost possible extent; to harass (tenants) by such exaction of rent. *n.* An apparatus for torture consisting of a framework on which the victim was laid, his wrists and ankles being tied to rollers which were turned so as to stretch him, to the extent sometimes of dislocating the joints. **rack-rent,** *n.* An exorbitant rent, approaching the value of the land. *v.t.* To extort such a rent from (a tenant, land, etc.). **rack-renter,** *n.* A landlord extorting such a rent; a tenant paying it. **racking** (1), *a.*

rack (2) (răk) [prob. rel. to prec., cp. Dut. *rek*, *rekke*, Dan. *række*, Swed. *räck*], *n.* An open framework or set of rails, bars, woven wire, etc., for placing articles on; a grating or framework of metal or wooden rails or bars for holding fodder for cattle, etc.; (*Mach.*) a bar or rail with teeth or cogs for engaging with a gear-wheel, pinion, or worm. *v.t.* To place on or in a rack; to fill (a rack) for a horse; to fasten (up) at a rack. *v.i.* To fill (up) a stable rack for a horse. **rack-railway,** *n.* A railway (usu. on a steep incline) with a cogged rail between the bearing rails. **rack-wheel,** *n.* A cog-wheel.

rack (3) (răk) [perh. from Scand., cp. Norw. and Swed. dial. *rak*, wreckage, Icel. *rek*, drift, *reka*, to drive, rel. to WREAK], *n.* Light vapoury clouds, cloud-drift; (perh. var. of WRACK) destruction, wreck. *v.i.* To fly, as cloud or vapour before the

R

wind. **to go to rack and ruin:** To fall completely into ruin.

rack (4) [ARRACK].

rack (5) (răk) [O. Prov. *arracar*, from *raca*, the stems, husks, dregs], *v.t.* To draw off (wine, etc.) from the lees. **racking-can, -cock, -engine, -faucet, -pump,** *n.* Kinds of vessel, tap, pump, etc., used in racking off wine.

rack (6) (răk) [etym. doubtful], *n.* A horse's mode of going in which both hoofs of one side are lifted from the ground almost or quite simultaneously, all four legs being off the ground entirely at times. *v.i.* To go in this manner (of a horse). **racker,** *n.* A horse that goes at a racking pace. **racking** (2), *a.*

rack (7) (răk) [etym. unknown], *n.* (*prov.*) The neck and spine of a fore-quarter of veal or mutton.

rackarock (răk' å rok) [RACK (1), (2), ROCK (1)], *n.* An explosive composed of chlorate of potassium and nitro-benzol.

racket (1) (răk' ėt) [F. *raquette*, perh. dim. from low L. *racha*, Arab. *rāha*, palm of the hand], *n.* A kind of bat, with a network of catgut instead of a blade, with which players at tennis or rackets strike the ball; a snow-shoe resembling this; (*pl.*) a game of ball resembling tennis, played against a wall in a four-walled court. *v.t.* To strike with or as with a racket.

racket (2) (răk' ėt) [prob. imit.], *n.* A clamour, a confused noise, a din; a commotion, a disturbance, a fuss; a frolic, a spree, uproarious gaiety, excitement, or dissipation; (*slang*) a scheme, a dodge, an underhand plan; an underhand combination; an organized illegal or unethical activity. *v.i.* To make a noise or din; to frolic, to revel, to live a gay life, to knock about. **to stand the racket:** To stand the expenses, to pay the score; to put up with the consequences; to get through without mishap. **racketer,** *n.* **racketeer,** *n.* Member of a gang engaged in systematic blackmail, extortion, etc. **racketing,** *n.* Confused, tumultuous mirth. **rackety,** *a.*

racking (1 and 2) [RACK (1 and 6)].

racking-can, etc. [RACK (5)].

rackle (răk' ėl) [etym. doubtful], *a.* (*Sc. and North.*) Hasty, rash; rough, vigorous, esp. in old age.

rack-rent [RACK (1)].

racloir (rak lwar') [Fr. *racler*, to scrape], *n.* (*Archæol.*) A flint implement used for scraping sideways.

raconteur (ra kon tĕr') [F., from *raconter*, to RECOUNT], *n.* A (good, skilful, etc.) story-teller.

racoon (rå koon') [Algonkin], *n.* A furry ring-tailed N. American carnivore of the genus *Procyon*, allied to the bears, esp. *P. lotor*.

racquet [RACKET (1)].

racy (rā' si) [RACE (2)], *a.* Having the characteristic qualities in high degree; strongly flavoured; smacking of the race, type or origin, tasting of the soil; lively, pungent, piquant, spirited; (*colloq.*) suggestive, bordering on the indecent. **racily,** *adv.* **raciness,** *n.*

Radar (rā' dar) [abbr. *ra*dio *d*etection *a*nd *r*anging], *n.* (*Radio.*) The employment of reflected or re-transmitted radio waves to locate the presence of objects and to determine their angular position and range.

raddle (1) (răd' ėl) [A.-F. *reidele*, O.F. *reddalle* (F. *ridelle*), a pole, the back rail of a cart], *n.* A lath, stick, or branch interwoven with others to form a fence, usu. plastered over with clay, etc.; a hurdle or hedge of twisted branches. *v.t.* To interweave, to twist (sticks, etc.) together.

raddle (2) [var. of RUDDLE (2)].

radial (rā' di ål) [RADIUS or RADIUM, -AL], *a.* Of, pertaining to, or resembling a ray, rays, or radii; extending or directed from a centre as rays or radii, divergent; having radiating parts, lines, etc.; of or pertaining to radium; (*Anat.*) of or pertaining to the radius of the forearm. *n.* (*Anat.*) A radiating part, bone, nerve, artery, etc. **radial artery,** *n.* (*Anat.*) Artery of the forearm, felt at the wrist when taking the pulse. **radial axle:** An axle so arranged as to take the position of a radius to a curve it is traversing on a railway line, etc. **radial axle-box:** An axle-box on a locomotive, etc., adapted for such motion. **radialize,** *v.t.* To cause to radiate as from a centre. **radialization** (-zā' shŭn), *n.* **radially,** *adv.* **radian,** *n.* (*Math.*) An arc equal in length to the radius of its circle; the angle subtending such an arc.

radiant (rā' di ånt) [L. *radians -ntem*, pres.p. of *radiāre*, as prec.], *a.* Emitting rays of light or heat; issuing in rays; (*fig.*) shining, beaming (with joy, love, etc.); splendid, brilliant; (*Bot.*) radiating, radiate. *n.* (*Astron.*) The point from which a star-shower seems to proceed; (*Opt.*) the point from which light or heat radiates; (*Geom.*) a straight line proceeding from a fixed pole about which it is conceived as revolving. **radiant heat,** *n.* (*Med.*) Heat by radiation, employed therapeutically in rheumatism by the use of electric lamps. **radiant point:** (*Astron. and Opt.*) A radiant. **radiance, *-ancy,** *n.* **radiantly,** *adv.*

Radiata (rā di ā' tå) [L., neut. pl. of *radiātus*, see foll.], *n.pl.* (*Zool.*) Cuvier's name for one of the great divisions of animals in which the organs are arranged round a central axis, as in the sea-anemone and the star-fish.

radiate (rā' di āt) [L. *radiātus*, p.p. of *radiāre*, from RADIUS], *v.i.* To emit rays of light or heat; to send out rays from or as from a centre; to issue and proceed in rays from a central point. *v.t.* To send out as rays or from a central point; to send forth in all directions, to disseminate. *a.* (-åt) Having rays or parts diverging from a centre, radiating; radially arranged, marked, etc., radially symmetrical; (*Zool.*) belonging to the *Radiata*. **radiate flower:** A composite flower in which the florets of the disk are radial and usu. ligulate. **radiately,** *adv.* **radiatiform** (-ā' ti fôrm), *a.* (*Bot.*) **radiation** (-ā' shŭn), *n.* The act of radiating or emitting rays; (*Phys.*) the transmission of heat, light, etc., from one body to another without raising the temperature of the intervening medium; travelling outwards, as long radii, to the periphery; a group of rays of the same wave-length. **radiation sickness:** (*Med.*) Illness caused by too great absorption of radiation in the body. **radiative** (rā' di å tiv), *a.* **radiato-,** *comb. form.*

radiator (rā' di ā tŏr), *n.* That which radiates; a vessel, chamber, or coil of pipes charged with hot air, water, steam, etc., for radiating heat in a building; (*Motor.*) a device for dissipating the heat absorbed by the cooling-water of the jacket.

radical (răd' i kål) [F., from late L. *rādīcālis*, from *rādix -īcis*, root], *a.* Pertaining to the root, source, or origin; inherent, fundamental; original, basic, primary; going to the root, thorough-going, extreme; belonging, pertaining, or according to the Radical party; (*Bot.*) arising from or close to the root; (*Math.*) of or pertaining to the root of a number or quantity; (*Philol.*) pertaining to a root, primary, underived. *n.* One promoting extreme measures or holding advanced views; a member of the Radical party or the more advanced section of the Liberal party; a fundamental principle; (*Philol.*) a root; (*Math.*) a quantity that is, or is expressed as, the root of another; the radical sign ($\sqrt{}$, $\sqrt[3]{}$, etc.); (*Chem.*) an element, atom, or group of atoms forming the base of a compound and not decomposed by the reactions that normally alter the compound. **radicalism,** *n.* **radicality** (-kăl' i ti), **radicalness,** *n.* **radicalize,** *v.t.* and *i.* **radicalization** (-zā' shŭn), *n.* **radically,** *adv.* Thoroughly, fundamentally, essentially.

radicate (răd' i kåt) [L. *rādīcātus*, p.p. of *rādīcāre*, as prec.], *a.* (*Bot.*) Having a root, rooted; (*Zool.*) having root-like organs of attachment (as some molluscs). **v.t.* (-kāt) To root, to plant firmly. **v.i.* To take root. **radicant,** *a.* (*Bot.*) Producing roots from the stem. **radication** (-kā' shŭn), *n.* **radicel** (răd' i sel), *n.* A rootlet. **radici-**, *comb. form.* **radicicolous** (răd i sik' ŏ lŭs), *a.* Infesting roots (as a variety of phyloxera). **radiciflorous** (-flôr' ŭs), *a.* Flowering from the root. **radiciform** (-dis' i fôrm), *a.* **radicivorous** (-siv' ŏ rŭs), *a.* Feeding on roots.

radicle (răd' i kĕl) [L. *rādīcula*, dim. of *rādix*], *n.* (*Bot.*) The part of an embryo that develops into the primary root; a small root, a rootlet; (*Anat.*) a root-like part of a nerve, vein, etc. **radicular** (ră dik' ū lăr), *a.* (*Bot., Anat., etc.*).

radio (rā' di ō) [RADIUM], *n.* Generic term applied to anything connected with wireless electricity; broadcasting; a wireless receiving set.

radio- (1) (rā' di ō) [RADIUM], *comb. form.* **radioactive** (rā di ō ăk' tiv), *a.* Having the property of emitting invisible rays that penetrate bodies opaque to light, affecting the electrometer, photographic plates, etc. **radioactivity** (-tiv' i ti), *n.* **radio beacon**, *n.* (*Radio.*) A transmitting station which sends out signals to aid navigators. **radio-astronomy**, *n.* The study of radio waves received from celestial objects. **radio-chemistry**, *n.* The chemistry of radioactive elements. **radio-dramatist**, *n.* One who writes dramas for broadcasting. **radio-element**, *n.* (*Phys.*) A chemical element with radioactive powers. **radio-frequency**, *n.* (*Radio.*) Frequency which is within the range for radio-transmission. **radio-frequency amplifier**, *n.* A high-frequency amplifier. **radio-frequency choke**, *n.* A coil presenting a high impedance to high-frequency alternating currents. **radio-frequency transformer**, *n.* A high-frequency transformer. **radiogenic** (-jĕn' ik), *a.* Produced by radioactivity; suitable for radio broadcasting. **radiogoniometer**, *n.* Adjustment of coils linking aerials in the Bellini-Tosi direction-finding system. **radiograph** (rā' di ŏ grăf), *n.* An actinograph; a negative produced by Röntgen rays; a print from this. *v.t.* To obtain a negative of by means of such rays. **radiographic** (-grăf' ik), *a.* **radiographically**, *adv.* **radiography** (-og' ră fi), *n.* **radio-isotope**, *n.* A radioactive isotope, produced in an atomic pile or in an atomic bomb explosion. **radio-location**, *n.* The employment of a radio-pulse and the time-delay of its reflection to ascertain the relative position in space of a reflecting object such as an aeroplane. **radiologist**, *n.* A medical practitioner specially trained in radiology. **radiology**, *n.* The branch of medical science concerned with radioactivity, X-rays and other diagnostic radiations. **radiometer** (rā di om' ĕ tĕr), *n.* An instrument for illustrating the conversion of radiant light and heat into mechanical energy. **radiometric** (-met' rik), *a.* **radio-micrometer** (-mī krom' ĕ tĕr), *n.* An instrument for measuring minute variations of heat, etc. **radiophone** (rā' di ŏ fōn), *n.* An instrument for the production of sound by means of radiant energy. **radiophonic** (-fon' ik), *a.* **radiophony** (of' ŏ ni), *n.* **radioscopy** (-os' kŏ pi), *n.* The examination of bodies by means of Röntgen rays. **radiosonde** (-sond), *n.* A miniature radio transmitter sent up in a balloon and dropped by parachute, for sending information of pressures, temperatures, etc. **radiotelegram** (-tel' ĕ grăm), *n.* A message sent by wireless telegraphy. **radiotelephony** (-tel ef' ŏ ni), *n.* Wireless telephony. **radio telescope**, *n.* (*Astron.*) An apparatus for collecting radio waves from outer space. **radio-therapy**, *n.* The treatment of disease by means of radiation, actinotherapy.

radio- (2) (rā' di ō) [RADIUS], *comb. form.* Radiate; pertaining to the outer bone of the forearm. **radiocarpal**, *a.* Pertaining to the radius and the wrist. **radiolarian**, *a.* (*Zool.*) Of or pertaining to the *Radiolaria*, a class of marine rhizopod protozoa emitting radiate filamentous pseudopodia, abounding in warm seas. *n.* An individual of the *Radiolaria.* **radiolite**, *n.* (*Palæont.*) A fossil bivalve from the chalk; (*Min.*) a variety of natrolite.

radish (răd' ish) [F. *radis*, from L. *rādīcem*, nom. *-dix*, see RADIX], *n.* A cruciferous plant, *Raphanus sativus*, cultivated for its root, which is eaten as a salad.

radium (rā' di ŭm) [as foll., -IUM], *n.* A highly radioactive metallic element resembling barium, obtained from pitchblende, discovered by Pierre and Marie Curie and G. Bémont in 1898.

radius (rā' di ŭs) [L., rod, spoke, ray], *n.* (*pl.* **-dii**) (*Anat.*) The shorter of the two long bones of the forearm; the corresponding bone in animals and birds; (*Math.*) the straight line from the centre of a circle or sphere to any point in the circumference; the length of this, half the diameter; a radiating line, part, object, etc., as a spoke; a circular area measured by its radius; (*Bot.*) the outer zone of a composite flower; a floret in this; a branch of an umbel. **the radius** or **the four-mile radius:** An area extending four miles in every direction from Charing Cross, London, beyond which cab-fares are higher. **radius vector:** (*pl.* **radii vectores**) (*Math.*) The distance from a fixed point to a curve; (*Astron.*) a line drawn from the centre of a heavenly body to that of a second revolving round it.

radix (rā' diks) [L., root], *n.* (*pl.* **radices**, rā' di sēz) A quantity or symbol taken as the base of a system of enumeration, logarithms, etc.; a source or origin; a root.

radon (rā' don), *n.* A gaseous radioactive element emitted by radium.

radula (răd' ū lă) [L., scraper, from *rādere*, to scrape, see RAZE], *n.* (*Zool.*) The odontophore or lingual ribbon of some molluscs.

raff (răf) [prob. from RIFF-RAFF], *n.* Sweepings, refuse; the rabble, the ruck, the lowest class; a person of this class, a rowdy. **raff-merchant**, *n.* A dealer in lumber, etc. **raffish**, *a.* Disreputable, disorderly, dissipated-looking. **raffishly**, *adv.* **raffishness**, *n.*

Raffaelesque, etc. [RAPHAELESQUE].

raffia (răf' i ă) [Malagasy], *n.* A Madagascar palm with a short stem and gigantic pinnate leaves; fibre prepared from these used for tying, ornamental work, etc.

raffish [RAFF].

raffle (1) (răf' ĕl) [M.E. and F. *rafle*, a game with dice], *n.* A kind of lottery in which an article is put up to be disposed of by lot among a number of persons each subscribing a like sum. *v.t.* To dispose of by means of a raffle. *v.i.* To engage in a raffle (for).

raffle (2) (răf' ĕl) [O.F. *rafle* (in *rifle ou rafle*), prob. rel. to RAFF], *n.* Rubbish, lumber; (*Naut.*) a tangle of cordage, gear, etc.

rafflesia (ră flē' zi ă) [after Sir T. *Raffles* (1781–1826)], *n.* (*Bot.*) A genus of very large stemless parasitic plants from Java and Sumatra.

raft (1) (raft) [Icel. *raptr* (cp. Swed. *raft*, Dan. *rafte*)], *n.* A number of logs, planks, etc., fastened together for transport by floating; a flat floating framework of planks or other material used for supporting or carrying persons, goods, etc., esp. as a substitute for a boat in a shipwreck, etc.; (*Am.*) a floating accumulation of driftwood, ice, etc., in a river. *v.t.* To transport on or as on a raft; to fasten together with a raft. *v.i.* To travel on a raft; to work a raft. **rafter** (2), **raftsman**, *n.* One who manages or works on a raft.

raft (2) (raft) [var. of RAFF], *n.* (*Am. colloq.*) A large number, a crowd, a lot.

rafter (1) (raf' tĕr) [A.-S. *ræfter*, cp. RAFT (1)], *n.* A sloping piece of timber supporting a roof or the framework on which the tiles, etc., of the roof are laid. *v.t.* To furnish with rafters; to plough with ridges by turning a strip over on the unploughed adjoining strip, to half-plough.

rafter (2) **raftsman** [RAFT (1)].

rafty (raf' ti) [etym. doubtful], *a.* (*prov.*) Damp, foggy; musty, stale, rancid.

rag (1) (răg) [cp. Icel. *rögg*, Norw. and Swed. *ragg*, rough hair], *n.* A fragment of cloth, esp. an irregular piece detached from a fabric by wear and tear; (*pl.*) tattered or shabby clothes; (*fig.*) a remnant, a scrap, the smallest piece (of anything); (*collect.*) torn fragments of cloth, linen, etc., used as material for paper, stuffing, etc.; (*contemp.*) a flag, a sail, a drop-curtain, a newspaper, etc. **raga-muffin,** *n.* A ragged, beggarly fellow. **raga-muffinly,** *adv.* **rag-and-bone man,** *n.* Itinerant dealer in household refuse. **ragbag,** *n.* A bag for scraps of cloth; (*colloq.*) a carelessly-dressed woman. **rag-bolt,** *n.* A bolt with jags on the shank to prevent its being easily withdrawn. *v.t.* To fasten with these. **rag-fair,** *n.* A market for or sale of old clothes. **ragman** (1), *n.* One who collects or deals in rags. **ragtag** or **ragtag and bobtail:** The riff-raff, the rabble. **rag-time,** *n.* (*Am.*) Irregular syncopated time in music, esp. in dances and negro melodies. **rag-wheel,** *n.* A wheel with a notched margin, a sprocket-wheel. **ragwort,** *n.* A yellow-flowered plant of the genus *Senecio.*

rag (2) (răg) [etym. doubtful], *n.* A hard, coarse, rough stone, usu. breaking up into thick slabs; a large roofing-slate with a rough surface on one side (also called **ragstone**).

rag (3) (răg) [cp. BALLYRAG], *v.t.* (*past & p.p.* **ragged**) To tease, irritate, or play rough practical jokes on; to rate, to reprove, to talk to severely. *n.* The act of ragging; a piece of boisterous and disorderly conduct.

ragamuffin, rag-bolt [RAG (1)].

rage (rāj) [F., late L. *rabia,* RABIES], *n.* Violent anger, fury; a fit of passionate anger; (*fig.*) extreme violence, vehemence, or intensity (of); a violent desire or enthusiasm (for); intense emotion, passion, or ardour; (*colloq.*) an object of temporary pursuit, enthusiasm, or devotion. *v.i.* To storm, to rave, to be furious with anger; to be violently incensed or agitated; to express anger or passion violently; to be violent, to be at the highest state of vehemence, intensity, or activity. *v.t.* *To enrage. **all the rage:** An object of general desire, quite the fashion. **rageful,** *a.* **ragefully,** *adv.* **rager,** *n.* (*Austral.*) A fierce old cow or bullock. **raging,** *a.* Acting with violence; angry, furious, frantic, vehement. *n.* Violence; fury. **ragingly,** *adv.*

ragged (răg′ėd) [RAG (1)], *a.* Rough, shaggy; broken, jagged, or uneven in outline or surface; disjointed, irregular, imperfect; lacking in uniformity, finish, etc.; harsh, dissonant; worn into rags, rent, tattered; wearing tattered clothes; shabby, poor, miserable in appearance. **ragged robin:** A crimson-flowered plant, *Lychnis floscuculi,* the petals of which have a tattered appearance. **ragged school:** (*Hist.*) A free school for the education of poor children. **raggedly,** *adv.* **raggedness,** *n.*

ragi (ra′ gi) [Hindi], *n.* An Indian food-grain, *Eleusine coracana.*

Raglan (răg′ lȧn) [Lord *Raglan,* 1788–1855], *n.* A loose overcoat with no seams on the shoulders, the sleeves going up to the neck.

ragman (1) [RAG (1)].

***ragman** (2) (răg′ mȧn) [etym. doubtful], *n.* A document or sealed instrument, especially the Ragman roll. **Ragman** or **Ragman's roll:** The list of the deeds by which the Scottish king (Balliol) and nobles vowed allegiance to Edward I in 1296.

ragout (rȧ goo′) [F. *ragout,* from *ragoûter,* to bring one's taste back (RE-, *goût,* GUST (2))], *n.* A stewed dish of small pieces of meat and vegetables, highly seasoned.

ragstone [RAG (2)].

raguly (răg′ ū li), ***raguled** [etym. doubtful, prob. rel. to RAG (1)], *a.* (*Her.*) Obliquely indented (of a bearing), having projections like lopped branches at the sides.

rag-wheel, ragwort [RAG (1)].

raid (rād) [Sc., from A.-S. *rād,* ROAD], *n.* A hostile or predatory incursion, esp. of mounted men moving with rapidity in order to surprise, a foray; a sudden invasion or descent, esp. of police or custom-house officers; an air raid. *v.t.* To make a raid upon. *v.i.* To make a raid. **raider,** *n.*

rail (1) (rāl) [O.F. *reille,* L. *rēgula,* RULE], *n.* A bar of wood or metal or series of such bars resting on posts or other supports, forming part of a fence, banisters, etc.; one of a continuous line of iron or steel bars, resting on sleepers, etc., laid on the ground, usu. forming one side of a pair of such lines constituting the track of a railway or tramway; one of a similar pair of lines serving as track for part of a machine; the railway as a means of travel or transportation; (*pl.*) railway shares. *v.t.* To enclose with rails; to furnish or fill with rails; to lay down rails upon; to send by rail. *v.i.* To travel by rail. **rail-car,** *n.* A motor-driven vehicle on railway lines. **rail-chair,** *n.* An iron socket or holder, fixed on a sleeper, to which a rail is fastened. **rail-fence,** *n.* A fence made of rails. **railhead,** *n.* A terminus; the farthest point to which rails have been laid. **railroad,** *n.* (*chiefly Am.*) A railway. *v.t.* (*Am.*) To force hurriedly to a conclusion. **rail-roader,** *n.* A person employed on a railway. **railer** (1), *n.* One who makes or fits rails. **railing** (1), *n.* A fence made of wooden or other rails; materials for railings; the laying of rails. **railless,** *a.*

rail (2) (rāl) [F. *railler,* etym. doubtful], *v.i.* To use abusive or derisive language to scoff (at or against). **v.t.* To effect by raillery, **railer** (2), *n.* One who rails or scoffs, **railing** (2), *a.* and *n.* **railingly,** *adv.* **raillery.** *n.* Good-humoured ridicule or pleasantry, banter.

rail (3) (rāl) [F. *râle,* etym. doubtful], *n.* A bird of the family *Rallidæ,* esp. of the genus *Rallus,* comprising *R. aquaticus,* the water-rail, and the corn-crake or landrail, *Crex pratensis.*

***rail** (4) (rāl) [etym. doubtful], *v.i.* To flow, to gush (down).

railer, railing, etc. [RAIL (1 and 2)].

raillery [RAIL (2)].

railway (rāl′ wā) [RAIL (1)], *n.* A road laid with a track formed of rails of iron or steel along which trains and vehicles are driven usu. by locomotives; a track laid with rails for the passage of heavy horse-vehicles, travelling-cranes, trucks, etc.; a system of tracks, stations, rolling-stock, and other apparatus worked by one company or organization. *v.i.* To make railways; to travel by rail. **British Railways:** The unification for nationalization of the principal railway systems in Great Britain under the Transport Act of 1947, which came into force 1 January, 1948. **Railway Bill:** A proposed Act of Parliament for constructing a new railway or conferring further powers on a railway company. **railway company:** A joint-stock company owning and managing a railway. **railway novel:** A light novel for reading on a journey by rail. **railway sub-office:** A place on a railway with a post-office subordinate to another office. **railway spine:** An affection caused by concussion of the spine in a railway accident. **railwayize,** *v.t.* **railwayless,** *a.*

raiment (rā′ mĕnt) [short for obs. *arrayment* (ARRAY, -MENT)], *n.* Dress, apparel, clothes.

rain (rān) [A.-S. *regn, rēn* (cp. Dut. and G. *regen,* Icel., Swed., and Dan. *regn*), whence *regnian,* to rain, *rēnig,* rainy], *n.* The condensed moisture of the atmosphere falling in drops; a fall of such drops; a similar fall or shower of liquid, dust, or bodies; (*pl.*) the rainy season in a tropical country; a rainy region of the Atlantic, 4–10° N. lat. *v.i.* To fall in drops of water from the clouds (*usu. impers.*); to fall in showers like rain. *v.t.* To pour down (rain); to send down in showers like rain. **to rain cats and dogs** [CAT (1)]. **rain-bird,** *n.* One of various birds supposed to foretell rain, esp. the green woodpecker. **rainbow,** *n.* A luminous arc showing the prismatic colours, appearing opposite the sun during rain, caused by the reflection, double refraction, and dispersion of the sun's rays passing through the drops. *a.* Coloured like the rainbow; many-coloured. **rainbow-tinted,** *a.* **rainbow trout:** A brightly-coloured Californian trout, *Salmo irideus.* **rain-box,** *n.* (*Theat.*) A device imitating the noise of rain. **rain-cloud,** *n.* A cloud producing rain, a nimbus. **rain-coat,** *n.* A waterproof coat or cloak for wearing in wet weather; (*Am.*) a mackintosh. **rain-doctor,** *n.* A wizard professing to cause rain by incantations. **raindrop,** *n.* A particle of rain. **rainfall,** *n.* The amount of rain which falls in a particular district in a given period; a shower of rain. **rain-gauge,** *n.* An instrument for measuring the amount of rain falling on a given surface. **rain-glass,** *n.* (*colloq.*) A barometer. **rain-maker** [RAIN-DOCTOR]. **rain-proof, -tight,** *a.* Impervious to rain. **rain-wash,** *n.* (*Geol.*) The movement of soil and stones effected by rain. **rain-water,** *n.* Water that has fallen in the form of rain. **rainless,** *a.* **rainy,** *a.* Characterized by much rain; showery, wet. **rainy day:** (*fig.*) A time of misfortune or distress, esp. pecuniary need. **rainily,** *adv.* **raininess,** *n.*

Rais (REIS) [(2)].

raise (rāz) [Icel. *reisa* (cp. Dan. *reise*, Swed. *resa*)], *v.t.* To cause to rise, to elevate; to cause to stand up, to set upright; to restore to life, to rouse, to excite, to stir up (against, upon, etc.); to erect, to build, to construct; to rear, to cause to grow, to breed; to produce, to create, to cause; to collect, to procure, to levy (money, etc.); to occasion; to set up, to suggest (a point, etc.); to advance, to promote, to heighten, to make higher or nobler, to cause to ascend; to make tender; to increase the amount of; (*Naut.*) to come in sight of (land, etc.). *n.* (*Am.*) A rise in salary. **to raise a blockade** or **siege:** To relinquish the attempt to take a place by blockade or siege. **to raise Cain:** To create a disturbance. **to raise cloth:** To put a nap on cloth. **to raise one's eyes:** To look upwards (to). **to raise the hat to** [HAT]. **to raise the wind:** (*slang*) To make a disturbance or commotion; to get hold of cash. **raised beach** [BEACH]. **raiser,** *n.* **raising-gig,** *n.* A machine for raising a nap on cloth. **raising-piece,** *n.* A piece of timber laid on a brick wall or frame to carry a beam or beams. **raising-plate,** *n.* A horizontal timber for carrying the heels of rafters.

raisin (rā′ zin) [O.F. *raizin* (F. *raisin*), pop. L. *racīmum*, L. *racēmum*, RACEME], *n.* A dried grape, the partially dried fruit of various species of vine.

raison d'être (rā zon dätr′) [F., reason of being], *n.* The reason for a thing's existence.

raisonné (rā′ zo nā) [F., p.p. of *raisonner*, to REASON], *a.* Arranged systematically (of a catalogue).

raj (raj) [Hindi], *n.* (*Ang.-Ind.*) Sovereignty, rule.

Rajah, Raja (ra′ jȧ) [Hindi, from Sansk. *rāj*, to reign, rel. to L. *rex*, king], *n.* An Indian king, prince, or tribal chief, a title of a dignitary or noble; a Malayan or Javanese chief. **Rajahship,** *n.*

Rajpoot (raj′ poot) [Hindi *rajpūt* (Sansk. *rāja*, see prec., *putra*, son)], *n.* One of an Indian warrior caste who claim descent from the Kshatriyas; one of a Hindu aristocratic class.

rake (1) (rāk) [A.-S. *raca* (cp. Dut. *raak*, G. *rechen*, Icel. *reka*)], *n.* An implement having a long handle with a cross-bar set with teeth, used for drawing loose material together, smoothing soil, etc.; a two-wheeled implement drawn by a horse for gathering hay together, etc.; a similar implement for collecting light articles. *v.t.* To collect or gather (up or together) with a rake; to scrape, scratch, smooth, clean, etc. (soil) with a rake; to search with or as with a rake, to scour, to ransack; to fire along the length of, to enfilade; to sweep (a ship, deck, line of soldiers, etc.) from end to end; to pass (of shot) from end to end of; (*fig.*) to command from end to end with the eye. *v.i.* To use or work with a rake; to search (about, etc.) with or as with a rake. ***rake-hell,** *n.* An utterly abandoned scoundrel, a rake (2). ***rake-helly,** *a.* **rake-off,** *n.* (*slang*) Commision on a job; more or less illicit profits from a job. **raker,** *n.* **raking,** *n.* The act of using or working with a rake; the amount of ground or quantity of material raked; that which is raked together (*usu. in pl.*).

rake (2) (rāk) [short for RAKE-HELL, see prec.], *n.* A dissolute or immoral man, a debauchee, a libertine. **v.i.* To lead a dissolute life. **rakish** (1), *a.* **rakishly,** *adv.* **rakishness,** *n.*

rake (3) (rāk) [etym. doubtful], *n.* Inclination, slope, esp. backward slope; projection of the stem or stern of a vessel beyond the extremities of the keel; the slope of a mast or funnel towards the stern; (*Theat.*) the slope of the stage, an auditorium. *v.i.* To slope backwards from the perpendicular. *v.t.* To give such an inclination to. **rakish** (2), *a.* (*Naut.*) With masts sharply inclined; apparently built for speed; smart-looking with a suggestion of the pirate or smuggler (prob. with alln. to RAKE (2)).

raki (rȧ kē′, răk′ i) [Turk. *rāqī*, brandy, spirit], *n.* An aromatic liquor made from spirit or grape-juice, usu. flavoured with mastic, used in the Levant.

rakish, etc. [RAKE (2 and 3)].

râle (ral) [F., from *râler*, etym. doubtful], *n.* A rattling sound in addition to that of respiration, heard with the stethoscope in lungs affected by disease.

rallentando (răl ėn tăn′ dō) [It., p.p. of *rallentare*, as RELENT], *adv.* (*Mus. direction*) Gradually slower.

rallier [RALLY (2)].

ralline (răl′ īn) [mod. L. *rallus*, RAIL (3)], *a.* (*Ornith.*) Of or pertaining to the *Rallidæ* or rails.

rally (1) (răl′ i) [F. *rallier* (RE-, *allier*, to ALLY)], *v.t.* To reunite, to bring (disordered troops) together again; to restore, to reanimate, to revive, to pull together. *v.i.* To reassemble, to come together again after a reverse or rout; to regain strength, to recover tone or spirit, to return to a state of health, vigour, or courage. *n.* The act of rallying or recovering order, strength, health, energy, etc.; an assembly, a reunion; (*Lawn-tennis, etc.*) rapid return of strokes. **rallying-point,** *n.* A spot or moment for making a rally.

rally (2) (răl′ i) [F. *railler*, to RAIL (2)], *v.t.* To attack with raillery; to banter, to chaff. *n.* Banter, raillery. **rallier,** *n.* **rallyingly,** *adv.*

ram (1) (răm) [A.-S. (cp. Dut. and O.H.G. *ram*, G. *ramme*, prob. rel. to Icel. *ramr*, strong)], *n.* A male sheep, a tup; a battering-ram; a battleship armed with a beak of steel at the bow for cutting into a hostile vessel; such a beak; the drop-weight of a pile-driver or steam-hammer; an hydraulic engine for raising water, lifting, etc.; a rammer; the compressing piston of an hydrostatic press; the plunger of a force-pump; (*Naut.*) a spar for driving planks, etc., by impact. *v.t.* (*past & p.p.* **rammed**) To beat, drive, press, or force (down, in, into, etc.) by heavy blows; to stuff, to compress, to force (into) with pressure; to make firm by ramming; to strike (a ship) with a ram; to drive or impel (a thing against, into, etc.) with violence. *v.i.* To beat, to pound, or hammer with or as with a rammer. **the Ram:** The constellation or zodiacal sign Aries. **ramrod,** *n.* A rod for forcing down the charge of a muzzle-loading gum. **ramroddy,** *a.* Stiff as a ramrod, uncompromising, formal. **ramrodism,** *n.* **ram's-horn,** *n.* A horn of a male sheep; a scroll-ornament like a ram's skull and horns; (*Fort.*) a semicircular work commanding a ditch; *an ammonite. **rammer,** *n.* One who or that which rams; an instrument for pounding, driving, etc.; a ramrod.

ram (2) (răm) [etym. doubtful], *n.* (*Naut.*) Length of a boat over all. **ram-line,** *n.* A small rope used for striking the centre-line of a vessel, as a guide in setting the frames, etc.

Ramadan (răm ȧ dan′) [Arab. (cp. Pers. and Turk. *Ramazān*), from *ramada*, to be hot], *n.* The ninth month of the Mohammedan year, the time of the great annual fast.

ramal (rā′ măl) [L. *rāmus*, branch, -AL], *a.* Of, pertaining to, or growing on a branch. ***ramage** (răm′ ȧj), *n.* (*collect.*) Branches. *a.* Having left the nest, hence wild, shy, untamed (of hawks).

rama-rama (ra′ mȧ ra′ mȧ) [Maori], *n.* A widely spread N. Zealand shrub.

ramble (răm′ bėl) [etym. doubtful], *v.i.* To walk or move about freely or aimlessly, to rove; to wander or be incoherent in speech, writing, etc. *n.* A roaming about; a walk for pleasure or without a definite object, a stroll. **rambler,** *n.* One who rambles about; a variety of climbing-rose. **rambling,** *a.* Wandering about; desultory, disconnected, irregular, straggling. **ramblingly,** *adv.*

rambustious [RUMBUSTIOUS].

rambutan (răm boo′ tȧn) [Malay, from *rambut*, hair], *n.* The red, hairy, pulpy fruit of a Malaysian tree, *Nephelium lappaceum.*

ramé (ra mā) [F., branched, from *rame*, L. *rāmus*, branch], *a.* (*Her.*) Attired.

rameal [RAMAL]. **ramee** [RAMIE].

ramekin (răm′ ė kin) [F. *ramequin*, etym. doubtful], *n.* A dish of cheese, eggs, breadcrumbs, etc., boiled in a small dish or mould.

ramentum (rȧ men′ tŭm) [L., from *rādere*, to RAZE], *n.* (*usu. in pl.* **-ta**) (*Bot.*) Thin membranous scales formed on leaves, stems, etc.; (*Path.*) debris of organic tissue discharged in some diseases. **ramentaceous** (-tā′ shŭs), *a.* (*Bot.*).

rameous (rā′ mė ŭs) [L. *rāmus*, branch, -EOUS], *a.* (*Bot.*) Of or belonging to branches.

rami, *pl.* [RAMUS].

ramicorn (răm′ i kôrn) [L. *rāmus*, branch, *cornu*, horn], *a.* (*Ent.*) Having ramified antennæ. *n.* (*Ornith.*) The horny sheath of the rami of the lower mandible.

ramie (răm′ i) [Malay *rāmī*], *n.* A bushy Chinese and E. Indian plant, *Bœhmeria nivea*, of the nettle family; the fine fibre of this woven as a substitute for cotton.

ramify (răm′ i fī) [F. *ramifier*, med. L. *rāmificāre* (L. *rāmus*, branch, *-ficāre*, *-facere*, to make)], *v.i.* To divide into branches or subdivisions, to branch out, to send out offshoots. *v.t.* To cause to divide into branches, etc. **ramification** (-kā′ shŭn), *n.* The act of ramifying; a subdivision in a complex system, structure, etc.; the production of figures like branches; (*Bot.*) the arangement of branches.

ram-line [RAM (2)]. **rammer** [RAM (1)].

rammish (răm′ ish) [RAM (1), -ISH], ***rammy,** *a.* Strong-smelling; rank. **rammishness,** *n.*

ramollissement (ra mol′ ēs man) [F., from *ramollir* (RE-, *amollir*, from *mou*, L. *mollis*, soft, cp. MOLLIFY)], *n.* (*Path.*) A morbid softening of some organ or tissue, esp. of the brain.

ramose (rȧ mōs′), ***ramous** (rā′ mŭs) [L. *rāmōsus*, from *rāmus*, branch], *a.* Branching; branched; full of branches.

ramp (1) (rămp) [O.F. *ramper*, to creep, crawl, climb, etym. doubtful], *v.i.* To rear or stand up on the hind-legs, with the forelegs raised (of an heraldic lion); to dash about, to rage, to storm; (*Arch.*) to ascend or descend to another level (of a wall). *v.t.* To build or provide with ramps. *n.* A slope or inclined plane or way leading from one level to another, esp. in the interior of a fortification; (*Arch.*) a difference in level between the abutments of a rampart arch; a sloping part in the top of a hand-rail, wall, coping, etc.; *the act of ramping; *a vulgar, badly-behaved woman.

ramp (2) (rămp) [etym. doubtful], *v.t.* (*slang*) To rob with violence; to force (one) to pay a bet, etc. *n.* A swindle. **ramper, rampman,** *n.* A swindler; a robber, a footpad.

rampage (răm pāj′) [etym. doubtful], *v.i.* To dash about, to storm, to rage, to behave violently or boisterously. *n.* Boisterous, excited, or violent behaviour. **on the rampage:** Violently excited; on a drunken spree. **rampageous** (-pā′ jŭs), *a.* **rampageously,** *adv.* **rampageousness,** *n.*

***rampallion** (răm păl′ i ŏn) [etym. doubtful], *n.* A rapscallion, a ruffian.

rampant (răm′ pȧnt) [F., pres.p. of *ramper*, to RAMP (1)], *a.* Standing upright on the hind legs, ramping (of the heraldic lion); unrestrained, aggressive, wild, violent; rank, luxuriant (of weeds, etc.); (*Arch.*) springing from different levels (of an arch). **rampant gardant:** (*Her.*) Rampant, with the animal looking full-faced. **rampant passant:** In the attitude of walking with the dexter fore-paw raised. **rampant regardant:** Rampant with the head looking backward. **rampancy,** *n.* **rampantly,** *adv.*

rampart (răm′ part) [F. *rempart*, from *remparer*, to fortify (RE-, EM-, *parer*, L. *parāre*, see PARRY)], *n.* An embankment, usu. surmounted by a parapet, round a fortified place, or such an embankment together with the parapet; (*fig.*) a defence. *v.t.* To fortify or defend with or as with a rampart.

ramper [RAMP (2)].

rampick, rampike (răm′ pik, -pīk) [etym. doubtful], *n.* (*prov. and Am.*) A dead or partly-decayed tree, a stump. **rampicked, -piked,** *a.*

rampion (răm′ pi ŏn) [prob. rel. to F. *rapiponce* or It. *ramponzolo*, etym. doubtful], *n.* A bell-flower, *Campanula rapunculus*, with red, purple, or blue blossoms.

ramplor (rămp′ lŏr) [Sc., prob. from RAMP (1)], *n.* A gay rover.

***rampire** [RAMPART]. **ramrod,** etc. [RAM (1)].

ramshackle (răm′ shăk′ ėl) [var. of obs. *ramshackled*, prob. from *ransackle*, freq. of RANSACK], *a.* In a crazy state, shaky, tumble-down, rickety. *v.t.* To construct in a ramshackle way. **ramshackly,** *a.* In bad repair.

ram's-horn [RAM (1)]. **ramskin** [RAMEKIN].

ramson (răm′ zŏn, -sŏn) [A.-S. *hramsan*, pl. of *hramsa* (cp. G., Dan., and Swed. *rams*, also Gr. *kromuon*)], *n.* (*usu. in pl.*) The broad-leaved garlic, *Allium ursinum*, or its bulbous root, eaten as a relish.

ram-stam (răm′ stăm) [Sc. (perh. RAM (1), *stam*, dial. var. of STAMP)], *a.* Reckless, precipitate, headstrong, forward. *adv.* Headlong, rashly, precipitately. *n.* A headstrong or hasty person.

ramulose, -lous (răm′ ū lōs, -lŭs) [L. *rāmulōsus*, from *rāmulus*, dim. of *rāmus*], *a.* Having many small branches. **ramuliferous** (-lif′ ėr ŭs), *a.* **ramulus** (răm′ ū lŭs), *n.* (*pl.* **-li,** -lī) A small branch or ramus. **ramuscule** (rȧ mŭs′ kūl), *n.* A small branch. **ramus** (rā′ mŭs), *n.* (*pl.* **rami,** rā′ mī) A branched or forked part or structure; (*Zool.*) the barb of a feather.

ran (1) (răn) [etym. unknown], *n.* A length of 20 cords of twine.

ran (2), *past* [RUN].

Rana (rā′ nȧ′) [L., frog.], *n.* (*Zool.*) A genus of batrachians comprising the frogs and toads.

rance (1) (rans) [etym. doubtful], *n.* A variegated kind of marble.

rance (2) (răns) [prob. from F. *ranche*], *n.* A rod, bar, or prop.

***rancescent** (răn ses′ ėnt) [L. *rancescens -ntem*, pres.p. of *rancescere*, cogn. with *rancidus*, RANCID], *a.* Becoming sour or rancid.

ranch (rănch), **rancho** (ran′ chō) [Sp. *rancho*, mess, a party eating together, prob. rel. to RANK (1)], *n.* (*Am.*) A farm for rearing cattle and horses; a house belonging to such a farm. *v.t.* To manage or work upon a ranch. **ranchman, rancher, *ranchero*** (ran châr′ ō), *n.* **rancheria** (ran chė rē′ ȧ), *n.* A house or hut of a ranchero or rancheros; a cluster of Indian huts.

rancid (răn′ sid) [L. *rancidus*], *a.* Having the taste or smell of stale oil or fat. **rancidify** (răn sid′ i fī), *v.t.* and *i.* **rancidity, rancidness,** *n.* **rancidly,** *adv.*

rancour (răng′ kŏr) [O.F., from L. *rancōrem*, nom. *-cor*, cogn. with prec.], *n.* Inveterate spite, resentment, or enmity, malignancy, deep-seated malice; (*fig.*) corruption, poison. **rancorous,** *a.* **rancorously,** *adv.*

rand (rănd) [A.-S., also Dut. and G., Swed. and Dan., cp. Icel. *rönd*], *n.* Orig. a border, edge, or margin, a strip of leather between the heel-piece of a boot or shoe; a thin inner sole; (*S. Afr.*) the highlands bordering a river-valley. **the Rand,** *n.* abbr. for Witwatersrand, the gold and diamond country in S. Africa of which Johannesburg is the centre.

randan (1) (răn′ dăn) [etym. doubtful], *n.* A boat worked by three rowers, the one amidships using two oars; this method of rowing a boat.

randan (2) (răn dăn′) [perh. rel. to RANDOM], *n.* (*slang*) A spree.

randem (răn′ dĕm) [from RANDOM after TANDEM], *a.* Having three horses harnessed tandem. *adv.* In this fashion. *n.* A team or a carriage driven thus.

randle-balk, -tree [RANNEL-TREE].

random (răn′ dŏm) [F. *randon*, from *randir*, to press forward, to gallop], *n.* Great speed or impetuosity. *a.* Done, made, etc., without calculation or method; left to chance. **at random:** At haphazard; without direction or definite purpose; *at great speed. **random shot:** A shot discharged without direct aim; orig. a shot fired at the extreme range attainable by elevating the muzzle of a gun. **randomly,** *adv.*

randy (răn′ di) [RAND (2), -Y], *a.* (*chiefly Sc.*). Loud-tongued, boisterous; disorderly, riotous; lustful, on heat. *n.* A sturdy beggar, a vagrant; a scold, a virago. **randiness,** *n.*

ranee (ra′ ni, ra′ nē) [Hindi *rānī*, Sansk. *rājnī*, fem. of *rājā*, RAJAH], *n.* A Hindu queen; the consort of a rajah.

rang, *past* [RING (2)].

rangatira (răng gȧ tē′ rȧ) [Maori], *n.* A Maori chieftain.

range (rānj) [O.F. *ranger, renger*, from *rang*, RANK (1)], *v.t.* To set in a row or rows; to arrange in definite order, place, company, etc., to array; to rank; to roam or pass over, along, or through; to sail along or about. *v.i.* To lie, extend, or reach; (*Ordnance*) to carry (a specified distance) in a particular direction; to rank, to be in place (among, with, etc.); to vary (from one specified point to another); to roam, to wander, to rove, to sail (along, etc.); (*Ordnance*) to go or be thrown (of a projectile). *n.* A row, rank, line, chain, or series; a stretch, a tract, esp. of grazing or hunting-ground; the area, extent, scope, compass, or sphere of power, activity, variation, etc.; (*Radio.*) a set of coils; the extreme horizontal distance attainable by a gun or a projectile; the distance between a gun and the object aimed at; a piece of ground with targets, etc., for firing practice; a cooking-stove or fire-place, usu. containing a boiler, oven, or ovens, hot-plate, etc. **to range oneself:** To adopt a more settled course of life, to settle down (as by marrying). **rangé** (ran zhā), *a.* (*Her.*) Set in order (of a number of charges). **range-finder,** *n.* An instrument for measuring the distance of an object to be fired at. **ranger,** *n.* One who ranges, a rover, a wanderer; the superintendent of a royal forest or park; a dog used to scour over ground; a Girl Guide of 16 and upwards; (*Am.*) a commando in the U.S. army; (*pl.*) a body of mounted troops. **rangership,** *n.* **rangy,** *a.* (*Am. colloq.*) Tall, wiry, strong; (*Austral.*) mountainous.

ranine (rā′ nīn) [RANA], *a.* (*Anat.*) Of or pertaining to the under side of the tip of the tongue, where *ranula* occurs; *(*Zool.*) pertaining to or like frogs. **raniform,** *a.* Frog-shaped. **ranivorous** (rȧ niv′ ŏ rŭs), *a.* Frog-eating.

rank (1) (răngk) [F. *ranc* (now *rang*), prob. from O.H.G. *hring, hrinc*, RING (1)], *n.* A row, a line, a row of soldiers ranged side by side, opp. to file; order, array; relative position, degree, standing, station, class; high station, dignity, eminence; relative degree of excellence, etc.; (*Chess*) a line of squares stretching across the board from side to side. *v.t.* To draw up or marshal in rank; to classify, to estimate, to give a (specified) rank to. *v.i.* To hold a (specified) rank; to have a place or position (among, with, etc.); (*Law*) to have a place on the list of claims on a bankrupt's estate. **rank and fashion:** People of high society. **rank and file:** Common soldiers; (*fig.*) ordinary people. **to take rank with:** To be placed on a level or be ranked with. **ranker,** *n.* One who disposes or arranges in ranks; a commissioned officer promoted from the ranks.

rank (2) (răngk) [A.-S. *ranc*, cp. Dut. *rank*, Icel. *rakka*, straight, slender], *a.* Luxuriant in growth, over-fertile, over-abundant; coarse, gross; rich, fertile; rancid, offensive, strong, evil-smelling; strongly marked, thorough, flagrant, arrant, utter; indecent, obscene. **adv.* Rankly. **rankly,** *adv.* **rankness,** *n.*

ranker [RANK (1)].

rankle (răng′ kĕl) [O.F. *rancler*, from *rancle, drancle*, an eruption or sore, med. L. *dracunculus*, dim. of *draco*, DRAGON], *v.i.* To be inflamed, to fester (of a wound, etc.); to be inflamed, to irritate, to cause pain (of resentment, etc.).

rankly [RANK (2)].

rankness [RANK (2)].

rannel-tree (răn′ ĕl trē) [Sc. and North., prob. Scand.], *n.* A horizontal beam or bar, esp. one fixed across an open chimney for hanging cooking-utensils, etc., on, also called **rannel-balk.**

ransack (răn′ săk) [Icel *rannsaka* (*rann*, house, *sækja*, to seek, cogn. with A.-S. *sēcan*, SEEK)], *v.t.* To search thoroughly, to rummage; to pillage, to plunder; *to ravish. **ransacker,** *n.*

ransom (răn′ sŏm) [O.F. *ranson* (F. *rançon*), L. *redemptiōnem*, nom. *-tio*, REDEMPTION], *n.* Release from captivity in return for a payment; a sum of money paid for such release or for goods captured by an enemy; (*euphem.*) blackmail; *(*Law*) a fine or sum paid for the pardon of some offence. *v.t.* To redeem from captivity or obtain the restoration of (property) by paying a sum of money; to demand or exact a ransom for, to hold to ransom; to release in return for a ransom; (*Theol.*) to redeem from sin, to atone for. **ransomable,** *a.* **ransomer,** *n.* **ransomless,** *a.*

rant (rănt) [M. Dut. *randten, ranten*, cp. G. *ranzen*, to spring or dance about], *v.i.* To use loud, bombastic, or violent language; to declaim or preach in a theatrical or noisy fashion. *n.* Bombastic or violent declamation; a tirade, a noisy declamation; inflated talk. **ranter,** *n.* One who rants; a declamatory preacher; (*pl.*) a nickname given to the Primitive Methodists. **ranterism,** *n.* **rantingly,** *adv.* **rantipole,** *n.* A wild, harum-scarum or romping person; a scold, a termagant. *a.* Wild, harum-scarum, rakish. *v.i.* To behave or go about in a boisterous or extravagant fashion. ***rantism,** *n.* Ranterism.

ranula (răn′ ū lȧ) [L., rānula, dim. of *rāna*, frog], *n.* A cystic tumour under the tongue, sometimes called frog-tongue. **ranular,** *a.*

ranunculus (rȧ nŭn′ kū lŭs) [L., dim. of *rāna*, frog], *n.* (*pl.* **-luses, -li,** -lī) (*Bot.*) A genus of plants including the buttercup. **ranunculaceous** (-lā′ shŭs), *a.*

ranz-des-vaches (rans dā vash) [French (Swiss), *ranz*, etym. doubtful, *des vaches*, of the cows], *n.* A melody or flourish blown on their horns by Swiss herdsmen to call their cattle.

rap (1) (răp) [prob. imit., cp. Swed. *rappa*, to beat, G. *rappeln*, to rattle], *v.t.* (*past & p.p.* **rapped**) To strike with a slight, sharp blow; to strike smartly; (*fig.*) to utter in a quick, abrupt way. *v.i.* To strike a sharp, quick blow, esp. at a door; to make a sharp, quick sound like a light blow. *n.* A slight, sharp blow; a sound like the blow from a knocker, the knuckles, etc., on a door; a similar sound made by some agency as a means of communicating messages at a spiritualistic séance. **to take the rap:** (*colloq.*) To take the blame for another. **rap on the knuckles:** A reproof, reprimand. **rapper,** *n.* One who raps; a spirit-rapper; a door-knocker.

rap (2) (răp) [etym. doubtful], *n.* A counterfeit Irish coin, passing for a halfpenny in the time of George I; (*fig.*) a thing of no value. **not worth a rap:** Worthless.

***rap** (3) (răp) [prob. rel. to Dan. *rappe*, Swed. *rappa*, G. *rappen*; prob. in later sense a back formation from RAPT], *v.t.* To snatch away, to seize by violence; to transport, to carry out of oneself.

rapacious (rȧ pā' shŭs) [L. *rapax -pācis*, from *rapere*, to seize, see RAPE (1)], *a.* Grasping, extortionate; given to plundering or seizing by force, predatory; living on food seized by force (of animals). **rapaciously,** *adv.* ***rapaciousness, rapacity** (rȧ păs' i ti), *n.*

rape (1) (rāp) [prob. from L. *rapere*, to seize], *v.t.* To ravish, to force (a woman); *to seize, to carry off. *n.* Carnal knowledge of a woman against her will, ravishing; seizing or carrying off by force. **rapist,** *n.* A ravisher (of women).

rape (2) (rāp) [prob. from A.-S., etym. doubtful], *n.* One of six divisions of the county of Sussex.

rape (3) (rāp) [L. *rāpum* or *rāpa*, turnip], *n.* A plant, *Brassica napus*, allied to the turnip, grown as food for sheep; a plant, *B. campestris oleifera*, grown on the Continent for its seed which yields oil, cole-seed. **wild rape:** Charlock. **rape-cake,** *n.* The compressed seeds and husks of rape after the oil has been expressed, used for feeding cattle and as manure. **rape-oil,** *n.* Oil obtained from the seed of *B. napus*. **rape-seed,** *n.* The seed of *B. napus*.

rape (4) (rāp) [F. *râpe*, med. L. *raspa*], *n.* The refuse stems and skins of grapes after the wine has been expressed, used to make vinegar; a large vessel used in making vinegar.

rap-full (răp' ful) [etym. doubtful], *a.* (*Naut.*) Full of wind (of a sail when close-hauled).

Raphaelesque (răf ā ĕl esk'), *a.* After the style of the Italian painter Raphael (1483–1520). **Raphaelism,** *n.* The idealistic principles of Raphael in painting. **Raphaelite,** *n.* [cf. PRERAPHAELITE.]

Raphanus (răf' ȧ nŭs) [L., from Gr. *raphanos*, radish], *n.* (*Bot.*) A genus of cruciferous plants typified by the radish. **raphania** (rȧ fā' ni ȧ), *n.* (*Path.*) A form of ergotism supposed to be due to the use of grain containing seeds of species of *Raphanus*.

raphe (rā' fi) [mod. L. and Gr.], *n.* (*Anat.*) A seam-like suture or line of union; (*Bot.*) a suture or line of junction, a median line or rib, a fibrovascular cord connecting the hilum of an ovule with the base of the nucleus.

raphia [RAFFIA].

raphilite (răf' i līt) [as foll. -LITE], *n.* (*Min.*) A tremolite.

raphis (rā' fis) [Gr. *raphis -idos*, needle], *n.* (*usu. in pl.* ***raphides***, -fi dēz) (*Bot.*) Needle-shaped transparent crystals found in the cells of plants.

rapid (răp' id) [L. *rapidus*, from *rapere*, to seize, see RAPE (1)], *a.* Very swift, quick, speedy; done, acting, moving, or completed in a very short time; descending steeply. *n.* (*usu. pl.*) A sudden descent in a stream, with a swift current. **rapid-fire:** Quick-firing (of guns). **rapid-firer,** *n.* **rapidity** (rȧ pid' i ti), ***rapidness,** *n.* **rapidly,** *adv.*

rapier (rā' pi ėr) [F. *rapière*, etym. doubtful], *n.* A light, narrow sword, used only in thrusting, a small-sword. **rapier-fish,** *n.* A sword-fish.

rapine (răp' in) [F. *rapine*, L. *rapīna*, from *rapere*, to seize], *n.* The act of plundering or carrying off by force; plunder, spoliation, robbery.

raploch (răp' lo*ch*) [Sc., etym. unknown], *n.* Coarse homespun. *a.* Coarse, homely.

rapparee (răp' ȧ rē) [Ir. *rapaire*, a noisy fellow, a robber], *n.* An Irish freebooter, or robber, esp. during the late 17th and the 18th centuries.

rappee (rȧ pē') [F. *râpé*, from *râper*, to RASP], *n.* A coarse kind of snuff.

rappel (ra pel) [F., from *rappeler*, to recall, as REPEAL], *n.* The beat of a drum calling soldiers to arms.

rapport (rȧ pôrt', ra' pôr) [F., from *rapporter* (RE-, AP-, *porter*, L. *portāre*, to carry)], *n.* Correspondence, sympathetic relationship, agreement, harmony.

rapprochement (ra prōsh' ma*n*) [F., from *rapprocher*], *n.* Reconciliation, re-establishment of friendly relations, esp. between nations.

rapscallion (răp skăl' yŏn) [RASCALLION], *n.* A rascal, a scamp, a good-for-nothing. *a.* Rascally.

rapt (răpt) [L. *raptus*, p.p. of *rapere*, to seize, see RAPE (1)], *a.* Transported, carried away by one's thoughts or emotions, enraptured, absorbed, engrossed. **raptor,** *n.* *A ravisher; (*Ornith.*) one of the *Raptores*.

Raptores (răp tôr' ēz) [L., pl. of *raptor*, as prec.], *n.* (*Ornith.*) An order of birds of prey containing the eagles, hawks, and owls. **raptorial,** *a.* and *n.* **raptorious,** *a.*

rapture (răp' chėr, răp' tyŭr) [RAPT, -URE], *n.* Ecstasy, transport, ecstatic joy; (*pl.*) a fit or transport of delight; *vehemence or violence of passion, etc.; *a fit, a paroxysm. **raptured, rapturous,** *a.* **rapturist,** *n.* An enthusiast. **rapturously,** *adv.*

rara avis [L., rare bird], *n.* A rarity, something very rarely met with.

rare (1) (râr) [L. *rārus*], *a.* Of sparse, tenuous, thin, or porous substance, not dense; exceptional, seldom existing or occurring, not often met with, unusual, scarce, uncommon; especially excellent, singularly good, choice, first-rate. **rare earth metals,** *n.pl.* (*Metall.*) A group of rare metals (in many of their properties resembling aluminium) which occur in some rare minerals. **rarely,** *adv.* **rareness,** *n.*

rare (2) (râr) [var. of *rear*, A.-S. *hrēr*], *a.* (*Am.*) Half-cooked, underdone; soft (of eggs). **rarebit** [WELSH RABBIT].

raree-show (râr' ė shō) [corr. of RARE (1), SHOW], *n.* A show carried about in a box, a peep-show.

rarefy (râr' ė fī) [obs. F. *raréfier*, L. *rārēfacere* (*rārus*, RARE (1), *facere*, to make)], *v.t.* To make rare, thin, porous, or less dense and solid; to expand without adding to the substance of; (*fig.*) to purify, to refine, to make less gross. *v.i.* To become less dense. **rarefaction** (-făk' shŭn), **rarefication** (-fi kā' shŭn), *n.* **rarefactive** (-făk' tiv), *a.* ***rarefiable,** *a.*

rareripe (râr' rīp) [var. of RATHE-RIPE], *a.* (*Am.*) Early ripe. *n.* An early fruit, esp. a variety of peach or an onion that ripens early.

rarity (râr' i ti) [F. *rarité*, L. *rāritātem*, nom. *-tas*, from *rārus*, RARE (1)], *n.* Rareness; tenuity; unusual excellence; a rare thing; a thing of exceptional value through being rare.

ras (răs) [Ethiop.], *n.* An Abyssinian governor or administrator.

rascal (răs-, ras' kȧl) [O.F. *rascaille*, *rescaille* (F. *racaille*), rabble, dreggs, outcasts], *n.* A mean rogue, a tricky, dishonest, or contemptible fellow, a knave, a scamp; applied playfully to a child, etc. *a.* Worthless, low, mean. **rascaldom, rascalism. rascality** (-kăl' i ti), *n.* **rascallion,** *n.* A rascal. **rascally** (răs-, ras' kȧ li), *a.*

rase [RAZE].

rash (1) (răsh) [cp. Dan. and Swed. *rask*, Dut. and G. *rasch*, quick, vigorous], *a.* Hasty, precipitate, impetuous, venturesome; reckless, thoughtless, acting or done without reflection. **rashling,** *n.* A rash person. **rashly,** *adv.* **rashness,** *n.*

rash (2) (răsh) [perh. from M.F. *rasche* (F. *rache*)], *n.* An eruption of spots or patches on the skin.

***rash** (3) (răsh) [form of obs. *arrache*, F. *arracher*, see RACE (5)], *v.i.* To snatch, to tear (away), to pull (down, out, etc.).

rasher (răsh' ėr) [from obs. *rash*, to cut, var. of RAZE, or rel. to RASH (1), with the sense rashly or hastily cooked], *n.* A thin slice of bacon or ham for frying.

rashling, rashly, rashness [RASH (1)].

raskolnik (răs kol' nik) [Rus., a schismatic], *n.* A dissenter from the Orthodox or Greek Church in Russia.

Rasores (rà sôr' ēz) [L., pl. of *rāsor*, from *rādere*, to scrape, see RAZE], *n.pl.* (*Ornith.*) An order of birds usu. called the *Gallinæ* of which the common fowl is the type, characterized by the toes ending in strong claws for scratching up seeds, etc. **rasorial,** *a.*

rasp (rasp) [O.F. *rasper* (F. *râper*), from Teut. (cp. O.H.G. *raspōn*, G. *raspeln*)], *v.t.* To rub down, scrape, or grate with a coarse, rough implement; to file with a rasp; (*fig.*) to irritate. *v.i.* To rub, to grate; to make a grating sound; (*fig.*) to grate (upon feelings, etc.). *n.* An instrument like a coarse file with projections or raised teeth for scraping away surface material. **raspatory,** *n.* (*Surg.*) A rasp for scraping the outer membrane from bones, etc. **rasper,** *n.* A rasp, a scraper; a rasping-machine; (*slang*) an unpleasant sort of person; an extraordinary person or thing. **raspingly,** *adv.*

raspberry (raz' bėr i) [obs. *rasp*, *raspis*, perh. rel. to RAPE (4)], *n.* The fruit of various species of *Rubus*, esp. *R. Idæus*, consisting of red or sometimes white or yellow drupes set on a conical receptacle; (*colloq.*) a rude derisive sound with the lips. **raspberry-cane,** *n.* A long woody shoot of this plant. **raspberry-vinegar,** *n.* A syrup prepared from raspberry juice.

rasse (răs' i, răs) [Javanese *rase*], *n.* A feline carnivore allied to the civet, inhabiting the E. Indies and S. China.

***rasure** (rā' zhūr) [F., from L. *rāsūra*, from *rādere*, to RAZE], *n.* The art of scraping or shaving; erasure.

rat (răt) [A.-S. *ræt* (cp. Dut. *rat*, G. *ratz*, F. *rat*)], *n.* One of the large rodents of the mouse family, esp. the black rat, *Mus rattus*, and *M. decumanus*, the grey, brown or Norway rat; (*Polit.*) one who deserts his party, a turncoat; (*colloq.*) a workman who works for less than the trade-union rate of wages, or who stands aloof from or works during a strike, a blackleg. *v.i.* (*past & p.p.* **ratted**) To hunt or kill rats (esp. of dogs); (*colloq.*) to play the rat in politics, in a strike, etc. **like a drowned rat:** Soaked to the skin. **rats!** (*slang*) An exclamation of incredulity or derision. **to smell a rat:** To be suspicious. **rat-catcher,** *n.* One who gets his living by catching rats. **ratsbane,** *n.* Poison for rats. **rat-snake,** *n.* An Indian snake, *Zamenis mucosus*, which preys on rats. **rat's-tail,** *n.* (*pl.* rat-tails). A thing, esp. a file, like the rail of a rat. **rat-tail,** *n.* An excrescence growing from the pastern to the middle of the shank of a horse; a disease in horses in which the hair of the tail is lost; a tail like a rat's. **rat-tailed,** *a.* **rat-trap,** *n.* A trap for catching rats; a rat-trap pedal. *a.* Applied to a cycle-pedal consisting of two parallel notched or toothed steel plates. **ratter,** *n.* **ratting,** *a.* and *n.* **ratty,** *a.* Infested with or characteristic of rats; (*slang*) annoyed, ill-tempered.

rata (ra' tà) [Maori], *n.* A large New Zealand forest tree of two species belonging to the myrtle family, having beautiful crimson flowers and yielding hard red timber.

ratable [RATEABLE, see RATE (1)].

ratafia (răt à fē' à) [F., etym. doubtful], *n.* A liqueur or cordial flavoured with the kernels of cherry, peach, almond, or other kinds of fruit; a sweet biscuit eaten with this.

ratal [RATE (1)]. **ratany** [RHATANY].

rataplan (răt' à plăn) [F., imit.], *n.* A noise like the rapid beating of a drum. *v.t.* To beat (a drum). *v.i.* To make a rataplan on a drum. **rat-a-tat** [RAT-TAT].

ratch (răch) [etym. doubtful, cp. G. *ratsche*, also F. *rochet*, whence prob. the form *ratchet*], *n.* A ratchet or ratchet-wheel. **ratchet,** *n.* A wheel or bar with inclined angular teeth, between which a pawl drops, permitting motion in one direction only; the pawl or detent that drops between the teeth of a ratchet-wheel. **ratchet-bar,** *n.* A bar with teeth into which a pawl drops to prevent motion in more than one direction. **ratchet-brace, -coupling, -drill, -jack, -lever, -punch, -wrench,** *n.* Various tools or mechanical appliances working on the principle of the ratchet-bar or wheel with a pawl. **ratch-, ratchet-wheel,** *n.* A wheel with toothed edge.

ratchel (răch' ėl) [etym. doubtful], *n.* (*prov.*) Fragments of stone lying above bed-rock; hard pan.

rate (1) (rāt) [O.F. from med. L. *rata*, fem. of L. *ratus*, p.p. of *rērī*, to think, to judge], *n.* The proportional measure of something in relation to some other thing, ratio, comparative amount, degree, etc.; a standard by which any quantity or value is fixed; valuation, price, value, relative, speed, etc.; a sum levied upon property for local purposes, distinguished from taxes which are for national purposes (*Am.* local tax); *rank or class, esp. of a ship of war. *v.t.* To estimate the value, relative worth, rank, etc., of; to fix the rank of (a seaman, etc.); to assess for local rates; to subject to payment of local rates; (*colloq.*) to consider, to regard as. *v.i.* To be rated or ranked (as). **at any rate:** In any case; even so. **at that rate:** If that is so. **to rate up:** (*Insurance*) To subject to a higher rate or premium in order to cover increased risks. **rate-book,** *n.* A book of rates or prices; a record of local valuations for assessment of rates. **rate-payer,** *n.* One who is liable to pay municipal rates. **ratal,** *n.* The amount on which local rates are assessed. **rateable** (rā' tàbl), *a.* Liable to be rated, subject to assessment for municipal rates; *capable of being rated or valued; proportional, estimated proportionally. **rateability** (-bil' i ti), *n.* **rateably** (rā' tà bli), *adv.* **rater,** *n.* One who rates or assesses. **-rater,** *n.* (*in comb.*) A ship or boat, esp. a yacht, of a specified rate.

rate (2) (rāt) [etym. doubtful], *v.t.* To chide angrily, to scold. *v.i.* To chide, to storm (at).

ratel (rā' tėl) [S. Afr. Dut., etym. doubtful], *n.* A nocturnal carnivore of the genus *Mellivora*, allied to the badger, with two species, *M. Indicus*, from India, and *M. Capensis*, the honey-badger of W. and S. Africa.

ratepayer, rater, etc. [RATE (1)].

rath (1) (rath) [Ir.], *n.* A prehistoric Irish hill-fort or eathwork.

rath (2) (rath), ***rathe** (1) (rā*th*) [A.-S. *hrathe*, adv. from *hræd*, a., quick], *adv.* Early, soon, quickly. *a.* Coming, appearing, ripening, etc., early or before the usual time; quick, speedy; pertaining to early morning. **rath-, rathe-ripe,** *a.* Ripening early. *n.* An early kind of apple, pea, etc.

Rathaus (răt' hous) [G. *Răt*, counsellor, cp. A.-S. *ræd*, counsel, *haus*, HOUSE], *n.* A town-hall in Germany.

rathe (1) [RATH (2)]. **rathe** (2) [RAVE (2)].

rather (ra' *th*ėr) [compar. of RATHE (1)], *adv.* Sooner, more readily or willingly, preferably, for choice; with more reason, more properly, rightly, or truly, more accurately; in a greater degree, to a greater extent; to a certain extent; slightly, somewhat; (*colloq.*) very much, assuredly; yes, certainly. **the rather:** By so much the more. **ratherish,** *adv.* (*Am.*). **ratherly,** *adv.* (*Sc.*).

ratify (răt′ i fī) [F. *ratifier*, med. L. *ratificāre* (*ratus*, RATE (1), *-ficāre*, *facere*, to make)], *v.t.* To confirm, to establish or make valid (by formal consent or approval). **ratification** (-kā′ shŭn), *n.* **ratifier,** *n.*

rating (1) (rā′ ting), *n.* The act of assessing, judging, renting, etc.; the amount fixed as a local rate; (*Naut.*) the class or grade of a seaman as stated in the ship's books; (*collect.*) (*pl.*) persons of a particular rating; a ship's crew.

rating (2) (rā′ ting), *n.* A scolding, a harsh reprimand.

rating (3) (rā′ ting), *n.* A limit on the conditions under which a device, equipment, apparatus, etc., will operate satisfactorily.

ratio (rā′ shi ō) [L., as RATE (1)], *n.* The relation of one quantity or magnitude to another of the same kind, measured by the number of times one is contained by the other, either integrally or fractionally; (*Motor.*) the relation existing between speeds of driving and driven gears, pulleys, etc. **turns ratio:** (*Elec.*) The ratio of the number of turns of wire in the primary winding of a transformer to the number in the secondary.

ratiocinate (răsh i os′ i nāt) [L. *ratiōcinātus*, p.p. of *ratiōcinārī*, as prec.], *v.i.* To reason or argue; to deduce consequences from premises or by means of syllogisms. **ratiocination** (-nā′ shŭn), *n.* **ratiocinative** (-os′ i nā tiv), *a.*

ration (răsh′ ŭn) [F., from L. RATIO], *n.* A fixed allowance of food served out for a given time; a portion of provisions, etc., allowed to one individual; (*pl.*) provisions, esp. food. *v.t.* To supply with rations; to put on fixed rations. **ration book,** *n.* Book issued periodically containing coupons, etc., authorising the holder to draw rations.

rational (1) (răsh′ ȯ nȧl) [L. *ratiōnālis*, as prec.], *a.* Having the faculty of reasoning, endowed with mental faculties; agreeable to reasoning, reasonable, sensible, not foolish, not extravagant; based on or conforming to what can be tested by reason; (*Math.*) of a number which can be expressed as the ratio of two integers; quantities. **rational dress:** A dress regarded as more sensible than the conventional one for women. ***rationable,** *a.* **rationally,** *adv.*

rationale (răsh ȯ nā′ li), *n.* A statement or exposition of reasons or principles; the logical basis or fundamental reason (of anything).

rationalism (răsh′ ȯn ȧ lizm), *n.* The determination of all questions of belief, esp. in religious matters, by the reason, rejecting supernatural revelation; (*Phil.*) the doctrine that reason supplies certain principles for the interpretation of phenomena that cannot be derived from experience alone. **rationalist,** *n.* **rationalistic** (-lis′ tik), *a.* **rationalistically.** *adv.* **rationality** (-năl′ i ti), ***rationalness** (răsh′ ȯ nȧl nės), *n.* The quality of being rational; the power of reasoning; reasonableness.

rationalize (răsh′ ȯn ȧ līz), *v.t.* To convert to rationalism; to interpret as a rationalist; to render rational or reasonable; (*Math.*) to clear (an equation, etc.) of radical signs. *v.i.* To think or act as a rationalist. **rationalization** (-zā′ shŭn), *n.* The act of rationalizing; (*Psych.*) the attempt to supply a conscious reason for an unconscious motivation in the explanation of behaviour. **rationalization of industry:** The systematic organization of industries, co-operation between employers and employees, and the extension of scientific methods to all phases of production.

rational (2) (răsh′ ȯ nȧl) [L. *ratiōnāle*, neut of *ratiōnālis*, as prec., translating Heb. *hōshen*, after Gr. *logeion*, oracle], *n.* A pectoral formerly worn by bishops in celebrating Mass; *the breastplate of the Jewish high-priest.

ratite (răt′ īt) [L. *ratis*, raft, -ITE], *n.* (*Ornith.*) Of or belonging to the genus *Ratitæ* or birds with a keelless sternum and abortive wings, comprising the ostrich, emu, cassowary, kiwi, moa, etc. **ratitous,** ***ratitate,** *a.*

ratline, ratling (răt′ lin, -ling) [etym. doubtful, perh. rel. to O.F. *raalingue*, small cords strengthening a sail, etc.], *n.* (*Naut.*) One of the small ropes extended across the shrouds on each side of a mast, forming steps or rungs.

ratoon (rȧ toon′) [Sp. *retoño*, shoot, sprout], *n.* A sprout from the root of a sugar-cane that has been cut down.

ratsbane [RAT (1)].

rattan (1) (rȧ tăn′) [Malay *rōtan*, from *rāut*, to pare], *n.* The long, thin, pliable stem of various species of E. Indian climbing palms of the genus *Calamus*; a switch or walking-stick of this material; (*collect.*) such stems used as material for building, etc.

rattan (2) (rȧ tăn′) [imit.], *n.* The beat of a drum, a rataplan.

rat-tat (răt tăt′) [imit.], *n.* A rapid knocking sound as of a knocker on a door.

ratteen (rȧ tēn′) [F. *ratine*, etym. doubtful], *n.* A thick quilted or twilled woollen stuff.

ratten (răt′ ėn) [etym. doubtful, perh. var. of obs. *ratton*, O.F. *raton*, RAT (1)], *v.t.* To annoy or molest by destroying, injuring, or taking away the tools or machinery of (a workman or employer) in a trade-union dispute, etc. *v.i.* To practise this method of persecution. **rattener,** *n.*

ratter [RAT (1)].

***rattinet** (răt i net′) [RATTEEN, -ET], *n.* A woollen stuff thinner than ratteen.

rattle (răt′ ėl) [M.E. *ratelen* (cp. Dut. *ratelen*, G. *rasseln*)], *v.i.* To make a rapid succession of sharp noises, as of things clattered together or shaken in a hollow vessel; to talk rapidly, noisily, or foolishly; to move, go, or act with a rattling noise; to run, ride, or drive rapidly. *v.t.* To cause to make a rattling noise, to make (a window, door, etc.) rattle; to utter, recite, play, etc. (off, away, etc.) rapidly; to stir (up); to cause to move quickly with noise, to drive fast; to scold. *n.* A rapid succession of sharp noises; an instrument, esp. a child's toy, with which such sounds are made; a rattling noise in the throat; rapid, noisy, or empty talk, chatter; an incessant chatterer; noise, bustle, racket, boisterous gaiety; the horny articulated rings in the tail of the rattlesnake, which make a rattling noise; a plant (**yellow rattle** and **red rattle**) having seeds that rattle in their cases. **rattle-bag, -box,** *n.* A bag or box with loose things inside for rattling. **rattle-brained, -headed, -pated,** *a.* Giddy, wild, empty-headed. **rattlesnake,** *n.* A snake of the American genus *Crotalus*, the tail of which is furnished with a rattle. **rattletrap,** *n.* A rickety object, esp. a vehicle; (*pl.*) valueless articles, rubbishy curios. *a.* Rickety, rubbishy. **rattlewort,** *n.* A plant of the genus *Crotalaria.* **rattler,** *n.* One who or that which rattles; (*slang*) a first-rate specimen. **rattling,** *a.* Making a rapid succession of sharp noises; (*colloq.*) brisk, vigorous; (*slang*) first-rate, excellent.

raucous (raw′ kŭs) [L. *raucus*], *a.* Hoarse, rough or harsh in sound. **raucity** (-si ti), *n.* **raucously,** *adv.*

***raught** [*past & p.p.* of REACH].

raupo (rou′ pō) [Maori], *n.* The giant bulrush of N. Zealand.

ravage (răv′ aj) [F., from *ravir*, to RAVISH], *n.* Devastation, ruin, havoc, waste; (*pl.*) devastating effects. *v.t.* To devastate; to spoil, to pillage. *v.i.* To make havoc. **ravager,** *n.*

rave (1) (rāv) [prob. from O.F. *raver*, var. of *rêver*, to dream (cp. REVERIE)], *v.i.* To wander in mind, to be delirious, to talk wildly, incoherently, or irrationally; to speak in a furious way (against, at, etc.); to act, move, or dash furiously, to rage; to be excited, to go into raptures (about, etc.). *v.t.* To utter in a wild, incoherent, or furious manner. *n.* The act of raving; a raving sound. **raver,** *n.* **ravingly,** *adv.*

rave (2) (rāv), ***rathe** (2) (rāth) [etym. doubtful], *n.* A cart-rail, esp. (*pl.*) a framework added to enable a larger load to be carried; (*Am.*) a vertical side-piece in a wagon, sleigh, etc.

ravel (răv′ ėl) [prob. from M. Dut. *ravelen*], *v.t.* (*past & p.p.* **ravelled**) To entangle, to confuse, to complicate, to involve; to untwist, to disentangle, to separate the component threads of; to fray. *v.i.* To become tangled; to become untwisted, unravelled, or unwoven; to fray (out); *to busy oneself with intricacies. **ravelling**, *n.* The act of entangling, confusing, etc.; the act of unravelling; anything, as a thread, separated in the process of unravelling. ***ravelly**, *a.* **ravelment**, *n.*

ravelin (răv′ ė lin) [F., from It. *rivellino*, earlier *ravellino*], *n.* (*Fort.*) A detached work with a parapet and ditch forming a salient angle in front of the curtain of a larger work.

raven (1) (rā′ vėn) [A.-S. *hræfn* (cp. Dut. *raaf*, G. *rabe*, Icel. *hrafn*, Dan. *ravn*)], *n.* A large, black, omnivorous British bird, *Corvus corax*, of the crow family. *a.* Resembling a raven in colour, glossy black.

raven (2) (răv′ ėn) [O.F. *raviner*, from L. *rapīna*, RAPINE], *v.t.* To devour with voracity; *to ravage, to plunder. *v.i.* To plunder; to go about ravaging; to prowl after prey; to be ravenous. **n.* Ravin. ***ravener**, *n.* **ravening**, *a.* and *n.*

ravenous (răv′ ė nůs) [O.F. *ravineux*, as prec.], *a.* Voracious, hungry, famished; furiously rapacious, eager for gratification. **ravenously**, *adv.* **ravenousness**, *n.*

***ravin** (răv′ in) [O.F. *ravine*, L. *rapīna*, RAPINE], *n.* Plundering, rapine, spoliation, ravaging; prey. **beast of ravin:** A beast of prey. ***ravined** (1), *a.* Ravenous.

ravine (rȧ vēn′) [F., orig. a torrent, as prec.], *n.* A long, deep hollow caused by a torrent, a gorge, a narrow gully or cleft. **ravined** (2), *a.*

ravingly [RAVE (1)].

ravish (răv′ ish) [F. *raviss-*, pres.p. stem of *ravir*, L. *rapere*, to seize, to snatch], *v.t.* To carry away, to enrapture, to transport (with pleasure, etc.); to violate, to rape; *to snatch away or carry off by force. **ravisher**, *n.* One who ravishes, rapes, or carries off by force. **ravishing**, *a.* Enchanting, charming, entrancing, transporting, filling one with rapture. **ravishingly**, *adv.* **ravishment**, *n.*

raw (raw) [A.-S. *hrēaw* (cp. Dut. *raauw*, G. *roh*, Icel. *hrār*, also L. *crūdus*, *cruor*, blood, Gr. *kreas*, raw flesh)], *a.* Uncooked; in the natural state; not wrought, not manufactured, requiring further industrial treatment; untrained, unskilled, inexperienced, undisciplined, immature, fresh; crude, untempered; having the skin off, having the flesh exposed, galled, inflamed, sore; cold and damp, bleak (of weather). *n.* A raw place on the body, a sore, a gall. **to touch on the raw:** To wound in a sensitive spot. **raw-boned**, *a.* Having bones scarcely covered with flesh, gaunt. **raw deal:** (*colloq.*) Unfair treatment. **raw-head**, *n.* A spectre or goblin. **raw-head and bloody-bones:** A death's-head and cross-bones; (*adj.*) applied to blood-and-thunder fiction, etc. **rawhide**, *n.* Untanned leather; a whip made of this. *v.t.* To whip with this. **raw material:** The material of any manufacturing process. **rawish**, *a.* ***rawly**, *adv.* **rawness**, *n.*

rax (răks) [A.-S. *raxan*, etym. doubtful], *v.i.* (*Sc. and North.*) To stretch or reach (out or up). *v.t.* To stretch or strain (oneself); to stretch (the hand) out.

ray (1) (rā) [O.F. *rai*, *ray*, nom. *rais*, L. RADIUS], *n.* A line or beam of light proceeding from a radiant point; (*Phys.*) a straight line along which radiant energy, esp. light or heat, is propagated; (*fig.*) a gleam, a vestige, or slight manifestation (of hope, enlightenment, etc.); one of a series of radiating lines or parts; (*Bot.*) the outer whorl of florets in a composite flower; (*Zool.*) one of the bony rods supporting the fin of a fish, one of the radial parts of a starfish or other radials. *v.t.* To shoot out (rays), to radiate. *v.i.* To issue or shine forth in rays. **Becquerel rays** [BECQUEREL]. **Röntgen rays** [RÖNTGEN]. **rayed**, *a.* **rayless**, *a.*

ray (2) (rā) [M.E. and O.F. *raye* (F. *raie*) L. *raia*], *n.* A large cartilaginous fish of various species of the genus *Raiæ*, allied to the sharks, with a flat disk-like body and a long, slender tail.

ray (3) (rā), *n.* (*Mus.*) The second note in the tonic sol-fa notation.

Rayah (rī′ ā) [Arab. *ra'ūjah*, flock, from *ra'ā*, to feed], *n.* A non-Mohammedan subject in Turkey.

rayed, rayless [RAY (1)]. ***rayle** [RAIL (2)].

rayon (rā′ ȯn) [F., from *rai*, RAY (1)], *n.* A radius, an area measured from a central point; artificial silk made from cellulose; *a ray, a beam. ***rayonnance**, *n.* Radiance. **rayonné** (rā yon ā), *a.* (*Her.*) Having radiating points or alternate projections and depressions.

raze (1) (rāz) [F. *raser*, pop. L. *rāsāre*, freq. of L. *rādere* (p.p. *rāsus*), to scrape], *v.t.* *To graze or shave; (*usu. fig.*) to wound slightly; to scratch (out); to erase, to obliterate; to demolish, to level with the ground, to destroy.

***raze** (2) [RACE (3), RAISE].

razee (rȧ zē′) [F. *rasée*, p.p. of prec.], *n.* A vessel cut down to a less number of decks. *v.t.* To reduce (a ship) in height thus.

razoo (rȧ zoo′) [Austral. slang], *n.* A farthing. **not a brass razoo:** Not a farthing.

razor (rā′ zȯr) [O.F. *rasor* (F. *rasoir*), late L. *rāsōrium*, from *rādere*, to RAZE], *n.* A cutting instrument for shaving off the hair of the beard or head. *v.t.* To shave with a razor; to shave; to cut (down) close. **razor-back**, *n.* A sharp back like a razor; (*Austral.*) a skinny bullock. *a.* Having a sharp back or ridge like a razor. **razor-backed**, *a.* **razor-bill**, *n.* A bird with a bill like a razor, esp. the razor-billed auk, *Alca torda*. **razor-billed**, *a.* **razor-edge**, *n.* The edge of a razor; a keen edge; (*fig.*) a sharp crest or ridge, as of a mountain; a critical situation, a crisis; a sharp line of demarcation, esp. between parties or opinions. **razor-fish**, *n.* A fish of the *Labridæ*, *Xyrichthis novacula* or *X. lineatus*. **razor-shell**, *n.* A bivalve mollusc with a shell like a razor. **razor-strop**, A leather pad on which a razor is sharpened. ***razorable**, *a.* Fit to be shaved.

***razure** [RASURE].

razzia (răz′ i ȧ) [F., from Algerian *ghāzīah*, var. of Arab. *ghazwah*, from *ghazw*, making *war*], *n.* A foray or incursion for the purpose of capturing slaves, etc., as practised by African Mohammedans.

razzle-dazzle (răz′ ėl dăz′ ėl) [redupl. of DAZZLE], *n.* (*colloq.*) Bewilderment, excitement, stir, bustle; intoxication. *v.t.* To dazzle, to daze; to bamboozle; to intoxicate. **on the razzle-dazzle:** On the spree.

re (1) (rā) [It., see GAMUT], *n.* (*Mus.*) The second note of a major scale; the second note of the scale of C major, D.

re (2) (rē) [L., abl. of *rēs*, thing, matter, affair], *prep.* (*Legal*) In the matter of; (*colloq.*) as regards, about.

re- [L., back, again], *pref.* Back, backward, back again; after, behind; un-; in return, mutually; again, again and again, afresh, anew, repeatedly; against, in opposition; off, away, down. **reabsorb** (rē ȧb sôrb′), *v.t.* To absorb anew or again. **reabsorption**, *n.* **reaccommodate** (rē ȧ kom′ ȯ dāt), *v.t.* To accommodate or adjust afresh or again. **reaccuse** (rē ȧ kūz′), *v.t.* To accuse again.

reach (1) (rēch) [A.-S. *rǣcan* (cp. Dut. *reiken*, G. *reichen*], *v.t.* To stretch out; to extend; to extend towards so as to touch, to extend as far as, to attain to, to arrive at, to hit, to affect; to hand, to deliver, to pass. *v.i.* To reach out, to extend; to reach or stretch out the hand; to make a reaching effort, to put forth one's powers, to be extended so as to touch, to have extent in time, space, etc.; to attain (to). *n.* The act or power of reaching;

extent, range, compass, power, attainment; an unbroken stretch of water, as between two bends. **reach-me-down,** *a.* Ready-made or second-hand (of clothes). *n.pl.* Ready-made or second-hand clothes. **reachable,** *a.* **reacher,** *n.*

***reach** (2) [RETCH].

reacquire (rē ȧ kwīr′), *v.t.* To acquire anew.

react (rė ăkt′), *v.i.* To act in response (to a stimulus, etc.); to have a reciprocal effect, to act upon the agent; to act or tend in an opposite manner, direction, etc.; (*Phys.*) to exert an equal and opposite force to that exerted by another body; (*Chem.*) to exert chemical action (*upon*). *v.t.* (rē ăkt′) To act again. **reaction,** *n.* Reciprocal action; the response of an organ, etc., to stimulation; (*Chem.*) the chemical action of one substance upon another; (*Phys.*) the equal and opposite force exerted upon the agent by a body acted upon; contrary action or condition following the first effects of an action; action in an opposite direction, esp. in politics after a reform movement, revolution, etc.; (*Radio.*) phenomenon obtained from a three-electrode valve whereby a small voltage on the grid is strengthened by the amplified currents flowing in the anode circuit. **reactionary,** *a.* Involving or tending towards reaction, esp. in politics, retrograde, conservative. *n.* A reactionary person. **reactionist,** *n.* **reactivate,** *v.t.* To restore to a state of activity. **reactive,** *a.* **reactively,** *adv.* **reactivity** (-tiv′ i ti), ***reactiveness,** *n.* **reactor** [NUCLEAR REACTOR].

read (rēd) [A.-S. *rǣdan* (cp. Dut. *raden*, G. *rathen*, Icel. *ratha*, Goth. *rēdan*, rel. to Sansk. *rāth*, to succeed)], *v.t.* (*past & p.p.* **read,** red) To perceive and understand the meaning of (printed, written, or other characters, signs, symbols, significant features, etc.), to peruse; to reproduce mentally or vocally or instrumentally (words, notes, etc., conveyed by symbols, etc.); to discover by observation; to interpret, to explain; to assume as implied in a statement, etc.; to see through; to learn or ascertain by reading; to study by reading; to bring into a specified condition by reading; to study for an examination; to indicate or register (of a meteorological instrument, etc.). *v.i.* To follow or interpret the meaning of a book, etc.; to pronounce (written or printed matter) aloud; to render written music vocally or instrumentally (well, easily, etc.); to acquire information (about); to study by reading; to mean or be capable of interpretation (in a certain way, etc.); to sound or affect (well, ill, etc.) when perused or uttered. *n.* An act of reading, a perusal. **to read between the lines** [LINE (1)]. **to read into:** To extract a meaning not explicit. **to read oneself in:** To enter upon an incumbency by the public reading of the Thirty-nine Articles. **to read out:** To read aloud; *to read through or to the end. **to read out of:** To expel from by the formal reading of a sentence or proclamation. **readable,** *a.* Worth reading, interesting, legible. **readableness, readability** (-bil′ i ti), *n.* **readably,** *adv.* **reader,** *n.* One who reads; one who reads much; a person employed by a publisher to read and report upon MSS., etc., offered for publication; a corrector of the press; a person appointed to read aloud, esp. parts of the Church service; a professional elocutionist; a lecturer in some Universities, Inns of Court, etc.; a text-book, a book of selections for translation, or a reading-book for schools. **readership,** *n.* **reading,** *a.* Addicted to reading, studious. *n.* The act, practice, or art of reading; the study or knowledge of books, literary research, scholarship, a public recital or entertainment at which selections, etc., are read to the audience; the form of a passage given by a text, editor, etc.; the way in which a passage reads, an interpretation, a rendering; an observation made by examining an instrument; the recital of the whole or part of a Bill as a formal introduction or measure of approval in a legislative assembly. **first reading:** The formal introduction of a Bill. **second reading:** A general approval of the principles of a Bill. **third reading:** The final acceptance of a Bill together with the amendments passed in committee. **reading-book,** *n.* A book of selections to be used as exercises in reading. **reading-desk,** *n.* A stand for books, etc., for the use of a reader, esp. in church, a lectern. **reading-glass,** *n.* A hand magnifying-glass. **reading-room,** *n.* A room in a library, club, etc., furnished with books, papers, etc., for the use of readers.

readdress (rē ȧ dres′) [RE-, ADDRESS], *v.t.* To put a new (esp. a corrected) address upon.

reader, reading [READ].

readily, readiness [READY].

readjourn (rē ȧd jĕrn), *n.* To adjourn again. **readjust** (rē ȧd jŭst′), *v.t.* To arrange or adjust afresh. **readjustment,** *n.* **readmit** (rē ȧd mit′), *v.t.* To admit again. **readmission** (-mish′ ŭn), **readmittance,** *n.* **readopt** (rē ȧ dopt), *v.t.* To adopt again. **readorn** (rē ȧ dôrn′), *v.t.* To adorn afresh.

ready (red′ i) [M.E. *redi*, *rædi*, prob. from A.-S. *gerǣde* (cp. O.H.G. *bireiti*, G. *bereit*, Dut. *bereid*), -Y, from conf. with A.-S. *-ig*], *a.* In a state of preparedness, fit for use or action; willing, apt, disposed, about (to); quick, prompt; able, expert, facile; at hand, within reach, handy, quickly available; (*Mil.*) held in the position preparatory to presenting and aiming (of a fire-arm). *adv.* In a state of preparedness, beforehand (*usu. in comb. with p.p.*). *n.* (*Mil.*) The position in which a fire-arm is held before presenting and aiming; (*slang*) ready money. *v.t.* *To make ready, to prepare; (*slang*) to pull (a horse) with a view to a handicap for another race. **to make ready:** To prepare; (*Print.*) to prepare a forme before printing. **to ready up:** (*Austral. colloq.*) To swindle. **ready-made,** *a.* Made beforehand, not made to order (esp. of clothing kept in standard sizes); selling ready-made articles (of a shop, etc.). **ready money:** Actual cash, ready to be paid down. **ready-money,** *a.* Conducted on the principle of payment on delivery. **ready-reckoner,** *n.* A book with tables of interest, etc., for facilitating business calculations. **ready-witted,** *a.* Quick of apprehension. **readily,** *adv.* Without trouble or difficulty, easily; willingly, without reluctance. **readiness,** *n.* The state of being ready, preparedness; willingness, prompt compliance; facility, ease, aptitude, quickness in acting.

reaffirm (rē ȧ fĕrm′), *v.t.* To affirm again. **reaffirmation** (-mā′ shŭn), *n.* **reafforest** (rē ȧ for′ ėst), *v.t.* To convert again into forest. **reafforestation** (-tā′ shŭn), *n.* **reagent** (rė ā′ jėnt), *n.* (*Chem.*) A substance used to detect the presence of other substances by means of their reaction; a force, etc., that reacts. **reagency,** *n.* Reciprocal action. **reaggravation** (rē ăg rȧ vā′ shŭn), *n.* (*R.-C. Ch.*) The last admonition, to be followed by excommunication.

***reaks** (rēks) [etym. doubtful, cp. FREAK], *n.pl.* Pranks, tricks, freaks.

real (1) (rē′ ȧl) [late L. *reālis*, from *rēs*, thing], *a.* Actually existing; not fictitious, affected, imaginary, apparent, theoretical, or nominal; true, genuine; not counterfeit, not spurious; having substantial existence, objective; (*Law*) consisting of fixed or permanent things, as lands or houses, opp. to personal; (*Phil.*) having an absolute and independent existence, opp. to nominal or phenomenal. **the real:** That which is actual, esp. as opposed to the ideal; the genuine thing. **real estate:** Landed property. **real presence:** The actual presence of the body and blood of Christ in the Eucharist. **really** (rē′ ȧl i), *adv.* In fact, in reality; (*colloq.*) positively, I assure you; is that so?

real (2) (rē′-, rā′ ȧl [Sp., from L. *rēgālis*, REGAL], *n.* (*pl.* ***reales,*** rā a′ lēz) A Spanish silver coin or money of account worth about 2½d. [see also REIS (1)].

realgar (rė ăl′ gar) [med. L., or F. *réalgar*, Arab. *rehj al-ghār*, powder of the mine or cave], *n.* Native disulphide of arsenic, also called red arsenic or red orpiment, used as a pigment and in the manufacture of fireworks.

realism (rē′ ȧ lizm) [REAL (1), -ISM], *n.* (*Phil.*) The scholastic doctrine that every universal or general idea has objective existence, opp. to nominalism and conceptualism; the doctrine that the objects of perception have real existence, opp. to idealism; the doctrine that in perception there is an immediate cognition of the external object; (*Art*) the practice of representing objects, persons, scenes, etc., as they are or as they appear to the painter, novelist, etc., opp. to idealism and romanticism. **realist,** *n.* A believer in realism; a practical person. **realistic** (-lis′ tik), *a.* Pertaining to realism; matter-of-fact, common-sense. **realistically,** *adv.*

reality (rė ăl′ i ti) [F. *réalité*, med. L. *realitātem*, nom. *-tas*], *n.* The quality of being real, actuality, actual existence, being, that which underlies appearances; truth, fact; that which is real and not counterfeit, imaginary, suppositious, etc.; the real nature (of).

realize (rē′ ȧ līz), *v.t.* To perceive as a reality; to apprehend clearly and vividly; to bring into actual existence, to give reality to; to present as real, to impress on the mind as real, to make realistic; to convert into money; to sell; to bring in, as a price. **realizable,** *a.* **realization** (-zā′ shŭn), *n.*

reallege (rē ȧ lej′), *v.t.* To allege again.

really, etc. [REAL (1)].

realm (relm) [O.F. *realme, reaume* (F. *royaume*), prob. through a pop. L. *rēgālimen*, from L. *rēgālis*, REGAL], *n.* A kingdom; (*fig.*) domain, region, sphere.

realtor (rē′ ăl tĕr), *n.* (*Am.*) Estate agent; dealer in land for development. **realty** (rē′ ăl ti), *n.* (*Law*) Real property; *reality.

ream (1) (rēm) [M.E. *rēm, rim*, through O.F. *rayme* or Dut. *riem*, from Arab. *rizmah*, bundle], *n.* 480 sheets or twenty quires of paper (often 500 or more sheets to allow for waste). **printer's ream:** 516 sheets.

ream (2) (rēm) [A.-S. *ryman*, cogn. with *rūm*, ROOM], *v.t.* To enlarge (a hole in metal); to turn the edge of (a cartridge-case) over; (*Naut.*) to open (a seam) for caulking. **reamer,** *n.* An instrument or tool used in reaming.

ream (3) (rēm) [A.-S. *rēam*, cp. Dut. *room*, G. *rahm*, Icel. *rjōmi*], *n.* (*chiefly Sc.*) Cream; froth or scum. **reamy,** *a.*

reanimate (rē ăn′ i māt), *v.t.* To restore to life; to revive, to encourage, to give new spirit to. **reanimation** (-mā′ shŭn), *n.* **reannex** (rē ȧ neks′), *v.t.* To annex anew; to reunite. **reannexation** (-nek sā′ shŭn), *n.* ***reanswer** (rė an′ sėr), *v.t.* To be equivalent to.

reap (rēp) [A.-S. *rīpan*], *v.t.* To cut with a scythe, sickle, or reaping-machine; to gather in (a harvest, etc.); to cut the harvest off (ground, etc.); (*fig.*) to obtain as return for labour, deeds, etc. *v.i.* To perform the act of reaping; to receive the consequences of labour, deeds, etc. **reaper,** *n.* One who reaps; a reaping-machine. **reaping-hook,** *n.* A sickle. **reaping-machine,** *n.*

reapparel (rē ȧ păr′ ėl), *v.t.* To clothe again. **reappear** (rē ȧ pēr′), *v.i.* To appear again. **reappearance,** *n.* **reapply** (rē ȧ plī′), *v.t.* To apply again. **reapplier,** *n.* **reapplication** (-kā′ shŭn), *n.* **reappoint** (rē ȧ point′), *v.t.* To appoint again. **reappointment,** *n.* **reapproach** (rē ȧ prōch′), *v.t.* To approach again.

rear (1) (rēr) [A.-S. *rǣran*, cogn. with RAISE, which has largely superseded it], *v.t.* To raise, to set up, to elevate to an upright position; to build, to erect, to uplift, to place or hold on high; to bring up, to breed, to educate; to raise, to cultivate, to grow; to raise from a prostrate position; *to rouse, to reanimate. *v.i.* To stand on the hind legs (of a horse). **rearer,** *n.*

rear (2) (rēr) [shortened from ARREAR], *n.* The back or hindmost part, esp. the hindmost division of a military or naval force; the back (of); a place or position at the back; (*colloq.*) a w.c., a latrine. *a.* Pertaining to the rear. **to bring up the rear:** To come last. **rear-admiral,** *n.* A naval officer next below the rank of vice-admiral. **rear-arch** (rēr′ arch) [REAR (2), ARCH (1)], *n.* (*Arch.*) An inner arch of a doorway or window-opening differing in size or form from the outer arch. **rear-guard,** *n.* A body of troops protecting the rear of an army. **rear-rank, -line,** *n.* The rank or line of a body of troops in the rear. **rearmost,** *a.* Coming or situated last of all. **rearward,** *n.* *The rear-guard; (*fig.*) those coming last; the rear. *a.* Situated in or towards the rear. *adv.* Rearwards. **rearwards,** *adv.* Towards the rear.

reargue (rė ar′ gū), *v.t.* To argue or debate afresh. **reargument,** *n.* **rearm** (rė arm′), *v.t.* To arm afresh, esp. with more modern weapons.

***rearmouse** (rēr′ mous) [A.-S. *hrēremūs* (*hrēre*, etym. doubtful, MOUSE)], *n.* A bat.

rearrange (rē ȧ rānj′), *v.t.* To arrange in a new order. **rearrangement,** *n.* **reascend** (rē ȧ send′), *v.t.* and *i.* To ascend again. **reascension** (-sen′ shŭn), *n.*

reason (rē′ zȯn) [O.F. *raisun* (F. *raison*), L. *ratiōnem*, nom. *-tio*, see RATIO], *n.* That which is adduced to support or justify, or serves as a ground or motive for an act, opinion, etc.; that which accounts for anything, a final cause; the premise of an argument, esp. the minor premise when stated after the conclusion; the intellectual faculties, esp. the group of faculties distinguishing man from brutes; the intuitive faculty which furnishes a priori principles, categories, etc.; the power of consecutive thinking, the logical faculty; good sense, judgment, sanity; sensible conduct; moderation; the exercise of the rational powers. *v.i.* To use the faculty of reason; to argue, esp. to employ argument (with) as a means of persuasion; to reach conclusions by way of inferences from premises. *v.t.* To debate, discuss, or examine by means of the reason or reasons and inferences; to assume, conclude, or prove by way of argument; to persuade or dissuade by argument; to set forth in orderly argumentative form. **by reason of:** Because, on account of, in consequence of. **in reason:** Within moderation; according to good sense. **to listen to reason:** To allow oneself to be persuaded. **to stand to reason:** To follow logically. **reasonable,** *a.* Endowed with reason; rational, reasoning, governed by reason; conformable to reason, sensible, proper; not extravagant, moderate, esp. in price, fair, not extortionate. **reasonableness,** *n.* **reasonably,** *adv.* **reasoner,** *n.* **reasoning,** *n.* The act of drawing conclusions from premises or using the reason; argumentation; a statement of the reasons justifying a course, opinion, conclusion, etc. **reasonless,** *a.*

reassemble (rē ȧ sem′ bėl), *v.t.* and *i.* To assemble or collect together again. **reassert** (rē ȧ sĕrt′), *v.t.* To assert anew. **reassertion,** *n.* **reassess** (rē ȧ ses′), *v.t.* To make a new assessment of. **reassessment,** *n.* **reassign** (rē ȧ sīn′), *v.t.* To assign again; to transfer back or to another what has been already assigned. **reassignment,** *n.* **reassume** (rē ȧ sūm′), *v.t.* To take up again; to revoke; to take upon oneself again; to resume. **reassumption** (-sŭmp′ shŭn), *n.* **reassure** (rē ȧ shoor′), *v.t.* To assure or confirm again; to restore to confidence, to give fresh courage to; to reinsure. **reassurance,** *n.* **reassurer,** *n.* **reassuring,** *a.* **reassuringly,** *adv.*

reata (rė a′ tȧ) [Sp., from *reatar*, to tie again (RE-, L. *aptāre*, to apply, see APT)], *n.* A lariat.

reattach (rē ȧ tăch′), *v.t.* To attach afresh. **reattachment,** *n.* **reattain** (rē ȧ tān′), *v.t.* To attain again. **reattainment,** *n.* **reattempt** (rē ȧ tempt′), *v.t.* To attempt afresh; *n.* A new attempt.

Réaumur (rā′ ō mur), *a.* Applied to the thermometer invented by the French physicist R. A. F. de Réaumur (1683–1757), or to his thermometric scale, the zero of which corresponds to freezing-point and 80° to boiling-point.

***reave** (rēv) [A.-S. *rēafian* (cp. Dut. *rooven*, G. *rauben*, Icel. *raufa*, also L. *-rup-*, *rumpere*, to break)], *v.t.* (*past & p.p.* **reaved,** *poet.* **reft)** To take (away or from) by force; to deprive (of) by force, to bereave. *v.i.* To pillage, to ravage. ***reaver,** *n.*

reavouch (rē à vouch'), *v.t.* To avouch again. **reawake** (rē à wāk'), *v.t.* and *i.* To awake again. **rebaptize** (rē băp tīz'), *v.t.* To baptize again. **rebaptizer,** *n.* **rebaptism** (-băp' tizm), **rebaptization** (-zā' shŭn), *n.* **rebaptist,** *n.* **rebarbarize** (rē bar' bà rīz), *v.t.* To reduce to barbarism again. **rebarbarization** (-zā' shŭn), *n.*

rebarbative (rē barb' à tiv) [F. *barbe*, a beard], *a.* Repellent, grim, forbidding; surly; unco-operative.

rebate (1) (rė bāt') [O.F. *rabattre* (RE-, *abattre*, to ABATE)], *v.t.* To make a deduction from, to abate; to reduce, to diminish; to make blunt, to dull; (*Her.*) to remove a portion of (a charge). (rē' bāt), *n.* A deduction, a drawback, a discount. **rebatement,** *n.*

rebate (2) (rė bāt') [etym. doubtful], *n.* (*prov.*) A kind of hard freestone.

rebate (3) (rė bāt', ră' bit) [RABBET].

rebato [RABAT].

Rebeccaite (rė bek' à īt) [*Rebecca* (the leader and his followers being called 'Rebecca and her daughters,' from a misapplication of Gen. xxiv. 60)], *n.* A member of an anti-turnpike association formed in Wales in 1843–44, who attempted to carry out their objects by violence. **Rebeccaism,** *n.*

rebeck (rē' bek) [O.F. *rebec*, var. of *rebebe*, Arab. *rebāb*], *n.* A mediæval three-stringed musical instrument played with a bow.

rebel (reb' ėl) [F. *rebelle*, L. *rebellem*, nom. *-lis*, rebellious (RE-, *bellum*, war)], *a.* Rebellious; pertaining to rebellion or to rebels. *n.* One who forcibly resists the established government or renounces allegiance thereto; one who resists authority or control. (rė bel'), *v.i.* (*past & p.p.* **rebelled)** To engage in rebellion (against); to revolt (against any authority or control); (*fig.*) to feel or show repugnance (against). **rebel-like,** *a.* ***rebeller,** *n.* **rebellion** (rė bel' yŏn), *n.* Organized resistance by force of arms to the established government; opposition to any authority. **rebellious,** *a.* Engaged in rebellion; defying or opposing lawful authority; disposed to rebel, refractory, insubordinate, difficult to manage or control. **rebelliously,** *adv.* **rebelliousness,** *n.*

rebellow (rē bel' ō), *v.i.* To bellow in return; to echo back loudly. *v.t.* To re-echo loudly. **rebind** (rē bīnd'), *v.t.* (*past & p.p.* **rebound)** (1)). To bind again; to give a new binding to. **rebirth** (rē bĕrth'), *n.* A second birth, esp. an entrance into a new sphere of existence, as in reincarnation. **rebite** (rē bīt'), *v.t.* To bite again, to apply acid, etc., again to an etched plate.

reboant (rē' bō ȧnt) [L. *reboans -ntem*, pres.p. of *reboāre* (*boāre*, to bellow)], *a.* Rebellowing, loudly resounding or re-echoing.

reboil (rē boil'), *v.i.* To boil again. **reborn** (rē bôrn'), *a.* Born again (esp. of spiritual life).

re-bound (1), *past & p.p.* [RE-BIND].

rebound (2) (rė bound') [O.F. *rebondir*], *v.i.* To bound back, to recoil (from a blow, etc.); to react, to recoil (upon); *to re-echo. **v.t.* To cause to rebound, to return (blows, etc.). *n.* The act of rebounding, a recoil; reaction (of feeling, etc.). **rebrace** (rē brās'), *v.t.* To brace again. **rebreathe** (rē brēth'), *v.t.* To breathe again.

rebuff (rė bŭf') [obs. F. *rebuffe*, It. *re-*, *ribuffo* (*buffo*, puff, imit. in orig.)], *n.* A rejection, a check (to an offer or to one who makes advances, etc.); a curt denial, a snub; a defeat, a sudden or unexpected repulse. *v.t.* (*past & p.p.* **rebuffed)** To give a rebuff to, to repel. **rebuild** (rē bild'), *v.t.* To build again, to reconstruct.

rebuke (rė būk') [A.-F. and O.North.F. *rebuker*, O.F. *rebuchier* (RE-, *bucher*, to beat, perh. orig. to lop, from *busche*, F. *bûche*, a log)], *v.t.* To reprove, to reprimand, to chide; to censure, to reprehend (a fault, etc.); *to repress, to repulse. *n.* The act of rebuking; a reproof. **rebukable,** *a.* **rebukeful,** *a.* **rebukefully,** *adv.* **rebukefulness,** *n.* **rebuker,** *n.* **rebukingly,** *adv.*

rebury (rē ber' i), *v.t.* To bury again.

rebus (rē' bŭs) [L., abl. pl. of *rēs*, thing (application obscure)], *n.* A picture or figure representing enigmatically a word, name, or phrase, usu. by objects suggesting words or syllables; (*Her.*) a device representing a proper name or motto in this way.

rebut (rė bŭt') [A.-F. *reboter*, O.F. *rebouter*, *-boter* (RE-, BOTER, to BUTT (4))], *v.t.* (*past & p.p.* **rebutted)** To thrust back, to check, to repel; (*Law*) to contradict or refute by plea, argument, or countervailing proof. **rebuttable,** *a.* **rebutment, rebuttal,** *n.* **rebutter,** *n.* One who rebuts; (*Law*) the answer of a defendant to a plaintiff's surrejoinder.

recalcitrant (rė kăl' si trȧnt) [F. *récalcitrant* or L. *recalcitrans -ntem*, pres.p. of *recalcitrāre* (RE-, *calcitrāre*, to strike with the heel, from *calx calcis*, heel)], *a.* Refractory, obstinately refusing submission. *n.* A recalcitrant person. **recalcitrance, -cy,** *n.* **recalcitrate,** *v.i.* To kick (against or at a proposal, etc.); to refuse compliance, to show resistance, to be refractory. **recalcitration** (trā' shŭn), *n.*

recalesce (rē kȧ les') [L. *recalescere* (RE-, *calescere*, to grow hot, freq. of *calēre*, to be warm)], *v.i.* To grow hot again (esp. of iron or steel which glows more brightly when certain temperatures are reached in the process of cooling). **recalescence,** *n.*

recall (rė kawl'), *v.t.* To call back; to summon to return; to bring back to mind, to recollect; to renew, to revive, to resuscitate; to revoke, to annul, to take back. *n.* A calling back; a summons to return; a signal calling back soldiers, a ship, etc.; the power of recalling, revoking, or annulling. **recallable,** *a.* **recallment,** *n.*

recant (rė kănt') [L. *recantāre* (RE-, *cantāre*, freq. of *canere*, to sing)], *v.t.* To retract, to renounce, to abjure; to disavow. *v.i.* To disavow or abjure opinions or beliefs formerly avowed, esp. with a formal acknowledgment of error. **recantation** (-tā' shŭn), *n.* **recanter,** *n.*

recapitulate (rē kȧ pit' ū lāt), *v.t.* To repeat in brief (as the principal heads of a discourse), to sum up, to summarize. **to re-cap,** *v.i.* To recapitulate, to go over once again. **recapitulation** (-lā' shŭn), *n.* **recapitulative** (-pit' ū lā tiv), **recapitulatory,** *a.*

recaption (rė kăp' shŭn), *n.* (*Law*) Recovery of goods, wife, child, etc., from one unlawfully withholding them; a writ for the recovery of damages by one who has been distrained twice. **recaptor** (rē kăp' tŏr), *n.* **recapture,** *n.* The act of recapturing; that which is recaptured. *v.t.* To capture again, to recover (a prize from the captor). **recarburize** (rē kar' bū riz), *v.t.* To carburize (steel) after decarbonization. **recarburizer,** *n.* **recarburization** (-za' shŭn), *n.* **recarry** (rē kăr' i), *v.t.* To carry back or again. **recarriage,** *n.* **recarrier,** *n.* **recast** (rē kast') [CAST (1)], *v.t.* To cast, found, or mould again; to fashion again, to remodel; to compute or add up again. *n.* That which has been recast; the process or result of recasting. **recaster,** *n.*

recce (rek' i), *n.* (*Mil.*) Reconnaissance.

recede (1) (rė sēd') [L. *recēdere* (RE-, *cēdere*, to go, see CEDE)], *v.i.* To go back or away (from); to be gradually lost to view by distance; to incline, slope, or trend backwards or away; to retreat, to withdraw (from); (*fig.*) to decline, to retrograde.

recede (2) (rē sēd'), *v.t.* To cede again, to restore to a former possessor.

receipt (rė sēt′) [M.E. *receit*, A.-F. *receite*, O.F. *recete*, *reçoite*, L. *recepta*, fem. p.p. of *recipere*, to RECEIVE], *n.* The act or fact of receiving or being received; that which is received, esp. money (*usu. in pl.*); a written acknowledgment of money or goods received; a recipe; *a place for officially receiving money; *the act of admitting, reception (as of guests); *a receptacle; *capacity, power of receiving. *v.t.* To give a receipt for; to write an acknowledgment of receipt on (a bill, etc.).

receive (rė sēv′) [A.-F. *receivre* (O.F. *reçoivre*), L. *recipere* (RE-, *capere*, to take)], *v.t.* To obtain, get, or take as a thing due, offered, sent, paid, or given; to be given, to be furnished or supplied with, to acquire; to accept with approval or consent, to admit, as proper or true; to admit to one's presence, to welcome, to entertain as guest, to encounter, to take or stand the onset of; to be a receptacle for; to understand, to regard (in a particular light); to accept (stolen goods) from a thief. *v.i.* To hold a reception of visitors or callers. **receivable,** *a.* **receivability** (-bil′ i ti), **receivableness,** *n.*

receiver (rė sēv′ ėr), *n.* One who receives; one who receives stolen goods, a fence; a receptacle, as a part of a telephonic or telegraphic apparatus for receiving messages or current, a vessel for receiving the products of distillation or for collecting gas, the bell-glass of an air-pump, etc.; (*Law*) an officer appointed to administer property under litigation, esp. that of bankrupts; (*Radio.*) an apparatus for the reception of wireless signals. **official receiver:** A person appointed by a bankruptcy court to receive the sums due to and administer the property of a bankrupt. **receiver-general,** *n.* An officer appointed to receive public revenues, now applied to an officer of the Duchy of Lancaster. **receiving-house, -office, -room,** etc., *n.* Places for the receipt of parcels, money, recruits, etc. **receiving-order,** *n.* An order from a bankruptcy court staying separate action against a debtor and placing his affairs in the hands of an official receiver. **receivership,** *n.*

re-celebrate (rē sel′ ė brāt), *v.t.* To celebrate again.

recency [RECENT].

recension (rē sen′ shŭn) [L. *recensio*, from *recensēre* (RE-, *censēre*, to review)], *n.* The act of revising; a critical revision of a text, a revised edition. **recensor,** *n.*

recent (rē′ sėnt) [F. *récent*, L. *recentem*, nom. *-cens*, etym. unknown], *a.* Of or pertaining to the present or time not long past; that happened, existed, or came into existence lately; late (of existence); modern, fresh, newly begun or established; (*Geol.*) pertaining to the existing epoch, Post-pliocene, Quaternary. **recency, recentness,** *n.* **recently,** *adv.*

receptacle (rė sep′ tȧkl) [F., from L. *receptāculum*, from *recept-*, p.p. stem of *recipere*, to RECEIVE], *n.* That which receives, holds, or contains; a vessel, space, or place of deposit; (*Bot.*) a part forming a support, as the portion of a flower on which the sexual organs are set, the axis of a flower cluster, etc. **receptacular** (-tăk′ ū lȧr), *a.*

***receptible** (rė sep′ tibl) [L. *receptibilis*, as foll.], *a.* Receivable. **receptibility** (-bil′ i ti), *n.*

reception (rė sep′ shŭn) [F., from L. *receptiōnem*, nom. *-tio*, from *recipere*, to RECEIVE, p.p. *receptus*], *n.* The act of receiving; the state of being received; receipt, acceptance, admission; the receiving, admitting, or accommodating of persons, esp. guests, new members of a society, etc.; a formal welcome; an occasion of formal or ceremonious receiving of visitors; the act or process of receiving (ideas or impressions) into the mind; mental acceptance, admission, or recognition (of a theory, etc.) **reception order,** *n.* (*Law*) The official order required for detention in a lunatic asylum. **reception-room,** *n.* A room for receptions; (*colloq.*) a room to which visitors are admitted, opposed to bedrooms, kitchen, etc. **receptionist,** *n.* Person at a hotel, or elsewhere, whose duty it is to receive and look after visitors.

receptive (rė sep′ tiv), *a.* Having ability or capacity to receive; quick to receive impressions, ideas, etc. **receptively,** adv. **receptiveness, receptivity** (-tiv′ i ti), *n.*

recess (rė ses′) [L. *recessus*, from p.p. of *recēdere*, to RECEDE (I)], *n.* Cessation or suspension of public or other business, a vacation; a part that recedes, a depression, indentation, hollow, niche, or alcove; a secluded or secret place, a nook; *the act of withdrawing or receding; (*Anat. and Bot.*) a depression, cavity, indentation, or fold.

recession (rė sesh′ ŭn), *n.* The act of receding, withdrawal, retirement; a receding part or object; (*Am.*) a slump. **recessional,** *a.* Pertaining to the recession of the clergy and choir from the chancel; *n.* A hymn sung during this ceremony. **recessive,** *a.* **recessive tendency,** *n.* (*Biol.*) The tendency possessed by one of the parents of a hybrid, which may not appear in the hybrid but may be transmitted to its descendants.

Rechabite (rek′ ȧ bīt), *n.* Orig. one of the descendants of Jonadab, son of Rechab, who bound themselves to abstain from wine; a member of a society of total abstainers called the Independent Order of Rechabites. **Rechabitism,** *n.*

recharge (rē charj′), *v.t.* To charge again; to put a new charge into; to make a new charge against; to charge or attack again or in return. *n.* A new charge or a charge in return. **recharter** (rē char′ tėr), *v.t.* To charter again; to give a new charter to.

réchauffé (rā shō fā) [F., p.p. of *réchauffer*, to warm up again (RE-, *chauffer*, CHAFE)], *n.* A dish warmed up again; (*fig.*) a rehash.

recheat (rė chēt′) [prob. from O.F. *rachater*, to rally], *v.i.* To blow a recheat. *n.* A call on the horn to rally the hounds in a deer hunt.

recherché (rė shâr′ shā) [F., p.p. of rechercher (RE-, *chercher*, to SEARCH)], *a.* (*fem.* **-chée**) Out of the common; rare, choice.

rechristen (rē krisn′), *v.t.* To christen again; (*fig.*) to give a new name to.

recidivist (rė sid′ i vist) [F. *récidiviste*, L. *recidīvus*, from *recidere* (RE-, *cadere*, to fall)], *n.* A relapsed or inveterate criminal, usu. one serving or who has served a second term of imprisonment. **recidivation** (-vā′ shŭn), **recidivism,** *n.*

recipe (res′ i pi) [L., imper. of *recipere*, to RECEIVE], *n.* A formula or prescription for compounding medical or other mixtures, a receipt; directions for preparing a dish; a remedy, expedient, device, or means for effecting some result.

recipient (rė sip′ i ėnt) [L. *recipiens -ntem*, pres.p. of *recipere*, to RECEIVE], *a.* Receiving; receptive. *n.* One who receives, a receiver. **recipiency,** *n.*

reciprocal (rė sip′ rō kȧl) [L. *reciprocus* (prob. RE-, back, *pro*, forward)], *a.* Acting, done, or given in return, mutual; mutually interchangeable, inversely correspondent, complementary; (*Gram.*) expressing mutual action or relation; *reflexive. *n.* (*Math.*) The quotient resulting from dividing unity by a quantity. **reciprocal ratio:** The ratio between the reciprocals of two quantities. **reciprocal terms:** (*Log.*) Terms having the same signification and therefore interchangeable. ***reciprocality** (-kăl′ i ti), *n.* Reciprocity. **reciprocally** (rė sip′ rō kȧl i), *adv.* **reciprocant,** *n.* (*Math.*) A differential invariant.

reciprocate (re sip′ rō kāt), *v.i.* To alternate, to move backwards and forwards; to return an equivalent, to make a return in kind. *v.t.* To give alternating or backward-and-forward motion to; to give and take mutually, to interchange; to give in return. **reciprocating engine:** An engine performing work with a part having reciprocating, not rotatory, motion. **reciprocating motion:** Backward-and-forward or up-and-down motion, as of a piston. **reciprocation** (-kā′ shŭn), *n.* The act of reciprocating; giving and returning; reciprocal motion. ***reciprocative** (rė sip′ rö kā tiv), *a.* **reciprocator,** *n.* **reciprocatory,** *a.* (*Mach.*) Reciprocating, opp. to rotatory.

reciprocity (res i pros′ i ti), *n.* The state of being reciprocal, reciprocation of rights or obligations; mutual action or the principle of give-and-take, esp. interchange of commercial privileges between two nations.

***recision** (rė sizh′ ŭn) [L. *recīsio*, from *recīdere* (RE-, *cædere*, to cut)], *n.* The act of cutting back, pruning.

recital (rė sī′ tål), *n.* The act of reciting; an enumeration or narrative of facts or particulars, a story; the part of a document formally stating facts, reasons, grounds, etc.; a public entertainment consisting of recitations; a musical performance, esp. by one person or the works of one person.

recitation (res i tā′ shŏn), *n.* The recital of a piece of prose or poetry, esp. the delivery of a composition committed to memory; a composition intended for recital.

recitative (rē sit′ å tiv), *n.* (*Mus.*) A style of rendering vocal passages intermediate between singing and ordinary speaking, as in oratorio and opera; a piece or part to be sung in recitative. *a.* Pertaining or suitable for recitative. *v.t.* To render in recitative. **recitatively,** *adv.*

recite (rė sīt′) [F. *réciter*, L. *recitāre* (RE-, *citāre*, to CITE)], *v.t.* To repeat aloud or declaim from memory, esp. before an audience; to narrate, to rehearse (esp. facts, etc., in a legal document); to quote, to cite; to enumerate. *v.i.* To give a recitation. **reciter,** *n.* One who recites; a book of selections, etc., for reciting.

recivilize (rē siv′ i līz), [RE-, CIVILIZE], *v.t.* To civilize again. **recivilization** (-zā′ shŭn), *n.*

reck (rek) [A.-S. *reccan* (cp. O.H.G. *ruohhen*, M.H.G. *ruochen*, Icel. *rækja*)], *v.t.* (*chiefly poet.*) To care, to heed. *v.i.* To have a care or thought (of); to trouble oneself, to be concerned, to be heedful. **reckless,** *a.* Careless, heedless; rash, venturesome; regardless, indifferent, neglectful, heedless (of). **recklessly,** *adv.* **recklessness,** *n.*

reckon (rek′ ŏn) [A.-S. *gerecenian* (cp. M.Dut. *rekenen*, G. *rechnen*, Icel. *reikna*), cogn. with prec.], *v.t.* To count, to add (up), calculate, or compute; to count or include (in or among), to regard (as), to account, to esteem, to consider (to be); (*Am.*) to be of the opinion, to 'calculate,' to 'guess' (that). *v.i.* To compute, to calculate, to settle accounts with; to rely, to count, to place dependence (upon); (*Am.*) to suppose, to believe, to 'guess,' to 'calculate.' **to reckon on:** To rely upon, to expect. **to reckon without one's host:** To underestimate. **reckoner,** *n.* **reckoning,** *n.* The act of calculating or counting; a statement of accounts or charges, a bill, esp. for liquor at a tavern, a score; a settling of accounts; (*Naut.*) an estimate or calculation of a ship's position. **day of reckoning:** The day of settling accounts; (*fig.*) the Day of Judgment. **dead reckoning** [DEAD]. **out of one's reckoning:** Mistaken in one's judgment or expectation.

reclaim (rė klām′) [O.F. *reclamer*, L. *reclāmāre*, to cry out against (RE-, *clāmāre*, to shout)], *v.t.* To bring back from error, vice, wildness, etc.; to reform, to tame, to civilize, to bring under cultivation; to demand back, to claim the restoration of; *to call back, to recall; *to bring back (a hawk) to the wrist. **v.i.* To cry out, to exclaim or protest; *to reform; to draw back. *n.* The act of reclaiming or being reclaimed, reclamation. **reclaimable,** *a.* **reclaimably,** *adv.* ***reclaimant,** *n.* One who remonstrates against anything. **reclaiming,** *a.* (*Law*) Appealing from a judgment. **reclamation** (rek lå mā′ shŭn), *n.*

réclame (rā klam) [F., from *reclamer*, see prec.], *n.* Notoriety; puffing, self-advertisement.

reclasp (rē klasp′), *v.t.* To clasp again.

recline (rė klīn′) [L. *reclīnāre* (RE-, *clīnāre*, to lean), see DECLINE], *v.t.* To lay or lean (one's body, head, limbs, etc.) back, esp. in a horizontal or nearly horizontal position. *v.i.* To assume or be in a leaning or recumbent posture, to lie down or lean back upon cushions or other supports; (*fig.*) to rely (upon). **a.* Reclining, recumbent. **reclinate** (rek′ li nāt), *a.* (*Bot.*) Inclined from an erect position, bending downwards. **reclination,** *n.* **recliner,** *n.*

reclose (rē klōz′), *v.t.* and *i.* To shut again. **reclothe,** *v.t.* To clothe again.

recluse (rė kloos′) [O.F. *reclus -cluse*, p.p. of *reclure*, L. *reclūdere* (RE-, *claudere*, to shut)], *a.* Retired from the world; solitary, secluded, retired, sequestered. *n.* One who lives retired from the world, esp. a religious devotee who lives in a solitary cell and practises austerity and self-discipline, a hermit, an anchorite or anchoress. ***reclusely,** *adv.* ***recluseness,** *n.* **reclusery** [RECLUSORY]. **reclusion** (-kloo′ zhŭn), *n.* **reclusive** (-kloo′ siv), *a.* **reclusory,** *n.* A hermitage.

recoal (rē kōl′), *v.t.* To furnish with a fresh supply of coal. *v.i.* To take in a fresh supply of coal (of a steamship). **recoat** (rē kōt′), *v.t.* To coat again (with paint, etc.).

recognition (rek ŏg nish′ ŭn) [L. *recognitio*, from *recognit-*, p.p. stem of *recognoscere*, to RECOGNIZE], *n.* Act of recognizing; state of being recognized; acknowledgment, notice taken; a perceiving as being known. ***recognitor** (-kog′ ni tŏr), *n.* One of a jury at an assize or inquest. **recognitory,** *a.*

recognizance (rė kog′ ni zåns, re kon′ i zåns) [A.-F. *reconisaunce*, O.F. *recoignisance*, as foll.], *n.* (*Law*) A bond or obligation entered into in a court or before a magistrate to perform a specified act, fulfil a condition, etc. (as to keep the peace or appear when called upon); a sum deposited as pledge for the fulfilment of this; *recognition, avowal; *a badge or token.

recognize (rek′ ŏg nīz) [O.F. *reconoistre* (F. *reconnaître*), L. *recognoscere* (RE-, *cognoscere*, to COGNOSCE)], *v.t.* To know again; to recall the identity of; to acknowledge, to admit the truth, validity, existence, etc., of. *v.i.* (*Am.*) To enter into recognizances. **recognizable** (rek ŏg nīz′ åbl), *a.* **recognizability** (-bil′ i ti), *n.* **recognizably** (-nīz′ å bli), *adv.* **recognizant** (rė kog′ ni zånt), *a.* **recognizer** (rek′ ŏg nī zėr), *n.*

recoil (rė koil′) [O.F. *reculer* (RE-, *cul*, L. *culum*, nom. *-lus*, the posterior)], *v.i.* To start or spring back; to rebound; to shrink back, as in fear or disgust; to be driven back; to retreat. **v.t.* To drive back. *n.* The act of recoiling; a rebound; the act or feeling of shrinking back, as in fear or disgust. **recoil escapement,** *n.* (*Clock.*) An escapement in which after each beat the escape-wheel recoils slightly. **recoiler,** *n.* **recoilingly,** *adv.* **recoilment,** *n.*

recoin (rē koin′), *v.t.* To coin over again. **recoinage,** *n.* **recoiner,** *n.*

recollect (1) (rē kŏ lekt′), *v.t.* To gather together again; to collect or compose (one's ideas, thoughts, or feelings); to summon up, to rally, to recover (one's strength, spirit, etc.). *v.i.* To come together again.

recollect (2) (rek ŏ lekt′) [L. *recollectus*, p.p. of *recolligere*, after F. *récolliger*], *v.t.* To recall to memory, to remember, to succeed in recalling the memory of. *v.i.* To succeed in remembering. **recollection** (-lek′ shŭn), *n.* The act or power of recollecting; a memory, a reminiscence; the period of past time over which one's memory extends. **recollective,** *a.*

Recollect (3) (rek′ ŏ lekt) [as prec. or from F. *récollet*], *n.* A member of an Observantine branch of the Franciscan order, founded in Spain in 1500, characterized by strictness of rule and devotional contemplation or recollection.

recolonize (rē kol′ ŏ nīz), *v.t.* To colonize afresh. **recolonization** (-zā′ shŭn), *n.* **recolour** (rē kŭl′ ŏr), *v.t.* To colour again. **recombine** (rē kŏm bīn′), *v.t.* To combine again. **recombination**

(-nā' shŭn), *n.* **recomfort** (rē kŭm' fȯrt), *v.i.* To comfort or console again; to give new strength to ***recomforture,** *n.* **recommence** (rē kȯ mens'), *v.t.* and *i.* To begin again. **recommencement,** *n.*

recommend (rek ȯ mend') [from F. *recommender*, var. of *recommander*, or med. L. *recommendāre* (RE-, *commendāre*, to COMMEND)], *v.t.* To commend to another's notice, use, or favour, esp. to represent as suitable for an office or employment; to advise (a certain course of action, etc.); to render acceptable or serviceable (of qualities, etc.); *to give or commend (one's soul, a person, etc.) in charge (to God, etc.). **recommendable,** *a.* **recommendableness, recommendability** (-bil' i ti), *n.* **recommendably,** *adv.* **recommendation** (-dā' shŭn), *n.* The act of recommending; a quality or feature that tends to procure a favourable reception, a ground of approbation; (*colloq.*) a letter recommending a person for an appointment, etc. **recommendatory** (-men' dȧ tȯr i), *a.* **recommender,** *n.*

recommission (rē kȯ mish' ŭn), *v.t.* To commission anew. **recommit** (rē kȯ mit'), *v.t.* To commit again; to refer back (to a committee, etc.). **recommitment, recommittal,** *n.* **recommunicate** (rē kȯ mū' ni kāt), *v.t.* To communicate anew. **recompact** (rē kȯm păkt'), *v.t.* To join together again.

recompense (rek' ȯm pens) [O.F. *recompenser*, late L. *recompensāre* (RE-, *compensāre*, to COMPENSATE)], *v.t.* To make a return or give an equivalent for, to requite, to repay (a person, a service, an injury, etc.); to indemnify, to compensate (for), to make up (for); *to atone for. *n.* That which is given as a reward, compensation, requital, or satisfaction (for a service, injury, etc.). **recompensation** (rē kom pėn sā' shŭn), *n.* (*Sc. Law*) A counter-plea of compensation to a defender's plea of compensation from the pursuer. **recompenser,** *n.* **recompensive,** *a.*

recompile (rē kȯm pīl'), *v.t.* To compile again. **recompilation** (-lā' shŭn), *n.* **recompose** (rē kȯm pōz'), *v.t.* To compose or put together again; to rearrange; to restore the composure of, to tranquillize again. **recomposition** (-zish' ŭn), *n.* **recompound** (rē kȯm pound'), *v.t.* To compound afresh.

reconcile (rek' ȯn sīl) [F. *réconcilier*, L. *reconciliāre* (RE-, *conciliāre*, to conciliate)], *v.t.* To restore to friendship after an estrangement; to make content, acquiescent, or submissive (to); to harmonize, to make consistent, or compatible (with); to adjust, to settle (differences, etc.); (*R.-C. Ch.*) to purify or restore (a desecrated church, etc.) to sacred uses. **reconcilable,** *a.* **reconcilability** (-bil' i ti), ***reconcilableness,** *n.* **reconcilably,** *adv.* **reconcilement, reconciliation** (-ā' shŭn), *n.* **reconciler,** *n.* **reconciliatory** (-sil' i ȧ tȯr i), *a.*

recondense (rē kȯn dens'), *v.t.* and *i.* To condense again. **recondensation** (-sā' shŭn), *n.*

recondite (rek' ȯn dīt) [L. *reconditus*, p.p. of *recondere* (RE-, *condere*, to hide, see CONDIMENT)], *a.* Out of the way, abstruse, little known, obscure; pertaining to abstruse or special knowledge, profound; hidden, secret. **reconditely,** *adv.* **reconditeness,** *n.* ***reconditory** (-kon' di tȯr i), *n.* A repository.

recondition (rē kȯn dish' ȯn), *v.t.* To repair, to make as new.

reconduct (rē kȯn dŭkt'), *v.t.* To conduct back again. **reconfirm** (rē kȯn fĕrm'), *v.t.* To confirm or ratify again. **reconjoin** (rē kon join'), *v.t.* To join together again.

reconnaissance (rė kon' ȧ sȧns) [F., from *reconnaître*, late form of foll.], *n.* The act of reconnoitring, a preliminary examination or survey, esp. of a tract of country or a coast-line in war-time to ascertain the position of the enemy, the strategic features, etc.; a detachment of soldiers or sailors performing this duty. **reconnaissance in force:** A reconnaissance by a large body of troops or vessels of war.

reconnoitre (rek ȯ noi' tėr) [F., now *reconnaître*, L. *recognoscere*, to RECOGNIZE], *v.t.* To make a reconnaissance of to make a preliminary examination or survey of. *v.i.* To make a reconnaissance. **reconnoitrer,** n.

reconquer (rē kong' kėr), *v.t.* To conquer again; to regain. **reconquest,** *n.* **reconsecrate** (rē kon' sė krāt), *v.t.* To consecrate afresh. **reconsecration** (-krā' shŭn), *n.* **reconsider** (rē kon sid' ėr), *v.t.* To consider again (esp. with a view to rescinding); to review, to revise. **reconsideration** (-ā' shŭn), *n.* **reconsolidate** (rē kon sol' i dāt), *v.t.* and *i.* To consolidate again. **reconsolidation** (-dā' shŭn), *n.* **reconstitute** (rē kon' sti tūt), *v.t.* To constitute again; to give a new constitution to. **reconstituent** (-kȯn stit' ū ėnt), *a.* and *n.* **reconstitution** (-kon sti tū' shŭn), *n.* **reconstruct** (-kȯn strŭkt'), *v.t.* To construct again; to rebuild. **reconstruction,** *n.* The act or process of reconstructing; (*Am. Hist.*) the process by which the Southern States which had seceded from the Union were restored to Federal rights and privileges, after the Civil War of 1861–5. **reconstructionary,** *a.* **reconstructive,** *a.* **reconstructively,** *a.* **reconvalescent** (rē kon vȧ les' ėnt), *a.* Becoming convalescent or healthy again. **reconvalescence,** *n.* **reconvene** (rē kȯn vēn'), *v.t.* and *i.* To convene or assemble again. **reconvention** (rē kȯn ven' shŭn), *n.* (*Law*) A counter-action brought by the defendant in a suit against the plaintiff. **reconvert** (rē kȯn vĕrt'), *v.t.* To convert again. **reconversion,** *n.* **reconvey** (rē kȯn vā'), *v.t.* To convey back; to restore to a former owner. **reconveyance,** *n.*

record (1) (rė kȯrd') [O.F. *recorder*, L. *recordāre*, *-dārī* (RE-, *cor cordis*, heart)], *v.t.* To register, to write an account of, to set down permanent evidence of, to imprint deeply on the mind; (*Radio.*) to reproduce an item or programme; (*Gramophone*) to make a record; to go over, to rehearse; *(of birds) to sing over (a tune). **v.i.* To sing or warble a tune (of birds). **recording,** *a.* Registering waveforms arising from sound sources, or the readings of meteorological and other instruments making a record automatically.

record (2) (rek' ȯrd), *n.* A written or other permanent account or statement of a fact or facts; a register, a report, a minute or minutes of proceedings, a series of marks made by a recording instrument; a cylinder, disk, etc., or similar device with indentations, etc., for reproducing sound in a gramophone; (*Law*) an official report of proceedings, judgment, etc., to be kept as authentic legal evidence, or an official memorial of particulars, pleadings, etc., to be submitted as a case for decision by a court; the state of being recorded, testimony, attestation; the past history of a person's career, esp. as an index of character and abilities; the authentic register of performances in any sport; hence, the best performance or the most striking event of its kind recorded; a portrait, monument, or other memento of a person, event, etc. **court of record:** A court whose proceedings are officially recorded and preserved as evidence. **off the record:** In confidence, not said officially. **on record:** Recorded, esp. with legal authentication. **to beat** or **break the record:** To surpass all former achievements or events of the kind. **record-breaker,** *n.* **record-breaking,** *a.* and *n.* **Record Office,** *n.* Official repository for state papers. **recordable,** *a.* ***recordation** (-dā' shŭn), *n.* Remembrance.

recorder (rė kȯr' dėr), *n.* One who or that which records; a magistrate having a limited criminal and civil jurisdiction in a city or borough and presiding over quarter-sessions; a recording-apparatus; a vertical form of flageolet or flute. **recordership,** *n.*

recount (1) (rė kount') [O.F. *reconter* (RE-, COUNT (1))], *v.t.* To relate in detail, to narrate. **recountal, *recountment,** *n.*

recount (2) (rē kount'), *v.t.* To count over again. *n.* A new count.

recoup (rė koop′) [F. *recouper* (RE-, *couper*, to cut, see COUP (1))], *v.t.* To reimburse, to indemnify (oneself) for a loss or expenditure; to compensate, to make up for (a loss, expenditure, etc.); (*Law*) to keep back (a part of something due). *v.i.* (*Law*) To make such a deduction. **recoupé, recouped** (rė koo′ pā, -koopt′), *a.* (*Her.*) Couped, clean-cut. **recouper,** *n.* **recoupment,** *n.*

recourse (rė kôrs′) [F. *recours*, L. *recursum*, nom. *-us* (RE-, *cursus*, COURSE)], *n.* Resorting or applying (to) as for help; a source of help, that which is resorted to; *recurrence, flowing back. **to have recourse to:** To go to for advice, help, etc., esp. in emergency. **v.i.* To go back, to return (to). ***recourseful,** *a.*

recover (1) (rė kŭv′ ėr) [O.F. *recovrer* (F. *recouvrer*), L. *recuperāre*, to RECUPERATE], *v.t.* To regain, to repossess oneself of, to win back; to make up for, to retrieve; to save (the by-products of an industrial process); to bring (a weapon) back after a thrust, etc.; (*Law*) to obtain by legal process; *to bring back to health, consciousness, life, etc. *v.i.* To regain a former state, esp. after sickness, misfortune, etc.; to come back to consciousness, life, health, etc.; (*Law*) to be successful in a suit; (*Fencing, Boxing, etc.*) to come back to a posture of defence. *n.* (*Fencing, etc.*). The position of a weapon or the body after a thrust, etc.; the act of coming back to this. **recoverable,** *a.* **recoverableness,** *n.* ***recoveree** (-ė rē′), *n.* (*Law*) The person against whom a judgment is obtained in recovery. **recoverer,** *n.* (*Law*) The person who obtains such a judgment. **recovery,** *n.* The act of recovering or the state of having recovered; restoration to health after sickness, etc.; (*Law*) the obtaining of the right to something by the judgment of a court.

re-cover (2) (rē kŭv′ ėr), *v.t.* To cover again, to put a new covering on.

recreant (rek′ rė ȧnt) [O.F., pres.p. of *recroire*, to yield in trial by combat (RE-, *croire*, L. *crēdere*, to believe, to entrust)], *a.* Craven, cowardly. *n.* One who has yielded in combat, one who has begged for mercy, a coward, a mean-spirited wretch, an apostate, a deserter. **recreancy,** *n.* **recreantly,** *adv.*

recreate (1) (rek′ rė āt) [L. *recreātus*, p.p. of *recreāre*], *v.t.* To refresh after toil; to divert, to entertain, to amuse. *v.i.* To take recreation. **recreation** (1) (-ā′ shŭn), *n.* The act of refreshing oneself or renewing one's strength after toil; amusement, diversion; an amusing or entertaining exercise or employment. **recreation ground:** A communal open space in an urban area. **recreational, recreative** (rek′ rė ā tiv), *a.* Refreshing, reinvigorating. **recreatively,** *adv.* **recreativeness,** *n.*

re-create (2) (rē krė āt′), *v.t.* To create anew. *a.* (*Poet.*) Re-created. **re-creation** (2) (ā′ shŭn), *n.* **re-creator** (rē krė ā′ tȯr), *n.* **re-creative,** etc. [RECREATE (1)].

recrement (rek′ rė mėnt) [F. *récrément*, L. *recrēmentum*, from *recernere* (RE-, *cernere*, to sift)], *n.* Useless matter separated from that which is useful, refuse; (*Physiol.*) fluid separated from the blood and absorbed into it again, as gastric juice, saliva, etc. **recremental** (-men′ tȧl), **-mentitial, -titious** (-tish′ ȧl, -ŭs), *a.*

recriminate (rė krim′ i nāt) [med. L. *recrīminātus*, p.p. of *recrīminārī* (RE-, L. *crīminārī*, to CRIMINATE)], *v.i.* To retort an accusation, to bring counter-charges against. *v.t.* To accuse in return. **recrimination** (-nā′ shŭn), *n.* **recriminative** (-krim′ i nā tiv), **recriminatory,** *a.* **recriminator,** *n.*

recross (rē kros′), *v.t.* and *i.* To cross or pass over again. **recrucify** (rē kroo′ si fī), *v.t.* To crucify again.

recrudesce (rē krŭ des′) [L. *recrūdescere* (RE-, *crūdescere*, to become raw, from *crūdus*, raw)], *v.i.* To open, break out, or become raw or sore again.

recrudescence (rē kroo des′ ėns), *n.* The state of becoming sore again; a relapse, a breaking-out again; (*Bot.*) the production of a young shoot from a ripened spike, etc.; (*loosely*) a renewal, a reappearance. **recrudescent,** *a.*

recruit (rė kroot′) [F. *recruter*, from obs. *recrute*, a recruit, prov. form of *recrue*, fem. p.p. of *recroître* (RE-, *croître*, O.F. *creistre*, L. *crescere*, to grow, to INCREASE)], *v.t.* To enlist (persons, esp. soldiers or sailors, or airmen); to supply (an army, regiment, crew, etc.) with recruits, to replenish with fresh supplies, to fill up gaps, etc.; to restore to health, to refresh, to reinvigorate. *v.i.* To gain new supplies; to seek to recover health; to act as a recruiting-officer, etc. *n.* A service man newly enlisted; (*fig.*) one who has newly joined a society, etc.; *a new supply, a recruitment. **recruital, recruitment,** *n.* **recruiter,** *n.* One who recruits. **recruiting-officer, -party, -sergeant,** *n.* Persons engaged in enlisting recruits.

recrystallize (rē kris′ tȧ līz), *v.t.* and *i.* To crystallize again. **recrystallization** (-za′ shŭn), *n.*

rectal (rek′ tȧl), *a.* (*Anat.*) Pertaining to the rectum.

rectangle (rek′ tăng gėl) [F., from late L. *rectangulus* (*rectus*, straight, *angulus*, ANGLE (2))], *n.* A plane rectilinear quadrilateral figure with four right-angles. **rectangled,** *a.* Having an angle or angles of 90°. **rectangular,** *a.* Shaped like a rectangle; rectangled; placed or having parts placed at right angles. **rectangularity** (-lăr′ i ti), *n.* **rectangularly,** *adv.*

rectify (rek′ ti fī) [F. *rectifier*, late L. *rectificāre* (L. *recti-*, *rectus*, right, *-ficāre*, *facere*, to make)], *v.t.* To set right, to correct, to amend, to adjust; to reform, to supersede by what is right or just, to abolish; (*Chem.*) to refine or purify (spirit, etc.) by repeated distillations and other processes; (*Geom.*) to determine the length of (an arc, etc.); (*Elec.*) to transform (an alternating current) into a continuous one. **rectifiable,** *a.* **rectification** (-kā′ shŭn), *n.* Rectifying in all its senses; (*Radio.*) the conversion of an alternating current into a direct current. **rectifier,** *n.*

rectigrade (rek′ ti grād) [L. *recti-*, *rectus*, straight, *gradus*, GRADE], *a.* (*Ent.*) Walking in a straight line; belonging to the *Rectigradæ*, a class of spiders that walk straight forward.

rectilinear, rectilineal (rek ti lin′ ė ȧr, -ȧl) [late L. *rectilīneus* (as prec., *līnea*, LINE (1))], *n.* Consisting of, lying or proceeding in a straight line; straight; bounded by straight lines. **rectilineally, rectilinearly,** *adv.* **rectilinearity** (-ăr′ i ti), *n.*

rectiserial (rek ti sēr′ i ȧl) [L. *recti*, *rectus*, straight, SERIAL], *a.* (*Bot.*) Arranged in a straight line, esp. in vertical ranks (of leaves).

rectitis (rek tī′ tis), *n.* (*Path.*) Inflammation of the rectum. **rectitic** (-tit′ ik), *a.*

rectitude (rek′ ti tūd) [F., from late L. *rectitūdo*, from L. *rectus*, right], *n.* Uprightness, rightness of moral principle, conformity to truth and justice; *freedom from error, correctness.

recto (rek′ tō) [L. *recto* (*folio*), on the right (leaf)], *n.* The right-hand page of an open book (**usu.** that odd numbered), opp. to verso.

recto- [RECTUM].

rector (rek′ tȯr) [L., ruler, from *regere* (p.p. *rectus*), to rule], *n.* A parson or incumbent of a parish whose tithes are not impropriate; the head of a religious institution, university, incorporated school, etc.; *a director, a ruler. **Lord Rector** [LORD]. **rectorate, rectorship,** *n.* **rectorial** (-tôr′ i ȧl), *a.* **rectory** (rek′ tȯr i), *n.* The benefice or living of a rector with all its rights, property, etc.; the house of a rector. **rectress,** *n.* A female ruler or governor.

rectoscope, recto-uterine, etc. [RECTUM].

rectrix (rek′ triks) [L., fem. of RECTOR], *n.* (*pl.* **rectrices**) A rectress; the quill-feathers in a bird's tail which guide its flight.

rectum (rek′ tŭm) [L., neut. of *rectus*, straight], *n.* (*pl.* **-ta**) (*Anat.*) The lowest portion of the large intestine extending to the anus. **recto-**, *comb. form.* **rectocele** (rek′ tō sēl), *n.* (*Path.*) Prolapse of the anus with protrusion. **rectoscope**, *n.* (*Surg.*) A speculum for examining the rectum. **recto-uterine** (-ū′ tėr in), *a.* (*Anat.*) Of or pertaining to the rectum and the uterus. **recto-vaginal** (-văj′ i nȧl), *a.* Of or pertaining to the rectum and the vagina.

rectus (rek′ tŭs) [L., straight], *n.* (*pl.* **-ti**, -tī) (*Anat.*) One of various straight muscles, esp. of the abdomen, thigh, neck, and eyes.

re-cultivate (rē kŭl′ ti vāt), *v.t.* To cultivate afresh. **re-cultivation** (-vā′ shŭn), *n.*

recumbent (rė kŭm′ bėnt) [L. *recumbens -ntem*, pres.p. of *recumbere* (RE-, *cumbere*, to lie)], *a.* Lying down, reclining; (*fig.*) inactive, idle. **recumbence**, **recumbency**, *n.* **recumbently**, *adv.*

recuperate (rė kū′ pėr āt) [L. *recuperātus*, p.p. of *recuperāre*, var. of *reciperāre*, form of *recipere*, to RECEIVE], *v.t.* To recover, to regain (health, strength, etc.); to restore to health. *v.i.* To recover (from sickness, loss of power, etc.). ***recuperable**, *a.* **recuperation** (-ā′ shŭn), *n.* **recuperative** (rė kū′ pėr ȧ tiv), ***recuperatory**, *a.* **recuperator**, *n.*

recur (rė kėr′) [L. *recurrere* (RE-, *currere*, to run)], *v.i.* (*past & p.p.* **recurred**) To return, to go back to in thought, etc.; to come back to one's mind; to happen again, to happen repeatedly; (*Math.*) to be repeated indefinitely. **recurring** (rė kėr′-, -kŭr′ ing), *a.* Happening or being repeated. **recurring decimals:** Figures in a decimal fraction that recur over and over again in the same order. **recurrence** (rė kŭr′ ėns), ***recurrency**, *n.*

recurrent (re kŭ′ rėnt), *a.* Returning, recurring, esp. at regular intervals; (*Anat.*) turning in the opposite direction (or veins, nerves, etc.), running in an opposite course to those from which they branch. *n.* A recurrent nerve or artery, esp. one of the laryngeal nerves. **recurrently**, *adv.*

***recure** (rė kūr′) [L. *recūrāre*], *v.t.* To cure, to heal; to recover, to retrieve. *n.* Recovery.

recurve (rė kėrv′) [L. *recurvāre*], *v.t.* To bend backwards. **recurvate** (-vȧt), *a.* Recurved, reflexed. **v.t.* (-vāt) To bend back. **recurvation** (rē kėr vā′ shŭn), **recurvature** (-kėr′ vȧ tyŭr), *n.* **recurvirostег** (-vi ros′ tėr), *n.* A bird with the beak bent upwards as the avocet. **recurvirostral**, *a.* ***recurvity** (-kėr′ vi ti), *n.* **recurvo-**, *comb. form.* **recurvous**, *a.*

recusant (rek′ ū zȧnt, rė kū′ zȧnt) [L. *recusans -ntem*, pres.p. of *recusāre*, to refuse, to object (RE-, *causa*, CAUSE)], *a.* Obstinately refusing to conform, esp. (*Eng. Hist.*) to attend the services of the Established Church. *n.* One who refuses to submit or comply, esp. one who refused to attend the services of the Established Church. **recusance**, **-cy**, *n.* ***recusation** (rek ū zā′ shŭn), *n.* The act of objecting against a judge on the score of prejudice, etc. **recusative** (rė kū′ zȧ tiv), *a.* ***recuse**, *v.t.* To object against, to renounce, esp. to object against a judge.

recut (rē kŭt′), *v.t.* To cut again.

red (1) (red) [A.-S. *read* (cp. Dut. *rood*, G. *roth*, Icel. *rauthr*, also L. *rufus*, *ruber*, Gr. *eruthros*, Sansk. *rudhira-*)], *a.* Of a bright warm colour, as blood, usually including crimson, scarlet, vermilion, etc., of the colour at the least refracted end of the spectrum or that farthest from the violet; (*fig.*) flushed, stained with blood; revolutionary, anarchistic; (*fig.*) a sign of danger. *n.* A red colour or a shade of this; the red colour in roulette, etc.; the red ball at billiards; a red pigment; red clothes; (*fig.*) a revolutionary, an extreme radical, an anarchist; *one of the three former divisions of the British fleet (the others being the white and the blue). **to paint the town red:** To have a riotous time. **to put out the red carpet:** To give an impressive welcome. **to see red:** To become enraged. **red admiral** [ADMIRAL]. **red-and-black**, *n.* Rouge-et-noir. **red-backed**, *a.* **red-backed shrike:** The butcher-bird, *Lanius collurio.* **red-backed spider:** (*Austral.*) A venomous spider with red spots on its back. **red bark:** A variety of cinchona. **red-bearded, -bellied, -berried, -billed**, *a.* Having a red beard, belly, berries, etc. **red-blind**, *a.* Colour-blind with regard to red. **red-blindness**, *n.* **red book:** A book, orig. bound in red, containing a list of the peerage, civil servants, etc. **redbreast**, *n.* The robin, *Erythacus rubecula.* **red-breasted**, *a.* **redbrick university:** One of the newer provincial universities. **redbud**, *n.* The Judas-tree, *Cercis Canadensis.* **redcap**, *n.* A popular name for any small bird with a red head, esp. the goldfinch; a person wearing a red cap. **red-capped**, *a.* **red cent**, *n.* (*Am. colloq.*) A trifle of money. **Red Centre:** (*Austral.*) The interior of the continent. **red-chalk**, *n.* Ruddle. **red-cheeked**, *a.* **red-coat**, *n.* A British soldier, so called from the scarlet tunics worn by line regiments. **red-coated**, *a.* **red cross:** St. George's Cross, the English national emblem. **Red Cross Society:** An international society or organization having a red cross as emblem, for the provision of ambulance and hospital service for the wounded in time of war, and to assist in severe epidemics and national disasters in peace time, in accordance with the Geneva convention of 1864. **red deer:** A large species of deer with reddish coat and branching antlers (*Cervus elaphus*), still wild in the Scottish Highlands, Exmoor, etc.; the Virginia deer, *Cariacus Virginianus.* **red-drum**, *n.* The red-fish, *Sciæna ocellata.* **red ensign**, *n.* A red flag with the Union Jack in one corner, used as the ensign of the British Merchant Navy. **red-eye**, *n.* An animal, bird, etc., with a red iris; the name of several American fishes, also of the European *Leuciscus erythropthalmus*, with scarlet lower fins; (*Austral.*) a black cicada with red eyes. **red-eyed**, *a.* **red eyes:** Bloodshot eyes; with lids red and inflamed with weeping. **red-fish**, *n.* The name of various American fishes, including the red-drum, *Sciæna ocellata*, the blue-back salmon, *Oncorhyncus nerka*, etc.; a male salmon in the spawning season. **red flag:** The symbol of revolution or of anarchism; (*fig.*) a danger signal. **red grouse** [GROUSE (1)]. **red-gum**, *n.* An eruption of red pimples in infants, caused by dentition; an Australian eucalyptus of various species yielding reddish resin. **red-handed**, ***red-hand**, *a.* Having hands red with blood; (caught) in the very act (originally of homicide). **red hat**, *n.* A cardinal's hat; a staff officer. **red herring:** Herring dried and smoked. **to draw a red herring across the track:** (*fig.*) To distract attention by starting an irrelevant discussion. **red-hot**, *a.* Heated to redness; (*fig.*) excited, furious, wildly enthusiastic. **red-hot poker:** The flame-flower. **Red Indian**, *n.* A North American Indian. **red lattice:** A lattice window painted red, formerly the sign of a tavern. **red-lattice phrases:** Pot-house talk. **red lead:** Red oxide or lead used as a pigment. **red-legged**, *a.* Having red legs (of birds). **red-legs**, *n.* A name for various red-legged birds; the bistort. **red-letter**, *a.* Marked with red letters. **red-letter day:** An auspicious or memorable day, because saints' days were so marked in the calendar. **red man** [REDSKIN]. **red meat**, *n.* Beef and mutton. **redpole, -poll**, *n.* A popular name for two species of *Fringillidæ* from the red hue of their heads, esp. the greater redpole, the male linnet; (*pl.*) red-haired polled cattle. **red rag:** (*fig.*) Anything that excites rage as a red object is supposed to enrage a bull. **red rattle** [RATTLE]. **red ribbon:** The ribbon worn by members of the Order of the Bath, hence, membership of this. **red-rumped**, *a.* **red sanders:** Red sandalwood. ***red-sear**, *v.i.* To crack when too hot, as iron under the hammer. **redshank**, *n.* The red-legged sand-piper, *Tringa totanus*; *(*pl.*) a Celtic Highlander of Scotland, also applied to the native Irish (from their going barelegged). **red-short**, *a.* Hot-short. **red-shouldered**, *a.* **Redskin**, *n.* A N. American Indian. **red snow:** Snow reddened by a minute alga, *Protococcus nivalis*, frequent in Arctic and Alpine regions. **red**

spider: A mite infesting vines and other hot-house plants. **redstart** [A.-S. *steort*, tail], *n.* A red-tailed migratory song-bird, *Phœnicurus phœnicurus.* **red-streak,** *n.* A kind of cider apple. **red-tape,** *n.* Extreme adherence to official routine and formality (from the red tape used in tying up official documents). *a.* Characterized by this. **red-tapery, red-tapism,** *n.* **red-tapist,** *n.* **red-top,** *n.* (*Am.*) A kind of bent grass. **Red Triangle,** *n.* The emblem of the Y.M.C.A. **red-water,** *n.* Hæmaturia in cattle and sheep, the most marked symptom of which is the red urine. **red weed:** The corn poppy; herb Robert and other plants. **redwing,** *n.* A variety of thrush, *Turdus musicus*, with red on the wings. **redwood,** *n.* A name of various trees and their timber, esp. the gigantic Californian *Sequoia sempervirens.* **redden,** *v.t.* To make red. *v.i.* To become red, esp. to blush. **reddish, reddy,** *a.* **reddishness,** *n.* **redly,** *adv.* **redness,** *n.*

red (2) [REDD]. ***red** (3), *past* [READ].

red- [L. RE-, before vowels in words of L. orig.], *pref.*

-red [A.-S. *rǣdan*], *suf.* Condition, as in *hatred, kindred.*

redaction (rė dăk′ shŭn) [F. *rédaction*, late L. *redactiōnem*, nom. *-tio*, from *redigere* (RED-, *agere*, to bring), p.p. *redactus*], *n.* Reduction to order, esp. revising, rearranging, and editing a literary work; a revised or rearranged edition. **redact** (rė dăkt′), *v.t.* To reduce to a certain form, esp. a literary form, to edit, to prepare for publication. ***redacteur*** (rā dăk tur), **redactor** (-dăk′ tȯr), *n.* One who redacts, an editor.

redan (rė dăn′) [F., for *redent* (RE-, DENT, tooth)], *n.* (*Fort.*) A work having two faces forming a salient towards the enemy.

***redargue** (rė dar′ gū) [F. *rédarguer*, L. *redarguere* (RED-, ARGUE)], *v.t.* (*Sc.*) To refute, to disprove. ***redargution** (-gū′ shŭn), *n.*

redbreast, etc. [RED (1)].

redd (red) [etym. doubtful, cp. Dut. *redden*], *v.t.* (*Sc.*) To clear, to make clear; to clean out, to get rid of; to adjust, to clear up, to put in order, to tidy, to make ready; to interfere between, to separate (combatants, etc.), to settle (a quarrel). **to redd up:** To put in order. **redder,** *n.* **redding-blow, -stroke,** *n.* A blow received by one interfering in a quarrel. **redding-comb,** *n.* A hair-comb.

redden, etc. [RED (1)].

***reddition** (rė dish′ ŭn) [F. *reddition*, or L. *redditio*, from *reddere*, to RENDER], *n.* Restitution; surrender; translation, version, explanation. ***redditive,** *a.*

reddle [var. of RUDDLE].

***rede** (rēd) [A.-S. *rǣd*, from *rǣdan*, see READ], *n.* Counsel, advice; resolve, intention, plan; a tale, a story; a saying, a motto. *v.t.* To counsel, to advise; to read or interpret (a riddle, etc.).

redecorate (rē dek′ ȯ rāt), *v.t.* To decorate afresh. **redecoration** (-rā′ shŭn), *n.* **rededicate** (rē ded′ i kāt), *v.t.* To dedicate anew. **rededication** (-kā′ shŭn), *n.* **rededicatory** (-ded i kā′ tȯr i), *a.*

redeem (rė dēm′) [F. *redimer*, L., *redimere* (RED-, *emere*, to buy), p.p. *redemptus*], *v.t.* To buy back, to recover by paying a price; (*Law*) to recover (mortgaged property), to discharge (a mortgage), to buy off (an obligation, etc.); to perform (a promise); to recover from captivity by purchase, to ransom; to deliver, to save, to rescue, to reclaim; (*Theol.*) to deliver from sin and its penalty; to atone for, to make amends for; to make good. **redeemability** (-bil′ i ti), **redeemableness,** *n.* **reedeemable,** *a.* **redeemer,** *n.* One who redeems, esp. Christ, the Saviour of the world.

redeliver (rē dė liv′ ėr), *v.t.* To deliver back, to restore, to free again; to repeat, to report. **redeliverance, redelivery,** *n.* **redemand** (rē dė mand′), *v.t.* To demand again or back. **redemise** (rē dė mīz′), *v.t.* (*Law*) To transfer (an estate, etc.) back. *n.* A retransfer.

redemption (rė demp′ shŭn) [F., from L. *redemptiōnem*, nom. *-tio*, from *redimere*, to REDEEM], *n.* The act of redeeming or the state of being redeemed, esp. salvation from sin and damnation by the atonement of Christ; release by purchase, ransom; reclamation (of land, etc.); purchase (of admission to a society, etc.); (*fig.*) that which redeems. **redemptioner,** *n.* (*Am. Hist.*) An emigrant to the United States who sold his services for a certain time to pay his passage-money, etc. ***Redemptionist,** *n.* A member of an order devoted to the redemption of Christian slaves in the hands of the Infidels. **redemptive, *redemptory,** *a.* ***redemptor,** *n.* A redeemer. **Redemptorist,** *n.* A member of a R.-C. congregation of missionary priests founded at Naples in 1732 by St. Alfonso Liguori.

redeployment (rē de ploi′ mėnt), *n.* Improved internal arrangements in a factory, etc., as a means to improving output.

redescend (rē dė send′), *v.t.* and *i.* To descend again. **redescribe** (rē dė skrīb′), *v.t.* To describe again. **redescription** (-skrip′ shŭn), *n.* **redetermine** (rē dė tĕr′ min), *v.t.* and *i.* To determine again. **redetermination** (-nā′ shŭn), *n.* **redevelop** (rē dė vel′ ȯp), *v.t.* (*Phot.*) To develop again. **redevelopment,** *n.*

redia (rē′ di ȧ) [mod. L., after Francesco *Redi* (1626–95), It. naturalist], *n.* (*pl.* ***rediæ***) (*Zool.*) An asexual stage in certain trematode worms such as the liver-fluke.

redif (rė dif′) [Turk, and Arab.], *n.* The first Turkish reserve; a soldier in this.

redigest (rē di jest′), *v.t.* To digest again. **redigestion,** *n.*

redingote (red′ ing gōt) [F., corr. of RIDING-COAT], *n.* (*in France*) A woman's long double-breasted coat; orig. a similar coat worn by men.

redintegrate (rė din′ tė grāt) [L. *redintegrātus*, p.p. of *redintegrāre*], *v.t.* To restore to completeness, to make united or perfect again; to renew, to re-establish. **a.* (-grȧt) Redintegrated. **redintegration** (-grā′ shŭn), *n.*

redirect (rē di rekt′), *v.t.* To direct again; to re-address. **redirection,** *n.* ***redisburse** (rē dis bĕrs′), *v.* To pay back again, to refund. ***redisbursement,** *n.* **rediscover** (rē dis kŭv′ ėr), *v.t.* To discover afresh. **rediscovery,** *n.* **redispose** (rē dis pōz′), *v.t.* To dispose again. **redisposition** (-zish′ ŭn), *n.* **redisseisin** (rē di sē′ zin), *n.* (*Law*) A writ to recover seizin of lands or tenements, a second disseisin. **redisseisor,** *n.* **redissolve** (rē di zolv′), *v.t.* and *i.* To dissolve again. **redissoluble** (-dis′ ȯl ŭbl), **redissolvable** (-zol′ vȧbl), *a.* **redissolution** (-lū′ shŭn), *n.* **redistribute** (rē dis trib′ ūt), *v.t.* To distribute again. **redistribution** (-bū′ shŭn), *n.* **redivide** (rē di vīd′), *v.t.* To divide again. **redivision** (-vizh′ ŭn), *n.*

***redivivous** (red i vī′ vŭs) [L. *redivīvus* (*redi-*, RED-, *vīvus*, living)], *a.* Revived, or tending to revive; come to life again.

redolent (red′ ȯ lėnt) [O.F., L. *redolentem* nom. *-lens*, pres.p. of *redolēre* (RED-, *olēre*, to smell)], *a.* Giving out a strong smell; (*fig.*) suggestive, reminding one (of); esp. of *fragrant odours. **redolence,** *n.*

redondilla (rā don dē′ lyȧ) [Sp., dim. of *redonda*, fem. of *redondo*, round], *n.* A Spanish stanza in trochaics, the first and fourth and the second and third lines of which rhymed with each other.

redouble (rė dŭb′ ėl) [F. *redoubler*], *v.t.* To double again; to increase by repeated additions, to intensify, to multiply; to fold back. *v.i.* To become increased by repeated additions, to grow more intense, numerous, etc.; to be repeated, to re-echo.

redoubt (rė dout′) [F. *redoute*, It. *redott*, L. *reductus*, retired (later, a secret place, a refuge), p.p. of *redūcere*, to REDUCE], *n.* A detached outwork or field-work enclosed by a parapet without flanking defences.

redoubtable (rė dou′ tå bėl) [O.F. *redoutable*, from *redouter*, to fear], *a.* Formidable; valiant. ***re-doubted,** *a.* Dreaded.

redound (rė dound′) [F. *rédonder*, L. *redundāre*, to overflow (RED-, *undāre*, from *unda*, wave)], *v.i.* To have effect, to conduce or contribute (to one's credit, etc.); to result (to), to act in return or recoil (upon); *to be in excess, to be redundant.

redowa (red′ ō vå) [F. and G., from Boh. *reydovák*, from *reydovati*, to whirl round], *n.* A Bohemian round dance of two forms, one resembling a waltz the other a polka.

redpole, etc. [RED (1)].

redraft (rē draft′), *v.t.* To draft or draw up a second time. *n.* A second draft. **redraw** (rē draw′), *v.t.* To draw again. *v.i.* To draw a fresh bill of exchange to cover a protested one. **redrawer,** *n.*

redress (1) (rē dres′), *v.t.i.* To dress again.

redress (2) (rė dres′), *v.t.* To set straight or right again, to readjust, to rectify; to remedy, to amend, to make reparation for; *to repair, to mend; *to re-erect, to set upright again. *n.* Redressing of wrongs or oppression; reparation; rectification. **redressable,** *a.* Capable of being redressed. **redresser,** *n.* ***redressive,** *a.* **redressment,** *n.*

redshank, etc. [RED (1)].

reduce (rė dūs′) [L. *redūcere* (RE-, *dūcere*, to bring), p.p. *reductus*], *v.t.* To bring to an original or a specified condition; to bring back (to); to modify so as to bring (into another form, a certain class, etc.), to make comformable (to a rule, formula, etc.); to bring by force (to a specified condition, action, etc.), to subdue, to conquer; to bring down, to lower, to degrade, to diminish, to weaken; (*Math.*) to change from one denomination to another; (*Sc. Law*) to set aside or annul by judicial action. **to reduce to the ranks:** To degrade to the rank of private soldier. **reducement,** *n.* **reducent,** *a.* and *n.* **reducer,** *n.* **reducible,** *a.* **reducibility** (-bil′ i ti), **reducibleness,** *n.* **reducibly,** *adv.* ***reduct** (rė dŭkt′), *v.t.* To reduce or bring (to or into).

reduction (rė dŭk′ shŭn), *n.* The act of reducing; the state of being reduced; a conquest; a decrease, a diminution; a reduced copy of anything; the process of making this; (*Arith.*) the process of finding an equivalent expression in terms of a different denomination; (*Phot.*) the process of reducing the opacity of a negative, etc.; (*Chem.*) a term applied to any process whereby an electron is added to an atom. **reduction to absurdity:** Proof of the truth of a proposition by showing that its contrary has absurd consequences; (*colloq.*) an absurd conclusion.

redundant (rė dŭn′ dånt) [L. *redundans -ntem*, pres.p. of *redundāre*, to REDOUND], *a.* Superfluous, excessive, superabundant; using more words than are necessary, pleonastic, tautological; exuberant, copious, luxuriant. **redundance, -cy,** *n.* **redundantly,** *adv.*

reduplicate (rė dū′ pli kāt) [med. L. *reduplicātus*, p.p. of *reduplicāre* (RE-, *duplicāre*, to DUPLICATE)], *v.t.* To redouble, to repeat; (*Gram.*) to repeat a letter or syllable to form a tense. *a.* (-kåt) Doubled, repeated. *n.* A duplicate. **reduplication** (-kā′ shŭn), *n.* The act of doubling or repeating; (*Gram.*) the repetition of a syllable or other part of a word; the part so repeated; (*Anat. and Zool.*) the doubling or folding back of a part or organ. **reduplicative** (-dū′ pli kå tiv), *a.*

reduviid (rė dū′ vi id) [mod. L. *Reduvius*, -ID], *a.* (*Ent.*) Belonging to the *Reduviidæ*, a family of predaceous bugs. *n.* A bug of this family. **reduvioid,**, *a.* and *n.*

redwing, redwood, etc. [RED (1)].

re-dye (rē dī′), *v.t.* To dye again.

ree (1) (rē) [var. of REEVE (3)], *n.* The female ruff.

ree (2) (rē) [Sc., etym., doubtful], *a.* Excited, wild, esp. with drink; delirious.

ree (3) [REIS (1)].

reebok (rē′ bok) [Dut., ROEBUCK], *n.* (*S. Afr.*) A small S. African antelope, *Pelea capreola.*

re-echo (rē ek′ ō), *v.t.* To echo again; to return the sound, to resound. *v.i.* To echo again; to reverberate.

***reechy** (rē′ chi) [var. of REEKY], *a.* Smoky; dirty, foul; rancid.

reed (rēd) [A.-S. *hrēod* (cp. Dut. and G. *riet*)], *n.* The long straight stem of certain water or marsh plants belonging to the genus *Phragmites* or the genera *Arundo* and *Ammophila*; (*collect.*) these as material for thatching, etc.; a musical pipe made of this, a shepherd's pipe; (*fig.*) pastoral poetry; a thin strip of metal or wood inserted in an opening in a musical instrument, set in vibration by a current of air to produce the sound; hence, a musical instrument or organ-pipe constructed with this (*usu. in pl.*); (*Weaving*) an implement or part of a loom for separating the threads of the warp and beating up the weft; (*Arch.*) a semicircular moulding, usu. in parallel series (*usu. in pl.*). *v.t.* To thatch with reed; to fit (an organ-pipe, etc.) with a reed; (*Arch.*) to decorate with reeds. **broken reed,** *n.* An unreliable person. **reed-babbler, -warbler, -wren,** *n.* A common European bird, *Acrocephalus scirpaceus.* **reed-bird,** *n.* The bobolink. **reed-grass,** *n.* Any of the reeds or any grasses of similar habit. **reed-mace,** *n.* The bulrush. **reed-organ,** *n.* A musical instrument with a keyboard the sounds of which are produced by reeds of the organ type. **reed-pipe,** *n.* A reeded organ-pipe; a musical pipe made of a reed. **reed-stop,** *n.* An organ-stop controlling a set of reed-pipes. ***reeden,** *a.* Consisting or made of reeds. **reeding,** *n.* A semi-cylindrical moulding or series of these; milling on the edge of a coin. **reedless,** *a.* **reedling,** *n.* The bearded titmouse. **reedy,** *a.* Abounding in reeds; like a reed; sounding like a reed, thin, sharp in tone. **reediness,** *n.*

re-edify (rē ed′ i fī), *v.t.* To rebuild; (*fig.*) to reconstruct, to re-establish. **re-edification** (-kā′ shŭn), *n.*

re-edit (rē ed′ it), *v.t.* To edit afresh.

reef (1) (rēf) [prob. from Dut. *rif*, Icel. *rif*, perh. cogn. with RIB], *n.* A ridge of rock, coral, sand, etc., in the sea at or near the surface of the water; (*Mining*) a lode or vein of auriferous quartz, or the bed-rock left after the removal of the diamantiferous portion. **reefy,** *a.* Abounding in reefs.

reef (2) (rēf) [Icel. *rif*, see prec.], *n.* One of the horizontal portions across the top of a square sail or the bottom of a fore-and-aft sail, which can be rolled up or wrapped and secured in order to shorten sail. *v.t.* To reduce the extent of a sail by taking in a reef or reefs; to take in a part of (a bowsprit, top-mast, etc.) in order to shorten it. **to take in a reef:** To reef a sail; (*fig.*) to proceed with caution or in moderation. **reef-knot,** *n.* A square or symmetrical double knot. **reef-line,** *n.* A small rope passing through eyelet-holes for reefing a sail. **reefer** (1), *n.* One who reefs; a reef-knot; a reefing-jacket; (*Naut. slang*) a midshipman. **reefing-jacket,** *n.* A stout, close-fitting double-breasted jacket.

reefer (2), *n.* A marijuana cigarette.

reek (rēk) [A.-S. *rēc* (cp. Dut. *rook*, G. *rauch*, Icel. *reykr*), whence *rēocan*, Dut. *rieken*, G. *rauchen*, to smoke], *n.* Smoke; vapour, steam, fume; a foul, stale, or disagreeable odour, a foul atmosphere. *v.i.* To emit smoke, vapour, or steam; to smoke, to steam, to emit fumes; to give off a disagreeable odour; to be steamy, sweaty, or smeared with foul moisture. **Auld Reekie,** *n.* Edinburgh. **reeky,** *a.* Smoky; filthy, dirty.

reel (1) (rēl) [A.-S. *hrēol*], *n.* A rotatory frame, cylinder, or other device on which thread, cord, wire paper, etc. can be wound, either in the process of manufacture or for winding and unwinding as required; a quantity of material wound on a reel; a bobbin (*Am.* a spool); (*Cinema.*) the spool on which a film is wound; a portion of film, usually 1,000 ft.; (*colloq.*) the film itself. *v.i.* To wind on a reel; to unwind or take (off) a reel. **to reel in** *or* **up:** To wind (thread, a line, etc.) on a reel; to draw (a fish, etc.) towards one by using a reel. **to reel off:** To unwind or pay out from a reel; (*fig.*) to tell (a story) fluently and without a hitch. **to reel up:** To wind up entirely on a reel. **reel-check,** *n.* A contrivance for checking the motion of a fishing-line pulled off the reel by a fish, etc. **reel-cotton,** *n.* Sewing-cotton or thread wound on reels or spools. **reel-line,** *n.* An angler's line wound on a reel, esp. the back part as distinguished from the casting-line. **reel-plate,** *n.* A metal plate on an angler's reel fitting into a groove, etc. on a fishing-rod. **reeler,** *n.* **reeling-machine,** *n.* A machine for winding up thread, cotton, etc.

reel (2) (rēl) [perh. rel. to prec.], *v.i.* To stagger, to sway; to go (along) unsteadily; to have a whirling sensation, to be dizzy, to swim; to be staggered, to rock, to give way. *n.* A staggering or swaying motion or sensation. **reelingly,** *adv.*

reel (3) (rēl) [perh. from REEL (2)], *n.* A lively Scottish dance in which the couples face each other and describe figures of 8; a piece of music for this. *v.i.* To dance a reel.

re-elect (rē ė lekt′), *v.t.* To elect again. **re-election** (-lek′ shŭn), *n.* **re-elevate** (rē el′ ė vāt), *v.t.* To elevate again. **re-elevation** (-vā′ shŭn), *n.* **re-eligible** (rē el′ i jibl), *a.* Capable of being re-elected to the same position. **re-eligibility** (-bil′ i ti), *n.* **re-embark** (rē ėm bark′), *v.t.* and *i.* To embark again. **re-embarkation** (-kā′ shŭn), *n.* **re-embattle** (rē ėm băt′l′), *v.t.* To array again for battle. **re-embody** (rė ėm bod′ i), *v.t.* To embody again. **re-embrace** (rē ėm brās′), *v.t.* To embrace again. *n.* A second embrace. **re-emerge** (rē ė mĕrj′), *v.i.* To emerge again. **re-emergence, re-emersion,** *n.* **re-emergent,** *a.* **re-enable** (rē ė nābl′), *v.t.* To make able again. **re-enact** (rē ė năkt′), *v.t.* To enact again. **re-enactment,** *n.* **re-endow** (rē ėn dou′), *v.t.* To endow again. **re-enforce** (rē ėn fôrs′), *v.t.* To give fresh or additional force or strength to; to strengthen a part, esp. a support; to reinforce. *n.* A reinforce. **re-engage** (rē ėn gāj′), *v.t.* and *i.* To engage again. **re-engagement,** *n.* **re-engine** (rē en′ jin), *v.t.* To furnish with new engines. **re-enlist** (rē ėn list′), *v.t.* and *i.* To enlist again. **re-enter** (rē en′ tėr), *v.t.* and *i.* To enter again. **re-entrance,** *n.* **re-entrant,** *a.* Re-entering, pointing inward. *n.* A re-entrant angle, esp. in fortification, opp. to salient. **re-entry,** *n.* The act of re-entering; a new entry in a book, etc.; (*Law*) re-entering upon possession. **re-erect** (rē ė rekt′), *v.t.* To erect again. **re-erection,** *n.*

***reermouse** [REREMOUSE].

reest (1) (rēst) [Sc. and North., etym. doubtful], *v.t.* To dry or smoke (bacon, fish, etc.), to cure. *v.i.* To become smoke-dried.

reest (2) (rēst) [Sc. and North., prob. var. of REST or a form of Sc. *arreest*, ARREST], *v.i.* To stop, to refuse to go on, to balk (of a horse, etc.). **reesty,** *a.*

re-establish (rē ės tăb′ lish) [RE-, ESTABLISH], *v.t.* To establish anew, to restore. **re-establisher,** *n.* **re-establishment,** *n.*

reeve (1) (rēv) [A.-S. *gerēfa*, etym. doubtful (not rel. to GRAF, GRAVE (4)], *n.* (*Hist.*) A chief officer or magistrate of a town or district, holding office usually under the king but sometimes by election; (*Canada*) the presiding officer of a township or village council; *a bailiff, a steward.

reeve (2) (rēv) [prob. from Dut. *reven*, to REEF (2)], *v.t.* (*past* & *p.p.* **rove, reeved**) (*Naut.*) To pass (the end of a rope, a rod, etc.) through a ring, a hole in a block, etc.; to fasten (a rope, etc.) round some object by this means.

reeve (3) (rēv) [etym. obscure, cp. RUFF (2)], *n.* The female of the ruff.

re-examine (rē ėg zăm′ in) [RE-, EXAMINE], *v.t.* To examine again. **re-examination** (-nā′ shŭn), *n.* **re-exchange** (rē eks chānj′), *v.t.* To exchange again. *n.* (*Comm.*) A renewed exchange; the difference in the value of a bill of exchange occasioned by its being dishonoured in a foreign country where it was payable. **re-exhibit** (rē ėg zib′ it), *v.t.* To exhibit again. **re-exist** (rē ėg zist′), *v.t.* To exist again. **re-existence,** *n.* **re-existent,** *a.* **re-export** (rē ėk spôrt′), *v.t.* To export again; to export after having been imported; *n.* (-ek′ spôrt). A commodity re-exported. **re-exportation** (-tā′ shŭn), *n.* **reface** (rē fās′), *v.t.* To put a new face or surface on. **refacing,** *n.* **refashion** (rė făsh′ ŭn), *v.t.* To fashion anew. **refashioner,** *n.* **refashionment,** *n.* **refasten** (rē fasn′), *v.t.* To fasten again.

refection (rė fek′ shŭn) [F. *réfection*, L. *refectiōnem*, nom. *-tio* (RE-, FACTION)], *n.* Refreshment by food; a light meal, a repast. **refect** (rė fekt′), *v.t.* To refresh with food; to restore after fatigue. **refective,** *a.* and *n.* **refectory,** *n.* A room or hall where meals are taken in religious houses, etc.

refer (rė fĕr′) [O.F. *referer*, L. *referre* (RE-, *ferre*, to bear)], *v.t.* (*past* & *p.p.* **referred**) To trace back, to assign (to a certain cause, source, class, place, etc.); to hand over (for consideration and decision); to send or direct (a person) for information, etc.; to commit (oneself) to another's favour, etc. *v.i.* To apply for information; to appeal, to have recourse; to cite, to allude, to direct attention (to); to be concerned with, to have relation (to). **referable** (ref′ ėr ȧbl), *a.* **referential** (ref ėr en′ shȧl), *a.* ***referment,** *n.* **referrible** [REFERABLE]. **referred sensation:** Pain or other sensation localized at a different point from the part actually causing it.

referee (ref ė rē′), *n.* One to whom a point or question is referred; a person to whom a matter in dispute is referred for settlement or decision, an arbitrator, an umpire. *v.i.* To act as a referee (in football, etc.).

reference (ref′ ėr ėns), *n.* The act of referring; relation, respect, correspondence; allusion, directing of attention (to); a note or mark referring from a book to another work or from the text to a commentary, diagram, etc.; that which is referred to; a person referred to for information, evidence of character, etc., a referee; a testimonial. *v.t.* (*usu. in p.p.*) To furnish (a work) with cross-references, references to authorities, etc. **cross-reference** [CROSS (1)]. **in** *or* **with reference to:** With regard to, as regards, concerning. **without reference to:** Irrespective of, regardless of. **reference Bible:** A Bible with cross-references in the margin. **work** or **book of reference:** An encyclopædia, dictionary, or the like, consulted when occasion requires, not for continuous reading. ***referendary** (-en′ dȧr i), *n.* A referee; an adviser, an assessor; an officer in a papal, royal, or imperial Court who formerly delivered answers to petitions, etc. **reference library:** A library where books may be consulted but not borrowed.

referendum (ref er en′ dum), *n.* The submission of a political question to the whole electorate for a direct decision by general vote.

reffo (ref′ ō) [REFUGEE], *n.* (*Austral. colloq.*) A political refugee from Europe.

***refigure** (rē fig′ ŭr) [RE-, FIGURE], *v.t.* To figure or represent anew. **refill** (rē fil′), *v.t.* To fill again. *n.* (rē′ fil) That which is used to refill; a fresh fill (as of lead for a pocket-pencil, tobacco for a pipe, etc.). **refind** (rē fīnd′), *v.t.* To find again.

refine (rė fīn′) [RE-, FINE (2)], *v.t.* To clear from impurities, defects, etc., to purify, to clarify; to free from coarseness, to educate, to polish, to cultivate the taste, manners, etc., of; to make (a statement, idea, etc.) more subtle, complex, or abstract; to transform or modify into a subtler or more abstract form. *v.i.* To become pure or clear; to become polished or more highly cultivated in talk, manners, etc.; to affect subtlety of thought or language; to draw subtle distinctions (upon). **refinable,** *a.* **refined,** *a.* Freed from impurities; highly cultivated, elegant, polished. **refinedly** (-ĕd li), *adv.* **refinedness,** *n.*

refinement (rė fīn′ mėnt), *n.* The act or process of refining; the state of being refined; elegance of taste, manners, language, etc.; high culture, polish; elaboration (of luxury, etc.); affected subtlety; a subtle distinction or piece of reasoning.

refiner (rė fī′ nėr), *n.* One who refines, esp. a person whose business it is to refine metals, etc.; an apparatus for purifying coal-gas, etc.; one who invents superfluous subtleties or distinctions. **refinery,** *n.*

refit (rē fit′), *v.t.* To make fit for use again, to repair, to fit out anew (esp. a ship). *v.i.* To repair damages (of ships). *n.* The repairing or renewing of what is damaged or worn out, esp. the repairing of a ship. **refitment,** *n.*

reflect (rė flekt′) [L. *reflectere* (RE-, *flectere*, to bend), p.p. *reflexus*], *v.t.* To turn or throw (light, heat, sound, an electric body, etc.) back, esp. in accordance with certain physical laws; to mirror, to throw back an image of; (*fig.*) to reproduce exactly, to correspond in features or effects; to cause to accrue or to cast (honour, disgrace, etc.) upon; *to bend, fold, or turn back. *v.i.* To throw back light, heat, sound, etc.; to turn the thoughts back, to think, to ponder, to meditate; to remind oneself (that); to bring shame or discredit (upon). **to reflect on:** To cast censure or blame upon. **reflectible,** *a.* **reflectingly,** *adv.* Casting censure or reflections (upon); reproachfully. **reflection, *reflexion,** *n.* The act of reflecting; the state of being reflected; that which is reflected; rays of light, heat, etc. or an image thrown back from a reflecting surface; reconsideration; the action or process by which the mind takes cognizance of its own operations; continued consideration, thought, meditation; a thought, idea, comment, or opinion resulting from deliberation; censure, reproach (brought or cast upon, etc.); that which entails censure or reproach (upon); reflex action. **reflectional,** *a.* **reflectionless,** *a.* **reflective,** *a.* Throwing back an image, rays of light, heat, etc.; pertaining to or concerned with thought or reflection; meditative, thoughtful; taking cognizance of mental operations; *(*Gram.*) reflexive; *reflected; *reflex, reciprocal. **reflectively,** *adv.* **reflectiveness,** *n.* **reflector,** *n.* One who or that which reflects, esp. a reflecting surface that throws back rays of light, heat, etc., usu. a polished, concave surface, as in a lamp, lighthouse, telescope, surgical or other instrument, etc.; (*fig.*) any one or anything that reflects or reproduces impressions, feelings, etc. **reflecting telescope:** (*Astron.*) A telescope in which the object glass is replaced by a polished reflector, from which the image is magnified by an eye-piece.

reflex (rē′ fleks) [L. *reflexus*, p.p. of *reflectere*, to reflect (whence late L. *reflexus -ūs*, a reflex)], *a.* Turned backward; introspective; reactive, turned back upon itself, or the source, agent, etc.; (*Bot.*) bent back, recurved; (*Painting*) reflected, lighted by reflected light; (*Physiol.*) produced independently of the will under stimulus from impressions on the sensory nerves; (*Gram.*) reflexive. *n.* A reflection; a reflected image, reproduction, or secondary manifestation; a reflex action; reflected light, colour, etc.; (*Painting*) a part of a picture represented as illuminated by the reflected light or colour of other parts. *v.t.* (rė fleks′) To bend or fold back, to recurve; *to reflect. **conditioned reflex,** *n.* (*Psych.*) A behaviouristic mechanism or reaction by which the emotions may be organized in the education of an individual. **reflex action,** *n.* The involuntary contraction of a muscle in response to stimulus from without the body. **reflex camera,** *n.* (*Phot.*) A camera in which the main lens is used as a view-finder. **reflexible,** *a.* **reflexibility** (-bil′ i ti), *n.* ***reflexity,** *n.* **reflexive,** *a.* (*Gram.*) Denoting action upon the agent; implying action by the subject upon itself or himself; referring back to the grammatical subject; reflective. **reflexive verb:** A verb that has for its direct object a pronoun which stands for the agent or subject. **reflexively,** *adv.* **reflexiveness,** *n.* **reflexly,** *adv.*

reflexion [REFLECT].

refloat (rē flōt′), *v.t.* and *i.* To float again. **reflorescence** (rē flō res′ ėns), *n.* A second florescence. **reflorescent,** *a.* **reflourish** (rē flŭr′ish) [RE-, FLOURISH], *v.i.* To flourish anew. **reflow** (rē flō′), *v.i.* To flow back; to ebb. *n.* A reflowing, a reflux; the ebb (of the tide). **reflower** (rē flou′ ėr), *v.i.* To flower again.

refluent (ref′ lu̇ ėnt) [L. *refluens -ntem*, pres.p. of *refluere* (RE-, *fluere*, to flow)], *a.* Flowing back; ebbing. **refluence,** *n.* **reflux** (rē′ flŭks), *n.* A flowing back; a return, an ebb.

refold (rē fōld′), *v.t.* To fold again. **refoot** (rē fut′), *v.t.* To put a new foot to (a stocking, etc.). **reforest** (rē for′ ėst), *v.t.* To reafforest. **reforestation** (-tā′ shŭn), *n.* **reforge** (rē fôrj′), *v.t.* To forge over again; to refashion.

reform (rė fôrm′) [F. *reformer*, L. *reformāre*], *v.t.* To change from worse to better by removing faults, imperfections, abuses, etc.; to improve, to amend, to redress, to cure, to remedy. *v.i.* To amend one's habits, morals, conduct, etc.; to abandon evil habits, etc. *n.* The act of reforming; an alteration for the better, amendment, improvement, reformation, correction of abuses, etc., esp. in parliamentary representation. **Reform Acts,** *n.pl.* Acts passed in 1832, 1867, and 1884 for enlarging the electorate and reforming the constitution of the House of Commons. **reform school,** *n.* (*Am.*) A reformatory. **reformable,** *a.*

re-form (rē fôrm′), *v.t.* To form again or anew. **re-formation** (rē fôr mā′ shŭn), *n.* **reformer,** *n.*

***reformado** (ref ŏr mā′ dō), ***reformade** [Sp., from L. *reformātus*, p.p. of *reformāre*, to REFORM (1), *reformado*], *n.* (*Mil.*) An officer deprived of his command by the disbanding or re-forming of his company, but retaining his rank and usu. his pay; a volunteer serving without a commission but with the rank of officer.

reformation (ref ŏr mā′ shŭn) [F., from L. *reformātiōnem*, nom. *-tio*, from *reformāre*, to REFORM (1)], *n.* The act of reforming; the state of being reformed; redress of grievances or abuses, esp. a thorough change or reconstruction in politics, society, or religion. **the Reformation:** The great religious revolution in the 16th cent. which resulted in the establishment of the Protestant Churches. **reformational,** *a.* **reformative** (rė fôr′ mȧ tiv), *a.* Tending to produce reformation. **reformatory,** *a.* Reformative. *n.* An institution for the detention and reformation of juvenile offenders.

reformed (rė fôrmd′), *a.* Corrected, amended, purged of errors and abuses. **Reformed Church:** One of the Protestant Churches that adopted Calvinistic doctrines and polity, distinguished from Lutheran Churches.

reformer (re fôr′ mėr), *n.* One who effects a reformation; one who favours political reform; one who took a leading part in the Reformation of the 16th cent. ***reformist,** *n.*

refortify (rē fôr′ ti fī), *v.t.* To fortify anew. **refound** (rē found), *v.t.* To found anew, to recast.

refract (rė frăkt′) [L. *refractus*, p.p. of *refringere* (RE-, *frangere*, to break)], *v.t.* To deflect or turn (a ray of light, etc.) from its direct course (of water, glass, or other medium differing in density from that through which the ray has passed). **refracted,** *a.* Deflected from a direct course, as a ray of light or heat; (*Bot., Zool., etc.*) bent back at an acute angle. **refraction,** *n.* The deflection that takes place when a ray of light, heat, etc. passes at any other angle than a right angle from the surface of one medium into another medium of different density. **astronomical refraction:** The deflection of a luminous ray proceeding from a heavenly body not in the zenith to the eye of a spectator on the earth, due to the refracting power of the atmosphere. **double refraction:** The splitting of a ray of light, heat, etc. into two polarized rays which may be deflected differently on entering certain materials, *e.g.* most crystals. **refractional, refractive,** *a.* **refractor,** *n.* A refracting medium, lens, or telescope. **refracting telescope:** (*Astron.*) The earliest form of telescope, in which the image of an object is received direct through a converging lens and magnified by an eye-piece.

refractory (rė frăk′ tȯr i) [L. *refractārius*, as prec.], *a.* Perverse, contumacious, obstinate in opposition or disobedience, unmanageable; (*Med.*) not amenable to ordinary treatment; (*Metal.*) not easily fused or reduced, not easily worked; (*Psychophysiology*) tardily responsive to stimulus (of nerves, etc.). *n.* A piece of refractory ware used in a kiln with a flux for glazing pottery; *a refractory person. **refractorily,** *adv.* **refractoriness,** *n.*

refracture (rē frăk′ tyủr), *v.t.* To fracture again.

***refragable** (ref′ rȧ gȧbl) [med. L. *refragābilis* from L. *refragārī*, see IRREFRAGABLE], *a.* Refutable. ***refragability** (-bil′ i ti), *n.*

refrain (1) (rė frān′) [O.F., from *refraindre*, pop. L. *refrangere*, L. *refringere*, to REFRACT], *n.* The burden of a song, a phrase or line usu. repeated at the end of every stanza.

refrain (2) (rė frān′) [O.F. *refrener*, L. *refrēnāre* (RE-, *frēnum*, bit, curb)], *v.t.* To hold back, to restrain, to curb (oneself, one's tears, etc.). *v.i.* To forbear; to abstain (from an act or doing). ***refrainment,** *n.*

reframe (rē frām′), *v.t.* To frame again, to fashion anew.

refrangible (rė frăn′ jibl) [pop. L. *refrangibilis*, from *refrangere*, see REFRAIN (1)], *a.* Capable of being refracted. **refrangibility** (-bil′ i ti), ***refrangibleness,** *n.*

refresh (rė fresh′) [O.F. *refreschir*], *v.t.* To make fresh again; to reanimate, to reinvigorate; to revive or restore after depression, fatigue, etc.; to freshen up (one's memory); to restore, to repair; (*colloq.*) to give (esp. liquid) refreshments to; *to give a sensation of coolness to. *v.i.* (*colloq.*) To take (esp. liquid) refreshment. **refresher,** *n.* One who or that which refreshes; an extra fee paid to counsel when a case is adjourned or continued from one term or sitting to another; (*colloq.*) a drink. **refresher course:** A course to bring up to date knowledge of a particular subject. **refreshing,** *a.* Reinvigorating, reanimating. **refreshingly,** *adv.* **refreshingness,** *n.* **refreshment,** *n.* The act of refreshing; the state of being refreshed; that which refreshes, esp. (*pl.*) food or drink. **refreshment room:** A room at a railway station, etc. for the supply of refreshments.

refrigerate (rė frij′ ėr āt) [L. *refrīgerātus*, p.p. of *refrīgerāre* (RE-, *frīgus -goris*, cold)], *v.t.* To make cool or cold; to freeze or keep at a very low temperature in a refrigerator, so as to preserve in a fresh condition. **refrigerant,** *a.* Cooling, allaying heat. *n.* That which cools or refreshes; a medicine for allaying fever or inflammation. **refrigeration** (-ā′ shŭn), *n.* **refrigerative** (rė frij′ ėr ȧ tiv), *a.* and *n.*

refrigerator (rė frij′ e rā tȯr), *n.* An apparatus for keeping meat and other provisions in a frozen state or at a very low temperature, in order to preserve their freshness. **refrigeratory,** *a.* Cooling. *n.* A vessel attached to a still for condensing vapour; a refrigerator.

refringent (rė frin′ jėnt) [L. *refringens -ntem*, pres.p. of *refringere*, to REFRACT], *a.* Refractive. **refringency,** *n.*

reft, *past & p.p.* [REAVE].

refuge (ref′ ūj) [F., from L. *refugium* (RE-, *fugium*, from *fugere*, to flee)], *n.* Shelter or protection from danger or distress; a place, thing, person, or course of action that shelters or protects from danger, distress, or calamity; a stronghold, a retreat, a sanctuary, a house of refuge; an expedient, a subterfuge; a raised area in the middle of a road forming a safe place for crossers to halt at. *v.t.* To give refuge to. *v.i.* To take refuge. **city of refuge:** (*Bibl.*) One of six cities in the Holy Land appointed as places of refuge to one who had unintentionally committed manslaughter. **house of refuge:** A charitable institution for the destitute and homeless.

refugee (ref ū jē′), *n.* One who flees to a place of refuge, esp. one who takes refuge in a foreign country in time of war or persecution or political commotion.

refulgent (rė fŭl′ jėnt) [L. *refulgens -ntem*, pres.p. of *refulgēre* (RE-, *fulgēre*, to shine)], *a.* Shining brightly, brilliant, radiant, splendid. **refulgence, *-gancy,** *n.* **refulgently,** *adv.*

refund (rė fŭnd′) [L. *refundere*, to pour back (RE-, *fundere*, see FOUND (1))], *v.t.* To pay back, to repay, to restore; to reimburse. *v.i.* To make repayment. *n.* (rē′ fŭnd). **refunder,** *n.* **refundment,** *n.*

refurbish (rē fĕr′ bish), *v.t.* To furbish up anew. **refurnish** (rē fĕr′ nish), *v.t.* To furnish anew; to supply with new furniture.

refusal (rė fūz′ ȧl), *n.* The act of refusing; denial of anything solicited, demanded, or offered; the choice or option of taking or refusing something before it is offered to others.

refuse (1) (rė fūz′) [O.F. *refuser*, prob. through a pop. L. *refūsāre*, from L. *refundere*, see REFUND, p.p. *refūsus*], *v.t.* To decline to do, yield, grant, etc.; to deny the request of; to decline to jump over (a ditch, etc.); to fail to take, to repel (a dye, etc.); *to disown. *v.i.* To decline to comply; to fail to jump (of a horse); (*Cards*) to be unable to follow suit. ***refusable,** *a.*

refuse (2) (ref′ ūs) [prob. O.F. *refus*, *refuse*, p.p. of prec.], *a.* Refused, rejected; valueless. *n.* That which is refused or rejected as worthless; waste or useless matter. **refuse tip:** A place where refuse is heaped or disposed of, (*Am.* a dump).

re-fuse (rē fūz′), *v.t.* To fuse or melt again. **refusion** (rē fū′ zhŭn), *n.*

refute (rė fūt′) [F. *refuter*, L. *refūtāre*, see CONFUTE], *v.t.* To prove (a statement, argument, etc.) false or erroneous, to disprove; to prove wrong, to rebut in argument, to confute. **refutable** (ref′ ū-, rė fū′ tȧbl), *a.* **refutal, refutation** (-tā′ shŭn), *n.* **refutatory** (-fū′ tȧ tȯr i), *a.* **refuter,** *n.*

regain (rė gān′) [F. *regagner* (RE-, GAIN (1))], *v.t.* To recover possession of; to reach again; to gain anew, to recover.

regal (1) (rē′ gȧl) [L. *rēgālis*, from *rex rēgis*, king], *a.* Pertaining to or fit for a king, or kings. *n.* Kingly, royal, magnificent. **regally,** *adv.*

***regal (2)** (rē′ gȧl) [F. *régale*, perh. from prec.], *n.* A small portable reed-organ held in the hands, in use in the 16th and 17th cents. (*often in pl. form, as a pair of regals*).

regale (rė gāl′) [F. *régaler*, It. *regalare*, etym. doubtful], *v.t.* To entertain sumptuously; to delight, to gratify (with something rich or choice). *v.i.* To feast, to fare sumptuously (on). **n.* A choice repast, a feast, a sumptuous entertainment. **regalement,** *n.* **regaler,** *n.*

regalia (1) (rė gā′ li ȧ) [L., neut. pl. of *rēgālis*, REGAL (1)], *n.pl.* *The prerogatives and rights of a sovereign; the insignia of royalty, esp. the emblems worn or displayed in coronation ceremonies, etc.

regalia (2) (rė gā′ li ȧ) [Sp., royal privilege, as prec.], *n.* A Cuban cigar of superior quality.

regalism (rē′ gȧ lizm), *n.* The doctrine of the royal supremacy in ecclesiastical affairs. **regality** (rė găl′ i ti), *n.* Royalty, kingship; sovereign jurisdiction; an attribute of royalty; (*Sc.*) a territorial distinction formerly conferred on a noble by the king; a monarchical state, a kingdom.

regally [REGAL (1)].

regard (rė gard′) [F. *regarder*], *v.t.* To look at, to observe, to notice; to give heed to, to pay attention to, to take into account; to value, to pay honour to, to esteem; to look upon or view in a specified way or with fear, reverence, etc., to consider (as); to concern; to affect, to relate to. *v.i.* To look; to pay attention. *n.* A look, a gaze; observant attention, heed, care, consideration; esteem, kindly or respectful feeling; reference, relation; (*pl.*) compliments, good wishes. **as regards:** Regarding. **in** or **with regard to:** Regarding; as touching. ***regardable,** *a.* **regardant,** *a.* (*Her.*) Looking backward; observant, watchful. **regarder,** *n.* **regardful,** *a.* **regardfully,** *adv.* **regardfulness,** *n.* **regarding,** *prep.* Respecting, concerning. **regardless,** *a.* Heedless, careless, negligent. *adv.* (*colloq.*) Regardless of expense, lavishly dressed. **regardlessly,** *adv.* **regardlessness,** *n.*

regather (rē găth′ ėr), *v.t.* and *i.* To gather or collect again.

regatta (rė găt′ ȧ) [It., orig. contention], *n.* A race-meeting at which yachts or boats contend for prizes.

regelate (rē jė lāt′) [RE-, L. *gelātus*, p.p. of *gelāre*, to freeze], *v.i.* To freeze together again; to unite into a mass by freezing together (of fragments of ice, snow, etc.) with moist surfaces in contact at a temperature not lower than 32° F (0° C). **regelation** (-lā shŭn), *n.*

regency (rē′ jėn si) [REGENT], *n.* *Rule, government, control; the office, commission, or government of a regent; a body entrusted with the office or duties of a regent; the period of office of a regent or a body so acting. **the Regency:** (*Eng. Hist.*) The period (1810–20) when George, Prince of Wales, was regent for George III.

regenerate (rė jen′ ėr āt) [L. *regenerātus*, p.p. of *regenerāre* (RE-, *generāre*, to GENERATE)], *v.t.* To change fundamentally and reform the moral and spiritual nature of; to impart fresh vigour or higher life to; to generate anew, to give new existence to; (*Theol.*) to cause to be born again, to renew the heart of by the infusion of divine grace; to convert. *a.* (-ăt) Regenerated, renewed; reformed, converted. **regeneracy, regenerateness, regeneration** (-ā′ shŭn), *n.* **baptismal regeneration:** (*Theol.*) Spiritual regeneration or new birth as the consequence of baptism. **regenerative** (-jen′ ėr ȧ tiv), **regeneratory,** *a.* **regeneratively,** *adv.*

regenerator (rē jen′ ėr ā tŏr), *n.* One who or that which regenerates; a device in furnaces, hot-air engines, and gas-burners, by which the waste heat is applied to the incoming current of air or combustible gas. **regeneratrix,** *n.*

regenesis (rē jen′ ė sis), *n.* The state of being born again or reproduced.

regent (rē′ jėnt) [F., from L. *regentem*, nom. *-gens*, pres.p. of *regere*, to rule], *a.* Exercising the authority of regent; *governing, ruling, controlling. *n.* A person appointed to govern a kingdom during the minority, absence, or disability of a sovereign; *(*Oxf. and Camb.*) a Master of Arts presiding over deputations, etc.; (*Am.*) a member of the governing body of a State University; *a ruler, a governor. **regentess,** *n.* **regent bird** or **oriole:** An Australian bower-bird, *Sericulus melinus*, having beautiful plumage. **regentship,** *n.*

regerminate (rē jĕr′ mi nāt), *v.i.* To germinate anew. **regermination** (-nā′ shŭn), *n.*

***regest** (rė jest′) [late L. *regesta*, neut. pl. p.p. of *regerere* (RE-, *gerere*, to carry on)], *n.* A register.

regicide (rej′ i sīd) [F. *régicide* (L. *rex rēgis*, king, -CIDE)], *n.* The killing or one who takes part in the killing of a king. **the Regicides:** Those taking part in the trial and execution of Charles I (1649). **regicidal** (-sī′ dȧl), *a.*

Régie (rā zhē′) [F., from *régir*, L. *regere*, see REGENT], *n.* The revenue department in some Continental States having sole control of the importation of tobacco, and sometimes of salt.

regild (rē gild′), *v.t.* To gild again.

regime (rė zhēm′) [F. *régime*, L. REGIMEN], *n.* Mode, conduct, or prevailing system of government or management; the prevailing social system or general state of things. ***ancien régime*** (an syan rā zhēm): The system of government and society prevailing in France before the Revolution of 1789.

regimen (rej′ i mėn) [L., from *regere*, to rule], *n.* (*Med.*) The systematic management of food, drink, exercise, etc., for the preservation or restoration of health; *rule, orderly government; (*Gram.*) the syntactical dependence of one word on another, government, *a regime, a prevailing system of government.

regiment (rej′ i mėnt) [F., from L. *regimentum*, as prec.], *n.* A body of soldiers forming the largest permanent unit of the army, usu. divided into two battalions comprising several companies or troops, and commanded by a colonel; *rule, government; *regimen. *v.t.* (rej′ i ment) To form into a regiment or regiments; to organize into a system of bodies or groups. **regimental** (-men′ tȧl), *a.* Of or pertaining to a regiment. *n.pl.* Military uniform. **regimentally,** *adv.* **regimentation** (-tā′ shŭn), *n.* Organization into a regiment or a system of groups, etc.

regina (rė jī nȧ) [L., fem. of *rex rēgis*, king], *n.* A reigning queen. **reginal,** *a.*

region (rē′ jŭn) [A.-F. *regiun*, L. *regiōnem*, nom. *-gio*, from *regere*, to rule, to direct], *n.* A tract of land, sea, space, etc., of large but indefinite extent having certain prevailing characteristics, as of fauna or flora; a part of the world or the physical or spiritual universe (*often in pl.*); a district, a sphere, a realm; a civil division of a town or district; one of the strata into which the atmosphere or the sea may be divided; a part of the body surrounding an organ, etc. **the infernal, lower,** or **nether regions:** Hell, Hades, the realm of the dead. **upper regions:** The higher strata of the atmosphere or the sea; the sky; heaven. **regional,** *a.* **regionalism,** *n.* Sectionalism on a regional basis. **regionalist,** *n.* **regionalistic** (-lis′ tik), *a.* **regionally,** *adv.* **regionary** (rē′ jŏ nȧr i), *a.* Regional. *n.* An account of the regions of Rome. **regioned, regionic** (-jon′ ik), *a.*

register (rej′ is tėr) [F. *registre* or med. L. *registrum*, var. of *regestrum*, late L. *regesta*, pl. REGEST], *n.* An official written record; a book, roll, or other document in which such record is kept; an official or authoritative list of names, facts, etc., as of births, marriages, deaths, persons entitled to vote at elections, shipping, etc.; an entry in such a record or list; registration; a mechanical device for registering automatically the number of persons entering a public building, or the movements of a gauge or other instrument, a recording indicator; a contrivance for regulating the admission of air or heat to a room, ventilator, fire-place, etc.; the range or compass of a voice or instrument; a particular portion of this; a sliding device in an organ for controlling a set of pipes; (*Print.*) precise correspondence of lines, etc., on one side of the paper to those on the other; (*Colour-print.*) exact overlaying of the different colours used; (*Phot.*) correspondence of the surface of a sensitized film to that of the focusing-screen. *v.t.* To enter in a register; to record as in a register; to cause to be entered in a register, esp. (a letter, etc.) at a post office for special care in transmission and delivery; to record, to indicate (of an instrument); (*Print., Phot., etc.*) to cause to correspond precisely. *v.i.* To enter one's name in or as in a register; to express an emotion facially; (*Print, etc.*) to be in register; (*Artil.*) to carry out experimental shoots in order to ascertain the exact range. **in register:** Exactly corresponding (of printed matter, photographic and colour plates, etc.). **parish register** [PARISH]. **register office:** An office at which a register is kept. **registrable,** *a.* **registrant,** *n.* One registering, esp. a trade-mark, etc.

registrar (rej′ is trar), *n.* An official keeper of a register or record; an official charged with keeping registers of births, deaths, and marriages. **Registrar-General.** *n.* A public officer who superintends the registration of births, deaths, and marriages. **registrarship,** *n.* **registrary,** *n.* The registrar of Cambridge University. **registration** (-trā′ shŭn), *n.*

registry (rej′ is tri), *n.* An office or other place where a register is kept; registration; a register. **registry office:** An employment agency for domestic servants; a registrar's office where marriages, etc., are performed.

regium donum (rē′ ji ŭm dō′ nŭm) [L., royal gift]: An annual grant of public money formerly made in favour of the income of the Presbyterian clergy in Ireland (commuted 1869); a similar grant made at various dates to other Nonconformist clergy.

regius (rē′ ji ŭs) [L., royal from *rex rēgis*, king], *a.* Royal; appointed by the sovereign. **Regius Professor:** One of several professors at Oxford and Cambridge Universities whose chairs were founded by Henry VIII; or in Scottish Universities whose chairs were founded by the Crown.

reglet (reg′ lėt) [F. *réglet*, dim. of *règle*, L. *rēgula*, RULE], *n.* (*Print.*) A strip of wood, less than type high, used for separating pages, filling blank spaces, etc.; (*Arch.*) a flat, narrow band separating moulding, etc.

regma (reg′ må) [Gr. *rhēgma*, fracture], *n.* (*pl.* **-mata**) (*Bot.*) A dry fruit made up of several cells that dehisce when ripe. **regmacarp,** *n.* A dry dehiscent fruit.

regnal (reg′ nål) [med. L. *regnālis*, from *regnum*, see REIGN], *a.* Of or pertaining to a reign. **regnal day:** The anniversary of a sovereign's accession. **regnal year,** *n.* (*Law*) The year of a reign dating from the sovereign's accession (used in dating state documents). **regnant,** *a.* Reigning, ruling, exercising regal authority; predominant, prevalent. **regnancy,** *n.*

regorge (rē gôrj′), *v.t.* To disgorge, to vomit up; to swallow back again. *v.i.* To gush or flow back (from a river, etc.). ***regrade** (rė grād′) [L. *gradī*, to go], *v.i.* To go back, to retire. **regraft** (rē graft′), *v.t.* To graft again. **regrant** (rē grant′), *v.t.* To grant anew; *n.* A renewed or fresh grant.

regrate (rė grāt′) [O.F. *regrater* (F. *regratter*), (prob. RE-, *gratter*, to GRATE (2))], *v.t.* To buy up (corn, provisions, etc.) and sell again in the same or a neighbouring market so as to raise the prices. **regrater,** *n.*

regrede (rė grēd′) [L. *regredī* (RE-, *gradī*, to go), cp. REGRADE], *v.i.* To go back to retrograde.

regress (rē′ gres) [L. *regressus*, p.p. of *regredī*, to REGREDE], *n.* Passage back, return, regression. *v.i.* (rė gres′) To move back, to return. **regression** (rė gresh′ ŭn), *n.* Retrogradation; reversion to type; the turning back of a curve upon itself. **regressive,** *a.* **regressively,** *adv.* **regressiveness,** *n.*

regret (rė gret′) [F., from *regretter*, O.F. *regrater*, etym. doubtful], *n.* Distress or sorrow for a disappointment, loss, or want; grief, repentance, or remorse for a wrong-doing, fault, or omission (esp. in offering an apology); vexation, annoyance, disappointment. *v.t.* (*past & p.p.* **regretted)** To be distressed or sorry for (a disappointment, loss, etc.); to regard (a fact, action, etc.) with sorrow or remorse. **regretful,** *a.* **regretfully,** *adv.* **regretfulness,** *n.* **regrettable,** *a.* **regrettably,** *adv.*

regroup (rē groop′), *v.t.* To group again. **regrow** (rē grō′), *v.t.* To grow again. **regrowth,** *n.* **reguerdon** (rė gĕr′ dȯn), *v.t.* To reward, to recompense. *n.* Reward, recompense.

regulable [REGULATE].

regular (reg′ ū lår) [O.F. *reguler* (F. *régulier*), L. *rēgulāris*, from *rēgula*, rule], *a.* Conforming to or governed by rule, law, type, or principle; systematic, methodical, consistent, symmetrical, unvarying, harmonious, normal; acting, done, or happening in an orderly, uniform, constant, or habitual manner, not casual, fortuitous, or capricious; conforming to custom, etiquette, etc., not infringing conventions; duly authorized, properly qualified; (*Gram.*) conforming to the normal type of inflection; (*Math.*) governed throughout by the same law, following consistently the same process; (*Geom.*) having the sides and angles equal; (*Mil.*) belonging to the standing army, opp. to territorials, yeomanry, etc.; (*Eccles.*) belonging to a religious or monastic order; complete, thorough, out-and-out, unmistakable. *n.* A soldier belonging to a permanent army; one of the regular clergy; (*colloq.*) a person permanently employed or constantly attending (as a customer, etc.). **regularity** (-lăr′ i ti), *n.* **regularize,** *v.t.* **regularization** (-zā′ shŭn), *n.* **regularly,** *adv.*

regulate (reg′ ū lāt) [late L. *regulātus*, p.p. of *regulāre*, as prec.], *v.t.* To adjust, control, or order by rule; to subject to restrictions; to adjust to requirements, to put or keep in good order; to reduce to order. **regulable,** *a.* **regulation** (-lā′ shŭn), *n.* The act of regulating; the state of being regulated; a prescribed rule, order, or direction. *a.* (*colloq.*) Prescribed by regulation; formal, normal, accepted, ordinary, usual. **regulative** (reg′ ū lå tiv), *a.*

regulator (reg′ ū lā tȯr), *n.* One who or that which regulates; a clock keeping accurate time, used for regulating other timepieces; the lever of a watch or other contrivance for regulating or equalizing motion. **regulator valve,** *n.* (*Mach.*) A valve in a locomotive which controls the supply of steam to the cylinders.

regulus (reg′ ū lŭs) [L., dim. of *rex rēgis*, king, prob. applied to antimony on account of its readiness to combine with gold], *n.* (*Metal.*) The purer mass of a metal that sinks to the bottom when ore is being smelted, an intermediate product retaining to a greater or less extent the impurities of the ore; (*Ornith.*) a genus of warblers containing the crested wren; (*Astron.*) a star in the constellation Leo. **reguline,** *a.* (*Metal.*).

regurgitate (rė gĕr′ ji tāt) [med. L. *regurgitātus*, p.p. of *regurgitāre* (RE-, L. *gurges -gitis*, eddy, whirlpool)], *v.t.* To throw or pour back again. *v.i.* To gush or be poured back. **regurgitant,** *a.* **regurgitation** (-tā′ shŭn), *n.*

rehabilitate (rē hå bil′ i tāt), *v.t.* To restore to a former rank, position, office, or privilege, to reinstate; to re-establish one's character or reputation; to make fit after disablement, imprisonment, etc., for making a living or playing a part in the life of society. **rehabilitation** (-tā′ shŭn), *n.* Re-establishment of character or reputation; (*Med.*) the branch of occupational therapy which deals with the restoration of the maimed or unfit to a place in society. **rehandle** (rē hăndl′), *v.t.* To handle or deal with again. **rehash** (rē hăsh′), *v.t.* To work over again; to re-model, esp. in a perfunctory or ineffective manner. *n.* Something stated or presented under a new form.

rehear (rē hēr′), *v.t.* To hear a second time; (*Law*) to try over again. **rehearing,** *n.* A second hearing; (*Law*) a retrial.

rehearse (rė hĕrs′) [O.F. *rehereer*, to harrow over again (RE-, HEARSE)], *v.t.* To repeat, to recite; to relate, to recount, to enumerate; to recite or practise (a play, musical performance, part, etc.) before public performance. **rehearsal,** *n.* The act of rehearsing; a preparatory performance of a play, etc. **rehearser,** *n.*

reheat (rē hēt′), *v.t.* To heat again. **reheater,** *n.* An apparatus for reheating, esp. in an industrial process. **reheel** (rē hēl′), *v.t.* To heel (a stocking, etc.) again. **rehouse** (rē houz′), *v.t.* To house anew. **rehumanize** (rē hū′ må nīz), *v.t.* To humanize again. **rehypothecate** (rē hī poth′ ė kāt), *v.t.* To hypothecate again; to pledge again. **rehypothecation** (-kā′ shŭn), *n.*

rei [REIS (1)].

Reich (rīch) [G., kingdom], *n.* The German realm considered as an empire made up of subsidiary states. **Reichsrat** (rīchs′ rat), *n.* The old Austrian parliament.

Reichstag (rīchs′ tag) [G. (as prec., *tag*, day)], *n.* The parliament of the German Reich; the parliament of the Trans-leithan division of Austria and Hungary; *the Diet of the North German Confederation, etc.

reify (rē′ i fī) [L. *rēs*, *rĕī*, thing, -FY], *v.t.* To make concrete, to treat as real. **reification** (-kā′ shŭn), *n.*

reign (rān) [M.E. and O.F. *regne*, L. *regnum*, from *regere*, to rule], *n.* Supreme power, sovereignty, dominion; rule, sway, control, influence; the period during which a sovereign reigns; *a kingdom, realm, sphere. *v.i.* To exercise sovereign authority, to be a king or queen; to predominate, to prevail.

reignite (rē ig nīt′), *v.t.* To ignite again. **reillume, reillumine** (rē il ūm′, -ū′ min), *v.t.* To light up again, to illumine again. **reillumination** (-nā′ shŭn), *n.* **reimburse** (rē im bĕrs′), *v.t.* To repay (one who has spent money); to refund (expenses, etc.). **reimbursable,** *a.* **reimbursement,** *n.* **reimburser,** *n.* **reimplant** (rē im plant′), *v.t.* To implant again. **reimplantation** (-tā′ shŭn), *n.* **reimport** (rē im pôrt′), *v.t.* To import again after exportation. **reimportation** (-tā′ shŭn), *n.* **reimpose** (rē im pōz′), *v.t.* To impose again. **reimposition** (-zish′ ŭn), *n.* **reimpress** (rē im pres′), *v.t.* To impress anew. **reimpression** (-presh′ ŭn), *n.* **reimprint** (-print′), *v.t.* To imprint again; to reprint. **reimprison** (re im priz′ ŏn), *v.t.* To imprison again. **reimprisonment,** *n.*

rein (rān) [O.F. *rene*, *reine*, *resne* (F. *rêne*), prob. through a late L. *retina*, from L. *retinēre* (RE-, *tenere*, to hold)], *n.* A long narrow strip, usu. of leather, attached at each end to a bit for guiding and controlling a horse or other animal in riding or driving; (*fig.*) means of restraint or control (*often in pl.*). *v.t.* To check, to control, to manage with reins; to pull (in or up) with reins; (*fig.*) to govern, to curb, to restrain. *v.i.* To obey the reins. **to give rein** or **the reins to:** To leave unrestrained; to allow (a horse) to go its own way. **to take the reins:** To assume guidance, direction, office, etc. **reinsman,** *n.* (*Am.*) A driver [REINS].

reinaugurate (rē in aw′ gū rāt), *v.t.* To inaugurate anew. **reincarnate** (rē in kar′ nāt), *v.t.* To incarnate anew. **reincarnation** (-nā′ shŭn), *n.* Metempsychosis. **reincense** (rē in sens′), *v.t.* To incense anew. **reincite** (rē in sīt′), *v.t.* To incite anew. **reincorporate** (rē in kôr′ pŏ rāt), *v.t.* To incorporate again. **reincorporation** (-rā′ shŭn), *n.* ***reincrease** (rē in krēs′), *v.t.* and *i.* To increase again.

reindeer (rān′ dēr) [Icel. *hreinn* (in *hreindȳri*), -DEER], *n.* A deer, *Rangifer tarandus*, now inhabiting the sub-arctic parts of the northern hemisphere, domesticated for the sake of its milk and as a draught animal. **reindeer-lichen, -moss,** *n.* A lichen, *Cladonia rengiferina*, which forms the winter food of the reindeer.

reinfect (rē in fekt′), *v.t.* To infect again. **reinfection,** *n.*

reinforce (rē in fôrs′), *v.t.* To add new strength to; to strengthen or support with additional troops, ships, etc.; to strengthen by adding to the size, thickness, etc., to add a strengthening part; to enforce again. *n.* The thicker part of a gun, that next the breech; a reinforcing or strengthening part, band, etc. **reinforced concrete:** Concrete given great tensile strength by the incorporation of rods, etc., of iron, etc., ferro-concrete. **reinforcement,** *n.* The act of reinforcing; the state of being reinforced; anything that reinforces; additional troops, ships, etc. (*usu. in pl.*).

reinform (rē in fôrm′), *v.t.* To inform again; to invest with form again. **reinfuse** (rē in fūz′), *v.t.* To infuse again. **reingratiate** (rē in grā′ shi āt), *v.t.* To ingratiate (oneself) again. **reinhabit** (rē in hăb′ it), *v.t.* To inhabit again. **reink** (rē ink′), *v.t.* To ink again.

reinoculate (rē in ok′ ū lāt), *v.t.* To inoculate again. **reinoculation** (-lā′ shŭn), *n.*

***reins** (rānz) [O.F., from L. *rēnes*], *n.pl.* The kidneys; the loins (formerly supposed to be the seat of the affections and passions).

reinscribe (rē in skrīb′), *v.t.* To inscribe again. **reinsert** (rē in sĕrt), *v.t.* To insert again. **reinsertion,** *n.*

reinsman [REIN].

reinspect (rē in spekt′), *v.t.* To inspect again. **reinspection,** *n.* **reinspire** (rē in spīr′), *v.t.* To inspire again. **reinstall** (rē in stawl′), *v.t.* To install again. **reinstalment,** *n.* **reinstate** (rē in stāt′), *v.t.* To restore, to replace (in a former position, state, etc.); to replace, to repair (property damaged by fire, etc.). **reinstatement, reinstation,** *n.* **reinstruct** (rē in strukt′), *v.t.* To instruct again or in turn. **reinstruction,** *n.* **reinsure** (rē in shoor′), *v.t* To insure against insurance risks. **reinsurance,** *n.* **reinsurer,** *n.* **reintegrate** (rē in′ tĕ grāt), *v.t.* To redintegrate. **reintegration** (-grā′ shŭn), *n.* **reinter** (rē in tĕr′), *v.t.* To inter or bury again. **reinterment,** *n.* **reinterrogate** (rē in ter′ ŏ gāt), *v.t.* To interrogate again. ***reinthrone** (rē in thrōn′), *v.t.* To enthrone again, to replace on a throne. **reintroduce** (rē in trŏ dūs′), *v.t.* To introduce or bring back into again. **reintroduction** (-dŭk′ shŭn), *n.* **reinvent** (rē in vent′), *v.t.* To invent again. **reinvention,** *n.* **reinvest** (rē in vest′), *v.t.* To invest again. **reinvestment,** *n.* **reinvestigate** (rē in ves′ ti gāt), *v.t.* To investigate again. **reinvestigation** (-gā′ shŭn), *n.* **reinvigorate** (rē in vig′ ŏ rāt), *v.t.* To reanimate; to give fresh vigour to. **reinvigoration** (-ā′ shŭn), *n.* **reinvite** (rē in vīt), *v.t.* To invite again. **reinvolve** (rē in volv′), *v.t.* To involve again.

reis (1) (rās) [Port., sing. *ree*, *rei*, correctly REAL (2)], *n.pl.* A Portuguese and Brazilian money of account, the thousandth part of a milreis.

Reis (2) (rās) [Arab., from *rās*, head], *n.* A head, a chief, a governor; a captain of a boat, etc. ***Reis Effendi:*** The title of a former Turkish state officer acting as chancellor and minister of foreign affairs.

reissue (rē is′ ū, -ish′ ū), *v.t.* and *i.* To issue again. *n.* A second issue. **reissuable,** *a.*

***reiter** (rī′ tĕr) [G., from *reiten*, to RIDE], *n.* A German trooper or cavalry soldier, esp. in the religious wars of the 16th and 17th cents.

reiterate (rĕ it′ ĕr āt), *v.t.* To repeat again and again. **reiteratedly,** *adv.* **reiteration** (-ā′ shŭn), *n.* **reiterative** (-it′ ĕr ă tiv), *a.* Expressing or characterized by reiteration. *n.* A word or part of a word repeated so as to form a reduplicated word.

***reive, reiver** [REAVE].

reject (rĕ jekt′) [from F. *rejecter* (now *rejeter*) or L. *rējectus*, p.p. of *rēicere* (RE-, *jacere*, to throw)], *v.t.* To put aside, to discard, to cast off; to refuse to accept, receive, grant, etc., to deny (a request, etc.); to repel, to cast up again, to vomit. *n.* (rē′ jekt) Something that has been rejected. **rejectable,** *a.* **rejecter, -tor,** *n.* **rejection** (-jek′ shŭn), *n.* **rejective,** *a.* ***rejectment,** *n.* **rejectamenta,** *n.pl.* Matter rejected, refuse, excrements.

rejoice (rĕ jois′) [O.F. *rejoiss-*, pres.p. stem of *rejoir* (F. *rejouir*)], *v.t.* To make joyful, to gladden. *v.i.* To feel joy or gladness in a high degree; to be glad (that or to); to delight or exult (in); to express joy or gladness; to make merry. **rejoicer,** *n.* **rejoicing,** *n.* Joyfulness; the expression of joyfulness, making merry, celebrating a joyful event (*usu. in pl.*). **rejoicingly,** *adv.*

rejoin (rĕ join′) [F. *rejoin-*, stem of *rejoindre*], *v.t.* To join again; to join together again, to reunite after separation. *v.i.* To come together again; to answer to a reply, to retort; (*Law*) to answer a charge or pleading, esp. as the defendant to the plaintiff's replication. **rejoinder,** *n.* An answer to a reply a retort; a reply or answer in general; (*Law*) the answer of a defendant to the plaintiff's replication. ***rejoindure,** *n.*

rejoint (rē joint'), *v.t.* To reunite the joints of; to fill up the joints of (stone-, brick-work, etc.) with new mortar, to point. ***rejourn** (rė jĕrn'), *v.t.* To adjourn. **rejudge** (rē jŭj'), *v.t.* To judge again; to re-examine.

rejuvenate (rė joo' vė nāt) [RE-, L. *juvenis*, young, -ATE], *v.t.* To make young again. *v.i.* To become young again. **rejuvenation** (-nā' shŭn), *n.* **rejuvenator** (-joo' vė nā tör), *n.* **rejuvenesce** (rė joo vė nes'), *v.i.* To grow young again; (*Biol.*) to acquire fresh vitality (of cells). *v.t.* To give fresh vitality to. **rejuvenescence,** *n.* **rejuvenescent,** *a.* **rejuvenize** (-joo' vė nīz), *v.t.* and *i.*

rekindle (rē kin' dėl), *v.t.* To kindle again; (*fig.*) to inflame or rouse anew. *v.i.* To take fire again (*lit.* and *fig.*). **relabel** (rē lā' bėl), *v.t.* To label again. **relaid,** *past & p.p.* [RE-LAY (2)].

relais (rė lā') [F.], *n.* (*Fort.*) A narrow space between a rampart and the ditch, for keeping earth from falling into the latter.

reland (rē lănd'), *v.t.* and *i.* To land again.

relapse (rė lăps') [L. *relapsus*, p.p. of *relābī* (RE-, *lābi*, to slip)], *v.i.* To fall or slip back (into a former bad or vicious state or practice), esp. into illness after partial recovery; to fall away after moral improvement, conversion, or recantation. *n.* A falling or sliding back into a former bad state, esp. in a patient's state of health after partial recovery. **relapser,** *n.* **relapsing fever:** An epidemic infectious fever characterized by frequent relapses.

relate (rė lāt') [F. *relater*, med. L. *relātāre*, from *relātus*, p.p. of *referre*, see REFER], *v.t.* To tell, to narrate, to recount; to bring into relation or connexion (with); to ascribe to as source or cause, to show a relation (with). *v.i.* To have relation or regard (to); to refer (to). **relatable,** *a.* **related,** *a.* Connected or allied by blood or marriage. **relatedness,** *n.* **relater,** *n.*

relation (rė lā' shŭn), *n.* The act of relating; that which is related; a narrative, an account, a story; respect; the condition of being related or connected; the way in which a thing stands or is conceived in regard to another as dependence, independence, similarity, difference, correspondence, contrast, etc.; connexion by blood or marriage, kinship; a person so connected, a relative, a kinsman or kinswoman; (*Law*) the laying of an information before the Attorney-General by a person bringing an action. **relational,** *a.* Having, pertaining to, or indicating relation; having kinship. **relationally,** *adv.* **relationship,** *n.* The state of being related; connexion by blood, etc., kinship. **relationless,** *a.*

relative (rel' ȧ tiv) [F. *relatif*, *-tive*, L. *relatīvus*, as prec.], *a.* Being in relation to something, involving or implying relation, correlative; resulting from relation, proportioned to something else, comparative; not absolute but depending on relation to something else; having mutual relation, corresponding, related; relevant, pertinent, closely related (to); having reference, relating; (*Gram.*) referring or relating to another word, sentence, or clause, called the antecedent. *n.* A person connected by blood or marriage, a kinsman or kinswoman, a relation; (*Gram.*) a relative word, esp. a pronoun; (*Phil.*) something relating to or considered in relation to another thing, a relative term. **relatival** (-ti' vȧl), *n.* (*Gram.*) **relatively** (rel' ȧ tiv li), *adv.* In relation to something else; comparatively. **relativeness, relativity** (-tiv' i ti), *n.* **relativity of knowledge:** The doctrine that knowledge is of and through relations only. **relativity theory,** *n.* A theory enunciated by Albert Einstein founded on the postulate that velocity is relative, and developing the Newtonian conception of space, time, motion, and gravitation. **relativism,** *n.* (*Phil.*) The doctrine that existence is not absolute but relative to the thinking mind, relativity of knowledge. **relativist,** *n.*

relator (rė lā' tör), *n.* (*Law*) An informer, a complainant, esp. one who institutes proceedings by way of a relation or information to the Attorney-General; a relater.

relax (rė lăks') [L. *relaxāre* (RE-, *laxus*, LAX)], *v.t.* To slacken, to loosen; to allow to become less tense or rigid; to enervate, to enfeeble, to make languid; to make less strict or severe, to abate, to mitigate; to relieve from constipation; to relieve from strain or effort. *v.i.* To become less tense, rigid, stern, or severe; to grow less energetic; to take relaxation. ***relaxable,** *a.* **relaxant,** *a.* (*Med.*) Relaxing; *n.* A relaxing medicine. **relaxation** (rel ak sā' shŭn), *n.* The act of relaxing; the state of being relaxed; a diminution of tension, severity, application, or attention; cessation from work, indulgence in recreation, amusement; (*Law*) remission of a penalty, etc. **relaxative,** *a.*

relay (rė lā') [O.F. *relais*, from *relayer*, to relay, etym. doubtful], *n.* A supply of fresh horses, men, hounds, etc., to relieve others when tired; a supply of anything to be ready when required. *v.t.* (*Teleg.*) A contrivance for strengthening a current by means of a local battery in transmitting messages to an unusually long distance; (*Radio.*) to broadcast signals or a programme received from another station. **relay race,** *n.* (*Sport*) A race between teams each member of which runs a certain distance.

re-lay (rē lā'), *v.t.* To lay again.

release (rė lēs') [O.F. *relesser*, *relaisser*, var. of *relâcher*, L. *relaxāre*, to RELAX], *v.t.* To set free from restraint, to liberate; to deliver from pain, care, trouble, grief, or other evil; to free from obligation or penalty; to make information public; (*Law*) to surrender, to quit, to remit (a right, debt, claim, etc.). *n.* Liberation from restraint, pain, care, obligation, or penalty; a discharge from liability, responsibility, etc.; (*Law*) surrender or conveyance of property or right to another; the instrument by which this is carried out; (*Mach., etc.*) a handle, catch, or other device by which a piece of mechanism is released. ***releasable,** *a.* **releasee** (rė lē sē'), *n.* (*Law*) A person to whom property is released. ***releasement** (rė lēs' mėnt), *n.* **releaser,** *n.* **releasor,** *n.* (*Law*) One releasing property or a claim to another.

relegate (rel' ė gāt) [L. *relegātus*, p.p. of *relegāre* (RE-, *legāre*, to send)], *v.t.* To send away, to banish; to consign or dismiss (usu. to some inferior position, etc.); to refer, commit, or hand over (to). **relegable,** *a.* **relegation** (-gā' shŭn), *n.*

relent (rė lent') [etym. obscure, perh. through F. *ralentir*, to slacken; ult. from RE-, L. *lentus*, soft], *v.i.* To become less harsh, severe, or obdurate; to give way to compassion, to yield. ****v.t.*** To abate, to give up, to relinquish; to cause to relent; to repent. *n.* Relenting; slackening or remission of speed. **relentingly,** *adv.* **relentless,** *a.* Merciless, pitiless. **relentlessly,** *adv.* **relentlessness,** *n.*

re-let (rē let'), *v.t.* To let again.

relevant (rel' ė vȧnt) [med. L. *relevans -ntem*, orig. pres.p. of L. *relavāre* (RE-, *levāre*, to raise)], *a.* Pertinent, applicable, bearing on the matter in hand, apposite; (*Sc. Law*) legally sufficient. **relevance, -cy,** *n.* **relevantly,** *adv.*

reliable (rė lī' ȧbl), *a.* That may be relied on; trustworthy. **reliability** (-bil' i ti), **reliableness,** *n.* **reliably,** *adv.* **reliance** (rė lī' ȧns), *n.* Confident dependence (upon), trust; a ground of confidence. **reliant,** *a.*

relic (rel' ik) [O.F. *relique*, L. *reliquiæ*, pl., remains, as foll.], *n.* Some part or thing remaining after loss or decay of the rest, a remnant, a fragment, a scrap, a survival, a trace; something remaining or kept in remembrance of a person, esp. a part of the body or other object religiously cherished from its having belonged to some saint; a keepsake, a souvenir, a memento; (*pl.*) a dead body, a corpse, remains. **relic-monger,** *n.* One who trades in relics.

relict (rel' ikt) [O.F. *relicte* or L. *relicta*, p.p. of *relinquere* (RE-, *linquere*, to leave)], *n.* A widow; *a survivor, a survival, a relic. ***relicted** (rė lik′ tėd), *a.* (*Law*) Left uncovered by the recession of water (of land). ***reliction,** *n.*

relief (1) (rė lēf′) [O.F. *relef*, from *relever*, to RELIEVE], *n.* Alleviation of pain, grief, discomfort, etc.; that which alleviates; assistance given to people in poverty or distress, esp. under the Poor Law; redress of a grievance, etc., esp. by legal remedy; release from a post or duty by a person or persons acting as substitute; such a substitute; assistance in time of stress or danger, raising of the siege of a besieged town; an army or detachment carrying this out; (*fig.*) anything that breaks monotony or relaxes tension. **comic relief:** Dialogue, incidents, or scenes of a comic nature alleviating the stress in a tragic play or story. **indoor, outdoor relief,** *n.* Poor-relief given in the workhouse or at home. **relief works:** Public works organized for the unemployed, refugees, etc.

relief (2) (rė lēf′) [It. *rilievo*, from *rilevare*, L. *relevāre*, to RELIEVE, assim. to prec.], *n.* The projecting of carved or moulded figures or designs from a surface in approximate proportion to the objects represented; a piece of sculpture, moulding, etc., with the figures, etc. projecting; (*Painting*) apparent projection of forms and figures due to drawing, colouring, and shading; distinctness of contour, clearness, vividness. **relief-map,** *n.* One in which hills and valleys are shown by prominences and depressions (usu. in exaggerated proportion) instead of contour-lines. **relief-printing,** *n.* Printing by letterpress or blocks as dist. from lithography.

relieve (rė lēv′) [O.F. *relever*, L. *relevāre* (RE-, *levāre*, to raise, from *levis*, light)], *v.t.* To alleviate, mitigate, to relax, to lighten; to free wholly or partially from pain, grief, discomfort, etc.; to remove a grievance from, esp. by course of law or by legislation; to release from a post, duty, responsibility, etc., esp. to take turn on guard; to raise the siege of; (*colloq.*) to take away, to deprive one of; to break or mitigate monotony, dullness, etc.; to give relief or prominence to, to bring out or make conspicuous by contrast. **to relieve nature:** To defecate. **relievable,** *a.* **relievo** [RILIEVO]. **reliever,** *n.* **relieving arch:** One constructed in a wall to take the weight off a part underneath. **relieving-officer,** *n.* An officer appointed by the guardians to superintend the relief of the poor in a parish or union.

relight (rē līt′), *v.t.* To light, kindle, or illumine afresh. *v.i.* To take fire again.

religieuse (rė lē zhėrz) [F., RELIGIOUS], *n.* A nun. ***religieux*** (rė lē zhėr), *n.* A monk.

religion (rė lij′ ŭn) [A.-F. *religiun* (F. *religion*), L. *religiōnem*, nom. *-gio*, perh. rel. to *religāre*, to bind (acc. to Skeat from *religens*, fearing the gods, opp. to *negligens*, NEGLIGENT)], *n.* Belief in a superhuman being or beings, esp. a personal God, controlling the universe and entitled to worship and obedience; the feelings, effects on conduct, and the practices resulting from such belief; a system of faith, doctrine, and worship; (*colloq.*) spiritual awakening, conversion; (*fig.*) devotion, sense of obligation; (*Eccles.*) the monastic state, the state of being bound by religious vows. **to get religion:** To be converted. ***religionary,** *a.* **religionism,** *n.* A profession or affectation of religion, the outward practice of religion; excessive or exaggerated religious zeal. **religionist,** *n.* **religionize,** *v.t.* To make religious, to imbue with religion. *v.i.* To profess or display religion. **religionless,** *a.* **religiose** (rē lij′ i ōs), *a.* Morbidly affected with religious emotion. **religiosity** (-os′ i ti), *n.* Religious sentimentality or emotionalism. **religious** (rė lij′ ŭs), *a.* Imbued with religion; pious, devout; of or pertaining to religion; bound by vows to a monastic life, belonging to a monastic order; (*fig.*) conscientious, rigid, strict. *n.* One bound by monastic vows. **religious house:** A house for monks or nuns, a monastery, a convent. **religiously,** *adv.* In a religious manner; (*colloq.*) scrupulously. **religiousness,** *n.*

reline (rē līn′), *v.t.* To line again, to give a new lining to.

relinquish (rė ling′ kwish) [O.F. *relinquiss-*, pres.p. stem of *relinquir*, L. *relinquere* (RE-, *linquere*, to leave)], *v.t.* To forsake, to abandon, to resign; to quit, to desist from; to give up a claim to, to surrender. **relinquent,** *a.* and *n.* **relinquisher,** *n.* **relinquishment,** *n.*

reliquary (rel′ i kwȧ ri) [F. *reliquaire*, from *relique*], *n.* A depository for relics, a casket for keeping a relic or relics in. ***reliquaire*** (rel i kwâr′) [F.], *n.* A reliquary. ***relique** [RELIC].

reliquiæ (rė lik′ wi ē) [L.], *n.pl.* Remains; (*Geol.*) fossil remains of organisms; (*Bot.*) withered leaves remaining on plants.

relish (rel′ ish) [M.E. and O.F. *reles*, var. of *relais*, that left behind, from *relesser*, see RELEASE], *n.* The effect of anything on the palate, taste, distinctive flavour, esp. a pleasing taste or flavour; something taken with food to give a flavour, a condiment; enjoyment of food, etc., gusto, appetite, zest, fondness, liking; a slight admixture or flavouring, a smack, a trace (of). *v.t.* To give agreeable flavour to, to make piquant, etc.; to partake of with pleasure, to like; to be gratified by, to enjoy. *v.i.* To have a pleasing taste; to have a flavour, to taste or smack (of); to affect the taste (well, etc.) **relishable,** *a.*

re-listen (rē lis′ ėn), *v.i.* To listen again. **relive** (rē liv′), *v.i.* To live again, to revive. *v.t.* To live over again; *to animate, to revive. **reload** (rē lōd′), *v.t.* To load again. *v.i.* To load a fire-arm again. **relocate** (rē lō kāt′), *v.t.* and *i.* To locate again. **relocation** (-kā′ shŭn), *n.* The act of relocating; (*Sc. Law*) renewal of a lease without a fresh agreement. ***relucent** (rė loo′ sėnt) [L. *relūcent -ntem* (LUCENT)], *a.* Refulgent, bright, shining.

reluctant (rė lŭk′ tȧnt) [L. *reluctans -ntem*, pres.p. of *reluctārī* (RE-, *luctārī*, to struggle)], *a.* Struggling or resisting, unwilling, averse, disinclined (to), doing, done, or granted unwillingly. **reluct,** *v.i.* To be disinclined; to show reluctance or resistance (at or against). **reluctance, *-ancy,** *n.* **reluctantly,** *adv.* **reluctate,** *v.i.* To reluct. **reluctation** (-tā′ shŭn), *n.*

relume (rė lūm′), **relumine,** *v.t.* To light again, to rekindle; to make bright or light up again.

rely (rė lī′) [O.F. *relier*, L. *religāre* (RE-, *ligāre*, to bind)], *v.i.* To trust or depend (upon) with confidence.

remain (rė mān′) [O.F. *remaindre*, L. *remanēre* (RE-, *manēre*, to stay)], *v.i.* To stay behind or be left over after use, separation, destruction, etc.; to survive; to continue in a place or state; to last, to abide, to continue, to endure; to continue (to be). *n.* (*usu. pl.*) That which remains behind; a dead body, a corpse; literary productions published after one's death; ruins, relics.

remainder (rė mān′ dėr), *n.* Anything left over after a part has been taken away, the rest, the residue; (*Arith.*) the quantity left over after subtraction, the excess remaining after division; (*Law*) an interest in an estate limited to take effect and be enjoyed after a prior estate is determined; (*Bookselling*) copies left unsold of an edition after the demand has ceased and offered at a reduced price. *v.t.* To offer such copies of (a book) at a reduced price. **remainder-man,** *n.* (*Law*) One to whom an estate in remainder is devised.

remake (rē māk′), *v.t.* To make again or anew. **reman** (rē măn′), *v.t.* To man (a ship, gun, etc.) again; to equip with a new complement of men.

remanation (rem ȧ nā′ shŭn) [L. *remānāre* (RE-, *mānāre*, to flow)], *n.* Flowing back, reabsorption (as of a soul in the universal spirit).

remand (rė mand′) [O.F. *remander*, late L. *remandāre* (RE-, *mandāre*, to commit)], *v.t.* To send back (to); to recommit in custody after a partial hearing. *n.* The act of remanding; the state of being remanded. **remand home:** (*Law*) A place of detention for young persons awaiting trial. **remandment,** *n.*

remanent (rem′ å nėnt) [L. *remanens -ntem,* pres.p. of *remanēre,* to REMAIN], *a.* Remaining, left behind, surviving; (*Sc.*) remaining over, additional. **remanence,** *n.* **remanet** (rem′ å nėt) [L., 3rd sing. of *remanēre,* as prec.], *n.* A remainder; (*Law*) a cause postponed to another term; (*Parl.*) a Bill deferred to another session.

remargin (rē mar′ jin), *v.t.* To give a fresh margin to (a page, etc.).

remark (rė mark′) [F. *remarquer* (RE-, *marquer,* to MARK (1))], *v.t.* To take notice of, to observe with particular attention, to perceive; to utter by way of comment, to comment (upon); *to distinguish. *n.* The act of noticing, observation; an observation, a comment; (*colloq., usu. in pl.*) anything said, conversation; (*Engraving,* also ***remarque***) a distinguishing mark indicating the particular state of an engraved plate, usu. as a marginal sketch. **remark-proof,** *n.* A proof bearing such a mark. **remarkable,** *a.* Worthy of special observation or notice, notable; unusual, extraordinary, striking. **remarkableness,** *n.* **remarkably,** *adv.* **remarker,** *n.*

re-mark (rē mark′), *v.t.* To mark again.

remarque [REMARK].

remarry (rē măr′ i), *v.t.* and *i.* To marry again. **remast** (rē mast′), *v.t.* To furnish with a new mast or masts. **remasticate** (rē măs′ ti kāt), *v.t.* To chew over again. **remastication** (-kā′ shŭn), *n.*

remblai (ran blā) [F., from *remblayer,* to embank], *n.* (*Fort.*) The material used to form a rampart or embankment.

Rembrandtesque (rem brån tesk′), *a.* In the style or resembling the effects of the Dutch painter Rembrandt van Rijn (1609–69), esp. in chiaroscuro. **Rembrandtish** (rem′ brån tish), *a.*

remeant (rē′ mė ånt) [L. *remeans -ntem,* pres.p. of *remeāre* (RE-, *meāre,* to pass)], *a.* Coming back, returning.

remeasure (rē mezh′ ŭr), *v.t.* To measure again.

remedy (rem′ ė di) [A.-F. *remedie* (F. *remède*), L. *remedium* (RE-, *medērī,* to heal)], *n.* That which cures a disease; medicine, healing treatment; that which serves to remove, counteract, or repair any evil; redress, reparation. *v.t.* To cure, to heal; to repair, to rectify, to redress. **remediless** (rem′ ė di-, rė med′ i lės), *a.* **remedilessly,** *adv.* **remedilessness,** *n.* **remediable** (rė mē′ di åbl), *a.* **remediableness,** *n.* **remediably,** *adv.* **remedial,** *a.* Affording, containing, or intended for a remedy. **remedial training:** The attempt to make delinquents or mental defectives as useful members of the community as possible. **remedially,** *adv.* ***remediate,** *a.*

remelt (rē melt′), *v.t.* To melt again.

remember (rė mem′ bėr) [O.F. *remembrer,* late L. *rememorārī* (RE-, *memor,* mindful)], *v.t.* To bear or keep in mind, not to forget, to know by heart; to recall to mind, to recollect; to keep in mind with gratitude, reverence, or respect; (*colloq.*) to convey a greeting from; to be good to, to make a present to, to tip; *to remind. **to remember oneself:** To bethink oneself (of). **rememberable,** *a.* **rememberability** (-bil′ i ti), *n.* **rememberably,** *adv.* ***rememberer,** *n.*

remembrance (re mem′ brǎns), *n.* The act of remembering; memory; the time over which memory extends; the state of being remembered; a recollection, a memory; that which serves to recall to or preserve in memory; a keepsake, a memento, a memorial; (*pl.*) regards, greetings; *admonition. **Remembrance Day:** The Sunday nearest the 11th November, when the fallen in the two World Wars are remembered, also called Armistice Day. **remembrancer,** *n.* One who or that which puts in mind; a reminder, a memento; an officer of the Court of Exchequer, now only the **Queen's** or **King's Remembrancer,** whose business is to collect debts due to the sovereign. **City Remembrancer:** An officer of the City of London representing the City Corporation before parliamentary committees, etc.

remerge (rē mĕrj′), *v.t.* To merge again.

remex (rē′ mėks) [L., rower, from *rēmus,* oar], *n.* (*pl. **remiges***) (*Ornith.*) One of the quill feathers of a bird's wings. **remiform** (rem′ i fôrm), *a.* Oar-shaped. **remigial** (rė mij′ i ål), *a.*

remigrate (rem′ i-, rē mī′ grāt) [L. *remigrātus,* p.p. of *remigrāre* (RE-, MIGRATE)], *v.i.* To migrate back again, to return to a former place or state. **remigrant,** *n.* (*Ent.*) An aphid that returns to the tree that was its former host. **remigration** (-grā′ shŭn), *n.*

remind (rė mīnd′), *v.t.* To put in mind (of); to cause to remember (to do, etc.). **reminder,** *n.* ***remindful,** *a.*

reminiscence (rem i nis′ ėns) [late L. *reminiscentia,* from *reminiscī* (RE-, *men-,* stem of *meminī,* I remember, cogn. with MIND)], *n.* The act or power of remembering or recalling past knowledge; that which is remembered; (*pl.*) a collection of personal recollections of past events; (*fig.*) something reminding or suggestive (of). **reminiscent,** *a.* Recalling past events to mind; of the nature of or pertaining to reminiscence; reminding or suggestive (of). *n.* One who records reminiscences. **reminiscential** (-sen′ shål), **reminiscitory** (-nis′ i tór i), *a.* **reminiscently,** *adv.*

remint (rē mint′), *v.t.* To mint over again.

remiped (rem′ i ped) [F. *rémipède* (L. *rēmi-, rēmus,* oar, *pes pedis,* foot)], *a.* (*Zool.*) Having oar-like feet. *n.* A small crustacean or aquatic insect with oar-like feet.

remise (rė mēz′) [F., from *remettre,* to REMIT], *n.* (*Law*) A release of property; *a coach-house; *a carriage from a livery-stable; (*Fencing*) a thrust following up one that misses before the opponent has time to recover. *v.t.* To surrender, to release or grant back; (*Fencing*) to make a remise.

remiss (rė mis′) [L. *remissus,* p.p. of *remittere,* to REMIT], *a.* Careless or lax in the performance of duty or business; heedless, negligent; slow, slack, languid. **remissible** (rė mis′ ibl), *a.* That may be remitted, admitting of remission. **remissibility** (-bil′ i ti), *n.* **remissly,** *adv.* **remissness,** *n.* ***remissful,** *a.*

remission (rė mish′ ŭn) [O.F., from L. *remissiōnem,* nom. *-sio,* as prec.], *n.* The act of remitting; the remitting or discharge of a debt, penalty, etc.; forgiveness, pardon; abatement, diminution, relaxation; remittance (of money, etc.). **remissive, remissory,** *a.* Remitting, relieving, abating; forgiving. **remissly, remissness** [REMISS].

remit (rė mit′) [L. *remittere* (RE-, *mittere,* to send), p.p. *remissus*], *v.t.* (*past & p.p.* **remitted**) To send or put back; to transmit (cash, bills, etc.); to refer or submit, to send back for consideration, to refer to a lower court; to defer, to put off; to relax, to slacken, to mitigate, to desist from partially or entirely; to refrain from exacting, etc., to forgo, to discharge from (a fine, penalty, etc.); to pardon, to forgive. *v.i.* To become less intense, to abate. **remitment,** *n.* Remittance (of money). **remittal,** *n.* A giving up, a surrender; remission from one court to another; remission (for offences, etc.). **remittance,** *n.* The act of remitting money, bills, or the like, in payment for goods, etc.; the sum so remitted; *a consignment of goods. **remittance-man,** *n.* An emigrant depending on remittances from home for his living. **remittee** (rė mit ē′), *n.* One receiving a remittance. **remittent** (rė mit′ ent), *a.* (*Path.*) Having alternate increase and decrease of intensity. *n.* A malarial fever marked by alternate increase and decrease of intensity.

remitter (rė mit′ ėr) [O.F., as prec.], *n.* (*Law*) Remission to the more valid of two titles to an estate in favour of the holder entering in possession by the inferior title; remission to another court. **remittitur** (re mit′ it er), *n.* (*Law*) An order sending back a case to an inferior court; a surrender of damages in order to avert further litigation on appeal.

remnant (rem′ nȧnt) [M.E. and O.F. *remenant*, pres.p. of *remanoir*, *-manoir*, to REMAIN], *n.* That which is left after a larger part has been separated, lost or destroyed; the remainder; the last part of a piece of cloth, etc., esp. a portion offered at a reduced price; a scrap, a fragment, a surviving trace.

remodel (rē mod′ ėl), *v.t.* (*past & p.p.* **remodelled**) To model again; to refashion. **remodify** (rē mod′ i fī), *v.t.* To modify again. **remodification** (-kā′ shŭn), *n.* ***remollient** (rė mol′ i ėnt), *a.* Mollifying, softening. *n.* An emollient. ***remolten,** *p.p.* [REMELT]. **remonetize** (rē mon′-, -mŭn′ ė tīz), *v.t.* To reinstate (a metal, etc.) as legal currency. **remonetization** (-zā′ shŭn), *n.*

remonstrance (rė mon′ strȧns) [O.F., from med. L. *remonstrāre* (RE-, L. *monstrāre*, to show)], *n.* The act of remonstrating; an expostulation, a protest; a formal representation or protest against public grievances, etc. **the Grand Remonstrance:** The statement of grievances presented by Parliament to Charles I in 1641. **remonstrant,** *a.* Containing or of the nature of remonstrance, expostulatory; *pertaining to the Arminian party in the Dutch Church. *n.* One who remonstrates; *(*pl.*) the Dutch Arminians who in 1610 presented to the States of Holland a remonstrance formulating their points of departure from Calvinism. **remonstrantly,** *adv.*

remonstrate (rė mon′ strāt), *v.t.* To say or state in remonstrance. *v.i.* To make a remonstrance. **remonstratingly,** *adv.* **remonstration** (rem ȯn strā′ shŭn), *n.* **remonstrative** (rė mon′ strȧ tiv), **remonstratory,** *a.* **remonstrator** (-strā′ tȯr), *n.*

remontant (rė mon′ tȧnt) [F., pres.p. of *remonter*, to REMOUNT], *a.* Blooming more than once in the season (of roses). *n.* A rose blooming more than once in the season.

remora (rem′ ȯ rȧ) [L., orig. hindrance, impediment (RE-, *mora*, delay)], *n.* A sucking-fish, *Echeneis remora*, having a suctorial disk for attaching itself to sharks, sword-fishes, etc., and believed by the ancients to have the power of stopping ships in this way.

remorse (rė mȯrs′) [O.F. *remors*, late L. *remorsus*, from *remordere* (RE-, *mordere*, to bite, p.p. *morsus*)], *n.* The pain caused by a sense of guilt, bitter repentance; compunction, reluctance to commit a wrong or to act cruelly. ***remord** (rė mȯrd′), *v.t.* To cause remorse to. **remordent,** *a.* ***remordency,** *n.* **remorseful,** *a.* **remorsefully,** *adv.* **remorsefulness,** *n.* **remorseless,** *a.* **remorselessly,** *adv.* **remorselessness,** *n.*

remote (rė mōt′) [L. *remōtus*, p.p. of *removēre*, to REMOVE], *a.* Far off, distant in time or space; not closely connected or related, separated, different, alien, foreign; out-of-the-way, retired, sequestered; slight, inconsiderable, least (*usu. in superl.*). **remote control:** Electric or radio control of apparatus, etc. from a distance. **remotely,** *adv.* **remoteness,** *n.* ***remotion,** *n.*

remould (rē mōld′), *v.t.* To mould, fashion, or shape anew. **remount** (rē-, rė mount′), *v.t.* To mount again, to reascend; to mount or set up (a gun, etc.) again; to supply (a regiment, etc.) with fresh horses. *v.i.* To mount a horse again; to make a fresh ascent; to go back (to a date, source, etc.). *n.* (rē′ mount) A fresh horse for riding on; a fresh mount or setting.

remove (rė moov′) [O.F. *remouvoir*, *-movoir*, L. *removēre* (RE-, *movēre*, to MOVE)], *v.t.* To move from a place; to move to another place; to take away, to get rid of; to transfer to another post or office, to dismiss. *v.i.* To go away (from), esp. to change one's place of abode. *n.* A degree of difference or gradation; a dish removed to give place to another, or the dish brought on in its place; a class or form (in some public schools); removal, change of place or position, departure; *distance, esp. between stopping-places on a stage-road. **once or twice removed:** Separated by one or two intervals of relationship. **removable,** *a.* Able to be moved; liable to removal. *n.* A removable official, esp. formerly in Ireland holding office during the pleasure of the Government. **removability** (-bil′ i ti), *n.* **removal,** *n.* The act of removing or displacing; change of place, site, or abode; dismissal; (*euphem.*) murder. ***removedness,** *n.* The state of being removed or estranged. **remover,** *n.* One who removes, esp. one whose business is to remove furniture from one house to another.

remunerate (rė mū′ nėr āt) [L. *remūnerātus*, p.p. of *remūnerāre*, *-erārī* (RE-, *mūnus*, gift)], *v.t.* To reward, to recompense, to pay for a service, etc.; to serve as recompense or equivalent (for or to). ***remunerable,** *a.* ***remunerability** (-bil′ i ti), *n.* **remuneration** (-ā′ shŭn), *n.* **remunerative** (rė mū′ nėr ȧ tiv), **remuneratory,** *a.* Producing a due return for outlay; paying, profitable. **remuneratively,** *adv.* **remunerativeness,** *n.*

remurmur (rė mėr′ mŭr) [L. *remurmurāre*], *v.t.* To utter back in murmurs. *v.i.* To return a murmuring echo. ***remutation** (rē mū tā′ shŭn), *n.* The act of changing back again.

Renaissance (rė nā′ sȧns, ren′ ā sans) [F., from *renaître* (RE-, *naître*, to be born), cp. RENASCENCE], *n.* The revival of art and letters in the 14th–16th cent.; the period of this; the style of architecture or of painting that was developed under it; any revival of a similar nature.

renal (rē′ nȧl) [late L. *rēnālis*, from *rēn*, kidney], *a.* (*Anat.*) Pertaining to the kidneys.

rename (rē nām′), *v.t.* To name anew, to give a new name to.

renascent (rė nȧs′ ėnt) [L. *renascens -ntem*, pres.p. of *renascī* (RE-, *nascī*, to be born)], *a.* Coming into being again; pertaining to the Renaissance. **renascence,** *n.* Rebirth, renewal, a springing into fresh life; the Renaissance. ***renascible,** *a.*

rencounter (ren koun′ tėr), **rencontre** (ren kon′ tėr, ran kontr) [F. *rencontre*, from *rencontrer* (RE-, ENCOUNTER)], *n.* A hostile meeting or collision, an encounter, a combat, a duel, a skirmish; an unexpected meeting or encounter. **v.t.* To fall in with unexpectedly; to meet in combat. *v.i.* To come together, to clash; to meet an enemy unexpectedly.

rend (rend) [A.-S. *rendan*, cp. O.Fris. *renda*], *v.t.* (*past & p.p.* **rent** (1)) To tear, pull, or wrench (off, away, apart, asunder, etc.); to split or separate with violence; to make (laths) by splitting wood; (*fig.*) to lacerate, to cause anguish to. *v.i.* To be or become torn or pulled apart. **render** (1), *n.*

render (2) (ren′ dėr) [O.F. *rendre*, pop. L. *rendere*, var. of L. *reddere* (RE-, *dare*, to give)], *v.t.* To give in return; to pay or give back; to give up, to surrender; to bestow, to give, to pay, to furnish; to present, to submit, to hand in; to reproduce, to express, to represent, to interpret, to translate, to perform, to execute; to make, to cause to be; to boil down, to melt and clarify (fat); to give the first coat of plaster to. *n.* A return, a payment in return; the first coat of plaster on a wall, etc.; *a surrender; *a statement, a declaration. **renderset,** *v.t.* To coat (a wall) with two coats of plaster; *a.* Consisting of two such coats; *n.* The laying on of two such coats. **renderable,** *a.* **renderer,** *n.* **rendering,** *n.* A return; a translation, a version; interpretation, execution (of a piece of music, a dramatic part, etc.); the first coat of plaster on brickwork, etc.

rendezvous (ron′ dā voo) [F. *rendez-vous*, render or betake yourselves], *n.* (*pl.* unchanged, -vooz) A place appointed for assembling, esp. of troops or warships; a place agreed upon for meeting; a place of common resort; *a resort, a shift; *a refuge, a retreat. *v.i.* To meet or assemble at a rendezvous.

rendition (ren dish′ ŭn) [obs. F., from *rendre*], *n.* Surrender, giving up; translation, interpretation; execution, performance, rendering (of music, etc.).

renegade, ***renegado** (ren′ ė gād, -gā′ dō) [Sp. *renegado*, med. L. *renegātus*, p.p. of *renegāre* (RE-, *negāre*, to deny)], *n.* An apostate, esp. from

Christianity; a deserter; a turncoat. *v.i.* To turn renegade. **renegation** (-gā' shŭn), *n.*

renegue (rė nēg') [med. L. *renegāre*, see prec.], *v.i.* (*Cards*) To fail to follow suit, to revoke; *to make denial. **v.t.* To deny, to renounce, to refuse, to decline. **reneguer,** *n.*

renerve (rē nĕrv'), *v.t.* To put fresh nerve or vigour into.

renew (rė nū'), *v.t.* To make new again or as good as new, to renovate; to restore to the original or a sound condition; to make fresh or vigorous again, to reanimate, to revivify, to regenerate; to repair, to patch up, to replace; to make do, or say over again, to recommence, to repeat; to grant a further period of (a lease, patent, mortgage, etc.); to obtain such a grant. *v.i.* To become young or new again; to grow again; to begin again. **renewable,** *a.* **renewability** (-bil' i ti), *n.* **renewal** (-nū' ăl), *n.* The act of renewing; the state of being renewed; revival, regeneration; a fee paid for continuance of anything. ***renewedly,** *adv.* ***renewedness,** *n.* **renewer,** *n.*

***renfierce** (renfērs'), *v.t.* To render fierce. ***renforce** (ren fôrs') [F. *renforcer* (ENFORCE)], *v.t.* To reinforce; to force (to do). **renidify** (rē nid' i fī), *v.i.* To build another nest. **renidification** (-kā' shŭn), *n.*

reniform (rē' ni fôrm) [L. *rēn rēnis*, kidney, -FORM], *a.* (*Anat.*) Kidney-shaped.

***renitence,** ***renitency** (rē nī'-, ren' i tėns, -i), [obs. F. *rénitence*, from *rénitent*, L. *renitentem*, nom. *-tens*, pres.p. of *renītī* (RE-, *nītī*, to struggle)], *n.* Resistance, esp. of a body to pressure; moral resistance, reluctance, disinclination. ***renitent,** *a.*

rennet (1) (ren' ėt) [M.E., from *renne*, to RUN], *n.* Curdled milk from the stomach of an unweaned calf, etc., or an aqueous infusion of the stomach-membrane of the calf, used to coagulate milk; a similar preparation from seeds or other vegetable sources. **rennin,** *n.* An enzyme with the power of coagulating the protein in milk.

rennet (2) (ren' ėt) [F. *reinette*, prob. dim. of *reine*, queen (Skeat prefers *rainette*, dim. of *raine*, frog, see RANA, with alln. to the speckled skin)], *n.* A name for several varieties of apple, esp. pippins.

renominate (rē nom' i nāt), *v.t.* To nominate again. **renomination** (-nā' shŭn), *n.*

renounce (rė nouns') [F. *renoncer*, L. *renuntiāre* (RE-, *nuntiare*, from *nuntius*, messenger, see NUNCIO)], *v.t.* To declare against, to reject or cast off formally, to repudiate, to disclaim, to disown; to forsake, to abandon; to forswear, to abjure; to give up, to withdraw from; (*Law*) to decline or resign a right or trust; (*Cards*) to fail to follow suit through having none left of that suit. *v.i.* (*Cards*) To fail thus to follow suit. *n.* Such failure to follow suit. **renouncement, renouncer,** *n.*

renovate (ren' ŏ vāt) [L. *renovātus*, p.p. of *renovāre* (RE-, *novus*, new)], *v.t.* To make new again; to restore to a state of soundness or vigour; to repair. **renovation** (-vā' shŭn), *n.* **renovator** (ren' ŏ vā tŏr), *n.*

renown (rė noun') [M.E. and A.-F. *renoun*, O.F. *renon* (F. *renommée*), from *renoumer*, *renomer*, L. *renomināre*, see RENOMINATE], *n.* Exalted reputation, fame, celebrity. *v.t.* To make renowned or famous. **renowned** (rė nound'), *a.* **renownedly** (rė noun' ėd li), *adv.* ***renowner,** *n.* A braggart, a boaster. ***renownless,** *a.* Inglorious.

rent (1), *past & p.p.* [REND].

rent (2) (rent) [from obs. v. *rent*, var. of REND], *n.* A tear, slit, or breach, an opening made by rending or tearing asunder; a cleft, a fissure, a chasm; (*fig.*) a schism, a separation brought about by violent means.

rent (3) (rent) [O.F. *rente*, prob. through pop. L. *rendita*, var. of *reddita*, fem. p.p. of *reddere*, to RENDER (2)], *n.* A sum of money payable periodically for the use of lands, tenements, etc.; payment for the use of any kind of property. *v.t.* To occupy, hold in tenancy, or use in return for rent; to let for rent; to impose rent upon; to hire. *v.i.* To be let (at a certain rent); to hire. **rent-charge,** *n.* A periodical charge on land, etc., granted by deed to some person other than the owner. **rent-day,** *n.* The day on which rent is due. **rent-free,** *a.* Exempted from the payment of rent. *adv.* Without payment of rent. **rent-roll,** *n.* A schedule of a person's property and rents; a person's total income from this source. **rentable,** *a.* **rental,** *n.* The total income from rents of an estate; a rent-roll; (*Sc.*) a favourable rent or lease to a 'kindly' tenant. *v.t.* (*Sc.*) To let or hold (land) on a rental. **rentaller,** *n.* **renter** (1), *n.* One who holds an estate or tenement by paying rent; a tenant; the proprietor of a seat in a theatre. **rentless,** *a.*

rente (ra*n*t) [F.], *n.* Income, revenue; (*pl.*) interest or annuities from French government stocks; the stock themselves. ***rentier*** (ra*n* tyā), *n.* A person drawing his income from *rentes* or investments.

renter (2) (ren' tėr) [F. *rentrer*, var. of *rentraire*], *v.t.* To fine-draw; to sew together (the edges of two pieces of cloth) without doubling them, so that the seam is scarcely visible. **renterer,** *n.*

renuent (ren' ū ėnt) [L. *renuens -ntem*, pres.p. of *renuere* (RE-, *nuere*, to nod)], *a.* (*Anat.*) Throwing back the head (applied to muscles which perform this function).

renule (ren' ūl) [dim. of L. *rēn*, kidney, see RENIFORM], *n.* (*Anat.*) A renal lobule or small kidney (as in some animals).

renumber (rē nŭm' bėr), *v.t.* To number again.

renunciation (rė nŭn si ā' shŭn) [L. *renuntiātio*, from *renuntiāre*, to RENOUNCE], *n.* The act of renouncing; a declaration or document expressing this; self-denial, self-sacrifice, self resignation. ***renunciance,** *n.* **renunciant,** *a.* and *n.* **renunciative, -tory** (-nŭn' shȧ tiv, -tŏr i), *a.*

renverse (ren vĕrs') [O.F. *renverser* (RE-, *enverser*, from *envers*, L. *inversus*, see INVERSE)], *v.t.* To reverse, to turn the other way; to overthrow, to upset. **renversé, renverse** (ra*n* ver sā, ra*n* vers), *a.* (*Her.*) Inverted, reversed.

reobtain (rē ob tān'), *v.t.* To obtain again. **reobtainable,** *a.* **reoccupy** (rē ok' ū pī), *v.t.* To occupy again. **reoccupation** (-pā' shŭn), *n.* **reopen** (rē ō' pėn), *v.t.* and *i.* To open again. **reordain** (rē ôr dān'), *v.t.* To ordain again; to appoint or enact again. **reordination** (-di nā' shŭn), *n.* **reorder** (rē ôr' dėr), *v.t.* To put in order again, to rearrange; to order or command again. **reorganize** (rē ôr' gȧ nīz), *v.t.* To organize anew. **reorganizer,** *n.* **reorganization** (-zā' shŭn), *n.* **reorient** (rē ôr' i ėnt), *a.* (*poet.*) Rising again.

rep (1) (rep) [F. *reps*, etym. unknown], *n.* A textile fabric of wool, cotton, or silk, with a finely-corded surface. **repped,** *a.* Having a surface like rep.

rep (2) [REPERTORY THEATRE].

rep (3) (rep) abb. (commercial) Representative.

repacify (rē păs' i fī), *v.t.* To pacify again. **repack** (rē păk'), *v.t.* To pack again. **repacker,** *n.* **repaganize** (rē pā' gȧ nīz), *v.t.* To make pagan again. *v.i.* To become pagan again. **repaid,** *past & p.p.* [REPAY]. **repaint** (rē pānt'), *v.i.* To paint again.

repair (1) (rė pâr') [O.F. *repairer*, late L. *repatriāre* (RE-, *patria*, one's native land)], *v.i.* To go, to betake oneself, to resort (to). *n.* A place to which one goes often or which is frequented by many people; a haunt, a resort.

repair (2) (rė pâr') [O.F. *reparer*, L. *reparāre* (RE-, *parāre*, to make ready)], *v.t.* To restore to a good or sound state after dilapidation or wear; to make good the damaged or dilapidated parts of, to renovate, to mend; to remedy, to set right, to make amends for; *to revive, to recreate. *n.* Restoration to a sound state; good or comparative condition. **in repair** or **in good repair:** In sound working condition. **in bad repair** or **out of repair:** In a dilapidated condition, needing repair. **repairable** [REPARABLE]. **repairer,** *n.* ***repairment,** *n.*

repand (rė pănd′) [L. *repandus* (RE-, *pandus*, bent)], *a.* (*Bot.*) Having an uneven, wavy, or sinuous margin. **repando-,** *comb. form.* ***repandous,** *a.*

repaper (rē pā′ pėr), *v.t.* To paper (walls, etc.) again.

reparable (rep′ ȧ rȧbl) [F., from L. *reparābilis*, from *reparāre*, to REPAIR (2)], *a.* Capable of being made good, put in a sound state, or repaired. **reparation** (-rā′ shŭn) *n.* The act of repairing or restoring; the state of being repaired; satisfaction for wrong or damage, amends, compensation; (*pl.*) repairs. **reparative** (rep′ ȧr-, rė păr′ ȧ tiv), *a.*

repartee (rep ȧr tē′) [F. *repartie*, fem. p.p. of *repartir*, to start again (RE-, *partir*, to PART (2))], *n.* A smart or witty rejoinder, a witty retort. **v.i.* To make repartees.

repartition (rep ȧr-, rē par tish′ ŭn), *n.* Distribution, allotment; a fresh distribution or allotment. **repass** (rē pas′), *v.t.* To pass again; to go past again; to recross. *v.i.* To pass in the opposite direction; to pass again (into, through, etc.). **repassage** (rē păs′ ȧj), *n.*

repast (rė past′) [O.F., from *repaistre* (F. *repaître*) (RE-, L. *pascere*, to feed, see PASTURE)], *n.* A meal; food, victuals; the act of taking food; *repose. *v.i.* To feed, to feast (upon, etc.). ***repasture,** *n.* Food, a repast.

repatriate (rė pā′ tri āt) [late L. *repatriātus*, p.p. of *repatriāre* (RE-, *patria*, one's country)], *v.t.* To restore to one's country. *v.i.* To return to one's country. **repatriation** (-ā′ shŭn), *n.*

repay (rė pā′) [O.F. *repayer*], *v.t.* (*past & p.p.* **repaid**) To pay back, to refund; to return, to deal (a blow, etc.) in retaliation or recompense; to pay (a creditor, etc.), to make recompense for, to requite. *v.i.* To make a repayment or requital. **repayable,** *a.* **repayment,** *n.*

repeal (rė pēl′) [A.-F. *repeler*, O.F. *rapeler* (RE-, *apeler*, to APPEAL)], *v.t.* To revoke, to rescind, to annul; *to recall, to summon back; to recall or retract. *n.* Abrogation, revocation, annulment. **repealable,** *a.* ***repealability** (-bil′ i ti), ***repealableness,** *n.* **repealer,** *n.* One who repeals; one who advocates repeal, esp. (*Hist.*) one who advocated a repeal of the Union between Great Britain and Ireland in the time of the liberator O'Connell. **repealist,** *n.*

repeat (rė pēt′) [F. *repeter*, L. *repetere* (RE-, *petere*, to seek)], *v.t.* To do, make, or say over again; to reiterate; to recite, to rehearse; to reproduce, to imitate. *v.i.* To do something over again; to recur, to happen again; to strike over again the last hour or quarter-hour struck (of a watch, etc.); to rise to the mouth, to be tasted again (of food). *n.* Repetition, esp. of a song or other item on a programme; (*Mus.*) a passage to be repeated, a sign indicating this; (*Comm.*) a supply of goods corresponding to the last; the order for this. **repeatable,** *a.* **repeatedly,** *adv.* **repeater,** *n.* One who repeats; a repeating fire-arm; a watch or clock striking the hours and parts of hours when required; a repeating signal, etc.; (*Arith.*) an indeterminate decimal in which the same figures continually recur in the same order. **repeating-circle,** *n.* (*Astron.*) A reflecting instrument for measuring angular distances. **repeating-decimal** [RECURRING]. **repeating rifle:** One constructed usu. with a magazine, to fire several shots without reloading.

repel (rė pel′) [L. *repeller* (RE-, *peller*, to drive, p.p. *pulsus*)], *v.t.* (*past & p.p.* **repelled**) To drive or force back, to check the advance of; to repulse, to ward off; to keep at a distance; (of fluids, etc.) to refuse to mix with (each other); to tend to drive back, to be repulsive or antagonistic to. **repellence, -ency,** *n.* **repellent,** *a.* Repelling or tending to repel; repulsive. *n.* That which repels; (*Path.*) a remedy causing morbid fluids to recede from a tumescent part. **repellently,** *adv.* **repeller,** *n.*

repent (1) (rē′ pėnt) [L. *rēpens*, *-ntem*, pres.p. of *rēpere*, to creep], *a.* (*Bot.*, *Zool.*, *etc.*) Creeping, esp. along the ground and rooting.

repent (2) (rė pent′) [F. *repentir* (RE- L. *pœnitēre*, to make contrite, see PENITENT)], *v.i.* To feel sorrow, regret, or pain for something done or left undone, esp. to feel such sorrow for sin as leads to amendment, to be penitent or contrite; to be sorry; *to grieve, to mourn. *v.t.* To feel contrition or remorse for, to regret; to affect (oneself) with penitence. **I repent me** or **it repents me:** I feel penitence or regret (that). **repentance,** *n.* **repentant,** *a.* **repentantly, repentingly,** *adv.* **repenter,** *n.*

repeople (rē pē′ pėl), *v.t.* To people anew.

repercussion (rē pėr kŭsh′ ŭn) [F. *répercussion* or L. *repercussiōnem*, nom. *-sio*, from *repercutere* (RE-, *percutere*, to PERCUSS)], *n.* The act of driving or forcing back; recoil; echo, reverberation; (*Mus.*) frequent repetition of the same subject, note, chord, etc. ***repercuss** (rē pėr kŭs′), *v.t.* **repercussive,** *a.* Driving back, repellent; causing reverberation; driven back; reverberated. *n.* (*Med.*) A repellent.

repertoire (rep ėr twar′) [F. *répertoire*, as foll.], *n.* A stock of musical pieces, songs, etc., that a person or company is ready to perform.

repertory (rep′ ėr tȯ ri) [L. *repertōrium*, from *reperīre* (p.p. *repertus*), to find (RE-, O.L. *parīre*, L. *parere*, to produce)], *n.* A place in which things are so disposed that they can be readily found; a storehouse, a collection, a magazine, esp. of information, statistics, etc.; a repertoire. **repertory theatre:** A theatre served by a stock or permanent company prepared to present a number of different plays.

reperuse (rē pė rooz′), *v.t.* To peruse again. **reperusal,** *n.*

repetend (rep ė tend′) [L. *repetendum*, ger. of *repetere*, to REPEAT], *n.* Something repeated, a recurring word or phrase; a refrain; (*Arith.*) that part of a repeating decimal which keeps recurring.

repetition (rep ė tish′ ŭn) [O.F. *repeticion* (F. *répétition*), L. *repetitiōnem*, nom. *-tio*, as prec.], *n.* The act of repeating, iteration; recital from memory; that which is repeated, a piece set to be learnt by heart; a copy, a reproduction, a replica; (*Mus.*) the ability of a musical instrument to repeat a note in rapid succession. **repetitional, -ary, repetitious, repetitive** (rė pet′ i tiv), *a.* **repetitiously** (-tish′ ŭs li), **repetitiousness, repetitiveness** (-pet′ i tiv nės), *n.*

repiece (rē pēs′), *v.t.* To piece together again.

repine (rė pīn′), *v.i.* To fret oneself, to be discontented (at); to murmur; to complain, to grumble. **n.* Repining. **repiner,** *n.* **repiningly,** *adv.*

repique (rė pēk′) [F. *repic*], *n.* (*Piquet*) The scoring of 30 points on cards alone before playing. *v.t.* To make a repique against. *v.i.* To make a repique.

replace (rė plās′), *v.t.* To put back again in place; to take the place of, to succeed; to be a substitute for; to supersede, to displace; to put a substitute in place of, to fill the place of (with or by); to put in a fresh place; *to repay, to refund. **replaceable,** *a.* **replacer,** *n.* **replacement,** *n.* One that replaces; a substitute. **replacing-switch,** *n.* (*Railway*) A contrivance placed on the line to enable derailed vehicles to mount the rails again.

replant (rē plant′), *v.t.* To plant (a tree, etc.) again; to re-establish, to resettle; to plant (ground) again. **replantation** (tā′ shŭn), *n.* **repleader** (rė plē′ dėr) [F. *replaider*], *n.* (*Law*) A second pleading; the right of pleading again. ***repledge** (rė plej′) [O.F. *repleger*], *v.t.* (*Sc. Law*) To take (a prisoner or cause) from the jurisdiction of one court to that of another on the pledge that justice shall be done.

replenish (rė plen′ ish) [O.F. *repleniss-*, pres.p. stem of *replenir* (RE-, L. *plēnus*, full)], *v.t.* To fill up again; to fill completely; to stock abundantly; *to occupy completely; *to finish, to perfect. *v.i.* To become filled. **replenisher,** *n.* **replenishment,** *n.*

replete (rė plēt′) [F. *replet, -plète,* L. *replētus,* p.p. of *replēre* (RE-, *plēre,* to fill)], *a.* Completely filled; abundantly supplied or stocked (with); filled to excess, sated, gorged (with). **repletion,** *n.* The state of being replete; eating and drinking to satiety; surfeit; fullness of blood, a plethoric condition. ***repletive, repletory,** *a.* **repletively,** *adv.*

replevy (rė plev′ i) [A.-F. and O.F. *replevir* (RE-, *plevir,* etym. doubtful, cp. PLEDGE)], *v.t.* (*Law*) To recover possession of (distrained goods) upon giving security to submit the matter to a court and to surrender the goods if required. *n.* A replevin. **repleviable, replevisable,** *a.* **replevin,** *n.* An action for replevying; the writ by which goods are replevied.

replica (rep′ li kȧ) [It., from *replicare,* to REPLY], *n.* A duplicate of a picture, sculpture, etc., by the artist who executed the original; an exact copy, a facsimile.

replicate (rep′ li kȧt) [L. *replicātus,* p.p. of *replicāre* (RE-, *plicāre,* to fold)], *a.* (*Bot.*) Folded back on itself. *n.* (*Mus.*) A tone one or more octaves above or below a given tone. *v.t.* (-kāt) To fold back on itself; (*Mus.*) to add a replicate to (a tone); *to reproduce, to make a replica of; *to repeat; *to reply. **replicatile,** *a.* (*Ent.*) Capable of being folded back (of a wing). **replication** (-kā′ shŭn), *n.* A reply, a rejoinder; (*Law*) the reply of a plaintiff to the defendant's plea; an echo, a repetition, *a copy, an imitation; (*Mus.*) a replicate. **replicative** (rep′ li kȧ tiv), *a.* (*Bot.*)

replier [REPLY].

replum (rep′ lŭm) [L., a bolt], *n.* (*pl.* **-pla**) (*Bot.*) The central process or placenta remaining after the valves of a dehiscent fruit have fallen away.

replume (rē ploom′), *v.t.* To preen or rearrange.

replunge (rē plŭnj′), *v.t.* and *i.* To plunge again. *n.* The act of plunging again. **replunger,** *n.*

reply (rė plī′) [O.F. *replier,* L. *replicāre* (RE-, *plicāre,* to fold, cp. REPLICATE)], *v.i.* To answer, to respond, to make answer orally, in writing, or by action; (*Law*) to plead in answer to a defendant's plea. *v.t.* To return as in answer; to answer (that, etc.). *n.* The act of replying; that which is said, written, or done in answer, a response.

repoint (rē point′), *v.t.* and *i.* To point again. **repolish** (rē pol′ ish), *v.t.* To polish again. **repone** (rė pōn′) [L. *repōnere* (*pōnere,* to place), cp. REPOSE (1)], *v.t.* To replace, to rehabilitate; (*Sc. Law*) to restore to a former position; *to reply. **repopulate** (rē pop′ ū lāt), *v.t.* To populate again.

report (rė pôrt′) [O.F. *reporter,* L. *reportāre* (RE-, *portāre,* to bring)], *v.t.* To bring back as an answer; to give an account of, to describe or to narrate, esp. as an eye-witness; to state as a fact or as news; to prepare a record of, esp. for official use or for publication; to take down in full or to summarize (a speech, sermon, etc.); to announce, to make a formal or official statement about, to certify; to give information against. *v.i.* To make or tender a report; to act as a reporter; to report oneself (at a certain place, etc.). *n.* That which is reported, esp. the formal statement of the result of an investigation, trial, etc.; a detailed account of a speech, meeting, etc., esp. for publication in a newspaper; common talk, popular rumour; fame, repute, accepted character; end-of-term statement of a pupil's work and behaviour at school; a loud noise, esp. of an explosive kind. **report stage:** (*Parl.*) The stage of progress with a Bill in the House of Commons when a committee has reported. **to report a Bill to the House:** (*Parl.*) To state that the Committee has finished its consideration of a Bill (between the 2nd and 3rd readings). **to report oneself:** To report that one has arrived at one's place of duty, etc. **to report progress:** (*Parl.*) To state what has been done on a Bill up to the time being. **reportable,** *a.* **reportage,** *n.* Gossip.

reporter (rė pôr′ tėr), *n.* One who reports; one who draws up official statements of law proceedings and decisions of legislative debates; one who reports public meetings, etc., for a newspaper. **reporterism, reportership,** *n.* ***reportingly,** *adv.* **reportorial** (-tôr′ i ȧl), *a.*

repose (1) (rė pōz′) [L. *repos-,* p.p. stem of *repōnere* (RE-, *pōnere,* to place, p.p. *positum*), assim. to foll.], *v.t.* To place, to put (confidence, etc. in). **reposal,** *n.*

repose (2) (rė pōz′) [F. *reposer,* late L. *repausāre* (RE-, *pausāre,* to PAUSE, conf. with L. *pōnere,* see prec.)], *v.t.* To lay (oneself, etc.) to rest, to rest; to refresh with rest; to place at rest, to cause to rest or recline. *v.i.* To rest; to lie at rest; to be laid or be in a recumbent position, esp. in sleep or death; to rest or be supported (on). *n.* The act of resting or being at rest; rest, cessation of activity, excitement, toil, etc.; sleep, quiet, tranquillity, calmness, composure, ease of manner, etc.; (*Art.*) restful effect; quietude, moderation and harmony of colour and treatment. **altar of repose:** (*R.-C.Ch.*) The altar upon which the Blessed Sacrament is reserved from Maundy Thursday to Good Friday. **reposedness,** *n.* **reposeful,** *a.* **reposefully,** *adv.* **reposefulness,** *n.*

reposit (rė poz′ it) [L. *repositus,* p.p. of *repōnere,* to REPONE], *v.t.* To lay up; to deposit, as in a place of safety. **reposition** (-zish′ ŭn), *n.* **repositor** (rė poz′ i tôr), *n.* (*Surg.*) An instrument for replacing (used for prolapsus).

repository (rė poz′ i tôr i), *n.* A place where things are deposited for safety or preservation; a depository, a museum, a store, a magazine, a shop, a warehouse, a vault, a sepulchre; (*fig.*) a person to whom a secret, etc., is confided.

repossess (rē pȯ zes′), *v.t.* To possess again. **repossession** (-zesh′ ŭn), *n.* **repot** (rė pot′), *v.t.* To put (a plant) into a fresh pot.

repoussé (rė poo′ sā) [F., p.p. of *repousser* (RE-, *pousser,* to PUSH)], *a.* Formed in relief by hammering from behind (of ornamental metal work). *n.* Metal work ornamented in this way. **repoussage** (rė poo sazh′), *n.*

repp, repped [REP (1)].

reprehend (rep rė hend′) [L. *reprehendere* (RE-, *prehendere,* to seize, cp. COMPREHEND), p.p. *reprehensus*], *v.t.* To find fault with; to censure, to blame; *to convict of fallacy. **reprehender,** *n.* **reprehensible,** *a.* **reprehensibleness,** *n.* **reprehensibly,** *adv.* **reprehension,** *n.* ***reprehensive, *-sory,** *a.*

represent (rep rė zent′) [O.F. *representer,* L. *repræsentāre*], *v.t.* To present to or bring before the mind by describing, portraying, imitating, etc.; to serve as a likeness of, to depict (of a picture, etc.); to set forth, to state (that), to describe (as), to make out (to be); to enact (a play, etc.) on the stage, to personate, to play the part of; to serve as symbol for, to stand for, to be an example or specimen of; to take the place of as deputy, substitute, etc.; to act as agent or spokesman for, esp. in a representative chamber; (*Psych.*) to bring a mental image of (an event, object, etc.) before the mind. **representable,** *a.* **representer,** *n.* **representment,** *n.*

representation (rep rė zen tā′ shŭn), *n.* The act of representing; a dramatic performance; a statement of arguments, etc.; the system of representing bodies of people in a legislative assembly; the rights, status, or functions of a representative; representatives collectively. **proportional representation:** An electoral system by which minorities are represented in proportion to their numbers. **representational,** *a.* **representationism,** *n.* The doctrine that the immediate object in perception is only an idea, image, or other representation of the external thing. **representationist,** *n.*

representative (rep rė zen′ tȧ tiv), *a.* Serving to represent or symbolize, able or fitted to represent, typical; presenting the general characters of; similar or corresponding to other species, etc., living elsewhere; acting as agent, delegate, deputy, etc.; consisting of delegates, etc.; based on representation by delegates; presenting images or ideas to the mind. *n.* One who or that which represents; an example, a specimen, a typical instance or embodiment; an agent, deputy, or substitute, esp. a person chosen by a body of electors; (*Law*) one who stands in the place of another as heir, etc. **representative government**, *n.* System of government by representatives elected by the people. **House of Representatives,** *n.* The lower house of the U.S. Congress. **representatively,** *adv.* **representativeness,** *n.*

repress (rė pres′) [L. *repressus*, p.p. of *reprimere* (RE-, *premere*, to PRESS (1))], *v.* To restrain, to keep under restraint; to put down, to suppress, to quell; to prevent from breaking out, etc. ***represser,** *n.* **repressible,** *a.* **repressive** (-pres′ iv), *a.* **repressively,** *adv.*

repression (rė presh′ ůn), *n.* The act of repressing; (*Psych.*) unconscious exclusion from the thoughts of complexes and processes which are painful.

reprieve (rė prēv′) [from obs. *repry*, to remand, A.-F. and O.F. *repris*, p.p. of *reprendre* (RE-, L. *prehendere*, to seize, see COMPREHEND)], *v.t.* To suspend the execution of for a time; to grant a respite to; (*fig.*) to rescue, to save (from); *to set free, to acquit. *n.* The temporary suspension of a sentence on a prisoner; the warrant authorizing this; a respite. ***reprieval,** *n.*

reprimand (rep′ ri mand) [F. *réprimande, reprimende*, from *reprimer*, to REPRESS], *n.* A severe reproof, a rebuke, esp. a public or official one. *v.t.* (rep ri mand′) To reprove severely, to rebuke, esp. publicly or officially.

reprint (rē print′), *v.t.* To print (a book, etc.) again; to print (letterpress, etc.) over again; *to renew the impression of (a word, mark, etc.). *n.* (rē′ print) A new edition or impression of a printed work without considerable alteration of the contents.

reprisal (rė prī′ zål) [O.F. *reprisaille* (cp. F. *représaille*, It. *ripresaglia*), from foll.], *n.* The act of seizing from an enemy by way of indemnification or retaliation; that which is so taken; any act of retaliation.

reprise (rė prīz′) [F., fem. of *repris*, p.p. of *reprendre*, see REPRIEVE], *n.* (*Law*) A yearly rent-charge or other payment out of a manor and lands (*usu. in pl.*); (*Mus.*) a refrain, a repeated phrase, etc.; *a resumption or renewal of action; *a reprisal.

reprize (rē prīz′), *v.t.* To prize anew.

reproach (rė prōch′) [F. *reprocher*, etym. doubtful (perh. from a pop. L. *repropriāre*, from L. *prope*, near, cp. as APPROACH, or from L. as APPROVE)], *v.t.* To censure in opprobrious terms, to upbraid; to find fault with (something done); *to disgrace. *n.* Censure mingled with opprobrium or grief; a rebuke, a censure; shame, infamy, disgrace; an object or cause of scorn or derision. **reproachable,** *a.* ***reproachableness,** *n.* **reproachably,** *adv.* **reproacher,** *n.* **reproachful,** *a.* Containing or expressing reproach; upbraiding, opprobrious, abusive; shameful, infamous, base. **reproachfully,** *adv.* **reproachfulness,** *n.* **reproachingly,** *adv.* **reproachless,** *a.* **reproachlessness,** *n.*

reprobate (rep′ rō bāt) [L. *reprobātus*, p.p. of *reprobāre*, see REPROVE], *a.* Abandoned to sin, lost to virtue or grace; depraved. *n.* One who is abandoned to sin; a wicked, depraved wretch. *v.t.* (-bāt) To express disapproval and detestation of, to condemn severely; to abandon to wickedness and eternal punishment; *to disallow, to reject. ***reprobacy,** ***reprobance,** ***reprobateness,** *n.* ***reprobater,** *n.* **reprobation** (-bā′ shůn), *n.* ***reprobationer,** *n.* (*Theol.*) One who believes in the doctrine of the reprobation of the non-elect. **reprobative, reprobatory** (rep′ rō bā tiv, -tôr i), *a.*

reproduce (rē prō dūs′), *v.t.* To produce again; to copy. **reproducer,** *n.* **reproducible,** *a.* **reproduction** (-dŭk′ shůn), *n.* **reproductive, -tory,** *a.* **reproductively,** *adv.* **reproductiveness, reproductivity** (-tiv′ i ti), *n.* **repromulgate** (rē prō′ můl gāt), *v.t.* To promulgate anew.

reproof (rė proof′) [O.F. *reprove*, from *reprover*, L. *reprobāre*, to disapprove (RE-, *probāre*, to PROVE)], *n.* An expression of blame; censure, blame, reprehension; disproof. **reprove** (rė proov′), *v.t.* To rebuke, to censure, esp. to one's face, to chide; *to convict; *to disprove. *to refute. **reprovable,** *a.* ***reprovableness,** *n.* ***reprovably,** *adv.* ***reproval,** *n.* **reprover,** *n.* **reprovingly,** *adv.*

reprovision (rē prō vizh′ ůn), *v.t.* To provision (a ship, etc.) afresh. **reprune** (rē proon′), *v.t.* To prune again.

reps [var. of REP (1)].

reptant (rep′ tånt) [L. *reptans -ntem*, pres.p. of *reptāre*, freq. of *rēpere*, to creep], *a.* (*Nat. Hist.*) Creeping. **reptation** (-tā′ shůn), *n.* **reptatory** (rep′-), *a.*

reptile (rep′ tīl, -til) [F., from late L. *reptilis*, from *rēpere*, to creep, p.p. *reptus*], *a.* Creeping, crawling, moving on the belly or on small, short legs; (*fig.*) grovelling, servile, mean, base. *n.* A crawling animal; one of the *Reptilia*, a class of animals comprising the snakes, lizards, turtles, crocodiles, etc.; (*fig.*) a grovelling, mean, base person. **reptilian** (-til′ i ån), *a.* and *n.* **reptiliferous** (-lif′ ėr ůs), *a.* (*Geol.*) Containing fossil reptiles. **reptiliform** (rep til′ i fôrm), **reptilious, reptiloid** (rep′ ti loid), *a.* **reptilivorous** (-liv′ ō růs), *a.* Devouring reptiles.

republic (rė pŭb′ lik) [F. *république*, L. *rēspublica* (*rēs*, thing, concern, PUBLIC)], *n.* A State or a form of political constitution in which the supreme power is vested in the people or their elected representatives, a commonwealth. **republic of letters** [LETTER]. **republican,** *a.* Pertaining to or consisting of a republic; characteristic of the principles of a republic; believing in or advocating these; (*Ornith.*) social, nesting in large companies. *n.* One who favours or advocates a republican form of government; a member of the Republican party in the U.S.A. **Republican Party:** The alternative political party to the Democratic in the government of the U.S.A. **republicanism,** *n.* **republicanize,** *v.t.*

republish (rē pŭb′ lish), *v.t.* To publish again; to print a new edition of. ***republisher,** *n.* **republication** (-kā′ shůn), *n.*

repudiate (rė pū′ di āt) [L. *repudiātus*, p.p. of *repudiāre*, from *repudium*, divorce (RE-, *pud-*, stem of *pudēre*, to feel shame)], *v.t.* To refuse to acknowledge, to disown, to disclaim (a debt, etc.); to disavow, to reject, to refuse to admit, accept, recognize, etc.; to cast off, to put away, to divorce (one's wife). *v.i.* To repudiate a public debt (of a State). ***repudiable,** *a.* **repudiation** (-ā′ shůn), *n.* **repudiationist,** *n.* One in favour of repudiating a public debt. **repudiator** (-pū′ di ā tôr), *n.*

repugn (rė pūn′) [F. *répugner*, L. *repugnāre* (RE-, *pugnāre*, to fight)], *v.i.* To oppose, to resist, to strive (against); *(*fig.*) to be repugnant (to) or inconsistent (with). *v.t.* To combat, to oppose, to strive against.

repugnance, repugnancy (re pŭg′ nåns, -si), *n.* Antipathy, dislike, distaste, aversion; inconsistency, incompatibility, or opposition, of mind, disposition, statements, ideas, etc. **repugnant,** *a.* **repugnantly,** *adv.*

repullulate (rė pŭl′ ū lāt) [L. *repullulāre*], *v.i.* To sprout, shoot, or bud again; (*Path.*) to break out again, to recur, to reappear (of a disease or morbid growth). **repullulation** (-lā′ shůn), *n.* **repullulescent** (-les′ ėnt), *a.*

repulse (rė pŭls′) [L. *repulsus*, p.p. of *repellere* (RE-, *pellere*, to drive)], *v.t.* To repel, to beat or drive back, esp. by force of arms; (*fig.*) to reject, esp. in a churlish manner, to rebuff, to snub; to defeat in argument. *n.* The act of repulsing; the state of being repulsed; a rebuff, a refusal, a failure, a disappointment. **repulser,** *n.* **repulsion** (-pŭl′ shůn), *n.*

The act of repulsing; the state of being repulsed; (*Phys.*) the tendency of certain bodies to repel each other, opp. to attraction; (*fig.*) dislike, repugnance, aversion. **repulsive, repulsory,** *a.* Acting so as to repel; unsympathetic, forbidding; repellent, loathsome, disgusting; (*Phys.*) acting by repulsion. **repulsively,** *adv.* **repulsiveness,** *n.*

repurchase (rē pĕr′ chȧs), *v.t.* To purchase back or again. *n.* The act of buying again; that which is so bought. ***repure** (-pūr′), **repurify,** *v.t.* To make pure again.

reputable (rep′ ū tȧ bėl), *a.* Being in good repute; respectable, creditable. **reputableness,** *n.* **reputably,** *adv.*

reputation (rep ū tā′ shŭn) [L. *reputātio,* from *reputāre,* to REPUTE], *n.* The estimation in which one is generally held, repute; good estimation, good fame, credit, esteem, respectability; *estimation, consideration; character or repute; the repute, honour, or credit derived from favourable public opinion or esteem. **reputative,** *a.* Putative. ***reputatively,** *adv.*

repute (rė pūt′) [F. *réputer,* L. *reputāre* (RE-, *putāre,* to think)], *v.t.* To think, to account, to reckon; (*chiefly in p.p.*) to consider, to report, to regard (as). *n.* Reputation, fame; character attributed by public report. **reputed,** *a.* Generally regarded (usu. with implication of doubt, etc.). **reputed pint:** A bottle of beer, etc., sold as holding a pint but not guaranteed as such. **reputedly,** *adv.* ***reputeless,** *a.*

request (rė kwest′) [O.F. *requeste* (RE-, QUEST)], *n.* An expression of desire or the act of asking for something to be granted or done; a petition; that which is asked for; the state of being demanded or sought after; *an inquiry. *v.t.* To ask (that); to address a request to. ***requestant, requester,** *n.*

requicken (rē kwik′ ėn), *v.t.* To quicken again, to reanimate.

requiem (rē′ kwi ėm, rek′ wi ėm) [L., rest (the first word of the introit *Requiem æternam dona ies, Domine*)], *n.* A mass for the repose of the soul of a person deceased; the musical setting of this, a dirge; *repose, rest, quiet.

requiescat (rek wi es′ kăt) [L. *requiescat in pace,* let him (or her) rest in peace], *n.* A wish or prayer for the repose of the dead.

require (rė kwīr′) [O.F. *requerre* (F. *requérir*), assim. to L. *requīrere* (RE-, *quærere,* to seek)], *v.t.* To ask or claim as a right or by authority, to order; to demand (something of a person), to insist (on having, that, etc.); to have need of, to call for imperatively, to depend upon for completion, etc. *v.i.* To be necessary. **requirable,** *a.* **requirement,** *n.* That which is required; an essential condition; *the act of requiring, a requisition. ***requirer,** *n.*

requisite (rek′ wi zit) [L. *requīsītus,* p.p. of *requīrere,* as prec.], *a.* Required by the nature of things, necessary for completion, etc., indispensable. *n.* That which is required; a necessary part or quality. ***requisitely,** *adv.* **requisiteness,** *n.*

requisition (rek wi zish′ ŭn) [F. *réquisition,* L. *requīsītiōnem,* nom. *-tio,* as prec.], *n.* The act of requiring or demanding; application made as of right; a formal and usu. written demand or request for the performance of a duty, etc.; an authoritative order for the supply of provisions, etc., esp. a military order to a town, etc.; the state of being called upon or put in use. *v.t.* To make a formal or authoritative demand for, esp. for military purposes; to make such a demand upon (a town, etc.); to take upon requisition, to call in for use; (*Am.*) to indent. **requisitionist,** *n.* One who makes a requisition. ***requisitive** (rė kwiz′ i tiv), *a.* and *n.* ***requisitory,** *a.*

requite (rė kwīt′) [RE-, *quite,* var. of QUIT], *v.t.* To repay, to make return to, to recompense; to give or deal in return; to make return for; to reward, to avenge. **requital,** *n.* **requiter,** *n.*

rerail (rē rāl′), *v.t.* To put (rolling stock) on the rails again. **re-read** (rē rēd′), *v.t.* To read or peruse again.

reredos (rēr′ ė dos) [M.E. *rere,* REAR (2), F. *dos.* L. *dorsum,* back], *n.* (*pl.* **-doses**) The ornamental screen at the back of an altar; the back of an open hearth, a fire-back.

resaddle (rē săd′ ėl), *v.t.* and *i.* To saddle again. **resail** (rē sāl′), *v.t.* To sail (a race, etc.) again. *v.i.* To sail back again. **resale** (rē sāl′), *n.* A second sale; a sale at second hand. ***resalute** (rē sȧ loot′), *v.t.* To salute again; to salute in return.

rescind (rė sind′) [F. *rescinder,* L. *rescindere* (RE-, *scindere,* to cut, p.p. *scissus*)], *v.t.* To annul, to cancel, to revoke, to abrogate; *to cut off or away. **rescission** (-sizh′ ŭn), *n.* **recissory** (-sis′ ȯ ri), *a.*

***rescribe** (rė skrīb′) [L. *rescribere* (RE-, *scrībere,* to write)], *v.t.* To write again, to rewrite; to write back.

rescript (rē′ skript) [L. *rescriptum,* neut. p.p. of prec.], *n.* (*Rom. Law*) The answer or decision of a Roman emperor to a question or appeal, esp. on a point of jurisprudence; a Pope's written reply to a question of canon law, morality, etc.; an edict, a decree, an order, or official announcement; something rewritten, the act of rewriting; a palimpsest. ***rescription,** *n.* ***rescriptive,** *a.* ***rescriptively,** *adv.*

rescue (res′ kū) [O.F. *rescoure* (F. *recourre*) (ult. RE-, L. *excutere,* EX- *cutere, quatere,* to shake)], *v.t.* To deliver from confinement, danger, evil, or injury; forcible seizure (*Law*) to liberate by unlawful means from lawful custody, to recover (property, etc.) by force. *n.* Deliverance from confinement, danger, evil, or injury; forcible seizure (of a person, property, etc.) from the custody of the law. **rescuable,** *a.* **rescuer,** *n.*

research (rė sĕrch′) [F. *recerche* (now *recherche*), *n.* Diligent and careful inquiry or investigation; (*pl.*) systematic study of phenomena, etc., a course of critical investigation. *v.i.* To make researches. *v.t.* To make careful and systematic investigation into. **researcher,** *n.*

reseat (rē sēt′), *v.t.* To seat again; to replace (a person) in a seat; to furnish (a church, etc.) with new seats; to provide (a chair, pair of trousers, etc.) with a new seat.

resect (rė sekt′) [L. *resectus,* p.p. of *resecāre* (RE-, *secāre,* to cut)], *v.t.* (*Surg.*) To excise a section of an organ or part; to cut or pare down, esp. the articular extremity of a bone. **resection,** *n.*

reseda (rė sē′ dȧ) [L., prob. imper. of *resedāre,* to assuage (first word of a charm for allaying tumours)], *n.* (*Bot.*) A genus of plants containing the mignonette and dyer's weed; a pale or greyish green (usu. in F. form ***réséda***).

reseek (rē sēk′), *v.t.* To seek again. **reseize** (rē sēz′) [O.F. *resaisir* (F. *ressaisir*)], *v.t.* To seize again; to take possession of (disseized lands and tenements); *to reinstate. ***reseizer,** *n.* ***reseizure,** *n.* **resell** (rē sel′), *v.t.* To sell again.

resemble (rė zem′ bėl) [O.F. *resembler* (F. *ressembler*) (RE-, *sembler,* L. *similāre, simulāre,* from *similis,* SIMILAR)], *v.t.* To be like, to be similar to; to have features, nature, etc., like those of; *to liken, to compare, *to imitate, to counterfeit. **v.i.* To be similar (to). ***resemblable,** *a.* **resemblance,** *n.* **resemblant,** *a.*

resend (rē send′), *v.t.* To send back or again.

resent (rė zent′) [F. *ressentir* (RE-, *sentir,* L. *sentire,* to feel)], *v.t.* To regard as an injury or insult; to feel or show displeasure or indignation at; to cherish bitter feelings about; *to perceive by the senses, to be sensibly affected by. *v.i.* To feel indignant. **resenter,** *n.* **resentful,** *a.* **resentfully,** *adv.* **resentfulness,** *n.* **resentingly,** *adv.* ***resentive,** *a.* **resentment,** *n.*

reservation (rez ėr vā′ shŭn), *n.* The act of reserving; that which is reserved; the booking of accommodation in an hotel, train, ship, etc.; (*Am.*) a tract of land reserved for native Indian tribes or for public use; (*R.-C. Ch.*) the reserving of the right of nomination to benefices, of the power of absolution, or of a portion of the consecrated elements of the Eucharist; an expressed or tacit limitation, exception, or qualification. **mental reservation:** An unexpressed qualification or exception radically affecting or altering the meaning of a statement, oath, etc.

reserve (rė zěrv') [O.F. *reserver*, L. *reservāre* (RE-, *servāre*, to keep)], *v.t.* To keep back for future use, enjoyment, treatment, etc., to hold over, to postpone, to keep in store; to retain for oneself or another, esp. as an exception from something granted; to keep or set apart; (*R.-C. Ch.*) to retain the right of nomination to a benefice for the Pope; to set apart (a case) for absolution by the Pope, a bishop, etc.; to retain a portion of the consecrated elements of the Eucharist; (*in p.p.*) to set apart for a certain fate, to destine; *to preserve. *n.* That which is reserved; a sum of money or a fund reserved, esp. by bankers, to meet any demand; a reservation of land; (*Mil.*) troops kept for any emergency, such as to act as reinforcements or cover a retreat; a part of the military or naval forces not embodied in the regular army and navy, but liable to be called up in case of emergency; a member of these forces, a reservist; the state of being reserved or kept back for a special purpose; mental reservation, exception or qualification; a limitation attached to a price, etc.; an award to an exhibit entitling it to a prize if another should be disqualified; reticence, self-restraint, caution in speaking or action. **in reserve:** Reserved from and ready for use in emergency. **without reserve:** (Offered for sale) to the highest bidder without the condition of a reserve price. **reserve price:** A price below which no offer will be accepted. ***reservative** (rė zěr' vȧ tiv), *a.* ***reservatory,** *n.* A receptacle, a reservoir. **reservist,** *n.* A member of the military or naval reserve.

reserved (rė zěrvd'), *a.* Reticent, backward in communicating one's thoughts or feelings, undemonstrative, distant; retained for a particular use, person, etc. **reserved list:** A list of naval officers not on active service but liable to be called up in emergency. **reserved sacrament,** *n.* (*Eccles.*) Portion of the consecrated elements reserved after communion, for adoration. **reservedly** (rė zěr' vėd li), *adv.* **reservedness,** *n.*

reservoir (rez' ėr vwar) [F. *réservoir*, late L. *reservātorium*, as prec.], *n.* A receptacle in which a quantity of anything, esp. fluid, may be kept in store; a receptacle of earthwork or masonry for the storage of water in large quantity; a part of an implement, machine, animal or vegetable organ, etc., acting as a receptacle for fluid; (*fig.*) a reserve supply or store of anything. *v.t.* To collect or store in a reservoir.

reset (1) (rē set') [RE-, SET (1)], *v.t.* To set (type, a jewel, etc.) again. *n.* (*Print.*) Matter set up again. **resettable,** *a.*

***reset** (2) (rė set') [O.F. *recet*, L. *receptum*, p.p. of *recipere*, to RECEIVE], *n.* The receiving of stolen goods; (*Sc. Law*) the act of harbouring an outlaw or criminal. *v.t.* (*Sc. Law*) To receive (stolen goods); to harbour (an outlaw, etc.). *v.i.* To receive stolen goods. **resetter,** *n.* **resettle** (rē set' ėl), *v.t.* and *i.* To settle again. **resettlement,** *n.* **reshape** (rē shāp'), *v.t.* To shape again. **reship** (rē ship'), *v.t.* and *i.* To ship again. **reshipment,** *n.* **reshuffle** (rē shŭf' ėl), *v.t.* To shuffle again. *n.* The act of reshuffling.

***resiant** (rez' i ȧnt) [O.F. *reseant*, pres.p. of *reseoir*, L. *residēre*, to RESIDE], *a.* Residing, resident. *n.* A resident. ***resiance,** *n.*

reside (rė zīd') [F. *résider*, L. *residēre* (RE-, *sedēre*, to sit)], *v.i.* To dwell permanently or for a considerable length of time, to have one's home (at); to be in official residence; (of qualities, rights, etc.) to inhere, to be vested (in), *to be precipitated, to sink.

residence (rez' i dėns), *n.* The act or state of residing in a place; the act of living or remaining where one's duties lie; the place where one dwells, one's abode; (*colloq.*) a house of some size or pretensions. **Residency,** *n.* Formerly the official residence of a minister resident in India.

resident (res' i dėnt), *a.* Residing; having a residence, esp. official quarters in connexion with one's duties; (*Ornith.*) non-migratory; inherent; *fixed, firm. *n.* One who dwells permanently in a place as dist. from a visitor. **residenter,** *n.* (*Sc.*) A resident.

residential (rez i den' shȧl), *a.* Suitable for residence or for residences; pertaining to residence. **residentiary,** *a.* Maintaining or bound to an official residence. *n.* An ecclesiastic bound to an official residence.

residue (rez' i dū) [A.-F. (F. *résidu*), L. *residuum*, nom. *-duus*, remaining, as prec.], *n.* That which is left or remains over; the rest, the remainder; that which remains of an estate after payment of all charges, debts, and particular bequests; residuum. **residual,** *a.* Of the nature of a residue or residuum; remaining after a part has been taken away; (*Math.*) left by a process of subtraction; remaining unexplained or uneliminated. *n.* (*Math.*) A residual quantity, a remainder; the difference between the computed and the observed value of a quantity at any given moment, a residual error. **residuary,** *a.* Pertaining to or forming a residue, residual, remaining; pertaining to the residue of an estate. **residuary legatee:** One to whom is bequeathed the residue of an estate after deduction of all charges, debts, and specific legacies. **residuation** (rė' zid ū ā' shŭn), *n.* (*Math.*) The process of finding a residual. **residuum** (rė zid' ū ŭm), *n.* (*pl.* **-dua**) That which is left after any process of separation or purification, esp. (*Chem.*) after combustion, evaporation, etc.; (*Math.*) the remainder left by subtraction or division, a residual error; the lowest classes, the dregs of society.

re-sign (rē sīn'), *v.t.* To sign again.

resign (rė zīn') [O.F. *resigner*, L. *resignare*, to unseal (RE-, *signāre*, to seal, see SIGN)], *v.t.* To give up, to surrender, to relinquish; to hand over (to or unto); to renounce, to abandon; to yield, to submit, to reconcile (oneself, one's mind, etc., to). *v.i.* To give up office, to retire (from). **resignation** (rez ig nā' shŭn), *n.* The act of resigning, esp. an office; a document announcing this; the state of being resigned, patience, acquiescence, submission, esp. to the Divine will. **resigned** (rė zīnd'), *a.* Submissive, patiently acquiescent or enduring; surrendered, given up. **resignedly** (rė zī' nėd li), *adv.* ***resignee** (rez i nē'), **resigner,** *n.* ***resignment,** *n.*

resile (rė zīl') [obs. F. *resiler*, L. *resilēre* (RE-, *salīre*, to leap)], *v.i.* To spring back, to rebound, to recoil; to resume the original shape after compression, stretching, etc.; to show elasticity (*lit.* and *fig.*). **resilience, -cy** (rė zil' i ėns, -ėn si), *n.* **resilient,** *a.* ***resilition,** *n.*

resin (rez' in) [F. *résine*, L. *rēsīna*, rel. to Gr. *rhētinē*], *n.* An amorphous inflammable vegetable substance secreted by plants and usu. obtained by exudation, esp. from the fir and pine; a similar substance obtained by the chemical treatment of various vegetable products. **mineral resin:** A resin obtained from minerals, as asphalt or bitumen. ***resinaceous** (-nā' shŭs), *a.* **resiniferous** (-nif' ėr ŭs), **resiniform** (rez' i ni fôrm), *a.* **resinify,** *v.t.* and *i.* **resinification** (-kā' shŭn), *n.* **resino-,** (*comb. form*). **resino-electric,** *a.* Capable of being negatively electrified, as amber and other resins. **resinoid** (rez' i noid), *a.* and *n.* **resinol,** *n.* A colourless resinous alcohol, retinol. **resinolic** (-nol' ik), *a.* **resinous,** *a.* Pertaining to or resembling resin; obtained from resin; (*Elec.*) negative. **resinously,** *adv.* **resinousness,** *n.* **resiny,** *a.*

resipiscence (res i pis' ėns) [L. *resipiscentia*, from *resipicere* (RE-, *sapere*, to be wise, see SAPIENT)], *n.* Wisdom after the fact; recognition of error, etc. **resipiscent,** *a.*

resist (rė zist') [O.F. *resister*, L. *resistere* (RE-, *sistere*, redupl. of *stare*, to stand)], *v.t.* To stand or strive against, to act in opposition to, to endeavour to frustrate; to oppose successfully, to withstand, to stop, to repel, to frustrate, to be proof against; to be disagreeable to. *v.i.* To offer resistance. *n.* A substance applied to a surface, etc., to prevent the action of a chemical agent, such as the mordant used in dyeing calico. **resistant,** *n.* (also *a.*). A resister. **resister,** *n.* **passive resister:** A person refusing on conscientious grounds to perform an action or to pay a tax or rate, esp. the education rate. **resistible,** *a.* **resistibility** (-bil' i ti), **resistibleness,** *n.* **resistibly, resistingly,** *adv.* **resistive,** *a.* **resistless,** *a.* **resistlessly,** *adv.* **resistlessness,** *n.* **resistor,** *n.* (*Elec.*) A resisting device.

resistance (re zis' tȧns), *n.* The act or power of resisting; opposition, refusal to comply; that which hinders or retards, esp. the opposition exerted by a fluid to the passage of a body; the opposition exerted by a substance to the passage of electric current, heat, etc. through it; (*Med.*) the natural power to withstand disease; (*Elec.*) a resistance-coil, etc.; (*Psych.*) an unconscious mental barrier against bringing the unconscious to light. **resistance-coil,** *n.* (*Elec.*) A coil of insulated wire used to offer resistance to a current. **Resistance Movement:** An underground organization of civilians and others in an enemy-occupied country directed to sabotaging the invaders' plans and rendering their position as difficult as possible. **passive resister** [PASSIVE]. **resistor,** *n.* An electronic component with a specified resistance.

resolder (rē sol' dėr), *v.t.* To solder again. **resoluble** (rē sol' ūbl), *a.* Capable of being dissolved again.

resolute (rez' ȯ loot, -lūt) [L. *resolūtus*, p.p. of *resolvere*, see foll.], *a.* Having a fixed purpose, determined, constant in pursuing an object, firm, decided, unflinching, bold. **n.* A determined person, a desperado. *v.i.* (*Am. slang*) To draw up and pass resolutions. **resolutely,** *adv.* **resoluteness,** *n.*

resolution (rez ȯ lū' shȯn, rez ȯ loo' shŭn), *n.* The act or process of resolving or separating anything into the component parts, decomposition, analysis; (*Mech.*) analysis of a force into two or more jointly equivalent, as in a parallelogram of forces; (*Path.*) the disappearance of inflammation without production of pus; (*Mus.*) the conversion of a discord into a concord; the substitution of two short syllables for a long one; mental analysis, solution of a problem, etc.; a formal proposition, statement of opinion, or decision by a legislative or corporate body or public meeting; a proposition put forward for discussion and approval; a resolve, a settled purpose; resoluteness, determination, firmness and boldness in adhering to one's purpose. ***Resolutioner,** *n.* A member of the party in Scotland supporting the resolutions passed in 1650 admitting to service in the army opposing Cromwell all who were not excommunicated or professed enemies to the Covenant. **resolutionist,** *n.* One who makes or supports a resolution. **resolutive** (rez' ȯ loo-, -lū tiv), *a.* Having the power or tending to resolve, dissolve, or relax; (*Med.*) a drug or application for resolving or dispersing morbid matter. ***resolutory,** *a.*

resolve (rė zolv') [L. *resolvere* (RE-, *solvere*, to loosen, see SOLVE)], *v.t.* To separate into the component parts; to dissolve, to analyse, to disintegrate, to dissipate; to reduce to the constituent parts or elements; to analyse mentally, to solve, to explain, to clear up, to answer; to convert (into) by analysis; (*Med.*) to cause to disperse or pass away without suppuration; (*Mus.*) to convert (a discord) into concord; to make up one's mind, to decide, to determine on; to pass by vote a resolution that; to cause (a person) to decide or determine; *to relax. *v.i.* To separate into the component parts, to dissolve, to break up, to be analysed; (*Med.*) to pass away without suppuration; (*Mus.*) to be converted from discord into concord; to make one's mind up, to decide or determine (upon); to pass a resolution. *n.* A resolution, a firm decision or determination; resoluteness, firmness of purpose; (*Am.*) a resolution by a deliberative assembly. **resolvable,** *a.* **resolvability** (-bil' i ti), ***resolvableness,** *n.* **resolved** (rė zolvd'), *a.* Determined, resolute. **resolvedly** (-zol' vėd li), *adv.* ***resolvedness,** *n.* **resolvent,** *a.* Having the power of resolving, dissolving, or disintegrating. *n.* That which has the power of resolving, esp. a chemical substance, drug, or medical application, a discutient. **resolver,** *n.*

resonance (rez' ȯ nȧns) [as foll.], *n.* The quality or state of being resonant; (*Eng.*) the specially large vibration of a body when a force of suitable frequency is applied to it; (*Elec. and Radio.*) the sympathetic oscillation of current in a circuit at a particular frequency.

resonant (rez' ȯ nȧnt) [L. *resonans -ntem*, pres.p. of *resonāre* (RE-, *sonāre*, to SOUND (2))], *a.* Capable of returning sound; re-echoing, resounding; having the property of prolonging or reinforcing sound, esp. by vibration; (of sounds) prolonged or reinforced by vibration or reverberation; (*Elec.*) responding audibly to electric waves of a corresponding length. *n.* A nasal consonant. **resonance,** *n.* **resonantly,** *adv.* **resonate,** *v.i.*

resonator (rez' ȯ nā tȯr), *n.* An acoustic instrument, usu. consisting of a chamber responding to a particular note, used for detecting this note in a complex sound; anything that augments sounds by resonance; various appliances for this; (*Elec.*) a conductor exhibiting electric resonance; an apparatus for detecting Hertzian waves, esp. a receiving apparatus in wireless telegraphy.

resorb (rė sôrb') [L. *resorbēre* (RE-, *sorbēre*, to drink in, p.p. *sorptus*)], *v.t.* To absorb again. **resorbence,** *n.* **resorbent,** *a.* **resorption,** *n.* **resorptive,** *a.*

resorcin (rė zôr' sin) [RES-IN, ORCIN], *n.* A crystalline compound orig. obtained by the action of potash or galbanum and other resins but now usually by synthesis, used as a dye-stuff and in medicine.

resorption, resorptive [RESORB].

resort (rė zôrt') [O.F. *resortir* (F. *ressortir*), to come out, etym. doubtful], *v.i.* To go, to repair, to betake onself; to have recourse, to apply, to turn to (for aid, etc.). *n.* The act of frequenting a place; the state of being frequented; the place frequented; recourse; that to which one has recourse, an expedient; a concourse, a company, a meeting. **last resort:** That to which one comes for aid or relief when all else has failed; the final tribunal; a final attempt. **resorter,** *n.*

re-sort (rē sôrt'), *v.t.* To sort again.

resound (rė zound') [RE-, SOUND (2), after F. *resonner*, cp. RESONANT], *v.i.* To ring, to re-echo, to reverberate (with); to be filled with sound (of a place); to be re-echoed, to be repeated, reinforced, or prolonged (of sounds, instruments, etc.); to be noised abroad, to make a sensation (of news, events, etc.). *v.t.* To sound again; to return the sound of; to spread the fame of. **n.* An echo, a resonance. **resoundingly,** *adv.*

resource (rė sôrs') [F. *ressource*, from O.F. *ressourdre*, from L. *resurgere* (RE-, *surgere*, to rise)], *n.* A means of aid, support, or safety; an expedient, a device; (*pl.*) means of support and defence, esp. of a country; capacity for finding or devising means; fertility in expedients, practical ingenuity; *possibility of being aided. **resourceful,** *a.* **resourcefully,** *adv.* **resourcefulness,** *n.* **resourceless,** *a.* **resourcelessness,** *n.*

re-speak (rē spēk'), *v.t.* To speak again; to echo back.

respect (rė spekt') [F., from L. *respectus*, p.p. of *respicere* (RE-, *specere*, to look)], *n.* Relation, regard, reference; attention, heed (to), regard (to or of); particular, aspect, point; esteem, deferential regard, demeanour, or attention; (*pl.*) expressions of esteem sent as a complimentary message. *v.t.* To esteem, to regard with deference; to treat with consideration, to spare from insult, injury, interference, etc.; to relate or have reference to [see RESPECTING]; *to heed, to regard. ***in respect of:** In comparison with. **in respect to:** With regard to. **to pay one's respects:** To send a message of esteem or compliment. **respectable,** *a.* Worthy of respect, of good repute; of fair social standing, honest, decent, not disreputable; fairly good, tolerable, passable; not mean, not inconsiderable, above the average in number, quantity, merit, etc. **respectability** (-bil' i ti), **respectableness,** *n.* The quality or character of being respectable; one who is respectable. **respectably,** *adv.* **respecter,** *n.* **respecter of persons:** One who pays undue consideration to and is biased by wealth and station. **respectful,** *a.* Showing respect. **respectfully,** *adv.* **respectfulness,** *n.* **respecting,** *prep.* In regard to, in respect of. **respective,** *a.* Relating severally to each of those in question, several, comparative, relative. **respectively,** *adv.* ***respectless,** *a.* Disrespectful; regardless, heedless; impartial.

respell (rē spel'), *v.t.* To spell again.

respire (rė spīr') [F. *respirer*, L. *respīrāre* (RE-, *spīrāre*, to breathe)], *v.i.* To breathe; to inhale or take air into and exhale it from the lungs; to recover breath; (*fig.*) to recover hope, spirit, etc.; (*fig.*) to be alive; *to take rest, as after toil. *v.t.* To inhale and exhale, to breathe out, to emit (perfume, etc.). **respirable** (res' pir-, rė spīr' ȧbl), *a.* Capable of being respired; fit to be breathed; *that can respire. **respirability** (-bil' i ti), **respirableness,** *n.* **respiration** (-ā' shŭn), *n.* The act or process of breathing; one act of inhaling and exhaling; (*Bot.*) the absorption of oxygen and emission of carbon dioxide by plants. **respirato-,** *comb. form.* **respirator** (res' pi rā tŏr), *n.* A contrivance of gauze or other filtering material worn over the mouth or mouth and nose to exclude injurious matter or to protect the lungs from the sudden inspiration of cold air; a gas-mask. **respiratory,** *a.* **respiratory disease:** (*Path.*) Any disease involving an organ concerned in respiration. **respirometer** (res pi rom' ė tėr), *n.* An instrument for measuring respiration; an apparatus for supplying a diver with air for breathing.

respite (res' pit) [O.F. *respit*, from L., as RESPECT], *n.* A temporary intermission of labour, effort, suffering, etc., esp. a delay in the execution of a sentence; an interval of rest or relief, a reprieve. *v.t.* To relieve by a temporary cessation of labour, suffering, etc.; to grant a respite to, to reprieve; to suspend the execution of (a sentence); to postpone, to defer, to delay; (*Mil.*) to suspend from pay, to keep back (pay); *to save or prolong (one's life). **respiteless,** *a.*

resplendent (rė splen' dėnt) [L. *resplendens -ntem*, pres.p. of *resplendēre* (RE-, *splendēre*, to shine, to glitter)], *a.* Shining with brilliant lustre; vividly or gloriously bright. **resplendence, -cy,** *n.* **resplendently,** *adv.*

respond (rė spond') [O.F. *respondre* (F. *répondre*), L. *respondēre* (RE-, *spondēre*, to pledge, p.p. *sponsus*)], *v.i.* To answer, to make reply (esp. of a congregation returning set answers to a priest); to perform an act or show an effect in answer or correspondence to; to react (to an external irritation or stimulus); to be responsive, to show sympathy or sensitiveness (to); *to correspond, to suit, to be analogous. *v.t.* To answer, to say in response; (*Am.*) to satisfy by payment. *n.* An anthem or versicle sung in response, a responsory; (*Arch.*) a half-column or half-pier in a wall supporting the impost of an arch. **respondent,** *a.* Giving response, answering; responsive (to); in the position of defendant. *n.* One who answers; one who maintains a thesis in reply; one who answers in a suit at law, a defendant, esp. in a divorce case. ***respondence, *-cy,** *n.* ***respondentia*** (res pŏn den' shi ȧ), *n.* A loan upon a cargo repayable provided that the goods arrive safely.

response (rė spons') [O.F., from L. *responsum*, neut. p.p. of *respondēre*, to RESPOND], *n.* The act of answering; that which is answered in word or act, an answer, a reply, a retort; a versicle or other portion of a liturgy said or sung in answer to the priest, a responsory. ***responsal,** *n.* A response; a responsory; a reaction, feeling, movement, etc., called forth by an external stimulus, influence, etc.

responsible (re spon' si bėl), *a.* Answerable, liable, accountable (to or for); morally accountable for one's actions, able to discriminate between right and wrong; respectable, trustworthy; involving responsibility. **responsibility** (-bil' i ti), ***responsibleness,** *n.* The state of being responsible, as for a person, trust, etc.; ability to act according to the laws of right and wrong; that for which one is responsible. **responsibly,** *adv.*

responsion (re spon' shŏn), *n.* A response; (*Ox. Univ. pl.*) the first of three examinations for the degree of B.A.

responsive (re spon' siv), *a.* Answering or inclined to answer; of the nature of an answer; reacting to stimulus; responding readily, sympathetic, impressionable. **responsively,** *adv.* **responsiveness,** *n.*

responsory (re spon' sȯ ri), *n.* (*Eccles.*) An anthem said or sung alternately by the soloist and a choir after one of the lessons. *a.* Of, pertaining to, or of the nature of a response.

ressaldar, risaldar (rės al dar') [Hind.], *n.* The captain of a troop in Indian cavalry.

rest (1) (rest) [A.-S. *rest, ræst* (cp. Dut. *rust*, G. *raste*, Icel. *röst*), whence *ræstan*, to rest (cp. Dut. *rusten*, G. *rasten*)], *n.* Cessation from bodily or mental exertion or activity, repose, sleep; freedom from care, disturbance, or molestation, peace, tranquillity; a period of such cessation or freedom, esp. a brief pause or interval; a place of quiet and repose; a stopping-place, a place for lodging; a shelter for cabmen, sailors, etc.; that on which anything stands or is supported, a prop, a support, a device for steadying a rifle on in taking aim, for supporting the cutting-tool in a lathe, etc.; a long cue with a cross-piece at one end used as a support for a billiard cue in playing; (*Mus.*) an interval of silence, the sign indicating this; (*Prosody*) a pause in a verse, a cæsura; (*fig.*) death; *stay, abode, residence. *v.i.* To cease from exertion, motion, or activity; to be relieved from toil or exertion, to repose; to lie in sleep or death, to lie buried; to be still, to be without motion; to be free from care, disturbance, or molestation, to be tranquil, to be at peace; to be allowed to lie fallow (of land); to lie; to be spread out; to be supported or fixed, to be based, to lean, to recline, to stand (on); to depend, to rely (upon); to trust or put one's confidence (in God, etc.); (of eyes) to be fixed, to be directed steadily (upon); to remain; (*U.S.A.*) (of an attorney) to call no more evidence. *v.t.* To cause to cease from exertion; to give repose to, to lay at rest; (*in p.p.*) to refresh by resting; to give (oneself rest); to place for support, to base, to establish, to lean, to lay, to support. **at rest:** Reposing; not in motion; still; not disturbed, agitated, or troubled; (*euphem.*) dead, in the grave. **to lay to rest:** To bury. **to rest with:** To be left in the hands of. **rest-balk,** *n.* A ridge left unploughed between furrows; *v.t.* To plough so as to leave these. **rest-cure,** *n.* (*Med.*) Seclusion and repose (usu. in bed) as a method of treatment for nervous disorders. **rest-day,** *n.* A day of rest, esp. from marching; Sunday. **rest-house,** *n.* (*Ang.-Ind.*) A dawk-bungalow. **restful,** *a.* Inducing rest, soothing, free from disturbance; at rest, quiet. **restfully,** *adv.* **restfulness,** *n.* **resting-place,** *n.* A place for rest; (*fig.*) the grave. **restless,** *a.* Not resting, never still, agitated, uneasy, fidgety, unsettled, turbulent; not affording sleep, sleepless. **restlessly,** *adv.* **restlessness,** *n.*

rest (2) (rest) [F. *reste*, from *rester*, L. *restāre* (RE-, *stāre*, to stand)], *n.* That which is left, the remaining part or parts, the residue, the remainder; the others; (*Banking*) a reserve fund, a balance or surplus fund for contingencies; (*Comm.*) a balancing, a stock-taking and balancing; (*Tennis*) a continuous series of quick returns of the ball. *v.i.* To remain, to stay, to continue (in a specified state); *to be left, to remain over. **all the rest:** All that remains, all the others. **for the rest** or **as for the rest:** As regards the remaining persons, matters, or things, as regards anything else.

***rest** (3) (rest) [form of ARREST], *n.* A support for the butt of a lance in charging, fixed to the right side of mediæval armour. *v.t.* (*prov.*) To arrest; to stop, to check.

restamp (rē stămp'), *v.t.* To stamp again. **restart** (rē start'), *v.t.* and *i.* To start afresh. **restate** (rē stāt'), *v.t.* To state again or express differently.

restaurant (res' tò rȧnt, res tō ran) [F., from *restaurer*, to RESTORE], *n.* A place for refreshment; an eating house. **restaurant car:** (*Rail.*) A dining-car. ***restaurateur*** (res tō rȧ tĕr), *n.* The keeper of a restaurant. ***restauration,** *n.* Restoration, reinstatement.

***restem** (rē stem'), *v.t.* To stem again.

restful, etc. [REST (1)].

rest-harrow (rest' hăr ō) [REST (3), HARROW (1)], *n.* A shrubby pink-flowered plant, *Ononis arvensis*, also called cammock, with a tough woody root, arresting the prongs of the harrow, whence the name.

restiform (res' ti fôrm) [L. *restis*, cord, -FORM], *a.* (*Anat.*) Rope- or cord-like (applied to two bundles of fibrous matter connecting the *medulla oblongata* with the cerebellum). **restiform body:** Either of these bundles.

resting-place [REST (1)].

restitution (res ti tū' shùn) [O.F., from L. *restitutiōnem*, nom. *-tio*, from *restituere* (RE-, *statuere*, to set up)], *n.* The act of restoring something taken away or lost; making good, reparation, indemnification; restoration to a former state or position; (*Phys.*) the resumption of its former shape by an elastic body. **restitution of all things:** (*Theol.*) The final restoration of things to their original state of perfection. **restitution of conjugal rights:** (*Law*) A matrimonial cause. **Restitutionist,** *n.* One of a Christian sect in New England believing in the restitution of all things.

restive (res' tiv) [formerly *restiff*, O.F. *restif*, from *rester*, to REST (3)], *a.* Unwilling to go forward, standing still, halting, unruly, refractory (of a horse); restless, fidgety, impatient of control, unmanageable. **restively,** *adv.* **restiveness,** *n.*

restock (rē stok'), *v.t.* To stock again.

restoration (res tò rā' shùn), *n.* The act of restoring; a building, etc., restored to its supposed original state; a skeleton of an extinct animal built up of its remains; a drawing, model, or other representation of a building, extinct animal, etc., in its supposed original form; (*Theol.*) the restitution of all things [see RESTITUTION]. **the Restoration:** the return of Charles II in 1660 and the re-establishment of the monarchy after the Commonwealth; the return of the Bourbons to France in 1814. **restorationism,** *n.* The doctrine of the final restoration of all men to happiness and sinlessness in the future life. **restorationist,** *n.*

restorative (re stôr' ȧ tiv), *a.* Tending to restore health, strength, etc. *n.* Food, drink, a medicine, etc., for restoring strength, vigour, etc., a stimulant, a tonic. **restoratively,** *adv.* **restorer,** *n.*

restore (rė stôr') [O.F. *restorer*, L. *restaurāre* (RE-, *sta-*, root of *stāre*, to stand, cp. G. *stauros*, stake)], *v.t.* To bring back to a former state, to repair, to reconstruct; to put back, to replace, to return; to bring back to health, to cure; to bring back to a former position, to reinstate; to bring into existence or use again, to re-establish, to renew; to reproduce (a text or part of a text) by emendation, conjecture, etc.; to represent (an extinct animal, mutilated picture, ruin, etc.) as it is supposed to have been originally; to give back, to make restitution of. **n.* Restoration. **restorable,** *a.*

re-strain (rē strān'), *v.t.* To strain again.

restrain (rė strān') [O.F. *restraign-*, pres.p. stem of *restraindre* (F. *restreindre*), L. *restringere* (RE-, *stringere*, to draw tight, p.p. *strictus*)], *v.t.* To hold back, to check, to curb; to keep under control, to repress, to hold in check, to restrict; to confine, to imprison; *to forbear. **restrainable,** *a.* **restrainedly,** *adv.* **restrainer,** *n.* ***restrainment,** *n.* **restraint,** *n.* The act of restraining; the state of being restrained; check, repression, control, self-repression, avoidance of excess; constraint, reserve; restriction, limitation; abridgment of liberty, confinement, esp. in an asylum.

restrengthen (rē streng' thėn), *v.t.* To strengthen anew.

restrict (rė strikt') [L. *restrictus*, see RESTRAIN (2)], *v.t.* To limit, to confine, to keep within certain bounds. **restriction,** *n.* **restrictive,** *a.* **restrictedly, restrictively,** *adv.*

restrike (rē strīk'), *v.t.* To strike again. ***restringe** (rė strinj') [L. *restringere*, see RESTRAIN (2)], *v.t.* To restrict; to affect with costiveness; to astringe. ***restringent,** *a.* Astringent. *n.* An astringent medicine. **restuff** (rē stŭf'), *v.t.* To stuff anew.

***resty** (res' ti) [var. of RESTIVE], *a.* Restive; indolent, lazy.

result (rė zŭlt') [F. *résulter*, L. *resultāre* (RE-, *saltāre*, freq. of *salīre*, to leap)], *v.i.* To be the actual or follow as the logical consequence, to ensue; to have an issue, to terminate or end (in); (*Am.*) to decide. *n.* Consequence, issue, outcome, effect; a quantity, value, or formula obtained from a calculation. **resultance,** *n.* **resultant,** *a.* Following as a result; resulting from the combination of two factors, agents, etc. *n.* That which results; (*Mach.*) the force resulting from the combination of two or more forces acting in different directions at the same point, ascertained by a parallelogram of forces. **resultful,** *a.* **resultless,** *a.*

resume (rė zūm') [O.F. *resumer*, L. *resūmere* (RE-, *sūmere*, to take, p.p. *sumptus*)], *v.t.* To take back, to take again, to reoccupy, to recover; to begin again, to recommence, to go on with after interruption; to sum up, to recapitulate, to make a résumé of. *v.i.* To continue after interruption, to recommence. **resumable,** *a.*

résumé (rez' ū mā) [F., p.p. of *résumer*, to RESUME], *n.* A summary, a recapitulation, a condensed statement, an abstract.

resummon (rē sŭm' ȯn), *v.t.* To summon again; to convene again. **resummons,** *n.*

resumption (rė zŭmp' shùn) [L. *resumptio*, from *resūmere*, to RESUME], *n.* The act of resuming. **resumptive,** *a.*

resupinate (rė sū' pi nȧt) [L. *resupīnātus*, p.p. of *resupīnāre* (RE-, *supīnāre*, to make SUPINE)], *a.* (*Bot.*). Inverted, apparently upside-down. **resupination** (-nā' shùn), *n.* ***resupine** (rē sū pīn'), *a.* Lying on the back, supine.

resurge (rė sĕrj') [L. *resurgere* (RE-, *surgere*, to rise)], *v.i.* To rise again. **resurgence,** *n.* **resurgent,** *a.* Rising again, rising from the dead. *n.* One who rises from the dead.

resurrect (rez ů rekt') [see foll.], *v.t.* (*colloq.*) To bring back to life; to bring again into vogue or currency, to revive; to exhume.

resurrection (rez ů rek' shùn) [O.F., from late L. *resurrectiōnem*, nom. *-tio*, from *resurgere*, to RESURGE], *n.* A rising again from the dead, esp. the rising of Christ from the dead, and the rising of all the dead at the Last Day; the state of being risen again; the future state; a springing again into life, vigour, vogue, or prosperity; exhumation, resurrecting, body-snatching. **resurrection-man, resurrectionist,** *n.* A body-snatcher. **resurrection-pie,** *n.* (*facet.*) A pie made of remains of previous meals. **resurrectional,** *a.*

resurvey (rē sûr vā'), *v.t.* To survey again; to read and examine again. *n.* (rē sěr' vā) A renewed survey.

resuscitate (rė sŭs' i tāt) [L. *resuscitātus*, p.p. of *resuscitāre* (RE-, SUS-, *citāre*, to CITE)], *v.t.* To revive, to restore from apparent death; to revivify, to restore to vigour, animation, usage, etc. *v.i.* To revive, to come to life again. ***a.** (-tȧt) Restored to life. ***resuscitable,** *a.* **resuscitant,** *a.* and *n.* **resuscitation** (-tā' shŭn), *n.* **resuscitative** (rė sŭs' i tȧ tiv), *a.* **resuscitator** (-tā tȯr), *n.*

ret (ret) [etym. obscure, cp. Dut. *reten*, Swed. *röta*, Norw. *röyta*, rel. to ROT], *v.t.* (*past & p.p.* **retted**) To subject (flax, etc.) to the action of retting. *v.i.* To be spoilt by wet (of hay). **rettery,** *n.* **retting,** *n.* The act or process of steeping flax or hemp to loosen the fibre from the woody portions.

retable (rė tā' bėl) [Fr. *rétable*, after med. L. *retrotabulum*], *n.* (*Eccles.*) A shelf, ledge, or panelled frame above the back of an altar for supporting ornaments.

retail (rē' tāl) [O.F. *retail*, *retaille*, from *retailler*, to cut off a piece (RE-, *tailler*, see TAILOR)], *n.* The sale of commodities in small quantities; a dealing out in small portions. *a.* Pertaining to selling by retail. *v.t.* (rė tāl') To sell in small quantities; to tell (a story, etc.) in detail, to recount, to retell, to spread about. *v.i.* To be sold by retail (at or for a specified price). **retailer,** *n.* ***retailment,** *n.*

retain (rė tān') [O.F. *retenir*, L. *retinēre* (RE-, *tenēre*, to hold)], *v.t.* To hold or keep possession of, to keep; to continue to have, to maintain, to preserve; to hire, to engage the services of (esp. counsel) by paying a preliminary fee; to hold back, to keep in place; to remember. **retainable,** *a.* **retainer,** *n.* One who or that which retains; an attendant, a follower, esp. of a feudal chieftain; (*Law*) an agreement by which an attorney acts in a case; a preliminary fee paid (esp. to a counsel) to secure his services. **retaining fee:** A retainer. **retaining force:** (*Mil.*) A body of troops stationed to keep part of an enemy from interfering with large movements. **retaining wall:** A massive wall built to support and hold back the earth of an embankment, a mass of water, etc.

retake (rē tāk'), *v.t.* To take again; to recapture.

retaliate (rė tăl' i āt) [L. *retāliātus*, p.p. of *retāliāre* (RE-, *tāliāre*, from *tālis*, such, cp. *tālio*, retaliation)], *v.t.* To return like for like, esp. evil for evil, to return or retort in kind. *v.i.* To return like for like, to make reprisals. **retaliation** (-ā' shŭn), *n.* The act of retaliating; (*Polit. Econ.*) the imposition of import duties by one country against another which imposes duties on imports from the country first mentioned. **retaliative, -tory** (rē tăl' i ȧ tiv, -tor i), *a.*

retard (rė tard') [F. *retarder*, L. *retardāre* (RE-, *tardus*, slow)], *v.t.* To cause to move more slowly; to hinder, to impede, to check, restrain, or delay the growth, advance, arrival, or occurrence of. *v.i.* To be delayed; to happen or arrive abnormally late. *n.* Delay, retardation. **retardation** (-dā' shŭn), *n.* **retardative, -tory** (rė tar' dȧ tiv, -tȯr i), *a.* **retarder,** *n.* **retardment,** *n.*

retch (rēch, rech) [A.-S. *hrǣcan*, from *hrāca*, spittle (cp. Icel. *hrækja*, from *hrāki*, spittle)], *v.i.* To make an effort to vomit; to strain, as in vomiting. *n.* The act or sound of retching.

retell (rē tel'), *v.t.* (*past & p.p.* **retold**) To tell again.

retention (re ten' shŭn) [O.F. from L. *retentiōnem*, nom. *-tio*, from *retinēre*, to RETAIN], *n.* The act of retaining; the state of being retained; confinement; the power of retaining, esp. ideas in the mind; (*Med.*) failure to evacuate urine, etc., power of retaining food, etc. ***retent** (rė tent'), *n.* That which is retained. **retentive,** *a.* **retentively,** *adv.* **retentiveness,** *n.*

retenue (rė tė nu') [F., p.p. of *retenir*, see prec.], *n.* Reserve, self-restraint.

retepore (rē' tė pôr) [L. *rēte*, rel. *porus*, PORE (1)], *n.* Any individual of the *Retepora*, a genus of zoophytes.

retiary (rē' shi ȧ ri) [L. *rētiārius*, gladiator armed with a net, from *rēte*, net], *a.* Retiform; weaving or using nets. *n.* A geometrical or net-making spider; ***a** gladiator armed with a net.

reticent (ret' i sėnt) [L. *reticens -ntem*, pres.p. of *reticēre* (RE-, *tacēre*, to be silent)], *a.* Reserved in speech; not disposed to communicate one's thoughts or feelings; keeping back something; inclined to keep one's own counsel; silent, taciturn. **reticence,** ***-cy,** *n.* **reticently,** *adv.*

reticle (ret' i kėl) [L. *rēticulum*, dim. of *rēte*, net], *n.* A net-work of fine lines, etc., drawn across the focal plane of a telescope to facilitate the accurate location of an object.

reticular (re tik' ū lȧr) [RETICLE], *a.* Having the form of a net or net-work; formed with interstices, retiform. **reticularly,** *adv.* ***recticulary,** *a.* **reticulate** (-lāt), *v.t.* To make or divide into or arrange in a network, to mark with fine intersecting lines. *v.i.* To be divided into or arranged in a network. *a.* (-lȧt) Formed of or resembling network. **reticulately,** *adv.* **reticulation** (-lā' shŭn), *n.* **reticulato-,** *comb. form.* **reticulose** (rė tik' ū lōs), *a.* **reticulo-,** *comb. form.*

reticule (ret' i kūl) [F., as prec.], *n.* A kind of bag, orig. of net-work; a lady's handbag; a reticle; (*Astron.*) the Reticulum.

reticulum (rė tik' ū lŭm), *n.* (*pl.* **reticula**) (*Anat.*) The second stomach of ruminants; a net-like or reticulated structure, membrane, etc.; (*Astron.*) a southern constellation.

retiform (rē' ti fôrm) [L. *rēte*, net, -FORM], *a.* Reticulated

retina (ret' i nȧ) [med. L., prob. from L. *rēte*, net], *n.* (*pl.* **-næ**) A net-like layer of sensitive nerve-fibres and cells behind the eyeball in which the optic nerve terminates. **retinal,** *a.* **retinitis** (ret i nī' tis), *n.* (*Path.*) Inflammation of the retina.

retinaculum (ret i năk' ū lŭm) [L., from *retinēre*, to RETAIN], *n.* (*pl.* **-la**) (*Anat.*) A connecting band or cord; (*Ent.*) an apparatus in some insects controlling the sting; an apparatus by which the wings of insects are interlocked in flight.

retinalite (ret' i nȧ līt) [Gr. *rhētinē*, RESIN, -LITE], *n.* (*Min.*) A variety of serpentine with a resinous lustre. **retinite,** *n.* Pitch-stone. ***retinoid,** *a.* **retinol,** *n.* A liquid hydrocarbon obtained from resin, used in pharmacy, etc.

retinitis [RETINA].

***retinoid, retinol** [RETINALITE].

retinoscopy (ret i nos' kȯ pi), *n.* Examination of the retina with the ophthalmoscope. **retinoscopic** (-skop' ik), *a.* **retinoscopically,** *adv.*

retinue (ret' i nū) [M.E. and O.F. *retenue*, p.p. of *retenir*, to RETAIN], *n.* The attendants on a prince or other distinguished person; a train, a suite.

retire (rė tīr') [O.F. *retirer* (RE-, *tirer*, to draw, from Teut.)], *v.i.* To withdraw, to go away, to fall back, to retreat, to recede; to withdraw from business to a private life; to resign one's office or appointment, to cease from or withdraw from active service; to go to or as to bed; to go into privacy or seclusion. *v.t.* To cause to retire or resign; to order (troops) to retire; to withdraw (a bill or note) from circulation or operation. *n.* (*Mil.*) A signal (to troops) to retire; *retirement, seclusion. **retired,** *a.* Private, withdrawn from society; given to privacy or seclusion; secluded, sequestered; having given up business, etc. **retired list:** A list of retired officers, etc., usu. on half-pay. ***retiredly** (-tīr' ėd li), *adv.* **retiredness,** *n.* **retirement,** *n.* **retiring,** *a.* Unobtrusive, not forward, unsociable. **retiringly,** *adv.* **retiringness,** *n.* **retiring-room,** *n.* A room for withdrawing into, esp. a lavatory.

retold, *past & p.p.* [RETELL].

***retorsion** [var. of RETORTION].

retort (1) (rė tôrt′) [F. *retorte*, med. L. *retorta*, as foll.], *n.* A vessel with a bulb-like receptacle and a long neck bent downwards used for distillation of liquids, etc.; a large receptacle of fire-clay, iron, etc., of analogous shape, used for the production of coal-gas. *v.t.* To purify (mercury, etc.) by treatment in a retort.

retort (2) (rė tôrt′) [L. *retortus*, p.p. of *retorquēre* (RE-, *torquēre*, to twist)], *v.t.* To turn or throw back; to turn (an argument, accusation, etc.) on or against the author; to pay back (an attack, injury, etc.) in kind; to say, make, or do, by way of repartee, etc. *v.i.* To turn an argument or charge against the originator or aggressor. *n.* The turning of a charge, taunt, attack, etc., against the author or aggressor; a sharp rejoinder, a repartee. ***retorted,** *a.* Recurved, bent or twisted back. **retorter,** *n.* **retortion** (-tôr′ shŭn), *n.* Bending, turning, or twisting back; the act of retorting; (*International Law*) retaliation by a State on the subjects of another without actual war. ***retortive,** *a.*

•**retoss** (rē tos′), *v.t.* To toss back or again. **retouch** (rē tŭch′), *v.t.* To touch again; to improve (a photograph, picture, etc.) by new touches. *n.* A second touch given to a picture, etc. **retoucher,** *n.* **retouchment,** *n.* **retrace** (rė trās′), *v.t.* To trace back to the beginning, source, etc.; to go over (one's course or track) again; (*fig.*) to go over again in memory, to try to recollect; to trace (an outline) again. **retraceable,** *a.*

retract (rė trăkt′) [L. *retractus*, p.p. of *retrahere* (RE-, *trahere*, to draw), later senses from *retractāre*, to revoke, freq. of *retrahere*], *v.t.* To draw back or in; to take back, to revoke, to recall, to recant, to disavow, to acknowledge to be false or erroneous. *v.i.* To withdraw, to shrink back; to withdraw or recall a declaration, promise, concession, etc. **retractable, retractile,** *a.* **retractability** (-bil i ti), **retractility** (-til′ i ti), *n.* **retractation** (-tā′ shŭn), *n.* The act of retracting, disavowing, or recanting. **retraction** (rė trăk′ shŭn), *n.* The act or process of drawing in; the act of retracting; retractation. **retractive,** *a.* Serving to retract or draw in. **retractor,** *n.* (*Anat.*) A muscle used for drawing back; (*Surg.*) an instrument or bandage for holding back parts in the way of an operator; (*Fire-arms*) a contrivance for withdrawing cartridge-cases from the breech.

•**retrait** (rė trāt′) [It. *ritratto*, as prec.], *n.* A picture, a portrait.

retral (rē′ trål) [RETRO-, -AL], *a.* Situated at the back, posterior, hinder; bending backward.

retransfer (rē trăns fĕr′), *v.t.* To transfer again. *n.* An act of retransferring. **retransform** (rē trăns fôrm′), *v.t.* To transform anew. **retransformation** (-mā′ shŭn), *n.* **retranslate** (rē trăns lāt′), *v.t.* To translate again; to translate back again to the original language. **retranslation** (-lā′ shŭn), *n.* **retraxit** (rė trăk′ sit) [L., he withdrew, as RETRACT], *n.* (*Law*) The voluntary withdrawing of a suit by the plaintiff. **retread** (rē tred′), *v.t.* To tread again. *n.* (*Austral.*) A re-enlisting soldier; a retired man who re-enters his employment.

retreat (rė trēt′) [O.F. *retret*, *-trete* (F. *retraite*), p.p. of *retraire*, L. *retrahere*, to RETRACT], *n.* The act of withdrawing or retiring, esp. the retiring of an army before an enemy; a signal for such retirement; (*Mil.*) a drum-beat at sunset; a state of retirement or seclusion; a period of retirement; a place of retirement, security, privacy, or seclusion; a lurking-place, a lair, a refuge, an asylum for lunatics, inebriates, aged persons, etc.; (*Eccles.*) retirement for meditation, prayer, etc. *v.i.* To move back, to retire, esp. before an enemy or from an advanced position; to withdraw to a place of privacy, seclusion, or security; to recede. *v.t.* To cause to retire; (*Chess*) to move (a piece) back.

retrench (rė trench′) [F. *retrencher*, obs. var. of *retrancher* (RE-, TRENCH)], *v.t.* To cut down, to reduce, to curtail, to diminish; to shorten, to abridge, to cut out or pare down; (*Mil.*) to furnish with a retrenchment. *v.i.* To curtail expenses, to make economies. **retrenchment,** *n.* The act of retrenching; a work constructed within or behind another to prolong a defence.

retrial (rē trī′ ål), *n.* A new trial.

retribution (ret ri bū′ shŭn) [O.F. *retribucion*, *-tion*, L. *retribūtiōnem*, nom. *-tio*, from *retribuere* (RE-, *tribuere*, to assign)], *n.* Recompense, a suitable return, esp. for evil; requital, vengeance; (*Theol.*) the distribution of rewards and punishments in the future life. ***retribute** (rė trib′ ūt, ret′ ri būt), *v.t.* **retributive, -tory** (rė trib′ ū-), *a.* **retributor,** *n.*

retrieve (rė trēv′) [O.F. *retroev-*, a stem of *retrover* (RE-, *trouver*, to find, see TROVER and CONTRIVE (1))], *v.t.* To find and bring in (esp. of a dog bringing in dead or wounded game); to recover by searching or recollecting, to recall to mind; to regain (that which has been lost, impaired, etc.); to rescue (from); to restore, to re-establish (one's fortunes, etc.); to remedy, to make good, to repair. *v.i.* To bring in dead or wounded game (of a dog). **retrievable,** *a.* **retrievably,** *adv.* ***retrieval,** *n.* ***retrievement,** *n.* **retriever,** *n.* A dog usu. of a special breed, trained to fetch in game that has been shot.

retrim (rē trim′) [RE-, TRIM], *v.t.* To trim again.

retro- [L., behind, backwards], *pref.* Backwards, back; in return; (*Anat. etc.*) behind. **retroact** (rē trō ăkt′) [L. *retroactus*, p.p. of *retroagere* (ACT)], *v.i.* To act backwards or in return; to act retrospectively, to react. **retroaction** (-ăk′ shŭn), **retroactivity** (-tiv′ i ti), *n.* **retroactive,** *a.* **retroactively,** *adv.* **retrocede** (rē trō sēd′) [L. *retrōcēdere* (*cēdere*, to yield, to go back, see CEDE)], *v.t.* To cede back again, to restore (territory, etc.). *v.i.* (ret′ rō-, rē′ trō sēd). To move backward; to recede; (*Path.*) to shift to an inner part of the body (of gout). **retrocedent, retrocessive** (-ses′ iv), *a.* **retrocession** (ret rō sesh′ ŭn), *n.* **retrochoir** (rē′ trō kwīr) [CHOIR], *n.* A part of a cathedral or other large church east of or beyond the high altar. **retrocognition** (ret rō kog nish′ un), *n.* An extrasensory knowledge of the past. **retroflected** (rē trō-, ret rō flek′ tėd), **retroflex, -flexed** (rē′ trō-, ret′ rō fleks, -flekst) [med. L. *retroflexus*, p.p. of *retroflectere* (*flectere*, to bend)], *a.* Turned or curved backward. **retroflexion** (-flek′ shŭn), *n.* **retrofract, -fracted** (rē′ trō-, ret′ rō frăkt, -ėd) [cp. REFRACT], *a.* (*Bot.*) Bent back so as to look as if broken.

retrograde (ret′ rō grād) [L. *retrōgradus*, from *retrōgradī*, to go backward (RETRO-, *gradī*, to go)], *a.* Going, moving, bending, or directed backwards; inverted, reversed; declining, degenerating, deteriorating; (*Astron.*) applied to the motion of a planet relatively to the fixed stars when it is apparently from east to west; *opposite, contrary. *n.* A backward movement or tendency, deterioration, decline; a degenerate person. *v.i.* To move backward; to decline, to deteriorate, to revert, to recede; (*Astron.*) to move or appear to move from east to west relatively to the fixed stars. **v.t.* To turn back, to cause to go backward. **retrogradation** (-grå dā′ shŭn), *n.* Retrogression; (*Astron.*) backward or apparently backward motion of a planet in the zodiac or relatively to the fixed stars.

retrogress (ret′ rō-, rē trō gres) [L. *retrōgressus*, p.p. of *retrōgradī*, as prec.], *v.i.* To go backward, to retrograde; to degenerate. **retrogression** (-gresh′ ŭn), *n.* **retrogressive** (-gres′ iv), *a.* **retrogressively,** *adv.*

retromingent (rē trō-, ret rō min′ jėnt) [RETRO-, L. *mingens -ntem*, pres.p. of *mingere*, to make water], *a.* (*Path.*) Discharging the urine backwards. *n.* An animal that discharges the urine backwards. **retroposition** (-pō zish′ ŭn), *n.* Displacement in a backward direction. **retropulsion** (-pŭl′ shŭn), *n.* Shifting of a disease from an external to an internal part; a locomotory disease characterized by a tendency to make the patient walk backwards. **retropulsive** (-pŭl′ siv), *a.* **retrorse** (rė trôrs′) [L. *retrorsus* (*versus*, p.p. of *vertere*, to turn)], *a.* Turned or bent backwards, reverted. **retrorsely,** *adv.*

retrospect (ret′ rō-, rē′ trō spekt) [L. *retrospectus*, p.p. of *retrospicere* (RETRO-, *specere*, to look)], *n.* A looking back on things past; view of, regard to, or consideration of previous conditions, etc.; a review of past events. *v.i.* To look or refer back (to). *v.t.* To view or consider retrospectively. **retrospection** (-spek′ shŭn), *n.* **retrospective** (-spek′ tiv), *a.* In retrospection; viewing the past; applicable to what has happened; licensing, condoning, or condemning a past action. **retrospectively,** *adv.*

retroussé (rė troo′ sā) [F., p.p. of *retrousser*], *a.* Turned up at the end (of the nose).

retrovert (rē trō vĕrt′) [late L. *retrovertere* (RETRO-, *vertere*, to turn, p.p. *versus*)], *v.t.* To turn back, esp. (*Path.*) of the womb. **retroversion** (-vĕr′ shŭn), *n.* **retrovision** (-vizh′ ŭn), *n.* The power of looking back, esp. of seeing unknown events in the past.

retry (rē trī′), *v.t.* To try again.

rettery, retting [RET].

returf (rē tĕrf′), *v.t.* To turf again.

return (rė tĕrn′) [O.F. *returner* (F. *retourner*)], *v.i.* To come or go back, esp. to the same place or state; to revert, to happen again, to recur; *to answer, to retort. *v.t.* To bring, carry, or convey back; to give, render, or send back; to repay, to put or send back or in return, to requite; to say in reply, to retort; to report officially; to elect; (*Cards*) to play a card of the same suit as another player has led. *n.* The act of coming or going back; the act of giving, paying, putting, or sending back; that which is returned; an official account or report; a sheriff's report on a writ or a returning officer's announcement of a candidate's election; the act of electing or returning; the state of being elected; the proceeds or profits on labour, investments, etc. (*often in pl.*); a return bend in a pipe, etc.; (*Arch.*) a receding part of a façade, etc., a part of a hood-moulding, etc., bending in another direction; (*Games, Fencing, etc.*) a stroke, thrust, etc., in return; a return match or game; (*Law*) the rendering back or delivery of a writ, precept, or execution to the proper officer or court; (*pl.*) a mild kind of tobacco, orig. refuse of tobacco. **in return:** In reply or response; in requital; sent, given, etc., back. **many happy returns:** A birthday greeting. **to return a lead:** (*Cards*) To lead from the same suit. **to return thanks:** To offer thanks; to answer a toast. **return-day,** *n.* (*Law*) The day on which the defendant is to appear in court, or the sheriff is to return his writ. **return game** or **match:** A second meeting of the same clubs or teams. **return-ticket,** *n.* A ticket for a journey to a place and back again; the return-half of such a ticket. **returnable,** *a.* **returner,** *n.* **returning officer:** The presiding officer at an election. **returnless,** *a.*

retuse (rė tūs′) [L. *retūsus*, p.p. of *retundere* (RE-, *tundere*, to beat)], *a.* (*Bot., Ent., etc.*) Having a round end with a depression in the centre.

reunion (rē ū′ nyŏn) [F. *réunion* (RE-, UNION)], *n.* The act of reuniting; the state of being reunited; a meeting or social gathering, esp. of friends, associates, or partisans. **reune,** *v.i.* (*Am. college slang*) To hold a reunion. *v.t.* To reunite. **reunent,** *a.* **reunionism,** *n.* A movement for reunion of the Anglican and Roman Catholic Churches. **reunionist,** *n.* **reunite** (rē ū nīt′), *v.t.* To join again after separation; to reconcile after variance. *v.i.* To become united again. ***reunition** (-nish′ ŭn), *n.* ***reunitive** (rē ū′ ni tiv), *a.*

re-urge (rē ĕrj′), *v.t.* To urge again. **re-use** (rē ūz′), *v.t.* To use again. *n.* (-ūs′) The act of using again. **revaccinate** (rē văk′ si nāt), *v.t.* To vaccinate again.

rev (rev) [abbr. REVOLUTION], *v.t.* and *i.* (*Motor.*) To run an engine quickly.

revalenta (rev ȧ len′ tȧ) [altered from *ervalenta*, from L. *ervum lens*, LENTIL], *n.* A preparation from lentil meal, used for invalids, etc.

revalorization (rē văl ôr ī zā′ shŭn), *n.* (*Econ.*) Restoration of the value of currency.

revanche (re vansh) [F.], *n.* Revenge, return match.

reveal (1) (rė vēl′) [O.F. *reveler*, L. *revēlāre* (RE-, *vēlāre*, from *vēlum*, VEIL)], *v.t.* To make known by supernatural or divine means; to disclose, to divulge (something secret, private, or unknown), to betray; to allow to appear. *n.* *Revelation. **revealable,** *a.* **revealer,** *n.* **revealingly,** *adv.* **revealment,** *n.*

reveal (2) (rė vēl′) [earlier *revale*, from O.F. *revaler* (RE-, *valer*, *avaler*, to VAIL (1))], *n.* The depth of a wall as revealed in the side of an aperture, doorway, or window.

réveillé (rė vā′ lyi, rė vel′ i) [F. *réveillez*, awake, pl. imper. of *réveiller* (RE-, *veiller*, L. *vigilāre*, to watch, see VIGIL)], *n.* (*Armed services*) A morning signal by drum or bugle for men to rise.

revel (rev′ ėl) [O.F. *reveler*, L. *revellāre*, to revel], *v.i.* (*past & p.p.* **revelled**) To make merry, to feast, to carouse; to be boisterously festive; to take unrestrained enjoyment (in). *v.t.* To spend or waste in revelry. *n.* An act of revelling, a carouse, a merry-making. **revel-rout,** *n.* Tumultuous festivity; a band of revellers. **reveller,** *n.* ***revelment, revelry,** *n.*

revelation (rev ė lā′ shŭn) [M.E. and O.F. *revelacion*, L. *revēlātiōnem*, nom. *-tio*, from *revēlāre*, to REVEAL (1)], *n.* The act of revealing, a disclosing of knowledge or information; that which is revealed, esp. by God to man; the title of the last book of the New Testament, the Apocalypse; (*fig.*) an astonishing disclosure. **revelational,** *a.* **revelationist,** *n.* One who believes in divine revelation; the author of the Apocalypse. **revelative, -tory** (rev′ ė lā tiv, -tôr i), *a.*

reveller, *revelment, revelry [REVEL].

revenant (rev′ e nănt) [F., from *revenir*, L. *revenīre* (RE-, *venīre*, to come)], *n.* One who returns from the grave or from exile, esp. a ghost.

revendication (rė ven di kā′ shŭn) [F.], *n.* (*International Law*) A formal claim for the surrender of rights, esp. to territory. **revendicate** (rė ven′ di kāt), *v.t.*

revenge (rė venj′) [O.F. *revenger* (RE-, *venger*, to VENGE)], *v.t.* To exact satisfaction or retribution for, to requite, to retaliate; to avenge or satisfy (oneself) with such retribution or retaliation; to inflict injury on in a malicious spirit. *v.i.* To exact vengeance. *n.* Retaliation, requital, retribution or spiteful return for an injury; a means, mode, or act of revenging; the desire to inflict revenge, vindictiveness. **revengeful,** *a.* **revengefully,** *adv.* **revengefulness,** *n.* **revengeless,** *a.* **revengement,** *n.* **revenger,** *n.* **revengingly,** *adv.*

revenue (rev′ en ū), *n.* Income, esp. from a considerable amount or many forms of property (*often in pl.*); the annual income of a State, derived from taxation, customs, excise, etc.; the department of the Civil Service collecting this; *return, reward. **inland revenue** [INLAND]. **revenue-cutter,** *n.* A vessel employed to prevent smuggling. **revenue-officer,** *n.* A customs officer. **revenue-tax,** *n.* One for raising revenue not to affect trade, opp. to protective.

reverberate (rė vĕr′ bėr āt) [L. *reverberātus*, p.p. of *reverberāre* (RE-, *verberāre*, to beat, from *verber*, a scourge)], *v.t.* To send back, to re-echo, to reflect (sound, light, or heat); *to drive or force back, to repulse. *v.i.* To be driven back or to be reflected (of sound, light, heat); to resound, to re-echo; to rebound, to recoil. ***reverb,** *v.t.* ***reverberant,** *a.* ***reverberative,** *a.* **reverberation** (-ā′ shŭn), *n.* **reverberator** (rė vĕr′ bėr ā tôr), *n.* A reflector; a reflecting lamp; a reverberating furnace. **reverberatory** (re vĕr′ bėr ȧ tôr i), *a.* Producing or acting by reverberation. *n.* A reverberatory-furnace or kiln, in which metal or other material is exposed to the action of flame and heat which are thrown back from a vaulted roof, etc.

revere (rė vēr′) [F. *révérer*, L. *reverērī* (RE-, *verērī*, to fear)], *v.t.* To regard with awe mingled with affection, to venerate.

reverence (rev′ ėr ėns), *n.* The act of revering, veneration; a feeling of or the capacity for feeling this; *an act or gesture of respect, an obeisance, a bow, a curtsy (*now vulg. or facet.*); a title given to the clergy (in *his reverence*, etc.). *v.t.* To regard or treat with reverence, to venerate. ***to do reverence to:** To treat with reverence. **saving your reverence:** (*facet.*) With all respect to you. **reverencer,** *n.*

reverend (rev′ ėr ėnd), *a.* Worthy or entitled to reverence or respect, esp. as a title of respect given to clergymen; (a dean is addressed as **Very Reverend,** a bishop as **Right Reverend,** and an archbishop as **Most Reverend**).

reverent (rev′ ėr ėnt), *a.* Feeling or expressing reverence; submissive, humble. **reverential,** *a.* **reverentially,** *adv.* **reverently** (rev′ ėr ėnt li), *adv.*

reverie (rev′ ėr i) [F. *rêverie*, from *rêver*, to dream, etym. doubtful, cp. RAVE], *n.* Listless musing; a day-dream, a loose or irregular train of thought; (*Mus.*) a dreamy musical composition; *a wild or fantastic conceit, a vision, a delusion.

revers (rė vâr′) [F. as foll.], *n.* A part of a coat, bodice, etc., turned back so as to show the lining.

reverse (rė vĕrs′) [O.F. *revers*, L. *reversus*, p.p. of *revertere* (RE-, *vertere*, to turn)], *a.* Turned backward, inverted, reversed, upside down; having an opposite direction, contrary. *n.* The contrary, the opposite; the back surface (of a coin, etc.), the opposite of obverse; a complete change of affairs for the worse, a check, a defeat; *a back-handed stroke or thrust in fencing. *v.t.* To turn in the contrary direction, to turn the other way round, upside down, or inside out; to invert, to transpose; to cause to have a contrary motion or effect; to revoke, to annul, to nullify; *to remove; *to recall, to bring back (to). *v.i.* To change to a contrary condition, direction, etc.; (*Motor.*) to put a car into the reverse gear; (*Dancing*) to begin to turn in the opposite direction. **on the reverse:** (*Motor.*) With the car moving backwards. **reverse battery** or **fire:** A battery or fire directed at the rear or from the rear of the enemy. **reversal,** *n.* **reversed,** *a.* Turned in a reverse direction; changed to the contrary; made or declared void; (*Bot.*) resupinate; (*Conch.*) applied to the spire of a shell turning from right to left. **reversedly** (rė vĕr′ sėd li), *adv.* ***reverseless,** *a.* Not to be reversed. **reversely,** *adv.* **reverser,** *n.* One who reverses; (*Sc. Law*) one borrowing on a mortgage of land. **reversi** (rė vĕr′ si), *n.* A game played by two persons on a draughtboard with pieces differently coloured above and below, which may be reversed; *an obsolete card-game in which the player wins who takes fewest tricks. **reversible,** *a.* **reversibility** (-bil′ i ti), *n.* **reversion** (rė vĕr′ shŭn), *n.* Return to a former condition, habit, etc.; (*Biol.*) the tendency of an animal or a plant to revert to ancestral type or characters; (*Law*) the returning of an estate to the grantor or his heirs after a particular period is ended; the right of succeeding to an estate after the death of the grantee, etc.; a sum payable upon some event, as a death, esp. an annuity or life assurance; the right or expectation of succeeding to an office, etc., on relinquishment by the present holder. **reversional, reversionary,** *a.* **reversionally,** *adv.* **reversioner,** *n.* One who holds the reversion to an estate, etc. **reverso,** *n.* The left-hand page of an open book, usu. even-numbered.

revert (rė vĕrt′) [O.F. *revertir*, L. *revertere*, as prec.], *v.t.* To turn (esp. the eyes) back; *to reverse. *v.i.* To return, to go back, to fall back, to return (to a previous condition, habits, type, etc., esp. to a wild state); to recur, to turn the attention again (to); (*Law*) to come back by reversion to the possession of the former proprietor. *n.* A return; one who or that which reverts, esp. to a previous faith. **revertant,** *a.* (*Her.*) Bent back, esp. like the letter S. **reverter,** *n.* One who or that which reverts; (*Law*) reversion. **revertible,** *a.* ***revertive,** *a.* ***revertively,** *adv.*

***revest** (rė vest′) [O.F. *revestir* (F. *revêtir*), late L. *revestīre*], *v.t.* To clothe, to attire; to robe; to reinvest. *v.i.* (*Law*) To vest or take effect again, to return to a former owner. ***revestiary, revestry,** *n.* A vestry.

revet (rė vet′) [F. *revêtir*, as prec.], *v.t.* (*past & p.p.* **revetted**) To face (a wall, scarp, parapet, etc.) with masonry. **revetment,** *n.*

revictual (rē vi tėl′), *v.t.* To victual again.

review (rė vū′), *v.t.* To view again; to look back on, to go over in memory, to revise; to survey, to look over carefully and critically; to write a critical review of; to hold a review of, to inspect. *v.i.* To write reviews. *n.* A repeated examination, a reconsideration, a second view; a retrospective survey; a revision, esp. by a superior court of law; a critical account of a book, etc.; a periodical publication containing essays and criticisms; a display or a formal or official inspection of military or naval forces. **court of review:** One to which sentences and decisions are submitted for judicial revision. **review order:** (*Mil.*) Parade uniform and arrangement; (*fig.*) full dress, full rig. **reviewable,** *a.* ***reviewage, reviewal,** *n.* **reviewer,** *n.* One who reviews, esp. books.

revigorate (rė vig′ ŏ rāt) [F. *revigorer*, med. L. *revigorāre* (RE-, L. *vigor*, VIGOUR)], *v.t.* To reinvigorate.

revile (rė vīl′) [O.F. *reviler*], *v.t.* To address with opprobrious or scandalous language, to abuse, to vilify. *v.i.* To be abusive, to rail. **n.* Abuse. **revilement,** *n.* **reviler,** *n.* **revilingly,** *adv.*

***revindicate** (rė vin′ di kāt), *v.t.* To vindicate again; to reclaim, to restore. ***revindication** (-kā′ shŭn), *n.*

revise (rė vīz′) [F. *reviser* (RE-, *viser*, L. *vidēre*, to see, p.p. *vīsus*)], *v.t.* To look over, to re-examine for correction or emendation; to correct, alter, or amend. *n.* A revision; a proof-sheet in which corrections made in rough proof have been embodied; a revised form or version. **revisable,** *a.* **revisal, revision** (rė vizh′ ŭn), *n.* **Revised Version,** *n.* (*Eccles.*) The revision of the Authorized Version of the Bible, made in 1870–84. **reviser, revisor,** *n.* **revisership,** *n.* **revising barrister** [BARRISTER]. **revisional, -ary, revisory** (re vī′ zŏ ri), *a.* **revisionist,** *n.* One in favour of revision; a reviser of the Bible; a right-wing political party in Israel; (*Pol.*) one who believes in the broadening and evolution of the theories of Marxism.

revisit (rē viz′ it), *v.t.* To visit again; *to revise. *n.* A further visit. **revisitation** (-tā′ shŭn), *n.*

revisor, revisory [REVISE].

revitalize (rē vī′ tȧ līz), *v.t.* To vitalize again. **revitalization** (-zā′ shŭn), *n.*

revival (re vī′ vȧl), *n.* The act of reviving; the state of being revived; return or recovery of life, consciousness, vigour, activity, or vogue; a renaissance; a religious awakening, esp. a movement for the renewal of religious fervour by means of special services, etc. **revivalism,** *n.* **revivalist,** *n.*

revive (rė vīv′) [F. *revivre*, L. *revīvere* (RE-, *vīvere*, to live)], *v.i.* To return to life, consciousness, health, vigour, activity, vogue, etc.; to gain new life or vigour; to recover from a state of obscurity, neglect, or depression; to come back to the mind again, to reawaken. *v.t.* To bring back to life, consciousness, vigour, etc.; to re-animate; to resuscitate, to renew, to renovate, to reawaken, to re-establish, to re-encourage; (*Chem.*) to restore or reduce to its natural or metallic state. **revivable,** *a.* **revivably,** *adv.* **reviver,** *n.* One who or that which revives; a preparation for renovating leather, cloth, etc.; (*slang*) a drink, a stimulant. **revivingly,** *adv.*

revivify (rē viv′ i fī) [F. *revivifier*, late L. *revivificāre*], *v.t.* To restore to life; to reanimate, to reinvigorate, to put new life into; (*Chem.*) to revive. **revivification** (-kā′ shŭn), *n.* **revivingly** [REVIVE]. **reviviscent** (rev i vis′ ėnt) [L. *reviviscens -ntem*, pres.p. of *revīviscere*], *a.* Recovering life and strength, reviving. **reviviscence, -cy,** *n.* **revivor** (rė vī′ vŏr), *n.* (*Law*) The reviving of a suit that has been abated by death, etc.

revoke (rė vōk′) [O.F. *revoquer*, L. *revocāre* (RE-, *vocāre*, to call)], *v.t.* To annul, to cancel, to repeal, to rescind; *to recall; *to withdraw, to take back. *v.i.* (*Cards*) To fail to follow suit when this is possible. *n.* The act of revoking at cards. **revocable,** *a.* **revocability** (-bil′ i ti), **revocableness,** *n.* **revocably,** *adv.* **revocation** (rev ō kā′ shŭn), *n.* **revocatory** (rev′ ō kȧ tŏr i), *a.* ***revokement,** *n.*

revolt (rė vōlt′, -volt′) [F. *révolte*, from *révolter*, M.It. *revoltare* (It. *rivoltare*) (RE-, L. *volutāre*, freq. of *volvere*, to roll, p.p. *volūtus*)], *v.i.* To renounce allegiance, to rise in rebellion or insurrection, to turn away (from); to be repelled (by), to feel disgust (at), to turn away in loathing (from), to feel repugnance (at); *to desert; *to be faithless. *v.t.* To repel, to nauseate, to disgust; *to turn back. *n.* A renunciation of allegiance and subjection; a rebellion, a rising, an insurrection; a change of sides; *revulsion. **revolter,** *n.* **revolting,** *a.* Causing disgust, repulsion, or abhorrence. **revoltingly,** *adv.*

revolute (1) (rev′ ō lūt, -loot) [L. *revolūtus*, p.p. of *revolvere* (RE-, *volvere*, to roll)], *a.* (*Bot. etc.*) Rolled backwards from the edge.

revolution (rev ō lū′-, -loo shŭn) [M.E. and O.F. *revolucion* (F. *révolution*), L. *revolūtiōnem*, nom. *-tio*, from *revolvere*, to REVOLVE], *n.* The act or state of revolving; the circular motion of a body on its axis, rotation; the motion of a body round a centre; a complete rotation or movement round a centre; the period of this; a round or cycle of regular recurrence or succession; a radical change or reversal of circumstances, conditions, relations, or things; a fundamental change in government, esp. by the forcible overthrow of the existing system and substitution of a new ruler or political system. **American Revolution:** The successful revolt of the thirteen American colonies from Great Britain in the War of Independence (1775–81). **French Revolution:** The overthrow of the French monarchy in 1789 and the succeeding years. **Russian Revolution:** The overthrow of the Tsarist régime by the Bolshevists and the establishment of a socialist republic, in 1917. **the Revolution:** That by which James II was driven from the English throne in 1688. **revolute** (2) (rev′ ō loot), *v.i.* **revolutionary,** *a.* Pertaining to or tending to produce a revolution in government; *pertaining to rotation. *n.* A revolutionist. **revolutionism,** *n.* **revolutionist,** *n.* An advocate of revolution; one who takes an active part in a revolution. **revolutionize,** *v.t.*

revolve (rė volv′) [L. *revolvere* (RE-, *volvere*, to roll)], *v.t.* To turn round; to move round a centre, to rotate; to move in a circle, orbit, or cycle; to roll along; *to return. *v.t.* To cause to revolve or rotate; to turn over and over in the mind, to meditate on, to ponder over. ***revolvency,** *n.* **revolver,** *n.* One who or that which revolves; a pistol having a revolving breech cylinder by which it can be fired several times without reloading.

revue (rė vū′) [F.], *n.* A music-hall entertainment with songs, dances, etc., representing topical characters, events, fashions, etc.

revulsion (rė vŭl′ shŭn) [F. *révulsion*, L. *revulsiōnem*, nom. *-sio*, from *revellere* (RE-, *vellere*, to pull, p.p. *vulsus*)], *n.* A sudden or violent change or reaction, esp. of feeling; (*Med.*) reduction of a disease in one part of the body by treatment of another part, as by counter-irritation; *violent withdrawal from something. **revulsive,** *a.* Causing or tending to cause revulsion. *n.* (*Med.*) An application causing revulsion, a counter-irritant. **revulsor,** *n.* (*Med.*) An apparatus for the alternate application of heat and cold.

reward (rė wôrd′) [A.-F. and O. North. F. *rewarder*, O.F. *reguarder*, to REGARD], *v.t.* To repay, to requite, to recompense (a service or offence, a doer or offender). *n.* That which is given in return for good or evil done or received; a recompense, a requital, retribution; a sum of money offered for the detection of a criminal or for the restoration of anything lost. **reward claim:** (*Austral.*) Land awarded to a miner who discovers gold in a new area. **rewardable,** *a.* **rewardableness,** *n.* **rewardably,** *adv.* **rewarder,** *n.* **rewardfulness,** *n.* **rewardingly,** *adv.* **rewardless,** *a.*

rewa-rewa (rē′ wȧ rē′ wȧ) [Maori], *n.* The N. Zealand honeysuckle.

re-weigh (rē wā′), *v.t.* To weigh again. **rewin** (rē win′), *v.t.* To win again or back. **reword** (rē wĕrd′), *v.t.* To put into words again; to repeat; to re-echo; to put into new words. **rewrite** (rē rīt′), *v.t.* To write over again.

rex (reks) [L.], *n.* A reigning king.

reynard (ren′ ȧrd, rā′ nȧrd) [O.F. *Renart*, name of the fox in the mediæval 'Roman de Renart,' from Teut. (cp. O.H.G. *Reginhart*)], *n.* A proper name for the fox.

rhabarbarate (rȧ bar′ bȧ rȧt) [med. L. *rhabarbarum*, RHUBARB, -ATE], *n.* (*Chem.*) A salt of rhabarbaric acid. **rhabarbaric** (-băr′ ik), *a.* Of or pertaining to rhubarb. **rhabarbarin** (-bar′ bȧ rin), *n.* Rhabarbaric acid, a crystalline compound derived from rhubarb, senna-leaves, etc.

rhabdite (răb′ dīt) [Gr. *rhabdos*, rod, -ITE], *n.* (*Zool.*) A smooth, rod-like body found in the epidermis of tubellarian worms. **rhabditic** (-dit′ ik), *a.* **rhabdoid,** *a.* Rod-like. *n.* (*Bot.*) A needle-shaped body found in the cells of certain irritative plants, as the sundew. **rhabdoidal** (-doi′ dȧl), *a.* Rod-like; (*Anat.*) applied to the sagittal suture connecting the two parietal bones. ***rhabdology** (-dol′ ō ji) [-LOGY], *n.* Rhabdomancy. **rhabdomancy** (răb′ do măn si), *n.* Divination by a rod, esp. the discovery of minerals, underground streams, etc., with the divining-rod. **rhabdomancer,** *n.* **rhabdomantic** (-măn tik), *a.*

rhachis, rhachitis, etc. [RACHIS].

Rhadamanthine (răd ȧ măn′ thīn) [L. *Rhadamanthus*, judge in Hades], *a.* Rigorously just and severe.

Rhætian (rē′ shȧn), *a.* Pertaining to the ancient Roman district of Rhætia, embracing the Grisons and part of Tyrol, or the people inhabiting this. *n.* Rhæto-Romanic. **Rhætic,** *a.* (*Geol.*) Of or pertaining to the Rhætian Alps (applied to the group of strata between the Lias and Trias developed there and also in England); *n.* The Rhætic formation or strata. **Rhæto-Romanic, -Romansch** (-rō măn′ ik, -măns′), *a.* (*Philol.*) Belonging to the Romance peoples of S.E. Switzerland and Tyrol or their dialects, esp. Romansch and Ladin. *n.* The Rhæto-Romanic language.

rhamphoid (răm′ foid) [G. *rhamphos*, curved beak], *a.* Beak-shaped. **rhamphorhyncus** (răm fō ring′ kŭs) [Gr. *rhunchos*, beak], *n.* (*Palæont.*) A pterodactyl of the Jurassic period. **rhamphotheca** (răm fō thē′ kȧ), *n.* (*Ornith.*) The horny integument of the beak.

rhapontic (rȧ pon′ tik) [mod. L. *rhaponticum* (*Rha*, see RHUBARB, PONTIC (1))], *n.* A species of rhubarb, *Rheum Rhaponticum*.

rhapsode (răp′ sōd) [Gr. *rhapsōdos* (*rhaptein*, to sew, ODE)], *n.* An ancient Greek reciter of epic poems, esp. one of a professional school who recited the Homeric poems.

rhapsody (răp′ sō di), *n.* A high-flown, enthusiastic composition or utterance; (*Mus.*) an irregular and emotional composition, esp. of the nature of an improvisation; (*Gr. Ant.*) an epic poem, or a portion of this for recitation at one time by a rhapsodist. **rhapsodic, -al,** *a.* Of or pertaining to rhapsody; (*fig.*) irregular, disconnected; high-flown, extravagant. **rhapsodically,** *adv.* **rhapsodist,** *n.* A rhapsode; any professional reciter or improvisor of verses; (*fig.*) one who writes or speaks rhapsodically. **rhapsodize,** *v.t.i.*

rhatany (răt' å ni) [Port. *ratanhia* or Sp. *ratania*, Quichua, *ratañа*], *n.* A Peruvian shrub, *Krameria triandra*, or its root, from which an extract is obtained used in medicine and for adulterating port wine.

rhea (1) (rē' å) [Gr., daughter of Uranos and Gea, and wife of Kronos], *n.* (*Zool.*) A genus of birds containing the S. American three-toed ostriches; a bird of this genus.

rhea (2) (rē' å) [Assamese], *n.* The ramie plant.

rheic (rē' ik) [F. *rhéique* (RHE-UM (2), -IC)], *a.* (*Chem.*) Of or derived from rhubarb. **rhein,** *n.* Rheic acid, an orange-coloured liquid obtained from rhubarb.

rhematic (rē măt' ik) [Gr. *rhēmatikos*, from *rhēma -atos*, word], *a.* Pertaining to the formation of words, esp. verbs. **n.pl.* The science of propositions.

Rhemish (rē' mish), *a.* Of or pertaining to Rheims (applied esp. to an English translation of the New Testament by R.-C. students in 1582).

Rhenish (ren' ish), *a.* Pertaining to the Rhine or Rhineland. *n.* Rhine-wine.

rhenium (rē' ni ŭm) [L. *Rhenus*, the Rhine], *n.* A metallic element occurring in certain platinum and molybdenum ores.

rheo- [Gr. *rheos*, stream, current, rel. to *rheein*, to flow], *comb. form.* (*Elec.*) Pertaining to a current.

rheostat (rē' ō stăt), *n.* A variable resistance for adjusting and regulating an electric current. **rheostatic,** *a.*

rheotropism (rē' ō trōp izm), *n.* (*Bot.*) The tendency in growing plant-organs exposed to running water to dispose their longer axes either in the direction of or against the current.

rhesus (rē' sŭs) [L., from Gr. *Rhēsos*, a king of Thrace], *n.* (*Zool.*) One of the macaques, *Macacus rhesus*, an Indian monkey, held sacred in some parts of India. **rhesus (Rh.) factor:** (*Biol.*) An antigen substance occurring in the red blood corpuscles of most human beings and many mammals (*e.g.* the rhesus monkey). **Rh. positive** or **Rh. negative** are where this substance is present, or absent.

Rhetian, Rhetic, etc. [RHÆTIAN].

rhetor (rē' tôr) [L., from Gr. *rhētor*, rel. to *eirein*, to speak, perf. *eirēka*], *n.* (*Gr. and Rom. Ant.*) A teacher or professor of rhetoric; a professional orator, a mere orator.

rhetoric (ret' ŏ rik) [O.F. *rethorique* (F. *rhétorique*), L. *rhētorica*, Gr. *rhētorikē technē*, rhetorical art, from prec.], *n.* The art of effective speaking or writing, the rules of eloquence; a treatise on this; the power of persuading by looks or acts; the use of language for effect or display, esp. affected or exaggerated oratory or declamation. **rhetorical** (rė tor' i kăl), *a.* Pertaining to or of the nature of rhetoric; designed for effect or display, florid, showy, affected, declamatory. **rhetorical question:** One put merely for the sake of emphasis and requiring no answer. **rhetorically,** *adv.* **rhetorician** (ret ŏ rish' ăn), *n.* ***rhetorize,** *v.i.*

rheum (1) (room) [O.F. *reume*, L. *rheuma*, Gr. *rheuma -atos*, stream, from *rheu-*, root of *rheein*, to flow], *n.* The thin serous fluid secreted by the mucous glands as tears, saliva, or mucus; (*poet.*) tears; *moisture; (*Path.*) mucous discharge, catarrh; (*pl.*) rheumatic pains.

rheum (2) (rē' ŭm) [mod. L., from Gr. *rhēon*], *n.* (*Bot.*) A genus of plants comprising the rhubarbs.

rheumatic (roo măt' ik) [L. *rheumaticus*, Gr. *rheumatikos*], *a.* Pertaining to, of the nature of, suffering from, or subject to rheumatism. **rheumatically,** *adv.* **rheumatics,** *n.pl.* (*colloq.*) Rheumatism.

rheumatism (roo' mă tizm), *n.* (*Path.*) An inflammatory disease affecting muscles and joints of the human body, and attended by swelling and pain. **rheumatismal** (-tiz' măl), *a.* Rheumatic. **rheumato-,** *comb. form.* **rheumatoid,** *a.* **rheumatoid arthritis,** *n.* Disease of the synovial tissues of the joints. **rheumatology** (-ol' ō ji), *n.* The study of rheumatism. **rheumophthalmia** (roo mof thăl' mi å), *n.* Rheumatic inflammation of the sclerotic membrane.

rhinal (rī' năl) [RHINO-], *n.* (*Anat.*) Of or pertaining to the nose or nostrils.

rhinalgia (rī năl' ji å), *n.* (*Path.*) Nasal neuralgia.

rhinanthin (rī năn' thin), *n.* (*Chem.*) A glucoside obtained from *Rhinanthus major*.

Rhinanthus (rī năn' thŭs), *n.* (*Bot.*) A genus of scrophulariaceous plants containing the yellow-rattle.

rhinarium (rī nâr' i ŭm), *n.* (*Ent.*) The anterior part of the clypeus in an insect.

rhine (1) (rīn) [prob. from A.-S. *ryne*, cogn. with RUN], *n.* (*W. of England*) A large ditch or drain.

Rhine (2) (rīn) [German river], *a.* Pertaining to or derived from the Rhine or its bordering regions. **rhinestone,** *n.* (*Min.*) A species of rock crystal; a colourless artificial gem cut to look like a diamond. **Rhine wine,** *n.* A wine made from grapes grown in the neighbourhood of the Rhine.

rhine (3) (rīn) [formerly *rine hemp*, G. *reinhanf*, clean hemp], *n.* A superior quality of Russian hemp.

rhinencephalon (rī nen sef' å lon) [RHIN-, ENCEPHALON], *n.* (*Anat.*) The olfactory lobe of the brain. **rhinencephalic** (-făl' ik), **rhinencephalous** (-sef' å lŭs), *a.*

rhinestone [RHINE (2)].

rhinitis (rī nī' tis) [RHIN-, -ITIS], *n.* (*Path.*) Inflammation of the nose.

rhino (1) (rī' nō) [etym. doubtful], *n.* (*slang*) Money, coin.

rhino (2) (rī' nō), *n.* A rhinoceros.

rhino- [Gr. *rhis rhinos*, nose], *comb. form.* Pertaining to the nose or nostrils. **rhinobatid** (rī nob' å tid) [Gr. *batos*, ray], *n.* (*Ichthyol.*) A shark-like ray. **rhinocaul** (rī' nŏ kawl), *n.* (*Anat.*) The peduncle of the olfactory bulb of the brain.

rhinoceros (rī nos' ėr ŏs) [late L., from Gr. *rhīnokerōs* (RHINO-, *kerōs*, *keras*, horn)], *n.* (*pl.* **-oses**) A large pachydermatous quadruped, now found only in Africa and S. Asia, with one or two horns on the nose. **rhinoceros-bird,** *n.* The African beef-eater or ox-pecker, *Buphaga Africana*. **rhinocerical** (-ser' i kăl), **rhinoceroid, rhinocerotic** (-sė rot' ik), **rhinocerotiform,** *a.* **rhinocerotoid** (-ser' ŏ toid), *a.* and *n.*

rhinolith (rī' nŏ lith) [RHINO-, -LITH], *n.* (*Path.*) Nasal calculus. **rhinology** (rī nol' ŏ ji), *n.* The branch of science dealing with the nose and nasal diseases. **rhinological** (-loj' i kăl), *a.* **rhinologist** (-nol' ŏ jist), *n.* **rhino-pharyngeal** (rī nŏ fă rin' jė ăl), *a.* Pertaining to the nose and the pharynx. **rhino-pharyngitis** (-jī' tis), *n.* **rhinoplasty** (rī' nŏ plăs ti), *n.* (*Surg.*) An operation for restoring an injured nose. **rhinoplastic** (-plăs' tik), *a.* **rhinorrhœa** (rī nŏ rē' å), *n.* Discharge of blood from the nose. **rhinoscleroma** (-sklė rō' mă), *n.* A disease affecting the nose, lips, etc., with a tuberculous growth. **rhinoscope** (rī' nŏ skōp), *n.* An instrument for examining the nasal passages. **rhinoscopic** (-skop' ik), *a.* **rhinoscopy** (rī nos' kŏ pi), *n.*

rhipido- [Gr. *rhipis rhipidos*, fan], *comb. form.* Having fan-like processes. **rhipidoglossal** (rip i dŏ glos' ăl) [Gr. *glōssa*, tongue], *a.* Belonging to the *Rhipidoglossa*, a division of gasteropods having an odontophore with several median and many marginal teeth.

rhipipteran (ri pip' tėr ăn) [Gr. *rhipis*, fan, *pteron*, wing], *a.* (*Ent.*) Fan-winged. *n.* One of the *Rhipiptera*, an order of insects. **rhipipterous,** *a.*

rhiz-, rhiza-, rhizo- [Gr. *rhiza*, root], *comb. form.* Pertaining to a root; having roots or root-like processes. **rhizanth** (rī' zănth) [Gr. *anthos*, flower], *n.* (*Bot.*) A plant flowering or seeming to flower from the root. **rhizanthous** (-zăn' thŭs), *a.* **rhizic** (rī' zik), *a.* (*Math.*) Of or pertaining to the root of an equation. **rhizocarp** (rī' zō karp) [Gr. *karpos*, fruit], *n.* A plant of the group *Rhizocarpeæ* (now *Marsileaceæ*). **rhizocarpean** (-kar' pē ăn), *a.* **rhizocarpic, -carpous,** *a.* Having a perennial root but a stem that withers annually. **rhizocephalan** [Gr. *kephalē*, head], *n.* (*Zool.*) One of the *Rhizocephala*, a sub-order of parasitic crustaceans related to the cirripeds. **rhizocephalous,** *a.* **rhizodont** (rī' zō dont), *a.* Having teeth rooted and anchylosed with the jaw (as crocodiles); *n.* A rhizodont reptile. **rhizogen** (rī' zō jĕn), *n.* (*Bot.*) A plant parasitic on the roots of another plant. **rhizogenic** (-jen' ik), ***-genetic** (-jē net' ik), *a.* Root-producing. **rhizoid** (rī' zoid), *a.* Root-like. *n.* A filiform or hair-like organ serving for attachment, in mosses, etc.

rhizome (rī' zōm), **rhizoma** (rī zō' mȧ) [Gr. *rhizōma*, from *rhizoun*, to cause to take root, from *rhiza*, root], *n.* (*Bot.*) A prostrate, thickened, root-like stem, sending roots downwards and yearly producing aerial shoots, etc. **rhizomatous** (-zom' ȧ tŭs), *a.* **rhizomorph** (rī' zō môrf), *n.* A root-like mycelial growth by which some fungi attach themselves to higher plants. **rhizomorphoid, -phous** (-môr' foid, -fŭs), *a.*

rhizophagous (rī zof' ȧ gŭs) [RHIZO-, Gr. *phagein*, to eat], *a.* Feeding on roots; pertaining to the *Rhizophaga*, a sub-order of marsupials comprising the wombat. **rhizophagan,** *a.* and *n.* **rhizophore** (rī' zō fôr) [-PHORE], *n.* (*Bot.*) A root-like structure bearing the roots in species of *Selaginella*. **rhizophorous** (-zof' ō rŭs), *a.* Root-bearing. **rhizopod** (rī' zō pod) [Gr. *pous podos*, foot], *n.* (*Zool.*) An animalcule of the class *Rhizopoda*, the lowest division of the protozoa, comprising those with pseudopodia used for locomotion and the ingestion of food; (*Bot.*) the mycelium of fungi. *a.* Of or pertaining to the *Rhizopoda*. **rhizopodal** (-zop' ō dăl), **rhizopodic** (-pod' ik), **rhizopodous** (-zop' ō dŭs), *a.*

rhodanic (rō dăn' ik) [Gr. *rhodon*, rose, -IC], *a.* (*Chem.*) Producing a rose-red colour with ferric salts. **rhodanic acid:** Sulphocyanic acid. **rhodanate** (rō' dȧ nāt), *n.* Sulphocyanate.

Rhodes Scholar (rōdz skol' ăr) [Cecil *Rhodes* (1853–1902)], *n.* Scholarships at Oxford founded under the will of Cecil Rhodes for students from the British Commonwealth and U.S.A.

Rhodian (1) (rō' di ăn), *a.* Pertaining to Rhodes, an island in the Ægean Sea. *n.* An inhabitant or native of Rhodes.

rhodian (2), **rhodian-wood** [RHODIUM (1)].

rhodinol (rō' di nōl, -nol) [Gr. *rhodinos*, made of roses, as foll., -OL], *n.* (*Chem.*) An alcohol occurring in geranium- and rose-oil.

rhodium (1) (rō' di ŭm) [mod. L., neut. of *rhodius*, rose-like, from Gr. *rhodon*, rose], *n.* The Jamaica rosewood; the hard, white, scented wood of either of two shrubby convolvuluses growing in the Canary islands, also called rhodium- or rhodian-wood. **oil of rhodium:** An oil obtained from this. **rhodian** (2), *a.*

rhodium (2) (rō' di ŭm) [Gr. *rhodon*, rose, -IUM], *n.* (*Chem.*) A greyish-white metallic element belonging to the platinum group. **rhodic, rhodous,** *a.*

rhodo- [Gr. *rhodon*, rose], *comb. form.* Rose-like; scented like a rose. **rhodocrinite** (rō dō krin' īt), *n.* (*Palæont.*) One of a Palæozoic family of encrinites, the *Rhodocrinidæ* or rose-encrinites. **rhodocrinid** (rō dok' ri nid), **rhodocrinoid,** *a.* and *n.*

rhododendron (rō dō den' drŏn) [late L. and Gr. (RHODO-, *dendron*, tree)], *n.* A genus of evergreen shrubs akin to the azaleas, with brilliant flowers; a shrub of this genus.

rhodonite (rō' dō nīt) [G. *rhodonit* (Gr. *rhodon*, rose)], *n.* (*Min.*) A rose-pink silicate of manganese.

rhodophyl (rō' dō fil) [RHODO-, Gr. *phullon*, leaf], *n.* (*Bot.*) The compound pigment giving red algæ their colour. **rhodophyllous** (-fil' ŭs), *a.* **rhodopsin** (rō dop' sin) [Gr. *opsis*, sight], *n.* (*Physiol.*) A purplish pigment found in the retina, visual purple.

Rhodora (rō dôr' ȧ) [Gr. *rhodon*, rose], *n.* (*Bot.*) A N. American flowering shrub, *R. Canadensis*, belonging to the family *Ericaceæ*, growing in boggy ground.

rhodous [RHODIUM (2)].

rhœadic (rē ăd' ik) [Gr. *rhoias -ados*, a kind of poppy, -IC], *a.* Derived from the red poppy, *Papaver rhœas*. **rhœadic acid:** A compound found in the flowers of this, the principle of their colouring-matter. **rhœadine** (rē' ȧ din), *n.* An alkaloid obtained from the red poppy.

rhomb (rom, *before a vowel* romb) [F. *rhombe*, L. *rhombus*, Gr. *rhombos*], *n.* An oblique parallelogram, with equal sides; (*Cryst.*) a rhombohedron. **rhomb-spar,** *n.* A perfectly crystallized variety of dolomite. **rhombic,** *a.* **rhombiform,** *a.* **rhombo-,** *comb. form.* **rhombohedron** (rom bō hē' drŏn, -hed' rŏn), *n.* (*pl.* **-dra**) A solid figure bounded by six equal rhombs. **rhombohedral,** *a.* **rhomboid** (rom' boid), *n.* A parallelogram the adjoining sides of which are not equal and which contains no right angle; (*Anat.*) a rhomboid muscle. *a.* Having the shape or nearly the shape of a rhomboid. **rhomboid ligament:** (*Anat.*) A ligament connecting the first rib and the end of the clavicle. **rhomboid muscle:** Either of two muscles connecting the vertebral border of the scapula with the spine. **rhomboidal** (rom boi' dăl), *a.* **rhomboidally,** *adv.* **rhomboideum** (rom boi' dē ŭm), *n.* (*pl.* **-dea**) (*Anat.*) A rhomboid ligament.

rhombus (rom' bŭs), *n.* (*pl.* **rhombi**) A rhomb; (*Zool.*) a genus of flat-fishes containing the turbot, brill, etc.

rhotacism (rō' tȧ sizm) [Gr. *rhōtakizein*, to rhotacize, from *rhō*, the letter *r*, -ISM], *n.* Exaggerated or erroneous pronunciation of the letter *r*, burring; (*Philol.*) the change of *s* into *r*, as in Indo-European languages. **rhotacize,** *v.i.*

rhubarb (roo' barb) [O.F. *reubarbe* (F. *rhubarbe*), med. L. *rheubarbum*, *rheubarbarum*, altered from *rhabarbarum* (*rha barbarum*, foreign *Rha*, the Volga)], *n.* Any herbaceous plant of the genus *Rheum*, esp. *R. rhaponticum*, the English, French, common, or garden rhubarb, the fleshy and juicy leaf-stalks of which are cooked when young as a substitute for fruit; the roots of several Oriental species of *Rheum*, usu. called East Indian, Russia, or Turkey rhubarb, from which purgative medicines are prepared. **rhubarby,** *a.*

rhumb (rŭm) [from F. *rumb* or Sp. *rhumbo*, L. RHOMBUS], *n.* (*Naut.*) A line cutting all the meridians at the same angle, such as a ship would follow sailing continuously on one course; any one of the 32 principal points of the compass; the angular distance, 11° 15′, between any successive pair of these. **rhumbline,** *n.*

rhyme, rime (1) (rīm) [O.F. *rime*, L. *rhythmum*, nom. *-mus*, Gr. *rhuthmos*, RHYTHM, first form assim. to RHYTHM], *n.* A correspondence of sound in the final accented syllable or group of syllables of a line of verse with that of another line, consisting of identity of the vowel sounds and of all the consonantal sounds but the first; verse characterized by rhyme (*sing. or pl.*); poetry, verse; a word rhyming with another. *v.i.* To make rhymes, to versify; to make a rhyme with another word or verse; (*fig.*) to be in accord, to harmonize (with). *v.t.* To put into rhyme; to pass or waste (time, etc.) in rhyming. **without rhyme or reason:** Inconsiderately, thoughtlessly; unreasonable, purposeless. **rhyme royal:** A seven-lined decasyllabic stanza rhyming *a b a b b c c*, so called because employed by James I of Scotland in the *King's Quhair*. **rhymeless,** *a.* **rhymelessness,** *n.* **rhymer, rhymester, rhymist,** *n.* ***rhymic,** *a.*

rhynch-, rhyncho- [Gr. *rhunchos*, snout], *comb. form.* Having a snout or snout-like process. **rhynchocephalian** (ring kō sė fā′ li ȧn) [Gr. *kephalē*, head, -AN], *a.* (*Zool.*) Belonging to the *Rhyncocephalia*, an almost extinct order of reptiles; *n.* A reptile of this order. **rhyncocœle** (ring′ kō sēl) [Gr. *koilos*, hollow]. *a.* Belonging to the *Rhynchocœla*, a section of turbellarians comprising the nemerteans. **rhynchocœlous,** *a.* **rhyncholite** (ring′ kō līt) [-LITE], *a.* (*Palæont.*) A fossil beak of a tetrabranchiate cephalopod. **rhynchonella** (ring kō nel′ ȧ), *n.* (*Conch.*) A brachiopod of the genus *Rhynchonellidæ*. **rhynchophore** (ring′ kō fôr) [-PHORE], *n.* (*Ent.*) One of the *Rhynchophora*, a division of tetramerous beetles containing the weevils or snout-beetles. **rhyncophoran,** *a.* and *n.* **rhynchophorous,** *a.* **rhynchosaur** (ring′ kō sawr), **rhynchosauros** (-saw′ rŭs) [Gr. *sauros*, lizard], *n.* (*Palæont.*) A genus of edentulous saurians from the Devonian strata.

rhyolite (rī′ ō līt) [G. *rhyolit* (Gr. *rhuax*, stream, -LITE)], *n.* (*Petrol.*) An igneous rock of structure showing the effect of lava-flow, composed of quartz and orthoclase with other minerals. **rhyolitic** (-lit ik), *a.*

rhyparographer (rī′ pȧ rog′ rȧ fėr) [late L. *rhyparographus*, Gr. *rhuparographos* (*rhuparos*, filthy, -GRAPHER)], *n.* A painter of squalid subjects. **rhyparographic** (-grăf′ ik), *a.* **rhyparography** (-rog′ rȧ fi), *n.*

rhysimeter (rī sim′ ė tėr) [Gr. *rhusis*, flowing, rel. to *-rheein*, to flow, -METER], *n.* An instrument for measuring the velocity of a fluid or the speed of a ship.

rhythm (ri*th*m, rithm) [F. *rithme* (now *rhythme*), L. *rhythmus*, Gr. *rhuthmos*, from *rhu-*, root of *rheein*, to flow], *n.* Movement characterized by action and reaction or regular alternation of strong and weak impulse, stress, accent, motion, sound, etc.; metrical movement determined by the regular recurrence or harmonious succession of groups of long and short or stressed and unstressed syllables called feet; the flow of words in verse or prose characterized by such movement; (*Mus.*) the regulated succession of notes according to duration; structural system based on this; (*Art*) correlation of parts in an harmonious whole; (*Physics and Nat. Hist.*) alternation of strong and weak states or movements. **rhythmic, -al** (ri*th*′ mik, -ȧl), *a.* **rhythmically,** *adv.* **rhythmist,** *n.* **rhythmless** (ri*th*m′ lės), *a.*

ria (rē′ a) [Sp., rivermouth], *n.* (*Geog.*) A long, narrow inlet into the sea-coast.

riant (rī′ ȧnt) [F. pres.p. of *rire*, L. *ridēre*, to laugh], *a.* (*fem.* ***riante***) Smiling, cheerful, gay. ***riancy,** *n.*

rib (rib) [A.-S. *ribb* (cp. Dut. *rib*, G. *rippe*, Icel. *rif*, Norw. *riv*)], *n.* One of the bones extending outwards and forwards from the spine, and in man forming the walls of the thorax; a ridge, strip, line, etc., analogous in form or function to this; a curved timber extending from the keel for supporting the side of a ship, etc.; a raised moulding or groin on a ceiling or vaulted roof; a timber or iron beam helping to support a bridge; a hinged rod forming part of an umbrella-frame; a purlin; a ridge for stiffening a casting, etc.; a main vein in a leaf; a spur of a mountain; (*facet.*) a wife, in allusion to Eve. *v.t.* (*past & p.p.* **ribbed**) To furnish with ribs; to mark with ribs or ridges; to enclose with ribs; to rafter or half-plough; (*Am. slang*) to tease. **rib-grass, -wort,** *n.* The narrow-leaved plantain, *Plantago lanceolata*. **rib-roast,** *v.t.* (*slang*) To beat soundly, to thrash. **rib-roaster,** *n.* (*slang*) A heavy blow on the body. **rib-vaulting,** *n.* **ribbed,** *a.* **ribbing,** *n.* A system or arrangement of ribs, as in a vaulted roof, etc.; a method of ploughing, raftering or half-ploughing. **ribless,** *a.* **false ribs,** *n.pl.* (*Anat.*) The lower five pairs of ribs. **floating ribs,** *n.pl.* The two lowest pairs of ribs.

ribald (rib′ ȧld) [O.F. *ribaud* (F. *ribaut*), a low ruffian, etym. doubtful], *n.* A low, coarse, or indecent fellow, esp. one using scurrilous language. *a.* Scurrilous, coarse, licentious, lewd (of language). ***ribaldish, *ribaldrous,** *a.* **ribaldry,** *n.*

riband [RIBBON].

ribband (rib′ ȧnd) [var. of prec. or from RIB, BAND (2)], *n.* (*Shipbuilding*) A strip, scantling, or spar temporarily attached lengthwise to the body of a ship to hold the ribs in position; a piece of timber used in launching, as a stop, guide, etc., or in the construction of pontoons, gun-platforms, etc.

ribble-rabble (rib′ ėl răb′ ėl), *n.* Rabble; a rabble, a mob; meaningless talk, a rigmarole.

ribbon (rib′ ŏn) [F. *riban* (now *ruban*), etym. doubtful], *n.* A narrow woven strip or band of silk, satin, etc., used for ornamenting dress, etc.; such a strip or band worn as distinctive mark of an order, college, club, etc.; a narrow strip of anything; (*pl.*) driving-reins. **ribbon development,** *n.* Urban extension in the form of a single depth of houses along roads radiating from the town. **ribbon-fish,** *n.* A long, narrow, flattish fish of various species. **ribbon-grass,** *n.* An American grass, *Phalaris arundinacea picta*, grown for ornamental purposes in gardens. **Blue Ribbon,** *n.* The Order of the Garter; a teetotal badge; the highest distinction for creating a record. **ribboned,** *a.* Wearing or adorned with ribbons (*usu. in comb.*).

Ribes (rī′ bēz) [med. L., from Arab. *rībās*, sorrel], *n.* (*Bot.*) The genus comprising the currant and gooseberry plants.

Ribston pippin (rib′ stŏn pip′ in), *n.* A choice variety of apple first cultivated in England at Ribston Park, Yorkshire.

Ricardian (ri kar′ di ȧn), *a.* Of or pertaining to the political economist David Ricardo (1772–1823) or his opinions. *n.* A follower of Ricardo.

rice (rīs) [O.F. *riz*, It. *riso*, L. *oryza*, Gr. *oruza*, prob. from O.Pers.], *n.* The white grain or seeds of *Oryza sativa*, an E. Indian aquatic grass extensively cultivated in warm climates for food. **rice-bird,** *n.* The Java sparrow; the bobolink. **rice-biscuit,** *n.* **rice milk,** *n.* Milk boiled and thickened with rice. **rice-paper,** *n.* A paper made from the pith of the Formosan *Aralia papyrifera*, and used by Chinese artists for painting on.

rich (rich) [A.-S. *rīce* (cp. Dut. *rijk*, G. *reich*, Icel. *rīkr*), rel. to L. *rex*, king, perh. ult. drived from it], *a.* Wealthy, having large possessions, abounding (in resources, productions, etc.); abundantly supplied with; producing ample supplies; fertile, abundant, well-filled; valuable, precious, costly; elaborate, splendid; abounding in qualities pleasing to the senses, sweet, luscious, high-flavoured, containing much fat, oil, sugar, spices, etc.; vivid, bright; mellow, deep, full, musical (of sounds); comical, funny, full of humorous suggestion. ****v.t.*** To enrich. ***richen,** *v.t.* and *i.* **riches, *richesse,** *n.* (*usu. as pl.*). Abundant possessions, wealth, opulence, affluence. **richly,** *adv.* In a rich manner, abundantly, thoroughly. **richness,** *n.*

Richardsonian (rich ȧrd sō′ ni ȧn), *a.* Of or resembling the work or style of the novelist Samuel Richardson (1689–1761). *n.* A follower or admirer of Richardson.

Ricinus (ris′ i nŭs) [L.], *n.* (*Bot.*) A genus of plants comprising the castor-oil plant. **ricinic** (ri sin′ ik), **ricinoleic** (-lē′ ik), **ricinolic** (-nol′ ik), *a.* (*Chem.*) Derived from castor-oil.

rick (1) (rik) [A.-S. *hrēac* (cp. Dut. *rook*, Icel. *hraukr*)], *n.* A stack of corn, hay, etc., regularly built and thatched. *v.t.* To make or pile into a rick. **rick-barton, -yard,** *n.* Space on a farm reserved for ricks. **rick-stand,** *n.* A platform of short pillars and joists for keeping a rick above the ground.

rick (2) [WRICK].

rickets (rik′ ėts) [perh. rel. to prec., supposed by F. Glisson, med. writer (1597–1677), to be corr. from RACHITIS], *n.* A disease of children consisting in the softening of the bones, esp. the spine, bow-legs, emaciation, etc., owing to lack of mineral matter in the bones. **rickety,** *a.* Affected with or of the nature of rickets; feeble in the joints; shaky, unsteady, tumble-down, fragile, unsafe.

rickshaw [JINRICKSHA].

ricochet (rik' ŏ shā, -shet) [F., etym. doubtful], *n.* A bounding or skipping of a stone, cannon ball, or bullet over water or other flat surface; the act of aiming so as to produce this, or a hit so made. *v.i.* (*past & p.p.* **ricochetted** (rik' ō shăd)) To skip or bound in this manner. *v.t.* To aim at or hit thus.

rictus (rik' tŭs) [L., p.p. of *ringī*, to open the mouth wide], *n.* (*pl.* **rictuses,** or **rictūs**) The expanse of a person's or animal's open mouth, gape; (*Bot.*) the opening of a two-lipped corolla.

rid (1) (rid) [Icel. *rythja*, conf. with REDD], *v.t.* (*past* **ridded, rid,** *p.p.* **rid, *ridded**) To free, to clear, to disencumber (of); *to deliver, to save (from, etc.); *to redd; *to drive away; *to destroy by violence. *a.* Free, clear. **to be** or **get rid of:** To free oneself or become free from. **riddance,** *n.*

***rid,** (2), **ridden,** *p.p.* [RIDE].

riddle (1) (rid' ĕl) [A.-S. *rædels*, from *rædan*, to READ (cp. Dut. *raadsel*, G. *rätsel*)], *n.* A question or proposition put in ambiguous language to exercise the ingenuity; a puzzle, conundrum, or enigma; any person, thing or fact of an ambiguous, mysterious, or puzzling nature. *v.i.* To speak in riddles. *v.t.* To solve, to explain (a riddle, problem, etc.); to express in a riddle or riddles (*usu. in p.p.*); to be a riddle to. **riddler,** *n.* **riddlingly,** *adv.*

riddle (2) (rid' ĕl) [A.-S. *hriddel, hridder*, from *hrīd-*, to shake (cp. G. *reiter*, also L. *crībrum*)], *n.* A coarse sieve for sifting gravel, cinders, etc., or washing ore. *v.t.* To pass through a riddle, to sift; (*fig.*) to perforate with holes, as with shot; to assail with arguments, questions, facts, etc. **riddlings,** *n.pl.* Screenings, siftings.

riddler, riddlingly [RIDDLE (1)].

ride (rīd) [A.-S. *rīdan* (cp. Dut. *rijdan*, G. *reiten*, Icel. *rīthā*, Dan. *ride*)], *v.i.* (*past* **rode, *rid,** *p.p.* **ridden, *rid**) To sit and be carried along, as on a horse, cycle, public conveyance, etc., esp. to go on horseback; to practise horsemanship; to float, to seem to float; to lie at anchor; to be supported, to be on something, esp. in motion; to project, to overlap; to work (up); to serve for riding; to be in a (specified) condition for riding. *v.t.* To sit on and be carried along by (a horse, etc.); to traverse on a horse, cycle, etc.; to execute or accomplish this; to cause to ride, to give a ride to; (*fig.*) to be upborne by, to float over; to oppress, to tyrannize, to domineer (over). *n.* The act of riding; a journey on horseback or in a public conveyance; a road for riding on, esp. through a wood; a district under an excise-officer. **to ride and tie:** To ride and walk alternately (of two persons having only one horse). **to ride down:** To overtake by riding; to trample on in riding. **to ride for a fall:** To go recklessly. **to ride hard:** (*Naut.*) To pitch violently when at anchor. **to ride to death:** To overdo. **to ride to hounds:** To hunt. **to ride out:** (*Naut.*) To come safely through (a storm, etc.). **to take for a ride:** (*Am. slang*) To kidnap and murder; to play a trick on. **ridable,** *a.* **rider,** *n.* One who rides, esp. on a horse; an additional clause to a document, act, etc., an opinion, recommendation, etc., added to a verdict; a subsidiary problem, a corollary, an obvious supplement; (*Naut.*) an additional timber or plate for strengthening the framework of a ship (*usu. in pl.*); a rope overlying or crossing another; (*Curling*) a stone dislodging another. **riderless,** *a.* **riding** (1), *n.* The act or state of one who rides; a road for riding on, esp. a grassed track through or beside a wood. **riding-habit,** *n.* A woman's costume for riding on horseback. **riding-hood,** *n.* A hood formerly worn by women when travelling. **riding light,** *n.* (*Naut.*) Light shown by a ship at anchor. **riding-master,** *n.* One who teaches riding, an officer superintending the instruction of troopers in the riding-school. **riding-school,** *n.* A place where riding is taught. **riding-whip,** *n.* A whip with a short lash used by riders on horseback.

rideau (ri dō') [F., curtain], *n.* (*Fort.*) An eminence commanding a fortified place; a mound or ridge covering a camp from hostile approach.

rider, etc. [RIDE].

ridge (rij) [A.-S. *hrycg* (cp. Dut. *rug*, G. *rücken*, Icel. *hryggr*, Dan. *ryg*)], *n.* The long horizontal angle formed by the junction of two slopes; an elevation of the earth's surface long in comparison with its breadth; a long and narrow hill-top or mountain-crest; a continuous range of hills or mountains; a strip of ground thrown up by a plough or other implement; the spine of an animal; (*Meteor.*) a tongue of high pressure on a weather map. *v.t.* To break (a field, etc.) into ridges; to plant in ridges; to mark or cover with ridges. *v.i.* To gather into or be marked with ridges. **ridge-piece, -plate,** *n.* A horizontal timber along the ridge of a roof. **ridge-pole,** *n.* A ridge-piece; the horizontal pole of a long tent. **ridge-way,** *n.* A road or way along a ridge. **ridgelet,** *n.* **ridgy,** *a.*

ridicule (rid' i kūl) [L. *ridiculus*, laughable, from *rīdēre*, to laugh], *n.* Words or actions intended to express contempt and excite laughter; derision, mockery; *ridiculousness. *v.t.* To treat with ridicule; to laugh at; to make fun of; to expose to derision. **ridiculer,** *n.* **ridiculous** (ri dik' ū lŭs), *a.* **ridiculously,** *adv.* **ridiculousness,** *n.*

riding (1) [RIDE].

riding (2) (rī' ding) [orig. *thriding* (THIRD, -ING)], *n.* One of the three administrative divisions of Yorkshire.

ridotto (ri dot' ō) [It., from med. L. *reductus*, orig. p.p. of *redūcere*, to REDUCE], *n.* An entertainment consisting of singing and dancing, esp. a masked ball.

riem (rēm) [Dut., cp. RIM (2)], *n.* (*S. Afr.*) A raw-hide strap or thong.

rieve, river [REAVE].

rifacimento (ri fās i men' tō) [It., from *rifare* (RE-, L. *facere*, to make)], *n.* (*pl.* **ti-,** -tē) A recast of a literary work, etc.

rife (rīf) [late A.-S. *rȳfe* (cp. Icel. *rīfa*, Dut. *rijf*)], *a.* Occurring in great quantity, number, etc., current, prevalent, abundant. ***rifely,** *adv.* **rifeness,** *n.*

riffle (rif' ĕl) [etym. doubtful], *n.* (*Gold-min.*) A groove, channel, slab, block or cleat set in an inclined trough, sluice, or cradle for arresting the particles of auriferous sand, etc.; (*Am.*) a timber or plank forming part of a fish-ladder; an obstruction in a stream; a scour.

riffler (rif' lĕr) [F. *rifloir*, from *rifler*, to RIFLE], *n.* A file with curved ends for working in shallow depressions, etc.

riffraff (rif' răf) [formerly *riff and raff*, F. *rif et raf*, prob. from Teut. (cp. M.Dut. *rijf ende raf*)], *n.* The rabble.

rifle (rī' fĕl) [O.F. *rifler*, to scrape, scratch, strip, plunder (cp. L.G. *rifeln*, G. *riefeln*, Dan. *rifle*, Swed. *reffla*)], *v.t.* To search and rob; to plunder, to pillage, to strip; to snatch and carry off; to furnish (a fire-arm or the bore or barrel of a fire-arm) with spiral grooves in order to give a rotary motion to the projectile. *v.i.* To shoot with a rifle. *n.* A musket or carbine having the barrel spirally grooved so as to give a rotary motion to the projectile; (*pl.*) troops armed with rifles. **rifle-bird,** *n.* An Australian bird (*Ptilorrhis paradisea*) with velvety black plumage. **rifle-brigade,** *n.* A brigade comprising several British regiments of infantry. **rifle-corps,** *n.* **rifle-man,** *n.* **rifle-pit,** *n.* A trench or pit forming a projection for riflemen. **rifle-shot,** *n.* The distance a rifle will carry; a marksman with the rifle. **rifler,** *n.* A robber, a plunderer. **rifling,** *n.* The spiral grooves in the bore of a fire-arm which cause the rotation of the projectile fired.

rift (rift) [from Scand. (cp. Dan. and Norw. *rift*, Icel. *ript*, from *rīfa*, to RIVE)], *n.* A cleft, a fissure; a wide crack, rent, or opening, made by riving or splitting; a break in cloud. *v.t.* (*past & p.p.* **riven**)

To cleave, to split, to rive. *v.i.* To break open. **rift in the lute,** *n.* The start of discord. **riftless,** *a.* **rifty,** *adv.*

rig (1) (rig) [etym. doubtful, Norw. and Swed. *rigga*, may be from Eng.], *v.t.* (*past & p.p.* **rigged**) To furnish or fit (a ship) with spars, gear, or tackle; to dress, clothe, or fit (up or out); to put together or fit (up) in a hasty or make-shift way. *v.i.* (*Naut.*) To be rigged. *n.* The way in which the masts and sails of a ship are arranged; (*colloq.*) the style or look of a person's clothes, etc.; an outfit, a turn-out. **rig-out, -up,** *n.* Dress, outfit; appearance or look as regards this. **rigger,** *n.* One who rigs vessels; a band-wheel having a slightly curved rim. **rigging,** *n.* The system of tackle, ropes, etc., supporting the masts, and controlling the sails, etc., of a ship; (*Aviat.*) the adjustment or alignment of the components of an aeroplane. **rigging-loft,** *n.* A large room or gallery where rigging is fitted; (*Theat.*) a space over the stage in a theatre from which the scenery is worked.

rig (2) (rig) [etym. doubtful], *n.* A swindling scheme, a corner, a dodge, a trick; a prank, a frolic, a practical joke; *a wanton, a strumpet. *v.t.* To manipulate fraudulently; to hoax, to trick. **v.i.* To play the wanton. **to rig the market:** To manipulate the market so as to raise or lower prices for underhand purposes. **to run the rig:** To indulge in practical joking. ***riggish,** *a.*

rig (3) (*Sc. and North.*) [RIDGE].

***rigadoon** (rig ȧ doon′) [F. *rigaudon, rigodon*, etym. doubtful, perh. from *Rigaud*, name of a dancing-master], *n.* A lively dance performed by one couple; the music for this.

***rigation** (ri gā′ shŭn) [L. *rigātio*, from *rigāre*, cp. IRRIGATE], *n.* Irrigation.

rigescent (ri jes′ ėnt) [L. *rigenscens -ntem*, pres.p. of *rigescere*, incept. of *rigēre*, to be stiff], *a.* Growing stiff, rigid, or numb. **rigescence,** *n.*

rigger, rigging, etc. [RIG (1)].

riggish [RIG (2)].

right (rīt) [A.-S. *riht* (cp. Dut. *regt*, G. *recht*, Icel. *rettr*), cogn. with L. *rectus*, rel. to *reg-*, root of *regere*, to rule], *a.* Required by or acting, being, or done in accordance with truth and justice; equitable, just, good, proper, correct, true, fit, suitable, most suitable, the preferable, the more convenient; sound, sane, well; properly done, placed, etc., not mistaken, satisfactory; real, genuine, veritable; on or towards that side of the body which is to the south when the face is to the sunrise; straight; direct; formed by lines meeting perpendicularly; not oblique, involving or based on a right-angle or angles (of cones, pyramids, cylinders, etc.). *adv.* In accordance with truth and justice, justly, equitably, rightly; aright, exactly, correctly, properly, satisfactorily, well; very, quite, to the full; to or towards the right hand; straight; all the way to, completely. *n.* That which is right or just; fair or equitable treatment; the cause or party having justice on its side; just claim or title, esp. a claim enforceable at law, justification; that which one is entitled to; (*pl.*) proper condition, correct or satisfactory state; (*colloq.*) the right hand; the right-hand side, part, or surface of anything; a thing, part, etc., pertaining or corresponding to this; the party sitting on the right of the president in a foreign legislature, usu. the more conservative party. *v.t.* To set in or restore to an upright, straight, correct, or proper position, to correct, to make right, to rectify; to do justice to, to vindicate, to rehabilitate; to relieve from wrong or injustice. *v.i.* To resume a vertical position. **all right:** (*colloq.*) Correct, satisfactory, in good condition, safe, etc.; yes. **in her own right,** *adv.* By right independent of marriage. **right and left:** In all directions; on both sides; with both hands, etc. **right away, right off:** At once, immediately. **right-down,** *a.* Thorough, thorough-paced; thoroughly. **right of way:** The right established by usage or by dedication to the public to use a track, path, road, etc., across a person's land; (*Am.*) permanent way of a railway. **right oh! right you are:** (*colloq.*) Forms of assent, approval, etc. **to put** or **set to rights:** To arrange, to put in order. **to right the helm:** To place it amidships. **to serve one right:** To be thoroughly well deserved. **right-about,** *n.* The opposite direction, the reverse, to the opposite direction. **right-angle,** *n.* An angle formed by two lines meeting perpendicularly. **right-angled,** *a.* Having a right-angle or angles. **at right angles:** Placed at or forming a right angle. **right hand:** The hand on the right side, esp. as the better hand; position on or direction to this side; (*fig.*) one's best or most efficient assistant, aid, or support. **right-hand,** *a.* Situated on or towards the right hand; (*fig.*) denoting one whose help is most useful or necessary. **right-hand man:** A soldier placed on this side; one's best assistant, aid, etc. **right-handed,** *a.* Using the right-hand more readily than the left; clever, dexterous; used by or fitted for use by the right hand (of tools, etc.); turning to the right (of the thread of a screw, etc.). **right-hander,** *n.* A blow with the right hand. **right-handedness,** *n.* **right-hearted,** *a.* **right honourable:** A title given to peers, peeresses, privy councillors, etc. **right line:** A straight line. **right-minded,** *a.* Properly, justly, or equitably disposed. **right-mindedness,** *n.* **right whale:** A true whale, one yielding the best whalebone, etc. **rightable,** *a.* ***righten,** *v.t.* **righter,** *n.* **rightful,** *a.* Just, equitable, fair; entitled, holding, or held by legitimate claim. **rightfully,** *adv.* **rightfulness,** *n.* **rightist,** *n.* (*Pol.*) A conservative, an adherent of the right in politics. **rightless,** *a.* **rightly,** *adv.* Justly, fairly, equitably; honestly, uprightly; correctly, accurately, properly. **rightness,** *n.* **rightward,** *a.* and *adv.* **right-wing:** (*Pol.*) Conservative, opp. to left-wing.

righteous (rī′ tyŭs, rī′ chŭs) [A.-S. *rightwīs* (RIGHT, WISE (1) or -WISE)], *a.* Just, upright, morally good; equitable, deserved, justifiable, fitting. **righteously,** *adv.* **righteousness,** *n.*

rightful, rightly, etc. [RIGHT].

rigid (rij′ id) [L. *rigidus*], *a.* Stiff, not easily bent, not pliant, unyielding; rigorous, strict, punctilious, inflexible, harsh, stern, austere. **rigid airship,** *n.* (*Aviat.*) An airship in which the envelope is attached to a framework of hoops and girders. **rigidity** (ri jid′ i ti), **rigidness,** *n.* **rigidly,** *adv.* **rigidulous** (ri jid′ ū lŭs), *a.* (*Bot.*) Rather stiff.

rigmarole (rig′ mȧ rōl) [prob. corr. of RAGMAN-ROLL], *n.* A long unintelligible story; loose disjointed talk. *a.* Consisting of rigmarole, incoherent.

***rigol** (rī′ gol) [It. *rigolo*, dim. of *rigo, riga*, O.H.G. *rīga*, line], *n.* A circle; a ring.

rigor (rig′ ŏr, rī′ gôr) [L., RIGOUR], *n.* (*Path.*) A feeling of chill, a shivering attended with stiffening, etc., premonitory of fever, etc.; (*Zool.*) a state of rigidity assumed by certain animals and commonly known as 'shamming dead'. **rigor mortis:** The stiffening of the body following death.

rigour (rig′ ŏr) [O.F., from L. *rigōrem*, nom. *-or*, from *rigēre*, to be stiff], *n.* Strictness, exactness in enforcing rules; stiffness or inflexibility of opinion, doctrine, observance, etc., austerity of life; sternness, harshness, asperity; inclemency of the weather, etc., hardship, distress; (*pl.*) harsh proceedings, severities. **rigorism,** *n.* **rigorist,** *a.* and *n.* **rigorous,** *a.* Strict, precise, severe, stern, inflexible; logically accurate, precise, stringent; inclement, harsh. **rigorously,** *adv.* **rigorousness,** *n.*

Rigsdag (rigz′ dag) [Dan. *rige*, kingdom, *dag*, DAY], *n.* The Danish parliament.

Rig-Veda (rig vā′ dȧ) [Sansk. *ric*, praise, *veda*, knowledge], *n.* The oldest and most original of the Vedas.

rigwiddy (rig′ wid i) [Sc. (RIG (3), WITHY)], *n.* A band, orig. of twisted withes, going over a horse's back to support the shafts. *a.* Deserving the rope (or gallows).

Riksdag (riks′ dag) [Swed., cp. RIGSDAG], *n.* The Swedish parliament.

rile (rīl) [va. of ROIL], *v.t.* To make angry, to vex, to irritate.

rilievo (rē lyā' vō) [It., RELIEF (2)], *n.* (*pl.* **-vi**, **-vē**) Raised or embossed work, relief.

rill (ril) [cp. L.G. and G. *rille*. Dut. *ril*], *n.* A small brook, a rivulet; (*Astron.*) a rille. *v.i.* To issue or flow in a small stream. **rille**, *n.* (*Astron.*) A furrow, trench, or narrow valley on the moon. **rillet**, *n.*

rillettes (ri lets') [F.], *n.pl.* A tinned preparation of minced chicken, ham, goose-fat, spices, etc.

rim (1) (rim) [A.-S. *rima* (cp. Icel. *rime*, *rimi*, strip, ridge)], *n.* An outer edge, border, or margin, esp. of a vessel or other circular object; a ring or frame; the peripheral part of the framework of a wheel, between the spokes and the tire; (*Naut.*) the surface (of the water). *v.t.* (*past & p.p.* **rimmed**) To form or furnish with a rim; to serve as rim to, to edge, to border. **rim-fire**, *a.* Having the detonating fulminate in the rim not the centre (of a cartridge). **rim-brake**, *n.* One acting on the rim not the hub of a wheel. **rimless**, *a.* **rimmed**, *a.* Having a rim (*usu. in comb.*).

***rim** (2) [A.-S. *reoma* (cp. Dut. *riem*, G. *riemen*, strap, thong)], *n.* The peritoneum or inner membrane (of the belly).

rime (1) [RHYME].

rime (2) (rīm) [A.-S. *hrīm* (cp. Dut. *rijm*, Icel. *hrīm*, O.F. *rime*)], *n.* Hoar-frost. *v.t.* To cover with rime. *v.i.* To congeal into rime. **rimy**, *a.*

rimose, -mous (rī' mōs, -mŭs) [L. *rīmōsus*, from *rīma*, chink], *a.* Full of chinks or cracks, as the bark of trees. ***rimoscity** (-mos' i ti), *n.*

rimple (rim' pėl) [cp. A.-S. *hrimpan*, also RUMPLE], *n.* A wrinkle, a fold. *v.t.* To wrinkle, to pucker, to ripple. *v.i.* To become wrinkled or rippled.

rimu (rē moo') [Maori], *n.* The red pine of N. Zealand.

rimy [RIME (2)].

rin, rinabout (*Sc.*) [RUN].

rind (rīnd) [A.-S., cp. Dut. *run*, G. *rinde*], *n.* The outer coating of trees, fruits, etc.; bark, peel, husk, skin. *v.t.* To strip the rind from. **rinded**, *a.* Having rind (*in comb.* as *coarse-rinded*).

rinderpest (rin' dėr pest) [G. *rinder*, pl. of *rind*, OX, PEST], *n.* A malignant contagious disease attacking ruminants, esp. oxen, cattle-plague.

ring (1) (ring) [A.-S. *hring* (cp. Dut. and G. *ring*, Icel. *hringr*)], *n.* A circlet; a circlet of gold, etc., worn usu. on a finger as an ornament, token, etc.; anything in the form of the circumference of a circle; a line, mark, moulding, space, or band round or the rim of a circular or cylindrical object; a concentric band of wood formed by the annual growth of a tree; a group or concourse of people, things, etc., arranged in a circle; a circular space, enclosure, or arena for prize-fighting, circus-riding, etc.; a combination of persons acting selfishly in concert for commercial or political ends; (*Austral.*) scene of a two-up game. *v.t.* (*past* **ringed**; *p.p.* **ringed**) To put a ring round; to encircle, to enclose, to hem in; to fit with a ring; to cut a ring of bark from (a tree). *v.i.* (*past* **ringed**; *p.p.* **ringed**) To form a ring; to rise in spirals (of a bird). **the ring:** Bookmakers or pugilists; the prize-ring, pugilism. **to make rings round:** To outstrip easily. **ring-bark**, *v.t.* (*Hort.*) To cut a ring of bark from a tree in order to check growth, kill it or induce it to fruit. **ring-bolt**, *n.* A bolt with a ring or eye at one end for fastening a rope to. **ring-bone**, *n.* A morbid deposit of bony matter on the pastern-bones of a horse. **ring-carrier**, *n.* A go-between. **ring-dial**, *n.* A pocket sundial in the form of a ring. **ring-dove**, *n.* A wood-pigeon. **ring-fence** [FENCE]. **ring-finger**, *n.* The third finger of the left hand, on which the wedding-ring is placed. **ring-formed**, *a.* Circular. **ring-leader**, *n.* The leader of a riot, mutiny, etc. **ring-lead**, *v.t.* To conduct as ringleader. **ringlet**, *n.* A small ring; a ring-shaped mark, object, moulding, etc.; a curl, a curly lock of hair; a satyrid butterfly, *Hipparchia hyperanthus*. **ringleted, ringlety**, *a.* **ring-lock**, *n.* A lock opened by the right combination of several rings. **ring-man**, *n.* A bookmaker. **ring-master**, *n.* The manager of a circus performance. **ring-money**, *n.* (*Ant.*) Metal rings supposed to have been used as money by the late Celts. **ring-neck**, *n.* A ring plover; the ring-necked duck; (*Austral.*) a variety of parakeet. **ring-necked**, *a.* Having a band or bands of colour round the neck. **ring-net**, *n.* A portable net expanded by means of a hoop, for catching butterflies, etc.; a variety of salmon-net; a variety of lace. **ring-ouzel**, *n.* A thrush-like bird, *Turdus torquatus*, allied to the blackbird, having a white band on the breast. **ring-snake**, *n.* The grass-snake; a harmless American snake. ***ring-streaked**, *a.* Streaked with bands of colour. **ringtail**, *n.* (*Naut.*) An additional sail set abaft the spanker or driver; the female of the hen-harrier. **ring-tailed**, *a.* Having the tail marked with rings or bands of colour. ***ring-time**, *n.* The time for marrying. **ring-wall**, *n.* A wall round an estate, etc. (cp. RING-FENCE]. **ringworm**, *n.* A skin-disease, *Tinea tonsurans*, caused by a white fungus, usu. affecting children. **ringed**, *n.* Having, encircled by, or marked with a ring or rings (*often in comb.*); annular. **ringer** (1), *n.* A quoit falling round the pin; a curling-stone in the ring; a fox running in a ring during a hunt; (*Racing*) a horse raced under the name of another horse; (*Austral.*) the fastest shearer in a shearing-shed. **ringie**, *n.* (*Austral.*) The keeper of a two-up school. **ringless**, *a.*

ring (2) (ring) [A.-S. *hringan* (cp. Dut. and G. *ringen*, Icel. *hringja*), prob. imit.], *v.i.* (*past* **rang**, *p.p.* **rung**) To give a clear vibrating sound, as a sonorous metallic body when struck; to re-echo, to resound, to reverberate, to continue to sound; to have a sensation as of vibrating metal, to tingle (of the ears); to give a summons or signal by ringing. *v.t.* To cause to ring; to sound (a knell, peal, etc.) on a bell or bells; to utter, to repeat; to summon, signal, announce, proclaim, celebrate, etc., by ringing; to usher (in or out); to fling (a coin) down so as to make it ring in order to test it. *n.* The sound of a bell or other resonant body; the act of ringing a bell; a set of bells tuned harmonically; a ringing sound, a continued or reverberated sound; the quality of resonance; the characteristic sound of a voice, statement, etc. **to ring down:** (*Theat.*) to lower the curtain. **to ring false** or **true:** To sound counterfeit or genuine (of or as of coin tested by throwing it on the counter). **to ring off:** To signal the end of a conversation on the telephone by a ring. **to ring the changes** [CHANGE]. **to ring up:** To call or seek communication with on the telephone; (*Theat.*) to raise the curtain. **ringing-engine**, *n.* A pile-driving engine with a falling weight worked by ropes. **ringer** (2), *n.* One who rings church bells; a device for ringing a bell, a bell-pull. **ringing**, *a.* Sounding like a bell; sonorous, resonant. *n.* A sound of or as of a bell.

ringent (rin' jėnt) [L. *ringens -ntem*, pres.p. of *ringere*, to gape], *a.* (*Bot.*) Irregular and gaping (of a flower or corolla).

ringer, ringing [RING (1 & 2)]. **ringleader, ringlet, ringworm**, etc. [RING (1)].

rink (ringk) [prob. rel. to RANK (1) or RING (1)], *n.* A piece of ice marked off for the game of curling; a division of a side so playing; a prepared floor for skating with roller-skates, or a sheet of natural or artificial ice for ordinary skating. *v.i.* To skate on a rink. **rinker**, *n.*

rinse (rins) [F. *rincer*, etym. doubtful], *v.t.* To wash, to cleanse, esp. with a second application of clean water; to clean (out, away, etc.) by rinsing. *n.* The act of rinsing. **rinser**, *n.*

riot (rī' ŏt) [O.F. *riote*, whence, *rioter*, to riot (cp. It. *riotta*), etym. doubtful], *n.* A disturbance, an outbreak of lawlessness, a tumult, an uproar; turbulent behaviour, wanton or unrestrained conduct, loose living, profligacy, a revel; revelry; (*fig.*) unrestrained indulgence in something, luxuriant growth, lavish display; (*Law*) a tumultuous disturbance of the peace by three or more persons. *v.i.* To take part in a riot; to revel, to behave or live licentiously. *v.t.* To pass or spend (time, money, etc.) in rioting or dissipation. **Riot Act:** An Act enjoining riotous persons to disperse on pain of being treated as felons. **to read the riot Act:** To warn a riotous assembly to disperse before ordering the military or police to fire. **to run riot:** To act without control or restraint (orig. of hounds following a false scent); (*fig.*) to grow luxuriantly. **rioter,** *n.* ***riotise,** *n.* Riotousness. **riotous,** *a.* **riotously,** *adv.* **riotousness, *riotry,** *n.*

rip (1) (rip) [prob. from Scand. (cp. Norw. and Swed. dial. *ripa*, Dan. *rippe*)], *v.t.* (*past & p.p.* **ripped**) To tear or cut forcibly (out, off, up, etc.); to rend, to split; to saw (wood) with the grain; to take out or away by cutting or tearing; to make a long tear or rent in; to undo the seams of; to open (up) for examination or disclosure; to make (a passage, opening, etc.) by ripping; to utter (an oath, etc.) with violence. *v.i.* To come or be torn forcibly apart, to tear; to go (along) at a great pace. *n.* A rent made by ripping, a tear. **rip cord,** *n.* (*Aviat.*) A cord which, upon being pulled by the wearer, releases a parachute from its pack. **rip-saw,** *n.* One for sawing along the grain. **ripper,** *n.* One who rips or tears; a rip-saw; (*slang*) a first-class person or thing. **ripping,** *a.* (*slang*) Excellent, first-class, fine, splendid. **rippingly,** *adv.* (*slang*).

rip (2) (rip) [etym. doubtful, perh. var. of *rep*, short for REPROBATE], *n.* A scamp, a rake; a cheat; a worthless horse, a screw.

rip (3) [etym. doubtful, perh. from RIP (1)], *n.* An eddy, an overfall, a stretch of broken water.

riparian (rī pâr' i ȧn) [L. *rīpārius*, from *rīpa*, bank], *a.* Pertaining to the banks of a river. *n.* An owner of property on the banks of a river.

ripe (rīp) [A.-S. *rīpe* (cp. Dut. *rijp*, G. *reif*), whence *rīpian*, to ripen], *a.* Ready for reaping or gathering; mature, come to perfection in growth, fully developed, mellow, fit for use, ready or in a fit state (for); resembling ripe fruit, rosy, rounded, luscious; (*slang*) drunk. *v.t.* and *i.* To ripen. **ripely,** *adv.* **ripen,** *v.t.* and *i.* **ripeness,** *n.*

ripieno (ri pyā' nō) [It. (*ri-*, RE-, *pieno*, L. *plēnus*, full)], *a.* Additional, supplemental. *n.* A *ripieno* player or instrument. **ripienist,** *n.*

ripost (ri pōst') [F. *riposte*, It. *risposta*, repartee], *n.* (*Fencing*) A quick lunge or thrust in return; (*fig.*) a quick reply, a retort, a repartee; a counterstroke.

ripper, ripping, etc. [RIP (1)].

ripple (1) (rip' ėl) [cp. Dut. *repel* (v. *repelen*), G. *riffel* (v. *riffeln*)], *n.* A large comb for cleaning the seeds from flax. *v.t.* To clean with a ripple.

ripple (2) (rip' ėl) [etym. doubtful], *v.i.* To run in small waves or undulations; to sound as water running over a rough surface. *v.t.* To agitate or cover with small waves or undulations. *n.* The ruffling of the surface of water; a wavelet, an undulation (of water, hair, etc.); a sound as of rippling water. **ripple-mark,** *n.* (*Sc. and Am.*) A mark as of ripples or wavelets on sand, mud, rock, etc. **ripple-marked,** *a.* **ripplet,** *n.* **ripplingly,** *adv.* **ripply,** *a.*

riprap (rip' răp) [redupl. of RAP (1)], *n.* (*Am.*) A foundation of loose stones, as in deep water or on a soft bottom; a firework giving a succession of loud reports.

rip-saw [RIP (1)]. ***ript** [RIPPED, see RIP (1)].

Ripuarian (rip ū âr' i ȧn) [med. L. *Ripuārius*, perh. from L. *rīpa*, bank], *a.* Of or pertaining to the ancient Franks dwelling near the Rhine; applied to their code of laws. *n.* A Ripuarian Frank.

riro-riro (rē' rō rē' rō) [Maori], *n.* The grey warbler of N. Zealand, the N. Zealand wren.

rise (rīz) [A.-S. *rīsan*, cp. Dut. *rijzen*, G. *reisen*, Icel. *rīsa*, O.H.G. *rīsan*], *v.i.* (*past* **rose,** *p.p.* **risen,** riz' ėn) To move upwards, to ascend, to leave the ground, to mount, to soar; to get up from a lying, kneeling, or sitting posture or out of bed, to become erect, to stand up; to cease from sitting, to adjourn; to come to life again; to swell or project upwards; to increase, to become lofty, or tall; to be promoted, to thrive; to increase in energy, force, intensity, value, price, etc.; to slope up; to arise, to come into existence, to originate; to come to the surface, to come into sight; to become audible; to break into insurrection, to revolt, to rebel (against). *v.t.* To make (a fish) rise; (*Naut.*) to see a ship rise above the horizon. *n.* The act of rising; ascent, elevation; an upward slope, the degree of this; a hill, a knoll; source, origin, start; increase or advance in price, value, power, rank, age, prosperity, height, amount, salary, etc.; promotion, upward progress in social position, advancement; the rising of a feeding fish to the surface; the vertical part of an arch, step, etc.; appearance above the horizon, rising (of the sun, etc.). **riser,** *n.* One who rises; the vertical part of a step, etc. **to take a rise out of one:** To make a person angry, to play a trick on him. **rising,** *n.* A mounting up or ascending; a resurrection; a revolt, an insurrection; (*prov.*) a protuberance, a tumour, a knoll; (*prov.*) a large spring of water. **rising-again,** *n.* Resurrection. **rising butt:** A butt-hinge so shaped that it causes the door to close automatically.

rishi (rish' i) [Sansk.], *n.* A seer, a saint, an inspired poet, esp. one of the seven sages said to have communicated the Vedas to mankind.

risible (riz' i bėl) [F., from late L. *rīsibilis*, from *rīdēre*, to laugh], *a.* Inclined to laugh; exciting laughter. **risibility** (-bil' i ti), ***risibleness,** *n.* **risibly,** *adv.*

rising [RISE].

risk (risk) [F. *risque*, It. *risco*], *n.* Hazard, chance of harm, injury, loss, etc. *v.t.* To expose to risk or hazard; to venture on, to take the chances of. **to run a risk:** To incur a hazard; to encounter danger. ***risker,** *n.* **riskful, risky,** *a.* Dangerous, hazardous; venturesome, daring; [F. ***risqué -quée***] suggestive of indecency, indelicate. **riskily, riskiness,** *n.* **riskless,** *a.*

Risorgimento (rē zôr ji men' tō) [It., RESURRECTION], *n.* The rising of the Italian peoples against Austrian and Papal dominion, culminating in the unification of Italy in 1870.

***risorial** (rī sôr' i ȧl) [L. *rīsor*, laughter, from *rīdēre*, to laugh, -IAL], *a.* Pertaining to or causing laughter.

risotto (ri zot' ō) [It.], *n.* An Italian dish of rice, onions, butter, and broth, with cheese, chicken, etc.

risp (risp) [Icel. *rispa*], *v.t.* (*Sc.*) To rasp, to grate. *v.i.* To make a rasping or grating noise.

risqué, risquée [RISKY].

rissole (rē' sōl, ris' ōl) [F., from O.G. *roussole*, perh. from L. *russeolus*, reddish, from *russus*, red], *n.* A ball of minced meat, fish, etc., fried with bread-crumbs, etc.

ritardando (rē tar dan' dō) [It., from *ritardare*, to RETARD], *adv.* (*Mus. direction*) Slower.

rite (rīt) [L. *rītus*], *n.* A religious or solemn prescribed act, ceremony, or observance; (*pl.*) the prescribed acts, ceremonies, or forms of worship of any religion. **riteless,** *a.*

ritornello (rē tôr nel' ō), **ritornel** (rit ôr nel') [F. *ritournelle*, It. *ritornello*, dim. of *ritorno*, RETURN], *n.* (*Mus.*) A brief prelude, interlude, or refrain.

****ritter*** [REITER].

ritual (rit' ū ȧl) [F., from L. *rītuālis*, from *rītus*, RITE], *a.* Pertaining to, consisting of, or involving rites. *n.* A prescribed manner of performing divine service; performance of rites and ceremonies, esp. in an elaborate or excessive way; a book setting forth the rites and ceremonies of a particular Church; (*pl.*) ritual observances.

ritualism (rit' ū ȧ lizm), *n.* A system of ritual or prescribed forms of worship, as dist. from a system leaving these to the discretion of the minister, etc.; punctilious or exaggerated observance of ritual; Tractarianism; the ornate service of High Anglicans. **Ritualist,** *n.* **ritualistic** (-lis' tik), *a.* **ritualistically,** *adv.* **ritualize** (rit' ū ȧ līz), *v.t.* and *i.* **ritually,** *adv.*

***rivage** (rī' vȧj) [F., from *rive*, L. *rīpa*, bank], *n.* A bank, a shore, a coast.

rival (rī' vȧl) [F., from L. *rīvālis*, orig. on the same stream, from *rīvus*, stream], *n.* One's competitor for something, esp. a woman's love; one striving to surpass another in a quality, pursuit, etc., an emulator. *a.* Being a rival, having the same claims or pretensions, emulous. *v.t.* (*past & p.p.* **rivalled**) To vie with, to emulate, to strive to equal or surpass. *v.i.* To vie, to stand in rivalry (with). **rivalling,** *pres.p.* ***rivality** (rī văl' i ti), **rivalry, rivalship,** *n.*

rive (rīv) [Icel. *rīfa*, cp. Dan. *rive*, Swed. *rifva*], *v.t.* (*p.p.* **riven,** rivn, ***rived,** rīvd) To tear, split, cleave, or rend asunder; to wrench or rend (away, from, off, etc.); to split; to make (shingles, slats, etc.) by splitting. *v.i.* To be split asunder; to be easily split. **n.* A rift, a rent, a tear.

***rivel** [A.-S. *ge-riflian*, extant only in *rifelede*, wrinkled, etym. doubtful], *v.t.* To wrinkle, to pucker; to shrivel (up). *v.i.* To wrinkle, to crumple. *n.* A wrinkle. **rivelling,** *pres.p.*

riven [RIVE].

river (riv' ėr) [A.-F. *rivere*, O.F. *riviere*, pop. L. *rīpāria*, from *rīpa*, bank (cp. RIPARIAN)], *n.* A large stream of water flowing in a channel over a portion of the earth's surface and discharging itself into the sea, a lake, a marsh, or another river; (*fig.*) a large and abundant stream, a copious flow. **river-bed, -channel,** *n.* **river-crab,** *n.* A freshwater crab belonging to the genus *Thelphusa.* **river-craft,** *n.* Small craft plying only on rivers. **river-god,** *n.* A deity presiding over or personifying a river. **river-hog,** *n.* An African wild hog of the genus *Potamochœrus*, inhabiting river banks, etc. **river-horse,** *n.* The hippopotamus. **river-side,** *n.* The ground along the bank of a river. *a.* Built on or pertaining to this. **riverain** (-ān), *a.* Of or pertaining to a river; living on or near a river. *n.* One who lives on or near a river. **riverine** (-īn), *a.* Pertaining to or resembling a river; riparian. **rivered,** *a.* Having a river or rivers (*usu. in comb.*). **riverless,** *a.*

rivet (riv' ėt) [F., from *river*, to clinch, etym. doubtful], *n.* A short bolt, pin, or nail, usu. with a flat head at one end, the other end being flattened out and clinched by hammering, used for fastening metal plates, etc., together. *v.t.* (*past & p.p.* **riveted**) To join or fasten together with a rivet or rivets; to clinch; (*fig.*) to fasten firmly; to fix (attention, eyes, etc., upon); to engross the attention of. **riveter,** *n.*

rivière (riv' i âr) [F. RIVER], *n.* A necklace of gems, usu. of several strings.

rivose (ri-, rī vōs') [late L. *rīvōsus*, from *rīvus*, stream], *a.* (*Ent.*) Marked with sinuous furrows.

rivulet (riv' ū lėt) [perh. through L. *rīvulus*, dim. from *rīvus*, as prec.], *n.* A streamlet; one of the *Geometridæ*, a family of moths.

rivulose (riv' ū lōs) [as prec.], *a.* (*Bot.*) Rivose.

rix-dollar (riks' dol ȧr) [Dut. *rijksdaler* (now *-daalder*), G. *reichsthaler* (*reich*, RICH, THALER)], *n.* A name for several Continental silver coins or money of account in the 16th–19th cents., ranging in value from 2s. 3d. to 4s. 6d.

rizzar (riz' âr) [Sc., from obs. F. *ressoré*, *rizzared* (RE-, *sorer*, to dry, to make red)], *v.t.* To dry (haddocks, etc.) in the sun. *n.* A rizzared haddock.

roa (rō' ȧ) [Maori], *n.* The large, brown kiwi.

roach (1) (rōch) [O.F. *roche*, *roce*, perh. from Teut. (cp. G. *roche*, A.-S. *reohhe*)], *n.* A freshwater fish allied to the carp (*Leuciscus rutilus*).

roach (2) (rōch) [etym. doubtful], *n.* (*Naut.*) The upward curve in the foot of a square sail; (*Am.*) a horse's mane cut short and standing up stiff. *v.t.* To cut (a sail) with a roach; (*Am.*) to cut (a horse's mane) so that it will stand up stiff.

road (rōd) [A.-S. *rād*, from *rīdan*, to RIDE], *n.* A track or way for travelling on, esp. a broad strip of ground suitable for riders, vehicles, or foot-passengers, forming a public line of communication between places, a highway; way of going anywhere, route, course; a roadstead. **on the road:** Passing, travelling. **rule of the road:** A regulation governing the methods of passing each other for vehicles, etc., on the road or vessels on the water. **the road:** The highway. **to take the road:** To set out. ***to take to the road:** To become a highwayman. **road bed,** *n.* (*Rail.*) The foundation upon which the sleepers bearing the rails are laid. **road-book,** *n.* A guide-book describing roads, distances, etc. **road-hog,** *n.* A motorist or cyclist paying no regard to the convenience of other people using the road. **road house,** *n.* An inn on a highway, usually away from a town or village, which caters for motorists. **road-man,** *n.* A man who keeps roads in repair. **road-metal,** *n.* Broken stones for road-making. **road-sense,** *n.* The instinct of a driver or pedestrian whereby he is able to cope with a traffic emergency or avoid an accident. **roadside,** *n.* The border of a road; *a.* Pertaining to this, situated or growing there. **roadway,** *n.* The central part of a highway, used by vehicles, horses, etc.; the part of a bridge, railway, etc., used for traffic. **roadworthy,** *a.* Fit for use or travel (of a horse, car, etc.). **roadless,** *a.*

roadstead (rōd' sted), *n.* A place where ships may ride at anchor at some distance from the shore.

roadster (rōd' stėr), *n.* A horse fitted for, or employed in travelling; a cycle or motor-car suitable for the road, opposed to a racer; (*Am.*) a two-seater automobile; a coach-driver; (*Naut.*) a vessel that works by tides and waits the turn of the tide in some roadstead.

roadway, roadworthy [ROAD].

roam (rōm) [etym. doubtful], *v.i.* To wander about without any definite purpose, to rove, to ramble. *v.t.* To range, to wander, to rove over. **roamer,** *n.*

roan (1) (rōn) [O.F. (cp. It. and Sp. *roano*, Port. *ruão*), etym. unknown], *a.* Of a bay, sorrel, or dark colour, with spots of grey or white thickly interspersed; a mixed colour having a decided shade of red. *n.* A roan colour, a roan animal, esp. a horse.

roan (2) (rōn) [perh. from *Rouen*, France], *n.* A soft flexible leather made of sheepskin tanned with sumach.

roan (3) [ROWAN].

roar (rôr) [A.-S. *rārian* (cp. G. *raren*, M.Dut. *reeren*, G. *rehren*), prob. imit.], *v.i.* To make a loud, deep, hoarse, continued sound, as a lion; to make a confused din like this (of a person in rage, distress, or loud laughter, the sea, thunder, guns, a conflagration, etc.); to make a noise in breathing (of a diseased horse); to resound, to re-echo, to be full of din (of a place). *v.t.* To shout, say, sing, or utter with a roaring voice. *n.* A loud, deep, hoarse, continued sound as of a lion, etc.; a confused din resembling this; a burst of mirth or laughter. **roarer,** *n.* One who roars; a broken-winded horse. **roaring,** *a.* Shouting, noisy, boisterous, stormy; (*colloq.*) brisk, active. *n.* A loud, continued, or confused noise; a peculiar sound emitted during respiration by some horses, due to disease in the air-passages. **the roaring forties** [FORTY].

roast (rōst) [O.F. *rostir* (F. *rôtir*), from Teut. (cp. O.H.G. *rōsten*, from *rōst*, grate, grid-iron)], *v.t.* To cook by exposure to the direct action of radiant heat, esp. at an open fire or (incorrectly) to bake in an oven; to dry and parch (coffee beans, etc.) by exposure to heat; to heat excessively or violently; to heat highly (ore, etc.) without fusing, to drive out impurities; (*colloq.*) to banter, quiz, chaff, or tease unmercifully. *v.i.* To dress meat by roasting; to be roasted. *a.* Roasted. *n.* The act or operation of roasting; that which is roasted, roast meat, or a dish of this; (*Am.*) a roast joint. **to rule the roast:** To take the lead or mastery. **roaster,** *n.* One who or that which roasts; a contrivance for roasting coffee, a kind of oven for roasting; a furnace for roasting ore; a pig, or other animal, or potato, etc., for roasting. **roasting-jack,** *n.* A contrivance for turning a spit.

rob (rob) [O.F. *robber*, *rober*, rel. to REAVE], *v.t.* (*past & p.p.* **robbed**) To despoil of anything by unlawful violence or secret theft; to plunder, to pillage, to deprive, to strip (of); *to steal. *v.i.* To commit robbery. **robber,** *n.* **robber-baron,** *n.* A mediæval baron exacting tribute by oppressive means. **robber-crab,** *n.* One of the hermit-crabs. **robber-gull,** *n.* The skua. **robbery,** *n.* The act or practice of robbing; (*Law*) the felonious taking of goods or money from the person of another by violence or by putting him in fear.

robbo (rob' ō), *n.* (*Austral.*) A broken-winded horse, a decrepit horse.

robe (rōb) [O.F., cogn. with ROB (1), cp. A.-S. *rēaf*, spoil, clothing, G. *raub.* Icel. *rauf*, booty], *n.* A loose outer garment; a dress, gown, or vestment of state, rank, or office (*often in pl.*); a lady's gown, dress, or costume, esp. in one piece; a long outer garment for an infant in long clothes; (*Am.*) a dressed buffalo or other skin used as a covering in a carriage, etc. *v.t.* To invest with a robe or robes; to clothe, to dress. *v.i.* To put on a robe or dress. **gentlemen of the robe:** The legal profession; lawyers. ***robe de chambre*** (rōb dė shambr): A dressing-gown or morning-dress.

Robert (rob' ėrt) [F., personal name, from Teut.], *n.* The herb Robert (*see* HERB); (*colloq.*) a policeman; *a waiter.

robin (rob' in) [O.F., fam. for ROBERT], *n.* A small warbler, the redbreast, also called robin redbreast; (*Am.*) a thrush. **Robin Goodfellow:** A merry domestic fairy, famous for mischievous pranks. **robin-run-in-the-hedge,** *n.* The ground-ivy, bindweed, and other trailers or climbers. **robinet,** *n.* (*prov.*) A robin; (*Naut.*) a faucet, stop, or cock.

Robinia (rȯ bin' i ȧ) [from Jean *Robin* (1550–1629), French botanist], *n.* (*Bot.*) A genus of leguminous shrubs or trees including the false acacia.

roble (rōbl) [Sp. and Port., from L. *rōbur*, oak], *n.* The Californian white-oak, *Quercus lobata*; a W. Indian catalpa; a Chilean beech, *Fagus obliqua.*

roborant (rō' bȯ rȧnt) [L. *rōborans -ntem*, pres.p. of *rōborāre*, to strengthen, from *rōbur-boris*, strength], *a.* (*Med.*) Strengthening. *n.* A strengthening medicine. ***roborate,** *v.i.* **roburite** (rō' bŭr it), *n.* A powerful flameless explosive.

robot (rō' bot) [Karel Capek's play "R.U.R." (1923)], *n.* A man-like mechanism; a machine acting in a human manner; (*fig.*) a brutal, mechanically efficient person who is devoid of sensibility; (*fig.*) traffic lights.

Rob Roy canoe (rob roi) [pen-name of J. MacGregor (1825–92)], *n.* A canoe with double-bladed paddle, invented by MacGregor.

robust (rō bŭst') [F. *robuste*, L. *rōbustus*, as prec.], *a.* Strong, hardy, vigorous, capable of endurance, having excellent health and physique; sturdy, hardy (of plants); requiring muscular strength, invigorating (of exercise, sports, discipline, etc.); sinewy, muscular; (*fig.*) mentally vigorous, firm, self-reliant. **robustious,** *a.* Boisterous, rough, noisy. **robustly,** *adv.* **robustness,** *n.*

roc (rok) [F. *rock*, Arab. *rokh*, *rukh*], *n.* A fabulous bird of immense size and strength.

rocambole (rok' ȧm bōl) [F., etym. doubtful], *n.* A plant allied to the leek, *Allium scorodoprasum*, Spanish garlic.

Roccella (rok sel' ȧ) [mod. L., from O.F. *orchel*, ORCHIL], *n.* (*Bot.*) A genus of shrubby lichens containing the orchil. **roccellate,** *n.* (*Chem.*) A salt of roccellic acid. **roccellic,** *a.* **roccellin,** *n.* A dye obtained from orchil.

***Rochelle** (rȯ shel'), *n.* A wine exported from the French seaport La Rochelle; Rochelle-powder or salt. **Rochelle-powder,** *n.* Seidlitz-powder. **Rochelle-salt,** *n.* A tartrate of soda and potash, used as Epsom salt.

roches moutonnées (rōsh moo tȯ nā) [F., rocks rounded like the backs of sheep], *n.pl.* (*Geol.*) Rocks ground down by glacial action so as to present a rounded appearance on the side from which the flow came.

rochet (1) (roch' ėt) [O.F. *rochet*, *roket*, from Teut. (cp. Dut. *rok*, G. *rock*, A.-S. *rocc*)], *n.* A vestment like a surplice open at the sides, worn by bishops and abbots.

rochet (2) (roch' ėt) [O.F. *rouget*, from *rouge*, red] *n.* The red gurnard.

rock (1) (rok) [O.F. *roke*, *roque*, *roche*, etym. doubtful], *n.* The solid matter constituting the earth's crust or any portion of this; any solid, indurated, or stony part of this, a mass of it, esp. forming a hill, promontory, islet, cliff, etc.; a detached block of stone, a boulder; (*Am.*) a stone; a hard sweetmeat of various kinds; (*fig.*) anything on which one may come to grief; a defence, asylum, or refuge. **on the rocks:** (*slang*) Poor, hard up. **Rock of Ages:** Christ. **the Rock:** Gibraltar. **rock-alum,** *n.* A superior variety of alum, also called Roman alum. **rock-basin,** *n.* A hollow occupied by a lake, etc., in rock, usually attributed to glacial action. **rock-bottom,** *n.* The lowest stratum reached in excavating, mining, etc.; (*fig.*) the lowest point. *a.* (*slang*) Lowest (*of prices*). **rock-bound,** *a.* Hemmed in by rocks. **rock-butter,** *n.* An impure efflorescence oozing from some alum shales. **rock-cake,** *n.* Bun with a hard rough surface. **rock-candy,** *n.* Candy in hard crystals. **rock-cod,** *n.* A gadoid fish allied to the cod; a cod caught on a rocky bottom. **rock-cork,** *n.* A cork-like variety of asbestos. **rock-crystal,** *n.* The finest and most transparent kind of quartz, usu. found in hexagonal prisms. **rock-dove** [ROCK-PIGEON]. **rock English:** The mixed patois spoken at Gibraltar. **rock fever:** Malta or Mediterranean fever, common at Gibraltar. **rock-fish,** *n.* The black goby; a name for several wrasses, etc. **rock-goat,** *n.* The ibex. **rock-hewn,** *a.* Hewn or quarried from the rock. **rock-hopper,** *n.* The crested penguin. **rock-leather** [ROCK-CORK]. **Rock Lizard:** a British-born native of Gibraltar. **rock-oil,** *n.* Petroleum. **rock-pigeon,** *n.* The European wild pigeon, *Columba livia*, supposed to be the ancestor of the domesticated varieties. **rock-rabbit,** *n.* A hyrax, esp. *Hyrax Capensis.* **rock-rose,** *n.* The cistus. **rock-ruby,** *n.* A variety of garnet. **rock salmon:** Dogfish or other coarse fish disguised for the market. **rock-salt,** *n.* Salt found in stratified beds. **rock-shelter,** *n.* A cave, etc., used, as a shelter by primitive man. **rock-silk** [ROCK-CORK]. **rock-snake,** *n.* Any species of the genus *Python*, or the Australian genus *Morelia.* **rock-soap,** *n.* A greasy silicate of aluminium used as a crayon, etc. **rock-tar,** *n.* Petroleum. **rockwood** [ROCK-CORK]. **rock-work,** *n.* A rockery. **rockery,** *n.* A pile of rocks, stones, and earth, with places for Alpine and other plants; a display of rocks. **rockless,** *a.* **rocklet,** *n.* **rocklike,** *a.*

rock (2) (rok) [A.-S. *roccian*, cp. G. *rücken*], *v.t.* To move backwards and forwards; to cause a cradle to move to and fro; hence, to soothe, to lull to sleep; to shake, to cause to sway or reel; to work a gold-miner's cradle or other rocking apparatus; to shake or sift in a cradle. *n.* An act or spell of rocking; rocking motion. *v.i.* To move backwards and forwards; to sway, to reel; to move as a gold-miner's cradle. **off one's rocker:** (*slang*) Crazy. **rock an' roll, rock and roll:** An energetic dance to swing music. **rockaway,** *n.* (*Am.*) A four-wheeled two-seated carriage with a standing top. **rocker,** *n.* One who or that which rocks; a curved piece of wood on which a cradle, etc., rocks; a gold-miner's cradle; a low skate with a convexly-curved blade; (*Mach.*) applied to various devices and fittings having a rocking motion. **rocking-chair,** *n.*

A chair with a seat that rocks, usu. a chair mounted on rockers. **rocking-horse,** *n.* **rocking-shaft,** *n.* A shaft rocking, instead of revolving, on its bearings, usu. for conveying horizontal motion. **rocking-stone,** *n.* A stone so balanced on a natural pedestal that it can be rocked. **rocking-tool,** *n.* An instrument used in mezzotinting to give the plate a burr.

***rock** (3) (rok) [cp. Icel. *rokkr,* M. Dut. *rocke,* Dut. *rok,* G. *rocken*], *n.* A distaff.

rock-alum, -basin, -bottom, -bound, -butter, -candy, -cork, etc. [ROCK (1)].

rocket (1) (rok' ėt) [F. *roquette,* It. *ruchetta,* dim. of *ruca,* L. *ērūca*], *n.* A name for some species of *Hesperis, Brassica,* and other *Cruciferæ,* some used for salads, etc., and others as garden flowers.

rocket (2) (rok' ėt) [F. *roquet,* It. *rocchetta,* dim. of *rocca,* ROCK (3)], *n.* A firework consisting of a cylindrical case of metal or paper filled with a mixture of explosives and combustibles, used for display, signalling, conveying a line to stranded vessels, and in warfare; (*Mil.*) a device with a warhead containing high explosive and propelled by the mechanical thrust developed by gases generated through the use of chemical fuels. *v.t.* To fire at or bombard with rockets. *v.i.* To fly straight up or to fly fast and high (as a pheasant). **rocket range:** A place for testing rocket projectiles. **rocketry,** *n.* The scientific study of rockets. **rocketer,** *n.* A pheasant, etc., that flies straight up in the air when flushed.

rock-fish, -goat, etc. [ROCK (1)].

rockling (rok' ling), *n.* A small gadoid fish, esp. the sea-loach.

rocky (1) (rok' i), *a.* Full of or abounding with rocks; consisting of or resembling rock; (*fig.*) solid; rugged, hard, stony, obdurate.

rocky (2) (rok' i) [ROCK (2), -Y], *a.* (*colloq.*) Unsteady, tottering, fragile. **rockily,** *adv.* Unsteadily. **rockiness,** *n.*

rococo (rō kō' kō) [F., prob. coined from *rocaille,* ROCKERY], *n.* A florid, debased kind of ornamentation (in architecture, furniture, etc.) flourishing under Louis XIV and XV in the 17th and 18th cents.; design or ornament of an odd, eccentric, or freakish kind. *a.* In this style; debased, eccentric, quaint, antiquated.

rod (rod) [A.-S. *rodd,* cp. Icel. *rudda,* rel. to ROOD], *n.* A straight, slender piece of wood, a stick, a wand; this or a bundle of twigs, etc., as an instrument of punishment; punishment; a baton, a sceptre; a fishing-rod; an enchanter's wand; a slender bar of metal, esp. forming part of machinery, etc.; a unit of lineal measure, equal to 5½ yards; (*Am. slang*) a revolver; (*Anat.*) a rod-like body or structure; *a tribe, a race. **a rod in pickle:** Trouble or punishment in store. **Napier's rods** [NAPIER'S BONES]. **rodded,** *a.* **rodless,** *a.* **rodlet,** *n.* **rodlike,** *a.* **rodman, rodster,** *n.* An angler.

rode (1), *past* [RIDE]. ***rode** (2) [ROAD].

rode (3) (rōd) [?], *v.i.* (*Ornith.*) To fly in the evening, as woodcocks.

rodent (rō' dėnt) [L. *rōdens -ntem,* pres.p. of *rōdere,* to gnaw], *a.* Gnawing; (*Zool.*) pertaining to the *Rodentia.* *n.* Any animal of the order *Rodentia,* having two (or sometimes four) strong incisors and no canine teeth, comprising the squirrel, beaver, rat, etc. **rodential** (rō den' shål), *a.*

rodeo (rō dā' ō) [Sp., from *rodear,* to go round], *n.* (*Am.*) A driving together or rounding-up of all the cattle on a ranch; an outdoor entertainment involving this.

rodless, rodlet, rodlike, rodman [ROD].

rodomontade (rod ō mon tād') [F., from *Rodomont, Rodomonte,* leader of the Saracens in Ariosto's 'Orlando Furioso'], *n.* Brag, bluster, rant. *v.i.* To boast, to bluster, to rant. *a.* Bragging, boastful. ***rodomont** (rod' ō mont), *n.* A vain boaster.

rodster [ROD].

roe (1) (rō) [A.-S. *rāha,* cp. Icel. *rā,* Dut. *ree,* G. *reh*], *n.* A small species of deer, *Capreolus capræa.* **roebuck,** *n.* The male roe. **roedeer,** *n.* The roe.

roe (2) (rō) [cp. M.Dut. and M.L.G. *roge,* O.H.G. *rogo*], *n.* The mass of eggs forming the spawn of fishes, amphibians, etc., called the hard roe; the sperm or milt, called the soft roe. **roe-stone,** *n.* Oolite.

roentgen [RÖNTGEN].

rogation (rō gā' shůn) [L. *rogātio,* from *rogāre,* to ask], *n.* (*usu. in pl.*) A solemn supplication or litany, chanted in procession on Rogation Days; (*Rom. Ant.*) a law submitted by the consul or tribune for adoption by the people. **Rogation Days:** The Monday, Tuesday, and Wednesday preceding Ascension Day. **Rogation Sunday:** That preceding Ascension Day. **Rogation Week:** The week comprising these.

Roger (roj' ėr) [O.F., a personal name, prob. from Teut.], **n.* A ram; a rogue. **jolly Roger:** The pirate's flag. **Roger** or **Sir Roger de Coverley:** A country dance; music for this.

rogue (rōg) [16th cent. cant], *n.* A knave, a rascal, a scamp, a trickster, a swindler; a playful term of endearment for a child or a waggish person; a vicious wild animal, esp. an elephant; a shirking or vicious racehorse or hunter; (*Bot.*) an inferior or intrusive plant among seedlings; (*Biol.*) a variation from the standard type of variety; *a vagrant. *v.t.* To practise roguery upon; to weed out (inferior plants) from among seedlings. **v.i.* To play the rogue. **rogue-buffalo, elephant,** etc., *n.* **rogue's march, tattoo,** or **walk:** A march, etc., played in drumming a disgraced soldier out of the regiment. **roguery,** *n.* **rogueship,** *n.* **roguish,** *a.* Mischievous, high-spirited, saucy. **roguishly,** *adv.* **roguishness,** *n.*

roil (roil) [perh. from obs. F. *ruiler,* to mix up mortar, cp. RILE], *v.t.* To render turbid, as by stirring or shaking up sediment; to make angry, to irritate, to rile.

***roinish** (roi' nish) [obs. *roin,* F. *rogne,* scab, scurf, etym. unknown, -ISH], *a.* Scabby, scurvy, paltry, vile.

roister (roi' stėr) [F. *rustre,* a ruffian, var. of *ruste,* L. *rusticus,* RUSTIC], *v.i.* To behave turbulently or uproariously, to revel boisterously. **n.* A roisterer. ***roist,** *v.i.* **roisterer,** *n.* One who roisters, a swaggering, turbulent, noisy fellow.

***rokelay** (rōk' lā) [F. *roquelaire,* var. of ROGUELAURE], *n.* A woman's short cloak, worn in the 18th cent.

Roland (rō' lånd) [paladin and nephew of Charlemagne, comrade of Oliver], *n.* A blow for a blow, an effective retort, a story capping another, usu. in the phrase **a Roland for an Oliver.**

rôle (rōl) [F., ROLL], *n.* A part or character taken by an actor; any part or function one is called upon to perform.

roll (1) (rōl) [O.F. *roler, roller,* It. *rololare,* from L. *rotula,* dim. of *rota,* wheel], *v.t.* To send, push, or cause to move along by turning over and over on its axis; to cause to rotate; to cause to revolve between two surfaces; to knead, press, flatten, or level with or as with a roller or rollers; to enwrap (in), to wrap (up in); to form into a cylindrical shape by wrapping round and round or turning over and over; to carry or impel forward with a sweeping motion; to carry (oneself along) with a swinging gait; to convey in a wheeled vehicle; to utter with a prolonged, deep, vibrating sound. *v.i.* To move along by turning over and over and round and round; to revolve; to move along on wheels; to be conveyed (along) in a wheeled vehicle; to move or slip about with a rotary motion (of eyes, etc.); to wallow about; to sway, to reel, to go from side to side; to move along with such a motion; (*Naut.*) (of a ship) to turn back and forth on her longitudinal axis; (*Aviat.*) to make a full corkscrew revolution about the longitudinal axis; to undulate or sweep along; to be formed into a cylindrical shape by turning over upon itself; to grow into a cylindrical or spherical shape by turning over and over; to spread (out) under a roller; to give a prolonged deep vibratory sound. **to roll in:** To come in quantities, or numbers. **to roll up:** To wind into a cylinder; (*colloq.*) to assemble, to come up. **rolling-mill,** *n.* A factory in which metal is rolled out by machinery into plates, sheets, bars, etc. **rolling-pin,** *n.* A hard wooden roller used by cooks for rolling out dough, pastry, etc. **rolling-press,** *n.* A machine by which pressing, calendering, etc., is effected by means of rollers. **rolling-stock:** The carriages, vans, locomotives, etc., of a railway. **rolling stone:** A person who cannot settle down.

roll (2) (rōl), *n.* Anything rolled up, a cylinder of any flexible material formed by or as by rolling or folding over on itself; a small loaf of bread; a document, an official record, a register, a list, esp. of names, as of solicitors, soldiers, schoolboys, etc.; a cylindrical or semi-cylindrical mass of anything; a fold, a turned-back edge, a convex moulding, a volute; a roller; a rolling motion or gait; a resounding peal of thunder, etc.; a continuous beating of a drum with rapid strokes. **Master of the Rolls:** The head of the Record Office, an ex-officio judge of the Court of Appeal and member of the Judicial Committee. **to strike off the rolls:** To remove from the official list of qualified solicitors. **roll-call,** *n.* (*Mil.*) The act of calling over a list of names at muster. **roll film,** *n.* (*Phot.*) Film wound on a spool. **roll-moulding,** *n.* (*Arch.*) A convex moulding. **roll-on,** *n.* A step-in elastic corset that fits by stretching. **roll-top desk:** A desk with a flexible cover sliding in grooves.

roller (rō′ lėr), *n.* One who or that which rolls; a cylindrical body turning on its axis, employed alone or forming part of a machine, used for smoothing, spreading out, crushing, etc.; a long, heavy, swelling wave; (*Surg.*) a long, broad bandage, rolled up for convenience; any bird of the genus *Coracias*, remarkable for their habit of turning somersaults in the air; a tumbler pigeon. **roller-bearings,** *n.pl.* (*Mach.*) Bearings comprised of strong steel rollers for giving a point of contact. **roller-coaster,** *n.* A switchback railway at an amusement park. **roller-skate,** *n.* A skate mounted on wheels or rollers for skating on asphalt, etc. **roller-skating,** *n.* **roller-towel,** *n.* An endless towel hung on a roller.

rollick (rol′ ik) [etym. doubtful], *v.i.* To behave in a careless, merry fashion; to frolic, to revel, to be merry or enjoy life in a boisterous fashion. *n.* A frolic, a spree, an escapade. **rollicking, rollicksome,** *a.* **rollickingly,** *adv.* **rollickingness, rollicksomeness,** *n.*

rollock (*prov.*) [ROWLOCK].

roly-poly (rō′ li pō′ li) [prob. a redupl. of ROLL], *a.* Round, plump, podgy. *n.* A pudding made of a sheet of paste, spread over with jam, rolled up, and boiled; a plump or dumpy person, esp. a child; *a name for various ball-games. **roly-poly grass,** *n.* (*Austral.*) A ball-like grass of Central Australia that is blown about hither and thither.

rom (rom) [Romany, man], *n.* (*pl.* ***roma***) A male gipsy, a Romany.

Romaic (rȯ mā′ ik) [Gr. *Rōmaikos*, from *Rōmē*, L. *Rōma*, Rome], *n.* The vernacular language of modern Greece. *a.* Of, pertaining to, or expressed in the modern Greek vernacular. **Romaika,** *n.* The modern Greek national dance.

romal (rȯ māl′) [Hind. and Pers. *rūmāl*], *n.* An East Indian silk or cotton fabric; orig. a handkerchief worn as a head-dress, etc.

Roman (rō′ mȧn) [L. *Rōmānus*], *a.* Pertaining to the city of Rome or its territory or people; denoting numerals expressed in letters, not in figures; denoting ordinary upright characters used in print as distinct from italic or gothic; of or pertaining to the Roman Catholic Church, papal. **Roman architecture:** A style of architecture in which the Greek orders are combined with the use of the arch, distinguished by its massive character and abundance of ornament. **Roman candle** [CANDLE]. **Roman Catholic,** *a.* Of or pertaining to the Church of Rome. *n.* A member of this Church. **Roman Catholicism,** *n.* **Roman Empire:** The empire established by Augustus, 27 B.C., divided A.D. 395 into the Western or Latin and Eastern or Greek Empires. **Roman fever:** Malaria once prevalent at Rome. **Roman nose:** One with a high bridge, an aquiline nose.

romance (rȯ măns′) [O.F. *romanz*, prob. through a pop. L. *rōmānicē*, adv. from *Rōmānicus*, ROMANIC], *n.* A mediæval tale, usu. in verse, orig. in early French or Provençal, describing the adventures of a hero of chivalry; a story, usu. in prose, rarely in verse, with characters, scenery, and incidents more or less remote from ordinary life; fiction of this character; the spirit or atmosphere of imaginary adventure, chivalrous or idealized love, strangeness and mystery; an episode, love-affair, or series of facts having this character; a fabrication, a fiction, a falsehood; (*Mus.*) a short composition of simple character, usu. suggestive of a love-song; one of the languages, esp. Old French, sprung from the Latin spoken in the old European provinces of ancient Rome. *a.* Pertaining to these languages or the peoples speaking them. *v.i.* To tell romantic or extravagant stories; to make false, exaggerated, or imaginary statements. **romancer,** *n.* A writer or composer of romances; one who romances, exaggerates, or draws the long bow. **romanceless,** *a.* **romancist,** *n.* A writer of romances.

Romanes (rō′ mȧ nėz) [Romany, from *Romano*, see ROMANY], *n.* The gipsy language.

romanesque (rō mȧ nesk′), *a.* (*Arch.*) A general term for the styles of architecture that succeeded the Roman and lasted till the introduction of Gothic; Romance. *n.* Romanesque architecture; any of the Romance languages.

Romanic (rō măn′ ik) [L. *Rōmānicus*, from *Rōmānus*, ROMAN], *a.* Derived from Latin; Romance (of languages or dialects), derived or descended from the Romans; (*Print.*) in roman type. *n.* Romance.

Romanish (rō′ mȧ nish), *a.* Of, pertaining to, or characteristic of the Church of Rome. **Romanism,** *n.* **Romanist,** *n.* **Romanistic** (-nis′ tik), *a.*

Romanity (rȯ măn′ i ti), *n.* The spirit or influence of Roman civilization and institutions. **romanize** (rō′ mȧ nīz), *v.t.* To make Roman in character; to subject to the authority of ancient Rome; to Latinize; to convert to the Roman Catholic religion. *v.i.* To use Latin words or idioms; to conform to Roman Catholic opinions. **romanization** (-zā′ shŭn), *n.* **romanizer,** *n.* **Romano-,** *comb. form.*

Romansch (rȯ mansh′) [native, as ROMANCE], *n.* and *a.* The Rhæto-Romanic language of part of E. Switzerland.

romantic (rȯ măn′ tik) [F. *romantique*, from O.F. *romant*, ROMAUNT], *a.* Pertaining to, of the nature of, or given to romance; imaginative, visionary, poetic, extravagant, fanciful; fantastic, unpractical, chimerical, quixotic, sentimental (of conduct, etc.); wild, picturesque, suggestive of romance (of scenery, etc.); pertaining to the movement in literature and art tending away from the moderation, harmonious proportion, and sanity of classicism towards the unfettered expression of ideal beauty and grandeur. *n.* A romantic poet, novelist, etc.; (*pl.*) high-flown talk or ideas. **romantically,** *adv.* **romanticism** (-sizm), *n.* The quality or state of being romantic; the reaction from classical to mediæval forms and to the unfettered expression of romantic ideals which originated in Germany about the middle of the 18th century, and reached its culmination in England and France in the first half of the 19th century. **romanticize,** *v.t.* and *i.* **romanticness,** *n.*

Romany (rom′ ȧ ni) [native *Roman*, fem. and pl. of *Romano*, from ROM], *n.* A gipsy; (*collect.*) gipsies, the gipsies; the gipsy language.

***romaunt** (rȯ mawnt′) [O.F. *romant*, var. of *romanz*, ROMANCE], *n.* A romance, a tale of chivalry.

Rome (rōm) [L. *Rōma*, city and ancient State in Italy], *n.* The Roman Empire; the Church of Rome. ***Rome-penny, *Rome-scot,** *n.* (*Sc.*) Peter's-penny. **Romewards,** *a.* and *adv.* **Romeward,** *adv.* Tending towards Roman Catholicism. **Romic,** *a.* and *n.* (*Phon.*) Applied to an adaptation of the Roman alphabet devised by Dr. H. Sweet to represent sounds phonetically. **Romish,** *a.* (*depreciatory*) Belonging to, or tending towards Roman Catholicism.

romp (romp) [var. of RAMP (1)], *v.i.* To play or frolic roughly or boisterously; (*slang*) to go rapidly (along, past, etc.) with ease. *n.* A child or girl fond of romping; rough or boisterous play. **to romp in or home:** To win easily. **rompish, rompy,** *a.* **rompishly,** *adv.* **rompishness,** *n.*

rompu (rom′ pu) [F., p.p. of *rompre*, L. *rumpere*, to break], *a.* (*Her.*) Broken.

ronde (rond) [F., fem. of *rond*, ROUND (2)], *n.* (*Print.*) An upright angular form of type imitating handwriting.

rondeau (ron′ dō) [F., var. of foll.], *n.* A poem in iambic verse of eight or ten syllables and ten or thirteen lines, with only two rhymes, the opening words coming twice as a refrain; (*Mus.*) a rondo.

rondel (ron′ dĕl) [F., dim. of *rond*, ROUND (2)], *n.* A particular form of rondeau, usu. of thirteen or fourteen lines with but two rhymes throughout; *a round tower. **rondelet,** *n.* A poem of seven lines with a refrain, usu. repeating words from the opening.

rondelle (ron del′) [F., as prec.], *n.* A circular piece, disk, pane of glass, etc.; (*Foundry*) a crust or scale forming on molten metal in cooling.

rondo (ron′ dō) [It., from F. RONDEAU], *n.* A musical composition having a principal theme which is repeated after each subordinate theme, often forming part of a symphony, etc.

***rondure** (ron′ dūr) [F. *rondeur*, from *rond*, ROUND (2)], *n.* A circle, a circular or spherical outline or thing.

***rong** [RUNG (2)]. ***ronnion** [RUNNION].

Röntgen rays (runt′ gĕn rāz) [W. K. von *Röntgen* (1845–1923), the discoverer], *n.pl.* A form of radiant energy penetrating most substances opaque to ordinary light, employed for photographing hidden objects and for therapeutic treatment of lupus, cancer, etc., also known as X-rays. **röntgen, roentgen,** *n.* The international unit of quantity of X- or Gamma-rays.

roo (roo), *n.* (*Austral. colloq.*) A kangaroo.

rood (rood) [A.-S. *rōd*, cogn. with ROD], *n.* The cross of Christ, a crucifix, esp. one set on a rood-beam or screen; a measure of land, usu. the fourth part of a statute acre; (*fig.*) a small quantity of land. **rood-beam,** *n.* A beam across the arch opening into a choir, supporting the rood. **rood-loft,** *n.* A gallery over the rood-screen. **rood-screen,** *n.* A stone or wood screen between the nave and choir, usu. elaborately designed and decorated with carving, etc., orig. supporting the rood.

roof (roof) [A.-S. *hrōf*, cp. Dut. *roef*, Icel. *hrōf*], *n.* The upper covering of a house or other building; the covering or top of a vehicle, etc.; any analogous part, as of a furnace, oven, etc.; the palate; (*fig.*) the top of a mountain; a covering, a canopy; a house, shelter, etc. *v.t.* To cover with or as with a roof; to be the roof of; to shelter. **roof garden,** *n.* A garden of plants and shrubs growing in soil-filled receptacles on a flat roof. **roof-tree,** *n.* The ridge-pole of a roof; (*fig.*) a roof, a house. **roofage,** *n.* **roofer,** *n.* **roofing,** *n.* **roofless,** *a.* **roofy,** *a.*

rooinek (roo′ i nek) [S. Afr. Dut., red neck], *n.* Nickname for a British soldier; a European immigrant; a greenhorn.

rook (1) (ruk) [A.-S. *hrōc* (cp. Dut. *roek*, G. *ruch*, Icel. *hrōkr*), prob. imit., cp. Gr. *krōzein*, to caw], *n.* A gregarious British bird, *Corvus frugilegus*, of the crow family with glossy black plumage; (*fig.*) a cheat, a swindler, a sharper, esp. at cards, dice, etc. *v.t.* To cheat, to swindle; (*slang*) to charge extortionately. **rookery,** *n.* A wood or clump of trees where rooks nest; a colony of rooks; a place frequented by seabirds or seals for breeding; a colony of seals, etc.; (*fig.*) an old tenement or low neighbourhood densely populated, esp. as a resort of thieves, sharpers, etc. **rookie,** *n.* (*slang*) A raw recruit. **rooklet, rookling,** *n.* **rooky,** *a.*

rook (2) (ruk) [O.F. *roc*, *rock*, ult. from Pers. *rukh*], *n.* The castle at chess.

room (1) (room) [Assamese], *n.* A deep blue dye, from a plant of the genus *Ruellia.*

room (2) (rum) [A.-S. *rūm* (cp. G. *raum*, Dan. and Swed. *rum*, also Dut. *ruim* and Icel. *rūmr*, spacious)], *n.* Space regarded as occupied or available for occupation, accommodation, capacity, vacant space or standing-ground; opportunity, scope; a portion of space in a building enclosed by walls, floor and ceiling; (*pl.*) apartments, lodgings, accommodation for a person or family. *v.i.* (*Am.*) To occupy rooms, to lodge. *v.t.* (*Am.*) To accommodate, to lodge (guests). **to give, leave, or make room:** To withdraw so as to leave space for other people. **roomed,** *a.* Having rooms (*usu. in. comb.* as *six-roomed*). **roomer,** *n.* (*Am.*) A lodger. **roomful,** *n.* **roomy,** *a.* Having ample room; spacious, extensive. **roomily,** *adv.* **roominess,** *n.*

roon (run) [Sc. etym. doubtful], *n.* A rim, a strip, a shred.

roop [ROUP].

roost (1) (roost) [A.-S. *hrōst*, cp. Dut. *roest*], *n.* A pole or perch for birds to rest on; a place for fowls to sleep in at night; (*fig.*) a resting-place, a room, esp. a bedroom. *v.i.* To perch on or occupy a roost, to sleep on a roost; to be lodged for the night. *v.t.* To provide with a roost or a resting-place. **at roost:** Perched or sleeping on the roost; (*fig.*) in bed. **rooster,** *n.* The domestic cock.

roost (2) (roost) [Icel. *rost*], *n.* A powerful tidal current, esp. off the Orkney and Shetland Islands.

root (1) (root) [late A.-S. and Icel. *rōt*, rel. to L. *rādix* and WORT], *n.* The descending part of a plant which fixes itself in the earth and draws nourishment therefrom; (*pl.*) the ramifying parts, rootlets or fibres into which this divides, or the analogous part of an epiphyte, etc.; a young plant for transplanting; an esculent root; the part of an organ or structure that is embedded; (*fig.*) the basis, the bottom, the fundamental part, or that which supplies origin, sustenance, means of development, etc.; (*Philol.*) the elementary, unanalysable part of a word as distinguished from its inflexional forms and derivatives; (*Mus.*) the fundamental note of a chord; (*Math.*) the quantity or number that, multiplied by itself a specified number of times, yields a given quantity. *v.i.* To take root. *v.t.* To cause to take root: (*fig.*) to fix or implant firmly (to the spot); to pull or dig (up) by the roots. **to take or strike root:** To become planted and send out living roots or rootlets. **root and branch:** Utterly, radically. **to root out:** To uproot; to extirpate. **root-bound,** *a.* Fixed to the earth by roots; immovable. **root-crop,** *n.* A crop of plants with esculent roots. **root-leaf,** *n.* A leaf apparently growing immediately from the root, but really from a part of the stem underground. **root-stock,** *n.* A rhizome; the original source or primary form of anything. **rootage,** *n.* **rootedly,** *adv.* **rootedness,** *n.* **rootery,** *n.* A pile of roots and stumps for growing plants in. **rootless,** *a.* **rootlet,** *n.* A small root, a radicle. **rooty,** *a.*

root (2) (root) [A.-S. *wrōtan*, from *rōt*, ROOT (1)], *v.t.* To dig, turn, or grub (up) with the snout, beak, etc. *v.i.* To turn up the ground in this manner in search of food; to hunt (up or out), to rummage (about, in, etc.); (*Am.*) to cheer, to shout encouragements to. **rooter,** *n.* One who roots up, an extirpator; (*Am.*) one who cheers, a partisan. *n.* **rootle,** *v.t.* and *i.*

rooti, rooty (roo′ ti) [Hind.], *n.* Bread, food.

rope (rōp) [A.-S. *rap* (cp. Dut. *reep*, G. *reif*, Icel. and Norw. *reip*, Swed. *rep*)], *n.* A stout cord of twisted fibres of hemp, flax, cotton, etc., or wire; a general name for cordage, over one inch in circumference; a series of things strung together in a line; (*fig.*) a halter for hanging a person; a slimy or gelatinous formation in beer, etc. *v.t.* To tie, fasten or secure with a rope; to enclose or close (in) with rope; to pull (a horse) so as to avoid winning a race; (*Mountaineering*) to fasten (persons) together or to tie (a person on) with a rope. *v.i.* To form threads or filaments (of glutinous matter in liquid); (*Mountaineering*) to put a rope on. **rope of sand:** A feeble or delusive bond. **the ropes:** (*slang*) Those enclosing a prize-ring, etc. **to give** (a person) **plenty of rope** or **rope enough:** To allow (him) freedom of action with a view to his committing an irreparable blunder or indiscretion. **to know the ropes:** To be well acquainted with the circumstances, methods and opportunities in any sphere. **rope-dancer,** *n.* One who performs feats on the tight rope. **rope-dancing,** *n.* **rope-ladder,** *n.* A ladder made of two ropes connected by rungs usu. of wood. **rope's-end,** *n.* A short piece of rope used for flogging, esp. on shipboard. **rope-walk,** *n.* A long piece of ground where ropes are twisted. **rope-walker,** *n.* A rope-dancer. **rope-yarn,** *n.* A yarn composed of fibres for making rope; (*fig.*) a small thing or part, a mere trifle. **ropeable,** *a.* (*Austral. colloq.*) Wild, intractable; angry, out of temper, irascible. **ropery,** *n.* A rope-walk; *(*fig.*) roguery. **ropy,** *a.* Resembling a rope; glutinous, viscid. **ropiness,** *n.* **roping-pole,** *n.* (*Austral.*) A pole with a noose attached, for catching cattle.

Roquefort (rōk′ fôrt, rôk′ fôr) [orig. made at *Roquefort*], *n.* French cheese made from goats' and ewes' milk.

roquelaure (rok′ ė lôr) [Duc de *Roquelaure*], *n.* A short cloak for men worn in the 18th cent.

roquet (rō′ kā) [from CROQUET], *v.t.* (*Croquet*) To make one's ball strike another; to strike another ball (of one's ball). *v.i.* To make this stroke. *n.* This stroke or a hit with it.

***roral, *-ic** (rôr′ ȧl, ik) [L. *rōs rōris*, dew, -AL, -IC], *a.* Pertaining to or like dew; dewy. ***roriferous** (rȯ rif′ ėr ŭs), *a.* Producing dew or moisture.

rorqual (rôr′ kwȧl) [F., from Norw. *röyrkval* (*reythr*, red, *kval*, whale)], *n.* A whale with dorsal fins, one of the genus *Balænoptera*.

rorty (rôr′ ti) [etym. unknown], *a.* (*slang*) Of the best, fine, most satisfactory.

rosace (rō′ zās) [F., from ROSE (1)], *n.* A rose-shaped centre-piece or other ornament; a rose-window.

rosaceous (rō zā′ shŭs) [L. *rosāceus*, rose-coloured, from *rosa*, ROSE (1)], *a.* (*Bot.*) Pertaining to the *Rosaceæ* of which the rose is the type; rose-like. **rosacean,** *n.* **rosaniline** (rō zăn′ i lin), *n.* (*Chem.*) A compound having powerful basic properties derived from aniline; a salt of this used as a dye-stuff under the names aniline red, magenta, etc. **rosarian** (rȯ zâr′ i ȧn), *n.* A rose-fancier. **rosarium,** *n.* A rose-garden.

rosary (rō′ zȧ ri) [L. *rosārium*, rose-garden, late L., chaplet, from *rosa*, ROSE (1)], *n.* A rose-garden, a rose-plot; (*R.-C. Ch.*) a form of prayer in which 3 sets of 5 decades of aves, each decade preceded by a paternoster and followed by a gloria, are repeated; this series of prayers; a string of beads by means of which account is kept of the prayers uttered; *a chaplet, a garland. **Rosarian,** *n.* A member of the Fraternity of the Rosary.

Roscian (rosh′ i ȧn), *a.* Of or after the manner of Roscius Gallus, the Roman actor.

***roscid** (ros′ id) [L. *rōscidus*, from *rōs*, dew], *a.* Dewy.

rose (1) (rōz) [A.-S. *rose*, L. *rosa*, prob. ult. from Gr. *rhodea, rhodon*], *n.* Any plant or flower of the genus *Rosa*, consisting of prickly bushes or climbing and trailing shrubs bearing single or double flowers, usu. scented, of all shades of colour from white and yellow to dark crimson; one of various other flowers or plants (with distinctive adjective or phrase) having some resemblance to the rose; a light crimson or pink colour; a complexion of this colour (*often in pl.*); a device, rosette, knot, ornament, or other object shaped like a rose; a perforated nozzle for a hose or watering-pot; a rose-window; a rose-shaped ornament on a ceiling; a circular card, disk, or diagram with radiating lines, used in a mariner's compass, etc.; erysipelas. *a.* Coloured like a rose, pink or pale red. *v.t.* (*chiefly in p.p.*) To make rosy. **a bed of roses:** A luxurious place. **under the rose:** In secret; privately, confidentially. **Wars of the Roses:** The civil wars (1455–85) between the Houses of Lancaster and York, who respectively took a red and a white rose as their emblems. **rose-acacia,** *n.* The locust tree, *Robinia hispida.* **rose-apple,** *n.* A tropical tree of various species of the genus *Eugenia* cultivated for its foliage, flowers, and fruit. **rose-bay,** *n.* The great willow-herb, *Epilobium angustifolium*; the azalea; the oleander; the rhododendron. **rose-bud,** *n.* A flower-bud of a rose; (*fig.*) a young girl, (*Am.*) a debutante. *a.* Like a rose-bud (of a mouth). **rose-bug,** *n.* An American beetle destructive to roses. **rose-campion,** *n.* A garden plant with crimson flowers of the genus *Agrostemma.* **rose-chafer,** *n.* A European beetle, *Cetonia aurata*, infesting roses. **rose-cheeked,** *a.* **rose-colour,** *n.* A deep pink; (*fig.*) an attractive outlook or state of affairs. **rose-coloured,** *a.* (*fig.*) Attractive, encouraging; sanguine, optimistic. **rose-cut,** *a.* Cut with a flat surface below and a hemispherical or pyramidal part above covered with facets (of diamonds, etc.). **rose-diamond,** *n.* A diamond so cut. **rose-drop,** *n.* A lozenge flavoured with rose-essence; an ear-ring; a skin-disease characterized by red blotches, grog-blossom. **rose-engine,** *n.* A machine or an attachment to a lathe for producing curved patterns. **rose-gall,** *n.* A gall on the dog-rose, produced by an insect. **rose-hued,** *a.* **rose-leaf,** *n.* A petal (or leaf) of a rose; (*fig.*) a slight drawback to general satisfaction. **rose-mallow,** *n.* The hollyhock, a plant of the genus *Hibiscus.* ***rose-noble,** *n.* An old English gold coin, with the impression of a rose, worth 6s. 8d. **rose of Jericho:** A small annual cruciferous plant of N. Africa and the Levant, having fronds that expand with moisture, also called the resurrection plant. **rose of May:** The white narcissus. **rose of Sharon:** An Eastern plant sometimes identified with the meadow saffron, the cystus, and the polyanthus narcissus; a species of St. John's wort. **rose-pink,** *n.* A pigment composed of whiting dyed with Brazil-wood. **rose-quartz,** *n.* A rose-red variety of quartz. **rose-rash** [ROSEOLA]. **rose-root,** *n.* A species of stonecrop, *Sedum rhodiola*, with a fragrant root. **rose-water,** *n.* Perfume made from rose leaves; (*fig.*) gentle treatment. *a.* Affectedly delicate, fine, or sentimental. **rose-window,** *n.* A circular window filled with tracery branching from the centre, usu. with mullions arranged like the spokes of a wheel. **rosewood,** *n.* A hard close-grained fragrant wood of a dark-red colour obtained chiefly from various species of *Dalbergia.* **rosewood oil:** Oil obtained from a species of rosewood.

rose (2), *past* [RISE].

roseate (rō′ zė ȧt) [L. *roseus*, rosy, from *rosa*, ROSE (1)], *a.* Rose-coloured, rosy; (*fig.*) smiling, promising, optimistic. **roseal** (rō′ zė ȧl), *a.* **roseately,** *adv.* **roselet,** *n.*

rose-bud, rose-leaf, etc. [ROSE (1)].

roselite (rō′ zė līt) [Gustav *Rose* (1798–1873), German mineralogist, -LITE], *n.* (*Min.*) A rare native arsenate of cobalt and calcium found in rose-red crystals.

rosella, roselle (rȯ zel′ ȧ, -zel′), *n.* The E. Indian hibiscus, called in the W. Indies red sorrel; (*Austral.*) a variety of brightly-coloured parakeet.

rosemary (rōz′ mȧ ri) [orig. *rosmarine*, O.F. *rosmarin* [F. *romarin*), late L. *rōsmarīnum* (*rōs*, dew, *marīnus*, MARINE)], *n.* An evergreen fragrant shrub, *Rosmarinus officinalis*, of the mint family, leaves of which yield a perfume and oil, and are used in medicine, etc.; *a funeral emblem signifying remembrance.

roseo- [L. *roseus*, from *rosa*, ROSE (1)], *comb. form.* (*Chem.*) Rose-red (applied to certain salts and alkalis).

roseola (rō zē′ ō lȧ) [dim. of ROSE (1)], *n.* A non-contagious febrile disease with rose-coloured spots, German measles; a rash occurring in measles, etc.

rosery (rō′ zėr i), *n.* A place where roses grow, a rose-plot, a rosarium.

***roset** (1) (rō zet′), *n.* A rose-red pigment; a rosette.

roset (2) (*Sc.*) [var. of ROBIN].

Rosetta stone (rō zet′ ȧ stōn), *n.* A basalt stele with an inscription in hieroglyphics, demotic characters, and Greek, discovered at Rosetta, in Egypt, in 1799, furnishing a key to Egyptian hieroglyphics. **Rosetta wood:** A finely-veined East Indian wood, of a bright orange-red.

rosette (rō zet′) [F.], *n.* A rose-shaped ornament, knot, or badge; a bunch of ribbons, worsted, strips of leather, etc., arranged concentrically more or less as the petals of a rose; a carved or painted ornament in the conventional form of a rose.

rosewood, etc. [ROSE (1)].

Rosicrucian (rō zi kroo′ shȧn) [L. *rosa crucis* (rose of the cross), from *Rosenkreuz*, -AN], *n.* A member of a secret society devoted to the study of occult science, which became known to the public early in the 17th cent., and was alleged to have been founded by a German noble, Christian Rosenkreuz, in 1484. *a.* Of or pertaining to Rosenkreuz or this society. **Rosicrucianism,** *n.*

***rosier** [F.], *n.* A rose-bush.

rosily [ROSY].

rosin (roz′ in) [var. of RESIN], *n.* Resin, esp. the solid residue left after the oil has been distilled from crude turpentine. *v.t.* To rub, smear, etc., with rosin, esp. to apply it to the strings of a fiddle or fiddle-bow. **rosiny,** *a.*

rosinante (roz in ăn′ ti) [horse in *Don Quixote*], *n.* A worn-out horse, a jade.

rosiness [ROSY].

***rosmarine** (1) (ros′ mȧ rēn) [see ROSEMARY], *n.* Rosemary; sea-dew, sea-spray.

***rosmarine** (2) (ros′ mȧ rēn) [Dan. *rosmar*], *n.* The walrus.

Rosolio (rō zō′ li ō) [It. (L. *rōs*, dew, *sōlis*, gen. of *sōl*, sun)], *n.* A cordial made from raisins, spirit, etc., in Italy and S. Europe; a Maltese red wine.

ross (ros) [prob. from Scand. (cp. Norw. dial. *ros*, *rus*)], *n.* (*Am.*) The rough scaly surface of the bark of certain trees; (*Sc.*) refuse of plants, loppings from trees, etc. *v.t.* To strip the ross from; to cut (bark) up for tanning.

rossignol (ros′ i nyōl) [F., from It. *rossignuolo*, ult. from L. *lusciniola*, dim. of *luscinia*], *n.* (*Canada*) The song-sparrow; *the nightingale.

rostellum (ros tel′ ŭm) [L., dim. of ROSTRUM], *n.* (*pl.* **-la**) (*Bot.*) An elevated portion of the stigma in orchids; any small beak-shaped process; that part of the seed which descends and forms the root, a radicle; (*Zool.*) a beak-like part or process, as the protruding fore part of the head in tapeworms, the mouth-part of lice, etc. **rostellar, rostellate, rostelliform** (-tel′ i fôrm), *a.*

roster (ros′ tėr) [Dut. *rooster*, list, orig. grid-iron, from *roosten*, to ROAST], *n.* A list showing the order of rotation in which officers, companies, or regiments are to perform their turns of duty.

rostrum (ros′ trŭm) [L., beak, cogn. with *rōdere*, to gnaw, cp. RODENT], *n.* (*pl.* **-tra**) (*Rom. Ant.*) The beak or prow of a war-galley; a platform (decorated with beaks of captured galleys) in the Roman forum from which public orations, etc., were delivered; hence, a platform, a pulpit; (*Nat. Hist.*) a beak, bill, beak-like snout, part, or process; (*Surg.*) a curved forceps with beak-like jaws. **rostral,** *a.* (*Nat. Hist.*) Pertaining to, situated on, or resembling, a rostrum or beak; (*Rom. Ant.*) decorated with the beaks of war-galleys or representations of these (of columns, etc.). **rostrate, -trated,** *a.* (*Nat. Hist.*) Furnished with or ending in a process resembling a bird's beak; (*Rom. Ant.*) rostral. **rostriferous** (-trif′ ėr ŭs), *a.* **rostriform** (ros′ tri fôrm), *a.* **rostro-,** *comb. form.* **rostroid,** *a.* **rostrulum,** *n.* The beak or mouth-parts of a flea, etc.

rosulate (rō zū′ lāt) [ROSE], *a.* (*Bot.*) With leaves making a small rosette.

rosy (rō′ zi), *a.* Resembling a rose; blooming; (*fig.*) favourable, auspicious. *n.* (*slang*) Red wine; (*Pugil.*) blood. **rosily,** *adv.* **rosiness,** *n.*

rot (rot) [A.-S. *rotian* (cp. Dut. *rotten*, Icel. *rotna*, from *rot*)], *v.i.* (*past & p.p.* **rotted**) To decay, to decompose by natural change, to putrefy; to be affected with sheep-rot; (*fig.*) to become effete or morally corrupt, to pine away; (*slang*) to talk banteringly. *v.t.* To cause to rot, to decompose, to make putrid; (*colloq.*) to confound, to spoil; to chaff, to banter. *n.* Putrefaction, rottenness; dry-rot; a malignant liver-disease in sheep, etc.; (*colloq.*) nonsense, rubbish.

rota (rō′ tȧ) [L., wheel], *n.* A list of names, duties, etc., a roster; (*R.-C. Ch.*) the supreme court deciding on ecclesiastical and secular causes. **rotal,** *a.*

rotary (rō′ tȧ ri) [late L. *rotārius*, from prec.], *a.* Rotating on its axis; acting or characterized by rotation. *n.* A rotary machine. **Rotary Club,** *n.* A local business club for mutual benefit and service. **Rotarian,** *n.* A member of a Rotary Club. **rotary machine,** *n.* (*Print.*) A printing press in which the printing surface is a revolving cylinder. **rotaplane** [GYROPLANE]. **rotary pump,** *n.* (*Mach.*) A pump in which the liquid is delivered at low pressure by means of shaped rotating members. **rotagravure,** *n.* (*Print.*) A process of photogravure-printing on a rotary machine.

rotate (rō tāt′) [ROTA], *v.i.* To revolve round an axis or centre; to act in rotation. *v.t.* To cause (a wheel, etc.) to revolve; to arrange (crops, etc.) in rotation. *a.* (rō′ tāt) Wheel-shaped (of a calyx, corolla, etc.). **rotable,** *a.* **rotation** (rō tā′ shŭn), *n.* The act of rotating, rotary motion; alternation, recurrence, regular succession. **rotational,** *a.* **rotative** (rō′ tȧ tiv), **rotatory,** *a.* **rotator** (rō tā′ tôr), *n.* That which moves in or gives a circular motion; (*Anat.*) a muscle imparting rotatory motion.

rote (1) (rōt) [etym. doubtful, said to be rel. to ROUTE], *n.* Mere repetition of words, phrases, etc. without understanding; mechanical routine, memory, or knowledge. *v.t.* To repeat from memory; *to learn by rote.

***rote** (2) (rōt) [O.F., prob. from Celt., cp. CROWD (2)], *n.* A mediæval musical instrument like a fiddle.

rother (roth′ ėr) [A.-S. *hrīther*, *hrȳther*, cp. Dut. *rund*, G. *rind*], *n.* An ox. ***rother-beast,** *n.*

rotifer (rō′ ti fėr) [ROTA, L. *-fer*, -FEROUS], *n.* (*pl.* **-fers**) (*Zool.*). One of the *Rotifera*. **rotifera** (rō tif′ ėr ȧ), *n.pl.* The wheel-animalcules, a group of minute aquatic animals with swimming organs appearing to have a rotary movement. **rotiferal, rotiferous,** *a.* **rotiform** (rō′ ti fôrm), *a.* (*Bot.*) Wheel-shaped, rotate.

Rotodyne (rō′ tō dīn), *n.* Proprietary name of a type of aircraft combining the vertical lift of a helicopter and the flight of an aeroplane.

rotor (rō′ tôr) [ROTA], *n.* (*Aviat.*) Name given to any system of revolving planes that produce lift; (*Elec.*) the rotating part of an electric machine. **rotaplane** [GYROPLANE]. **rotorcraft,** *n.* An aircraft deriving its lift from rotors. **Rotovator,** *n.* Trade name of a rotary cultivator.

rotten (rot′ ėn) [prob. from Icel. *rotinn* (cp. Swed. *rutten*), cogn. with ROT and RET], *a.* Decomposed, decayed, decaying, tainted, putrid, fetid; unsound, liable to break, tear, etc.; morally corrupt, effete, unhealthy, untrustworthy, defective; affected with sheep-rot; (*colloq.*) poor or contemptible in quality, disagreeable, annoying. **rottenstone,** *n.* A friable siliceous limestone used for polishing. **rottenly,** *adv.* **rottenness,** *n.* **rotter,** *n.* (*slang*) A good-for-nothing or undesirable person.

rotula (rō′ tū lȧ) [L., dim. of ROTA], *n.* (*pl.* **-læ**) (*Anat.*) The knee-cap or patella; (*Zool.*) one of the radial parts of the oral skeleton of a sea-urchin. **rotular, rotuliform** (-tū′ li fôrm), *a.*

rotund (rȯ tŭnd′) [L. *rotundus*, ROUND], *a.* Rounded (of the mouth in speaking); orotund, sonorous, magniloquent (of speech or language); round, circular, spherical; plump, well-rounded. **rotunda,** *n.* A circular building, hall, etc., esp. with a dome. **rotundante,** *a.* **rotundi-,** *comb. form.* **rotundifolious** (-fō′ li ŭs), *a.* (*Bot.*) Having round leaves. **rotundity,** *n.* **rotundo-,** *comb. form.* **rotundo-ovate** (-ō′ vȧt), *a.* Of a roundish egg-shape.

roturier (rō tu′ ryā) [F., from *roture*, prob. from L. *ruptūra*, RUPTURE], *n.* A plebeian.

rouble (roobl) [F., from Rus. *ruble*], *n.* The Russian monetary unit, a silver coin worth about 2s. ½d.

roué (roo′ ā) [F., p.p. of *rouer*, to break on the wheel, L. *rotāre*, to ROTATE], *n.* A rake, a debauchee.

rouge (roozh) [F., from L. *rubeus* (cp. *ruber*, *rufus*, also RED)], *n.* A cosmetic prepared from safflower, *Carthamus tinctorius*, used to colour the cheeks or lips; red oxide of iron used for polishing metal, glass, etc. **a.* Red. *v.t.* To colour with rouge. *v.i.* To colour (one's cheeks, etc.) with rouge. **Rouge Croix** (-krwa), **Rouge Dragon:** The titles of two pursuivants in the English College of Arms. ***rouge et noir*** (-ā nwar′): A gambling card-game played by a 'banker' and a number of persons on a table marked with four diamonds, two red and two black.

rough (rŭf) [A.-S. *rūh* (cp. Dut. *ruig*, G. *rauh*, Dan. *ru*)], *a.* Having an uneven, broken, or irregular surface, having prominences or inequalities, not smooth, level, or polished; shaggy, hairy, of coarse texture; rugged, hilly, hummocky; harsh to the senses, astringent, discordant, severe; violent, boisterous, tempestuous; turbulent, disorderly; harsh or rugged in temper or manners; cruel, unfeeling; rude, unpolished; lacking finish or completeness, not completely wrought, crude; approximate, not precise or exact, general. *adv.* Roughly, in a rough manner. *n.* A rough or unfinished state; rough ground; (*Golf*) the ground to right and left of the fairway; a rough person, a rowdy; a spike put in a horseshoe to prevent slipping; (*Austral.*) a variety of salmon; (*collect.*) rough or harsh experiences, hardships. *v.t.* To make rough, to roughen; to furnish (a horse or horseshoe) with roughs or spikes; to plan or shape (out) roughly; to break in (a horse) esp. for military purposes. **to cut up rough:** To be upset, to grow quarrelsome. **to rough in:** To outline, to draw roughly. **to rough it:** To put up with hardships; to live without the ordinary conveniences. **rough-and-ready,** *a.* Hastily prepared, without finish or elaboration; provisional, good enough for the purpose. **rough-and-tumble,** *a.* Disorderly, irregular, boisterous, haphazard. *n.* An irregular fight, contest, scuffle, etc. **rough ashlar,** *n.* (*Build.*) A block of building-stone as taken from the quarry. **rough-cast,** *v.t.* To form or compose roughly; to coat (a wall) with coarse plaster. *n.* A rough model or outline; a coarse plastering, usu. of lime and gravel, for outside walls, etc. *a.* Formed roughly, without revision or polish. **rough draft:** A rough sketch. **rough-draw,** *v.t.* To draw roughly. **rough-dry,** *v.t.* To dry without smoothing or ironing. **rough-hew,** *v.t.* To hew out roughly; to give the first crude form to. **rough-hewn,** *a.* Rugged, rough, unpolished. **rough house,** *n.* (*slang*) Horse-play, a scrimmage. **rough-neck,** *n.* (*Am. colloq.*) A rowdy, a hooligan. **rough-rider,** *n.* A horse-breaker; a bold skilful horseman able to ride unbroken horses; an irregular horse-soldier. **rough-hound,** *n.* A dog-fish. **rough-shod,** *a.* Shod with roughened shoes. **to ride rough-shod over:** To treat in a domineering way. **rough-wrought,** *a.* Worked only as regards the initial stages. **roughage,** *n.* (*Diet.*) Food materials containing a considerable quantity of cellulose, which resist digestion and promote peristalsis. **roughen,** *v.t.* and *i.* **rougher,** *n.* One who works in the rough, or in the rougher stages of a process, etc. **roughish,** *a.* **roughly,** *adv.* **roughness,** *n.*

roulade (roo lad′) [F., from *rouler*, to ROLL], *n.* (*Mus.*) A run of notes on one syllable, a flourish.

rouleau (roo lō′) [F., from RÔLE], *n.* (*pl.* ***-leaux***) A small roll, esp. a pile of coins done up in paper.

roulette (roo let′) [F., dim. of *rouelle*, dim. of *roue*, L. *rota*, wheel], *n.* A game of chance played with a ball on a table with a revolving disk; a wheel with points for making dotted lines, used in engraving, perforating stamps, etc.; (*Math.*) a curve that is the locus of a point rolling on a curve.

rounce (rouns) [Dut. *ronse*, *ronds*], *n.* (*Print.*) The handle by which the bed of a printing-press is run in and out under the platen.

rouncival (roun′ si vȧl) [perh. from *Roncesvalles* in the Pyrenees], *n.* The marrowfat pea.

***round** (1) (round) [A.-S. *rūnian*, from *rūn*, mystery, cogn. with RUNE], *v.i.* and *t.* To whisper.

round (2) (round) [O.F. *rund*, *rond*, *round* (F. *rond*), L. *rotundus*, from *rota*, wheel], *a.* Spherical, circular, cylindrical, or approximately so; convexly curved in contour or surface, full, plump, not hollow, corpulent; going and returning to the same point, with circular or roughly circular course or motion; continuous, unbroken; plain, open, frank, candid, fair; quick, smart, brisk (of pace, etc.); full-toned, smooth, flowing (of sounds, etc.); liberal, ample, large, considerable; composed of tens, hundreds, etc., esp. evenly divisible by ten. *n.* A round object, piece, slice, etc.; a ladder-rung, a circle, sphere, or globe; a thick cut from the joint (of beef); that which goes round, circumference, extent; a circular course, a circuit, a heat, a cycle, a recurrent series, a bout, a spell, an allowance, a series of actions, etc., in which all participate; (*Mil.*) a single shot fired from a firearm or gun; ammunition for this; (*Sculp.*) the state of being completely carved out in the solid, opp. to relief; (*Mil.*) a watch making a circuit of inspection, the circuit so made; (*Mus.*) a piece of music sung by several voices each taking it up in succession. *adv.* On all sides so as to encircle; so as to come back to the same point; to or at all points on the circumference, or all members of a party, etc.; by a circuitous route; with rotating motion. *prep.* On all sides of; so as to encircle; to or at all parts of the circumference of; in all directions from (in the relation of a body to its axis or centre). *v.t.* To make round or curved; to pass, go, or travel round; to collect together, to gather (up); to fill out, to complete; to pronounce fully and smoothly; *to surround. *v.i.* To grow or become round; to go the rounds, as a guard; (*chiefly Naut.*) to turn round. **to come or get round one:** (*colloq.*) To take advantage of by flattery or deception. **to round off:** To shape (angles, etc.) to a round of less sharp form. **to round on:** To turn upon, to attack; to peach upon (of an informer). **to round to:** (*Naut.*) To turn toward the wind, in order to heave to. **round about:** In or as in a circle round, all round; circuitously, indirectly; in an opposite direction. **roundabout,** *a.* Circuitous, indirect, loose; encircling; plump, stout; *ample, extensive. *n.* A merry-go-round; a circuitous or indirect journey, way, course, etc.; a device at a cross-roads whereby traffic circulates in one direction only; a circumlocution. **round arm:** (*Cricket*) A style of bowling in which the arm turns at shoulder level. **round-backed,** *a.* Having a round or curved back. **round-dance,** *n.* A dance in which the performers are ranged or move in a circle, esp.

a waltz. **round game:** One played round a table; one in which there are a number of players but no sides or partners. **round-hand,** *n.* Writing in which the letters are round and full; a style (of bowling at cricket) with the arm swung more or less horizontally. **Round-Head,** *n.* A term applied by the Cavaliers during the Great Civil War to the Parliamentarians, from their wearing their hair cut short. *a.* Pertaining to the Parliamentarians. **round-house,** *n.* *A lock-up; (*Naut.*) a cabin on the after part of the quarterdeck, esp. on sailing ships; this part of the deck. **round-ridge,** *v.t.* To plough into round ridges. **round robin:** A petition with the signatures placed in a circle so that no name heads the list. **round-shouldered,** *a.* Bent forward so that the back is rounded. **roundsman,** *n.* One sent round by a tradesman to collect orders; (*Am.*) a policeman making a round of inspection. **in round numbers:** Approximately. **round table conference:** A conference at which all parties are on an equal footing. **round-top,** *n.* A platform formerly round, as the top of a mast. **round tower:** A high narrow tower, tapering from the base upwards, usu. with a conical top (frequent in Ireland, esp. near an ancient church or monastery. **round trip,** *n.* (*Am.*) A return journey, there and back. **round-turn,** *n.* (*Naut.*) One turn of a rope round a timber, etc. **round-up,** *v.t.* To gather (horses, cattle, etc.) together. *n.* A gathering together of cattle, etc., for branding, etc.; a herd so rounded-up. **roundel,** *n.* *A circle, anything of a round shape; a round disk, panel, heraldic circular charge, etc.; a rondel or rondeau; *a round dance. **roundelay,** *n.* A simple song, usu. with a refrain; a bird's song; a round dance.

rounder (roun′ dėr), *n.* One who or that which rounds, esp. a tool used in bookbinding, a wheelwright's plane, etc.; (*slang*) one who makes the rounds; a complete run through all the bases in rounders; (*pl.*) a game with a short bat and a ball, between two sides, with four bases to which a player hitting the ball has to run without being hit by it.

rounding (roun′ ding), *a.* Becoming round, nearly round. *n.* The act of making or turning round; (*Naut.*) material wrapped round a rope to save chafing. **rounding machine,** *n.* A machine of various kinds for cutting things round, shaping barrel-heads, rounding the backs of books, etc. **rounding-tool,** *n.* **roundish,** *a.* **roundishness,** *n.* ***roundlet,** *n.* **roundly,** *adv.* In a round or roundish form; bluntly, straightforwardly, plainly, emphatically. **roundness,** *n.*

roup (1) (roop) [etym doubtful], *n.* A disease of poultry.

roup (2) (roup) [Sc. and North., cp. Icel. *raupa*], *v.i.* To cry, to shout. *v.t.* To sell by auction. *n.* Hoarseness; a sale by auction. **articles of roup:** The laws regulating sales by auction. **roupy,** *a.* Hoarse.

rouse (1) (rouz) [etym. doubtful, perh. rel. to RUSH (2)], *v.t.* To raise or startle (game) from a covert; to wake; to excite to thought or action; to provoke, to stir (up), to agitate; (*Naut.*) to haul (in) with vigour. *v.i.* To wake or be wakened; to start up; to be excited or stirred (up) to activity, etc. *n.* (*Mil.*) The reveille. **rouser,** *n.* One who or that which rouses; anything that excites or startles; an implement for stirring up beer in brewing; (*slang*) a thumping lie. **rousing,** *a.* Having power to rouse, awaken, or excite; (*slang.*) outrageous, startling, astonishing. **rousingly,** *adv.*

***rouse** (2) (rouz) [prob. from CAROUSE], *n.* A draught of liquor, a bumper; a carouse.

rouseabout (rouz′ á bout), *n.* (*Austral.*) An odd-job man in a shearing-shed or on a station.

rouser, rousing, etc. [ROUSE (1)].

Rousseauism (ru sō′ izm) *n.* The views or teaching of the French writer Jean Jacques Rousseau (1712–78) on education, ethics, politics, religion, etc. **Rousseauan** (-sō′ án), **Rousseauesque** (esk′).

Roussillon (ru sē′ yon) [the former province of *Roussillon*, France], *n.* A red wine from the south of France.

roust (roust) [prob. var. of ROUSE (1)], *v.t.* (*prov.*) To rouse, to rout (out). **roustabout,** *n.* (*Am.*) A labourer on river-steamers, wharves, etc.; (*Am. and Austral.*) a casual labourer.

rout (1) (rout) [O.F. *route*, a troop, company, etc.], *n.* A crowd, a miscellaneous or disorderly concourse; (*Law*) an assembly and attempt of three or more people to do an unlawful act upon a common quarrel; a riot, a brawl, an uproar, a disturbance; an utter defeat and overthrow; a disorderly and confused retreat of a defeated army, etc.; *a large evening party. *v.t.* To defeat utterly and put to flight. **to put to rout:** To overthrow completely. **rout-cake,** *n.* A rich cake orig. for use at routs. **rout-seat,** *n.* A long, light seat hired out for use at receptions, etc. **routable,** *a.* ***routous,** *a.*

rout (2) (rout) [var. of ROOT (2)], *v.t.* To root (up or out); to turn, fetch, drive, etc. (out of bed, house, etc.); to gouge, to scoop, to tear (up, etc.). *v.i.* To root (about).

rout (3) (rout) [Sc. and North., from Scand. (cp. Icel. *rauta*, Norw. *ruta*), rel. to prec.], *v.i.* To bellow, to roar (of cattle, etc.); to make a loud noise (of the sea, etc.).

route (root, *Mil.* rout) [F., from L. *rupta*, broken (way), fem. p.p. of *rumpere*, to break], *n.* The course, way or road travelled or to be travelled; (*Mil.*) the order to march. ***en route:*** On the way. **route-march,** *n.* (*Mil.*) A long exercise march. **route-step,** *n.* An easy step allowed in long marching.

router (rou′ tėr) [ROUT (2), -ER], *n.* A plane used in cutting grooves, mouldings, etc. *v.t.* To cut (away) or hollow out with this. **router-gauge, -plane, -saw,** *n.* Tools used in cutting grooves for the insertion of mouldings, etc. **routing-machine, -tool,** *n.*

routh (routh) [Sc., etym. doubtful], *n.* Plenty. *a.* Abundant, plentiful. **routhly,** *a.*

routine (roo tēn′) [F.], *n.* A course of procedure, business, or official duties, etc., regularly pursued; any regular habit or practice. **routineer** (-nēr′), **routiner** (roo tē′ nėr), *n.* **routinism,** *a.* **routinist,** *n.*

routing-machine, etc. [ROUTER].

rove (1), *past* [REAVE].

rove (2) (rōv) [etym. doubtful, perh. rel. to Icel. *rāfa* or (acc. to Skeat) to Dut. *rooven*, to rob], *v.i.* To wander, to ramble, to roam; (*Angling*) to troll with live-bait; *(*Archery*) to shoot at a chance mark or for distance, etc. *v.t.* To wander over, through, etc. *n.* The act of roving; a ramble. **rove-beetle,** *n.* A beetle also called the devil's coach-horse. **rover,** *n.* A pirate, a sea-robber, a freebooter; a wanderer; a fickle person; (*Croquet*) a ball that has gone through all the hoops but not pegged out, the person playing this; (*Archery*) a mark chosen at random, a mark for long-distance shooting. **Rovers,** *n.pl.* An organization of older lads, of which Boy Scouts may become members on reaching the age of 16. **to shoot at rovers:** To shoot at random. **rovingly,** *adv.* **rovingness,** *n.* **roving-shot,** *n.*

rove (3) (rōv) [etym. doubtful], *v.t.* To draw out slivers of wool, cotton, etc., from a carding-machine before spinning into thread; to pass through an eye or aperture; to ravel out. *n.* A slightly-twisted sliver of wool, cotton, etc. **roving-frame, -machine, -plate, -reel,** *n.* Machinery used in the operations of twisting fibres, etc., into thread in the manufacture of worsted, thread, etc.

rovingly, rovingness [ROVE (2)].

row (1) (rō) [A.-S. *rāw*, cp. Dut. *rij*, G. *reihe*], *n.* A series of persons or things in a straight or nearly straight line; a line, a rank. **The Row,** *n.* Rotten Row, in Hyde Park.

row (2) (rō) [A.-S. *rōwan* (cp. Dut. *roeijen*, Icel. *rōa*, M.H.G. *rüejen*, also L. *rēmus*, Gr. *eretmon*, oar)], *v.t.* To propel by oars; to convey by rowing. *v.i.*

To row a boat; to labour with an oar; to be impelled by oars. *n.* A spell at rowing; an excursion in a row-boat. **to row down:** To overtake by rowing, esp. in a bumping race. **row-, rowing-boat,** *n.* A boat propelled by rowing. **rowlock** (rŭl′ ŏk), *n.* A crotch, notch, or other device on the gunwale of a boat serving as a fulcrum for an oar (*Am.* oarlock). **row-port,** *n.* A small port cut near the water's edge for the use of sweeps in a small vessel. **rower,** *n.*

row (3) (rou) [etym. doubtful, prob. orig. slang], *n.* (*colloq.*) A noisy disturbance, a noise, a din, a commotion, a tumult, a quarrel, a shindy. *v.t.* To rate, to scold, to reprimand; to rag. *v.i.* To make a row. **row-de-dow** (-dou′), *n.* A hubbub, a din.

rowan (rou′-, rō′ ăn) [Sc. and O.North.F., from Scand. (cp. Swed. *röun*, Dan. *rön*, Icel. *reynir*)], *n.* The mountain-ash, *Pyrus aucuparia*. **rowan-tree,** *n.*

rowdy (rou′ di), *n.* A noisy, rough or disorderly fellow (*Am.* rough-neck). *a.* Rough, riotous, blackguardly. **rowdiness, rowdyism,** *n.* **rowdyish,** *n.*

rowel (rou′ ĕl) [O.F. *rouel*, dim. of *roue*, L. *rota*, wheel], *n.* A spiked disk or wheel on a spur; a roll of hair, silk, etc., or a piece of rubber, leather, etc., with a hole in the centre for placing under a horse's skin to discharge purulent matter. *v.t.* To insert a rowel in (a horse, etc.). **rowelling-scissors,** *n.* Scissors used for inserting rowels.

rower, rowlock [ROW (2)].

roxburghe (roks′ bŭr ŏ) [Duke of *Roxburghe* (1740–1804)], *n.* A style of bookbinding comprising plain leather back, usu. gilt-lettered, cloth or paper sides, gilt top, and the other edges untrimmed.

royal (roi′ ăl) [O.F. *roial*, L. *rēgālis*, REGAL], *a.* Of, pertaining to, suitable to, or befitting a king or queen; under the patronage or in the service of a king or queen; regal, kingly, princely; noble, magnificent, majestic; surpassingly fine, on a great scale, splendid, first-rate. *n.* A stag with a head of twelve or more points; (*Naut.*) a royal mast or sail next above the topgallant; (*colloq.*) a royal personage. **blood royal:** The royal family. **Burgh Royal** [BURGH]. **rhyme royal** [RHYME]. ***the Royals:** The first regiment of foot in the British service, the Royal Scots. **Royal Arch:** A superior degree in Freemasonry. **royal blue,** *n.* A deep blue. **royal fern:** The flowering fern, *Osmunda regalis*. **royal paper:** A size of paper 20 × 25 in. for printing, 19 × 24 for writing. **royal road,** *n.* (*fig.*) An easy way. **royal standard,** *n.* Flag with the royal arms. ***royalet,** *n.* A petty king. **royalist,** *n.* An adherent or supporter of royalism or of monarchical government, esp. a supporter of the royal cause in the Great Civil War. *a.* Supporting monarchical government; belonging to the Royalists. **royalism,** *n.* **royalistic** (-lis′ tik), *a.* **royalize** (roi′ ă līz), *v.t.* **royally,** *adv.*

royalty (roi′ ăl ti), *n.* The office or dignity of a king or queen, sovereignty; royal rank, birth, or lineage; kingliness; a royal person or persons; a member of a reigning family (*usu. in pl.*); a right or prerogative of a sovereign (*usu. in pl.*); a share of profits paid to a landowner for the right to work a mine, to a patentee for the use of an invention, to an author on copies of books sold, etc.; a royal manor; (*Sc., pl.*) the bounds of a royal burgh.

***royne** [ROUND (2)]. ***roynish** [ROINISH].

royster, etc. [ROISTER].

Royston crow (roi′ stŏn krō) [*Royston*, Herts, CROW (1)], *n.* The grey or hooded crow, *Corvus cornix*.

rua (roo′ ă) [Maori], *n.* A storage pit for edible roots, etc.

rub (1) (rŭb) [M.E. *rubben* (cp. L.G. *rubben*), etym. doubtful], *v.t.* (*past & p.p.* **rubbed**) To apply friction to, to move one's hand or other object over the surface of; to polish, to clean, to scrape, to graze; to slide or pass (a hand or other object) along, over or against something; to take an impression of (a design) with chalk and graphite on paper laid over it; to remove by rubbing; to affect (a person or feelings, etc.) as by rubbing. *v.i.* To move or slide along the surface of, to grate, to graze, to chafe (against, on, etc.); to get (along, on, through, etc.) with difficulty. *n.* The act or a spell of rubbing; (*fig.*) a hindrance, an obstruction, a difficulty, a pinch; *a sarcasm, a jibe. **to rub along:** To manage, just to succeed. **to rub down:** To bring to smaller dimensions or a lower level by rubbing; to clean or dry by rubbing. **to rub in:** To force in by friction; (*colloq.*) to enforce or emphasize (a grievance, etc.). **to rub the wrong way:** To irritate. **to rub out:** To remove or erase by friction. **to rub up:** To polish, to burnish; to mix into a paste, etc., by rubbing; to freshen (one's recollection of something). **rubbing-machine,** *n.* A machine with rollers between which linen is rubbed in cleansing. **rubbing-post,** *n.* A post for cattle to rub themselves against. **rubbing-stone, rubstone,** *n.* A stone used to sharpen instruments; a whetstone.

rub (2) [short for RUBBER (2)].

rub-a-dub (rŭb′ ă dŭb) [imit.], *n.* The sound of a rapid drum-beat. *v.i.* To make this sound.

rubber (1) (rŭb′ ĕr), *n.* One who or that which rubs; an instrument used for rubbing; a rubstone; a part of a machine that rubs, grinds, polishes, etc., a masseur or masseuse.

rubber (2) (rŭb′ ĕr), *n.* India-rubber or caoutchouc; a piece of india-rubber for erasing pencil marks, etc. **rubbers,** *n.pl.* Galoshes, rubber over-shoes. **rubber-cloth,** *n.* Cloth coated with this. **rubber-gauge,** *n.* A contrivance for determining the amount of rubber required to make a given article. **rubberless,** *n.*

rubber (3) (rŭb′ ĕr) [etym. doubtful], *n.* A series of three games at whist, bridge, back-gammon, etc.; two games out of three, or the game that decides the contest.

rubbing-machine, -post, etc. [RUB (1)].

rubbish (rŭb′ ish) [M.E. *robows*, A.F. *robeux*, prob. pl. of foll.], *n.* Waste, broken, or rejected matter, refuse (*Am.* junk); trash, nonsense. **rubbishing, rubbishy,** *a.*

rubble (rŭb′ ĕl) [prob. from Scand. (cp. Icel. *rubb rubbr*, Norw. *rubl*)], *n.* Rough, broken fragments of stone, etc.; (*Geol.*) disintegrated rock, waterworn stones; rubble-work. **rubble-stone,** *n.* The upper fragmentary and decomposed portion of a mass of rock. **rubble-work,** *n.* Masonry composed of irregular fragments of stone, or in which these are used for filling in. **rubbly,** *a.*

rubefy (roo′ bė fī) [F. *rubéfier*, L. *rubefacere* (*rubēre*, to be red, *facere*, to make)], *v.t.* To make red; (*Med.*) to act on (the skin) as a counter-irritant. **rubefacient** (roo bė fā′ shĕnt), *a.* Making red. *n.* A counter-irritant causing redness of the skin. **rubefaction** (-făk′ shŭn), *n.* **rubescent,** *a.* Turning pink or red.

rubella (rŭ bel′ ă) [dim. of L. *rubellus*, reddish], *n.* (*Path.*) German measles. ***rubeola*** (rŭ bē′ ŏ lă), *n.* Rubella; *measles; (*Vet.*) swine fever.

rubescent [RUBIFY].

Rubia (roo′ bi ă) [L.], *n.* (*Bot.*) A genus of plants containing the madder. **rubiaceous** (-ā′ shŭs), *a.* (*Bot.*) **rubiacic** (-ăs′ ik), *a.* (*Chem.*) **rubian** (roo′ bi ăn), *n.* (*Chem.*) The colouring principle of madder root. **rubianic** (-ăn′ ik), *a.*

rubicel (roo′ bi sel) [F. *rubicelle*, prob. dim. of *rubis*, RUBY], (*Min.*) A yellowish or orange-red transparent spinel ruby.

Rubicon (roo′ bi kŏn) [small stream in Italy, bounding the province of Cæsar, who crossed it before the war with Pompey, exclaiming, "The die is cast!"], *n.* (*Piquet*) The winning of the game before one's opponent has scored 100 points. *v.t.* To defeat (one's opponent) thus. **to cross the Rubicon:** To take a decisive step.

rubicund (roo′ bi kŭnd) [F. *rubicond*, L. *rubicundus*, from *rubēre*, to be red], *a.* Ruddy, rosy, red-faced. **rubicundity** (-kŭn′ di ti), *n.*

rubidium (rū bid′ i ŭm) [L. *rubidus*, red, as prec., -IUM], *n.* A silvery-white metallic element belonging to the potassium group.

rubied [RUBY]. **rubify** [RUBEFY].

rubiginous (rū bij′ i nŭs) [L. *rūbīgo -gīnis*, rust], *a.* Rusty or brownish-red in colour.

***rubious** (roo′ bi ŭs) [RUBY, -OUS], *a.* Ruby-coloured. ***rubor**, *n.* Redness, ruddiness.

rubric (roo′ brik) [F. *rubrique*, L. *rubrīca*, from *ruber*, red], *n.* A title, chapter-heading, or direction printed in red or distinctive lettering, esp. a liturgical direction in the Prayer Book, etc.; *such an entry of a saint's name in a calendar, hence, a calendar of saints. *v.t.* To rubricate. *a.* Red, marked with red; pertaining to or enjoined by the rubrics. **rubrical**, *a.* **rubrically**, *adv.* **rubricate**, *v.t.* To mark, distinguish, or illuminate with red; to furnish with a rubric or rubrics. **rubrication** (-kā′ shŭn), *n.* **rubricator** (roo′ bri kā tŏr), *n.* **rubrician** (rū brish′ ăn), ***rubricist** (roo′ brisist), *n.* One versed in or adhering strictly to the rubrics. **rubricism**, *n.* ***rubrisher**, *n.* A rubricator.

rubstone [RUB (1)].

Rubus (roo′ bŭs) [L., as foll.], *n.* A genus of rosaceous shrubs comprising the blackberry, raspberry, etc.

ruby (roo′ bi) [O.F. *rubi*, *rubis*, ult. from L. *rub-*, stem of *rubeus*, red], *n.* A precious stone of a red colour, a variety of corundum; (*Am.*) an agate; the colour of ruby, esp. a purplish red; (*fig.*) red wine; (*Pugil.*) blood; a red pimple, a carbuncle; (*pl.*) red lips; (*Print.*) a size of type between nonpareil and pearl. *a.* Of the colour of a ruby. *v.t.* To make red or ruby-coloured. **ruby-glass**, *n.* A purplish-red glass coloured by oxides of iron, tin, lead, copper, etc. **ruby-tail**, *n.* A brilliant fly with bluish-green back and red abdomen, also called the golden wasp. **rubied**, *a.*

ruche (roosh) [F., bee-hive], *n.* A quilled or ruffled strip of gauze, lace, silk, or the like. **ruched**, *a.* **ruching**, *n.*

ruck (1) (rŭk) [prob. cogn. with RICK], *n.* A heap, a rick, a pile; a multitude, a crowd, esp. the mass of horses left behind by the leaders in a race; the common herd.

ruck (2) (rŭk) [Icel. *hrukka*, cp. Norw. *rukka*], *n.* A crease, a wrinkle, a fold, a plait. *v.t.* To wrinkle, to crease. **ruckle** (1), *n.*, *v.t.* and *i.*

ruckle (2) (rŭk′ ĕl) [prob. from Scand. (cp. Norw. *rukla*)], *v.i.* To make a rattling or gurgling noise. *n.* A rattling or gurgling noise, esp. in the throat, a death-rattle.

rucksack (ruk′ săk) [G. (*rucken*, dial., back, SACK (1))], *n.* A bag or valise carried loosely on the back by means of straps, for a pedestrian's or climber's necessaries.

ructions (rŭk′ shŭnz) *n.pl.* (*colloq.*) A commotion, a disturbance, a row.

Rudbeckia (rŭd bek′ i ă) [Olaus *Rudbeck* (1630–1702), Swedish botanist], *n.* (*Bot.*) A genus of N. American plants of the aster family, also called the cone-flowers.

rudd (rŭd) [prob. from obs. *rud*, A.-S. *rudu*, cogn. with RED], *n.* A fish, *Leuciscus erythrophthalmus*, akin to the roach, also called the red-eye.

rudder (rŭd′ ĕr) [A.-S. *rōther* (cp. Dut. *roer*, G. *ruder*, Swed. *roder*), cogn. with ROW (2)], *n.* A flat wooden or metal framework or solid piece hinged to the stern-post of a boat or ship and serving as a means of steering; (*Aviat.*) a vertical moving surface in the tail of an aeroplane for providing directional control and stability; a kind of paddle for stirring malt in the mash-tub; (*fig.*) a principle, etc., which guides, governs, or directs the course of anything. **rudder-band, -brace, -case, -chain, -head, -hole, -post, -tackle, -wheel,** *n.* Parts of the rudder, its supports, or the apparatus controlling it. **rudder bar**, *n.* (*Aviat.*) The foot control of the rudder in an aeroplane. **rudderless**, *a.*

ruddily, ruddiness [RUDDY].

ruddle (1) [var. of RADDLE (1)].

ruddle (2) (rŭd′ ĕl) [as RUDD], *n.* A variety of red ochre used for marking sheep. *v.t.* To colour or mark with ruddle. **ruddle-man**, *n.* One who digs or deals in ruddle.

ruddock (rŭd′ ŏk) [A.-S. *rudduc*, rel. to RUDD], *n.* The redbreast.

ruddy (rŭd′ i) [A.-S. *rudig* (cp. Icel. *rothi*), from *rudu*, cogn. with *rēad*, RED (1)], *a.* Of a red or reddish colour; of a healthy complexion, fresh-coloured; (*slang*) bloody. *v.t.* To make ruddy. *v.i.* To grow red. **ruddily**, *adv.* **ruddiness**, *n.*

rude (rood) [F., from L. *rudem*, nom. *-dis*], *a.* Simple, primitive, crude, uncultivated, uncivilized, unsophisticated, unrefined; coarse, rough, rugged; unformed; coarse in manners, uncouth; impolite, uncivil, insolent, offensive, insulting; violent, boisterous, ungentle, tempestuous; hearty, robust, strong. ***rude-growing**, *a.* Rough, wild. **rudely**, *adv.* **rudeness**, *n.* **rudish**, *a.*

***ruderal** (roo′ dĕr ăl) [L. *rūdera*, pl. of *rūdus*, broken stones], *a.* (*Bot.*) Growing on rubbish. ***ruderate**, *v.t.* To pave with small stones. **ruderation** (-ā′ shŭn), *n.*

Rudesheimer (roo′ dĕs hī mĕr) [*Rudesheim*, in Nassau], *n.* A white Rhine wine.

rudiment (roo′ di mĕnt) [F., from L. *rudīmentum*, from *rudis*, RUDE], *n.* An elementary or first principle of knowledge, etc. (*usu. in pl.*); (*pl.*) the undeveloped or imperfect form of something, a beginning, a germ; a partially-developed, aborted, or stunted organ, structure, etc., a vestige. **rudimentary, *-tal**, *a.* **rudimentarily**, *adv.* **rudimentariness**, *n.*

rudish [RUDE].

rue (1) (roo) [F., from L. *rūta*, Gr. *rhutē*], *n.* A plant of the genus *Ruta*, esp. *R. graveolens*, a shrubby evergreen plant, of rank smell and acrid taste, formerly used as a stimulant, etc., in medicine.

rue (2) (roo) [A.-S. *hrēowan* (cp. Dut. *rouwen*, G. *reuen*), rel. to Icel. *hryggr*, grieved], *v.t.* To grieve or be sorry for, to regret, to repent of. **v.i.* To be sorry, to be penitent or regretful. **n.* Sorrow, regret, repentance, compassion. **rueful**, *a.* **ruefully**, *adv.* **ruefulness**, *n.* **rueing**, *pres.p.*

rufescent (rū fes′ ĕnt) [L. *rūfescens -ntem*, pres.p. of *rūfescere*, from *rūfus*, reddish], *a.* Reddish; tinged with red. **rufescence**, *n.*

ruff (1) (rŭf) [O.F. *roffle*, *roufle*, perh. corr. of *triomphe*, cp. TRUMP (2)], *n.* *An old game at cards; the act of trumping when one cannot follow suit. *v.t.* and *i.* To trump thus.

ruff (2) (rŭf) [prob. shortened from RUFFLE], *n.* A broad plaited or fluted collar or frill of linen or muslin worn by both sexes, esp. in the 16th cent.; anything similarly puckered or plaited, as the top of a loose boot turned over; a growth like a ruff, as the ring of feathers round the necks of some birds; a bird, *Philomachus pugnax*, of the sandpiper family (perh. from the conspicuous ruff in the male in the breeding season); a breed of pigeons related to the jacobin. **ruffed**, *a.* Having a ruff.

ruff (3) (rŭf) [var. of ROUGH], *v.t.* To heckle (flax, etc.); to nap (a hat). **ruffer**, *n.*

ruffe (rŭf) [prob. from ROUGH], *n.* A small fresh-water fish, *Acerina cernua*, related to and resembling the perch.

ruffian (rŭf′ i ăn) [O.F., cp. It. *ruffiano*, etym. doubtful], *n.* A low, lawless, brutal fellow, a bully, rough, or desperado ready for any crime; a robber, a murderer; *a pander. *a.* Ruffianly. **v.i.* To act the ruffian; to rage. **ruffianage, -dom, -hood**, *n.* ***ruffianish**, *a.* **ruffianism**, *n.* **ruffianly**, *a.*

ruffle (rŭf′ ĕl) [M.E. *ruffelen*, etym. doubtful, cp. Dut. *roffelen*, L.G. *ruffelen*, E. Fris. *ruffeln*], *v.t.* To disorder, to disturb the smoothness or order of, to rumple, to disarrange; to annoy, to disturb, to upset, to discompose. *v.i.* To grow rough or turbulent, to play or toss about loosely, to flutter; to swagger, to bluster (about); *to contend, to fight. *n.* A strip or frill of fine plaited or goffered lace, etc., attached to some part of a garment, esp. at the neck or wrist; a ruff or fluted collar; a ripple on water; a low, vibrating beat of the drum; *a disturbance, a commotion, a dispute. ***rufflement,** *n.* **ruffler,** *n.* A bully, a swaggerer; an attachment to a sewing-machine for making ruffles.

rufous (roo' fŭs) [L. *rūfus*], *a.* Of a brownish or yellowish red. **rufi-, rufo-,** *comb. form.*

rug (rŭg) [prob. from Scand. (cp. Norw. dial. *rugga*, Swed. *rugg*, tangled hair, Icel. *rögg*, cp. RAG (1))], *n.* A thick, heavy wrap, coverlet, etc., usu. woollen with a thick nap or of skin with the hair or wool left on; a carpet or floor-mat of similar material; (*Am.*) a carpet; *a shaggy variety of dog. ***rug-headed,** *a.* Having shaggy hair. **rugging,** *n.* Material for making rugs.

ruga (roo' gȧ) [L.], *n.* (*pl.* **-gœ**) (*Nat. Hist.*) A wrinkle, crease, fold, or ridge. **rugate** (roo' gȧt), **rugose** (ru gōs', roo' gōs), **rugous** (roo' gŭs), *a.* Wrinkled, ridged, corrugated. **rugosely,** *adv.* **rugosity** (-gos' iti), *n.* **rugulose** (roo gū lōs'), ***rugulous** (roo' gū lŭs), *a.* Finely wrinkled, slightly rugose. **rugulosity** (-los' i ti), *n.*

Rugby (rŭg' bi) [Warwickshire town with public school], *n.* and *a.* (*Sport.*) A game of football (15 to each side) in which players are allowed to use their hands in carrying the ball and holding their opponents; also called **Rugby football** or **rugger.**

rugged (rŭg' ėd) [prob. from Scand., cp. RUG and ROUGH], *a.* Having a surface full of inequalities, extremely uneven, broken, and irregular; rocky, craggy, of abrupt contour; ragged, shaggy, unkempt; strongly marked (of features); harsh, grating (of sounds); rough in temper, stern, unbending, severe; rude, unpolished; tempestuous, turbulent (of weather, waves, etc.). **ruggedly,** *adv.* **ruggedness,** *n.* ***ruggy,** *a.* (*prov.*) Rough, shaggy.

rug-headed, rugging [RUG].

rugose, rugosity, rugulose, etc. [RUGA].

ruin (roo' in) [F. *ruine*, L. *ruīna*, from *ruere*, to fall], *n.* A disastrous change or state of wreck or disaster, overthrow, downfall; a cause of destruction, downfall, or disaster, havoc, bane; the state of being ruined; the remains of a structure, building, city, etc., or (*fig.*) a person, etc., that has become demolished or decayed (*often in pl.*). *v.t.* To bring to ruin; to reduce to ruin, to dilapidate; to destroy, to overthrow, to subvert; to seduce (a woman). **v.i.* To fall violently; to fall into ruins; to come to ruin. ***ruinate,** *v.t.* and *i.* **ruination** (-nā' shŭn), *n.* **ruiner,** *n.* **ruinous,** *a.* Fallen into ruin, dilapidated; causing ruin, baneful, destructive, pernicious. **ruinously,** *adv.* **ruinousness,** *n.*

rule (rool) [A.-F. *reule*, O.F. *riule* (F. *règle*), L. *rēgula*, whence *rēgulāre*, to rule, to REGULATE], *n.* The act of ruling or the state of being ruled, government, authority, sway, direction, control; that which is established as a principle, standard, or guide of action or procedure; a line of conduct, a regular practice, an established custom, canon, or maxim; method, regularity; an authoritative form, direction, or regulation, or a body of laws or regulations, to be observed by an association, religious order, etc., and its individual members; a strip of wood, ivory, metal, etc., usu. graduated in inches and fractions of an inch, used for linear measurement; (*Math.*) a prescribed formula, method, etc., for solving a problem of a given kind; (*Law*) an order, direction, or decision by a judge or court, usu. with reference to a particular case only; (*Print.*) a thin metal strip for separating columns, headings, etc. *v.t.* To govern, to manage, to control; to curb, to restrain; to be the rulers, governors, or sovereign of; to lay down as a rule or as an authoritative decision; to mark (paper, etc.) with straight lines. *v.i.* To exercise supreme power (usu. over); to decide, to make a decision; to stand at or maintain a certain level (of prices). **as a rule:** Usually, generally. **to rule out:** To exclude. **to work to rule:** To strike in a passive way, slowing down work by observing every rule and regulation most carefully and deliberately whether applicable to the situation or not. **rule absolute:** (*Law*) A rule following a rule nisi making this no longer conditional. **rule of three:** (*Arith.*) Simple proportion. **rule of thumb:** Practice or experience, as dist. from theory, as a guide in doing anything. ***rulable,** *a.* Capable of being ruled; (*Am.*) permissible, correct. **ruleless,** *a.* **ruler,** *n.* One who rules or governs; an instrument with straight edges or sides, used as a guide in drawing straight lines. **rulership,** *n.*

ruling (roo' ling), *n.* An authoritative legal decision, esp. with regard to a special case.

rullion (rŭl' i ŏn) [Sc. var. of obs. *rilling*, *riveling*, A.-S. *rifeling*], *n.* A shoe of undressed hide; (*fig.*) a virago.

rum (1) (rŭm) [formerly *rumbo*, *rumbullion* (now, in Devon dial., a great tumult)], *n.* A spirit distilled from fermented molasses or cane-juice. **rum-blossom, -bud,** *n.* A grog-blossom. **rum-punch, -shrub, -toddy,** *n.* **rum-runner,** *n.* A smuggler of intoxicants during the era of Prohibition in U.S.A.

rum (2) (rŭm) [perh. ident. with 16th cent. cant, *rum*, a fine treat], *a.* (*colloq.*) Strange, singular, odd, queer. **rummy** (1), *a.* **rumly, rummily,** *adv.* **rumminess, rumness,** *n.*

rumb [RHUMB].

rumba (rŭm' ba) [Sp.], *n.* (*Dancing*) A complex Cuban dance.

rumble (rŭm' bėl) [M.E. *romblen* (cp. Dut. *rommelen*, G. *rummeln*, Dan. *rumle*), prob. of imit. orig.], *v.i.* To make a low, heavy, continuous sound, as of thunder, heavy vehicles, etc.; to move (along) with such a sound; to mutter, to grumble; (*slang*) to see through. *v.t.* To cause to move with a rumbling noise; to utter with such a sound. *n.* A rumbling sound; a seat or place for luggage behind the body of a carriage. **rumble-gumption** (*Sc.*) [RUMGUMPTION]. **rumble-seat,** *n.* (*Am.*) A dicky. **rumble-tumble,** *n.* A rumble or seat behind a vehicle; a rumbling vehicle; a commotion. **rumbler,** *n.* **rumbling,** *a.* and *n.* **rumblingly,** *adv.* **rumbly,** *a.*

***rumbo, *rumbullion** [RUM (1)].

rumbustious (rŭm bŭs' ti ŭs) [prob. corr. of ROBUSTIOUS], *a.* (*colloq.*) Boisterous, turbulent, rampageous.

rumen (roo' mėn) [L., throat], *n.* (*pl.* **-mina**) The first cavity of the complex stomach of a ruminant.

rumgumption (rŭm gŭm' shŭn) [GUMPTION], *n.* (*chiefly Sc.*) Common sense.

ruminant (roo' mi nȧnt) [L. *rūminans -ntem*, pres.p. of *rūminārī*, to ruminate, from RUMEN], *a.* and *n.* **Ruminantia** (-năn' shi ȧ), *n.pl.* (*Zool.*) A division of herbivorous animals with a complex stomach serving for chewing the cud, comprising the ox, camel, deer, etc. **ruminantly,** *adv.* **ruminate,** *v.i.* To chew over the cud; (*fig.*) to muse, to meditate. *v.t.* To chew over again; (*fig.*) to ponder over. **rumination** (-nā' shŭn), *n.* **ruminative** (roo' mi nā tiv), *a.* **ruminatively,** *adv.* **ruminator,** *n.*

rummage (rŭm' ȧj) [F. *arrumage* (now *arrimage*), from *arrumer* (*arrimer*), etym. doubtful], *v.t.* *To stow, to arrange (goods in a ship); to make a careful search in, to ransack, esp. by throwing the contents about; to find (out) or fetch (up) by such searching; *to disarrange or throw into disorder by searching. *v.i.* To make careful search. *n.* The act of rummaging, a search, esp. of a vessel by a customs officer; miscellaneous things got by rummaging, lumber, **odds and ends. rummage-sale,** *n.* A sale of miscellaneous articles, esp. in aid of charity. **rummager,** *n.*

rummer (rŭm′ ėr) [W. Flem. *rummer*, *rommer*, cp. Dut. *romer*, G. *römer*], *n.* A large glass or drinking cup.

rummy, rumness [RUM (2)].

rummy (2) (rŭm′ i) [?], *n.* (*Cards*) A simple game played with two packs.

rumour (roo′ mŏr) [A.-F., from L. *rūmōrem*, nom. *-mor*], *n.* Popular report, hearsay, common talk; a current story without any known authority; *a confused noise. *v.t.* To report or circulate as a rumour. **rumorous,** *a.* ***rumourer,** *n.*

rump (rŭmp) [prob. from Scand. (cp. Icel. *rumpr*, Swed. and Norw. *rumpa*, Dan. *rumpe*)], *n.* The end of the backbone with the adjacent parts, the posteriors, the buttocks (usu. of beasts and birds or contemptuously of human beings); (*fig.*) the fag- or tail-end of anything; **the Rump:** (*Hist.*) The remnant of the Long Parliament, after the expulsion of those favourable to Charles I by Pride's Purge in 1648, or after its restoration in 1659. ***rump-fed,** *a.* Fed on rump, or fat in the rump. **rumpless,** *a.* **rump-steak,** *n.* A beef-steak cut from the rump.

rumple (rŭm′ pėl) [cp. RIMPLE], *v.t.* To wrinkle, to make uneven, to crease, to disorder. **n.* A fold, a crease, a wrinkle.

rumpus (rŭm′ pŭs) [etym. doubtful], *n.* A disturbance, an uproar, a row.

rumpy (rŭm′ pi) [RUMP, -Y], *n.* A Manx tailless cat.

run (rŭn) [M.E. *rinnen*, *rennen*, A.-S. *rinnan* (also *iernan*), perh. affected by Icel. *rinna* (cp. Dut. and G. *rennen*)], *v.i.* (*past* **răn**, *p.p.* **run**) To move or pass over the ground by using the legs more quickly than in walking, esp. with a springing motion, so that both feet are never on the ground at once; to amble, trot, or canter (of horses, etc.); to flee, to try to escape; to make a run at cricket; to compete in a race; to seek election, etc.; to move or travel rapidly; to be carried along violently; to move along on or as on wheels; to revolve; to be in continuous motion, to be in action or operation; to go smoothly; to glide, to elapse; to flow; to fuse, to melt; to flow (with), to be wet, to drip, to emit liquid, mucus, etc.; to go, to ply; to spread rapidly; to move from point to point, to rove; to extend, to take a certain course, to proceed, to go on, to continue; to pass or develop (into, etc.); to tend, to incline; to be current; to be allowed to wander or grow (wild). *v.t.* To cause to run or go; to cause to pass, penetrate, etc., to thrust with; to drive, to propel; to pursue, to chase, to hunt; to press (hard) in a race, competition, etc.; to accomplish by running, to perform or execute (a race, an errand, etc.), to follow or pursue (a course, etc.); to keep going, to manage, to conduct, to carry on, to work, to operate; to introduce or promote the election of (a candidate); to discharge, to flow with; to cast, to found, to mould; to smuggle; to incur, to expose oneself to; to allow a bill, etc., to accumulate before paying. *n.* The act of running, an act or spell of running; a trip, a short excursion; the running of two batsmen from one wicket to the other in cricket without either's being put out; a complete circuit of the bases by a player in baseball, etc.; a continuous course, period of operation, series, or succession; a succession of demands (on a bank, etc.); a rapid fall (of a barometer, etc.); the ordinary succession, trend, or general direction, the way things tend to move; (*Am.*) a ladder in a stocking; general nature, character, class, or type; a batch, flock drove, or shoal of animals, fish, etc., in natural migration; a periodical passage or migration; an habitual course, a regular track (of certain animals), a burrow; a grazing-ground; an enclosure for fowls; free use or access, unrestricted enjoyment; (*Mus.*) a roulade; (*Shipbuilding*) the after part of a ship's bottom where it tapers towards the stern. **at a run:** Running. **in the long run:** Eventually. **on the run:** In flight. **the run of mankind:** The generality or the average kind of people. **to run after:** To pursue with attentions; to cultivate, to devote oneself to; to chase. **to run against:** To fall in with. **to run at:** To rush at, to attack. **to run away:** To flee, to abscond, to elope. **to run down:** To stop through not being wound up; to become enfeebled by overwork, etc.; to pursue and overtake; to search for and discover; to disparage, to abuse; (*Naut.*) to run against and sink. **to run into:** To incur, to fall into; to collide with; to reach (a specified number, amount, etc.). **to run in:** To drive (cattle, etc.) in; to call, to drop in; (*colloq.*) to arrest, to take to prison; (*Football*) to carry the ball over the opponent's goal line and touch down. **to run on:** To talk volubly or incessantly; to be absorbed by (of the mind); (*Print.*) to continue without a break. **to run to:** To extend to. **to run out:** To come to an end. **to run over:** To review or examine cursorily; to recapitulate; to overflow; to pass, ride, or drive over. **to run riot** [RIOT]. **to run the show:** (*slang*) To manage; to have the control of in one's own hands. **to run through:** To go through or examine rapidly; to take, deal with, spend, etc., one after another, to squander; to pervade; to transfix; to strike out by drawing a line through. **to run upon:** To dwell on, to be absorbed by; to meet suddenly and accidentally. **to run up:** To grow rapidly; to increase quickly; to accumulate (a debt, etc.) to force up (prices, etc.); to build in a hasty manner. **with a run:** Suddenly, precipitately. **runabout,** *a.* Wandering, roving. *n.* A runabout person; (*prov.*) a pedlar; a light motor-car; (*pl.*) (*Austral.*) cattle let loose to graze at will, wild cattle. **runaway,** *n.* One who flies from danger, restraint or service; a deserter, a fugitive; a bolting horse. *a.* Breaking from restraint; fleeing as a runaway. **runaway marriage or match:** One involving elopement. **run-in,** *n.* (*Football*) The act of running in.

runagate (rŭn′ ȧ găt) [O.F. *renegat*, *renegade* (assim. to RUN, AGATE (2))], *n.* A renegade, a fugitive; a wanderer, a vagabond.

runcible (rŭn′ si bėl) [nonsense word invented by Edward Lear], **runcible spoon,** *n.* A three-pronged fork hollowed out like a spoon and with one of the prongs having a cutting edge.

runcinate (rŭn′ si nȧt) [L. *runcīna*, plane (taken to mean saw), -ATE], *a.* (*Bot.*) Toothed like a saw, with the teeth or lobes inclining backwards.

rundale (rŭn′ dăl) [RUN, obs. *dale*, var. of DOEL (2)], *n.* (*chiefly Ir.*) Joint occupation of detached pieces of land.

***rundle** (rŭn′ dėl) [var. of ROUNDEL], *n.* A round, a ball, a ring, a roundel; a rung of a ladder; something round an axis, as the drum of a capstan. ***rundlet** (1) [RUNLET (1)]. ***rundlet** (2) [RUNLET (2)].

rune (roon) [Icel. *rūn*, cogn. with A.-S. *rūn*, secret, mystery, see ROUND (1)], *n.* A letter or character of the earliest Teutonic alphabet or furthorc, formed from the Greek alphabet by modifying the shape to suit carving, used chiefly by the Scandinavians and Anglo-Saxons; (*fig.*) any mysterious mark or symbol; a canto or division in Finnish poetry; (*pl.*) ancient lore or poetry expressed in runes. **rune-craft,** *n.* **rune-staff,** *n.* A magic staff carved with runes. **runer,** *n.* **runic,** *a.* Of, pertaining to, consisting of, or cut in runes; pertaining to the ancient Scandinavians (esp. of monuments, ornaments, etc.). *n.* A runic inscription; a style of type of even thickness and compressed form. **runology** (ru nol′ ŏ ji), *n.* **runologist,** *n.*

rung (1) (rŭng) [A.-S. *hrung*, cp. Dut. *hronge*, L.G. *runge*], *n.* A stick or bar forming a step in a ladder; a rail or spoke in a chair, etc.; (*Naut.*) a floor-timber in a ship.

rung (2), *past & p.p.* [RING (2)].

runic [RUNE].

***runlet** (1) (rŭn′ lėt) [M.E. and O.F. *rondelet*, dim. of *ronde*, ROUND (2)], *n.* A barrel or cask, esp. for wine, varying considerably in capacity.

runlet (2) (rŭn′ lėt) [RUN, -LET], *n.* A small stream, a runnel.

runnable (rŭn′ ȧ bėl), *a.* That can be run, esp. of a stag fit for the chase.

runnel (rŭn′ ėl) [A.-S. *rynel*, dim. of RUN], *n.* A rivulet, a little brook; a gutter.

runner (rŭn′ ėr), *n.* One who runs; a racer, a messenger, a scout, a spy; one who solicits custom, etc., an agent, a collector, a tout; a smuggler; *a police officer, a detective; that on which anything runs, revolves, slides, etc.; the blade of a skate; a piece of wood or metal on which a sleigh runs; a groove, rod, roller, etc., on which a part slides or runs, esp. in machinery; a sliding ring, loop, etc., on a strap, rod, etc.; a rope run through a single block with one end attached to a tackle-block and the other armed with a hook; a revolving millstone; a creeping stem thrown out by a plant, such as a strawberry, tending to take root; a twining or climbing plant, esp. a kidney bean; a cursorial bird, esp. the water-rail; a longer strip of carpet for a passage, etc. **runner-up,** *n.* The unsuccessful competitor in a final.

running (rŭn′ ing), *n.* The act of one who or that which runs; smuggling; power of running; chance of winning a race, etc.; discharge from a sore. *a.* Moving at a run; kept for a race; flowing; discharging matter; following in succession. *adv.* In succession. **to make the running:** To set the pace. **four, five times running:** Four, five times in succession. **in** or **out of the running:** Having or not having a chance of winning. **running-board,** *n.* (*Motor.*) The footboard of a motor-car. **running commentary:** An oral description, usu. by broadcasting, of an event in progress, *e.g.* a race. **running fight:** A fight between one pursuing and one pursued. **running-fire,** *n.* A continuous fire of artillery or musketry. **running gear:** The wheels, axles, etc., of a vehicle, etc. **running hand:** Cursive or flowing handwriting. **running jump:** One taken with a preliminary run. **running postman,** *n.* (*Austral.*) A Tasmanian trailing-plant. **running powers:** Power granted to a railway company to run trains over the line of another company. **running rigging:** All the rigging except the shrouds and other fixed ropes, etc. **running title:** The title of a book used as a head-line throughout.

***runnion** (rŭn′ yŭn) [perh. from obs. *roin*, see ROINISH], *n.* A mangy, scabby animal; a scurvy person; a drab.

runology, runologist [RUNE].

runt (rŭnt) [etym. doubtful], *n.* An ox or bullock of a small breed, esp. Welsh or Highland; a large variety of domestic pigeon; any animal stunted in growth; a dwarf; a boor, an uncouth person; (*Sc.*) a hag; (*prov.*) an old decayed stump. **runtish, runty,** *a.*

runway (rŭn′ wā), *n.* The way, channel, groove, etc., in which anything runs, slides, etc.; the run of an animal; the channel of a stream; a fowl-run; (*Aviat.*) a prepared track, usually concrete, on an aerodrome for the landing and taking-off of aeroplanes.

rupee (ru pē′) [Hind. *rūpiyah*, from Sansk. *rūpya*, wrought silver], *n.* An East Indian silver coin and money of account, now worth about 1s. 4d.

rupestral (ru pes′ trål) [mod. L. *rūpestris*, from *rūpes*, rock], *a.* Growing on or inhabiting rocks. **rupestrean, rupestrine,** *a.*

rupia (roo′ pi å) [Gr. *rhupos*, dirt], *n.* (*Path.*) A severe skin disease characterized by pustules succeeded by ulcerating scabs.

rupture (rŭp′ tyůr) [F., from L. *ruptūra*, from *rumpere*, to break, p.p. *ruptus*], *n.* The act of breaking or the state of being broken or violently parted, a break, a breach; a breach or interruption of concord or friendly relations; (*Path.*) hernia. *v.t.* To burst, to break, to separate by violence; to sever (a friendship, etc.); to affect with hernia. *v.i.* To suffer a breach or disruption. **ruptile,** *a.* (*Bot.*) Bursting, breaking open, esp. irregularly. ***ruption,** *n.* **ruptive,** *a.* **rupturable,** *a.*

rural (roor′ ål) [F., from L. *rūrālis*, from *rus rūris*, the country], *a.* Pertaining to the country as distinguished from town; pastoral, agricultural; suiting or resembling the country, rustic. **rural dean:** A clergyman, ranking below an archdeacon, charged with the inspection of a district. **ruralism, ruralist,** *n.* **rurality** (-ăl′ i ti), **ruralness,** *n.* **ruralize,** *v.i.* and *t.* **ruralization** (-zā′ shůn), *n.* **rurally,** *adv.* **ruridecanal** (roor i dė kā′ nål, -dek′ å năl), *a.* Pertaining to a rural dean or deanery.

Ruritania (roo ri tăn′ yå) [name invented by Anthony Hope], *n.* A fictitious state in S.E. Europe, scene of great adventures; an imaginary kingdom.

ruru (roo′ roo) [Maori], *n.* The morepork.

rusa (roo′ så) [Malay], *n.* A large East Indian deer.

ruscus (rŭs′ kůs) [L. *ruscum*], *n.* (*Bot.*) A genus of shrubby evergreen plants containing the butcher's broom.

ruse (rooz) [F., from *ruser*, perh. rel. to RUSH (2)], *n.* A stratagem, artifice, trick, or wile.

ruse de guerre (dė gâr′): A war stratagem. **rusé** (roo′ zā), *a.* (*fem.* **-sée,** -zā) Wily, sly, cunning.

rush (1) (rŭsh) [A.-S. *risc*, *rysc*, cp. Dut. and G. *rusch*], *n.* A plant with long thin stems or leaves, of the order *Juncaceæ*, growing mostly on wet ground, used for making baskets, mats, seats for chairs, etc., and formerly for strewing floors; a stem of this plant; (*fig.*) something of little or no worth. *v.t.* To strew with rushes; to furnish with a rush seat. **rush-bearing,** *n.* A northern country festival when rushes and garlands are carried to strew the floor of a church. **rush-bottomed,** *a.* Having a seat made of rushes. **rush-candle,** *n.* A small candle made of the pith of a rush dipped in tallow. **rushlight,** *n.* A rush-candle; any weak flickering light. **rush-lily,** *n.* A plant of the genus *Sisyrinchium* with rushy leaves and blue flowers. **rushlike,** *a.* **rushy,** *a.*

rush (2) (rŭsh) [A.-F. *russher*, O.F. *reusser*, *ruser*, perh. from a pop. L. *refūsāre*, see REFUSE (1)], *v.t.* To drive, urge, force, or push with violence and haste, to hurry; to take by sudden assault; to surmount, to pass, to seize and occupy, with dash or suddenness; (*colloq. in p.p.*) to cheat, to swindle; (*colloq.*) to charge in price. *v.i.* To move or run impetuously or precipitately; to enter or go (into) with undue eagerness or lack of consideration; to run, flow, or roll with violence and impetuosity. *n.* The act of rushing; a violent or impetuous movement, advance, dash, or onslaught; a sudden movement or thronging of people (to a gold-field, etc.); (*Cinema*) the first print from a film; (*colloq.*) extreme pressure or stress of work; a violent demand (for) or run (on) a commodity, etc. **rusher,** *n.* **rush hours:** Hours when traffic is very congested owing to people going to or leaving work.

rushy [RUSH (1)].

rusk (rŭsk) [Sp. or Port. *rosca*, twist or roll of bread], *n.* A piece of bread or cake crisped and browned in the oven; a light cake or sweetened biscuit.

Ruskinian (rŭs kin′ i ån), *n.* According to the teaching of John Ruskin (1819–1900), writer on art and social matters. *n.* A follower of Ruskin's teaching. **Ruskinese** (-nēz′), *n.* The style of Ruskin.

Russ (rŭs) [Rus. *Rusi*], *n.* A Russian; the Russian language.

russel (rŭs′ ėl) [etym. doubtful], *n.* A twilled woollen or cotton fabric or rep, also called **russel-cord.**

russet (rŭs′ ėt) [O.F. *rousset*, dim. of *rous* (F. *roux*), L. *russus*, red], *a.* Of a reddish-brown colour; *coarse, homespun, rustic, homely, simple. *n.* *A coarse homespun cloth worn by peasants; a reddish-brown colour; a rough-skinned reddish or brownish variety of apple. **russeting,** *n.* A russet apple. **russety,** *a.*

russia, russia leather (rŭsh′ å le*th*′ ėr) [name of country, see foll], *n.* A soft leather made from hides prepared with birch-bark oil, used in bookbinding, etc.

Russian (rŭsh′ ån) [med. L. *Russiānus*], *a.* Pertaining to Russia. *n.* A native of Russia; the Russian language. **Russianize,** *v.t.* **Russify,** *v.t.* **Russification** (-kā' shŭn), *n.* **Russo-,** *comb. form.* **Russophil** (rŭs' ō fil), *n.* A friend or admirer of Russia or the Russians. *a.* Friendly to Russia. **Russophilism** (rŭs of' i lizm), *n.* **Russophobe,** *n.* An enemy of Russia or the Russians. *a.* Hating or hostile to Russia. **Russophobia** (-fō' bi ȧ), *n.*

rust (rŭst) [A.-S. *rūst* (cp. Dut. *roest*, G. and Swed. *rost*, Dan. *rust*) rel. to RED], *n.* The red incrustation on iron or steel caused by its oxidation when exposed to air and moisture; any similar incrustation on metals; any corrosive or injurious accretion or influence; (*fig.*) a dull or impaired condition due to idleness, etc.; (*Bot.*) a plant disease caused by parasitic fungi of the order *Uredinales*, blight; any of these fungi. *v.i.* To contract rust; to be oxidated; to be attacked by blight; (*fig.*) to degenerate through idleness or disuse. *v.t.* To affect with rust, to corrode; to impair by idleness, disuse, etc. **rust-coloured,** *a.* **rustless,** *a.* **rusty,** *a.* Covered with or affected with or as with rust; rust-coloured; faded, discoloured by age; antiquated in appearance; harsh, husky (of the voice); (*fig.*) impaired by disuse, inaction, neglect, etc. **rustily,** *adv.* **rustiness,** *n.*

rustic (rŭs' tik) [L. *rusticus*, from *rus*, the country], *a.* Pertaining to the country, rural; like or characteristic of country people, unsophisticated, simple, artless; rude, unpolished; awkward, uncouth, clownish; of rude workmanship, coarse, plain. **rustic work:** Woodwork made of roughly-trimmed trunks, branches, etc.; masonry with a rough surface and chamfered joints. **rustically,** ***rusticly,** *adv.* **rusticity** (-tis' i ti), *n.*

rusticate (rŭs' ti kāt), *v.i.* To retire or to dwell in the country. *v.t.* To suspend for a time from residence at a University, as a punishment; (*in p.p.*) to countrify; to give a rough surface and chamfered joints to (masonry). **rustication** (-kā' shŭn), *n.*

rustle (rŭs' ėl) [imit., cp. Dut. dial. and L.G. *russeln*], *v.i.* To make a quick succession of small sounds like the rubbing of silk or dry leaves; to move or go along with this sound; (*Am.*) to steal cattle. *v.t.* To cause to make this sound. *n.* A rustling. **rustler,** *n.* One who or that which rustles; (*Am.*) a pushing, bustling person; (*Am.*) a cattle thief. **rustlingly,** *adv.*

rut (1) (rŭt) [O.F. *rut*, *ruit*, ult. from L. *rugītus*, from *rugīre*, to roar], *n.* The sexual excitement or heat of deer and some other animals; the noise made by the males at this time. *v.i.* (*past & p.p.* **rutted**) To be moved by this. *v.t.* To cover in copulation.

rut (2) (rŭt) [etym. doubtful], *n.* A sunken track made by wheels or vehicles; a hollow, a groove; (*fig.*) a settled habit or course of procedure. *v.t.* (*past & p.p.* **rutted**) To make ruts in. **rutty,** *a.*

ruta-baga (roo' tȧ bā' gȧ) [F., prob. from Swed.], *n.* The Swedish turnip.

ruth (rooth) [RUE (1), -TH], *n.* Mercy, pity, compassion, tenderness.

Ruthene (ru thēn') [med. L. *Rutheni*, *Ruteni*, rel. to *Rusi*, see RUSS], *n.* A member of the Little Russian race dwelling in Czechoslovakia and Russia. *a.* Ruthenian. **Ruthenian,** *n.* A Ruthene, a member of the Ruthenian Church; the language of the Ruthenes. *a.* Pertaining to the Ruthenes, their language, etc.

ruthenium (ru thē' ni ŭm) [*Ruthenia*, Czechoslovakia, as prec.], *n.* A white, spongy metallic element of the platinum group. **ruthenic** (-then' ik), **ruthenious** (-thē' ni ŭs), *a.* **ruthenio-,** *comb. form.*

ruthless (rooth' lės) [RUTH, -LESS], *a.* Pitiless, merciless, cruel, barbarous. ***ruthful,** *a.* **ruthlessly,** *adv.* **ruthlessness,** *n.*

rutile (roo' til) [F., from L. *rutilus*, red], *n.* (*Min.*) Red dioxide of titanium.

***ruttish** (rŭt' ish) [RUT (1), -ISH], *a.* Lustful, libidinous, lewd. ***ruttishness,** *n.*

-ry [shortened form of -ERY], *suf.* As in *Englishry*, *poultry*, *yeomanry*.

rye (rī) [A.-S. *ryge* (cp. Icel. *rūgr*, Dan. *rug*, also Dut. *rogge*, G. *roggen*)], *n.* The seeds or grain of *Secale cereale*, a cereal allied to wheat, used to make the black bread of some Continental countries; the plant bearing this; (*Am. colloq.*) rye whisky. **rye-grass,** *n.* One of various grasses of the genus *Lolium*, cultivated for fodder grass.

rye-peck (rī' pek) [etym. doubtful], *n.* An iron-shod pole used for driving into the bed of a stream to moor a punt, etc.

ryot (rī' ŏt) [Hind. *rāiyat*, *as* RAYAH], *n.* A Hindu peasant or cultivator of the soil.

S

S, s, the nineteenth letter and the fifteenth consonant of the English alphabet (*pl.* **Ss, S's, Esses**) is a voiceless sibilant, with a hard sound, as in *sin*, *so*, the sound of *z*, as in *music*, *muse*, etc., of *sh* in *sugar*, *mission*, and of *zh* in *measure*, *vision*; an S-shaped object or curve. **collar of SS** [COLLAR].

sabadilla (săb ȧ dil' ȧ) [Sp. *cebadilla*, dim. of *cebada*, barley], *n.* A Mexican and Central American liliaceous plant yielding acrid seeds from which veratrine is obtained; the barley-like seeds of this.

Sabæan (sȧ bē' ȧn) [L. *Sabæus*, Gr. *Sabæos*, from Arab. *Saba'*, Sheba], *n.* One of the ancient people of Yemen. *a.* Of or pertaining to this people.

Sabaism (sā' bȧ izm) [Heb. *çābā*, host, -ISM], *n.* The worship of the stars or the host of heaven. **Sabaistic** (-is' tik), *a.*

Sabaoth (săb' ā oth) [Heb. *çabāōth*, pl. of *çābā*, army], *n.* (*Bibl.*) Hosts, armies (in the title 'Lord God of Sabaoth').

Sabbatarian (săb' ȧ târ' i ȧn) [L. *Sabbatārius*, as foll.], *n.* A Jew who strictly observes the seventh day of the week; a Christian who observes Sunday as a Sabbath, as the Seventh-day Baptists, or who is specially strict in its observance. *a.* Observing or inculcating the observance of the Sabbath or Sunday. **Sabbatarianism,** *n.*

Sabbath (săb' ȧth) [L. *Sabbatum*, from Gr. *Sabbaton*, Heb. *shabbāth*, from *shābath*, to rest], *n.* The seventh day of the week, set apart for rest and divine worship; the Christian Sunday; (*fig.*) a time of rest. **witches' Sabbath:** A midnight assembly of witches, wizards, and demons, supposed to be convoked by the devil. **Sabbath-breaker,** *n.* One who profanes the Sabbath. **Sabbath-breaking,** *n.* **Sabbath Day:** The Jewish Sabbath (Saturday); Sunday. **Sabbathless,** *a.* **Sabbatic, -al** (sȧ băt' ik, -ȧl), *a.* Pertaining to or befitting the Sabbath. **Sabbatical year:** Every seventh year, during which the Hebrews were not to sow their fields or prune their vineyards, and were to liberate slaves and debtors; the year's leave of absence granted every seven years to a university professor. **Sabbatically,** *adv.* ***Sabbatine** (săb' ȧ tīn), *a.* **Sabbatism,** *n.* **Sabbatismal** (-tiz' mal), *a.* **Sabbatize,** *v.t.* To keep as or turn into a Sabbath. *v.i.* To keep the Sabbath.

Sabean, etc. [SABÆAN, SABIAN].

Sabellian (sȧ bel' i ȧn) [late L. *Sabelliānus* (*Sabellius*, -AN)], *a.* Pertaining to Sabellianism. *n.* A follower of Sabellius, an African priest of the 3rd cent., who taught that the persons of the Trinity are only different manifestations of one divine person. **Sabellianism,** *n.* The doctrines of Sabellius.

sabelline (sȧ bel' īn) [med. L. *sabellīnus*, from *sabellum*, SABLE], *a.* Pertaining to the sable; coloured like its fur.

Sabian (sā′ bi ăn) [Arab. *çabi'*, prob. to baptize], *n.* A member of an ancient sect who are classed in the Koran with Mohammedans, Jews, and Christians as worshippers of the true God; (*erron.*) a star-worshipper. *a.* Pertaining to Sabianism. **Sabianism,** *n.* The religion of the Sabians; (*erron.*) Sabaism.

Sabine (săb′ īn) [L. *Sabīnus*], *n.* One of an ancient Italian race inhabiting the central Apennines. *a.* Of or pertaining to this people.

sable (sā′ bėl) [O.F., from Slav., cp. Rus., Pol., and Czech, *sobol*], *n.* A small Arctic and sub-Arctic carnivorous quadruped, *Mustela zibellina*, allied to the marten, the brown fur of which is very highly valued; its skin or fur; a painter's brush made of its hair; (*Her.*) black; (*poet.*) black, esp. as the colour of mourning; (*pl.*) mourning garments. *a.* Black, dark, gloomy. *v.t.* To make dark or dismal. **sable-coloured,** *a.* Black. **sable-stoled, sable-vested,** *a.* Clothed in sables. **sabled, sably,** *a.*

sabot (săb′ ō) [F., etym. doubtful], *n.* A wooden shoe, usu. made in one piece, worn by peasantry, etc., in France, Belgium, etc.; a wooden-soled shoe; (*Ordnance*) a wooden disk fastened to a spherical projectile or a metal cap on a conical one to make these fit the gun-bore; (*Mech.*) a cap or shoe for protecting the end of a pile, etc.

sabotage (săb′ ȯ tazh), *n.* The operation of cutting shoes or sockets for railway-lines; malicious damage to a railway, industrial plant, machinery, etc., as a protest by discontented workmen, or as a non-military act of warfare. **saboteur** (săb ȯ ter′), *n.* One who commits sabotage.

Sabra (sa′ bra) [Heb.], *n.* An Israeli born in Israel.

sabre (sā′ bėr) [F., earlier *sable*, G. *sābel*, *sabel*, cp. Hung. *száblya*, Pol. *szabla*], *n.* A cavalry sword having a curved blade; (*pl.*) cavalry. *v.t.* To cut or strike down or kill with the sabre. **sabre-bill, -wing,** *n.* S. American birds. **sabre-fish,** *n.* The silver eel, *Trichiurus lepturus.* **sabre-toothed lion** or **tiger:** A large extinct feline mammal, *Machairodus*, with long upper canines. **sabretache** (săb′ ėr tăsh), *n.* A cavalry officer's leather pocket suspended on the left side from the sword-belt. **sabreur** (sa brur′), *n.* One who fights with the sabre, a cavalry-man.

sabulous (săb′ ū lŭs) [L. *sabulōsus*, from *sabulum*, sand], *a.* Sandy, gritty; (*Med.*) applied to gritty particles in the body, sediment in urine, etc. ***sabulosity** (-los′ i ti), *n.* **saburra** (să bŭr′ ă), *n.* (*Path.*) Foul granular matter accumulated in the stomach through indigestion. **saburral,** *a.* **saburration** (săb ū rā′ shŭn), *n.* (*Med.*) The application of hot sand as a bath.

sac (1) (săk) [A.-S. *sacu*, dispute, lawsuit], *n.* (*Hist.*) A right or privilege, such as that of holding a court, granted to a lord of a manor by the Crown.

sac (2) (săk) [F., from L. *saccus*, SACK], *n.* A pouch, a cavity or receptacle in an animal or vegetable; a pouch forming the envelope of a tumour, cyst, etc. **saccate, sacciform** (-si fôrm), *a.* **sacco-,** *comb. form.*

saccade (să kad′) [F., etym. unknown], *n.* A sudden check of a horse with the reins; a strong pressure of a violin bow against the strings.

saccate [SAC (2)].

saccharine, saccharin (săk′ ă rin) [F. *saccharin* (Gr. *sacchar-on*, sugar, -INE)], *n.* An intensely sweet compound obtained from toluene, a product of coal-tar, used for sweetening food for persons suffering from gout, rheumatism, diabetes, etc. *a.* Pertaining to sugar; having the qualities of sugar. **saccharate,** *n.* A salt of saccharic acid. **saccharic** (să kăr′ ik), *a.* Pertaining to or obtained from sugar. **saccharic acid:** An acid produced by the action of nitric acid on dextrose, etc. **sacchariferous** (-rif′ ėr ŭs), *a.* Producing sugar. **saccharify** (să kăr′ i fī), ***saccharize** (săk′ ă rīz), *v.t.* To convert into sugar. **saccharimeter** (-rim′ ė tėr), *n.* An instrument for determining the quantity of sugar in solutions by means of polarized light. **saccharimetry,** *n.* **saccharo-,** *comb. form.* **saccharo-colloid** (-kol′ oid) [COLLOID], *n.* Any one of the cellulose group of carbohydrates. **saccharomyces** (săk ă rō mī′ sēz), *n.* A genus of fungi comprising the yeasts. **saccharite** (săk′ ă rīt), *n.* (*Min.*) A white or whitish granular variety of feldspar. **saccharoid,** *a.* (*Geol.*) Having a granular structure. *n.* A sugar-like substance. ***saccharometer** [SACCHARIMETER]. **saccharose,** *n.* Any one of the group of sugars turning the plane of polarized light to the right and differentiated from the glucose group. **saccharous,** *a.* **saccharum,** *n.* An invert sugar obtained from cane sugar; (*Bot.*) a genus of grasses comprising the sugar-cane.

sacciform, sacco- [SAC (2)].

saccule (săk′ ūl) [L. *sacculus*, dim. of *saccus*, SAC (2)], *n.* A small sac, a cyst. **saccular, sacculate, -ated,** *a.* **sacculation.**

sacellum (să sel′ ŭm) [L. dim. of *sacrum*, shrine, neut. of *sacer*, holy], *n.* (*pl.* **-la**) (*Rom. Ant.*) A small sanctuary, usu. roofless, containing an altar; (*Eccles.*) a chapel, a shrine.

sacerdotal (săs ėr dō′ tăl) [L. *sacerdōtālis*, from *sacerdōs -dōtis*, priest (*sacer*, holy, *dōs dōtis*, cogn. with *dare*, to give)], *a.* Pertaining to priests or the priesthood; priestly; attributing sacrificial power and supernatural or sacred character to priests. ***sacerdocy** (săs′ ėr dō si), *n.* Sacerdotalism; the priestly office. **sacerdotage** (-dō′ taj), *n.* Sacerdotalism; devotion to or the devotees of the priesthood. **sacerdotalism,** *n.* **sacerdotalist,** *n.* **sacerdotalize,** *v.t.* **sacerdotally,** *adv.*

sachem (sā′ chėm, săch′ ėm) [N.Am.Ind.], *n.* A chief of certain tribes of N. American Indians; (*fig.*) a magnate, a prominent man; (*U.S.A.*) one of the governing officers of the Tammany Society in New York City. **sachemship,** *n.*

sachet (săsh′ ā) [F., dim. of SAC], *n.* A small ornamental bag or other receptacle for perfumes in the form of powder.

sack (1) (săk) [A.-S. *sacc*, L. *saccus*, Gr. *sakkos*, Heb. *saq*], *n.* A large, usu. oblong bag of strong coarse material, for holding corn, raw cotton, wool, etc.; the quantity a sack contains, as a unit of measure and weight; a sack together with its contents; a loose garment, gown, or appendage to a dress, of various kinds, a sacque; a loose-fitting waistless dress; dismissal. *v.t.* To put into a sack; to give the sack to; to beat in a race, etc. **to give** (one) or **to get the sack:** To dismiss or be dismissed. **sackcloth,** *n.* Sacking; this worn formerly in token of mourning or penitence. **sack-race,** *n.* A race in which the competitors are tied up to the neck in sacks. ***Sack-Friar** or ***Sacked-Friar,** *n.* A member of an order of 13th cent. mendicant friars who wore sackcloth. **sackful,** *n.* **sacking,** *n.* Coarse stuff of which sacks, bags, etc., are made.

sack (2) (săk) [prob. from prec., cp. F. *saccager*, It. *saccheggiare*], *v.t.* To plunder or pillage (a place taken by storm); to rifle, to ransack, to loot. *n.* The pillaging of a captured place; (*poet.*) plunder, booty. ***sackage,** *n.* **sacker,** *n.*

sack (3) (săk) [orig. *wyne seck*, F. *vin sec*, dry wine], *n.* An old name for various white wines, esp. those from Spain and the Canaries. **sack-posset, -whey,** *n.* Beverages made of sack, milk, etc.

sackage [SACK (2)].

sackbut (săk′ bŭt) [F. *saquebote*, prob. conf. with O.North.F. *saqueboute*, a lance with a hook], *n.* *A bass trumpet with a slide like the modern trombone; (*Bibl.*) an Aramaic musical stringed instrument.

sackcloth [SACK (1)]. **sacker** [SACK (2)].

sackful, sacking [SACK (1)].

sackless (săk′ lės) [A.-S. *saclēas* (SAC (1), -LESS)], *a.* Innocent; peaceable, simple, feeble-minded.

sacque (săk) [prob. var. of SACK (1)], *n.* A loose-fitting woman's gown; a loose-fitting coat hanging from the shoulders.

sacra, sacral [SACRUM].

sacrament (săk′ rȧ mĕnt) [F. *sacrement*, L. *sacrāmentum*, orig. military oath, from *sacrāre*, to make sacred, from *sacer sacris*, SACRED], *n.* A religious rite instituted as an outward and visible sign of an inward and spiritual grace (applied by the Eastern and R.-C. Churches to baptism, the Eucharist, confirmation, matrimony, penance, holy orders, and extreme unction, and by most Protestants to the first two of these); the Lord's Supper, the Eucharist; the consecrated elements; a sacred token, symbol, influence, etc.; (*Rom. Ant.*) a military oath; hence a solemn oath or engagement. *v.t.* To bind by an oath (*usu. in p.p.*). **sacramental** (-men′ tȧl), *a.* Pertaining to or constituting a sacrament; bound by oath, consecrated. *n.* A rite or observance ancillary or analogous to the sacraments. **sacramentalism,** *n.* The doctrine of the spiritual efficacy of the sacraments. **sacramentalist,** *n.* **sacramentality** (-tăl′ i ti), *n.* **sacramentally,** *adv.* **sacramentarian** (-târ′ i ȧn), *a.* Relating to the sacraments or the Sacramentarians. *n.* One holding extreme or 'high' doctrines regarding the spiritual efficacy of the sacraments; *one of the German reformers of the 16th century who opposed the Lutheran view of the sacraments and regarded them as merely signs and symbols. **sacramentarianism,** *n.* ***sacramentary,** *a.* Pertaining to a sacrament or to the Sacramentarians. *n.* An ancient book of ritual in the Western Church, containing the rites for Mass and for the administration of the sacraments generally, etc.; a Sacramentarian.

sacrarium (1) (sȧ krâr′ i ŭm) [L., from *sacer -cris*, SACRED], *n.* (*pl.* **-ia**) (*Rom. Ant.*) A sacred place where sacred things were kept, esp. the room in the house where the penates were kept, or the adytum of a temple; (*Eccles.*) the sanctuary of a church; (*R.-C. Ch.*) a piscina.

sacrarium (2) (sȧ krâr′ i ŭm) [from SACRUM], *n.* (*Ornith.*) The complex sacrum of a bird.

sacré (sa′ krā) [F., *sacré*, SACRED, int.], *v.i.* To say *sacré*, to swear.

sacred (sā′ krĕd) [p.p. of M.E. *sacren*, O.F. *sacrer*, L. *sacrāre*, to consecrate, from *sacer -cris*, holy], *a.* Dedicated to religious use, consecrated; dedicated or dear to a divinity; set apart, reserved, or specially appropriated (to); pertaining to or hallowed by religion or religious service, holy; sanctified by religion, reverence, etc., not to be profaned, inviolable. **sacred beetle:** A scarab. **Sacred College,** *n.* The collegiate body of cardinals in the Roman Catholic Church. **sacredly,** *adv.* **sacredness,** *n.*

sacrifice (săk′ ri fīs) [F., from L. *sacrificium* (*sacer -cris*, holy, SACRED, *facere*, to make)], *n.* The act of offering an animal, person, etc., esp. by immolation, or the surrender of a valued possession to a deity, as an act of propitiation, atonement, or thanksgiving; that which is so immolated or given up, a victim, an offering; (*Theol.*) the Crucifixion as Christ's offering of Himself; the Eucharist as a renewal of this or as a thanksgiving; (*fig.*) the giving up of anything for the sake of another person, object, or interest; the sale of goods at a loss; a great loss or destruction (of life, etc.). *v.t.* To offer to God or to a deity as a sacrifice; to surrender for the sake of another person, object, etc., to devote; (*colloq.*) to sell at a much reduced price. ***sacrifical,** *a.* ***sacrificant** (sȧ krif′ i kȧnt), **sacrificator** (săk′ ri fi kā tŏr), *n.* One who offers a sacrifice. ***sacrificatory,** *a.* **sacrificer** (săk′ ri fī sėr), *n.* **sacrificial** (-fish′ ȧl), *a.* **sacrificially,** adv.

sacrilege (săk′ ri lĕj) [O.F., from L. *sacrilegium*, from *sacrilegus*, a sacrilegious person (*sacer -cris*, SACRED, *legere*, to gather, to steal)], *n.* The violation or profanation of sacred things, esp. larceny from a consecrated building; *the alienation of Church property to lay uses. **sacrilegious** (-lē′ jŭs), *a.* **sacrilegiously,** *adv.* ***sacrilegiousness,** **sacrilegist,** *n.*

sacring (sā′ kring) [M.E. *sacren*, see SACRED, -ING], *n.* Consecration, esp. of the elements in the Mass, and of bishops, kings, etc. **sacring-bell,** *n.* The sanctus bell.

sacrist (sā′ krist) [O.F. *sacriste*, L. *sacrista*, from *sacer -cris*, SACRED], *n.* An officer in charge of the sacristy of a church or religious house with its contents. **sacristan** (săk′ ri stȧn), *n.* A sacrist; *a sexton. **sacristy,** *n.* An apartment in a church in which the vestments, sacred vessels, books, etc., are kept.

sacro-, sacro-costal, etc. [SACRUM].

sacrosanct (sā′ krō-, săk′ rō săngkt) [L. *sacrosanctus* (*sacro- sacer*, SACRED, *sanctus*, see SAINT)], *a.* Inviolable by reason of sanctity. **sacrosanctity,** *n.*

sacrum (sā′ krŭm) [L., neut. of *sacer*, holy], *n.* (*pl.* **-cra**) (*Anat.*) A composite bone formed by the union of vertebræ at the base of the spinal column, constituting the dorsal part of the pelvis. **sacral,** *a.* **sacro-,** *comb. form.* **sacro-costal** (sā krō kos′ tȧl), *a.* Pertaining to the sacrum and of the nature of a rib. *a.* A sacro-costal part. **sacro-iliac** (il′ i ăk), *a.* Pertaining to the sacrum and the ilium. **sacro-pubic** (-pū′ bik), *a.* Pertaining to the sacrum and the pubis.

sad (săd) [A.-S. *sæd*, sated, cp. Dut. *zat*, G. *satt*, also L. *satis*], *a.* Sorrowful, mournful; expressing sorrow; causing sorrow, unfortunate; lamentable, bad, shocking; (*prov.*) heavy, not well raised (of bread); *dull, dark-coloured. **sad-eyed, -faced, -hearted,** *a.* (*poet.*) Sorrowful or looking sorrowful. **sad-iron,** *n.* A solid smoothing iron. **sadden,** *v.t.* To make sad; (*Dyeing, etc.*) to tone down (a colour, etc.) by certain chemicals. *v.i.* To become sad. **saddish,** *a.* **sadly,** *adv.* **sadness,** *n.*

saddle (săd′ ėl) [A.-S. *sadol* (cp. Dut. *zadel*, G. *sattel*, Icel. *söthull*), whence *sadelian* (cp. Dut. *zadelen*, G. *satteln*), prob. rel. to SIT], *n.* A seat placed on an animal's back, to support a rider or load; a similar seat on a cycle, agricultural machine, etc.; an object resembling a saddle; a joint of mutton, etc., including the loins; a supporting piece in various machines, suspension-bridges, gun-mountings, tackle, etc.; a depressed part of a ridge between two summits, a col; (*Geol.*) a raised and symmetrical anticlinal fold. *v.t.* To put a saddle on; to put (a burden) on; to load or burden (with a duty, etc.). **saddleback,** *n.* A roof or coping sloping up at both ends or with a gable at each end; a saddle-backed hill; a name for various fish, moths, birds, etc., esp. the hooded crow. *a.* Saddlebacked. **saddlebacked,** *a.* Having a low back with an elevated neck and head (of a horse); curving up at each end. **saddle-bag,** *n.* One of a pair of bags connected by straps slung across a horse, etc., from the saddle; a kind of carpeting woven in imitation of Persian saddle-bags for camels. **saddle-bow,** *n.* The pommel. **saddle-cloth,** *n.* A cloth laid on a horse under the saddle, a housing. **saddle-corporal, -sergeant,** *n.* A regimental saddler. **saddle-pillar,** *n.* The saddle support of a cycle. **saddle-spring,** *n.* The spring of a cycle saddle. **saddle-tree,** *n.* The frame of a saddle; the tulip-tree. **saddleless,** *a.* **saddler** (săd′ lėr), *n.* A maker or dealer in saddles and harness; (*Mil.*) a non-commissioned officer in charge of the harness in a cavalry regiment. **saddlery,** *n.*

Sadducee (săd′ ū sē) [L. *Sadducæi*, pl., from Gr. *Saddoukaioi*, prob. from *Zadok*, name of High Priest], *n.* One of a sect among the Jews, arising in the 2nd cent. B.C., who adhered to the written law to the exclusion of tradition, and denied the resurrection from the dead, existence of spirits, etc. **Sadducean** (-sē′ ȧn), *a.* **sadduceeism,** *n.*

sadism (sa′ dizm) [F. *sadisme*, from the Marquis de *Sade* (1740–1814), French writer], *n.* Sexual perversion characterized by a passion for cruelty. **sadist,** *n.*

sad-iron, sadly, sadness [SAD].

safari (să far′ i) [Ar. *safar*, a journey], *n.* A hunting expedition.

safe (sāf) [M.E. and O.F. *sauf*, L. *salvus*, whole, uninjured], *a.* Free or secure from danger, damage, or evil; uninjured, unharmed, sound; affording security; not dangerous, hazardous, or risky; cautious, prudent, trusty; unfailing, certain, sure; no longer dangerous, secure from escape or from doing harm. *n.* A receptacle for keeping things safe, a steel fire-proof and burglar-proof receptacle for valuables, a strong-box; a cupboard or other receptacle for keeping meat and other provisions in. **safe-conduct,** *n.* An official document or passport ensuring a safe passage, esp. in a foreign country or in time of hostilities. **v.t.* To conduct safely. **safe deposit,** *n.* A specially-constructed building or basement with safes for renting. **safe-keeping,** *n.* The act of keeping or preserving in safety; secure guardianship; custody. **safely,** *adv.* **safeness.**

safeguard (sāf′ gard), *n.* One who or that which protects; a proviso, precaution, circumstance, etc., that tends to save loss, trouble, danger, etc.; a safe-conduct, a passport. **v.t.* To make safe or secure by precaution, stipulation, etc. **safeguarding,** *n.* (*Econ.*) Protecting specified home industries against foreign competition by customs duties.

safety (sāf′ ti), *n.* The state of being safe, freedom from injury, danger, or risk; safe-keeping or custody; (*colloq.*) a safety-bicycle. **safety-bicycle,** *n.* A low bicycle with wheels of equal size. **safety-catch, safety-lock,** *n.* A lock that cannot be picked easily; a device in a firearm to prevent accidental discharge. **safety curtain:** (*Theat.*) A fire-proof curtain that cuts off the stage from the audience. **safety-fuse,** *n.* A fuse that allows an explosive to be fired without danger to the person igniting it. **safety-lamp,** *n.* A miner's lamp protected by wire or gauze so as not to ignite fire-damp. **safety-match,** *n.* A match that ignites only on a surface treated with a special ingredient. **safety-pin,** *n.* A pin with a part for keeping it secure and guarding the point. **safety-razor,** *n.* One mounted on a handle with a guard to prevent cutting the skin. **safety-valve,** *n.* A valve on a boiler automatically opening to let steam escape to relieve pressure and prevent explosion; (*fig.*) any harmless means of relieving anger, excitement, etc.

saffian (săf′ i ȧn) [Rus. *safiyanu*], *n.* Leather prepared from goatskin or sheepskin tanned with sumac and dyed yellow or red.

safflower (săf′ lou ėr) [Dut. *saffloer*, O.F. *saffleur*, obs. It. *saffiore*], *n.* A thistle-like plant, *Carthamus tinctorius*, with orange flowers yielding a dye, used in rouge, etc.

saffranin [SAFFRON].

saffron (săf′ rȯn) [O.F. *safran*, Arab. *za'farān*], *n.* Colouring matter prepared from the stigmas of *Crocus sativus*, the autumnal crocus, used for colouring and flavouring; this plant; the colour deep orange; the meadow saffron, *Colchicum autumnale*; the bastard saffron or safflower. *a.* Saffron-coloured, deep yellow. *v.t.* To make yellow; to tinge with saffron. **saffrony,** *a.* **safranin,** *n.* (*Chem.*) One of a series of basic compounds derived from coal-tars and used in dyeing; the colouring-matter of saffron.

sag (săg) [prob. of Scand. orig. (cp. Dan. and Norw. *sakke*, Dut. *zakken*)], *v.i.* (*past & p.p.* **sagged**) To droop, to sink, to yield or give way esp. in the middle, under weight or pressure; to bend, to hang sideways; to decline (of prices, esp. of stocks); (*Naut.*) to drift to leeward. *v.t.* To cause to give way, bend, or curve sideways. *n.* The act or state of sagging or giving way; the amount of this; (*Naut.*) a sideways drift or tendency to leeward. **saggy,** *a.*

saga (sa′ gȧ) [Icel., cogn. with SAW (2)], *n.* A mediæval prose narrative recounting family or public events in Iceland or Scandinavia, usu. by contemporary or nearly contemporary native writers; a story of heroic adventure; a series of books relating the history of a family.

sagacious (sȧ gā′ shŭs) [L. *sagax -ācis* (rel. to *sagīre*, to perceive)], *a.* Intellectually keen or quick to understand or discern, intelligent, perspicacious, shrewd, wise; characterized by wisdom and discernment (of policy, etc.); sensible, quick-scented (of animals). **sagaciously,** *adv.* **sagaciousness, sagacity** (-găs′ i ti), *n.*

sagamore (săg′ ȧ môr) [N.Am.Ind. *sagamo*], *n.* A N. American Indian chief, a sachem.

sagan (sā′ gȧn) [Heb.], *n.* The deputy of the Jewish high priest.

sagapenum (săg ȧ pē′ nŭm) [late L., from Gr. *sagapēnon*], *n.* A gum resin obtained from *Ferula Persica*, formerly used to relieve spasms.

sage (1) (sāj) [M.E. and A.-F. *sauge*, L. *salvia*], *n.* A grey-leaved aromatic plant of the genus *Salvia*, esp. *S. officinalis*, formerly much used in medicine, now employed in cookery. **sage-brush,** *n.* A shrubby plant of various species of *Artemisia*, abounding in sterile regions in the western U.S.A. **sage-cheese,** *n.* Cheese flavoured and coloured with layers of or an infusion of sage. **sage-cock, -grouse,** *n.* The largest of the American grouse, *Centrocercus urophasianus*, frequenting the sage-brush regions. **sage-green,** *n.* A greyish green. **sagy,** *a.*

sage (2) (sāj) [F., ult. from pop. L. *sapius*, from *sapere*, to be wise], *a.* Wise, discreet, prudent; judicious, well-considered; grave, serious- or solemn-looking. *n.* A man of great wisdom, esp. one of past times with a traditional reputation for wisdom. **sagely,** *adv.* **sageness,** *n.* **sageship,** *n.*

sagene (1) (sȧ jēn′) [L. *sagēna*, Gr. *sagēnē*, cp. SEINE], *n.* A fishing-net.

sagene (2) (sa′ zhen) [Rus.], *n.* A Russian measure of length, about 7 English feet.

saggar (săg′ ȧr) [perh. corr. of SAFEGUARD], *n.* A vessel of fire-proof pottery in which delicate porcelain is enclosed while in a kiln. **saggar-house,** *n.*

saggy [SAG].

sagitta (sȧ jit′ ȧ) [L., arrow], *n.* (*Geom.*) The versed sine of an arc; (*Zool.*) a genus of small transparent pelagic worms; (*Astron.*) a northern constellation. **sagittal,** *a.* Pertaining to or resembling an arrow. **Sagittarius** (târ′ i ŭs), *n.* The Archer, the ninth sign of the zodiac, which the sun enters 22 Nov. **sagittary** (săj′ i tȧr i), *n.* A centaur; sagittarius; (*Shak.*) perh. the arsenal at Venice. **a.* Pertaining to arrows. **sagittate,** *a.* (*Nat. Hist.*) Shaped like an arrow-head. **sagittiferous** (-tif′ ėr ŭs), *a.* **saggittilingual** (-lin′ gwȧl), *a.* Having an arrow-like tongue.

sago (sā′ gō) [Malay *sāgu*], *n.* (*pl.* **sagos**) The soft inner portion of the trunk of several palms or cycads, the starch of which is separated and used as food.

sagum (sā′ gŭm) [L.], *n.* (*pl.* **-ga**) The military cloak worn by ancient Roman soldiers.

sagy [SAGE (1)].

sahib (sa′ ib) [Hind. from Arab. *ṣāḥib*, friend, companion], *n.* The title used in India and Persia in addressing Europeans; (*colloq.*) a gentlemanly man.

sahlite (sa′ līt) [from *Sahla*, in Sweden], *n.* A green variety of pyroxene.

sai (sī) [Tupi-Guarani *çahy*], *n.* A S. American monkey, *Cimia capucina*.

saic (sā′ ik) [F. *saïque*, Turk. *shāīqā*], *n.* A Levantine sailing-vessel.

said, *past & p.p.* [SAY (1)].

saiga (sā′-, sī′ gȧ) [Rus.], *n.* An antelope, *Saiga Tartarica*, of the steppes of Eastern Europe and Western Asia.

sail (sāl) [A.-S. *segel, segl* (cp. Dut. *zeil*, G. *segel*, Icel. *segl*)], *n.* A piece of canvas or other fabric spread on rigging to catch the wind, and cause a ship or boat to move in the water; (*collect.*) some or all of a ship's sails; a ship or vessel; (*collect.*) a specified number of ships in a squadron, etc.; an excursion by sail or (*loosely*) by water; anything like a sail in form or function; the arm of a windmill; the dorsal fin of some fish; a wing. *v.i.* To move or be driven forward by the action of the wind upon sails; to be conveyed in a vessel by water; to set sail; to pass gently (along), to float (as a bird), to glide; to go along in a stately manner. *v.t.* To pass over in a ship, to navigate; to perform by sailing; to manage the navigation of (a ship); to cause to sail, to set afloat. **to make sail:** To set sail; to extend an additional quantity of sail. **to set sail:** To begin a voyage. **to shorten sail:** To reduce the amount of sail spread. **to strike sail:** To lower sails suddenly; (*fig.*) to give way, to submit. **under sail:** With sails spread. **sail-arm,** *n.* An arm of a windmill. **sailcloth,** *n.* Canvas, etc., for making sails; a kind of dress-material. **sail-fish,** *n.* A fish with a large dorsal fin, as the sword-fish or the basking shark. **sail-loft,** *n.* A large apartment where sails are cut out and made. **sail-room,** *n.* An apartment on board ship where spare sails are stowed. **sail-yard,** *n.* A horizontal spar on which sails are extended. ***sailable,** *a.* **sailer,** *n.* A ship (with reference to her power or manner of sailing). **sailing-master,** *n.* An officer whose duty it is to navigate a yacht, etc. **sailless,** *a.* **full sail:** With all sail set and a fair wind.

sailor (sā′ lŏr), *n.* A seaman, a mariner, esp. one of the crew as dist. from an officer. **good, bad sailor,** *n.* One who is not, or who is, liable to be seasick. **sailor-hat,** *n.* A flat-crowned narrow-brimmed straw hat worn by women, or one with a turned-up brim for children. **sailor-man,** *n.* (*colloq.*) A seaman. **sailor's-knot:** A kind of reef-knot used in tying a neck-tie. **sailor-like, sailorly,** *a.* **sailoring,** *n.* **sailorless,** *a.*

***sain** (1) (sān) [A.-S. *segnian*, L. *signāre*, to SIGN], *v.t.* To make the sign of the cross on; to bless, to guard from evil by divine or supernatural power.

***sain** (2), *p.p.* [SAY (1)].

sainfoin (sān′ foin) [F. *sainfoin*, L. *sānum*, SANE, *fænum*, hay], *n.* A leguminous herb, *Onobrychis sativa*, resembling clover, grown for fodder.

saint (sānt, as *pref.* sȧnt) [O.F., from L. *sanctus*, p.p. of *sancīre*, to make holy, rel. to *sacer*, SACRED], *a.* Holy (esp. of persons canonized or recognized by the Church as pre-eminently holy and deserving of veneration). *n.* A person eminent for piety and virtue, a holy person; one of the blessed in heaven; one canonized by the Church; (*pl.*) the name used by the Mormons and members of some other sects in speaking of themselves. *v.t.* To canonize; to regard or address as a saint. *v.i.* To act as a saint. **St. Andrew's cross** [CROSS]. **St. Anthony's fire, St. Elmo's fire** [FIRE]. **St. Bernard** or **St. Bernard dog:** A large and powerful breed of dog kept by the monks of the Hospice in the Great St. Bernard Pass to rescue travellers. **Saint-John's-wort,** *n.* (*Bot.*) Any species of the genus *Hypericum*. **St. Martin's summer:** A spell of mild weather in late autumn. **St. Monday:** Monday turned into a holiday by workmen. **St. Vitus's dance** [DANCE]. **saint's-bell,** *n.* The sanctus-bell. **saint's day:** A day dedicated to the commemoration of a particular saint, esp. the patron saint of a church, school, etc. **Saint Stephen's:** The British parliament (so named from the chapel within the precincts of the Houses of Parliament). **St. Valentine's day** [VALENTINE]. **saintdom, sainthood,** *n.* **saintlike, saintly,** *a.* **saintliness,** *n.* **sainting,** *n.* **saintship,** *n.* **sainted,** *a.* Canonized; gone to heaven; holy, pious.

St.-Simonian (sānt-, sȧnt si mō′ ni ȧn), *n.* An adherent of the Comte de St.-Simon (1760–1825), who advocated the establishment of State ownership and distribution of earnings according to capacity and labour. *a.* Of or pertaining to his doctrines. **St.-Simonianism, -Simonism** (-sī′ mŏ nizm), *n.* **St.-Simonist, -Simonite,** *n.*

sair, etc. (*Sc.*) [SERVE, SORE].

***saith,** *3rd sing.* [SAY (1)].

saithe (sāth) [Sc., from Icel. *seithr*, cp. Gael. *saigh*], *n.* The coal-fish.

sajou (sȧ zhoo′) [F., also *sajouassu*, Tupi-Guarani *sauiassu*], *n.* A small South American monkey, one of the sapajous or the capuchin monkeys.

sake (sāk) [A.-S. *sacu*, SAC (1)], *n.* End, purpose; desire of obtaining; account, reason, cause. **for old sake's sake:** In memory of days gone by. **for the sake of:** Because of, out of consideration for. **for God's sake:** A solemn adjuration.

saké (săk′ ā) [Jap.], *n.* A fermented liquor made from rice.

saker (sā′ kėr) [F. *sacre*, Sp. and Port. *sacro*, Arab. *çaqr*], *n.* A large falcon used in hawking, esp. the female; *a small piece of artillery. **sakeret,** *n.* The male of the saker, which is smaller than the female.

saki (sa′ ki) [F., prob. from Tupi-Guarani *çahy*, SAI], *n.* Any monkey of the S. American genera *Pithecia* or *Brachiurus*.

sakieh (săk′ i ė) [Arab. *sāqiyah*, fem. pres.p. of *saqā*, to irrigate], *n.* An apparatus used in Egypt for raising water, consisting of a vertical wheel or wheel and chain carrying pots or buckets.

sal (1) (săl) [L.], *n.* (*Chem. and Pharm.*) Salt (used only with qualifying word). **sal alembroth** (-ȧ lem′ brŏth): A compound of corrosive sublimate of mercury and sal-ammoniac. **sal-ammoniac,** *n.* Ammonia. ***sal-gem,** *n.* Rock salt. **sal-prunella** (-prŭ nel′ ȧ), *n.* Nitrate of potash fused and cast into cakes or balls. **sal-seignette** (-sā nyet′), *n.* Rochelle salt. **sal-soda,** *n.* Impure carbonate of soda, washing soda. **sal volatile** (-vŏ lăt′ i li): An aromatic solution of ammonium carbonate.

sal (2) (sal, sawl) [Hindi], *n.* A large Indian timber tree.

salaam (sȧ lam′) [Arab. *salam*], *n.* A ceremonious salutation or obeisance among Orientals. *v.t.* To make a salaam.

salable [SALE].

salacious (sȧ lā′ shŭs) [L. *salax -ācis*, cogn. with *salīre*, to leap], *a.* Lustful, lecherous. **salaciously,** *adv.* **salaciousness, salacity** (-lăs′ i ti), *n.*

salad (săl′ ȧd) [O.F. *salade*, O.It. *salata*, pop. L. *salāta*, p.p. of *salāre*, to salt, from SAL (1)], *a.* A dish of vegetables or fruit with dressing, etc., so as to be eaten raw; any herb or other vegetable suitable for eating raw. **salad-cream, -dressing,** *n.* A mixture of oil, vinegar, mustard, etc., for dressing salads. **salad days:** The time of youth and inexperience. **salad-oil,** *n.* A superior quality of olive-oil. **salading,** *n.* Herbs, etc., for salads.

salal (săl′ ȧl) [Chinook], *n.* An evergreen shrub, *Gaultheria shallon*, of California, etc., bearing grape-like edible berries.

salamander (săl′ ȧ măn dėr) [F. *salamandre*, L. and Gr. *salamandra*], *n.* A lizard-like animal anciently believed to live in fire; a spirit or genie fabled to live in fire; (*fig.*) any one who can stand great heat, a soldier who is unperturbed under fire; various implements and utensils used in a heated state; (*Zool.*) an amphibian of the family *Urodela*. **salamandrian** (-măn′ dri ȧn), **salamandrine,** *a.* **salamandroid,** *a.* and *n.*

salame (sa la′ mā) [It.], *n.* A highly-seasoned Italian sausage.

salangane (săl′ ȧng gān) [F., from Luzon *salamga*], *n.* A Chinese swallow that builds edible nests.

salary (săl′ ȧ ri) [A.-F. *salarie* (F. *salaire*), L. *salārium*, orig. salt-money given to soldiers, from SAL (1)], *n.* Fixed pay given periodically for work not of a manual or mechanical kind. *v.t.* To pay a salary to. **salaried,** *a*,

sale (sāl) [A.-S. *sala*, prob. from Icel. *sala*, cogn. with SELL], *n.* The act of selling; the exchange of a commodity for money or other equivalent; an auction; a disposal of a shop's remaining goods at reduced prices; demand, market. **sales resistance:** Apathy or opposition of a prospective customer requiring persuasiveness by the salesman. **bill of sale** [BILL (3)]. **saleroom,** *n.* A room in which goods are sold, an auction-room. **sale-work,** *n.* Work made for sale; work done in a perfunctory way. **sale of work:** A sale of needle-work, etc., for charitable purposes. **saleable, salable,** *a.* **saleableness, saleability** (-bil' i ti), *n.* **salesman, -woman,** *n.* A person employed to sell goods, esp. in a shop. **salesmanship,** *n.* The art of selling, skill in persuading prospective purchasers. **sales talk:** Persuasive or attractive arguments to influence a possible purchaser.

***salebrous** (săl' ė brůs) [late L. *salebrōsus*, from L. *salebra*, ruggedness], *a.* Rough, rugged, uneven.

salep (săl' ėp) [F. and Turk., from Arab. *tha' leb*], *n.* A farinaceous meal made from the dried roots of *Orchis mascula* and other orchidaceous plants.

saleratus (săl ė rā' tůs) [mod. L. *sal aerātus*, aerated salt], *n.* An impure bicarbonate of potash or soda, much used as baking powder.

sale-room, salesman, -woman [SALE].

Salian (1) (sā' li ån) [L. *Salii*, from *salīre*, to leap, -AN], *a.* (*Rom. Ant.*) Pertaining to the Salii or priests of Mars.

Salian (2) (sā' li ån) [late L. *Salii*, the tribe, -AN], *a.* Of or pertaining to a Frankish tribe on the lower Rhine to which the ancestors of the Merovingians belonged. *n.* One of this tribe. **Salic** (săl' ik), *a.* Salian. **Salic law** (1) or **code:** A Frankish law-book written in Latin extant during the Merovingian and Crolingian periods. **Salic** (or **Salique) law** (2) (så lēk'): A law derived from this excluding females from succession to the throne, esp. as the fundamental law of the French monarchy.

salicet (săl' i set) [as foll.], *n.* An organ-stop with a note like that of a willow-pipe. **salicetum** (-sē' tům), *n.* A garden or arboretum of willows.

salicin (săl' i sin) [F. *salicine* (L. *salix -icis*, willow)], *n.* (*Chem.*) A bitter crystalline compound obtained from the bark of willows and poplars, used medicinally. **salicional,** *n.* Salicet. **salicyl,** *n.* The hypothetical radical of salicylic acid. **salicylate** (så lis' i låt), *n.* A salt of salicylic acid. *v.t.* (-lāt) To salicylize. **salicylic** (-sil' ik), *a.* Derived from the willow; belonging to a series of benzene derivatives of salicin; derived from salicylic acid. **salicylize** (så lis' i līz), *v.t.* To impregnate with salicylic acid. **salicylism,** *n.* **salicylous,** *a.*

salient (sā' li ėnt) [L. *saliens -ntem*, pres.p. of *salīre*, to leap], *a.* Leaping, jumping, springing; pointing or projecting outwards; shooting out (of water); conspicuous, prominent, noticeable; (*Her.*) represented in a leaping posture. *n.* A salient angle; (*Fortif. and Mil.*) a portion of defensive works or of a line projecting towards the enemy. **salience, -ency,** *n.* **saliently,** *adv.*

Salientia (săl i en' shå), *n.* (*Zool.*) An order of *Amphibia*, including frogs and toads.

saliferous (så lif' ėr ůs) [L. *sal salis*, SAL, -FEROUS], *a.* Bearing or producing salt (of strata). **saliferous system:** The Triassic rocks, from the deposits of salt. ***salify** (săl' i fī), *v.t.* and *i.* To form a salt. **salifiable,** *a.* **salification** (-ka' shůn), *n.*

saline (sā' līn) [SAL (1), -INE], *a.* Consisting of or partaking of the qualities of salt; containing or impregnated with salt or salts. *n.* A salt-lake, -spring, etc.; a salt-pan, salt-works, etc.; a saline substance, esp. a purgative. **salina** (så lī' nå), *n.* A salt-marsh; salt-works. ***salineness, salinity** (så lin' i ti), *n.* ***saliniferous** [SALIFEROUS]. **salino-**, *comb. form.* **salinometer** (-nom' ė tėr), *n.* An instrument for ascertaining the density of brine in the boilers of marine steam-engines. **salinoterrene** (-tė rēn'), *a.* Consisting of a salt and earth. ***salinous** (så lī' nůs), *a.*

Salique [SALIC, see SALIAN (2)].

saliva (så lī' vå) [L.], *n.* An odourless, colourless, somewhat viscid liquid consisting of secretions of the salivary and mucous glands into the mouth, spittle. ***salival,** *a.* **salivant** (săl' i vånt), *a.* Exciting salivation. *n.* A medicine exciting salivation. **salivary** (să' li vå ri), *a.* **salivate,** *v.t.* (*Med.*) To excite an unusual secretion and discharge of saliva, usually by the use of mercury. *v.i.* To secrete or discharge saliva in excess. **salivation** (-vā' shůn), *n.* ***salivous** (så lī' vůs), *a.*

Salix (săl' iks) [L.], *n.* (*Bot.*) A genus of trees containing the willow.

salle (sal) [F., from Teut., cp. A.-S. *sæl*, G. *saal*], *n.* A hall, a spacious room. ***salle à manger:*** (a man zhā) A dining-room. ***salle d'attente:*** (da tant) A waiting-room at a railway-station.

sallee (săl' ē) [Austral. abor.], *n.* Name given to several kinds of acacia; a species of eucalyptus.

Sallee-man (săl' i măn) [*Sallee*, port in Morocco, MAN], *n.* A Moorish pirate or pirate-ship, also called **Sallee rover.**

sallenders (săl' ėn dėrz) [F. *solandre*, etym. doubtful], *n.pl.* A dry scabby inflammation in the hock-joint of a horse's hind-leg.

***sallet** (săl' ėt) [earlier *salade*, F. *salade*, It. *celata*, prob. from L. *cælāta*, fem. p.p. of *cælāre*, to engrave or chase (a helmet)], *n.* A light hemispherical, crestless helmet with the back curving away, worn by 15th-cent. foot-soldiers.

sallow (1) (săl' ō) [A.-S. *sealh* (cp. Icel. *selja*, O.H.G. *salaha*, also L. *salix*, Gr. *helikē*)], *n.* A willow-tree, esp. one of the low shrubby varieties; a willow-shoot, an osier; any of various moths feeding on willows. **sallowy,** *a.*

sallow (2) (săl' ō) [A.-S. *salu* (cp. M.Dut. *salu*, Icel. *sölr*, O.H.G. *salo*)], *a.* Of a sickly-yellowish or pale-brown colour. *v.t.* To make sallow. **sallowish,** *a.* **sallowness,** *n.*

sally (1) (săl' i) [F. *saillie*, from *saillir*, to rush out, L. *salīre*, to leap], *n.* A sudden rushing out or sortie of troops from a besieged place against besiegers; an issuing forth, an excursion; an ebullition of spirits, etc., an outburst, a flight of fancy or wit, a bantering remark, etc.; *an act of levity, an escapade. *v.i.* To rush out suddenly (of troops); to go (out or forth) on a journey, excursion, etc.; *to leap or come out suddenly. **sally-port,** *n.* (*Fort.*) A postern or passage for making sallies from.

sally (2) (săl' i) [?], *n.* The part of a bell-ringer's rope covered with wool for holding; the first movement of a bell when set for ringing. **sally-hole,** *n.* The hole through which the bell-rope is passed.

Sally-lunn (săl' i lŭn) [*Sally Lunn*, who hawked them at Bath, *c.* 1800], *n.* A sweet tea-cake eaten hot and buttered.

salmagundi (săl må gŭn' di) [F. *salmagondis*, etym. doubtful], *n.* A dish of chopped meat, anchovies, eggs, oil, vinegar, etc.; a multifarious mixture, a medley, a miscellany.

salmiac (săl' mi åk), *n.* Native sal-ammoniac.

salmis (săl' mē) [F., prob. from SALMAGUNDI], *n.* A ragout, esp. of game-birds stewed with wine and other ingredients.

salmon (săm' ȯn) [M.E. and A.-F. *saumoun* (O.F. and F. *saumon*), L. *salmōnem*, nom. *-mo*], *n.* A larger silvery, pink-fleshed fish of the genus *Salmo*, esp. *S. salar*, an anadromous fish, fished both for food and sport. *a.* Salmon-coloured. **salmon-colour,** *n.* The colour of salmon flesh, pink. **salmon-coloured,** *a.* **salmon-ladder, -leap, -pass, -stair, -weir,** *n.* A series of steps, zigzags, or other contrivances to enable salmon to get past a dam or waterfall. **salmon-parr** [PARR]. **salmon-peal,** *n.* A salmon weighing less than 2 lb. **salmon-trout,** *n.* An anadromous fish, *Salmo trutta*, resembling the salmon but smaller. ***salmonet,** *n.* A samlet. **salmonoid** (săl' mȯ noid), *a.* and *n.*

salon (sa' lon) [F., from It. *salone*, augmented form of *sala*, SALLE], *n.* A reception-room, esp. in a great house in France; a periodical reunion of eminent personages in the reception-room, esp. of a Parisian lady; (*pl.*) fashionable circles. **the Salon:** An annual exhibition of pictures, etc., esp. that held at Paris.

saloon (sȧ loon′) [from prec.], *n.* A large room or hall, esp. one suitable for social receptions, public entertainments, etc.; a large cabin for (usu. first-class) passengers on board ship; (*Motor.*) a closed motor-car with no internal partitions; a saloon-carriage; (*Am.*) a drinking-bar, a public-house; a public room applied to some specified purpose (*usu. in comb.*, as *dancing-saloon, hairdressing-saloon*). **saloon bar:** The more reserved bar in a public-house. **saloon car,** *n.* (*Motor.*) An enclosed car (*Am.* a sedan). **saloon-carriage,** *n.* A large railway-carriage without compartments, often arranged as a drawing-room. **saloon-pistol, -rifle,** *n.* Fire-arms suitable for short-range practice in a shooting saloon.

saloop (sȧ loop′) [var. of SALEP], *n.* An infusion of sassafras, etc., formerly used with milk and sugar as a beverage instead of tea or coffee; salep.

Salopian (sȧ lō′ pi ȧn) [*Salop*, Shropshire, from A.-F. *Sloppesberie*, corr. of A.-S. *Scrobbesbyrig*, Shrewsbury], *n.* A native of Shropshire. *a.* Pertaining to Shropshire.

salpicon (săl′ pi kŏn) [F. and Sp., from *salpicar*, to pickle], *n.* Stuffing made of chopped meat and vegetables.

Salpiglossis (săl pi glos′ is) [Gr. *salpinx -ngos*, trumpet, *glōssa*, tongue], *n.* A genus of S. American herbaceous plants with handsome flowers.

salpingitis (săl pin jī′ tis) [Gr. *salpinx -ngos*, trumpet, -ITIS], *n.* (*Path.*) Inflammation of the Eustachian or the Fallopian tubes. **salpingitic** (-jit′ ik), *a.* **salpinx,** *n.* The Eustachian or the Fallopian tube.

salse (săls) [F., from It. *salsa*, orig. a volcano at Salsuolo, near Modena], *n.* A mud-volcano.

salsify (săl′ si fi) [F. *salsifis*, etym. doubtful], *n.* A composite plant, *Tragopogon porrifolius*, the purple goat's-beard, the root of which is eaten.

salsilla (săl sil′ ȧ) [Sp., dim. of *salsa*, SAUCE], *n.* The tubers of *Bomarea edulis* and *B. salsilla*, eaten in the West Indies.

Salsola (săl′ sō lȧ) [It., dim. of *salso*, SALT, a.], *n.* (*Bot.*) A genus of herbs and shrubby plants comprising the saltworts. **salsolaceous** (-lā′ shŭs), *a.*

salt (sawlt) [A.-S. *sealt* (cp. Dut. *zout*, G. *salz*, Icel., Dan., and Swed. *salt*, also L. *sal*, Gr. *hals*)], *n.* Chloride of sodium, used for seasoning and preserving food, obtained from sea-water or brine by evaporation or in crystalline form in beds of various geological age; that which gives flavour; relish, piquancy, pungency, wit, repartee, brilliance in talk, etc.; a salt-cellar; (*colloq.*) a sailor; a salt-marsh or salting; (*Chem.*) a compound formed by the union of basic and acid radicals, an acid the hydrogen of which is wholly or partially replaced by a metal; a salt or other chemical substance used as a medicine; (*pl.*) smelling salts. *a.* Impregnated or flavoured with or tasting of salt, saline; cured with salt; living or growing in salt water; pungent (of wit, etc.); bitter (of grief); indecent, salacious. *v.t.* To sprinkle or season with salt; to cure or preserve with salt; to make salt; (*Phot.*) to treat (paper, etc.) with a solution of a salt. *v.i.* To deposit salt from a saline substance. **salt bath,** *n.* (*Metall.*) A bath of molten salts used in the hardening or tempering of steel. **salt-box,** *n.* A wooden box for holding salt; (*slang*) a prison-cell. **salt-bush,** *n.* (*Austral.*) A shrubby plant of the goose-foot family on which stock feed. **not worth one's salt:** Worthless, not worth keeping. **salt of the earth:** One of the utmost worth. **salt-cake,** *n.* Crude sulphate of soda, prepared for the use of glass- and soap-makers. **salt-cat,** *n.* A mixture of salt, gravel, cummin seed, and stale urine given to pigeons. **salt-cellar** [A.-F. *saler*, O.F. *saliere* (*salière*), salt-cellar, assim. to CELLAR], *n.* A vessel for holding salt at table. **salt-glaze,** *n.* A glaze produced on pottery by putting salt into the kiln after firing. ***salt-horse, salt-junk,** *n.* Dry salt beef for use at sea. **salt-lick,** *n.* A place to which cattle resort to lick ground impregnated with salt. **salt-marsh,** *n.* Land liable to be overflowed by the sea, esp. used for pasturage or for collecting salt. **salt-mine,** *n.* A mine for rock-salt. **salt-pan,** *n.* A shallow depression near the sea in which sea-water is evaporated in order to obtain salt a vessel in which brine is evaporated at salt-works. **salt-pit,** *n.* A pit where salt is obtained. **salt-rheum,** *n.* *A running cold; (*Am.*) a vague term for almost all non-febrile cutaneous eruptions. **salt water:** Sea-water. **salt-water,** *a.* Living in or pertaining to the sea. **salt-works,** *n.* A factory for making salt. **salt-wort,** *n.* One of various plants of the genus *Salsola* or *Salicornia*, growing in salt-marshes and on seashores. **above the salt:** At the higher part of a table, above the salt-cellar. **Attic salt** [ATTIC (1)]. **below the salt:** Among the less distinguished company. **in salt:** Sprinkled with salt or steeped in brine for curing. **salt of lemon** [LEMON]. **to eat one's salt:** To accept one's hospitality. **to salt a mine:** To put pieces of ore, etc., in position so as to represent it as profitable to work. **to salt an account,** etc.: To put down excessively high prices. **with a grain of salt:** With doubt or reserve. **salter,** *n.* One who salts (fish, etc.); one who makes or sells salt; a workman at a salt-works. **saltern,** *n.* A salt manufactory; a series of pools for evaporating sea-water. **saltiness,** *n.* **salting,** *n.* The application of salt for preservation, etc.; (*pl.*) salt-lands, a salt-marsh. **saltish,** *a.* **saltishly,** *adv.* **saltishness,** *n.* **saltless,** *a.* **saltness,** *n.* **salts,** *n.pl.* (*colloq.*) Smelling-salts; a name for various chemical salts, as Epsom salts. **salty,** *a.* Saltish; witty.

saltant (săl′ tȧnt) [L. *saltans -ntem*, pres.p. of *saltāre*, freq. of *salīre*, to leap], *a.* (*Her.*) Salient (of figures of small animals); leaping.

saltarello (săl tȧ rel′ ō) [It., from *saltare*, prec.], *n.* An Italian or Spanish dance characterized by sudden skips; the music for such dance.

saltation (săl tā′ shŭn) [L. *saltātio*, from *saltāre*, see SALTANT], *n.* A leaping or bounding; an abrupt transition or variation; (*Path.*) a palpitation or beating. **saltatorial** (-tôr′ i ȧl), **saltatorian, saltatorious, saltatory** (săl′ tȧ tŏr i), *a.*

saltigrade (săl′ ti grād) [L. *saltus*, leap, from *saltāre*, see SALTANT, *-gradus*, walking], *a.* Formed for leaping (of legs). *n.* One of the *Saltigrada*, a family of spiders that approach their prey stealthily and suddenly spring on it.

***saltimbanco** (săl tim băng′ kō) [It. (*saltare*, as prec., BANCO (2))], *n.* A mountebank, a quack.

saltire (săl′ tīr) [M.E. *sawtire*, O.F. *sauteoir, -toir*, a stile, L. *saltātōrium*, SALTATORY], *n.* (*Her.*) An ordinary in the form of a St. Andrew's cross or the letter X. **saltire-wise,** adv.

saltpetre (sawlt pē′ tėr) [M.E. and O.F. *salpetre*, med. L. *salpetra* (L. *sal petræ*, salt of the rock), assim. to SALT], *n.* Potassium nitrate; nitre. **saltpetrous,** *a.*

saltus (săl′ tŭs) [L., leap, cp. SALTIGRADE], *n.* A sudden starting aside, breach of continuity, or jumping to a conclusion.

salubrious (sȧ lū′ bri ŭs) [L. *salūbris*, -OUS], *a.* Promoting health, wholesome (of climate, etc.). **salubriously,** *adv.* **salubriousness, salubrity,** *n.*

***salue** [SALUTE].

Saluki (sa loo′ ki) [Arab.], *n.* A Persian greyhound.

salutary (săl′ ū tȧr i) [L. *salūtāris*, from *salus -ūtis*, health], *a.* Promoting good effects, beneficial, profitable; *salubrious, wholesome. **salutarily,** *adv.* **salutariness,** *n.*

salute (sȧ lūt′, -loot′) [L. *salūtāre*, as prec., to wish health to], *v.t.* To greet with a gesture or words of welcome, respect, or recognition; to accost or welcome (with a bow, kiss, oath, volley, etc.); to honour by the discharge of ordnance; to meet (the eye, etc.); *to hail (as king, etc.); *to kiss, esp. at meeting or parting. *v.i.* To perform a salute. *n.* A gesture of welcome, homage, recognition, etc., a salutation; (*Mil. and Nav.*) a prescribed method of doing honour or paying a compliment or respect, as discharge of ordnance, dipping colours, presenting arms, etc.; the attitude taken by a soldier, sailor, etc., in giving a salute; (*Fencing*) a conventional series of movements performed before engaging; *a kiss.

salutation (săl ū tā′ shŭn), *n.* The act of saluting; that which is said or done in the act of greeting; words of greeting or communicating good wishes or courteous inquiries; a salute. **salutational,** *a.* **salutatorian** (-tôr′ i ȧn), *n.* (*Am.*) A student who pronounces the salutatory. **salutatory** (sȧ lū′ tȧ tŏr i), *a.* Pertaining to or of the nature of a salutation; (*Am.*) pertaining to a salutatory. *n.* (*Am.*) An oration delivered by a student at commencement in colleges; *an audience-chamber, esp. in a church or monastery. **salutatorily,** *adv.* **saluter,** *n.*

***salutiferous** (săl ū tif′ ėr ŭs) [L. *salutifer* (*salus -ūtis*, health, -FERROUS)], *a.* Health-giving. **salutiferously,** *adv.*

salvable (săl′ vȧ bėl) [L. *salv-āre*, to SAVE, -ABLE], *a.* Capable of being saved. **salvableness, salvability** (-bil′ i ti), *n.* **salvably,** *adv.*

salvage (săl′ vȧj) [O.F., from *salver* (F. *sauver*), to SAVE], *n.* The act of saving (a ship, goods, etc.) from shipwreck, capture, fire, etc.; compensation allowed for such saving; property so saved. *v.t.* To save from wreck, capture, fire, etc. **salvage-money,** *n.*

Salvarsan (săl var′ sȧn), *n.* (*Med.*) The proprietary name of a compound used as an injection for the treatment of syphilis, anthrax, and other microbic diseases.

salvation (săl vā′ shŭn) [M.E. and O.F. *sauvacion* (F. *salvation*), L. *salvātionem*, nom. *-tio*, from *salvāre*, to SAVE], *n.* The act of saving from destruction; deliverance, preservation, esp. of the soul or of believers from sin and its consequences; that which delivers, preserves, etc. **Salvation Army:** A religious organization on a military pattern working among the poorer classes. **Salvationism,** *n.* **Salvationist,** *n.* ***salvatory** (săl′ vȧ tŏr i), *a.* Saving or tending to save or preserve. *n.* A repository, a safe.

salve (1) (sălv) [A.-S. *sealf* (cp. Dut. *zalf*, G. *salbe*), in later verbal senses partly from L. *salvāre*, to SAVE or SALVAGE], *n.* A healing ointment; anything that soothes or palliates. *v.t.* To dress or anoint with a salve; to soothe, to ease; to palliate, to make good; to save, to vindicate (one's honour, etc.); to salvage.

salve (2) (săl′ vē) [L., hail, imper. of *salvēre*, to be well], *n.* (*R.-C. Ch.*) An antiphon beginning with the words *Salve Regina*, 'hail, holy Queen,' addressed to the Virgin; music for this.

salver (săl′ vėr) [F. *salve*, a tray on which things were presented to a king, from Sp. *salva*, tasting of food before serving, from *salvar*, L. *salvāre*, to SAVE], *n.* A tray, usu. of silver, brass, electro-plate, etc., on which visiting-cards, etc., are presented by servants. **salver-shaped,** *a.*

Salvia (săl′ vi ȧ) [L., SAGE (1)], *n.* (*Bot.*) A genus of labiate plants comprising the common sage and many cultivated species with brilliant flowers.

salvo (1) (săl′ vō) [It. *salva*, salutation, prob. as SALVE (2)], *n.* (*pl.* **-voes, -vos**) A discharge of guns, etc., as a salute; (*fig.*) a volley of cheers, etc.; a concentrated fire of artillery, etc.

salvo (2) (săl′ vō) [L., abl. of *salvus*, SAFE], *n.* (*pl.* **-vos**) A saving clause, a proviso; a mental reservation, an evasion, an excuse; an expedient to save one's reputation, etc.

salvor (săl′ vŏr, -vôr), *n.* A person or ship effecting salvage.

sam, sammy (săm, -i) [etym. doubtful], *v.t.* To damp or dry skins partially in process of manufacture, so as to temper them.

samara (săm′ ȧ rȧ) [L.], *n.* (*Bot.*) A fruit with indehiscent dry cells elongated into wing-like expansions.

Samaritan (sȧ măr′ i tȧn), *a.* Pertaining to Samaria; applied to the archaic Hebrew characters in which the Samaritan Pentateuch, a recension of the Hebrew Pentateuch, was written. *n.* A native or inhabitant of Samaria; the language of Samaria; one adhering to the Samaritan religious system; (*fig.*) a kind, charitable person, in allusion to the 'good Samaritan' of the parable (Luke x. 30–37).

Sama-Veda (sa′ mȧ vā′ dȧ) [Sansk.], *n.* The third of the four Vedas, mainly made up of extracts from hymns in the Rig-Veda.

samba (săm′ bȧ), *n.* A Brazilian native dance; a ballroom dance in imitation of this.

sambo (săm′ bō) [Sp. *zambo*, prob. orig. bandy-legged, from L. *scambus*, Gr. *skambos*, crooked], *n.* A half-breed, esp. the offspring of a Negro and a mulatto; nickname for a Negro.

Sam Browne (săm′ broun) [Sir *Samuel Browne* (1824–1901)], *n.* (*Mil.*) A belt with a light strap over the right shoulder.

sambuke (sam′ būk), **sambuca** (săm bū′ kȧ) [L. *sambuca*, Gr. *sambukē*, cogn. with Aramaic *sabbekā*], *n.* An ancient musical stringed instrument of high-pitched tone.

sambur (săm′ bŭr) [Hindi *sābar, sāmbar*], *n.* A large deer or elk from the hill-country of India, *Axis Aristotelis*.

same (sām) [Icel. *same*, a., or A.-S. *same*, adv. (*cp.* O.H.G. and Goth. *sama*, also Gr. *homos*, L. *similis*), cogn. with Sansk. *sawa*], *a.* Identical; not other, not different; identical or similar in kind, quality, degree, etc.; exactly alike, indifferent; just mentioned, aforesaid; unchanged, unchanging, uniform, monotonous. **all the same:** Nevertheless; notwithstanding what is said, done, altered, etc. **at the same time:** Nevertheless, still. **sameness,** *n.*

Samian (sā′ mi ȧn) [L. *Samius*, Gr. *Samios*, from *Samos*, isle in the Ægean], *a.* Pertaining to Samos. **Samian earth:** A kind of bole or marl from Samos. **Samian ware:** (*Ant.*) Red or black pottery made from this or similar earth.

samiel (sā′ mi ėl) [Turk. *samyel*, from *sam*, Arab. *samm*, cp. SIMOOM], *n.* The simoom.

samisen (săm′ i sen) [Jap., from Chin. *sanhsien* (*san*, three, *hsien*, string)], *n.* A Japanese three-stringed guitar-like instrument played with a plectrum.

samite (săm′ īt) [O.F. *samit*, med. L. *samitum*, *examitum*, Gr. *hexamiton* (*hex*, six, *mitos*, a thread)], *n.* A rich mediæval silk fabric with a warp, each thread of which was of six strands.

samlet (săm′ lėt), *n.* A young salmon.

sammy [SAM].

Samnite (săm′ nīt) [L. *Samnītes*], *n.* One of an ancient Italian people eventually subjugated by the Romans. *a.* Of or pertaining to them.

Samoan (sȧ mō′ ȧn), *n.* A native or the language of Samoa. *a.* Pertaining to Samoa.

samovar (săm′ ŏ var) [Rus. *samovaru*, self-boiler, prob. from Tatar], *n.* A Russian tea-urn with burning charcoal in an inner tube.

Samoyed (săm′ ŏ yed) [Rus. *Samoyedu*], *n.* A member of a Mongolian race inhabiting middle Siberia; their language; a breed of white sledge-dog. **Samoyedic** (-yed′ ik), *a.* Pertaining to such race. *n.* Their language.

samp (sămp) [Algonkin *nasamp*], *n.* (*Am.*) Maize coarsely ground or made into porridge.

sampan (săm′ păn) [Chin. (*san*, three, *pan*, board)], *n.* A Chinese flat-bottomed river boat, frequently used for habitation.

samphire (săm′ fīr) [formerly *sampire*, F. *herbe de St. Pierre*, St. Peter's herb], *n.* A herb, *Crithmum maritimum*, growing on sea-cliffs, the aromatic leaves of which are pickled as a condiment.

sample (sam′ pėl) [orig. *essample*, var. of EXAMPLE],

n. A part taken or offered as illustrating the whole, a specimen, an example, a pattern, a model. **sample-room,** *n.* A room where samples are shown; (*Am. slang*) a grog-shop. *v.t.* To take samples of, to test, to try; to have an experience of; to present samples of.

sampler (sam′ plėr), *n.* A piece of embroidered work done as a specimen of skill. **samplery,** *n.*

Samson (săm′ sȯn) [L. and Gr. *Sampsōn,* Heb. *Shimshōn*], *n.* A man of abnormal strength (Judges xiv. 6 *passim*). **samson's post:** (*Naut.*) A pillar resting on the kelson and passing through the hold or between decks; an upright in whalers for fastening the harpoon-rope to.

Samurai (săm′ u rī) [Jap.], *n.* (*pl. unchanged*) A member of the military caste under the feudal régime, or a military retainer; now, an army officer.

sanative (săn′ å tiv) [med. L. *sānātivus,* from *sānāre,* to heal, from *sānus,* SANE], *a.* Healing, tending to cure, curative. ***sanable,** *a.* ***sanability** (-bil′ i ti), ***sanableness,** *n.*

sanatorium (săn å tôr′ i ŭm), *n.* (*pl.* **sanatoria**) An institution for the treatment of chronic diseases, especially pulmonary tuberculosis; a place to which people resort for the sake of their health; an institution for invalids, esp. convalescents, (*Am.* **sanitarium**). **sanatory** (săn′-), *a.*

sanbenito (săn bė nē′ tō) [Sp. (*San Benito,* St. Benedict)], *n.* A penitential garment painted with a red St. Andrew's cross worn by heretics who recanted, or painted over with flames and figures of devils, worn at an *auto-da-fé* by persons condemned by the Inquisition.

sancho (săng′ kō) [Ashanti *osanku*], *n.* A rude W. African musical instrument like a guitar.

sanctify (săngk′ ti fī) [M.E. *seintefie,* O.F. *saintifier* (F. *sanctifier*), late L. *sanctificāre* (*sanctus,* holy, *-ficāre, facere,* to make)], *v.t.* To make holy, to consecrate; to set apart or observe as holy; to purify from sin; to give a sacred character to, to sanction, to make inviolable; to render productive of holiness. **sanctification** (-kā′ shŭn), *n.* **sanctifier,** *n.*

sanctimony (săngk′ ti mō ni) [O.F. *sanctimonie,* L. *sanctimōnia,* from *sanctus,* holy], *n.* Affectation of piety, sanctimoniousness. **sanctimonious** (-mō′ ni ŭs), *a.* Making a show of piety or saintliness. **sanctimoniously,** *adv.* **sanctimoniousness,** *n.*

sanction (săngk′ shŭn) [F., from L. *sanctiōnem,* nom. *-tio,* from *sancīre,* to render sacred, see SAINT], *n.* The act of ratifying, ratification, confirmation by superior authority; a provision for enforcing obedience, a penalty or reward; anything that gives binding force to a law, etc.; countenance, support, encouragement conferred by usage, etc.; (*Ethics*) that which makes any rule of conduct binding. *v.t.* To give sanction to, to authorize, to ratify; to countenance, to approve; to enforce by penalty, etc. **sanctionable,** *a.* ***sanctionary,** *a.* **sanctionless,** *a.*

sanctity (săngk′ ti ti) [O.F. *sainctetė* (F. *sainteté*), L. *sanctitātem,* nom. *-tas,* from *sanctus,* SAINT], *n.* The state of being holy, holiness; spiritual purity, saintliness; sacredness, inviolability; (*pl.*) sacred things, feelings, etc. **sanctitude,** *n.* Holiness, saintliness; sacredness.

sanctuary (săngk′ tū å ri) [A.-F. *saintuarie,* O.F. *sainctuarie* (F. *sanctuaire*), L. *sanctuārium,* as prec.], *n.* A holy place; a church, temple, or other building or enclosure devoted to sacred uses, esp. an inner shrine or most sacred part of a church, etc., as the part of a church where the altar is placed; (*Hist.*) a church or other consecrated place in which debtors and malefactors were free from arrest; any similar place of immunity, an asylum, a refuge; immunity, protection; a place where deer, birds, etc., are left undisturbed. ***sanctuarize,** *v.t.*

sanctum (săngk′ tŭm) [L., neut. of foll.], *n.* (*pl.* **-ta**) A sacred or private place; (*colloq.*) a private room, den, or retreat. **sanctum sanctorum:** The holy of holies in the Jewish temple; (*colloq.*) one's sanctum.

sanctus (săngk′ tŭs) [L., holy], *n.* The liturgical phrase 'Holy, holy, holy,' in Latin or English; the music for this. **sanctus-bell,** *n.* A bell, usu. in a turret or bell-cote over the junction of nave and chancel, rung at the Sanctus before the Canon of the Mass.

sand (sănd) [A.-S., cp. Dut. *zand,* G. *sand,* Icel. *sandr,* Swed. and Dan. *sand*], *n.* Comminuted fragments of rock, esp. of chert, flint, etc., reduced almost to powder; a particle of this; (*pl.*) tracts of sand, stretches of beach, or shoals or submarine banks of sand; (*pl.*) particles of sand in an hour-glass; (*pl. fig.*) the time one has to live; (*Am. slang*) grit, endurance, pluck. *v.t.* To sprinkle or treat with sand; to mix sand with to adulterate; to cover or overlay with or bury under sand; to drive (a ship) on a sand-bank. **the sands are running out:** (*fig.*) The end is approaching. **sand-bag,** *n.* A bag or sack filled with sand, used in fortification for making defensive walls, as ballast, for stopping crevices, draughts, etc., as a cushion for supporting an engraver's plate, as a weapon for stunning a person, etc. *v.t.* To strike or fell with a sand-bag. **sand-bank,** *n.* A bank or shoal of sand, esp. in the sea, a river, etc. **sand-bath,** *n.* A vessel containing hot sand used for heating, tempering, etc. **sand-blast,** *n.* A jet of sand used for engraving and cutting glass, etc. **sand-blight,** *n.* (*Austral.*) An eye affection caused by sand. **sand-box,** *n.* A box containing sand carried by a locomotive, etc., for sprinkling the rails when slippery; (*Golf*) a box for sand used in teeing; a box with a perforated top formerly used for sprinkling paper with sand to dry up ink. ***sand-boy,** *n.* A boy carting or hawking sand. **sand-crack,** *n.* A fissure in the hoof of a horse, liable to cause lameness; a crack or flaw in a brick due to defective mixing. **sand-eel,** *n.* An eel-like fish of the genus *Ammodytes.* **sand-flood,** *n.* A mass of sand borne along in a desert. **sand-fly,** *n.* A species of midge; an angler's fly. **sand-glass,** *n.* An hour-glass. **Sandgroper,** *n.* (*Austral.*) A Western Australian. **sand-heat,** *n.* Heat imparted by warmed sand in chemical operations. **sand-hopper,** *n.* A crustacean, *Talitrus locusta.* **sand-martin,** *n.* A small swallow, *Hirundo riparia,* which makes its nest in sand-banks, etc. **sand-iron,** *n.* (*Golf*) A club used for lifting the ball from sand. **sand-man,** *n.* A being in fairy-lore who makes children sleepy by casting sand in their eyes. **sand-paper,** *n.* A paper or thin cloth coated with sand, used for smoothing wood, etc.; *v.t.* To rub or smooth with this. **sand-pipe,** *n.* (*Geol.*) A deep cylindrical hollow, filled with sand and gravel, penetrating chalk. **sandpiper,** *n.* A popular name for several birds haunting sandy places, chiefly of the genera *Tringa* and *Totanus*; (*Austral.*) the rainbow bird. **sand-pump,** *n.* A pump used for extracting wet sand from a drill-hole, caisson, etc. **sand-shoe,** *n.* A light shoe, usu. of canvas with a rubber sole, for walking on sands. **sandstone,** *n.* Stone composed of an agglutination of grains of sand. **sand-storm,** *n.* A storm of wind carrying along volumes of sand in a desert. **sand-worm,** *n.* The lug-worm. **sandwort,** *n.* Any plant of the genus *Arenaria,* low herbs growing in sandy soil. **sanded,** *a.* Sprinkled with sand; filled, covered, or dusted with sand; *of a sandy colour; sand-blind.

sandal (1) (săn′ dål) [F. *sandale,* L. *sandalium,* Gr. *sandalion*], *n.* A kind of shoe consisting of a sole secured by straps passing over the instep and round the ankle; a strap for fastening a low shoe. **sandalled,** *a.* Wearing sandals; fitted or fastened with a sandal.

sandal (2) (săn′dål) [med. L. *sandalum,* Gr. *sandalon,* Arab. *sandal,* prob. from Sansk. *chandana*], *n.* Sandalwood. **sandalwood,** *n.* The fragrant wood of various trees of the genus *Santalum,* esp. *S. album,* much used for cabinet work.

sandarach (săn′ dȧ răk) [L. *sandaraca*, Gr. *sandarakē*, etym. doubtful], *n.* A whitish-yellow gum-resin obtained from a N.W. African tree, *Callitris quadrivalvis*; realgar. **sandarach-tree,** *n.*

***sand-blind** (sănd′ blīnd) [prob. corr. of *sam-blind* (A.-S. *sam-*, cogn. with SEMI-, BLIND)], *a.* Half-blind, dim-sighted.

Sandemanian (săn dė mā′ ni ȧn), *n.* A follower of Robert Sandeman (1718–81) the Glassite.

sanderling (săn′ dėr ling) [etym. doubtful], *n.* A small wading-bird, *Crocethia alba.*

sanders, sanders-wood [SANDALWOOD, see SANDAL (2)].

sandiness [SANDY].

sandiver (săn′ div ėr) [prob. corr. of O.F. *sain de verre* (*suin, suint*, exudation, from *suer*, to sweat, *de verre*, of glass)], *n.* A saline scum rising to the surface of fused glass in the pot.

sandpiper, sandstone [SAND].

sandwich (sănd′ wich) [after the 4th Earl of *Sandwich* (1718–92)], *n.* Two thin slices of bread and butter with meat, etc., between them. *v.t.* To put, lay, or insert between two things of a dissimilar kind. **sandwich-man,** *n.* A man carrying two advertisement boards hung from his shoulders, one in front and one behind.

sandwort [SAND].

sandy (1) (săn′ di), *a.* Consisting of or abounding in sand; of the colour of sand, yellowish-red (of hair), having hair of this colour; (*Am. slang*) plucky, brave, having plenty of grit or sand; (*fig.*) shifting, unstable. **sandiness,** *n.* **sandyish,** *a.*

Sandy (2) (săn′ di) [Sc., fam. for *Alexander*], *n.* (*colloq.*) A Scotsman.

***sandyx** (săn′ diks) [L., from Gr. *sandux*], *n.* A red pigment prepared by calcining carbonate of lead.

sane (sān) [L. *sānus*]. *a.* Sound in mind, not deranged; sensible, reasonable (of views), *healthy, sound physically. **sanely,** *adv.* ***saneness,** *n.*

sang (1), *past* [SING]. **sang** (2) (*Sc.*) [var. of SONG].

sanga, sangar (săng′ gȧ) [Hind. *sunga*], *n.* A breastwork or wall of loose stones built for defensive purposes by Indian hill-tribes.

sangaree (săng gȧ rē′) [Sp. *sangria*, ult. from L. *sanguis*, blood], *n.* Wine and water sweetened and spiced, and usually iced. *v.t.* To make wine with this.

sang-de-bœuf (san dė buf) [F., blood of a bullock], *n.* A dark-red colour such as that of some old Chinese porcelain. *a.* Of this colour.

sangfroid (san frwa) [F., cold blood], *n.* Coolness, calmness, composure in danger, etc.

***sanglier** (san′ li ėr) [O.F., ult. from L. *singulāris*, solitary, see SINGULAR], *n.* A wild boar.

sangraal, -greal [GRAIL].

sangrado (săng gra′ dō) [a physician in Le Sage's 'Gil Blas'], *n.* A medical practitioner whose chief resource is blood-letting; a quack.

sanguification (săng gwi fi kā′ shůn) [L. *sanguis*, blood], *n.* The formation of blood, the conversion of chyle into blood. **sanguiferous** (săng gwif′ ėr ůs), *a.* Conveying blood. **sanguifier** (săng′-), *n.* **sanguifluous** (-gwif′ lu ůs), *a.* Running with blood. **sanguify** (săng′ gwi fī), *v.i.* To produce blood.

sanguinary (săng′ gwi nȧr i) [L. *sanguinārius*, from *sanguis -uinis*, blood], *a.* Attended with bloodshed or carnage; delighting in bloodshed, bloodthirsty, murderous. **sanguinarily,** *adv.* **sanguinariness,** *n.*

sanguine (săng′ gwin) [F. *sanguin*, L. *sanguineum*, nom. *-us*, as prec.], *a.* Having the colour of blood; ruddy, florid (of the complexion); formerly said of a temperament supposed to be due to the predominance of blood over the other humours; hopeful, cheerful, confident, optimistic, ardent, enthusiastic; full of blood, plethoric; *composed of blood; *sanguinary. *n.* Blood colour, deep red; a crayon of this colour prepared from iron oxide; a drawing with this. *v.t.* To stain with blood; to colour red. **sanguinely,** *adv.* **sanguineness,** *n.* **sanguineous** (-gwin′ ė ůs), *a.* Pertaining to, forming, or abounding in blood; of a blood colour; full-blooded, plethoric; ***sanguine.** ***sanguinity,** *n.* Sanguineness; consanguinity. **sanguinivorous** (-niv′ ȯ růs), **sanguivorous** (-gwiv′ ȯ růs), *a.* Feeding on blood. **sanguinolent** (-gwin′ ȯ lėnt), *a.* Of blood; bleeding, suffering from hæmorrhage. ***sanguinolence,** *n.* **sanguisorb** (săng′ gwi sôrb), *n.* (*Bot.*) A plant of the rosaceous genus *Sanguisorba*, containing the burnet, formerly used as a styptic.

Sanhedrin (săn′ ė drin) [late Heb., from Gr. *sunedrio* (SYN-, *hedra*, seat)], *n.* The supreme court of justice and council of the Jewish nation, down to A.D. 425, consisting of 71 priests, elders and scribes.

sanicle (săn′ i kėl) [O.F., from med. L. *sānicula*, from *sānus*, SANE], *n.* A small woodland plant of the umbelliferous genus *Sanicula*, allied to the parsley.

sanies (sā′ ni ēz) [L.], *n.* (*Path.*) A thin fetid discharge, usu. stained with blood, from sores or wounds. **sanious,** *a.*

sanify (săn′ i fī) [L. *sānus*, SANE], *v.t.* To make healthy or more sanitary.

sanitary (săn′ i tȧr i) [cp. F. *sanitaire*, from L. *sānitas*, see foll.], *a.* Relating to or concerned with the preservation of health, pertaining to hygiene; hygienic. **sanitary towel,** *n.* An absorbent pad used for menstruation. **sanitary wallpaper,** *n.* Varnished wallpaper that can be sponged. **sanitarian** (-târ′ i ȧn), *n.* and *a.* **sanitarily** (săn′-), *adv.* **sanitariness,** *n.* **sanitarist,** *n.* **sanitarium** [SANATORIUM]. **sanitate,** *v.t.* To improve the sanitary condition of. *v.i.* To carry out sanitary measures. **sanitation** (-tā′ shůn), *n.* **sanitationist,** *n.*

sanity (săn′ i ti) [L. *sānitas*, from *sānus*, SANE], *n.* Saneness, mental soundness; reasonableness; moderation.

sanjak (săn′ jăk) [Turk.], *n.* An administrative subdivision of a Turkish vilayet or province.

sank, *past* [SINK].

sans (sănz, san) [F., from L. *sine*, without], *prep.* (*Shakespeare*) Without. ***sans-culotte*** (san ku lot′, sănz kū lot′), *n.* One without breeches; (*pl.*) applied generally to the republicans in the French Revolution; *a.* Republican, revolutionary. **sansculottic,** *a.* **sans-culottism,** *n.* **sans serif:** (*Print.*) Without serifs; a type without serifs.

Sanskrit (săn′ skrit) [Sansk. *saṃskṛta* (*sam*, together, cp. SAME, *kṛta*, made)], *n.* The ancient language of the Hindu sacred writings, the oldest of the Indo-European group. **Sanskritic** (-skrit′ ik), *a.* **Sanskritist** (săn′-), *n.*

Santa Claus (săn′ tȧ klawz′) [Am., from Dut. *Sint Klaas*, St. Nicholas], *n.* A fabulous white-bearded old man bringing presents at Christmas and putting them in children's stockings made popular in England in the late 19th cent.

santal (săn′ tȧl) [F., from med. L. *santalum*, Gr. *santalon*, as SANDAL (2)], *n.* Sandal-wood. **santalaceous** (-lā′ shůs), *a.* (*Bot.*). **santalic** (-tăl′ ik), *a.* (*Chem.*). **santalin** (săn′ tȧ lin), *n.* The colouring matter of red sandalwood.

santir (săn tēr′) [Arab., corr. of Gr. *psaltērion*, PSALTERY], *n.* An Eastern form of dulcimer played with two sticks.

santolina (săn tȯ lī′ nȧ) [prob. var. of SANTONICA], *n.* (*Bot.*) A genus of fragrant shrubby composite plants allied to the camomile.

santon (săn′ ton) [F. or Sp., from *santo*, SAINT], *n.* A Mohammedan hermit, a dervish.

santonica (săn ton′ i kȧ) [L., fem. adj., pertaining to the *Santones*, a people of Aquitania], *n.* The unexpanded flower-heads of an Oriental species of

Artemisia or wormwood, used as an anthelmintic. **santonin** (săn′ tȯ nin), *n.* (*Chem.*) The bitter principle of this. **santoninic** (-nin′ ik), *a.*

Saorstat Eireann (sā ŏr′ stath ā′ ri ėn) [Ir.], *n.* (*Pol.*) The Irish Free State.

sap (1) (săp) [A.-S. *sæp* (cp. Dut. *sap*, G. *saft*), prob. cogn. with L. *sapa*, must, new wine], *n.* The watery juice or circulating fluid of living plants; the sapwood or alburnum of a tree; (*fig.*) vital fluid, strength, vigour. *v.t.* (*past & p.p.*) **sapped.** To draw off sap; (*fig.*) to exhaust the strength or vitality of. **sap-colour,** *n.* An expressed vegetable colour inspissated by evaporation for the use of painters. **sap-green,** *n.* A pigment obtained from the juice of blackthorn berries; the colour of this; *a.* Of this colour. **sap-head,** *n.* A softhead, a ninny. **sap-lath,** *n.* A lath of sapwood. **sap-rot,** *n.* Dry-rot. **sap-tube,** *n.* (*Bot.*) A vessel conducting sap. **sap-wood,** *n.* The soft new wood next the bark, alburnum. **sapful,** *a.* **sapless,** *a.* **sapling,** *n.* A young tree; (*fig.*) a youth. **sappy,** *a.* **sappiness,** *n.*

sap (2) (săp) [F. *sapper*, from O.F. *sappe* (F. *sape*) or It. *zappa*, late L. *sappa*, spade], *v.t.* To undermine; to approach by mines, trenches, etc.; to render unstable by wearing away the foundation; (*fig.*) to subvert or destroy insidiously. *v.i.* To make an attack or approach by digging trenches or undermining. *n.* The act of sapping; a deep ditch, trench, or mine for approach to or attack on a fortification; (*fig.*) insidious undermining or subversion of faith, etc.

sap (3) (săp) [prob. from prec.], *v.i.* (*Schoolboy slang*) To be studious, to grind. *n.* A hard-working student, a plodder; a tiring piece of work, a grind.

sapajou (săp′ å joo) [F., said to be a Cayenne word], *n.* A small S. American prehensile-tailed monkey of genus *Cebus*, often kept as a pet.

sapan-wood (săp′ ȧn wud) [Dut. *sapan*, Malay *sapang*, wood], *n.* A brownish-red dyewood obtained from trees of the genus *Cæsalpinia*, esp. *C. sappan*, from Southern Asia and Malaysia.

sapful, sap-green, sap-head [SAP (1)].

saphena (så fē′ nå) [med. L., from Arab. *çāfin*], *n.* (*Anat.*) Either of two prominent veins of the leg. **saphenal, saphenous,** *a.*

sapid (săp′ id) [L. *sapidus*, from *sapere*, to taste], *a.* Possessing flavour that can be relished, savoury; not insipid, vapid, or uninteresting. **sapidity** (så pid′ i ti), ***sapidness,** *n.*

sapient (sā′ pi ėnt) [L. *sapiens -ntem*, pres.p. of *sapere*, to be wise, as prec.], *a.* Wise, sagacious, sage (usu. ironical). **sapience,** *n.* **sapiently,** adv. **sapiential** (-en′ shål), *a.* Of or conveying wisdom. **sapiential books:** (*Bibl.*) Proverbs, Ecclesiastes, Ecclesiasticus, The Book of Wisdom, etc.

sapi-utan (săp i oo′ tăn) [Malay, wild ox], *n.* The wild ox of Celebes.

sapless, sapling [SAP (1)].

sapodilla (săp ȯ dil′ å) [Sp. *zapotilla*, dim. of *zapote*, Mex. *zapotl*], *n.* The edible fruit of a large evergreen tree, *Achras sapota*, growing in the West Indies and Central America; the tree itself; its durable wood.

saponaceous (săp ȯ nā′ shŭs) [L. *sāpo -pōnis*, soap, -ACEOUS], *a.* Soapy; resembling, containing, or having the qualities of soap.

Saponaria (să pon âr′ i å), *n.* (*Bot.*) An order of plants comprising the soapworts.

saponify (så pon′ i fī), *v.t.* To convert into soap by combination with an alkali; *v.i.* To turn into soap thus (of oil, fat, etc.). **saponifiable,** *a.* **saponification,** *n.*

saponin (săp′ ȯ nin), *n.* (*Chem.*) A glucoside obtained from the soapwort, horse-chestnut, etc.

saponule (săp′ ȯn ūl), *n.* A soap-like compound formed by the action of an alkali on an essential oil.

sapor (sā′ pŏr) [L., from *sapere*, to taste], *n.* Taste; distinctive flavour. ***saporific** (-rif′ ik), *a.* Producing taste or savour. ***saporous** (sā′ pȯ rŭs), *a.* ***saporosity** (-ros′ i ti), *n.*

sapper (săp′ ėr) [SAP (2), -ER], *n.* One who saps; (*colloq.*) an officer or private of the Royal Engineers.

sapphic (săf′ ik) [L. *Sapphicus*, Gr. *Sapphikos*, from *Sapphō*], *a.* Pertaining to Sappho, a Lesbian poetess (*c.* 600 B.C.); applied to a stanza or metre used by her, esp. a combination of three pentameters followed by a dipody. *n.pl.* Sapphic verses or stanzas. **sapphism,** *n.* Unnatural erotic relations between women.

sapphire (săf′ īr) [F. *saphir*, L. *saphīrus*, Gr. *sappheiros*, prob. from Semitic (cp. Heb. *sappīr*)], *n.* Any transparent blue variety of corundum; an intense and lustrous blue, azure; a S. American humming-bird with blue throat. *a.* Sapphire-blue. **sapphirine,** *a.* Having the qualities, esp. the colour of sapphire. *n.* A mineral of a pale blue colour, esp. a silicate of alumina and magnesia or a blue spinel.

sappy, sappiness [SAP (1)].

sapr-, sapro- [Gr. *sapros*, rotten], *comb. form.* **sapræmia** (så prē′ mi å) [Gr. *haima*, blood], *n.* (*Path.*) Septic poisoning. **sapræmic,** *a.* **saprogenic** (-jen′ ik), *a.* Producing or produced by putrefaction. **saprolegnia** (-leg′ ni å) [Gr. *legnon*, border], *n.* A genus of fungi infesting fishes, and causing a destructive salmon disease. **saprolegnious,** *a.* **saprophagan** (så prof′ å gån), *n.* (*Ent.*) A lamellicorn beetle living on decomposed vegetable matter. **saprophagous** (så prof′ å gŭs), *a.* **saprophile** (săp′ rȯ fīl), *n.* A bacterium feeding on decomposed matter. **saprophilous** (så prof′ i lŭs), *a.* **saprophyte** (săp′ rȯ fīt), *n.* A vegetable organism growing on decaying organic matter. **saprophytic** (-fit′ ik), *a.* **saprophytically,** *adv.* **saprophytism** (săp′-) *n.* **saprostomus** (så pros′ tȯ mŭs) [Gr. *stoma*, mouth], *n.* (*Path.*) Foulness of breath. **saprostomous,** *a.*

sap-rot, sap-tube [SAP (1)].

sapsago (săp sā′ gō) [corr. of G. *schabzieger* (*schaben*, to grate, *zieger*, cheese)], *n.* A greenish hard cheese flavoured with melilot, made in Switzerland.

sapucaya (sa poo kā′ yå) [Braz.], *n.* A South American tree bearing an edible nut. **sapucaya-nut,** *n.*

sap-wood [SAP (1)].

sar (sar) [F., var. of *sargo*, L. *sargus*], **sargo,** *n.* A fish of the genus *Sargus* comprising the sea-breams.

saraband (săr′ å bănd) [F. *sarabande*, Sp. *zarabanda*, prob. from Moorish], *n.* A slow and stately Spanish dance; a piece of music for this in strongly accented triple time.

Saracen (săr′ å sėn) [late L. *Saracēnus*, late Gr. *Sarakēnos*, prob. from *Arab.*], *n.* A nomad Arab of the Syro-Arabian desert in the times of the later Greeks and Romans; a Moslem or Arab at the time of the Crusades. **Saracenic** (-sen′ ik), *a.*

Saratoga (săr å tō′ gå) [*Saratoga* Springs, New York State], *n.* A variety of lady's large travelling trunk sometimes called a **Saratoga trunk.**

sarcasm (sar′ kăzm) [late L. *sarcasmus*, late Gr. *sarkazmos*, from *sarkazein*, to tear flesh, as SARCO-], *n.* A bitter, taunting, ironical, or wounding remark; bitter irony or invective. **sarcast,** *n.* A sarcastic speaker, etc. **sarcastic, *-al** (-kăs′ tik, -ål), *a.* **sarcastically,** *adv.*

sarcelle (sar sel′) [O.F. *cercelle*, ult. from L. *querquedula*], *n.* A teal or a long-tailed duck allied thereto.

sarcenchyme (sar seng′ kīm) [*sarc-*, SARCO-, after PARENCHYME], *n.* The gelatinous tissue of some higher sponges. **sarcenchymatous** (-kī′ må tŭs), *a.*

sarcenet (sar′ sė net) [A.-F. *sarzinett*, O.F. *sarcenet*, prob. dim. of *sarzin*, SARACEN], *n.* A thin, fine soft-textured silk used chiefly for linings, ribbons, etc.

Sarcina (sar′ si-, sar sī′ nå) [L., bundle, from *sarcīre*, to mend], *n.* (*pl.* *-næ*) (*Bot.*) A genus of bacteria or schizomycetous fungi in which the cocci break up into cuboidal masses. **sarcinæform** (-sī′ ni fôrm), **sarcinic** (-sin′ ik), *a.*

sarcine (sar′ sīn) [G. *sarkin* (*sarc-*, SARCO-, -INE)], *n.* (*Chem.*) A nitrogenous compound existing in the juice of flesh.

sarco- [Gr. *sarx sarkos*, flesh], *comb. form.*

sarcobasis (sar kob′ ȧ sis), *n.* (*Bot.*) A fleshy gynobase.

sarcoblast (sar′ kō blast), *n.* (*Biol.*) A germinating particle of protoplasm. **sarcoblastic,** *a.*

sarcocarp (sar′ kō karp), *n.* (*Bot.*) The fleshy part of a drupaceous fruit.

sarcocele (sar′ kō sēl), *n.* (*Path.*) Fleshy enlargement of the testicle.

sarcocol (sar′ kȯ kol), *n.* A gum-resin imported from Arabia and Persia.

sarcocolla (sar kō kol′ ȧ), *n.* Sarcocol; (*Bot.*) a genus of S. African shrubs of the order *Penæaceæ*, from which this was formerly supposed to be obtained.

sarcode (sar′ kōd), *n.* (*Biol.*) Animal protoplasm. **sarcodal, sarcodic,** *a.*

sarcoderm (sar′ kō dĕrm), *n.* (*Bot.*) An intermediate fleshy layer in certain seeds.

sarcody (sar′ kō di), *n.* (*Bot.*) Conversion into fleshiness.

sarcoid (sar′ koid), *a.* Resembling flesh. *n.* A particle of sponge tissue.

sarcolemma (sar kō lem′ ȧ), *n.* (*Anat.*) The tubular membrane sheathing muscular tissue. **sarcolemmic,** *a.*

sarcology (sar kol′ ȯ ji), *n.* The branch of anatomy treating of the soft parts of the body. **sarcological** (-loj′ i kȧl), *a.* **sarcologist,** *n.*

sarcoma (sar kō′ mȧ) [Gr. *sarkōma*, from *sarcoun*, to become fleshy, from *sarx*, SARCO-], *n.* (*pl.* **-mata**) (*Path.*) A tumour composed of fleshy tissue; (*Bot.*) a fleshy disk. **sarcomatosis** (-tō′ sis), *n.* Sarcomatous degeneration. **sarcomatous** (-kō′ mȧ tůs), *a.*

sarcophagus (sar kof′ ȧ gůs) [L., from Gr. *sarkophagos* (SARCO-, Gr. *phagein*, to eat)], *n.* (*pl.* **-gi,** -jī) (*Gr. Ant.*) A kind of stone used for coffins, as it was believed to consume the flesh of those buried in it in a few weeks; a stone coffin, esp. one of architectural or decorated design. **sarcophagal, sarcophagous,** *a.* Feeding on flesh; of or like a sarcophagus. **sarcophagon,** *n.* (*Ent.*) An insect of the order *Sarcophaga*, a flesh-fly. **sarcophagy** (-ji), *n.* The practice of eating flesh.

sarcoplasm (sar′ kȯ plăzm), *n.* (*Anat.*) The substance between the columns of muscle-fibre.

sarcoptes (sar kop′ tēz) [Gr. *koptein*, to cut], *n.* (*Zool.*) A genus of acaridans comprising the itch-mites; a mite of this genus. **sarcoptic,** *a.*

sarcosis (sar kō′ sis) [Gr. *sarkōsis*, from *sarkoun*, as SARCOMA], *n.* A fleshy tumour, sarcoma. ***sarcotic** (-kot′ ik), *a.* Producing flesh. *n.* A sarcotic medicine. **sarcotome** (sar′ kȯ tōm), *n.* (*Surg.*) An instrument for cutting through the tissues of the body. **sarcous** (sar′ kůs), *a.* Composed of flesh or muscle.

sard (sard) [F. *sarde*, L. *sarda*, SARDIUS], *n.* A precious stone, a variety of cornelian. **sardachate** (sar′ dȧ kāt), *n.* A variety of agate containing layers of cornelian. **sardine** (2) (sar′ dīn), *n.* (*Bibl.*) Prob. the sardius.

sardelle (sar del′) [It. *sardella*, dim. of *sarda*, SARDINE (1)], *n.* A small Mediterranean clupeoid fish like and prepared as the sardine.

sardine (1) (sar dēn′) [F., from It. *sardina*, L. *sardina*, late Gr. *sardēnē*, Gr. *sarda*], *n.* A fish, *Clupea pilchardus*, caught off Brittany and Sardinia, and cured and preserved in oil; other small fish preserved in the same way.

sardine (2) [SARD].

Sardinian (sar din′ yȧn, -i ȧn), *a.* Pertaining to the island or the former kingdom of Sardinia. *n.* A native or inhabitant of Sardinia.

sardius (sar′ di ůs) [L., from G. *sardios*, from *Sardeis*, Sardis], *n.* A precious stone mentioned in Scripture, perhaps the sard or the sardonyx.

sardonic (sar don′ ik) [F. *sardonique*, L. *Sardonicus*, *Sardonius*, Gr. *Sardonios*, Sardinian (as if in alln. to the effects of a Sardinian plant in contorting the face), for *Sardonios*, etym. doubtful], *a.* Unnatural, forced, affected, insincere; sneering, malignant, bitterly ironical (of laughter, etc.). **sardonian** (-dō′ ni ȧn), *a.* and *n.* **sardonically,** *adv.*

sardonyx (sar′ dȯ niks) [L., from Gr. *sardonux*], *n.* A variety of onyx composed of white chalcedony alternating with layers of sard.

sargasso (sar găs′ ō) [Port. *sargaço*], *n.* The gulf-weed, *Sargassum bacciferum.* **Sargasso Sea:** A part of the Atlantic abounding with this.

sargo [SAR].

sari, saree (sa′ rē) [Hind.], *n.* A Hindu woman's dress.

sarigue (sa′ rēg) [F., from Port. *sarigué*, Braz. *sarigueya*], *n.* A S. American opossum, *Didelphys opossum.*

sark (sark) [A.-S. *serc* or Icel. *serkr*, cp. Swed. *sărk*, Dan. *særk*], *n.* (*Sc.*) A shirt or chemise. *v.t.* To clothe with a sark; to cover (a roof) with sarking. **sarking,** *n.* Thin boards for lining, esp. a roof under slates.

sarkinite (sar′ ki nīt) [Gr. *sarkinos*, fleshy, see SARCINE, -ITE], *n.* (*Min.*) A red arsenate of manganese.

Sarmatian (sar mā′ shȧn), *a.* Pertaining to ancient Sarmatia, now Poland and part of Russia, or its people; (*poet.*) Polish. *n.* An inhabitant of Sarmatia; (*poet.*) a Pole.

sarmentose, -tous (sar men′ tōs, -tůs) [L. *sarmentōsus*, from *sarmentum*, twigs, brushwood], *a.* (*Bot.*) Having or producing runners. **sarmentum,** *n.* (*pl.* **-ta**) A prostrate shoot rooting at the nodes, a runner.

sarong (sȧ rong′) [Malay *sārung*, from Sansk. *sāranga*, variegated], *n.* A garment worn by men and women in the Malay Archipelago.

saros (sâr′ os) [Gr.], *n.* (*Astron.*) A cycle of 18 years 10⅔ days in which solar and lunar eclipses repeat themselves.

sarothrum (sa rō′ thrům) [Gr. *sarotron*, a broom], *n.* (*Zool.*) The pollen brush on the leg of a honey-bee.

***sarplier** (sar′ pli ėr) [A.-F. *sarpler*, O.F. *sarpillere* (F. *serpillière*), etym. doubtful], *n.* A sack or bale of wool containing 80 tods; coarse sacking or packing cloth.

Sarracenia (săr ȧ sē′ ni ȧ) [after Dr. D. *Sarrazen* of Quebec, *c.* 1700], *n.* (*Bot.*) A genus of insectivorous plants with pitcher-shaped leaves.

***Sarrasin** [SARACEN].

sarrusophone (sȧ rŭs′ ȯ fōn) [M. *Sarrus*, inventor (*c.* 1860), -PHONE], *n.* A brass musical instrument resembling an oboe with a metal tube.

sarsaparilla (sar sȧ pȧ ril′ ȧ) [Sp. *zarzaparrilla* (*zarza*, bramble, *-parrilla*, perh. dim. of *parra*, vine)], *n.* The dried roots of various species of *Smilax*, much used in medicine as an alterative and tonic; a plant of this genus.

sarsen (sar′ sėn) [prob. var. of SARACEN], *n.* A sandstone boulder such as those that bestrew the chalk downs of Wiltshire. **sarsen-boulder, -stone,** *n.*

sarsenel [SARCENEL].

sarsenet (sar′ sėn et) [O.F. *sarzinett*], *n.* (*Textiles*) A kind of fine, soft silk.

sartage (sar′ tȧj) [O.F., from *sarter*, to clear ground, from *sart*, med. L. *sartum*, neut. p.p. of

L. *sartire*, to hoe], *n.* The clearing of woodland for agricultural purposes.

sartorial (sar tôr' i ăl) [L. *sartōrius*, from *sartor*, mender, tailor, from *sarcīre*, to patch], *a.* Pertaining to a tailor.

sartorius (sar tôr' i ŭs), *n.* (*Anat.*) A muscle of the thigh that helps to flex the knee.

sash (1) (săsh) [formerly *shash*, a strip worn as a turban, from Arab. *shāsh*, muslin], *n.* An ornamental band or scarf worn round the waist or over the shoulder, frequently by men as a badge or part of a uniform. **sashed** (1), *a.*

sash (2) (săsh) [corr. of CHASSIS], *n.* A frame of wood or metal holding the glass of a window; a sliding light in a greenhouse, etc. *v.t.* To furnish with sashes. **sash-cord, -line,** *n.* Stout cord attached to a sash and the weights balancing it. **sash-frame,** *n.* The frame in which a sash slides up and down. **sash-pocket,** *n.* The space in which the weights balancing the sash are hung. **sash-window,** *n.* A window having a movable sash or sashes. **sashed** (2), **sashless,** *a.*

sasin (săs' in) [Nepalese], *n.* The common Indian antelope, *Antilope cervicapra.*

sasine (sā' sin) [var. of SEISIN], *n.* (*Sc. Law.*) The act of giving legal possession of feudal property; the instrument by which this is effected.

sass, sassy (*Am. colloq.*) [SAUCE, SAUCY].

sassaby (să sā' bi) [native name], *n.* A large S. African antelope, *Alcelaphus lunatus*, the bastard hartebeest.

sassafras (săs' ă frăs) [Sp. *sasafras*, etym. doubtful, perh. from SAXIFRAGE], *n.* A small N. American tree, *Sassafras officinale*, of the laurel family; the dried bark of its root used as an aromatic stimulant.

Sassanian (să sā' ni ăn) [Pers. *Sāsān*], *a.* Of or pertaining to the Sassanids. *n.* A Sassanian king. **Sassanid** (săs' ă nid), *n.* One of the descendants of Sasan, ancestor of the last national dynasty of Persia (A.D. 226–642). *a.* Sassanian.

Sassenach (săs' ĕ năch) [Gael. and Ir., SAXON], *n.* A Saxon, an Englishman. *a.* English.

sassoline (săs' ŏ lin) [G. *sassolin* (*Sasso*, Tuscany, -INE)], *n.* (*Min.*) A native triclinic form of boric acid.

sastra [SHASTER].

sat, *past & p.p.* [SIT].

Satan (sā' tăn), **Satanas** (săt' ă năs) [L. and Gr. *Satān, Satanās*, Heb. *Sātān*, enemy, adversary], *n.* The arch fiend, the devil. **satanic, -al** (să tăn' ik, -ăl), *a.* Pertaining to, emanating from, or having the qualities of Satan; devilish, infernal. **Satanic School:** Southey's description of Byron, Shelley, etc.; applied to other writers charged with deliberate impiety or satanism. **satanically,** *adv.* **satanism** (sā' tă nizm), *n.* A diabolical disposition, doctrine, or conduct; the deliberate pursuit of wickedness; Satan-worship; the characteristics of the Satanic School. **satanist,** *n.* **satanize,** *v.t.* **satanology** (-nol' ŏ ji), *n.* Study of or a treatise on doctrines relating to the devil. **satanophany** (-nof' ă ni), *n.* A visible manifestation of Satan. ***satanophobia** (-fō' bi ă), *n.* Morbid dread of Satan.

satara (săt' ă ră, să ta' ră) [town in India], *n.* A heavy, horizontally-ribbed woollen or broad-cloth.

satchel (săch' ĕl) [M.E. and O.F. *sachel*, L. *saccellum*, nom. *-lus*, dim. of *saccus*, SACK (1)], *n.* A small bag suspended by a strap passing over one shoulder, esp. for school children to carry books, etc., in. **satchelled,** *a.*

sate (1) (sāt) [O.F. *satier*, to SATIATE, or from A.-S. *sadian*, to make SAD, assim. to this], *v.t.* To satisfy the appetite or desire of; to satiate, to surfeit, to glut, to cloy. **sateless,** *a.* (*poet.*).

***sate** (2), *past* [SIT].

sateen (să tēn') [from SATIN], *n.* A glossy woollen or cotton fabric made in imitation of satin.

sateless [SATE (1)].

satellite (săt' ĕ līt) [F., from L. *satellitem*, nom. *-telles*, guard, attendant], *n.* A secondary planet revolving round a primary one; an obsequious follower, dependant, or henchman. **satellite state:** (*Pol.*) A country subservient to a greater power. **satellite town:** A small town dependent upon a larger town in the vicinity. **earth satellite:** An artificial satellite containing scientific instruments, etc., projected into space, where it revolves round the earth. The first was launched from Russia, 4 October, 1957.

satiate (sā' shi āt) [L. *satiātus*, p.p. of *satiāre*, from *sat, satis*, see SATISFY], *v.t.* To satisfy the desire or appetite of; to sate, to glut, to surfeit. ****a.*** Sated, glutted, cloyed. **satiable,** *a.* **satiation** (sā shi-, -si ā' shŭn), *n.* **satiety** (să tī' ĕ ti), *n.* The state of being sated or glutted; excess of gratification producing disgust; *sufficiency, fullness, overabundance.

satin (săt' in) [F., prob. through late L. *sētīnus*, silken, from L. *sēta*, silk, orig. bristle], *n.* A silken fabric with an overshot woof and a highly-finished glossy surface on one side only. *a.* Made of or resembling this, esp. in smoothness. *v.t.* To give (paper, etc.) a glossy surface like satin. **white satin,** *n.* The plant honesty. **satin-bird,** *n.* An Australian bower-bird, *Ptilonorhyncus violaceus.* **satin-finish,** *n.* A lustrous polish given to silverware with a metallic brush. **satin-flower,** *n.* Honesty; the greater stitchwort. **satin-gypsum,** *n.* A fibrous gypsum used by lapidaries. **satin-paper,** *n.* A fine, glossy writing-paper. **satin-spar,** *n.* A finely fibrous variety of aragonite, calcite, or gypsum. **satin-stitch,** *n.* A stitch in parallel lines giving the appearance of satin. **satin-stone** [SATIN-GYPSUM]. **satin-wood,** *n.* An ornamental cabinet wood of various species from the East and West Indies. **satiné** (sa tē' nā), *n.* A variety of satin-wood from Guiana. **satinet** (săt i net'), *n.* A thin satin; a glossy fabric made to imitate satin. **satining-machine,** *n.* A machine for giving (paper, etc.) a satiny surface. **satinize,** *v.t.* **satiny,** *a.*

satire (săt' īr) [F., from L. *satira, satura* (*lanx satura*, full dish, medley), rel. to *satur, satis*, see SATISFY], *n.* A composition, orig. a medley in verse, now either in verse or prose, in which wickedness or folly or individual persons are held up to ridicule; ridicule, sarcasm, or the use of ridicule, irony, and invective ostensibly for the chastisement of vice or folly. **satiric, -al** (-tir' ik, -ăl), *a.* **satirically,** adv. **satiricalness,** *n.* **satirist** (săt' i rist), *n.* One who writes or employs satire. **satirize,** *v.t*

satisfy (săt' is fī) [O.F. *satisfier*, L. *satisfacere* (*satis*, enough, *facere*, to make, p.p. *factus*)], *v.t.* To supply or gratify to the full; to content, to gratify, to please (*usu. in p.p.*); to pay (a debt, etc.); to fulfil, to comply with; to be sufficient for, to meet the desires or expectations of; (*Math.*) to fulfil the conditions of; to free from doubt; to convince; to meet (a doubt, objection, etc.) adequately. *v.i.* To give satisfaction; to make payment, compensation, or reparation, to atone. **satisfaction** (-făk' shŭn), *n.* The act of satisfying; the state of being satisfied; gratification, contentment, payment of a debt, fulfilment of an obligation; reparation, compensation, amends; atonement, performance of penance. **satisfactory,** *a.* Giving satisfaction, sufficient, adequate, meeting all needs, desires, or expectations; relieving the mind from doubt; atoning; making amends. **satisfactorily,** *adv.* **satisfactoriness,** *n.* **satisfiable,** *a.* **satisfier,** *n.* **satisfying,** *a.* **satisfyingly,** *adv.*

satrap (sā' trăp, săt' răp) [L. *satrapa, satrapes*, Gr. *satrapēs*, O.Pers. *khsatrapāvā* (*khsatra*, province, *pa-*, to protect)], *n.* A governor of a province under the ancient Persian empire, a viceroy; a governor, a ruler of a dependency, etc., esp. one who affects despotic ways. **satrapess,** *n.* **satrapal, satrapial** (-trā' pi ăl), **satrapic, -al** (-trăp' ik, -ăl), *a.* **satrapy** (săt'-), *n.*

Satsuma (săt′ sū mȧ) [Japanese district], *a.* Applied to a cream-coloured variety of Japanese pottery, usu. called **Satsuma ware.**

saturate (săt′ ū rāt) [L. *saturātus*, p.p. of *saturāre*, from *satur*, cogn. with *satis*, enough], *v.t.* To soak, impregnate, or imbue thoroughly; to fill or charge (a body, substance, gas, fluid, etc., with another substance, fluid, electricity, etc.) so that it will hold no more. *a.* (-rȧt) Intense, deep (of colours); (*poet.*) saturated. **saturable,** *a.* **saturant,** *a.* Saturating. *n.* A substance neutralizing acidity or alkalinity. **saturater** (săt′ ū rā tėr), *n.*

saturation (săt ū rā′ shŭn), *n.* The state of being saturated; (*Chem.*) the fusing of one body with another until the receiving body has reached repletion point; (*Magnetism*) the point at which increasing magnetizing force fails to increase any further the flux-density of the magnet. **saturation current,** *n.* (*Elec.*) The maximum value of current that can be carried.

Saturday (săt′ ŭr dā) [A.-S. *Sæter-dæg* (*Sæternes*, L. *Saturni*, of SATURN, *dies*, DAY)], *n.* The seventh day of the week.

Saturn (săt′ ŭrn) [L. *Saturnus*, prob. from *sa-* or *se-* (*serere*, to sow)], *n.* (*Rom. Ant.*) An ancient Italian god of agriculture, usually identified with the Greek Kronos, father of Zeus, under whose sway the world was in the golden age; (*Astron.*) the sixth of the major planets in distance from the sun; (*Alch.*) lead. **Saturnalia** (-nā′ li ȧ), *n.pl.* (*Rom. Ant.*) An annual festival in December in honour of Saturn, regarded as a time of unrestrained licence and merriment; (*fig.*) a season or occasion of unrestrained revelry. **saturnalian,** *a.* **saturnian** (sȧ tĕr′ ni ȧn), *a.* Pertaining to the god Saturn or the golden age; happy, virtuous, distinguished for purity; of or pertaining to the planet Saturn; denoting the accentual metre of early Latin poetry. *n.* An inhabitant of Saturn; (*pl.*) saturnian verses. **saturnic,** *a.* (*Path.*) Affected with lead-poisoning.

saturnine (săt′ ĕr nīn), *a.* Orig. born under the influence of the planet Saturn; dull, phlegmatic, gloomy, morose; (*Path., old Chem., etc.*) pertaining to lead or lead-poisoning. **saturninely,** *adv.* **saturnism** (săt′-), *n.* Lead-poisoning. **saturnist,** *n.* A saturnine person.

saturnite (săt′ ĕr nīt), *n.* (*Min.*) A mineral substance containing lead.

satyagraha (sa tya′ gra ha) [Sansk. *satya*, faithful, *agraha*, obstinacy], *n.* (*Pol.*) Non-violent resistance to authority.

satyr (săt′ ir) [L. *satyrus*, Gr. *saturos*], *n.* (*Gr. Myth.*) An ancient sylvan deity represented with the legs of a goat, budding horns, and goat-like ears, identified by the Romans with the fauns; a lascivious or brutish man; the orang-outang. **satyral,** *n.* (*Her.*) A monster with a human head and parts of various animals. **satyric, *-al** (sȧ tir′ ik, -ȧl), *a.* **satyric drama:** A burlesque play with a chorus of satyrs, usually following a trilogy.

satyriasis (săt i rī′ ȧ sis), *n.* (*Path.*) A diseased and unrestrained venereal appetite in men.

satyrid (săt′ i rid), *n.* (*Ent.*) One of the *Satyridæ*, a family of butterflies.

Satyrium (sȧ tir′ i ŭm), *n.* (*Bot.*) A genus of tropical orchids with flowers in dense spikes.

sauce (saws) [F., from pop. L. *salsa*, fem. of *saisus*, salt, from SAL], *n.* A preparation, usu. liquid, taken with foods to improve the relish; (*fig.*) anything that gives piquancy or makes palatable; (*colloq.*) sauciness, impertinence, impudence, cheek. *v.t.* (*fig.*) To flavour, to make piquant or pungent; to be saucy or impudent; to treat with sauce, to season. **sauce-alone,** *n.* The hedge garlic. **sauce-boat,** *n.* A table-vessel for holding sauce. **sauce-box,** *n.* (*colloq.*) An impudent person, esp. a child. **saucepan,** *n.* A metal pan or pot, usu. cylindrical with a long handle, for boiling or stewing; orig. a pan for cooking sauces. **sauceless,** *a.*

saucer (saw′ sėr), *n.* A shallow china vessel for placing a cup on and catching spillings; any small flattish vessel, dish, or receptacle of similar use. **saucer-eye,** *n.* A large, round, staring eye. **saucer-eyed,** *a.* **saucerful,** *n.* **saucerless,** *a.*

saucisse (sō′ sēs), ***saucisson*** (sō′ sē son) [F., SAUSAGE], *n.* (*Fort.*) A long tube of gunpowder, etc., for firing a charge; a long fascine.

saucy (saw′ si), *a.* Pert, impudent, insolent to superiors, cheeky; smart, sprightly, piquant; fastidious, dainty. **saucily,** *adv.* **sauciness,** *n.*

sauerkraut (sour′ krout) [G.], *n.* A German dish of chopped cabbage compressed with salt until it ferments.

sauger (saw′ gėr) [etym. doubtful], *n.* The smaller American pike-perch, *Stizostedion Canadense.*

saugh, sauch (*Sc.*) [SALLOW (1)].

saul [var. of SAL (2); Sc., var. of SOUL].

***saulie** (saw′ li) [Sc., etym. doubtful], *n.* A hired mourner.

sault (sō, soo) [O.F., from L. *saltus*, from *salīre*, to leap], *n.* (*F. Canadian*) A rapid on a river.

saunders [SANDERS]. **saunt** (*Sc.*) [SAINT].

saunter (sawn′ tėr) [perh. through A.-F. *sauntrer*, from med. L. *exadventūrāre* (EX-, ADVENTURE)], *v.i.* To wander about idly and leisurely; to walk leisurely (along). *n.* A leisurely ramble or stroll; a sauntering gait. **saunterer,** *n.* **saunteringly,** *adv.*

saurian (saw′ ri ȧn) [Gr. *saura*, *sauros*, lizard, -IAN], *a.* Pertaining to or resembling the *Sauria*, an order of reptiles formerly including the crocodiles and lizards, but now the lizards alone. *n.* A lizard or lizard-like creature, esp. one of the extinct forms as the ichthyosaurus and plesiosaurus. **sauro-,** *comb. form.* **saurodont,** *n.* One of the *Saurodontidæ*, an extinct family of fishes of the Cretaceous age. *a.* Of or pertaining to this family. **saurognathous** (saw rog′ nȧ thŭs), *a.* (*Ornith.*) Having a palate similar to that of the lizards. **saurognathism,** *n.* **sauroid,** *a.* and *n.* **saurophagous** (saw rof′ ȧ gŭs) [-PHAGOUS], *a.* Feeding on lizards and other reptiles. **sauropod** (saw′ rō pod), *n.* One of the *Sauropoda*, an extinct order of gigantic herbivores. **sauropodous** (-rop′ ō dŭs), *a.* ***sauropsida*** (saw rop′ si dȧ) [Gr. *opsis*, appearance], *n.pl.* (*Zool.*) One of Huxley's three great primary groups of vertebrata, comprising birds and reptiles. **sauropsidan,** *a.* and *n.* **saururæ** (saw roor′ ē) [Gr. *ouros*, tail], *n.pl.* (*Palæont.*) An extinct sub-class of birds having lizard-like tails. **saururous,** *a.* ***saurus,** *n.* (*pl* **-ri**) A saurian.

saury (saw′ ri) [etym. doubtful, perh. rel. to prec.], *n.* A sea-fish, *Scomberesox saurus*, with elongated body ending in a beak.

sausage (sos′ ȧj) [F. *saucisse*, late L. *salsicia*, from *salsus*, SAUCE], *n.* A popular article of food consisting of pork or other meat minced, seasoned, and stuffed into a length of animal's gut or a similar receptacle; a length of this between two ligatures. **sausage balloon,** *n.* (*Mil.*) An observation balloon shaped like an inflated sausage. **sausage-cutter, -filler, -grinder, -machine,** *n.* Appliances used in manufacturing sausages. **sausage-meat,** *n.* Meat used for stuffing sausages, esp. cooked separately as stuffing, etc. **sausage-roll,** *n.* Sausage meat enclosed in pastry and baked.

saussurite (saw′ sū rīt) [H. B. de *Saussure* (1740–99), the discoverer], *n.* (*Min.*) An impure white, grey, or green silicate formed by alteration from feldspar. **saussuritic** (-rit′ ik), *a.*

saut (*Sc.*) [SALT].

sauté (sō′ tā) [F., p.p. of *sauter*, to leap], *a.* (*fem.* **-*tée***, *pl.* **-*tés*, -*tées***) Lightly fried.

Sauterne (sō târn′) [district on the Garonne, France], *n.* A white Bordeaux wine.

sauve qui peut (sōv kē pĕr) [F., save himself who can], *int.* and *n.* Each for himself.

savable, etc. [SAVE].

savage (săv′ ȧj) [O.F. *salvage*, L. *silvāticus*, from *silva*, wood], *a.* Uncultivated, wild; uncivilized, in a primitive condition, fierce, brutal, cruel, violent, furious; (*colloq.*) extremely angry, enraged; (*Her.*) nude, unclad. *n.* A human being in a primitive state, esp. a member of a nomadic tribe living by hunting and fishing; a person of extreme brutality or ferocity, a brute, a barbarian. *v.t.* To bite, tear, or trample (of horses); *to make wild or savage. **savagely,** *adv.* **savagedom, savageness, savagery, savagism,** *n.*

savanna (sȧ văn′ ȧ) [Sp. *sabana*, prob. from Carib.], *n.* An extensive treeless plain covered with low vegetation, esp. in tropical America. **savanna bird,** or **s. blackbird:** The W. Indian *Crotophaga ani.* **savanna flower:** An evergreen shrub of various species of *Echites.*

savant (sa′ van) [F., orig. p.p. of *savoir*, to know], *n.* A man of learning, esp. an eminent scientist.

savate (sa′ vat) [F., from It. *ciabatta*, etym. doubtful], *n.* The French method of boxing in which the feet are used as well as the hands.

save (sāv) [F. *sauver*, L. *salvāre*, from *salvus*, SAFE], *v.t.* To preserve, rescue, or deliver as from danger, destruction, or harm of any kind; to deliver from sin, to preserve from damnation; to keep undamaged or untouched; to keep from being spent or lost; to reserve and lay by, to husband, to refrain from spending; to spare, to exempt (*with double object*); to obviate, to prevent; to prevent or obviate the need of; to take advantage of; to be in time for, to catch. *v.i.* To be economical, to avoid waste or undue expenditure. *prep.* Except, saving; leaving out, not including. *conj.* Unless. *n.* (*Football, etc.*) The act of preventing opponents from scoring; something saved, an economy. **save-all,** *n.* Anything that prevents things from being wasted; a contrivance to hold a candle-end in a candlestick; (*Naut.*) a strip of canvas laced to a sail to catch a light wind. **savable,** *a.* **saver,** *n.* (*usu. in comb.*, as *life-saver*). **saving,** *a.* Preserving from danger, loss, waste, etc.; economical, frugal; reserving or expressing a reservation, stipulation, etc. *n.* The act of economizing; that which is saved, an economy (*usu. in pl.*); an exception, a reservation. *prep.* Save, except; with due respect to. **savingly,** *adv.* ***savingness,** *n.* **savings bank:** A bank receiving small deposits and usu. devoting any profits to the payment of interest.

saveloy (săv′ ĕ loi) [corr. of F. *cervelas*, It. *cervelatta*, from *cervello*, L. CEREBELLUM], *n.* A highly-seasoned dried sausage of salted pork (orig. of brains).

savin (săv′ in) [A.-S. *safine*, O.F. *savine*, L. *sabīna*, SABINE], *n.* An evergreen bush or low tree, *Juniperus Sabina*, with bluish-green fruit, yielding an oil used medicinally.

saviour (sā′ vyŭr) [O.F. *saveor*, *salveor*, L. *salvātōrem*, nom. *-tor*, from *salvāre*, to SAVE], *n.* One who preserves, rescues, or redeems. **our** or **the Saviour:** Christ, the Redeemer of mankind.

savoir faire (săv war fâr′) [F., to know what to do], *n.* Quickness to do the right thing; tact; presence of mind.

savonette (săv′ ō net) [F. (now *savonnette*), dim. of *savon*, L. *sāpo*, soap], *n.* A toilet preparation of various kinds. **savonette-tree,** *n.* A W. Indian tree the bark of which is used as a substitute for soap.

savory (sā′ vŏ ri) [O.F. *savereie*, L. *saturēia*], *n.* A plant of the aromatic genus *Satureia*, esp. *S. hortensis*, used in cookery.

savour (sā′ vŏr) [O.F., from L. *sapōrem*, nom. *sapor*, from *sapere*, to taste], *n.* Flavour, taste, relish; characteristic quality; (*fig.*) suggestive quality, smack or admixture (of); *smell, perfume. *v.t.* To give a flavour to; *to have the flavour or to smack of; *to like, to relish; *to discern. *v.i.* To have a particular smell or flavour, to smack (of); to perceive, to relish, to enjoy the savour of. **savourily,** *adv.* **savouriness,** *n.* **savourless,** *a.* **savoury,** *a.* Having a pleasant savour; palatable, appetizing; free from offensive smells. *n.* A savoury dish, usu. one served as an appetizer or digestive.

savoy (sȧ voi′) [district in France], *n.* A hardy variety of cabbage with wrinkled leaves.

Savoyard (sȧ voi′ ȧrd), *n.* A native of Savoy; one connected with or an habituee of the Savoy Theatre in the days of the Gilbert and Sullivan operas (1875–96). *a.* Of Savoy.

savvy (săv′ i) [corr. of Sp. *sabe*, know, ult. from L. *sapere*, to be wise], *v.t.* and *i.* To know, to understand. *n.* Understanding, knowingness, cleverness.

saw (1) (saw) [A.-S. *saga* (cp. Dut. *zaag*, G. *säge*, Icel. *sög*), cogn. with L. *secāre*, to cut], *n.* A cutting-instrument, usu. of steel, with a toothed edge, worked by hand, or in circular, ribbon, or other form as part of machinery; a machine comprising such a part or parts; a tool or implement used as a saw; (*Zool.*) a serrated part or organ. *v.t.* (*past* **sawed,** *p.p.* **sawn**) To cut with a saw; to form or make with a saw; to make motions in as of one sawing; to make cuts in the back of a book to receive the threads in sewing. *v.i.* To use a saw; to make motions of one sawing. **saw-bill,** *n.* A tropical or sub-tropical American bird, the motmot, with serrated mandibles. **saw-bones,** *n.* (*slang*) A surgeon. **saw-doctor,** *n.* A machine for cutting teeth in a saw. **sawdust,** *n.* Small fragments of wood produced in sawing, used for packing, etc. **saw-fish,** *n.* A fish of the genus *Pristis*, with an elongated, saw-like snout. **saw-fly,** *n.* A hymenopterous insect of the genus *Tenthredo*, furnished with a saw-like ovipositor. **saw-gin,** *n.* A cotton-gin with saw-teeth. **sawmill,** *n.* A mill with machinery for sawing timber. **sawpit,** *n.* A pit over which timber is sawed, one man standing above and the other below the log. **saw-set, -wrest,** *n.* A tool for slanting the teeth of a saw alternately outward. **saw-whet,** *n.* A small N. American owl, *Nyctale Acadica*, with a harsh cry. **sawwort,** *n.* Any plant of the genus *Serratula*, having serrated leaves yielding a yellow dye. **sawing-horse,** *n.* A rack on which logs are laid for sawing. **sawyer,** *n.* One employed in sawing timber into planks, or wood for fuel; a wood-boring larva; (*Am.*) a tree fallen into a river and swept along, sawing up and down in the water; (*N. Zealand*) a kind of grasshopper, the weta.

saw (2) (saw) [A.-S. *sagu*, cogn. with SAY (1)], *n.* A saying, a proverb, a familiar maxim; *a tale, a recital.

saw (3) *past* [SEE (1)].

sawder (saw′ dĕr) [corr. of SOLDER], *n.* Blarney, flattery.

Sawney (saw′ ni) [prob. *Sandy*, corr. of *Alexander*], *n.* A nickname for a Scotsman; a simpleton.

sawwort, sawyer, etc. [SAW (1)].

sax (1) (săks) [A.-S. *seax*, knife, cp. Icel. and O.H.G. *sax*], *n.* A slate-cutter's chopping and trimming tool with a point for making holes.

sax (2) (*Sc.*) [SIX].

saxatile (săk′ sȧ til, -tīl) [F., from L. *saxātilis* from *saxum*, rock], *a.* Pertaining to or living among rocks.

saxe (săks) [F. *Saxe*, Saxony], *n.* An albumenized photographic paper made in Saxony. **saxe-blue** [SAXON-BLUE].

saxhorn (săks′ hôrn) [Adolphe *Sax*, inventor (*c.* 1845), HORN], *n.* A brass musical wind-instrument with a long winding tube, a wide opening, and several valves.

saxicavous (săk si kā′ vŭs) [L. *saxi-*, *saxum*, rock, *cavāre*, to hollow], *a.* Hollowing out stone; belonging to the *Saxicava*, a genus of rock-boring molluscs. **saxicoline** (săk sik′ ō lin), *a.* Inhabiting or growing among rocks, saxatile. **saxicolous,** *a.*

saxifrage (săk′ si frāj) [F., from L. *saxifraga*, spleenwort (*saxi-*, *saxum*, rock, *frag-*, root of *frangere*, to break)], *n.* Any plant of the genus *Saxifraga* (so called because formerly esteemed good for stone in the bladder), consisting largely of Alpine or rock plants with tufted, mossy, or encrusted foliage and small flowers. **saxifragaceous** (-gā' shùs), *a.* ***saxifrageous**, *a.* Breaking or destroying stone or calculi. ***saxifragant**, *a.* and *n.*

Saxon (săk' sòn) [F., from late L. *Saxonēs*, pl., from A.-S. *Seaxan*, from *seax*, see SAX, rel. to L. *saxum*, rock], *n.* One of a Teutonic race from northern Germany who conquered England in the 5th and 6th cent.; an Anglo-Saxon; the old Saxon or the Anglo-Saxon language; a native of modern Saxony. *a.* Pertaining to the Saxons, their country, or language; Anglo-Saxon; pertaining to Saxony or its inhabitants. **Saxon-blue**, *n.* Indigo dissolved in sulphuric acid, used by dyers. **Saxondom**, *n.* **Saxonism**, *n.* **Saxonist**, *n.* **Saxonize**, *v.t.* and *i.*

Saxony (săk' sò ni) [*Saxony*, in Germany], *n.* A fine wool or woollen material produced in Saxony.

saxophone (săk' sò fōn) [A. *Sax*, see SAXHORN, -PHONE], *n.* A brass musical wind-instrument with a single reed used as a powerful substitute for the clarinet. **saxtuba**, *n.* A bass saxhorn.

say (1) (sā) [A.-S. *secgan*, cp. Icel. *segja*, Dan. *sige*, G. *sagen*], *v.t.* (*past & p.p.* **said**, **sed**, ***3rd sing. pres.** **saith**, seth) To utter in words, to speak; to recite, to rehearse, to repeat; to tell, to affirm, to assert, to state; to allege, to report; to promise; to suppose, to assume; to give as an opinion or answer, to decide. *v.i.* To speak, to talk, to answer. *n.* What one says or has to say, an affirmation, a statement; (*colloq.*) one's turn to speak. **it is said** or **they say:** It is generally reported or rumoured. **that is to say:** In other words. **say-so**, *n.* A dictum, a positive assertion. **says (sez) you!** *int.* (*slang*) An expression of incredulity. **saying**, *n.* That which is said; a maxim, an adage, a saw.

***say** (2) (sā) [O.F. *saie*, L. *saga*, pl. of *sagum*, Gr. *sagos*, military cloak], *n.* A fine thin serge; a kind of silk or satin.

***say** (3), ***sayer** [ASSAY, ASSAYER].

sayette (sā et') [F., dim. of *saie*, SAY (2)], *n.* A mixed fabric of silk and wool or silk and cotton.

sbirro (zbēr' ō) [It.], *n.* (*pl.* **-ri**, -rē) An Italian policeman; a police spy.

***'sblood** (zblŭd) [euph. for *God's blood*], *int.* An oath or imprecation.

scab (skăb) [Dan. and Swed. *skabb* (cp. A.-S. *sceab*, *scæb*)], *n.* An incrustation formed over a sore, etc., in healing, a cicatrice; a highly-contagious skin-disease resembling mange, attacking horses, cattle, and esp. sheep; one of various fungoid plant-diseases; (*fig.*) *a paltry dirty fellow; a workman who refuses to join in a strike or who takes the place of a striker, a blackleg. *v.i.* To form a scab, to cicatrize. **scabmite**, *n.* The itch-mite. **scabbed**, **scabby**, *a.* **scabbily**, *adv.* **scabbiness**, *n.*

scabbard (skăb' ard) [M.E. *scauberc*, A.-F. *escaubers*, pl., prob. from Teut.], *n.* The sheath of a sword or similar weapon. *v.t.* To put into a scabbard, to sheathe. **scabbard fish**, *n.* A small silvery sea-fish with a blade-like body.

scabble [var. of SCAPPLE].

scaberulous [SCABROUS].

scabies (skā' bi ēz) [L., from *scabere*, to scratch], *n.* (*Path.*) The itch, a contagious skin-disease.

scabious (skā' bi ùs) [L. *scabiōsus*, as prec.], *a.* Consisting of or covered with scabs; affected with itch. *n.* A plant of the herbaceous genus *Scabiosa*, having involucrate heads of blue, pink, and white flowers.

scabrous (skā' brùs) [L. *scabrōsus*, from *scaber*, cogn. with prec.], *a.* Rough, rugged, or uneven; scurfy; thorny; (*fig.*) awkward to handle, approaching the indelicate, risky. **scaberulous** (skȧ ber' ū lùs), *a.* (*Bot.*) Somewhat scabrous. **scabridity** (-brid' i ti), **scabrousness**, *n.*

scad (1) (skăd) [etym. unknown], *n.* The horse-mackerel.

scad (2) (skăd) [perh. var. of SHAD], *n.* The fry of salmon.

scad (3) (*Sc.*) [SCALD (1)].

scaff (skăf) [Sc., etym. doubtful], *n.* Food; (*fig.*) the rabble, the riff-raff. **scaff-raff**, *n.*

scaffold (skăf' òld) [O.North.F. *escafaut*, O.F. *escadafault* (F. *échafaud*), (perh. EX-, It. *catafalco*, CATAFALQUE)], *n.* A temporary structure of poles and ties supporting a platform for the use of workmen building or repairing a house or other building; a temporary raised platform for the execution of criminals; *a platform, or stage for shows or spectators; (*Anat.*, *Embryology*, *etc.*) the bony framework of a structure, esp. one to be covered by developed parts. *v.t.* To furnish with a scaffold; to uphold, to support. ***scaffoldage**, *n.* Scaffolding. **scaffolder**, *n.* **scaffolding**, *n.* A scaffold for builders, shows, pageants, etc.; (*Anat.*, *etc.*) scaffold; materials for scaffolds.

scaglia (ska' li ȧ) [It., SCALE (2)], *n.* A red, white, or grey Italian limestone corresponding to the chalk. **scagliola** (skăl yō' lȧ), *n.* A hard, polished plaster, coloured in imitation of marble.

scaith (*Sc.*) [SCATHE].

scalable (skā' lȧbl), *a.* That may be scaled.

***scalade**, ***scalado** [ESCALADE].

scalar (skā' lȧr) [L. *scālāris*, from *scāla*, SCALE (3)], *a.* (*Bot.*) Scalariform; (*Math.*) of the nature of a scalar. *n.* (*Math.*) A pure number, esp. the term in a quaternion that is not a vector. **scalariform** (skȧ lăr' i fôrm), *a.* (*Bot.*, *Zool.*, *etc.*) Ladder-shaped (of the structure of cells, vessels, veins, etc.).

scald (1) (skawld) [O.North.F. *escalder*, O.F. *eschalder*, L. *excaldāre* (EX-, *calidus*, hot)], *v.t.* To burn with or as with a hot liquid or vapour; to clean (out) with boiling water; to cook lightly in hot water or steam; to raise (milk) nearly to boiling point. *n.* An injury to the skin from hot liquid or vapour. **scalder**, *n.* **scalding**, *n.* **scalding-hot**, *n.* Hot enough to scald.

scald (2) (skawld) [Icel. *skald*], *n.* An ancient Norse poet or reciter of poems, a bard. **scaldic**, *a.*

scald (3) (skawld) [orig. *scalled*, see SCALL], *a.* Affected with scall. **scald-head**, *n.* An affection of the scalp.

scalder, **scalding** [SCALD (1)].

scaldic [SCALD (2)].

scaldino (skăl dē' nō) [It., from *scaldare*, to warm, from L. as SCALD (1)], *n.* (*pl.* **-ni**, -nē) A small earthenware brazier used for warming the hands, etc.

scale (1) (skāl) [O.F. *escale*, O.H.G. *scala* (A.-S. *scealu*, cogn. with foll., G. *schale*)], *n.* One of the thin horny plates forming a protective covering on the skin of fishes and reptiles; a modified leaf, bract, hair, feather, disk, husk or other structure resembling this; a scab, a carious coating, an incrustation; a small plate or flake of metal, etc. *v.t.* To strip the scales off. *v.i.* To form scales; to come off in scales; (*Sc.*) to disperse, to scatter; (*Austral.*) to ride on a tram or bus without paying the fare. **scale-armour**, *n.* Armour made of small plates overlapping each other like the scales of a fish. **scale-board**, *n.* A thin board for the back of a picture, etc. **scale-fern**, *n.* The ceterach. **scale-winged**, *a.* Having the wings covered with scales, lepidopterous. **scale-work**, *n.* An arrangement of overlapping scales, imbricated work. **scaled**, *a.* Having scales (*usu. in comb.* as *thick-scaled*). **scaleless**, *a.* **scaly**, *a.* **scaliness**, *n.*

scale (2) (skāl) [O.F. *escale*, cup, Icel. *skāl*, bowl (cp. Dut. *schaal*), cogn. with prec.], *n.* The dish of a balance; (*pl.*) a simple balance. *v.t.* To amount to in weight; *to weigh in scales.

scale (3) (skāl) [L. *scāla*, ladder, cogn. with *scandere*, to climb], *n.* Anything graduated or marked with lines or degrees at regular intervals, as a scheme for classification, gradation, etc.; a basis for a numerical system in which the value of a figure depends on its place in the order; a system of correspondence between different magnitudes, relative dimensions; a set of marks or a rule or other instrument marked with these showing exact distances, proportions, values, etc., used for measuring, calculating, etc.; (*Mus.*) all the tones of a key arranged in ascending or descending order according to pitch. *v.t.* To climb by or as by a ladder; to clamber up; to draw or otherwise represent to scale or proper proportions. *v.i.* To have a common scale, to be commensurable. **scaling-ladder,** *n.* A ladder used in storming fortified places.

scalene (skȧ lēn′) [late L. *scalēnus*, Gr. *skalēnos*, prob. rel. to *skolios*, crooked], *a.* Having no two sides equal (of triangles); having the axis inclined to the base (of a cone or cylinder), *n.* A scalene triangle or muscle. **scalenohedron** (-hē′ drȯn), *n.* (*Cryst.*) A hemihedral form of the hexagonal or the tetragonal system with eight similar and equal scalene triangles as faces. **scalenohedral,** *a.* **scalenum,** *n.* A scalene triangle. **scalenus,** *n.* (*pl.* **-ni**) (*Anat.*) One of a series of irregularly triangular muscles at the neck.

scaliness [SCALE (1)].

scaling-ladder [SCALE (3)].

scalion (skăl′ i ȯn) [O.North.F. *escalogne*, SHALLOT], *n.* A variety of onion or shallot.

***scall** (skawl) [Icel. *skalli*, cp. Swed. *skallig*, bald], *n.* A scabby or scaly eruption, esp. of the scalp. **a.* Mean, scurvy, paltry, low. **scalled-head** [SCALD-HEAD, SCALD (3)].

scallop (skol′-, skăl′ ȯp) [O.F. *escalope*, from Teut. (cp. M.Dut. *schelpe*), cogn. with SHELL], *n.* A bivalve mussel of the genus *Pecten* with ridges and flutings radiating from the middle of the hinge and an undulating margin; a single shell of this worn as a pilgrim's badge; such a shell or a small shallow dish or pan used for cooking and serving oysters, mince, etc. in; (*pl.*) an ornamental undulating edging cut like that of a scallop-shell. *v.t.* To cut or indent the edge of thus; to cook in a scallop. **scallop-shell,** *n.* **scalloping,** *n.* **scalloping-tool,** *n.*

scallywag (skăl′ i wăg) [corr. of *Scalloway*, Shetland], *n.* A poor, ill-conditioned, or undersized animal (orig. of Shetland ponies); a scamp, a scapegrace.

scalp (skălp) [prob. Scand. (cp. M.Swed. *skalp*, Icel. *skālpr*, sheath), cogn. with SCALLOP], *n.* The top of the head; the skin of this with the hair belonging to it, torn off by North American Indians as a trophy of victory; (*poet.*) a bare hill-top; a whale's head without the lower jaw. *v.t.* To tear or take the scalp from; to cut the top part, layer, etc., off (anything); to flay, to lay bare; (*fig.*) to criticize or abuse savagely; (*Am.*) to buy and sell at less than the recognized price; to take small profits on (stocks, etc.). *v.i.* (*Am.*) To take small profits to minimize risk. **scalp-lock,** *n.* A solitary tuft of hair left on the shaven crown of the head as a challenge by the warriors of some American tribes. **scalper,** *n.* One who scalps; (*Am.*) a ticket tout. **scalping-iron,** *n.* (*Surg.*) A raspatory. **scalping-knife,** *n.* **scalpless,** *a.*

scalpel (skăl′ pėl) [L. *scalpellum*, dim. of *scalprum*, knife, from *scalpere*, to scrape], *n.* A small knife used in surgical operations and anatomical dissections.

scalper, etc. [SCALP].

scalpriform (skăl′ pri fôrm) [L. *scalpri-*, *scalprum*, see SCALPEL, -FORM], *a.* Chisel-shaped (as the teeth of rodents).

***scamble** (skăm′ bėl) [prob. rel. to SHAMBLE and SCRAMBLE], *v.i.* To scramble or struggle (for, after, etc.); to get (through or along) somehow. *v.t.* To mangle, to maul; to waste, to squander. *n.* A scramble; a struggle. **scambler,** *n.* ***scamblingly,** *adv.*

scammony (skăm′ ȯ ni) [O.F. *scammonie*, L. *scammōnia*, Gr. *skammōnia*], *n.* An Asiatic convolvulus, *C. scammonia*; a purgative gum-resin from the root of this. **scammonic** (-mon′ ik), *a.* (*Chem.*). ***scammoniate** (-mō′ ni ăt), *a.* and *n.*

scamp (1) (skămp) [prob. as SCAMPER], *n.* A worthless fellow, a knave, a rogue. **scampish,** *a.*

scamp (2) (skămp) [prob. var. of SCANT], *v.t.* To do or execute (work, etc.) in a careless manner or with bad material.

scamper (skăm′ pėr) [orig. to run away, O.North.F. *escamper*, (EX-, L. *campus*, field)], *v.i.* To run rapidly, hastily, or impulsively; *to run away. *n.* A hasty run; (*fig.*) a hurried excursion, a hurried tour.

scampi (skam′ pē) [It.], *n.pl.* Large Italian prawns.

scampish [SCAMP (1)].

scan (skăn) [L. *scandere*, to climb (*d* prob. conf. with -ED)], *v.t.* (*past & p.p.* **scanned**) To count or test the metrical feet or the syllables of (a line of verse); to examine closely or intently, to scrutinize; (*T.V.*) to traverse an area with electronic beams [SCANNING]; *(*Spens.*) to climb. *v.i.* To be metrically correct, to agree with the rules of scansion.

scandal (skăn′ dȧl) [M.E. *scandle*, O.North.F. *escandle* (F. *scandale*), L. *scandalum*, Gr. *skandalon*, snare, stumbling-block], *n.* Indignation, offence, or odium at some act or conduct, esp. as expressed in common talk; reproach, shame, disgrace; malicious gossip, aspersion of character; (*Law*) a defamatory statement, esp. of an irrelevant nature; an affront. **v.t.* To speak scandal of; to defame, to traduce. **scandalize,** *v.t.* To offend by improper or outrageous conduct, to shock; (*vulg.*) to talk scandal about. **scandal-monger,** *n.* One who disseminates scandal. **scandalous,** *a.* **scandalously,** *adv.* **scandalousness,** *n.* ***scandalum magnatum*** (-măg nā′ tum) [med. L. *magnātum*, gen. pl. of *magnas*, MAGNATE], *n.* (*Law*) Defamation of high personages of the realm.

scandent (skăn′ dĕnt) [L. *scandens -ntem*, pres.p. of *scandere*, to climb], *a.* Climbing, as ivy.

Scandinavian (skăn di nā′ vi ȧn), *a.* Pertaining to Scandinavia (Norway, Sweden, Denmark, and Iceland), its language, or literature. *n.* A native of Scandinavia; (*collect.*) the languages of Scandinavia.

scandium (skăn′ di ŭm) [obs. *Scandia*, Scandinavia], *n.* (*Chem.*) A rare metallic element discovered in certain Swedish yttrium metals.

scanning (skăn′ ing), *n.* (*T.V.*) The continuous traversing of a picture by a beam of light or of electrons, for the purpose of transmitting the image. **scanning beam,** *n.* The beam of light or electrons with which an image is scanned for television. **scanning disk,** *n.* A disk with a spiral of holes with or without lenses, used for dividing the transmitted picture into a series of narrow strips.

scansion (skăn′ shŭn) [L. *scansio*, from *scandere*, to SCAN], *n.* The act of scanning verse; a system of scanning.

Scansores (skăn sôr′ ēz) [mod. L., as prec.], *n.pl.* (*Ornith.*) Climbing-birds, an order containing the cuckoos, woodpeckers, parrots, trogons, etc. **scansorial,** *a.* Climbing, adapted for climbing; belonging to the *Scansores*. *n.* Any bird of the order *Scansores*.

scant (skănt) [Icel. *skamt*, short], *a.* Not full, large, or plentiful; scarcely sufficient, not enough, deficient; short (of); *sparing, stingy. **v.t.* To limit, to skimp, to stint; to dole out grudgingly. *v.i.* (*Naut.*) To fail, to decrease in force, to become unfavourable (of the wind). **scantly,** *adv.* **scanty,** *a.* **scantily,** *adv.* **scantiness,** *n.*

scantle (skăntl) [perh. from SCANTLING], *v.t.* To divide into small pieces, to partition. *n.* A gauge by which slates are cut; a small kind of slate.

scantling (skănt′ ling) [M.E. *scantilone*, O.North.F. *escantillon* (F. *échantillon*), etym. doubtful (perh.

EX-, CANTLE)], *n.* *A specimen, a sample, a pattern; a small quantity or portion; a rough draft or sketch; a beam less than 5 in. in breadth and thickness; the sectional measurement of timber, the measurement of stone in all three dimensions; a set of fixed dimensions, esp. in shipbuilding; a trestle for a cask.

scantly, scantness, scanty [SCANT].

scape (1) (skāp) [L. *scapus*, cogn. with SCEPTRE], *n.* The spring or shaft of a column; (*Bot.*) a leafless radical stem bearing the fructification; (*Ent.*) the basal part of an antenna; (*Ornith.*) the shaft of a feather. **scapeless,** *a.* **scapiform,** *a.* **scapiferous** (skà pif' ėr ůs), *a.* Bearing a scape.

scape (2) (skāp) [ESCAPE]. **scapegoat,** *n.* (*Bibl.*) A goat on whose head the high priest laid the sins of the people and then sent it away into the wilderness; (*fig.*) one made to bear blame due to another. **scapegrace,** *n.* A graceless, good-for-nothing person, esp. a child.

scapeless [SCAPE (1)].

scapement [ESCAPEMENT].

scaph-, scapho- [Gr. *skaphē*, boat], *comb. form.* Boat-shaped. **scapha** (skā' fà) [L.], *n.* (*Anat.*) The scaphoid fossa of the helix of the ear. ***scaphism** [-ISM], *n.* An ancient punishment among the Persians in which the victim was confined in a hollow tree, the limbs being smeared with honey to attract insects. **scaphite** (skaf' īt) [-ITE], *n.* (*Palæont.*) A cephalopod of the fossil genus *Scaphites.* **scaphocephalic** (-se făl' ik) [Gr. *kephale*, head, -IC], *a.* (*Path.*) Having a boat-shaped skull, owing to premature union of the parietal bones at the sagittal suture. **scaphocephalous** (-sef' à lůs), *a.* **scaphocephalus, scaphocephaly,** *n.* **scaphoid** (skăf' oid) [-OID], *a.* (*Anat.*) Boat-shaped. *n.* A scaphoid bone. **scaphoid bone:** A bone of the carpus, and one of the tarsus.

scapiform, scapiferous [SCAPE (1)].

scapinade (skăp i nād') [*Scapin* in Molière's 'Les Fourberies de Scapin'], *n.* A rascally trick, a piece of roguery.

scapolite (skăp' ŏ līt) [G. *skapolith* (Gr. *skapos*, cp. SCAPE (1), -LITE)], *n.* (*Min.*) One of a group of tetragonal silicates of calcium, aluminium, and sodium.

scapple (skăp' ėl) [O.F. *escapeler*, to dress timber], *v.t.* To reduce (stone) to a level surface without smoothing.

scapula (skăp' ū là) [late L., sing. of L. *scapulæ*], *n.* (*pl.* **-læ**) (*Anat.*) The shoulder-blade. **scapular,** *a.* Pertaining to the scapula or shoulder. *n.* (*R.-C. Ch.*) A vestment usu. consisting of two strips of cloth worn by certain religious orders across the shoulders and hanging down the breast and back; an adaptation of this worn as a badge of affiliation to a religious order; (*Surg.*) a bandage for the shoulder-blade; (*Ornith.*) any of a series of feathers springing from the base of the humerus in birds, and lying along the side of the back. ***scapulary,** *n.* (*R-C. Ch.*) A scapular. **scapulated,** *a.* (*Ornith.*) Having the scapular feathers conspicuous, esp. by their white colour. **scapulimancy,** *n.* Divination by a shoulder-blade. **scapulo-,** *comb. form.* **scapulo-humeral,** *a.* Pertaining to the scapula and the humerus. **scapulo-ulnar,** *a.* Pertaining to the scapula and the ulnus.

scapus [SCAPE (1)].

scar (1) (skar) [O.F. *escare*, L. and Gr. *eschara*, hearth, scar of a burn], *n.* A mark left by a wound, burn, ulcer, etc., a cicatrice; (*Nat. Hist.*) the mark left by the fall of a leaf, stem, seed, deciduous part, etc.; (*fig.*) the effects of a grief, crime, etc. *v.t.* To mark with a scar or scars. *v.i.* To form a scar, to cicatrize. **scarless,** *a.* **scarred, scarry,** *a.* **scarring,** *n.*

scar (2) (skar) [Icel. *sker*, SKERRY, cogn. with SHEAR], *n.* A crag, a cliff, a precipitous escarpment.

scar (3) [SCARUS].

scarab (skăr' àb) [F. *scarabée*, L. *scarabæus*], *n.* An ancient Egyptian sacred beetle; a seal or gem cut in the shape of a beetle, worn as an amulet by the Egyptians; *a beetle. **scarabæus** (-bē' ůs), *n.* (*pl.* **-bæi,** -bē' ī) (*Ent.*) A genus of beetles typical of the *Scarabæidæ.* **scarabæid,** *a.* Of or pertaining to the *Scarabæidæ*, a family of beetles comprising the cockchafer. *n.* A beetle of this family. **scarabæist,** *n.* **scarabæoid,** *a.* and *n.* ***scarabee,** *n.* A scarab.

scaramouch (skăr' à mouch) [It. *Scaramuccia*, a personage in old Italian comedy, characterized by great boastfulness and poltroonery], *n.* A poltroon and braggart.

scarbroite (skar' brō īt) [*Scarbro', Scarborough*], *n.* (*Min.*) A clayey hydrous silicate of alumina found near Scarborough.

scarce (skârs) [O.North.F. *escars* (cp. It. *scarso*), perh. from late L. *scarpsus, excarpsus*, L. *excarptus* (EX-, *carptus*, p.p. of *carpere*, to pluck)], *a.* Infrequent, seldom met with, rare, uncommon; insufficient, not plentiful, scantily supplied; *parsimonious. *adv.* Hardly, scarcely. **to make oneself scarce:** To keep out of the way; to be off, to decamp. **scarcely,** *adv.* Hardly, barely, only just; with difficulty; not quite (used as a polite negative). **scarceness, scarcity,** *n.* Deficiency; rareness; a dearth (of); a famine; *parsimoniousness, stinginess.

scarcement (skârs' mėnt) [etym. doubtful], *n.* (*Sc.* and *North.*) A set-off in a wall, or a plain flat ledge resulting from this.

scare (skâr) [prob. from M.E. *skerren*, Icel. *skjarr*, shy, timid], *v.t.* To frighten, to alarm, to strike with sudden fear; to drive (away) through fear. *n.* A sudden fright, a panic, esp. an unreasonable state of terror of invasion, epidemic, etc. **scarecrow,** *n.* A rude figure set up to frighten birds away from crops, etc.; a bugbear; (*fig.*) a shabby or absurd-looking person, a guy. **scaremonger,** *n.* One who gets up scares, esp. by circulating unfounded reports, etc. **scary,** *a.*

scarf (1) (skarf) [perh. from Dut. *scherf*, a shred, or O.North.F. *escarpe*, O.F. *escharpe*, cp. SCRIP and SCRAP], *n.* (*pl.* **scarfs, scarves**) A long strip of some material worn round the neck and shoulders or as a sash; a neckcloth or neck-tie; a stole. *v.t.* To clothe or cover with or as with a scarf; to wrap (around or about) as a scarf; *to blindfold. **scarf-pin, -ring,** *n.* A pin or ring, usu. of gold, used to fasten a neck-tie. **scarf-skin,** *n.* The outer layer of skin, the cuticle. **scarf-wise,** *adv.* Used or worn as a scarf, baldric-wise. **scarfed,** *a.*

scarf (2) (skarf) [perh. from Swed. *skarfva*, from *scarf*, a seam, cogn, with prec.], *v.t.* To join the ends of (timber) by means of a scarf-joint; to flench (a whale). *n.* A joint made by bevelling or notching so that the thickness is not increased, and then bolting or strapping together; a cut, a groove. **scarf-joint,** *n.* **scarf-weld,** *n.* A welded joint between two pieces of metal. **scarfing,** *n.* **scarfing-machine,** *n.*

scarf (3) (skarf) [Icel. *skarfr*, cp. Norw. and Swed. *skarf*], *n.* (*Sc.*) A cormorant.

scarfing [SCARF (2)].

scarify (skâr' i fī) [F. *scarifier*, L. *scarīficāre*, Gr. *skariphasthai*, from *skariphos*, pencil, style, cogn. with L. *scrībere*, to write], *v.t.* (*Surg.*) To scratch or make slight incisions in; to stir (soil); (*fig.*) to pain, to torture, to criticize mercilessly. **scarification** (-kā' shůn), *n.* **scarificator** (skâr' i fi kā tŏr), *n.* A surgical instrument with lancet-points used in scarifying. **scarifier,** *n.* One who scarifies; a scarificator; an implement or machine for stirring up soil, etc.

scarious, -iose (skâr' i ůs, -ōs) [F. *scarieux* (acc. to C.O.D. from L. *scaria*, thorny shrub)], *a.* (*Bot.*) Membranous and dry (of bracts, etc.).

scarlatina (skar là tē' nà) [It. *scarlattina*], *n.* Scarlet fever.

scarless [SCAR (1)].

scarlet (skar′ lėt) [O.F. *escarlate* (F. *écarlate*), Pers. *saqalāt*, scarlet cloth], *n.* A bright red colour tending towards orange; cloth or dress of this colour, esp. official robes or uniform. *a.* Of a scarlet colour; dressed in scarlet. **scarlet admiral:** A butterfly, the red admiral. **scarlet-bean** [SCARLET RUNNER]. **scarlet hat:** A cardinal's hat; (*fig.*) the rank of cardinal. **scarlet fever:** An infectious fever characterized by the eruption of red patches on the skin. **scarlet rash:** Roseola. **scarlet runner:** A trailing bean, *Phaseolus multiflorus*, with scarlet flowers. **scarlet woman:** Worldliness or sensuality; pagan or papal Rome (see Rev. xvii. 4–5).

scaroid [SCARUS].

scarp (1) (skarp) [O.F. *escarpe*, It. *scarpa*, perh. from O.H.G. *scarpēn*, cp. SHARP], *n.* A steep or nearly perpendicular slope; (*Fort.*) the interior slope of the ditch at the foot of the parapet. *v.t.* To cut down so to be steep or nearly perpendicular; (*in p.p.*) precipitous, abrupt.

scarp (2) (skarp) [O.North.F. *escarpe*, SCARF (1)], *n.* (*Her.*) A diminutive of the bend sinister, half its width.

***scarpines** (skar′ pēns) [It. *scarpino*, dim. of *scarpa*, shoe], *n.pl.* An instrument of torture similar to the boot.

scart (skart) [Sc., var. of SCRAT], *v.t.* To scratch, to scrape; to scribble. *n.* A scratch; a mark, a dash, a stroke; a puny or miserly person.

Scarus (skâr′ ŭs) [L., from Gr. *skaros*], *n.* (*pl.* **-ri**) A genus of sea-fishes containing the parrot-wrasses; a parrot-fish. **scaroid,** *a.* and *n.*

scary [SCARE].

scat (1) (skăt) [Icel. *skattr*, cp. A.-S. *sceatt*], *n.* (*Scand. Hist.*) Tax, tribute; (*Orkney and Shetland*) a land-tax from an odaller to the Crown. **scat field, hold,** or **land:** Land subject to this.

scat (2) (skăt) [perh. imit.], *n.* (*prov.*) A blow; the noise of a blow or hit; a brisk shower or squall. **scatty,** *a.* Showery; (*colloq.*) silly.

scatch (1) (skăch) [O.North.F. *escache* (F. *échasse*), see SKATE (2)], *n.* (*usu. in pl.*) A stilt.

scatch (2) (skăch) [It. *scaccia*], *n.* A kind of bridle-bit.

scathe (skāth) [Icel. *skatha*, cp. Swed. *skada*, Dan. *skade*, A.-S. *scathan*, G. and Dut. *schaden*, also Gr. *askēthēs*, unharmed], *n.* Hurt, harm, injury. *v.t.* To hurt, to harm, to injure, to destroy. ***scatheful,** *a.* ***scathefulness,** *n.* **scatheless,** *a.* **scathing,** *a.* Hurtful, harmful; very bitter or severe, withering (of sarcasm, etc.). **scathingly,** *adv.*

scatology (skă tol′ ŏ ji) [Gr. *skatos*, gen. of *skōr*, dung, -LOGY], *n.* (*Palæont.*) The study of fossil excrement or coprolites. **scatological** (-loj′ i kăl), *a.* **scatomancy** (skăt′ ŏ măn si), **scatoscopy** (skă tos′ kŏ pi), *n.* Divination or diagnosis by means of fæces. **scatophagous** (skă tof′ ă gŭs), *a.* Feeding on dung.

scatter (skăt′ ėr) [M.E. *scateren*, freq. of SCAT (3), cogn. with Gr. *skedannunai*, to scatter, Sansk. *skhad*, to cut], *v.t.* To throw loosely about, to fling or send broadcast; to strew, to bestrew; to disperse, to rout, to dissipate, to diffuse. *v.i.* To disperse; to be dispersed or routed; to be dissipated or diffused. **scatter-brain,** *n.* A giddy, heedless person. **scatter-brained,** *a.* **scattered,** *a.* Irregularly situated, not together; widely apart. **scatteringly,** *adv.* ***scattering,** *n.* A vagabond. **scatter-mouch** [altered from SCARAMOUCH]. **scattery,** *a.*

scatty [SCAT (3)].

***scaturient** (skă tūr′ i ėnt) [L. *scatūriens -ntem*, pres.p. of *scatūrīre*, from *scatere*, to flow], *a.* Gushing out, as from a fountain.

scaud (*Sc.*) [SCALD (1), SCOLD].

scaup (skawp) [var. of SCALP], *n.* A sea-duck of the genus *Aythya*, esp. *A. marila*, found in the northern regions. **scaup-duck,** *n.*

scauper (skaw′ pėr) [prob. var. of SCALPER], *n.* A wood-engraver's gouge-like tool.

scaur (*Sc.*) [SCAR (2), SCARE].

scaurie (skaw′ ri) [cp. Norw. *skaare*, Icel. *skāre*], *n.* (*Orkney and Shetland*) A young gull.

***scavage** (skăv′ ăj) [A.-F. *scawage*, from *escauwer*, to inspect, Flem. *scauwen*, A.-S. *scēawian*, to SHOW], *n.* A duty formerly exacted of merchant-strangers on goods offered for sale in London and other towns.

scavenger (skăv′ ėn jėr) [orig. *scavager*, collector of scavage, from prec.], *n.* A man employed to clean the streets by sweeping, scraping, and carrying away refuse; an animal feeding on carrion, etc.; a child employed in a spinning-mill to collect loose cotton; (*fig.*) any one willing to do 'dirty work' or delighting in filthy subjects. **scavenge,** *v.t.* and *i.* **scavengery,** *n.* **scavenger-beetle, -crab,** *n.* A beetle or crab feeding on carrion. **scavenger's daughter** [travesty of *Skevington*]: An instrument of torture for compressing the body, invented by Leonard Skevington or Skeffington, Lieutenant of the Tower, under Henry VIII.

scazon (skā′ zŏn) [L., from Gr. *skazōn*, orig. pres.p. of *skazein*, to limp], *n.* (*Pros.*) A satiric metre of a limping character, esp. an iambic trimeter ending with a spondee or trochee, a choliamb. **scazontic** (-zon′ tik), *a.*

***scelerate** (sel′ ėr ăt) [L. *scelerātus*, from *scelus -eris*, wickedness (cp. F. *scélérat*)], *n.* A scoundrel, a wretch.

scelides (sel i dēz) [mod. L., from Gr. *skelos*, leg], *n.pl.* (*Zool.*) The posterior limbs of a mammal. **scelidate,** *a.* **scelidosaur,** *n.* (*Palæont.*) A dinosaur of the Jurassic genus *Scelidosaurus*. **scelidosaurian** (-saw′ ri ăn), *a.* and *n.* **scelidosauriform,** *a.* **scelidosauroid** (-dō saw′ roid), *a.* and *n.* **scelidothere** (sel′ i dŏ thēr), *n.* A S. American megatherian edentate mammal.

scelp [SKELP].

scena (shā′ nă) [It., from L. *scēna*, SCENE], *n.* (*pl.* ***-ne,*** -nā) A scene or a long elaborate solo in opera.

scenario (se na′ ri ō, she na′ ri ō) [It.], *n.* A sketch or outline of the scenes and main points of a play, a skeleton libretto; (*Cinema.*) the script with dialogue and directions for the producer during the actual shooting.

scend (*Naut.*) [SEND].

scene (sēn) [L. *scēna*, Gr. *skēnē*, tent, stage], *n.* The stage in a Greek or Roman theatre; hence, the stage, the theatre, the place where anything occurs or is exhibited as on a stage; the place in which the action of a play or story is supposed to take place; one of the painted frames, hangings, or other devices used to give an appearance of reality to the action of a play; a division of a play comprising so much as passes without change of locality or break of time, or, in French drama, without intermediate entrances or exits; a description of an incident, situation, etc., from life; a striking incident, esp. an exhibition of feeling or passion; a landscape, a view, regarded as a piece of scenery. **behind the scenes:** At the back of the stage; in possession of facts, etc., not generally known. **change of scene:** Change of surroundings by travel. **scene-dock,** *n.* A place near the stage in a theatre for storing scenery. **scene-painter,** *n.* One who paints scenery for theatres. **scene-painting,** *n.* **scene-shifter,** *n.* A person employed in a theatre to move scenery.

scenery (sē′ nė ri), *n.* (*collect.*) The various parts or accessories used on the stage to represent the actual scene of an action; picturesque views presented by natural features.

scenic, scenical (sen′ ik, -ăl), *a.* Of or pertaining to the stage; picturesque, arranged for effect, dramatic, theatrical. **scenic railway:** A switch-back railway at a fun-fair (*Am.* a roller-coaster).

scenography (sė nog′ ră fi) [Gr. *skēnographia* (prec., -GRAPHY)], *n.* The representation of an object in perspective. **scenograph** (sē′ nȯ grăf), **scenographer** (-nog′ rȧ fėr), *n.* **scenographic** (-grăf′ ik), *a.* **scenographically,** *adv.*

scent (sent) [orig. *sent*, F. *sentir*, L. *sentīre*, to perceive], *v.t.* To perceive by smell; to recognize the odour of; (*fig.*) to begin to suspect; to trace or hunt (out) by or as by smelling; to perfume. *v.i.* To exercise sense of smell; *to give forth a smell. *n.* Odour, esp. of a pleasant kind; the odour left by an animal forming a trail by which it can be followed by hounds; pieces of paper left as a trail in a paper-chase; (*fig.*) a clue; a liquid essence containing fragrant extracts from flowers, etc., a perfume; the sense of smell, esp. the power of recognizing or tracing things by smelling. **scent-bag,** *n.* An external pouch-like scent-gland, as in the musk-deer; a bag containing aniseed, etc., used to leave a track of scent for hounds to follow. **scent-bottle,** *n.* A bottle for holding perfume. **scent-gland,** *n.* A gland secreting an odorous substance, as in the musk-deer, civet, etc. **scent-organ,** *n.* **scented,** *a.* Having a scent (*usu. in comb.*, as *keen-scented*). ***scentful,** *a.* Highly scented; having a quick scent. **scentless,** *a.*

sceptic (skep′ tik) [F. *sceptique*, L. *scepticus*, Gr. *skeptikos*, from *skeptesthai*, to examine], *n.* One who doubts the truth of the Christian religion or of any revealed religion; an agnostic; (*pop.*) an atheist; a person of a questioning, doubting, or incredulous habit of mind; one who casts doubt on any statement, theory, etc., esp. in a cynical manner; one who questions or denies the possibility of attaining knowledge of truth; an adherent of philosophical scepticism, a Pyrrhonist. *a.* Sceptical. **scepsis,** *n.* Scepticism, sceptical philosophy; the attitude of philosophic doubt. **sceptical,** *a.* Pertaining to or characteristic of a sceptic; doubting or denying the truth of revelation, or the possibility of knowledge; given to doubting or questioning, incredulous. **sceptically,** *adv.* ***scepticalness, scepticism** (-sizm), *n.* **scepticize,** *v.i.* To act as a sceptic.

sceptre (sep′ tėr) [M.E. and O.F. *ceptre, sceptre*, L. *scēptrum*, Gr. *skēptron*, from *skēptein*, to prop], *n.* A staff or baton borne by a sovereign as a symbol of authority; (*fig.*) royal authority. *v.t.* (*in p.p.*) To invest with a sceptre or with royal authority. **sceptreless,** *a.*

***schediasm** (skē′ di ăzm) [Gr. *schediasma*, from *schediazein*, to do a thing at once, from *schedon*, near], *n.* Something done off-hand; an extemporized or hasty writing.

schedule (shed′ ūl, *Am.* sked′ ūl) [M.E. and O.F. *cedule*, from late L. *scedula, schedula*, dim. of L. *scheda*, strip of papyrus, Gr. *schidē*, splint, from *schizein*, to cleave], *n.* A written or printed table, list, catalogue, or inventory, usu. appended to a document. *v.t.* To enter in a schedule, to make a schedule or list of. **schedulize,** *v.t.*

Scheelite (shē′ līt) [K. W. *Scheele* (1742–86), Swedish chemist, -ITE], *n.* (*Min.*) A vitreous variously-coloured tungstate of calcium.

scheiner (shī′ nėr) [name of inventor], *n.* Term applied to the principle on which the different speeds of English photographic film are gauged.

schema (skē′ mȧ) [L., from Gr. *schēma -atos*, from *schē-*, base of *schēsō*, fut. of *echein*, to have], *n.* (*pl.* *-ata*) A scheme, summary, outline, or conspectus; a chart or diagram; (*Log.*) the abstract figure of a syllogism; (*Rhet.*) a figure of speech; (*Kant*) the form, type, or rule under which the mind applies the categories to the material of knowledge furnished by sense-perception. **schematic** (skė măt′ ik), *a.* **schematically,** *adv.* **schematize** (skē′ mȧ tīz), *v.t.* To formulate; to apply the Kantian categories to. **schematism,** *n.*

scheme (skēm) [L. SCHEMA], *n.* A plan, a project, a proposed method of doing something; a contrivance, an underhand design; a table or schedule of proposed acts, events, etc., a syllabus; a systematic statement, representation, diagram, or arrangement of facts, objects, principles, etc.; a table of classification. *v.t.* To plan, to design, to contrive, to plot. *v.i.* To form plans. **schemer,** *n.* **scheming,** *a.* Given to forming schemes. ***schemist,** *n.* **schematist,** *n.* One given to forming schemes, a projector.

scheme-arch (skēm′ arch) [etym. doubtful], *n.* An arch of circular form less in extent than a semicircle; the part of a three-centre or elliptical arch having a wider radius.

schepen (skā′ pen) [Dut., cp. O.H.G. *sceffin*], *n.* A Dutch alderman or magistrate.

scherzo (skĕrt′ sō) [It., from Teut. (cp. G. *scherz*, sport)], *n.* (*pl.* *-zi*, -sē) A light playful movement in music, usu. following a slow one, in a symphony or sonata. ***scherzando*** (skĕrt săn′ dō), *adv.* (*Mus. direction*) Playfully.

***schesis** (skē′ sis) [Gr. *schesis*, cogn. with SCHEME], *n.* (*pl.* -ses) Relation, condition with regard to other things; disposition or state of the body. ***schetic,** *a.* Constitutional; habitual.

schiavone (skya vō′ nā) [It.], *n.* (*Ant.*) A 17th-cent. basket-hilted broadsword, so called because the Schiavoni or Slav bodyguards of the Doge were armed with it.

Schiedam (skē dam′) [town where made], *n.* Hollands gin.

schiller (shil′ ėr) [G.], *n.* (*Min.*) The peculiar bronze-like sheen or iridescence characteristic of certain minerals. **schiller-spar, schillerite,** *n.* A rock allied to diallage which has undergone schillerization. **schillerization** (-zā′ shŭn), *n.* A process by which minute crystals are deposited in other minerals so as to produce this peculiar sheen. **schillerize,** *v.t.*

schindylesis (skin di lē′ sis) [Gr. *schindulēsis*], *n.* (*Anat.*) An articulation in which a thin part of one bone fits into a groove in another. **schindyletic** (-let′ ik), *a.*

schipperke (skip′ ĕr kė) [Dut., little boatman], *n.* A small black variety of lapdog.

schisiophone (shiz′ i ȯ fōn) [Gr. *schisis schiseōs*, from *schizein*, to cleave, -PHONE], *n.* An instrument comprising a hammer and induction-balance for detecting flaws in iron rails.

schism (sizm) [F. *schisme*, late L. and Gr. *schisma*, from *schizein*, to split], *n.* A split or division in a community; division in a Church, esp. secession of a part or separation into two Churches; the sin of causing such division. **schismatic** (-măt′ ik), *a.* and *n.* **schismatical,** *a.* **schismatically,** *adv.* ***schismaticalness,** *n.* **schismatist** (siz′ mȧ tist), *n.* **schismatize,** *v.t.* and *i.* **schismless,** *a.*

schist (shist) [F. *schiste*, L. and Gr. *schistos*, easily split, as prec.], *n.* A rock of a more or less foliated or laminar structure, tending to split easily. **schistaceous** (-tā′ shŭs), *a.* Slate-grey. **schistoid** (shis′ toid), **schistose, schistous,** *a.* Of the nature or structure of schist.

schiz-, schizo- [Gr. *schizein*, to cleave], *comb. form.* Marked by a cleft or clefts; tending to split. **Schizanthus** (skī zăn′ thŭs) [Gr. *anthos*, flower], *n.* (*Bot.*) A genus of annual plants from Chile with much-divided leaves and showy flowers. **schizocarp** (skī′ zȯ karp), *n.* (*Bot.*) A fruit splitting into several one-seeded portions without dehiscing. **schizocarpic -pous** (-kar′ pik, -pŭs), *a.* **schizocœle** (skī′ zȯ sēl) [Gr. *koilos*, hollow], *n.* (*Zool.*) A perivisceral cavity produced by a splitting of the mesoblast of the embryo. **schizocœlous** (-sē′ lŭs), *a.* **schizodon** (skī′ zȯ don) [Gr. *odous, odontos*, tooth], *n.* A genus of S. American rodents having a molar with folds meeting in the middle.

schizogenesis (skit zō jen′ ė sis), *n.* Reproduction by fission. **schizogenic, schizogenetic** (-net′ ik), *a.* **schizogenetically,** *adv.* **schizogony** (-zog′ ȯ ni), *n.* Schizogenesis. **schizognathous** (skī zog′ nȧ thŭs) [Gr. *gnathos*, jaw], *n.* (*Ornith.*) Having the bones of the palate cleft from the vomer and each other, as in the gulls, plovers, etc. **schizognathism,** *n.* **schizomycete** (skī′ zȯ mi sēt)

[MYCETES], *n.* (*Bot.*) One of the *Schizomycetes*, a class of microscopic (usu. unicellular) vegetable organisms allied to the algæ and comprising bacilli, bacteria, microbes, etc. **schizomycetous,** *a.*

schizophrenia (skit zō frē′ ni ȧ), *n.* (*Path.*) A form of insanity characterized by a double orientation involving a loss of contact with reality; dementia præcox.

schizopod (skit′ zō pod) [Gr. *pous podos*, foot], *n.* (*Zool.*) One of the *Schizopoda*, a sub-order of podophthalmate crustaceans with the feet apparently cleft. **schizopodous** (-zop′ ȯ dŭs), *a.* **schizothecal** (-thē′ kȧl) [Gr. *thēkē*, case], *a.* (*Ornith.*) Having the tarsus divided by scutellation or reticulation.

Schläger (shlā′ gėr) [G., from *schlagen*, to beat], *n.* A German student's duelling sword, pointless, but with sharpened edges towards the end.

Schloss (shlos) [G.], *n.* A castle (in Germany).

schmelze (shmelt′ sė) [G. *schmelz*, enamel, cp. SMELT (1)], *n.* One of various kinds of coloured glass, esp. that coloured red and used to flash white glass.

Schnapps (schnăps) [G., from Dut. *snaps*, mouthful, from *snappen*, to SNAP], *n.* Hollands gin.

Schneiderian (shnī dēr′ i ȧn) [C. V. *Schneider* (1610–80), German anatomist], *a.* (*Anat.*) Applied to the mucous membrane of the nose, first investigated by Schneider.

Schnorkel (shnôr′ kėl) [G.], *n.* (*Nav.*) A device for enabling submarines to take in air when at periscope depth.

scholar (skol′ ȧr) [A.-F. *escoler* (F. *écolier*), cp. A.-S. *scolere* (SCHOOL (2), -ER), assim. to late L. *scholāris*], *n.* A learned person, esp. one with a profound knowledge of literature; (*Univ.*) an undergraduate on the foundation of a college and receiving assistance from its funds, usu. after a competitive examination; a person acquiring knowledge, a (good or apt) learner; a disciple; (*pop.*) a pupil, a student, a schoolboy or schoolgirl. **scholarlike,** *a.* **scholarly,** *a.* Befitting a scholar; learned. **adv.* As befits a scholar. **scholarship,** *n.* High attainments in literature or science; education, instruction; education, usu. with maintenance, free or at reduced fees, granted to a successful candidate after a competitive examination; the emoluments so granted to a scholar.

scholastic (skȯ lăs′ tik) [L. *scholasticus*, Gr. *scholastikos*, from *scholazein*, to be at leisure, see SCHOOL], *a.* Pertaining to school, schools, Universities, etc.; educational, academic, pedagogic, pedantic; pertaining to or characteristic of the schoolmen of the Middle Ages; given to precise definitions and logical subtleties. *n.* A schoolman of the Middle Ages; one characterized by the method and subtlety of the schoolman; a mere scholar, an academic person; a Jesuit of the third grade. **scholastically,** *adv.* **scholasticism,** *n.*

scholiast (skō′ li ăst) [Gr. *scholiastēs*, from *scholiazein*, to write *scholia*], *n.* A commentator, esp. an ancient grammarian who annotated the classics. **scholiastic** (-ăs′ tik), *a.* **scholium,** *n.* (*pl.* **-lia**) A marginal note, esp. an explanatory comment on the Greek and Latin authors by an early grammarian.

school (1) (skool) [Dut., cp. SHOAL (2)], *n.* A shoal of fish, porpoises, etc. *v.i.* To form a school. **school-fish,** *n.* A fish that usually appears in shoals, esp. the menhaden. **school-whale,** *n.*

school (2) (skool) [A.-F. *escole*, L. *schola*, Gr. *scholē*, rest, leisure, philosophy, lecture-place], *n.* An institution for education or instruction, esp. one for instruction of a more elementary or a less liberal kind than that given at Universities; the building or buildings of this; the body of pupils; a session or time during which teaching is carried on; a lecture-room; a seminary in the Middle Ages for teaching logic, metaphysics, and theology; (*pl.*) the mediæval Universities, professors, teaching, etc.; scholasticism; (*Univ.*) any of the branches of study with separate examinations taken by candidates for honours; the hall where such examinations are held; (*pl.*) the examination itself; the body of disciples or followers of a philosopher, artist, etc., or of adherents of a cause, principle, system of thought, etc.; (*Mus.*) a book of instruction, a manual; (*fig.*) any sphere or circumstances serving to discipline or instruct. *v.t.* To instruct, to educate; to discipline, to bring under control; to send to school; *to chide, to admonish. (In U.S.A. a **public school** is one provided by the state; a **private school** is what is known in England as a public school; a **preparatory school** is one for older children from either of above where they attend before going to university.) **board-school** [BOARD]. **continuation school:** A school for those who have left the elementary school and are continuing their education in their leisure from work. **evening school** [NIGHT-SCHOOL]. **grammar-school** [GRAMMAR]. **high school:** A secondary school or any school of a kind superior to the elementary or primary schools. **mixed school:** A school at which boys and girls are educated together. **night-school** [NIGHT]. **public school** [PUBLIC]. **ragged school** [RAGGED]. **secondary school** [SECONDARY]. **Sunday school** [SUNDAY]. **technical school** [TECHNICAL]. **school board:** A public body elected to provide for the elementary instruction of children in their district (1870–1902). **school-book,** *n.* A book for use in schools. **schoolboy,** *n.* A boy attending a school. *a.* Pertaining to schoolboys. **school-dame,** *n.* (*Am.*) A schoolmistress; the keeper of a dame-school. **school-divine,** *n.* One who adopts scholastic theology. **school-divinity,** *n.* **schoolfellow,** *n.* One who attends the same school. **schoolgirl,** *n.* A girl attending school. **schoolhouse,** *n.* A building used as a school; the dwelling-house of a schoolmaster or schoolmistress; the headmaster's house or the chief boarding-house at a public school. **school-ma'am, -marm,** *n.* (*Am. colloq.*) A schoolmistress. **schoolman,** *n.* A teacher or professor in a mediæval University; one versed in the theology, logic, or metaphysics of the mediæval schools or the niceties of academical disputation. **schoolmaster,** *n.* A chief or assistant male teacher in a school; a pedagogue; (*fig.*) one who or that which trains or disciplines. **schoolmate,** *n.* One attending the same school. **school-miss,** *n.* A schoolgirl; (*fig.*) an inexperienced or bashful girl. **schoolmistress,** *n.* A woman who teaches in a school, esp. a headmistress. **schoolroom,** *n.* A room where teaching is given, in a school, house, etc. **school-teacher,** *n.* One who teaches, esp. in a primary school. **schoolable,** *a.* **schooling,** *n.*

schooner (skoo′ nėr) [Clydesdale *scoon*, *scon*, to skim along, to glide swiftly (rel. to SHUNT), -ER (assim. to Dut. derivative *schooner*)], *n.* A vessel with two or more masts with fore-and-aft rigging; (*Am.*) a large emigrant-wagon or van; a tall glass for beer or ale.

schorl (shôrl) [F., from G. *schörl*], *n.* Black tourmaline.

schottische (shȯ tēsh′, shot′ ish) [G., Scottish], *n.* A dance resembling a polka; the music for it.

schout (skout) [Dut., cogn. with A.-S. *sculthēta*, *scyldhæta*], *n.* A municipal officer in the Netherlands and Dutch colonies.

Schwenkfelder (shwenk′ fel dėr), *n.* A member of a Protestant sect founded in Silesia in the 16th cent. by Caspar Schwenkfeld (1496–1561). **Schwenkfeldian** (-fel′ di ȧn), *a.* and *n.* **Schwenkfeldianism,** *n.*

sciagraph, sciamachy, sciametry, etc. [SKIAGRAPH, SKIAMACHY, SKIAMETRY].

sciatheric (sī ȧ ther′ ik) [late Gr. *skiathērikos*, from Gr. *skiathēros*, sundial (*skia*, shadow, *thēran*, to catch)], *a.* Of or pertaining to a sundial. **sciatherically,** *adv.*

sciatic (sī ăt′ ik) [F. *sciatique*, late L. *sciaticus*, L. *ischiadicus*, Gr. *ischiadikos*, from *ischias -ados*, pain in the loins, from *ischion*, socket of the thigh-bone], *a.* Pertaining to the hip; of or affecting the sciatic nerve; of the nature of or affected by sciatica. **sciatica,** *n.* Neuralgia of the hip and thigh; pain in the great sciatic nerve. **sciatically,** *adv.*

science (sī′ ėns) [F., from L. *scientia*, from *scīre*, to know], *n.* *Knowledge; systematized knowledge; a department of systematized knowledge, a system of facts and principles concerning any subject; the pursuit of such knowledge or the principles governing its acquirement; exceptional skill due to knowledge and training, as distinguished from natural ability, esp. in pugilism; *a trade or occupation. **science fiction:** Sensational fiction dealing with space travel, life on one of the planets, etc. **mental science:** Psychology, mental philosophy. **moral science** [MORAL]. **natural** or **physical science** [NATURAL]. **pure science:** Science based on self-evident truths, as logic, mathematics, etc. **the dismal science:** Political economy of the old-fashioned deductive kind. ***scienter*** (sī en′ tėr), *adv.* (*Legal*) With knowledge, wittingly, deliberately. **sciential** (-en′ shål), *a.* **scientially,** *adv.*

scientific (sī ėn tif′ ik), *a.* Pertaining to, used, or engaged in science; treating of or devoted to science; made or done according to the principles of science, systematic, exact; skilful, expert (esp. of pugilism, etc.). **scientifically,** *adv.* **scientism,** *n.* **scientist,** *n.*

scilicet (sī′ li sėt) [L. (*scīre licet*, it is permitted to know)], *adv.* To wit, *videlicet*, namely.

Scilla (sil′ å) [L., from Gr. *skilla*], *n.* (*Bot.*) A genus of bulbous liliaceous plants containing the squills. **scillitin,** *n.* (*Chem.*) The active principle of *Scilla maritima*.

Scillonian (sī lō′ ni ån), *n.a.* A native of, or pertaining to the Scilly Isles.

scimitar (sim′ i tår) [orig. O.F. *cimiterre*, It. *scimitarra*, prob. from Pers. *shimshīr*], *n.* A short Oriental sword, single-edged, curved, and broadest towards the point.

scincoid (sing′ koid) [L. *scinc-us*, SKINK (1), -OID], *a.* Of, pertaining to, or resembling the *Scincidæ* or skinks. *n.* A skink-like lizard. **scincoidian** (sing koi′ di ån), *a.* and *n.*

scintilla (sin til′ å) [L.], *n.* A spark; an atom. **scintillate** (sin′ ti lāt), *v.i.* To emit sparks; to sparkle, to twinkle. **scintillant,** *a.* **scintillation** (-lā′ shůn), *n.* ***scintillescent** (-les′ ėnt), *a.* **scintillometer** (-lom′ ė tėr), *n.* An instrument attached to a telescope for measuring the amount of scintillation of a star; an instrument for measuring radioactivity.

sciography [SKIAGRAPHY].

sciolist (sī′ ȯ list) [L. *sciolus*, smatterer, dim. of *scius*, knowing, from *scīre*, to know], *n.* One who knows many things superficially, a smatterer. **sciolism,** *n.* **sciolistic** (-lis′ tik), ***sciolous,** *a.*

sciolto (shol′ tō) [It.], *adv.* (*Mus. direction*) Freely, to one's taste; staccato.

sciomachy [SKIAMACHY].

sciomancy (sī′ ȯ măn si) [Gr. *skia*, shadow, -MANCY], *n.* Divination through the shades of the dead. **sciomantic** (-măn′ tik), *a.*

scion (sī′ ȯn) [F., perh. from *scier*, to saw, L. *secāre*, to cut], *n.* A shoot, esp. for grafting or planting; a descendant, a child.

scioptic, *-tric (sī op′ tik, -trik) [Gr. *skia*, shadow, -OPTIC, see also CATOPTRIC], *a.* Pertaining to the camera obscura or its use. ***scioptric ball:** A ball containing a lens used for producing luminous images in a darkened room. **sciopticon,** *n.* A kind of magic lantern. **scioptics,** *n.*

sciotheism (sī ȯ thē′ izm), *n.* Ghost-worship, esp. of departed ancestors.

sciotheric [SCIATHERIC].

scire facias (sī′ ri fā′ si ăs) [L., make (him) to know], *n.* (*Law*) A writ to enforce the execution of or annul judgments, etc.

scirocco [SIROCCO].

scirrhus (sir′-, skir′ ůs) [late L., from Gr. *skirros*, *skīros*, hardened swelling, from *skiros*, hard], *n.* (*Path.*) A hard tumour, esp. a hard cancer. **scirrhoid, scirrhous,** *a.* **scirrhosity** (-ros′ i ti), *n.*

scissel (sis′ ėl) [F. *cisaille*, from *ciseler*, to CHISEL], *n.* Metal clippings; the remainder of plates after disks have been punched therefrom in coining.

scissile (sis′ īl) [L. *scissilis*, from *scindere*, to cut, p.p. *scissus*], *a.* That may be cut. **scission** (sish′ ůn), *n.* The act of cutting or dividing; a division, separation, or split.

scissors (siz′ ȯrz) [M.E. *sisoures*, O.F. *cisoires*, L. *cīsōrium*, from *cīs-*, *cæs-*, p.p. stem of *cædere*, to cut], *n.pl.* A cutting instrument, consisting of two blades pivoted together and cutting objects placed between them, usu. **pair of scissors. scissors and paste:** Compilation, as distinguished from original literary work. **scissor,** *v.t.* To cut with scissors; to clip or cut (out) with scissors. **scissoring,** *n.* **scissor-beak, -bill,** *n.* A skimmer, a bird of the genus *Rhynchops*. **scissor-bird, -tail,** *n.* An American tyrant-flycatcher. **scissors-grinder,** *n.* (*Austral.*) A kind of fly-catcher. **scissor-tooth,** *n.* A tooth working against another like a scissor-blade, in certain carnivora. **scissorwise,** *adv.* ***scissure** (sish′ yůr), *n.* A longitudinal opening made by cutting; a cut, a fissure.

sciurine (sī′ ū rin) [L. *sciūrus*, Gr. *skiouros* (*skia*, shadow, *oura*, tail)], *a.* Pertaining to or resembling the squirrel family. *n.* A squirrel. **sciuroid** (sī ūr′ oid), *a.*

Sclav, Sclavonian, etc. [SLAV, etc.].

scler-, sclero- [Gr. *sklēros*, dry, hard], *comb. form.* **sclera** (sklēr′ å), *n.* (*Anat.*) The sclerotic. **sclerenchyma** (sklēr eng′ ki må) [Gr. *enchuma*, infusion, see PARANCHYMA], *n.* (*Bot.*) The tissue forming the hard parts of plants, such as the walls of nuts, fruit-stones, etc.; (*Zool.*) the calcareous tissue in coral. **schlerenchymatous** (-ki′ må tůs), *a.*

scleriasis (skle rī′ å sis), *n.* (*Path.*) Hardening or induration of tissue. **sclerite** (sklēr′ īt), *n.* (*Zool.*) One of the definite component parts of the hard integument of various invertebrates. **scleritic** (-it′ ik), *a.* **scleritis** [SCLEROTITIS].

scleroderm (skle′ rō dĕrm), *n.* (*Zool.*) A hardened integument or exo-skeleton, esp. of corals; a fish of the family *Sclerodermi*, having hard scales. **scleroderma, -dermia** (-dĕr′ må, -mi å), *n.* (*Path.*) A chronic induration of the skin. **sclerodermatous, sclerodermic,** *a.* **sclerodermite,** *n.* One of the hard segments of the body in crustaceans. **sclerodermitic** (-mit′ ik), *a.* **sclerogen** (sklēr′ ȯ jėn), *n.* The hard matter deposited in the cells of certain plants, as the ivory-nut. **sclerogenous** (-oj′ ė nůs), *a.* **scleroid** (sklēr′ oid), *a.* (*Bot. and Zool.*) Hard in texture. **scleroma** (sklēr ō′ må), *n.* (*pl.* **-omata**) (*Path.*) Hardening of cellular tissue, scleriasis. **scleromeninx** (-mē′ ninks) [MENINX], *n.* (*Anat.*) The *dura mater*.

sclerosis (skle rō′ sis), *n.* (*Bot.*) Hardening of a cell-wall by the deposit of sclerogen; (*Path.*) morbid thickening of a tissue. **sclerosed,** *a.* **scleroskeleton** (-skel′ ė tȯn), *n.* The skeletal parts resulting from ossification of tendons, ligaments, etc. **scleroskeletal, sclerosteous** (-os′ tė ůs), *a.* **sclerotal** (sklēr ō′ tål), *n.* One of the bony plates of the sclerotic coat in some birds and reptiles; the sclerotic. *a.* Pertaining to the sclerotal; sclerotic.

sclerotic (skle rot′ ik), *a.* Hard, indurated (applied to the outer coat or tunic of the eye); of or affected with sclerosis. *n.* The firm white membrane forming the outer coat of the eye, the white of the eye; (*Med.*) a medicine hardening the parts to which it is applied. **sclerotitis** (-tī′ tis), *n.* (*Path.*) Inflammation of the sclerotic. **sclerotium** (sklēr ō′ ti ům), *n.* A compact tuberous mass formed on the mycelium of certain higher fungi, as ergot; (*Zool.*)

a cyst-like part of a plasmodium in the Mycetozoa. **sclerotioid,** *a.* Resembling a sclerotium. **sclerotized** (sklĕr′ ŏ tīzd), *a.* Indurated. **sclerotome** (sklĕr′ ŏ tōm), *n.* (*Surg.*) A knife used in cutting the sclerotic coat of the eye. **sclerotomy** (-ot′ ŏ mi), *n.* **sclerous** (sklē′ ŭs), *a.* Hard, indurated, ossified.

scobby (skob′ i) [North., etym. doubtful], *n.* (*prov.*) The chaffinch.

scobs (skobz) [L.], *n.* Sawdust, scrapings, shavings, filings; dross of metal, ivory, hartshorn, or other hard substance. **scobiform** (skō′ bi fôrm), *a.*

scoff (1) (skof) [prob. from Scand. (cp. M.Dan. *skof,* Icel. *skaup,* also O.Fris. *schof,* M.Dut. *schobben*), perh. rel. to SHOVE], *n.* An expression of contempt, derision, or mockery; a gibe, a taunt; an object of derision, a laughing-stock. *v.i.* To speak in derision or mockery, to mock or jeer (at). **v.t.* To mock, to ridicule, to deride. **scoffer,** *n.* **scoffingly,** *adv.*

scoff (2) (skof) [S.Afr.Dut.], *v.t.* (*slang*) To eat ravenously. *n.* Food.

scold (skōld) [M.E. *scolden,* cp. Dut. *schelden,* G. *schelten,* O.Fris. *skelda*], *v.i.* To find fault noisily or angrily; to rail (at). *v.t.* To chide or find fault with noisily or angrily; to chide, to rate, to rail at. *n.* A noisy, railing, nagging woman; a scolding. **scolder,** *n.* **scolding,** *a.* and *n.* **scoldingly,** *adv.*

scolex (skō′ lĕks) [Gr. *skōlēx,* worm), *n.* (*pl.* **scoleces** (skō lē′ sēz)) The larva or embryo in metagenesis, esp. the head of the tapeworm. **scolecid** (skŏ lē′ sid), *n.* One of the *Scolecida,* a class of worms including the turbellarians. **scoleciform, scolecoid** (-koid), *a.* **scolecite** (skol′ ĕ sīt), *n.* (*Bot.*) The vermiform body formed in the fructification of some fungi; (*Min.*) a hydrous silicate of aluminium and calcium.

scolion (skol′ i on) [Gr. *skolion*], *n.* (*Gr. Ant.*) An impromptu song sung by guests at a banquet.

scoliosis (skol i ō′ sis) [Gr. *skoliōsis,* from *skolios,* bent], *n.* (*Path.*) Lateral curvature of the spine. **scoliotic** (-ot′ ik), *a.*

scollop [SCALLOP].

Scolopax (skol′ ŏ păks) [L. and Gr.], *n.* (*Ornith.*) A genus of birds containing the snipe, woodcock, redshank, etc. **scolopaceous** (-pā′ shŭs), **scolopacine** (-lop′ ă sin), **scolopacoid** (-koid), *a.*

scolopendra, *scolopender (skol ŏ pen′ dră, -dĕr) [L. and Gr. *skolopendra*], *n.* (*Zool.*) A genus of myriapods containing the larger centipedes; a millipede or centipede; *(*Spens.,* **-der**) a fabulous marine animal. **scolopendriform, scolopendrine,** *a.*

scolopendrium (skol ŏ pen′ dri ŭm) [L., from Gr. *skolopendrion,* from a supposed resemblance to prec.], *n.* (*Bot.*) A genus of ferns containing the hart's tongue.

Scolytus (skol′ i tŭs) [mod. L. from Gr. *skoluptein,* to peel, to strip], *n.* (*Zool.*) A genus of bark-boring beetles. **scolytid,** *n.* **scolytoid,** *a.*

scomber (skom′ bĕr) [L., from Gr. *skombros*], *n.* (*pl.* **-bri,** -brī) (*Ichthyol.*) A genus of fish containing the mackerel. **scombrid,** *n.* **scombroid,** *a.* and *n.*

scomfish (skŭm′ fish) [Sc. for *discomfish,* corr. of DISCOMFIT], *v.t.* To suffocate, to stifle; to discomfit, to disconcert.

scon [var. of SCONE].

sconce (skons) [O.F. *esconse,* hiding-place, concealed light, dark-lantern, L. *absconsa,* fem. of *-sus,* var. of *absconditus,* p.p. of *abscondere,* to hide, cp. ABSCOND], *n.* A candle-holder fixed to a wall; the socket of a candlestick into which the candle is inserted; a block-house, a bulwark, a small detached fort; (*colloq.*) the head, the skull; (*fig.*) brains, sense; (*Univ.*) a fine for a light offence; a piece of ice-floe; *a lantern; *a shelter, a covering, a penthouse, a shed. *v.t.* To fortify with a sconce; (*Univ.*) to fine.

scone (skon, skōn) [cp. M.Dan. *skon-roggen,* muffin of bolted rye-flour (L.G. *schön,* fine, *roggen,* rye)], *n.* A soft thin cake of barley-meal or wheat-flour, usu. in small triangular pieces, cooked on a girdle.

scoop (skoop) [perh. through O.F. *escope,* from Swed. *skopa,* or M.Dut. *schōpe,* bailing-vessel, or M.Dut. *schoppe* (Dut. *schop*), shovel, cp. G. *schöpfen,* to draw water], *n.* A short-handled shovel-like implement for drawing together, lifting, and moving loose material such as coal, grain, sugar, potatoes, etc.; a large ladle or dipping-vessel; a gouge-like implement used by grocers, surgeons, etc.; the bucket of a dredging-machine; a coal-scuttle; the act or movement of scooping; the amount scooped at once; (*slang*) a large profit made in a speculation or competitive transaction; (*Journalist's slang*) the publication of a piece of sensational news in advance of rival journals; *a basin-like cavity. *v.t.* To ladle or dip (out) or to hollow (out) with a scoop; to lift (up) with a scoop; to scrape, gouge, or hollow (out); (*slang*) to gain (a large profit) by a deal, etc.; (*Journalist's slang*) to forestall (rival journals, etc.) with a piece of sensational news. **scoop-net,** *n.* A net so formed as to sweep the bottom of a river, etc. **scoop-wheel,** *n.* A wheel with buckets round is used to raise water or for dredging. **scooper,** *n.* One who or that which scoops; a tool used by engravers; a scooping.

scoot (skoot) [var. of SHOOT], *v.i.* To dart off, bolt, to scurry away. **scooter,** *n.* A two-wheeled toy vehicle on which a child can ride with one foot, propelling with the other; a similar larger vehicle with a seat and propelled by a motor. **scooterist,** *n.* A rider on a scooter.

scopa (skō′ pă) [L., in pl., twigs], *n.* (*pl.* **-pæ**) (*Ent.*) A brush-like tuft of bristly hairs as on the legs of bees. **scoparious** (-pâr′ i ŭs), **scopate** (skō′ pāt), **scopiform,** *a.* Brush-shaped; covered with brush-like hairs. **scopula** (skop′ ū lă), *n.* A small brush-like tuft on the legs of bees and spiders, a *scopa.* **scopulate, scopuliform** (-pū′ li fôrm), *a.* **scopiped, *scopulipede** (skop′ ū li ped, -pēd), *a.* Applied to certain solitary bees with a broom-like contrivance on the hind legs for collecting pollen.

scope (skōp) [prob. through It. *scopo,* from Gr. *skopos,* a watcher, a mark, rel. to *skeptesthai,* to look out], *n.* *A butt or mark; *end, aim, purpose or intention; range of action or observation, outlook, reach, sphere, extent or room for activity, etc.; outlet, opportunity, vent; (*Naut.*) length of cable at which a vessel rides; *extent of surface, etc. ***scopeful, scopeless,** *a.*

-scope [Gr. *skopos,* see prec.], *suf.* Denoting an instrument of observation, etc., as in *microscope, spectroscope.* **-scopic,** *suf.* Pertaining to this or to observation, etc., as in *microscopic, spectroscopic.* **-scopy,** *suf.* Observation by the instrument, etc., specified, as in *microscopy, spectroscopy.*

scopelid (skop′ ĕ lid) [Gr. *skopelos,* -ID], *n.* (*Ichthyol.*) A fish of the deep-water, teleostean group *Scopelidæ.* **scopeloid,** *a.* and *n.*

scopiform, scopiped [SCOPA].

scopolamine (skō pol′ ă mīn), *n.* (*Med.*) Hyoscine hydrobromide, a hypnotic drug used, among other purposes, with morphia for producing twilight sleep.

scops (skops) [Gr. *skōps*], *n.* A genus of owls having erect tufts of feathers on the side of the head. **scops-eared,** *a.* **scops-owl,** *n.*

scopula, scopuliped, etc. [SCOPA].

scorbutic (skôr bū′ tik) [obs. *scorbute* (F. *scorbut*), low L. *scorbūtus,* scurvy, prob. from L.G., cp. SCURF], *a.* Pertaining to, like, or affected with scurvy. *n.* A person affected with scurvy. **scorbutically,** *adv.*

scorch (skôrch) [O.F. *escorcher,* late L. *excorticāre* (EX-, L. *cortex -ticis,* bark)], *v.t.* To burn the outside of so as to injure or discolour without consuming, to singe, to parch, to dry or shrivel (up); to affect harmfully with or as with heat; *to burn.

v.i. To be parched, singed, or dried up with or as with heat; (*colloq.*) to go at an excessive rate of speed (esp. of a cyclist). *n.* A burn or mark caused by scorching; (*colloq.*) an act or spell of scorching. **scorching,** *a.* **scorchingly,** *adv.* **scorcher,** *n.* One who or that which scorches; (*slang*) a striking or staggering example, a stunner. **scorched earth:** A descriptive term for the destruction of everything in a country that might be of service to an invading army.

scordato [skôr da' tō) [It., from *scordare,* to be out of tune, for *discordare,* see DISCORD], *a.* (*Mus.*) Put out of tune. **scordatura** (-toor' å), *n.* An intentional departure from normal tuning to secure special effects.

score (skôr) [A.-S. *scor,* twenty, Icel. *skor,* twenty, notch, cogn. with SHEAR], *n.* A notch or mark on a tally; a reckoning orig. kept on a tally, esp. a running account for liquor marked up against a customer's name at a tavern; an account, a bill, a debt; (*fig.*) anything laid up or recorded against one, a grudge; the points made by a player or side in certain games; the record of this; a mark from which a race starts, competitors fire in a shooting-match, etc.; a weight of 20 or 21 lb. used in weighing pigs and cattle; (*Naut.*) a groove in a block, etc., for receiving a strap; a line drawn or scratched through writing, etc.; a copy of a musical work in which all the component parts are shown, either fully or in a compressed form, so called from the line orig. drawn through all the staves; twenty, a set of twenty; (*pl.*) large numbers; account, category, head, reason; (*slang*) a remark, etc., in which one scores off another person. *v.t.* To mark with notches, cuts, scratches, lines, etc.; to gash, to groove, to furrow; to make or mark (lines, etc.); to mark (out) with lines; to mark (up) or enter in a score; to register (a point, a win, etc.) in cricket, etc.; (*Mus.*) to arrange in score, to orchestrate; to arrange for an instrument; (*Cinema.*) to prepare the sound-script for a film. *v.i.* To keep a score; to win points, advantages, etc. **to pay off old scores:** To pay some one out or have revenge for an offence of old standing. **to score off:** (*colloq.*) To get the better of; to triumph over in argument, repartee, etc. **scorer,** *n.* **scoring,** *n.*

scoria (skôr' i å) [L., from Gr. *skōria,* refuse, from *skōr,* dung], *n.* (*pl.* **-iæ**) Cellular lava or ashes; the refuse of fused metals, dross. **scoriaceous** (-ā' shŭs), *a.* **scorify** (skôr' i fī), *v.t.* To reduce to dross; to assay (metal) by fusing its ore in a scorifier with lead and borax. **scorification** (-kā' shŭn), *n.* **scorifier** (skôr-), *n.* **scoriform,** *a.*

scorn (skôrn) [from M.E. *scorn,* O.F. *escorne,* perh. from *escorner,* to deprive of horns (EX-, L. *cornu,* horn), or M.E. *scarn,* O.F. *escarn,* O.H.G. *skern,* mockery, sport], *n.* Contempt, disdain; mockery, derision; a subject or object of extreme contempt. *v.t.* To hold in extreme contempt or disdain, to regard as unworthy, paltry, or mean. **to laugh to scorn:** To deride, to mock. ***to take** or **think scorn:** To disdain, to scorn. **scorner,** *n.* **scornful,** *a.* **scornfully,** *adv.* **scornfulness,** *n.*

scorodite (skor' ŏ dīt) [G. *skorodit, skorod-on,* garlic, -ITE], *n.* (*Min.*) A native arsenate of iron.

scorpæna (skôr pē' nå) [mod. L., from Gr. *skorpaina,* prob. from *skorpios,* SCORPION], *n.* (*Ichthyol.*) A genus of acanthopterygian fishes, typical of the family *Scorpænidæ.* **scorpænid,** *n.* **scorpænoid,** *a.* and *n.*

scorper (skôr' pėr) [var. of SCAUPER], *n.* A gouging-tool for working in concave surfaces in wood, metal, or jewellery.

Scorpio (skôr' pi ō) [as foll.], *n.* A zodiacal constellation, and the eighth sign of the zodiac. **scorpioid,** *a.* (*Bot.*) Curled up like the end of a scorpion's tail and uncurling as the flowers develop. *n.* A scorpioid inflorescence.

scorpion (skôr' pi ŏn) [L. *scorpiōnem,* nom., *-pio,* Gr. *skorpios*], *n.* One of a genus of *Arachnida,* with claws like a lobster and a sting in the jointed tail; (*Bibl.*) a whip armed with points of iron; a form of ballista; the constellation Scorpio. **rock scorpion,** *n.* (*colloq.*) A native of Gibraltar. **scorpion-broom, -thorn,** *n.* A yellow-flowered broom from S. Europe, *Genista scorpius.* **scorpion-fish,** *n.* The sea-scorpion, a scorpænoid fish. **scorpion-fly,** *n.* A fly of the family *Panorpidæ,* named from the forceps-like point of the abdomen. **scorpion-grass, -wort,** *n.* The myosotis or forget-me-not. **scorpion-plant,** *n.* A Javan orchid with large spider-like flowers; scorpion-broom. **scorpion-, scorpion's-thorn,** *n.* Scorpion-broom.

***scorse** (skôrs) [etym. doubtful], *v.t.* and *i.* To barter, to exchange. *n.* Barter, exchange.

***scortatory** (skôr' tå tôr i) [from L. *scortātor,* fornicator, from *scortārī,* to be lewd, from *scortum,* whore], *a.* Pertaining to or consisting in lewdness.

scorza (skôr' zå) [G., prob. from Wallachian name], *n.* (*Min.*) An arenaceous variety of epidote.

Scorzonera (skôr zŏ nēr' å) [It., perh. from *scorzone,* a snake], *n.* (*Bot.*) A genus of herbs the roots of some species of which are used as a vegetable; a plant of this genus, esp. the salsify.

scot (1) (skot) [O.F. *escot,* Icel. *skot,* cp. A.-S. *sceot,* Dut. *schot,* G. *schoss,* SHOT (3)], *n.* A payment, an assessment, a tax. **scot and lot:** A town or parish tax levied according to ability to pay. **to pay scot and lot:** To settle outstanding accounts, obligations, etc. **scot-free,** *a.* Free from payment, untaxed; (*fig.*) unpunished; unhurt, safe.

Scot (2) (skot) [A.-S. *Scottas,* pl.], *n.* A native of Scotland; (*pl.*) orig., a Gaelic tribe migrating to Scotland from Ireland in the 5th or 6th cent.

Scotch (1) (skoch), **Scottish** (skot' ish), **Scots** (skots), *a.* Pertaining to Scotland, its people, language, or literature. *n.* The people of Scotland; the Scottish dialect or dialects of English; Scotch whisky; a glass of this. **Scotch and English:** Prisoner's-base. **Scotch-barley,** *n.* Pot or husked barley. **Scotch broth,** *n.* A clear broth containing barley and chopped vegetables. **Scotch cap:** A brimless woollen cap, either a Balmoral or a Glengarry. **Scotch catch** or **snap:** A short note followed by a long note in two played to the same beat. **Scotch fir** [FIR]. **Scotch mist:** A wet dense mist; fine drizzle. **Scotch terrier,** *n.* A breed of dog characterized by short legs and a rough coat. **Scotch thistle:** One of various thistles regarded as the Scottish national emblem, esp. *Carduus lanceolatus* or *C. nutans.* **Scotch whisky:** Whisky with a flavour of peat-reek, orig. distilled in Scotland. **Scotchman,** (*Sc.*). **Scotsman,** *n.* **Scotchman grass,** *n.* (*N. Zealand*) A variety of grass with sharp points. **Scotchness,** *n.* **Scotchwoman,** (*Sc.*). **Scotswoman,** *n.* **Scotice** (skot' i si), *adv.* In a or the Scottish manner. **Scoto-** (1), *comb. form.* **Scots,** *a.* (*Sc.*) Scottish. **Scotticism,** *n.* **Scotticize,** *v.t.* and *i.* **Scottify,** *v.t.*

scotch (2) (skoch) [M.E. *scocche,* prob. from SCORE], *v.t.* To cut with narrow incisions; to wound slightly, to cripple, to disable. *n.* A slight cut or incision; a mark for hopping from. **scotched-collops,** *n.* Beef cut into small pieces and stewed in a stew-pan. **scotch-hopper** [HOPSCOTCH, see HOP (1)].

scotch (3) (skoch) [etym. doubtful], *n.* A block for a wheel or other round object. *v.t.* To block, wedge, or prop (a wheel, barrel, etc.) to prevent rolling; to frustrate (a plan, etc.).

scoter (skō' tėr) [etym. doubtful], *n.* A large sea-duck of the genus *Œdemia.*

scotia (skō' ti å) [Gr. *skotia,* darkness, cp. SCOTO-], *n.* (*Arch.*) A hollow moulding in the base of a column.

Scotism (skō' tizm), *n.* The scholastic philosophy of Johannes Duns Scotus (d. 1308). **Scotist,** *a.* and *n.*

Scotland Yard (skot' lånd yard') [locality in London], *n.* The headquarters of the London Metropolitan Police; (*fig.*) the Criminal Investigation Department of the police; police detectives.

Scoto- (1) [SCOT (2)].

scoto- (2) [Gr. *skotos*, dullness], *comb. form.*

scotodinia (skot ō din′ i à), *n.* (*Path.*) Dizziness, vertigo, with dimness of vision.

scotograph (skŏt′ ō grăf), *n.* An instrument for writing in the dark or by the blind.

scotoma, scotomy (skot ō′ mà, -mi), *n.* (*Path.*) A defect in the field of vision; dizziness or swimming of the head with dimness of sight.

scotoscope (skot′ ō skōp), *n.* A night-glass.

Scots, Scotsman, Scotticism, Scottish, Scotticize, etc. [SCOTCH (1)].

scoundrel (skoun′ drĕl) [etym. unknown], *n.* An unprincipled person, a thorough-paced rogue, a rascal, a villain. *a.* Base, villainous, unprincipled. **scoundreldom, scoundrelism,** *n.* **scoundrelly,** *a.*

scoup (skoup) [Sc., etym. doubtful], *v.i.* To bound, trip, caper, or scamper.

scour (1) (skour) [prob. through M.Dut. *schūren*, O.F. *escurer*, pop. L. *excūrāre* (EX-, *cūrāre*, to CURE (1))], *v.t.* To clean, polish, or brighten by friction; to remove or clean (away, off, etc.) by rubbing; to flush or clear out; to pass swiftly through or over (of water, etc.); to purge violently. *v.i.* To clean; to be scoured or cleaned (well, easily, etc.); to be purged to excess. *n.* A swift, deep current; a rapid; the clearing action of this; dysentery in cattle; a cleanser for various fabrics. **scourer,** *n.*

scour (2) (skour) [O.F. *escourre*, L. *excurrere* (EX-, *currere*, to run)], *v.i.* To rove, to range; to skim, to scurry; to search about. *v.t.* To move rapidly over, esp. in search.

scourge (skĕrj) [A.-F. *escorge* (F. *écourgée*), ult. from L. *excoriāre*, to strip the skin off (EX-, *corium*, hide)], *n.* A whip with thongs used as an instrument of punishment; (*fig.*) any means of inflicting punishment, vengeance, or suffering; a pestilence or plague. *v.t.* To whip with or as with a scourge; to afflict, to harass, to chastise. **scourger,** *n.*

scout (1) (skout) [O.F. *escoute*, eavesdropper, from *escouter* (F. *écouter*), to listen, L. *auscultāre*, see AUSCULTATION], *n.* One sent out to bring in information, esp. one employed to watch the movements, etc., of an enemy; the art of watching or bringing in such information, a scouting expedition; a boy scout; (*Oxf. Univ.*) a college servant; *(*Cricket*) a fielder. *v.i.* To act as a scout. **Boy Scout:** A member of an organization, established in Great Britain by Lord Baden-Powell in 1908, which quickly spread to most parts of the world, for training and disciplining boys. **scout-master,** *n.* The leader of a group of Boy Scouts; a person in charge of a troop of scouts.

scout (2) (skout) [perh. from Scand. (cp. Icel. *skuti*, a taunt, rel. to *skjōta*, to SHOOT)], *v.t.* To treat with contempt and disdain, to reject contemptuously.

scout (3) (skout) [etym. doubtful], *n.* (*prov.*) The guillemot; the razor-billed auk.

scow (skou) [Dut. *schouw*], *n.* (*chiefly Am.* and *Ir.*) A large flat-bottomed, square-ended boat. *v.t.* To transport in a scow.

scowl (skoul) [M.E. *scoulen*, Dan. *skule*, cp. Icel. *skolla*, to skulk], *v.i.* To frown, to look sullen or ill-tempered. **v.t.* To repel, drive, or bear (down) by frowning or looking sullen. *n.* An angry frown; a look of sullenness, ill-temper, or discontent. **scowlingly,** *adv.*

scrabble (skrăb′ ĕl) [var. of SCRAPPLE], *v.i.* To make irregular or unmeaning marks; to scrawl, to scribble; (*Bibl.*) to scramble, to scrape, or grope (about) as if to obtain something. *v.t.* To scribble on or over.

scrag (skrăg) [cp. Norw. *skragg*, a poor creature, Dan. *skrog*, carcase, a poor creature, N.Fris. *skrog*, a lean man], *n.* Anything thin, lean, or shrivelled; a lean or bony person or animal; a lean or bony piece of meat, esp. the lean end of neck of mutton. *v.t.* (*slang*) To wring the neck of, to throttle; to kill by hanging; (*Football*) to tackle by the neck. **scrag-necked,** *a.* Having a long, thin neck. **scragged, scraggy,** *a.* **scraggedness, scragginess,** *n.* **scraggily,** *adv.*

scraich, scraigh (skrāch) [Sc., imit.], *v.i.* To make a harsh cry, to screech, to scream. *n.* A harsh cry.

scram (1) (skrăm) [var. of SHRAM], *v.t.* (*prov. in p.p.*) To benumb, to shram. *a.* Small, puny, withered, shrunken.

scram (2) (skrăm) [SCRAMBLE], *int.* (*slang*) Get out of it! Go away!

scramble (skrăm′ bĕl) [prob. var. of SCRABBLE], *v.i.* To climb or move along by clambering, crawling, wriggling, etc., esp. with the hands and knees; to seek or struggle (for, after, etc.) in a rough-and-tumble manner. *v.t.* To prepare (eggs) by breaking into a pan and stirring up during cooking (*Am.* buttered eggs); (*Radio.*) to make a radiotelephonic conversation unintelligible without the code by altering the frequencies. *n.* The act of scrambling; a climb or walk over rocks, etc., or in a rough-and-tumble manner; a rough or unceremonious struggle for something. **scrambler,** *n.* One who scrambles; (*Radio.*) a device to obtain secrecy in wireless telephone conversations.

scran (skrăn) [etym. doubtful], *n.* (*prov.*) Broken victuals; scraps, refuse. *v.t.* To collect or gather up scran. **bad scran to you!** (*Ir.*) Bad luck to you!

scranch (skrawnch) [prob. imit.], *v.t.* To grind with the teeth, to crunch.

scrannel (skrăn′ ĕl) [cp. Norw. and Swed. dial. *skran*], *a.* Thin, slender, feeble, reedy (of a voice, etc.). **scranky** (*Sc.*), **scranny,** *a.* (*prov.*) Lean, thin, meagre.

scrap (1) (skrăp) [Icel. *skrap*, SCRAPE], *n.* A small detached piece, a bit, a fragment; a picture, paragraph, etc., cut from a newspaper, etc., for preservation; (*collect.*) refuse, waste, esp. old pieces of discarded metal collected for melting down, etc.; (*pl.*) bits, odds-and-ends, leavings; (*usu. in pl.*) refuse of fat from which the oil has been expressed. *v.t.* (*past & p.p.* **scrapped**) To make scrap of, to consign to the scrap-heap; to condemn and discard as worn out, obsolete, etc. **scrapbook,** *n.* A blank book into which pictures, cuttings from newspapers, etc., are pasted for preservation. **scrap-cake,** *n.* Fish-scrap compressed into cakes. **scrap-heap,** *n.* A heap of scrap-metal; (*lit.* or *fig.*) a rubbish-heap. **scrap iron** or **metal:** Scrap. **scrappy,** *a.* **scrappily,** *adv.* **scrappiness,** *n.*

scrap (2) (skrăp) [etym. doubtful], *n.* (*slang*) A fight, a scuffle, a contest. *v.i.* To engage in a contest, esp. with fisticuffs. **scrapper,** *n.* **scrapping-match,** *n.*

scrape (skrāp) [M.E. *scrapien*, Icel. *skrapa* (cp. Dan. *skrabe*, Dut. *schrapen*), cogn. with A.-S. *screpan*, to scratch], *v.t.* To rub the surface of with something rough or sharp; to abrade, smooth, or shave thus, to remove, to clean (off, out, etc.) thus; to erase; to rub or scratch (out); to excavate or hollow (out) by scraping; to draw or rub along with a scraping noise; to collect or get together by scraping; to save or amass with difficulty or by small amounts. *v.i.* To rub the surface of something with a rough or sharp instrument; to abrade, to smooth, to clean something thus; to rub (against something) with a scraping or rasping noise; to make such a noise; to get through (an opening, examination, etc.) by a close shave; to be saving or parsimonious; to play awkwardly on a violin, etc.; to make an awkward bow with a drawing back of the foot. *n.* The act, sound, or effect of scraping; an awkward bow with a drawing back of the foot; an awkward predicament, esp. one due to one's own conduct. **to scrape acquaintance with:** To contrive to make the acquaintance of. **to scrape along:** (*colloq.*) To keep going somehow. **to scrape away:** To abrade, to reduce by scraping. **to scrape the barrel** [BARREL]. **to scrape down:** To scrape away; to scrape from head to foot; to silence or put down by scraping the feet. **scraper,** *n.* One who scrapes; an instrument for scraping, esp. for cleaning the dirt off one's boots before entering a house; an awkward fiddler; a miser; (*Archæol.*) a prehistoric flint implement used for scraping skins, etc. **scraping,** *n.*

***scrapple** (skrăp′ėl) [freq. of SCRAPE], *v.t.* To scrape, to use a scrapple. *n.* A tool used for scraping, raking, etc.

scrappy, etc. [SCRAP (1)].

***scrat** (skrăt) [M.E. *scratten*, perh. from Swed. *kratta*, to scrape, cp. G. *kratzen*], *v.t.* and *i.* To scratch, to rake with the fingers, claws, etc.

scratch (1) (skrăch) [prob. from prec. and M.E. *cracchen*, M.Dut. *kratsen*], *v.t.* To tear or mark the surface of lightly with something sharp; to wound slightly; to rub or scrape with the nails; to hollow out with the nails or claws; to erase, to obliterate, to score (out, through, etc.); to expunge (esp. the name of a horse in a test of entries for a race); to cancel a match, game, etc.; to form by scratching; to scrape (up or together). *v.i.* To use the nails or claws in tearing, scraping, marking, hollowing out, etc.; to rub or scrape one's skin with the nails; to scrape the ground as in searching. *n.* (*pl.* **-ches**) A mark made by scratching; a slight wound; a sound of scratching; an act or spell of scratching; a scratch-wig; a mark from which competitors start in a race, or a line across a prize-ring at which boxers begin; (*pl.*) a horse-disease characterized by scabs or chaps between the heel and pastern-joint. *a.* Got together at haphazard, multifarious, nondescript. **to come up to the scratch, to toe the scratch:** To be ready when wanted; to stand the test. **to start from scratch:** To start from the very beginning, with no advantage. **to scratch along:** (*slang*) To scrape along. **scratch-pad,** *n.* (*Am.*) A scribbling block. **scratch-wig,** *n.* A wig covering a bald part of the head. **scratcher,** *n.* One who or that which scratches; a bird that scratches for food; one of the *Rasores*. ***scratchingly,** *adv.* **scratchings,** *n.pl.* (*prov.*) Refuse strained out of melted lard. **scratchy,** *a.* Consisting of or characterized by scratches, irregular, rough; making a noise like scratching; (*Sport*) scratch, irregular, heterogeneous (of a team, etc.). **scratchily,** *adv.* **scratchiness,** *n.*

Scratch (2) (skrăch) [cp. Icel. *skratte*, O.H.G. *scrato*, goblin], *n.* The Devil, usu. **Old Scratch.**

scrattle (skrăt′ėl) [freq. of SCRAT], *v.i.* (*prov.*) To keep scratching or scraping; to shuffle or scramble (along).

scraw (skraw) [Ir. and Gael. *sgrath*], *n.* (*Ang.-Ir.*) A turf, a sod.

scrawl (skrawl) [perh. var. of SCRABBLE], *v.t.* To draw, write, or mark clumsily, hurriedly, or illegibly, to scribble. *v.i.* To scribble on or mark (over or all over) with illegible writing, etc. *n.* A piece of hasty, clumsy, or illegible writing. **scrawler,** *n.* **scrawly,** *a.*

scrawny [var. of SCRANNY].

scray (skrā) [W. *ysgräen* or *ysgräell*, cp. F. *screau*], *n.* The tern or sea-swallow.

screak (skrēk) [Icel. *skrækja*, prob. imit.], *v.i.* (*prov.*) To shriek, to screech; to creak. *n.* A shriek, a screech; a creaking.

scream (skrēm) [cp. Icel. *skræma*, to scare, to terrify], *v.i.* To make a shrill, piercing, prolonged cry as if in extreme pain or terror; to give out a shrill sound, to whistle, hoot, or laugh loudly. *v.t.* To utter or say in a screaming tone. *n.* A loud, shrill, prolonged cry, as of one in extreme pain or terror; (*slang*) something excruciatingly funny. **screamer,** *n.* One who or that which screams, esp. the swift; any bird of the South American semi-aquatic family *Palamedeidæ*, from their harsh cry. **screamingly,** *adv.* **screamy,** *a.* **screamily,** *adv.* **screaminess,** *n.*

scree (skrē) [Icel *skritha*, landslip, from *skrītha*, to glide, cp. A.-S. *scrithan*], *n.* Loose fragments or débris of rock on a steep slope; a slope covered with this.

screech (skrēch) [M.E. *scriken*, *schriken*, from Icel. as SCREAK], *v.i.* To scream out with a sharp, harsh, shrill voice; to make a shrill, strident noise. *v.t.* To utter or say with such a voice. *n.* A shrill, harsh cry as of terror or pain. **screech-hawk,** *n.* (*prov.*) The night-jar. **screech-martin,** *n.* The swift, also called the screecher. **screech-owl,** *n.* An owl, *Tyto alba*, that screeches instead of hooting. **screecher,** *n.* **screechy,** *a.*

screed (skrēd) [North. var. of SHRED], *n.* A long harangue or tirade; a strip of mortar or wood put on a wall, etc., that is to be plastered, as a guide to evenness of surface, etc.; a piece, a fragment, a strip; a long and tedious piece of writing; (*prov.*) a border, a frill; (*Sc.*) a rent, a tear. **screeding,** *n.* The final rendering of concrete to get a smooth surface.

screen (skrēn) [M.E. *scren*, O.F. *escren* (F. *écran*), prob. from O.H.G. *skrank*, barrier (cp. G. *shranke*)], *n.* A partition separating a portion of a room or of a church from the remainder, esp. one between the choir and the nave or ambulatory; a movable piece of furniture, usu. consisting of light framework covered with paper, cloth, etc., used to shelter from excess of heat, draught, etc.; anything serving to shelter, protect, or conceal; a sheet on which images can be projected from a magic-lantern, etc.; a board or structure on which notices, etc., can be posted; a coarse sieve or riddle, esp. for assorting coal; (*Elec.*) a body affording a shield against electric or magnetic induction; (*Phot.*) a device for modifying the effect of light passing through a lens; (*Cinema.*) the white surface upon which a picture is projected; moving pictures collectively. *v.t.* To shelter or protect from inconvenience, injury, hurt or pain, to shield; to hide, to conceal wholly or partly; to sift, to riddle. **screening-machine,** *n.* A machine for sifting and assorting coal, etc. **screenings,** *n.pl.* Small stuff or refuse separated by screening.

screeve (skrēv) [perh. through It. *scrivare*, from L. *scrībere*, to write], *v.t.* (*slang*) To write. *v.i.* To write or draw with coloured chalk, etc., on pavements; to write begging letters.

screw (1) (skroo) [formerly *scrue*, O.F. *escroue* (F. *écrou*), etym. doubtful], *n.* A cylinder with a spiral ridge or groove round its outer surface (called a male or exterior screw) or round its inner surface (called a female or internal screw), esp. a male screw used for fastening boards, etc., together; a male or female screw forming part of a tool, mechanical applicance, or machine and conveying motion to another part or bringing pressure to bear; a screw-propeller; a screw steamer; a turn of a screw; a sideways motion or tendency like that of a screw, a twist; a twisted-up paper (of tobacco, etc.); (*slang*) a stingy person; (*colloq.*) salary; (*slang*) a prison warder. *v.t.* To fasten, secure, tighten, or compress with a screw or screws; to turn (a screw); to turn round or twist as a screw; (*fig.*) to press hard, to oppress, esp. by exactions, to grind; to extort, to squeeze (money, etc., out of); to twist, to contort, to distort. *v.i.* To turn as a screw; to twist, to move obliquely or spirally, to swerve. **differential screw** [DIFFERENTIAL]. **endless screw** [ENDLESS]. **to have a screw at:** (*Austral. colloq.*) To take a look at. **to have a screw loose:** To be slightly crazy. **to put the screw on:** (*slang*) To put pressure on. **to screw up:** To tighten up with or as with a screw; to fasten with a screw or screws; to shut (a person) in thus; to twist. **to screw up courage:** To summon up resolution. **screw-coupling,** *n.* A collar with threads for joining pipes, etc., together. **screw-cutter,** *n.* A tool for cutting screws. **screw-driver,** *n.* A tool like a blunt chisel for turning screws. **screw-eye,** *n.* A screw with a loop instead of a slotted head, for attaching cords to picture-frames, etc. **screw-gear,** *n.* An endless screw or worm for working a cogwheel, etc. **screw-jack,** *n.* A lifting-jack with a screw rotating in a nut; a dentist's implement for pressing teeth apart, etc. **screw-pile,** *n.* A pile armed with a screw-point, sunk by turning instead of hammering. **screw-pine,** *n.* Any tree of the

East Indian genus *Pandanus*, with leaves clustered spirally. **screw-press,** *n.* A press worked by means of a screw. **screw-propeller** [PROPELLER]. **screw steamer:** A steamer driven by a screw-propeller. **screw-wrench,** *n.* A tool for gripping the head of a large screw or nut; a wrench with jaws worked by a screw. **screwable,** *a.* **screwed,** *a.* (*slang*) Drunk, tipsy. **screwer,** *n.*

screw (2) (skroo) [var. of SCREW], *n.* A broken-down or vicious horse. **screwy,** *a.*

scribal, *scribaceous [SCRIBE].

scribble (1) (skrib' ėl) [SCRIBE, -LE], *v.i.* To write hastily, illegibly, or without regard to correctness of handwriting or composition; (*disparagingly*) to be a journalist or author. *v.t.* To write hastily, carelessly, or without regard to correctness. *n.* Hasty or careless writing; a scrawl; something written hastily or carelessly. **scribblement,** *n.* **scribbler** (1), *n.* **scribble-scrabble,** *n.* Scribble, scrawling; *a scribbler; *v.t.* To scribble. **scribbling-paper,** *n.* Paper for making hasty notes on. **scribblingly,** *adv.*

scribble (2) (skrib' ėl) [Swed. *skrubbla*, freq. of *skrubba*, to SCRUB], *v.t.* To card roughly; to pass through a scribbler. **scribbler** (2), **scribbling-machine,** *n.* A carding-machine used for the first rough process in preparing wool, cotton, etc.

scribe (skrīb) [L. *scrība*, from *scrībere*, to write], *n.* A writer, a penman; a secretary, a copyist; (*Bibl.*) an ancient Jewish writer or keeper of official records, one of a class of commentators, interpreters, and teachers of the sacred law; a pointed instrument for marking lines on wood, bricks, etc., a scriber. *v.t.* To mark with a scriber; to mark and fit one piece to the edge of another. **scriber, scribing-awl, -iron, -tool,** *n.* A tool used for marking lines, etc. **scribing-compasses,** *n.pl.* Compasses used for scoring circles, etc. **scribal, *scribaceous** (-bā' shŭs), *a.* **scribedom, scribism,** *n.*

scrieve (skrēv) [Sc., prob. from Icel. *skrefa*, to stride], *v.i.* To stride along swiftly.

scriggle (skrig' ėl) [onomat.], *v.i.* (*prov.*) To wriggle, to writhe, to squirm. *n.* A wriggling movement.

scrim (skrim) [etym. doubtful], *n.* Strong cotton or linen cloth used for lining in upholstery.

scrimmage (skrim' aj) [var. of SKIRMISH], *n.* A tussle, a confused or rough-and-tumble struggle, a skirmish; (*Rugby Football*) a scrummage.

scrimp (skrimp) [cp. Swed. and Dan. *skrumpen*, shrivelled, G. *schrumpfen*, cogn. with A.-S. *scrimman*], *v.t.* To make small, scant, or short; to limit or straiten, to skimp. *v.i.* To skimp, to be niggardly. *a.* Scanty, narrow. *adv.* Scarcely, barely. *n.* (*Am.*) A niggard, a pinching miser. **scrimply,** *adv.* **scrimpily,** *adv.* **scrimpiness,** *n.* **scrimpness,** *n.* **scrimpy,** *a.*

scrimshank (skrim' shăngk) [etym. unknown], *v.i.* (*slang*) To avoid work, to get out of doing one's duty.

scrimshaw (skrim' shaw) [prob. a surname], *v.t.* To decorate (ivory, shells, etc.) with carvings and coloured designs. *v.i.* To produce decorated work of this kind. *n.* A piece of such work.

scrip (1) (skrip) [SCRIPT] *n.* Orig. a writing, a list, as of names, a schedule; a provisional certificate of stock subscribed to a bank or company; (*collect.*) such certificates. **scrip-holder,** *n.*

scrip (2) (skrip) [A.-S. *scripp*, cp. Icel. *skreppa*, rel. to SCRAP (1)], *n.* A small bag, a wallet or satchel. ***scrippage** [cp. BAGGAGE], *n.* (*Shak.*) That which is contained in a scrip.

script (skript) [O.F. *escript* (F. *écrit*), L. *scriptum*, something written, neut. p.p. of *scrībere*, see SCRIBE], *n.* A piece of writing; handwriting as dist. from print; printed cursive characters, type in imitation of writing; handwriting in imitation of type; (*Law*) a writing, an original document. **scription,** *n.* **scriptorium** (-tôr' i ŭm), *n.* (*pl.* **-ria**) A writing-room, esp. in a monastery. **scriptorial,** *a.* ***scriptory** (skrip'-), *a.* Written, not oral; used for writing. *n.* A scriptorium. **script writer:** (*Cinema.*) One who prepares drafts for plays.

scripture (skrip' chŭr) [M.E. from O.F. *escripture*, L. *scriptūra*, as prec.], *n.* A sacred writing or book, esp. the Bible, esp. the books of the Old and New Testament without the Apocrypha; a passage from the Scriptures; *an inscription. **v.* To write. **scriptural,** *a.* Pertaining to, derived from, based upon, or contained in the Scriptures. **scripturalism,** *n.* **scripturalist, *scripturist,** *n.* **scripturally,** *adv.* **scripturalness,** *n.* **Scripture-reader,** *n.* One employed to read the Scriptures publicly. **Holy Scripture** or the **Scriptures:** The Bible.

***scritch** (skrich) [imit. cp. SCREECH], *v.i.* To screech. *n.* A screech. **scritch-owl** [SCREECH-OWL].

scrive [SCRIBE].

***scrivener** (skriv' ė nėr) [M.E. *scriveyn*, O.F. *escrivain* (F. *écrivain*), It. *scrivano*, late L. *scrībānus*, SCRIBE, -ER], *n.* One whose business was to draw up contracts or other documents, a notary; a financial agent, a broker, a money-lender.

scrobe (skrōb) [L. *scrobis*, trench], *n.* (*Ent.*) A groove, as that receiving the base of the antennæ in weevils. **scrobicule,** *n.* (*Biol.*) A small pit or depression. **scrobicular** (skrō' bik' ū lăr), **scrobiculate, -lated, scrobiculous** (-bik' ū lŭs), *a.* ***scrobiculus*** (*pl.* ***-li***) [SCROBICULE].

scrofula (skrof' ū là) [L., orig. dim. of *scrōfa*, breeding sow], *n.* A constitutional state, usu. hereditary, tending to the development of glandular swellings and consumption, also called king's evil. **scrofulous,** *a.* **scrofulously,** *adv.* **scrofulousness,** *n.*

scrog (skrog) [etym. doubtful], *n.* (*chiefly Sc.*) A stunted bush; brushwood, undergrowth, thicket; (*Her.*) a branch of a tree. **scrogged, scroggy,** *a.*

scroll (skrōl) [formerly *scrowl*, dim. of M.E. *scrowe*, *scroue*, O.F. *escroue*, from Teut. (cp. M.Dut. *schroode*, O.H.G. *scrōt*, strip) SHRED], *n.* A roll of paper or parchment; an ancient book or volume in this form; *a schedule, a list, a catalogue; a convolved or spiral ornament more or less resembling a scroll of parchment, as a volute, the curved head of a violin, etc., a band or ribbon bearing an inscription, a flourish, or tracery consisting of spiral lines; (*Her.*) the ribbon upon which a motto is inscribed. *v.t.* To roll up like a scroll; to decorate with scrolls; to enter in a scroll. *v.i.* To curl up like a scroll. **scroll-gear** [SCROLL-WHEEL]. **scroll-head,** *n.* A volute-shaped timber at a ship's bow. **scroll-saw,** *n.* A fret-saw for cutting scrolls. **scroll-wheel,** *n.* A disk-shaped wheel with cogs arranged spirally on one surface causing variation of speed. **scroll-work,** *n.* Ornamental work in spiral lines, esp. cut out with a scroll-saw.

scroop (skroop) [imit.], *v.i.* To make a harsh, grating or creaking noise. *n.* Such a noise.

Scrophularia (skrof ū lâr' i à) [mod. L. from med. L. *scrophula*, SCROFULA], *n.* (*Bot.*) A genus of plants typical of the *Scrophulariaceæ*, containing the figwort. **scrophulariaceous** (-ā' shŭs), *a.*

scrotum (skrō' tŭm) [L.], *n.* (*pl.* **-ta**) (*Anat.*) The pouch enclosing the testes in the higher mammals. **scrotal, scrotiform,** *a.* **scrotitis** (-tī' tis), *n.* (*Path.*) Inflammation of the scrotum. **scrotocele** (skrō' tō sēl), *n.* A scrotal hernia.

scrouge (skrouj) [etym. doubtful, perh. from SCREW], *v.t.* (*prov.*) To press against, to squeeze or crowd (in). **scrouger,** *n.* One who scrouges; (*Am. slang*) a beggar.

scrounge (skrounj) [etym. doubtful], *v.t.* (*colloq.*) To pilfer, to cadge. **scrounger,** *n.*

scrub (skrŭb) [M.E. *scrobben*, M.Dan. *skrubbe* (cp. Swed. *skrubba*, Dut. *schrobben*, also SHRUB (2))], *v.t.* (*past & p.p.* **scrubbed**) To rub hard with something coarse and rough, esp. with soap and water used with a scrubbing-brush for the purpose of cleaning or scouring. *v.i.* To clean, scour, or brighten things by rubbing thus; (*fig.*) to work hard and penuriously, to drudge. *n.* A tract of brushwood, undergrowth, or stunted trees; a stunted tree, bush, etc.; a worn-out brush or broom; a paltry, stingy person; something mean or despicable; the act of scrubbing. *a.* Mean, paltry, petty, niggardly, contemptible. **scrub-bird,** *n.* An Australian passerine bird, *Atrichia clamosa.* **scrub-cattle:** (*Austral.*) Cattle that have run wild and deteriorated. **scrub fowl:** (*Austral.*) One of the mound-builder birds. **scrub-rider:** (*Austral.*) One who goes out in search of scrub cattle. **scrub turkey,** *n.* (*Austral.*) The lowan or mallee mound bird. **scrub-oak,** *n.* A name for several North American dwarf oaks. **scrub-woman,** *n.* (*Am.*) A charwoman. **scrubber,** *n.* One who or that which scrubs; a scrubbing-brush; a gas-purifier for removing tar and ammonia by spraying with water; (*Austral.*) a bullock that has run wild. **scrubbing-board,** *n.* A ribbed board used in washing for rubbing clothes on. **scrubbing-brush,** *n.* A stiff brush for scrubbing floors, etc. **scrubby, *scrubbed,** *a.* Mean, stunted, insignificant; covered with brushwood; rough, unshaven. **scrubbiness,** *n.* **the Scrubs:** (*colloq.*) Wormwood Scrubs prison.

scruff (skrŭf) [formerly *scuft,* Icel. *skopt* (*skoft*), hair of head], *n.* The nape or back of the neck, esp. as grasped by a person dragging another.

scruffy [SCURRY].

scrum, scrummage (skrŭm′ ȧj) [var. of SCRIMMAGE], *n.* (*Rugby Football*) A regular struggle between the forwards of both sides grappling in a compact mass with the ball on the ground in the middle. **scrum half:** The half-back who puts the ball into the scrum.

scrumptious (skrŭmp′ shůs) [perh. orig. mean. stingy, from SCRIMP], *a.* (*colloq.*) First-class, stylish, delicious; *fastidious.

scrunch [var. of CRUNCH].

scruple (skroo′ pėl) [F. *scrupule,* L. *scrūpulum,* nom. *-lus,* dim. of *scrūpus,* sharp stone], *n.* A weight of twenty grains, the third part of a dram (apothecaries' weight); *a small quantity, a tiny fraction, a particle; (*fig.*) doubt, objection, or hesitation from conscientious motives. *v.i.* To have scruples, to doubt, to hesitate, to be reluctant (to do, etc.). *v.t.* To doubt, hesitate, or demur, to question the correctness or propriety of. ***scrupler, scrupulist,** *n.* **scrupulous** (skroo′ pū lůs), *a.* Influenced by scruples; careful, cautious, extremely conscientious, punctilious, precise, exact; *captious, inclined to object or demur. **scrupulously,** *adv.* **scrupulosity** (-los′ i ti), **scrupulousness,** *n.*

scrutator (skroo tā′ tôr) [L., as foll.], *n.* One who scrutinizes, a close inquirer. ***scrutable,** *a.*

scrutineer (skroo ti nēr′), *n.* One who acts as examiner in a scrutiny of votes.

scrutinize (skroo′ ti nīz), *v.t.* To examine narrowly or minutely. **scrutinizer,** *n.,* **scrutinizingly,** *adv.*

scrutiny (skroo′ ti ni) [late L. *scrūtinium,* from *scrūtārī,* to search carefully, from *scrūta,* broken pieces, cogn. with SHRED], *n.* Close observation or investigation; minute inquiry; critical examination; an official examination of votes given at an election to verify the correctness of a declared result.

scruto (skroo′ to) [etym. doubtful], *n.* (*Theat.*) A trap-door with springs, made flush with the stage, for rapid disappearances, etc.

***scrutoire** [ESCRITOIRE].

scry (skrī) [DESCRY], *v.t.* To crystal-gaze; to descry.

scud (skŭd) [Norw. *skudda,* allied to SHOOT], *v.i.* To run or fly swiftly; (*Naut.*) to run fast before a gale with little or no sail spread. *v.t.* To move swiftly over. *n.* The act or a spell of scudding; loose, vapoury clouds driven swiftly by the wind; a light passing shower. **scudder,** *n.*

scudo (skoo′ dō) [It., from L. *scūtum,* shield], *n.* (*pl.* ***-di,*** -dē) An old Italian silver coin and money of account, worth about 4s.

scuff (1) (skŭf) [etym. doubtful, cp. Swed. *skuffa,* Icel. *skūfa,* to SHOVE, perh. conf. with SCRUFF or SCURF in some senses], *v.i.* To drag or scrape with the feet in walking, to shuffle. *v.t.* (*Sc.*) To scrape or wear with the feet; to touch lightly, to graze. *n.* (*Sc.*) The act or noise of scuffing with the feet; a scuffle; a gust. **scuffed, scuffy,** *a.* (*chiefly Sc.*) Worn, shabby.

scuff (2) [SCRUFF].

scuffle (skŭf′ ėl) [freq. of SCUFF (1)], *v.i.* To fight or struggle in a rough-and-tumble way; *to shuffle, to scrape with the feet. *n.* A confused and disorderly fight or struggle. **scuffler,** *n.*

sculduddery (skŭl dŭd′ ėr i) [Sc., etym. doubtful], *n.* Lewdness, bawdry, obscenity; (*Am., usu.* **skulduggery**) malversation, plotting, conspiracy.

sculk, etc. [SKULK].

scull (skŭl) [etym. doubtful], *n.* One of a pair of short oars used by one person for propelling a boat, an oar used with twisting strokes over the stern; one who sculls a boat. *v.t.* To propel (a boat) by a scull or sculls. *v.i.* To propel a boat thus. **sculler,** *n.* One who sculls; a boat rowed thus.

scullery (skŭl′ ėr i) [O.F. *escuelier,* L. *scutellārius,* dish-keeper, from *scutella,* see SCUTTLE, -ERY], *n.* A place where dishes, pots, and other utensils are washed up.

***scullion** (skŭl′ i ǒn) [O.F. *escouillon, escouvillon,* Sp. *escobillon,* sponge for a cannon, from *escobilla,* sponge, dim. of *escoba,* L. *scōpa,* pl. *scōpæ,* a besom], *n.* A boy who cleans pots, dishes, etc., a kitchen drudge. ***scullionly,** *a.*

sculp (skŭlp) [short for SCULPTURE], *v.t.* (*colloq.*) To carve, to sculpture.

sculpin (skŭl′ pin) [perh. corr. of obs. *scorpene,* SCORPÆNA], *n.* A name for various American sea-fish with large spiny heads.

sculpture (skŭlp′ chůr) [F., from L. *sculptūra,* from *sculpere,* to carve], *n.* The art of cutting, carving, modelling, or casting wood, stone, clay, or metal into representations of natural objects in round or in relief; a carved figure; (*collect.*) carved work; (*Nat. Hist.*) raised or sunk markings on a shell, elytrum, etc. *v.t.* To represent in or by sculpture; to ornament with sculpture. **sculpt,** *v.t.* (*colloq.*) **sculptor, -tress,** *n.* One who sculptures. **sculptural, sculpturesque** (skŭlp tū resk′), *a.* **sculpturally,** *adv.*

scum (skŭm) [Dan. *skum* (cp. Icel. *skūm,* G. *schaum*), rel. to SKIM], *n.* Impurities that rise to the surface of liquid, esp. in fermentation or boiling; the scoria of molten metal; froth, foam, or any film of floating matter; (*fig.*) refuse, offscourings, the vile and worthless part (of). *v.t.* To clear of scum, to skim. *v.i.* To rise as scum, to form a scum; to become covered with scum. **scummer,** *n.* **scummings,** *n.pl.* Skimmings. **scummy,** *a.*

scumble (skŭm′ bėl) [freq. of prec.], *v.t.* To cover (an oil-painting) lightly with opaque or semi-opaque colours so as to soften the outlines; to prepare a painted wall for re-painting.

scuncheon (skŭn′ chůn) [extension of SCONCE], *n.* (*Arch.*) A bevelling, splay, or elbow in a window-opening, etc.; arching, etc., across the angles of a square tower supporting a spire.

scunner (skŭn′ ėr) [Sc., etym. doubtful], *v.t.* To disgust, to nauseate. *v.i.* To feel loathing, to be sickened. *n.* Loathing, disgust.

scupper (skŭp′ ėr) [prob. from O.F. *escope,* SCOOP], *n.* (*Naut.*) A hole or tube through a ship's side to carry off water from the deck. *v.t.* To sink, to do for. **scupper-hole,** *n.* **scupper-hose, -shoot,** *n.* A spout hanging from a scupper to carry the water clear of the side. **scupper-nail,** *n.* A short nail with a broad, flat head for nailing on scupper-hose, etc.

scuppernong (skŭp′ ėr nong) [river in N. Carolina], *n.* (*Am.*) A variety of the fox-grape, *Vitis vulpina.*

scur [SKIRR].

scurf (skĕrf) [A.-S. (cp. Swed. *skorf*, Icel. *skurfur*), rel. to *sceorfan*, to scarify], *n.* Flakes or scales thrown off by the skin, esp. of the head; any loose scaly matter adhering to a surface. **scurfiness,** *n.* **scurfy,** *a.*

scurrilous (skŭr' i lŭs), ***scurrile** (skŭr' il) [L. *scurrilis*, from *scurra*, buffoon], *a.* Using or expressed in low, vulgar, grossly abusive, or indecent language. **scurrilously,** *adv.* **scurrility** (-ril' i ti), **scurrilousness,** *n.*

scurry (skŭr' i) [perh. from obs. *scurrier*, a scout, as SCOUR (2)], *v.i.* To go with great haste, to hurry, to scamper, *n.* An act or the noise of scurrying.

scurvy (skĕr' vi) [SCURFY], *a.* Mean, paltry, base, shabby, contemptible. *n.* A diseased condition of the blood characterized by swollen gums, extravasation of blood, and general debility, arising esp. among those on shipboard from deficiency of vegetable diet and the use of salt meat. **scurvy-grass** [corr. of CRESS], *n.* A plant, *Cochlearia officinalis*, used as a remedy for scurvy. **scurvied,** *a.* **scurvily,** *adv.* **scurviness,** *n.*

scut (skŭt) [cp. Icel. *skott*], *n.* A short tail, as of a hare, rabbit, or deer.

scuta [SCUTUM].

scutage (skū' tȧj) [med. L. *scūtāgium*, from *scūtum*, shield (cp. O.F. *escuage*)], *n.* (*Feudal Law*) Money paid by a tenant in lieu of personal attendance on his lord in war.

scutal, scutate [SCUTUM].

scutch (skŭch) [O.F. *escoucher*, *escousser*, perh. from Scand. (cp. Norw. *skoka*, scutcher)], *v.t.* To dress (cotton, flax, etc.) by beating. *n.* A scutcher; coarse tow separated from flax by scutching. **scutch-blade, -rake, scutcher, scutching-sword,** *n.* An implement of various kinds used in scutching flax.

scutcheon (skŭch' ŏn) [ESCUTCHEON], *n.* An escutcheon; a cover or frame for a keyhole; a name-plate. **scutcheoned,** *a.*

scutellum (skū tĕl' ŭm) [dim. of SCUTUM], *n.* (*pl.* **-la**) (*Nat. Hist.*) A small shield, plate, scale, or horny segment. **scutellar, scutellate, scutellated,** *a.* **scutellation** (-lā' shŭn), *n.* **scutelliform** (-tel' i fôrm), *a.* Shield-shaped.

scutiger (skū' ti jėr) [SCUTUM], *n.* (*Zool.*) A centipede of the genus *Scutigera* or the family *Scutigeridae*. **scutigerous,** *a.*

scutiped (skū' ti ped) [SCUTUM], *a.* (*Ornith.*) Having scutellate tarsi.

scuttle (1) (skŭtl) [A.-S. *scutel*, dish, L. *scutella*, salver, dim. of *scutra*, tray, platter], *n.* A metal or other receptacle for carrying or holding coals, esp. for a fire-place, usu. called a coal-scuttle. **scuttleful,** *n.*

scuttle (2) (skŭtl) [O.F. *escoutilles*, pl. hatches (cp. F. *écoutille*), Sp. *escotilla*, from *escotar*, to cut out round the neck, from *escote*, tucker, from Teut. (cp. Dut. *schoot*, G. *schooss*, bosom)], *n.* A hole with a movable lid or hatch in a wall or roof or the deck or side of a ship; the lid or hatch covering this. *v.t.* To cut holes through the bottom or sides of (a ship); to sink by cutting such holes. **scuttle-butt, -cask,** *n.* A cask of drinking-water, usu. with a hole for dipping through, and kept on deck. **scuttler** (1), *n.*

scuttle (3) (skŭtl) [orig. *scuddle*, freq. of SCUD], *v.i.* To hurry along, to scurry; to make off, to bolt. *n.* A hurried run or gait, a hasty flight, a bolt. **scuttler** (2), *n.*

scutum (skū' tŭm) [L., from *sku-*, to cover, cogn. with sky], *n.* (*pl.* **-ta**) (*Rom. Ant.*) The shield of the heavy-armed Roman legionaries; (*Nat. Hist.*) a shield-like plate, scale, or bony segment as of the armour of a crocodile, turtle, etc.; (*Anat.*) the knee-pan. **scutal, scutate,** *a.* **scutiform,** *a.* **scutulum,** *n.* (*pl.* **-la**) A shield-shaped scale or scab, esp. in ringworm of the scalp. **scutulate,** *a.*

scye (sī) [Sc. dial.], *n.* (*Tailoring*) The opening of a coat, etc., where the sleeve is inserted.

Scylla (sil' ȧ) [L., from Gr. *Skulla*], *n.* A rock on the Italian shore of the Straits of Messina, facing Charybdis, described by Homer as a monster devouring sailors. **Scylla and Charybdis:** Alternative risks, escape from one of which entails danger from the other.

***scymitar** [SCIMITAR].

scyphus (sī' fŭs) [L., from Gr. *skuphos*], *n.* (*pl.* **-phi, -fī**) (*Gr. Ant.*) A bowl-shaped footless cup with two handles; (*Bot.*) a cup-shaped part or organ. **scyphiform, scyphose,** *a.*

scytale (sit' ȧ lē) [Gr. *skutalē*, staff], *n.* (*Gr. Ant.*) A staff of a special form used for sending dispatches; a method of sending secret messages by writing on a strip of parchment wound about such a staff so that it was legible only when wound about a staff of similar form.

scythe (sīth) [A.-S. *sīthe* (cp. Dut. *zeis*, Icel. *sigthr*, L.G. *saged*), cogn. with L. *secāre*, to cut], *n.* A long curved blade with a crooked handle used for mowing or reaping; a curved blade projecting from the axle of an ancient war-chariot. *v.t.* To cut with a scythe. **scytheman,** *n.* One who uses a scythe, a mower; *one of an irregular body of troops armed with scythes. **scythe-stone,** *n.* A whetstone for sharpening scythes. **scythed,** *a.*

Scythian (sith' i ȧn), *a.* Pertaining to ancient Scythia, the region north of the Black Sea, the Caspian, and the Sea of Aral, or the ancient race inhabiting it. *n.* One of this race; the Scythian language. **Scythic** (sith' ik), *a.* **Scythism,** *n.* **Scytho-,** *comb. form.*

***'sdeath** (zdeth) [short for GOD'S DEATH], *int.* An exclamation of impatience, anger, etc.

se- [L., away from, apart, without], *pref.* As in *secede*, *secure*.

sea (sē) [A.-S. *sǣ*, cp. Dut. *zee*, G. *see*, Icel. *sær*], *n.* The body of salt water covering the greater part of the earth's surface, the ocean; a definite part of this, or a very large enclosed body of (usu. salt) water; the swell or motion of the sea, a great wave, a billow; the set or direction of the waves; (*fig.*) a vast quantity or expanse, an ocean, a flood (of people, troubles, etc.). *a.* Of, pertaining to, living, growing, or used in, on, or near the sea, marine, maritime. **at full sea:** At high tide; (*fig.*) at the acme or culmination. **at sea:** On the open sea; out of sight of land; (*fig.*) perplexed, uncertain, wide of the mark. **brazen sea** [MOLTEN SEA (see below)]. **half-seas over:** Half-tipsy. **high seas** [HIGH]. **over** or **beyond seas:** To or in countries separated by sea. **the four seas:** Those surrounding Great Britain on the N., E., W., and S. **to go to sea, to follow the sea:** To become or to be a sailor. **to put to sea:** To leave port or land. **the molten sea:** The brazen laver of the Mosaic ritual (see 1 Kings vii. 25). **The Seven Seas,** *n.pl.* The North and South Atlantic, the North and South Pacific, the Indian, the Arctic and the Antarctic oceans. **sea-acorn,** *n.* A barnacle. **sea-anchor** [DRAG-ANCHOR]. **sea-anemone,** *n.* A popular name for an actinia. **sea-angel,** *n.* The angel-fish. **sea-ape,** *n.* The sea-fox; the sea-otter. **sea-bank,** *n.* The shore; a bank built to keep out the sea. **sea-bar,** *n.* The sea-swallow or tern. **sea-bass** [BASS (2)]. **sea-bat,** *n.* A flying fish; a fish of the genus *Platax*, from the length of its dorsal and ventral fins. **sea-bear,** *n.* A polar bear; the N. Pacific fur-seal. **sea-beat, -beaten,** *a.* Beaten by the waves. **sea-bells,** *n.* A species of bindweed growing on the shore. **sea-belt,** *n.* A species of fucus with belt-like fronds. **sea-bird,** *n.* **sea-board,** *n.* Land bordering on the sea; the sea-coast; the seashore. *a.* Bordering on the sea. **sea-boat,** *n.* A ship (with regard to her sea-going qualities). **sea-borne,** *a.* Conveyed by sea. **sea-bow,** *n.* A bow like a rainbow produced in sea-spray. **sea-boy,** *n.* A boy employed on board a sea-going vessel. **sea-breach,** *n.* Irruption of the sea through an embankment. **sea-bread,** *n.* Ship-biscuit. **sea-breeze,** *n.* A breeze blowing from the sea, usually by day in alternation with a land-breeze at night. **sea-calf,** *n.* The common seal. **sea-campion,** *n.* A plant of the pink family, *Silene maritima.* **sea-canary,** *n.* The white whale (from its whistling). **sea-cap,** *n.* A cap to be worn on shipboard; the cap of a wave; (*Am.*) a large basket-shaped sponge. **sea-captain,** *n.* The captain of a vessel, as dist. from a military officer; a great commander or admiral. **sea-card,** *n.* The card of the mariner's compass; a map or chart. **sea-change,** *n.* Transformation or transmutation produced by the sea. **sea-coal,** *n.* Coal (orig. brought from Newcastle by sea) as distinct from charcoal. **sea-coast,** *n.* **sea-cob,** *n.* A black-backed sea-gull. **sea-cock,** *n.* A valve through which the sea can be admitted into the hull of a ship. **sea-colander,** *n.* An olive-coloured seaweed with perforated fronds. **sea-cow,** *n.* Any of the *Sirenia*; a walrus. **sea-crow, -cormorant, -drake,** *n.* Local names for the laughing gull, *Larus ridibundus,* and other sea-birds. **sea-cucumber,** *n.* A holothurian such as the trepang. **sea-devil,** *n.* The angler-fish; any holothurian, esp. the bêche-de-mer. **sea-dog,** *n.* The common seal; the dog-fish; (*fig.*) an old sailor, esp. of the Elizabethan era. **sea-dragon,** *n.* Applied to various fishes having some resemblance to a dragon. **sea-eagle,** *n.* The osprey; various fishing-eagles and other large sea-birds. **sea-ear,** *n.* An ormer or mollusc of the genus *Haliotis.* **sea-egg,** *n.* A sea-urchin. **sea-elephant,** *n.* The largest of the seals, *Macrorhinus elephantinus,* the male of which has a short proboscis. **sea-fan,** *n.* A coral of the genus *Gorgonia,* having fan-like branches. ***seafarer,** *n.* A sailor, a seaman. **seafaring,** *a.* Following the occupation of a sailor; *n.* The occupation of a sailor. **sea-fennel,** *n.* Samphire. **sea-fight,** *n.* A naval engagement. **sea-flower,** *n.* The sea-anemone. **sea food:** Edible salt-water shellfish. **sea-fowl,** *n.* **sea-fox,** *n.* The long-tailed shark, *Alopias vulpes.* **sea front,** *n.* The part of a town that faces the sea. **sea-gauge,** *n.* A self-registering apparatus for taking deep-sea soundings; the draught of a ship. **sea-gherkin** [SEA-CUCUMBER]. **sea-gilliflower,** *n.* The sea-pink. **sea-girt,** *a.* Surrounded by the sea. **sea-god, -deity,** *n.* A deity supposed to preside over the sea. **sea-goddess,** *n.* **sea-going,** *a.* Making foreign voyages, as opp. to coasting; seafaring. ***sea-gown,** *n.* A gown with short sleeves worn at sea. **sea-green,** *n.* A faint bluish-green. *a.* Of this colour. **sea-gudgeon,** *n.* The black goby, *Gobius niger.* **sea-gull,** *n.* **sea-hare,** *n.* A mollusc of the genus *Aplysia.* **sea-hedgehog,** *n.* A sea-urchin. **sea-hog,** *n.* The common porpoise. **sea-horse,** *n.* The walrus; the hippocampus; a fabulous animal, half horse and half fish, harnessed to the chariot of a sea-god. **sea-island cotton:** A fine variety of cotton originally grown on the islands of the coasts of Georgia, South Carolina, and Florida. **sea-kale,** *n.* A cruciferous plant, *Crambe maritima,* grown as a culinary vegetable for its young shoots. **sea-king,** *n.* (*poet.*) A viking or piratical Scandinavian chieftain. **sea-lark, -laverock,** *n.* The ringed plover; other sea-birds. **sea-lavender,** *n.* Any species of *Limonium,* esp. *Statice limonium.* **sea-lawyer,** *n.* (*Naut.*) A sailor given to arguing and criticizing; a shark. **sea-legs,** *n.pl.* Ability to walk on the deck of a vessel at sea on a stormy day. **sea-lemon,** *n.* A yellow oval gasteropod of the genus *Doris.* **sea-leopard,** *n.* A spotted seal from the South Pacific and Antarctic. **sea-letter,** *n.* A document from the custom-house carried by a neutral ship in time of war, specifying the nature of the cargo, etc. **sea-level,** *n.* A level continuous with that of the surface of the sea at mean tide, taken as a basis for surveying, etc. (in Britain at Newlyn, Cornwall). **sea-lily,** *n.* A crinoid. **sea-line,** *n.* The horizon at sea. **sea-lion,** *n.* A large-eared seal, esp. of the genus *Otaria*; (*Her.*) a fabulous animal, half lion and half fish. **Sea Lord,** *n.* (*Pol.*) One of four naval Lords of the Admiralty. **sea-magpie,** *n.* The sea-pie (1). **sea-maid,** *n.* A mermaid, a sea-nymph. **seaman,** *n.* (*pl.* **-men**) A mariner, a sailor, esp. one below the rank of officer; a person able to navigate a ship, a navigator. **seaman-like, seamanly,** *a.* **seamanship,** *n.* **sea-mark,** *n.* An elevated object, such as a lighthouse or beacon, serving as a guide to vessels at sea. **sea-mat,** *n.* A polyzoan forming a flat matted coral. **sea-melon,** *n.* A holothurian such as the sea-cucumber. **seamew,** *n.* A sea-gull. **sea-mile,** *n.* A geographical mile. **sea-monster,** *n.* A huge sea-creature, natural or mythical. **sea-moss,** *n.* A moss-like coralline or seaweed; corrageen. **sea-mouse,** *n.* An iridescent sea-worm, *Aphrodite aculeata.* **sea-needle,** *n.* The garfish, *Belone vulgaris.* **sea-nettle,** *n.* A jelly-fish. **sea-onion,** *n.* The squill. **sea-otter,** *n.* A marine otter, *Enhydra marina,* of the shores of the N. Pacific. **sea-owl,** *n.* The lump. **sea-pad,** *n.* The starfish. **sea-pass** [SEA-LETTER]. **sea-peach, -pear,** *n.* Peach-, or pear-shaped kinds of ascidians. **sea-pen,** *n.* A feather-shaped polyp. **sea-pheasant,** *n.* The pintail duck. **sea-pie** (1), *n.* The oyster-catcher, *Hæmatopus ostralegus.* **sea-pie** (2), *n.* A sailors' dish of crust and meat in alternate layers, baked together. **sea-piece,** *n.* A picture representing a scene at sea. **sea-pig,** *n.* A porpoise; a dugong. **sea-pike,** *n.* The garfish; the hake; other fish of a similar kind. **sea-pilot,** *n.* A sea-pie (1). **sea-pink,** *n.* Thrift, *Armeria maritima.* **sea-plane,** *n.* (*Aviat.*) An aeroplane fitted with floats to enable it to take off from and alight on the water. **sea-plane carrier,** *n.* (*Nav.*) A warship that is fitted with a deck from which planes can operate. **seaport,** *n.* A town with a harbour on the coast. **sea-pumpkin,** *n.* A sea-melon. **sea-purse,** *n.* The leathery envelope in which sharks and rays deposit their eggs. ***sea-rat,** *n.* A pirate. **sea-raven,** *n.* A deep-sea sculpin from the Western Atlantic; a cormorant. **sea-risk,** *n.* Hazard of injury or loss at sea. **sea-roll,** *n.* A holothurian. **sea-robber,** *n.* A pirate. **sea-robin,** *n.* The red gurnard. **sea-room,** *n.* Room to handle a ship without danger of running ashore or of collision. **sea-rosemary,** *n.* The sea-lavender. **sea-rover,** *n.* A pirate; a piratical vessel. **sea-salt,** *n.* Salt obtained from sea-water by evaporation. **seascape,** *n.* A sea-piece. **sea-scorpion,** *n.* Any fish of the genus *Scorpæna*; the sculpin, *Cottus scorpius.* **sea-serpent,** *n.* A sea-snake; a creature of immense size and serpentine form, believed by mariners to inhabit the depths of the ocean. **Sea Scouts,** *n.pl.* A maritime branch of the Boy Scouts. **sea-shore,** *n.* The shore, coast, or margin of the sea; (*Law*) the space between high- and low-water mark; land adjacent to the sea. **sea-sick,** *a.* Suffering from sea-sickness. **sea-sickness,** *n.* A peculiar functional disturbance characterized by nausea and vomiting, bought on by the motion of a ship. **seaside,** *n.* A place or district close to the sea, esp. a watering-place. *a.* Bordering on the sea. **sea-sleeve,** *n.* A cuttle-fish. **sea-slug,** *n.* (*Zool.*) A trepang. **sea-snail,** *n.* A snail-like marine gasteropod; a slimy fish of the family *Liparididæ,* the unctuous sucker. **sea-snake,** *n.* A venomous marine snake of the family *Hydrophidæ* inhabiting the Indian Ocean and other tropical seas; (*poet.*) the sea-serpent. **sea-snipe,** *n.* The snipe-fish; the dunlin. **sea-squirt,** *n.* An ascidium. **sea-sunflower,** *n.* A sea-anemone. **sea-swallow,** *n.* The tern. **sea-tang, -tangle,** *n.* A seaweed of the genus *Laminaria.* **sea-term,** *n.* A word or phrase peculiar to seamen. **sea-toad,** *n.* The toad-fish; the angler-fish; the sculpin. **sea-trout,** *n.* The salmon-trout, bull-trout, and some other fishes. **sea-unicorn,** *n.* The narwhal. **sea-urchin,** *n.* An echinus. **sea-wall,** *n.* A wall or embankment for protecting land against encroachment by the sea. **sea-way,** *n.* (*Naut.*) A ship's progress; a clear way for a ship at sea. **seaweed,** *n.* Any alga or other plant growing in the sea. **sea-weeded, -weedy,** *a.* **sea-whip,** *n.* A whip-shaped coral. **sea-whipcord,** *n.* A variety of sea-weed. **sea-wife,** *n.* A variety of wrasse. **sea-wolf,** *n.* A viking; a pirate; a large voracious fish, esp. the wolf-fish, *Anarrhicas lupus*; *a sea-elephant. **seaworthy,** *a.* In a fit state to go to sea (of a ship). **seaworthiness,** *n.* **sea-wrack,** *n.* Coarse seaweed, esp. thrown up by the waves. **seaward,** *a.* Directed or situated towards the sea. *adv.* Towards the sea. *n.* A seaward side or aspect. **seawards,** *adv.*

seal (1) (sēl) [A.-S. *seolh*, cp. Icel. *selr*, Dan. *sæl*, Swed. *själ*], *n.* A carnivorous amphibious marine mammal of various species of the family *Phocidæ*, having flipper-like limbs adapted for swimming and thick fur; applied to allied mammals belonging to the family *Otariidæ*, distinguished by having visible external ears, comprising the sea-bear, sea-lion, and fur-seals. *v.i.* To hunt seals. **seal-fishery,** *n.* **seal-rookery,** *n.* **sealskin,** *n.* The under-fur of the fur-seal, esp. prepared for use as material for jackets, etc.; a sealskin garment. **sealer,** *n.* A ship or man engaged in seal-hunting.

seal (2) (sēl) [O.F. *seel* (F. *sceau*), L. *sigillum*, cogn. with *signum*, SIGN], *n.* A die or stamp having a device, usu. in intaglio, for making an impression on wax or other plastic substance; a piece of wax, lead, or other material stamped with this and attached to a document as a mark of authenticity, etc., or to an envelope, package, box, etc., to prevent its being opened without detection, etc.; the impression made thus on wax, lead, etc.; a stamped wafer- or other mark affixed to a document in lieu of this; (*fig.*) any act, gift, or event regarded as authenticating, ratifying, or guaranteeing; a symbolic, significant, or characteristic mark or impress; (*Plumbing*) anything used to prevent the escape of gas, etc., esp. water in the trap of a drain-pipe preventing the ascent of foul-air. *v.t.* To affix a seal to; to stamp with a seal or stamp, esp. as a mark of correctness or authenticity; to fasten with a seal; to close hermetically, to shut up; to close (the lips, etc.) lightly; to confine securely; to fix or secure with plaster, etc.; (*fig.*) to confirm; to ratify, to certify; to set a mark on, to designate or destine irrevocably. **Fisher's Seal:** The papal privy seal with a device showing St. Peter fishing. **Great Seal:** The official seal of the United Kingdom used to seal treaties, writs summoning Parliament, and other State documents of great importance. **Privy Seal** [PRIVY]. **seal-pipe,** *n.* A dip-pipe. **seal-ring,** *n.* A finger-ring with a seal. **seal-wort,** *n.* Solomon's seal. ***sealing-day,** *n.* A day for ratification or confirmation. **sealing-wax,** *n.* A composition of shellac and turpentine with a pigment used for sealing letters, etc.

sealskin [SEAL (1)]. **seal-wort** [SEAL (2)].

sealyham (sē′ li hăm) [village in Pembrokeshire], *n*, A breed of Welsh terrier.

seam (1) (sēm) [A.-S. (cp. Dut. *zoom*, G. *saum*. Icel. *saumr*), rel. to SEW], *n.* A ridge or other visible line of junction between two parts or things, esp. two pieces of cloth, etc., sewn together, planks fitted edge to edge, or sheet-metal lapped over at the edges; (*Anat.*) a suture; a mark of separation, a crack, a fissure; a line on the surface of anything, esp. the face, a wrinkle, a cicatrix, a scar; (*Geol.*) a thin layer separating two strata; a thin stratum of coal; (*Am.*) a piece of sewing. *v.t.* To join together with or as with a seam; to mark with a seam, furrow, scar, etc.; (*Knitting*) to make ridges in (stockings, etc.). **seam-, seaming-lace,** *n.* Galloon, braid, etc., used to cover the seams in upholstery. **seam-presser,** *n.* A heavy iron used by tailors for pressing seams; an implement used to flatten down the ridges after ploughing. ***seam-rent,** *n.* A rent along a seam. *a.* Ragged. **seamer, seaming-machine,** *n.* A sewing-machine for making seams. **seaming-plough:** A seam-presser. **seamless,** *a.* ***seamster, *sempster** (sēm′ stėr, semp′ stėr), *n.* One who sews. **seamstress, sempstress,** *n.* A woman whose occupation is to sew. **seamy,** *a.* Showing the seams. **seamy side:** The side of a garment showing the seams; (*fig.*) the disreputable or worst side of life, etc.

***seam** (2) (sēm) [F. *saim*, ult. from L. *sagīna*, fattening, fatness], *n.* Fat, grease; hog's lard.

seam (3) (sēm) [A.-S. *sēam*, O.H.G. *soum*, med. L. *sauma*, Gr. *sagma*, pack-saddle], *n.* (*now prov.*) A horse-load measure of 8 bushels of corn, 6–8 pecks of sand, etc.; a cart-load, usu. 3 cwt. of hay or 2 cwt. of straw.

Seanad Eireann (shăn′ ăd ār′ ėn) [Ir.], *n.* The upper house, or senate, of the parliament of Eire.

séance (sā′ ans) [F., a sitting, from O.F. *seoir*, L. *sedēre*, to sit], *n.* A session, as of a society, deliberative body, etc.; a meeting for exhibiting, receiving, or investigating spiritualistic manifestations.

sear (1), **sere** (2) (sēr) [A.-S. *sēar* (cp. O.Dut. *sore*, also Gr. *auos*, for *sausos*, dry, and AUSTERE), whence *sēarian*, to sear], *a.* Dried up, withered (of leaves, etc.). *v.t.* To burn or scorch the surface of to dryness and hardness; to cauterize; (*fig.*) to brand; to make callous or insensible; *to wither up, to blast. **seared,** *a.* Hardened, insensible, callous. **searedness,** *n.*

sear (2) [SERE (1)].

***searce** (sĕrs) [M.E. *saarce*, O.F. *saas* (F. *sas*), ult. as SETACEOUS], *n.* A sieve, a strainer. *v.t.* To sift.

search (sĕrch) [M.E. *serchen*, O.F. *cercher* (F. *chercher*), *circāre*, to go round, from CIRCUS], *v.t.* To go over and examine for what may be found or to find something; to explore, to probe; to look for, to seek (out). *v.i.* To make search, inquiry, or investigation. *n.* The act of seeking, looking, or inquiring; investigation, exploration, inquiry, quest, examination. **search me!** *int.* How should I know? I have no idea. **right of search:** The right claimed by a belligerent nation to board neutral vessels and examine their papers and cargo for contraband. **searchlight,** *n.* An electric arc-light or other powerful illuminant concentrated into a beam that can be turned in any direction for lighting channels, discovering an enemy, etc. **search-party,** *n.* One going out to search for a lost, concealed, or abducted person or thing. **search-warrant,** *n.* A warrant granted by a Justice of the Peace, authorizing entry into a house, etc., to search for stolen property, etc. **searchable,** *a.* ***searchableness,** *n.* **searcher,** *n.* **searching,** *a.* Making search or inquiry; penetrating, thorough, minute, close. *n.* Examination; minute inquiry. **searchingly,** *adv.* **searchingness,** *n.* **searchless,** *a.*

season (sē′ zŏn) [O.F. *seson* (F. *saison*), L. *satiōnem*, nom. *-tio*, from *serere*, to sow], *n.* One of the four divisions of the year, spring, summer, autumn, winter; a period of time of a specified or indefinite length; the period of the greatest activity of something, or when it is in vogue, plentiful, at its best, etc.; a favourable opportunity, fit, suitable, or convenient time; (of a mammal) period of being on heat; seasoning; a season ticket. *v.t.* To make sound or fit for use by preparation, esp. by tempering, maturing, acclimatizing, inuring, habituating, or hardening; to render palatable or give a higher relish to by the addition of condiments, etc.; to make more piquant or pleasant, to add zest to; to mitigate, to moderate, to qualify (justice with mercy, etc.). *v.i.* To become inured, habituated, accustomed, etc.; to become hard and dry (of timber). **in season:** In vogue; in condition for shooting, hatching, use, mating, eating, etc.; (of a mammal) on heat; at a fit or opportune time. **in season and out of season:** At all times, continuously or indiscriminately. **season-ticket,** *n.* A railway or other ticket, usu. issued at a reduced rate, valid for any number of journeys, etc., for the period specified. **seasonable,** *a.* Occurring or done at the proper time, suitable to the season, opportune. **seasonableness,** *n.* **seasonably,** *adv.* **seasonal,** *a.* **seasonally,** *adv.* **seasoner,** *n.* **seasoning,** *n.* Anything added to food to make it more palatable; anything that increases enjoyment. **seasonless,** *a.*

seat (sēt) [M.E. *sete*, Icel. *sæti*, cogn. with SIT], *n.* That on which one sits or may sit, a chair, bench, stool, etc.; the part of a chair, etc., on which a person's weight rests in sitting, or of a machine or other structure on which another part or thing is supported; the buttocks or the part of trousers, etc., covering them; the place where anything is, location, site, situation; a country residence, a mansion; the right of sitting, esp. in a legislative body; manner or posture of sitting. *v.t.* To cause to sit down, to place or set on a seat; to assign seats to; to provide (a church, etc.) with seats; to provide (a chair, trousers, etc.) with a seat; to settle, to locate, to install, to establish, to fix in place. **v.i.* To rest; to settle. **seat-back,** *n.* A loose ornamental covering for the back of a chair, etc. **seat-earth,** *n.* A bed of clay, etc., underlying a coal-seam. **seatage,** *n.* **seated,** *a.* Sitting. **seater,** *n.* (*usu. in comb.* as *two-seater*). **seating,** *n.* **seatless,** *a.*

***seax** [SAX (1)].

sebaceous (sė bā′ shŭs) [L. *sēbāceus*, from *sēbum*, tallow], *a.* Fatty; made of, containing, conveying, or secreting fatty or oily matter (esp. of glands, ducts, follicles, etc.). **sebacic** (-băs′ ik), *a.* (*Chem.*) **sebacic acid:** An acid derived from various oils. **sebate** (sē′ bāt), *n.* A salt of this. **sebiferous** (-bif′ ėr ŭs), **sebific,** *a.* **seborrhœa** (seb ȯ rē′ ȧ), *n.* (*Path.*) Stearrhœa. **seborrhœic,** *a.* **sebum** (sē′ bŭm), *n.* (*Physiol.*) The fatty matter secreted by the sebaceous glands, which lubricates the hair, etc.

Sebat (sē′ băt) [Heb. *sh'baṭ*], *n.* The fifth month of the Jewish civil year and the eleventh of the ecclesiastical year, corresponding to part of Jan. and Feb.

sebesten (sė bes′ tėn) [Arab. *sebastān*, Pers. *sapistān*], *n.* The drupaceous fruit of an Assyrian or Indian tree, *Cordia myxa* or *C. latifolia*, used medicinally now only in the East.

sebiferous, seborrhœa, sebum, etc. [SEBACEOUS].

***sebilla** (sė bil′ ȧ) [F. *sébile*], *n.* A wooden bowl used for holding sand and water in the process of cutting marble.

sec (sek) [F., from L. *siccus*], *a.* Dry (of wines, etc.).

secability (sek ȧ bil′ i ti) [late *secābilitas*, from *secāre*, to cut], *n.* Capability of being cut or divided into parts.

Secale (sė kā′ li) [L.], *n.* (*Bot.*) A genus of cereals containing the rye-plant.

secant (sē′ kȧnt, sek′ ȧnt) [L. *secans -ntem*, pres.p. of *secāre*, to cut], *a.* Cutting; dividing into two parts. *n.* (*Math.*) A straight line intersecting a curve, esp. a radius of a circle drawn through the second extremity of an arc of this and terminating in a tangent to the first extremity; the ratio of this to the radius. **secant of an angle:** The ratio of the hypotenuse to the base of a right-angled triangle formed by drawing a perpendicular to either side of the angle.

secateurs (sek′ ȧ tėrs) [F.], *n.pl.* Pruning-scissors.

secco (sek′ ō) [It.], *a.* (*Mus.*) Plain, unadorned. *n.* Tempera-painting.

secede (sė sēd′) [L. *sēcēdere* (SE, *cedere*, to go, p.p. *cessus*)], *v.i.* To withdraw from fellowship, association, or communion, esp. with a Church. **seceder,** *n.* One who secedes; (*pl.*) those who seceded from the Scottish Church in 1733.

secern (sė sėrn′) [L. *sēcernere* (SE-, *cernere*, to separate)], *v.t.* To separate, to distinguish; (*Physiol.*) to excrete. **secernment,** *a.* Secretory; *n.* A secretory organ; a drug, etc., promoting secretion. **secernment,** *n.*

secesh, secesher [SECESSION].

secession (sė sesh′ ŭn) [L. *sēcessio*, SECEDE], *n.* The act of seceding. **secesh,** *a.* and *n.* (*Am. colloq.*) Secessionist. **secesher,** *n.* **secessionism,** *n.* **secessionist,** *n.* A seceder or advocate of secessionism, esp. one who took part with the Southern States in the American Civil War of 1861–5. ***secessive** (-ses′ iv), *a.* Retired, secluded.

seckel (sek′ ėl) [*Seckel*, of Pennsylvania, who introduced it], *n.* A small, pulpy variety of pear.

seclude (sė klood′) [L. *sēclūdere* (SE-, *claudere*, to shut)], *v.t.* To shut up or keep (a person, place, etc.) apart or away from society or resort; to cause to be solitary or retired. **secludedly,** *adv.* ***secluse,** *a.* **seclusion** (-kloo′ zhŭn), *n.* **seclusive** (-kloo′ siv), *a.*

second (1) (sek′ ŏnd) [F., from L. *secundus*, orig. following, from *sequī*, to follow], *a.* Immediately following the first in time or place; next in value, authority, rank, or position; secondary, inferior, other, additional, supplementary, subordinate, derivative; (*Mus.*) lower in pitch. *n.* The next after the first in rank, importance, etc.; a second-class in an examination, etc.; a person taking this; another or an additional person or thing; one who supports another, esp. one who attends on the principal in a duel, pugilistic encounter, etc.; the sixtieth part of a minute of time or angular measurement; (*colloq.*) a very short time; (*pl.*) goods of second quality, esp. coarse, inferior flour, or bread made from this; (*Mus.*) the interval of one tone between two notes, either a whole tone or a semitone; the next tone above or below; two tones so separated combined together; a lower part added to a melody when arranged for two voices or instruments; (*colloq.*) an alto. *v.t.* To forward, to promote, to support; to support (a resolution) formally to show that the proposer is not isolated. **second advent:** The return of Christ to establish His personal reign on earth. **second-adventist,** *n.* A premillenarian. **second-best,** *a.* Of second quality. **second chamber:** The upper house in a legislative body having two chambers. **second childhood:** Senile dotage. **second-class,** *a.* Of second or inferior quality, rank, etc., second-rate. **second coming:** The second advent. **second floor,** *n.* The second from the ground-floor. (In *Am.* the term is applied to the first story.) **second-hand,** *a.* Not primary or original; not new, sold or for sale after having been used or worn; dealing in second-hand goods. **second-pair back or front:** A room in the back or front of the house on the floor two flights of stairs above the ground-floor. **second-rate,** *a.* Of inferior quality, size, value, etc. **second sight:** The power of seeing things at a distance in space or time as if they were present, claimed by some Scottish Highlanders. **secondly,** *adv.* In the second place.

second (2) (se kŏnd′), *v.t.* (*Mil.*) To retire an officer temporarily without pay in order that he may take a civil or other appointment; to transfer an officer temporarily to another regiment or arm of the service.

secondary (sek′ on dȧ ri), *a.* Coming next in order of place or time to the first; not primary, not original, derivative, supplementary, subordinate; of the second or of inferior rank, importance, etc.; (*Astron.*) revolving round a primary planet; (*Geol.*) between the tertiary formation above and the primary below, Mesozoic. *n.* A delegate or deputy; a cathedral dignitary of secondary rank; a secondary planet, a satellite; (*Geol.*) the secondary epoch or formation; (*Zool.*) a feather on the second joint of a bird's wing; a hind wing in an insect. **secondarily,** *adv.* **secondariness,** *n.* **secondary cell,** *n.* (*Elec.*) A cell that can be recharged by driving an electric current through it in the reverse direction. **secondary colours** [COLOUR]. **secondary education** or **school:** That provided for children who have received an elementary education. **secondary electrons,** *n.pl.* (*Radio.*) The electrons which the anode of a thermionic valve emits when the primary electrons strike it with a high velocity. **secondary winding,** *n.* (*Elec.*) A coil in which the current in the primary winding induces the electric current.

seconde (se′ gond) [F.], *n.* (*Fencing*) A position in parrying or lungeing.

secondo (se kon′ dō) [It.], *n.* (*Mus.*) The second part or the second performer in a duet.

secrecy (sē′ kre si), *n.* The state of being secret, concealment; the quality of being secretive, secretiveness; solitude, retirement, seclusion.

secret (sē′ krėt) [O.F., from L. *sēcrētus*, p.p. of *sēcernere*, to SECERN], *a.* Concealed from notice, kept private, hidden, not to be revealed or exposed, privy; unseen, occult, mysterious; given to secrecy, secretive, close, reserved, reticent; secluded, private. *n.* Something to be kept back or concealed; a thing kept back from general knowledge; a mystery, something that cannot be explained; the explanation or key to this; secrecy; (*pl.*) the parts of the body that are usually concealed; (*R.-C. Ch.*) a prayer in a low tone recited by the celebrant at Mass. **in secret:** Secretly, privately. **an open secret:** Something known generally. **secret service:** A Government service for obtaining information or other work of which no account is given to the public; espionage. **secret-service money:** Money expended on this. **secretage,** *n.* A process of preparing furs. **secretly,** *adv.* **secretness,** *n.*

secretaire (sek rė târ′) [F. *secrétaire*, as foll.], *n.* An escritoire, a bureau.

secretary (sek′ rė târ i) [F. *secrétaire*, late L. *sēcrētārius*, orig. a confidential officer, as SECRET], *n.* An officer appointed by a company, firm, society, etc., to conduct its correspondence, keep its records, and represent it in business transactions, etc.; a person employed by another to assist in literary work, correspondence, etc., usu. called private secretary; a minister in charge of a Government department, usu. called Secretary of State; an escritoire; a secretary-bird; *a confidant, a confidential manager, friend, etc. **secretary of an embassy** or **legation:** The principal assistant or deputy of an ambassador. **under-secretary:** One of two secretaries attached to a Secretary of State. **secretary-bird,** *n.* A South African bird, *Serpentarius secretarius*, preying on snakes, etc. (named from its pen-like tufts stuck in the ear). **secretarial** (-târ′ i ăl), *a.* **secretariat** (sek re târ′ i ăt), *n.* The post of a secretary; an administrative office building.

secrete (sė krēt′) [L. *sēcrētus*, SECRET], *v.t.* To conceal, to hide; to keep secret; (*Physiol.*) to separate from the blood, sap, etc., by the process of secretion. **secretion,** *n.* The act of secreting or concealing; (*Physiol.*) the process of separating materials from the blood, sap, etc., for the service of the body or for rejection as excreta; any matter thus secreted, as mucus, gastric juice, urine, etc. **secretional, -ary,** *a.* ***secretitious** (-tish′ ŭs), **secretor,** *n.* **secretory,** *a.*

secretive (sė krē′ tiv), *a.* Given to secrecy, reserved, uncommunicative; (*Physiol.*) promoting or causing secretion. **secretively,** *adv.* **secretiveness,** *n.*

secretly, secretness [SECRET].

secretor, secretory [SECRETE].

sect (1) (sekt) [O.F. *secte*, L. *secta*, a following, faction (med. L. suite, suit, costume), from *sequī*, to follow], *n.* A body of persons who have separated from a larger body, esp. an established Church, on account of philosophical or religious differences; a religious denomination, a nonconformist Church (as regarded by opponents); the body of adherents of a particular philosopher, school of thought, etc.; *a party, a faction; *a class or kind. **sectarial** (-târ′ i ăl), *a.* **sectarian,** *a.* and *n.* **sectarianism,** *n.* **sectarianize,** *v.t.* ***sectarist** (sek′ tă rist), *n.* **sectary,** *n.* A member of a sect; (*Hist.*) a Dissenter, esp. an Independent or Presbyterian in the epoch of the Great Civil War. ***sectator** (-tā′ tŏr), *n.* A follower, adherent, or disciple; a secretary.

***sect** (2) (sekt) [prob. from L. *sectum*, neut. p.p. of *secāre*, to cut], *n.* (*Shak.*) A cutting, a scion.

sectant (sek′ tănt) [*sect-um*, see prec., -ANT], *n.* (*Geom.*) A portion of space separated by three intersecting planes but extending to infinity.

sectile (sek′ til, -tīl) [F., from L. *sectilis*, as foll.], *a.* Capable of being cut.

section (sek′ shŭn) [F., from L. *sectiōnem*, nom. -*tio*, from *secāre*, to cut, p.p. *sectus*], *n.* Separation by cutting; that which is cut off or separated, a part, a portion; one of a series of parts into which anything naturally separates or is constructed so as to separate for convenience in handling, etc.; a division or sub-division of a book, chapter, statute, etc.; the sign § indicating such a division, a section-mark; a distinct part of a country, people, community, class, etc.; (*Nat. Hist.*) a group, a sub-genus; (*Mil.*) a subdivision of a half-company; (*Am.*) one of the portions of a square of 640 acres into which public lands are divided; a thin slice of any substance prepared for microscopic examination; a cutting of a solid figure by a plane, or the figure so produced; a vertical plan of a building, etc., as it would appear upon an upright plane cutting through it. *v.t.* To divide or arrange in sections; to represent in sections. **section-mark,** *n.* The sign §. **sectional,** *a.* **sectionalism,** *n.* **sectionalize,** *v.t.* **sectionally,** *adv.*

sector (sek′ tŏr) [L., orig. cutter, as prec. (late L., sector)], *n.* (*Geom.*) A portion of a circle or other curved figure included between two radii and an arc; a mathematical rule consisting of two hinged arms marked with sines, tangents, etc.; (*Mil.*) a section of a battle front. **sector of a sphere:** A solid figure generated by the revolution of a plane sector round one of the radii. **sectoral,** *a.* **sectorial** (-tôr′ i ăl), *a.* (*Zool.*) Denoting a tooth on each side of either jaw, adapted for cutting like scissors with the corresponding one, as in many carnivora; sectoral. *n.* A sectorial tooth.

secular (sek′ ū lăr) [O.F. *seculier*, L. *sæculāris*, from *sæculum*, generation, age, perh. cogn. with *serere*, to sow], *a.* Pertaining to the present world, or to things not spiritual or sacred, not ecclesiastical or monastic; worldly, temporal, profane; lasting, extending over, occurring in, or accomplished during a century, an age, or a very long period of time; pertaining to secularism. *n.* A layman; a Roman Catholic priest bound only by the vow of chastity and belonging to no regular order; a church official who is not ordained. **secularism,** *n.* The state of being secular; applied by George Jacob Holyoake to an ethical system founded on natural morality and opposed to religious education or ecclesiasticism. **secularist,** *a.* and *n.* **secularity** (-lăr′ i ti), ***secularness,** *n.* **secularize** (sek′ ū lă rīz), *v.t.* **secularization** (-zā′ shŭn), *n.* **secularly,** *adv.*

secund (sek′ ŭnd, sē′ kŭnd) [L., SECOND], *a.* (*Bot., etc.*) Arranged all on one side of the rachis (of flowers, etc.). **secundly,** *adv.*

secundine (sek′ ŭn din, -dīn) [late L. *secundīnæ*, pl., as prec.] *n.* (*Obstetrics*) The placenta and other parts connected with the fœtus, ejected after parturition, the after-birth (*often in pl.*); (*Bot.*) the membrane immediately surrounding the nucleus.

secundogeniture (sė kŭn dō jen′ i tūr) [L. *secundō*, abl. of *secundus*, SECOND, GENITURE], *n.* The right of inheritance belonging to a second son.

secure (sė kūr′) [L. *sēcūrus* (SE-, *cūra*, care)], *a.* Free from danger, risk, or apprehension; safe from attack, impregnable; reliable, confident, certain, sure (of); in safe keeping, safe not to escape; *overconfident, unsuspecting. *v.t.* To make safe or secure; to put into a state of safety from danger; to fasten, to close securely, to enclose or confine securely; to make safe against loss, to guarantee payment of; to get, to obtain, to gain possession of; (*Surg.*) to compress (a vein, etc.) to prevent bleeding. **to secure arms:** To hold rifles muzzle downwards with the lock under the armpit as a protection from rain. **securable,** *a.* **securely,** *adv.* ***secureness,** *n.* Security. ***securer,** *n.*

securi- [L. *secūris*, axe], *comb. form.* **securifer** (sė kū′ ri fėr) [L. *fer*, -FEROUS], *n.* (*Ent.*) One of the *Securifera*, or phyllophagous hymenoptera, a sandfly. **securiferous** (-rif′ ėr ŭs), *a.* **securiform** (sė kū′ ri fôrm), *a* Axe-shaped. **securipalp** (sė kū′ ri pălp) [PALP], *n.* (*Ent.*) A beetle of the division *Securipalpi*.

securite (sek′ ū rīt) [SECURE, -ITE], *n.* A high explosive composed of nitrated hydrocarbons, used chiefly for blasting.

security (sė kū′ ri ti) [F. *sécurité*, L. *sēcūritātem*, nom. -*tas*, from *sēcūrus*, SECURE], *n.* The state of being or feeling secure; freedom from danger or risk, safety; certainty, assurance, over-confidence; that which guards or secures; a pledge, a guarantee; something given or deposited as a pledge for payment of a loan, fulfilment of obligation, etc., to be forfeited in case of non-performance; one who becomes surety for another; a document constituting evidence of debt or of property, a certificate of stock, a bond, etc. **Security Council:** (*Pol.*) A body of the United Nations charged with the maintenance of international security and peace. **security risk:** (*Pol.*) A person whose political views, etc., make him unsafe for employment by the State.

sedan (sė dăn′) [town in France], *n.* A covered chair for one person, carried by two men by means of a pole on each side, also called **sedan-chair**; (*Motor.*) a closed car with a single compartment for driver and passengers, a saloon car.

sedate (sė dāt′) [L. *sēdātus*, p.p. of *sēdāre*, causal of *sedēre*, to sit], *a.* Composed, calm, tranquil, staid, not impulsive. **sedately,** *adv.* **sedateness,** *n.*

sedative (sed′ ȧ tiv), *a.* Allaying nervous irritability, soothing, assuaging pain. *n.* A sedative medicine, influence, etc.

sedentary (sed′ ėn tȧ ri) [F. *sédentaire*, L. *sedentārius*, from *sedēre*, to sit], *a.* Sitting; accustomed or inclined, or obliged by occupation, to sit a great deal; involving or requiring much sitting; caused by sitting much; (*Zool.*) not migratory, attached to one place, not free-moving; belonging to the *Sedentariæ*; *motionless, inactive, tranquil. *n.* A sedentary person; (*Zool.*) one of the *Sedentariæ*, a tribe of spiders which rest motionless till the prey is entangled in the web. ***sedent** (sē′ dėnt), *a.* Sitting, inactive, quiet. **sedentarily,** *adv.* **sedentariness,** *n.*

sederunt (sė dēr′ ŭnt) [L. they sat, as prec.], *v.i.* (*Law*) Were present at the sitting of a court, etc. *n.* A sitting of a court, etc.; (*Sc.*) a long session of conversation. **Act of Sederunt:** (*Sc. Law*) An ordinance regulating procedure in the Court of Session.

sedge (sej) [A.-S. *secg*, cp. L.G. *segge*, rel. to SAW (1), L. *secāre*, to cut], *n.* A coarse grass-like plant of the genus *Carex*, usu. growing in marshes or beside water; any coarse grass growing in such spots; a sedge-fly. **sedge-bird, -warbler, -wren,** *n.* A reed-warbler, *Acrocephalus scirpaceus*, haunting sedgy places. **sedge-fly,** *n.* A caddis or May-fly; an imitation of this, used by anglers. ***sedged, sedgy,** *a.*

sedigitate [SEXDIGITATE].

sedilia (sė dil′ i ȧ) [L., pl. of *sedīle*, cogn. with *sedēre*, to sit], *n.pl.* (*Arch.*) A series of (usu. three) stone seats, usu. canopied and decorated, on the south side of the chancel in churches, for the priest, deacon, and sub-deacon.

sediment (sed′ i mėnt) [O.F. from L. *sedimentum*, as prec.], *n.* The matter which subsides to the bottom of a liquid; lees, dregs, settlings. **sedimentary,** *a.* **sedimentary rocks:** (*Geol.*) Rocks or strata laid down as sediment from water. **sedimentation** (-tā′ shŭn), *n.*

sedition (sė dish′ ŭn) [O.F., from L. *sēditiōnem*, nom. *-tio* (L. *sed-*, SE-, *īre*, to go, supine *-itum*)], *n.* Agitation, disorder, or commotion in a State, not amounting to insurrection; conduct tending to promote treason or rebellion. ***seditionary,** *a.* and *n.* ***seditioner, -ist,** *n.* **seditious** (sė dish′ ŭs), *a.* **seditiously,** *adv.* **seditiousness,** *n.*

seduce (sė dūs′) [L. *sēdūcere* (SE-, *dūcere*, to lead, p.p. *ductus*)], *v.t.* To lead astray, to entice from rectitude or duty, esp. to induce a woman to a surrender of chastity. ***seducement,** *n.* **seducer,** *n.* **seducible,** *a.* **seducing,** *a.* **seducingly,** *adv.*

seduction (sė dŭk′ shŭn), *n.* The act of seducing, esp. of persuading a woman to surrender her chastity; the state of being seduced; that which seduces, an enticement, an attraction, a tempting or attractive quality, a charm. **seductive,** *a.* **seductively,** *adv.* **seductiveness, seductress,** *n.*

sedulous (sed′ ū lŭs) [L. *sēdulus*, from *sēdulō*, honestly, diligently (SE-, *dolō*, abl. of *dolus*, guile)], *a.* Assiduous, constant, steady, and persevering in business or endeavour; industrious, diligent. **sedulity** (-dū′ li ti), **sedulousness,** *n.* **sedulously,** *adv.*

Sedum (sē′ dŭm) [L. houseleek], *n.* (*Bot.*) A genus of fleshy-leaved plants including the stonecrop, orpine, etc.

see (1) (sē) [A.-S. *sēon*, cp. Dut. *zien*, G. *sehen*, Icel. *sjā*, Dan. and Swed. *se*], *v.t.* (*past* **saw,** *p.p.* **seen**) To perceive by the eye; to discern, to descry, to observe, to look at; to perceive mentally, to understand, to apprehend, to have an idea of; to witness, to experience, to go through, to have knowledge of; to imagine, to picture to oneself; to call on, to pay a visit to, to grant an interview to, to receive; to escort, to attend, to conduct (a person home, etc.); (*Poker, etc.*) to accept (a challenge, bet, etc., or person offering this). *v.i.* To have or exercise the power of sight; to discern, to comprehend; to inquire, to make an investigation (into); to reflect, to consider carefully; to ascertain by reading; to take heed; to give attention; to make provision for; to look out; to take care (that); (*imper.*) to refer to. **let me see:** A formula asking for time to consider or reflect. **to be well** (or **ill**) **seen in:** To be versed (or not versed) in. **to see about:** To give attention to; to make preparations, etc.; a polite form of refusal. **to see after:** To take care of. **to see daylight:** (*colloq.*) To begin to comprehend. **to see fit, good:** To think advisable. **to see life:** To gain experience of the world, esp. by dissipation. **to see off:** To escort on departure. **to see over:** To inspect. **to see through:** To penetrate, not to be deceived by; to persist in a task, etc., until it is finished; to help (a person) through a difficulty, danger, etc. **to see the light:** To be born; (*fig.*) to realise the truth. **to see to:** To look after. **to see it that:** To take care that. **see-bright,** *n.* The clary. **seeable,** *a.* **seeing,** *conj.* Inasmuch as, since, considering (that). **seer,** *n.* One who sees; one who foresees, a prophet. **seership,** *n.*

see (2) (sē) [O.F. *se*, *sed*, L. *sēdes*, from *sedēre*, to sit], *n.* The diocese or jurisdiction of a bishop or archbishop. **Holy See:** The Papacy, the papal Court.

seecatch (sē′ kăch) [Alaskan or Aleutian native], *n.* (*pl.* **seecatchie**) An adult male fur-seal.

seecawk (sē′ kawk) [N.Am.Ind.], *n.* The skunk.

seed (sēd) [A.-S. *sæd* (cp. Dut. *zaad*, G. *saat*, Icel. *sæthi*, Dan. *sæd*, Swed. *säd*), cogn. with SOW (1)], *n.* The mature fertilized ovule of a flowering plant, consisting of the embryo germ, or reproductive body and its covering; (*collect.*) seeds, esp. in quantity for sowing; the male fertilizing fluid, semen; the germ from which anything springs, first principle, beginning or source; (*Bibl.*) progeny, offspring, descendants, *birth, descent. *v.t.* To sow or sprinkle with seed; to remove the seeds from (fruit, etc.); (*Tennis*) to arrange the draw in a tournament so that the best players do not meet in the early rounds; to classify a good player in this way. *v.i.* To sow seed; to run to seed. **to run to seed:** (*fig.*) To become shabby; to lose self-respect. **seed-bud,** *n.* (*Bot.*) An ovule. **seed-cake,** *n.* A sweet cake containing aromatic seeds, esp. caraway. **seed-coat,** *n.* (*Bot.*) The integument of a seed. **seed-coral,** *n.* Coral in small seed-like pieces. **seed-corn, -grain,** *n.* Corn set aside for sowing. **seed-eater,** *n.* A granivorous bird. **seed-fish,** *n.* One ready to spawn. **seed-lac,** *n.* Lac dried. **seed-leaf, -lobe,** *n.* A cotyledon or primary leaf. **seed-leap, -lop,** *n.* The vessel in which a sower carries seed. **seed-oyster,** *n.* Oyster-spat. **seed-pearl,** *n.* A small seed-like pearl. **seed-plot,** *n.* A piece of ground on which seeds are sown; (*fig.*) a nursery or hotbed (of seditions, etc.). **seedsman,** *n.* One who deals in seeds. **seed-time,** *n.* The season for sowing. **seed-vessel,** *n.* The pericarp.

seed-wool, *n.* Raw cotton from which the seeds have not yet been removed. **seeded,** *a.* **seeder,** *n.* A seed-drill or other device for planting seeds; a device for removing the seeds from raisins, etc.; a seed-fish. ***seedful, seedless,** *a.* **seedling,** *a.* Raised from seed. *n.* A plant reared from seed. ***seedness,** *n.* Seed-time. **seedy,** *a.* Abounding in seeds; run to seed; having a peculiar flavour, derived from weeds among the vines (of some French brandies); (*colloq.*) shabby, down-at-heel; off colour, as after a debauch; out of sorts. **seedily,** *adv.* **seediness,** *n.* Shabbiness, near poverty; a state of poor health.

seek (sēk) [A.-S. *sēcan* (cp. Dut. *zoekan,* G. *suchen,* Icel. *sækja,* also L. *sāgīre,* to perceive, Gr. *hēgeisthai,* to lead)], *v.t.* (*past & p.p.* **sought,** sawt) To go in search of; to try to find, to look for; to ask, to solicit (a thing of a person); to aim at, to try to gain, to pursue as an object; to search (a place, etc., through), to resort to. *v.i.* To make search or inquiry (after or for); to endeavour, to try (to do). **to seek:** Wanting, deficient; not found yet. **sought-after,** *a.* In demand, much desired or courted. **seeker,** *n.* One who seeks, an inquirer; (*Hist.*) a member of an English sect of the time of Cromwell, somewhat akin to the Quakers. **Seekerism,** *n.*

***seel** (sēl) [O.F. *siller, ciller,* from *cil,* eyelid, L. CILIA], *v.t.* To close the eyes of (a hawk), or close (its eyes) by threads drawn through the lids; (*fig.*) to hoodwink.

***seely** (sē′ li) [A.-S. *sǣlig* in *gesǣlig,* from *sǣl,* SELE, cp. SILLY], *a.* Lucky, fortunate; blessed, pious; innocent; poor, miserable, defenceless; mean, trifling; foolish. ***seeliness,** *n.*

seem (sēm) [A.-S. *sēman,* to conciliate, cogn. with SAME], *v.i.* To give the impression of being, to be apparently though not in reality; to appear (to do, to have done, to be true or the fact that); to be evident or apparent (impers.). ***v.t.** To befit. **it seems:** It appears, it is reported (that).

seeming (sē′ ming), *a.* Appearing, apparent, but not real; apparent and perhaps real; *becoming, seemly. *n.* Appearance, semblance, esp. when false; *fair appearance; *estimation, opinion. ***seeming-virtuous,** *a.* **seemingly,** *adv.* **seemingness,** *n.* ***seemless,** *a.* Unseemly.

seemly (sēm′ li) [M.E. *semlish,* Icel. *sæmiligr* (*sæmr,* becoming, from *samr,* SAME, -LY)], *a.* Becoming, decent; suited to the occasion, purpose, etc. ***adv.** In a seemly manner. **seemliness,** *n.*

seen, *p.p.* [SEE (1)].

seep (sēp) [A.-S. *sipian,* rel. to SIP], *v.i.* To soak, to percolate, to ooze.

seer-fish (sēr′ fish) [*seer,* corr. of Port. *serra,* saw, FISH], *n.* An E. Indian scombroid fish.

seersucker (sēr′ sŭk ėr) [corr. of Pers. *shīr o shakkar,* milk and sugar], *n.* A thin blue-and-white striped fabric of linen or linen and silk.

see-saw (sē′ saw) [redupl. of SAW (1)], *n.* A game in which two persons sit one on each end of a board balanced on a support in the middle and move alternately up and down (*Am.* teeter); the board so used (*Am.* teeter-board); alternate or reciprocating motion. *a.* Moving up and down or to and fro. *v.t.* To cause to move in a see-saw fashion. *v.i.* To play at see-saw; to move up and down or backwards and forwards; to act in a vacillating manner.

seethe (sēth) [A.-S. *sēothan,* cp. Dut. *zieden,* G. *sieden,* Icel. *sjotha*], *v.t.* (*past* **seethed,** ***sod,** *p.p.* **seethed,** ***sod, sodden**) To boil; to prepare by boiling or steeping in hot liquid. *v.i.* To be in a state of ebullition; (*fig.*) to be agitated, to bubble over. **seether,** *n.*

seg (1) (seg) [etym. unknown], *n.* (*prov.*) A bull castrated when full grown.

seg (2) (*prov.*) [SEDGE]. **segar** [CIGAR].

seggar [SAGGAR].

segment (seg′ mėnt) [L. *segmentum,* from *secāre,* to cut], *n.* A portion cut or marked off as separable, a section, a division, esp. one of a natural series (as of a limb between the joints, the body of an articulate animal, a fruit or plant organ divided by clefts, etc.); (*Geom.*) a part cut off from any figure by a line or plane. *v.i.* To divide or be divided into segments; to undergo cleavage. *v.t.* To divide into segments; (*in p.p.*) to compose of segments. **segmental, -ary, -ate** (-men′ tȧl, -tar i, -tȧt), *a.* **segmentally,** *adv.* **segmentation** (-tā′ shŭn), *n.*

segolate, segholate (seg′ ŏ lāt) [Heb. *segōl,* name of vowel-point ∵, -ATE], *a.* (*Heb. Gram.*) Disyllabic with a short unaccented vowel in the last syllable. *n.* A segolate noun.

***segreant** (seg′ rė ȧnt) [etym. doubtful], *a.* (*Her.*) Erect, rampant, or salient (of a griffin).

segregate (seg′ rė gāt) [L. *sēgregātus,* p.p. of *sēgregāre* (SE-, *grex gregis,* flock)], *v.t.* To separate from others, to set apart, to isolate; (*Sci.*) to place in a separate class. *v.i.* (*Mendelism*) To become separated into dominants, hybrids, etc.; (*Cryst.*) to separate from a mass and collect about nuclei and lines of fracture. *a.* (-gȧt) *Separate, set apart, select; (*Zool.*) simple, solitary, not compound. **segregable,** *a.* **segregation** (-gā′ shŭn), *n.* The act of segregating; separation of a community on racial grounds. **segregationist,** *n.* A believer in racial segregation. **segregative** (seg′ rė gā tiv), *a.*

seguidilla (seg i dil′ yȧ) [Sp., dim of *seguida,* a continuation, from *seguir,* L. *sequī,* to follow], *n.* A lively Spanish dance in triple time; the music for this.

seiche (sāsh) [Swiss F., prob. G. *seiche,* sinking], *n.* An undulation, somewhat resembling a tidal wave, in the water of the Lake of Geneva and other Swiss lakes, perhaps due to disturbance of atmospheric pressure or to subterranean movements. **seichometer** (sā shom′ ė tėr), *n.* An instrument for measuring seiches.

Seid (sād, sēd) [Arab. *seyid,* prince], *n.* A descendant of Mohammed through his daughter Fatima and his nephew Ali.

Seidlitz powder (sed′ lits) [village in Bohemia with mineral spring], *n.* A mild aperient, composed of a mixture of Rochelle salt and bicarbonate of soda and finely-powdered tartaric acid, mixed separately in water to form an effervescing drink. **Seidlitz water:** A sparkling mineral water of the same composition as that of the Seidlitz spring.

seigneur (sān yėr), ***seignior*** (sē′ nyôr) [F., as SENIOR], *n.* (*F. Hist.*) A feudal lord; (*Canada*) the holder of a seigneury. ***droit de seigneur:*** A feudal manorial right to the first night with a tenant's bride. ***grand seigneur:*** A great nobleman; a person of high rank. **the grand seignior** [GRAND SIGNIOR, see GRAND]. **seigneurial** (-nūr′ i ȧl), *a.* **seigneury** (sē′ nyėr i), *n.* (*F. Hist.*) The territory or lordship of a *seigneur*; (*Canada*) an estate formerly held on a feudal tenure; the mansion of a *seigneur*. **seigniorage** (sē′ nyŏ rȧj), *n.* Something claimed by the sovereign or by a feudal superior as a prerogative, esp. an ancient right of the Crown to a percentage on bullion brought to the mint to be coined; the profit derived from issuing coins at a rate above their intrinsic value; a royalty. **seigniorial** [SEIGNEURIAL]. ***seigniorize,** *v.t.* and *i.* **seigniorship, *seigniority** (-or′ i ti), *n.* **seigniory** (sē′ nyŭr i), *n.* Feudal lordship; power as sovereign lord; the territory or domain of a feudal lord; (*It. Hist.*) the municipal council of an Italian republic.

seil [SILE].

seine (sān, sēn) [F., from L. *sagēna,* Gr. *sagēnē*], *n.* A large fishing-net with floats at the top and weights at the bottom for encircling. *v.t.* To catch with this. *v.i.* To fish with it. **seine-gang,** *n.* A body of men working a seine. **seine-roller,** *n.* A roller over which it is hauled. **seiner,** *n.*

seise (sēz) [SEIZE], *v.t.* (*Law*) To put in possession of (*usu. in p.p.*). **to be** or **stand seised of:** To have in legal possession. **seisable,** *a.* **seisin,** *n.* Possession of land under a freehold; the act of taking possession; the thing possessed. **seisor,** *n.*

seismic, seismal (sīz′ mik, -mȧl) [Gr. *seism-as*, earthquake, from *seiein*, to shake, -IC, -AL], *a.* Of, pertaining to, or produced by an earthquake. **seismo-,** *comb. form.* **seismogram,** *n.* A record given by a seismograph. **seismograph** [-GRAPH], *n.* An instrument for recording the period, extent, and direction of the vibrations of an earthquake. **seismographer** (-mog′ rȧ fėr), *n.* **seismographic, -al** (-grăf′ ik, -ȧl), *a.* **seismography** (-mog′ rȧ fi), *n.* **seismology** (-mol′ ȯ ji) [-LOGY], *n.* The study or science of earthquakes. **seismological** (-loj′ i kȧl) *a.* **seismologically,** *adv.* **seismologist** (-mol′ ȯ jist), *n.* **seismometer** (-mom′ ė tėr) [-METER], *n.* A seismograph; a seismoscope. **seismometry,** *n.* **seismometric, -al** (-met′ rik, -ȧl), *a.* **seismoscope** (sīz′ mȯ skōp) [-SCOPE], *n.* A simple form of seismograph. **seismoscopic** (-skop′ ik), *a.* **seismotic** (-mot′ ik), *a.* Seismic.

seity (sē′ i ti) [med. L. *sēitas*, from L. *sē*, oneself], *n.* Selfhood.

seize (sēz) [O.F. *seisir*, *saisir*, to put in possession of, late L. *sacīre*, to take possession of, perh. from Teut. and cogn. with SET (1)], *v.t.* To grasp or lay hold of suddenly, to snatch, to take possession of by force; to grasp mentally, to comprehend; (*fig.*) to come upon, to affect suddenly and forcibly; (*Naut.*) to fasten, to lash with cord, etc.; (*Law*) to seise; to take possession of; to impound, to confiscate. *v.i.* To lay hold (upon); (*Mech.*) to jam, to become stuck. **seizer,** *n.* **seizin,** etc. [SEISIN, see SEISE]. **seizing-up:** (*Mach.*) The locking or partial welding together of sliding surfaces from lack of lubrication. **seizure,** *n.* The act of seizing; a sudden attack, as of a disease.

sejant (sē′ jȧnt) [A.-F. *seiant*, pres.p. of *seier*, O.F. *seoir*, L. *sedēre*, to sit], *a.* (*Her.*) Sitting with the forelegs erect.

sejugous (sē′ ju gůs) [L. *sējugis* (*sē-*, SEX-, *jugum*, yoke)], *a.* (*Bot.*) Having six pairs of leaflets.

***sejunction** (sė jŭngk′ shůn) [L. *sējunctio* (SE-, JUNCTION], *n.* The act of disjoining; separation.

sekos (sē′ kos) [Gr.], *n.* (*Gr. Ant.*) A sacred enclosure, as the shrine or adytum of a temple.

sel (*Sc.*) [SELF].

selachian (sė lā′ ki ȧn) [Gr. *selachos*], *n.* A fish of the group *Selachii* comprising the sharks, dog-fishes, etc. *a.* Pertaining to this group. **selachoid** (sel′ ȧ koid), *a.* and *n.*

Selaginella (sel ȧ ji nel′ ȧ) [L. dim. of *selāgo -ginis*, club-moss], *n.* (*Bot.*) A genus of evergreen moss-like cryptogamic plants many of which are cultivated for ornamental purposes.

selah (sē′ lȧ) [Heb.], *n.* (*Bibl.*) A word occurring in the Psalms and in Habakkuk, always at the end of a verse, variously interpreted as indicating a pause, a repetition, the end of a strophe, etc.

selamlik (sė lam′ lik) [Turk.], *n.* The part of a Mohammedan house assigned to the men.

***selcouth** (sel′ kooth) [A.-S. *selcouth* (as foll., COUTH)], *a.* Rare, strange, marvellous.

seldom (sel′ dȯm) [A.-S. *seldan*, *-don*, *-dom* (*seld*, *-om*, dat. pl.), cp. Dut. *zelden*, G. *selten*, Icel. *sjaldān*], *adv.* Rarely, not often. **a.* Rare. ***seld,** *a.* and *n.* ***seld-shown,** *a.* ***seldomness,** *n.*

***sele** (sēl) [A.-S. *sæl*, cp. Icel. *sæll*, happy, also SILLY], *n.* Happiness, good fortune; occasion, opportunity.

select (sė lekt′) [L. *sēlectus*, p.p. of *sēligere* (SE-, *legere*, to choose)], *a.* Chosen, picked out, choice; taken as superior to or more suitable than the rest; strict in selecting new members, etc., exclusive, more valuable. *v.t.* To choose, to pick out (the best, etc.). **select committee,** *n.* (*Polit.*) Members of parliament specially chosen to examine a particular question and to report on it. ***selectedly,** *adv.* **selection,** *n.* The act of selecting; the right or opportunity of selecting, choice; that which is selected; (*Biol.*) a natural or artificial process of sorting out organisms suitable for survival; (*Austral.*) [FREE SELECTION]. **selective,** *a.* **selectively,** *adv.* **selectivity,** *n.* (*Radio.*) The efficiency of a wireless receiver in separating the different broadcasting stations. **selectman,** *n.* One of a board of officers chosen annually by the freemen of towns in New England to manage local affairs. **selectness,** *n.* **selector,** *n.* One who selects; (*Austral.*) a settler who takes up a piece of select land.

selen-, selenio, seleno- [G. *selen* or SELENIUM, or Gr. *Selēnē*, the moon], *comb. form.* Pertaining to or containing selenium; pertaining to the moon.

selenate (sel′ e nȧt), *n.* (*Chem.*) A salt of selenic acid.

selenic (se len′ ik), *a.* Contained in or derived from selenium; of or derived from the moon.

selenide (se′ le nīd), *n.* (*Chem.*) A compound of selenium with an element or radical.

selenite (se′ le nīt), *n.* (*Min.*) A transparent variety of gypsum or sulphate of lime; (*Chem.*) a salt of selenious acid; an inhabitant of the moon. **selenitic,** *a.* **selenitiferous,** *a.*

selenium (sė lē′ ni ŭm) [Gr. *Selēnē*, the moon, -IUM], *n.* (*Chem.*) A non-metallic element obtained as a by-product in the manufacture of sulphuric acid, similar in chemical properties to sulphur and tellurium, utilized for its varying electrical resistance in light and darkness. ***seleniuret** [SELENIDE].

selenocentric (sė lē nȯ sen′ trik) [SELENO-, CENTRIC], *a.* Referred to, seen from, or measured from the moon as centre. **selenodont** [Gr. *odous odontos*, tooth], *a.* (*Zool.*) Having crescent-shaped ridges (of molar teeth); pertaining to the *Selenodonta*. *n.* A selenodont mammal. **selenography** (sel ė nog′ rȧ fi), *n.* A description of the moon and its phenomena; the art of delineating the face of the moon. **selenograph** (sė lē′ nȯ grăf), *n.* **selenographer** (-nog′ rȧ fėr), *n.* **selenographic, -al** (-grăf′ ik, -ȧl), *a.* **selenology** (-nol′ ȯ ji), *n.* The branch of astronomical science treating of the moon. **selenological** (-loj′ i kȧl), *a.* **selenologically,** *adv.* **selenologist** (-nol′ ȯ jist), *n.* **selenotropic** (-trop′ ik) [F. *sélénotropique* (Gr. *tropos*, from *trepein*, to turn, -IC)], *a.* (*Bot.*) Curving towards the moon (of plant organs). **selenotropism, -tropy** (-not′ rȯ pizm, -rȯ pi), *n.*

Seleucid (sė lū′ sid) [L. *Seleucidēs*, Gr. *Seleukidēs* (*Seleukos*, -ID)], *n.* (*pl.* **-cids, -cidæ**) A member of the dynasty ruling Syria c. 312–64 B.C., founded by Seleucus. *a.* Pertaining to the Seleucidæ. **Seleucidan,** *a.*

self (self) [A.-S., cp. Dut. *zelf*, G. *selbe*, Icel. *sjālfr*, Dan. *selv*, Swed. *sjelf*], *n.* (*pl.* **selves**) The individuality of a person or thing, as the object of reflexive consciousness or action; one's individual person; one's private interests, etc.; furtherance of these; a flower of a uniform or of the original wild colour. *a.* *Same; uniform, pure, unmixed (of colour); self-coloured; of one piece or the same material throughout. **selfdom, selfhood, selfness,** *n.* **selfish,** *a.* Attentive only to one's own interests; not regarding the interests or feelings of others; actuated by or proceeding from self-interest. **selfishly,** *adv.* **selfishness,** *n.* **selfless,** *a.* Having no regard for self, unselfish. **selflessness,** *n.*

self- [prec.], *comb. form.* Expressing (1) direct or indirect reflexive action, as in *self-command*; (2) action performed independently, or without external agency, as in *self-acting*, *self-fertilization*; (3) action or relation to the self, as in *self-conscious*, *self-suspicious*; (4) uniformity, naturalness, etc., as in *self-coloured*, *self-glazed*. **self-abandonment,** [SELF (1)], *n.* **self-abasement,** *n.* **self-abhorrence,** *n.* **self-abnegation,** *n.* **self-absorbed** [SELF- (3)], *a.* **self-absorption,** *n.* **self-abuse** [SELF- (1)], *n.* Masturbation. **self-accusation,** *n.* **-accusatory,** *a.* **-accused,** *n.* and *a.* **-accuser,** *n.*

-accusing, *a.* **self-acting,** *a.* **-action,** *n.* **self-activity** [SELF- (2)], *n.* **self-adjusting** [SELF (1)], *a.* **self-adjustment,** *n.* **self-admiration,** *n.* **self-advancement,** *n.* ***self-affairs** [SELF- (2)], *n.pl.* One's own business. ***self-affected,** *a.* In love with oneself. ***self-affrighted,** *a.* Frightened at oneself. **self-aggrandizement** [SELF- (1)], *n.* **self-amendment,** *n.* **self-appointed,** *a.* **self-appointment,** *n.* **self-appreciation,** *n.* **self-approval,** *n.* **self-approbation,** *n.* **self-asserting, -assertive,** *a.* **-assertion,** *n.* **self-assumed** [SELF- (2)], *a.* ***self-assumption** [SELF- (3)], *n.* Self-conceit. **self-begot, -begotten, -born** [SELF- (1)], *a.* Begotten by or born of oneself or one's own powers. **self-betrayal** [SELF- (1)], *n.* **self-binder** [SELF- (2)], *n.* A reaping-machine with an automatic binding device; this device. **self-blinded** [SELF- (1)], *a.* ***self-bounty** [SELF- (2)], *n.* Inherent kindness and benevolence. **self-centred** [SELF- (3)], *a.* Interested solely in oneself and one's own affairs, egotistic. ***self-charity** [SELF- (3)], *n.* Love of oneself. **self-closing** [SELF- (1), CLOSING], *a.* **self-cocking,** *a.* Cocking automatically (of a gun or gun-hammer). **self-collected** [SELF- (3)], *a.* Self-possessed, composed. **self-colour** [SELF- (4)], *n.* A colour uniform throughout; a pure or unmixed colour; a colour not changed by cultivation. **self-coloured,** *a.* **self-command** [SELF- (1)], *n.* Self-control. **self-communion** [SELF- (3)], *n.* Meditation, mental converse with oneself. **self-complacent,** *a.* Pleased with oneself. **self-complacency,** *n.* **self-conceit,** *n.* **self-conceited,** *a.* **self-condemned** [SELF- (1)], *a.* **self-condemnation,** *n.* **self-confident** [SELF- (3)], *a.* **self-confidence,** *n.* **self-confidently,** *adv.* **self-conscious,** *a.* Conscious of one's actions, behaviour, situation, etc., esp. as observed by others; (*Phil.*) conscious of one's own activities, states, etc.; able to reflect on these. **self-consciousness,** *n.* **self-consistent,** *a.* **self-consistency,** *n.* **self-constituted** [SELF- (1)], *a.* **self-consumed, -consuming,** *a.* **self-contained,** *a.* Reserved, not communicative; complete in itself. **self-contempt,** *n.* **self-contemptuous,** *a.* **self-content** [SELF- (3)], *n.* **self-contented,** *a.* **self-contradiction** [SELF- (1)], *n.* **self-contradictory,** *a.* **self-control,** *n.* Power of controlling one's feelings, impulses, etc. **self-convicted,** *a.* **self-created,** *a.* Brought into existence by one's own power or vitality. **self-creation,** *n.* **self-critical,** *a.* **self-criticism,** *n.* **self-culture,** *n.* ***self-danger** [SELF- (3)], *n.* Danger arising from oneself. **self-deceiver** [SELF- (1)], *n.* **self-deceit, -deception,** *n.* **self-defence,** *n.* The act of defending one's own person, property, or reputation. **the art of self-defence:** Boxing. **self-delusion,** *n.* **self-denial,** *n.* Refusal to gratify one's own appetites or desires; self-abnegation. **self-denying,** *a.* **self-dependent** [SELF- (3)], *a.* **self-dependence,** *n.* **self-depreciation** [SELF- (1)], *n.* **self-depreciative,** *a.* **self-despair** [SELF- (3)], *n.* **self-destroying** [SELF- (1)], *a.* **self-destruction,** *n.* Suicide. **self-determination,** *n.* Determination of one's own will, as opp. to fatalism; (*Pol.*) the right of a group (local or racial) to decide to what state it will adhere; the liberty of a state to determine its own form of government. **self-determined, -determining,** *a.* **self-development,** *n.* **self-devotion,** *n.* **self-discipline,** *n.* **self-disparagement,** *n.* **self-display,** *n.* **self-distrust,** *n.*

selfdom [SELF].

self-educated [SELF- (1)], *a.* **self-education,** *n.* **self-effacement,** *n.* **self-elect, self-elected,** *n.* Elected by oneself or (as a committee) by its own members, co-opted. **self-election,** *n.* **self-elective,** *a.* **self-esteem,** *n.* **self-estimation,** *n.* **self-evident** [SELF- (3)], *a.* Obvious of itself, not requiring proof or demonstration. **self-evidently,** *adv.* **self-examination** [SELF- (1)], *n.* **self-executing,** *a.* Providing for its own enforcement independently of other legislation (of a law). **self-existent** [SELF- (3)], *a.* Existing independently, underived, unconditioned. **self-existence,** *n.* **self-faced** [SELF- (4)], *a.* Having its natural face, unhewn (of stone). **self-feeder** [SELF- (1)], *n.* A machine, furnace, etc., that feeds itself. **self-feeding,** *a.* **self-fertile** [SELF- (3)], *a.* Fertilized by their own pollen (of plants). **self-fertility,** *n.* **self-fertilized, -fertilizing,** *a.* **self-flattery** [SELF- (1)], *n.* **self-forgetful,** *a.* Oblivious of self, unselfish. **self-forgetfulness,** *n.* **self-generating,** *a.* **self-glazed** [SELF (4)], *a.* Covered with glaze of uniform colour. **self-glorification** [SELF (1)], *n.* **self-governing,** *a.* Controlling oneself; autonomous. **self-government,** *n.* **self-gratulation,** *n.* **self-heal,** *n.* A plant having healing virtues, esp. *Prunella vulgaris.* **self-help,** *n.* The act or practice of attaining one's ends without help from others. **self-helpful,** *a.*

selfhood [SELF].

self-humiliation [SELF- (1)], *n.* **self-immolation,** *n.* Sacrifice of self. **self-important** [SELF- (3)], *a.* Important in one's own conceit, pompous. **self-importance,** *n.* **self-imposed** [SELF- (2)], *a.* **self-impotent,** *a.* (*Bot.*) Unable to fertilize itself. **self-induction** [SELF- (3)], *n.* (*Elec.*) Production of an induced current in a circuit by the variation of the current in that circuit. **self-inductive,** *a.* **self-indulgent** [SELF- (1)], *a.* Gratifying one's inclinations, etc. **self-indulgence,** *n.* **self-inflicted** [SELF- (3)], *a.* **self-interest,** *n.* One's personal advantage; absorption in selfish aims. **self-interested,** *a.* **self-invited** [SELF- (1)], *a.* **self-involved** [SELF- (3)], *a.* Wrapped up in oneself.

selfish, etc. [SELF].

self-justification [SELF- (1)], *n.* **self-knowing,** *a.* **self-knowledge,** *n.* **self-laudation,** *n.*

selfless, etc. [SELF].

self-love [SELF- (1)], *n.* Undue regard for oneself or one's own interests; selfishness; conceit. **self-luminous** [SELF- (2)], *a.* Shining by its own light. **self-made** [SELF- (1)], *a.* Successful, wealthy, etc., through one's own exertions. **self-mastery,** *n.* **self-mortification,** *n.* **self-moved, -moving,** *a.* **self-motion,** *n.* **self-murder,** *n.* **self-murderer,** *n.*

self-opinion [SELF- (3)], *n.* **self-opinioned, -opinionated,** *a.* Conceitedly or obstinately adhering to one's own views. **self-partial,** *a.* **self-partiality,** *n.* **self-pity** [SELF- (1)], *n.* **self-pleasing,** *a.* **self-poised** [SELF- (2)], *a.* **self-pollution** [SELF- (1)], *n.* Self-abuse. **self-possessed,** *a.* Calm, imperturbable, having presence of mind. **self-possession,** *n.* **self-preservation,** *n.* Preservation of oneself from injury; the instinct impelling one to this. **self-profit** [SELF- (3)], *n.* Self-interest. **self-propagating** [SELF- (1)], *a.* **self-raker** [SELF- (2)], *n.* A reaping-machine automatically gathering corn into sheaves for binding. **self-realization** [SELF- (1)], *n.* Full development of one's faculties. **self-recording** [SELF- (2)], *a.* Self-registering. **self-regard** [SELF- (1)], *n.* Consideration or respect for oneself. **self-regarding,** *a.* **self-registering** [SELF- (2)], *a.* Recording its movements, etc., automatically (of a scientific instrument, etc.). **self-regulating** [SELF- (1)], *a.* **self-reliant** [SELF- (3)], *a.* **self-reliance,** *n.* **self-renunciation** [SELF- (1)], *n.* Self-sacrifice. **self-repression,** *n.* **self-reproach,** *n.* **self-reproachful,** *a.* **self-reproof,** *n.* **self-reproving,** *a.* **self-repugnant** [SELF- (3)], *a.* Self-contradictory, inconsistent. **self-respect** [SELF- (1)], *n.* Due regard for one's character and position; observing a worthy standard of conduct. **self-respectful, -respecting,** *a.* **self-restrained,** *a.* **self-restraint,** *n.* **self-revealing,** *a.* **self-revelation,** *n.* **self-reverence,** *n.* Self-respect, esp. in a spiritual sense. **self-righteous** [SELF- (3)], *a.* Pharisaical. **self-righteousness,** *n.* **self-righting** [SELF- (1)], *a.* Righting itself when capsized. **self-sacrifice,** *n.* Surrender or subordination of one's own interests and desires to those of others. **self-sacrificing,** *a.* **selfsame** [SELF- (4)], *a.* Exactly the same, absolutely identical. **self-satisfaction**

[SELF- (3)], *n.* Conceit. **self-satisfied,** *a.* **self-scorn** [SELF- (1)], *n.* Self-contempt. **self-seeker** [SELF- (3)], *n.* One selfishly pursuing his own interests. **self-seeking,** *a.* and *n.* **self-service:** Of a restaurant, shop, etc., where the customer helps himself and pays a cashier on leaving. **self-sown,** *a.* Growing from seed sown naturally by the parent plant. **self-starter,** *n.* (*Motor.*) An automatic device for starting a motor car. **self-sterile** [SELF- (2)], *a.* Incapable of self-fertilization. **self-sterility,** *n.* **self-styled** [SELF- (1)], *a.* Assuming a name or title oneself without authorization, would be, pretended. **self-substantial** [SELF- (3)], *a.* Consisting of one's own substance. **self-sufficient, -sufficing,** *a.* Capable of fulfilling one's own desires, etc., without aid; conceited, overbearing. **self-sufficiency,** *n.* **self-suggestion,** *n.* Suggestion arising reflexively within the self, esp. in hypnotic states. **self-support** [SELF- (1)], *n.* **self-supporting,** *a.* **self-surrender,** *n.* **self-sustained, -sustaining,** *a.* **self-taught,** *a.* ***self-tempted,** *a.* **self-torment, -torture,** *n.* **self-tormenting,** *a.* **self-tormentor,** *n.* **self-trust,** *n.* Reliance on oneself. **self-violence** [SELF- (3)], *n.* Violence to oneself, esp. suicide. **self-will,** *n.* Obstinacy. **self-willed,** *a.* **self-winding** [SELF- (1)], *a.* Winding itself automatically (of a clock, etc.). **self-worship,** *n.* ***self-wrong** [SELF- (3)], *n.* Wrong done by a person to himself.

Seljuk (sel jook') [Turk. *seljūq*], *n.* One of the Turkish family descended from the chieftain Seljuk, who furnished Mohammedan dynasties in Central and W. Asia during 11th–13th cent. **Seljukian,** *a.* and *n.*

sell (1) (sel) [A.-S. *sellan* (cp. *selja*, O.H.G. *saljan*), cogn. with SALE], *v.t.* (*past & p.p.* **sold**) To transfer or dispose of (property) to another for an equivalent in money; to yield or give up (one's life, etc.) exacting some return; to be a regular dealer in; to surrender, betray, or prostitute for a price, reward, or bribe; (*slang*) to disappoint, to cheat, to play a trick upon; to inspire others with a desire to possess. *v.i.* To be a shopkeeper or dealer; to be purchased, to find purchasers. *n.* (*slang*) A disappointment, a fraud. **to sell off:** To sell the remainder of (goods); to clear out stock, esp. at reduced prices. **to sell one a pup:** (*slang*) To swindle. **to sell out:** To sell off (one's stock, etc.); to dispose of (one's shares in a company, etc.); to betray. **sell-out,** *n.* A betrayal. **to sell up:** To sell the goods of (a debtor) to pay his debt. **to be sold on:** To be enthusiastic about. **seller,** *n.* **seller's market:** One in which demand exceeds supply and sellers make the price. **selling race,** *n.* A horse-race the winner of which is sold by auction.

sell (2) (sel) [M.E. and O.F. *selle*, L. *sella*, cogn. with *sedēre*, to sit], *n.* A seat, a throne; a saddle. **selliform,** *a.* Saddle-shaped.

sellanders [SALLENDERS].

seller [SELL (1)]. **selliform** [SELL (2)].

Sellotape (sel' ō tāp), *n.* Proprietary name of a cellulose adhesive tape for mending, binding, etc.

seltzer (selt' sėr) [corr. of *Selters*, town of Nassau], *n.* An effervescing mineral water, also **seltzer water. seltzogene,** *n.* A gazogene.

selvage [SELVEDGE], *n.* **selvaged,** *a.* **selvagee** (sel vȧ jē'), *n.* (*Mil. and Nav.*) A rope or ring made of spun yarns, etc., laid parallel and secured by lashings.

selvedge (sel' vėj) [M.Dut. *selfegge* (SELF, EDGE)], *n.* The edge of cloth woven so as not to unravel; a narrow strip of different material woven along the edge of cloth, etc., and removed or hidden in seaming; the edge-plate of a lock with an opening for the bolt.

selves, *n.pl.* [SELF].

semantics (se măn' tiks) [Gr. *semantikos*, significant], *n.pl.* Semasiology, the study of the meanings of words as distinct from their derivations.

semaphore (sem' ȧ fôr) [F. *sémaphore* (Gr. *sēma*, sign, *pherein*, to bear)], *n.* An apparatus for signalling by means of oscillating arms or flags or the arrangement of lanterns, etc. **semaphoric, -al,** *a.* **semasphere,** *n.* An electric aerostatic signalling apparatus.

semasiology (se măz i ol' ŏ ji) [Gr. *sēmasia*, signification, as prec.], *n.* The department of philology concerned with meaning. **semasiological** (-loj' i kȧl), *a.* **semasiologically,** *adv.* **semasiologist,** *n.*

semasphere [SEMAPHORE].

sematic (sė măt' ik) [Gr. *sēma -matos*, sign, -IC], *a.* Of the nature of a sign, significant, esp. of markings on animals serving to attract, to warn off enemies, etc. **sematography** (sem ȧ tog' rȧ fi), *n.* The use of signs or symbols instead of letters in writing. **sematology** (sem ȧ tol' ŏ ji), *n.* The science of signs as expressions of thought, etc.; semasiology.

sematrope (sem' ȧ trōp), *n.* A form of heliograph.

***semblable** (sem' blȧ bėl) [O.F., as foll.], *a.* Like, similar, seeming. *n.* (One's) like or fellow. ***semblably,** *adv.*

semblance (sem' blȧns) [O.F., from *sembler*, L. *simulāre*, see SIMULATE], *n.* External appearance, seeming; a mere show; a likeness, an image. ***semblant,** *a.* Like, resembling; apparent. *n.* Resemblance, appearance; demeanour, expression; seeming, outward aspect. ***semblative,** *a.*

semé (sem' ā) [F., p.p. of *semer*, L. *sēmināre*, to sow, from SEMEN], *a.* (*Her.*) Applied to a field, or charge, strewn over with figures, as stars, crosses, etc.

semeiography (sē mī og' rȧ fi) [Gr. *sēmeion*, sign, -GRAPHY], *n.* (*Med.*) The description of the symptoms of disease. **semeiology** (-ol' ŏ ji), *n.* The science of signs; (*Med.*) the branch of pathology dealing with symptoms. **semeiological** (-loj' i kȧl), *a.* **semeiotic, -al** (-ot' ik, -ȧl), *a.* Pertaining to symptoms, symptomatic. **semeiotics,** *n.* Semeiology.

semen (sē' mėn) [L., seed, cogn. with *serere*, to sow], *n.* The fertilizing fluid produced by the generative organs of a male animal.

semester (sė mes' tėr) [F. *semestre*, L. *semestris* (*se-*, *sex*, six, *mensis*, month)], *n.* A college half-year in German, some American, and other Universities.

semi- [L., cp. Gr. *hēmi-*, A.-S. *sam-*, Sansk. *sāmi-*, prob. cogn. with SAME], *pref.* Half; partially, imperfectly. **semi-acid** (sem i ăs' id), *a.* Subacid. **semi-annual,** *a.* Occurring every six months; half-yearly. **semi-annually,** *adv.* **semi-annular,** *a.* Semicircular. **Semi-Arian** (-âr' i ȧn), *n.* One of a branch of Arians who held that the Son was of like substance with the Father, but not consubstantial with him. **Semi-Arianism,** *n.* **semi-attached,** *a.* Partially attached; semi-detached. **semi-barbarous,** *a.* Half-barbarous. **semi-barbarism,** *n.* **semibreve** (sem' i brēv), *n.* (*Mus.*) A note equal to half a breve, a whole note. **semi-bull,** *n.* A bull issued by a Pope between his election and coronation. **semi-centennial,** *a.* Happening, celebrated, etc., at the end of every fifty years. **semi-chorus,** *n.* One sung by only a half or portion of the choir; a chorus to be rendered thus. **semi-choric,** *a.* **semicircle** (sem' i sĕr' kėl), *n.* A half circle. **semicircular,** *a.* **semi-circled,** *a.* **semicolon,** *n.* A mark (;) used in punctuation, now usu. intermediate in value between the period and the comma. **semi-column,** *n.* (*Arch.*) An engaged column of semicircular section. **semi-columnar,** *a.* **semi-conductor,** *n.* A substance whose electrical resistivity lies between those of metals and insulators, and decreases with rise of temperature. **semi-conscious,** *a.* Half-conscious. ***semicope,** *n.* A mediæval clerical vestment; a half cloak. **semi-cylinder,** *n.* Half of a cylinder divided along the plane of its axis. **semi-cylindric, -al,** *a.* **semi-detached,** *a.* Partially detached (chiefly of houses built in pairs). **semidiameter,** *n.* Half a diameter. ***semi-diaphanous,** *a.* Imperfectly transparent. **semi-diurnal,** *a.* Consisting of, pertaining to, or lasting half a day or in half the time between the rising and setting of a heavenly body. **semi-dome,** *n.* A half-dome, usu. a structure like a dome divided vertically. **semi-elliptical,** *a.* Shaped like half an ellipse divided by either axis. **semi-final,** *n.* (*Sport*) The match or round before the final. **semifluid,** *a.* Imperfectly fluid. *n.* A semifluid substance. **semifused,** *a.* In a half-molten condition. **semihiant,** *a.* Half-open (of lips). **semi-hiatus,** *n.* **semi-infidel,** *a.* Half-infidel. **semi-infinite,** *a.* Limited in one direction and extending to infinity in the other. **semiligneous,** *a.* Partly woody, woody below, herbaceous above. **semilunar,** *a.* Resembling or shaped like a half-moon or crescent. *n.* A semilunar bone. ***semilunary, *-nate,** *a.* **semi-menstrual,** *a.* Half-monthly. ***semi-metal,** *n.* An element having metallic properties but non-malleable. **semi-metallic,** *a.* **semi-monthly,** *a.* Occurring twice a month; issued at half-monthly intervals. **semi-mute,** *a.* Without the power of speech or having it poorly developed. *n.* A semi-mute person.

seminal (sem' i nȧl) [O.F., from L. *sēminālis*, from SEMEN], *a.* Of or pertaining to semen or reproduction; germinal propagative. ***seminality** (-năl' i ti), *n.* **seminally,** *adv.*

seminar (sem' i nar) [G., as foll.], *n.* (*Univ.*) A group of students undertaking an advanced course of study or research together, usu. under the guidance of a professor.

seminary (sem' i nȧr i) [L. *sēminārium*, seed-plot, as foll.], *n.* A place of education, a school, academy, or college, esp. a foreign R.-C. school for training priests. **seminarist,** *n.* ***seminarian** (-nâr' i ȧn), *a.* and *n.*

semination (sem i nā' shŭn) [L. *sēminātio*, from *sēmināre*, to sow, from SEMEN], *n.* The natural dispersal of seeds by plants. ***seminate** (sem' i nāt), *v.t.* **seminiferous** (-nĭf' ėr ŭs), *a.* Bearing or producing seed; conveying semen. ***seminific, -al,** *a.* Producing seed or semen.

semiography, -logy, etc. [SEMEIOGRAPHY].

semi-official (sem i ȯ fish' ȧl) [SEMI, OFFICIAL], *a.* Partly or virtually official. **semi-officially,** *adv.* **semi-opal,** *n.* A non-opalescent variety of opal. **semi-opaque,** *a.* Partly opaque. **semi-opacity,** *n.* **semi-osseous,** *a.* Partially ossified. **semi-oval,** *a.* Semi-elliptical. **semi-oviparous,** *a.* Imperfectly viviparous, producing young only partially developed beyond the egg, as the marsupials. **semi-palmate,** *a.* Half-webbed, as the toes of many shore-birds. **semiparabola,** *n.* A curve of such a nature that the powers of its ordinates are to each other as the next lower powers of its abscissæ. **semi-parabolic,** *a.* **semi-ped** (semi' i ped) [L. *sēmipes -pedis* (SEMI-, *pes pedis*, foot)], *n.* (*Pros.*) A half foot. **Semi-Pelagian,** *n.* One of those in the 5th cent. who maintained a doctrine midway between the predestination inculcated by Augustine and the free-will taught by Pelagius. **Semi-Pelagianism,** *n.* **semi-penniform,** *a.* Penniform on one side only. **semi-piscine,** *a.* Partly resembling a fish. **semi-plume,** *n.* A feather with a stiff stem but a downy web. **semi-plumaceous,** *a.* **semi-precious,** *a.* (*Jewel.*) Valuable, but not regarded as a precious stone. **semi-quadrate,** *n.* The aspect of two planets when distant 45° from each other. **semiquaver,** *n.* (*Mus.*) A note of half the duration of a quaver. **semi-rotary,** *a.* Capable of turning half round. **semi-Saxon,** *a.* Intermediate between Anglo-Saxon and English, pertaining to the early period of Middle English, *c.* 1150–1250. *n.* The semi-Saxon language. **semi-sex,** *n.* (*Biol.*) A group in a bisexual species capable of breeding with other groups. **semi-sexual,** *a.* **semi-sextile,** *n.* (*Astron.*) The aspect of two planets when distant from each other 30° or one-twelfth of a circle. **semi-smile,** *n.* A half or forced smile. **semi-solid,** *a.* So viscous as to be almost solid.

semita (sem' i tȧ) [L., path, way], *n.* (*Zool.*) A band of minute tubercles in some sea-urchins.

Semite (sem' īt, sē' mīt) [late L. and Gr. *Sēm*], *n.* A descendant of Shem, or a member of one of the races (including Hebrews, Phœnicians, Aramæans, Assyrians, Arabs, and Abyssinians) reputed to be descended from Shem. *a.* Semitic. **Semitic** (sė mit' ik), *a.* Pertaining to the Semites or their languages. *n.* One of the Semitic group of languages. **Semiticize, Semitize** (sem' i tīz), *v.t.* **Semitization** (-zā' shŭn), *n.* **Semitism** (sem' i-, sē' mī tizm), *n.* **Semitist,** *n.*

semitone (sem' i tōn) [SEMI-, TONE], *n.* (*Mus.*) An interval equal to half a major tone on the scale. **semitonal, semitonic** (-ton' ik), *a.* **semitonically,** *adv.* **semitontine,** *n.* A form of tontine assurance allowing surrender-value before the expiration of the tontine period. **semi-transparent,** *a.* Almost transparent. **semi-transparency,** *n.* **semi-tropical,** *a.* Partly within or bordering on the tropics. **semi-tubular,** *a.* Having the shape of a tube divided lengthwise. **semi-uncial,** *a.* Half-uncial, between uncial and cursive (of letters). **semi-vitreous,** *a.* Partially vitreous. **semi-vitrify,** *v.t.* **semi-vitrification,** *n.* **semi-vocal,** *a.* **semivowel,** *n.* A sound having the character of both vowel and consonant as *w* and *y*; sometimes applied to consonants like *l*, *m*, *r*, and *z*, that are not mute; a character representing such. **semi-weekly,** *a.* Occurring, issued, etc., twice a week.

semmit (sem' it) [Sc., var. of SAMITE], *n.* A vest or undershirt.

semnopithecus (sem nȯ pi thē' kŭs) [Gr. *semnos*, sacred, *pithekos*, ape], *n.* (*Zool.*) A genus of Asiatic monkeys having long limbs and tails; a monkey of this genus. **semnopitherine,** *a.* **semnopithacoid,** *a.* and *n.*

semolina (sem ȯ lē' nȧ), **semola** (sem' ȯ lȧ) [It. *semolino*, dim. of *semola*, bran, L. *simila*, fine wheat-flour], *n.* The hard grains of wheat left after bolting, used for puddings, etc.

sempervirent (sem pėr vī' rėnt) [L. *semper*, always, *virens -ntem*, pres.p. of *virēre*, to be green, from *vis*, pl. *vires*, strength], *a.* Evergreen.

sempervivum (sem pėr vī' vŭm) [L., neut. of *sempervīvus* (as prec., *vīvus*, living)], *n.* (*Bot.*) A genus of fleshy plants of the family *Crassulaceæ* containing the house-leeks.

sempiternal (sem pi tĕr' nȧl) [O.F. *sempiternel*, L. *sempiternus* (*sempi-*, *semper*, always), *-ternus*, cp. *nocturnus*], *a.* Everlasting, eternal, endless. ***sempitern** (sem' pi tėrn), *n.* **sempiternous** (-tĕr' nŭs), *a.* **sempiternally,** *adv.* **sempiternity,** *n.*

semple (*Sc.*) [SIMPLE].

semplice (sem' pli chā) [It.], *adv.* (*Mus.*) Simply, plainly, without embellishment.

sempre (sem' prā) [It., from L. *semper*, always], *adv.* (*Mus.*) In the same manner throughout.

***sempster, sempstress** [SEAM (1)].

semuncia (sė mŭn' shȧ) [L. (SEMI-, UNCIA)], *n.* (*Rom. Ant.*) A coin equal to half an uncia. **semuncial,** *a.*

sen (sen) [Jap.], *n.* A Japanese coin of copper or bronze worth about half a halfpenny.

senarius (sė nâr' i ŭs) [L., as (*sēnī*, six each)], *n.* (*L. Pros.*) A verse of six feet, esp. the iambic trimeter. **senary** (sē' nȧ ri), *a.* Containing six units; by sixes.

senate (sen' ȧt) [O.F., *senat*, L. *senātum*, nom. *-tus*, from *sen-*, base of *senex*, old], *n.* An assembly or council performing legislative or administrative functions; the State council of the ancient Roman republic and empire of ancient Athens, Lacedæmon, etc., of the free cities of the Middle Ages, etc.; the upper legislative house in various bicameral parliaments, as of the U.S.A. and France;

the governing body of the Universities of Cambridge and London; (*fig.*) any venerable deliberative or legislative body. **senate-house,** *n.* A building in which a senate meets. **senator,** *n.* A member of a senate. **senatorial** (-tôr′ i ȧl), *a.* **senatorially,** *adv.* **senatorship,** *n.* ***senatus*** (sė nā′ tŭs), *n.* The ancient Roman senate; the governing body of a University. **Senatus Consultum:** A decree of the Roman Senate; (*F. hist.*) a decree of Napoleon I.

send (send) [A.-S. *sendan*, cp. Dut. *zenden*, G. *senden*, Icel. *sende*], *v.t.* (*past & p.p.* **sent**) To cause or bid to go or pass or to be conveyed or transmitted to some destination; to cause to go (in, up, off, away, etc.); to propel, to hurl, to cast; to cause to come or befall, to grant, to bestow, to inflict; to cause to be, to bring about. *v.i.* To dispatch a messenger; (*Naut.*) to pitch or plunge deeply into the trough of the sea. *n.* (*Naut.*) The impetus or drive of the sea; the act of sending or pitching into the trough of the sea. **to send down:** (*Univ.*) To rusticate. **to send for:** To require the attendance of a person or the bringing of a thing; to summon; to order. **to send forth** or **out:** To put forth; to emit. **sender,** *n.* **send-off,** *n.* A start as on a race; a leave-taking, a friendly demonstration to one departing on a journey.

sendal (sen′ dȧl) [O.F. *sendal*, *cendal*, low L. *cendalum*, Sansk. *sindhu-*, pertaining to the Indus or Scinde], *n.* A light, thin silken fabric used in the Middle Ages for costly attire, banners, etc.

sender, send-off [SEND].

Seneca (sen′ ė kȧ) [name of tribe of N. Am. Indians forming one of the 'Six Nations' or Iroquois confederacy], *a.* Of or pertaining to Seneca Lake, New York. ***Seneca oil:** Crude petroleum, so called because first found near this.

senecan (sen′ ė kȧn) [L. Annæus *Seneca* (*d.* A.D. 65), Roman stoic, dramatist, etc.], *a.* Of, pertaining to, or in the style of Seneca.

Senecio (sė nē′ shi ō) [mod. L., from *senex*, old man], *n.* A genus of composite plants, with about 500 species, containing the groundsel, ragwort, etc. **senecioid,** *a.*

senega, -ka (sen′ ė gȧ, -kȧ) [N.Am.Ind. *Seneca* Indians], *n.* (*Med.*) The dried root of the Seneca snake-root *Polygala senega*, used as an expectorant, etc.

senescent (sė nes′ ėnt) [L. *senescens -ntem*, pres.p. of *senescere*, from *senex*, old], *a.* Growing old. **senescence,** *n.*

seneschal (sen′ ė shȧl) [O.F., from Teut. (cp. Goth. *sins*, cogn. with L. *senex*, old, *skalks*, servant)], *n.* An officer in the houses of princes and high dignitaries in the Middle Ages having the superintendence of feasts and domestic ceremonies, sometimes dispensing justice; a steward or major-domo. **seneschalship,** *n.*

sengreen (sen′ grēn) [A.-S. *sin- grēne* (*sin*, ever, GREEN)], *n.* The house-leek or sempervivum.

senhor (sā nyôr′) [Port.], *n.* (*fem.* **-ra**) The Portuguese title corresponding to the English Mr. or sir.

senile (sē′ nīl, nil) [L. *senīlis*, see foll.], *a.* Pertaining to or proceeding from the infirmities, etc., of old age. **senility** (-nil′ i ti), *n.* Old age; (*Biol.*) condition of exhaustion due to racial old age.

senior (sē′ nyȯr) [L. older, comp. of *senex senis*, old], *a.* Older, elder (appended to names (**sen., sr.**) to denote the elder of two persons with identical names, esp. father and son), older or higher in rank or service. *n.* One older than another; one older or higher in rank, service, etc.; (*Am.*) a student in his third or fourth year; *an aged person. **Senior Service:** The Royal Navy. **senior wrangler, optime:** (*Camb. Univ.*) First in first class of mathematical tripos. **seniority** (-ni or′ i ti), *n.* **seniory,** *n.*

senna (sen′ ȧ) [It. *sena*, Arab. *sanā*], *n.* The dried, purgative leaflets of several species of cassia.

sennachie (sen′ ȧ *chi*) [Gael. *seanachaidh*], *n.* (*Sc. Highlands and Ir.*) One learned in tradition and clan genealogy; a reciter of old romances.

***sennet** (sen′ ėt) [O.F. *segnet*, dim. of *seing*, L. *signum*, SIGN], *n.* (*Elizabethan Theatre*) A trumpet-signal for stage entrances and exits.

***sen-night** (sen′ īt) [contr. of SEVEN-NIGHT], *n.* A week.

sennit (sen′ ėt) [prob. contr. of SEVEN-KNIT], *n.* (*Naut.*) Braided cordage, made from 3–9 strands for gaskets, packing, etc.

senocular (sė nok′ ū lȧr) [L. *sēnī*, six each, OCULAR], *a.* Having six eyes, as some spiders. **senoculate,** *a.*

Senonian (sė nō′ ni ȧn) [F. *sénonian* (L. *Senon-ēs*, a people in central Gaul, -IAN)], *a.* (*Geol.*) A division of the upper Cretaceous in France and Belgium.

señor (sen yôr′) [Sp.] (*fem.*, ***-ora, -orita,*** -yō rē′ tȧ), *n.* The Spanish form of address, equivalent to Mr., Mrs., Miss, sir, madam, etc.

***sens** [SENSE, SINCE].

sensation (sen sā′ shŭn) [med. L. *sensātio*, from late L. *sensātus*, *sensate*, from L. *sensus*, SENSE], *n.* The mental state or affection resulting from the excitation of an organ of sense, the primary element in perception or cognition of an external object; the content of such a mental state or affection, a state of excited feeling or interest, esp. affecting a number of people; the thing or event exciting this. **to create a sensation:** To cause surprise and excitement. ***sensate** (sen′ sȧt), *a.* Perceived by the senses. *v.t.* (-sāt′) To perceive by the senses. **sensational,** *a.* **sensationally,** *adv.* ***sensationary,** *a.* **sensationalism,** *n.* The employment of sensational methods in literary composition, political agitation, etc.; (*Phil.*) the theory that all knowledge is derived from sensation. **sensationalist,** *n.*

sense (sens) [F. *sens*, L. *sensum*, nom. *-sus*, feeling, from *sentīre*, to feel, p.p. *sensus*], *n.* One of the five faculties by which sensation is received through special bodily organs (sight, hearing, touch, taste, smell), also the muscular sense giving a sensation of physical effort; the faculty of sensation, perception, or ability to perceive through the senses, sensitiveness; bodily feeling, sensuousness; intuitive perception, comprehension, appreciation; consciousness, conviction (of); sound judgment, sagacity, common sense, good mental capacity; meaning, signification; general feeling or judgment, consensus of opinion; (*pl.*) normal command or possession of the senses, sanity. *v.t.* To be aware of, to perceive by the senses. **in one's senses:** Sane. **out of one's senses:** Insane. **to make sense:** To be intelligible. **sense-body, -capsule, -cell, -centre, -filament, -hair, -organ,** *n.* A bodily part or organ concerned in the production of sensation. **sense-impression,** *n.* An impression on the mind through the medium of sensation. **sense-perception,** *n.* **senseful,** *a.* Significant. **senseless,** *a.* Incapable of sensation, insensible; contrary to reason, foolish, nonsensical. **senselessly,** *adv.* **senselessness,** *n.*

sensible (sen′ si bėl) [F., from late L. *sensibilis*, as prec.], *a.* Perceptible by the senses; appreciable, acting with or characterized by good sense or judgment, judicious, reasonable; having perception (of); *capable of sensation, easily affected, sensitive (to). *n.* That which is sensible or perceptible. **sensibleness,** *n.* **sensibly,** *adv.* **sensifacient** (-fā′ shi ėnt), **sensific** (-sif′ ik), **sensificatory** (-kā′ tȯr i), **sensigenous** (-sij′ ė nŭs), *a.* Producing sensation. **sensiferous** (-sif′ ėr ŭs), *a.* **sensify** (sen′ si fī), *v.t.* **sensile** (sen′ sil, -sīl), *a.* **sensism, -sist** [SENSATIONALISM, -IST].

sensibility (sen si bil′ i ti), *n.* Capacity to see or feel; susceptibility of impression; acute or delicate susceptibility, over-sensitiveness (often in pl.).

sensitive (sen′ si tiv) [O.F. *sensitif*, *-tive*, med. L. *sensitīvus*, as prec.], *a.* Of or depending on the senses, sensory; readily or acutely affected by external influences; impressible, delicately susceptible, excitable, or responsive; (*Phot.*) susceptible to the action of light. **sensitive plant:** A plant, *Mimosa pudica* or *M. sensitiva*, the leaves of which shrink from the touch. **sensitively,** *adv.* **sensitiveness, sensitivism,** *n.* **sensitivity** (-tiv' i ti), *n.* **sensitize,** *v.t.* (*Phot.*) To render (paper, etc.) sensitive. **sensitization** (-zā' shŭn), *n.* **sensitizer,** *n.* **sensitometer** (-tom' ė tėr), *n.* (*Photo.*) An apparatus for determining the sensitiveness of plates, films, etc.

sensorium (sen sôr' i ŭm) [late L., as prec.], *n.* (*pl. -ria*) The seat or organ of sensation, the brain; the nervous system, comprising the brain, spinal cord, etc.; the grey matter of these. **sensorial,** *a.* **sensory** (sen' sŏr i), *a.* Sensorial. *n.* The sensorium.

sensual (sen' shu ăl, -sū ăl) [late L. *sensuālis*, as prec.], *a.* Pertaining to or affecting the senses, carnal as dist. from spiritual or intellectual; pertaining or devoted to the indulgence of the appetites or passions, esp. those of sex, voluptuous, lewd; (*Phil.*) pertaining or according to sensationalism; *pertaining to sense or sensation, sensory. **sensualism, sensuality** (-ăl' i ti), ***sensualness,** *n.* **sensualist,** *n.* **sensualistic** (-lis' tik), *a.* **sensualize** (sen' shu-, -sū ă līz), *v.t.* **sensualization** (-zā' shŭn), *n.* **sensually,** *adv.*

sensuous (sen' sū ŭs) [L. *sensu-s*], *a.* Pertaining to or derived from the senses; abounding in or suggesting sensible images; readily affected through the senses. **sensuously,** *adv.* **sensuousness,** *n.*

sent, *past & p.p.* [SEND].

sentence (sen' tėns) [O.F., from L. *sententia*, from *sentīre*, to feel], *n.* A series of words, containing a subject, predicate, etc., expressing a complete thought; a penalty or declaration of penalty upon a condemned person; a judicial decision, verdict; *a decision, judgment, or opinion; a pithy saying, a maxim, a proverb. *v.t.* To pronounce judgment on; to condemn to punishment; *to decree.

sententious (sen ten' shŭs), *a.* Abounding in pithy sentences, axioms, or maxims; terse, brief and energetic; pompous in tone. **sententiously, sententiousness,** *n.*

sentient (sen' shi ėnt) [L. *sentiens -ntem*, pres.p. of *sentīre*, to feel], *a.* Having the power of sense-perception; having sense of feeling. *n.* A sentient person or thing. **sentience,** *n.* **sentiently,** *adv.*

sentiment (sen' ti mėnt) [M.E. and O.F. *sentement*, med. L. *sentīmentum*, as prec.], *n.* Mental feeling, esp. one of the higher feelings or the sum of such feelings excited by æsthetic, moral, or spiritual ideas; a thought, view, or mental tendency derived from or characterized by emotion; the verbal expression of this; susceptibility to emotion, sensibility.

sentimental (sen ti men' tăl), *a.* Characterized by sentiment; swayed by emotion; mawkish; displaying unbalanced tenderness. **sentimentalism, sentimentality** (-tăl' i ti), *n.* Unreasonable or uncontrolled emotion; mawkishness. **sentimentalist,** *n.* **sentimentalize,** *v.i.* To affect sentimentality. **sentimentally,** *adv.*

sentinel (sen' ti nėl) [O.F. *sentinelle*, from It. *sentinella* or dim. of *sentine*, dim. of *sente*, L. *sēmita*, path], *n.* One who keeps watch to prevent surprise, esp. a soldier on guard; a sentinel-crab. *v.t.* To watch over, to guard; to set sentinels at or over. **sentinel-crab,** *n.* A crab with long eye-stalks found in the Indian and Pacific Oceans.

sentry (sen' tri) [perh. corr. of prec., or from O.F. *senteret*, from *sentier*, med. L. *sēmītārius*, from *sēmita*, as prec.], *n.* (*Mil.*) A sentinel; the duty of a sentinel. **sentry-box,** *n.* A shelter for a sentry. **sentry-go,** *n.* A sentry's duty of pacing to and fro.

senza (sent' så) [It.], *prep.* Without. ***senza tempo:*** Without strict time.

sepal (sep' ăl) [F. *sépale* (L. *sēpar-*, SEPARATE, assim. to PETAL)], *n.* (*Bot.*) One of the segments, divisions, or leaves of a calyx. **sepaline, sepaloid, sepalous,** *a.* **sepalody,** *n.* Reversion of petals, etc., into sepals by metamorphosis.

separate (sep' ȧ rāt) [L. *sēparātus*, p.p. of *sēparāre* (SE-, *parāre*, to arrange)], *v.t.* To disunite, to set or keep apart; to break up into distinct parts, to disperse; to come or be between, to be the boundary of. *v.i.* To part, to be disconnected, to withdraw (from); to disperse; to agree to live apart (of a married couple). *a.* (-rȧt) Disconnected, considered apart; distinct, individual; *disunited from the body. **separate estate:** The property of a married woman held independently of her husband. **separate maintenance:** An allowance made by a husband to a wife from whom he is separated by consent. **separability** (-bil' i ti), *n.* **separable,** *a.* ***separableness,** *n.* **separably,** *adv.* **separately,** *adv.* **separateness,** *n.* **separation** (-rā' shŭn), *n.* The act of separating or the state of being separated, esp. partial divorce, consisting of cessation of cohabitation between married persons. **separatist** (sep'-), *n.* One who secedes, esp. from a church, sect, or political party. **separatism,** *n.* **separator,** *n.* One who separates; a machine that separates the cream from milk.

separatrix (sep ȧ rā' triks), *n.* A separating mark, as a decimal point, or line marking off corrections in the margin of proof, the line of demarcation between light and shade in a picture, etc.

separatum (sep ȧ rā' tŭm), *n.* A reprint of one of a series of papers, etc.

sephardi (sė fär' di) [mod. Heb.], *n.* (*pl.* **-dim**) A Spanish or Portuguese Jew. **sephardic,** *a.*

sephen (sef' ėn) [Arab. *sapan*, shagreen], *n.* An Arabian sting-ray, the skin of which yields shagreen.

Sephira (sef' i rȧ) [Heb.], *n.* (*pl.* **Sephiroth**) One of the ten intelligences, attributes, or emanations of God, in the Cabbala. **Sephiric, Sephirothic** (-roth' ik), *a.*

sepia (sē' pi ȧ) [L. and Gr.], *n.* A dark brown pigment; this pigment prepared from the black secretion of the cuttle-fish; a cuttle-fish; a genus of cephalopodous molluscs containing this; a water-colour drawing in sepia. ***sepic,** *a.*

***sepiment** [DISSEPIMENT].

sepoy (sē poi) [perh. through Port. *sipae*, from Hind. and Pers. *sipāhī*, from *sipāh*, army], *n.* A native East Indian soldier disciplined in the European manner, esp. one in the former British Indian army.

seps (seps) [L. and Gr. *sēps*, from *sēpein*, to make rotten], *n.* A serpent-lizard, a genus of lizards of the family Scincidæ.

sepsine (sep' sēn), *n.* A poisonous compound found in decomposing yeast and various putrid substances; a ptomaine causing septic poisoning.

sepsis (sep' sis) [Gr. *sēpsis*, as prec.], *n.* (*Path.*) Putrefaction; infection from putrescent matter as in a festering wound, blood-poisoning.

sept (sept) [O.F. *septe*, var. of *secte*, SECT], *n.* A clan, a family.

septa (*pl.*) [SEPTUM].

septæmia [SEPTICÆMIA, see SEPTIC].

septal (sep' tăl), *a.* Of or pertaining to a septum or septa, or to a sept or septs.

septan (sep' tăn) [L. *sept-em*, seven], *a.* Recurring on the seventh day (of fever, ague, etc.). **septangle** [ANGLE (2)], *n.* A heptagon. **septangular** (-tăng' gū lȧr), *a.*

septarium (sep târ' i ŭm), *n.* (*pl.* **-ia**) (*Geol.*) A nodule of limestone, ironstone, etc., with radiating fissures in the middle filled with some extraneous deposit. **septarian,** *a.*

septate (sep' tāt) [late L. *sēptatus*, as prec.], *a.* (*Nat. Hist.*) Provided with or divided by a septum or septa, partitioned. **septation** (-tā' shŭn), *n.*

September (sep tem' bėr) [M.E. and O.F. *Septembre*, L. *September* (*septem*, seven, cp. DECEMBER)], *n.* The ninth month of the year (the seventh after

March, first month of the ancient Roman year). **Septembrist,** *n.* One of the Paris mob that massacred political prisoners in Sept. 1792.

septempartite (sep tėm par′ tīt) [*septem*, as prec., PARTITE], *a.* Divided into seven parts. **septemvir** (sep tem′ vir) [L. (*vir*), man], *n.* (*pl.* **-viri,** -vi rī) One of seven men forming a government, committee, etc. **septemvirate,** *n.*

septenarius (sep tė nâr′ i ŭs) [L., from *septēnī*, seven apiece, from *septem*, seven], *n.* (*pl.* **-rii,** -ri ī) A verse of seven feet, esp. a trochaic trimeter catalectic.

septenary (sep′ tė nȧr i) [as prec.], *a.* Consisting of or relating to seven; by sevens; lasting seven years. *n.* A set of seven years, things, etc. **septenate, -tenous,** *a.* (*Bot.*) Growing in sevens.

septennium (sep ten′ i ŭm) [L. (*septem*, seven, *annus*, year)], *n.* A period of seven years. **septennial,** *a.* **septennially,** *adv.*

***septentrion** (sep ten′ tri ŏn) [L. *septentrio*, pl. *-triōnes* (*septem*, seven, *triōnes*, pl. of *trio*, plough-ox)], *n.* The north; the Great Bear. *a.* Northern. **septentrional,** *a.* ***septentrionally,** *adv.*

septet (sep tet′) [G., from L. *septem*, seven], *n.* A group of seven, esp. singers, voices, instruments, etc.; a musical composition for seven performers.

septfoil (sept′ foil) [L. *sept-em*, seven, FOIL (1)], *n.* A figure of seven equal segments of a circle, used as a symbol of the seven sacraments, etc.; the tormentil *Potentilla tormentilla.*

septic, *-al (sep′ tik, -ȧl) [Gr. *sēptikos*, from *sēptos*, rotten, from *sēpein*, to cause to rot], *a.* (*Path.*) Causing or tending to promote putrefaction, not aseptic. *n.* A septic substance. **septic tank,** *n.* A tank in which sewage is partially purified by the action of bacteria. **septicæmia** (sep ti sē′ mi ȧ) [Gr. *haima*, blood], *n.* A morbid state of the blood caused by the absorption of poisonous or putrid matter. **septicæmic,** *a.* **septically,** *adv.* **septicidal** (sep′ ti sī′ dȧl), *a.* (*Bot.*) Taking place through the partitions (of the dehiscence of a fruit). **septicidally,** *adv.* **septicity** (-tis′ i ti), *n.* **septo-** (1), *comb. form.*

septifarious (sep ti fâr′ i ŭs) [late L. *septifarius* (*septem*, seven, cp. MULTIFARIOUS)], *a.* (*Bot.*) Turned seven different ways.

septiferous [SEPTUM].

septiform (1) (sep′ ti fôrm) [late L. *septiformis* (*septem*, seven, -FORM)], *a.* Sevenfold. (2) [SEPTUM]. **septifragal** (-tif′-) [L. *frag-*, root of *frangere*, to break, cp. FRAGILE], *a.* (*Bot.*) Breaking away from the partitions (of a mode of dehiscence in which the septa break away from the valves). **septilateral** (-lăt′ ėr ȧl), *a.* Seven-sided. **septillion** (-til′ yŭn), *n.* The seventh power of a million. **septillionth,** *a.* and *n.* **septimal** (sep′ ti mȧl), *a.* Of, relating to, or based on the number seven. **septime** (sep′ tim), *n.* The seventh parry in fencing. **septimole** (sep′ ti mōl), *n.* (*Mus.*) A group of seven notes to be played in the time of four or six.

septine [SEPSINE, see SEPSIS].

septinsular (sep tin′ sū lȧr) [L. *septem*, seven, INSULAR], *a.* Consisting of seven islands (applied to the Ionian Islands). **septisyllable** (-sil′ ȧbl), *n.* A word of seven syllables.

septo- (1) [SEPTIC].

septo- (2), *comb. form.* [SEPTUM].

septuagenarian (sep tū ȧ jė nâr′ i ȧn) [L. *septuāgēnārius*, from *septuāgēnī*, seventy each, from *septuāginta*, seventy], *n.* A person of 70 years of age, or between 69 and 80. *a.* Of such an age. **septuagenary** (-jē′ nȧ ri), *a.* Containing or consisting of seventy. **Septuagesima** (-jes′ i mȧ), *n.* The third Sunday before Lent, so called because about seventy days before Easter. ***septuagesimal,** *a.* Consisting of seventy.

Septuagint (sep′ tū ȧ jint) [L. *septuāginta*, seventy], *n.* A Greek version of the Old Testament including the Apocrypha (*c.* 3rd cent. B.C.), so called because, according to tradition, about seventy persons were employed on the translation.

septum (sep′ tŭm) [L., from *sē-*, *sæpīre*, to enclose, from *sēpes*, *sæpes*, hedge], *n.* (*pl.* **-ta**) (*Biol., etc.*) A partition as in a chambered cell, the cell of an ovary, between the nostrils, etc. **septiferous** (-tif′ ėr ŭs), *a.* Bearing septa. **septiform** (2), *a.* Shaped like a septum. **septo-maxillary** (-mak′ si lȧr i, -mȧk sil′ ȧ ri), *a.* (*Zool.*) Connected with a maxillary bone and a nasal septum. *n.* A small bone of this nature in some birds and fishes. **septonasal,** *a.* Forming a nasal septum. *n.* A septonasal bone. **septulum,** *n.* A small septum. **septulate,** *a.*

septuple (sep′ tūpl) [late L. *septuplus*, from *septem*, seven], *a.* Sevenfold. *n.* A set of seven things. *v.t.* and *i.* To multiply by seven. **septuplet,** *n.* A septimole.

sepulchre (sep′ ŭl kėr) [O.F. *sepulcre*, L. *sepulcrum* (*sepelīre*, to bury, p.p. *sepultus*, *-crum*, suf.)], *n.* A tomb, esp. one hewn in the rock or built in a solid and permanent manner; a burial-vault. **v.t.* To place in a sepulchre, to entomb. **sepulchral** (sė pŭl′ krȧl), *a.* Pertaining to burial, the grave, or to monuments raised over the dead; (*fig.*) suggestive of a sepulchre, grave, dismal, funereal. **sepulchrally,** *adv.*

sepulture (sep′ ŭl tyŭr) [O.F., from L. *sepultūra*, as prec.], *n.* Interment, burial; *a burial-place.

***sepurture** (sė pĕr′ tūr) [etym. doubtful], *a.* (*Her.*) Raised about the back and expanded (of wings).

seq. [SEQUENCE].

***sequacious** (sė kwā′ shŭs) [L. *sequax -ācis*, from *sequī*, to follow, -OUS], *a.* Following, inclined to follow; servile, ductile, pliant; logically consistent and coherent. **sequaciously,** *adv.* ***sequaciousness, *sequacity** (-kwăs′ i ti), *n.*

sequel (sē′ kwėl) [O.F. *sequele*, L. SEQUELA], *n.* That which follows; a succeeding part, a continuation (of a story, etc.); the upshot, consequence, or result (of an event, etc.).

sequela (sė kwē′ lȧ) [L., from *sequī*, to follow], *n.* (*pl.* **-læ**) (*Path.*) A morbid condition occurring as the consequence of some disease; an inference, a consequence; *an adherent.

sequence, *-cy (sē′ kwėns, -kwėn si) [O.F., from L. *sequentia*, from *sequens -ntis*, pres.p. of *sequī*, to follow], *n.* Succession, the process of coming after in space, time, etc.; a series of things following one another consecutively or according to a definite principle; (*Cards*) a run of cards; (*Mus.*) a succession of similar harmonious formations or melodic phrases at different pitches; (*Cinema.*) a scene in a film. **sequent,** *a.* **sequentes** (sė kwen′ tēz), **-tia** (-shȧ), *n.pl.* (And) the following (usu. as **seq.** or **seqq.**). **sequential** (sė kwen′ shȧl), *a.* **sequentially,** *adv.* **sequentiality** (-shi ăl′ i ti), *n.*

sequester (sė kwes′ tėr) [O.F. *sequestrer*, late L. *sequestrāre*, to surrender, to commit, from *sequester*, agent, trustee, from *sequī*, to follow], *v.t.* To set apart, to isolate, to seclude (esp. in p.p.); (*Law*) to separate (property, etc.) from the owner temporarily; to take possession of (property in dispute) until some case is decided or claim is paid; to confiscate, to appropriate. *v.i.* (*Law*) To renounce or decline any concern with the estate of a late husband (of a widow). *n.* *The act of sequestering; seclusion, isolation. ***sequestrable,** *a.* **sequestral** [SEQUESTRUM], **sequestrate** (sē′ kwės-, sė kwes′ trāt), *v.t.* (*Law*) To sequester. **sequestration** (-trā′ shŭn), *n.* **sequestrator** (sē′ kwės trā tŏr), *n.*

sequestrum (sė kwes′ trŭm) [med. L., as prec.], *n.* (*pl.* **-ra**) (*Path.*) A piece of dead and separated bone remaining in place. **sequestrotomy** (-trot′ ŏ mi), *n.* (*Surg.*) The removal of this. **sequestral,** *a.*

sequin (sē′ kwin) [F., from It. *zecchino*, from *zecca*, mint, Arab. *sikka*, die], *n.* (*Hist.*) A Venetian gold coin worth from 9s. 2d. to 9s. 6d.; a disk of metal, jet, etc., used as a trimming for dresses, etc.

Sequoia (sė kwoi′ ȧ) [Cherokee], *n*, A Californian genus of gigantic conifers, with two species.

sérac (sė răk') [Swiss F., orig. a cheese in the form of a cube], *n.* One of the large angular or tower-shaped masses into which a glacier breaks up at an ice-fall.

seraglio (sė ra' lyō) [It. *serraglio*, enclosure, from *serrare*, late L. *serare*, to bolt, to shut in, from L. *sera*, bolt, from *serere*, to bind, to join], *n.* A walled palace, esp. the old palace of the Sultan, with its mosques, government offices, etc., at Constantinople; a harem.

serai [CARAVANSERAI].

seralbumen, -min (sēr ăl bū' mėn, -min), *n.* (*Chem.*) A variety of albumen occurring in the serum of the blood.

serang (se răng') [Hind.], *n.* A boatman; leader of a lascar crew.

serape (sā ra' pā) [Mex.-Sp.], *n.* A Mexican blanket or shawl.

seraph (ser' ăf) [orig. *seraphin*, Heb. *serāphīm*, pl., from Arab. *sharaf*, high], *n.* (*pl.* **-aphs, -aphim**) An angel of the highest order. **seraphic, *-al** (sė răf' ik, -al), *a.* **seraphically,** *adv.*

seraphina (ser à fē' nà), **seraphine** (ser' a fēn) [prec., -INE], *n.* A form of harmonium (invented 1833) with reeds, a key-board, etc.

seraskier (ser às kēr') [F. *sérasquieur*, Turk. *ser'asker* (Pers. *ser*, head, Arab. *'asker*, army)], *n.* A Turkish commander, esp. the commander-in-chief or minister of war. ***seraskierate,*** *n.*

Serb, Serbian (sërb, sër' bi ȧn), *a.* Of or pertaining to Serbia, one of the federated republics of Yugoslavia, its people or its language. *n.* A native of Serbia; the Slav language of Serbia.

Serbonian (sėr bō' ni ȧn), *a.* (*Milton*) Applied to the Egyptian lake or bog of Serbonis in the Nile delta, in which whole armies were reported to have been swallowed up; (*fig.*) applied to a difficulty or complication from which there is no escape.

serdab (sër dab') [Pers.], *n.* A secret passage or cell in an ancient Egyptian tomb.

sere (1) (sēr) [O.F. *serre*, grasp, lock, from *serrer*, late L. *serāre*, to lock, see SERAGLIO], *n.* The pawl or catch of a gun- or pistol-lock holding the hammer at half or full cock.

sere (2) [SEAR (1)]. ***serecloth** [CERECLOTH].

serein (sā' răn) [F., as SERENE], *n.* A fine rain or snow falling from a clear sky after sunset, esp. in tropical regions.

serenade (ser e nād') [F. *sérénade*, It. *serenata*, orig. fem. p.p. of *serenare*, to make serene, see foll.], *n.* A song or piece of music played or sung in the open air at night, esp. by a lover beneath his lady's window; a nocturne, a serenata. *v.t.* To sing or play a serenade to or in honour of. *v.i.* To perform a serenade. **serenader,** *n.* **serenata** (-na' tȧ), *n.* A cantata or simple form of symphony, usu. with a pastoral subject, for the open air.

serendipity (se ren dip' i ti) [coined by Horace Walpole, after the fairy tale *The Three Princes of Serendip*], *n.* The happy knack of making unexpected and delightful discoveries by accident.

serene (sė rēn') [L. *serēnus*], *a.* Calm, fair, and clear (of the sky, atmosphere, etc.); placid, tranquil, undisturbed; applied as a title to certain Continental princes. **n.* Clearness, calmness; (*poet.*) a serene expanse of sky, etc. **v.t.* To make clear and calm. **Serene Highness:** Title accorded to certain European princelings. **all serene:** (*slang*) All right. **serenely,** *adv.* Calmly, quietly, deliberately. **serenity** (sė ren' i ti), ***sereneness,** *n.*

serf (sërf) [F., from L. *servus*, slave], *n.* A feudal labourer attached to an estate, a villein; (*fig.*) a slave, a drudge. **serfage, -dom, -hood, -ism,** *n.*

serge (sërj) [F., from L. *sērica*, fem. of *sēricus*, silken, orig. Chinese, from L. and Gr. *Sēres*, the Chinese], *n.* A strong and durable twilled cloth, usu. of worsted.

sergeant, (*Law*) **serjeant** (sar' jėnt) [O.F. *sergant*, *serjant* (F. *sergent*), late L. *servientem*, nom. *-iens*, orig. pres.p. of *servīre*, to SERVE], *n.* (*Mil.*) A non-commissioned officer ranking next above corporal, teaching drill, commanding small detachments, etc.; a police-officer ranking next below an inspector; a serjeant-at-law; *a bailiff, a constable. **colour-sergeant** [COLOUR]. **common serjeant:** A judicial officer of the Corporation of London. **Sergeant-, Serjeant-at-Arms,** *n.* An officer of the Houses of Parliament attending the Lord Chancellor or the Speaker, and carrying out arrests, etc.; an officer with corresponding duties attached to other legislative bodies; one of several Court and City officers with ceremonial duties. **serjeant-at-law,** *n.* Formerly a member of the highest order of barristers, abolished in 1877. **sergeant-fish,** *n.* A fish with lateral stripes resembling a chevron. **sergeant-major,** *n.* The chief sergeant of a regiment, of a squadron of cavalry, or of a battery of artillery. ***sergeantry, *-jeantry, *sergeanty, *-jeanty,** *n.* A form of feudal tenure. **grand sergeantry:** A form of tenure by special honorary service to the king. **petit** or **petty sergeantry:** A tenure by a rent or the rendering of some token, etc. **sergeantship, *sergeancy, serjeancy,** *n.*

sergette (sėr jet') [F.], *n.* A thin serge.

serial (sēr' i ȧl), *a.* Pertaining to, consisting of, or having the nature of a series. *n.* A serial story; a serial publication, a periodical. **seriality** (-ăl' i ti), *n.* **serially,** *adv.* **seriate** (-ȧt), **-ated** (-ā tėd), *a.* Arranged in a series or regular sequence. *v.t.* (-āt) To arrange thus. **seriately,** *adv.* ***seriatim*** (sēr-, ser i ā' tim), *adv.* In regular order; one point, etc., after the other. **seriation** (-ā' shŭn), *n.*

Seric (sēr' ik) [L. *sēricus*], *a.* (*poet.*) Chinese.

sericate (ser' i kȧt), **-cated** (-kā tėd), **sericeous** (sė rish' i ŭs) [late L. *sericeus*, silken, L. *sericum*, silk, as prec.], *a.* (*Nat. Hist.*) Pertaining to or consisting of silk; silky, downy, soft, and lustrous.

sericin (ser' i sin), *n.* (*Chem.*) A gelatinous substance contained in silk.

sericite (ser' i sīt), *n.* (*Min.*) A silky form of muscovite. *a.* Sericitic. **sericitic,** *a.*

sericterium (ser ik tēr' i ŭm), *n.* (*pl.* **sericteria**) (*Ent.*) The silk-spinning gland in silkworms.

sericulture (ser i kŭl' chŭr), *n.* The breeding of silkworms and the production of raw silk. **sericultural,** *a.* **sericulturist,** *n.*

seriema (ser i ē' mȧ) [Tupi-Guarani], *n.* A long-legged Brazilian and Paraguayan bird, the crested screamer.

series (sēr' i ēz, sēr' ēz) [L., from *serere*, to join together, cp. Gr. *eirein*, to bind], *n.* (*pl. unchanged*) A number, set, or continued succession of things similar to each other or each bearing a definite relation to that preceding it; a sequence, a row, a set; (*Bibliog.*) a set of volumes, parts, articles, periodicals, etc., consecutively numbered or dated or issued in the same format under one general title; (*Math.*) a number of terms each successive pair of which are related to each other according to a common law or mode of derivation, a progression; (*Elec.*) the connexion of two or more electric circuits so that the same current traverses all the circuits; (*Geol.*) a group of allied strata forming a subdivision of a system.

serif (ser' if) [etym. doubtful; perh. from Dut. and Flem. *schreef*, a line], *n.* (*Type*) One of the fine cross-lines at the top and bottom of letters.

Seriform (sēr' i fôrm) [L. *sēri-*, see SERIC, -FORM], *a.* Denoting a division of the Ugro-Finnish races comprising the Chinese, etc.

serin (ser' in) [F., etym. doubtful], *n.* A small green finch allied to the canary, *Serinus hortulanus.* **serinette** (ser i net'), *n.* A bird-call or bird organ.

seringa (sė ring' gȧ) [F. and Port., from L. SYRINGA], *n.* A Brazilian rubber-tree of various species.

serious (sēr' i ŭs) [O.F. *serieux*, late L. *sēriōsus*, L. *serius*, etym. doubtful], *a.* Grave, sober, sedate, thoughtful, earnest, not frivolous; of great importance, momentous; in earnest, not ironical or pretended, sincere; sincerely concerned about religious matters, esp. one's own salvation. **serio-**, *comb. form.* **serio-comic, -comical,** *a.* Mingling the serious and the comic; serious in meaning with the appearance of comedy, or comic with a grave appearance. **serioso** (ser i ō' sō), *adv.* (*Mus. direction*) With gravity, solemnly. **seriously,** *adv.* **seriousness,** *n.*

serjeant, etc. [SERGEANT].

***sermocination** (sėr mos i nā' shůn) [L. *sermōcinātio*, from *sermōcinārī*, from *sermo*, SERMON], *n.* (*Rhet.*) A form of prosopopœia in which the speaker holds a dialogue with himself asking and answering questions; *a conversation, discourse.

sermon (sěr' mȯn) [O.F., from L. *sermōnem*, nom. *-mo*, speech, discourse], *n.* A discourse founded on a text of Scripture delivered in church in exposition of doctrine or instruction in religion or morality; a similar discourse delivered elsewhere; a moral reflection; a serious exhortation or reproof. *v.t.* To deliver a sermon to; to lecture. ***sermoner,** *n.* **sermonet** (sěr'mȯ net), **sermonette** (-net'), *n.* **sermonic** (-mon' ik), *a.* **sermonize,** *v.i.* and *t.* **sermonizer,** *n.* **sermonology** (-nol' ȯ ji), *n.*

sero- [SERUM], *comb. form.* **sero-purulent** (sēr ȯ pū' rů lėnt) [PURULENT], *a.* (*Path.*) Composed of serum and pus. **sero-sanguinolent** (-săng gwin' ȯ lėnt) [SANGUINOLENT], *a.* Composed of serum and blood. **serotherapy** [SERUM].

seron (sē' rȯn), **seroon** (sė roon') [Sp. *seron*, from *sera*, basket], *n.* A bale or package (of figs, almonds, etc.) made up in a hide, etc.

serosity [SEROUS].

sérotine (ser' ȯ tīn) [F. *sérotine*, L. *sērōtina*, fem. of *-tus*, from *sērōm* adv., *sērus*, late], *n.* A small reddish bat, *Vesperugo serotinus*, flying in the evening.

serotinous (sė rot' i nus) [from L., as prec.], *a.* (*Bot.*) Appearing late in the season.

serous (sēr' ůs), *a.* Pertaining to or resembling serum; thin, watery; like whey. **serosity** (sė ros' i ti), *n.*

serpent (sěr' pėnt) [F., from L. *serpentem*, nom. *-pens*, orig. pres.p. of *serpere*, to creep, cogn. with Gr. *herpein*, to creep, and Sansk., *sarpa-*, snake], *n.* A reptile with an elongated scaly body and no limbs, a snake; a northern constellation; (*fig.*) a treacherous, insinuating person; an old-fashioned wind-instrument of serpentine form. **Pharaoh's serpent** [PHARAOH]. **sea-serpent** [SEA]. **serpent-charmer,** *n.* One who charms serpents, esp. with music. **serpent-charming,** *n.* **serpent-eater,** *n.* The secretary-bird. **serpent-grass,** *n.* The bistort. **serpent-lizard,** *n.* The seps. **serpent's-tongue,** *n.* The adder's tongue. **serpentaria** (-târ' i ȧ), **serpentary** (sěr' pėn tȧr i), *n.* The Virginian snake-root, *Æristolochia serpentaria*, the root of which is used for medicinal purposes. **serpentiform, serpent-like,** *a.* Serpentine. **serpentine** (-tīn), *a.* Pertaining to, resembling, or having the qualities of a serpent; coiling, winding, twisting, sinuous; subtle, wily, treacherous. *n.* A massive or fibrous rock consisting of hydrated silicate of magnesia richly coloured and variegated and susceptible of a high polish, used for making various ornamental articles. *v.i.* To wind in and out like a serpent; to meander. **serpentine-verse,** *n.* A verse beginning and ending with the same word. **serpentinely,** *adv.* ***serpentry,** *n.*

serpette (sėr pet') [F.], *n.* A hooked pruning-knife.

serpigo (sěr pī' gō) [med. L. *serpīgo -piginis*, from *serpere*, to creep, cp. HERPES], *n.* (*Path.*) A skin-disease, esp. a form of herpes or spreading ring-worm. **serpiginous** (-pij' i nůs), *a.*

serplath (*Sc.*) [SARPLIER].

serpolet (sěr' pȯ lėt) [F. and Prov., dim. of *serpol*, L. *serpullum*, *serpyllum*, Gr. *herpullon*], *n.* Wild thyme. **serpolet oil:** A fragrant oil obtained from *Thymus serpyllum.*

serpula (sěr' pū lȧ) [late L., small serpent], *n.* A brilliantly-coloured marine worm living in a contorted or spiral shell. **serpulan, serpulean** (-pū' lė ȧn), **serpulid** (sěr'-), **serpulidan,** *a.* and *n.* **serpuline,** *a.* and *n.* **serpulite,** *n.* (*Geol.*) A fossil serpula or similar formation. **serpuloid,** *a.*

serra (1) (ser' ȧ) [L., saw], *n.* (*Nat. Hist.*) A saw-like organ, part, or structure; a saw-fish; a Californian sea-fish.

serra (2) (*Port.*) [SIERRA].

serradilla (ser ȧ dil' ȧ) [Port., dim. of *serredo*, SERRATE], *n.* A species of clover grown for fodder.

serrate (ser' āt) [L. *serrātus*, from SERRA (1)], *a.* Notched on the edge, like a saw, serrated. *v.t.* (sė rāt') To cut into notches and teeth, to give a saw-like edge to (*usu. in p.p.*). **serration** (-rā' shůn), **serrature** (ser' ȧ tyůr), *n.*

serrato-, serri-, serro-, *comb. form.* **serricorn,** *a.* (*Ent.*) Having serrated antennæ. *n.* A serricorn beetle. **serriferous** (sė rif' ėr ůs), *a.* **serriform** (ser' i fôrm), *a.* **serriped,** *a.* (*Ent.*) Having serrated feet. **serrirostrate** (-ros trȧt), *a.* (*Ornith.*) Having a serrated bill. **serromotor** (ser ȯ mō' tor), *n.* A reversing-gear, with cogs, etc., used in marine steam-engines. **serrulate, -lated** (ser' ů lāt, -ėd), *a.* Finely serrate; having minute notches. **serrulation** (-lā' shůn), *n.*

serried (ser' ėd) [F. *serré*, p.p. of *serrer*, to close, from late L. *serāre*, see SERAGLIO], *a.* Close-packed, in compact order (esp. of soldiers). **serry,** *v.t.*

serriform, -ped, -rostrate, serromotor, serrulate, etc. [SERRATE].

serry [SERRIED].

Sertularia (sěr tū lâr' i ȧ) [mod. L. from L. *sertula*, dim. of *serta*, garland], *n.* (*pl.* **-iæ**) (*Zool.*) A genus of hydroids with the individual polyps set in a series of cup-like parts.

serum (sēr' ům) [L., whey, cp. Gr. *oros*, Sansk. *saras*, flowing], *n.* (*pl.* **serums, sera**) The thin transparent part that separates from the blood in coagulation, a constituent of milk and other animal fluids, lymph; (*Med.*) animal serum used as an antitoxin, etc. **serum therapy,** *n.* (*Med.*) The treatment or prevention of disease by injecting blood containing the appropriate anti-bodies.

serval (sěr' vȧl) [Native name], *n.* The African tiger-cat, *Felis serval.*

servant (sěr' vȧnt) [O.F., orig. pres.p. of *servir*, to SERVE], *n.* A person employed by another person or body of persons to work under direction for wages, an employee, esp. one living in the house of an employer and receiving board and lodging as part of the wages, a domestic; a devoted follower, one willing to perform the will of another. **civil servant,** *n.* An employee of the State. ***your humble servant:** Now usually only in ironically courteous reference to oneself. **your obedient servant:** A formal, esp. official mode of concluding a letter, followed by the signature. **servant-girl, -maid,** *n.* A female domestic servant. **servants' hall:** The room in a large domestic establishment where servants have their meals, etc., together.

serve (sěrv) [O.F. *servir*, L. *servīre*, from *servus*, slave], *v.t.* To act as servant to, to be in the employment of; to be useful to, to render service to; to be subservient or subsidiary to; to satisfy, to avail, to suffice; to supply, to perform (a purpose, function, etc.); to carry out the duties of, to do the work of (an office, etc.); to behave towards, to treat (well, ill, etc.); to dish (up), to bring to and set on table; to distribute to those at table; to furnish, to supply (a person with); to deliver (a summons, writ, etc.) in the manner prescribed by law; to throw or send (a ball, etc.); (of male animal) to mate with. *v.i.* To be employed, to perform the duties of or to hold an office, etc.; to perform a function, to take the place of, to be used as, to be a satisfactory substitute (for), to suffice, to avail; to be satisfactory, favourable, or suitable; to be in subjection; to deliver the ball in certain games; (*Eccles.*) to attend a celebrant at the altar. *n.* The act of or turn for serving at tennis, etc. **serving-maid,** *n.* A female servant. **serving-man,** *n.* A manservant. **to serve a mare:** To cover her (of a stallion, esp. one hired for the purpose). **to serve a rope:** (*Naut.*) To lash or whip a rope with thin cord to prevent fraying. **to serve a sentence:** To undergo the punishment prescribed. **to serve at table:** To act as waiter. **to serve one's time:** To serve one's sentence; to go through an apprenticeship; to hold an office, etc., for the full period. **to serve out:** To distribute portions of food to those at table; to have one's revenge on. **serves you right:** (*colloq.*) You've got your deserts. **server,** *n.* (*usu. in comb.* as *time-server*).

Servian [SERB].

service (1) (sĕr′ vis) [O.F., from L. *servitium*, as prec.], *n.* The act of serving; work done for an employer or for the benefit of another; a benefit or advantage conferred on some one; the state of being a servant, esp. the place or position of a domestic servant; a department of State or public work or duty, the organization performing this, or the persons employed in it; willingness to work or act; use, assistance; a liturgical form for worship, an office; a performance of this; a musical setting of a liturgical office or part of it; formal legal delivery, posting up, or publication (of a writ, summons, etc.); a set of dishes, plates, etc., required for serving a meal; that which is served at table; the act of serving the ball at tennis, etc.; maintenance work undertaken by the vendor after a sale. *v.t.* To repair or maintain a car, etc., after sale. **on service** or **in active service:** Engaged in actual duty in the army, navy, etc. **to see service:** To have experience, esp. as a soldier or sailor. **service area,** *n.* (*Radio*) An area served by a broadcasting station within which efficient transmission can be guaranteed. ***service-book,** *n.* A book containing the Church offices, esp. the Book of Common Prayer. **service dress,** *n.* (*Nav., Mil.*) Uniform other than full-dress. **service flat,** *n.* A flat for which an inclusive sum is charged for rent and full hotel service. **service-line,** *n.* (*Lawn Tennis*) One of two lines marking the limit within which the serve must fall. **service-pipe,** *n.* A pipe from the water- or gas-main to a building. **service road:** A minor road running alongside a main road and carrying local traffic. **service station:** A roadside establishment for giving service to motorists. **the Services:** Navy, Army and Air Force.

service (2) (sĕr′ vis) [M.E. *serves*, pl., from A.-S. *syrpe*, ult. from L. *sorbus*], *n.* The service-tree. **service-berry,** *n.* The June-berry or fruit of the shad-bush. **service-tree,** *n.* A European tree, *Pyrus Sorbus*, or *domestica*, with small pear-like fruit; the wild service-tree, *Pyrus torminalis*.

serviceable (sĕr′ vis à bėl), *a.* Able or willing to render service; useful, beneficial, advantageous; durable, fit for service; *obliging, officious. **serviceableness,** *n.* **serviceably,** *adv.*

***servient** (sĕr′ vi ėnt) [L. *serviens -ntem*, pres.p. of *servīre*, to SERVE], *a.* Subordinate; (*Law*) subject to an easement or servitude.

serviette (sĕr vi et′) [F., related to *servir*, to SERVE], *n.* A table-napkin.

servile (sĕr′ vīl, -vil) [O.F. from L. *servīlis*, from *servus*, slave], *a.* Of, pertaining to, or befitting a slave or slaves; slavish, abject, mean, cringing, fawning, menial, dependent; (*Gram.*) not belonging to the original root, not itself sounded but serving to modify the pronunciation of another (of letters like *e* in saleable or in singeing). **servilely,** *adv.* **servility** (-vil′ i ti), ***servileness,** *n.*

serving-maid, -man, [SERVE].

servitor (sĕr′ vi tŏr) [O.F., from late L. *servitōrem*, nom. *-tor*, from *servīre*, to serve], *n.* A male servant or attendant; (*poet.*) a follower, an adherent, a henchman; *(*Oxf. Univ.*) an undergraduate partly supported out of the college funds, who waited at table on the fellows and gentlemen-commoners.

servitude (sĕr′ vi tūd) [F., from L. *servitūdo*, as prec.], *n.* The condition of a slave, slavery, bondage; subjection to or as to a master; (*Law*) the subjection of property to an easement for the benefit of a person other than the owner or of another estate. ***serviture,** *n.* Servants collectively.

servo-mechanism (sĕr′ vō mek′ à nizm), *n.* A mechanical amplifier used primarily for reinforcing the physical effort in working the controls of an aircraft or vehicle, or of aiming artillery. **servo-assisted,** *a.* (Controls) aided by a servo-mechanism.

sesame (ses′ à mi) [F. *sésame*, ult. from Gr. *sesamon, -mē*, prob. of Oriental orig.], *n.* An East Indian annual herb of the genus *Sesamum*, with oily seeds used as food, as a laxative, etc. **open sesame:** A magic formula for opening a door, mentioned in the *Arabian Nights*; (*fig.*) a key to a mystery, etc. **sesamoid,** *a.* Shaped like a sesame-seed, nodular. *n.* A sesamoid bone, one of several small bones developed in tendons as in the knee-cap, the sole of the foot, etc.

sesban (ses′ băn) [F., from Pers. *sīsabān*], *n.* A tropical plant of the bean family, one species of which yields rope-fibre.

seseli (ses′ ė li) [med. L. and Gr.], *n.* A genus of white-flowered umbelliferous plants comprising the meadow-saxifrage.

sesqui- [L. (*semis*, half, *-que*, and), more by one half], *comb. form.* Denoting a proportion of 1½ to 1, or 3 to 2; (*Chem.*) denoting combinations of three atoms of one element with two of another. **sesquialter** (ses kwi awl′ tėr) [L. *alter*, second], *a.* In the proportion of 1½ to 1 or 3 to 2. *n.* A sesquialtera. **sesquialtera,** *n.* (*Mus.*) An interval with the ratio of 3 to 2, a perfect fifth; a rhythm in which three minims equal two minims preceding; a compound organ-stop. **sesquialteral, -alterate, -alterous,** *a.* **sesquiduple** (ses kwi dūpl′) [DUPLE]. **sesquiduplicate** (-dū′ pli kȧt), *a.* Denoting the ratio of 2½ to 1. **sesquipedal** (ses kwip′ ė dȧl, ses′ kwi ped ȧl) [L. *sesquipedālis* (PEDAL)], *a.* Measuring a foot and a half; sesquipedalian. *n.* A sesquipedalian person or thing. **sesquipedalian** (-dā′ li ȧn), *a.* Many-syllabled (of words); given to using long words. *n.* A sesquipedalian word. **sesquipedalianism, sesquipedality** (-dăl′ i ti), *n.* **sesquiplicate** (ses kwip′ li kȧt) [PLICATE], *a.* Having the ratio of a cube to a square. **sesquitertia** (-tĕr′ shi ȧ) [see TERTIAN], *n.* A ratio of 1⅓ to 1; (*Mus.*) an interval having this ratio, a perfect fourth. **sesquitertial, -tian,** *a.* **sesquitone** (ses′ kwi tōn), *n.* (*Mus.*) An interval of a tone and a half, a minor third.

***sessa** (ses′ ȧ) [perh. from F. *cessez*, CEASE], *int.* An exclamation prob. of encouragement.

sessile (ses′ īl, -il) [L. *sessilis*, from *sess-*, see foll], *a.* (*Bot., Zool.*) Attached by the base, destitute of a stalk or peduncle.

session (sesh′ ŭn) [F., from L. *sessiōnem*, nom. *-sio*, from *sedēre*, to sit, p.p. *sessus*], *n.* The act of sitting or being assembled; a sitting or meeting of a court, council, legislature, academic body, etc., for the transaction of business; the period during which such meetings are held at short intervals; the time of such meeting; the period from the meeting of Parliament till its prorogation or dissolution; the lowest court of the Presbyterian Church, called the Kirk-Session; *the enthronement of Christ on the right hand of the Father. **Court of Session,** *n.* (*Law*) The supreme civil court of justice in Scotland. **session-clerk,** *n.* The clerk of the Kirk-Session. **sessional,** *a.*

sesterce (ses′ tėrs), **sestertius** (ses tĕr′ shŭs) [F. *sesterce*, L. *sestertius*, orig. adj. (*semis*, SEMI-, TERTIUS)], *n.* (*pl.* **-ces, -tii,** -shi i) An ancient Roman silver (afterwards bronze) coin and money of account worth 2½ asses (about 2d.) **sestertium,** *n.*

(*pl.* **-tia**) An ancient Roman money of account equivalent to 1,000 sesterces.

sestet (ses tet′) [It. *sestetto*, dim. of *sesto*, L. *sextus*, sixth], *n.* (*Mus.*) A composition for six instruments or voices; the last six lines of a sonnet. ***sestetto***, *n.*

sestina (ses tē′ nȧ) [It., as prec.], *n.* A form of verse consisting of six six-lined stanzas with a final triplet, each stanza having the same terminal words to the lines but in different order.

set (1) (set) [A.-S. *settan*, causal of *sittan*, to SIT (cp. Dut. *zetten*, G. *setzen*, Icel. *setja*)], *v.t.* (*past & p.p.* **set**) To place, to put, to stand; to fix; to plant (usu. out); to bring, put, place, or station in a specified or right position, posture, direction, or state; to arrange or dispose for use, action, display, etc.; to apply (a thing to something else); to attach, to fasten, to join; to determine, to appoint, to settle, to establish; to cause to sit; to apply (oneself, one's energies, etc., to), to cause (to work, etc.); to present, to offer (an example, task, etc.); to stud, to make insertions in (a surface, etc.); to arrange, to compose (type); to fix the hair in waves, etc.; (*Mus.*) to adapt or fit (words, etc.) to music usu. composed for the purpose; (*Naut.*) to hoist, to spread (sail). *v.i.* To become solid, hard, or firm from a fluid condition, to congeal, to solidify; to take shape, to become fixed; to move, tend, or incline in a definite or specified direction; to mature, to develop (of flowers or fruit); to point (of a dog); to face one's partner (in dancing); to pass below the horizon; (*fig.*) to decline, to pass away. *a.* Fixed, unyielding, immovable; determined, intent (on or upon); rigid, motionless; stationary; established, prescribed; regular, in due form. **of set purpose:** Intentionally, deliberately. **set-fair**, *a.* Fine and settled (of the weather). **set piece:** A large firework built up with scaffolding; a set scene. **set scene:** (*Theat.*) A scene of more or less solid and permanent construction. **to set about:** To begin; to prepare or take steps (to do, etc.). **to set against:** To oppose; to balance (one thing) against another; to make (a person) unfriendly to or prejudiced against. **to set apart:** To separate, to reserve (for some special purpose). **to set aside:** To reserve; to reject; to annul, to quash. **to set at defiance:** To defy. **to set at ease:** To relieve of anxiety, fear, bashfulness, etc.; to make comfortable. **to set at naught** [NAUGHT]. **to set back:** To turn backwards, to reverse the movement of. **to set by:** To reserve; to lay by, to save. **to set by the compass:** To observe the compass bearings of. **to set by the ears** or **at loggerheads** [EAR (1)]. **to set down:** To put on the ground; to put in writing, to note; to attribute; to explain (as); to snub, to rebuke. **to set eyes on** [EYE (1)]. **to set fire to** [FIRE (1)]. **to set foot:** To tread (on). **to set forth:** To show, to demonstrate, to expound, to make known; to start (on a journey, etc.); *to recommend. **to set forward:** To promote, to help; to begin going forward. **to set free:** To release. **to set in:** To begin in a steady manner; to obtain vogue; to move steadily shoreward (of the tide); to become settled (of the weather). **to set in order:** To arrange, to adjust; (*fig.*) to reform. **to set little** or **much by:** To value little or highly. **to set off:** To make more attractive or brilliant by contrast; to act as a foil to; to beautify, to adorn; to place over against as an equivalent; to start (laughing, etc.); to set out. **to set on:** To incite, to instigate, to urge (to attack); to employ (on a task); to make an attack on. **to set oneself:** To apply oneself, to undertake; to resolve. **to sėt one's hand, seal,** etc.**:** To sign, seal, etc. (a document). **to set one's hand to:** To begin (a task). **to set on foot** [FOOT]. **to set out:** To mark off; to assign, to allot; to display, to expound, to state at length, to publish; to equip; to adorn, to embellish; to plant out; to lay (a stone, etc.) so as to project; to start (upon a journey, etc.). **to set over:** To put in authority over or in control of. **to set right:** To correct. **to set sail** [SAIL]. **to set store by** [BY]. **to set the heart** or **mind on** [HEART]. **to set the teeth:** To clench them; to be obstinate or determined. **to set the teeth on edge** [EDGE]. **to set to:** To apply oneself vigorously; to begin to fight. **to set to work:** To begin; to cause to begin working. **to set up:** To erect, to fix up, to post up or display; to raise, to exalt, to establish; to start a business (as); to cause to develop, to occasion; to begin to utter. **to set-up:** To compose (type); to put ('copy', etc.) in type.

set (2) (set) [O.F. *sette*, var. of *secte*, SECT, in some senses blended with prec.], *n.* A number of similar, related, or complementary things or persons, a collection, a group, a company, a clique; a number of things intended to be used together or required to form a whole; a clutch or sitting of eggs; a group of games played together, counting as a unit, esp. in lawn-tennis; the direction of a current, opinion, etc., drift, tendency, trend; confirmation, posture, pose, carriage; the way a dress, etc., sits; permanent inclination, bend, displacement, bias; the spread or deflection of the teeth of a saw alternately to right or left, the amount of this; the act of pointing at game, etc. (by a setter); a young plant for setting out, a shoot, a slip for planting; the last coat of plaster on a wall; (*Mining*) a mine or group of mines leased together, a distance set off for excavation, a timber framing for supporting the roof; (*Print.*) the amount of margin in type determining the distance between letters; (*Theat.*) a set scene; (*Cinema.*) a built-up scene; *the act of setting (of the sun, etc.). **dead set** [DEAD]. **to have a set on:** (*Austral.*) To intend mischief to. **set-back**, *n.* A check, an arrest; an overflow, a counter-current; a relapse. **set-down**, *n.* A rebuke, a snub, a rebuff. **set-off**, *n.* A thing set off against another, an offset, a counterpoise, a counter-claim; a decorative contrast, an embellishment; (*Arch.*) a ledge or sloping projection between the thicker part of a wall and a receding portion above; (*Print.*) an accidental transference of ink from one printed sheet to another. **set-out**, *n.* Beginning, start, outset; preparations or equipment; a display. **set-piece**, *n.* (*Theat.*) A carefully-prepared and usually elaborate performance. **set-square**, *n.* A right-angled triangular piece of wood, etc., used in mechanical drawing. **set-to**, *n.* A fight, esp. with the fists; a heated argument.

setaceous (sē tā′ shŭs) [L. *sēta*, bristle, -ACEOUS], *a.* Bristly; set with, consisting of, or resembling bristles. **setaceously**, *adv.* **setiferous** (-tif′ ėr ŭs), **setigerous** (-tij′-), **setiform** (sē′-), **setose**, ***setous**, *a.*

seton (sē′ tŏn) [F. *séton*, ult. from L. *sēta*, see SETACEOUS], *n.* A twist of silk, cotton, or similar material inserted in a wound to maintain an artificial issue and counter irritation, esp. in veterinary surgery.

setose, *-tous [SETACEOUS].

set-out, set-square [SET (2)].

sett [var. of SET (2)], *n.* A small rectangular block of stone used for road paving.

settee (1) (sė tē′) [prob. var. of SETTLE (1)], *n.* A long seat for several persons with a back; a short sofa for two.

settee (2) (sė tē′) [F. *scétie*, It. *saettia*, perh. from *saetta*, L. *sagitta*, arrow], *n.* A sharp-prowed, single-decked Mediterranean vessel with two or three masts, and lateen sails.

setter (set′ ėr), *n.* One who or that which sets (as type, gems, music to words, etc.); a large dog trained to point at game by standing rigid. **setter-on**, *n.* An instigator. **setter-up**, *n.* One who sets up, establishes, etc.

setterwort (set′ ėr wŏrt) [*setter*, etym. doubtful, WORT], *n.* The bear's foot or stinking hellebore, *Helleborus fœtidus.*

setting (set′ ing), *n.* The action of one who or that which sets; the result of this; solidification, hardening, concretion; the framing, etc., in which something (as a jewel) is set; the framing, surroundings, or environment of a thing, event, etc.; the scenery and other stage accessories of a play; a set of eggs; the music to which words, a song, etc,. are fitted. **setting-board**, *n.* A board for mounting entomological specimens on. **setting-box,** *n.* A case in which these are arranged as shelves. **setting-coat,** *n.* A finishing coat of plaster. **setting-stick,** *n.* A stick used in type-setting.

settle (1) (set′ėl) [A.-S. *setl* (cp. Dut. *zettel,* G. *sessel*), cogn. with SIT], *n.* A long, high-backed seat or bench for several persons.

settle (2) (set′ ėl) [A.-S. *setlan,* as prec., combined with *sahtlian,* to reconcile, from *saht,* Icel. *sætl,* peace], *v.t.* To place firmly, to put in a permanent or fixed position, to establish; to cause to sit down or to become fixed; to determine, to decide; to plant with inhabitants, to colonize; to settle in as colonists; to cause to sink or subside, to precipitate; to clear of dregs; to deal with, to dispose of, to finish with, to do for; to adjust and liquidate (a disputed account); to pay (an account); to secure (property, an income, etc., on); to arrange, to adjust, to accommodate (a quarrel, dispute, etc.). *v.i.* To sit down, to alight; to cease from movement, agitation, etc.; to become motionless, fixed, or permanent; to take up a permanent abode, mode of life, etc., to become established, to become a colonist (in); to subside, to sink to the bottom; to become clarified; to determine, to resolve (upon); to adjust differences, claims, or accounts. **to settle down:** To become regular in one's mode of life, to become established. **to settle up:** To pay what is owing. **settling-day,** *n.* A day for the settling-up of accounts, esp. on the Stock Exchange. **settlings,** *n.pl.* Sediment, lees, dregs. **settlor,** *n.* (*Law*) One who makes a settlement.

settlement (set′ ėl mėnt), *n.* The act of settling; the state of being settled; a subsidence; a place or region newly settled, a colony; a community or group of persons living together, esp. in order to carry out social work among the poor; (*Law*) the conveyance of property or creation of an estate to make provision for the support of a person or persons or for some other object; the property so settled. **Act of Settlement:** An Act (passed 1701) settling the succession to the Crown of Britain on Sophia of Hanover and her heirs.

settler (set′ lėr), *n.* One who settles, esp. a colonist; (*slang*) a knock-down blow, a decisive argument, etc. **settler's clock:** (*Austral.*) The Kookaburra. **settler's matches:** (*Austral.*) Pieces of dry bark used as tinder.

set-to [SET (2)]. **set-up** [SET (1)].

setwall (set′ wawl) [M.E. *zedewal,* A.-F. *zedewale,* O.F. *citoual,* as ZEDOARY], *n.* Valerian; *the root of an E. Indian plant, *Curcuma zedoaria,* used as a drug.

seven (sev′ ėn) [A.-S. *seofon* (cp. Dut. *zeven,* G. *sieben,* Icel. *sjö,* Dan. *syv,* L. *septem,* Gr. *hepta,* Sansk. *saptan*)], *n.* The sum of one and six; the cardinal number next above six; the figure 7 or vii; a set of seven persons or things, esp. a card with seven pips. *a.* Consisting of one more than six. **seven deadly sins:** Pride, covetousness, lust, gluttony, anger, envy, sloth. **seven dolours:** Seven sorrowful experiences in the life of the Virgin Mary. **seven-league boots:** Magical boots enabling the wearer to go seven leagues at a stride. **seven wise men** or **sages of Greece:** Seven ancient Greeks renowned for practical wisdom, Periander of Corinth, Pittacus of Mitylene, Thales of Miletus, Solon of Athens, Bias of Priene, Chilon of Sparta, and Cleobulus of Lindus. **seven wonders of the world:** The Pyramids, the Hanging Gardens of Babylon, the Temple of Diana at Ephesus, the tomb of Mausolus of Caria, the Colossus of Rhodes, the statue of Zeus by Phidias, and the Pharos of Alexandria. **seven-up,** *n.* (*Am.*) A card game, all-fours. **sevenfold,** *a.* and *adv.* **sevenfolded,** *a.* **seven-knit** [SENNIT]. **seven-night** [SENNIGHT]. **seventeen,** *n.* The sum of seven and ten; the number 17 or xvii. *a.* Consisting of seven and ten. **seventeenth,** *a.* and *n.* **seventh,** *a.* Coming next after the sixth. *n.* The next after the sixth; a seventh part; the seventh day of the month; (*Mus.*) the interval between a given tone and the seventh above it (inclusively) on the diatonic scale, a combination of these two. **Seventh Day Adventists:** A sect that believes in the imminent second advent of Christ and observes Saturday as the sabbath. **seventh part:** One of seven equal parts. **seventhly,** *adv.*

seventy (sevn′ ti) [A.-S. *seofontig* (SEVEN, -TY)], *n.* Seven times ten; the number 70 or lxx. *a.* Consisting of or amounting to seven times ten. **the seventy:** The translators of the Septuagint; the seventy evangelists mentioned in Luke x. 1–24; the Jewish Sanhedrin. **seventy-four,** *n.* (*Hist.*) A warship with 74 guns. **seventieth,** *a.* and *n.*

sever (sev′ ėr) [O.F. *sevrer,* L. *sēparāre,* to SEPARATE], *v.t.* To part, to separate, to disjoin; to divide, to cleave, to sunder; to cut or break off (apart from the whole); to keep distinct or apart; to conduct or carry on independently. *v.i.* To separate, to part. **severable,** *a.* **severance,** *n.*

several (sev′ ėr ǎl) [O.F., from late L. *sēparāpe,* as prec.], *a.* Separate, distinct, individual, single, particular; not common, not shared with others, pertaining to individuals; consisting of a number, more than two but not many. *n.* A few, an indefinite number, more than two but not many; an enclosed piece of ground, pasture or field; *an individual or particular person or thing. ***severality** (-ǎl′ i ti), *n.* **severally,** *adv.* **severalty,** *n.* (*Law*) Exclusive tenure or ownership.

severance [SEVER].

severe (sė vēr′) [O.F., from L. *sevērus*], *a.* Rigorous, strict, austere, harsh, merciless; trying, hard to endure or sustain; distressing, bitter, painful; grave, serious, sedate; rigidly conforming to rule, unadorned, restrained. **severely,** *adv.* **severity** (-ver′ i ti), *n.*

Sèvres (sāvr) [town in Seine-et-Oise, France], *n.* Porcelain made at Sèvres, also called **Sèvres porcelain.**

sew (1) (sō) [A.-S. *siwian* (cp. Icel. *sȳja,* O.H.G. *siwan*), cogn. with L. *suere,* Gr. *kas-suein,* Sansk. *sīv*], *v.t.* (*p.p.* **sewn, sewed**) To fasten together by thread worked through and through with a needle; to make, mend, close up, attach, fasten on or in, etc., by sewing. *v.i.* To work with a needle and thread. **to be sewed up:** To be mended, closed up, fastened in, or enclosed by sewing; (*slang*) to be done up, exhausted, or nonplussed; to be intoxicated. **sewer** (3), *n.* **sewing-machine,** *n.* A machine for stitching, etc.; driven by a treadle or a crank turned by hand, or electrically. **sewing-press,** *n.* A framework used in sewing books, when binding.

***sew** (2) [SUE].

sewage [SEWER (1)].

sewer (1) (sū′ ėr) [O.F. *seuwiere, seweria,* sluice (EX-, L. *aqua,* water), cp. med. L. *exaquātōrium*], *n.* A channel, underground conduit, or tunnel for carrying off the drainage and liquid refuse of a town, etc. **sewer-gas,** *n.* Foul air from a sewer. **sewer-rat,** *n.* The common brown rat. **sewage,** *n.* The waste matter carried off through the sewers. *v.t.* To manure with sewage. **sewage-farm,** *n.* A farm equipped with apparatus for the disposal of sewage and its utilization as manure. **sewerage,** *n.* The system of draining by means of sewers; (*collect.*) the sewers, drains, etc., of a town, etc.; *sewage.

***sewer** (2) (sū′ ėr) [O.F. *asseour,* from *asseoir,* L. *assidēre* (AS-, *sedēre,* to sit)], *n.* An officer who arranged the dishes at a feast, placed the guests, etc.

sewer (3) (sō′ ėr) [SEW (1)].

sewin (sū′ in) [etym. doubtful], *n.* A variety of sea- or salmon-trout.

sewing-machine, -press, sewn [SEW (1)].

sex (seks) [F. *sexe,* L. *sexum,* nom. *-us,* perh. cogn. with *secāre,* to cut], *n.* The sum total of the physiological, anatomical and functional characteristics which distinguish male and female; the quality of being male and female; (*collect.*) males or females, men or women. **sex appeal,** *n.* Sexual attractiveness; the mental and physical traits that make a man attractive to a woman, or vice versa. **sex determination,** *n.* The factors which decide whether a particular organism will evolve into a male or a female. **the sex:** (*colloq.*) Women. **the sterner sex:** Men. **sex chromosome,** *n.* The chromosome responsible for the initial determination of sex. **sexology,** *n.* The science dealing with the sexes and their relationships. **sexed, sexless,** *a.* **sexlessness,** *n.*

sex-, sexa- [L. *sex*, six], *comb. form.* Containing six; sixfold. **sexagenarian** (sek sȧ jė nâr′ i ȧn) [L. *sexāgēnārius*, from *sexāgēnī*, sixty each, from *sexāginta*, sixty], *a.* Sixty years of age or between 59 and 70. *n.* A sexagenarian person. **sexagenary** (seks ȧ jen′ ȧ ri), *a.* Of or pertaining to sixty; sexagesimal; sexagenarian. *n.* A sexagenarian; a thing composed of sixty parts.

Sexagesima (sek sȧ jes′ i mȧ) [L., fem. of *sexagēsimus*, sixtieth, from *sexāginta*, sixty], *n.* The second Sunday before Lent, so called as being about the sixtieth day before Easter, usu. **Sexagesima Sunday. sexagesimal,** *a.* Sixtieth; pertaining to sixty; proceeding by or based on sixties. **sexagesimally,** *adv.*

sexangle (sek′ săng gėl) [L. *sexangulus* (SEX-, ANGLE (2))], *n.* A hexagon. **sexangled, sexangular,** *a.* **sexangularly,** *adv.* **sexcentenary** (-sen′ tė nȧr i, -sen tē′ nȧ ri), *a.* Pertaining to or consisting of 600 years. *n.* A 600th anniversary. **sexdigitate** (seks dij′ i tȧt), *a.* Having six fingers or toes on a limb. **sexennial** (sek sen′ i ȧl), *a.* Occurring once every six years; lasting six years. **sexennially,** *adv.* **sexfid** (seks′ fid), **sexifid,** *a.* Six-cleft. **sexfoil,** *n.* A six-leaved flower, a six-lobed leaf; an architectural or other ornament of six-lobed foliation. **sexillion** [SEXTILLION]. **sexisyllable** (sek si sil′ ȧbl), *n.* A word of six syllables. **sexisyllabic** (-lăb′ ik), *a.* **sexivalent, sexvalent** (-vā′ lėnt), *a.* (*Chem.*) Having a valency or combining power of six. **sexlocular** (-lok′ ū lȧr), *a.* (*Bot.*) Having six cells.

sexless, sexology, etc. [SEX].

sexpartite (seks par′ tīt), *a.* Divided into six.

sext (sekst) [F. *sexte*, med. L. *sexta*, orig. fem. of L. *sextus*, sixth], *n.* (*R.-C. Ch.*) The office for the sixth hour or noon.

sextain (sek′ stān) [L. *sext-us*, sixth, after QUATRAIN], *n.* A stanza of six lines, a sestina.

sextant (sek′ stȧnt) [L. *sextans*, *-ntem*, from *sextus*, sixth], *n.* The sixth part of a circle; an instrument used in navigation and surveying for measuring angular distances or altitudes. **sextantal** (-tăn′ tȧl), *a.*

sextet [SESTET].

sextic (seks′ tik) [L. *sext-us*, sixth, from *sex*, see SIX, -IC], *a.* (*Math.*) Of the sixth degree or order. *n.* A sextic quantic, equation, or curve.

sextile (sek′ stīl, -stil) [L. *sextilis*, from *sextus*, sixth], *a.* (*Astrol.*) Denoting the aspect of two planets when distant from each other 60°. *n.* A sextile aspect.

sextillion (seks til′ yȯn) [L. *sex*, SIX, after MILLION], *n.* The sixth power of a million, represented by 1 followed by 36 ciphers; (*Am. and Fr.*) the seventh power of a thousand, 1 followed by 21 ciphers.

sexto (sek′ stō) [L. *sex*, SIX], *n.* (*pl.* **-tos**) A book formed by folding sheets into six leaves each. **sextodecimo** (-des′ i mō), *n.* A book formed by folding sheets into sixteen leaves each; a sheet of paper folded thus.

sexton (sek′ stȯn) [M.E. *sekesteyn*, corr. of SACRISTAN], *n.* An officer having the care of a church, its vessels, vestments, etc., and frequently acting as parish-clerk and a grave-digger. **sexton-beetle,** *n.* A beetle that buries carrion to serve as a nidus for its eggs. **sextonship,** *n.*

sextuple (sek′ stūpl) [from L. *sextus*, after QUADRUPLE, etc.], *a.* Six times as many. *n.* A sextuple amount. *v.t.* and *i.* To multiply by six.

sexual (sek′ sū ȧl) [late L. *sexuālis*, from *sexus*, SEX], *a.* Of, pertaining to, or based on sex or the sexes or on the distinction of sexes; pertaining to generation or copulation, venereal. **sexual selection,** *n.* (*Zool.*) A method of selection based on the struggle for mating which, according to one school of thought, accounts for the origin of secondary sexual characteristics. **sexualist,** *n.* **sexuality** (-ăl′ i ti), *n.* **sexually,** *adv.* **sexualize,** *v.t.* **sexualization** (-zā′ shȯn), *n.*

sforzando, sforzato (sfôrt zăn′ dō) [It., from *sforzare*, to FORCE], *adv.* (*Mus. direction*) Emphatically, with sudden vigour.

sgraffito [GRAFFITO].

shabby (shăb′ i) [A.-S. *scæb*, *sceab*, SCAB, -Y], *a.* Ragged, threadbare; in ragged or threadbare clothes; mean, paltry, despicable. **shabbily,** *adv.* **shabbiness,** *n.* **shabbyish,** *a.*

shabrack (shăb′ răk) [G. *schabracke*, Turk. *chāprāq*], *n.* The housing of a cavalry saddle.

shack (1) (shăk) [etym. doubtful], *n.* (*prov.*) An idler, a vagabond; a worthless horse. *v.i.* To idle, to loaf; (*Am.*) to hibernate (of a bear).

shack (2) (shăk) [etym. doubtful], *n.* A rude cabin or shanty, esp. one built of logs.

shack (3) (shăk) [var. of SHAKE], *n.* (*now prov.*) Grain fallen from the ear and used after harvest for feeding pigs, etc.; the right to send pigs, etc., to feed on this, or right of winter pasturage on another's land. *v.t.* To turn (pigs, etc.) into stubble; (of animals) to feed on (stubble).

shackle (shăk′ ėl) [A.-S. *sceacul* (cp. Icel. *skökull*, Swed. *skakel*, carriage-pole), rel. to SHAKE], *n.* A fetter, gyve, or handcuff; the bow of a padlock; a coupling link; an insulating spool or support for a telegraph wire; (*pl.*) fetters, restraints, impediments. *v.t.* To chain, to fetter; to restrain, to impede, to hamper; (*Am.*) to couple (railway carriages). **shackle-bolt,** *n.* A bolt passing through holes in a shackle to fasten it; a bolt with a shackle at the end. **shackle-bone,** *n.* (*Sc.*) The wrist. **shackle-joint,** *n.* A joint composed of ring-like parts in some fishes.

shad (shăd) [A.-S. *sceadda* (cp. G. and Gael. *sgaden*), etym. doubtful], *n.* A name for several anadromous deep-bodied food-fish, esp. the American or white shad. **shad-bush,** *n.* The June-berry, *Amelanchier Canadensis.*

shaddock (shăd′ ȯk) [Capt. *Shaddock*, who took it to the West Indies], *n.* The large orange-like fruit of a Malayan and Polynesian tree, *Citrus decumana.*

shade (shād) [A.-S. *scæd*, *sceadu* (cp. Dut. *schaduw*, G. *schatten*, Ir. and Gael. *sgath*, also Gr. *skotos*), cogn. with SKY], *n.* Obscurity or partial darkness caused by the interception of the rays of light; gloom, darkness; a place sheltered from the sun, a secluded retreat (*often in pl.*); the dark or darker part of a picture; a screen for protecting from or moderating light, esp. a covering for a lamp, or a shield worn over the eyes; (*Am.*) a window blind; a glass cover for protecting an object; a colour; gradation of colour, esp. with regard to its depth or its luminosity; (*fig.*) a scarcely perceptible degree, a small amount; something unsubstantial, unreal, or delusive; the soul after its separation from the body, a spectre; (*pl.*) the abode of spirits, Hades; (*pl.*) wine and spirit or beer vaults. *v.t.* To shelter or screen from light or heat; to cover, to obscure, to darken; to darken (an object in a picture) so as to show gradations of colour or effects of light and shade; to graduate as to light and shade or colour; to cause to pass or blend with another colour. *v.i.* To pass off by degrees or blend (with another colour). **shadeless,** *a.* ***shader,** *n.* **shadily,** *adv.* **shadiness** [SHADY]. **shading,** *n.*

shadoof (shȧ doof) [Arab. *shādūf*], *n.* A water-raising contrivance consisting of a long pole with bucket and counterpoise, used on the Nile, etc.

shadow (shăd′ ō) [A.-S. *sceadu*, see SHADE], *n.* Shade; a patch of shade; the dark figure of a body projected on the ground, etc., by the interception of light; (*fig.*) an inseparable companion; darkness, obscurity, privacy; protection, shelter; the dark part of a picture, room, etc.; a reflected image, (*fig.*) an imperfect or faint representation, an adumbration, a type; a dim foreshadowing, a premonition; a faint trace, the slightest degree; something unsubstantial or unreal; a phantom, a ghost. *v.t.* To darken, to cloud; to set (forth) dimly or in outline, to adumbrate, to typify; to watch secretly, to spy upon, to dog. **shadow boxing:** Boxing against an imaginary opponent when training. **shadow cabinet,** *n.* (*Pol.*) A group of leading members of a party out of office which settles the programme to be followed if or when they get into power. **shadow mark:** (*Archæol.*) The trace of an ancient site as observed from the air. **shadowless,** *a.* **shadowy,** *a.* **shadowiness,** *n.*

shady (shā′ di), *a.* Sheltered from the light and heat of the sun; casting shade; shunning the light, disreputable, of equivocal honesty; (*colloq.*) declining, later. **shadily,** *adv.* **shadiness,** *n.*

shaft (shaft) [A.-S. *sceaft*, spear-shaft, orig. shaved, from *scafan*, to SHAVE (cp. Dut. *schacht*, G. *schaft*, Icel. *skapt*)], *n.* The slender stem or stock of a spear, arrow, etc.; an arrow; anything more or less resembling this, as a ray (of light), a bolt or dart (of lightning, ridicule, etc.); a column between the base and the capital; a small column in a cluster or in a window-joint; a stem, a stalk, a trunk; the scape of a feather; any long, straight, and more or less slender part; the handle of a tool; one of the bars between a pair of which a horse is harnessed; a large axle, arbor, or long cylindrical bar, esp. rotating and transferring motion; a well-like excavation, usu. vertical, giving access to a mine; the tunnel of a blast-furnace; an upward vent to a mine, tunnel, etc. **shaft-horse,** *n.* A horse harnessed between the shafts. **shafted,** *a.* **shafting,** *n.* A system of shafts for the transmission of power. **shaftless,** *a.* ***shaftment** (1), *n.* The feathered part of an arrow. **shaftsman,** *n.* One employed in sinking shafts. **shafty,** *a.* Long, compact, and strong, in the staple (of wool).

shaftment (2) (shăft′ ment) [A.-S. *sceaftmund* (SHAFT, *mund*, hand)], *n.* A measure of about six inches; the distance from the tip of the thumb to the further side of the extended hand.

shag (shăg) [A.-S. *sceacga* (cp. Icel. *skegg*, beard, *skaga*, to jut)], *n.* A rough coat of hair, a bushy mass; cloth having a long coarse nap; strong tobacco cut into fine shreds; the crested cormorant, *Phalacrocorax aristotelis*. *a.* Shaggy. ***shag-eared,** *a.* Having shaggy ears. ***shag-haired,** *a.* ***shagged, shaggy,** *a.* Rough-haired, hairy, hirsute; coarse, tangled, unkempt; overgrown with trees or coarse vegetation, scrubby, rugged. **shaggily,** *adv.* **shagginess,** *n.*

shagreen (shȧ grēn′) [var. of CHAGRIN], *n.* A kind of leather with a granular surface prepared without tanning from the skins of horses, asses, camels, sharks, and seals, usu. dyed green; the skins of various sharks, rays, etc., covered with hard papillæ, used for polishing, etc.

shagroon (shȧ groon) [uncertain], *n.* (*N. Zealand*) An original settler, esp. at Canterbury; one of non-European origin.

shah (sha) [Pers.], *n.* The sovereign of Persia.

shaheen (shȧ hēn′) [Hind. and Pers., from prec.], *n.* An Indian falcon.

shahi (sha′ i) [Pers., royal, as prec.], *n.* A Persian copper coin worth about $\frac{5}{8}$d.; *a small Persian silver coin.

shaitan (shā tan′) [Arab., from Heb. SATAN], *n.* The devil; an evil spirit; an evil person or animal.

shake (shāk) [A.-S. *sceacan*, cp. Icel. and Swed. *skaka*, Dan. *skage*], *v.t.* (*past*, **shook,** shuk, *p.p.* **shaken**) To move forcibly or rapidly to and fro or up and down; to cause to tremble or quiver; to shock, to convulse, to agitate, to disturb; to brandish, to weaken the stability of, to impair, to shatter (*lit. or fig.*); to trill; to upset another's composure; to cause another to doubt; (*Austral. slang*) to steal. *v.i.* To move quickly to and fro or up and down, to tremble, to totter, to shiver; to quiver, to rock; to change the pitch or power of the voice, to make trills; (*Am.*) to shake hands. *n.* The act or an act of shaking; a jerk, a jolt, a shock, a concussion; the state of being shaken, agitation, vibration, trembling; a trill; a glass of milk, or milk and egg shaken up; a crack in growing timber. **to shake hands:** [HAND (1)]. **to shake off:** To get rid of by shaking, to cast off. **to shake one's head:** To move the head from side to side in token of refusal, dissent, disapproval, etc. **no great shakes:** (*slang*) Of no great account. **to shake down:** To bring down (fruit, etc.) by shaking; to cause (grain, etc.) to settle into a compact mass; to become compact; to settle down into a comfortable or harmonious state. **shake-down,** *n.* A makeshift bed. **shakeable,** *a.* **shaker** (1), *n.*

Shaker (2) (shā′ kėr), *n.* One of an American religious sect, founded in Manchester, who hold that Christ's second advent has already taken place (named from their religious dances). **Shakeress,** *n.* **Shakerism,** *n.*

Shakespearean (shāk spēr′ i ȧn), *a.* Pertaining to or resembling Shakespeare or his style. **Shakespeareana** (-an′ ȧ), *n.pl.* **Shakespeareanism,** *n.*

shakily, shakiness [SHAKY].

shako (shăk′ ō) [F., from Hung. *csako*], *n.* (*pl.* **-kos**) A military cylindrical hat, usu. flat-topped, with a peak in front, usu. tilting forward, and decorated with a pompom, plume, or tuft.

shaky (shā′ ki), *a.* Liable to shake, unsteady, rickety, unstable, tottering; (*fig.*) of doubtful integrity, solvency, ability, etc. **shakily,** *adv.* **shakiness,** *n.*

shale (1) (shāl) [G. *schale*, cogn. with obs. Eng. *shale*, shell, var. of SCALE (1)], *n.* A laminated argillaceous rock resembling soft slate, often containing much bitumen. **shaly,** *a.*

***shale** (2) [SHELL].

shall (shăl) [A.-S. *sceal*, past of *sculan*, to owe (cp. Dut. *zal*, G. *soll*, Icel. *skal*), cogn. with *scyld*, G. *schuld*, and prob. L. *scelus*, guilt], *v.aux.* (*2nd sing.* **shalt,** *past and subj.* **should,** shud, **shouldst, shouldest**) Used to express simple futurity or a conditional statement (*now only in 1st pers.*); to express a command, intention, promise, permission, etc. (*in 2nd and 3rd pers.*); to express future or conditional obligation, duty, etc., or to form a conditional protasis, etc. (*in any person*).

shalloon (shȧ loon′) [F. *Châlons*-sur-Marne], *n.* A light worsted fabric used for linings, etc.

shallop (shăl′ ȯp) [F. *chaloupe*, Dut. *sloep*, sloop], *n.* A light open boat.

shallot (shȧ lot′) [O.F. *eschalote* (F. *échalote*), corr. of *escalogne*, L. *escalōnia*, fem. of *-ius*, from *Ascalon* in Palestine], *n.* A plant, *Allium Ascalonicum*, allied to garlic with similar but milder bulbs.

shallow (shăl′ ō) [M.E. *schalowe*, perh. rel. to A.-S. *sceald* (cp. Icel. *skālgr*, wry, also SHOAL (1), SHELVE (2))], *a.* Not having much depth; (*fig.*) superficial, trivial, silly. *n.* A shallow place, a shoal. *v.i.* To become shallow or shallower. *v.t.* To make shallow. **shallow-brained, *-pated,** *a.* Weak-minded. **shallow-hearted,** *a.* Incapable of deep or sincere feeling. **shallowly,** *adv.* **shallowness,** *n.*

***shalm, *shalmic** [SHAWM].

shalt, *2nd pers. sing.* [SHALL].

shaly [SHALE].

sham (shăm) [var. of SHAME], *v.t.* (*past & p.p.* **shammed**) To feign, to make a pretence of; *to cheat, to trick. *v.i.* To feign, to pretend. *n.* An imposture, a false pretence, a fraud, one who or that which pretends to be some one or something else. *a.* Feigned, pretended, counterfeit. **sham fight:** A mimic battle for training or showing off troops. **to sham Abraham** [ABRAHAMIC]. **shammer,** *n.*

Shamanism (sha' må-, shăm' å nizm) [perh. from Pers. *shaman*, idolator, -ISM], *n.* A form of religion based on the belief in good and evil spirits which can be influenced by shamans, prevailing among Siberian and N. American tribes. **Shaman** (sha' mån, shăm' ån), *n.* A priest, exorcist, or medicine man among Shamanists. **Shamanist,** *n.* and *a.* **Shamanistic** (-nis' tik), *a.*

shamble (shăm' bėl) [etym. doubtful, cp. SCAMBLE and SCAMPER], *v.i.* To walk in an awkward, shuffling or unsteady manner. *n.* A shambling walk or gait. **shambling,** *a.*

shambles (shăm' bėlz) [pl. of obs. *shamble*, A.-S. *scamel*, L. *scamellum*, stool, dim. of *scamnum*, bench, step, cogn. with Gr. *skēptein*, to prop], *n.pl.* (*usu. as sing.*) A butcher's slaughter-house; (*fig.*) a place of carnage or execution; utter confusion; (*now prov.*) butchers' stalls, a meat-market.

shame (shām) [A.-S. *sceamu*, *scamu* (cp. G. *scham*, Dan. *skam*, Icel. *skömm*) whence *sceamian*, *scamian*, to shame], *n.* A painful feeling due to consciousness of guilt, degradation, humiliation, etc.; the instinct to avoid this, the restraining sense of pride, modesty, decency, decorum; a state of disgrace, discredit, or ignominy; anything that brings reproach, a disgrace; (*colloq.*) an unfairness. *v.t.* To make ashamed; to bring shame on, to cause to blush or feel disgraced; to disgrace; *to mock at. **v.i.* To be ashamed. **shame!** *int.* That is unfair! Disgraceful! **to put to shame:** To humiliate by exhibiting better qualities. ***shame-proof,** *a.* Insensible to shame. **shamefaced, *shamefast** [A.-S. *scamfæst* (EAST (1))], *a.* Bashful, shy, easily confused or abashed, modest, retiring. **shamefacedly** (-fāst li, -fā sėd li), *adv.* **shamefacedness, *shamefastness,** *n.* **shameful,** *a.* **shamefully,** *adv.* **shamefulness,** *n.* **shameless,** *a.* Immodest. **shamelessly,** *adv.* **shamelessness,** *n.* ***shamer,** *n.*

shammer [SHAM].

shammy, shamoy (*colloq.*) [CHAMOIS].

shampoo (shăm poo') [Hind. *chāmpnā*, to press, to shampoo], *v.t.* To squeeze, rub, and massage the body of after a hot bath; to lather, wash, and rub the head of. *n.* The act of shampooing; any substance used for this.

shamrock (shăm' rok) [Ir. *seamrog*], *n.* A species of trefoil forming the national emblem of Ireland.

***shan** (1) (shăn), ***shand** (shănd) [etym. doubtful], *n.* (*Sc.*) Base coin. *a.* Mean, shabby, worthless.

Shan (2) (shăn) [native name], *n.* One of a Taic people living on the borders of N. Siam, E. Burma, and Yunnan. *a.* Pertaining to the Shans.

shandry (shăn' dri) [etym. doubtful], *n.* (*prov.*) A light cart or trap. **shandrydan,** *n.* A kind of hooded chaise; (*fig.*) a ramshackle conveyance.

shandygaff (shăn' di găf), **shandy** [etym. doubtful], *n.* A mixture of beer and ginger-beer.

Shanghai (shăng hī') [town in China], *v.t.* To drug and ship as a sailor while stupefied; to kidnap; (*Austral.*) a catapult.

shank (shăngk) [A.-S. *sceanca*, *scanca* (cp. Dut. *schonk*, Dan. and Swed. *skank*), perh. rel. to SHAKE], *n.* The leg, esp. the part from the knee to the ankle; the shin-bone; a bird's tarsus; the shaft of a column; the straight part of an instrument, tool, etc., connecting the acting part with the handle, a shaft, a stem, a tag, etc. *v.i.* To be affected or fall (off) with decay in the footstalks. **shank-painter,** *n.* (*Naut.*) A painter for fastening an anchor to the side of a vessel. **Shanks's mare:** One's legs for walking as opp. to riding, etc. **shanked,** *a.* Having a shank (*esp. in comb.*, as *short-shanked*).

shanker [CHANCRE].

shanny (shăn' i) [etym. unknown], *n.* The smooth blenny.

shan't (*colloq.*) [SHALL, NOT (1)].

shantung (shăn tŭng') [province in China], *n.* (*Textiles*) A plain fabric woven in coarse silk yarns.

shanty (1) (shăn' ti) [etym. doubtful], *n.* A rude hut or cabin; a hastily-built or rickety building; (*Austral.*) a low public-house, a grog-shop.

shanty (2) [CHANTEY].

shape (shāp) [A.-S. *scieppan* (p.p. *gescapen*), cp. G. *schaffen*, to create, also -SHIP], *v.t.* (*p.p.* **-ed, *-en**) To form, to create, to construct; to make into a particular form, to mould, to fashion; to adapt, to fit, to adjust, to make conform (to); to regulate, to direct; to conceive, to conjure up. *v.i.* To take shape, to come into shape, to develop (well, ill, etc.); to become fit or adapted (to). *n.* The outward form, figure, configuration, or contour; outward aspect, guise, appearance; concrete form, embodiment, realization; definite, fit, or orderly form or condition; kind, sort; an image, an appearance, an apparition; a pattern, a mould, a confection shaped in a mould. **shapeable,** *a.* **shaped,** *a.* Having a shape (*usu. in comb.*, as *square-shaped*). **shapeless,** *a.* Having no regular form; lacking in symmetry; *deformed. **shapelessly,** *adv.* **shapelessness,** *n.* **shapely,** *a.* Well-formed, well-proportioned; having beauty or regularity. **shapeliness,** *n.* **shaper,** *n.*

shard (shard), **sherd** (shĕrd) [A.-S. *sceard*, cogn. with SHEAR, SHARE (1)], *n.* A potsherd; the wing-case of a beetle; *a gap in a hedge; *a boundary. *v.t.* and *i.* To break or flake off. ***shard-born,** *a.* Born on shards (of beetles).

share (1) (shâr) [A.-S. *scearu*, from *sceran*, to SHEAR], *n.* A part or portion detached from a common amount or stock; a part to which one has a right or which one is obliged to contribute, a fair or just portion; a lot, an allotted part, esp. one of the equal parts into which the capital of a company is divided. *v.t.* To divide into portions, to distribute among a number, to apportion; to give away a portion of; to partake of, to have, or endure, with others, to participate in. *v.i.* To have a share or shares (in), to be a sharer or sharers (with), to participate. **deferred shares:** Those on which a reduced or no dividend is paid until a fixed date or contingent event. **preference** or **preferred shares** [PREFERENCE]. **to go shares:** To divide equally with others. **sharebroker,** *n.* A dealer in shares. **shareholder,** *n.* One who holds a share or shares in a joint-stock company, etc. **share-list,** *n.* A list of the current prices of shares. **sharer,** *n.*

share (2) (shâr) [A.-S. *scear*, from *sceran*, to SHEAR], *n.* A plough-share; a blade of a cultivator, seeder, etc. **share-beam,** *n.* The part of a plough to which the share is fixed.

shark (shark) [etym. doubtful, perh. from L. *carcharus*, Gr. *karcharias*, from *karcharos*, jagged (in alln. to its teeth)], *n.* A selachoid sea-fish of various species with lateral gill openings and an inferior mouth, mostly large and voracious and armed with formidable teeth; (*fig.*) a grasping, rapacious person; a rogue, a swindler. *v.i.* To play the part of a shark or swindler. *v.t.* To gain or pick (up) by underhand, fraudulent, or disreputable means; to swallow greedily. **shark-bait,** *n.* (*Austral. colloq.*) A bather or surfer who goes too far out to sea.

sharn (sharn) [A.-S. *scearn*, cogn. with SHARE (1), SHEAR], *n.* (*Sc.*) The dung of cattle.

sharp (sharp) [A.-S. *scearp* (cp. Dut. *scherp*, G. *scharf*, Icel. *skarpr*), perh. rel. to SCRAPE], *a.* Having a keen edge or fine point; terminating in a point or edge; peaked, pointed, edged; angular, abrupt; clean-cut, clearly outlined or defined; (*fig.*) pungent, acid, sour; gritty (of sand); shrill, biting, piercing; harsh, sarcastic, acrimonious, severe, painful, intense; acute, keen-witted; vigilant, attentive, alert, penetrating; alive to one's interests, unscrupulous, dishonest, underhand; quick, speedy, energetic, brisk, vigorous, impetuous; (*Phon.*) surd, voiceless; (*Mus.*) above the true pitch, esp. a semitone higher. *adv.* Punctually, exactly; at a sharp angle; above the true pitch. *n.* A long and slender sewing-needle; (*Mus.*) a note a semitone above the true pitch; the sign (♯) indicating this. *v.t.* To raise the pitch of (a note); to mark with a ♯. *v.i.* To swindle, to cheat. **sharp-cut,** *a.* Clearly outlined, well-defined. **sharp practice:** (*colloq.*) Underhand or questionable dealings. ***sharp-set,** *a.* Ravenous. **sharp-shooter,** *n.* A skilled marksman. **sharp-shooting,** *n.* **sharp-sighted,** *a.* Having keen sight; sharp-witted. **sharp-witted,** *a.* Having a keen wit, judgment, or discernment. **sharpen,** *v.t.* and *i.* To make sharp. **sharpener,** *n.* **sharper,** *n.* One who or that which sharpens; (*colloq.*) a swindler, a rogue; one who lives by his wits. **sharply,** *adv.* **sharpness,** *n.*

shaster, -tra (shăs′ tėr, -trȧ) [Hind. *shāstr,* Sansk. *shastra*], *n.* Any of the Vedas and other Brahmanic scriptures.

shatter (shăt′ ėr) [var. of SCATTER], *v.t.* To break up at once into many pieces; to smash, to shiver; (*fig.*) to destroy, to dissipate, to overthrow, to ruin. *v.i.* To break into fragments. ***shatter-brained, -pated,** *a.* Mentally disordered. **shatters,** *n.pl.* Fragments into which anything is smashed. ***shattery,** *a.*

shaucle (shaw*ch*l) [cp. Icel. *skjālgr,* wry, squinting], *v.t.* (*Sc.*) To deform, to distort; to wear awry. *v.i.* To shuffle, to shamble, to limp.

shave (shāv) [A.-S. *sceafan, scafan* (cp. Dut. *schaven,* G. *schaben,* Icel. *skafa*), cogn. with L. *scabere,* to scratch, Gr. *skaptein,* to dig], *v.t.* To remove hair from (the face, a person, etc.) with a razor; to remove (usu. off) from a surface with a razor; to pare or cut thin slices off the surface of (leather, wood, etc.); to pass by closely with or without touching, to brush past, to graze. *v.i.* To shave oneself. *n.* The act of shaving or the process of being shaved; a knife for shaving, paring, or scraping, esp. a blade with a handle at each end for shaving hoops, etc.; a thin slice; (*fig.*) a narrow escape or miss; (*slang*) a swindle; a doubtful report. **shavegrass,** *n.* The scouring-rush, *Equisetum hyemale.* ***shaveling,** *n.* A man shaved (used contemptuously for a monk or friar). **shaver,** *n.* A barber; a humorous fellow, a wag; **dry shaver,** *n.* An electric razor. **shavie,** *n.* (*Sc.*) A trick, a prank. **shaving,** *n.* The act of one who shaves; a thin slice pared off. **shaving-basin, -bowl, -brush, -cup:** Utensils employed for lathering the face before shaving. **shaving-horse,** *n.* A bench with a clamp for holding wood, slate, etc., to be shaved.

Shavian (shā′ vi ȧn), *a.* Of or in the manner of George Bernard Shaw (1856–1950). *n.* A follower of Shaw.

shaw (shaw) [A.-S. *scaga* (cp. Icel. *skōgr,* Swed. *skog,* Dan. *skov*), rel. to SHAG], *n.* A thicket, a small wood.

shawl (shawl) [Pers. *shāl,* cp. F. *châle*], *n.* A square or oblong garment worn chiefly by women as a loose wrap for the upper part of the person. *v.t.* To wrap with a shawl. **shawl-dance,** *n.* An Oriental dance in which the performer waves a shawl. **shawl-pattern,** *n.* A variegated pattern with a design characteristic of Oriental shawls. **shawlless,** *a.*

shawm (shawm) [O.F. *chalemie* (cp. *chalemelle, chalumeau,* also *chaume,* straw), L. *calamus,* Gr. *kalamos,* reed], *n.* An ancient wind instrument similar to the clarionet.

shay (shā) [from CHAISE, taken as pl.], *n.* (*prov. or facet.*) A chaise.

shaya root [CHAY ROOT]. **shayk** [SHEIKH].

she (shē) [A.-S. *sēo,* fem. of *se,* def. article (cp. Dut. *zij,* G. *sie,* Icel. *sū, sā,* Gr. *hē,* Sansk. *sā*)], *pron.* (*obj.* **her,** *poss.* **her, hers**) The female person, animal, or personified thing mentioned or referred to. *n.* A female; *a woman. *a.* Female (*esp. in comb.,* as *she-cat, she-devil, she-goat, etc.*).

shea (shē, shē′ ȧ) [Native name], *n.* A tropical African tree, *Bassia Parkii,* yielding a kind of butter.

sheading (shē′ ding) [var. of SHED (1), -ING], *n.* Any one of the six divisions of the Isle of Man.

sheaf (shēf) [A.-S. *scēaf* (cp. Dut. *shoof,* G. *schaub,* Icel. *skauf*), cogn. with SHOVE], *n.* (*pl.* **-ves**) A quantity of things bound or held together lengthwise, esp. a bundle of wheat, oats, barley, etc. *v.t.* To collect and bind into sheaves, to sheave. **sheafy,** *a.*

sheal, shealing, etc. [SHEEL, SHIEL, SHEILING].

shear (shēr) [S.-S. *sceran* (cp. Dut. and G. *scheren,* Icel. *skera,* also Gr. *keirein*), cogn. with SCAR (1), SHARD (1), SHORT, etc.], *v.t.* (*past* **sheared, *shore,** *p.p.* **shorn, sheared**) To cut or clip with shears; to reduce or remove nap from (cloth, etc.) by clipping; to remove (wool, etc.) thus; (*fig.*) to fleece, to plunder, to strip; *to cut (usu. off) with a sword, etc.; to reap. *v.i.* To use shears; to cut, to penetrate; (*Mech.*) to undergo a shear. *n.* (*pl.*) A cutting-instrument with two large blades crossing each other like scissors and joined together by a spring; (*Mech.*) a strain caused by pressure upon a solid body in which the layers of its substance move in parallel planes; (*Geol.*) alteration of structure by transverse pressure; (*pl.*) [SHEERS]. **shear-bill,** *n.* The scissor-bill or skimmer. **shearer,** *n.* One who shears sheep. **shear-legs** [SHEERS]. **shearling,** *n.* A sheep that has been shorn once. **shearman,** *n.* One employed to shear metal; *one who shears cloth. **shear steel:** Blister-steel, heated, rolled, etc., to improve the quality.

shearwater (shēr′ wôr ter), *n.* (*Zool.*) A bird of the genus *Procellaria,* esp. *P. puffinus,* the Manx shearwater allied to the petrels.

sheat-fish (shēt′ fish) [A.-S. *scēola,* trout, rel. to SHOOT, FISH], *n.* A large cat-fish, *Silurus glanis,* the largest European freshwater fish.

sheath (shēth) [A.-S. *scæth,* cp. Dut. *scheede,* G. *scheide,* Icel. *skeithir,* Dan. *skede*], *n.* A case for a blade, weapon, or tool, a scabbard; (*Nat. Hist.*) an envelope, a case, a cell-covering, investing tissue, membrane, etc.; a structure of loose stones for confining a river within its banks; a contraceptive appliance. **sheath-knife,** *n.* A large case-knife. **sheath-winged,** *a.* (*Ent.*) Having the wings encased in elytra, coleopterous. **sheathe** (shē*th*), *v.t.* To put into a sheath; to protect by a casing or covering; to hide, to conceal. **to sheathe the sword:** To make peace. **sheathing,** *n.* That which sheathes, esp. a metal covering for a ship's bottom. **sheathless,** *a.* ***sheathy,** *a.*

sheave (1) (shēv) [var. of SHIVE], *n.* The grooved wheel in a block or pulley over which the rope runs. **sheave-hole,** *n.* (*Naut.*) A groove or channel in which to fix a sheave.

sheave (2) [from SHEAF], *v.t.* To gather into sheaves, to sheaf. **sheaved,** *a.* Put up in sheaves; (*Shak.*) prob. made of straw.

sheaves, *pl.* [SHEAF].

shebang (shė băng′) [etym. unknown], *n.* (*Am. slang*) A store, a saloon, gaming-house, etc.; a brothel; business, concern, affair.

shebeen (shė bēn′) [Ir.], *n.* A low public-house; an unlicensed house where excisable liquors are sold.

shechinah [SHEKINAH].

shed (1) (shed) [A.-S. *scēadan, scādan,* to separate, to scatter (cp. G. *scheiden,* also L. *scindere,* Gr. *schizein,* to cleave, to split)], *v.t.* (*past & p.p.* **shed**) To pour out, to let fall, to drop, to spill, to effuse; to throw off, to emit, to diffuse, to spread around; *to sprinkle, to intersperse. *v.i.* To cast off seed, a covering, clothing, etc. *n.* A division, a parting; the ridge of a hill; a divide, a watershed; (*Weaving*) the opening between the warp threads in a loom through which the shuttle carries the weft. **shedder,** *n.*

shed (2) (shed) [var. of SHADE], *n.* A slight simple building, usu. a roofed structure with the ends or ends and sides open; a hovel, a hut. **shedding,** *n.*

***sheel** (shēl) [rel. to A.-S. *scalu*, shell, husk], *v.t.* To shell, to husk. **sheeling** (1), *n.*

sheeling (2) [SHIELING].

sheen (shēn) [A.-S. *scēne* (cp. Dut. *schoon*, G. *schön*), not rel. to SHINE], *a.* *Beautiful, bright, shining. *n.* Brightness, splendour, lustre, glitter. **sheeny,** *a.*

sheep (shēp) [A.-S. *sceāp*, cp. Dut. *schaap*, G. *schaf*, O.H.G. *scaf*], *n.* (*pl. unchanged*) A gregarious ruminant animal of the genus *Ovis*, esp. the domesticated *O. aries*, or any of its numerous breeds, reared for the sake of their flesh and wool; sheepskin used as a leather; (*pl.*) God's people, as the flock of the Good Shepherd; (*pl.*) the members of a minister's flock; (*fig.*) a timid, subservient, unoriginal person, a bashful or embarrassed person. **black sheep,** *n.* (*fig.*) A disreputable person. **sheep-biter,** *n.* A dog that worries sheep; *a petty thief, a thievish or rascally person. **sheep-bot,** *n.* A bot-fly infesting sheep. ***sheep-cote** [SHEEP-FOLD]. **sheep-dip, -wash,** *n.* A preparation for killing vermin or preserving the wool on sheep. **sheep-dog,** *n.* A breed of heavy, rough-coated, short-tailed dogs employed by shepherds; a collie. **sheep-faced,** *a.* Sheepish, bashful. **sheep-fold,** *n.* A pen or enclosure for sheep. **sheep-hook,** *n.* A shepherd's crook. **sheep-louse, -tick,** *n.* An insect parasitic on sheep. **sheep-market,** *n.* A place where sheep are sold. **sheep-master,** *n.* An owner of sheep. **sheep-pen** [SHEEP-FOLD]. **sheep-pox,** *n.* An eruptive contagious disease resembling smallpox, affecting sheep. **sheep-run,** *n.* A large tract of land for pasturing sheep. **sheep's-bit,** *n.* A plant with blue flowers like the scabious. **sheep's eye,** *n.* (*usu. in pl.*) A bashful or diffident look; a wishful glance. **sheep's head:** The head of a sheep; an important food-fish, *Sargus ovis*, abundant on the Atlantic coasts of the United States. **sheep-shearer,** *n.* One who shears sheep. **sheep-shearing,** *n.* **sheepskin,** *n.* The skin of a sheep, esp. used as a coat or rug; leather prepared therefrom, used for bookbinding, etc.; parchment made therefrom or a document or diploma of this. **sheep-tick** [SHEEP-LOUSE]. **sheep-track,** *n.* A path trodden by the feet of sheep. **sheep-walk,** *n.* Land for pasturing sheep, usu. of less extent than a sheep-run. **sheep-wash** [SHEEP-DIP]. **sheepish,** *a.* Like a sheep; bashful, diffident, timid. **sheepishly,** *adv.* **sheepishness,** *n.*

sheepshank (shēp' shăngk), *n.* (*Naut.*) A hitch used to shorten a rope temporarily.

sheepskin (shēp' skin), *n.* The skin of a sheep, esp. used as a coat or rug; leather prepared therefrom, used for bookbinding, etc.; parchment made therefrom or a document or diploma of this.

sheer (1) (shēr) [Icel. *skærr*, cogn. with *skīna*, to SHINE, and A.-S. *skir*], *a.* Pure, unmixed, simple, mere, absolute, bitter, downright; perpendicular, unbroken by a ledge or slope; very thin, diaphanous (of fabrics). *adv.* Vertically, plumb; entirely, outright.

sheer (2) (shēr) [Dut. *scheren*, to SHEAR], *v.i.* (*Naut.*) To deviate from a course; to start aside, to shy (of a horse). *n.* The upward curvature of a vessel toward the bow and stern; the position of a ship riding at single anchor; a swerving or curving course. **to sheer off:** To move off, to go away.

sheers (shērz) [var. of SHEAR], *n.pl.* An apparatus consisting of two masts, or legs, secured at the top, for hoisting heavy weights, esp. in dockyards, also called **sheer-legs. sheer-hulk,** *n.* A dismantled hull of a vessel fitted with sheers for hoisting out and putting in the masts of other ships, etc.

sheerwater [SHEARWATER].

sheet (shēt) [A.-S. *scēte*, *scyte*, rel. to and blended with *scēat*, a corner, a fold, from *scēotan*, to shoot], *n.* A thin, flat, broad piece of anything, esp. a rectangular piece of linen or cotton used in a bed to keep the blankets, etc., from a sleeper's body; a piece of metal, etc., rolled out, hammered, fused, etc., into a thin sheet, a piece of paper of a regular size, esp. complete as it was made, reckoned as the 24th part of a quire; a newspaper; a broad expanse or surface; (*Naut.*) a rope attached to the clew of a sail for moving, extending it, etc. *v.t.* To cover, wrap, or shroud in a sheet or sheets; to form into sheets. **in sheets:** Not bound (of a book). **three sheets in the wind:** (*Naut. slang*) Drunk. **to sheet home:** To secure a sail with the sheet. **sheet-anchor** [orig. *shoot-anchor*, one to be shot out], *n.* A large anchor, usu. one of two carried outside the waist of a ship for use in emergencies; (*fig.*) a chief support, a last refuge. **sheet-copper, -iron, -lead, -metal,** etc. Metal rolled out, hammered, or fused into thin sheets. **sheet-glass,** *n.* **sheet-lightning,** *n.* Lightning in wide extended flashes. **sheeting,** *n.*

sheikh (shāk, shēk) [Arab.], *n.* The head of a Bedouin family, clan, or tribe. **Sheikh ul Islam:** The grand mufti or head of the Mohammedan hierarchy in Turkey.

shekel (shek' ėl) [Heb. *sheqel*, from *shāqal*, to weight], *n.* A Hebrew weight of $\frac{1}{50}$ of a mina; a silver coin of this weight, worth about 2s. 4d.; (*pl.*) money, riches.

Shekinah (shė kī nȧ) [Heb. from *shākan*, to dwell], *n.* The visible presence of Jehovah above the mercy-seat in the Tabernacle and Solomon's Temple.

sheldrake (shel' drāk) [A.-S. *scild*, SHIELD (cp. G. *schildern*, to paint, with alln. to plumage), DRAKE], *n.* A large wild duck with vivid plumage of the genus *Tadorna* or *Cascarca*, esp. *Tadorna tadorna*, breeding on sandy coasts. **sheld-duck, shell-duck,** *n.* The female of this.

shelf (shelf) [A.-S. *scylfe*, cogn. with SCALE (1) and SHELL], *n.* (*pl.* **-ves**) A horizontal board or slab set in a wall or forming one of a series in a bookcase, cupboard, etc., for standing vessels, books, etc., on; a projecting layer of rock, a ledge; a reef, a shoal, a sandbank. **on the shelf:** Put aside, discarded. **shelfful,** *n.*

shell (shel) [A.-S. *scell* (cp. Dut. *schel*, Icel. *skel*), cogn. with SCALE (1)], *n.* A hard outside covering, as of a nut, egg, testaceous animal, etc., a husk, a pod, a wing-case or elytron, a pupa case, an exoskeleton, a carapace, etc.; the framework or walls of a house, ship, etc., with the interior removed or not yet built; the outline of a plan, etc.; (*Am.*) a cartridge-case; a light, long, and narrow racing-boat; an inner coffin; a hollow projectile containing a bursting-charge, missiles, etc., exploded by a time or percussion fuse; a case of the paper or other material containing the explosive in fireworks, cartridges, etc.; an intermediate form in some schools; (*poet.*) a lyre, orig. a stringed tortoise shell; (*fig.*) mere outer form or semblance. *v.t.* To strip or break off the shell from; to take out of the shell; to cover with a shell or with shells; to throw shells at, to bombard. *v.i.* To come away or fall (off) in scales; to cast the husk or shell. **shell-back,** *n.* (*Naut. slang*) An old sailor. **shell-drake** [SHELDRAKE]. **shell-bark,** *n.* Either of two kinds of hickory. **shellfish,** *n.* Any aquatic mollusc or crustacean having a shell. **shell-heap, -mound,** *n.* A kitchen-midden. **shell-jacket,** *n.* (*Mil.*) An undress or fatigue jacket. **shell-lime,** *n.* Lime obtained by burning sea-shells. **shell-out,** *n.* A variety of pool played on the billiard-table. **to shell out.** (*slang*) To pay up, to pay the required sum. **shell-proof,** *a.* Impenetrable to shells, bomb-proof. **shell-shock,** *n.* (*Path.*) A type of neurotic condition resulting from some violent shock of horror, disgust or fear, the memory of which is suppressed. **shell-work,** *n.* Work composed of or ornamented with shells. **shelled,** *a.* (*usu. in comb.* as *hard-shelled*). **shell-less,** *a.*

shellac (shė lăk') [SHELL, LAC (1)], *n.* A thermoplastic resin obtained by purifying the resinous excreta of certain jungle insects. It is used, e.g., in the manufacture of gramophone records. *v.t.* To varnish with this. **shellacking,** *pres.p.*

Shelta (shel' tȧ) [etym. doubtful], *n.* A secret

jargon made up largely of Gaelic or Irish words, used by tinkers, beggars, etc.

shelter (shel′ tėr) [M.E. *sheld-trume*, A.-S. *scild-trume* (SHIELD, *truma*, hand, rel. to *trum*, firm)], *n.* Anything that covers or shields from injury, danger, heat, wind, etc.; being sheltered, security; a place of safety; a light building affording protection from the weather to persons, instruments, etc.; an air-raid shelter. *v.t.* To shield from injury, danger, etc.; to protect, to cover; to conceal, to screen. *v.i.* To take shelter (under). **shelterer,** *n.* **shelterless,** *a.* ***sheltery,** *a.*

shelty, -tie (shel′ ti) [prob. from Icel. *Hjalti*, Shetlander], *n.* A Shetland pony; any pony; a Shetlander.

shelve (1) (shelv), *v.t.* To place on a shelf or shelves; (*fig.*) to put aside, to defer indefinitely; to fit with shelves. **shelving** (1), *n.* **shelvy,** *a.* Projecting, overhanging.

shelve (2) (shelv) [cp. Icel. *shelgjask*, to be askew, also SHOAL (1)]. *v.i.* To slope gradually. **shelving** (2), *a.*

shelves (*pl.*) [SHELF].

shemozzle (she moz′ ėl) [Yiddish-German], *n.* (*slang*) An uproar, a violent row.

***shend** (shend) [A.-S. *scendan*, cp. Dut. *schenden*, G. *Shänden*], *v.t.* (*past & p.p.* **shent**) To disgrace, to put to shame; to hurt, to mar, to ruin, to destroy; to surpass.

she-oak (shē′ ōk), *n.* An Australian tree of the genus *Casuarina*.

Sheol (shē′ ōl, -ŏl) [Heb., from *shā′al*, to dig], *n.* (*Bibl.*) The place of the dead, often translated "hell" in the Authorized Version.

shepherd (shep′ ėrd) [A.-S. *scēaphyrde*, SHEEP, HERD (2)], *n.* One employed to tend sheep at pasture; (*fig.*) a pastor, a Christian minister. *v.t.* To tend, as a shepherd; to drive or gather together; (*Austral.*) to preserve legal rights on a mining claim (*n.* One who holds such a claim). **Good Shepherd:** Jesus Christ. **shepherd's clock:** (*Austral.*) The kookaburra. **shepherd's crook,** *n.* A long staff armed with an iron crook, used to catch or hold sheep. **shepherd's knot:** The tormentil. **shepherd's needle:** A plant, also called Venus's comb, *Scandix Pecten*; the cranes-bill. **shepherd's pie,** *n.* Cooked minced meat, covered with mashed potatoes and baked in an oven; (*Am.* hash). **shepherd's plaid,** *n.* Black-and white checked cloth. **shepherd's purse:** A common cruciferous weed, *Capsella bursa-pastoris*. **shepherd's rod:** The teasel. **shepherd's staff:** The common mullein. **shepherdess,** *n.* ***shepherdly,** *a.* **shepherdship,** *n.* **sheppy,** *n.* (*prov.*) A sheep-cote.

Sheraton (sher′ ȧ tȯn) [Thomas *Sheraton* (1751–1806)], *a.* Applied to furniture of a severe style designed and introduced into England by Sheraton towards the end of the 18th cent.

sherbet (shĕr′ bėt) [Pers., from Arab. *shariba*, to drink, cp. SYRUP], *n.* An oriental cooling drink, made of diluted fruit juices.

sherd [SHARD].

sherif (shė rēf′) [Arab. *sherif*, lofty], *n.* A descendant of Mohammed through his daughter Fatima and Hassan Ibn Ali; the chief magistrate of Mecca.

sheriff (sher′ if) [A.-S. *scīr-gerēfa* (SHIRE, REEVE (1))], *n.* The chief Crown officer of a county or shire charged with the keeping of the peace, the execution of writs, sentences, etc., the conduct of elections, etc., usu. called **high sheriff**; in London, Bristol, Norwich and Nottingham the sheriffs are civic authorities; (*Am.*) an elected county official responsible for keeping the peace, etc. **sheriff-clerk,** *n.* (*Sc.*) The registrar of the sheriff's court. **sheriff-deputy,** *n.* (*Sc.*) An officer appointed by the Crown acting as chief local judge in a county. **sheriff's officer,** (*Sc.*) **sheriff officer:** An officer appointed to execute the sheriff's writs, to distrain, etc. **sheriff-substitute,** *n.* (*Sc.*) The acting sheriff in a county or city who hears cases in the first instance subject to appeal to the sheriff-deputy. **sheriffalty, sheriffdom, sheriffhood, sheriffship,** *n.* [SHRIEVALTY].

Sherpa (shĕr′ pa), *n.* One of a mountaineering Tibetan people living in the Himalayas.

sherry, *sherris (sher′ i, -is) [*Xeres*, now Jerez de la Frontera, in Spain], *n.* A Spanish white wine from Xeres or S. Spain. **sherry-cobbler** [COBBLER].

Shetland (shet′ lȧnd) [group of islands to the north-east of Scotland], *n.* A Shetland pony. **Shetland lace:** An ornamental openwork trimming made of woollen yarn. **Shetland pony:** A very small variety of the horse with flowing mane and tail, peculiar to Shetland.

sheuch, sheugh (shu*ch*) [Sc. and North. var. of SOUGH (2)], *n.* A trench, ditch, or drain. *v.t.* To plough, to furrow.

sheva (shė va′) [Rabbinic Heb. *shewā*], *n.* The Hebrew sign (:) put under a consonant to denote the absence of a following vowel sound; (*Phon.*) a neutral vowel-sound.

shew, etc. (*Sc. and Bibl.*) [var. of SHOW].

shiah, shiite (shē′ ȧ, -īt) [Arab. *shi'a*, sect], *n.* A member of the great Mohammedan sect (cp. SUNNI, see SUNNA) who regard Ali as the first rightful imam or caliph and reject the three Sunni caliphs. **shiism,** *n.*

shibboleth (shib′ ō lėth) [Heb.], *n.* A word used as a test to distinguish the Ephraimites from the Gileadites, the former calling it *sibboleth* (Judges xii); (*fig.*) a criterion, test, or watchword of a party, etc.; an old-fashioned or discredited doctrine, etc.

shicer (shī′ sėr), *n.* (*Austral. colloq.*) A crook, a welsher; a useless mine.

shicker (shik′ ėr), *n.* (*Austral. colloq.*) Drink, excessive drinking.

shiel [SHIELING].

shield (shēld) [A.-S. *scild*, cp. Dut. and G. *schild*, Icel. *skjlödr*, perh. rel. to SHELL and SCALE (1)], *n.* A broad piece of defensive armour made of wood, leather, or metal, usu. carried on the left arm to protect the body, a buckler; a wooden screen or framework or a metal plate used in tunnelling, machinery, etc., as a protection to men working a gun, etc.; a shield-like part in an animal or a plant; (*Her.*) an escutcheon or field bearing a coat of arms; (*fig.*) defence, a protection, a defender; (*Am.*) a sheriff's or detective's badge. *v.t.* To screen or protect with or as with a shield. **shield-fern,** *n.* A fern of the genus *Aspidium* having shield-shaped covers protecting the fruit-dots. **shieldless,** *a.* **shieldlessly,** *adv.* ***shieldlessness,** *n.*

shieling (shē′ ling), **shiel** (shēl) [North. M.E. *shāle*, *schele*, perh. from Icel. *skjōl*, shelter, rel. to SKY], *n.* (*Sc.*) A hut used by shepherds, sportsmen, etc.; a small house or cottage; a piece of summer pasturage.

shier, shiest [SHYER, SHYEST, see SHY (1) and (2)].

shift (shift) [A.-S. *sciftan*, to divide (cp. Dut. *schiften*, Icel. *skipta*, Swed. *skifta*)], *v.t.* To move from one position to another; to change the position of; to change (one thing) for another; *to change (one's clothes). *v.i.* To move or be moved about; to change place or position; to change into a different place, form, state, etc.; to change one's dress; to resort to expedients, to do the best one can, to manage, to contrive; to prevaricate, to practise evasion. *n.* A shifting, a change of place, form, or character; a substitution of one thing for another, a vicissitude; a change of clothing; a relay of workmen; the period of time for which a shift of men work; a chemise; a device, a contrivance, an expedient; a dodge, a trick, an artifice, an evasion. **to make shift:** To manage, to contrive (to do, to get on, etc.). **to shift about:** To turn right round, to prevaricate; to be shifted from side to side. **to shift off:** To get rid of, to defer.

shiftable, *a.* **shifter,** *n.* **shiftingly,** *adv.* **shiftless,** *a.* Incompetent, incapable, without forethought. **shiftlessly,** *adv.* **shiftlessness,** *n.* **shifty,** *a.* Dishonest, sly, unreliable. **shiftily,** *adv.* **shiftiness,** *n.*

shiite, etc. [SHIAH].

shikar (shi kar′) [Hind.], *n.* Hunting, sport, game. **shikari, shikaree,** *n.* A hunter.

shillelagh (shi lē′ lȧ) [place in co. Wicklow, Ireland], *n.* (*Ang.-Ir.*) An oak or blackthorn sapling used as a cudgel.

shilling (shi′ ling) [A.-S. *scilling* (cp. Dut. *schelling,* G. *schilling,* Icel. *skillingr*), perh. from Teut. *skel-,* to divide, cp. SKILL], *n.* A British silver coin and money of account, equal in value to twelve pence or one-twentieth of a pound sterling. **to take the King's** or **Queen's shilling:** To enlist (with alln. to the former practice of giving recruits a shilling as token of a contract).

shilly-shally (shil′ i shăl′ i) [reduplicate of SHALL I], *v.i.* To act in an irresolute manner, to hesitate; to be undecided. *n.* Irresolution, hesitation; foolish trifling.

shilpit (shil′ pit) [Sc., etym. doubtful], *a.* Weak, insipid, washy (of drink); weakly, puny (of a person).

shily [SHYLY, see SHY (1)].

shim (shim) [etym. doubtful], *n.* A wedge, piece of metal, etc., used to tighten up joints, fill in spaces, etc. *v.t.* To fill in, wedge, or fit with this.

shimmer (shim′ ėr) [A.-S. *scymrian,* freq. of *scīmian,* to shine (cp. Dut. *schemeren,* G. *schimmern*)], *v.i.* To emit a faint or tremulous light; to glimmer, beam, or glisten faintly. *n.* A faint or tremulous light.

shimmy (*colloq.*) [CHEMISE].

shin (shin) [A.-S. *scinu* (cp. Dut. *scheen,* G. *schiene*), prob. cogn. with SKIN], *n.* The forepart of the human leg between the ankle and the knee. *v.i.* (*past & p.p.* **shinned**) To climb up (a tree, etc.) by means of the hands and legs alone; to trudge, to trot; (*Am. slang*) to borrow money in a hurry. *v.t.* To kick on the shins; to climb. **shin-bone,** *n.* The tibia. **shin-guard,** *n.* A padded guard for the shin worn at football, etc.

shindig (shin′ dig) [SHINDY], *n.* A social function, a ball or dance.

shindy (shin′ di) [perh. corr. of SHINNY or SHINTY], *n.* A row, a disturbance, a rumpus, a brawl.

shine (shīn) [A.-S. *scinan,* cp. Dut. *schijnen,* G. *scheinen,* Icel. *skīna*], *v.i.* (*past & p.p.* **shone,** shon) To emit or reflect rays of light; to be bright, to beam, to glow; to be brilliant, eminent, or conspicuous; to be lively or animated. *v.t.* (*past & p.p.* **shined**). To cause to shine, to make bright, to polish; (*Am.*) to clean shoes, etc. *n.* (*colloq.*) Fair weather, sunshine, brightness, lustre; (*slang*) a row, a shindy. **shiner,** *n.* One who or that which shines; (*slang*) a coin, esp. a sovereign; a popular name for several silvery fishes. **to take a shine to:** To like at first sight. **shiny,** *a.* **shininess,** *n.*

shingle (1) (shing′ gėl) [corr. of *shindle,* L. *scindula,* from *scindere,* to split (cp. G. *schindel*)], *n.* A thin piece of wood used as a roof-covering; a method of cutting a woman's hair. *v.t.* To roof with shingles; (*Hairdressing*) to trim a woman's hair to follow the lines of the head at the back. **shingler,** *n.* **shingling,** *n.* **shingly** (1), *a.*

shingle (2) (shing′ gėl) [cp. Norw. *singl*], *n.* Coarse rounded gravel on the seashore. **shingle-trap,** *n.* A groin. **shingly** (2), *a.*

shingles (shing′ gėlz) [O.F. *cengle,* L. *cingulum,* girth, from *cingere,* to gird], *n.pl.* A cutaneous disease, *Herpes zoster,* which spreads round the body like a girdle.

shingly [SHINGLE (1) and (2)].

shinny (shin′ i) [Sc. and North., perh. from the cry *shin ye*], *n.* A game resembling hockey; the club used in this.

shintiyan, -tyan (shin′ ti ȧn) [Arab.], *n.* The loose trousers worn by Mohammedan women.

Shinto (shin′ tō) [Jap., from Chin. *chin tao,* way of the gods], *n.* The religious belief of the people of Japan prior to the introduction of Buddhism; a species of nature- and hero-worship. **Shintoism,** *n.* **Shintoist,** *n.*

shinty (shin′ ti) [SHINNY], *n.* Shinny; a shindy.

shintyan [SHINTIYAN]. **shiny** [SHINE].

ship (ship) [A.-S. *scip* (cp. Dut. *schip,* G. *schiff,* Icel. *skip*), cogn. with SKIFF, Gr. *skaphos*], *n.* (*fem.*) A large sea-going vessel, esp. one with three or more square-rigged masts; (*Aviat. slang*) an aeroplane. *v.t.* (*past & p.p.* **shipped**) To put on board a ship; to send, take, or carry in a ship; to engage for service on board a ship; to fix (a mast, rudder, etc.) in the proper place on a ship; to send (goods) by any recognized means of conveyance. *v.i.* To embark on a ship; to engage for service as a sailor. **ship of the desert:** A camel. **ship of the line:** A warship suitable for taking its place in a line of battle. **ship-biscuit,** *n.* A hard coarse kind of bread or biscuit used on shipboard, hard-tack. **shipboard,** *n.* The deck or side of a ship. **on shipboard:** On board ship. **ship-breaker,** *n.* A contractor who breaks up old ships. **ship-broker,** *n.* One who transacts all necessary business for a ship when in port; a marine insurance agent. **shipbuilder,** *n.* A shipwright; a naval architect. **shipbuilding,** *n.* **ship-canal,** *n.* A canal along which ocean-going vessels can pass. **ship-chandler,** *n.* One who deals in cordage, canvas, and other commodities for fitting out ships. **ship-chandlery,** *n.* **ship-fever,** *n.* Typhus. **ship-load,** *n.* The quantity of cargo, passengers, etc., that a ship carries. **shipman,** *n.* A sailor; the captain or master of a ship. **shipmaster,** *n.* The master, captain, or commander of a vessel. **shipmate,** *n.* One who serves or sails in the same ship, esp. a fellow-sailor. **ship-money,** *n.* (*Hist.*) A tax formerly charged on the ports, towns, cities, boroughs, and counties of England for providing certain ships for the navy. **shipowner,** *n.* One who owns a ship or ships or shares therein. **ship-rigged,** *n.* Having three or more square-rigged masts. **shipshape,** *adv.* In a seaman-like manner, in good order. *a.* Well-arranged, neat, trim. **ship's husband,** *n.* One who attends to the repairs, provisioning, and other necessaries of a ship, a ship-broker. ***ship-tire,** *n.* A head-dress either shaped like a ship or having streamers, for women. **ship-way,** *n.* A timber structure forming an inclined way for building or launching ships. **shipworm,** *n.* A bivalve that bores into ship's timbers, piles, etc. **shipwreck,** *n.* The destruction or loss of a ship, by foundering, striking a rock, or other cause; (*fig.*) destruction, ruin. *v.t.* To cause to suffer shipwreck; to ruin. *v.i.* To suffer shipwreck; to be ruined. **shipwright,** *n.* A shipbuilder. **shipyard,** *n.* A yard, etc., where ships are built. **shipment,** *n.* The act of shipping; goods or commodities shipped, a consignment. **shipped,** *a.* Put on board a ship; *provided with ships. **shipper,** *n.* One who ships or sends goods by a common carrier.

shipping (ship′ ing), *a.* Pertaining to ships. *n.* The act of putting on board ship, sending goods, etc.; ships collectively, esp. the ships of a country or port; tonnage; sailing. **to take shipping:** To embark on board ship. **shipping-articles,** *n.pl.* Articles of agreement between the captain of a vessel and his crew as to wages, etc. **shipping-bill,** *n.* An invoice of goods shipped. **shipping-master,** *n.* An official superintending the signing of shipping articles, paying off of men, etc.

-ship [A.-S. *-scipe,* cogn. with SHAPE], *suf.* Denoting state, condition, the quality of being so-and-so; status, office, tenure of office; skill in the capacity specified; as in *fellowship, friendship, judgeship, ladyship, marksmanship, scholarship.*

shippo (ship′ ō) [Jap., from Chin. *ts'ih pao* (*ts'ih,* seven, *pao*, jewel)], *n.* Japanese cloisonné enamel ware.

shippon (shiɔ′ ŏn) [A.-S. *scypen* (SHOP, -EN)], *n.* (*prov.*) A cattle-shed, a byre.

shipshape, ship-way, ship-worm, shipwreck, shipwright, shipyard [SHIP].

shiralee (shi rȧ lē′) [Austral.], *n.* A swag, a tramp's bundle. **to hump a shiralee:** To carry a burden.

Shiraz (shi raz′) [city in Persia], *n.* A wine from Shiraz.

shire (shīr) [A.-S. *scīr*, etym. doubtful; not rel. to SHEAR (I) or SHARE (I)], *n.* A territorial division of Britain, a county. **the shires:** Midland counties noted for fox-hunting, esp. Leicestershire, Northamptonshire, and Rutland; the counties whose names end in '-shire.' **shireman,** *n.* An inhabitant of the shires; *a sheriff. **shire-horse,** *n.* A large breed of draught horse, orig. raised in the midland shires. **shire-moot,** *n.* (*Hist.*) A deliberative assembly of the people of a shire in Anglo-Saxon times; afterwards a county court held twice a year before the ealdorman, etc. ***shire-reeve,** *n.* A sheriff.

shirk (shĕrk) [prob. var. of SHARK], *v.t.* To avoid or get out of unfairly. *v.i.* To avoid the performance of work or duty. *n.* One who shirks. **shirker,** *n.* ***shirky,** *a.*

shirr (shĕr) [etym. doubtful], *n.* An elastic cord or thread inserted in cloth, etc., to make it elastic; a gathering or fulling. *v.t.* To draw (a sleeve, dress, etc.) into gathers by means of elastic threads; (*Am.*) to bake eggs in a buttered dish.

shirt (shĕrt) [from A.-S. *scyrte*, from *scort*, SHORT, or the cogn. Icel. *skyrta*, SKIRT], *n.* A loose garment of linen, cotton, wool, silk, or other material, extending from the neck to the thighs, and usu. showing at the collar and wristbands, worn by men and boys under the outer clothes; a woman's blouse with collar and cuffs; (*fig.*) a lining or inner casing. **boiled shirt:** (*slang*) A man's evening clothes. **Black Shirts:** Italian fascists, or their British imitators. **Brown Shirts:** German Nazis. **Red Shirts:** Soldiers of the Garibaldian campaigns in Italy. **in one's shirt sleeves:** With one's coat off. **shirt-front,** *n.* The part of a shirt covering the breast, esp. if stiffened and starched; a dicky. **shirt-waist,** *n.* A woman's shirt or blouse belted at the waist. **shirted,** *a.* **shirting,** *n.* **shirtless,** *a.* **shirty,** *a.* (*slang*) Cross, ill-tempered. **to put one's shirt on:** (*colloq.*) To bet all one has.

shit (shit) [O.N. *skita*, cp. Dut. *schijten*], *v.i.* (*vulg.*) (*past & p.p.* **shat**) To empty the bowels. *n.* Ordure, excrement.

shittim (shit′ im) [Heb.], *n.* The wood of the shittah tree (prob. an acacia) used in constructing the ark of the covenant and the tabernacle. **shittah,** *n.*

shive (shīv) [M.E. *schīve* (cp. Dut. *schijf*, G. *scheibe*, Icel. *skīfa*), see also SHEAVE (I)], *n.* (*prov.*) A thin slice; a thin fragment, a splinter, a billet, etc.; a flat cork, a thin bung.

shiver (I) (shiv′ ėr) [dim. of prec.], *n.* A small fragment, a sliver, a shive; a species of blue slate; (*Naut.*) a sheave, a pulley. *v.t.* and *i.* To break into shivers. **shiver-spar,** *n.* A slaty carbonate of lime. **shivery** (I), *a.*

shiver (2) (shiv′ ėr) [M.E. *chiveren*, perh. rel. to QUIVER (2), cp. Norw. and Swed. dial., *kippa*], *v.i.* To tremble or shake, as with fear, cold, or excitement. *n.* The act of shivering, a shivering movement. **the shivers:** A feeling or movement of horror; a chill, ague. **shiveringly,** *adv.* **shivery** (2), *a.*

shivoo (shi voo′) [Austral. slang], *n.* A party, an entertainment, a do.

shoal (I) (shōl) [var. of SHALLOW], *a.* Shallow, of little depth (of water). *n.* A shallow, a submerged sand-bank. *v.i.* To become shallower. **shoaly,** *a.* **shoaliness,** *n.*

shoal (2) (shōl) [A.-S. *scolu*, cp. SCHOOL (I)], *n.* A large number, a multitude, a crowd, esp. of fish moving together. *v.i.* To form a shoal or shoals (of fish).

shoat (shōt) [prob. var. of SHOT], *n.* (*Am.*) A young hog.

shock (I) (shok) [prob. through F. *choc*, from O.H.G. *scoc* (cp. Dut. *schok*, Icel. *skykkr*), cogn. with SHAKE], *n.* A violent collision of bodies, a concussion, an impact, a blow, a violent onset; a sudden and violent sensation, as that produced on the nerves by a discharge of electricity; (*Path.*) prostration brought about by a violent and sudden disturbance of the system; (*fig.*) a sudden mental agitation, a violent disturbance (of credit, etc.). *v.t.* To give a violent sensation of disgust, horror, or indignation to; to shake or jar by a sudden collision. *v.i.* To behave or appear in an improper or scandalous fashion; (*poet.*) to collide. **shock-absorber,** *n.* (*Motor.*) An apparatus to neutralize the shock of axle-springs on recoil. **shock tactics,** *n.pl.* (*Mil.*) Action relying on weight of impact. **shock therapy:** (*Med.*) The treatment of certain mental and other cases by administering an electric shock. **shock troops,** *n.pl.* (*Mil.*) Selected soldiers employed on tasks requiring exceptional endurance and courage. **shocker,** *n.* (*colloq.*) Something that shocks, esp. a sensational story; a staggering specimen or example of anything. **shocking,** *a.* Causing a shock; disgraceful; dreadful. **shockingly,** *adv.* **shockingness,** *n.*

shock (2) (shok) [cp. M.Dut. *shocke*, Swed. *shock*, prob. rel. to prec.], *n.* A collection of sheaves of grain, usu. twelve but varying in number. *v.i.* To collect sheaves into shocks.

shock (3) (shok) [prob. var. of SHAG, or rel. to prec.], *n.* A thick, bushy mass or head of hair; a dog with shaggy hair, esp. a poodle. *a.* Shaggy. **shock-dog,** *n.* **shock-headed,** *a.*

shocker, shocking [SHOCK (I)].

shod, *past & p.p.* [SHOE]

shoddy (shod′ i) [prob. from A.-S. *sceādan*, to SHED (I)], *n.* Fibre obtained from old cloth torn to pieces and shredded; inferior cloth made from a mixture of this with new wool, etc.; anything of an inferior, sham, or adulterated kind. *a.* Made of shoddy; inferior, not genuine, sham.

shoe (shoo) [A.-S. *sceō*, *scōh*, *scō* (cp. Dut. *schoen*, G. *schuh*, Icel. *skōr*, Swed. and Dan. *sko*)], *n.* An outer covering for the foot, esp. one distinguished from a boot by not coming up to the ankles; (*Am.*) a boot; a metallic rim or plate nailed to the hoof of a horse, ox, or ass, to preserve it from wear and damage; anything resembling a shoe in form or function, as a socket, ferrule, wheel-drag or parts fitted to implements, machinery, etc., to take friction, thrust, etc.; (*Rail.*) the apparatus by which a tractor collects current from a live rail. *v.t.* (*past & p.p.* **shod**) To furnish (esp. a horse) with shoes; to cover at the bottom or tip. **another pair of shoes:** A different matter or state of things altogether. **to be in another's shoes:** To be in another's place or plight. **to die in one's shoes:** To meet with a violent death, esp. by hanging. **dead man's shoes:** An inheritance; a position left vacant by death. **shoe-black,** *n.* A man or boy earning his living by cleaning the shoes of passers-by. **shoe-buckle,** *n.* A buckle for fastening a shoe over the instep. **shoe-horn,** *n.* A device to assist one in putting on a shoe. **shoe-lace,** *n.* A string of cotton, etc., for fastening on a shoe. **shoe-latchet,** *n.* (*Bibl.*) A string or strap for fastening a shoe. **shoe-leather,** *n.* Leather for making shoes; (*fig.*) shoes. **shoemaker,** *n.* **shoe-string,** *n.* A shoe-lace; (*colloq.*) an inadequate or barely adequate sum of money. **shoe-tie,** *n.* **shoeing,** *pres.p.* **shoeless,** *a.* **shoer,** *n.* One who makes or puts on shoes; a farrier.

shog (shog) [M.E. *shogge*, SHOCK (I)], *v.t.* (*prov.*) To shake, to agitate. *v.i.* To bump or jog (along); *to clear (off). *n.* A shake; a jerk.

shogun (shō′ gun) [Jap., general], *n.* The hereditary commander-in-chief of the army and virtual ruler of Japan under the feudal regime, abolished in 1868. **shogunate,** *n.*

shone, *past & p.p.* [SHINE].

shoo (shoo) [instinctive sound], *int.* Begone; be off. *v.t.* To drive (fowls, etc., away) by crying 'shoo.' *v.i.* To cry 'shoo.'

shook (1), *past* [SHAKE].

shook (2) (shuk) [prob. var. of SHOCK (2)], *n.* A set of staves and headings for a cask ready for setting up; a set of boards for a box, etc. *v.t.* To pack in shooks.

***shoon,** *n.pl.* [SHOE].

shoot (shoot) [A.-S. *scotian*, to shoot, dart, rush (intr.) *scēotan*, shoot or throw (tr.) (cp. Dut. *schieten*, G. *schiessen*, Icel. *skjōta*)], *v.i.* (*past & p.p.* **shot**) To dart, rush, or come (out, along, up, etc.) swiftly; to sprout, to put out buds, etc., to extend in growth; to protrude, to project, to jut out; to discharge a missile, esp. from a fire-arm; to hunt game, etc., thus. *v.t.* To propel, let fly, discharge, eject, or send with sudden force; to cause (a bow, fire-arm, etc.) to discharge a missile; to hit, wound, or kill with a missile from a bow, fire-arm, etc.; to hunt thus over (ground, an estate, etc.); to pass swiftly through, over, or down; to protrude, to push out; to put forth; (*Cinema.*) to take pictures; (*Football*) To kick at a goal. *n.* A young branch, sprout, or sucker; an inclined plane or trough down which water, goods, etc., can slide, a chute, a rapid; a place where rubbish can be shot; a shooting-party, match, or expedition, a hunt. **shoot!** *int.* (*Am.*) Speak out! Say it! **to shoot ahead:** To get swiftly to the front in running, swimming, etc. **to shoot the sun:** (*Naut.*) To take the sun's altitude at noon with a sextant. **shootable,** *a.* **shooter,** *n.* One who or that which shoots (*usu. in comb.*, as *six-shooter*); (*Cricket*) a ball that darts along the ground without bouncing. **shooting,** *n.* The act of discharging fire-arms or arrows; a piece of land rented for shooting game; the right to shoot over an estate, etc. **shooting-box,** *n.* A small house or lodge for use during the shooting season. **shooting-brake:** (*Motor.*) A car to carry passengers and luggage, etc. **shooting-iron,** *n.* (*Am. slang*) A fire-arm; a revolver. **shooting-gallery, shooting-range,** *n.* A piece of ground or an enclosed space with targets and measured ranges for practice with fire-arms. **shooting-star:** An incandescent meteor shooting across the sky. **shooting-stick,** *n.* A walking-stick that may be adapted to form a seat. **shot silk** [SHOT (1)].

shop (shop) [A.-S. *sceoppa*, stall, booth (cp. L.G. *schup*, med. O.H.G. *scopf*, whence F. *échoppe*)], *n.* A building in which goods are sold by retail, (*Am.* a store); a building in which a manufacture, craft, or repairing is carried on; (*fig.*) one's business, profession, etc., or talk about this; (*slang*) a berth, a job. *v.i.* (*past & p.p.* **shopped**) To visit shops for the purpose of purchasing goods. *v.t.* (*colloq.*) To discharge from employment; to inform against to the police. **the Shop:** (*slang*) The Royal Military Academy, Woolwich. **all over the shop:** (*colloq.*) Scattered around. **to shut up shop:** To give up doing something. **to talk shop:** To talk about one's occupation. **shop assistant,** *n.* One who serves in a retail shop. **shop-bell,** *n.* An automatic bell giving notice of the entry of a customer. **shop-board,** *n.* A bench on which work is done, esp. by tailors. **shop-boy, -girl,** *n.* One employed in a shop. **shopkeeper,** *n.* The owner of a shop, a tradesman who sells goods by retail. **shoplifter,** *n.* One who steals from a shop under pretence of purchasing. **shoplifting,** *n.* **shopman,** *n.* A shop-keeper or a man employed to assist in a shop. **shop steward,** *n.* A trade union's representative in a plant or department elected by the membership to carry out union duties, adjust grievances, collect dues, and solicit new members. He is usually an employee. **shop-walker,** *n.* A person employed in a large shop to direct customers, etc. **shop-worn,** *a.* Faded, soiled, etc., by exposure in a shop. **shopper,** *n.* **shopping,** *n.* **shoppy,** *a.*

shore (1) (shôr) [A.-S. *score*, from *sceran*, to SHEAR], *n.* The land on the borders of a large body of water, the sea, a lake, etc.; (*Law*) the land between high- and low-water marks. **shoreless,** *a.* **shoreward,** *a.* and *adv.*

shore (2) (shôr) [M.E. *schore* (cp. M.Dut. *schōre*, Dut. *schoor*, Icel. *skortha*), etym. doubtful], *n.* A prop, a stay; a support for a building or a vessel on the stocks. *v.t.* To support or hold (up) with shores. **shoring,** *n.*

shore (3), *past* [SHEAR].

shorl [SCHORL].

***shorling** (shôr′ ling) [SHORE (3) or SHORN, -LING], *n.* (*prov.*) A newly-shorn sheep; wool shorn from a living sheep, opp. to morling.

shorn, *p.p.* [SHEAR].

short (shôrt) [A.-S. *sceort*, cogn. with SHEAR (cp. L. *curtus*, CURT, Gr. *keirēin*, to cut)], *a.* Measuring little in linear extension, not long; not extended in time or duration, brief; below the average in stature, not tall; not coming up to a certain standard; deficient, scanty, defective, in want (of); breaking off abruptly; brief, concise, abrupt, curt; brittle, friable, crumbling or breaking easily; (*colloq.*) neat, undiluted; (*Phon. and Pros.*) not prolonged, unaccented (of vowels and syllables); (*Comm., Stock Exchange, etc.*) not having goods, stocks, etc., in hand at the time of selling; not in hand (of stocks, etc.), sold. *adv.* Abruptly, at once; so as to be short or deficient. *n.* A short syllable or vowel, or a mark (◡) indicating that a vowel is short; (*Elec.*) a short circuit; (*Cinema.*) a single-reel film. (*pl.*) small-clothes, breeches cut short at the knees; the bran and coarse part of meal mixed together. *v.t.* To shorten; to make of no effect. **in short:** Briefly, in few words. **the long and the short of it:** [LONG (1)]. **to come short:** To be deficient, to fail. **to cut** or **bring** or **pull up short:** To check or pause abruptly. **to fall short** [FALL]. **to run short:** To exhaust the stock in hand (of a commodity). **to sell short:** To sell (stocks) for future delivery. **to stop short:** To come to a sudden stop; to fail to reach the point aimed at. **to be taken short:** To be seized with sudden motion of the bowels. **shortbread, shortcake,** *n.* A brittle, dry cake made with much butter and sugar. **short circuit,** *n.* (*Elec.*) An accidental crossing of two conductors carrying a current by another conductor of negligible resistance, which shortens the route of the current. **short-circuit,** *v.t.* To form or introduce a short circuit; (*fig.*) to dispense with intermediaries. **short-coat,** *n.* (*in pl.*) Clothes worn by an infant when too old for long clothes; *v.t.* To put into short-coats. **short-coming,** *n.* A failure of performance of duty, etc.; a falling short of supply, produce, etc. **short-dated,** *a.* Having only a little time to run (of a bill, note, etc.). **short-handed,** *a.* Short of workmen, helpers, etc. **short-lived** (-livd), *a.* Not living or lasting long, brief. **short rib:** A false rib. **short sea:** Short broken waves. **short sight:** Inability to see clearly at a distance, myopia; (*fig.*) lack of foresight. **short-sighted,** *a.* **short-sightedly,** *adv.* **short-sightedness,** *n.* **short-spoken,** *a.* Curt and abrupt in speech. **short supply,** *n.* General shortage of a commodity. **short-tempered,** *a.* Having little self-control, irascible. **short-waisted,** *a.* Having the waist high up (of a dress). **short waves,** *n.pl.* (*Radio.*) Electro-magnetic waves of a wavelength of 50 metres or less. **short-winded,** *a.* Easily put out of breath. **short-windedness,** *n.* Affected with shortness of breath. **shortish,** *a.* **shortly,** *adv.* **shortness,** *n.*

shortage (shôrt′ ij), *n.* A deficiency; the amount of this.

shorten (shôr′ tėn), *v.t.* To make short in time, extent, etc.; to curtail; to reduce the amount (of sail spread); *v.i.* To become short, to contract. **shortener,** *n.* **shortening,** *n.*

shorthand (shôrt′ hănd), *n.* A system of contracted writing used for reporting, etc., stenography.

shorthorn (shôrt′ hôrn), *n.* One of a breed of cattle with short horns.

shot (1) (shot) [A.-S. *gesceot*, from *scēotan*, to SHOOT], *n.* A missile for a fire-arm, esp. a solid or non-explosive projectile; the act of shooting; the discharge of a missile from a fire-arm or other weapon; an attempt to hit an object with such a missile; (*Cinema.*) the film taken between the starting and stopping of the camera; (*fig.*) a stroke at various games; an attempt to guess, etc.; the distance reached by a missile, the range of a fire-arm, bow, etc.; a marksman; (*pl.* **shot**) a small lead pellet, a quantity of which are used in a charge or cartridge for shooting game. *a.* Having a changeable colour, as shot silk. *v.t.* (*p.p.* **shotted**) To load or weight with shot. **a shot in the arm:** (*Med.*) A hypodermic injection. **big shot,** *n.* (*colloq.*) An important person. **shot-belt,** *n.* A belt with pouches, etc., for carrying shot. **shot-gun,** *n.* A light gun for firing small-shot. **shot-hole,** *n.* A hole made by a shot. **shot-proof,** *a.* Impenetrable to shot. **shot silk:** Silk with warp and weft of different colours, chatoyant silk. **shot-tower,** *n.* A tower in which shot is made by pouring molten lead through a rotating sieve at the top and letting it fall into water at the bottom. **shot-window,** *n.* A window projecting from a wall.

shot (2) (shot) [var. of SCOT (1)], *n.* A reckoning. **shot-free** [SCOT-FREE].

***shotten** (shotn) [p.p. of SHOOT], *a.* Having ejected the spawn (of a herring, etc.); (*prov.*) curdled; sour.

shough [SHOCK (3)].

should, *past* [SHALL].

shoulder (shōl′ dėr) [A.-S. *sculdor* (cp. Dut. *schouder*, G. *schulter*, Swed. *skuldra*), etym. doubtful], *n.* The part of the body at which the arm, foreleg, or wing is attached to the trunk; (*fig., pl.*) one's power to sustain burdens, responsibility, etc.; (*pl.*) the upper part of the back; the fore-quarter of an animal cut up as meat; anything resembling a shoulder; a projecting part of a mountain, tool, etc.; (*Fort.*) the obtuse angle formed by the face and flank of a bastion; (*Am.*) the verge of a road. *v.t.* To push with the shoulder; to jostle, to make (one's way) thus; to take on one's shoulders; to accept a responsibility; (*Mil.*) to carry vertically (a rifle, etc.) at the side of the body. **shoulder to shoulder:** (Standing in rank) with shoulders nearly touching (of soldiers); (*fig.*) with hearty co-operation, with mutual effort. **shoulder-belt,** *n.* A baldric, bandolier, etc., passing across the shoulder. **shoulder-blade, -bone,** *n.* The scapula. **shoulder-brace,** *n.* An arrangement of straps for correcting a child's tendency to stoop. ***shoulder-clapper,** *n.* One who claps another on the shoulder, a bailiff. **shoulder-knot,** *n.* An ornamental knot of ribbons, etc., worn on the shoulder by livery servants. **shoulder-of-mutton sail:** A triangular fore-and-aft sail with a boom at the bottom. ***shoulder-shotten, -slipped,** *a.* Strained in the shoulder. **shoulder-slip,** *n.* **shoulder-strap,** *n.* A strap worn over the shoulder, esp. by soldiers, bearing the initials or number of the regiment, etc.; one of two strips of cloth that suspend a garment from the shoulders. **shouldered,** *a.* Having shoulders (*usu. in comb.*, as *broad-shouldered*).

shout (shout) [etym. doubtful], *n.* A loud, vehement, and sudden call or outcry of joy, triumph, or the like. *v.i.* To utter a loud cry or call; to speak at the top of one's voice; (*Austral. colloq.*) to buy a round of drinks. *v.t.* To utter with a shout; to say at the top of one's voice. **shouter,** *n.*

shove (shŭv) [A.-S. *scūfan*, cp. Dut. *schuiven*, G. *schieben*, Icel. *skūfa*], *v.t.* To push, to move forcibly along; to push against, to jostle. *v.i.* To push; to make one's way (along, etc.) by pushing; to jostle. *n.* A strong or hard push. **to shove off:** To push off from the shore, etc.; (*slang*) to go away.

shovel (shŭv′ ėl) [A.-S. *scofl* (*scof-*, base of prec., -LE)], *n.* An implement, usu. resembling a broad spade, consisting of a wide blade with a handle, used for shifting loose material. *v.t.* (*past & p.p.* **shovelled**) To shift, gather together, or take up and throw with a shovel. **shovel-hat,** *n.* A hat with a broad brim turned up at the sides, worn by English Church dignitaries. **shovel-head, -nose,** *n.* A popular name for kinds of sturgeon, sharks, etc. **shovelful,** *n.* **shoveller,** *n.* One who shovels; the spoon-bill duck, *Spatula clypeata.*

shovel-board (shŭv′ ėl bôrd) [orig. *shoveboard*], *n.* A game played (now usu. on a ship's deck) by shoving wooden disks with the hand or a mace towards marked compartments.

show, shew (shō) [A.-S. *scēawian*, to see, to point out (sp. Dut. *schouwen*, G. *schauen*, Dan. *skue*), cogn. with L. *cavēre*, to take heed, Gr. *koein*, to observe], *v.t.* (*past & p.p.* **shown, *showed**) To cause or allow to be seen, to disclose, to offer to view, to exhibit, to expose, to reveal; to give, to bestow, to offer; to make clear, to point out, to explain, to demonstrate, to prove; to cause (a person) to see or understand; to conduct (round or over a house, etc.). *v.i.* To become visible or noticeable, to appear; to have a specific appearance. *n.* The act of showing; outward appearance, semblance, pretence; display, ostentation, parade, pomp; a spectacle, a pageant, a display, an entertainment, an exhibition, esp. one of a petty kind shown for money; (*slang*) an opportunity, a chance, a concern, a business. **to give one a fair show:** To let one have a chance. **to show fight:** Not to give in without resistance. **to give the show away:** To let out the real nature of something pretentious; to blab. ***to show forth:** To display, to make manifest. **to show off:** To set off, to show to advantage; to make a display of oneself, one's talents, etc. **to show up:** To expose; to be clearly visible; to be present. **to show one's hand:** (*fig.*) To disclose one's designs (orig. of cards). **show-boat,** *n.* A Mississippi steamboat fitted as a theatre. **show-bread, shew-bred,** *n.* Twelve loaves (one for each tribe) displayed by the Jewish priests in the Temple, and renewed every Sabbath. **show-case,** *n.* A glass case for exhibiting specimens, articles on sale, etc. **show-down,** *n.* (*colloq.*) A revelation of the true facts. **show-girl,** *n.* An actress chosen for her looks rather than her ability. **showman,** *n.* The manager or proprietor of a menagerie, circus, etc. **showmanship,** *n.* The showman's art; the ability to display goods, etc., most attractively. **show-place,** *n.* A place tourists, etc., go to see. **show-room,** *n.* A room where goods are set out for inspection. **show-window,** *n.* **shower** (1), *n.* **showing,** *n.* **showy,** *a.* Ostentatious, gaudy. **showily,** *adv.* **showiness,** *n.*

shower (2) (shou′ ėr) [A.-S. *scūr*, cp. Dut. *schoer*, G. *schauer*, Icel. *skūr*], *n.* A fall of rain, hail, or snow of short duration; a brief fall of arrows, bullets, etc.; a copious supply (of). *v.t.* To sprinkle or wet with a shower; to discharge or deliver in a shower. *v.i.* To fall in a shower. **shower-bath,** *n.* A bath in which a shower of water descends on one's head from a sprayer. **showerless,** *a.* **showery,** *a.* **showeriness,** *n.*

shram (shrăm) [cp. A.-S. *scrimman*, to be drawn up (of limbs)], *v.t.* (*prov., in p.p.*) To benumb or cause to shrink (of cold).

shrank, *past* [SHRINK].

shrapnel (shrăp′ nėl) [Gen. Henry Shrapnel (1761–1842), inventor], *n.* Bullets enclosed in a shell with a small charge for bursting in front of the enemy and spreading in a shower; shell-splinters from a high-explosive shell.

shred (shred) [A.-S. *screade* (cp. M.Dut. *schroode*, G. *schrot*), doublet of SCREED], *n.* A piece torn off; a strip, a rag, a fragment, a bit, a tiny particle. *v.t.* (*past & p.p.* **shredded**) To tear or cut into shreds. **shredding,** *n.* **shredless,** *a.* **shreddy,** *a.*

shrew (shroo) [A.-S. *scrēawa*, shrew-mouse], *n.* A bad-tempered, scolding woman, a virago; a shrew-mouse. **shrew-mole,** *n.* A N. American mole of the genus *Scalops* or *Scapanus*. **shrew-mouse,** *n.* A small nocturnal insectivorous mammal, *Sorex vulgaris*. **shrewish,** *a.* **shrewishly,** *adv.* **shrewishness,** *n.*

shrewd (shrood) [M.E. *schrewed*, p.p. of *schrewen*, to curse, as prec.], *a.* Astute, sagacious, discerning; *wicked, vixenish, shrewish, troublesome, spiteful. **shrewdly,** *adv.* **shrewdness,** *n.*

shriek (shrēk) [var. of SCREECH], *v.i.* To utter a sharp, shrill, inarticulate cry; to scream, to screech, as in a sudden fright; to laugh wildly. *v.t.* To utter with a shriek. *n.* A sharp, shrill, inarticulate cry. **shrieker,** *n.*

shrievalty (shrē′ vȧl ti) [SHERIFF, *-alty*, as in COMMONALTY], *n.* The office or jurisdiction of a sheriff; the tenure of this. ***shrieve,** *n.* A sheriff.

shrift (shrift) [A.-S. *scrift*, from *scrīfan*, to SHRIVE], *n.* Confession to a priest; (*fig.*) absolution, esp. of one about or appointed to die. **short shrift:** Summary treatment.

shrike (shrīk) [A.-S. *scrīc*, cp. SCREECH, from its cry], *n.* A bird of the family *Laniidæ*, especially *Lanius colluris*, the butcher-bird, feeding on insects and small birds, and having the habit of impaling them on thorns for future use.

shrill (shril) [cp. SKIRL, L.G. *schrell*, G. dial. *schrill*], *a.* High-pitched and piercing in tone, sharp, acute; noisy, importunate. *n.* A shrill sound. *v.i.* To utter a piercing sound; to sound shrilly. *v.t.* To cause to utter in a shrill tone. **shrill-gorged, -tongued, -voiced,** *a.* **shrillness,** *n.* **shrilly** (shril′ li), *adv.*

shrimp (shrimp) [cogn. with SCRIMP and SHRINK], *n.* A slender long-tailed edible crustacean, allied to the prawn; (*fig.*) a dwarfish person. **shrimper,** *n.*

shrine (shrīn) [A.-S. *scrin*, L. *scrīnium*, writing-chest, cogn. with *scribere*, to write], *n.* A chest or casket in which sacred relics were deposited; a tomb, altar, chapel, etc., of special sanctity; (*fig.*) a place hallowed by its associations. *v.t.* To place in a shrine.

shrink (shringk) [A.-S. *scrincan*, cp. M.Dut. *schrinken*, Swed. *skrynka*], *v.i.* (*past* **shrank,** *p.p.* **shrunk,** *part.a.* **shrunken**) To grow smaller, to contract, to shrivel; to give way, to recoil; to flinch. *v.t.* To cause to shrink, to make smaller. **to shrink on:** To put (a tire, etc.) on in a heated condition so that it may become firmly fixed in contracting. **shrinkable,** *a.* **shrinkage,** *n.* **shrinker,** *n.* **shrinking,** *n.* **shrinkingly,** *adv.*

shrive (shrīv) [A.-S. *scrīfan*, from L. *scribere*, to write], *v.t.* (**past* **shrove,** **p.p.* **shriven**) To receive the confession of; to confess, impose penance on, and absolve; to confess (oneself) and receive absolution. *v.i.* To confess, impose penance, and administer absolution. ***shriver,** *n.* A confessor. **shriving time:** Time in which to make confession.

shrivel (shriv′ ėl) [cogn. with Swed. dial. *skryvla*], *v.i.* To contract, to wither, to become wrinkled. *v.t.* To cause to contract or become wrinkled. **shrivelling,** *pres.p.*

shriven, shriver, shriving time [SHRIVE].

shroff (shrof) [corr. of *sarof*, Pers. and Hind. *çarāf*, from *çarafa*, to exchange], *n.* An East-Indian banker or money-changer. *v.t.* To examine (coins) and separate the good from the debased.

shroud (shroud) [A.-S. *scrūd* (cp. Icel. *skrūth*, Dan., Norw., and Swed. *skrud*), cogn. with SHRED], *n.* A winding sheet; (*fig.*) anything that covers or conceals; (*Naut.*, *pl.*) ropes extending from the lower mast-heads to the sides of the ship, serving to steady the masts; (*Aviat.*) the ropes from a parachute to its burden. *v.t.* To dress for the grave; (*fig.*) to cover, disguise, or conceal. **shroudless,** *a.* ***shroudy,** *a.* Affording shelter.

shrove, **past* [SHRIVE].

Shrovetide (shrōv′ tīd), *n.* The period before Lent, when people went to confession, and afterwards made merry. **Shrove Tuesday:** The day before Ash Wednesday. **shroving,** *n.* The festivities of Shrovetide.

***shrow** [SHREW].

shrub (1) (shrŭb) [Arab. *sharāb* or *shurb*, drink], *n.* A drink composed of the sweetened juice of lemons or other fruit with spirit.

shrub (2) (shrŭb) [A.-S. *scrybb*, cp. Norw. *skrubba*, SCRUB], *n.* A woody plant smaller than a tree with branches proceeding directly from the ground without any supporting trunk. **shrubbery,** *n.* A plantation of shrubs. **shrubby,** *a.* **shrubbiness,** *n.* **shrubless,** *a.*

shrug (shrŭg) [cp. Dan. *skrugge*, Swed. *skrukka*, cogn. with SHRINK], *v.t.* (*past & p.p.* **shrugged**) To draw up (the shoulders) to express dislike, doubt, etc. *v.i.* To draw up the shoulders. *n.* This gesture.

shrunk, *p.p.*, **shrunken,** *p.p.* and *a.* [SHRINK].

shuck (shŭk) [etym. doubtful], *n.* (*chiefly Am.*) A shell, husk, or pod; (*pl.*) something utterly valueless. *v.t.* To remove the shell, etc., from. **shuck off:** To strip off. **shucker,** *n.* **shucks,** *int.* Expressive of contempt, etc.

shudder (shŭd′ ėr) [M.E. *schuderen*, cp. M.Dut. *schudden*, E.Fris. *schüdden*, G. *schüttern*], *v.i.* To shiver suddenly as with fear; to tremble, to quake, to shrink. *n.* A sudden shiver or trembling. **shudderingly,** *adv.*

shuffle (shŭf′ ėl) [var. of SCUFFLE], *v.t.* To shift or shove to and fro or from one to another; to move (cards) over each other so as to mix them up; to mix (up), to throw into disorder; to put aside, to throw (off); to put or throw (on) hastily. *v.i.* To change the relative positions of cards in a pack; to shift ground; to prevaricate; to move (along) with a dragging gait. *n.* The act of shuffling; a shuffling movement of the feet, etc.; the shuffling of cards; a mix-up, a general change of position; an evasive or prevaricating piece of conduct. **shuffle-cap,** *n.* A game in which money is shaken in a cap. **shuffler,** *n.* **shufflingly,** *adv.*

shun (shŭn) [A.-S. *scunian*, etym. doubtful], *v.t.* (*past & p.p.* **shunned**) To avoid, to eschew, to keep clear of.

shunt (shŭnt) [from prov., to turn aside, M.E. *shunten*, A.-S. *scyndan*, to hasten], *v.t.* To turn (a train, etc.) on to a side track; (*fig.*) to get rid of, suppress, or defer discussion or consideration of; to get (a person) out of the way, or keep (a person) inactive. *v.i.* To turn off on to a side track (of a train, etc.). *n.* The act of shunting; (*Elec.*) a conductor joining two points of a circuit through which part of the current may be diverted. **shunter,** *n.*

shut (shŭt) [A.-S. *scyttan*, cogn. with SHOOT, from shooting the bolt], *v.t.* (*past & p.p.* **shut**) To close by means of a door, lid, cover, etc.; to cause (a door, lid, cover, etc.) to close an aperture; to keep (in or out) by closing a door; to bar (out), to exclude, to keep from entering or participating in; to bring (teeth, etc.) together. *v.i.* To become closed; to come together (of teeth, scissor-blades, etc.). **to shut down:** To pull or push down (a window-sash, etc.); to stop working (of a factory). **to shut in:** To confine; to encircle; to prevent egress or prospect from. **to shut off:** To stop the inflow or escape of (gas, etc.) by closing a tap, etc.; to separate. **to shut out:** To exclude, to bar out; to prevent the possibility of. **to shut to:** To close (a door); to shut (of a door). **to shut up:** To close all the doors, windows, etc., of a house; to close and fasten up (a box, etc.); to put away in a box, etc.; to confine; (*colloq.*) to stop, to make an end; to confute, to silence. **shut up!** (*int.*) Be quiet! Stop talking!

shutter (shŭt′ er), *n.* One who or that which shuts; a cover of wooden battens, or panels, or metal slats for sliding, folding, rolling, or otherwise fastening over a window to exclude light, burglars, etc.; a device for admitting and cutting off light to a photographic lens; (*Cinema.*) a device in the camera, and in the projector, for cutting off light while the film is moved intermittently; a contrivance for closing the swell-box of an organ. **shutterless,** *a.*

shuttle (shŭt′ ėl) [A.-S. *scyttel*, bolt, cogn. with SHUT and SHOOT], *n.* A boat-shaped contrivance enclosing a bobbin used by weavers for passing the thread of the weft between the threads of the warp; the sliding holder carrying the lower thread for making lock-stitches in a sewing machine. **shuttle service:** (*Transport*) Rail or other service running to and fro between two points. **shuttlewise,** *adv.*

shuttlecock (shŭt′ ėl kok), *n.* A cork stuck with feathers which is struck to and fro with a battledore; the game of battledore and shuttlecock.

shy (1) (shī) [A.-S. *scēoh*, cp. Dan. *shy*, Dut. *schuw*, G. *scheu*], *a.* (*comp.* **shyer** (1), **shier,** *sup.* **shyest, shiest**) Easily frightened, fearful, timid; bashful, coy, shrinking from approach or familiarity; wary, cautious, suspicious; circumspect, careful, watchful (of); difficult to secure, understand, etc., elusive. *adv.* Short of, lacking. *v.i.* To start or turn aside suddenly (of a horse). *n.* The act of shying. **shyly,** *adv.* **shyness,** *n.*

shy (2) (shī) [etym. doubtful], *v.t.* and *i.* (*colloq.*) To fling, to throw. *n.* The act of shying. **shyer** (2), *n.*

shyster (shī′ stėr), *n.* A tricky or disreputable lawyer, esp. one who hangs about the lower courts, etc., to exploit petty criminals, etc.; (*colloq.*) a tricky person.

si (sē) [perh. from initials of *Sanctus Johannes*, see GAMUT], *n.* The seventh note of the diatonic scale.

sialogenous (sī å loj′ e nŭs) [as foll.], *a.* Resembling saliva.

sialogogue (sī′ å lō gōg) [F. (Gr. *sialon*, saliva, *agōgos*, leading, from *agein*, to lead)], *n.* (*Med.*) A medicine promoting salivary discharge. **sialoid,** *a.* Resembling saliva. **sialorrhœa** (-rē′ å), *n.* Excessive flow of saliva.

siamang (sī′ å măng) [Malay], *n.* A gibbon from the Malay peninsula and Sumatra.

Siamese (sī å mēz′), *a.* Of or pertaining to Siam or Thailand. *n.* A native of Siam; the Siamese language; (*collect.*) the Siamese people.

sib (sib) [A.-S., from *sib*, *sibb*, relationship, peace (cp. Icel. *sif*, G. *sippe*, affinity)], *a.* Related, akin. *n.* A brother or sister. **sibling,** *n.* One of two or more children having one or both parents in common. **sibship,** *n.* Being children of the same two parents.

Siberian (sī bēr′ i ån) [*Siberia*, -AN], *a.* Of or pertaining to Siberia. *n.* A native of Siberia.

sibilant (sib′ i lånt) [L. *sībilans -ntem*, pres.p. of *sībilāre*, from *sībilus*, a hissing, prob. imit. in orig.], *a.* Hissing; having a hissing sound. *n.* A letter which is pronounced with a hissing sound, as *s* or *z*. **sibilance, sibilancy,** *n.* **sibilate,** *v.t.* and *i.* **sibilation** (-lā′ shŭn), *n.*

sibling, sibship [SIB].

sibyl (sib′ il) [L. *Sibylla*, Gr. *Sibulla*, prob. rel. to L. *sapere*, to be wise], *n.* One of a number of women who prophesied in ancient times under the supposed inspiration of a deity; a prophetess, a sorceress; (*fig.*) a fortune-teller, a gipsy, an old hag. **sibylline** (si bil′ īn), *a.* Pertaining to or composed or uttered by a sibyl; prophetic, oracular, cryptic, mysterious. **sibylline books** or **oracles:** A collection of oracles of mysterious origin preserved by the ancient Romans and consulted by the senate in times of calamity or emergency. **sibyllism** (sib′ i lizm), *n.* **sibyllist,** *n.* **sibyllistic** (-lis′ tik), *a.*

sic (1) (*Sc.*) [SUCH].

sic (2) (sik) [L.], *adv.* Thus, so (usu. printed after a doubtful word or phrase to indicate that it is quoted exactly as in the original).

Sicanian (si kā′ ni ån) [L. *Sīcanius*, from *Sicāni*, pl., Gr. *Sikanoi*], *n.* One of the aboriginal inhabitants of Sicily, found there by the Sicels. *a.* Of or pertaining to them.

siccative (sik′ å tiv) [late L. *siccātivus*, from L. *siccāre*, to dry, from *siccus*, dry], *a.* Drying, causing to dry. *n.* A siccative substance, esp. one used with oil-paint. **siccity** (sik′ si ti), *n.* Absence of moisture; aridity, dryness.

sice (1) (sīs) [O.F. *sis*, SIX], *n.* The number six on dice.

sice (2) [SYCE]. ***sich** [SUCH].

Sicel (sis′ ėl), **Siculian** (si kū′ li ån) [Gr. *Sikeloi*, and Gr. *Sikuli*, pl.], *n.* A member of a race supposed to have entered Sicily about the 11th cent. B.C., a native as dist. from a Greek ancient Sicilian. *a.* Of or pertaining to the Sicels. **Siceliot** (si sel′ i ŏt), *n.* An ancient Greek settler in Sicily; *a.* Of or pertaining to the Siceliots. **Siculo-,** *comb. form.*

Sicilian (si sil′ i ån), *a.* Of or pertaining to Sicily or its inhabitants; *n.* A native of Sicily. **Sicilian Vespers:** A great massacre of the French in Sicily, which began at the first stroke of the vesper bell on Easter Monday in 1282. **siciliana** (si sil i a′ nå) [It.], *n.* A graceful dance of the Sicilian peasantry; the music for it. **sicilienne** (-en′) [F.], *n.* A fine ribbed silk or poplin.

sick (1) (sik) [A.-S. *sēoc*, cp. Dut. *ziek*, G. *siech*, Icel. *sjūkr*, Dan *syg*], *a.* Ill, affected by some disease, in bad health; affected with nausea, inclined to vomit; tending to cause sickness; disgusted, feeling disturbed, upset, pining (for, etc.); tired of; needing repair (of a ship); set apart for sick persons (of a room, quarters, etc.). *n.pl.* Those who are ill. **to be or feel sick:** To vomit or be inclined to vomit. **sick-bed,** *n.* A bed occupied by one who is ill; (*fig.*) the state of being ill. **sick benefit,** *n.* An allowance made by a club or trade union to a worker in case of illness. ***sick-brained,** *a.* Disordered in the brain. ***sick-fallen,** *a.* Struck down with sickness. **sick-leave,** *n.* Leave of absence on account of illness. **sick-list,** *n.* A list of persons, esp. in a regiment, ship, etc., laid up by sickness. **on the sick-list:** Laid up by illness. **sicken,** *v.i.* To grow ill, to show symptoms of illness; to feel disgust (at). *v.t.* To make sick; to affect with nausea; to disgust. **sickener,** *n.* **sickening,** *a.* Disgusting, offensive; (*colloq.*) annoying. **sickeningly,** *adv.* **sickish** (sik′ ish), *a.* **sickishly,** *adv.* **sickishness,** *n.* **sickly,** *a.* Habitually indisposed, weak in health, invalid, marked by sickness; languid, faint, weakly-looking; nauseating, mawkish. *adv.* In a sick manner. *v.t.* To make sickly; to give a sickly appearance to. **sickliness,** *n.* **sickness,** *n.*

sick (2) (sik) [SEEK], *v.t.* To incite to chase or attack, to urge to set upon.

sicker (sik′ ėr) [A.-S. *sicor*, ult. from L. *sēcūrus*, SECURE], *a.* (*now Sc.*) Sure, certain, firm. *adv.* Surely; certainly. *v.t.* To make sure or certain. ***sickerly,** *adv.*

sickle (sik′ ėl) [A.-S. *sicol*, L. *secula*, cogn. with *secāre*, to cut], *n.* An implement with a long curved blade set on a short handle, used for reaping, lopping, etc.; a reaping-hook. **sickle-bill,** *n.* A bird of various species with a sickle-shaped bill. **sickle-feather,** *n.* One of the long curved feathers of a cock's tail. **sickle-man,** *n.* **sickled,** *a.*

sickly, sickness [SICK (1)].

Siculian, etc. [SICEL].

Sida (sī′ då) [Gr. *sidē*], *n.* A genus of plants containing the Indian mallows, many of which yield fibre used for cordage, etc.

side (sīd) [A.-S. *sīde* (cp. Dut. *zijde*, G. *seite*, Icel. *sītha*), prob. rel. to *sīd*, spacious], *n.* One of the bounding surfaces (or lines) of a material object, esp. a more or less vertical inner or outer surface (as of a building, a room, a natural object, etc.); such a surface as dist. from the top and bottom, back and front, or the two ends; the part of an object, region, etc., to left or right of its main axis or part facing one; either surface of a plate, sheet, layer, etc.; the part of a person or animal on the right hand or left, esp. that between the hip and shoulder; direction or position, esp. to right or left, in relation to a person or thing; an aspect or partial view of a thing; one of two opposing bodies, parties, or sects; one of the opposing views or causes represented by them; line of descent through father or mother; (*Billiards*) a twist or spin given to the ball; (*slang*) swagger, bumptiousness, swank. *v.i.* To take part with, to put oneself on the side of. *a.* Situated at or on the side, lateral; being from or towards the side, oblique, indirect. **to choose sides:** To select parties for competition in a game. **side-arms,** *n.pl.* Weapons as swords or bayonets carried at the side. **side-band,** *n.* (*Radio.*) The band of frequencies on either side of the carrier frequency, caused by modulation. **sideboard,** *n.* A flat-topped table or cabinet placed at the side of a room to support decanters, dining utensils, etc. **side-bone,** *n.* One of the small bones under the wings of a fowl, easily separated in carving; ossification of the cartilage in the pasterns of a horse. **side-burns,** *n.pl.* (*Am.*) Short whiskers. **side-car,** *n.* A small jaunting-car; (*Motor.*) a car with seats attached to the side of a motor-cycle; a kind of cocktail. **side-dish,** *n.* A supplementary dish at dinner, etc. **side-issue,** *a.* A subsidiary matter. **side-light,** *n.* Light admitted into a building, etc., from the side; (*fig.*) an incidental illustration (of a subject, etc.). **side-line,** *n.* An incidental branch of business. **side-note,** *n.* A marginal note as dist. from a foot-note. **side-piercing,** *a.* Heart-rending. **side-saddle,** *n.* A saddle, esp. for a woman, for sitting sideways on a horse. **side-show,** *n.* A subordinate show, business affair, etc. **side-slip,** *n.* A skid; a slip or shoot from a plant; (*fig.*) an illegitimate child; (*Aviat.*) a movement of an aeroplane downwards and outwards from its true course; (*Theat.*) a groove at the wings for moving scenery on and off the stage. *v.i.* To skid, to slip sideways (esp. of bicycles and motor-cars). **sidesman,** *n.* A church officer assisting the churchwarden. **side-splitting,** *a.* Convulsing (of laughter, a joke, etc.). **side-splitter,** *n.* **side-step,** *n.* A step or movement to one side; a step at the side of a carriage, etc. **side-stroke,** *n.* A stroke delivered sideways or upon the side of a thing. **side-track,** *n.* (*chiefly Am.*) A siding. *v.t.* To turn into a siding, to shunt; (*fig.*) to get rid of, to shelve, to defer indefinitely. **side-view,** *n.* A view from the side, a profile. **side-walk,** *n.* (*chiefly Am.*) A pavement at the side of the road. **side-wind,** *n.* A wind from the side; (*fig.*) an indirect influence, agency, etc. **sided,** *a.* (*usu. in comb.*, as *many-sided*). **sidedly,** *adv.* **sidedness,** *n.* **sideless,** *a.* ***sideling,** *a.* Sloping, slanting, inclined; *n.* A slope. *adv.* Sideways; obliquely; indirectly. **sidelong,** *adv.* Obliquely; laterally. *a.* Oblique. **sider,** *n.* One who sides with a particular party, etc. **sideward,** *adv.* and *a.* **sidewards,** *adv.* **sideways, sidewise,** *adv.* **siding,** *a.* Taking sides. *n.* The act of taking sides; a short line of metals beside a railway line used for shunting and joining this at one end.

sidereal (sī dēr′ i ȧl) [L. *sīderius*, from *sīdus -deris*, star], *a.* Pertaining to the fixed stars or the constellations; starry; measured or determined by the apparent motion of the stars. **sidereal day:** The time between two successive upper culminations of a fixed star or of the vernal equinox, about four minutes shorter than the solar day. **sidereal month:** The mean period required by the moon to make a circuit among the stars, amounting to 27·32166 days. **sidereal time:** Time as measured by the apparent diurnal motion of the stars. **sidereal year:** The time occupied by a complete revolution of the earth round the sun, longer than the tropical year. **sideral** (sī′ dėr ȧl), *a.* Sidereal.

siderite (sid′ ėr īt, sī dēr′ īt) [F., from L. and G. *sidērītēs*, from *sidēros*, iron], *n.* (*Min.*) A rhombohedral carbonate of iron; an iron meteorite; a blue variety of quartz.

siderography (sid ėr-, sī dėr og′ rȧ fi) [Gr. *sidēros*, iron, -GRAPHY], *n.* The art or process of engraving on steel. **siderographic, -al** (-grăf′ ik, -al), *a.* **siderographist** (-og′ rȧ fist), *n.*

siderolite (sid′ ėr ō līt, sīd′ ėr-), *n.* A meteorite consisting partly of stone and partly of iron.

sideromancy (si′ dėr ō măn si), *n.* Divination by means of straws burnt on red-hot iron.

sideroscope (si′ dėr ō skōp). *n.* An instrument for detecting minute degrees of magnetism.

siderostat (si′ dėr ō stăt), *n.* An astronomical instrument by which a star under observation is kept within the field of the telescope. **siderostatic,** *a.*

sideroxylon (sid ėr oks′ i lon), *n.* (*Bot.*) A genus of tropical trees and shrubs of the family *Sapotaceæ*, with very hard and heavy wood.

siding [SIDE].

sidle (sī′ dėl) [back-formation, from SIDELING], *v.i.* To go or move sideways; (*fig.*) to fawn, to cringe.

siege (sēj) [M.E. and A.-F. *sege*, O.F. *siege*, ult. from L. *sedes*, seat], *n.* The process of besieging or the state of being besieged; the operations of an army before or round a fortified place to compel surrender; a seat, a fixed place or station; *excrement. **siege-basket,** *n.* A gabion. **siege-gun,** *n.* A heavy cannon adapted for breaching fortifications, etc. **siege-piece,** *n.* A siege-gun; a coin issued at a place in a state of siege. **siege-train,** *n.* Artillery and other materials carried by an army for siege purposes.

Sienese (sē ė nēz′), *a.* Of or pertaining to Siena, a city of Italy. *n.* A native of Siena; a member of the Sienese school of painters (13th and 14th cents.).

sienite [SYENITE].

sienna (si en′ ȧ) [It. *terra di Siena*, earth of Siena], *n.* A pigment composed of a native clay coloured with iron and manganese, known as raw or burnt sienna according to the mode of preparation.

sierra (si er′ ȧ) [Sp., from L. *serra*, saw], *n.* A long serrated mountain-chain; (*Astron.*) a chromosphere.

siesta (si es′ tȧ) [Sp., from L. *sexta hora*, sixth hour], *n.* A short midday sleep, esp. in hot countries.

sieve (siv) [A.-S. *sife*, cp. Dut. *zeef*, G. *sieb*], *n.* An instrument for separating the finer particles of substances from the coarser by means of meshes or holes through which the former pass and the others are retained; a coarse-plaited basket; (*fig.*) a talkative or indiscreet person. *v.t.* To sift.

siffle (sif′ ėl) [F. *siffler*, late L. *siffilāre*, form of L. *sibilāre*, see SIBILANT], *v.i.* To whistle; to hiss. *n.* A sibilant *râle*. **siffleur** (si flĕr′), *n.* The mountain marmot; a whistling artiste.

sift (sift) [A.-S. *siftan*, from SIEVE], *v.t.* To separate into finer and coarser particles by means of a sieve; to separate (from, out, etc.); to sprinkle (sugar, flour, etc.) as with a sieve; to examine minutely, to scrutinize, to analyse critically. *v.i.* To fall or be sprinkled as from a sieve (of light snow, etc.). **sifter,** *n.* (*usu. in comb.*, as *sugar-sifter*).

sigh (sī) [A.-S. *sīcan* (cp. Swed. *sucka*, Dan. *sukke*), prob. imit.], *v.i.* To draw a deep, long respiration, as an involuntary expression of grief, fatigue, relief, etc.; to yearn (for); to make a sound like sighing. *v.t.* To utter with sighs. *n.* The act or sound of sighing. **sigher,** *n.* **sighingly,** *adv.*

sight (sīt) [A.-S. *gesihth* (cp. Dut. *gezigt*, G. *sicht*), from *sēon*, to SEE], *n.* The faculty of seeing; the act of seeing; vision, view; range of vision; point of view, estimation; visibility; that which is seen, a spectacle, a display, a show, esp. something interesting to see; a device on a fire-arm, optical instrument, etc., for enabling one to direct it accurately to any point; (*colloq.*) a great quantity (of); a strange object, a fright. *v.t.* To get sight of, to espy, to discover by seeing; to adjust the sights of; to aim by means of sights. **at or on sight:** As soon as seen; immediately; on presentation for payment. **in sight:** Visible. **to lose sight of:** To cease to see; to overlook; to forget. **out of sight:** Where it cannot be seen; disappeared; forgotten.

sight-reader, *n.* One who reads (music, etc.) at sight. **sight-reading,** *n.* **sight-seeing,** *n.* Seeing the sights or notable features of a place. **sightseer,** *n.* **sighted,** *a.* (*usu. in comb.*, as *short-sighted*). **sightless,** *a.* Wanting sight, blind; invisible. **sightlessly,** *adv.* **sightlessness,** *n.* **sightly,** *a.* Pleasing to the eye, not unsightly. **sightliness,** *n.* **sightworthy,** *a.* Worth seeing. **sightsman,** *n.* One who reads music readily at sight; a guide, a cicerone.

sigil (sij′ il) [late L. *sigillum*, dim. of L. *signum*, SIGN], *n.* A seal, a signet; *an astrological or occult sign. **sigillaria** (-lâr′ i å), *n.* (*Geol.*) A genus of fossil cryptogamic trees found largely in coal formations. **sigillate** (sij′ i låt), *a.* (*Bot.*) Marked with seal-like impressions; decorated with stamped marks (of pottery). **sigillography** (-log′ rå fi) [-GRAPHY], *n.* The study or science of seals. **sigillographer,** *n.* **sigillographical** (-grăf′ i kål), *a.*

sigma (sig′ må) [Gr.], *n.* The name of the Greek letter Σ, σ, or S, equivalent to *s*. **sigmate** (sig′ måt), *a.* Sigma- or S-shaped. *v.t.* To add *s* or a sigma to. **sigmatic** (-măt′ ik), *a.* (*Gram.*) Formed with a sigma (of certain tenses, etc.). **sigmatism,** *n.* Imperfect or peculiar utterance of the sound *s*. **sigmoid,** *a.* (*chiefly Anat.*) Curved like the sigma or the letter *s*; having a double or reflexed curve; *n.* Such a curve. **sigmoidal** (-moi′ dål), *a.* Sigmoid.

sign (sīn) [M.E. and O.F. *signe*, L. *signum*], *n.* A mark expressing a particular meaning; a conventional mark used for a word or phrase to represent a mathematical process (as + or −), etc.; a symbol, a token, a symptom or proof (of), esp. a miracle as evidence of supernatural power; a password, a secret formula, motion, or gesture by which confederates, etc., recognize each other; a motion, action, or gesture used instead of words to convey information, commands, etc.; a device usu. painted on a board displayed as a token or advertisement of a trade, esp. by innkeepers; one of twelve ancient divisions of the zodiac named after the constellations formerly in them but now not corresponding through the precession of the equinoxes. *v.t.* To mark with a sign, esp. with one's signature, initials, or an accepted mark as an acknowledgment, guarantee, ratification, etc.; to convey (away) by putting one's signature to a deed, etc.; to engage or to be taken (on) as an employee by signature; to order, request, or make known by a gesture; to write (one's name) as signature. *v.i.* To write one's name as signature. **to sign off:** To stop work for the time; to discharge from employment; (*Radio.*) to leave off broadcasting. **sign-board,** *n.* A board on which a tradesman's sign or advertisement is painted. **sign manual:** A signature written by a person's own hand. **sign-painter,** *n.* One who paints sign-boards, etc. **signpost,** *n.* A post supporting a sign, esp. as a mark of direction at crossroads, etc. **signable,** *a.* **signer,** *n.*

signal (sig′ nål) [F., from late L. *signāle* (SIGN, -AL)], *n.* A sign agreed upon or understood as conveying information, esp. to a person or persons at a distance; (*fig.*) an event that is the occasion for some action; (*Rail.*) a semaphore or coloured light to indicate whether the line is clear or otherwise. *v.t.* (*past & p.p.* **signalled**) To make signals to; to convey, announce, order, etc., by signals. *v.i.* To make signals. *a.* Distinguished from the rest, conspicuous, noteworthy, extraordinary. **signal-box,** *n.* (*Rail.*) The cabin from which signals and points are worked. **signal-fire,** *n.* A fire intended to act as a signal. **signalman,** *n.* (*Rail.*) One who works the signals. **signaller,** *n.* **signally,** *adv.* **signal post:** (*Rail.*) A tall post bearing signalling arms. **signal off, on:** The signal for or against a train proceeding.

signalize (sig′ nå līz), *v.t.* To make signal or remarkable; to point out or indicate particularly.

signature (sig′ nå tyůr) [F., from med. L. *signātūra*, from *signāre*, to SIGN], *n.* The name, initials, or mark of a person written or impressed with his own hand; a distinguishing letter or number at the bottom of the first page of each sheet of a book; such a sheet after folding; (*Mus.*) the signs of the key and rhythm placed at the beginning of a staff to the right of the clef; all such signs including the clef; a significant mark, sign, or stamp. **signature tune:** (*Theat., Radio., etc.*) A distinctive piece of music played at the beginning or end of a variety turn, or of a band's performance. ***signation** (sig nā′ shůn), *n.* A sign; a signature; signing with the cross. **signatory, *-tary,** *a.* Having signed, bound by signature; *pertaining to a seal, used in sealing. *n.* One who signs, esp. as representing a State.

signet (sig′ nět) [F., dim. of *signe*, SIGN], *n.* A small seal, esp. for use in lieu of or with a signature as a mark of authentication; such a seal used by the English or Scottish sovereigns either privately or for certain official purposes. **signet-ring,** *n.* A finger-ring set with a seal.

significance, significancy (sig nif′ i kåns, -kåns i), *n.* The quality of being significant, expressiveness; meaning, real import; importance, moment, consequence. **significant,** *a.* Meaning something; expressing or suggesting something more than appears on the surface; meaning something important, weighty, noteworthy, not insignificant. **n.* A sign, a token. **significantly,** *adv.*

signification (sig ni fi kā′ shůn), *n.* The act of signifying; that which is signified, the precise meaning, sense, or implication (of a term, etc.).

significative (sig nif′ i kå tiv), *a.* Conveying a meaning or signification; serving as a sign or evidence (of), significant. **significatively,** *adv.* **significativeness,** *n*

signify (sig′ ni fī) [F. *signifier*, L. *significāre* (SIGN, -FY)], *v.t.* To make known by signs or words; to communicate, to announce; to be a sign of, to mean, to denote; to matter. *v.i.* To be of consequence. **significator,** *n.* One who or that which signifies; (*Astrol.*) the planet ruling a house. **significatory,** *a.* and *n.*

signior [SIGNOR, also GRAND SIGNIOR].

signiory [SEIGNORY].

signor (sē′ nyôr), ***signora*** (sē nyôr′ å), ***signorina*** (sē nyô rē′ nå) [It., as SENIOR, cp. SEIGNEUR], *n.* Italian titles of address, etc., corresponding to the English sir, madam, Mr., Mrs., and Miss.

sike (sīk) [A.-S. *sīc*, cp. Icel. *sīk*], *n.* (*Sc. and North.*) A small stream of water; a ditch, a channel.

Sikh (sēk) [Hind., from Sansk. *sishya*, disciple], *n.* One of a Hindu religious (monotheistic) and military community, founded in the 16th cent. in the Punjab.

silage [ENSILAGE].

sile (sīl) [prob. from Icel., cp. Norw. and Swed. *sil*], *n.* (*now prov.*) A strainer. *v.t.* To strain, esp. milk.

silence (sī′ lėns) [F., from L. *silentium*, from *silēre*, to be silent], *n.* The state of being silent, taciturnity, absence of noise, stillness; the fact of not mentioning a thing, secrecy; absence of mention, oblivion. *v.t.* To make silent, esp. by refuting with unanswerable arguments; to stop from sounding; to compel to cease firing. **silencer,** *n.* One who or that which silences; a device for reducing or muffling noise fitted to fire-arms, the exhaust of a motor on a vehicle, etc.

Silene (sī lē′ nē) [mod. L., from SILENUS], *n.* (*Bot.*) A genus of caryophyllaceous plants comprising the catch-fly, etc.

silent (sī′ lėnt), *a.* Not speaking, not making any sound, noiseless, still; not pronounced (of a letter); not loquacious, taciturn, making no mention, saying nothing (about); **n.* A time of silence. **silent partner:** One having no voice in the management of a business. **silentiary** (sī len′ shi år i), *n.* One appointed to maintain silence in a court, etc.; one sworn to secrecy in affairs of State, esp. a confidential officer of the Byzantine court. **silently,** *adv.* **silentness,** *n.*

Silenus (sī lē′ nůs) [L., from Gr. *Seilēnos*, attendant and tutor of Bacchus and oldest of the satyrs], *n.* (*fig.*) A riotous and drunken old man.

silesia (si-, sī lē′ shi å) [orig. made in *Silesia*, Germany], *n.* A name for kinds of linen cloth used for blinds, dress-linings, etc.

silex (sī′ leks) [L., flint], *n.* Flint; silica.

silhouette (sil u et′) [Etienne de *Silhouette* (1709–67), French minister of finance, whose name became a synonym for anything cheap], *n.* A portrait in profile or outline, usu. black on a white ground or cut out in paper, etc.; the outline of a figure as seen against the light or cast as a shadow. *v.t.* To represent or cause to be visible in silhouette.

silica (sil′ i kå) [from L. *silex -licis*, see SILEX], *n.* (*Chem.*) A hard, crystalline silicon dioxide, occurring in various mineral forms, esp. as sand, flint, quartz, etc. **silicate,** *n.* A salt of silicic acid. **silicated,** *a.* Combined or impregnated with silica; coated with silica. **siliceous** (-lish′ ůs), **silicic** (-lis′ ik), **siliciferous** (-sif′ ėr ůs), *a.* **silici-, silico-,** *comb. form.* **silicify,** *v.t.* To convert into or impregnate with silica, to petrify. *v.i.* To become or be impregnated with silica. **silicification** (-kā′ shůn), *n.* **silicium** (si lish′ i ům), *n.* Silicon. **silicon** (sil′ i kon), *n.* A non-metallic semiconducting element usu. occurring in combination with oxygen as quartz or silica, and next to oxygen the most abundant of the elements. **silicones,** *n.pl.* Water-repellant oils of low melting-point, the viscosity of which changes little with temperature; used as lubricants, constituents of polish, etc. **silicone rubber,** *n.* A synthetic rubber stable up to comparatively high temperatures. **silicosis,** *n.* (*Path.*) An occupational disease of the lungs occasioned by the inhalation of silica dust.

silicle (sil′ i kėl) ***silicula*** (si lik′ ū lå) [F. *silicule* or L. *silicula*, dim. of foll.], *n.* (*Bot.*) A short siliqua or seed-pod. **siliculose** (-lōs′), *a.*

siliqua (sil′ i kwå) [L.], *n.* (*Bot.*) A dry, elongated pericarp or pod containing the seeds, as in plants of the mustard family; (*Anat.*) a pod-like envelope. **silique** (si lēk′), *n.* (*Bot.*) A siliqua. **siliquiform** (si lik′ wi fôrm), *a.* **siliquose** (sil′ i kwōs), **siliquous** (-kwůs), *a.*

silk (silk) [A.-S. *seolc*, L. *sēricum*, see SERICATE], *n.* A fine, soft, glossy fibre spun by the larvæ of certain moths, esp. the common silkworm, *Bombyx mori*; similar thread spun by the silk-spider and other arachnids; cloth made of silk; (*pl.*) varieties of this or garments made of it; the silky lustre seen in some gems. *a.* Made of silk, silken, *silky. **to take silk:** To exchange a stuff gown for one of silk, esp. to become a K.C. or Q.C. **silk-cotton,** *n.* The silky covering of the seed-pods of the bombax and other trees. **silk-gland,** *n.* A gland in the silkworm, certain spiders, etc., secreting silk. **silkman,** *n.* A maker of or dealer in silk. **silk-mercer,** *n.* **silk-mill,** *n.* **silk-reel, -winder,** *n.* A reel used for winding the raw silk from the cocoon. **silk-spider,** *n.* A spider spinning a silky substance, esp. *Nephela plumipes.* **silk-thrower, -throwster,** *n.* One who winds, twists, or throws silk to prepare it for weaving. **silk-weaver,** *n.* **silkworm,** *n.* The larva of *Bombyx mori* or allied moths which enclose their chrysalis in a cocoon of silk. **silkworm gut:** A fine gut used for angling, drawn from the glands of the silkworm. **silken,** *a.* **silky,** *a.* Like silk, glossy, soft; silken. **silky oak,** *n.* An Australian tree yielding wood suitable for furniture, fittings, etc. **silkiness,** *n.*

sill (sil) [A.-S. *syll*, cp. Icel. *syll, svill,* Swed. *syll*, Dan. *syld*], *n.* A block or timber forming a basis or foundation in a structure, esp. a slab of timber or stone at the foot of a door or window; the top level of a weir; (*Geol.*) a sheet of intrusive igneous rock between other strata.

sillabub (sil′ å bŭb) [orig. *sillibouk* (perh. SILLY, merry, dial. *bouk*, belly)], *n.* A dish made by mixing wine or cider with cream or milk and thus forming a soft curd.

siller (sil′ ėr), *n.* (*Sc.*) Silver; money.

Sillery (sil′ ėr i) [village in Marne department, France], *n.* A sparkling, dry champagne from Sillery or the neighbourhood.

sillograph (sil′ ō grăf) [L. *sillographus*, Gr. *sillographos* (*sillos*, satirical poem)], *n.* A writer of satires. **sillographer, -phist** (-log′ rå fėr, -fist), *n.*

sillometer (si lom′ ė tėr) [F. *siller*, to run ahead, -METER], *n.* An instrument for measuring the speed of a ship, esp. without a log-line.

sillon (sil′ on) [F., furrow], *n.* (*Fort.*) A defensive work raised in the middle of a very wide ditch.

silly (sil′ i) [A.-S. *sǣlig*, happy, fortunate (cp. Dut. *zalig*, G. *selig*, Icel. *sæll*, blessed)], *a.* Foolish, fatuous, weak-minded; showing want of judgment, unwise, imprudent; mentally weak, imbecile; *innocent. simple-minded, guileless; *merry, happy, blessed. **sillily,** *adv.* **silliness,** *n.*

silo (sī′ lō) [Sp., from L. *sīrus*, Gr. *siros*], *n.* (*pl.* **silos**) A store-pit or air-tight chamber for pressing and preserving green fodder; a tall construction in which grain, etc., can be stored. *v.t.* To put in a silo; to convert into ensilage.

silphium (sil′ fi ům) [L., from Gr. *silphion*], *n.* A plant of the Mediterranean region the juice of which was used by the ancients as a condiment and as a medicine; a genus of American resinous herbs of the aster family.

silphology (sil fol′ ō ji) [Gr. *silphē*, beetle], *n.* (*Biol.*) The science of larval forms.

silt (silt) [M.G. *silte*, cp. M.Swed. *sylta*, mud, Dan. *sylt*, Norw. *sylta*, salt-marsh, G. *sülze*, brine], *n.* Fine sediment deposited by water. *v.t.* To choke or fill (up) with silt. *v.i.* To be choked (up) with silt.

Silurian (1) (sī-, si lūr′ i ån), *a.* Of or pertaining to the Silures, an ancient British people inhabiting South Wales; (*Geol.*) of or pertaining to the Silurian. *n.* (*Geol.*) The lowest sub-division of the Palæozoic strata, next above the Cambrian (well developed in S. Wales where these strata were first examined). **Silurist,** *n.* Belonging to or native of this region (applied to the poet Henry Vaughan, 1622–95).

Silurus (si lūr′ ůs) [L., from Gr. *Silouros*], *n.* (*Ichthyol.*) A genus of fishes typical of the *Siluridæ*, containing the sheat-fish. **silurian** (2), *n.* **silurid, siluridan, silurine, siluroid,** *a.* and *n.*

silvan [SYLVAN].

silver (sil′ vėr) [A.-S. *seolfor* (cp. Dut. *zilver*, G. *silber*, Icel. *silfr*), etym. doubtful], *n.* A precious ductile and malleable metallic element of a white colour; domestic utensils, implements, etc., made of this; silver coin; salts of silver employed in photography; the colour or lustre of or as of silver. *a.* Made of silver; resembling silver, white or lustrous like silver; soft and clear in tone (esp. of bells); of second-best quality or rank. *v.t.* To coat or plate with silver; to coat with tin-foil amalgamated with quicksilver; to give a silvery lustre to; to tinge (hair) with white or grey. **silver-bath,** *n.* A solution of nitrate of silver for sensitizing photographic plates. **silver-beater,** *n.* One who beats silver into thin sheets. **silver bream,** *n.* An edible Australian fish. **silver collection:** A collection at concerts, etc., where nothing smaller than silver is taken. **silver fir:** A tall species of fir, *Abies pectinata*, with silvery bark and two white lines on the underside of the leaves. **silver-fish,** *n.* A silvery fish of various species, esp. a white variety of gold-fish. **silver-foil,** *n.* Silver-leaf. **silver-fox,** *n.* A variety of common fox with black fur mixed with silver. **silver-gilt,** *a.* Silver or silverware gilded; an imitation gilding of silver-foil varnished with yellow lacquer. **silver-haired,** *a.* **silver-leaf,** *n.* Silver beaten out into thin leaves or plates; a disease of plum trees. **silver lining,** *n.* (*fig.*) The bright side of trouble. **silver paper,** *n.* Tin-foil. **silver plate:** Silver-ware. **silver-plated,** *a.* **silver-point,** *n.* A silver-pointed pencil; a sketch with this; the process of drawing with it. **silver-**

print, *n.* A print from a photographic negative on paper sensitized with a silver salt. **silver-printing,** *n.* **silver ring,** *n.* (*Racing*) A cheap enclosure at a race-course. **silver sand,** *n.* Fine, white sand. **silver screen:** (*fig.*) The cinematograph. **silver-side,** *n.* The upper and choicer part of a round of beef. **silver-smith,** *n.* A maker of or worker in silver articles. **silver-stick,** *n.* A court official (a field-officer of the Life Guards) attending the sovereign on state occasions. **silver thaw,** *n.* Icy surface caused by a hard frost following immediately after a thaw. **silver-tongued,** *a.* Eloquent. **silverware,** *n.* Articles of silver, esp. table utensils. **silver-weed,** *n.* A silvery-leaved plant, *Potentilla anserina.* ***silverize,** *v.t.* **silverless,** *a.* **silver-like,** *a.* **silverly,** *adv.* With the appearance of silver; with a soft clear sound. ***silvern,** *a.* **silvery,** *a.* **silveriness,** *n.*

simar, simarre [CYMAR].

Simaruba (sim å roo' bå) [prob. Guiana native name], *n.* A genus of tropical American trees; a tree of this genus; simaruba-bark. **simaruba-bark,** *n.* The bark of *Simaruba amara,* used as a tonic or astringent, esp. in cases of dysentery, etc. **simarubaceous** (-bā' shủs), *a.*

Simeonite (sim' ė ō nīt) [Charles *Simeon* (1759–1836) of Cambridge, distinguished for his evangelism], *n.* A follower of Simeon; a low Churchman.

Simia (sim' i å) [L., ape], *n.* (*pl.* ***-miæ***) (*Zool.*) A genus of anthropoid apes containing the orang-utan. ***simiad, *simial, simioid, simious,** *a.* **simian,** *a.* and *n.*

similar (sim' i lår) [F. *similaire,* L. *similis,* like], *a.* Like, having a resemblance (to); resembling (each other); alike; (*Geom.*) made up of the same number of parts arranged in the same manner. *n.* That which resembles something else; (*pl.*) similar things. **similarity** (-lăr' i ti), *n.* **similarly,** *adv.*

simile (sim' i li), *n.* A comparison of two things which have some strong point of resemblance, esp. as an illustration or poetical figure.

similitude (si mil' i tūd), *n.* Likeness, resemblance, outward appearance; comparison, simile, metaphor; counterpart.

similor (sim' i lôr) [F. (L. *simil-is,* SIMILAR, F. *or,* gold)], *n.* A gold-coloured alloy of copper and zinc used for cheap jewelry.

simioid, simious [SIMIA].

simitar [SCIMITAR].

simmer (sim' ėr) [cp. Dan. *summe,* G. *summen,* to hum, -ER], *v.i.* To boil gently; to be just below boiling-point; to be on the point of bursting into laughter, anger, etc. *v.t.* To boil gently; to keep just below boiling-point. *n.* A state of simmering.

simnel (sim' nėl) [O.F. *simenel,* late L. *siminellus,* fine bread, from L. *simila,* the finest wheat flour, rel. to Gr. *semidalis*], *n.* A rich cake, boiled, or boiled and baked, and ornamented with scallops, formerly eaten on Mid-Lent Sunday, Easter, and Christmas Day.

simoniac, etc. [SIMONY].

Simon Pure (sī' mȯn pūr) [character in Mrs. Centlivre's 'A Bold Stroke for a Wife' (1718)], *n.* The genuine article, the real person.

simony (si' mȯ ni) [F. *simonie,* late L. *simōnia,* from *Simon* Magus, who wished to buy the gift of the Holy Ghost with money (Acts viii. 18)], *n.* The buying or selling of ecclesiastical preferment. **simoniac** (si mō' ni ăk), *n.* One guilty of simony. **simoniacal** (-nī' å kål), *a.* Guilty of simony; of the nature of or obtained by simony. **Simonian,** *n.* A follower of Simon Magus, regarded as the first heretic. ***simonious,** *a.* **Simonist** (sī' mȯ nist), *n.*

simoom (si moom') [Arab. *samūm,* from *samma,* to poison], *n.* A hot dry wind blowing over the desert, esp. of Arabia, raising great quantities of sand and causing intense thirst.

simous (sī' mủs) [L. *sīmus,* Gr. *simos*], *a.* Having a flat nose; *concave.

simpai (sim' pī) [native name], *n.* A small black-crested monkey of Sumatra.

simper (sim' pėr) [cp. Norw. *semper,* smart, Dan. dial. *semper,* Swed. *sipp,* prim], *v.i.* To smile in an affected manner, to smirk. *n.* An affected smile or smirk. **simperer,** *n.* **simperingly,** *adv.*

simple (sim' pėl) [F., from L. *simplicem,* nom. *-plex,* onefold (*sim-,* cp. *semel,* once, *simul,* at once, *singulī,* one by one, *-plic-,* as in *plicāre,* to fold)], *a.* Consisting of only one thing; uncompounded, unmingled, all of one kind, not analysable, not subdivided, elementary; not complicated, not complex; not elaborate, not adorned, not sumptuous; plain, homely, humble, of low degree; insignificant, trifling; unaffected, unsophisticated, natural, artless, sincere; clear, intelligible; weak in intellect, silly, inexperienced, ignorant; absolute, mere. *n.* Something not mixed or compounded; a medicinal herb or a medicine made from it. **simple addition:** (*Arith.*) Addition of numbers all of the same denomination. **simple-hearted,** *a.* **simple interest:** Interest upon the principal only, paid at given periods. **simple-minded,** *a.* Frank, devoid of duplicity, unsuspecting. **simple-mindedness,** *n.* ***simpleness,** *n.* Simplicity. **simplex,** *a.* Simple, not compound. *n.* A simplex word. ***simpler,** *n.* One who gathers simples, a herbalist. ***simplesse,** *n.* Simplicity. **simpleton,** *n.* A silly, gullible, or feeble-minded person. **simplicity** (-plis' i ti), *n.* ***simpliciter,*** *adv.* Absolutely without limitation or qualification. **simplify** (sim' pli fī), *v.t.* To make simple; to make simpler or easier to understand. **simplification** (-kā' shủn), *n.* **simplism,** *n.* Affectation of simplicity. ***simplist,** *n.* A simpler. **simplistic** (-plis' tik), *a.* **simply,** *adv.*

simulacrum (sim ū lā' krủm) [L., from *simulāre,* to SIMULATE], *n.* (*pl.* **-cra**) An image, a shadowy representation, a semblance; a mere pretence, a sham.

simulate (sim' ū lāt) [L. *simulātus,* p.p. of *simulāre,* from *similis,* SIMILAR], *v.t.* To assume the likeness or mere appearance of; to counterfeit, to feign, to imitate, to put on, to mimic. **a.* (-låt) Simulated, feigned, false. **simulant,** *a.* **simulance,** *n.* ***simular,** *n.* One who simulates, a pretender. *a.* Simulated, pretended, specious, false. **simulation** (-lā' shủn), *n.* **simulative** (sim'-), *a.* **simulatively,** *adv.* **simulator,** *n.*

simultaneous (sim ủl tā' nė ủs) [late L. *simultāneus* (*simultim,* adv., from L. *simul,* together, -ANEOUS)], *a.* Happening, done, or acting at the same time. **simultaneity** (-nē' i ti), *n.* **simultaneousness,** *n.* **simultaneously,** *adv.*

simurg (si moorg') [Pers. *sīmurgh*], *n.* (*Pers. Myth.*) A fabulous bird of enormous size.

sin (1) (sin) [A.-S. *synn,* cp. Dut. *zonde,* G. *sünde,* Icel., Dan., and Swed. *synd*], *n.* Transgression of duty, morality, or the law of God; wickedness, moral depravity; a transgression; a breach of etiquette, sensible behaviour, etc.; *a sin-offering; *the embodiment of sin. *v.i.* (*past & p.p.* **sinned**) To commit sin; to offend (against). **like sin:** (*colloq.*) Hard, vigorously. **mortal sin:** Deliberate sin that deprives the soul of divine grace. **original sin** [ORIGINAL]. **seven deadly sins** [SEVEN]. ***sin-born,** *a.* **sin-bred,** *a.* Produced from sin. **sin-eater,** *n.* One who took on himself the sins of a deceased person by eating beside the corpse. **sin-offering,** *n.* A sacrifice to atone for sin. ***sin-worn,** *a.* Worn by sin. **sinful,** *a.* **sinfully,** *adv.* **sinfulness,** *n.* **sinless,** *a.* **sinlessly,** *adv.* **sinlessness,** *n.* **sinner,** *n.*

***sin** (2) [SITHEN].

Sinaitic (sī nå it' ik), *a.* Pertaining to or given at Mount Sinai or the peninsula of Sinai.

Sinanthropus (sin' ăn thrō' pus) [Gr. *Sinæ,* the Chinese; *anthropos,* a man], *n.* An ape-like man of the type discovered in remains found in China.

Sinapis (si nā′ pis) [L., from Gr. *sinēpi*, mustard], *n.* A genus of crucifers with five species from the seeds of which mustard is prepared. **sinapic** (si năp′ ik), *a.* **sinapine** (sin′ å pin), *n.* (*Chem.*) An organic base, existing as sulphocyanate in the seed of *Sinapis alba*, white mustard. **sinapisine** (si năp′ i sin), *n.* A white crystalline substance obtained from black mustard seed. **sinapism** (sin′ å pizm), *n.* A mustard plaster.

since (sins) [M.E. *sithens*, thence, A.-S. *siththan* (*sith*, after, *thon*, that)], *adv.* After or from a time specified or implied till now; at some time after such a time and before now; from that time before this, before now, ago. *prep.* From the time of; throughout or during the time after; after and before now. *conj.* From the time that or when, during the time after that; inasmuch as; because.

sincere (sin sēr′) [O.F., from L. *sincērus*, pure, sincere], *a.* Being in reality as in appearance or profession; not feigned or put on, genuine, honest, undissembling, frank. **sincerely,** *adv.* **sincereness,** *n.* **sincerity** (-ser′ i ti), *n.*

sinciput (sin′ si pŭt) [L. SEMI-, *caput*, head], *n.* The upper part of the head, esp. from the forehead to the coronal suture. **sincipital** (-sip′ i tål), *a.*

sind (sīnd) [Sc., etym. doubtful], *v.t.* To rinse; to wash down (drink, food, etc.). *n.* A rinsing; a draught.

sine (1) (sīn) [L. *sinus*, curve], *n.* (*Trig.*) The straight line drawn from one extremity of an arc perpendicular to the diameter passing through the other extremity. **sine of an angle:** The ratio of the length of the line opposite the angle to the length of the hypotenuse in a right-angled triangle.

sine (2) [SYNE].

sinecure (sī′ nė-, sin′ ė kūr) [L. *sine cura*, without care], *n.* An ecclesiastical benefice without cure of souls; any paid office with few or no duties attached. **sinecurism,** *n.* **sinecurist,** *n.*

sinew (sin′ ū) [A.-S. *sinu*, *seono* (cp. Dut. *zenuw*, G. *sehne*, Icel. *sin*), cp. HOX], *n.* A tendon, a fibrous cord connecting muscle and bone; (*pl.*) muscles; (*fig.*) that which gives strength or power. *v.t.* To knit strongly together; to strengthen or furnish with sinews. **the sinews of war:** Money. **sinew-shrunk,** *a.* Having the sinews under the belly shrunk by excessive fatigue (said of a horse). **sinewed,** *a.* **sinewless,** *a.* **sinewy,** *a.* **sinewiness,** *n.*

sinfonia (sin fō nē′ å) [It.], *n.* (*Mus.*) A symphony.

sing (sing) [A.-S. *singan*, cp. Dut. *zingen*, G. *singen*, Icel. *syngja*], *v.i.* (*past* **sang,** ***sung,** *p.p.* **sung**) To utter words in a tuneful manner, to render a song vocally, to make vocal melody; to emit sweet or melodious sounds; to make a murmuring sound (of a kettle, etc.); (*fig.*) to relate something in numbers or verse, to compose poetry. *v.t.* To utter (words, a song, tune, etc.) in a tuneful or melodious manner; to celebrate in verse or poetry; (*fig.*) to celebrate; to accompany with singing; to greet, acclaim, usher (in or out), etc., with singing. **to sing out:** To call out loudly, to shout. **singable,** *a.* **singer** (sing′ ėr), *n.* **singing-bird,** *n.* ***singing-book,** *n.* A book containing music for singing. **singing-man,** *n.* One employed to sing; a chorister. **singing-master,** *n.* One who teaches singing. **singing-voice,** *n.* The voice as used in singing. ***singing-woman,** *n.* **singingly,** *adv.*

singe (sinj) [A.-S. *sengan*, cp. Dut. *zengen*, G. *sengen*, cogn. with Icel. *sangr*, burnt, singed], *v.t.* To burn slightly; to burn the surface of or the tips of (hair, etc.); to scorch; to burn bristles, etc., off (an animal carcase); (*fig.*) to harm slightly. *n.* A slight burn; (*fig.*) a slight injury. **singeing-machine, -plate,** *n.* An appliance for burning the superfluous nap off cloth, etc.

Singhalese [CINGALESE].

single (sing′ gėl) [late L. *singulus*, from L. *singulī*, one by one], *a.* Consisting of one only; particular, individual, separate, solitary, alone, unaided; unmarried; simple, not compound, not complicated, not combined with others; performed by one or by one on each side; designed for use by or with one person, thing, etc.; sincere, not double-minded, ingenuous, consistent; (*Bot.*) not double, not clustered. *n.* A single round, game, a hit for one run, etc.; (*Rail.*) a ticket for one journey only; (*pl.*) twisted threads of raw silk. *v.t.* To pick out from among others. **single-acting,** *a.* Working by means of steam acting on one side of the piston only (of a steam-engine). **single blessedness:** The state of being unmarried. **single-breasted,** *a.* Having only one thickness of cloth over the breast, with one set of buttons, holes, etc.; not overlapping. **single-deck,** *a.* Descriptive of an omnibus or tram with accommodation on one level only. **single-entry** [ENTRY]. **single-eyed,** *a.* Intent on one purpose only; sincere. **single-fire,** *a.* Not intended to be reloaded (of a cartridge). **single-handed,** *a.* Done without assistance; unassisted, alone; using only one hand (of a player in certain games, etc.). *adv.* Without assistance. **single-hearted, single-minded,** *a.* Single-eyed; free from duplicity. **single-mindedly,** *adv.* **single-mindedness,** *n.* **single-loader,** *n.* A breech-loading rifle without a magazine. **single phase:** (*Elec.*) An alternating current-supply using two wires. **single-stick,** *n.* A long stick formerly used in a kind of fencing; fencing with this, cudgel-play. **singleness,** *n.* **singleton** (sing′ gėl tŏn), *n.* A single card of any particular suit in a player's hand at whist, etc. **singly,** *adv.*

singlet (sing′ glet), *n.* An under-shirt, a vest.

singsong (sing′ song), *a.* Sung, recited, etc., in monotone or monotonous rhythm. *n.* Monotonous cadence or rhythm; an impromptu concert, esp. by amateur vocalists. *v.t.* and *i.* To speak, recite, or utter in a monotonous style.

singspiel (sing′ spēl, zing′ shpēl) [G. (*singen*, to SING, *spiel*, play)], *n.* A dramatic entertainment in which the action is expressed in alternate dialogue and song.

singular (sing′ gū lår) [M.E. *singuler*, F. *singulier*, L. *singulāris*, as SINGLE], *a.* Single, individual, standing alone, out of the usual course, strange, remarkable, extraordinary, distinguished; peculiar, odd, eccentric; (*Gram.*) denoting or referring to one person or thing; not plural. *n.* The singular number; a word denoting this. **singularism,** *n.* **singularist,** *n.* One who affects singularity. **singularity** (-lăr′ i ti), *n.* **singularize,** *v.t.* To alter a word that looks like a plural (as *pease*) to the singular form (as *pea*). **singularization** (-zā′ shŭn), *n.* **singularly,** *adv.*

singult** (sing′ gŭlt) [L. *singultus*], *n.* A sob. ***singultus (sing gŭl′ tŭs), *n.* (*Path.*) Hiccups, hiccuping. ***singultous,** *a.*

Sinhalese [CINGALESE].

Sinic (sin′ ik) [med. L. *sinicus*, from late L. *Sīnæ*, the Chinese], *a.* Chinese. **Sinicism,** *n.* **Sinicize, Sinify,** *v.t.* **Sinicization, Sinification,** *n.*

sinical (sin′ i kål), *a.* Pertaining to a sine or sines.

Sinicism, Sinicize, Sinify, etc. [SINIC].

sinister (sin′ is tėr) [F. *sinistre*, L. *sinistrum*, nom. *-tor*, left], *a.* (*Her.*) On the left side (of a shield, etc.), the side to the right of the observer; ill-omened, inauspicious, ill-looking, malignant, malevolent, villainous. **sinisterly,** *adv.* ***sinistrad,** *adv.* Sinistrally. **sinistral** (si nis′ trål), *a.* With a whorl turning to the left (said of a spiral shell); sinistrous. **sinistrally,** *adv.* **sinistro-,** *comb. form.* **sinistro-cerebral,** *a.* (*Anat.*) Of or situated in the left cerebral hemisphere. **sinistrorse** (sin′ is trôrs), *a.* Directed towards the left; (*Bot.*) twining to the left. **sinistrorsal** (-trôr′ sål), *a.* **sinistrorsally,** *adv.* **sinistrous** (sin′ is trŭs), *a.* Being on, pertaining to, directed towards, or inclined to the left; ill-omened, unlucky, sinister; *wrong, perverse, absurd. **sinistrously,** *adv.*

sink (singk) [A.-S. *sincan* (cp. Dut. *zinken*, G. *sinken*, Dan. *synke*, also Sansk., *sich*, to sprinkle)], *v.i.* (*past* sank, *sunk, *p.p.* sunk, *part.a.* sunken) To go downwards, to descend, to fall gradually; to disappear below the surface or the horizon; to fall or descend by force of gravity; to decline to a lower level of health, morals, etc.; to deteriorate; to subside, to droop, to despond; to expire or come to an end by degrees; to become lower in intensity, pitch, value, price, etc.; to become shrunken or hollow, to slope downwards, to recede; to go deep or deeper into, to penetrate, to be impressed into, to be absorbed. *v.t.* To cause to sink; to submerge in a fluid, to send below the surface; to excavate, to make by excavating; to cause to disappear; to put out of sight, to conceal, to suppress, to lose sight of; to allow to fall or droop; to lower, to degrade, to ruin; to reduce, to diminish, to lessen the value of; to invest unprofitably, to lose, to waste, to squander. *n.* A stone, porcelain, or metal basin or rectangular trough for receiving slops, waste water, etc.; a receptacle for filth (*usu. fig.*); a pool, marsh, or rock-basin into which a stream disappears; (*Theat.*) a stage-trap through which scenery is raised and lowered. **sink-hole,** *n.* A hole in a sink for the water to discharge through; a hole or series of holes in limestone strata through which water sinks below the surface. **sinkable,** *a.* **sinker,** *n.* One who or that which sinks; a weight used to sink a fishing-line, net, etc. **sinking-fund,** *n.* A fund set aside for the reduction of a public debt. ***sinking-ripe,** *a.* Ready to fall off.

***sink-a-pace** [CINQUEPACE, see CINQUE].

sinker, sinking-fund, etc. [SINK].

sinless, etc., **sinner** [SIN (1)].

sinnet [SENNIT].

Sinn Fein (shin fān′) [Ir., ourselves], *n.* (*Pol.*) An Irish revolutionary party formed in 1905 by the coalescence of all the Irish separatist organizations. **Sinn Feiner,** *n.* A member of Sinn Fein.

sinology (si nol′ ŏ ji) [Gr. *Sinæ*, late L. *Sinæ*, see SINIC, -LOGY], *n.* Knowledge of the Chinese language, literature, etc. **sinological** (-log′ i kăl), *a.* **sinologist** (-nol′ ŏ jist), **sinologue** (sin′ ŏ log), *n.*

sinopite (sin′ ō pīt), *n.* (*Min.*) A ferruginous quartz found in Hungary.

sinople (sin′ ŏpl) [O.F., from L. and Gr. *Sinōpis*, from *Sinōpe*, Greek colony on the Euxine], *n.* (*Her.*) Vert, green; a red earth formerly used as a pigment. **sinopic** (-nop′ ik), *a.*

sinsyne (sin sin′) [Sc. and North. (SIN (2), SYNE)], *adv.* Since then.

sinter (sin′ tĕr) [G., CINDER], *n.* A calcareous or siliceous rock precipitated from mineral waters.

Sinto, Sintu, etc. [SHINTO].

sintoc (sin′ tok) [Malay *sintoq*], *n.* A tree of Sumatra, Java, and Borneo, with aromatic bark.

sinuate (sin′ ū ăt) [L. *sinuātus*, p.p. of *sinuāre*, as foll.], *a.* Bending, curving, or winding in and out (esp. of the edges of leaves, etc.). ***v.i.** (-āt) To wind or creep in and out. **sinuated,** *a.* **sinuately,** *adv.* **sinuation** (-ā′ shŭn), *n.*

sinuosity (sin ū os′ i ti), *n.* The quality of being sinuous; a bend or series of bends and curves.

sinuoso-, *comb. form.* [as SINUATE].

sinuous (sin′ ū ŭs), *a.* Bending in and out; winding, serpentine, tortuous. **sinuously,** *adv.*

sinupallial, sinupalliate (sin ū păl′ i ăl, -ăt) *a.* (*Conch.*) Having a deeply incurved pallial line; of or pertaining to the *Sinupalliata*, a division of bivalves with a posterior sinus in the pallial impression for the passage to and fro of the pallial siphons.

sinus (sī′ nŭs) [L., a curve, a recess], *n.* (*Anat., Zool., etc.*) A cavity or pouch-like hollow, esp. in bone or tissue; (*Path.*) a fistula; (*Bot.*) a rounded recess or curve, as in the margin of a leaf.

-sion [L. *-siōnem*, nom. *-sio*, cp. -ION].

Sioux (soo, sū) [F., from N. Am. Ind.], *n.* A tribe or family of N. American Indians comprising the Dakotas, or a member of this. *a.* Pertaining to the Sioux.

sip (sip) [A.-S. *sypian*, cogn. with *sūpan*, to SUP (cp. M.Dut. *sippen*, Swed. dial. *syppa*)], *v.t.* and *i.* (*past & p.p.* sipped) To drink or imbibe in small quantities. *n.* A very small draught of liquid. **sipper,** *n.* **sippet,** *n.* A small piece of toast or fried bread garnishing a dish of mince, etc.; a small piece of bread or other food soaked in broth, etc.

sipahee, sipahi [SEPOY].

sipe [SEEP]. **siphilis** [SYPHILIS].

siphon (sī′ fŏn) [F., from L. *sīphōnem*, nom. *-pho*, Gr. *siphōn*, pipe], *n.* A curved tube having one branch longer than the other, used for conveying liquid over the edge of a cask, tank, etc., through the force of atmospheric pressure; a siphon-bottle; (*Zool.*) a suctorial or other tubular organ, esp. in cephalopods gasteropods, etc. *v.t.* To convey or draw off by a siphon. *v.i.* To flow by a siphon. **siphon-bottle,** *n.* A bottle for holding aerated water, discharging through a siphon-like tube through the pressure of the gas. **siphon-gauge,** *n.* A gauge in the form of a bent tube indicating variations of pressure in a reservoir by the height of a column of mercury. **siphon-trap,** *n.* A trap in the emptying pipe of sinks, baths and water-closets in which a water seal prevents the reflux of foul gases. **siphonage,** *n.* **siphonal, siphonic** (-fon′ ik), *a.* **Siphonaptera,** *n.* (*Zool.*) An order of wingless insects represented by the fleas. **siphonet** (sī′-), *n.* One of the abdominal tubes through which the honey-dew is exuded by an aphis. **siphoniferous** (-nif′ ĕr ŭs), *a.* **siphoniform** (-fon′ i fôrm), *a.* **siphonophore** (sī′ fŏn ŏ fôr), *n.* One of the *Siphonophoridæ*, variously regarded as a colony of medusoid zooids or as a single individual composed of a cluster of tubular organs. **siphonophoran** (-nof′ ŏr ăn), *a.* and *n.* **siphuncle** (sī′ fŭnkl), *n.* The tube connecting the chambers of the shell in many cephalopods; the suctorial or other tubes in insects, etc. **siphuncular, siphunculated,** *a.* **siphunculus,** *n.* (*pl.* **-li,** -lī).

sipper, sippet [SIP].

sipylite (sip′ i līt) [L. *Sipyl-us*, Gr. *Sipulos*, one of the children of Niobe, -ITE], *n.* (*Min.*) A niobite of erbium.

sir (sĕr) [SIRE], *n.* A term of courteous or formal address to a man; a title prefixed to the names of baronets and knights and formerly clergymen; *a lord, a gentleman.

sircar [SIRKAR].

sirdar (sĕr′ dar) [Hind. (Pers. *sar*, head, *-dār*, holding)], *n.* (*E.Ind.*) A chieftain, leader, or commander; (*Egypt*) the former commander-in-chief of the army.

sire (sīr) [O.F., earlier *senre*, L. SENIOR], *n.* A title used in addressing a king or a sovereign prince; a father, a progenitor; the male parent of a beast, esp. a stallion. *v.t.* To beget (beasts, esp. stallions).

siren (sī′ rĕn) [L. *sīrēn*, Gr. *seirēn*], *n.* (*Gr. Myth.*) A sea-nymph, half-woman and half-bird, one of several dwelling on a rocky isle and luring sailors to shipwreck by their singing; a charming or seductive woman, esp. a dangerous temptress; a sweet singer; an apparatus for producing a loud sound by means of a rotating perforated disk through which steam or compressed air is emitted; a sirenian; one of the *Sirenidæ*, a genus of American eel-like amphibians, with two anterior feet and permanent branchiæ. *a.* Of or as of a siren; bewitching, fascinating. **siren suit:** A suit in one piece and closed with a zip-fastening.

sirenian (sī rē′ ni ăn) [as prec., -AN], *n.* One of the *Sirenia*, an order of marine herbivorous mammals, allied to the whales, but having the fore limbs developed into paddles, comprising the manatees and dugongs. *a.* Of or pertaining to the *Sirenia*.

sirgang (sĕr′ gang) [E.Ind.], *n.* A brilliant green Indian magpie or jackdaw, *Cissa Chinensis*.

siriasis (si rī′ ă sis) [Gr. *seiriasis*, from *seiriān*, to be hot], *n.* (*Path.*) Sunstroke; (*Med.*) a sun-bath.

sirih (sir′ i) [Malay], *n.* Betel-leaf.

Sirius (sir′ i ŭs) [Gr. *seirios*, cogn. with *seiriasis*, see SIRIASIS], *n.* The dog-star.

sirloin (sĕr′ loin) [orig. *surloine*, O.F. *surlonge* (*sur*, over, *longe*, LOIN)], *n.* The loin or upper part of the loin of beef.

***sirname** [SURNAME].

***sir-reverence** (sĕr rev′ ėr ėns) [corr. of SAVE REVERENCE], *n.* The phrase 'save reverence' used apologetically; human ordure; a lump of this.

sirocco (si rok′ ō), ***siroc** [It. *sirocco*, Arab. *sharq*, east], *n.* A hot oppressive wind blowing from northern Africa across to Italy, etc.; applied generally to a sultry southerly wind in Italy.

sirrah (sir′ ȧ) [Prov. *sira*, F. *sire*, SIRE], *n.* Fellow, sir (a term of address used in anger or contempt).

sirup, etc. [SYRUP].

sirvente (sir vant′) [F., from *servir*, L. *servīre*, to SERVE], *n.* A form of lay, usu. satirical, used by the mediæval trouvères and troubadours.

Sisal (sis′ ȧl), *a.* Of or obtained from Sisal, a port in Yucatan. **Sisal-grass, -hemp,** *n.* The fibre of the American aloe used for cordage, etc.

siscowet (sis′ kŏ et) [Ojibwa], *n.* A great lake trout found in Lake Superior.

***siserary** (sis er âr′ i) [corr. of CERTIORARI], *n.* An effective stroke, a blow; *a certiorari. ***with a siserary:** (*colloq.*) With a vengeance.

siskin (sis′ kin) [M.Dut. *cijsken*, L.G. *zieske*, Pol. *czyzik*], *n.* A small migratory song-bird, *Carduelus spinus*, allied to the goldfinch, the aberdevine.

siskiwit, -kowet [SISCOWET].

sissy (sis′ i) [SISTER], *n.* An effeminate fellow. *a.* Effeminate.

sist (sist) [L. *sistere*, to cause to stand, from *stāre*, to stand], *v.t.* (*Sc. Law*) To stop, to stay; to summon. *n.* A stay of proceedings.

sister (sis′ tėr) [A.-S. *sweoster*, *swuster* (cp. Dut. *zuster*, G. *schwester*, Icel. *systir*, also L. *soror*, Sansk. *svasā*)], *n.* A female born of the same parents as another; applied to a half-sister, a sister-in-law, or a foster-sister, also to a very close female friend; a senior nurse, one in charge of a hospital ward; a female member of the same society, community, etc., esp. of a religious community; a female fellow-Christian or member of the human race; any thing, quality, etc., closely resembling another. *v.i.* To be closely allied or to have a sisterly resemblance (to). *v.t.* To be sister to; to resemble closely. **half-sister** [HALF]. **sister-hook,** *n.* (*Naut.*) One of a pair of hooks opening to receive a rope, etc., and overlapping. **sister-in-law,** *n.* A husband's or wife's sister; a brother's wife. **sister of mercy:** A member of a sisterhood. **sisterhood,** *n.* The state of being a sister, the relation of sisters; a community of women bound together by vows, co-operation in charitable work, etc. **sisterless,** *a.* **sister-like,** *adv.* **sisterlike, -ly,** *a.* **sisterliness,** *n.*

sistrum (sis′ trŭm) [L., from Gr. *seistron*, from *seiein*, to shake], *n.* A jingling instrument used by the ancient Egyptians in the worship of Isis.

Sisyphean (sis i fē′ ȧn) [from *Sisuphos*, one of the Titans, condemned to push up a hill a stone that everlastingly rolled back again], *a.* Unceasingly or fruitlessly laborious.

Sisyrinchium (sis i ring′ ki ŭm) [Gr. *sus*, swine, *rhunchos*, snout], *n.* (*Bot.*) A genus of grass-like plants with blue or yellow flowers of the iris family.

sit (sit) [A.-S. *sittan* (cp. Dut. *zitten*, G. *sitzen*, Icel. *sitja*, also L. *sedēre*, Gr. *hezesthai*, Sansk. *sad*)], *v.i.* (*past & p.p.* **sat**) To set oneself or be in a resting posture with the body nearly vertical supported on the buttocks; to be in a resting posture (of birds and various beasts); to perch, to roost; to cover eggs in order to hatch, to brood; to be in a specified position, quarter, etc.; to be situated; to suit, to fit (of clothes, etc.); to rest or weigh (on); to take a position, to pose (for one's portrait, etc.); to meet, to hold a session; to hold or occupy a seat (on) a deliberative body or in a specified capacity (as in judgment); to take up a position, to encamp (before) so as to besiege; *to remain, to abide. *v.t.* To cause to sit, to set; to place (oneself) in a seat; to hold or keep a sitting position on (a horse, etc.); to be a candidate for an examination. **to sit down:** To place oneself on a seat after standing; to begin a siege; to take up a permanent abode. **sit-down strike,** *n.* A form of protest in which operatives go to the scene of their work but refuse to work. **to sit for:** To take an examination; to represent a constituency in parliament; to pose for a portrait. **to sit on:** To hold a meeting, discussion, or investigation over; (*slang*) to repress severely, to snub. **to sit out:** To sit out of doors; to sit apart from (a dance, etc.); to sit till the end of (a concert, etc.); to stay longer than (other visitors): **to sit pretty:** (*colloq.*) To be favourably placed. **to sit tight:** (*colloq.*) To hold firm and do nothing. **to sit under:** To attend the ministrations of (a clergyman). **to sit up:** To rise from a recumbent position; to sit with the body erect; not to go to bed. **to make one sit up:** To astonish or disconcert one; to stir one up to action. **sitter,** *n.* One who sits, esp. for a portrait; a hen that sits well, badly, etc. **baby-sitter** [BABY]. **sitting,** *a.* and *n.* The action of the verb TO SIT; a session, a meeting for business; the time during which one sits; a seat in a church, etc., allotted to one person; a clutch of eggs for hatching; posing for a portrait. **sitting-room,** *n.* A room for sitting in, a parlour; room or space for persons sitting.

sitar (si tar′) [Hind.], *n.* (*Ang.-Ind.*) An Indian musical instrument resembling the guitar.

site (sīt) [F., from L. *situs*], *n.* Local position, situation; ground on which anything, esp. a building, stands, has stood, or will stand. ***sited,** *a.* Situated; having a site.

sitfast (sit′ fast), *a.* Stationary. *n.* An ulcerated, horny sore on a horse's back under the saddle.

***sith** (sith), ***sithen** (si*th*′ ėn) [A.-S., see SINCE], *conj.* Since; seeing that.

sitiology, sitology (sit i ol′-, si tol′ ŏ ji) [Gr. *sitos*, food, *sition*, bread, -LOGY], *n.* Dietetics. **sitiomania** (-mā′ ni ȧ), *n.* Morbid repugnance to food. **sitiophobia** (-fō′ bi ȧ), *n.* The refusal to take food.

sitter, sitting [SIT].

situated, *situate (sit′ ū ā tėd, -ȧt) [late L. *situātus*, p.p. of *situāre*, to locate, from situs, SITE], *a.* Placed or being in a specified situation, condition, or relation.

situation (sit ū ā′ shŭn), *n.* The place in which something is situated, position, locality; position of affairs or circumstances, esp. a critical juncture in a story or play; a paid office, post, or place, esp. of a domestic servant.

sitz-bath (sits′ bath) [G. *sitzbad* (*sitzen*, to sit, BATH)], *n.* A bath in which one sits; a bath taken thus.

Siva (sē′ vȧ) [Hind., from Sansk. *çiva*, auspicious], *n.* The god associated with Brahma and Vishnu in the Hindu triad, known as the destroyer and reproducer of life. **Sivaistic** (-is′ tik), *a.* **Sivaite** (sē′ vȧ īt), *n.*

Sivan (si van′) [Heb.], *n.* The third month of the Jewish ecclesiastical year comprising part of June and July.

sivatherium (siv ȧ thēr′ i ŭm) [SIVA, Gr. *thēron*, wild beast], *n.* (*Palæont.*) A gigantic four-horned fossil ruminant found in N. India.

six (siks) [A.-S. (cp. Dut. *zes*, G. *sechs*, Icel., Dan., and Swed. *sex*, also L. *sex*, Gr. *hex*, Sansk, *shash*)], *a.* One more than five. *n.* The number or the symbol representing this, 6, vi; a playing-card with six pips; the face of a die bearing the six; (*pl.*) candles made six to the pound; boots, shoes, etc., of No. 6 size. **at sixes and sevens:** In disorder or confusion. **six-footer,** *n.* (*colloq.*) A person six feet high. **sixain,** *n.* A six-line stanza. **sixer,** *n.* Anything representing, worth, or equal to six, esp. a hit for six runs at cricket. **sixfold,** *a.* and *adv.* **sixpence,** *n.* A cupro-nickel coin of the value of six pennies. **sixpenny,** *a.* Worth or priced at sixpence. **six-shooter,** *n.* (*colloq.*) A six-chambered revolver. **sixte** (sikst), *n.* (*Fencing*) A parry in which the hand is opposite the right breast and the point of the sword raised and a little to the right. **sixteen** (siks tēn′), *a.* Consisting of six and ten. *n.* This number or the symbol representing it, 16, xvi. **sixteenmo,** *n.* Sexto-decimo. **sixteenth,** *a.* and *n.* **sixth** (siksth), *a.* Next in order after the fifth; being one of six equal parts; *n.* A sixth part; the sixth form in a school; (*Mus.*) the interval between a tone and the sixth (inclusively) above or below it on the diatonic scale; a note separated from another by this interval; a tone and its sixth sounded together. **sixthly,** *adv.* In the sixth place. **sixty,** *a.* Ten times six. *n.* This number or the symbol representing it, 60, lx. **sixty-miler,** *n.* (*Austral.*) A coastal tramp steamer, a small trading vessel. **sixtieth** (siks′ ti ėth), *a.* and *n.*

sizable (sī′ zăbl), *a.* Of considerable size.

sizar (sī′ zȧr) [SIZE (1), -ER], *n.* A student at Cambridge University or Trinity College, Dublin, who pays lower fees than the ordinary students, and formerly acted as servitor.

size (1) (sīz) [orig. short for ASSIZE], *n.* Measurement, extent, dimensions, magnitude; one of a series of standard grades or classes with which garments and other things are divided according to their relative dimensions; a sizer for pearls; *a standard of weight or measurement; (*Camb. Univ.*) a specific allowance of food and drink from the buttery, a ration; (*slang*) quality, character, condition (of any one or anything). *v.t.* To sort or arrange according to size; to cut or shape to a required size. *v.i.* (*Camb. Univ.*) To order food or drink from the buttery. **to size up:** To form a rough estimate of the size of; (*colloq.*) to judge the capacity (of a person). **sized,** *a.* (*usu. in comb.* as *small-sized*). **sizer** (1), *n.* An appliance, usu. consisting of a perforated plate or screen, for sorting out bullets, pearls, etc., according to size. **sizing** (1), *n.* The act of sorting or arranging according to size; (*Camb. Univ.*) a size.

size (2) (sīz) [It. *sisa*, short for *assisa*, painter's size, as ASSIZE], *n.* A gelatinous solution used to glaze surfaces, stiffen fabrics, etc. *v.t.* To coat, glaze or prepare with size. **sizer** (2), **sizing** (2), **sizy,** *a.* **siziness,** *n.*

sizel [SCISSEL].

sizer [SIZE (1), (2)].

sizzle (siz′ ėl) [imit.], *v.i.* To make a hissing noise as of frying. *n.* Such a noise.

sjambok (zhăm′ bok) [S.Afr. Dut., from Malay (*chābok*, Pers. *chābuk*, alert, a horse-whip)], *n.* A short heavy whip, usu. of rhinoceros hide. *v.t.* To flog with this.

skain [SKEIN].

***skainsmate** (skānz′ māt) [etym. unknown], *n.* (*Shak.*) A comrade, a boon companion.

skald [SCALD (2)].

skat (skăt) [G., from It. *scarto*], *n.* A game somewhat like piquet, played chiefly by Germans.

skate (1) (skāt) [Icel. *skata*, cp. Norw. *skata*, Dan. *skade*], *n.* A fish of the genus *Raia*, distinguished by having a long pointed snout.

skate (2) (skāt) [formerly *schates*, *scates*, Dut. *schaats*, pl. *schaatsen*, O.F. *eschace* (F. *échasse*), stilt, L.G. *schake*, SHANK], *n.* A device consisting of woodblock or steel attached under the boot with a steel blade or runner underneath to enable one to glide over ice; a similar block or frame with wheels underneath for gliding over a smooth floor. *v.i.* To move over ice, etc., on skates. *v.t.* To cut (figures) on skates. **to skate over thin ice:** To talk about or deal with a ticklish question. **skater,** *n.* **skating rink,** *n.* A place with an artificial floor or sheet of ice for skating.

skean (skēn) [Gael. *sgian*, knife, cp. O.Ir. *scīan*], *n.* A long knife or dagger. **skean-dhu** (-doo) [Gael. *dhu*, black], *n.* A knife or dagger worn by Scottish Highlanders, usu. worn in the stocking.

skedaddle (skė dăd′ ėl), *v.i.* To run away, as in a panic. *n.* A hasty flight, retreat, or dispersal.

skee [SKI].

skeel (skēl) [Icel. *skjōla*], *n.* (*Sc.*) A wooden bucket, tub, or other vessel for holding milk.

skeely (*Sc.*) [SKILLY (1)].

skeet (skēt) [etym. doubtful], *n.* (*Naut.*) A long-handled scoop or shovel used for throwing water on the decks, etc.

skeg (skeg) [Icel. *skegg*, cp. Norw. *skjegg*, Swed. *skägg*, Dan. *skjæg*, beard], *n.* A bearded variety of oats; (*Naut.*) a knee uniting the stern-post and keel of a boat.

skegger (skeg′ ėr) [etym. doubtful], *n.* A little salmon.

skein (skān) [O.F. *escaigne*, prob. from Celt. (cp. Ir. *sgainne*, Gael. *sgeinnidh*)], *n.* A quantity of yarn, silk, wool, cotton, etc., wound in a coil which is folded over and knotted; a flock of wild geese, swans, etc., in flight; (*fig.*) a tangle.

skelder (skel′ dėr) [Cant, etym. doubtful], *v.i.* To beg; to get a living thus. *v.t.* To swindle, to take in, to cheat.

skeleton (skel′ ė tȯn) [Gr., a mummy, orig. neut. of *skeletos*, dried up, from *skellein*, to dry, to parch], *n.* The bones of a person or animal dried, preserved, and fastened together in the posture of the living creature; a very lean person; (*Biol.*) the hard supporting or protective framework of an animal or vegetable body, comprising bones, cartilage, shell, and other rigid parts; the supporting framework of any structure; the essential portions, the nucleus (of an organization); an outline or rough draft. **family skeleton** or **skeleton in the cupboard:** An unpleasant or distressing domestic secret. **skeleton-drill,** *n.* Drill carried out by a small number of men representing companies, battalions, etc. **skeleton-key,** *n.* A key with most of the inner bits removed, used for picking locks. **skeleton type:** Type characterized by thin strokes. **skeletal,** *a.* (*Anat.*) Pertaining to the skeleton. **skeleto-,** *comb. form.* **skeletography** (-tog′ ră fi), *n.* The science of describing the skeleton. **skeletology** (-tol′ ŏ ji), *n.* The branch of anatomy treating of the skeleton. **skeletonize** (skel′-), *v.t.* To reduce to or as to a skeleton framework or outline.

skelloch (skel′ och) [imit.], *v.i.* (*Sc.*) To shriek, to squeal, to yell, to make a shrill noise. *n.* Such a cry or noise.

***skellum** (skel′ ŭm) [Dut. *schelm*, cp. G. *schelm*, Icel. *skelmir*], *n.* A rogue, a scoundrel.

skelly (1) (skel′ i) [prob. from Icel., cp. Norw. *skjegla*, A.-S. *sceolh*, squint], *v.i.* (*Sc.*) To squint.

skelly (2) (skel′ i) (*Sc.*) [SKERRY].

skelp (skelp) [Sc., from Gael. *sgealp*, a slap], *n.* A blow, a smack; a squall, a sudden shower. *v.t.* To strike, to slap.

skelter [HELTER-SKELTER].

skene [SKEAN].

skep (skep) [Icel. *skeppa*, cp. Dut. *schepel*, G. *scheffel*, basket], *n.* A basket or similar receptacle of wicker, wood, etc.; a beehive of straw or wicker.

skeptic, etc. [SCEPTIC].

skerrick (ske′ rik) [Austral.], *n.* A tiny amount. **there's not a skerrick left:** There's not anything whatever left.

skerry (sker′ i) [Orkney, from Icel. *sker*, cp. SCAR (2)], *n.* A rocky islet in the sea; a reef.

sketch (skech) [Dut. *schets*, It. *schizzo*, L. *schedius*, Gr. *schedios*, hasty, off-hand, cogn. with *schein*, to hold], *n.* A rough, hasty, unfinished, or tentative delineation; a preliminary study, a rough draft, an outline, a short account without details; a play, descriptive article, musical composition, etc., of a brief, unelaborated, or slight character. *v.t.* To make a sketch of; to present in rough draft or outline without details. *v.i.* To make a sketch or sketches. **sketch-block,** *n.* A pad of drawing-paper for making sketches on. **sketch-book,** *n.* A book for sketching in; a collection of descriptive essays, etc. **sketchable,** *a.* **sketcher,** *n.* **sketchy,** *a.* **sketchily,** *adv.* **sketchiness,** *n.*

skew (skū) [prob. from M.Dut. *schouwen*, to avoid (cp. G. *scheuen*, also ESCHEW, SHY (1))], *v.i.* To move sideways, to turn aside, to swerve; to squint, to look askance. *a.* Oblique, twisted, turned askew; (*Math.*) distorted, unsymmetrical. *n.* An oblique course, position, or movement; a squint; a sloping coping, or a stone supporting the coping of a gable. **skew-back,** *n.* A stone, plate, or course of masonry at the top of an abutment taking the spring of an arch. **skewness,** *n.* **skew bridge:** A bridge having an arch or arches set obliquely to the abutments. **skew curve:** A curve not in one plane. **skew-wheel,** *n.* A gear wheel with oblique teeth. **skew-whiff,** *a.* Askew, to one side.

skewbald (skū′ bawld), *a.* Piebald with spots of white and another colour than black.

skewer (skū′ ėr) [var. of obs. *skiver*, SHIVER (1)], *n.* A pin of wood or iron for holding meat together; (*facet.*) a sword. *v.t.* To fasten with a skewer; to pierce with or as with a skewer.

ski (shē, skē) [Norw., from Icel. *skīth*, billet of wood, snow-shoe], *n.* (*pl.* **skis**) A long narrow snow-shoe or sleigh consisting of a narrow runner fastened one to each foot and used for sliding over snow. *v.i.* To slide on skis. **ski-ing,** *pres.p.*

skiagraphy (skī ăg′ rȧ fi) [F. *sciagraphie*, L. and Gr. *skiagraphia* (*skia*, shadow, -GRAPHY)], *n.* The art of drawing objects with correct shading; a photograph by Röntgen rays; a sciagraph; (*Astron.*) the art of finding the hour by the shadow of the sun, moon, or stars; dialling. **skiagraph** (skī′ ȧ grăf), *n.* A photograph by Röntgen rays; a vertical section of a building showing the interior. **skiagraphic, -al** (-grăf′ ik, -ȧl), *a.* **skiagraphically,** *adv.*

skiamachy (skī ăm′ ȧ ki), *n.* A sham fight, a visionary fight; a fight with a shadow.

skiametry (skī ăm′ e tri), *n.* The theory of eclipses; the measurement of eclipses; the science of skiagraphs mathematically considered.

skiascopy (skī ăs′ kŏ pi), *n.* A method of measuring the refractive power of the eye by projecting light into it from a small mirror, the shadow-test.

skid (skid) [cp. Icel. *skīth*, SKI, also M.E. *shide*, A.-S. *scid*, a thin piece of wood, rel. to SHEATH], *n.* One of a pair of parallel timbers for supporting a barrel, boat, etc.; a timber or frame used to prop a vessel during building, etc.; a plank or log used for sliding heavy things on; a skid-pan or other device acting as a brake; the act of skidding, a slip on muddy ground. *v.t.* (*past & p.p.* **skidded**) To place on or support with a skid or skids; to check or brake with a skid. *v.i.* (of wheels or vehicles) To slip sideways; to revolve rapidly without progressing. **skid-pan,** *n.* A shoe or drag usu. put under a wheel as a brake on a slope, etc.

skiey [SKYEY].

skiff (1) (skif) [F. *esquif*, It. *schifo*, prob. from O.H.G. *skif* (cp. G. *schiff*), SHIP], *n.* A small light boat. *v.t.* To row or scull in a skiff.

skiff (2) (skif) [etym. doubtful], *a.* (*prov.*) Awkward, clumsy; distorted. **skiffy,** *a.*

skiffle (skif′ ėl), *n.* Sort of music played by a **skiffle group,** a band composed of players on a variety of unconventional instruments.

skill (skil) [Icel. *skil*, discernment, from *skilja*, to separate, distinguish, cogn. with SHELL and SCALE (1)], *n.* Familiar knowledge of any art or science combined with dexterity; expertness, practical mastery. *†v.t.* To understand; to be skilled in. *†v.i.* To have discernment or understanding; to matter, to signify. **†it skills not:** It matters not; it avails not. **skilful,** *a.* Having or showing skill, expert, adept; clever, adroit, dexterous, †reasonable. **skilfully,** *adv.* **skilfulness,** *n.* **skilled,** *a.* Having skill, skilful. **†skilless,** *a.* Destitute of skill; ignorant (of). **skilly** (1), *a.* (*Sc.*).

skillet (skil′ ėt) [O.F. *escuellette*, dim. of *escuelle*, L. *scutella*, dim. of *scutra*, dish (cp. SCUTTLE (1))], *n.* A metal pan or kettle, with a long handle and usu. short legs, for boiling water, etc.

skilling (1) (skil′ ing) [etym. doubtful], *n.* An outhouse, a lean-to, a shed.

skilling (2) (skil′ ing) [Dan., Norw., and Swed., cp. Dut. *schelling*], *n.* A former Scandinavian copper money of account, worth about ½d.

skilly (1) [SKILL].

skilly (2), **†skilligalee** (skil′ i, -gȧ lē′) [etym. doubtful], *n.* (*slang*) Thin broth, soup, or gruel, esp. as used in prisons, workhouses, etc.

skim (skim) [from SCUM, cp. DINT and DENT (1), FILL (1) and FULL (1)], *v.t.* (*past & p.p.* **skimmed**) To clear the scum, etc., from the surface of; to take (cream, etc.) from the surface of a liquid; to touch lightly or nearly touch the surface of, to graze; to glance over or read superficially. *v.i.* To pass lightly and rapidly over or along a surface; to glance (over) rapidly and superficially. *n.* Scum; the thick matter which forms on the surface of a liquid. **skim-milk,** *n.* Milk from which the cream has been skimmed. **skimmer,** *n.* One who or that which skims; a perforated ladle for skimming; a bird of the N. American genus *Rhynchops*, which skims small fishes from the water with its lower mandible. **skimming,** *n.* **skimmingly,** *adv.*

skimmington (skim′ ing tȯn) [perh. from SKIMMING, *-ton*, as in pers. names, e.g. *Washington*], *n.* A mock procession, ridiculing a henpecked husband, unfaithful wife, etc., once common in villages (often with a woman in the attitude of beating a man with a skimming-ladle, whence the name).

skimp (skimp) [perh. from Icel. *skemma*, to shorten, from *skamr*, short], *v.t.* To supply in a niggardly manner, to stint (a person, provisions, etc.). *v.i.* To be stingy or parsimonious. **skimpingly,** *adv.* **skimpy,** *a.*

skin (skin) [Icel. *skinn*, cogn. with G. *schinden*, to skin, to flay], *n.* The natural membranous outer covering of an animal body; the hide or integument of an animal removed from the body, with or without the hair; a vessel made of the skin of an animal for holding liquids; the outer layer or covering of a plant, fruit, etc.; (*fig.*) the outside layer of a wall, the planking or plates of a vessel; (*Elec.*) the outer layers of a conductor which serve to transmit current at high frequencies. *v.t.* (*past & p.p.* **skinned**) To strip the skin from, to flay, to peel; (*slang*) to strip (oneself) or take off (a garment); to cover (over) with or as with skin. *v.i.* To become covered (over) with skin, to cicatrize. **by the skin of one's teeth:** Very narrowly, by a close shave. **to save one's skin:** To escape injury. **to get under one's skin:** To interest or annoy one intensely. **skin current,** *n.* (*Elec.*) A current transmitted by the outer layer only of a conductor. **skin-diver,** *n.* One who dives deep wearing no protective clothing, esp. a pearl-diver. **skin effect,** *n.* (*Elec.*) The tendency of an alternating current to be diffused over the surface of a conductor instead of being equally distributed over the whole area. **skin-game,** *n.* A swindle; robbery by business methods. **skin-grafting,** *n.* (*Surg.*) The transfer of skin from a sound to a diseased or injured part. **skin-wool,** *n.* Wool from a dead sheep. **skin-deep,** *a.* Superficial, not deep. **skinflint,** *n.* A niggardly person, a miser. **skinful,** *n.* (*slang*) As much as the stomach will hold (esp. of liquor). **skinless,** *a.* **skinned,** *a.* (usu. in comb., as *thin-skinned*). **skinner,** *n.* One who skins; one who deals in skins, a furrier. **skinny,** *a.* Consisting only of a skin, very lean or thin. **skinniness,** *n.*

skink (skingk) [F. *scinc* (now *scinque*), L. *scincus*, Gr. *skinkos*], *n.* A small African and Syrian lizard formerly esteemed in medicine.

skip (1) (skip [M.E. *skippen* (cp. Norw. and Swed. dial. *skopa*, also Icel. *skoppa*, to spin)], *v.i.* (*past & p.p.* **skipped**) To move about with light bounds, hops, or capers, esp. by shifting rapidly from one foot to another; to frisk, to gambol; to jump repeatedly over a skipping-rope passed rapidly over the head and under the feet; to pass rapidly from one thing to another; to make omissions; (*slang*) to make off hurriedly, to bolt (off); to go over with a bound; to pass over without notice, to omit. *n.* A light leap or spring, esp. from one foot to the other; (*Radio.*) a belt of inaudibility; (*T.C.D.*) a college-servant, a scout. **skip-jack,** *n.* A jumping toy made from the wish-bone of a fowl; one of various kinds of fish, beetles, etc., that move with skips; an upstart, *a conceited fop. ***skip-kennel,** *n.* One who skips gutters, a lackey, a footboy. **skippable,** *a.* **skipper** (1), *n.* One who skips; a young, thoughtless person; the cheese-maggot; a skip-jack; one of the lepidopteran family *Hesperidæ*, from their short, jerky flight. **skipping-rope,** *n.* A rope used by children in the game of skipping. **skippingly,** *adv.*

skip (2) (skip) [var. of SKEP], *n.* (*Eng.*) A bucket for moving spoil or materials, working from a crane; a box for hoisting coal or mineral up a mine shaft.

skipper (1) [SKIP (1)].

skipper (2) (skip' ėr) [Dut. *schipper* (*schip*, SHIP, -ER)], *n.* A sea captain, esp. the master of a merchant vessel; the captain of a team or side. **skipper's daughters:** White-crested waves.

skippet (skip' ėt) [dim. of SKIP (2)], *n.* A flat round box for holding the seal attached to a document; *a small boat.

skippingly, skipping-rope [SKIP (1)].

skirl (skĕrl) [Sc., var. of SHRILL], *v.i.* To make a shrill noise like that of the bagpipes; to shriek. *n.* A shrill cry or noise.

skirmish (skĕr' mish) [O.F. *eskermiss-*, stem of *eskermir*, to fence; from O.H.G. *scirman*, from *scirm* (cp. G. *schirm*, shelter, cover)], *n.* A slight or irregular fight, esp. between small parties or troops in scattered formation; a desultory combat; (*fig.*) a light contest in debate, etc. *v.i.* To fight in a slight, desultory or preliminary way, or in scattered formation or small parties. **skirmisher,** *n.*

skirr (skĕr) [prob. rel. to SCOUR (2)], *v.t.* To pass over rapidly, as on horseback, to scour. *v.i.* To move rapidly, to scud.

skirret (skir' ėt) [M.E. *skyrwyt*, prob. from O.F. *eschervis*, Sp. *chirivia*, Arab. *karawiyā*, CARAWAY], *n.* A species of water-parsnip, *Sium sisarum*, the tuberous root of which was formerly eaten as a relish.

skirt (skĕrt) [M.E. *skyrt*, Icel. *skyrta*, shirt], *n.* The part of a coat or other garment hanging below the waist; a woman's outer garment shaped like a petticoat, hanging from the waist; (*slang*) a woman, a girl; the edge of anything, a border, a margin; (*pl.*) the extremities or outer parts. *v.t.* To lie or go along or by the edge of; to border; to edge or border (with). *v.i.* To lie or move (along, round, on) the border or outskirts. **skirt-dance,** *n.* A dance in which the performer waves long, flowing skirts about in graceful undulations. **skirt-dancer,** *n.* **skirt-dancing,** *n.* **skirter,** *n.* One who skirts, esp. a dog that runs wide of the pack. **skirting, skirting-board,** *n.* A board running round the wall of a room at the bottom. **skirtings,** *n.pl.* (*Austral.*) The inferior parts of wool.

skit (skit) [prob. var. of foll.], *n.* A satirical piece, lampoon, or burlesque of a trifling kind.

skite (skīt) [Sc., prob. from Icel. *skȳt*, stem of *skjōta*, to SHOOT], *v.i.* To dart aside, to slip off, to scoot; (*Austral. colloq.*) to boast. *n.* A sharp blow, esp. in a slanting direction; a skit; a contemptible person.

skitter (skit' ėr) [prob. freq. of prec.], *v.i.* To glide, skim, or skip rapidly, esp. along a surface; (*Am.*) to fish by drawing a spoon-bait, etc., along the surface.

skittish (skit' ish), *a.* Excitable, nervous, easily frightened (of horses); capricious, uncertain, coquettish, wanton, too lively. **skittishly,** *adv.* **skittishness,** *n.*

skittle (skit' ėl) [Dan. *skyttel*, an earthen ball used in child's game, as SHUTTLE], *n.* One of the blocks or pins set up to be thrown at in ninepins. *v.i.* To play at ninepins. **skittle-alley, -ground,** *n.* **skittle-ball,** *n.*

skive (skīv) [Icel. *skīfa*, cogn. with SHIVE], *v.t.* To split (leather) into thin layers; to shave or pare (hides). **skiver,** *n.* A paring-tool for leather; a thin leather split from a sheep-skin, used for book-binding.

skivvy (ski' vi), *n.* (*vulg.*) A servant maid, a general servant.

skof (skof) [S. African, Dut. *schoft*, a meal], *n.* Food, a meal.

skrik (skrik) [S. African, Dut.], *n.* Fright.

skua (skū' à) [Icel. *skūfr*, *skūmr* (cp. *skūmi*, shade, Norw. and Swed. *skum*, dull, dusky)], *n.* A dark-coloured predatory sea-bird allied to the gulls.

skulduggery (skŭl dŭg' ė ri) [?], *n.* (*colloq.*) Underhand trickery.

skulk (skŭlk) [Dan. *skulk* (cp. Swed. *skolka*, Dut. *schuilen*)], *v.i.* To lurk, to withdraw and conceal oneself; to lie concealed, to move about furtively; to sneak away, esp. from duty, work, danger, etc. *n.* One who skulks, a skulker. **skulker,** *n.*

skull (skŭl) [M.E. *skulle*, *scolle* (cp. Swed. dial. *skulle*, Norw. *skult*), cogn. with SCALE (2)], *n.* The bony case enclosing the brain, the skeleton of the head, the cranium. **skull-cap,** *n.* A light, brimless cap fitting closely to the head, esp. worn indoors to protect against draughts; the sinciput; a plant of the genus *Scutellaria* with blue, helmet-shaped flowers. **skull and crossbones:** A representation of a human skull surmounting two crossed thigh-bones, used as an emblem of death. **skulled,** *a.* (*usu. in comb.*, as *thick-skulled*). **skull-less,** *a.*

skullbanker (skŭl' băng kėr) [Austral.], *n.* A loafer, a ne'er-do-well, a tramp.

skunk (skŭngk) [Abenaki (Algonkin) *segongw*], *n.* A N. American carnivorous quadruped, *Mephitis mephitica*, with bushy tail and white stripes down the back, which when irritated ejects a fetid secretion from the anal glands; (*fig.*) a base, low fellow; (*Am. slang*) a defeat (at cards, etc.). *v.t.* (*Am. slang*) To defeat completely. **skunk-bird, -blackbird,** *n.* The bobolink.

Skupshtina (skup' shtē na) [Serb.], *n.* (*Pol.*) The old Serbian parliament.

sky (skī) [Icel. *sky* (cp. A.-S. *scēo*, cloud, *scuwa*, shadow), cogn. with SCUM, SHOWER, L. *obscūrus*, OBSCURE], *n.* The apparent vault of heaven, the firmament; the upper region of the atmosphere, the region of clouds; a climate; (*pl.*) the celestial regions, the heavens; *a cloud. *v.t.* To hit (a ball) high into the air; to hang (a picture) in the top tier at an exhibition. **sky-blue,** *a.* and *n.* ***sky-born, -bred,** *a.* (*poet.*) Of heavenly or divine origin. **sky-colour,** *n.* **sky-high,** *a.* or *adv.* High as the sky, very high. **sky-lark,** *n.* A lark, *Alauda arvensis*, that flies singing high into the air. *v.i.* (*slang*) To lark, to frolic, to play practical jokes, etc. **skylight,** *n.* A window set in a roof or ceiling in the same plane. **sky-pilot,** *n.* (*slang*) A clergyman, a priest, a preacher. **sky-planted,** *a.* Placed in the sky. **sky-rocket,** *n.* A rocket fired high in the air. **skysail,** *n.* A light sail set above the royal in a square-rigged ship. **skyscape,** *n.* A picture or view chiefly of the sky or clouds. **sky-scraper,** *n.* A very high building, chimney, signboard, etc.; a triangular skysail. **sky-line,** *n.* Outline against the sky of the configuration of the land. **sky-sign, sky-writing,** *n.* A pattern, which can be in the form of writing, traced in the air by smoke discharged from an aeroplane. ***sky-tinctured,** *a.* Coloured like the sky. **skyey, skyish,** *a.* **skyless,** *a.* **skyward,** *a.* and *adv.* **skywards,** *adv.*

Skye (skī) [Isle of *Skye*], *n.* A small rough-haired variety of Scotch terrier with long body and short legs, also called **Skye terrier.**

skyey, skylight, etc. [SKY].

skyr (skĕr) [Icel.], *n.* A dish of curd.

skyscape, sky-scraper, etc. [SKY].

slab (1) (slăb) [etym. doubtful, cp. O.F. *esclape*, splinter (*es-*, EX-, L.G. *klappen*, to cleave noisily, cp. G. *klaffen*, to split)], *n.* A thin, flat, regularly-shaped piece of anything, esp. of fissile sandstone; the outside piece sawn from a log in squaring the side; (*Austral.*) a plank. *v.t.* (*past & p.p.* **slabbed**) To saw slabs from (a log, etc.); to square (a tree) in order to saw it into planks; to cover or line with slabs. **slab-sided,** *a.* Having flat sides; (*Am.*) tall or long and lank. **slab-stone,** *n.* A flag-stone. **slabbing-gang,** *n.* A series of saws held in two sets for cutting timber into slabs, etc. **slabbing-machine,** *n.*

***slab** (2) (slăb) [prov. *slab*, puddle, Icel. *slabb*, mire (cp. Swed. dial. and Norw. *slabb*, M.Dan. *slab*)], *a.* Thick, slimy, viscous, sticky. *n.* Ooze, mud, slime. ***slabby,** *a.* ***slabbiness,** *n.* The state of being slabby.

slabber, etc. [SLOBBER].

slack (1) (slăk) [A.-S. *sleac* (cp. Icel. *slakr*, Swed. and Dan. *slak*, O.H.G. *slah*), cogn. with LAG and LAX], *a.* Not drawn tight, loose; limp, relaxed, careless, listless, remiss, not zealous, eager, or active; tardy, sluggish, dull. *adv.* In a slack manner; insufficiently. *n.* The part of a rope that hangs loose; a slack period in trade, etc.; small coal, screenings; (*pl.*) trousers, esp. as worn in the navy; women's trousers. *v.t.* and *i.* To slacken; (*colloq.*) to be lazy. **slack in stays:** (*Naut.*) Slow in going about. **to slack away** or **off:** To loosen, to reduce the tension on (a rope, etc.). **to slack up:** To slow down (a train) before stopping. **slack-bake,** *v.t.* To bake (bread, etc.) slightly, to underbake. **slacken,** *v.i.* To become slack. *v.t.* To cause to be slack, to relax; to slake (lime). **slacker,** *n.* A thing that slackens; (*colloq.*) a shirker, a lazy fellow. **slackly,** *adv.* **slackness,** *n.*

slack (2) (slăk) [Icel. *slakki*, cp. Norw. *slakke*], *n.* (*Sc. and North.*) A hollow, a dip, a dell; a bog, a morass.

slackwater (slăk′ waw′ ter), *n.* The interval between the flux and the reflux of the tide.

slade (slād) [A.-S. *slæd*, cp. Norw. dial. *slad*, Dan. and G. dial. *slade*], *n.* (*prov.*) A little valley or dell, a dingle; a flat piece of low moist ground.

slae (*Sc.*) [SLOE].

slag (slăg) [Swed. *slagg*, cp. Norw. *slagga*, to flow over, G. *schlacke*, slag], *n.* The fused refuse or dross separated in the reduction of ores; volcanic scoria. *v.i.* To form a slag, to combine in a slaggy mass. *v.t.* To convert into slag. **slaggy,** *a.*

slain, *p.p.* [SLAY (1)].

slaister (slā′ stėr) [Sc., etym. doubtful], *n.* A dirty or repulsive mess; the act of making this. *v.t.* To plaster up, to daub. *v.i.* To do anything in a dirty, slovenly way.

slake (1) (slāk) [A.-S. *slacian*, from *slæc*, *sleac*, SLACK (1)], *v.t.* To quench, to assuage, to satisfy, to appease; to mix (lime) with water so as to form a chemical combination. *v.i.* To become slaked (of lime). **slakeless,** *a.*

slake (2) (slāk) [Icel. *sleikja*, also Norw.], *v.t.* (*Sc.*) To lick, to bedaub, to smear. *n.* A smear, a lick.

slalom (sla′ lŏm) [Norw.], *n.* A ski-race down a course marked with artificial obstacles.

slam (slăm) [cp. Norw. *slemba*, Icel. *slambra*, prob. imit. in orig.], *v.t.* (*past & p.p.* **slammed**) To shut suddenly with a loud noise; to put (a thing down) thus; (*slang*) to hit, to thrash, to defeat completely; (*whist, etc.*) to beat by winning every trick. *v.i.* To shut violently or noisily (of a door). *n.* A noise as of the violent shutting of a door; (*whist, etc.*) the winning of every trick in a game.

***slammakin, -merkin** (slăm′ ȧ-, -ėr kin) [etym. doubtful], *n.* (*prov.*) A slatternly woman. *a.* Slatternly, untidy.

slander (slan′ dėr) [O.F. *esclander*, L. *scandalum*, SCANDAL], *n.* A false report maliciously uttered to injure a person; defamation, calumny; (*Law*) false defamatory language or statements. *v.t.* To injure by the malicious utterance of a false report, to defame falsely. **slanderer,** *n.* **slanderous,** *a.* **slanderously,** *adv.* **slanderousness,** *n.*

slang (1) (slăng) [prob. from Norw. *sleng*, slinging, from *slengja*, to SLING], *n.* Words or language used colloquially but not regarded as correct English; the special language or dialect of a particular class, cant, jargon; cheek, abuse, violent language; a short weight or measure; a hawker's licence. *v.i.* To use slang. *v.t.* To use slang to; to abuse. **slangy,** *a.* **slangily,** *adv.* **slanginess,** *n.*

slang (2) (slăng) [prob. from Dut. *slang*, snake], *n.* (*Cant*) A chain, esp. a watch-chain; (*pl.*) fetters.

slank [SLINK].

slant (slant) [prob. through M.E. *slenten*, *sclenten*, from Norw. *slenta*], *v.i.* To slope; to incline from or be oblique to a vertical or horizontal line. *v.t.* To cause to slant. *a.* Sloping, oblique; inclined from a horizontal or perpendicular line. *n.* A slope; inclination from the vertical or horizontal; (*fig.*) an oblique censure or sarcasm; (*colloq.*) an angle of approach, information concerning; (*Naut.*) a slight breeze. **slantendicular** (-dik′ ū lȧr), *a.* (*slang*) Oblique, slanting. **slantingly,** *adv.* **slantly, -ways, -wise,** *adv.*

slap (1) (slăp) [cp. L.G. *slapp*, imit. of sound], *v.t.* (*past & p.p.* **slapped**) To strike with the open hand, to smack. *n.* Such a blow. *adv.* As with a sudden blow, plump, bang. **slap in the face:** A rebuff. **slap-bang,** *adv.* Suddenly, violently, headlong. **slap-dash,** *adv.* In a careless, rash, impetuous manner. *a.* Hasty, impetuous, careless, happy-go-lucky. *n.* Rough and random work; rough-cast. *v.t.* To rough-cast. **slap-jack,** *n.* A flap-jack. **slapstick,** *n.* (*Theat.*) A comedian's stick so constructed as to make a loud noise when striking someone. *a.* Broad comedy or farce in which furniture is broken, clothes are torn, etc. **slap-up,** *a.* First-rate, smart, stylish.

slap (2) (slăp) [cp. Dut. and L.G. *slop*, G. *schlupf*], *n.* (*Sc.*) A breach, a gap in a fence, etc.; a narrow pass or cleft between hills; a passage left open at fixed times in a salmon-cruive; the period during which this is left open.

slape (slāp) [Icel. *sleipr*, cp. Norw. *sleip*], *a.* (*North.*) Slippery, smooth; crafty, hypocritical. **slape-face,** *n.* **slape-haired,** *a.*

slash (slăsh) [O.F. *esclachier* (*es-*, EX-, M.H.G. *klecken*, to break noisily, from *klac*, noise), perh. conf. with *esclicier*, to SLICE], *v.t.* To cut by striking violently at random; to make long incisions or narrow gashes in, to slit; (*usu. in p.p.*) to make slits in (sleeves, etc.) to show the lining; to lash (with a whip, etc.); (*Mil.*) to fell (trees) so as to make an abatis. *v.i.* To strike (at, etc.) violently and at random with a knife, sword, etc.; to lash (out at, etc.). *n.* A long cut, slit, or incision; a slashing cut. **slasher,** *n.*

slat (1) (slăt) [M.E., var. of foll.], *n.* A thin narrow strip, usu. of wood, used in Venetian blinds, crates, etc. **slatted,** *a.* **slatting,** *n.*

slat (2) (slăt) [etym. doubtful], *v.t.* To fling, to dash, to slap, to jerk; to beat, to bang. *v.i.* To beat, to bang; to flap violently (of sails). *n.* A sharp blow, a violent flap.

slatch (slăch) [var. of SLACK (1)], *n.* (*Naut.*) The slack of a rope; a spell of fine weather.

slate (1) (slāt) [M.E. *slat*, *sclat*, O.F. *esclat* (F. *éclat*), from *esclater*, to break to pieces, late L.

exclapitāre (EX-, L.G. *klappen*, to CLAP)], *n.* A fine-grained laminated rock easily splitting into thin, smooth, even slabs; a slab or trimmed piece of this, esp. for use as a roofing-tile; a tablet of slate, usu. framed, for writing on; (*Am.*) a preliminary list of candidates liable to revision. *v.t.* To cover or roof with slates. **slate-axe,** *n.* A slater's sax. **slate-black, -blue, -grey,** *a.* Of the dark, blue, or grey colour characteristic of slate. **slate-club,** *n.* A small friendly society which provides relief, Christmas dinners, etc., from weekly subscriptions paid by the members. **slate-colour,** *n.* **slate-coloured,** *a.* **slate-pencil,** *n.* A piece of soft slate for writing on slates with. **slater,** *n.* One who manufactures slates; one who slates roofs; (*Sc.*) a wood-louse. **slaty,** *a.* **slatiness,** *n.*

slate (2) (slāt) [etym. unknown; prob. conn. with prec.], *v.t.* To criticize savagely, to abuse, to berate.

slattern (slăt' ėrn) [from obs. *slatter*, to be wasteful or untidy, freq. of obs. *slat*, to splash, cp. Icel. *sletta*], *n.* An untidy or sluttish woman. **slatternly,** *a.* **slatternliness,** *n.*

slaty [SLATE (1)].

slaughter (slaw' tėr) [Icel. *slātr*, slaughtering, meat, cogn. with SLAY (1)], *n.* Wholesale or indiscriminate killing, butchery, carnage; the killing of beasts for market. *v.t.* To kill wantonly or ruthlessly, to massacre; to kill for the market. **slaughterhouse,** *n.* A place where beasts are slaughtered, a shambles; (*fig.*) a scene of great destruction of life. **slaughterman,** *n.* One who kills beasts for market; a slayer, a destroyer. **slaughterer,** *n.* ***slaughterous,** *a.* ***slaughterously,** *adv.*

Slav (slav, slăv) [F. *Slave* or G. *sklave*, med. L. *Slavus*, *Sclavus*, or late Gr. *sklabos*, *sklabēnos*, from Slavonic], *n.* One of an Aryan race inhabiting eastern Europe, comprising the Russians, Poles, Serbo-Croatians, Bulgarians, Slovenes, etc. *a.* Slavonic. **Slavdom, Slavism,** *n.* **Slavic,** *a.* Slavonic, *n.* The Slavonic language. **Slavonian** (slȧ vō' ni ȧn), *a.* Of or pertaining to the Slav race or to Slavonia, a part of the Austrian province of Croatia-Slavonia. *n.* The Slav language; a member of the Slav race; an inhabitant of Slavonia. **Slavonic** (-von' ik), *a.* and *n.* **Slavonicize,** *v.t.* **Slavophil** (slăv' ȯ fil) [-PHIL], *n.* **Slavophobe** [-PHOBE], *n.*

slave (slāv) [F. *esclave*, med.L. *sclavus*, a SLAV captive], *n.* One who is the property of and bound to obedience to another; one who is entirely under the influence (of) or a helpless victim (to); one who works like a slave, a drudge; a person of slavish mind, a mean, abject person. *v.i.* To toil like a slave, to drudge. ***slave-born,** *a.* Born in slavery or of slave parents. **slave-driver,** *n.* An overseer of slaves at their work; an exacting taskmaster. **slave-grown,** *a.* Produced by slave labour. **slave-holder,** *n.* One who owns slaves. **slave-holding,** *a.* **slave-hunt,** *n.* An expedition for capturing persons to be sold into slavery; a hunt for fugitive slaves. **slave-hunter,** *n.* **slave-ship,** *n.* A vessel engaged in the slave-trade. **slave State:** One of the Southern States of N. America in which slavery flourished. **slave-trade,** *n.* The trade of procuring, buying, and selling slaves. **slave-trader,** *n.* **slave-like,** *a.* **slaver** (1), *n.* One who deals in slaves; a slave-ship. **slavery** (1), *n.* **slavey,** *n.* (*slang*) A maid-servant, a household drudge.

slaver (2) (slăv' ėr) [Icel. *slafra* (cp. L.G. *slabbern*)], *v.i.* To let saliva flow from the mouth, to slabber, to dribble. *v.t.* To let saliva dribble upon or over. *n.* Saliva dribbling from the mouth; (*fig.*) abject flattery. **slaverer,** *n.* **slavery** (2) *a.*

slavery (1) [SLAVE]; (2) [SLAVER (2)].

slavey [SLAVE].

Slavic, etc. [SLAV].

slavish (slā' vish), *a.* Pertaining to or characteristic of a slave; subservient, servile, base, abject, ignoble; entirely imitative, devoid of originality; consisting in drudgery. **slavishly,** *adv.* **slavishness,** *n.*

slavocracy (slā vok' rȧ si), *n.* Slave owners collectively, esp. as a dominating political or social power. **slavocrat** (slā' vȯ krăt), *n.*

Slavonian, Slavonic, etc. [SLAV].

slaw (slaw) [Dut. *slaa*, SALAD], *n.* Sliced cabbage served as a salad.

slay (1) (slā) [A.-S. *slēan* (cp. Dut. *slaan*, G. *schlagen*, Icel. *slā*)], *v.t.* (*past* **slew,** sloo, *p.p.* **slain**) To put to death, to kill. **slayer,** *n.*

slay (2), **sley** (slā) [A.-S. *slege*, cogn. with SLAY (1)], *n.* (*prov.*) A weaver's reed.

***sleave** (slēv) [A.-S. *slǣfan*, cogn. with *slīfan*, to SLIVE (see O.E.D.)], *v.t.* To separate or divide (threads, etc.). *n.* Knotted, entangled, or unspun silk, floss-silk. ***sleaved,** *a.*

sleazy, sleezy (slē' zi) [etym. doubtful], *a.* Thin, wanting in substance, flimsy; slatternly. **sleaziness,** *n.*

sled (sled), **sledge** (1) (slej) [M.E. *slede*, M. Dut. *sledde* (Dut. *slede*), cp. Icel. *slethi*, Swed. *släde*, Dan *slæde*, cogn. with SLIDE (2nd form assim. to foll.)], *n.* A vehicle on runners instead of wheels used for hauling loads, etc., esp. over snow or ice; a sleigh; a toboggan. *v.t.* To carry or convey on a sled. *v.i.* To travel in a sled. ***sledded,** *a.* Mounted on a sled.

sledge (2) (slej) [A.-S. *slecge* (cp. Dut. *slegge*, Icel. *sleggja*), cogn. with SLAY (1)], *n.* The heavy hammer of a blacksmith, wielded by both hands, usu. **sledgehammer.**

sleek (slēk) [Icel. *slīkr*, cp. Dut. *slijk*, G. *schlick*, grease], *a.* Smooth, glossy (of fur, skin, etc.); (*fig.*) oily, unctuous, smooth-spoken. *v.t.* To make (hair, etc.) sleek; (*fig.*) to make pleasant or less disagreeable. **sleekly,** *adv.* **sleekness,** *n.* **sleek-headed,** *a.* **sleekstone,** *n.* A smoothing stone. **sleeky,** *a.*

sleep (slēp) [A.-S. *slǣpan*, *slēpan* (cp. Dut. *slapen*, G. *schlafen*), from *slǣp*, rel. to G. *schlaff*, loose], *v.i.* (*past & p.p.* **slept**) To take rest in sleep, to be asleep; to be or lie dormant, inactive, or in abeyance; to be dead; to spin rapidly and smoothly so as to seem motionless (of a top). *v.t.* To rest in (sleep); to furnish with accommodation for sleeping, to lodge. *n.* A state of rest in which consciousness is almost entirely suspended, the body relaxed, and the vital functions are inactive, occurring normally to men and animals once every twenty-four hours; a similar state much prolonged in hibernating and æstivating animals; (*fig.*) torpor, rest, quiet, death. **to sleep in:** To sleep on the premises; to oversleep. **to sleep on it:** To postpone making a decision until the morrow. **sleep-walker,** *n.* A somnambulist. **sleep-walking,** *n.* **sleepless,** *a.* **sleeplessly,** *adv.* **sleeplessness,** *n.*

sleeper (slē' pėr), *n.* One who sleeps; (*Rail.*) a wooden beam or other support for the rails; (*colloq.*) a sleeping-car.

sleeping (slē' ping), *a.* Asleep. *n.* The act of sleeping. **sleeping-bag,** *n.* A bag of some warm material sewn on three sides, in which one can sleep independent of bedding. **sleeping-car,** *n.* A railway-car fitted up with berths for sleeping in. **sleeping-draught,** *n.* An opiate. **sleeping-partner:** A partner having no share in the management (*Am.* a silent partner). **sleeping-sickness:** A disease characterized by fever and mental and physical lethargy, almost always fatal, endemic in tropical Africa, and caused by a parasite *Trypanosoma Gambiense.*

sleepy (slē' pi), *a.* Inclined to sleep, drowsy, somnolent; dull, lazy, indolent, habitually inactive; tending to induce sleep; (of pears and other fruit) beginning to decay. **sleepy sickness,** *n.* (*Path.*) Encephalitis lethargica, acute inflammation of certain portions of the brain, causing drowsiness and eventual mental disease. **sleepily,** *adv.* **sleepiness,** *n.*

sleet (slēt) [cp. E.Fris. *slaite*, Norw. *slūtr*, hail, G. *schlosse*, hailstone], *n.* Hail or snow mingled with rain. *v.i.* To snow or hail with a mixture of rain. **sleety,** *a.* **sleetiness,** *n.*

sleeve (slēv) [A.-S. *slyf*, rel. to SLIP], *n.* The part of a garment that covers the arm; a tube, pipe, or cylindrical sheath enclosing a revolving shaft, connecting lengths of pipe, etc. **to have up one's sleeve:** To hold secretly in reserve or in readiness for action. **to laugh in one's sleeve** [LAUGH]. **sleeve-button, -link,** *n.* A fastening, usu. of two buttons linked together, for the wrist-band. **sleeve-coupling,** *n.* A sleeve for connecting lengths of piping, etc. **sleeve-nut,** *n.* A long union with a right-hand and a left-hand screw-thread at the ends for drawing together and connecting pipes, shafts, etc. **sleeved,** *a.* Having sleeves. **sleeveless,** *a.* **sleever,** *n.* (*Austral. colloq.*) A long drink.

sleezy [SLEAZY].

***sleided** (*Shak.*) [var. of SLEAVED].

sleigh (slā) [form of SLED], *n.* A vehicle mounted on runners for driving over snow or ice. **sleigh-bell,** *n.* A small bell hung on a sleigh or its harness. **sleighing,** *n.*

sleight (slīt) [Icel. *slægth*, from *slægr*, SLY], *n.* Dexterity, skill in manipulating things; a trick so dexterously performed as to escape detection. *a.* Deceitful, artful. **sleight of hand:** Legerdemain, juggling.

slender (slen′ dėr) [M.E. *slendre*, O.F. *esclendre*, M.Dut. *slinder*, cp. G. *schlendern*, to saunter (prob. cogn. with SLIDE)], *a.* Small in circumference or width as compared with length; thin, slim; slight, scanty, meagre, inadequate, small, poor; feeble, not strong. **slenderly,** *adv.* **slenderness,** *n.*

slept, *past & p.p.* [SLEEP].

sleuth (slooth) [var. of SLOT (2)], *n.* The track of man or beast as known by the scent; (*colloq.*) a detective, esp. an amateur detective. **sleuth-hound,** *n.* A bloodhound.

slew (1) *past* [SLAY (1)].

slew (2) [SLUE]. **sley** [SLAY (2)].

slice (slīs) [M.E. *sclice*, O.F. *esclice*, from *esclicier*, to slit, from Teut., cogn. with SLIT], *n.* A broad thin piece cut off, esp. from bread, etc.; a part, share, etc., separated or allotted from a larger quantity; an implement used for slicing, a broad thin knife for taking fish, etc., from a frying-pan or for serving it; a fire shovel, a spatula. *v.t.* To cut (*usu.* up) into broad, thin pieces; to cut (off) slices from; to cut, to divide; (*Golf*) to strike a ball with a drawing motion. *v.i.* To make a cut or motion as in slicing something. **slicer,** *n.* One who or that which slices; a broad flat-bladed knife or other implement.

slick (slik) [var. of SLEEK], *a.* Smooth, sleek; (*fig.*) oily, smooth of speech, etc.; (*colloq.*) dexterous, adroit; neatly or deftly performed; clever, smart, specious. *adv.* Smoothly, deftly, smartly; quickly, immediately. **slicker,** *n.* (*Am.*) A waterproof.

slickenside, -sides (slik′ ėn sīd, -sīdz) [prov. *slicken*, SLICK, SIDE], *n.* (*Min.*) A specular galena found in Derbyshire limestone; (*Geol.*) a polished and grooved rock surface produced by friction, as in faults, the sides of a vein, etc.

***slidder** (slid′ ėr) [A.-S. *sliderian*, freq. from *slid-*. *slīdan*, to SLIDE], *v.i.* To slip, to slide. **sliddery,** *a.*

slide (slīd) [A.-S. *slīdan*, cp. L.G. *sliddern*, G. *schlittern*, freq. from *slid-*], *v.i.* (*past & p.p.* **slid,** **p.p.* **slidden**) To move smoothly along a surface with continuous contact, to glide, to slip, esp. to glide over ice, snow, or other slippery surface, without skates; to pass (away, into, etc.) smoothly, gradually, or imperceptibly. *v.t.* To cause to move smoothly along with a slippery motion. *n.* A thing, piece, or part that slides, as a glass carrying a picture used in a magic-lantern or an object to be viewed in a microscope, the part in front of the negative in a photographic plate-holder, a part serving to open or close an aperture in a steam-engine, instrument, etc.; a surface, series of grooves, guide-bars, etc., on which a part slides; an inclined plane, shute, etc.; a polished track on ice on which persons slide; a prepared slope for coasting or tobogganing; the act of sliding; a smooth and easy passage; (*Mus.*) a series of tones passing smoothly one into another. **slide-rule** [SLIDING-RULE]. **slide-way,** *n.* An inclined plane, shute, etc. **slidable,** *a.* **slider,** *n.* **sliding-keel,** *n.* A centre-board. **sliding-rule,** *n.* **slide rule,** *n.* A device, consisting of one rule sliding within another, whereby several arithmetical processes can be performed mechanically. **sliding-scale,** *n.* A scale of duties, prices, etc., varying directly or inversely according to fluctuations of value or other conditions. **sliding-seat,** *n.* A seat moving with the rower's body so as to lengthen the stroke, esp. in racing-boats.

***slight** (1) [SLEIGHT].

slight (2) (slīt) [M.Dut. *slicht*, cp. O.L.G. *sligt*, G. *schlicht*, Icel. *slēttr*], *a.* Inconsiderable, insignificant; small in amount, intensity, etc.; inadequate, paltry, superficial, negligible; slender, slim; frail, flimsy, weak; *foolish. *n.* An act of disregard, disrespect, or neglect. *v.t.* To treat as of little importance, to disregard; to treat disrespectfully, to put a slight upon; *to throw, as of no value. **slighter,** *n.* **slightingly,** *adv.* **slightish,** *a.* **slightly,** *adv.* **slightness,** *n.* ***slightly,** *a.*

slily [SLYLY].

slim (slim) [cp. M.Dut. *slim*, sly, G. *schlimm*, bad, cunning], *a.* Slender, thin, of slight shape or build; (*colloq.*) cunning, crafty, clever in outwitting. *v.i.* (*past & p.p.* **slimmed**) To adopt devices such as dieting and exercises in order to keep the body slim. **slimming,** *n.* **slimly,** *adv.* **slimmish,** *a.* **slimness,** *n.* **slimsy,** *a.* (*Am.*) Flimsy, frail.

slime (slīm) [A.-S. *slīm*, cp. Dut. *slijm*, G. *schleim*, Icel. *slīm*, also L. *līmus*, mud], *n.* A soft, glutinous, or viscous substance, esp. soft, moist, and sticky earth. *v.t.* To smear or cover with slime. **slime pit,** *n.* A pit of liquid asphalt or bitumen. **slimy,** *a.* Consisting of or of the nature of slime; covered with or abounding in slime; slippery; (*fig.*) repulsively mean, dishonest, cringing, or obsequious. **slimily,** *adv.* **sliminess,** *n.*

sling (1) (sling) [Icel. *slyngva*, cp. G. *schlingen*, to wind, twist, sling], *v.t.* (*past & p.p.* **slung**) To throw, to hurl, esp. from a sling; to suspend in or as in a swing, to hang so as to swing; to hoist by means of a sling. *v.i.* To hurl missiles with or as with a sling; to move swiftly or violently. *n.* A short leather strap having a string at each end for hurling a small missile by hand; a band, loop, or other arrangement of rope, chains, straps, etc., for suspending, hoisting, or transferring anything; a band for supporting an injured limb. **sling your hook!** (*slang*) go away! **sling-cart,** *n.* A cart for carrying heavy loads suspended from its axle-tree. **sling-shot,** *n.* A heavy weight attached to a strap or cord, used as a weapon, esp. by criminals; (*Am.*) a catapult. **sling-stone,** *n.* A stone for throwing from a sling. **slinger,** *n.*

sling (2) (sling) [prob. from G. *schlingen*, to swallow], *n.* (*Am.*) Toddy, esp. made with gin.

slink (1) (slingk) [A.-S. *slincan*, cp. G. *schleichen*], *v.i.* (*past & p.p.* **slunk,** **past* **slank**) To steal or sneak away in a furtive, ashamed, or cowardly manner. **slinky** (sling′ ki), *a.* Sinuous, slender.

slink (2) (slingk) [prob. var. of SLING (1)], *v.i.* To miscarry, to produce young prematurely (of beasts). *v.t.* To cast prematurely (of beasts). *a.* Born prematurely (of an animal or its flesh). *n.* An animal, esp. a calf, born immaturely; its flesh.

slip (slip) [M.E. *slippen* (cp. Dut. *slippen*, G. *schleifen*), cogn. with A.-S. *slūpan*, also with L. *lūbricus*, slippery], *v.i.* (*past & p.p.* **slipped**) To slide, to glide; to slide unintentionally or out of place, to miss one's footing; to move, go, or pass unnoticed, furtively, or quickly; to get away, become free, or escape thus; to commit a small mistake or oversight; to go (along) swiftly. *v.t.* To cause to move in a sliding manner; to put (on or off) or to insert (into) with a sliding, stealthy, hasty, or careless motion; to let loose, to unleash; to escape or free oneself from; to give birth to prematurely; to dislocate (a bone); to cut a slip from. *n.* The act or state of slipping; an unintentional error, a small offence, a lapse, an indiscretion; a garment, etc., easily slipped on or off, as a loose petticoat, underskirt, pillow-case; a leash for a dog or hounds; an inclined plane, dock, or movable structure on which vessels are built, repaired, or laid up temporarily; a long narrow strip of paper, wood or other material; a galley-proof on such a strip of paper; a long, narrow space, passage, alley, etc.; a cutting for planting or grafting; (*fig.*) a scion, a descendant; (*Theat., pl.*) that part from which the scenes are slipped on, the part where actors stand before coming on the stage. **to give the slip:** To escape from, to evade. **to slip up:** To make a mistake. **slip-board,** *n.* A board sliding in grooves. **slip-carriage,** *n.* A railway carriage detached at a station from an express train in motion. **slip-knot,** *n.* A knot that slips up and down the string, etc., on which it is made, a running knot. **slip proof,** *n.* (*Print.*) A proof taken from a galley of type matter. **slip-rope,** *n.* (*Naut.*) A rope, usu. with both ends on board, for casting loose easily. **slipshod,** *a.* Wearing shoes down at heel; (*fig.*) careless, slovenly. **slipslop,** *a.* Slipshod, poor, feeble, jejune. *n.* Feeble, sloppy, or mawkish writing, talk, etc.; weak drink. **slipstream,** *n.* (*Aviat.*) The stream of air behind an air-screw. **slipway,** *n.* A slip for the repair or laying up of vessels; (*Aviat.*) an inclined pathway along which seaplanes can be hauled into or out of the water. **slippy,** *a.* (*colloq.*) Slippery; quick, sharp, wide awake. **slippiness,** *n.*

slipper (slip′ ėr), *n.* One who or that which slips or lets slip; a loose shoe easily slipped on or off for wearing indoors; a skid or shoe for braking a wheel. *v.t.* To beat with a slipper. **slipper-bath,** *n.* A bath with covered end, roughly resembling a slipper. **slipper-wort,** *n.* The calceolaria. **slippered,** *a.* Wearing slippers. **slippering,** *a.*

slippery (slip′ er i), *a.* So smooth, wet, muddy, etc. as to cause slipping, not allowing a firm footing; difficult to hold, elusive, not to be depended on, shifty, artful, cunning; risky, suggestive, lewd. **slipperily,** *adv.* **slipperiness,** *n.*

slips (slips), *n.pl.* Bathing-drawers; (*Cricket*) the ground on the off side behind the wicket or a fielder stationed here.

***slish** (slish) [var. of SLASH], *n.* A slash, a slit.

slit (slit) [A.-S. *slītan*, cp. Icel. *slīta*, Dut. *slijten*, G. *schleissen, schlitzen*], *v.t.* (*past & p.p.* **slit**) To cut lengthways; to cut into long pieces or strips; to make a long cut in. *n.* A long cut or narrow opening. **slit-trench:** (*Mil.*) A narrow trench for one or two men. **slitter,** *n.* **slitting-mill,** *n.* A machine or mill in which metal is cut into strips for making nails, etc.; a machine for slitting gems, a slicer.

slither (slitħ′ ėr) [var. of SLIDDER], *v.i.* (*colloq.*) To slip, to slide unsteadily (along, etc.).

sliver (sliv′ ėr) [dim. of obs. *slive*, a slip, from A.-S. *slīfan*, to cast off (in *tō-slāf*)], *n.* A piece of wood or similar material torn off, a splinter; a strip cut out of a fish for bait; a fleecy strand or twist pulled out from wool or other textile fibre. *v.t.* To tear or divide into long, thin pieces; to cut or break off as a sliver. *v.i.* To split, to splinter, to break to slivers.

slobber (slob′ ėr) [var. of SLUBBER], *v.i.* To let saliva run from the mouth, to drivel; (*fig.*) to talk or behave in a maudlin manner. *v.t.* To wet with saliva, to drivel over; (*fig.*) to make a mess of, to bungle. *n.* Saliva or spittle running from the mouth, drivel. **slobbery,** *a.* **slobberiness,** *n.*

slocken (slok′ ėn) [Icel. *slokna*, cp. Norw. *slokna, slokkna*, Swed. *slockna*], *v.t.* (*Sc. and North.*) To quench, to extinguish (*lit. and fig.*).

sloe (slō) [A.-S. *slā*, cp. Dut. *slee*, G. *schlehe*, Dan. *slaaen*], *n.* The fruit of the blackthorn, *Prunus spinosa*, or the shrub bearing it.

slog (slog) [etym. doubtful], *v.t.* and *i.* To hit vigorously and at random, esp. in batting or with the fists; to work hard. *n.* Such a stroke; a spell of hard work. **slogger,** *n.*

slogan (slō′ gȧn) [Gael. *sluagh-ghairm* (*sluagh*, host, *gairm*, outcry)], *n.* The war-cry of the old Highland clans; a political catchword; a catchy advertising phrase or word.

sloid (sloid) [Swed. *slöjd*, skill, cogn. with SLEIGHT], *n.* A system of manual training, esp. in woodwork, originating in Finland, applied to elementary education.

sloom (sloom) [etym. doubtful], *n.* (*prov.*) A layer of clay or shale between coal-seams.

sloop (sloop) [Dut. *sloep*, L.G. *sluup*, from *slupen*, to glide along, cogn. with SHALLOP], *n.* A fore-and-aft rigged vessel with one mast; (*Nav.*) a steam- or petrol-driven patrol boat. **sloop-rigged,** *a.*

slop (1) (slop) [A.-S. *sloppe, slyppe*, in *cū slyppe*, see COWSLIP, rel. to SLIP], *n.* Water or other liquid carelessly thrown about; (*pl.*) dirty water, liquid refuse; (*pl.*) liquid food, weak or non-alcoholic liquors. *v.t.* (*past & p.p.* **slopped**) To spill or allow to overflow; to soil by spilling liquid upon; to make sloppy. *v.i.* To spill, to overflow the side of a vessel. **to slop over:** (*fig.*) To be too effusive, to gush. **slop-basin, -bowl,** *n.* A basin for emptying the dregs of cups, etc., into at table. **slop-pail,** *n.* A pail for bedroom slops. **sloppy,** *a.* Wet, splashed, covered with spilt water or puddles; (*fig.*) slovenly, done carelessly; weakly sentimental, maudlin. **sloppily,** *adv.* **sloppiness,** *n.*

slop (2) (slop) [Icel. *sloppr*, cogn. with SLIP], *n.* (*Naut. pl.*) Ready-made clothing, bedding, etc., sold cheap to sailors; *(*pl.*) wide loose knickerbockers or trousers. **slop-seller, -shop,** *n.*

slop (3) (slop) [slang], *n.* A policeman.

slope (slōp) [M.E., *cogn.* with SLIP], *n.* An inclined surface, line, or direction, an incline, a declivity or acclivity, ground whose surface makes an angle with the horizon; the degree of such inclination; (*Mil.*) the position of a rifle when carried on the shoulder. *v.i.* To be inclined at an angle to the horizon, to lie obliquely, to slant; (*slang*) to run away, to clear off. *v.t.* To place or form with a slope, to hold or direct obliquely. ***slope-wise, slopingly,** *adv.*

slosh (slosh), *v.t.* (*colloq.*) To strike hard; to spread paint, etc., thickly. *n.* A heavy blow.

slot (1) (slot) [perh. from O.F. *esclot*, pit of the breast or stomach], *n.* A groove, channel, depression, or opening, esp. in timber or a machine for some part to fit into; the aperture into which coins are put in a slot-machine. *v.t.* (*past & p.p.* **slotted**) To make a slot in. **slot-machine,** *n.* An automatic apparatus with a small aperture into which coins are put to cause articles to be delivered, a telephone to be made available, etc. **slotted,** *a.* **slotter,** *n.* **slotting-machine,** *n.* One for making slots, mortises, etc.

slot (2) (slot) [A.F. and O.F. *esclot*, Icel. *sloth*, cp. SLEUTH], *n.* The track of a deer. *v.t.* To track by the slot. **slot-hound,** *n.* A sleuth-hound.

slot (3) (slot) [M.E., cp. M.Dut. *slot*, G. SCHLOSS], *n.* (*Sc. and North.*) A bar or bolt fastening a door; a metal rod, bar, etc.

sloth (slōth) [M.E. *slouthe*, A.-S. *slǣwth*, from *slāw*, SLOW], *n.* Laziness, indolence, sluggishness; a S. American arboreal mammal of the edentate group *Tardigrada*, characterized by its slow and awkward movements on the ground. **slothful,** *a.* **slothfully,** *adv.* **slothfulness,** *n.*

slouch (slouch) [Icel. *slōkr*, cp. Norw. *slōk*, slouching fellow, cogn. with SLACK], *n.* An ungainly or negligent drooping attitude, gait, or movement; a downward bend of the hat-brim; (*slang*) an awkward, slovenly, or incapable fellow, worker, or piece of work; a slouch-hat. *v.i.* To droop or hang down carelessly; to stand or move in a loose, negligent, or ungainly attitude. *v.t.* To bend the brim of (a hat) so that it hangs down on one side;

(*slang*) to perform negligently or incompetently. **slouch-hat,** *n.* A hat with the brim hanging down on one side. **slouchy,** *a.* **slouchiness,** *n.*

slough (1) (slou) [A.-S. *slōh,* cogn. with G. *schlingen,* to devour], *n.* A place full of mud, a bog, a quagmire; (*Am.*) a marsh, a swamp, a small bayou. **sloughy** (slou′ i), *a.*

slough (2) (slŭf) [M.E. *sloh,* etym. doubtful, cp. L.G. *slu, sluwe,* husk, covering, perh. rel. to SLEEVE], *n.* The cast skin of a snake; the covering or other part cast off by any animal; dead tissue separating from a living part, a scab. *v.t.* To cast off (a skin, dead tissue, etc.). *v.i.* To peel and come (off, away, etc.); to cast off slough.

Slovak (slō vak′, slō′ vák) [Czech], *n.* One of a Slav race inhabiting the north of Hungary. *a.* Of or pertaining to the Slovaks. **Slovakian** (slō văk′ i ån), *a.*

sloven (slŭv′ ėn) [M.E. *sloveyn* (perh. M.Dut. *slof,* Flem. *sloef,* -EN)], *n.* One who is careless of dress or negligent of cleanliness; an untidy, careless, lazy person. **slovenly,** *a.* and **adv.* **slovenliness, *slovenry,** *n.*

Slovene (slō vēn′) [Gr. *Sklabēnos,* see SLAV], *n.* One of a Slav race inhabiting Carinthia, Styria, and Carniola. **Slovenian,** *a.* Of or pertaining to the Slovenes. *n.* Their language.

slow (slō) [A.-S. *slāw,* cp. Dut. *sleeuw,* Icel. *slær*], *a.* Not quick, of small velocity, moving at a low speed; taking a long time in doing, going, proceeding, growing, etc.; not prompt; tardy, backward; not hasty, not precipitate, behind the right time; stupid, dull; tedious, lifeless. *adv.* Slowly. *v.i.* To slacken speed, to go slower (*usu.* up or down). *v.t.* To reduce the speed of. **slowcoach,** *n.* One who is slow in moving, acting, deciding, etc.; a dull person; one behind the times. **slow-gaited,** *a.* **slow-match,** *n.* A fuse burning slowly for igniting explosives. **slow-motion,** *a.* (*Cinema.*) Descriptive of a film the motion of which through the projector has been greatly slowed down. ***slow-sighted,** *a.* ***slow-winged,** *a.* **slow-witted,** *a.* **slowly,** *adv.* **slowness,** *n.*

slow-worm (slō′ wĕrm) [A.-S. *slā-wyrm* (prob. *slā, slah,* from *slēan,* to SLAY, WORM, from its being formerly supposed to be venomous)], *n.* A small limbless snake-like lizard, *Anguis fragilis,* the blind-worm.

sloyd [SLOID].

slub (slŭb) [etym. doubtful], *n.* A slightly twisted roll or sliver of wool. *v.t.* To form into slubs, in preparation for spinning.

slubber (slŭb′ ėr) [cp. Dan. *slubbre,* to slaver, also L.G. *slubbern,* to lap up, to scamp], *v.t.* (*prov.*) To do lazily, carelessly, or bunglingly; to stain, to daub, to soil. **slubberingly,** *adv.*

sludge (slŭj) [M.E. *sluche,* etym. doubtful], *n.* Mud, mire, slush; an oozy or slimy mixture, as of ore and water; (*Naut.*) small floating pieces of ice or snow. **sludgy,** *a.*

slue (sloo) [etym. doubtful], *v.t.* and *i.* To turn, twist, or swing (round, about, etc.) as on a pivot. *n.* Such a turn or twist.

slug (slŭg) [orig. sluggard, from obs. *slug,* M.E. *sluggen* (cp. Dan. *slug,* Swed. *sloka,* Norw. *sloka,* to SLOUCH)], *n.* A shell-less air-breathing gasteropod, very destructive to plants; [perh. from SLOG] a roughly-shaped bullet; a small, roughly-rounded lump of metal; (*Print.*) a strip of type-metal for spacing, etc., a line of type from a linotype machine. **v.i.* To be sluggish. **v.t.* To make sluggish; to retard. ***slug-a-bed,** *n.* One who indulges in lying in bed.

sluggard (slŭg′ árd), *n.* A person habitually lazy. **a.* Sluggish, lazy. ***sluggardize,** *v.t.* **sluggish,** *a.* Habitually lazy, dull, inactive; slow in movement, inert, torpid. **sluggishly,** *adv.* **sluggishness,** *n.*

slug-horn (slŭg′ hôrn), *n.* (*poet.*) A corr. of 'slogan', but incorrectly thought by Chatterton and Browning to be a kind of trumpet.

sluice (sloos) [M.E. *scluse,* O.F. *escluse,* late L. *exclūsa,* flood-gate, orig. fem. p.p. of *exclūdere,* to EXCLUDE], *n.* A waterway with a valve or hatch by which the level of a body of water is controlled; a sluice-gate or flood-gate; the stream above, below, or passing through a flood-gate; (*fig.*) a source, a vent, an opening. *v.t.* To flood or drench by means of a sluice or sluices; to let out by a sluice; to drench, to wash thoroughly, to rinse. *v.i.* To pour out through or as through a sluice. **sluice-gate, -valve,** *n.* **sluice-way,** *n.* ***sluicy,** *a.*

slum (1) (slŭm) [Cant., etym. doubtful], *n.* A low squalid neighbourhood in a town. *v.i.* (*past & p.p.* **slummed**) To visit slums for philanthropic purposes. **slummer,** *n.* **slummy,** *a.*

slum (2) (slŭm), *n.* The non-lubricating part of crude oil; the sticky residue of lubricating oil.

slumber (slŭm′ bėr) [M.E. *slumeren,* freq. of *slumer* (from n. *slume,* A.-S. *slūma,* slumber), cp. Dut. *sluimeren,* G. *schlummern,* Swed. *slumra*], *v.i.* To sleep, esp. lightly. *v.t.* To waste (time away) in sleep. *n.* Light sleep. **slumberer,** *n.* **slumberingly,** *adv.* **slumberless,** *a.* **slumberous, *slumbery,** *a.* **slumberously,** *adv.*

slummock (slŭm′ ŏk) [etym. unknown], *v.i.* To swallow greedily; to move or speak clumsily. *n.* A slut, a slattern.

slump (1) (slŭmp) [cp. Dan. *slumpe,* Norw. and Swed. *slumpa,* to fall; prob. imit.], *v.i.* (*prov.*) To fall or sink suddenly, as through ice or into a bog; to come down, to collapse (of prices, prosperity, interest in a matter, etc.). *n.* A heavy fall or decline, a collapse (of prices, etc.). **slumpy,** *a.* (*prov.*) Marshy, boggy.

slump (2) (slŭmp) [Sc., from L.G., cp. Dut. *slomp*], *n.* The gross amount, the lump. *v.t.* To lump together.

slung, *past & p.p.,* **slung-shot** [SLING (1)].

slunk, *past & p.p.* [SLINK (1 and 2)].

slur (slĕr) [M.Dut. *sleuren,* to trail], *v.t.* (*past & p.p.* **slurred**) To soil, to sully; to calumniate; to speak slightingly of; to pass lightly over; to pronounce indistinctly; (*Mus.*) to sing or play legato. *v.i.* To speak or articulate indistinctly; to pass lightly or slightingly (over). *n.* A stain, a stigma, a reproach or disparagement; a blurred impression in printing; a slurring in pronunciation or singing; (*Mus.*) a curved line (◡ ◠) placed over or under notes, denoting that they are to be played or sung legato. **slurred,** *a.*

slurry (slŭr′ i) [obs. *slur,* fluid mud, cogn. with prec., -Y], *n.* A thin, fluid paste made by mixing certain materials (esp. cement) with water, used in repairing the linings of converters, etc., the inequalities on the inner surface of pottery.

slush (slŭsh) [perh. from Norw. *slush* or var. of SLUDGE], *n.* Liquid mud, sludge; half-melted snow; (*slang*) worthless talk or writing, piffle. *v.t.* To throw slush over, to soak or bedaub with slush; to wash thoroughly, to sluice. **slushy,** *a.*

slut (slŭt) [cp. Swed. dial. *slåta,* Norw. *slott,* Dan. *slatte*], *n.* A dirty, slovenly woman, a slattern; (*contemp.*) a girl; (*Am.*) a bitch. **sluttery,** *n.* **sluttish,** *a.* **sluttishly,** *adv.* **sluttishness,** *n.*

sly (slī) [M.E. *sleigh,* Icel. *slægr,* cogn. with SLAY], *a.* Crafty, cunning, stealthily artful; underhand, not open or frank; playfully roguish, knowing, arch. **on the sly:** Slyly, in secret, on the quiet. **slyboots,** *n.* A sly, artful person. **slyly,** *adv.* **slyness,** *n.*

slype (slīp) [var. of SLIP], *n.* A covered passage between the transept of a cathedral and the chapter-house, deanery, etc.

smack (1) (smăk) [A.-S. *smæc,* cp. M.Dut. *smac,* L.G. *smakk,* Swed. *smak,* G. *geschmack*], *n.* A slight taste or flavour; a suggestion, trace, tincture, or dash (of); a smattering. *v.i.* To have a taste or flavour (of), to taste well or ill (of food, etc.).

smack (2) (smăk) [M.Dut. *smacke,* cp. L.G. *smakk,*

perh. rel. to SNAKE, cp. A.-S. *snacc*], *n.* A one-masted vessel, like a sloop or cutter, used in fishing, etc. **smacksman,** *n.*

smack (3) (smăk) [prob. onomat., cp. Swed. *smacka*, Dan. *smække*, to bang, to slam], *n.* A quick, smart report as of a blow with something flat, a crack of a whip, etc.; a blow with the flat of the hand, a slap; a loud kiss. *v.t.* To strike with the flat of the hand, to slap; to separate (the lips) with a sharp noise; to crack (a whip). *v.i.* To make a sharp noise as of opening quickly (of the lips); to crack (of a whip); to kiss loudly. *adv.* Suddenly, plump, directly. **to smack one's lips over:** To gloat over; to relish. **smacker,** *n.* A noisy kiss; a resounding blow; (*slang*) a pound (money). **smacking,** *a.* (*slang*) Brisk, lively.

small (smawl) [A.-S. *smæl*, cp. Dut., Dan., and Swed. *smal*, G. *schmal*], *a.* Deficient or relatively little in size, degree, power, amount, number, etc.; of less dimensions than the standard kind, belonging to the smaller kind; of minor importance, slight, trifling, petty; concerned or dealing with business, etc., of a restricted or minor kind; of low degree, poor, humble, plebeian; unpretentious; paltry, mean, ignoble, narrow-minded. *adv.* Quietly, in a low voice; humbly, in a humiliated manner; *little, slightly. *n.* The slender part of anything, especially of the back; (*pl.*) small clothes; (*Oxf. Univ.*) Responsions; a slate size 12 × 8 ins. **to feel small:** To feel humiliated. **small-arms,** *n.pl.* Portable fire-arms, as rifles, pistols, etc., as distinguished from cannon. **small beer:** Beer of a mild, light quality. **to chronicle small beer:** To speak consequentially of trivial matters. **small capitals:** Capitals lower in height than the regular capitals of the same fount. ***small-clothes,** *n.pl.* Knee-breeches. **small coal:** Coal not in lumps or large pieces. **small craft:** Vessels of small size. **small fry:** An insignificant person. **small hand:** Ordinary writing as opp. to text-hand. **small holding,** *n.* A portion of land of limited area and rental let, usually by county authorities, to agricultural workers for cultivation. **small holder,** *n.* Tenant of a small holding. **small hours:** The time from midnight till 3 or 4 A.M. **small-minded,** *a.* Restricted in outlook, petty. **small-mindedness,** *n.* **smallpox,** *n.* Variola, a contagious, feverish disease, characterized by eruptions on the skin. **small talk:** Light conversation, gossip. **smallish,** *a.* **smallness,** *n.*

smallage (smawl' āj) [small, F. *ache*, L. *apium*, parsley], *n.* Wild celery, *Apium graveolens*.

small-arms, smallpox, etc. [SMALL].

smalt (smawlt) [F., from It. *smalto*, from Teut., cp. G. *schmalz*, cogn. with SMELT (1)], *n.* A blue glass coloured with cobalt, used in a pulverized state as a pigment. **smaltine, -tite** (smawl' tin, -tīt), *n.* (*Min.*) Tin-white or grey cobalt.

***smaragd** (smăr' ăgd), ***smaragdus** (smă răg' dŭs) [O.F. *smaragde*, L. *smaragdus*, EMERALD], *n.* An emerald. **smaragdine,** *a.* **smaragdite,** *n.* (*Min.*) A green variety of hornblende.

smarmy (smar' mi) [onomat.], *a.* (*colloq.*) Sleek and smooth; having a wheedling manner.

smart (smart) [A.-S. *smeortan* (cp. Dut. *smarten*, G. *schmerzen*, Swed. *smarta*, also L. *modēre*, to bite, Gr. *smerdaleos*, terrible)], *v.i.* To feel or give or cause a sharp pain, to rankle; to feel wounded. *adv.* Smartly. *n.* A sharp, lively pain, a stinging sensation; a feeling of irritation; distress, anguish; smart-money. *a.* Stinging, pungent, keen, severe, poignant; vigorous, lively, brisk; acute, clever, intelligent, ingenious; quick at repartee, impertinently witty; shrewd, wide-awake, sharp; spruce, well groomed, stylish, fashionable. **Smart Aleck,** *n.* A know-all. **smart-money,** *n.* Money paid to buy oneself off from an unpleasant engagement, etc.; money allowed to soldiers and sailors for injuries received in service; excessive damages. **smart-ticket,** *n.* A certificate entitling one to smart-money. **smarten,** *v.t.* and *i.* **smartly,** *adv.* **smartness,** *n.*

smartweed (smart' wēd), *n.* (*Bot.*) The water-pepper, *Polygonum hydropiper*.

smash (smăsh) [prob. onomat.], *v.t.* To break to pieces by violence, to shatter; to hit with a crushing blow; (*fig.*) to overthrow completely, to rout, to crush. *v.i.* To break to pieces; to go bankrupt; (*colloq.*) to collide or crash (into); (*slang*) to utter base coin. *n.* A breaking to pieces; a break up, a collapse; a disaster; bankruptcy, ruin; (*slang*) an iced and flavoured beverage of brandy or other spirit. *adv.* With a smash. **smash-and-grab,** *a.* Descriptive of a theft where a shop window is broken and goods within hurriedly grabbed. **smasher,** *n.* One who or that which smashes; (*slang*) something of staggering size, quality, effectiveness, etc. **smashing,** *a.* (*colloq.*) Very fine, wonderful.

smatter (smăt' ėr) [etym. doubtful], *v.i.* To talk superficially or ignorantly; to have a slight knowledge of. **v.t.* To chatter about. *n.* A smattering. **smatterer,** *n.* **smattering,** *n.* A slight superficial knowledge.

smear (smēr) [A.-S. *smerien* (cp. Dut. *smeren*, G. *schmieren*, Icel. *smyrja*), from *smeru*, fat, cogn. with Gr. *muron*, ointment], *v.t.* To rub or daub with anything greasy or sticky; to rub (writing, etc.) so as to blur; (*fig.*) to soil, to pollute; to besmirch the name of someone. *v.i.* To make a smear; to be blurred. *n.* A stain or mark made by smearing. **smeary,** *a.* **smeariness,** *n.*

smectite (smek' tīt) [Gr. *smēktis*, cogn. with SMEGMA, -ITE], *n.* A clay resembling fuller's earth.

Smectymnuan (smek tim' nū ȧn) [*Smectymnuus*, name coined from initials of the Puritans S. Marshall, E. Calamy, T. Young, M. Newcomen, and W. Spurstow, authors of a reply to Bishop Hall's 'Humble Remonstrance to the High Court of Parliament,' 1641], *n.* One of these authors. *a.* Of or pertaining to or characteristic of them or their opinions.

smeddum (smed' ŭm) [A.-S. *smedima*, etym. doubtful], *n.* Fine powder, insecticide powder; (*Mining*) fine sifted or ground particles of ore; (*Sc.*) spirit, mettle, go.

smee (smē) [cp. Dut. *smient*], *n.* The smew, widgeon, or pochard.

smegma (smeg' mȧ) [Gr. *smēgma*, soap, from *smēchein*, to wipe], *n.* A sebaceous soapy secretion found in the folds of the skin. **smegmatic** (-măt' ik), *a.* Soapy, detersive, cleansing. *n.* A cleanser, a detergent.

smell (smel) [M.E. *smel*, v. *smelen* (cp. Dut. *smeulen*, L.G. *smelen*, to SMOULDER)], *n.* The sense by which odours are perceived; the sensation or the act of smelling; that which affects the organs of smell, scent, odour; a bad odour, a stench. *v.t.* (*past & p.p.* **smelt** (3), ***smelled**) To perceive the odour of; to inhale the odour of anything with the nose; to detect by means of scent; to hunt, trace, or find (out) by or as by the scent. *v.i.* To affect the sense of smell, to give out an odour (of, etc.); to suggest, to indicate, to smack (of); to have the sense of smell; to stink. ***smell-feast,** *n.* A parasite, a sponger. **smellable,** *a.* **smeller,** *n.* One who smells; (*slang*) the nose, a hit on the nose. **smelling-bottle,** *n.* A small bottle or phial for holding smelling-salts. **smelling-salts,** *n.* (*pl.*) An aromatic preparation of ammonium carbonate used in cases of faintness, etc. **smell-less,** *a.* **smelly,** *a.* (*colloq.*) Malodorous.

smelt (1) (smelt) [cp. M.Dut. *smelten*, G. *schmelzen*, Dan. *smelta*, O.H.G. *smelzen*], *v.t.* To fuse (an ore) so as to extract the metal; to extract (metal) from ore thus. **smelter,** *n.* **smeltery,** *n.* **smelting-furnace,** *n.*

smelt (2) (smelt) [A.-S., cp. *smeolt*, smooth], *n.* A small food-fish, *Osmerus eperlanus*, allied to the salmon.

smelt (3) *past & p.p.* [SMELL].

smerk, smerky [SMIRK].

smew (smū) [var. of obs. *smee, smeath,* SMOOTH], *n.* A small merganser or diving-duck, *Mergus albellus.*

smiddy (*Sc.*) [SMITHY].

smift (smift) [etym. doubtful], *a.* (*Mining*) A slow-match or fuse.

smilax (smī' lăks) [Gr.], *n.* A genus of climbing shrubs many species of which yield sarsaparilla; a S. African twining plant resembling these.

smile (smīl) [M.E. *smīlen* (cp. O.H.G. *smīlen,* M.H.G. *smielen*), cogn. with L. *mīrāri,* to wonder, and Gr. *meidân,* to smile], *v.i.* To express kindness, love, pleasure, amusement, or contempt by an instinctive lateral and upward movement of the lips and cheeks; to look gay, cheerful, or favourable (of the weather, fortune, etc.). *v.t.* To express by or as by a smile; to bring or drive (into, out of, away, etc.) thus. *n.* The act of smiling; a gay, cheerful, or favourable expression, aspect, or disposition. **smileless,** *a.* **smiler,** *n.* ***smilet,** *n.* A little smile. **smilingly,** *adv.* **smilingness,** *n.*

smirch (smĕrch) [extension of M.E. *smeren,* to SMEAR], *v.t.* To soil, to smear, to stain, to defile, to defame.

smirk (smĕrk) [A.-S. *smercian,* cp. M.H.G. *smieren, smielen,* to SMILE], *v.i.* To smile affectedly, to simper. *n.* An affected smile, a simper. *a.* (*prov.*) Smart, spruce. **smirky,** *a.*

smirr [SMUR].

smite (smīt) [A.-S. *smītan,* cp. Dut. *smijten,* G. *schmeissen,* M.Swed. *smita*], *v.t.* (*past* **smote,** ***smit,** *p.p.* **smitten,** ***smit**) To strike, to deal a severe blow to; to inflict defeat or disaster upon; (*usu. in p.p.*) to strike or affect (with a feeling, disease, etc.). *v.i.* To strike, to knock, to come (on, against, etc.) with force. *n.* A blow. **smiter,** *n.*

smith (smith) [A.-S., cp. Dut. *smid,* G. *schmied,* Icel. *smithr,* Dan. and Swed. *smed*], *n.* One who works in metals, esp. one who forges iron with the hammer; (*fig.*) one who makes or effects anything. **smithery,** *n.* The trade or occupation of a smith; a smithy. **smithy** (smith' i), *n.* A blacksmith's shop. **smithing** (smith' ing), *n.*

smitham (smith' ăm) [var. of SMEDDUM].

smithereens (smith ėr ēnz') [dim. of prov. *smithers,* etym. doubtful], *n.pl.* Little bits, tiny fragments.

smithery, smithy, etc. [SMITH].

Smithsonian (smith sō' ni ăn), *a.* Of or pertaining to the institution for the diffusion of knowledge founded by J. L. M. Smithson (*c.* 1765–1829) at Washington, D.C.

smithsonite (smith' sŏ nīt) [as prec.], *n.* (*Min.*) Silicate of zinc; (*Am.*) carbonate of zinc.

smitten, *p.p.* [SMITE], (*colloq.*) Enamoured.

smock (smok) [A.-S. *smoc,* cogn. with *smūgan,* to creep into, cp. SMUGGLE], *n.* A smock-frock; *a woman's undergarment, a chemise. ***smock-faced,** *a.* Having an effeminate appearance or complexion. **smock-frock,** *n.* A coarse garment resembling a shirt, worn by farm labourers over their other clothes. **smock-mill,** *n.* A windmill in which a rotating cap carries the sales. ***smock-race,** *n.* A race run by women with a smock for prize. **smocking,** *n.* Honeycomb work such as that decorating the front of a smock. **smockless,** *a.*

smog (smog), *n.* A smoky fog.

smoke (smōk) [A.-S. *smoca* (cp. Dut. *smook,* G. *schmauch*), rel. to *smēocan,* cogn. with Gr. *smuchein,* to smoulder], *n.* Volatile products of combustion, esp. carbonaceous and other matter in the form of visible vapour escaping from a burning substance; (*fig.*) anything ephemeral or unsubstantial; the act of smoking a tobacco-pipe, cigar, etc.; (*slang*) a cigarette. *v.i.* To emit smoke; to emit vapour, steam, etc., to reek; to send smoke into a room, to fail to draw (of a chimney, etc.); to draw into the mouth or inhale and exhale the smoke of tobacco, etc.; (*Austral. colloq.*) To decamp, to escape. *v.t.* To apply smoke to; to blacken, colour, cure, flavour, suffocate, destroy, cleanse, etc., with smoke; to draw with the mouth or inhale and exhale the smoke of (tobacco, etc.); to make (oneself sick, etc.) by this; (*slang*) to suspect, to become aware of. **to smoke out:** To investigate thoroughly. **smoke-oh,** *n.* (*Austral. colloq.*) A break from work. **smoke-ball, smoke bomb,** *n.* A projectile containing a composition that emits a dense smoke, for concealing military movements, etc.; a ball emitting a puff of smoke when struck, used in trap-shooting; a vessel giving off medicated vapour for inhalation in asthma, etc. **smoke-bell,** *n.* A bell-shaped glass hung over a lamp, etc., to prevent its smoking the ceiling. **smoke-black,** *n.* Lamp-black. **smoke box,** *n.* (*Rail.*) The chamber through which smoke and gases pass from the boiler tubes to the funnel. **smoke-consumer,** *n.* An apparatus for oxidizing the unoxidized matter in smoke. **smoke-consuming,** *a.* **smoke-dried,** *a.* Cured by smoking. **smoke-jack,** *n.* An apparatus for turning a roasting-spit by using the current of hot air in a chimney. **smoke-plant, -tree,** *n.* An ornamental shrub or tree with long, feathery fruit stalks. **smoke-rocket,** *n.* A device for generating smoke in drain-pipes so as to reveal leakages. **smoke-screen,** *n.* A dense volume of smoke produced by chemicals and liberated to conceal the movements of ships, troops, etc., from the enemy. **smoke shell** [SMOKE BOMB]. **smoked herring:** (*Am.*) A kipper. **smoke-stack,** *n.* A funnel, esp. on a steamer. **smokable,** *a.* **smokeless,** *a.* **smoker,** *n.* One who smokes tobacco; one who dries, cures, fumigates, etc., with smoke; (*colloq.*) a smoking-carriage, a smoking-concert. **smoker's heart, smoker's throat:** Affections of the heart and throat due to excessive smoking. **smoking-cap, jacket,** *n.* A cap or jacket, usu. decorated with fringe, etc., worn when smoking. **smoking-car, -carriage, -room,** *n.* A railway-carriage, etc., reserved for smokers. **smoking-concert,** *n.* A concert at which smoking is permitted. **smoky,** *a.* **smokily,** *adv.* **smokiness,** *n.*

smolder [SMOULDER].

smolt (smōlt) [perh. from A.-S. *smolt,* serene, shining], *n.* A salmon in its second year when it acquires its silvery scales.

smooth (smooth) [A.-S. *smethe* (rare *smōth*)], *a.* Having a continuously even surface, free from roughness, projections, or indentations; not hairy; unruffled (of water); free from obstructions or impediments; not harsh (of sound, taste, etc.); equable, calm, pleasant, bland, suave, polite, flattering. *v.t.* To make smooth; to free from harshness, discomforts, obstructions, etc.; to extenuate, to soften, to cloak (over). *v.i.* To become smooth. *n.* The act of smoothing. **smooth ashlar,** *n.* (*Build.*) A block of stone dressed ready for use. **smooth-bore,** *a.* Not rifled; *n.* A smooth-bore gun. **smooth breathing:** (*Gr. Gram.*) Sounded without the aspirate (of vowels); a sign marking this. **smooth-chinned,** *a.* Beardless. **smooth-faced,** *a.* Beardless; having a suave, specious, flattering appearance or expression. **smooth-shaven,** *a.* Cut or clipped smooth. **smooth-spoken, -tongued,** *a.* Polite, plausible, flattering. ***smoothen,** *v.t.* and *i.* **smoother,** *n.* **smoothing-iron,** *n.* A polished iron implement for smoothing linen. **smoothing-plane,** *n.* A short plane, finely set, for finishing. **smoothly,** *adv.* **smoothness,** *n.*

smore (*Sc.*) [SMOTHER].

smorzando (smôrt săn' dō), ***smorzato*** (-sa' tō) [It. pres.p. and p.p. of *smorzare,* to extinguish], *adv.* (*Mus.*) A direction that the passage is to be played so as to fade or die away gradually.

smote, *past* [SMITE].

smother (smŭth' ėr) [M.E. *smorther,* from A.-S. *smorian,* to choke, stifle, cp. Dut. *smooren,* G. *schmoren,* cogn. with SMOKE and SMOULDER], *n.* A stifling cloud of dust, smoke, vapour, etc.; a smouldering state. *v.t.* To suffocate, to stifle; to kill by suffocation, etc.; to keep (a fire) down by covering it with ashes, etc.; to hide, to suppress, to keep from being divulged. *v.i.* To be suffocated, to be prevented from breathing freely. **smotherable,** *a.* **smotheration** (-ā′ shŭn), *n.* **smotheringly,** *adv.* **smothery,** *a.* **smotheriness,** *n.*

smouch [SMUTCH].

smoulder (smōl′ dėr) [M.E. *smolderen*, from *smolder*, smoke, cogn. with SMELL and SMOTHER], *v.i.* To burn in a smothered way without flame; (*fig.*) to exist in a suppressed or latent condition. *n.* A smouldering state. ***smouldery,** *a.* Smothery.

smouse (smous) [Dut. *smous*, prob. from Jewish *schmuoss*, news, talk, from Heb.], *n.* (*S. Afr.*) An itinerant trader.

smudge (smŭj) [M.E. *smogen*, cogn. with SMUT], *v.t.* To smear or blur (writing, drawing, etc.); to make a dirty smear, blot, or stain on; (*fig.*) to soil, to smirch, to defile, to sully (purity, reputation, etc.); (*Am.*) to fumigate so as to drive mosquitoes away. *v.i.* To become smeared or blurred. *n.* A dirty mark, a smear, a blur; (*Am.*) a smouldering fire for driving away mosquitoes, etc.

smug (1) (smŭg) [cp. M.Dan. *smug*, smooth, L.G. *smuk*, G. *schmuck*, neat, spruce], *a.* Self-satisfied, complacently respectable. *n.* A smug person, esp. (*Univ. slang*) an unclubbable, non-athletic, non-sporting person. **smugly,** *adv.* **smugness,** *n.*

smug (2) (smŭg) [etym. doubtful], *v.t.* (*slang*) To seize, to filch, to run off with; to hush up. *v.i.* To crib.

smuggle (smŭg′ ėl) [L.G. *smuggeln* (cp. Dan. *smöge*, Icel. *smuga*, lurking-hole), cogn. with SMOCK], *v.t.* To import or export illegally without paying the customs duties; to convey or introduce clandestinely. **smuggler,** *n.* **smuggling,** *n.*

smur (smĕr) [etym. doubtful], *n.* (*chiefly Sc.*) Fine misty rain, drizzle. *v.i.* (*past & p.p.* **smurred**) To drizzle.

smut (smŭt) [cp. L.G. *schmutt*, G. *schmutz*, Swed. *smuts*], *n.* A particle of soot or other dirt, a mark or smudge made by this; a disease of corn due to parasitic fungi; (*fig.*) obscene or ribald talk, language, stories, etc. *v.t.* (*past & p.p.* **smutted**) To stain or mark with smut; to infect with smut; (*fig.*) to blacken, to tarnish. *v.i.* To be attacked by smut (of corn). **smutty,** *a.* **smuttily,** *adv.* **smuttiness,** *n.*

smutch [SMUDGE].

Smyrniot (smĕr′ ni ŏt), *a.* Of or pertaining to Smyrna. *n.* A native or inhabitant of Smyrna.

snack (snăk) [var. of SNATCH], *n.* A slight, hasty meal. **snack-bar,** *n.* A counter in a public house, etc., where light refreshments can be bought and consumed. **to go snacks:** To go shares.

snaffle (snăf′ ėl) [cp. Dut. *snavel*, muzzle, G. *schnabel*, bill, snout], *n.* A bridle-bit with a joint in the middle and usu. with cheek-pieces at the ends, also **snaffle-bit.** *v.t.* (*colloq.*) To purloin.

snag (snăg) [prob. from Scand. (cp. Norw. dial. *snag*, Icel. *snagr*), perh. rel. to KNAG], *n.* A jagged projection, as the stumpy base of a branch left in pruning, a branch broken off, a knot, a stump of a tooth; (*Am.*) the trunk of a tree fixed at one end in the bottom of a river; (*fig.*) an unexpected or concealed difficulty, an obstacle; (*Austral. slang*) a sausage. *v.t.* To run or damage (a vessel) on a snag; to clear of snags; (*prov.*) to lop or prune (a tree). **snagged, snaggy,** *a.* **snagger,** *n.*

snail (snāl) [A.-S. *snægl*, dim. of *snaca*, SNAKE], *n.* A gasteropodous mollusc of various species, usu. bearing a shell, feeding on vegetation, and often very destructive to garden crops; a snail-shell; (*fig.*) a sluggish person. **snail-clover, -trefoil,** *n.* A variety of medick, lucerne, or sainfoin. **snail-fish,** *n.* A sea-snail. **snail-like,** *a.* and *adv.* ***snail-paced, snail-slow,** *a.* **snail-wheel,** *n.* A rotating part of a clock, usu. spiral or snail-shaped in outline, with notches determining the number of strokes to be given in striking. **snailery,** *n.* A place where edible snails are cultivated. **snaily,** *n.* (*Austral.*) A bullock with large curved horns.

snake (snāk) [A.-S. *snaca* (cp. L.G. *snake*, Icel. *snākr*, Dan. *snog*), cogn. with SNEAK], *n.* A serpent, esp. the common British and other harmless kinds; a snake-like lizard or amphibian; (*fig.*) a sneaking, treacherous person. **snake in the grass:** (*fig.*) A treacherous person. **snake-charmer,** *n.* A serpent-charmer. **snake-charming,** *n.* **snake-fence,** *n.* (*Am.*) A zigzag fence. **snake juice:** (*Austral. colloq.*) Strong drink, gin, whisky. **snake-lizard,** *n.* A lizard with rudimentary legs. **snake-root,** *n.* The root of various American plants supposed to be a specific for snake-bites; one of these plants. **snake-stone,** *n.* An ammonite. **snake's-head,** *n.* The fritillary. **snake-weed,** *n.* The bistort. **snakish, snake-like, snaky,** *a.*

snap (snăp) [prob. from M.Dut. *snappen*, cp. G. *schnappen*, Dan. *snappe*, cogn. with SNAFFLE], *v.t.* (*past & p.p.* **snapped**) To bite, try to bite, or snatch (at); to make a sharp, quick sound, like a crack or slight explosion; to break or part suddenly with such a noise; (*fig.*) to speak sharply or spitefully. *v.t.* To seize suddenly, to snatch; (*fig.*) to interrupt or take (up) in the midst of a speech, etc.; to cause (a whip, the fingers, etc.) to make a sharp crack or report; to break with such a noise; to shut (to) or bring (together) thus; (*colloq.*) to photograph instantaneously. *n.* The act of snapping; the sound produced by this; the spring catch of a bracelet, purse, etc.; a sudden spell of severe weather, a crisp gingerbread cake; a children's round game of cards; a snapshot; (*colloq.*) vigour, briskness, dash, go; (*Theat.*) a short casual engagement as actor. *a.* Done, taken, etc., suddenly, offhand, or by surprise. **to snap out of it:** (*colloq.*) To change one's mood; to take a more reasonable attitude. **snap-bolt, -hook, -link, -lock, -ring,** *n.* Devices closing and fastening automatically with a spring. **snap division,** *n.* (*Pol.*) A surprise division in Parliament, engineered to the discomfiture of opponents. **snap vote:** A vote taken unexpectedly, esp. in Parliament. **snapper,** *n.* ***snapper-up,** *n.* One who picks things up stealthily, a thief. **snapping-turtle,** *n.* A fierce and voracious N. American fresh-water turtle, *Chelydra serpentina.* **snappish,** *a.* Given to snapping or biting, given to sharp replies, spiteful, irascible. **snappishly,** *adv.* **snappishness,** *n.* **snappy,** *a.* Snappish; irritable, cross; (*colloq.*) brisk, sharp, lively.

snapdragon (snăp′ drăg ŏn), *n.* (*Bot.*) A plant of the genus *Antirrhinum*, with a flower opening like a dragon's mouth; a game of snatching raisins from a dish of burning spirit.

***snaphance** (snăp′ hăns) [Dut.], *n.* The spring-lock of a fire-arm; a musket or other fire-arm fitted with this.

snapshot (snăp′ shot), *n.* An instantaneous photograph; a photograph taken without preparation or posing.

snar [SNARL (1)].

snare (snâr) [A.-S. *snear*, cp. Dut. *snaar*, G. *schnur*, Icel. *snara*, string], *n.* A trap, usu. consisting of a noose, for catching birds or other animals; (*fig.*) a trick, stratagem, or allurement by which one is brought into difficulty, defeat, disgrace, sin, etc.; a string of gut, wire, or hide stretched inside the head of a drum to make a rattling sound when the head is struck. *v.t.* To catch in a snare; to ensnare, entrap, or inveigle. **snarer,** *n.* (*usu. in comb.* as *bird-snarer*).

snarky (snar′ ki) [as foll.], *a.* Irritable, short-tempered.

snarl (1) (snarl) [orig. *snar*, M.Dut. *snarren*, to trawl, cp. G. *schnarren*, Swed. *snarra*, to make guttural noises, prob. imit.], *v.i.* To growl in a sharp tone, as an angry dog; to speak in a harsh, surly, or savage manner. *v.t.* To express or say (out) with a snarl. *n.* A sharp-toned growl; a savage remark or exclamation. **snarler,** *n.* **snarlingly,** *adv.* **snarly,** *a.*

snarl (2) (snarl) [SNARE], *n.* A tangle, a knot of hair, thread, etc.; (*fig.*) an entanglement, embarrassing difficulty. *v.t.* To entangle; to flute or emboss (metal-ware) by hammering the inside with a snarling-iron. *v.i.* To become entangled. **snarling-iron,** *n.*

snatch (snăch) [M.E. *snacchen*, cogn. with SNACK and SNECK (1) (cp. Dut. *snakken*)], *v.t.* To seize suddenly, eagerly, or without permission or ceremony; (*fig.*) to seize and remove or rescue (from, away, etc.). *v.i.* To try to seize, to make a sudden motion (at) as if to seize. *n.* An act of snatching, a grab (at); that which is snatched; a short spell of talk, song, rest, work, etc. **snatch-block,** *n.* (*Naut.*) A single block with an opening in one cheek to receive the bight of a rope. **snatchable,** *a.* **snatcher,** *n.* (*often in comb.* as *body-snatcher*). **snatchily, *snatchingly,** *adv.* **snatchy,** *a.*

snath, snathe (*Am.*) [SNEAD].

snead (snēd) [A.-S. *snǣd*, etym. doubtful], *n.* The long curved handle of a scythe.

sneak (snēk) [A.-S. *snīcan*, to creep, cogn. with SNAKE (cp. Icel. *snikja*, to hanker after)], *v.i.* To creep, slink, or steal (about, away, off, etc.), as if afraid or ashamed to be seen; to behave in a mean, cringing, cowardly, or underhand way; (*schoolboy slang*) to tell tales. *v.t.* (*slang*) To steal. *n.* One who sneaks; (*schoolboy slang*) a tale-bearer; (*Cricket*) a ball bowled along the ground. ***sneak-cup,** *n.* One who sneaks away from his cup or liquor; a mean, servile creature. **sneak-thief,** *n.* A pilferer, one who steals from open windows or doors. ***sneaker,** *n.* **sneakers,** *n.pl.* (*colloq.*) Rubber-soled shoes. **sneakingly,** *adv.*

***sneap** (snēp) [earlier *snape*, Icel. *sneypa*, to outrage, to snub], *v.t.* To reprove, to snub; to nip, to pinch. *n.* A reprimand, a check, a snub.

sneb [SNIB (1 and 2)].

sneck (1) (snek) [Sc., cp. SNACK and SNATCH], *n.* A latch or catch. *v.t.* and *i.* To latch, to fasten, to lock (up). **sneck-bend,** *n.* A shape of fish-hook in which the point is inclined to one side. **snecked,** *a.*

sneck (2) (snek) [etym. doubtful, cp. SNICK], *v.t.* To cut. *n.* A cut.

sneer (snēr) [M.E. *sneren*, cp. N.Fris. *sneere*, M.Dan. *snarre*, rel. to SNARL (1)], *v.i.* To show contempt by a smile or grin; to scoff, to jibe. *v.t.* To utter or express with a sneer; to treat or put (down, etc.) with a sneer. *n.* A grimace or verbal expression of contempt or derision. **sneerer,** *n.* **sneeringly,** *adv.*

sneeshing (snē' shing) [Sc. and North. (SNEEZE, -ING)], *n.* Snuff.

sneeze (snēz) [M.E. *snesen*, A.-S. *fnēosan* (cp. Dut. *fniezen*, Icel. *fnasa*, also Gr. *pneein*, to breathe)], *v.i.* To eject air, etc., through the nostrils audibly and convulsively, owing to irritation of the inner membrane of the nose. *n.* The act of sneezing. **not to be sneezed at:** Not to be despised, worth consideration. **sneezewort,** *n.* The wild pellitory, *Achillea ptarmica*. **sneezer,** *n.* **sneezy,** *a.*

snell (1) (snel) [A.-S. *snel*, cp. L.G. and O.H.G. *snel*, G. *schnell*, Icel. *snjallr*], *a.* (*now Sc.*) Active, keen, smart, severe, stinging, pungent.

snell (2) (snel) [etym. doubtful], *n.* A short line or snood, usu. of gut, for attaching fish-hooks to a line.

snib (1) (snib) [etym. doubtful], *n.* (*Sc.*) A bolt or catch. *v.t.* (*past & p.p.* **snibbed**) To fasten with this; (*fig.*) to catch.

snib (2) (snib) [from Scand., cogn. with SNUB], *v.t.* (*now chiefly Sc.*) To rebuke, to reprimand, to check. *n.* A rebuke, a snub.

snick (snik) [etym. doubtful], *v.t.* To cut, to nick, to snip; (*Cricket*) to hit (the ball) lightly with a glancing stroke. *n.* A slight cut, nick, or notch; (*Cricket*) a light glancing hit. **snickersnee** [prob. corr. of obs. *snick or snee*, a fight with knives], *n.* A big knife, esp. a bowie.

***snicker** (snik' ėr) [imit., cp. SNIGGER], *v.i.* To snigger; to neigh, to nicker. *n.* A snigger.

snide (snīd) [etym. doubtful], *a.* (*slang*) Sham, bogus. *n.* Sham jewellery, etc.

Snider (snī' dėr) [Jacob *Snider* (1820–66), inventor], *n.* An early form of breech-loading rifle.

sniff (snif), ***snift** (snift) [M.E. *sneven*, cp. Dan. *snive*, Icel. *snippa*, M.Dan. *snifte*, imit. in orig.], *v.i.* To draw air audibly up the nose (often as an expression of contempt). *v.t.* To draw (*usu.* up) with the breath; to smell, to perceive by sniffing. *n.* The act of sniffing; that which is sniffed in. **sniffy,** *a.* (*colloq.*) Given to sniffing, disdainful. **snifting valve:** A valve in a steam cylinder for the escape of air. **snifty,** *a.* (*Am. slang*) Having an agreeable smell.

snig (snig) [etym. doubtful], *n.* A small eel.

snigger (snig' ėr) [var. of SNICKER], *v.i.* To laugh in a half-suppressed manner. *n.* A suppressed laugh.

sniggle (snig' ėl) [from SNIG, etym. doubtful], *v.i.* To fish for eels by thrusting the bait into their holes. *v.t.* To catch thus.

snip (snip) [cp. Dut. and L.G. *snippen*, G. *schnippen*, cogn. with SNAP], *v.t.* (*past & p.p.* **snipped**) To cut or clip off sharp with shears or scissors. *v.i.* To make such a cutting movement (*usu.* at). *n.* The act or movement of snipping; a cut with scissors or shears; a small piece snipped off; (*slang*) a tailor; (*colloq.*) a certainty, a bargain. ***snip-snap,** *n.* Dialogue characterized by quick repartee. *a.* Short and smart. **snipper,** *n.* **snipper-snapper,** *n.* (*prov.*) A pert, insignificant fellow. **snippet, snipping,** *n.* A small bit snipped off; (*pl.*) scraps, fragments (of news, etc.). **snippety, snippy,** *a.* **snippetiness,** *n.*

snipe (snīp) [Icel. *snīpa*, cp. Dut. *snip*, G. *schnepfe*, cogn. with SNAP], *n.* A long-billed marsh- and shore-bird of the genus *Gallinago*, esp. the British *G. cœlestis*; *(*fig.*) a block-head, a fool. *v.i.* To shoot or hunt snipe; (*Mil.*) to pick off members of the enemy, usu. from cover. *v.t.* To shoot in this manner. **sniper,** *n.*

snipper, snippet, snippety, etc. [SNIP].

snitch (snich) [etym. doubtful], *v.i.* (*slang*) To inform, to peach. *n.* The nose.

snivel (sniv' ėl) [M.E. *snevelen*, cogn. with A.-S. *snofl*, mucus, cp. SNUFF (1), SNUFFLE], *v.i.* (*past & p.p.* **snivelled**) To run at the nose; to cry or fret with snuffling; (*fig.*) to be affectedly tearful. *n.* Mucus running from the nose; audible or affected weeping; (*fig.*) hypocrisy, cant. **sniveller,** *n.* ***snivelly,** *a.*

snob (snob) [etym. doubtful], *n.* A journeyman cobbler; a vulgar person who apes gentility, cultivates or truckles to those of higher social position, or regards the claims of wealth and position with an exaggerated and contemptible respect; (*Austral.*) the last sheep shorn in a day's work; *(*Univ.*) a townsman (as opp. to a gownsman); *a shoemaker. **snobbery, snobbishness, snobbism,** *n.* **snobbish, snobby,** *a.* **snobbishly,** *adv.* **snobling,** *n.* **snobocracy** (-ok' rȧ si), *n.* **snobography** (-og' rȧ fi), *n.*

snod (snŏd) [Sc., etym. doubtful], *a.* Neat, tidy, trim; smooth, sleek; snug. *v.t.* To make snod, to put in order.

snood (snood) [A.-S. *snōd*, from *snā-*, to spin, cogn. with SNARE], *n.* A fillet or ribbon formerly worn round the hair in Scotland by unmarried girls; a crocheted net to contain a woman's back hair; a gut- or hair-line by which a fish-hook is fastened to the main line. **snooded,** *a.*

snook (1) (snook) [Dut. *snoek*, pike], *n.* The tropical American *Centropomus undecimalis*, and various kinds of sea-fish used for food.

snook (2) (snook) [etym. doubtful], *n.* (*usu. in pl.*) A gesture of derision. **to cock a snook:** To put the thumb to the nose and spread the fingers.

snooker (snoo' kėr) [etym. doubtful], *n.* A game resembling pool or pyramids played on a billiard-table.

snool (snool) [etym. doubtful], *n.* (*Sc.*) A mean-spirited submissive person. *v.i.* To submit abjectly, to knuckle under. *v.t.* To keep down, to snub.

snoop (snoop) [Dut. *snoepen*], *v.i.* To go about in an inquisitive or sneaking manner, to pry. **snooper,** *n.* A prying busybody.

snooty (snoo′ ti), *a.* (*colloq.*) Supercilious.

snooze (snooz) [etym. doubtful, prob. onomat.], *v.i.* To take a short sleep, esp. in the day. *v.t.* To pass or waste (time) in slumber or indolence. *n.* A short sleep, a nap. **snoozer,** *n.*

snore (snôr) [prob. imit.], *v.i.* To breathe through the mouth and nostrils with a hoarse noise in sleep. *v.t.* To pass (time) in snoring or sleeping. *n.* The act or sound of snoring. **snorer,** *n.*

snort (snôrt) [M.E. *snorten*, prob. imit. (cp. prec., also L.G. *snurten*, Dut. *snorken*, Swed. *snarka*)], *v.i.* To force air violently and loudly through the nostrils like a frightened or excited horse; to make a noise like this; *to snore. *v.t.* To utter or throw (out) with a snort. *n.* The act or sound of snorting. **snorter,** *n.* One who or an animal that snorts; (*colloq.*) a boisterous wind; anything of extraordinary size, excellence, violence, etc.; an abusive or violent letter. **snortingly,** *adv.*

snot (snot) [A.-S. *gesnot* (cp. L.G. *snotte*, Dut. and Dan. *snot*), cogn. with SNOUT], *n.* (*vulg.*) Mucus from the nose; a low or contemptible person. **snotter** (1), *n.* A turkey-cock's wattles; (*Sc.*) snot. *v.i.* To snivel, to weep. **snotty,** *a.* *n.* (*Nav. slang*) A midshipman. **snottily,** *adv.* **snottiness,** *n.*

snotter (2) (snot′ ėr) [etym. doubtful], *n.* (*Naut.*) A becket, eye, or collar, esp. one forming the lower support of a sprit.

snout (snout) [M.E. *snute*, cogn. with A.-S. *snȳtan*, to blow the nose (cp. Dut. *snuit*, G. *schnauze*, Swed. *snut*)], *n.* The projecting nose or muzzle of a beast; (*contemp.*) the nose, a nozzle; a projecting front, as of a glacier, a cliff, a war-ship's ram, etc. **snouted,** *a.* (*usu. in comb.*, as *long-snouted*). **snouty,** *a.*

snow (1) (snō) [A.-S. *snāw*, Dut. *sneeuw*, G. *schnee*, Dan. *snee*, Icel. *snæo*, also L. *nix nivis*, Gr. *nipha*], *n.* Watery vapour in the atmosphere frozen into crystals and falling to the ground in flakes; a fall of this (*often in pl.*); anything resembling snow, esp. in whiteness; (*Am. slang*) cocaine. *v.i.* (*impers.*) Snow falls. *v.t.* To cover, sprinkle, or block (up) with snow; to send or scatter down as snow. **snowball,** *n.* A round mass of snow pressed together in the hands and flung as a missile; a round pudding or confection of various kinds; a fund to which each subscriber secures others. *v.t.* To pelt with snowballs. *v.i.* To throw snowballs. **snowball-tree,** *n.* The sterile-flowered variety of guelder-rose. **snow-blind,** *a.* Partially or totally blinded, usu. temporarily, through the glare of reflected light from the surface of snow. **snow-blindness,** *n.* **snow-blink** [ICEBLINK, see ICE], **snow-bound,** *a.* Imprisoned or kept from travelling by snow. **snow-broth,** *n.* Snow and water mixed. **snow-capped,** *a.* Crowned with snow. **snow-drift,** *n.* A mass of snow accumulated by the wind. **snow-fall,** *n.* A fall of snow; the amount of snow falling in a given place during a given time, as measured in a rain- or snow-gauge. **snow-field,** *n.* An expanse of snow, esp. in polar or lofty mountain regions. **snow-grouse,** *n.* The ptarmigan. **snow-leopard,** *n.* The ounce. **snow-line,** *n.* The lowest limit of perpetual snow on mountains, etc. **snow-on-the-mountains,** *n.* The arabis, N. American spurge and other plants with white flowers or leaves. **snow-owl** [SNOWY-OWL]. **snow-plant** [RED SNOW, see RED]. **snow-plough,** *n.* An implement used to clear a road or railway track of snow. **snow-shoe,** *n.* A long, light, racket- or ski-shaped frame worn to prevent sinking when walking on snow. **snow-slip,** *n.* An avalanche. **snow-storm,** *n.* A heavy fall of snow, esp. accompanied by wind. **to snow under:** To overwhelm (with work, etc.). **snow-white,** *a.* **snow-wreath,** *n.* A heap of drifted snow. **snowless,** *a.* **snow-like,** *a.* and *adv.* **snowy,** *a.* White like snow; abounding with snow; covered with snow; spotless, unblemished. **snowy-owl,** *n.* A white, black-barred northern owl, *Nyctea Scandiaca.* **snowily,** *adv.* **snowiness,** *n.*

***snow** (2) (snō) [Dut. *snauw*, or L.G. *snaw*, etym. doubtful], *n.* A brig-rigged vessel, with supplementary mast just abaft the mainmast carrying a trysail.

snowberry (snō′ be ri), *n.* (*Bot.*) The N. American shrub, *Symphoricarpus racemosus*, the W. Indian *Chiococca racemosa*, and other white-berried ornamental shrubs.

snowbird (snō′ bĕrd), *n.* (*Zool.*) A small finch, bunting or sparrow, esp. the **snow-bunting,** a northern finch, *Plectrophanex nivalis*, visiting Britain in winter.

snowdrop (snō′ drop), *n.* (*Bot.*) A bulbous plant, *Galanthus nivalis*, with a white flower appearing in early spring.

snowflake (snō′ flāk), *n.* A fleecy particle of falling snow; (*Bot.*) a plant of the genus *Leucoium*, a European flower resembling the snowdrop.

snowman (snō′ măn), *n.* A big snowball shaped like a man. **The Abominable Snowman:** A supposedly sub-human creature whose tracks are alleged to have been found in the snows of the Himalayas, the yeti.

snub (snŭb) [Icel. *snubba*, to chide, cp. Dan. *snubbe*, to nip off], *v.t.* (*past & p.p.* **snubbed**) To check, to rebuke with sarcasm or contempt, to slight in a pointed or offensive manner; (*Naut.*) to stop (a cable, ship, etc.) suddenly, esp. by tying a rope round a snubbing-post; *to stunt, to nip. *n.* An act of snubbing, a check, a rebuff; a snub-nose. **snub-nose,** *n.* A short flat nose. **snub-nosed,** *a.* **snubbing-post,** *n.* A stout post or bollard for winding a rope round to check a ship's motion. **snubbingly,** *adv.*

***snudge** (snŭj) [prob. rel. to SNUG], *v.i.* To lie close and still. *n.* A miser; a sneak.

snuff (1) (snŭf) [prob. from M.Dut. *snuffen*, to clear the nose, prob. cogn. with M.Dut. *snuyven* (Dut. *snuiven*)], *v.t.* To draw in through the nostrils, to sniff, to scent. *v.i.* To sniff; to take snuff; *to take offence. *n.* A sniff; powdered tobacco inhaled through the nose; medicinal powder taken thus. **up to snuff:** (*slang*) Knowing, sharp, not easily imposed upon. **snuff-box,** *n.* **snuff-mill,** *n.* A mill for grinding snuff; (*Sc.*) a snuff-box. **snuff-taker,** *n.* **snuff-taking,** *n.* **snuffer,** *n.* **snuffy,** *a.* **snuffiness,** *n.*

snuff (2) (snŭf) [etym. doubtful, cp. prov. *snop*, to crop shoots, cogn. with SNUB], *n.* The charred part of the wick in a candle or lamp. *v.t.* To trim (a wick, candle, etc.) by removing this. **to snuff out:** To extinguish by or as by snuffing; (*slang*) to die, also **to snuff it.** **snuff-dish, -tray,** *n.* **snuffers,** *n.pl.* A scissor-like instrument for trimming away snuff.

snuffle (snŭf′ ėl), *v.i.* To breathe noisily or make a sniffing noise as when the nose is obstructed; to talk through the nose; (*fig.*) to snivel, to whine, to talk or preach in a canting style. *v.t.* To utter or sing through the nose or in a canting manner. *n.* The act or sound of snuffling; obstruction of the nostrils by mucous nasal catarrh. **snuffler,** *n.* **snufflingly,** *adv.*

snuffy, snuffiness [SNUFF (1)].

snug (snŭg) [cp. L.G. *snügger*, Dan. *snugg*, neat, tidy, smooth, short-haired], *a.* Lying close, sheltered, and comfortable; cosy, comfortable; compact, trim, well secured; *not exposed to view. **v.i.* To lie close, to nestle, to snuggle. **snuggery,** *n.* A snug place, as a bar-parlour, one's 'den,' etc.

snuggle (snŭg′ ėl), *v.i.* To move or lie close (up to) for warmth. *v.t.* To draw close to one, to cuddle.

so (sō) [A.-S. *swā*, cp. Dut. *zoo*, G. *so*, Icel. *svā*, Dan. *saa*], *adv.* and *conj.* In such a manner or to such an extent, degree, etc. (with *as* expressed or understood); in the manner or to the extent, degree, intent, result, etc. (with *that* or *but*); on condition or provided (that); (*colloq.*) extremely, very; for this reason, therefore, accordingly; (*ellipt.*) thus, this, that, as follows; in such a case, or state. *int.* (also **soh**) stand still, quiet, steady, stop. **or so:** Or thereabouts. **so-and-so,** *n.* An indefinite person or thing. **so be it:** Let it be thus (in affirmation, resignation, etc.). **so-called,** *a.* Usually called thus (with implication of doubt). **and so forth** or **so on** [FORTH]. **so help me God** [HELP]. **so long!** *int.* Au revoir, good-bye. **so much as:** However much, to whatever extent. **so-so,** *a.* Indifferent, middling, mediocre. *adv.* Indifferently. **so what?** What about it?

soak (sōk) [A.-S. *socian*, cogn. with SUCK], *v.t.* To suck (in or up), to absorb (liquid); to put in liquid to become permeated, to steep, to wet thoroughly, to drench; (*slang*) to overcharge, to make (a person) pay. *v.i.* To lie in liquid so as to become permeated, to steep, to penetrate, to permeate (into, through, etc.); to drink excessively, to tipple. **soak-hole,** *n.* (*Austral.*) Part of a stream where sheep are penned to be washed. **soakage,** *n.* **soakaway,** *n.* A hole dug in the ground to allow drainage to percolate into the soil; (*Austral.*) low-lying land where water is retained. **soaker,** *n.* One who or that which soaks; a heavy drinker; a heavy shower. **soaking,** *a.* and *n.*

soap (sōp) [A.-S. *sāpe*, cp. Dut. *zeep*, G. *seipe*, also L. *sēbum*, tallow], *n.* An unctuous compound of a fatty acid and a base, usu. soda or potash, used for washing and cleansing. *v.t.* To rub or wash with soap. **soft soap,** *n.* A semi-liquid soap made with potash, used for scrubbing; (*fig.*) flattery. *v.t.* To flatter. **soap-boiler,** *n.* A maker of soap. **soap-bubble,** *n.* A thin inflated film of soapy water, formed accidentally or by blowing into a pipe containing soap-suds. **soap-suds,** *n.pl.* Water impregnated with soap. **soap-works,** *n.* **soapy,** *a.* Of the nature of or resembling soap; smeared with soap; (*fig.*) unctuous, flattering. **soapily,** *adv.* **soapiness,** *n.*

soapberry (sōp' be ri), *n.* (*Bot.*) The fruit of *Sapindus saponaria* and related shrubs and trees, used as soap.

soapstone (sōp' stōn), *n.* (*Geol.*) Steatite.

soapwort (sōp' wĕrt), *n.* (*Bot.*) A trailing herbaceous plant, *Saponaria officinalis*, the juice of which forms a lather with water.

soar (sôr) [F. *essorer*, prob. from a pop. L. *exaurare* (EX-, *aura*, air)], *v.i.* To fly aloft, to rise, sail, or float at a great height (of a bird, etc.); (*fig.*) to rise or mount intellectually or morally. *n.* A towering flight. **soaringly,** *adv.*

sob (sob) [M.E. *sobben*, prob. imit., perh. rel. to A.-S. *siofian*], *v.i.* (*past & p.p.* **sobbed**) To catch the breath in a convulsive manner, as in violent weeping. *v.t.* To utter with a sob or sobs. *n.* A convulsive catching of the breath, as in weeping. **sob sister,** *n.* (*Am. slang*) A woman who writes sentimental news articles. **sob stuff,** *n.* (*slang*) Conversation, literature, or drama, displaying extreme sentimentality. **sobbingly,** *adv.*

sober (sō' bėr) [F. *sobre*, L. *sōbrius* (*sō-*, SE-, *ēbrius*, drunk), see EBRIETY], *a.* Not drunk; temperate in the use of alcoholic liquors, etc.; moderate, well-balanced, sane; self-possessed, dispassionate; serious, solemn, sedate; subdued, quiet (of colours, etc.). *v.t.* To make sober. *v.i.* To become calm, quiet, or grave. ***sober-blooded,** *a.* **sober-minded,** *a.* **sobermindedness,** *n.* **sobersides,** *n.* A person of sober, serious disposition. ***sober-suited,** *a.* (*poet.*) Clad in sober colours. **soberly,** *adv.* **soberness,** *n.* **sobriety** (sō brī' ė ti), *n.*

soboles (sob' ō lēz) [L.], *n.* (*Bot.*) A creeping or underground stem, a sucker.

Sobranje (sō bra' nyė) [Bulg.], *n.* The National Assembly of Bulgaria.

sobriety [SOBER].

sobriquet (sō' bri kā) [F., etym. doubtful], *n.* A nickname; an assumed name.

***soc** (sok), **soke** (sōk) [A.-S. *sōcn*, cogn. with SEEK (cp. Icel. *sōkn*, Norw. *sokn*, Dan. *sogn*, parish, Goth. *sōkns*, enquiry)], *n.* The right of holding a local court; a district under such jurisdiction. ***socage,** *n.* A feudal tenure by any certain and determinate service distinct from military tenure and villainage. ***socager,** *n.*

soccer [SOCKER]. **so-called** [SO].

sociable (sō' shȧ bėl) [F., from L. *sociābilis*, from *sociāre*, to accompany, from *socius*, companion, rel. to *sequī*, to follow], *a.* Fit or inclined to associate or be friendly, companionable, affable; of a friendly, not stiff or formal, character (of a party, etc.). *n.* An open carriage with side seats facing each other; a tricycle for two riders side by side; a seat with an S-shaped back for two persons to sit side by side and face each other. **sociability** (-bil' i ti), **sociableness,** *n.* **sociably,** *adv.*

social (sō' shȧl) [F., from L. *sociālis*, as prec.], *a.* Of or pertaining to society or to the intercourse or mutual relations of mankind; living in communities, gregarious, not solitary, tending to associate with others, fitted for existence in an organized, co-operative system of society; sociable, companionable, consisting in friendly converse, convivial. *n.* A social gathering. **Social Credit:** The doctrine of a school of economists that the returns of industry are mostly unearned increment which, with all interest, should be returned to the public. **social democrat:** A member of a political party aiming at the gradual improvement of society by the adoption of Socialist reforms, esp. a member of the Socialist party in Germany. **social science:** Sociology. **social security:** Freedom from want and from unemployment, guaranteed by the state. **the social evil:** Prostitution. **sociality** (sō shi ăl' i ti), *n.* **socialite,** *n.* (*Am. colloq.*) An aspirant to fashionable society. **socialize,** *v.t.* **socialization** (-zā' shŭn), *n.* **socially,** *adv.*

Socialism (sō' shȧ lizm) [SOCIAL, -ISM], *n.* The doctrine that the political and economic organization of society should be based on the subordination of the individual to the interests of the community, involving the collective ownership of the sources and instruments of production, democratic control of industries, co-operation instead of individual private gain, state distribution of the products instead of payment by wages, free education, etc. **Socialist,** *n.* and *a.* **Socialistic,** *a.* **Socialistically,** *adv.*

socialite, sociality, socialize, etc., **socially** [SOCIAL].

society (sȯ sī' ė ti) [F. *société*, L. *societātem*, nom. *-tas*, from *socius*, see SOCIAL], *n.* A social community; the general body of persons, communities, or nations constituting civilized mankind regarded as a family or community; social organization, civilization; the privileged and fashionable classes of a community; a body of persons associated for some common object, an association; companionship, fellowship. **Society of Friends,** *n.* The religious body of Quakers. **Society of Jesus,** *n.* The R.C. order of Jesuits. **society journal:** A newspaper or periodical chronicling the events of fashionable society. **society verse:** Poetry of a light, witty, fanciful, or gently satirical kind.

Socinian (sȯ sin' i ȧn) [Faustus and Lælius *Socinus*, 16th-cent. Ital. theologians, -IAN], *n.* A follower of Faustus and Lælius Socinus, who taught a form of unitarianism. *a.* Pertaining to these or their teachings. **Socinianism,** *n.*

sociology (sō shi ol' ȯ ji) [F. *sociologie*], *n.* The science of the evolution and constitution of human society. **sociological,** *a.* **sociologically,** *adv.* **sociologist,** *n.*

sock (1) (sok) [A.-S. *socc*, L. *soccus*, a shoe worn by comic actors], *n.* A short stocking; a removable inner sole; the light shoe worn by classic comic actors, hence (*fig.*) comedy. **sock-suspender,** *n.*

A light garter to keep a sock in place (*Am.* a garter). **to pull up one's socks:** To make a vigorous effort.

sock (2) (sok) [etym. doubtful], *v.t.* (*slang*) To fling, to throw; to hit with a blow or missile. *n.* A hit, a blow, esp. with a missile.

sock (3) (sok) [etym. doubtful], *n.* (*schoolboy slang*) Food, esp. sweets, pastry, etc., tuck.

sock (4) (sok) [O.F. *soc*, perh. from Celt.], *n.* (*Sc.*) A ploughshare.

socker (sok′ ėr) [corr. of ASSOCIATION], *n.* (*colloq.*) Association football [see FOOTBALL].

socket (sok′ ėt) [M.E. and O.F. *soket*, dim. of *soc*, SOCK (4) (O.E.D.); dim. of *souche*, tree-stump, from Teut. (Skeat)], *n.* A natural or artificial hollow place or fitting adapted for receiving and holding another part or thing, esp. an implement, revolving tool, limb, head of an instrument, etc. **socket-joint** [BALL AND SOCKET JOINT, see BALL (1)], *n.* **socketed,** *a.*

socle (sō′ kėl) [G., from *zoccolo*, L. *socculus*, dim. of *soccus*, SOCK (1)], *n.* (*Arch.*) A plain, low, rectangular block or plinth, forming a base for a statue, column, etc.

Socotrine (sok′ ŏ trin, sō′ kŏ trīn), *a.* Pertaining to Socotra, an island in the Indian Ocean. *n.* A native or inhabitant of Socotra. **Socotrine aloes:** A drug obtained from the juice of *Aloe Socotrina.*

Socratic, *-al (sŏ krăt′ ik, -ål), *a.* Of, pertaining to, or according to Socrates, Greek philosopher (B.C. 469–399). *n.* An adherent of Socrates or his philosophy. **Socratic irony** [IRONY (2)]. **Socratic method:** The dialectical method of procedure by question and answer introduced by Socrates. **Socratically,** *adv.* **Socratism,** *n.*

sod (1) (sod) [cp. M.Dut. *sode*, Dut. *zode*, perh. cogn. with SEETHE, cp. foll.], *n.* Surface soil filled with the roots of grass, etc., turf, sward; a piece of this cut away. *v.t.* To cover with sod.

***sod** (2), *past & p.p.* [SEETHE].

sod (3) [SODOMITE].

soda (sō′ då) [It., prob. fem. of *sodo, solido*, glasswort, prob. from L. as SOLID], *n.* Carbonate or bicarbonate of sodium, esp. in the crystalline form used in washing, etc.; applied to other compounds of sodium; (*colloq.*) soda-water. **soda-fountain,** *n.* A vessel in which soda-water is kept under pressure and from which it can be drawn. **soda-jerker:** (*Am.*) A barman for soft drinks. **soda-water,** *n.* An effervescent drink composed of water charged with carbonic acid, formerly generated from sodium bicarbonate.

sodalite (sō dȧ līt′), *n.* (*Min.*) A vitreous silicate of sodium and aluminium.

sodality (sŏ dăl′ i ti) [F. *sodalité*, L. *sodālitas*, from *sodālis*, comrade], *n.* A fellowship, a confraternity, esp. (*R.-C. Ch.*) a charitable association.

sodden (sodn) [p.p. of SEETHE], *a.* Soaked, saturated; not properly baked, heavy, doughy (of bread, etc.); bloated and stupid, esp. with drink. *v.t.* To soak, to saturate, esp. with drink. *v.i.* To become sodden. **soddenness,** *n.*

sodium (sō′ di ŭm) [SOD-A, -IUM], *n.* A silver-white metallic element, the base of soda. **sodium bicarbonate,** *n.* Baking soda. **sodic,** *a.*

sodomite (sod′ ŏ mīt) [Gr. *Sodomitēs*, inhabitant of Sodom], *n.* A homosexual, one addicted to sodomy, Genesis xix. 5. **sodomitical** (-mit′ i kål), *a.* **sodomy,** *n.* Unnatural sexual intercourse, esp. between male persons.

soever (sō ev′ ėr), *adv.* Appended, sometimes as a suf. and sometimes after an interval, to pronouns, adverbs, or adjectives to give an indefinite or universal meaning.

sofa (sō′ fȧ) [prob. through F., from Arab. *suffah*], *n.* A long stuffed couch or seat with raised back and ends. **sofa-bedstead,** *n.* A sofa that can be extended so as to serve as a bedstead.

soffit (sof′ it) [F. *soffite*, It. *soffitta*, ceiling, fem. of *soffitto*, p.p. (SUB-, L. *figere*, to FIX)], *n.* The under surface of a cornice, lintel, balcony, arch, etc.

sofi, sofism [SUFI].

soft (sawft, soft) [A.-S. *sōfte*, adv. (*sēfte*, a.), cp. G. *sanft*, Dut. *zacht*, also Gr. *hēmeros*, mild, Sansk. *sāmen*, mildness], *a.* Yielding easily to pressure, easily moulded, cut, or worked, malleable, pliable, plastic, opp. to hard; affecting the senses in a mild, delicate, or gentle manner; smooth to the touch, not rough or coarse; not hot or cold, mild, genial; not brilliant, glaring, or abrupt (of colours, outlines, etc.); not loud or harsh, low-toned; free from mineral salts, suitable for washing (of water); gentle or mild in disposition, yielding, conciliatory; impressionable, sympathetic, compassionate; weak, timorous, effeminate; silly, simple; (*colloq.*) amorous, spoony; (*prov.*) wet, rainy; (*Phon.*) not guttural or explosive, sibilant (as *c* in *cede* or *g* in *gem*), voiced (as *b*, *d*, and *g*); (*slang*) easy (of a job). *adv.* Softly, gently, quietly. *n.* A silly, weak-minded person. *int.* Gently! stop! hush! **soft currency:** (*Fin.*) A currency that is unstable owing to the uncertainty of its gold backing. **soft-headed, -witted,** *a.* Silly. **soft-hearted,** *a.* Tender-hearted, compassionate; weak, cowardly. **soft-heartedness,** *n.* **soft palate,** *n.* (*Anat.*) The posterior part of the palate terminating in the uvula. **soft soap:** Semi-liquid soap made with potash; (*fig.*) flattery, blarney. **soft-soap,** *v.t.* To flatter for some ulterior object. **soft-spoken,** *a.* Speaking softly; mild, affable, conciliatory. **soft valve,** *n.* (*Radio.*) A thermionic valve in which the gas is not completely exhausted. **soft drinks,** *n.pl.* Non-intoxicant beverages. **soft goods,** *n.pl.* Textiles. **soft water,** *n.* Rain water; water free from mineral salts. **soften** (sawfn), *v.t.* To make soft or softer; to palliate, to mitigate, tone down. *v.i.* To become soft or softer. **softener,** *n.* **softish,** *a.* **softly,** *adv.* **softness,** *n.* **softy,** *n.* A silly, weak-minded person.

softa (sof′ tȧ) [Turk., from Pers. *sūhtah*, lighted], *n.* A student of Mohammedan theology and sacred law.

soften, softish, softly, softy, etc. [SOFT].

soggy (sog′ i) [etym. doubtful], *a.* Soaked, sodden, thoroughly wet. **sogginess.**

soh [SO].

soho (sŏ hō′) [A.-F., prob. instinctive], *int.* A sportsman's hallo; soh.

soi-disant (swa dē zan′) [F., *soi*, L. *se*, self, *disant*, pres.p. of *dire*, L. *dīcere*, to say], *a.* Self-styled, pretended.

soigné (swa′ nyā) [F.], *a.* Well-turned-out, elegant, exquisite in taste.

soil (1) (soil) [A.-F., prob. from L. *solium*, seat, or late L. *solea*, sole, ground, conf. with *solum*, ground], *n.* The ground, esp. the top stratum of the earth's crust whence plants derive their mineral food; land, country. **soilless** (1), *a.*

soil (2) (soil) [A.-F. *soyler*, O.F. *soillier*, *suillier* (F. *souiller*), prob. from *soil*, a boar's soil, L. *suillus*, pertaining to swine, from *sus*, pig (cp. SULLY)], *v.t.* To make dirty; to sully, to tarnish, to pollute. *n.* A dirty spot, stain, taint, or defilement; any foul matter, filth, refuse, dung, compost; a marshy or miry place to which a hunted boar or deer resorts for refuge. **soil-pipe,** *n.* A pipe from a water-closet, etc. ***soil-less** (2), *a.* ***soilure,** *n.* Pollution.

soil (3) (soil) [perh. from prec., or from O.F. *soeler* (F. *soûler*), to satiate, ult. from L. *satullus*, dim. of *satur*, full], *v.t.* To feed (cattle, etc.) with green food, in order to fatten, orig. to purge.

soirée (swa′ rā) [F., orig. evening, from L. *sērus*, late], *n.* An evening party or gathering for conversation and social intercourse, discussion, etc., usu. with music.

sojourn (sŭj′-, soj′ ŭrn, sō′ jŭrn) [O.F. *sojourner* (F. *séjourner*), (SUB-, L. *diurnāre*, to stay, from *diurnus*,

DIURNAL)], *v.i.* To stay or reside (in, among, etc.) temporarily. *n.* A temporary stay or residence. **sojourner, sojournment,** *n.*

***soke** [SOC].

soko (sō′ kō) [native name], *n.* An anthropoid ape described by Livingstone as living west of Lake Tanganyika.

sol (1) (sol) [L.], *n.* The sun; (*Her.*) or, gold.

sol (2) (sol) [L. *sol-ve*, see GAMUT], *n.* (*Mus.*) The fifth tone of the diatonic scale; the syllable noting such tone.

***sol** (3) (sol) [F.], *n.* An obsolete coin and money of account in France, etc., later superseded by the sou.

sola (1) (sō′ lȧ) [Hind. *solā*, Hindi *sholā*], *n.* The hat-plant or sponge-wood or its pith. **sola topee** [TOPEE].

***sola** (2) [cp. SOHO, HALLO], *int.* Here! stop!

solace (sol′ ȧs) [O.F. *solaz*, L. *sōlācium*, cogn. with *sōlārī*, to console], *n.* Comfort in grief, trouble, etc., consolation, compensation; *happiness, pleasure. *v.t.* To comfort or console, in trouble, etc. ***solacement,** *n.*

solan, solan goose (sō′ lȧn goos) [Icel. *sūla*, perh. *ond*, goose], *n.* The gannet, *Sula bassana.*

***solander** [SALLENDERS].

solano (sō la′ nō) [Sp., from L. *Solānus*, from SOL (1)], *n.* A hot, oppressive S.E. wind in Spain.

solanum (sȯ lā′ nŭm) [late L.], *n.* (*Bot.*) A large genus of plants, containing the potato, egg-plant, nightshade, etc. **solanaceous** (sō lȧ nā′ shŭs), *a.* **solanine** (sol′ ȧ nin), *n.* A poisonous alkaloid found in several species of Solanum.

solar (sō′ lȧr) [L. *sōlāris*, from SOL (1)], *a.* Pertaining to, proceeding from, or determined by the sun. **solar flowers:** Flowers that open and shut daily at determinate hours. **solar myth:** A myth supposed to be an allegory or symbolic narrative of solar phenomena. **solar plexus:** (*Anat.*) The epigastric plexus. **solar system:** The sun and the various heavenly bodies revolving about it.

solarism (sō′ lȧ rizm), *n.* The doctrine that mythology is chiefly derived from solar myths. **solarist,** *n.*

solarium (sō lâr′ i ŭm), *n.* A room or building constructed for the enjoyment of, or therapeutical exposure of the body to, the rays of the sun.

solarize (sō′ lȧ rīz), *v.t.* (*Phot.*) To expose (a plate) too long. *v.i.* To be spoiled by over-exposure. **solarization** (-zā′ shŭn), *n.*

solatium (sȯ lā′ shi ŭm) [L., SOLACE], *n.* (*pl.* **-tia**) Compensation for suffering or loss.

sold (1), *past & p.p.* [SELL (1)].

***sold** (2) [O.F. *soude*, *soulde*, L. *soldum*, pay, prob. from SOLIDUS], *n.* Pay, remuneration.

soldado (sol da′ dō) [Sp., from *soldo*, prec.], *n.* A soldier.

***soldan,** etc. [SULTAN].

soldanella (sol dȧ nel′ ȧ) [It., etym. doubtful], *n.* An Alpine plant of the primrose family with blue, pink, or rarely white flowers, esp. *S. Alpina*, the blue moonwort.

solder (so′ dėr, sol′ der, sō′ der) [M.E. *soudur*, *soudre*, O.F. *soudure*, from *souder*, L. *solidāre*, to make firm, as foll.], *n.* A fusible alloy for uniting the edges, etc., of less fusible metals; (*fig.*) anything that cements or unites. *v.t.* To unite with or as with solder. **soldering-bolt, -iron,** *n.* A tool used hot for applying solder.

soldier (sōl′ jėr) [O.F., from late L. *soldārius* (SOLD (2), -ARY)], *n.* A man engaged in military service, esp. a private or non-commissioned officer; a man of military skill or experience; an able commander; a soldier-ant, -beetle, or -crab; (*colloq.*) a shirk, a malingerer. *v.i.* To go or serve as a soldier; (*colloq.*) to shirk, to malinger. **old soldier:** An experienced, knowing, or crafty person; (*slang*) a bottle that has been drained, a cigar-end, a well-chewed quid. **soldier-ant,** *n.* One of the asexual fighting ants of a community of termites. **soldier-beetle,** *n.* A reddish beetle that preys on the larvæ of other insects. **soldier-crab,** *n.* A species of hermit-crab. **soldier-like, -ly,** *a.* and *adv.* **soldier of fortune:** A military adventurer; one who lives on his wits. **soldiership,** *n.* **soldiery,** *n.* Soldiers collectively; a body of soldiers.

soldo (sol′ dō) [It.], *n.* (*pl.* ***-di***, -dē) A small Italian coin worth ½d.

sole (1) (sōl) [A.-S., from L. *solea*, from *solum*, the ground], *n.* The flat under side or bottom of the foot; the part of a boot or shoe under the foot, esp. the part in front of the heel; the bottom or lower part (of a plane, a ploughshare, the head of a golf-club, various engines, etc.). *v.t.* To furnish (a boot, etc.) with a sole. **sole-leather,** *n.* **sole-plate,** *n.* The bed-plate of a machine etc.

sole (2) (sōl) [L. *solea*, see prec.], *n.* A flat-fish of various species highly esteemed as food.

sole (3) (sōl) [A.-F., from O.F. *sol*, L. *sōlum*, nom. *-lus*], *a.* Single, only, unique, alone in its kind; (*Law*) unmarried; *solitary, alone. **solely,** *adv.*

solecism (sol′ ė sizm) [L. *solœcismus*, Gr. *soloikismos*, from *soloikos*, speaking incorrectly (*Soloi*, in Cilicia, where the Attic colonists spoke bad Greek, *-oikos*, dwelling)], *n.* A deviation from correct idiom or grammar; a breach of good manners, an impropriety. ***solecist,** *n.* **solecistic, -al** (-sis′ tik′, -ȧl), *a.* ***solecize,** *v.i.*

solely [SOLE (3)].

solemn (sol′ ėm) [M.E. and O.F. *solempne*, L. *sōlemnis*, *sollennis*, prob. from *sollus*, whole, entire, cp. Gr. *holos*], *a.* Performed with or accompanied by rites, ceremonies, or due formality; awe-inspiring, impressive; grave, serious, momentous; formal, affectedly grave, self-important, pompous. **solemnly,** *adv.* **solemnness, solemness,** *n.*

solemnity (so lem′ ni ti), *n.* Solemnness, impressiveness; affected gravity or formality; a rite or ceremony, esp. one performed with religious reverence (*often in pl.*).

solemnize (sol′ ėm nīz), *v.t.* To dignify or to celebrate with solemn formalities or ceremonies; to make solemn. **solemnization** (-ni-, -nī zā′ shŭn), *n.* **solemnizer,** *n.*

solen (sō′ lėn) [L., from Gr. *sōlēn*], *n.* A bivalve mollusc, the razor-fish. **solenacean** (-nā′ shi ȧn), *a.* and *n.* **solenaceous,** *a.* **solenite** (sō′ lė nīt), *n.* A fossil solen. **soleno-,** *comb. form.* **solenostomatous** (sȯ lē nȯ stom′ ȧ tŭs) [Gr. *stoma*, mouth], *a.* (*Zool.*) Of or belonging to the *Solenostomi*, a sub-order of lophobranchiate fishes with a spinous dorsal fin and ventral fins.

solenoid (sō′ lė noid, sȯ lē′ noid) [F. *solenoïde* (prec., -OID)], *n.* (*Elec.*) A magnet consisting of a cylindrical coil traversed by an electric current. **solenoidal** (-noi′ dȧl), *a.* **solenoidally,** *adv.*

solenostomatous [SOLEN].

soleus (sȯ lē′ ŭs, sō′ lė ŭs) [from L. *solea*, SOLE (1)], *n.* (*Anat.*) A muscle of the calf of the leg beneath the gastrocnemius, helping to extend the foot.

sol-fa (sol fa′) [SOL (2), FA], *v.i.* To sing the notes of the musical scale up or down to the syllables *do* (or *ut*), *re*, *mi*, *fa*, *sol*, *la*, *si*. *v.t.* To sing (a musical composition) thus. *n.* Solmization.

solfatara (sol fȧ ta′ rȧ) [It., from *solfo*, sulphur], *n.* A volcanic vent emitting sulphurous gases.

solfeggio (sol fej′ ō) [It., from SOL-FA], *n.* (*pl.* **-gi, -gios**) A singing exercise in solmization; solmization, sol-fa.

solferino (sol fė rē′ nō) [It., from the battle of *Solferino*, 1859, the year of its discovery], *n.* The purplish-red colour of rosaniline, a deep pink aniline colour or dye.

soli, *n.pl.* [SOLO].

solicit (sȯ lis′ it) [O.F. *soliciter*, L. *sollicitāre*, from *sollicitus*, SOLICITOUS], *v.t.* To make earnest or importunate request for; to make earnest or persistent requests or appeals to, to importune (esp. of beggars, prostitutes, etc.). *v.i.* To make earnest or importunate appeals. **solicitant,** *a.* and *n.* **solicitation** (-tā′ shŭn), *n.*

solicitor (sŏ lis′ i tŏr) [O.F. *soliciteur* (prec.)], *n.* A legal practitioner authorized to advise clients and prepare causes for barristers but not to appear as advocate in the higher courts; *one who solicits. **Solicitor-General,** *n.* A law officer of the British Crown ranking next to the Attorney-General, appointed by the Government in power to advise and represent it in legal matters. **solicitorship,** *n.*

solicitous (sŏ lis′ i tŭs) [L. *sōlicitus, sollicitus* (perh. *sollus*, see SOLEMN, *citus*, p.p. of *ciēre*, to CITE)], *a.* Anxious, concerned, apprehensive, disturbed (about, for, etc.); eager (to). **solicitously,** *adv.* **solicitousness, solicitude,** *n.*

solid (sol′ id) [O.F. *solide*, L. *solidum*, nom. *-dus*, cogn. with Gr. *bolos*, Sansk. *sarva(s)*, whole], *a.* Composed of particles closely cohering, dense, compact; not hollow, devoid of cavities, interstices, or crevices, not porous; firm, unyielding, stable, rigid; sound, substantial, not flimsy; (*fig.*) real, genuine, reliable, well-grounded; the same throughout, homogeneous; (*fig.*) thinking, feeling, or acting unanimously; (*Geom.*) of three dimensions, cubic; (*Print.*) having no leads between the lines. *n.* A rigid, compact body; (*Geom.*) a body or magnitude possessing length, breadth, and thickness. **solid matter,** *n.* (*Print.*) Type matter without leads or cast on its own body size. ***solidare,** *n.* (*Shak.*) A small coin. **solidity** (sŏ lid′ i ti), **solidness,** *n.* **solidly,** *adv.*

solidarity (so li dăr′ i ti), *n.* Cohesion, mutual dependence; community of interests, feelings, responsibilities, etc.

solidary (so′ li dà ri), *a.* United in nature, interests, etc.

solidify (sŏ lid′ i fī), *v.t.i.* To make or become solid. **solidifiable,** *a.* **solidification,** *n.*

solidism (sol′ i dizm), *n.* (*Med.*) The theory that refers all diseases to alterations of the solid parts of the human body. **solidist,** *n.*

solidungular (sol i dŭng′ gū lȧr), *a.* Solid-hoofed, soliped. **solidungulate,** *a.*

solidus (sol′ i dŭs) [late L., as prec.], *n.* (*pl.* **-di,** -dī) A shilling (in abbrev. *s.*); the stroke (/) standing for this (as in 2/6); (*Hist.*) a Roman gold coin introduced by Constantine.

solifidian (sō li fid′ i ȧn) [L. *sōli-*, *sōlus*, SOLE (3), *fides*, faith, -IAN], *n.* One who maintains that faith without works is sufficient for salvation. **solifidianism,** *n.*

soliloquy (sŏ lil′ ŏ kwi) [L. *sōliloquium* (as prec., *loquī*, to speak)], *n.* A talking to oneself; a speech or discourse, esp. in a play, uttered to oneself, a monologue. **soliloquize,** *v.i.* **soliloquist,** *n.*

soliped (sol′ i ped) [O.F. *solipede*, L. *solidipes -pedis* (SOLID, L. *pes pedis*, foot)], *a.* Solidungulate. *n.* A solidungulate. ***solipedal,** ***-dous,** *a.* Soliped.

solipsism (sol′ ip sizm) [L. *soli-*, *solus*, SOLE (3), *ipse*, self, -ISM], *n.* (*Metaph.*) The theory that the only knowledge possible is that of oneself, absolute egoism. **solipsist,** *n.* A believer in solipsism.

solisequious (sō li sē′ kwi ŭs) [L. *sōl sōlis*, SOL (1), *sequī*, to follow], *a.* (*Bot.*) Following the course of the sun.

solitaire (sol i târ′) [F., as foll.], *n.* A gem set singly, in a stud, ear-ring, etc.; a game played by one person on a board with hollows and marbles, holes and pegs, etc.; a card game for one player, patience; an American rock-thrush and other birds; an extinct bird, *Pezophaps solitarius*, allied to the dodo; *a hermit, a recluse.

solitary (sol′ i tȧr i) [A.-F. *solitaire* (F. *solitaire*), L. *sōlitārius* (*sōlitas*, loneliness, from *sōlus*, SOLE (3))], *a.* Living or being alone, lonely, not gregarious; passed or spent alone; unfrequented, sequestered, secluded; single, individual, sole. *n.* One who lives in solitude, a recluse. **solitarily,** *adv.* **solitariness,** *n.* **solitude,** *n.* Loneliness, seclusion; a lonely place.

solivagant (sŏ liv′ ȧ gȧnt) [L. *sōlivagus* (*sōlus*, SOLE (1), *vagārī*, to wander, pres.p. *vagans -ntem*)], *a.* Wandering alone. **solivagous,** *a.*

solive (sŏ lēv′) [O.F., etym. doubtful], *n.* A joist or intermediate timber.

sollar (sol′ ȧr) [A.-S. *solor*, L. SOLARIUM], *n.* *An upper room, attic, garret, or loft, esp. in a church or belfry; (*Min.*) a platform or raised floor in a mine.

solleret (sol′ ĕr et) [O.F., dim. of *soler* (F. *soulier*), shoe], *n.* (*Ant.*) A steel shoe worn with mediæval armour.

solmization (sol mi zā′ shŭn) [F., from *solmiser* (SOL (2), MI, -IZE)], *n.* The association of certain syllables with the notes of the musical scale, a recital of the notes of the gamut, solfaing. **solmizate** (sol′-), *v.i.*

solo (sō′ lō) [It., as SOLE (3)], *n.* (*pl.* **solos, soli**) A composition or passage played by a single instrument or sung by a single voice, usu. with an accompaniment; solo whist, a call in this game; (*Motor.*) a motor-cycle without a side-car attached. **solo flight,** *n.* (*Aviat.*) A flight by a single person. **soloist,** *n.* **solo whist:** A card game for four persons somewhat resembling whist.

Solomon (sol′ ŏ mŏn) [King of Israel], *n.* (*fig.*) A very wise man. **Solomon's seal:** A plant, *Polygonatum multiflorum*, with drooping white flowers and a root-stalk marked with scars which are said to account for the name. **Solomonic** (-mon′ ik), *a.*

Solon (sō′ lŏn) [ancient Athenian lawgiver], *n.* (*fig.*) A sage, esp. a wise law-maker.

so long (sō long′) [possibly corr. of SALAAM], *int.* (*colloq.*) Good-bye.

solstice (sol′ stis) [F., from L. *sōlstitium* (SOL (1), *-stitium*, from *statum*, neut. p.p. of *sistere*, to cause to stand)], *n.* The time (about 21 June and 22 Dec.) at which the sun is farthest from the celestial equator (north in summer and south in winter). **solstitial** (-stish′ ȧl), *a.*

soluble (sol′ ū bĕl) [F., from L. *solūbilis*, from *solvere*, to SOLVE], *a.* Capable of being dissolved in a fluid; capable of being solved. **solubility** (-bil′ i ti), *n.* The noun of soluble; (*Chem.*) the number of grams of substance required to saturate 100 grams of solvent.

solum (sō′ lŭm) [L.], *n.* (*Sc. Law*) Ground, soil, a piece of ground.

solus, fem. ***sola*** (sō′ lŭs, -lȧ) [L., SOLE (3)], *a.* Alone (used esp. in stage directions).

solution (sŏ loo′-, -lū′ shŭn) [F., from L. *solūtiōnem*, nom. *-tio*, as foll.], *n.* The liquefaction of a solid or gaseous body by mixture with a liquid; the liquid combination so produced; (*Cycling*) a liquid-rubber preparation used for sticking patches to tires; the resolution or act or process of solving a problem, difficulty, etc.; the correct answer to a problem, etc.; separation, dissolution, disintegration. **solute** (sŏ loot′, -lūt′), *a.* **solutionist,** *n.* A professional solver of newspaper puzzles and problems.

Solutrian (so lū′ tri ȧn) [Solutre, France], *a.* (*Palæont.*) Pertaining to the period of Upper Palæolithic culture between the Aurignacian and Magdalenian periods, including flint and bone instruments and carvings on stone.

solve (solv) [L. *solvere*], *v.t.* To resolve or find an answer to (a problem, etc.); to clear up, to settle, to put an end to; to dissolve. **solvable,** *a.* **solvability** (-bil′ i ti), *n.* **solver,** *n.*

solvent (sol′ vent) [L. *solvens -ntem*, pres.p. of *solvere*, prec.], *a.* Having the power to dissolve;

able to pay all just debts or claims. *n.* A liquid that can dissolve a substance, a menstruum. **solvency,** *n.*

solver [SOLVE].

soma (1) (sō' mȧ) [Gr. *soma*, the body, a dead body], *n.* (*Biol.*) The axial part of the body, *i.e.* without the limbs; the body as distinct from the germ cells; (*Theol.*) the body as distinguished from soul and spirit.

soma (2) (sō' mȧ) [Sansk.], *n.* An intoxicating liquor used in connexion with ancient Vedic worship; the plant from the juice of which it was made.

somatic, somatical (sō măt' ik, -ȧl), *a.* Pertaining to the body, corporeal, physical. *n.pl.* Somatology. **somatic cell,** *n.* A non-reproductive cell of the parent body.

somato- *comb. form.* **somatogenic** (sō mȧ tȯ jen' ik), *a.* (*Biol.*) Originating in the body of an organism, opp. to external. **somatology** (sō mȧ tol' ȯ ji) [-LOGY], *n.* The science of organic bodies, esp. human anatomy and physiology; *physics. **somatological** (-loj' i kȧl), *a.* **somatologist** (-tol' ȯ jist), *n.* **somatome** (sō' mȧ tōm), *n.* One of the segments of which a body is composed, a somite.

sombre (som' bėr) [F. (perh. EX-, or SUB-, L. *umbra*, shade)], *a.* Dark, gloomy. **sombrely,** *adv.* **sombreness,** *n.* ***sombrous** (som' brŭs), *a.*

sombrero (som brâr' ō) [Sp. from *sombra*, shade, as prec.], *n.* A wide-brimmed hat worn largely in America, esp. Mexico.

***sombrous** [SOMBRE].

some (sŭm) [A.-S. *sum* (cp. Icel. *sumr*, Dan. *somme*, pl., O.H.G. *sum*), cog. with SAME], *a.* An indeterminate quantity, number, etc. of; an appreciable if limited amount, etc., of; a considerable quantity, etc., of; a certain, a particular but not definitely known or specified (person or thing). *adv.* About, approximately; (*colloq.*) to some extent. *pron.* A particular but undetermined part or quantity; certain not definitely known or unspecified ones. **somebody,** *n.* Some person; a person of consequence. ***somedeal,** *adv.* In some degree, somewhat. **somehow,** *adv.* In some indeterminate way; in some way or other; by some indeterminate means. **some one:** Somebody. **something,** *n.* Some indeterminate or unspecified thing; some quantity or portion if not much; a thing of consequence or importance. *adv.* In some degree. **something like** [LIKE (1)]. **sometime,** *adv.* Once, formerly, at one time. *a.* Former, late. **sometimes,** *adv.* At some times. **someway,** *adv.* In some way. **somewhat,** *adv.* To some extent, rather. *n.* A certain amount or degree; something. **somewhen,** *adv.* (*affected*) At some indeterminate time. **somewhere,** *adv.* In some unknown or unspecified place; in some place or other. ***somewhile,** *adv.* At some indeterminate time, sometimes. *a.* Sometime, former. ***somewhither,** *adv.* To some indeterminate place.

-some [A.-S. *-sum* (cp. Dut. *-zaam*, G. *-sam*, Icel. *-samr*), as prec.], *suf.* Forming adjectives, full of, as in *gladsome, troublesome, winsome.*

somebody, -deal, -how [SOME].

somersault, *somerset (sŭm' ėr sawlt, -set) [O.F. *sombresaut*, Prov. *sobresaut* (L. *suprā*, above, *saltum*, nom. *-tus*, a leap)], *n.* A leap in which one turns heels over head and alights on one's feet. *v.i.* To make a somersault.

something, -time, -what, etc. [SOME].

somite (sō' -mīt) [Gr. *sōma*, body, -ITE], *n.* A segment of the body in an animal, esp. of an articulate or vertebrate, a somatome. **somitic** (sȯ mit' ik), *a.*

somnambulism (som năm' bū lizm) [L. *somnus*, sleep, *ambul-āre*, to walk, -ISM], *n.* The act of walking or performing other actions in sleep or a condition resembling sleep; the mental affection causing this. ***somnambulant,** *a.* and *n.* ***somnambulate,** *v.i.* ***somnambulation** (-lā' shŭn), *n.* **somnambulist,** *n.* **somnambulistic** (-lis' tik), *a.*

somniferous (som nif' ėr ŭs) [L. *somnifer* (*somni-, somnus*, see prec., -FEROUS)], *a.* Causing or inducing sleep. **somnific** (-nif, ik), *a.* **somniloquism, *-quence, somniloquy** (som nil' ȯ kwizm, -kwėns, -kwi) [L. *loquī*, to talk], *n.* The act or habit of talking in one's sleep. **somniloquist,** *n.* **somniloquous,** *a.* **somnipathy** (som nip' ȧ thi) [-PATHY], *n.* Hypnotic sleep. **somnipathist,** *n.*

somnolent (som' nō lėnt) [earlier and O.F. *sompnolent*, L. *somnolentus* (*somno-, somnus*, sleep, suf. *-lentus*)], *a.* Sleepy, drowsy; inducing sleep; (*Path.*) a morbid dreamy condition. **somnolence, -lency,** *n.* **somnolently,** *adv.* **somnolism,** *n.* A sleepy condition produced by hypnotism.

son (sŭn) [A.-S. *sunu*, cp. Dut. *zoon*, G. *sohn*, Icel. *sunr, sonr*, O.H.G. *sunu*], *n.* A male child in relation to a parent or parents; (*fig.*) a descendant; a form of address used by an old person to a youth, a priest or teacher to a disciple, etc.; (*fig.*) a native of a country; an inheritor, exponent, or product of (a quality, art, occupation, etc.). **the Son or the Son of Man:** Christ, the Messiah. **son-in-law,** *n.* The husband of one's daughter. **sonless,** *a.* **sonny,** *n.* (*fam.*) A term of endearment. **sonship,** *n.* The state of being a son.

sonant (sō' nȧnt) [L. *sonans -ntem*, pres.p. of *sonāre*, to SOUND (2)], *a.* Capable of being sounded continuously, intonated, voiced, not surd (as the vowels and the consonants *b, d, g, j, m, n, v, th, z*). *n.* A voiced letter or sound. **sonance, -nancy,** *n.*

sonata (sȯ na' tȧ) [It., from L. *sonāta*, fem. p.p. as prec.], *n.* An instrumental composition, esp. for the piano, usu. in three or four movements in different rhythms. **sonatina** (son ā tē' nȧ), *n.* A short or simple sonata.

song (song) [A.-S. *sang, song*, cp. Dut. *zang*, G. and Dan. *sang*, Icel. *söngr*, rel. to SING], *n.* Musical or modulated utterance with the voice, singing; a melodious utterance, as the musical cry of a bird; a musical composition accompanied by words for singing; an instrumental piece of a similar character; a short poem intended or suitable for singing, esp. one set to music; (*fig.*) poetry, verse. **going for an old song:** Selling for a trifle. **nothing to make a song about:** Hardly worth mentioning. **song-bird, -sparrow, -thrush,** *n.* A bird that sings. ***song-craft,** *n.* The art of composing songs. **songless,** *a.* **songster,** *n.* One skilled in singing; a song-bird. **songstress,** *n.*

sonifer (son' i fėr) [L. *sonus*, SOUND (2), *-fer*, -FEROUS], *n.* An instrument with a receiver and tube for enabling deaf persons to hear. **soniferous** (sȯ nif' ėr ŭs), *a.* Producing or conveying sound.

sonnet (son' ėt) [F., from It. *sonetto*, dim. of *sono*, L. *sonus*, SOUND (2)], *n.* A poem of fourteen iambic pentameter lines, usu. consisting of an octave rhyming *a b b a a b b a*, and a sestet with three rhymes variously arranged. **sonneteer,** *n.* A writer of sonnets. *v.i.* To compose sonnets.

sonnite [SUNNITE]. **sonny** [SON].

sonobuoy (son' ō boi) [L. *sonus*, sound; BUOY], *n.* A buoy fitted with instruments for detecting submarines and communicating observations by radio to surface vessels, etc.

sonometer (sȯ nom' ė tėr), *n.* An instrument for testing or measuring the intensity of sounds, testing hearing of deaf persons, etc.

sonorous (sȯ nôr' ŭs) [L. *sonōrus*, from *sonor sonōris*, sound, from *sonāre*, to SOUND (2)], *a.* Giving out sound, resonant; loud sounding, sounding rich or full; high sounding, impressive. **sonorescent** (sō nȯ res' ėnt), *a.* Giving out sounds in response to pulsations of radiant light or heat. **sonorescence,** *n.* **sonorific** (son ȯ-, sō nȯ rif' ik), *a.* Producing sound, stridulating (esp. of insects). **sonority, sonorousness,** *n.* **sonorously,** *adv.*

sonsy (son' si) [Sc. and Ir. *sonse*, Gael. *sonas*, good fortune, -Y], *a.* Happy or jolly-looking, buxom, well-favoured, plump; good-natured, tractable (of animals).

soochong [SOUCHONG].

sook (sook), *n.* (*Austral. colloq.*) A timid fellow, a coward.

sool (sool), *v.t.* (*Austral. colloq.*) To set a dog on to attack.

soon (soon) [A.-S. *sōna*, cp. O.Sax and O.H.G. *sān*, Goth. *suns*], *adv.* In a short time from now or after a specified time, early; quickly, readily, easily, willingly. **as soon:** As willingly. **as** or **so soon as:** At the moment that; immediately after; not later than. **sooner or later:** Sometime or other; inevitably.

soop (soop) [Icel. *sōpa*, cogn. with A.-S. *swāpan*, to SWEEP], *v.t.* (*Sc.*) To sweep.

soot (sut) [A.-S. *sōt*, cp. Icel. *sōt*, Dan. *sod*, Swed. *sot*], *n.* A black substance composed of carbonaceous particles rising from fuel in a state of combustion and deposited in a chimney, etc. *v.t.* To cover, manure, or soil with soot. **sootless,** *a.* **sooty,** *a.* **sootily,** *adv.* **sootiness,** *n.*

***sooterkin** (soot' ėr kin) [etym. doubtful], *n.* A false birth fabled to be produced by Dutch women through sitting over their stoves; (*fig.*) an abortive proposal or scheme.

***sooth** (sooth) [A.-S. *sōth*, for *santh* (cp. Icel. *sannr*, Swed. *sann*), from root *es-*, to be], *n.* Truth, reality, *cajolery, blandishment. **a.* True; truthful. ***soothfast,** *a.* Truthful; loyal, steadfast.

soothe (sooth) [A.-S. *gesōthian*, to confirm, to assent to, as prec.], *v.t.* To calm, to tranquillize; to soften, to mitigate, to assuage; to humour, to flatter, to gratify. **soother,** *n.* **soothingly,** *adv.*

soothsayer (sooth' sā ėr) [SOOTH, SAY (1), -ER], *n.* A prognosticator, a diviner. **soothsay,** *v.i.*

sop (sop) [A.-S. *sopp* (cp. Icel. *soppa*), cogn. with SUP], *n.* Anything steeped or dipped and softened in milk, broth, gravy, etc., and intended to be eaten; (*fig.*) something given to pacify (in alln. to the legendary sop to Cerberus, the watch-dog of Hades). *v.t.* (*past & p.p.* **sopped**) To dip or steep in broth, etc.; to take (*usu.* up) by absorption. *v.i.* To be thoroughly wet or soaked. **sop-, sops-in-wine,** *n.* A pink, esp. the clove-pink. **soppy,** *a.* Wet through; (*slang*) maudlin, sentimental, weak-minded. **soppiness,** *n.*

Sopherim (sō' fėr im) [Heb.], *n.pl.* The scribes as copyists and interpreters of the Jewish law. **sopheric** (sȯ fer' ik), *a.*

sophism (sof' izm) [O.F. *sophisme*, L. and Gr. *sophisma*, from *sophizein*, to instruct, from *sophos*, wise], *n.* A specious but fallacious argument. **sophistic, -al** (sȯ fis' tik, -ȧl), *a.* **sophistically,** *adv.* **sophistry** (sof' is tri), *n.*

sophist (sof' ist), *n.* One of a class of men in ancient Athens who taught philosophy, dialectic, rhetoric, etc., for pay; a fallacious reasoner, a quibbler.

sophister (sof' is tėr), *n.* (*Camb. Univ.*) A student in his second year (**junior sophister**) or third year (**senior sophister**).

sophisticate (so fis' ti kāt) [as prec.], *v.t.* To envelop or obscure with sophistry; to mislead or delude thus; to alter or garble (a text, etc.) in order to support one's arguments, etc.; to make spurious by admixture, to adulterate; to deprive of simplicity, to make perverted, affected, or artificial. *v.i.* To be sophistical. **sophisticated,** *a.* Worldly-wise; self-assured from a superficial mental capacity. **sophistication** (-kā' shŭn), *n.* **sophisticator** (sȯ fis' ti kā tȯr), *n.*

sophistry [SOPHISM].

Sophoclean (sof ȯ klē' ȧn) [L. *Sophoclēus*, Gr. *Sophokleios* (*Sophocles*, -AN)], *a.* Pertaining to or characteristic of Sophocles, the Greek tragic poet.

sophomore (sof' ȯ môr) [from prec., -ER, or Gr. *soph-os*, wise, *mōros*, foolish], *n.* (*Am. Univ.*) A student in his second year. **sophomoric, -al** (-mor' ik, -ȧl), *a.* **sophomorically,** *adv.*

Sophora (sȯ fôr' ȧ) [Arab. *sofāra*, from *asfar*, yellow], *n.* (*Bot.*) A genus of trees, herbs, or shrubs of the bean family, many of which are cultivated for ornamental purposes.

***sopite** (sō pīt') [L. *sōpītus*, p.p. of *sōpīre*], *v.t.* To put to sleep; to quiet, to settle, to quash. *a.* Put to sleep; settled.

soporific (sō pȯ-, sop ȯ rif' ik) [L. *sopor*, *sopōris*, sleep, -FIC], *a.* Causing or tending to cause sleep. *n.* A soporific medicine. **soporiferous, soporose, soporous** (sop ȯ rif' ėr ŭs, sop' ȯ rōs, -rŭs), *a.* **soporiferousness,** *a.*

soprano (sȯ pra' nō) (It., from late L. *superānus*, SOVEREIGN], *n.* (*pl.* **-nos, -ni,** -nē) A female or boy's voice of the highest kind; a singer having such a voice; a musical part for such voices. **sopranist,** *n.*

sora (sôr' ȧ) [prob. from native], *n.* The Carolina rail, a bird haunting the N. American marshes and esteemed as food.

Sorb (sôrb) [G. *Sorbe*, var. of *Serbe*, SERB], *n.* One of a Slavonic race in Lusatia, E. Saxony, a Wend; the language of this race.

sorb (sôrb) [F. *sorbe*, L. *sorbus*], *n.* The service-tree; its fruit, also called **sorb-apple. sorbate,** *n.* (*Chem.*) A salt of sorbic acid. **sorbic,** *a.* Contained in or derived from mountain-ash or rowan berries. **sorbin,** *n.* A sugar obtained from these.

sorbefacient (sôr bė fā' shėnt) [L. *sorbē-re*, to ABSORB, -FACIENT], *a.* (*Med.*) Promoting absorption. *n.* A substance or preparation promoting absorption.

sorbet (sôr' bėt) [F., as SHERBERT], *n.* An ice flavoured with fruit juice, spirit, etc.; sherbet.

sorbic, sorbin [SORB].

Sorbonne (sôr bon'), *n.* A theological college founded by Robert de Sorbon *c.* 1250, afterwards the faculty of theology in the University of Paris; the buildings formerly occupied by this, originally built by Richelieu, now seat of the faculties of science and literature in the University of Paris.

sorcerer (sôr' sėr ėr) [M.E. *sorser*, O.F. *sorcier*, late L. *sortiārius*, from *sortiāre*, to cast lots, from L. *sors sortis*, lot], *n.* One who uses magic, witchcraft, or enchantments, a wizard. **sorceress,** *n.* ***sorcerous,** *a.* **sorcery,** *n.*

sordavalite (sôr' dȧ vė līt) [Swed. *sordawalit*, *Sordavala*, Finland], *n.* (*Min.*) A vitreous silicate of alumina and magnesia found in diabase.

sordid (sôr' did) [F. *sordide*, L. *sordidus*, from *sordes*, dirt, filth], *a.* Mean, base, ignoble, vile; avaricious, niggardly; (*Bot.*) dirt-coloured; *foul, squalid. ***sordes,** *n.* Foul matter, filth, esp. (*Path.*) foul discharges, excretions, etc. **sordidly,** *adv.* **sordidness,** *n.*

sordine (sôr' dēn, -din) [It. *sordino*, L. *surdus*, deaf, see SURD], *n* A contrivance for deadening the sound of a musical instrument, a mute, a damper.

sore (1) (sôr) [A.-S. *sār*, cp. Dut. *zeer*, Icel. *sārr*, G. *sehr*, sorely, very], *a.* Tender and painful to the touch, esp. through disease or irritation; mentally distressed, aggrieved, vexed; easily annoyed; touchy; causing annoyance, irritating, exasperating; *sharp, severe, grievous, heavy. *adv.* Sorely, grievously, severely, intensely. *n.* A sore place on the body where the surface is bruised, broken, or inflamed as by a boil, ulcer, etc.; (*fig.*) a subject, etc., that excites resentment, remorse, etc. **sorely,** *adv.* **soreness,** *n.*

sore (2) (sôr) [O.F. *sor*, from L.G. *soor*, dried, withered (cp. Dut. *zoor*), cogn. with SEAR (1) and SERE (2)], *n.* (*Shak.*) A buck of the fourth year.

soredium (sȯ rē' di ŭm) [mod. L., from Gr. *sōros*, heap], *n.* (*pl.* **-dia**) (*Bot.*) One of the reproductive buds or cells in lichens. **soredial, -ate, sorediferous** (-dif' ėr ŭs), *a.*

***sorehon** [SORN]. **sorel** [SORREL (2)].

sorely, soreness [SORE].

***sorex** (sôr' ėks) [L. cogn. with Gr. *hurax*, HYRAX],

n. (*pl.* **sorices**) A genus of small rodents containing the shrews; a shrew-mouse.

sorghum (sôr′ gŭm) [mod. L., from F. *sorgho*, etym. doubtful], *n.* A genus of plants containing the Indian millet, durra, etc., much cultivated in the U.S. for fodder, etc.

soricine (sor′ i sin) [L. *sōricinus*, from *sōrex sōricis*, see SOREX], *a.* Shrew-like; of or pertaining to the *Soricidæ* or shrew-mice.

sorites (sȯ rī′ tēz) [L., from Gr. *sōratēs*, from *sōros*. heap], *n.* A series of syllogisms so connected that the predicate of one forms the subject of that which follows, the subject of the first being ultimately united with the predicate of the last; a sophistical argument in this form.

sorn (sôrn) [earlier *sorren*, *sorehon*, O.Ir. *sorthan*, free quarters], *v.i.* (*Sc.*) To obtrude oneself on others for board and lodging, to sponge. **sorner,** *n.*

sororal (sȯ rôr′ ȧl) [F. (L. *soror*, sister, -AL)], *a.* Pertaining to or characteristic of a sister or sisters. **sororial,** *a.* **sororicide** (-sīd) [-CIDE], *n.* The murder of a sister; the murderer of a sister. **sororicidal** (-sī′ dȧl), *a.* **sorority** (-rôr′ i ti), *n.* A body or association of women, a sisterhood. **sororize,** *v.t.*

sorosis (sȯ rō′ sis) [mod. L. (Gr. *sōros*, heap, -OSIS)], *n.* (*Bot.*) A fleshy fruit formed by the cohesion of numerous flowers, etc., as the pineapple.

sorrel (1) (sor′ ėl) [O.F. *sorel* (F. *surelle*), from M.H.G. *sūr*, SOUR], *n.* A herb with acid leaves, *Rumex acetosa*, allied to the dock.

sorrel (2) (sor′ ėl) [O.F. *sorel*, dim. of *sor*, sorrel horse, see SORE (2)], *a.* Of a reddish or yellowish-brown. *n.* This colour; a horse or other animal of this colour; a buck of the third year.

sorrily, sorriness [SORRY].

sorrow (sor′ ō) [M.E. *sorwe*, A.-S. *sorg* (cp. Dut. *zorg*, G. *sorge*, Icel., Dan., and Swed. *sorg*)], *n.* Mental pain or distress from loss, disappointment, etc., grief, sadness; an event or thing causing this, an affliction, a misfortune; mourning, lamentation. *v.i.* To grieve; to lament. **sorrower,** *n.* **sorrowful,** *a.* **sorrowfully,** *adv.* **sorrowfulness,** *n.* ***sorrowless,** *a.*

sorry (sor′ i) [A.-S. *sārig* (*sār*, SORE (1), -Y)], *a.* Feeling grief for some loss, etc., regretful; poor, paltry, pitiful, despicable. **sorrily,** *adv.* **sorriness,** *n.*

sort (sôrt) [O.F. *sorte*, L. *sortem*, nom. *sors*, lot, chance, condition], *n.* A number (of things, etc.) having the same or similar qualities, a class, kind, or species; fashion, way, manner; (*Print.*) a letter or other piece of type considered as part of a fount. *v.t.* To separate into sorts, classes, etc.; to select from a number; to arrange postal matter for delivery. *to suit, to adapt, to fit. **v.i.* To consort, to be adapted, to agree or accord (with). **a good sort:** An attractive, companionable person. **out of sorts:** Not in one's usual health, not very well; (*Print.*) out of type of a particular letter. **sortable,** *a.* ***sortance,** *n.* Suitableness, agreement. **sorter,** *n.* One who sorts; post office employee who sorts letters ready for distribution. **sortment,** *n.*

sortes (sôr′ tēz) [L., see prec.], *n.pl.* A kind of divination by the chance selection of a passage in a book, etc.

sortie (sôr′ ti) [F., fem. p.p. of *sortir*, to go out], *n.* A sally, as from a besieged place.

sortilege (sôr′ ti lėj) [O.F. (F. *sortilège*), med. L. *sortilegium*, from L. *sortilegus*, diviner (*sors sortis*, lot, *legere*, to choose)], *n.* Divination by drawing lots.

***sortment** [SORT].

sorus (sôr′ ŭs) [Gr. *sōros*, heap], *n.* (*pl.* **sori,** sō′ rī) A heap, group, or cluster, esp. of spore-cases; patches on the fronds of ferns.

S O S (es ō es′) [Morse letters], *n.* and *v.i.* Radio code signal calling for help.

so-so [SO].

sostenuto (sos tė nū′ tō) [It., p.p. of *sostenere*, to SUSTAIN], *adv.* (*Mus. direction*) In steadily sustained manner.

sot (sot) [M.E., prob. from O.F. (F. *sot sotte*), cp. M.Dut. *zot*. M.H.G. *sot*], *n.* An habitual drunkard, one habitually muddled with excessive drinking; *a fool, a blockhead. *v.i.* To tipple. **sottish,** *a.* **sottishly,** *adv.* **sottishness,** *n.*

Sotadean (sō tȧ dē′ ȧn), *a.* and *n.* Sotadic. **Sotadic** (sȯ tăd′ ik), *a.* Of, pertaining to, or in the manner or style of versification of Sotades, an ancient Greek poet famous for coarseness and scurrility. *n.* A Sotadic poem or verse; (*Pros.*) a catalectic tetrameter in *Ionics a minore* (see IONIC (2) under IONIAN).

soteriology (sȯ tēr i ol′ ȯ ji) [Gr. *sōtēria*, salvation, from *sōtēr*, saviour, cogn. with *sōzein*, to save], *n.* The doctrine of salvation; the science of hygiene.

Sothic (soth′ ik, sō′ thik) [Gr. *Sōthis*, *Sīrius*, the dogstar, from Egypt.], *a.* (*Egypt. Ant.*) Denoting a cycle or period of 1460 Sothic years or 1461 ordinary years, or a year of 365¼ days, opp. to the ordinary Egyptian year of 365 days. **Sothiac, -al** (sō′ thi ăk, -ȧl), *a.*

sotnia (sot′ ni ȧ) [Rus. *sotniya*, hundred, cogn. with L. *centum*], *n.* A Cossack squadron.

sou (soo) [F., from O.F. *sol*, L. *solidum*, cp. SOLD (2)], *n.* A French copper coin, formerly $\frac{1}{12}$ of a livre; the 5-centime piece.

soubrette (soo bret′) [F., from Prov. *soubreto*, fem. of *soubret*, affected, from *soubra*, to put on one side], *n.* A waiting-maid, esp. one of a meddlesome, intriguing, mischievous character in a comedy.

soubriquet [SOBRIQUET].

souchong (soo′ shong) [F., from Chinese (Canton) *siu-chung* (*siu*, small, *chung*, sort)], *n.* A black tea made from the youngest leaves.

souffle (soofl) [F., from *souffler*, L. *sufflare* (SUF-, *flāre*, to blow)], *n.* (*Path.*) A low whispering or murmur heard in the auscultation of an organ, etc.

soufflé (soo′ flā) [F., p.p. of *souffler*, see prec.], *n.* A light dish made of beaten whites of eggs, etc. *a.* Made light and frothy.

sough (1) (sŭf, sou, *Sc.* soo*ch*) [A.-S. *swōgan*, prob. imit. in orig., cp. Goth. *ufswōgjan*], *v.i.* To make a murmuring, sighing sound, as the wind. *n.* Such a sound.

sough (2) (sŭf) [etym. doubtful], *n.* A drain, a sewer, a water-channel, esp. a tunnel for draining a mine.

sought, *past & p.p.* [SEEK].

soul (sōl) [A.-S. *sāwel*, *sāwl*, cp. Dut. *ziel*, G. *seele*, Dan. *sjæl*, Swed. *själ*], *n.* The spiritual part of a person; (*fig.*) a spiritual being; the moral and emotional part of a person; the intellectual part of a person, consciousness; the vital principle and mental powers possessed by man in common with lower animals; the essential or animating or inspiring force or principle, the life, the energy in anything; the heart; spirit, courage; a disembodied spirit; (*fam.*) a human being, a person. **The Souls:** A cultural society coterie formed in London in the late 19th century. **soul bell:** A passing-bell. ***soul-curer,** *n.* A parson. ***soul-fearing,** *a.* Appalling. ***soul-scott, -shot,** *n.* A funeral duty paid to the church of the parish. **souled,** *a.* (*usu. in comb.*, as *high-souled*). **soulful,** *a.* Rich in, satisfying, or expressing the spiritual, emotional, or higher intellectual qualities. **soulfully,** *adv.* **soulfulness,** *n.* **soulless,** *a.* **soullessly,** *adv.* **soullessness,** *n.*

sound (1) (sound) [A.-S. *sund*, cp. Dut. *gezond*, G. *gesund*, Dan. and Swed. *sund*], *a.* Whole, unimpaired, free from injury, defect, or decay; not diseased or impaired, healthy; based on truth or reason, valid, correct; solvent; thorough. *adv.* Soundly, fast (asleep). **soundly,** *adv.* **soundness,** *n.*

sound (2) (sound) [M.E. *soun*, F. *son*, L. *sonus*, whence *sonāre*, F. *sonner*, to sound], *n.* The sensation produced through the organs of hearing; that which causes this sensation, the vibrations affecting the ear, esp. those of a regular and continuous nature as opp. to noise; a specific tone or note; an articulate utterance corresponding to a particular vowel or consonant; hearing distance, ear-shot. *v.i.* To make or give out sound; (*fig.*) to convey a particular impression by or as by sound. *v.t.* To cause to sound, to utter audibly; to give a signal for by sound; to cause to resound, to make known, to proclaim; to test by sound. **sound barrier:** The shock wave produced when a moving body attains the speed of sound, *i.e.* 764 miles per hour at sea level, with variations for temperature. **sound-board** [SOUNDING-BOARD]. **sound-bell,** *n.* The thick curved edge against which the tongue strikes in a bell. **sound-box,** *n.* (*Acous.*) A box opening on one side into a horn and containing a diaphragm actuated by an armature and needle. **sound-film,** *n.* (*Cinema.*) A combination of the projection of a cinematograph film and the synchronised sounds proper to it. **sound-hole,** *n.* An opening in the belly of some stringed musical instruments. **sound-post,** *n.* An upright supporting the belly of a violin, etc., and transmitting sound-vibrations to the back. **sound-proof,** *a.* Impenetrable to sound. **sound-track,** *n.* (*Cinema.*) The portion along the side of a film which bears the continuous recording of the accompanying sound.

sound (3) (sound) [A.-S. *sund*, cp. G., Icel., Dan., and Swed. *sund*, allied to SWIM], *n.* A narrow passage of water, as a strait connecting two seas; the swimming-bladder of a fish; a cuttle-fish.

sound (4) (sound) [F. *sonder*, prob. from Scand. *sund*], *v.t.* To measure the depth of (a sea, channel, water in a ship's hold, etc.) with a sounding-line or rod; (*fig.*) to test, to examine, to endeavour to discover (intentions, feelings, etc.); (*Med.*) to test or examine by means of a probe, etc. *v.i.* To use the line and lead to ascertain the depth of water; (*fig.*) to dive deeply (of a whale, etc.). *n.* An instrument for exploring cavities of the body, a probe.

sounder (soun' dėr), *n.* That which causes or emits a sound; a rod for probing depth, etc.; a herd of wild swine; a young wild boar.

sounding (1) (soun' ding), *a.* Making or giving out sound; sonorous, resonant, noisy; (*fig.*) plausible, imposing, high-flown. **sounding-board,** *n.* A canopy-like structure of wood or metal placed over a pulpit, etc., to reflect sound towards the audience; a board for enhancing the sounds in various musical instruments.

sounding (2) (soun' ding), *n.* The act of measuring the depth of water; (*pl.*) a part of the sea where the bottom can be reached by sounding; (*pl.*) measurements of depth taken thus. **sounding-rod,** *n.* A graduated iron rod, used to ascertain the depth of water in a ship's hold.

soundless (sound' les), *a.* Without a sound, silent; unfathomable.

soup (soop) [F. *soupe*, from *souper*, to SUP], *n.* A liquid food made from meat, fish, or vegetables. **in the soup:** (*slang*) In difficulties, in trouble. **soup-kitchen,** *n.* A public establishment for supplying soup to the poor gratis or at a nominal charge. **soup-maigre** (soop māgr'), *n.* Thin soup, made without meat. **soup-plate,** *n.* **soup-ticket,** *n.* A ticket entitling one to soup at a soup-kitchen. **soupy,** *a.*

soupçon (soop so*n*) [F., as SUSPICION], *n.* A mere trace, taste, or flavour (of).

sour (sour) [A.-S. *sūr*, cp. Dut. *zuur*, G. *sauer*, Icel. *sūrr*, Swed. *sur*, Dan. *suur*], *a.* Sharp or acid to the taste, tart; tasting thus through fermentation, rancid; harsh of temper, crabbed, morose, peevish. *v.t.* To make sour. *v.i.* To become sour. **sour-dock,** *n.* The common sorrel. ***sour-eyed,** *a.* **sour-gourd,** *n.* The fruit of the baobab, *Adansonia digitata* or *G. Gregorii*. **souring,** *n.* A process of bleaching with acid, etc.; *anything used to make sour or acid; (*prov.*) a crab-apple. **sourish,** *a.* **sourly,** *adv.* **sourness,** *n.*

source (sôrs) [O.F. *sorse*, p.p. of *sordre* (F. *sourdre*), L. *surgere*, to rise, see SURGE], *n.* The spring or fountain-head from which a stream of water proceeds; (*fig.*) original, first cause, producer, etc.

sourdine [SORDINE].

sourdough (sour' dō) [SOUR, DOUGH], *n.* (*Canada*) An old-timer.

sourock (sou' rok) [SOUR, -OCK], *n.* (*Sc.*) Sorrel.

souse (sous) [O.F. *sorse*, SAUCE, combined in some senses with obs. *sorse*, to swoop, as SOURCE], *n.* Pickle made with salt; anything steeped or preserved in pickle, esp. mackerel and herring; a dip or plunging into water. *adv.* With sudden descent, plump, slap. *v.t.* To pickle; to plunge into or drench thoroughly with water, etc. *v.i.* To plunge into water. **soused,** *a.* (*slang*) Drunk.

soutache (su tash) [F., from Hung. *szuszak*, a curl, a lock], *n.* A narrow, ornamental braid.

soutane (soo tan', -tān') [F., from It. *sottana*, L. *subtus*, under], *n.* A priest's cassock.

souteneur (soo' ten ěr) [Fr., from *soutenir*, to support], *n.* A prostitute's lover living on her immoral earnings, a pimp.

souter (soo' tėr) [A.-S. *sūtere*, L. *sūtor*, from *suere*, see SEW (1)], *n.* (*now Sc.*) A shoemaker, a cobbler.

south (south) [A.-S. *sūth* (cp. Dut. *zuid*, G. *sud*, Icel. *suthr*, *sunnr*, O.H.G. *sund*), perh. rel. to SUN], *n.* That one of the four cardinal points of the compass directly opposite to the north; a southern part or region, esp. the Southern States of America; a wind from the south. *a.* Situated in the south; facing in a southern direction; coming from the south (of the wind). *adv.* Towards the south; from the south (of the wind). *v.t.* To move towards the south; to cross the meridian (of the moon). **Southdown,** *a.* Of or pertaining to the South Downs, Sussex; *n.* A breed of hornless sheep originating here. **south-east,** *n.* The point of the compass equally distant from the south and the east; *a.* Pertaining to or coming from the S.E.; *adv.* Towards the S.E. **south-easter,** *n.* A S.E. wind. **south-easterly,** *a.* and *adv.* **south-eastern,** *a.* **souther,** *n.* A S. wind. **southerly** (sŭ*th*' ėr li), *a.* and *adv.* Tending towards the south. **southerliness,** *n.* **southerly buster,** *n.* (*Austral.*) An unexpected and violent squall from the south. **southing** (south' ing), *n.* The act of going south or passing the meridian; (*Astron.*) the transit of the moon or a star across the meridian; (*Naut.*) difference of latitude towards the south. **southmost,** *a.* **southron** (sŭ*th*' ròn), *a.* (*Sc.*) Belonging to the south, esp. English; *n.* An Englishman. **southward** (south' wȧrd), *adv.* and *a.* **southwards,** *adv.* **south-west,** *n.* and *a.* **southwester,** (*Naut.*) **sou'wester,** *n.* A wind from the S.W.; a waterproof hat with a wide brim hanging down behind, worn by sailors, etc. **southwesterly,** *a.* and *adv.* **south-western,** *a.*

southern (sŭ*th*' ėrn), *a.* Of or pertaining to or situated in or towards the south; coming from the south. *n.* A Southerner. **Southern Cross** [CROSS (1)]. **southern-wood,** *n.* A shrubby species of wormwood, *Artemisia abrotanum*. **Southerner,** *n.* An inhabitant or native of the south, esp. of the Southern States of U.S.A. ***southernly,** *adv.* **southernmost,** *a.*

souvenir (soo' vė nēr) [F., orig. to remember, L. *subvenīre* (SUB-, *venīre*, to come)], *n.* A keepsake, a memento.

sovereign, sovran (sov' rȧn) [M.E. *soverein*, O.F. *soverain*, late L. *superānus* (*super-*, suf. *-ānus*), assim. to REIGN], *a.* Supreme; possessing supreme power, dominion, or jurisdiction; royal; efficacious, effectual (as a remedy). *n.* A supreme ruler, a king, an emperor, a monarch; an English gold coin, value 20s. ***sovereignly,** *adv.* **sovereignty,** *n.*

soviet (sov' yet) [Rus. council], *n.* (*Pol.*) A council elected by workers and inhabitants of a district in Russia; a council selected by a number of these; the all-Russian congress of delegates from these latter.

Sovnarkom (sov′ nar kom) [from Rus. Soviem Narodnik Kommissarov], *n.* (*Pol.*) The council of people's commissars in Russia, with the direct management of government affairs.

sow (1) (sō) [A.-S. *sāwan* (cp. Dut. *zaaijen*, G. *säen*, Icel. *sā*, also L. *serere*)], *v.t.* (*past* **sowed,** *p.p.* **sown, sowed**) To scatter (seed) for growth; to scatter seed over (ground, etc.); to scatter over, to cover thickly with; to disseminate, to propagate. *v.i.* To scatter seed for growth. **sower,** *n.* **sowing,** *n.*

sow (2) (sou) [A.-S. *sugu*, *sū* (cp. Dut. *zog*, G. *sau*, Icel. *sȳr*, Dan. and Swed. *so*, also L. *sūs*, Gr. *hus*, *sus*), from root *su-*, to produce, cogn. with SWINE], *n.* A female pig; a sow-bug; (*Metal.*) the main channel for molten iron leading to the pigs; a block of iron solidified in this. **sowback,** *n.* A long ridge of boulder-clay, etc. **sow-bug,** *n.* A species of wood-louse. **sowbread,** *n.* A cyclamen, esp. *C. Europæum.* **sow-thistle,** *n.* A plant of the genus *Sonchus*, with toothed leaves and milky juice.

sowens (sou′ ėnz, soo′ ėnz) [Gael. *súghan*, *súbhan*, from *súgh*, *súbh*, sap], *n.* (*Sc.*) A kind of flummery made from the husks of oats.

sowff (souf) [earlier *solf*, O.F. *solfier*, from SOL-FA]. *v.t.* (*Sc.*) To whistle or hum (a tune, etc.) softly.

***sowl** (soul) [etym. doubtful], *v.t.* To drag about, to tug, to pull by the ears.

sowth [SOWFF].

soya bean (soi′ yȧ bēn) [Jap. *si-yan*; Chin. *shi-yu*], *n.* A leguminous herb, *Glycine soja*, originally cultivated in Japan as a principal ingredient of a piquant sauce called Soy, in more recent years grown in Manchuria as a source of oil for making margarine, or for the flour made from the bean itself.

sozzled (soz′ ėld) [onomat.], *a.* Blind drunk.

spa (spa, spaw) [town in Belgium], *n.* A mineral spring; a place where there is such a spring.

space (spās) [O.F. *espace*, L. *spatium*], *n.* Continuous extension or any quantity or portion of this; an interval between points, etc.; an interval of time; (*Print.*) a thin piece of type-metal used to separate words; (*Mus.*) one of the degrees between the lines of the staff. *v.t.* To set so that there will be spaces between; to put the proper spaces between (words, lines, etc.). **space-bar,** *n.* A bar or key in a typewriter for making spaces between words. **space charge,** *n.* (*Radio.*) An accumulation of charge set up by the stream of electrons from the filament of a thermionic valve, which has a tendency to check the flow of electrons. **space-platform, space-station:** A platform planned in outer space to serve as a landing-stage in space travel. **spaceship,** *n.* A craft for travelling through outer space. **space-suit,** *n.* Clothing specially adapted for space travel. **space-time,** *n.* (*Phys.*) The four-dimensional manifold or continuum which, in accordance with Einstein's theory of relativity, is the result of fusing time with three-dimensional space. **space-writer,** *n.* A journalist paid according to the space his articles occupy in print. **space-writing,** *n.* **spacer,** *n.* **spacial** [SPATIAL]. **spacing,** *n.*

spacious (spā′ shůs), *a.* Having ample room; capacious, roomy, wide, extensive. **spaciously,** *adv.* **spaciousness,** *n.*

spadassin (spȧ dăs′ in) [F. from It. *spadaccino*, from *spada*, sword, see foll.], *n.* A bravo, a hired bully.

spade (1) (spād) [A.-S. *spædu*, *spadu* (cp. Dut., Dan. and Swed. *spade*, G. *spate*, also Gr. *spathē*, whence L. *spatha*, It. *spada*, sword)], *n.* An implement for digging, having a broad blade fitted into a long handle, and worked with both hands and one foot; a tool of similar form employed for various purposes; a playing-card with a figure or figures shaped like a heart with a small triangular handle; (*pl.*) this suit of cards. *v.t.* To dig with a spade; to cut (a whale) with a spade. **to call a spade a spade:** To be outspoken, not to mince matters. **spade-bayonet,** *n.* A broad-bladed bayonet, which may be used in digging. ***spade-bone,** *n.* The shoulder-blade. **spade-guinea,** *n.* A guinea (minted 1787–99) having a shield like the spade on cards on the reverse. **spade-husbandry,** *n.* Cultivation by means of deep digging with the spade. **spadeful,** *n.* **spadework,** *n.* (*fig.*) Tiresome preliminary work.

spade (2) (spād) [SPADO], *n.* A eunuch; a gelded beast.

spadille (spȧ dil′) [F., from L. *espadilla*, dim. of *spada*, sword, see SPADE (1)], *n.* The ace of spades in ombre and quadrille.

spadix (spā′ diks) [L. and Gr., from *spaein*, to draw out, to rend], *n.* (*pl.* **-dices,** -di sēz) An inflorescence in which the flowers are closely arranged around a fleshy rachis and surrounded by a spathe. **spadiceous** (spā dish′ ůs), *a.*

spado (spā′ dō) [L., from Gr. *spadon*, cogn. with prec.], *n.* (*Law*) One who has not the power of procreation.

spae (spā) [Icel. *spā*, etym. doubtful], *v.t.* (*Sc.*) To foretell. **spaeman, -wife, -woman, spaer** (spā′ ėr), *n.* A diviner, a fortune-teller.

spaghetti (spȧ get′ i) [It., pl. dim. of *spago*, cord], *n.* A string-like variety of macaroni.

***spagyric** (spȧ jir′ ik) [F. *spagirique*, mod. L. *spagiricus*, prob. invented by Paracelsus], *a.* Pertaining to alchemy. *n.* An alchemist. ***spagyrical,** *a.* ***spagyrist** (spăg′ i rist), *n.*

spahi (spa′ i) [Turk. *sipāhī*, SEPOY], *n.* A Turkish irregular horse-soldier; a native Algerian cavalry-soldier in the French army.

***spake,** *past* [SPEAK].

spale (spāl) [Sc., etym. doubtful, cp. SPALL (2)], *n.* A splinter, a chip, a thin strip, a shred (*lit. and fig.*).

***spall** (1) (spawl) [It. *spalla*, L. SPATULA], *n.* The shoulder.

spall (2) (spawl) [etym. doubtful, cp. M.E. *speld*, splinter, Dut. *spald*, pin, M.Dut. *spalden*, G. *spalten*, to split], *n.* A chip, splinter, or flake. *v.t.* To break up (ore) for sorting. *v.i.* To splinter, to chip. **spalder,** *n.*

spalpeen (spăl′ pēn) [Ir. *spailpin*], *n.* A scamp, a rascal.

spalt (spawlt) [G., from *spalten*, to SPALL], *n.* A white scaly mineral used as a flux for metals.

Spam (spăm), *n.* Proprietary name of a make of tinned chopped spiced ham.

span (1) (spăn) [A.-S. *spannan* (cp. Dut. and G. *spannen*, Icel. *spenna*, also Gr. *spaein*, to draw)], *v.t.* (*past & p.p.* **spanned**) To extend from side to side of (a river, etc.); to measure with one's hand expanded; (*Naut.*) to make fast (booms, etc.) with ropes. *v.i.* To progress by distinct stretching movements as a span-worm. *n.* The space from the end of the thumb to the end of the little finger when extended, esp. as a measure, nine inches; a brief space of distance or time; the space from end to end of a bridge, etc.; the horizontal distance between the supports of an arch; (*Naut.*) a rope having both ends fastened for taking a purchase in the loop; (*Am.*) a pair of horses, usu. matched in colour, etc., harnessed side by side; (*S. Afr.*) a yoke or team of oxen, etc. ***span-counter,** *n.* A game for two persons, with counters, in which a piece of money is won if another is thrown within a span of it. **span-long,** *a.* Of the length of a span. **span-roof,** *n.* An ordinary roof with two sloping sides. **span-worm,** *n.* The larva of a geometer moth. **spanless,** *a.* Measureless.

span (2), *past* [SPIN].

spanæmia (spȧ nē′ mi ȧ) [Gr. *spanos*, *spanios*, scanty, *haima*, blood], *n.* (*Path.*) Poorness of blood shown by deficiency of the red corpuscles. **spanæmic,** *a.*

spancel (spăn′ sĕl) [cp. Dut. and L.G. *spansel*], *n.* (*prov.*) A rope for hobbling a cow, horse, etc. *v.t.* To hobble with this.

spandrel (spăn′ drĕl) [etym. doubtful], *n.* The space between the shoulder of an arch and the rectangular moulding, etc., enclosing it, or between the shoulders of adjoining arches and the moulding, etc.

spang (spăng) [Sc. and North., etym. doubtful], *v.i.* To leap, to bound. *v.t.* To fling, to hang (down). *n.* A leap, a bound.

spangle (spăng′ gĕl) [M.E. *spangel*, dim. of obs. *spang*, A.-S. *spang*, a metal clasp, cp. M.Dut. and G. *spange*, rel. to Gr. *sphingein*, to bind lightly], *n.* A small disk of glittering metal or other material, used for ornamenting dresses, etc.; any small sparkling object. *v.t.* To set or adorn with spangles. **spangler,** *n.* **spangly,** *a.*

Spaniard (spăn′ yărd) [alt. of M.E. *Spaynyell*, as foll.], *n.* A native of Spain; (*N. Zealand*) a prickly, bushy grass.

spaniel (spăn′ yĕl) [M.E., from O.F. *espagneul*, Sp. *español*, Spanish, from *España*, L. *Hispania*, Spain], *n.* A popular name for a class of dogs, distinguished chiefly by large drooping ears, long silky coat, and a gentle disposition; (*fig.*) a servile, cringing person.

Spanish (spăn′ ish), *a.* Of or pertaining to Spain. *n.* The Spaniards; their language. **Spanish-bayonet** [BAYONET]. **Spanish-black, -brown,** etc., *n.* Various pigments. **Spanish broom:** A Mediterranean shrub, *Spartium junceum*, with rush-like branches. **Spanish-fly,** *n.* A cantharis. **Spanish fowl:** A breed of domestic fowl of a glossy black colour. **Spanish-grass,** *n.* Esparto grass. **Spanish main** [MAIN (2)].

spank (spăngk) [prob. onomat.], *v.t.* To strike with the open hand, to slap, esp. on the buttocks; to urge along thus. *v.i.* To move briskly along, esp. at a pace between a trot and a gallop. *n.* A sounding blow with the open hand, a slap, esp. on the buttocks. **spanker,** *n.* One who spanks; a fast horse; (*colloq.*) an exceptionally fine specimen, a stunner; (*Naut.*) a fore-and-aft sail set by two spars on the after-side of the mizen-mast. **spanking,** *a.* That spanks; (*colloq.*) dashing, brisk, stunning; strong (of a breeze).

spanner (spăn′ ĕr), *n.* One who or that which spans; an instrument for tightening up or loosening the nuts on screws, a wrench; a brace, connecting rod, etc., in a bridge, steam-engine, etc.; a span-worm.

span-new (spăn′ nū) [Icel. *spānnyr* (*spānn*, chip, *nyr*, NEW], *a.* (*prov.*) Quite new, brand new.

spar (1) (spar) [M.E. *sparre* (cp. Dut. *spar*, G. *sparren*, Icel. *sperri*, Dan. and Swed. *sparre*), perh. cogn. with SPEAR], *n.* A round timber, a pole, esp. used as a mast, yard, boom, shears, etc. **spar-deck,** *n.* The upper deck of a vessel stretching from stem to stern.

spar (2) (spar) [A.-S. *spær*], *n.* A name for various lustrous minerals occurring in crystalline or vitreous form. **sparry,** *a.*

spar (3) (spar) [perh. O.F. *esparer*, to strike out with the heels, perh. from Teut. and rel. to SPUR, SPURN], *v.i.* (*past & p.p.* **sparred**) To move the arms about in defence or offence as in boxing; to strike out, esp. with protected spurs (of cocks); (*fig.*) to engage in a contest of words, etc. *n.* A boxing-match; a cock-fight; (*fig.*) a wordy contest. **sparrer,** *n.* **sparring-match,** *n.* **sparring-partner,** *n.* (*Boxing*) A boxer with whom one in training practises; (*fig.*) a partner.

sparable (spăr′ ȧ bĕl) [corr. of SPARROW, and BILL (1)], *n.* A headless nail for boot-soles.

spare (spâr) [A.-S. *spær*, whence *sparian*, to spare (cp. Icel. *sparr*, G. *spärlich*, also Dut. and G. *sparen*, Icel. and Swed. *spara*), prob. cogn. with L. *parcere*, to spare], *a.* Meagre, scanty, frugal; that can be spared, kept in reserve, available for use in emergency, etc. *v.t.* To use frugally, to be chary of using; to refrain from using; to dispense with; to refrain from inflicting upon; to refrain from punishing, injuring, destroying, etc.; *to forbear (to). *v.i.* To live sparingly or frugally. **spare-rib,** *n.* A piece of pork consisting of the ribs with but little meat. **sparely,** *adv.* **spareness,** *n.* **sparer,** *n.* **sparingly,** *adv.* **sparingness,** *n.*

sparger (spar′ jĕr) [obs. *sparge*, L. *spargere*, to sprinkle, -ER], *n.* A sprinkling-apparatus used in brewing.

sparhawk [SPARROW-HAWK].

sparingly, sparingness [SPARE].

spark (1) (spark) [A.-S. *spearca*, cp. M.Dut. *sparcke*, L.G. *sparke*, Icel. *spraka*, to crackle, prob. imit.], *n.* An incandescent particle thrown off from a burning substance; (*fig.*) a brilliant point, facet, gleam, etc.; a flash of wit, a particle of life or energy; (*Elec.*) the luminous effect of a disruptive discharge. *v.i.* To give out sparks; (*Elec.*) to produce sparks at the point of broken continuity in a circuit. **to make the sparks fly:** To start a violent quarrel, to cause a row. **spark coil,** *n.* (*Radio.*) An instrument for producing a high electromotive force from a supply of low E.M.F. **spark frequency,** *n.* (*Radio.*) The number of spark discharges per second. **spark gap,** *n.* (*Radio.*) An apparatus consisting of two or more electrodes between which an electric discharge occurs in a spark transmitter. **spark-plug:** (*Am.*) A sparking-plug. **spark system,** *n.* (*Radio.*) The oldest form of wireless telegraphy in which a condenser is charged from an induction coil and discharged through an inductance coil in series with a spark gap. **spark transmitter,** *n.* (*Radio.*) A set which uses the discharge of a condenser through a spark gap to supply its radio-frequency power. **sparking-plug,** *n.* A device for igniting the explosive mixture in the cylinder of a motor-engine. **sparkless,** *n.* **sparklet,** *n.* **sparks,** *n.* (*Naut. slang*) The wireless operator on board ship.

spark (2) (spark) [perh. from prec., or var. of SPRACK], *n.* A gay young fellow; a gallant, a beau. *v.i.* To play the spark. **sparkish,** *a.*

sparkle (spar′ kĕl) [dim. of SPARK (1)], *n.* A gleam, a glittering, glitter, brilliance. *v.i.* To emit sparks; to glisten, to glitter, to twinkle; to emit carbon dioxide in little bubbles (of some wines, mineral waters, etc.). **sparkler,** *n.* Something that sparkles; (*slang*) a diamond. **sparklingly,** *adv.*

sparling (spar′ ling) [O.F. *esperlinge* (F. *éperlan*), from Teut., cp. G. and Dut. *spiering*], *n.* (*Sc. and North*). A smelt.

***sparre** [SPAR (1)].

sparrer, sparring-match [SPAR (3)].

sparrow (spăr′ ō) [A.-S. *spearwa* (cp. Icel. *spörr*, Dan. *spurv*, Swed. *sparf*), cogn. with SPAR (3)], *n.* A small brownish-grey bird of the genus *Passer*, esp. *P. domesticus*, the house-sparrow. **sparrow-grass** [corr. of ASPARAGUS]. **sparrow-hawk,** *n.* A small hawk, *Accipiter nisus*, preying on small birds, etc.

sparry [SPAR (2)].

sparse (spars) [L. *sparsus*, p.p. of *spargere*, to scatter], *a.* Thinly scattered, set or occurring at considerable intervals, not dense. **sparsely,** *adv.* **sparseness, sparsity,** *n.*

Spartan (spar′ tăn), *n.* A native of Sparta; (*fig.*) one bearing pain, enforcing discipline, etc., like a Spartan. *a.* Of or pertaining to Sparta or the Spartans; like a Spartan.

sparterie (spar′ tĕr i) [F., from Sp. *esparteria*, from ESPARTO], *n.* Articles manufactured from esparto.

spasm (spăzm) [F. *spasme*, L. *spasmus*, Gr. *spasmos*, from *spaein*, to draw out], *n.* A convulsive and involuntary muscular contraction; a sudden or convulsive act, movement, etc.; a violent and generally fruitless effort. **spasmodic, -al** (-mod′ ik, -ăl), *a.* **spasmodically,** *adv.* **spastic** (spăs′ tik), *a.* Spasmodic. *n.* (*Med.*) A sufferer from cerebral palsy. **spasticity** (-tis′ i ti), *n.*

spat (1) (spăt) [prob. from *spat*, stem of SPATTER], *n.* The spawn of shell-fish, esp. oysters. *v.i.* To spawn. *v.t.* To deposit (spawn).

spat (2) (spăt) [short for SPATTERDASH], *n.* (*usu. in pl.*) A short gaiter fastening over and under the shoe.

spat (3) *past* [SPIT (2)].

spatangus (spȧ tăng′ gŭs) [mod. L., from Gr. *spatangēs*], *n.* (*Zool.*) (*pl.* **-tangi, -tăn′ jī**) A genus of heart-shaped sea-urchins. **spatangoid,** *a.* and *n.*

spatchcock (spăch′ kok) [said to be short for *dispatch-cock* (acc. to C.O.D. perh. conf. with SPITCHCOCK)], *n.* A fowl killed and immediately cooked. *v.t.* To insert or interpolate (a phrase, etc.) hurriedly.

spate (spāt) [etym. doubtful], *n.* A heavy flood, especially in a mountain stream.

spathe (spāth) [L. *spatha*, Gr. *spathē*, a broad blade, sword, etc.], *n.* (*Bot.*) A large bract or pair of bracts enveloping the spadix. **spathaceous** (spȧ thā′ shŭs), **spathose** (spā′ thōs), *a.*

spathic (spăth′ ik) [G. *spath*, spar, -IC], *a.* Resembling spar, esp. in cleavage. **spathiform,** *a.*

spatial (spā′ shȧl), *a.* Of, or relating to space. **spatiality** (-ăl′ i ti), *n.* **spatially,** *adv.*

spatter (spăt′ ėr) [freq. of *spat*, cogn. with prov. *spat*, to spit], *v.t.* To scatter or splash (water, etc.) about; to sprinkle or splash with water, mud, etc.; (*fig.*) to asperse, to defame. *v.i.* To sprinkle drops of saliva, etc., about; to be scattered about thus. *n.* A shower, a sprinkling, a pattering. **spatterdash,** *n.* (*usu. in pl.*) A legging or gaiter for protecting against mud, etc.

spatula (spăt′ ū lȧ) [L., dim. of *spatha*, SPATHE], *n.* A broad knife or trowel-shaped tool used for spreading plasters, working pigments, etc.; a surgeon's instrument of similar form. **spatule,** *n.* A broad, spatuliform part, as in the tail of many birds. **spatular, -late, -liform,** *a.*

spavin (spăv′ in) [O.F. *esparvin*, prob. through a late L. *sparvānus*, from O.H.G. *sparwe*, SPARROW, with alln. to bird-like motion of a spavined horse], *n.* A disease in horses affecting the hock-joint. **blood** or ***bog spavin:** Distension of the hock-joint by effusion of synovial fluid. **bone spavin:** A deposit of bony matter ultimately uniting the bones. **spavined,** *a.*

***spawl** (spawl) [etym. doubtful], *v.i.* To eject saliva with force, to spit.

spawn (spawn) [O.F. *espandre*, L. *expandere*, to EXPAND], *v.t.* To deposit or produce (eggs, young, etc., of fish, amphibians, etc.); (*contemp.*) to bring forth (of human beings). *v.i.* To deposit eggs (of fish, etc.); (*usu. contemp.*) to issue, to be brought forth, esp. in abundance. *n.* The eggs of fish, frogs, and molluscs; white fibrous matter from which fungi are produced; (*contemp.*) offspring. **spawner,** *n.*

spay (spā) [prob. through O.F., from late L. *spadāre*, from SPADO], *v.t.* To castrate, to destroy the ovaries of female animals.

speak (spēk) [A.-S. *sprecan*, later *specan* (cp. Dut. *spreken*, G. *sprechen*, also Icel. *spraka*, SPARK (1))], *v.i.* (*past* **spoke, *spake,** *p.p.* **spoken**) To utter articulate sounds or words in the ordinary tone as dist. from singing; to talk, to converse; to deliver a speech or address; (*fig.*) to be highly expressive or lifelike (of a picture, etc.). *v.t.* To utter articulately; to make known, to tell, to declare; to talk or converse in a language; (*fig.*) to show, to reveal (to be, etc.); (*Naut.*) to hail and communicate with (a ship). **speak-easy,** *n.* (*Am. slang*) A shop where illicit liquor was sold during the time of Prohibition. **to speak fair:** To address in a conciliating manner. **to speak of:** To mention. **to speak out** or **up:** To speak loud; to speak without constraint, to express one's opinion freely. **to speak to:** To address; to speak in support or confirmation of. **to speak volumes:** To be of great or peculiar significance (for, etc.). **to speak well for:** To furnish favourable evidence of. **speakable,** *a.* **speaker,** *n.* One who speaks, esp. one who delivers a speech; an officer presiding over a deliberative assembly (esp. the House of Commons). **speakership,** *n.* **speaking,** *a.* Animated, vivid (of a likeness). **strictly speaking:** (*colloq.*) In the strict sense of the words. **speaking-trumpet,** *n.* A trumpet used for intensifying the sound of the voice, as in giving commands, hailing ships, etc. **speaking-tube,** *n.* A tube for conveying the sound of the voice between parts of a building, etc.

spear (spēr) [A.-S. *spere* (cp. Dut. and G. *speer*, Icel. *spjör*), perh. cogn. with SPAR (1)], *n.* A weapon with a pointed head on a long shaft; a sharp-pointed instrument with barbs, for stabbing fish, etc. *v.t.* To pierce, kill, or capture with a spear. *v.i.* To shoot into a long stem. **spear-grass,** *n.* Grass of various species having long, sharp leaves. **spear-head,** *n.* The pointed end of a spear; (*fig.*) the person or group leading a thrust, or attack. **spearman,** *n.* One armed with a spear.

spearmint (spēr′ mint), *n.* (*Bot.*) The garden mint, *Mentha viridis.*

spear-thistle (spēr′ thisl), *n.* (*Bot.*) A common thistle, *Carduus lanceolatus.*

spearwort (spēr′ wĕrt), *n.* (*Bot.*) A popular name for several species of ranunculus.

spec (spek) (*colloq.*) [short for SPECULATION, SPECIFICATION].

special (spesh′ ȧl) [shortened from ESPECIAL or directly from L. *speciālis*, as foll.], *a.* Particular, peculiar, not ordinary or general; designed for a particular purpose or occasion. *n.* A person or thing designed for a special purpose, etc.; a special train, constable, edition of a newspaper, etc. **special constable** [CONSTABLE]. **special delivery:** (*Am.*) Express delivery. **special election:** (*U.S.A.*) A by-election. **special pleading:** (*Law*) The allegation of special or new matter; (*colloq.*) specious or unfair argument. **special verdict:** A verdict stating the facts but leaving the decision to be determined by the court. **specially,** *adv.*

specialist (spe′ shȧ list), *n.* One who devotes himself to a particular branch of a profession, etc. **specialistic,** *a.* **specialism,** *n.*

speciality (spesh i ăl′ i ti), *n.* A special characteristic or feature, a peculiarity; a special pursuit, occupation, commodity, etc. **specialty,** *n.*

specialize (spesh′ ȧ līz), *v.t.* To differentiate, limit, or apply to a specific use, function, purpose, or meaning. *v.i.* To become differentiated, adapted, or applied thus; to employ oneself as or train oneself for a specialist. **specialization** (-zā′ shŭn), *n.*

specie (spē′ shē, -shi ē) (from L. *in speciē*, in kind (as foll.)], *n.* Coin as dist. from paper money.

species (spē′ shēz, -shi ēz) [L., appearance, sort, from *specere*, to look], *n.* (*Nat. Hist.*) A group of organisms (subordinate to a genus) generally resembling each other and capable of reproduction; (*Log.*) a group of individuals having certain common attributes and designated by a common name (subordinate to a genus); (*colloq.*) a kind, a sort, a variety; (*Law*) the form or shape given to any material.

specific (spė sif′ ik) [F. *specifique*, L. *specificus* (as prec., -IC)], *a.* Clearly specified or particularized, explicit, definite, precise; pertaining to, characterizing, or particularizing a species; distinctive, peculiar, special. *n.* An efficacious medicine, remedy, agent, etc. **specific gravity** [GRAVITY]. **specific heat** [HEAT]. **specifically,** *adv.* ***specificate** [SPECIFY].

specification (spes i fi kā′ shŭn), *n.* The act of specifying; an article or particular specified; a detailed statement of particulars, esp. of materials, work, workmanship to be undertaken or supplied by an architect, builder, manufacturer, etc.; a detailed description of an invention by an applicant for a patent; (*Law*) the production of a new commodity out of materials belonging to another person. **specificity** (-fis' i ti), **specificness** (spė sif' ik nės), *n.*

specify (spes' i fī), *v.t.* To mention expressly, to name distinctively; to include in a specification; *to distinguish from anything else. **specifiable,** *a.*

specimen (spes' i mėn) [L., from *specere*, to look], *n.* A part or an individual intended to illustrate or typify the nature of a whole or a class, an example, an illustration, an instance.

speciology (spē shi ol' ȯ ji), *n.* The branch of biology treating of the nature and origin of species. **speciological** (-loj' i kȧl), *a.*

specious (spē' shŭs) [F. *specieux*, L. *speciōsus*, from *specere*, to see], *a.* Apparently right or fair, plausible; *pleasing to the eye, showy. **speciously,** *adv.* **speciosity** (-os' i ti), **speciousness,** *n.*

speck (1) (spek) [A.-S. *specca*, cp. L.G. *spaken*, to be spotted, M.Dut. *spickelen*, to speckle], *n.* A small spot, fleck, stain, or blemish; a minute particle of rottenness, etc. *v.t.* To mark with a speck or specks. **speckless,** *a.* **specky,** *a.*

speck (2) (spek) [Dut. *spek*, cp. G. *speck*, A.-S. *spic*, bacon, lard], *n.* Blubber or fat, esp. of whales, seals, etc. **specksioneer** (spek shȯ nēr'), *n.* A chief harpooner.

speckle (spek' ėl) [dim. of SPECK (1)], *n.* A small spot, stain, or patch of colour, light, etc. *v.t.* To mark with speckles. **speckledness,** *n.*

specksioneer [SPECK (2)]. **specky** [SPECK (1)].

spectacle (spek' tȧ kėl) [F., from L. *spectāculum*, from *specere*, to look], *n.* A show, something exhibited to the view; a pageant, an object, a sight; (*pl.*) an optical instrument, consisting of a lens for each eye mounted in a light frame for resting on the nose and ears, used to assist the sight, often called a pair of spectacles. **spectacled,** *a.*

spectacular (spek tăk' ū lȧr), *a.* Of the nature of a spectacle; marked by great display; dramatic; thrilling. **spectacularly,** *adv.*

spectator (spek tā' tȯr) [L., from *spectāre*, to behold, from *specere*, to look], *n.* One who looks on, esp. at a show or spectacle. **spectatorial** (-tôr' i ȧl), *a.* **spectatorship,** *n.* **spectatress, -trix,** *n.*

spectre (spek' tėr) [O.F., from L. SPECTRUM], *n.* An apparition, a ghost. **spectre-bat, -crab, -insect, -lemur, -shrimp,** *n.* A bat, crab, etc., having an exceedingly thin or diaphanous body. **spectral,** *a.* Ghostlike, of or pertaining to ghosts; of or pertaining to the spectrum. **spectrally,** *adv.*

spectro- [SPECTRUM], *comb. form.* **spectrograph** (spek' trȯ grăf) [-GRAPH], *n.* An apparatus for photographing or otherwise reproducing spectra. **spectrogram,** *n.* **spectrographic** (grăf' ik), *a.* **spectrography** (-trog' rȧ fi), *n.* **spectrology** (-trol' ȯ ji) [-LOGY], *n.* The science of spectral analysis. **spectrological** (-loj' i kȧl), *a.* **spectrologically,** *adv.* **spectrometer** (-trom' ė tėr) [-METER], *n.* An instrument for measuring the angular deviation of a ray of light passing through a prism. **spectrometric** (-met' rik), *a.* **spectrophone** (spek' trȯ fōn) [PHONE], *n.* An adaptation of the spectroscope in which visual observation is superseded by perception of a succession of sounds

spectroscope (spek' trȯ skōp) [prec., -SCOPE], *n.* An instrument for forming and analysing the spectra of rays emitted by bodies. **spectroscopic, -al** (-skop' ik, -ȧl), *a.* **spectroscopically,** *adv.* **spectroscopist** (-tros' kȯ pist), *n.* **spectroscopy,** *n.*

spectrum (spek' trŭm) [L., a vision, an image, from *specere*, to look], *n.* An image produced by the decomposition of rays of light or other radiant energy by means of a prism, in which the parts are arranged according to their refrangibility; an image persisting on the retina after the eyes are removed. **spectrum** or **spectral analysis:** Chemical analysis with the spectroscope.

specular [SPECULUM].

speculate (spek' ū lāt) [L. *speculātus*, p.p. of *speculārī*, to behold, from *specula*, a watch-tower, as foll.], *v.i.* To pursue an inquiry or form conjectures or views by consideration in the mind, to theorize; to make purchases, investments, etc., on the chance of profit. **speculation** (-lā' shŭn), *n.* The act or practice of speculating; a mental inquiry, train of thought, or series of conjectures about a subject; a speculative business transaction, investment, or undertaking; a game in which the players speculate on the value of their cards. **speculative** (spek' ū lȧ tiv), *a.* **speculatively,** *adv.* **speculativeness,** *n.* **speculator, *speculatist,** *n.* ***speculatory,** *a.*

speculum (spek' ū lŭm) [L., mirror, from *specere*, to look], *n.* (*pl.* **-la**) (*Surg.*) An instrument for dilating passages of the body, to facilitate inspection; a mirror, esp. one of polished metal used as a reflector in a telescope; (*Ornith.*) a lustrous spot or coloured area on the wing of certain birds, also an ocellus. **specular,** *a.* **specular iron:** A bright crystalline variety of hæmatite.

sped, *past & p.p.* [SPEED].

speech (spēch) [A.-S. *spǣc*, *sprǣc*, see SPEAK], *n.* The faculty or act of uttering articulate sounds or words; that which is spoken, an utterance, a remark; a public address, an oration; the language or dialect of a nation, etc.; the sounding-quality of a musical instrument, esp. of an organ-pipe. **speech-day,** *n.* The annual day for presenting prizes in schools, etc. **speech-maker,** *n.* One who speaks much in public. **speech-making,** *n.* **speech-reading,** *n.* The interpretation of speech by observation of the lips, as by deaf-mutes. **speechify,** *v.i.* (*usu. contemp.*) To make a speech or speeches, to harangue. **speechifier,** *n.* **speechless,** *a.* Unable to speak, silent, esp. through emotion; dumb; (*colloq.*) drunk. **speechlessly,** *adv.* **speechlessness,** *n.*

speed (spēd) [A.-S. *spēd* (whence *spēdan*, v.), from *spōwan*, to succeed (cp. Dut. *spoed*, O.H.G. *spuot*, *spōt*, success, *spuon*, to prosper, also L. *spatium*, SPACE, *spēs*, hope)], *n.* Rapidity, swiftness, celerity, rate of motion; the ratio of the distance covered to the time taken by a moving body; *success, prosperity. *v.i.* (*past & p.p.* **sped**) To move rapidly, to hasten; to succeed, to prosper, to fare (well, ill, etc.). *v.t.* To promote, to make prosperous, to cause to succeed; to cause to go fast, to urge to send at great speed; (*past & p.p.* **speeded**) to regulate the speed of, to set (an engine, etc.) at a fixed rate of speed; *to get rid of, to kill, to execute, to ruin. **speedboat,** *n.* (*Naut.*) A light boat driven at great speed by a motor-engine. **speed-cop,** *n.* A police motor-cyclist checking motorists on the highway. **speed limit,** *n.* The legal limit of speed for a road vehicle. **speedometer,** *n.* A device attached to a vehicle to indicate its speed in miles per hour. **speed-way** [DIRT TRACK]. **speedwell,** *n.* A flowering herb, one of various species of *Veronica*. **speeder,** *n.* ***speedful,** *a.* ***speedfully,** *adv.* **speedy,** *a.* **speedily,** *adv.* **speediness,** *n.*

speer, speir (spēr) [A.-S. *spyrian*, to follow a track, cogn. with SPOOR], *v.i.* and *t.* (*Sc.*) To question, to inquire, to ask.

speiss (spīs) [G. *speise*, orig. food, It. *spesa*, from L. as EXPENSE], *n.* A compound of arsenic, nickel, copper, etc., produced in the smelting of lead, etc.

spek-boom (spek' bōm) [S. Afr. Dut. *spek*, fat meat, *boom*, tree], *n.* A large shrub, *Portulacaria Afra*, the purslane-tree.

spelæan (spė lē' ȧn) [L. *spēlaeum*, Gr. *spēlaion*, cave, -AN], *a.* Of or pertaining to a cave or caves. **spelæology** (spe lē ol' ȯ ji) [-LOGY], *n.* The study or exploration of caves. **spelæologist,** *n.*

spelding (spel' ding) [A.-S. *speld*, splinter], *n.* (*Sc.*) A small fish split and dried in the sun.

spelk (spelk) [A.-S. *spelc*, cp. Dut. *spalk*], *n.* (*Sc.*

and North.) A splint; a spike used in thatching; a rod in a loom.

spell (1) (spel) [A.-S. *spel*, *spell*, cp. Icel. *spjall*, O.H.G. *spel*, narrative, story, cogn. with foll.], *n.* A series of words used as a charm, an incantation; occult power, fascination, mysterious charm. **spell-bound,** *a.* Under the influence of a spell.

spell (2) (spel) [O.F. *espeler*, cp. Dut. *spelen*, A.-S. *spellian*, from prec.], *v.t.* (*past & p.p.* **spelled, spelt**) To say or write the letters forming (a word); (*fig.*) to read or decipher with difficulty; to puzzle (out or over); to form a word (of letters); (*fig.*) to mean, to import, to portend. *v.i.* (*fig.*) To read. **speller,** *n.* One who spells; a spelling-book. **spelling,** *n.* The act of one who spells; orthography. **spelling-bee,** *n.* A competition in spelling. **spelling-book,** *n.* A book for teaching to spell.

spell (3) (spel) [A.-S. *spelian*, perh. cogn. with *spilian*, to play, cp. G. *spielan*, and *spiel*], **v.t.* To take the turn of at work, to relieve. *n.* A turn of work; a short period.

spelt (1) (spelt) [A.-S., from late L. *spelta*], *n.* A variety of wheat cultivated in S. Europe, etc., called also German wheat.

spelt (2), *past & p.p.* [SPELL (2)].

spelter (spel′ tėr) [from Teut. (cp. Dut. and G. *spiauter*), rel. to PEWTER], *n.* (*Comm.*) Zinc.

***spence** (spens) [O.F. *despense*, DISPENSE, or *espense*, EXPENSE], *n.* A buttery, a larder.

Spencean scheme (spen′ si ȧn) [Thomas *Spence* (1750–1814)], *n.* (*Econ.*) A scheme of land nationalization by which parishes would own the land and rent it out to farmers and small-holders.

spencer (1) (spen′ sėr) [Earl *Spencer* (1758–1834)], *n.* A short overcoat or jacket, for men or women.

spencer (2) (spen′ sėr) [etym. doubtful], *n.* (*Naut.*) A fore-and-aft sail set abaft the fore- or main-mast.

Spencerism (spen′ sėr izm) [Herbert *Spencer* (1820–1903)], *n.* The philosophical teaching of Spencer, briefly, the explanation of the universe by the necessary laws of mechanics, also known as the synthetic philosophy. **Spencerian** (-sēr′ i ȧn), *a.* **Spencerianism,** *n.*

spend (spend) [A.-S. *spendan*, late L. *dispendere*, to weigh out, see DISPENSE], *v.t.* (*past & p.p.* **spent**) To pay out (money, etc.); to consume, to use up; to pass (time); to squander, to waste; to wear out, to exhaust; (*Naut.*) to lose (a mast). *v.i.* To expend money; to waste away, to be consumed. **spendthrift,** *a.* Prodigal, wasteful. *n.* A prodigal or wasteful person. **spendable,** *a.* **spender,** *n.*

Spenserian (spen sēr′ i ȧn) [Edmund *Spenser* (1552–1599), poet, -IAN], *a.* Of or pertaining to Spenser. *n.* A Spenserian stanza, as used in his *Faerie Queene* or in Byron's *Childe Harold.*

spent, *past & p.p.* [SPEND], *a.* Exhausted, burnt out.

***sperket** [SPIRKET (1)].

sperm (1) (spĕrm) [F. *sperme*, from L. and Gr. *sperma*, from *speirein*, to sow], *n.* The male seminal fluid of animals.

sperm (2) (spĕrm) [short of SPERMACETI], *n.* A whale yielding spermaceti, a sperm-whale or cachalot; spermaceti. ***sperm-oil,** *n.* **sperm-whale,** *n.*

spermaceti (spĕr mȧ sē′ ti) [L., *sperma*, SPERM (1), *cētī*, gen. of *cetus*, Gr. *kētos*, whale], *n.* A white, fatty, brittle substance, existing in solution in the oily matter in the head of the sperm-whale, used for candles, ointments, etc.

spermary (spĕr′ mȧ ri), ***spermarium*** (spĕr mâr′ i ŭm) [mod. L. from L. *sperma*, SPERM (1)], *n.* (*pl.* **-ries, -ria**) The male spermatic gland, testicle, or other organ. **spermatheca** (-thē′ kȧ) [Gr. *thēkē*, respository], *n.* A receptacle in female insects and other invertebrates for spermatozoa.

spermatic (spĕr măt′ ik) [F. *spermatique*, L. *spermaticus*, from *sperma -matos*, SPERM (1)], *a.* Consisting of, pertaining to, or conveying sperm or semen; of or pertaining to the spermary. **spermatism** (spĕr′ mȧ tizm), *n.* The emission of semen; spermism. **spermatist,** *n.* **spermatize,** *v.i.*

spermato- [SPERM (1)], *comb. form.* **spermatoblast** (spĕr′ mȧ tō blăst) [-BLAST], *n.* A cell from which a spermatozoon develops. **spermatocele** (-sēl) [-CELE], *n.* (*Path.*) A morbid distension of the testes. **spermatogenesis** (-jen′ ė sis) [GENESIS], *n.* The development of spermatozoa. **spermatogenetic** (-jė net′ ik), **spermatogenous** (tog′ ė nŭs), *a.* **spermatogeny,** *n.* **spermatoid** (spĕr′ mȧ toid), *a.*

spermatology (spĕr mȧ tól′ ō ji), *n.* The scientific study of sperm. **spermatological** (-loj′ i kȧl), *a.* **spermatologist** (-tol′ ō jist), *n.* **spermatophore** (spĕr′ mȧ tō fôr) [-PHORE], *n.* A capsule holding spermatozoa, in molluscs, etc.

spermatorrhea (spĕr măt ō rē′ a) [Gr. *rheein*, to flow], *n.* (*Path.*) Involuntary discharge of seminal fluid.

spermatozoon (spĕr mȧ tō zō′ on), *n.* (*pl.* **spermatozoa**) One of the minute living bodies in the seminal fluid essential to fecundation by the male. **spermatozoal, -zoan,** *a.* **spermatozoid,** *a.* and *n.* **spermic** (spĕr′ mik) [SPERMATIC]. **spermism,** *n.* The old theory that the spermatozoon alone is the germ of the future animal. **spermist,** *n.* **spermoblast** [SPERMATOBLAST]. **spermoderm,** *n.* (*Bot.*) The testa of a seed.

spermology (spĕr mol′ ō ji), *n.* The branch of botany dealing with seeds; spermatology. **spermological** (-loj′ i kȧl), *a.* **spermologist** (-mol′ ō jist), *n.* **spermophile** (spĕr′ mō fil) [-PHILE], *n.* An Arctic squirrel-like rodent. **spermophore** [-PHORE], *n.* (*Bot.*) The placenta in plants.

spew (spū) [A.-S. *speowan*, *spīwan* (cp. M.Dut. *spouwen*, G. *speien*, Icel. *spȳja*, also L. *spuere*, Gr. *ptuein*), imit. in orig.], *v.t.* To vomit; to cast out with abhorrence. *v.i.* To vomit; to droop at the muzzle through too rapid firing (of a gun). *n.* Vomit. **spewy,** *a.*

sphacelate (sfăs′ ė lāt) [Gr. *sphakelos*, gangrene, -ATE], *v.i.* To become gangrenous, to mortify. *v.t.* To affect with gangrene. **sphacelation** (-lā′ shŭn), *n.* ***sphacelus,*** *n.* Gangrene, necrosis.

sphær, sphæro- [Gr. *sphaira*, ball], *comb. form.* Circular, globular. **sphæridium** (sfē rid′ i ŭm), *n.* (*pl.* **-idia**) One of certain spheroidal bodies attached to parts of the sea-urchin. **sphærosiderite** (sfēr ō sī′ dėr īt) [SIDERITE], *n.* (*Min.*) A variety of siderite occurring in spheroidal masses. **sphærulite** [SPHERULITE].

Sphagnum (sfăg′ nŭm) [Gr. *sphagnos*], *n.* (*Bot.*) A genus of cryptogams containing the bog- or peat-mosses. **sphagnous,** *a.*

sphen- [SPHENO].

sphendone (sfen′ dō nē) [Gr., sling], *n.* (*Gr. Ant.*) A sling-shaped band or fillet for supporting the back-hair worn by women of ancient Greece; the curved end of a stadium.

sphene (sfēn) [F. *sphène*, Gr. *sphēn*], *n.* (*Min.*) Titanite.

sphenic (sfen′ ik) [as foll.], *a.* Wedge-shaped.

spheno-, sphen-, *comb. form.* Pertaining to or resembling a wedge. **sphenethmoid** (sfē neth′ moid) [ETHMOID], *a.* Of or pertaining to the sphenoid and the ethmoid bone; applied to the girdle bone. *n.* The sphenethmoid bone or girdle bone at the base of the skull in batrachians. **Sphenodon** (sfē′ nō don) [Gr. *odous*, *odontos*, tooth], *n.* A genus of nocturnal lizard-like reptiles, now confined to New Zealand. **sphenogram** [-GRAM], *n.* A cuneiform character. **sphenographic** (-grăf′ ik), *a.* **sphenography** (-nog′ rȧ fi), *n.*

sphenoid (sfen′ oid), *a.* Wedge-shaped. *n.* A sphenoid bone; (Cryst.) a wedge-shaped crystal enclosed by four equal isosceles triangles. **sphenoid bone:** A wedge-shaped bone lying across the base of the skull. **sphenoidal,** *a.* **sphenoido-,** *comb. form.*

sphere (sfēr) [M.E. *spere*, O.F. *espere*, L. *sphæra*, Gr. *sphaira*, ball], *n.* A solid bounded by a surface every part of which is equally distant from a point within called the centre; a solid figure generated by the revolution of a semicircle about its diameter; a figure approximately spherical, a ball, a globe, esp. one of the heavenly bodies; a globe representing the earth or the apparent heavens; one of the spherical shells revolving round the earth as centre in which, according to ancient astronomy, the heavenly bodies were set; (*poet.*) the sky, the heavens; (*fig.*) field of action, influence, etc., scope, range, province, place, position. *v.t.* To enclose in or as in a sphere; to make spherical; to put among the celestial spheres. **celestial sphere:** The spherical surface on which the heavenly bodies appear to be. **doctrine of the spheres:** Spherics. **spheral,** *a.* Spherical; of or pertaining to the celestial spheres or the music of the spheres. **spheric** (sfer′ ik), *a.* Spheral; *spherical. **sphericity,** *n.* **spheriform,** *a.*

spherical (sfer′ i kȧl), *a.* Sphere-shaped, globular; relating to spheres. **spherical triangle:** A figure on the surface of a sphere bounded by the arcs of three great circles. **spherically,** *adv.* **sphericity** (sfė ris′ i ti), *n.*

spherics (sfer′ iks), *n.pl.* Spherical geometry and trigonometry.

spherograph (sfer′ ō grăf), *n.* A stereographic projection of the earth with meridians and lines of latitude, used for the mechanical solution of problems in navigation, etc.

spheroid (sfer′ oid), *n.* A body nearly spherical; a solid generated by the revolution of an ellipse about its minor axis (called an oblate spheroid) or its major axis (called a prolate spheroid). **spheroidal, -ic, -ical** (sfė roi′-), *a.* **spheroidally,** *adv.* **spheroidity, -icity** (-dis′ i ti), *n.*

spherometer (sfė rom′ e tėr), *n.* An instrument for measuring the radii and curvature of spherical surfaces.

spherule (sfer′ ūl), *n.* A small sphere. **spherular,** *a.*

spherulite (sfer′ ū līt), *n.* A rounded concretion occurring in various rocks; a radiolite.

sphex (sfeks) [Gr. *sphēx*], *n.* (*pl.* **spheges,** sfē′ jēz) A genus of digger-wasps; a wasp of this genus. **sphex-wasp, sphexide,** *n.*

sphincter (sfingk′ tėr) [L. and Gr., from *sphingein*, to bind tight], *n.* (*Anat.*) A muscle that contracts or shuts any orifice or tube. **sphincteral, -terial** (-tēr′ i ȧl), **-teric** (-ter′ ik), *a.*

sphinx (sfingks) [L. and Gr., prob. of foreign etym., pop. as prec.], *n.* (*Gr. Ant.*) A winged monster, half woman and half lion, said to have devoured the inhabitants of Thebes till a riddle she had proposed should be solved, and on its solution by Œdipus to have flung herself down and perished; (*Egypt. Ant.*) a figure with the body of a lion and a human or animal head; (*fig.*) a taciturn or enigmatic person; a hawk-moth; a variety of baboon.

sphragistics (sfrȧ jis′ tiks) [Gr. *sphragistikos*, from *sphragis*, seal], *n.pl.* (*usu. as sing.*) The study of engraved seals.

sphygmic [SPHYGMOGRAPH].

sphygmograph (sfig′ mȯ grăf) [Gr. *sphugmos*, pulse, from *sphuzein*, to beat, to throb, -GRAPH], *n.* An instrument for recording the movements of the pulse. **sphygmogram,** *n.* **sphygmographic** (-grăf′ ik), *a.* **sphygmography** (-mog′ rȧ fi), *n.* **sphygmology** (-mol′ ȯ ji) [-LOGY], *n.* The branch of physiology concerned with the pulse. **sphygmomanometer** (-nom′ ė tėr), *n.* An instrument for measuring the tension of blood in an artery. **sphygmophone** (sfig′ mȯ fōn) [-PHONE], *n.* An instrument for enabling one to hear the action of the pulse. **sphygmoscope** [SCOPE], *n.* An instrument for rendering the movements of the pulse visible. **sphygmus,** *n.* (*Physiol.*) A pulse, a pulsation. **sphygmic,** *a.*

***spial** (spī′ ȧl) [ESPIAL]. A spy, a scout; close watch.

spica (spī′ kȧ) [L., ear of corn, spike], *n.* (*Bot.*) A spike; (*Surg.*) a spiral bandage with the turns reversed. **spicate, spicated, spiciform** (spī′ si fôrm), *a.* (*Bot.*).

spice (spīs) [O.F. *espice*, L. *speciēs*, kind, late L. spice], *n.* Any aromatic and pungent vegetable substance used for seasoning food; (*fig.*) a flavour, a touch, a trace. *v.t.* To season with spice. **spice-bush, -wood,** *n.* The wild allspice, *Benzoin odoriferum*, an American shrub. ***spicer,** *n.* **spicery,** *n.* **spicy,** *a.* Flavoured with spice; abounding in spices; (*fig.*) pungent, piquant; suggestive, indelicate; showy, smart. **spicily,** *adv.* **spiciness,** *n.*

spiciform [SPICA]. **spicily, spiciness** [SPICE].

spick-and-span (spik′ ȧnd spăn′) [SPIKE, AND, SPOON], *a.* New and fresh, fresh and smart.

spicknel [SPIGNEL].

spicule (spī′ kūl) [L. *spīculum*, dim. of SPICA], *n.* A small sharp needle-shaped body, such as the calcareous or siliceous spikes in sponges, etc.; (*Bot.*) a small or subsidiary spike. **spicular, -late, spiculiform,** *a.* **spiculiferous** (-lif′ ėr ŭs), **-ligerous,** *a.* **spiculum,** *n.* (*pl.* **-ula**) (*Zool.*) A spicule; a needle-like process, organ, etc.

spicy [SPICE].

spider (spī′ dėr) [A.-S. for *spinther*, *spinner*, see SPIN], *n.* An eight-legged arachnid of the order *Arachneida*, usu. furnished with a spinning apparatus utilized by most species for making webs to catch their prey; an arachnid resembling this; a spider-like thing, esp. a three-legged frying-pan, grid-iron, frame, etc. **spider-catcher,** *n.* A bird of the Indian genus *Arachnothera*; the wall-creeper. **spider-crab,** *n.* A crab with long thin legs. **spider-line,** *n.* A filament of spider's web used in the reticle of astronomical instruments, etc. **spider-monkey,** *n.* A monkey belonging to the American genus *Ateles* or *Eriodes* with long limbs and slender bodies. **spider-wasp,** *n.* A wasp that stores its nest with other insects and spiders. **spider's web, spider-web,** *n.* **spider-like,** *a.* and *adv.* **spidery,** *a.*

Spiegeleisen (spē′ gėl īzn) [G. *spiegel*, mirror, SPECULUM, *eisen*, iron], *n.* A white variety of cast-iron containing manganese, used in making Bessemer steel.

spiel (spēl) [G., a game], *n.* (*Am. colloq.*) A speech, a showman's patter. *v.i.* To reel off patter. **spieler,** *n.* (*Austral.*) A card-sharper, a trickster.

spiffy (spif′ i) [etym. doubtful], *a.* (*slang*) Smartly dressed, spruce.

spiflicate (spif′ li kāt) [etym. doubtful], *v.t.* (*slang*) To smash, to crush, to do for. **spiflication** (-kā′ shŭn), *n.*

spignel (spig′ nėl) [etym. doubtful], *n.* An umbelliferous plant, *Meum athamanticum*, with an aromatic root used in medicine, and finely cut, ornamental leaves.

spigot (spig′ ŏt) [prob. from O.Prov. *espigot*, dim. of *espiga*, L. SPICA], *n.* A peg or plug for stopping the vent-hole in a cask; the turning-plug in a faucet; a faucet, a tap.

spike (spīk) [perh. from Scand. (cp. Icel. *spīk*, Swed. *spik*), cogn. with SPOKE (I), in some senses from L. SPICA], *n.* A pointed piece of metal, as one of a number fixed on the top of a railing, fence, or wall, or worn on boots to prevent slipping; any pointed object, a sharp point; a large nail or pin, used in structures built of large timbers, on railways, etc.; an inflorescence having flowers sessile along a common axis; spike-lavender. *v.t.* To fasten with spikes; to furnish with spikes; to sharpen to a point; to pierce or impale; to fasten on with a spike or spikes; to plug the touch-hole (of a cannon) with a spike; (*Am.*) to lace a drink with spirits. **spike-lavender,** *n.* French lavender, *Lavandula spica.* **spike-nail,** *n.* **spikelet,** *n.* (*Bot.*). **spiky,** *a.*

spikenard (spīk' nard) [O.F. *spiquenard* (L. SPICA, *nardī*, gen. of *nardus*, NARD)], *n.* A herb, *Nardostachys atamansi*, related to the valerian; an ancient and costly aromatic ointment prepared chiefly from the root of this; one of various vegetable oils.

spile (spīl) [cp. Dut. *spijl*, L.G. *spile*, bar, spile, G. *speiler*, skewer, cogn. with SPIRE], *n.* A small wooden plug, a spigot; a large timber driven into the ground to protect a bank, etc., a pile. *v.t.* To pierce (a cask) with a hole and furnish with a spile.

spill (1) (spil) [etym. doubtful, perh. rel. to SPILE], *n.* A slip of paper or wood used to light a candle, lamp, etc.

spill (2) (spil) [A.-S. *spillan*, to destroy, Icel. *spilla*, cp. Swed. *spilla*, A.-S. *spildan*, prob. cogn. with prec.], *v.t.* (*past & p.p.* **spilt, spilled**) To suffer to fall or run out of a vessel; to shed; (*Naut.*) to empty (the belly of a sail) of wind; (*colloq.*) to throw out of a vehicle or from a saddle; *to ruin, to destroy. *v.i.* To run or fall out (of liquid); to be destroyed, to perish. *n.* A tumble, a fall, esp. from a vehicle or saddle. **to spill the beans:** (*slang*) To divulge a secret, to tell the truth. **spillway,** *n.* A passage for the overflow of water from a reservoir, etc. **spiller,** *n.* One that spills; a trawl-line; a small seine used to take the fish out of a larger one. **spilling-line,** *n.* A rope for spilling the wind out of a square sail to enable it to be reefed. ***spilth,** *n.* That which is spilt; over-plus, excess of supply.

spillikin (spil' i kin) [prob. dim. of SPILL (1)], *n.* A small peg or pin of bone, wood, etc., used in certain games.

spilosite (spī' lō sīt) [Gr. *spilos*, spot, -ITE], *n.* (*Min.*) A greenish schistose rock spotted with chlorite concretions or scales.

spilt, spilth [SPILL (2)].

spilus (spī' lŭs) [Gr. *spilos*, spot], *n.* (*Path.*) A spot or mole on the skin, a *nævus*.

spin (spin) [A.-S. *spinnan* (cp. Dut. and G. *spinnen*, Icel. and Swed. *spinna*), cogn. with SPAN (1)], *v.t.* (*past* **spun, span,** *p.p.* **spun**) To draw out and twist (wool, cotton, etc.) into threads; to make (yarn, etc.) thus; to produce (a web, cocoon, etc.) by drawing out a thread of viscous substance (of spiders, etc.); (*fig.*) to tell, compose, etc., at great length; to make (a top, etc.) rotate rapidly; to shape in a lathe, etc.; to fish with a revolving bait; (*slang*) to reject after examination. *v.i.* To draw out and twist cotton, etc., into threads; to make yarn, etc., thus; to whirl round; to turn round quickly; to fish with a spinning bait; (*fig.*) to go along with great swiftness. *n.* The act or motion of spinning, a whirl; (*colloq.*) a brief run, row, ride, etc., at a brisk pace; (*Aviat.*) a rapid diving descent accompanied by a continued gyration of the aeroplane; (*Austral.*) fortune, luck. **spin-drier,** *n.* A machine that dries washing to the point of being ready for ironing by forcing out the water by centrifugal force. **to spin a yarn:** To tell a story. **to spin out:** To compose or tell (a yarn, etc.) at great length; to prolong, to protract; to spend (time) in tedious discussion, etc. **spinner,** *n.* One who spins; a machine for spinning thread; one who shapes things in a lathe; a spider, a spinneret; (*Austral.*) the man who tosses the coin in two-up. **spinnery,** *n.* A spinning-mill. ***spinning-house,** *n.* A house of correction in which women of loose character were obliged to spin, beat hemp, etc. **spinning-jenny,** *n.* A mechanism invented by Hargreaves in 1767 for spinning several strands at once. **spinning-mill,** *n.* A factory where spinning is carried on. **spinning-wheel,** *n.* A wheel driven by the foot or hand, formerly used for spinning wool, cotton, or flax.

spinach (spin' ăj) [O.F. *espinache*, *espinage*, Sp. *espinaca*, Arab. *aspanātch*, prob. from Pers.], *n.* An annual herb of the genus *Spinacia*, esp. *S. oleracea*, with succulent leaves cooked as food; other herbs similarly used. **spinach-beet,** *n.* A variety of beet of which the leaves are eaten as spinach. **spinaceous** (spi nā' shŭs), *a.*

spinal (spī' năl) [late L. *spīnālis*, from *spīna*, SPINE], *a.* Pertaining to the spine. **spinal column:** The backbone. **spinal cord** or **marrow:** A cylindrical structure of nerve-fibres and cells within the vertebral canal and forming part of the central nervous system.

spindle (spin' dėl) [A.-S. *spinl*, from *spinnan*, to SPIN], *n.* A pin or rod in a spinning-wheel for twisting and winding the thread; a rod used for the same purpose in hand-spinning; a pin bearing the bobbin in a spinning-machine; a rod, axis, or arbor which revolves or on which anything revolves; (*fig.*) a slender object or person. *v.i.* To grow into a long slender stalk, shape, etc. **spindle-legged, -shanked,** *a.* Having long, thin legs. **spindle-legs, -shanks,** *n.pl.* **spindle-shaped,** *a.* Tapering from the middle towards both ends, fusiform. **spindle side:** The female side in descent. **spindle-tree,** *n.* A shrub or small tree, *Euonymus Europæus*, the hard wood of which is used for spindles, pins, skewers, etc. **spindle-whorl,** *n.* (*Ant.*) A small perforated disk, usu. of baked clay, formerly used to weight a spindle.

spindrift (spin' drift) [var. of *spoon-drift*, (L. *spūma*, loom, DRIFT)], *n.* Fine spray blown up from the surface of water.

spine (spīn) [O.F. *espine* (F. *épine*), L. *spīna*, thorn, backbone], *n.* The backbone; (*Bot.*) a sharp, stiff woody process; a sharp ridge, projection, outgrowth, etc.; (*Print.*) the back of a book, usually bearing the title and the author's name. **spined,** *a.* **spineless,** *a.* Without a spine; (*fig.*) of weak character, lacking decision. **spinescent** (spīnes' ėnt), *a.* (*Bot.*) Tending to be spinous; spinous, thorny. **spinescence,** *n.* **spinicerebrate** (spī ni ser' i brāt) [CEREBELLUM], *a.* Having a brain and spinal cord. **spiniferous** (spī nif' ėr ŭs) [-FEROUS], **spinigerous** (-nij' ėr ŭs) [-GEROUS], *a.* **spinoid,** *a.* **spinose** (spī nōs', spī' nōs), **spinous,** *a.* **spinosity** (-nos' i ti), *n.* **spiny,** *a.* **spininess,** *n.*

spinel (spi nel', spin' ėl) [O.F. *espinel*, dim. of *espine*, prec.], *n.* (*Min.*) A vitreous aluminate of magnesium, of various colours, crystallizing isometrically; other minerals of similar structure.

spinet (spi net', spin' ėt) [M.F. *espinette*, It. *spinetta*, dim. of *spina*, thorn, SPINE], *n.* An obsolete musical instrument, similar in construction to but smaller than the harpsichord.

spinicerebrate, spiniferous, etc. [SPINE].

spinifex (spī' ni feks) [L. *spīna*, SPINE, *-fex*, maker, from *facere*, to make], *n.* A coarse, spiny Australian grass growing in the sandhills, etc., of the Australian steppes and often covering enormous areas of ground.

spink (spingk) [prob. imit. of cry; cp. Gr. *spingos*, from *spizein*, to chirp], *n.* (*prov.*) A finch, esp. the chaffinch.

spinnaker (spin' ă kėr) [perh. from *Sphinx*, name of a yacht], *n.* A large jib-shaped sail carried opposite the mainsail on the mainmast of a racing-yacht.

spinner [SPIN].

spinneret (spin' ėr et) [SPIN], *n.* (*Zool.*) The spinning organ of a spider through which the silk issues; the orifice through which liquid cellulose is projected to form threads of rayon or artificial silk.

spinney (spin' i) [O.F. *espinei*, *espinoye* (F. *épinaie*), L. *spīnētum*, from *spīna*, thorn, SPINE], *n.* A small wood with undergrowth, a copse.

spinning-house, -jenny, -mill, etc. [SPIN].

spinode (spī' nōd), *n.* (*Geom.*) A stationary point on a curve, a cusp.

spinoid, spinose, etc. [SPINE].

Spinozism (spi nō' zizm), *n.* The monistic system of Baruch de Spinoza (1632–77), a Spanish Jew, who resolved all being into extension and thought, which he considered as attributes of the Sole Substance, God. **Spinozist,** *n.* **Spinozoistic** (-zis' tik), *a.*

spinster (spin′ stėr) [SPIN, -STER], *n.* An unmarried woman. **spinsterhood,** *n.*

spinthariscope (spin thăr′ i skōp) [Gr. *spintharis,* spark, -SCOPE], *n.* An instrument for showing the rays emitted by radium by the scintillations caused by their impact against a fluorescent screen. **spinthariscopic** (-skop′ ik), *a.*

***spinthere** (spin′ thēr) [F. *spinthère,* Gr. *spinthēr*], *n.* (*Min.*) Sphene.

spinule (spī′ nūl) [L. *spīnula,* dim. of *spīna,* SPINE], *n.* A minute spine. **spinuliferous** (-lif′ ėr ŭs), *a.* **spinulose, -lous** (spī nū lōs′, spī′ nū lŭs), *a.*

spiny [SPINE].

spiracle (spīr′ ȧ kėl) [F., from L. *spīrāculum,* from *spīrāre,* to breathe], *n.* A breathing-hole, esp. in the lower animals; a vent-hole for lava, etc. **spiracular, -late** (spī răk′ ū lȧr, -lȧt), **spiraculiform** (-kū′ li fôrm), *a.*

spiræa (spī rē′ ȧ) [L., from Gr. *speiraia,* meadow-sweet, from *speira,* SPIRE (2)], *n.* A flowering plant belonging to a genus of *Rosaceæ* including the meadow-sweet.

spiral (spīr′ ȧl) [F., from L. *spīrālis*], *a.* Forming a spire, spiral, or coil; continually winding about and receding from a centre; continually winding, as the thread of a screw. *n.* A spiral curve, formation, spring, or other object; (*Aviat.*) a continuous banked turn made during a glide with the motor stopped, or ticking over. **spirality** (spi răl′ i ti), *n.* **spirally,** *adv.* **spiraled,** *a.*

spirant (spīr′ ȧnt) [L. *spirans -ntem,* pres.p. of *spīrāre,* to breathe], *n.* A consonant in the articulation of which breath is not wholly stopped, a continuable sound (opp. to explosive), as *f, v, h, th,* etc.

spiration (spī rā′ shŭn) [L. *spīrātio,* from *spīrāre,* to breathe], *n.* (*Theol.*) The procession of the Holy Ghost.

spire (1) (spīr) [A.-S. *spīr,* cp. Dut. and G. *spier,* Dan. *spire,* Swed. *spira*], *n.* A tapering, conical, or pyramidal structure, esp. the tapering portion of a steeple; a stalk of grass, the tapering part of a tree above the point where branching begins. *v.i.* To shoot up like a spire. *v.t.* To furnish with a spire or spires. **spiry** (1), *a.*

spire (2) (spīr) [F., from L. *spīra,* Gr. *speira,* coil], *n.* A spiral, a coil; a single turn in this, a whorl, a twist. **spiry** (2), *a.*

spirifer (spīr′ i fėr) [L. *spīra,* SPIRE (2), *-fer,* bearing], *n.* (*Palæont.*) An extinct genus of brachiopods with spiral appendages. **spiriferous** (spī rif′ ėr ŭs), *a.*

Spirillum (spi ril′ ŭm) [dim. of L. *spīra,* SPIRE (2)], *n.* (*pl.* **-la**) (*Biol.*) A genus of bacteria having a spiral structure; a bacterium of this genus. **spirillar, spirilliform,** *a.*

spirit (spir′ it) [O.F. *espirit* (F. *esprit*), L. *spīritum,* nom. *-tus,* from *spīrāre,* to breathe], *n.* The immaterial part of man, the soul; this as not connected with a physical body, a disembodied soul, a ghost; an incorporeal or supernatural being, a sprite, an elf, a fairy, a person considered with regard to his peculiar qualities of mind, temper, etc.; a person of great mental or moral force; vigour of mind or intellect; vivacity, energy, ardour, enthusiasm; temper, disposition; mental attitude, mood, humour (*often in pl.*); real meaning or intent; actuating principle, pervading influence, peculiar quality or tendency; (*usu. pl.*) distilled alcoholic liquors, as brandy, whisky, etc.; (*Pharm.*) a solution (of a volatile principle) in alcohol. *v.t.* To animate, to inspirit; to convey (away, off, etc.) secretly and rapidly. **the Spirit, the Holy Spirit:** The Third Person of the Trinity. **spirit or spirits of wine:** Pure alcohol. **spirit-duck,** *n.* The buffle-head and other ducks that dive with striking rapidity. **spirit-lamp,** *n.* A lamp burning alcohol (*Am.* an alcohol lamp). **spirit-level,** *n.* An instrument used for determining the horizontal by an air-bubble in a tube containing alcohol. **spirit-rapper,** *n.* One professing to communicate with spirits by means of raps on a table, etc. **spirit-rapping,** *n.* **spirit room,** *n.* (*Naut.*) The pay-master's store-room, formerly for spirituous liquors. **spirited,** *a.* Full of spirit, fire, or life, animated, lively, courageous (*usu. in comb.,* as *high-spirited*). **spiritedly,** *adv.* **spiritedness,** *n.* ***spiritful,** *a.* **spiritism** [SPIRITUALISM]. **spiritist** [SPIRITUALIST]. **spiritless,** *a.* **spiritlessly,** *adv.* **spiritlessness,** *n.* **spiritoso** (-tō′ sō) [It.], *adv.* (*Mus. direction*) In a spirited manner. ***spiritous,** *a.* Refined, pure; ardent, active; spirituous. ***spiritousness,** *n.*

spiritual (spir′ i tū ȧl) [M.E. and O.F. *spirituel,* late L. *spīrituālis,* from *spiritus,* prec.], *a.* Pertaining to or consisting of spirit; immaterial, incorporeal; pertaining to the soul or the inner nature; derived from or pertaining to God, pure, holy, sacred, divine, inspired; pertaining to sacred things, not lay or temporal. *n.* A type of hymn sung by Negroes of the southern U.S.A. **spirituality** (-ăl′ i ti), *n.* Immateriality, incorporeity; the quality of being spiritual or unworldly; that which belongs to the Church, or to an ecclesiastic on account of a spiritual office. **spiritualize,** *v.t.* **spiritualization** (-zā′ shŭn), *n.* **spiritualizer,** *n.* **spiritually,** *adv.* **spiritualness,** *n.*

spiritualism (spir′ i tū ȧ lizm), *n.* A system of professed communication with departed spirits, chiefly through persons called mediums; (*Phil.*) the doctrine that the spirit exists as distinct from matter or as the only reality, opp. to materialism. **spiritualist,** *n.* **spiritualistic** (-lis′ tik), *a.*

spirituelle (spir i tū el′) [F., fem. of *spirituel,* SPIRITUAL], *a.* Characterized by refinement, grace, or delicacy of mind (esp. of women).

spirituous (spir′ i tū ŭs) [prob. through F. *spiritueux,* from L.], *a.* Containing spirit, alcoholic, distilled as distinguished from fermented. **spirituousness,** *n.*

spiritus (spīr′ i tŭs) [L., SPIRIT] *n.* (*Gr. Gram.*) A breathing. ***spiritus asper:*** A rough breathing or aspirate, in Greek marked (ʽ). ***spiritus lenis:*** A smooth breathing, in Greek (ʼ), denoting the absence of an aspirate.

spirket (1) (spěr′ kėt) [E. Anglian, etym. doubtful], *n.* (*prov.*) A stout hooked peg, esp. for hanging harness on.

spirket (2) (spěr′ kėt) [etym. unknown], *n.* (*Shipbuilding*) A space forward or aft between floor-timbers. **spirketing,** *n.* The inside planking between the top of the water-ways and the port-sills.

spirochæta (spī rō kē′ tȧ) [Gr. *speira,* a coil; *chaite,* a bristle], *n.* (*Bacter.*) A genus of spiral-shaped bacteria which includes the causative agents of syphilis, relapsing fever, and epidemic jaundice.

spirograph (spīr′ ȯ grăf) [L. *spīro,* I breathe, -GRAPH], *n.* An instrument for recording the movement in breathing. **spirometer** (-om′ ė ter) [-METER], *n.* An instrument for measuring the capacity of the lungs. **spirometric** (-met′ rik), *a.* **spirometry,** *n.* **spirophore** (spīr′ ȯ fôr) [-PHORE], *n.* An instrument for inducing respiration when animation is suspended. **spiroscope** (spī′ rō skōp), *n.* A spirometer.

spirt [SPURT (1 and 2)].

Spirula (spīr′ ū lȧ) [dim. of L. *spīra* [SPIRE (2)], *n.* A genus of tropical cephalopods having a flat spiral shell.

spiry [SPIRE (1 and 2)].

***spissated** (spis′ a tėd) [L. *spissātus,* p.p. of *spissāre,* from *spissus,* thick, compact], *a.* Thickened, inspissated. ***spissitude,** *n.*

spit (1) (spit) [A.-S. *spitu,* cp. Dut. *spit,* G. *spiess,* Dan. *spīd,* Swed. *spētt*], *n.* A long pointed rod on which meat for roasting is rotated before a fire; a point of land or a narrow shoal extending into the sea; a spade; a spadeful. *v.t.* To fix (meat) upon a spit; to pierce, to transfix.

spit (2) (spit) [A.-S. *spittan,* cogn. with *spætan,* and prob. with Icel. *spyta,* Dan. *spytte,* Swed. *spotta,* rel. to SPOUT], *v.t.* (*past & p.p.* **spat, *spit**) To eject (saliva, etc.) from the mouth; to utter in a violent or spiteful way. *v.i.* To eject saliva from the mouth; to make a spitting noise (of an angry cat); (*fig.*) to drizzle (of rain). *n.* Spittle, saliva; spitting; the spawn of certain insects; likeness, counterpart. **spitfire,** *n.* An irascible person, esp. a woman. **spitter,** *n.* **spittle** (1), *n.* Saliva, esp. ejected from the mouth. **spittoon** (spi toon′), *n.* A receptacle for spittle.

***spital** (spit′ ȧl) [M.E. *spittal*, var. of HOSPITAL], *n.* A hospital, a lazar-house. ***spital-house,** *n.*

spitch-cock (spich′ kok) [perh. from M.H.G. *spiz*, SPIT (1), G. *kochen*, to cook], *v.t.* To split and broil (an eel, etc.). *n.* An eel split and broiled.

spite (spīt) [short for DESPITE], *n.* Ill will, malice, malevolence; rancour, a grudge. *v.t.* To thwart maliciously; to vex or annoy. **in spite of, spite of:** Notwithstanding. **spiteful,** *a.* **spitefully,** *adv.* **spitefulness,** *n.*

spitfire [SPIT (2)].

spitter, spittle (1) [SPIT (2)].

***spittle** (2) [SPITAL].

spittoon [SPIT (2)].

spitz (spits) [G.], *n.* A sharp-muzzled breed of dog, called also Pomeranian.

spiv (spiv) [etym. unknown], *n.* A hanger-on in dubious circles; a man cheaply over-dressed without apparent occupation; one who dresses flashily; a petty black-market dealer.

splanç hnic (splăngk′ nik) [Gr. *splanchnikos*, from *splanchna*, entrails], *a.* Pertaining to the bowels. **splanchnography** (-nog′ rȧ fi) [-GRAPHY], *n.* Descriptive splanchnology. **splanchnology** (-nol′ ȯ ji) [-LOGY], *n.* The branch of medical science dealing with the viscera. **splanchnoskeleton** (-skel′ ė tȯn), *n.* The skeletal parts connected with the sense organs or viscera. **splanchnotomy** (-not′ ȯ mi) [-TOMY], *n.* Dissection of the viscera.

splash (splăsh) [*s-*, F. *es-*, EX- PLASH (2)], *v.t.* To bespatter with water, mud, etc.; to dash (liquid, etc., about, over, etc.); to make (one's way) thus; (*colloq.*) to spend recklessly. *v.i.* To dash water or other liquid about; to be dashed about in drops, to dabble, to plunge; to move or to make one's way (along, etc.) thus. *n.* The act of splashing; water or mud splashed about; a noise as of splashing; a spot or patch of liquid, colour, etc.; a white toilet-powder. **to make a splash:** (*slang*) To make a sensation, display, etc. **splash-board,** *n.* A guard in front of a vehicle to protect the occupants from mud. **splasher,** *n.* One who or that which splashes; a guard over the wheels of locomotives; a splash-board; a screen hung behind a wash-stand to keep splashes off the wall. **splashy,** *a.*

splatter (splăt′ ėr), *v.i.* To make a continuous splash or splashing noise. *v.t.* To utter thus, to sputter. **splatterdash,** *n.* A stir, a commotion; (*pl.*) spatterdashes.

splay (splā) [var. of DISPLAY], *v.t.* To form (a window-opening, etc.) with oblique sides; to dislocate (esp. the shoulder-bone of a horse). *n.* An oblique surface, side, or widening of a window, etc. *a.* Turned outwards. **splay-foot,** *n.* A broad, flat foot turned outwards. **splay-footed,** *a.* **splay-mouth,** *n.* A wide, distorted mouth. **splay-mouthed,** *a.*

spleen (splēn) [L. and Gr. *splēn*], *n.* A soft vascular organ situated to the left of the stomach in most vertebrates having some action on the blood; (*fig.*) spitefulness, ill temper; low spirits, melancholy. **spleen-wort,** *n.* A fern of the genus *Asplenium*, formerly supposed to be a specific for spleen. **spleenful, spleenish, spleeny,** *a.* **spleenfully, spleenishly,** *adv.* **spleenless,** *a.*

splen- [Gr. *splēn*, prec.], *comb. form.* **splenalgia** (splė năl′ ji ȧ) [Gr. *algos*, pain], *n.* Pain in or near the spleen. **splenalgic,** *a.*

splendid (splen′ did) [L. *splendidus*, from *splendēre*, to shine], *a.* Magnificent, gorgeous, sumptuous; glorious, illustrious; brilliant, lustrous, dazzling; (*colloq.*) fine, excellent, first-rate. **splendent,** *a.* Shining, lustrous, brilliant; very conspicuous; splendid. **splendidly,** *adv.* **splendiferous** (splen dif′ ėr ŭs), *a.* (*facet.*) Splendid. ***splendorous,** *a.* **splendour,** *n.*

splenetic (splė net′ ik) [late L. *splēnēticus*, from L. *splēn*, SPLEEN], *a.* Of or pertaining to the spleen; affected with spleen; peevish, ill-tempered. *n.* A person affected with spleen; a medicine for disease of the spleen. **splenetically,** *adv.*

splenial [SPLENIUS].

splenic (splen′ ik) [L. *splēnicus*, Gr. *splēnikos*, from *splēn*, SPLEEN], *a.* Pertaining to or affecting the spleen. **splenitis** (splė nī′ tis), *n.* Inflammation of the spleen. **splenitic** (-nit′ ik), *a.*

splenius (splē′ ni ŭs) [Gr. *splēnion*, bandage], *n.* (*Anat.*) A muscle extending in two parts on either side of the neck serving to bend the head backwards. **splenial,** *a.* Of or pertaining to this; (*Surg.*) splint-like.

splenization (splē ni zā′ shŭn) [F. *splénisation*], *n.* Conversion of a portion of the lung into tissue resembling the spleen.

splenology (splė nol′ ȯ ji) [SPLEEN], *n.* Scientific study of the spleen. **splenological** (-loj′ i kȧl), *a.* **splenotomy** (-not′ ȯ mi) [-TOMY], *n.* The dissection of or an incision into the spleen.

splent [SPLINT].

spleuchan (sploo′ *ch*ăn) [Gael. *spliùchan*], *n.* (*Sc.*) A small bag, pouch, or purse, esp. a tobacco-pouch.

splice (splīs) [Dut. *splitsen*, to splice, from *splijten*, to SPLIT (cp. Dan. *splidse*, Swed. *splissa*, G. *splissen*, to splice)], *v.t.* To unite (two ropes, etc.) by interweaving the strands of the ends; to unite (timbers, etc.) by bevelling, overlapping, and fitting the ends together; (*colloq.*) to unite in marriage. *n.* A union of ropes, timbers, etc., by splicing; (*Cinema.*) the point of juncture between two pieces of film. **to splice the main-brace** [BRACE].

spline (splīn) [etym. doubtful], *n.* A flexible strip of wood or rubber used in laying down large curves in mechanical drawing; (*Mach.*) a key fitting into a slot in a shaft and wheel to make these revolve together; the slot itself.

splint (splint) [M.Dut. *splinte*, cp. Dut., G., Dan., Swed., and Norw. *splint*], *n.* A thin piece of wood or other material used to keep the parts of a broken bone together; a thin strip of wood used in basket-making, etc.; a splint-bone; a callous tumour on the splint-bone of a horse. *v.t.* To secure or support with splints. **splint-bone,** *n.* One of two small bones extending from the knee to the fetlock in the horse; (*Anat.*) a fibula. **splint coal:** A slaty variety of cannel coal.

splinter (splin′ tėr) [M.Dut., rel. to prec.], *n.* A thin piece broken, split, or shivered off. *v.t.* To split, shiver, or rend into splinters; to support with splinters. *v.i.* To split or shiver into splinters. **splintery,** *a.* **splinter-bar,** *n.* A cross-bar in front of a vehicle to which the traces are attached or which supports the springs. **splinter-bone,** *n.* The splint-bone. **splinter party:** (*Pol.*) A small group that has broken away from its parent party. **splinter-proof,** *a.* Proof against the splinters of bursting shells.

split (split) [M.Dut. *splitten*, rel. to Dut. *splijten*, G. *spleissen*], *v.t.* (*past & p.p.* **split**) To break, cleave, tear, or divide, esp. longitudinally or with the grain; to divide into two or more parts, thicknesses, etc.; to divide into opposed parties; to divide (one's vote or votes) between different candidates; to cause to ache or throb. *v.i.* To be broken or divided, esp. longitudinally or with the grain; to break up, to go to pieces; to divide into opposed parties; (*slang*) to betray the secrets of, to inform (on); (*colloq.*) to burst with laughter. *n.* The act or result of splitting; a crack, rent, or fissure; a separation into opposed parties, a rupture, a schism;

something split, a split osier for basket-work, a single thickness of split hide, etc.; one of the strips or splints forming the reed of a loom; (*pl.*) an acrobat's feat of sitting down with the legs stretched out right and left; (*slang*) a half bottle of soda water; a half glass of liquor. **to split hairs** [HAIR]. **to split the infinitive:** To insert a word between *to* and the verb, as *to completely defeat*. **split-pease,** *n.* Pease husked and split. **split pin,** *n.* (*Mach.*) A pin with a divided end which is splayed apart to keep the pin in place. **split ring,** *n.* A metal ring so constructed that keys can be put on it or taken off. **split-stuff,** *n.* (*Austral.*) Timber sawn into lengths and split into planks. **splitter,** *n.* One who splits; (*Austral.*) a timber cutter who prepares posts for fencing.

splodge (sploj), **splotch** (sploch) [perh. onomat.], *n.* A daub, a blotch, an irregular stain. **splotchy,** *a.*

splore (splôr) [etym. doubtful], *n.* (*Sc.*) A noisy frolic, a carousal, a spree.

splotch, splotchy [SPLODGE].

splurge (splĕrj) [Am., onomat.], *v.i.* To show off, to make a blustering effort. *n.* The act of splurging.

splutter (splŭt′ ėr) [imit.], *v.t.* and *i.* To sputter. *n.* A sputter, a noise, a fuss. **splutterer,** *n.*

spode (spōd), *n.* Porcelain made by the potter Josiah Spode (1754–1827). **spode-ware,** *n.*

*__spodium__ (spō′ di ŭm) [L., from Gr. *spodion*, dim. of *spodos*, ashes, dust], *n.* Fine powder obtained from calcined bone and other substances. ***spodomancy** (spod′ ō măn si) [-MANCY], *n.* Divination by ashes. ***spodomantic,** *a.*

spodumene (spod′ ū mēn) [F. *spodumène*, G. *spodumen*, Gr. *spodoumenos*, p.p. of *spodousthai*, to be turned to ashes, from *spodos*, ash], *n.* (*Min.*) a monoclinic silicate of aluminium and lithium.

spoffish (spof′ ish) [etym. doubtful], *a.* (*slang*) Fussy, officious. **spoffy,** *a.*

spoil (spoil) [O.F. *espoillier*, L. *spoliāre*, from *spolium*, a skin stripped off, (*in pl.*) booty], *v.t.* (*past & p.p.* **spoilt, spoiled**) To mar, to vitiate, to impair the goodness, usefulness, etc., of; to impair the character of by over-indulgence; *to plunder, to deprive (of) by violence. *v.i.* To decay, to deteriorate through keeping (of perishable food); (*colloq.*) to be eager or over-ripe (for a fight). *n.* (*usu. in pl. or collect.*) Plunder, booty; (*fig.*) offices, honours, or emoluments acquired as the result of a party victory, esp. in the U.S.; waste material obtaining in mining, quarrying, excavating, etc.; pillage, spoliation, rapine. **spoil-five,** *n.* A card game in which unless a player makes three out of five possible tricks the hand is 'spoiled.' **spoilsman,** *n.* (*Am.*) A politician working for a share of the spoils; a supporter of the spoils system. **spoilage,** *n.* (*Print.*) Spoilt paper from the presses. **spoiler,** *n.* ***spoilful,** *a.* Rapacious. **spoil-sport,** *n.* A person who interferes with another's pleasure.

spoke (1) (spōk) [A.-S. *spāca* (cp. Dut. *speek*, G. *speiche*), rel. to SPIKE], *n.* One of the members connecting the hub with the rim of a wheel; a rung of a ladder; a stick for preventing a wheel from turning in descending a hill; (*Naut.*) one of the radial handles of a steering-wheel. *v.t.* To furnish with spokes; to check (a wheel) with a spoke. **to put a spoke in one's wheel:** To thwart him. **spoke-shave,** *n.* A plane with a handle at each end for dressing spokes, curved work, etc.

spoke (2), *past*, **spoken,** *p.p.* [SPEAK].

spokesman (spōks′ măn), *n.* One who speaks for another or others.

spole [SPOOL].

spoliation (spō li ā′ shŭn) [F., from L. *spoliātiōnem*, nom. *-tio*, from *spoliāre*, to SPOIL], *n.* Robbery, pillage, the act or practice of plundering, esp. of neutral commerce, in time of war; (*Law*) destruction, mutilation, or alteration of a document to prevent its use as evidence; (*Eccles.*) taking the emoluments of a benefice under an illegal title.

***spoliate** (spō′ li āt), *v.t.* **spoliator,** *n.* **spoliatory,** *a.*

spondee (spon′ dē) [L. *spondēus*, Gr. *spondeios*, from *spondai*, a solemn treaty, pl. of *spondē*, libation], *n.* A metrical foot of two long syllables. **spondaic** (-dā′ ik), *a.*

spondulics (spon dū′ liks) [etym. unknown], *n.* (*slang*) Money, cash.

spondyl, -dyle (spon′ dil) [F. *spondyle*, L. *spondylus*, Gr. *sphondulos*], *n.* A vertebra. **spondylitis** (-lī′ tis), *n.* Inflammation of the vertebræ. **spondylo-,** *comb. form.*

sponge (spŭnj) [A.-S., from L. *spongia*, Gr. *spongia*, *-gos*, cogn. with FUNGUS], *n.* A marine animal with pores in the body-wall; the skeleton or part of the skeleton of a sponge or colony of sponges, esp. of a soft, elastic kind used as an absorbent in bathing, cleansing, etc.; any sponge-like substance or implement; dough for baking before it is kneaded; sponge-cake; a kind of mop for cleaning a cannon-bore after a discharge; a parasite, a sponger. *v.t.* To wipe, wet, or cleanse with a sponge; to obliterate, to wipe (out) with or as with a sponge; to absorb, to take (up) with a sponge; (*fig.*) to extort or obtain by parasitic means. *v.i.* To suck in, as a sponge; (*fig.*) to live parasitically or by practising mean arts (on). **to throw up the sponge:** To acknowledge oneself beaten; to give up the contest (orig. of a boxer on the tossing of the sponge into the air by his second as token of defeat). **sponge-cake,** *n.* A light, spongy cake. **sponge cloth,** *n.* Loosely-woven fabric with a wrinkled surface. **spongelet,** *n.* **spongeous, spongiform, spongious, spongoid** (spong′ goid), **spongy,** *a.* **sponginess,** *n.* **sponger,** *n.* One who or that which sponges; a mean parasite. **sponging-house,** *n.* A house where persons arrested for debt were lodged temporarily before being put in prison. **spongiole,** *n.* (*Bot.*) The spongy extremity of a radicle, a spongelet. **spongiopiline** (spŭn ji ō pī′ lin, -lin) [Gr. *pilos*, felt, -INE], *n.* A substitute for a poultice, made of sponge and fibre on a rubber backing. **spongology** (spong gol′ ō ji) [-LOGY], *n.* The scientific study of sponges. **spongologist,** *n.*

***sponsal** (spon′ săl) [L. *sponsālis*, from *sponsus*, SPOUSE], *a.* Pertaining to marriage.

sponsible (*prov.*) [RESPONSIBLE].

sponsion (spon′ shŭn) [L. *sponsio*, from *spondēre*, to promise, p.p. *sponsus*], *n.* The act of becoming surety for another; (*International Law*) an act or engagement on behalf of a state by an agent not specially authorized.

sponson (spon′ sŏn) [etym. doubtful], *n.* A projection from the sides of a vessel, as before and abaft a paddle-box, for a gun on a warship, or to support a bearing, etc.; (*Aviat.*) a device attached to the wings of a hydroplane to give it steadiness when resting on the water.

sponsor (spon′ sŏr) [L. (*spons-*, see SPONSION, -OR)], *n.* A surety, one who undertakes to be responsible for another; a godfather or godmother; an advertiser who pays for the insertion of advertisements of his goods introduced into radio or television programmes. **sponsorial** (-sôr′ i ăl), *a.* **sponsorship,** *n.*

spontaneous (spon tā′ nė ŭs) [L. *spontāneus*, from *sponte*, of one's own accord], *a.* Arising, occurring, done, or acting without external cause; not due to external constraint or suggestion, voluntary; not due to conscious volition or motive; instinctive, automatic, involuntary; self-originated, self-generated. **spontaneity** (-tă nē′ i ti), *n.* **spontaneousness** (-tā′ nė ŭs nės), *n.* **spontaneously,** *adv.*

spontoon (spon toon′) [F. *sponton*, It. *spontone*, from *punto*, point], *n.* A kind of half-pike or halberd borne by British infantry officers in the 18th cent.

spoof (spoof) [onomat.], *v.t.* To hoax, to fool.

spook (spook) [Dut., cp. G. *spuk*], *n.* A ghost. **spookish, spooky,** *a.*

spool (spool) [M.Dut. *spoele* (perh. through O.North.F. *espole*), cp. Dut. *spoel*, G. *spule*], *n.* A small cylinder for winding thread, photographic film, etc., on; the central bar of an angler's reel; (*Am.*) a reel (of cotton, etc.). *v.t.* To wind on a spool.

***spoom** (spoom) [earlier *spoon*, etym. doubtful], *v.i.* To sail fast, to scud. **spooming,** *a.* (*Keats*) Spuming, foaming.

spoon (1) (spoon) [A.-S. *spōn*, chip, splinter (cp. Dut. *spaan*, G. *span*, Icel. *spānn*, *spōnn*, also Gr. *sphēn*, wedge)], *n.* A domestic utensil consisting of a shallow bowl on a stem or handle, used for conveying liquids or liquid food to the mouth, etc.; an implement or other thing shaped like a spoon, as an oar with the blade curved lengthwise, a golf-club with a lofted face, a spoon-bait, etc. *v.t.* To take (up, etc.) with a spoon; (*Cricket, etc.*) to hit a ball (*usu.* up) with little force. *v.i.* To fish with a spoon-bait. **spoon-bait,** *n.* A spoon-shaped piece of bright metal with hooks attached used as a revolving lure in fishing. **spoon-beak, -bill,** *n.* A bird with a broad, flat bill, esp. of the genus *Platalea.* **spoon-fed,** *a.* Pampered. **spoon-food, -meat, -victuals,** *n.* Liquid food, food for infants. **spoon-net,** *n.* A small landing-net used by anglers. **spoonful,** *n.* (*pl.* **spoonfuls**).

spoon (2) (spoon) [prob. from *spoony* (SPOON (1), -Y)], *n.* A silly fellow; a mawkish or foolishly demonstrative lover. *v.i.* To indulge in demonstrative love-making. **spoony,** *a.* **spoonily,** *adv.* **spooniness,** *n.*

spoonerism (spoo' nėr izm) [Rev. W. A. *Spooner* (1844–1930), Warden of New College, Oxford], *n.* Accidental or facetious transposition of the initial letters or syllables of words. *e.g.* "I have in my breast a half-warmed fish."

spoor (spoor) [Dut., cogn. with SPEER], *n.* The track of a wild animal. *v.i.* To follow a spoor.

sporadic, *-al (spȯ răd' ik, -ȧl) [Gr. *sporadikos*, from *sporas -ados*, from *speirein*, to sow], *a.* Separate, scattered, occurring here and there or irregularly. **sporadically,** *adv.* **sporadicalness,** *n.*

sporan [SPORRAN].

sporange, sporangium (spȯ rănj', -i ŭm) [Gr. *spora*, spore, *angeion*, vessel], *n.* (*Bot.*) (*pl.* **-ges, -gia**) A spore-case. **sporangial,** *a.* **sporangiferous** (-jif' ėr ŭs), *a.* **sporation** (-rā' shŭn), *n.* The formation of spores.

spore (spôr) [Gr. *spora*, sowing, as SPORADIC], *n.* (*Bot.*) The reproductive body in a cryptogam, usu. composed of a single cell not containing an embryo; (*Biol.*) a minute organic body that develops into a new individual, as in protozoa, etc.; (*fig.*) a germ. **sporo-,** *comb. form.* **sporocarp** (spô' ȯ karp), *n.* A fructification containing spores or sporangia. **sporocyst** (-sist), *n.* (*Zool.*) A cyst containing spores or an encysted organism giving rise to spores. **sporocystic** (-sis' tik), *a.* **sporogenesis** (spo rō jen' e sis), *n.* Spore formation. **sporophore** (spôr' ȯ fôr), *n.* A spore-bearing branch, process, etc. **sporosac,** *n.* A sac-shaped gonophore in certain Hydrozoa.

sporran (spor' ȧn) [Gael.], *n.* A pouch, usu. covered with fur, hair, etc., worn by Highlanders in front of the kilt.

sport (spôrt) [short for DISPORT], *n.* Diversion, amusement; fun, jest, pleasantry; game, pastime, esp. athletic or outdoor pastime, as hunting, shooting, fishing, racing, running, etc.; (*fig.*) an animal or plant deviating remarkably from the normal type. *v.i.* To play, to divert oneself; to trifle, to jest, to make merry (with a person's feelings, etc.); (*Biol.*) to vary remarkably from the normal type. *v.t.* To wear or display in an ostentatious manner. **to make sport of:** To jeer at, to ridicule. **sporter,** *n.* ***sportful,** *a.* ***sportfully,** *adv.* ***sportfulness,** *n.* **sporting,** *a.* **sportive,** *a.* Gay, frolicsome, playful. **sportively,** *adv.* **sportiveness,** *n.* **sportless,** *a.*

sportsman (spôrts' mȧn), *n.* One skilled in or devoted to sports, esp. hunting, shooting, fishing, etc.; (*fig.*) one who acts fairly towards opponents or who faces good or bad luck with equanimity. **sportsmanlike,** *a.* **sportsmanship,** *n.* **sportswoman,** *n.*

sporule (spor' ūl) [F., dim. of SPORE], *n.* A spore, esp. a small or secondary spore. **sporular,** *a.* **sporulation,** *n.* **sporuliferous** (-lif' ėr ŭs), *a.*

spot (spot) [M.E. (cp. E. Fris. *spot*, M.Dut. *spotten*, Icel. *spotte*, Norw. *spott*) cogn. with SPOUT], *n.* A small mark or stain, a speck, a blot; (*fig.*) a stain on character or reputation; a small part of a surface of distinctive colour or texture; a small extent of space; a particular place, a definite locality; a sea-fish, esp. the red-fish, marked with a spot; a breed of domestic pigeon; (*Billiards*) a mark near the top of a billiard-table on which the red ball is placed; a spot-stroke. *v.t.* (*past & p.p.* **spotted**) To mark, stain, or discolour with a spot or spots; (*fig.*) to sully, to blemish (one's reputation); (*colloq.*) to pick out, to notice, to detect; to place on the spot at billiards. *v.i.* To become or be liable to be marked with spots. **on the spot:** At once, without change of place; alert, wideawake (of persons). **spot-ball,** *n.* (*Billiards*) A white ball marked with a black spot. **spot-barred,** *a.* (*Billiards*) Denoting a game in which the spot-stroke is not allowed more than twice in succession. **spot cash:** (*colloq.*) Money down. **spot-cotton** or **wheat:** Cotton or wheat on the spot for immediate delivery. **spot-light,** *n.* (*Theat.*) An apparatus for throwing a concentrated beam of light on an actor on the stage; the patch of light thus thrown. **spot-stroke,** *n.* (*Billiards*) A winning-hazard off the red ball when on the spot. **spotted fever:** Cerebro-spinal meningitis, characterized by spots on the skin. **spotted gum,** *n.* (*Austral.*) A Eucalyptus tree, marked on the bark with spots. **spotless,** *a.* **spotlessly,** *adv.* **spotlessness,** *n.* **spottedness,** *n.* **spotter,** *n.* Observer trained to detect the approach of enemy aircraft. **spotty,** *a.* **spottiness,** *n.*

spouse (spouz) [M.E. *spuse*, O.F. *spus*, *spuse*, var. of *éspus* (F. *epoux*), L. *sponsus*, p.p. of *spondēre*, to promise], *n.* A husband or wife. **spousal,** *a.* Pertaining to marriage; nuptial, matrimonial. ***n.** (*usu. in pl.*) Marriage, nuptials. **spouseless,** *a.*

spout (spout) [M.E. *spouten* (cp. Dut. *spuiten*, Swed. *sputa*, *spruta*), prob. by-form of SPROUT], *v.t.* To pour out or discharge with force or in large volume; (*fig.*) to utter or recite in a declamatory manner. *v.i.* To pour out or issue forcibly or copiously, to declaim. *n.* A short pipe, tube, or channelled projection for carrying off water from a gutter, conducting liquid from a vessel, shooting things into a receptacle, etc.; a shoot or lift in a pawnbroker's shop; a continuous stream, jet, or column of water, etc.; a water-spout; a whale's spiracle or spout-hole. **up the spout:** At the pawnbroker's, in pawn. **spouter,** *n.* **spoutless,** *a.*

sprack (sprăk) [etym. doubtful; perh. from Icel. *sprækr*, *sparkr*, lively], *a.* (*prov.*) Brisk, smart, alert, sprightly, spruce.

sprackle (sprăk' ėl) [Sc., etym. doubtful], *v.i.* To clamber, to climb with difficulty.

sprag (1) (sprăg) [etym. doubtful], *n.* A billet of wood, esp. a prop for the roof of a mine; a billet of wood for locking the wheel of a vehicle. *v.t.* To support with sprags.

sprag (2) (sprăg) [etym. doubtful], *n.* (*prov.*) A young salmon; a half-grown cod.

sprain (sprān) [O.F. *espreindre*, L. *exprimere* (EX-, *premere*, to PRESS], *v.t.* To twist or wrench the muscles or ligaments of (a joint) so as to injure without dislocation. *n.* Such a twist or wrench or the injury due to it.

spraints (sprānts) [O.F. *espraintes*, as prec.], *n.pl.* The dung of an otter.

sprang, *past* [SPRING].

sprat (sprăt) [A.-S. *sprott*, cp. Dut. *sprot*, also A.-S.

sprot, *sprota*, SPROUT], *n.* A small food-fish, *Clupea sprattus*, of the herring tribe; applied to the young of the herring and to other small fish. *v.i.* To fish for sprats. **spratter**, *n.*

sprattle (sprăt′ ėl) [Sc., cp. Swed. *sprattla*], *v.i.* To scramble, to struggle. *n.* A scramble, a struggle.

sprawl (sprawl) [A.-S. *spreawlian*, cp. Norw. *sprala*, Dan. *sprælle*], *v.i.* To lie or stretch out the body and limbs in a careless or awkward posture; to straggle, to be spread out in an irregular or ungraceful form. *v.t.* To open out or deploy (troops) irregularly. **sprawler**, *n.*

spray (1) (sprā) [cp. L.G. *sprei*, drizzle, M.Dut. *sprayen*, G. *sprühen*, to drizzle], *n.* Water or other liquid flying in small, fine drops; a medical disinfectant, or other liquid applied in fine particles with an atomiser. *v.t.* To throw or apply in the form of spray; to treat with a spray; (*Metal.*) to coat a surface by spraying with molten metal. **sprayer**, *n.* **sprayey** (1), *a.*

spray (2) (sprā) [etym. doubtful], *n.* A small branch or sprig, esp. with branchlets, leaves, flowers, etc., used as a decoration; an ornament resembling a sprig of leaves, flowers, etc. **sprayey** (2), *a.*

spread (spred) [A.-S. *sprǣdan*, cp. Dut. *spreiden*, G. *spreiten*], *v.t.* (*past & p.p.* **spread**) To extend in length and breadth by opening, unrolling, unfolding, flattening out, etc.; to scatter, to diffuse, to disseminate, to publish; to cover the surface of; (*fig.*) to display to the eye or mind. *v.i.* To be extended in length and breadth; to be scattered, diffused, or disseminated. *n.* The act of spreading; breadth, extent, compass, expansion; diffusion, dissemination; (*colloq.*) a meal set out, a feast. **spread-eagle**, *n.* (*Her.*) An eagle with wings and legs extended; (*colloq.*) a fowl split open lengthwise and broiled; (*Naut.*) a seaman lashed with outstretched limbs to the rigging for punishment. *v.t.* To fix (a person) for punishment thus. *a.* Bombastic; bombastically patriotic (with alln. to the eagle on U.S.A. coins). **spread-eagleism**, *n.* **spread-over**, *n.* A system for adjusting the legal hours of work to particular circumstances or needs. **spreader**, *n.*

spreagh (sprech) [var. of obs. *spreath*, Gael. *spréidh*], *n.* (*Sc.*) A foray, a raid; plunder, booty, esp. stolen cattle. **spreaghery**, *adv.*

spree (sprē) [etym. doubtful], *n.* A lively frolic, esp. with drinking. *v.i.* To go on the spree.

***sprent** (sprent) [p.p. of obs. *sprenge*, A.-S. *sprengan*, causal of *springan*, to SPRING], *a.* Sprinkled, besprent (with).

sprig (sprig) [etym. doubtful], *n.* A small branch, twig, or shoot; an ornament resembling this; a small headless nail or brad; an offshoot, a scion, a young fellow (*usu. disparagingly*). *v.t.* To ornament with sprigs; to drive small brads into. **spriggy**, *a.*

sprightly (sprīt′ li), *a.* Lively, spirited, gay, vivacious. ***spright** [SPRITE]. ***sprightful**, *a.* ***sprightfully**, *adv.* ***sprightless**, *a.* ***sprightliness**, *n.*

spring (1) (spring) [A.-S. *springan*, *sprincan*, cp. Dut. and G. *springen*, Icel. *springa*, to burst], *v.i.* (*past* **sprang**, *p.p.* **sprung**) To leap, to bound, to jump; to move suddenly by or as by the action of a spring; to rise, to come (up) from or as from a source, to arise, to originate, to appear, esp. unexpectedly; to warp, to split (of wood, etc.). *v.t.* To cause to move, fly, act, etc., suddenly by or as by releasing a spring; to cause (a mine) to explode; to cause (timber, etc.) to warp, crack, or become loose; to develop (a leak) thus (of a vessel). *n.* A leap; a backward movement as from release from tension, a recoil, a rebound; the starting of a plank, seam, leak, etc.; elastic force; an elastic body or structure, usu. of bent or coiled metal used to prevent jar, to convey motive power in a watch, etc.; (*fig.*) a source of energy, a cause of action, a motive; a natural issue of water from the earth, a fountain; (*fig.*) a source, an origin. **spring-balance**, *n.* A balance weighing objects by the tension of a spring. **spring-beam**, *n.* A beam of wide span without intermediate support; an elastic bar used as a spring in a tilt-hammer, jig-saw, etc. **spring-bed, -mattress**, *n.* One in which the mattress consists of a series of spiral springs set in a frame. **spring-board**, *n.* A springy board giving impetus in leaping, diving, etc. **spring-carriage, -cart**, *n.* One mounted on springs. **spring-gun**, *n.* A gun fired by the stumbling of a trespasser, etc., against a wire controlling its trigger. **spring-halt**, *n.* A convulsive movement of a horse's hind legs in walking. **spring-pole**, *n.* An elastic pole acting as a spring, in machinery, etc. **spring-tail**, *n.* An insect having bristles on its under side enabling it to leap. **spring tide:** A high tide occurring a day or two after the new or the full moon; (*poet.*) springtime. **spring washer**, *n.* (*Mach.*) A washer consisting of one or two coils of spiral-spring form, used to prevent nuts from becoming slack with vibration. **springer** (spring′ ėr), *n.* One who or that which springs; a spaniel used to rouse game; the springbok; the grampus; (*Arch.*) the part or stone where the curve of an arch begins; the rib of a groined roof; the lowest stone of a gable-coping. **springless**, *a.* **springlet**, *n.* **springy**, *a.* Elastic, like a spring. **springiness**, *n.*

spring (2) (spring) [as prec.], *n.* The first of the four seasons of the year, that preceding summer (about 21st March–22nd June); (*fig.*) the early part, youth. **springtime, springtide**, *n.* The season of spring. **springlike**, *a.*

***springal** (spring′ ål) [prec., F. *-ald*, O.H.G. *-wald*, cp. HERALD], *n.* A youth.

springbok (spring′ bok) [S. Afr. Dut. (SPRING, bok, BUCK (1))], *n.* A S. African gazelle, *Antilope euchore*, that leaps in play and when alarmed.

springe (sprinj) [M.E., var. of SPRING], *n.* A noose, a snare, usu. for small game. *v.t.* To catch in this.

springer, springless, springy, etc. [SPRING].

sprinkle (spring′ kėl) [formerly *sprenkle*, prob. freq. from A.-S. *sprengan*, causal of *springan*, to SPRING], *v.t.* and *i.* To scatter in small drops or particles. *n.* A sprinkling, a light shower.

sprinkler (spring′ klėr), *n.* That which sprinkles; a system of fire-extinction in which the fusing by heat of certain connexions in a system of pipes releases streams of water.

sprint (sprint) [prob. cogn. with SPURT (2)], *v.t.* and *i.* To run at one's topmost speed. *n.* A short run thus. **sprint-race**, *n.* **sprint-runner**, *n.* **sprinter**, *n.*

sprit (sprit) [A.-S. *sprēot*, pole, cogn. with SPROUT], *n.* (*Naut.*) A small spar set diagonally from the mast to the top outer corner of a sail. **spritsail**, *n.*

sprite (sprīt) [M.E., as SPIRIT], *n.* A fairy, an elf. **spritely**, etc. [SPRIGHTLY].

sprocket (sprok′ ėt) [etym. doubtful], *n.* One of a set of teeth on a wheel, etc., engaging with the links of a chain; a sprocket-wheel. **sprocket-wheel**, *n.* A wheel set with sprockets.

sprod (sprod) [etym. doubtful], *n.* (*prov.*) A salmon in its second year.

sprout (sprout) [A.-S. *sprūtan*, cp. Dut. *spruiten*, G. *spriessen*, cogn. with SPOUT and SPURT (2)], *v.i.* To shoot forth, to develop shoots, to germinate; to grow, like the shoots of plants. *v.t.* To cause to put forth sprouts or to grow. *n.* A new shoot on a plant; (*pl.*) Brussels sprouts.

spruce (1) (sproos) [prob. from O.F. *Pruce*, G. *Preussen*, Prussia (orig. applied to Prussian leather)], *a.* Neat, trim, smart. *v.t.* To smarten (*usu.* up). **sprucely**, *adv.* **spruceness**, *n.*

spruce (2) (sproos) [G. *sprossen*, sprouts (in *sprossenfichte*, sprouts-fir, or fir from which sprouts-beer was brewed), assim. to prec.], *n.* Spruce-fir. **spruce-beer**, *n.* A fermented liquor made from the leaves and small branches of the spruce-fir. **spruce-fir**, *n.* A pine of the genus *Picea*.

sprue (1) (sproo) [etym. doubtful], *n.* A hole or

channel through which molten metal is poured into a mould; the corresponding projection in a casting.

sprue (2) (sproo) [Dut. *spruw*, thrush], *n.* (*Path.*) A tropical disease characterized by diarrhœa, anæmia, and wasting.

sprug (sprŭg) [etym. doubtful], *n.* (*prov.*) The common sparrow.

spruik (sprook), *v.i.* (*Austral. colloq.*) To speak in public, to make a speech. **spruiker,** *n.* A barker at a fair-booth.

spruit (sproo′ it) [S. Afr. Dut.], *n.* (*S. Afr.*) A small tributary stream, esp. one dry in summer.

sprung, *p.p.* [SPRING].

spry (sprī) [cp. Swed. dial. *sprygg*], *a.* Active, lively; sharp, wideawake.

spud (spŭd) [M.E. *spudde*, cp. Dan. *spyd*, M.Dan. *spjud*, Swed. *spjut*, Icel. *spjōt*], *n.* A short spade-like tool for cutting up weeds by the root, etc.; a short and thick person or thing; (*colloq.*) a potato. *v.t.* To dig (up) or clear (out) with a spud. **spuddy,** *a.*

spue [SPEW].

spulyie, spulzie, spuilzie (spul′ yė) [Sc. var. of SPOIL].

spume (spūm) [L. *spūma*], *n.* Froth, foam. *v.i.* To froth, to foam. **spumescent, spumiferous** (-mif′ ėr ŭs), **spumous, spumy,** *a.* **spumescence, spuminess,** *n.*

spun (spŭn) [SPIN]. **spun glass,** *n.* Glass that is spun, when heated, into filaments that retain their pliancy when cold. **spun gold, silver,** *n.* Gold or silver thread spun for weaving. **spun silk,** *n.* Yarn made from silk waste and spun like woollen yarn.

spun yarn, *n.* (*Naut.*) Line made of twisted rope-yarns.

spunge, spunging-house, etc. [SPONGE].

spunk (spŭngk) [Ir. *sponc*, tinder, L. and Gr. *spongia*, SPONGE], *n.* Mettle, spirit, pluck; touch-wood, tinder; (*Sc.*) a match. **spunky,** *a.*

spur (spĕr) [A.-S. *spura*, *spora*, cp. Dut. *spoor*, G. *sporn*, Icel. *spori*, Dan. *spore*], *n.* An instrument worn on a horseman's heel having a sharp or blunt point or a rowel; (*fig.*) instigation, incentive, stimulus, impulse; a spur-shaped projection, attachment, or part, as the pointed projection on a cock's leg, or a steel point or sheath fastened on this in cock-fighting; the largest root of a tree; a ridge or buttress projecting from a mountain range; a wall crossing a rampart and connecting it to an interior work; a curved timber used in shipbuilding, etc.; the projecting part of a ship's ram; a tubular projection on the columbine and other flowers; a climbing-iron, etc. *v.t.* (*past & p.p.* **spurred**) To prick with spurs; to urge, to incite; to furnish with spurs. *v.i.* To ride hard. **to win one's spurs:** To gain knighthood; (*fig.*) to achieve distinction, to make oneself famous. **spur-gall,** *v.t.* To wound or gall with spurring; *n.* A place galled by the spur. **spur-royal,** *n.* A gold coin of James I having on the reverse a sun with rays, somewhat resembling a rowel. **spur-wheel,** *n.* A gear-wheel with radial teeth projecting from the rim. **spurless,** *a.* **spurrer,** *n.* **spurrier** (spŭr′ i ėr), *n.* One who makes spurs.

spurge (spĕrj) [A.-F., from O.F. *espurge*, from *espurger*, L. *expurgāre*, to EXPURGATE], *n.* A plant of the genus *Euphorbia* with milky and usu. acrid juice. **spurge-laurel,** *n.* A bushy evergreen shrub, *Daphne laureola*, with poisonous berries.

spurious (spūr′ i ŭs) [L. *spurius*], *a.* Not genuine, not proceeding from the true or pretended source, false, counterfeit; (*Biol.*) like an organ in form or function but physiologically or morphologically different. **spuriously,** *adv.* **spuriousness,** *n.*

spurling-line (spĕr′ ling līn) [etym. doubtful], *n.* (*Naut.*) A line from the steering-wheel to the tell-tale in the cabin.

spurn (spĕrn) [A.-S. *spornan*, *spurnan* (cp. Icel. *sperna*, also L. *spernere*), cogn. with SPUR], *v.t.* To thrust away, as with the foot; to reject with disdain; to treat with scorn. *v.i.* To show contempt (at). *n.* The act of spurning, scornful rejection. **spurner,** *n.*

spurrer, spurrier [SPUR].

spurry (spŭr′ i) [O.F. *spurrie*, late L. *spergula*, perh. from G.], *n.* A low annual weed of the genus *Spergule* of the family *Silenaceæ*.

spurt (1) (spĕrt) [M.E. *sprutten*, A.-S. *spryttan*, causal of *sprūtan*, to SPROUT], *v.i.* To gush out in a jet or sudden stream. *v.t.* To send or force out thus. *n.* A forcible gush or jet of liquid.

spurt (2) (spĕrt) [Icel. *sprettr*, cogn. with SPRINT], *n.* A sudden vigorous effort, esp. in racing. *v.i.* To make a spurt.

spurtle (1) (spĕr′ tėl), *v.t.* (*prov.*) To shoot or spurt in a scattering manner. ******n.* A small stream.

spurtle (2) (spĕr′ tėl) [etym. doubtful], *n.* (*Sc.*) A stirring-stick for porridge. **spurtle-blade,** *n.* A broadsword.

sputa, *pl.* [SPUTUM].

sputnik (spŭt′ nik, **spoot′** nik) [Rus., a travelling-companion], *n.* The name given by the Russians to an earth satellite.

sputter (spŭt′ ėr) [freq. of SPOUT], *v.i.* To emit saliva in scattered particles, to splutter; to speak in a jerky, incoherent, or excited way. *v.t.* To emit with a spluttering noise; to utter rapidly and indistinctly. *n.* Sputtering; confused, incoherent speech. **sputterer,** *n.* **sputteringly,** *adv.*

sputum (spū′ tŭm) [L., orig. p.p. or *spuere*, to spit], *n.* (*pl.* **-ta**) Spittle, saliva; (*Path.*) matter expectorated in various diseases.

spy (spī) [O.F. *espier*, to ESPY], *v.t.* To see, to detect, to discover, esp. by close observation; to explore or search (out) secretly; to discover thus. *v.i.* To act as a spy; to search narrowly, to pry. *n.* One sent secretly into an enemy's territory, esp. in disguise, to obtain information that may be useful in the conduct of hostilities; one who keeps a constant watch on the actions, movements, etc., of others. **spy-glass,** *n.* A small telescope. **spy-hole,** *n.* A peep-hole. ***spyism,** *n.*

squab (skwob) [cp. Swed. dial. *squabb*, loose, fat flesh, *squabba*, fat woman], *a.* Fat, short, squat. *adv.* With a heavy fall; plump. *n.* A short, fat person; a young pigeon, esp. unfledged; a stuffed cushion, a sofa padded throughout, an ottoman. *v.i.* To fall plump. **squab-pie,** *n.* A pie made of pigeon, apples, and onions. **squabby, *squabbish,** *a.*

squabble (skwob′ ėl) [cp. Swed. dial. *skvabbel*, dispute, *skvappa*, to chide, from *skvapp*, splash, imit.], *v.i.* To engage in a petty or noisy quarrel, to wrangle. *v.t.* (*Print.*) To disarrange (composed type). *n.* A petty or noisy quarrel, a wrangle. **squabbler,** *n.*

squacco (skwăk′ ō) [imit. of cry], *n.* A small crested heron of S. Europe, Asia, and Africa.

squad (skwod) [M.F. *esquadre* (F. *escadre*), It. *squadra*, SQUARE], *n.* A small number of men assembled for drill or inspection; a small party of people. **awkward squad:** A body of recruits not sufficiently drilled to take their place in the regimental parade.

squadron (skwod′ rŏn) [M.F. *esquadron*, It. *squadrone*, as prec.], *n.* A main division of a cavalry regiment, usu. consisting of two troops containing 120–200 men; a detachment of several war-ships employed on some particular service; (*Aviat.*) an R.A.F. formation of two or more flights. *v.t.* To arrange in squadrons. **squadron-leader,** *n.* (*Aviat.*) A commissioned officer in the R.A.F. equivalent in rank to a major in the army.

squail (skwāl) [etym. doubtful], *n.* A disk used in the game of squails; (*pl.*) a game played on a small table or board with disks which are snapped from the edge towards a mark in the centre. *v.t.* To pelt with a stick, etc. *v.i.* To throw a stick, etc. (at). **squailer,** *n.* A stick with a leaded knob for squailing birds, etc. **squail-board,** *n.*

squalid (skwɔl′ id) [L. *squālidus*, from *squālēre*, to be stiff, dirty, etc.], *a.* Dirty, mean, poverty-stricken. **squalidity** (skwȧ lid′ i ti), **squalidness, squalor,** *n.* **squalidly,** *adv.*

squall (skwawl) [Icel. *skvala*, cp. Swed. *skvala*, to gush out noisily, Gael. *sjal*, loud cry], *v.i.* and *t.* To cry out; to scream discordantly. *n.* A harsh, discordant scream, esp. of a child; a sudden, violent gust or succession of gusts of wind, esp. accompanied by rain, hail, snow, etc. **squaller,** *n.* **squally** (1), *a.*

squally (2) (skwaw′ li) [prob. SCALL, -Y], *a.* Badly or irregularly woven; (*prov.*) having bare patches (of a field of corn, etc.).

squaloid (skwā′ loid) [L. *squalus*, a sea-fish, prob. a shark], *a.* Resembling a shark; belonging to the *Squalidæ*, a family of sharks. **squaliform,** *a.*

squalor [SQUALID].

squama (skwā′ mȧ) [L.], *n.* (*pl.* **-mæ**) (*Nat. Hist.*) A scale or scale-like structure, feather, part of bone, etc. **Squamata,** *n.* (*Zool.*) An order of *Reptilia* which includes snakes and lizards. **squami-, squamo-,** *comb. form.* **squamiform, squamoid, squamose, squamous,** *a.* **squamiferous** (skwȧ mif′ ėr ŭs), **squamigerous** (-mij′ ėr ŭs), *a.* Scale-bearing. **squamulose,** *a.* Covered with small scales.

squander (skwon′ dėr) [prob. nasalized form of prov. *squatter*, *swatter*, Dan. *sqvatte*, to splash, cp. Icel. *skvetta*, to squirt], *v.t.* To spend wastefully; to dissipate by foolish prodigality. **squanderer,** *n.* **squanderingly,** *adv.*

square (skwâr) [O.F. *esquarre*, from p.p. of non-extant late L. *exquadrāre* (EX-, L. *quadrāre*, to make square, from *quadrus*, four-cornered, cogn. with *quatuor*, four)], *n.* A rectangle with equal sides; any surface, area, object, part, etc., of this shape; a rectangular division of a chess- or draught-board, window-pane, etc.; an open quadrilateral area surrounded by buildings, usu. laid out with trees, flower-beds, lawns, etc.; a block of buildings bounded by four streets; a body of infantry formed into a rectangular figure; an arrangement of words, figures, etc., with as many rows as columns (usu. reading alike perpendicularly or across); an L- or T-shaped instrument for laying out and testing right angles; (*fig.*) order, regularity, proper proportion; equity, fairness, honesty; the product of a quantity multiplied by itself; an area of 100 square feet as a measure of flooring, roofing, etc.; (*slang*) a conventional, old-fashioned person, one out of keeping with modern ways of thought. *a.* Having four equal sides and four right angles; rectangular; at right angles (to); broad with straight sides or outlines; (*fig.*) just, fair, honest; in proper order; evenly balanced, even, settled, complete, thorough, absolute; full, satisfactory *adv.* Squarely. *v.t.* To make square or rectangular; (*fig.*) to adjust, to bring into conformity (with or to); to make even, to settle, to pay; (*colloq.*) to bribe, to gain over thus; (*Math.*) to multiply (a number or quantity) by itself; (*Naut.*) to lay (a vessel's yards, etc.) at right angles to the plane of the keel. *v.i.* To be at right angles (with); (*fig.*) to conform precisely, to agree, to harmonize; to put oneself in an attitude for boxing. **on the square:** At right angles; fairly, honestly; descriptive of a Freemason. **to square off:** (*Austral.*) To apologise, to make excuses. **to square up:** To settle an account. **to square the circle:** To construct geometrically a square equal in area to a given circle; hence, to attempt impossibilities. **square dinkum:** (*Austral. colloq.*) Absolutely honestly. **square foot, inch,** etc.: One foot, inch, etc., squared, *i.e.* the area of a square, each side of which measures a foot, inch, etc. **square leg,** *n.* (*Cricket*) A fielder standing about 20 yards directly behind a batsman as he receives the bowling. **square measure:** A system of measures expressed in square feet, etc. **square number:** The product of a number multiplied by itself. **square-rigged,** *a.* Having the principal sails extended by horizontal yards suspended from the middle. **square root:** The quantity that, multiplied by itself, will produce the given quantity. **square-sail,** *n.* A four-cornered sail set on a yard, esp. on a fore-and-aft rigged vessel. **square-shouldered,** *a.* Having the shoulders held well up and back, opp. to sloping and round shoulders. **square-toed,** *a.* Having the toes (of the shoes) square; (*fig.*) precise. prim. **square-toes,** *n.* (*fig.*) A formal, precise person. **squarely,** *adv.* **squareness,** *n.* **squarer,** *n.* One who squares. **squarish,** *a.*

squarrose, -rous (skwor′ ōs, -ŭs) [said to be from late L. *squarrōsus*, perh. *squāmōsus* (SQUAMA, -OSE)], *a.* Rough with projecting scale-like processes.

squarson (skwar′ sŏn) [comb. of SQUIRE and PARSON], *n.* (*Facet.*) A clergyman who is also a landed proprietor.

squash (1) (skwosh) [prob. from M.E. *squachen*, O.F. *esquacher* (EX-, late L. *coacticāre*, from *coactus*, p.p. of *cōgere*, to drive together)], *v.t.* To crush, to press flat or into a pulp. *v.i.* To be crushed or beaten to pulp by a fall; to squeeze (into). *n.* A thing or mass crushed or squeezed to pulp; the fall of a soft body; the sound of this; (*fig.*) a throng, a squeeze; a game with rackets and balls played in a court. **squasher,** *n.* **squashy,** *a.* **squashiness,** *n.*

squash (2) (skwosh) [N. Am. Ind. *esquash*, green, raw], *n.* The fleshy, edible, gourd-like fruit of trailing plants of the genus *Cucurbita*; (*Am.*) a vegetable marrow.

squat (skwot) [O.F. *esquatir*, to flatten, crush (EX-, *quatir*, as SQUASH (1))], *v.i.* (*past & p.p.* **squatted**) To sit down or crouch on the haunches; to crouch, to cower (chiefly of animals); (*colloq.*) to sit; to settle on land without any title. *v.t.* To put (oneself) in a crouching posture; (*prov.*) to squash. *a.* Short, thick, dumpy; in a squatting position. *n.* A squatting posture; a squat person. **squattocracy,** *n.* (*Austral.*) Squatters as a corporate body.

squatter (skwot′ ėr), *n.* One who sits on his haunches; one who settles without a title, esp. on public or uncultivated land; (*Austral.*) one who leases land for pasturage from the Government, a stock-owner.

squaw (skwaw) [N. Am. Ind. *squa*], *n.* A N. American Indian woman or wife.

squawk (skwawk) [var. of foll.], *v.i.* To utter a loud, harsh cry. *n.* Such a cry.

squeak (skwēk) [cp. M.Swed. *sqwæka*, cp. Norw. *skvaka*, Icel. *skvakka*], *v.i.* To utter a sharp, shrill, usu. short cry; to break silence or secrecy. *v.t.* To utter with a squeak. *n.* A sharp, shrill sound; (*colloq.*) a narrow escape or margin, a close shave. **squeaker,** *n.* One who or that which squeaks; a young bird, esp. a pigeon; (*slang*) an informer, a traitor. **squeaky,** *a.* **squeakily,** *adv.*

squeal (skwēl) [M.Swed. *sqwæla*, freq. as prec.], *v.i.* To utter a more or less prolonged shrill cry as in pain, etc.; (*fig.*) to turn informer. *n.* A more or less prolonged shrill cry. **squealer,** *n.*

squeamish (skwē′ mish) [M.E. *skeymous*, A.-F. *escoymous*, etym. doubtful], *a.* Easily nauseated, disgusted or offended; fastidious, finical, hypercritical, excessively nice, prudish, unduly scrupulous. **squeamishly,** *adv.* **squeamishness,** *n.*

squeegee (skwē′ jē) [formerly *squilgee*, etym. doubtful], *n.* An implement, composed of a strip of rubber fixed to a handle for cleaning wet pavements, etc.; a similar implement, usu. with a rubber roller, used by photographers for squeezing and flattening. *v.t.* To sweep, smooth, etc., with a squeegee.

squeeze (skwēz) [A.-S. *cwīesan*, cp. L.G. *quōsen*], *v.t.* To press closely, esp. between two bodies or with the hand, so as to force juice, etc., out; to extract (juice, etc.) thus; to force (oneself, etc., into, out of, etc.); to extort money, etc., from, to harass by exactions; to exact (money, etc.) by extortion, etc.; to put pressure on, to oppress, to constrain by arbitrary or illegitimate means. *v.i.* To press, to push, to force one's way (into, through, etc.). *n.* The act of squeezing; pressure; a close embrace; a throng, a crush. **squeezable,** *a.* **squeezability** (bil' i ti), *n.* **squeezer,** *n.* One who or that which squeezes; (*pl.*) playing-cards marked at the top right-hand corner with the value to save spreading out in the hand.

squelch (skwelch) [perh. rel. to QUELL], *v.t.* To crush; (*fig.*) to silence, to extinguish, to discomfit; (*colloq.*) to make a noise as of treading in wet snow. *n.* A heavy blow; (*fig.*) a crushing retort; (*colloq.*) a squelching noise.

squib (skwib) [perh. from M.E. *squippen, swippen,* to move swiftly, Icel. *svipa,* to flash, cogn. with SWEEP], *n.* A firework emitting sparks and exploding with a bang, usu. thrown by the hand; a tube containing gunpowder for igniting a blasting-charge; a petty lampoon; (*Austral.*) a coward, a sneak. *v.i.* To write squibs. *v.t.* To satirize in a squib.

squid (skwid) [cp. Swed. dial. *skvitta,* Icel. *skvetta,* to squirt], *n.* A small kind of cuttle-fish; an artificial bait roughly imitating a fish. *v.i.* To fish with this.

squiffy (skwif' i) [onomat.], *a.* (*slang*) Slightly drunk.

squiggle (skwig' ėl) [prob. imit.], *v.i.* To squirm, to wriggle; (*prov.*) to shake a fluid about in the mouth; to make wriggly lines.

squill (skwil) [M.F. *squille,* L. *squilla,* Gr. *skilla*], *n.* A liliaceous plant, *Scilla maritima,* resembling the bluebell; the sliced bulb of this used as an expectorant, diuretic, etc. **squillitic** (-lit' ik), *a.*

squinancy-wort (skwin' ȧn si wĕrt) [obs. *squinancy,* var. of QUINSY, WORT], *n.* The small woodruff, *Asperula cynanchica.*

squinch (skwinch) [var. of SCONCE], *n.* An arch across the internal angle of a square tower to support the side of an octagonal spire, etc.

***squinny** (skwin' i) [SQUINT], *v.i.* (*Shak.*) To squint.

squint (skwint) [etym. uncertain], *v.i.* To look with the eyes differently directed; to be affected with strabismus; to look obliquely; to look with eyes half shut. *v.t.* To cause to squint; to shut or contract (the eyes) quickly; to keep (the eyes) half shut. *a.* Looking obliquely; looking askance. *n.* An affection of the eyes causing the axes to be differently directed, strabismus; a stealthy look, a sidelong glance; (*colloq.*) a look; a leaning (towards); a hagioscope. **squint-eye,** *n.* **squint-eyed,** *a.* **squinter,** *n.* **squintingly,** *adv.*

squire (skwīr) [ESQUIRE], *n.* A country gentleman, esp. the chief landowner in a place; a beau, a gallant; (*Hist.*) an attendant on a knight. *v.t.* To attend as a squire, to escort (a woman). **squirearchy,** *n.* Landed proprietors collectively; the political influence of, or government by these. **squirearch,** *n.* **squirearchal, -archical** (-ar' ki kȧl), *a.* **squireen** (skwī rēn'), *n.* A petty squire, esp. in Ireland. **squirehood, squireship,** *n.*

squirm (skwĕrm) [perh. from M.E. *quirr,* var. of WHIRR], *v.i.* To wriggle, to writhe about; to climb (up) by wriggling; (*fig.*) to display discomfort, embarrassment, etc. *n.* A wriggling movement; (*Naut.*) a twist in a rope.

squirrel (skwir' ėl) [O.F. *escuirel, escurel,* late L. *scūrellus,* dim. of *sciūrus,* Gr. *skiouros,* perh. shadow-tail (*skia,* shadow, *oura,* tail)], *n.* A brown or grey bushy-tailed rodent quadruped living chiefly in trees; a prairie-dog, also called barking-squirrel. **squirrel-fish,** *n.* A W. Indian and N. American seafish. **squirrel-tail,** *n.* Grass allied to barley with long hair-like awns.

squirt (skwĕrt) [cp. L.G. *swirtjen,* cogn. with WHIRR], *v.t.* To eject in a jet or stream from a narrow orifice. *v.i.* To be so ejected (of liquid). *n.* A syringe; a jet (of liquid); (*colloq.*) a pert, conceited fellow. **squirter,** *n.*

squitch-grass [QUITCH-GRASS].

stab (stăb) [M.E. *stabbe,* cp. Swed. dial. *stabbe,* Icel. *stabbi,* stump], *v.t.* (*past & p.p.* **stabbed**) To pierce or wound with a pointed weapon; to plunge (a weapon into); to inflict pain upon or to injure by slander, etc.; to roughen (a wall) with a pick to make it hold plaster. *v.i.* To aim a blow with or as with a pointed weapon (at). *n.* A blow or thrust with a pointed weapon; a wound inflicted thus; (*fig.*) a secret malicious injury. **stabber,** *n.* **stabbingly,** *adv.*

Stabat Mater (stā' băt mā' tėr, sta' băt ma' tėr) [L., the Mother was standing], *n.* A Latin hymn reciting the seven dolours of the Virgin at the Cross, beginning with these words; a musical setting of this.

stability (stȧ bil' i ti), *n.* The quality of being stable; (*Eng.*) the property of mechanical, electrical or aerodynamic systems that makes them return to a state of equilibrium after disturbance.

stabilize (stăb' i līz) [STABLE (1)], *v.t.* To make stable. **stabilization** (stăb i lī zā' shŭn), *n.* The act of stabilizing; (*Econ.*) the maintenance of purchasing power by fixing the value of currency in terms of gold.

stable (1) (stā' bėl) [O.F. *estable,* L. *stabilem,* nom. *-lis,* from *stāre,* to stand], *a.* Firmly fixed, established; not to be moved, shaken or destroyed easily; firm, resolute, constant, not changeable, unwavering; (*Chem.*) durable, not readily decomposed. **stable equilibrium,** *n.* (*Mech.*) The tendency of any body to recover equilibrium when moved. **stableness,** *n.* **stably,** *adv.*

stable (2) (stā' bėl) [O.F. *estable,* L. *stabilem,* as prec.], *n.* A building or part of a building for horses or (sometimes) cattle; (*fig.*) the race-horses belonging to a particular stable. *v.t.* To put or keep in a stable. *v.i.* To lodge in a stable (of horses, etc.). **stable-boy, -man,** *n.* One employed in a stable. **stable-companion,** *n.* (*fig.*) A person with whom one shares rooms, etc. **stabling,** *n.* Accommodation in a stable or stables.

***stablish** [ESTABLISH]. **stably** [STABLE (1)].

staccato (stȧ ka' tō) [It.], *adv.* (*Mus. direction*) With each note sharply distinct and detached, opp. to legato.

stachys (stăk' is) [L., from Gr. *stachus,* ear of corn], *n.* A genus of labiate plants with white or reddish spikes of flowers, also called the woundworts.

stack (stăk) [Icel. *stakkr,* Swed. *stack,* Dan. *stak*], *n.* A round or rectangular pile of corn in the sheaf, hay, straw, etc., usu. with a thatched top; a pile, a heap, esp. of an orderly kind; a pyramidal pile of rifles standing on their butts with the muzzles together; a measure of wood, 108 cubic ft.; (*colloq.*) a great quantity; a chimney, a funnel, a smoke-stack; a towering isolated mass of rock, esp. in Scotland, etc. *v.t.* To pile in a stack or stacks. **stack-stand,** *n.* A platform for supporting a stack of hay, etc. **stack-yard,** *n.* A yard for stacks.

stacte (stăk' tē) [L. and Gr., from *stazein,* to drip], *n.* One of the spices used by the ancient Jews in the preparation of incense.

stactometer (stăk tom' ė tėr) [Gr. *staktos,* as prec., -METER], *n.* A tube for measuring a liquid in drops.

***staddle** (stădl) [A.-S. *stathol,* foundation, base, cp. G. *stadel*], *n.* A prop or support; a small tree left standing; a stack-stand. *v.t.* To leave the staddles in (a wood that is being cut down). **staddle-roof,** *n.* A covering for a stack.

***stade** [STADIUM].

stadia (stā' di ȧ) [late L., from foll.], *n.* A temporary surveying-station; an instrument, usu. comprising a graduated rod and a telescope, for measuring distances. **stadiometer** (-om' ė tėr), *n.* A self-recording theodolite.

stadium (stā' di ŭm) [L., from Gr. *stadion,* from *sta-,* root of *histanai,* to stand], *n.* (*pl.* **-dia**) (*Gr. Ant.*) A measure of about 202 yds., the course for foot-races at Olympia; an enclosure, usu. an amphitheatre, where games can be watched by a large number of spectators; (*Med.*) a stage in a disease.

Stadtholder (stat'-, stăt' hōl dėr) [Dut. *stadhouder* (STEAD, HOLDER)], *n.* (*Hist.*) A viceroy, governor, or deputy-governor of a province or town in the Netherlands; the chief magistrate of the United Provinces. **Stadtholderate, -ship,** *n.*

staff (1) (staf) [A.-S. *stæf*, cp. Dut. *staf*, G. *stab*, Icel. *stafr*], *n.* (*pl.* **staffs,** stafs, **staves,** stāvz) A stick carried for help in walking, etc., or as a weapon; (*fig.*) support; a stick, rod, pole, etc., borne as an emblem of office or authority; a shaft, pole, etc., forming a support or handle, as a flagstaff; a rod used in surveying, etc., a cross-staff, a Jacob's staff; a rod-like appliance, instrument, part, fitting, etc.; (*Mil.*) a body of officers assisting an officer in command whose duties are concerned with a regiment or an army as a whole; a body of persons working under a manager, editor, etc.; (*Mus.*) a set of five parallel lines and spaces on or between which notes are written representing the pitch of tones. **staff-officer, -sergeant,** etc., *n.* One serving on a staff. **staff-notation,** *n.* (*Mus.*) Notation by the staff as dist. from sol-fa. **staff-work,** *n.* Organization.

staff (2) (staf) [perh. var. of STUFF], *n.* A composition of plaster of Paris, cement, etc., used as building-material, etc., esp. in temporary structures.

stag (stăg) [A.-S. *stagga*, Icel. *steggr*, he-bird, male animal], *n.* The male of the red deer, esp. from his fifth year; the male of other large deer; a bull castrated when nearly full-grown; (*slang*) an informer; (*Stock Exch.*) one who stags. *v.t.* (*slang*) To watch closely, to spy. *v.i.* (*Stock Exch.*) To apply for or to purchase stock or shares in a new issue solely with the object of selling at a profit immediately on allotment. **stag-beetle,** *n.* A beetle with large mandibles, in the male branching like stag's horns. **stag-evil,** *n.* Lockjaw in horses. **staghound,** *n.* A large hound used for hunting stags. **stag party,** *n.* (*colloq.*) A party for men only.

stage (stāj) [O.F. *estage* (F. *étage*), prob. through a L. *staticum*, from *stāre*, to stand], *n.* An elevated platform, as a scaffold for workmen erecting or repairing a building, a shelf on which objects may be exhibited or examined, etc.; a raised platform on which theatrical performances take place; (*fig.*) the theatre, the drama, the profession of an actor, actors collectively; (*fig.*) a scene of action; one of a series of regular stopping-places on a route; the distance between two such stations; a definite portion of a journey; (*fig.*) a point in a progressive movement, a definite period in development; a stage-coach. *v.t.* To put on the stage. **to go on the stage:** To become a professional actor or actress. **stage-coach,** *n.* A coach running regularly by stages for conveyance of parcels, passengers, etc. **stage-coachman, -driver,** *n.* **stage-craft,** *n.* The art of writing or staging plays. **stage-direction,** *n.* An instruction respecting the movements, etc., of actors in a play. **stage-door,** *n.* A door to a theatre for the use of actors, workmen, etc. **stage-effect,** *n.* Theatrical effect (*lit. and fig.*). **stage-fever,** *n.* Intense desire to become an actor. **stage-fright,** *n.* A fit of nervousness in facing an audience. **stage-manager,** *n.* One who superintends the scenic effects, etc., of a play. **stage-struck,** *a.* Smitten with stage-fever. **stage-whisper,** *n.* An audible aside; (*fig.*) something meant for the ears of others than the person ostensibly addressed. **stager,** *n.* A person of long experience in anything. **staging,** *n.* A scaffolding; the driving or running of stage-coaches; the act of putting a play on the stage. **stagy,** *a.* Theatrical, unreal. **staginess,** *n.*

staggard (stăg' ȧrd), *n.* A stag four years old.

stagger (stăg' ėr) [M.E. *stakeren*, Icel. *stakra*, freq. of *staka*, to push], *v.i.* To move unsteadily in standing or walking, to totter, to reel; to begin to give way, to waver, to hesitate. *v.t.* To cause to reel; to cause to hesitate; to shock with surprise, etc.; to set (the spokes of a wheel) alternately leaning in and out; to overlap, to place zig-zag; (of cross-roads, etc.) to site so as not to meet opposite one another; (of working hours, etc.) to arrange so as not to coincide with others. *n.* A staggering movement; (*pl.*) a disease affecting the brain and spinal cord in horses and cattle characterized by vertigo, etc.; (*fig.*) giddiness, vertigo. **staggerer,** *n.* One who staggers; a staggering blow, argument, etc. **staggeringly,** *adv.*

stagnate (stăg' nāt) [L. *stagnātus*, p.p. of *stagnāre*, from *stagnum*, pool], *v.i.* To cease to flow; to be without current, to be motionless; (*fig.*) to cease to be active, to become sluggish, inert, or dull. **stagnant** (-nȧnt), *a.* **stagnancy,** *n.* **stagnantly,** *adv.* **stagnation,** *n.*

staid (stād) [STAYED, p.p. of STAY (1)], *a.* Sober, steady, sedate. **staidly,** *adv.* **staidness,** *n.*

stain (stān) [M.E. *steinen*, as DISTAIN], *v.t.* To discolour, to soil, to sully; (*fig.*) to tarnish, to blemish (a reputation, etc.); to colour by means of a dye or other agent acting chemically or by absorption, opp. to painting; to impregnate (an object for microscopic examination) with a colouring matter affecting certain parts more powerfully than others; to dim, to obscure. *v.i.* To cause discoloration; to take stains. *n.* A discoloration; a spot of a distinct colour; a blot, a blemish. **stainable,** *a.* **stainer,** *n.* **stainless,** *a.* Without a stain, immaculate. **stainless steel,** *n.* A rustless alloy steel used for cutlery. **stainlessly,** *adv.* **stainlessness,** *n.*

stair (stâr) [A.-S. *stǣger* (cp. Dut. *steiger*, G. *steg*, Icel. *stigi*), from Teut. *steigan*, to climb, cogn. with Gr. *steichein*, to ascend, to go], *n.* One of a series of steps, esp. for ascending from one story of a house to another; a flight of stairs (*usu. in pl.*). **backstairs** [BACK]. **below stairs:** In the basement; in the servants' quarters or relating to their affairs. **flight** or **pair of stairs:** A set of stairs, as from one landing to another. **stair-carpet,** *n.* A narrow carpet used to cover the stairs. **staircase,** *n.* A flight of stairs with banisters, supporting structure, etc. **moving staircase** [ESCALATOR]. **stair-rod,** *n.* A rod for fastening a stair-carpet between two stairs. **stairway,** *n.* A staircase.

staith (stāth) [A.-S. *stæth*, bank, shore], *n.* (*prov.*) A landing-stage, a wharf, esp. a staging laid with rails from which coal-wagons, etc., may discharge their loads into vessels.

stake (stāk) [A.-S. *staca* (cp. M.Dut. and Swed. *stake*, Icel. *stjaki*, Dan. *stage*), cogn. with STACK], *n.* A stick or post pointed at one end and set in the ground, as a support, part of railing, etc.; a post to which persons condemned to death by burning were bound; (*fig.*) martyrdom; a prop or upright part or fitting for supporting a machine, etc., a tinsmith's small anvil that may be set in a bench; anything, esp. money, wagered on a competition or contingent event, esp. deposited with a stake-holder; (*pl.*) money competed for in a race, etc.; (*pl.*) a race for this; (*fig.*) anything contended for. *v.t.* To fasten, support, or protect with a stake or stakes; to mark (out or off) with stakes; to wager, to venture (on an event, etc.). **at stake:** In hazard, at issue, in question. **stake-holder,** *n.* One who holds the stakes when a wager is made. **stake-net,** *n.* A fishing-net stretched on stakes.

Stakhanovism (stăk hăn' ō vizm), *n.* A U.S.S.R. system for increasing production by utilizing each worker's initiative.

stalactite (stăl' ȧk-, stȧ lăk'-, -tīt) [F. (Gr. *stalaktos*, dripping, from *stalazein*, to drip)], *n.* A deposit of carbonate of lime, hanging from the roof of a cave, etc., in the form of a thin tube or a large icicle, produced by the evaporation of percolating water. **stalactic, stalactiform, stalactitic** (-tit' ik), *a.*

stalagmite (stăl' ȧg-, stȧ lăg'-, -mīt) [F. (Gr. *stalagmos*, dripping, as prec.)], *n.* A deposit of the same material as in a stalactite on the floor or walls of a cave. **stalagmitic** (-mit′ ik), *a.* **stalagmitically,** *adv.*

stale (1) (stāl) [O.F. *estaler*, to make water, from Teut., cogn. with STALL (1)], *a.* Not fresh, dry, musty; vapid or tasteless from being kept too long; (*fig.*) trite; (*Athletics*) in poor condition from overtraining. *n.* Urine of horses, etc. *v.t.* To make stale. *v.i.* To urinate (of horses). **stalely,** *adv.* **staleness,** *n.*

***stale** (2) (stāl) [A.-S. *stalu*, theft, see STEAL], *n.* A dupe; a laughing-stock.

stalemate (stāl māt) [perh. from M.E. *stal*, O.F. *estal*, a fixed position, cp. STALL (1), MATE (1)], *n.* (*Chess*) The position when the king, not actually in check, is unable to move without placing himself in check, and there is no other piece that can be moved. *v.t.* To subject to a stalemate; (*fig.*) to bring to a standstill.

stalk (1) (stawk) [A.-S. *stealcan*, perh. with feet uplifted, cp. *stealc*, high], *v.i.* To walk with high, pompous steps; to go stealthily, to steal (up to game) under cover. *v.t.* To pursue stealthily by the use of cover. *n.* The act of stalking game; a pompous gait. **stalker,** *n.* **stalking-horse,** *n.* A horse or figure like a horse behind which a sportsman conceals himself; (*fig.*) a mask, a pretence.

stalk (2) (stawk) [M.E. *stalke*, dim. of *stale*, A.-S. *stæla*, cp. Dut. *steel*], *n.* The stem or axis of a plant; the peduncle of a flower; the supporting peduncle of a barnacle, etc.; the stem of a wine-glass, etc.; a high factory chimney. **stalk-eyed,** *a.* Having the eyes set on peduncles (as certain crustaceans). **stalked,** *a.* (*usu. in comb.* as *thin-stalked*). **stalkless,** *a.* **stalklet,** *n.* **stalky,** *a.*

stall (1) (stawl) [A.-S. *steal*, *steall* (cp. Dut. *stal*, G. *stall*, Icel. *stallr*, O.H.G. *stal*), cogn. with STABLE (2), STEAD], *n.* A division or compartment for a horse, ox, etc., in a stable or byre; a booth or shed in a market, street, etc., or a bench, table, etc., in a building for the sale of goods; a finger-stall; a seat in the choir of a large church, enclosed at the back and sides and usu. canopied, for a clergyman, chorister, etc.; (*fig.*) a canonry, etc.; one of a set of seats in a theatre, usu. in the front part of the pit. *v.t.* To put or keep in a stall (esp. cattle for fattening); to furnish with stalls. *v.i.* To stick fast (in mire, etc.); (*Motor.*) to cease working suddenly (of the engine); (*Aviat.*) to allow an aeroplane to lose its forward impetus and thus deprive the planes of sustaining power if there is not airspace enough underneath it for recovering lift; to play for time; to be evasive. **to stall off:** To stave off. **to stall for time:** To postpone or hold off as long as possible. **stall-feed,** *v.t.* To fatten in a stall. **stallage,** *n.* The right of erecting a stall in a fair; the rent for this; accommodation for or by stalls.

stall (2) (stawl) [var. of STALE (2)], *n.* The confederate of a thief or pickpocket who diverts attention while the theft is committed and helps the thief to escape.

stallion (stăl′ yŏn) [O.F. *estalon* (F. *étalon*), cogn. with STALL (1)], *n.* An uncastrated male horse, esp. one kept for breeding purposes.

stalwart (stawl′ wĕrt) [A.-S. *stælwyrthe* (*stathol*, foundation, WORTH)], *a.* Strong in build, sturdy; stout, resolute. **stalwartly,** *adv.* **stalwartness,** *n.*

stamen (stā′ mĕn) [L. *stāmen -minis*, orig. warp in upright loom, from *stāre*, to stand], *n.* (*Bot.*) The pollen-bearing male organ of a flower. **stamened,** *a.* **staminal** (stăm′ i năl), **stamineous** (stă min′ ē ŭs), *a.* Of or pertaining to stamens. **staminate** (stăm′ i nāt), *a.* Having stamens but no pistils; having stamens. **staminiferous** (stăm i nif′ ĕr ŭs), *a.*

stamina (stăm′ i nă) [L., pl. of prec.], *n.* Strength, vigour, power of endurance.

staminal, etc. [STAMEN].

stammel (stăm′ ĕl) [prob. from obs. *stamin*, O.F. *estamine* (F. *étamine*), L. STAMEN], *n.* (*prov.*) A woollen cloth of a dull red colour; this colour.

stammer (stăm′ ĕr) [M.E. *stameren* (cp. A.-S. *stamm*, *stamor*, stammering, Dut. *stameren*, G. *stammern*), ult. from *sta-*, to stand], *v.i.* and *t.* To speak with halting articulation, nervous hesitation, or repetitions of the same sound; to stutter. *n.* A stammering utterance or vocal affection. **stammerer,** *n.* **stammeringly,** *adv.*

stamp (stămp) [A.-S. *stempen* (cp. Dut. *stampen*, G. *stampfen*, Icel. *stappa*, Swed. *stampa*, also Gr. *stembein*)], *v.t.* To make a mark or impression upon with a dye, pattern, etc.; to affix a stamp to; to impress (initials, etc.) upon something; (*fig.*) to impress deeply (on the memory, etc.); to bring (the foot, etc.) down heavily (*Am.* to stomp); to extinguish thus, to put (out); to crush by downward force or pressure; (*fig.*) to destroy. *v.i.* To strike the foot forcibly on the ground. *n.* The act of stamping; an instrument for stamping marks, designs, etc.; the mark made by this; an official mark set on things chargeable with some duty or tax, to show that such is paid; a small piece of paper officially stamped for affixing to letters, receipts, etc.; a label, imprint, or other mark certifying ownership, quality, genuineness, etc.; (*fig.*) distinguishing mark, impress, kind, sort; a downward blow with the foot; a blow with a stamping-machine; the block for crushing ore in a stamp-mill. **Stamp Act:** An Act dealing with stamp-duties, esp. that of 1765 imposing a duty on the American colonies, one of the causes of the Revolution. **stamp album,** *n.* A book to hold a postage-stamp collection. **stamp battery,** *n.* (*Mining*) A machine for crushing gold ores. **stamp-collector,** *n.* One who collects specimens of postage stamps; a collector of stamp-duties. **stamp-duty,** *n.* A duty imposed on certain legal documents. **stamp-mill,** *n.* A mill for crushing ore, fruit, etc. **stamper,** *n.*

stampede (stăm pēd′) [Sp. and Port. *estampido*, from *estampar*, to STAMP], *n.* A sudden fright causing horses or cattle to scatter and run; a sudden panic and flight (of troops, etc.); (*fig.*) any impulsive unreasoning movement on the part of a large number of persons. *v.i.* To take part in a stampede. *v.t.* To cause to do this.

stance (stăns) [O.F. *estance*, late L. *stantia*, see STANZA], *n.* (*Golf*) The position taken for a stroke; (*Sc.*) place, site, station.

stanch (stanch) [O.F. *estancher*, late L. *stancāre*, L. *stagnāre*, to STAGNATE], *v.t.* To prevent or stop the flow of (blood, etc., from a wound). **v.i.* To stop flowing. *a.* Loyal, constant, trustworthy (in this sense often spelt **staunch**). **stancher,** *n.* **stanchless,** *a.* **stanchly,** *adv.* **stanchness,** *n.*

stanchion (stăn′-, stan′ shŏn) [O.North.F. *estanchon* (F. *étançon*), dim. of *estance*, STANCE], *n.* A prop, post, pillar, etc., forming a support or part of a structure; a vertical bar or pair of bars for confining cattle in a stall. *v.t.* To fasten with a stanchion.

stand (stănd) [A.-S. *standan*, *stondan*, cp. Dut. *staan*, G. *stehen*, Icel. *standa*, Swed. *stā*, also L. *stāre*, Gr. *histanai*], *v.i.* (*past & p.p.* **stood, stud**) To be upon the feet; to be or become or remain erect; to be in a specified state, attitude, position, situation, rank, etc.; to have a specified height or stature; to be or remain in a stationary position, to cease from motion, to stop, to be or remain immovable, not to give way; to remain firm or constant, to abide, to endure, to persist; to hold good, to remain valid or unimpaired; to be motionless, to lie stagnant; to move into a specified position and remain in it; to hold a specified course, to steer; to point (of a setter); to become a candidate. *v.t.* To set in an erect or a specified position; to endure, to sustain, without giving way or complaining; to undergo (a trial, etc.); (*colloq.*) to sustain the expense of (a drink, etc.). *n.* A cessation of motion or progress, a stop, a halt, a state of inactivity, a standstill; the act of standing, esp. with firmness, in a fixed or stationary position, place, or station; resistance, etc.; a small frame or piece of furniture for supporting anything; a place in a town where cabs, etc., stand for hire; an erection for spectators to stand or sit on. **it stands to reason:** It is logically manifest (that). **stand of arms:** A complete outfit of arms and ammunition for one man. **to be at a stand:** To be perplexed; to be in doubt as to further progress. **to stand by:** To be present, to be a bystander; to look on passively; to uphold, to support firmly; to abide by; to stand near in readiness to act promptly as directed. **stand-by,** *n.* A thing or person to be confidently relied upon. **to stand down:** To withdraw; (of a committee) to be dissolved. **to stand fast:** To stay firm, to be unmoved. **to stand for:** To support the cause of; to represent, to imply; to offer oneself as a candidate for (*Am.* to run for *e.g.* Congress). **to stand good:** To remain valid. **to stand in:** (*Cinema.*) To take an actor's place in a scene until the cameras are ready; to deputize for. **stand-in,** *n.* (*Cinema.*) A minor actor who takes the place of a star in a scene until the cameras are ready. **to stand in with:** To have an understanding or community of interest with. **to stand off:** To keep at a distance; to move away; to suspend (an employee). **to stand off and on:** (*Naut.*) To tack in and out along shore. **to stand on:** To insist on (ceremony, etc.); (*Naut.*) to keep on the same course. **to stand out:** To project, to be conspicuous; to persist (in opposition against); to endure without giving way. **to stand over:** To be deferred. **to stand to:** To abide by; not to desert; to fall to, to set to work. **to stand to it:** To maintain (that). **to stand up:** To rise to one's feet; to be or remain erect. **to stand up for:** To maintain, to support, to take the part of. **to stand upon:** To stand on. **stand-offish,** *a.* Distant, reserved. **stand-offishly,** *adv.* **stand-offishness,** *n.* **stand-pipe,** *n.* An upright pipe serving as a hydrant, to provide a head of water for pressure, etc. **stand-point,** *n.* A point of view. **standstill,** *n.* A stoppage, a cessation of progress. **stand-up,** *a.* Upright (of a collar), manfully fought, unflinching, thorough. **stander,** *n.* **stander-by,** *n.* **standing,** *a.* Erect; not cut down; fixed, established, permanent, not temporary or for a special occasion; stagnant. *n.* The act of one that stands; station; relative place or position; repute, estimation, esp. good estimation, duration, existence. **standing army,** *n.* A peacetime army of professional soldiers. **standing orders:** Orders made by a deliberative assembly as to the manner in which its business shall be conducted. **standing rigging:** (*Naut.*) The fixed ropes and chains by which the masts, etc., are secured.

standard (stăn′ dȧrd) [O.F. *estandard,* from O.H.G. *standan,* to STAND, combined with O.F. *estendard,* from L. as EXTEND], *n.* A flag as the distinctive emblem of an army, government, etc.; a measure of extent, quantity, value, etc., established by law or custom as an example or criterion for others; any type, fact, thing, etc., serving as a criterion; the degree of excellence required for a particular purpose; comparative degree of excellence; (*Coinage*) the proportion of gold or silver and alloy fixed by authority; a grade of classification in elementary schools; an upright pillar, post, or other support; a tree or shrub growing on a single upright stem, or supported on its own stem. *a.* Recognized as a standard for imitation, comparison, etc. **standard-bearer,** *n.* A soldier carrying a standard. **standard lamp,** *n.* A movable lamp on a tall pedestal. **standard time,** *n.* The method of reckoning time from a conventionally-adopted meridian (for most purposes this is the meridian of Greenwich). **standardize,** *v.t.* **standardization,** *n.*

standing, etc. [STAND].

***standish** (stăn′ dish), *n.* A stand for ink, pens, etc.

standpoint, standstill, etc. [STAND].

stang (1) (stăng) [A.-S. *steng,* rel. to *stingan,* to pierce, to STING], *n.* (*prov.*) A wooden bar, pole, or shaft; a rood of land. **to ride the stang:** To be carried on a pole in derision, an old method of punishing obnoxious persons.

stang (2), *n.* (*Sc.*) [STING].

stanhope (stăn′ ŏp), *n.* A light open two- or four-wheeled carriage; an iron printing-press invented by the 3rd Earl Stanhope (1753–1816).

staniel (stăn′ yėl) [A.-S. *stāngiella* (STONE, *giellan,* to YELL)], *n.* A kestrel.

stank, *past* [STINK].

stannary (stăn′ ȧ ri) [late L. *stannāria,* from *stannum,* tin, perh. rel. to *stagnum,* pool, see STAGNATE], *n.* A tin-mine, tin-works; a tin-mining district. *a.* Pertaining to tin-mines, etc. **stannary courts:** Courts in Devon and Cornwall for regulating the tin-mines.

stannic (stăn′ ik), *a.* Pertaining to tin, esp. in its higher valence. **stannate,** *n.* A salt of stannic acid. **stanniferous,** *a.* **stanno-,** *comb. form.* **stannous,** *a.*

stanza (stăn′ zȧ) [It., from late L. *stantia,* abode, from *stāre,* to stand], *n.* A group of rhymed lines adjusted to each other in a definite scheme. **stanzaed, stanzaic** (-zā′ ik), *a.*

stapes (stā′ pēz) [med. L., stirrup, prob. from Teut.], *n.* (*Anat.*) The innermost of the three ossicles of the middle ear. **stapedial** (stȧ pē′ di ȧl), **stapediferous** (-dif′ ėr ŭs), *a.*

staphyle (stăf′ i lė) [Gr. *staphulē,* bunch of grapes], *n.* (*Anat.*) The uvula. **staphyline,** *a.* Shaped like a bunch of grapes; pertaining to the uvula. **staphylitis** (-lī′ tis), *n.* (*Path.*) Inflammation of the uvula.

staphylococcus (stăf′ il ō kok′ ŭs), *n.* (*Biol.*) A genus of micro-organisms (*cocci*) forming the bacteria most frequently found in cutaneous affections of a suppurative kind.

staphyloma (stăf i lō′ mȧ), *n.* (*pl.* **staphylomata)** A protrusion of any of the coats of the eye. **staphylomatous,** *a.*

staphylotomy (stăf i lot′ ō mi), *n.* (*Surg.*) The operation of cutting off the end of the uvula.

staple (1) (stā′ pėl) [A.-S. *stapul,* cp. Dut. *stapel,* G. *staffel,* step, rung, G. and Swed. *stapel,* heap, emporium, Dan. *stabel,* hinge, pile], *n.* A U-shaped piece of metal driven into a post, wall, etc., to receive part of a fastening or to hold wire, etc.; the box-like part receiving the bolt of a lock; a bent wire used in wire-stitching; the metal tube holding the reeds of musical instruments like the oboe. *v.t.* To fasten, attach, or support with staples. **stapling-machine,** *n.* A wire-stitching machine used by bookbinders; an appliance for stapling together papers.

staple (2) (stā′ pėl) [O.F. *estaple,* L.G. *stapel,* cogn. with prec.], *n.* The principal commodity sold or produced in any place, country, etc.; the chief material or substance of anything; raw material; the fibre of wool, cotton, etc., as a criterion of quality. *a.* Settled, marketable; chief, principal, main. *v.t.* To sort or classify (wool, etc.) according to staple. **stapler,** *n.*

star (star) [A.-S. *steorra,* cp. Dut. *ster,* G. *stern,* Icel. *stjarna,* Swed. *stjerna,* also L. *stella,* Gr. *astēr*], *n.* A celestial body appearing as a fixed point, esp. one of the fixed stars or those so distant that their relative position in the heavens appears constant; an object, figure, or device resembling a star, esp. one with radiating points used as an emblem or ornament; an asterisk (*); a white spot on the forehead of a horse, etc.; (*fig.*) a brilliant or prominent person, esp. an actor or singer; (*Astrol.*) a heavenly body regarded as having influence over a person's life. *v.t.* (*past & p.p.* **starred)** To set, spangle, or decorate with stars; to put an asterisk against (a name, etc.). *v.i.* To appear as a star (of an actor, singer, etc.). **Star-Chamber,** *n.* A court of civil and criminal jurisdiction at Westminster (abolished 1641) famous under Charles I for its arbitrary proceedings (named from the stars painted on the ceilings, or from certain Jewish covenants, called Starrs, said to have been deposited there). ***star-crossed,** *a.* Unfortunate. **star-drift,** *n.* The common proper motion of stars in the same region of the heavens. **star-finch,** *n.* The redstart.

starfish, *n.* An echinoderm, *Asterias rubens,* with five or more rays or arms. **star-gazer,** *n.* (*contemp.*) An astronomer or astrologer. **star-gazing,** *n.* **starlight,** *n.* The light of the stars. **starlit,** *a.* **star of Bethlehem:** A bulbous plant, *Ornithogallum umbellatum,* of the lily family with star-shaped white flowers striped outside with green. **Star of India,** *n.* A British order of chivalry reserved for recognition of services in India. **Star of Judah,** *n.* The yellow cloth star that persons of Jewish descent were forced by the Nazi government to wear on their clothes as a distinguishing mark. **Stars and Stripes,** *n.* The national flag of the U.S.A. **star-shell,** *n.* A shell bursting in the air and emitting luminous stars, used to light up an enemy's position. **star-spangled,** *a.* **star-stone,** *n.* A variety of sapphire. **starless,** *a.* **starlet,** *n.* **starlike, starry,** *a.* **starriness,** *n.*

starblind (star′ blīnd) [A.-S. *stær-blind, stær,* stiff, BLIND), cp. STARE and STARK], *a.* Seeing obscurely, partially blind.

starboard (star′ bôrd) [A.-S. *stēorbord* (*stēor,* rudder, as STEER (1))], *n.* The right-hand side of a vessel looking forward. *v.t.* To put or turn (the helm) to starboard; to make a vessel turn to starboard.

starch (starch) [M.E. *sterch,* strong, cp. A.-S. *stercan,* to stiffen, cogn. with STARK], *n.* A white, tasteless, odourless, amorphous compound, found in all plants except fungi, but especially in cereals, potatoes, beans, etc., an important constituent of vegetable foods, and used as a soluble powder to stiffen linen, etc.; (*fig.*) stiffness, preciseness, formality. *a.* Stiff, precise, prim. *v.t.* To stiffen with starch. **starchedly, starchly,** *adv.* **starchedness, starchness, starchiness,** *n.* **starcher,** *n.* **starchy,** *a.*

stare (stâr) [A.-S. *starian* (cp. Dut. *staren,* Icel. *stara,* also G. *starr,* stiff), prob. rel. to Gr. *stereos,* firm], *v.i.* To look with eyes fixed and wide open, as in admiration, surprise, horror, etc.; (*fig.*) to stand out, to be prominent. *v.t.* To affect by staring. *n.* A staring gaze. **to stare in the face:** To be obvious to. **starer,** *n.* **staringly,** *adv.*

stark (stark) [A.-S. *stearc* (cp. Dut. *sterk,* G. *stark,* Icel. *sterkr*), cogn. with prec.], *a.* Rigid, stiff; (*fig.*) stubborn, inflexible; complete, downright, sheer; (*poet.*) strong. *adv.* Wholly, absolutely.

stark-naked (stark nā′ kėd) [A.-S. *steort,* tail (cp. Dut. *stert,* G. *sterz,* Icel. *stertr,* also Gr. *storthē,* spike), NAKED], *a.* Quite naked.

starling (1) (star′ ling) [A.-S. *stær* (cp. G. *staar,* Icel. *stari, starri*)], *n.* A small black and brown speckled bird of the genus *Sturnus,* esp. *S. vulgaris.*

starling (2) (star′ ling) [cp. Dan. and Swed. *stor,* stake], *n.* An enclosure of piles round a bridge-pier, etc.

start (start) [M.E. *sterten,* cp. Dut. *storten,* G. *sturzen,* Dan. *styrte,* Swed. *störta,* to cast down, etc.], *v.i.* To make a sudden involuntary movement, as from fear, surprise, etc.; to move abruptly (aside, etc.); to shrink, to wince; to give way, to become loose, etc. (of timber, rivets, etc.); to set out, to begin a journey; to make a beginning (on a journey, etc.). *v.t.* To cause to start, to rouse; to originate, to set going; to set (people) working; to give the signal to (persons) to start in a race; (*colloq.*) to begin (work, etc.); to cause (timbers, etc.) to start; (*Naut.*) to draw (liquor) from, or draw liquor from (a cask). *n.* A sudden involuntary movement, as of fear, surprise, etc.; a spasmodic effort (*usu. in pl.*); the beginning of a journey, enterprise, etc., a setting-out; a starting-place; the amount of lead originally given to a competitor in a race, etc.; advantage gained in a race, business, etc. **by fits and starts** [FIT (1)]. **to start up:** To rise suddenly; to come into notice or occur to the mind suddenly; (of an engine) to start. **starter,** *n.* One who starts; one who gives the signal for starting a race, etc.; a horse or other competitor starting in a race. ***startful, startish,** *a.* Skittish, shy (of horses). **starting-point,** *n.* A point of departure. **starting-post,** *n.* A post from which competitors start in a race. ***startingly,** *adv.* By fits and starts.

startle (startl) [M.E. *stertlen,* freq. of prec.], *v.t.* To cause to start; to alarm, to shock. **startler,** *n.* **startling,** *a.* Surprising, alarming. **startlingly,** *adv.*

starve (starv) [A.-S. *steorfan,* to die, cp. *sterfan,* to kill, Dut. *sterven,* G. *sterben*], *v.i.* To perish or suffer severely from hunger; (*fig.*) to be in want or penury; (*fig.*) to suffer from the lack of mental or spiritual nutriment; (*prov.*) to die or suffer severely from cold; *to die, to perish. *v.t.* To cause to perish or be extremely distressed by lack of food; to force (into surrender, etc.) thus; to deprive of physical or mental nutriment; (*prov.*) to cause to perish or suffer severely from cold. **starvation** (-vā′ shůn), *n.* **starveling,** *a.* and *n.* **starvo,** *n.* (*Austral.*) A sausage, a saveloy.

starwort (star wôrt), *n.* A plant of the genus *Stellaria* or the genus *Aster.*

stasimon (stăs′ i mǒn) [Gr., as foll.], *n.* (*pl.* **-ma**) (*Gr. Ant.*) An ode sung by the entire chorus after the opening ode.

stasis (stăs′ is) [Gr., from *sta-,* root of *histanai,* to stand], *n.* (*Path.*) Stagnation of the blood, esp. in the small vessels or capillaries; (*Gr. Ch.*) one of the portions of the psalter read with a response by the choir.

state (stāt) [O.F. *estat,* L. STATUS], *n.* Condition, mode of existence, situation, relation to circumstances; a political community organized under a government, a commonwealth, a nation, the body politic; such a community forming part of a federal republic; civil government; dignity, pomp, splendour; *a throne, *a canopy; (*pl.*) the legislative body in Jersey or Guernsey. *a.* Of or pertaining to the State or body politic; used or reserved for ceremonial occasions. *v.t.* To set forth, esp. with explicitness and formality; to fix, to determine, to specify; (*Alg.*) to express the conditions of (a problem, etc.) in symbols. **to lie in state:** (of the dead) To lie in a coffin in some place where the public may come to visit as a token of respect. **state-craft,** *n.* Statesmanship. **State Department:** (*Pol.*) That part of the U.S. government responsible for the conduct of foreign affairs. **State paper:** A document relating to State affairs. **State rights:** (*U.S.*) Rights reserved by the individual States in the Union. **state room:** A room reserved for occasions of ceremony; a private sleeping apartment on a steamer, etc. **States General:** The legislative assembly in the Netherlands and in France before the Revolution. **State Socialism:** Management of the greater industrial enterprises by the State. **state-trial,** *n.* A trial for a political offence under prosecution by the State. **statable,** *a.* **statedly,** *adv.* **stateless,** *a.* (*Pol.*) Deprived by war or revolution, etc., of home, as well as political and all other rights in any state.

stately (stāt′ li), *a.* Grand, lofty, dignified, elevated, imposing. **stateliness,** *n.*

statement (stāt′ mėnt), *n.* The act of stating; that which is stated; a formal account, recital, or narration; a formal presentation of accounts.

stater (stā′ tėr) [Gr., from *sta-,* see STATIC], *n.* A coin of ancient Greece, esp. the standard gold coin of 20 drachmæ.

statesman (stāts′ mån), *n.* One versed in the art of government; one taking a leading part in the administration of the State; (*prov.*) a small landowner. **statesmanlike,** *a.* **statesmanship,** *n.*

static, statical (stăt′ ik, -ål) [Gr. *statikos*], *a.* Pertaining to bodies at rest or in equilibrium; acting as weight without producing motion. *n.* Static electricity usually produced by materials rubbing together. **statics,** *n.pl.* The branch of dynamics which treats of the relations between forces in equilibrium; (Radio.) atmospherics. **statically,** *adv.*

Statice (stăt′ i sē) [Gr. *statikē,* fem. of *statikos,* STATIC], *n.* A genus of plants containing the sea-lavender.

station (stā′ shŭn) [F., from L. *statiōnem*, nom. *-tio*, from *stāre*, to stand], *n.* The place where a person or thing stands, esp. an appointed or established place; a place where police, coastguards, naval or military forces, etc., have their headquarters, a military post; a place or building at which railway-trains stop for setting down or taking up passengers or goods (*Am.* a depot); position, occupation, standing, rank, esp. high rank; (*Surv.*) a point from which measurements are made, a standard distance, usu. a chain of 100 or 66 ft.; (*Austral.*) the ranch-house or homestead of a sheep-farmer; (*Eccles.*) a fixed fast (*Gr. Ch.*) on Wednesday and Friday or (*R.-C. Ch.*) on Friday; (*R.-C. Ch.*) a church to which a procession resorts for devotion; any of a series of 14 images or pictures in a church representing successive scenes in Christ's passion; (*Biol.*) the area inhabited by a particular organism, a habitat. *v.t.* To assign to or place in a particular station, to post. **station-bill,** *n.* (*Naut.*) A list of the appointed posts of a ship's company. **station-house,** *n.* A police-station. **station-master,** *n.* The official in charge of a railway-station. **station wagon:** (*Am.*) A shooting-brake. **stational,** *a.*

stationary (stā′ shŏ năr i) [L. *stationārius*, as prec.], *a.* Remaining in one place, not moving; intended to remain in one place, fixed, not portable; having no apparent movement in longitude (of planets); not changing in character, condition, magnitude, etc. *n.* One who is stationary, esp. (*pl.*) stationary troops. **stationariness,** *n.*

stationer (stā′ shŏ nėr) [orig. a bookseller, having a stall or stand, as prec.], *n.* One who sells papers, pens, ink, and writing-materials. **stationery,** *n.* **Stationery Office,** *n.* The government department for the preparation and issue of official books and documents.

statist (stăt′ ist), *n.* A statistician; *a politician.

statistics (stȧ tis′ tiks), *n.pl.* Numerical facts, arranged and classified, esp. respecting social conditions; (*as sing.*) the science of collecting, organizing, and applying statistics, also called **statistology** (stăt is tol′ ŏ ji). **statistic, -al,** *a.* **statistically,** *adv.* **statistician** (stăt is tish′ ȧn), *n.*

stative (stăt′ iv) [L. *stativus*, from *stāre*, to stand, p.p. *status*], *a.* (*Heb. Gram.*) Expressing past action, etc., as still continuing (of some verbs); (*Rom. Ant.*) pertaining to a fixed camp or military post.

statoblast (stăt′ ŏ blăst) [Gr. *statos*, fixed, from *sta-*, root of *histanai*, to stand, -BLAST], *n.* An internal bud developed in freshwater sponges and polyzoa.

stator (stā′ tŭr) [Gr. *statos*, fixed], *n.* (*Elec.*) The fixed part of an electrical generator.

statoscope (stăt′ ō skōp), *n.* An aneroid barometer with a large air reservoir for showing minute fluctuations of pressure.

statue (stăt′ ū) [O.F., from L. *statua*, from *statuere*, to cause to stand, as foll.], *n.* A representation of a person or animal sculptured or cast, usu. in marble or bronze, esp. about life-size. **statuary,** *a.* and *n.* **statued,** *a.* **statuesque** (-esk′), *a.* Having the dignity or beauty of a statue. **statuesquely,** *adv.* **statuesqueness,** *n.* **statuette** (-et′), *n.* A small statue.

stature (stăt′ ūr) [F., from L. *statūra*, upright posture, from *stāre*, to stand, p.p. *status*], *n.* The natural height of a body, esp. of man. **statured,** *a.* (*usu. in comb.*, as *lofty-statured*).

status (stā′ tŭs) [L., as prec.], *n.* Relative standing, rank, or position in society; (*Law*) legal position or relation to others.

statute (stăt′ ūt) [F. *statut*, L. *statūtum*, neut. p.p. of *statuere*, see STATUE], *n.* A law enacted by a legislative body; an ordinance of a corporation or its founder intended as a permanent law. **Statute of Westminster:** (*Pol.*) An Act passed by the U.K. parliament in 1931 recognizing the independent sovereign status of the self-governing dominions. **statute-book,** *n.* A book in which statutes are published. **statute-roll,** *n.* A statute-book; an engrossed statute. **statutable, statutory,** *a.* **statutably,** *adv.*

staunch, etc. [STANCH].

staurolite (staw′ rŏ līt) [Gr. *stauros*, cross, -LITE], *n.* (*Min.*) An orthorhombic ferrous silicate of aluminium occurring in cross-like twin crystals. **staurolitic** (-lit′ ik), *a.* **stauroscope** [-SCOPE], *n.* An instrument for observing the effects of parallel polarized light in crystals.

stave (stāv) [var. of STAFF, from M.E. dat. sing.], *n.* One of the curved strips forming the side of a cask, etc.; a strip of wood or other material used for a similar purpose; a stanza, a verse; (*Mus.*) a staff. *v.t.* (*past & p.p.* **staved, stove**) To break a hole in (a cask, boat, etc.); to make (a hole) thus; to furnish or fit with staves; to stop, avert, or ward (off). **staves,** *pl.* [STAFF and STAVE].

stavesacre (stāv′ zā kėr) [O.F. *stavesaigre*, *staphisaigre*, L. *staphisagria* (Gr. *staphis*, raisins, *agria*, wild)], *n.* A species of larkspur, *D. staphisagria*, the seeds of which are used as a poison for lice, etc.

stay (1) (stā) [O.F. *ester*, L. *stāre*, STAND (acc. to O.E.D.)], *v.i.* To continue in a specified place or state; to remain; to dwell or have one's abode temporarily (at, with, etc.); (*Sc.*) to live (at); to pause, to stand still; to tarry, to wait; to keep going or last out (in a race, etc.). *v.t.* To hinder, to stop (the progress, etc., of); to postpone, to suspend. *n.* The act of staying or dwelling; continuance in a place, etc.; a check, a restraint or deterrent; (*Law*) suspension of judicial proceedings. **to stay put:** To remain in one's place. **stayer** (1), *n.* **stay-at-home,** *a.* and *n.* Unenterprising.

stay (2) (stā) [O.F. *estayer*, to prop, *estaye*, prop, M. Dut. *stade*, *staeye*, O.H.G. *stata*, fit place or time, cogn. with STEAD], *n.* A support, a prop; (*pl.*) a corset. *v.t.* To prop (usu. up), to support. **stay-bar, -rod,** *n.* One used as a stay or support in a building, etc. **stay-lace,** *n.* One used in lacing a corset. **stay-maker,** *n.* A corset-maker. **stayer** (2), *n.* **stayless,** *a.*

stay (3) (stā) [perh. from A.-S. *stæg*, etym. doubtful, or prec.], *n.* (*Naut.*) A rope supporting a mast or spar. *v.t.* To support by stays; to put on the other tack. **in stays** or **hove in stays:** Going about from one tack to another (of a ship). **to miss stays:** To fail in tacking. **staysail** (stāsl), *n.* A sail extended by a stay.

stayer (1) [STAY (1)].

stayer (2), **stay-lace, -maker,** etc. [STAY (2)].

stead (sted) [A.-S. *stede* (cp. Dut. *stede*), cogn. with *stæth*, bank, Dut. *stad*, G. *stadt*, town, L. *statis*, Gr. *stasis*, and STAND], *n.* Place or room which another had or might have had. **in one's stead:** Instead of one. **to stand in good stead:** To be of service to.

steadfast (sted′ făst) [A.-S. *stedefæst*], *a.* Firm, resolute, unwavering. **steadfastly,** *adv.* **steadfastness,** *n.*

steady (sted′ i), *a.* Firmly fixed, not wavering; moving or acting in a regular way, uniform, constant; free from intemperance, irregularity, constant in mind, or conduct. *n.* A rest or support for keeping the hand, etc., steady. *v.t.* To make steady. *v.i.* To become steady. **steadily,** *adv.* **steadiness,** *n.*

steak (stāk) [M.E. *steike*, Icel. *steik*, from *steikja*, to roast on a spit, cogn. with STICK], *n.* A slice of beef, pork, etc., cut for broiling.

steal (stēl) [A.-S. *stelan*, cp. Dut. *stelen*, G. *stehlen*, Icel. *stela*], *v.t.* (*past* **stole,** *p.p.* **stolen**) To take away without right or permission, to take feloniously; to secure covertly or by surprise; to secure insidiously. *v.i.* To take anything feloniously; to go or come furtively or silently. **to steal a march on:** To be beforehand with, to get the start of. **stealer, stealingly,** *adv.*

stealth (stelth), *n.* Furtiveness, secrecy; secret procedure. **stealthy,** *a.* **stealthily,** *adv.* **stealthiness,** *n.*

steam (stēm) [A.-S. *stēam*, cp. Dut. *stoom*], *n.* Water in the form of vapour or the gaseous form to which it is changed by boiling; the visible mass of particles of water into which this condenses; any vaporous exhalation; (*fig.*) energy, force, go. *v.i.* To give off steam; to rise in steam or vapour; to move by the agency of steam. *v.t.* To treat with steam for the purpose of softening, melting, etc., esp. to cook by steam. **to let off steam:** (*fig.*) To relieve one's feelings. **to go under one's own steam:** To go by one's own efforts, to go without help. **steamboat,** *n.* A vessel propelled by steam. **steam-boiler,** *n.* A boiler in a steam-engine. **steam-box, -chest,** *n.* The box-shaped part through which steam is conveyed from the boiler to the cylinder. **steam-crane, -digger, -gun, -hammer, -plough, -whistle,** etc., *n.* One worked by steam. **steam-engine,** *n.* An engine worked by the pressure of steam on a piston moving in a cylinder, etc. **steam-gas,** *n.* Superheated steam. **steam-gauge,** *n.* An instrument attached to a boiler to indicate the pressure of steam. **steam-jacket,** *n.* A hollow casing round a cylinder, etc., for receiving steam to heat the latter. **steam navvy,** *n.* (*Mach.*) A mechanical excavator consisting of a large bucket working from a long beam. **steam-power,** *n.* Force applied by the agency of steam to machinery, etc. **steam roller,** *n.* (*Mach.*) A heavy roller propelled by steam, used in road-making and repairing. **steamship,** *n.* A ship propelled by steam. **steam-tug,** *n.* A small steam-vessel used for towing ships. **steam turbine,** *n.* (*Mach.*) A machine in which steam acts on moving blades attached to a drum. **steamer,** *n.* A vessel propelled by steam; a steam fire-engine; a receptacle for steaming articles, esp. for cooking food. **steamy,** *a.* **steaminess,** *n.*

stean, etc. [STEIN].

stearin (stē' ȧ rin) [F. *stéarine* (Gr. *stear*, fat)], *n.* A fatty compound contained in the more solid animal and vegetable fats; stearic acid as used for candles. **stearate,** *n.* **stearic** (stē ăr' ik), *a.* **stearrhœa** (-rē' ȧ), *n.* (*Path.*) An abnormal increase in the secretion from the oil-glands of the skin.

steatite (stē' ȧ tīt) [F. *stéatite* (foll., -ITE)], *n.* Massive talc, soapstone. **steatitic** (-tit' ik), *a.*

steato-, steat- [Gr. *stear, steatos*, fat], *comb. form.* **steatocele** (ste' ȧ tȯ sēl) [-CELE], *n.* A fatty tumour of the scrotum. **steatoma** (-tō' mȧ), *n.* A fatty encysted tumour. **steatomatous,** *a.* **steatopygous** (-top' i gůs) [Gr. *pugē*, rump], *a.* Characterized by fat buttocks (as the African Bushmen). **steatopygy,** *n.*

steed (stēd) [A.-S. *stēda*, cogn. with STUD (2)], *n.* A horse, esp. a war-horse.

steel (stēl) [A.-S. *style*, cp. Dut. *staal*, G. *stahl*, Icel. *stal*, Dan. *staal*], *n.* Iron combined with carbon in various proportions, remaining malleable at high temperatures and capable of being hardened by cooling; a sword; a steel rod with roughened surface for sharpening knives; a steel strip for stiffening a corset, etc. *v.t.* To cover, point, or face with steel; to harden (the heart, etc.). **steel-clad,** *a.* Clad in armour. **steel-engraving,** *n.* The art of engraving upon steel plates; an engraving on a steel plate; an impression from this. **steel-plated,** *a.* Plated with steel. **steel-wool,** *n.* Fine steel shavings bunched together for cleaning pots and pans. **steel-work,** *n.* **steel-worker,** *n.* **steelify,** *v.t.* **steely,** *a.* **steeliness,** *n.*

steelyard (stēl' yard) [mistrans. of L.G. *staalhof*, sample-yard (*staal*, sample, conf. with *staal*, STEEL), and YARD (2) an enclosure], *n.* A balance with unequal arms, the article weighed being hung from the shorter arm and a weight moved along the other till they balance.

steen [STEIN].

steenbok (stān'-, stēn' bok) [Dut., stone-buck, cp. G. *steinbock*], *n.* A small S. African antelope.

steening [STEINING].

steenkirk (stēn' kĕrk) [battle of *Steenkerke*, 3rd Aug. 1692], *n.* A lace cravat worn loose; applied also to wigs, buckles, and other articles of attire.

steep (1) (stēp) [A.-S. *stēap*, cp. Icel. *steypthr*, rel. to *steypa*, to overthrow, causal of *stūpa*, to stoop], *a.* Sharply inclined, sloping at a high angle; (*colloq.*) excessive, exorbitant (of prices, etc.). *n.* A steep slope; a precipice. **steepen,** *v.t.* and *i.* **steeply,** *adv.* **steepness,** *n.* **steepy,** *a.*

steep (2) (stēp) [M.E. *stepen*, Icel. *steypa*, to pour out or cast metals, see prec.], *v.t.* To soak in liquid; to wet thoroughly. *n.* The process of steeping; a liquid for steeping. **to steep in:** To impregnate or imbue with. **steeper,** *n.*

steepen, etc. [STEEP (1)]. **steeper** [STEEP (2)].

steeple (stē' pėl) [A.-S. *stypel*, as STEEP (1)], *n.* A lofty structure rising above the roof of a building, esp. a church tower with a spire. **steeple-crowned,** *a.* Having a tall, tapering crown (of a hat). **steeple-jack,** *n.* One who climbs steeples, etc., to do repairs, etc. **steepled,** *a.* **steeplewise,** *adv.*

steeplechase (stē' pėl chās), *n.* A horse-race across country in which hedges, etc., have to be jumped. **steeplechaser,** *n.* **steeplechasing,** *n.* and *a.*

steer (1) (stēr) [A.-S. *stēoran*, cogn. with *stēor*, rudder (cp. Dut. *sturen, stuur*, G. *steuern, steuer*)], *v.t.* To guide (a ship, aeroplane, motor-car, etc.) by a rudder, wheel, handle, etc.; to direct (one's course) thus. *v.i.* To guide a ship, etc., or direct one's course by or as by this means; to be steered (easily, etc.). **to steer clear of:** (*fig.*) To avoid. **steerable,** *a.* **steerage,** *n.* The part of a ship, usu. forward and on or below the main deck, allotted to passengers travelling at the lowest rate; the part of the berth-deck on a war-ship just forward of the ward-room, allotted as quarters to junior officers, etc.; the effect of the helm on a ship; *steering; *the stern. **steerage-way,** *n.* Sufficient motion of a vessel to enable her to answer the helm. **steerer,** *n.* **steering column,** *n.* (*Motor.*) A column carrying the steering-wheel at the top. **steering engine,** *n.* (*Naut.*) An engine for working the rudder of a ship. **steering lock,** *n.* (*Motor.*) The maximum angular amount which wheels can swivel from side to side. **steering-wheel, -gear,** *n.* The wheel or gear which controls the rudder of a ship, or the stub axles of the front wheels of a motor-car. **steersman,** *n.* One who steers. **steersmanship,** *n.*

steer (2) (stēr) [A.-S. *stēor*, cp. Dut. and G. *stier*, Icel. *stjörr*, also L. *taurus*, Gr. *tauros*], *n.* A young male of the ox kind, esp. a castrated bullock. **steerling,** *n.*

steerage, etc. [STEER (1)].

steeve (1) (stēv) [A.-S. *stīfian*, from *stīf*, STIFF], *v.i.* (*Naut.*) To have a certain angle of elevation (of a bowsprit). *v.t.* To give (a bowsprit) this. *n.* Such an angle.

steeve (2) (stēv) [O.F. *estiver*, L. *stipāre*, to press, cogn. with prec.], *n.* A spar or derrick for stowing cargo. *v.t.* (*Naut.*) To stow with a steeve.

steganography (steg ȧ nog' rȧ fi) [Gr. *steganos*, see foll., -GRAPHY], *n.* The art of secret writing or writing in cipher. **steganographist,** *n.*

steganopod (steg' ȧ nȯ pod) [Gr. *steganos*, covered, from *stegein*, to cover, *pous podos*, foot], *n.* Any individual of the *Steganopodes*, an order of birds with all the toes webbed, as the pelicans, frigate-birds, etc. *a.* Pertaining to this order. **steganopodan, -dous** (-nop' ȯ dȧn, -důs), *a.*

stegnosis (steg nō' sis) [Gr., from *stegnoein*, from *stegnos, steganos*, see STEGANOPOD], *n.* (*Path.*) Constriction of the pores and vessels; constipation. **stegnotic** (-not' ik), *a.* and *n.*

stein (stān) [A.-S. *stǣnan*, from *stān*, STONE], *v.t.* (*prov.*) To line (a well, etc.) with stones; (*Am.*) a drinking-mug. **steining,** *n.*

steinberger (stīn' bėr gėr) [G.], *n.* A Rhenish white wine from near Wiesbaden.

steinbock [STEENBOK].

stele (stē′ lē) [Gr.], *n.* (*pl.* **-læ**) (*Ant.*) An upright slab usu. with inscriptions and sculpture, for sepulchral or other purposes. **stelar, stelene,** *a.*

stelechite (stel′ ė kīt) [Gr. *stelechos*, stem, trunk], *n.* A fine quality of storax.

***stell** (stel) [A.-S. *stellan*, cogn. with STALL (1)], *v.t.* (*Shak.*) To place, to set.

stellar (stel′ ȧr) [late *stellāris*, from L. *stella*, star], *a.* Of or pertaining to stars. **Stellaria** (stė lâr′ i ȧ), *n.* A genus of tufted herbs containing the chickweeds or starworts. **stellate, -lated,** *a.* Star-shaped, radiating. **stellately,** *adv.* **stelliferous** (-lif′ ėr ůs), *a.* **stelliform,** *a.* **stellular, -late,** *a.* Set with or shaped like small stars.

stellion (stel′ yȯn) [L. *stellio -onis*, from *stella*, star], *n.* A lizard belonging to the family *Agamidæ.*

stem (1) (stem) [A.-S. *stæfn, stefn, stemn*, cp. Dut. *stam*, trunk, *steven*, prow, Icel. *stafn, stamn*, stem of ship, G. *stamm*, trunk, *steven*, stem of ship], *n.* The stock, stalk, or ascending axis of a tree, shrub, or other plant; the slender stalk or peduncle of a flower, leaf, etc.; an analogous part, as the slender part between the body and foot of a wine-glass, etc., the tube of a tobacco-pipe, the part by which a watch is attached to a chain, etc., the part of a noun, verb, etc., to which case-endings, etc., are affixed; (*fig.*) the stock of a family, a branch of a family; (*Shipbuilding*) the upright piece of timber or iron at the fore end of a vessel to which the sides are joined. *v.t.* (*past & p.p.* **stemmed**) To remove the stem or stems of. **to stem from:** To originate in. **from stem to stern:** From one end of the ship to the other. **stem-winder,** *n.* A watch which may be wound by the stem without a key. **stemless,** *a.* **stemlet,** *n.* **stemmed,** *a.* **stemmer,** *n.*

stem (2) (stem) [Icel. *stemma*, cp. G. *stemmen*], *v.t.* To draw up, to check, to hold back; (*fig.*) to make headway against.

stemless, stemmer, etc. [STEM (1)].

stemma (stem′ ȧ) [L., a wreath], *n.* (*Zool.*) A simple eye; one of the facets of a compound eye; an ocellus.

stemple (stem′ pėl) [etym. doubtful], *n.* A cross-bar serving as a step or support in the shaft of a mine.

stemson (stem′ sȯn) [STEM (1), *-son*, as in KELSON], *n.* A curved timber behind a vessel's apron, supporting the scarfs.

stench (stench) [A.-S. *stenc*, from *stincan*, to STINK], *n.* A foul or offensive smell. **stench-trap,** *n.* A trap in a sewer to prevent the escape of noxious gas. ***stenchy,** *a.*

stencil (sten′ sil) [prob. from O.F. *estenceler*, to sparkle, to cover with stars, from *estencele*, spark, as TINSEL], *n.* A thin plate of metal or other material out of which patterns have been cut for painting through the spaces on to a surface; a decoration, etc., produced thus. *v.t.* (*past & p.p.* **stencilled**) To paint (letters, designs, etc.) by means of a stencil; to decorate (a wall, etc.) thus. **stenciller,** *n.*

steno- [Gr. *stenos*, narrow], *comb. form.* **stenochrome** (sten′ ȯ krōm) [CHROME], *n.* A print taken at one impression from several differently-coloured blocks. **stenochromy** (stė nok′ rȯ mi), *n.*

stenograph (sten′ ȯ grăf), *n.* A character used in shorthand; a form of typewriter using stenographic characters. **stenographer** (stė nog′ rȧ fėr), **stenographist** (-nog′ rȧ fist), *n.* A shorthand writer. **stenography,** *n.* **stenotype** (sten′ ȯ tīp) [TYPE], *n.* A letter or combination of letters used in shorthand to represent a word or phrase. **stenotypic** (-tip′ ik), *a.* **stenotypy,** *n.*

stenosis [STEGNOSIS]. ***stent** [STINT].

Stentor (sten′ tôr, -tȯr) [L. and Gr. *Stentōr*, herald in Trojan war], *n.* A person with a loud, strong voice; a howling monkey, esp. the ursine howler. **stentorian** (-tôr′ i ȧn), *a.*

step (step) [A.-S. *steppan*, cogn. with STAMP, *n. stæpe*, cp. Dut. *stap* G. *stapfe*], *v.i.* To lift and set down a foot or the feet alternately, to walk a short distance in a specified direction; to walk or dance slowly or with dignity. *v.t.* To go through, perform, or measure by stepping; (*Naut.*) to insert the foot of (a mast, etc.) in a step. *n.* A single complete movement of one leg in the act of walking, dancing, etc.; the distance traversed in this; (*fig.*) a short distance; an action or measure taken in a series directed to some end; that on which the foot is placed in ascending or descending, a single stair or a tread in a flight of stairs; a rung of a ladder, a support for the foot in stepping in or out of a vehicle, a door-step, etc.; a foot-print; (*Aviat.*) a break in the outline at the bottom of a float or hull which assists in lifting it from the surface of the water; (*pl.*) a self-supporting step-ladder with fixed or hinged prop; (*fig.*) a degree or grade in progress, rank, or precedence; (*Carp., etc.*) a socket supporting a frame, etc., for the end of a mast, shaft, etc. **to step on it:** (*Am. slang*) To hurry, to increase speed. **step-down transformer,** *n.* (*Elec.*) A transformer for changing high-voltage supply to low-voltage supply; a **step-up transformer** performs the reverse operation. **step-ladder,** *n.* A ladder with flat treads or rungs. **stepped,** *a.* **stepper,** *n.* **stepping-stone,** *n.* A raised stone in a stream or swampy place on which one steps in crossing; (*fig.*) a means to an end. **step-wise,** *adv.*

step- [A.-S. *steop*, orphaned, cp. Dut. and G. *stief*, Icel. *stjūp-*, O.H.G. *stiufan*, to deprive of parents], *pref.* A prefix used to express relation only by the marriage of a parent. **stepbrother, -sister,** *n.* A stepfather's or stepmother's child by a former marriage. **stepchild, -daughter, -son,** *n.* The child of one's husband or wife by a former marriage. **stepfather, -mother, -parent,** *n.* The later husband or wife of one's parent. **stepmotherly,** *a.* Like a stepmother; (*fig.*) neglectful, unfeeling.

stephanite (stef′ ȧ nīt) [Archduke *Stephan* of Austria], *n.* (*Min.*) A metallic, black sulphantimonite of silver.

stephanotis (stef ȧ nō′ tis) [Gr. *stephanos*, wreath, *ous, ōtos*, ear], *n.* A tropical climbing plant with fragrant waxy flowers.

stepmother, etc. [STEP-].

stepney (step′ ni) [London borough], *n.* (*Motor.*) Spare wheel and tire carried on a car for use in the event of a puncture.

steppe (step) [Rus. *stepe*], *n.* A vast plain devoid of forest, esp. in Russia and Siberia.

stepping-stone, etc. [STEP].

stepsister, etc. [STEP-].

-ster [A.-S. *-estre* (comb. of *-es*, *-ter*, as in L. *minister*)], *suf.* Denoting an agent, as in *maltster, punster, songster*; denoting a female agent, as in *spinster.*

stercoraceous (stĕr kȯ rā′ shůs) [L. *stercus -coris*, dung, -ACEOUS], *a.* Pertaining to, composed of, or like dung. **stercoral,** *a.* **stercorary,** *a.* and *n.*

stere (stēr) [F. *stère*, as STEREO-], *n.* A cubic metre 35·3147589 cubic ft.

stereo [short for STEREOTYPE].

stereo- [Gr. *stereos*, stiff, solid], *comb. form.*

stereobate (ster′ e ō bāt), *n.* A solid substructure or base for a building.

stereo-chemistry (ster e ō kem′ is tri), *n.* Chemistry concerned with the composition of matter as exhibited in the relations of atoms in space.

stereochromy (ster e ō krō′ mi), *n.* Painting with pigments mixed with soluble or water-glass.

stereo-electric (ster e ō el ek′ trik), *a.* Denoting the electric current produced when two solids are brought together at different temperatures.

stereography (ster e og′ rȧ fi), *n.* The art of delineating solid forms on a plane. **stereographic,** *a.* **stereographically,** *adv.* **stereogram,** *n.*

stereome (ster′ e ōm), *n.* (*Bot.*) A strengthening

tissue composed of thick-walled, elongated prosenchymatous cells in vascular plants.

stereometer (ster e om′ ė tėr), *n.* An instrument for measuring the volume of solid bodies; an instrument for determining the specific gravity of liquids, powders, etc. **stereometric, -al,** *a.* **stereometry,** *n.*

stereophony (ster e of′ ȯ ni), *n.* The stereophonic reproduction of sound (the aural equivalent of stereoscopy). **stereophonic,** *a.*

stereopticon (ster i op′ ti kon), *n.* A double magic-lantern for producing dissolving views.

stereoptics (ster i op′ tiks), *n.* The science of stereoscopy.

stereoscope (ster′-, stēr′ ė ȯ skōp) [STEREO-, SCOPE], *n.* A binocular instrument for blending into one two pictures taken from slightly different positions, thus giving an effect of three dimensions. **stereoscopic, -al** (-skop′ ik, -ål), *a.* Giving the effect of solidity. **stereoscopy** (-os′ kȯpi), *n.*

stereotomy (ster ė ot′ ȯ mi) [STEREO-, -TOMY], *n.* The science or art of cutting solids into figures by certain sections. **stereotomic, -al** (-tom′ ik, -ål), *a.*

stereotrope (ster′ ė ȯ trōp) [Gr. *tropē*, turning, from *trepein*, to turn], *n.* An optical device for bringing pictures into relief and conveying the impression of continuous motion. **stereotropic** (-trop′ ik), *a.*

stereotype (ster′-, stēr′ ė ȯ tīp) [STEREO-, TYPE], *n.* A printing-plate cast from a mould taken from movable type. *v.t.* To take a stereotype of; (*fig.*) to fix or establish in unchangeable form. **stereotyper, -pist,** *n.* **stereotypography** (-pog′ rå fi), **-typy** (ster′-, stēr′ ė ȯ tī pi), *n.*

sterigma (stė rig′ må) [Gr. *stērigma -matos*, a support], *n.* (*Bot.*) A stalk or support. **sterigmatic** (-măt′ ik), *a.*

sterile (ster′ il, -il) [O.F., from L. *sterilem*, nom. *-lis*, cogn. with Gr. *stereos*, STEREO-, G. *starr*, rigid], *a.* Barren, unfruitful; not producing crops, fruit, young, etc.; containing no living bacteria, microbes, etc., sterilized; (*fig.*) destitute of ideas or sentiment. **sterility** (stė ril′ i ti), *n.* **sterilize,** *v.t.* To rid of living bacteria; to make sterile; to render incapable of procreation. **sterilization** (-ză′ shŭn), *n.* **sterilizer,** *n.*

sterlet (stĕr′ lėt) [F., from Rus. *sterlyadi*], *n.* A small sturgeon, *Acipenser ruthenus.*

sterling (stĕr′ ling) [perh. from A.-S. *steorling*, little star, or as STARLING (1)], *a.* Of standard value, genuine, pure (of coins and precious metals); (*fig.*) sound, of intrinsic worth, not showy. *n.* British (as distinct from foreign) money; genuine British money. **sterling area:** (*Fin.*) A group of countries that keep their reserves in sterling rather than in gold or dollars.

stern (1) (stĕrn) [A.-S. *styrne*, perh. rel. to Gr. *stereos*, STEREO-], *a.* Severe, grim, forbidding, austere; harsh, rigid, strict; ruthless, unyielding, resolute. **sternly,** *adv.* **sternness,** *n.*

stern (2) (stĕrn) [M.E. *stēorne*, Icel. *stjōrn*, steering, cogn. with STEER (1)], *n.* The hind part of a ship or boat; the rump or tail of an animal. **stern-chase,** *n.* A chase in which one vessel follows the other straight behind. **stern-chaser** [CHASE (1)]. **stern-fast,** *n.* A rope or chain mooring the stern to a wharf, etc. **stern foremost:** (Moving) with the stern in front. **stern-post,** *n.* A timber or iron post forming the central upright of the stern and usu. carrying the rudder. **stern-sheets,** *n.pl.* The space in a boat between the stern and the aftermost thwart. **sternway,** *n.* The movement of a ship backward. **stern-wheel,** *n.* A paddle-wheel at the stern of a river-steamer. **stern-wheeler,** *n.* ***sternage,** *n.* (*Shak.*) Steerage; the stern. **sterned,** *a.* (*usu. in comb.*, as *flat-sterned*). **sternmost,** *a.* **sternward,** *a.* and *adv.* **-wards,** *adv.*

stern-, sterno- [STERNUM], *comb. form.* **sternal** (stĕr′ nål), *a.* Pertaining to the sternum. **sternalgia** (-ăl′ ji å), *n.* Pain in the chest, esp. angina pectoris. **sternebra** (stĕr′ nė brå), *n.* One of the serial segments of the sternum of a vertebrate. **sterno-clavicular** (-klå vik′ ū lår) [CLAVICULAR], *a.* Pertaining to the sternum and the clavicle.

sternly, etc. [STERN (1)].

sternmost [STERN (2)].

sternum (stĕr′ nŭm) [L., from Gr. *sternon*], *n.* The breast-bone.

sternutation (stĕr nū tā′ shŭn) [L. *sternūtātio*, from *sternūtāre*, freq. of *sternuere*, to sneeze, cp. Gr. *ptarnusthai*], *n.* The act of sneezing, a sneeze. **sternutative** (-nū′ tå tiv), **sternutatory,** *a.* Causing (one) to sneeze. *n.* A sternutative substance, as snuff.

sternward, etc. [STERN (2)].

stertorous (stĕr′ tȯr ŭs) [L. *stertere*, to snore, -OR, -OUS], *a.* Characterized by deep snoring or snore-like sounds. **stertorously,** *adv.* **stertorousness,** *n.*

stet (stet) [L., 3rd sing. pres. subj. of *stāre*, to stand], *v.t.* (*Print.*) Let it stand (cancelling a previous correction); to write 'stet' against.

stethometer (stė thom′ ė tėr) [Gr. *stēthos*, breast, -METER], *n.* An instrument for measuring the movements of the chest during respiration. **stethograph** (steth′ ȯ grăf), *n.* An instrument recording the movements of the thorax during respiration. **stethographic** (-grăf′ ik), *a.*

stethoscope (steth′ ȯ skōp) [as prec., -SCOPE], *n.* An instrument used in auscultation of the chest, etc. *v.t.* To examine with this. **stethoscopic** (-skop′ ik), *a.* **stethoscopically,** *adv.* **stethoscopist** (stė thos′ kȯ pist), *n.* **stethoscopy,** *n.*

stetson (stet′ sȯn) [maker's name], *n.* A broad-brimmed slouch hat.

stevedore (stē′ vė dôr) [Sp. *estivador*, from *estivar*, L. *stīpāre*, see STEEVE (2)], *n.* One whose occupation is to load or unload ships.

stew (1) (stū) [M.E. *stuwen*, from *stuwe, stue*, O.F. *estuve*, bath, hot-house, cogn. with STOVE (1)], *v.t.* To cook by boiling slowly or simmering. *v.i.* To be cooked thus; (*fig.*) to be stifled or oppressed by a close atmosphere. *n.* Meat, etc., cooked by stewing; (*fig.*) a state of mental agitation or worry; *(*pl.*) a brothel (orig. a bath- or hot-house). **stew-pan, -pot,** *n.* A cooking-utensil for stewing.

stew (2) (stū) [M.E. *stewe* (cp. L.G. *stau*, dam, *stauen*, to dam), cogn. with STOW], *n.* A fish-pond or tank for keeping fish alive for the table; an artificial oyster-bed.

steward (stū′ ård) [A.-S. *stigweard* (STY (1), WARD)], *n.* A person employed to manage the property or affairs of another or other persons (esp. the paid manager of a large estate or household), or of the service of provisions, etc., in a college, club, etc.; a petty officer on shipboard in charge of provisions, cabins, etc.; one of the officials superintending a ball, show, public meeting, etc. **Lord High Steward:** An officer of State regulating precedence at coronations, etc. **stewardess,** *n.* ***stewardry** (*Sc.*), **stewartry, stewardship,** *n.*

Stewart Islander (stū′ årt ī′ lån der), *n.* (*N. Zealand*) A fine oyster found on that island.

sthenic (sthen′ ik) [Gr. *sthenos*, strength, -IC], *a.* (*Path.*) Exhibiting a morbid degree of energy or vital action.

stibium (stib′ i ŭm) [L., from Gr. *stibi*], *n.* (*Pharm.*) Antimony. **stibial,** *a.* **stibialism,** *n.* (*Path.*) Antimonial poisoning. **stibiated,** *a.*

stich (stik) [Gr. *stichos*], *n.* A metrical line, a verse; (*Bibl.*) a line of the Bible, esp. one of the rhythmic lines exhibiting the parallelism of the poetic books. **stichic,** *a.* **stichomancy** [-MANCY], *n.* Divination by passages taken at random in a book. **stichomyth, stichomythia** (-mith′ i å) [Gr. *stichomuthia* (MYTH)], *n.* Dialogue in alternate metrical lines, as in the ancient Greek drama. ***stichometry** (sti kom′ ė tri) [-METRY], *n.* Measurement of books, etc., by the number of lines; an appendix giving the number of stichs or lines in a book, etc. ***stichometric** (-met′ rik), *a.*

stick (stik) [M.E. *steken*, to pierce (cp. L.G. *steken*, G. *stechen*, also Gr. *stizein*, L. *instīgāre*, to INSTIGATE), coalescing with M.E. *stikien*, A.-S. *stician*, to stick, to be fixed, to prick, etc. (n. from A.-S. *sticca*, peg, rel. to *stician*)], *v.t.* (*past & p.p.* **stuck**) To thrust the point of (in, through, etc.); to fix or insert (into); to thrust (out or up); to protrude, to fix upright; to fix on or as on a point; to pierce, to stab, to set with something pointed; to cause to adhere to; to furnish (a plant) with a stick to climb on; to set or compose (type). *v.i.* To be inserted or thrust (into); to protrude, project, or stand (up, out, etc.); to become fixed, to adhere; to remain attached (to); to be inseparable, to be constant (to); to persist, to persevere; to be stopped, hindered, or checked; (*fig.*) to be perplexed or embarrassed; to have scruples or misgivings, to hesitate (at). *n.* A shoot or branch of a tree or shrub broken or cut off, or a slender piece of wood or other material used as a rod, wand, staff, baton, walking-cane, etc., or as part of something; anything resembling this in shape; a drum-stick, composing-stick, fiddle-stick, etc.; a number of bombs dropped in succession; (*Naut. facet.*) a mast, a spar; (*fig.*) an awkward, incompetent or stupid person; a thrust, a stab, a dig. **to stick at nothing:** Not to be deterred or feel scruples. **to stick one's neck out:** (*colloq.*) To invite trouble; to take a risk. **to stick out:** To protrude, to hold out, to resist. **to stick out for:** To demand, to insist upon. **to stick up:** To put up, to erect; to stand up, to be prominent; to paste or post up; (*slang*) to puzzle, to nonplus; (*Austral. slang*) to hold up, to bail up. **to stick up for:** To take the part of, to defend. **to stick up to:** To stand up against, to resist. **stick-in-the-mud,** *a.* Dull, slow, unprogressive; *n.* Such a person. **stick insect** [WALKING-STICK]. **sticker,** *n.* One who or that which sticks; a knife used by butchers; a bill-sticker; (*organ*) a rod connecting two reciprocating levers; (*Cricket*) a batsman who stays in long, making few runs. **stickful,** *n.* **sticking-place, -point,** *n.* The place where a screw, etc., becomes jammed; (*fig.*) hesitation.. **sticking-plaster,** *n.* An adhesive plaster for wounds, etc. **stickit,** *a.* (*Sc.*) Stuck; (*fig.*) spoiled. **stickit minister:** (*Sc.*) One who fails to get a pastorate. **sticky,** *a.* Tending to stick, adhesive; viscous, glutinous; (*colloq.*) difficult, painful. **stickily,** *adv.* **stickiness,** *n.* **stuck-up,** *a.* Standing up, erect, not turned down (of a collar); (*fig.*) puffed up, conceited, giving oneself airs.

stickle (1) (stik′ ėl) [prob. from M.E. *stightlen*, to be umpire, freq. from A.-S. *stihtan*, to arrange, to regulate], *v.i.* To contend pertinaciously for some trifle; *to interfere, to take part with one side or the other. **stickler,** *n.* One who stands out for trifles.

stickle (2) (stik′ ėl) [A.-S. *sticol*, high, steep], *n.* (*prov.*) A sharp run or shallow in a stream where the water is rough, a scour.

stickleback (stik′ ėl băk) [A.-S. *sticel*, prickle, from *stician*, to STICK], *n.* A small spiny-backed, fresh-water fish.

stickler [STICKLE (1)]. **sticky,** etc. [STICK].

stiff (stif) [A.-S. *stīf*, cp. Dut. *stijf*, Dan. *stiv*, Swed. *styf*, cp. STEEVE (2)], *a.* Rigid, not easily bent or moved; not pliant, not flexible, not yielding, not working freely; (*fig.*) obstinate, stubborn, firm, persistent; constrained, not easy, not graceful, awkward, formal, precise, affected; (*colloq.*) hard to deal with or accomplish; difficult; strong (of liquor); high (of prices); not fluid, thick and tenacious, viscous. *n.* (*slang*) A bill of exchange, negotiable money, forged paper; a corpse; (*racing*) a horse that is sure to lose. ***stiff-hearted,** *a.* **stiff-neck:** Rheumatism affecting the muscles of the neck. **stiff-necked,** *a.* Stubborn, self-willed. **stiff-neckedness,** *n.* **stiffen,** *v.t.* and *i.* To make or become stiff. **stiffener,** *n.* **stiffening,** *n.* **stiffish,** *a.* **stiffly,** *adv.* **stiffness,** *n.*

stifle (1) (stī′ fėl) [Icel. *stīfla*, freq. of *stiva*, to stiffen, cogn. with STIFF], *v.t.* and *i.* To smother, to suffocate. **stiflingly,** *adv.*

stifle (2) (stī′ fėl) [perh. from STIFF], *n.* The stifle-joint; a disease affecting this or the stifle-bone. **stifle-bone,** *n.* A horse's knee-pan or patella. **stifle-joint,** *n.* The joint of a horse's hind-leg between the femur and tibia.

stigma (stig′ mȧ) [L., from Gr. *stigma -matos*, from *stizein*, to brand], *n.* (*pl.* **-mas**) A mark formerly made with a branding-iron on slaves, criminals, etc.; (*fig.*) a mark of infamy, disgrace, etc.; (*Anat. and Zool.*) a natural mark or spot, a pore; (*Bot.*) the part of the pistil which receives the pollen; (*pl.* **stigmata**) (*Path.*) a small red spot on the skin from which blood oozes in excitement, etc.; (*R.-C. Ch.*) marks miraculously developed on the body, corresponding to the wounds of Christ. **Stigmaria** (-mâr′ i ȧ), *n.pl.* (*Palæont.*) The roots of species of Sigillaria and Lepidodendron found in the coal-measures. **stigmatic** (-măt′ ik), *a.* Pertaining to, like, or having stigmas or stigmata. **stigmatiform,** *a.* **stigmatiferous,** *a.* **stigmatically,** *adv.* **stigmatist** (stig′ mȧ tist), *n.* One on whom stigmata are said to be impressed. **stigmatize,** *v.t.* To mark with a brand of disgrace, etc.; (*R.-C. Ch. and Hypnotism*) to cause stigmata to appear on. **stigmatization** (-tī zā′ shŭn), *n.* **stigmatose,** *a.* (*Bot.*) Stigmatic. **stigmatosis** (-tō′ sis), *n.* (*Path.*) A spotty form of inflammation in the skin. **stigmatypy** (stig′ mȧ tī pi) [TYPE], *n.* A method of printing with points arranged to form pictures.

stilbite (stil′ bīt) [Gr. *stilbein*, to shine, -ITE], *n.* (*Min.*) A vitreous silicate of the zeolite group.

stile (1) (stīl) [A.-S. *stigel*, from *stīgan*, to climb], *n.* A series of steps or other contrivance by which one may get over or through a fence, etc.

stile (2) [STYLE (1 and 2)].

stiletto (sti let′ ō) [It., dim. of *stilo*, L. *stīlus*, STYLE (1)], *n.* (*pl.* **-tos**) A small dagger; a pointed instrument for making eyelet-holes, etc. *v.t.* To stab with a stiletto. **stiletto heel:** An excessively tapered heel for a woman's shoe.

still (1) (stil) [A.-S. *stille* (cp. Dut. *stil*, G. *still*, Dan. *stille*), rel. to *stillan*, to rest, cogn. with *stellan*, to place], *a.* At rest, motionless; quiet, calm; silent, noiseless, hushed; not effervescent (of liquors). *n.* Stillness, calm, quiet; (*Cinema.*) a picture made with a portrait camera for record or publicity purposes. *adv.* Now, then, or for the future, as previously; even till now or then, yet; nevertheless, all the same; *continually, habitually. *v.t.* To quiet, to calm; to silence; to appease. **v.i.* To grow calm. **still birth:** The bringing forth of a dead child; a child born dead. **stillborn,** *a.* **still life:** The representation of fruit, flowers, and other inanimate objects. ***still-vexed,** *a.* (*Shak.*) In continual agitation. ***stilly,** *adv.* **stillness,** *n.*

still (2) (stil) [L. *stillāre*, to drip; sometimes short for DISTIL], *n.* A vessel or apparatus employed in distillation, esp. of spirituous liquors, consisting of a boiler, a tubular condenser or worm enclosed in a refrigerator, and a receiver. *v.t.* To distil. **still-room,** *n.* A room for distilling; a store-room for liquors, preserves, etc. **stilliform,** *a.* Drop-shaped.

stillage (stil′ ȧj) [cp. STILLING], *n.* A frame, stool, bench, etc., for placing things on for draining, waiting to be packed up, etc.

stilliform [STILL (2)].

stilling (stil′ ing) [cp. L.G. *stelling*, G. *stellung*, from *stellen*, to place, cp. STILL (1)], *n.* A stand for a cask.

stillness, stilly [STILL (1)].

stilt (stilt) [M.E. *stilte*, Swed. *stylta* (cp. Dut. *stelt*, G. *stelze*), prob. cogn. with O.H.G. *stellan*, to place], *n.* A pole having a rest for the foot, used in pairs, to raise a person above the ground in walking; a long-legged, three-toed, shore-bird related to the plover. **stilt-bird, -plover,** *n.* The common stilt, *Himantopus candidus*. **stilted,** *a.* Raised on or as on stilts; (*fig.*) bombastic, inflated (of literary style, etc.); springing from vertical masonry set on the imposts (of an arch).

Stilton (stil′ tȯn), *n.* A rich, white, veined cheese, orig. made at Stilton, in Hunts.

stimulant (stim′ ū lȧnt) [L. *stimulans, -ntem*, pres.p. of *stimulāre*, to prick, from *stimulus*, goad], *a.* Serving to stimulate; (*Med.*) producing a quickly diffused and transient increase of vital energy. *n.* Anything that stimulates, esp. alcoholic liquor.

stimulate (stim′ ū lāt), *v.t.* To rouse to action or greater exertion; to spur on, to incite; to excite organic action. *v.i.* To act as a stimulus. **stimulation** (-lā′ shȯn), *n.* **stimulative** (stim′ ū lā tiv), *a.* **stimulator,** *n.* **stimulose,** *a.* (*Bot.*)

stimulus (stim′ ū lȯs), *n.* (*pl.* **stimuli**) That which stimulates; an incitement, a spur; (*Physiol.*) that which excites reaction in a nerve, etc.; (*Bot., etc.*) a sting; (*Med.*) a stimulant.

stimy [STYMY].

sting (sting) [A.-S. *stingan* (cp. Icel. and Swed. *stinga*, Dan. *stinge*), perh. rel. to STICK], *v.t.* (*past & p.p.* **stung**) To pierce or wound with a sting; (*fig.*) to cause acute physical or mental pain to; (*slang*) to cheat, to overcharge. *v.t.* To have or use a sting; to have an acute and smarting pain. *n.* A sharp-pointed defensive or offensive organ, often conveying poison, with which certain insects, scorpions, and plants are armed; the act of stinging; the wound or pain so caused; (*fig.*) any acute pain, ache, smart, stimulus, etc. **sting-bull, -fish,** *n.* The greater weaver, *Trachinus draco.* **sting-ray,** *n.* A tropical ray with a venomous spine on its tail. **stingaree** [STING-RAY]. **stinger,** *n.* One who, or that which, stings; a smarting blow. **stinging-nettle,** *n.* **stingless,** *a.*

stingily, stinginess [STINGY].

stingo (sting′ gō) [from STING], *n.* (*slang*). Strong ale.

stingy (stin′ ji) [STING, -Y], *a.* Close-fisted, meanly parsimonious, niggardly. **stingily,** *adv.* **stinginess,** *n.*

stink (stingk) [A.-S. *stincan*, cp. Dut. and G. *stinken*, Dan. *stinke*, Swed. *stinka*], *v.i.* (*past* **stank, stunk,** *p.p.* **stunk**) To emit a strong, offensive smell; (*fig.*) to have an evil reputation. *v.t.* To annoy with an offensive smell. *n.* A strong, offensive smell; (*slang*) a disagreeable exposure. **stink-ball, stink-pot,** *n.* A device holding a combustible mixture causing offensive fumes, for use in warfare. **stink-horn,** *n.* An evil-smelling fungus, esp. *Phallus impudicus.* **stink-stone,** *n.* A limestone or other rock emitting a fetid odour when struck. **stink-trap** [STENCH-TRAP]. **stinkard,** *n.* A stinking person, animal, etc.; the teledu; the skunk. **stinker,** *n.* A stinkard, a stinkpot. **stinking,** *a.* Emitting an offensive smell; (*fig.*) offensive, repulsive, objectionable. **stinkingly,** *adv.*

stint (stint) [A.-S. *styntan*, from *stunt*, dull, witless, cp. Icel. *stytta*, to shorten, from *stuttr*, short], *v.t.* To give or allow scantily or grudgingly; to supply scantily or grudgingly (with food, etc.). **v.i.* To cease, to leave off. *n.* Limit, bound, restriction; an allotted amount, quantity, turn of work, etc.; a small sandpiper, esp. the dunlin. **stintedness,** *n.* ***stinter,** *n.* **stintingly,** *adv.* **stintless,** *a.* Unstinted; abundant.

stipate (stī′ păt) [L. *stīpātus*, p.p. of *stīpāre*, to pack], *a.* (*Bot.*) Crowded, close-set.

stipe (stīp) [F., from L. *stīpes -pilis*], *n.* (*Bot. and Zool.*) A stalk, stem or stem-like support, also **stipes** (stī′ pēz, *pl.* **-pites,** -pi′ tēz). **stipel,** *n.* (*Bot.*) A secondary stipule at the base of a leaflet. **stipellate, stipiform, stipitate, stipitiform,** *a.*

stipend (stī′ pėnd) [L. *stipendium* (*stips, stipem*, gift in small coin, *pendere*, to pay)], *n.* A periodical payment for services rendered, a salary, esp. of a clergyman. **stipendiary** (sti pend′-), *a.* Performing services for or receiving a stipend. *n.* One receiving a stipend, esp. a paid magistrate.

stipes, stipitate, etc. [STIPE].

stipple (stip′ ėl) [Dut. *stippelen*, from *stippel*, dim. of *stip*, point, cp. G. *stift*, pin], *v.t.* and *i.* To engrave, paint, or draw by means of dots instead of lines, etc. *n.* This method; work produced thus. **stippler,** *n.*

stipulaceous, stipular, etc. [STIPULE].

stipulate (1) (stip′ ū lāt) [L. *stipulātus*, p.p. of *stipulārī*, from O.L. *stipulus*, firm, fast, cogn. with *stīpes*, post], *v.t.* To lay down or specify as essential to an agreement. *v.i.* To settle terms. **stipulation** (1) (-lā′ shȯn), *n.* **stipulator** (stip′ ū lā tȯr), *n.*

stipule (stip′ ūl) [L. *stipula*, dim. of *stipes*, STIPE], *n.* (*Bot.*) A small leaf-like appendage, usu. in pairs at the base of a petiole. **stipulaceous** (-lā′ shȯs), **stipular, -lary, -late** (2), **-liform** (stip′-), *a.* **stipulation** (2) (-lā′ shȯn), *n.*

stir (stĕr) [A.-S. *styrian*, cp. Dut. *storen*, G. *stören*, Icel. *styrr*, a stir], *v.t.* (*past & p.p.* **stirred**) To cause to move, to agitate, to disturb; to move vigorously, to bestir (oneself, etc.); to rouse (up), to excite, to animate, to inflame. *v.i.* To move, to be in motion, not to be still. *n.* Agitation, commotion, bustle, excitement; a movement; the act of stirring; (*slang*) prison. **stirabout,** *n.* Porridge. *a.* Active, bustling. **stirless,** *a.* **stirrer,** *n.* **stirring,** *a.* Moving; animating, rousing, exciting, stimulating. **stirringly,** *adv.*

stirk (stĕrk) [A.-S. *styric*, dim. of *stēor*, STEER (2)], *n.* (*prov.*) A yearling ox or cow.

stirps (stĕrps) [L.], *n.* (*pl.* **-pes,** -pēz) (*Law*) Stock, family, progenitor; (*Zool.*) a classificatory group. **stirpiculture,** *n.* Eugenics. **stirpicultural,** *a.*

stirrup (stir′ ȯp) [A.-S. *srīrāp* (*stīgan*, to climb, *rāp*, ROPE)], *n.* A horseman's foot-rest, usu. consisting of an iron loop suspended from the saddle by a strap; (*Naut.*) a rope with an eye for carrying a foot-rope. **stirrup-cup,** *n.* A parting cup on horseback. **stirrup-iron, stirrup-leather, -strap,** *n.* **stirrup-pump,** *n.* A portable hand-pump with a length of hose, to be worked by one or two persons.

stitch (stich) [A.-S. *stice*, from *stician*, see STICK (cp. *stich* and *stechen*)], *n.* A sharp intense pain in the side; a single pass of the needle in sewing; a single turn of the wool or thread round a needle in knitting; the link of thread, wool, etc., thus inserted. *v.t.* and *i.* To sew. **to stitch up:** To sew together or mend. **stitch-bird,** *n.* The N. Zealand honey-eater. **stitcher,** *n.* **stitchery,** *n.*

stitchwort (stich′ wĕrt), *n.* (*Bot.*) A plant of the genus *Alsine*, esp. two species with starry white flowers, common in hedges.

***stithy** (sti*th*′ i) [M.E. *stith*, Icel. *stethi*, anvil, -Y], *n.* A forge, a smithy. *v.t.* To forge on an anvil.

stiver (stīv′ ėr) [Dut. *stuiver*, a former Dutch coin], *n.* Any small coin.

stoa (stō′ ȧ) [Gr.], *n.* (*Gr. Ant.*) A portico.

stoat (stōt) [M.E. *stot*, male animal, stoat, cp. Icel. *stūtr*, Swed. and Norw. *stut*, bull, Dut. *stooten*, G. *stossen*, to push], *n.* The ermine, esp. in its summer coat; applied also to the weasel, ferret, etc.

stob (stob) [var. of STUB], *n.* (*Coal-mining*) A steel wedge used for bringing down coal; (*Sc.*) a small post, a stake, a stump.

***stoccade, *stoccado** (stȯ kad′, -ka′ dō) [It. *stoccata*, from *stocco*, rapier, G. *stock*, stick], *n.* A movement in fencing.

stock (1) (stok) [A.-S. *stocc*, cp. Dut. *stok*, G. *stock*, Icel. *stokkr*], *n.* The trunk or main stem of a tree or other plant; (*fig.*) a family, a breed, a line of descent, a distinct group of languages; (*Biol.*) a colony, an aggregate organism; a post, a butt, a stump; (*fig.*) a stupid, senseless person; the principal supporting or holding part of anything, the handle, block, base, body, etc.; liquor from boiled meat, bones, etc., used as a basis for soup; the aggregate of goods, raw material, etc., kept on hand for trade, manufacture, etc., or as a reserve store; the beasts on a farm (called live stock), or implements of husbandry and produce (called dead stock); (*Finance*) money lent to a government represented by certificates entitling the holders to fixed interest; the capital of a corporate company divided into shares entitling the holders to a proportion of the profits; (*pl.*) the shares of such capital; a stock-gillyflower; (*pl.*) a frame of timber with holes in which the ankles, and sometimes also the wrists, of petty offenders were formerly confined; (*pl.*) a timber framework on which a vessel rests during building; *a band of silk, leather, etc., worn as a cravat, now superseded by the collar, except in some uniforms. *a.* Kept in stock; habitually used, standing, permanent. *v.t.* To provide with goods, live stock, or other requisites; to keep in stock; to furnish with a handle, butt, etc.; *to put into the stocks, *v.i.* To take in supplies; to tiller. **fat stock,** *n.* Beasts in condition for slaughter as food. **live stock,** *n.* Domestic and draught animals; (*facet.*) verminous insects. **in stock:** On hand. **on the stocks:** In preparation. **to take stock:** To make an inventory of goods, etc., on hand; (*fig.*) to survey one's position, prospects, etc.; to examine, to form an estimate (of a person, etc.). **stock-book,** *n.* A book recording quantities of goods received and disposed of. **stock-breeder,** *n.* One who raises live stock. **stock-broker,** *n.* One engaged in the purchase and sale of stocks on commission. **stock-broking,** *n.* **stock company:** (*Theat.*) The actors working a repertory company. **stock exchange:** The place where stocks or shares are publicly bought and sold. **stock-farmer,** *n.* One who raises live stock. **stock-gillyflower,** *n.* A fragrant, bright-flowered herbaceous plant, *Matthiola incana.* **stock-holder,** *n.* A proprietor of stock in the public funds or shares in a stock company; (*Austral.*) a grazier. **stock-in-trade,** *n.* Goods, tools, and other requisites of a trade, etc.; (*fig.*) resources, capabilities. **stock-jobber,** *n.* A dealer who speculates in stocks so as to profit by fluctuations of price and acts as an intermediary between buying and selling stock-brokers. **stock-jobbing, -jobbery,** *n.* **stock-list,** *n.* A publication giving current prices, etc., of stocks. **stock-man,** *a.* (*Austral.*) One in charge of live stock, also called a **stock-keeper. stock-market,** *n.* A stock exchange or the business transacted there; a cattle-market. **stock-pile,** *v.t.* To accumulate commodities, esp. reserves of raw materials. **stock-pot,** *n.* A pot for storing stock for soup. **stock-rider,** *n.* (*Austral.*) A herdsman in charge of stock. **stock-still,** *a.* Motionless. **stock-taking,** *n.* **stock-whip,** *n.* A short-handled whip with a long lash for herding cattle. **stock-yard,** *n.* An enclosure with pens, etc., for cattle at market, etc. ***stockish,** *a.* Stupid, dull. **stockist,** *n.* (*Comm.*) One who keeps certain goods in stock. **stockless,** *a.* **stocky,** *a.* Thick-set, short and stout, stumpy. **stockily,** *adv.* **stockiness,** *n.*

***stock** (2) [STOCCADO].

stockade (stȯ kād′) [Sp. *estacada,* from *estaca,* M.Dut. *stake,* see STAKE, assim. to STOCK (1)], *n.* A line or enclosure of posts or stakes. *v.t.* To surround or fortify with a stockade.

stockdove (stok′ dŭv), *n.* The European wild pigeon, *Columba œnas,* smaller and darker than the ring-dove.

stockfish (stok′ fish), *n.* Cod, ling, etc., split open and dried in the sun without salting.

stockinet (stok′ i net) [dim. of foll.], *n.* An elastic knitted material for undergarments, etc.

stocking (stok′ ing) [dim. of STOCK (1), in sense of trunk or docked part, earlier *stocks,* short for *netherstocks,* the *upper-stocks* being the knee-breeches], *n.* A close-fitting covering for the foot and leg (*usu. in pl.*); an elastic covering used as a support for the leg in cases of varicose veins, etc. **stocking-frame, -loom, -machine,** *n.* **stockingless,** *a.*

stockish, stocky, etc. [STOCK (1)].

stodgy (stoj′ i) [etym. doubtful], *a.* Heavy, stiff, indigestible (of food); crammed, lumpy (of a bag, etc.); (*fig.*) dull, heavy, matter-of-fact (of books, etc.). **stodge,** *n.* (*slang*) Food, esp. stodgy food; *v.i.* To feed, to stuff. **stodginess,** *n.*

stoep (stoop) [S. Afr. Dut.], *n.* (*S. Afr.*) An open, roofed platform in front of a house.

Stoic (stō′ ik) [L. *Stoicus,* Gr. *Stoikos,* from STOA, with ref. to the *Stoa Poikilē,* painted porch, at Athens, where Zeno taught], *n.* A philosopher of the school founded by Zeno *c.* 308 B.C., teaching that virtue is the highest good, and that the passions and appetites should be rigidly subdued. *a.* Stoical. **stoical,** *a.* **stoically,** *adv.* **stoicalness, stoicism** (stō′ i sizm), *n.*

stoichiology (stoik i ol′ ȯ ji) [Gr. *stoicheion,* dim. of *stoichos,* post, -LOGY], *n.* The doctrine of elements or fundamental processes, laws, etc. **stoichiometry** (-om′ ė tri) [-METRY], *n.* The branch of chemistry treating of chemical combination in definite proportions, the mathematics of chemistry. **stoichiometric, -al** (-met′ rik, -ăl), *a.*

stoke (stōk) [back-formation from Dut., STOKER (*stoken,* to make fire, prob. from M.Dut. *stock,* stick or poker, -ER)], *v.t.* To tend (a furnace, esp. of a steam-engine). *v.i.* To act as stoker. **stoke-hold,** *n.* The compartment where the furnaces are tended, esp. on ship-board. **stoke-hole,** *n.* The mouth of a furnace; an aperture in a blast-furnace, etc., for a stirring tool and adding fuel; a stoke-hold. **stoker,** *n.* A man who stokes a furnace.

stole (1) (stōl) [L. *stola,* Gr. *stolē,* from *stellein,* to array], *n.* (*Rom. Ant.*) The outer garment of a Roman matron; (*Eccles.*) a narrow band of silk, etc., worn over both shoulders by priests, and by deacons over the left shoulder; a band of fur, etc., worn round the neck by women.

stole (2) [STOLON].

stole (3), *past,* **stolen,** *p.p.* [STEAL].

***stole** (4) [var. of STOOL], *n.* A privy. **groom of the stole:** The first lord of the bed-chamber.

stolid (stol′ id) [L. *stolidus*], *a.* Dull, impassive, phlegmatic, stupid. **stolidity** (stȯ lid′ i ti), **stolidness,** *n.* **stolidly,** *adv.*

stolon (stō′ lȯn) [L. *stolo -onis*], *n.* A trailing or prostrate shoot that takes root and develops a new plant; an underground shoot in mosses developing leaves. **stolonate, stoloniferous** (-nif′ ėr ŭs), *a.*

stoma (stō′ mȧ) [Gr.], *n.* (*pl.* **stomata**) A minute orifice, a pore; (*Bot.*) an aperture for respiration in a leaf. **stomatic** (stȯ măt′ ik), **stomatiferous** (-tif′ ėr ŭs), *a.* **stomapod** (stom′ ȧ pod) [Gr. *pous podos,* foot], *n.* Any member of the *Stomapoda,* a sub-order of podophthalmate crustaceans with gills attached to natatory feet.

stomach (stŭm′ ȧk) [M.E. *stomak,* O.F. *estomac,* L. *stomachum,* nom. *-us,* Gr. *stomachos,* dim. of STOMA], *n.* A digestive cavity formed by a dilatation of the alimentary canal, or (in certain animals) one of several such cavities; (*loosely*) the belly, the abdomen; (*fig.*) appetite, inclination, liking; *anger, resentment, sullenness, haughtiness, arrogance. *v.t.* To accept as palatable; (*fig.*) to put up with, to brook. **stomach-ache,** *n.* An abdominal pain. **stomach-pump,** *n.* A suction- and force-pump for withdrawing the contents of the stomach, also used as an injector. **stomach-staggers,** *n.* Apoplexy in horses due to paralysis of the stomach. **stomachal,** *a.* **stomacher,** *n.* An ornamental covering for the breast and upper abdomen worn by women in the 15th–17th cents. **stomachful,** *n.* **stomachic** (stȯ măk′ ik), *a.* Pertaining to the stomach; exciting the action of the stomach or aiding digestion. *n.* A stomachic medicine.

stomatitis (stō mȧ tī′ tis) [STOMA], *n.* Inflammation of the mouth. **stomatogastric,** *a.* Pertaining to the mouth and the stomach. **stomatology,** *n.* The science of diseases of the mouth.

stomp (stomp), *v.t.* and *i.* (*Am.*) To stamp with the feet.

stone (stōn) [A.-S. *stān*, cp. Dut. *steen*, G. *stein*, Icel. *steinn*], *n.* A piece of rock, esp. a small one, a pebble, cobble, or piece used in road-making, etc.; rock as material for building, paving, etc.; a piece of this shaped and prepared for a specific purpose, as a millstone, grindstone, tombstone, etc.; a gem, usu. called a precious stone; a calculus, the disease calculus; a testicle (*usu. in pl.*); the seed of a grape, etc., the hard case of the kernel in a drupe or stone-fruit, a hailstone; a measure of weight of 14 lb. *a.* Made of stone or a hard material like stone. *v.t.* To pelt with stones; to face, wall, or pave with stone; to free (fruit) from stones. **to leave no stone unturned:** To use all available means to effect an object. **stone age:** The period in which primitive man used implements of stone, not metal. **stone-axe,** *n.* A stone-cutter's axe with two blunt edges. **stone-blind,** *a.* Perfectly blind. **stone-boiling,** *n.* A primitive method of making water boil by putting hot stones into it. **stone-borer,** *n.* A mollusc that bores into stone. **stone-break,** *n.* Saxifrage. **stone-cast** [STONE'S CAST]. **stone-chat, -chatter,** *n.* The wheatear. **stone-coal,** *n.* Anthracite. **stone-cold,** *a.* Quite cold. **stone-coral,** *n.* Massive as distinguished from branched coral. **stone-crop,** *n.* Any species of *Sedum*, esp. *S. acre.* **stone-curlew,** *n.* The thick-knee curlew. **stone-cutter,** *n.* One whose occupation is to cut stones for building, etc. **stone-cutting,** *n.* **stone-dead,** *a.* Dead as a stone. **stone-deaf,** *a.* Quite deaf. **stone-dresser,** *n.* **stone-eater** [STONE-BORER]. **stone-fern,** *n.* Ceterach. **stone-fly,** *n.* An insect with aquatic larvæ harbouring under stones, used as bait for trout. **stone-fruit,** *n.* A fruit with seeds covered by a hard shell, as peaches, plums, etc., a drupe. ***stone-horse,** *n.* An uncastrated stallion. **stone man:** A small cairn marking a track, etc. **stone-mason,** *n.* One who dresses stones or builds with stone. **stone-parsley,** *n.* A hedge parsley, *Sison Amomum*, the meadow saxifrage. **stone-pine,** *n.* The Mediterranean pine with a spreading top. **stone-pit,** *n.* A stone quarry. **stone-pitch,** *n.* Hard, inspissated pitch. **stone-plover** [STONE-CURLEW]. **stone-rag,** *n.* A lichen, *Parmelia saxatilis.* **stone-rue,** *n.* Wall-rue. **stone-snipe,** *n.* A large N. American snipe. **stone-still,** *a.* Perfectly still. **stone-wall:** (*Austral.*) To obstruct parliamentary business by making long speeches; (*Cricket*) to stay in batting without trying to make runs. **stone-ware,** *n.* Pottery made from clay and flint or a hard siliceous clay. **stone-work,** *n.* Masonry. **stonewort,** *n.* The stone-parsley and other plants. **stone's cast** or **throw:** The distance a stone can be thrown by hand. **stoned,** *a.* (*usu. in comb.*, as *hard-stoned.*) **stoneless,** *a.* **stony,** *a.* Pertaining to, made or consisting of, abounding in or resembling stone; (*fig.*) hard, cruel, pitiless; impassible; obdurate, perverse; (*slang*) destitute or nearly destitute of money. **stony-hearted,** *a.* **stonily,** *adv.* **stoniness,** *n.*

stood, *past & p.p.* [STAND].

stooge (stooj) [onomat.], *n.* A butt, a confederate, a decoy; a subordinate.

stook (stuk) [cp. L.G., Dan., and Swed. dial. *stuke*], *n.* (*chiefly Sc.*) A bundle of sheaves set up. *v.t.* To set up in stooks.

stool (stool) [A.-S. *stōl*, cp. Dut. *stoel*, G. *stūhl*, Icel. *stōll*, cogn. with STAND], *n.* A seat without a back, for one person, usu. with three or four legs; a low bench for kneeling or resting the feet on; the seat used in evacuating the bowels; an evacuation; the stump of a timber-tree from which shoots are thrown up; a plant or stock from which young plants are produced by layering, etc. *v.i.* To shoot out stems from the root; to evacuate the bowels. **stool of repentance:** A cutty-stool. **stool-pigeon,** *n.* A pigeon used as a decoy; a decoy.

stoop (1) (stoop) [A.-S. *stūpian* (cp. M.Dut. *stuypen*, Icel. *stūpa*), cogn. with STEEP (1 and 2)], *v.i.* To bend the body downward and forward; to have an habitual forward inclination of the head and shoulders; (*fig.*) to condescend, to lower, to bring oneself down (to); *to pounce, to swoop. *v.t.* To incline (the head, shoulders, etc.) downward and forward. *n.* The act of stooping; an habitual inclination of the shoulders, etc.; *the swoop of a bird on its prey. **stoopingly,** *adv.*

stoop (2) [STOEP]. **stoop** (3) [STOUP].

stoor (stoor) [cogn. with STIR], *v.t.* (*prov.*) To stir up; to pour out. *v.i.* To rise in clouds (of dust or smoke). *n.* Dust flying about; stir, commotion.

stop (stop) [A.-S. *stoppian*, in *forstoppian*, from late L. *stuppāre*, from *stūpa*, *stuppa*, tow (cp. Gr. *stupē*, *stuppē*)], *v.t.* (*past & p.p.* **stopped**) To close by filling or obstructing, to stanch, to plug (up); to fill a crack, a cavity in a tooth, etc.; to impede; to cause to cease moving, going, working, or acting (or from moving, etc.); to prevent the doing or performance of; to keep back, to cut off, to suspend; (*Mus.*) to press a string, close an aperture, etc. (of an instrument) so as to alter the pitch. *v.i.* To come to an end, to come to rest; to discontinue, to cease or desist (from); (*colloq.*) to stay, to remain temporarily, to sojourn; to punctuate. *n.* The act of stopping or the state of being stopped, a cessation, a pause, an interruption; a punctuation mark indicating a pause; a block, peg, pin, etc., used to stop the movement of something at a particular point; (*Mus.*) the pressing down of a string, closing of an aperture, etc., effecting a change of pitch; a key, lever, or other device employed in this; a set of pipes in an organ having tones of a distinct quality; a knob bringing these into play; (*Opt., etc.*) a perforated diaphragm for regulating the passage of light; (*Phon.*) a sound produced by closure of the mouth, a mute consonant. **to stop a gap** [GAP]. **to stop down:** (*Phot.*) To reduce the area of (a lens) transmitting light, by means of a diaphragm. **to stop over:** To break one's journey. **stopcock,** *n.* A tap, a faucet. **stopgap,** *n.* A temporary substitute or expedient. **stop-press,** *a.* Applied to news inserted in a paper after the printing has commenced. **stop-watch,** *n.* A watch, an additional hand of which can be stopped by a special device at any second or fraction of a second, used for timing races, etc. **stoppage,** *n.* **stopper,** *n.* One who or that which stops; a plug, a stopple; (*Naut.*) a rope, plug, clamp, etc., for checking the motion of a cable, etc. *v.t.* To close or secure with a stopper.

stopping (stop′ ing), *n.* Material for filling a cavity in a tooth; the operation of stopping a tooth; plastic material for filling holes and cracks in wood, etc., before painting.

stopple (stop′ ėl), *n.* That which stops or closes the mouth of a vessel, a stopper, plug, bung, etc.; *v.t.* To close with a stopple.

storage [STORE].

storax (stôr′ ăks) [L., from Gr. *sturax*], *n.* A balsamic vanilla-scented resin obtained from *Styrax officinalis*, formerly used in medicine, etc.; the tree itself.

store (stôr) [O.F. *estor*, late L. *staurum*, *instaurum*, from *instaurāre* (IN-, *staurāre*, see RESTORE)], *n.* A stock laid up for drawing upon; an abundant supply, plenty, abundance (*often in pl.*); a place where things are laid up or kept for sale, a storehouse, a warehouse; a large establishment where articles of various kinds are sold; (*Am.*) a shop; (*pl.*) articles kept on hand for special use, esp. ammunition, arms, military and naval provisions, etc., a supply of such articles. *v.t.* To accumulate or lay (usu. up or away) for future use; to stock or supply (with); to deposit in a warehouse, etc., for safe keeping; to hold or keep in (as water, etc.). **in store:** In reserve; ready for use; on hand; **to set store by:** To value highly. **store cattle:** Cattle for fattening. **storehouse,** *n.* A place where things are stored up, a warehouse, granary, repository, etc.; (*fig.*) a great quantity. **storekeeper,** *n.* One who has the charge of stores; (*Am.*) a shopkeeper. **store-room,** *n.* **store-ship,** *n.* A supply-vessel for a fleet, etc. **storable,** *a.*

storage (stôr′ ij), *n.* The act of storing, warehousing, etc.; the price paid for or the space reserved for this; the control of a water-supply. **storer,** *n.*

storey [STORY (2)].

storiated [HISTORIATED].

storied (1) [STORY (2)]; (2) [STORY (1)].

storiology, etc. [STORY (1)].

stork (stôrk) [A.-S. *storc*, cp. Dut. *stork*, G. *storch*, Icel. *storkr*, also Gr. *torgos*], *n.* A long-necked, long-legged wading-bird of the genus *Ciconia*, allied to the heron, esp. the white or house-stork *C. alba*, nesting on buildings. **stork's-bill,** *n.* A plant of the genus *Erodium* allied to the crane's-bill. **King Stork:** An oppressive ruler (alln. to Æsop's Fables).

storm (stôrm) [A.-S. (cp. Dut., Swed., and Dan. *storm*, G. *sturm*, Icel. *stormr*), cogn. with STIR], *n.* A violent disturbance of the atmosphere attended by wind, rain, snow, hail, or thunder and lightning, a tempest; (*fig.*) a violent disturbance or agitation of society life, the mind, etc., a tumult, commotion, etc.; a violent outburst (of cheers, etc.); a direct assault on a fortified place. *v.i.* To rage (of wind, rain, etc.); (*fig.*) to bluster, to fume, to behave violently. *v.t.* To take by storm. **a storm in a teacup:** A fuss about nothing. **storm and stress** [trans. of G. *Sturm und Drang*]: A period of unrest, ferment, and revolt, in life, literature, etc. **storm-beat, -beaten,** *a.* Beaten or injured by storms. **storm-belt,** *n.* A zone where storms are frequent. **storm-bird,** *n.* The stormy petrel. **storm-bound,** *a.* Stopped or delayed by storms. **storm-centre,** *n.* The place of lowest pressure in a cyclonic storm; (*fig.*) a place, etc., liable to violent disturbance. **storm-cock,** *n.* The mistle-thrush, fieldfare, or green wood-pecker. **storm-cone** [STORM-SIGNAL]. **storm-drum** [STORM-SIGNAL]. **storm-finch,** *n.* The stormy petrel. **storm-glass,** *n.* A sealed tube containing an alcoholic solution of camphor, etc., which is affected by changes of temperature, and was formerly used as a weather-glass. **storm-proof,** *a.* **storm-sail,** *n.* A sail of smaller size and stouter canvas, for heavy weather. **storm-signal,** *n.* A signal usu. consisting of a hollow drum and cone of canvas, hoisted as warning of an approaching storm, the positions of the drum and cone indicating the probable direction of the wind. **storm-trooper,** *n.* A semi-military member of the Nazi party. **stormer,** *n.* **stormful,** *a.* **stormfulness,** *n.* **storming-party,** *n.* A party told off to lead an assault. **stormless,** *a.*

stormy (stôr′ mi), *a.* Characterized by storms; tempestuous; (*fig.*) violent, vehement, passionate. **stormy petrel:** The petrel. **stormily,** *adv.* **storminess,** *n.*

stornello (stôr nel′ ō) [It.], *n.* A form of improvised folk-song, usu. composed of two lines.

Storthing (stôr′ ting) [Norw. *stor*, great, *thing*, meeting], *n.* The Norwegian parliament.

story (1) (stôr′ i) [A.-F. *storie*, O.F. *estoire*, L. *historia*, HISTORY], *n.* A narrative or recital in prose or verse, of actual or fictitious events, a tale, short novel, romance, anecdote, legend, or myth; the plot or incidents of a novel, epic, or play; a series of facts of special interest connected with a person, place, etc.; an account of an incident, experience, etc.; a descriptive article in a newspaper; (*childish*) a falsehood, a fib; *history. **story-book,** *n.* A book containing a story or stories. **story-teller, -writer,** *n.* **story-telling,** *n.* **storied** (2), *a.* (*poet.*) Adorned with scenes from or celebrated in stories or history. **storiology** (-ol′ ŏ ji) [LOGY], *n.* The science of folk-lore. **storiologist,** *n.*

story (2) (stôr′ i) [L. *historia*, HISTORY, as above; but the line of sense-development is uncertain; not conn. with STORE], *n.* A horizontal division, a set of rooms on the same floor. **story-post,** *n.* An upright supporting a beam on which rests a floor or wall. **storied** (1), *a.* (*usu. in comb.*, as *three-storied*).

stot (stot) [M.E., see STOAT], *n.* A bullock, a steer; *a horse, a stallion.

***stound** (stound) [A.-S. *stund*, cp. Icel. *stund*, O.H.G. *stunt*, *stunta*], *n.* A certain length of time; a point of time, hour, season.

stoup (stoop) [Icel. *staup*, cp. Dut. *stoop*, G. *stauf*, Icel. *steap*], *n.* *A flagon, a drinking-vessel; a basin for holy water.

***stour** (stour) [O.F. *estour*, *estor*, O.H.G. *stōr*], *n.* A battle, a tumult; a paroxysm.

stoush (stoush), *n.* (*Austral. colloq.*) A fight, a brawl.

stout (stout) [O.F. *estout*, M.Dut. *stolt*, stout (cp. G. *stolz*, proud), perh. from L. *stultus*, stupid], *a.* Strong, sound, sturdy, stanch, well-built, lusty, vigorous, brave, resolute, intrepid; corpulent, bulky, fleshy. *n.* A malt liquor, very strong porter. **stout-hearted,** *a.* **stout-heartedly,** *adv.* **stout-heartedness,** *n.* **stoutish,** *a.* **stoutly,** *adv.* **stoutness,** *n.*

stovaine (stō′ vā ēn) [F.], *n.* (*Chem.*) Amylocaine hydrochloride, a local anæsthetic used largely for spinal operations.

stove (1) (stōv) (orig. a bath or hot-house, A.-S. *stofa* (cp. M.Dut. *stove*, G. *stube*, Icel. *stofa*, *stufa*), prob. rel. to STEW (1)], *n.* An apparatus, wholly or partially closed, in which fuel is burned for heating, cooking, etc.; a drying-room for explosives, etc.; an oven for heating the blast of a blast-furnace; a hot-house in which a high temperature is maintained. *v.t.* To heat, dry, force, etc., in a stove. **stove-pipe,** *n.* A pipe for conducting smoke, etc., from a stove to a chimney. **stove-pipe hat:** A high silk hat.

stove (2), *past* [STAVE].

***stover** (stō′ vėr, stŭv′ ėr) [O.F. *estover*, see ESTOVERS], *n.* Fodder for cattle.

stow (stō) [A.-S. *stōwigan*, from *stōw*, place, cogn. with STAND], *v.t.* To put or pack (often away) in a suitable or convenient place or position; to pack or fill compactly with things. **stow it:** (*slang*) Drop it! stop (joking, etc.). **stowaway,** *n.* One who conceals himself on a vessel in order to get a free passage. **stowage,** *n.* **stower,** *n.*

stown (*Sc.*) [STOLEN].

strabismus (stră biz′ mŭs) [Gr. *strabismos*, from *strabos*, crooked], *n.* (*Path.*) Squinting, a squint. **strabismal, -mic,** *a.* **strabotomy** (-bot′ ŏ mi) [-TOMY], *n.* The operation of cutting the muscle or muscles distorting the eyeball to cure squinting. **strabotome** (străb′ ŏ tōm), *n.* A knife for use in this operation.

straddle (străd′ ėl) [earlier *striddle*, freq. of STRIDE], *v.i.* To stand or walk with the legs wide apart; (*fig.*) to trim, to sit on the fence. *v.t.* To stand or sit astride of this. *n.* The act of straddling; the distance between the legs of one straddling; (*Stock Exch.*) a contract securing the right of either a put or call. **straddle-legged,** *a.* **straddler,** *n.*

Stradivarius (străd i vâr′ i ŭs), *n.* A stringed instrument, esp. a violin made by Antonio Stradivari of Cremona (1644–1737).

strae (strā) [Sc. var. of STRAW (1)], *n.* Straw. **strae death:** Death in one's bed (orig. on one's straw), opp. to a violent death.

strafe (straf) [G. *strafen*, to punish], *v.t.* To bombard heavily; to punish severely; to do a serious and deliberate injury to.

straggle (străg′ ėl) [perh. freq. of M.E. *straken*, to roam], *v.i.* To wander away from the main body or direct course; to get dispersed; to spread irregularly (of plants, etc.). **straggler,** *n.* **stragglingly,** *adv.* **straggly,** *a.*

straight (strāt) [A.-S. *streht*, p.p. of *streccan*, to STRETCH], *a.* Extending uniformly in one direction, not bent, curved, or crooked; upright, honest, not deviating from truth or fairness, correct, accurate, right; level, even; unobstructed, uninterrupted; undiluted; (*colloq.*) reliable, trustworthy, authoritative; (*Am.*) (of a drink) undiluted. *n.* A straight part, piece, or stretch of anything. *adv.* In a straight line; directly, without deviation; immediately, at once. (*colloq. int.*) Really? **to keep a straight face:** To refrain from smiling. **straight away, straight off:** At once, without delay. **straight-edge,** *n.* A strip of metal or wood having one edge straight, used as a ruler, etc. **straightforward,** *a.* Straight; upright, honest, frank, open. **straighten,** *v.t.* To make straight. **straightener,** *n.* **straightly,** *adv.* **straightness,** *n.* **straight part,** *n.* (*Theat.*) A normal part as opp. to a character part. ***straightway,** *adv.* Forthwith, at once.

straik (1 and 2) (*Sc.*) [STROKE (1), v. and n., and p.p. of STRIKE].

strain (1) (strān) [M.E. *streinen*, O.F. *estraign-*, stem of *estraindre*, L. *stringere*, see STRINGENT], *v.t.* To stretch tight; to exert to the utmost; to weaken, injure, or distort by excessive effort or over-exertion; to force beyond due limits; to apply (rules, etc.) beyond the proper scope or intent; to press closely, to embrace; to constrain, to make unnatural, artificial, or uneasy; to purify from extraneous matter by passing through a colander or other strainer; to remove (solid matter) by straining (out). *v.i.* To exert oneself, to make violent efforts (after, etc.); to pull or tug (at); to be filtered, to percolate. *n.* The act of straining, a violent effort, a pull, tension; an injury, distortion, or change of structure, caused by excessive effort, exertion, or tension; impulse, feeling; a song, a tune, a melody, a piece of poetry; (*fig.*) tone, spirit, manner, style, pitch. **strainer,** *n.* A filter; a sieve, colander.

strain (2) (strān) [A.-S. *strēon*], *n.* Race, stock, family, breed; natural tendency or disposition.

strait (strāt) [A.-F. *estreit*, O.F. *estroict* (F. *étroit*), L. *strictum*, STRICT], *a.* Narrow, confined, restricted, tight; *strict, rigorous. *n.* A narrow passage of water between two seas (*usu. in pl.*); a trying position, distress, difficulty (*usu. in pl.*). **strait-jacket, -waistcoat,** *n.* A garment usu. without sleeves, for confining the arms of violent lunatics, etc. **strait-laced,** *a.* Laced or braced tightly: (*fig.*) puritanically strict in morals or manners. **straiten,** *v.t.* **straitly,** *adv.* **straitness,** *n.*

strake (1) (strāk) [var. of STREAK], *n.* A continuous line of planking or plates from stem to stern of a vessel.

***strake** (2), *p.p.* [STRIKE].

strake (3) (*Sc.*) [STROKE (2)].

stramash (strȧ măsh') [etym. doubtful, cp. O.F. *estramaçon*, It. *stramazzone*, a cut with a sword], *n.* (*Sc.*) A disturbance, a fray, a struggle. *v.t.* To strike, beat, or bang; to break, to destroy.

stramineous (strȧ min' i ŭs) [L. *strāmineus*, from *strāmen -inis*, straw, from *sternere*, to strew], *a.* Straw-coloured; consisting of straw, light, or worthless like straw.

stramonium (strȧ mō' ni ŭm) [etym. doubtful], *n.* A drug prepared from the thorn-apple, *Datura stramonium*, used for asthma.

strand (1) (strănd) [A.-S., cp. Dut., G., Swed., and Dan. *strand*, Icel. *strönd*], *n.* A shore or beach of the sea, lake, or large river. *v.t.* To run or force aground; (*in p.p.*) to bring to a standstill or into straits, esp. from lack of funds. *v.i.* To run aground. **The Strand,** *n.* One of the principal London thoroughfares, from the City to Westminster. **stranded,** *p.p.* In difficulties; without resources.

strand (2) (strănd) [O.North.F. *estran*, O.H.G. *streno* (cp. G. *strähne*), cord], *n.* One of the twists or parts of which a rope, etc., is composed. *v.t.* To break a strand (of a rope).

strange (strānj) [O.F. *estrange* (F. *étrange*), L. *extrāneus*, EXTRANEOUS], *a.* Foreign; not one's own; not well known, unfamiliar, new; unusual, singular, extraordinary, queer, surprising, unaccountable; fresh or unused (to), unacquainted, awkward. **strangely,** *adv.* **strangeness,** *n.*

stranger (strān' jėr), *n.* One from another place; foreigner; a guest, a visitor; a person unknown (to one); one ignorant or unaccustomed (to); (*Law*) one not privy or party to an act.

strangle (străng' gel) [O.F. *estrangler*, L. *strangulāre*, Gr. *strangalizein*, from *strangalē*, halter, from *strangos*, twisted], *v.t.* To kill by compressing the windpipe, to choke, to throttle; (*fig.*) to suppress, to stifle. **strangler,** *n.* **stranglehold,** *n.* A deadly grip. **strangles,** *n.pl.* An infectious catarrh affecting horses, etc.

strangulate (străng' gū lāt) [L. *strangulātus*, p.p. as prec.], *v.t.* To strangle, esp. (*Surg.*) to compress a blood-vessel, intestine, etc. **strangulation,** *n.*

strangury (străng' gū ri) [L. *strangūria*, Gr. *strangouria* (*stranx- gos, ouron*, urine)], *n.* A disease characterized by pain in passing the urine, which is excreted in drops; (*Hort.*) an abnormal condition produced in plants by bandaging. **strangurious,** *a.*

strap (străp) [A.-S. *stropp* (cp. Dut. *strop*), L. *struppus* (cp. Gr. *strophos*, cogn. with *strephein*, to twist)], *n.* A long, narrow strip of leather, or similar material, usu. with a buckle, for fastening about things; a strip, band, or plate for holding parts together; a shoulder-strap; a strop; (*Bot.*) a strap-shaped blade or part, a ligula. *v.t.* (*past & p.p.* **strapped**) To fasten (*often* down, up, etc.) with a strap; to beat with a strap; to sharpen, to strop. **the strap:** Chastisement with a strap. **strap-hanger,** *n.* (*colloq.*) A standing passenger in an omnibus or train. **strap-oil,** *n.* A thrashing. **strap-shaped,** *a.* **strap-work,** *n.* Ornamentation in the form of crossed or interlacing bands. **strapper,** *n.* One who uses a strap; a tall, strapping person. **strapping,** *a.* Tall, lusty, strong, muscular.

***strappado** (strȧ pā' dō) [It. *strappata*, from *strappare*, to pull, G. Swiss *strapfen*, prob. from Dut. *straffen*, to punish, from *straf*, severe], *n.* The old punishment of drawing up an offender by a rope and letting him fall to the end of this. *v.t.* To torture or punish thus.

strapper, etc. [STRAP].

strass (străs) [Joseph *Strasser*, inventor], *n.* Paste for making false gems.

strata, *pl.*, **stratal** [STRATUM].

stratagem (străt' ȧ jem) [O.F. *stratageme*, L. and Gr. *stratēgēma*, from *stratēgein*, to act as general (*stratos*, army, *agein*, to lead)], *n.* An artifice, trick, or manœuvre for deceiving an enemy.

strategic, -al (strȧ tē' jik, -tej' ik, -ȧl) [Gr. *strategikos*, as prec.], *a.* Pertaining to, used in, or of the nature of strategy. **strategically,** *adv.* **strategics,** *n.*

strategy (străt' e ji) [as. prec.], *n.* The art of war, generalship, esp. the art of directing military movements so as to secure the most advantageous positions and combinations of forces. **strategist,** *n.* **strategus** (strȧ tē' gŭs), *n.* (*pl.* **-gi,** -ji) (*Gr. Hist.*) A military commander, esp. one of the board of ten at Athens.

strath (străth) [Gael. *srath*, rel. to STRATUM], *n.* A wide valley through which a river runs. **strathspey** (străth spā') [valley of the *Spey*], *n.* A Scottish dance slower than a reel; music for this.

stratify (străt' i fī) [F. *stratifier* (STRATUM, -FY)], *v.t.* To form or arrange in strata. **straticulate** (strȧ tik' ū lȧt), *a.* (*Geol.*) Arranged in numerous thin strata. **stratification** (-kā' shŭn), *n.*

stratigraphy (strȧ' tig' rȧ fi), *n.* The branch of geology dealing with the classification, nomenclature, etc., of stratified rocks. **stratigraphic,** *a.*

strato-cirrus [CIRROSTRATUS].

stratocracy (strȧ tok' rȧ si) [Gr. *stratos*, army, -CRACY], *n.* Military government; government by a military class.

strato-cumulus [CUMULO-STRATUS].

stratosphere (străt' ō sfēr), *n.* The upper layer of atmosphere extending upwards from about 6 miles above the earth's surface in which the temperature does not decrease with the height.

stratum (strā′ tŭm) [L. orig. neut. p.p. of *sternere*, to strew], *n.* (*pl.* **-ta**) A bed or layer of matter spread out horizontally, esp. by the action of water. **stratal, stratiform,** *a.*

stratus (strā′ tŭs) [as prec.], *n.* (*pl.* **-ti,** -tī) A continuous horizontal sheet of cloud.

***straught,** *past & p.p.* [STRETCH].

stravaig (stra vāg′) [O.F. *estravaguer*, late L. *extrāvagārī*, see EXTRAVAGANT], *v.i.* To roam about idly, to ramble.

straw (1) (straw) [A.-S. *strēaw* (cp. Dut. *stroo*, G. *stroh*, Icel. *strā*), cogn. with STRATUM], *n.* The dry, ripened stalk or stalks of certain species of grain, esp. wheat, rye, oats, etc.; such a stalk or a piece of one; (*fig.*) anything proverbially worthless; (*colloq.*) a straw-hat. **v.t.* To strew. ***in the straw:** Lying-in, in childbed. **man of straw** [MAN]. **straw-board,** *n.* A millboard or thick cardboard made from straw. **straw-colour,** *n.* A pale yellow. **straw-coloured,** *a.* **straw-hat,** *n.* A hat made of plaited straw. **straw vote,** *n.* (*Pol.*) An unofficial ballot test of opinion. **straw-worm,** *n.* The caddis-worm. **strawy,** *a.*

***straw** (2), **strawed,** *past & p.p.* [STREW].

strawberry (straw′ bĕr i) [as prec.], *n.* A low, stemless perennial plant of the genus *Fragaria* bearing a fleshy red fruit with small achenes on the surface; the fruit of this. **strawberry leaves:** A dukedom (the coronet of a duke being ornamented with eight strawberry leaves). **strawberry-mark,** *n.* A soft reddish birthmark. **strawberry-tree,** *n.* An evergreen arbutus, *A. unedo*, bearing a strawberry-like fruit.

stray (strā) [O.F. *estraier*, from L. *strāta*, STREET], *v.i.* To wander from the direct or proper course, to go wrong, to lose one's way; to wander from the path of rectitude. *n.* Any domestic animal that has gone astray; a straggler, a waif. *a.* Gone astray; straggling, occasional, sporadic. **strayer,** ***strayling,** *n.*

streak (strēk) [M.E. *streke*, from Scand. (cp. Swed. *streck*) or A.-S. *strica*, STROKE (1) (cp. G. *strich*), cogn. with STRIKE], *n.* An irregular line or long narrow mark of a distinct colour from the ground. *v.t.* To mark with streaks. **yellow streak:** A strain of cowardice. **streaky,** *a.* **streakily,** *adv.* **streakiness,** *n.*

stream (strēm) [A.-S. (cp. Dut *stroom*, G. *strom*, Icel. *straumr*), from Teut. *streu-*, cogn. with Sansk. *sru*, Gr. *rheein*, to flow], *n.* A body of flowing water or other fluid; a river, a brook; a steady flow, a current, a drift; anything in a state of continuous progressive movement, a moving throng, etc. (*often in pl.*). *v.i.* To flow, move, or issue in or as a stream; to pour out or emit liquid abundantly; to float, hang, or wave in the wind, etc. *v.t.* To pour out or flow with liquid abundantly. **stream line,** *n.* The direction of an air current or of the particles of air impinging on a moving body; the shape given to aircraft, motors, etc., in order to cause the minimum of resistance. **streamless,** *a.* **streamlet,** *n.* **streamy,** *a.*

streamer (strē′ mėr), *n.* A long, narrow flag or ribbon, a pennon; a column of light shooting across the sky.

street (strēt) [A.-S. *strǣt*, L. *strāta* (*via*), paved (way), fem. p.p. of *sternere*, cp. STRATUM], *n.* A road in a city or town with houses on one side or on both. **on the street:** Living by prostitution. **not in the same street with:** (*colloq.*) Not to be compared with. **street arab** [ARAB]. **street-orderly,** *n.* A scavenger. **streets ahead of:** (*colloq.*) Far in advance of, much better than. **street-car,** *n.* (*Am.*) A tram. **street-sweeper,** *n.* A person or a machine that sweeps streets. **street-walker,** *n.* A common prostitute. **street-walking,** *n.* **streetward,** *a.* and *adv.*

***streight, *streightly,** etc. [STRAIT].

strength (strength) [A.-S. *strengthu*, from *strang*, STRONG], *n.* The quality of being strong; muscular force; firmness, solidity; amount or proportion of the whole number (of an army, ships, etc.). **on the strength:** (*Mil.*) On the muster-roll. **on the strength of:** In reliance on; on the faith of. **strengthen,** *v.t.* To make strong or stronger. *v.i.* To increase in strength. **strengthener,** *n.* **strengtheningly,** *adv.* **strengthless,** *a.*

strenuous (stren′ ū ŭs) [L. *strēnuus*, cp. Gr. *strēnēs*, strong, *stereos*, STEREO-], *a.* Energetic, vigorous, zealous, ardent; eagerly persistent. **strenuously,** *adv.* **strenuousness,** *n.*

Strephon (stref′ ŏn) [shepherd in Sidney's 'Arcadia'], *n.* A fond or languishing lover.

strepitoso (strep i tō′ zō) [It., from L. *strepitus*, noise, from *strepere*, to make a noise], *adv.* (*Mus. direction*) In a noisy, impetuous manner.

streptococcus (strep tō kok′ ŭs) [Gr. *streptos*, twisted; *kokkus*, a grain], *n.* (*pl.* **-i**) (*Bacter.*) A genus of bacteria consisting of spherical organisms in chains of varying length.

streptomycin (strep tō mī′ sin), *n.* An antibiotic against bacteria immune to penicillin.

stress (stres) [O.F. *estrecier*, pop. L. *strictiāre*, see DISTRESS], *n.* Constraining or impelling force; tension, pressure, violence; weight, importance, or influence; emphasis, accent; (*Mech.*) force exerted upon or between the parts of a body. *v.t.* To lay the stress or accent on; to subject to stress or force. **stressless,** *a.*

stretch (strech) [A.-S. *streccan*, from *stræc*, strong, violent (cp. Dut. *strekken*, G. *strecken*, also L. *stringere*, and Gr. *straggos*, twisted), cogn. with STRING, STRONG], *v.t.* To draw out, to extend, to extend in any direction or to full length; to tighten, to draw tight; to extend lengthwise, to straighten; to cause to extend, to hit so as to prostrate; to distend, to strain; to do violence to; to exaggerate. *v.i.* To be extended in length or breadth; to have a specified extension, to reach; to be drawn out or admit of being drawn out; to extend or straighten one's body or limbs. *n.* The act of stretching or state of being stretched; extent or reach; a reach, sweep, or tract (of land, water, etc.); (*Naut.*) the distance covered in one tack; period of a prison sentence. **at a stretch:** At one go; continuously. **to stretch a point:** To go beyond what might be expected. **stretcher,** *n.* One who or that which stretches; a litter or other appliance for carrying a disabled person in a recumbent position; (*Build.*) a brick or stone laid lengthwise in a course in a wall; a cross-piece in a boat for a rower to press his feet against. **stretcher-bond,** *n.* (*Build.*) A form of bond in which nothing but stretchers are used, though the joints come against the middles of the bricks in the contiguous course. **stretching course:** (*Build.*) A course of stretchers. **stretchy,** *a.* **stretchiness,** *n.*

strew (stroo) [A.-S. *strēowian*, from *strēaw*, STRAW (1)], *v.t.* (*p.p.* **strewn, strewed**) To scatter, to spread thus; to cover by scattering or by being scattered over. ***strewment,** *n.*

stria (strī′ à) [L.], *n.* (*pl.* **striæ**) A superficial furrow, a thin line or groove, mark, or ridge. **striate** (strī′ āt), *a.* Marked with striæ. *v.t.* (stri āt′). **striately,** *adv.* **striation** (strī ā′ shŭn), **striature** (strī′ à tyŭr), *n.*

strick (strik) [cogn. with STRIKE], *n.* (*prov.*) A straight-edge for levelling grain, etc.

stricken, *p.p.* [STRIKE].

strickle (strik′ ėl) [dim. of STRICK], *n.* A straight-edge for levelling grain in a measure; a templet; a straight-edge for sharpening curved blades.

strict (strikt) [L. *strictus*, p.p. of *stringere*, see STRINGENT], *a.* Enforcing or observing rules precisely, not lax; rigorous, severe, stringent; defined or applied exactly, accurate, precise. **strictly,** *adv.* **strictness,** *n.*

stricture (strik′ chŭr), *n.* A censure, a sharp criticism; (*Path.*) a contraction of duct or channel, as of the urethra. **strictured,** *a.*

stride (strīd) [A.-S. *strīdan*, cp. L.G. *strīden*, Dut. *strijden*, to stride, to strive, G. *streiten*, to strive], *v.i.* (*past* **strode,** *p.p.* **stridden, strid)** To walk with long steps; to straddle. *v.t.* To pass over in one step; to bestride. *n.* A long or measured step or the distance covered by this.

strident (strī′ dėnt) [L. *strīdens -ntem*, pres.p. of *strīdēre*, to creak], *a.* Sounding harsh, grating. **stridently,** *adv.* **stridor,** *n.* A harsh, creaking noise as that made by grasshoppers.

stridulate (strid′ ū lāt), *v.i.* To make a shrill creaking noise (esp. of cicadas and grasshoppers by rubbing hard parts of their body together). **stridulant, stridulous, stridulatory,** *a.* **stridulation** (-lā′ shŭn), *n.* **stridulator** (strid′-), *n.*

strife (strīf) [O.F. *estrif*, Icel. *strīth*, cogn. with STRIDE], *n.* Contention, conflict, hostile struggle. ***strifeful,** *a.*

strig (strig) [from foll.], *n.* (*prov.*) The footstalk of a flower, leaf, etc. *v.t.* To strip (fruit) etc., of this.

striga (strī′ gȧ) [L., a swath, rel. to *stringere*, to bind], *n.* (*pl.* **-gæ,** -jē) (*Bot.*) A short stiff hair, bristle, or hair-like scale; (*Arch.*) a fluting on a column. **strigose, -gous,** *a.* (*Bot.*).

Strigidæ (strī′ ji dē) [mod. L., from L. *strix strigis*, Gr. *strinx*, owl, from *strizein*, to screech], *n.pl.* A family of raptorial birds containing the owls.

strigil (strij′ il) [L. *strigilis*, rel. to *stringere*, to graze], *n.* (*Ant.*) A skin-scraper used in baths.

strike (strīk) [A.-S. *strīcan*, to go (cp. Dut. *strijken*, G. *streichen*, Icel. *strjūka*, to stroke, rub, smooth, etc.), cogn. with L. *stringere*, to graze], *v.t.* (*past* **struck,** *p.p.* **struck, stricken)** To hit, to deliver a blow or blows upon; to deliver, to deal, to inflict (a blow, etc.); to afflict (*usu. in p.p.*); to drive, to send (a ball, etc.) with force; to produce, make, form, effect, or bring into a particular state by a stroke, as to ignite (a match), to stamp or mint (a coin), to blind, to deafen, etc.; to make (a bargain); to cause (a bell, etc.) to sound; to notify by sound; to cause to penetrate, to thrust (into); to hook (a fish) by jerking the tackle upwards; to effect forcibly, to impress strongly, to occur suddenly to the mind of; to cause (a cutting, etc.) to take root; to lower (sails, a flag, tent, etc.); to surrender by lowering (a flag, etc.); to leave off (work), esp. to enforce a demand for higher wages, etc.; to level corn, etc., in (a measure) by scraping off the surplus; to determine (a balance, average, etc.); to assume (an attitude); (*colloq.*) to discover, to come across. *v.i.* To hit, to deliver a blow or blows (upon); to collide, to dash (against, upon, etc.); to be driven on shore, a rock, etc.; to sound (the time) by a stroke (of a bell, etc.); to lower sails, flag, etc., in token of surrender, etc.; to take root; to leave off work to enforce a demand for higher wages, etc.; to arrive suddenly, to happen (upŏn); to enter or turn (into a track, etc.); (*Geol.*) to extend in a particular direction (of strata). *n.* The act of striking for an increase of wages, etc.; a straight-edge for levelling something, as a measure of grain; (*Geol.*) the horizontal direction of an outcrop. ***to strike hands** [HAND (1)]. **to strike lucky:** To be fortunate. **to strike off:** To remove, separate, dislodge, etc., by a blow; to erase, to strike out; to print. **to strike out:** To produce by striking; to blot out, to efface, to expunge; to devise, to contrive; to make vigorous strokes (in skating, swimming, etc.); to hit from the shoulder (in boxing). **to strike up:** To drive up with a blow; to begin to play or sing; to enter into, to start (a conversation, etc.). **well stricken in years:** Advanced in age. **strike-a-light,** *n.* A device for obtaining light by means of a flint, etc. **strike-breaker,** *n.* A blackleg; worker brought in to replace one out on strike. **strike-pay,** *n.* An allowance for subsistence from a trade-union to workmen on strike. **striker,** *n.* One who or that which strikes, esp. a workman on strike.

striking (strī′ king), *a.* Surprising, forcible, impressive, noticeable. **strikingly,** *adv.* **strikingness,** *n.*

string (string) [A.-S. *streng*, cogn. with STRONG], *n.* Twine, a fine line, usu. thicker than thread and thinner than cord; a length of this or strip of leather, tape, or other material, used for tying, fastening, binding together, connecting, etc.; a string-like fibre, tendon, nerve, etc.; a piece of wire, catgut, etc., yielding musical sounds or notes when caused to vibrate in a piano, violin, etc.; (*pl.*) the stringed instruments in an orchestra; a cord or thread upon which anything is strung, hence a series of things or persons connected together or following in close succession; (*Billiards*) the apparatus for keeping the score, the score itself; (*Racing*) the horses under training at a particular stable. *v.t.* (*past & p.p.* **strung)** To furnish with a string or strings; to fasten the string on (a bow); (*fig.*) to make (nerves, etc.) tense (*usu. in p.p.*); to thread on a string; to strip (beans, etc.) of strings or fibres. *v.i.* To become stringy; (*Billiards*) to send the ball against the top cushion and back to decide which player is to begin. **no strings attached:** (*colloq.*) With no conditions or restrictions. **to have two strings to one's bow** [BOW (1)]. **to pull strings:** To exert influence unobtrusively. **string-band,** *n.* A band of stringed instruments. **string-bean,** *n.* (*Am.*) A runner bean, a french bean. **string-board,** *n.* A timber receiving the ends of stairs in a staircase. **string-course,** *n.* A projecting horizontal band or moulding running along a building. **string-halt** [SPRING-HALT]. **string-piece,** *n.* A supporting timber forming the edge of a framework, esp. of a floor; a string-board. **string quartette, quartet,** *n.* (*Mus.*). A combination of four string instruments, *viz.* two violins, a viola, and a violoncello; music written for this combination. **stringed,** *a.* **stringer,** *n.* One who strings; a string-board; a long horizontal member in a structural framework. **stringless,** *a.* **stringy** (string′ i), *a.* Consisting of strings or small threads, fibrous, ropy, viscous. **stringy-bark,** *a.* A name for many of the Australian gum-trees, from their fibrous bark. **stringiness,** *n.*

stringendo (strin jėn′ dō) [It., as foll.], *adv.* (*Mus.*) In accelerated time.

stringent (strin′ jėnt) [L. *stringens -ntem*, pres.p. of *stringere*, to draw tight, p.p. *strictus*], *a.* Strict, precise, binding, rigid, hampered, tight, unaccommodating (of the money-market, etc.). **stringency, stringentness,** *n.* **stringently,** *adv.*

stringer, stringless, stringy, etc. [STRING].

strip (1) (strip) [A.-S. *strȳpan*, cp. Dut. *stroopen*, G. *streifen*], *v.t.* (*past & p.p.* **stripped)** To pull the covering from, to denude, to skin, to peel, to husk, to clean; to deprive (of), to despoil, to plunder; to remove (clothes, bark, rigging, branches, etc.); to milk (a cow) to the last drop. *v.i.* To take off one's clothes, to undress; to come away in strips; to have the thread torn off (of a screw), to be discharged without spin (of a projectile). **strip-tease,** *n.* (*Theat.*) A music-hall or cabaret turn in which an actress partially or wholly undresses herself. **stripper,** *n.* **strippings,** *n.pl.* The last milk drawn from a cow.

strip (2) (strip) [prob. var. of foll.], *n.* A long, narrow piece. **comic strip,** *n.* A row of humorous drawings in a newspaper presenting in sequence some comic incident. **strip-leaf,** *n.* Tobacco stripped of the stems.

stripe (strīp) [prob. from M.Dut. *strijpe*, cp. Norw. *stripa*, L.G. *stripe*, G. *streifen*], *n.* A long, narrow band of a distinctive colour or texture; (*Mil.*) a chevron; *a stroke with a whip, scourge, etc. *v.t.* To mark with stripes; *to lash, to scourge. **stripy,** *a.* **stripiness,** *n.*

stripling (strip′ ling) [dim. of prec.], *n.* A youth, a lad.

strive (strīv) [O.F. *estriver*, from *estrif*, STRIFE], *v.i.* (*past* **strove,** strōv, *p.p.* **striven,** striv′ ėn) To make efforts, to endeavour earnestly, to struggle;

to contend, to vie, to emulate; to quarrel (with each other). **striver,** *n.* **strivingly,** *adv.*

strob (strob) [Gr. *strobos*, twisting, from *strephein*, to turn], *n.* (*Mech.*) The angular velocity of one radian per second. **stroboscope** (strob' ŏ skōp) [-SCOPE], *n.* An instrument for observing periodic motion by making the moving body visible at certain points. **stroboscopic, -al** (skop' ik, -ăl), *a.* **stroboscopically,** *adv.*

strobile (strob' il), **strobilus** (strŏ bī' lŭs) [Gr. *strobilos*, cogn. with *strephein*, to turn], *n.* A multiple fruit such as a pine-cone. **strobilaceous** (strob i lā' shŭs), **strobiliform** (strŏ bil' i fôrm), **strobiline** (strob' i līn), *a.*

stroboscope, etc. [STROB].

strode, *past* [STRIDE].

stroke (1) (strōk) [A.-S. *strāc*, from *strican*, to STRIKE], *n.* The act of striking, a blow; the impact, shock, noise, etc., of this; a sudden attack (of disease, affliction, etc.), a sudden onset of paralysis; a single movement of something, esp. one of a series of recurring movements, as of the heart, an oar, wing, piston, etc.; the length, manner, rate, etc., of such a movement; a mark made by a single movement of a pen, pencil, etc.; a stroke-oar. *v.t.* To act as stroke for (a boat or crew). **stroke-oar,** ***strokesman,** *n.* The aftermost oarsman in a boat who sets the time of the stroke for the rest. **stroker,** *n.* **strokingly,** *adv.*

stroke (2) (strōk) [A.-S. *strācian*, from *strāc*, see prec.], *v.t.* To pass the hand over the surface of caressingly. *n.* The act of stroking. **to stroke the wrong way:** To ruffle, to annoy.

stroll (strōl) [etym. doubtful], *v.i.* To walk leisurely or idly, to saunter. *v.t.* To saunter or ramble on foot. *n.* A leisurely ramble. **stroller,** *n.*

stroma (strō' mă) [Gr. *strōma*, bed, cogn. with *strōnnunai*, to spread], *n.* (*pl.* **-mata**) The framework of tissue of an organ or cell. **stromatic** (strŏ măt' ik), *a.*

stromatology (strō mă tol' ō ji), *n.* (*Geol.*) The history of the successive formation of stratified rocks.

stromb (stromb) [mod. L. *strombus*, Gr. *strombos*, pine-cone, cogn. with *strephein*, to turn], *n.* A gasteropod of the genus Strombus or the family *Strombidæ*, chiefly found in tropic seas; a shell of this used for ornament. **strombiform, stromboid,** *a.* **strombite,** *n.* A fossil stromb. **strombuliform,** *a.* (*Bot.*) Twisted spirally like a screw. **Strombus,** *n.* A genus of marine gasteropods.

strong (strong) [A.-S. *strang* (cp. Dut. and Dan. *streng*, Icel. *strangr*, Swed. *sträng*, G. *streng*, strict), cogn. with L. *stringere*, see STRICT], *a.* *comp.* **stronger** (strong' gĕr); (*super.*) **strongest** (strong' gĕst). Able to exert great force, powerful, muscular, able, capable; acting with great force, vigorous, forcible, energetic; having great powers of resistance or endurance; healthy, robust, hale, firm, tough, solid; having great numbers, resources, etc.; having a specified number of men, etc.; having a powerful effect on the senses, loud and penetrating, glaring, pungent, ill-smelling, intoxicating, heady; (*Gram.*) forming inflexions by internal vowel-change, and not by addition of a syllable (as *strike, struck, stride, strode*). **going strong:** (*slang*) Prospering, getting on famously, in good form or spirits. **to go it strong:** (*slang*) To act or behave in a violent, reckless, or defiant way. **strong drink,** or **waters:** Alcoholic liquors. **stronghold,** *n.* A fortress, a fastness; (*fig.*) a refuge. **strong meat,** *n.* (*fig.*) Theories or doctrines demanding courageous thought. **strong-minded,** *a.* Having a vigorous mind; having a virile mind (esp. as applied to women claiming equality with men). **strong-mindedly,** *adv.* **strong-mindedness,** *n.* **strongish,** *a.* **strongly,** *adv.*

strontia (stron' shă) [*Strontian*, Argyleshire, where first found], *n.* An oxide of strontium the nitrate of which is used to produce a red light in pyrotechny. **strontian,** *n.* and *a.* **strontianite,** *n.* A carbonate of strontia.

strontium (stron' shi ŭm), *n.* A yellowish metallic element, resembling calcium. **strontium 90,** *n.* Strontium with atomic weight of 90. A radioactive product of nuclear fission which tends to accumulate in bones.

***strook,** *past* [STRIKE]. (*Milton.*)

strop (strop) [var. of STRAP], *n.* A strip of leather, etc., for sharpening razors, etc., on. *v.t.* To sharpen with or on a strop.

strophanthus (strō făn' thŭs) [Gr. *strophos*, a twisted band; *anthos*, a flower], *n.* A genus of tropical gamopetalous small trees or shrubs. **strophanthin,** *n.* (*Med.*) A poisonous drug made from strophanthus seeds, used as arrow-poison; its medicinal uses are similar to those of digitalis.

strophe (strof' i, strō' fi) [Gr. *strophē*, orig. a turning, from *strephein*, to turn], *n.* The turning of the chorus from right to left in an ancient Greek drama; a part of the ode (consisting of strophe, antistrophe, and epode) sung whilst so turning, esp. the first part, the strophe proper. **strophic,** *a.*

strophiole (strof' i-, strō' fi ōl) [L. *strophiolum*, dim. of *strophium*, Gr. *strophion*, dim. of *strophos*, a band, as prec.], *n.* (*Bot.*) An aril-like appendage attached to the hilum of some seeds. **strophiolate,** *a.*

***strossers** [TROUSERS]. **strove,** *past* [STRIVE].

***strow** [STREW]. ***stroy** [DESTROY].

struck, *past* & *p.p.* [STRIKE].

structure (strŭk' tyŭr) [F., from L. *structūra*, from struere, to build, *p.p. structus*], *n.* A combination of parts, as a building, machine, organism, etc., esp. the supporting or essential framework; the manner in which a complex whole is constructed, put together, or organically formed; the arrangement of parts, organs atoms, etc., in a complex whole. **structural,** *a.* **structurally,** *adv.* **structured,** *a.* (*usu. in comb.*, as *loose-structured*) **structureless,** *a.*

struggle (strŭg' ĕl) [M.E. *strogelen*, cp. Swed. dial. *strug*, contention, Norw. *stru*, refractory], *v.i.* To make violent movements; to put forth great efforts, esp. against difficulties or opposition; to strive (to); to contend (with or against); to make one's way (along, etc.) against difficulties, opposition, etc. *n.* An act or spell of struggling; a strenuous effort; a fight or contest, esp. of a confused character. **struggler,** *n.* **strugglingly,** *adv.*

struldbrug (strŭld' brŭg) [coined by Swift], *n.* One of a class of immortals, in Swift's *Gulliver's Travels*, born with a mark on the forehead and kept at the public expense after the age of eighty.

strum (strŭm) [imit.], *v.t.* and *i.* To play noisily or carelessly, to thrum on a stringed instrument. *n.* Strumming.

struma (stroo' mă) [L., from *struere*, to build], *n.* (*pl.* **-mæ**) (*Path.*) Scrofula; (*Bot.*) a cushion-like swelling on a petiole, etc. **strumose, strumous,** *a.* **strumousness,** *n.*

strumpet (strŭm' pĕt) [prob. from O.F. *strupe*, *strupre*, concubinage, L. *stuprum*, defilement], *n.* A prostitute, a harlot. *v.t.* To debauch.

strung, *past* & *p.p.* [STRING].

strut (1) (strŭt) [M.E. *strouten*, prob. from Dan. *strutte* (cp. Swed. dial. *strutta*), cogn. with L.G. *strutt*, rigid], *v.i.* To walk with a pompous, conceited gait. *n.* Such a gait. **strutter,** *n.* **struttingly,** *adv.*

strut (2) (strŭt) [cogn. with prec.], *n.* A timber or iron beam inserted in a framework so as to keep other members apart, a brace. *v.t.* To brace with a strut or struts.

Struthio (stroo' thi ō) [L., from Gr. *strouthiōn*, from *strouthos*, sparrow], *n.* A genus of cursorial birds, containing the ostrich. **struthious,** *a.*

strychnine (strik' nin, -nīn) [L. *strychnos*, Gr. *struchnos*, nightshade, -INE], *n.* A highly poisonous alkaloid obtained from species of *Strychnos*, esp. *S. nux vomica*, used in medicine as a stimulant, etc. ***strychnia,** *n.* **strychnic,** *a.* **strychninism, strychnism,** *n.*

stub (stŭb) [A.-S. *stybb*, cp. Dut. *stobbe*, Icel. *stubbi*, Dan. *stub*, also Gr. *stupos*], *n.* The stump of a tree, tooth, etc.; a stump, end, or remnant of anything; a cheque counterfoil; (*Am.*) a counterfoil. *v.t.* (*past & p.p.* **stubbed**) To grub up by the roots; to clear of stubs; to strike one's toe against something. **stub-iron,** *n.* Iron made from old horseshoe nails, used for gun-barrels, etc. **stubbed, stubby,** *a.* **stubbedness, stubbiness,** *n.*

stubble (stŭb' ėl) [M.E. *stobil*, O.F. *estoubie*, late L. *stupula*, L. *stipula*, see STIPULE], *n.* The stumps of wheat, barley, etc., covering the ground after harvest; (*fig.*) short, bristly hair, whiskers, etc. **stubble-fed,** *a.* Fed on the grass growing amongst stubble, split grain, etc. **stubbly, *stubbled,** *a.*

stubborn (stŭb' ȯrn) [M.E. *stoburn*, *stiborn*, prob. from A.-S. *stybb*, STUB], *a.* Unreasonably obstinate, not to be persuaded; obdurate, inflexible, intractable, refractory. **stubbornly,** *adv.* **stubbornness,** *n.*

stucco (stŭk' ō) [It., from O.H.G. *stucchi*, crust (cp. G. *stück*, A.-S. *stycce*, piece), *cogn.* with STOCK (1)], *n.* Fine plaster for coating walls or moulding into decorations in relief; any plaster used for coating the outside of buildings. *v.t.* To coat with stucco. **stuccoer,** *n.*

stuck, *past & p.p.* [STICK].

stud (1) (stŭd) [A.-S. *studu*, a post, cp. Dan. and Swed. *stöd*, Icel. *stoth*, G. *stütze*, prop.], *n.* A large-headed nail, knob, head of a bolt, etc., esp. fixed as an ornament; an ornamental button for wearing in a shirt-front, etc.; a cross-piece in a link of chain-cable; a stud-bolt; a small spindle, pin, or dowel, in a lathe, watch, etc.; a post or scantling to which laths are nailed in a partition. *v.t.* (*past & p.p.* **studded**) To set with studs or ornamental knobs; to set thickly, to bestrew. **stud-bolt,** *n.* A bolt with a thread for screwing into a fixed part at one end and having a nut screwed on it at the other.

stud (2) (stŭd) [A.-S. *stōd* (cp. Icel. *stōth*, Dan. *stod*, G. *gestüt*), cogn. with STAND], *n.* A number of horses kept for riding, racing, breeding, etc. **stud-book,** *n.* A register of pedigrees of horses or cattle. **stud-farm,** *n.* A farm where horses are bred. **stud-horse,** *n.* A stallion.

studding sail (stŭnsl) [etym. doubtful], *n.* An additional sail set beyond the leech of a square sail in light winds.

student (stū' dėnt) [L. *studens -dentis*, pres.p. of *studēre*, see STUDY], *n.* A person engaged in study, esp. one receiving instruction at a University, college, or other institution for higher education or technical training; (*Am.*) a schoolboy or girl; a studious person; a person receiving an annual grant for study or research from a foundation, etc. **studentship,** *n.*

studiedly [STUDY].

studio (stū' di ō) [It., from L. *studium*, STUDY], *n.* The working-room of a sculptor, painter, photographer, etc.; the sound-proof room in which gramophone records are made; (*Radio & T.V.*) the place from which musical and other programmes are broadcast; (*Cinema.*) a room or building used for making films.

studious (stū' di ůs) [F. *studieux*, L. *studiōsus*, as foll.], *a.* Devoted to study; eager, diligent, anxious (to do something); careful, observant (of); studied, deliberate, intended. **studiously,** *adv.* **studiousness,** *n.*

study (stŭd' i) [A.-F. and O.F. *estudie*, L. *studium*, eagerness, zeal, whence, med L. *studiāre*, O.F. *estudier*, F. *étudier*, to study], *n.* Mental application to books, art, science, etc., the pursuit of knowledge; something that is studied or worth studying; a sketch or other piece of work done for practice or as a preliminary design for a picture, etc.; (*Mus.*) a composition designed to test or develop technical skill; (*Theat.*) one who learns a part; a room devoted to study, literary work, etc.; a reverie, a fit of musing; earnest endeavour, watchful attention; the object of this. *v.t.* To apply the mind to for the purpose of learning; to inquire into, to investigate; to contemplate, to consider attentively; to commit to memory; to apply thought and pains to, to be zealous for; (*in p.p.*) deliberate, premeditated, intentional. *v.i.* To apply oneself to study, esp. to reading; to meditate, to cogitate, to muse; to be assiduous, diligent, or anxious (to do). **studied,** *a.* Deliberate, intentional. **studiedly,** *adv.*

stufa (stoo' fȧ) [It.], *n.* A jet of steam issuing from a fissure of the earth.

stuff (stŭf) [O.F. *estoffe* (F. *étoffe*), L. *stuppa*, *stūpa*, see STOP], *n.* The material of which anything is made or may be made; the fundamental substance, essence, or elements of anything; household goods, furniture, utensils, etc.; a textile fabric, esp. woollen, as opp. to silk or linen; (*fig.*) worthless matter, nonsense, trash. *v.t.* To cram, to pack, to fill or stop (up); to fill (a fowl, etc.) with stuffing or seasoning for cooking; to fill the skin of (a dead animal) so as to restore its natural form; to fill with food; to cram, press, ram, or crowd into a receptacle, confined space, etc.; (*fig.*) to fill with ideas, notions, nonsense, etc.; (*colloq.*) to impose on, to hoax. *v.i.* To cram oneself with food. **stuffed shirt:** (*facet.*) A pompous fellow. **stuffer,** *n.* **stuffing,** *n.* **stuffing-box,** *n.* A chamber packed with stuffing so as to be air-tight or water-tight, in which a piston-rod, etc., can work freely.

stuffy (stŭf' i), *a.* Ill-ventilated, close, fusty; strait-laced; (*Am.*) sulky. **stuffiness,** *n.*

stuggy, (*prov.*) [STOCKY].

stultify (stŭl' ti fī) [L. *stulti-*, *stultus*, foolish, -FY], *v.t.* To render absurd, to cause to appear self-contradictory, inconsistent, or ridiculous; (*Law*) to allege or prove to be insane. **stultification** (-kā' shůn), *n.* **stultifier,** *n.* ***stultiloquence, *-quy** (stŭl til' ȯ kwėns, -kwi) [L. *stultiloquentia* (*loquī*, to talk)], *n.* Foolish talk. ***stultiloquent,** *a.*

stum (stŭm) [Dut. *stom*, orig. a., quiet, cp. G. *stumm*, dumb], *n.* Unfermented grape-juice, must. *v.t.* To prevent (wine) from fermenting by treating with an antiseptic.

stumble (stŭm' bėl) [M.E. *stumblen*, freq. of *stum-*, cogn. with prec. and STAMMER], *v.i.* To trip in walking or to strike the foot against something without falling, to have a partial fall; to fall into a blunder, to act, move, or speak blunderingly; to come (upon) by chance; (*fig.*) to feel misgivings, to boggle (at). ***v.t.** To cause to stumble; to confound, to puzzle. *n.* An act of stumbling. **stumbler,** *n.* **stumbling-block,** *n.* An obstacle, an impediment, a cause of difficulty, hesitation, etc. **stumblingly,** *adv.*

stumer (stū' mėr) [etym. unknown], *n.* (*Racing*) A disappointing horse; a failure; (*colloq.*) a cheque that has no money to back it; a returned cheque.

stump (stŭmp) [Icel. *stumpr* (cp. Dan. and Swed. *stump*, Dut. *stomp*, G. *stumpf*), cogn. with STAMP and STUB], *n.* The part left in the earth after a tree has fallen or been cut down; any part left when the rest of a branch, limb, tooth, etc., has been cut away, amputated, destroyed, or worn out, a stub, a butt; (*Cricket*) one of the three posts of a wicket; (*facet., pl.*) the legs; a pointed roll of leather or paper used to rub down the strong lines of a crayon or pencil drawing, etc. *v.i.* To walk stiffly, awkwardly, or noisily, as on wooden legs; to make stump-speeches, to go about doing this. *v.t.* To work upon (a drawing, etc.) with a stump; to go about (a district) making stump speeches; to put out (the batsman) at cricket by touching the wicket while he is out of the crease; (*colloq.*) to pose, to put at a loss; (*slang*) to pay (up) at once. **on the stump:** Going about making political speeches. **to stump up:** To pay up; to produce the money required. **stump-orator,** *n.* **stump-oratory,** *n.* **stump-speech,** *n.* A speech from some improvised platform, orig. a tree-stump; an electioneering speech. **stump-tail,** *n.* (*Austral.*) A short-tailed lizard. **stumper,** *n.* **stumpy,** *a.* Short, thick-set, stocky; full of stumps, stubby.

stun (stŭn) [A.-S. *stunian*, to make a din, cp. Icel. *stynja*, G. *stöhnen*, to groan, also Gr. *steinein*], *v.t.* (*past & p.p.* **stunned**) To daze or deafen with noise; to render senseless with a blow; to stupefy, to overpower. **stunner,** *n.* One who or that which stuns; (*slang*) something astonishing or first-rate. **stunning,** *a.* (*slang*) Wonderfully good, fine, etc.

Stundist (stoon′ dist) [G. *stunde*, hour, lesson (from their meetings)], *n.* A member of a body of Russian dissenters from the Orthodox Church who base their creed and practices on the Bible as translated into Russian in 1861. **Stundism,** *n.*

stung, *past & p.p.* [STING].

stunk, *past & p.p.* [STINK].

stunsail, stuns'l (*Naut.*) [STUDDING-SAIL].

stunt (1) (stŭnt) [A.-S., dull, obtuse (cp. Icel. *stuttr*, short), cogn. with STINT], *v.t.* To check in growth or development, to dwarf, to cramp. *n.* A check in growth; a stunted animal or thing.

stunt (2) (stŭnt) [etym. unknown], *n.* A performance serving as a display of strength, skill, or the like; a feat; a thing done to attract attention; (*Aviat.*) a feat of aerobatics.

stupa (stū′ pă) [Sansk., see TOPE (3)], *n.* A tope.

stupe (stūp) [L. *stūpa*, STUFF], *n.* A compress of flannel or other soft material used in fomentations, etc. *v.t.* To treat with this, to foment.

stupefy (stū′ pė fī) [F. *stupéfier*, L. *stupefacere* (*stupēre*, to be amazed, *facere*, to make)], *v.t.* To make stupid or senseless; to deprive of sensibility. **stupefacient** (-fā′ shėnt), *a.* and *n.* **stupefaction** (-făk′ shŭn), *n.* **stupefactive** (stū′ pė făk tiv), *a.* **stupefier,** *n.*

stupendous (stū pen′ dŭs) [L. *stupendus*, from *stupēre*, to be amazed], *a.* Astounding in magnitude, force, degree, etc., marvellous, amazing, astonishing. **stupendously,** *adv.* **stupendousness,** *n.*

stupeous, stupose (stū′ pė ŭs, -pōs) [L. *stūpeus*, from *stūpa*, STUPE (1)], *a.* (*Nat. Hist.*) Having long, loose scales or tufts of filament or hair like tow.

stupid (stū′ pid) [F. *stupide*, L. *stupidus*, from *stupēre*, see STUPEFY], *a.* In a state of stupor, stupefied; dull of apprehension, wit, or understanding, obtuse; senseless, nonsensical. **stupidity** (-pid′ i ti), **stupidness,** *n.* **stupidly,** *adv.*

stupor (stū′ pŏr) [L., as prec.], *n.* A dazed condition, torpor, deadened sensibility.

stupose [STUPEOUS].

***stuprate** (stū′ prāt) [L. *stuprātus*, p.p. of *stuprāre*, to defile, from *stuprum*, dishonour, lewdness], *v.t.* To ravish, to violate, to debauch. ***stupration** (-prā′ shŭn), ***stuprum,** *n.*

sturdy (1) (stĕr′ di) [O.F. *estourdi*, p.p. of *estourdir* (F. *étourdir*), to astound, to amaze], *a.* Robust, lusty, vigorous, hardy. **sturdy beggar:** An able-bodied vagrant or tramp. **sturdily,** *adv.* **sturdiness,** *n.*

sturdy (2) (stĕr′ di) [O.F. *estourdie*, giddiness, as prec.], *n.* A disease in sheep characterized by giddiness caused by a tape-worm in the brain. **sturdied,** *a.*

sturgeon (stĕr′ jŏn) [O.F. *esturgeon*, med. L. *sturiōnem*, nom. *-rio*, O.H.G. *sturjo*, cp. A.-S. *styria*, G. *stör*], *n.* A large anadromous fish of the genus *Acipenser*, characterized by bony scales, esp. *A. sturio*, which yields caviare and isinglass.

sturniform (stĕr′ ni fôrm) [L. *sturnus*, starling, -FORM], *a.* Like a starling; belonging to the *Sturnidæ*, a family of birds containing the starlings. **sturnoid,** *a.*

stutter (stŭt′ ėr) [freq. of obs. *stut*, M.E. *stoten*, cp. Dut. *stotteren*, G. *stottern*, also G. *stossen* and L. *tundere*, to beat], *v.i.* To keep hesitating or repeating sounds spasmodically in the articulation of words. *v.t.* To utter thus (*usu.* out). *n.* This act or habit. **stutterer,** *n.* **stutteringly,** *adv.*

sty (1) (stī) [A.-S. *stīgo* (cp. Icel. *stīa*, *stī*, Dan. *sti*, Swed. *stia*, O.H.G. *stīga*, cattle-pen), prob. from *stīgan*, to climb], *n.* (*pl.* **sties**) A pen or enclosure for swine; a mean or filthy habitation; a place of debauchery. *v.t.* To shut up in or as in a sty. *v.i.* To live in or as in a sty.

sty (2) (stī) [prob. from A.-S. *stīgend*, pres.p. of *stīgan*, to rise], *n.* A small inflamed swelling on the edge of the eyelid.

Stygian (stij′ i ăn), *a.* Pertaining to the river Styx; (*fig.*) gloomy, impenetrable (of darkness).

style (1) (stīl) [M.E. and O.F. *stile*, L. *stilus*, sometimes written *stylus*, assim. to foll.], *n.* A pointed instrument used by the ancients for writing on wax-covered tablets; a writing-instrument or other thing shaped like this, an etching-needle, a graver, a blunt-pointed surgical instrument, a pointed or styloid projection, cusp, or process in a bone, etc.; (*fig.*) manner of writing, expressing ideas, speaking, behaving, doing, etc., as dist. from the matter expressed or done; (*loosely*) sort, kind, make, pattern; the general characteristics of literary diction, artistic expression, or mode of decoration, distinguishing a particular people, person, school, period, etc.; (*Rhet.*) the proper expression of thought in language; (*colloq.*) manner or form of a superior or fashionable character, fashion, distinction; mode of designation or address, title, description. *v.t.* To designate, to describe formally by name and title. **new style:** The Gregorian method of reckoning dates (introduced 1582). **old style:** The Julian method, in vogue before this. **stylar,** *a.* Of or pertaining to a style for writing, etc. **styliform,** *a.* **stylish,** *a.* Fashionable in style, smart, showy. **stylishly,** *adv.* **stylishness,** *n.* **stylist,** *n.* A writer having or cultivating a good style. **stylistic** (-lis′ tik), *a.* **stylistically,** *adv.*

style (2) (stīl) [Gr. *stulos*, pillar], *n.* The gnomon of a sun-dial; (*Bot.*) the prolongation of an ovary, bearing the stigma.

style (3) [STILE (1)].

stylet (stī′ lėt) [O.F., from It. STILETTO], *n.* A long pointed instrument, a stiletto; (*Surg.*) the stiffening wire of a catheter; a probe.

stylist, etc. [STYLE (1)].

stylite (stī′ līt) [late Gr. *stulitēs*, from *stulos*, STYLE (2)], *n.* A mediæval recluse who lived on the top of a pillar.

stylo- *comb. form* [STYLE (2)].

stylobate (stī′ lō bāt) [Gr. *stulobatēs* (STYLE (2), *bainein*, to stand)], *n.* A continuous base for a range of columns.

stylograph (stī′ lō grăf) [STYLO-, see STYLE (1), -GRAPH], *n.* A pen with a tubular point fed with ink from a reservoir in the shaft. **stylographic** (-grăf′ ik), *a.* **stylographically,** *adv.* **stylography** (stī log′ ră fi), *n.* The art, process, etc., of using a style or stylograph.

stylo-hyoid (stī lō hī′ oid), *a.* (*Anat.*) Pertaining to the styloid process of the temporal bone and the hyoid bone.

styloid (stī′ loid), *a.* Style-like. *n.* The styloid process, a spine projecting from the base of the temporal bone. **stylospore** (stī′ lō spôr) [SPORE], *n.* (*Bot.*) A pycnidiospore.

stylus (stī′ lŭs) [STYLE (1)], *n.* A pointed instrument for writing by means of carbon paper, a style; (*Gramophone*) the cutter in a recording-head.

stymie (stī′ mi) [etym. doubtful], *n.* (*Golf*) The position when an opponent's ball lies between the player's ball and the hole. *v.t.* To hinder by a stymie.

styptic (stip′ tik) [F. *styptique*, L. *stypticus*, Gr. *stuptikos*, from *stuphein*, to contract, prob. cogn. with STOP], *a.* That stops bleeding; *astringent. *n.* A preparation that arrests bleeding. **stypticity** (-tis′ i ti), *n.*

styrax (stī′ răks) [L., from Gr. *sturax*], *n.* A tree or shrub of the genus *Sturax*, species of which yield benzoin and storax.

Styrian (stir′ i ȧn), *a.* Pertaining to Styria, a province of Austria. *n.* A native of Styria.

Styx (stiks) [L., from Gr. *Stux -gos*], *n.* The river of Hades over which Charon ferries the departed souls.

suable (sū′ ȧbl), *a.* Capable of being sued. **suability** (-bil′ i ti), *n.*

suasion (swā′ zhŭn) [F., from L. *suāsiōnem*, nom. *-sio*, from *suādēre*, to persuade, p.p. *suāsus*, cogn. with foll.], *n.* Persuasion as opp. to compulsion. **suasive** (swā′ siv), *a.* **suasively,** *adv.*

suave (swāv, swav) [F., from L. *suāvis*, cogn. with SWEET], *a.* Agreeable, bland, gracious, polite. **suavely,** *adv.* **suavity** (swăv′ i ti), *n.*

sub (sŭb) [short for SUBALTERN, etc.], *n.* (*colloq.*) A subaltern, subordinate, sub-editor, etc.; a subscription. *v.i.* To act as a substitute or as a sub-editor; to receive pay in advance on account of wages due later.

sub- [L. *sub-*, pref., *sub*, prep., under], *pref.* Under, situated below; from below, upward; denoting inferior or subordinate position; slightly, rather; (*Chem.*) less than normal; (*Math.*) denoting the inverse of a ratio. In cases where no definition is given reference should be made to the unprefixed word in its proper place in the dictionary. **subabdominal** (sŭb ăb dom′ i nȧl), *a.* Situated below the abdomen. **subacid** (-ăs′ id), *a.* Slightly acid or sour; *n.* A subacid substance. **subacrid** (-ăk′ rid), *a.* ***subact** (-ăkt′), *v.t.* To subdue, to reduce. ***subaction,** *n.* **subacute** (-ȧ kūt′), *a.* **subaerial** (-ā ĕr′ i ȧl), *a.* (*Geol.*) Being, acting, or produced in the open air, as opp. to submarine, subterranean, etc. **subaerially,** *adv.* **subaerialist,** *n.* One who ascribes the chief inequalities of the earth's surface to subaerial causes. **sub-agent** (-ā′ jėnt), *n.* One employed by an agent. **sub-agency,** *n.*

subalpine (sŭb ăl′ pīn) [SUB-, ALPINE], *a.* Pertaining to elevated regions not above the timber-line.

subaltern (sŭb′ ȧl tėrn) [F. *subalterne*, med. L. *subalternus* (SUB-, *alternus*, see ALTERNATE)], *a.* Subordinate; of inferior rank; (*Log.*) particular, ranking below universal. *n.* (*Mil.*) A junior officer, one below the rank of captain. **subalternant, subalternate** (-tĕr′ nȧnt, -nȧt), *a.* and *n.* **subalternation** (-nā′ shŭn), *n.*

subapennine (sŭb ăp′ ė nīn) [SUB-, *Apennine*], *a.* Situated at the base of the Apennine mountains. **subapostolic** (-ăp ȯs tol′ ik), *a.* Pertaining to the period succeeding that of the apostles. **subaquatic** (-ȧ kwăt′ ik), *a.* Partially aquatic; subaqueous. **subaqueous** (-ā′ kwė ŭs), *a.* Being or formed under water. **subarctic,** *a.* Pertaining to the region bordering on the Arctic. **subastral** (-ăs′ trȧl), *a.* Terrestrial.

subaudition (sŭb aw dish′ ŭn) [L. *subauditio*, from *subaudīre* (SUB-, *audīre*, to hear)], *n.* The act of understanding something not expressed; something implied but not expressed.

subaxillary (sŭb ăk′ si lȧr i) [SUB-, AXILLARY], *a.* Situated beneath the armpit or the wing-cavity, or under the axil formed by a petiole and stem, etc. **sub-base,** *n.* (*Arch.*) The lowest part of a base horizontally divided; (*Elec.*) a base placed under a machine.

subbing (sŭb′ ing), *n.* (*colloq.*) The act of working as a substitute; the advancement of a portion of wages during piece-work; the work of sub-editing (a newspaper).

subcaudal (sŭb kaw′ dȧl) [SUB-, CAUDAL], *a.* Situated under the tail. **subcelestial** (-sė les′ ti ȧl), *a.* Terrestrial. **subcentral** (-sen′ trȧl), *a.* Situated under the centre; nearly central. **subcerebral** (-ser′ ė brȧl), *a.* **subclass** (sŭb′ klas), *n.* **subclavate** (-klăv′ ȧt), **-clavian** (-klā′ vi ȧn), **clavicular** (-klȧ vik′ ū lȧr), *a.* Situated under the clavicle. **subcommission** (-kȯ mish′ ŭn), *n.* **subcommissioner,** *n.* **sub-committee,** *n.* A small committee appointed from among its members by a larger committee to consider and report on a particular matter. **subconcave** (-kon′ kāv), *a.* Slightly concave. **subconical** (-kon′ i kȧl), *a.*

subconscious (sŭb kon′ shŭs), *a.* Slightly or partially conscious. **the subconscious:** (*Psych.*) That part of the field of consciousness which at any given moment is outside the range of one's attention; the accumulation of past conscious experiences which are forgotten or for the moment are out of one's thoughts. **subconsciously,** *adv.* **subconsciousness,** *n.*

subcontinent (sŭb kon′ ti nėnt), *n.* (*Geog.*) A region large enough to be a continent though itself forming part of a yet larger continent. **subcontinuous** (-tin′ ū ŭs), *a.* **subcontract** (-kon′ trăkt), *n.* A contract sublet from another. **subcontract** (-kon trăkt′), *v.t.* and *i.* **subcontractor,** *n.* **subcontrary** (-kon′ trȧ ri), (*Log.* and *Geom.*) Contrary in an inferior degree; *n.* A subcontrary proposition. **subcontrariety** (-trȧ rī′ ė ti), *n.* **subconvex** (-kon′ veks), *a.* **subcordate,** *a.* **subcostal** (-kos′ tȧl), *a.* **subcranial** (-krā′ ni ȧl), *a.* **subcrystalline** (-kris′ tȧ lin), *a.* **subcutaneous** (-kū tā′ nė ŭs), *a.* **subcutaneously,** *adv.* **subcuticular** (-kū tik′ ū lȧr), *a.* **subcylindrical** (-si lin′ dri kȧl), *a.* **subdeacon** (-dē′ kȯn), *n.* **subdeaconry, subdeaconship,** *n.* **subdean** (sŭb′ dēn), *n.* **subdeanery** (-dē′ nėr i), *n.* **subdecanal** (-dė kā′ nȧl), *a.* **subdecuple** (-dek′ ūpl), *a.* Containing one part of ten. **subdelirium** (-dė lir′ i ŭm), *n.* A mild or intermittent form of delirium. **subdentate** (-den′ tȧt), *a.* **subdermal** (-dĕr′ mȧl), **subdiaconate** (-dī ăk′ ȯ nȧt), *n.*

subdititious (sŭb di tish′ ŭs) [L. *subdititius, -cius*, from *subdere* (SUB-, *dare*, to put)], *a.* Inserted surreptitiously, foisted in.

subdivide (sŭb di vīd′) [L. *subdivīdere*], *v.t.* and *i.* To divide again or into smaller parts. **subdivisible** (-viz′ ibl), *a.* **subdivision** (-vizh′ ŭn), *n.*

subdominant (sŭb dom′ i nȧnt), *a.* (*Mus.*) The tone next below the dominant, the fourth of the scale. **subdorsal** (-dôr′ sȧl), *a.* **subdouble** (-dŭbl′), *a.* In the ratio of one to two.

subduable, subdual [SUBDUE].

***subduce, *subduct** (sŭb dūs′, -dŭkt′) [L. *subdūcere* (SUB-, *dūcere*, to lead, p.p. *ductus*)], *v.t.* To withdraw, to take away, to subtract. ***subduction** (-dŭk′ shŭn), *n.*

subdue (sŭb dū′) [M.E. *soduen*, from p.p. *sodued*, O.F. *subduz*, pl., subdued, prob. through a late L. *subdutus*, L. *subditus*, p.p. of *subdere*, see SUBDITITIOUS], *v.t.* To conquer, to reduce to subjection, to vanquish, to overcome; to tame, to render gentle or mild; to tone down, to soften, to make less glaring. **subduable,** *a.* **subdual** (-dū′ ȧl), **subduement,** *n.* **subduedness** (-dū′ ėd nės), *n.* **subduer,** *n.*

subduple (sŭb′ dūpl), *a.* In the ratio of one to two. **subduplicate** (-dū′ pli kȧt), *a.* Expressed by the square root. **sub-edit,** *v.t.* To prepare manuscript for printing. **sub-editor,** *n.* **subepidermal** (-ep i dĕr′ mȧl), *a.* **subequal** (-ē′ kwȧl), *a.* Nearly equal, esp. of quantities in a group of which none equals the sum of any two others. **subequilateral** (-ek wi lăt′ ėr ȧl), *a.* **suberect** (-ė rekt′), *a.*

subereous (sū bĕr′ ė ŭs), **suberic** (sū ber′ ik) [L. *sūber*, cork, -OUS], *a.* Of the nature or texture of, pertaining to or derived from cork. **suberin,** *n.* A form of cellulose found in cork. **suberose** (1), **suberous** (sū′ bė rōs, -ŭs), *a.*

suberose (2) (sŭb ė rōs′), *a.* (*Bot.*) Slightly erose. **subfamily** (-făm′ i li), *n.* **subfebrile** (-fē′ bril), *a.* **subfue** (-fū′), *v.t.* **subfuedation** (-dā′ shŭn), *n.* **subflavour** (-flā′ vȯr), *n.* **subflora** (-flôr′ ȧ), *n.* **subform** (sŭb fôrm′), *n.* **subfluvial** (-floo′ vi ȧl), *a.* **subfusc, subfuscous** (sŭb fŭsk′, -ŭs) [L. *fuscus*, FUSCOUS], *a.* **subgelatinous** (-jė lăt′ i nŭs), *a.* **subgenus** (-jē′ nŭs), *n.* **sub-generic** (-jė ner′ ik), *a.* **subglacial** (-glā′ shȧl), *a.* **subglobular**

(-glob' ū lȧr), *a.* **subgranular** (-grăn' ū lȧr), *a.* **sub-group** (-groop'), *n.* **sub-head, -heading** (-hed', -ing), *n.* A heading, often explanatory, beneath the main heading of a book, article, etc. **subhepatic** (-hė păt' ik), *a.* **subhimalayan** (-hi ma' lā ȧn), *a.* **sub-human** (-hū' mȧn), *a.* **sub-humeral** (-hū' mėr ȧl), *a.* **subimago** (-i mā' gō), *n.* (*Ent.*) A stage in the metamorphosis of certain insects preceding the imago. **subindicative** (-in dik' ȧ tiv), *a.* **subinfeudation** (-in fū dā' shŭn), *n.* **subinspector** (-in spek' tȯr), *n.* **subintestinal** (-in tes' ti nȧl), *a.*

subintrant (sŭb in' trȧnt) [late L. *subintrans, -ntem,* pres.p. of *subintrāre* (SUB-, *intrāre,* ENTER)], *a.* (*Path.*) Characterized by paroxysms that succeed each other so rapidly as to be almost continuous.

sub-irrigation (-ir i gā' shŭn), *n.* Irrigation beneath the surface; partial irrigation.

***subitaneous** (sŭb i tā' nė ŭs) [L. *subitāneus,* SUDDEN], *a.* Sudden, hasty. **subitaneousness,** *n.*

subitamente (soo bē ta men' tā) [It.], *adv.* (*Mus.*) Suddenly.

subjacent (sŭb jā' sėnt) [L. *subjacens -ntem,* pres.p. of *subjacēre* (SUB-, *jacēre,* to lie)], *a.* Underlying; lower in position.

subject (sŭb' jėkt) [M.E. and O.F. *suget* (F. *sujet*), assim. to L. *subjectus,* p.p. of *subjicere* (SUB-, *jacere,* to cast)], *a.* Being under the power, control, or authority of another; exposed, liable, prone, disposed (to); dependent, conditional; *submissive; *lower in position, subjacent. *n.* One under the dominion or political rule of a person or State, one owing allegiance to a sovereign, a member of a State as related to the sovereign or Government; that which is treated or to be treated in any specified way, as the topic under consideration, the theme of discussion or description, or artistic expression or representation; the leading phrase or motif in music; a dead body for dissection, etc.; the cause or occasion (for); a person regarded as subject to any specified disease, mental affection or tendency, psychic influence, etc.; (*Log.*) that member of a proposition about which something is predicated; (*Gram.*) the noun or its equivalent about which something is affirmed, the nominative of a sentence; (*Metaph.*) the ego, as distinguished from the object or non-ego, the mind, the conscious self; the substance or substratum to which attributes must be referred. *v.t.* (sŭb jekt') To subdue, to reduce to subjection (to); to expose, to make liable. **subject to:** Conditional upon (ratification, etc.); (*colloq.*) conditionally upon. **subject-heading,** *n.* A heading in an index, catalogue, etc., under which references are given. **subject-matter,** *n.* The object of consideration, discussion, etc. **subject-object,** *n.* The immediate object in thought as distinguished from an external thing. **subjection** (-jek' shŭn), *n.*

subjective (sŭb jek' tiv), *a.* Concerned with or proceeding from the consciousness or the ego as opp. to objective or external things; due to the individual mind, fanciful, imaginary; (*Art*) characterized by the prominence given to the individuality of the author or artist. **subjectively,** *adv.* **subjectiveness, subjectivity** (-tiv' i ti), *n.* **subjectivism,** *n.* The doctrine that human knowledge is purely subjective, and therefore relative. **subjectivist, *subjectist** (sŭb'-), *n.* **subjectless,** *a.*

subjoin (sŭb join') [O.F. *subjoign-,* stem of *subjoindre,* L. *subjungere* (SUB-, *jungere,* to join, p.p. *junctus*)], *v.t.* To add at the end, to append, to affix. ***subjoinder,** *n.* **subjoint** (sŭb' joint), *n.* A secondary joint.

subjugate (sŭb' jụ gāt) [L. *subjugātus,* p.p. of *subjugāre,* to bring under the yoke (SUB-, *jugum,* cogn. with YOKE)], *v.t.* To subdue, to conquer, to bring into subjection, to enslave. **subjugable,** *a.* **subjugation** (-gā' shŭn), *n.* **subjugator** (sŭb' jụ gā tȯr), *n.*

subjunctive (sŭb jŭngk' tiv) [L. *subjunctīvus,* from *subjunct-,* see SUBJOIN], *a.* Denoting the mood of a verb expressing condition, hypothesis, or contingency. *n.* The subjunctive mood. **subjunctively,** *adv.*

sub-kingdom (sŭb' king dȯm), *n.* A primary division of the animal or vegetable kingdom. **sublanceolate** (-lăn' sė ō lȧt), *a.* **sublapsarian** (-lap sâr' i ȧn), *a.* Infralapsarian. **sublapsarianism,** *n.*

sublate (sŭb' lāt) [L. *sublātus* (SUB-, *lātus,* p.p. of *tollere,* to take away)], *v.t.* (*Log.*) To treat as untrue, to deny, opp. to posit. **sublation** (-lā' shŭn), *n.*

sublease (sŭb' lēs), *v.t.* and *n.* **sublessee** (-lė sē'), *n.* **sublessor** (-les' ȯr), *n.* **sublet** (sŭb let'), *v.t.* To let property already rented or held on lease. **sub-librarian** (-lī brâr' i ȧn), *n.* **sub-lieutenant** (-lef ten' ȧnt), *n.*

sublimate (sŭb' li māt) [L. *sublimātus,* p.p. of *sublimāre,* as foll.], *v.t.* To convert (a solid substance) by heat to the state of vapour and to solidity again by cooling; (*fig.*) to refine, to purify, to etherealize. **sublimated,** *a.* *n.* (-mȧt) The product of sublimation. **corrosive sublimate** [CORROSIVE]. **sublimation** (-mā' shŭn), *n.* The result of sublimating; (*Psych.*) the diversion by the subject himself of certain instinctive impulses, esp. sexual, into altruistic channels. **sublimatory** (sŭb li mā' tȯr i), *a.* and *n.*

sublime (sụ blīm') [F., from L. *sublīmis* (perh. SUB-, *līmen,* lintel, reaching up to the lintel)], *a.* Of the most lofty or exalted nature, characterized by grandeur, nobility, or majesty, inspiring awe; (*iron.*) unconquerable, indifferent to criticism (of conceit, etc.). *v.t.* To sublimate; to elevate, to purify; to make sublime. *v.i.* To be sublimated; to be elevated or purified; to become sublime. *a.* Exalted, raised aloft; *haughty; high in excellence; exalted by lofty or noble qualities; elevated in manner or expression; elate, excited. ***Sublime Porte*** [PORTE]. **sublimely,** *adv.* **sublimer,** *n.* **sublimeness, sublimity** (-lim' i ti), *n.*

subliminal (sŭb lim' i nȧl), *a.* Not reaching the threshold of consciousness, hardly perceived; pertaining to subconsciousness. **subliminal advertising:** Advertising directed to and acting on the unconscious. **sublineation** (-lin ā' shŭn), *n.* **sublingual** (-ling' gwȧl), *a.* **sublittoral** (-lit' ȯr ȧl), *a.* ***sublunar, sublunary** (-lū' nȧr, -i), *a.* Situated beneath the moon, pertaining to this world, mundane. **submammary** (-măm' ȧ ri), *a.* Situated under the *mammæ.*

submarine (sŭb mȧ rēn'), *a.* Situated, acting or growing beneath the surface of the sea. *n.* (sŭb' mȧ rēn), A vessel that may be submerged. **submariner** (sŭb mă' ri nėr), *n.* A sailor in a submarine. **submaxillary** (-măk' si lȧ ri), *a.* **submedian** (-mē' di ȧn), *a.* Situated next to the median line. **submembranous** (-mem brā' nŭs), *a.* **submental** (-men' tȧl) [MENTAL (2)], *a.* **submetallic** (-mė tăl' ik), *a.*

submerge (sŭb mĕrj') [F. *submerger,* L. *submergere* (SUB-, *mergere,* to dip, p.p. *mersus*)], *v.t.* To put under water, etc., to flood, to inundate; (*fig.*) to overwhelm. *v.i.* To sink under water, etc. **submergence,** *n.* **submerse** (-mĕrs'), *v.t.* (*chiefly p.p. in Bot.*) To submerge. *a.* Being or growing under water. **submersible,** *a.* and *n.* **submersion** (-mĕr' shŭn), *n.*

submission, submissive, etc. [SUBMIT].

submit (sŭb mit') [L. *submittere* (SUB-, *mittere,* to send, p.p. *missus*)], *v.t.* To yield or surrender (oneself); to present or refer for consideration, decision, etc.; to put forward deferentially. *v.i.* To yield, to surrender, to give in; to be submissive. **submitter,** *n.* ***submiss** (-mis), *a.* Submissive. **submission** (-mish' ŭn), *n.* The act of submitting; the state of being submissive; compliance, obedience, resignation, meekness. **submissive,** *a.* **submissively,** *adv.* **submissiveness,** *n.*

submontane (sŭb mon' tān) [SUB-, MONTANE], *a.* Situated at the foot of a mountain or range of mountains. **submultiple** (-mŭl' tipl), *a.* and *n.* **submuscular** (-mŭs' kū lȧr), *a.* **subnarcotic**

(-nar kot′ ik), *a.* **subnasal** (-nā′ zȧl), *a.* **subnatural** (-năt′ yụr ȧl), *a.* **subneural** (-nūr′ ȧl), *a.* Situated beneath a neural axis, etc. **subnivean** (-niv′ ė ȧn), *a.* Situated beneath the snow. **subnodal** (-nō′ dȧl), *a.*

subnormal (sŭb nôr′ mȧl), *a.* Less than normal, below the normal standard. **subnubilar** (-nū′ bi lȧr), *a.* Situated beneath the clouds. **suboccipital** (-ŏk sip′ i tȧl), *a.* **suboceanic** (-ō shė ăn′ ik), *a.* **subocellate** (-ŏ sel′ ȧt), *a.* **suboctave** (-ok′ tȧv), *n.* **suboctuple** (-ok′ tūpl), *a.* Containing one part in eight. **subocular** (-ok′ ū lȧr), *a.* **subopercular** (-ō pĕr′ kū lȧr), *a.* **suboperculum,** *n.* **suborbital** (-ôr′ bi tȧl), *a.* **suborder** (-ôr′ dėr), *n.* (*Zool. and Bot.*) A subdivision of an order. **subordinal,** *a.* **subordinary,** *n.* (*Her.*).

subordinate (sụ bôr′ di nȧt) [med. L. *subordinātus*, p.p. of *subordināre* (SUB-, *ordo -dinem*, ORDER)], *a.* Inferior in order, rank, importance, power, etc.; subject, subservient, subsidiary (to). *n.* A person working under another or inferior in official standing. *v.t.* (-nāt) To make subordinate; to treat or consider as of secondary importance; to make subject or subservient (to). **subordinately,** *adv.* **subordinateness,** *n.* **subordination** (-nā′ shŭn), *n.* **subordinationism,** *n.* The doctrine of the priority of the first to the second and third Persons of the Trinity as regards order (the orthodox view) or as regards essence (the Arian view). **subordinative** (-ôr′ di nȧ tiv), *a.*

suborn (sụ bôrn′) [F. *suborner*, L. *subornāre* (SUB-, *ornāre*, to furnish, to incite)], *v.t.* To procure by underhand means, esp. bribery, to commit perjury or other criminal act. **subornation** (-nā′ shŭn), *n.* **suborner,** *n.*

suboval (sŭb ō′ vȧl), *a.* Nearly oval. **subovate** (-ō′ vȧt), *a.* **subpanation** (-pȧ nā′ shŭn) [cp. IMPANATION], *n.* (*Theol.*) The doctrine that the body and blood of Christ are locally and materially present in the Eucharist under the form of the bread and wine. **subparietal** (-pȧ rī′ ė tȧl), *a.* **subperitoneal** (-per i tō′ nė ȧl), *a.* **subpermanent** (-pĕr′ mȧ nėnt), *a.* **subpleural** (-ploo′ rȧl), *a.*

subpoena (sŭb pē′ nȧ) [L., under penalty], *n.* A writ commanding a person's attendance in a court of justice under a penalty. *v.t.* To serve with such a writ.

subpolar (sŭb pō′ lȧr), *a.* Adjacent to one of the poles; (*Astron.*) lying under a celestial pole. **subprefect** (-prē′ fėkt), *n.* **sub-prefecture,** *n.* **subprior** (-prī′ ŏr), *n.* **subprovince** (-prov′ ins), *n.* **subpubic** (-pū′ bik), *a.* **subpulmonary** (-pŭl′ mŏ nȧ ri), *a.* **subquadrate** (-kwod′ rȧt), *a.* **subquadruple** (-kwod′ rupl), *a.* In the ratio of one to four. **subquintuple** (-kwin′ tūpl), *a.* **subramose** (-rā′ mōs), *a.* **subreader** (-rē′ dėr), *n.* An assistant reader in the Inns of Court. **subregion** (sŭb′ rē jŭn), *n.* **subregional** (-rē′ jŭn ȧl), *a.*

subreption (sŭb rep′ shŭn) [L. *subreptio*, from *subripere* (SUB-, *rapere*, to seize)], *n.* The act of obtaining something by surprise or fraudulent representation.

subrogation (sŭb rō gā′ shŭn), *n.* The substitution of one person in the place of another with succession to his rights to a debt, etc. **sub-sacral** (-sā′ krȧl), *a.* **sub-saturated** (-săt′ ū rā tėd), *a.* **subsaturation** (-rā′ shŭn), *n.* **subscapular** (-skăp′ ū lȧr), *a.*

subscribe (sŭb skrīb′) [L. *subscrībere* (SUB-, *scrībere*, to write)], *v.t.* To write (one's name, etc.) at the end of a document, etc.; to sign (a document, promise, etc.); to contribute (an annual or other specified sum to or for a fund, object, etc.); to publish by securing subscribers beforehand; *to characterize. *v.i.* To write one's name at the end of a document; (*fig.*) to assent (to an opinion, etc.); to engage to pay a contribution, to allow one's name to be entered in a list of contributors; to undertake to receive and pay for a newspaper, book, etc.; *to yield, to surrender. **subscribable,** *a.* **subscriber,** *n.* **subscription** (-skrip′ shŭn), *n.* The act of subscribing; a contribution to a fund, etc.; a membership fee (*Am.* dues); raising money from subscribers. **subscript** (sŭb′ skript), *a.* (*Gr. gram.*) Written underneath (of the iota (ι) written below ᾳ, ῃ, ῳ).

subsection (sŭb sek′ shŭn) [SUB-, SECTION], *n.* A subdivision of a section.

subsellium (sŭb sel′ i ŭm) [L. (SUB-, *sella*, seat)], *n.* (*pl.* **-lia**) A misericord. **subsensible** (-sen′ sibl), *a.* **subseptuple** (-sep′ tūpl), *a.*

subsequent (sŭb′ sė kwėnt) [L. *subsequens -ntem*, pres.p. *subsequī* (SUB-, *sequī*, to follow)], *a.* Coming immediately after, in time or order; following, succeeding, posterior (to). **subsequence,** ***-quency,** *n.* **subsequently,** *adv.*

subserve (sŭb sĕrv′) [L. *subservīre* (SUB-, *servīre*, to SERVE)], *v.t.* To serve as a means or instrument in promoting (an end, etc.). **subservient,** *a.* Useful as an instrument or means; obsequious, servile. **subservience, -ency,** *n.* **subserviently,** *adv.*

subsessile (sŭb ses′ il), *a.* Nearly sessile. **subsextuple** (-seks′ tūpl), *a.* In the ratio of one to six.

subside (sŭb sīd′) [L. *subsīdere* (SUB-, *sīdere*, to settle, cogn. with *sedēre*, to sit)], *v.i.* To sink, to fall in level, to settle (of lees, etc.); to sink in, to collapse; (*fig.*) to settle down, to abate, to become tranquil. **subsidence** (sŭb sī′ dėns, sŭb′ si dėns), *n.*

subsidiary (sŭb sid′ i ȧ ri) [L. *subsidiārius*, as foll.], *a.* Aiding, auxiliary, supplemental; pertaining to or of the nature of a subsidy; tributary. *n.* A subsidiary person or thing, an auxiliary, an accessory. **subsidiarily,** *adv.*

subsidy (sŭb′ si di) [M.E. and A.-F. *subsidie*, L. *subsidium* (SUB-, *sedēre*, to sit)], *n.* (*Hist.*) Pecuniary aid granted by Parliament to the sovereign for purposes of State, a tax to defray special expenses; a sum paid by one government to another, usu. to meet the expenses of a war; a contribution by the State, a public corporation, etc., to a commercial or charitable undertaking of benefit to the public. **subsidize,** *v.t.*

subsist (sŭb sist′) [F. *subsister*, L. *subsistere* (SUB-, *sistere*, causal of *stāre*, to stand)], *v.i.* To exist, to remain in existence; to live, to have means of living, to find sustenance, to be sustained (on); to inhere. *v.t.* To maintain, to support. **subsistence,** *n.* **subsistence allowance, money,** *n.* An advance of wages, or a special payment, made to enable an employee to meet immediate needs; a payment for food, etc., made in addition to salary or wages. **subsistent,** *a.*

subsoil (sŭb′ soil), *n.* The stratum of earth immediately below the surface-soil. **subsonic,** *a.* Pertaining to speeds less than that of sound. **subspecies** (-spē′ shēz), *n.* **subspecific** (-spė sif′ ik), *a.* **sub-spherical** (-sfer′ i kȧl), *a.* **subspherically,** *adv.* **subspinous** (-spī′ nŭs), *a.* **substage** (sŭb′ stāj), *n.* An apparatus underneath the stage of a microscope carrying the condenser, etc.

substance (sŭb′ stȧns) [F., from L. *substantia* (SUB-, *stāre*, to stand)], *n.* That of which a thing consists; matter, material, as opp. to form; the essence, the essential part, pith, gist, or main purport; that which is real, solidity, firmness, solid foundation; material possessions, property, wealth, resources; (*Phil.*) the permanent substratum in which qualities and accidents are conceived to inhere, the self-existent ground of attributes and phenomena.

substantial (sŭb stăn′ shȧl), *a.* Having substance, real, actually existing, not illusory; solid, stout, strongly constructed, durable; possessed of substance, having sufficient means, well-to-do, financially sound; of considerable importance, value, extent, amount, etc.; material, practical, virtual; *n.* (*usu. pl.*) The essential parts, reality. **substantialism,** *n.* The doctrine that there are substantial realities underlying phenomena. **substantialist,** *n.* **substantiality** (-ăl′ i ti), *n.* **substantialize,** *v.t.* and *i.* **substantially,** *adv.*

substantiate (sŭb stăn′ shi āt), *v.t.* To make real

or actual; to establish, to prove, to make good (a statement, etc.). **substantiation** (-ā′ shŭn), *n.*

substantive (sŭb′ stăn tiv) [M.E. and F. *substantif*, L. *substantivus*, as prec.], *a.* Expressing real existence; having substance or reality, having or pertaining to the essence or substance of anything; independently existent, not merely implied inferential, or subsidiary; (*Mil.*) permanent (rank). *n.* A noun or part of a sentence used as a noun. **substantival** (-tī′ văl), *a.* **substantivally, substantively,** *adv.*

sub-station (sŭb′ stā shŭn) [SUB-, STATION], *n.* A subsidiary station. **substernal** (-stĕr′ năl), *a.*

substitute (sŭb′ sti tūt) [F. *substitut*, L. *substitūtus*, p.p. of *substituere* (SUB-, *statuere*, see STATUTE)], *n.* A person or thing put in the place of or serving for another. *v.t.* To put in the place of another person or thing. **substitution** (-tū′ shŭn), *n.* **substitutional, -ary, substitutive** (sub′ sti tū tiv), *a.* **substitutionally,** *adv.*

***substractor** (sŭb străk′ tŏr) [erron. for SUBTRACTOR], *n.* (*Shak.*) A detractor. **substratosphere** (sŭb străt′ ō sfêr), *n.* The atmospheric region below the stratosphere and over $3\frac{1}{2}$ miles above the earth. **substratum** (sŭb strā′ tŭm) [L., neut. p.p. of *substernere* (SUB-, STRATUM)], *n.* (*pl.* **-ta**) That which underlies anything; a layer or stratum lying underneath, subsoil; the ground or basis (of phenomena, etc.).

substruction, substructure (sŭb strŭk′ shŭn, -tyŭr), *n.* An under-structure or foundation. **substructural** (-strŭk′ tū răl), *a.* **substyle** (sŭb′ stīl), *n.* The line on which the style or gnomon of a dial stands. **substylar,** *a.* **subsulphate** (-sŭl′ fāt), *n.* A basic sulphate.

subsultus (sŭb sŭl′ tŭs) [L., p.p. of *subsilīre* (SUB-, *salīre*, to spring)], *n.* (*Path.*) A convulsive muscular twitching. **subsultive,** *a.*

subsume (sŭb sūm′) [SUB-, L. *sūmere*, to take (p.p. *sumptus*)], *v.t.* To include under a more general class or category. **subsumption** (-sŭmp′ shŭn), *n.* **subsumptive,** *a.*

subtangent (sŭb tăn′ jėnt), *n.* The portion of the axis of a curve intercepted between an ordinate and a tangent both drawn from the same point. **subtemperate** (-tem′ pėr ăt), *a.* **subtenant** (-ten′ ănt), *n.* A tenant holding property from one who is himself a tenant. **subtenancy,** *n.*

subtend (sŭb tend′) [L. *subtendere* (SUB-, *tendere*, to stretch, p.p. *tensus*)], *v.t.* To extend under or be opposite to (of a chord relatively to an arc, or the side of a triangle to an angle). **subtense,** *n.* That which subtends.

subtepid (sŭb tep′ id), *a.* Somewhat tepid.

subter- [L., under, less than, opp. to SUPER-], *pref.*

subterfuge (sŭb tėr fūj) [F., from late L. *subterfugium* (SUBTER-, *fugere*, to flee)], *n.* A shift, an evasion, a prevarication, employed to avoid an inference, censure, etc.

subterposition (sŭb tėr pŏ zish′ ŭn), *n.* Position under something else, esp. of strata.

subterranean, -terraneous (sŭb tė rā′ nė ăn, -ŭs) [L. *subterrāneus* (SUB-, *terra*, earth, -ANEOUS)], *a.* Underground. ***subterrene,** *a.* **subterraneously,** *adv.* **subterrestrial** (-res′ tri ăl), *a.*

subthoracic (sŭb thŏ răs′ ik), *a.* Situated below the thorax.

subtile (sŭb til, sŭt′ ėl) [M.E. *sobil*, O.F. *sutil*, L. *subtilem*, nom. *-lis* (prob. finely-woven, SUB-, *tela*, web)], *a.* Tenuous, thin, extremely fine; *subtle. ***subtilely,** *adv.* **subtility,** *n.* **subtilize,** *v.t.* and *i.* **subtilization** (-zā′ shŭn), *n.* **subtilty** *n.*

sub-title (sŭb′ tī′ tėl), *n.* An additional or subsidiary title to a book, etc.; a half-title, usu. placed before the title page in books; (*Cinema.*) the caption to a film.

subtle (sŭt′ ėl) [SUBTILE], *a.* Rarefied, attenuated, delicate, hard to seize, elusive; making fine distinctions, acute, discerning; ingenious, skilful, clever; artful, cunning, crafty, insidious. **subtlety** (sŭtl′ ti), *n.* **subtly** (sŭt′ li), *adv.*

subtonic (sŭb ton′ ik), *n.* (*Mus.*) The note next below the tonic. *a.* (*Phon.*) Sonant. **subtopia** (sŭb tō′ pi ă), *n.* Unsightly suburbs, ill-planned rural or urban areas. **subtorrid** (-tor′ id), *a.*

subtract (sŭb trăkt′) [L. *subtractus*, p.p. of *subtrahere* (SUB-, *trahere*, to draw)], *v.t.* To take away (a part, quantity, etc.) from the rest, to deduct. **subtracter,** *n.* **subtraction** (-trăk′ shŭn), *n.* **subtractive,** *a.* **subtrahend** (sŭb′ tră hend), *n.* The number or quantity to be subtracted from another.

subtriangular (sŭb trī ăng′ gū lăr), *a.* Approximately triangular. **sub-tribe** (sŭb′ trīb), *n.* **subtriple** (-tripl), *a.* Containing one part of three. **subtriplicate** (-trip′ li kăt), *a.* **subtropical** (-trop′ i kăl), *a.* Characterized by features common to both the temperate and tropical zones; pertaining to the regions near the tropics. **subtropics,** *n.pl.* **subtype** (sŭb′ tīp), *n.*

subulate (sŭb′ ū lăt) [L. *subula*, awl, -ATE], *a.* Awl-shaped. **subuliform,** *a.*

subungulate (sŭb ŭng′ gū lăt), *a.* Hoofed, but having several digits.

suburb (sŭb′ ŭrb) [A.-F. and O.F. *suburbe*, L. *suburbium* (SUB-, *urbs urbis*, city)], *n.* An outlying part of a city or town. **suburban,** *a.* Pertaining to a suburb; (*fig.*) descriptive of an outlook on life limited by certain narrow conventions.

subursine (sŭb ĕr′ sin), *a.* Somewhat bear-like in structure, etc. **sub-variety** (-vă rī′ ė ti), *n.*

subvene (sŭb vēn′) [F. *subvenir*, L. *subvenire* (SUB-, *venīre*, to come)], *v.i.* To happen so as to aid or effect a result. **subvention** (-ven′ shŭn), *n.* A grant in aid, a subsidy.

subvert (sŭb vĕrt′) [F. *subvertir*, L. *subvertere*, (SUB-, *vertere*, to turn, p.p. *versus*)], *v.t.* To overthrow, to destroy, to overturn; to corrupt, to pervert. ***subverse** (-vĕrs′), *v.t.* **subversion** (-vĕr′ shŭn), *n.* **subversive,** *a.* **subverter,** *n.* **subvertible,** *a.*

subvertebral (sŭb vĕr′ tė brăl), *a.* Situated under the vertebræ. **subvertical** (-vĕr′ ti kăl), *a.* **subvirile** (-vir′ il), *a.* Deficient in manhood or vigour. **subvitalized** (-vī′ tă līzd), *a.* **subvitreous** (-vit′ rė ŭs), *a.* **subvocal** (vō′ kăl), *n.* and *a.* Subtonic.

subway (sŭb′ wā), *n.* An underground passage, tunnel, conduit, etc.; (*Am.*) an underground railway.

suc- [SUB-], *pref.* (before *c*).

succades (sŭ kādz′) [L. *succ-us*, juice, -ADE], *n.pl.* (*Comm.*) Fruit candied and preserved in syrup.

succedaneum (sŭk sė dā′ nė ŭm) [L. *succēdāneus*, as foll.], *n.* (*pl.* **-nea**) That which (or *rarely* who) is used instead of something else, a substitute. **succedaneous,** *a.*

succeed (sŭk sēd′) [F. *succéder*, L. *succedere* (SUC-, *cēdere*, see CEDE, p.p. *cessus*)], *v.t.* To follow, to come after (in time or order), to be subsequent to; to take the place previously occupied by, to be heir or successor to. *v.i.* To follow in time or order, to be subsequent (to); to be the heir or successor (to an office, estate, etc.); to be successful, to attain a desired object, to end prosperously. ***succeeder,** *n.*

succentor (sŭk sen′ tŏr) [late L., from L. *succinere* (SUC-, *canere*, to sing), p.p. *succentus*], *n.* A deputy precentor; the leading bass in a choir.

success (sŭk ses′) [O.F. *succes*, L. *successum*, nom. *-sus*, from *succedere*, to succeed], *n.* The act of succeeding, favourable result, attainment of what is desired or intended, esp. of worldly prosperity; *the issue or result of an undertaking. **successful,** *a.* **successfully,** *adv.* **successfulness,** *n.* ***successless,** *a.* ***successlessly,** *adv.* ***successlessness,** *n.* **successor,** *n.*

succession (sŭk sesh′ ŭn) [F., from L. *successiōnem*, nom. *-sio*, as prec.], *n.* A following in order; a series of things following in order; the act or right of succeeding to an office or inheritance; the order in which persons so succeed; (*Biol.*) the order of descent in the development of species. **succession duty:** A tax on property to which a person succeeds by the death of the owner. **successional,** *a.* **successionally,** *adv.*

successive (sŭk ses′ iv) [F. *successif*, fem. *-ve*, med. L. *successīvus*, from L. *successus*, SUCCESS], *a.* Following in order or uninterrupted succession, consecutive; *hereditary, legitimate. **successively,** *adv.* **successiveness,** *n.*

***succiduous** (sŭk sid′ ū ŭs) [L. *succiduus*, from *succidere* (SUC-, *cadere*, to fall)], *a.* On the point of falling; falling.

succiferous (sŭk sif′ ėr ŭs) [L. *succus*, juice, -FEROUS], *a.* (*Bot.*) Producing or conveying sap.

succin (sŭk′ sin) [late L. *succinum*, from *succus*, see prec.], *n.* Amber. **succinic** (-sin′ ik), *a.* Derived from or contained in amber. ***succinous** (sŭk′ si nŭs), *a.* **succinate,** *n.* A salt of succinic acid. **succinite,** *n.* Amber; a yellow variety of garnet.

succinct (sŭk singkt′) [L. *succinctus*, p.p. of *succingere* (SUC-, *cingere*, to gird)], *a.* Compressed into few words, brief, concise. **succinctly,** *adv.* **succinctness,** *n.*

succinic, succinite, etc. [SUCCIN].

succivorous (sŭk siv′ ŏ rŭs) [L. *succus*, juice, VOROUS], *a.* Feeding on sap (of insects, etc.).

succory [corr. of CHICORY].

succose (sŭk′ ōs) [L. *succ-us*, juice], *a.* Juicy, sappy.

succotash (sŭk′ ŏ tăsh) [N.Am.Ind.], *n.* (*Am.*) A dish composed of green maize and beans cooked together.

succour (sŭk′ ŏr) [O.F. *sucurre*, L. *succurrere* (SUC-, *currere*, to run, p.p. *cursus*)], *v.t.* To come to the aid of; to help or relieve in difficulty or distress. *n.* Aid in time of difficulty or distress; *(*pl.*) reinforcements. **succourer,** *n.* **succourless,** *a.*

succuba, -bus (sŭk′ ū bȧ, -bŭs) [L., from *succumbere* (SUC-, *cumbere*, to lie)], *n.* (*pl.* **-bæ, -bi**) A demon believed to assume the shape of a woman and have sexual intercourse with men in their sleep. **succubate,** *v.t.* **succubine,** *a.*

succulent (sŭk′ ū lėnt) [F., from L. *succulentus*, from SUCCUS], *a.* Juicy; (*Bot.*) thick and fleshy (of plants, stems, etc.). **succulence,** *n.* **succulently,** *adv.*

succumb (sŭ kŭm′) [L. *succumbere* (SUC-, *cumbere* to lie)], *v.i.* To cease to resist, etc., to give way; to yield, to submit (to force, etc.); to die. **succumbent,** *a.*

succursal (sŭ kĕr′ sȧl) [F. *succursale* (*église*), subsidiary (church), from med. L. *succursus*, SUCCOUR], *a.* Auxiliary (of a chapel of ease).

succus (sŭk′ ŭs) [L., also *sūcus*, juice, sap], *n.* (*pl. succi*) (*Physiol.*) A juice or fluid secretion; (*Med.*) the expressed juice of a plant.

succuss (sŭ kŭs′) [L. *succussus*, p.p. of *succutere* (SUC-, *quatere*, to shake)], *v.t.* To shake suddenly, esp. (*Med.*) in diagnosis. ***succussation** (sŭk ȧs ā′ shŭn), *n.* A shaking, a succussion; a trot, trotting. **succussion** (-kŭsh′ ŏn), *n.* A shaking; a shock; a shaking of the thorax to detect pleural effusion. **succusive,** *a.*

such (sŭch) [A.-S. *swylc* (*swā*, so, *līc*, LIKE, -LY), cp. Dut. *zulk*, G. *solch*, Icel. *slīkr*, Swed. *slik*], *a.* Of that, or the same, or the like kind or degree (as); of the kind or degree mentioned or implied; being the same in quality, degree, etc.; so great, intense, etc. (*usu.* as or that); (with adj.) so. *pron.* Such a person, persons, or things (as); (*colloq.*) the same, they or them. **such and such:** Certain, some. ***such as:** Those who. **such-like,** *a.* Of such a kind; *pron.* (*colloq.*) things of that sort.

suck (sŭk) [A.-S. *sūcan*, cp. L. *sugere*, p.p. *suctus*], *v.t.* To draw (milk, etc.) into the mouth by the action of the lips or lips and lungs; to imbibe, to drink in, to absorb (up or in), to acquire, to gain; to engulf, to draw (in); to draw liquid from with or as with the mouth; to dissolve thus. *v.i.* To draw liquid, etc., in by suction; to draw milk, nourishment, etc., in thus. *n.* An act or spell of sucking, suction; force of suction; a small draught or drink. **suck-in,** *n.* (*slang*) A deception, a fiasco.

sucker (sŭk′ ėr), *n.* One who or that which sucks; a sucking-pig; a newly-born whale; a fish that sucks in food or has a suctorial mouth, esp. one of the N. American *Catostomidæ*; the piston of a suction-pump; a pipe or tube through which anything is drawn by suction; a sucking-disk; (*Biol.*) an organ, such as an acetabulum, acting on the same principle, a suctorial organ; (*Bot.*) a shoot from a root or a subterranean part of a stem; (*slang*) a sweet, a lollipop; (*slang*) a ready dupe, a gullible fellow. *v.t.* To strip suckers from.

sucking (sŭk′ ing), *a.* Deriving nourishment from the breast; not yet weaned; (*fig.*) young and inexperienced. **sucking-bottle,** *n.* An infant's feeding-bottle. **sucking-disk,** *n.* A disk of leather, rubber, etc. adhering firmly to a smooth surface when wetted. **sucking-pig,** *n.* A pig not yet weaned.

suckle (sŭk′ ėl) [freq. of SUCK], *v.t.* To give suck to. **suckling,** *n.* A child or animal not yet weaned.

sucrose (sū′ krōs) [F. *sucre*, SUGAR, -OSE], *n.* Cane-sugar or sugar of a similar chemical composition.

suction (sŭk′ shŭn) [F., from L. *suct-us*, p.p. of *sugere*, to SUCK], *n.* The act or process of sucking; the production of a vacuum in a confined space causing fluid to enter, or a body to adhere to something, under atmospheric pressure. **suction-chamber, -pipe,** *n.* **suction-pump,** *n.* The common pump, in which water is forced up by atmospheric pressure. **suctorial** (-tôr′ i ȧl), *a.*

sudamina (sū dăm′ i nȧ) [pl. of late L. *sudāmen*, from L. *sudāre*, to sweat], *n.pl.* (*Path.*) Minute transparent vesicles arising from a disorder of the sweat-glands. **sudaminal,** *a.*

Sudanese (soo′ dȧ nēz), *a.* Of or pertaining to the Republic of the Sudan, the region of Central Africa south of Egypt. *n.* An inhabitant of the Sudan (*also pl.*).

sudation (sū dā′ shŭn) [L. *sūdātio*, from *sūdāre*, cogn. with SWEAT], *n.* Sweating, sweat. **sudarium** (sū dâr′ i ŭm), *n.* A cloth for wiping away sweat, esp. that of St. Veronica miraculously impressed with the face of Christ at the Crucifixion. **sudatorium** (-tôr′ i ŭm), *n.* (*pl.* **-ia**) A hot-air bath. **sudatory** (sū′ dȧ tŏr i), *a.* Exciting perspiration; *n.* A sudatorium.

sudd (sŭd) [Arab.], *n.* A floating mass of vegetation, trees, etc., obstructing navigation in the White Nile.

sudden (sŭd′ ėn) [M.E. and O.F. *sodain*, L. *subitāneus*, from *subitus*, sudden, from *subīre*, to come up (SUB-, *īre*, to come)], *a.* Happening unexpectedly, without warning; instantaneous, abrupt, swift, rapid; *precipitate, rash, choleric. **on or of a sudden:** Suddenly; unexpectedly. **suddenly,** *adv.* **suddenness,** *n.*

sudoriferous (sū dŏ rif′ ėr ŭs) [L. *sūdōrifer* (*sūdor -dōris*, sweat, FEROUS)], *a.* Secreting perspiration (of glands). **sudorific,** *a.* Causing perspiration. *n.* A sudorific drug.

Sudra (soo′ drȧ) [Hind., from Sansk. *çūdra*], *n.* A member of the lowest of the four great Hindu castes.

suds (sŭdz) [lit., things sodden, see SEETHE], *n.pl.* Soapy water forming a frothy mass.

sue (sū) [O.F. *suir* (F. *suivre*), late L. *sequere*, L. *sequī*, to follow], *v.t.* To prosecute or to pursue a claim (for) by legal process; to entreat, to petition. *v.i.* To take legal proceedings (for); to make entreaty or petition (to or for). **to sue out:** To petition for and obtain (a writ, pardon, etc.).

suède (swād) [F., SWEDE], *n.* Undressed kid (*often as adj.*).

suet (sū′ ėt) [dim. from O.F. *seu*, L. *sebum*, *tallow*], *n.* The hard fat about the kidneys and loins of oxen, sheep, etc. **suety,** *a.*

suf- [SUB-], *pref.* (before *f*).

suffer (sŭf′ ėr) [O.F. *suffrir*, L. *sufferre* (SUF-, *ferre*, to bear)], *v.t.* To experience, to undergo (something painful, disagreeable, or unjust); to endure, to sustain, to support (unflinchingly, etc.); to tolerate, to put up with; to permit, to allow. *v.i.* To undergo pain, grief, injury, loss, etc.; to undergo punishment, esp. to be executed. **sufferable,** *a.* **sufferableness,** *n.* **sufferably,** *adv.* **sufferance,** *n.* Negative consent, toleration, allowance, tacit or passive permission; *suffering; *endurance, patience, submissiveness. **on sufferance:** Merely tolerated. **sufferer,** *n.* **suffering,** *n.* **sufferingly,** *adv.*

suffete (sŭf′ ēt) [L. *suffes, sūfes, -ētis*, from Punic, cp. Heb. *shôphet*, judge], *n.* One of the two chief executive magistrates of ancient Carthage.

suffice (sŭ fīs′) [M.E. *suffisen*, O.F. *suffis-*, stem of *suffire*, L. *sufficere* (SUF-, *facere*, to make)], *v.i.* To be enough, to be adequate or sufficient (for or to do, etc.). *v.t.* To be enough for, to content, to satisfy; *to supply or provide. **sufficiency** (-fish′ ėn si), *n.* The quality of being sufficient; an adequate supply (of); a competence; adequate qualification, competence, efficiency. **sufficient,** *a.* Enough, adequate, sufficing (for); *competent, fit, qualified (in ability, resources, etc.); self-sufficient. *n.* (*colloq.*) Enough, a sufficiency. **sufficiently, sufficingly,** *adv.* ***suffisance,** *n.*

suffix (sŭf′ iks) [L. *suffixus*, p.p. of *suffigere* (SUF-, *figere*, to FIX, p.p. *fixus*)], *n.* A letter or syllable appended to a word. *v.t.* (sŭ fiks′) To add as a suffix, to append. **suffixal, suffixion** (-fik′ shŭn), *n.*

***sufflate** (sŭ flāt′) [L. *sufflātus*, p.p. of *sufflāre* (SUF-, *flāre*, to blow)], *v.t.* To blow up, to inflate; (*fig.*) to inspire.

suffocate (sŭf′ ŏ kāt) [L. *suffōcātus*, p.p. or *suffōcāre* (SUF-, *fōcāre*, from *fauces*, pl., throat)], *v.t.* To choke, to kill by stopping respiration; to smother, to stifle; to cause difficulty of respiration to. *v.i.* To be or feel suffocated. **a.* Suffocated. **suffocatingly,** *adv.* **suffocation** (-kā′ shŭn), *n.* **suffocative** (suf′ ŏ kā tiv), *a.*

suffragan (sŭf′ rȧ gȧn) [M.E., from F. *suffragant*, med. L. *suffrāgans -ntem*, pres.p., or *suffrāgāneus*, from L. *suffrāgārī*, to vote for, as foll.], *a.* Assisting (said of a bishop consecrated to assist another bishop or of any bishop in relation to the metropolitan). *n.* A suffragan or auxiliary bishop. **suffraganship,** *n.*

suffrage (sŭf′ rȧj) [F., from L. *suffrāgium*, perh. from *suffrāgo -gīnis*, ankle-bone (used for voting) or perh. orig. a potsherd, from *suffringere*, to break], *n.* A vote in support of an opinion, etc., or of a candidate for office; approval, consent; the right to vote, esp. in parliamentary elections; (*Eccles.*) a short intercessory prayer by the congregation, esp. one of the responses in the Litany. **suffragette** (-jet′), *n.* A female agitator for women suffrage. **suffragist** (sŭf′ rȧ jist), *n.* An advocate of extension of the suffrage, esp. to women. **suffragism,** *n.*

suffrutex (sŭf′ rŭ teks) [SUF-, L. *frutex -ticis*, shrub, prob. cogn. with Gr. *bruein*, to sprout], *n.* An undershrub. **suffrutescent** (-tes′ ėnt), **suffruticose** (sŭ froo′ ti kōs), *a.*

***suffumigate** (sŭ fū′ mi gāt) [SUF-, FUMIGATE], *v.t.* To apply fumes or smoke to (parts of the body). ***suffumigation** (-gā′ shŭn), *n.*

suffuse (sŭ fūz′) [L. *suffūsus*, p.p. of *suffundere* (SUF-, *fundere*, to pour)], *v.t.* To overspread, as from within (of a blush, fluid, etc.). **suffusion** (-fū′ zhŭn), *n.*

sufi (soo′ fi) [Arab. *sūfī*, pure, wise], *n.* A Mohammedan pantheistic philosopher and mystic. **sufic,** *a.* **sufism,** *n.*

sug- [SUB-], *pref.* (*before g*).

sugar (shug′ ȧr) [M.E. *sugre*, F. *sucre*, Sp. *azucar*, Arab. *sakkar*, *sokkar*, Pers. *shakar*, Sansk. *çarkarā*, gravel, candy, whence Gr. *sacharon*, L. *saccharum*], *n.* A sweet, crystalline substance obtained from the expressed juice of various plants, esp. the sugar-cane and the beet; any substance resembling sugar, esp. in taste; (*Chem.*) one of various sweet or sweetish soluble carbohydrates, such as glucose, saccharose, lactose, etc.; (*fig.*) flattering or seductive words, esp. used to mitigate or disguise something distasteful. *v.t.* To sweeten, cover, or sprinkle with sugar; (*fig.*) to mitigate, disguise, or render palatable. **sugar-bean,** *n.* A variety of kidney-bean. **sugar-beet,** *n.* A variety of common beet from which sugar is extracted. **sugar-berry,** *n.* (*Am.*) The hackberry. **sugar-candy,** *n.* Candy. **sugar-cane,** *n.* A very tall grass, *Saccharum officinalum*, with jointed stems from 8 to 20 feet high, from the juice of which sugar is made. **sugar-daddy,** *n.* (*Am. slang*) A well-to-do elderly man who spends money on a young girl. **sugar-gum,** *n.* A large Australian eucalyptus with sweet foliage. **sugar-house,** *n.* A building in which sugar is made. **sugar-loaf** [LOAF (1)]. **sugar-maple,** *n.* An American tree, *Acer saccharum*, the sap of which yields sugar. **sugar-mill,** *n.* A mill for expressing the juice from sugar-canes. **sugar-mite,** *n.* One infesting unrefined sugar. **sugar of lead:** Acetate of lead. **sugar-orchard,** *n.* A small plantation of maples for making sugar. **sugar, planter,** *n* **sugar-plum,** *n.* A sweetmeat, esp, boiled sugar formed into a ball, etc. **sugar-refiner.** *n.* **sugar-refinery,** *n.* **sugar-squirrel,** *n.* (*Austral.*) A small opossum. **sugar-tongs,** *n.pl.* A pair of small tongs for lifting lumps of sugar at table. **sugar-tree** [SUGAR-MAPLE]. **sugarer,** *n.* **sugarless,** *a.* **sugary,** *a.* **sugariness,** *n.*

suggest (sŭ jest′) [L. *suggestus*, p.p. of *suggerere* (SUG-, *gerere*, to bring)], *v.t.* To cause (an idea, etc.) to arise in the mind; to propose (a plan, idea, etc.) for consideration. **suggester,** *n.* **suggestible,** *a.* That may be suggested; readily yielding to hypnotic suggestion. **suggestion,** *n.* The act of suggesting; that which is suggested, a hint, a prompting, an insinuation; insinuation of an idea or impulse to a receptive mind or the mind of a hypnotized person; the spontaneous calling up of an associated idea in the mind. **suggestive,** *a.* Containing suggestion; tending to suggest thoughts, etc., esp. of a prurient nature. **suggestively,** *adv.* **suggestiveness,** *n.*

suicide (sū′ i sīd) [L. *suī*, of oneself, gen. of *se*, self, -CIDE], *n.* The act of intentionally taking one's own life; (*fig.*) any self-inflicted action of a disastrous nature; a person who takes his own life intentionally. **suicidal** (-sī′ dȧl), *a.* **suicidally,** *adv.* ***suicidism** (sū′ i si dizm), *n.*

suilline (sū′ i lin, -līn) [L. *suillus*, from *sus suis*, swine], *a.* Hog-like. *n.* One of the hog family.

suint (sū′ int, swint) [F., from Teut., cogn. with SWEAT], *n.* The natural grease of wool.

suit (sūt) [F. *suite*, med. L. *secūta*, from *secut*, p.p. stem of *sequī*, to follow], *n.* The act of suing, petition, request; courtship; a legal prosecution or action for the recovery of a right, etc.; one of the four sets in a pack of cards; those cards in a hand belonging to one of these; a set of outer clothes for a male person (usu. jacket, waistcoat, and trousers or breeches), esp. when made of the same cloth; a woman's costume; a set (of sails or other articles used together). *v.t.* To adapt, to accommodate, to make fitting (to); to satisfy, to please, to meet the desires, etc., of; to agree with, to befit, to be appropriate to. *v.i.* To agree, to accord, to correspond (with); to be convenient. **to follow suit:** (*Cards*) To play a card of the suit led; (*fig.*) to follow an example. **suit case,** *n.* A small travelling case. **suitable,** *a.* Suited, fitting, convenient, proper, becoming. **suitability** (-bil′ i ti), **suitableness,** *n.* **suitably,** *adv.*

suite (swēt) [F., see prec.], *n.* A company, a retinue; a set (of rooms, furniture, etc.); (*Mus.*) a series of instrumental compositions, orig. of dance-tunes.

suitor (sū′ tȯr), *n.* A petitioner, an applicant; a wooer, a lover; (*Law*) a party to a suit.

suivez (swē′ vā) [F., imper. of *suivre*], *v.i.* (*Mus. direction*) Follow (to accompanist to adapt his time to the soloist).

sulcate, *-cated (sŭl′ kȧt, -kā tėd) [L. *sulcātus*, p.p. of *sulcāre*, from *sulcus*, furrow], *a.* Having longitudinal furrows, grooves, or channels.

sulfa drugs, *n.* Collective name given to sulphonamides.

sulk (sŭlk) [from *sulky*, from *sulkenness*, A.-S. *solcennes* in *āsolcennes* (*solcen*, slothful)], *v.i.* To be sulky. *n.* A fit of sulkiness (*usu. in pl.*). **sulky,** *a.* Sullen, morose, ill-humoured, resentful. *n.* A light, two-wheeled vehicle for a single person. **sulkily,** *adv.* **sulkiness,** *n.*

sullage (sŭl′ ij) [F. *souiller*, to soil], *n.* Filth, refuse; sewage; silt.

sullen (sŭl′ ėn) [M.E. and O.F. *solain*, SOLE (3)], *a.* Persistently ill-humoured, morose, sour-tempered, cross; dismal, forbidding, unpropitious, baleful. *n.pl.* The sulks. **sullenly,** *adv.* **sullenness,** *n.*

sully (sŭl′ i) [A.-S. *sylian*, from *sol*, mud (prob. with mixture of O.F. *soillier*, to SOIL (2))], *v.t.* To soil, to tarnish; to defile, to disgrace. *v.i.* To be soiled or tarnished. *n.* A spot, a blemish.

sulph-, sulpho- [SULPH-UR], *comb. form.* **sulphamic** (sŭl făm′ ik) [AMIC], *a.* Of or derived from an amic acid of sulphuric acid. **sulphanilamide** (sŭl făn il′ ȧ mīd), *n.* (*Med.*) Para-aminobenzene sulphonamide, a drug administered orally and by injection for combating streptococcal and other bacterial diseases. **sulph-antimonic,** *a.* Derived from an antimonic sulphide. **sulph-antimonate,** *n.* **sulph-antimonious,** *a.* **sulph-antimonite,** *n.*

sulphate (sŭl′ fāt), *n.* A salt of sulphuric acid. **sulphate of copper:** Blue vitriol; **of iron:** green vitriol; **of magnesium:** Epsom salts; **of sodium:** Glauber salts; **of zinc:** white vitriol. **sulphatic** (-făt′ ik), *a.*

sulphide (sŭl′ fīd), *n.* A compound of sulphur, with an element or radical.

sulphite (sŭl′ fīt), *n.* A salt of sulphurous acid.

sulphonal (sŭl′ fō năl), *n.* A crystalline compound used for hypnotic and anæsthetic purposes.

sulphonamides (sŭl fon′ ȧ mīdz), *n.pl.* A group of drugs used therapeutically on account of their powerful antibacterial action.

sulphovinic (sŭl fō vin′ ik), *a.* Denoting an acid obtained from sulphuric acid and alcohol.

sulphur (sŭl′ fụr) [L.], *n.* A pale-yellow non-metallic element, insoluble in water, occurring in crystalline or amorphous forms, used in the manufacture of gunpowder, matches, vitriol, etc., brimstone; one of various pale-yellow butterflies. *a.* Of the colour of sulphur, pale-yellow. **sulphur-ore,** *n.* Iron pyrites. **sulphur-spring,** *n.* A spring of water impregnated with sulphur or sulphide, etc. **sulphurate** (sŭl′ fū rāt), *v.t.* To impregnate with or subject to the action of sulphur, esp. in bleaching. **sulphuration** (-ā′shŭn), *n.* **sulphurator** (sŭl′ fū rā tȯr), *n.* **sulphureous** (-fūr′ ė ŭs), *a.* Consisting of or having the qualities of sulphur; sulphur-coloured. **sulphureously,** *adv.* **sulphureousness,** *n.* ***sulphuret** (sŭl′ fū rėt), *n.* A sulphide. **sulphuretted** (-ret′ ėd), *a.* Saturated, impregnated, or combined with sulphur. **sulphuric** (-fūr′ ik), *a.* Derived from or containing sulphur, esp. in its highest valence. **sulphuric acid:** Oil of vitriol. **sulphurize** (sŭl′ fū rīz), *v.t.* To sulphurate. **sulphurization** (-zā′ shŭn), *n.* **sulphurous** (sŭl′ fū rŭs), *a.* Containing sulphur in its lower valence; sulphureous. **sulphury,** *a.*

sultan (sŭl′ tȧn) [F., from Arab. *sultān*], *n.* A Mohammedan sovereign, esp. a former ruler of Turkey; a bird of the water-hen family with splendid blue and purple plumage; a white-crested variety of domestic fowl, orig. from Turkey. **sultana** (-ta′ nȧ), *n.* The wife, mother, or daughter of a sultan; the mistress of a king, prince, etc.; a kind of raisin grown in Smyrna; an American sultan-bird. **sultanate** (sŭl′ tȧ nȧt), *n.* **sultaness,** *n.* **sultanic** (-tăn′ ik), *a.* ***sultanry, sultanship,** *n.*

sultry (sŭl′ tri) [var. of obs. *sweltry*, from SWELTER], *a.* Very hot, close, and heavy; oppressive. **sultrily,** *adv.* **sultriness,** *n.*

sum (sŭm) [M.E. and F. *somme*, L. *summa*, orig. fem. of *summus*, super. of *superus*, higher, see SUPER-], *n.* The aggregate of two or more numbers, magnitudes, quantities, or particulars, the total; substance, essence, summary; a particular amount of money; an arithmetical problem or the process of working it out. *v.t.* (*past & p.p.* **summed**) To add, collect, or combine into one total or whole (*usu.* up); to put in a few words, to condense (*usu.* up). *v.i.* To recapitulate (*usu.* up). **sumless,** *a.* Innumerable, countless.

sumac (sū′-, shoo′ măk) [F., from Sp. *zumaque*, Arab. *summāq*], *n.* A tree or shrub of the genus *Rhus*, the dried and powdered leaves of which are used in tanning, dyeing, etc.

summary (sŭm′ ȧ ri) [L. *summārium*, from *summa*, SUM], *a.* Condensed into narrow compass or few words, abridged, concise, compendious; done briefly or unceremoniously. *n.* An abridged or condensed statement, an epitome. **summarily,** *adv.* **summarize,** *v.t.* To make or be a summary of. **summarist,** *n.* **summation** (sủ mā′ shŭn), *n.* The act or process of making a sum, addition.

summer (1) (sŭm′ ėr) [A.-S. *sumor* (cp. Dut. *zomer*, G. *sommer*, Icel. *sumar*), cogn. with Sansk. *samā*, year], *n.* That season of the year when the sun shines most directly upon a region, the warmest season of the year; (*pl.*) years of age. *a.* Pertaining to or used in summer. *v.i.* To pass the summer. *v.t.* To feed or keep (cattle, etc.) during the summer. **Indian summer** [INDIAN]. **St. Martin's summer** [SAINT]. **summer-house,** *n.* A light building in a garden, for shade, etc., in summer. **summer lightning:** Sheet lightning seen too far off for the thunder to be heard. **summer time,** *n.* The official time of one hour in advance of Greenwich mean time that comes into force between stated dates in the summer, by virtue of the Summer Time Act of 1916. **summering,** *n.* An early variety of apple. **summerless,** *a.* **summerly,** **summery,** *a.*

summer (2) (sŭm′ ėr) [F. *sommier*, L. *sagmarius*, from L. and Gr. *sagma*, packsaddle], *n.* A heavy horizontal beam or girder; a lintel, a breast-summer; a large stone laid on a column as beginning of an arch, vault etc.

summering, etc. [SUMMER (1)].

summersault, -set [SOMERSAULT].

summit (sŭm′ it) [F. *sommet*, dim. of O.F. *som*, L. *summum*, neut. of *summus*, see SUM], *n.* The highest point, the top, the vertex; utmost elevation, degree, etc. **summit-level,** *n.* The highest level. **summit conference:** (*Pol.*) A conference between heads of states. **summitless,** *a.*

summon (sŭm′ ȯn) [O.F. *somoner*, L. *submonēre*, (SUB-, *monēre*, to warn)], *v.t.* To call, cite, or command to meet or attend, esp. to appear in court; to call upon (to surrender, etc.); to call (up courage, etc.). **summoner,** *n.*

summons (sŭm′ ȯnz), *n.* (*pl.* **summonses**) The act of summoning; an authoritative call or citation, esp. to appear before a court or judge. *v.t.* (*colloq.*) To serve with a summons, to summon.

sump (sŭmp) [cp. Swed. and Dan. *sump*, Dut. *somp*, G. *sumpf*], *n.* A well in the floor of a mine, to collect water for pumping; (*Motor.*) receptacle for lubricating oil in the crank-case (called in *Am.* an oil-pan); (*Metal.*) a pit to collect metal at its first fusion; a pond at a salt-works.

sumph (sŭmf) [etym. doubtful], *n.* (*prov.*) A blockhead, a simpleton.

sumpitan (sŭm′ pi tȧn) [Malay], *n.* A Malay blow-pipe. **sumpit,** *n.* A poisoned arrow blown from this.

sumpsimus (sŭmp′ si mŭs) [L., 1st pl. perf. of *sumere*, to take], *n.* A correct expression displacing a common but inaccurate one.

sumpter (sŭmp′ tėr) [O.F. *sommetier*, packhorse driver, prob. through a late L. *sagmatārius*, from Gr. *sagma -atos*, burden, see SUMMER (2)], *n.* An animal employed to carry packs, a baggage-horse, etc.; a driver of this. **sumpter-horse, -mule,** etc., *n.*

sumption (sŭmp′ shŭn) [L. *sumptio*, from *sumere*, to take, p.p. *sumptus*], *n.* (*Log.*) The major premise of a syllogism.

sumptuary (sŭmp′ tū ăr i) [L. *sumptuārius*, as foll.], *a.* Pertaining to or regulating expenditure. **sumptuary law** or **edict:** One restraining private excess in dress, luxury, etc.

sumptuous (sŭmp′ tū ŭs) [F. *somptueux*, L. *sumptuōsus*, from *sumptus -tūs*, expense, cost], *a.* Costly, expensive; showing lavish expenditure; splendid, magnificent. **sumptuously,** *adv.* **sumptuousness,** *n.*

sun (sŭn) [A.-S. *sunne* (cp. Dut. *zon*, G. *sonne*, Icel. *sunna*), cogn. with Goth. *sauil*, Icel. *sōl*, L. *sōl*], *n.* The heavenly body round which the earth revolves and which gives light and heat to the earth and other planets of the solar system; the light or warmth of this, sunshine, a sunny place; a fixed star that has satellites and is the centre of a system; (*poet.*) a day, a sunrise; a sun-burner; anything splendid or luminous, or a chief source of light, honour, etc. *v.t.* (*past & p.p.* **sunned**) To expose to the rays of the sun. *v.i.* To sun oneself. **place in the sun:** A favourable situation, scope for action, etc. **to have the sun in one's eyes:** To be intoxicated. **to see the sun:** To be alive. **to take** or (*slang*) **shoot the sun:** (*Naut.*) To ascertain the sun's altitude in order to determine the latitude. **under the sun:** In the world, on earth. **sun and planet** [PLANET-GEAR]. **sunbath,** *n.* Exposure of the naked body to the sun, insolation. **sunbeam,** *n.* A ray of sunlight. **sun-bird,** *n.* Any of the *Nectariniidæ*, small birds of brilliant metallic plumage with a striking resemblance to humming-birds. **sunblind,** *n.* A window-shade. **sunbonnet,** *n.* A large bonnet of light material with projections at the front and sides and a pendant at the back. **sun-bow,** *n.* A rainbow formed by sunlight on spray, etc. **sunburn,** *n.* Tanning or inflammation of the skin due to exposure to the sun. **sunburned, -burnt,** *a.* **sun-burner,** *n.* A concentric group of gas-jets, incandescent lamps, etc., usu. with a reflector, for throwing light from a ceiling, etc. **sun-burst,** *n.* A strong or sudden burst of sunlight. **sundew,** *n.* A low, hairy, insectivorous bog-plant of the genus *Drosera*. **sun-dial** [DIAL]. **sun-dog** [DOG]. **sundown,** *n.* Sunset. **sundowner,** *n.* (*Austral. slang*) A tramp who times his arrival at sundown in order to get a night's lodging. **sun-dried,** *a.* Dried in the sun. **sunfish,** *n.* A large fish of various species with a body like a sphere truncated behind. **sunflower,** *n.* A plant of the genus *Helianthus*, esp. *H. annuus*, with yellow-rayed flowers. **sun-glasses,** *n.pl.* Darkened glasses for protecting the eyes from glare. **sun-god,** *n.* The sun worshipped as a deity. **sun-hat, -helmet,** *n.* A light hat with a broad brim, etc., to protect from the sun. **sun-lamp,** *n.* A lamp that gives out ultra-violet rays for curative or other purposes. **sunlight,** *n.* **sunlit,** *a.* **sun-myth,** *n.* A solar myth. **Sun of righteousness:** Christ. **sunproof,** *a.* **sunrise, -rising,** *n.* The first appearance of the sun above the horizon; the time of this. **sun-rose,** *n.* A rock-rose; a plant of the genus *Helianthemum*. **sunset, -setting,** *n.* The disappearance of the sun below the horizon; the time of this; (*fig.*) the decline (of life, etc.). **sunshade,** *n.* A parasol, awning, blind, etc., used as a protection against the sun. **sunshine,** *n.* The light of the sun; the space illuminated by this; (*fig.*) warmth, brightness, cheerfulness, favourable influence. **sunshine roof,** *n.* (*Motor.*) A car roof with a sliding panel. **sunshiny,** *a.* **sunspot,** *n.* A dark patch sometimes seen on the surface of the sun. **sunstroke,** *n.* A cerebral affection akin to apoplexy, due to exposure to the sun in hot weather. **sunstricken,** *a.* **sunstruck,** *a.* **sunup,** *n.* (*Am.*) Sunrise. **sun-worship,** *n.* **sun-worshipper,** *n.* **sunless,** *a.* **sunlessness,** *n.* **sunlike,** *a.* **sunny,** *a.* Bright with or warmed by sunlight; (*fig.*) bright, cheerful, cheery, genial; proceeding from the sun. **sunnily,** *adv.* **sunniness,** *n.*

sundae (sŭn′ dā) [etym. unknown], *n.* An ice-cream containing fragments of nuts and various fruits.

Sunday (sŭn′ dā, -di) [A.-S. *sunnan dæg*, day of the sun], *n.* The first day of the week, the Lord's Day, the Christian Sabbath. **month of Sundays:** An indefinitely long period. **Sunday best:** (*colloq.*) Best clothes for use on Sundays. **Sunday school,** *n.* A school held on Sundays for religious instruction.

sunder (sŭn′ dėr) [A.-S. *sundrian*, from *sundor*, asunder (cp. Icel. *sundra*, Dan. *söndre*, G. *sondern*)], *v.t.* To part, to separate; to keep apart. *v.i.* To be separated. **in sunder:** Apart, in two. **sunderance,** *n.*

sundown, sundowner, etc. [SUN].

sundry (sŭn′ dri) [A.-S. *syndrig*, as SUNDER], *a.* Several, divers, various. *n.pl.* Matters, items, or miscellaneous articles, too trifling or numerous to specify.

sung, *past & p.p.* [SING].

sunk, sunken, *p.p.* [SINK].

sunn (sŭn) [Hind. *san*], *n.* An E. Indian plant cultivated for its fibres, also called **sunn-hemp.**

Sunna (sŭn′ ȧ) [Arab.], *n.* The traditional part of the Mohammedan law, based on the sayings or acts of Mohammed, accepted as of equal authority to the Koran by orthodox Mohammedans or the Sunni but rejected by the Shiites. **Sunni** (sŭn′ i), *n.* **Sunnite,** *a.* and *n.*

sunny, sunrise, sunshine, etc. [SUN].

sup (sŭp) [A.-S. *sūpan* (cp. Dut. *zuipen*, L.G. *supen*, Icel. *sūpa*, O.H.G. *sūfan*), partly from O.F. *souper*, see SUPPER], *v.t.* (*past & p.p.* **supped**) To take (soup, etc.) in successive sips or spoonfuls. *v.i.* To take in liquid food by sips or spoonfuls; to take supper. *n.* A mouthful (of liquor, soup, etc.).

sup- [SUB-], *pref.* (*before p.*).

supawn (sū pawn′) [N.Am.Ind.], *n.* (*Am.*) A dish or pudding composed of boiled Indian corn.

super (sū′ pėr) [short for SUPERNUMERARY], *n.* (*Theat.*) A supernumerary actor. *a.* (*colloq.*) Superlative, excellent.

super- [L. *super-*, pref., *super*, prep., orig. compar. of *sub*, see SUB- (cp. Gr. *huper*, Sansk. *hupari*)], *pref.* Over, above; above in position, on the top of; over in degree or amount, excessive, exceeding, more than, transcending; besides, in addition; of a higher kind In cases where no definition is given reference should be made to the unprefixed word in its proper place in the dictionary.

superable (sū′ pėr ȧbl) [L. *superābilis*, from *superāre*, as prec.], *a.* That may be overcome, conquerable. **superableness,** *n.* **superably,** *adv.*

superabound (sū pėr ȧ bound′), *v.i.* To be more than enough. **superabundance** (-bŭn′ dȧns), *n.* **superabundant,** *a.* **superabundantly,** *adv.* **superacidulated** (-ȧ sid′ ū lā tėd), *a.* **superadd** (-ăd′), *v.t.* **superaddition** (-ȧ dish′ ŭn), *n.* **superaltar** (sū′ pėr awl tėr), *n.* A consecrated slab used to place on an unconsecrated altar. **superanal** (-ā′ nȧl), *a.* **superangelic** (-ăn jel′ ik), *a.*

superannuate (sū pėr ăn′ ū āt) [SUPER-, L. *annus*, year, cp. ANNUAL], *v.t.* To dismiss, discard, disqualify, or incapacitate on account of age; to pension off on account of age. **superannuation** (-ā′ shŭn), *n.*

superation (sū pėr ā shŭn) [L. *superātio*, from *superāre*, to go over, from *super*, SUPER-], *n.* (*Astron.*) The apparent passing of one planet by another in longitude

superb (sū pĕrb′) [F. *superbe*, L. *superbus* (*super*, see SUPER-, *fu-*, stem of *fuī*, I was)], *a.* Grand, majestic, imposing, magnificent, splendid, stately; (*colloq.*) first-rate. **superbly,** *adv.* **superbness,** *n.*

super-calendered (sū pėr kăl′ ėn dėrd), *a.* Highly finished (of paper). **supercanopy** (-kăn′ ȯ pi), *n.* **supercargo** (-kar′ gō), *n.* An officer in a merchant-ship who superintends sales, etc. **supercelestial** (-sė les′ ti ǎl), *a.* **supercharge** (-charj′), *v.t.* (*Her.*) To superimpose on another charge; *n.* (sū′ pėr charj) One charge borne upon another. **supercharger,** *n.* (*Mach.*) A mechanism in an internal-combustion engine which provides for the complete filling of the cylinder with explosive material when going at high speed.

superciliary (sū pėr sil′ i ȧr i) [as foll.], *a.* Pertaining to or situated above the eyebrows.

supercilious (sū pėr sil′ i ůs) [L. *superciliōsus*, from *supercilium*, see CILIA (with alln. to raising the eyebrows)], *a.* Contemptuous, overbearing, haughtily indifferent, arrogant, disdainful. **superciliously,** *adv.* **superciliousness,** *n.* **supercivilized** (-siv′ i līzd), *a.* **superclass** (sū′ pėr klas), *n.* **supercolumnar** (-kȯ lŭm′ nȧr), *a.* Having one order of columns placed over another. **supercolumniation** (-ā′ shůn), *n.* **supercool** (sū′ pėr kool), *v.t.* To cool (a liquid) below its freezing-point without solidification. **supercretaceous** (-krė tā′ shůs), *a.* (*Geol.*) Above the cretaceous strata. ***superdainty** (-dān′ ti), *a.* **superdominant** (-dom′ i nȧnt), *n.* (*Mus.*) The tone above the dominant, the sixth note of the diatonic scale. **super-ego,** *n.* (*Psych.*) The unconscious inhibitory morality in the mind which criticizes the ego and condemns the unworthy impulses of the id. **supereminent** (-em′ i nėnt), *a.* **supereminence,** *n.* **supereminently,** *adv.*

supererogation (sū pėr er ȯ gā′ shůn) [late L. *superērogātio*, from *superērogāre*, to pay out beyond what is expected], *n.* Performance of more than duty requires. **works of supererogation:** 'Voluntary works, besides, over, and above God's Commandments.' **supererogate** (-er′ ȯ gāt), *v.i.* **supererogatory** (-ė rog′ ȧ tȯr i), *a.*

***superessential** (sū pėr ė sen′ shǎl), *a.* (*Phil.*) Transcending mere essence (of the Absolute). **superethical** (-eth′ i kǎl), *a.* **superexalt** (-ėg zawlt′), *v.t.* **superexaltation** (-tā′ shůn), *n.* **superexcellent** (-ek′ sė lėnt), *a.* **superexcellence,** *n.* **superfamily** (-fǎm′ i li), *n.* **superfatted** (-făt′ ėd), *a.* Containing excess of fatty matter relatively to alkali (of soap). **superfecundation** (-fek ůn dā′ shůn), *n.* Superfœtation.

superficial (sū pėr fish′ ǎl) [as foll.], *a.* Pertaining to or lying on the surface; not penetrating deep; not deep or profound, shallow. **superficiality** (-ăl′ i ti), **superficialness,** *n.* **superficially,** *adv.*

superficies (sū pėr fish′ i ēz) [L.], *n.* A surface; its area.

superfine (sū′ pėr fīn), *a.* Exceedingly fine, surpassing in fineness, of extra quality; over-refined. **superfineness,** *n.*

superfluous (sū pĕr′ floo ůs) [L. *superfluus* (SUPER-, *fluere*, to flow)], *a.* More than is necessary or sufficient, excessive, superabundant, redundant. **superfluity** (-floo′ i ti), **superfluousness,** *n.* **superfluously,** *adv.*

superfœtation (sū pėr fē tā′ shůn), *n.* The conception of a second embryo during the gestation of the first. **superfrontal** (-frun′ tǎl), *a.* Pertaining to the upper part of the frontal lobe of the brain. *n.* The part of an altar-cloth covering the top. **superfunction** (-funk′ shůn), *n.* **superfunctional,** *a.* **superheat** (-hēt′), *v.t.* To heat to excess, esp. to heat (steam) above the boiling-point of water. **superheater,** *n.* **super-heterodyne,** *n.* (*Radio.*) A receiver with a high degree of selectivity. **superhive** (sū′ pėr hīv), *n.* A removable upper story to a hive. **superhuman** (-hū′ mȧn), *a.* **superhumanly,** *adv.* **superhumeral** (-hū′ mėr ǎl), *n.* Something worn upon the shoulders, as an archbishop's pallium, or a Jewish sacerdotal ephod. **superimpose** (-im pōz′), *v.t.* To lay upon something else. **superimposition** (-pō zish′ ůn), *n.* **superimpregnation** (-im preg-nā′ shůn), *n.* Superfœtation. **superincumbent** (-in kŭm′ bėnt), *a.* Lying or resting on something. **superinduce** (-in dūs′), *v.t.* To bring in as an addition, to superadd. **superinduction** (-dŭk′ shůn), *n.* **superinstitution** (-in sti tū′ shůn), *n.* One institution upon another, as of an incumbent to a benefice already occupied.

superintend (sū pėr in tend′) [L. *superintendere* (SUPER-, *intendere*, see INTEND)], *v.t.* To have or exercise the management or oversight of; to direct, to control. **superintendence,** *n.* **superintendent,** *n.* One who superintends; a police officer ranking above an inspector.

superior (sū pēr′ i ȯr) [O.F. *superieur*, L. *superiōrem*, nom. *-or*, compar. of *superus*, high (from *super*, above, see SUPER-)], *a.* Upper, of higher position, class, grade, rank, excellence, degree, etc.; better or greater relatively (to); of a quality above the average; of wider application (of a class, etc.); situated near the top, or in the higher part; above being influenced by or amenable (to). *n.* A person superior to one or to others, one's better; the head of a monastery, convent, or other religious house. **superioress,** *n.* **superiority** (-or′ i ti), *n.*

superjacent (sū pėr jā′ sėnt) [SUPER-, JACENT], *a.* Lying on or above something.

superlative (sū pĕr′ lȧ tiv) [L. *superlatīvus*, from *superlātus*, exaggerated (SUPER-, *lātus*, p.p. of *ferre*, to carry)], *a.* Raised to the highest degree, consummate, supreme; (*Gram.*) expressing the highest or utmost degree. *n.* The superlative degree; a word or phrase in the superlative degree. **superlatively,** *adv.* **superlativeness,** *n.*

***superlunar, -nary** (sū pėr lū′ nȧr, -i), *a.* Above the moon, not mundane. **superman** (sū′ pėr măn), *n.* A hypothetical superior being, esp. one advanced in intellect and morals; an overman. **supermarket** (sū′ pėr mar kėt), *n.* A large, self-service store where food and domestic goods are sold. **supermedial** (-mē′ di ǎl), *a.* **supermolecule** (-mol′ ė kūl), *n.* A compound molecule or combination of molecules acting as a physical unit. **supermundane** (-mŭn′ dān), *a.* Above or superior to worldly things. **supernaculum** (-năk′ ū lům) [mod. L. *naculum*, G. *nagel*, NAIL (I)], *n.* Wine or liquor of the choicest quality. *adv.* To the last drop (lit., on the nail, from the custom of pouring the last drop on the thumb-nail). ***supernacular,** *a.*

supernal (sū pĕr′ nǎl) [M.F. *supernel* (L. *supern-us*, -AL)], *a.* Of a loftier kind, nature, or region; celestial, heavenly, divine, lofty.

supernatant (sū pėr nā′ tant), *a.* Floating on the surface. **supernatation** (-nȧ tā′ shůn), *n.*

supernatural (sū pėr năt′ ū rǎl), *a.* Existing by, due to, or exercising powers above the forces of nature, outside the sphere of natural law. **supernaturalism,** *n.* Belief in the supernatural. **supernaturalist,** *n.* **supernaturalistic** (-lis′ tik), *a.* **supernaturalize,** *v.t.* **supernaturally,** *adv.* **supernaturalness,** *n.* **supernormal** (-nôr′ mǎl), *a.* **supernumerary** (-nū′ mėr ȧr i), *a.* Being in excess of a prescribed or customary number. *n.* A supernumerary person or thing, esp. (*Theat.*) a person appearing on the stage without a speaking part. **super-nutrition** (-nū trish′ ůn), *n.* **superoccipital** (-ok sip′ i tǎl), *a.* **superoctave** (-ok′ tȧv), *n.* (*Organ*) A coupler causing a note to sound an octave higher than the key struck; an organ-stop a fifteenth above the principal. **superorder** (-ôr′ dėr), *n.* **superordinal,** *a.* **superiordinary,** *a.* **superordinate,** *a.* **superordination** (-nā′ shůn), *n.* The ordination of a person to fill an office not yet vacant; (*Log.*) the relation of a universal proposition to a particular proposition that it includes. **superorganic** (-găn′ ik), *a.* Superior or external to the organism, psychical; pertaining to a higher grade of organism, social.

superoxygenation (-ok si jė nā′ shŭn), *n.* **superparasite** (-păr′ ȧ sīt), *n.* **superparasitic** (-sit′ ik), *a.*

superphosphate (sū pėr fos′ fāt), *n.* A phosphate containing the greatest amount of phosphoric acid that can combine with the base. **superphysical** (-fiz′ i kȧl), *a.* **superpose** (sū pėr pōz′), *v.t.* To lay over or upon something. **superposable,** *a.* **superposition** (-pȯ zish′ ŭn), *n.* ***superpraise** (-prāz′), *v.i.* **super-royal** (-roi′ ȧl), *a.* Larger than royal (denoting a size of printing paper 27½ × 20½ in.). **supersacral** (-sā′ krȧl), *a.* **supersalt** (sū′ pėr sawlt), *n.* An acid salt. **supersaturate** (-săt′ ū rāt), *v.t.* **supersaturation** (-rā′ shŭn), *n.* **superscribe** (sū′ pėr skrīb) [L. *scrībere*, to write], *v.t.* ***superscript,** *a.* and *n.* **superscription** (-skrip′ shŭn), *n.* Written at the top or outside (of a letter, inscription, etc.).

supersede (sū pėr sēd′) [O.F. *superseder*, to leave off, to desist, L. *supersedēre* (SUPER-, *sedēre*, to sit, p.p. *sessus*)], *v.t.* To put a person or thing in the place of, to set aside, to annul; to take the place of, to displace, to supplant. **supersedeas** (-sē′ dė ȧs), *n.* (*Law*) A writ to stay proceedings, etc. **supersedence, supersedure, supersession** (-sesh′ ŭn), *n.* **supersensible** (-sen′ sibl), *a.* **supersensitive,** *a.* **supersensual,** *a.* **supersensuous,** *a.* ***superserviceable** (-sėr′ vis ȧbl), *a.* Over officious. **supersolid** (-sol′ id), *a.* A solid of more than three dimensions.

supersonic (sū pėr son′ ik), *a.* Pertaining to sound waves with such a high frequency that they are inaudible; above the speed of sound.

superstition (sū pėr stish′ ŭn) [F., from L. *superstitiōnem*, nom. *-tio*, standing over, amazement (SUPER-, *stat*, p.p. stem of *stāre*, to stand)], *n.* Credulity regarding the supernatural, the occult, or the mysterious; ignorant or unreasoning dread of the unknown; a religion, particular belief or practice originating in this, esp. a belief in omens, charms, etc. **superstitious,** *a.* **superstitiously,** *adv.* **superstitiousness,** *n.*

superstratum (sū pėr strā′ tŭm), *n.* (*pl.* **-ta**) A stratum resting on another. **superstruction, -structure** (-strŭk′ shŭn, -tyŭr), *n.* **superstructural,** *a.* **supersubstantial** (-sŭb stăn′ shȧl), *a.* **supersubtle** (-sŭtl′), *a.* **supersubtlety,** *n.* **supertax,** *n.* (*Fin.*) A graduated tax in addition to the income tax, levied on incomes above a certain level, since 1929 known as surtax. **supertelluric** (-tel ūr′ ik), *a.* **supertemporal** (1) (-tem′ pȯ rȧl), *a.* Situated in the upper part of the temporal region of the head. **supertemporal** (2), *a.* Transcending time. **superterrene** (-tė rēn′), **superterrestrial** (-tė res′ tri ȧl), *a.* **supertonic** (-ton′ ik), *n.* (*Mus.*) The note next above the tonic in the diatonic scale. **supertuberation** (-tū bėr ā′ shŭn), *n.* The production of young tubers from old ones while still growing.

supervene (sū pėr vēn′) [L. *sūpervenīre* (SUPER-, *vēnīre*, to come)], *v.i.* To come or happen as something extraneous or additional **supervenient,** *a.* **supervention** (-ven′ shŭn), *n.*

supervise (sū pėr vīz′) [L. *supervīsum*, supine of *supervidēre* (SUPER-, *vidēre*, to see)], *v.t.* To have oversight of, to oversee, to superintend. **supervision** (-vizh′ ŭn), *n.* **supervisor** (sū′ pėr vī zȯr), *n.* **supervisory,** *a.*

supinate (sū′ pi nāt) [L. *supīnātus*, p.p. of *supīnāre*, as foll.], *v.t.* To turn the palm of (the hand) upward. **supinator** (sū′ pi nā tȯr), *n.* Either of two muscles which do this. **supination** (-nā′ shŭn), *n.* The placing or holding of the palm of the hand upward or forward.

supine (sū pīn′) [L. *supīnus*, from *sup-*, *sub*, under, see SUB-], *a.* Lying on the back of with the face upward; negligent, indolent, listless, careless. *n.* (*Lat. Gram.*) A verbal noun formed from the p.p. stem and ending in *-um* (1st supine) or *-u* (2nd supine). **supinely,** *adv.* **supineness,** *n.*

suppedaneum (sŭp ė dā′ nė ŭm) [late L. (SUP-, L. *pes pedis*, foot)], *n.* (*pl.* **-ea**) A foot-rest on a cross or crucifix. ***suppedaneous,** *a.* Placed or being under the feet.

supper (sŭp′ ėr) [O.F. *soper*, *super* (F. *souper*), from *soper*, L.G. *supen*, cogn. with SUP], *n.* The last meal of the day, unless dinner is the last. **the Lord's Supper:** Holy Communion. **supperless,** *a.*

supplant (sŭ plant′) [O.F. *supplanter*, L. *supplantāre* (SUP-, *plantāre*, from *planta*, sole of foot)], *v.t.* To take the place of or oust, esp. by craft or treachery. ***supplantation** (-tā′ shŭn), *n.* **supplanter,** *n.*

supple (sŭp′ ėl) [M.E. and F. *souple*, L. *supplicem*, nom. *-plex* (SUP- *plic-*, base of, *plicāre*, to fold)], *a.* Pliant, flexible, easily bent; yielding, compliant, soft, submissive, obsequious, servile. *v.t.* To make pliant or flexible; to make compliant. *v.i.* To become pliant. **supple-jack,** *n.* A tough climbing shrub, from which walking-sticks are made. **suppleness,** *n.* **supply** (1) (sŭp′ li), *adv.*

supplement (sŭp′ li mėnt) [F. *supplément*, L. *supplēmentum*, from *supplēre* (SUP-, *plēre*, to fill)], *n.* An addition supplying deficiencies; an addition to a book or newspaper; (*Math.*) the angle that added to another will make the sum two right angles. *v.t.* (-ment′) To make additions to; to complete by additions. **supplemental, -ary** (-men′ tȧl, -tȧ ri), *a.* **supplementation** (-tā′ shŭn), *n.* **suppletory** (sŭp′-), *a.*

suppleness [SUPPLE].

suppliant (sŭp′ li ȧnt) [F., pres.p. of *supplier*, as foll.], *a.* Entreating, supplicating; expressing entreaty or supplication. *n.* A humble petitioner. **suppliance** (sŭp′ li ȧns), *n.* **suppliantly,** *adv.*

supplicate (sŭp′ li kāt) [L. *supplicātus*, p.p. of *supplicāre*, as SUPPLE], *v.t.* To beg or ask for earnestly and humbly; to address in earnest prayer; to beg humbly (to grant, etc.). *v.i.* To petition earnestly, to beseech. ***supplicant,** *a.* Suppliant; *n.* A suppliant. ***supplicantly,** *adv.* Like a suppliant. **supplicatingly,** *adv.* **supplication** (-kā′ shŭn), *n.* **supplicatory** (sŭp′ li kā tȯr i), *a.*

supply (1) (sŭp′ li) [SUPPLE].

supply (2) (sŭ plī′) [O.F. *supploier* (F. *suppléer*), L. *supplēre* (SUP-, *plēre*, to fill)], *v.t.* To furnish with what is wanted, to provide (with); to furnish, to provide; to serve instead of; to fill (the place of), to make up for (a deficiency, etc.). *n.* The act of supplying things needed; that which is supplied; a sufficiency of things required; necessary stores or provisions (*often in pl.*); (*pl.*) a grant of money by Parliament to meet the expenses of government, an allowance; one who supplies a place, a substitute. **supply and demand** [DEMAND]. **supplier,** *n.*

support (sŭ pôrt′) [F. *supporter*, L. *supportāre* (SUP-, *portāre*, to carry)], *v.t.* To bear the weight of, to hold up, to sustain, to keep from yielding or giving way, to give strength or endurance to; to furnish with necessaries, to provide for; to give assistance to, to advocate, to defend, to back up, to second; to bear out, to substantiate, to corroborate; to bear; to endure, to put up with; to keep up, to be able to carry on; to maintain; to act as, to represent (a character, etc.). *n.* The act of supporting or the state of being supported; one who or that which supports; aid, countenance, assistance; subsistence, livelihood. **supportable,** *a.* **supportableness,** *n.* **supportably,** *adv.* ***supportance,** *n.* **supporter,** *n.* One who or that which supports or maintains; (*Her.*) a figure on each side of a shield, etc., appearing to support it. **supportless,** *a.*

suppose (sŭ pōz′) [F. *supposer* (SUP-, *poser*, to POSE (1))], *v.t.* To lay down without proof, to assume by way of argument or illustration; to imagine, to believe; to take to be the case, to accept as probable, to surmise; to believe (to exist); to involve or require as a condition, to imply. **supposable,** *a.* **supposedly,** *adv.* **supposer,** *n.* **supposition** (sŭp ȯ zish′ ŭn), *n.* **suppositional,** *a.* **suppositionally,** *adv.*

supposititious (sŭ poz i tish′ ŭs) [L. *supposītīcius*,

from *supposit-*, p.p. stem of *suppōnere*, to substitute (SUP-, *pōnere*, to put)], *a.* Substituted for something else, not genuine, spurious. **supposititiously,** *adv.* **supposititiousness,** *n.*

suppositive (sů poz′ i tiv) [as prec.], *a.* Including or implying supposition. *n.* A conjunction implying supposition. **suppositively,** *adv.*

suppository (sů poz′ i tòr i) [late L. *suppositorium*, as prec.], *n.* A medicinal body introduced into an internal passage, as the vagina or rectum, and left to dissolve.

suppress (sů pres′) [L. *suppressus*, p.p. of *supprimere* (SUP-, *premere*, to press)], *v.t.* To put down, to overpower, to subdue, to quell; to keep in or back, to withhold, to stifle, to repress; to keep back from disclosure or circulation, to conceal. **suppressible,** *a.* **suppresser,** *n.* **suppression** (-presh′ ůn), *n.* **suppressionist,** *n.* **suppressive,** *a.* **suppressor,** *n.* One who suppresses; (*T.V.*) a device for preventing electrical interference in television reception.

suppurate (sŭp′ ū rāt) [L. *suppūrātus*, p.p. of *suppūrāre* (SUP-, *pūrāre*, from *pur-*, base of PUS)], *v.i.* To generate pus, to fester. **suppuration** (-rā′ shůn), *n.* **suppurative** (sŭp′ ū rā tiv), *a.*

supra- [L. *suprā-*, pref. *suprā*, prep. and adv., above, for *superā*, abl. of *superus*, higher, from *super*, see SUPER-], *pref.* Above, over, super-; beyond. **supraciliary** [SUPERCILIARY]. **supraclavicular** (sū prå klå vik′ ū lår), *a.* Situated above the clavicle. **supracondylar, -loid** (-kon′ di lår, -loid), *a.* Situated above the condyle. **supracostal,** *a.* Lying or situated above or outside the ribs. **supradorsal,** *a.* (*Anat.*) On the back; above the dorsal surface. **supralapsarian** (-lăp sâr′ i ån), *n.* A higher Calvinist, one believing that election and rejection were decreed before the Fall; *a.* Pertaining to supralapsarianism. **supralapsarianism,** *n.* The belief and doctrines of the supralapsarians. **supralateral** (-lăt′ ėr ål), *a.* **supralunar** (-lū′ når), *a.* **supramaxillary** (-măk′ si lår i), *a.* Of or pertaining to the upper jaw; *n.* The upper maxillary bone. **supramundane** (-mŭn′ dān), *a.* **supranational** (sū prå năsh′ ŏn ål), *a.* Overriding national sovereignty. **supraorbital,** *a.* Being above the eye-socket. **supra-renal** (-rē′ nål), *a.* Situated above the kidneys. **supraposition** [SUPERPOSITION]. **supraprotest** (-prō′ test), *n.* Acceptance or payment of a bill of exchange by a person not a party to it after protest for non-acceptance or non-payment. **suprascapular, -lary** (-skăp′ ū lår, -lår i), *a.* Situated above the shoulder-blade. **suprasensible** [SUPERSENSIBLE]. **supraspinal** (-spī′ nål), *a.*

supreme (sū prēm′) [F., from L. *suprēmus*, superl. of *superus*, see SUPRA-], *a.* Highest in authority or power; highest in degree or importance, utmost, extreme, greatest possible; last, final. **the Supreme:** God. **Supreme Court of Judicature** [JUDICATURE]. **supremacy** (sū prem′ å si), *n.* The quality or state of being supreme; the highest authority or power. **Oath of Supremacy** [OATH]. **supremely,** *adv.*

sur- [O.F., from L. SUPER-], *pref.* Super-, as in *surcingle*, *surface*, *surfeit*.

sura (soo′ rå) [Arab., step], *n.* A chapter of the Koran.

***suraddition** (sĕr å dish′ ůn), *n.* (*Shak.*) Something added.

surah (sū′ rå) [prob. as SURAT], *n.* A soft, twilled, usu. self-coloured silk material.

sural (sū′ rål) [L. *sūra*, calf]. Pertaining to the calf of the leg.

surat (su răt′), *n.* Coarse, short cotton grown near Surat, India; cloth made from this.

surbase (sĕr′ bās) [SUR-, BASE (2)], *n.* The cornice or moulding at the top of a pedestal or base. **surbased,** *a.* **surbed** (-bed′), *v.t.* To set (a stone) on edge in relation to the grain.

surcease (sėr sēs′) [A.-F. *sursise*, fem. of *sursis*, p.p. of *surseer*, F. *surseoir*, L. *supersedēre*, to SUPERSEDE], *n.* Cessation. *v.i.* To cease.

surcharge (sůr charj′) [A.-F. (SUR-, CHARGE)], *v.t.* To overload, to overburden, to overfill; to put an extra charge on, to overcharge; to show an omission in (an account) for which credit should be allowed; to impose payment of (a sum) or on (a person) for amounts in official accounts disallowed by an auditor. *n.* An excessive load, burden, or charge; an overcharge; an amount surcharged on official accounts; another valuation or other matter printed on a postage- or revenue-stamp, a stamp so treated; an additional charge imposed as a penalty for false returns of income or other taxable property. **surcharger,** *n.* ***surchargement,** *n.*

surcingle (sĕr′ sing gėl) [M.E. and O.F. *surcengle* (SUR-, *cengle*, girth, L. *cingula*, belt, from *cingere*, to gird)], *n.* A belt or girth put round the body of a horse, etc., for holding a saddle or blanket on its back; the girdle of a cassock. *v.t.* To put a surcingle on; to fasten with this.

surcoat (sĕr′ kōt) [A.-F. *surcote*], *n.* An outer coat, esp. a loose robe worn over armour; an outer jacket worn by women (14th–16th cent.).

surculus (sĕr′ kū lůs) [L.], *n.* (*pl.* **-li, -lī**) (*Bot.*) A shoot rising from a root-stock, a sucker. **surculigerous** (-lij′ ėr ůs), **surculose, -lous,** *a.*

surd (sĕrd) [L. *surdus*, deaf], *a.* (*Math.*) Not capable of being expressed in rational numbers; (*Phon.*) uttered with the breath and not with the voice. *n.* An irrational quantity; (*Phon.*) a surd consonant, as *p*, *f*, *s*, opp. to the vocals *b*, *v*, *z*. **surdity,** *n.*

sure (shoor) [O.F. *sur*, *seur*, L. *sēcūrus*, SECURE], *a.* Certain, confident, undoubting; free from doubts (of); positive, believing, confidently trusting (that); infallible, stable, certain (to); safe, reliable, trustworthy, unfailing; unquestionably true; certain (of finding, gaining, etc.). **adv.* Surely, certainly; (*Am.*) yes. **sure enough:** In reality, not merely expectation. **to be sure:** (*colloq.*) Without doubt, certainly, of course. **to make sure:** To make certain, to ascertain; to make secure. **to make sure of** [MAKE (2)]. **well, I'm sure:** An exclamation of surprise. **sure-footed,** *a.* Not liable to stumble or fall (*lit. or fig.*). **sureness,** *n.*

surely (shoor′ li), *adv.* Securely, safely; certainly (frequently used by way of asseveration or to deprecate doubt); undoubtedly.

surety (shoor′ ti), *n.* A person undertaking responsibility for payment of a sum, discharge of an engagement, or attendance in court by another, a guarantor; a pledge deposited as security against loss or damage or for payment or discharge of an engagement, etc.; *certainty. **suretyship,** *n.*

surf (sĕrf) [formerly *suffe*, prob. var. of SOUGH (1)], *n.* The swell of the sea breaking on the shore, rocks, etc.; the foam of this. **surf-bird,** *n.* A plover-like bird of the Pacific coasts of America, akin to the sandpiper. **surf-board,** *n.* A board on which a bather can ride on the surf of incoming waves. **surf-boat,** *n.* A strong and buoyant boat for use in surf. **surf-boatman,** *n.* **surf-duck,** *n.* A scoter. **surfy,** *a.*

surface (sĕr′ fås) [F.], *n.* The exterior part of anything that has length and breadth, the outside, the superficies; (*Geom.*) that which has length and breadth but not thickness; (*fig.*) that which is apparent at first view or on slight consideration. *v.t.* To put a surface on; to smooth, to polish. **surface-man,** *n.* One employed in keeping the permanent way of a railway in order; a mine-worker employed at the surface. **surface-printing,** *n.* Printing from a relief surface as distinguished from an incised surface. **surface-tension,** *n.* The tension of a liquid causing it to act as an elastic enveloping membrane tending to contract to the minimum area, as seen in the bubble, the drop, etc. **surface-water,** *n.* Water collecting on the surface of the ground. **surfaced,** *a.* **surfacer,** *n.* **surficial** (-fish′ ål), *a.* **surficially,** *adv.*

surfeit (sĕr′ fet) [A.-F. *surfet*, O.F. *sorfait*, p.p. of *sorfaire* (SUR-, *faire*, L. *facere*, to do)], *n.* Excess, esp. in eating and drinking; oppression resulting thence, satiety, nausea. *v.t.* To feed to excess, to overload, to cloy. **surfeit water:** A highly alcoholic drink taken in small amounts to counteract the effect of over-eating. **surfeiter,** *n.*

surficial, etc. [SURFACE].

surfy [SURF].

surge (sĕrj) [F. *surgir*, L. *surgere*, *surrigere* (*sur-*, SUB-, *regere*, to direct)], *v.i.* To swell, to heave, to move up and down (of waves). *n.* A large wave, a billow, a swell, a heaving and rolling motion. ***surgeful, *surgent, *surgy,** *a.* ***surgeless,** *a.*

surgeon (sĕr′ jŏn) [contr. of CHIRURGEON], *n.* A medical practitioner treating injuries, deformities, and diseases by manual procedure; a practitioner holding the diploma of the Royal College of Surgeons; a general practitioner; a medical officer in the army, navy, or a military hospital; a surgeon-fish. **surgeon-fish,** *n.* A sea-fish of the genus *Teuthis*, with lance-like spines at the tail. **surgeoncy, surgeonship,** *n.*

surgery (sĕr′ jėr i), *n.* The treatment of injuries, deformities, or diseases by manual operation; a surgical office, consulting-room, or dispensary. **surgical,** *a.* **surgically,** *adv.*

***surgy** [SURGE].

suricate (sū′ ri kāt) [native], *n.* A small S. African burrowing carnivore *Suricata tetradactyla*, allied to the weasel, and often domesticated as a mouser.

Surinam-toad (sūr i nam′ tōd) [*Surinam* in Dutch Guiana], *n.* A S. American toad-like amphibian.

surlily, etc. [SURLY].

surloin [SIRLOIN].

surly (sĕr′ li) [SIR, -LY], *a.* Churlish, rude, gruff, uncivil. **surlily,** *adv.* **surliness,** *n.*

surmaster (sĕr′ mas tėr), *n.* A master next in rank to the headmaster in some schools.

surmise (sůr mīz′) [O.F., fem. of *surmis*, p.p. of *surmettre* (SUR-, *mettre*, to put, from L. *mittere*, to send, p.p. *missus*)], *n.* A supposition on slight evidence, a guess, a conjecture. *v.t.* To guess, to imagine, with but little evidence; to conjecture, to suspect. *v.i.* To conjecture, to guess, to suppose. **surmisable,** *a.* **surmiser,** *n.*

surmount (sůr mount′) [F. *surmonter* (SUR-, MOUNT)], *v.t.* To overcome, to vanquish, to rise above; to overtop, to cap (*usu. in p.p.*); to surpass. **surmountable,** *a.* **surmountableness,** *n.* **surmounter,** *n.*

surmullet (sůr mŭl′ ėt) [O.F. *surmulet* (*sur*, *sor*, SORREL (2), MULLET)], *n.* The red mullet, *Mullus surmuletus.*

surname (sĕr′ nām) [F. *surnom* (SUR-, *nom*, L. NOMEN, assim. to NAME)], *n.* A name added to the Christian name; orig. an appellation signifying occupation, etc., or a nickname ultimately becoming hereditary, a family name. *v.t.* To call by a surname; to give a surname to. **surnominal** (-nom′ i nȧl), *a.*

surpass (sůr pas′) [F. *surpasser*], *v.t.* To excel, to go beyond in amount, degree, etc. **surpassable,** *a.* **surpassing,** *a.* Excellent in an eminent degree. **surpassingly,** *adv.* **surpassingness,** *n.*

surplice (sĕr′ plis) [F. *surplis*, med. L. *superpelliceum* (SUPER-, *pelliceum*, L. *pellicius*, PELISSE)], *n.* A loose, flowing vestment of white linen, with full sleeves, worn by the clergy and choristers in the English church at divine service. ***surplice-fee,** *n.* A fee paid to the clergy for occasional duties, as marriages, churchings, and funerals. **surpliced,** *a.*

surplus (sĕr′ plůs) [F.], *n.* That which remains over, excess beyond what is used or required; the balance in hand after all liabilities are paid, the residuum of an estate after all debts and legacies are paid. **surplusage,** *n.*

surprise (sůr prīz′) [O.F., fem. of *surpris*, *sorpris*, *p.p.* of *sur-*, *sorprendre* (SUR-, *prendre*, L. *prehendere*, to take)], *n.* A taking unawares or unprepared; emotion excited by something sudden or unexpected, astonishment, an event exciting this, something unexpected. *v.t.* To come or fall upon suddenly and unexpectedly, esp. to attack unawares; to strike with astonishment, to be contrary to or different from expectation; to shock, to scandalize (*usu. in p.p.*); to disconcert, to lead or drive unawares (into an act, etc.). **surprisal,** *n.* **surprisedly, surprisingly,** *adv.* **surpriser,** *n.* **surprising,** *a.* **surprisingness,** *n.*

surrealism (sū rē′ ȧl izm) [F. *surrealisme*], *n.* (*Art*) An artistic and literary movement of the twentieth century which aimed at expressing the subconscious activities of the mind by presenting images with the chaotic incoherency of a dream. **surrealist,** *n.*

surrebut (sŭr ė bŭt′), *v.i.* (*Law*) To reply to a defendant's rebutter (of a plaintiff). **surrebutter,** *n.* The plaintiff's reply to the defendant's rebutter [cp. SURREJOINDER].

surrejoin (sŭr ė join′), *v.i.* (*Law*) To reply to a defendant's rejoinder (of a plaintiff). **surrejoinder,** *n.* The reply of the plaintiff to a defendant's rejoinder [cp. SURREBUTTER].

surrender (sů ren′ dėr) [O.F. *surrendre*], *v.t.* To yield up to the power or control of another; to give up possession of, esp. upon compulsion or demand; to yield (oneself) to any influence, habit, emotion, etc. *v.i.* To yield something or to give oneself up into the power of another, esp. to an enemy in war; to give in, to yield, to submit; to appear in court in discharge of bail, etc. *n.* The The act of surrendering or the state of being surrendered. **surrenderee,** *n.* (*Law*) One to whom an estate is surrendered. **surrenderer,** *n.* ***surrendry,** *n.*

surreptitious (sŭr ėp tish′ ůs) [L. *surrepticius*, from *surripere*, to purloin (*sur-*, SUB-, *rapere*, to snatch), p.p. *surreptus*], *a.* Done by stealth or fraud; secret, clandestine. **surreptitiously,** *adv.*

surrogate (sŭr′ ō gȧt) [L. *surrogātus*, p.p. of *surrogāre*, to elect as substitute (*sur-*, SUB-, *rogāre*, to ask)], *n.* A deputy, esp. of a bishop or his chancellor, for granting marriage licences and probates. **surrogateship,** *n.* **surrogatum** (-gā′ tům), *n.* (*Sc. Law*) A substitute.

surround (sů round′) [O.F. *soronder*, *surunder*, to overflow (SUR-, over, L. *undāre*, to flow, cp. ABOUND, conf. with ROUND)], *v.t.* To lie or be situated all round, to encompass, to environ, to encircle, to invest, to enclose. *n.* The floor-covering, or staining of floorboards, between the skirting and the carpet. **surroundings,** *n.* (*pl.*) Things around a person or thing, environment, circumstances.

***sursize** (sůr sīz′) [O.F. *sursise*, see SURCEASE], *n.* (*Feud. Law*) A penalty for not paying castle-guard rent on the appointed day.

sursolid (sůr sol′ id) [SUR-, SOLID], *a.* (*Math.*) Of the fifth degree. *n.* The fifth power of a quantity.

surtax (sĕr′ tăks), *n.* An additional tax; an additional income tax imposed in 1929 in place of the super-tax on all incomes above a certain amount; *v.t.* (sėr tăks′) To impose a surtax.

***surtout** (sůr too′) [F. (SUR-, *tout*, all, L. *tōtum*, nom. *-tus*, whole)], *n.* A man's overcoat, esp. one like a frock-coat.

surveillance (sůr vā′ lȧns) [F., from *surveiller* (SUR-, *veiller*, L. *vigilāre*, to watch, see VIGIL)], *n.* Oversight, close watch, supervision.

survey (sůr vā′) [A.-F. *surveier* (SUR-, O.F. *veeir*, L. *vidēre*, to see)], *v.t.* To look over, to take a general view of, to view with a scrutinizing eye; to examine closely; to examine and ascertain the condition, value, etc., of; to determine by accurate observation and measurement the boundaries, extent, position, contours, etc., of (a tract of country, coast, estate, etc.), *n.* (sẽr′ vā) The act or process of surveying; a general view; a careful examination, inspection, or scrutiny; an account based on this; the operation of surveying land, etc.; a department carrying this on; a map, plan, etc., recording the results of this; (*Am.*) a district for the collection of customs. **surveyable,** *a.* **surveying,** *n.* **surveyor,** *n.* One who surveys, esp. one who measures land; an inspector (of customs, weights and measures, etc.); *an overseer. **surveyorship,** *n.*

survive (sủr vīv′) [F. *survivre,* L. *supervīvere* (SUPER-, *vīvere,* to live)], *v.t.* To live longer than, to outlive, to outlast; to be alive after, to live through, to outlive or outlast (an event, period, etc.). *v.i.* To be still alive or in existence. **survival,** *n.* The act of surviving; a person, thing, custom, opinion, etc., surviving into a new state of things. **survival of the fittest:** (*Biol.*) The preservation of forms of life that have proved themselves best adapted to their environment, the process or result of natural selection. **survivor,** *n.* **survivorship,** *n.*

sus- [SUB-], *pref.* (before *p, t,* and some L. derivatives in *c*).

susceptible (sủ sep′ ti bėl) [F., from L. *suscipere* (SUS-, *capere,* to take), p.p. *susceptus*], *a.* Admitting (of); capable of being influenced or affected, accessible, liable (to); impressionable, sensitive, touchy. **susceptibility** (-bil′ i ti), **susceptibleness,** *n.* **susceptibly,** *adv.* **susceptive,** *a.* Readily receiving impressions, etc., susceptible; receiving emotional impressions. **susceptiveness, susceptivity** (-tiv′ i ti), **susceptor,** *n.* ***suscipient** (-sip′ i ėnt), *a.* ***suscipiency,** *n.*

***suscitate** (sŭs′ i tāt) [L. *suscitātus,* p.p. of *suscitāre* (SUS-, *citāre,* to CITE)], *v.t.* To rouse, to excite. ***suscitation** (-tā′ shủn), *n.*

susi (soo′ si) [Hind.], *n.* An E. Indian striped cotton and silk fabric.

suspect (sủs pekt′) [F. *suspecter,* L. *suspectāre,* from *suspectus,* suspicious, p.p. of *suspicere* (SUS-, *specere,* to look)], *v.t.* To imagine to exist, to have an impression of the existence of without proof, to surmise, to be inclined to believe to be guilty but upon slight evidence, to doubt the innocence of, to distrust; to hold to be uncertain, to doubt, to mistrust. *v.i.* To be suspicious. (sŭs′ pekt) *a.* Suspected, under suspicion, suspicious; doubtful, uncertain. *n.* A person suspected of crime, etc. **suspectable,** *a.* **suspectedly,** *adv.* ***suspectless,** *a.*

suspend (sủs pend′) [F. *suspendre,* L. *suspendere* (SUS-, *pendere,* to hang), p.p. *suspensus*], *v.t.* To hang up, to hang from something above; to sustain (of the particles of a body, fluid, etc.); to cause to cease for a time, to intermit, to defer, to debar temporarily from a privilege, etc. **to suspend payment:** To be unable to meet one's financial engagements. **suspender,** *n.* One who or that which suspends; (*pl.*) attachments to hold up socks or stockings; (*Am.*) braces. **suspensible,** *a.* **suspensibility** (-bil′ i ti), *n.*

suspense (sủs pens′) [F. *suspens,* suspended, L. *suspensus,* see prec.], *n.* A state of uncertainty, doubt, or apprehensive expectation or waiting; (*Law*) a temporary cessation of a right, etc. **suspensible,** etc. [SUSPEND]. **suspension** (-pen′ shủn), *n.* The act of suspending; the state of being suspended. **suspension-bridge,** *n.* A bridge sustained by flexible supports passing over a tower or elevated pier and secured at each extremity. **suspensive, suspensory,** *a.* Having power to suspend; uncertain, doubtful. **suspensively,** *adv.* **suspensor,** *n.* **suspensorium** (-sôr′ i ủm), *n.* (*pl.* **-ria**) A supporting ligament, part, etc., esp. the bone or bones by which the lower jaw is suspended from the cranium in vertebrates.

suspicion (sủs pish′ ủn) [O.F. *souspeçon* (F. *soupçon*), L. *suspitiōnem,* nom. *-tio,* from *suspicere,* to SUSPECT], *n.* The act or feeling of one who suspects; belief in the existence of wrong or guilt on inadequate proof, doubt, mistrust; (*fig.*) a very slight amount. **suspicionless,** *a.* **suspicious,** *a.* Inclined to suspect; entertaining suspicion; exciting or likely to excite suspicion. **suspiciously,** *adv.* **suspiciousness,** *n.*

***suspire** (sủs pīr′) [O.F. *souspirer,* L. *suspirāre* (SUB-, *spirāre,* to breathe)], *v.i.* To sigh; to breathe. **suspiration** (sŭs pi rā′ shủn), *n.*

sustain (sủs tān′) [O.F. *sustenir* (F. *soutenir*), L. *sustinēre* (SUS-, *tenēre,* to hold)], *v.t.* To bear the weight of, to hold up, to keep from falling; to bear up against or under; to stand, to undergo without yielding; to experience, to suffer; to enable to bear, to keep from failing, to strengthen, to encourage, to keep up; to maintain, to uphold, to establish by evidence; to support, to confirm, to bear out, to substantiate. **sustainable,** *a.* **sustainer,** *n.* A person who, or a thing that, sustains; the principal motor in a rocket.

sustenance (sŭs′ te nảns), *n.* That which sustains, the nourishing element in food; food, subsistence; the act of sustaining.

sustentaculum (sŭs ten tăk′ ū lủm), *n.* (*Zool., etc.*) A supporting part, tissue, etc. **sustentacular,** *a.*

sustentation (sŭs ten tā′ shủn), *n.* Support, maintenance. **sustentation fund,** *n.* A fund to assist indigent clergy. **sustentator, sustentor,** *n.*

susurrant, -rous (sủ sŭr′ ảnt, -ủs) [L. *susurrans -ntem,* pres.p. of *susurrāre,* from *susurrus,* whisper], *a.* Whispering, rustling, murmuring. **susurration** (sŭs ủ rā′ shủn), **susurrus** (-sŭr′ ủs), *n.*

***sutile** (sū′ til, -tīl) [L. *sūtilis,* from *suere,* to sew], *a.* Done or made by stitching.

sutler (sŭt′ lėr) [Dut. *zoetelaar,* from *zoetelen,* cp. G. *sudeln,* to sully (cogn. with SUDS and SEETHE)], *n.* A person who follows an army and sells provisions, liquor, etc. **sutlership,** *n.* **sutlery,** *n.*

sutor (sū′ tȯr) [L., from *suere,* to sew], *n.* A cobbler. **sutorial** (-tôr′ i ảl), *a.*

Sutra (soo′ trả) [Sansk.], *n.* A rule, a precept, an aphorism; (*pl.*) Brahminical books of rules, doctrine, etc.

suttee (sủ tē′) [Sansk. *satī,* virtuous wife], *n.* A Hindu custom by which the widow was burnt on the funeral pyre with her dead husband; a widow so burnt. **suteeism,** *n.*

suttle (sŭt′ ėl) [var. of SUBTLE], *a.* Taken after the tare has been deducted and the tret has yet to be allowed. *n.* Suttle weight.

suture (sū′ tyủr) [F., from L. *sūtūra,* from *suere,* to sew, p.p. *sūtus*], *n.* The junction of two parts by their margins as if by sewing, esp. of the bones of the skull; the uniting of the edges of a wound by stitching. *v.t.* To unite by a suture. **sutural, sutured,** *a.* **suturally,** *adv.* **suturation** (-ā′ shủn), *n.*

suzerain (sū′ zė rān, -rin) [F., from *sus,* L. *susum, sursum,* above, after *suverain,* SOVEREIGN], *n.* A feudal lord, a lord paramount; a State having sovereignty or control over another. **suzerainty,** *n.*

svelt (svelt) [F., from It. *svelto*], *a.* Slender, lissom (esp. of a woman's figure).

swab (swob) [back-formation from *swabber,* Dut. *zwabber,* drudge, from *zwabberen,* to do dirty work, cp. G. *schwabbern,* prob. cogn. with *schwappen,* to spill], *n.* A mop for cleaning floors, decks, the bore of a gun, etc.; (*Med.*) a small piece of cotton-wool or gauze used for removing blood, etc., and dressing wounds; (*Naut. slang*) an officer's epaulet, a lubber, a clumsy fellow. *v.t.* (*past & p.p.* **swabbed**) To rub, wipe, or clean with a swab or mop. **swabber,** *n.*

Swabian (swā′ bi ản), *a.* Of or pertaining to Swabia. *n.* A native of Swabia.

swaddle (swod′ ėl) [A.-S. *swethel,* swaddling-band, from *swathu,* SWATH], *v.t.* To wind or swathe in a bandage, wrap, or wraps. **swaddler,** *n.* (*Irish slang*) A Protestant, a Methodist. **swaddling-bands, -clothes, *-clouts,** *n.pl.*

Swadeshi (swa dā′ shi) [Hind.], *n.* (*Pol.*) A movement in India for favouring the development of home industries.

swag (swăg) [cp. Norw. *svagga*, cogn. with SWAY], **v.i.* To hang loose and heavy; to sag. *n.* Booty obtained by robbery, esp. burglary; (*Austral.*) a pack or bundle, baggage. **swag-bellied,** *a.* Having a large prominent belly. **swag-belly,** *n.* **swag-man,** *n.* (*Austral.*) A man who carries his swag about with him in search of work, **swag-shop,** *n.* (*slang*) A shop where cheap and trashy goods are sold.

swage (1) (swāj) [F. *suage*, etym. doubtful], *n.* A tool for shaping wrought-iron, etc., by hammering or pressure. *v.t.* To shape with a swage. **swage-block,** *n.* A heavy iron block or anvil with grooves, etc., used for shaping metal.

***swage** (2) (*Milton*) [ASSUAGE].

swagger (swăg′ ėr) [freq. of SWAG], *v.i.* To walk, strut, or go (about, etc.) with an air of defiance, self-confidence, or superiority; to talk in a blustering, boastful, or hectoring manner. *v.t.* To bluster or bluff (a person into, out of, etc.). *n.* A swaggering walk, gait, or behaviour; bluster, dash, self-conceit. *a.* (*colloq.*) Smart, fashionable, swell. **swagger-cane, -stick,** *n.* A short cane with metal head carried by soldiers. **swagger-coat,** *n.* A loose coat made on full lines that sways when the wearer walks. **swaggerer,** *n.* **swaggeringly,** *adv.*

swagman, -shop [SWAG].

Swahili (swa hē′ li) [Arab. *Waswahili*, coast people], *n.* A Bantu people and language of Zanzibar and the adjoining coast.

swain (swān) [Icel. *sveinn*, cp. A.-S. *swān*], *n.* (*poet.*) A young rustic; a country gallant; a male lover. ***swainish,** *a.* ***swainishness,** *n.*

swallow (1) (swol′ ō) [A.-S. *swalewe* (cp. Dut. *zwaluw*, G. *schwalbe*, Icel. *svala*), cogn. with SWELL], *n.* A small, swift, migratory bird of the genus *Hirundo*, with long, pointed wings and forked tail; a swift or other bird resembling the swallow. **one swallow does not make summer:** A warning against jumping to conclusions. **swallow-fish,** *n.* The sapphirine gurnard, *Trigla hirundo*. **swallow-tail,** *n.* A deeply-forked tail, a butterfly with such a tail, also a humming-bird; the points of a burgee; a dove-tail; a swallow-tailed coat, a dress-coat (*sing. or pl.*). **swallow-tailed,** *a.* With deeply-forked tail.

swallow (2) (swol′ ō) [M.E. *swolowen*, A.-S. *swelgan*, cp. Dut. *zwelgen*, G. *schwelgen*, Icel. *svelgja*], *v.t.* To take through the throat into the stomach; to absorb, to engulf, to overwhelm, to consume (up); (*fig.*) to accept with credulity; to accept without resentment, to put up with; to retract, to recant. *v.i.* To perform the action of swallowing. *n.* The gullet or œsophagus; the amount swallowed at once; a swallow-hole. **swallow-hole,** (*prov.*) **swallet,** *n.* An opening in limestone into which a stream or streamlet runs. **swallowable,** *a.* **swallower,** *n.*

swam (swăm), *past* [SWIM].

swami (swa′ mi) [Sans. *svamin*, master], *n.* A Hindu religious teacher.

swamp (swomp) [cp. SUMP, Dut. *zwamp*; perh. rel. to A.-S. *swamm*, G. *schwamm*, sponge], *n.* A tract of wet, spongy land, a bog, a marsh. *v.t.* To cause (a boat, etc.) to be filled with or to sink in water; to plunge or sink into a bog; (*fig.*) to overwhelm, to render helpless with difficulties, numbers, etc. *v.i.* To fill with water, to sink, to founder. **swamp gum,** *n.* (*Austral.*) A variety of eucalyptus growing in swamps. **swamp oak,** *n.* The casuarina. **swamp-ore,** *n.* Bog-iron ore. **swamp sparrow,** *n.* (*N. Zealand*) The fern-bird. **swampy,** *a.*

swan (swon) [A.-S. (cp. Dut. *zwaan*, G. *schwan*, Icel. *svanr*), perh. cogn. with Sansk. *swan*, L. *sonāre*, to SOUND (2)], *n.* A large, web-footed aquatic bird of the genus *Cygnus*, with a long neck and usu. white plumage, noted for its grace in the water; the constellation *Cygnus*; (*fig.*) a poet, a singer (with alln. to the swan-song). **swan-herd,** *n.* One who tends swans, esp. a royal officer superintending swan-marks. **swan-hopping** [SWAN-UPPING]. **swan-maiden,** *n.* (*Folk-lore*) A maiden able to take the shape of a swan. **swan-mark,** *n.* A mark on a swan showing ownership, usu. a notch on the upper mandible. **swan-marker,** *n.* **swan-neck,** *n.* A pipe, tube, rail, etc., curved like a swan's neck, esp. the end of a discharge-pipe. **swansdown,** *n.* Down obtained from a swan; a thick cotton cloth with a downy nap on one side. **swan-shot,** *n.* A large size of shot. **swanskin,** *n.* A swan's skin with the feathers on; a soft, fine-twilled flannel. **swan-song,** *n.* The song traditionally believed to be sung by a dying swan; (*fig.*) the last or dying work, esp. of a poet. **swan-upping,** *n.* The annual inspection and marking of Thames swans. **swanlike,** *a.* **swannery,** *n.*

swank (1) (swăngk) [etym. doubtful], *v.i.* (*slang*) To swagger, to show off, to bluster. *n.* Swagger, bluster. **swanky,** *a.* Showing off, showy.

swank (2) (swăngk) [etym. doubtful], *n.* (*Sc.*) Slender, slim; agile, supple. **swankie,** *n.* An active fellow.

swap (swop) [prob. from obs. *swap*, M.E. *swappen*, to strike], *v.t.* and *i.* (*past & p.p.* **swapped**) To exchange, to barter. *n.* An exchange, a barter. **swapping,** *a.* Large, strapping.

swape (swāp) [var. of SWEEP], *n.* (*prov.*) A pump-handle; a long oar or sweep; a pole for lifting water from a well, a sconce. **swape-well,** *n.*

Swaraj (swa raj′) [Sansk. *svaraj*, self-ruling], *n.* (*Pol.*) Home rule for India; agitation to secure it.

sward (swôrd) [A.-S. *sweard*, skin, cp. Dut. *zwoord*, G. *schwarte*, Icel. *svörthr*, skin, hide], *n.* A surface of land covered with thick short grass; turf. **swarded, swardy,** *a.*

***sware,** *past* [SWEAR].

swarf (swarf) [O.N. file-dust], *n.* Grit, metal filings, chips, grindings.

swarm (1) (swôrm) [A.-S. *swearm* (cp. Dut. *zwerm*, G. *schwarm*, Icel. *svarmr*), perh. cogn. with Sansk. *svr*, to sound, L. *susurrus*, see SUSURRANT], *n.* A large number of small animals, insects, people, etc., esp. when moving in a confused mass; (*pl.*) great numbers; a cluster of honey-bees issuing from a hive with a queen-bee and seeking a new home. *v.i.* To collect together in readiness for emigrating, to leave (or go out of) a hive in a swarm (of bees); to congregate, to throng, to be exceedingly numerous; to move (about, etc.) in a swarm; (of places) to be thronged or overcrowded (with). **swarm-cell, -spore,** *n.* A zoospore.

swarm (2) (swôrm) [etym. doubtful], *v.t.* and *i.* To climb (up a tree, rope, pole, etc.) by embracing it with the arms and legs.

***swart** (swôrt) [A.-S. *sweart* (cp. Dut. *zwart*, G. *schwarz*, Icel. *svartr*), cogn. with L. *sordidus*, SORDID], *a.* Of a black or dark colour; swarthy.

swarthy (swôr′ *thi*) [obs. *swarth*, var. of SWART], *a.* Dark or dusky in complexion. **swarthily,** *adv.* **swarthiness,** *n.*

swash (swosh) [imit., cp. Swed. dial. *svasska*], *v.i.* To make a noise as of splashing water; to wash or splash about (of water); to strike noisily or violently. *v.t.* To strike noisily or violently. *n.* A washing or splashing of water; a blustering noise, a vapouring. **swash-buckler,** *n.* A bully, a bravo. **swash letter,** *n.* (*Print.*) An ornamental italic capital with tails and flourishes. **swash-plate,** *n.* An inclined disk on a revolving axis transmitting an up-and-down motion to a bar. **swasher,** *n.*

swastika (swăs′ ti kȧ) [Sansk., fortunate (*su*, well, *asti*, being)], *n.* A fylfot or gammadion.

swat (swot) [onomat.], *v.t.* To crush (a fly).

swatch (swoch, swăch) [?], *n.* A sample of cloth.

swath (swawth, swoth, swā*th*) [A.-S. *swæth*, *swathu*, track (cp. Dut. *zwaad*, G. *schwad*, swath, L.G. *swade*, scythe, Norw. *swada*, to slice off)], *n.* A row or ridge of grass, corn, etc., cut and left lying on the ground; the space cut by a scythe, machine, etc., in one course.

swathe (swāth) [M.E. *swathen*, cp. *swethel*, SWADDLE, perh. as prec.], *v.t.* To bind or wrap in a bandage, cloth, bandages, etc. *n.* A bandage, a wrapping.

sway (swā) [M.E. *sweyen*, cp. Dan. *svaie*, Norw. *svaga*, Swed. *svaja*, to jerk], *v.i.* To move backwards and forwards, to swing, to oscillate irregularly; to be unsteady, to waver, to vacillate; to lean or incline to one side or in different directions; *to bear rule, to govern. *v.t.* To cause to oscillate, waver, or vacillate; to cause to incline to one side; to bias; to influence, to control, to rule. *n.* Rule, dominion, control; the act of swaying, a swing. **sway-backed, swayed,** *a.* Having the back hollowed, strained, or weakened (of horses).

sweal (swēl) [A.-S. *swēlan* (cp. G. *schwelen*), cogn. with SULTRY], *v.i.* (*prov.*) To burn away slowly; to melt and run (of a candle). *v.t.* To dress (a hog) by singeing the bristles off.

swear (swâr) [A.-S. *swerian* (cp. Dut. *zweren*, G. *schwören*, Icel. *sverja*, Swed. *svara*, to answer), cogn. with SWARM (1)], *v.i.* (*past* **swore, *sware,** *p.p.* **sworn,** swôrn) To affirm solemnly invoking God or some other sacred person or object as witness or pledge, to take an oath; to appeal (to) as witness of an oath; to use profane language; to give evidence on oath; to promise on oath. *v.t.* To utter or affirm with an oath, to take oath (that); to cause to take oath, to administer an oath to, to bind by an oath; to declare, to vow, to promise, or testify upon oath; to utter profanely. *n.* An act or spell of swearing; a profane oath. **to swear by:** (*colloq.*) To have or profess great confidence in. **to swear in:** To induct into office with the administration of an oath. **to swear off:** To renounce solemnly.

sweat (swet) [A.-S. *swat* (cp. Dut. *zweet*, G. *schweiss*, Icel. *sveiti*, also Sansk. *svēda-*, Gr. *hidrōs*, L. *sūdor*)], *n.* The moisture exuded from the skin of an animal, perspiration; moisture exuded from or deposited in drops on any surface; the act or state of sweating; (*fig.*) labour, toil, exertion, a spell of exercise; drudgery, toil, hard labour; a state of anxiety, a flurry; (*colloq.*) an old soldier. *v.i.* To exude sweat, to perspire; to emit moisture; to exude (of moisture); (*fig.*) to be in a flurry or state of anxiety, panic, etc., to smart; to toil, to labour, to drudge; to be sweated; to carry on business on the sweating-system. *v.t.* To emit as sweat; to make (an animal, etc.) sweat by exertion; to employ at starvation wages, to exact the largest possible amount of labour from at the lowest pay, by utilizing competition; to bleed, to subject to extortion; to subject (hides, tobacco, etc.) to fermentation; to wear away (coins) by friction, etc.; to remove sweat from (horses, etc.) with a scraper. **sweaty,** *a.* **sweatily,** *adv.* **sweatiness,** *n.*

sweater (swet′ ėr), *n.* A thick woollen garment like a jersey put on after exercise; a woollen pull-over; one or that which causes to sweat.

sweating (swet′ ing), *a.* Causing or enduring sweat. **sweating-bath,** *n.* A vapour-bath for exciting sweat. **sweating-iron,** *n.* A scraper for removing sweat from horses. **sweating-room,** *n.* A sudatorium, esp. in a Turkish bath; a room for sweating superfluous moisture from cheese. **sweating-sickness,** *n.* A form of malaria epidemic in the 15th and 16th cent. **sweating system:** The practice of employing operatives at starvation wages in unhealthy conditions and for long hours.

Swede (swēd), *n.* A native or inhabitant of Sweden. **swede,** *n.* A Swedish turnip, *Brassica rutabaga* (*Am.* a rutabaga).

Swedenborgian (swē dėn bôr′ ji ȧn) [Emanuel Swedenborg (1688–1772), Swedish philosopher and mystic], *a.* Of or pertaining to Swedenborg or Swedenborgianism. *n.* A member of the Swedenborgian or New Church, or a believer in the doctrines of Swedenborg. **Swedenborgianism,** *n.*

Swedish (swē′ dish), *a.* Pertaining to Sweden or its inhabitants. *n.* The language of the Swedes.

sweeny (swē′ ni) [etym. doubtful], *n.* Atrophy of a muscle, esp. of the shoulder in horses.

sweep (swēp) [M.E. *swepen*, from *swǣp-*, stem of A.-S. *swāpan*, to SWOOP], *v.i.* (*past & p.p.* **swept**) To glide or move along with a strong, swift continuous motion; to range unchecked (of the eye); to extend continuously (of land, a curve, etc.); to go with a stately motion. *v.t.* To carry (along, away, etc.) with powerful or unchecked force; to move swiftly and powerfully over, across, or along, to range, to scour; to pass over in swift survey (of the eyes, etc.); to pass over destructively; to rake, to enfilade, to clear (of mines, etc.); to dredge (the bottom of a river, etc.); to clear dirt, etc., from or clean with or as with a broom, etc.; to collect or gather (up) with or as with a broom; to propel with sweeps; to cause to move with a sweeping motion. *n.* The act of sweeping; a clearance, a riddance; a sweeping motion, a sweeping curve, direction, piece of road, etc.; the range, reach, or compass of a sweeping motion or of an instrument, weapon, implement, etc., having this motion; a long oar used to propel barges or sailing-vessels in a calm; a swape; a chimney-sweeper; (*fig.*) a blackguard; a sweepstake. **to make a clean sweep:** To get rid of entirely. **to sweep the board:** To win everything. **sweep-back,** *n.* (*Aviat.*) The angle relatively to the axis at which an aircraft wing is set back. **sweep-net,** *n.* A sweep-seine; a butterfly-net. **sweep-seine,** *n.* A long seine used for sweeping a large area. **sweeper,** *n.* One who sweeps; a carpet-sweeper; (*Austral.*) a worker in the woolsheds, a 'broomie'; (*Austral. colloq.*) a slow train. **sweeping,** *a.* That sweeps; wide-ranging, comprehensive; *n.pl.* Things collected by sweeping; (*fig.*) rubbish, refuse, litter. **sweepingly,** *adv.* **sweepingness,** *n.*

sweepstake, sweepstakes (swēp′ stāk, -s), *n.* A gaming transaction in which a number of persons stake sums on an event, esp. on a horse-race, the total amount being divided among the winning betters.

sweet (swēt) [A.-S. *swēte*, cp. Dut. *zoet*, G. *süsz*, Icel. *sætr*, Sansk. *svad*, to please, L. *suāvis*, Gr. *hēdus*, sweet], *a.* Having a taste like that of honey or sugar; pleasing to the senses; fragrant; pleasant or melodious in sound; refreshing, restful; fresh, not salt or salted, not sour, bitter, stale, or rancid; (*Am.*) (of butter) fresh, unsalted; (*fig.*) pleasant to the mind, agreeable, delightful; charming, amiable, gracious, lovable, dear, beloved. *n.* A sweet thing; a sweetmeat (*Am.* a candy); (*pl.*) sweet dishes, as tarts, puddings, ices, etc.; (*pl.*) the course at dinner after the joint; (*pl.*) sweet scents, fragrance; the sweetness or the sweet part of anything; (*pl.*) pleasures, delights, pleasant experiences; dear one, darling. *adv.* Sweetly. ***sweet-and-twenty:** (*Shak.*) Young and charming. **to be sweet on:** To be in love with; to be very fond of. **to have a sweet tooth:** To be fond of sweet things. **sweetbread,** *n.* The pancreas or thymus-gland, esp. of a calf or sheep, used as food. **sweet-brier** [BRIER]. **sweet course:** (*Am.*) dessert. **sweet-flag** [SWEET-RUSH]. **sweet-gale** [GALE (3)], *n.* The bog myrtle. **sweetheart,** *n.* A lover, male or female; *v.i.* To be love-making. **sweet-john,** *n.* The narrow-leaved variety of sweet-william. **sweetmeat,** *n.* An article of confectionery, usu. consisting wholly or principally of sugar, a sugar-plum, a bonbon; a fruit candied with sugar. **sweet-oil,** *n.* Olive oil. **sweet-pea,** *n.* An annual leguminous climbing plant *Lathyrus odoratus*, with showy flowers. **sweet-potato,** *n.* A tropical climbing plant, *Batatas edulis*, with an edible root. **sweet-root,** *n.* Liquorice-root. **sweet-rush,** *n.* A flag, *Acorus calamus*, with an aromatic root-stock used in medicine, confectionery, etc. **sweet-scented,** *a.* **sweet-shop,** *n.* A shop where sweets are sold (*Am.* a candy-store). **sweet-sop,** *n.* A tropical American tree, *Anona squamosa*, allied to the custard-apple, with sweet, pulpy fruit. **sweet-tempered,** *a.*

sweet violet: The scented or wood-violet, *Viola odorata*. **sweet-water,** *n.* A sweet, watery variety of white grape. **sweet-william,** *n.* A perennial species of pink, *Dianthus barbatus*, with dense clusters of showy and fragrant flowers. **sweet-willow,** *n.* The sweet-gale. **sweet-wood,** *n.* The true laurel, *Laurus nobilis*; applied to other trees and shrubs of the family *Lauraceæ*. ***sweet-wort,** *n.* Any plant of a sweet taste. **sweeten,** *v.t.* and *i.* To make sweet. **sweetener,** *n.* **sweetening,** *n.* **sweeting,** *n.* A sweet variety of apple; *a term of endearment. **sweetish,** *a.* **sweetishness,** *n.* **sweetly,** *adv.* **sweetness,** *n.* **sweety,** *n.* (*Childish*) A sweetmeat, a lollypop; a term of endearment.

swell (swel) [A.-S. *swellan* (cp. Dut. *zwellen*, G. *schwellen*, Icel. *svella*), perh. cogn. with Gr. *saluein*, to surge], *v.i.* (*p.p.* **swollen,** swō′ lėn, **swelled**) To dilate or increase in bulk or extent, to expand; to rise up from the surrounding surface, to bulge, to belly (out); to become greater in volume, strength, or intensity; to rise in altitude; (*fig.*) to be puffed up, to be elated, to strut, to be inflated with anger, etc. *v.t.* To increase the size, bulk, volume, or dimensions of; to inflate, to puff up. *n.* The act or effect of swelling; rise, increase, augmentation; a succession of long, unbroken waves in one direction, as after a storm; a bulge, a bulging part; (*Mus.*) an increase followed by a decrease in the volume of sound; a combined crescendo and diminuendo; a contrivance for gradually increasing and diminishing sound in an organ, etc.; a swell-organ; (*colloq.*) a person of high standing or importance, a showy, dashing, or fashionable person. *a.* (*colloq.*) Characterized by showiness or display, smart, foppish, dandified; of distinction; (*Am. colloq.*) excellent, fine. **swell-blind,** *n.* One of the movable slats forming the front of a swell-box. **swell-box,** *n.* A chamber containing the pipes of a swell-organ. **swell-mob** [MOB (1)]. **swell-organ,** *n.* An organ or partial organ with the pipes enclosed in a swell-box. **swelled head:** (*fig.*) Conceit. **swelldom,** *n.* **swelling,** *n.* The act of expanding, etc., or the state of being swollen or augmented; (*Path.*) an unnatural enlargement or tumefaction of a part. **swellish,** *a.* (*colloq.*).

swelter (swel′ tėr), ***swelt** (swelt) [A.-S. *sweltan* (cp. Icel. *svelta*, Goth. *swiltan*, O.H.G. *schwelzan*, to be consumed), cogn. with SWEAL], *v.i.* To be hot, moist, and oppressive, to cause faintness, languor, or oppression (of the weather, etc.); to be overcome and faint with heat; to sweat profusely. *n.* (*colloq.*) A sweltering condition. **swelteringly,** *adv.* **sweltry,** *a.*

swept, *past* & *p.p.* [SWEEP].

swerve (swěrv) [A.-S. *sweorfan*, to rub, file, polish (cp. Dut. *zwerven*, to swerve, Icel. *sverfa*, to file)], *v.i.* To turn to one side, to deviate, to diverge from the direct or regular course. *v.t.* To cause to diverge, to deflect. *n.* The act of swerving, a sudden divergence or deflection.

swift (swift) [A.-S., from *swīfan*, to move quickly (cp. Icel *svīfa*, O.H.G. *sweibōn*), cogn. with SWEEP], *a.* Moving with great rapidity, fleet, rapid, quick, speedy, ready, prompt, expeditious; passing rapidly, soon over, brief, unexpected, sudden. *adv.* Swiftly. *n.* A small, long-winged insectivorous bird of the family *Micropodiæ*, esp. *Apus apus*, closely resembling the swallow; the common newt; a ghost-moth; the sail of a windmill. **swift-footed, -handed, -heeled, -winged,** *a.* Running, acting, flying, etc., with swiftness. **swifter,** *n.* (*Naut.*) A rope used to fasten, hold, or tighten something. **swiftlet,** *n.* **swiftly,** *adv.* **swiftness,** *n.*

swig (swig) [perh. from A.-S. *swelgan*, SWALLOW (2)], *v.t.* and *i.* To drink in large draughts. *n.* A large or deep draught of liquor.

swill (swil) [A.-S. *swillian*, to wash, cp. Icel. *skyla*], *v.t.* To wash, to rinse; to drink greedily. *v.i.* To drink to excess. *n.* A rinsing; liquid food, hog-wash; *liquor taken in excess. **swiller,** *n.* **swillings,** *n.pl.* Hog-wash.

swim (swim) [A.-S. *swimman* (cp. Dut. *zwemmen*, G. *schwimmen*, Icel. *svimma*), blended with A.-S. *swīma*, a swoon (cp. Dut. *zwijm*, Icel. *svimi*, G. *schwindel*)], *v.i.* (*past* **swam,** *p.p.* **swum**) To float or be supported on water or other liquid; to move progressively in the water by the motion of the hands and feet, or fins, tail, etc.; to glide along; to be drenched or flooded (with water, etc.); to seem to reel or whirl round one; to have a feeling of dizziness; *to overflow, to abound. *v.t.* To pass, traverse, or accomplish by swimming; to compete in (a race); to cause (a horse, boat, etc.) to swim or float; to bear up, to float (a ship, etc.). *n.* The act or a spell of swimming; a pool or run frequented by fish in a river; the swimming-bladder; (*fig.*) the main current of life, business, etc. **swim-bladder** [SWIMMING-BLADDER]. **swim-suit,** *n.* Bathing costume. **swimmable,** *a.* **swimmer,** *n.* **swimmeret,** *n.* One of the appendages of a crustacean serving as a swimming-organ. **swimming-bath,** *n.* A bath for swimming in. **swimming-bell,** *n.* A bell-shaped swimming-organ, as of a jelly-fish. **swimming-belt,** *n.* A belt stuffed with cork, etc., for helping a learner to swim. **swimming-bladder,** *n.* The air-bladder or sound of a fish. **swimmingly,** *adv.* Smoothly, easily, without impediment.

swindle (swin′ dėl) [from *swindler*, G. *schwindler*, extravagant projector, from *schwindeln*, to be dizzy, from *schwindel*, see prec.], *v.t.* and *i.* To cheat; to defraud grossly or deliberately. *n.* The act or process of swindling; a gross fraud or imposition, a fraudulent scheme; (*colloq.*) a thing that is not what it pretends to be, a deception, a fraud. **swindler,** *n.* ***swindlery,** *n.* **swindlingly,** *adv.*

swine (swīn) [A.-S. *swīn* (cp. Dut. *zwijn*, G. *schwein*, Icel *svīn*), perh. orig. adj., cp. L. *suīnus*, pertaining to swine, from *sus*, sow], *n.* (*pl. unchanged*) An ungulate omnivorous mammal of the family *Suidæ*, esp. the genus *Sus*, a pig, a hog; (*fig.*) a greedy, vicious, or debased person. **swine-bread,** *n.* The truffle; the sowbread. **swine-fever, -plague,** *n.* An infectious lung-disease affecting the pig. **swine-herd,** *n.* One who tends swine. **swine-pox,** *n.* A form of chicken-pox affecting swine. **swine's-snout,** *n.* The dandelion. **swinish,** *a.* **swinishly,** *adv.* **swinishness,** *n.*

swing (swing) [A.-S. *swingan*, cp. Swed. *svinga*, Dan. *svinge*, G. *schwingen*], *v.i.* (*past* **swung,** ***swang,** *p.p.* **swung**) To move to and fro, as a body suspended by a point or one side, to sway, hang freely as a pendulum, to oscillate, to rock; to turn on or as on a pivot, to move or wheel (round, etc.) freely; to go with a swaying, undulating, or rhythmical gait or motion; to go to and fro in a swing; to be hanged. *v.t.* To cause to move to and fro, to sway, to oscillate; to wave to and fro, to brandish; to cause to turn or move round, as on a pivot; to cause to go to and fro in a swing. *n.* The act or state of swinging; a swinging or oscillating motion; a swinging gait or rhythm; the compass or sweep of a moving body; free course, unrestrained liberty, a seat suspended by ropes, etc., in which a person or thing may swing to and fro; a spell of swinging in this. **in full swing:** In full activity or operation. **to swing the lead:** To trump up an excuse for evading a duty. **swing-back,** *n.* An arrangement for adjusting the screen and plate-holder at the back of a camera at different angles. **swing-boat,** *n.* A boat-shaped carriage for swinging in at fairs, etc. **swing-bridge,** *n.* A draw-bridge opening by turning horizontally. **swing music, swing:** A style of playing jazz in which the basic melody and rhythm persist through individual interpretations of the theme, impromptu variations, etc. **swing-plough,** *n.* A plough without wheels. **swing-wheel,** *n.* The wheel driving a clock-pendulum, corresponding to the balance-wheel of a watch. **swinger,** *n.* **swingingly,** *adv.*

swinge (swinj) [A.-S. *swengan*, causal of *swingan*, prec.], *v.t.* To strike hard, to beat, to thrash. *n.* The sweep of anything in motion; a heavy blow; sway, rule. ***swinge-buckler,** *n.* A bully; a swash-buckler. **swingeing,** *a.* Thumping, huge. ***swingeingly,** *adv.*

swingle (swing′ gėl) [M.E. *swingelen*, freq. from A.-S. *swingan*, to beat, to SWING], *v.t.* To clean (flax) by beating with a swingle. *n.* A wooden instrument for beating flax to separate the woody parts from the fibre. **swingle-bar, -tree,** *n.* The cross-bar pivoted in the middle to which the ends of a horse's traces are attached. **swingling-tow,** *n.* The coarse part of flax.

swinish, etc. [SWINE].

***swink** (swingk) [A.-S. *swincan*, perh. cogn. with SWING], *v.i.* To labour, to toil. *v.t.* To tire or exhaust with labour. *n.* Labour, toil, drudgery. ***swinker,** *n.*

swipe (swīp) [A.-S. *swipian, swippan*, cogn. with SWEEP], *v.i.* and *t.* To hit with great force, in cricket, golf, etc.; to drink off, to gulp down. *n.* A hard, swiping blow, esp. at cricket; (*in pl., colloq.*) thin, washy, or inferior beer. **swiper,** *n.*

***swire** (swīr) [A.-S. *swīra, swēora*, neck], *n.* A depression between two hills or peaks, a saddle, a col.

swirl (swĕrl) [cp. Norw. *svirla*, freq. of *sverra*, to hum, to whirl; cogn. with SWARM (I)], *v.i.* To form eddies, to whirl about. *v.t.* To carry (along, down, etc.) with an eddying motion. *n.* A whirling motion, an eddy; the furious rush of a fish through water, or the disturbance so caused.

swish (swish) [imit.], *v.i.* To make a whistling sound in cutting through the air; to move with such a sound. *v.t.* To make such a whistling movement with (a cane, lash, etc.); to strike or cut (off) with such a sound; to flog, to thrash, esp. with a birch. *n.* A whistling sound, movement, or blow; a stroke with a birch, etc. *a.* (*slang*) Smart, elegant.

Swiss (swis), *a.* Of or pertaining to Switzerland or its inhabitants. *n.* A native or inhabitant or the people of Switzerland. **Swiss Guards:** Mercenaries formerly employed as bodyguards in France, Naples, etc., and still at the Vatican.

switch (swich) [M. Dut. *swick* (cp. L.G. *swikk*, G. *swecke*, tack, peg, *zwecken*, to prick), cogn. with TWITCH], *n.* A small flexible twig or rod; a tress of hair tied up at one end; a mechanism for diverting railway trains or vehicles from one line to another, or for completing or interrupting an electric circuit, transferring current from one wire to another, etc. *v.t.* To lash or beat with a switch; to move, whisk, or snatch (away, etc.) with a jerk; to shift (a train, etc.) from one line to another; to turn (on or off) with a switch; to connect or disconnect (a user of a telephone) thus. *v.i.* To move or swing with a careless or jerking movement, to whisk; to cut (off) connexion on a telephone, etc. **switch-board,** *n.* A board on which switches are fixed controlling electric or telephonic circuits. **switch-man,** *n.* A man in charge of railway switches, a shunter.

switchback (swich′ băk), *n.* A zigzag railway for ascending or descending steep inclines; a railway on which the vehicles are carried over a series of ascending inclines by the momentum of previous descents, used for amusement at fairs, etc. (*Am.* a roller-coaster).

switchel (swich′ ėl) [etym. doubtful], *n.* (*Am.*) A drink of molasses and water, flavoured with rum, etc.

swither (swi′ *th*er) [?], *v.i.* To hesitate.

Switzer (swit′ zėr), *n.* A Swiss.

swivel (swiv′ ėl) [A.-S. *swīfan*, see SWIFT, with agent suf. -LE], *n.* A link or connexion comprising a ring and pivot or other mechanism allowing the two parts to revolve independently; a support allowing free horizontal rotation; a swivel-gun. *v.i.* and *t.* (*past & p.p.* **swivelled**) To turn on a swivel or pivot. **swivel-eye,** *n.* A squinting eye. **swivel-eyed,** *a.* **swivel-gun,** *n.* A gun mounted on a pivot. **swivel-hook, -joint,** etc., *n.*

swizzle (swiz′ ėl) [perh. rel. to SWIG], *v.t.* and *i.* (*prov.*) To drink immoderately, to bib. *n.* A mixed drink of various kinds; a fraud. **swizzle-stick,** *n.* A stick with a brush-like end for frothing drinks.

swob, etc. [SWAB].

swollen, *swoln, *p.p.* [SWELL].

swoon (swoon) [M.E. *swownen, swoghenen*, from A.-S. *swogan*, see SOUGH (I)], *v.i.* To fall into a fainting fit; (*fig.*) to sink or die away (of music, etc.). *n.* The act of swooning, a faint. **swooningly,** *adv.*

swoop (swoop) [A.-S. *swāpan*, to rush (cp. Icel. *sveipa*, G. *schweifen*, to rove), cogn. with SWEEP], *v.i.* To descend upon prey, etc., suddenly as a hawk, to come (down) upon, to attack suddenly from a distance. *v.t.* To fall on suddenly and seize, to snatch (up). *n.* A sudden plunge of or as of a bird of prey on its quarry; a sudden descent, attack, seizing, or snatching; (*colloq.*) a snatching up of all at once.

swop [SWAP].

sword (sôrd) [A.-S. *sweord* (cp. Dut. *zwaard*, G. *schwert*, Icel. *sverth*), etym. doubtful], *n.* An offensive weapon, usu. consisting of a long blade fixed in a hilt with a guard for the hand, used for cutting or thrusting; (*fig.*) the power of the sword, military power, sovereignty; war, destruction in war, death. **fire and sword:** Rapine, destruction by invaders, etc. **to put to the sword:** To kill (esp. of victors or captors). **sword-arm,** *n.* The right arm. **sword-bayonet,** *n.* A sword-shaped bayonet. **sword-bearer,** *n.* An officer who carries a sword of State. **sword-belt,** *n.* A belt from which a sword is slung. **sword-bill,** *n.* A S. American humming-bird with a long sword-shaped bill. **sword-blade,** *n.* **sword-cane,** *n.* A hollow walking-stick enclosing a long, pointed blade. **sword-cut,** *n.* A cut or scar inflicted by a sword. **sword-dance,** *n.* A dance in which swords are brandished or clashed together or in which women pass under crossed swords; a Highland dance performed over two swords laid crosswise on the floor. **sword-fish,** *n.* A sea-fish of the genus *Xiphias*, allied to the mackerel, having the upper jaw prolonged into a formidable swordlike weapon. **sword-flag,** *n.* The yellow flag, *Iris pseudacorus*. **sword-grass,** *n.* A species of sedge with swordlike leaves. **sword-guard,** *n.* The part of a sword-hilt protecting the hand. **sword-hand,** *n.* The right hand. **sword-knot,** *n.* A ribbon or tassel tied to the hilt of a sword, orig. used for securing it to the wrist. ***sword-law,** *n.* Government by the sword. **sword-lily,** *n.* The gladiolus. **sword of justice:** Judicial authority. **sword of State:** A sword carried before the sovereign, etc., on ceremonial occasions. **Sword of the Spirit:** The word of God; a R.-C. organization for promoting piety. **sword-play,** *n.* A combat between gladiators, fencing; (*fig.*) repartee. **sword-player,** *n.* **sword-shaped,** *a.* **swordsman,** *n.* One who carries a sword; one skilled in the use of the sword. **swordsmanship,** *n.* **swordstick,** *n.* A sword-cane. **sworded,** *a.* Girt or armed with a sword. ***sworder,** *n.* A swordsman; a cut-throat. **swordless,** *a.* **sword-like,** *a.* **swordproof,** *a.*

swore, *past*, **sworn,** *p.p.* [SWEAR].

swot (swot) [var. of SWEAT], *v.i.* and *t.* (*colloq.*) To study hard. *n.* Hard study; a piece of hard work; one who studies hard.

***swound** [SWOON].

swum, *p.p.* [SWIM].

swung, *past & p.p.* [SWING].

swy (swī), *n.* (*Austral. colloq.*) The game of two-up.

sybarite (sib′ å rīt), *n.* An inhabitant of Sybaris, an ancient Greek colony in S. Italy, noted for effeminacy and voluptuousness; an effeminate and luxurious person. *a.* Sybaritic. **sybaritic, *-al** (-rit′ ik, -ål), *a.* **sybaritism** (sib′ å rīt izm), *n.*

sybil [SIBYL].

sycamine (sik′ å min) [L. *sȳcamīnus*, Gr. *sukaminos*,

perh. from Heb. *shiqmāh*, SYCAMORE], *n.* The black mulberry-tree.

sycamore (sik' ȧ môr) [var. of SYCOMORE], *n.* A medium-sized tree, *Acer pseudo-platanus*, allied to the maple and plane, also called sycamore-maple. **sycamore-fig**, *n.* The Egyptian sycamore, *Ficus sycomorus*. **sycamore-maple**, *n.* The sycamore, *Acer pseudo-platanus*.

sycee (sī sē') [Chin. *si sze*, fine silk], *n.* Pure uncoined silver cast into ingots, usu. bearing the seal of a banker or assayer, and used in China by weight as a medium of exchange, also called **sycee silver**.

sychnocarpous (sik nō kar' pŭs) [Gr. *suchnos*, many, *karpos*, fruit], *a.* (*Bot.*) Bearing fruit more than once before dying, perennial.

sycomore (sik' ō môr) [L. *sȳcomorus*, Gr. *sukomoros*, perh. as SYCAMINE, assim. to *sukon*, fig, *morom*, mulberry], *n.* A Syrian and Egyptian fig-tree, *Ficus sycomorus*, the sycamore fig, called also the Egyptian or Oriental sycamore.

syconium (sī-, si kō' ni ŭm) [mod. L., from Gr. *sukon*, fig], *n.* (*pl.* **-nia**) (*Bot.*) A multiple fruit developed from a fleshy receptacle having numerous flowers, as in the fig.

sycophant (sik' ō fănt) [L. *sȳcophanta*, Gr. *sukophantēs*, etym. doubtful, said to mean orig. an informer against persons exporting figs or plundering the sacred fig-trees (*sukon*, fig, *phainein*, to show)], *n.* A servile flatterer, a parasite; *an informer, a slanderer. *v.i.* and *t.* To play the sycophant. **sycophancy**, *n.* **sycophantic** (-făn' tik), *a.* **sycophantish**, *a.* **sycophantism**, ***sycophantry**, *n.* **sycophantize**, *v.i.*

sycosis (sī-, si kō' sis) [Gr. *sukōsis*, fig-like ulcer (*suk-on*, fig, -OSIS)], *n.* (*Path.*) A pustular eruption or inflammation of the scalp or bearded part of the face, barber's itch.

Sydneysider (sid ni sī' dėr), *n.* (*Austral.*) A resident of Sydney. **Sydney silkie**, *n.* (*Austral.*) A little, long-haired dog.

syenite (sī' ė nīt) [L. *Syēnītes lapis*, stone of *Syene*, Egypt], *n.* A granular igneous rock consisting of orthoclase and hornblende, with or without quartz. **syenitic** (-nit' ik), *a.*

syl- [SYN-], *pref.* (*before l*).

syllable (sil' ȧ bėl) [M.E. and O.F. *sillabe*, L. *syllaba*, Gr. *sullabē* (SYL-, *lab-*, base of *lambanein*, to take), assim. to PRINCIPLE, etc.], *n.* A sound forming a word or part of a word, containing one vowel sound, with or without a consonant or consonants, and uttered at a single effort or vocal impulse; (*fig.*) the least expression or particle of speech. *v.i.* To pronounce by syllables, to articulate; (*poet.*) to utter, to speak. **syllabary**, *n.* A catalogue of characters representing syllables; (*collect.*) such characters serving the purpose of an alphabet in certain languages. **syllabic** (si lăb' ik), *a.* Pertaining to or consisting of a syllable or syllables; having each syllable distinctly articulated; representing the sound of a whole syllable, opp. to alphabetic. **syllabically**, *adv.* **syllabicate**, **syllabify**, **syllabize** (sil' ȧ bīz), *v.t.* To separate into or pronounce by syllables. **syllabication**, **syllabification** (-kā' shŭn), *n.* **syllabled**, *a.* (*usu. in comb.* as *two-syllabled*).

syllabub [SILLABUB].

syllabus (sil' ȧ bŭs) [late L., from late Gr. *sullabos*, as SYLLABLE], *n.* (*pl.* **-buses**) A list, outline, summary, abstract etc., giving the principal heads of a course of lectures, teaching, etc., hours of attendance, etc.; (*R.-C. Ch.*) a summary of points decided by the Curia, esp. the list of heretical doctrines, etc., forming the appendix to the encyclical letter *Quanta cura* of Pius IX in 1864.

syllepsis (si lep' sis) [L., from Gr. *sullēpsis*, comprehension (SYL-, *-lēpsis*, from *lambanein*, see SYLLABLE)], *n.* (*pl.* **-ses**, -sēz) The application of a word in both the literal and the metaphorical senses at once, as in 'Doth sometimes counsel take and sometimes tea'; the connexion of a verb or adjective with two nouns, with only one of which it is in syntactical agreement, as in 'Neither he nor I am there.' **sylleptic** (-lep' tik), *a.* **sylleptically**, *adv.*

syllogism (sil' ō jizm) [M.E. and O.F. *silogime*, L. *syllogismum*, nom. *-mus*, Gr. *sullogismos*, from *sullogizesthai*, to reason (SYL-, *logos*, reason)], *n.* A form of argument consisting of three propositions, a major premise or general statement, a minor premise or instance, and a third deduced from these called the conclusion. **syllogistic** (-jis' tik), *a.* **syllogistically**, *adv.* **syllogize**, *v.i.* and *t.* **syllogization** (-zā' shŭn), *n.* **syllogizer**, *n.*

sylph (silf) [F. *sylphe*, prob. from Gr. *silphē*, some beetle or grub], *n.* An elementary being inhabiting the air, intermediate between material and immaterial beings; a graceful and slender girl; a S. American humming-bird with a long, brilliantly-coloured tail. **sylph-like**, *a.* ***sylphid**, *a.* and *n.* **sylphine**, *a.*

sylvan (sil' văn) [L. *syl-*, *silvanus*, from *silva*, wood], *a.* Pertaining to a wood or forest; growing in woods; (*fig.*) rural, rustic. *n.* A deity of the woods, a satyr; a rustic.

sylvanite (sil' vȧ nīt), *n.* (*Min.*) A gold or silver tellurid.

sylvate (sil' vāt), *n.* (*Chem.*) A salt of sylvic acid.

sylvic (sil' vik), *a.* Of or derived from wood (applied to an acid obtained from resin).

sylviculture (sil' vi kŭl chŭr), *n.* Arboriculture, forestry.

sym- [SYN-], *pref.* (*before b, m, or p*).

symbion (sim' bi ŏn) [Gr. *sumbiōn*, pres.p. of *sumbiōnai* (SYM-, *biōnai*, from *bios*, life)], *n.* (*Biol.*) An organism living in a state of symbiosis. **symbiosis** (-bi ō' sis), *n.* The vital union or partnership of certain organisms, such as the fungus and alga in lichens. **symbiotic** (-ot' ik), *a.* **symbiotically**, *adv.*

symbol (sim' bŏl) [F. *symbole*, L. *symbolum*, Gr. *sumbolon*, token, pledge, from *sumbollein* (SYM-, *ballein*, to throw)], *n.* An object typifying or representing something by resemblance, association, etc., a type, an emblem; a mark, character, or letter accepted as representing or signifying some thing, idea, relation, process, etc., as the letters of the alphabet, those representing chemical elements, the signs of mathematical relations, etc. *v.t.* To symbolize. **symbolic**, **-al** (-bol' ik, -ăl), *a.* **symbolically**, *adv.* **symbolicalness**, *n.* **symbolics**, *n.* **symbolism** (sim' bō lizm), *n.* **symbolist**, *n.* **symbolistic** (-lis' tik), *a.* **symbolize**, *v.t.* To be the symbol of, to typify; to represent by symbols; to treat as symbolic, not literal, to make symbolic or representative of something; *to make to agree in properties. *v.i.* To use symbols; *to agree, to harmonize. **symbolization** (-zā' shŭn), *n.* **symbolizer**, *n.* **symbology** (-bol' ō ji), ***-bolology** (-bō lol' ō ji), *n.* **symbological** (-loj' i kăl), *a.* **symbologist** (-bol' ō jist), *n.* **symbolatry** (-bol' ȧ tri), **symbololatry** (-bō lol' ȧ tri) [-LATRY], *n.* Symbol-worship.

symmetry (sim' ė tri) [F. *symmetrie*, L. *symmetria*, Gr. *summetria*, from *summetros*, commensurate (SYM-, *metron*, measure)], *n.* Due proportion of the several parts of a body or any whole to each other, congruity, parity, regularity, harmony; arrangement of parts on either side of a dividing line or point so that the opposite parts are exactly similar in shape and size; (*Anat.*, *etc.*) regularity of structure so that opposite halves exactly correspond; (*Bot.*) regularity of number in sepals, petals, stamens, etc., each whorl comprising the same number or multiples of this. **symmetral**, **symmetric**, **-al** (si met' rik, -ăl), *a.* **symmetrically**, *adv.* **symmetricalness**, *n.* **symmetrist** (sim' ė trist), ***symmetrian** (-met' ri ăn), **symmetrician** (-trish' ăn), *n.* **symmetrize**, *v.t.* **symmetrization** (-zā' shŭn), *n.* **symmetrophobia** (-fō' bi ȧ) [-PHOBIA], *n.*

symmorph (sim' ôrf) [Gr. *summorphos* (SYM-, *morphē*, form)], *n.* A character differing from another or others in form but representing the same idea.

sympathy (sim′ på thi) [F. *sympathie*, L. *sympathīa*, Gr. *sumpatheia*, from *sumpathēs*, sympathetic (SYM-, *pathein*, *paschein*, to suffer)], *n.* The quality of being affected with the same feelings as another, or of sharing emotions, affections, inclinations, etc., with another person, animal, etc.; fellow-feeling, agreement, accord (with); compassion (for); (*Physiol.*) response of an organ or part to an affection in another without actual transmission of the cause; (*Phys.*) the relation between inanimate bodies by which the vibration of one sets up a corresponding vibration in another; *the tendency of inanimate bodies to mutual attraction, influence, etc.

sympathetic (sim på thet′ ik), *a.* Pertaining to, expressive of, or due to, sympathy; having sympathy or common feeling with another, sympathizing; being in sympathy or agreement, concordant; (*Physiol.*) proceeding from sympathy, due to pain or injury in another organ or part; (*Phys.*) produced by impulses from other vibrations (of acoustic, electrical, and other vibrations). **sympathetic-ink,** *n.* A colourless ink writing in which is made visible by heat or other agency. **sympathetically,** *adv.* **sympatheticism,** *n.* A morbid tendency to be sympathetic. **sympathism** (sim′ på thizm), *n.* Immediate communication of subjective emotions.

sympathize (sim′ på thīz), *v.i.* To have or express sympathy with another, as in pain, pleasure, etc.; to be of the same disposition, opinion, etc. **sympathizer, *sympathist,** *n.*

sympetalous (sim pet′ å lŭs) [SYM-, PETALOUS], *a.* (*Bot.*) Gamopetalous. **symphenomenon** (sim fė nom′ ė nŏn), *n.* (*pl.* **-na**) A phenomenon resembling or accompanying another exhibited by the same object. **symphenomenal,** *a.*

symphony (sim′ fŏ ni) [O.F. *symphonie*, L. *symphōnia*, Gr. *sumphōnia* from *sumphōnos*, agreeing in sound (SYM-, *phōnē*, sound)], *n.* A complex and elaborate composition for an orchestra, usu. consisting of four varied movements; *consonance or harmony of sounds. **symphonic** (-fon′ ik), **symphonious** (fō′ ni ŭs), *a.* **symphonist** (sim′ fŏ nist), *n.* ***symphonize,** *v.i.* and *t.* To harmonize.

symphoricarpous (sim fŏr i kar′ pŭs) [Gr. *sumphorein*, to join together (SYM-, *pherein*, to bear), *karpus*, fruit], *a.* (*Bot.*) Bearing several fruits clustered together. **symphylous** (sim′ fi lŭs) [Gr. *phulē*, tribe], *a.* (*Ent.*) Of the same race. **symphyllous** (-fil′ ŭs) [Gr. *phullon*, leaf], *a.* (*Bot.*) Gamophyllous.

symphynote (sim′ fi nōt) [*symphy-*, SYMPHYO-, Gr. *nōton*, back], *a.* (*Conch.*) Soldered together at the hinge (of the valves of some river mussels).

symphyo- [*sumphuēs*, grown together (SYM-, *phuein*, to grow], *comb. form.* **symphyogenesis** (sim fi ŏ jen′ ė sis) [GENESIS], *n.* (*Bot.*) The formation of an organ or part by the growing together of parts previously separate. **symphyogenetic** (-jė net′ ik), *a.*

symphysis (sim′ fi sis) [Gr., as prec.], *n.* (*Anat.*) The union of two parts of the skeleton by growing together or the intervention of cartilage; (*Bot.*) the growing together or union of two parts. **symphyseal** (-fis′ ė ăl), *a.* **symphysia,** *n.* A malformation produced by the union of parts previously separate. **symphytism** (sim′ fi tizm), *n.* (*Gram.*) The coalescence of word-elements.

sympiesometer (sim pi ė zom′ ė tėr) [Gr. *sumpiezein* (SYM-, *piezein*, to squeeze), -METER], *n.* An instrument for measuring the pressure or velocity of a current of water; a barometer in which atmospheric pressure is measured by the compression of a small quantity of gas behind a column of liquid.

symploce (sim′ plŏ si) [Gr. *sumplokē* (SYM-, *plekein*, to twine)], *n.* (*Rhet.*) The repetition of a word or phase at the beginning and of another at the end of successive clauses.

sympodium (sim pō′ di ŭm) [SYM-, Gr. *pous podos*, foot], *n.* (*pl.* **-dia**) (*Bot.*) A false axis or stem composed of superimposed branches.

symposiarch (sim pō′ zi ark), *n.* The president or director of a feast; a toast-master; (*fig.*) the leading spirit of a social or convivial meeting.

symposium (sim pō′ zi ŭm) [L., from Gr. *symposion* (SYM-, *po-*, base of *pinein*, to drink, cp. *posis*, drink)], *n.* (*pl.* **-ia**) (*Gr. Ant.*) A drinking together, a convivial party usu. following a banquet, with music, dancing, etc.; a drinking party; a discussion, esp. a series of brief articles expressing the views of different writers, in a magazine, etc. **symposiac,** *a.* and *n.* **symposial,** *a.*

symptom (simp′ tŏm) [O.F. *symptome*, L. *symptōma*, Gr. *sumptōma*, *-matos*, a chance, a casualty, from *sumpiptein* (SYM-, *piptein*, to fall)], *n.* A perceptible change in the appearance or functions of the body indicating disease; (*fig.*) a sign, a token, an indication. **symptomatic, -al** (-măt′ ik, -ăl), *a.* **symptomatically,** *adv.* **symptomatology** (-tol′ ŏ ji) [-LOGY], *n.*

symptosis (simp tō′ sis) [Gr., as prec.], *n.* (*Math.*) A meeting of polars at the same point with reference to different loci; (*Gram.*) a coming together of vowels, a hiatus.

syn- [Gr. *sun-*, pref. *sun*, prep. with], *pref.* With; together; alike. **synacmy** (si năk′ mi) [Gr. *akmē*, maturity], *n.* (*Bot.*) The simultaneous maturity of the stigmas and anthers of a flower. **synacmic,** *a.* **synacral** (si nā′ krăl) [Gr. *akros*, top], *a.* (*Geom.*) Having as common vertex (of the faces of a polyhedron). **synadelphic** (sin å del′ fik) [Gr. *adelphos*, brother], *a.* Working or acting together (of the members or organs of a body). **synæresis** (si nēr′ ė sis) [L., from Gr. *sunairesis* (*hairein*, to take)], *n.* (*Gram.*) The contraction of two vowels or syllables into one. **synæsthesia** (-ēs thē′ zi å) [cp. HYPERÆSTHESIA], *n.* Sensation experienced at a point distinct from the point of stimulation.

synagogue (sin′ å gog) [F., from L. *synagōga*, Gr. *sunagōgē* (SYN-, *agein*, to bring)], *n.* A Jewish congregation for religious instruction and observances; a building or place of meeting for this. **synagogal, synagogical** (-goj′ i kăl), *a.*

synalepha (sin å lē′ få) [Gr. *sunaloiphē* (SYN-, *aleiphein*, to smear)], *n.* A blending of two syllables into one, esp. by the suppression of a final vowel before an initial vowel. **synalgia** (si năl′ ji å) [Gr. *-algia algos*, pain], *n.* (*Path.*) Sympathetic pain. **synallagmatic** (sin å lăg măt′ ik) [Gr. *sunallagmatikos* (*allassein*, to exchange)], *a.* Imposing reciprocal obligations (applied to a contract or treaty). **synangium** (si năn′ ji ŭm) [Gr. *angeion*, vessel], *n.* (*pl.* **-gia**) (*Bot.*) The boat-shaped sorus composed of sporangia in some ferns; (*Zool.*) an arterial trunk. **synantherous** (si năn′ thėr ŭs) [ANTHER, -OUS], *a.* (*Bot.*) Having the anthers growing together. **synanthous** (si năn′ thŭs) [Gr. *anthos*, flower], *a.* Having flowers and leaves appearing at the same time. **synaphea** (sin å fē′ å) [Gr. *sunapheia* (*haptein*, to join)], *n.* (*Anc. Pros.*) Continuity between lines or portions of lines in verse, esp. when the last syllable of a line is made long or elided by synalepha with the initial syllable of the next. ***synarchy** (sin′ ăr ki) [Gr. *sunarchia* (*archein*, to rule)], *n.* Joint sovereignty. **synarthrosis** (sin ar thrō′ sis) [ARTHROSIS, see ARTHRO-], *n.* (*pl.* **-ses,** -sēz) Articulation not permitting motion, as in sutures, symphysis, etc. **synarthrodial** (-thrō′ di ăl), *a.* ***synaxis** (si năk′ sis) [Gr. *sunaxis* (*agein*, to lead)], *n.* (*Ch. Hist.*) A congregation, esp. one assembled to partake of the Lord's Supper. **syncarp** (sin′ karp) [Gr. *karpos*, fruit], *n.* (*Bot.*) An aggregate fruit, as the blackberry. **syncarpous** (sin kar′ pŭs), *a.* (*Bot.*) **syncategorematic** (sin kăt ė gôr ė măt′ ik) [Gr. *sunkatēgorēmatikos* (CATEGOREMATIC)], *a.* (*Log.*) Denoting words that can express only parts of terms, as adverbs, prepositions, etc. **synchondrosis** (sin kŏn drō′ sis) [Gr. *sunchondrōsis* (*chondros*, cartilage)], *n.* The almost immovable articulation of bones by means of cartilage, as in the vertebræ. **synchoresis** (sin kō rē′ sis) [Gr. *sunchoresis* (*choros*, space)], *n.* (*Rhet.*) A concession made for the purpose of retorting more effectively.

synchromesh gear (sin′ krō mesh gēr), *n.* (*Motor.*) A system of gearing in which the drive and driving members are automatically synchronized before engagement, thus avoiding shock and noise in changing gear.

synchronism (sin′ krō nizm) [Gr. *sunchronismos* (SYN-, *chronos*, time, -ISM)], *n.* Concurrence of two or more events in time, coincidence, simultaneousness; a tabular arrangement of historical events or personages according to their dates. **synchronal, synchronous,** *a.* **synchronistic** (-nis′ tik), *a.* **synchronistically, synchronously,** *adv.*

synchronize (sin′ krō nīz), *v.i.* To concur in time, to happen at the same time; (*Cinema.*) to secure exact timing in the co-ordination of sound and picture. *v.t.* To cause to agree in time. **synchronization** (-zā′ shŭn), *n.* **synchronizer,** *n.*

synchronology (sin krō nol′ ō ji), *n.* Comparative chronology.

synchysis (sin′ ki sis) [Gr. *sunchusis*, confusion (SYN-, *cheein*, to pour)], *n.* (*Path.*) A disease of the eye caused by cholesterine floating in the vitreous humour; *confusion, derangement; a confused arrangement of words in a sentence.

synclastic (sin klăs′ tik) [SYN-, Gr. *klastos*, broken], *a.* (*Math.*) Having uniform curvature, convex or concave in every direction. **synclinal** (klī′ năl, sing′ kli năl), *a.* (*Geol.*) Sloping downward towards a common point or line, opp. to anticlinal. **syncline** (sing′ klīn), *n.* A synclinal flexure or axis.

syncopate (sin′ kō pāt) [L. *syncopātūs*, p.p. of *syncopāre*, orig. to swoon, as foll.], *v.t.* To contract (a word) by omitting one or more letters or syllables from the middle; (*Mus.*) to begin (a note or tone) on an unaccented and continue with an accented beat. **syncopation** (-pā′ shŭn), *n.*

syncope (sin′ kō pē) [L. *syncopē*, Gr. *sunkopē* (SYN-, *koptein*, to strike)], *n.* The elision of a letter or syllable from the middle of a word; (*Path.*) fainting, swooning; (*Mus.*) syncopation; the correspondence of several notes in one voice-part with one in another. **syncopal, -copic** (-kop′ ik), **-coptic** (-kop′ tik), *a.* **syncopist,** *n.* **syncopize,** *v.t.* To syncopate.

syncotyledonous (sin kot i lē′ dō nŭs) [SYN-, COTYLEDONOUS], *a.* (*Bot.*) Having the cotyledons united.

syncretism (sin′ krē tizm) [Gr. *sunkrētismos*, from *sunkrētizēin* (SYN-, *krētizēin*, etym. doubtful)], *n.* The attempted reconciliation of various philosophic or religious schools or systems of thought, as against a common opponent. **syncretic** (sin krē′ tik, -kret′ ik), *a.* and *n.* **syncretist** (sin′ krē tist), *n.* **syncretistic** (-tis′ tik), *a.* **syndactyl, -ous** (sin dăk′ til, -ŭs) [SYN-, Gr. *daktūlos*, finger], *a.* Having the digits united, as in webbed feet. **syndactylism,** *n.* **syndesmosis** (sin dez mō′ sis) [Gr. *sundesmos* (*desmos*, bond, from *deein*, to bind)], *n.* Articulation of bones by ligaments. **syndesmography** (-mog′ ră fi) [-GRAPHY], *n.* **syndesmology** (-mol′ ō ji) [-LOGY], *n.* **syndesmotic** (-mot′ ik), *a.* **syndesmotomy** (-mot′ ō mi) [-TOMY], *n.* The dissection or anatomy of the ligaments. **syndetic** (-det′ ik) [cp. ASYNDETON], *a.* Serving to connect, copulative.

syndic (sin′ dik) [F., from L. *syndicus*, Gr. *sundikos* (SYN-, *dikē*, justice)], *n.* An officer or magistrate invested with varying powers in different places and times; (*Camb. Univ.*) a member of a special committee of the senate.

syndicalism (sin′ di kă lizm) [prec., -AL, -ISM], *n.* The economic doctrine that all the workers in any trade or industry should participate in the management and control and in the division of the profits, and that in order to bring about this condition the workers in different trades should federate together and enforce their demands by sympathetic strikes. **syndicalist,** *n.*

syndicate (sin′ di kăt) [med. L. *syndicātus*], *n.* A body of syndics, esp. at Cambridge; an association of persons or firms formed to promote some special interest. *v.t.* (sin′ di kāt) To combine in a syndicate; to manage by means of a syndicate. **syndication** (-kā′ shŭn), *n.*

***syndrome** (sin′ drō mi) [Gr. *sundromē* (SYN-, *dramein*, to run)], *n.* Concurrence; (*Med.*) the aggregate of symptoms characteristic of any disease.

syne (sīn) [Sc., SINCE], *adv.* Long ago.

synecdoche (si nek′ dō ki) [L., from Gr. *sunekdochē* (SYN-, *ek*, out, *dechesthai*, to receive)], *n.* A rhetorical figure by which a part is put for the whole or the whole for a part. **synecdochical** (-dok′ i kăl), *a.*

synechia (sin ē kī′ ă) [Gr. *sunecheia* (SYN-, *echein*, to have, to hold)], *n.* (*Path.*) Morbid adhesion of the iris to the cornea or to the capsule of the crystalline lens. **synechiology** (-ek i ol′ ō ji) [-LOGY], *n.* (*Phil.*) The doctrine of connexion by causation or spatial and temporal relations. **synechiological** (-loj′ ik ăl), *a.* **synectic** (-ek′ tik), *a.* Connecting together things of different nature.

synecphonesis (sin ek fō nē′ sis) [Gr. *sunekphōnēsis* (SYN-, *ek-*, out, *phōnein*, to sound)], *n.* Synæresis.

synedral (si ned′ răl), **synedrous** (sin′ ē drŭs) [Gr. *sunedros* (SYN-, *hedra*, seat)], *a.* (*Bot.*) Growing on the angles of a stem. **synema** (si nē′ mă) [Gr. *nēma*, thread], *n.* (*Bot.*) The column of combined filaments in a monadelphous flower.

synergism (sin′ ĕr jizm) [Gr. *sunergos* (SYN-, *ergos*, work), -ISM], *n.* The doctrine that human energy co-operates with divine grace in the work of salvation. **synergastic** (-ĕr găs′ tik), *a.* Formed by co-operative effort or work. **synergetic** (-jet′ ik), *a.* Working together, co-operative (of muscles). **synergist,** *n.* **synergistic** (-jis′ tik), *a.* **synergy** (sin′ ĕr ji), *n.* Combined action; correlation between different organs, etc.

synesis (sin′ ē sis) [Gr. *sunesis*, understanding (SYN-, *hienai*, to send)], *n.* (*Gram.*) Construction according to the sense rather than syntax.

syngenesious, -an (sin jē nē′ si ŭs, -ăn) [foll., -OUS, -AN], *a.* (*Bot.*) Having the anthers cohering; cohering into a tube (of anthers).

syngenesis (sin jen′ ē sis), *n.* The theory that the embryo is the product of both male and female; reproduction by the union of the ovum and the spermatozoon. **syngenetic** (-jē net′ ik), *a.* ***syngraph** (sin′ grăf) [-GRAPH], *n.* A writing signed by both or all the parties concerned.

synizesis (sin i zē′ sis) [Gr. *sunizēsis* (SYN-, *hizein*, to seal)], *n.* (*Gram.*) The combination into one syllable in pronunciation of two vowels that cannot make a diphthong; (*Path.*) blindness caused by a closure of the pupil.

synocha (sin′ ō kă) [Gr. *sunochos*, lasting (SYN-, *echein*, to hold)], *n.* (*Path.*) Inflammatory continued fever. **synochal, synochoid,** *a.* **synochus,** *n.* A continued fever; mixed fever.

synod (sin′ ŏd) [F. *synode*, L. *synodum*, nom. *-dus*, Gr. *sunodos* (SYN-, *hodos*, way)], *n.* An ecclesiastical council; (*Presbyterian*) a council intermediate between the presbyteries and the General Assembly; a deliberative assembly, a meeting for discussion; (*Astron.*) a conjunction of heavenly bodies. **synodal, synodic, -al** (si nod′ ik, -ăl), *a.* **synodically,** *adv.*

synœcious (si nē′ shŭs) [Gr. *sunoikia* (SYN-, *oikos*, house), -OUS], *a.* (*Bot.*) Having male and female organs in the same inflorescence or receptacle.

***synomosy** (si nom′ ō si) [Gr. *sunōmosia* (SYN-, *ommunai*, to swear)], *n.* (*Gr. Ant.*) A secret brotherhood or political club bound by oath, a conspiracy.

synonym (sin′ ȯ nim) [F. *synonime*, L. *synōnyma*, Gr. *sunōnumos*, of like meaning or name (SYN-, *onuma -atos*, name)], *n.* A word having the same meaning as another of the same language; a word denoting the same thing but differing in some senses or in range of application. **synonymatic** (-măt′ ik), **synonymic** (-nim′ ik), *a.* Of or pertaining to synonymy. **synonymicon** (sin ȯ nim′ i kȯn), *n.* A dictionary of synonyms. **synonymics,** *n.* Synonymy. **synonymist,** *n.* **synonymity** (-nim′ i ti), *n.* **synonymize** (si non′ i mīz), *v.t.* To express by synonyms or a synonym. **synonymy,** *n.* A system of synonyms; a treatise on synonyms; synonymity.

synonymous (si non′ i mŭs), *a.* Expressing the same thing by a different word or words; conveying the same idea. **synonymously,** *adv.*

synopsis (si nop′ sis) [L., from Gr. *sunopsis* (SYN-, *opsis*, seeing, from *op-*, to see)], *n.* (*pl.* **-ses,** -sēz) A general view, a conspectus, a summary. **synoptic** (-nop′ tik), *a.* Of the nature of a synopsis, affording a general view; *n.* One of the synoptic gospels. **synoptic gospels:** Those of Matthew, Mark, and Luke. **synoptical,** *a.* **synoptically,** *adv.* **synoptist,** *n.* One of the writers of the synoptic gospels.

synosteography (sin os tė og′ rȧ fi) [SYN-, Gr. *osteon*, bone, -GRAPHY], *n.* A description of the articulations of the body. **synosteology** (-ol′ ȯ ji) [-LOGY], *n.* The science of or a treatise on these. **synosteosis** (-ō′ sis), *n.* (*Anat.*) Union of different parts of the skeleton by means of bone. **synosteotome** (-os′ tė ȯ tōm), *n.* A knife for the dissection of joints. **synosteotomy** (-ot′ ȯ mi) [-TOMY], *n.*

synovia (si nō′ vi ȧ) [SYN-, L. *ovum*, egg], *n.* An albuminous lubricating fluid secreted in the synovial membranes of the joints. **synovial,** *a.* Pertaining to or secreting synovia. **synovitis** (sin ȯ vī′ tis), *n.* Inflammation of a synovial membrane.

syntax (sin′ tăks) [F. *syntaxe*, late L. *syntaxis*, Gr. *suntaxis* (SYN-, *tascein*, to arrange)], *n.* The part of grammar that deals with the due arrangement of words or the construction of sentences. **syntactic** (-tăk′ tik), *a.* Of, pertaining to, or according to the rules of syntax; *n.pl.* (*Math.*) The branch of mathematics treating of the number of ways of putting things together, as permutations, combinations, etc. **syntactically,** *adv.*

synteresis (sin tėr ē′ sis) [Gr. *sunteresis*, watching closely], *n.* (*Theol.*) The habit of mind which enables one to make primary moral judgments, conscience; remorse.

synthermal (sin thĕr′ mȧl) [SYN-, THERMAL], *a.* Having the same temperature.

synthesis (sin′ thė sis) [L., from Gr. *sunthesis* (SYN-, *thesis*, putting, see THESIS], *n.* (*pl.* **-ses,** -sēz) The putting of two or more things together, combination, composition; the building up of a complex whole by the union of elements, esp. the process of forming concepts, general ideas, theories, etc.; (*Gram.*) the formation of compound words by means of composition and inflexion, as opp. to analysis which employs prepositions, etc.; (*Surg.*) the union of broken or divided parts. **synthetic, -al** (-thet′ ik, -ȧl), *a.* Pertaining to or consisting in synthesis. **synthetically,** *adv.* **synthesize, -tize** (sin′ thė sīz, -tīz), *v.t.* **synthesist, -tist,** *n.*

syntonic (sin ton′ ik) [Gr. *suntonous* (SYN-, *teinein*, to stretch)], *a.* Harmonized or tuned to each other (of transmitters and receivers in wireless telegraphy); (*Anc. Mus.*) intense in quality, syntonous (of the diatonic scale). **syntonize,** *v.t.* **syntonization, syntonism, syntony,** *n.* **syntonizer,** *n.* **syntonous,** *a.* (*Anc. Mus.*) Having the quality of intensity.

syntropic (sin trop′ ik) [SYN-, Gr. *trepein*, to turn], *a.* (*Anat.*) Turning or pointing in the same direction (of vertebræ, etc.).

sypher (sī′ fėr) [etym. doubtful], *v.t.* To join (planks, etc.) with bevelled and overlapping edges so as to leave a flush surface. **sypher-joint,** *n.*

syphilis (sif′ i lis) [F., from mod. L. *Syphilus*, shepherd in a poem by Frascatorio (16th cent.)], *n.* An infectious venereal disease due to a micro-organism introduced into the system by direct contact or due to heredity, having three stages; primary syphilis, affecting the genitals, etc., secondary syphilis, attacking the skin and mucous membranes, and tertiary syphilis, spreading to the muscles, bones, and brain. **syphilitic** (-lit′ ik), **syphilous,** *a.* **syphilize,** *v.t.* **syphilization** (-zā′ shŭn), *n.* **syphilo-,** *comb. form.* **syphiloid,** *a.* **syphilology** (-lol′ ȯ ji) [-LOGY], *n.*

syphon [SIPHON]. **syren** [SIREN].

Syriac (sir′ i ăk) [L. *Syriacus*, Gr. *Suriakos*, from *Suria*, from *Suros*, Syrian], *a.* Pertaining to Syria or its language. *n.* The language of the ancient Syrians, western Aramaic. **Syrian,** *a.* and *n.* A native of, or pertaining to, Syria.

syringa (si ring′ gȧ) [SYRINX (the stems being formerly used for the stems of Turkish pipes)], *n.* The mock-orange, Philadelphus; (*Bot.*) a genus of plants containing the lilacs.

syringe (si′ rinj) [O.F. *seringue*, L. *syringem*, nom. *-inx*, from Gr. SYRINX], *n.* A cylindrical instrument with a piston used to draw in a quantity of liquid by suction and eject it in a stream, spray, or jet, a squirt. *v.t.* To water, spray, or cleanse with a syringe. **syringeful,** *n.*

syrinx (sir′ inks) [L., from Gr. *surinx -ingos*, reed, shepherd's pipe], *n.* (*pl.* **syringes,** si rin′ jēz) (*Anat.*) The Eustachian tube; (*Ornith.*) the inferior larynx, a modification of the trachea where it joins the bronchi, the organ of song in birds; (*Surg.*) a fistula; a Pan-pipe; (*Ant.*) a narrow gallery cut in the rock in ancient Egyptian tombs. **syringeal** (si rin′ jė ȧl), *a.* (*Ornith.*). **syringitis** (-jī′ tis), *n.* Inflammation of the Eustachian tube. **syringo-,** *comb. form.* **syringotomy** (-got′ ȯ mi) [-TOMY], *n.* The operation of cutting for fistula.

Syro- [Gr. *Suros*, see SYRIAC], *comb. form.* **Syro-arabian** (sīr ȯ ȧ rā′ biȧn), *a.* Pertaining to or comprising Syriac and Arabic. **Syro-phœnician** (-fė nish′ i ȧn), *a.*

syrtis (sĕr′ tis) [L., from Gr. *surtis*, from *surein*, to draw along], *n.* (*pl.* **-tes,** -tēz) A quicksand. **syrtic,** *a.*

syrup (sir′ ŭp) [O.F. *syrop* (F. *sirop*), Arab. *sharāb*, beverage, see SHERBET], *n.* A saturated solution of sugar in water, usu. combined with fruit-juice, etc. for use in cookery, as a beverage, etc., or with a medicinal substance; the uncrystallizable fluid separated from sugar-cane juice in the process of refining molasses, treacle. **syrupy,** *a.*

syssarcosis (sis ȧr kō′ sis) [Gr. *sussarkōsis* (SYN-, *sarkoein*, from *sarx sarkos*, flesh)], *n.* The connexion of the parts of the skeleton by intervening muscle.

syssitia (si sit′ i ȧ) [Gr. *sussitia*, pl. of *sussition* (SYN-, *sitos*, food)], *n.pl.* (*Gr. Ant.*) The public meals for men and youths among the Spartans and other Dorians, held to promote simplicity and discipline and to inculcate patriotism.

systaltic (sis tăl′ tik) [late L. *systalticus*, Gr. *sustaltikos* (SYN-, *stellein*, to place)], *a.* Alternately contracting and dilating, pulsatory (of the heart).

***systasis** (sis′ tȧ sis) [Gr. *sustasis* (SYN-, *histanai*, see STASIS)], *n.* A political union or confederation.

systatic (sis tăt′ ik) [Gr. *sustatikos*, as prec.], *a.* Commendatory (of a letter, etc.); affecting several sensory faculties at the same time.

system (sis′ tėm) [L. *systēma*, Gr. *sustēma -matos* (SYN-, *stē-*, to set, from *sta-*, see STASIS)], *n.* Co-ordinated arrangement, organized combination, organization, method; a co-ordinated body of principles, facts, theories, doctrines, etc.; a logical grouping, a method or plan of classification; a co-ordinated arrangement or organized combination of things or parts, for working together, performing a particular function, etc.; any complex and co-ordinated whole; any organic structure taken as a whole, as the animal body, the universe, etc. **The System,** *n.* (*Austral. hist.*) The whole question of transportation, including the treatment of convicts. **system-maker, -monger,** *n.* One given to forming systems. **systematic, -*al** (-măt′ ik, -ăl), *a.* Methodical; done, formed, or arranged on a regular plan, not haphazard. **systematically,** *adv.* **systematics,** *n.pl.* Systematology. **systematist,** *n.* **systematize,** *v.t.* **systematization** (-zā′ shŭn), *n.* **systematizer,** *n.* **systemic** (si stem′ ik), *a.* Pertaining to the bodily system as a whole. **systemically,** *adv.* **systemless,** *a.* **systematology** (-tol′ ŏ ji) [-LOGY], *n.*

systole (sis′ tŏ lė) [Gr. *sustolē*, from *sustellein*, to draw together, see SYSTALTIC], *n.* (*Physiol.*) The contraction of the heart impelling the blood outwards, alternating with diastole. **systolic** (-tol′ ik), *a.*

systyle (sis′ tīl) [late L. *systylos*, Gr. *sustulos* (SYN-, STYLE (2))], *a.* With columns set only two diameters apart. **systylous** (sis′ ti lŭs), *a.* (*Bot.*) Having the styles united.

***syth, sythe** (1) [SITH].

***sythe** (2) [SCYTHE].

syzygy (siz′ i ji) [L. *syzygia*, Gr. *suzugia*, from *suzengnunai*, to yoke together (SYN-, *zugon*, yoke)], *n.* The conjunction or opposition of any two of the heavenly bodies, esp. of a planet with the sun; (*Biol. etc.*) conjunction or union. **syzygetic** (-jet′ ik), *a.* **syzygetically,** *adv.*

T

T, t, the twentieth letter and the sixteenth consonant (*pl.* **Ts, T's, Tees**), is a hard voiceless dental mute; followed by *h* it has two distinct sounds, surd or breathed, as in *think, thank, thought* (shown in this dictionary by 'th'), representing the A.-S. *þ*, and sonant or vocal, as in *this that, though* (shown here by '*th*'), representing the A.-S. *ð*. *n.* A T-shaped thing or part. *a.* T-shaped (*usu. in comb.*, as *T-bar, -piece, -square*, etc.). **to a T:** Exactly, to a nicety.

ta (ta) [etym. doubtful], *int.* (*Infantile*) Thank you.

Taal (tal) [Dut., language], *n.* S. African Dutch.

tab (tăb) [prob. rel. to TAPE], *n.* A small flap, tag, tongue, etc., as the flap of a shoe, the tag or tip of lace, etc. **to keep tab:** To keep a watch-out.

tabard (tăb′ ărd) [O.F., etym. doubtful], *n.* *A coarse outer garment worn by the poorer classes; an outer garment worn over armour; a herald's sleeveless coat blazoned with the arms of the sovereign. ***tabarder,** *n.*

tabaret (tăb′ ȧ rėt) [etym. doubtful], *n.* A fabric of alternate satin and watered-silk stripes used for upholstery.

tabasheer (tăb ȧ shēr′) [Hind. and Arab. *tabāshīr*], *n.* A hydrated opaline silica deposited in the joints of the bamboo, used in the E. Indies as a medicine.

tabbinet [TABINET].

tabby (tăb′ i) [F. *tabis*, Sp. *tabi*, Arab. '*utābī*], *n.* Silk or other stuff with a watered surface; a garment of this; a tabby-cat; a cat, esp. a female cat; (*fig.*) a gossipy old maid or old woman; a kind of concrete made with lime, shells, and gravel, or stones. *v.t.* To give a wavy or watered appearance to. *a.* Wavy, watered. **tabby-cat,** *n.* A grey or brownish cat with dark stripes.

tabefaction (tăb ė făk′ shŭn) [L. *tābefactio*, from *tābefacere* (*tābēre*, from TABES, *facere*, to make)], *n.* Wasting away from disease, emaciation. **tabefy** (tăb′ ė fī), *v.i.* and *t.*

tabellion (tȧ bel′ i ŏn) [F., from late L. *tabelliōnem*, nom. *-lio*, from *tabella*, dim. of *tabula*, TABLE], *n.* A notary or official scribe under the Roman empire and in France before 1761.

taberdar (tăb′ ėr dar) [var. of TABARDER], *n.* A scholar of Queen's College, Oxford.

tabernacle (tăb′ ėr năk ėl) [F., from L. *tabernāculum*, tent, dim. of *taberna*, hut], *n.* A tent, booth, or other building of light construction, and usu. movable, used as a habitation, temple, etc.; (*fig.*) the human body as the temporary abode of the soul; a tent-like structure used by the Jews as a sanctuary before settlement in Palestine; a nonconformist place of worship; an ornamental receptacle for the consecrated Elements or the pyx; (*Arch.*) a canopy, canopied stall or niche, a canopy-like structure over a tomb, etc.; (*Naut.*) a socket or hinged post for unstepping the mast on a river-boat. *v.i.* To dwell in or as in a tabernacle, to sojourn. *v.t.* To give shelter to. **Feast of Tabernacles:** An autumn feast of the Jews in memory of the sojourn in the wilderness. **tabernacle-work,** *n.* Carved canopies and tracery over a pulpit, stall, etc. **tabernacular,** *a.*

tabes (tā′ bēz) [L., cogn. with Gr. *tēkein*, to melt, and THAW], *n.* Wasting away, emaciation; a wasting disease. **tabescence** (tȧ bes′ ėns), *n.* **tabescent, tabetic** (tȧ bet′ ik), **tabic** (tăb′ ik), **tabid,** *a.* **tabidly,** *adv.* **tabidness, tabitude,** *n.*

tabinet (tăb′ i nėt) [prob. dim. of TABBY, said by French to be from M. *Tabinet*, French refugee who introduced the manufacture to Ireland], *n.* A watered fabric of silk and wool, used for window-curtains, etc.

tablature (tăb′ lȧ tyŭr, -chŭr) [F., from foll.], *n.* A painting on a wall or ceiling; a picture; (*fig.*) a vivid description, mental image, etc.; (*Mus.*) an old system of notation for instruments of the lute and violin class.

table (tā′ bėl) [O.F., from L. *tabula*, a board, a table], *n.* An article of furniture consisting of a flat surface resting on one or more supports, used for serving meals upon, working, writing, playing games, etc.; this used for meals; (*fig.*) the food served upon it, fare, cuisine; the company sitting at a table; a table or board adapted for a particular game (*usu. in comb.*, as *billiard-table*); either half of a backgammon-table; (*pl.*)* the game of backgammon; a part of a machine or machine-tool on which the work is put to be operated on; any apparatus consisting of a plane surface; a slab of wood or other material; such a slab with writing or an inscription; hence, the contents of such writing, etc.; a list of numbers, references, or other items arranged systematically, esp. in columns; a flat surface, a plateau; the flat face of a gem; (*Arch.*) a flat surface, usu. rectangular, a horizontal band of moulding. *v.t.* (*Parl.*) To lay (a Bill, etc.) on the table; to fit (timbers) together with alternate feathers and grooves to prevent separation or slipping; (*Naut.*) to strengthen (a sail) with wide hems. **at table:** Taking a meal. **to lay or lie on the table:** (*Parl.*) To defer or be deferred indefinitely. **to turn the tables:** To reverse the conditions or relations. **the twelve tables:** The Roman laws inscribed on 12 (orig. 10) tablets by the Decemvirs 451 B.C., the foundation of Roman jurisprudence. **table-beer,** *n.* Beer for drinking at meals. **table-book,** *n.* An ornamental book for keeping on a table. **table-cloth,** *n.* A cloth, usu. of white linen, for covering a table, esp. at mealtimes. **table-cover,** *n.* A cloth, usu. coloured, for covering a table at other times. **table-cut,** *a.* Cut with a flat face (of gems). **table d'hôte** (tabl dōt′) [F., host's table], *n.* (*pl.* **tables-**) A hotel or restaurant meal at fixed price, limited to certain dishes arranged by the proprietor. **table-knife,** *n.* A knife for use at meals. **table-land,** *n.* A plateau. **table-linen,** *n.* (*collect.*) Table-cloths, napkins, etc. **table-lifting, -moving, -rapping, -turning,** etc., *n.* Making a table rise, move, or turn over without apparent cause, as by spiritualistic agency. **table-money,** *n.* An allowance to general and flag officers for hospitality; a charge to members of clubs for use of the dining-room. **table-talk,** *n.* Talk at table or meals; familiar conversation, miscellaneous chat. **table-turning** [TABLE-LIFTING]. **table-ware,** *n.* Dishes, plates, knives, forks, etc., for use at meals. **tableful,** *n.* ***tabler,** *n.* **tabling,** *n.*

tableau (tăb′ lō) [F., dim. of prec.], *n.* (*pl.* **-eaux**) A picture; a striking or vivid representation or effect. **tableau vivant:** (*pl.* **tableaux vivants**) A motionless group of performers dressed and arranged to represent some scene or event.

tablespoon (tā′ bėl spoon), *n.* A large spoon four times the size of a teaspoon and holding a fluid oz. **tablespoonful,** *n.*

tablet (tăb′ lėt) [O.F. *tablete* (F. *tablette*), dim. of TABLE], *n.* A thin flat piece of wood, ivory, or other material for writing on; (*pl.*) a set of these; a small table or slab, esp. used as a memorial; a small flat piece or cake of medicinal or other substance. **tablette,** *n.* A flat, projecting coping-stone, on a wall, etc.

tablier (ta blyā) [F., from L. *tabulārium*, from *tabula*, TABLE], *n.* A small apron or apron-like part of a woman's dress.

tabling [TABLE].

tabloid (tăb′ loid), *n.* (*Med.*) Proprietary name for a compressed dose of a drug; (*Am.*) a popular newspaper; a cheap, sensational newspaper.

taboo (tȧ boo′) [Maori *tapu*], *n.* A custom among the Polynesians, etc., of prohibiting the use of certain persons, places or things; (*fig.*) ban, prohibition. *a.* Banned, interdicted, prohibited. *v.t.* To put under taboo; to forbid the use of or intercourse with.

***tabor** (tā′ bȯr) [O.F. *tabour* (F. *tambour*), Arab. *tambūr*, lute, drum], *n.* A small drum used to accompany the pipe. ***taborer,** *n.* ***taboret, *taborine,** *n.*

tabouret (tăb′ ȯ ret) [O.F., dim. of prec.], *n.* A small seat, usu. without arms or back; an embroidery frame; a needle-case.

tabular (tăb′ ū lȧr) [L. *tabula*], *a.* In the form of a table, having a broad flat surface; formed in laminæ or thin plates; set forth, arranged in, or computed from tables. ***tabularize,** *v.t.* **tabularly,** *adv.* **tabulate** (-lāt), *v.t.* To reduce to or arrange (figures, etc.) in tabular form; to shape with a flat surface. *a.* (-lȧt) Table-shaped, broad and flat; arranged in laminæ. **tabulation** (-lā′ shŭn), *n.* **tabulator** (tăb′ ū lā tȯr), *n.* An attachment to a typewriter to facilitate tabulation work.

tacamahac (tăk′ ȧ mȧ hăk) [native name], *n.* A resinous exudation from various S. American trees; the balsam poplar.

tac-au-tac (tăk ō tăk′) [F., imit.], *n.* (*Fencing*) The parry combined immediately with the riposte; a series of attacks and parries in swift succession.

tace (tā′ sē) [imper. L. *tacere*, to be silent], Be silent!

tache (tăsh) [O.F., as TACK], *n.* A freckle, a blotch on the skin; a spot, stain, or blemish; (*Bibl.*) a catch, a fastening.

tacheometer [TACHYMETER].

tachometer (tȧ kom′ ė tėr) [Gr. *tachos*, speed, -METER], *n.* An instrument for indicating the speed of rotation of a revolving shaft. **tachometry,** *n.*

tachygraphy (tȧ kig′ rȧ fi) [Gr. *tachus*, SWIFT, cp. prec., -GRAPHY], *n.* Shorthand, stenography, esp. one of the ancient Greek or Roman systems. **tachygrapher,** *n.* **tachygraphic, -al** (-grăf′ ik, -ȧl), *a.*

tachylyte (tăk′ i līt), *n.* (*Geol.*) A black, vitreous basalt. **tachylytic,** *a.*

tachymeter (tȧ kim′ ė tėr), *n.* A surveying-instrument for measuring distances rapidly. **tachymetry,** *n.*

tacit (tăs′ it) [L. *tacitus*, silent, from *tacēre*, to be silent], *a.* Implied but not expressed, understood, existing though not stated. **tacitly,** *adv.*

taciturn (tăs′ i tŭrn) [F. *taciturne*, from L. *taciturnus*, as prec.], *a.* Habitually silent, reserved. **taciturnity** (-tĕr′ ni ti), *n.* **taciturnly,** *adv.*

tack (tăk) [O.North.F. *taque* (O.F. *tache*), fastening, nail, peg. E.Fris. and Dan. *takke*, pointed thing (cp. L.G. *takk*, G. *zacke*, point, prong, Dut. *tak*, twig)], *n.* A small, sharp, flat-headed nail; a stitch, esp. one of a series of long, rapid stitches for fastening temporarily; (*Naut.*) a rope by which the forward lower corner of certain sails is fastened; the part of a sail to which such rope is fastened; the course of a ship as determined by the position of her sails; the act of tacking or changing direction to take advantage of a side-wind, etc.; (*fig.*) course of action, policy; stickiness, tackiness; (*Sc. Law*) a letting contract, a lease, land or pasturage leased; (*colloq.*) food, fare. *v.t.* To fasten with tacks; to stitch together in a hasty manner; to annex, to append (to or on to). *v.i.* To change the course of a ship by shifting the tacks and position of the sails; (*fig.*) to alter one's conduct or policy. **to come down to brass tacks:** To face realities, to state facts. **hard tack:** Ship's biscuit. **tacker,** *n.* One who tacks; one who makes additions. **tacket,** *n.* (*Sc.*) A clout-nail.

tacking (tăk′ ing), *n.* The act of one who tacks; (*Parl.*) attaching a clause with a different object to a Bill in order to enable this to pass the House of Lords; (*Law*) the right of a mortgagee to priority of a subsequent mortgage over an intermediate one of which he had no notice.

tackle (tăk′ ėl) [prob. from M.L.G. or Dut. *takel*, from M.L.G. *taken*, to TAKE, to lay hold of], *n.* Apparatus, esp. of ropes, pulleys, etc., for lifting, hoisting, etc., or for working spars, sails, etc.; a windlass or winch with its ropes, etc.; the implements, gear, or outfit for carrying on any particular work or sport. *v.t.* To grapple with; (*Football*) to seize hold of and stop, to collar; (*colloq.*) to set to work vigorously upon; to secure or make fast with tackle. **tackling,** *n.* (*collect.*) Tackle.

tacksman (tăks′ mȧn), *n.* (*Sc.*) One who holds a tack or lease of land from another.

tacky (tăk′ i), *a.* Sticky. **tackiness,** *n.*

tact (tăkt) [L. *tactus*, -*tūs*, touch, from *tactus*, p.p. of *tangere*, see TANGENT], *n.* An intuitive sense of what is fitting or right, or adroitness in doing or saying the proper thing; (*Mus.*) the stroke in beating time. **tactful,** *a.* **tactfully,** *adv.* **tactfulness,** *n.* **tactless,** *a.* **tactlessly,** *adv.* **tactlessness,** *n.*

tactics (tăk′ tiks) [Gr. *taktika*, neut. pl. of *taktikos*, from *taktos*, ordered, from *tassein*, to arrange], *n.* (*sing. or pl.*) The art of manœuvring military or naval forces, esp. in actual contact with the enemy; (*pl.*) procedure or devices to attain some end. **tactical,** *a.* **tactically,** *adv.* **tactician** (-tish′ ȧn), *n.*

tactile (tăk′ til, -tīl) [F., from L. *tactilis* (TACT, -ILE)], *a.* Of, pertaining to, or perceived by the sense of touch. **tactility** (-til′ i ti), *n.* ***taction,** *n.* **tactual,** *a.* **tactually,** *adv.*

tadpole (tăd′ pōl) [M.E. *tadpolle* (TOAD, POLL, head)], *n.* The larva of an amphibian, esp. of a frog or toad, before the gills and tail disappear.

tael (tāl) [Malay *tahil*], *n.* A Chinese weight of 1½ oz., and a silver monetary unit, value about 5s. 10d. **Haikwan** or **Customs tael:** A Chinese silver coin, value about 3s. 0⅜d.

ta'en, *contr.* [TAKEN].

tænia (tē′ ni ȧ) [L., from Gr. *tainia*, from *teinein*, to stretch], *n.* (*Arch.*) A band or fillet separating the Doric frieze from the architrave; (*Anat.*) a band or ribbon-like part; (*Zool.*) a genus of internal parasites containing the tapeworm. **tænioid,** *a.*

tafferel (tăf′ ėr ėl) [Dut. *tafereel*, dim. of *tafel*, from L. as TABLE], *n.* (*Naut.*) The upper part of a ship's stern.

taffeta (tăf' ė tȧ) [F. *taffetas*, It. *taffetà*, Pers. *tāftah*, from *tāftan*, to twist], *n.* A light, thin, glossy silk fabric; applied also to silk and linen or silk and wool fabrics.

taffrail (tăf' rāl, -rȧl) [corr. of TAFFEREL], *n.* The rail round a ship's stern.

Taffy (1) (tăf' i) [Welsh pron. of *Davy*, short for *David*], *n.* (*colloq.*) A Welshman.

taffy (2) [TOFFEE].

tafia (tăf' i ȧ) [native name], *n.* A variety of rum distilled from molasses.

tag (tăg) [cp. Swed. *tagg*, prickle, Norw. *tagge*, tooth, also TACK], *n.* Any small appendage, as a metal point at the end of a lace; a loop for pulling a boot on; a label, esp. one tied on; a loose or ragged end or edge; a loose tuft of wool on a sheep; the tail or tip of the tail of an animal; anything tacked on at the end; the refrain of a song, the closing speech in a play addressed to the audience; a well-worn phrase or quotation; a children's game in which the players try to escape being touched by one. *v.t.* (*past & p.p.* **tagged**) To fit, furnish, or mark with a tag; to furnish with tags or trite phrases; to attach (to, on to, or together); to touch in the game of tag; (*colloq.*) to follow closely or persistently (after). **tag-rag** [RAGTAG, see RAG (1)]. **tagtail**, *n.* A worm with a coloured tail; a hanger-on, a sycophant. **tagger**, *n.* One who tags, esp. the pursuer in the game of tag; (*pl.*) thin tin-plate or sheet iron.

Tagetes (tȧ jē' tēz) [mod. L., from L. *Tages*, Etruscan divinity], *n.* A genus of showy American plants of the aster family comprising the French and African marigolds.

tahona (tȧ hō' nȧ) [Sp.], *n.* (*Am.*) A grinding-mill for silver-ore, worked by means of a horse or mule.

Taic [THAI].

taigle (tā' gėl, teg' ėl) [prob. from Scand., cp. Swed. dial. *taggla*, to disarrange], *v.t.* (*Sc.*) To hinder, to delay; to embarrass, to entangle. *v.i.* To delay, to linger, to tarry, to dawdle.

taiaha (tī a' ha) [Maori], *n.* A chieftain's walking-stick, a wand of office.

taihoa (tī hō' ȧ) [Maori], *n.* A phrase meaning 'Wait!'

tail (1) (tāl) [A.-S. *tægl*, *tægel*, cp. Icel. *tagl*, Swed. *tagel*, G. *zegel*], *n.* The hindmost part of an animal, esp. when it extends beyond the rest of the body; anything resembling this in shape or position, as a prolongation of the body of or a pendant or appendage to anything, the slender end or luminous train of a comet, the stem of a note in music, the skirt of a coat (*usu. in pl.*); (*Aviat.*) the horizontal unit at the rear of an aeroplane; the hind or lower or inferior part of anything, as the exposed end (of a tile or slate in a roof), the unexposed end (of a brick or tile in a wall), the lower end of a stream or pool; a retinue, a suite, a queue; (*Turkey*) a horse-tail formerly carried before a pasha. *v.t.* To furnish with a tail; (*colloq.*) to remove the tails or ends from; to join (on to another thing); to insert one end of (a timber, etc.) into a wall, etc.; (*colloq.*) to fasten something to the tail of a dog, etc. *v.i.* To follow closely (after); (*Austral.*) to herd sheep or cattle; to fall behind or drop (away or off) in a scattered line; to swing (up and down stream) with the tide (of a vessel). **to tail away, off:** To dwindle. **tail of the trenches:** The part where the advancing party begins to break ground. **to turn tail:** To turn one's back; to run away. **tail-board**, *n.* The hinged or sliding board at the back of a cart, wagon, etc. **tail-coat**, *n.* A coat with tails or the skirt divided at the back, a morning or evening coat. **tail-end**, *n.* The fag-end. **tail-gate**, *n.* The lower gate of a canal-lock. **tail-light**, *n.* (*Motor.*) A red warning light at the rear of a motor-car. **tail-piece**, *n.* An ornamental design at the end of a chapter or section of a book; a triangular block in a violin, etc., to which the strings are attached. **tail-pipe**, *n.* The suction-pipe in a pump. **tailplane**, *n.* (*Aviat.*) The fixed horizontal portion of the tail of an aeroplane. **tail-race**, *n.* The part of a mill-race below a water-wheel. **tail-skid**, *n.* (*Aviat.*) A device to take the weight at the rear end of an aeroplane's fuselage while taxi-ing. **tail-spin**, *n.* (*Aviat.*) A vertical, nose-foremost dive by an aeroplane, during which it describes a spiral. **tailed**, *a.* (*usu. in comb.*, as *long-tailed*) **tailing**, *n.* The action of one that tails; the part of a stone or brick inserted into a wall; (*pl.*) the refuse part of ore, grain, etc. **tail-less**, *a.*

tail (2) (tāl) [F. *taille*, as TALLY], *n.* Limitation of ownership, limited ownership; an estate of inheritance limited to a person and the heirs of his body. **tailage** [TALLAGE].

tailed, tailless [TAIL (1)].

tailor (tā' lōr) [O.F. *tailleor*, *taillour*, from *tailler*, to cut, see TAIL (2)], *n.* One whose occupation is to cut out and make men's clothes. *v.i.* To work as a tailor. *v.t.* To make clothes for (*usu. in p.p.*, as *well-tailored*); (*slang*) to kill (a bird, etc.) in a bungling fashion. **tailor-bird**, *n.* An oriental bird that sews together leaves to form its nest. **tailor-made**, *a.* Made by a tailor, well cut and close-fitting (of women's outer clothes). **tailoress**, *n.* **tailoring**, *n.* **tailorize**, *v.t.*

tailye, tailzie (*Sc.*) [TAIL (2)].

tain (tān) [F., tinfoil, from *étain*, tin], *n.* Tin-foil for backing mirrors.

taint (tānt) [F. *teint*, p.p. of *teindre*, L. *tingere*, to tinge, perh. conf. with ATTAINT], *n.* A trace of decay, unsoundness, disease, etc.; a corrupting influence, infection; a stain, a blemish, a disgrace. *v.t.* To imbue or infect with a noxious, poisonous, or corrupting element; to sully, to tarnish. *v.i.* To be infected or affected with incipient putrefaction. **taintless**, *a.* **taintlessly**, *adv.* ***tainture**, *n.*

taipo (tī' pō) [Maori], *n.* A devil, an evil spirit; a surveyor's instrument, a theodolite.

taisch (tāsh) [Gael. *taibhs*, cp. O.Ir. *taidbse*, phantasm], *n.* (*Folklore*) The premonitory sound of the voice of a person about to die heard at a distance; a wraith, a vision of second-sight.

tait (tāt) [Austral. abor.], *n.* A long-snouted phalanger, *Tarsipes*, of Western Australia.

taj (taj) [Pers.], *n.* A crown, a head-dress of distinction, esp. a tall cap worn by Mohammedan dervishes.

takahe (ta ka' hē) [Maori], *n.* The notornis.

takapu (ta ka' poo) [Maori], *n.* The N. Zealand gannet.

take (tāk) [late A.-S. *tacan*, Icel. *taka*, cogn. with TACK], *v.t.* (*past* **took**, tuk, p.p. **taken**) To lay hold of, to grasp, seize, capture, catch, arrest, gain possession of, win, captivate, transport, charm, etc.; to carry off, to remove, carry away, carry with one, convey, conduct, extract, exact, withdraw, extort, etc.; to receive, obtain, procure, acquire, consume, appropriate, to assume; to accept, hold, adopt, select, receive and retain, submit to, put up with; to ascertain by inquiry, weighing, measuring, etc.; to understand, apprehend, grasp, suppose, consider, infer, conclude, interpret; to be infected with, to contract, to be affected with, to feel, to experience; to bear in a specified way, to regard (as); to perform (an action, etc.); to undertake the duties of; to photograph. *v.i.* To deduct something from, to derogate, to detract; to have a desired effect, to work, to operate; to come out well (in a photograph); to please, to be popular (with); to be attracted or inclined (to); to betake oneself (to); to be attracted by a bait. *n.* The act of taking; that which is taken; the amount (of fish, etc.) taken at one catch or in one season; takings; (*Print.*) the amount of copy taken at one time; (*Cinema.*) a scene that has been filmed. **take-in**, *n.* A deception, a fraud, an imposition. **take-off**, *n.* Caricature; the spot from which one's feet leave the ground in leaping; (*Croquet*) a stroke by which a player sends his own ball forward and touches another ball without shifting it; (*Aviat.*) the rising of an aircraft into the air. **to take a back seat** [BACK (1)]. **to take account of:** To pay attention to, to consider. **to take advantage of:** To make use of circumstances to the prejudice of; to use to advantage. **to take after:** To resemble, physically, mentally, etc. **to take aim:** To direct a missile, etc. **to take back:** To withdraw, to retract. **to take care:** To be careful, cautious, or vigilant. **to take care of:** To look after, to provide for. **to take down:** To write down; to swallow, to gulp down; to take apart, to pull to pieces; to humiliate, to humble. **to take effect** [EFFECT]. **to take fire:** To ignite; (*fig.*) to become excited. **to take for:** To mistake for. **to take from:** To deduct from; to diminish, to lessen, to derogate. **to take heed** [HEED]. **to take hold of:** To seize. **to take in:** To admit, to receive; to undertake, to do (washing, typewriting, etc.); to include, to comprise; to contract, to furl (sails); to understand, to receive into the mind, to accept as true; to deceive, to cheat. **to take in hand** [HAND]. **to take into one's head:** To seize the idea or belief (that), to resolve (to). **to take it:** To accept misfortune or punishment. **to take it out of:** (*colloq.*) To get revenge, compensation, or satisfaction from; to exhaust the strength or freshness of. **to take leave** [LEAVE (1)]. **to take oath:** To swear (that). **to take off:** To remove; to carry away; to deduct (from); to drink off, to swallow; to mimic, to ridicule; to jump (from); (*Aviat.*) to begin flight. **to take on:** To engage (workmen, etc.); to undertake (work, etc.); (*colloq.*) to be violently affected, to be upset. **to take one up on:** To accept a person's challenge. **to take out:** To remove (a stain, etc.); to bring, lead, or convey out; to obtain for oneself, to procure; to copy. **to take over:** To assume the management, ownership, etc., of. **take-over bid:** (*Fin.*) An offer to purchase enough shares to obtain control of a company. **to take place:** To happen, to occur. **to take root:** To strike root. **to take the air** [AIR]. **to take the field** [FIELD]. **to take to:** To resort to; to form a habit or liking for. **to take to heart** [HEART]. **to take up:** To lift (up); to receive into a vehicle; to enter upon, to begin; to pursue; to occupy, to engage, to engross; to arrest, to take into custody; to accept; to pick up and secure; to take possession of; to criticize. **to take upon:** To assume. **to take up with:** To associate with. **taker,** *n.* One who takes, esp. one who accepts a bet. **taking,** *a.* That takes; pleasing, alluring, attractive; infectious. *n.* The act of one that takes; capture, arrest; a state of agitation; (*pl.*) money taken; receipts. **takingly,** *adv.* **takingness,** *n.*

takhaar (tak' har), *n.* [S. Afr.] A man from the wilds, an uncouth fellow.

takin (tā' kin) [native name], *n.* A hollow-horned, goat-like antelope inhabiting the Mishmi Hills of S.E. Tibet.

talapoin (tăl' ȧ poin), *n.* A Buddhist priest or monk in Siam, Burma, Ceylon, etc.; an African monkey, *Cercopithecus talapoin.*

talaria (tȧ lâr' i ȧ) [L., pl. of *tālāris*, from TALUS], *n.pl.* (*Ant.*) The winged boots or sandals of Hermes, Iris, etc.

talbot (tawl' bȯt) [prob. from the surname], *n.* A large variety of hound, usu. white with large pendulous ears and massive jaws, formerly used for tracking and hunting.

talbotype (tawl' bȯ tīp) [W. H. Fox *Talbot* (1800–1877), scientist], *n.* A process invented by Fox Talbot in 1840 of producing a latent image upon sensitized paper, the basis of the photographic process.

talc (tălk) [F., from Arab. *talq*], *n.* (*Min.*) A fibrous, greasy magnesium silicate occurring in prisms and plates, used as a lubricator etc.; (*colloq.*) mica. **talcite** (tăl' kīt), *n.* A massive variety of talc. **talcky, talcoid, -ose, -ous,** *a.* **talcum powder,** *n.* (*Med.*) Powdered magnesium silicate.

tale (tăl) [A.-S. *tæl*, number, *talu*, story (cp. TAAL, Icel. *tal*, story, *tala*, number), cogn. with TELL], *n.* A narrative, an account, a story, true or fictitious, esp. an imaginative or legendary story; an idle or malicious report; *a number, a total, a reckoning. **talebearer,** *n.* One who spreads malicious reports. **tale-bearing,** *n.* **tale-teller,** *n.* ***taleful,** *a.*

Talegalla (tăl ė găl' ȧ) [F. *talégalle*, Malagasy *talèva*, L. *gallus*, cock], *n.* (*Ornith.*) A genus of birds comprising the brush-turkey and allied megapods of Australia and New Guinea; a bird of this genus, esp. the brush-turkey.

talent (tăl' ėnt) [F., from L. *talentum*, Gr. *talanton*, balance, a talent, cogn. with *talas -ntos*, enduring, cp. L. *tollere*, to lift], *n.* A weight and denomination of money in ancient Greece, Rome, Assyria, etc. differing in various countries at different times (the later Attic talent was 56 lb. 14 oz. troy, and was worth from £200 to £250); a particular aptitude, gift, or faculty; mental capacity of a superior order; persons of talent. **talented,** *a.* Endowed with talents or ability. **talentless,** *a.*

tales (tā' lēz) [L., pl. of *tālis*, such (first word of writ)], *n.* (*Law*) A writ for summoning jurors to make up a deficiency; a list of such as may be thus summoned. **to pray a tales:** To pray that the number of jurymen may be completed. **talesman** (tālz'-, tā' lēz mȧn), *n.* A person thus summoned.

taliacotian (tăl i ȧ kō' shȧn), *a.* Pertaining to the Italian anatomist Tagliacozzi (*d.* 1599). **taliacotian operation:** The operation of forming a new nose by taking a graft from the arm or forehead, dissevered only after union has taken place.

talion (tăl' i ȯn) [F., from L. *tāliōnem*, nom. *-lio*, from *tālis*, see TALES], *n.* The law of retaliation. **talionic** (-on' ik), *a.*

taliped (tăl' i ped) [TAL-US, L. *pes pedis*, foot], *a.* Club-footed; (*Zool.*) having the feet twisted into a peculiar position (of the sloth). **talipes** (-pēz), *n.* Club-foot; the sloth-like formation of the feet.

talipot (tăl' i pot) [Hind. *tālpāt*], *n.* An E. Indian fan-palm.

talisman (tăl' is-, -iz mȧn) [F. and Sp., from It. *talismano*, Arab. *tilsam*, Gr. *telesma*, payment, late Gr. mystery, from *teleein*, to accomplish, to pay, from *telos*, end], *n.* A charm, an amulet, a magical figure, cut or engraved under superstitious observance of the heavens, to which wonderful effects were ascribed; (*fig.*) something producing wonderful effects. **talismanic** (-măn' ik), *a.*

talk (tawk) [M.E. *talken*, freq. of A.-S. *tal-*, see TALE], *v.i.* To speak; to utter words; to converse, to communicate ideas or exchange thoughts in spoken words; to have the power of speech; to make sounds as in speech. *v.t.* To express in speech; to converse about, to discuss; to speak, to use (a specified language); to persuade or otherwise affect by talking. *n.* Conversation, chat; a subject of conversation; gossip, rumour. **to talk at:** To talk, esp. offensively, about (a person) in his presence. **to talk away:** To spend or use up (time) in talking. **to talk big:** To boast. **tall talk,** *n.* (*colloq.*) Exaggeration. **talk-down,** *n.* (*Aviat.*) A method of guiding an aircraft in to land by transmitting navigational instructions from a radar station by the runway. **to talk down:** To silence by loud or persistent talking. **to talk of:** To discuss; to mention; (*colloq.*) to suggest. **to talk out:** (*Pol.*) To kill a motion by discussing it until the time of adjournment. **to talk over:** To discuss at length; to persuade or convince by talking. **to talk to:** To speak to; (*colloq.*) to remonstrate with, to reprove. **talkative,** *a.* Given to talking. **talkatively,** *adv.* **talkativeness,** *n.* **talkee-talkee** (taw' ki taw' ki), *n.* A barbarous lingo, esp. the broken English of negroes, etc. **talker,** *n.* **talking,** *a.* That talks; able to talk. **talking film, talkie,** *n.* (*Cinema.*) A sound film. **talking point:** A matter to be talked about.

tall (tawl) [prob. of Celtic orig., cp. W. and Corn. *tal*; obs. *tall*, serviceable, valiant, is from A.-S. *getæl*, swift, prompt, cp. O.H.G. *gizal*, quick], *a.*

High in stature, above the average height; having a specified height; (*slang*) extravagant, boastful, exorbitant, excessive. **tall order:** An exacting, or unreasonable, demand. **tallness,** *n.*

tallage, talliage (tăl′ ȧj, -i ȧj) [O.F. *taillage*, from *tailler*, to cut, see TAIL (2)], *n.* (*Eng. Hist.*) A tax levied by the king (abolished 1340).

tallat, tallet (tăl′ ȧt) [W. *taflawd*, *taflod*, med. L. *tabulāta*, orig. fem. p.p. of *tabulāre*, to board, to floor, from L. *tabula*, TABLE], *n.* A hay-loft.

tallboy (tawl′ boi), *n.* A high chest of drawers, often on legs.

talliage [TALLAGE]. **tallier** [TALLY].

tallith (tăl′ ith) [Heb.], *n.* A scarf worn by Jews during prayer.

tallow (tăl′ ō) [M.E. *talgh*, cp. M.Dut. *talgh*, Dut. *talk*, L.G., Dan., and Swed. *talg*, Icel. *tōlgr*], *n.* A substance composed of the harder or less fusible fats, chiefly of animals, esp. beef- or mutton-fat, used for making candles, soap, etc. *v.t.* To grease or smear with tallow; to fatten, to cause to have a large quantity of tallow. **tallow-candle,** *n.* **tallow-chandler** [CHANDLER], *n.* One who makes or deals in tallow-candles. **tallow-face,** *n.* A person with a pale complexion. **tallow-faced,** *a.* **tallow-tree,** *n.* One of various trees yielding vegetable tallow. **tallower,** *n.* **tallowish, tallowy,** *a.*

tally (tăl′ i) [F. *taille*, notch, incision, as TAIL (2)], *n.* A stick in which notches are cut as a means of keeping accounts; such a notch or mark, a score; a reckoning, an account; anything made to correspond with something else, a counterpart, a duplicate (of); a mark registering number (of things received, delivered, etc.); such a number used as a unit of reckoning; a label or tag for identification. *v.t.* To score as on a tally, to record, to register; (*Naut.*) to put (a sheet, etc.) aft. *v.i.* To agree, to correspond (with). **tallier, tallyman,** *n.* One who keeps a tally; one who keeps a tally-shop. **tally-shop,** *n.* A shop at which goods are sold on the tally system. **tally system:** The system of giving and receiving goods on credit, to be paid for by regular instalments.

tally-ho (tăl′ i hō′) [prob. from F. *taïaut*], *int.* and *n.* The huntsman's cry to hounds. *v.i.* To utter this cry. *v.t.* To urge on (hounds) thus.

talma (tăl′ mȧ) [F. J. *Talma* (1763–1826), F. tragedian], *n.* A long cape or cloak, worn by men or women early in the 19th cent.

talmi-gold (tăl′ mi gōld) [G., orig. a trade-name], *n.* A brass alloy, sometimes plated, used to imitate gold in cheap jewellery.

Talmud (tăl′ mụd) [late Heb. from *lāmad*, to teach], *n.* The body of Jewish civil and religious law not comprised in the Pentateuch, including the Mishna and the Gemara. **Talmudic, -al** (-mŭd′ ik, -mū′ dik, -ȧl), *a.* **Talmudist** (tăl′ mụ dist), *n.* **Talmudistic** (-dis′ tik), *a.*

talon (tăl′ ȯn) [F., heel, late L. *tālōnem*, nom. *tālo*, L. TALUS], *n.* A claw, esp. of a bird of prey; the projection on a lock-bolt against which the key presses; the heel of a sword-blade; the cards left in the pack after dealing; (*Arch.*) an ogee moulding. **taloned,** *a.*

talpa (tăl′ pȧ) [L., mole], *n.* (*Path.*) An encysted tumour, a wen; (*Zool.*) the genus of insectivorous animals typified by the common mole.

talus (tā′ lụs) [L., ankle, heel], *n.* (*Anat.*) The ankle bone; (*Path.*) talipes; the slope or inclination of a wall, etc., tapering towards the top; (*Geol.*) a mass or sloping heap of fragments accumulated at the base of a cliff.

tamable (tā′ mȧbl), *a.* Capable of being tamed. **tamability** (-bil′ i ti), **tamableness,** *n.*

tamale (tam a′ le) [Sp. *tamal*], *n.* A Mexican dish of maize and meat highly seasoned.

tamandua (tȧ măn′ dū ȧ), **tamanoir** (tam a nwar′) [Tupi-Guarani *tamandua*, whence F. *tamanoir*], *n.* A genus or subgenus of tropical American ant-eaters.

tamanu (ta′ mȧ noo) [Tahitian], *n.* A large E. Indian and Polynesian tree, *Calophyllum inophyllum*, yielding tacamahac.

tamara (tăm′ ȧ rȧ) [E. Ind.], *n.* A condiment used largely in Italy, consisting of powdered cinnamon, cloves, coriander, aniseed, and fennel-seeds.

tamarack (tăm′ ȧ răk) [N.Am.Ind.], *n.* The American or black larch; a N. American pine, *Pinus Murrayana.*

tamarin (tăm′ ȧ rin) [native name], *n.* A S. American marmoset, esp. *Midas rosalia.*

tamarind (tăm′ ȧ rind) [M.F., from Sp. *tamarindo*, Arab. *tamr*, ripe date, *Hind*, India], *n.* A tropical tree, *Tamarindus Indica*; its pulpy leguminous fruit, used in making cooling beverages and as a laxative.

tamarisk (tăm′ ȧ risk) [L. *tamariscus*], *n.* An evergreen shrub of the genus *Tamarix*, with slender feathery branches and white and pink flowers.

tamasha (tȧ ma′ shȧ), *n.* (*colloq.*) A show, a public function.

Tambaroora, Tambaroora muster, *n.* (*Austral.*) An old game in Queensland, etc., to decide who shall pay for drinks.

tambour (tăm′ bȯr) [F., see TABOR], *n.* A drum, esp. a bass drum; a circular frame on which silk, etc., is embroidered; silk or other stuff embroidered thus; (*Arch.*) a cylindrical stone, as one of the courses of the shaft of a column, a drum; a ceiled vestibule in a porch, etc., for preventing draughts; (*Fort.*) a palisade defending an entrance. *v.t.* and *i.* To embroider with or on a tambour.

tambourine (tăm bȯ rēn′) [F., dim. of prec.], *n.* A small drum-like instrument composed of a hoop with parchment stretched across one head and loose jingles in the sides, played by striking with the hand, etc.; a Provençal tabor or drum; a dance accompanied by this and the pipe; the music for such a dance.

tame (tām) [A.-S. *tam*, whence *temian*, v. (cp. Dut. *tam*, G. *zahm*, Dan. and Swed. *tam*, also L. *domāre*, Gr. *damaein*, to tame)], *a.* Having lost its native wildness; domesticated, not wild; tractable, docile; subdued, spiritless; dull, insipid; (*colloq.*) cultivated, produced by cultivation. *v.t.* To make tame; to domesticate, to make docile; to subdue, to humble. **tameless,** *a.* **tamely,** *adv.* **tameness,** *n.* **tamer,** *n.*

Tamil (tăm′ il) [native name], *n.* A Dravidian language spoken in S. India and Ceylon.

tamis (tăm′ is) [F.], *n.* A sieve or strainer of cloth.

tamma (tam′ a) [Austral. abor.], *n.* A variety of wallaby.

Tammany tăm′ ȧ ni) [*Tammany* Hall, meeting-place, named after Indian chief *Tamanend*], *n.* A political organization in New York affiliated to the Democratic party, also called *Tammany Hall* or *Tammany Society*; (*fig.*) political corruption. **Tammanyism,** *n.*

tam-o'-shanter (tăm ȯ shăn′ tėr) [Burns's poem *Tam o' Shanter*], *n.* A cap fitted closely round the brows but wide and full above.

tamp (tămp) [etym. doubtful], *v.t.* To fill up (a blast-hole) with rammed clay above the charge; to ram down (railway ballast, road-metal, etc.). **tamping,** *n.*

tampan (tăm′ pȧn) [native name], *n.* A S. African tick with venomous bite.

tamper (tăm′ pėr) [var. of TEMPER], *v.i.* To meddle (with); to interfere illegitimately, esp. to alter documents, etc., to adulterate, or employ bribery. **tamperer,** *n.*

tampion (tăm′ pi ȯn) [var. of TAMPOON], *n.* A stopper for the mouth of a gun; a stopper for the top of an organ-pipe.

tampon (tăm′ pȯn) [O.F., also *tapon*, from *tampe*, *tape*, Dut. *tap*, bung], *n.* A plug of lint, etc., used for stopping hæmorrhage. *v.t.* To plug with this.

tam-tam [TOM-TOM].

tan (1) (tăn) [F. *tan* (whence *tanner*, to tan), G. *tanne*, fir-tree, O.H.G. *tanna*, fir, oak], *n.* The bark of the oak or other trees, bruised and broken in a mill and used for tanning hides; the colour of this, yellowish brown; bronzing of the complexion. *a.* Tan-coloured. *v.t.* (*past & p.p.* **tanned**) To convert (raw hide) into leather by steeping in an infusion of tannin or by the action of some mineral or chemical salt; to make brown by exposure to the sun; to subject (nets, sails, artificial marble, etc.) to a hardening process; (*colloq.*) to flog, to thrash. *v.i.* To become sunburned. **tan-balls,** *n.pl.* Spent tan compressed into balls for fuel. **tan-bed,** *n.* (*Hort.*) A bed made of tan. **tan-liquor, -ooze, *-pickle,** *n.* An infusion used in tanning. **tan-stove,** *n.* A hot-house with a bark-bed. **tan-yard,** *n.* A tannery. **tannable,** *a.* **tannage,** *n.* **tanner** (1), *n.* **tannery,** *n.* **tanning,** *n.*

tan (2) [abbrev. for TANGENT].

tanager (tăn′ ȧ jėr) [Tupi-Guarani *tangara*], *n.* An American bird of the family *Tanagridæ*, related to the finches, usu. with brilliant plumage. **tanagrine, tanagroid,** *a.*

tandem (tăn′ dėm) [L., at length], *adv.* With two horses harnessed one behind the other; (harnessed) one behind the other. *n.* A vehicle with two horses so harnessed; a cycle for two riders one behind the other. *a.* Harnessed or arranged thus.

tanekaha (ta nē ka′ ha) [Maori], *n.* A N. Zealand pine with straight-grained wood.

tang (1) (tăng) [M.E., sting, cogn. with foll.], *n.* A strong taste or flavour, a twang; a distinctive quality. **tangy** (tăng′ i), *a.*

tang (2) (tăng) [Icel. *tangi*, cogn. with TONGS], *n.* A projecting piece, tongue, etc., as the shank of a knife, chisel, etc., inserted into the haft. *v.t.* To furnish with a tang.

tang (3) (tăng) [imit.], *v.t.* To make a ringing, twanging noise. *v.t.* To cause to sound thus; to bring (bees) together by clanging pieces of metal together. *n.* A ringing or twanging noise.

tang (4) (tăng) [see TANGLE], *n.* One of various seaweeds.

tangent (tăn′ jėnt) [L. *tangens -ntem*, pres.p. of *tangere*, to touch], *a.* Meeting at a single point without intersecting it (even if produced). *n.* A straight line meeting a circle or curve without intersecting it (even if produced). **tangent of an angle:** (*Trig.*) The ratio of the perpendicular subtending the angle in a right-angled triangle to the base. **to go** or **fly off at a tangent:** To diverge suddenly from a course of thought or action. **tangency,** *n.* **tangential** (-jėn′ shȧl), *a.* **tangentially,** *adv.*

Tangerine (tăn jėr ēn′), *a.* Of or pertaining to Tangiers. *n.* A native of Tangiers; a small, red-skinned orange from Tangiers.

tanghin (tăng′ gin) [F., from Malagasy *tangena*], *n.* A Madagascan tree, *Tanghinia venenifera*, the fruit of which has a poisonous kernel, formerly used in trial by ordeal; this poison.

tangible (tăn′ ji bėl) [F., from late L. *tangibilis*, from *tangere*, to touch], *a.* Perceptible by touch; definite, capable of realization, not visionary; (*Law*) corporeal. **tangibility** (-bil′ i ti), **tangibleness,** *n.* **tangibly,** *adv.*

tangle (tăng′ gėl) [conn. with Dan. *tang*, cp. Swed. *täng*, Icel. *thang*, dim. *thōngull*, seaweed], *v.t.* To knot together or intertwine in a confused mass; to entangle, to ensnare, to entrap; to complicate. *v.i.* To become thus knotted together or intertwined. *n.* A confused mass of threads, etc., intertwined; (*fig.*) a state of confusion; a device for dredging up delicate forms of marine life; various kinds of seaweed. **tangle-foot,** *n.* (*Am. slang*) Intoxicant, bad whisky. **tanglesome, tangly,** *a.* **tanglingly,** *adv.*

tango (tăng′ gō) [Am. Sp.], *n.* A dance of a complicated kind for couples, a development of the chica.

tangram (tăng′ grȧm) [etym. doubtful], *n.* A Chinese puzzle consisting of a square cut into several differently shaped pieces which have to be fitted together.

tangy [TANG (1)].

tanist (tăn′ ist) [Ir. *tanaiste*, heir to a prince, from *tan*, territory], *n.* (*Anc. Ir.*) The elected heir presumptive to a chief. **tanistry,** *n.* An ancient Irish tenure of lands and chieftainship, successors being appointed by election from the chief's kin.

tanjib (tăn′ jib) [Hind.], *n.* A kind of figured muslin made in Oudh.

tank (tăngk) [Port. *tanque* (cp. Sp. *estanque*), from late L. as STANCH (1)], *n.* A cistern or vessel of large size for holding liquid, gas, etc.; a reservoir for water; an excavation in which water collects; the part of a locomotive-tender containing the supply of water for the boiler; (*Mil.*) a heavily-armoured motor vehicle running on caterpillar tractors and carrying guns of various calibres. **tank-car, -ship, -steamer, -vessel,** *n.* One carrying a tank or tanks, one for carrying oil, etc. **tank-engine,** *n.* A locomotive with a water-tank over the boiler, and without a tender. **tankage,** *n.* Storage in tanks; a charge for this; the cubic capacity of a tank or tanks; the residuum from rendering refuse fats, etc., used as a fertilizer.

tanka (tăng′ kȧ) [Chin. *tan*, egg (prob. name of tribe), Cantonese *ka*, people], *n.* (*collect.*) The descendants of an aboriginal tribe now living in boats or by the waterside at Canton. **tanka-boat,** *n.*

tankard (tăng′ kȧrd) [F. *tanquard*, M.Dut. *tanckaert*], *n.* A large drinking-vessel, usu. of metal and often with a cover.

tanker (tăng′ ker), *n.* (*Naut.*) A specially-built steamer or motor vessel fitted with tanks for carrying a cargo of oil; (*Aviat.*) an aircraft for refuelling other aircraft in the air.

tannable, etc. [TAN (1)]. **tannate** [TANNIC].

tanner (1) [TAN (1)].

tanner (2) (tăn′ ėr) [etym. doubtful], *n.* (*slang*) Sixpence.

tannic (tăn′ ik) [TAN, -IC], *a.* Pertaining to or derived from tan. **tannate,** *n.* (*Chem.*). **tanniferous** (tȧ nif′ ėr ŭs), *a.*

tannin (tăn′ in), *n.* Tannic acid, an astringent substance obtained from oak-bark, etc., used in tanning leather, making writing-ink, etc., and in medicine.

tanrec, tenrec (tăn′-, ten′ rėk) [F. *tanrec*, Malagasy *tàndraka*], *n.* A small insectivorous mammal, *Centetes ecaudatus*, from Madagascar, allied to the hedgehog.

tansy (tăn′ zi) [O.F. *tanasie*, *athanasie*, L. and Gr. *athanasia*, immortality, see ATHANASY], *n.* A yellow-flowered perennial herb, *Tanacetum vulgare*, with much-divided, bitter, aromatic leaves.

tantalize (tăn′ tȧ līz) [TANTALUS], *v.t.* To tease or torment by holding out some desirable object and continually disappointing by keeping it out of reach. **tantalism, tantalization** (-zā′ shŭn), *n.* **tantalizer,** *n.* **tantalizingly,** *adv.*

tantalum (tăn′ tȧ lŭm) [from foll.], *n.* A rare, silvery-white metallic element, used with other refractory metals for filaments in electric lamps.

Tantalus (tăn′ tȧ lŭs) [L., from Gr. *Tantalos*], *n.* (*Gr. Myth.*) A son of Zeus, condemned to stand up to his chin in water, which perpetually shrank away when he attempted to quench his thirst; (*Zool.*) a genus of wading-birds allied to the ibis; a spirit-stand in which the decanters remain in sight but are secured by a lock. **tantalus-cup,** *n.* A scientific toy consisting of a figure of a man in a cup, illustrating the principle of the siphon.

tantamount (tăn′ tȧ mount) [A.-F. *tant amunter*, to amount to so much], *a.* Equivalent (to) in value or effect.

tantara (tăn ta′ rȧ) [imit.], *n.* A quick succession of notes on a trumpet, hunting-horn, etc.

***tantivy** (tăn′ ti vi, tăn tiv′ i) [prob. imit.], *n.* A hunting-cry; rushing movement, a furious gallop, great speed. *adv.* Swiftly, speedily. *v.i.* To hasten, to rush, to speed.

tantony (tăn′ tȯ ni) [corr. of *St. Anthony*, patron of swine-herds], *n.* The smallest pig in a litter, usu. **tantony pig.**

tantra (tăn′ trȧ) [Sansk. orig. thread], *n.* One of a class of later Sanskrit religious text-books dealing chiefly with magical powers. **tantrism,** *n.* **tantrist,** *n.*

tantrum (tăn′ trŭm) [perh. from W. *tant*, passion, impulse], *n.* A burst of ill-temper, a fit of passion.

tanzib (tan zēb′) [Pers. (*tan*, body, *zib*, adornment)], *n.* A fine variety of muslin, usu. figured, made in Oudh.

Taoiseach (tē′ shȧ*ch*) [Ir.]. The Prime Minister of Eire.

Taoism (tā′ ō izm, tou′ izm) [Chin. *tao*, way, -ISM], *n.* The Chinese religious system based on the teachings of Lao-tze (b. 604 B.C.). **Taoist,** *n.* **Taoistic** (-is′ tik), *a.*

tap (1) (tăp) [F. *taper*, *tapper*, prob. from Teut. (cp. L.G. and G. *tappen*, Icel. *tapsa*), prob. imit.], *v.t.* To strike lightly or gently; to strike lightly with; to apply leather to the heel of (a shoe). *v.i.* To strike a gentle blow. *n.* A light or gentle blow, a rap; the sound of this; a piece of leather put on the heel of a shoe; (*pl.*) a military signal for putting lights out in quarters. **tapper** (1), *n.*

tap (2) (tăp) [A.-S. *tæppa*, cp. Dut. *tap*, G. *zappen*, Icel. *tappi*, O.H.G. *zapho*], *n.* A cock for drawing water or other fluid through (*Am.* a faucit or spigot); a faucet, a spigot; a plug or bung for closing a hole in a cask, etc.; (*fig.*) liquor of a particular brew or quality; (*colloq.*) a tap-room; a tool for cutting female or internal screw-threads. *v.t.* (*past & p.p.* **tapped**) To pierce (a cask, etc.) so as to let out a liquid; to let out or draw off (a liquid) thus; to furnish with a tap or cock; (*Surg.*) to draw (fluid) from a person's body, to draw fluid from (a person) thus; (*fig.*) to get into connexion with (a country, etc.) by way of trade, etc.; to divert current from (a wire), to intercept (a message); to make an internal screw in. **on tap:** Tapped (of a cask, etc.); ready to be drawn (of liquor). **tap-bolt,** *n.* A bolt with a head on one end and a thread on the other for screwing into some fixed part. **tap-dancing,** *n.* Solo dancing with rhythmical beat of heels and toes. **tap-room,** *n.* A room where liquor is drawn for drinking. **tap-root,** *n.* The main root of a plant penetrating straight downwards for some depth. **tappable,** *a.* That may be tapped (of rubber-trees, etc.). **tapper** (2), *n.* **tapping,** *n.* **tapster** [A.-S. *tæppestre* (-STER)], *n.* One who serves liquor in a bar.

tap (3) (*Sc.*) [TOP].

tapa (ta′ pȧ) [native name], *n.* A kind of tough cloth-like paper made from the bark of a tree, used by the Polynesians for clothes, nets, etc.

tapadero (ta pȧ dâr′ ō) [Sp., cover, from *tapar*, to stop up, to cover], *n.* A leather guard worn in front of the stirrup in California.

tape (tāp) [A.-S. *tæppe*, L. *tapēte*, cp. TAPPET and TAPESTRY], *n.* A narrow strip of woven linen, cotton, etc., used for tying things together, in dressmaking, book-binding, etc.; such a strip stretched across a race-course at the winning-post; a tape-line or tape-measure; a continuous strip of paper on which messages are recorded by a recording telegraph; a strong flexible band rotating on pulleys in printing and other machines; (*slang*) spirituous liquor. *v.t.* To furnish, fasten, or tie up with tapes; to bind (sections of a book) with tape bands. **red tape** [RED]. **tapeless,** *a.* **tape-line, -measure,** *n.* A tape or strip of metal, marked with inches, etc., for measuring, usu. coiled in a round flat case. **tape-machine,** *n.* A telegraphic instrument that records news, stock prices, etc. **tape recorder,** *n.* An electronic apparatus for recording music, etc., on **magnetic tape,** *i.e.* plastic tape coated with magnetic powder which can be magnetized in patterns corresponding to recorded music, speech, etc. **tapeworm,** *n.* A cestoid worm infesting the alimentary canal of man and other vertebrates.

taper (tā′ pėr) [A.-S. *tapor*, cp. Ir. *tapar*, W. *tampr*], *n.* A small wax-candle; anything giving a very feeble light; tapering form. *a.* (*poet.*) Growing smaller gradually towards one end. *v.i.* To become taper or gradually smaller towards one end. *v.t.* To make taper. **tapering,** *a.* **taperingly,** *adv.* **taperness,** *n.* **taperwise,** *adv.*

tapestry (tăp′ ės tri) [F. *tapisserie*, from *tapisser*, to furnish with tapestry, from TAPIS], *n.* A textile fabric in which the wool is supplied by a spindle instead of a shuttle, with designs applied by stitches across the warp; any ornamental fabric with designs applied in this manner. *v.t.* To hang with or as with tapestry. **tapestried,** *a.*

tapetum (tȧ pē′ tŭm) [late L., from L. *tapēte*, carpet], *n.* (*pl.* **-ta**) (*Bot.*) A layer of cells lining the cavity of anthers in flowering plants or of the sporangia in ferns; (*Anat.*) a portion of the choroid membrane of the eye in certain vertebrates.

tapeworm [TAPE].

tapioca (tăp i ō′ kȧ) [Port., from Tupi-Guarani *tipioka*, cassava-juice], *n.* A starchy, granular substance produced by beating cassava, forming a light farinaceous food.

tapir (tā′ pir) [Tupi-Guarani *tapīra*], *n.* An ungulate herbivorous, swine-like mammal of the family *Tapiridæ*, allied to the rhinoceros, with a short, flexible proboscis. **tapiroid,** *a.* and *n.*

tapis (tȧ pē′, tăp′ is) [F., tapestry, from med. L. *tapētium*, Gr. *tapētion*, dim. of *tapēs-pētos*], *n.* Tapestry (formerly used as a table-covering). **to be or come on the tapis:** To be or come under consideration.

tappable [TAP (2)]. **tapper** [TAP (1 and 2)].

tappet (tăp′ ėt) [perh. dim. of TAP (1)], *n.* A projecting arm or lever imparting intermittent motion to some part in machinery. **tappet-loom,** *n.* One in which the heddles are worked by tappets. **tappet-motion, -rod, -wheel,** *n.*

tapping [TAP (2)].

tappit (tăp′ it) [Sc. var. of *topped* (TOP, -ED)], *a.* Topped, crested. **tappit hen:** A hen with a top-knot or tuft; a drinking-vessel holding a Scotch quart or about three English quarts.

tapsalteerie, tapsie-teerie (*Sc.*) [TOPSY-TURVY].

tapsman (*Sc.*) [TOPSMAN].

tapster [TAP (2)].

tapu [TABOO].

tar (1) (tar) [A.-S. *teoru* (cp. Dut. *teer*, Icel. *tjara*, Dan. *tjære*, Swed. *tjära*), cogn. with TREE], *n.* A thick, dark, viscid oily liquid produced by the dry distillation of organic bodies and bituminous minerals. *v.t.* (*past & p.p.* **tarred**) To cover with tar. **tarred with the same brush:** Having the same bad characteristics. **to tar and feather:** To smear with tar and then cover with feathers, a punishment inflicted usually by rioters. **tar macadam,** *n.* (*Eng.*) A mixture of tar and road metal giving a smooth, dustless surface. **tar-water,** *n.* A cold infusion of tar, formerly used as a medicine; a tarry ammoniacal water obtained in the process of purifying coal-gas. **tarry** (1), *a.*

tar (2) (tar) [short for TARPAULIN], *n.* (*colloq.*) A sailor.

tara (ta′ rȧ) [native name], *n.* The tara-fern. **tara-fern,** *n.* The New Zealand and Tasmanian edible fern, *Pteris esculenta*.

taradiddle [TARRADIDDLE].

taraire (ta rī′ rē) [Maori], *n.* A white-wood N. Zealand tree.

tarakihi (ta ra kē′ hē) [Maori], *n.* An edible fish from N. Zealand waters.

tarantass (tăr ȧn tăs′) [Rus. *tarantasu*], *n.* A large four-wheeled carriage without springs.

tarantella (tăr ȧn tel′ ȧ) [It., from *Taranto*, L. *Tarentum*, S. It. town], *n.* A rapid Neapolitan dance in triplets for one couple; the music for such a dance.

tarantula (tȧ răn′ tū lȧ), *n.* A large, venomous spider of S. Europe, esp. *Lycosa tarantula*, whose bite was formerly supposed to produce **tarantism** (tă′ rȧn tizm), an epidemic dancing mania.

tarata (ta ra′ ta) [Maori], *n.* The lemon-wood tree of N. Zealand.

taratantara (tăr ȧ tăn′ tȧ rȧ) [imit.], *n.* The sound of a trumpet, bugle, etc.

taraxacum (tȧ răk′ sȧ kŭm) [mod. L., prob. from Arab. or Pers.], *n.* A genus of plants containing the dandelion; a plant of this family; a drug prepared from this. **taraxacin** (-răk′ sȧ sin), *n.* A bitter principle believed to be the basis of this drug.

tarboosh (tar boosh′) [Arab. *tarbūsh*], *n.* A brimless cap or fez, usu. red.

tardamente (tar dȧ men′ tā) [It.], *adv.* (*Mus.*) Slowly.

tardigrade (tar′ di grād) [L. *tardigradus* (*tardus*, slow, *gradī*, to walk)], *a.* (*Zool.*) Slow-moving. *n.* One of the *Tardigrada*, a division of edentates containing the sloths.

tardy (tar′ di) [F. *tardif*, L. *tardus*], *a.* Moving slowly, slow, sluggish; late, behindhand, dilatory; reluctant. **tardily,** *adv.* **tardiness,** *n.*

tare (1) (târ) [M.E., cp. M.Dut. *terwe*, Dut. *tarwe*, wheat], *n.* A vetch, esp. *Vicia sativa*, the common vetch; (*Bibl.*) a weed, perh. darnel.

tare (2) (târ) [F., from Sp. *tara*, Arab. *tarhah*, rejected, from *taraha*, to fling], *n.* An allowance for the weight of boxes, wrapping, etc. in which goods are packed; the weight of a motor vehicle without fuel, load, or equipment; (*Chem.*) the weight of the vessel in which a substance is weighed. *v.t.* To ascertain the amount of tare of.

***tare** (3), *p.p.* [TEAR (1)].

target (tar′ gėt) [O.F. *targuete*, dim. of *targue*, var. *targe* (cp. Icel. *targa*, A.-S. *targe*, O.H.G. *zarga*)], *n.* An object set up as a mark to be fired at in archery, musketry, etc., orig. a circular pad of twisted straw, etc. painted with concentric bands surrounding a bull's eye; the objective of an air-raid; (*colloq.*) the aim, sum of money, etc., to be reached by a combined effort; (*fig.*) any person or thing made the object of attack, criticism, etc., a butt; (*Elec.*) the anti-cathode used in a discharge-tube to set up X-rays; (*Railway*) a small signal at a switch, etc.; *a shield, a buckler, esp. a small round one. ***targe** (tarj), *n.* **targeted,** *a.* **targeteer** (tar gė tēr′), *n.* A soldier armed with a target.

Targum (tar′ gŭm) [Chaldee, interpretation], *n.* One of various ancient Aramaic versions or paraphrases of the Old Testament Scriptures. **Targumic** (-gū′ mik), **Targumistic** (-mis′ tik), *a.* **Targumist** (tar′ gŭ mist), *n.*

tariff (tăr′ if) [O.F. *tariffe*, arithmetic, Sp. *tarifa*, Arab. *ta'rīf*, information, from *'irf*, knowledge, from *'arafa*, to know], *n.* A list or table of duties or customs payable on the importation or export of goods; a duty on any particular kind of goods; a law imposing such duties; a table of charges. *v.t.* To draw up a list of duties on (goods); to price, to put a valuation on. **tariff reform:** The removal of defects or abuses in the tariff, esp. the introduction of protective duties on imports into Great Britain; (*Am.*) free trade or approximation to this

tarlatan (tar′ lȧ tȧn) [F. *tarlatane*, etym. doubtful], *n.* A fine, transparent muslin.

tarn (tarn) [Icel. *tjörn*, gen. *tjarnar*, Swed. dial. *tjärn*, *tärn*], *n.* A small mountain lake.

tarnish (tar′ nish) [F. *terniss-*, stem of *ternir*, M.H.G. *ternen*, cp. O.H.G. *tarnan*, to obscure, to darken, from *tarni*, secret], *v.t.* To diminish or destroy the lustre of; to sully, to stain. *v.i.* To lose lustre. *n.* Loss of lustre, a stain, a blemish; (*Min.*) the film of discoloration forming on the exposed face of a mineral. **tarnishable,** *a.*

taro (târ′ ō) [native name], *n.* A tropical plant of the arum family, esp. *Colocasia esculenta* and *C. macrorhiza*, the roots of which are used as food by Pacific islanders.

taroc, tarot (tăr′ ō) [F. *tarots*, spotted cards, It. *tarrocchi*, etym. doubtful], *n.* A figured playing-card, one of a pack of 78, used in an old (orig. Italian) card-game; this game.

tarpan (tar′ pȧn) [Tatar], *n.* A small wild horse of the steppes of Russia and Tartary.

tarpaulin (tar paw′ lin) [TAR (1), *palling*, covering, from PALL (1)], *n.* A canvas-cloth coated with tar or other waterproof compound; a sailor's broad-brimmed tarred or oiled hat; (*colloq.*) a sailor.

Tarpeian (tar pē′ ȧn), *a.* Relating to *Tarpeia*, said to have been buried at the foot of the Tarpeian rock. **Tarpeian rock:** A cliff in ancient Rome from which state criminals were hurled.

tarpon (tar′ pȯn) [etym. doubtful], *n.* A large and powerful game-fish, *Megalops atlanticus*, of the herring family common in West Indian and Western Atlantic waters.

tarradiddle (tăr ȧ didl′) [etym. doubtful], *n.* (*colloq.*) A lie, a fib.

tarragon (tăr′ ȧ gȯn) [Sp. *taragona*, Arab. *tarkhūn*, Gr. *drakōn*, DRAGON], *n.* A perennial herb, *Artemisia dracunculus*, allied to wormwood, used in cookery, etc. **tarragon vinegar:** Vinegar flavoured with tarragon.

***tarras** (tăr′ ȧs) [Dut. *tarasse*, *terras*, now *tras*, cp. O.F. *terrace*], *n.* A rock containing abundant fragments of pumice and other volcanic matter, found on the Rhine, used for making cement, etc.; such cement used for lining cisterns, etc.

***tarre** (tar) [as TARRY (2)], *v.t.* To incite; to urge (on).

tarrock (tar′ ȯk) [etym. doubtful], *n.* The young kittiwake; the tern; the guillemot.

tarry (1) (tar′ ri) [TAR (1)].

tarry (2) (tăr′ i) [M.E. *tarien*, to irritate, to delay, A.-S. *tergan*, to vex (influenced by M.E. *targen*, O.F. *targer*, late L. *tardicāre*, L. *tardāre*, to delay, from *tardus*, see TARDY)], *v.i.* To stay, to remain behind; to wait; to linger, to delay, to be late. *v.t.* To wait for. ***tarriance,** *n.* ***tarrier,** *n.*

tarsal, tarsi [TARSUS].

tarsia (tar′ si ȧ) [It.], *n.* An Italian mosaic or inlaid woodwork.

tarsier (tar′ si ėr) [F., from foll.], *n.* A small arboreal tarsioid lemur with very large eyes and ears.

tarsus (tar′ sŭs) [Gr. *tarsos*, flat surface], *n.* (*pl.* **-si, -sī**) The set of bones (seven in man) between the lower leg and the metatarsus, the ankle; the shank of a bird's leg; the terminal segment in the leg of an insect or crustacean; a plate of connective tissue in the eyelid. **tarsal, tarsioid,** *a.* **tarso-,** *comb. form.* **tarsometatarsal** (-met ȧ tar′ sȧl), *a.* Pertaining to the tarsus and the metatarsus. **tarsometatarsus,** *n.*

tart (1) (tart) [A.-S. *teart*, prob. cogn. with TEAR (1)], *a.* Sharp to the taste, acid; (*fig.*) biting, cutting, piercing. **tartish,** *a.* **tartly,** *adv.* **tartness,** *n.*

tart (2) (tart) [O.F. *tarte*, prob. var. of *tourte*, *torte*, L. *torta*, fem. p.p. of *torquēre*, to twist], *n.* A pie containing fruit; a piece of pastry with jam, etc. (*Am.* a pie); (*slang*) a girl, esp. one of doubtful character. **tartlet,** *n.*

tartan (1) (tar′ tăn) [etym. doubtful], *n.* A woollen fabric cross-barred with stripes of various colours forming patterns distinguishing the various Highland clans; the pattern on this; a garment, esp. a plaid, made of it; (*fig.*) a Highlander or a Highland regiment. *a.* Consisting, made of, or like tartan.

tartan (2), **tartane** (tar′ tăn) [F. *tartane*, perh. from Arab. *taridah*], *n.* A small Mediterranean one-masted vessel with bowsprit and lateen sail.

tartar (1) (tar′ tăr) [F. *tartre*, late L. *tartarum*, Arab. *durd*, dregs, tartar of wine], *n.* Partially purified argol, the impure tartrate of potassium deposited from wines; cream of tartar; a yellowish incrustation of calcium phosphate deposited on the teeth. **cream of tartar** [CREAM]. **tartar emetic:** A tartrate of potassium and antimony used as an emetic and purgative. **tartareous** (-târ′ ė ŭs), **tartaric** (tăr′ ik), **tartarous** (tar′ tȧ rŭs), *a.* **tartarize,** *v.t.* **tartarization** (-zā′ shŭn), *n.* **tartrate,** *n.* A salt of tartaric acid.

Tartar (2) (tar′ tăr), **Tatar** (ta′ tăr) [Pers. *Tātār*], *a.* Of or pertaining to Tartary or the races comprising Turks, Cossacks, and Kirghis Tartars. *n.* A native of Tartary or a member of this group of races; (*fig.*) a person of an intractable, irritable temper or more than one's match. **to catch a Tartar:** To find an opponent stronger than was expected.

Tartarean [TARTARUS.]

tartareous, -ric, tartarize, etc. [TARTAR (1)].

Tartarus (tar′ tȧ rŭs) [L., from Gr. *Tartaros*], *n.* (*Gr. Myth.*) A deep abyss below Hades where the Titans were confined; the abode of the wicked in Hades. **Tartarean** (târ′ ė ăn), *a.*

tartish, tartly, etc. [TART (1)].

tartlet [TART (2)]. **tartrate** [TARTAR (1)].

Tartuffe (tar tuf′) [F., a character in Molière's *Tartuffe*], *n.* A hypocritical pretender. **Tartuffish,** *a.* **Tartuffism,** *n.*

task (task) [O.North.F. *tasque*, O.F. *tasche* (F. *tâche*), late L. *tasca*, TAX], *n.* A definite amount of work imposed; a lesson to be learned at school; a piece of work undertaken voluntarily. *v.t.* To impose a task upon; to strain, to overtax. **to take to task:** To reprove, to reprimand. **taskmaster, taskmistress, *tasker,** *n.* One who imposes a task. **task force,** *n.* (*Nav.*) A temporary naval attack unit organized for a specific action. **task-work,** *n.* Work imposed or performed as a task.

taslet (tăs′ lėt) [dim. of TASSE], *n.* A tasse, a tassel.

Tasmanian (tăz mā′ ni ăn), *a.* Of or pertaining to Tasmania. *n.* A native or inhabitant of Tasmania. **Tasmanian devil,** *n.* (*Zool.*) The dasyure, a fierce, cat-like marsupial. **Tasmanian tiger,** *n.* A wolf-like, carnivorous marsupial, the thylacine, now almost extinct.

tasmanite (tăz′ mȧ nīt), *n.* (*Min.*) A resinous mineral found in some Tasmanian shales.

tass (tăs) [O.F. *tasse*, goblet, later, cup, prob. from Arab. *tass*, basin], *n.* A cup, a goblet; a small draught.

***tasse** (tăs) [O.F.], *n.* (*usu. in pl.*) One of a series of overlapping plates hanging from the corslet as a sort of kirtle to protect the thighs.

tassel (1) (tăs′ ėl) [O.F. *tasel*, *tassel*, It. *tassello*, med. L. *tassellus*, etym. doubtful], *n.* A pendent ornament, usu. composed of a tuft of threads, cords, silk, etc. attached to the corners of cushions, curtains, etc.; the pendent head of a flower, esp. the staminate inflorescence on Indian corn; a small ribbon of silk sewn into a book as a marker; a torsel. *v.t.* To furnish or adorn with tassels; to remove the tassels from (Indian corn) to strengthen the plant.

***tassel** (2) [TERCEL].

taste (tāst) [O.F. *taster*, to handle, feel, taste (F. *tâter*), L. *taxāre*, from *tag-*, base of *tangere*, to touch], *v.t.* To try the flavour of by taking into the mouth; to perceive the flavour of; to experience; (*colloq.*) to eat a little of; *to enjoy, to relish. *v.i.* To take or eat a small portion of food, etc., to partake (of); to have experience (of); to have a smack or flavour (of). *n.* The sensation excited by the contact of various soluble substances with certain organs in the mouth, flavour; the sense by which this is perceived; the act of tasting; a small quantity tasted, drunk or eaten, a bit taken as a sample; the mental faculty or power of apprehending and enjoying the beautiful and the sublime in nature and art, or of appreciating and discerning between the degrees of artistic excellence; manner, style, execution, as directed or controlled by this; an inclination, a predilection (for). **tastable,** *a.* **tasteful,** *a.* Having, characterized by, or done with good taste. **tastefully,** *adv.* **tastefulness,** *n.* **tasteless,** *a.* Having no flavour, insipid; vapid, dull; lacking æsthetic taste. **tastelessly,** *adv.* **tastelessness,** *n.*

taster (tās′ tėr), *n.* One who tastes, esp. one employed to test the quality of teas, liquors, etc., by tasting, orig. one employed to taste food and drink before it was served; an implement for cutting a small cylindrical sample from cheese, a small cup used by a wine-taster, etc.

tasty (tās′ ti), *a.* Savoury, toothsome; (*colloq.*) in good taste. **tastily,** *adv.*

tat (1) (tăt) [cp. M.Swed. *tätte*, Dan. dial. *tat*, Norw. *taatt*, thread, strand], *v.t.* (*past & p.p.* **tatted**) To make by knotting. *v.i.* To make tatting. *n.* Knotted work or lace used for edging, etc., also called **tatting.**

tat (2) (tat) [Hindi], *n.* A coarse East Indian canvas or matting, esp. gunny.

tat (3) [TATTY]. **tat** (4) [TATTOO (3)].

ta-ta (ta ta) [instinctive sound], *int.* (*Childish*) Goodbye!

Tatar [TARTAR (2)].

tate (tāt) [Sc., etym. doubtful], *n.* A small portion, tuft, handful, or scrap of anything, esp. of wool, hair, etc.

tater (tā′ tėr) (*vulg.*) [POTATO].

tatler [TATTLE].

tatou, tatu (ta′ tu) [S. Am. native], *n.* An armadillo.

tatter (tăt′ ėr) [cp. Icel. *tötrar*, L.G. *taltern*, rags, E.Fris. *talte*, rag], *n.* A rag; a torn and hanging piece or shred. **tatterdemalion** (-dė mā′ li ŏn), *n.* A ragged fellow. **tattered, tattering, tattery,** *a.*

tatting [TAT (1)].

tattle (tăt′ el) [freq. of obs. *tat*, imit.], *v.i.* To chatter, to gossip; to tell tales or secrets. *n.* Prattle, gossip, idle talk. **tattler,** *n.* One who tattles, a gossip; a sandpiper. ***tattlery,** *n.* **tattingly,** *adv.*

tattoo (1) (tȧ too′) [Dut. *taptoe* (TAP (2), *toe*, put to, closed), signal for closing tavern taps], *n.* The beat of drum recalling soldiers to their quarters; a military pageant, esp. by night. *v.i.* To beat the tattoo.

tattoo (2) (tȧ too′) [Tahitian *tatau*], *v.t.* To mark (the skin) by pricking and inserting pigments. *n.* A mark or pattern so produced. **tattooage,** *n.* **tattooer,** *n.*

tattoo (3) (tŭt′ oo) [Hind.], *n.* A native-bred pony.

tatty (tăt′ i) [Hind. *tatti*], *n.* A matting of cuscus-grass for hanging in doorways and other openings, usu. kept wet to cool the air. *a.* (*slang*) Untidy.

tatu [TATOU].

tau (taw) [Gr.], *n.* The Greek letter τ; a tau cross; the American toad-fish *Batrachus tau*. **tau cross:** A cross shaped like a T, a St. Anthony's cross.

taught, *past & p.p.* [TEACH].

taunt (1) (tawnt) [from O.F. *tanter*, *tenter*, L. *tentāre*, to TEMPT, or from F. *tant*, L. *tantum*, so much], *v.t.* To reproach or upbraid sarcastically or contemptuously. *n.* A bitter or sarcastic reproach. **taunter,** *n.* **tauntingly,** *adv.*

taunt (2) (tawnt) [from obs. *ataunt*, in full rig, F. *autant*, as much, cp. prec.], *a.* (*Naut.*) Tall (of masts) [ATAUNTO].

taurine (taw' rīn) [L. *taurīnus*, from TAURUS], *a.* Bull-like; bovine; of or pertaining to Taurus. **tauriform,** *a.* **tauromachy** (taw rom' ȧ ki) [Gr. *machē*, fight], *n.* Bull-fighting; a bull-fight.

Taurus (taw' rŭs) [L., from Gr. *tauros*], *n.* The Bull, the second zodiacal constellation; the second sign of the zodiac.

taut (1) (tawt) [M.E. *togt*, *toght*, prob. p.p. of *togen*, to TOW (1)], *a.* (*Naut.*) Tight, tense, not slack; in good order, trim. **tauten,** *v.t.i.* To make taut, to become taut.

taut (2) (tawt) [Sc., etym. doubtful], *v.t.* and *i.* To tangle, to mat (esp. of hair).

tauto- [Gr., for *to auto*, the same], *comb. form.* **tautochrone** (taw' tȯ krōn) [Gr. *chronos*, CHRONO-], *n.* A curve such that a heavy body rolling down it from a state of rest will always reach the same point in the same time from whatever point it starts. **tautochronism** (-tok' rȯ nizm), *n.* **tautochronous,** *a.*

tautog (taw tog') [Narragansett, *taut-anog*], *n.* A food-fish common on the Atlantic coast of the United States, the American black-fish.

tautology (taw tol' ȯ ji) [L. and Gr. *tautologia*], *n.* Repetition of the same thing in different words. **tautologic, -al** (-loj' ik, -ȧl), *a.* **tautologically,** *adv.* **tautologist** (-tol' ȯ jist), *n.* **tautologize,** *v.i.* ***tautologous** (-gŭs), *a.* **tautophony** (taw tof' ȯ ni) [Gr. *phōnē*, sound], *n.* Repetition of the same sound.

tavern (tăv' ĕrn) [F. *taverne*, L. *taberna*, hut, tavern], *n.* A public-house, an inn. ***taverner,** *n.* ***taverning,** *n.*

taw (1) (taw) [A.-S. *tawian*, cp. Dut. *touwen*, to curry, O.H.G. *zouwan*, to make, to prepare], *v.t.* To dress or make (skins) into leather with mineral agents, as alum, instead of tannin. **tawer,** *n.* **tawery,** *n.*

taw (2) (taw) [etym. doubtful], *n.* A game at marbles; the line from which to play in this; a marble.

tawa (ta' wa) [Maori], *n.* A N. Zealand tree the wood of which is used for box-making.

tawahi (ta wa' hē) [Maori], *n.* The N. Zealand penguin.

tawdry (taw' dri) [from *St. Audrey* (corr. of *Etheldrida*, founder of Ely cathedral), whose fair was held in the Isle of Ely, etc., on 17th Oct.], *a.* Showy without taste or elegance; gaudy. *n.* Tasteless or worthless finery. **tawdrily,** *adv.* **tawdriness,** *n.*

tawer, tawery [TAW (1)].

tawhai (ta' wī) [Maori], *n.* One of the N. Zealand beeches.

tawhiri (ta wī' rē) [Maori], *n.* The N. Zealand pittosporum.

tawny (taw' ni) [M.E. *tanny*, F. *tanné*, p.p. of *tanner*, to TAN (1)], *a.* Brownish-yellow, tan-coloured. **tawniness,** *a.*

tawpie, tawpy (taw' pi) [Sc., prob. from Scand.], *n.* A foolish, thoughtless girl or woman. *a.* Foolish, silly, thoughtless.

taws, tawse (tawz) [prob. pl. of obs. *taw*, lash, from TAW (1)], *n.* (*chiefly Sc.*) A leather strap, usually with the end cut into thin strips, used as an instrument of punishment; a lash.

tax (tăks) [F. *taxe*, from *taxer*, L. *taxāre*, from *tag-*, base of *tangere*, to touch], *n.* A compulsory contribution levied on persons, property, or businesses to meet the expenses of government or other public services; (*fig.*) a heavy demand, requirement, strain, etc. *v.t.* To impose a tax on; (*fig.*) to lay a heavy burden or strain upon, to make demands upon; to charge (with an oversight, etc.); (*Law*) to fix amounts of (costs, etc.); (*Bibl.*) to register for payment of tribute. **tax-cart, taxed cart:** A light spring-cart for agricultural purposes, etc., on which a reduced tax was charged. **tax-collector, -gatherer,** *n.* **tax-free,** *a.* Exempt from taxation. **tax-payer,** *n.* **taxability** (-bil' i ti), *n.* **taxable,** *a.* **taxableness,** *n.* **taxably,** *adv.* **taxation** (tăk' sā' shŭn), *n.* **taxer,** *n.* **taxing master,** *n.* (*Law*) The official who assesses costs of actions.

taxi (tăk' si) [short for TAXIMETER], *n.* (*colloq.*) A motor-cab fitted with a taximeter, also called **taxi-cab.** *v.i.* (*Aviat.*) (Of an aircraft) to travel along the ground. **taxi-stand:** A cab rank.

taxidermy (tăk' si dĕr mi) [TAXIS, DERM], *n.* The art of preparing and mounting the skins of animals so that they resemble the living forms. **taxidermal** (-dĕr' mȧl), **taxidermic,** *a.* **taxidermist,** *n.*

taximeter (tăk sim' ė tėr) [F. *taximètre* (*taxe*, TAX, -METER)], *n.* An automatic instrument fitted in a cab for registering distances and indicating fares.

taxin (tăk' sin) [L. *tax-us*, Gr. *taxos*, yew, -IN], *n.* A resinous substance extracted from yew leaves.

taxis (tăk' sis) [Gr., from *tassein*, to arrange], *n.* (*Gr. Ant.*) A division of hoplites, etc.; (*Gram. and Rhet.*) order, arrangement; (*Zool., etc.*) classification; (*Surg.*) methodical application of manual pressure to restore parts to their places.

taxonomy (tăk son' ȯ mi) [F. *taxonomie* (prec., Gr. *nom-*, from *nemein*, to deal out)], *n.* The department of natural history treating of the principles of classification; classification; also called **taxology.** **taxonomic, -al** (-nom' ik, -ȧl), *a.* **taxonomically,** *adv.* **taxonomist,** *n.*

***tayout** [TALLY-HO].

tazza (tăt' sȧ) [It.], *n.* (*pl.* ***-ze***, -sā) A flattish or saucer-shaped cup, esp. one on a high foot.

tchick (chik) [imit.], *n.* A sound made by pressing the tongue against the palate and withdrawing it quickly. *v.i.* To make this sound, as in urging a horse.

tea (tē) [Chin. (Amoy) *tē* (pron. tā), *ch'a*], *n.* The dried and prepared leaves of *Thea Sinensis* or *T. Assamica*, a small evergreen tree or shrub of the camellia family; the tea-plant; a decoction or infusion of tea-leaves for drinking; a light afternoon or a more substantial evening meal at which tea is served; an infusion or decoction of other vegetable or animal substances for drinking, esp. for medicinal purposes. *v.i.* To take tea. *v.t.* To supply with tea. **green tea,** *n.* Tea roasted while fresh. **high tea, meat tea,** *n.* A cooked evening meal at which tea is drunk. **Russian tea,** *n.* Tea drunk with lemon instead of milk. **tea-caddy** [CADDY]. **tea-cake,** *n.* A light cake, often toasted for eating at tea. **tea-canister,** *n.* **tea-chest,** *n.* A box lined with thin sheet-lead, in which tea is imported; *a tea-caddy. **tea-cloth,** *n.* A table-cloth for tea; a dish-cloth. **tea-cup,** *n.* A small cup for drinking tea from. **teacupful,** *n.* **tea-dealer,** *n.* **tea-drinker,** *n.* **tea-fight,** *n.* (*colloq.*) A tea-party. **tea-garden,** *n.* A garden where tea and other refreshments are served to the public. **tea-gown,** *n.* A woman's loose gown for wearing at afternoon tea. **tea-kettle,** *n.* A kettle for boiling water to make tea. **tea-leaf,** *n.* A leaf of tea or the tea-plant; (*pl.* **-leaves**) such leaves after infusion. **tea meeting,** *n.* A religious meeting at which there is an interval for tea and social chatter. **tea-party,** *n.* A party at which tea is served. **tea-plant,** *n.* *Thea Sinensis* or *T. Assamica.* **teapot,** *n.* A vessel in which tea is infused. **tea-room,** *n.* A restaurant where afternoon teas are provided. **tea rose,** *n.* A rose with scent supposed to resemble tea. **tea-saucer, -service, -set, -spoon,** *n.* Utensils used in serving tea. **teaspoonful,** *n.* The quantity contained in a teaspoon; a quarter of a fluid oz. **tea-table,** *n.* **tea-taster,** *n.* One whose business it is to test and sample tea by the taste. **tea-things,** *n.pl.* (*colloq.*) Cups, saucers, etc. for tea. **tea-tray,** *n.* **tea-tree,** *n.* The tea-plant or shrub; one of the Australian myrtaceous plants, Melaleuca, Leptospermum etc., that furnished a tea substitute for early settlers. **tea-urn,** *n.* A vessel for supplying hot water for tea, or tea in large quantities.

teach (tēch) [A.-S. *tǣcan*, cogn, with TOKEN], *v.t.* (*past & p.p.* **taught,** tawt) To cause (a person, etc.) to learn (to do) or acquire knowledge or skill in, to instruct or train in; to impart knowledge or information concerning (a subject, etc.), to give lessons in; to impart instruction to, to educate; to explain, to show, to disclose, to make known. *v.i.* To perform the duties of a teacher; to give instruction. **teachable,** *a.* That may be taught (of a subject, etc.); apt to learn, docile. **teachableness,** *n.* **teacher,** *n.* **teachership,** *n.* **teaching,** *n.* The act of one who teaches; that which is taught, doctrine. ***teachless,** *a.*

teagle (tēgl) [North. var. of TACKLE], *n.* (*prov.*) A hoisting-apparatus, a lift.

teak (tēk) [Port. *teca*, Malayalam *tekka*], *n.* A large E. Indian tree, *Tectona grandis*, yielding a heavy timber that does not crack, warp, shrink, or corrode iron, used largely for shipbuilding, etc.; this timber.

teal (tēl) [M.E. *tele*, cp. M.Dut. *teelingh*], *n.* A small freshwater duck of the genus *Nettion* or *Querquedula*.

team (tēm) [A.-S. *tēam*, family, team (cp. Dut. *toom*, G. *zaum*, bridle, Icel. *taumr*, rein), cogn. with TOW (1)], *n.* Two or more horses, oxen, etc., harnessed together; a number of persons working together, forming a side in a game, etc. *v.t.* To harness or join together in a team; to haul, convey, etc., with a team; to sublet (work, etc.,) to a contractor who employs teams of workmen. **teamster,** *n.* One who drives a team. **teamwise,** *adv.* **team-work,** *n.* Co-operation.

teapoy (tē′ poi) [Hind. *tīn*, three, Pers. *pēē*, *pāī*, foot, *sipāī*, assim. to TEA], *n.* A small three- or four-legged table for holding a tea-service, etc.

tear (1) (târ) [A.-S. *teran*, cp. Goth. *gatairan*, G. *zehren*, to destroy, Icel. *tæra*, to consume, also Gr. *derein*, to flay], *v.t.* (*past* **tore,** tôr, ***tare,** târ, *p.p.* **torn,** tôrn) To pull forcibly apart, to rend; to lacerate; to make (a rent, tear, wound, etc.) thus; to pull violently (away, out, etc.); to drag, remove, or sever thus. *v.i.* To pull violently (at); to part or separate on being pulled; to rush, move, or act with violence. *n.* A rent. **that's torn it:** (*slang*) That's spoiled it. **to tear one's hair:** To be overcome with grief; to be very puzzled. **tearer,** *n.* **tearing,** *a.* (*colloq.*) Violent, furious, tremendous.

tear (2) (tēr) [A.-S. *tēar*, *tær* (cp. Icel. *tār*, Dan. *taar*, Goth. *tagr*, also Gr. *dakru*, L. *lacrima*, O.L. *dacrima*)], *n.* A drop of the saline liquid secreted by the lachrymal glands, moistening the eyes or flowing down in strong emotion, etc.; a drop of liquid; a solid, transparent drop or drop-like object. **tear-drop,** *n.* **tear-duct,** *n.* The nasal duct. ***tear-falling,** *a.* Shedding tears, tender, pitiful. **tear gas,** *n.* A poison gas that affects the lachrymal ducts and causes violent watering of the eyes. **tear-shell,** *n.* A shell that on explosion liberates gases that irritate the lachrymatory glands. **tear-stained,** *a.* **tearful,** *a.* Shedding tears. **tearfully,** *adv.* **tearfulness,** *n.* **tearless, teary,** *a.*

tease (tēz) [A.-S. *tæsan*, to pluck, pull (cp. M.Dut. *teesen*, Dan. *tæse*)], *v.t.* To pull apart or separate the fibres of; to comb or card (wool or flax); to annoy, to irritate, to vex with petty requests, importunity, jesting, or raillery; to importune (to do something). *n.* One who teases or irritates thus. **teaser,** *n.* One who or that which teases; a machine for teasing wool, etc.; (*colloq.*) an awkward question, problem, or situation, a poser. **teasingly,** *adv.*

teasel (tē′ zèl) [A.-S. *tæsl*, *tæsel*, from prec.], *n.* A plant with large burs or heads covered with stiff, hooked awns, which are used for raising a nap on cloth; this bur or head; a machine used as a substitute for this. *v.t.* To dress with teasels. **teaseler,** *n.*

teat (tēt) [M.E. and O.F. *tete* (F. *tette*), L.G. *titte* (cp. M.Dut. *titte*, G. *zitze*, A.-S. *tit*, also Gr. *titthē*)], *n.* The nipple of the female breast through which milk is drawn; the pap of a woman; the dug of a beast; a projection or appliance resembling this. **teated,** *a.* **teatlike,** *a.*

Tebeth (teb′ ėth) [Heb.], *n.* The tenth month of the Jewish ecclesiastical year, comprising parts of December and January.

Tebilise (teb′ i līz), *v.t.* Proprietary name of a method of treating cotton and linen fabrics to prevent creasing and shrinking.

tec (*slang*) [DETECTIVE].

technic (tek′ nik) [Gr. *technikos*, from *technē*, art], *a.* Technical. *n.* Technique, technics.

technical (tek′ ni kȧl), *a.* Of or pertaining to the mechanical arts; of or pertaining to any particular art, science, business, etc., **technicality** (-kăl′ i ti), *n.* Technicalness; a technical term, expression, etc., **technically,** *adv.* **technicalness,** *n.*

technician, technicist (tek nish′ ȧn, tek′ ni sist), *n.* One skilled in the technical side of a subject, a technical expert.

Technicolor (tek′ ni kŭl ėr), *n.* Proprietary name for a colour cinematograph process.

technicon (tek′ ni kȯn), *n.* A gymnastic apparatus for training the hands of organists, pianists, etc.

technics (tek′ niks), *n.* The doctrine of arts in general; technical rules, terms, methods, etc.

techniphone (tek′ ni fōn), *n.* A dumb piano for exercise in fingering.

technique (tek nēk′), *n.* A mode of artistic performance or execution; mechanical skill in art, craft, etc.

technocracy (tek nok′ rȧ si), *n.* Government by technical experts.

technology (tek nol′ ō ji), *n.* The science of the industrial arts; the terminology of an art or science. **technologic, technological,** *a.* **technologist,** *n.*

techy, etc. [TETCHY].

tecnology (tek nol′ ȯ ji) [Gr. *teknon*, child, -LOGY], *n.* The scientific study of children; a treatise on children, their diseases, etc., **tecnonymy** (tek non′ i mi) [Gr. *onuma*, name], *n.* The custom of naming the parent from the child. **tecnonymous,** *a.*

tectology (tek tol′ ȯ ji) [G. *tektologie* (Gr. *tektōn*, carpenter, -LOGY)], *n.* Morphology dealing with the organism as a group of organic individuals, structural morphology. **tectological** (-loj′ i kȧl), *a.*

tectonic (tek ton′ ik) [L. *tectonicus*, Gr. *tektonikos*, from *tektōn*, *-tonos*, carpenter], *a.* Of or pertaining to building or construction; (*Geol.*) structural. **tectonics,** *n.* The art of constructing buildings, vessels, implements, etc., for use and beauty.

tectorial (tek tôr′ i ȧl) [L. *tectōrius*, from *tec-*, p.p. stem of *tegere*, to cover], *a.* Forming a covering (esp. of a membrane of the ear). **tectorium,** *n.* (*pl.* **-ia**). **tectrices** (tek′ tri sēz), *n.pl.* (*Ornith.*) The feathers covering the wing or tail.

ted (ted) [prob. from an A.-S. *teddan* (cp. Icel. *tethja*, past *tadda*, to spread manure, from *tath*, manure)], *v.t.* (*past & p.p.* **tedded**) To turn over and spread (hay) so as to expose to the sun and air. **tedder,** *n.* An implement to do this.

teddy-bear (ted i bâr′) [Theodore (*Teddy*) Roosevelt (1858–1919)], *n.* A stuffed toy bear; the koala. **Teddy boy:** A type of hysterical adolescent seeking self-expression by affecting clothes reminiscent of the late Edwardian period, and frequently by unruly behaviour.

Tedesco (te des′ kō) [It., from Teut., cp. A.-S. *thēodisc*, G. *deutsch*], *a.* and *n.* (*pl.* **-chi,** -kē) German (used in connexion with painting, etc.).

Te Deum (tē dē′ ŭm) [from the first words '*Te Deum* laudamus,' We praise Thee, O God], *n.* A hymn of praise sung at morning service or as a special **thanksgiving**; a musical setting for this; a thanksgiving service at which it is sung.

tedious (tē′ di ŭs) [late L. *tædiōsus*, from *tædium*; from *tædet*, it wearies], *a.* Tiresome, wearisome; monotonous, fatiguing. **tediously,** *adv.* **tediousness, tedium,** *n.*

tee (1) (tē) [T], *n.* The letter T; a T-shaped pipe, joint, etc.; a mark for quoits, curling-stones, etc.; (*Golf*) a small pile of sand or a rubber cone from which the ball is played at the commencement of each hole. *v.t.* To put the ball on this. **to tee off:** To play from this; (*fig.*) to begin.

tee (2) (tē) [Burmese *h'ti*, umbrella], *n.* An umbrella-shaped finial surmounting a tope or pagoda.

teem (1) (tēm) [A.-S. *tȳman*, *tīeman*, from *tēam*, or TEAM], **v.t.* To bring forth (off-spring); to be prolific; to be stocked to overflowing. **teemer,** *n.*

teem (2) (tēm) [Icel. *tæma*, from *tōmr*, empty, cp. TOOM], *v.t.* To pour out (esp. molten metal); to empty. *v.i.* (*prov.*) To pour (down) as rain, etc.

***teen** (tēn) [A.-S. *tēona*, whence *tēonian*, to irritate (cp. Icel. *tjōn*, damage)], *n.* Grief, vexation, anger, resentment. *v.t.* To vex, to provoke.

-teen [A.-S. *-tȳne*, *tīen*, TEN], *suf.* Denoting the addition of ten (in numbers 13–19). **-teenth** [-TEEN, -TH], *suf.* Forming ordinal numbers from the cardinals 13–19.

teens (tēnz) [from prec.], *n.pl.* The years of one's age from 13 to 19. **teenager** (tēn āj′ ėr), *n.* An adolescent in his or her teens.

teeny (*childish*) [TINY].

teetee (1) (tē′ tē) [Maori], *n.* (*New Zealand*) The diving petrel.

teetee (2) (tē′ tē) [S. Am. native], *n.* A small S. American monkey of the genus *Callithrix* or *Chrysothrix*.

teeter (tē′ tėr) [var. of TITTER, M.E. *titer*, Icel. *titra*, to shake], *v.i.* (*chiefly Am.*) To see-saw; to move to and fro unsteadily, to sway. *v.t.* To move to and fro, to tip up, to tilt. *n.* A see-saw.

teeth, *pl.* [TOOTH].

teethe (tēth) [from prec.], *v.i.* To cut or develop teeth. **teething,** *n.*

teetotal (tē tō′ tål) [redupl. of TOTAL], *a.* Of, pertaining to, pledged to, or advocating total abstinence from intoxicants; (*colloq.*) entire, complete. **teetotalism,** *n.* **teetotaller,** *n.* **teetotally,** *adv.*

teetotum (tē tō′ tŭm) [for *T-totum*, take all (T, L. *tōtum*, the whole), marked on one of the sides], *n.* A toy, orig. four-sided, turning like a top, used in a game of chance.

teff (tef) [Abyssinian], *n.* The chief Abyssinian cereal, *Eragrostis Abyssinica*, yielding flour used in Abyssinia for bread, elsewhere used as a fodder-plant.

teg (tĕg) [etym. doubtful, cp. Swed. *tacka*, ewe], *n.* A female fallow-deer; a doe in the second year; a young sheep.

tegmen (teg′ men) [L., var. *tegimen*, *tegumen*, from *tegere*, to cover], *n.* (*pl.* **-mina**) A covering of an organ or part in an animal or plant. **tegminal,** *a.* **tegmentum** [TEGUMENTUM].

tegular (teg′ ū lår) [L., *tegula*, tile, as prec., -AR], *a.* Pertaining to, resembling, or consisting of tiles. **tegularly,** *adv.* **tegulated,** *a.*

tegument (teg′ ū mėnt) [O.F., from L. *tegumentum*, as prec.], *n.* A protective covering, envelope, or membrane in animals. **tegumental** (-men′ tål), **tegumentary,** *a.* **tegumentum,** *n.* (*pl.* **-ta**).

tehee (tė hē′) [imit.], *n.* A restrained laugh, a titter. *v.i.* To laugh frivolously or contemptuously; to titter.

Te igitur (tē ij′ i tŭr) [L., thee, therefore], *n.* The first two words of the canon of the Mass; the book containing this.

teil (tēl) [O.F. (F. *tille*), L. *tilia*], *n.* The lime-tree or linden. **teil-tree,** *n.*

teind (tēnd) [M.E. *tende*, cogn. with TITHE], *n.* (*Sc.*) A tithe.

teinoscope (tī′ nō skōp) [Gr. *teinein*, to stretch, -SCOPE], *n.* An optical instrument, consisting of two prisms so combined that the chromatic aberration of light is corrected, and the linear dimensions of objects are increased or diminished.

teknology, teknonymy, etc. [TECNOLOGY].

tela (tē′ lå) [L.], *n.* (*Anat.*) A web, a web-like membrane, structure, etc. **telar, telary,** *a.*

telamon (tĕl′ å mŏn) [L., from Gr. *Telamōn*, mythical hero], *n.* (*pl.* **-mones,** -mō ′nēz) (*Arch.*) A male figure serving as a column or pilaster.

telautograph (tel aw′ tō grăf) [TELE-, AUTOGRAPH], *n.* A telegraph reproducing writing, etc., at a distance. **telautogram,** *n.* **telautographic** (-grăf′ ik), *a.* **telautography** (-tog′ rå fi), *n.*

tele- (1) [Gr. *tēle-*, pref. from *tēle*, adv., far off], *comb. form.* **telebarometer** (tel ė bå rom′ ė tėr) [BAROMETER], *n.* An instrument showing the barometric pressure at a distance. **telebarograph** (-băr′ ō grăf), *n.* **telecommunication,** *n.* Communication at a distance, *e.g.* by cable, telephone, radio, etc.

tele- (2) [abbrev. TELEVISION]. **telecast** (tel′ i kast), *n.* A programme or item broadcast by television. **telefilm,** *n.* A cinema film transmitted by television. **telegenic** (tel i jen′ ik), *a.* Suitable for television. **teleprompter,** *n.* An apparatus that enables a speaker on television to see his text without this being visible to the viewers. **telerecording,** *n.* A recording for broadcasting by television.

teledu (tel′ ė dū) [Javanese], *n.* The stinking badger, *Mydaus meliceps*, of Java and Sumatra.

Telefunken system (tel e fŭng′ kėn) [TELE-, G. *funken*, sparks], *n.* (*Radio.*) An early form of wireless on the spark system.

telega (tė lā′ gå) [Rus. *telêjga*], *n.* A four-wheeled springless Russian cart.

telegony (tel eg′ ō ni) [Gr. *tele*, far, *gonos*, offspring], *n.* (*Zool.*) The supposed influence that a female's first mate has on her offspring by subsequent mates.

telegram (tel′ ė grăm), *n.* A communication sent by telegraph.

telegraph (tel′ ė grăf) [TELE-, GRAPH], *n.* An apparatus or device for transmitting messages or signals to a distance, esp. by electrical agency; a telegraph-board; *a telegram. *v.t.* To transmit (a message, etc.,) by telegraph; to signal in any way. *v.i.* To send a message by telegraph; to signal (to, etc.). **telegraph-table,** *n.* A board on which the names of horses in a race, cricket-scores, etc. are displayed. **telegraph-cable, -line, -pole, -post, -wire,** *n.* A cable, wire, support, etc., used in establishing telegraphic connexion. **telegraph-plant,** *n.* An E. Indian plant of the bean family the leaves of which have a spontaneous jerking movement. **telegrapher, telegraphist** (tė leg′ rå fėr, -fist), *n.* **telegraphist's cramp** [MORSE-KEY PARALYSIS]. **telegraphic** (-grăf′ ik), *a.* Pertaining to the telegraph; sent by telegraph; suitable for the telegraph, brief, concisely worded. **telegraphically,** *adv.* **telegraphophone** (-grăf′ ō fōn) [-PHONE], *n.* An instrument for reproducing phonographic sounds or records at a distance. **telegraphy** (tė leg′ rå fi), *n.* The art or practice of communicating by telegraph or of constructing or managing telegraphs.

telekinesis (tel ė ki nē′ sis) [TELE-, Gr. *kinesis*, motion, see KINESI-], *n.* (*Psychics*) The movement of ponderable bodies at a distance and without the interposition of a material cause. **telekinetic** (-net′ ik), *a.*

telemark (tel′ e mark) [district in Norway], *n.* (*Sport*) A swinging turn in skiing.

telemeter (tė lem′ ė tėr) [TELE-, -METER], *n.* An

instrument for determining distances, used in surveying, artillery practice, etc. **telemetric** (-met′ rik), *a.* **telemetry,** *n.*

teleology (tel ē ol′ ȯ ji) [Gr. *telos teleos*, end, -LOGY], *n.* The doctrine of final causes. **teleologic, -al** (-loj′ ik, -ȧl), *a.* **teleologically,** *adv.* **teleologist,** *n.*

teleosaurus (tel ė ȯ saw′ rŭs) [Gr. *teleos*, complete, see prec., *sauros*, lizard], *n.* (*Palæont.*) A Mesozoic genus of fossil saurians. **teleostean** (-os′ tė ȧn) [Gr. *osteon*, bone], *a.* Of or belonging to the *Teleostai*, an order of osseous fishes.

telepathy (tė lep′ ȧ thi), *n.* Communication between minds at a distance without the agency of the senses, thought-transference, mind-reading. **telepathic** (-păth′ ik), *a.* **telepathically,** *adv.* **telepathist,** *n.* **telepathize,** *v.t.* and *i.*

telephone (tel′ ė fōn), *n.* An instrument for transmitting sounds to distances by a wire or cord, esp. by electrical agency. *v.t.* To transmit by means of a telephone. *v.t.* To speak thus (to). **telephone-booth:** (*Am.*) A call-box, a telephone kiosk. ***telepheme** (-fēm) [Gr. *phēmē*, voice], *n.* A telephonic message. **telephonic** (-fon′ ik), *a.* **telephonically,** *adv.* **telephonist** (tė lef′ ȯ nist), *n.* **telephony,** *n.*

telephote (tel′ ė fōt) [TELE-, Gr. *phōs phōtos*, light], *n.* A device for reproducing pictures at a distance. **telephoto** [TELEPHOTOGRAPHIC]. **telephotograph** (tel ė fō′ tȯ grăf), *n.* A picture reproduced at a distance, as by a telephote; a picture obtained by telephotography; *v.t.* To photograph thus. **telephotographic** (-grăf′ ik), *a.* **telephotography** (-tog′ rȧ fi), *n.* The act or process of photographing objects beyond the limits of ordinary vision. **telephoto lens,** *n.* (*Phot.*) A lens of long focal length, for obtaining photographs of very distant objects.

teleprinter (tel i prin tėr), *n.* A telegraphic apparatus with a keyboard transmitter and a type-printing receiver, whereby messages are received in printed form.

telescope (tel′ ė skōp) [TELE-, -SCOPE], *n.* An optical instrument for increasing the apparent size of distant objects. *v.t.* To drive or force (sections, trains, etc.,) into each other, like the sliding sections of a telescope. *v.i.* To move or be forced into each other thus. **telescopic** (-skop′ ik), *a.* **telescopically,** *adv.* **telescopiform,** *a.* **telescopist** (tė les′ kȯ pist), *n.* **telescopy,** *n.*

teleseme (tel′ ė sēm) [TELE-, Gr. *sēma*, sign], *n.* A system of electric transmitters with an annunciator used for signalling from different rooms in an hotel, etc.

***telesia** (tė les′ i ȧ) [Gr., pl. neut. of *telesios*, completing], *n.* A mineral composed of crystallized alumina, a sapphire.

telespectroscope (tel ė spek′ trȯ skōp) [TELE-, SPECTROSCOPE], *n.* An instrument for spectroscopic examination of the heavenly bodies. **telestereoscope** (-ster′ ė ȯ skōp), *n.* An optical instrument presenting distant objects in relief.

***telestick** (tė les′-, tel′ ės tik) [Gr. *telos*, end, *stichos*, row, verse], *n.* A poem in which the final letters of each line make up a word or words.

telethermograph (tel ė thĕr′ mȯ grăf) [TELE-, THERMOGRAPH], *n.* A self-registering telethermometer; a record made by this. **telethermometer** (-thėr mom′ ė tėr), *n.* A thermometer registering at a distance by electrical means.

teletype (tel′ e tīp), *n.* (*Elec.*) The sending by direct keyboard and the type-printing of telegraph messages.

teleutospore (tė lū′ tȯ spôr) [Gr. *teleutē*, completion, from *telos*, end, SPORE], *n.* A spore produced at the end of the season of fructification in the rust-fungi or *Uredinales.*

teleview (tel′ ē vū) [TELE-, VIEW], *v.t.*, *v.i.* To view with a television receiver. **televiewer,** *n.*

televise (tel′ ė vīz) [TELE-, VISION], *v.t.* To transmit by television.

television (tel′ e vi zhȯn) [TELE-, VISION], *n.* The transmission by radio or other means of visual images so that they are displayed on a cathode-ray tube screen. A rapid succession of such images gives a visual impression of an event as it actually occurs. **televisor** (tel′ ė vī zôr), *n.* A television receiver.

telic (tel′ ik) [Gr. *telos*, see prec., -IC], *a.* (*Gram.*) Expressing end or purpose; purposive.

tell (tel) [A.-S. *tellan*, from *talu*, TALE], *v.t.* (*past & p.p.* **told,** tōld) To relate, to recount; to make known, to express in words, to communicate, to divulge; to inform, to assure; to order, to bid, to direct; to distinguish, to ascertain; *to count, to enumerate. *v.i.* To give information or an account (of); (*colloq.*) to inform, to tattle; to produce a marked effect. **to tell off:** To count off; to select or detach on some special duty; (*colloq.*) to scold. **to tell one's beads:** To recite the rosary. **to tell the tale:** (*colloq.*) To tell a piteous story. **all told:** All included. **tellable,** *a.* **teller,** *n.* One who tells; one who numbers or counts, esp. one of four appointed to count votes in the House of Commons; an officer in a bank, etc., appointed to receive or pay out money. **tellership,** *n.* **telling,** *a.* **tellingly,** *adv.* **you're telling me:** (*colloq.*) You are telling me something I know all about.

telltale (tel′ tāl), *a.* Telling tales; given to telling tales conveying information. *n.* One who tells tales, esp. about the private affairs of others; (*fig.*) a sign, an indication, a token; any automatic device for giving information as to condition, position, etc.; (*Naut.*) an index in front of the wheel or in the cabin to show the position of the tiller.

tellural (tė lūr′ ȧl) [L. *tellus -lūris*, the earth, -AL], *a.* Of or pertaining to the earth. **tellurian,** *n.* An inhabitant of the earth; **a.* Tellural. **telluric** (1), *a.* **tellurion,** *n.* An apparatus for illustrating the real and apparent movements of the earth, the phenomena of eclipses, day and night, the seasons, etc.

tellurium (tė lūr′ i ŭm) [as prec., -IUM], *n.* A rare silvery-white non-metallic element found in association with gold, silver, and bismuth. **tellurate** (tel′ ū rȧt), *n.* A salt of telluric acid. **telluret,** *n.* **telluretted,** *a.* **telluride,** *n.* **telluric** (2) (tė lūr′ ik), **tellurous,** *a.* **telluriferous** (tel ū rif′ ėr ŭs), *a.* **tellurite,** *n.* (*Min.*) Native oxide of tellurium; (*Chem.*) a salt of tellurous acid.

telly (tel′ i), *n.* (*colloq.*) Television.

telotype (tel′ ȯ tīp) [Gr. *telos*, end, TYPE], *n.* A printing electric telegraph; a telegram printed by this.

telpher (tel′ fėr) [for *telephore* (TELE-, -PHORE)], *n.* A form of suspended monorail on which a truck runs, carrying its load hanging below the level of the truck and rail. **telpherline, -way,** *n.* **telpherage,** *n.* Transportation of this nature, operated usually by electricity.

telson (tel′ son) [Gr., limit], *n.* The last somite or joint in the abdomen of crustacea.

Telugu (tel′ u goo) [native name], *n.* The most extensive of the Dravidian languages, spoken on the Coromandel coast of India.

temenos (tem′ ė nos) [Gr., from *tem-*, base of *temnein*, to cut], *n.* (*Gr. Ant.*) A sacred enclosure, esp. the precinct of a temple.

temerarious (tem ė râr′ i ŭs) [L. *temerārius*, from *temere*, rashly], *a.* Rash, reckless, headstrong; careless, done at random. **temerariously,** *adv.* **temerity** (tė mer′ i ti), *n.* Excessive rashness, recklessness. ***temerous** (tem′ ė rŭs), *a.*

Tempean (tem pē′ ȧn) [L. and Gr. *Tempē*, -AN], *a.* Of or like Tempe, a beautiful vale in Thessaly, much praised by classic poets; delightful, lovely.

temper (tem′ pėr) [A.-S. *temprian*, L. *temperāre*, from *tempus -poris*, time, season], *v.t.* To mix in due proportion; to bring (clay, etc.,) to a proper consistency by mixing, kneading, etc.; to bring (steel, etc.,) to a proper degree of hardness by heating and cooling; (*fig.*) to qualify by admixture, to modify, to moderate, to tone down, to mitigate; (*Mus.*) to adjust the tones of (an instrument) according to a particular temperament. *v.i.* To be tempered. *n.* Disposition of mind, esp. as regards the passions or emotions; composure, self-command; anger, irritation, passion; the state of a metal as regards hardness and elasticity; condition or consistency (of a plastic mixture as mortar). **temperable,** *a.* **temperative,** *a.* **tempered,** *a.* **temperedly,** *adv.* (*usu. in comb.* as *hot-tempered, hot-temperedly*). **temperer,** *n.*

tempera (tem′ pėr å) [It.], *n.* Painting in distemper.

temperament (tem′ pėr å mėnt) [L. *temperāmentum*, as prec.], *n.* Individual character as determined by the reaction of the physical upon the mental constitution, natural disposition (formerly supposed to be determined by the relative predominance of certain humours, and classified as sanguine or full-blooded, lymphatic or phlegmatic, bilious, and melancholic); (*Mus.*) the adjustment of the tones of an instrument to fit the scale in any key, esp. by a compromise in the case of instruments of fixed intonation, as an organ or piano. **temperamental** (-men′ tål), *a.* Resulting from or connected with temperament; having an erratic or neurotic temperament.

temperance (tem′ pėr åns) [O.F., from L. *temperantia*, as prec.], *n.* Moderation, self-restraint, esp. in the indulgence of the appetites and passions; moderation in the use of intoxicants; (incorr.) total abstinence. **temperance hotel:** One in which alcoholic liquors are not supplied.

temperate (tem′ pėr åt) [L. *temperātus*, p.p. of *temperāre*, to TEMPER], *a.* Moderate, self-restrained; abstemious; not liable to excess of heat or cold, mild (of climate). **temperately,** *adv.* **temperateness,** *n.*

temperative [TEMPER].

temperature (tem′ pėr å tūr, -chėr) [F., from L. *temperātūra*, as TEMPERATE], *n.* Degree of sensible heat or cold in a body or the atmosphere, esp. as registered by the thermometer; (*colloq.*) body temperature above normal.

tempered, etc. [TEMPER].

tempest (tem′ pėst) [O.F. *tempeste* (F. *tempête*), L. *tempestātem*, nom. *-tas*, weather, from *tempus*, time], *n.* A violent storm of wind, esp. with heavy rain, hail, or snow; (*fig.*) violent tumult or agitation. **tempestuous,** *a.* **tempestuously,** *adv.* **tempestuousness,** *n.*

Templar (tem′ plår) [A.-F. *templer*, O.F. *templier*, med. L. *templārius*, from *templum*, TEMPLE (1)], *n.* A member of a religious and military order (the Knights Templars), founded in the 12th cent., for the protection of pilgrims to the Holy Land; a lawyer or a law-student having chambers in the Temple, in London; a member of the 'Good Templars.'

template [TEMPLET].

temple (1) (tem′ pėl) [A.-S. *templ*, L. *templum*, cogn. with TEMENOS], *n.* An edifice dedicated to the service of some deity or deities, esp. of the ancient Egyptians, Greeks, or Romans; one of the three successive buildings that were the seat of Jewish worship at Jerusalem; a place of public Christian worship, esp. a Protestant church in France; (*London*) two Inns of Court, on the ancient site of the Temple, the establishment of the Knights Templars; (*Bibl., etc.*) a place in which the divine presence specially resides.

temple (2) (tem′ pėl) [O.F. *temples*, L. *tempora*, pl. of *tempus*, time], *n.* The flat portion of the head between the forehead and ear. **temporal** (2), *a.*

temple (3) (tem′ pėl) [F., see foll.], *n.* An attachment in a loom for keeping the fabric stretched.

templet (tem′ plėt) [F., dim. of *temple*, L. *templum*, a small timber], *n.* A pattern, gauge, or mould, usu. of thin wood or metal, used as a guide in shaping, turning, or drilling; a short timber or stout stone placed in a wall to distribute the pressure of beams, etc.

tempo (tem′ pō) [It., from L. *tempus*, see foll.], *n.* (*Mus.*) Quickness or rate of movement, time.

temporal (1) (tem′ pŏ rål) [O.F., from L. *temporālis*, from *tempus -poris*, time], *a.* Pertaining to this life; secular; (*Gram.*) pertaining to or expressing time. **temporal lords:** The peers of the realm, as distinguished from the archbishops and bishops. **temporal power:** That of the Pope or the Church in temporal as distinguished from ecclesiastical affairs. **temporally,** *adv.* **temporalness,** *n.* **temporality,** *n.* The laity; a temporality.

temporal (2) [TEMPLE (2)].

temporality (tem pŏ răl′ i ti), *n.* A secular possession esp. (*pl.*) the revenues of a religious corporation or an ecclesiastic; temporalness.

temporary (tem′ pŏ rå ri) [L. *temporārius*, as TEMPORAL (1)], *a.* Lasting or intended only for a time or a special occasion. **temporarily,** *adv.* **temporariness,** *n.*

temporize (tem′ pŏ rīz), *v.i.* To pursue an indecisive, procrastinating, or time-serving policy; to comply with or humour or yield to the requirements of time and occasion; to trim; *to delay. **temporization** (-zā′ shŭn), *n.* **temporizer,** *n.* **temporizingly,** *adv.*

tempt (tempt) [O.F. *tenter*, *tempter*, L. *tentāre*, *temptāre*, freq. of *tenēre*, to hold], *v.t.* *To put to trial or proof; to incite or entice (to something or to do); to attract, to allure, to invite; *to provoke, to defy; *to attempt. **temptable,** *a.* **temptability** (-bil′ i ti), *n.* **temptation** (-tā′ shŭn), *n.* **tempter,** *n.* One who tempts; the devil. **temptingly,** *adv.* **temptress,** *n.*

***temse** (tems, temz) [A.-S. *temes* (in *temes -pile*), cp. Dut. *teems*, N. Fris. *tems*], *n.* A sieve. **temse-bread, -loaf,** *n.* Bread made of flour better sifted than common flour.

***temulent** (tem′ ū lėnt) [L. *tēmulentus*, from *tēm-*, cp. *tēmētum*, strong drink], *a.* Intoxicated, drunk; intoxicating. ***temulence, *-lency,** *n.*

ten (ten) [A.-S. *tiēn*, *tȳn* (Anglian *tēn*), (cp. Dut. *tien*, G. *zehn*, Icel. *tiu*, also L. *decem*, Gr. *deka*)], *n.* The sum of one and nine; twice five, 10, x; a playing-card with ten pips. *a.* One more than nine. **tenfold,** *a.* and *adv.* **tenpence,** *n.* **tenpenny,** *a.* Priced or sold at tenpence. **tenpenny nail:** A large nail orig. costing 10*d.* per 100. **ten-pins,** *n.* (*Am.*) A game played with ten pins in a skittle-alley. **tenth,** *a.* and *n.* **tenthly,** *adv.*

tenable (ten′ åbl) [F., from *tenir*, L. *tenēre*, to hold], *a.* Capable of being held, retained, or maintained against attack. **tenability** (-bil′ i ti), *n.* **tenableness,** *n.*

tenace (ten′ ās) [F., as foll], *n.* (*Whist, etc.*) The best and third best cards of a suit held in the same hand. **minor tenace:** The second and fourth best cards thus held.

tenacious (tė nā′ shŭs) [L. *tenax-ācis*, from *tenēre*, to hold], *a.* Holding fast; inclined to hold fast, obstinate, unyielding; retentive; adhesive, sticky; highly cohesive, tough. **tenaciously,** *adv.* **tenaciousness, tenacity** (tė năs′ i ti), *n.*

tenaculum (ten ăk′ ū lŭm), *n.* (*pl.* **tenacula**). A surgeon's finely-hooked instrument for seizing blood-vessels, etc.

tenail, *tenaille (tė nāl′) [F. *tenaille*, L. TENACULUM], *n.* (*Fort.*) A low outwork in the enceinte ditch in front of the curtain between two bastions.

tena koe (tē′ nä kō′ ē [Maori], *n.* The Maori greeting.

tenancy (ten′ ån si), *n.* The holding of lands, etc.; the period of such holding.

tenant (ten′ ånt) [O.F., pres.p. of *tenir*, see TENABLE], *n.* A person holding a land or tenement from a landlord; (*Law*) one holding lands or tenements by any kind of title; a defendant in a real action; (loosely) an occupant, a dweller, an inhabitant. *v.t.* To hold as tenant; to occupy. **tenant at will:** (*Law*) One who holds possession of lands at the will of the owner or lessor. **tenant-farmer,** *n.* One cultivating land leased from the owner. **tenant-right,** *n.* The right allowed by custom to a well-behaved tenant not to be liable to injurious increase of rent or to be deprived of tenancy without compensation. **tenantable,** *a.* Fit for occupation by a tenant. **tenantableness,** *n.* **tenantless,** *a.* **tenantry,** *n.* (*Collect.*) Tenants.

tench (tench) [O.F. *tenche* (F. *tanche*), L. *tinca*], *n.* A freshwater fish, *Tinca tinca* or *vulgaris*, of the carp family.

tend (1) (tend) [A.-F. *tendre*, L. *tendere*, to stretch (p.p. *tensus, tentus*), cogn. with TENABLE], *v.i.* To move, hold a course, or be directed (in a certain direction, etc.); to have a bent, inclination, or attitude, to aim, to conduce (to).

tend (2) (tend) [shortened from ATTEND], *v.t.* To attend, to watch, to look after, to take charge of; (*Naut.*) to watch (a vessel at anchor) so as to prevent her fouling the anchor and chain at the turn of the tide. *v.i.* To attend, to wait (upon). ***tendance,** *n.* **tendency** [TEND (1)].

tendency (ten' den si), *n.* Bent, drift, inclination, disposition.

tendentious (ten den' shus), *a.* With an underlying purpose, intended to further a cause.

tender (1) (ten' dėr) [TEND (2)], *n.* One who tends; a carriage attached to a locomotive carrying the supply of fuel, water, etc.; a vessel attending a larger one, to supply provisions, carry despatches, etc.

tender (2) (ten' dėr) [F. *tendre*, to TEND (1)], *v.t.* To offer, to present for acceptance; to offer in payment. *v.i.* To make a tender (to do certain work or supply goods, etc.). *n.* An offer for acceptance; an offer in writing to do certain work or supply certain articles, at a certain sum or rate; (*Law*) a formal offer of money or other things in satisfaction of a debt or liability; (*Am.*) a bid. **legal tender** [LEGAL].

tender (3) (ten' dėr) [M.E. and O.F. *tendre*, L. *tenerum*, nom. *tener*], *a.* Easily impressed, broken, bruised, etc., soft, delicate, fragile, weakly, frail; sensitive, easily pained or hurt, susceptible to pain, grief, etc., impressible, sympathetic; loving, affectionate, fond; careful, solicitous, considerate (of), requiring to be treated delicately or cautiously, ticklish. **tender-eyed,** *a.* Having gentle eyes; *weak-eyed. **tenderfoot,** *n.* (*Am. and Austral. slang*) A new-comer in the bush, etc., a novice; one of the lowest grade of Boy Scouts. **tender-hearted,** *a.* Having great sensibility, or susceptibility. **tender-heartedly,** *adv.* **tender-heartedness,** *n.* ***tender-hefted,** *a.* Tender-hearted. **tender-loin,** *n.* The tenderest part of the loin in beef or pork; (*Am.*) the undercut, fillet; (*Am.*) an unsavoury quarter of New York City. **tender-minded,** *a.* **tenderling,** *n.* **tenderly,** *adv.* **tenderness,** *n.*

tendon (ten' dŏn) [F., from med. L. *tendōnem*, nom. *-do*, from L. *tendere*, to stretch], *n.* One of the strong bands or cords of connective tissue forming the termination or connexion of the fleshy part of a muscle. **tendinous, tendonous,** *a.*

tendril (ten' dril) [etym. doubtful, prob. from L. as prec.], *n.* A leafless organ by which a plant clings to another body for support. **tendrilled,** *a.*

tenebræ (ten' ė brē) [L., darkness], *n.pl.* (*R.-C. Ch.*) The office of matins and lauds for the last three days in Holy Week. **tenebrific** (-brif' ik), *a.* Causing or producing darkness. ***tenebrosity** (-bros' i ti), *n.* ***tenebrous** (ten' ė brŭs), *a.* Dark, gloomy.

tenement (ten' ė mėnt) [O.F. from med. L. *tenementum*, from *tenēre*, to hold], *n.* An apartment or set of apartments used by one family; a dwelling-house; (*fig.*) a dwelling-place, a habitation; (*Law*) any kind of permanent property that may be held, as lands, houses, etc. **tenement-house,** *n.* A house let out in tenements, esp. in a poor district. **tenemental, tenementary** (-men' tăl, -tăr i), *a.*

tenendum (ten en' dŭm) [L.], *n.* (*pl.* **tenenda**) (*Law*) The cause in a deed in which the tenure is defined.

****tenesmus*** (tė nĕz' mŭs) [med. L., from Gr. *teinesmos*, from *teinein*, to stretch, to strain], *n.* An impotent desire, accompanied by effort and straining, to evacuate the bowels, usu. the result of inflammation in the rectum. ***tenesmic,** *a.*

tenet (ten' ėt, tē' net) [L., he holds, see TENEMENT], *n.* An opinion, principle, doctrine, or dogma held by a person or school.

tenfold [TEN]. **tenoid** [TÆNIOID].

tenner (ten' ėr), *n.* (*colloq.*) A ten-pound note.

tennis (ten' is) [M.E. *tenetz, tenys*, perh. from O.F. *tenez*, hold, take, as foll.], *n.* A game for two, three, or four persons played by striking a ball to and fro with rackets over a net stretched across a walled court; lawn-tennis. **lawn tennis,** *n.* A game for two (singles) or four (doubles) simpler than tennis and omitting the wall. **table tennis,** *n.* An indoor game resembling lawn tennis but played on a table; ping-pong. **tennis-arm, -elbow, -knee,** *n.* An arm, etc., strained or sprained in tennis-playing. **tennis-ball,** *n.* **tennis-court,** *n.*

tenon (ten' ŏn) [F., from *tenir*, L. *tenēre*, to hold], *n.* The projecting end of a piece of timber fitted for insertion into a mortise, etc. *v.t.* To cut a tenon on; to join by a tenon. **tenon-saw,** *n.* A thin saw with a strong brass or steel back used for cutting tenons, etc. **tenon-machine,** *n.* **tenoner,** *n.*

tenor (ten' ŏr) [M.E. and O.F. *tenour*, L. *tenōrem*, nom. *-or*, a holding on, (later) melody or canto fermo, from *tenēre*, to hold], *n.* A settled course, tendency, or direction; general purport or drift (of thought, etc.); (*Law*) the exact purport or meaning, also an exact transcript or copy; (*Mus.*) the highest of male chest voices between baritone and alto; the part for this; one with a tenor voice; an instrument, esp. the viola, playing a part between bass and alto. *a.* Pertaining to or adapted for singing or playing the tenor part. **tenor-clef,** *n.* The C clef placed upon the fourth line of the stave. ***tenore*** (tė nôr' ā) [It.], *n.* (*pl.* **-ti** -ē). **tenorino** (ten ŏ rē' nō) [It., dim. of prec.], *n.* (*pl.* **-ni,** -nē) A falsetto tenor voice or singer; an artificial soprano. **tenorist,** *n.*

tenotomy (tė not' ŏ mi) [Gr. *tenōn*, tendon, -TOMY], *n.* The cutting of a tendon.

tenpence, tenpenny, etc. [TEN].

tenrec [TANREC].

tense (1) (tens) [O.F. *tens* (F. *temps*), L. *tempus*, time], *n.* (*Gram.*) A form taken by a verb to indicate the time, and also the continuance or completedness, of an action. **tenseless,** *a.*

tense (2) (tens) [L. *tensus*, p.p. of *tendere*, see TEND (1)], *a.* Stretched tight, strained to stiffness (*lit. and fig.*). **tensely,** *adv.* **tenseness, tensity,** *n.* **tensible,** *a.* **tensibility** (-bil' i ti), *n.*

tensile (ten' sīl, -sil), *a.* Of or pertaining to tension; capable of extension. **tensility,** *n.*

tension (ten' shŭn), *n.* The act of stretching or the state of being stretched; strain, stress, effort; mental strain, stress, or excitement; (*Mech.*) stress tending to draw asunder the particles of a body, as in a belt, sheet, etc., that is being pulled; the expansive force of a gas or vapour. **tension-rod,** *n.* A rod in a structure preventing the spreading of opposite members. **tensional,** *a.* ***tensive,** *a.*

tenson (tan son, ten' sŏn) [F., from It. *tenzone*, as TENSION], *n.* A contention in verse between troubadours; a subdivision of a poem sung by one of them.

tensor (ten' sŏr), *n.* (*Anat.*) A muscle that stretches or tightens a part.

tent (1) (tent) [O.F. *tente*, L. *tenta*, pl. of *tentum* neut. p.p. of *tendere*, to stretch], *n.* A portable shelter consisting of canvas or other flexible material stretched over and supported on poles. *v.t.* To cover with or lodge in a tent. *v.i.* To encamp in a tent. **bell tent,** *n.* A circular tent supported on a central pole. **tent bed,** *n.* A bed with curtains which hang from a central point, in the style of a tent. **tented,** *a.* **tenter** (1), *n.* **tentful,** *n.* **tent-wise,** *adv.* **tent-fly,** *n.* A loose piece of canvas, etc., fastened over the ridge-pole to shelter a tent from sun and rain. **tent-maker,** *n.* **tent-peg, -pin,** *n.* A peg or pin fixed in the ground for fastening down the ropes stretching a tent. **tent-pegging,** *n.* The cavalry sport or exercise of pulling out tent-pegs with a lance while at full gallop.

tent (2) (tent) [O.F. from *tenter*, to probe, see TEMPT], *n.* (*Surg.*) A small roll of lint, sponge, etc., inserted in a wound, ulcer, etc., to keep it open. *v.t.* To keep open with a tent.

tent (3) (tent) [Sp. *vino tinto*, deep-coloured wine (*tinto*, L. *tinctus*, see TINGE)], *n.* A Spanish wine of a deep red colour, used for sacramental purposes.

tent (4) (tent) [Sc. and North., var. of TEND (2)], *v.i.* To watch, to take heed. *v.t.* To take care of, to tend. **tenter** (2), *n.*

tentacle (ten' tȧ kėl) [from L. *tentāre*, see TEMPT, after SPECTACLE, etc.], *n.* A long slender organ of touch, prehension, or locomotion, a feeler, as an arm of a cuttle-fish; (*Bot.*) a sensitive hair. **tentacled,** *a.* **tentacular** (-tăk' ū lȧr), **tentaculate, -lated, -loid,** *a.* **tentaculiferous, -ligerous** (-lif'-, -lij' ėr ŭs). Bearing, or producing, tentacles. **tentaculiform** (-tăk' ū li fôrm), *a.* **tentaculum** (*pl.* **-ula**), *n.*

tentative (ten' tȧ tiv) [med. L. *tentātīvus*, from *tentāre*, see TEMPT], *a.* Consisting or done as a trial or essay, experimental. *n.* An experiment, a trial, a conjecture. ***tentation** (-tā' shŭn), *n.* Trial, temptation. **tentatively,** *adv.*

tenter (1 and 2) [TENT (1) and (4)].

tenter (3) (ten' tėr) [prob. through an A.-F. and O.F. *tentour*, from *tendere*, to stretch], *n.* A frame or machine for stretching cloth to dry or make it set even and square; a tenter-hook. **tenter-hook,** *n.* One of a set of hooks used in stretching cloth on the tenter. **on tenter-hooks:** (*fig.*) In a state of suspense and anxiety.

tenth, etc. [TEN].

***tentigo** (ten tī' gō) [L.], *n.* Priapism, lecherousness. ***tentiginous** (-tij' i nŭs), *a.*

tentorium (ten tôr' i ŭm) [L., from *tendere*, see TENT (1)], *n.* (*Anat.*) A membranous partition stretched across the cranium between the cerebrum and the cerebellum.

***tenture** (ten' tūr) [F., ult. from L. *tendere*, to stretch, p.p. *tentus*], *n.* Wall-hangings, wall-paper.

tenuity (tė nū' i ti) [F. *ténuité*, L. *tēnuitātem*, nom. *-tas*, from *tenuis*, thin], *n.* Thinness, slenderness; rarity; (*fig.*) meagreness. **tenuifolious** (ten ū i fō' li ŭs), *a.* (*Bot.*) Having thin or narrow leaves. **tenuiroster** (-ros' tėr), *n.* One of the *Tenuirostres*, a group of insessorial birds with long, slender bills. **tenuirostral,** *a.* **tenuis** (ten' ū is), *n.* (*Gr. Gram.*) One of the hard or surd mutes, *k, p, t.*

tenuous (ten' ū ŭs), *a.* Thin, slender, small, minute; rare, rarefied, subtle, over-refined.

tenure (ten' ūr) [A.-F. and O.F., from med. L. *tenitūra*, *tenūra*, cp. TENOR], *n.* The act, manner, or right of holding property, esp. real estate; the manner or conditions of holding; the period or term of holding.

tenuto (tė noo' tō) [It., held, from L. as prec.], *a.* (*Mus.*) Sustained, held on for the full time, opp. to staccato.

teocalli (tē ȯ kăl' i) [Mex. *teotl*, god, *calli*, house], *n.* A pyramidal mound or structure, usu. surmounted by a temple, used for worship by the aborigines of Mexico, Central America, etc.

tepefy (tep' ė fī) [L. *tepefacere* (*tepēre*, see TEPID, *facere*, to make)], *v.t.* To make tepid. *v.i.* To become tepid. **tepefaction** (-făk' shŭn), *n.*

tephrite (tef' rīt) [L. *tephrītis* (Gr. *tephra*, ashes, -ITE)], *n.* (*Min.*) A volcanic rock allied to basalt. **tephritic** (tė frit' ik), **tephritoid** (tef' ri toid), *a.* **tephromancy,** *n.* Divination by the inspection of sacrificial ashes.

tepid (tep' id) [L. *tepidus*, from *tepēre*, to be warm], *a.* Moderately warm; lukewarm. **tepidarium** (-dâr' i ŭm), *n.* (*pl.* **-ia**) (*Rom. Ant.*) The room between the frigidarium and the caldarium in a Roman bath; a boiler in which the water was heated. **tepidity** (tė pid' i ti), **tepidness,** *n.* **tepidly,** *adv.*

ter (tĕr) [L.], *adv.* Thrice, three times.

teraphim (ter' ȧ fim) [Heb.], *n.pl.* Household gods or idols among the Jews consulted as oracles.

teratogeny (ter ȧ toj' ė ni) [Gr. *teras -atos*, monster, -GENY], *n.* (*Biol. etc.*) The production of monsters or abnormal growths. **teratogenic** (-jen' ik), *a.* **teratoid,** *a.*

teratology (ter ȧ tol' ō ji), *n.* The branch of biology dealing with monsters and malformations; a work on the marvellous, a marvellous tale, etc. **teratological** (-loj' i kȧl), *a.* **teratologist** (-tol'-), *n.*

teratosis (ter ȧ tō' sis), *n.* (*Path.*) Monstrosity.

terbium (tĕr' bi ŭm) [*Ytterby*, in Sweden, cp. ERBIUM, -IUM], *n.* (*Chem.*) A rare metallic element found in association with erbium and yttrium.

terce [TIERCE]. **tercel** [TIERCEL].

tercentenary (tĕr sen' tė-, -sėn tē' nȧ ri) [TER, CENTENARY], *a.* Comprising 300 years. *n.* A 300th anniversary.

tercet (tĕr' sėt) [It. *terzetto*, dim. of *terzo*, L. TERTIUS], *n.* (*Pros. and Mus.*) A triplet.

tercine (tĕr' sin) [F., from *tiers*, or L. *tertius*, third], *n.* (*Bot.*) A layer supposed to form a third coat in certain ovules.

terebinth (ter' ė binth) [L. *terebinthus*, Gr. *terebinthos*], *n.* The turpentine-tree, *Pistacia terebinthus*, from which Chian turpentine is obtained; its resin. **terebene** (-bēn) [-ENE], *n.* A liquid hydrocarbon obtained by treating oil of turpentine with sulphuric acid, used as an antiseptic, disinfectant, etc., **terebinthine** (-bin' thin), *a.* Pertaining to or partaking of the qualities of terebinth or turpentine. **terebic** (tė reb' ik), *a.*

terebra (ter' ė brȧ) [L., borer (from *terere*, to pierce), whence *terebrāre*, to bore], *n.* (*pl.* **-bræ, -brē**) [*Ent.*] An ovipositor adapted for boring. **terebrate,** *v.t.* To bore. **terebrant,** *a.* and *n.* ***terebration** (-brā' shŭn), *n.* **Terebratula** (-brăt' ū lȧ), *n.* (*pl.* **-læ, -lē**) (*Zool.*) A genus of brachiopods, largely extinct. **terebratular, terebratuliform** (-brȧ tū' li fôrm), *a.* **terebratulid,** *n.* **terebratulite,** *n.* A fossil species of Terebratula. **terebratuloid,** *a.* and *n.*

teredo (tėr ē' dō) [L., from Gr. *terēdōn*, from *teirein*, to bore], *n.* A mollusc that bores into submerged timber, the ship-worm. **teredine** (ter' ė din, -dīn), *n.*

terek (ter' ėk) [name of river in Caucasus], *n.* A species of sandpiper, *Terekia cinerea*, with the bill curved slightly upward, frequenting E. Asia.

Terentian (tė ren' shi ȧn), *a.* Of, pertaining to, or in the style of the Roman dramatist Terence.

terete (tė rēt') [L. *teres -retis*, from *terere*, see TEREBRA], *a.* Rounded, cylindrical, and smooth.

tergal (tĕr' gȧl) [L. *tergum*, back], *a.* Of or pertaining to the back or a tergite. ***tergant** (-gȧnt), ***tergiant** (-jȧnt), *a.* (*Her.*) Showing the back part.

tergeminate (tėr jem' i nȧt) [L. *tergeminus* (TER, *geminus*, see GEMINATE)], *a.* (*Bot.*) Having a pair of leaflets on each of two secondary petioles and at the base.

tergiferous (ter jif' ėr ŭs) [L. *tergum*, back, -FEROUS], *a.* (*Bot.*) Bearing or carrying on the back, as ferns their seeds. **tergite** (tĕr′ jit), *n.* The upper or dorsal plate of a somite or segment of an articulate animal, also called **tergum** (*pl.* **-ga**).

tergiversate (tĕr′ ji vėr sāt) [L. *tergiversatus*, p.p. of *tergiversārī* (*tergum*, back, *versārī*, freq. of *vertere*, to turn), *v.i.* To practise evasions or subterfuges, to equivocate; to change sides. **tergiversation** (sā′ shŭn), *n.* **tergiversator** (tĕr′ ji vėr sā tôr), *n.*

tergum [TERGIFEROUS].

term (tĕrm) [O.F. *terme*, L. *terminum*, nom. *-us*, cp. Gr. *terma*, limit], *n.* A limit, a boundary; a limited period; (*Univ., schools, Law, etc.*) the period during which instruction is regularly given or the courts are in session; an appointed day or date; (*Law*) an estate to be enjoyed for a fixed period; a word having a definite and specific meaning; (*pl.*) language or expressions used; (*pl.*) conditions, stipulations, price, charge, rate of payment; relative position, relation, footing; (*Log.*) a word or group of words that may be the subject or predicate of a proposition; (*Math.*) the antecedent or consequent of a ratio; one of the parts of an expression connected by the plus or minus signs. *v.t.* To designate, to call, to denominate. **to come to terms:** To conclude an agreement (with); to yield, to give way. **to bring to terms:** To force or induce to accept conditions. **termer, -or,** *n.* (*Law*) One who has an estate for a term of years or for life. **terms of reference:** The specific points which a committee or other body is charged to decide. ***termless,** *a.* Unlimited, boundless. **termly,** *a.* Occurring every term. *adv.* Term by term; every term; periodically.

terma (tĕr′ mȧ) [Gr., see prec.], *n.* (*pl.* ***-ata***) (*Anat.*) A thin layer of grey matter at the front of the third ventricle of the brain. **termatic** (-măt′ ik), *a.* and *n.*

termagant (tĕr′ mȧ gȧnt) [M.E. *Tervagant*, O.F. *Tervagan*, It. *Trivigante* (per. L. *tri-*, TER, *vagans, -ntem*, pres.p. of *vagārī*, to wander, with ref. to Selene or the Moon), name of an idol or deity whom the Saracens are represented in mediæval romances as worshipping], *n.* A shrewish, abusive, violent woman. *a.* Violent, boisterous, turbulent, shrewish. **termagancy,** *n.* ***termagantly,** *adv.*

termatic [TERMA]. **termer** [TERM].

termes (tĕr′ mēz) [L., from *ter-ere*, Gr. *teirein*, to rub, to bore], *n.* (*pl.* ***termites,*** tĕr′ mi tēz) A termite.

terminable, etc. [TERMINATE].

terminal (tĕr′ mi nȧl) [L. *terminālis*, from TERMINUS], *a.* Pertaining to or forming a boundary, limit, or terminus; forming or situated at the end of a series or part. *n.* That which terminates; a limit, an extremity, an end, esp. one of the free ends of an electrical conductor from a battery, etc., ***terminalia*** (tĕr mi nā′ li ȧ), *n.pl.* (*Rom. Ant.*) A festival celebrated annually on 23rd Feb. in honour of Terminus, the god of boundaries. **terminally,** *adv.*

terminate (tĕr′ mi nāt) [L. *terminātus*, p.p. of *termināre*, from TERMINUS], *v.t.* To bound, to limit; to form the extreme point or end of; to put an end to. *v.i.* To stop, to end (in, etc.). *a.* Limitable, limited, bounded; (*Math.*) finite. **terminable,** *a.* Capable of being terminated; having a given term or period. **terminableness,** *n.* **termination** (-nā′ shŭn), *n.* **terminational,** *a.* **terminative** (tĕr′ mi nā-, -nȧ tiv), **terminatory,** *a.* **terminatively,** *adv.* **terminator** (-nā tôr), *n.* One who or that which terminates; (*Astron.*) the dividing-line between the illuminated and the dark part of a heavenly body.

terminer [DYER].

terminism (tĕr′ mi nizm), *n.* (*Theol.*) The doctrine that there is a limited period in each man's life for repentance and grace; (*Phil.*) nominalism. **terminist,** *n.*

terminology (tĕr mi nol′ ȯ ji) [as prec. -LOGY], *n.* The science of the correct use of terms; (*collect.*) the terms used in any art, science, etc., **terminological** (-loj′ i kȧl), *a.* **terminological inexactitude,** *n.* (*facet.*) A lie. **terminologically,** *adv.*

terminus (tĕr′ mi nŭs) [L., see TERM], *n.* (*pl.* **-ni**) A boundary, a limit, a boundary-mark; the station at the end of a railway or important branch; (*Rom. Ant.*) the god of boundaries; a figure of the upper portion of the human body, terminating in a block or pillar; *a final point, goal, or end.

termite (tĕr′ mīt) [L. *termes -mitis*, woodworm, cogn. with TEREDO], *n.* A white ant. **termitarium** (-târ′ i ŭm), **termitary** (tĕr′-), *n.* A nest of or cage for termites.

termless, termor, etc. [TERM].

tern (1) (tĕrn) [prob. from Dan. *terne*, cp. Icel. *therna*, Swed. *tärna*], *n.* A gull-like sea-bird of the genus *Sterna*, slenderly-built, with narrow, sharp-pointed wings. **ternery,** *n.*

tern (2) (tĕrn) [L. *ternī*, by threes, from TER], *a.* Ternate. *n.* A set of three, esp. three lottery numbers winning a large prize if won together; the prize thus won. **ternal, ternary,** *a.* Proceeding by or consisting of three. *n.* A group of three, a triad. **ternate,** *a.* Arranged in threes, esp. in whorls of three (of leaflets, etc.). **ternately,** *adv.*

terne (tĕrn) [F., dull, tarnished], *n.* Sheet-iron coated with an alloy of tin and lead; inferior tin-plate. **terne-plate,** *n.*

ternery [TERN (1)].

terpene (tĕr′ pēn) [obs. *terp-*, TURP-ENTINE, -ENE], *n.* (*Chem.*) One of various isomeric oily hydrocarbons derived chiefly from coniferous plants. **terpin,** *n.* A derivative of oil of turpentine and other terpenes.

Terpsichorean (tĕrp si kȯ rē′ ȧn), *a.* Pertaining to Terpsichore the Muse of dancing; dancing.

terra (ter′ ȧ) [It. and L.], *n.* Earth. **terra-cotta,** *n.* A hard, unglazed pottery used as a decorative building-material, for statuary, etc.; a statue or figure in this; the brownish-orange colour of terra-cotta. **terra firma:** Dry land. **terra incognita:** Unknown country. **terra japonica:** Gambier.

terrace (1) (ter′ ȧs) [O.F., from It. *terraccia, terrazza*, from prec.], *n.* A raised level space or platform, artificially constructed or natural; a row of houses, esp. running along the side of a slope; (*Geol.*) an old shore-line or raised beach. *v.t.* To form into or furnish with terraces.

***terrace** (2) [TARRAS].

terrain (ter ān′) [F., TERRENE], *n.* A region, a tract, an extent of land of a definite geological character; a tract of country which is the scene of operations.

terramara (ter ȧ ma′ rȧ) [It. TERRA *amara*, bitter earth (L. *amārus*, bitter)], *n.* (*pl.* **-re,** -rā) An earthy deposit of various kinds, usu. composed of bones, phosphates, and mineral matter, used as a fertilizer; a deposit in parts of S. Europe containing prehistoric remains, analogous to that of the kitchen-middens.

terraneous (te rā′ ni ŭs), *a.* (*Bot.*) Growing on land.

terrapin (ter′ ȧ pin) [Algonkin], *n.* A freshwater tortoise, esp. the N. American saltmarsh or diamond-back terrapin, highly esteemed for food.

terraqueous (ter ā′ kwė ŭs) [TERRA, AQUEOUS], *a.* Consisting of land and water, as the globe.

terrene (1) (tė rēn′) [L. *terrēnus*, from TERRA], *a.* Pertaining to the earth, earthy; terrestrial. **terrenely,** *adv.*

***terrene** (2) [TERRINE].

terreplein (târ′ plān) [F. (*terre*, as prec., *plein*, PLAIN (1))], *n.* (*Fort.*) The upper surface of the rampart where guns are mounted; the level surface about a fieldwork.

terrestrial (tė res′ tri ȧl) [L. *terrestris*], *a.* Pertaining to or existing on the earth, not celestial; consisting of land, not water; living on the ground, not aquatic, arboreal, etc.; pertaining to this world, worldly. **terrestrial magnetism,** *n.* The magnetic properties possessed by the earth as a whole, which actuate the magnetic compass. **terrestrially,** *adv.*

terret (ter' ėt) [etym. doubtful], *n.* One of the rings or loops on harness through which the driving-reins pass.

terrible (ter' i bėl) [O.F., from L. *terribilis,* from *terrēre,* to terrify], *a.* Causing terror or dread; awful, formidable, terrifying, appalling, shocking; (*colloq.*) excessive, extreme. **terribleness,** *n.* **terribly,** *adv.*

terricolous (tė rik' ȯ lùs) [L. terricola, earth-dweller (TERRA, *colere,* to dwell)], *a.* Living on or in the earth; pertaining to the *Terricolæ,* a group of annelids comprising the earthworms.

terrier (1) (ter' i ėr) [F., from med. L. *tarrārius,* from TERRA], *n.* A small active dog of various breeds with an instinct for pursuing its quarry underground; (*colloq.*) a member of the Territorial Army.

terrier (2) (ter' i ėr) [F. *papier terrier,* as prec.], *n.* A book or roll in which the lands of private persons or corporations are described by site, boundaries, acreage, etc.

terrific (tė rif' ik) [L. *terrificus* (*terrēre,* to frighten, -FIC)], *a.* Causing terror; frightful, terrible. **terrifically,** *adv.* Frighteningly; (*colloq.*) exceedingly, surprisingly. **terrify** (ter' i fī), *v.t.* To strike with terror, to frighten.

terrigenous (tė rij' ė nùs) [L. *terrigena,* earth-dweller], *a.* Produced by or derived from the earth.

terrine (tė rēn') [F., TUREEN], *n.* An earthenware jar containing some table-delicacy, sold with its contents.

territorial (ter i tôr' i ȧl) [as foll., -AL], *a.* Pertaining to territory; limited to a given district; of or pertaining to the Territorial Army; (*U.S.*) pertaining to a Territory or the Territories. *n.* (*colloq.*) A member of the Territorial Army. **Territorial Army:** A military force established in 1907 for home defence to supersede the militia, yeomanry, and volunteers. **territorial waters:** The area of sea, usu. three miles out, adjoining the coast and adjudged to be under the jurisdiction of the country occupying that coast. **territorialize,** *v.t.* **territorially,** *adv.* **territoried,** *a.*

territory (ter' i tȯr i) [L. *territōrium,* from TERRA], *n.* The extent of land within the jurisdiction of a particular sovereign, state, or other power; a large tract of land; (*U.S.*) a division of the country not yet granted full State rights or admitted into the Union.

terror (ter' ȯr) [M.E. *terrour,* F. *terreur,* L. *terrōrem,* nom. *-or,* from *terrēre,* to frighten], *n.* Extreme fear; an object of fear; (*colloq.*) an exasperating nuisance, bore, troublesome child, etc., **king of terrors:** Death. **Reign of Terror:** The bloodiest period of the French Revolution (April 1793–July 1794). **terror-stricken, -struck,** *a.* Terrified, paralysed with fear. **terrorist,** *n.* One who rules or advocates rule by intimidation, as a Russian nihilist, etc., **terrorism,** *n.* **terroristic** (-ris' tik), *a.* **terrorize,** *v.t.* **terrorization** (-zā' shùn), *n.*

terry (ter' i) [etym. doubtful], *n.* A pile fabric in which the loops are not cut. **terry-velvet,** *n.*

Ter-sanctus (tĕr sănk' tùs) [L. TER, *sanctus,* holy], *n.* (*Eccles.*) The Trisagion.

terse (tĕrs) [L. *tersus,* p.p. of *tergere,* to wipe], *a.* Concise, pithy, neat and compact (of style). **tersely,** *adv.* **terseness,** *n.*

tertial (tĕr' shȧl) [from L., as foll.], *a.* Pertaining to the tertiary feathers. *n.* One of the tertiary feathers.

tertian (tĕr' shȧn) [M.E. *terciane,* L. *tertiānus,* from TERTIUS], *a.* Occurring or recurring every third day. *n.* A fever or ague, the paroxysms of which recur every other day.

tertiary (tĕr' shȧ ri) [L. *tertiārius,* as prec.], *a.* Of the third order, rank, or formation; (*Geol.*) pertaining to the Tertiary. *n.* One of the feathers attached to the proximal joint of a bird's wing; (*Geol.*) the third geological period, following the Secondary or Mesozoic; (*R.-C.*) a member of the third order of a monastic body.

tertiate (tĕr' shi āt) [L. *tertiātus,* p.p. of *tertiāre,* as prec.], *v.t.* *To do for the third time; (*Mil.*) to examine the thickness of the metal of (a gun) by measuring at three or more points.

tertius (tĕr' shùs) [L., third, cp. TER], *a.* Third (of the name).

teru-tero (ter' u ter' ō) [S. Am. native, imit. of cry], *n.* The Cayenne lapwing, *Vanellus Cayannensis.*

Terylene (ter i lēn'), *n.* Proprietary name of a synthetic textile material.

terza rima (târt' sȧ rē' mȧ) [It., third (as TERTIUS) rhyme], *n.* (pl. ***-ze, -me,*** -sā, ma) A form of triplet in iambic decasyllables or hendecasyllables rhyming *ababcb,* employed by Dante in the *Divina Commedia.*

terzetto (târt set' ō) [It., see TERCET], *n.* A short composition for three performers or singers.

tessellated (tes ė lā' tėd) [L. *tessellātus,* from *tessela,* dim. of foll.], *a.* Composed of tesseræ, inlaid; (*Nat. Hist.*) coloured or marked in checkered squares. **tessellar,** *a.* **tessellation** (-lā' shùn), *n.*

tessera (tes' ėr ȧ) [L., from Gr. *tessares,* four], *n.* (*pl.* **-seræ**) A small cubical piece of marble, earthenware, etc., used in mosaics. **tesseral,** *a.* Of or composed of tesseræ; (*Cryst.*) isometric. **tessular,** *a.* (*Cryst.*) Tesseral.

test (1) (test) [O.F. (F. *têt*), L. *testum,* cp. TESTA], *n.* A vessel used in refining gold and silver, a cupel; a critical trial or examination; a means of trial, a standard, a criterion; judgment, discrimination; (*Chem.*) a substance employed to detect one or more of the constituents of a compound; a removable hearth in a reverberatory furnace. *v.t.* To put to the test, to try, to prove by experiment; to try severely, to tax (one's endurance, etc.); (*Chem.*) to examine by the application of some reagent; (*Metal.*) to refine in a cupel. **Test Act:** An Act of 1672 (repealed in 1828) requiring persons holding office, receiving pay from the Crown, etc., to take the Oaths of Allegiance and Supremacy, receive the sacrament, etc., **test case,** *n.* (*Law*) A case taken to trial in order that the court shall decide some question that affects other cases. **test match,** *n.* (*Sport*) A cricket match forming one of a series of international matches. **test-paper,** *n.* Bibulous paper saturated with a chemical solution that changes colour when exposed to the action of certain chemicals. **test-tube,** *n.* A narrow glass tube closed at one end, used in chemical tests. **testable** (1), *a.* **tester** (1), *n.* One who or that which tests. **testing,** *n.*

test (2) (test) [O.F. *tester,* L. *testārī,* from *testis,* witness], *v.t.* To attest, to verify. *v.i.* (*Sc. Law*) To attest a will or other deed.

test (3) (test) [L. TESTA], *n.* A shell, a hard covering or exoskeleton.

testa (tes' tȧ) [L., potsherd, tile, etc.], *n.* (*pl.* ***testæ***) The outer integument of a seed; a test.

testable (1) [TEST (1)].

testable (2) (tes' tȧbl) [O.F., from L. *testābilis,* from *testārī,* see TESTATE], *a.* (*Law*) That may be given in evidence; that may be devised or bequeathed.

Testacea (tes tā' shi ȧ) [L. *testaceus,* from TESTA], *n.pl.* An order of protozoans having shells, shell-bearing invertebrates excluding crustaceans. **testacean,** *a.* and *n.* **testaceous,** *a.* **testacel** (tes' tȧ sel), *n.* Any species of the *Testacella,* a genus of carnivorous slugs; a member of the *Testacella.* **testaceology** (-shė ol' ȯ ji) [-LOGY], *n.*

testacy (tes' tȧ si), *n.* The state of being testate.

testament (tes′ tȧ mėnt) [O.F., from L. *testāmentum*, from *testārī*, to testify, see TESTATE], *n.* A solemn instrument in writing by which a person disposes of his personal estate after death, a will; one of the two main divisions of the Scriptures; (*colloq.*) a copy of the New Testament. **New Testament:** The portion of the Bible dealing with the Christian dispensation composed after the birth of Christ. **Old Testament:** The portion treating of the old or Mosaic dispensation. **testamentary** (-men′ tȧ rĭ), ***testamental,** *a.* **testamentarily,** *adv.* ***testamentation** (-tā′ shŭn), *n.* ***testamur*** (tes tā′ mŭr) [L., we testify], *n.* A certificate that a student has passed an examination.

testate (tes′ tāt) [L. *testātus*, p.p. of *testāri*, see prec.], *a.* Having made and left a will. *n.* One who has left a will in force. **testation** (-tā′ shŭn), *n.* **testator** (-tā′ tŏr), *n.* **testatrix,** *n.*

tester (1) [TEST (1)].

tester (2) (tes′ tėr) [M.E. and O.F. *testre*, L. *testa*, late L., head], *n.* A canopy, esp. over a four-post bedstead.

***tester** (3) (tes′ tėr) [corr. of earlier *teston*, O.F. *teston*, as prec.], *n.* A shilling of Henry VIII; (*colloq.*) a sixpence. ***testern,** *v.t.* (*Shak.*) To present with a tester.

testes, *pl.* [TESTIS].

testicle (tes′ ti kėl) [L. *testiculus*, dim. of TESTIS], *n.* One of the two glands which secrete the seminal fluid in males. **testicular, testiculate,** *a.*

testify (tes′ ti fī) [F. *testifier*, L. *testificāre* (*testis*, witness, *-ficāre*, *facere*, to make)], *v.i.* To bear witness (to, against, concerning, etc.); (*Law*) To give evidence. *v.t.* To bear witness to; to attest; to affirm or declare; to be evidence or serve as proof of. ***testificate** (-tif′ i kȧt), *n.* (*Sc. Law*) A solemn written assertion. **testification** (-kā′ shŭn), *n.* **testifier, *testificator** (tes′ tif i kā tŏr), *n.*

testily [TESTY].

testimonial (tes ti mō′ ni ȧl) [F., from late L. *testimoniālis*, from *testimonium*, see foll.], **a.* Relating to or consisting of testimony; intended as a testimonial. *n.* A certificate of character, services, qualifications, etc., of a person; a gift formally (and usu. publicly) presented to a person as a token of esteem and acknowledgment of services, etc. **testimonialize,** *v.t.*

testimony (tes′ ti mŏ ni) [L. *testimonium*, from *testis*, witness], *n.* A solemn declaration or statement; (*Law*) a statement under oath or affirmation; evidence, proof, confirmation; a solemn declaration of approval or protest; (*Bibl.*) the law as set forth in the two tables, the decalogue, the word of God, the Scriptures. **v.t.* To prove by evidence, to attest.

testiness [TESTY]. **testing** [TEST (1)].

testis (tes′ tis) [L., etym. doubtful], *n.* (*pl.* **-tes,** -tēz). (*Anct.*) A testicle; a round organ or part resembling this.

***testril** (*Shak.*) [corr. of TESTER (2)].

testudo (tes tū′ dō) [L. *testūdo -dinis*, from TESTA], *n.* (*Rom. Ant.*) A screen or penthouse formed by shields held above their heads and overlapping by soldiers advancing to the attack of a fortress; any similar screen, esp. one used by miners working in places liable to cave in; a genus of tortoises. **testudinal,** *a.* Pertaining to or resembling the tortoise. **testudinarious** (-nâr′ i ŭs), *a.* Mottled like tortoiseshell. **testudinated, -dinate,** *a.* Shaped or arched like the back of a tortoise. **testudineous** (-din′ ė ŭs), *a.* Resembling the shell of a tortoise.

testy (tes′ ti) [M.E. and A.-F. *testif*, from O.F. *teste* (F. *tête*), head], *a.* Irritable, peevish, pettish, petulant. **testily,** *adv.* **testiness,** *n.*

tetanus (tet′ ȧ nŭs) [L., from Gr. *tetanos*, redupl. from *ten-*, stem of *teinein*, to stretch], *n.* A disease marked by long-continued spasms of voluntary muscles, esp. those of the jaws, as in lock-jaw.

tetanic (tė tăn′ ik), *a.* Pertaining to or characteristic of tetanus. *n.* A medicine acting on the muscles through the nerves, as strychnine. **tetanize** (tet′ ȧ nīz), *v.t.* **tetanization** (-zā′ shŭn), *n.* **tetanoid,** *a.* **tetany,** *n.* An intermittent tetanoid affection.

tetchy (tech′ i) [etym. doubtful], *a.* Fretful, irritable, touchy. **tetchily,** *adv.* **tetchiness,** *n.*

tête-à-tête (tāt′ a tāt′) [F., head to head], *a.* Private, confidential. *adv.* In private or close confabulation. *n.* A private interview, a close or confidential conversation; a sofa for two persons, esp. with seats facing in opposite directions so that the occupants face one another.

tether (te*th*′ ėr) [M.E. *tedir*, cp. Icel. *tjōthr*, Swed. *tjuder*, M.Dut. *tūder*, Dut. *tuier*], *n.* A rope or halter by which a grazing animal is prevented from moving too far; (*fig.*) prescribed range, scope. *v.t.* To confine with or as with a tether.

tetra- [Gr., from *tettares*, four], *comb. form.* **tetrabranchiate** (tet rȧ brăng′ ki ȧt) [BRANCHIATE], *a.* Having four branchiæ or gills. **tetrachord** (tet′ rȧ kôrd) [CHORD], *n.* (*Mus.*) A scale series of half an octave, esp. as used in ancient music. **tetrachordal** (-kôr′ dȧl), *a.* **tetrachotomous** (-kot′ ŏ mŭs) [cp. DICHOTOMOUS], *a.* Separated into four branches, series, etc., doubly dichotomous. **tetrachotomy,** *n.* **tetract** (tet′ răkt) [Gr. *aktis -tinos*, ray], *a.* (*Zool.*) Having four rays or branches, as a sponge-spicule; *n.* A four-rayed sponge-spicule. **tetractinal, -nose** (tė trăk′ ti nȧl, -nōs), *a.* ***tetractine,** *a.* and *n.* **tetracyclic** (-sik′ lik) [CYCLIC], *a.* (*Bot.*) Having four circles or whorls.

tetrad (tet′ răd) [Gr. *tetras -ados*, as TETRA-], *n.* The number four; a collection, group, or set of four things (*Chem.*) an atom or element that can unite with or replace four atoms of hydrogen. **tetradic** (tė trăd′ ik), *a.*

tetradactyl (tet rȧ dăk′ til) [Gr. *tetradaktulos* (TETRA-, *daktūlos*, finger)], *n.* (*Zool.*) An animal having four digits on each limb. *a.* Tetradactylous. **tetradactylous,** *a.* Having four digits on each limb. **tetradecapod** (-dek′ ȧ pod) [DECAPOD], *a.* Having fourteen feet; of or pertaining to the *Tetradecapoda*, an order of crustaceans with seven pairs of feet; *n.* One of the *Tetradecapoda*. **tetradecapodon** (-dė kăp′ ŏ dŏn), *a.* and *n.* **tetradecapodous,** *a.* **tetragon** (tet′ rȧ gŏn) [Gr. *tetragōnon*, -GON], *n.* A plane figure having four angles. **tetragonal** (tė trăg′ ŏ nȧl), *a.* **tetragram** (tet′ rȧ grăm) [-GRAM], *n.* A word of four letters; (*Geom.*) a quadrilateral figure. **tetragrammaton** (-grăm′ ȧ tŏn), *n.* The group of four letters representing the name Jehovah or some other sacred word. **tetragynian** (-jin′ i ȧn), **tetragynous** (-trăj′ i nŭs) [Gr. *gunē*, female], *a.* (*Bot.*) Having four pistils.

tetrahedron (tet rȧ hē′ dron) [Gr. *hedra*, base], *n.* (*Geom.*) A solid figure bounded by four planes, esp. equilateral, triangular faces. **tetrahedral,** *a.* **tetrahedroid,** *n.* **tetrahexahedron** (-hek sȧ hē′ drŏn) [HEXAHEDRON], *n.* A solid bounded by twenty-four equal faces, four corresponding to each face of the cube. **tetrahexahedral,** *a.* **tetralogy** (tė trăl′ ŏ ji) [-LOGY], *n.* A collection of four dramatic works, esp. (*Gr. Ant.*) a trilogy or three tragedies, followed by a satyric piece. **tetrameral, tetramerous** (tė trăm′ ėr ȧl, -ŭs) [Gr. *tetramerēs* (*meros*, part)], *a.* Consisting of four parts. **tetrameter** (tė trăm′ ė tėr) [L. *tetrametrus*, Gr. *tetrametros* (-METER)], *n.* A verse consisting of four measures. **tetramorph** (tet′ rȧ môrf) [Gr. *morphē*, form], *n.* (*Art*) The union of the attributes of the four evangelists in one composite figure. **tetrandrous, *-drian** (tė trăn′ drŭs, -dri ȧn) [Gr. *anēr andros*, male], *a.* (*Bot.*) Having four stamens. **tetrapetalous** (tet rȧ pet′ ȧ lŭs) [PETALOUS], *a.* (*Bot.*) Having four petals. **tetraphyllous** (-fil′ ŭs) [Gr. *phullon*, leaf], *a.* Having four leaves.

tetrapla (tet′ rȧ plȧ) [Gr. *tetraplā*, neut. of *tetraplous* (TETRA-, *-ploos*, -fold)], *n.* An edition containing four versions, esp. Origen's edition of the four Greek versions of the Old Testament.

tetrapod (tet′ rȧ pod) [TETRA-, Gr. *pous podos*, foot], *a.* Having four feet or limbs; belonging to the *Tetrapoda*, a division of butterflies with only four perfect legs. *n.* A four-footed animal, esp. one of the *Tetrapoda.* **tetrapodous** (tė trăp′ ȯ dŭs), *a.* **tetrapody,** *n.* (*Pros.*) A group or a verse of four feet. **tetrapolitan** (-pol′ i tȧn) [from Gr. *tetrapolis* (*polis*, city), after METROPOLITAN], *a.* Of or pertaining to a group of four towns. **Tetrapolitan Confession:** The confession of faith submitted to the Diet of Augsburg in 1530 from Strasburg, Memmingen, Constance, and Lindau. **tetrapterous** (tė trăp′ tėr ŭs) [Gr. *pteron*, wing], *a.* Having four wings or wing-like appendages, as certain fruits. **tetrapteran,** *a.* Tetrapterous; *n.* A tetrapterous insect. **tetraptote** (tet′ răp tōt) [Gr. *ptōsis*, case], *n.* (*Gram.*) A noun which has four cases only.

tetrarch (tet′ rark, tē′ trark) [late L. *tetrarcha*, L. and Gr. *tetrarchēs* (TETRA-, *archein*, to rule)], *n.* A governor of the fourth part of a province under the Roman empire, also a tributary prince; the commander of a subdivision of the ancient Greek phalanx. **tetrarchate, tetrarchy,** *n.* **tetrarchical** (tė trar′ ki kȧl), *a.*

tetraspermous (tet rȧ spĕr′ mŭs) [TETRA-, Gr. *sperma*, seed], *a.* (*Bot.*) Having four seeds. **tetraspore** (tet′ rȧ spôr) [SPORE], *n.* A group of four spores asexually produced, as in some algæ. **tetrastich** (tet′ rȧ stik) [Gr. *stichos*, row], *n.* A stanza, poem, or epigram consisting of four lines of verse. **tetrastyle** (tet′ rȧ stīl) [STYLE (2)], *a.* Having four pillars; *n.* A building, portico, etc., having four pillars. **tetrasyllable** (-sil′ ȧbl) [SYLLABLE], *n.* A word of four syllables. **tetrasyllabic** (-lăb′ ik), *a.* **tetratheism** (-thē′ izm) [THEISM], *n.* (*Theol.*) The doctrine that the Godhead comprises four elements, the three persons of the Trinity and a divine essence from which each of these proceeds.

tetrode (tet′ rōd), *n.* A thermionic valve containing four electrodes.

***tett** [TEAT].

tetter (tet′ ėr) [A.-S. *teter*, cp. Sansk. *dadru*], *n.* A name applied to several cutaneous diseases. *v.t.* To affect with tetter. **tetterwort,** *n.* The greater celandine, *Chelidonium majus.*

tettix (tet′ iks) [Gr.], *n.* A cicada or tree-cricket; (*Ent.*) a genus of *Acridiidæ* or short-horned grasshoppers; (*Gr. Ant.*) an ornament in the form of a *tettix* worn in the hair.

Teucrian (tū′ kri ȧn) [L. *Teucri*, from Gr. *Teukros*, king of Troy], *a.* Of ancient Troy or the Troad. *n.* An ancient Trojan.

teucrium (tū′ kri ŭm) [L., from Gr. *teukrion*, as prec.], *n.* The germander.

Teuton (tū tȯn) [L. *Teutoni, Teutonēs*, from Teut., cp. Goth. *thiuda*, people, G. *deutsch*, German], *n.* Orig. one of a German tribe, first mentioned as dwelling near the Elbe, *c.* 300 B.C.; a member of any Teutonic race. **Teuto-,** *comb. form.* **Teutonic** (-ton′ ik), *a.* Pertaining to the Teutons; pertaining to the Germanic peoples, including Scandinavians, Anglo-Saxons, etc., as well as the German races. *n.* The language or languages of the Teutons collectively. **Teutonic languages:** A group of Aryan or Indo-European languages including High and Low German and the Scandinavian languages. **Teutonicism** (-ton′ i sizm), **Teutonism** (tū′ tȯ nizm), *n.* **Teutonize,** *v.t.* **Teutonization** (-zā′ shŭn), *n.*

tew [TAW (1)].

tewel (tū′ ėl) [M.E. and O.F. *tuel* (F. *tuyan*), from Teut., cp. Dut. *tuit*, G. *tüte*, pipe], *n.* A pipe, a chimney, a tuyere.

text (tekst) [M.E. and F. *texte*, L. *textus -tūs*, style, later the Scriptures, from *texere*, to weave], *n.* The original words of an author, esp. as opp. to a translation, commentary, etc.; a verse or passage of Scripture, esp. one selected as the theme of a discourse; a subject, a topic; text-hand. **text-book,** *n.* A standard book for a particular branch of study; a manual of instruction. **text-hand,** *n.* A large style of handwriting (from the practice of writing the text in a larger hand than the commentary).

textile (tek′ stil, -stīl) [L. *textilis*, as prec.], *a,* Woven; suitable for weaving; pertaining to weaving. *n.* A woven fabric. **textorial** (-tôr′ i ȧl), *a.* Pertaining to weaving.

textual (tek′ stū ȧl) [M.E. and F. *textuel*, as TEXT]. *a.* Pertaining to or contained in the text. **textualist,** *n.* One who adheres strictly to the text. **textualism,** *n.* **textually,** *adv.* **textuary,** *a.* and *n.*

texture (tek′ styŭr, teks′ chŭr) [F., from L. *textūra*, from *textus*, TEXT], *n.* The particular arrangement or disposition of threads, filaments, etc., in a woven fabric; the disposition of the constituent parts of any body, structure, or material; (*Biol.*) the structure of tissues, tissue; (*Art.*) the representation of the surface of objects in works of art. **textural,** *a.* **textureless,** *a.*

-th [from var. Teut. suffixes, in second sense from A.-S. *-tha, -the*, cp. Gr. *-tos*, L. *-tus*], *suf.* Forming abstract names [cp. -NESS], as *filth, wealth*; forming ordinal numbers, as *fifth, fiftieth.*

thack (thăk) [A.-S. *thæc*, THATCH, whence *thacian*, to thatch], *n.* (*now prov.*) Thatch; (*Sc.*) the thatching on a rick or stack. **thack and rape:** (*Sc.*) The covering of straw on a rick, etc., and the strawwythes securing this. **under thack and rape:** (*fig.*) Snug, comfortable.

Thai (tī), *a.* Of or pertaining to Thailand, formerly known as Siam; Siamese. *n.* The language of Thailand.

thaive [THEAVE].

thalamus (thăl′ ȧ mŭs) [L., from Gr. *thalamos*], *n.* (*Gr. Ant.*) An inner room, the women's apartment, a nuptial chamber; (*Anat.*) the place at which a nerve originates, or is supposed to originate, esp. the optic thalamus; (*Bot.*) the receptacle of a flower. **thalamic** (thȧ lăm′ ik), *a.* **thalamifloral** (thăl ȧ mi flôr′ ȧl), *a.* (*Bot.*) Having the petals, stamens, etc., inserted on the thalamus. **thalamium** (thȧ lā′ mi ŭm), *n.* (*pl.* **-mia**) A spore-case in algæ; a form of hymenium in some fungi.

thalassic (thȧ lăs′ ik) [F. *thalassique* (Gr. *thalassa*, the sea, -IC)], *a.* Of or pertaining to the sea, marine. **thalassocracy** (thăl ȧ sok′ rȧ si) [-CRACY], *n.* Naval supremacy, sea-power. **thalassocrat** (thȧ lăs′ ȯ krăt), *n.* **thalassography** (-sog′ rȧ fi) [-GRAPHY], *n.* **thalassographer,** *n.* **thalassographic** (-grăf′ ik), *a.*

thaler (ta′ lėr) [G., see DOLLAR], *n.* An old German silver coin worth about 3s.

Thalia (thȧ lī′ ȧ) [L., from Gr. *Thaleia*, from *thallein*, to bloom], *n.* The Muse of comedy and pastoral poetry. **Thalian** (thȧ lī′ ȧn, thā′ li ȧn), *a.*

Thalictrum (thȧ lik′ trŭm) [L., from Gr. *thaliktron*], *n.* (*Bot.*) A genus of ranunculaceous herbs containing the meadow-rues.

thallium (thăl′ i ŭm) [Gr. *thall-os*, see foll., -IUM], *n.* A rare soft, white, crystalline metallic element, the spectrum of which contains a bright-green line (whence the name), used in alloys and glassmaking. **thallic, thallous,** *a.*

thallochlore (thăl′ ō klôr), *n.* The green colouring matter of lichens.

thallogen, thallophyte (thăl′ ō jen, -fīt) [as foll.], *n.* One of a class of plants the lowest in organization, consisting of those whose vegetative body is a thallus, comprising the algæ, fungi, and lichens. **thallogenic** (-jen′ ik), **thallogenous** (-loj′ ė nŭs), **thallophytic** (-fit′ ik), *a.*

thallus (thăl′ ŭs) [L., from Gr. *thallos*, from *thallein*, to bloom], *n.* (*Bot.*) A plant-body without true root, stem, or leaves. **thalliferous** (thȧ lif′ ėr ŭs), *a.* **thalloid,** *a.*

than (*th*ȧn, *th*ăn) [A.-S. *thanne, thonne, thænne*, THEN], *conj.* Used after adjectives and adverbs expressing comparison, such as *more*, *better*, *worse*, *rather*, etc., to introduce the second member of a comparison.

thanage [THANE].

thanat-, thanato- [Gr. *thanatos*, death], *comb. form.* **thanatism** (thăn' ȧ tizm), *n.* The doctrine of annihilation at death. **thanatist,** *n.* **thanatognomonic** (-tog nō mon' ik), *a.* Indicative of death. **thanatography** (-tog' rȧ fi), *n.* An account of a person's death. **thanatoid,** *a.* Resembling death; apparently dead; (*Zool.*) poisonous, deadly. **thanatology** (-tol' ō ji), *n.* The scientific study of death. **thanatophidia** (-fid' i ȧ) [OPHIDIA], *n.pl.* (*Zool.*) The venomous snakes. **thanatophobia** (thă năt ō fō' bi ȧ), *n.* A morbid fear of death. **thanatopsis** (thă nă top' sis), *n.* A view, or contemplation, of death.

thane (thān) [A.-S. *thegen*, *thegn* (cp. Icel. *thegn*, G. *degen*, O.H.G. *degan*), cogn. with Gr. *teknon*, child], *n.* (*A.-S. Hist.*) A freeman holding land by military service and ranking between ordinary freemen and the nobles. **thanage,** *n.* Thaneship; the land held by a thane; the tenure of this. **thanedom, thanehood, thaneship,** *n.*

thank (thăngk) [A.-S. *thanc*, *thonc*, thought, grace (cp. Dut. and G. *dank*, Icel. *thökk*), whence *thancian*, cp. Dut. and G. *danken*], *n.* (*now pl.*) An expression of gratitude; a formula of acknowledgment of a favour, kindness, benefit, etc. *v.t.* To express gratitude (to or for); to make acknowledgment to for a gift, offer, etc. (often used ironically, esp. as a contemp. refusal). **thank you:** A formula expressing thanks, polite refusal, etc. **thank-offering,** *n.* An offering made as an expression of gratitude, esp. a Jewish sacrifice of thanksgiving. ***thank-worthy,** *a.* **thankful,** *a.* Grateful; expressive of thanks. **thankfully,** *adv.* **thankfulness,** *n.* **thankless,** *a.* Insensible to kindness, ungrateful; not deserving thanks, unprofitable. **thanklessly,** *adv.* **thanklessness,** *n.* **thanksgiver,** *n.* **thanksgiving,** *n.* The act of returning thanks or expressing gratitude, esp. to God; a form of words expressive of this; (*Bibl.*) a thank-offering. **Thanksgiving Day:** (*U.S.*) A day set apart annually for thanksgiving to God for blessings enjoyed individually and nationally (since 1941 the fourth Thursday in Nov.).

Thapsia (thăp' si ȧ) [L. and Gr., prob. from *Thapsus*, in Sicily], *n.* (*Bot.*) A genus of umbelliferous herbs of the Mediterranean region, comprising *T. garganica*, the deadly carrot, used by the Algerians as a panacea, and three other species.

that (*thȧt*, *thăt*) [A.-S. *thæt*, orig. neut. of THE], *a.* (*pl.* **those,** *thōz*) The (person or thing) specifically designated, pointed out, implied, or understood; (correlated with *this*) the more remote or less obvious of two things; such (usu. followed by *as*). *pron.* The person or thing specifically designated, pointed out, implied, or understood; who or which (now usu. demonstratively and introducing a restrictive or defining clause). *adv.* In such a manner, to such a degree. *conj.* Introducing a clause, stating a fact or supposition; implying purpose, so that, in order that; implying result, consequence, etc.; implying reason or cause, on the ground that, because, since.

thatch (thăch) [A.-S. *thæc* (cp. Dut. *dak*, G. *dach*, Icel. *thak*, also Gr. *tegos*, roof, L. *tegere*, to cover), whence *theccan*, to thatch], *n.* A roof-covering of straw, rushes, reeds, etc. *v.t.* To cover with this. **thatcher,** *n.* **thatching,** *n.*

thaumasite (thaw' mȧ sīt) [Gr. *thaumas-ios*, wonderful, as foll., -ITE], *n.* (*Min.*) A dull white, translucent compound of calcium.

thaumatrope (thaw' mȧ trōp) [Gr. *thauma*, wonder, *-tropos*, turning, from *trepein*, to turn], *n.* An optical toy consisting of a disk with figures on opposite sides which appear to combine and perform movements when the disk is rotated.

thaumaturge (thaw' mȧ tĕrj) [med. L. *thaumaturgus*, Gr. *thaumatourgos* (*thauma -atos*, wonder, *-ergos*, working)], *n.* A worker of miracles; a wonder-worker, a magician or conjurer. **thaumaturgic, -al** (-tĕr' jik, -ȧl), *a.* **thaumaturgist** (thaw' mȧ tĕr jist), *n.* **thaumaturgy,** *n.*

thaw (thaw) [A.-S. *thāwian*, cp. Dut. *dooijen*, G. *tauen*, Icel. *theyja*], *v.i.* To melt, dissolve, or become liquid (of ice, snow, etc.); to become so warm as to melt ice or snow (of weather); (*fig.*) to relax one's stiffness, to unbend, to become genial. *v.t.* To melt, to dissolve; (*fig.*) to infuse warmth or geniality into. *n.* The act of thawing or the state of being thawed; warm weather that thaws. **thawless,** *a.* **thawy,** *a.*

the (*thė*, *thē*) [A.-S. *the*, fem. *theo*, neut. *thæt* (earlier *sē*, *sēo*, *thæt*), instrumental case *thy*], *a.* Applied to a person or thing or persons or things already mentioned, implied, or definitely understood; used before a singular noun to denote a species; prefixed to adjectives used absolutely, giving them the force of a substantive; before nouns expressing a unit to give distributive force (as '4d. the pint'); emphatically (*thē*) to express uniqueness (as '*the* famous Duke of Wellington'), *adv.* Used before adjectives and adverbs in the comparative degree, to that extent, to that amount, by so much.

theandric (thē ăn' drik) [Gr. *theandrikos* (*theos*, god, *anēr andros*, man)], *a.* Relating to or existing by the union of divine and human nature in Christ.

theanthropic, -al (thē ȧn throp' ik, -ȧl) [Gr. *theos*, god, *anthrōpos*, man], *a.* Being both human and divine; tending to embody deity in human forms. **theanthropism** (-ăn' thrō pizm), *n.*

thearchy (thē' ar ki) [Gr. *theos*, god, *-archia*, rule, from *archein*, to rule], *n.* Government by God or gods; a body, class, or order of gods or deities.

theater [THEATRE].

Theatine (thē' ȧ tīn) [mod. L. *Theatīnus*, from *Theate* or *Teate*, anc. name of Chieti, a city of the Abruzzi, Italy], *n.* A member of a congregation of regular clerks, founded in 1524 by John Peter Caraffa, Archbishop of Chieti. *a.* Of or pertaining to this order.

theatre, (*Am.* **theater**) (thē' ȧ tėr) [O.F., from Gr. *theatron*, from *theasthai*, to behold, from *thea*, view], *n.* A building for dramatic spectacles, a play-house; a room, hall, etc., with a platform at one end, and seats arranged in ascending tiers, used for lectures, demonstrations, etc.; the room in a hospital, etc. used for operations; (*fig.*) the drama, the stage; the place or scene of an action, event, etc.; matter suitable to be staged. **theatre organ,** *n.* (*Mus.*) A type of organ usu. electrically wind-controlled, with effects of most instruments of an orchestra, employed for entertainment purposes in cinemas and theatres. ***theatric.**

theatrical (the ăt' ri kȧl), *n.* Of or pertaining to the theatre; befitting the stage, dramatic; suitable or calculated for display, pompous, showy; befitting or characteristic of actors, stagy, affected. **theatricalism, theatricality** (-kăl' i ti), *n.* **theatricalize,** *v.t.* **theatrically,** *adv.* **theatricals,** *n.pl.* Dramatic performances, esp. private.

theatrophone (the ăt' rō fōn), *n.* A telephone connected with a theatre, etc., enabling persons to hear performances without being present.

theave (thēv), **thaive** (thāv) [etym. unknown], *n.* (*chiefly Midland*) A ewe of the first or second year.

thebaine (thē' bā in), *n.* (*Chem.*) A poisonous crystalline alkaloid obtained from opium.

Theban (thē' bȧn) [L. *Thēbānus*, from *Thēbæ*, Gr. *Thebai*], *a.* Pertaining to ancient Thebes (in Greece or in Egypt). *n.* A native or inhabitant of Thebes. **Theban year:** The Egyptian year of 365¼ days. **Thebaid** (thē' bā id), *n.* The territory of Egyptian Thebes.

theca (thē' kȧ) [L., from Gr. *thēkē*], *n.* (*pl.* **-cæ,** -kē) (*Bot., Zool., etc.*) A sheath, a case. **thecal, thecate,** *a.* **theciferous** (thē sif' ėr ŭs) [-FEROUS], *a.* **theciform** (thē' si fôrm), *a.* **thecodont** [Gr. *odous* *odontos*, tooth], *a.* Pertaining to the *Thecodontia*, an order of extinct saurians having the teeth in distinct sockets; *n.* One of the Thecodontia. **thecophore,** *n.* A receptacle bearing *thecæ*; (*Bot.*) the stalk of an ovary.

thee (*th*ē), *obj.* [THOU].

theek, theik (*Sc. and North.*) [THATCH].

theft (theft) [A.-S. *thīefth, thēofth, thēoft*], *n.* The act of thieving or stealing; larceny; that which is stolen. **theftuous,** *a.* (*Sc.*). **theftuously,** *adv.*

thegn, etc. [THANE].

theic (thē′ ik) [mod. L. *thea*, TEA, -IC], *n.* An excessive tea-drinker. **theiform,** *a.* **theine** (thē′ in), *n.* An organic base occurring in tea, caffeine. **theism** (1), *n.* A morbid condition resulting from excessive tea-drinking.

theik [THEEK].

their, theirs (*th*âr, *th*ârz), *poss.* [THEY].

theism (1) [THEIC].

theism (2) (thē′ izm) [Gr. *theos*, god, -ISM], *n.* Belief in a God, as opp. to atheism; belief in a righteous God supernaturally revealed, as opp. to Deism. **theist,** *n.* **theistic, -al** (thē is′ tik, -ȧl), *a.*

them (*th*ėm, *th*em), *obj.* [THEY].

theme (thēm) [L. *thema*, Gr. *thema -atos*, from *the-*, root of *tithenai*, to put], *n.* A subject on which a person writes or speaks; short dissertation or essay by a student, schoolboy, etc., on a certain subject; the part of a noun or verb remaining unchanged by inflexions; (*Mus.*) a melodic subject usu. developed with variations; (*Log.*) the subject of thought. **thematic** (thė măt′ ik), *a.* **thematic catalogue:** (*Mus.*) A catalogue giving the opening theme of each piece of music. **thematically,** *adv.*

Themis (them′ is, thē′ mis) [L. and Gr., law, as prec.], *n.* The Greek goddess of Justice or Law; one of the asteroids.

themselves (*th*ėm selvz′) [THEM, SELVES], *pron.* The emphatic and reflexive form of the third plural personal pronoun.

then (*th*en) [M.E. *thenne*, A.-S. *thanne, thonne, thænne* (cogn. with THAT, THE), cp. THAN], *adv.* At that time; afterwards, soon after, after that, next; at another time. *conj.* In that case; therefore; consequently; this being so, accordingly. *a.* (*colloq.*) Of or existing at that time. *n.* That time, the time mentioned or understood.

thenar (thē′ nar) [Gr. *thenar*], *n.* (*Anat.*) The palm, the sole. *a.* Of or pertaining to the palm of the hand or the sole of the foot.

thence (*th*ens) [M.E. *thennes* (*thenne*, -ES), A.-S. *thanon, thonan*, cogn. with THAT, THE], *adv.* From that place; for that reason, from that source; from that time. **thenceforth, thenceforward,** *adv.* From that time onward.

theo- [Gr. *theos*, god], *comb. form.*

Theobroma [thē ō brō′ mȧ) [Gr. *broma*, food], *n.* (*Bot.*) A genus of tropical trees, one of which, *T. cacao*, yields cocoa and chocolate. **theobromic,** *a.*

theobromine (thē ō brō′ mīn), *n.* (*Chem.*) A bitter alkaloid resembling caffeine contained in the seeds of *T. cacao.*

theocracy (thē ok′ rȧ si), *n.* Government by the immediate direction of God or through a sacerdotal class; a state so governed. **theocrat,** *n.* **theocratic, theocratical,** *a.* **theocratist,** *n.*

theocrasy (thē ok′ rȧ si) [CRASIS], *n.* Mixed worship of different gods, polytheism; the union of the soul with God in contemplation.

Theocritean (thē ok ri tē′ ȧn), *a.* Of, pertaining to, or in the style of the Greek pastoral poet Theocritus; pastoral, idyllic, Arcadian.

theodicy (thē od′ i si) [F. *théodicée* (THEO-, Gr. *dikē*, justice)], *n.* A vindication of divine justice in respect to the existence of evil. **theodicean** (-sē′ ȧn), *n.*

theodolite (thē od′ ō līt) [etym. doubtful], *n.* A portable surveying-instrument for measuring horizontal and vertical angles. **theodolitic** (-lit′ ik), *a.*

Theodosian (thē ō dō′ shi ȧn), *a.* Of or pertaining to the emperor Theodosius, esp. Theodosius II, who issued a code of Roman law (A.D. 438).

theogony (thē og′ ō ni) [L. and Gr. *theogonia* (THEO-, *gonia*, from *gen-*, to beget)], *n.* The genealogy of the gods; a poem treating of this. **theogonic** (-gon′ ik), *a.* **theogonist,** *n.*

theology (thē ol′ ō ji) [M.E. and O.F. *theologie*, L. and Gr. *theologia* (THEO-, -LOGY)], *n.* The science of God and His attributes and relations to the universe; the science of religion, esp. Christianity. **natural theology:** The science dealing with the knowledge of God as derived from His works. **theologian** (-lō′ ji ȧn), ***theologist, *theologue** (thē′ ō log), *n.* One versed in theology; a professor of theology. **theological** (-loj′ i kȧl), *a.* **theologically,** *adv.* **theologaster** (thė ol ō găs′ tėr), *n.* A pretender to a knowledge of theology. **theologize** (thē ol′ ō jīz), *v.t.* ***theologizer,** *n.*

theomachy (thė om′ ȧ ki) [L. and Gr. *theomachia* (THEO-, *-machia*, fighting)], *n.* A combat against or among the gods. **theomachist,** *n.* **theomancy** (thē′ ō măn si) [Gr. *theomanteia* (-MANCY)], *n.* Divination. **theomania** (thē ō mā′ ni ȧ) [-MANIA], *n.* Religious insanity; a delusion that one is God. **theomaniac,** *n.* **theomorphic** (thē ō môr′ fik) [Gr. *morphē*, form], *n.* Having the form or semblance of God, opp. to anthropomorphic. **theomorphism,** *n.*

theopaschite (thē ō păs′ kīt) [late L. *theopaschita*, Gr. *theopaschites* (*paschein*, to suffer)], *n.* A member of a sect who affirmed that in the crucifixion and passion the godhead had suffered. **theopaschist,** *n.* **theopaschitally,** *adv.* **theopaschitic** (-kit′ ik), **theopaschitism,** *n.* **theopathy** (thė op′ ȧ thi) [-PATHY], *n.* Emotion excited by the contemplation of God. **theopathetic** (pȧ thet′ ik), *a.* **theophany** (thė of′ ȧ ni) [L. *theophania*, Gr. *theophania* (*ephainein*, to show)], *n.* The manifestation or appearance of God to man. **theophanic** (făn′ ik), *a.* **theophilanthropy** (thē ō fi lăn′ thrō pi) [PHILANTHROPY], *n.* A system of deism promulgated in France in 1796, based on adoration of God and love of man and intended to take the place of Roman Catholicism. **theophilanthropic** (fil ȧn throp′ ik), *a.* **theophilanthropism** (-lăn′ thrō pizm), *n.* **theophilanthropist,** *n.* **theopneusty** (thē ȯp nū′ sti) [Gr. *theopneustos*, inspired (*pnein*, to blow)], *n.* Divine inspiration. **theopneustic,** *a.*

theorbo (thė ôr′ bō) [It. *tiorba*, etym. doubtful (cp. F. *théorbe*)], *n.* A stringed instrument resembling a two-necked lute used in the 16th–17th cents. **theorbist,** *n.*

theorem (thē′ ō rėm) [late L. and Gr. *theōrēma*, from *theōrein*, to behold], *n.* A proposition to be proved; a principle to be demonstrated by reasoning; (*Math.*) a rule or law, esp. one expressed by symbols, etc. **theorematic, -al** (-măt′ ik, -ȧl), *a.* **theorematist** (-rem′ ȧ tist), *n.*

theoretic, -al (thē ō ret′ ik, -ȧl) [late L. *theōrēticus*, Gr. *theōretikos*, from *theōrētos*, as foll.], *a.* Pertaining to or founded on theory not facts or knowledge, not practical, speculative. **theoretically,** *adv.* **theoretics,** *n.* The speculative parts of a science. **theoretician** (-tish′ ȧn), *n.*

theoric (thė or′ ik) [M.E. *theorike*, O.F. *theorique*, Gr. *theōrikos*, from *theōrein*, to behold, to contemplate], *a.* (*Gr. Ant.*) Pertaining to the public spectacles; theoretic. ***n.** Theory. **theorist,** etc. [THEORY].

theory (thē′ ō ri) [A.F. *theorie*, L. and Gr. *theōria*, as prec.], *n.* Supposition explaining something, esp. a generalization explaining phenomena as the results of assumed natural causes; a speculative idea of something; mere hypothesis; speculation, abstract knowledge; an exposition of the general principles of a science, etc.; a body of theorems illustrating a particular subject. **theorist,** *n.* One who theorizes; one given to forming theories. **theorize,** *v.i.* **theorization** (-zā′ shŭn), *n.* **theorizer,** *n.*

theosophy (thē os′ ȯ fi) [med. L. and late Gr. *theosophia* (THEO-, *sophos,* wise)], *n.* A form of speculation, mysticism, or philosophy aiming at the knowledge of God by means of intuition and contemplative illumination or by direct communion; a term commonly applied to a system founded in U.S.A., in 1875, which claims to show the unity of all religions in their esoteric teaching, manifested by occult phenomena. **theosoph** (thē′ ȯ sof), **theosopher, -phist** (thė os′ ȯ fer, -fist), *n.* **theosophic, -al** (-sof′ ik, -ȧl), *a.* **theosophism** (thē os′ ȯ fizm), *n.* **theosophistical** (-fis′ ti kȧl), *a.* **theosophize** (thē os′ ȯ fīz), *v.i.*

theotechny (thē′ ȯ tek ni) [THEO-, *technē,* art], *n.* The supernatural machinery of a literary composition. **theotechnic** (thē ȯ tek′ nik), *a.*

Theotokos (thė ot′ ȯ kos) [Gr. (THEO-, Gr. *-tokos,* bringing forth, rel. to *tiktein,* to bear)], *n.* The God-bearer (a title of the Virgin Mary, cp. DEIPAROUS).

Therapeutæ (ther ȧ pū′ tē) [L., from Gr. *therapeutai,* from *therapeuein,* to wait on (also to heal), from *theraps -apos,* servant], *n.pl.* A sect of Egyptian Jews in the 1st cent. A.D. who gave themselves up to contemplation of God.

therapeutic (ther ȧ pū′ tik) [as prec.], *a.* Pertaining to the healing art; curative. *n.pl.* The branch of medical science dealing with the treatment of disease and the action of remedial agents in both health and disease. **therapeutical,** *a.* **therapeutically,** *adv.* **therapeutist,** *n.* **therapy** (ther′ ȧ pi), *n.* (*Med.*) Therapeutics, the treatment of disease from a curative and preventive point of view.

there (*th*âr, *th*ėr) [A.-S. *thǣr, thēr* (cp. Dut. *daar,* G. *da,* Icel. *thar,* Dan. and Swed. *der*), cogn. with THAT, THE], *adv.* In or at that place, point, or stage; to that place, thither, frequently used before the verb in interrogations, negative sentences, etc. *n.* That place. *int.* Expressing direction, confirmation, triumph, alarm, etc. **all there:** (*slang*) Wide awake, fully competent, knowing all about it. **not all there:** (*colloq*) Imbecile, mentally deficient. **here and there** [HERE]. **thereabout, -bouts** (-ȧ bout′, -s), *adv.* Near that place, number, degree, etc. **thereafter** (-af′ tėr), *adv.* After that; according to that. **thereanent** (-ȧ nent′), *adv.* (*Sc.*) As regards that matter. **thereat** (ăt′), *adv.* At that place; thereupon; on that account. **thereby** (*th*âr bī), *adv.* By that means; in consequence of that; thereabouts. ***therefor** (-fôr′), *adv.* For that object. **therefore** (*th*âr′ fôr), *adv.* For that reason, consequently, accordingly. **therefrom** (-from′), *adv.* From this or that time, place, etc. **therein** (-in′), *adv.* In that or this time, place, respect, etc. **thereinafter** (-af′ tėr), *adv.* Later in the same (document, etc.). **thereinbefore** (-bė fôr′), *adv.* Earlier in the same (document, etc.). ***thereinto** (-in′ tụ), *adv.* Into that place or matter. **thereof** (-ov′), *adv.* Of that or it. **thereon** (-on′), *adv.* On that or it. ***thereout** (-out′), *adv.* Out of that or this. **thereto** (-too′), *adv.* To that or this; besides, over and above. ***thereunder** (-ŭn′ dėr), *adv.* Under that or this. ***thereunto** (-ŭn′ tụ), *adv.* To that or this, thereto. **thereupon** (-ụ pon′), *adv.* In consequence of that; immediately after or following that; *upon that. **therewith** (-wi*th*′), *adv.* With that; thereupon. **therewithal** (-wi *th*awl′), *adv.* With all this, besides.

theriac (thēr′ i ăk) [late L. *thēriaca, thēriacē,* Gr. *thēriakē,* orig. fem. a. from *thērion,* dim. of *thēr,* wild beast], *n.* An antidote against the bite of poisonous animals. **theriacal** (thė rī′ ȧ kȧl), *a.*

therianthropic (thēr i ȧn throp′ ik) [Gr. *thērion,* see prec., *anthropos,* man], *a.* Of or pertaining to deities represented as half man and half beast or to their worship. **therianthropism** (-ăn′ thrȯ pizm), *n.* **theriomancy** (-măn′ si) [-MANCY], *n.* Divination by observing the movements of animals. **theriomorphic, -phous** (-môr′ fik, -fùs) [Gr. *morphē,* form], *a.* Having the form of a beast. **theriotomy** (-ot′ ȯ mi) [-TOMY], *n.* Zootomy.

therm (thĕrm) [Gr. *thermē,* heat], *n.* (*Phys.*) The unit of heat, being the quantity of heat required to raise 1 lb. of water from 60° F. to 61° F. The *Mean British Thermal Unit* is $\frac{1}{180}$th part of the quantity of heat required to raise the temperature of 1 lb. of water from 32° F. to 212° F.

thermæ (thĕr′ mē) [L.], *n.pl.* Hot springs or baths, esp. the public baths of the ancient Romans. **thermal,** *a.* Of or pertaining to heat or thermæ. **thermal springs:** Hot springs. **thermally,** *adv.* ***thermatology** [THERMOLOGY]. **thermic,** *a.*

Thermidor (thĕr mi dôr′, tĕr mi dôr′) [as prec., Gr. *dōron,* gift], *n.* The eleventh month of the French Republican year, 19 July–17 Aug. **Thermidorian** (-dôr′ i ȧn), *n.* One of those who aided or favoured the overthrow of Robespierre and the Jacobins on 9 Thermidor, 1794.

thermionics (thĕr mi on′ iks) [Gr. *thermos,* warm, ION], *n.* (*Phys.*) The science dealing with the emission of electrons from hot bodies; the study of the behaviour of these electrons in a vacuum. **thermionic valve,** *n.* (*Radio.*) A vacuum tube in which a stream of electrons flows from one electrode to another and is controlled by one or more other electrodes.

thermite (thĕr′ mīt) [G. *thermit* (Gr. *thermē,* heat, -ITE)], *n.* A mixture of finely-divided aluminium and a metallic oxide, esp. of iron, producing intense heat on combustion.

thermo- [Gr. *thermos,* warm, see THERM], *comb. form.* **thermo-barometer** (thĕr mȯ bȧ rom′ ė tėr), *n.* An apparatus for measuring atmospheric pressure by the boiling-point of water. **thermo-chemistry,** *n.* The branch of chemistry dealing with the relations between chemical reactions and the heat liberated or absorbed. **thermo-electric,** *a.* **thermo-electricity** (-tris′ i ti), *n.* Electricity generated by differences of temperature. **thermo-electrometer** (-trom′ ė tėr), *n.* An instrument for ascertaining the heating power of an electric current. **thermo-magnetism** (-măg′ nė tizm), *n.* Magnetism as modified or produced by the action of heat. **thermomagnetic** (-net′ ik), *a.*

thermod (thĕr′ mod), *n.* The odic force of heat.

thermodynamics (thĕr mo dī năm′ iks), *n.* The science dealing with the relations between heat and mechanical work.

Thermogene (thĕr′ mō jēn), *n.* Proprietary name of a form of medicated cotton-wool.

thermogenesis (thĕr mō jen′ ė sis), *n.* The production of heat, esp. of animal heat. **thermogenetic, thermogenic,** *a.*

thermograph (thĕr′ mō grăf), *n.* An instrument for automatically recording variations of temperature. **thermogram,** *n.*

thermometer (thĕr mom′ ė tėr), *n.* An instrument for measuring temperature, usu. by the expansion or contraction of a column of mercury or alcohol in a graduated tube of small bore with a bulb at one end. **thermometric, -al,** *a.* **thermometrically,** *adv.* **thermometry,** *n.*

thermomotive (thĕr mō mō′ tiv), *a.* Of or relating to motion produced by heat.

thermomotor (thĕr mō mō′ tȯr), *n.* A heat-engine, esp. one driven by hot air.

thermonuclear (thĕr mō nū′ kle ȧr), *a.* Used of the fusion of nuclei, as in **thermonuclear reaction,** which is the fusion of nuclei at very high temperatures, as in the hydrogen bomb.

thermopile (thĕr′ mō pīl), *n.* A thermo-electric battery, esp. one employed to measure small quantities of radiant heat.

thermoplastic (thĕr mō plăs′ tik), *n.* A plastic which softens under heat without undergoing any chemical change, and can therefore be heated repeatedly. **thermosetting plastic,** *n.* A plastic which softens initially under heat but subsequently hardens and become infusible and insoluble.

Thermos (thĕr′ mos), *n.* Protected trade-name of a type of vacuum flask.

thermoscope (thĕr′ mō skōp), *n.* An instrument for indicating differences of temperature without measuring them. **thermoscopic,** *a.*

thermostat (thĕr′ mō stăt), *n.* A self-acting apparatus for regulating temperatures. **thermostatic,** *a.*

thermotaxis (thĕr mō tăks′ is), *n.* (*Biol.*) The reaction of an organism to heat stimulus.

thermotic (thĕr mot′ ik), *a.* Of, pertaining to, or resulting from heat. **thermotics,** *n.* The science of heat.

thermotype (thĕr′ mō tīp), *n.* An impression obtained by wetting the object, as a section of wood, with dilute acid, printing from this, and developing by heat.

theroid (thēr′ oid) [Gr. *thēr*, see THERIAC, -OID], *a.* Having animal propensities, esp. of certain idiots.

therology (thēr ol′ ŏ ji) [*thēr*, as prec., -LOGY], *n.* The science of mammals, mammalogy. **therologist,** *n.*

thesaurus (thē saw′ rŭs) [L., from Gr. *thēsauros*, TREASURE], *n.* (pl. **-i,** -ī) A cyclopædia or lexicon; a collection of words, phrases, literary examples, etc.

these, *pl.* [THIS].

thesis (thē′ sis) [L., from Gr. *thesis*, from *the-*, root of *tithenai*, to set], *n.* (*pl.* **theses,** -sēz) A proposition advanced or maintained; an essay or dissertation, esp. one submitted by a candidate for a degree, etc.; a school or college exercise; (*Log.*) an affirmation, as opp. to an hypothesis: (*Pros.*, thes′ is) the unaccented part of a metrical foot, opp. to arsis.

Thesmophoria (thes mŏ fôr′ i ȧ) [Gr. from *thesmophoros* (*thēsmos*, law, *-phoros*, bearing, rel. to *pherein*, to bear), an epithet of Demeter], *n.pl.* (*Gr. Ant.*) A Greek festival celebrated by married women in honour of Demeter. **thesmophorian,** *a.*

thesmothete (thes′ mŏ thēt) [Gr. *thesmothetēs* (*thesmos*, law, *the-*, as THESIS)], *n.* A lawgiver; (*Gr. Ant.*) one of the six inferior archons at Athens.

Thespian (thes′ pi ȧn), *a.* Pertaining to Thespis, traditional Greek dramatic poet; relating to tragedy or the drama. *n.* An actor.

theurgy (thē′ ŭr ji) [late L. *theurgia*, Gr. *theourgia* (*theos*, god, *ergon*, work)], *n.* Divine or supernatural agency, esp. in human affairs; supernatural as distinguished from natural magic. **theurgic, -al** (thē ĕr′ jik, -ȧl), *a.* **theurgist,** *n.*

thew (thū) [A.-S. *thēaw*, habit, cp. O.H.G. *thau*, *dau*, discipline, etym. doubtful], *n.* (*usu. in pl.*) Muscles, sinews; strength, vigour; *manners, mental qualities. **thewed, thewy,** *a.* **thewless,** *a.*

they (*th*ā) [A.-S. *thā*, pl. of THE, THAT], *pron.* (*obj.* **them,** *poss.* **their,** *absol.* **theirs**) The plural of the third personal pronoun (*he*, *she*, or *it*). **they say:** People say, it is said.

thibet [TIBET].

thick (thik) [A.-S. *thicce*, cp. Dut. *dik*, G. *dick*, Icel. *thykkr*], *a.* Having great or specified extent or depth from one surface to the opposite; arranged, set or planted closely, crowded together, close packed or abounding (with), following in quick succession; dense, inspissated, turbid, muddy, impure, cloudy, foggy; (*fig.*) dull, stupid; indistinct, muffled (of articulation, etc.); (*colloq.*) very friendly, familiar. *adv.* Thickly; in close succession; indistinctly. *n.* The thickest part. **a bit thick:** Unreasonable. **through thick and thin:** Under any conditions, undauntedly, resolutely. ***thick-coming,** *a.* Following in quick succession. **thick ear,** *n.* (*fig.*) A blow on the ear. **thickhead,** *n.* A blockhead; (*Austral.*) a bird of the Pachycephalidæ family, akin to the flycatchers. **thick-headed,** *a.* **thick-knee,** *n.* The stone-plover. **thick-lipped,** *a.* ***thick-pleached,** *a.* Closely interwoven. **thick-set,** *a.* Planted, set or growing close together; solidly built, stout, stumpy. *n.* A thick-set hedge; *a thicket. **thick-skinned,** *a.* Not sensible to taunts, reproaches, etc. **thick-skin,** *n.* **thick-skull,** *n.* **thick-skulled, -witted,** *a.* **thick 'un:** (*slang*) A sovereign, one pound. **thicken,** *v.t.* and *i.* **thickening,** *n.* **thicket** [A.-S. *thiccet*], *n.* A thick growth of small trees, bushes, etc. **thickish,** *a.* **thickly,** *adv.*

thickness (thik′ nes), *n.* The state of being thick; extent from upper surface to lower, the dimension that is neither length nor breadth; a sheet or layer of cardboard, etc.

thief (thēf) [A.-S. *thēof*, cp. Dut. *dief*, G. *dieb*, Icel. *thjōfr*], *n.* (*pl.* **thieves**) One who steals, esp. furtively and without violence; (*prov.*) a projecting piece of wick in a candle causing it to gutter. **thief-catcher, -taker,** *n.* One whose business is to arrest thieves. **thieve** [A.-S. *gethēofian*], *v.i.* To practise theft; to be a thief. *v.t.* To take by theft. **thieves' Latin** [LATIN]. **thievery, thievishness,** *n.* **thievish,** *a.* **thievishly,** *adv.*

thig (thig) [A.-S. *thicgan*, to take (food, etc.), cp. O.S. *thiggian*, to beg, O.H.G. *dikken*], *v.t.* (*now Sc.*) To beg, to get by begging. *v.i.* To beg; to live by begging. **thigger,** *n.*

thigh (thī) [A.-S. *thēoh*, *thēo*, cp. Dut. *dij*, Icel. *thjō*, O.H.G. *dioh*], *n.* The thick, fleshy portion of the leg between the hip and knee in man; the corresponding part in other animals. **thigh-bone,** *n.* The principal bone in the thigh, the femur.

***thilk** (*th*ilk) [M.E. *thilke* (THE, ILK)], *a.* That, the same. *n.* That person or thing.

thill (thil) [A.-S. *thille*, plank, flooring, cogn. with DEAL (2)], *n.* The shaft of a cart, carriage or other vehicle. **thill-horse, thiller,** *n.* The horse between the thills.

thimble (thim′ bėl) [A.-S. *thȳmel*, thumb-stall], *n.* A cap of metal, etc., worn to protect the end of the finger in sewing; a sleeve or short metal tube; a ferrule; (*Naut.*) an iron ring having an exterior groove worked into a rope or sail to receive another rope or lanyard. **thimble-case,** *n.* **thimbleful,** *n.* As much as a thimble holds; a very small quantity. **thimblerig,** *n.* A sleight-of-hand trick with three thimbles and a pea, persons being challenged to bet under which cover is the pea. *v.t.* To cheat by means of thimblerigging; *v.i.* To practise this. **thimblerigger,** *n.*

thin (thin) [A.-S. *thynne*, cp. Dut. *dun*, G. *dünn*, Icel. *thunnr*, also L. *tenuis*, Gr. *tanaos*], *a.* Having the opposite surfaces close together, of little thickness, slender; not close-packed, not dense; sparse, scanty, meagre; lean, not plump; not full, scant, bare; flimsy, easily seen through. *adv.* Thinly. *v.t.* (*past & p.p.* **thinned**) To make thin; to make less crowded; to remove fruit, flowers, etc., from (a tree or plant) to improve the rest. *v.i.* To become thin or thinner; to waste away. **thin-skinned,** *a.* Sensitive, easily offended. **thinly,** *adv.* **thinness,** *n.* **thinnish,** *a.*

thine (*th*īn) [THY].

thing (1) (thing) [A.-S., *thing*, cause, sake, office, reason, council (cp. Dut. and G. *ding*, Icel. *thing*, Dan. and Swed. *ting*)], *n.* Any object or thought; whatever exists or is conceived to exist as a separate entity, esp. an inanimate object as distinguished from a living being; an act, a fact, affair, circumstance, etc.; (*colloq.*) a person or other animate object regarded with commiseration, disparagement, etc.; (*pl.*) clothes, belongings, luggage, etc., **the thing:** The proper thing (to do, etc.). **to have a thing about:** To have an unaccountable prejudice or fear about. **one of those things:** A happening that one cannot do anything about. **to make a good thing of:** To make a profit out of. **thingumajig, thingumabob, thingummy,** *n.* (*colloq.*) A thing, what d'you call it.

thing (2) (thing) [Icel., prec.], *n.* A Scandinavian public assembly, esp. a legislative body.

think (thingk) [A.-S. *thencan*, *thencean* (cp. G. *denken*, Icel. *thekkja*, Dan. *tænke*), cogn. with THANK], *v.t.* (*past & p.p.* **thought** (1), thawt) To regard or examine in the mind, to reflect, to ponder (over, etc.); to consider, to be of opinion, to believe; to design, to intend; to effect by thinking; (*colloq.*) to remember, to recollect. *v.i.* To exercise the mind actively, to reason; to meditate, to cogitate, to consider (on, about, etc.). **to think better of:** To change one's mind. **to think of:** To have in mind, to conceive, to imagine; to call to mind, to remember; to have a particular opinion or feeling about, to esteem. **to think out:** To devise; to solve by long thought. **thinkable,** *a.* **thinker,** *n.* **thinking,** *a.* and *n.* **thinkingly,** *adv.*

thinly, etc. [THIN].

thio- [Gr. *theion*, sulphur], *comb. form.* (*Chem.*) **thiosulphuric** (thī ō sŭl fūr' ik), *a.* Applied to an acid corresponding to sulphuric acid in which one atom of oxygen is replaced by one of sulphur. **thiosulphate,** *n.*

third (thĕrd) [A.-S. *thridda*, from *thrī*, THREE], *a.* Coming next after the second. *n.* One of three equal parts (of anything); the sixtieth part of a second of time or angular measurement; (*Mus.*) an interval between a tone and the next but one on the diatonic scale; a tone separated by this interval; the consonance of two such tones; (*pl.*) the third part of a deceased husband's estate, sometimes assigned as her share to the widow. ***third-borough,** *n.* (*Shak.*) An under-constable. **third-class, -rate,** *a.* Of the class coming next to the second; inferior, worthless. **third degree,** *n.* (*Am.*) A severe cross-examination by the police to extort a confession. **third programme:** (*facet.*) Highbrow, intellectual, in allusion to the 3rd Programme of the B.B.C. **third-rail system,** *n.* (*Rail.*) A system of traction in which current is fed to the electric locomotive from an insulated conductor rail. **thirdly,** *adv.*

***thirl** (thĕrl) [A.-S. *thyrlian*, from *thyrel*, a hole, from *thurh*, THOROUGH], *v.t.* To pierce through, to perforate. *n.* A hole, an aperture.

thirst (thĕrst) [A.-S. *thurst* (cp. Dut. *dorst*, G. *durst*, Icel. *thorsti*), whence *thyrstan*, cp. Dut. *dorsten*, G. *dürsten*, cogn. with L. *torrēre*, Gr. *tersesthai*, to dry up], *n.* The uneasiness or suffering caused by want of drink; desire for drink; (*fig.*) eager longing or desire. *v.i.* To feel thirst (for or after). **thirstless,** *a.* **thirsty,** *a.* Feeling thirst; dry, parched; (*colloq.*) exciting thirst. **thirstily,** *adv.* **thirstiness,** *n.*

thirteen (thir tēn') [A.-S. *thrēotēne* (THREE, -TEEN)], *a.* Consisting of one more than twelve. *n.* The sum of ten and three; 13, xiii. **thirteenth,** *a.* and *n.*

thirty (thĕr' ti) [A.-S. *thrītig*, *thrittig* (THREE, -TY)], *a.* Thrice ten. *n.* The sum of this; 30, xxx. **thirtieth,** *a.* and *n.* Tenth after the twentieth.

this (*this*) [A.-S. *thes*, fem. *theos*, neut. *this* (cp. Dut. *deze*, G. *dieser*, Icel. *thessi*), cogn. with THAT, THE], *a.* or *pron.* (*pl.* **these,** *thēz*) Used to denote the person or thing that is present or near in place or time, or already mentioned, implied, or familiar. **this and that:** (*colloq.*) Random and usu. unimportant subjects of conversation. **thisness,** *n.* Hæcceity.

thistle (this' ėl) [A.-S. *thistel*, cp. Dut. and G. *distel*, Icel. *thistill*], *n.* A plant of several genera of the aster family with prickly stems, leaves, and involucres. **Order of the Thistle:** A Scottish order of knighthood instituted in 1687 and revived in 1703. **thistly,** *a.*

thither (*thith'* ėr) [A.-S. *thider*, *thyder*, cogn. with THAT, cp. HITHER], *adv.* To that place; to that end, point, or result. ***thitherward, -wards,** *adv.*

thlipsis (thlip' sis) [Gr., from *thlibein*, to press], *n.* Constriction of blood-vessels by external compression.

tho' [THOUGH].

thole (1) (thōl) [A.-S. *thol*, cp. Dut. *dol*, Icel. *thollr*, tree, peg, thole], *n.* A pin in the gunwale of a boat serving as fulcrum for the oar, also called **thole pin.**

thole (2) (thōl) [A.-S. *tholian*, cp. Icel. *thola*, O.H.G. *dolēn*, Goth. *thulan*, also L. *tollere*, Gr. *tlēnai*], *v.t.* To suffer, to endure; to permit, to put up with; to bear, to undergo.

***tholobate** (thol' ō bāt) [Gr. *tholos*, *-balos*, from *bainein*, to go], *n.* (*Arch.*) The substructure on which a cupola is based. **tholus** (thō' lŭs), *n.* (*pl.* **-li,** -lī) A dome, cupola, or lantern.

Thomism (tō' mizm), *n.* The scholastic philosophy and theology of St. Thomas Aquinas (1227–74). **Thomist,** *a.* and *n.* **Thomistic** (-mis' tik), *a.*

thong (thong) [A.-S. *thwang* (cp. Icel. *thvengr*), cogn. with TWINGE], *n.* A strip of leather used as a whip-lash, for reins, or for fastening anything. *v.t.* To fit or furnish with a thong; to fasten or thrash with a thong.

Thor (thôr) [Icel. *Thorr*], *n.* The ancient Scandinavian god of thunder, war, and agriculture. **Thor's hammer:** A flint implement.

thoracic, etc. [THORAX].

thoral (thôr' ăl) [med. L. *thorus*, L. *torus*, bed], *a.* Pertaining to the marriage-bed.

thorax (thôr' ăks) [L., from Gr. *thōrāx* *-akos*], *n.* (*pl.* **thoraces,** thō rā' sēz) The part of the trunk between the neck and the abdomen; the middle division of the body of insects; (*Gr. Ant.*) a breast-plate, cuirass, or corselet. **thoracic** (thō răs' ik), *a.* **thoraci-, thoracico-, thoraco-,** *comb. form.*

thorium (thôr' i ŭm), *n.* A rare metallic element found chiefly in thorite. **thoria,** *n.* Oxide of thorium. **thoric** (thôr' ik), **thorinic** (thō rin' ik), *a.* ***thorinum,** *n.* Thorium. **thorite,** *n.* A massive dark hydrous silicate of thorium, found in Norway.

thorn (thôrn) [A.-S., cp. Icel. *thorn*, Dut. *doorn*, G. *dorn*], *n.* A spine, a sharp-pointed process, a prickle; a thorny shrub, tree, or herb (*usu. in comb.* as *blackthorn*, *whitethorn*); (*fig.*) an annoyance, a trouble, a care; the A.-S. letter þ (th). **a thorn in one's side:** A constant source of trouble. **thorn-apple,** *n.* A plant with prickly seed-capsules, *Datura stramonium*. **thornback,** *n.* The British ray or skate, *Raja clavata*, the back and tail of which are covered with spines. **thorn-bill, -tail,** *n.* A name for various humming-birds. **thorn-bush,** *n.* ***thornless,** *a.* **thorny,** *a.*

thorough (thŭr' ō) [THROUGH], *a.* Complete, perfect, not superficial. *n.* (*Hist.*) The uncompromising absolutist policy of Strafford, under Charles I. **thorough-brace,** *n.* A strap passing between two C-springs to support the body of a vehicle. **thorough-paced,** *a.* Trained to all paces (as a horse); (*fig.*) thorough-going, out-and-out. **thorough-pin,** *n.* A dropsical swelling in the hollow of a horse's hough. **thoroughly,** *adv.* **thoroughness,** *n.*

thoroughbass (thŭr' ō bās), *n.* (*Mus.*) A bass part accompanied by shorthand marks, usu. figures, written below the stave, to indicate the harmony; this method of indicating harmonies; the science of harmony.

thoroughbred (thŭr' ō bred), *a.* Of pure breed; high-spirited, mettlesome. *n.* A thoroughbred animal, esp. a horse.

thoroughfare (thŭr' ō fâr), *n.* A passage through from one street, etc., to another, an unobstructed road or street; a road or street for public traffic.

thoroughgoing (thŭr ō gō' ing), *a.* Going or ready to go to any lengths; thorough, uncompromising.

thorp, thorpe (thôrp) [A.-S. *thorp*, cp. Dut. *dorp*, G. *dorf*, Icel. *thorp*], *n.* A village, a hamlet (esp. in place-names).

those, *pl.* [THAT].

thou (*thou*) [A.-S. *thū*, cp. G., Dan., and Swed. *du*, Icel. *thū*, L. *tu*, Gr. *su*, *tu*], *pron.* (*obj.* **thee,** *thē*) The second personal pronoun singular, denoting the person spoken to (now used only in addresses to the Deity and in poetry). ***v.t.*** To address as 'thou.' *v.i.* To use 'thou' instead of 'you.'

though (*thō*) [M.E. *thogh*, Icel. *thō*, cp. Dut. and G. *doch*, A.-S. *thēah*, *thæh*, *thāh*], *conj.* Notwithstanding that; even if; granting or supposing that; (*ellipt.*) and yet; however. **as though:** As if.

thought (1), *past & p.p.* [THINK].

thought (2) (thawt) [A.-S. *thōht*, as prec.], *n.* The act or process of thinking; reflection, serious consideration, meditation; deep concern or solicitude; the faculty of thinking or reasoning; that which is thought; a conception, an idea, a reflection, a judgment, conclusion, etc.; (*pl.*) one's views, ideas, opinions, etc., **a thought:** (*colloq.*) A very small degree, etc., a shade, somewhat. **happy thought:** An apposite or timely suggestion, idea, etc., **thought-reader,** *n.* One who perceives by telepathy what is passing in another person's mind. **thought-reading,** *n.* ***thought-sick,** *a.* Uneasy with sad reflections. **thought-transference,** *n.* Telepathy. **thought-wave,** *n.* A telepathic undulation or vibration. **thoughted,** *a.* Having a (usu. specified kind of) thought or thoughts. **thoughtful,** *n.* **thoughtfully,** *adv.* **thoughtfulness,** *n.* **thoughtless,** *a.* **thoughtlessly,** *adv.* **thoughtlessness,** *n.*

thousand (thou' zȧnd) [A.-S. *thūsend* (cp. Dut. *duizend*, G. *tausend*, Icel. *thūsund*), etym. *doubtful*], *a.* and *n.* Ten hundred, 1000, M.; a great many. **thousand-legs,** *n.* A millepede or centipede. **thousand-fold,** *a.* and *adv.* **thousandth,** *a.* and *n.*

***thowel, *thowl** [THOLE (1 and 2)].

thowless (*Sc.*) [THEWLESS].

thrall (thrawl) [M.E. *thral*, Icel. *thræll* (cp. Dan. *træl*, Swed. *träl*), cogn. with A.-S. *thrægan*, to run], *n.* A slave, a serf; bondage, thraldom. *a.* I. thrall. *v.t.* To enthral, to enslave. **thraldom,** *n.*

thrang (thrăng) [THRONG], *a.* (*Sc.*) Thronged, busy.

thrap (thrăp) [etym. doubtful], *v.t.* (*Naut.*) To bind, tie, or fasten (round, about, etc.).

thrapple [THROPPLE].

thrash (thrăsh), **thresh** (thresh) [A.-S. *therscan*, cp. Dut. *dorschen*, G. *dreschen*, Icel. *threskja*], *v.t.* To beat out or separate the grain from (corn, etc.); to beat soundly, esp. with a stick or whip; to overcome, to defeat, to conquer. *n.* A thrashing. **to thrash out:** To discuss, consider, or examine thoroughly. **thrasher** (1), **thresher,** *n.* One who thrashes; the fox-shark. **thrashing,** *n.* **thrashing-floor,** *n.* A floor or area on which grain is thrashed out. **thrashing-machine, -mill,** *n.*

thrasher (2) (thrăsher) [prob. var. of THRUSH (1)], *n.* (*Am.*) A N. American songbird of the genus *Harporhyncus*, resembling the thrush, esp. the brown thrasher, *H. rufus*, common in the Eastern States.

thrasonical (thrȧ son' i kȧl), *a.* [*Thraso*, the braggart in Terence's comedies, -ICAL], *a.* Bragging, boastful. **thrasonically,** *adv.*

thratch, etc. (*Sc.*) [FRATCH].

thrave (thrāv) [from Scand., cp. Icel. *threfi*, Norw. *treve*, Swed. *trafue*], *n.* (*Sc.*) Twenty-four sheaves or two stooks of corn.

thrawn (thrawn) [THROW], *a.* (*Sc.*) Twisted; perverse.

thread (thred) [A.-S. *thræd*, from *thrāwan*, to THROW (cp. Dut. *draad*, G. *draht*, Icel. *thrāthr*)], *n.* A slender cord consisting of two or more yarns doubled or twisted; a single filament of cotton, silk, wool, etc., esp. Lisle thread; anything resembling this; a fine line of colour, etc.; a thin seam or vein; the spiral on a screw; (*fig.*) a continuous course (of life, etc.). *v.t.* To pass a thread through the eye or aperture of; to string (beads, etc.,) on a thread; (*fig.*) to pick (one's way) or to go through an intricate or crowded place, etc.; to streak (the hair) with grey, etc.; to cut a thread on (a screw). **thread and thrum:** Good and bad together, all alike. **threadbare,** *a.* Worn so that the thread is visible, having the nap worn off; (*fig.*) worn, trite, hackneyed. **threadbareness,** *n.* **thread-mark,** *n.* A mark produced by coloured silk fibres in banknotes to prevent counterfeiting. **thread-paper,** *n.* Soft paper for wrapping up thread. **threadworm,** *n.* A thread-like nematode worm, esp. one infesting the rectum of children. **threader,** *n.* **threadlike,** *a.* and *adv.* **thready,** *a.* **threadiness,** *n.*

threap (thrēp) [A.-S. *threapian*, to rebuke], *v.t.* (*Sc.* and *North.*) To assert with pertinacity; to persist; to contradict. *v.i.* To quarrel, to wrangle, *n.* Persistence, stubborn insistence; contradiction.

threat (thret) [A.-S. *thrēat*, crowd, trouble, threat, from *āthrēotan*, to afflict (cp. Icel. *thrjōta*, cogn. with L. *trūdere*, to push)], *n.* A declaration of an intention to inflict punishment, loss, injury, etc., a menace; (*Law*) such a menace as may interfere with freedom, business, etc., or a menace of injury to life, property, or reputation. **threaten,** *v.t.* To use threats to; to announce intention (to inflict injury, etc.); to announce one's intention to inflict (injury, etc.). *v.i.* To use threats; to have a threatening appearance. **threatener,** *n.* **threateningly,** *adv.* ***threatful,** *a.*

three (thrē) [A.-S. *thrēo*, *thrī*, cp. Dut. *drie*, G. *drei*, Icel. *thrīr*, also L. *trēs*, Gr. *treis*], *a.* Consisting of one more than two, 3, III. *n.* One more than two; the figure representing this. **rule of three** [RULE]. ***three F's:** The demands of the Irish Land League—free sale, fixity of tenure, free rent. **three R's:** Reading, writing, and arithmetic. **three-colour process:** The printing of coloured illustrations by the superposition of the three primary colours. **three-cornered,** *a.* Having three corners or angles. **three-decker,** *n.* A vessel carrying guns on three decks; a pulpit in three stories. **three dimensional:** Giving the effect of being seen or heard in three dimensions. **three-handed,** *a.* Having three hands; for three players (of some card-games). **three-headed,** *a.* **three-master,** *n.* A vessel, esp. a schooner, with three masts. **threepence** (threp-, thrip' ėns, thrē' pens), *n.* The sum of threepence. **threepenny,** *a.* **threepenny bit:** A small coin value threepence. **three-per-cents,** *n.pl.* Bonds or securities bearing interest at three per cent, esp. Government bonds. **three-phase,** *a.* (*Elec.*) A term applied to an alternating-current system in which the currents flow in three separate circuits. ***three-pile,** *n.* The finest kind of velvet. ***three-piled,** *a.* Having a thick, rich pile; of first-rate quality; exaggerated, high-flown. **three-ply,** *a.* Having three strands, thicknesses, etc.; plywood of three layers. **three-quarter,** *a.* Of three-fourths the usual size or number; showing three-fourths of the face, or going down to the hips (of portraits). **threescore,** *a.* Sixty. *n.* The age of sixty. **three-fold,** *a.* and *adv.* **threesome,** *a.* Threefold, triple. *n.* A party of three; (*Golf*) a game for three. **three-star,** *a.* Indicating a brandy of high grade.

thremmatology (threm ȧ tol' ŏ ji) [Gr. *thremma -atos*, nursling, from *trephein*, to nourish, -LOGY], *n.* The branch of biology dealing with the breeding of animals and plants.

threnody (thren' ŏ di), **threnode** (thrē' nōd) [Gr. *thrēnōdia* (*thrēnos*, dirge, *ōidē*, see ODE)], *n.* A song of lamentation; a poem on the death of a person. ***threne,** *n.* A threnody. **threnetic, -al** (thrė net' ik, -ȧl), **threnodial** (-nō' di ȧl), **threnodic** (-nod' ik), *a.* **threnodist** (thren' ŏ dist), *n.*

threpsology (threp sol' ŏ ji) [Gr. *threpsis*, nutrition, from *trephein*, to nourish, -LOGY], *n.* The science of nutrition of living organisms.

thresh, thresher, etc. [THRASH].

threshold (thresh' ōld) [A.-S. *therscold* (THRESH, suf. doubtful)], *n.* The stone or plank at the bottom of a doorway; (*fig.*) an entrance, a doorway, a beginning.

threw, *past* [THROW].

thrice (thrīs) [M.E. *thries*], *adv.* Three times; (*fig.*) very much. **thrice-favoured,** *a.* Highly favoured.

***thrid**, *v.t.* [var. of THREAD].

thridacium (thri dā′ shi ŭm) [mod. L., from Gr. *thridax -akos*, lettuce], *n.* The inspissated juice of lettuce, used as a sedative.

thrift (thrift) [Icel. *thrīfa*, to seize, to THRIVE], *n.* Frugality; good husbandry, economical management; the sea-pink. *Armeria, maritima.* **thriftless,** *a.* **thriftlessly,** *adv.* **thriftlessness,** *n.* **thrifty,** *a.* Frugal, careful, economical. **thriftily,** *adv.* **thriftiness,** *n.*

thrill (thril) [A.-S. *thyrlian*, from *thȳrel*, bore, from *thurh*, THROUGH], *v.t.* To penetrate; to affect with emotion so as to give a sense as of vibrating or tingling; to go through one (of emotion). *v.i.* To penetrate, vibrate, or quiver (through, along, etc., of emotion); to have a vibrating, shivering, or tingling sense of emotion. *n.* An intense vibration, shiver or wave of emotion; (*Med.*) a vibratory or tremulous resonance observed in auscultation; (*slang*) anything exciting. **thriller,** *n.* A sensational novel. **thrillingly,** *adv.* **thrillingness,** *n.*

thrips (thrips) [Gr., wood-worm], *n.* A minute insect of the genus *Thrips* or allied genus injurious to plants, esp. grain.

thrive (thrīv) [M.E. *thriven*, Icel. *thrīfa*, to seize, cp. Swed. *trifvas*, Dan. *trives* (reflex.), to thrive], *v.i.* (*past*, **throve, thrived,** *p.p.* **thriven, thrived**) To prosper, to be fortunate, to be successful; to grow vigorously. **thriver,** *n.* **thrivingly,** *adv.* **thrivingness,** *n.*

thro′ [THROUGH].

throat (thrōt) [A.-S. *throte* (cp. G. *drossel*, O.H.G. *drozza*), perh. cogn. with Dut. *strot*, throat, Icel. *throti*, swelling, from *thrūtna*, to swell, cp. THROPPLE], *n.* The front part of the neck, containing the gullet and windpipe; the gullet, the pharynx, the windpipe, the larynx; a throat-shaped inlet, opening, or entrance, a narrow passage, strait, etc.; (*Naut.*) the crotch of a gaff where it rests against the mast. *v.t.* To groove or channel. **sore throat:** An inflamed condition of the membraneous lining of the gullet, etc., usu. due to a cold. **throated,** *a.* **to cut one another's throats:** To engage in a ruinous competition. **to cut one's own throat:** (*fig.*) To adopt a suicidal policy. **to lie in one's throat:** To lie outrageously. **throaty,** *a.* Guttural; having a large or prominent throat. **throatiness,** *n.*

throatwort (thrōt′ wĕrt), *n.* (*Bot.*) The nettle-leaved bell-flower *Campanula trachelium.*

throb (throb) [M.E. *throbben*, prob. imit.], *v.i.* (*past & p.p.* **throbbed**) To beat rapidly or forcibly (of the heart or pulse); to vibrate, to quiver. *n.* A strong pulsation, a palpitation. **throbbingly,** *adv.*

throe (thrō) [M.E. *throwe*, Icel. *thrā*, cp. A.-S. *thrōwian*, to suffer], *n.* A violent pain, a pang, esp. (*pl.*) the pains of child-birth. *v.i.* To be in agony.

Throgmorton Street (throg môr′ tŏn) [street in the City of London], *n.* (*colloq.*) The Stock Exchange; Stock Exchange operations.

thrombosis (throm bō′ sis) [Gr., from *thrombousthai*, to become clotted, from *thrombos*, thrombus], *n.* (*Path.*) Local coagulation of the blood in the heart or a blood-vessel. **thrombotic** (-bot′ ik), *a.* **thrombin,** *n.* An enzyme concerned in the clotting of blood. **thrombus,** *n.* The clot of blood closing a vessel in thrombosis.

throne (thrōn) [M.E. and O.F. *trone*, L. *thronum*, nom. *-us*, Gr. *thronos*, seat, support], *n.* A royal seat, a chair or seat of State for a sovereign, bishop, etc.; (*fig.*) sovereign power; one of the third order of angels. *v.t.* To enthrone. *v.i.* To sit on a throne. **thronal,** *a.* **throneless,** *a.*

throng (throng) [A.-S. *gethrang*, from *thringan*, to crowd (cp. Dut. and G. *drang*, Icel. *thröng*)], *n.* A multitude of persons or living things pressed close together, a crowd. *v.i.* To crowd or press together; to come in multitudes. *v.t.* To crowd, to fill to excess; to fill with a crowd; to press or impede by crowding upon.

thropple (throp′ ĕl) [etym. doubtful, cp. THROAT], *n.* The throat, the windpipe, the gullet.

throstle (thros′ ĕl) [A.-S., cp. M.H.G. *trostel*, also THRUSH (1), L. *turdus*], *n.* The songthrush, *Turdus musicus*; a machine for continuously twisting and winding wool, cotton, etc. **throstling,** *n.* A swelling in the throat in cattle.

throttle (throt′ ĕl) [dim. of THROAT], *n.* The windpipe, the gullet, the throat; a throttle-valve. *v.t.* To choke, to strangle; to shut off, reduce or control (the flow of steam in a steam-engine or of explosive mixture to an internal-combustion engine). **throttle-valve,** *n.* A valve regulating such flow.

through (throo) [A.-S. *thurh*, *thuruh* (cp. Dut. *door*, G. *durch*), cogn. with Goth. *thairh*], *prep.* From end to end of, from side to side of, between the sides or walls of; over the whole extent of, in the midst of, throughout; by means, agency, or fault of, on account of. *adv.* From end to end or side to side, from beginning to end; up to and including; to a final issue; (*Am.*) finished, done with. *a.* Going through or to the end, proceeding right to the end or destination, esp. (of train, railway or steamboat tickets, etc.) over several companies' lines. **all through:** All the time, throughout. **through and through:** Through again and again; searchingly. **to be through with:** (*colloq.*) To have finished. **to carry through** [CARRY]. **to fall through** [FALL]. **to go through, to go through with** [GO (1)]. ***through-fare, through-going** (*Sc.*) [THOROUGHFARE]. **throughither** (throo′ ith ĕr), *a.* and *adv.* (*Sc.*) Confused, muddled, unmethodical. ***throughly** [THOROUGHLY]. **throughout,** *adv.* Right through, in every part; from beginning to end. *prep.* Right through, from beginning to end of.

throve, *past* [THRIVE].

throw (thrō) [A.-S. *thrāwan*, to twist, to hurl, cp. G. *drehen*, Dut. *draaien*, to twist, to twirl], *v.t.* (*past* **threw,** throo, *p.p.* **thrown,** thrōn) To fling, to hurl, to cast, esp. to a distance with some force; to cast down, to cause to fall, to prostrate; to drive, to impel to dash; to make (a cast) with dice; to turn or direct quickly or suddenly (the eyes, etc.); to put on (clothes, etc.) hastily or carelessly; to cast off (the skin, as a snake); to bring forth (young, of rabbits, etc.); to twist, to wind into threads; to shape on a potter's wheel. *v.i.* To hurl or fling a missile (at, etc.); to cast dice. *n.* The act of throwing, a cast; a cast of the dice; the distance to which a missile is thrown; the extent of motion (of a crank, etc.); a device for giving rapid rotation to a machine; (*Geol.*) a faulting, a dislocation, the extent of dislocation. **to throw away:** To cast from one; to reject carelessly; to spend recklessly, to squander; to lose through carelessness or neglect. **to throw back:** To reflect, as light, etc.; to revert (to ancestral traits). **to throw down:** To overturn; to lay (oneself) down prostrate. **to throw in:** To interject, to interpolate; to put in without extra charge, to add as a contribution or extra. **to throw in one's hand:** To give up a job, etc., as hopeless. **to throw off:** To cast off, to get rid of, to abandon, to discard; to produce without effort. **to throw oneself on:** To commit oneself to the protection, favour, etc., of. **to throw open:** To open suddenly and completely; to make freely accessible. **to throw out:** To cast out, to reject; to emit; to give utterance to, to suggest; to cause (a building, etc.) to stand out or project. **to throw over:** To abandon, to desert. **to throw up:** To raise or lift quickly; to abandon, to resign; to vomit. **throw-off,** *n.* The start (of a race, etc.). **throw-stick,** *n.* A short curved stick for throwing, a boomerang. **thrower,** *n.* **throwing,** *n.* (*Ceram.*) The operation of shaping clay on a potter's wheel.

throwback (thrō′ băk), *n.* A reversion to an earlier type; (*Cinema.*) a scene from the past breaking into the present.

throwster (thrō′ stĕr), *n.* One who throws silk.

thrum (1) (thrŭm) [Icel. *thruma*, to rattle, to thunder, cogn. with DRUM (1)], *v.i.* (*past & p.p.* **thrummed**) To play carelessly or unskilfully (on a stringed instrument); to tap, to drum monotonously (on a table, etc.). *v.t.* To play (an instrument) thus; to tap or drum on. *n.* The act or sound of such drumming or playing.

thrum (2) (thrŭm) [A.-S. *tungethrum*, cp. Icel. *thrömr*, edge, Dut. *dreum*, G. *trumm*], *n.* The fringe of warp-threads left when the web has been cut off, or one of such threads; loose thread, fringe, etc., a tassel; (*pl.*) coarse or waste yarn. *v.t.* To cover or trim with thrums. **thrummy,** *a.*

thrush (1) (thrŭsh) [A.-S. *thrysce*, cp. G. *dross l*, O.H.G. *drosca*, also THROSTLE], *n.* A bird of the family *Turdidæ*, esp. the song-thrush or throstle, *Turdus musicus*.

thrush (2) (thrŭsh) [cp. Dan. *tröske*, Swed. *törsk*, also Norw. *frosk*, prob. ident. with *frosk*, frog], *n.* A vesicular disease of the mouth and throat, usu. affecting children; an inflammatory affection of the frog in the feet of horses.

thrusher [THRASHER (2)].

thrust (thrŭst) [M.E. *thrusten*, *thrysten*, Icel. *thrysta*, perh. cogn. with L. *trūdere*], *v.t.* To push suddenly or forcibly; to stab. *v.i.* To make a sudden push (at); to stab (at); to force or squeeze (in, etc.). *n.* A sudden or violent push; an attack as with a pointed weapon, a stab; force exerted by one body against another, esp. horizontal outward pressure, as of an arch against its abutments. **to thrust one's self in:** To intrude; to interfere. **to thrust through:** To pierce. **thrust-hoe,** *n.* A hoe worked by pushing. **thruster,** *n.*

thud (thŭd) [cp. A.-S. *thyddan*, to strike, to thrust], *n.* A dull sound as of a blow on something soft. *v.i.* (*past & p.p.* **thudded**) To make a thud; to fall with a thud.

thug (thŭg) [Hindi *thag*, *thug*], *n.* One of a fraternity of religious assassins in India (suppressed 1828–35); a cut-throat, a ruffian. **thuggee, thuggery, thuggism,** *n.*

Thuja [THUYA].

Thule (thū′ lē) [L., from Gr. *Thoule*], *n.* The name given by the voyager Pytheas of Massilia to the northernmost land he reached, variously identified with the Shetlands, Iceland, Norway, etc. **ultima Thule:** (*fig.*) A very remote place. **thulite,** *n.* A rose-red variety of zoisite. **thulium** (thū′ li ŭm), *n.* (*Metal.*) One of the rarest metallic elements, a member of the rare earth group.

thumb (thŭm) [A.-S. *thūma* (cp. Dut. *duim*, G. *daumen*, Swed. *tumme*), cogn. with TUMID], *n.* The short thick digit of the human hand; the corresponding digit in animals. *v.t.* To handle, perform, or play awkwardly; to soil or mark with the thumb. *v.i.* To thrum. **one's fingers all thumbs:** Fumbling, clumsily. **rule of thumb:** A rough, practical method. **to thumb a lift:** To get a lift from a passing car by signalling with up-raised thumb. **under one's thumb:** Completely under one's power or influence. **thumb index,** *n.* (*Print.*) An index in which the letters are printed on the fore-edge, spaces being cut away from preceding pages to expose them to sight. **thumb-latch,** *n.* One with a broad-ended lever for pressing down with the thumb. **thumb-mark,** *n.* A mark made with a dirty thumb. **thumb-nut,** *n.* A nut with wings for screwing up with the thumb. **thumb-print** [FINGERPRINT]. **thumb-screw,** *n.* A screw adapted to be turned with the finger and thumb; an old instrument of torture for compressing the thumb. **thumb-stall,** *n.* A case, sheath, or covering for an injured or sore thumb. **thumb-tack,** *n.* (*Am.*) A drawing-pin. **thumbed,** *a.* **thumbikins, *thumbkins,** *n.pl.* A thumb-screw. **thumbless,** *a.* **thumbs up!** *int.* (*colloq.*) An indication of success. **thumb-nail sketch,** *n.* A brief, vivid description.

thummim [URIM].

thump (thŭmp) [imit.], *v.t.* To strike with something giving a dull sound, esp. with the fist. *v.i.* To beat, to knock, to hammer (on, at, etc.). *n.* A blow giving a dull sound; the sound of this. **thumper,** *n.* One who or that which thumps; (*colloq.*) anything very large, excellent, or remarkable. **thumping,** *a.* (*colloq.*) Very large.

thunder (thŭn′ dėr) [A.-S. *thunor* (cp. Dut. *donder*, G. *donner*, Icel. *thōrr*), whence *thunrian*, cogn. with L. *tonāre*, to thunder, Gr. *stenein*, to groan], *n.* The sound following a flash of lightning, due to the disturbance of the air by the electric discharge; a thunderbolt; (*fig.*) a loud noise; a vehement denunciation or threat. *v.i.* To make the noise of thunder; to make a loud noise; to make loud denunciations, etc. *v.t.* To emit or utter as with the sound of thunder. **thunderbolt,** *n.* An electric discharge with lightning and thunder; a supposed missile or mass of heated matter formerly believed to be discharged in this; (*fig.*) an irresistible force, hero, a daring denunciation, etc. **thunder-clap, -crack, -peal,** *n.* **thunder-cloud,** *n.* A cloud from which lightning and thunder are produced. **thunder-dart,** *n.* A thunderbolt. **thunder-shower, -storm,** *n.* A storm with thunder. **thunder-struck,** *a.* Struck by lightning; amazed, astounded. **thunderer,** *n.* One who thunders; (*facet.*) applied to *The Times* newspaper in the mid-nineteenth cent. **thundering,** *a.* Producing thunder or a loud sound like thunder; (*slang*) extreme, remarkable, tremendous, out-and-out. *adv.* Unusually, remarkably, tremendously. **thunderingly,** *adv.* **thunderless, thunderous, thundery,** *a.* **thunderously,** *adv.*

thurible (thūr′ i bėl) [L. *thūribulum*, from *thūs*, *thūris*, frankincense, Gr. *thuos*, from *thuein*, to sacrifice], *n.* A censer. **thurifer,** *n.* One who carries a censer. **thuriferous** (thū rif′ ėr ŭs), *a.* Producing frankincense. **thurification,** *n.* The act of burning incense.

Thursday (thĕrz′ dā, -di) [A.-S. *Thūres* (*Thunres*) *dæg*, Icel. *thōrs-dagr*, Thor's day, after *dies Jovis*, Jupiter's day], *n.* The fifth day of the week.

thus (1) (*th*ŭs) [A.-S., cp. O.Fris. and O.S. *thus*, Dut. *dus*, prob. cogn. with THAT], *adv.* In this manner; in the way indicated or about to be indicated; accordingly; to this extent. **thusness,** *n.* (*humo.*). ***thuswise,** *adv.*

thus (2) (thus, thoos) [L., see THURIBLE], *n.* Resin of the spruce-fir, etc.; frankincense.

***Thuya*, Thuja** (thū′ yȧ) [Gr. *thuia*], *n.* A genus of coniferous trees or shrubs, also called arbor-vitæ.

thwack [WHACK].

thwaite (thwāt) [Icel. *thveit*, paddock, a piece cut off, cogn. with A.-S. *thwītan*, to WHITTLE], *n.* A piece of ground reclaimed and converted to tillage.

thwart (thwôrt) [M.E., from Icel. *thvert*, cp. A.-S. *thwerh*, *thweorh*, perverse], *a.* Transverse, oblique. ***prep.** Across, athwart. *n.* A transverse plank in a boat serving as seat for a rower. *v.t.* To cross, to frustrate. **thwarter,** *n.* **thwartingly, *thwartly,** *adv.* ***thwartness,** *n.* **thwartship,** *a.* and *adv.* (*Naut.*) Across the vessel.

thy (*th*ī) [A.-S. *thīn*, gen. of *thū*, THOU (cp. Icel. *thinn*, Dan. and Swed. *din*, G. *dein*)], *pron.* and *a.* (*before vowels usu. and absolutely* **thine**) Of or pertaining to thee (poss. corresponding to THOU).

thyine (thī′ in) [L. *thyīnus*, Gr. *thuinos*, from *thua*, THUYA], *a.* (*Bibl.*) Applied to a kind of wood and a tree (Rev. xviii. 12), perh. the African conifer, *Callitris quadrivalvis*.

thylacine (thī′ lȧ sin) [F. (Gr. *thulakos*, pouch)], *n.* The Tasmanian zebra-wolf, *Thylacinus cynocephalus*, the largest predatory marsupial now living.

thyme (tīm) [O.F. *tym* (F. *thym*), L. *thymum*, nom. *-us*, Gr. *thumos*], *n.* Any plant of the genus *Thymus*, esp. the garden thyme, *T. vulgaris*, a pungent aromatic herb used in cookery.

thymol (thī′ mol), *n.* (*Chem.*) A phenol obtained from oil of thyme, used as an antiseptic.

thymus (thī′ mŭs) [Gr. *thumos*], *n.* (*pl.* **-mi, -mi**) A gland situated in the lower region of the neck, usu. degenerating after infancy.

thyroid (thī′ roid) [Gr. *thureoeidēs* (*thureos*, shield, from *thura*, door, -OID)], *a.* Shield-shaped; of or connected with the thyroid gland or cartilages; (*Zool.*) having a shield-shaped marking; (*Bot.*) peltate. *n.* The thyroid body or gland; the thyroid cartilage; a thyroid artery. **thyroid body** or **gland:** A large ductless organ consisting of two lobes situated on each side of the larynx and the upper part of the windpipe, of obscure function, but giving rise to goitre when it becomes enlarged. **thyroid cartilage:** A large cartilage in the larynx, called in man the Adam's apple. **thyroid extract,** *n.* (*Med.*) An extract prepared from the thyroid glands of oxen, sheep and pigs, and employed therapeutically. **thyro-,** *comb. form.*

thyrsus (thĕr′ sŭs) [L., from Gr. *thursos*], *n.* (*pl.* **-si, -sī**) (*Gr. Ant.*) A spear or shaft wrapped with ivy or vine branches and tipped with a fir-cone, an attribute of Bacchus; (*Bot.*) an inflorescence consisting of a panicle with the longest branches in the middle. **thyrse,** *n.* **thyrsoid,** *a.*

Thysanuran (this à nūr′ ăn) [Gr. *thusanos*, tassel, *oura*, tail], *a.* Belonging to the *Thysanura*, a division of wingless insects comprising the springtails. *n.* One of these insects. **thysanuriform,** *a,*

thyself (*thī* self′), *pron.* A reflexive and emphatic form used after or instead of 'thou.'

tiake (tē a′ kē) [Maori], *n.* The jack-bird or saddleback.

tiara (ti a′ rà) [L. and Gr., prob. from Pers.], *n.* The head-dress of the ancient Persian kings, resembling a lofty turban; the triple crown worn by the Pope as a symbol of his temporal, spiritual, and purgatorial power; hence, the papal dignity; a jewelled coronet or headband worn as an ornament by women. ***tiar** (tī′ ăr), *n.* **tiara'd,** *a.*

***tib** (tib) [short for *Isabel*], *n.* The ace of trumps in the game of gleek; a low woman, a prostitute.

tibet, thibet (ti bet′) [*Tibet*, in Central Asia], *n.* A cloth made of goat's hair or in imitation of this; a garment of this material. **Tibetan** (ti be′ tăn), *a.* Of or pertaining to the country of Tibet; *n.* An inhabitant of that country.

tibia (tib′ i à, tī′ bi à]) [L.), *n.* (*pl.* **-biæ, -bias**) The shinbone, the anterior and inner of the two bones of the leg; the fourth joint of the leg in an arthropod; a pipe or flute. **tibial,** *a.* **tibio-,** *comb. form.*

tic (tik) [F., prob. from Teut.], *n.* An habitual convulsive twitching of muscles, esp. of the face, tic douloureux. **tic douloureux:** Facial neuralgia characterized by spasmodic twitching.

tice (1) (tīs), *n.* (*Cricket*) A yorker.

***tice** (2) [ENTICE].

tick (1) (tik) [A.-S. *ticia*, cp. M.Dut. *teke*, G. *zecke*], *n.* A name for various parasitic acarids infesting some animals and occasionally man.

tick (2) (tik) [formerly *teke*, L. *thēca*], *n.* A cover or case for the filling of mattresses and beds; the material for this, usu. strong striped cotton or linen cloth, also called **ticking.**

tick (3) (tik) [shortened from TICKET], *n.* (*colloq.*) Credit, trust. *v.i.* To give credit.

tick (4) (tik) [M.E. *tek*, a light touch, prob. imit., cp. Dut. *tik*, whence *tikken*, Norw. *tikka*], *v.i.* To make a small regularly recurring sound like that of a watch or clock. *v.t.* To mark (off) with a tick. *n.* The sound made by a going watch or clock; a small mark used in checking items. **to tick over:** (*Motor.*) The engine to run slowly with gear disconnected. **tick-tack,** *n.* A recurring, pulsating sound; (*Racing*) a code of signalling employed by bookmakers whereby their agents can keep them informed of the betting odds. **ticker,** *n.* (*colloq.*) A watch.

ticket (tik′ ĕt) [M.E. *etiquet*, O.F. *etiquet*, *estiquette*, ticket, bill, from G. *stecken*, to STICK], *n.* A card or paper with written or printed contents entitling the holder to admission to a concert, etc., conveyance by train, etc., or other privilege; a tag or label giving the price, etc. of a thing it is attached to; (*slang*) a visiting-card; the correct thing; (*Mil. colloq.*) discharge from the Army; (*Naut. colloq.*) a master's certificate; (*Aviat. colloq.*) a pilot's certificate; (*Am.*) the list of candidates put up by a party, hence the principles or programme of a party. *v.t.* To put a ticket on. **ticket-day,** *n.* The day before settling-day on the Stock Exchange when the brokers and jobbers learn the amount of stocks and shares that are passing between them and are due for settlement, and the names of the actual purchasers. **ticket of leave:** The term formerly applied to a licence to a prisoner to be at large under certain restrictions before the expiration of the sentence. **ticket-of-leave man:** A person holding this. **ticket-porter,** *n.* A licensed porter wearing a ticket or badge of identification. **ticket-punch,** *n.* A punch for cancelling or marking tickets. **ticket-writer,** *n.* An expert in window-card lettering.

ticking [TICK (2)].

tickle (tik′ ĕl) [M.E. *tikelen*, freq. of TICK (4)], *v.t.* To touch lightly so as to cause a thrilling sensation usually producing laughter; (*fig.*) to please, to gratify, to amuse. *v.i.* To feel the sensation of tickling. *n.* The act or sensation of tickling. *a.* (*prov.*) Ticklish, uncertain. **tickler,** *n.* One who or that which tickles; something difficult to deal with.

ticklish (tik′ lish), *a.* Sensible to the feeling of tickling; difficult, critical, precarious, needing tact or caution. **ticklishly,** *adv.* **ticklishness,** *n.*

tid (tid) [var. of TIDE], *n.* (*Sc.*) The right time or condition (for sowing or other agricultural operation).

tidal [TIDE].

tidbit [TITBIT].

tiddle [TITTLE (2)].

tiddler (1) (tid′ lĕr) [corr. of TITTLEBAT], *n.* (*Childish*) A stickleback. **tiddling,** *n.* Fishing for these.

tiddler (2) (tid′ lĕr) [*tiddle*, var. of TITTLE (2)], *n.* (*slang*) A feather or other instrument for tickling a person in order to tease.

tiddly (tid′ li), *a.* (*colloq.*) Slightly drunk, drunk. *n.* An intoxicating drink.

tiddlywinks (tid′ li wingks) [etym. doubtful], *n.* A game in which players snap small bone or ivory disks into a tray.

***tiddy** (tid′ i) [etym. doubtful], *n.* The four of trumps in the game of gleek.

tide (tīd) [A.-S. *tīd*, time, hour, cp. Dut. *tijd*, G. *zeit*, Icel. *tīth*, Dan. and Swed. *tid*], *n.* Time, season, hour; a regular period of time (for a day's work, etc.); the alternate rise and fall of the sea, due to the attraction of the sun and moon; (*fig.*) a rush of water, a flood, a torrent, a stream; the course or tendency of events. *v.i.* (*Naut.*) To work in or out of a river or harbour by the help of the tide. **to tide over:** To surmount difficulties by the help of circumstances. **tide-gate,** *n.* A gate for admitting vessels at high tide and retaining the water at low tide. **tide-gauge,** *n.* An instrument showing or registering the rise and fall of the tide. **tide-lock,** *n.* A lock between the tide-water of a harbour and an enclosed basin. **tide-mill,** *n.* A mill driven by a wheel set in motion by the tide. **tide-waiter,** *n.* A custom-house officer who boards ships entering port in order to enforce customs regulations. **tideway,** *n.* The channel in which the tide runs; the ebb or flow of the tide in this. **tidesman,** *n.* A tide-waiter. **tidal** (tī′ dăl) [TIDE, -AL], *a.* Pertaining or relating to the tides; periodically rising and falling or ebbing and flowing, as the tides. **tidal basin, dock,** or **harbour:** One in which the level of the water rises or falls with the tide. **tidal river:** One in which the tides act a long way inland. **tidal wave:** A wave following the sun and moon from east to west and causing the tides; (*incorr.*) a large wave due to an earthquake, etc.; (*fig.*) a great movement of popular feeling. **tideless,** *a.*

tidings (tī′ dingz) [M.E. *tidinde*, Icel. *tīthindi*, cp. A.-S. *tiding*, as prec.], *n.pl.* News, intelligence, a report.

tidy (tī′ di) [orig. seasonable, TIDE, -Y], *a.* Orderly, in becoming order, neat, trim; (*colloq.*) considerable, pretty large; fairly well. *n.* A knitted covering for a chair-back, etc. *v.t.* To make tidy, to put in order. **tidily,** *adv.* **tidiness,** *n.*

tie (tī) [M.E. *tigen*, A.-S. *tīegan*, from *tēag*, *tēah*, bond, rope, etc., from *tēon*, to pull (cp. Icel. *tang*, tie)], *v.t.* (*pres.p.* **tying**) To fasten with a cord, etc., to secure, to attach, to bind; to arrange together and draw into a knot, bow, etc.; to bind together, to unite; to confine, to restrict, to bind (down, etc.); (*Mus.*) to unite (notes) by a tie. *v.i.* To be exactly equal (with) in a score. *n.* Something used to tie things together; a neck-tie; a bond, an obligation; a beam or rod holding parts of a structure together; (*Mus.*) a curved line placed over two or more notes to be played as one; (*fig.*) an equality of votes, score, etc., among candidates, competitors, etc.; a match between any pair of a number of players or teams; (*Am.*) a railway sleeper. **to tie up:** To fasten securely to a post, etc.; to restrict, to bind by restrictive conditions. **tie-beam,** *n.* A horizontal beam connecting rafters. **tie-up,** *n.* (*Am.*) A deadlock, a standstill, esp. in business or industry, through a strike, etc. **tie-wig,** *n.* A wig tied behind with ribbon. **tied house:** A public house bound to obtain its supplies of beer or other liquor from one firm. **tier** (1) (tī′ ėr), *n.*

tier (2) (tēr) [O.F. *tire*, prob. from Teut.], *n.* A row, a rank, esp. one of several rows placed one above another. *v.t.* To pile in tiers.

tierce (tērs) [F. *tiers*, fem. *tierce*, L. *tertius*, third], *n.* A cask of 42 gallons, or one-third of a pipe; a sequence of three cards of the same suit; (*Fencing*) the third position for guard, parry, or thrust; (*Mus.*) a third; (*Eccles.*) the office for the third hour; (*Her.*) a field divided into three parts of different tinctures.

tiercel (tēr′ sėl) [O.F., dim. of *tiers*, prec.], *n.* A male falcon.

tiercet [TERCET].

tiers état (tyârz ė ta′) [F., third estate], *n.* The third estate of the realm, the commonalty.

tiff (1) (tif) [cp. Norw. *tev*, a sniff, a scent, Icel. *thefa*, to sniff], *n.* A small draught of liquor; a fit of peevishness, a slight quarrel. *v.t.* To sip, to drink. *v.i.* To be pettish; (*Ang.-Ind.*) to take tiffin.

tiff (2) (tif) [M.E. *tiffen*, O.F. *tiffer*, *atiffer*, from Teut. (cp. Dut. *tippen*, to cut, to clip)], *v.t.* (*prov.*) To dress, to deck, to prank.

tiffany (tif′ ȧ ni) [O.F. *tiffanie*, THEOPHANY (orig. a Twelfth Night dress)], *n.* A kind of thin silk-like gauze.

tiffin (tif′ in), *n.* (*Ang.-Ind.*) A lunch or light repast between breakfast and dinner. *v.i.* To take this.

tig (tig) [perh. var. of TICK (4)], *v.t.* To touch in the game of tig. *v.i.* (*Sc.*) To give light touches. *n.* A children's game in which one pursues and touches another who in turn pursues until he can touch someone.

tige (tēzh) [F., from L. TIBIA], *n.* (*Arch.*) The shaft of a column; (*Bot.*) a stem or stalk.

tiger (tī′ gėr) [M.E. and O.F. *tigre*, L. and Gr. *tigris*, perh. from O.Pers. *tighri*, arrow, in alln. to its swiftness], *n.* A large Asiatic carnivorous feline mammal, *Felis tigris*, tawny with black stripes; applied to other large feline animals as the American tiger or jaguar, the red tiger or cougar, etc.; (*colloq.*) a swaggering ruffian, a bully; (*slang*) a liveried groom attending a person in a light vehicle. **tiger-beetle,** *n.* A predaceous beetle with striped or spotted wing-cases. **tiger-cat,** *n.* A wild cat of various species; (*Austral.*) the dasyure. **tiger-flower,** *n.* A plant of the genus *Tigridia*, spotted with orange and yellow. **tiger-footed,** *a.* Swift as a tiger. **tiger-lily,** *n.* A lily, *Lilium tigrinum*, with orange-spotted flowers. **tiger-moth,** *n.* One of the *Arctiidæ*, with streaked hairy wings. **tiger's-eye,** *n.* A gem with brilliant chatoyant lustre. **tiger's-foot,** *n.* A plant of the genus *Ipomæa*. **tiger-wood,** *n.* A wood imported from British Guiana for cabinet-making. **tigerish,** *a.* **tigress,** *n.* **tigrine,** *a.*

tight (tīt) [M.E. *tigt*, Icel. *thēttr*, cp. Swed. *tät*, Dan. *tæt*, N.Fris. *tacht*], *a.* Compactly built or put together, not leaky; impervious, impermeable (*often in comb.* as *water-tight*); drawn, fastened, held, or fitting closely; tense, stretched to the full, taut; (*fig.*) neat, trim, compact; (*Am.*) close-fisted, parsimonious; (*Comm.*) cramped, straitened; not easily obtainable (of money); (*colloq.*) awkward, difficult; (*slang*) drunk. *adv.* Tightly. **tight-fisted,** *a.* Mean, stingy. **tight-rope,** *n.* A rope stretched between two points upon which an acrobat walks, dances, etc. **tighten,** *v.t.* and *i.* **tightener,** *n.* **tightly,** *adv.* **tightness,** *n.* **tights,** *n.pl.* Clothes fitting tightly to the body worn by actors, acrobats, etc.

tigon (tī′ gon), *n.* (*Zool.*) The offspring of a tiger and a lioness.

tigress, tigrine [TIGER].

tihore (tē hō rē) [Maori], *n.* The N. Zealand flax.

tika (tē′ ka) [Hind.], *n.* The red mark on the forehead of a Hindu woman.

tike (tīk) [M.E., from Icel. *tīk*, cp. Swed. *tik*, Norw. *tik*], *n.* (*prov.*) A dog, a cur; a low fellow.

tiki (tī′ kē) [Maori, god], *n.* A greenstone neck ornament; a small wooden image.

tilbury (til′ bůr i) [name of a London coachbuilder], *n.* An old form of gig.

tilde (til′ dė) [Sp., var. of *titulo*, TITLE], *n.* A diacritical sign (~) put over *n* and sometimes *l* to show when this should be pronounced as if followed by *y*.

tile (tīl) [A.-S. *tigele*, L. *tēgula*, from *tegere*, to cover], *n.* A thin slab of baked clay, used for covering roofs, paving floors, constructing drains, etc.; a similar slab of porcelain or other material used for ornamental paving; (*colloq.*) a silk hat. *v.t.* To cover with or as with tiles; (*Freemasonry*) to secure against intrusion by stationing the tiler at the door; (*fig.*) to bind to secrecy. **to have a tile loose:** To be eccentric, half-crazy. **tile-drain,** *n.* A drain made of tiles. **tile-kiln,** *n.* **tilestone,** *n.* An argillaceous stone, esp. from the uppermost group of the Silurian formation, used for tiling. **tiler,** *n.* One who makes or lays tiles; (*Freemasonry*) the door-keeper of a lodge. **tilery,** *n.* **tiling,** *n.*

tiliaceous (til i ā′ shůs) [L. *tilia*, linden, -ACEOUS], *a.* Allied to or resembling the linden or lime-tree.

tilka [TIKA].

till (1) (til) [A.-S. *tilian*, *teolian*, to labour, to strive for, to till, from *til*, good, goodness], *v.t.* To cultivate. **tillable,** *a.* **tillage,** *n.* **tiller** (1), *n.*

till (2) (til) [Icel. *til*, cp. Dan. *til*, Swed. *till*, G. *ziel*, purpose], *prep.* Up to, up to the time of, until. *conj.* Up to the time when. **till now:** Up to the present time. **till then:** Up to that time.

till (3) (til) [earlier and prov. *tiller*, drawer, from M.E. *tillen*, A.-S. *tyllan* (in *fortyllan*), to draw], *n.* A money-drawer in a counter.

till (4) (til) [etym. doubtful], *n.* (*Geol.*) An unstratified clay containing boulders, pebbles, sand, etc., deposited by glaciers. **tilly,** *a.*

tiller (1) [TILL (1)].

tiller (2) (til′ ėr) [M.E. *tillen*, see TILL (3), -ER], *n.* The lever on the head of a rudder by which this is turned. **tiller-chain, -rope,** *n.* One connecting the tiller with the steering-wheel.

tiller (3) (til′ ėr) [A.-S. *telgor*, *tealgor*, from *telga*, cp. Dut. *telg*], *n.* The shoot of a plant springing from the base of the original stalk; a sucker; a sapling. *v.i.* To put forth tillers.

tilt (1) (tilt) [A.-S. *teld*, cp. M.Dut. *telde, telte*, G. *zelt*, Icel. *tjald*, Dan. *telt*], *n.* A covering for a cart or wagon; an awning over the stern-sheets of a boat, etc. *v.t.* To cover with a tilt.

tilt (2) (tilt) [M.E. *tilten*, from A.-S. *tealt*, unsteady (cp. Icel. *tölta*, to amble, Norw. *tylta*, to go tiptoe, Swed. *tulta*, to waddle)], *v.i.* To heel over, to tip, to be in a slanting position; to charge with a lance, to joust, as in a tournament. *v.t.* To raise at one end, to cause to heel over, to tip, to incline; to thrust or aim (a lance); to hammer or forge with a tilt-hammer. *n.* An inclination from the vertical, a slanting position; a tilting, a tournament, a charge with the lance; a tilt-hammer; a contrivance, usu. of crossed sticks, for showing a bite in angling through ice. **full tilt:** At full speed or full charge, with full force. **tilt-hammer,** *n.* A large hammer on a pivoted lever, usu. worked by steam or water-power. **tilt-yard,** *n.* A place for tilting. **tilter,** *n.*

tilth (tilth) [A.-S. (TILL (1), -TH)], *n.* Tillage, cultivation; the depth of soil tilled.

timbal, tymbal (tim' bȧl) [F. *timbale*, It. *timballo*, Arab. *tabl*, drum, cp. ATABAL], *n.* A kettle-drum.

timbale (tan bal') [F.], *n.* A dish of fowl or fish pounded and mixed with white of egg, cream, etc., and moulded.

timber (tim' bėr) [A.-S. (cp. Dut. and Swed. *timmer*, G. *zimmer*, room, timber, Icel. *timbr*), cogn. with Gr. *demein*, to build], *n.* Wood suitable for building, carpentry, etc.; (*collect.*) trees yielding wood suitable for constructive purposes, trees generally (*Am.* lumber); a piece of wood prepared for building, esp. one of the curved pieces forming the ribs of a ship; (*Hunting slang*) fences, hurdles, etc. *v.t.* To furnish or construct with timber; to cover with trees (*in p.p.*). **timber-cart,** *n.* A vehicle with high wheels fitted for stringing logs and carrying lengthwise. **timber-head,** *n.* (*Naut.*) A timber rising above the deck for belaying ropes, etc. **timber-toes,** *n.* (*colloq.*) A wooden-legged person. **timber-yard,** *n.* A yard where timber is stored, etc. **timbered,** *a.* Wooded (*usu. in comb.*, as *well-timbered*). **timbering,** *n.* The using of timber; temporary timber supports for the sides of an excavation.

timbre (tim' bėr, tanbr) [F., from O.F. *tymbre*, L. *tympanum*], *n.* The quality of tone distinguishing particular voices, instruments, etc., due to the individual character of the sound-waves.

timbrel (tim' brėl) [M.E. dim. of *timber*, as prec.], *n.* An ancient instrument like the tambourine.

time (tīm) [A.-S. *tīma* (cp. Icel. *tīmi*, Dan. *time*, Swed. *timme*), cogn. with TIDE], *n.* The general relation of sequence or continuous or successive existence; duration or continuous existence regarded as divisible into portions or periods, a particular portion of this; a period characterized by certain events, persons, manners, etc., an epoch, an era (*sometimes in pl.*); a portion of time allotted to one or to a specific purpose, the time available or at one's disposal; the period of an apprenticeship, of gestation, of a round at boxing, etc.; a portion of time as characterized by circumstances, conditions of existence, etc.; a point in time, a particular moment, instant, or hour; a date, a season, an occasion, an opportunity; time as reckoned by conventional standards, as sidereal time, solar time, etc.; (*Gram.*) the relation of a verb as regards past, present, or future, or as regards tenses; (*Mus.*) the relative duration of a note or rest; rate of movement, tempo; style of movement, rhythm; (*Pros.*) duration of a vowel, syllable, etc., in pronunciation. *v.t.* To adapt to the time or occasion; to do, begin, or perform at the proper season; to regulate as to time; to ascertain or mark the time, duration, or rate of; to measure, as in music. *v.i.* To keep time (with). **time and motion study:** Investigation into the motions and time taken for them of manual workers, with a view to increasing production. **to pass the time of day:** To greet, to say 'good-day' to. **apparent time, solar time:** Time as reckoned by the apparent motion of the sun. **at the same time** [SAME]. **at times:** At intervals, now and then. **from time to time** [FROM]. **Greenwich time** [GREENWICH]. **in good time:** At the right moment; early; fortunately, happily (*often iron.*). **in time:** Not too late; early enough; in course of time; sometime or other, eventually; in accordance with the time, rhythm, etc. **mean time:** An average of apparent time. **quick time** [QUICK]. **sidereal time:** Time shown by the apparent diurnal revolutions of the stars. **time-bomb,** *n.* A bomb set to explode at some prearranged time after falling. **time enough:** Soon enough. **time of day:** The hour by the clock; a greeting appropriate to this; (*slang*) the latest aspect of affairs. **time out of mind, time immemorial:** Time beyond legal memory. **to beat time** [BEAT]. **to lose time:** To delay. **what time:** (*poet.*) When. **time-ball,** *n.* A ball dropped from the top of a staff at an observatory at a prescribed instant of time, usu. 1 P.M. **time-bargain,** *n.* An agreement to buy or sell stock, etc., at a certain time. ***time-bill,** *n.* A time-table. **time-book, -card, -sheet,** *n.* One specifying or recording hours of work for workmen, etc. **time-expired,** *a.* Applied to soldiers whose period of service is completed. **time-fuse,** *n.* A fuse in a shell, etc., graduated to ignite the charge at a certain time. **time-honoured,** *a.* Of venerable age. **time-keeper,** *n.* A clock, watch, or chronometer; a person who records time, esp. of workmen. **time lag,** *n.* The interval that elapses between cause and result. **time-limit,** *n.* The period within which a task must be completed. **timepiece,** *n.* A clock or watch. **time-server,** *n.* One who suits his conduct, opinions, and manners to those in power. **time-serving,** *a.* and *n.* **time-serving man,** *n.* A soldier in the regular army. **time-signal,** *n.* A signal issued by an observatory or broadcasting station to indicate the exact time. **time-table,** *n.* A printed list of the times of departure and arrival of trains, etc.; a record of times of employés, school-lessons, etc.; a table containing the relative value of every note in music. **time-work,** *n.* Work paid for by time, opp. to piece-work. **time-worn,** *a.* Antiquated, dilapidated. **timeful,** *a.* Seasonable, timely, early. ***timeless,** *a.* Untimely, premature; without end. ***timelessly,** *adv.* **timer,** *n.* **timing,** *n.* Reckoning the time taken; (*Mech.*) the precise instant at which ignition occurs in an internal-combustion engine, and at which the valves open and close; the controlling mechanism for this. **timist,** *n.* One who keeps time in music.

timely (tīm' li), *a.* Seasonable, opportune, early, premature. **timeliness,** *n.* **timeous, timous,** *a.* (*Sc.*) **timeously, timously,** *adv.*

***timenoguy** (tī men' ȯ gī) [etym. unknown], *n.* (*Naut.*) A rope or spar stretched across a place to prevent fouling of rigging.

timid (tim' id) [F. *timide*, L. *timidus*, from *timēre*, to fear], *a.* Easily frightened, shy. **timidity** (tim id' i ti), **timidness,** *n.* Habitual shyness or cowardice. **timidly,** *adv.*

timing, timist [TIME].

timocracy (ti mok' rȧ si) [Gr. *timokratia* (*timē*, honour, -CRACY)], *n.* A form of government in which a certain amount of property is a necessary qualification for office. **timocratic** (-krăt' ik), *a.*

Timon (tī' mȯn) [Gr. *Timōn*, a Greek misanthrope, hero of Shakespeare's play 'Timon of Athens'], *n.* A misanthrope.

***timoneer** (tī mȯ nēr') [F., from It. *timoniere*, from *timon*, helm, L. *tēmōnem*, nom. *tēmo*, a helm], *n.* A helmsman; one on the lookout who directs a helmsman.

timorous (tim' ȯ rŭs) [med. L. *timorōsus*, from L. *timor*, fear, from *timēre*, to fear], *a.* Fearful, timid. ***timoroso*** (tim ȯ rō' sō) [It.], *adv.* (*Mus. direction*) With hesitation. **timorously,** *adv.* **timorousness,** *n.*

Timothy grass (tim′ ŏ thi gras) [*Timothy* Hanson, an American through whom it first came into use, *c.* 1720], *n.* A valuable fodder-grass, *Phleum pratense.*

timous, etc. [TIMELY].

timpano (tim′ pȧ nō) [It., from L. *tympanum*], *n.* (*pl.* **-ni,** -nē) An orchestral kettle-drum.

***timwhisky** (tim wisk′ i) [*tim,* etym. doubtful, WHISKY (2)], *n.* A high light chaise for one horse or two horses driven tandem.

tin (tin) [A.-S., cp. Dut., Icel., and Dan. *tin,* G. *zinn*], *n.* A lustrous white metal easily beaten into thin plates, much used for cooking utensils, etc., esp. in the form of thin plates of iron coated with tin; a pot or other utensil made of this (*Am.* a can); (*slang*) money. *v.t.* (*past & p.p.* **tinned**) To coat or overlay with tin; to preserve (meat, fruit, etc.) in tins (*Am.* to can). **a little tin god:** A person of local, undeserved importance. **tin fish,** *n.* (*Nav. slang*) A torpedo. **tinfoil,** *n.* Tin or a tin-like alloy beaten into foil for wrapping tobacco and other articles; *v.t.* To coat or cover with this. **tin hat,** *n.* A steel shrapnel helmet. **tinman, tinsmith,** *n.* One who makes articles of tin or tin-plate. **tin-opener,** *n.* An implement for opening air-tight tins of preserved meat, fruit, etc. **tin-pan alley:** The source of popular music; the source of cheap sentimental songs. **tin-plate,** *n.* Iron-plate coated with tin. *v.t.* To coat with tin. **tin-stone,** *n.* Native oxide of tin, the commonest form of tin ore. **tintack,** *n.* A carpet tack, tack coated with tin. **tin-type,** *n.* Ferrotype. **tinware,** *n.* (*collect.*) Vessels or utensils of tin or tin-plate. **tinner,** *n.* **tinny,** *a.*

tinamou (tin′ ȧ moo) [F., from S. Am. native name], *n.* A S. American quail-like gallinaceous game-bird.

tincal, -kal (ting′ kȧl) [Malay *tingkal*], *n.* (*Comm.*) Borax in the crude state.

tinchel (tin′ *ch*ĕl, ting′ kĕl) [Gael. *timchioll,* circuit, compass], *n.* A circle of hunters surrounding a wide piece of ground and gradually collecting the deer.

tinct (tingt), *v.t.* To tincture, to paint. *n.* A colour, stain, or tint.

tinction (ting′ shŭn), *n.* Colouring-material; the act or process of colouring; (*Med.*) a modification of a remedy by admixture, etc.

tinctorial (ting tôr′ i ȧl), *a.* Pertaining to colour or dyes; colouring.

tincture (tingk′ tyŭr, -chėr) [L. *tinctūra,* from *tingere,* to TINGE, p.p. *tinctus*], *n.* An alcoholic or other solution of some principle, usu. vegetable, used in medicine; a tinge or shade (of colour), a tint; (*fig.*) a slight taste or flavour, a spice (of); (*Her.*) one of the colours, metals, or furs used in emblazoning. *v.t.* To imbue with a colour or tint, to tinge; to flavour; to give a flavour or tinge (of some quality, etc.). ***tinct,** *v.t.* To tincture, to tint. *n.* A stain, colour, or tint. *a.* Tinctured. **tinction,** *n.* Colouring-material; the act or process of colouring; (*Med.*) a modification of a remedy by admixture, etc. **tinctorial** (tingk tôr′ i ȧl), *a.* Pertaining to colour or dyes; colouring.

tinder (tin′ dėr) [A.-S. *tyndre,* from *tendan,* to kindle], *n.* Any dry, very combustible substance, esp. charred linen, used to kindle fire from a spark. **tinder-box,** *n.* A box furnished with tinder, flint, and steel, for this purpose. **tinder-like, tindery,** *a.*

tine (tīn) [A.-S. *tind,* cp. Icel. *tindr,* Swed. *tinne,* also L. *dens dentis,* tooth], *n.* The prong, point, or spike of an antler, fork, harrow, etc. **tined,** *a.*

tinea (tin′ ė ȧ) [L., worm, moth], *n.* A clothes-moth; a genus of moth some species of which in the larval stage are very destructive to clothes; (*Path.*) ringworm.

tinfoil [TIN].

ting (ting) [imit.], *n.* A tinkling sound, as of a small bell. *v.i.* To make this sound. **ting-a-ling,** *n.*

tinge (tinj) [L. *tingere,* cogn. with Gr. *tengein,* to wet], *v.t.* To colour slightly, to stain (with); (*fig.*) to modify the character or qualities of. *n.* A slight admixture of colour, a tint; (*fig.*) a smack, flavour. **tinger,** *n.* **tingible,** *a.* **tinging, tingeing,** *a.*

tingle (ting′ gĕl) [M.E. *tinglen,* freq. from TING], *v.i.* To feel a stinging, prickly sensation; to give this sensation.

tinker (ting′ kėr) [M.E. *tinkere,* from *tinken,* see foll.], *n.* An itinerant mender of pots, kettles, pans, etc.; a rough-and-ready worker or repairer; the act of tinkering, patching, botching. *v.t.* To mend pots, kettles, etc.; to mend, alter, or patch up in a rough-and-ready way, or in a clumsy, makeshift, or ineffective manner. *v.i.* To work thus (at). **tinkerly,** *a.* **tinkler** (1), *n.* (*Sc.*).

tinkle (ting′ kĕl) [M.E. *tinklen,* freq. of *tinken,* to ring, of imit. orig.], *v.i.* To make a succession of sharp, metallic sounds as of a bell. *v.t.* To cause to tinkle, to ring. *n.* Such a sound. **tinkler** (2), *n.* Such a sound. **tinkler** (2), *n.* One who or that which tinkles; (*slang*) a small bell.

tinman, tinner [TIN].

tinnitus (ti nī′ tŭs) [L., from *tinnīre,* to ring], *n.* (*Path.*) Ringing in the ears.

tinny, etc. [TIN].

tinsel (tin′ sĕl) [O.F. *estincelle* (F. *étincelle*), L. *scintilla,* spark], *n.* Brass, tin, or other lustrous metallic substance beaten into thin sheets and used in strips, disks, or spangles to give a sparkling effect to dresses, hangings, etc.; a fabric adorned with this; a cloth composed of silk and silver; superficial brilliancy or display. *a.* Gaudy, showy, superficially fine. *v.t.* To adorn with tinsel. **tinselly,** *a.* ***tinselry,** *n.*

tin-stone [TIN].

tint (tint) [from TINCT], *n.* A variety of colour, esp. one produced by admixture with another colour, esp. white; a slight tinge (of another colour); (*Engraving*) an effect of shading or texture obtained by a close series of parallel lines. *v.t.* To give a tint or tints to; to tinge. **tint-block,** *n.* A block with a design for printing in faint colour as a background. **tint-tool,** *n.* A tool for engraving parallel lines, etc. **tinter,** *n.* One who or that which tints; an engraving-tool or machine for tinting; a plain lantern-slide of one colour. **tintless,** *a.* **tintometer** (-tom′ ė tėr), *n.* An instrument or a scale of colours for determining tints. **tinty,** *a.* Inharmoniously tinted.

tintack [TIN].

tintinnabulum (tin ti năb′ ū lŭm) [L., from *tintinnāre,* redupl. from *tinnīre*], *n.* (*pl.* **-la**) A bell, esp. a small tinkling one for signalling, fitting to harness, etc.; a ringing, tinkling, or jingling of bells, plates, etc. **tintinnabular, -lary, *-lous,** *a.* **tintinnabulation** (-lā′ shŭn), *n.*

tintless, tintometer, etc. [TINT].

tinware [TIN].

tiny (tī′ ni) [formerly *tine, tyne,* something small, etym. doubtful], *a.* Very small. **tinier, tiniest,** *comp.* and *superl.*

-tion [L. *-tiōnem,* accus. sing. of nouns in *-tio,* cp. -ION], *suf.* Denoting action or condition, as *mention, expectation, vacation.*

tip (1) (tip) [M.E. *typ,* cp. Dut., Dan., and Swed. *tip*], *n.* The point, end, or extremity, esp. of a small or tapering thing; a small piece or part attached to anything to form a point or end, as a ferrule or shoe-tip; a brush used in laying on gold-leaf. *v.t.* (*past & p.p.* **tipped**) To put a tip on; to form the tip of. **tiptoe,** *adv.* On the tips of the toes; *v.i.* To walk or stand on tiptoe. **tip-top,** *n.* The highest point, the very best; *a.* Of the very best. *adv.* In a first-rate way. **tip-topper,** *n.*

tip (2) (tip) [M.E. *tippen* (cp. Swed. *tippa*), cogn. with TAP (2)], *v.t.* To cause to lean, to tilt (up, over, etc.); to overturn, to upset; to discharge (the contents of a cart, vessel, etc.) thus; to strike lightly, to tap, to touch; (*colloq.*) to give a small gratuity to; (*slang*) to toss or throw lightly, to give; (*Sport. slang*) to give private information to about a horse, etc. *v.i.* To lean over, to tilt; to upset. *n.* A small present in money; private information, esp. for betting purposes; a slight touch, push, or hit; a place where rubbish is discharged. **to tip in:** (*Print.*) To insert a loose plate by pasting the back margin to the page following. **to tip off:** To give a warning hint. **to tip the wink:** (*colloq.*) To hint, to inform furtively. **tip-car, -cart,** *n.* One constructed with a pivot for tipping over, (*Am.* a dump-truck). **tip-cat,** *n.* A game with a piece of wood pointed at both ends which is hit with a stick; the tapering piece of wood. **tipper** (1), *n.*

***tipper** (2) (tip′ ėr) [name of Sussex brewer, d. 1785], *n.* A kind of ale the flavour of which was said to be due to its being brewed with brackish water.

tippet (tip′ ėt) [A.-S. *tæppet*, L. *tapēte*, Gr. *tapēs -etos*, carpet], *n.* A fur or cloth covering for the neck and shoulders, worn over the dress by women, footmen, etc.; an ecclesiastical vestment; part of the official costume of judges, etc.

tipple (tip′ ėl) [freq. of TIP (1), cp. Norw. *tipla*, from *tippa*, to drip, from *tipp*], *v.i.* To drink alcoholic liquors habitually. *v.t.* To sip repeatedly; to drink (alcoholic liquors) habitually. *n.* Strong drink; one's favourite beverage. **tippler,** *n.* **tippling-house,** *n.*

tipstaff (tip′ staf), *n.* A metal-tipped staff carried by a sheriff's officer; a sheriff's officer.

tipster (tip′ stėr), *n.* One who supplies tips about races, etc.

tipsy (tip′ si) [prob. rel. to TIP (1), cp. Swiss *tipseln*, to fuddle oneself], *a.* Fuddled, partially intoxicated, proceeding from or inducing intoxication. **tipsy-cake,** *n.* A sponge cake soaked in wine served with custard. **tipsily,** *adv.* **tipsiness,** *n.*

tiptoe, tip-top [TIP (1)].

Tipula (tip′ ū lȧ) [L. *tippula*, water-spider], *n.* (*Ent.*) A genus of dipterous insects containing the crane-flies. **tipularian** (-lâr′ i ȧn), **tipulid** (tip′ ū lid), **tipulidan** (ti pū′ li dȧn), *a.* and *n.* **tipulary, tipulideous** (-lid′ ė ŭs), *a.*

tirade (ti rād′)[F., from It. *tirata*, p.p. of *tirare*, late L. *tīrāre*, to draw, to pull], *n.* A long, vehement speech, declamation, or harangue, esp. of censure or reproof; (*Mus.*) a diatonic run filling an interval between two notes.

tirailleur (tē ra yĕr′, tir ȧ loor′) [F., from *tirailler*, to skirmish, from *tirer*, to shoot], *n.* A skirmisher, a sharpshooter.

tirasse (tē ras′) [F., from *tirer*, to draw], *n.* (*Organ*) A pedal-coupler.

tire (1) (tīr) [M.E *tiren*, *teorian*, A.-S. *tyrigan*, etym. doubtful], *v.t.* To exhaust the strength of by toil or labour; to fatigue, to weary; to exhaust the patience or attention. *v.i.* To become weary or exhausted. **tiredness,** *n.* **tireless** (1), *a.* Unwearied, untirable. **tirelessly,** *adv.* **tiring,** *a.*

tire (2), **tyre** (tīr) [etym. doubtful, perh. from foll.], *n.* A band of iron, steel, rubber, etc., placed round the rim of a wheel to strengthen it or reduce vibration, etc. **tired,** *a.* (*usu. in comb.*, as *rubber-tired*). **tireing,** *n.* **tireless** (2), *a.* **tire-smith,** *n.*

***tire** (3) (tīr) [contr. of ATTIRE], *n.* A head-dress; attire generally. *v.t.* To attire, to adorn, to dress. ***tirewoman,** *n.* One employed to dress another. ***tiring-house, -room,** *n.* A dressing-room, esp. in a theatre.

***tire** (4) (tīr) [O.F. *tirer*, see TIRADE], *v.t.* To pull to pieces, to rend. *v.i.* To seize upon and tear prey; to gloat (over).

tireless, etc. [TIRE (1 and 2)].

tiresome (tīr′ sŏm), *a.* Fatiguing, tiring; wearisome, tedious, annoying. **tiresomely,** *adv.* **tiresomeness,** *n.*

tirl (tĕrl) [Sc., var. of TWIRL], *v.i.* To quiver, to vibrate; to make a rattling noise. *v.t.* To strip; to lay bare; to unclothe; to unroof. *n.* A twirl, a twist; a turn; a wheel resembling a lantern-wheel used in a mill. **tirl-mill,** *n.* **tirlie-whirlie,** *n.* A whirligig; an ornament consisting of irregularly interlacing lines. *a.* Tortuous, intricate, irregular.

Tirolese (ti rō lēz′), *a.* Pertaining to Tirol. *n.* A native of Tirol.

Tironian (tī rō′ ni ȧn) [L. *Tiro -ōnis*, freedman and amanuensis of Cicero], *a.* Pertaining to a system of shorthand attributed to Tiro.

tirra-lirra (tir′ ȧ lir′ ȧ) [O.F. *tirelire*, imit.], *n.* A warbling sound as of a lark, horn, etc.

***tirret** [TERRET].

***tirrit** (tir′ it) [prob. corr. of TERROR], *n.* (*Shak.*) A fright, an upset.

tirrivee (tir i vē′) [etym. doubtful], *n.* (*Sc.*) An ill-tempered outburst, a tantrum.

tirwit (tĕr′ wit) [imit. of cry], *n.* The lapwing.

'tis (tiz) [short for IT IS].

tisane (ti zan′) [PTISAN]. **tisic,** etc. [PHTHISIS].

Tishri (tish′ ri), **Tisri** (tiz′ ri) [Heb. *tishrī*], *n.* The first month of the Hebrew civil and the seventh of the ecclesiastical year, corresponding to parts of September and October.

tissue (tish′-, tis′ ū) [F. *tissu*, p.p. of *tistre*, now *tisser*, L. *texere*, to weave], *n.* Any fine, gauzy, or transparent woven fabric; (*Biol.*) a fabric of cells and their products, forming the elementary substance of plant and animal organs; (*fig.*) a fabrication, a connected series (of lies, accidents, etc.). *v.t.* To form into tissue; to interweave, to variegate. **tissue-paper,** *n.* A thin, gauzy, unsized paper, used for wrapping articles, protecting engravings, etc. **tissued,** *a.*

tit (1) (tit) [Icel. *tittr*, bird, something small, cp. Norw. *tita*], *n.* A titmouse; a titlark; *a small horse; *a child, a girl; *a bit, a morsel. **titbit,** *n.* A delicate or dainty morsel. **titlark,** *n.* A small bird of the genus *Anthus*, esp. *Anthus pratensis*, the meadow-pipit. **titling** (1), *n.* A titmouse; a titlark. **titmouse** [A.-S. *māse*, a name for several small birds], *n.* (*pl.* **-mice**) A small insectivorous bird of the sub-family *Parinæ*, usu. nesting in holes in tree-trunks.

tit (2) (tit) [perh. corr. of TIP (2)], *n.* A tap, a slight blow. **tit for tat** [perh. *tip for tap*]: Blow for blow, retaliation.

tit (3) (tit) [A.-S., cp. TEAT], *n.* A teat.

Titan (tī′ tȧn) [L. and Gr., cogn. with Sansk. *tithā*, fire], *n.* (*Gr. Myth.*) One of the twelve children of Uranus and Ge of gigantic size and strength; the sun-god as the offspring of Hyperion, one of the Titans; a person of superhuman strength or genius. *a.* Titanic. **Titanesque** (-nesk′), **Titanic** (1) (-tăn′ ik), *a.* **Titaness,** *n.* **Titano-** (1), *comb. form.*

titanium (tī tā′ ni ŭm) [prec.], *n.* A dark-grey metallic element found in small quantities in various minerals. **titanate,** *n.* A salt of titanic acid. **titanic** (2) (tī tăn′ ik), *a.* Of quadrivalent titanium. **titaniferous** (-nif′ ėr ŭs), *a.* **titanite** (tī′ tȧ nīt), *n.* (*Min.*) An intensely hard titano-silicate of calcium, sphene. **titano-** (2), *comb. form.* **titanous,** *a.*

titbit [TIT (1)].

tithe (tīth) [A.-S. *tēodha* (TEN, -TH), whence *tēothian*], *n.* The tenth part of anything; a tax of one-tenth, esp. of the yearly proceeds from land and personal industry, payable for the support of the clergy and Church. *v.t.* To impose tithes upon. **tithe barn.** A barn in which the parson stored his corn and other tithes. **tithe-pig,** *n.* One pig out of ten set apart for tithe. **tithable,** *a.* **tither,** *n.* **tithing,** *n.* The taking or levying of tithes; a civil division consisting of ten householders living near each other bound as sureties for each other's good behaviour. ***tithing-man,** *n.* The chief man of a tithing; a peace-officer; an under-constable.

***tithonic** (ti-, tī thon′ ik) [Gr. *Tithōn-os*, husband of Eos, dawn, -IC], *a.* Pertaining to or denoting those rays of light which produce chemical effects, actinic.

titi (tē′ tē) [Maori], *n.* The N. Zealand diving petrel.

titian (tish′ ȧn) [It. artist *Titian* (1477–1576)], *a.* Reddish-brown in colour.

titillate (tit′ i lāt) [L. *titillātus*, p.p. of *titillāre*, to tickle], *v.t.* To tickle; to excite or stimulate pleasurably. **titillation** (-lā′ shůn), *n.*

titivate (tit′ i vāt) [prob. arbitrary], *v.t.* and *i.* To dress up, to adorn, to make smart.

titlark [TIT (1)].

title (tī′ tėl) [O.F., from L. *titulum*, nom. *-us*], *n.* An inscription serving as a name or designation, esp. of a book, chapter, poem, etc.; the entire contents of the title page of a book; a book or publication; a brief part of this containing the essentials; a title page; the distinguishing formula at the head of a legal document, statute, etc.; a division of a document, treatise, etc., including caption and text, as arranged for reference; a personal appellation denoting office, nobility, distinction, or other qualification; (*Law*) the right to ownership of property; the legal evidence of this; a title-deed; an acknowledged claim; the grounds of this; fineness, esp. of gold, expressed in carats; (*Eccles.*) a source of income and a fixed sphere of duty required as a condition precedent to ordination; (*Rome*) a church or parish. **title-deed,** *n.* A legal instrument giving the evidence of a person's right to property. **title page:** The page at the beginning of a book giving the subject, author's name, etc. **title-rôle,** *n.* (*Theat.*) The character or part from whose name the title of a piece is taken. **titled,** *a.* Bearing a title of nobility. **titleless,** *a.* **titling** (2), *n.* The act of impressing the title on the back of a book.

titling (1) [TIT (1)]; (2) [TITLE].

titmouse [TIT (1)].

Titoism (tē′ tō izm), *n.* (*Pol.*) The kind of Communism introduced by Marshal Tito in Yugoslavia as opposed to that of Russia.

titrate (tī′ trāt, tit′ rāt) [F. *titre*, TITLE, -ATE], *v.t.* To determine the amount of a particular constituent in a solution by adding a known quantity of another chemical capable of reacting upon it. **titration** (-trā′ shůn), *n.*

titter (tit′ ėr) [M.E. *titeren*, freq. of *tit-*, imit.], *v.i.* To laugh in a restrained manner, to giggle. *n.* A restrained laugh. **titterer,** *n.*

tittie (1) (tit′ i) [perh. childish dim. of SISTER], *n.* (*Sc. colloq.*) A sister.

tittie (2) [childish dim. of TIT (3)].

tittle (1) (tit′ ėl) [M.E. *titel*, a small line over a word, etc. (cp. TILDE), as TITLE], *n.* A particle, an iota.

tittle (2) (tit′ ėl) [prob. var. of TICKLE], *v.t.* and *i.* (*prov.*) To tickle.

tittlebat [STICKLEBACK].

tittle-tattle (tit′ el tăt′ ėl) [redupl. from TATTLE], *n.* Gossip. *v.i.* To gossip.

tittup (tit′ ůp) [etym. doubtful], *v.i.* (*colloq.*) To go, act, or behave in a lively manner, to prance, to frisk. *n.* A tittuping action or movement. **tittupy,** *a.*

titubation (tit ū bā′ shůn) [L. *titubātis*, from *titubāre*, to totter], *n.* (*Path.*) Nervousness shown by perpetual change of position or fidgetiness.

titular (tit′ ū lȧr) [L. *titul-us*], *a.* Existing in name or in title only, or holding a title without the office or duties attached, nominal; of, pertaining to, or held in virtue of a title; conferring a title. *n.* One who holds the title of an office or benefice without the authority or duties pertaining to it. **titularly,** *adv.* **titulary,** *a.* and *n.*

tiver (tiv′ ėr) [A.-S. *tēafor*, cp. Icel. *taufr*, secret writing, sorcery], *n.* (*prov.*) A red ochre used for marking sheep. *v.t.* To mark (a sheep) with tiver.

tizzy (tiz′ i) [corr. of TESTER (3)], *n.* (*slang*) A sixpence.

tmesis (mē′ sis) [L. and Gr., from Gr. *temnein*, to cut], *n.* (*Gram.*) The separation of the parts of a compound word by inserting one or more words between.

to (tò, tu, too) [A.-S. *tō*, cp. Dut. *toe*, G. *zu*, Rus. *do*], *prep.* In a direction towards (a place, person, thing, state, or quality); as far as; no less than in comparison with, in respect of, in correspondence with; concerning; in the relation of, for, as; preceding the indirect object or the person or thing affected by the action, etc.; the sign of the infinitive mood, expressing futurity, purpose, consequence, etc., limiting the meaning of adjectives, or forming verbal nouns; (*ellipt.*) denoting the infinitive of a verb mentioned or understood. *adv.* Towards the condition or end required; into the normal condition, esp. to a standstill or a state of adjustment; ***forward, on. to and fro** [FRO].

***to-** [A.-S. *to-*, cp. G. *zer-*, also L. DIS-], *pref.* Expressing disjunction or disruption, as in *to-break*, *to-burst*.

toad (tōd) [A.-S. *tādige*, etym. doubtful], *n.* A tailless amphibian like a frog, usu. with a warty body, terrestrial except during breeding; (*fig.*) a repulsive or detestable person. **toad-eater,** *n.* An obsequious parasite, a sycophant. **toad-eating,** *a.* and *n.* **toad-fish,** *n.* A batrachoid fish of the Atlantic coast of N. America. **toad-flax,** *n.* A perennial herb of the genus *Linaria*, usu. with yellow or bluish personate flowers. **toad-in-the-hole:** A piece of beef, sausage, or the like, baked in batter. **toad-spit,** *n.* Cuckoo-spit. ***toad-spotted,** *a.* Spotted like a toad; (*fig.*) polluted.

toadstone (tōd′ stōn) [G. *todtes gestein*, dead stone], *n.* A stone coloured and shaped somewhat like a toad, or supposed to have been found in the body of a toad, formerly worn as a talisman; an igneous rock of Carboniferous age, occurring in veins and sheets in limestone, named from its barrenness in metalliferous ores.

toadstool (tōd′ stool), *n.* An umbrella-shaped fungus, esp. a poisonous mushroom.

toady (tō′ di), *n.* A toad-eater. *v.t.* To fawn upon, to play the toady to. **toadyish,** *a.* **toadyism,** *n.*

toast (tōst) [M.E. *tost*, from *toster*, to toast, L. *torrēre*, to parch, p.p. *tostus*], *n.* A slice of bread browned at the fire, eaten dry, buttered, or with some other dish; a drinking or a call for drinking to the health of some person, cause, sentiment, etc., (from the old custom of putting toast in liquor perh. through an incident recorded in *The Tatler*); the person or other object of this; a woman often toasted. *v.t.* To brown (bread), cook (bacon, etc.), or warm (the feet, etc.) at an open fire; to drink to the health or in honour of. *v.i.* To be toasted. **toast-master,** *n.* An official who announces the toasts at public dinners, etc. **toast-rack,** *n.* A table-utensil for holding slices of toast. **toast and water** or **toast-water,** *n.* A cooling drink made by pouring boiling water on toast. **toaster,** *n.* **toasting-fork,** *n.* A fork to hold bread, etc., for toasting. ***toasting-iron,** *n.* (*facet.*) A sword.

toa-toa (tō′ ȧ tō′ ȧ) [Maori], *n.* A red-wood N. Zealand tree.

tobacco (tò băk′ ō) [Sp. *tabaco*, prob. from native name of pipe], *n.* A plant of American origin of the genus *Nicotiana*, with narcotic leaves which are used, after drying and preparing, for smoking, chewing, snuff, etc.; the leaves of this, esp. prepared for smoking. **tobacco-cutter,** *n.* A knife for cutting plug-tobacco; a device for shredding tobacco. **tobacco-heart,** *n.* Smoker's heart. **tobacco-pipe,** *n.* A pipe used in smoking tobacco. **tobacco-plant,** *n.* **tobacco-pouch,** *n.* A pouch for carrying a small quantity of tobacco in. **tobacco-stopper,** *n.* A plug for pressing down tobacco in a pipe. **tobacconist,** *n.* A dealer in tobacco.

tobine (tō′ bin) [G. *tobin*, Dut. *tabijn*, TABBY], *n.* A stout twilled silk used for dresses.

toboggan (tŏ bog′ ăn) [Algonkin], *n.* A long low sled used for sliding down snow- or ice-covered slopes. *v.i.* To slide on a toboggan. **toboggan-shoot, -slide,** *n.* A prepared course for tobogganing, on a hillside or a timber structure. **tobogganer, *-ist,** *n.* **tobogganing,** *n.*

toby (tō′ bi) [personal name, *Tobias*], *n.* A mug or jug shaped like an old man wearing a three-cornered hat.

toby-man (tō′ bi măn) [prob. Shelta *tobar*, road, MAN], *n.* (*slang*) A highwayman.

toccata (tŏ ka′ tă) [It., p.p. of *toccare*, to TOUCH], *n.* (*Mus.*) A composition orig. designed to exercise the player's touch. **toccatella** (-tel′ ă), **toccatina** (-tē′ nă), *n.* A short or easy toccata.

tocher (to*ch*′ ėr) [Gael. *tochar*], *n.* (*Sc.*) A woman's dowry. *v.t.* To give a dowry to. **tocherless,** *a.*

toco, toko (tō′ kō) [perh. from Gr. *tokos*, see foll.], *n.* (*slang*) Corporal punishment, castigation.

tocology (tŏ kol′ ŏ ji) [Gr. *tokos*, birth, from *tiktein*, to bring forth, -LOGY], *n.* Obstetrics.

tocsin (tok′ sin) [M.F. *toquesing* (O.F. *toquer*, to TOUCH, *sing*, SIGNAL)], *n.* An alarm-bell; the ringing of an alarm-bell, an alarm-signal.

***tod** (tod) [Icel. *toddi*, tod or wool, cp. Dut. *todde*, G. *zolle*, rag], *n.* A bush, esp. of thick ivy; a bunch, a mass; an old weight for wool, usu. 28 lb.; a fox, from his bushy tail.

to-day, today (tŏ dā′) [A.-S. *todæge*, for or on (this) day], *adv.* On or during this or the present day; at the present day. *n.* This day.

toddle (tod′ ėl) [var. of TOTTER], *v.i.* To walk with short unsteady steps, as a child; to walk in a careless or leisurely way, to saunter. *v.t.* To walk (a certain distance, etc.) thus. *n.* A toddling walk; a saunter, a stroll. **toddler,** *n.* (*colloq.*) A toddling child.

toddy (tod′ i) [Hind. *tāḍi*, *tāṛi*, from Hind. and Pers. *tār*, palm], *n.* A juice obtained by tapping certain palms which by fermentation makes an intoxicating liquor; a beverage of spirit and hot water sweetened.

to-do (tŏ doo′), *n.* Ado, commotion.

tody (tō′ di) [L. *tōdus*], *n.* A small W. Indian insectivorous bird allied to the American kingfishers.

toe (tō) [A.-S. *tā*, cp. Dut. *teen*, G. *zehe*, Icel. *tā*, Dan. *taa*], *n.* One of the five digits of the foot, the part of a boot, stocking, etc., covering the toes; the fore part of the hoof of a horse, etc.; the calk in the front of a horse-shoe; a projection from the foot of a buttress, etc., to give it greater stability; the end of the head of a golf-club; the lower end or a projecting part in a shaft, spindle, rod, lever, organ-pipe, etc. *v.t.* To touch (a line, mark, etc.) with the toes; to furnish (socks, shoes, etc.) with toes; (*Golf*) to strike (a ball) with the toe of a club; (*slang*) to kick. **to toe in** or **out:** To turn the toes in or out in walking, etc. **to toe the line:** To conform, to bow to discipline. **to turn up one's toes:** (*fig.*) To die. **toed,** *a.* (*usu. in comb.*, as *three-toed*). **toeless,** *a.* **toe-ragger,** *n.* (*Austral.*) A tramp.

toff (tof) [etym. doubtful], *n.* (*slang*) A swell, a dandy, a person of consequence.

toffee, toffy (tof′ i) [F. and Malay *tafia*, see RATAFIA], *n.* A sweetmeat made of boiled sugar or molasses and butter (*Am.* taffy).

to-fore (tŏ fōr′) [A.-S. *tōforan*], *prep.* and *adv.* Before.

toft (toft) [late A.-S., *from* Icel. *topt*, pron. 'toft'], *n.* A homestead; (*Law*) a place where a messuage has stood; (*prov.*) a hillock or knoll. ***toftman,** *n.* One occupying a toft. **toftstead,** *n.*

tog (tog) [perh. from foll.], *n.* (*slang*) (*usu in pl.*) Clothes. *v.t.* (*past & p.p.* **togged**) To dress (up or out), esp. in one's best. **long togs:** (*Naut.*) Shore-clothes. **toggery,** *n.*

toga (tō′ gă) [L., cogn. with *tegere*, to cover], *n.* A loose flowing robe, the principal outer garment of an ancient Roman citizen. **toga prætexta** [PRÆTEXTA]. **toga virilis** (vi rī′ lis) [L. *virilis*, VIRILE]: The toga assumed by the ancient Roman at the age of 14. **togaed** (tō′ găd), ***togated** (tŏ gā′ tėd), ***toged,** *a.*

together (tŏ ge*th*′ ėr) [A.-S. *tōgædere* (TO, *gador*, together, see GATHER)], *adv.* In company or union, conjointly, unitedly; in the same place or at the same time; into union, so as to unite or be joined; without cessation or intermission.

toggery [TOG].

toggle (tog′ ėl) [prob. dim. of *tog*, cogn. with TUG], *n.* (*Naut.*) A pin put through a loop or eye at the end of a rope for securing this; a cross-piece for securing a watch-chain; the barb of a toggle-iron; a toggle-joint; (*pl.*) a kind of rope ladder made with a single rope having cross-pieces fastened in the middle. **toggle-harpoon, -iron,** *n.* A harpoon with a movable barb pivoted so as to turn in the animal's flesh. **toggle-joint,** *n.* A knee-joint formed by two plates hinged together so as to change the direction of pressure from vertical to horizontal. **toggle-press,** *n.* A press acting by means of toggle-joints.

togue (tōg) [from native name], *n.* The great N. American lake trout.

toho (tŏ hō′), *int.* (*Sport*) A call to a pointer or setter to halt.

toheroa (tō hō′ ra) [Maori], *n.* An edible mollusc on the N. Zealand shores.

tohu-bohu (tō′ hu bō′ hu) [Heb. *thōhū wabhōhū*, emptiness and desolation], *n.* Confusion, chaos.

toil (1) (toil) [A.-F. *toiler*, to strive, prob. from O.F. *toillier*, to mix, to trouble, L. *tudiculāre*, from *tudicula*, machine for bruising olives, dim. of *tudes*, mallet, cogn. with *tundere*, to beat], *v.i.* To labour with pain and fatigue of body or mind; to move or progress painfully or laboriously. *v.t.* To fatigue or wear out with toil. *n.* Hard and unremitting work, labour, drudgery. **toil-worn,** *a.* Worn with toil. **toiler,** *n.* **toilful, toilsome,** *a.* **toilfully, toilsomely,** *adv.* **toilless,** *a.* **toilsomeness,** *n.*

toil (toil) (2) [F. *toile*, see foll.], *n.* (*now in pl.*) A net or snare.

toile (twal) [F., from L. TELA], *n.* Cloth.

toiler [TOIL (1)].

toilet (toi′ lėt) [F. *toilette*, dim. of TOILE], *n.* The act or process of dressing, etc.; style or fashion of dress; dress, costume; a dressing-table or toilet-table, with looking-glass, etc.; a cover for this; a water-closet; (*Med.*) the cleansing of a part after an operation, etc. **to make one's toilet:** To dress, arrange one's hair, etc. **toilet-cover,** *n.* A cloth usu. fringed with lace, etc., for a toilet-table. **toilet-paper,** *n.* Soluble paper for use in a water-closet. **toilet-service, -set,** *n.* A set of utensils for a toilet-table. **toilet-soap,** *n.* **toilet-table,** *n.* A dressing-table with looking-glass, etc.

toilful, etc. [TOIL (1)].

toilinet, toilinette (twa li net′) [dim. of TOILE], *n.* A fabric of silk and cotton with woollen filling.

toise (toiz) [F., ult. from L. *tensa*, orig. neut. pl. p.p. of *tendere*, see TENSE (2)], *n.* An old French measure of length = about 6½ ft.

Toison d'or (twa zon dôr′) [F. *toison*, fleece (L. *tonsiōnem*, nom. *-sio*, from *tondere*, to shear), *d'or*, of gold], *n.* The Golden Fleece, esp. as the Spanish and Austrian order of knighthood.

Tokay (tŏ kā′), *n.* A rich aromatic wine made at Tokay in Hungary; a white grape from which it is made.

token (tō′ kėn) [A.-S. *tācen*, *tācn* (cp. Dut. *teeken*, G. *zeichen*, Icel. *tākn teikn*), cogn. with TEACH], *n.* Something representing or recalling another thing, event, etc.; a sign, a symbol; an evidence, an indication, a symptom; a memorial of love or friendship, a keepsake; a sign proving authenticity; a piece of metal like a coin, formerly issued by tradesmen, banks, etc., representing money of greater intrinsic value. *v.t.* To make known, to betoken; to mark, to betroth. **by the same token:** In corroboration. **more by token** [MORE (1)]. **token payment,** *n.* A small payment made to indicate that the debt or obligation is not repudiated. **tokenless,** *a.*

toko [TOCO].

tola (tō′ lȧ) [Hind.], *n.* A unit of weight for gold and silver, usu. about 180 gr. Troy.

tolbooth [TOLL (1)].

told, *past & p.p.* [TELL].

Toledo (tȯ lē′ dō), *n.* A sword or sword-blade made at Toledo in Spain. **Toledan,** *a.* and *n.*

***tole** [TOLL (2)].

tolerable (tol′ ėr ȧbl), *a.* Endurable, supportable; passable, fairly good. **tolerableness,** *n.* **tolerably,** *adv.*

tolerance (tol′ ėr ȧns), *n.* The act or state of toleration; permissible variation in weight, dimension, fitting, etc.

tolerant (tol′ ėr ȧnt), *a.* Showing toleration. **tolerantly,** *adv.*

tolerate (tol′ ėr āt) [L. *tolerātus*, p.p. of *tolerāre*, cogn. with *tollere*, to bear, cp. Gr. *tlēnai*, to suffer], *v.t.* To suffer, to endure, to permit by not preventing or forbidding; to abstain from judging harshly or condemning (persons, religions, votes, opinions, etc.); to sustain, to endure (pain, toil, etc.); (*Med.*) to sustain (a drug, etc.) with impunity. **toleration** (-ā′ shŭn), *n.* The act of tolerating; the spirit of tolerance; recognition of the right of private judgment in religious matters and of freedom to exercise any forms of worship. **tolerationist,** *n.* **tolerator** (tol′ ėr ā tȯr), *n.*

toll (1) (tōl) [A.-S. *toll, toln* (cp. Dut. *tol*, G. *zoll*, Icel. *tollr*), perh. from late L. *tollōnium, telōnium*, Gr. *telōnion*, toll-house, from *telos*, tax], *n.* A tax or duty charged for some privilege, service, etc., esp. for the use of a road, bridge, market, etc.; a portion of grain taken by a miller as compensation for grinding. *v.i.* To pay toll; to take toll. **v.t.* To levy or collect (a toll). **toll-bar, -gate,** *n.* A gate or bar placed across a road to stop passengers or vehicles till toll is paid. **tolbooth, tollbooth** (tol′-, tōl′ buth), *n.* (*Sc.*) A town jail; orig. a temporary structure for the collection of market-tolls. **toll-bridge,** *n.* A bridge where toll is charged for passing over it. **toll-dish,** *n.* A vessel for measuring the proportion of grain paid as toll. ***toll-gatherer, -man,** *n.* **toll-house,** *n.* The house at a toll-gate occupied by a toll-collector. **tollable,** *a.* **tollage,** *n.* **toller** (1), *n.*

toll (2) (tōl) [M.E. *tollen*, to attract, to entice, etym. doubtful], *v.t.* To cause (a bell) to sound with strokes slowly and uniformly repeated; to give out (a knell, etc.) with a slow, measured sound (of a bell, clock, etc.); to ring on account of. *v.i.* To sound or ring (of a bell) with slow, regular strokes. *n.* A tolling or a stroke of a bell. **toll call,** *n.* (*Teleph.*) A call between toll exchanges. **toll exchange,** *n.* (*Teleph.*) A short-distance trunk system installed in London and elsewhere; (*Am.*) an exchange for long-distance calls. **toller** (2).

***toll** (3) (tōl) [A.-S. *toller*, L. *tollere*], *v.t.* (*Law*) To take away; to annul.

tollable, tollage, etc. [TOLL (1)].

toller (1) and (2) [TOLL (1) and (2)].

tolt (tōlt) [A.-F. *tolte*, med. L. *tolta*, from *tollere*, to TOLL (3)], *n.* (*Law*) A writ transferring a cause from a court-baron to a county court.

Toltec (tol′ tek) [Mex.], *n.* One of a legendary race said to have ruled in Mexico during the 7th–11th cent., before the Aztecs. *a.* Of or pertaining to this race.

tolu (tȯ loo′) [Santiago de *Tolu*, seaport in Colombia], *n.* A balsam derived from a S. American tree, *Toluifera balsamum.*

toluate (tol′ ū ȧt), *n.* A salt of toluic acid.

toluene (tol′ ū ēn), *n.* A liquid compound belonging to the aromatic series derived from coal-tar. **toluic,** *a.*

tom (tom) [short for *Thomas*], *n.* A male animal, esp. a tom-cat. **long tom:** A long gun of large bore; (*Naut.*) a long swivel-gun carried amidships. **Old Tom:** A strong variety of gin. **Tom and Jerry:** A hot drink of rum and water with eggs beaten up, etc. **Tom, Dick, and Harry:** Average commonplace people; any taken at random. **tomboy,** *n.* A romping girl, a hoyden; *a boisterous boy. **tom-cat,** *n.* A male cat. **tom-fool,** *n.* A ridiculous fool, a trifler. *v.i.* To play the fool, to act nonsensically. **tomfoolery,** *n.* **tom-noddy,** *n.* A blockhead, a dolt; the puffin. **Tom Thumb,** *n.* (*fig.*) A midget. **tom-tit,** *n.* A small bird, a tit, esp. a titmouse.

tomahawk (tom′ ȧ hawk) [Algonkin], *n.* A N. American Indian battle-axe or hatchet with a stone, horn, or steel head. *v.t.* To strike or kill with a tomahawk; (*fig.*) to criticize or review savagely; (*Austral.*) to cut a sheep when shearing.

tomalley (tȯ măl′ i) [var. of TOURMALINE], *n.* The soft, fatty, greenish so-called liver of the lobster.

toman (tȯ man′) [Pers. *tūmān*], *n.* A Persian gold coin worth about 7s. 2d.

tomato (tȯ ma′ tō) [Sp. and Port. *tomate*, Mex. *tomatl*], *n.* (*pl.* **-toes**) The red or yellow pulpy edible fruit of a trailing plant, *Lycopersicon lycopersicum*, of the nightshade family or *Solanaceæ*, orig. S. American and formerly called the love-apple; the plant itself.

tomb (toom) [O.F. *tumbe* (F. *tombe*), L. and Gr. *tumba*, prob. cogn. with TUMULUS], *n.* A grave; a vault for the dead; a sepulchral monument. *v.t.* To bury, to entomb. **tombless,** *a.* **tombstone,** *n.* A stone placed as a memorial over a grave.

tombac, tomback (tom′ băk) [F. *tombac*, Port. *tambaca*, Malay *tambaga*, Sansk. *tāmrakam*, copper], *n.* One of various copper and zinc alloys.

tombola (tom′ bȯ lȧ) [It., from *tombolare*, to TUMBLE], *n.* A form of lottery in which each of a given set of numbers must be drawn to win a prize.

tomboy, tom-cat, etc. [TOM].

tom-cod (tom kod), *n.* A gadoid fish, esp. *Microgadus tomcod*, common on the Atlantic coast of the U.S.A.; applied to other fish.

tome (tōm) [F., from L. *tomum*, nom. *-us*, Gr. *tomos*, section, from *temnein*, to cut], *n.* A volume, esp. a ponderous one.

tomentum (tȯ men′ tŭm) [L. wool-stuffing], *n.* (*Bot.*) A pubescence consisting of matted woolly hairs; (*Anat.*) the inner surface of the *pia mater*, flocculent with tiny vessels. **tomentose, -ous,** *a.*

tom-fool, etc. [TOM].

***tomin** (tō′ min) [Sp., from Arab. *tomn*, one-eighth], *n.* A jeweller's weight of 12 gr.

tommy (tom′ i) [fam. form. of TOM], *n.* A British private soldier (from *Tommy Atkins*, of disputed orig.); (*slang*) bread, food, provisions, esp. carried by workmen or given to them in lieu of wages; this method of payment, the truck system; a form of wrench; a rod inserted in a box-spanner. **soft tommy:** (*Naut.*) Soft bread, opp. to hard tack. **tommy-gun,** *n.* A short-barrelled, quick-firing firearm. **tommy rot,** *n.* (*colloq.*) Nonsense. **tommy-shop,** *n.* A shop or other place where the truck system is in force.

to-morrow, tomorrow (tȯ mor′ ō) [TO, MORROW, as TO-DAY], *n.* The next day after to-day, the morrow. *adv.* On or during this.

tompion (1) (tom′ pi ȯn) [var. of TAMPION], *n.* A lithographic inking-pad; a tampon; a tampion.

***tompion** (2) (tom′ pi ȯn), *n.* A watch (properly one made by Thomas Tompion (1639–1713) a London clockmaker, or one of the same type).

tom-tit [TOM].

tom-tom (tom' tom) [Hindi, *tam-tam*, imit.], *n.* A native drum used in India, Africa, etc. *v.i.* To beat this.

-tomy [Gr. *-tomia*, from *temnein*, to cut], *suf.* Used chiefly of surgical operations as in *phlebotomy*, *tracheotomy*.

ton (1) (tŭn) [var. of TUN], *n.* A measure of weight 20 cwt. or 2240 lb. av.; (*Am.*) 2000 lb. av.; a measure of capacity (for timber or cargo on shipboard, 40 cubic ft.; stone, 16 cubic ft.; wheat, 20 bushels; lime, 40 bushels); (*colloq.*) a great weight, a great quantity. **-tonner,** *comb. form.* A ship of a specified tonnage, as a 3000-*tonner*. **metric ton:** 1000 kilograms, 2204·62 lb. av. **register ton:** 100 cubic ft. **short ton:** 2000 lb. av.

ton (2) (ton) [F., TONE], *n.* The prevailing fashion or mode. **tonish,** *a.* **tonishness,** *n.* **tony** (1) (tō' ni), *a.* (*slang*).

tonal (tō' năl), *a.* Pertaining to tone or tonality. **tonality** (tò năl' i ti), *n.* (*Mus.*) The character or quality of a tone or tonal system; a system of tones, a key; (*Painting*) the general colour-scheme of a picture. **tonally,** *adv.*

to-name (too' nām), *n.* (*Sc.*) A distinguishing name added to a surname; a nickname.

tondo (ton' dō) [It., from L. *rotundus*, ROUND (2)], *n.* A majolica plate with a wide decorated rim. **tondeno** (-dē' nō), *n.* A tondo with a bowl-like centre; (*Arch.*) an astragal.

tone (tōn) [M.E. and F. *ton*, L. *tonum*, nom. *-us*, Gr. *tonos*, from *teinein*, to stretch], *n.* Sound, with reference to pitch, quality, and volume; a musical sound; modulation or inflexion of the voice to express emotion, etc.; (*fig.*) general disposition, temper, mood, prevailing sentiment, spirit; (*Mus.*) timbre; an interval of a major second; an ancient psalm-tune, esp. one of the Gregorian tones; (*Gram.*) syllabic stress; (*Chromatics*) degree of luminosity of a colour; (*Painting*) the general effect of a picture, esp. as regards colour and luminosity, the tint or shade of colour; (*Phot.*) the shade or colour of a print; (*Physiol.*) healthy general condition of the bodily organs, tissues, etc. *v.t.* To give tone or quality to; (*Mus.*) to tune; (*Phot.*) to modify the colour of a photographic picture by a chemical bath. *v.i.* To harmonize in colour, tint, etc.; to receive a particular tone or tint. **to tone down:** To subdue, to soften (the tint, tone, pitch, intensity, etc., of); to modify, to reduce, to soften (a statement, demands, etc.); to become softer, less emphatic, etc. **tone arm,** *n.* The tube that connects the sound-box of a gramophone to the horn. **tone poem,** *n.* (*Mus.*) An orchestral composition in one movement which illustrates a train of thought external to the music. **tone-wheel,** *n.* (*Radio.*) A high-speed commutator used for the reception of continuous waves. **toned,** *a.* **toneless,** *a.* **tonometer** (tò nom' è tėr) [-METER], *n.* A tuning-fork or other instrument for determining the pitch of a tone; an instrument for measuring strains in liquids.

tong (tong) [Chin. *t'ang*, a meeting-place], *n.* A Chinese secret society.

tonga (tong' gȧ) [Hindi *tanga*], *n.* A light two-wheel cart for four persons.

tongs (tongz) [A.-S. *tange*, sing. (cp. Dut. and Dan. *tang*, G. *zange*, Icel. *tōng*), cogn. with Gr. *daknein*, to bite], *n.pl.* An implement consisting of two limbs, usu. connected near one end by a pivot, used for grasping coals, etc., usu. called **a pair of tongs.**

tongue (tŭng) [A.-S. *tunge* (cp. Dut. *tong*, G. *zunge*, Icel. and Swed. *tunga*), cogn. with L. *lingua*, O.L. *dingua*], *n.* A fleshy muscular organ in the mouth, used in tasting, swallowing, and (in man) speech; the tongue of an ox, sheep, etc., as food; a tongue-shaped thing or part; the clapper of a bell; the pin in a buckle; a piece of leather closing the gap in the front of a laced shoe; the index of a scale or balance; a vibrating slip in the reed of a flageolet and other instruments; a pointed rail in a railway-switch; a projecting edge for fitting into a groove in matchboard; a long low promontory, a long narrow inlet; (*fig.*) speech, utterance, the voice; manner of speech; a language; hence a nation, a race. *v.t.* To modify (the sounds of a flute, etc.) with the tongue; to put a tongue on (matchboard, etc.); (*poet.*) to speak; *to reproach, to reprove. *v.i.* To use the tongue in playing some wind instruments. **the gift of tongues:** The power of speaking in unknown tongues, esp. as miraculously conferred on the Apostles on the day of Pentecost. **to give tongue** [GIVE (1)]. **to hold one's tongue** [HOLD (1)]. **with one's tongue in one's cheek:** Ironically. **tongue-bit,** *n.* A bit with a plate to prevent a horse from getting his tongue over the mouth-piece. **tongue-bone,** *n.* The hyoid bone. **tongue-tie,** *n.* Shortness of frænum impeding movement of the tongue. **tongue-tied,** *a.* Impeded in speech by this; (*fig.*) afraid of or prevented from speaking freely. **tongued,** *a.* (*usu. in comb.*, as *loud-tongued*). **tongueless,** *a.* **tonguelet,** *n.*

tonic (ton' ik) [Gr. *tonikos* (TONE, -IC)], *a.* Invigorating, bracing; of or pertaining to tones; (*Mus.*) pertaining to or founded on the key-note; (*Phonet.*) denoting a voiced sound; stressed; (*Path.*) pertaining to tension, unrelaxing (of spasms). *n.* A tonic medicine; (*Mus.*) the key-note. **Tonic Sol-fa** [SOL-FA]: A system of musical notation in which diatonic scales are written always in one way (the key-note being indicated), the tones being represented by syllables or initials, and time and accents by dashes and colons. **tonic sol-faist** (-fa' ist): One versed in or advocating this system. **tonicity** (tò nis' i ti), *n.* The state of being tonic; tone; elasticity or contractility of the muscles.

to-night, tonight (tò nīt'), *n.* The present night; the night of to-day. *adv.* On or during this.

tonish, etc. [TON (2)].

tonite (tō' nīt) [L. *ton-āre*, to thunder], *n.* A powerful explosive prepared from gun-cotton.

Tonka bean (tong' kȧ bēn) [Guiana *tonka*], *n.* The fruit of a S. American tree, *Dipterix odorata*, the fragrant seeds of which are used in perfumery.

tonnage (tŭn' ăj), *n.* The carrying capacity or internal cubic capacity of a vessel expressed in tons; the aggregate freightage of a number of vessels, esp. of a country's merchant marine; a duty on ships, formerly assessed on tonnage, now on dimensions. **tonnage-deck,** *n.* The upper of two decks, the second from below of three or more.

tonneau (ton' ō, tò nō') [F., cask], *n.* The after part of a motor-car containing the back seats.

-tonner [TON (1)].

tonometer [TONE].

tonsil (ton' sil) [F. *tonsille*, L. *tonsilla*, a sharp stake, (*pl.*) tonsils, prob. dim. of *tonsa*, oar], *n.* Either of two organs situated in the hinder part of the mouth on each side of the fauces. **tonsillar, tonsillitic** (-lit' ik), *a.* **tonsillitis** (-lī' tis), *n.* Inflammation of the tonsils.

tonsorial (ton sôr' i ȧl) [L. *tonsōrius*, from *tonsor -sōris*, barber, from *tondere*, to shave, p.p. *tonsus*], *a.* Pertaining to a barber or his art.

tonsure (ton' shûr) [F., from L. *tonsūra*, as prec.], *n.* The shaving of the crown (as in the R.-C. Ch.) or of the whole head (as in the Gr. Ch.) on admission to the priesthood or a monastic order; (*fig.*) admission into holy orders. *v.t.* To shave the head of, to confer the tonsure on.

tontine (ton tēn') [F., from Lorenzo *Tonti*, It. banker, originator, *c.* 1653], *n.* A form of annuity in which the shares of subscribers who die are added to the profits shared by the survivors, the last of whom receives the whole amount.

tonus (tō' nŭs) [L., TONE], *n.* Tonicity; (*Path.*) a tonic spasm.

tony (1) [TON (2)].

***tony** (2) (tō' ni) [short for *Antony*], *n.* A simpleton.

too (too) [TO], *adv.* In excessive quantity, degree, etc.; more than enough; as well, also, in addition, at the same time; moreover; (*colloq.*) extremely, superlatively. **too-too,** *a.* Gushing, affected, sentimental.

tooart (too′ årt) [native name], *n.* A W. Australian tree, *Eucalyptus gomphocephala*, yielding an intensely hard and durable wood valuable for shipbuilding.

took, *past* [TAKE].

tool (tool) [A.-S. *tōl* (cp. Icel. *tōl*, pl.), cogn. with *tawian*, see TAW (1)], *n.* A simple implement, esp. one used in manual work; a machine used in the making of machines; (*fig.*) anything used as an instrument or apparatus in one's occupation or profession; a person employed as an instrument or agent, a cat's paw; (*Bookbinding*) a hand-stamp or design used in tooling; (*vulg.*) the penis. *v.t.* (*Bookbinding*) To impress designs on (a book-cover); (*slang*) to drive (a coach, team of horses, etc.). *v.i.* (*Bookbinding*) To work with a tool; (*slang*) to drive, to ride. **tool-holder,** *n.* A device for pressing the tool against the work in a lathe; a handle for use with various tools. **tool-post, -rest,** *n.* A device for supporting or holding the tool in a lathe. **tooler,** *n.* One who or that which tools; a stone-mason's broad chisel. **tooling,** *n.*

toolache (too′ lăch) [Austral. abor.], *n.* Grey's wallaby, now extinct.

toom (toom) [M.E. *tom*, Icel. *tōmr*, cp. Swed. and Dan. *tom*], *a.* (*Sc.*) Empty. *v.t.* To empty.

toon (toon) [Hind. *tun*], *n.* A large E. Indian tree, *Toona ciliata*, with close-grained red wood.

toot (1) (toot) [cp. M.Swed. and Norw. *tuta*, Icel. *thjōta*, L.G. *tuten*, M.Dut. *tuyten*, of imit. orig.], *v.i.* To make a noise with an instrument or the mouth like that of a horn; to give out such a sound; to call (of grouse). *v.t.* To sound (a horn, etc.) thus; to give out (a blast, etc.) on a horn. *n.* A tooting sound or blast. **tooter,** *n.*

toot (2) (toot) [A.-S. *tōtian*, see TOUT (1)], *v.i.* (*prov.*) To peep about, to spy; to stand out, to be prominent. **toot-hill,** *n.* A look-out hill, a natural or artificial hillock formerly used as a watch-tower.

tooth (tooth) [A.-S. *tōth*, cp. Dut. *tand*, G. *zahn*, Icel. *tönn*, also L. *dens dentis*, Gr. *odous odontos*], *n.* (*pl.* **teeth**) One of the hard dense structures, originating in the epidermis, growing in the mouth or pharynx of vertebrates, and used for mastication; a false or artificial tooth made by a dentist; (*Nat. Hist.*) a tooth-like projection on the margin of a leaf, etc.; a projecting pin, point, cog, etc.; (*fig.*) a discriminating taste, a palate. *v.t.* To furnish with teeth; to indent. *v.i.* To interlock. **in the teeth of:** In spite of; in direct opposition to; in the face of (the wind). **long in the tooth:** Elderly, old (as in horses). **to cast in one's teeth** [CAST (1)]. **to one's teeth:** To one's face; in open opposition. **tooth and nail:** With all one's power. **to set the teeth on edge** [EDGE]. **to show one's teeth:** To adopt a threatening attitude. **a sweet tooth:** A liking for sweet things. **tooth-ache,** *n.* Pain in the teeth. **tooth-bill,** *n.* The tooth-billed pigeon of Samoa. **tooth-billed,** *a.* (*Ornith.*) Having tooth-like processes on the bill. **tooth-brush,** *n.* A brush for the teeth. **tooth-comb,** *n.* A fine-toothed comb. **tooth-edge,** *n.* The tingling sensation in the teeth excited by grating sounds, etc. **tooth ornament** (*Arch.*) [DOG'S-TOOTH]. **tooth-paste, -powder,** *n.* Paste or powder for cleaning the teeth. **toothpick,** *n.* A pointed instrument of bone, quill, etc., for removing particles of food, etc., from between the teeth. **toothlet,** *n.* **toothy,** *a.* Having prominent teeth.

toothful (tooth′ fụl), *n.* A small draught of liquor, etc.

toothing (too′ thing), *n.* Fitting with teeth; projecting stones or bricks left in the end of a wall for bonding it to a continuation. **toothing-plane,** *n.* A plane for scoring the under-surface of a veneer.

toothsome (tooth′ sụm), *a.* Palatable, pleasing to the taste. **toothsomely,** *adv.* **toothsomeness,** *n.*

toothwort (tooth′ wẽrt), *n.* (*Bot.*) A herb, *Lathræa squamaria*, allied to the broom-rape, with tooth-like scales on the root-stock; the shepherd's purse, *Capsella bursa-pastoris*, and other plants.

tootle (too′ tẹl) [freq. of TOOT (1)], *v.i.* To toot gently or continuously, as on a flute; (*colloq.*) to amble, to trot.

top (1) (top) [A.-S., cp. Dut. and Dan. *top*, Icel. *toppr*, Swed. *topp*, G. *zopf*, tuft, tree-top], *n.* The highest part or point of anything, the summit; the upper side or surface; the upper part of a shoe, etc.; the cover of a carriage, etc.; (*Am.*) the hood of a motor-car; the head of a page in a book; the part of a plant above ground; the uppermost part of a jointed fishing-rod; the crown of the head; the upper end or head of a table; the highest position, place, rank, etc.; the highest degree, the apex, the culmination, the height; (*Naut.*) a platform round the head of a lower mast, forming an extended base for securing the topmast shrouds; (*pl.*) metal buttons plated or washed only on the face. *v.t.* (*past & p.p.* **topped**) To remove the top or extremity of (a plant, etc.); to put a top or cap on; to cover the top of; to rise to the top of, to surmount; to excel, to surpass, to be higher than; to be (of a specified height); (*Naut.*) to tip (a yard) so as to bring one end above the other. *a.* Being on or at the top or summit; highest in position, degree, etc. **to top off** or **up:** To complete by putting the top or uppermost part to; to finish, to complete. **to go over the top:** To go to the attack. **to top up:** To fill up (with petrol, oil, etc.). **big top,** *n.* A big circus tent. **top-boot,** *n.* A boot having high tops, usu. of distinctive material and colour. **top-coat,** *n.* An overcoat. **top dog,** *n.* (*colloq.*) The uppermost fellow, the boss. **top-dress,** *v.t.* To manure on the surface, as distinguished from digging or ploughing in. **top-dressing,** *n.* **topgallant** (top-, tọ găl′ ănt), *a.* (*Naut.*) Applied to the mast, rigging, and sail, next above the topmast. **top-hamper,** *n.* (*Naut.*) The light upper sails and rigging; tackle, anchors, casks, etc., encumbering the deck. **top-hat,** *n.* A tall silk hat. **top-heavy,** *a.* Having the top or upper part too heavy for the lower; (*colloq.*) intoxicated. **top-hole,** *a.* (*slang*) Excellent, first-rate. **top-knot,** *n.* An ornamental knot or bow worn on the top of the head; a tuft or crest growing on the head. **top-lantern, -light,** *n.* One displayed from the mizen-top of a flagship. **top-level,** *a.* At the highest level. **topman,** *n.* (*Naut.*) A man stationed in one of the tops; a top-sawyer. **topmast,** *n.* The mast next above the lower mast. ***top-proud,** *a.* Excessively proud. **topsail** (topsl), *n.* A square sail next above the lowest sail on a mast; a fore-and-aft sail above the gaff. **top-sawyer,** *n.* The one in the upper position in pit-sawing; a person in a high or superior position; a first-rate man in anything. **top secret,** *n.* A secret of the highest importance. **top-sides,** *n.pl.* (*Naut.*) The sides of a vessel above the water-line. **topsman,** *n.* (*Sc. or prov.*) A head servant, bailiff or overseer; a chief drover; (*slang*) a hangman. **top-soil,** *n.* The upper layer of soil; *v.t.* To remove this from (a piece of ground). **top-soiling,** *n.* ***top-ful,** *a.* High, lofty. **topless,** *a.* **topmost,** *a.* Highest, uppermost. **topper,** *n.* One who or that which tops; fruit, etc., of better quality put at the top in a basket, etc.; (*slang*) a top-hat. **topping,** *a.* (*slang*) Very fine, excellent. **topping-up,** *n.* (*Elec.*) The addition of distilled water to the accumulator cell to compensate for loss by evaporation. **toppingly,** *adv.*

top (2) (top) [late A.-S. *topp*, ult. from M.H.G. *topf*, cogn. with DIP], *n.* A wooden or metal toy, usu. conical- or pear-shaped, made to rotate with great velocity on a metal point underneath, by the rapid unwinding of a string or spring or with the hand.

toparch (top′ ark) [Gr. *toparchēs* (*topos*, place, *-archēs*, ruler, from *archein*, to rule)], *n.* The ruler or chief man in a place or country, a petty king. **toparchy,** *n.* A little state or country governed by a toparch.

topaz (tō′ păz) [O.F. *topaze*, L. *topazus*, *topazion*, Gr. *topazos*, *topazion*, cp. Sansk. *tapas*, fire, from *tap*, to shine], *n.* A transparent or translucent fluosilicate of aluminium, usu. white or yellow, but sometimes green, blue, red, or colourless, valued as a gem; a large and brilliant humming-bird. **topazolite** (tō păz′ ō līt), *n.* A yellow or green variety of garnet resembling topaz.

top-boot, -coat, -dress, etc. [TOP (1)].

tope (1) (tōp) [Tamil *toppu*], *n.* A grove, esp. of mango-trees.

tope (2) (tōp) [Hindi *top*, corr. from Sansk. *stūpa*, mound], *n.* A Buddhist monument in the form of a dome, tower, or mound, usu. containing relics.

tope (3) (tōp) [perh. from F. *tôpe* (from *tôper*, to cover a stake in dicing), as an int. 'accepted! agreed!' afterwards a drinking phrase; or from Teut. as TOP (1), in alln. to putting the tops of the thumbs together and crying *topp*], *v.i.* To drink alcoholic liquors excessively or habitually, to tipple. **toper,** *n.* A tippler, a heavy drinker.

tope (4) (tōp) [prob. Cornish], *n.* A small shark of the genus *Galeus*, the dog-fish.

***topful, topgallant** [TOP (1)].

toph (tōf), **tophus** (tō′ fŭs) [L. *tōphus*, TUFA], *n.* Calcareous matter deposited round the teeth and at the surface of the joints in gout. **tophaceous** (tō fā′ shŭs), *a.*

Tophet (tō′ fĕt) [Heb. *tōpheth*], *n.* A place in the valley of Hinnom, S.E. of Jerusalem, once used for idolatrous worship, and afterwards for the deposit of the city refuse, to consume which fires were continually kept burning; (*fig.*) hell.

topi, topee (tō′ pi, tō′ pē) [Hind., hat], *n.* A sun-hat, a pith helmet. **sola topi,** *n.* A helmet made of sola pith.

topia (tō′ pi à) [L., fancy gardening, from Gr. *topos*, place], *n.* (*Rom. Ant.*) Mural decoration for interiors, usu. consisting of fanciful landscapes, trees, etc. **topiary,** *a.* Shaped by cutting or clipping. **topiary art:** The art of cutting and clipping trees, shrubs, etc., into fanciful shapes. **topiarian** (-âr′ i ǎn), *a.*

topic (top′ ik) [F. *topiques*, L. *topica*, Gr. *topika*, topics, neut. pl. of *topikos*, local, from *topos*, place], *n.* The subject of a discourse, argument, literary composition, or conversation; (*Med.*) a remedy for external application to a particular part of the body. **topical,** *a.* Pertaining to or of the nature of a topic comprising or consisting of allusions, esp. to current or local topics; local, esp. (*Med.*) of a particular part of the body. **topical-song,** *n.* A song dealing with topics of the day. **topically,** *adv.*

topless, topman, etc. [TOP (1)].

topography (tō pog′ rà fi) [F. *topographie*, late L. and Gr. *topographia* (*topos*, place, -GRAPHY)], *n.* The detailed description of particular places; representation of local features on maps, etc.; the artificial or natural features of a place or district; (*Anat.*) the mapping of the surface or the anatomy of particular regions of the body. **topographer,** *n.* **topographic, -al** (-grăf′ ik, -ǎl), *a.* **topographically,** *adv.*

topolatry (tō pol′ à tri) [Gr. *topos*, place, -LATRY], *n.* Excessive veneration for or attachment to a place. **topology** (tō pol′ ō ji) [-LOGY], *n.* The art of aiding the memory by associating things with places. **toponomy** (tō pon′ ō mi) [Gr. *onoma*, Æolic *onuma*, name], *n.* The science of place-names; a register of place-names of a district, etc. **toponymy** (-i mi), *n.* (*Anat.*) The naming of regions of the body.

topper, topping, etc. [TOP (1)].

topple (top′ ĕl) [freq. of TOP (1)], *v.i.* To totter and fall; to project as if about to fall. *v.t.* To cause to topple, to overturn.

topsail, top-sawyer, etc. [TOP (1)].

topsy-turvy (top si tĕr′ vi) [acc. to Skeat from TOP (1), so, obs. *terve*, allied to A.-S. *tearflian*, to turn, to roll over, cp. L.G. *tarven*, O.H.G. *zerben*], *adv.* and *a.* Upside down; in an upset or disordered condition. *n.* A topsy-turvy state. *v.t.* To turn topsy-turvy; to throw into confusion. **topsy-turviness, topsy-turvydom, topsy-turvyism,** *n.*

toque (tōk) [F., prob. from Breton *tok*, cp. W. *toc*], *n.* A small, brimless, close-fitting bonnet; a cap or head-dress, usu. small and close-fitting, worn at various periods by men and women; a monkey with a cap-like bunch of hair.

tor (tôr) [A.-S. *torr*, W. *tor*, knob, cogn. with L. *turris*, whence W. *twr*, tower], *n.* A prominent hill or rocky peak, esp. on Dartmoor and in Derbyshire.

-tor [-OR, after *t*, L. p.p. stems], *suf.* Denoting the agent, as in *inspector*, *orator*.

torah (tôr′ à) [Heb.], *n.* The Divine will or counsel, the Mosaic law; the Pentateuch; the ten commandments.

torc [TORQUE].

torch (tôrch) [M.E. and F. *torche*, late L. *tortica*, from *torquēre*, to twist, p.p. *tortus*], *n.* A light made of resinous wood, twisted flax, hemp, etc., soaked in oil or tallow, for carrying in the hand; an oil, electric, or other lamp used for this purpose, esp. when raised aloft on a pole, etc.; a hand-lamp containing an electric battery and bulb, (*Am.* a flash-light). **torch-bearer,** *n.* **torch-dance,** *n.* A dance in which each performer carries a torch. **torch-fishing** or **torching,** *n.* Fishing at night by torch-light. **torch-light,** *n.* **torch-race,** *n.* A race among the ancient Greeks, in which the runners carried lighted torches. **torch-song,** *n.* (*Theat.*) A song sung with the spot-light trained on the singer. **torcher,** *n.*

torchon (tôr′ shŭn) [F. *torcher*, to wipe, as prec.], *n.* A dish-cloth, a clout. **torchon-board,** *n.* A board on which torchon-paper is stretched. **torchon-paper,** *n.* A rough-surfaced paper used for water-colours, etc.

torcular (tôr′ kū lăr) [L., a press, from *torquēre*, to twist], *n.* A surgeon's tourniquet.

tore (1), *past* [TEAR (1)].

tore (2) [TORUS].

tore (3) (tôr) [etym. unknown], *n.* (*prov.*) The dead grass that remains on mowing land in winter and spring.

torea (tō′ rĕ à) [Maori], *n.* The N. Zealand oyster-catcher.

toreador (tor ė à dôr′) [Sp., from *torear*, to fight bulls, from *toro*, L. *taurus*], *n.* A bull-fighter, esp. one who fights on horse-back.

toreutic (tō roo′ tik) [Gr. *toreutikos*, from *toreuein*, to bore, to chase], *a.* Pertaining to carved, chased, or embossed work, esp. in metal. *n.pl.* The art of this. **toreumatography** (-mà tog′ rà fi) [-GRAPHY], *n.* A description of or treatise on toreutics. ***toreumatology** (-tol′ ō ji) [-LOGY], *n.*

torfaceous (tôr fā′ shŭs) [TURF, -ACEOUS], *a.* (*Bot.*) Growing in bogs, mosses, etc. (of some plants).

torgoch (tôr′ goch) [W. *tor*, belly, *goch*, red], *n.* A red-bellied variety of char.

torii (tō′ ri ē) [Jap.], *n.* (*unchanged in pl.*) A delicately-built gateless gateway composed of two uprights with (usu.) three superimposed cross-pieces, usu. at the approach to a Shinto temple, etc.

torment (tôr′ mĕnt) [O.F. from L. *tormentum*, a machine for hurling stones, a rack, torment, from *torquēre*, to twist], *n.* Extreme pain or anguish of body or mind; a source or cause of this. *v.t.* (tôr ment′) To subject to torment, to afflict, to vex, to irritate; *to torture. **tormentingly,** *adv.* **tormentor,** *n.* One who or that which torments; a heavy harrow on wheels; (*Naut.*) a long fork for lifting meat from the coppers. **tormentress,** *n.* **tormentum,** *n.* (*pl.* **-ta**) An ancient war-engine, a catapult.

tormentil (tôr′ mĕn til) [F. *tormentille*, late L. *tormentilla*, perh. from prec. with ref. to curing toothache], *n.* A low herb, *Potentilla tormentilla*, with four-petalled yellow flowers, the astringent root-stock of which is used for medicine.

tormina (tôr′ mi nȧ) [L., from *torquēre*, see TORMENT], *n.* Severe griping pains in the bowels.

torn, *p.p.* [TEAR (1)].

tornado (tôr nā′ dō) [Sp. *tronada*, thunder-storm, from *tronar*, to thunder], *n.* (*pl.* **-does**) A storm of extreme violence covering a very small area at once, but progressing rapidly, usu. having a rotary motion with electric discharges, occurring in W. Africa and the United States at certain seasons.

***torneament** [TOURNAMENT].

toroa (tō′ rȧ) [Maori], *n.* A species of albatross.

toroidal (tȯ roi′ dȧl), *a.* Of or like a torus.

torous, *-ose (tôr′ ŭs, -ōs) [L. *torōsus* from TORUS], *a.* Muscular, knobby; (*Bot.*) cylindrical with protuberances at intervals.

torpedo (tôr pē′ dō) [L., numbness (also the fish), from *torpēre*, to be numb], *n.* (*pl.* **-does**) A long, cigar-shaped apparatus charged with explosive, used for attacking a hostile ship below the water-line; a submarine mine for defending harbours, etc.; a detonating fog-signal placed on a railway track to be exploded by the wheels of a train; a cartridge for exploding in an oil-well, etc.; a mine or shell buried in the way of a storming-party; a mixture of fulminate and grit exploded on the ground as a toy; an electric ray, a sea-fish having an electrical apparatus for disabling or killing its prey. *v.t.* To attack, blow up, or sink with a torpedo. **aerial torpedo,** *n.* A torpedo launched from an aircraft. **torpedo-boat,** *n.* A small swift vessel fitted for firing torpedoes. **torpedo-boat destroyer** [DESTROYER]. **torpedo-net,** *n.* A wire net hung round a ship to intercept torpedoes. **torpedo-tube,** *n.* (*Nav.*) A tube for the discharge of torpedoes. **torpedoist** (tôr pē′ dō ist), *n.*

torpid (tôr′ pid) [L. *torpidus*, from *torpēre*, to be numb], *a.* Having lost the power of motion or feeling; benumbed; dormant (of a hibernating animal); dull, sluggish, inactive. *n.* A second-class racing-boat at Oxford; (*pl.*) the Lenten races in which these compete. ***torpent,** *a.* Torpid. *n.* A torpifying medicine. ***torpescent** (-pes′ ėnt), *a.* ***torpescence,** *n.* **torpidity** (-pid′ i ti), **torpidness, torpor,** *n.* **torpidly,** *adv.* **torpify,** *v.t.* **torporific** (tôr pȯ rif′ ik), *a.*

torque (tôrk) [L. *torques*, from *torquēre*, to twist], *n.* A twisted necklace of gold or other metal, worn by the ancient Gauls, etc.; (*Mech.*) the movement of a system of forces causing rotation. **torquate, torquated,** *a.* (*Zool.*) Having a ring of distinctive colour about the neck. **torqued,** *a.* Twisted; (*Her.*) wreathed.

torrefy (tor′ ė fī) [L. *torrefacere* (*torrēre*, to parch, *facere*, to make)], *v.t.* To dry or parch; to roast (ores, etc.). **torrefaction** (-făk′ shŭn), *n.*

torrent (tor′ ėnt) [F., from L. *torrentem*, nom. *-rens*, pres.p. of *torrēre*, to parch], *n.* A violent rushing stream (of water, lava, etc.); (*fig.*) a flood (of abuse, passion, etc.). *a.* Rushing, impetuous. **torrential** (tȯ ren′ shȧl), *a.* **torrentially,** *adv.*

Torricellian (tor i chel′ i ȧn, -sel′ i ȧn), *a.* Pertaining to the Italian physicist and mathematician E. Torricelli (1608–47). **Torricellian tube:** The barometer. **Torricellian vacuum:** The vacuum above the mercury in this.

torrid (tor′ id) [F. *torride*, L. *torridus*, from *torrēre*, to parch], *a.* Dried up with heat, parched, scorching, very hot. **torrid zone:** The broad belt of the earth's surface included between the tropics. **torridity** (tȯ rid′ i ti), **torridness,** *n.*

torsade [TORSE (1)]. **torsal** [TORSE (2)].

torse (1) (tôrs) [F., also *torce*, ult. from L. *tors-*, p.p. stem of *torquēre*, to twist], *n.* (*Her.*) A wreath. **torsade** (tôr sād′), *n.* An ornamental twisted cord, ribbon, etc.

torse (2) (tôrs) [L. *torsus*, p.p. of *torquēre*, see prec.], *n.* (*Geom.*) A surface generated by a straight line continuously moving about some point or other in its length. **torsal,** *a.*

torse (3) [TORSO].

torsel (tôr′ sėl) [prob. var. of TASSEL], *n.* A twisted ornament, as a scroll; a block of wood fixed in a wall for a beam or joist to rest on.

torsion (tôr′ shŭn) [F., from L. *tortiōnem*, nom. *-tio*, from *torquēre*, to twist], *n.* The act of twisting or the state of being twisted; (*Mech.*) the force with which a body tends to return to its original state after being twisted; (*Surg.*) twisting of the cut end of an artery for checking hæmorrhage after an operation. **torsion balance:** An instrument for estimating very minute forces by the action of a twisted wire. **torsibility** (-bil′ i ti), *n.* **torsional,** *a.* **torsionally,** *adv.* **torsionless,** *a.*

torsk (tôrsk) [Dan. and Swed., cp. Icel. *thorskr*], *n.* A food-fish, *Brosmius brosme*, allied to the cod.

torso (tôr′ sō) [It., stump, stalk, from L. THYRSUS], *n.* (*pl.* **-sos**) The trunk of a statue or body without the head and limbs.

tort (tôrt) [F., wrong, harm, L. *tortum*, nom. *-tus*, p.p. of *torquēre*, to twist], *n.* (*Law*) A private or civil wrong; *mischief, injury, calamity. **tortious** (tôr′ shŭs), *a.* **tortiously,** *adv.*

torticollis (tôr ti kol′ is) [L. *tortus*, see prec., *collum*, neck], *n.* (*Path.*) A spasmodic affection of the neck-muscles, stiff-neck.

tortile (tôr′ til, -tīl) [L. *tortilis*, from *tortus*, see TORT], *a.* Twisted, wreathed, coiled, curved. **tortility** (-til′ i ti), *n.* ***tortive,** *a.* (*Shak.*).

tortilla (tôr tē′ lyȧ) [Sp., dim. of *torta*, TART (2)], *n.* A thin flat maize cake baked on an iron plate, the Mexican substitute for bread.

tortious, tortiously [TORT].

***tortive** [TORTILE].

tortoise (tôr′ tŭs) [M.E. *tortuce*, *tortu*, O.F. *tortue*, late L. *tortūca*, from *tortus*, see TORT], *n.* A terrestrial or freshwater turtle; (*Rom. Ant.*) a testudo. **tortoise-shell,** *n.* The mottled horny plates of the carapace of some sea-turtles, used for combs, ornaments, inlaying, etc.; *a.* Made of this; resembling this in marking and colour, mottled with red and black.

Tortrix (tôr′ triks) [mod. L., fem. of *tortor*, from *tort-*, p.p. stem of *torquēre*, to twist], *n.* A genus of British moths typical of the family *Tortricidæ*, called the leaf-rollers.

tortulous (tôr′ tū lŭs) [from late L. *tortula*, dim. of *torta*, twist, see TORT], *a.* (*Nat. Hist.*) Bulging out at intervals, moniliform.

tortuous (tôr′ tū ŭs) [M.E. and O.F. *tortuos* (F. *tortueux*), L. *tortūosus*, from *tortus*, twist, see TORT], *a.* Twisting, winding, crooked; (*fig.*) roundabout, devious, not open and straightforward. **tortuose,** *a.* (*Bot.*) **tortuosity** (-os′ i ti), *n.* **tortuousness,** *n.* **tortuously,** *adv.*

torture (tôr′ tyŭr, -chėr) [F., from L. *tortura*, as prec.], *n.* The infliction of extreme physical pain as a punishment or to extort confession, etc.; excruciating pain or anguish of mind or body. *v.t.* To subject to torture; (*fig.*) to wrest from the normal position; to distort; to pervert the meaning of (a statement, etc.). **torturable,** *a.* **torturer,** *n.* **torturingly,** *adv.* **torturous,** *a.*

torula (tor′ ū lȧ) [dim. of TORUS], *n.* (*Biol.*) A chain of spherical bacteria; (*Bot.*) a genus of microscopic yeast-like fungi, causing fermentation. **toruliform,** *a.* **torulose, -lous,** *a.* (*Bot.*) Having alternate swells and contractions like the growth of torula.

torus (tôr′ ŭs) [L., a prominence, a couch], *n.* (*pl.* **-ri,** -rī) A semi-circular projecting moulding, esp. in the base of a column; (*Bot.*) the receptacle or thalamus of a flower, the modified end of a stem supporting the floral organs; (*Anat.*) a rounded ridge.

***torve, *torvus** (tôrv′, -ŭs) [L. *torvus*, grim], *a.* Sour, stern, grim; of a severe countenance. ***torvid,** *a.* ***torvity,** *n.*

Tory (tôr′ i) [orig. an Irish moss-trooper, from Ir. *toiridhe*, from *toir*, pursuit], *n.* (*Hist.*) One of the party opposed to the exclusion of the Duke of York (James II) from the throne and to the Revolution of 1688; (*Pol.*) a member of the Conservative party; (*pl.*) this party. *a.* Pertaining to the Tories. **Tory Democrat:** A Conservative favouring some democratic reforms. **Toryism,** *n.*

-tory [-ORY, cp. -TOR], *suf.* Forming nouns and adjectives, as *factory*, *oratory*, *perfunctory*, *rotatory*.

tosh (1) (tosh) [etym. doubtful, cp. TUSH], *n.* (*slang*) Rubbish, nonsense.

tosh (2) (tosh) [O.F. *touse*, L. *tonsus*, clipped], *v.i.* To make tidy.

toss (tos) [Norw. *tossa*, cp. L.G. *teusen*], *v.t.* (*past & p.p.* **tossed,** *poet.* **tost**) To throw up with the hand, esp. palm upward; to throw, to pitch, to fling, with an easy or careless motion; to throw back (the head) with a jerk; to jerk; to throw about or from side to side, to cause to rise and fall, to agitate; to throw (up) a coin into the air to decide a wager, etc., by seeing which way it falls; hence, to settle a wager or dispute with (a person) thus; (*Mining*) to separate the heavy from the lighter parts of (tin ore) by agitating the slime. *v.i.* To roll and tumble about, to be agitated; to throw oneself from side to side. *n.* The act of tossing; the state of being tossed. **to take a toss:** To be thrown by a horse. **to toss off:** To swallow at a draught. **to toss up:** To toss a coin. **to win the toss:** To have something decided in one's favour by tossing up a coin. ***toss-pot,** *n.* A toper. **toss-up,** *n.* The tossing up of a coin; a doubtful point, an even chance. **tosser,** *n.* **tossily,** *adv.* (*colloq.*) Pertly, indifferently. **tossy,** *a.*

tot (1) (tot) [Icel. *tottr*, cp. Dan. *tot*], *n.* Anything small or insignificant, esp. a small child; (*colloq.*) a dram of liquor. **tottie,** *n.*

tot (2) (tot) [L., so many, or short for foll.], *n.* A sum in simple or compound addition. *v.t.* (*past & p.p.* **totted**) To add (up). *v.i.* To mount (up).

total (tō′ tal) [F., from late L. *tōtālis*, from *tōtus*, entire], *a.* Complete, comprising or constituting the whole; comprising everything; absolute, entire, thorough. *n.* The total sum or amount; the aggregate. *v.t.* (*past & p.p.* **totalled**) To ascertain the total of; to amount to as a total. *v.i.* To amount (to) as a total. **total abstinence** [see ABSTENTION]. **total warfare,** *n.* Warfare in which all available resources, military and civil, are employed. **totality** (tō tăl′ i ti), *n.* **totalitarian,** *a.* (*Pol.*) Permitting no rival parties or policies; controlling the entire national resources of trade, natural wealth, and man-power. **totalize** (tō′ tȧ līz), *v.t.* To total. *v.i.* To use a totalizer. **totalization,** *n.* **totally,** *adv.*

totalizator (tō tȧ lī zā′ tôr), *n.* (*Sport*) A contrivance for showing the total amount of bets staked on a race in order to divide the whole among those betting on the winner.

totara (tō ta′ ra) [Maori], *n.* The N. Zealand red pine.

tote (1) (tōt) [etym. doubtful], *v.t.* To carry, to bear, to lead, to haul. **to tote fair:** To act fairly. **tote-road,** *n.* A rough road for carriers.

tote (2) [TOTALIZATOR].

totem (tō′ tėm) [Algonkin], *n.* (*Ethnol.*) A natural object, usu. an animal, taken by primitive races as a badge or emblem of an individual or clan on account of a supposed relationship; an image of this. **totem-post,** *n.* A post on which totems are carved or hung. **totemic** (tō tem′ ik), **totemistic** (-mis′ tik), *a.* **totemism** (tō′ tėm izm), *n.* **totemist,** *n.*

tother (tŭdh′ ėr) [M.E. *thet* (THAT), OTHER], *a.* and *pron.* The other.

totient (tō′ shėnt) [L. *totiēs*, from *tot*, so many, after QUOTIENT], *n.* The number of totitives of a given number. **totitive** (tō′ ti tiv), *n.* A number less than another having with this no common divisor but unity.

totipalmate (tō ti păl′ māt) [L. *tōti-*, *tōtus*, whole, PALMATE], *a.* (*Ornith.*) Wholly webbed, steganopodous. **totipalmation** (-mā′ shŭn), *n.*

totitive [TOTIENT].

totter (tot′ ėr) [for *tolter*, freq. cogn. with M.E. *tulten*, *tilten*, TILT (2)], *v.i.* To walk or stand unsteadily, to stagger; to be weak, to be on the point of falling. **totterer,** *n.* **totteringly,** *adv.* **tottery,** ***totty,** *a.* **tottie** [TOT (1)].

toucan (tu kan′, too′ kăn) [Braz. *tucana* (Port. *tucano*)], *n.* A brilliantly-coloured tropical American bird with an enormous beak.

touch (tŭch) [M.E. *touchen*, O.F. *tuchier*, *tochier* (F. *toucher*), It. *toccare*, prob. of imit. orig.], *v.t.* To meet the surface of, to have no intervening space between at one or more points, to be in contact with, to come into contact with; to bring or put the hand or other part of the body or a stick, etc., into contact with; to cause (two objects) to come into contact; to put the hand to (the hat, etc.); to reach, to attain; to meddle, to interfere with; to injure slightly, to approach, to compare with; to impair; to concern, to relate to; to treat of hastily or lightly; to strike lightly, to tap, to play upon lightly, to mark or delineate lightly, to put (in) fine strokes with a brush, etc.; to be tangent to; to produce a mental impression on; to affect with tender feeling, to soften; to excite the anger of, to rouse, to irritate; (*slang*) to beg or borrow money. *v.i.* To come into contact (of two or more objects); to deal with or treat of (usu. with *on*) in a slight or hasty manner; to come to land, to call (at a port, etc.). *n.* The act of touching; the state of touching or being touched, contact; the junction of two bodies at the surface, so that there is no intervening space; the sense by which contact, pressure, etc., are perceived; a slight effort, a light stroke with brush or pencil; (*fig.*) a stroke, a twinge; a trace, a minute quantity, a tinge; characteristic manner or method of handling, working, executing, playing on the keys or strings of a musical instrument, etc.; the manner in which the keys of a piano, etc., respond to this; characteristic impress; intimate correspondence, intercourse, or communication, accord, sympathy; magnetization of a steel bar by contact with magnets; a test, a proof, a touchstone; (*Med.*) the exploring of organs, etc., by touch; (*Football*) the part of the field outside the touch-lines and between the goal-lines. **to touch down:** (*Rugby*) To touch the ground with the ball behind the opponent's goal; (*Aviat.*) to alight. **to touch lucky:** (*slang*) To have a stroke of luck. **to touch on** or **upon:** To allude to; to deal with (a subject, etc.) briefly. **to touch up:** To correct or improve by slight touches, to retouch; to strike or stimulate (a horse, etc.) gently. **touch-and-go,** *n.* A state of uncertainty. *a.* Highly uncertain, very risky or hazardous. **touch-down,** *n.* A touching down. **touch-hole,** *n.* The priming hole or vent of a gun. **touch-lines,** *n.pl.* (*Football*) The two longer or side boundaries of the field. **touch-me-not,** *n.* The plant noli-me-tangere. **touch-needle,** *n.* A needle of gold alloy of known composition employed in assaying other alloys by comparison of the marks made on the touchstone. **touchable,** *a.* **toucher,** *n.* One who or that which touches; (*slang*) a close shave, a narrow squeak. **touching,** *a.* Affecting, moving, pathetic. *prep.* Concerning, with regard to. **touchingly,** *adv.* **touchingness,** *n.*

touchpaper (tŭch′ pā pėr), *n.* Paper saturated with nitrate of potash for igniting gunpowder, etc.

touchstone (tŭch′ stōn), *n.* A dark stone, usu. jasper, schist, or basanite used in conjuction with touch-needles for testing the purity of gold and other alloys; (*fig.*) a standard, a criterion.

touchwood (tŭch′ wud), *n.* A soft white substance

into which wood is converted by the action of fungi, easily ignited and burning like tinder.

touchy (tŭch′ i) [corr. of TETCHY], *a.* Apt to take offence, irascible, irritable. **touchily,** *adv.* **touchiness,** *n.*

tough (tŭf) [A.-S. *tōh,* cp. Dut. *taai,* G. *zähe*], *a.* Flexible without being brittle; firm, strong, not easily broken; able to endure hardship; viscid, stiff, tenacious; stubborn, unyielding; laborious, difficult; (*colloq.*) hard, severe (of luck, etc.). *n.* (*Am.*) A rough, a murderous bully. **toughen,** *v.t.* and *i.* **toughish,** *a.* **toughly,** *adv.* **toughness,** *n.*

toupee (tu pē′) [F. *toupet,* dim. of O.F. *toup,* tuft, see TOP (1)], *n.* An artificial lock or curl of hair; a small wig.

tour (toor) [F., from *tourner,* to TURN], *n.* A journeying round from place to place in a district, country, etc.; an extended excursion or ramble; a circuit; a shift or turn of work or duty, *esp.* a period of duty on a foreign station. *v.i.* To make a tour. *v.t.* To make a tour through. **tourism,** *n.* Organized touring, esp. from or to a foreign country. **tourist,** *n.* **tourist class,** *n.* A superior type of third-class accommodation on ocean liners. **tourist ticket:** A railway or other return or circular ticket issued on special terms.

touraco (too′ rȧ kō) [F., from native name], *n.* A brilliantly-coloured African bird of the genus *Turacus corythaix.*

tourbillion (toor bil′ i ŏn) [F. *tourbillion,* whirlwind], *n.* A firework revolving in the air so as to represent a fiery scroll or spiral.

tourist [TOUR].

tourmaline (toor′ mȧ lēn) [F., from Cingalese *tōramalli*], *n.* (*Min.*) A black or coloured transparent or translucent silicate with electrical properties, some varieties of which are used as gems.

tournament (toor′-, tĕr′ nȧ mėnt) [M.E. *tornement,* O.F. *torneiement,* from *torneier,* to TOURNEY], *n.* A contest, exercise, or pageant in which mounted knights contested, usu. with blunted lances, etc.; any contest of skill in which a number of persons take part.

tournay (toor′ nā) [*Tournay,* in Belgium], *n.* A printed worsted material used in upholstery.

tourney (toor′ ni) [M.E. and O.F. *tornei,* from *torneier,* L. *tornāre,* to TURN], *n.* A tournament. *v.i.* To engage in a tournament.

tourniquet (toor′ ni ket) [F., from *tourner,* to TURN], *n.* An instrument for compressing an artery with a screw and checking hæmorrhage.

tournure (toor noor′) [F.], *n.* The curving outline or contour of a figure; characteristic outline or contour in a drawing, etc.; a pad worn by women to give the effect of well-rounded hips; the drapery at the back of a dress.

tousle (tou′ zėl) [freq. of *touse,* M.E. *tūsen,* cp. G. *zausen*], *v.t.* To pull about; to disarrange, to rumple, to dishevel, to put into disorder. *v.i.* To toss about, to rummage. *n.* A tousling, a romp; a tousled mass (of hair, etc.). ***touse,** *v.t.* To tousle; to tear at, to worry. **tously, tousy,** *a.*

tous-les-mois (too lā mwa′) [F., every month], *n.* A food starch got from the roots of species of canna, esp. *C. edulis,* a perennial Peruvian herb.

tout (1) (tout) [M.E. *tūten,* var. of *toten,* A.-S. *tōtian,* to project, to peep out, cp. TOOT (2)], *v.i.* To solicit custom in an obtrusive way; to observe secretly, to spy (esp. on horses in training for a race). *n.* One employed to tout; one who watches horses in training and supplies information. **touter,** *n.*

tout (2) (tout) [etym. doubtful], *v.t.* (*Sc.*) To annoy, to vex, to tease. *v.i.* To have a fit of ill humour. *n.* Such a fit; a slight illness.

tow (1) (tō) [A.-S. *togian,* cp. Icel. *toga,* O.H.G. *zogōn,* also L. *dūcere,* to lead, and Eng. TUG], *v.t.* To pull (a boat, ship, etc.) through the water by a rope, etc.; to pull a vehicle behind another; to drag (a net) over the surface of water to obtain specimens; to pull, to drag behind one. *n.* The act of towing; the state of being towed. **to take** or **have in tow:** To be towing; (*fig.*) to have under one's control, guidance, guardianship, etc. **towboat,** *n.* A tug; a boat, barge, etc., that is being towed. **tow-, towing-line, -rope,** *n.* A hawser or rope used in towing. **tow-, towing-net,** *n.* One for towing along the surface of water to collect specimens. **tow-, towing-path,** *n.* A track beside a canal or river for animals towing barges, etc. **towage,** *n.*

tow (2) (tō) [etym. doubtful, perh. from A.-S. *tow-,* spinning (in *towlīc,* fit for spinning)], *n.* The coarse broken part of hemp or flax after heckling, etc. **towy,** *a.*

towai (to′ wī) [Maori], *n.* A tree from which bark for tanning is obtained.

toward (1), **towards** (tȯ wôrd′, -z, twôrd, -z, tōrd, -z) [A.-S. *tōweard* (TO, -WARD)], *prep.* In the direction of; as regards, with respect to; for, for the purpose of; near, about. **adv.* In preparation, at hand.

***toward** (2) (tō′ ėrd) [as prec.], *a.* Docile, obedient; ready to learn or do, apt; *forward, advanced. ***towardly,** *a.* **towardliness, *towardness,** *n.*

towel (tou′ ėl) [M.E. *towaille,* O.F. *toaille* (F. *touaille*), O.H.G. *twahila, dwahila* (whence G. *zwehle*), from *twahan,* to wash, cp. A.-S. *thwēan*], *n.* A cloth for wiping and drying oneself on after washing, etc.; (*slang*) a cudgel, also called an oaken towel. *v.t.* (*past & p.p.* **towelled**) To wipe with a towel; (*slang*) to thrash. *v.i.* To wipe oneself with a towel. **towel-horse,** *n.* A wooden stand on which to hang towels. **towelling,** *n.* Material for making towels; (*slang*) a thrashing.

tower (tou′ ėr) [M.E. *tour, tūr* (late A.-S. *torr*), O.F. *tor* (F. *tour*), L. *turrem,* nom. *-ris,* Gr. *tursis, turris*], *n.* A structure lofty in proportion to the area of its base, and circular, square, or polygonal in plan, frequently of several stories, insulated, or forming part of a church, castle, or other large building; (*Elec.*) a pylon; (*fig.*) a place of defence, a protection. *v.i.* To rise to a great height, to soar; to be relatively high, to reach high (above). **towered,** *a.* **towering,** *a.* Very high, lofty; (*fig.*) violent, outrageous (of passion, etc.). **towery,** *a.*

town (toun) [A.-S. *tūn* (cp. Dut. *tuin,* Icel. *tūn,* G. *zaun,* hedge), cogn. with DUN (3)], *n.* A collection of dwelling-houses larger than a village, esp. one not constituted a city; this as contrasted with the country; the people of a town; the chief town of a district or neighbourhood, esp. London; *a collection of dwellings enclosed by a wall or other defence. **to go to town:** (*colloq.*) To let oneself go, to drop all reserve. **town and gown** [GOWN]. **town adjutant, town major:** A garrison officer appointed to maintain discipline. **town-clerk,** *n.* The clerk to a municipal corporation; the keeper of the records of a town. **town-council,** *n.* The governing body in a town. **town-councillor,** *n.* **town-crier** [CRIER]. **town hall:** A large public building for the transaction of municipal business, public meetings, and entertainments, etc. **town house:** A private residence in town, opp. to country house. **town-planning,** *n.* The regulating of the laying out or extension of a town with a view to securing the greatest advantages for public health, convenience, attractiveness, etc. **town-planner,** *n.* **town-talk,** *n.* The subject of general conversation. **townee** (tou′ nē), *n.* (*Univ. slang*) An inhabitant of a University town not connected with the University. **townish,** *a.* **townless,** *a.* **townlet,** *n.* **townsfolk,** *n.pl.* (*collect.*) The people of a town or city. **township,** *n.* A division of a large parish, comprising a village or town; (*Hist.*) the inhabitants of a parish, village, etc., regarded as a corporate body; (*Am.*) a territorial district subordinate to a county invested with certain administrative powers; (*Austral.*) any town or settlement, however small. **townsman,** *n.* An inhabitant of a town; one's fellow citizen. **townspeople,** *n.pl.* (*collect.*) **townward,** *a.* and *adv.* **townwards,** *adv.*

towy [TOW (2)].

tox-, toxi-, toxico- [see TOXIC], *comb. form.* **toxæmia** (tok sē' mi ȧ) [Gr. *haima*, blood], *n.* Blood-poisoning. **toxanæmia** (-ȧ nē' mi ȧ), *n.* Anæmia due to blood-poisoning.

toxic (tok' sik) [med. L. *toxicus*, from L. *toxicum*, Gr. *toxikon* (*pharmation*), poisonous (drug for arrows), from *toxa*, pl., arrows, from *toxon*, bow], *a.* Of or pertaining to poison; poisonous. **toxically,** *adv.* **toxicant,** *a.* Poisonous; *n.* A poison. **toxication** (-kā' shŭn), *n.* **toxicity** (tok sis' i ti), *n.* **toxicology** (-kol' ȯ ji) [-LOGY], *n.* The branch of medicine treating of poisons and their antibodies. **toxicologist,** *n.* **toxicological** (-loj' i kȧl), *a.* **toxicologically,** *adv.* **toxicomania** (-mā' ni ȧ) [-MANIA], *n.* A morbid desire for poison. **toxicosis** (-kō' sis) [-OSIS], *n.* A morbid state due to the action of toxic matter. **toxiphobia** (-fō' bi ȧ) [-PHOBIA], *n.* Unreasonable fear of being poisoned.

toxin (tok' sin), *n.* A poisonous compound causing a particular disease; any poisonous ptomaine.

toxophilite (tok sof' i līt) [Gr. *toxon*, bow, -PHIL, -ITE], *n.* One skilled in or devoted to archery. *a.* Pertaining to archery. **toxophilitic** (-lit' ik), *a.*

toy (toi) [etym. doubtful], *n.* A plaything, esp. for a child; something of an amusing or trifling kind, not serious or for actual use. *v.i.* To trifle, to amuse oneself, to sport, to dally. **toy dog, spaniel,** or **terrier:** A pigmy variety of dog kept as a curiosity or pet. **toyman,** *n.* One who deals in toys. **toy-shop,** *n.* A shop where toys are sold. **toyer,** *n.* **toyingly,** *adv.* **toyish,** *a.* Toy-like; *trifling, wanton. ***toyishly,** *adv.* ***toyishness,** *n.* ***toysome,** *a.* Disposed to toy; wanton.

***toze** (tōz) [M.E. *tosen*, cogn. with TEASE], *v.t.* To pull apart, to unravel, to card (wool, etc.); (*fig.*) to search or find out; (*Tin-mining*) to separate tin-ore by stirring the slime.

tra- [TRANS-], *pref.* As in *tradition*, *travesty*.

trabeate, trabeated (trā' bė āt, -ĕd) [L. *trabs -bem*, beam, -ATE], *a.* (*Arch.*) Furnished with an entablature. **trabeation** (-ā' shŭn), *n.* **trabecula** (trȧ bek' ū lȧ), *n.* (*Anat.*) A band or bar of connective tissue, esp. one forming the framework of an organ; (*Bot.*) a beam-like projection, cross-bar, etc. **trabecular, trabeculate, trabeculated,** *a.*

trace (1) (trās) [M.E. and O.F. *trays*, pl. of TRAIT], *n.* One of the two straps, chains, or ropes by which a vehicle is drawn by horses, etc. **in the traces:** In harness.

trace (2) (trās) [F., from *tracer*, O.F. *tracier*, L. *tractus*, p.p. of *trahere*, to draw], *n.* A mark left by a person or animal walking or thing moving, a track, a trail, a footprint, a rut, etc. (*usu. in pl.*); a token, vestige, or sign of something that has existed or taken place; a minute quantity. *v.t.* To follow the traces or track of; to note the marks and vestiges of; to ascertain the position or course of; to pursue one's way along; to delineate, to mark out; to sketch out (a plan, scheme, etc.); to copy (a drawing, etc.) by marking the lines on transparent paper or linen laid upon it. **traceable,** *a.* **traceability** (-bil' i ti), **traceableness,** *n.* **traceably,** *adv.* **tracer,** *n.* One who makes traces; a trace-horse; (*Biol.*) an artificially produced radioactive isotope introduced into the human body where its course can be followed by its radiations. **tracer bullet, shell,** *n.* (*Artill.*) A bullet or shell whose course is marked by a smoke trail or a phosphorescent glow. **tracery,** *n.* Ornamental open-work in Gothic windows, etc.; any decorative work or natural markings resembling this. **traceried,** *a.* **tracing,** *n.* **tracing-paper, cloth, -linen,** *n.* A thin transparent paper or linen used for copying drawings, etc., by tracing.

trachea (trȧ kē' ȧ, trā' kė ȧ) [L., from Gr. *tracheia*, orig. fem. of *trachus*, rough], *n.* (*pl.* **-cheæ**) The windpipe, the air-passage from the larynx to the bronchi and lungs; one of the tubes by which air is conveyed from the exterior in insects and arachnids; (*Bot.*) a duct, a vessel. **tracheal, trachean, tracheate** (trā'-), *a.* **trachearian** (-âr' i ȧn), **tracheary** (trā'-), *a.* Belonging to the *Trachearia*, a division of arachnids having tracheæ; *n.* One of this division. **tracheo-,** *comb. form.* **tracheocele** [-CELE], *n.* A tumour in the trachea, an enlargement of the thyroid gland. **tracheotomy** (-ot' ȯ mi) [-TOMY], *n.* The operation of making an opening into the windpipe. **trachitis** (trȧ kī' tis), *n.* Inflammation of the trachea.

trachelo- [Gr. *trachēlos*, neck], *comb. form.* **trachelo-occipital** (trȧ kē' lō ok sip' i tȧl) [OCCIPITAL], *a.* Pertaining to or connecting the nape of the neck and the cciput.

trachle (tra*chl*), **trauchle** (traw*chl*) [Sc., etym. doubtful], *v.t.* To tire, to fatigue, to wear out; to distress. *n.* Fatiguing toil; a wearisome effort. **trachly,** *a.*

trachoma (trȧ kō' mȧ) [Gr., roughness, from *trachus*, rough], *n.* (*Path.*) A disease of the eye characterized by papillary or granular excrescences on the inner surface of the lids.

trachyte (trăk' īt) [Gr. *trachutēs*, roughness, as prec.], *n.* A gritty-surfaced volcanic rock containing glassy feldspar crystals. **trachytic** (trȧ kit' ik), *a.*

tracing, etc. [TRACE (2)].

track (trăk) [O.F. *trac*, prob. from Teut. (cp. Dut. *treck*, TREK, from *trekken*, to pull)], *n.* A series of marks left by the passage of a person, animal, or thing, a trail; a series of footprints (*usu. in pl.*); a path, esp. one not constructed but beaten by use; a course, the route followed by ships, etc.; a race-course, a racing-path; a set of rails, a monorail, or a line of railway with single or double tracks; (*Am.*) a railway line; the groove in a gramophone record in which the needle travels; (*Mach.*) the endless band on which a tractor propels itself. *v.t.* To follow the track or traces of; to trace, to follow out (the course of anything); to tow. **beaten track,** *n.* The usual method; the ordinary way. **to make tracks:** To run away, to bolt, to decamp. **to track down:** To discover by tracking. **trackage,** *n.* (*collect.*) Railway-tracks; the right to use the tracks of another company; towage. **track-clearer,** *n.* A device fixed to an engine, car, mowing-machine, etc., for clearing the track in front and behind. **tracker,** *n.* **track-layer:** (*Am.*) A plate-layer. **trackless,** *a.* Pathless, unmarked by feet; untrodden, untravelled, leaving no track. **tracklessly,** *adv.* **tracklessness,** *n.*

tract (1) (trăkt) [L. *tractus -tūs*, from *trahere*, to draw, p.p. *tractus*], *n.* A region or area of land or water of a considerable but undefined extent; (*Anat.*) the region of an organ or system; a period (of time).

tract (2) (trăkt) [short for TRACTATE], *n.* A short treatise or pamphlet, esp. on religion or morals; (*R.-C. Ch.*) an anthem sung in place of the Alleluia.

tractable (trăk' tȧbl) [L. *tractābilus*, from *tractāre*, to TREAT], *a.* That may be easily led, managed, or controlled; docile, manageable. **tractability** (-bil' i ti), *n.* **tractableness,** *n.* **tractably,** *adv.*

Tractarian (trăk târ' i ȧn), *n.* One of the authors of 'Tracts for the Times' (1833–41) enunciating the principles of the Oxford Movement; an adherent of this, a High Churchman. *a.* Pertaining to Tractarianism. **Tractarianism,** *n.* Reaction towards primitive Catholicism and against rationalism, as taught by the Tractarians.

tractate (trăk' tāt) [L. *tractātus*, orig. p.p. of *tractāre*, to TREAT], *n.* A treatise.

tractile (trăk' tīl), *a.* Capable of being drawn out.

traction (trăk' shŭn) [F., from L. *tractiōnem*, nom. *-tio*, from *trahere*, to draw, p.p. *tractus*], *n.* The act of drawing something along a surface; the state of being so drawn; contraction. **traction-engine,** *n.* A locomotive for drawing heavy loads on ordinary roads. **traction-wheel,** *n.* The wheel to which the force is applied in a locomotive, etc. **tractional,** *a.*

tractor (trăk′ tȯr), *n.* A self-propelling vehicle capable of drawing other vehicles, farm implements, etc. **tractor plane,** *n.* An aeroplane propelled by an airscrew designed to pull on its shaft. **tractor plough,** *n.* (*Agric.*) A plough with not more than five shares or coulters drawn by a tractor.

trade (trād) [M.L.G., track, cogn. with TREAD], *n.* A business, handicraft, or mechanical or mercantile occupation carried on for subsistence or profit, distinguished from agriculture, unskilled labour, the professions, etc.; the exchange of commodities, buying and selling, commerce; the amount of business done in a particular year, place, etc.; (*collect.*) persons engaged in a particular trade; (*colloq.*) a deal, a bargain (in business or politics); (*pl.*) the trade-winds; a track, a path, a way. *v.i.* To buy and sell, to barter, to exchange, to traffic, to deal (in); to carry on commerce or business (with); to carry merchandise (between, etc.); to buy and sell (political influence, patronage, etc.) corruptly. *v.t.* To sell or exchange in commerce, to barter. **to trade in:** To give in part payment. **to trade on:** To take advantage of. **Board of Trade:** A government department dealing with commercial and industrial affairs. **domestic** or **home trade:** That carried on within a country. **foreign trade:** Interchange of commodities by importation or exportation with other countries. **the Trade,** *n.* The brewing industry. **trade cycle,** *n.* (*Comm.*) The recurrent alternation of prosperity and depression in trade. **trade-hall,** *n.* A hall for the meetings of a trade-guild, etc. **trade-mark,** *n.* A registered symbol or name used by a manufacturer or merchant to guarantee the genuineness of goods. **trade name:** The name by which an article is called in the trade; the name of a proprietary article. **trade-price:** The price charged to dealers for articles to be sold again. **trade show,** *n.* (*Cinema.*) Advance show of a film to exhibitors and critics. **tradesman,** *n.* A retail dealer, a shopkeeper; a craftsman. **tradespeople,** *n.* (*collect.*) People engaged in trades, tradesmen and their families. **trade union,** *n.* An organized body of workmen in any trade, formed for the promotion and protection of their common interests. **trade-unionism,** *n.* **trade-unionist,** *n.* **trade-wind,** *n.* A wind blowing from the north or south toward the thermal equator and deflected in a westerly direction by the easterly rotation of the earth; (*pl.*) these and the anti-trades. ***traded,** *a.* (*Shak.*) Practised, versed, skilled. ***tradeful,** *a.* Busy in traffic, commercial. **tradeless,** *a.* **trader,** *n.* A person engaged in trade; a merchant, a tradesman; a vessel employed in trade.

tradition (trȧ dish′ ŭn) [M.E. and O.F. *tradicion*, L. *trāditiōnem*, nom. *-tio*, from *trādere*, to hand over], *n.* The handing down of opinions, practices, customs, etc., from ancestors to posterity, esp. by oral communication; a belief, custom, etc., so handed down; (*Theol.*) a doctrine believed to have divine authority but not found in Scripture, as the oral law said to have been given by God to Moses on Mount Sinai, the oral teaching of Christ not recorded in the New Testament; the acts and sayings of Mohammed not recorded in the Koran; (*Lit., Art, etc.*) the principles, maxims, etc., derived from the usage and experience of artists, dramatists, actors, etc.; (*Law*) formal delivery (of property). **traditional, traditionary, *traditive** (trăd′ i tiv), *a.* **traditionalism,** *n.* Adherence to tradition, esp. superstitious regard to tradition in religious matters; a philosophic system attributing human knowledge, esp. of religion and ethics, to revelation and tradition. **traditionalist, traditionist, *traditioner,** *n.* **traditionalistic** (-lis′ tik), *a.* **traditionally,** *adv.*

traditor (trăd′ i tȯr) [L., from *trādere*, see prec.], *n.* One of the early Christians who, to save their lives, gave up copies of the Scriptures or the goods of the Church to the persecutors.

traduce (trȧ dūs′) [L. *tradūcere* (TRA-, *dūcere*, to lead)], *v.t.* To defame, to calumniate, to misrepresent. **traducement,** *n.* **traducer,** *n.* **traducible,** *a.* **traducingly,** *adv.*

traducianist (trȧ dū′ shȧn ist) [late L. *trāduciānus*, from *trādux -ducis*, layer, shoot, as prec.], *n.* One who held that souls were transmitted by parents to children. **traducianism,** *n.*

traduction (trȧ dŭk′ shŭn) [O.F., from L. *trāductiōnem*, nom. *-tio*, as prec.], *n.* (*Log.*) The transference of conclusions from one order of reasoning or classification to another; *translation, a translation; *derivation or transmission by descent, propagation; traducement. **traductive,** *a.*

traffic (trăf′ ik) [F. *trafique* (*trafiquer*, to traffic), It. *traffico*, from *trafficare*, to traffic, etym. doubtful], *n.* The exchange of goods by barter or by the medium of money; trade, commerce; the trade (in a particular commodity, etc.); the transportation of persons, animals, or goods by road, rail, sea or air; the passing to and fro of persons, vehicles, etc., on a road, etc.; amount of goods or number of persons conveyed; *intercourse, dealings (with). *v.i.* (*p.p.* **trafficked,** *pres.p.* **trafficking**) To trade, to buy and sell goods, to have business (with). *v.t.* To barter. **traffic circle,** *n.* (*Am.*) A roundabout. **traffic lights,** *n.pl.* Coloured lights at street intersections to control the flow and direction of traffic. **trafficker,** *n.* **trafficless,** *a.*

trafficator (trăf′ i kā tȯr), *n.* (*Motor.*) Movable arm or flashing light on a car that indicates the driver's intention to turn to right or left.

tragacanth (trăg′ ȧ kănth) [F. *tragacanthe*, L. *tragacantha*, Gr. *tragakantha* (*tragos*, goat, ACANTHUS)], *n.* A whitish or reddish demulcent gum obtained from species of *Astragalus*, used in pharmacy, calico-printing, etc.; a low, spiny, leguminous shrub of this genus growing in S.W. Asia.

tragedian (trȧ jē′ di ȧn), *n.* A writer of tragedies; an actor in tragedy. **tragedienne** (trȧ jē di en′), *n.* An actress of tragedy.

tragedy (trăj′ ė di) [M.E. and O.F. *tragedie*, L. *tragœdia*, Gr. *tragōidia*, prob. *goat-song* (*tragos*, he-goat, *ōdē*, see ODE)], *n.* A drama in verse or elevated prose dealing with a lofty theme of a sad, pathetic, or terrible kind, usu. with an unhappy ending; tragedy personified, the Muse of Tragedy; a fatal or calamitous event, esp. a murder or fatal accident with dramatic accompaniments. **tragic, -al** (trăj′ ik, -ȧl), *a.* Of the nature or in the style of tragedy; characterized by loss of life; lamentable, sad, calamitous. **tragically,** *adv.* **tragicality, tragicalness,** *n.* **tragi-comedy** (-kom′ ė di), *n.* A drama in which tragic and comic scenes or features are mingled. **tragi-comic, -al,** *a.* **tragi-comicality,** *n.* **tragi-comically,** *adv.*

tragelaph (trăg′ ė lăf), **tragelaphus** (tra gel′ ȧ fŭs) [L. *tragelaphus*, Gr. *tragelaphos* (*tragos*, he-goat, *elaphos*, deer)], *n.* (*Myth.*) A fabulous animal, half goat, half stag; (*Zool.*) a genus of S. African antelopes, an animal of this genus. **tragelaphine** (-gel′ ȧ fīn), *a.*

tragic, tragi-comedy, etc. [TRAGEDY].

tragule (trăg′ ūl) [mod. L. *tragulus*, dim. of *tragus*, Gr. *tragos*, he-goat], *n.* A ruminant of the genus *Tragulus*, a chevrotain. **traguline** (-līn), *a.*

tragus (trā′ gŭs) [L., see prec.], *n.* (*pl.* **-gi,** -jī) (*Anat.*) A small process on the front of the orifice in the external ear.

traik (trāk) [Sc., etym. doubtful], *v.i.* To roam, to wander, to stray; to follow (after); to decline in health. *n.* A misfortune.

trail (trāl) [M.E. *trailen*, prob. from O.F. *trailler*, to tow, prob. ult. from L. *trāgula*, drag-net, sledge, from *trahere*, to draw], *v.t.* To drag along behind, esp. along the ground; to follow by the track or trail; to carry (a rifle, etc.) in a horizontal or oblique position in the right hand with the arm extended; to tread down (grass) to make a path.

v.i. To be dragged along behind, to hang down loosely or grow to some length along the ground, over a wall, etc. *n.* Anything trailing behind a moving thing, a train, a floating appendage, etc.; the end of a gun-carriage resting on the ground when the gun is unlimbered; a track left by an animal, etc.; the scent followed in hunting; a beaten track through forest or wild country. **trail-net,** *n.* A drag-net. **trailing edge,** *n.* (*Aviat.*) The rear edge of a streamlined body, or of a control surface.

trailer (trā′ lėr), *n.* One who or that which trails; a trailing plant; a light car, usu. two-wheeled, drawn behind a bicycle, etc.; any vehicle, sled, etc., drawn behind another; (*Am.*) a caravan; (*Cinema.*) a short film giving advance publicity to a forthcoming production.

train (trān) [F. *train*, m., retinue, series, and *traîne*, f., that which is trailed, from *traîner*, ult. from L. *trahere*, to draw], *n.* That which is drawn or dragged along behind; an extended part of a gown, robe, etc., trailing behind the wearer; the tail of a comet; a long trailing tail or tail-feathers of a bird; the trail of a gun-carriage; a retinue, a suite; a line or long series or succession of persons or things; a series of railway carriages or trucks drawn by an engine; a line of combustible material leading fire to a charge or mine; a set of wheels, pinions, etc., transmitting motion; process, orderly succession, progressive condition. *v.t.* To bring to a state of proficiency by prolonged instruction, practice, etc.; to instruct, to drill, to accustom (to perform certain acts or feats); to prepare by diet and exercise (for a race, etc.); to bring (a plant, etc.) by pruning, manipulation, etc., into a desired shape, position, etc.; to bring to bear, to aim (a cannon upon); *to entice, to allure (away, etc.); *to drag or draw along. *v.t.* To prepare oneself or come into a state of efficiency for (a race, match, etc.); to go by train. **to train fine:** To bring or be brought to a fine pitch of efficiency by training. **train of artillery:** A siege-train. **train-, trained-band,** *n.* A company of citizen soldiers organized at various dates during the 16th–18th cent. **train-bearer,** *n.* An attendant employed to hold up the train of a robe, etc. **train ferry,** *n.* (*Rail.*) A ferry on to which a train is run to be conveyed across water to a track on the farther side. **train-mile,** *n.* A mile travelled by a train, the unit of work in railway statistics. **trainable,** *a.* **trainee,** *n.* A person undergoing training. **trainer,** *n.* One who trains; esp. one who prepares men, horses, etc., for races, etc. **training,** *n.* **training-college, -school,** *n.* One for training teachers. **training-ship,** *n.* A ship for instructing boys in navigation, seamanship, etc.

train-oil (trān′ oil) [formerly *train*, *trane*, M.L.G, *trān*, M.Dut. *traen* (Dut. *traan*), orig. tear, resin], *n.* Oil obtained from the blubber or fat of whales.

traipse [TRAPES].

trait (trā, *Am.* trāt) [F., orig. p.p. of *traire*, L. *trahere*, to draw, p.p. *tractus*], *n.* A distinguishing or peculiar feature; a stroke, a touch (of).

traitor (trā′ tȯr) [M.E. and O.F. *traitre* (A.-F. and O.F. *traitour*, acc.), L. *trāditōrem*, nom. *-tor*, from *trādere*, to hand over (TRA-, *-dere*, *dare*, to give)], *n.* One who violates his allegiance; one guilty of disloyalty, treason, or treachery. **a.* Traitorous. **traitorous, *traitorly,** *a.* **traitorously,** *adv.* **traitorousness,** *n.* **traitress,** *n.*

trajectory (tră jek′ tȯr i) [L. *trājectus*, p.p. of *trājicere* (TRA-, *jacere*, to throw), -ORY], *n.* The path described by a body, comet, projectile, etc., under the action of given forces; a curve or surface cutting the curves or surfaces of a given system at a constant angle. ***traject** (tră jekt′), *v.t.* To transmit; to transport. *n.* (trăj′ ėkt) A ferry. ***trajection,** *n.*

tram (1) (trăm) [cp. L.G. *traam*, balk, beam, G. *trumm*, lump, slump, Norw. *tram*, door-step, Swed. dial. *tromm*, log], *n.* The shaft of a cart, wagon, or truck; a four-wheeled truck or car used in coal-mines; a line of beams or rails, a pair of which form a tramway; a tramway, a tram-car. *v.t.* (*past & p.p.* **trammed**) To convey or perform (a journey) in a tram-car. *v.i.* To go in a tram-car. **tram-car, *tramway-car,** *n.* **tram-line, tramway,** *n.* A street railway on which passenger-cars are drawn by horses, or by electricity, steam, or other mechanical power. **tram-road,** *n.* A road laid with tracks of timber, stone, or iron.

tram (2) (trăm) [M.F. *trame*, It. *trama*, L. *trāma*, weft], *n.* Silk thread made up of two or more strands twisted together, used for the weft of the finer kinds of silk goods.

tram-line, etc. [TRAM (1)].

trammel (trăm′ ėl) [M.E. *tramayle*, M.F. *tramail* (F. *trémail*), pop. L. *tramaculum*, *-la* (perh. TRI-, *macula*, mesh)], *n.* A net of various forms for catching fish, esp. a trammel-net; a shackle or fetter, esp. one used in teaching a horse to amble; a hook in a fire-place for pots, kettles, etc.; an instrument for drawing ellipses; a beam-compass; (*fig.*) anything restraining freedom or activity (usu. in *pl.*). *v.t.* (*past & p.p.* **trammelled**) To confine, to hamper, to restrict. **trammel-net,** *n.* A net formed by a combination of three seines, in which fish become entangled. **trammelled,** *a.* Confined, hampered; with white marks on the feet of one side (of a horse). **cross-trammelled,** *a.* With fore and hind feet so marked but on opposite sides. **trammeller,** *n.*

tramontane (tră mon′ tân, trăm on tān′) [It. *tramontana* (perh. through F.), L. *transmontānus* (TRANS-, *mons montis*, MOUNT)], *a.* Lying, situated, or coming from beyond the Alps (as seen from Italy); hence, foreign, barbarous. *n.* A tramontane person; the tramontana. **tramontana** (tra mon ta′ nâ), *n.* A name for the north wind in the Mediterranean; a cold and blighting wind in the Greek Archipelago.

tramp (trămp) [M.E., L.G., and G. *trampen*, cp. Dan. *trampe*, Swed. and Norw. *trampa*], *v.i.* To walk or tread heavily; to walk, to go on foot. *v.t.* To tread heavily on, to trample; to go over or traverse, or to perform (a journey, etc.) on foot; to hike. *n.* An act of tramping, the tread of persons, etc., walking or marching; the sound of this; a walk, a journey on foot; an itinerant beggar, a vagrant; (*Am. slang*) a harlot; a freight-vessel having no regular line; an iron plate worn to protect the sole of the boot in digging. **tramper,** *n.*

trample (trăm′ pėl) [freq. of TRAMP], *v.t.* To tread under foot, esp. in scorn, triumph, etc.; to tread down, to crush thus; (*fig.*) to treat with arrogance or contemptuous indifference. *v.i.* To tread heavily (on); (*fig.*) to tread (on) in contempt. *n.* The act or sound of trampling. **trampler,** *n.*

tran- [TRANS- before *s*], *pref.*

trance (trans) [O.F. *transe*, from *transir*, to depart, to die, to be numbed, L. *transīre* (TRANS-, *īre*, to go)], *n.* A state in which the soul seems to have passed into another state of being; ecstasy, rapture; a state of insensibility to external surroundings with suspension of some of the vital functions, catalepsy; the hypnotic state. *v.t.* (*poet.*) To entrance, to enchant. **trancedly** (tran′ sėd li), *adv.*

traneen (tră nēn′) [Ir. *traithnin*], *n.* The *Cynosurus cristatus*, crested dog's-tail grass. **not worth a traneen:** Not worth a rush.

trank (trăngk) [perh. from F. *tranche*, cutting], *n.* An oblong piece of skin from which the parts of a glove are cut.

tranquil (trăng′ kwil) [F. *tranquille*, L. *tranquillus*], *a.* Calm, peaceful, serene, quiet, undisturbed. **tranquillity** (-kwil′ i ti), **tranquilness,** *n.* **tranquillize,** *v.t.* **tranquillization** (-zā′ shŭn), *n.* **tranquillizer,** *n.* That which makes tranquil; (*Med.*) a sedative drug. **tranquillizingly,** *adv.* **tranquilly,** *adv.*

trans- [L., across, over, cross-wise; beyond, on or to the other side (of); through; into another state or place], *pref.*

transact (trăn zăkt′, -săkt′) [L. *transactus*, p.p. of *transigere* (TRANS-, *agere*, to act)], *v.t.* To do, to perform, to manage, to carry out. *v.i.* To do business, to conduct matters (with). **transaction,** *n.* The management or carrying out of a piece of business, etc.; that which has been transacted, a piece of business, an affair, a proceeding; (*pl.*) the reports of the proceedings of learned societies; (*Law*) adjustment of a dispute by mutual concessions, etc. **transactor,** *n.*

transalpine (trăn zăl′ pin, -pīn), *a.* Lying or situated beyond the Alps (usu. as seen from Italy). *n.* A person living beyond the Alps. **transatlantic** (trănz ȧt lăn′ tik), *a.* Lying or being beyond the Atlantic; crossing the Atlantic.

transcend (trăn send′) [O.F. *transcender*, L. *transcendere* (TRAN-, *scandere*, to climb)], *v.t.* and *i.* To rise above, to surpass, to excel, to exceed; to pass or be beyond the range, sphere, or power (of human understanding, etc.).

transcendent (trăn send′ ėnt), *a.* Excelling, surpassing, supremely excellent; (*Scholastic Phil.*) applied to concepts higher or of wider signification than the categories of Aristotle; (*Kantian Phil.*) beyond the sphere of knowledge or experience; above and independent of the material universe. *n.* That which is transcendent. **transcendence, -dency,** *n.*

transcendental (trăn sen den′ tȧl), *a.* (*Kant.*) Transcendent, beyond the sphere of experience; belonging to the a priori elements of experience, implied in and necessary to experience; explaining matter and the universe as products of mental conception; transcending ordinary ideas; abstruse, speculative, vague, obscure; (*Math.*) not capable of being produced by the fundamental operations of algebra, addition, multiplication, etc. *n.* A transcendent concept. **transcendentalism,** *n.* The state of being transcendental; a transcendental philosophy, as that of Schelling. **transcendentalist,** *n.* **transcendentally,** *adv.*

transcontinental (trănz kon ti nen′ tȧl), *a.* Extending or travelling across a continent.

transcribe (trăn skrīb′) [L. *transcrībere* (TRAN-, *scrībere*, p.p. *scriptus*)], *v.t.* To copy in writing, to write out in full (shorthand notes, etc.); (*Radio.*) to record for broadcasting. **transcriber,** *n.* **transcript** (trăn′ skript), *n.* A written copy. **transcription** (-skrip′ shŭn), *n.* What is transcribed; (*Mus.*) the arrangement of a vocal composition for an instrument, or the readjustment of a composition for another instrument. **transcriptional, transcriptive,** *a.*

transcurrent (trănz kŭr′ ėnt) [L. *transcurrens -ntem*, pres.p. of *transcurrere* (TRANS-, *currere*, to run)], *a.* Running or passing across or transversely. **transducer** (tranz du′ ser), *n.* (*Elec.*) A power-transforming device for which the input and output are of different kinds, electrical, acoustic, optical, etc., *e.g.* loudspeaker, microphone, photoelectric cell, etc. ***transduction** (trănz dŭk′ shŭn) [L. *transductio*, from *trans-* (*dūcere*, to lead)], *n.* A carrying or leading across. **transductor,** *n.* That which carries or leads across; (*Anat.*) a muscle of the great toe. **transect** (trăn′ sekt) [as SECT (2)], *v.t.* To cut across; (*Anat.*) to dissect transversely. **transection** (-sek′ shŭn), *n.*

transenna (trăn sen′ ȧ) [L., grating, lattice], *n.* A metal or stone lattice, etc., enclosing a shrine.

transept (trăn′ sept) [TRAN-, SEPTUM], *n.* Either of the transverse arms extending north and south in a cruciform church.

transfer (trăns fĕr′) [L. *transferre* (TRANS-, *ferre*, to bear)], *v.t.* (*past & p.p.* **transferred**) To convey, remove, or shift from one place or person to another; to make over the possession of; to convey (a design, etc.) from one surface to another, esp. in lithography; to remove (a picture, etc.) from a wall, etc., to canvas or other surface. *n.* (trăns′ fėr) The removal or conveyance of a thing from one person or place to another; (*Law*) the act of conveying a right, property, etc., from one person to another; the deed by which this is effected; that which is transferred; a design conveyed or to be conveyed from paper, etc., to some other surface; a soldier transferred from one regiment, troop, etc., to another. **transfer-book,** *n.* A register of transfers of stocks, shares, etc. **transfer-day,** *n.* An official day for the transfer of consols, etc., at the Bank of England. **transfer-ink,** *n.* Lithographic ink for transferable drawing, writing, etc., on lithographic stone, transfer-paper, etc. **transfer-paper,** *n.* Prepared paper for receiving impressions and transferring to stone. **transferable** (trăns′ fėr-, trăns fĕr′ ȧbl), *a.* **transferability** (-bil′ i ti), *n.* **transferee** (trăns fė rē′), *n.* **transference** (trăns′-), *n.* **transferrer** (-fĕr′ ėr), *n.* **transferential** (-en′ shȧl), *a.*

transfiguration (trăns fig ū rā′ shŭn) [F., from L. *transfigūrātiōnem*, nom. *-tio*, from *transfigūrāre* (TRANS- *figūrāre*, to change the figure of, from *figūra*, figure)], *n.* A change of form or appearance, esp. that of Christ on the Mount (Matt. xvii. 1–9); a festival on 6 Aug. in commemoration of this. **transfigure,** *v.t.* To change the outward appearance of, esp. so as to elevate and glorify.

transfix (trăns fiks′) [L. *transfixus*, p.p. of *transfīgere* (TRANS-, *fīgere*, to fix)], *v.t.* To pierce through, to impale. **transfixion,** *n.* The act of transfixing; (*Surg.*) amputation by piercing and cutting outwards.

***transfluent** (trăns floo′ ėnt) [L. *transfluens -ntem*, pres.p. of *transfluere* (TRANS-, *fluere*, to flow)], *a.* Flowing across or through, esp. (*Her.*) of water represented as flowing through a bridge.

transform (trăns fôrm′) [F. *transformer*, L. *transformāre* (TRANS-, *formāre*, to form)], *v.t.* To change the form, shape, or appearance of, to metamorphose; to change in disposition, character, etc. **transformable,** *a.* **transformative,** *a.*

transformation (trăns fôr mā′ shŭn), *n.* The act of transforming; the state of being transformed, a metamorphosis, a transmutation; (*Phys.*) a change from solid to liquid or liquid to gaseous form or the reverse; (*Math.*) the change of a figure or expression with another equivalent to it; (*Physiol.*) the change in the blood in its passage through the capillaries of the vascular system; (*Path.*) a morbid change of tissue into a form not proper to that particular part. **transformation-scene,** *n.* A scene in a pantomime in which the principal characters are supposed to be transformed into the chief characters of the harlequinade.

transformer (trăns fôrm′ ėr), *n.* One or that which transforms; (*Elec.*) a device which changes the current and voltage of an alternating electrical supply. The product of current and voltage remains almost unchanged.

transformism (trăns′ fôrm izm), *n.* The theory of the development of one species from another; the theory that complex animals were developed from organisms originally free, united into a colony and then into organs of a differentiated whole. **transformist,** *n.* **transformistic** (-mis′ tik), *a.*

trans-frontier (trăns frŭn′-, -fron′-, -tēr) [TRANS-, FRONTIER], *a.* Situated, living, or done beyond the frontier.

transfuse (trăns fūz′) [L. *transfūsus*, p.p. of *transfundere* (TRANS-, *fundere*, to pour)], *v.t.* To cause to pass from one vessel, etc., into another; (*Med.*) to transfer (blood) from the veins of one person or animal to those of another; to inject (a liquid) into a blood-vessel or cavity to replace loss or wastage. ***transfusible,** *a.* **transfusion** (-fū′ zhŭn), *n.* **transfusionist,** *n.* **transfusive** (-fū′ siv), *a.*

transgress (trăns-, trănz gres′) [L. *transgressus*, p.p. of *transgredī* (TRANS-, *gradī*, to walk)], *v.t.* To break, to violate, to infringe. *v.i.* To offend by violating a law or rule, to sin. **transgression** (-gresh′ ŭn), *n.* **transgressive,** *a.* **transgressively,** *adv.* **transgressor,** *n.*

tranship (tran ship′) [TRAN-, SHIP], *v.t.* To transfer from one ship, vehicle, etc., to another. **transhipment,** *n.*

***transhuman** (trănz hū′ mȧn) [TRANS-, HUMAN], *a.* Superhuman. **transhumanize,** *v.t.* **transhumanation** (-nā′ shŭn), *n.*

transhume (trănz hūm′) [TRANS-, L. *humus*, ground], *v.t.i.* To move to or from winter to summer or summer to winter pastures. **transhumance,** *n.*

transient (trăn′ si ėnt, -zi ėnt, -shėnt) [L. *transiens*, pres.p. of *transīre* (TRANS-, *īre*, to go)], *a.* Not lasting or durable; transitory, momentary, hasty, brief; (*Mus.*) passing, serving merely to connect or introduce; (*Am.*) (of a hotel guest) staying one night only. **transience, -ency, transientness,** *n.* **transiently,** *adv.*

***transilient** (trăn sil′ i ėnt) [L. *transiliens -ntem*, pres.p. of *transilīre* (TRAN-, *salīre*, to leap)], *a.* Springing or extending across, spanning. ***transilience,** *n.* An abrupt transition.

transilluminate (trăns i lū′ mi nāt), *v.t.* (*Med.*) To send a powerful light through an organ or part in diagnosis. **transillumination** (-nā′ shŭn), *n.*

transire (trăn sīr′ ē) [L., TRANS-, *īre*, to go], *n.* A custom-house warrant authorizing the removal of dutiable goods.

transistor (trăn zis′ tor), *n.* A device made primarily of a semi-conductor (germanium or silicon) capable of giving current and power amplification. It has uses similar to a thermionic triode.

trans-isthmian (trănz is′-, ist′ mi ȧn), *a.* Extending across an isthmus.

transit (trăn′ sit) [L. *transitus -tūs*, from *transīre*, see TRANSIRE], *n.* The act of passing, conveying, or being conveyed, across, over, or through; conveyance; a line of passage, a route; (*Astron.*) the apparent passage of a heavenly body over the meridian of a place; the passage of a heavenly body across the disk of another, esp. of Venus or Mercury across the sun's disk; a transit-compass or instrument. *v.t.* To pass across the disk (of the sun, etc.). **transit-circle, -instrument,** *n.* An instrument for observing transits across a meridian. **transit-compass,** *n.* A surveying instrument for measuring horizontal angles. **transit-duty,** *n.* Duty paid upon goods passing through a country.

transition (trăn sizh′ ŭn), *n.* Passage or change from one place, state, or action to another; a change in architecture, painting, literature, etc.; (*Mus.*) a change from one key to another or from the major to the relative minor; (*Rhet.*) a passing from one subject to another. **transition stage** or **period,** *n.* The stage or period of transition in art, etc. **transitional, -ary,** *a.* **transitionally,** *adv.*

transitive (trăn′ si tiv) [late L. *transitivus*], *a.* (*Gram.*) Expressing an action passing over from a subject to an object, having a direct object (of verbs). **transitively,** *adv.* **transitiveness,** *n.*

transitory (trăn′ si tŏr i) [O.F. *transitoire*, late L. *transitōrius*, as prec.], *a.* Lasting but a short time, transient, not durable, short-lived. **transitorily,** *adv.* **transitoriness,** *n.*

translate (trăn slāt′) [O.F. *translater*, L. *translātus*, p.p. of *transferre*, to TRANSFER], *v.t.* To render or express the sense of (a word, passage, or work) into or in another language; (*fig.*) to interpret, to express in clearer terms; to express, paraphrase, or convey (an idea, etc.) from one art or style into another; to remove from one office to another (esp. a bishop to another see); to convey to heaven without death; *to transform; (*Mech.*) to move (a body) so that all parts follow the same direction, to give motion without rotation; (*Teleg.*) to retransmit (a message); *to transport, to enrapture. *v.i.* To be engaged in translation. **translatable,** *a.* **translation** (-lā′ shŭn), *n.* **translational,** *a.* **translator,** *n.* **translatory,** *a.* **translatress,** *n.*

Trans-Leithan (trans lī′ thȧn) [TRANS-, *Leitha*, tributary of Danube, part of boundary between Austria and Hungary], *a.* Hungarian or Magyar, opp. to cis-Leithan.

transliterate (trăns lit′ ėr āt) [TRANS-, L. *litera*, LETTER], *v.t.* To represent (words, sounds, etc.) in the corresponding or approximately corresponding characters of another language. **transliteration** (-ā′ shŭn), *n.* **transliterator** (trăns lit′ ėr ā tŏr), *n.*

translucent (trăns lū′ sėnt) [L. *translūcens -ntem*, pres.p. of *translūcēre* (TRANS-, *lūcēre*, to shine, see LUCID)], *a.* Allowing light to pass through but not transparent; (*loosely*) transparent. **translucence -cency,** *n.* ***translucid,** *a.*

translunary (trănz lū′ nȧ ri) [TRANS-, LUNARY], *a.* Situated beyond the moon, opp. to sublunary; (*fig.*) ethereal, visionary. **transmarine** (trănz mȧ rēn′) [MARINE], *a.* Situated beyond the sea. ***transmew** [TRANSMUTE].

transmigrate (trănz′ mi grāt, -mī′ grāt) [L. *transmigrātus*, p.p. of *transmigrāre* (TRANS-, MIGRATE)], *v.i.* To pass from one body into another (of the soul), to undergo metempsychosis; to pass from one place, country, or jurisdiction to another, to migrate. **transmigrant,** *n.* One who transmigrates, a migrant; an alien passing through one country on the way to another. **transmigrant,** *a.* **transmigration** (-grā′ shŭn), *n.* **transmigrationism,** *n.* The doctrine of metempsychosis. **transmigrator** (trănz′ mi grā tŏr), *n.* **transmigratory** (trănz mī′ grȧ tŏr i), *a.*

transmit (trănz mit′) [L. *transmittere* (TRANS-, *mittere*, to send)], *v.t.* (*past & p.p.* **transmitted**) To send, transfer, convey, or communicate from one person or place to another; to suffer to pass through, to act as a medium for, to conduct. **transmissible, *-mittable,** *a.* **transmissibility** (-bil′ i ti), *n.* **transmission** (-mish′ ŭn), *n.* The act of transmitting; (*Elec.*) the conveying of electrical energy from place to place; (*Radio.*) the radiation of ether waves; signals sent out by a transmitter; (*Motor.*) the gear by which power is conveyed from the engine to the live axle. **transmissive** (-mis′ iv), *a.* **transmitter,** *n.* A person or thing that transmits: (*Elec.*) any form of machine that transmits telegraphic messages; (*Radio.*) the apparatus required for radiating a signal.

transmogrify (trănz mog′ ri fī) [TRANS-, *mogrify*, appar. an arbitrary coinage], *v.t.* (*colloq.*) To transform, esp. as if by magical means. **transmogrification** (-kā′ shŭn), *n.*

transmontane (trănz mon′ tān, trănz mon tān′), *a.* Situated beyond the mountains; tramontane.

***transmove** (trănz moov′), *v.t.* To transform, to transmute.

transmute (trănz mūt′) [L. *transmūtāre* (TRANS-, *mūtāre*, to change)], *v.t.* To change from one form, nature, or substance into another; to transform (into). **transmutable,** *a.* **transmutability** (-bil′ i ti), *n.* **transmutably,** *adv.* **transmutative,** *a.* **transmuter,** *n.*

transmutation (trăns mū tā′ shŭn), *n.* The act of transmuting; the state of being transmuted; (*Alch.*) the change of base metals into gold or silver; (*Biol.*) the change of one species into another; (*Geom.*) the reduction of one figure or body into another of the same area or content. **transmutationist,** *n.* One who believes in the transmutation of species. **transmutative** (-mū′ tȧ tiv), *a.* **transmuter,** *n.*

transnormal (trănz nôr′ mȧl) [TRANS-, NORMAL], *a.* Beyond what is normal. **transoceanic** (-ō shė ăn′ ik) [OCEANIC], *a.* Situated or coming from beyond the ocean; crossing the ocean.

transom (trăn′ sŏm) [M.E. *traunsum*, prob. corr. of L. *transtrum*, from *trans*, see TRANS-], *n.* A horizontal bar of wood or stone across a window or other opening; a horizontal bar across the top of a doorway separating it from the fan-light; (*Am.*) a fanlight; one of the beams bolted across the stern-post of a ship, supporting the after-end of the deck; a horizontal piece connecting the cheeks of a gun-carriage; a beam across a saw-pit; the vane of a cross-staff. **transom-window,** *n.* A window divided by a transom; a window over the transom of a door. **transomed,** *a.*

transpadane (trăns′ pȧ dān) [L. *transpadānus* (TRANS-, *Padus*, Po)], *a.* Situated beyond the River Po (from Rome).

transparency (trăns păr′ ėn si), *n.* Transparentness; a thing that is transparent, esp. a picture, inscription, photograph, etc., painted on glass, muslin, or other transparent or semi-transparent material, to be exhibited by means of light shining through it.

transparent (trăns pâr′ ėnt) [F., from med. L. *transpārentum*, nom. *-ens*, pres.p. of *transpārēre* (TRANS-, *pārēre*, to appear)], *a.* Having the property of transmitting rays of light without diffusion, so that objects may be distinctly seen through; (*fig.*) easily seen through; plain, evident, clear; frank, sincere. **transparence, transparentness,** *n.* **transparently,** *adv.* ***transpicuous** (trăn spik′ ū ŭs), *a.* Transparent.

transpierce (trăns pērs′), *v.t.* To pierce through.

transpire (trăn spīr′) [TRAN-, L. *spīrāre*, to breathe], *v.t.* To emit through the excretory organs (of the skin or lungs), to emit as vapour, to exhale. *v.i.* To be emitted through the excretory organs, to pass off as vapour (of perspiration, etc.); (*fig.*) to leak out, become known; (*improperly*) to happen. **transpirable,** *a.* **transpiration** (-ā′ shŭn), *n.* **transpiratory** (-spīr′ ȧ tȯr i), *a.*

transplant (trăns plant′) [F. *transplanter*, L. *transplantāre*], *v.t.* To remove and plant in another place; to remove from one place and establish in another; (*Surg.*) to transfer (living tissue) from one part or person to another. **transplantable,** *a.* **transplantation** (-tā′ shŭn), *n.* **transplanter,** *n.* One who or that which transplants; a machine for removing trees with earth and replanting; a tool for taking up plants thus.

transpontine (trăns pon′ tīn) [TRANS-, L. *pons pontis*, bridge], *a.* Belonging to the Surrey side of London or the part across London Bridge; melodramatic, from the plays formerly in vogue there.

transport (1) (trăns pôrt′) [F. *transporter*, L. *transportāre* (TRANS-, *portāre*, to carry)], *v.t.* To carry or convey from one place to another; to remove (a criminal) to a penal colony; (*chiefly in p.p.*) to carry away by powerful emotion, to entrance, to ravish. **transportable,** *a.* That may be transported; involving transportation (of an offence). **transportability** (-bil′ i ti), *n.* ***transportance,** *n.* **transportedly,** *adv.* **transporter,** *n.* **transporter bridge,** *n.* (*Eng.*) A device for carrying road traffic across a river on a moving platform. **transportingly,** *adv.*

transport (2) (trăns′ pôrt), *n.* Transportation, conveyance from one place to another; a transport ship or aircraft; *a transported convict or one sentenced to transportation; (*fig.*) ecstasy. **transport ship** or **vessel:** One used to carry troops, munitions of war, stores, etc. **transport-worker,** *n.* A worker on any system of transport.

transportation (trăns pôr tā′ shŭn), *n.* The act of transporting or conveying; the state of being transported; conveyance; carriage of persons or things from one place to another; banishment to a penal colony.

transpose (trăns pōz′) [M.E. *transposen*, F. *transposer* (TRANS-, POSE (1))], *v.t.* To cause to change places; to change the natural order or position of (words or a word) in a sentence; (*Alg.*) to transfer from one side of an equation to the other, changing the sign; (*Mus.*) to write or play in a different key. **transposal, transposition** (-pȯ zish′ ŭn), *n.* The act of transposing; the state of being transposed. **transpositional, transpositive** (-poz′ i tiv), *a.*

***transprint** (trănz print′) [TRANS-, PRINT], *v.t.* To reprint from another book or place; to print out of place.

trans-ship [TRANSHIP].

transubstantiate (trăn sŭb stăn′ shi āt) [med. L. *transubstantiātus*, p.p. of *transubstantiāre* (TRAN-, *substantia*, SUBSTANCE)], *v.t.* To change the substance of. **transubstantiation** (-ā′ shŭn), *n.* Change from one substance into another, a change of essence; (*Theol.*) conversion of the whole substance of the bread and wine in the Eucharist into the body and blood of Christ. **transubstantiative** (-stăn′ shi ȧ tiv), *a.*

transude (trăn sūd′) [F. *transsuder* (TRANS-, L. *sūdāre*, to sweat)], *v.i.* To pass or ooze through the pores or interstices of a membrane, etc. **transudation** (-dā′ shŭn), *n.* **transudatory** (-sū′ dȧ tȯr i), *a.*

transverse (trănz vĕrs′) [L. *transversus*, p.p. of *transvertere* (TRANS-, *vertere*, to turn)], *a.* Lying, being, or acting across or in a cross direction; *collateral. *n.* That which is transverse, esp. a transverse muscle. *v.t.* To lie or pass across; *to overturn; to thwart, to cross. **transversal,** *a.* Transverse; running or lying across. *n.* A straight line cutting a system of lines; (*Anat.*) a transversalis. **transversalis** (-sā′ lis), *n.* A transverse muscle, one lying across other parts. **transversally, transversely,** *adv.* **transverso-,** *comb. form.*

transvestism (trănz vest′ izm), *n.* The adoption of clothing and manners properly belonging to the opposite sex.

Transylvanian (trăn sil vā′ ni ȧn) [*Transylvania*], *a.* Of or belonging to Transylvania, in Rumania.

trant (trănt) [from TRANTER, cp. med. L. *trāvetārius*, etym. doubtful], *v.i.* (*prov.*) To work as a tranter. **tranter,** *n.* A local carrier, huckster, or pedlar.

trap (1) (trăp) [A.-S. *treppe*, cp. M.Dut. *trappe*, W.Flem. *traap*, O.F. *trape*], *n.* A contrivance for catching game, vermin, and other animals, consisting of a pitfall, enclosure, or mechanical arrangement, esp. with a door or lid closing with a spring, often baited; (*fig.*) a trick or artifice for misleading or betraying a person, an ambush, a stratagem; a device for suddenly releasing a bird or propelling an object into the air to be shot at; the game of trap-ball, the wooden instrument used in this game; a U-shaped bend or other contrivance in a soil-pipe, etc., for sealing this with a body of liquid and preventing the return flow of foul gas; a two-wheeled vehicle on springs; a trap-door; (*slang*) a policeman; (*slang*) the mouth. *v.t.* (*past & p.p.* **trapped**) To catch in or as in a trap; to furnish (a drain) with a trap; to stop or hold (gas, etc.) in a trap; to make trap-doors in (a stage). *v.i.* To catch animals in traps; to be stopped or impeded (of steam, etc., in a pipe). **trap-ball,** *n.* A children's game played with a wooden device having a pivoted bar for sending a ball into the air on being hit with a bat. **trap-cellar,** *n.* The space under the stage in a theatre. **trap-door,** *n.* A door in a floor or roof opening and shutting like a valve. **trapper,** *n.* One who traps animals, esp. for furs; one in charge of air-doors in mines. **trappy,** *a.* (*colloq.*) Treacherous, tricky. **trappiness,** *n.*

trap (2) (trăp) [Swed. *trapp*, from *trappa*, stair], *n.* (*Geol.*) A dark igneous rock, esp. a variety of dolerite or basalt, presenting a columnar or stair-like aspect; (*Sc.*) a movable ladder.

trap (3) (trăp) [F. *drap*, cloth, etym. doubtful], **n.* A cloth for a horse's back, a trapping, a caparison. *v.t.* To adorn, to caparison. **trappings,** *n.pl.* Ornamental harness or housing; (*fig.*) decorations, adornments, esp. those pertaining to an office, etc., finery. **traps,** *n.pl.* One's personal belongings, luggage, baggage.

trapes (trāps) [rel. to obs. *trape*, perh. from M.Dut. *trappen*, to tramp], *v.i.* To gad about in a slatternly manner; to trudge, to drag along wearily. *n.* A slattern; a trapesing.

trapeze (trȧ pēz′) [F. *trapèze*, L. *trapezium*, Gr. *trapezion*, dim. of *trapeza*, table (*tra-*, *tetra*, four, *peza*, foot, cogn. with *pous podos*)], *n.* An apparatus consisting of a suspended bar on which gymnasts perform swinging, balancing, and other feats; a trapezium. **trapezial,** *a.* Trapeziform; (*Anat.*) of the trapezium. **trapezian,** *a.* (*Cryst.*). **trapeziform,** *a.* **trapezium,** *n.* (*pl.* **-zia, -ziums**) A quadrilateral figure no two or only two sides of which are parallel; (*Anat.*) the outermost bone of the distal row in the carpus. **trapezoid** (trăp′ ẻ zoid), *a.* Trapeziform. *n.* A quadrilateral only two or no two of whose sides are parallel. **trapezoidal** (-zoi′ dȧl), *c.*

trappean, trappoid, etc. [TRAP (2)].

trapper, trappy, etc. [TRAP (1)].

trappings, traps [TRAP (3)].

Trappist (trăp′ ist) [La *Trappe*], *n.* A member of a Cistercian order, following the strict rule of La Trappe, a monastery founded at Soligny-la-Trappe, France, in 1140. **Trappistine** (-tin, -tīn), *n.* One of an order of nuns allied to the Trappists; a liqueur made by the Trappists.

trash (1) (trăsh) [etym. doubtful], *n.* Any waste or worthless matter, refuse, rubbish; (*Am.*) domestic refuse; loppings of trees; bruised sugar-canes; a rubbishy article or production of any kind. *v.t.* To lop. **trash-can:** (*Am.*) A dust-bin. **trashery, trashiness,** *n.* **trashily,** *adv.* **trashy,** *a.*

***trash** (2) (trăsh) [etym. doubtful], *v.t.* To check, to hold in with a leash. *n.* A leash.

***trash** (3) (trăsh) [cp. Swed. *traska,* Norw. *traske*], *v.t.* To tire, to wear out.

trauchle [TRACHLE].

trauma (traw′ mȧ) [Gr. *trauma -atos,* wound], *n.* (*Path.*) A wound or external injury; the morbid condition produced by this. **traumatic** (-măt′ ik), *a.* Pertaining to or adapted to the cure of wounds. *n.* A medicine for wounds. **traumatism** (traw′ mȧ tizm), *n.* **traumato-,** *comb. form.*

travail (trăv′ āl) [O.F., *from travailler,* to toil, prob. from late L. *trepālium,* instrument of torture (*trēs,* three, *pālus,* stake, PALE (1))], *n.* Painful toil, painful exertion or effort; the pangs of childbirth. *v.i.* To toil painfully; to suffer the pangs of childbirth. **v.t.* To harass, to tire.

trave (trāv) [O.F., from L. *trabam,* nom. *trabs*], *n.* (*prov.*) *A cross-beam; a wooden frame for confining a restive horse while it is being shod.

travel (trăv′ ėl) [var. of TRAVAIL], *v.i.* (*past & p.p.* **travelled**) To make a journey, esp. to distant or foreign lands; to move (along, in, up and down, etc.) of a machine or part; to move, to go, to pass through space; to make journeys as a commercial traveller for securing orders, etc. *v.t.* To journey over; to cause to travel. *n.* The act of travelling; (*pl.*) an account of travelling, usu. in distant countries; the length of stroke, the range or scope, of a piston, etc. **travel-soiled, -stained, *-tainted, -worn,** *n.* Soiled or worn with travel. **travelled,** *a.* Having travelled; experienced in travelling. **traveller,** *n.* One who travels; a commercial traveller; (*Austral.*) a swag-man; (*Naut.*) an iron ring, etc., sliding on a spar, rope, etc. **traveller's-joy,** *n.* The wild clematis, *C. vitalba.* **travelling expenses:** Expenses incurred by a commercial traveller, etc., and paid by the employers. **travelogue,** *n.* A lecture or talk of travel illustrated by cinematograph films.

traverse (trăv′ ėrs) [F. *travers -rse,* L. *transversus,* TRANSVERSE], **a.* Lying or being across, transverse; on a zigzag track (of sailing). **adv.* Athwart, crosswise. *n.* Anything, esp. a part of a building or mechanical structure, crossing something else; a gallery or loft communicating between opposite sides of a church or other large building; a mound or earthwork protecting a covered way, etc., from enfilading fire; (*Geom.*) a transversal; (*Naut.*) a zigzag line described by a ship owing to contrary winds, etc.; the act of traversing or travelling across; the sideways travel of part of a machine; a sideways movement of climbers on a mountain-side or precipice to avoid obstacles; (*Law*) a denial of a formal allegation by the opposite party; (*Ordnance*) the horizontal sweep of a gun; *anything that thwarts, a cross. *v.t.* To travel across; to make a traverse along (a cliff, etc.); to lie across or through; (*fig.*) to examine, consider, or discuss thoroughly; to thwart, to frustrate, to bring to naught; to plane (wood) across the grain; (*Law*) to deny (a plea or allegation); (*Ordnance*) to turn and point. *v.i.* To turn, as on a pivot; to make a traverse; to move or walk crosswise (of a horse). **traverse-table,** *n.* (*Naut.*) A circular board having holes and pegs to indicate the course by which the ship has been sailing during a traverse; a wheeled platform for shifting carriages, locomotives, etc., from one line to another. **traversable,** *a.* **traverser,** *n.* One who or that which traverses a traverse-table. **traversing,** *n.* (*Surveying*) A method of plane-table surveying by measured connected lines.

travertine (trăv′ ėr tin) [It. *travertino,* L. *Tiburtīnus,* from *Tībur,* Tivoli], *n.* A light-yellow porous rock formed by calcareous deposit from streams, hardening on exposure, used for building.

travesty (trăv′ ės ti) [F. *travesti,* p.p. of *travestir,* It. *travestire,* to disguise (TRA-, L. *vestīre,* to clothe)], *n.* A burlesque imitation; a ridiculous misrepresentation. *v.t.* To make a travesty of, to burlesque.

trawl (trawl) [etym. doubtful], *n.* A net, shaped like a flattened bag, for dragging along the sea-bottom; a trawl-line. *v.i.* To fish with a trawl-net. **trawl-boat,** *n.* **trawl-line,** *n.* A line of great length, with short lines carrying baited hooks, buoyed up at intervals, for deep-sea fishing. **trawl-net,** *n.* **trawler,** *n.* One who trawls; a fishing-vessel using a trawl-net. **trawling,** *n.*

tray (1) (trā) [A.-S. *trig,* perh. cogn. with TREE], *n.* A flat shallow vessel, used for holding or carrying small articles on; a shallow coverless box, esp. one forming a compartment in a trunk, etc. **trayful,** *n.*

tray (2) (trā) [var. of TREY], *n.* The third branch of a stag's horn.

treacherous (trech′ ėr ůs) [O.F. *trecheros, tricheros,* from *trecheur,* traitor, from *trechier, trichier, to* cheat, It. *treccare,* perh. from L. *trīcārī,* to make difficulties, from *tricæ,* wiles], *a.* Violating allegiance, disloyal, perfidious; deceptive, illusory. ***treacher, *treachetour,** *n.* **treacherously,** *adv.* **treacherousness, treachery,** *n.*

treacle (trē′ kėl) [M.E. and O.F. *triacle,* L. *thēriaca,* THERIAC], *n.* A syrup drained from sugar in refining; (*loosely*) molasses; a saccharine fluid consisting of the inspissated juices or decoctions of certain plants. **treacly,** *a.*

tread (tred) [A.-S. *tredan,* cp. Dut. *treden,* G. *treten,* Icel. *trotha,* Dan. *træde*], *v.i.* (*past* **trod,** trod, **trode,** trōd, *p.p.* **trodden,** trodn) To set the foot on the ground; to walk, to step, to go; (*fig.*) to deal (cautiously, etc.); to follow (in a person's footsteps); to copulate with a hen (of a male bird). *v.t.* To step or walk on; to crush with the feet; to trample on; to walk (a distance, journey, etc.); to dance (a measure, etc.); to copulate with, to cover (said of male birds). *n.* The act or manner of walking; the sound of walking, a footstep; the flat part of a stair or step; a piece of rubber, metal, etc., placed on this to reduce wear or noise; the part of a wheel that bears upon the ground; the part of a rail on which the wheels bear; the part of a sole that rests on the ground; the lateral distance between the pedals of a bicycle, etc.; the act of copulating in birds; the cicatricule of an egg. **to tread down:** To press down or crush with the feet; to trample on; to destroy. **to tread in:** To press in or into with the feet. **to tread on:** To trample on; to set the foot on; to follow closely. **to tread on one's toes:** (*fig.*) To offend one's susceptibilities. **to tread upon one's heels** [HEEL (1)]. **to tread out:** To press out (wine, etc.) with the feet; to extinguish by stamping on. **to tread under foot:** To destroy; to treat with scorn. **treadmill,** *n.* A mechanism, usu. in the form of a revolving cylinder driven by the weight of a person or persons, horses, etc., treading on movable steps on the periphery, formerly used as a punishment in prisons; (*fig.*) wearisome monotony or routine. **treader,** *n.*

treadle (tred′ ėl) [A.-S. *tredel* (TREAD, -LE)], *n.* A lever worked by the foot giving motion to a lathe, sewing-machine, bicycle, etc. *v.i.* To work this.

treadmill [TREAD].

***treague** (trēg) [med. L. *tregua*, Goth. *triggwa*, from *triggws*, true, cp. TRUCE], *n.* A truce.

treason (trē' zȯn) [M.E. *trayson*, A.-F. *treysoun*, O.F. *traïson* (F. *trahison*), L. *trāditiōnem*, TRADITION], *n.* A violation of allegiance by a subject against his sovereign or Government, esp. an overt attempt to subvert the Government; an act of treachery, a breach of faith. **constructive treason:** An act that may be legally interpreted as treason, though not intended or realized as such. **high treason:** Violation of allegiance to the sovereign or the State. **treason-felony,** *n.* The act of attempting to depose the sovereign, levying war to compel a change of measures, intimidating Parliament, or stirring up foreign invasion. **treasonable,** *a.* Consisting of or involving treason. **treasonableness,** *n.* **treasonably,** *adv.* ***treasonous,** *a.*

treasure (trezh' ůr) [O.F. *tresor*, L. THESAURUS], *n.* Precious metals in any form, or gems; a quantity of these hidden away or kept for future use, a hoard; accumulated wealth; anything highly valued, a precious or highly-prized thing, esp. if portable; a person greatly valued, a beloved person. *v.t.* To lay (up) as valuable, to hoard, to store (up); to prize, to lay (up) in the memory as valuable. **treasure-city,** *n.* (*Bibl.*) A city for stores and magazines. **treasure-house,** *n.* A building in which treasures or highly-valued things are kept. **treasure trove** (trōv) [A.-F. *tresor trové*, treasure found]: Money, gold, silver, plate, or bullion found hidden in the earth or private place, the owner thereof being unknown, but now becoming the property of the Crown.

treasurer (trezh' ėr ėr), *n.* One who has charge of a treasure or treasury; an officer who receives and disburses the public revenue from taxes, duties, etc.; one who has the charge of the funds of a company, society, club, etc. **treasurership,** *n.*

treasury (trezh' ė ri), *n.* A place or building in which treasure is stored; a place where the public revenues are kept; a Government Department in charge of the public revenue; the officers of this; a repository, a book, etc., full of information on any subject; (*Theat. slang*) weekly salary. **Treasury bench:** The front bench on the right hand of the Speaker in the House of Commons, appropriated to the First Lord of the Treasury, the Chancellor of the Exchequer, and other members of the ministry. **Treasury bill:** An instrument of credit issued by the Government as an acknowledgment of money lent by a private person for three, six or twelve months. **Treasury bond:** A Government promissory note running for a definite period not exceeding six years, bearing interest at a fixed rate, and redeemable at par; an Exchequer bond. **Treasury note:** A demand note issued by the Treasury; a currency note. **Treasury warrant:** A warrant or order for a sum disbursed by the Exchequer.

treat (trēt) [M.E. *treten*, F. *traiter*, L. *tractāre*, to handle, freq. of *trahere*, to draw], *v.t.* To act or behave to or towards; to deal with or manipulate for a particular result, to apply a particular process to, to subject to the action of a chemical agent, etc.; to handle or present or express (a subject, etc.) in a particular way; to supply with food, drink, or entertainment at one's expense, esp. to supply (electors) with these in order to secure votes; to discuss, to discourse (of); to arrange terms (with). *n.* An entertainment, esp. out of doors, given to school-children, etc.; an unusual pleasure or gratification. **to stand treat:** (*colloq.*) To pay for drinks, etc. **treatable,** *a.* **treater,** *n.*

treatise (trē' tiz), *n.* A literary composition expounding, discussing, and illustrating some particular subject in a thorough way.

treaty (trē' ti), *n.* An agreement formally concluded and ratified between different States; an agreement between persons, etc.; negotiation, the act of treating for the adjustment of differences, etc. **treaty port,** *n.* (*Pol.*) A seaport kept open by treaty to foreign commerce.

treble (treb' ėl) [O.F., from pop. L. *trīplus*, TRIPLE], *a.* Triple, threefold; soprano. *n.* A soprano voice, singer, or part. *v.t.* To multiply by three. *v.i.* To become threefold. ***trebleness,** *n.* **trebly,** *adv.*

trebuchet (treb' ů shet, trā bu shā) [O.F., from *trebucher*, to overturn, to tumble (TRANS-, *buc*, trunk, O.H.G., *buk*, belly, cp. G. *bauch*)], *n.* A mediæval military engine for hurling stones; a delicate balance for weighing small articles; a kind of trap for small birds; a cucking-stool.

trecento (trā chen' tō) [It., short for *mil trecento*, one thousand three hundred], *n.* The 14th century as characterized by a distinctive style of Italian literature and art.

treddle [TREADLE].

***tredille, *tredrille** (trė dil', -dril') [L. *tre-*, *trēs*, three, after QUADRILLE], *n.* A card-game for three persons.

tree (trē) [A.-S. *treo* (cp. Icel. *trē*, Dan. *træ*, Swed. *trä*), cogn. with Gr. *drus*, oak, *doru*, spear, Sansk. *dru*, tree], *n.* A perennial woody plant rising from the ground with a single supporting trunk or stem; a thing resembling a tree, esp. in having a stem and branches; a family or genealogical tree; a gibbet; a cross of crucifixion; a diagram with branching lines; a timber beam or framework, as an axle-tree, swingle-tree, etc.; a boot-last. *v.t.* To drive or force to take refuge in a tree. **family tree,** *n.* A genealogy, pedigree. **at the top of the tree:** Having attained the highest position in a profession, etc. **up a tree:** (*fig.*) In a fix, cornered. **tree of knowledge:** A tree in the Garden of Eden, the fruit of which gave knowledge of good and evil (Gen. iii.). **tree of life:** A tree in the Garden of Eden of which Adam and Eve were forbidden to eat (Gen. ii. 9); the arbor-vitæ. **tree-agate,** *n.* A variety of agate with dendritic markings. **tree-calf,** *n.* A brown calf binding with a conventional tree-like design. **tree-fern,** *n.* A fern with a vertical rhizome like a tree-trunk. **tree-frog,** *n.* A frog with arboreal habits. **treeless,** *a.*

treen (trēn) [Manx], *n.* An obsolete territorial division in the Isle of Man, the third of a tithe.

treenail (trē' nāl, tren' ėl), *n.* A pin or peg of hard wood used in fastening timbers, esp. in ship-building.

trefle (tref' ėl) [F., as foll.], *n.* A mine with three chambers.

trefoil (trē' foil, tref' oil) [A.-F. *trifoil*, L. *trifolium* (TRI- *folium*, leaf)], *n.* A plant with three leaflets or three-lobed leaves, esp. of the genus *Trifolium*, as the clover, the black medick, etc.; a three-lobed or three-cusped ornament in window-tracery, etc.; any object in this shape. **trefoiled,** *a.*

trehala (trė ha' lȧ) [Turk. *tiqālah*], *n.* A kind of manna formed by the substance of the cocoons of a coleopterous insect in Asia Minor, also called Turkish or Syrian manna or **trehala-manna.**

treillage (trā' lȧj) [F., from *treille*, see TRELLIS], *n.* A light frame of posts and rails to support espaliers; a trellis.

trek (trek) [Dut. *trekken*, cp. O.H.G. *trechan*, to draw], *v.i.* (*S. Afr.*) To draw a vehicle or load (of oxen); to travel by ox-wagon; to journey, esp. in search of a new settlement. *n.* A journey with a wagon; a stage or day's march. **trekker,** *n.*

trellis (trel' is) [M.E. and O.F. *trelis*, ult. from L. *trilix -līcis* (TRI-, *līcium*, thread, thrum) combined later with O.F. *treille*, late L. *trichila*, bower, arbour, etym. doubtful], *n.* Open-work of strips of wood crossing each other and nailed together, used for verandas, summer-houses, etc.; a lattice, a grating; a summer-house, screen, or other structure made of this. *v.t.* To interlace into a trellis; to furnish with trellis.

trematode (trem' ȧ tōd) [Gr. *trēmatōdēs*, from *trēma*, hole], *a.* Pertaining to the *Trematoda*, an order of parasitic worms containing the flukeworms. **trematoid,** *a.* and *n.*

tremble (trem' bėl) [F. *trembler*, pop. L. *tremulāre*, from *tremulus*, TREMULOUS], *v.i.* To shake involuntarily, as with fear, cold, weakness, etc.; to be in a state of fear or agitation; to be alarmed (for); to totter, to oscillate, to quaver. *n.* The act or state of trembling; fear. ***tremblement,** *n.* *A trembling; (*Mus.*) a trill or shake. **trembler,** *n.* One who trembles; (*Elec.*) an automatic vibrator for making or breaking a circuit; an electric bell. **tremblingly,** *adv.* **trembly,** *a.*

tremellose (trem' ė lōs) [mod. L. *tremella*, dim. of *tremula*, fem. of *tremulus*, see prec.], *a.* (*Bot.*) Tremulous, jelly-like, gelatinous (of some fungi).

tremendous (trė men' dŭs) [L. *tremendus*, from *tremere*, to tremble], *a.* Terrible, dreadful; of overpowering magnitude, violence, etc.; (*colloq.*) extraordinary, considerable. **tremendously,** *adv.* **tremendousness,** *n.*

tremolando (trem ŏ lan' dō) [It.], *adv.* (*Mus.*) Tremulously. **tremolant** [TREMULANT], *n.*

tremolite (trem' o līt) [Val *Tremola*, N. Italy], *n.* (*Min.*) A calcium magnesium metasilicate crystallizing in the monoclinic system. **tremolitic** (-lit' ik), *a.*

tremolo (trem' ŏ lō) [It.], *n.* A tremulous or quavering effect in singing, playing, etc.; an organ or harmonium stop producing a vibrating tone.

tremor (trem' ŏr) [M.E. and O.F. *tremour*, L. *tremōrem*, nom. *-or*, from *tremere*, to tremble], *n.* A trembling, shaking, or quivering; a thrill. **tremorless,** *a.*

tremulous (trem' ū lŭs) [L. *tremulus*, from *tremere*, to tremble], *a.* Trembling, shaking, quivering; timid, irresolute, wavering. **tremulously,** *adv.* **tremulousness,** *n.* **tremulant,** *a.* Tremulous. *n.* (*Mus.*) A tremolo; an organ-stop for producing this.

trench (trench) [M.E. and O.F. *trenche* (F. *tranche*), from *trenchier* (F. *trancher*), prob. ult. from L. *truncāre*, to TRUNCATE], *n.* A long, narrow cut or deep furrow in the earth, a ditch, esp. a long narrow ditch, usu. with a parapet formed by the excavated earth, to cover besieging troops, etc. *v.t.* To cut a trench or trenches in (ground, etc.); to turn over (ground) by cutting a successive series of trenches and filling in with the excavated soil; to ditch; to cut a furrow or groove (in wood, etc.); to cut military trenches against. *v.i.* To cut or dig a trench or trenches; (*fig.*) to encroach (on). **to open the trenches:** To begin to dig or to form trenches or lines of approach. **trench-cart,** *n.* A low hand-cart for carrying ammunition, etc., in trenches. **trench coat,** *n.* A heavy, lined macintosh crossing over in front and furnished with belt and storm sleeves. **trench fever,** *n.* (*Path.*) A remittent or relapsing fever affecting men living in trenches, etc., and transmitted by the excrement of lice. **trench foot,** *n.* (*Path.*) A gangrenous condition of the foot caused by prolonged standing in cold water. **trench mortar,** *n.* (*Artill.*) A mortar used for throwing bombs. **trench-, trenching-plough,** *n.* A plough for cutting deep furrows. **trencher** (1), *n.*

trenchant (tren' chănt) [O.F., pres.p. of *trenchier*, see prec.], *a.* Sharp, keen; cutting, biting, incisive. **trenchancy,** *n.* **trenchantly,** *adv.*

trencher (2) (tren' chėr) [A.-F. *trenchour* (F. *tranchoir*), from *trenchier*, as TRENCH], *n.* A wooden plate, now used for cutting bread upon; *(*fig.*) the pleasures of the table, a trencher-cap. **trencher-cap,** *n.* A college cap with a flat top, a mortar-board. **trencher-friend, -mate,** *n.* A table-friend, a parasite. **trencher-man,** *n.* A (good or bad) feeder or eater.

trend (trend) [M.E. *trenden*, A.-S. *trendan*, cp. O.Fris., Dan., and Swed. *trind*, round], *v.i.* To extend or lie along in a particular direction; to incline; to bend (away, etc.); (*fig.*) to have a general tendency or direction. *n.* General tendency, bent, or inclination.

trental (tren' tăl) [O.F., from med. L. *trentāre*, from L. *triginta*, thirty], *n.* (*R.C. Ch.*) A series of thirty masses for the dead.

trepan (1) (trė păn') [F. *trepan*, med. L. *trepanum*, Gr. *trupanon*, borer], *n.* A surgeon's cylindrical saw for removing portions of the skull. *v.t.* To perforate with a trepan. **trepanation** (trep ȧ nā' shŭn), **trepanning,** *n.*

trepan (2) (trė păn') [formerly *trapan*, prob. a slang derivative from TRAP (1)], *v.t.* To entrap, to ensnare; to inveigle (into); to cheat, to swindle. **n.* A decoy; a stratagem, a snare.

trepang (trė păng') [Malay, *tripang*], *n.* The sea-slug or bêche-de-mer.

trephine (trĕ fēn', -fīn') [F. *tréphine*, TREPAN], *n.* An improved trepan with a centre-pin. *v.t.* To operate on with this.

trepidation (trep i dā' shŭn) [F., from L. *trepidātiōnem*, nom. *-tio*, from *trepidāre*, to bustle, from *trepidus*, agitated], *n.* A state of alarm, excitement, or agitation; a trembling of the limbs, as in paralysis; *a slow oscillation of the ecliptic, formerly supposed to account for the precession of the equinoxes; *vibratory motion. ***trepid,** *a.* Agitated.

trespass (tres' pȧs) [M.E. and O.F. *trespas*, from *trespasser* (F. *trépasser*), med. L. *transpassāre* (TRANS-, *passāre*, to PASS)], *n.* A transgression against law, duty, etc., an offence, a sin; (*Law*) a wrongful act involving injury to the person or property of another, any transgression other than treason, misprision of treason, or felony. *v.i.* To commit an illegal intrusion (upon the property or personal rights of another); (*fig.*) to intrude, encroach, or make undue claims (upon); *to transgress (against). **trespass-offering,** *n.* A sacrifice to atone for a trespass under the Mosaic law. **trespasser,** *n.*

tress (tres) [M.E. and F. *tresse*, med. L. *tricia*, *trica*, Gr. *tricha*, three-fold], *n.* A lock or plait of hair, esp. from the head of a girl or woman; (*pl.*) hair. *v.t.* To arrange in tresses. **tressed, tressy,** *a.*

tressure (tresh' ŭr) [O.F., as prec.], *n.* (*Her.*) A diminutive of the orle, usually borne double and emblazoned with fleurs-de-lis.

trestle (tres' ėl) [O.F. *trestel* (F. *tréteau*), pop. L. *transtellum*, *transtillum*, dim. of *transtrum*, TRANSOM], *n.* A movable frame for supporting a table, platform, etc., usu. consisting of a pair of divergent legs, fixed or hinged; an open braced framework of timber or iron for supporting the horizontal portion of a bridge, etc.; (*Naut.*) a trestle-tree; (*pl.*) the props or shores of a ship in process of building, etc. **trestle-bridge,** *n.* **trestle-table,** *n.* A table formed of boards supported on movable trestles. **trestle-tree,** *n.* (*Naut.*) Either of a pair of horizontal fore-and-aft timbers fixed to a lower mast to support the cross-trees. **trestle-work,** *n.*

tret (tret) [perh. from O.F. *traite*, transportation, TRACT (1)], *n.* An allowance to purchasers of goods of certain kinds for damage or deterioration during transit (usu. 4 lb. in every 104 lb.).

trevally (tre văl' i), *n.* (*Austral.*) The silver bream.

trevet [TRIVET].

trews (trooz) [var. of TROUSERS], *n.pl.* (*Sc.*) Trousers, esp. made of tartan. **trewsman,** *n.* A Highlander wearing these.

trey (trā) [A.-F. *treis*, *trei* (F. *trois*), L. *trēs*], *n.* The three at cards or dice. Cp. TRAY (2).

tri- [L. and Gr. *tri-*, three, from L. *trēs*, Gr. *treis*], *pref.* Three; three times; triple.

triable (trī' ȧbl) [A.F.], *a.* That may be tried or tested. **triableness,** *n.*

triacontahedron (trī ȧ kon tȧ hē' drŏn) [Gr. *triakonta*, thirty, *hedra*, base], *n.* A solid figure or a crystal having thirty sides. **triacontahedral,** *a.*

triact (trī′ ȧkt) [TRI-, Gr. *aktis -tinos*, ray], *a.* Having three rays, as a sponge-spicule. **triactinal, triactine** (-ăk′ ti nȧl, -tin), *a.*

triad (trī′ ȧd) [late L. and Gr. *trias triados*, from *treie*, three], *n.* A collection of three; (*Welsh Lit.*) a composition in which statements, etc., are grouped in threes; (*Chem.*) an element or radical with a combining power of three; (*Mus.*) a chord of three notes; a common chord. **triadic** (-ăd′ ik), *a.*

triadelphous (trī′ ȧ del′ fŭs) [TRI-, Gr. *adelphos*, brother], *a.* (*Bot.*) Having the stamens in three bundles.

triage (trī′ ȧj) [F.], *n.* Refuse of coffee-beans.

trial (trī′ ȧl) [O.F. (TRY, -AL)], *n.* The act or process of trying or testing; experimental treatment; a test, an examination, an experiment; that which tries or tests strength, endurance, and other qualities; hardship, trouble, suffering, etc.; (*Law*) the judicial examination and determination of the issues in a cause between parties before a judge, judge and jury, or a referee. **trial balance:** A comparison of the debit and credit totals in double-entry book-keeping. ***trial-fire,** *n.* (*Shak.*) A fire for trying or proving. **trial-trip,** *n.* A test trip by a new vessel to show her capabilities.

trialism (trī′ ȧ lizm), *n.* The doctrine or principle of threefold union, as of body, soul, and spirit in man; (*Polit.*) a union of three States, as of the German, Hungarian, and Slav portions of the former Austro-Hungarian empire.

triandria (trī ăn′ dri ȧ) [TRI-, Gr. *anēr andros*, male], *n.pl.* (*Bot.*) A Linnæan class consisting of plants with hermaphrodite flowers having three stamens. **triandrian, -drous,** *a.*

triangle (trī′ ăng gėl) [F., from L. *trangulum*, neut. adj. (TRI-, *angulus*, ANGLE (2))], *n.* A figure, esp. a plane figure, bounded by three lines, esp. straight lines; a drawing-implement or other thing or ornament of this shape; (*Naut.*) a combination of three spars lashed together at the top for shifting weights; (*Mus.*) a steel rod bent into a triangle and sounded by striking with a steel rod; (*Astron.*) a northern constellation; *a frame formed by three halberds to which a person was tied up to be flogged. **eternal triangle,** *n.* (*fig.*) The complicated situation of a married couple and the lover of one of them. **triangular** (-ăng′ gū lȧr), *a.* Having the shape of a triangle; three-cornered. **triangular compasses,** *n.pl.* Compasses with three legs. **triangularity** (-lăr′ i ti), *n.* **triangularly,** *adv.* **triangulate** (-lāt), *v.t.* To make triangular; to divide into triangles. esp. (an area) in surveying; to ascertain by this means. *a.* (-lȧt) (*Zool.*) Marked with triangles. **triangulation** (-lā′ shŭn), *n.* **triangulately,** *adv.*

triapsal, -apsidal (trī ăp′ sȧl, -ăp′ si dȧl), *a.* (*Arch.*) Having three apses. **triarch** (trī′ ark) [Gr. *triarchos -archos*, from *archein*, to rule], *n.* The ruler of one of three divisions of a country. **triarchy,** *n.*

***triarian** (trī âr′ i ȧn) [L. *triārii*, pl. from TRI-, -AN], *a.* Occupying the third rank or place; (*Rom. Ant.*) denoting the veteran Roman soldiers who were stationed in the third rank from the front in order of battle. *n.* One of the triarian soldiers.

Trias (trī′ ȧs) [late L. and Gr., TRIAD], *n.* (*Geol.*) The division of strata between the Carboniferous and the Jurassic (divided in Germany into three groups, whence the name). **Triassic,** *a.* and *n.*

triaxal, -axial (trī ăk′ sȧl, -si ȧl), *a.* (*Geom., etc.*) Having three axes. **triatomic** (trī ȧ tom′ ik) [ATOMIC], *a.* Having three atoms (of a molecule).

tribadism (trī′ bȧd izm) [Gr. *tribas -ados*, a lewd woman, -ISM], *n.* Unnatural vice between women, Lesbianism.

tribal (trī′ bȧl) [TRIBE, -AL], *a.* Belonging or pertaining to a tribe. **tribally,** *adv.* **tribalism,** *n.*

tribasic (trī bā′ sik), *a.* (*Chem.*) Having three atoms of hydrogen replaceable by a base or basic radical.

tribble (trib′ ėl) [etym. doubtful], *n.* A horizontal drying-frame used in paper-making.

tribe (trīb) [M.E. and O.F. *tribu*, L. *tribus*, etym. doubtful], *n.* A group of people ethnologically related and forming a community or a political division; (*Rom. Ant.*) one of the three ancient divisions of the Roman people later increased to 35; a group claiming common descent or affinity, a clan or group of clans, esp. a group of savage clans under a chief; a number of persons of the same character, profession, etc. (*usu. contemp.*); (*Bot. and Zool.*) a more or less indefinite group of plants or animals, usu. above a genus and below an order.

triblet (trib′ lėt) [formerly *tribolet*, F. *triboulet*, etym. doubtful], *n.* A mandrel used in forging tubes, nuts, and rings, etc.

tribometer (trī bom′ ė tėr) [F. *tribomètre* (Gr. *tribos*, rubbing, from *tribein*, to rub, -METER)], *n.* A sled-like apparatus for measuring sliding friction.

tribrach (trib′ răk) [L. *tribrachys*, Gr. *tribrachus* (TRI-, *brachus*, short)], *n.* A metrical foot of three short syllables. **tribrachic** (-brăk′ ik), *a.*

tribrachial (trī brā′ ki ȧl), *n.* A three-armed tool or implement.

tribulation (trib ū lā′ shŭn) [M.E. and O.F. *tribulacion*, late L. *trībulātiōnem*, nom. *-tio*, from *trībulāre*, to rub, to oppress, from *trībulum*, threshing-sledge, from *terere*, to rub, p.p. *trītus*], *n.* Severe affliction, suffering, distress.

tribunal (trī-, tri bū′ nȧl) [L., from foll.], *n.* A court of justice; a board of arbitrators, etc.; a seat or bench for judges, magistrates, etc., a judgment-seat.

tribune (1) (trib′ ūn) [M.E. and O.F. *tribun*, L. *tribūnus*, from *tribus*, TRIBE], *n.* (*Rom. Hist.*) One of two (later ten) representatives elected by the people to protect their rights and liberties against the patricians, also, one of various civil, fiscal, and military officers; (*fig.*) a champion of popular rights and liberties. **tribunate, tribuneship,** *n.* **tribunicial** (-nish′ ȧl), **-cian, -tial,** *a.*

tribune (2) (trib′ ūn) [F., from med. L. *tribūna*, tribunal, as prec.], *n.* A raised floor for the curule chairs of the magistrates in the apse of a Roman basilica; a bishop's throne in an apse, hence, an apse containing this; a platform; a rostrum, a pulpit.

tributary (trib′ ū tȧr i) [L. *tribūtārius*, as foll.], *a.* Paying or subject to tribute; subsidiary, contributory; serving to increase a larger stream. *n.* A tributary person or State; a tributary stream. **tributarily,** *adv.* **tributariness,** *n.*

tribute (trib′ ūt) [L. *tribūtum*, neut. of *tribūtus*, p.p. of *tribuere*, to give, to pay], *n.* A sum of money or other valuable thing paid by one prince or State to another in token of submission, for peace or protection, or by virtue of a treaty; the state of being under obligation to pay this; (*fig.*) a contribution, gift, or offering (of praise, etc.); (*Mining*) a share of ore paid to a miner under the system of tribute-work. **tribute-money,** *n.* **tribute-work,** *n.* (*Mining*). **tributer,** *n.* (*Mining*). One doing tribute-work.

tricala [TREHALA].

tricapsular (trī kăp′ sū lȧr) [TRI-, CAPSULAR], *a.* (*Bot.*) Having three capsules. **tricarpous** (-kar′ pŭs) [Gr. *karpos*, fruit], *a.* (*Bot.*) Having three carpels. **tricaudate** (-kaw′ dȧt) [CAUDATE], *a.* Having three tail-like processes.

trice (1) (trīs) [M.E. *tricen*, *trisen*, M.Dut. *trîsen* (cp. Dut. *trijsen*, G. *triezen*, to hoist)], *v.t.* (*Naut.*) To haul; to tie (up).

trice (2) (trīs) [prob. from prec.], *n.* An instant. **in a trice:** In a moment.

Tricel (trī′ sel), *n.* Proprietary name of a partly synthetic textile fibre used in dress fabrics.

***tricennial** (trī sen′ i ȧl) [L. *tricenni-um*, (TRICES, thirty times, *annus*, year), -AL], *a.* Of or pertaining to thirty years; occurring once in every thirty years.

tricentenary [TERCENTENARY].

tricephalous (trī sef′ ȧ lu̇s), *a.* Three-headed.

triceps (trī seps) [L. (TRI-, *-ceps*, from *caput*, head)], *a.* Three-headed (of muscles). *n.* A three-headed muscle, esp. the large muscle at the back of the upper arm.

tricerion (trī sēr′ i ŏn) [late Gr. *trikērion* (TRI-, *kēros*, wax)], *n.* (*Gr. Ch.*) A three-branched candlestick symbolizing the Trinity, used by a bishop in benediction.

trichiasis (tri kī′ ȧ sis) [Gr., as foll.], *n.* (*Path.*) Entropion or inversion of the eyelashes; a disease of the kidneys in which filamentous matter is passed in the urine; a swelling of the breasts due to obstruction of milk-excretion in child-bearing women.

trichina (tri kī′ nȧ) [mod. L., from Gr. *trichinos*, a. from *thrix trichos*, hair], *n.* (*pl.* **-næ**) A hair-like nematode parasitic worm, infesting the intestine or muscles of pigs, man, etc. **trichiniasis** (trik i nī′ ȧ sis), **trichinosis** (-nō′ sis), *n.* (*Path.*) A disease due to the presence of trichinæ in the system. **trichinize** (trik′ i nīz), *v.t.* **trichinization** (-zā′ shu̇n), *n.* **trichinozed** (trik′ i nōzd), **trichinotic** (-not′ ik), **trichinous** (tri kī′ nu̇s), *a.*

trichite (trik′ īt, trī′ kīt) [G. *trichit* (Gr. *thrix trichos*, hair, -ITE)], *n.* (*Min.*) A minute hair-like form occurring in certain vitreous volcanic rocks; (*Zool.*) a minute fibril found in some sponge-spicules, a spicule composed of these.

trichiurid (trik i ūr′ id) [Gr. *thrix trichos*, hair, *oura*, tail], *n.* (*Ichthyol.*) One of the Trichiuridæ, a family of Scombroidean fishes with a ribbon-like body and a filamentous tail. **trichiuriform**, *a.* **trichiuroid**, *a.* and *n.*

Trichocephalus (trik ȯ sef′ ȧ lu̇s) [Gr. *thrix trichos*, hair, see CEPHAL-], *n.* (*Zool.*) A genus of nematode worms with filamentous heads, of which *Trichocephalus dispar* affects man, residing chiefly in the cæcum. **tricocephalid**, *n.* **trichocephaloid**, *a.*

trichogenous (tri koj′ ė nu̇s) [Gr. *thrix trichos*, hair, -GENOUS], *a.* Promoting the growth of the hair. **trichogen** (trī′ kȯ jėn), *n.* **trichology** (tri kol′ ȯ ji) [-LOGY], *n.* The study of the human hair. **trichological** (-loj′ i kȧl), *a.* **trichologist** (-kol′ ȯ jist), *n.*

trichoma (tri kō′ mȧ) [Gr. *trichōma*, from *trichoun*, to cover with hair, as prec.], *n.* (*Bot.*) One of the threads composing the thallus in filamentous algæ; (*Path.*) a disease of the hair, *plica*. **trichomatose**, *a.* Affected with this. **trichome** (trī′ kōm), *n.* (*Bot.*) A hair, filament, scale, prickle, or an outgrowth. **trichopathy** (tri kop′ ȧ thi) [-PATHY], *n.* Any disease of the hair. **trichopathic** (-păth′ ik), *a.*

trichopter (trī kop′ tėr) [Gr. *thrix trichos*, hair, *pteron*, wing], *n.* One of the *Trichoptera*, a group or sub-order of neuroptera containing the caddis-flies. **trichopteran**, *a.* and *n.* **trichopterous**, *a.*

trichord (trī′ kôrd) [Gr. *trichordos*], *a.* Having three strings to each note (esp. of pianos). *n.* A musical instrument with three strings.

trichotomy (tri-, trī kot′ ȯ mi) [Gr. *tricha*, triply, from *treis*, three, -TOMY], *n.* Division into three, esp. (*Theol.*) of the human being into body, soul, and spirit. **trichotomize**, *v.t.* **trichotomous**, *a.* **trichotomously**, *adv.*

trichroism (trī′ krȯ izm) [F. *trichroïsme* (Gr. *trichroos*, *-chrous*, three-coloured)], *n.* The property of exhibiting different colours in three different directions when viewed by transmitted light. **trichroic** (-krō′ ik), *a.*

trichromatic (trī krȯ măt′ ik), *a.* Three-coloured, having the normal three fundamental colour-sensations (of red, green, and purple). **trichromatism** (-krō′ mȧ tizm), *n.*

trick (trik) [O.F. *trique*, *triche*, from *trichier*, *trechier* (F. *tricher*), prob. from L., see TREACHEROUS], *n.* An artifice, an artful device or stratagem; a foolish or malicious act, a prank, a practical joke; a feat of dexterity, esp. of legerdemain or sleight of hand; an ingenious or peculiar way of doing something, a knack; a particular habit or practice, a mannerism, a personal peculiarity; (*Cards*) the whole number of cards played in one round; a round; a point gained as the result of a round; (*Naut.*) a turn or spell at the helm, usu. half a watch or two hours. *v.t.* To cheat, to deceive; to delude, to inveigle (into, out of, etc.); to dress, to deck (out or up). *v.i.* To practise trickery. **to know a trick worth two of that:** To know of some better expedient. **to trick out:** To decorate, to dress up. **trick-track** [TRIC-TRAC]. **trick-wig**, *n.* An actor's wig so contrived that the hair can be made to stand up on end. **tricker, trickster**, *n.* **trickery**, *n.* **trickish, tricky, tricksome**, *a.* **trickishly**, *adv.* **trickishness**, *n.* **trickily**, *adv.* **trickiness**, *n.* **tricksy**, *a.* Playful, sportive.

trickle (trik′ ėl) [M.E. *triklen*, acc. to Skeat for *striklen*, freq. from A.-S. *strīcan*, to sweep along, to STRIKE], *v.i.* To flow in drops or in a small stream. *v.t.* To cause to flow thus. *n.* A trickling; a small stream, a rill. **tricklet**, *n.* **trickly**, *a.*

triclinic (trī klin′ ik) [TRI-, Gr. *klinein*, to lean], *a.* (*Cryst.*) Having the three axes unequal and inclined at oblique angles.

triclinium (trī klin′ i u̇m, tri klī′ ni u̇m) [L., from Gr. *triklinion* (TRI-, *klinē*, couch)], *n.* (*pl.* **-ia**) (*Rom. Ant.*) A set of couches arranged round three sides of a dining-table; a dining-table furnished with this; a dining-room with this.

tricolour (trī′ kȯ lȯr, trik′ ȯ lėr) [F. *tricoleur*], *n.* A flag or banner having three colours, esp. arranged in equal stripes, as the national standard of France of blue, white, and red, divided vertically. *a.* Three-coloured. **tricoloured**, *a.*

triconsonantal (trī kon sȯ năn′ tȧl), *a.* Composed of or containing three consonants. **triconsonantalism**, *n.*

tricorn (trī′ kôrn) [F. *tricorne*, L. *tricornis* (TRI-, *cornu*, horn)], *a.* Having three horns. *n.* A three-cornered hat. **tricornered**, *a.* Three-cornered. ***tricornigerous** (-nij′ ėr u̇s) [-GEROUS], **tricornute** (-kôr′ nūt), *a.* **tricorporal, tricorporate** (-kôr′ pȯr ȧl, -ȧt) [CORPORAL (2)], *a.* (*Her., etc.*) Having three bodies. **tricostate** (-kos′ tāt) [COSTATE], *a.* Three-ribbed.

tricot (trē kō) [F., from *tricoter*, to knit], *n.* A hand-knitted woollen fabric or a machine-made imitation; a soft, ribbed cloth.

tricotyledonous (trī kot i lē′ dȯ nu̇s) [TRI-, COTYLEDONOUS], *a.* (*Bot.*) Having three cotyledons.

tricrotic (trī krot′ ik) [Gr. *trikrotos*], *a.* Having three distinct undulations for each beat (of the pulse, etc.), **tricrotous**, *a.*

tric-trac (trik′ trăk) [F., imit. of clicking sound], *n.* A complicated form of back-gammon.

tricuspid (trī kŭs′ pid) [L. *tricuspis -pidis* (TRI-, CUSP)], *a.* Having three cusps or points (of molar teeth, a valve of the heart, etc.). **tricuspidate, -dated**, *a.*

tricycle (trī′ si kėl), *n.* A three-wheeled cycle. *v.i.* To ride on this. **tricyclist**, *n.*

Tridacna (trī dăk′ nȧ) [mod. L., from Gr. *tridaknos*, eaten at three bites (TRI-, *daknein*, to bite)], *n.* (*Conch.*) A genus of bivalve molluscs, comprising the giant clam, having an extremely hard and massive shell and attaining a greater size than any other bivalve.

tridactyl, -tylous (trī dăk′ til, -u̇s) [Gr. *tridaktulos* (TRI-, *daktulos*, finger)], *a.* Having three fingers or toes.

tride (trīd) [F., etym. doubtful], *a.* Short and swift (of a horse's pace).

trident (trī′ dėnt) [L. *tridens -ntem* (TRI-, *dens dentem*, tooth)], *n.* A three-pronged implement or weapon, esp. a fish-spear; a three-pronged sceptre or spear, the emblem of Poseidon or Neptune as god of the sea. **tridental** (-den′ tăl), *a.* **tridentate** (tri den′ tāt), *a.* Having three teeth or prongs.

Tridentine (trī den′ tin) [med. L. *Tridentīnus*, from *Tridentum*, Trent, a city of Tyrol], *a.* Of, or pertaining to Trent or the Council held there 1545–63. *n.* One who accepts the decrees of the Council of Trent, a Roman Catholic.

tridigitate (trī dij′ i tāt), *a.* Tridactylous. **tridimensional** (tri di men′ shŏ năl) [DIMENSIONAL], *a.* Having three dimensions.

triduo (trē′ du ō), **triduum** (trī′ dū ŭm) [It. and Sp. *triduo*, L. *triduum* (TRI-, *dies*, day)], *n.* (*R.-C. Ch.*) A three days' service of prayer, etc. **triduan,** *a.* Lasting three days, happening every third day.

tridymite (trid′ i mīt) [G. *tridymit* (Gr. *tridumos*, threefold)], *n.* (*Min.*) A vitreous form of silica usu. occurring in small hexagonal tables composed of groups of three individual crystals.

tried, *p.p.* [TRY].

triennial (trī en′ i ăl) [L. *triennium* (TRI-, *annus*, year), -AL], *a.* Lasting for three years; happening every three years. *n.* A triennial plant, publication, etc.; every third anniversary of an event; (*R.-C. Ch.*) a mass for a dead person performed daily for three years. **triennially,** *adv.*

trier (trī′ ĕr), *n.* One who tries, examines, or tests in any way; one who keeps on endeavouring or persisting; a person appointed to determine whether a challenge to a juror or jurors is well founded.

trierarch (trī′ ĕr ark) [L. *triērarchus*, Gr. *triērarchos* (*triērēs*, trireme, -*archos*, from *archein*, to rule)], *n.* (*Gr. Ant.*) The commander of a trireme; a citizen appointed alone or with others to fit out and maintain a trireme. **trierarchal** (-ar′ kăl), *a.* **trierarchy** (trī′ ĕr ar ki), *n.* The office or duty of a trierarch; the duty of fitting out and maintaining a trireme.

trifacial (trī fā′ shăl), *a.* Three-fold and pertaining to the face (as the trigeminus). *n.* The trigeminus.

trifarious (trī fâr′ i ŭs), *a.* (*Bot.*) Arranged in three rows; facing three ways.

trifid (trī′ fid) [L. *trifidus* (TRI-, *fid*-, stem of *findere*, to cleave)], *a.* (*Bot. and Zool.*) Divided wholly or partially into three, three-cleft.

trifle (trī′ fĕl) [M.E. and O.F. *trufle*, var. of *truffe*, mockery, cheating, cp. It. *truffa*, etym. doubtful], *n.* A thing, matter, fact, etc., of no value or importance; (*fig.*) a small amount of money, etc.; a light confection of whipped cream or white of egg, with cake, jam, wine, etc.; a variety of pewter. *v.i.* To act or talk with levity; to sport, to jest, to fool. *v.t.* To waste, fritter, or fool away (time) in trifling. **to trifle with:** To treat with levity, disrespect, or lack of proper seriousness; to dally, to toy (with). **trifler,** *n.* **trifling,** *a.* **triflingly,** *adv.* **triflingness,** *n.*

trifloral (trī flôr′ ăl), *a.* (*Bot.*) Bearing three flowers. **triflorous,** *a.* **trifoliate, -ated** (-fō′ li ăt, -ā tĕd) [FOLIATE], *a.* (*Bot.*) Three-leaved, consisting of three leaflets. **trifoliolate,** *a.* Having three leaflets. **Trifolium,** *n.* A genus of low herbs containing the trefoils or clovers.

triforium (trī fôr′ i ŭm) [med. L. (TRI-, *foris*, door opening)], *n.* (*pl.* **-ia**) A gallery or arcade in the wall over the arches of the nave or choir, or sometimes the transepts, in a large church.

triform, -ed (trī′ fôrm, -fôrmd) [L. *triformis*], *a.* Having three shapes, parts, or divisions. **trifurcate, -cated** (trī fĕr′ kăt, -kā tĕd) [FURCATE], *a.* Having three branches or forks; trichotomous. *v.t.* and *i.* To divide into three.

trig (1) (trig) [etym. doubtful], *v.t.* To stop, check, or skid (a wheel). *n.* A wedge, block, etc., used for this.

trig (2) (trig) [Icel. *tryggr*, cp. Norw., Swed., and Dan. *trygg*], *a.* Neat, trim, spruce. *n.* A dandy. **trigly,** *adv.* **trigness,** *n.*

trigamous (trig′ ă mŭs) [Gr. *trigamos* (TRI-, *gamos*, marriage)], *a.* Married three times; having three wives or three husbands at once; (*Bot.*) having male, female, and hermaphrodite flowers on the same head. **trigamist,** *n.* **trigamy,** *n.*

trigeminal (trī jem′ i năl) [L. *trigeminus* (TRI-, *geminus*, born with another)], *a.* Threefold; (*Anat.*) of or pertaining to the trigeminus. *n.* The trigeminus. **trigeminus,** *n.* The fifth cranial or trifacial nerve dividing into the superior and inferior maxillary and the ophthalmic nerves.

trigger (trig′ ĕr) [formerly *tricker*, Dut. *trekker*, from *trekken*, to pull, cp. TREK], *n.* A catch or lever for releasing the hammer of a gun-lock; any similar device for releasing a spring, etc., in various forms of mechanism.

trigla (trig′ lă) [mod. L., from Gr. *triglē*], *n.* (*Ichthyol.*) A genus of fishes comprising the gurnard; a fish of this genus.

triglot (trī′ glot) [TRI-, Gr. *glotta*, tongue], *a.* Written in three languages.

triglyph (trī′ glif, trig′ lif) [L. *triglyphus*, Gr. *trigluphos* (TRI-, *gluphein*, to carve)], *n.* (*Arch.*) An ornament on a Doric frieze consisting of a tablet with three vertical grooves. **triglyphal, -ic, -ical** (-glif′ ăl, -ik, -i kăl), *a.*

trigon (trī′ gŏn) [L. *trigōnum*, Gr. *trigōnon* (TRI-, -*gōnos*, *gōnia*, angle)], *n.* A triangle; a set of three signs of the zodiac arranged at the angles of an equilateral triangle; a triangular instrument used in dialling; (*Gr. Ant.*) a ball-game with three players; a triangular harp or lyre, also called **trigonon** (tri gō′ nŏn). **trigonic** (-gon′ ik), *a.* **trigonal** (trig′ ŏ năl), *a.* Triangular, three-cornered; (*Math.*) denoting a system of trilinear co-ordinates. **trigonally,** *adv.* **trigonous,** *a.*

trigoneutic (trig ŏ nū′ tik) [TRI-, Gr. *goneuein*, to beget], *a.* (*Ent.*) Producing three broods in a year.

trigonic [TRIGON].

trigonometry (trig ŏ nom′ ĕ tri) [Gr. *trigōnon*, TRIGON, -METRY], *n.* The branch of mathematics treating of the relations of the sides and angles of triangles, and applying these to astronomy, navigation, surveying, etc. **trigonometer,** *n.* An instrument for the mechanical solution of plane right-angled triangles. **trigonometric, -al** (-met′ rik, -ăl), *a.* **trigonometrically,** *adv.*

trigonon, etc. [TRIGON].

trigram (trī′ grăm), *n.* A trigraph; (*Geom.*) a set of three straight lines in one plane not all intersecting in the same point. **trigrammatic** (-gră măt′ ik), **trigrammic** (-grăm′ ik), *a.* **trigraph,** *n.* A group of three letters representing a single sound. **trigynous** (trī′ ji nŭs) [Gr. *gunē*, female], *a.* (*Bot.*) Having three pistils. **trihedron** (-hē′ drŏn) [Gr. *hedra*, base], *n.* A figure having three sides. **trihedral,** *a.* **trijugate, -gous** (trī′ jŭ găt, -gŭs, trī joo′ găt, -gŭs) [JUGATE], *a.* (*Bot.*) Having three pairs of leaflets. **trike** (*colloq.*) [TRICYCLE]. **trilabe** (trī′ lāb) [Gr. *labein*, to hold], *n.* A three-pronged grasping instrument used in surgery. **trilaminar** (-lăm′ i năr) [LAMINAR], *a.* Having or consisting of three layers. **trilateral** (-lăt′ ĕr ăl) [LATERAL], *a.* Having three sides. **trilaterally,** *adv.* **trilemma** (-lem′ ă) [after DILEMMA], *n.* (*Log.*) A syllogism involving three alternatives. **trilinear** (-lin′ ĕ ăr) [LINEAR], *a.* Consisting of three lines. **trilingual, *-guar** (-ling′ gwăl, -gwăr) [LINGUAL], *a.* Pertaining to or expressed in three languages. **triliteral** (-lit′ ĕr ăl) [LITERAL], *a.* Consisting of or using three letters (esp. of Semitic roots); *n.* A triliteral word or root. **triliteralism, triliterality** (-ăl′ i ti), *n.* **trilith, trilithon** (trī′ lith, -ŏn) [Gr. *trilithon*, neut. of *trilithos* (*lithos*, stone)], *n.* A megalithic monument usu. consisting of two uprights supporting an impost. **trilithic** (-lith′ ik), *a.*

trilby (tril′ bi) [heroine of novel *Trilby*], *n.* A man's soft felt hat with a dent in the middle.

trill (1) (tril) [It. *trillāre*, imit.], *v.i.* To sing or give forth a sound with a tremulous vibration. *v.i.* To sing or utter with a quavering or shake. *n.* A tremulous or quavering sound; a consonant pronounced with a trilling sound, as *r*; (*Mus.*) a shake, a rapid alternation of two notes a tone or semitone apart.

***trill** (2) (tril) [cp. G. *trillen*, Norw. and Swed., *trilla*, and M.G. *trille*, to turn], *v.i.* To roll or flow in a small stream, to purl.

trilling (tril' ing) [TRI-, -LING], *n.* (*Cryst.*) A crystal composed of three individuals; any one child in a triplet.

trillion (tril' yȯn) [after MILLION], *n.* The product of a million raised to the third power; (*Am. & F.*) a million million. **trillionth,** *a.*

trilobate (trī lō' bȧt, trī' lō bȧt), **trilobated** (trī' lȯ bā tėd), **trilobed** (trī' lōbd) [LOBATE], *a.* Having three lobes. **trilobation** (-bā' shŭn), *n.* **trilobite** (trī' lȯ bīt), *n.* (*Palæont.*) One of a Palæozoic group of articulates with a three-lobed body. **trilobitic** (-lȯ bit' ik), *a.*

trilocular (-lok' ū lȧr) [LOCULUS], *a.* (*Nat. Hist.*) Having three cells or chambers.

trilogy (tril' ȯ ji) [Gr. *trilogia*)], *n.* (*Gr. Ant.*) A series of three tragedies, each complete in itself, but connected by the story or theme, and adapted for performance in immediate succession; a group of three plays, operas, novels, etc., each complete in itself, but similarly connected.

trim (trim) [A.-S. *trymian*, to make firm, to set in order, from *trum*, firm, stable], *v.t.* (*past & p.p.* **trimmed**) To put in good order, to make neat and tidy; to remove irregularities, excrescences, or superfluous or unsightly parts from; to cut, lop, or clip (those) away or off; to dress, to smooth, to plane (wood, boards, etc.); to put (a lamp, etc.) in order by clipping or renewing a wick, carbons, etc.; to decorate, to ornament (with trimmings, etc.); (*Naut.*) to adjust (sails, yards, etc.) to the wind; to adjust (a ship) by arranging the cargo, ballast, etc.; (*colloq.*) to reprove sharply, to chastise, to flog. *v.i.* To adopt a middle course, between parties, opinions, etc. *a.* Properly adjusted, in good order; well-equipped, neat, tidy, smart; *nice, fine. *n.* State of preparation or fitness, order, condition, esp. of a ship or her cargo, ballast, masts, etc.; (*Aviat.*) the angle at which an aeroplane flies in given conditions. **trimly,** *adv.* **trimmer,** *n.* One who or that which trims; an implement or machine for clipping timber, etc.; a joist into which others are framed; one who trims between parties, esp. in politics, a time-server. **trimming,** *n.* The act of one who trims; material sewn on a garment for ornament; (*colloq., pl.*) accessories to a dish. **trimness,** *n.*

trimensual (trī men' sū ȧl), **trimestrial** (-mes' tri ȧl) [L. *trimestus*, TRI-, *mensis*, month], *a.* Happening or issued every three months. **trimerous** (trī' mėr ŭs) [Gr. *trimerēs* (*meros*, part)], *a.* Having three parts, joints, members, etc. **trimeter** (trim' ė-, trī' mė tėr) [L. *trimetrus*, Gr. *tremetros* (-METRE)], *n.* A verse consisting of three measures of two feet each; *a.* Consisting of three measures. **trimetric, -al** (-met' rik, -ȧl), *a.* **trimethyl** (trī meth' il) [METHYL], *a.* (*Chem.*) Containing three methyl groups. **trimethylamine,** *n.* The tertiary amine of methyl, a frequent constituent of stale herring-brine.

trimonthly (trī mŭnth' li), *a.* Occurring every three months; lasting three months.

trimorphism (trī môr' fizm) [TRI-, Gr. *morphē*, form, -ISM], *n.* The existence in certain species of plants and animals of three distinct forms, colours, etc., esp. (*Bot.*) having flowers with pistils or stamens of three different relative lengths; (*Cryst.*) the property of crystallizing in three distinct forms. **trimorphic, -morphous,** *a.*

trine (trīn) [L. *trīnus*, from *trēs*, three], *a.* Threefold, triple; (*Astrol.*) pertaining to or in trine. *n.* A triad, a set of three; (*Theol.*) the Trinity; (*Astrol.*) the aspect of planets distant from each other 120°. **trinal, -ary,** *a.*

trinervate (trī nĕr' vȧt), *a.* (*Bot.*) Three-nerved, -veined, or -ribbed.

Tringa (tring' gȧ) [mod. L., from Gr. *trungas*], *n.* A genus of birds containing the sand-pipers. ***tring** (trinj), *n.* **tringine** (trin' jīn), **tringoid** (tring' goid), *a.*

tringle (tring' gėl) [F., etym. doubtful], *n.* A curtain-rod, a rod supporting the canopy of a bedstead; (*Arch.*) a small square ornament, esp. in a Doric triglyph.

trinitarian [TRINITY].

trinitrotoluene (trī nī trō tol' ū ēn), *n.* A chemical compound, usually known as T.N.T., largely used as a high explosive.

trinity (trin' i ti) [O.F. *trinite*, late L. *trīnitātem*, nom. *-tas*, from *trīnus*, TRINE], *n.* A group or union of three individuals, a triad; the state of being three or threefold; the union of three persons (the Father, the Son, and the Holy Ghost) in one Godhead; the doctrine of the Trinity; a symbolical representation of the Trinity frequent in art, as the triangle or three interlacing circles. **Trinity Brethren,** *n.pl.* Members of Trinity House. **Trinity House:** An association for licensing pilots, managing lighthouses, beacons, buoys, etc., in British waters. **Trinity Sunday:** The Sunday next after Whit-Sunday. **Trinitarian,** *a.* Of or pertaining to the doctrine of the Trinity; *n.* One who believes in this. **Trinitarianism,** *n.*

trinket (tring' kėt) [etym. unknown, perh. from M.E. *trenket*, O.North.F. *trenquet*, knife, from *trenquer*, var. of *tranchier*, to cut, see TRENCH], *n.* A small personal ornament of no great value as a jewel, esp. a ring; any small ornament or fancy article; *a small tool or implement; (*Naut.*) a topsail. ***trinketry,** *n.*

trinoctial (trī nok' shȧl) [TRI-, L. *nox noctis*, night, -AL], *a.* Lasting or comprising three nights. **trinodal** (trī nō' dȧl) [NODAL], *a.* (*Bot., Anat., etc.*) Having three nodes or joints. **trinomial** (-nō' mi ȧl) [L. *nōmen*, name], *a.* Consisting of three terms, esp. (*Alg.*) connected by the signs + or −; *n.* A trinomial name or expression. **trinomialism,** *n.* Trinomial nomenclature, esp. in biology. **trinomially,** *adv.*

trio (trē' ō) [It., from L. *trēs*, three], *n.* A set of three; (*Mus.*) a musical composition for three voices or three instruments; a set of three singers or players; the second part of a minuet, march, etc.; (*Piquet*) three aces, kings, queens, knaves, or tens.

triode (trī' ōd) [TRI-, (ELECTR)ODE], *n.* (*Radio.*) A thermionic valve with three electrodes.

triodion (trī ō' di ȯn) [Gr. *triōdion* (TRI-, *hodos*, way)], *n.* (*Gr. Ch.*) A book of offices for the services from Septuagesima to Easter.

trioecious (trī ō ē' shŭs) [Gr. *treis*, three; *oikos*, a house], *a.* (*Bot.*) Having male, female, and hermaphrodite flowers, each on different plants of the same species.

triole (trē ōl) [F., dim. of TRIO], *n.* (*Mus.*) A triplet.

triolet (trē' ȯ let) [F., dim. of TRIO], *n.* A poem of eight lines with two rhymes arranged *ab a a ab ab.*

trional (trī' ō năl), *n.* (*Med.*) A hypnotic drug prescribed in cases of mental disease and neurasthenia.

Triones (trī ō' nēz) [L., ploughing-oxen], *n.pl.* The seven chief stars of the Great Bear.

trionym (trī' ȯ nim) [TRI-, Gr. *onoma*, Æolic *onuma*, name], *n.* A name composed of three terms. **trionymal** (-on' i mȧl), *a.*

trior [TRIER].

trip (trip) [M.E. *trippen*, O.F. *treper*, *triper*, *tripper*, M.Dut. *trippen*, cp. Swed. *trippa*, Dan. *trippe*], *v.i.* (*past & p.p.* **tripped**) To move, step, walk, or run lightly or nimbly; to go lightly or evenly (of rhythm, etc.); to make a false step, to stumble; to catch the foot (over something) so as nearly to fall; to err, to go wrong; *to make an excursion. *v.t.* To cause to fall by catching or obstructing the feet, etc.; to catch or detect in a fault, mistake, or offence; (*Naut.*) to loosen (an anchor) from the bottom; to turn (a yard, etc.) from the horizontal to the vertical position; to release (a part of a machine) by unfastening. *n.* A light nimble step; a leaping movement of the feet; a short excursion, voyage, or journey; a sudden stroke or catch by which a wrestler trips up his antagonist; a stumble; a false step; a failure, a mistake; (*Naut.*) a single tack in plying to windward; the number of fish caught in one voyage. **trip-hammer,** *n.* A tilt-hammer. **trippant,** *a.* (*Her.*) Walking or trotting. **tripper,** *n.* One who trips or moves easily and nimbly; a dancer; one who trips up another; one who goes on a trip, an excursionist. **trippingly,** *adv.*

tripartite (trī par′ tīt, trip′ ȧr tīt) [TRI-, L. *partītus,* p.p. of *partīrī,* to divide, from *pars partis,* PART], *a.* Divided into three parts; having three corresponding parts or copies; made or concluded between three parties. **tripartitely,** *adv.* **tripartition** (-tish′ ůn), *n.*

tripe (trip) [F. (cp. Sp. and Port. *tripa,* It. *trippa*), etym. doubtful], *n.* A part of the stomach of ruminating animals prepared for food; (*vulg., usu. in pl.*) the entrails, the belly; (*slang*) poor writing, silly stuff. **tripe-de-roche** (trēp dė rōsh) [F., rock-tripe], *n.* A vegetable substance obtained from various lichens and eaten in emergency as food by hunters in N. America. **tripe-man, tripe-seller,** *n.* **tripery,** *n.*

***tripedal** (trip′ ė dȧl)]L. *tripedalis* (TRI-, *pes pedis,* foot)], *a.* Having three feet.

***tripennate** [TRIPINNATE].

tripersonal (trī pěr′ sȯ nȧl) [TRI-, PERSONAL], *a.* Consisting of three persons (esp. of the Godhead). **tripersonalism,** *n.* The doctrine of the Trinity. **tripersonalist,** *n.* A believer in this. **tripersonality** (-năl′ i ti), *n.* **tripetalous** (-pet′ ȧ lůs) [PETALOUS], *a.* (*Bot.*) Having three petals. **triphane** (trī′ fān) [Gr. *phainein,* to shine], *n.* Spodumene. **triphthong** (trif′ thong) [after DIPHTHONG], *n.* A combination of three vowels forming one sound. **triphthongal** (-thong′ gȧl), *a.* **triphyllous** (tri fil′ ůs) [Gr. *phullon,* leaf], *a.* (*Bot.*) Three-leaved. **Triphysite** (trif′ i sīt) [Gr. *phusis,* nature, -ITE], *n.* One of a Spanish sect of the 7th cent. who held that Christ has three natures, human, divine, and a third derived from the union of these. **tripinnate** (-pin′ ȧt) [PINNATE], *a.* Triply pinnate. **tripinnately,** *adv.* **triplane** (trī′ plān) [PLANE (3)], *n.* An aeroplane with three supporting planes.

triple (trip′ ėl) [F., from L. *triplus* (TRI-, *-plus,* cogn. with *plēnus,* full)], *a.* Consisting of three parts or three things united, three-fold; multiplied by three. *v.t.* To treble, to make threefold; to alter (a steam-engine) to triple expansion. *v.i.* To be three times as large or as many. **triple crown:** The crown or tiara worn by the Pope. **triple-crowned,** *a.* **triple-expansion engine,** *n.* (*Mach.*) An engine in which the steam expands successively in high, intermediate, and low pressure cylinders, all of which work on the same shaft. **triple-headed,** *a.* **triple time:** (*Mus.*) Time of three beats, or three times three beats in a bar. **triplet,** *n.* A set or group of three; (*colloq.*) each of three children at a birth; three verses rhyming together; (*Mus.*) three notes performed in the time of two; (*Naut., pl.*) three links of chain between the cable and the anchor-ring. **triplex,** *n.* Triple-time; a composition in three parts; protected trade name of a laminated glass. **triplicate** (trip′ li kȧt), *a.* Made thrice as much or as many, threefold. *n.* A copy, document, or other thing corresponding to two others of the same kind. *v.t.* (-kāt) To make triplicate, to treble. **triplicate ratio:** The ratio of the cubes (of two quantities). **triplication** (-kā′ shůn), **triplicature** (trip′ li kȧ tūr), *n.* **triplicity** (-plis′ i ti), *n.* The state of being triple. **triply,** *adv.*

tripod (trī′ pod) [L. *tripus -podis,* Gr. *tripous -podos* (TRI-, *pous podos,* foot)], *n.* A three-legged stand, stool, utensil, seat, table, etc.; a three-legged support for a camera, etc.; (*Gr. Ant.*) a bronze altar at Delphi on which the Pythian priestess sat to deliver oracles; an imitation of this, esp. offered as a prize at the Pythian games. **tripodal,** *a.*

tripoli (trip′ ȯ li) [*Tripoli,* N. Africa], *n.* Rottenstone, a friable siliceous limestone.

tripos (trī′ pȯs) [L. *tripus,* TRIPOD], *n.* (*pl.* **-ses**) (*Camb. Univ.*) The examination for honours, a printed list (arranged in three grades) of the successful candidates.

tripotage (trē pot azh) [F.], *n.* A medley, a jumble.

trippant, tripper, trippingly [TRIP].

triptane (trip′ tān), *n.* (*Aviat.*) A very powerful fuel, trimethyl butane.

triptote (trip′ tōt) [Gr. *triptōtos* (TRI-, *ptōtos,* falling, from *piptein,* to fall)], *n.* (*Gram.*) A noun having three cases only.

triptych (trip′ tik) [Gr. *triptuchon,* neut. of *triptuchos* (TRI-, *ptuchē,* fold, from *ptussein,* to fold)], *n.* A picture, carving, or other representation, on three panels side by side, frequently used for altar-pieces; a group of three associated pictures, etc.; a writing-tablet in three leaves.

triptyque (trip′ tēk) [F.], *n.* (*Motor.*) Customs pass, made out in triplicate, for importing or exporting a car.

tripudium (trī pū′ di ům) [L., etym. doubtful], *n.* (*Rom. Ant.*) A religious dance; a favourable divination from the feeding of the sacred chickens. ***tripudiary,** *a.* ***tripudiation** (-ā′ shůn), *n.*

triquetra (trī kwēt′-, -kwet′ rȧ) [L., fem. of *triquetrus,* three-cornered (TRI-, *quetrus,* etym. doubtful)], *n.* An ornament composed of three interlacing arcs. **triquetrous, *-tral,** *a.* Three-sided, three-cornered, triangular; (*Bot.*) having three sharp angles.

triradial (trī rā′ di ȧl), **triradiate, -ated,** *a.* Having three rays or radiating branches.

trireme (trī′ rēm) [L. *trirēmis* (TRI-, *rēmus,* oar)], *n.* (*Class. Ant.*) A war-galley with three benches of oars.

trisagion (tri săg′ i ȯn, -sā′ gi ȯn) [Gr. *trisagios* (*tris,* thrice, from *treis,* three, *hagios,* holy)], *n.* A hymn with a threefold invocation of God as holy, in the liturgies of the Greek and Eastern Churches.

trisect (trī sekt′) [TRI-, L. *sectus,* p.p. of *secāre,* to cut], *v.t.* To divide into three (esp. equal) parts. **trisection** (-sek′ shůn), *n.* **trisepalous** (-sep′ ȧ lůs) [SEPALOUS], *a.* (*Bot.*) Having three sepals. **triserial, -iate** (-sēr′ i ȧl, -ȧt) [SERIAL], *a.* (*Anat., Bot., etc.*) Arranged in three rows. **trisinuate** (-sin′ ū ȧt) [SINUATE], *a.* Having three sinuses (of a margin, etc.). **triskelion** (-skel′ i ȯn) [Gr. *triskelēs* (*skelos,* leg)], *n.* A form of fylfot, usu. consisting of three human legs, bent, and joined at the thigh, as in the arms of the Isle of Man.

trismegistus (tris mė jis′ tůs) [Gr. *trismegistos* (*tris,* thrice, *megistos,* great)], *a.* Thrice great (epithet of Hermes).

trismus (triz′ můs) [Gr. *trismos,* from *trizein,* to squeak, to creak], *n.* Lock-jaw.

trisoctahedron (tris ok tȧ hē′ drȯn) [Gr. *tris,* thrice, OCTAHEDRON], *n.* A solid having twenty-four equal faces.

trispermous (trī spěr′ můs), *a.* (*Bot.*) Three-seeded.

trisplanchnic (tris plăngk′ nik) [Gr. *tris,* thrice, SPLANCHNIC], *a.* (*Anat.*) Of or pertaining to the three great viscera of the body, cranial, thoracic, and abdominal.

trisporous (tri spôr′ ůs), *a.* Having three spores. **trisporic** (-spôr′ ik), *a.*

***trist** (trist) [O.F. *triste,* L. *tristis*], *a.* Sad, gloomy. ***tristful,** *a.*

tristich (tris′ tik) [Gr. *tristichos* (*tris,* thrice) from *treis,* three, *stichos,* row)], *n.* (*Pros.*) A strophe or set of three lines. **tristichous**, *a*. (*Bot.*) Arranged in three vertical rows. **tristigmatic** (-tig măt' ik) [STIGMA], *a*. (*Bot.*) Having three stigmas. **tristylous** (-tī' lŭs) [STYLE (2)], *a*. (*Bot.*) Having three styles. **trisulcate** (trī sŭl' kȧt) [SULCATE], *a*. (*Bot.*) Having three furrows or grooves; (*Zool.*) having three digits or hoofs. **trisyllable** (tri-, trī sil' ȧbl) [SYLLABLE], *n*. A word of three syllables. **trisyllabic** (-lăb' ik), *a*. **trisyllabically**, *adv*. **tritagonist** (-tăg' ȯnist) [Gr. *tritagōnistēs* (*tritos*, third, *agōnistēs*, see AGONISTIC)], *n*. The third actor in a classical Greek play.

trite (trīt) [L. *trītus*, p.p. of *terere*, to rub], *a*. Worn out; commonplace, hackneyed, stale. **tritely**, *adv*. **triteness**, *n*.

triternate (trī tĕr' nȧt), *a*. (*Bot.*) Thrice ternate; divided and subdivided into 27 leaflets. **tritheism** (trī' thē izm) [THEISM], *n*. The doctrine that the three persons of the Trinity are each distinct Gods. **tritheist**, *n*. **tritheistic** (-is' tik), *a*.

Triticum (trit' i kŭm) [L., perh. from *trītus*, as TRITE], *n*. A genus of grasses including wheat.

Tritoma (trī tō' mȧ) [Gr. *tritomos*, thrice cut (*tris*, thrice, *temnein*, to cut)], *n*. (*Bot.*) A genus of liliaceous plants comprising the flame-flowers.

Triton (trī' tŏn) [L. and Gr.], *n*. (*Gr. Myth.*) A son of Poseidon (Neptune) by Amphitrite, or one of a race of minor sea-gods, represented as half man and half fish, and blowing a spiral shell; (*Zool.*) a genus of aquatic salamanders; a genus of gasteropod, containing the trumpet-shell. **a triton among the minnows**: One greater than his fellows.

tritone (trī' tōn), *n*. (*Mus.*) An augmented fourth, containing three whole tones. **tritubercular** (trī tū bĕr' kū lar) [TUBERCULAR], *a*. Having three tubercles or cusps (of teeth). **trituberculism**, *n*.

triturate (trit' ū rāt) [late L. *trītūrātus*, p.p. of *trītūrāre*, from *trītūra*, rubbing, as TRITE], *v.t.* To rub or grind down to a fine powder; to masticate with the molar teeth. **triturable**, *a*. **trituration** (-ā' shŭn), *n*. **triturator** (trit' ū rā tȯr), *n*. **triturium, -torium** (tri tūr'-, -tôr' i ŭm), *n*. (*pl.* **-ia**) A vessel for separating liquids of different densities.

triumph (trī' ŭmf) [M.E. and O.F. *triumphe*, L. *triumphum*, nom. *-us*, Gr. *thriambos*, hymn to Bacchus], *n*. (*Rom. Ant.*) A pageant in honour of a victorious general who entered the city in a solemn procession, followed by religious ceremonies; the state of being victorious; victory, success; joy or exultation for success. *v.i.* To enjoy a triumph; to gain a victory, to prevail (over); to boast or exult (over); to exult. **triumphal** (-ŭm' fȧl), *a*. Of or pertaining to a triumph. **n*. A token of victory. **triumphal arch**: An arch built to celebrate a victory or other notable event. **triumphant**, *a*. Victorious, successful; exultant. **triumphantly**, **triumphingly**, *adv*. **triumpher** (trī' ŭm fėr), *n*.

triumvir (trī ŭm' vĕr) [L. (*trium*, gen. of *trēs*, three, *vir*, man)], *n*. (*pl.* ***triumvirs, -viri*** (-vi rī) (Rom. *Hist.*) Any one of three men united in office, esp. a member of the first or second triumvirate. **triumviral**, *a*. **triumvirate**, *n*. The office of a triumvir; a group of triumvirs; a coalition of three men in office or authority, esp. the first triumvirate, of Pompey, Julius Cæsar, and Crassus in 60 B.C., or the second, of Mark Antony, Octavian, and Lepidus, in 43 B.C.; a party or set of three men. ***triumviry**, *n*.

triune (trī' ūn) [TRI-, L. *ūnus*, one], *a*. Three in one. **triunity**, *n*.

trivalent (trī' vȧ-, triv' ȧ lėnt), *a*. (*Chem.*) Having a valency or combining power of three. **trivalence**, **trivalvular** (trī văl' vū lȧr) [VALVULAR], *a*. Having three valves. **trivalve** (trī' vălv), *a*. and *n*. **trivertebral** (-vĕr' tė brȧl) [VERTEBRAL], *a*. Consisting of three vertebræ.

trivet (triv' ėt) [formerly *trevet*, A.-S. *trefet*, L. *tripēs -pedem* (TRI-, *pēs pedis*, foot)], *n*. A three-legged stand, esp. a metal tripod or movable bracket for supporting cooking-vessels at a fire. **right as a trivet**: (*colloq.*) Firm, stable; hence in first-rate health, circumstances, position, etc.

trivia (triv' i ȧ) [see foll.], *n.pl.* Trifles, inessentials.

trivial (triv' i ȧl) [F., from L. *triviālis*, ordinary, from *trivium*, cross-roads (TRI-, *via*, way)], *a*. Of little value or importance; trifling; inconsiderable; commonplace, ordinary; (*Bot. and Zool.*) common, popular, not scientific (of names of plants, etc.). **trivialism, triviality** (-ăl' i ti), **trivialness**, *n*. **trivialize**, *v.t.* **trivially**, *adv*. **trivium** (triv' i ŭm), *n*. (*Mediæval schools*) The first three liberal arts: grammar, rhetoric, and logic.

tri-weekly (trī wēk' li), *a*. Happening, issued, or done three times a week.

-trix [L., fem. of -TOR], *suf*. Denoting a feminine agent, as in *executrix*, *testatrix*.

trizone (trī' zōn), *n*. (*Pol.*) The British, American and French zones of occupation in Germany after the 1939–45 war. **trizonal**, *a*.

troat (trōt) [imit.], *n*. The cry of a buck in rutting time. *v.i.* To cry thus.

trocar (trō' kȧr) [F. (*trois*, three, *carre*, L. *quadra*, square)], *n*. An instrument for draining an internal part of fluid, used in dropsy, hydrocele, etc.

trochaic [TROCHEE]. **trochal** [TROCHE].

trochanter (trȯ kăn' tėr) [Gr. from *trechein*, to run], *n*. (*Anat.*) Any one of several bony processes on the upper part of the thigh-bone; (*Ent.*) the second joint of the leg of an insect.

troche (trōk, trōch, trōsh) [Gr. *trochos*, wheel, as prec.], *n*. (*Med.*) A lozenge, usu. circular, of medicinal substance. **trochal** (trō' kȧl), *a*. Wheel-shaped, rotiform.

trochee (trō' kē) [L. *trochæus*, Gr. *trochaios*, running, as prec.], *n*. A metrical foot of two syllables, long and short. **trochaic** (trȯ kā' ik), *a*. and *n*.

trochil, -us (trok' il, -ŭs) [Gr. *trochilos*, from *trechein*, to run], *n*. An Egyptian plover said by the ancients to enter the mouth of crocodiles and feed on parasites; a variety of humming-bird; a crested warbler.

***trochite** (trok' īt) [Gr. *troch-os*, wheel, as prec. -ITE], *n*. The wheel-like joint of the stalk of an encrinite.

trochiter (trok' i tėr) [var. of TROCHANTER], *n*. The greater tuberosity of the humerus for the insertion of several muscles.

trochlea (trok' lė ȧ) [L., from Gr. *trochalia*, pulley, from *trechein*, to run], *n*. (*pl.* **-eæ**) (*Anat.*) A pulley-like part or surface, esp. that of the humerus articulating with the ulna. **trochlear**, *a*. (*Anat. and Bot.*). **trochleate**, *a*. (*Bot.*).

trochoid (trok' oid, trō' koid) [Gr. *trochoeidēs* (*trochos*, see TROCHE, -OID)], *a*. (*Anat.*) Rotating on its own axis, pivotal; (*Geom.*) trochoidal. *n*. (*Geom.*) A curve generated by a point in the plane of one curve rolling upon another; (*Anat.*) a trochoid joint. **trochoidal** (trȯ koi' dȧl), *a*. (*Geom.*). **trochometer** (-kom' ė tėr), *n*. An hodometer.

troco (trō' kō) [Sp. *truco*], *n*. An old game played on a lawn with wooden balls and a spoon-shaped cue, lawn-billiards.

trod, trodden, *trode [TREAD].

troglodyte (trog' lȯ dīt) [F., from L. *trōglodyta*, Gr. *trōglodutēs* (*trōglē*, cave, *duein*, to enter)], *n*. A cave-dweller. **troglodytic, -al** (-dit' ik, -ȧl), *a*. **troglodytism** (trog' lȯ dī tizm), *n*.

trogon (trō' gȯn) [Gr., pres.p. of *trōgein*, to gnaw], *n*. One of a family of tropical American insectivorous birds, with brilliant plumage.

Troic (trō' ik) [L. *Trōicus*, Gr. *Trōikos*, from *Trōia*, Troy], *a*. Trojan.

troika (troi' kȧ) [Rus.], *n*. A team of three horses harnessed abreast; a travelling-carriage drawn by this.

Trojan (trō' jȧn) [L. *Trōjānus*, from *Trōja*, *Trōia*], *a.* Pertaining to ancient Troy. *n.* An inhabitant of ancient Troy; (*fig.*) a person of pluck or determination; *a boon companion.

troke (*Sc.*) [TRUCK (1)].

troll (1) (trōl) [O.F. *troller, trauler,* G. *trollen,* to roll, to stroll, cp. M.Dut. *drollen*], *v.t.* To sing the parts of (a song) in succession; to roll or reel out (a song) in a careless manner; to fish (water) by trailing or spinning a revolving bait, esp. behind a boat. *v.i.* To fish thus; to sing in a free and easy way. *n.* A song the parts of which are sung in succession, a round, a catch; a reel on a fishing-rod; a spinning bait, a spoon-bait, etc. **to troll the bowl:** To pass it round. **troller,** *n.*

troll (2) (trōl) [Icel., cp. Swed. *troll,* Dan. *trold*], *n.* (*Scand. Myth.*) A giant or giantess endowed with supernatural powers; later, a familiar but impish dwarf.

troller [TROLL (1)].

trolley, trolly (1) (trol′ i) [TROLL (1)], *n.* A four-wheeled truck or low car, esp. one the body of which can be tilted over; a costermonger's cart; a grooved wheel on a pole used for conveying current to the motor on electric railways, tramways, etc. **trolley bus,** *n.* An omnibus deriving its motive power through a trolley from overhead wires. **trolley-car,** *n.* (*Am.*) A tramcar. **trolley-lace** [TROLLY (2)]. **trolley-pole,** *n.* **trolley-system,** *n.* The system of working electric railways, tramways, etc., by means of trolleys.

***troll-madam, *trol-my-dames** [F. *trou-madame*], *n.* An old English game like bagatelle, also called pigeon-holes or nine-holes.

trollol (tro lol′), *v.t.* and *i.* To sing in a jovial way, to troll.

trollop (trol′ ȯp) [etym. obscure], *n.* A careless, slovenly woman, a slattern; a woman of bad character. **trollopy,** *a.*

trolly (1) [TROLLEY].

trolly (2) (trol′ i) [cogn. with Flem. *tralje, traalje,* lattice, network], *n.* A kind of lace with the pattern outlined by thick thread or a number of threads combined. **trolly-lace,** *n.*

trombone (trom bōn′) [It., from *tromba,* trumpet], *n.* A large and powerful wind-instrument of the trumpet kind usu. played by means of a sliding tube. **tromba** (trom′ bȧ), *n.* A trumpet. **trombonist,** *n.*

trommel (trom′ ėl) [Gr., drum], *n.* (*Mining*) A rotating cylindrical sieve for cleaning and sizing ore.

tromometer (trȯ mom′ ė tėr) [Gr. *tromos,* trembling, from *tremein,* to tremble, -METER], *n.* An instrument for measuring earth tremors. **tromometric** (-met′ rik), *a.*

trompe (tromp) [F., TRUMP (1)], *n.* An apparatus worked by a descending column of water for producing a blast in a furnace.

tron (tron) [A.-F. *trone,* ult. from L. *trutina,* pair of scales, cp. Gr. *trutanē*], *n.* (*Sc.*) A weighing-machine consisting of a beam or balance for weighing heavy goods. **tron-pound, *tron-weight,** *n.* An ancient Scottish standard of weight (about 21 to 28 oz. av.) used for certain home products.

trona (trō′ nȧ) [Arab.], *n.* (*Min.*) A native hydrous carbonate of soda.

tronc (trongk) [F., collecting box], *n.* System whereby waiters and other employees in a restaurant share in the tips.

troop (troop) [F. *troupe,* O.F. *trope* (cp. Sp. *tropa,* It. *truppa*), etym. doubtful], *n.* An assemblage of persons or animals, a crowd, a company; (*pl.*) soldiers; a band or company of performers, a troupe; (*Mil.*) the unit of cavalry formation, usu. consisting of sixty troopers, commanded by a captain; a particular beat of the drum as a signal to march. *v.i.* To come together, to assemble, to come thronging (up, together, etc.); to move (along a way, etc.) in a troop; to hurry (off, etc.). *v.t.* To form (a squadron, etc.) into troops. **troop-horse,** *n.* **troop-ship,** *n.* A transport for soldiers. **trooper,** *n.* A cavalry-soldier; a private in a cavalry regiment; a troop-ship; (*Austral.*) a mounted policeman. **trooping the colour:** A ceremonial parade at which the colour is carried between the files of troops.

troopial (troo′ pi ȧl) [F. *troupiale,* from *troupe,* TROOP], *n.* An American bird of the genus *Icterus,* in some respects resembling the starling.

tropæolum (trȯ pē′ ȯ lŭm) [mod. L., from Gr. *tropaios,* turning, as foll], *n.* One of a genus of South American climbing plants containing the Indian-cress or nasturtium.

trope (trōp) [F., from L. *tropus,* Gr. *tropos,* turn, trope, from *trepein,* to turn], *n.* A figurative use of a word.

trophesy, etc [TROPHIC].

trophi (trȯ′ fī) [mod. L., pl. of *trophus,* Gr. *trophos,* nurse, as foll.], *n.pl.* (*Ent.*) The parts of the mouth in insects.

trophic (trof′ ik) [Gr. *trophē,* nourishment, from *trephein,* to nourish], *a.* Pertaining to nutrition. **trophesy,** *n.* (*Path.*) Deranged nutrition due to nervous disorder. **trophesial** (trȯ fē′ si ȧl), *a.*

tropho-, *comb. form.* [as prec.] **trophotropism** (trȯ fot′ rȯ pizm), *n.* (*Bot.*) The movement of the organs of a growing plant toward or away from nutrient substances, induced by the chemical nature of its surroundings. **trophotropic** (-trop′ ik), *a.*

Trophonian (trȯ fō′ ni ȧn), *a.* Pertaining or relating to the Grecian architect Trophonius, said traditionally to have built the celebrated temple of Apollo at Delphi.

trophy (trō′ fi) [F. *trophée,* L. *tropæum,* Gr. *tropaion,* neut. a. from *tropē,* defeat, from *trepein,* to turn], *n.* (*Gr. Ant.*) A pile of arms and other spoils taken from a vanquished enemy and set up on the battle-field to commemorate a victory; (*Rom. Ant.*) a more permanent memorial imitating this decorated with captured arms, beaks of ships, etc., or representations of these; anything preserved as a memorial of victory or success; an ornamental group of typical or symbolical objects placed on a wall, etc. **trophied,** *a.*

tropic (trop′ ik) [F. *tropique,* late L. *tropicum,* nom. *-cus,* Gr. *tropikos kuklos,* the tropic circle, from *tropē,* solstice, turning, from *trepein,* to turn], *n.* Either of the two parallels of latitude situated at 23° 27′ from the equator, the northern called the **tropic of Cancer,** and the southern the **tropic of Capricorn;** (*pl.*) the regions of the torrid zone between these; (*Astron.*) either of the corresponding parallels of declination on the celestial sphere. *a.* Of or pertaining to the tropics, tropical. **tropic-bird,** *n.* A tern-like bird of the natatorial genus *Phaëthon.* **tropical,** *a.* Pertaining to, lying within, or characteristic of the tropics; (*fig.*) passionate, fervent; of the nature of a trope, figurative, metaphorical. **tropical month:** (*Astron.*) The mean period of the moon's passing through 360° of longitude, *i.e.* 27 days, 7 hours, 43 min., 4·7 secs. **tropical year:** A solar year. **tropically,** *adv.* **tropicopolitan** (-pol′ i tȧn) [see COSMOPOLITAN], *a.* Inhabiting and confined to the tropics; *n.* A tropicopolitan animal or plant.

tropism (trōp′ izm) [Gr. *tropos,* turn], *n.* (*Physiol.*) The direction of growth in a plant or other organism that is due to an external stimulus.

tropology (trȯ pol′ ȯ ji), *n.* The use of tropical or figurative language; interpretation of the Scriptures in a figurative sense. **tropist** (trō′ pist), *n.* One who deals in tropes; one who explains the Scriptures by tropes. **tropological** (trop ȯ loj′ i kȧl), *a.* **tropologically,** *adv.*

troposphere (trō′ pō sfēr) [Gr. *tropos,* a turn, SPHERE], *n.* (*Meteor.*) The hollow sphere of atmosphere surrounding the earth, bounded by the stratosphere, in which temperature varies and the weather functions. **tropopause,** *n.* The boundary between the troposphere and the stratosphere.

troppo (trop′ ō) [It., too much], *adv.* (*Mus.*) Too much, excessively.

***trossers** [TROUSERS].

trot (trot) [M.E. *trotten*, F. *trotter*, etym. doubtful, perh. from L. *tolūtim*, at a trot, from *tollere*, to lift, through late L. *tolūtārius*, trotting], *v.i.* (*past & p.p.* **trotted**) To move at a steady rapid pace (of a horse or other quadruped) by simultaneously lifting one fore-foot and the hind-foot of the opposite side alternately with the other pair, the body being unsupported at intervals; to run with short brisk strides. *v.t.* To cause to trot; to cover (a distance, etc.) by trotting. *n.* The pace, motion, or act of a horse, etc., in trotting; a brisk steady pace; a dance; a toddling child; a term of endearment; *an old woman. **to trot out:** (*colloq.*) To bring forward. **trotter,** *n.* One who or that which trots, esp. a horse trained for fast trotting; (*pl.*) sheep's or other animals' feet used as food.

troth (trōth) [A.-S. *trēowth*, TRUTH], *n.* Faith, fidelity, truth. **troth-plight,** *a.* Betrothed, affianced.

trottoir (trot′ war) [F., from *trotter*, to TROT], *n.* The pavement at the side of a street, etc.

troubadour (troo′ bȧ door) [F., from Prov. *trobador*, from *trobar* (F. *trouver*, to find), prob. through a pop. L. *tropāre*, to compose poetry, from *tropus*, TROPE], *n.* One of a class of lyric poets who flourished in Provence in the 11th cent., writing in the *langue d'oc* chiefly of love and chivalry.

trouble (trŭb′ ėl) [O.F. *troubler*, *trubler*, from L. *turbula*, dim. of *turba*, crowd], *v.t.* To agitate, to disturb; to annoy, to molest; to distress, to afflict; to inconvenience, to put to some exertion or pains. *v.i.* To be agitated or disturbed; to take trouble or pains. *n.* Affliction, distress, worry, perplexity, annoyance, misfortune; labour, exertion, inconvenience. **to ask for trouble:** (*slang*) To lack caution. **to get into trouble:** *v.i.* To incur censure or punishment; to become pregnant. **troubler,** *n.* **troublesome** (trŭbl′ sȯm), *a.* Giving trouble; annoying, vexatious; tiresome, wearisome, importunate. **troublesomely,** *adv.* **troublesomeness,** *n.* ***troublous,** *a.* Full of commotion; disturbed, agitated, disorderly.

trough (trof, trawf) [A.-S. *trog* (cp. Dut., G., and Icel. *trog* Dan. *trug*, Swed. *träg*), cogn. with TREE], *n.* A long, narrow, open receptacle of wood, iron, etc., for holding water, fodder, etc., for domestic animals, kneading dough, washing ore, etc.; a deep narrow channel, furrow, or depression (in land, the sea, etc.).

trounce (trouns) [O.F. *trons*, TRUNCHEON], *v.t.* To beat severely. **trouncing,** *n.*

troupe (troop) [F., TROOP], *n.* A company of actors, performers, etc. **trouper,** *n.* A member of such a company.

troupial [TROOPIAL].

trous-de-loup (troo dė loo) [F., wolf-holes], *n.pl.* Pits with a pointed stake in each, as a defence against cavalry.

trouser (trou′ zėr) [prob. Ir. *triubhas*, but cp. F. *trousses*, breeches, bundles, see TRUSS], *n.* A two-legged outer garment reaching from the waist to the ankles, mostly worn by men and boys (*usu. in pl.*). **trousered,** *a.* **trousering,** *n.* Cloth for making trousers.

trousse (troos) [F.], *n.* A set of small (esp. surgical) instruments in a sheath or case.

trousseau (troo′ sō, troo sō′) [F., bundle, O.F. *troussel*, dim. of *trousse*, TRUSS], *n.* (*pl.* **-eaux**) The clothes and general outfit of a bride.

trout (trout) [A.-S. *truht*, L. *tructa*, Gr. *trōkkēs*, from *trōgein*, to gnaw], *n.* A freshwater game-fish, *Salmo fario*, allied to but smaller than the salmon. *v.i.* To fish for trout. **trout-coloured,** *a.* White, with spots of black, bay, or sorrel. **trout-stream,** *n.* **troutlet, -ling,** *n.* **trouty,** *a.*

trouvère (troo vâr′) [F., from *trouver*, see TROUBADOUR], *n.* One of the mediæval poets of N. France, composers chiefly of narrative poems.

trove [SEE TREASURE].

trover (trō′ vėr) [O.F. (F. *trouver*), see CONTRIVE], *n.* (*Law*) The acquisition or appropriation of any goods; an action for the recovery of personal property wrongfully converted by another to his own use.

***trow** (trō, trou) [A.-S. *trūwian*, *trēowian*, cogn. with *trēowe*, TRUE], *v.t.* and *i.* To think, to suppose, to believe.

trowel (trou′ ėl) [M.E. *truel*, F. *truelle*, late L. *truella*, dim. of *trua*, ladle], *n.* A flat-bladed, usu. pointed, tool used by masons, etc., for spreading mortar, etc.; a scoop-shaped tool used in digging up plants, etc. *v.t.* To apply or dress with a trowel. **to lay it on with a trowel:** To flatter grossly.

troy (troi) [prob. from *Troyes*, town S.E. of Paris], *n.* A system of weights (12 oz. av. to 1 lb.) used chiefly in weighing gold, silver, and gems, also called **troy weight.**

truant (troo′ ȧnt) [A.-F. *truaunt*, W. *truan*, wretched, cp. Ir. *trogha*, miserable, Gael. *truaghan*, a wretched creature], *a.* Shirking, idle, loitering. *n.* One who shirks or neglects duty; an idler, a loiterer; a child who stays away from school without leave. *v.i.* To play truant. **to play truant:** To stay away from school without leave. **truant-school,** *n.* An industrial school for children who habitually play truant. **truancy,** *n.* **truantly,** *adv.*

Trubenise (troo′ ben īz) *v.t.* Proprietary name of a method to stiffen fabrics with cellulose acetate.

truce (troos) [M.E. *triwes*, *treowes*, pl., from A.-S. *trēow*, compact, faith, see TRUE], *n.* A temporary cessation of hostilities; an agreement to cease hostilities; an armistice; (*fig.*) a temporary intermission, alleviation, or respite. **truce-breaker,** *n.* **truceless,** *a.*

Trucial Coast (troo′ si ȧl), *n.* (*Pol.*) A strip on the coast of the Persian Gulf including seven independent states under British protection by treaties of 1820, 1853, and 1892.

truck (1) (trŭk) [M.E. *trukken*, A.-F. *troquier* (F. *troquer*), from O.F. *troque*, barter, W.Flem. *trok*, sale, *trokken*, to procure goods, cogn. with TREK], *v.t.* and *i.* To exchange; to barter; to peddle, to hawk. *n.* Exchange of commodities; barter; commodities suitable for barter, small wares; traffic; intercourse, dealings; the truck system; (*colloq.*) rubbish. **Truck Acts:** Acts investigating or suppressing the truck system (passed 1831, '87, and '96). **truck farmer:** (*Am.*) A market-gardener. **truck shop:** A shop where the truck system is carried on, a tommy shop. **truck system:** The practice of paying wages in goods instead of money. ***truckage** (1), *n.*

truck (2) (trŭk) [L. *trochus*, Gr. *trochos*, wheel, from *trechein*, to run, or perh. short for foll.], *n.* A strong, usu. four-wheeled vehicle for conveying heavy goods; an open railway wagon; a low barrow with two small wheels used by porters, etc., for moving luggage, etc., at railway stations, in warehouses, etc.; a framework and set of wheels for supporting the whole or part of a railway carriage, etc.; (*Naut.*) a small wooden disk at the top of a mast with holes for the halyards, etc.; *a small tireless wheel; (*Am.*) a motor lorry. *v.t.* To convey on a truck. **truck-bolster,** *n.* A cross-beam in a car-truck supporting one end of the car. **truckage** (2) *n.*

truckle (trŭk′ ėl) [from TROCHLEA; cp. prec.], *v.i.* Orig. to sleep in a truckle-bed; hence, to give way obsequiously (to the will of another); to cringe, to be servile (to). **truckle-bed,** *n.* A low bed on castors or wheels for rolling under another; a trundle-bed. **truckler,** *n.*

truculent (trŭk′ ū-, troo′ kū lėnt) [O.F., from L. *truculentum*, nom. *-tus*, from *trux trucis*, savage], *a.*

Savage, ferocious, barbarous, violent. **truculence, -lency,** *n.* **truculently,** *adv.* In a truculent manner.

trudge (trŭj) [F. *trucher*, to beg, prob. from Teut. (cp. Dut. *troggelen*, also Icel. *thrūga*, Swed. *truga*, Dan. *true*, to press)], *v.i.* and *t.* To travel on foot esp. with labour and fatigue. *n.* A walk of this kind.

trudgeon, trudgen (trŭj' ŏn) [John *Trudgen* (fl. 1860–70) who introduced it], *n.* (*Swimming*) A stroke with the arms brought over the head alternately, and ordinary leg action.

true (troo) [A.-S. *trēowe, trȳw*, cp. Dut. *trouw*, G. *treu*, Icel. *tryggr, trūr*], *a.* Conformable to fact or reality, not false or erroneous; in accordance with appearance, not deceptive, counterfeit, or spurious, genuine; in accordance with right or law, legitimate, rightful; corresponding to type or standard; in perfect tune (of a voice, etc.); faithful, loyal, constant; *not given to falsehood, veracious, truthful, honest. *v.t.* To make true, exact, or accurate. *adv.* Truly. **true bill:** A bill of indictment endorsed by a grand jury as sustained by the evidence. **true blue** [BLUE]. **true-born,** *a.* Of legitimate birth; such by birth or blood. **true-bred,** *a.* Of genuine or right breed. ***true-derived,** *a.* Legitimate. ***true-disposing,** *a.* Just. **true-hearted,** *a.* **true-heartedness,** *n.* **true-love,** *n.* One truly loved or loving; one's sweetheart. **true-love** or **true-lover's knot,** *n.* A kind of double knot with two interlacing bows on each side and two ends. **true to type:** Normal, what might be expected. ***truepenny,** *n.* An honest fellow.

truffle (trŭf' ėl, trū' fėl) [O.F. *trufle*, prob. from L. TUBER], *n.* A fleshy fungus of the genus *Tuber*, used for seasoning, etc. **truffle-dog,** *n.* A dog trained to find truffles.

trug (trŭg) [etym. doubtful], *n.* A wooden basket used by gardeners, greengrocers, etc.; a wooden milk-pail; a hod for mortar.

truism (troo' izm), *n.* A self-evident or unquestionable truth; an obvious statement, a platitude.

***trull** (trŭl) [G. *trulle, trolle*, cogn. with TROLL (2) and DROLL], *n.* A strumpet, a drab.

truly (troo' li), *adv.* Sincerely, in accordance with truth, accurately; genuinely; in reality; faithfully, honestly, loyally; *really, indeed. **yours truly:** Conventional formal ending to a letter.

trumeau (troo mō) [F.], *n.* (*pl.* **-eaux**) A piece of wall, a pier or pillar, between two openings or dividing a doorway.

trump (1) (trŭmp) [O.F. *trompe* (whence *tromper*, to play on this, to deceive), O.H.G. *trumpa*, from O.Slav., cp. Rus. *truba*, Pol. *trabas*], **n.* A trumpet. **v.t.* To impose (a thing) upon by fraud. **Last Trump:** The end of the world. **to trump up:** To fabricate, to concoct.

trump (2) (trŭmp) [F. *triomphe*, a card-game, TRIUMPH], *n.* Any card of a suit ranking for the time being above the others; (*colloq.*) a good fellow; a generous or reliable person. *v.t.* To take with a trump. *v.i.* To play a trump-card. ***to put to one's trumps:** To reduce to one's last expedient. **trump-card,** *n.* The card turned up to determine which suit is to be trumps; any card of this suit; (*fig.*) an infallible expedient.

trumpery (trŭm' pė ri), *n.* Worthless finery; rubbish. *a.* Showy but worthless, delusive, rubbishy.

trumpet (trŭm' pėt [O.F. *trompette*, dim. of TRUMP (1)], *n.* A musical wind instrument, usu. consisting of a long, straight, curved, or coiled tube with a wide termination, usu. of brass, with a cup-shaped mouthpiece; a thing resembling this in shape, as a funnel; the horn of a gramophone; an ear-trumpet; a reed-stop in an organ; a sound of or as of a trumpet. *v.t.* To proclaim by or as by sound of trumpet. *v.i.* To make a loud sound as of a trumpet (esp. of the elephant). **to blow one's own trumpet:** To boast. **Feast of Trumpets:** A Jewish festival celebrating the beginning of the year. **trumpet-call,** *n.* A call by sound of trumpet; (*fig.*) an imperative call to action. **trumpet-conch, -shell,** *n.* A gasteropod with a turreted shell often used as a trumpet. **trumpet-fish,** *n.* *Centriscus scolopax*, from its elongated tubular snout. **trumpet-flower,** *n.* A plant with large tubular flowers. **trumpet-major,** *n.* The head trumpeter in a cavalry regiment. **trumpet-tongued,** *a.* Proclaiming loudly, as with the voice of a trumpet. **trumpeter,** *n.* One who sounds a trumpet, esp. a soldier giving signals on the trumpet in a cavalry regiment; (*fig.*) one who proclaims, publishes, or denounces; a variety of the domestic pigeon, with a prolonged coo; a S. American bird allied to the cranes; a N. American swan; an Australian edible fish.

truncal [TRUNK].

truncate (trŭng' kāt) [L. *truncātus*, p.p. of *truncāre*, from *truncus*, TRUNK], *v.t.* To cut the top or end from; (*Cryst.*) to replace an angle by a plane. *a.* Cut short, truncated; (*Bot.*) terminating abruptly, as if a piece had been cut off. **truncately,** *adv.* **truncation** (-kā' shŭn), **truncature** (trŭng' kȧ tūr), *n.*

truncheon (trŭn' shŏn, -chŏn) [O.North.F. *tronchon*, O.F. *tronçon*, dim. of *tronc*, TRUNK], *n.* A short staff, club, or cudgel; a baton, a staff of authority. *v.t.* To beat with a truncheon. ***truncheoneer** (-nēr'), *n.*

trundle (trŭn' dėl) [M.F. *trondeler*, L.G. *tröndeln*, cogn. with TREND], *n.* A small broad wheel, a castor; a lantern-wheel; a low-wheeled vehicle, a truck; a truckle-bed. *v.t.* and *i.* To roll. **trundle-head,** *n.* The head of a capstan. **trundle-tail,** *n.* A curled tail; a dog with a curled tail.

trunk (trŭngk) [F. *tronc*, L. *truncum*, nom. *-us*, stem, piece cut off], *n.* The main stem of a tree, opp. to the branches or roots; the body of an animal apart from the limbs, head, and tail; the main body of anything; a trunk-line; the shaft of a column; a box or chest with a hinged lid for packing clothes, etc., in for travel; (*Am.*) the boot of a motor-car; a ventilating shaft, conduit, chute, flume, etc.; a hollow cylinder in which a connecting-rod works, in marine and other steam-engines; the proboscis of an elephant or any analogous organ; (*pl.*) trunk-hose. **trunk call,** *n.* A long-distance telephone call. **trunk-drawers,** *n.pl.* Drawers cut off at the knees. **trunk exchange,** *n.* (*Teleph.*) An exchange connected by trunk lines to other trunk exchanges. **trunk-hose,** *n.pl.* Wide breeches extending from the waist to the middle of the thigh, worn in the 16th–17th cent. **trunk-line,** *n.* The main line of a railway, canal, telephone, etc. **trunk road,** *n.* A road maintained by the Ministry of Transport. **trunkful,** *n.* **trunkless,** *a.* **truncal,** *a.*

trunnion (trŭn' yŏn) [F. *trognon*, dim. of *tron*, *tronc*, prec.], *n.* One of the cylindrical projections from the sides of a cannon or mortar; a hollow gudgeon on which the cylinder oscillates in some steam-engines, and through which the steam enters. **trunnioned,** *a.*

truss (trŭs) [O.F. *trusser*, *trosser*, from L. THYRSUS], *v.t.* To support or brace with a truss; to fasten (a fowl or the wings of a fowl, etc.) with a skewer or twine before cooking; *to tie, tighten, or fasten up (one's clothes, etc.); (*fig.*) to hang (a criminal); *to seize (of hawks, etc.). *n.* A timber or iron supporting and strengthening structure in a roof, bridge, etc.; a large corbel; (*Naut.*) a heavy iron securing a lower yard to the mast; (*Surg.*) a padded belt or other apparatus worn round the body for preventing or compressing a hernia; a bundle (56 lb.) of old, (60 lb.) of new hay, or (36 lb.) of straw; a compact terminal cluster of flowers. **to truss up:** To make up in to a bundle; to bind or tie up; to hang. **truss-beam,** *n.* **trussbridge,** *n.*

trust (trŭst) [M.E., cp. O. Fris. *trāst*, Icel. *traust*, Dan. and Swed. *tröst*, G. *trost*, comfort, consolation], *n.* Confident reliance on or belief in the integrity, veracity, justice, friendship, power, protection, etc., of a person or thing; confidence, firm expectation (that); the person or thing on which reliance is placed; reliance on (assumed honesty, etc.) without examination; commercial credit; (*Law*) confidence reposed in a person to whom property is conveyed for the benefit of another; the right to or title in such property as distinct from its legal ownership; the property or thing held in trust; the legal relation between such property and the holder; something committed to one's charge or care; the obligation of one who has received such a charge; (*Comm.*) a combination of a number of businesses or companies under one general control for the purpose of defeating competition, creating a monopoly, etc. *v.t.* To place confidence in, to believe in, to rely upon; to believe, to have a confident hope of expectation; to commit to the care of a person, to entrust; to entrust (a person with a thing); to give credit to. *v.i.* To have trust or confidence; to sell goods on credit. **National Trust,** *n.* A body formed for the purchase and preservation of places of historic interest and natural beauty. **trust deed:** An instrument of conveyance that creates a trust. **trust-house:** A public house owned by a trust company and not by a brewer. **trustable,** *a.* **trustee** (trŭs tē'), *n.* One to whom property is committed in trust for the benefit of another; one of a body of men, often elective, managing the affairs of an institution. **trusteeship,** *n.* **truster,** *n.* **trustful,** *a.* Full of trust; trusting, confiding. **trustfully,** *adv.* **trustfulness,** *n.* **trustingly,** *adv.* **trustless,** *a.* Not worthy of trust; faithless. **trustlessness,** *n.* **trustworthy,** *a.* Deserving of trust or confidence. **trustworthiness,** *n.* **trusty,** *a.* Trustworthy, reliable; not liable to fail in time of need. *n.* A prisoner trusted with a certain amount of liberty to do jobs, etc. **trustily,** *adv.* **trustiness,** *n.*

truth (trooth, *pl.* troothz) [A.-S. *trēowthu*, from *trēowe*, TRUE], *n.* The state or quality of being true; conformity to fact or reality; that which is true, a fact, a verity; honesty, veracity, sincerity; fidelity, constancy; true religion. **in truth, *of a truth:** In reality, in fact, truly. **truth-teller,** *n.* **truthful,** *a.* Habitually speaking the truth, veracious, reliable, conformable to truth. **truthfully,** *adv.* **truthfulness,** *n.* **truthless,** *a.* False; faithless, unreliable. **truthlessness,** *n.*

truttaceous (trŭ tā' shŭs), *a.* Related to or resembling trout.

try (trī) [M.E. *trien*, F. *trier*, late L. *trītāre*, to triturate, from *trītus*, TRITE], *v.t.* (*past & p.p.* **tried**) To test, to examine by experiment; to determine the qualities, etc., of by reference to a standard; to find out by experiment or experience; to attempt, to endeavour (to do, etc.); to subject to a severe or undue test, to strain; to subject to hardship, suffering, etc., as if for a test, to afflict; to investigate (a charge, issue, etc.) judicially, to subject (a person) to judicial trial; to prove or settle by a test or experiment; to smooth (a roughly-planed board) with a trying-plane, etc., to secure a perfectly level surface; to purify, to refine (metals, etc.) by melting, etc. *v.i.* To endeavour, to make an attempt, to put forth efforts. *n.* (*colloq.*) An attempt; (*Rugby*) the right to carry the ball and try to kick a goal from in front. **to try for:** To aim at; to attempt to secure; to apply for. **to try on:** To put (clothes) on to see if they fit; (*slang*) to attempt (it with), to see how much a person will tolerate. **to try out:** To test. **try-sail** (trī' sĕl, trīsl), *n.* A fore-and-aft sail set on a gaff abaft the foremast and mainmast. **triable,** *a.* **try-, trying-square,** *n.* A carpenter's square with a wooden stock and steel limb.

Trygon (trī' gŏn) [Gr. *trugōn*], *n.* A genus of rays armed with a spine on the tail; a sting-ray.

tryma (trī' mȧ) [Gr. *truma*, hole, from *truein*, to rub], *n.* (*pl.* **-mata**) A drupe-like fruit the outer wall of the pericarp of which is dehiscent, as in the walnut.

trypanosome (trī' păn ō sōm) [Gr. *trupanon*, a borer; *soma*, a body], *n.* (*Zool.*) One of the *Trypanosomata*, an order of flagellate infusorians infesting the blood of man and pathogenic to him. The parasite is spread by the tsetse fly and causes sleeping-sickness, etc.

trypograph (trī' pō grăf) [Gr. *trupan*, to bore, -GRAPH], *n.* A stencil made by writing with a stylus on a sheet of prepared paper laid on a roughened surface so as to produce a series of minute holes. **trypographic** (-grăf' ik), *a.*

trypsin (trip' sin) [Gr., from *tribein*, to rub], *n.* (*Chem.*) A ferment contained in the pancreatic juice, etc. **tryptic,** *a.* **tryptone,** *n.* A peptone formed during digestion by the action of trypsin on proteins.

tryst (trīst trist) [O.F. *triste*, *tristre*, a watching-station in hunting, cogn. with TRUST], *n.* An appointed meeting, an appointment; a rendezvous. *v.t.* To agree to meet; to appoint (a time or place) for meeting. **trysting-day,** *n.* **trysting-place,** *n.*

Tsar (tsar, zar) [Rus. *tsari*, L. *Cæsar*], *n.* The title of the former Emperors of Russia. **Tsarevich,** *n.* The son of a Tsar. **Tsarevna** (-ev' nȧ), *n.* The daughter of a Tsar. **Tsarina** (-ē' nȧ), **Tsaritza** (-it' sȧ), *n.* The wife of a Tsar; an Empress of Russia.

tsetse (set' si) [native name], *n.* A South African fly, *Glossina morsitans*, the bite of which is often fatal to cattle, horses, dogs, etc., and transmits to man the trypanosomes of sleeping-sickness.

tsung-tuh (tsung' too) [Chin.], *n.* A Chinese viceroy or governor of a province.

tuan (too' ȧn) [Austral. abor.], *n.* A flying-squirrel.

tuart, touart (too' art) [Austral. abor.], *n.* The W. Australian eucalyptus, *E. gomphocephala.*

tuatara (too ȧ ta' ra) [Maori], *n.* The largest N. Zealand reptile, the lizard-like Sphenodon, now the last survivor of the class Rhyncocephalia.

tub (tŭb) [M.Dut. *tobbe*, *dobbe*, etym. doubtful], *n.* An open wooden (usu. round) vessel constructed of staves held together by hoops, used for washing, holding butter, etc.; the amount (of butter, etc.) that a packing-tub holds; a small cask; a sponge-bath, a bath in a tub; (*Mining*) a bucket, box, or truck for bringing up ore, etc.; a short clumsy boat; a boat for practising rowing in. *v.t.* (*past & p.p.* **tubbed**) To place or set in a tub; to bathe in a tub. *v.i.* To take a bath in a tub; to row in a tub. **tub-thumper,** *n.* (*colloq.*) A ranting preacher. **tub-wheel,** *n.* A bowl-shaped water-wheel analogous to a turbine; a rotating drum for washing leather, etc. **tubbing,** *n.* **tubbish,** *a.* **tubful,** *n.* **tubby,** *a.* Tub-shaped, corpulent; (*Mus.*) sounding like an empty tub when struck, wanting resonance.

tuba (tū' bȧ) [L., trumpet], *n.* (*pl.* **-bæ**) A brass wind-instrument of the saxhorn kind, with a low pitch; a powerful reed-stop in an organ.

tube (tūb) [F., from L. *tubum*, nom. *-us*, cogn. with prec.], *n.* A long hollow cylinder for the conveyance of fluids and various other purposes, a pipe; a cylindrical vessel of thin flexible metal for holding pigment, etc.; the main body of a wind-instrument; the central portion of a heavy gun round which the jackets are fixed by shrinking; (*colloq.*) a tubular electric railway; (*Am.*) a radio valve; (*Anat.*) a tubular vessel in an animal or plant for conveying air, fluids, etc. *v.t.* To furnish with or enclose in a tube or tubes. **tube-flower,** *n.* An ornamental E. Indian shrub, *Clerodendron siphonanthus*, of the vervain family. **tube railway,** *n.* An underground electric railway running in a tubular tunnel. **tubewell,** *n.* A pipe with a sharp point and perforations just above this for driving into the ground to obtain water from a depth. **tubal, tubar,** *a.* **tubing,** *n.*

tuber (tū' bĕr) [L., hump, lump, swelling, tumour, truffle, cogn. with TUMID], *n.* A short, thick portion of an underground stem, set with eyes or modified buds, as in the potato; a genus of subterranean fungi, containing the truffle; (*Anat.*) a swelling or prominence. **tuberiferous** (-if' ĕr ŭs), *a.* **tuberiform** (tū'-), *a.* **tuberosity, tuberousness,** *n.*

tuberous, *a.* Having prominent knobs or excrescences; like or bearing tubers.

tubercle (tū′ bėr kėl) [F., from L. *tūberculum*, dim. of prec.], *n.* A small prominence, esp. in bone; a small granular non-vascular tumour or nodule formed within the substance of an organ as the result of morbid action, due to a bacillus, tending to set up degeneration, pulmonary consumption, etc.; (*Bot.*) a small tuber; a warty excrescence. **tubercled, tubercular** (tū bĕr′ kū lȧr), **tuberculate, -lated, tuberculoid, tuberculose, -lous,** *a.* **tuberculation** (-lā′ shŭn), *n.* Formation of tubercles; a system of tubercles; the state of being tuberculous. **tubercularize, tuberculize,** *v.t.* To infect with tuberculosis. **tuberculization,** *n.*

tuberculin (tū bĕr′ kū lin), *n.* A ptomaine produced by the action of the tubercle-bacillus; a fluid used hypodermically in the diagnosis of tuberculosis.

tuberculosis (tū bĕr kū lō′ sis), *n.* A diseased condition characterized by the presence of tubercles in the tissues, esp. pulmonary tuberculosis or consumption. **tuberculosed,** *a.*

tuberiferous, etc. [TUBER].

tuberose (tū′ bėr ōs), *a.* **Tuberous.** *n.* (*often, but incorr., pron.* tūb′ rōz) A bulbous plant, *Polianthes tuberosa*, with fragrant white flowers.

tuberosity [TUBER].

tubi- [L. *tubus*, TUBE], *comb. form.* ***tubicen** (tū′ bi sėn) [L. (*canere*, to sing)], *n.* (*pl.* **-cines**) A trumpeter. ***tubicinate** (tū bis′ i nāt), *v.i.* To sound a trumpet. **tubicolous** (tū bik′ ȯ lŭs) [L. *colere*, to cultivate], *a.* Inhabiting a tubular case. **tubiform,** *a.*

tubular (tū′ bū lȧr) [L. *tubulus*, dim. of *tubus*, TUBE], *a.* Tube-shaped; having or consisting of a tube or tubes; sounding like air passing through a tube (of breathing). **tubular boiler:** One in which the water circulates in a number of pipes in contact with a fire. **tubular bridge:** One consisting of a large rectangular tube through which a roadway or railway passes. **tubulate, -lated,** *a.* **tubule,** *n.* A small pipe or fistular body. **tubuliform** (-bū′ li fôrm), *a.* **tubulose, tubulous,** *a.*

tuck (1) (tŭk) [M.E. *tukken*, L.G. *tukken, tokken*, cogn. with TOUCH], *v.t.* To press close together or press, fold, or roll the loose ends or parts of compactly (up, in, etc.); to wrap or cover (up or in) closely or snugly; to gather up, to fold or draw together or into small compass; to push or press, to cram, to stuff, to stow (away, into, etc.); to gather or stitch (a dress, etc.) in folds; (*slang*) to hang (a criminal up). *v.i.* To make tucks; to be got rid of by tucking away (of loose cloth, etc.). *n.* A horizontal fold in a dress, etc., esp. one of a series made for ornament or to dispose of loose material; a tuck-net; (*Naut.*) the after part of a ship where the ends of the bottom planks meet; (*slang*) food, esp. sweets, pastry, etc. **tucker** (1), *n.* (*Austral.*) Food. **to tuck in:** To eat greedily. **tuck-in, -out,** *n.* A hearty meal, a spread. **tuck-net, -seine,** *n.* A net or seine used for removing fish from a larger net. **tuck-shop,** *n.* (*slang*) A pastry-cook's or confectioner's shop.

tuck (2) (tŭk) [TUCKET], *n.* The beat or roll of a drum; a blast or flourish on a trumpet; a tucket.

***tuck** (3) (tŭk) [M.F. *étoc, estoc*, It. *stocco*, G. STOCK (1)], *n.* A long, narrow sword, a rapier.

tuckahoe (tŭk′ ȧ hō) [N.Am.Ind.], *n.* An underground fungus dug up in parts of the southern U.S.A.; an inhabitant of the poorer parts of Virginia supposed to live on this.

tucker (1) (tŭk′ er) [TUCK (1)].

tucker (2) (tŭk′ ėr), *n.* One who or that which tucks; an ornamental frilling of lace or muslin round the top of a woman's dress, covering the neck and shoulders, worn in 17th-18th cents.

***tucket** (tŭk′ ėt) [O.North.F. *touquet*, It. *toccata*, fem. p.p. of *toccare*, to TOUCH], *n.* A flourish on a trumpet, a fanfare. ***tucket sonance:** (*Shak.*) The sound of the tucket.

tucum (too′ kŭm) [Braz.], *n.* A South American palm, *Astrocaryum vulgare*, yielding a fibre used for cordage, etc.

-tude [L. *-tūdinem*, nom. *-tūdo*], *suf.* Forming abstract nouns, as *altitude, beatitude, fortitude.*

Tudor (tū′ dȯr), *a.* Pertaining to the English royal line (from Henry VII to Elizabeth), founded by Owen Tudor of Wales, who married the widow of Henry V, or to their period. **Tudor flower:** A trefoil ornament used in the Tudor style. **Tudor rose:** A five-lobed flower adopted as badge by Henry VII. **Tudor style:** The late Perpendicular style in Gothic architecture.

Tuesday (tūz′ dā, -di) [A.-S. *Tīwes dæg*, day of the god of war (*Tīw*, cogn. with L. *deus*, Gr. *Zeus*)], *n.* The third day of the week.

tufa (tū′ fȧ) [It. for *tufo*, L. *tōphus*, a soft, sandy stone, cp. Gr. *tophos*], *n.* A soft calcareous rock deposited by springs and streams. **tufaceous** (-fā′ shŭs), *a.*

tuff (tŭf) [F. *tuf*, It. *tufo*, see prec.], *n.* An earthy, sometimes fragmentary, deposit of volcanic materials of the most heterogeneous kind.

tuft (tŭft) [F. *touffe*, from Teut. (cp. Swed. dial. *tuppa*, Icel. *toppr*, G. *zopf*)], *n.* A cluster, a bunch, a collection of hairs, threads, feathers, etc., held or fastened together at one end; (*Anat.*) a bunch of small blood-vessels, etc.; (*colloq.*) a goatee, an imperial; *a young nobleman at a university, from the tuft or gold tassel formerly worn on his cap. *v.t.* To separate into tufts; to adorn with or as with tufts; to pass thread through (a mattress, etc.) at regular intervals and fasten a button or tuft in the depression thus made. *v.i.* To grow in tufts. **tuft-hunter,** *n.* One who courts the society of titled persons. **tuft-hunting,** *n.* **tufted, tufty,** *a.*

tug (tŭg) [M.E. *toggen*, perh. from Icel. *tog*, rope, cogn. with TOW (1)], *v.t.* To pull or draw with great effort or with violence; to haul, to tow. *v.i.* (*past & p.p.* **tugged**) To pull violently (at). *n.* The act or a spell of tugging; a vigorous or violent pull; a violent effort, a severe struggle; a small powerful steam-vessel for towing others; a loop hanging from the saddle in harness supporting a shaft or trace. **tug-carrier, -chain, -iron, -slide, -spring,** *n.* A part of the harness used in fastening the traces to the shafts, etc. **tug of war:** A contest between two sets of persons pulling a rope from opposite ends across a line marked on the ground; (*fig.*) a final struggle. **tugger,** *n.* ***tuggingly,** *adv.*

tui (too′ ē) [Maori], *n.* The parson-bird.

***tuille** (twēl) [O.F. (cp. F. *tuile*, TILE), L. *tugula*, TILE], *n.* A steel plate protecting the thighs, hanging from the tasses. ***tuillette** (twė let′), *n.* A small tuille protecting the hips.

tuism (tū′ izm) [L. *tū*, thou, -ISM], *n.* The theory that all thought is directed to a second person or to one's future self as such.

tuition (tū ish′ ŭn) [F., from L. *tuitiōnem*, nom. *-tio*, from *tuēri*, to watch, to guard, p.p. *tuitus*], *n.* Teaching, instruction, esp. in a particular subject or group of subjects as dist. from education; a fee for this. **tuitional, tuitionary,** *a.*

Tula-metal (tū′ lȧ met′ ȧl) [*Tula*, town in Russia, METAL], *n.* An alloy of silver, copper, and lead, used in niello work. **Tula-work,** *n.* Niello work.

tulchan, -chin (tŭl′ *ch*an, *-ch*in) [etym. doubtful], *n.* (*Sc.*) A calfskin stuffed with straw put beside a cow at milking time to induce a free flow of milk.

tulip (tū′ lip) [F. *tulippe*, It. *tulipa, tulipano*, Turk. *tulbend, dulbend*, TURBAN], *n.* Any plant of the genus *Tulipa*, bulbous plants of the lily family, with gorgeous bell-shaped flowers of various colours. **tulip-tree,** *n.* A large N. American tree, *Liriodendron tulipifera*, of the magnolia family, bearing greenish-yellow tulip-like flowers. **tulipist,** *n.* **tulipomania** (-mā′ ni ȧ), *n.* A craze for the cultivation or acquisition of tulips which arose in Holland about 1634.

tulle (tool, tul), *n.* A fine silk net, used for veils, etc., orig. manufactured in the French city of Tulle.

Tullian (tŭl′ i an) [Marcus *Tullius* Cicero, Roman statesman and orator], *a.* Of, pertaining to, or in the style of Cicero.

tulwar (tŭl′ wȧr) [Hind.], *n.* A curved sabre used by the Sikhs and some tribes of N. India.

tum, tum-tum (2) (tŭm, tŭm′ tŭm) [imit.], *n.* The sound of a stringed musical instrument like the banjo.

tumata Kuru (too ma ta ko′ roo) [Maori], *n.* A spiny shrub with usable wood.

tumble (tŭm′ bėl) [M.E. *tumblen*, freq. from A.-S. *tumbian*, cp. Dut. *tuimelen*, G. *taumeln*, *tummeln*, Swed. *tumla*, Dan. *tumle*], *v.i.* To fall (down, etc.) suddenly or violently; to roll or toss about; to walk, run, or move about, in a careless or headlong manner; to perform acrobatic feats, esp. without special apparatus. *v.t.* To toss or fling forcibly to throw or push (down, etc.); to cause to tumble or fall; to throw into disorder, to rumple. *n.* A fall; a state of disorder; an acrobatic feat, esp. a somersault. **to tumble home:** (*Naut.*) To incline inwards (of the sides of ships) from the line of greatest breadth. **to tumble in:** (*Carp.*) To fit (a piece of timber) into another; (*Naut.*) to tumble home; (*colloq.*) to go to bed, to turn in. **to tumble to:** (*slang*) To understand, to comprehend. **tumbledown,** *a.* Dilapidated. **tumbling,** *n.* **tumbling-barrel, -box,** *n.* A revolving box, etc., in which castings are cleaned by friction. **tumbly,** *a.*

tumbler (tŭm′ blėr), *n.* One who or that which tumbles; one who performs somersaults, an acrobat; a variety of pigeon, from its habit of turning over in flight; a toy that turns somersaults; a stemless drinking-glass, orig. with a rounded base, so that it fell on the side when set down; a spring-latch (usu. one of several) in a lock, that engages a bolt unless lifted by the key; a part of the lock in a fire-arm attached to the hammer and engaging with the trigger. **tumbler switch,** *n.* A simple form of switch used for electric light connexions. **tumblerful,** *n.*

tumbrel (tŭm′ brėl) [O.F. *tumbrel*, *tumberel*, from *tomber*, to fall, cogn. with prec.], *n.* A two-wheeled cart for carrying ammunition and tools for mining and sapping; a dung-cart; (*prov.*) a large willow rack for feeding sheep in winter.

tumid (tū′ mid) [L. *tumidus*, from *tumēre*, to swell], *a.* Swollen, enlarged, distended; (*fig.*) pompous, bombastic, turgid. **tumescent** (mes′ ėnt), *a.* **tumescence,** *n.* **tumidity** (-mid′ i ti), **tumidness,** *n.* **tumidly,** *adv.* **tumefy** (tū′ mi fī), *v.t.* To cause to swell; to inflate. *v.i.* To swell; to rise in or as in a tumour. **tumefacient** (-fā′ shėnt), *a.* **tumefaction** (-făk′ shŭn), *n.*

tummy [corr. of STOMACH].

tumour (tū′ mȯr) [F. *tumeur*, L. *tumōrem*, nom. *-or*, as TUMID], *n.* A swelling on some part of the body, esp. if due to a morbid growth.

tump (1) (tŭmp) [cp. W., Gael., and Ir. *tom*], *n.* A hillock, a mound. *v.t.* (*prov.*) To form a mass of earth round (a plant).

tump (2) (tŭmp) [etym. doubtful], *v.t.* (*Am.*) To draw (the carcass of a deer, etc.) home. **tump-line,** *n.* A strap worn round the forehead or breast by Canadian voyageurs, etc., to steady a load carried on the back.

tum-tum (1) (tŭm′ tŭm) [prob. imit.], *n.* A West Indian dish of boiled plantain beaten soft; a tom-tom.

tumult (tū′ mŭlt) [F. *tumulte*, L. *tumultus*, as foll.], *n.* The commotion, disturbance, or agitation of a multitude, esp. with a confusion of sounds; a confused outbreak or insurrection; uproar, stir, riot; excitement, agitation, or confusion of mind. **tumultuary, tumultuous,** *a.* **tumultuously, tumultuarily,** *adv.* **tumultuousness, tumultuariness,** *n.* ***tumultuation,** *n.*

tumulus (tū′ mū lŭs) [L., from *tumēre*, to swell], *n.* (*pl.* **-li**) A mound of earth, sometimes combined with masonry, usually sepulchral, a barrow. **tumular, *tumulary, tumulose, tumulous,** *a.*

tun (tŭn) [A.-S. *tunne*, cp. Dut. *ton*, G. *tonne*, Icel. and Swed. *tunna*], *n.* A large cask, esp. for alcoholic liquors; a wine-measure, 252 galls.; a brewer's fermenting-vat. *v.t.* To put (liquor) into a tun. ***tun-bellied,** *a.* **tun-belly,** *n.* **tun-dish,** *n.* A funnel, orig. of wood. **tunnage,** *n.* A tax on imported wine levied on each cask or tun, usu. coupled with [POUNDAGE].

tuna (tū′ nȧ) [Sp.], *n.* (*Zool.*) The Californian tunny, *Thunus saliens.*

tunable, etc. [TUNE].

tundra (toon′ drȧ) [Rus.], *n.* A marshy treeless plain in the north of Siberia and Russia, covered largely with mosses and lichens.

tune (tūn) [A.-F. *tun* (F. *ton*), L. *tonum*, nom. *-us*, TONE], *n.* A melodious succession of musical tones forming a coherent whole, an air, a melody, esp. as a setting for a song, hymn, etc.; correct intonation in singing or playing; proper adjustment of an instrument for this; (*fig.*) concord, agreement, harmony, frame of mind, mood. *v.t.* To put in tune; (*fig.*) to adjust, to adapt, to attune; (*poet.*) to sing, to produce (a song, music, etc.); (*Mach.*) to adjust a machine, esp. an aeroplane or motor, so as to obtain the maximum of efficiency in motion. *v.i.* To come or be in harmony; to utter or express musically. **to the tune of:** (*colloq.*) To the sum or amount of. **to tune in:** (*Radio.*) To adjust a circuit to obtain resonance at a required frequency. **tunable,** *a.* **tunableness,** *n.* **tunably,** *adv.* **tuneful,** *a.* Melodious, musical. **tunefully,** *adv.* **tunefulness,** *n.* **tuneless,** *a.* Not in tune; unmusical, inharmonious; (*fig.*) silent, without voice. **tuned circuit,** *n.* (*Radio.*) An oscillatory circuit adjusted to yield resonance at a required wave-length. **tuner,** *n.* One who tunes, esp. one whose occupation is to tune musical instruments. **tuning condenser,** *n.* (*Radio.*) A variable condenser embodied in a tuning circuit. **tuning-crook,** *n.* A hook in a cornet or other brass wind-instrument for varying the fundamental pitch. **tuning-fork,** *n.* A two-pronged steel instrument giving a fixed note when struck, used to measure the pitch of musical tones, etc. **tuning-hammer,** *n.* A hammer-shaped wrench for tuning pianofortes, harps, etc. **tuning note,** *n.* (*Radio.*) A prolonged note issued by a transmitting station to enable listeners to tune in.

tungsten (tŭng′ stėn) [Swed. (*tung*, heavy, *sten*, STONE)], *n.* A heavy, greyish-white metallic element of unusually high melting point. **tungstic,** *a.* **tungstate,** *n.* A salt of tungstic acid.

Tungus (tun guz′) [native name], *n.* One of a people belonging to a Turanian group occupying parts of Siberia and China. **Tungusian,** *a.* **Tungusic,** *a.* and *n.*

tunic (tū′ nik) [A.-S. *tunece*, L. *tunica*], *n.* (*Ant.*) A short-sleeved body-garment reaching nearly to the knees, worn by the ancient Greeks and Romans; a mediæval surcoat worn over armour; a modern loose coat or short overskirt gathered in or belted at the waist, now worn only by women and children; a military jacket; (*Anat.*) a membrane or envelope covering some part or organ; (*Bot.*) a membranous skin. **tunicary,** *n.* A tunicate.

tunicate (tū′ ni kȧt), *a.* Having or covered with a tunic. *n.* Any individual of the order *Tunicata*, a division of Metazoa, forming a connecting-link between the Vertebrata and the Invertebrata, many of them in the larval state being furnished with a notochord, which atrophies in the adult. **tunicated,** *a.*

tunicle (tū′ nik ėl), *n.* A small, fine, or delicate tunic, a fine integument; (*Eccles.*) a close-fitting vestment worn by deacons, and by R.-C. cardinals, bishops, and abbots with the dalmatic.

tuning-crook, etc. [TUNE].

tunnage [TUN].

tunnel (tŭn′ ėl) [O.F. *tonnel* (F. *tonneau*), dim. of *tonne,* TUN], *n.* An artificial underground passage or gallery, esp. one under a hill, river, etc., for a railway, road, or canal; a passage dug by a burrowing animal; a mining level, an adit; a main flue of a chimney. *v.t.* (*past & p.p.* **tunnelled**) To make a tunnel through (a hill, etc.); to shape like a tunnel; to catch in a tunnel-net. *v.i.* To cut or make a tunnel. **tunnel diode,** *n.* (*Elec.*) A semi-conductor diode capable of giving åa amplification. **tunnel-net,** *n.* A net with a wide mouth narrowing towards the other end.

tunny (tŭn′ i) [F. *thon,* L. *thunnus,* Gr. *thunnos*], *n.* A large scombroid sea-fish, *Orcynus thynnus,* chiefly caught in the Mediterranean.

tup (tŭp) [M.E. *tuppe,* cp. Swed. and Norw. *tupp,* cock, Dan. *top,* cock's crest, Icel. *toppr,* crest, TOP], *n.* A ram or male sheep; the striking-part of a steam-hammer. *v.t.* and *i.* To butt, as a ram; to cover, as a ram.

Tupaia (tū pā′ yȧ) [from Malay], *n.* (*Zool.*) A genus of small insectivorous squirrel-like mammals, the tree-shrews, from S.-E. Asia and Malaysia.

tupelo (tū′ pė lō) [native name], *n.* A N. American tree of the genus *Nyssa,* esp. the black- or sour-gum; the wood of this.

Tupi-Guarani (tū′ pē gwa ra′ nē) [native name], *n.* A S. American race or stock dwelling in the Amazon region; their language.

tupong (too pong) [*Austral. abor.*], *n.* A variety of flat-head fish in S. Australia.

tuque (tūk) [F.-Canadian, var. of TOQUE], *n.* A Canadian cap made by tucking in one end of a knitted cylindrical bag both ends of which are closed.

Turanian (tū rā′ ni ȧn) [*Turan,* mythical founder of the Turkish race], *a.* Applied to certain Asiatic languages that are neither Aryan nor Semitic, esp. the Ural-Altaic group.

turban (tĕr′ bȧn) [F., earlier *turbant,* It. *turbante,* Turk. *tulbend, dulbend,* Pers. *dulband,* prob. from Hindi], *n.* An Oriental head-dress consisting of a sash or scarf wound round the cap; woman's head-dress imitating this worn in England and France in the early 19th cent.; a narrow-brimmed or brimless hat worn by women and children; the whorls of a univalve shell. **turban-shell,** *n.* A gasteropod of the genus *Turbo*; a shell of this. **turbaned,** *a.*

turbary (tĕr′ bȧ ri) [O.F. *torberie,* late L. *turbāria,* from O.H.G. *zurba,* TURF], *n.* (*Law*) The right of digging turf on another's land; a place where turf or peat is dug.

Turbellaria (tĕr bė lâr′ i ȧ) [mod. L., from L. *turba,* crowd], *n.pl.* (*Zool.*) A genus of flat-worms with ciliated skin and without a body-cavity, the planarians. **turbellarian,** *a.* and *n.* **turbellariform,** *a.*

turbid (tĕr′ bid) [L. *turbidus,* from *turbāre,* to disturb, from *turba,* crowd], *a.* Muddy, discoloured, thick; (*fig.*) disordered, unquiet, disturbed. **turbidity** (-bid′ i ti), **turbidness,** *n.* **turbidly,** *adv.*

***turbillion** (tu̇r bil′ i ȯn) [F. *tourbillon,* dim. of O.F. *tourbille,* ult. from L. *turbo,* see TURBINE], *n.* A vortex, a whirl.

turbinate (tĕr′ bi nȧt) [L. *turbinatus,* as foll.], *a.* Top-shaped, like an inverted cone; spiral, whorled; spinning like a top. **turbinal, turbiniform** (-bin′ i fôrm), **turbinoid,** *a.* **turbination** (-nā′ shu̇n), *n.*

turbine (tĕr′ bin, -bīn) [F., from L. *turbinem,* nom. *turbo,* wheel,top, whirlwind, as prec.], *n.* A water-wheel or motor enclosed in a case or tube in which a flowing stream acts by direct impact or reaction upon a series of vanes or buckets; a similar wheel or motor driven by steam or air; a vessel propelled by a turbine.

turbit (tĕr′ bit) [etym. doubtful], *n.* A variety of domestic pigeon with a flattened head and short beak.

Turbo (tĕr′ bō) [L., see TURBINE], *n.* (*Zool.*) A genus of gasteropods with turbinate shells, typical of the family *Turbinidæ.*

turbo- [abbrev. TURBINE], **turbo-jet engine,** *n.* An engine with a turbine-driven compressor for supplying compressed air to the combustion chamber. **turbo-prop, turbo-propeller,** *n.* (*Aviat.*) An engine with a turbine-driven propeller.

turbot (tĕr′ bȯt) [F., from L. *turbo,* see TURBINE], *n.* A large European flat-fish, *Psetta maxima,* with bony tubercles, highly valued as food.

turbulent (tĕr′ bū lėnt) [F., from L. *turbulentus,* as TURBID], *a.* Disturbed, tumultuous; insubordinate, disorderly. **turbulence, *-lency,** *n.* **turbulently,** *adv.*

Turcism (tĕr′ sizm), *n.* The religion, manners, or character of the Turks. **Turco,** *n.* An Algerian sharp-shooter in the French army. **Turcoman** [TURKOMAN]. **Turcophil** [-PHIL], *n.* A lover of Turkey and the Turks. **Turcophilism,** *n.* **Turcophobe** [-PHOBE], *n.*

turd (tĕrd) [A.-S. *tord*], *n.* (*vulg.*) A lump of excrement or dung.

Turdus (tĕr′ du̇s) [L.], *n.* A genus of passerine birds of the family *Turdidæ,* comprising the thrush, blackbird, ring-ouzel, redwing, and fieldfare. **turdiform, turdine** (-dīn, -din), **turdoid,** *a.*

tureen (tu-, tū rēn′) [orig. *terreen,* TERRINE], *n.* A deep covered dish or vessel for holding soup.

turf (tĕrf) [A.-S., cp. Dut. *turf,* Icel. and Swed. *torf,* Dan. *törv*], *n.* (*pl.* **turfs, turves**) Surface earth filled with the matted roots of grass and other small plants; a piece of this, a sod; (*colloq.*) green-sward, growing grass; peat. *v.t.* To cover or line with turfs or sods. **to turf out:** (*colloq.*) To throw out, to eject forcibly. **the turf:** The race-course; the occupation or profession of horse-racing. **turf-clad,** *a.* Covered with turf. **turf-drain,** *n.* A pipe-drain constructed of turfs. **turf-man,** *n.* A turfite. ***turfen,** *a.* **turfiness,** *n.* **turfy,** *a.* **turfite,** *n.* One devoted to or making a living by horse-racing. **turfless,** *a.*

turgid (tĕr′ jid) [L. *turgidus,* from *turgēre,* to swell], *a.* Swollen, bloated, morbidly distended, tumid; (*fig.*) pompous, inflated, bombastic. **turgescent** (-jes′ ėnt), *a.* ***turgent,** *a.* **turgescence,** *n.* **turgidity** (-jid′ i ti), **turgidness,** *n.* **turgidly,** *adv.*

turion (tūr′ i ȯn) [L. *turiōnem,* nom. *-io*], *n.* A young scaly shoot rising from the ground, as in asparagus. **turioniferous** (-nif′ ėr u̇s), *a.*

Turk (tĕrk) [F. *Turc,* med. L. *Turcus,* Pers. *Turk*], *n.* One of the Mohammedan race ruling in Turkey, an Ottoman or Osmanli; a member of the Mongolo-Tatar race from which this is derived; a Mohammedan; a Turkish horse; (*fig.*) a troublesome person, esp. a boy. **Turk's-cap,** *n.* A martagon lily; the melon-cactus. **Turk's-head,** *n.* A brush on a long handle for cleaning cornices, etc.; a circular or elliptical pan for baking cakes; an ornamental knot.

Turkey (1) (tĕr′ ki), *n.* The country of the Turks. **Turkey carpet:** A soft velvety woollen carpet, orig. made in Turkey. **Turkey leather:** Leather tawed with oil before the hair is removed. **Turkey red:** A brilliant red dye orig. obtained from madder; cotton cloth dyed with this. **Turkey-rhubarb,** *n.* Medicinal rhubarb. **Turkey-stone,** *n.* Novaculite; turquoise.

turkey (2) (tĕr′ ki) [as prec. (from the belief that the bird came from Turkey)], *n.* A large gallinaceous bird of the genus *Meleagris,* allied to the pheasant, orig. introduced from America; (*Austral.*) the wild turkey, the Callegalla or brush turkey, and the mallee-bird or sand turkey. **turkey-buzzard, -vulture,** *n.* An American vulture, *Cathartes.* **turkey-cock,** *n.* A male turkey; (*fig.*) a conceited, pompous person. **turkey-corn,** *n.* Maize. **turkey-poult,** *n.* A young turkey. **turkey-trot,** *n.* A round dance with little or no bending of the knees and a swing of the body. **to**

talk turkey: (*Am.*) To come to the point, to talk facts.

***turkis** [TURQUOISE].

Turkish (tĕr′ kish), *a.* Pertaining to Turkey or the Turks. *n.* The language of the Turks. **Turkish bath:** A hot-air bath in which one is sweated, washed, rubbed, massaged, etc., and conducted through a series of cooling-rooms. **Turkish carpet** [TURKEY CARPET]. **Turkish delight:** A gelatinous sweetmeat.

***turkois** [TURQUOISE].

Turkoman (tĕr′ kō mȧn) [med L. *Turco-*, *Turcus*, TURK, MAN], *n.* (*pl.* **-mans**) A member of any of the Turkish or Tatar hordes living in Turkestan or the adjoining regions of Persia, Afghanistan, and Russia.

turlough (tĕr′ lòch) [Ir. *turloch* (*tur*, dry, LOCH)], *n.* A hollow tract of land in Ireland liable to flooding, esp. by subterranean streams.

***turm** (tĕrm) [L. *turma*], *n.* A troop of horse. ***turma**, *n.* (*pl.* **-mæ**) (*Rom. Ant.*) A body of cavalry; the tenth part of the wing of a legion.

turmalin [TOURMALINE].

turmeric (tĕr′ mė rik) [corr. of F. *terre-merite*, perh. corr. of Arab. *kurkum*, CURCUMA], *n.* An E. Indian plant, *Curcuma longa*, of the ginger family; the powdered rhizome of this used as dye-stuff, a stimulant, or a condiment, esp. in curry. **turmeric-paper**, *n.* Unsized white paper saturated with turmeric used as a test for alkalis, which change the colour from yellow to red.

turmoil (tĕr′ moil) [etym. doubtful, perh. from MOIL], *n.* Commotion, disturbance, tumult. **v.t.* To trouble, to agitate.

turn (tĕrn) [A.-S. *turnian*, *tyrnan* (cp. O.F. *torner*, F. *tourner*), L. *tornāre*, from *tornus*, lathe, Gr. *tornos*], *v.t.* To cause to move round on or as on an axis, to give a rotary motion to; to cause to go, move, aim, point, look, etc., in a different direction; to shift or change the sides of, to invert, to reverse; (*fig.*) to look at the different sides of, to revolve in the mind; to perform (a somersault); to apply or devote to a different purpose or object, to give a new direction to; to bend, to adapt, to change in form, condition, nature, etc.; to cause to become, to convert, to transform, to transmute; to translate, to paraphrase; to pass, go, or move to the other side of, to go round; to pass round the flank of (an army) so as to attack it from the flank or rear; to hand over; to bend back, to blunt (a knife-edge, etc.); to cause to ferment, to make sour; to nauseate, to infatuate, to unsettle, to make giddy; to cause to go, to send, to put (out, etc.); to shape in a lathe or on a potter's wheel; (*fig.*) to give a shapely form to, to mould, to round (a sentence, etc.). *v.i.* To have a circular or revolving motion, to rotate, to revolve, to move round or about; to move the body, face, or head in a different direction, to change front from right to left, etc.; to change in posture, attitude, or position; to return; to take a particular direction; to be changed in nature, form, condition, etc.; to become sour or spoiled; to become unsettled, infatuated, or giddy; to become nauseated; to result, to terminate; to undergo the process of turning on the lathe. *n.* The act of turning, rotary motion; a revolution; the state of being turned; a change of direction, position, or tendency, a deflexion; a bend, a curve, a winding, a corner; a single round or coil of a rope, etc.; a change, a vicissitude; a short walk, a stroll, a promenade; a performance, bout, or spell (of doing something), an occasion, opportunity, or time (for doing something) coming in succession to each of a number of persons; succession, alternation, rotation; (*colloq.*) a nervous shock; (*fig.*) shape, form, mould, character, disposition, temper; (*Mus.*) a melodic embellishment consisting of the principal tone with those above and below it; (*pl.*) the menses; (*Print.*) an inverted type put temporarily in place of a missing letter. **by turns:** Alternately; at intervals. **done to a turn:** Cooked exactly right. **a good turn:** A welcome service. **ill turn** [ILL]. **in turn:** In order of succession, in rotation. **on the turn:** Just turning (of the tide); beginning to go sour. **to serve one's turn:** To serve one's purpose; to help or suit one. **to take turns:** To take each one's place at work, etc., alternately. **to turn about:** To turn the face in another direction; to turn round. **to turn adrift:** To unmoor (a boat) and allow to float away; (*fig.*) to cast off. **to turn again:** To return. **to turn aside:** To deviate; to divert, to avert. **to turn down:** To fold or double down; to lower (gas) by turning the tap; to lay (a card) face downwards; (*colloq.*) to reject. **to turn in:** To direct or incline inwards; to fold or double in; to send, put, or drive in; (*colloq.*) to go to bed. **to turn off:** To deflect; to deviate; to dismiss; to shut off the supply of (water, gas, etc.) by turning the tap; to achieve, to produce, to accomplish; to hang (a criminal). **to turn on:** To open a way to (gas, etc.) by turning the tap; to direct, to aim; to retort, to hinge or depend upon; to attack. **to turn one's hand:** To apply oneself. **to turn out:** To drive out, to expel, to point or to cause to point outwards; to turn (pockets, etc.) inside out; (of a room) to clean thoroughly; to bring to view; to produce, as the result of labour; to prove to be the case; (*colloq.*) to get out of bed. **to turn over:** To change the position of, to invert, to reverse; to transfer (to), to put under other control; to cause to turn over, to upset; to do business to the amount of. **to turn round:** To face about; to adopt new views, attitude, policy, etc. **to turn tail:** To retreat ignominiously. **to turn to:** To be directed towards; to apply oneself to. **to turn turtle:** To turn topsy-turvy, to turn completely over. **to turn up:** To bring to the surface; to place (a card, etc.) with the face upwards; to tilt up; to find and refer to (a passage) in a book; to point upwards; to come to the surface; to happen; to make one's appearance. **to turn upon:** To turn on. **turn and turn about:** Alternately, successively. **turn-bench**, *n.* A small portable lathe, used by watchmakers. **turn-buckle**, *n.* A coupling for metal rods, etc. allowing adjustment of length. **turn-cap**, *n.* A chimney cowl turning round with the wind. **turn-coat**, *n.* One who turns his coat; one who deserts his party or principles. **turncock**, *n.* One who turns water on or off from a main. **turn-down**, *a.* Folded or doubled down. **turn indicator**, *n.* (*Aviat.*) A gyroscopic instrument which indicates any deviation in the course of an aircraft. **turnkey**, *n.* One who has the charge of the keys of a prison, a warder. **turn-out**, *n.* A turning out for duty; a quitting of employment, as of workmen coming out on strike; a strike; an assembly, a large party; a showy or well-appointed equipage; a quantity of articles or products manufactured in a given time. **turn-over**, *n.* An upset; a semicircular pie or tart made by turning over half the crust; the amount of money turned over in a business in a given time; an article filling a column and continued on the next page. **turn-screw**, *n.* A screw-driver. **turnsole** [SOL (1)], *n.* A plant supposed to turn with the sun. **turnspit**, *n.* A person who turns a spit; a variety of dog, allied to the terrier, formerly employed to turn spits. **turnstone**, *n.* A bird, *Arenaria interpres*, allied to the plover. **turn-table**, *n.* A platform rotating in a horizontal plane used for shifting rolling-stock from one line of rails to another; (*Gramophone*) the rotating table which supports a record while being played. **turn-up**, *n.* (*colloq.*) A disturbance. **turner**, *n.* One who turns, esp. one who turns articles in a lathe; a variety of tumbler-pigeon. **turnery**, *n.* **turning**, *n.* The act of one who or of that which turns; a bend, a corner, the point where a road meets another; such a road. **turning-point**, *n.* The point in place, time, etc., on or at which a change takes place, the decisive point.

turnip (tĕr′ nip) [perh. TURN, or F. TOUR, A.-S. *næp*, L. *nāpus*, turnip], *n.* A plant of the genus *Brassica*, with a fleshy globular root used as a vegetable and for feeding sheep. **turnip-fly**, *n.* An insect, *Athalia centifoliæ* or *Anthomyia radicum*, destructive to turnips.

turnpike (tĕrn′ pīk), *n.* A gate set across a road to stop carriages, etc., from passing till the toll is paid, orig. a frame set with spikes to prevent passage; a turnpike road. **turnpikeman,** *n.* A collector of tolls at a turnpike. **turnpike road:** A road on which turnpikes or toll-gates were established.

turnstile (tĕrn′ stīl), *n.* A post with four horizontal revolving arms, set at the entrance to an enclosure, building, etc., allowing persons to pass only after the toll is paid.

turpentine (tĕr′ pėn tīn) [M.E. and M.F. *turpentine*, L. *terebinthinus*, Gr. *terebinthinos*, from *terebinthos*, TEREBINTH], *n.* An oleoresin exuding naturally or from incisions in several coniferous trees, esp. the terebinth, used for mixing paints, varnishes, etc., and in medicine; oil or spirit of turpentine, popularly called **turps.** *v.t.* To put turpentine in; to saturate with turpentine. **turpentine-tree,** *n.* The terebinth. **turpentinic** (-tin′ ik), *a.*

turpeth (tĕr′ pėth) [O.F. *turbith*, Arab. and Pers. *turbid*, purge], *n.* The root of an E. Indian plant, *Ipomæa turpethum*, used as a drastic purgative.

turpinite (tĕr′ pi nīt) [M. *Turpin*, manufacturer, -ITE], *n.* A violent explosive containing picric acid and giving off poisonous fumes.

turpitude (tĕr′ pi tūd) [F., from L. *turpitūdo*, from *turpis*, base], *n.* Baseness, depravity.

turps [TURPENTINE].

turquoise (tĕr′ koiz, -kwoiz) [O.F., fem. of *turquois*, Turkish, see TURK], *n.* A sky-blue or bluish-green translucent or opaque precious stone. **turquoise-green,** *n.* A pale greenish-blue.

turret (tŭr′ ėt) [F. *tourette*, dim. of *tour*, TOWER], *n.* A small tower attached to a building, and rising above it; a low flat cylindrical or conical armoured tower, usu. revolving, so that the guns command a wide radius on a warship, tank or fort; (*Hist.*) a high wheeled structure used for attacking a castle, etc. **turret clock,** *n.* A tower clock in which the movement is separate from the dials. **turret-gun,** *n.* A gun for use in a turret. **turret-ship,** *n.* A warship with a turret or turrets. **turreted,** *a.* **turriculate, -lated** (tů rik′ ū lát, -lā tėd), *a.* Having a long spire (of shells).

***turribant** [TURBAN].

turtle (1) (tĕr′ tėl) [A.-S., from L. *turtur*, prob. imit. of coo], *n.* The turtle-dove. **turtle-dove,** *n.* The common wild dove, esp. *Turtur communis*, noted for its soft cooing and its affection for its mate and young.

turtle (2) (tĕr′ tėl) [corr. of Port. *tartaruga* or Sp. *tortuga*, late L. *tortūca*, TORTOISE], *n.* A marine reptile encased in a carapace, like a tortoise, with flippers used in swimming; a chelonian, esp. the green turtle, *Chelonia mydes*, used for soup; turtle-soup. *v.i.* To fish or hunt for turtles. **to turn turtle** [TURN]. **turtleback,** *n.* An arched covering over part of a ship's deck, esp. at the bows, and sometimes the stern, as a protection against heavy seas. **turtle-cowry,** *n.* A large dappled cowry. **turtle-shell,** *n.* Tortoise-shell, esp. the darker and less valuable kind, used for inlaying; a turtle-cowry. **turtle-soup,** *n.* Rich soup made from fatty parts of the turtle. **turtle-stone,** *n.* A septarium. **turtler,** *n.*

turves, *pl.* [TURF].

Tuscan (tŭs′ kån), *a.* Pertaining to Tuscany. *n.* A native or the language of Tuscany; the Tuscan order. **Tuscan order:** (*Arch.*) The simplest of the five classic orders, a Roman modification of Doric.

***tush** (1) (tŭsh) [cp. TUT (1)], *int.* An expression of contempt or impatience.

tush (2) (tŭsh) [var. of TUSK], *n.* A long pointed tooth, esp. a horse's canine tooth.

tusk (tŭsk) [A.-S. *tusc*, *tux*, cp. O.Fris. *tusk*, *tosch*, Icel. *toskr*], *n.* A long pointed tooth, esp. one protruding from the mouth as in the elephant, narwhal, etc.; a tooth-like point, spike, projection, etc., as in a harrow, lock, etc. *v.t.* To gore, mangle, or root up with tusks. **tusked, tusky,** *a.* **tusker,** *n.* An elephant or wild boar with well-developed tusks.

tuskar (tŭs′ kår) [Icel. *torfskeri* (TURF, *skera*, to cut)], *n.* (*Orkney and Shetland*) An iron tool with a wooden handle for cutting peat.

tussis (tŭs′ is) [L., cough], *n.* (*Path.*) A cough. **tussal, tussicular** (tů sik′ ū lår), **tussive,** *a.*

tussle (tŭs′ ėl) [var. of TOUSLE], *v.i.* To struggle, to scuffle (with or for). *n.* A struggle, a scuffle.

tussock (tŭs′ ók) [cp. Swed. dial. *tuss*, wisp of hay], *n.* A clump, tuft, or hillock of growing grass; a tuft or lock of hair, etc.; a tussock-moth. **tussock-grass,** *n.* A grass, *Dactylis cæspitosa*, forming tufts five to six feet high, growing in Patagonia and the Falkland Islands. **tussock-moth,** *n.* A bombycid moth the larvæ of which bear tufts of hair. **tussocker,** *n.* (*N. Zealand.*) A sun-downer. **tussocky,** *a.*

tussore, tussur, tusser (tŭs′ ôr, -ŭr, -ėr) [Hind. *tassar*, from Sansk. *tassara*, shuttle], *n.* An Indian silkworm moth, *Antherea mylitta*, feeding on the jujube tree, etc., or a Chinese oak-feeding silkworm moth, *A. pernyi*; a strong, coarse silk obtained from these.

tut (1) (tŭt) [instinctive sound], *int.* and *n.* An exclamation of impatience, rebuke, or contempt. *v.i.* To make this exclamation.

tut (2) (tŭt) [etym. doubtful], *n.* (*Mining*) A job. *v.i.* To work by the job, to do piece-work. **tut-work,** *n.*

tutamen (tū tā′ mėn) [L., from *tuērī*, to look after, to keep safe], *n.* (*pl.* **-mina**) (*Anat.*) A guard, a protection, a protecting part.

tutelage (tū′ tė lȧj) [L. *tūtēla*, guardianship], *n.* Guardianship; the state of being under a guardian; the period of this. **tutelar, -lary,** *a.* Having the care or protection of a person or thing, protective; pertaining to a guardian.

tutenag (tū′ tė năg) [F. *tutenague*, prob. from Arab. and Pers. *tūtiyā*, TUTTY], *n.* A white alloy of copper; zinc or spelter from China or the E. Indies.

tutiorism (tū′ shi ór izm) [L. *tūtior*, comp. of *tūtus*, safe], *n.* (*R.-C. Theol.*) The doctrine that in cases of moral doubt the course should be followed that seems the safer or more in accord with the letter of the law; mitigated rigorism. **tutiorist,** *a.* and *n.*

tutor (tū′ tór) [M.E. *tutour*, F. *tuteur*, L. *tūtōrem*, nom. *-tor*, from *tuēri*, to look after, p.p. *tūtus*], *n.* A private teacher, esp. one having the general care and instruction of a pupil in preparation for a university, etc.; (*Eng. Univ.*) an officer directing the studies of undergraduates in a college and charged with discipline, etc.; (*Law*) a guardian of a minor. *v.t.* To act as a tutor to; to instruct, to teach; to train; to discipline, to correct. **tutorage,** *n.* **tutoress,** *n.* **tutorial** (-tôr′ i ál), *a.* **tutorially,** *adv.* **tutorship,** *n.*

tutsan (tŭt′ sån) [O.F. *toutesaine* (*toute*, L. *tōtum*, nom. *-us*, all, *saine*, *sānus*, sound, SANE)], *n.* A species of St. John's wort, *Hypericum androsæmum*, formerly held to be a panacea for wounds, etc.

tutti (tut′ i) [It., pl. of *tutto*], *adv.* (*Mus. direction*) All together. *n.* A composition or passage for singing or performing thus.

tutti-frutti (tut′ i frut′ i) [It., all fruits, cp. prec. and FRUIT], *n.* A confection, as ice-cream, made of or flavoured with different fruits.

tutty (tŭt′ i) [M.E. and O.F. *tutie*, Arab. and Pers. *tūtiyā*], *n.* An impure oxide of zinc collected from the flues of smelting furnaces, used as polishing-powder.

tutu (1) (too′ too) [Maori], *n.* A New Zealand shrub or small tree from the berries of which a wine like claret is obtained, the wineberry shrub.

tutu (2) (too′ too) [F.], *n.* A ballet-dancer's short, stiff skirt that spreads outwards.

tut-work [TUT (2)].

tuum (tū′ ŭm) [L., neut. of *tuus*], *n.* Thine, yours; thy or your property.

tuxedo (tŭks ē′ dō) [New York club], *n.* (*Am.*) A dinner jacket.

tuyère (too yâr′, twi yâr, twĕr) [F., from *tuyau*, TEWEL], *n.* The blast-pipe or nozzle in a furnace, forge, etc.

tuzz (tŭz) [etym. doubtful, cp. TUSSOCK], *n.* (*prov.*) A tuft, a lock, a wisp (of wool, hair, etc.); a posy, a nosegay. **tuzzi-muzzy,** *a.* Tangled, shaggy. *n.* A posy. ***tuzzy,** *n.*

twa (twaw) (*Sc.*) [TWO].

twaddle (twŏd′ ėl) [formerly, *wattle*, var. of TATTLE], *v.i.* To talk unmeaningly; to prate, to chatter. *n.* Unmeaning talk, silly chatter, nonsense. **twaddler,** *n.* **twaddly,** *adv.*

twain (twān) [A.-S. *twegen*, masc., see TWO], *a.* Two. *n.* A pair, a couple. **in twain:** In two, asunder.

twal (*Sc.*) [TWELVE].

twang (1) (twăng) [var. of TANG (1)], *v.i.* To make a ringing metallic sound as by plucking the string of a musical instrument; to play (on) thus; to speak or be uttered with a nasal sound. *v.t.* To cause to sound with a twang; to play (an instrument) thus; to utter or pronounce with a nasal sound. *n.* Such a ringing metallic sound; a nasal tone (in speaking, etc.); (*prov.*) a tang, a disagreeable flavour. **twangle,** *v.i.* and *t.*

twang (2) (*Sc.*) [TWINGE].

twankay (twăng′ kā) [Chin., name of river], *n.* A variety of green tea.

'twas (twoz) [short for IT WAS].

twayblade (twā′ blād), *n.* An orchid with two broad, ovate, radical leaves, and green or purplish flowers.

tweak (twēk) [M.E. *twikken*, A.-S. *twiccian*, cp. G. *zwicken* and TWITCH], *v.t.* To pinch and twist or pull with a sudden jerk, to twitch. *n.* A sharp pinch or pull, a twitch.

tweed (twēd) [prob. from erroneous reading of TWEEL], *n.* A twilled woollen or wool-and-cotton fabric with unfinished surface, used chiefly for outer garments.

tweedle (twē′ dėl) [perh. var. of TWIDDLE], *n.* The sound of a fiddle. **v.t.* To handle carelessly, to trifle with; to play (a fiddle). **tweedledum and tweedledee:** Distinction without difference.

tweel (*Sc.*) [TWILL].

'tween (twēn) [short for BETWEEN], *adv.* and *prep.* Between. **'tween-decks,** *a.* Between decks; *n.* Space between decks. **tweeny,** *n.* (*colloq.*) A servant assisting two others, esp. the cook and housemaid.

tweezer (twē′ zėr) [obs. *tweese*, a small case for instruments, F. *étui*, -ER], *n.* (*in pl.*) Small pincers for picking up minute things, plucking out hairs, etc., usually called a pair of tweezers. *v.t.* To pluck out or pick up with these. **tweezer-case,** *n.*

twelfth (twelfth) [A.-S. *twelfta*, from foll.], *a.* Next after the eleventh. *n.* One of twelve equal parts; (*Mus.*) an interval of an octave and a fifth. **the twelfth:** 12th August, when grouse-shooting begins. **Twelfth cake:** A large cake prepared for Twelfth-night festivals. **Twelfth Day:** The twelfth day after Christmas, the festival of the Epiphany, 6 Jan. **Twelfth Night:** The eve of this, 5 Jan. **twelfthly,** *adv.*

twelve (twelv) [A.-S. *twelf* (*twā*, TWO, *lif*, *cogn.* with LEAVE (2))], *a.* Consisting of the sum of two and ten. *n.* The sum of two and ten, 12, xii. **the Twelve:** The twelve Apostles. **twelvemo,** *n.* Duodecimo, 12mo. **twelvemonth,** *n.* A year. ***twelvepence,** *n.* A shilling. **twelvepenny,** *a.* **twelvescore,** *n.* Twelve times twenty; twelve score yards, a common length for a shot in archery.

twenty (twen′ ti) [A.-S. *twentig* (*twegen*, TWAIN, -TY)], *a.* Twice ten, 20, xx; a considerable but indefinite number. *n.* The number of twice ten. **twentieth,** *a.* and *n.* **twentyfold,** *a.* and *adv.* **twenty-fourmo,** *n.* A sheet folding into 24 leaves; a book, etc., having 24 leaves to the sheet. **twenty-mo,** *n.*

'twere (twĕr) [short for IT WERE].

twerp, twirp (twĕrp) [etym. unknown], *n.* (*slang*) A contemptible fellow, a cad.

***twibill** (twī′ bil) [A.-S. (*twi*, two, double, as foll., BILL (2))], *n.* A double-bladed battle-axe; a mattock with an axe-shaped back. ***twiblade** [TWAYBLADE].

twice (twīs) [M.E. *twies*, A.-S. *twiges*, gen. of *twā*, TWO], *adv.* Two times; doubly. **twice-told,** *a.* Related twice; well-known, hackneyed. **twicer,** *n.* (*Print.*) One who is both compositor and pressman.

twiddle (twid′ ėl) [cp. Norw. *tvidla*, var. of *tvilla*, *tvirla*, TWIRL], *v.t.* To twirl idly; to fiddle with. *v.i.* To twirl; to fiddle or trifle (with). **to twiddle one's thumbs:** To sit idle. **twiddling-line,** *n.* (*Naut.*) A string attached to a compass-gimbal for starting it playing freely.

twifold (twī′ fōld) [*twi-*, see TWIBILL, -FOLD], *a.* and *adv.* Twofold.

twig (1) (twig) [A.-S. (cp. Dut. *twijg*, G. *zweig*), cogn. with TWO], *n.* A small shoot or branch of a tree, bush, etc., a branchlet; a divining rod; (*Anat.*) a small branch of an artery or other vessel; (*Elec.*) a small distributing conductor. **twigged,** *a.* ***twiggen,** *a.* Made of twigs or wicker. **twiggy,** *a.* **twigless,** *a.*

twig (2) (twig) [perh. from Ir. *tuigim*, I understand], *v.t.* (*past & p.p.* **twigged**) (*colloq.*) To understand, to comprehend, to catch the drift of; to see, to notice.

twilight (twī′ līt) [M.E. (A.-S. *twi-*, see TWIBILL, LIGHT (1))], *n.* The diffused light from the sky appearing a little before sunrise and after sunset; a faint light, shade, obscurity; (*fig.*) indistinct or imperfect perception, revelation, or knowledge. *a.* Pertaining to, happening, or done in the twilight; dim, shady, obscure. *v.t.* To illumine dimly. **twilight of the gods:** (*Norse Myth.*) A conflict in which the gods were overcome and the world destroyed. **twilight sleep,** *n.* (*Med.*) A state of semi-consciousness produced by administering scopolamine and morphine in which labour pains are mitigated and forgotten when over.

twill (twil) [A.-S. *twilīc*, cogn. with G. *zwillich*, two threaded (*twi-*, TWO, *-līc*, perh. from L. *bilix*, BI-, *līcium*, thread)], *n.* A fabric in which the weft-threads pass alternately over one warp-thread and then under two or more, producing diagonal ribs or lines. *v.t.* To weave thus. **twilly,** *n.* A cotton-cleaning or willowing machine.

twin (1) (twin) [M.E., from A.-S. *getwinne* (cp. Icel. *tvinnr*), cogn. with TWO], *a.* Being one of two born at a birth; being one of a similar or closely related pair of things, parts, etc.; double, twofold; (*Bot.*) growing in pairs or divided into two equal parts. *n.* One of two children or young produced at a birth; a person or thing very closely resembling or related to another; an exact counterpart; (*Cryst.*) a compound crystal having symmetrical halves separated by a plane that is not a plane of symmetry. *v.t.* To couple, to pair (with); to pair, to mate. *v.i.* To bring forth twins; to be born at the same birth; to be mated or paired (with). **dissimilar, binovular twins,** *n.pl.* Twins proceeding from the fertilization of two oocytes. **identical, uniovular twins,** *n.pl.* Twins that have developed from a single oocyte. **the twins:** (*Astron.*) Gemini. **twin-born,** *a.* **twinflower,** *n.* A tiny creeping evergreen, *Linnæa borealis*, with thread-like stalks and fragrant flowers. **twin-screw,** *n.* A steamer with two propellers twisted in opposite directions. ***twinling,** *n.* A twin lamb. ***twinner,** *n.* **twin set,** *n.* A jumper and cardigan made to match. **twinship,** *n.*

twin (2) (twin) [from prec.], *v.t.* (*Sc.*) To divide, to part in twain, to separate; to deprive of, to sever. **v.i.* To be separated, to part; to be divided or parted in twain.

twine (1) (twīn) [M.E. *twinen*, from A.-S. *twīn*, twisted thread (cp. Dut. *twijn*, G. *zwirn*, Icel. *tvinni*), cogn. with TWO], *v.t.* To twist; to form (thread, etc.) by twisting together; to wind or coil round, to embrace; to form by interweaving. *v.i.* To be interwoven; to entwine, to coil (about, round, etc.); to wind, to meander. *n.* A twist, a convolution, a coil; the act of twining or entwining; an interlacing, a tangle; strong string made of two or three strands twisted together. **twiner,** *n.* **twiningly,** *adv.*

***twine** (2) [TWIN (2)].

twinflower [TWIN (1)].

twinge (twinj) [A.-S. *twengan*, cp. Dut. *dwingen*, G. *zwingen*, Icel. *thvinga*, Dan. *tvinge*, to constrain, to compel], *v.t.* To affect with a sharp, sudden pain. *n.* A sharp, sudden, shooting pain; (*fig.*) a pang, as of remorse or sorrow.

twinkle twing' kėl) [A.-S. *twinclian*, freq. of v. represented by obs. *twink*, var. of *twiccan*, to TWITCH], *v.i.* To shine with a broken quivering light, to gleam fitfully, to sparkle; to appear and disappear in rapid alternation, to move tremulously; to open and shut rapidly, to blink, to wink. *v.t.* To flash or emit (light) in rapid gleams. *n.* A tremulous gleam, a sparkle; a glimmer; a blink, a wink; a rapid tremulous movement. ***twink,** *v.i.* To twinkle; to wink; *n.* A twinkle, a wink. **twinkling,** *n.* A twinkle; (*fig.*) the time of this, an instant.

***twinling,** etc. [TWIN (1)].

twinter (twin' tėr) [A.-S. *twiwintre* (*twi-*, TWO, WINTER)], *n.* (*prov.*) A beast two years old.

***twire** (twīr) [etym. obscure, cp. Bavarian *zwiren*, M.H.G. *zwieren*], *v.i.* (*Shak.*) To twinkle; to glance shyly or slyly, to peep, to peer. *n.* A sly look, a leer.

twirk (*Sc.*) [TWITCH (1)].

twirl (twĕrl) [freq. from A.-S. *thweran*, to turn, cp. Norw. *tvirla*], *v.t.* To cause to rotate rapidly, esp. with the fingers, to spin; to whirl (round); to twiddle, to twist, to curl (the moustache, etc.). *v.i.* To revolve or rotate rapidly, to whirl (round). *n.* A rapid circular motion; a quick rotation; a twist, a curl, a flourish.

twirp [TWERP].

***twissel** (twisl) [A.-S. *twisel*, cogn. with TWO, cp. foll.], *a.* Double, twofold. *n.* A twofold fruit; anything double or twofold. **twissel-tongued,** *a.*

twist (twist) [M.E. *twisten*, from A.-S. *twist*, rope (in *mæst-twist*, mast-rope), cogn. with TWO], *v.t.* To wind a thread, filament, strand, etc., round another; to form (a rope or threads, etc., into a rope, etc.) thus, to intertwine (with or in with); to give a spiral form to by turning the ends in opposite directions; to wrench, to distort; (*fig.*) to pervert, to misrepresent; to twine, to wreathe; to cause (a ball) to rotate while following a curved path; to make (one's way) in a winding manner. *v.i.* To be turned or bent round and round upon itself; to be or grow in a spiral form; to move in a curving, winding, or irregular path; to writhe, to squirm. *n.* The act or manner of twisting or the state of being twisted; a quick or vigorous turn, a whirling motion given to a ball, etc.; a sharp bend; (*fig.*) a peculiar tendency, a bent, an idiosyncrasy; the degree of inclination of rifle grooves; (*Phys.*) a twisting strain; the angle or degree of torsion of a rod, etc.; forward motion combined with rotation; thread, cord, string, rope, etc., made from twisted strands, esp. strong silk thread or cotton yarn; a twisted roll of bread; twisted tobacco; (*colloq.*) hunger. **twistable,** *a.* **twister,** *n.* One who or that which twists; a ball delivered with a twist at cricket, billiards, etc.; the inner part of the thigh on which a good horseman sits; (*colloq.*) a poser; (*slang.*) a cheat, a rogue.

twit (twit) [M.E. *atwīten*, A.-S. *ætwītan* (AT, *wītan*, to blame, cogn. with *wītan*, to know, Goth. *wertjan*, to reproach, L. *vidēre*, to see)], *v.t.* (*past & p.p.* **twitted**) To reproach, taunt, or upbraid (with some fault, etc.). **twitter** (2). **twittingly,** *adv.*

twitch (1) (twich) [M.E. *twicchen*, var. of *twikken*, to TWEAK], *v.t.* To pull with a sudden or sharp jerk; to snatch. *v.i.* To pull or jerk (at); to move with a spasmodic jerk or contraction. *n.* A sudden pull or jerk; a sudden involuntary contraction of a muscle, etc.; a cord twisted by a stick, fastened to the upper lip of a refractory horse for controlling it. **twitcher,** *n.* One who or that which twitches; (*pl.*) *tweezers.

twitch (2) (*prov.*) [QUITCH].

twite (twīt) [prob. imit. of its chirp], *n.* The mountain-linnet, *Carduelis flavirostris.*

twitter (1) (twit' ėr) [M.E. *twiteren*, freq. of *twit*, imit.], *v.i.* To utter a succession of short, tremulous, intermittent notes; to chirp; (*prov.*) to have a tremulous motion of the nerves, to be agitated. *v.t.* To utter with tremulous, intermittent sounds. *n.* Such a succession of sounds, a chirping; (*colloq.*) a state of excitement or nervous agitation (also **twitteration**). **twitter-bone,** *n.* An excrescence on a horse's hoof.

twitter (2), **twittingly** [TWIT].

twit-twat (twit twot) [imit. of chirp], *n.* A sparrow.

'twixt [short for BETWIXT].

twizzle (twizl) [prob. cogn. with TWIST], *v.i.* (*prov.*) To twist round and round, to spin.

two (too) [A.-S. *twegen* (fem. *twā*, neut. *tu*), cp. Dut. *twee*, G. *zwei*, Icel. *tveir*, also L. and Gr. *duo*, Sansk. *dva*], *a.* One more than one, 2, ii. *n.* The sum of one and one. **in two:** Into two parts; asunder. **one or two:** A few. **to put two and two together:** To draw inferences. **two-edged,** *a.* Having an edge on both sides (of a knife, etc.); (*fig.*) cutting both ways. **two-faced,** *a.* Having two faces; (*fig.*) deceitful, insincere. **twofold,** *a.* Double; *adv.* Doubly. **two-foot,** *a.* (*colloq.*) Measuring two feet. **two-handed,** *a.* Having two hands; having to be used with both hands; played, worked, etc., by two persons; using both hands with equal dexterity, ambidextrous. **two-headed,** *a.* **two-line,** *a.* (*Print.*) Having a depth of body double that of the size specified. **two-pair,** *a.* Second-floor. **twopence** (tŭp' ėns), *n.* The sum of two pence; a small silver coin of this value, now issued only as Maundy money. **twopenny** (tŭp' ė ni), *a.* Worth twopence; (*fig.*) cheap, worthless, common, vulgar. **twopenny-halfpenny,** *a.* Worth or costing twopence-halfpenny; paltry, insignificant. **two-ply,** *a.* Having two strands (as cord) or two thicknesses (as carpets, cloth, etc.). **two-sided,** *a.* Having two sides or aspects. **twosome,** *a.* Applied to any act, as a dance, a game at golf, etc., performed by two persons. *a.* A dance, game, etc., for two persons. **two-speed,** *a.* Giving or adapted to two rates of speed. **two-step,** *n.* (*Dancing*) A kind of round dance to march or polka time. **two-tongued,** *a.* Double-tongued, deceitful. **two-up,** *n.* An Australian gambling game in which two pennies are tossed in the air and bets made on whether they fall two heads or two tails. The game is also called swy. **two-way,** *a.* Arranged to allow a fluid to flow in either of two channels; (*Math.*) having a double mode of variation.

twyer [TUYÈRE].

-ty [F. *-té*, L. *-tātem*, nom. *-tas*], *suf.* Forming abstract nouns as *bounty*, *cruelty*, *fealty*; [A.-S. *-tig*, cogn. with TEN, Goth. *tigjus*, also Gr. *dekas*, decade, from *deka*, ten], as in *fifty*, *twenty*.

Tyburn (tī' bûrn) [an historic place of execution near the site of the Marble Arch, London], *a.* Of or pertaining to Tyburn. **Tyburn ticket:** A certificate exempting from certain parochial offices, etc., formerly granted to a successful prosecutor for felony, then a capital crime. **Tyburn tippet:** A halter. **Tyburn tree:** The gallows.

Tychonic (tī kon′ ik), *a.* Of or pertaining to the Danish astronomer Tycho Brahe (1546–1601) or his system of astronomy.

tycoon (tī koon′) [Jap. *taikun*, great prince], *n.* A title assumed by the shogun of Japan, from 1854 to 1868; (*fig.*) a financial, commercial or political magnate.

***tye, tying** [TIE].

tyke [TIKE].

tylarus (til′ ȧ-, tī′ lȧ rŭs) [mod. L., from Gr. *tulos*, knot], *n.* (*pl.* ***-ri***, -rī) (*Ornith.*) One of the fleshy pads of the toes in birds.

tyler [TILER].

tylopod (tī′ lō pod) [Gr. *tulos*, knot, *pous podos*, foot], *n.* Having the digits enclosed in a cutaneous pad, as the camels. *n.* A tylopod animal. **tylopodous** (-lop′ ō dŭs), *a.*

tylosis (tī lō′ sis) [Gr., from *tuloein*, to make callous, as prec.], *n.* (*Bot.*) A growth in the cavity of a duct intruding from the wall of a contiguous cell; (*Path.*) inflammation of the eyelids with thickening and hardening of the margins. **tylotic** (-lot′ ik), *a.*

tylote (tī′ lōt) [Gr. *tulōtos*, as prec.], *n.* A cylindrical spicule, in a sponge, knotted at each end.

***tymbal** [TIMBAL].

tymp (timp) [short for foll.], *n.* A casting or block of refractory material formerly used as the crown of the opening in front of the hearth of a blast-furnace; (*Mining*) a short horizontal roof-timber.

tympan (tim′ pȧn) [F., from L. TYMPANUM], *n.* A frame stretched with paper, cloth or parchment, used for equalizing the pressure in some printing-presses; any thin sheet or membrane tightly stretched; a tympanum; a drum (*pl.* **tympani**, -nī).

tympanites (tim pȧ nī′ tēz), *n.* (*Path.*) Distension of the abdomen, due to the accumulation of air in the intestine, etc. **tympanitic,** *a.*

tympanitis (tim pȧ nī′ tis), *n.* (*Path.*) Inflammation of the lining membrane of the middle ear.

tympanum (tim′ pȧ nŭm) [L., from Gr. *tumpanon*, drum], *n.* (*pl.* **-na**) The middle ear; the tympanic membrane or ear-drum; the lower end of the trachea in ducks, etc., modified into a resonance-cavity; (*Arch.*) a triangular area, usu. recessed, in a pediment, the space between the lintel of a doorway and the arch enclosing it; a door-panel; a form of tread-mill. **tympanic** (-păn′ ik), *a.* Like a drum; acting like a drum-head; (*Anat.*) pertaining to the tympanum. ***tympany** (tim′ pȧ ni), *n.* Tympanites; (*fig.*) conceit, bombast.

tynewald, tynwald (tin′ wawld) [Icel. *thingvöllr* (*thing*, assembly, *völlr*, field, cp. WEALD)], *n.* The legislature of the Isle of Man.

type (tīp) [F., from L. *typum*, nom. *-us*, Gr. *tupos*, blow, stamp, character, from *tuptein*, to strike], *n.* A distinguishing mark, a symbol, an emblem, an image; any person or thing that stands as an illustration, pattern, characteristic example, or representative specimen of another thing or class of things; a prophetic similitude; (*Biol.*) a general form or structure common to a number of individuals; an organism exhibiting the essential characteristics of its group; (*Chem.*) a compound, such as hydrochloric acid, water, ammonia, or methane, illustrating other compounds by analogy; (*Art*) an original conception, object, or work of art, serving as a model or guide to later artists; any of a class of objects embodying the characteristics of a group or class, esp. as a model, pattern, or exponent (of beauty or other qualities); (*Print.*) a piece of metal or hard wood bearing a letter or character usu. in relief, for printing with; (*collect.*) a set or quantity or kind of these; the device on a medal, coin, etc. *v.t.* To prefigure, to be a type of; to typewrite. **in type:** (*Print.*) Set in type. **type-bar,** *n.* A line of type cast in one piece by a linotype machine, etc.; a bar carrying a letter in a typewriter. **type-founder,** *n.* One who casts types. **type-foundry,** *n.* **type-high,** *a.* Of the standard height of type or the proper height for printing. **type-metal,** *n.* An alloy of lead, antimony, and tin, used for making printing-type. **typescript,** *n.* Typewritten matter. **type-setter,** *n.* A compositor. **type-setting,** *n.* and *a.*

typewriter (tīp′ rī tėr), *n.* A machine for producing printed characters as a substitute for handwriting; (*incorr.*) a typist. **typewrite,** *v.t.* and *i.* To write with this. **typewriting,** *n.* **typewritten,** *a.*

Typha (tī′ fȧ) [mod. L., from Gr. *tuphē*, the plant cat's-tail], *n.* A genus of marsh plants comprising the cats'-tails. **typhaceous** (-fā′ shŭs), *a.*

typhlitis (tif lī′ tis) [Gr. *tuphlos*, blind, -ITIS], *n.* (*Path.*) Inflammation of the cæcum. **typhlitic** (-lit′ ik), *a.* **typhlo-,** *comb. form.*

typhoid (tī′ foid) [TYPHUS, -OID], *a.* Pertaining to or resembling typhus. *n.* Typhoid fever, an infectious fever characterized by an eruption of red spots on the chest and abdomen, severe intestinal irritation, inflammation, diarrhœa, etc., enteric. **typhoidal** (-foi′ dȧl), *a.* **typhomalarial** (-mȧ lâr′ i ȧl), *a.* Malarial with typhoidal symptoms. **typhomania** (-mā′ ni ȧ), *n.* The low muttering delirium characteristic of typhus and typhoid fever. **typhonia** (-fō′ ni ȧ), *n.* A form of sleepless and delirious stupor characteristic of typhus.

typhoon (tī′ foon′) [Chin. *tai foong*, big wind], *n.* A violent cyclonic hurricane occurring in the China Seas. **typhonic** (-fon′ ik), *a.*

typhus (tī′ fŭs) [L., from Gr. *tuphos*, smoke, stupor], *n.* A contagious fever marked by an eruption of dark purple spots, great prostration, stupor and delirium. **typhous,** *a.*

typic (tip′ ik) [L. *typicus*, Gr. *tupikos*, from *tupos*, TYPE], *a.* Figurative, typical. **typic fever:** A fever regular in its attacks or of a particular type. **typical,** *a.* Of the nature of or serving as a type; representative, emblematic, symbolical (of); embodying the characters of a group, class, etc.; characteristic (of). **typically,** *adv.* **typicalness,** *n.*

typify (tip′ i fī), *v.t.* To represent by a type; to betoken, to prefigure; to be a type of, to exemplify. **typification,** *n.* **typifier,** *n.*

typist (tī′ pist), *n.* One who types letters, etc.

typo (tī′ pō), *n.* (*colloq.*) A typographer.

typograph (tī′ pō grăf), *n.* A machine formerly used for making and setting type.

typography (tī pog′ rȧ fi), *n.* The art of printing; the arrangement, character, or appearance of printed matter. **typographer,** *n.* **typographic, -al** (-grăf′ ik, -ȧl), *a.* **typographically,** *adv.*

typolite (tī′ pō līt), *n.* A stone impressed with the figure of a plant or animal, a fossil.

typolithography (tī pō lith og′ rȧ fi), *n.* The process of printing from lithographic stones which have previously received transferred impressions from type. **typolithographic,** *a.*

typology (tī pol′ ō ji), *n.* The doctrine of interpretation of types, esp. those of the Scriptures.

typonym (tī′ pō nim), *n.* (*Biol.*) The name based on a type. **typonimal** (tī pon′ i mȧl), *a.* **typonimic** (tī pō nim′ ik), *a.*

typtology (tip tol′ ō ji) [Gr. *tuptein*, to strike, -LOGY], *n.* The practice or science of spirit-rapping. **typtological** (-loj′ i kȧl), *a.* **typtologist,** *n.*

tyrannicide (ti răn′ i sīd) [F., from L. *tyrannicīda* (TYRANT, -CIDE)], *n.* The act of killing a tyrant; one who kills a tyrant. **tyrannicidal** (-sī′ dȧl), *a.*

tyrannize (tir′ ȧ nīz) [TYRANT, -IZE], *v.i.* To act the tyrant; to rule despotically or oppressively (over). *v.t.* To rule (a person, etc.) despotically. **tyrannous,** *a.* **tyrannously,** *adv.* **tyranny,** *n.* Arbitrary, despotic, or oppressive exercise of power; an arbitrary or oppressive act; the office or rule of a tyrant; the period of this; harshness, severity.

tyrannosauros (tī răn ō sôr′ ŭs) [Gr. *turannos*, a tyrant; *saura*, a lizard], *n.* (*Palæont.*) A genus of carnivorous dinosaurs, about 40 ft. in length.

tyranny [TYRANNIZE].

tyrant (tīr′ ȧnt) [M.E. *tirant*, O.F. *tiran*, *tirant*, L. *tyrannum*, nom. *-us*, Gr. *turannos*], *n.* An oppressive or cruel ruler or master; an oppressor, a despot, an autocrat, esp. (*Hist.*) one obtaining power by usurpation; an arbitrary or despotic ruler. **tyrannical** (tī-, ti răn′ i kȧl), *a.* Acting like or characteristic of a tyrant; despotic, arbitrary, imperious. **tyrannically,** *adv.* **tyrannicalness,** *n.*

tyre [TIRE (2)].

Tyrian (tir′ i ȧn), *a.* Pertaining to ancient Tyre; having the colour of Tyrian dye, purple. *n.* A native or inhabitant of Tyre. **Tyrian dye:** A purple dye formerly prepared from shellfish, esp. species of *Murex*.

tyriasis (ti rī′ ȧ sis) [Gr. *tur-os*, cheese, -ASIS], *n.* (*Path.*) A form of elephantiasis; tyroma. **tyroma** (tī rō′ mȧ), *n.* Falling off of the hair through a fungoid growth at the roots.

tyro (tīr′ ō) [L. *tiro*, a newly enlisted soldier], *n.* A beginner, a novice. **tirocinium** (-sin′ i ŭm), *n.* Apprenticeship, novitiate, pupilage.

Tyrolese [TIROLESE].

tyroma [TYRIASIS].

tyrotoxicon (tīr ō tok′ si kȯn) [Gr. *turos*, cheese *toxikon*, poison, see TOXIC], *n.* A ptomaine contained in putrid milk, cheese, etc.

Tyrrhene (tir′ ēn), **Tyrrhenian** (ti rē′ ni ȧn) [L. *Tyrrhēnus*, Gr. *Turrhēnos*], *a.* Etruscan. *n.* An Etrurian, Etruscan, or Tuscan.

Tyrtæan (tir tē′ ȧn), *a.* Of, pertaining to, or in the style of the Greek martial poet Tyrtæus (*c.* 650 B.C.).

***tythe** [TITHE].

Tzar, etc. [TSAR].

tzetze [TSETSE].

Tzigany (tsig′ ȧ ni) [Hung.], *a.* Of or pertaining to the Hungarian gipsies or their music. *n.* An Hungarian gipsy.

U

U, u, the twenty-first letter and the fifth vowel (*pl.* **Us, U's, Ues**), has five principal sounds; (1) as in *rule*, rool; (2) as in *bull*, bul; (3) as in *but*, bŭt; (4) as in *bur*, bĕr; (5) as in *due*, dū; U [initial of Upper], *a.* (*colloq.*) Of words, phrases, behaviour, etc., associated with the so-called Upper Classes. **U-boat** (ū bōt) [G. *unterseeboot*], *n.* A German submarine. **U-film,** *n.* (*Cinema.*) A film passed by the British Board of Film Censors for universal exhibition.

Uachtaran na h-Eireann (oo ėch dė ran nė hā r ėn) [Ir.], *n.* The President of Eire.

***uberty** (ū′ bėr ti) [L. *ūbertas*, from *ūber*, rich, fertile], *n.* Fruitfulness, fertility. ***uberous,** *a.*

ubiety (ū bī′ ė ti) [L. *ubī*, where, -TY], *n.* The state of being in a particular place; the relation of locality, whereness.

ubiquity (ū bik′ wi ti) [F. *ubiquité*, from L. *ubīque*, wherever, everywhere, from *ubī*, where], *n.* The quality or state of being everywhere or in an indefinite number of places at the same time, omnipresence. **ubiquitarian** (-târ′ i ȧn), *n.* (*Theol.*) A believer in the omnipresence of Christ's body, esp. with reference to the Eucharist; *a.* Of or pertaining to ubiquitarianism. **ubiquitarianism,** *n.* **ubiquitary, ubiquitous,** *a.* **ubiquitously,** *adv.* **ubiquitousness,** *n.*

udal, udaller [ODAL].

udder (ŭd′ ėr) [A.-S. *ūder* (cp. Dut. *uijer*, G. *euter*, Icel. *jūgr*, for *jūdr*), cogn. with L. *ūber*, Gr. *outhar*, Sansk. *ūdhar*], *n.* The milk-secreting organ of a cow, ewe, etc.; *a teat, a dug. **uddered,** *a.* **udderless,** *a.*

udometer (ū dom′ ė tĕr) [L. *ūdus*, wet, moist, -METER], *n.* A rain-gauge. **udometric** (-met′ rik), *a.* **udomograph** (-dom′ ȯ grăf) [-GRAPH], *n.* A self-registering rain-gauge.

ugh (u) [instinctive sound], *int.* An exclamation of disgust or horror.

ugly (ŭg′ li) [Icel. *uggligr* (*uggr*, fear, -LY)], *a.* Unpleasing to the sight, not beautiful; unsightly, ungraceful, not comely; (*fig.*) morally repulsive, unpleasant; suggesting evil; awkward, cantankerous, threatening, formidable. **uglify,** *v.t.* **uglily,** *adv.* **ugliness,** *n.*

Ugrian, Ugric (oo-, ū gri ȧn, -grik) [tribal name], *a.* Finnic. **Ugro-,** *comb. form.*

Uhlan (oo′-, ū lȧn) [G. and Pol. *ulan*, Turk. and Tatar *oglān*, son, lad], *n.* A cavalryman armed with a lance, in the old German and some other Continental armies.

uitlander (oo′ it lan der) [Dut., an outlander], *n.* An immigrant into the Transvaal.

ukase (ū kās′) [F., from Rus. *ukazu*], *n.* An edict or decree of the Imperial Russian Government.

ukelele (ū kė lā′ li) [Hawaiian], *n.* A small four-stringed instrument resembling a guitar.

ulcer (ŭl′ sėr) [M.F. *ulcere*, L. *ulcus -ceris*, sore, Gr. *helkos*, wound, sore], *n.* An open sore on the outer or inner surface of the body accompanied by a secretion of pus or other discharge; (*fig.*) a source of corruption or moral pollution. **ulcerable,** *a.* **ulcerate,** *v.t.* To affect with or as with an ulcer. *v.i.* To form an ulcer; to become ulcerous. **ulceration** (-ā′ shŭn), *n.* **ulcerative** (ŭl′ sėr ȧ tiv), *a.* **ulcered, ulcerous,** *a.* **ulcerously,** *adv.* **ulcerousness,** *n.*

-ule [L. *-ulus*, *-ula*, *-ulum*], *dim. suf.* As in *globule*, *pustule*.

ulema (oo′ lė mȧ) [Arab., pl. of *alim*, learned], *n.* (*collect.*) The body of Moslem doctors of law and interpreters of the Koran in a country, esp. in Turkey.

Ulex (ū′ lėks) [L.], *n.* A genus of thorny shrubs of the bean family comprising the furze, whin, or gorse.

uliginose (ū lij′ i nōs) [L. *ūlīginōsus*, from *ūlīgo -ginis*, moisture], *a.* (*Bot.*) Growing in swampy or muddy places; *muddy, slimy.

ulitis (ū lī′ tis) [Gr. *oula*, pl., the gums, -ITIS], *n.* (*Path.*) Inflammation of the gums.

ullage (ŭl′ ȧj) [Prov. *ulhage*, from *ulha*, to fill (cp. O.F. *eullier*, *ouillier*), from L. *oculus*, eye, orifice], *n.* The quantity that a cask wants of being full.

ulla-lulla (ŭl′ ȧ lŭl′ ȧ) [Ir.], *n.* A keen, a cry of lamentation.

ulmaceous (ŭl mā′ shŭs) [L. *ulm-us*, elm, -ACEOUS], *a.* Pertaining to or characteristic of the elm.

ulmin (ŭl′ min), *n.* (*Chem.*) A black alkaline, gummy substance contained in excrescences on the elm and other trees, and in vegetable mould. **ulmic, ulmous,** *a.*

Ulmus (ŭl′ mŭs), *n.* L., *n.* (*Bot.*) A genus of trees containing the elms.

ulna (ŭl′ nȧ) [L., elbow, cogn. with Gr. *ōlenē*], *n.* (*pl.* **-næ**) The larger and longer of the two bones of the fore-arm. **ulnad,** *adv.* Toward the ulna. **ulnar,** *a.* **ulno-,** *comb. form.*

Ulodendron (ū lȯ den′ drȯn) [Gr. *oulē*, scar, *dendron*, tree], *n.* (*Palæont.*) A genus of fossil trees with lepidodendroid cortical scars and large discoid scars left by the falling cones.

ulosis (ū lō′ sis) [Gr. *oulē*, scar, -OSIS], *n.* (*Med.*) Cicatrization.

ulotrichi (ū lot′ ri kī) [mod. L. (Gr. *oulos*, woolly, *thrix trichos*, hair)], *n.pl.* The woolly-haired races of mankind, one of Huxley's three great divisions. **ulotrichan,** *a.* and *n.* **ulotrichous,** *a.*

ulster (ŭl′ stėr) [province of Ireland], *n.* A long, loose overcoat for men or women, usu. with a belt, originally made of Ulster frieze.

ulterior (ŭl tēr′ i ŏr) [L., comp. of *ulter*, adj., whence adv. *ultra*, see ULTRA-], *a.* Lying beyond or on the other side of any line or boundary; more remote or distant; not at present in view, under consideration, or pertinent; not yet disclosed, unavowed. **ulteriorly,** *adv.*

ultimate (ŭl′ ti mȧt) [L. *ultimātus*, p.p. of *ultimāre*, from *ultimus*, superl., as prec.], *a.* Last, final, beyond which there is nothing existing or possible; incapable of further analysis; fundamental, elementary, primary; *farthest, most remote. **ultimately,** *adv.* **ultimateness,** *n.*

ultimatum (ŭl ti mā′ tŭm), *n.* A final proposal, statement of conditions, or concession, the rejection of which may involve rupture of diplomatic relations and a declaration of war; anything final, essential, or fundamental. ***ultimation,** *n.*

ultimo (ŭl′ ti mō), *adv.* (*Comm. correspondence*) Last month.

ultimogeniture (ŭl ti mō jen′ i chŭr), *n.* Inheritance by the youngest son, borough-English.

ultra (ŭl′ trȧ) [see foll.], *a.* Extreme, advocating extreme views or measures; uncompromising, extravagant. *n.* An extremist. **ultraism** (ŭl′ trȧ izm), *n.* **ultraist,** *n.*

ultra- [L., beyond, on the other side of; excessively; beyond the normal, reasonable, etc., orig. abl. fem. of O.L. *ulter*, adj.], *pref.* **ultra-classical** (ŭl trȧ klăs′ i kȧl) [CLASSICAL], *a.* Extravagantly classical in style, etc. **ultra-conservative,** *a.* Extravagantly conservative.

ultramarine (ŭl trȧ mȧ rēn′) [It. *oltra marino*], *a.* Situated, being, or lying beyond the sea. *n.* A deep-blue pigment formerly obtained from lapis lazuli; the colour of this.

ultramontane (ŭl trȧ mon′ tān) [ULTRA-, MONTANE], *a.* Being or lying beyond the mountains, esp. the Alps, esp. on the Italian side; hence, supporting the absolute power and infallibility of the pope. *n.* One who resides south of the Alps; a supporter of ultramontanism. **ultramontanism** (ŭl trȧ mon′ tȧ nizm), *n.* (*R.-C. Ch.*) The principle that all ecclesiastical power should be concentrated in the hands of the pope, in contradistinction to the independent development of national Churches. **ultramontanist,** *n.*

ultramundane (ŭl trȧ mŭn′ dān), *a.* External to the world or the solar system; pertaining to the supernatural or another life. **ultra-Protestant,** *a.* **ultra-religious,** *a.* **ultra-sensual,** *a.* **ultra-short waves,** *n.pl.* (*Radio.*) Electromagnetic waves below 10 metres in wavelength. **ultra-tropical** (-trop′ i kȧl), *a.* Situated beyond or hotter than the tropics. **ultra-violet rays,** *n.pl.* (*Phys.*) Actinic rays belonging to that portion of the spectrum which is beyond violet. They are used therapeutically to improve metabolism and in the treatment of bone diseases.

ultromotivity (ŭl trō mō tiv′ i ti) [L. *ultro*, of one's own accord, MOTIVITY], *n.* The power of spontaneous movement or action. ***ultroneous** (ŭl trō′ nė ŭs), *a.* Voluntary, spontaneous. ***ultroneously,** *adv.*

ululate (ū′ lū-, ŭl′ ū lāt) [L. *ululātus*, p.p. of *ululāre*, cp. Gr. *oluluzein*, imit.], *v.i.* To howl, as a dog or wolf, to hoot. **ululant,** *a.* **ululation** (-lā′ shŭn), *n.*

umbel (ŭm′ bėl) [L. *umbella*, parasol, dim. of *umbra*, shade], *n.* An inflorescence in which the flower-stalks spring from one point and spread like the ribs of an umbrella forming a flattish surface, as in the parsley family. **umbellal, -lar, umbellate, -lated, umbelliferous** (-lif′ ėr ŭs), *a.* **umbellet, umbellule,** *n.* **umbellifer** (-bel′ i fėr), *n.*

umber (ŭm′ bėr) [F. *ombre*, in *terre d'ombre*, It. *terra d'ombra*, L. *umbra*, shadow], *n.* A dark-brown pigment derived from a mineral ferric oxide containing manganese; a grayling; the umber-bird or umbrette. *a.* Of the colour of umber, dark, dusky. *v.t.* To colour with or as with umber. **burnt umber:** Umber heated so as to produce a much redder brown. **raw umber:** This in the natural state. **umber-bird,** *n.* The umbrette. **umbery,** *a.*

umbilical (ŭm bil′ i kȧl) [L. *umbilīc-us*, navel, cogn. with Gr. *omphalos*, -AL], *a.* Of, or pertaining to, or situated near the navel; central. **umbilical cord:** The rope-like structure of vessels and connective tissue connecting the fœtus with the placenta. **umbilicate, -ed,** *a.* **umbilication** (-kā′ shŭn), *n.* **umbilicus** (ŭm bi lī′ kŭs), *n.* The navel; (*Nat. Hist.*) a navel-shaped depression or other formation, the hilum; a depression at the axial base of some univalve shells; (*Rom. Ant.*) the ornamental boss at each end of the stick on which a manuscript was rolled. **umbiliferous** (-lif′ ėr ŭs), *a.* **umbiliform** (-bil′ i fôrm), *a.*

umbles (ŭmblz) [M.E. *noumbles*, O.F. *nombles*, corr. of *lomble*, L. *lumbulum*, nom. *-us*, dim. of *lumbus*, LOIN], *n.pl.* The entrails of a deer [cp. HUMBLE-PIE].

umbo (ŭm′ bō) [L., cogn. with *umbilīcus*, UMBILICAL], *n.* (*pl.* **-bos, -bones,** -bōz, -bō nēz) The boss or projecting point in the centre of a shield; (*Nat. Hist.*) a boss, knob, prominence, or elevation. **umbonal, umbonate, umbonic** (-bon′ ik), *a.*

umbra (ŭm′ brȧ) [L., shadow], *n.* (*pl.* ***-bræ***) The part of the shadow of a planet, etc., esp. the earth or moon, in which the light of the sun is entirely cut off, the dark central portion of a sun-spot; (*Rom. Ant.*) a guest brought by an invited person, a parasite. **umbral,** *a.* **umbrated,** *a.* (*Her.*) Shadowed, adumbrated. **umbriferous** (-brif′ ėr ŭs), ***umbrose,** *a.* ***umbrosity** (-bros′ i ti), *n.*

umbraculum (ŭm brăk′ ū lŭm) [L., dim. of prec.], *n.* (*pl.* **-la**) (*Bot.*) An umbrella-shaped appendage, as the capitulum of the sporophore in some liverworts. **umbraculate, umbraculiferous** (-lif′ ėr ŭs), *a.* **umbraculiform** (-brăk′ ū li fôrm), *a.*

umbrage (ŭm′ braj) [F. *ombrage*, from *ombre*, L. UMBRA], *n.* A sense of injury, offence; *shade; that which affords a shade. **umbrageous** (-brā′ jŭs), *a.* Shady, shaded. **umbrageously,** *adv.* **umbrageousness,** *n.* Shadiness.

umbral, umbrated [UMBRA].

umbrella (ŭm brel′ ȧ) [It. *umbrella*, *ombrella*, dim. of *ombra*, L. UMBRA], *n.* A light screen of silk, cotton, or other fabric, stretched on a folding frame of radiating ribs on a stick, for holding above the head as a protection against rain or sun; the umbrella-shaped disk of a medusa used as a swimming organ; an umbrella-shell; (*fig.*) a protection, a cover. **umbrella-bird,** *n.* A South American bird of the genus *Cephalopterus*, with a large erectile spreading crest. **umbrella bush,** *n.* A species of acacia. **umbrella grass,** *n.* (*Austral.*) An Australian millet. **umbrella-shell,** *n.* A tropical gasteropod with an umbrella-like shell. **umbrella-stand,** *n.* A stand for holding umbrellas, in an entrance hall, etc. **umbrella-tree,** *n.* A small magnolia with flowers and leaves in an umbrella-like whorl at the ends of the branches. **umbrellaed,** *a.*

umbrette (ŭm bret′) [F. *ombrette*, dim. of *ombre*, as prec.], *n.* An African bird, *Scopus umbretta*, allied to the storks and herons.

Umbrian (ŭm′ bri ȧn), *a.* Of or pertaining to Umbria, in Central Italy, esp. of the school of painting to which Raphael and Perugino belonged; the language of Umbria, one of the principal Italic dialects. *n.* A native of ancient Umbria.

umbriferous, *umbrose [UMBRA].

umiak (oo′ myăk) [Eskimo], *n.* An Eskimo boat made of skins stretched on a framework, paddled by women.

umlaut (um′ lout) [G. *um*, about, *laut*, sound], *n.* Change of the vowel in a syllable through the influence of an *i* or *u* (usu. lost or modified) in the following syllable; (*Print.*) the diæresis mark used over German vowels. *v.t.* To sound with or modify by umlaut.

umpire (ŭm′ pīr) [M.E. *nompere*, O.F. *nomper* (NON-, PEER (1)), peerless, odd, in the sense of odd man (cp. ADDER, APRON)], *n.* A person chosen to enforce the rules and settle disputes in a game, esp. cricket or hockey; a person chosen to decide a question in controversy; (*Law*) a third person called in to settle a disagreement between arbitrators. *v.t.* To act as umpire in or for. *v.i.* To act as umpire. **umpirage, umpireship,** *n.*

umpteen (ŭm tēn′) [analogy with thirteen, etc.], *a.* Any number.

umquhile (ŭm whīl′) [M.E. *umwhile*, at times], *a.* and *adv.* (*Sc.*) Formerly, late, whilom.

'un (ŭn), *pron.* (*colloq.*) [ONE].

un- [A.-S.], *pref.* (1) Giving a negative sense to adjectives, adverbs, and nouns; (2) used with verbs to denote reversal or annulment of the action of the simple verb (sometimes ambiguous, thus *unrolled* may mean 'not rolled', or 'opened out after having been rolled up'). Since there is no limit to the use of this prefix the meaning of words not given in the following selection can be ascertained by reference to the simple verb, adjective, etc. **unabashed** (ŭn ȧ băsht′), *a.* Not abashed; shameless. **unabated** (-bā′ tėd), *a.* ***unability** [INABILITY], *n.* **unable** (-ābl′), *a.* Not able (to); not having sufficient power or ability; incapable, incompetent; *weak, helpless. **unabolished** (-bol′ isht), *a.* **unabridged** (-brijd′), *a.* **unacademic** (-ăk ȧ dem′ ik), *a.* **unaccented** (-ăk sen′ tėd), *a.* **unacceptable** (-sep′ tȧbl), *a.* **unacceptableness, unacceptability** (-bil′ i ti), *n.* **unaccommodating** (-kom′ ȯ dā ting), *a.* **unaccompanied** (-kŭm′ pȧ nid), *a.* Unattended; (*Mus.*) without accompaniment. **unaccomplished** (-kom′ plisht), *a.* Unfinished, not carried out or effected; lacking accomplishments. **unaccountable** (-koun′ tȧbl), *a.* Not accountable or responsible; inexplicable. **unaccountability** (-bil′ i ti), **unaccountableness,** *n.* **unaccountably,** *adv.* **unaccoutred** (-ȧ koo′ tėrd), *a.* **unaccredited** (-kred′ i tėd), *a.* **unaccustomed** (-kŭs′ tȯmd), *a.* **unachievable** (-chē′ vȧbl), *a.* **unachieved,** *a.* ***unaching** (-ā′ king), *a.* Painless. **unacknowledged** (-nol′ ejd), *a.* Not acknowledged, not recognized. **unacknowledging,** *a.* Ungrateful. **unacquainted** (-kwān′ tėd), *a.* **unacquaintance, unacquaintedness,** *n.* **unacquirable** (-kwīr′ ȧbl), *a.* **unacquired,** *a.* **unactable** (-ăk′ tȧbl), *a.* Not capable of being acted; unfit for representation. **unacted,** *a.* **unadaptable** (-dăp′ tȧbl), *a.* **unadapted,** *a.* Unfitted (for). **unaddicted** (-dik′ tėd), *a.* **unaddressed** (-drest′), *a.* **unadjudged** (-jŭjd′), *a.* **unadjusted** (-jŭs′ tėd), *a.* **unadministered** (-min′ is tėrd), *a.* **unadmired** (-ȧd mīrd′), *a.* **unadmonished** (-mon′ isht), *a.* **unadopted,** *a.* Not adopted; (of road, etc.) not taken over by the local authority. **unadorned** (-dôrnd′), *a.* Not adorned, without decoration. **unadulterate, -ated** (-dŭl′ tėr ȧt, -ā tėd), *a.* Not adulterated, unmixed; pure, genuine. ***unadventurous** (-ăd ven′ tū rŭs), *a.* **unadvised** (-ȧd vīzd′), *a.* Not advised; not prudent or discreet, rash. **unadvisable,** *a.* **unadvisability** (-bil′ i ti). **unadvisableness,** *n.* **unadvisedly** (vī′ zėd li), *adv.* **unadvisedness,** *n.* **unaffected** (-ȧ fek′ tėd), *a.* Not influenced or affected; without affectation, sincere, genuine. **unaffectedly,** *adv.* **unaffectedness,** *n.* **unaffiliated** (-fil′ i ātėd), *a.* **unafflicted** (-flik′ tėd), *a.* ***unafraid** (-ȧ frād′), *a.* **unaggressive** (-gres′ iv), *a.* **unaided** (-ā′ dėd), *a.* **unalarmed** (-ȧ larmd′), *a.* **unalienable,** etc. [INALIENABLE].

***unalist** (ū′ nȧ list) [L. *unus*, one, after PLURALIST], *n.* A person holding only one benefice.

unallowable (ŭn ȧ lou′ ȧbl), *a.* That cannot be allowed. **unalloyed** (-loid′), *a.* **unalterable** (-awl′ tėr ȧbl), *a.* **unalterability** (-bil′ i ti), **unalterableness,** *n.* **unalterably,** *adv.* **unaltered,** *a.* **unamazed** (-ȧ māzd′), *a.* **unambiguous** (-ăm big′ ū ŭs), *a.* Plain, clear. **unambiguously,** *adv.* **unambiguousness,** *n.* **unambitious** (-ăm bish′ ŭs), *a.* **unambitiously,** *adv.* **unambitiousness,** *n.* **unamenable** (-ȧ mē′ nȧbl), *a.* **unamendable** (-men′ dȧbl), *a.* **un-American** (-ȧ mer′ i kȧn), *a.* Not American; alien to or incompatible with American ideas or feelings. **unamiable** (-ā′ mi ȧbl), *a.* Not amiable; ill-natured; repellent, unpleasant. **unamiability** (-bil′ i ti), **unamiableness,** *n.* **unamiably,** *adv.* **unamused** (-ȧ mūzd′), *a.* **unamusingly,** *adv.* **unanalysable** (-ăn ȧ lī′ zȧbl), *a.* **unanalysed** (-ăn′ ȧ līzd), *a.* **unanchor** (-ăng′ kȯr), *v.t.* and *i.* ***unaneled** (-ȧ nēld′) [M.E. *aneled*, p.p. of *anelian* (ON-, A.-S. *ele*, L. *oleum*, OIL)], *a.* Not having received extreme unction. **unanimated** (-ăn′ i mā tėd), *a.*

unanimous (ū năn′ i mŭs) [L. *ūnanimus* (*ūnus*, one, *animus*, mind)], *a.* Being all of one mind, agreeing in opinion; formed, held, or expressed with one accord. **unanimity** (-nim′ i ti), **unanimousness,** *n.* **unanimously,** *adv.*

unannounced (ŭn ȧ nounst′), *a.* Not announced. **unanswerable** (-an′ sėr ȧbl), *a.* That cannot be satisfactorily answered or refuted. **unanswerability** (-bil′ i ti), **unanswerableness,** *n.* **unanswerably,** *adv.* **unanswered,** *a.* **unanticipated** (-ăn tis′ i pā tėd), *a.* **unapocryphal** (-ȧ pok′ ri fȧl), *a.* True, genuine. **unapostolic** (-ăp ȯ stol′ ik), *a.* Not in accordance with apostolic usage or authority. **unappalled** (-ȧ pawld′), *a.* **unapparel** (-ȧ păr′ ėl), *v.t.* To unclothe. **unapparelled,** *a.* **unapparent** (-ȧ păr′-, -pâr′ ėnt), *a.* **unappeasable** (-ȧ pē′ zȧbl), *a.* **unappeased,** *a.* **unappetizing** (-ăp′ ė tī zing), *a.* **unappetizingly,** *adv.* **unapplied** (-ȧ plīd′), *a.* **unappreciated** (-prē′ shi ā tėd), *a.* **unappreciative,** *a.* **unapprehended** (-ăp rė hen′ dėd), *a.* **unapprehensible,** *a.* **unapprehensive,** *a.* **unapprehensiveness,** *n.* **unapprised** (-ȧ prīzd′), *a.* **unapproachable** (-prō′ chȧbl), *a.* **unapproachability** (-bil′ i ti), **unapproachableness,** *n.* **unapproachably,** *adv.* **unappropriated** (-prō′ pri ā tėd), *a.* **unapproved** (-ȧ proovd′), *a.* **unapproving,** *a.* **unapprovingly,** *adv.* **unapt** (-ăpt′), *a.* **unaptly,** *adv.* **unaptness,** *n.* **unarm** (-arm′), *v.t.* and *i.* To disarm. **unarmed,** *a.* **unarmoured,** *a.* **unarranged** (-ȧ rānjd′), *a.* **unarrayed** (-ȧ rād′), *a.* **unarrested** (-ȧ res′ tėd), *a.* ***unartful** (-art′ fŭl), *a.* ***unartfully,** *adv.* **unartificial** (-ar ti fish′ ȧl), *a.* Not artificial; natural. **unartificially,** *adv.* **unartistic** (-ar tis′ tik), *a.* **unascendable** (-sen′ dȧbl), *a.* **unascended,** *a.* **unascertainable** (-ăs ėr tā′ nȧbl), *a.* **unascertained,** *a.* **unashamed** (-ȧ shāmd′), *a.* **unasked** (-askt′), *a.* **unaspirated** (-ăs′ pi rā tėd), *a.* **unaspiring** (-ȧ spīr′ ing), *a.* **unaspiringly,** *adv.* **unassailable** (-ȧ sā′ lȧbl), *a.* Incapable of being assailed; incontestable. **unassailed,** *a.* **unassayed** (-ȧ sād′), *a.* **unassignable** (-sī′ nȧbl), *a.* **unassigned,** *a.* **unassimilated** (-sim′ i lā tėd), *a.* **unassisted** (-sis′ tėd), *a.* **unassuming** (-sū′ ming), *a.* Not arrogant or presuming; modest. **unassured** (-shoord′), *a.* **unatoned** (-ȧ tōnd′), *a.* **unattached** (-tăcht′), *a.* Not attached; (*Law*) not seized for debt; not belonging to any particular club, regiment, etc. **unattainable** (-tā′ nȧbl), *a.* **unattainableness,** *n.* **unattainted** (-tān′ tėd), *a.* **unattempted** (-temp′ tėd), *a.* **unattended** (-ten′ dėd), *a.* **unattested** (-tes′ tėd), *a.* **unattire,** *v.t.* and *i.* To undress (esp. of ceremonial robes). **unattractive** (-trăk′ tiv), *a.* **unattractively,** *adv.* **unattractiveness,** *n.* **unaugmented** (-awg men′ tėd), *a.* ***unauspicious** [INAUSPICIOUS]. **unauthentic** (-then′ tik), *a.* **unauthenticated,** *a.* **unauthenticity** (-tis′ i ti), *n.* **unauthoritative** (-thor′ i tā tiv), *a.* **unauthorized** (-aw′ thȯ rīzd), *a.* **unavailable** (-ȧ vā′ lȧbl), *a.* **unavailableness,** *n.* **unavailing,** *a.*

Ineffectual; vain, useless. **unavailingly** (-vā′ ling li), *adv.* **unavenged** (-venjd′), *a.* **unavoidable** (-voi′ dȧbl), *a.* Inevitable; that cannot be made null or void. **unavoidableness,** *n.* **unavoidably,** *adv.* **unavoided,** *a.* **unavowed** (-voud′), *a.* **unaware** (-wâr′), *a.* Not aware, ignorant (of); careless, inattentive; *adv.* Unawares. **unawares,** *adv.* Without warning; by surprise, unexpectedly; undesignedly. **at unawares:** Unexpectedly. **unbacked** (-băkt′), *a.* Not taught to bear a rider, unbroken (of a horse); unsupported, having no backers; without a back (of a seat, etc.). **unbag** (-băg′), *v.t.* To let out of a bag. **unbailable** (-bā′ lȧbl) [BAIL (1)], *a.* **unbaked** (-bākt′), *a.* **unbalance** (-băl′ ȧns), *v.t.* To throw off one's balance. **unbalanced,** *a.* Not balanced; not in equipoise; not brought to an equality of debit and credit; without mental balance, unsteady, erratic. **unballast** (-băl′ ȧst), *v.t.* To discharge or empty of ballast. **unballasted,** *a.* Not furnished with ballast; unsteady. **unbank** (-bănk′), *v.t.* To remove the ashes, etc., from a banked-up fire, to make it burn freely. **unbankable,** *a.* (*Comm.*) Not receivable at a bank. **unbaptized** (-băp tīzd′), *a.* **unbar** (-bar′), *v.t.* To remove a bar or bars from; to unfasten, to open. **unbarbed** (-barbd′), *a.* Not furnished with barbs; *not shaven, untrimmed. **unbarbered** (-bar′ bėrd), *a.* Unshaven. **unbarricade** (-băr′ i kād), *v.t.* ***unbated** (-bā′ tėd), *a.* Unabated, undiminished, unblunted. **unbathed** (-bā*th*d′), *a.* **unbattered** (-băt′ ėrd), *a.* ***unbay** (-bā′) [BAY (3)], *v.t.* To release from restraint; to open. **unbear** (-bâr′), *v.t.* To take off or slacken the bearing-rein. **unbearable,** *a.* Not to be borne, intolerable. **unbearably,** *adv.* **unbearded** (-bĕr′ dėd), *a.* **unbeaten** (-bētn′), *a.* Not beaten; not conquered or surpassed; untrodden. **unbeautiful** (-bū′ ti fůl), *a.* Not beautiful; ugly. **unbecoming** (-bė kŭm′ ing), *a.* Not becoming, not suited (to); not befitting; improper, indecorous, indecent. **unbecomingly,** *adv.* **unbecomingness,** *n.* **unbed** (-bed′), *v.t.* To rouse from bed. **unbedded,** *a.* Not yet brought to bed, virgin. **unbefitting** (-bė fit′ ing), *a.* **unbefriended** (-fren′ dėd), *a.* **unbegot, unbegotten** (-got′, -ėn), *a.* Not begotten; self-existent. **unbeguile** (-gīl′), *v.t.* To undeceive. **unbegun** (-gŭn′), *a.* ***unbeholden** (-hōl′ dėn), *a.* Unseen. **unbeknown** (-bė nōn′), **-knownst** (-nōnst′), *a.* (*colloq.*) Not known; unknown (to); *adv.* Without the knowledge of. **unbelief** (-bė lēf′), *n.* The withholding of belief; incredulity; scepticism; disbelief (in, esp. divine revelation). **unbelievable,** *a.* **unbeliever,** *n.* **unbelieving,** *a.* **unbeloved** (-lŭvd′), *a.* **unbelt** (-belt′), *v.t.* **unbend** (-bend′), *v.t.* (*past & p.p.* **-bent**) To change or free from a bent position; to straighten; to relax from exertion, tension, or constraint, etc.; (*Naut.*) to unfasten (sails) from the yards and stays; to cast loose or untie (a cable or rope); *v.i.* To become straightened; to relax from constraint, formality, etc.; to be affable, to condescend. **unbending,** *a.* Unyielding, resolute, inflexible; yielding oneself to relaxation or amusement; affable, condescending. **unbendingly,** *adv.* **unbendingness,** *n.* **unbeneficed** (-ben′ ė fist), *a.* **unbeseem** (-bė sēm′), *v.t.* To be unbecoming (to). **unbeseemingly,** *adv.* **unbesought** (-sawt′), *a.* **unbespoken** (-spō′ kėn), *a.* **unbestowed** (-stōd′), *a.* **unbias** (-bī′ ȧs), *v.t.* To set free from bias. **unbiased,** *a.* **unbiblical** (-bib′ li kȧl), *a.* Not in or according to the Bible. ***unbid, unbidden** (-bidn′), *a.* Not commanded; not called for, spontaneous; uninvited. **unbigoted** (-big′ ȯ tėd), *a.* **unbind** (-bīnd′), *v.t.* (*past & p.p.* **-bound**) To untie, to unfasten; to release from a binding; to free from bonds, to release. **unbishop,** *v.t.* To depose from the office of bishop. **unbitt** (-bit′), *v.t.* (*Naut.*) To remove the turns of (a rope, etc.) from the bitts. **unbitted,** *a.* Not restrained with a bit, unbridled; (*Naut.*) not fastened round the bitts. **unblamable** (-blā′ mȧbl), *a.* **unblamableness,** *n.* **unblamably,** *adv.* **unblamed,** *a.* **unbleached** (-blēcht′), *a.* **unblemished** (-blem′ isht), *a.* ***unbless** (-bles′), *v.t.* To make unhappy. **unblest,** *a.* **unblindfold** (-blīnd′ fōld), *v.t.* **unblock** (-blok′), *v.t.* **unblooded** (-blŭd′ ėd), *a.* Not thoroughbred. **unbloody,** *a.* Not stained with blood; not accompanied with bloodshed; not bloodthirsty. **unblotted** (-blot′ ėd), *a.* Not blotted; not blotted out. **unblown** (-blōn′), *a.* Not blown (as a trumpet); yet in bud, not yet in flower; not inflated or distended with wind. **unblushing** (-blŭsh′ ing), *a.* Shameless, barefaced, impudent. **unblushingly,** *adv.* **unblushingness,** *n.* **unbodied** (-bod′ id), *a.* Freed from the body; (*poet.*) incorporeal, immaterial. **unboiled** (-boild′), *a.* **unbolt** (-bōlt′), *v.i.* To undo the bolts of; to unfasten, to open. **unbolted** (1), *a.* Not fastened by a bolt. **unbolted** (2), *a.* Not bolted or sifted (of flour, etc.); *(*fig.*) gross, unrefined. **unbone** (-bōn′), *v.t.* To remove the bones from (meat). **unbonnet** (-bon′ ėt), *v.i.* To take off the cap or bonnet (esp. as a salutation); to uncover the head; *v.t.* To remove the bonnet from. **unbonneted,** *a.* **unbookish** (-buk′ ish), *a.* **unboot** (-boot′), *v.t.* **unborn** (-bôrn′), *a.* **unbosom** (-buz′ ům), *v.t.* To disclose (one's feelings, etc.); *v.i.* To disclose one's secret feelings, opinions, or intentions; to open one's heart. **unbound,** *past & p.p.* [UNBIND]. **unbounded** (-boun′ dėd), *a.* Boundless, not bounded (by); infinite, not subject to check or control. **unboundedly,** *adv.* **unboundedness,** *n.* **unbowed** (-boud′), *a.* Not bowed; (*fig.*) unconquered. **unbrace** (-brās′), *v.t.* To remove or relax the braces of; to free from tension, to loosen, to relax. **unbraid** (-brād′), *v.t.* To separate the strands of; to unweave, to disentangle. **unbreathed** (-brē*th*d′), *a.* Not breathed; *unexercised. **unbred** (-bred′), *a.* Not well bred, rude; (*Shak.*) unbegotten. **unbreech** (-brēch′), *v.t.* To unfasten or remove the breech of (a cannon, etc.). **unbreeched,** *a.* Not wearing breeches. **unbribable** (-brī′ bȧbl), *a.* **unbridle** (-brīdl′), *v.t.* To remove the bridle from; (*fig.*) to set free from restraint. **unbridled,** *a.* Freed from the bridle; unrestrained, unruly, ungovernable, insolent. **unbroken** (-brō′ kėn), *a.* Not broken; not subdued; uninterrupted, regular; not violated; not broken in, not accustomed to the saddle, etc.; not opened up by the plough. **unbrotherly** (-brŭ*th*′ ėr li), *a.* **unbrotherliness,** *n.* ***unbrute** (-broot′), *v.t.* To free from the nature of a brute. **unbuckle** (-bŭkl′), *v.t.* To unfasten the buckle of. ***unbuild** (-bild′), *v.t.* To demolish, to raze. ***unbundle** (-bŭndl′), *v.t.* To unpack, to disclose, to reveal, to confess. **unburden** (-bĕr′ dėn), *v.t.* To free from a load or burden; (*fig.*) to relieve (the mind, etc.) by disclosing or confession. **unburdened,** *a.* **unburied** (-ber′ id), *a.* **unburned, -burnt** (-bĕrnd′, -bĕrnt′), *a.* **unbusinesslike** (-biz′ nės līk), *a.* **unbutton** (-bŭt′ ȯn), *v.i.* To unfasten the buttons of; *v.t.* To undo one's buttons; (*colloq.*) to talk without restraint. **uncage** (-kāj′), *v.t.* **uncalled** (-kawld′), *a.* **uncalled for:** Not necessary; not asked for, gratuitous, impertinent. **uncandid** (-kăn′ did), *a.* **uncanny** (-kăn′ i), *a.* Not canny, weird, mysterious; incautious, rash, dangerous. **uncanonical** (-kȧ non′ i kȧl), *a.* **uncanonically,** *adv.* **uncanonicalness,** *n.* **uncanonized** (-kăn′ ȯ nīzd), *a.* **uncap** (-kăp′), *v.t.* To remove the cap or cover from; *v.i.* To remove one's cap or hat (in salutation). **uncape** (-kāp′), *v.t.* To take the hood from (a hawk). **uncapped** (-kăpt′), *a.* **uncared-for** (-kârd′ for), *a.* Not cared for, neglected. **uncarpeted** (-kar′ pė tėd), *a.* **uncart** (-kart′), *v.t.* To unload from a cart. **uncase** (-kās′), *v.t.* To take out of a case or covering; (*fig.*) to reveal, to disclose; to unfurl (the colours of a regiment); **v.i.* (*Shak.*) To undress. **uncastrated** (-kăs trā′ tėd), *a.* **uncatalogued** (-kăt′ ȧ logd), *a.* **uncate** (ŭng′ kȧt) [see UNCINATE], *a.* Hooked. **uncaused** (-kawzd′) [UN-, CAUSE], *a.* Not caused; self-existent. **uncauterized** (-kaw′ tėr īzd), *a.* **unceasing** (-sē′ sing), *a.* Not ceasing, incessant, continual. **unceasingly,** *adv.* **unceremonious** (-ser ė mō′ ni ůs), *a.* Without ceremony, formality, or courtesy; familiar, brusque, abrupt. **unceremoniously,** *adv.* **unceremoniousness,** *n.* **uncertain** (-sĕr tȧn), *a.* Not certain; not sure; doubtful; not certainly or precisely known; not to be relied on; undecided, changeable, fickle, capricious. **uncertainly,** *adv.* **uncertainty,** *n.* **uncertificated** (-sėr tif′ i kā tėd), *a.* **unchain** (-chān′), *v.t.* **unchallengeable** (-chăl′ ėnj ȧbl), *a.* **unchallenged,** *a.* **unchancy** (-chan′ si), *a.* (*Sc.*) Unlucky; uncanny; unseasonable, inconvenient; dangerous. **unchangeable** (-chānj′ ȧbl), *a.* **unchangeableness,** *n.* **unchangeably,** *adv.* **unchanging,** *a.* **unchangingly,** *adv.* **uncharge** (-charj′), *v.t.* To free from a charge or load; to withdraw a charge from, to acquit of blame. **unchariot** (-chăr′ i ȯt), *v.t.* To turn out of a chariot. **uncharitable** (-chăr′ i tȧbl), *a.* Not harmonizing with Christian feeling; harsh, censorious. **uncharitableness,** *n.* **uncharitably,** *adv.* **uncharnel** (-char′ nėl), *v.t.* (*poet.*) To exhume. **uncharted** (-char′ tėd), *a.* Not marked on a chart; unmapped. **unchartered** (-char′ tėrd), *a.* **unchary** (-châr′ i), *a.* **unchaste** (-chāst′), *a.* **unchastely,** *adv.* **unchastity** (-chăs′ ti ti), *n.* **unchastened** (-chā′ sėnd), *a.* **unchecked** (-chekt′), *a.* Not checked or repressed; unrestrained, uncontrolled; not examined. ***unchild** (-chīld′), *v.t.* To bereave of children; to make unfilial. **unchivalrous** (-shiv′-, -chiv′ ȧl rŭs), *a.* **unchivalrously,** *adv.* **unchristian** (-kris′ tyȧn), *a.* Not Christian, heathen; not according to or befitting the spirit of Christianity; **v.t.* To make unchristian. **unchristianize,** *v.t.* **unchristianly,** *a.* **unchristianness,** *n.* **unchurch** (-chĕrch), *v.t.* To expel from a Church; to excommunicate; to deprive of the character or standing of a Church.

uncial (ŭn′ shȧl) [L. *unciālis,* from *uncia,* inch, ounce], *a.* Denoting a kind of majuscule writing somewhat resembling modern capitals used in manuscripts of the 4th–8th cents. *n.* An uncial letter or manuscript.

uncinate (ŭn′ si nȧt) [late L. *uncinātus,* from *uncinus,* L. *uncus,* hook], *a.* (*Bot.*) Hooked at the end; (*Anat., etc.*) having a hooked appendage. **uncinal, unciferous** (-sif′ ėr ŭs), **unciform** (ŭn′-), *a.*

uncircumcised (ŭn sĕr′ kŭm sīzd), *a.* Not circumcised; not Jewish; (*fig.*) heathen, unholy, profane. **uncircumcision** (-sizh′ ŭn), *n.* **the uncircumcision:** (*Bibl.*) The Gentiles. **uncircumscribed** (-sĕr′ kŭm skrībd), *a.* **uncircumstantial** (-sĕr kŭm stăn′ shȧl), *a.* Not circumstantial, not given or considered in detail. **uncivil** (-siv′ il), *a.* Not civil, discourteous, ill-mannered; (*poet.*) rude, boisterous; *uncivilized. **uncivilly,** *adv.* **uncivilized** (-siv′ i līzd), *a.* **unclad** (-klăd′), *a.* **unclaimed** (-klāmd′), *a.* **unclasp** (-klasp′), *v.t.* To unfasten the clasp of. **unclass** (-klas′), *v.t.* To degrade from one's proper class.

uncle (ŭng′ kėl) [A.-F. (cp. F. *oncle*), L. *avunculum,* nom. *-us,* double dim. of *avus,* grandfather], *n.* The brother of one's father or mother; the husband of one's aunt; (*Am.*) an elderly man (a friendly mode of address); (*slang*) a pawnbroker. **Uncle Sam:** The Government or a typical representative of the U.S.A. **uncleship,** *n.*

unclean (ŭn klēn′), *a.* Not clean; foul, dirty; lewd, unchaste; (*Jewish Law*) not ceremonially clean. **uncleanness,** *n.* **uncleanly** (-klen′ li), *a.* **uncleanliness,** *n.* **unclench** (-klench′), *v.t.* and *i.* **unclerical** (-kler′ i kȧl), *a.* **unclew** (-kloo′), *v.t.* To unwind, untie, or undo. **unclinch** (klinch′), *v.t.* **uncloak** (-klōk′), *v.t.* and *i.* **unclog** (-klog′), *v.t.* To remove a clog from; to disencumber, to free. **uncloister** (-kloi′ stėr), *v.t.* To release from a cloister; to set at liberty. **unclose** (-klōz′), *v.t.* and *i.* To open. **unclothe** (-klōth′), *v.t.* **unclouded** (-kloud′ ėd), *a.* Not obscured by clouds; clear, bright. **unclubbable** (-klub′ ȧbl), *a.* **unco** (ŭng′ kō) [Sc., var. of UNCOUTH], *a.* Strange, extraordinary. *n.* A strange or surprising person or thing. *adv.* Remarkably, very. **uncock** (-kok′), *v.t.* To let down the hammer of (a gun, etc.) without exploding the charge. **uncoffined** (-kof′ ind), *a.* Not laid in a coffin. **uncogitable** (-koj′ i tȧbl), *a.* Beyond the reach of thought. **uncoif** (-koif′), *v.t.* To take the coif or head-covering off. **uncoil** (-koil′), *v.t.* and *i.* To unwind. **uncoined** (-koind′), *a.* Not coined; *(*fig.*) unfeigned, genuine. **uncoloured** (-kŭl′ ȯrd), *a.* Not coloured; (*fig.*) told with simplicity or without exaggeration, unvarnished. **uncolt** (-kōlt′), *v.t.* To unhorse. **uncombed** (-kōmd′), *a.* **uncomeatable** (-kŭm ăt′ ȧbl), *a.* (*colloq.*) That cannot be come at; not attainable, not obtainable. **uncomely** (-kŭm′ li), *a.* **uncomeliness,** *n.* **uncomfortable** (-kŭm′ fȯr tȧbl), *a.* **uncomfortably,** *adv.* **uncommercial** (-kȯ mĕr′ shȧl), *a.* Not consistent according to commercial principles or usage. **uncommitted** (-kȯ mit′ ėd), *a.* (*Pol.*) Standing outside major political groupings. **uncommon** (-kom′ ȯn), *a.* Not common, unusual, remarkable, extraordinary. **uncommonly,** *adv.* Remarkably, to an uncommon degree. **uncommonness,** *n.* **uncommunicative** (-kȯ mū′ ni kȧ tiv), *a.* Reserved, taciturn. **uncommunicatively,** *adv.* **uncommunicativeness,** *n.* ***uncompanied** (-kŭm′ pȧ nid), *a.* Unaccompanied; (*fig.*) unmatched. **uncompanionable** (-kȯm păn′ yȯn ȧbl), *a.* Unsociable. **uncomplaining** (-plā′ ning), *a.* **uncomplainingly,** *adv.* **uncomplaisant** (-plā zȧnt), *a.* **uncomplaisantly,** *adv.* **uncomplicated** (-kom′ pli kā tėd), *a.* **uncomplimentary** (-kom pli men′ tȧ ri), *a.* **uncompounded** (-kȯm poun′ dėd), *a.* **uncomprehensive** (-kom prė hen′ siv), *a.* Not comprehensive; *unable to comprehend; *incomprehensible. **uncompromising** (-kom′ prȯ mī zing), *a.* Not compromising or admitting of compromise; determined, rigid, inflexible, strict. **uncompromisingly,** *adv.* **unconcealed** (-kȯn sēld′), *a.* **unconcern** (-kȯn sĕrn′), *n.* Absence of concern or anxiety; indifference, apathy. **unconcerned,** *a.* Not concerned (in or with); free from anxiety. **unconcernedly** (-sĕr′ nėd li), *adv.* **uncondemned** (-kȯn demd′), *a.* **uncondensable** (-den′ sȧbl), *a.* **uncondensed,** *a.* **unconditional** (-kȯn dish′ ȯ nȧl), *a.* Not conditional; absolute. **unconditionality** (-năl′ i ti), **unconditionalness,** *n.* **unconditionally,** *adv.* **unconditioned,** *a.* **unconfinable** (-fī′ nȧbl), *a.* That cannot be confined; unbounded. **unconfined,** *a.* **unconfinedly,** *adv.* **unconfirmed** (-fĕrmd′), *a.* **unconformable** (-fôr′ mȧbl), *a.* **unconformability** (-bil′ i ti), **unconformableness,** *n.* **unconformably,** *adv.* **uncongenial** (-jē′ ni ȧl), *a.* **uncongenially,** *adv.* **unconnected** (-nek′ tėd), *a.* **unconquerable** (-kong′ kėr ȧbl), *a.* **unconquerably,** *adv.* **unconquered,** *a.* **unconscientious** (-kon shi en′ shŭs), *a.* **unconscientiously,** *adv.* **unconscientiousness,** *n.* **unconscionable** (-kon′ shȯ nȧbl), *a.* Not reasonable, inordinate; not influenced or restrained by conscience; (*Law*) grossly unfair, inequitable. **unconscionableness,** *n.* **unconscionably,** *adv.* **unconscious** (-kon′ shŭs), *a.* Not conscious, ignorant, unaware (of); temporarily deprived of consciousness; not perceived by the mind. *n.* (*Psych.*) A term which includes all processes which cannot be made conscious by an effort of the will. **unconsciously,** *adv.* **unconsciousness,** *n.* **unconsecrated** (-kon′ sė krā tėd), *a.* **unconsenting** (-kȯn sen′ ting), *a.* **unconsidered** (-kȯn sid′ ėrd), *a.* Not taken into consideration. ***unconstant** [INCONSTANT]. **unconstitutional** (-kon sti tū′ shȯ nȧl), *a.* Not authorized by or contrary to the principles of the constitution. **unconstitutionality** (-năl′ i ti), *n.* **unconstitutionally,** *adv.* **unconstrained** (-kȯn strānd′), *a.* **unconstrainedly** (-strā′ nėd li), *adv.* **unconsumed** (-kȯn sūmd′), *a.* **uncontainable** (-tā′ nȧbl), *a.* **uncontaminated** (-tăm′ i nā tėd), *a.* **uncontemplated** (-kon′ tėm plā tėd), *a.* Not contemplated or expected. **uncontested** (-kȯn tes′ tėd), *a.* **uncontracted** (-kȯn trăk′ tėd), *a.* **uncontradicted** (-kon trȧ dik′ tėd), *a.* **uncontrollable** (-kȯn trō lȧbl), *a.* Unmanageable. **uncontrollableness,** *n.* **uncontrollably,** *adv.* **uncontrolled,** *a.* **uncontrolledly** (-trō′ lėd li), *adv.* **uncontroversial** (-kon trȯ vėr′ shȧl), *a.* **uncontroversially,** *adv.* **uncontroverted** (-kon′ trȯ vėr tėd), *a.* **unconventional** (-kȯn ven′ sho nȧl), *a.* Not fettered by convention or usage; informal, free and easy, bohemian. **unconventionality** (-năl′ i ti), *n.* **unconventionally,** *adv.* **unconversable** (-kȯn vĕr′ sȧbl), *a.* Not free in conversation, reserved. **unconversant** (-kon′ vėr sȧnt), *a.* Not conversant or familiarly acquainted (with). **unconverted** (-kȯn vĕr′ tėd), *a.* **unconvertible,** *a.* **unconvinced** (-vinst′), *a.* **unconvincing,** *a.* **uncooked** (-kukt′), *a.* **uncord** (-kôrd′), *v.t.* To take the cord from; to unbind. **uncork** (-kôrk′), *v.t.* To take the cork out of; (*fig.*) to give vent to (one's feelings, etc.). **uncorroborated** (-kȯ rob′ ȯ rā tėd), *a.* **uncorroded** (-rō′ dėd), *a.* **uncorrupted** (-rŭp′ tėd), *a.* **uncorruptible,** *a.* **uncountable** (-koun′ tȧbl), *a.* **uncounted,** *a.* **uncountenanced** (-koun′ tė nȧnst), *a.* **uncouple** (-kŭpl′), *v.t.* To disconnect; to let loose, to release. **uncourtly** (-kôrt′ li), *a.* **uncourtliness,** *n.* **uncouth** (-kooth′) [A.-S. *uncūth* (*cūth*, p.p. of *cunnan*, to know, see CAN (2))], *a.* Awkward, clumsy; outlandish, odd, ungainly; *ignorant. **uncouthly,** *adv.* **uncouthness,** *n.* **uncovenanted** (-kŭv′ ė nȧn tėd), *a.* Not bound by a covenant; not promised or secured by a covenant. **Uncovenanted Civil Service:** A branch of the East Indian Civil Service the members of which passed no examination, might resign at pleasure, and received no pension. **uncover** (-kŭv′ ėr), *v.t.* To remove a covering from; to divest of covering; to make known, to disclose; to expose (a line of troops behind) by wheeling to right or left; *v.i.* To take off the hat, in salutation. **uncoveted** (-kŭv′ ė tėd), *a.* **uncowl** (-koul′), *v.t.* *uncreate (-krė āt′), *v.t.* To blot out of existence; *a.* (ŭn′ krė āt) Uncreated. **uncreated** (-krė ā′ tėd), *a.* Not yet created; existing independently of creation. **uncritical** (-krit′ i kȧl), *a.* Not critical, not inclined to criticize; not according to the rules of criticism. **uncritically,** *adv.* **uncross** (-kros′), *v.t.* To change from a crossed position. **uncrossed,** *a.* Not crossed (as a cheque); not opposed. **uncrown** (-kroun′), *v.t.* To discrown, to depose, to dethrone. **uncrowned,** *a.* Discrowned; not yet crowned; having the power without the title of king.

unction (ŭngk′ shŭn) [F., from L. *unctiōnem*, nom. *-tio*, from *ungere*, to anoint, p.p. *unctus*], *n.* The act of anointing with oil or an unguent, as a symbol of consecration or for medical purposes; that which is used in anointing, an unguent or ointment; (*fig.*) anything soothing or ingratiating; a quality in speech conveying deep religious or other fervour; effusive or affected emotion, gush; relish, gusto; (*Theol.*) grace. **unctuous,** *a.* Greasy, oily, soapy to the touch; full of unction; (*fig.*) oily, effusive, hypocritically or affectedly fervid. **extreme unction** [EXTREME]. **unctuously,** *adv.* **unctuousness,** *n.*

***uncular** [AVUNCULAR].

unculled (ŭn kŭld′), *a.* Not culled; not separated. **uncultivable** (-kŭl′ ti vȧbl), *a.* **uncultivated,** *a.* **uncultured,** *a.* **uncurb** (-kĕrb′), *v.t.* **uncurbed,** *a.* Unrestrained. **uncurl** (-kĕrl′), *v.t.* and *i.* **uncurtailed** (-kûr tāld′), *a.* **uncurtain** (-kĕr′ tȧn), *v.t.* To remove the curtain from, to reveal.

uncus (ŭng′ kŭs) [L., hook], *n.* (*pl.* **-ci,** -sī) (*Nat. Hist.*) A hook, claw, or hook-like part or appendage.

uncushioned (ŭn kush′ ȯnd), *a.* Not cushioned or padded. **uncustomed** (-kŭs′ tȯmd), *a.* Not subject to customs duty; not having paid duty. **uncut** (-kŭt′), *a.* Not cut; having the margins untrimmed (of leaves or a book). **undam** (-dăm′), *v.t.* **undamaged** (-dăm′ ȧjd), *a.*

undate, undated (1) (ŭn′ dāt, -dā tėd) [L. *undātus*, p.p. of *undāre*, from *unda*, wave], *a.* Having a wavy surface, undulate. **undé** (ŭn′ dā), *a.* (*Her.*) Wavy.

undated (2) (ŭn dā′ tėd), *a.* Not dated. **undaunted** (-dawn′ tėd), *a.* Not daunted; fearless. **undauntedly,** *adv.* **undauntedness,** *n.* ***undeaf** (-def′), *v.t.* (*Shak.*) To cure of deafness. **undebated** (-dė bā′ tėd), *a.* **undebauched** (-dė bawcht′), *a.*

undecagon (ŭn dek′ ȧ gȯn) [L. *undecim* eleven, Gr. *gōnia*, angle], *n.* A plane figure having eleven angles and eleven sides.

undeceive (ŭn dė sēv′), *v.t.* To free from deception or error; to open the eyes of. **undeceived,** *a.*

undecennary (ŭn dė sen′ ȧ ri), **undecennial** (-sen′ i ȧl) [L. *undecim*, eleven, after CENTENARY and CENTENNIAL], *a.* Pertaining to a period of eleven years; celebrated or occurring once in every eleven years.

undecided (ŭn dė sī′ dėd), *a.* Not decided or settled; irresolute, wavering. **undecidedly,** *adv.* **undecipherable** (-dė sī′ fėr ȧbl), *a.* ***undecisive** [INDECISIVE]. ***undeck** (-dek′), *v.t.* To divest of ornaments. **undecked,** *a.* Not adorned; not furnished with a deck. **undeeded** (-dē′ dėd), *a.* (*Law*) Not transferred by deed; *not signalized by any great action. **undefended** (-dė fen′ dėd), *a.* **undefiled** (-fīld′), *a.* Not defiled; pure. **undefined** (-fīnd′), *a.* Not defined; indefinite, vague. **undeify** (-dē′ i fī), *v.t.* **undelegated** (-del′ ė gā tėd), *a.* **undelivered** (-dė liv′ ėrd), *a.* **undemanded** (-man′ dėd), *a.* **undemonstrated** (-dem′ ȯn strā tėd), *a.* **undemonstrative** (-dė mon′ strȧ tiv), *a.* Not demonstrative; not exhibiting strong feelings; reserved. **undeniable** (-dė nī′ ȧbl), *a.* Not capable of being denied; indisputable; (*colloq.*) decidedly good, excellent. **undeniably,** *adv.* **undenominational** (-nom i nā′ shȯ nȧl), *a.* Not sectarian. **undenounced** (-nounst′), *a.* **undependable** (-pen′ dȧbl), *a.* Not to be depended on. **undeplored** (-plôrd′), *a.* **undepraved** (-prāvd′), *a.* **undepreciated** (-prē′ shi ā tėd), *a.* **undepressed** (-prest′), *a.* **undeprived** (-prīvd′), *a.*

under (ŭn′ dėr) [A.-S. (cp. Dut. *onder*, G. *unter*, Icel. *undir*, Swed. and Dan. *under*), cogn. with L. *infrā*, beneath], *prep.* In or to a place or position lower than, below; at the foot or bottom of; covered by, on the inside of, beneath the surface of; (*fig.*) beneath the appearance or disguise of; inferior to or less than in quality, rank, degree, number, amount, etc.; subject to, subordinate or subservient to; governed, controlled, or directed by; liable to, on condition or pain of, in accordance with; by virtue of; in the time of; attested by; planted or sown with. *adv.* In a lower or subordinate place, condition, or degree. *a.* Lower, inferior, subordinate. **under age:** Not of full age. **under arms** [ARM (2)]. **under a cloud:** Out of favour. **under fire** [FIRE (1)]. **under sail** [SAIL]. **under sentence:** Having received sentence or judgment. **under the breath:** In a low voice; very softly. **under the rose** [ROSE (1)]. **under way** [WAY].

under- [prec.], *pref.* Under, below (the substantive to which it is prefixed); underneath, beneath, lower than, in position, rank, etc., subordinate; insufficiently, incompletely, immaturely. Only a selection of compounds with this prefix is given; others can be explained by reference to the simple adjective, noun, or verb. **underact** (ŭn dėr ăkt′), *v.t.* To act or play inadequately. **underagent** (-ā′ jėnt), *n.* A subordinate agent. **underbear** (-bâr′) [BEAR (2)], *v.t.* To support, to endure; to face, to live. **underbearer** (ŭn′ dėr bâr ėr), *n.* One who supports the corpse at a funeral. **underbid** (-bid′), *v.t.* To bid less than (as at an auction). **underbitten** (-bit′ ėn), *a.* Not bitten in deep enough for printing (of etched lines on a copper plate). **underboard** (ŭn′ dėr bôrd) [cp. ABOVE-BOARD], *adv.* Secretly, underhandedly. **underbred** (-bred′), *a.* Not thoroughbred; ill-bred. **underbrush** (ŭn′ dėr brŭsh), *n.* Undergrowth, underwood; *v.t.* To clear of this. **underbuy** (ŭn dėr bī′), *v.t.* To buy something at a lower price than that offered at; to buy for less than the proper value. **undercarriage,** *n.* (*Aviat.*) The main alighting gear of an aircraft. **undercharge** (-charj′), *v.t.* To charge less than the fair price for, or put an insufficient charge in (a gun, etc.). **under-clay** (ŭn′ dėr klā), *n.* A bed of clay found under coal seams. **underclerk** (-klark), *n.* **under-clerkship,** *n.* **undercliff,** *n.* **underclothes,** *n.pl.* Clothes worn under others, esp next to the skin. **underclothing,** *n.*

under-cover (ŭn' der kŭv er), *a.* Done in secret. ***undercrest,** *v.t.* To support or wear, as a crest. **undercroft,** *n.* A vault, esp. under a church or large building, a crypt. **undercurrent,** *n.* A current running below the surface; (*fig.*) a secret or unapparent tendency or influence; (*Mining*) a large shallow box beside a main hydraulic sluice, with a steeper inclination, aiding to save gold from the finer material. **undercut** (ŭn dėr kŭt'), *v.t.* To cut under (coal, etc.) so as to remove it easily; to cut away the material beneath (a carved design) to give greater relief; to make a price lower than that of a competitor; (*Golf*) to hit (a ball) so as to make it rise high. *n.* (ŭn' dėr kŭt) The act or effect of undercutting; a blow upward; the under side of a sirloin, the tenderloin. **under-develop** (-dė vel' ŏp), *v.t.* To develop insufficiently. **underditch** (ŭn' dėr dich), *v.t.* To cut a deep ditch in, to drain the surface. **underdo** (-doo'), *v.i.* To do inadequately; to cook insufficiently. **underdone** (-dŭn'), *a.* Insufficiently cooked. **underdose** (-dōs'), *v.t.* To dose insufficiently; *n.* (ŭn' dėr dōs). **underdrain** (ŭn' dėr drān), *n.* A drain below the surface of the ground; *v.t.* (-drān') To drain thus. **underdraw** (-draw'), *v.t.* To represent inadequately. **underdress** (-dres'), *v.t.* and *i.* To dress insufficiently or too plainly. **underestimate** (-es' ti māt), *v.t.* To estimate at too low a rate; *n.* (-măt) An inadequate estimate. **underestimation** (-mā' shŭn), *n.* **under-expose** (-ek spōz'), *v.t.* (*Phot.*) **under-exposure** (-spō' zhŭr), *n.* **underfeed** (-fēd'), *v.t.* and *i.* **underfired** (-fīrd'), *a.* Insufficiently baked (of pottery). **underflow** (ŭn' dėr flō), *n.* An undercurrent. **underfoot** (-fut'), *adv.* Under the feet; beneath: *v.t.* To shore up, to underpin. **undergarment** (ŭn' dėr gar mėnt), *n.* One worn under others. **undergear** (ŭn' dėr gēr), *n.* Undergarments. **underglaze** (-glāz'), *a.* (*Ceramics*) Suitable for painting with before the glaze is applied. **undergo** (-gō'), *v.t.* (*past* **-went,** *p.p.* **-gone**) To experience, to pass through, to suffer; to bear up against, to endure with firmness. **undergrade** (ŭn' dėr grād), *a.* Having the truss below the roadway (as in a deck-bridge). **undergraduate** (-grăd' ū ăt), *n.* A member of a University who has not yet taken a degree. **undergraduateship,** *n.* **underground** (ŭn' dėr ground), *a.* Situated below the surface of the earth; obscure, secret, unperceived by those in authority. *n.* That which is underground; an underground railway. *adv.* (-ground') Below the surface of the earth. **undergrove** (-grōv), *n.* A grove or plantation overshadowed by larger trees. **undergrown** (-grōn'), *a.* **undergrowth** (ŭn' dėr grōth), *n.* Small trees or shrubs, growing under larger ones. **underhand** (ŭn dėr hănd'), *adv.* Secretly, not openly, clandestinely; slyly, unfairly, by fraud; with the hand underneath (of bowling). *a.* (*attributively*) (ŭn' dėr hănd). Clandestine, secret; sly, unfair, fraudulent; (of bowling) with the hand underneath both the elbow and the ball. **underhanded** (-hăn' dėd), *a.* Underhand. **underhandedly,** *adv.* **underhandedness,** *n.* **underhew** (-hū'), *v.t.* To hew less than is proper, esp. to hew (logs, etc.) so as to leave waste wood that should be cut away and convey a misleading impression of the cubic contents. **underhold** (ŭn' dėr hōld), *n.* (*Wrestling*) A hold round the body with the arms underneath one's opponent's. **underhung** (-hŭng', *attributively* ŭn' dėr hŭng), *a.* Projecting beyond the upper jaw (of the lower jaw); having the lower jaw projecting before the upper. **under-king** (ŭn' dėr king), *n.* **underlap** (-lăp') [cp. OVERLAP], *v.t.* To be folded or extend under the edge of. **underlay** (1) (ŭn dėr lā') [LAY (1)], *v.t.* (*past & p.p.* **-laid**) To lay something under. *v.i.* (*Mining*) To incline from the perpendicular (of a vein); *n.* (ŭn' dėr lā) Inclination of a vein; (*Print.*) a piece of paper, etc., placed beneath type, etc., to bring it to the proper level for printing. **underlay** (2), *past* [UNDERLIE]. **under-lease** (ŭn' dėr lēs), *n.* A sublease. **under-let** (-let'), *v.t.* To let below the proper value; to sublet. **underletter,** *n.* **under-letting,** *n.* **underlie** (-lī') [LIE (2)], *v.t.* (*past* **-lay,** *p.p.* **-lain**) To lie under or beneath; to be the basis or foundation of. **underline** (-līn'), *v.t.* To mark with a line underneath, esp. for emphasis. *n.* (ŭn' dėr līn) An announcement of a subsequent theatrical performance at the foot of a play-bill. **underlinen** (-lin' ėn), *n.* Linen underclothing. **underling** (ŭn' dėr ling) [-LING (1)], *n.* An inferior agent or assistant. **underlooker** (ŭn' dėr luk ėr), *n.* An underviewer. **underman** (-măn'), *v.t.* To furnish (a ship) with less than the proper complement of men. **undermasted** (-mas' tėd), *a.* **undermentioned** (-men' shŭnd), *a.* Mentioned below or later. **undermine** (-mīn'), *v.t.* To dig a mine or excavation under; to render unstable by digging away the foundation of; (*fig.*) to injure by clandestine or underhand means; to wear away (one's strength, etc.) by imperceptible degrees. **underminer,** *n.* **undermost** (ŭn' dėr mōst), *a.* Lowest in place, position, rank, etc. ***undern** [A.-S.], *n.* The third hour of the day, 9 A.M.; the period from this to noon; noon, as the time of the principal meal. **underneath** (-nēth'), *adv.* and *prep.* Beneath, below. **undernote** (ŭn' dėr nōt), *n.* A subdued note, an undertone. **under-pass** (ŭn' dėr pas), *n.* A road passing under a railway or another road. **underpay** (-pā'), *v.t.* (*past & p.p.* **-paid**) To pay inadequately. **underpin** (-pin'), *v.t.* To support (a wall, overhanging bank of earth, etc.) by propping up with timber, masonry, etc. **underpinning,** *n.* **underplay** (-plā'), *v.t.* To play (a part) inadequately; *v.i.* To play a low card whilst one holds a higher one of the same suit; *n.* (ŭn' dėr plā) The act of underplaying. **underplot** (ŭn' dėr plot), *n.* A subordinate plot in a play, novel, etc. **underpraise** (ŭn dėr prāz'), *v.t.* To praise less than is deserved. **underprivileged,** *a.* Belonging to the less-privileged class of society. **underprize** (-prīz'), *v.t.* To value below one's merits. **underproduction** (-dŭk' shŭn), *n.* Lower or less production than the normal or the demand. **underproof** (ŭn' dėr proof), *a.* Containing less alcohol than proof spirit. **underprop** (-prop'), *v.t.* To prop or support underneath. **underquote** (-kwōt'), *v.t.* To offer at lower prices than; to offer (goods, etc.) at lower prices than others. **underrate** (-rāt'), *v.t.* To rate or estimate too low. **under-reckon** (-rek' ŏn), *v.t.* **under-ripe** (-rīp'), *a.* **underrun** (-rŭn'), *v.t.* To run beneath, to pass under. **underscore** (-skôr'), *v.t.* To underline. **under-secretary** (sek' rė tȧr i), *n.* **under-secretaryship,** *n.* **undersell** (-sel'), *v.t.* To sell cheaper than. **underseller,** *n.* **under-servant** (-sěr' vȧnt), *n.* **underset** (1) (-set'), *v.t.* To support underneath by a prop, masonry, etc. **underset** (2) (ŭn' dėr set), *n.* (*Naut.*) A current of water below the surface in a direction contrary to that of the wind or surface water. **under-sheriff** (-sher' if), *n.* A deputy-sheriff. **undershirt** (ŭn' dėr shěrt), *n.* (*Am.*) A vest or singlet. **undershot** (ŭn' dėr shot), *a.* Driven by water passing under it (of a water-wheel). **undershoot,** *n.* (*Aviat.*) Falling short of the mark in landing. **undershrub** (-shrŭb), *n.* A plant of shrubby habit, but smaller than a shrub. **undersign** (-sīn'), *v.t.* To sign under or at the foot of. **the undersigned:** The person or persons signing a document, etc. **undersized** (-sīzd'), *a.* Below the normal or average size. ***underskinker** (-sking' kėr), *n.* An assistant tapster. **underskirt** (ŭn' dėr skěrt), *n.* A skirt worn under another. **underslung,** *a.* (*Motor.*) Descriptive of a chassis with the frame below the axles. **undersoil** (-soil), *n.* Subsoil. **undersong** (-song), *n.* A subordinate strain; (*fig.*) an underlying meaning; *the accompaniment of a song. **undersparred** (-spard'), *a.* Not adequately equipped with spars (of a ship).

understand (ŭn dėr stand') [A.-S. *understandan* (UNDER-, STAND)], *v.t.* (*past & p.p.* **-stood,** ***-standed**) To take in, know, or perceive the meaning of; to comprehend fully, to have complete apprehension of, to perceive the force or significance of; to suppose to mean, to take as meant or implied, to gather, assume, or infer from information received; to supply (a word, explanation, etc.)

mentally. *v.i.* To have or exercise the power of comprehension; to be informed or told, to hear. **understandable,** *a.* **understanding,** *a.* Intelligent; sensible. *n.* The act of one who understands; comprehension; the power or faculty of apprehension; the faculty of thinking or of apprehending relations and drawing inferences; discernment; clear insight and intelligence in practical matters; union of minds or sentiments, accord; an informal agreement or compact. **understandingly,** *adv.*

understate (ŭn dėr stāt′), *v.t.* To represent as less, inferior, etc., than the truth. **understatement,** *n.* **understock** (-stok′), *v.t.* To furnish (a shop, etc.) with insufficient stock. **understood,** *past & p.p.* [UNDERSTAND]. **understrapper** (ŭn′ dėr străp ėr), *n.* An inferior or subordinate agent. **understrapping,** *a.* **under-stratum,** *n.* **understudy,** *v.t.* To study (a part) in order to play it if the usual actor is unable; to study the acting of (an actor or actress) thus; *n.* One who studies a part or actor thus.

undertake (ŭn dėr tāk′) [M.E. *undertaken*], *v.t.* (*past* **-took,** *p.p.* **-taken**) To take upon oneself, to assume, to engage in, to enter upon (a task, enterprise, responsibility, etc.); to engage oneself, to promise (to do); to guarantee, to affirm, to answer for it (that); *to engage with in combat, etc. *v.i.* To promise, to be guarantee (for); (*colloq.*) to manage funerals.

undertaker (ŭn′ dėr tā kėr), *n.* One who undertakes; a tradesman who manages funerals; (*Hist.*) a person undertaking certain political offices, esp. one of those who undertook to manage the House of Commons for the King in 1614, the settlers who undertook to hold the lands forfeited to the Crown in Ireland in the 16th–17th cents., etc.

undertaking (ŭn dėr tā′ king), *n.* The act of one who undertakes any business; that which is undertaken, a task, an enterprise, an agreement, a promise, a stipulation.

under-tenant (ŭn′ dėr ten ȧnt), *n.* A tenant under another tenant. **under-tenancy,** *n.* **undertimed** (-tīmd′), *a.* Under-exposed. **undertint** (ŭn′ dėr tint), *n.* A subdued tint. **undertone,** *n.* A low or subdued tone, esp. in speaking; a subdued colour an undertint. **undertook,** *past* [UNDERTAKE]. **undertrump** (-trŭmp′), *v.t.* To play a lower trump than (another person or another trump played). **undertow** (ŭn′ dėr tō), *n.* A backward current opposite to that on the surface, an underset, esp. the backward flow under waves breaking on a shore. **undervalue** (-văl′ ū), *v.t.* To value too low; to despise. **undervaluation** (-ā′ shŭn), *n.* **undervaluer,** *n.* **undervest** (ŭn′ dėr vest), *n.* **underviewer** (-vū ėr), *n.* The overseer of the underground workings in a coal-mine. **underwear** (ŭn′ dėr wâr), *n.* Clothes worn underneath others, underclothing; the wearing of these. **underwent,** *past* [UNDERGO]. **underwing,** *n.* A nocturnal moth with conspicuous markings on the hind or under wings. **underwood,** *n.* Undergrowth. **underwork** (ŭn dėr wěrk′), *v.t.* To work for a lower price than, to undercut; *v.i.* To work inadequately; *n.* (ŭn′ dėr wŏrk) Subordinate or inferior work. **underworld,** *n.* The nether world, the infernal regions; the antipodes; the earth as the sublunary sphere; (*colloq.*) the lowest, esp. criminal, classes of society.

underwrite (ŭn dėr rīt′), *v.t.* To execute and deliver (a policy of marine insurance); to engage to buy all the stock in (a new company, etc.) not subscribed for by the public; to write beneath, to subscribe. *v.i.* To act as an underwriter, to practise marine insurance. **underwriter,** *n.* **underwriting,** *n.* **underwrought** (-rawt′), *a.* Insufficiently wrought.

undescried (ŭn dė skrīd′), *a.* Not descried. **undeserved** (-zěrvd′), *a.* **undeservedly** (-zěr′ vėd li), *adv.* **undeserving,** *a.* **undeservingly,** *adv.* **undesignated** (-dez′ ig nā tėd), *a.* **undesigned** (-dė zīnd′), *a.* Not designed, unintentional. **undesignedly** (-zī′ nėd li), *adv.* **undesignedness,** *n.* **undesigning,** *a.* **undesirable** (-zīr′ ȧbl), *a.* Not desirable; unpleasant, inconvenient; *n.* An undesirable person. **undesirability** (-bil′ i ti), **undesirableness,** *n.* **undesirably,** *adv.* **undesired,** *a.* Not desired; not asked for. **undesirous,** *a.* Not desirous (of). **undetachable** (-tăch′ ȧbl), *a.* **undetected** (-tek′ tėd), *a.* **undetermined** (-těr′ mind), *a.* Not determined, not decided, not fixed; irresolute; indeterminate. **undeterred** (-těrd′), *a.* **undeveloped** (-vel′ ŏpt), *a.* **undeviating** (-dē′ vi ā ting), *a.* **undeviatingly,** *adv.* **undevout** (-dė vout′), *a.* **undevoutly,** *adv.* **undid,** *past* [UNDO]. **undifferentiated** (-dif ėr en′ shi ā tėd), *a.* **undiffused** (-di fūzd′), *a.* **undigested** (-jes′ tėd), *a.* **undignified** (-dig′ ni fīd), *a.* Not dignified; not consistent with one's dignity. **undiluted** (-di lū′ tėd), *a.* **undiminished** (-min′ isht), *a.* **undimmed** (-dimd′), *a.*

undine (ŭn dēn′) [L. *unda*, wave, -INE], *n.* A female water sprite without a soul, but capable of obtaining one by marrying a mortal and bearing a child; (*Med.*) a form of eye-irrigator. **undinal** (-dē′ nȧl), *a.*

undiplomatic (ŭn dip lō măt′ ik), *a.* Not diplomatic. **undirected** (-di rek′ tėd), *a.* **undiscerned** (-di zěrnd′), *a.* **undiscernible,** *a.* **undiscerning,** *a.* **undiscerningly,** *adv.* **undischarged** (-dis charjd′), *a.* **undisciplined** (-dis′ i plind), *a.* **undisclosed** (-klōzd′), *a.* **undiscomfited** (-kŭm′ fi tėd), *a.* **undisconcerted** (-kŏn sěr′ tėd), *a.* ***undiscording** (-kôr′ ding) [DISCORD], *a.* Not disagreeing or discordant. **undiscouraged** (-kŭr′ ajd), **undiscoverable, undiscovered** (-kŭv′ ėrd), *a.* **undiscoverably,** *adv.* **undiscriminating** (-krim′ i nā ting), *a.* **undiscriminatingly,** *adv.* **undiscussed** (-kŭst′), *a.* **undisguised** (-gīzd′), *a.* Not disguised; open, frank, plain. **undisguisedly** (-gī′ zėd li), *adv.* **undisheartened** (-har′ tėnd), *a.* **undismayed** (-mād′), *a.* **undispelled** (-peld′), *a.* **undispersed** (-pěrst′), *a.* **undisplayed** (-plād′), *a.* **undisputed** (-pū′ tėd), *a.* **undissected** (-sek′ tėd), *a.* **undissembled** (-sembld′), *a.* **undissembling,** *a.* **undissolved** (-solvd′), *a.* **undistinguishable** (-ting′ gwish ȧbl), *a.* **undistinguishably,** *adv.* **undistinguishableness,** *n.* **undistinguished,** *a.* **undistorted** (-tôr′ tėd), *a.* **undistracted** (-trăk′ tėd), *a.* **undistressed** (-trest′), *a.* **undistributed** (-trib′ ū tėd), *a.* (chiefly *Log.*) Not distributed. **undisturbed** (-těrbd′), *a.* **undisturbedly** (-těr′ bėd li), *adv.* **undiversified** (-dī věr′ si fīd), *a.* **undiverted** (-věr′ tėd), *a.* **undivided** (-di vī′ dėd), *a.* **undividedly,** *adv.* **undivorced** (-vôrst′), *a.* **undivulged** (-vŭljd′), *a.* **undo** (-doo′), *v.t.* (*past* **-did,** *p.p.* **-done**) To reverse (something that has been done), to annul; to unfasten, to untie; to unfasten the buttons, garments, etc., of (a person); to bring ruin, to destroy, to corrupt. **undoer,** *n.* **undoing,** *n.* **undock** (-dok′), *v.t.* To take or bring out of dock. **undomesticate** (-dȯ mes′ ti kāt), *v.t.* **undomesticated,** *a.* **undone** (-dŭn′) [p.p. of UNDO], *a.* Not done; unfastened; ruined, destroyed.

undose (ŭn′ dōs) [L. *undōsus*, from *unda*, wave], *a.* Wavy, undulating.

undoubted (ŭn dou′ tėd), *a.* Not called in question, not doubted; unsuspected. **undoubtedly,** *adv.* Without doubt. **undoubting,** *a.* **undoubtingly,** *adv.* **undrape** (-drāp′), *v.t.* To remove drapery from, to uncover. **undraped,** *a.* **undreamed** (-drēmd′), **undreamt** (-dremt′), *a.* **undreamed-of,** *a.* Not thought of. **undress** (ŭn dres′), *v.t.* To divest of clothes, to strip; to take the dressing, bandages, etc., from (a wound, etc.). *v.i.* To undress oneself. *n.* Ordinary dress, opp. to full dress or uniform; negligent attire. *a.* Pertaining to everyday dress; (*fig.*) commonplace. **undressed,** *a.* **undrinkable** (-dring′ kȧbl), *a.* **undue** (-dū′), *a.* Excessive, disproportionate; not yet due; improper; illegal. **unduly,** *adv.*

undulate (ŭn′ dū lȧt) [L. *undulātus*, from *unda*, wave], *a.* Wavy, bending in and out or up and down. *v.i.* (-lāt) To have a wavy motion; to rise and fall (of water). **undulately,** *adv.* **undulatingly,** *adv.* **undulation** (-lā′ shŭn), *n.* The act of undulating; a wavy or sinuous form or motion, a gentle rise and fall, a wavelet; (*Path.*) a wave-like movement of a fluid in a cavity of the body. **undulationist,** *n.* One who believes in the undulatory theory. **undulatory** (ŭn dū lā′ tȯr i), *a.* Having an undulating character; rising and falling like waves; pertaining or due to undulation. **undulatory theory:** The theory that light is propagated through the ether by a wave-like motion imparted to the ether by the molecular vibrations of the radiant body. **undulous,** *a.*

unduly [UNDUE].

undurable (ŭn dūr′ ȧbl), *a.* **undurably,** *adv.* **undutiful** (-dū′ ti fụl), *a.* **undutifully,** *adv.* **undutifulness,** *n.* **undying** (-dī′ ing), *a.* Unceasing, immortal. **undyingly,** *adv.* **unearned** (-ĕrnd′), *a.* Not earned. **unearned increment:** Increase in the value of land due to increased population, etc., not to labour or expenditure on the part of the owner. **unearth** (-erth′), *v.t.* To pull or bring out of the earth; to cause (a fox, etc.) to leave his earth; to dig up; (*fig.*) to bring to light, to find out. **unearthly** (-erth′ li), *a.* Not earthly; not of this world, supernatural; weird, ghostly. **unearthliness,** *n.* **uneasy** (-ē′ zi), *a.* Restless, troubled, anxious, uncomfortable, ill at ease; difficult; awkward, stiff, constrained. ***unease,** *n.* **uneasily,** *adv.* **uneasiness,** *n.* **uneatable** (-ē′ tȧbl), *a.* **uneaten,** *a.* **unecclesiastical** (-ė klē zi ăs′ ti kȧl), *a.* **uneclipsed** (-klipst′), *a.* **uneconomical** (-ē kȯ nom′ i kȧl), *a.* **unedified** (-ed′ i fīd), *a.* **unedifying,** *a.* **unedited** (-ed′ i tėd), *a.* **uneducated** (-ed′ ū kā tėd), *a.* **uneffaced** (-ė fāst′), *a.* **uneffected** (-fek′ tėd), *a.* **unelaborated** (-lăb′-), *a.* **unelated** (-ė lā′ tėd), *a.* **unelected** (-lek′ tėd), *a.* **unelucidated** (-lū′ si dā tėd), *a.* **unemancipated** (-măn′ si pā tėd), *a.* **unembarrassed** (-ėm băr′ ȧst), *a.* **unemotional** (-mō′ shȯ nȧl), *a.* **unemotionally,** *adv.* **unemphatic** (-ėm făt′ ik), *a.* **unemphatically,** *adv.* **unemployed** (-ploid′), *a.* Not in use; out of work; *n.* A person out of work; (*collect.*) workless persons generally. **unemployable,** *a.* and *n.* **unemployment,** *n.* **unemployment benefit,** *n.* Payment to an unemployed worker under the National Insurance Act. **unempowered** (-pou′ ėrd), *a.* **unemptied** (-emp′ tid), *a.* **unenclosed** (-ėn klōzd′), *a.* **unencumbered** (-kŭm′ bėrd), *a.* Not encumbered; having no liabilities on it (of an estate, etc.). **unending** (-en′ ding), *a.* Having no end, endless. **unendorsed** (-ėn dôrst′), *a.* **unendowed** (-doud′), *a.* **unendurable** (-dūr′ ȧbl), *a.* **unendurably,** *adv.* **unenforced** (-fôrst′), *a.* **unenfranchised** (-frăn′ chīzd), *a.* **unengaged** (-gājd′), *a.* **un-English** (-ing′ glish), *a.* Not English; not characteristic or worthy of Englishmen. **unenjoyable** (-ėn joi′ ȧbl), *a.* **unenlightened** (-lī′ tėnd), *a.* **unenrolled** (-rōld′), *a.* **unenslaved** (-slāvd′), *a.* **unentangle** (-tăngl′), *v.t.* To disentangle. **unenterprising** (-en′ tėr prī zing), *a.* **unenterprisingly,** *adv.* **unenterprisingness,** *n.* **unentertaining** (-tā′ ning), *a.* **unentertainingly,** *adv.* **unentertainingness,** *n.* **unenthusiastic** (-thū zi ăs′ tik), *a.* **unenviable** (-en′ vi ȧbl), *a.* **unenviably,** *adv.* **unenvied,** *a.* **unequable** (-ē′ kwȧbl), *a.* **unequal** (-ē′ kwȧl), *a.* **unequalize,** *v.t.* **unequalled,** *a.* **unequally,** *adv.* **unequipped** (-ė kwipt′), *a.* **unequivocal** (-kwiv′ ȯ kȧl), *a.* Not equivocal, not ambiguous; plain, manifest. **unequivocally,** *adv.* **unequivocalness,** *n.* **unerased** (-ė rāzd′), *a.* **unerring** (-ĕr′ ing), *a.* Committing no mistake; not missing the mark, certain, sure. **unerringly,** *adv.* **unescapable** (-ė skā′ pȧbl), *a.* **unespied** (-spīd′), *a.* **unessayed** (-sād′), *a.* **unessential** (-ė sen′ shȧl), *a.* Not essential, not absolutely necessary; not of prime importance; *n.* Some thing or part not absolutely necessary or indispensable. **unestablished** (-stăb′ lisht), *a.* **unestimated** (-es′ ti mā tėd), *a.* **unestranged** (-strānjd′), *a.* **unevangelical** (-ē vȧn jel′ i kȧl), *a.* **unevaporated** (-ė văp′ ȯ rā tėd), *a.* **uneven** (-ē′ vėn), *a.* Not even, level, or smooth; not uniform, regular, or equable; not divisible by 2 without a remainder, odd. **unevenly,** *adv.* **unevenness,** *n.* **uneventful** (-ė vent′ fụl), *a.* **unexamined** (-ėg zăm′ ind), *a.* **unexampled** (-ėg zampld′), *a.* Not exampled; having no parallel; unprecedented. **unexcelled** (-ėk seld′), *a.* **unexceptionable** (-ėk sep′ shȯ nȧbl), *a.* Not exceptionable; to which no exception can be taken; unobjectionable, faultless. **unexceptionableness,** *n.* **unexceptionably,** *adv.* **unexcised** (-ėk sīzd′), *a.* Not liable to excise. **unexclusive** (-skloo′ siv), *a.* **unexclusively,** *adv.* **unexecuted** (-ek′ sė kū tėd), *a.* **unexemplified** (-ėg zem′ pli fīd), *a.* **unexercised** (-ek′ sėr sīzd), *a.* **unexhausted** (-ėg zaw′ stėd), *a.* **unexpected** (-ėk spek′ tėd), *a.* **unexpectedly,** *adv.* **unexpectedness,** *n.* **unexpensive** (-spen′ siv), *a.* **unexpiated** (-ek′ spi ā tėd), *a.* **unexpired** (-ėk spīrd′), *a.* Not having come to an end or termination. **unexplained** (-splānd′), *a.* **unexplored** (-splôrd′), *a.* **unexposed** (-spōzd′), *a.* **unexpounded** (-spoun′ dėd), *a.* **unexpressed** (-sprest′), *a.* **unexpressive,** *a.* **unexpurgated** (-ek′ spụr gā tėd), *a.* **unextended** (-ėk sten′ dėd), *a.* Not extended; occupying no assignable space; having no dimensions. **unextinguishable** [INEXTINGUISHABLE]. **unface** (-fās′), *v.t.* **unfadable** (-fā′ dȧbl), *a.* **unfading,** *a.* **unfadingly,** *adv.* **unfadingness,** *n.* **unfailing** (-fā′ ling), *a.* Not liable to fail or run short; unerring, infallible; reliable, certain. **unfailingly,** *adv.* **unfailingness,** *n.* **unfair** (-fâr′), *a.* Not fair; not equitable, not impartial; dishonourable, fraudulent. **unfairly,** *adv.* **unfairness,** *n.* **unfaithful** (-fāth′ fụl), *a.* Not faithful; adulterous. ***unfaith,** *n.* **unfaithfully,** *adv.* **unfaithfulness,** *n.* **unfallen** (-faw′ lėn), *a.* **unfaltering** (-fawl′ tėr ing), *a.* **unfalteringly,** *adv.* **unfamiliar** (-fȧ mil′ yȧr), *a.* Not familiar. **unfamiliarity** (-i ăr′ i ti), *n.* **unfamiliarly,** *adv.* **unfashionable** (-făsh′ ȯ nȧbl), *a.* **unfashionableness,** *n.* **unfashionably,** *adv.* **unfashioned,** *a.* Not fashioned by art; shapeless. **unfasten** (-fasn′), *v.t.* **unfathered** (-fa′ *th*ėrd), *a.* Not acknowledged by its father or author; (*poet.*) fatherless. **unfatherly,** *a.* **unfathomable** (-făth′ ȯm ȧbl), *a.* **unfathomableness,** *n.* **unfathomably,** *adv.* **unfathomed,** *a.* **unfatigued,** *a.* Not fatigued or tired. **unfavourable** (-fā′ vȯr ȧbl), *a.* **unfavourableness,** *n.* **unfavourably,** *adv.* **unfearing** (-fēr′ ing), *a.* **unfearingly,** *adv.* **unfeasible** (-fē′ zibl), *a.* **unfeathered** (-fe*th*′ ėrd), *a.* Not feathered; unfledged. **unfed** (-fed′), *a.* **unfeed,** *a.* Not retained by a fee. **unfeeling** (fē′ ling), *a.* Insensible; hard-hearted, cruel. **unfeelingly,** *adv.* **unfeelingness,** *n.* **unfeigned** (-fānd′), *a.* **unfeignedly** (-fā′ nėd li), *adv.* **unfelt** (-felt′), *a.* Not felt, not perceived. **unfeminine** (-fem′ i nin), *a.* **unfenced** (-fenst′), *a.* Not enclosed by a fence; not fortified. **unfermented** (-fėr men′ tėd), *a.* **unfertile** (-fĕr′ tīl, -til), *a.* **unfertilized** (-ti līzd), *a.* **unfetter** (-fet′ ėr), *v.t.* To free from fetters or restraint. **unfettered,** *a.* **unfeudalize** (-fū′ dȧ līz), *v.t.* **unfigured** (-fig′ ėrd), *a.* Not marked with figures. **unfile** (-fīl′), *v.t.* To take (a document, etc.) from a file. **unfilial** (-fil′ i ȧl), *a.* **unfilially,** *adv.* **unfilled** (-fild′), *a.* **unfiltered** (-fil′ tėrd), *a.* **unfinished** (-fin′ isht), *a.* **unfit** (-fit′), *a.* Not fit (to do, to be, for, etc.); improper, unsuitable; *v.t.* To make unfit or unsuitable; to disqualify. **unfitly,** *adv.* **unfitness,** *n.* **unfitted,** *a.* Not fitted; unfit; not fitted up, not furnished with fittings. **unfitting,** *a.* **unfittingly,** *adv.* **unfix,** *v.t.* **unfixed,** *a.* **unflagging,** *a.* **unflattering** (-flat′ ėr ing), *a.* **unflatteringly,** *adv.* **unflavoured** (-flā′ vȯrd), *a.* **unfledged** (-flejd′), *a.* Not yet fledged; (*fig.*) undeveloped, immature. **unfleshed** (-flesht′), *a.* Not having shed or tasted blood (of a sword or hound); (*fig.*) unseasoned. **unflinching** (-flinch′ ing), *a.* **unflinchingly,** *adv.* **unfold** (-fōld′), *v.t.* To open the folds of; to spread out; to discover, to reveal; to display; *v.i.* To spread open, to expand, to develop. **unforced** (-fôrst′), *a.* Not forced, not constrained; natural, easy. **unfordable** (-fôr′ dȧbl), *a.* **unforeseen** (-fȯr sēn′), *a.* **unforgettable** (-fȯr get′ ȧbl), *a.* **unforgivable** (-giv′ ȧbl), *a.* **un-**

forgiven, *a.* **unforgiving,** *a.* **unforgivingly,** *adv.* **unforgivingness,** *n.* **unforgotten** (-fôr got' ėn), *a.* **unform** (-fôrm'), *v.t.* To unmake. **unformed,** *a.* Devoid of form, shapeless, amorphous, structureless; not yet fully developed, immature. **unformulated** (-fôr' mū lā tėd), *a.* **unfortified** (-fôr' ti fīd), *a.* **unfortunate** (-fôr' tū nȧt), *a.* Not fortunate, unlucky, unhappy; *n.* One who is unfortunate, esp. a prostitute. **unfortunately,** *adv.* **unfound** (-found'), *a.* **unfounded** (-foun' dėd), *a.* Having no foundation of fact or reason, groundless; not yet established. **unframe** (-frām'), *v.t.* **unfrequent** (-frē' kwėnt), *a.* **unfrequented** (-frė kwen' tėd), *a.* ***unfriend** (-frend'), *n.* An enemy. **unfriended,** *a.* Without a friend or friends. **unfriendly,** *a.* **unfriendliness,** *n.* **unfrock** (-frok'), *v.t.* To take the frock or gown from; hence, to deprive of the character and privileges of a priest. **unfruitful** (-froot' fu̇l), *a.* **unfruitfully,** *adv.* **unfruitfulness,** *n.* **unfulfilled** (-fu̇l fild'), *a.* **unfunded** (-fŭn' dėd), *a.* Not funded, floating (of a debt, etc.). **unfurl** (-fĕrl'), *v.t.* and *i.* To open or spread out (a sail, banner, etc.). **unfurnished** (-fĕr' nisht), *a.* Not furnished (with); without furniture. **unfused** (-fūzd'), *a.* Not fused, not melted. **ungainly** (-gān' li) [M.E. *ungeniliche* (Icel. *gegn*, serviceable, see GAIN (2), -LY)], *a.* Clumsy, awkward. **ungainliness,** *n.* **ungallant** (-găl' ȧnt), *a.* Not gallant, not courteous to women. **ungalvanized** (-găl' vȧ nīzd), *a.* **ungarbled** (-garbld'), *a.* **ungarnered** (-gar' nėrd), *a.* **ungarnished** (-gar' nisht), *a.* Not garnished, not adorned. **ungauged** (-gājd'), *a.* **ungear** (-gēr'), *v.t.* To strip of gear; to throw out of gear. **ungenerous** (-jen' ėr ŭs), *a.* **ungenerously,** *adv.* **ungenial** (-jē' ni ȧl), *a.* **ungenteel** (-jen tēl'), *a.* **ungenteelly,** *adv.* **ungentle** (-jentl'), *a.* Not gentle, harsh, rude, unkind; ill-bred. **ungentleness,** *n.* **ungently,** *adv.* **ungentlemanly** (-jentl' mȧn li), *a.* Not becoming a gentleman; rude, ill-bred. **ungentlemanliness,** *n.* **unget-at-able,** *a.* and *adv.* Difficult of access. **ungild** (-gild'), *v.t.* To remove the gilding from. ***ungilded,** ***ungilt,** *a.* Not gilded. **ungird** (-gĕrd'), *v.t.* (*past & p.p.* **-girt**) To undo or remove a girdle from; to unbind. **unglaze** (-glāz'), *v.t.* To deprive of glazing. **unglazed,** *a.* Deprived of glazing; not glazed. **unglove** (-glŭv'), *v.t.* **unglue** (-gloo'), *v.t.* **unglutted** (-glŭt' ėd), *a.* **ungodly** (-god' li), *a.* **ungodlily,** *adv.* **ungodliness,** *n.* **ungovernable** (-gŭv' ėr nȧbl), *a.* Not governable; unruly, wild, passionate, licentious. **ungovernably,** *adv.* **ungown** (-goun'), *v.t.* **ungraceful** (-grās' fu̇l), *a.* Not graceful; clumsy, inelegant. **ungracefully,** *adv.* **ungracefulness,** *n.* **ungracious** (-grā' shŭs), *a.* Wanting in graciousness; discourteous, rude, unmannerly, offensive. **ungraciously,** *adv.* **ungraduated** (-grăd' ū ā tėd), *a.* **ungrammatical** (-grȧ măt' i kȧl), *a.* Not according to the rules of grammar. **ungrammatically,** *adv.* **ungrateful** (-grāt' fu̇l), *a.* **ungratefully,** *adv.* **ungratefulness,** *n.* **ungratified** (-grăt' i fīd), *a.* **ungrounded** (-groun' dėd), *a.* Unfounded, baseless. **ungrudging** (-grŭj' ing), *a.* **ungrudgingly,** *adv.*

ungual (ŭng' gwȧl) [L. *unguis*, nail, claw], *a.* Of, pertaining to, or having a nail, claw, or hoof. **unguicular** (-gwik' ū lȧr), **unguiculated, unguiferous** (-gwif' ėr ŭs), **unguiform** (ŭng' gwi fôrm), *a.*

unguarded (ŭn gar' dėd), *a.* Not guarded; careless, incautious; incautiously said or done. **unguardedly,** *adv.*

unguent (ŭng' gwėnt) [L. *unguentum*, from *unguere*, to anoint, pres.p. *unguens -ntis*], *n.* Any soft composition used as an ointment or for lubrication. **unguentary** (ŭng gwent' ȧ ri), *a.*

unguicular, etc. [UNGUAL].

ungula (ŭng' gū lȧ) [L., dim. of *unguis*, see UNGUAL], *n.* (*pl.* **-læ**) A hoof, claw, or talon; (*Surg.*) a hook-shaped instrument for extracting a dead fœtus from the womb; (*Math.*) the portion of a cone or cylinder included between the base and a plane intersecting it obliquely. **ungular,** *a.*

Ungulata (-lā' tȧ), *n.pl.* A division of mammals comprising those with hoofs. **ungulate,** *a.* Hoofed; hoof-shaped; belonging to the Ungulata; *n.* An ungulate animal.

ungum (ŭn gŭm'), *v.t.* To loosen (a thing fastened with gum); to remove the gum from. **unhackneyed** (-hăk' nid), *a.* **unhair** (-hâr'), *v.t.* **unhallow** (-hăl' ō), *v.t.* To profane, to desecrate. **unhallowed,** *a.* **unhampered** (-hăm' pėrd), *a.* **unhand** (-hănd'), *v.t.* To take the hand or hands off; to let go from one's grasp. **unhandsome** (-hăn' sȯm) *a.* Not handsome; not generous, petty, ungracious. **unhandsomely,** *adv.* **unhandsomeness,** *n.* **unhandy,** *a.* Not handy; clumsy, awkward, inconvenient. **unhandily,** *adv.* **unhandiness,** *n.* **unhang** (-hăng'), *v.t.* To take from a hanging position; to strip of hangings. **unhanged, unhung** (-hŭng'), *a.* Not hanged; not punished by hanging. **unhappy** (-hăp' i), *a.* Not happy, miserable, wretched; unlucky, unfortunate. **unhappily,** *adv.* **unhappiness,** *n.* **unharmed** (-harmd'), *a.* **unharness** (-har' nės), *v.t.* To remove harness from; *to divest of armour. **unhasp** (-hasp'), *v.t.* To unfasten from the hasp. **unhat** (-hăt'), *v.t.* **unhatched** (-hăcht'), *a.* Not hatched (of eggs). **unhealthful** (-helth' fu̇l), *a.* **unhealthfully,** *adv.* **unhealthfulness,** *n.* **unhealthy,** *a.* **unhealthily,** *adv.* **unhealthiness,** *n.* **unheard** (-hĕrd'), *a.* Not heard. **unheard of:** Not heard of; unprecedented. **unheeded** (-hē' dėd), *a.* Not heeded; disregarded, neglected. **unheedful,** *a.* **unheedfully,** *adv.* **unheeding,** *a.* ***unhelm** (-helm'), *v.t.* To divest of a helm or helmet. **unhelpful** (-help' fu̇l), *a.* **unhelpfully,** *adv.* **unhemmed** (-hemd'), *a.* **unheralded** (-her' ȧl dėd), *a.* **unheroic** (-hė rō' ik). *a.* **unhesitating** (-hez' i tā ting), *a.* **unhesitatingly,** *adv.* **unhidden** (-hid' ėn), *a.* **unhindered** (-hin' dėrd), *a.* **unhinge** (-hinj'), *v.t.* To take (a door) off the hinges; to unsettle (the mind, etc.). **unhinged,** *a.* **unhistoric, -al** (-his tor' ik, -ȧl), *a.* **unhitch** (-hich'), *v.t.* To unfasten or release from a hitch. **unhive** (-hīv'), *v.t.* **unholy** (-hō' li), *a.* Not holy, not hallowed; impious, wicked; (*colloq.*) hideous, frightful. **unholily,** *adv.* **unholiness,** *n.* **unhonoured** (-on' ȯrd), *a.* **unhook** (-huk'), *v.t.* To remove from a hook; to open or undo by disengaging the hooks of. **unhoop** (-hoop'), *v.t.* **unhoped** (-hōpt'), *a.* Not hoped for; unexpected, beyond hope. **unhorse** (-hôrs'), *v.t.* To remove from horseback; to take the horses out of. **unhouse** (-houz'), *v.t.* To drive from a house; to deprive of shelter. **unhouseled,** *a.* Not having received the sacrament. **unhuman** (-hū' mȧn), *a.* Not human. **unhurt** (-hĕrt'), *a.* **unhusk** (-hŭsk'), *v.t.*

uni- [L. *unus*, one], *comb. form.* **uniarticulate** (ū ni ar tik' ū lȧt) [ARTICULATE], *a.* Single-jointed.

Uniat, Uniate (ū' ni ȧt, -āt) [Rus. *uniyatŭ*, as prec.], *n.* A member of any community of Oriental Christians acknowledging the supremacy of the Pope but retaining its own liturgy, rites, and ceremonies. *a.* Of or pertaining to the Uniats.

uniaxal, -axial (-ū ni ăk' sȧl, -si ȧl) [UNI-, AXIAL], *a.* Having a single axis. **uniaxially,** *adv.* **unicameral** (-kăm' ėr ȧl) [CAMERA], *a.* Consisting of a single chamber (of a legislative body). **unicapsular** (-kăp sū lȧr), *a.* (*Bot.*) Having but a single capsule. **unicellular** (-sel' ū lȧr), *a.* Consisting of a single cell. **unicolour, -ed** (-kŭl' ȯr, -ȯrd), *a.* Of one colour.

unicorn (ū' ni kôrn) [A.-F. *unicorne*, L. *ūnicornem*, nom. *-cornis* (UNI-, *cornu*, horn)], *n.* A fabulous animal like a horse, with a long, straight, tapering horn; (*Bibl.*) a two-horned animal, perh. the urus (a mistranslation of Heb. *re'em*); (*Her.*) a one-horned horse with a goat's beard and lion's tail; a unicorn-fish, -bird, -beetle, -moth, or -shell; a coaching-team consisting of a pair of horses with a third horse in front. **sea-unicorn, unicorn-fish, -whale,** *n.* The narwhal, *Monodon monoceros.* **unicorn-beetle,** *n.* A large beetle with a single horn on the prothorax. **unicorn-bird,** *n.* The horned screamer. **unicorn-moth,** *n.* A North

American moth the caterpillar of which has a horn-like prominence on the back. **unicorn-shell,** *n.* A gasteropod with a prominent spine on the tip of the shell. **unicornous** (-kôr′ nŭs), *a.* One-horned.

unicostate (ū ni kos′ tāt) [UNI-, COSTATE], *a.* Having one principal rib or nerve; (*Bot.*) having a midrib. **unicuspid** (-kŭs′ pid) [CUSP], *a.* One-cusped; *n.* A unicuspid tooth. **unicycle** (ū′ ni sīkl) [CYCLE], *n.* A single-wheeled velocipede. **unifacial** (-fā′ shăl) [FACIAL], *a.* Having but one face.

unification, unifier [UNIFY].

uniflorous (ū ni flôr′ ŭs) [UNI-, FLOROUS], *a.* (*Bot.*) Bearing but a single flower. **unifoliar** (-fō′ li ăr), **unifoliate, unifoliolate** [FOLIAR], *a.* (*Bot.*) Consisting of one leaf or leaflet.

uniform (ū′ ni fôrm) [F. *uniforme,* L. *ūniformem,* nom. *-mis* (UNI-, -FORM)], *a.* Having always one and the same form, appearance, quality, character, etc., always the same, not varying, not changing, homogeneous; conforming to one rule or standard, applying or operating without variation for time or place. *n.* A dress of the same kind and appearance as that worn by other members of the same body, esp. the regulation dress of soldiers, sailors, etc. **uniformity** (-fôr′ mi ti), *n.* The quality or state of being uniform; consistency, sameness. **Act of Uniformity:** An Act, esp. that of 1662, prescribing the form of public prayers, administration of the sacraments, and other rites in the Church of England. **Uniformitarian** (-târ′ i ăn), *n.* One who believes that there has been essential uniformity of cause and effect throughout the physical history of the world, opp. to catastrophism. **Uniformitarianism,** *n.* **uniformly,** *adv.*

unify (ū′ ni fī) [med. L. *ūnificāre* (UNI-, L. *-ficāre, facere,* to make)], *v.t.* To make a unit of; to regard as one; to reduce to uniformity. **unification** (-kā′ shŭn), *n.* **unifier,** *n.*

Unigenitus (ū ni jen′ i tŭs) [mod. L., only-begotten (UNI-, L. *genitus,* p.p. of *gignere,* to beget, cp. GENIUS)], *n.* The bull of Clement XI. condemning Jansenism (1713), named from its initial word. **unigenital,** *a.* Only-begotten.

unilabiate (ū ni lā′ bi āt) [UNI-, LABIATE], *a.* (*Bot.*) Having a single lip (of flowers). **unilateral** (-lăt′ ėr ăl) [LATERAL], *a.* Arranged on or turned towards one side only; applied by one side or party only. **unilaterally,** *adv.* **uniliteral** (-lit′ ėr ăl) [LITERAL], *a.* Consisting of only one letter.

unilluminated (ŭn i lū′-, -loo′ mi nā tėd), *a.* Not illuminated; dark; (*fig.*) ignorant. **unillumined** (-mind), *a.* **unillustrated** (-il′ ŭs trā tėd), *a.*

unilocular, -loculate (ū ni lok′ ū lăr, -lok′ ū lāt) [UNI-, LOCULAR], *a.* Having or consisting of a single cell or chamber.

unimaginable (ŭn i măj′ i năbl), *a.* That cannot be imagined; inconceivable. **unimaginably,** *adv.* **unimaginative,** *a.* **unimaginativeness,** *n.* **unimagined,** *a.* **unimpaired** (-im pârd′), *a.* **unimpassioned** (-păsh′ ŭnd), *a.* **unimpeachable** (-pē′ chăbl), *a.* **unimpeachability** (-bil′ i ti), **unimpeachableness,** *n.* **unimpeached,** *a.* **unimpeded** (-pē′ dėd), *a.* **unimportance** (-pôr′ tăns), *n.* **unimportant,** *a.* **unimposing** (-pō′ zing), *a.* **unimpressionable** (-presh′ ŏ năbl), *a.* **unimpressive** (-pres′ iv), *a.* **unimpressively,** *adv.* **unimpressiveness,** *n.* **unimproved** (-proovd′), *a.* Not improved; not tilled. **unimproving,** *a.* **unimpugned** (-pūnd′), *a.* **unindexed** (-in′ dekst), *a.* **unindicated** (-in′ di kā tėd), *a.* **uninflammable** (-in flăm′ ăbl), *a.* **uninflated** (-flā′ tėd), *a.* **uninflicted** (-flik′ tėd), *a.* **uninfluenced** (-in′ flŭ ĕnst), **uninfluential** (-in flŭ en′ shăl), *a.* **uninformed** (-in fôrmd′), *a.* **uninhabitable** (-hăb′ i tăbl), *a.* **uninhabited,** *a.* **uninitiated** (-i nish′ i ā tėd), *a.* **uninjured** (-in′ jŭrd), *a.* **uninspired** (-in spīrd′), *a.* **uninstigated** (-in′ sti gā tėd), *a.* **uninstructed** (-in strŭk′ tėd), *a.* **uninstructive,** *a.* **uninstructively,** *adv.* **uninsulated** (-in′ sū lā tėd), *a.* **uninsured** (-in shoord′), *a.* **unintelligent** (-tel′ i jėnt), *a.* **unintelligently,** *adv.* **unintelligible** (-tel′ i jibl), *a.* **unintelligibility,** *n.* **unintelligibly,** *adv.* **unintentional** (-ten′ shŏ năl), *a.* **unintentionally,** *adv.* **uninterested** (-in′ tėr ės tėd), *a.* **uninteresting,** *a.* **uninterestingly,** *adv.* **unintermittent** (-in tėr mit′ ėnt), *a.* **unintermittently,** *adv.* **unintermitting,** *a.* **unintermittingly,** *adv.* **uninterpretable** (-in tĕr′ prė tăbl), *a.* **uninterred** (-in tĕrd′), *a.* **uninterrupted** (-in tė rŭp′ tėd), *a.* **uninterruptedly,** *adv.* **uninventive** (-ven′ tiv), *a.* **uninventively,** *adv.* **uninvestigated** (-ves′ ti gā tėd), *a.* **uninvited** (-vī′ tėd), *a.* **uninviting,** *a.* Not inviting, not attractive, repellent. **uninvitingly,** *adv.* **uninvoked** (-vōkt′), *a.* **uninvolved** (-volvd′), *a.*

union (ū′ nyŏn) [F., from late L. *ūniōnem,* nom. *-io,* from *ūnus,* one], *n.* The act of uniting; the state of being united; junction, coalition; agreement or concord of mind, will, affection, or interests; a combination of parts or members forming a whole, an amalgamation, a confederation, a league; (*Med.*) the growing together of parts separated by injury; two or more parishes consolidated for administration of the Poor Laws; a workhouse established by this; an amalgamation of parishes for ecclesiastical control; an association of non-conformist (esp. Congregational or Baptist) Churches for co-operative action or management; (*Gt. Brit. and N. Ir.*) a device emblematic of union borne in the upper corner next the staff of a flag; this used as a flag, called a **union jack** or **union flag. Union of Soviet Socialist Republics (U.S.S.R.),** *n.* (*Pol.*) English form of the official title of the government of Russia. **union suit:** (*Am.*) An undergarment combining vest and long pants, men's combinations. **union workhouse** [WORKHOUSE].

unionism (ū ni ŏn izm), *n.* The principle of combining, esp. the system of combination among workmen engaged in the same occupation or trade, and (*Polit.*) the principles of the Unionist party. **unionist,** *n.* A member of a trade-union; a promoter or advocate of trade-unionism; a member of a political party formed to uphold the legislative union between Great Britain and Ireland and to oppose Home Rule; (*Am.*) an opponent of secession before and during the American Civil War. **unionistic** (-nis′ tik), *a.*

uniparous (ū nip′ ȧ rŭs) [UNI-, L. *parere,* to bring forth], *a.* Bringing forth normally but one at a birth; (*Bot.*) having one axis or stem. **unipartite** (ū ni par′ tīt) [PARTITE], *a.* Not divided. **uniped** (ū′ ni ped) [L. *pes, pedis,* foot], *a.* Having only one foot; *n.* A one-footed animal. **unipersonal** (-pĕr′ sŏ năl), *a.* Existing in one person (of the Deity); (*Gram.*) used only in one person. **uniplanar** (-plā′ năr), *a.* Lying or occurring in one plane. **unipolar** (-pō′ lăr), *a.* (*Biol.*) Having but one pole (of nerve-cells, etc.); (*Elec.*) exhibiting but one kind of polarity. **unipolarity** (-pŏ lăr′ i ti), *n.*

unique (ū nēk′) [F., from L. *ūnicum,* nom. *-cus,* as prec.], *a.* Having no like or equal; unmatched, unparalleled. *n.* A unique person or thing. **uniquely,** *adv.* **uniqueness,** *n.*

uniradiate, -diated (ū ni rā′ di āt, -di ā tėd), *a.* Having only one ray or arm. **uniserial** (-sēr′ i ăl), *a.* (*Bot.*) Arranged in one row. **unisexual** (-sek′ sū ăl), *a.* Of one sex only; not hermaphrodite, having only one kind of sexual organs, stamens or pistils. **unisexually,** *adv.*

unisolated (ŭn ī′ sŏ lā tėd), *a.* Not isolated.

unison (ū′ ni zŏn) [M.F. *unisson,* med. L. *ūnisonus* (UNI-, *sonus,* SOUND (2))], *n.* (*Mus.*) Coincidence of sounds proceeding from equality in rate of vibrations, unity of pitch; an interval of one or more octaves; the act or state of sounding together at the same pitch; concord, agreement, harmony. *a.* Sounding together; coinciding in pitch; sounding alone. **unisonal, -nant, -nous,** *a.* **unisonance,** *n.*

unisulcate (ū ni sŭl′ kāt) [UNI-, SULCATE], *a.* Having but one groove or furrow.

unit (ū′ nit) [short for UNITY], *n.* A single person, thing, or group, regarded as one and individual for the purposes of calculation; each one of a number of things, persons, etc., forming a plurality; a quantity adopted as the standard of measurement or calculation, a quantity represented by the number one.

Unitarian (ū ni târ′ i ȧn), *n.* A member of a Christian body that rejects the doctrine of the Trinity; a monotheist; one who advocates unity or unification, esp. in politics. *a.* Pertaining to the Unitarians. **Unitarianism,** *n.* **Unitarianize,** *v.t.* **unitary** (ū′ ni tȧr i), *a.* Of or pertaining to a unit or units; of the nature of a unit, whole, integral; (*Phil.*) monistic.

unitate (ū′ ni tāt), *n.* (*Math.*) The remainder after dividing a number by any digit.

unite (ū nīt′) [L. *ūnītus*, p.p. of *ūnīre*, from *ūnus*, one], *v.t.* To join together so as to make one; to combine, to conjoin, to amalgamate; to cause to adhere, to attach together. *v.i.* To become one; to become consolidated, to combine, to coalesce, to agree, to co-operate. **United Brethren:** The Moravians. **United Free Church,** *n.* (*Eccles.*) A Presbyterian church in Scotland formed in 1900 by the union of the Free Church of Scotland and the United Presbyterian Church. It was united with the Church of Scotland in 1929. **United Kingdom** [KINGDOM]. **United Nations:** An international organization of 57 sovereign states, founded in 1945. "to save succeeding generations from the scourge of war." **United Provinces:** Holland, Zealand, Utrecht, Guelderland, Groningen, Friesland, and Overyssel united in 1579 in the Union of Utrecht. **United States:** A federal union or republic of sovereign States, esp. that of N. America. **unitedly,** *adv.* **uniter,** *n.* **unitism** (ū′ ni tizm), *n.* Monism. **unitive,** *a.* **unitize,** *v.t.*

unity (ū′ ni ti) [A.-F. *unité*, L. *ūnitātem*, nom. *-tas*, from *ūnus*, one], *n.* The state or condition of being one or individual, oneness, as opp. to plurality or division; the state of being united, union; an agreement of parts or elements, harmonious interconnexion, structural coherence; concord, agreement, harmony; a thing forming a coherent whole; (*Math.*) the number one, a factor that leaves unchanged the quantity on which it operates; (*Drama, etc.*) the condition that the action of a play should be limited to the development of a single plot, that the supposed time should coincide with the actual duration of the play or to a single day, and that there should be no change of scene (called the three dramatic unities of action, time, and place); (*Law*) a joint tenancy of two or more persons; joint possession by one person of two estates in the same property.

univalent (ū niv′ ȧ lent), *a.* (*Chem.*) Having a valence or combining power of one. **univalence, -ency,** *n.* **univalve** (ū′ ni vălv), *a.* Having only one valve. *n.* A univalve mollusc. **univalvular,** *a.*

universal (ū ni vĕr′ sȧl) [F. *universel*, L. *ūniversālis*, as foll.], *a.* Of or pertaining to the whole world or all persons or things in the world or in the class under consideration; common to all cases, unlimited, all-embracing, general; applicable to all purposes or conditions; (*Log.*) predicable of all the individuals of a class, opp. to particular. *n.* (*Log.*) A universal proposition; (*Phil.*) a universal concept; a thing or nature predicable of many. **universal coupling** or **joint:** A device for connecting two parts or things allowing freedom of movement in any direction. **universal time:** (*Astron.*) A method of reckoning time based on mean midnight at Greenwich. **universalism,** *n.* The quality of being universal; (*Theol.*) the doctrine that all men will eventually be saved. **universalist,** *a.* and *n.* **universalistic** (-lis′ tik), *a.* **universality, *universalness,** *n.* **universalize,** *v.t.* **universalization,** *n.* **universally,** *adv.*

universe (ū′ ni vĕrs) [F. *univers*, L. *ūniversum*, neut. of *universus*, combined into a whole (UNI-, *versus*, p.p. of *vertere*, to turn)], *n.* The aggregate of existing things; all created things viewed as constituting one system or whole, the cosmos, including or excluding the Creator; all mankind; (*Log.*) all the objects that are the subjects of consideration. **universology** (-sol′ o ji) [-LOGY], *n.* The science dealing with everything in the universe, or with all pertaining to human relations, etc. **universological** (-loj′ i kȧl), *a.* **universologist,** *n.*

university (ū ni vĕr′ si ti) [A.-F. *université*, a school for universal knowledge, L. *ūniversitātem*, nom. *-tas*, a whole, a universe, from prec.], *n.* An educational institution for both instruction and examination in the higher branches of knowledge with the power to confer degrees, usu. comprising subordinate colleges, schools, etc.; the members of this collectively; (*colloq.*) a team or crew representing a university, as distinguished from a college team, etc. **University Extension** [EXTENSION].

univocal (ū niv′ ō kȧl), *a.* Having only one meaning (of a word); (*Mus.*) having unison of sounds. **univocally,** *adv.* **univocation** (-kā′ shŭn), *n.* Agreement of name and meaning.

unjoin (ŭn join′), *v.t.* To disjoin. **unjoint** (-joint′), *v.t.* To disjoint, to separate the joints. **unjust** (-jŭst′), *a.* Not just; not conformable to justice. **unjustly,** *adv.* **unjustifiable** (-jŭs ti fī′ ȧbl), *a.* **unjustifiableness,** *n.* **unjustifiably,** *adv.* **unkempt** (-kempt′) [M.E. *kempt*, *kembed*, p.p. of *kemben*, A.-S. *cemban*, to comb], *a.* Uncombed; rough, unpolished. **unkennel** (-ken′ ĕl), *v.t.* To release or drive out from a kennel; to let loose. **unkind** (-kīnd′), *a.* Not kind, harsh, hard, cruel. **unkindly,** *adv.* **unkindness,** *n.* **unking** (-king′), *v.t.* **unkingly,** *a.* **unkink** (-kingk′), *v.t.* and *i.* **unkneaded** (-nē′ dĕd), *a.* **unknightly** (-nīt′ li), *a.* **unknightliness,** *n.* **unknit** (-nit′), *v.t.* **unknot** (-not′), *v.t.* **unknowable** (-nō′ ȧbl), *a.* **unknowability** (-bil′ i ti), **unknowableness,** *n.* **unknowably,** *adv.* **unknowing,** *a.* Not knowing; ignorant or unaware (of). **unknowingly,** *adv.* **unknown** (-nōn′), *a.* Not known; untold, incalculable, inexpressible; (*Math.*) unascertained (of quantities in equations, etc.). **unlabelled** (-lā bĕld), *a.* **unlaboured** (-lā′ bŏrd), *a.* Not produced by labour, untilled, unworked; spontaneous, natural, easy (of style, etc.). **unlace** (-lās′), *v.t.* To loose or unfasten by undoing the lace or laces of. **unlade** (-lād′), *v.t.* **unladylike** (-lā′ di līk), *a.* **unlaid,** *a.* Not laid; not having parallel watermarks (of paper); not suppressed. **unlamented** (-lȧ men′ tĕd), *a.* **unlash** (-lăsh′), *v.t.* (*Naut.*) To unfasten (something lashed). **unlatch** (-lăch′), *v.t.* To unfasten the latch of (a door, etc.). **unlawful** (-law′ fŭl) *a.* **unlawfully,** *adv.* **unlawfulness,** *n.* **unlay** (-lā′), *v.t.* (*Naut.*) To untwist rope, etc. **unlearn** (-lĕrn′), *v.t.* To forget the knowledge of; to expel from the mind (that which has been learned), to get rid of (a vice, etc.). **unlearned** (1) (-lĕrnd′), **-learnt,** *a.* Not learnt. **unlearned** (2) (-lĕr′ nĕd), *a.* Not learned. **unlearnedly,** *adv.* **unlearnedness,** *n.* **unleavened** (-lev′ ĕnd), *a.*

unless (ŭn les′) [formerly *onless* (ON, LESS)], *conj.* If it be not the case that; except when.

unlettered (ŭn let′ ĕrd), *a.* Illiterate. **unlicensed** (-lī′ sĕnst), *a.* **unlicked** (-likt′), *a.* Not licked into shape; unmannered, rough, rude. **unlike** (-līk′), *a.* Not like; dissimilar; *improbable. **unlikeness,** *n.* **unlikely,** *a.* Improbable; unpromising; *adv.* Improbably. **unlikelihood, unlikeliness,** *n.* **unlimber** (-lim′ bĕr), *v.t.* **unlimited,** *a.* Not limited; having no bounds, indefinite, unmeasured, unnumbered; unconfined, unrestrained. **unlimitedly,** *adv.* **unlimitedness,** *n.* **unline** (-līn′), *v.t.* To remove the lining from. **unlink** (-lingk′), *v.t.* **unliquidated** (-lik′ wi dā tĕd), *a.* **unlisted** (-lis′ tĕd), *a.* Not on the list. **unlit** (-lit′), *a.* **unload** (-lōd′), *v.t.* To discharge the load from; to discharge (a load); to withdraw the charge from (a gun, etc.); (*Stock Exchange*) to sell heavily; *v.i.* To discharge a load or freight; (*Stock Exchange*) to sell stock, etc., freely. **unlocated** (-lō kā′ tĕd), *a.* **unlock** (-lok′), *v.t.* To unfasten the lock of (a door, box, etc.); (*fig.*) to disclose. **unlodge** (-loj′), *v.t.* To dislodge. **unlooked-for** (-lukt′ fŏr), *a.* Not looked for, unexpected. **unloose** (-loos′), *v.t.* To unfasten, to loose; to set at liberty. **unloosen,** *v.t.* **unlopped** (-lopt′), *a.* **unlord** (-lôrd′), *v.t.* **unlovable** (-lŭv′ ȧbl), *a.* **unloved,** *a.* **unlovely,** *a.* Not lovely; not beautiful or attractive. **unloveliness,** *n.* **unloverlike,** *a.* **unloving,** *a.* **unlovingly,** *adv.* **unlucky** (-lŭk′ i), *a.* Not lucky or fortunate; unsuccessful, unfortunate; disastrous; inauspicious, ill-omened. **unluckily,** *adv.* **unluckiness,** *n.* **unmade** (-mād′), *a.* **unmaidenly,** *a.* **unmailable** (-mā′ lȧbl), *a.* Incapable of being sent by post. **unmaimed,** *a.* **unmaintainable** (-mȧn tā′ nȧbl), *a.* **unmake,** *v.t.* To destroy; to annihilate; to depose. **unmalleable** (-măl′ ė ȧbl), *a.* **unmalleability** (-bil′ i ti), *n.* **unman** (-măn′), *v.t.* To deprive of courage or fortitude; to deprive of men. **unmanageable** (-măn′ ȧ jȧbl), *a.* Not manageable; not easily controlled. **unmanful** (-măn fûl), *a.* **unmanfully,** *adv.* **unmanlike** (-măn′ līk), *a.* Not like a man; effeminate, childish. **unmanly,** *a.* **unmanliness,** *n.* **unmannerly** (-măn′ ėr li), *a.* Not mannerly; rude, ill-bred. **unmannerliness,** *n.* **unmantle** (-măntl′), *v.t.* **unmarked** (-markt′), *a.* Not marked; not noticed, unobserved. **unmarketable** (-mar′ kė tȧbl), *a.* **unmarriageable** (-măr′ ȧ jȧbl), *a.* **unmarriageableness,** *n.* **unmarried,** *a.* **unmartial** (-mar′ shȧl), *a.* **unmasculine** (-măs′ kū lin), *a.* **unmask** (-mask′), *v.t.* To remove the mask from; to expose; *v.i.* To take one's mask off; to reveal oneself. **unmasticable** (-măs′ ti kȧbl), *a.* **unmatchable** (-măch′ ȧbl), *a.* **unmatched,** *a.* **unmated** (-mā′ tėd), *a.* **unmatured** (-mȧ tūrd′), *a.* **unmeaning,** *a.* Having no meaning; senseless. **unmeaningly,** *adv.* **unmeaningness,** *n.* **unmeant** (-ment′), *a.* Not meant, not intended. **unmeasured** (-mezh′ ůrd), *a.* Not measured; indefinite, unlimited, unmeasurable. **unmechanical** (-mė kăn′ i kȧl), *a.* ***unmeet** (-mēt′), *a.* Not meet, not suitable (for, to do, etc.). ***unmeetly,** *adv.* ***unmeetness,** *n.* **unmelodious** (-mė lō′ di ůs), *a.* **unmelodiously,** *adv.* **unmelodiousness,** *n.* **unmelted** (-mel′ tėd), *a.* **unmendable** (-men′ dȧbl), *a.* **unmentionable** (-men′ shȯ nȧbl), *a.* Not mentionable, not fit to be mentioned; *n.pl.* (*facet.*) Trousers, inexpressibles. **unmentionableness,** *n.* **unmerchantable** (-mĕr′ chȧn tȧbl), *a.* **unmerciful** (-mĕr′ si fûl), *a.* **unmercifully,** *adv.* **unmercifulness,** *n.* **unmerited** (-mer′ i tėd), *a.* **unmethodical** (-mė thod′ i kȧl), *a.* **unmetrical** (-met′ ri kȧl), *a.* Not metrical; not according to the rules or requirements of metre. **unmetrically,** *adv.* **unmew** (-mū′), *v.t.* (*poet.*) To release from confinement, etc.; to set free. **unmilitary** (-mil′ i tȧr i), *a.* **unmindful** (-mīnd′ fûl), *a.* Not mindful, heedless (of). **unmindfully,** *adv.* **unmindfulness,** *n.* **unminted** (-min′ tėd), *a.* **unmirthful** (-mĕrth′ fûl), *a.* **unmirthfully,** *adv.* **unmistakable** (-mis tā′ kȧbl), *a.* That cannot be mistaken; manifest, plain. **unmistakably,** *adv.*; **unmitigated** (-mit′ i gā tėd), *a.* Not mitigated; unqualified, unconscionable. **unmixed** (-mikst′), *a.* **unmodern** (-mod′ ėrn), *a.* **unmodernized,** *a.* **unmodified** (-mod′ i fīd), *a.* **unmodulated** (-mod′ ū lā tėd), *a.* **unmolested** (-mȯ les′ tėd), *a.* **unmonk** (-mŭngk), *v.t.* **unmoor** (-moor′), *v.t.* To loose the moorings of, to unanchor; to release partially by weighing one of two or more anchors; *v.i.* To weigh anchor. **unmoral** (-mŏr′ ȧl), *a.* Non-moral. **unmorality** (-mȯ răl′ i ti), *n.* **unmortgaged** (-môr′ gȧjd), *a.* **unmortise** (-môr′ tis), *v.t.* **unmotherly** (-mŭ*th*′ ėr li), *a.* **unmould** (-mōld′), *v.t.* To change the form of. **unmounted** (-moun′ tėd), *a.* Not on horseback; not mounted (of a drawing, gem, etc.). **unmourned** (-môrnd′), *a.* **unmoved** (-moovd′), *a.* Not moved; not changed in purpose, unshaken, firm; not affected, not having the feelings excited. **unmoving,** *a.* Motionless; unaffecting. **unmown** (-mōn′), *a.* **unmuffle** (-mŭfl′), *v.t.* To remove a muffler from; *v.i.* To remove a muffler from one's face, etc. **unmurmuring** (-mĕr′ můr ing), *a.* Not complaining. **unmurmuringly,** *adv.* **unmusical** (-mū′ zi kȧl), *a.* Not pleasing to the ear, discordant; not interested or vested in music. **unmusicality** (-kăl′ i ti), *n.* **unmusically,** *adv.* **unmutilated,** *a.* **unmuzzle** (-mŭzl′), *v.t.* **unnail** (-nāl′), *v.t.* **unnamable** (-nā′ mȧbl), *a.* **unnamed,** *a.* **unnational** (-năsh′ ȯ nȧl), *a.* **unnatural** (-năt′ ū rȧl), *a.* Not natural; contrary to nature; monstrous, inhuman; artificial, forced, strained, affected. **unnaturalize,** *v.t.* To make unnatural. **unnaturalized,** *a.* Not naturalized, alien. **unnaturally,** *adv.* **unnaturalness,** *n.* **unnavigable** (-năv′ i gȧbl), *a.* **unnecessary** (-nes′ ė sar i), *a.* Not necessary; needless, superfluous; *n.* (*usu. in pl.*) That which is unnecessary. **unnecessarily,** *adv.* **unneeded** (-nē′ dėd), *a.* **unneedful,** *a.* **unnegotiable** (-nė gō′ shȧbl), *a.* **unneighbourly** (-nā′ bȯr li), *a.* **unneighbourliness,** *n.* **unnerve** (-nĕrv′), *v.t.* To deprive of nerve, strength, or resolution. **unnerved,** *a.* **unnest** (-nest′), *v.t.* **unnoted** (-nō′ tėd), *a.* Not heeded. **unnoticed** (-nō′ tist), *a.* **unnourished** (-nŭr′ isht), *a.* **unnumbered** (-nŭm′ bėrd), *a.* Not marked with numbers; countless.

U.N.O. United Nations Organization.

unobjectionable (ŭn ob jek′ shȯn ȧbl), *a.* **unobjectionably,** *adv.* **unobliging** (-ȯ blī′ jing), *a.* **unobliterated** (-ȯb lit′ ėr ā tėd), *a.* **unobscured** (-ȯb skūrd′), *a.* **unobservant** (-ȯb zĕr′ vȧnt), *a.* **unobserved** (-zĕrvd′), *a.* **unobserving,** *a.* **unobstructed** (-ȯb strŭk′ tėd), *a.* **unobtainable** (-ȯb tā′ nȧbl), *a.* **unobtrusive** (-ȯb troo′ siv), *a.* **unobtrusively,** *adv.* **unobtrusiveness,** *n.* **unoccupied** (-ok′ ū pīd), *a.* **unoffending** (-ȯ fen′ ding), *a.* Not offending; harmless, innocent. **unoffered** (-of′ ėrd), *a.* **unofficial** (-ȯ fish′ ȧl), *a.* **unofficially,** *adv.* **unofficinal** (-fis′ i nȧl), *a.* **unopened** (-ō′ pėnd), *a.* **unopposed** (-ȯ pōzd′), *a.* **unordained** (-ȯr dānd′), *a.* **unorganized** (-ôr′ gȧ nīzd), *a.* **unoriginal** (-ȯ rij′ i nȧl), *a.* Not original, derived; not possessed of originality. **unoriginated** (-ȯ rij′ i nā tėd), *a.* **unornamental** (-ôr nȧ men′ tȧl), *a.* Not ornamental; plain, ugly. **unornamented** (-ôr′ nȧ mėn tėd), *a.* **unorthodox** (-ôr′ thȯ doks), *a.* **unostentatious** (-os tėn tā′ shůs), *a.* **unostentatiously,** *adv.* **unostentatiousness,** *n.* **unowned** (-ōnd′), *a.* **unpacified** (-păs′ i fīd), *a.* **unpack,** *v.t.* To open and take out the contents of; to take (things) out of a package, etc. **unpaged** (-pājd′), *a.* Not having the pages numbered. **unpaid** (-pād′), *a.* Not paid, not discharged (of a debt, etc.); not having received the payment due; acting gratuitously. **the great unpaid:** Unpaid magistrates, etc. **unpaid for:** Not paid for; taken on credit. **unpaired** (-pârd′), *a.* Not paired, not matched. **unpalatable** (-păl ȧ tȧbl), *a.* **unpalatably,** *adv.* **unparalleled** (-pâr′ ȧ leld), *a.* Not paralleled; unequalled, unprecedented. **unpardonable** (-par′ dȯ nȧbl), *a.* **unpardonableness,** *n.* **unpardonably,** *adv.* **unpared** (-pârd′), *a.* **unparental** (-pȧ ren′ tȧl), *a.* **unparented** (-pâr′ ėn tėd), *a.* **unparliamentary** (-par li men′ tȧ ri), *a.* Contrary to the rules or usages of Parliament (esp. of language). **unparliamentarily,** *adv.* **unparliamentariness,** *n.* **unpatented** (-păt′ ėn tėd, -pā′ tėn tėd), *a.* **unpatriotic** (-pā tri-, -păt ri ot′ ik), *a.* **unpatriotically,** *adv.* **unpatronized** (-păt′ rȯ nīzd), *a.* **unpaved** (-pāvd′), *a.* **unpawned** (-pawnd′), *a.* **unpeaceful** (-pēs′ fûl), *a.* **unpedantic** (-pė dăn′ tik), *a.* **unpedigreed** (-ped′ i grēd), *a.* **unpeeled** (-pēld′), *a.* **unpeg** (-peg′), *v.t.* To take out the pegs from; to open or unfasten thus. **unpen,** *v.t.* **unpensioned** (-pen′ shȯnd), *a.* **unpeople** (-pēpl′), *v.t.* To empty of inhabitants. **unperceived** (-pėr sēvd′), *a.* **unperch** (-pĕrch′), *v.t.* To drive from a perch. **unperforated** (-pĕr′ fȯ rā tėd), *a.* **unperformed** (-pėr fôrmd′), *a.* **unperjured** (-pĕr′ jůrd), *a.* **unpersuadable** (-pėr swā′ dȧbl), *a.* **unpersuaded,** *a.* **unpersuasive,** *a.* **unperturbed** (-pėr tĕrbd′), *a.* **unperused** (-pė roozd′), *a.* Not perused; not read through. **unperverted** (-pėr vĕr′ tėd), *a.* **unphilosophical** (-fil ȯ sof′ i kȧl), *a.* Not in a philosophic way; lacking philosophy. **unphilosophically,** *adv.* **unphilosophicalness,** *n.* **unpick** (-pik′), *v.t.* To loosen, take out, or open, by picking; to unfasten or open with a pick. **un-**

picked, *a.* Not picked; not picked out or selected. **unpicturesque** (-pik tyů resk′), *a.* **unpiloted** (-pī′ lǒt ėd), *a.* **unpin** (-pin′), *v.t.* To remove the pins from; to unfasten (something held together by pins). **unpitied** (-pit′ id), *a.* **unpitying,** *a.* **unpityingly,** *adv.* **unplaced** (-plāst′), *a.* Not placed; not holding a place, esp. under government; not among the first three at the finish of a race. **unplagued** (-plāgd′), *a.* **unplait,** *v.t.* **unplaned** (-plānd′), *a.* **unplanned** (-plănd′), *a.* **unplanted** (-plan′ tėd), *a.* **unplastered** (-plas′ tėrd), *a.* **unplastic,** *a.* **unplated** (-plā′ tėd), *a.* **unplausible** (-plaw′ zibl), *a.* **unplausibly,** *adv.* **unplayable** (-plā′ ȧbl), *a.* **unpleasant** (-plez′ ȧnt), *a.* Not pleasant; disagreeable. **unpleasantly,** *adv.* **unpleasantness,** *n.* The quality of being unpleasant; a slight disagreement. **unpleased** (-plēzd′), *a.* **unpleasing,** *a.* **unpleasingly,** *adv.* **unpledged** (-plejd′), *a.* **unpliable** (-plī′ ȧbl), *a.* **unpliably,** *adv.* **unpliant,** *a.* **unpliantly,** *adv.* **unploughed** (-ploud′), *a.* **unplucked** (-plukt′), *a.* **unplug** (-plŭg′), *v.t.* **unplumbed** (-plŭmd′), *a.* **unpoetical** (-pȯ et′ i kȧl), *a.* **unpoetically,** *adv.* **unpoeticalness,** *n.* **unpointed** (-poin′ tėd), *a.* Not having a point; not punctuated; not having the vowel-points or diacritical marks; not pointed (of masonry). **unpolished** (-pol′ isht), *a.* **unpolitical** (-pȯ lit′ i kȧl), *a.* Not related to or interested in politics. **unpolled** (-pōld′), *a.* Not polled, not having registered one's vote. **unpolluted** (-pȯ lū′ tėd), *a.* **unpopular** (-pop′ ū lȧr), *a.* Not popular; not enjoying the public favour. **unpopularity** (-lăr′ i ti), *n.* **unpopularly,** *adv.* **unportioned** (-pôr′ shŭnd), *a.* Not portioned, portionless. **unpossessed** (-pȯ zest′), *a.* Not possessed; not in possession (of). **unposted** (-pō′ stėd), *a.* Not posted (of a letter, etc.); not posted up; without information. **unpractical** (-prăk′ ti kȧl), *a.* Not practical (of a person, proposal, etc.). **unpracticality** (-kăl′ i ti), *n.* **unpractically,** *adv.* **unpractised** (-prăk′ tist), *a.* Not put in practice; unskilful, inexperienced. **unpraised** (-prāzd′), *a.* ***unpreach** (-prēch′), *v.t.* To recant (something preached). **unprecedented** (-pres′ ė dėn tėd), *a.* Being without precedent, unparalleled. **unprefaced** (-pref′ ȧst), *a.* **unprejudice** (-prej′ ū dis), *n.* Freedom from prejudice. **unprejudiced,** *a.* **unprelatical** (-prė lăt′ i kȧl), *a.* **unpremeditated** (-prė med′ i tā tėd), *a.* Not premeditated, not planned beforehand; unintentional. **unpremeditatedly,** *adv.* **unpreoccupied** (-prė ok′ ū pīd), *a.* **unprepared** (-prė pârd′), *a.* Not prepared, impromptu; not ready (for, etc.). **unpreparedness,** *n.* **unprepossessing** (-prē pȯ zes′ ing), *a.* **unprescribed** (-prė skrībd′), *a.* **unpresentable** (-prė zen′ tȧbl), *a.* Not presentable; not fit to be seen. **unpresuming** (-zū′ ming), *a.* **unpresumptuous** (-zŭmp′ tū ŭs), *a.* **unpretending** (-ten′ ding), *a.* **unpretendingly,** *adv.* **unpretentious** (-ten′ shŭs), *a.* **unpretentiously,** *adv.* **unpretentiousness,** *n.* **unpreventable** (-ven′ tȧbl), *a.* **unpriced** (-prīst′), *a.* Having the price or prices not fixed, quoted, or marked up; priceless. **unpriest** (-prēst′), *v.t.* To deprive of the character or position of a priest. **unpriestly,** *a.* **unprimed** (-prīmd′), *a.* **unprince** (-prins′), *v.t.* **unprincely,** *adv.* **unprincipled** (-prin′ sipld), *a.* Not dictated by moral principles; destitute of principle, immoral. **unprinted** (-prin′ tėd), *a.* **unprivileged** (-priv′ i lėjd), *a.* ***unprizable** (-prī′ zȧbl), *a.* Invaluable, inestimable; valueless; worthless, despised. **unprized,** *a.* **unprobed** (-prōbd′), *a.* **unproclaimed** (-prȯ klāmd′), *a.* **unprocurable** (-prȯ kūr′ ȧbl), *a.* **unproductive** (-prȯ dŭk′ tiv), *a.* **unproductively,** *adv.* **unproductiveness,** *n.* **unprofaned** (-prȯ fānd′), *a.* **unprofessional** (-prȯ fesh′ ȯ nȧl), *a.* Not pertaining to one's profession; contrary to the rules or etiquette of a profession; not belonging to a profession. **unprofitable** (-prof′ i tȧbl), *a.* **unprofitableness,** *n.* **unprofitably,** *adv.* **unprogressive** (-prȯ gres′ iv), *a.* Not progressive, conservative. **unprogressiveness,** *n.* **unprohibited** (-prȯ hib′ i tėd), *a.* **unprolific** (-prȯ lif′ ik), *a.* **unpromising** (-prom′ i sing), *a.* Not promising success. **unprompted** (-promp′ tėd), *a.* Of one's own free will or initiative. **unpromulgated** (-prō′ mŭl gā tėd), *a.* **unpronounceable,** *a.* **unprop** (-prop′), *v.t.* To deprive of support. **unpropagated** (-prop′ ȧ gā tėd), *a.* **unprophetic** (-prȯ fet′ ik), *a.* **unpropitious** (-prȯ pish′ ŭs), *a.* **unpropitiously,** *adv.* **unpropitiousness,** *n.* **unproportional** (-pôr′ shȯ nȧl), *a.* Not in proportion, disproportionate. **unproposed** (-pōzd′), *a.* **unpropped** (-propt′), *a.* **unprosperous** (-pros′ pėr ŭs), *a.* **unprosperously,** *adv.* **unprosperousness,** *n.* **unprotected** (tek′ tėd), *a.* **unprotecting,** *a.* **unprotested** (-tes′ tėd), *a.* **unprovable** (-proo′ vȧbl), *a.* **unproved,** ***-proven** (-prōvn′), *a.* **unprovided** (-prȯ vī′ dėd), *a.* Not provided; not furnished (with supplies, etc.); *not prepared, not ready. **unprovoked** (-prȯ vōkt′), *a.* Having received no provocation; not instigated. **unpruned** (-proond′), *a.* Not pruned. **unpublished** (-pŭb′ lisht), *a.* Not made public; not published (of books, etc.). **unpunctual** (-pŭnk′ tū ȧl), *a.* **unpunctuality** (-ăl′ i ti), *n.* **unpunctually,** *adv.* **unpunctuated** (-pŭnk′ tū ā tėd), *a.* **unpunishable** (-pŭn′ i shȧbl), *a.* Not punishable. **unpunished,** *a.* **unpurchasable,** *a.* **unpurchased** (-pĕr′ chȧst), *a.* **unpurified** (-pūr′ i fīd), *a.* **unquailing** (-kwā′ ling), *a.* **unquailingly,** *adv.* **unqualified** (-kwol′ i fīd), *a.* Not qualified; not fit, not competent; not having passed the necessary examination, etc.; not qualified legally; not limited by conditions or exceptions, absolute. **unqualifiedly** (-fī ėd li), *adv.* **unquarried** (-kwor′ id), *a.* **unqueen** (-kwēn′), *v.t.* To depose from the position of queen. **unquelled** (-kweld′), *a.* **unquenchable** (-kwen′ chȧbl), *a.* **unquenchably,** *adv.* **unquenched,** *a.* **unquestionable** (-kwes′ tyȯ nȧbl), *a.* Not to be questioned or doubted, indisputable. **unquestionably,** *adv.* **unquestioned,** *a.* Not called in question, not doubted; having no questions asked, not interrogated. **unquestioning,** *a.* Not questioning, not doubting; implicit. **unquestioningly,** *adv.* **unquiet** (-kwī′ ėt), *a.* Restless, uneasy, agitated. **unquietly,** *adv.* **unquilted** (-kwil′ tėd), *a.* **unquotable** (-kwō′ tȧbl), *a.* **unquoted,** *a.* **unransomed** (-răn′ sȯmd), *a.* **unravaged** (-răv′ ȧjd), *a.* **unravel** (-răv′ ėl), *v.t.* To separate the threads of; to disentangle, to untwist; (*fig.*) to solve, to clear up (the plot of a play, etc.); *to throw into confusion or disorder; *v.i.* To be disentangled; to be opened up or revealed. **unravelment,** *n.* **unrazored** (-rā′ zȯrd), *a.* Unshaven; *beardless. **unreachable** (-rē′ chȧbl), *a.* **unread** (-red′), *a.* Not read; not well-read, unlearned, illiterate. **unreadable** (-rē′ dȧbl), *a.* **unreadableness,** *n.* **unready** (-red′ i), *a.* Not ready; not prompt to act, etc. **unreal** (-rē′ ȧl), *a.* Not real; unsubstantial, visionary, imaginary. **unreality** (-ăl′ i ti), *n.* **unreally,** *adv.* **unrealizable** (-lī′ zȧbl), *a.* **unrealized** (-rē′ ȧ līzd), *a.* **unreaped** (-rēpt′), *a.* **unreason** (-rē′ zȯn), *n.* Want of reason; folly, absurdity. **unreasonable,** *a.* Not reasonable; exorbitant, extravagant, absurd; not listening to reason; *irrational, brute. **unreasonableness,** *n.* **unreasonably,** *adv.* **unreasoned,** *a.* Not reasoned or thought out rationally. **unreasoning,** *a.* Not reasoning; foolish; not having reasoning faculties. **unreasoningly,** *adv.* **unrebuked** (-rė būkt′), *a.* **unrecallable** (-kaw′ lȧbl), *a.* **unrecanted** (-kăn′ tėd), *a.* **unreceived** (-rė sēvd′), *a.* **unreciprocated** (-sip′ rȯ kā tėd), *a.* **unreckoned** (-rek′ ȯnd), *a.* **unreclaimed** (-rė klāmd′), *a.* Not reclaimed; unregenerate. **unrecognizable** (-rek′ ȯg nīz ȧbl), *a.* **unrecognizably,** *adv.* **unrecognized,** *a.* Not recognized; not acknowledged. **unrecompensed** (-rek′ ȯm penst), *a.* **unreconciled** (-rek′ ȯn sīld), *a.* **unrecorded** (-rė kôr′ dėd), *a.* **unrectified** (-rek′ ti fīd), *a.* Not corrected. **unredeemed** (-rė dēmd′), *a.* Not redeemed, not fulfilled; not taken out of pawn; not recalled by payment of the value; not counterbalanced by any redeeming quality, unmitigated. **unredressed** (-rė drest′), *a.* **unreel** (-rēl′), *v.t.* To unwind; *v.i.* To become unwound. **unreeve** (-rēv′), *v.t.* (*Naut.*) To withdraw a rope from a block, dead-eye, etc.; *v.i.* To become unrove. **unrefined** (-rė fīnd′), *a.* Not refined; not purified; of unpolished manners, taste, etc. **unreflecting** (-flek' ting), *a.* **unreflectingly,** *adv.* **unreformable** (-fôr' mȧbl), *a.* **unreformed,** *a.* **unrefreshed** (-fresht'), *a.* **unrefuted** (-fū' tėd), *a.* **unregal** (-rē' gȧl), *a.* **unregarded** (-rė gar' dėd), *a.* **unregardful,** *a.* **unregenerate** (-jen' ėr ȧt), *a.* **unregistered** (-rej' is tėrd), *a.* **unregretted** (-rė gret' ėd), *a.* **unregulated** (-reg' ū lā tėd), *a.* Not reduced to order. **unrehearsed** (-rė hĕrst'), *a.* **unreined** (-rānd'), *a.* Not held in check by the rein; (*fig.*) unrestrained, unbridled. **unrelated** (-rė lā' tėd), *a.* **unrelaxed** (-lăkst'), *a.* **unrelaxing,** *a.* **unrelenting** (-len' ting), *a.* **unrelentingly,** *adv.* **unrelentingness,** *n.* **unreliable** (-lī' ȧbl), *a.* **unreliability** (-bil' i ti), **unreliableness,** *n.* **unreliably,** *adv.* **unrelieved** (-rė lēvd'), *a.* **unremembered** (-mem' bėrd), *a.* **unremitting** (-mit' ing), *a.* Not relaxing; incessant, continued. **unremittingly,** *adv.* **unremunerative** (-mū' nėr ȧ tiv), *a.* Not profitable. **unrenewed** (-nūd'), *a.* **unrenounced** (-nounst'), *a.* **unrepair** (-pâr'), *n.* Disrepair, dilapidation. **unrepealed** (-pēld'), *a.* **unrepentant** (-pen' tȧnt), *a.* **unrepentance,** *n.* **unrepented,** *a.* **unrepining** (-pī' ning), *a.* **unrepiningly,** *adv.* **unreplenished** (-plen' isht), *a.* **unreported** (-pôr' tėd), *a.* **unrepresentative** (-rep rė zen' tȧ tiv), **unrepresented** (-rep' rė zen tėd), *a.* **unrepressed** (-rė prest'), *a.* ***unreproachable,** *a.* **unreproachful** (-prōch' fůl), *a.* **unreproved** (-proovd'), *a.* **unrequited** (-kwī' tėd), *a.* Not requited; not recompensed. **unrescinded** (-sin' dėd), *a.* **unresented** (-zen' tėd), *a.* **unresenting,** *a.* **unresentingly,** *adv.* **unreserve** (-zĕrv'), *n.* Lack of reserve, frankness, candour. **unreserved,** *a.* Not reserved; open, frank; given, offered, or done without reservation. **unreservedly** (-zĕr' vėd li), *adv.* **unreservedness,** *n.* **unresisted** (-zis' tėd), *a.* **unresisting,** *a.* **unresistingly,** *adv.* **unresolved** (-zolvd'), *a.* Not resolved, undecided, irresolute; unsolved, not cleared up. **unrespected** (-spek' tėd), *a.* **unrespited** (-res' pi tėd), *a.* **unresponsive** (-spon' siv), *a.* **unrest** (-rest'), *n.* Restlessness, agitation, disquiet, uneasiness, unhappiness. **unrestful,** *a.* **unrestfully,** *adv.* **unrestfulness,** *n.* **unresting,** *a.* **unrestingly,** *adv.* **unrestored** (-rė stôrd'), *a.* **unrestrainable** (-strā' nȧbl), *a.* **unrestrainably,** *adv.* **unrestrained,** *a.* **unrestrainedly** (-strā' nėd li), *adv.* **unrestraint,** *n.* **unrestricted** (-strik' tėd), *a.* **unrestrictedly,** *adv.* **unretarded** (-tar' dėd), *a.* **unretentive** (-ten' tiv), *a.* **unretracted** (-trăk' tėd), *a.* **unrevealed** (-vēld'), *a.* **unrevenged** (-venjd'), *a.* **unreversed** (-vĕrst'), *a.* **unrevised** (-vīzd'), *a.* **unrevoked** (-vōkt'), *a.* **unrewarded** (-wôr' dėd), *a.* **unrhetorical** (-tor' kȧl), *a.* **unrhymed** (-rīmd'), *a.* **unrhythmic, -al** (-rit*h*' mik, -ȧl), *a.* **unridable** (-rī' dȧbl), *a.* **unridden** (-rid' ėn), *a.* **unriddle** (-ridl'), *v.t.* To solve, to interpret, to explain. **unrifled,** *a.* Not robbed or plundered; not rifled (of a gun, etc.). **unrig** (-rig'), *v.t.* (*Naut.*) To strip of rigging. ***unright** (-rīt'), *n.* A wrong; *a.* Unjust. **unrighted,** *a.* **unrighteous** (-rī' tyůs, -chůs), *a.* Not righteous, not just; contrary to justice or equity; evil, wicked, sinful. **unrighteously,** *adv.* **unrighteousness,** *n.* **unrip,** *v.t.* To rip open, to undo or unfasten by ripping. **unripe** (-rīp'), *a.* Not ripe; not mature; premature. **unripeness,** *n.* **unrivalled** (-rī' vȧld), *a.* Having no rival; unequalled, peerless. **unrivet** (-riv' ėt), *v.t.* **unrobe** (-rōb'), *v.t.* and *i.* **unroll** (-rōl'), *v.t.* To unfold (a roll of cloth, etc.); to display, to lay open; *v.i.* To be unrolled; to be displayed. **unromanize** (-rō' mȧ nīz), *v.t.* **unromantic** (-rȯ măn' tik), *a.* **unromantically,** *adv.* **unroof** (-roof'), *v.t.* To strip the roof off. **unroot** (-root'), *v.t.* To tear up by the roots; to extirpate, to eradicate. **unroyal** (-roi' ȧl), *a.* Not royal; not becoming a sovereign. **unroyally,** *adv.*

UNRRA (ŭn' ra) [initials of United Nations Relief and Rehabilitation Administration], *n.* (*Pol.*) A body authorized by the Atlantic Charter to organize relief and rehabilitation to peoples freed from enemy occupation after the World War of 1939–45.

unruffled (ŭn rŭf' ėld), *a.* Not ruffled, unperturbed. **unruled** (-roold'), *a.* Not governed; not ruled with lines (of paper, etc.). **unruly** (-roo' li) [RULE- -LY], *a.* Not submitting to restraint; lawless, turbulent, ungovernable. **unsaddle** (-sădl'), *v.t.* To remove the saddle from; to unseat; *v.i.* To unsaddle one's horse. **unsafe** (-sāf'), *a.* Dangerous, perilous, risky; not to be trusted. **unsafely,** *adv.* **unsafeness,** *n.* **unsaid** (-sed'), *a.* Not said, unspoken. **unsaintly** (-sānt' li), *a.* **unsalaried** (-săl' ȧ rid), *a.* **unsaleable** (-sā' lȧbl), *a.* **unsaleability** (-bil' i ti), **unsaleableness,** *n.* **unsalted** (-sawl' tėd), *a.* **unsanctified** (-sănk' ti fīd), *a.* **unsanctioned** (-sănk' shůnd), *a.* **unsanitary** (-săn' i tȧr i), *a.* Unhealthy. **unsated** (-sā' tėd), *a.* **unsatisfactory** (-săt is făk' tȯr i), *a.* **unsatisfactorily,** *adv.* **unsatisfactoriness,** *n.* **unsatisfied** (-săt' is fīd), *a.* **unsatisfying,** *a.* **unsatisfyingly,** *adv.* **unsaturated** (-săt' ū rā tėd), *a.* **unsaved** (-sāvd'), *a.* **unsavoury** (-sā' vȯr i), *a.* Unattractive, repellent, disgusting; *tasteless, insipid. **unsavourily,** *adv.* **unsavouriness,** *n.* **unsay** (-sā'), *v.t.* To retract or withdraw (what has been said). **unsayable,** *a.* **unscalable** (-skā' lȧbl), *a.* That cannot be climbed. **unscannable** (-skăn' ȧbl), *a.* That cannot be scanned. **unscared** (-skârd'), *a.* **unscarred** (-skard'), *a.* **unscathed** (-skā*th*d), *a.* Not scathed, uninjured. **unscented** (-sen' tėd), *a.* **unscheduled** (-shed' ūld), *a.* **unscholarly** (-skol' ȧr li), *a.* **unschooled** (-skoold'), *a.* **unscientific** (-si ėn tif' ik), *a.* **unscientifically,** *adv.* **unscorched** (-skôrcht'), *a.* **unscoured** (-skourd'), *a.* **unscourged** (-skĕrjd'), *a.* **unscramble,** *v.t.* To make a scrambled message intelligible. **unscreened** (skrēnd'), *a.* **unscrew** (-skroo'), *v.t.* To withdraw or loosen (a screw); to unfasten thus. **unscriptural** (-skrip' tū rȧl), *a.* Not in conformity with the Scriptures. **unscripturally,** *adv.* **unscrupulous** (-skroo' pū lůs), *a.* Having no scruples of conscience; unprincipled. **unscrupulously,** *adv.* **unscrupulousness,** *n.* **unsculptured** (-skŭlp' tūrd), *a.* Not adorned with sculpture; bearing no inscription; (*Zool.*) smooth. **unseal** (-sēl'), *v.t.* To break or remove the seal of; to open. **unsealed,** *a.* Not sealed; having the seal broken. **unseam** (-sēm'), *v.t.* To rip open at a seam. **unsearchable** (-sĕr' chȧbl), *a.* Incapable of being searched out, inscrutable. **unsearched,** *a.* **unseasonable** (-sē' zȯ nȧbl), *a.* **unseasonableness,** *n.* **unseasonably,** *adv.* **unseasoned,** *a.* **unseat** (-sēt'), *v.t.* To remove from one's seat; to throw from one's seat on horseback; to deprive of a seat in the House of Commons. **unseated,** *a.* Thrown from or deprived of a seat; not furnished with seats; having no seat. **unseaworthy** (-sē' wȯr *th*i), *a.* **unseaworthiness,** *n.* **unseconded** (-sek' ȯn dėd), *a.* **unsectarian** (-sek târ' i ȧn), *a.* **unsectarianism,** *n.* **unsecured** (-sė kūrd'), *a.* **unseduced** (-dūst'), *a.* **unseductive** (-dŭk' tiv), *a.* **unseeing** (-sē' ing), *a.* Blind; unobservant, unsuspecting. ***unseel** (-sēl') [SEEL], *v.t.* To open the eyes of (a hawk, etc.); to enlighten. **unseem** (-sēm'), *v.i.* Not to seem. **unseemly** (-sēm' li), *a.* Not seemly; unbefitting, unbecoming; **adv.* In an unseemly manner. **unseemliness,** *n.* **unseen** (-sēn'), *a.* Not seen; invisible; not seen previously (as a piece to be translated). **the unseen:** The world of spirits. **unseizable** (-sē' zȧbl), *a.* **unselect** (-sė lekt'), *a.* Not select, mixed, miscellaneous. **unself** (-self'), *v.t.* To divest of individuality. **unselfish** (-sel' fish), *a.* Regarding or prompted by the interests of others rather than one's own. **unselfishly,** *adv.* **unselfishness,** *n.* **unseminared** (sem' i nȧrd) [see SEMINARY], *a.* Without sexual capacity, impotent, emasculated. **unsensational** (-sen sā' shȯ nȧl), *a.* **unsent** (-sent'), *a.* **unsentenced,** *a.* **unsentimental** (-men' tȧl), *a.* **unseparated** (-sep' ȧ rā tėd), *a.* **unserviceable** (-sĕr' vi sȧbl), *a.* **unserviceableness,** *n.* **unserviceably,** *adv.* **unset** (-set'), *v.t.* To take from its setting; *a.* Not set (of a gem, trap, the sun, etc.). **unsettle** (-setl'), *v.t.* To change from a settled state or position; to make uncertain or fluctuating; to derange, to disturb; **v.i.* To become unsettled.

unsettled, *a.* Not settled, fixed, or determined; undecided, hesitating; changeable; having no fixed abode; not occupied, uncolonized; unpaid. **unsevered** (-sev′ ėrd), *a.* **unsex** (-seks′), *v.t.* To deprive of the qualities of sex (esp. of a woman). **unshackle** (-shăkl′), *v.t.* **unshaded** (-shā′ dėd), *a.* **unshadowed** (-shăd′ ōd), *a.* **unshaken** (-shā′ kėn), ***unshaked** (-shākt′), *a.* Not shaken; not moved in resolution; firm, steady. **unshakable,** *a.* ***unshape,** *v.t.* To throw out of regular form; to disorder, to derange. **unshapely** (-shāp′ li), *a.* Misshapen. ***unshapen,** *a.* Deformed, shapeless. **unshared** (shârd′), *a.* **unshaven** (-shā′ vėn), *a.* **unsheathe** (-shēth′), *v.t.* To draw from its sheath. **unshead** (-shed′), *a.* **unsheltered** (-shel′ tėrd), *a.* **unship** (-ship′), *v.t.* To unload from a ship; to disembark; (*Naut.*) to remove from the place where it is fixed or fitted; *v.i.* (*Naut.*) To become unshipped (of an oar, tiller, etc.). **unshipped,** *a.* **unshocked** (-shokt′), *a.* **unshod** (-shod′), *a.* **unshoe** (-shoo′), *v.t.* **unshorn** (-shôrn′), *a.* Not shorn, clipped, or shaven. **unshot** (-shot′), *v.t.* To take the shot out of (a gun, etc.). **unshown** (-shōn′), *a.* **unshrinkable** (-shring′ kȧbl), *a.* That will not shrink (of flannel, etc.). **unshrinking,** *a.* Not recoiling, undaunted, unhesitating. **unshrinkingly,** *adv.* ***unshriven** (-shriv′ ėn), *a.* Not absolved. **unshroud** (-shroud′), *v.t.* **unshrunk** (-shrŭnk′), *a.* **unshut** (-shŭt), *a.* **unshuttered,** *a.* **unsifted** (-sif′ tėd), *a.* **unsighted** (-sī′ tėd), *a.* Not sighted, not seen; invisible; unfurnished with sights (of a gun, etc.). **unsightly** (-sīt′ li), *a.* Unpleasing to the sight, ugly. **unsightliness,** *n.* **unsigned** (-sīnd′), *a.* **unsilvered** (-sil′ vėrd), *a.* **unsinged** (-sinjd′), *a.* **unsinning** (-sin′ ing), *a.* **unsisterly** (-sis′ tėr li), *a.* **unsisterliness,** *n.* **unsized** (-sīzd′), *a.* Not sized, not stiffened. **unskilful** (-skil′ fŭl), *a.* **unskilfully,** *adv.* **unskilfulness,** *n.* **unskilled,** *a.* Destitute of skill or special knowledge or training; produced without or not requiring special skill or training. **unslaked** (-slākt′), *a.* **unsleeping** (-slē′ ping), *a.* **unsling** (-sling), *v.t.* (*Naut.*) To take (a yard, a cask, etc.) off the slings. **unslumbering** (-slŭm′ bėr ing), *a.* Sleepless, vigilant. **unsmirched** (-smĕrcht′), *a.* **unsmoked** (-smōkt′), *a.* **unsociable** (-sō′ shȧbl), *a.* **unsociability** (-bil′ i ti), **unsociableness,** *n.* **unsociably,** *adv.* **unsocial** (-sō′ shȧl), *a.* **unsoiled** (-soild′), *a.* **unsolaced** (-sol′ ȧst), *a.* **unsold** (-sōld′), *a.* **unsolder** (-sol′ dėr), *v.t.* **unsoldierly** (-sōl′ dyėr-, -jėr li), *a.* **unsolicited** (-sȯ lis′ i tėd), *a.* **unsolicitous** (-lis′ i tŭs), *a.* **unsolid,** *a.* **unsolidity** (-sȯ lid′ i ti), *n.* **unsolvable** (-sol′ vȧbl), *a.* **unsolved** (-solvd′), *a.* **unsoothed** (-soothd′), *a.* **unsophistical** (-fis′ ti kȧl), *a.* **unsophisticated,** *a.* Simple, artless, free from artificiality, inexperienced; not corrupted or adulterated, pure, genuine. **unsophisticatedness,** *n.* **unsorted** (-sôr′ tėd), *a.* **unsought** (-sawt′), *a.* **unsound** (-sound′), *a.* Not sound; weak, decayed; unreliable; diseased; ill-founded, not valid, fallacious. **unsoundly,** *adv.* **unsoundness,** *n.* **unsounded** (-soun′ dėd), *a.* Not sounded or fathomed. **unsoured** (-sourd′), *a.* **unsown** (-sōn′), *a.* **unsparing** (-spâr′ ing), *a.* Liberal, profuse, lavish; unmerciful. **unsparingly,** *adv.* **unsparingness,** *n.* **unspeak** (-spēk′), *v.t.* To retract, to unsay. **unspeakable,** *a.* Unutterable, inexpressible, beyond expression. **unspeakably,** *adv.* **unspeakableness,** *n.* **unspecified** (-spes′ i fīd), *a.* **unspeculative** (-spek′ ū lȧ tiv), *a.* **unspent** (-spent′), *a.* **unsphere** (-sfēr′), *v.t.* To remove from its sphere. **unspilt** (-spilt′), *a.* **unspiritual** (-spir′ i tū ȧl), *a.* **unspirituality** (-ăl′ i ti), *n.* **unspiritually,** *adv.* **unspliced** (-splīst′), *a.* **unspoiled, -spoilt** (-spoild′, -spoilt′), *a.* **unspoken** (-spō′ kėn), *a.* **unspontaneous** (-spon tā′ nė ŭs), *a.* **unsporting** (-spôr′ ting), *a.* **unsportsmanlike** (-spôrts′ mȧn līk), *a.* Unbecoming a sportsman. **unspotted** (-spot′ ėd), *a.* Free from spots; (*fig.*) unblemished, uncontaminated; faultless, perfect. **unsprung,** *a.* Not equipped with springs. **unsquared** (-skwârd′), *a.* **unsquire** (-skwīr′), *v.t.* To degrade from the rank or deprive of the title of squire. **unstable** (-stābl′), *a.* **unstaid** (-stād′), *a.* **unstained** (-stānd′), *a.* Not stained; (*fig.*) unblemished, unsullied. **unstamped** (-stămpt′), *a.* Not having a stamp affixed. **unstarched** (-starcht′), *a.* **unstartled** (-startld′), *a.* **unstated** (-stā′ tėd), *a.* **unstatesmanlike** (-stāts′ mȧn līk), *a.* **unstatutable** (-stăt′ ū tȧbl), *a.* Not warranted by statute law. **unstatutably,** *adv.* **unsteadfast** (-sted′ fȧst), *a.* **unsteadfastly,** *adv.* **unsteadfastness,** *n.* **unsteady** (-sted′ i), *a.* Not steady, not firm; changeable, variable; unstable, precarious; (*colloq.*) irregular in habits or conduct. **unsteadily,** *adv.* **unsteadiness,** *n.* **unsteel** (-stēl′), *v.t.* To soften, to disarm. **unstep** (-step′), *v.t.* (*Naut.*) To take out of a step or socket. **unstick** (-stik′), *v.t.* **unstigmatized** (-stig′ mȧ tīzd), *a.* **unstimulated** (-stim′ ū lā tėd), *a.* **unstinted** (-stin′ tėd), *a.* **unstirred** (-stĕrd′), *a.* **unstitch** (-stich′), *v.t.* To open by unpicking the stiches of. **unstock** (-stok′), *v.t.* To deplete of stock; to take the stock from (a gun, etc.). **unstocked,** *a.* Not stocked (with). **unstop,** *v.t.* To free from obstruction; to remove the stopper from, to open. **unstopped,** *a.* **unstored** (-stôrd′), *a.* **unstrained** (-strănd′), *a.* Not strained, not filtered; not subjected to strain; not forced; easy, natural. **unstrap** (-străp′), *v.t.* To unfasten or remove the strap or straps of. **unstratified** (-străt′ i fīd), *a.* **unstressed** (-strest′), *a.* Unaccented. **unstring** (-string), *v.t.* (*past & p.p.* **-strung**) To take away the string or strings of; to loosen; to loosen the string or strings of; to relax the tension of (nerves, etc.); to remove (pearls, etc.) from a string. **unstuck,** *a.* (*slang*) Disarranged, disorganized. **unstudied** (-stŭd′ id), *a.* Not studied; easy, natural. **unstuffed** (-stŭft′), *a.* **unstung** (-stŭng′), *a.* **unsubdued** (-sŭb dūd′), *a.* **unsubjugated** (-sŭb′ jū gā tėd), *a.* **unsubmissive** (-sŭb mis′ iv), *a.* **unsubmissively,** *adv.* **unsubmissiveness,** *n.* **unsubscribed** (-skrībd′), *a.* **unsubstantial** (-stăn shȧl), *a.* Not substantial; not very solid; unreal. **unsubstantiality** (-ăl′ i ti), *n.* **unsubstantially,** *adv.* **unsubstantiated** (-stăn′ shi ā tėd), *a.* **unsubstantiation** (-ā′ shŭn), *n.* **unsuccess** (-sŭk ses′), *n.* **unsuccessful,** *a.* **unsuccessfully,** *adv.* **unsugared** (-shug′ ȧrd), *a.* **unsuitable** (-sū′ tȧbl), *a.* **unsuitability** (-bil′ i ti), **unsuitableness,** *n.* **unsuitably,** *adv.* **unsuited,** *a.* Not suited, not fit or adapted (for or to). **unsullied** (-sŭl′ id), *a.* **unsummed** (-sŭmd′), *a.* **unsummoned** (-sŭm′ ȯnd), *a.* **unsung** (-sŭng′), *a.* Not sung; (*poet.*) not celebrated in verse. **unsunned,** *a.* Not shone upon by the sun. **unsupplied** (-sŭ plīd′), *a.* **unsupported** (-pôr′ ted), *a.* **unsuppressed** (-prest′), *a.* **unsure** (-shoor′), *a.* **unsurgical** (-sĕr′ ji kȧl), *a.* **unsurmised** (-sŭr mīzd′), *a.* **unsurmountable** (-moun′ tȧbl), *a.* **unsurmounted,** *a.* **unsurpassable,** *a.* **unsurpassably,** *adv.* **unsurpassed** (-past′), *a.* **unsurrendered** (-ren′ dėrd), *a.* **unsurveyed** (-vād′), *a.* **unsusceptible** (-sep′ tibl), *a.* **unsuspected** (-spek′ tėd), *a.* **unsuspectedly,** *adv.* **unsuspecting,** *a.* **unsuspectingly,** *adv.* ***unsuspicion,** *n.* **unsuspicious** (-spish′ ŭs), *a.* **unsuspiciously,** *adv.* **unsuspiciousness,** *n.* **unsustainable** (-stā′ nȧbl), *a.* **unsustained,** *a.* **unswaddle** (-swodl′), *v.t.* **unswallowed** (-swol′ ōd), *a.* **unswathe** (-swāth′), *v.t.* **unswayed** (-swād′), *a.* Not swayed, biased, or influenced. **unswear** (-swâr′), *v.t.* To recant (something sworn to); to deny by oath. ***unsweet** (-swēt′), *a.* **unsweetened,** *a.* **unswept** (-swept′), *a.* **unswerving** (-swĕr′ ving), *a.* **unswervingly,** *adv.* **unsworn** (-swôrn′), *a.* Not sworn; not bound by an oath. **unsymbolical** (-sim bol′ i kȧl), *a.* **unsymmetrical** (-si met′ ri kȧl), *a.* Wanting in or out of symmetry. **unsymmetrically,** *adv.* **unsymmetry** (-sim′ ė tri), *n.* **unsystematic** (-sis tė măt′ ik), *a.* **untack** (-tăk′), *v.t.* To undo (something that has been tacked); to disjoin. **untainted** (-tān′ tėd), *a.* **untalented** (-tăl′ ėn tėd), *a.* **untamable** (-tā′ mȧbl), *a.* **untamableness,** *n.* **untamed,** *a.* **untangle** (-tăngl′), *v.t.* To disentangle. **untanned** (-tănd′), *a.* **untarnishable** (-tar′ ni shȧbl), *a.* **untarnished,** *a.* **untasked** (-taskt′), *a.* **untasted** (-tā′ stėd), *a.* **untaught** (-tawt′), *a.* Not instructed, illiterate;

ignorant. **untaxed** (-tăkst′), *a.* ***unteach** (-tēch′), *v.t.* To cause to be forgotten or unlearned. **unteachable,** *a.* **unteachableness,** *n.* **untearable** (târ′ ȧbl), *a.* **untechnical** (-tek′ ni kȧl), *a.* **untemper** (-tem′ pėr), *v.t.* To take away the temper of (of steel, etc.). **untempered,** *a.* Not moderated or controlled. **untempted** (-temp′ tėd), *a.* **untenable** (-ten′ ȧbl), *a.* **untenability** (-bil′ i ti), **untenableness,** *n.* **untenably,** *adv.* **untenantable** (-ten′ ȧn tȧbl), *a.* Not in suitable condition for a tenant. **untenanted,** *a.* **untended** (-ten′ dėd), *a.* **untender** (-ten′ dėr), *a.* Not tender, unkind. **untendered** (-ten′ dėrd), *a.* Not offered. **unterrified** (-ter′ i fīd), *a.* **untested** (-tes′ tėd), *a.* **untether** (-te*th*′ ėr), *v.t.* **unthanked,** *a.* **unthankful,** *a.* **unthankfully,** *adv.* **unthankfulness,** *n.* **unthatched** (-thăcht′), *a.* **unthink** (-think′), *v.t.* To retract in thought. **unthinkable,** *a.* Incapable of being thought or conceived; (*colloq.*) highly improbable. **unthinking,** *a.* Heedless, careless; done without thought or care. **unthinkingly,** *adv.* **unthought** (-thawt′), *a.* Not remembered or thought (of). **unthoughtful,** *a.* **unthoughtfulness,** *n.* **unthrashed** (-thrăsht′), *a.* **unthread** (-thred′), *v.t.* To take a thread out of (a needle, etc.); to find one's way out of (a maze, etc.). **unthreaded,** *a.* Not threaded. **unthreshed** (-thresht′), *a.* **unthrift** (ŭn thrift′), *n.* Unthriftiness; a prodigal, a spendthrift; *a.* (ŭn thrift′) Unthrifty. **unthrifty** (-thrif′ ti), *a.* **unthriftily,** *adv.* **unthriftiness,** *n.* **unthrone** (-thrōn′), *v.t.* **unthwarted** (-thwôr′ tėd), *a.* **untidy** (-tī′ di), *a.* **untidily,** *adv.* **untidiness,** *n.* **untie** (-tī′), *v.t.* To undo (a knot); to unfasten. **untied,** *a.*

until (ŭn til′) [M.E. var. of UNTO], *prep.* Till.

untiled (ŭn tīld′), *a.* Not covered with tiles. **untillable** (-til′ ȧbl), *a.* **untilled,** *a.* **untimbered** (-tim′ bėrd), *a.* **untimely** (-tīm′ li), (*Sc.*) **untimous,** *a.* Unseasonable, inopportune; premature; **adv.* Unseasonably, prematurely. **untimeliness,** *n.* **untin** (-tin′), *v.t.* **untinctured** (-tingk ′tūrd), *a.* **untinged** (-tinjd′), *a.* **untired** (-tīrd′), *a.* Not tired, not wearied. **untiring,** *a.* **untiringly,** *adv.* **untithed** (-tī*th*d′), *a.* Not subjected to tithes. **untitled** (-tītld′), *a.*

unto (ŭn′ tu) [O.Fris. and O.S. *und*, to, TO], *prep.* To.

untold (ŭn tōld′), *a.* Not told, revealed, or communicated; not counted, innumerable. **untormented** (-tȯr men′ tėd), *a.* **untorn** (-tôrn′), *a.* **untortured** (-tôr′ tūrd), *a.* **Untouchable,** *n.* A Hindoo belonging to one of the most degraded castes or to no caste. **untouched** (-tŭcht′), *a.* **untoward** (-tō′ ȧrd), *a.* Unlucky, unfortunate, awkward; froward, perverse, refractory. ***untowardly,** *adv.* **untraceable** (-trā′ sȧbl), *a.* **untraced,** *a.* **untracked** (-trăkt′), *a.* **untraded** (-trā′ dėd), *a.* **untragic** (-trăj′ ik), *a.* **untrained** (-trānd′), *a.* **untrammelled** (-trăm′ ėld), *a.* **untransferable** (-trăns′ fėr ȧbl), *a.* That cannot or is not permitted to be transferred. **untranslatable** (-trăns lā′ tȧbl), *a.* **untranslatability** (-bil′ i ti), **untranslatableness,** *n.* **untranslatably,** *adv.* **untranslated,** *a.* **untransportable** (-pôr′ tȧbl), *a.* **untravelled** (-trăv′ ėld), *a.* Not having travelled; not travelled over. **untraversed** (-trăv′ ėrst), *a.* **untried** (-trīd′), *a.* **untrimmed** (-trimd′), *a.* **untrod, -trodden** (-trod′, -ėn), *a.* **untroubled** (-trŭbld′), *a.* Not disturbed by care, sorrow, business, etc.; calm, unruffled. **untrue** (-troo′), *a.* Not in accordance with facts, false, not faithful, disloyal, inconstant; not conforming to the correct standard. **untruly,** *adv.* **untruss** (-trŭs′), *v.t.* **untrussed,** *a.* **untrustworthy** (-trŭst′ wȯr *th*i), *a.* **untrustworthiness,** *n.* **untruth** (-trooth′), *n.* Contrariety to truth; a falsehood, a lie; want of veracity; faithlessness. **untruthful,** *a.* **untruthfully,** *adv.* **untruthfulness,** *n.* **untuck** (-tŭk′), *v.t.* To unfold or undo, as a tuck. **untune** (-tūn′), *v.t.* To put out of tune; to make discordant. **untunable,** *a.* **untuneful,** *a.* **untunefully,** *adv.* **unturned** (-tĕrnd′), *a.* **untutored** (-tū′ tȯrd), *a.* Uninstructed; raw, crude. **untwine** (-twīn′), *v.t.* and *i.* **untwist** (-twist′), *v.t.* and *i.* **unurged,** *a.* **unused** (-ūzd′), *a.* **unusual** (-ū′ zhū ȧl), *a.* Not usual; uncommon, strange, remarkable. **unusually,** *adv.* **unusualness,** ***unusuality** (-ū ăl′ i ti), *n.* **unutilized** (-ū′ ti līzd), *a.* **unutterable** (-ŭt′ ėr ȧbl), *a.* Unspeakable, inexpressible, indescribable, ineffable. **unutterably,** *adv.* **unuttered,** *a.* **unvaccinated** (-văk′ si nā tėd), *a.* **unvalued** (-văl′ ūd), *a.* Not esteemed; not appraised, not estimated; invaluable, inestimable. **unvanquished** (-văng′ kwisht), *a.* **unvaried** (-văr′ id), *a.* **unvarnished** (-var′ nisht), *a.* Not covered with varnish; (*fig.*) not embellished, plain, simple. **unvarying** (-vâr′ i ing), *a.* **unvaryingly,** *adv.* **unveil** (-vāl′), *v.t.* To remove a veil or covering from, esp. with public ceremony from a statue, etc.; (*fig.*) to reveal, to disclose; *v.i.* To take one's veil off; to be revealed. **unvenerable** (-ven′ ėr ȧbl), *a.* **unvenomous** (-ven′ ȯ mŭs), *a.* **unventilated** (-ven′ ti lā tėd), *a.* **unveracious** (-vė rā′ shŭs), *a.* Untruthful. **unveracity** (-răs′ i ti), *n.* **unverifiable** (-ver′ i fī ȧbl), *a.* **unverified,** *a.* **unversed** (-vĕrst′), *a.* Not versed or skilled (in). **unvexed** (-vekst′), *a.* **unvictualled** (-vitld′), *a.* **unvindicated** (-vin′ di kā tėd), *a.* **unviolated** (-vī ȯ lā tėd), *a.* **unvisited** (viz′ i tėd), *a.* **unvitiated** (-vish′ i ā tėd), *a.* Not corrupted; pure. **unvoiced** (-voist′), *a.* Not spoken, not uttered; (*Phon.*) not voiced. **unvote** (-vōt′), *v.t.* To retract or cancel by voting. **unvouched,** *a.* Not attested, not vouched (for). **unvowelled** (-vou′ ėld), *a.* **unwake** (-wākt′), **unwakened** (-wā′ kėnd), *a.* **unwalled** (-wawld′), *a.* **unwanted** (-won′ tėd), *a.* **unwarlike** (-wawr′ līk), *a.* **unwarmed** (-wawrmd′), *a.* **unwarned** (-wawrnd′), *a.* **unwarp** (-wawrp′), *v.t.* To restore from a warped condition. **unwarped,** *a.* **unwarrantable** (-wor′ ȧn tȧbl), *a.* Not defensible or justifiable, inexcusable; improper, illegitimate. **unwarrantableness,** *n.* **unwarrantably,** *adv.* **unwarranted,** *a.* Not authorized; not guaranteed. **unwary** (-wâr′ i), *a.* **unwarily,** *adv.* **unwariness,** *n.* **unwashed** (-wosht′), *a.* Not washed. **the great unwashed:** The mob, the rabble. **unwasted** (-wā′ stėd), *a.* **unwatched** (-wocht′), *a.* **unwatchful,** *a.* **unwatchfulness,** *n.* **unwatered** (-waw′ tėrd), *a.* Not watered, not furnished with water, not diluted, not irrigated. **unwavering** (-wā′ vėr ing), *a.* Steady, steadfast, firm. **unwaveringly,** *adv.* **unweaned** (-wēnd′), *a.* **unwearable** (-wâr′ ȧbl), *a.* **unwearied** (-wēr′ id), *a.* **unweariedly** (-wēr′ i ėd li), *adv.* **unweary,** *a.* **unwearying,** *a.* **unwearyingly,** *adv.* **unweave** (-wēv′), *v.t.* To undo (something that has been woven); to separate the threads of. **unwed, unwedded** (-wed′ ėd), *a.* **unweeded** (-wē′ dėd), *a.* ***unweeting** [UNWITTING]. **unweighed** (-wād′), *a.* **unwelcome** (-wel′ kȯm), *a.* **unwelcomed,** *a.* **unwell** (-wel′), *a.* Not well; sick, indisposed. **unwept** (-wept′), *a.* Not lamented, not mourned. **unwhipped** (-hwipt′), *a.* **unwhispered** (-hwis′ pėrd), *a.* **unwhitened** (-hwī′ tėnd), *a.* **unwhitewashed,** *a.* **unwholesome** (-hōl′ sȯm), *a.* **unwholesomely,** *adv.* **unwholesomeness,** *n.* **unwieldy** (-wēl′ di), *a.* That cannot be easily wielded; bulky, ponderous, clumsy. **unwieldily,** *adv.* **unwieldiness,** *n.* **unwifely** (-wīf′ li), *a.* **unwill** (-wil′), *v.t.* To will the reverse of. ***unwilled,** *a.* **unwilling** (-wil′ ing), *a.* Not willing; averse, reluctant, undesirous (of, to, for, etc.); involuntary. **unwillingly,** *adv.* **unwillingness,** *n.* **unwind** (-wīnd′), *v.t.* (*past & p.p.* **-wound,** -wound) To pull out (something that has been wound); to free from entanglement; *v.i.* To become unwound. **unwinged** (-wingd′), *a.* **unwinking,** *a.* Watchful, vigilant. **unwisdom** (-wiz′ dȯm), *n.* Lack of wisdom; folly. **unwise** (-wīz′), *a.* Not wise, without judgment; foolish. **unwisely,** *adv.* **unwished** (-wisht′), *a.* Not desired; not sought (for). **unwithdrawn** (-*with* drawn′), *a.* **unwithered** (-wi*th*′ ėrd), *a.* **unwithering,** *a.* ***unwithstood** (-*with* stud′), *a.* **unwitnessed** (-wit′ nėst), *a.* ***unwitting** (-wit′ ing) [WIT (I)], *a.* Unconscious, unintentional, inadvertent. **unwittingly,** *adv.* **unwomanly** (-wum′ ȧn li), *a.* **unwon** (-wŭn′), *a.* **unwonted** (-wōn′ tėd), *a.* Not accustomed. **unwontedly,** *adv.* **unwontedness,** *n.* **unwooded** (-wud′ ėd), *a.* **unwooed** (-wood′), *a.* **unwork** (-wĕrk′), *v.t.* To undo, to destroy. **unworkable,** *a.* **unworkmanlike,** *a.* **unworldly** (-wĕrld′ li), *a.* Not worldly, spiritually minded; pertaining to spiritual things. **unworldliness,** *n.* **unworn** (-wôrn′), *a.* Not impaired by use. **unworshipped** (-wĕr′ shipt), *a.* **unworthy,** *a.* Not worthy, not deserving (of); not becoming, not seemly, discreditable. **unworthily,** *adv.* **unworthiness,** *n.* **unwound** (-wound), *past & p.p.* [UNWIND]. **unwounded** (-woon′ dėd), *a.* **unwoven** (-wō′ vėn), *a.* **unwrap** (-răp′), *v.t.* **unwreaked** (-rēkt′), *a.* **unwreath** (-rēth′), *v.t.* **unwrinkle** (-rinkl′), *v.t.* and *i.* **unwritable** (rī′ tȧbl), *a.* **unwritten** (-rit′ ėn), *a.* Not written; traditional; not distinctly expressed, not written upon, blank. **unwritten law:** That not formulated in statutes, etc., esp. that homicide is justifiable in certain circumstances, *e.g.* defence of one's honour. **unwrought** (-rawt′), *a.* **unwrung** (-rŭng′), *a.* Not pinched or galled. **unyielding** (-yēl′ ding), *a.* Unbending, stiff; firm, obstinate. **unyieldingly,** *adv.* **unyieldingness,** *n.* **unyoke** (yōk′), *v.t.* To loose from or as from a yoke; *v.i.* To give over work. **unyoked** (-yōkt), *a.* Freed or loosed from the yoke; not yoked; *(*fig.*) licentious, unrestrained. **unyouthful** (-ūth′ fủl), *a.* **unzealous** (-zel′ ủs), *a.*

up (ŭp) [A.-S. *ūp, ūpp* (cp. Dut. *op*, G. *auf*), cogn. with Gr. *hupo*, under, Sansk. *upa*, near, under, and Eng. OVER], *adv.* To a higher place, position, degree, amount, rank, musical pitch, etc.; to London, to a capital, university, a place farther north, or other place regarded as higher; to or in an erect or standing posture or a position or condition for action, out of bed, on one's legs, in the saddle; in arms, in a state of proficiency; above the horizon; so as to be level with, as high or as far as, equal (to); completely, entirely, effectually. *prep.* From a lower to a higher place or point of; in an ascending direction on or along, towards the higher part of; towards the interior of; at or in a higher part of. *a.* Moving, sloping, or directed towards a higher or more central part; towards the capital. *n.* That which is up. **time is up:** The allotted time is past; the appointed moment has arrived. **to come up with:** To overtake. **up-and-coming:** Enterprising, alert, keen. **up and doing:** Active and busy. **up and down:** Here and there; in one place and another; from one place to another; in every direction. **up the pole:** Eccentric, crazy. **up-end,** *v.t.* To stand on end, to raise on one end. **ups and downs:** Rises and falls, undulations; vicissitudes, changes of fortune. **up to:** To an equal height with; equal to; (*slang*) to be incumbent upon. **up to anything:** (*colloq.*) Ready for any devilment, sport, etc. **up to date:** (*colloq.*) Recent, abreast of the times. **up to snuff:** (*colloq.*) Knowing, cunning, acute, sharp. **what's up:** What is going on?

up- [prec.], *pref.*

upanishad (oo pa′ ni-, -păn′ i shăd) [Sansk.], *n.* One of the philosophical treatises forming the third division of the Vedas.

upas (ū′ pȧs) [Malay, poison], *n.* The upas-tree; the poisonous sap of this and other Malaysian trees; (*fig.*) corrupting or pernicious influence. **upas-tree,** *n.* A Javanese tree, *Antiaris toxicaria*, the acrid milky juice of which contains a virulent poison, used for poisoning arrows, and formerly believed to destroy animal or vegetable life in its immediate neighbourhood.

upbear (ŭp bâr′), *v.t.* (*past* **-bore,** *p.p.* **-borne,** -bôrn) To bear or lift up; to sustain aloft; to support. **upbind** (-bīnd′), *v.t.* To bind or fasten up. **upblaze** (-blāz′), *v.i.* To blaze up.

upbraid (ủp brād′) [A.-S. *upbregdan*, to lay hold of, to upbraid (UP-, BRAID (I))], *v.t.* To charge; to reproach (with); to reprove with severity. *v.i.* To chide. **upbraider,** *n.* **upbraidingly,** *adv.* ***upbray** (-brā′), *v.t.* To upbraid, to abuse. *n.* Reproach, abuse.

upbringing (ŭp′ bring ing), *n.* Bringing up, education. ***upbrought** (-brawt′), *a.* **upbuild** (-bild′), *v.t.* **upburst** (ŭp′ bĕrst), *n.* A bursting up. **upby** (ŭp′ bī), *adv.* (*Sc.*) A little farther up, up the way. **upcast** (-kast′), *v.t.* To cast or throw up; *a.* (ŭp′ kast, *predicatively* ŭp kast′) Directed upwards, cast up. *n.* A casting or throwing upwards; (*Mining*) the shaft by which air ascends after ventilating a mine. ***upcheer** (ŭp chēr′), *v.t.* To encourage, to inspirit. ***upcoil** (-koil′), *v.t.* and *i.* To coil up. **up-country** (ŭp′ kủn tri), *adv.* and *a.* Towards the interior of a country, inland. ***upcurl** (-kĕrl′), *v.t.* and *i.* ***upfill** (-fil′), *v.t.* To fill up. ***upgather** (-găth′ ėr), *v.t.* To gather up; to contract. **upgrowth** (ŭp′ grōth), *n.* The act or process of growing up; that which grows up. ***upgrow,** *v.i.* ***upgush** (-gŭsh′), *v.t.* ***uphand** (ŭp′ hănd), *a.* Lifted by hand. ***upheap** (-hēp′), *v.t.* **upheave** (-hēv′), *v.t.* To lift up from beneath. *v.i.* To heave up. **upheaval,** *n.* The act or process of heaving up; (*Geol.*) an elevation of part of the crust of the earth; (*fig.*) a violent disturbance, revolution, etc. **upheld,** *past & p.p.* [UPHOLD]. **uphill** (ŭp′ hil), *a.* Leading or going up a hill; (*fig.*) difficult, arduous, severe; *adv.* (ŭp hil′) In an ascending direction, upwards. ***uphoard** (-hôrd′), *v.i.*

uphold (ŭp hōld′), *v.t.* To hold up, to keep erect; to support, to sustain, to maintain; to defend; to approve, to countenance. **upholder,** *n.*

upholster (ŭp hōl′ stėr) [from UPHOLSTERER, formerly *upholdster, upholder* (UP-, HOLDER, HOLD, -STER)], *v.t.* To furnish with curtains, carpets, furniture, etc.; to furnish or adorn (chairs, etc.) with stuffing, cushions, coverings, etc.; to cover (with, etc.). **upholsterer,** *n.* **upholstery,** *n.*

uphroe (ū′ frō) [Dut. *juffrouw*, young woman (*jung*, YOUNG, *vrouw*, woman)], *n.* (*Naut.*) A long wooden block pierced with holes for reeving a cord, esp. for adjusting an awning.

upkeep (ŭp′ kēp), *n.* Maintenance. **upland** (ŭp′ lȧnd), *n.* The higher part of a district (*sing.* or *pl.*); *a.* Situated on or pertaining to the uplands. ***uplay** (-ā′), *v.t.* ***uplean** (-lēn′), *v.i.* **uplift** (-lift′), *v.t.* To lift up, to raise. *n.* (ŭp′ lift) An uplifting or upheaval; (*colloq.*) spiritual improvement, edification. *a.* Uplifted. ***uplook** (-luk′), *v.t.* **uplying** (ŭp′ lī ing), *a.* **upmaking** (ŭp′ mā king), *n.* A filling of planks, etc., inserted between a ship's bottom and the bilge-ways before launching. ***up-lock** (-lok′), *v.t.* To lock up. ***upmost,** *a.* Uppermost, topmost.

upon (ủ pon′) [A.-S. *uppon, uppan* (UP, ON)], *prep.* and *adv.* On.

upper (ŭp′ ėr) [comp. of UP], *a.* Higher in place; superior in rank, dignity, etc. *n.* The part of a boot or shoe above the sole. **upper case:** (*Print.*) The case holding capitals, reference marks, etc. **upper deck,** *n.* (*Naut.*) The full-length deck of a ship above the water-level. **upper hand:** Superiority, mastery. **The Upper House:** The House of Lords. **the upper ten (thousand):** Claimants to social superiority; the aristocracy. **upper works:** (*Naut.*) The parts above the water when a ship is in proper trim for a voyage. **uppermost,** *a.* Highest in place, rank, authority, etc.; predominant. *adv.* In the highest place; on, at, or to the top.

uppish (ŭp′ ish), *a.* Self-assertive, pretentious, putting on airs, snobbish. **uppishly,** *adv.* **uppishness,** *n.*

upraise (ŭp rāz′), *v.t.* To raise up; to lift. **uprear** (-rēr′), *v.t.*

upright (ŭp′ rīt, *predicatively*, -rīt′), *a.* Erect, perpendicular; righteous, honest, not deviating from moral rectitude. *adv.* Erect, vertically. *n.* An upright timber, pillar, post, or other part of a structure; an upright piano, etc. **uprightly,** *adv.* **uprightness,** *n.*

***uprise** (ŭp rīz′), *v.i.* (*past* **-rose,** -rōz, **-risen,** -riz′ ėn) To rise up. *n.* (ŭp′ rīz) An uprising. **uprising,**

n. The act of rising up, esp. from bed; an insurrection, a rising, a riot. ***uprist,** *past.*

uproar (ŭp′ rôr) [Dut. *oproer* (UP, *roeren*, to stir, cp. G. *rühren*, A.-S. *hreran*, Swed. *röra*, Dan. *röre*, Icel. *hræra*)], *n.* A noisy tumult, a violent disturbance, bustle and clamour. **v.i.* To make an uproar. **uproarious,** *a.* **uproariously,** *adv.* Noisily; hilariously. **uproariousness,** *n.*

***uproll** (ŭp rōl′), *v.t.* To roll up. **uproot** (ŭp root′), *v.t.* To tear up by or as by the roots. **uprose,** *past* [UPRISE]. ***uprouse,** *v.t.* **uprush** (ŭp′ rŭsh), *n.* ***upsend** (-send′), *v.t.* To send, cast, or throw up.

upset (ŭp set′), *v.t.* To overturn; to put out of one's normal state, to put out of sorts; to shorten and thicken (a tire or other metal object) by hammering or pressure. *v.i.* To be overturned. *n.* (ŭp′ set) The act of upsetting; the state of being upset. **upset price:** The lowest price at which property is offered for sale by auction, a reserve price.

upshot (ŭp′ shot) [UP-, SHOT, p.p. of SHOOT], *n.* The final issue, result, or conclusion (of a matter).

upside-down (ŭp′ sīd doun′) [M.E. *up so down*, up as it were down], *adv.* and *a.* With the upper part under; (*fig.*) in complete disorder and confusion.

***upspring** (ŭp′ spring), *n.* A leap in the air; an upstart. **v.i.* (-spring′) To spring up. **up-stage,** *a.* (*colloq.*) Stand-offish, supercilious. **upstair** (ŭp′ stâr), *a.* Pertaining to or in an upper story. **upstairs** (-stârz′), *adv.* In or to an upper story. ***upstand** (-stănd′), *v.i.* (*past* **-stood**). **upstart** (ŭp′ start), *n.* One who rises suddenly from a humble position to wealth, power, or consequence; one who assumes an arrogant bearing. ***upstay** (-stā′), *v.t.* To sustain, to support. **up-stream** (ŭp strēm′), *adv.* Against the stream; *a.* (ŭp′ strēm) Moving or directed up-stream. **upstroke** (ŭp′ strōk), *n.* An upward line in writing. ***upswarm** (-swôrm′), *v.t.* To raise in swarms; *v.i.* To rise in swarms. ***upswell** (-swel′), *v.i.* **uptake** (ŭp′ tāk), *n.* The act of lifting or taking up; (*Sc.*) understanding, apprehension; (*Min.*) the uptake shaft. *(-tāk′), *v.t.* To take up; to succour. **quick in the uptake:** Quick-witted, mentally alert. **uptake shaft:** (*Min.*) A shaft for the upward passage of air from underground. **uptear** (-târ′), *v.t.* **upthrow** (ŭp′ thrō), *n.* A throwing up, an upheaval; (*Geol.*) the upward displacement on one side of a fault. **upthrust** (ŭp′ thrŭst), *n.* (*Geol.*) An upheaval. ***uptie** (-tī′), *v.t.* To tie up; to twist. **uptown** (ŭp′ toun), *a.* Situated in, living in, or belonging to the upper part of a town; (*Am.*) the residential area of a town or city. ***uptrain** (-trān′), *v.t.* To bring up, to educate. **upturn** (-tĕrn′), *v.t.* To turn up, esp. in ploughing.

upward (ŭp′ wȧrd), *a.* Directed, turned, or moving towards a higher place. **upwardly,** *adv.* Upwards. **upwards,** *adv.* Towards a higher place, in an upward direction; towards the source or spring; more. **upwards of:** More than.

***upwell** (ŭp wel′), *v.i.* To well up. **upwhirl** (-hwĕrl′), *v.t.* **upwind** (-wīnd′), *v.t.* **upwrought** (-rawt′), *a.*

uræmia (ū rē′ mi ȧ) [mod. L. (Gr. *ouron*, urine, *haima*, blood)], *n.* (*Path.*) A morbid condition caused by the retention of urea and other noxious substances in the kidneys and bladder. **uræmic,** *a.*

uræum (ū rē′ ŭm) [mod. L., from Gr. *ouraion*, neut. of *ouraios* from *oura*, tail], *n.* (*pl.* **-æa**) (*Ornith.*) The posterior half of a bird.

uræus (ū rē′ ŭs) [Gr. *ouraios*, from *oura*, tail], *n.* The serpent emblem worn on the head-dress of ancient Egyptian divinities and kings.

Ural-Altaic (ūr′ ȧl ăl tā′ ik), *a.* Of or pertaining to the Ural and Altaic mountain ranges or the people inhabiting them; (*Philol.*) denoting a family of Mongoloid, Finnic, and allied languages of agglutinative structure spoken in N. Europe and Asia.

Uralite (ūr′ ȧ līt) [*Ural*, as prec., -ITE], *n.* (*Min.*) A pyroxene resembling hornblende in specific gravity and cleavage. **uralitic** (-lit′ ik), *a.* **uralization** (-zā′ shŭn), *n.* Metamorphic change of pyroxene or augite to hornblende.

Urania (ū rā′ ni ȧ) [L., from Gr. *Ourania*, the heavenly one, fem. of *ouranios*, from *ouranos*, see URANUS], *n.* (*Gr. Myth.*) The muse of astronomy. **Uranian,** *a.*

uranium (ū rā′ ni ŭm) [URAN-US, -IUM], *n.* A rare, heavy, white, hexad metallic element found in pitchblende, etc. It is radioactive and fissionable, as in the first atom bomb. **uranium bomb,** *n.* An atom bomb using uranium (not plutonium or hydrogen) as explosive. **uranic** (-răn′ ik), **uranous** (ūr′ ȧ nŭs), *a.* **uranite,** *n.* (*Min.*) Uranium copper phosphate, an ore of uranium. **uranitic** (-nit′ ik), *a.*

uranography (ūr ȧ nog′ rȧ fi) [*urano-*, from foll., -GRAPHY], *n.* Descriptive astronomy. **uranographic, -al** (-graf′ ik, -ȧl), *a.* **uranographist** *n.* **uranology** (-nol′ ȯ ji) [LOGY], *n.* Astronomy. **uranometry** (-nom′ ė tri) [-METRY], *n.* The measurement of the heavens or of stellar distances; a map of the heavens showing the relative positions and apparent magnitudes of the stars. **uranoscopy** (-nos′ kȯ pi) [-SCOPY], *n.* Observation of the heavenly bodies.

Uranus (ūr′ ȧ nŭs) [Gr. *ouranos*, heaven], *n.* (*Gr. Myth.*) The most ancient of all the Greek gods, son of Ge and father of Kronos or Saturn and the Titans; (*Astron.*) a planet situated between Saturn and Neptune, discovered by Sir William Herschel in 1781.

urare [CURARE].

urate (ūr′ ȧt), *n.* (*Chem.*) A salt of uric acid. **uratic** (ū răt′ ik), *a.* **uratoma** (-tō′ mȧ), *n.* (*Path.*) A deposit of urates in the joints or tissues. **uratosis** (-tō′ sis), *n.* A morbid condition due to this.

urbacity (ĕr băs′ i ti) [as foll.] Excess of civic pride.

urban (ĕr′ bȧn) [L. *urbānus*, from *urbs urbis*, city], *a.* Of or pertaining to, situated or living in a city or town. **urban district:** A district comprising a small town or towns with a small aggregate population or not yet incorporated as a borough. **urbanize,** *v.t.*

urbane (ŭr bān′) [as prec.], *a.* Courteous, polite, suave, refined, polished. **urbanely,** *adv.* **urbanity** (-băn′ i ti), *n.*

urceolus (ŭr sē′ ȯ lŭs) [L. *urceolus*, dim. of *urceus*, pitcher], *n.* (*pl.* **-li,** -lī) (*Bot.*) A pitcher- or urn-shaped organ; (*Zool.*) the external case or sheath of a rotifer. **urceolar, -late** (ĕr′ sė ȯ lȧr, -lāt), *a.* (*Bot.*) Pitcher-shaped, with a swelling body and contracted orifice.

urchin (ĕr′ chin) [M.E. *urchon*, O.North.F. *herichun* (F. *hérisson*), ult. from L. *ēricius*, from *ēr*, hedgehog, cogn. with Gr. *chēr*], *n.* A roguish, mischievous boy, a youngster, a child; a sea-urchin; *a hedgehog; *an elf, a fairy. *a.* Elfin, roguish.

Urdu (oor′ doo) [Hind., camp. as arising in the camps, etc., as a means of communication between the Mohammedans and the conquered Hindus], *n.* The Hindustani language.

***ure** (ūr) [O.F. *eure*, *uevre* (F. *œuvre*), L. *opera*, work], *n.* Practice, use.

-ure [F., from L. *-ūra*, added to p.p. stems of verbs], *suf.* Forming abstract nouns, as *censure, portraiture, seizure.*

urea (ū rē′ ȧ) [Gr. *ouron*, urine], *n.* (*Chem.*) A soluble crystalline compound contained in urine, esp. of mammals. **ureal,** *a.* **ureameter** (-ăm′ ė tėr) [-METER], *n.* An apparatus for determining the amount of urea in the urine.

Uredo (ū rē′ dō) [L. *ūrēdo, -dinis*, blight, from *urere*, to burn], *n.* (*Bot.*) A form-genus or stage typical of the *Uredinales*, or rust-fungi, a group of higher fungi that are destitute of sexual organs and are parasitic on plants. **uredineous** (-din′ ė ŭs), *a.* **uredospore** (ū rē′ dȯ spôr), *n.* A non-sexual spore in rust-fungi. **uredosporic** (-spor′ ik), *a.* **uredosporiferous** (-spȯ rif′ ėr ŭs), *a.*

***-uret** [*-ur* (SULPH-UR), -ET], *suf.* (*Chem.*) A suffix for compounds or derivatives now superseded by -IDE.

ureter (ū rē′ tėr) [Gr. *ourētēr*, from *ourein*, to make water], *n.* The duct conveying the urine from the kidneys into the bladder. **ureteritis** (-ī′ tis), *n.* Inflammation of the ureter.

urethra (ū rē′ thrȧ) [L., from Gr. *ourēthra*, as prec.], *n.* (*pl.* **-thræ**) The duct by which the urine is discharged from the bladder. **urethral,** *a.* **urethritis** (-thrī′ tis), *n.* Inflammation of the urethra. **urethro-,** *comb. form.* **urethrocele** (ū rē′ thrȯ sēl) [-CELE], *n.* **urethroscope** (ū rē′ thrō skōp), *n.* An instrument for examining the interior of the urethra. **urethrotomy** (-throt′ ȯ mi) [-TOMY], *n.* Incision of the urethra.

uretic [DIURETIC].

urge (ĕrj) [L. *urgēre*, cogn. with Gr. *heirgein*, to repress, Eng. WREAK], *v.t.* To drive; to impel; to force onwards; to press earnestly with argument, entreaty, etc., to importune; to press the acceptance or adoption of, to insist on.

urgency (ĕr′ jėn si), *n.* The quality or state of being urgent; pressure of necessity, esp. as a plea for giving a matter precedence in a deliberative assembly.

urgent (ĕr′ jėnt), *a.* Pressing, demanding early attention; demanding or soliciting with importunity. **urgently,** *adv.* **urger,** *n.*

uric [URINE].

Urim and Thummim (ūr′ im, thŭm′ im) [Heb. *ūrīm*, pl. of *ūr*, light, *tummīm*, pl. of *tom*, perfection], *n.pl.* Objects connected with the breastplate of the Jewish high-priest, apparently of oracular nature.

urinal (ūr′ i nȧl, ū rī′ nȧl), *a.* Toilet-vessel or fixed receptacle for the use of persons passing urine; a public or private room, building, enclosure, etc., containing these; a glass receptacle for holding urine for medical inspection.

urine (ūr′ in) [F., from L. *ūrīna*, cogn. with Gr. *ouron*, Sansk. *vāri*, water, A.-S. *wær*, the sea], *n.* A pale-yellow fluid with an acid reaction secreted from the blood by the kidneys, stored in the bladder, and discharged through the urethra, the chief means for the removal of nitrogenous and saline matters resulting from the decay of tissue. **uric,** *a.* **uric acid:** A white, tasteless and inodorous, almost insoluble compound found chiefly in excrement of birds and reptiles, and in small quantities in the urine of mammals. **urinary,** *a.* Pertaining to urine. *n.* A reservoir for urine, etc., for manure. **urinate,** *v.i.* To pass urine. **urination** (-nā′ shŭn), *n.* **urinative** (ūr′ i nā tiv), *a.* Provoking the discharge of urine; diuretic. **uriniferous** (-nif′ ėr ŭs), *a.* **urino-,** *comb. form.* **urinogenital** [GENITO-URINARY]. **urinology** (-nol′ ȯ ji) [-LOGY], *n.* The branch of medical science dealing with the urine, etc. **urinometer** (-nom′ ė tėr), *n.* An instrument for ascertaining the specific gravity of urine. **urinometric** (-met′ rik), *a.* **urinometry** (-nom′ ė tri), *n.* **urinoscopy** (-nos′ kȯ pi) [-SCOPY], *n.* Uromancy. **urinous,** *a.*

urite (ūr′ īt) [Gr. *oura*, tail, -ITE], *n.* The ventral portion of an abdominal segment in arthropods.

urman (ĕr′ mȧn) [Siberian], *n.* A large tract of swampy coniferous forest country in Siberia.

urn (ĕrn) [F. *urne*, L. *urna*], *n.* A vase with a foot and usually a rounded body formerly used for preserving the ashes of the dead, for holding water, as a measure, and other purposes; (*fig.*) something in which the remains of the dead are preserved, a grave; a vase-shaped vessel with a tap, and usually a spirit-lamp or other heater, for keeping tea, coffee, bouillon, etc., hot. *v.t.* To enclose in or as in an urn. **urn-shaped,** *a.* **urnful,** *n.*

uro- (1) [Gr. *oura*, tail], *comb. form.*

uro- (2) [URINO-], *comb. form.*

urochord (ūr′ ȯ kôrd) [URO- (1), CHORD], *n.* The notochord of larval ascidians and some tunicates; an individual of the *Urochordata* or *Tunicata.*

urocyst (ūr′ ȯ sist) [URO- (2), CYST], *n.* The urinary bladder. **urocystic** (-sis′ tik), *a.*

urogenital [GENITO-URINARY]. **urology** [URINOLOGY, etc., see URINE]. **uromancy** (ūr′ ȯ măn si) [-MANCY], *n.* Determination of disease by inspection of the urine, also called urinoscopy.

uropod (ū′ rō pod) [URO- (1), Gr. *podos*, a foot], *n.* (*Zool.*) An abdominal appendage of the *Malacostraca* division of the Crustacea.

uropygium (ūr ȯ pij′ i ŭm) [URO- (1), Gr. *pugē*, rump], *n.* (*Ornith.*) The terminal part of the body or the rump. **uropygial,** *a.* **uropyloric** (-pī lor′ ik) [PYLORIC], *n.* Pertaining to the posterior part of the pyloric division of the stomach in some crustaceans. **urosacral** (-sā′ krȧl) [SACRAL], *a.* Pertaining to the caudal and the sacral parts of the vertebral column.

uroscopy [URINOSCOPY, see URINE].

urosome (ūr′ ȯ sōm) [URO- (1), Gr. *sōma*, body], *n.* The abdomen or post-thoracic division of the body of an arthropod; the terminal somatome of a vertebrate. **urosthene** (ūr′ ȯs thēn) [Gr. *sthenos*, strength], *n.* An animal with a powerful or highly developed tail, as a cetacean. **urosthenic** (-thēn′ ik), *a.* **urostyle** (ūr′ ȯ stīl), *n.* A bone forming the posterior extremity of the vertebral column in the tailless amphibians. **urostylar** (-stī′ lȧr), *a.*

urotoxic (ūr ȯ tok′ sik) [URO- (2), TOXIC], *a.* Denoting the poisonous nature and effects of urinary matter carried into the system. **urotoxicity** (-tok sis′ i ti), *n.* **urotoxin,** *n.* A poison normally excreted by the urine. **urotoxy** (ūr′ ȯ tok si), *n.*

urry (ŭr′ i) [cp. Gael. *uir*, earth], *n.* (*prov.*) A blue or black clay lying close to a vein of coal.

Ursa (ĕr′ sȧ) [L., she-bear], *n.* (*Astron.*) The Bear. **Ursa Major:** The constellation, the Great Bear. **Ursa Minor:** The Little Bear. **ursiform,** *a.* Like a bear. **ursine** (sīn, -sin), *a.* Pertaining to or resembling a bear; (*Ent.*) thickly covered with bristles (of some caterpillars).

urson (ĕr′ sȯn) [var. of URCHIN], *n.* A N. American porcupine, *Erethizon dorsatus.*

Ursuline (ĕr′ sū lin, -līn) [St. *Ursula*, -INE], *n.* One of an order of nuns founded in 1537, devoted chiefly to nursing and the education of girls. *a.* Belonging to this.

urticaceous (ĕr ti kā′ shŭs) [L. *urtica*, nettle, -ACEOUS], *a.* (*Bot.*) Of or having the character of nettles. **urticaria** (ĕr ti kâr′ i a), *n.* (*Path.*) Nettle-rash. **urticate** (ĕr′ ti kāt), *v.t.* To sting with or as with nettles; to whip a benumbed or paralytic limb with nettles to restore feeling. **urtication** (-kā′ shŭn), *n.*

urubu (oo′ ru boo) [native name], *n.* The Central American black vulture.

urus (ūr′ ŭs) [L., from Gr. *ouros*], *n.* An extinct wild ox, *Bos urus* or *primigenius*, the aurochs.

us [I (2) and WE].

usage (ū zij), *n.* The manner of using or treating, treatment; customary or habitual practice, esp. as authorizing a right, etc.; (*Law*) a uniform and recognized practice; *conduct, behaviour.

usance (ū′ zȧns), *n.* A period of time allowed for payment of a foreign bill of exchange.

use (1) (ūs) [A.-F. and O.F. *us*, L. *ūsus -ūs*, from *utī*, to use (in legal senses from A.-F. *oes*, L. *opus*, employment, need)], *n.* The act of using; the state of being used; employment in or application to a purpose; occasion, need, or liberty to use; the quality of being useful or serving a purpose; utility, serviceableness, custom, practice, wont, usage; a form of ritual, etc., peculiar to a church, diocese, or country; (*Law*) enjoyment of the benefit or profit of lands and tenements held by another in trust for the beneficiary. **in use:** Being employed; in customary practice. **use and wont:** Common or customary practice. **useful** (ūs′ fŭl), *a.* Of use, serving a purpose; producing or able to produce; good, beneficial profitable, advantageous; (*slang*) clever, competent, highly satisfactory. **usefully,** *adv.* **usefulness,** *n.* **useless,** *a.* Not of use, serving no useful end or purpose; unavailing, ineffectual; (*slang*) out of sorts, unfit. **uselessly,** *adv.* **uselessness,** *n.*

use (2) (ūz), *v.t.* To employ, to apply to a purpose, to put into operation; to turn to account, to avail oneself of; to treat in a specified way; to consume or exhaust as material, to wear out; to make a practice of; (*usu. in p.p.*) to accustom, to habituate, to inure. *v.i.* (*usu. in past*) To be accustomed, to be wont, to make it one's constant practice to. **usable** (ū′ zȧbl), *a.* Capable of being used. **user** (ū′ zėr) (1), *n.* One who uses. **user** (2), *n.* (*Law*) Continued use or enjoyment of a thing.

usher (ŭsh′ ėr) [F. *huissier*, L. *ostiārium*, from *ostium*, door], *n.* An officer or servant acting as door-keeper (esp. in a court or public hall), or whose business it is to introduce strangers or to walk before a person of rank; an under-teacher or assistant in a school; a seat-attendant at a cinema, theatre, etc. *v.t.* To act as usher to; to introduce, as a forerunner or harbinger, bring or show (in, etc.). **usherette,** *n.* Woman usher at a cinema or theatre. **ushership,** *n.*

usquebaugh (ŭs′ kwė ba, -baw) [Ir. *uisge beatha* (*uisge*, water, see WHISKY (1), *beatha*, life, cogn. with Gr. *bios*, L. *vīta*)], *n.* Whisky; an Irish liqueur made of brandy, spices, etc.

Ustilago (ŭs ti lā′ gō) [late L., from *ustus*, p.p. of *ūrere*, to burn], *n.* A genus of parasitic fungi typical of the smut-fungi. **ustilaginous** (-lăj i nůs), *a.*

ustion (ŭs′ tyůn) [L. *ustio*, from *urere*, to burn, p.p. *ustus*], *n.* The act of burning; the state of being burned; (*Surg.*) cauterization. ***ustorious,** *a.* Having the quality of burning. **ustulate,** *a.* Scorched or coloured as if by fire. **ustulation** (-lā′ shůn), *n.* The act of burning, scorching, drying, etc., esp. the burning of wine.

usual (ū′ zhū ȧl) [L. *ūsuālis*, from *ūsus*, USE], *a.* Such as ordinarily occurs, customary, habitual, common, ordinary, frequent. **usually,** *adv.* **usualness,** *n.*

usucaption, -capion (ū zū kăp′ shůn, -kāp′ yůn) [L. *ūsūcapio -ōnis* (*ūsū*, by use, see USE, *capere*, to take)], *n.* (*Law*) The acquisition of the title or right to property by uninterrupted possession for a certain term of years.

usufruct (ū′ zū frŭkt) [L. *ūsusfructus* (USE, *fructus*, FRUIT)], *n.* Right to the use and enjoyment of property belonging to another without waste or destruction of its substance. *v.t.* To hold in or subject to usufruct. **usufructuary** (-frŭk′ tū ȧ ri), *n.* One who has usufruct. *a.* Relating to or of the nature of a usufruct.

usurer (ū′ zhůr ėr) [O.F. *usurier*, med. L. *ūsūrārius*, from L. *ūsūra*, use, enjoyment, interest, from *ūsus*, USE], *n.* One who lends money at exorbitant interest. ***usuring,** **usurious** (ū′ zhėr ing, ū zhoor′-, -zūr i ůs), *a.* Practising usury, exacting exorbitant interest; pertaining to or of the nature of usury. **usuriously,** *adv.* **usuriousness,** *n.* **usury** (ū′ zhů ri), *n.* The practice of lending money at exorbitant interest, esp. higher than that allowed by law; exorbitant interest; *lending at interest or the taking of interest.

usurp (ū zěrp′) [F. *usurper*, L. *ūsurpāre*, to employ, to acquire, etym. doubtful], *v.t.* To seize or take possession of without right. **v.i.* To encroach (upon). **usurpation** (-pā′ shůn), *n.* ***usurpatory** (ū zěr′ pȧ tȯr i), *a.* **usurper,** *n.* **usurping,** *adv.*

usury [USURER].

ut (ut) [L., see GAMUT], *n.* (*Mus.*) The first or key note in Guido's musical scale, now usu. superseded by do (see DO (2)).

***utas** (ū′ tȧs), ***utis** [M.E. *utas*, A.-F. *utaves*, O.F. *oitauves*, pl. of *oitauve*, L. *octava*, eighth, from *octo*, eight], *n.* The octave or eight days of a feast; merriment, festivity.

utensil (ū ten′ sil) [M.F. *utensile*, L. *ūtensilia*, utensils, from *ūtensilis*, fit for use, from *ūtī*, to USE], *n.* An implement, an instrument, esp. one used in cookery or domestic work.

uterine (ū′ tėr īn, -in) [M.F. *uterin*, fem. *-ine*, late L. *uterīnus*, from L. *uterus*, womb], *a.* Pertaining to the womb; born of the same mother but not the same father. **uteritis** (-ī′ tis), *n.* Inflammation of the womb. **utero-,** *comb. form.* **uterogestation** (-jes tā′ shůn), *n.* The development of the embryo within the uterus. **uteromania** (-mā′ ni ȧ), *n.* Nymphomania. **uterus,** *n.* (*pl.* **-ri**) The womb.

utilitarian (ū til i târ′ i ȧn), *a.* Of or pertaining to utility or to utilitarianism. *n.* An advocate of utilitarianism. **utilitarianism,** *n.* The ethical doctrine that actions are right in proportion to their usefulness or as they tend to promote happiness; the doctrine that the end and criterion of public action is the greatest happiness of the greatest number.

utility (ū til′ i ti) [F. *utilité*, L. *ūtilitātem*, nom. *-tas*, from *ūtilis*, useful, from *ūtī*, to USE], *n.* Usefulness, serviceableness; that which is useful; utilitarianism, the greatest happiness of the greatest number; (*Theat.*) a utility-man; a form of goods definitely planned to fit in with a rationing scheme; goods mass-produced to standard designs. **utility-man,** *n.* An actor employed to take unimportant parts as required.

utilize (ū′ ti līz), *v.t.* To make use of, to turn to account. **utilizable,** *a.* **utilization,** *n.*

utmost (ŭt′ mōst) [A.-S. *ūtemest*, double, superlative of *ūt*, OUT], *a.* Being or situated at the farthest point or extremity; farthest, extreme, greatest, ultimate. *n.* The utmost extent or degree.

Utopia (ū tō′ pi ȧ) [lit. nowhere, coined by Sir Thomas More as title of his book (published 1516) describing an imaginary island with a perfect social and political system (Gr. *ou*, not, *topos*, place)], *n.* A place or state of ideal perfection; a book describing such. **Utopian,** *a.* Pertaining to or resembling Utopia; ideal, perfect or highly desirable but impracticable. *n.* An inhabitant of Utopia; an ardent but visionary political or social reformer. **Utopianism,** *n.*

utricle (ū′ tri kėl) [F., from L. *ūtriculus*, dim. of *ūter*, leather bag or bottle], *n.* (*Biol.*) A cell of an animal or plant; (*Anat.*) a sac-like cavity, esp. one in the labyrinth of the inner ear. **utricular** (-trik′ ū lȧr), *a.*

utter (1) (ŭt′ ėr) [A.-S. *utter a*, comp. of *ūt*, OUT], *a.* Complete, total, perfect, entire; absolute, unconditional. **utter barrister:** A junior barrister not allowed to plead within the bar. **utterly,** *adv.* **uttermost,** *a.* **utterness,** *n.*

utter (2) (ŭt′ ėr) [M.E. *uttren*, as prec., cp. A.-S. *ūtian*, from *ūt*, OUT], *v.t.* To give forth audibly; to give expression to; to put notes, base coin, etc., into circulation; *to put forth, to give vent to, to emit. **utterable,** *a.* **utterance,** *n.* The act of uttering; vocal expression; speech, words; power of speaking. **utterer,** *n.* **utterly,** etc. [UTTER (1)].

uva (ū′ vȧ) [L., bunch of grapes], *n.* (*Bot.*) A succulent indehiscent fruit with a central placenta, as a grape. **uvea** (ū′ vė ȧ), *n.* (*Anat.*) The inner coloured layer of the iris. **uveal,** *a.* **uveous,** *a.* Resembling a grape; (*Anat.*) uveal.

uvula (ū′ vū lȧ) [mod. L., dim. of prec.], *n.* (*pl.* **-læ**) A fleshy body hanging from the posterior margin of the soft palate; one of two similar processes in the bladder and the cerebellum. **uvular,** *a.*

uxorious (ŭk sôr′ i ůs) [L. *uxōrius*, from *uxor*, wife], *a.* Excessively or foolishly fond of one's wife, doting. **uxorial,** *a.* Of or pertaining to a wife; uxorious. **uxoricide** [-CIDE], *n.* Wife-murder; a wife-murderer. **uxoriously,** *adv.* **uxoriousness,** *n.*

Uzbeg (ŭz′ beg) [native name], *n.* A member of one of the Turkish races of Turkestan.

V

V, v, the twenty-second letter, and the seventeenth consonant (*pl.* **Vs, V's, Vees**), is a voiced labio-dental spirant or fricative, produced by the junction of the lower lip and upper teeth, corresponding to the voiceless *f*, which is similarly produced; (*Roman numeral*) 5. **V.E. Day:** The day, 8 May, 1945, on which hostilities in Europe in World War II officially ceased. **V.J. Day:** The corresponding day (2 September, 1945) when hostilities against Japan ceased.

va (va) [It.], *v.i.* (*Mus. direction*) Go on.

vacant (vā' kȧnt) [F., from L. *vacans -ntem*, pres.p. of *vacāre*, to be empty], *a.* Unfilled, empty, unoccupied; unemployed, at leisure; unintelligent, empty-headed, silly, inane. **vacancy,** *n.* The state of being vacant, emptiness; mental vacuity, idleness, inanity; empty space, a gap, a chasm; an unfilled or vacant post or office. **vacantly,** *adv.*

vacate (vȧ kāt'), *v.t.* To make vacant, to give up occupation or possession of; to annul, to make void.

vacation (vȧ kā' shŭn), *n.* The act of vacating; a period of cessation of legal or other business, or of studies at university, etc.; a holiday.

vaccinate (văk' si nāt) [F. *vaccin*, vaccine, L. *vaccīnus*, a., from *vacca*, cow], *v.t.* To inoculate with vaccine to procure immunity from smallpox, or with the modified virus of any disease so as to produce a mild form of it and prevent a serious attack. **vaccination** (-nā' shŭn), *n.* **vaccinationist,** *n.* **vaccinnator,** *n.* **vaccine** (văk' sin), *a.* Of, pertaining to, or obtained from cows; of or pertaining to vaccination. *n.* The virus of cowpox prepared for use in vaccination; any agent used for inoculation and immunization. **vaccine-farm,** *n.* A place where heifers are inoculated for the production of vaccine. **vaccine-point,** *n.* A sharp point used for introducing vaccine. **vaccinal, vaccinic** (-sin' ik), *a.* **vaccinia** (-sin' i ȧ), *n.* Cowpox, esp. as produced by inoculation. **vaccinifer,** *a.* A person or animal from whose body vaccine is obtained.

vacillate (văs' i lāt) [L. *vacillātus*, p.p. of *vacillāre*], *v.i.* To sway to and fro, to waver; to oscillate from one opinion or resolution to another, to be irresolute. ***vacillant,** *a.* **vacillatingly,** *adv.* **vacillation** (-lā' shŭn), **vacillancy,** *n.*

vacuist (văk' ū ist), *n.* One who holds the doctrine of empty spaces between the molecules of matter, opp. to a plenist.

vacuole (văk' ū ōl), *n.* (*Biol.*) A minute cavity in an organ, tissue, etc., containing air, fluid, etc. **vacuolar, vacuolate,** *a.*

vacuous (văk' ū ŭs) [L. *vacuus*, rel. to *vacāre*, see VACANT], *a.* Empty, unfilled, void; unintelligent, blank, expressionless. ***vacuousness,** *n.* ***vacuate** [EVACUATE]. ***vacuation** [EVACUATION]. **vacuity** (vȧ kū' i ti), *n.*

vacuum (văk' ū ŭm) [L., neut. of prec.], *n.* (*pl.* **-ms, -ua**) A space completely devoid of matter; a space or vessel from which the air has been exhausted to the furthest possible extent by an air-pump or analogous means; a partial diminution of pressure, as in a suction-pump, below the normal atmospheric pressure. **vacuum-brake,** *n.* A continuous train-brake in which the pressure applying the brakes is caused by the exhaustion of the air from a bellows pulling the brake-rod as it collapses. **vacuum-cleaner,** *n.* A machine for removing dirt by suction. **vacuum flask,** *n.* A flask constructed with two walls between which is a vacuum, for the purpose of keeping the contents hot or cold. **vacuum-gauge,** *n.* A gauge indicating the pressure consequent on the production of a vacuum. **vacuum pump,** *n.* An air-pump used to remove air or other gas, and so create a vacuum. **vacuum tube,** *n.* (*Am.*) An electronic valve.

***vade** (*Shak.*) [FADE].

vade-mecum (vā' di mē' kŭm) [L., go with me], *n.* A pocket companion or manual for ready reference.

vadium (vā' di ŭm) [med. L., from L. *vas vadis*, surety], *n.* (*Sc. Law*) A bailment of personal property as security for a loan.

vagabond (văg' ȧ bŏnd) [F., from late L. *vagabundus*, from *vagārī*, to wonder], *a.* Wandering about, having no settled habitation, nomadic; driven or drifting to and fro, aimless. *n.* One who wanders about without any settled home, a wanderer, esp. an idle or disreputable one, a vagrant; (*colloq.*) a scamp, a rogue. **vagabondage, vagabondism,** *n* **vagabondish,** *a.* **vagabondize,** *v.i.*

vagary (vȧ gâr' i) [perh. directly from L. *vagārī*, see prec.], *n.* A whimsical idea, an extravagant notion, a freak. ***vagarious, *vagarish,** *a.* **vagarity** (-găr' i ti), *n.*

vagina (vȧ jī' nȧ) [L.], *n.* A sheath, a sheath-like envelope or organ; (*Anat.*) the genital passage of a female from the vulva to the uterus; (*Arch.*) the upper part of a terminus from which the figure seems to issue; (*Bot.*) a sheath or semi-tubular part, as at the base of a stem. **vaginal** (vȧ jī' nȧl, văj' i nȧl), **vaginate, -nated,** *a.* **vagini-, vagino-,** *comb. form.* **vaginipennate** (văj i ni pen' ȧt), *a.* (*Ent.*) Sheath-winged; coleopterous. **vaginismus,** *n.* (*Path.*) Spasmodic contraction of the vaginal sphincters. **vaginitis** (-nī' tis), *n.* Inflammation of the vagina. **vaginotomy** (-not' ŏ mi) [-TOMY], *n.* Incision of the vagina.

vagitus (vȧ jī' tŭs) [L.], *n.* (*Obstetrics*) The first cry of a new-born infant.

vagrant (vā' grȧnt) [formerly *vagarant*, A.-F. *wakerant*, O.F. *waucrant*, pres.p. of *walcrer*, from Teut., cogn. with O.H.G. *walkan*, to walk about, to full cloth, see WALK (confused with L. *vagārī*, see VAGUE)], *a.* Wandering about without a settled home; itinerant, strolling; roving, unrestrained; *unsteady, inconstant. *n.* A wanderer, an idle person, a vagabond, a tramp; (*Law*) a person wandering about begging or without visible means of subsistence. **vagrancy,** *n.* **vagrantly,** *adv.* ***vagrom** [distortion of VAGRANT], *a.*

vague (vāg) [from obs. v. to wander, F. *vaguer*, L. *vagārī*, from *vagus*, wandering], *a.* Indistinct, of doubtful meaning or application, ambiguous, indefinite, ill-defined; *vagrant. **vaguely,** *adv.* **vagueness,** *n.*

***vagus** (vā' gŭs) [L., see prec.], *a.* Wandering; (*Anat.*) out of place.

***vail** (1) (vāl) [shortened from AVALE], *v.t.* To lower (a topsail, etc.) or doff (one's cap, etc.), esp. in token of respect or submission. *v.i.* To yield, to give place.

***vail** (2) (vāl) [shortened from AVAIL], *n.* (*usu. in pl.*) Money given to servants by visitors as a gratuity; a tip, esp. for a corrupt purpose.

***vail** (3) [VEIL].

vain (vān) [F., from L. *vānum*, nom. *-us*, empty, vain], *a.* Empty, unsubstantial, unreal, worthless; fruitless, ineffectual, unavailing; unproductive, unprofitable; fallacious, deceitful; proud of petty things or of trifling attainments, conceited, self-admiring; foolish, silly. **in vain:** To no purpose; ineffectually. **vainglory** (-glôr' i), *n.* Excessive vanity; vain pomp or show; pride, boastfulness. **vainglorious,** *a.* **vaingloriously,** *adv.* **vaingloriousness,** *n.* **vainly,** *adv.* ***vainness,** *n.*

vair (vâr) [F., from L. *varius*, variegated, VARIOUS], *n.* (*Her.*) A fur represented by shield-shaped figures of argent and azure alternately.

Vaishnava (vīsh' nȧ vȧ) [Sansk.], *n.* One of the great sects of reformed Brahmins who worship Vishnu as supreme among the Hindu gods.

Vaisya (vīs' yȧ) [Sansk. *vaiçya*, from *viç*, settler], *n.* The third of the four chief Hindu castes; a member of this.

vaivode [VOIVODE].

valance (văl′ ȧns) [prob. from *Valence* in France], *n.* A short curtain; the hanging round the frame or tester of a bedstead; a damask fabric of silk, etc., for covering furniture.

vale (1) (văl) [M.E. and F. *val*, L. *vallem*, nom. *-lis*], *n.* (*poet.*) A valley; a little trough or channel. **Vale of tears:** (*fig.*) Human life, existence, the world.

vale (2) (vā′ lē) [L., farewell, imper. of *valēre*, to be strong], *int.* and *n.* Farewell.

valediction (văl ė dik′ shŭn) [L. *valēdictus*, p.p. of *valēdīcere* (VALE (2), *dīcere*, to say)], *n.* A bidding farewell; a farewell, an adieu. **valedictorian** (-tôr′ i ȧn), *n.* (*Am.*) A student who delivers a valedictory. **valedictory** (-dik′ tŏr i), *a.* Bidding farewell; pertaining to or of the nature of a farewell. *n.* A parting address or oration esp. at graduation in an American university.

valence (vā′ lėns) [late L. *valentia*, strength, from *valēre*, to be strong], *n.* (*Chem.*) The combining or replacing power of an element or radical reckoned as the number of monovalent elements it can replace or combine with.

Valenciennes (va la*n* syen′, văl′ ėn sēns) [*Valenciennes* in France], *n.* Valenciennes lace: a composition used in pyrotechnics. **Valenciennes lace:** A fine variety of lace the design of which is made with and of the same thread as the ground.

valency (vā′ lėn si) [VALENCE], *n.* (*Chem.*) A unit of combining capacity; valence.

valentine (văl′ ėn tīn), *n.* A sweetheart chosen on St. Valentine's day; a letter or picture of an amatory or satirical kind sent to a person of the opposite sex on St. Valentine's day. **St. Valentine's day:** 14 Feb., commemorating the day when St. Valentine was beheaded by the Romans and when birds were supposed to begin to mate.

Valentinian (văl ėn tin′ i ȧn), *a.* Of or pertaining to Valentinus, an Egyptian Gnostic of the 2nd century, or his teachings. *n.* A disciple of Valentinus.

valerian (vȧ lēr′ i ȧn) [O.F. *valeriane*, late L. *valēriana*, etym. doubtful], *n.* An herbaceous plant of the genus *Valeriana* with clusters of pink or white flowers; a preparation from the root of *V. officinalis* used as a mild stimulant, etc. **valerate** (văl′ ėr ȧt), *n.* A salt of valeric acid. **valeric** (vȧ ler′ ik), *a.*

valet (văl′ ėt) [F., var. of VARLET], *n.* A manservant who attends on his master's person; an iron-pointed stick or goad used in training horses. *v.t.* (*p.* **valeted**) To act as valet to. ***valet de chambre*** (văl ā dė shambr′): A valet. ***valet de place*** (-dė plas′): A courier or local guide.

valetudinarian (văl ė tū di nâr′ i ȧn) [F. *valétudinaire*, L. *valētūdinārius*, from *valētūdo -dinis*, health, from *valēre*, to be well], *a.* Sickly, infirm, delicate; seeking to recover health; morbidly anxious about one's state of health. *n.* An invalid; a valetudinarian person. **valetudinarianism,** *n.* **valetudinary** (-tū′ di nȧr i), *a.* and *n.* One who is morbidly anxious about his state of health; to be in such a condition.

Valhalla (văl hăl′ ȧ) [Icel. *valhöll*, gen. *valhallar*, hall of the slain (*valr*, slain, HALL)], *n.* The palace of immortality where the souls of heroes slain in battle were carried by the valkyries; a building used as the final resting-place of the great men of a nation, esp. the Temple of Fame, near Ratisbon, built by Louis I of Bavaria, 1830.

valiant (văl′ yȧnt, -i ȧnt) [O.F. *valant* (F. *vaillant*), pres.p. of *valoir*, to be worth, L. *valēre*, to be strong], *a.* Brave, courageous, intrepid. ***valiance, *valiantness,** *n.* **valiantly,** *adv.*

valid (văl′ id) [F. *valide*, L. *validus*, a prec.], *a.* Well-grounded, sound, cogent, logical, incontestable; (*Law*) legally sound, sufficient, and effective, binding. **validate,** *v.t.* To make valid, to ratify, to confirm, to make binding. **validation** (-dā′ shŭn), *n.* **validity** (vȧ lid′ i ti), **validness,** *n.* **validly,** *adv.*

valise (vȧ lēs′) [F., from late L. *valisia*, etym. doubtful], *n.* A bag or case, usu. of leather, for holding a traveller's clothes, etc., esp. one for carrying in the hand, a small portmanteau; (*Am.*) a suit-case.

valkyrie (văl′ kir i) [Icel. *valkyrja*, chooser of the slain (*valr*, slain, *-kyrja*, chooser, from *kjōsa*, cogn. with CHOOSE)], *n.* One of twelve maidens of Valhalla who were sent by Odin to select those destined to be slain in battle and to conduct their souls to Valhalla. **Valkyrian** (-kir′ i ȧn), *a.*

***vallancy** (văl′ ȧn si) [VALANCE], *n.* A large wig that shaded the face, worn in the 17th cent.

vallar, vallated, etc. [VALLUM].

vallecula (vȧ lek′ ū lȧ) [late L., dim. of *vallis*, VALE (1)], *n.* (*pl.* **-læ**, -lē) (*Anat., Bot., etc.*) A groove or furrow.

valley (văl′ i) [O.F. *valee* (F. *vallée*), from *val*, VALE (1)], *n.* A depression in the earth's surface bounded by hills or mountains, and usu. with a stream flowing through it; any hollow or depression between higher ground or elevations of a surface; the internal angle formed by two inclined sides of a roof.

vallonia (vȧ lō′ ni ȧ) [It., from Gr. *balanos*, oak], *n.* The large acorn-cup of the vallonia oak, used for dyeing, tanning, ink-making, etc. **vallonia oak:** An evergreen oak, *Quercus ægilops*, of the Greek Archipelago, etc.

vallum (văl′ ŭm) [L.], *n.* (*Rom. Ant.*) A rampart, an agger; (*Anat.*) an eyebrow. **vallar, *vallary, vallated,** *a.* **vallation** (-lā′ shŭn), *n.*

valonia [VALLONIA].

valorize (văl′ ŏr īz) [L. *valere*, to be worth, -IZE], *v.t.* (*Fin.*) To increase or stabilize the price of an article by an officially organized scheme.

valour (văl′ ŏr) [O.F. *valor*, *-lur* (F. *valeur*), L. *valōrem*, nom. *-or*, from *valēre*, to be strong, to be worth], *n.* Personal bravery, courage, esp. as displayed in fighting; prowess. **valorous,** *a.* **valorously,** *adv.*

valse (vawls) [F., WALTZ], *n.* A waltz.

valuable (văl′ ū ȧbl), *a.* Having great value, worth, or price, costly, precious; capable of being valued or appraised; (*colloq.*) worthy, estimable. **valuableness,** *n.* **valuably,** *adv.*

valuation (văl ū ā′ shŭn), *n.* The act of valuing or appraising; estimation of the value of a thing; estimated value or worth, the price placed on a thing. **valuator,** (văl′ ū ā tŏr), *n.* An appraiser.

value (văl′ ū) [F., fem. of *valu*, p.p. of *valoir*, to be worth, L. *valēre*, see VALOUR], *n.* Worth, the desirability of a thing, esp. as compared with other things; the qualities that are the basis of this; worth estimated in money or other equivalent, the market price; the equivalent of a thing; valuation, estimation, appreciation of worth; meaning, signification, import; (*Mus.*) the relative duration of a tone as indicated by the note; (*Painting*) the relation of the parts of a picture to each other with regard to light and shade, apart from colour; (*Math.*) the amount or quantity denoted by a symbol or expression; (*Biol.*) rank in classification. *v.t.* To estimate the value of, to appraise; to esteem, to rate highly, to prize; *to be worth; *to reckon at. **commercial, economic, exchange,** or **exchangeable value, value in exchange:** The value in terms of other commodities, the purchasing power of a commodity in the open market; the market price as determined by economic laws. **valueless,** *a.* Of no value, worthless, futile. **valuelessness,** *n.* **valuer,** *n.* One who values, an appraiser, esp. of property, jewellery, etc.

valuta (văl ū ta) [It., value], *n.* (*Fin.*) The definitive money with which it can be demanded that State payments due to individuals shall be paid; the value of one currency in terms of another.

valve (vălv) [F., from L. *valva*, leaf of a folding door, cogn. with *volvere*, to roll, to turn round], *n.* An automatic or other contrivance for opening or closing a passage or aperture so as to permit or prevent passage of a fluid, as water, gas, or steam; (*Anat.*) a membranous part of a vessel or other organ preventing the flow of liquids in one direction and allowing it in the other; (*Bot.*) one of the segments into which a capsule dehisces, either half of an anther after its opening; (*Radio.*) abbrev. for electronic or thermionic valve; a vacuum tube or bulb containing electrodes and exhibiting sensitive control by one or more electrodes of the current flowing between the others, (*Am.* a tube); (*Conch.*) one of the parts or divisions of a shell; *one of the leaves of a folding door. **valve box, chamber,** *n.* (*Mach.*) The chamber in which a valve works. **valve face,** *n.* (*Mach.*) The sealing surface of a valve. **valve-gear,** *n.* The mechanism operating a valve. **valve-oscillator,** *n.* (*Radio.*) An electrical circuit on which oscillations are maintained by a valve. **valve-seating,** *n.* (*Mach.*) That part of an internal-combustion engine which is in working contact with the valve face when the valve is shut. **valve voltmeter,** *n.* (*Radio.*) An electrical circuit, containing valves, used to measure voltages. **valval,** *a.* (*Bot.*) **valvar, valvate,** *a.* Like a valve; (*Bot.*) descriptive of petals which meet at the margins only. **valved,** *a.* (*usu. in comb.* as *three-valved*). **valveless,** *a.* **valvelet, valule,** *n.* A little valve. **valviferous** (-vif′ ėr ůs) [-FEROUS], *a.* **valviform, valvular,** *a.* **valvular disease,** *n.* (*Path.*) Disordered action of the heart owing to defects in the cardiac valves.

***vambrace** (văm′ brās) [M.F. *avant-bras* (AVANT-, *bras*, arm)], *n.* Armour for the arm from the elbow to the wrist.

vamose (vȧ mōs′) [Sp. *vamos*, let us go, L. *vādimus*, we go, from *vādere*, to go], *v.i.* (*Am. slang*) To decamp, to be gone, to be off. *v.t.* To decamp from.

vamp (1) (vămp) [M.E. *vaumpe, vampay, vauntpe*, M.F. *avant-pied* (AVANT-, *pied*, foot)], *n.* The part of a boot or shoe upper in front of the ankle seams; (*fig.*) a patch intended to give a new appearance to an old thing; (*Mus.*) an improvised accompaniment. *v.t.* To put a new vamp on (a boot, etc.); to give a new appearance to, to furbish (up); (*Mus.*) to improvise an accompaniment to. *v.i.* To improvise accompaniments. **vamper,** *n.*

vamp (2) (vămp) [VAMPIRE], *n.* (*colloq.*) An adventuress, a woman who exploits her charms to take advantage of men. *v.t.* To fascinate, to exploit men.

vampire (văm′ pīr) [F., from G. *vampyr*, Serbian *vampir*, prob. from Turk.], *n.* A ghost of a heretic, criminal, or other outcast, supposed to leave the grave at night and suck the blood of sleeping persons; (*fig.*) one who preys upon others, a bloodsucker; a bat of the genus *Desmodus*, which sucks the blood of man and the lower animals, esp. while they are asleep; (*Theat.*) a small double spring-door used for sudden entrances and exits. **vampiric** (-pir′ ik), *a.* **vampirism** (văm′ pi rizm), *n.* Belief in vampires; blood-sucking; (*fig.*) extortion.

***vamplate** (văm′ plāt) [F. *avant-plate* (AVANT-, PLATE)], *n.* An iron plate fixed on a lance as a guard for the hand.

van (1) (văn) [short for VANGUARD], *n.* The foremost division of an army or fleet, the advance-guard; the front of an army or the leading ships of a fleet in battle; (*fig.*) the leaders of a movement, the forefront.

van (2) (văn) [shortened from CARAVAN], *n.* A large vehicle, usu. covered, for conveying furniture, etc.; a closed railway-carriage for luggage or for the guard. *v.t.* (*past & p.p.* **vanned**) To convey in a van.

van (3) (văn) [F., from L. *vannum*, nom. -*us*, FAN], *n.* *A fan or machine for winnowing grain; *a wing; (*Mining*) a test of the quality of ore by washing on a shovel, etc. *v.t.* To test (ore) thus. **vanner,** *n.*

vanadium (vȧ nā′ di ům) [mod. L., from *Vanadis*, a Scand. goddess], *n.* A rare, silver-white metallic element, used to give tensile strength to steel and, in the form of its salts, to produce an intense permanent black colour. **vanadate** (văn′ ȧ dāt), *n.* A salt of vanadic acid. **vanadic** (vȧ năd′ ik), **vanadous** (văn′ ȧ důs), *a.* **vanadinite,** *n.* A mineral composed of vanadate and lead chloride.

***vancourier** [AVANT-COURIER, see **AVANT-**].

Vandal (văn′ dȧl) [L. *Vandalus*, from Teut. (cp. A.-S. *Wendle*, pl., cogn. with G. *wandeln*, to WANDER)], *n.* One of a Teutonic race from the shores of the Baltic that overran Gaul, Spain, and N. Africa and Rome in the 5th century, destroying works of art, etc.; (*fig.*) one who wilfully or ignorantly destroys or disfigures a work of art, etc. **Vandalic** (-dăl′ ik), *a.* **vandalism,** *n.*

Vandemonian (văn de mō′ ni ȧn) [Van Dieman's Land, or Tasmania], *n.a.* An inhabitant of or relating to Tasmania; (*Austral. hist.*) a convict in Tasmania.

vandyke (văn dīk′), *n.* A picture by Sir Anthony Van Dyck (1599–1641); any one of the series of points forming an ornamental border to lace, linen, etc.; a collar or cape with these points. *a.* Applied to the style of dress, esp. ornamented with vandykes, worn by the figures in Van Dyck's portraits. *v.t.* To cut the edge of (linen, etc.) into vandykes. **vandyke beard:** A pointed beard. **vandyke brown:** A reddish-brown colour or pigment. **vandyke cape** or **collar:** One ornamented with vandykes.

vane (vān) [A.-S. *fana*, small flag (cp. Dut. *vaan*, G. *fahne*, Icel. *fāni*, Swed. *fana*, Dan. *fane*), cogn. with L. *pannus*, cloth, PANE], *n.* A weathercock, flag, or arrow pointing in the direction of the wind; a similar device on an axis turned by a current of water, etc., as in a meter; a fin on a bomb to ensure its falling on its war-head; the arm of a windmill; the blade of a propeller, etc.; a horizontal part on a surveyor's levelling-staff for moving up and down to the line of sight of the telescope; the sight on a quadrant, compass, etc.; the broad part of a feather; (*Naut.*) a slender streamer used to show the direction of the wind, a dog-vane. **vaned,** *a.* **vaneless,** *a.*

Vanessa (vȧ nes′ ȧ) [etym. doubtful], *n.* (*Ent.*) A genus of butterflies with notched wings, comprising the Red Admiral, Camberwell Beauty, etc.

vang (văng) [Dut., from *vangen*, to catch, cogn. with FANG], *n.* (*Naut.*) Either of a pair of guy-ropes running from the peak of a gaff to the deck to steady it.

vangee (văn′ jē) [etym. doubtful], *n.* (*Naut.*) A contrivance comprising a barrel and crank-brakes for working a ship's pumps.

vanguard (văn′ gard) [O.F. *avant-warde*, -*garde* (AVANT-, GUARD)], *n.* The troops who march in the front or van of an army, an advance-guard, the van.

vanilla (vȧ nil′ ȧ) [Sp. *vainilla*, small pod, dim. of *vaina*, case, sheath, pod, L. VAGINA], *n.* A genus of tall, epiphytal orchids, natives of tropical Asia and America, bearing fragrant flowers; the fruit of *V. planifolia* and other species yielding the vanilla of commerce; an extract from this used for flavouring ices, syrups, etc. **vanillate,** *n.* (*Chem.*) **vanillic,** *a.* **vanillism,** *n.* (*Path.*) An eruptive, itching skin-disease prevalent among persons handling vanilla-pods, due to an insect.

vanish (văn′ ish) [M.E. *vanissen*, prob. through A.-F. *evaniss-*, pres.p. stem of *evanir*, O.F. *esvanir*, L. *ēvānescere*, from *vānus*, empty, VAIN], *v.i.* To disappear suddenly; to become imperceptible, to be lost to sight, to face away, to dissolve; to pass away, to pass out of existence; (*Math.*) to become zero. **vanishing cream,** *n.* A cosmetic which is rapidly absorbed into the pores leaving no trace of grease. **vanishing fraction:** A fraction that reduces to zero for a particular value of the variable which enters it. **vanishing point:** (*Perspective*)

The point in which all parallel lines in the same plane tend to meet.

vanity (văn′ i ti) [F. *vanité,* L. *vānitātem,* nom. *-tas,* from *vānus,* VAIN], *n.* The quality or state of being vain; empty pride, conceit of one's personal attainments or attractions; ostentation, show; emptiness, futility, unreality, worthlessness; that which is visionary, unreal, or deceptive. **vanity bag:** A small ornamental hand-bag carried by women, usu. containing powder-puff, mirror, etc.

vanner [VAN (3)].

vanquish (văng′ kwish) [M.E. *venkissen,* O.F. *veinquiss-,* pres.p. stem of *veinquir, veincre* (F. *vaincre*), L. *vincere*], *v.t.* To conquer, to overcome, to subdue, to refute. **vanquishable,** *a.* **vanquisher,** *n.* ***vanquishment,** *n.*

vantage (van′ tȧj) [short for ADVANTAGE], *n.* Advantage; a situation, condition, or opportunity favourable to success; (*Lawn-tennis*) the point scored by either side after deuce or five all. *v.t.* To profit to advantage. **vantage-ground,** *n.* Superiority of position or place.

***vanward** [VANGUARD].

vapid (văp′ id) [L. *vapidus,* cogn. with VAPOUR], *a.* Insipid, flat, spiritless. **vapidity** (-pid′ i ti), **vapidness,** *n.* **vapidly,** *adv.*

vaporable, vaporific, vaporize, etc. [VAPOUR].

vapour (vā′ pȯr) [F. *vapeur,* L. *vapōrem,* nom. *-por* (whence *vaporāre,* to steam), cogn. with Gr. *kapnos,* smoke, and VAPID], *n.* Moisture in the air, light mist; (*loosely*) any visible diffused substance floating in the atmosphere; (*Phys.*) the gaseous form of a substance that is normally liquid or solid; (*fig.*) an unreal or unsubstantial thing, a vain imagination; (*Med.*) a remedial preparation applied by inhaling; *empty brag, swagger; *(*pl.*) depression of spirits, hypochondria. *v.i.* To give out vapour; to boast, to brag, to bluster. **vapour-bath,** *n.* The application of vapour or steam to the body in a close place; the room or apparatus for this. **vapour-burner,** *n.* The apparatus for vaporizing a liquid, etc. **vapour-engine,** *n.* One driven by an elastic fluid other than steam. **vapour trail,** *n.* A white trail of condensed vapour left in the sky after the passage of an aircraft. **vaporiferous** (if′ ėr ůs), **vaporific, vaporiform** (vā′ pȯr i fôrm), *a.* **vaporimeter** (-im′ ė tėr) [-METER], *n.* An instrument for measuring the pressure of vapour. **vaporize,** *v.t.* To convert into vapour; *v.i.* To be converted into vapour. **vaporizer,** *n.* **vaporable, vaporizable,** *a.* **vaporization** (-zā′ shůn), *n.* **vaporability** (-bil′ i ti), *n.* **vaporole,** *n.* (*Med.*) A thin glass capsule containing a volatile drug for inhalation or fumigation. **vaporous, vapoury,** *a.* **vaporosity** (-os′ i ti), **vaporousness,** *n.* **vaporously,** *adv.* ***vapourer,** *n.* A braggart, a bully. ***vapouringly,** *adv.* **vapourish,** *a* Full of vapours, hypochondriac, splenetic. **vapourishness,** *n.*

vapulation (văp ū lā′ shůn) [L. *vāpulāre,* to be flogged], *n.* A flogging. ***vapulatory,** *a.*

vaquero (va kâr′ ō) [Sp., from med. L. *vaccārius,* from L. *vacca,* cow], *n.* (*Mexico and U.S.*) A herdsman, a cowherd.

vara (va′ rȧ) [Sp., VARE], *n.* A Spanish-American measure of length, about 33 in.

Varangian (vȧ ran′ ji ȧn) [med. L. *Varingus,* Icel. *Væringi,* confederate, from *vārar,* oaths, cogn. with L. *vērus,* true], *n.* One of the Norse sea-rovers in the 8th to 12th cent. who ravaged the coasts of the Baltic and conquered part of Russia. **Varangian Guard:** The body-guard of the Byzantine emperors, formed partly of Varangians.

Varanus (văr′ ȧ nůs) [mod. L., from Arab. *waran,* lizard], *n.* (*Zool.*) A genus of lizards comprising the monitors.

***vare** (vâr) [Sp. *vara,* ult. from L. *vārus,* crooked], *n.* A wand or staff of office.

varec (văr′ ėk) [F. *varech,* cogn. with WRECK, cp. Swed. *vrak*], *n.* An impure carbonate of soda made in Brittany.

vari- [L. *varius,* VARIOUS], *comb. form.*

variable (vâr′ i ȧbl) [F., from late L. *variābilis,* from *variāre,* to VARY], *a.* Capable of varying, liable to change; changeable, unsteady, fickle, inconstant; able to be varied, adapted, or adjusted; (*Math.*) quantitatively indeterminate, susceptible of continuous change of value, esp. assuming different values while others remain constant; (*Astron.*) applied to stars whose apparent magnitudes are not constant; (*Biol.*) tending to variations of structure, function, etc. *n.* That which is variable; (*Math.*) a variable quantity; (*Naut.*) a shifting wind, (*pl.*) the region between the northerly and southerly trade-winds. **variable condenser,** *n.* (*Elec.*) A condenser whose capacity is constantly and easily adjustable. **variable mu valve,** *n.* (*Radio.*) An electronic valve in which the degree of current control varies with the amount of current. **variability** (-bil′ i ti), **variableness,** *n.* **variably,** *adv.*

variance (vâr′ i ȧns) [L. *variāntia,* as prec.], *n.* The state of being variant, disagreement, difference of opinion, dissension, discord; (*Law*) disagreement between the allegations and proof or between the writ and the declaration. **variant,** *a.* Showing variation, differing in form, character, or details; tending to vary, changeable. *n.* A variant form, reading, type, etc.

variation (vâr i ā′ shůn) [F., from L. *variātiōnem,* nom. *-tio,* as prec.], *n.* The act, process, or state of varying; alteration, change, modification, deviation, mutation; the extent to which a thing varies; (*Gram.*) inflexion; (*Astron.*) deviation of a heavenly body from the mean orbit or motion; (*Phys.*) the angle of deviation from true north or of declination of the magnetic needle; (*Biol.*) the deviation in structure or function from the type or parent form; (*Math.*) the relation between the changes of quantities that vary as each other; permutation; (*Mus.*) a repetition of a theme with fanciful elaborations and changes of form. **variate,** *v.t.* **variational,** *a.* **variative** (vâr′ i ā tiv), *a.* **variator,** *n.*

varicated, etc. [VARIX].

varicella (văr i sel′ ȧ) [dim. of VARIOLA], *n.* Chicken-pox. **varicellar, varicelloid,** *a.*

varices, *n.pl.* [VARIX].

varicoloured (vâr-, văr′ i kŭl ȯrd) [VARI-, COLOUR], *a.* Variously coloured, variegated, parti-coloured. **varicorn** (văr′ i kôrn) [L. *cornu,* horn], *a.* Having diversiform antennæ. *n.* A varicorn beetle.

varicose (văr′ i kōs) [L. *varicōsus,* from VARIX], *a.* Permanently dilated, affected with varix (said of veins); intended for the cure of varices; varicated. **varicocele** [-CELE], *n.* A tumour formed by varicose veins of the spermatic cord. **varicosed,** *a.* **varicosity** (-kos′ i ti), *n.* ***varicous** [VARICOSE].

varied [VARY].

variegate (vâr′ i gāt, văr′ i ė gāt) [L. *variegātus,* p.p. of *variegāre* (VARI-, *agere,* to drive, to make)], *v.t.* To diversify in colour, to mark with patches of different hues; to dapple, to chequer. **variegation** (-gā′ shŭn), *n.*

variety (vȧ rī′ ė ti) [F. *varieté,* L. *varietātem,* nom. *-tas,* from *varius,* VARIOUS], *n.* The quality or state of being various; diversity, absence of sameness or monotony, many-sidedness, versatility; a collection of diverse things; a minor class or group of things differing in some common peculiarities from the class they belong to; a kind, a sort, a thing of such a sort or kind; (*Biol.*) an individual or group differing from the type of its species in some transmittable quality but usually fertile with others of the species, a sub-species. **variety entertainment** or **show:** An entertainment consisting of singing, dancing, acrobatic turns, conjuring, etc. **variety theatre:** One for variety shows, a music-hall. **varietal,** *a.* **varietally,** *adv.* **variform** (vâr′ i form), *a.* Varying in form, of different shapes. ***variformed,** *a.*

a. **vario-coupler** (vâr′ i ō kŭp′lėr), *n.* (*Elec.*) An apparatus comprising two inductance coils, one rotating within the other, which is used for indirect magnetic coupling.

variola (vȧ rī′ ȯ lȧ) [med. L., dim. from L. *varius*, VARIOUS], *n.* Smallpox. **variolar, variolic** (-ol′ ik), **variolous** (vȧ rī′ ȯ lŭs), *a.* **variolation** (vâr i ȯ lā′ shŭn), *n.* Inoculation with smallpox virus. **variole** (vâr′ i ōl), *n.* A shallow pit-like depression, a *foveola.* **variolate, -lated,** *a.* **variolite** *n.* (*Min.*) A variety of spherulitic basalt with a surface resembling skin marked with smallpox. **varioloid,** *a.* Resembling or of the nature of smallpox; *n.* A mild form of smallpox, esp. as modified by previous inoculation.

variorum (vâr i ôr′ ŭm) [L., gen. of *varius*, see foll.], *a.* With notes of various commentators inserted (of an edition of a work). **variorum edition,** *n.* An edition of a classic, etc., with comparisons of texts and notes by various editors and commentators.

various (vâr′ i ŭs) [L. *varius*], *a.* Differing from each other, diverse; divers, several; variable; uncertain, not uniform. **variously,** *adv.* **variousness,** *n.*

varix (vâr′ iks) [L., prob. from VARUS (2)], *n.* (*pl.* **-ices, -i sēz**) A permanent dilatation of a vein or other vessel; a varicose vessel; (*Conch.*) one of the ridges traversing the whorls of a univalve shell. **varicated** (vâr′ i kā tėd), *a.* (*Conch.*) Having varices. **varication** (-kā′ shŭn), *n.*

varlet (var′ lėt) [O.F. *varlet, vaslet,* dim. of VASSAL], *n.* A page, an attendant preparing to be a squire; a menial, a knave, a rascal. ***varletry,** *n.* The rabble, the crowd.

varmint (var′ mint) [corr. of VERMIN], *n.* (*prov.*) A troublesome or mischievous person or animal.

varnish (var′ nish) [F. *vernis,* etym. doubtful, whence *vernisser, vernir,* to varnish], *n.* A thin resinous solution for applying to the surface of wood, metal, etc., to give it a hard, transparent, shiny coating; any lustrous or glossy appearance on the surface of leaves, etc.; the lustrous surface or glaze of pottery, etc.; (*fig.*) superficial polish, gloss, palliation, whitewash. *v.t.* To cover with varnish; (*fig.*) to give an improved appearance to, to gloss over, to whitewash. **varnish-tree,** *n.* Any tree from which the material for varnish is obtained. **varnisher,** *n.* **varnishing-day,** *n.* A day before the opening of an exhibition when artists are allowed to varnish or retouch their pictures.

varry (văr′ i) [var. of VAIR], *n.* (*Her.*) A strip of vair used as a bearing. **varriated** (-ā′ tėd), *a.* Crenellated, in the form of a battlement with merlons and crenelles.

varsal (var′ sȧl) [corr. of UNIVERSAL], *a.* (*colloq.*) Universal.

varsity (var′ si ti) [corr. of UNIVERSITY], *n.* (*colloq.*) University.

varsovienne (var sō vyen′) [F., from *Varsovie,* Warsaw], *n.* A dance imitating the mazurka; music for this.

vartabed (var′ tȧ bed), *n.* One of an Armenian order of teaching clergy.

varus (1) (vâr′ ŭs) [L., knock-kneed], *n.* A variety of club-foot in which the foot is bent inwards; also called talipes varus [see TALIPES]; a knock-kneed person.

varus (2) (vâr′ ŭs) [L., blotch, pimple], *n.* Acne.

***varvel** (var′ vėl) [var. of VERVELLE], *n.* A metal ring bearing the owner's name attached to the jesses of a hawk. ***varveled,** *a.* (*Her.*) Having varvels attached.

vary (vâr′ i) [F. *varier,* L. *variāre,* from *varius,* VARIOUS], *v.t.* (*past & p.p.* **varied**) To change, to alter in appearance, form, or substance; to modify, to diversify; (*Mus.*) to make variations of (a melody, etc.). *v.i.* To be altered in any way; to undergo change; to be different or diverse, to differ, to be of different kinds; (*Math.*) to increase or decrease proportionately with or inversely to the increase or decrease of another quantity.

vas (văs) [L., vessel], *n.* (*pl.* **vasa,** vā′ sȧ) (*Anat.*) A vessel or duct. **vas deferens,** *n.* (*Anat.*) The spermatic duct. **vasal** (vā′ sȧl), *a.*

vascular (văs′ kū lȧr) [VASCULUM], *a.* Of, consisting of, or containing vessels or ducts for the conveyance of blood, chyle, sap, etc.; containing or rich in blood-vessels. **vascularity** (-lăr′ i ti), *n.* **vascularize,** *v.t.* **vascularization** (-zā′ shŭn), *n.* **vascularly,** *adv.* **vasculiform,** *a.* **vasculose,** *a.* Vascular. *n.* The substance forming the chief constituent of the vessels of plants.

vasculum (văs′ kū lŭm) [L., dim. of VAS], *n.* (*pl.* **-la**) A botanist's collecting-case, usu. of tin; (*Anat.*) a small vessel, a vas; the penis.

vase (vaz, vāz, *Am.* vās, vawz) [F. *vase,* L. *vasum,* vase, vessel, cogn. with VAS], *n.* A vessel of pottery, etc., of various forms but usu. circular with a swelling body and a foot or pedestal, applied to various ornamental and other purposes; a sculptured ornament in imitation of an ancient vase, used to decorate cornices, gate-posts, monuments, etc.; (*Arch.*) the bell of a Corinthian or Composite capital. **vase-painting,** *n.* The decoration of vases with pigments, esp. as practised by the ancient Greeks. **vaseful,** *a.*

vaseline (văs′ e lēn), *n.* Protected trade name for a yellow, soft, medicated paraffin jelly employed as a lubricant, etc.

vasi-, vaso- [VAS], *comb. form.* (*Physiol.*) **vasiform** (văs′ i fôrm), *a.* Having the form of a vas. **vasoconstrictor** (-kȯn strik′ tȯr), *a.* Causing constriction of a blood-vessel (of nerves). **vasoconstriction,** *n.* **vasodilator** (-di lā′ tȯr), *a.* Causing dilatation of a vessel; *n.* A nerve or drug causing this. **vasodilatation** (-tā′ shŭn), *n.* **vasomotor** (-mō′ tȯr), *a.* Causing constriction or dilatation in a vessel. *n.* A vasomotor agent or drug. **vasomotorial** (-tôr′ i ȧl), *a.* **vasosensory** (-sen′ sȯr i), *a.* Supplying sensation to the vessels.

vassal (văs′ ȧl) [F., from med. L. *vassallus vassus,* from Celt. (cp. Bret. *gwaz,* W. and Corn. *gwas,* O. Ir. *foss,* servant)], *n.* One holding land under a superior lord by feudal tenure, a feudatory; a slave, a humble dependant, a low wretch. *a.* Servile. **vassalage,** *n.* The state or condition of a vassal; the obligation of a vassal to feudal service; servitude, dependence; a fief; vassals collectively; *prowess in arms. ***vassalry,** *n.* Vassals collectively.

vast (vast) [F. *vaste,* L. *vastus,* empty, waste, vast], *a.* Of great extent, immense, huge, boundless; very great in numbers, amount, degree, etc. *n.* (*poet.*) A boundless expanse. **vastly,** *adv.* **vastness,** ***vastidity** (-tid′ i ti), ***vastitude,** *n.* ***vasty,** *a.*

vastus (văs′ tŭs) [as prec.], *n.* (*Anat.*) A large muscular mass on the outer or inner surface of the thigh.

vat (văt) [formerly *fat,* A.-S. *fæt* (cp. Dut. *vat,* G. *fass,* Icel. and Swed. *fat,* Dan. *fad*), cogn. with Dut. *vatten,* G. *fassen,* to catch, to contain], *n.* A large tub, tank, or other vessel used for holding mash or hop-liquor in brewing and in many manufacturing operations in which substances are boiled or steeped. *v.t.* (*past & p.p.* **vatted**) To put into or treat in a vat.

Vatican (văt′ i kȧn), *n.* The palace of the Pope on the Vatican hill in Rome; (*fig.*) the papal government. **Vatican Council:** The 20th Œcumenical Council (1869–70) at which the infallibility of the Pope when speaking ex cathedra was affirmed. **Vaticanism,** *n.* The term applied by W. E. Gladstone to the pretensions of the Holy See to infallibility, etc.

***vaticide** (văt′ i sīd) [L. *vātes vātis,* prophet, -CIDE], *n.* The murder or murderer of a prophet.

vaticinate (vȧ tis′ i nāt) [L. *vāticinātus*, p.p. of *vāticinārī* (*vāti-*, see prec., *canere*, to sing)], *v.t.* and *i.* To prophesy. ***vaticinal,** *a.* **vaticination** (-nā′ shŭn), *n.* A prophecy. **vaticinator** (vȧ tis′ i nā tȯr), *n.* A prophet.

vaudeville (vōd′ vil) [F., corr. of *Vau* (*Val*) *de Vire*, Valley of the Vire], *n.* A slight dramatic sketch or pantomime interspersed with songs and dances; a miscellaneous series of sketches, songs, etc., a variety entertainment; a French popular song with a refrain, a topical song; orig. a comic or convivial song, such as those of Olivier Basselin, poet, born in the Val de Vire (*d.* 1418). **vaudeville theater:** (*Am.*) A music-hall. **vaudevillist,** *n.* A writer of vaudevilles.

Vaudois (1) (vō dwa′) [F.], *a.* Of or pertaining to the canton of Vaud. *n.* (*pl. unchanged*) An inhabitant of Vaud (Switzerland); the Vaudois dialect.

Vaudois (2) (vō dwa′) [F., from med. L. *Valdenses*, WALDENSES], *a.* Of or pertaining to the Waldenses. *n.* (*pl. unchanged*) One of the Waldenses.

vault (1) (vawlt) [M.E. and O.F. *voute*, fem. of *volt*, vaulted, L. *volūtus*, p.p. of *volvere*, to roll], *n.* An arched roof, a continuous arch or semi-cylindrical roof, a series of arches connected by radiating joints; an arched chamber, esp. underground; a cellar; a place of interment built of masonry under a church or in a cemetery; (*fig.*) any vault-like covering or canopy, as the sky; (*Anat.*) an arched roof of a cavity. *v.t.* To cover with, or as with, a vault or vaults; to construct in the form of a vault. ***vaultage,** *n.* Vaulted work; a vaulted room. **vaulting,** *n.* ***vaulty,** *a.* Arched; concave.

vault (2) (vawlt) [M.E. *volter*, as prec.], *v.i.* To leap, to spring, esp. with the hands resting on something or with the help of a pole. *v.t.* To leap over thus. *n.* Such a leap. **vaulting-horse,** *n.* A wooden horse or frame for vaulting over in a gymnasium. **vaulter,** *n.*

vaunt (vawnt) [F. *vanter*, late L. *vānitāre*, freq. from *vānus*, VAIN], *v.i.* To boast, to brag. *v.t.* To boast of; *to display. *n.* A boast. **vaunter,** *n.* ***vauntful,** *a.* **vauntingly,** *adv.*

***vaunt-courier,** etc. [see AVANT-].

vavasour (văv′ ȧ sȯr, -soor) [O.F. *vavassour*, med. L. *vassus vassōrum*, VASSAL of vassals], *n.* A vassal holding land from a great vassal and having other vassals under him. ***vavasory,** *n.* The tenure or lands of a vavasour.

***vaward** [VANWARD].

Veader (vē′-, vā ȧ dar) [Heb. (*ve*, and, ADAR)], *n.* A supplementary or intercalary month inserted by the Hebrews every third year after the month Adar.

veal (vēl) [O.F. *veēl* (F. *veau*), L. *vitellum*, nom. *-lus*, dim. of *vitelus*, calf, cogn. with Gr. *italos*, calf, *etos*, year, L. *vetus*, old, cp. WETHER], *n.* The flesh of a calf as food. **veal-skin,** *n.* A skin-disease with shiny white tubercles, usu. on the ears, neck, and face. **vealy,** *a.*

vector (vek′ tȯr) [L., carrier, from *vehere*, to carry, p.p. *vectus*], *n.* (*Math.*) A line in space or in a diagram representing the magnitude and direction of a quantity; (*Biol.*) as agent (such as an insect) that carries a virus disease from one host to another. *v.t.* (*Aviat.*) To direct aircraft to a particular point. **vector quantity,** *n.* A quantity having both magnitude and direction (*e.g.* velocity), but not temperature. **vectorial** (-tȏr′ i ȧl), *a.*

Veda (vā′ dȧ) [Sansk., knowledge], *n.* The ancient Hindu scriptures, divided into four portions or books (*the Rig-, Yajur-, Sâma-, and Artharva-Veda*). **Vedanga** (vā dang′ gȧ), *n.* A work supplementary or auxiliary to the Veda. **Vedanta** (vā dan′ tȧ), *n.* A system of philosophy founded on the Veda. **Vedantic,** *a.* **Vedantist,** *a.* and *n.* **Vedic,** *a.*

vedette (vė det′) [F., from It. *vedetta*, var. of *viduta*, fem. p.p. of *vedere*, L. *vidēre*, to see], *n.* A sentinel (usu. mounted) stationed in advance of an outpost; (*Nav.*) a small vessel used for scouting purposes, etc.

veer (vēr) [F. *virer*, late L. *virāre*, cp. *virola*, ring, L. *viriola*, bracelet, dim. of *viria*, in *viriæ*, armlets], *v.i.* To change its direction (of the wind), esp. in the direction of the sun; to shift, to change about, esp. in opinion, conduct, etc. *v.t.* (*Naut.*) To let out or slacken (a rope, etc.); to wear (a ship); *to shift, to change. **to veer and haul:** (*Naut.*) To pull tight and slacken alternately. **to veer away** or **out:** To slacken and let run. **veeringly,** *adv.*

vega (vā′ gȧ) [Sp.], *n.* (*Spain and Cuba*) A tract of flat, open land; (*Cuba*) a tobacco-field.

vegan (vē′ gȧn) [as foll.], *n.* One who believes in the use for food, clothing, etc., of vegetable products only, thus excluding dairy products, leather, etc. **veganic** (-găn′ ik), *a.*

vegetable (vej′ ė tȧbl) [F., from late L. *vegetābilis*, from *vegetāre*, to enliven, to quicken, from L. *vegetus*, lively, from *vegēre*, to move, to quicken, cogn. with VIGIL and VIGOUR], *n.* A plant, esp. a herb used for culinary purposes or for feeding cattle, etc. *a.* Pertaining to, of the nature of, or resembling, a plant; made of or pertaining to culinary vegetables. **vegetable-ivory** [IVORY]. **vegetable kingdom:** The division of organic nature comprising plants. **vegetable marrow:** The fruit of a species of gourd, *Curcurbita ovifera*, used as a culinary vegetable. **vegetable-mould,** *n.* Mould or soil consisting to a certain extent of decaying or decayed vegetation. **vegetable oil,** *n.* An oil obtained from seeds or plants. **vegetability** (-bil′ i ti), *n.*

vegetal (vej′ e tȧl), *a.* Pertaining to, or of the nature of plants; common to plants and animals (of the functions of nutrition, growth, circulation, secretions, etc.). *n.* A plant, a vegetable. **vegetality,** *n.*

vegetaline (vej′ e tȧ lin), *n.* A material imitating ivory, coral, etc., made by treating woody fibre with sulphuric acid.

vegetarian (vej e târ′ i ȧn), *n.* One who abstains from animal food, and lives on vegetable food, and, usu. eggs, milk, etc. **vegetarianism,** *n.*

vegetate (vej′ e tāt), *v.i.* To grow in the manner of a plant, to exercise the functions of a vegetable; (*fig.*) to live an idle, passive, monotonous life. **vegetation,** *n.* The act or process of vegetating; vegetables or plants collectively, plant-life; (*Bot.*) all the plants in a specified area; (*Path.*) an excrescence on the body. **vegetative,** *a.* **vegetatively,** *adv.* **vegetativeness,** *n.* **vegeto-,** *comb. form.*

vehement (vē′ ė mėnt) [O.F., from L. *vehementem*, nom. *-ens*, perh. from *vehere*, to carry, or *vē-*, apart from, *mens mentis*, mind], *a.* Proceeding from or exhibiting intense fervour or passion, ardent, passionate, impetuous; acting with great force, energy, or violence. **vehemently,** *adv.* **vehemence, *-mency,** *n.*

vehicle (vē′ i kėl) [L. *vehiculum*, from *vehere*, to carry], *n.* Any kind of carriage or conveyance for use on land, having wheels or runners; any liquid, etc., serving as a medium for pigments, medicinal substances, etc.; any person or thing employed as a medium for the transmission of thought, feeling, etc. **vehicular, *-lary, *-latory** (vē hik′-), *a.* ***vehiculate,** *v.t.* and *i.*

Vehmgericht (fām′ gė ri*ch*t) [G. *feme*, punishment, tribunal, *gericht*, judgment, law], *n.* (*pl.* **-gerichte**) A system of irregular tribunals existing in Germany, esp. Westphalia, during the 14th and 15th cents., trying civil cases by day and the more serious criminal cases at night in secret sessions; such a tribunal. **vehmic** (fā′ mik), *a.*

veil (vāl) [M.E. and O.F. *veile*, L. *vēlum*, whence *velāre*, O.F. *veiler*, to veil], *n.* A more or less transparent piece of cloth, muslin, etc., usu. attached to the head-dress, worn to conceal, shade, or protect the face; a curtain or other drapery for concealing or protecting an object; (*fig.*) a mask, a disguise, a pretext; (*Eccles.*) the scarf on a pastoral staff; (*Anat., etc.*) a velum; (*Mus.*) a slight huskiness or obscuration of voice, permanent or due to a cold, etc. *v.t.* To cover with a veil; to hide, to conceal, to disguise. **veiling,** *n.* **to take the veil:** To assume the veil according to the custom of a woman when she becomes a nun; to retire to a convent. **veilless,** *a.*

veilleuse (vā yẽrz) [F., fem. of *veilleur*, from *veiller*, L. *vigilāre*, to watch], *n.* A night-lamp, shaded and usu. artistically decorated.

vein (vān) [M.E. and F. *veine*, L. *vēna*], *n.* One of the tubular vessels in animal bodies conveying blood to the heart; (*loosely*) any blood-vessel; (*Ent. and Bot.*) a rib or nervure in an insect's wing or a leaf; (*Geol. and Mining*) a fissure in rock filled with material deposited by water; a seam of any substance; a streak or wavy stripe of different colour, in wood, marble, or stone; (*fig.*) a distinctive trait, tendency, or cast of mind; particular mood or humour. *v.t.* To fill or cover with, or as with veins. **veinstone,** *n.* The non-metalliferous part in a vein, gangue. **veinage, veining,** *n.* **veinless,** *a.* **veinlet,** *n.* **veinlike, veiny,** *a.*

velamen (vė lā′ mėn), ***velamentum*** (vel ȧ men′ tŭm) [L., from VELUM], *n.* (*pl.* ***-mina, -menta***) (*Anat.*) A membraneous covering or envelope, esp. of parts of the brain. **velamentous,** *a.* **velar** [VELUM]. **velarium** (vė lâr′ i ŭm), *n.* (*pl.* **-ia**) (*Rom. Ant.*) The great awning stretched over the seats in a theatre or amphitheatre as a protection against rain or sun; (*Anat. etc.*) a velum. **velation** [VELUM].

velarize (vel′ ȧr īz) [L. *velare*, to veil], *v.t.* To sound a guttural further back than the hard palate

velatura (vel ȧ toor′ ȧ) [It. from *velare*, to VEIL], *n.* The glazing of pictures by rubbing on a thin coating of colour with the hand.

veld, veldt (felt) [Dut. *veld*, FIELD], *n.* (*S. Afr.*) Open country suitable for pasturage, esp. the high treeless plains in N. Transvaal and N.-W. Natal.

veld-schoen (fel′ skoon) [Dut. *vel*, skin, *schoen*, shoe], *n.* A shoe made of raw hide.

veliferous, etc. [VELUM].

***velitation** (vel i tā′ shŭn) [L. *vēlitātio*, from *vēlitārī*, to skirmish, from *vēles*, light-armed soldier, a velite], *n.* A slight skirmish; a controversial skirmish, a brush. **velite** (vē′ līt), *n.* (*Rom. Ant.*) A light-armed soldier.

***velleity** (vė lē′ i ti) [med. L. *velleitas*, from *velle*, to wish], *n.* A low degree of desire or volition unaccompanied by effort.

vellicate (vel′ i kāt) [L. *vellicātus*, p.p. of *vellicāre*, from *vellere*, to pluck], *v.t.* and *i.* To twitch spasmodically. **vellication** (-kā′ shŭn), *n.* **vellicative** (vel′ i kā tiv), *a.*

vellon (vel yon′) [Sp.], *n.* A Spanish money of account, obsolete, but formerly equal to 2½d.

velloped (vel′ ŏpt) [prob. var. of DEWLAPPED], *a.* (*Her.*) Having gills or wattles.

vellum (vel′ ŭm) [M.E. *velim*, F. *velin*, L. *vitulinus*, of a calf, from *vitulus*, see VEAL], *n.* A fine parchment orig. made of calf-skin; a manuscript written on this. **vellum-paper,** *n.* Paper made to imitate vellum. **vellumy,** *a.*

veloce (vė lō′ chā) [It.], *adv.* (*Mus.*) With great quickness.

velocipede (vė los′ i pēd) [L. *vēlox*, as foll., *pēs pedis*, foot], *n.* Any kind of carriage propelled by the feet; an early form of cycle. ***velociman** [L. *manus*, hand], *n.* An early vehicle resembling a velocipede, but driven by hand. **velocipedist,** *n.*

velocity (vė los′ i ti) [F. *vélocité*, L. *vēlōcitātem*, nom. *-tas*, from *vēlox-lōcis*, swift, cogn. with *volāre*, to fly], *n.* Swiftness, rapidity, rapid motion; rate of motion, esp. of inanimate things. **velocimeter** (vel ō sim′ ė tėr) [-METER], *n.* An apparatus for measuring velocity.

velours, velure (vel oor′, vel ūre′) [F. *velours*, O.F. *velous*, med. L. *villōsus*, shaggy, from VILLUS], *n.* Velvet, velveteen, or other fabric resembling velvet; a pad of velvet or silk for smoothing a silk hat. *v.t.* To smooth with this. **veloutine** (vel u tēn′), *n.* A corded fabric of merino, etc. **velutinous** (vė lū′ ti nŭs), *a.* (*Nat. Hist.*) Velvety.

velum (vē′ lŭm) [L., sail, covering, from *vehere*, to carry], *n.* (*pl.* **-la**) (*Anat., etc.*) A membrane, a membranous covering envelope, etc., esp. the soft palate. **velar,** *a.* **velation** (vė lā′ shŭn), *n.* **veliferous** (-lif′ ėr ŭs), *a.* **veligerous,** *a.*

velveret (vel vėr et′), *n.* An inferior kind of velvet.

velvet (vel′ vėt) [A.-F. from late L. *velluētum*, ult. from L. VILLUS], *n.* A closely-woven fabric, usu. of silk, with a short, soft nap or cut pile on one side; the furry skin covering the growing antlers of a deer; (*slang*) money won by gambling or speculation. *a.* Velvety; as soft as velvet. **cotton velvet:** Velvet made with cotton back and silk face. ***velvet-guard,** *n.* Velvet trimmings; a person wearing such trimmings. **velvet-pile,** *n.* A pile like that of velvet; a fabric with such a pile. **velveted, velvety,** *a.* **velveteen** (-tēn′), *n.* A cotton velvet or cotton fabric with a velvet-pile; *n.pl.* (*slang*) a gamekeeper. **velveting,** *n.* The fine nap or pile of velvet; (*collect.*) velvet goods.

vena (vē′ nȧ) [L.], *n.* (*pl.* ***venæ***) A vein. **venal** (1), *a.* **venation** (vė nā′ shun), *n.* The arrangement of the veins on leaves, insects' wings, etc. **venational,** *a.*

venal (2) (vē′ nȧl) [O.F., from L. *vēnālis*, from *vēnus, vēnum*, sale], *a.* Ready to be bought over for lucre or to sacrifice honour or principle for sordid considerations; mercenary, hireling, sordid. **venality** (vė năl′ i ti), *n.* **venally,** *adv.*

venatic, -al (vė năt′ ik, -ȧl) [L. *venāticus*, from *venātus*, hunting, see VENERY (1)], *a.* Pertaining to or used in hunting; fond of the chase. **venatically,** *adv.* **venatorial** (ven ȧ tôr i ȧl), *a.*

venation [VENA].

vend (vend) [F. *vendre*, L. *vendere* (*vēnum*, see VENAL (2), *dare*, to give)], *v.t.* (*chiefly legal*) To sell; to offer (small wares) for sale (as a costermonger, etc.). **vendee** (-dē′), *n.* **vendor** (*Law*), **vender,** *n.* **vendible,** *a.* **vendibility** (-bil′ i ti), ***vendibleness,** *n.* ***vendibly,** *adv.* In a saleable manner. ***vendition,** *n.* ***vendue,** *n.* A public auction.

vendace (ven′ dās) [O.F. *vendese*, *vandoise*, etym. doubtful], *n.* A small and delicate white-fish, *Coregonus vandesius*, found in some lakes.

Vendéan (van dā ȧn), *a.* Of or pertaining to La Vendée, a western department of France. *n.* An inhabitant or native of La Vendée; a member of the Royalist party who revolted against the French republic in 1793–5.

vendee, etc. [VEND].

Vendemiaire (van dā myâr) [F., from L. *vindēmia*, vintage, from *vinum*, wine], *n.* The first month of the French revolutionary calendar (22 Sept.–21 Oct.).

vendetta (ven det′ ȧ) [It., from L. *vindicta*, revenge, see VINDICTIVE], *n.* A blood-feud, often carried on for generations, in which the family of a murdered or injured man seeks vengeance on the offender or any member of his family, prevalent esp. in Corsica, Sardinia, and Sicily; this practice; (*fig.*) a feud, private warfare or animosity.

vendible, *vendue, etc. [VEND].

veneer (vė nēr′) [G. *furniren*, to inlay, F. *fournir*, to FURNISH], *v.t.* To cover with a thin layer of fine or superior wood; to coat (pottery, etc.) with a thin coating; (*fig.*) to put a superficial polish on, to disguise, to gloss over. *n.* A thin layer of superior wood for veneering; (*fig.*) superficial polish. **veneer-cutter, -mill, -saw,** *n.* A machine, etc., for cutting veneers. **veneering,** *n.*

venenate (ven′ ė nāt) [L. *venēnātus*, p.p. of *venēnāre*, from *venēnum*, poison], *a.* Infected with poison. ***veneficial, -cious** (-fish′ ȧl, -ŭs), *a.*

Acting by poison or sorcery. **venenation** (-nā′ shŭn), *n.* **venenific** (-nif′ ik), **veneniﬂuous** (-nif′ loo ŭs), *a.*

venerable (ven′ ėr ȧ bėl) [O.F., from L. *venerābilis*, as foll.], *a.* Worthy of veneration; rendered sacred by religious or other associations; applied as a title to archdeacons (*Ch. of Eng.*), and to a person who has attained the first of three degrees in canonization (*R.-C. Ch.*). **venerability** (-bil′ i ti), **venerableness,** *n.* **venerably,** *adv.*

venerate (ven′ ėr āt) [L. *venerātus*, p.p. of *venerārī*, cogn. with VENUS and with Sansk. *van*, to serve, to honour], *v.t.* To regard or treat with profound deference and respect, to revere. **veneration** (-ā′ shŭn), *n.* **venerative** (ven′ ėr ā tiv), *a.* **venerator,** *n.*

venereal (vė nēr′ ė ȧl) [L. *venereus*, from VENUS], *a.* Pertaining to, or produced by sexual intercourse. **venereal disease,** *n.* (*Path.*) Disease conveyed by sexual intercourse, viz., gonorrhœa, syphilis, and chancroid. **venerean, venereous,** *a.* Lustful, libidinous; aphrodisiac. ***venereate,** *v.t.* **venereology** (ven ēr i ol′ ō ji), *n.* The study of venereal diseases.

venery (1) (ven′ ėr i) [O.F. *venerie*, from *vener*, L. *vēnārī*, to hunt], *n.* Hunting, the chase.

venery (2) [VENUS], *n.* Sexual indulgence.

venesect (ven′ ė sekt) [L. *vēna*, VEIN, *secāre*, to cut, p.p. *sectus*], *v.t.* and *i.* To phlebotomize. **venesection** (-sek′ shŭn), *n.*

Venetian (vė nē′ shȧn) [L. *Venetia*, country of the Veneti], *a.* Pertaining to the city or province of Venice, in N. Italy. *n.* A native or inhabitant of Venice; (*colloq.*) a venetian blind; (*pl.*) a heavy kind of tape or braid used in venetian blinds. **venetian blind:** A blind made of thin slats on braid or webbing arranged to turn so as to admit or exclude light. **venetian chalk:** French chalk. **Venetian glass:** A delicate ornamental glass-ware made at or near Venice. **Venetian lace:** A variety of point lace. **Venetian mast,** *n.* A pole painted spirally in two or more colours, used for street decorations. **venetian window:** A window with three separate apertures.

***venew, veney** (ven′ ū, -ė) [VENUE], *n.* A bout at fencing; a thrust or hit.

vengeance (ven′ jȧns) [F., from *venger*, to *avenge*, L. *vindicāre*, see VINDICATE], *n.* Punishment inflicted in return for an injury or wrong, retribution; *mischief, evil. **with a vengeance:** (*colloq.*) Forcibly, emphatically, undoubtedly, extremely. ***venge,** *v.t.* To avenge or revenge. ***vengeable,** *a.* **vengeful,** *a.* Vindictive, revengeful. **vengefully,** *adv.* **vengefulness,** *n.* ***vengement,** *n.* ***venger,** *n.* ***vengeress,** *n.*

venial (vē′ ni ȧl) [O.F., from late L. *veniālis*, from *venia*, grace, pardon], *a.* That may be pardoned or excused; (*R.-C. Ch.*) not mortal (of some sins). **veniality** (-ăl′ i ti), **venialness,** *n.* **venially,** *adv.*

Venice (ven′ is) [city in N. Italy], *a.* Venetian. **Venice glass:** Venetian glass.

Veni Creator (vē′ nī krė ā′ tŏr) [L.], *n.* A hymn beginning 'Veni Creator Spiritus,' 'Come Creator Spirit,' used in the Anglican and R.-C. Churches at Whitsuntide, ordinations, etc.

venison (ven′ zŏn) [O.F. *veneisun* (F. *venaison*), L. *vēnātiōnem*, nom. *-tio*, from *vēnārī*, to hunt, see VENERY], *n.* The flesh of the deer as food.

Venite (vė nī′ tē) [L., come ye], *n.* Psalm xcv., 'O come let us sing,' used as a canticle; a musical setting of the same.

venom (ven′ ŏm) [M.E. and O.F. *venim* (F. *venin*), L. *venēnum*, poison], *n.* A poisonous fluid secreted by serpents, scorpions, etc., and injected by biting or stinging; (*fig.*) spite, malignity, virulence; *poison. **a.* Venomous. *v.t.* To imbue with venom; to poison. **venom-mouthed,** *a.* Full of venom; spiteful. **venomed, venomous,** *a.* **venomously,** *adv.* **venomousness,** *n.*

venose, -nous (vē′ nōs, -nŭs) [L. *vēnōsus*, from *vēna*, VEIN], *a.* (*Physiol., etc.*) Pertaining to or contained in the veins; consisting of veins. **venosity** (vė nos′ i ti), *n.* Local excess of veins or of venous blood; deficient aeration of venous blood with afflux of this to the arteries. **venously,** *adv.*

vent (1) (vent) [formerly *fent*, F. *fente*, from *fendre*, L. *findere*, to cleave], *n.* A hole or aperture, esp. for the passage of air, water, etc., into or out of a confined place, as in the head of a barrel, to allow air to enter while liquid is being drawn; the flue of a chimney, a touch-hole, a finger-hole in a wind-instrument, a loophole, etc.; the opening of the cloaca, the anus in animals below mammals; a means or place of passage, escape, etc., an outlet, free play, utterance, expression, etc. *v.t.* To make a vent in; to give vent to; to utter, to pour forth. **vent-hole,** *n.* **vent-peg,** *n.* A peg for stopping a vent-hole in a barrel. **vent-plug,** *n.* A plug for stopping the vent of a gun; a vent-peg. **vent stack,** *n.* (*Build.*) A vertical pipe to carry sewer gas above the level of the house windows. **ventage,** *n.* **ventless,** *a.*

vent (2) (vent) [F. *venter*, to blow, from *vent*, L. *ventum*, nom. *-tus*, wind], *v.i.* To take breath (of a hunted animal, esp. an otter). *n.* The act of venting, esp. of coming to the surface to breathe, as an otter; scent, trail.

***vent** (3) (vent) [F. *vente*, from *vendre*, L. *vendere*, to VEND], *n.* Sale, market.

***ventail** [AVENTAIL].

venter (ven′ tėr) [L.], *n.* The belly, the abdomen, any large cavity containing viscera; (*Nat. Hist.*) an expanded or hollowed part or surface; (*Law*) the womb, hence, a mother.

ventiduct (ven′ ti dŭkt) [L. *ventus*, wind], *n.* A passage or conduit, esp. subterranean, for ventilation.

ventil (ven′ til) [L. *ventulus*, breeze, dim. of *ventus*, wind], *n.* (*Mus.*) A valve; a shutter for regulating the admission of air in an organ.

ventilate (ven′ ti lāt) [L. *ventilātus*, p.p. of *ventilāre*, to blow, winnow, ventilate, from *ventus*, wind], *v.t.* To supply with fresh air, to cause a circulation of air in (a room, etc.); to oxygenate (the blood); (*fig.*) to give publicity to, to throw open for discussion, etc. **ventilation** (-lā′ shŭn), *n.* **ventilative** (ven′ ti lā tiv), *a.* **ventilator,** *n.*

ventose (1) (ven′ tōs) [L. *ventōsus*, from *ventus*, wind], *a.* Windy, flatulent.

Ventose (2) (van tōz) [as prec.], *n.* The sixth month of the French revolutionary year (19 Feb.–20 March).

ventral (ven′ trȧl) [L. *ventrālis*, from VENTER], *a.* (*Anat., etc.*) Pertaining to the venter; pertaining to or situated on the anterior surface or point (of fins, etc.). **ventrally,** *adv.* **ventricose, *-cous** (ven′ tri kōs, -kŭs), *a.* Having a protruding belly; (*Bot.*) distended, inflated.

ventricle (ven′ tri kėl) [F. *ventricule*, L. *ventriculum*, nom. *-us*, dim. of VENTER], *n.* A cavity or hollow part in an animal body, in the heart and brain. **ventricular, -lous** (-trik′ ū lȧr, -lŭs), *a.*

ventricose [VENTRAL].

ventriculite (ven trik′ ū līt) [L. *ventricul-us*, see prec., -ITE], *n.* (*Palæont.*) One of a family of fossil sponges common in flint nodules.

ventriloquism (ven tril′ ŏ kwizm) [L. *ventriloquus* (*venter-tris*, see VENTER, *loquī*, to speak), -ISM], *n.* The act or art of speaking or producing sounds so that the sound appears to come not from the person speaking but from a different source. **ventriloquist,** *n.* **ventriloquy, ventrilocution** (-kū′ shŭn), *n.* **ventriloquize,** *v.i.* **ventriloquial** (-lō′ kwi ȧl), **ventriloquistic** (-kwis′ tik), **ventriloquous** (-tril′ ŏ kwŭs), *a.*

ventro-, *comb. form.* [VENTER]. **ventrosity** (ven tros′ i ti), *n.* Corpulence.

venture (ven′ tūr, -chŭr) [shortened from AD-

VENTURE], *n.* The undertaking of a risk, a hazard; an undertaking of a risky nature; a commercial speculation; a stake, that which is risked; *chance, hap, contingency. *v.t.* To expose to hazard or risk, to hazard, to stake; to dare, to brave. *v.i.* To dare; to have the courage or presumption (to do, etc.); to undertake a risk. **at a venture:** At random. **to venture on or upon:** To dare to enter upon or engage in, etc. ***venturer,** *n.* **venturesome,** *a.* **venturesomely,** *adv.* **venturesomeness,** *n.* **venturous, venturously,** *adv.* **venturousness,** *n.*

venue (1) (ven' ū) [F., coming, from *venir*, L. *venīre*, to come], *n.* (*Law*) The place or country where a crime is alleged to have been committed and where the jury must be empanelled and the trial held; the clause in an indictment indicating this. **change of venue:** Alteration of the place of trial, etc., to avoid riot, etc.

***venue** (2) [VENEW].

Venus (vē' nŭs) [L.], *n.* (*Rom. Myth.*) The goddess of love, esp. sensual love; a planet between the earth and Mercury, the brightest heavenly body after the sun and moon. **Mount of Venus:** (*Anat.*) The female pubes, *mons veneris*; (*Palmistry*) the elevation at the base of the thumb. **Venus's basin, bath,** or **cup:** The teasel. **Venus's comb:** An annual herb of the parsley family. **Venus's flytrap:** An insectivorous herb of the sundew family. **Venus's looking-glass:** A plant of the genus *Specularia*, esp. *S. speculum*. **Venus's slipper:** The lady's-slipper.

veracious (vė rā' shŭs) [L. *vērax -acis*, from *vērus*, true], *a.* Habitually speaking or disposed to speak the truth; characterized by truth and accuracy; true. **veraciously,** *adv.* **veracity** (-ăs' i ti), *n.*

veranda (vė răn' dȧ) [Port. *varanda*, prob. from *vara*, L. *vāra*, forked pole], *n.* A light external gallery or portico with a roof on pillars, along the front or side of a house.

veratrine (ver' ȧ trin), *n.* (*Chem.*) A highly poisonous amorphous compound obtained from hellebore and other plants, used as a local irritant in neuralgia, rheumatism, etc. **veretrate,** *n.* A salt of veratric acid. **veratric,** *a.* **veratrize,** *v.t.*

veratrum (vė rā' trŭm) [L.], *n.* The hellebore; (*Bot.*) a genus of plants containing the hellebore.

verb (vĕrb) [F. *verbe*, L. *verbum*, word, cogn. with WORD and Gr. *eirein*, to speak], *n.* (*Gram.*) That part of speech which predicates, a word that asserts something in regard to something else (the subject).

verbal (vĕr' bȧl), *a.* Of or pertaining to words; respecting words only, not ideas, etc.; literal, word for word; (*Gram.*) pertaining to or derived from a verb; (*colloq.*) oral, spoken, not written. *n.* A verbal noun, one derived from a verb, esp. Eng. words in -ING. **verbalist,** *n.* One who deals in words only; a literal adherent to or a minute critic of words. **verbalism,** *n.* **verbalize,** *v.t.* To convert or change into a verb. *v.i.* To use many words, to be verbose. ***verbality,** *n.* **verbalization** (-zā' shŭn), *n.* **verbally,** *adv.* **verbify,** *v.t.* **verbarium** (-bâr' i ŭm), *n.* A game in which the players form words from given letters, etc.

verbatim (vĕr bā' tim), *adv.* Word for word.

verbena (vėr bē' nȧ) [L., in pl. *verbēnæ*, sacred boughs, of olive, etc.], *n.* A large genus of plants of which *V. officinalis*, the common vervain, is the type. **verbenaceous** (-bė nā' shŭs), *a.*

***verberate** (vĕr' bėr āt) [L. *verberātus*, p.p. of *verberāre*, from *verber*, rod, cogn. with prec.], *v.t.* To beat, to strike. ***verberation** (-ā' shŭn), *n.*

verbiage (vĕr' bi āj) [F., from *verbe*, VERB], *n.* The use of many words without necessity, verbosity, wordiness. **verbicide** [-CIDE], *n.* (*facet.*) Word-slaughter; a word-slaughterer.

verbose (vĕr bōs), *a.* Using or containing more words than are necessary, prolix. **verbosely,** *adv.* **verboseness, verbosity** (-bos' i ti), *n.*

verdant (vĕr' dȧnt) [O.F., from L. *viridans -ntem*, pres.p. of *viridāre*, from *viridis*, green], *a.* Green; covered with growing plants or grass; fresh, flourishing; (*slang*) green, inexperienced, unsophisticated, easily taken in. **verdancy,** *n.* **verde antico** (vâr' di ăn tē' kō), *n.* An ornamental stone composed chiefly of serpentine, usu. green and mottled or veined; a green incrustation on ancient bronze. **verdantly,** *adv.* **verdée** (-dā), *a.* (*Her.*) Charged with flowers.

***verderer** (vĕr' dėr ėr) [A.-F. *verder*, late L. *viridārius*, forester, as prec.], *n.* A judicial officer who has charge of the royal forests.

verdict (vĕr' dikt) [M.E. and O.F. *verdit*, L. *vērē dictum* (*vērē*, truly, DICTUM)], *n.* The decision of a jury on an issue of fact submitted to them in the trial of any cause, civil or criminal; decision, judgment. **open verdict:** One reporting the commission of a crime without specifying the guilty person. **special verdict:** One in which specific facts are placed on record but the court is left to form conclusions on the legal aspects.

verdigris (vĕr' dė gris, -grēs) [M.E. *verdegrees, grese*, A.-F. *vert de Grece*, green of Greece (VERT (1), L. *Græcia*, Greece)], *n.* A green crystalline substance formed on copper by the action of dilute acetic acid, used as a pigment and in medicine; greenish rust on copper, etc.

verditer (vĕr' di tėr) [A.-F. *verd de terre*, green of earth (O.F. *verd*, see prec., F. *terre*, L. *terra*, earth)], *n.* A light-blue pigment prepared from copper nitrate treated with chalk or other calcium carbonate.

***verdoy** [VERDÉE].

verdure (vĕr' dyŭr) [F., from O.F. *verd*, L. *viridis*]. *n.* Greenness of vegetation, fresh vegetation or foliage. **verdured, verdurous,** *a.* **verdureless,** *a.*

***verecund** (ver' ė kŭnd) [L. *verēcundus*, from *vereor*, to feel awe], *a.* Bashful, modest. **verecundity** (-kŭn' di ti), *n.*

Verein (fė rīn') [G.], *n.* An association, union, or organization.

verge (1) (vĕrj) [F., from L. *virga*, twig, rod], *n*, The extreme edge, brink, border, or margin; the grass-edging of a bed or border; a rod, wand, or staff, carried as an emblem of authority, esp. before a bishop or other dignitary; (*Arch.*) the shaft of a column; the edge of the tiles projecting over a gable, etc.; (*Mach.*) a spindle, shaft, etc., in the mechanism of a watch, loom, and other machines.

verge (2) (vĕrj) [L. *vergere*, to bend, to incline], *v.i.* To approach, to come near, to border (on). **vergency,** *n.* The act of verging, being near; (*Opt.*) the reciprocal of the focal distance of a lens taken as a measure of the divergence or convergence of rays. ***vergent,** *a.* Drawing to a close.

vergee (vėr jē') [F., from VERGE (1)], *n.* (*Channel Islands*) A land measure, about four-ninths of an acre.

verger (vĕr' jėr), *n.* An officer carrying the verge or staff of office before a bishop or other dignitary; an official in a church acting as usher or as pew-opener. **vergership,** *n.*

veridical (vė rid' i kȧl) [L. *vēridicus* (*verus*, true, *dicere*, to say)], *a.* Truthful, veracious. **veridically,** *adv.* **veridicous,** *a.*

verify (ver' i fī) [O.F. *verifier*, med. L. *vērificāre* (*vērus*, true, *-ficāre, facere*, to make)], *v.t.* To confirm the truth of; to inquire into the truth of, to authenticate; to fulfil; (*Law*) to affirm under oath, to append an affidavit to (pleadings). **verifiable,** *a.* **verifiability** (-bil' i ti), *n.* **verification** (-kā' shŭn), *n.* **verifier,** *n.*

***verily** (ver' i li) [M.E. *veraily* (VERY, -LY)], *adv.* In very truth, assuredly.

verisimilitude (ver i si mil' i tūd) [M.F., from L. *vērisimilitūdo*, from *verisimilis* (*vēri*, gen. of *vērus*, true, *similis*, like)], *n.* The appearance of or resemblance to truth; probability, likelihood; something apparently true or a fact. ***verisimilar, *-lous,** *a.*

veritable (ver′ i tȧ bėl) [O.F., from *verité*, VERITY], *a.* Real, genuine; actual, true. **veritably,** *adv.*

verity (ver′ i ti) [O.F. *verité*, L. *vēritātem*, nom. *-tas*, from *vērus*, true], *n.* Truth, correspondence (of a statement) with fact; a true statement, truth; a thing really existent, a fact. **of a verity:** In truth, surely.

verjuice (vĕr′ joos) [F. *verjus* (O.F. *verd*, VERT (I), JUICE)], *n.* An acid liquid expressed from crab-apples, unripe grapes, etc., and used in cooking and for other purposes. **verjuiced,** *a.*

vermeil (vĕr′ mil) [F., VERMILION], *n.* Silver-gilt; a transparent varnish for giving a lustre to gilt; (*poet.*) vermilion.

Vermes (vĕr′ mēz) [L., pl. of *vermis*], *n.pl.* An obsolete division of animals comprising earth-worms, sea-worms, leeches, brachiopods, etc. **vermeology** (-ol′ ȯ ji) [-LOGY], *n.* Helminthology. **vermicide** (vĕr′ mi sīd) [-CIDE], *n.* A medicine or drug that kills worms, an anthelmintic. **vermicidal,** *a.* **vermicular** (vĕr mik′ ū lȧr), *a.* Of or pertaining to a worm; resembling the motion or track of a worm; tortuous, marked with intricate wavy lines (of reticulated work, etc.); worm-eaten in appearance; vermiform. **vermiculate** (-lȧt), *a.* Worm-eaten; vermicular; *v.t.* (-lāt) To decorate with vermicular lines or tracery. **vermiculation** (-lā′ shŭn), *n.* Motion after the manner of a worm, as in the peristaltic motion of the intestines; the art of vermiculating; vermiculated work; the state of being worm-eaten. **vermicule,** *n.* A small grub or worm. **vermiculose, *-lous,** *a.* Full of or containing worms or grubs; worm-eaten; worm-shaped, vermicular. **vermiform** (vĕr′ mi fôrm), *a.* Worm-shaped; having the form or structure of a worm; vermicular. **vermiform appendix:** (*Anat.*) A small worm-like organ of no known function situated at the extremity of the cæcum. **vermifuge** (-fūj), *n.* A medicine or drug that destroys or expels intestinal worms, an anthelmintic. **vermifugal,** *a.* **vermigrade,** *a.* Moving or crawling like a worm. **vermivorous** (-miv′ ȯ rŭs) [-VOROUS], *a.* Feeding on worms.

vermicelli (vĕr mi sel′ i, -chel′ i) [It., pl. of *vermicello*, dim. of *verme*, worm, as prec.], *n.* A wheaten paste in the form of long slender tubes or threads like macaroni.

vermicular, -form, -fuge, etc. [VERMES].

vermilion (vĕr mil′ yȯn) [F. *vermillon*, from *vermeil*, L. *vermiculus*, dim. of *vermis*, worm, see VERMES], *n.* A brilliant red pigment consisting of mercuric sulphide obtained by grinding cinnabar or by the chemical treatment of mercury and sulphur; the colour of this. *a.* Of a beautiful red colour. *v.t.* To colour with or as with vermilion. ***vermily,** *n.* and *a.*

vermin (vĕr′ min) [F. *vermine*, from L. *vermis*, see VERMES], *n.* A collective name for certain mischievous or offensive animals, as the smaller mammals or birds injurious to crops or game, noxious or offensive insects, grubs, or worms, esp. lice, fleas, etc.; (*fig.*) low, noxious, or repulsive persons. **vermin-killer,** *n.* **verminate,** *v.i.* To breed vermin, to become infested with parasites. **vermination** (-nā′ shŭn), *n.* **verminous,** *a.* **verminously,** *adv.*

vermuth (vâr′ moot, vĕr′ muth) [F. *vermouth*, G. *wermuth*, wormwood], *n.* A liqueur made of white wine flavoured with wormwood and other aromatic herbs.

vernacular (vĕr năk′ ū lȧr) [L. *vernāculus*, from *verna*, home-born slave], *a.* Native, indigenous, belonging to the country of one's birth (of language, idiom, etc.). *n.* One's native tongue; the native idiom or dialect of a place or country. **vernacularism,** *n.* **vernacularity** (-lăr′ i ti), *n.* **vernacularize,** *v.t.* **vernacularization** (-zā′ shŭn), *n.* **vernacularly,** *adv.*

vernal (vĕr′ nȧl) [L. *vernālis*, from *vernus*, pertaining to spring, from *ver*, spring, cogn. with Gr. *ear*, Icel. *vār*], *a.* Pertaining to, prevailing, done, or appearing in spring; (*fig.*) pertaining to youth. **vernal equinox** [EQUINOX]. **vernal grass:** A fragrant grass, *Anthoxanthum odoratum*, sown among hay. **vernally,** *adv.* **vernalization,** *n.* (*Bot.*) The wetting of seeds before sowing, in order to hasten flowering. ***vernant,** *a.* Flourishing in the spring. **vernation** (-nā′ shŭn), *n.* The arrangement of the young leaves within the leaf-bud.

vernier (vĕr′ ni ėr) [F., from Pierre *Vernier* (*c.* 1580–1637), inventor], *n.* A movable scale for measuring fractional portions of the divisions of the scale on a measuring instrument, a barometer, theodolite, etc.

veronal (ve′ rō nȧl) [uncertain etym.], *n.* A hypnotic drug, diethylbarbituric acid, also called barbitone.

Veronese (ver ȯ nēz′), *a.* Pertaining to Verona. *n.* A native or inhabitant of Verona.

veronica (vė ron′ i kȧ) [name of woman said to have wiped the sweat from Christ's face on the way to Calvary, corr. of Gr. *Berenikē*], *n.* A herb or shrub of the fig-wort family, with blue, purple, or white flowers, the speedwell; a handkerchief or cloth bearing a portrait of Christ, esp. that of St. Veronica said to have been miraculously so impressed.

verricule (ver′ i kūl) [L. *verriculum*, net, from *verrere*, to sweep], *n.* (*Ent.*) A dense tuft of upright hairs.

verruca (ver′ ụ kȧ) [L.], *n.* (*pl.* **-cæ,** -sē) A wart; (*Nat. Hist.*) a wart-like elevation. **verruciform** (vė roo′ si fôrm), **verrucose, -cous, verruculose** (-roo′ kū lōs), *a.* **verrugas** (vėr oo′ găs) [Sp.], *n.* A disease characterized by ulcerous tumours, endemic in Peru.

***versable** (vĕr′ sȧbl) [L. *versābilis* from *versāre*, to turn round, see VERSANT], *a.* Capable of being turned. ***versability** (-bil′ i ti), ***versableness,** *n.*

***versal** (*Shak.*) [short for UNIVERSAL].

versant (vĕr′ sȧnt) [F., from *verser*, L. *versāre*, freq. of *vertere*, to turn], *n.* An area of land sloping in one direction; general lie or slope. *a.* *Conversant, versed; (*Her.*) having the wings open.

versatile (vĕr′ sȧ tīl) [F. *versatil*, L. *versātilis*, as prec.], *a.* Turning easily, readily applying oneself to new tasks, occupations, subjects, etc., many-sided; changeable, variable, inconstant; (*Bot. and Zool.*) moving freely round or to and fro on its support (of anthers, antennæ, etc.). **versatilely,** *adv.* **versatility** (-til′ i ti), *n.*

verse (vĕrs) [A.-S. *fers*, L. *versus -sūs*, a turning, furrow, row, verse, from *vertere*, to turn, p.p. *versus*], *n.* A metrical line consisting of a certain number of feet; (*pop.*) a group of metrical lines, a stanza; metrical composition as distinguished from prose; a particular type of metrical composition; one of the short divisions of a chapter of the Bible; a short sentence in a liturgy, etc. *v.t.* To express in verse. *v.i.* To make verses. ***vers de société*** (vâr dė sō syā tā): Society verses [see SOCIETY]. **verseman, versemonger,** *n.* **verse-mongering,** *n.* **verselet,** *n.* ***verser,** *n.* A versifier. **verset,** *n.* A short organ interlude or prelude. **versicle,** *n.* A short verse, esp. one of a series recited in divine service by the minister alternately with the people. **versicular** (-sik′ ū lȧr), *a.* Pertaining to verses; relating to division into verses. **versify** (vĕr′ si fī), *v.t.* To turn (prose) into verse; to narrate or express in verse; *v.i.* To make verses. **versification** (-kā′ shŭn), *n.* **versifier,** *n.*

versed (vĕrst) [L. *versātus*, p.p. of *versārī*, to turn about, see VERSANT], *a.* Skilled, familiar, experienced, proficient (in); (*Trig.*) turned about, reversed (of sines).

verselet, verset, versicle, etc. [VERSE].

versicolour, -coloured (vĕr′ si kŭl′ ȯr, -ȯrd) [L. *versicolor* (*versi-*, *versāre*, to turn, COLOUR)], *a.* Having various colours, variegated; changeable from one colour to another, with differences of light. ***versiform** (vĕr′ si fôrm) [-FORM], *a.* Varying in form.

versify, etc. [VERSE].

version (vĕr′ shŭn) [F., from med. L. *versiōnem*, nom. *-sio*, from *vertere*, to turn, p.p. *versus*], *n.* That which is translated from one language into another, a translation; the act of translating, translation; a piece of translation, esp. the rendering of a passage into another language as a school exercise; a statement, account, or description of something from one's particular point of view; (*Obstetrics*) the turning of a child in the womb to facilitate delivery. **versional,** *a.*

verso (vĕr′ sō) [as prec.], *n.* A left-hand page of a book, sheet, etc.; the other side of a coin or medal to that on which the head appears.

verst (vĕrst) [Rus. *versta*], *n.* A Russian measure of length, 3500·64 ft., nearly two-thirds of a mile.

versus (vĕr′ sŭs) [L., towards, from *vertere*, to turn, p.p. *versus*], *prep.* Against.

***versute** (vĕr sūt′) [L. *versūtus*, as prec.], *a.* Crafty, wily.

vert (1) (vĕrt) [F., from L. *viridem*, nom. *-dis*, green], *n.* (*Law*) Everything in a forest that grows and bears green leaves; the right to cut green or growing wood; (*Her.*) the tincture green.

vert (2) (vĕrt) [-*vert*, in PERVERT or CONVERT], *v.i.* (*colloq.*) To change one's religion; to leave one Church for another. *n.* One who verts, a pervert or convert.

vertebra (vĕr′ tė brȧ) [L., from *vertere*, to turn], *n.* (*pl.* **-bræ**) One of the bony segments of which the spine or backbone consists. **vertebral,** *a.* **vertebrally,** *adv.* **vertebrata,** *n.pl.* (*Zool.*) A division of animals comprising those with a backbone, including mammals, birds, reptiles, amphibians, and fishes. **vertebrate,** *a.* and *n.* **vertebrated,** *a.* **vertebration** (-brā′ shŭn), *n.* **vertebro-,** *comb. form.*

vertex (vĕr′ tėks) [L., whirlpool, summit, from *vertere*, to turn], *n.* (*pl.* **-tices,** -ti sēz) The highest point, the top, summit, or apex; (*Astron.*) the point on the limb (of sun, moon, or planet) furthest above the observer's horizon; (*Geom.*) the point of an angle, cone, pyramid, etc.; (*Anat.*) the top of the arch of the skull.

vertical (vĕr′ ti kȧl), *a.* Of, pertaining to, or situated at the vertex or highest point; situated at or passing through the zenith; perpendicular to the plane of the horizon; (*Anat.*) of or pertaining to the vertex of the head. **vertical angles:** Either pair of opposite angles made by two intersecting lines. **vertical circle:** An azimuth-circle. **vertical fins:** Fins situated in the median line, the dorsal, anal, and caudal fins. **vertical plane:** A plane passing through the zenith perpendicular to the horizon. **verticality** (-kăl′ i ti), **verticalness,** *n.* **vertically,** *adv.*

verticil (vĕr′ ti sil) [L. *verticillus*, dim. of VERTEX], *n.* (*Bot., etc.*) A whorl, an arrangement of parts in a circle round a stem, etc. **verticillate, -lated** (-tis′ i lȧt, -lā tėd), *a.* **verticillately,** *adv.*

vertigo (vĕr′ ti gō) [L., as VERTEX], *n.* Giddiness, dizziness; a feeling as if one were whirling round. **vertiginous** (-tij′ i nŭs), *a.* **vertiginously,** *adv.* **vertiginousness,** *n.*

vertu [VIRTU].

Verulamian (ver ū lā′ mi ȧn) [L. *Verulamium*, *Verulam*, ancient town near site of St. Albans], *a.* Of or pertaining to Francis Bacon, Baron Verulam (1561–1626), philosopher; of or pertaining to St. Albans.

verules (ver′ ulz) [var. of VIROLES, pl. of VIROLE], *n.pl.* (*Her.*) A bearing composed of a number of concentric rings one inside the other. **veruled,** *a.*

vervain (vĕr′ vān) [M.E. and O.F. *verveine*, L. VERBENA], *n.* A wild plant or weed, with small purplish flowers, of the genus Verbena, esp. *V. officinalis*, formerly credited with medical and other virtues.

verve (vĕrv) [F., perh. from L. *verba*, words, see VERB], *n.* Spirit, enthusiasm, energy, esp. in literary or artistic creation.

***vervel** [VARVAL].

vervet (vĕr′ vėt) [etym. doubtful], *n.* A small S. African monkey, usu. black-speckled greyish-green, with reddish-white face and abdomen.

very (ver′ i) [M.E. *verrai*, O.F. *verai* (F. *vrai*), L. *verax -ācis*, see VERACIOUS], *a.* Real, true, actual, genuine, being what it seems or is stated to be, selfsame (now chiefly used intensively). *adv.* In a high degree; to a great extent; greatly, extremely, exceedingly.

Very light (vâr′ i līt) [name of inventor], *n.* (*Mil.*) A firework to produce a flare for lighting up the countryside.

vesania (vė sā′ ni ȧ) [L., from *vēsānus* (*vē*, not, *sānus*, SANE)], *n.* (*Path.*) Insanity.

vesica (vė sī′ kȧ) [L.], *n.* (*pl.* **-cæ,** -sē) A bladder, cyst, etc., the gall-bladder, the urinary bladder. **vesica piscis:** [L., fish-bladder] The elliptic aureole in which the Saviour and the saints were often depicted by early painters. **vesical** (ves′ i kȧl), *a.* **vesicant,** *n.* A blister-producing counter-irritant; a poison-gas that causes blisters. **vesicate** (-kāt), *v.t.* To raise vesicles or blisters on. **vesicant, vesicatory,** *a.* and *n.* **vesication** (-kā′ shŭn), *n.* **vesicle** (ves′ ikl), *n.* A small bladder or cavity, sac, cyst, bubble, or hollow structure. **vesico-,** *comb. form.* **vesicocele** (ves′ i kō sēl) [-CELE], *n.* (*Path.*) Hernia of the bladder. **vesicotomy** (-kot′ ŏ mi), *n.* **vesicular** (vė sik′ ū lȧr), **-late, -liferous** (-lif′ ėr ŭs), **-liform** (vė sik′ ū li fôrm), **-lose, -lous,** *a.* **vesiculation** (-lā′ shŭn), *n.* **vesiculo-,** *comb. form.*

vesper (ves′ pėr) [L., cogn. with HESPER], *n.* The evening star, Venus, appearing just after sunset; (*fig.*) evening; (*R.-C. Ch. and Gr. Ch., pl.*) the sixth of the seven canonical hours; the evening service. *a.* Pertaining to the evening or to vespers. **Sicilian Vespers** [SICILIAN]. **vesperal,** *n.* The part of the antiphonary containing the chants for vespers. **vesperian** (-pēr′ i ȧn), *a.* **vespertine** (ves′ pėr tīn, -tin), *a.* Of, pertaining to, or done in the evening; (*Zool.*) flying in the evening; (*Bot.*) opening in the evening; (*Astrol.*) descending towards the horizon at sunset.

vespertilio (ves pėr til′ i ō) [L., from VESPER], *n.* (*Zool.*) A genus of Cheiroptera comprising the common bat.

vespiary (ves′ pi ȧ ri) [from L. *vespa*, wasp, after APIARY], *n.* A nest of wasps, hornets, etc. **vespiform,** *a.* Resembling a wasp. **vespine,** *a.*

vessel (ves′ ėl) [A.-F., from O.F. *vaissel* (F. *vaisseau*), L. *vascellum*, dim. of VAS], *n.* A hollow receptacle, esp. for holding liquids, as a jug, cup, dish, bottle, barrel, etc.; a ship or craft of any kind, esp. one of some size; (*Anat.*) a tube, a duct, or canal in which the blood or other fluids are conveyed; (*Bot.*) a canal or duct formed by the breaking down of the partitions between cells; (*fig.*) a person regarded as receiving or containing (grace, wrath, etc.). **the weaker vessel:** Woman (1 Peter iii. 7). **vesselful,** *n.*

vessignon (ves′ ik-, -ig nŏn) [F., from L. VESICA], *n.* A soft swelling on a horse's leg, a wind-gall.

vest (vest) [L. *vestis*, garment, cogn. with Gr. *esthēs*, clothing, Sansk. *vas*, to put on, and Eng. WEAR (1)], *n.* (*Tailor, & Am.*) A waistcoat; an undergarment for the upper part of the body, a singlet, (*Am.* an undershirt); a close jacket formerly worn by women, now a (usu. V-shaped) piece on the front of the body or waist of a gown; *a garment, clothing, dress. *v.t.* (*poet.*) To clothe with or as with a garment; to invest or endow (with authority, etc.); to confer an immediate fixed right of present or future possession of (property in a person). *v.i.* (of property, right, etc.) To come or take effect (in a person). **vested,** *a.* Wearing vestments, robed; (*Her.*) clothed; (*Law*) held by or fixed in a person, not subject to contingency. **vesting,** *n.* Material for making vests. **vested interest,** *n.* A source of gain to which the owner considers himself entitled by custom and right. **vestiture,** *n.* (*Zool.*) Anything covering a surface, as hair, scales, etc.

Vesta (ves′ tȧ) [L., cogn. with Gr. *Hestia*], *n.* (*Rom. Myth.*) The goddess of the hearth and the hearth-fire; (*Astron.*) the 4th asteroid. **vesta,** *n.* A wax match igniting by friction. **vestal,** *a.* Pertaining to the goddess Vesta or the vestal virgins; (*fig.*) pure, chaste; *n.* A vestal virgin; (*fig.*) a woman of spotless chastity; a nun. **vestal virgin:** One of the virgin priestesses, vowed to perpetual chastity, who had charge of the temple of Vesta at Rome, and of the sacred fire which burned perpetually on her altar.

vestiary (ves′ ti ȧr i) [late L. *vestiārius*, from *vestis*, VEST], *a.* Pertaining to dress. *n.* A wardrobe, a robing-room.

vestibule (ves′ ti būl) [L. *vestibulum*, etym. doubtful], *n.* A small hall, lobby, or ante-chamber next the outer door of a house, from which doors open into the various inner rooms; a porch; a covered passage between the cars in a corridor train; (*Anat.*) a chamber, cavity, or channel communicating with others, as the central chamber of the labyrinth of the ear. **vestibule train:** (*Am.*) A corridor train. **vestibular, -late,** *a.* (*Anat.*). **vestibuled,** *a.*

vestige (ves′ tij) [F., from L. *vestigium*, footstep, etym. doubtful], *n.* The mark of a foot made in passing, a foot-print; a sign, a mark or trace of something no longer present or in existence; (*colloq.*) an atom, a particle; (*Biol.*) an organ or part that has degenerated and become nearly or entirely useless. **vestigial, vestigiary,** *a.*

vesting, vestiture [VEST].

vestment (vest′ ment) [M.E. *vestiment*, O.F. *vestement*, L. *vestīmentum*, from *vestīre*, to clothe, from *vestis*, see VEST], *n.* A garment, esp. a robe of state or office; any of the ritual garments of the clergy, choristers, etc., esp. a chasuble; an altar-cloth.

vestry (ves′ tri) [O.F. *vestiairie*, L. *vestiārium*, wardrobe, neut. of *vestiārius*, VESTIARY], *n.* A room or place attached to a church in which the vestments are kept and in which the clergy, choristers, etc., robe; a chapel or room attached to a non-liturgical church; a meeting of the ratepayers of a parish (called a common, general, or ordinary vestry) or of their elected representatives (called a select vestry) for dealing with parochial business, formerly exercising sanitary and other powers of local government, as such now superseded by the parish council. **vestry-clerk,** *n.* An officer appointed by a vestry to keep the accounts, etc. **vestryman,** *n.* A member of a vestry. **vestral,** *a.* **vestrydom,** *n.* Government by a vestry, esp. if corrupt or incompetent.

vesture (ves′ tyůr) [O.F. *vesteure*, late L. *vestītūra*, VESTITURE], *n.* (*poet.*) Dress, clothes, apparel; a covering. *v.t.* To clothe, to dress. **vestural,** *a.* **vesturer,** *n.* A person in charge of church vestments; the subtreasurer of a collegiate church or cathedral.

Vesuvian (vė sū′ vi ȧn), *a.* Pertaining to Vesuvius, a volcano near Naples, Italy; volcanic. *n.* A variety of fusee for lighting cigars, etc., in the open air; vesuvianite. **vesuvianite,** *n.* A vitreous brown or green silicate first found among the ejections of Vesuvius.

vet (vet) [VETERINARY], *n.* (*colloq.*) A veterinary surgeon.

vetch (vech) [M.E. and O.North.F. *veche*, O.F. *vece*, L. *vicia*], *n.* A plant of the genus *Vicia* of the bean family, including several wild and cultivated species used for forage, esp. the common vetch or tare. **vetchling,** *n.* A plant of the genus *Lathyrus*, allied to the vetches. **vetchy,** *a.*

veteran (vet′ ėr ȧn) [L. *veterānus*, from *vetus -teris*, old], *a.* Grown old or experienced, esp. in the military service; of or pertaining to veterans. *n.* One who has had long experience in any service, occupation, or art, esp. as a soldier; (*Am.*) an ex-service man. **veteranize,** *v.t.* To render veteran. *v.i.* (*Am.*) To re-enlist.

veterinary (vet′ ėr i nȧr i) [L. *veterīnārius*, from *veterīnæ bestiæ*, beasts of burden, perh. from *vetus -teris*, see prec.], *a.* Pertaining to treatment of the diseases of domestic animals, as oxen, horses, dogs, etc. *n.* A veterinary surgeon. **veterinarian** (-nâr′ i ȧn), *n.*

veto (vē′ tō) [L., I forbid], *n.* The power or right of a sovereign, president, or branch of a legislature to negative the enactments of another branch; the act of exercising such right; any authoritative prohibition, refusal, negative, or interdict. *v.t.* To refuse approval to (a Bill, etc.); to prohibit, to forbid. **suspensive** or **suspensory veto:** A veto that suspends but does not necessarily prevent the ultimate completion of a measure. **vetitive** (vet′ i tiv), *a.* **vetoist** (vē′ tō ist), *n.*

vettura (vė toor′ ȧ) [It., from L. *vectūra*, conveyance, from *vehere*, to convey, p.p. *vectus*], *n.* (*pl.* **-re,** -rā) An Italian four-wheeled carriage. ***vetturino*** (-rē′ nō), *n.* (*pl.* ***-ni***) One who lets out *vetture* for hire; one who drives a *vettura*.

***vetust** (vė tŭst′) [L. *vetustus*, from *vetus*, old], *a.* Old, ancient.

vex (veks) [F. *vexer*, L. *vexāre*], *v.t.* To cause trouble or annoyance to, to irritate; (*poet.*) to agitate, to throw (the sea, etc.) into commotion; *to grieve, to afflict. **vexation** (-sā′ shůn), *n.* The act of vexing or the state of being vexed, irritation, annoyance, trouble; that which causes irritation, an annoyance; a harassing by process of or under the cover of law. **vexatious,** *a.* **vexatiously,** *adv.* **vexatiousness,** *n.* **vexed** (vekst), *a.* Annoyed, worried, filled with vexation; much debated or contested (of a question or doctrine). **vexedly** (vek′ sėd li), **vexingly,** *adv.* **vexer,** *n.*

vexillum (vek sil′ ům) [L., from *vehere*, see VETTURA], *n.* (*Rom. Ant.*) A square flag carried by a vexillary, forming the standard of a maniple or *turma*; a turma or other body of troops under a separate vexillum; (*Bot.*) the large upper petal of a papilionaceous flower; (*Ornith.*) the web of a feather; (*Eccles.*) a flag or pennon on a bishop's staff, usu. wound round it; a processional banner or cross. **vexil,** *n.* (*Bot.*) **vexillar, -late,** *a.* **vexillary,** *a.* and *n.* ***vexillation** (-lā′ shůn), *n.* A company of troops under one standard.

via (vī ȧ) [L. *viā*, abl. of *via*, way], *adv.* By way of, through. **Via Lactea:** The Milky Way. ***via media*** [L. *medius*, middle]: A middle way, a mean between extremes.

viable (vī′ ȧbl) [F. *vie*, life], *a.* Capable of maintaining independent existence, able to survive; (*Bot.*) able to live in a particular climate. **viability,** *n.*

viaduct (vī′ ȧ dŭkt) [L. *via ducta* (VIA, ducta, fem. p.p. *dūcere*, to lead, to conduct)], *n.* A bridge-like structure, esp. one composed of masonry and a considerable number of arches carrying a road or railway over a valley, etc.

vial (vī′ ȧl) [O.F. *viole*, *fiole*, L. *phiala*, PHIAL], *n.* A small vessel, usu. cylindrical and of glass, for holding liquid medicines, etc.; a vessel, a bottle. *v.t.* To put into a vial or vials. **to pour out vials of wrath:** To take vengeance (in alln. to Rev. xvi.); to give vent to one's anger or resentment.

viameter (vī ăm′ ė tėr) [VIA, -METER], *n.* An hodometer.

viand (vī′ ȧnd) [F. *viande*, L. *vivenda*, things to live on, provisions, neut. pl. ger. of *vivere*, to live], *n.* (*usu. in pl.*) Articles of food, esp. meat, victuals.

viaticum (vī ăt′ i kům) [L., from VIA], *n.* (*Rom. Ant.*) A supply of provisions or an allowance of money for a journey granted to a magistrate, envoy, etc.; (*Eccles.*) the Eucharist as given to a person at the point of death. ***viatic,** *a.* Pertaining to a journey or travel. **viator** (-ā' tŏr), *n.* A traveller, a wayfarer. ***viatorially,** *adv.*

vibex (vī' bĕks) [L., weal, mark of a blow], *n.* (*pl.* **vibices,** -bi sēz) (*Path.*) A purple spot appearing on the skin in certain fevers.

vibraculum (vī brăk' ū lŭm) [mod. L., as foll.], *n.* (*pl.* **-la**) One of the filamentous whip-like appendages of many polyzoa, bringing particles of food within reach by their lashing movements. **vibracular,** *a.*

vibrant (vī' brȧnt), *a.* Vibrating, tremulous; resonant. **vibrancy,** *n.*

vibrate (vī' brāt, vī brāt') [L. *vibrātus*, p.p. of *vibrāre*, to shake, to brandish], *v.i.* To move to and fro rapidly, to swing, to oscillate; to thrill, to quiver, to throb; (*Phys.*) to move to and fro ceaselessly, esp. with great rapidity. *v.t.* To cause to swing, oscillate, or quiver; to measure (seconds, etc.) by vibrations or oscillations. **vibratile** (vī' brȧ til, -tīl), *a.* **vibratility** (-til' i ti), *n.* **vibrative** (vī' brȧ tiv), **vibratory,** *a.*

vibration (vī brā' shŭn), *n.* The act of vibrating; oscillation; (*Phys.*) rapid motion backward and forward, esp. of the parts of an elastic solid or of a liquid the equilibrium of which has been disturbed; one such complete movement. **vibrational,** *a.* **vibratiuncle** (-shi ŭnkl), *n.* A small vibration.

vibrato (vē bra' tō) [It.], *n.* (*Mus.*) A pulsating effect, esp. in singing, produced by the rapid variation of emphasis on the same tone.

vibrator (vī brā' tŏr), *n.* One who or that which vibrates; (*Elec.*) a vibrating reed used in harmonic telegraphy; (*Elec.*) a vibrating reed used to chop a continuous current and thus produce an alternating current; (*Mus.*) a reed, as in a reed-organ; (*Print.*) a roller with vibratory and rotary motion for distributing ink.

vibrio (vib' ri ō) [from L. *vibro*, I vibrate], *n.* (*Biol.*) A form of bacterium more or less screw-shaped with a filament at each end, as that causing Asiatic cholera.

vibrissa (vi bris' ȧ) [L., hair in the nostril, as prec.], *n.* (*pl.* **-sæ**) A stiff coarse hair or bristle in the nostrils of man and about the mouths of most mammals; one of the bristle-like feathers about the mouths of some birds, as the flycatchers; one of the bristles about the mouths of some flies.

vibro-, *comb. form.* **vibrogen** (vī' brȯ jĕn), *n.* (*Bot.*) Active cellular tissue in the cortex of certain tendrils, to which the movements of circumnutation are due. **vibroscope** (vī' brȯ skōp) [-SCOPE], *n.* An instrument for registering vibrations.

viburnum (vī bĕr' nŭm) [L.], *n.* A shrub or small tree of a genus containing the guelder rose and the laurustinus, etc., of the honeysuckle family.

vicar (vik' ȧr) [O.F. *vicaire*, L. *vicārius*, orig. a., deputed, from *vic-*, see VICE-], *n.* The priest of a parish the greater tithes of which belong to a chapter or a layman, he himself receiving the smaller tithe or a stipend. **lay vicar:** (*Ang. Ch.*) A cathedral officer who sings some portion of the service. **vicar apostolic:** (*R.-C. Ch.*) A titular bishop appointed where no episcopate has been established, etc. **Vicar of Bray,** *n.* A turncoat. **vicar choral:** (*Ang. Ch.*) A clerical or lay assistant in the choral part of a cathedral service. **Vicar of Christ,** *n.* One of the pope's titles. **vicar forane:** (*R.-C. Ch.*) A functionary appointed by a bishop with limited (chiefly disciplinary) jurisdiction over clergy, etc. **vicar-general,** *n.* (*R.-C. Ch.*) An officer appointed by a bishop as his assistant, esp. in matters of jurisdiction; (*Ang. Ch.*) an officer assisting a bishop or archbishop in ecclesiastical causes and visitations. **vicarage,** *n.* The benefice of a vicar; the house or residence of a vicar. ***vicarial** (vi kâr' i ȧl), *a.* **vicariate,** *a.* Having delegated power, vicarious. *n.* Delegated office or power; a vicarship, esp. the jurisdiction of a vicar apostolic.

vicarious (vi kâr' i ŭs), *a.* Deputed, delegated; acting on behalf of another; performed, done, or suffered for or instead of another. **vicariously,** *adv.*

vice (1) (vīs) [F., from L. *vitium*], *n.* An evil or immoral practice or habit; evil conduct, gross immorality, depravity; a fault, a blemish, a defect; a bad habit or trick in a horse; *the buffoon in the old morality plays.

vice (2) (vīs) [M.E., spiral staircase, F. *vis*, screw, L. *vītis*, vine], *n.* An instrument with two jaws, brought together by a screw or lever, between which an object may be clamped securely; (*fig.*) *a grip, a grasp. *v.t.* To secure in or as in a vice.

vice (3) (vī' sė) [as VICE-], *prep.* In place of.

vice (4) (vīs) (*colloq.*) [short for VICE-PRESIDENT, -CHAIRMAN, etc.].

vice- [L., abl. from gen. *vicis*, change, alteration (nom. sing. does not occur)], *pref.* Denoting one acting or qualified to act in place or as deputy of another or one next in rank. **vice-admiral,** *n.* A naval officer next in rank below an admiral, and next above a rear-admiral. **vice-admiralty,** *n.* **vice-agent,** *n.* **vice-chair,** *n.* The seat occupied by a vice-chairman, a vice-chairman. **vice-chairman,** *n.* **vice-chairmanship,** *n.* **vice-chamberlain,** *n.* The deputy of the Lord Chamberlain. **vice-chancellor,** *n.* A deputy-chancellor; (*Univ.*) an officer who discharges most of the administrative duties of a university; (*R.-C. Ch.*) the head cardinal of the branch of Chancery dealing with bulls and briefs; (*Law*) formerly a subordinate judge in Chancery. **vice-chancellorship,** *n.* **vice-consul,** *n.* **vice-consulship,** *n.* **vice-governor,** *n.* **vice-king,** *n.* A viceroy.

vicegerent (vīs ge' rėnt), *n.* (often incorr. called "viceregent") [F. (L. *gerens -ntem*, pres.p. of *gerere*, to carry on)], *a.* Having or exercising delegated power. *n.* An officer exercising delegated authority, a deputy. **vicegerency,** *n.*

vicenary (vis' ė nȧr i) [L. *vīcēnārius*, from *vīcēni*, twenty each, from *vīginti*, twenty], *a.* Consisting of or pertaining to twenty. **vicennial** (vī sen' i ȧl) [L. *annus*, year], *a.* Happening every twenty years; lasting twenty years.

vice-president (vīs prez' i dėnt) [VICE-, PRESIDENT], *n.* A deputy-president. **vice-presidentship, presidency,** *n.* **vice-principal,** *n.* ***vice-queen,** *n.* A woman acting as viceroy; the wife of a viceroy. **viceregal,** *a.* Viceroyal. **vice-reine** (-rān) [F., queen], *n.* The wife of a viceroy.

viceroy (vīs' roi) [VICE-, F. *roi*, king], *n.* A ruler acting with royal authority in a colony, dependency, etc. **viceroyal,** *a.* **viceroyalty, viceroyship,** *n.*

vice versa (vī' sė vĕr' sȧ) [VICE (3), L. *versa*, fem. p.p. of *vertere*, to turn], *adv.* The order or relation being inverted, the other way round.

Vichy (vē' shi), *n.* A town in the Allier Department, France. **Vichy Government,** *n.* The French government formed, after the capitulation of France in 1940, by Marshal Pétain, with its seat at Vichy. **Vichy Water,** *n.* An effervescent mineral water found at Vichy.

vicinage (vis' i nȧj) [F. *voisinage*, from *voisin*, L. *vīcīnus*, neighbouring, from *vīcus*, village, street (assim. to L.)], *n.* Neighbourhood, vicinity, surrounding places, environs; the state of being neighbours, neighbourliness. ***vicinal,** *a.* Near, neighbouring. **vicinity** (vi sin' i ti), *n.* The neighbourhood, the adjoining or surrounding district; the state of being near, proximity; near relationship (to).

vicious (vish' ŭs) [F. *vicieux*, L. *vitiōsus*, from *vitium*, VICE (1)], *a.* Characterized by some vice, fault, or blemish; faulty, imperfect, defective, incorrect, corrupt; contrary to moral principles or to rectitude; addicted to vice, depraved, wicked; spiteful, malignant. **viciously,** *adv.* **viciousness,** *n.*

vicissitude (vi-, vi sis' i tūd) [L. *vicissitūdo -dinis*, from *vicissim*, by turns, as VICE (3)], *n.* A change of condition, circumstances, or fortune, a mutation, a revolution; (*poet.*) regular change or mutation. **vicissitudinary, -dinous,** *a.*

victim (vik' tim) [F. *victime*, L. *victima*, cogn. with Goth. *weihan*, to consecrate, *weihs*, holy], *n.* A living creature sacrificed to some deity or in the performance of some religious rite; a person or thing destroyed or injured in the pursuit of some object; a dupe, a gull. **victimize,** *v.t.* To make a victim of; to dupe, to swindle. **victimization** (-zā' shŭn), *n.* **victimizer,** *n.*

victor (vik' tŏr) [L., from *vict-*, p.p. stem of *vincere*, to conquer], *n.* One who conquers in battle or wins in a contest. **victress,** *n.*

victoria (vik tôr' i ȧ) [Queen *Victoria* (1819–1837–1901), L., victory, as prec.], *n.* A four-wheeled carriage with a raised seat for the driver, seats for two persons over the back axle and a low seat for two persons over the front axle, and a falling top; a gigantic variety of water-lily; a variety of domestic pigeon. **Victoria Cross:** A British naval and military decoration in the shape of a Maltese cross, instituted by Queen Victoria (1856), bestowed for conspicuous bravery or devotion in the presence of the enemy. **Victorian** (vik tôr' i ȧn), *a.* Of, pertaining to, or flourishing or living in the reign of Victoria. *n.* A person, esp. a writer, living or flourishing then; a native of Victoria, Australia. **Royal Victorian Order:** An order established by Queen Victoria (1896), bestowed principally for distinguished services to the sovereign.

victorine (vik tȯ rēn') [fem. name], *n.* A woman's small fur tippet with long narrow ends in front; a variety of peach.

victorious (vik tôr' i ŭs), *a.* Having conquered in battle or any contest, triumphant, associated or connected with victory. **victoriously,** *adv.* **victoriousness,** *n.*

victory (vik' tȯ ri) [M.E. and O.F. *victorie*, L. *victoria*, as VICTOR], *n.* The defeat of an enemy in battle, or of an opponent in a contest; a Roman or Greek goddess of victory. **Victory sign,** *n.* The first and second fingers extended in the form of a V.

victress [VICTOR].

victual (vit' ėl) [M.E. and O.F. *vitaille*, L. *victūalia*, neut. pl. of *victuālis*, pertaining to nourishment from *victus*, food, from *vīvere*, to live], *n.* (*usu. in pl.*) Food, provisions. *v.t.* To supply or store with provisions. *v.i.* To lay in provisions; to take food, to eat. **victualler** (vit' ler), *n.* One who supplies victuals, esp. an innkeeper; a victualling-ship. **licensed victualler** [LICENCE]. **victualless,** *a.* **victualling-bill,** *n.* A custom-house warrant for the shipment of provisions for a voyage. **victualling-department, -office,** *n.* The office managing the supply of provisions to the navy. **victualling-ship,** *n.* A ship conveying provisions to other ships or to a fleet. **victualling-yard,** *n.* One, usu. adjoining a dockyard, where warships are provisioned.

vicugna, vicunia (vi koo' nyȧ) [Sp., from Peruvian, *vicuña*], *n.* A S. American animal, *Auchenia vicugna*, allied to the camel, a native of the Andean regions of Bolivia and N. Chile; (*Text.*) a fine cloth made of worsted yarn.

vidame (vē dam) [F., corr. of med. L. *vice-dominus* (VICE-, L. *dominus*, lord)], *n.* (*F. Hist.*) A minor noble holding lands under a bishop; a bishop's deputy in secular matters.

vide (vī' dē) [L. imper. of *vidēre*, to see], *v. imper.* See (in reference to a passage in a book, etc.).

videlicet (vi dē' li sėt) [L., for *vidēre licet*, it is allowable to see, one may see], *adv.* Namely, that is to say, to wit (usu. abbrev. to VIZ].

vidette [VEDETTE].

vidimus (vī' di-, vid' i mŭs) [L., we have seen, as VIDE], *n.* (*pl.* **-uses**) An examination or inspection of accounts, etc.; an abstract or summary.

***viduous** (vid' ū ŭs) [L. *viduus*, separated from], *a.* Widowed. ***viduage, *viduity** (vi dū' i ti), *n.* ***vidual,** *a.* **viduation** (-ā' shŭn), *n.*

vie (vī) [M.E. *vien*, shortened from *envien*, O.F. *envier*, L. *invītāre*, to INVITE], *v.i.* To strive for superiority; to contend, to rival; to be equal or superior (with or in). **vying,** *a.*

***vielle** [VIOL].

Viennese (vi ė nēz'), *a.* Pertaining to Vienna or its inhabitants. *n.* A native or the inhabitants of Vienna.

view (vū) [A.-F., from O.F. *veue*, fem. of *veu*, p.p. of *voir*, L. *vidēre*, to see], *n.* Survey or examination by the eye; range of vision; power of seeing; that which is seen, a scene, a prospect; a picture or drawing of this; an intellectual or mental survey; the manner or mode of looking at things, considering a matter, etc.; judgment, opinion, theory; intention, purpose, design; (*Law*) inspection by a jury, etc. *v.t.* To examine with the eye; to survey mentally or intellectually; to consider, to form a mental impression or judgment of; to watch television. **in view:** In sight. **in view of:** Considering, having regard to. **on view:** Open to public inspection. **view-point,** *n.* A point of view, an aspect. ***to the view:** So as to be seen by everybody. **view-hallo,** *n.* A huntsman's shout on seeing the fox break cover. **with a view to:** For the purpose of; with an eye to. **viewable,** *a.* **viewer,** *n.* **view-finder,** *n.* (*Phot.*) A device of mirrors in a camera which shows the view to be taken. **viewless,** *a.* (*poet.*) Invisible. **viewy,** *a.* Having peculiar or impracticable views, faddy, visionary. **viewiness,** *n.*

vigesimal (vī jes' i mȧl) [L. *vīgēsimus*, from *vīginti*, twenty], *a.* Twentieth. ***vigesimation** (-mā' shŭn), *n.* The putting to death of every twentieth man. **vigesimo,** *a.* and *n.* 20mo. (of books). **vigesimo-quarto,** *a.* and *n.* 24mo.

vigia (vi jē' ȧ) [Sp., look out], *n.* A warning of a rock, shoal, etc., on a hydrographical chart.

vigil (vij' il) [F. *vigile*, L. *vigilia*, from *vigil*, awake, from *vigēre*, to be lively], *n.* Keeping awake during the customary hours of rest, watchfulness; devotions on the eve of a festival, orig. the watch kept on the night before a feast; the eve of a festival; (*pl.*) nocturnal devotions. **vigilance,** *n.* The state of being vigilant; (*Path.*) insomnia. **vigilance committee:** A self-organized committee for maintaining order or inflicting summary justice in an ill-ordered community or district. **vigilante** (vij i lăn' tė), *n.* A member of a Vigilance Committee.

vigilant (vij' i lȧnt), *a.* Awake and on the alert; watchful, wary, circumspect. **vigilantly,** *adv.*

vigneron (vē' nye ron) [F.], *n.* A wine-grower.

vignette (vin yet') [F., dim. of *vigne*, VINE], *n.* (*Arch.*) An ornament of tendrils and vine-leaves; an ornamental flourish round a capital letter in a manuscript; an engraving not enclosed within a definite border, esp. on the title page of a book; a photograph, drawing, or other portrait showing the head and shoulders with a background shading off gradually. *v.t.* To shade off (a portrait, drawing, etc.) thus; to make a photograph or portrait of in this style. **vignetter, vignettist,** *n.*

vigoroso (vig ȯ rō' sō) [It., as foll.], *adv.* (*Mus.*) With energy.

vigour (vig' ŏr) [O.F. *vigur*, *vigor*, L. *vigōrem*, nom. *-or*, from *vigēre*, to be lively], *n.* Active physical or mental strength or energy; abounding vitality, vital force, robustness; exertion of strength, force, activity; forcibleness, trenchancy. **vigourless,** *a.* **vigorous,** *a.* **vigorously,** *adv.* **vigorousness,** *n.*

viking (vī' king, vik' ing) [Icel. *vīkingr* (prob. *vīg*, war, cogn. with *vincere*, to conquer, -ING)], *n.* A rover, freebooter, or pirate, esp. one of the Scandinavian warriors of the 8th–10th cent. **vikingism,** *n.*

Vilayet (vil ȧ yet') [Turk.], *n.* A province of the old Turkish empire.

vile (vīl) [M.E. and O.F. *vil*, L. *vīlis*, cheap, base], *a.* Worthless, morally base, depraved, despicable, abject, villainous, odious; (*colloq.*) disagreeable, abominable. **vilely,** *adv.* **vileness,** *n.*

vilify (vil′ i fī), *v.t.* To traduce, to defame; *to debase, to degrade, to make base. **vilification** (-kā′ shŭn), *n.* **vilifier,** *n.*

***vilipend** (vil′ i pend) [L. *vīlipendere* (VILE, L. *pendere*, to weigh)], *v.t.* To speak of disparagingly or contemptuously, to depreciate.

***vill** (vil) [as foll.], *n.* A small town or village, a hamlet; a parish or part of a parish.

villa (vil′ ȧ) [L., farm-house, from *vīcus*, village], *n.* A country house; a detached suburban house. **villadom,** *n.* Villas collectively; (*fig.*) the middle classes.

village (vil′ ij) [F., from L. *villāticus*, pertaining to a VILLA], *n.* A small assemblage of houses, smaller than a town or city and larger than a hamlet. *a.* Pertaining to a village; rustic, countrified. **villager,** *n.* An inhabitant of a village. ***villagery,** *n.*

villain (vil′ ȧn) [O.F. and M.E. *vilein*, servile, base, from late L. *villānus*, a farm-servant, as VILLA], *n.* A person guilty or capable of crime or great wickedness; a scoundrel, a wretch; (*colloq.*) a rogue, a rascal; *a rustic, a clown, a boor; (*Hist.*) a feudal serf, a bondsman attached to a feudal lord or to an estate. *a.* Pertaining to, composed of, or performed by a villain or villains. **villainage,** *n.* **villainous,** *a.* Worthy or characteristic of a villain; depraved, vile; (*colloq.*) very bad. **adv.* Pitifully, wretchedly. **villainously,** *adv.* **villainousness,** *n.* **villainy,** *n.*

villanelle (vil ȧ nel′) [F., from It. *villanella*, dim, from *villano*, rustic, as prec.], *n.* A poem in five tercets and a final quatrain on two rhymes.

Villarsia (vi lar′ si ȧ) [Dominique *Villars* (1745–1814). French botanist], *n.* (*Bot.*) A genus of marsh or aquatic plants of the order *Gentianaceæ* with yellow flowers.

villeggiatura (vi lej a toor′ ȧ) [It., from *villegiare*. to stay at a country seat, from L. VILLA], *n.* Retirement or a stay in the country.

villein, villeinage, etc. [VILLAIN, etc.].

villus (vil′ ŭs) [L., shaggy hair], *n.* (*pl.* **-li,** -lī) (*Anat.*) One of the short hair-like processes on certain membranes, as those on the inner surface of the small intestine; (*Bot., pl.*) long, close, soft hairs. **villiform, villoid, villose, -lous,** *a.* **villosity** (-los′ i ti), *n.*

vim (vim) [L., acc. of VIS], *n.* (*colloq.*) Energy, vigour.

viminal (vim′ i nȧl) [L. *vīminālis*, from *vīmen -minis*, twig, from *viēre*, to twist], *a.* Pertaining to, producing, or consisting of twigs or shoots. **vimineous** (vi min′ ė ŭs), *a.*

vinaceous (vī-, vi nā′ shŭs) [L. *vīnāceus*, from *vīnum*, wine], *a.* Pertaining to wine or grapes; of the nature or colour of wine.

vinaigrette (vin ȧ gret′) [F., dim. of *vinaigre*, VINEGAR], *n.* An ornamental bottle or perforated case of gold or other metal, etc., for holding aromatic vinegar, etc., a smelling-bottle. **vinaigrous** (vi nā′ grŭs), *a.* Sour, acid; (*fig.*) cross, crabbed.

vinasse (vi nas′) [F.], *n.* A residual product containing potassium salts from the wine-press or beets from which sugar has been extracted.

Vincentian (vin sen′ shȧn), *a.* Pertaining to or founded by St. Vincent de Paul (1577–1660). *n.* A member of a religious and charitable order founded by him, a Lazarist.

vincible (vin′ si bėl) [L. *vincibilis*, from *vincere*, to conquer], *a.* Capable of being conquered, not invincible. **vincibility** (-bil′ i ti), **vincibleness,** *n.*

vinculum (ving′ kū lŭm) [L., a bond, from *vincire*, to bind], *n.* (*pl.* **-la**) (*Alg.*) A straight line drawn over several terms to show that they are all alike to be added to or deducted from those preceding or following; (*Anat.*) a frænum; (*Print.*) a brace. ***vinculate,** *v.t.*

***vindemial** (vin dē′ mi ȧl) [late L. *vindēmialis*, from *vindēmia*, grape-harvest (*vinum*, wine, *demere*, to take)], *a.* Pertaining to a vintage or grape-harvest. ***vindemiate,** *v.i.* ***vindemiation** (-ā′ shŭn), *n.*

vindicate (vin′ di kāt) [L. *vindicātus*, p.p. of *vindicāre* (VIM or *vēnum*, favour, *dicāre*, to assert, from *dīcere*, to say)], *v.t.* To maintain (a claim, statement, etc.) against attack or denial; to defend (a person) against reproach, accusation, etc.; to prove to be true or valid, to defend, to establish, to justify, to uphold. **vindicable,** *a.* **vindicability** (-bil′ i ti), *n.* The state of being vindicable. **vindication** (-kā′ shŭn), *n.* **vindicative** (vin′ di kā tiv), *a.* **vindicator,** *n.* **vindicatress,** *n.* **vindicatory,** *a.* Tending to vindicate or justify; punitory.

vindictive (vin dik′ tiv) [shortened from VINDICATIVE, see prec., from conf. with L. *vindicta*, revenge], *a.* Revengeful; characterized or prompted by revenge. **vindictive damages:** Damages given to punish the defendant. **vindictively,** *adv.* **vindictiveness,** *n.*

vine (vīn) [F. *vigne*, L. *vīnea*, vineyard, from *vīnum*, wine, cogn. with Gr. *oinos*, wine, *oinē*, vine, cp. L. *vītis*, vine, *vīmen*, twig, from *viēre*, to twist], *n.* A slender climbing plant of the genus *Vitis*, esp. *V. vinifera*, the common or grape-vine; any plant with a slender climbing or trailing stem. **vine-borer,** *n.* One of various insects that injure vines by boring into the stems, twigs, etc. **vine-clad,** *a.* Covered with vines. **vine-disease,** *n.* Any disease attacking the grape-vine, esp. that caused by the phylloxera. **vine-dresser,** *n.* One who dresses, trims, or prunes vines. **vine-fretter,** *n.* A small insect infesting vines. **vined,** *a.* **viny,** *a.* **vinery,** *n.* A greenhouse for vines. **vineyard** (vin′ yȧrd), *n.* A plantation of grape-vines. **vini-,** *comb. form.* **vinic,** *a.* Pertaining to or derived from wine. **viniculture** (vin′ i kŭl tyŭr), *n.* The cultivation of grape-vines. **viniculturist,** *n.* **vinifacteur** [FACTOR], *n.* Any apparatus used for wine-making. **viniferous** (vi nif′ ėr ŭs) [-FEROUS], *a.* **vinificator,** *n.* An apparatus for condensing the alcoholic vapours from the fermenting must in wine-making. ***vinolent** (vin′ ō lėnt), *a.* Full of wine (of a bottle, etc.); drunk. **vinometer** (vī nom′ ė tėr), *n.* An instrument for measuring the percentage of alcohol in wine. ***vin ordinaire*** (van ôr dē nâr) [F.], *n.* Ordinary wine, a cheap wine, usu. red and usu. drunk mixed with water. **vinous, *-nose** (vī′ nŭs, -nōs), *a.* Of, pertaining to, or having the qualities of wine. **vinosity** (-nos′ i ti), *n.*

vinegar (vin′ ė gȧr) [F. *vinaigre* (*vin*, L. *vinum*, wine, *aigre*, see EAGER)], *n.* An acid liquid obtained by oxidation or acetous fermentation from wine, cider, etc., used as a condiment and as a preservative in pickling; (*fig.*) anything sour or soured (in disposition, etc.). *v.t.* To put vinegar on or into; (*fig.*) to make sour. **vinegar-eel,** *n.* A minute worm infesting vinegar, sour paste, etc. **vinegar-plant,** *n.* A microscopic fungus producing acetous fermentation. ***vinegarette** [VINAIGRETTE]. **vinegarish, vinegary,** *a.*

vinery, vineyard [VINE].

***vinewed** (vin′ ūd) [also *finewed*, p.p. from A.-S. *fynegian*, *fynian*, from *fynig*, mouldy], *a.* Mouldy.

vingt-et-un (vant ā ŭn) [F., twenty-one], *n.* A card game in which the object is to make the aggregate number of the pips on the cards as nearly as possible twenty-one without exceeding this.

vini-, vinic, vinous, etc. [VINE].

vintage (vin′ tāj) [M.E. *vindage*, *vendage*, F. *vendange*, L. *vindēmia*, see VINDEMIAL], *n.* The yield of a vineyard or vine-district for a particular season; the season of gathering grapes; the product of a particular year. *a.* Produced at some particular time, esp. of a past season. **vint,** *v.t.* To make (wine). **vintage wine,** *n.* Wine of a good vintage year. **vintager,** *n.* A grape-gatherer. **vintner,** *n.* A wine-merchant. **vintnery,** *n.* **viny** [VINE].

viol (vī′ ŏl) [F. *viole*, Prov. *viula*, late L. *vitula*, cp. FIDDLE], *n.* A mediæval stringed musical instrument, the predecessor of the violin; a violoncello or bass-viol. **viol class:** Instruments like the violin, violoncello, etc., played with a bow and having no frets, thus being capable of continuous gradation. ***viol de gamba** [VIOLA DA GAMBA].

viola (1) (vē ō′ lȧ) [It.], *n.* An instrument like a large violin, the alto or tenor violin; a viol. **viola da gamba** [It., leg-viol]: An early form of bass-viol. **violist,** *n.* A player on the viol or viola.

viola (2) (vī′ ȯ lȧ) [L., violet], *n.* A plant or flower of the genus containing the violet and pansy. **violaceous** (-lā′ shŭs), *a.* Of a violet colour; (*Bot.*) of the violet family.

violate (vī′ ȯ lāt) [L. *violatus*, p.p. of *violāre*, cogn. with VIS], *v.t.* To infringe or transgress, to break, to disobey (a law, obligation, duty, etc.); to treat irreverently, to profane, to desecrate; to do violence to, to outrage; to deflower by force, to ravish. **violable,** *a.* **violation** (-lā′ shŭn), *n.* **violative** (vī′ ȯ lā tiv), *a.* **violator,** *n.*

violence (vī′ ȯ lėns) [F., from L. *violentia*, as prec.], *n.* The state or quality of being violent; violent exercise of power; violent treatment; injury, outrage; vehemence, intensity, or impetuosity of feeling, action, etc.; (*Law*) the illegal exercise of physical force, an act of intimidation by the show or threat of force. **to do violence to:** To do a physical injury to, to outrage, to violate.

violent (vī′ ō lėnt), *a.* Acting with or characterized by the exertion of great physical force; vehement, impetuous, furious; intense, abrupt, immoderate; produced by or resulting from extraneous force or poison, not natural (of death, etc.); (*Law*) based on almost conclusive evidence (of an inference or presumption). **violently,** *adv.*

violet (vī′ ȯ lėt) [F. dim. of *viole*, VIOLA (2)], *n.* A plant or flower of the genus *Viola*, esp. the sweet violet, *V. odorata*, the dog violet, *V. canina*, and some other species with small blue, purple, or white flowers; a colour seen at the opposite end of the spectrum to red, produced by a slight mixture of red with blue; a small violet-coloured butterfly of various species. *a.* Of the colour of violet. **violet powder:** Toilet powder perfumed with orris-root. **violet-wood,** n. One of several kinds of wood, esp. king-wood and myall-wood. **violescent** (-les′ ėnt), *a.* Tending to a violet colour.

violin (1) (vī ȯ lin′) [It. *violino*, dim. of VIOLA (1)], *n.* A musical instrument of the viol class with four strings, played with a bow; a player on this. **violinist,** *n.*

violin (2) (vī′ ȯ lin) [VIOLA (2), -IN], *n.* An emetic substance contained in the common violet.

violinist [VIOLIN (1)]. **violist** [It. VIOL].

violoncello (vē ȯ lon chel′ ō), *n.* A four-stringed musical instrument of the viol class rested on the ground between the legs, a bass-viol. **violoncellist,** *n.* **violone** (vē ȯ lō′ nā), *n.* A mediæval double-bass viol; an organ-stop of string-like tone.

viper (vī′ pėr) [F. *vipère*, L. *vīpera*, perh. *vivipara*, see VIVIPAROUS], *n.* A venomous snake of the family *Viperidæ*, esp. the European viper or adder, the only poisonous British snake; (*fig.*) a mischievous or malignant person. **viper's bugloss:** The blue weed or blue thistle, *Echium vulgare*. **viper's-grass,** *n.* A perennial plant, *Scorzonera Hispanica*, of the aster family. **viperiform, viperine, viperish, viperoid, viperous,** *a.*

virago (vi rā′ gō) [L., man-like maiden, from *vir*, man], *n.* An impudent, turbulent woman; a termagant; *a woman of masculine strength and courage. ***viraginian** (-jin′ i ȧn), **viraginous** (vi răj′ i nŭs), *a.* ***viraginity** (-jin′ i ti), *n.*

viral (vī′ rȧl), *a.* Pertaining to virus.

***vire** (vĕr) [O.F., from L. *viria*, ring], *n.* A heavy crossbow-bolt; (*Her.*) an annulet.

virelay (vir′ ė lā) [O.F. *virelai*, from *virer*, to turn, to VEER], *n.* An old form of French verse with two rhymes to a stanza and usu. a refrain.

vireo (vir′ ė ō) [L.], *n.* An American passerine insectivorous singing-bird.

virescent (vi res′ ėnt) [L. *virescens -ntem*, pres.p. of *virescere*, incept. of *virēre*, to be green], *a.* (*Bot.*) Green, tending to become green, viridescent; abnormally green (of petals, etc.). **virescence,** *n.*

virgate (vĕr′ gȧt) [L. *virgātus*, from *virga*, rod], *a.* Long, straight, and erect, rod-like. ***n.** An old measure for land.

Virgilian (vĕr jil′ i ȧn) [Maro Publius *Vergilius*, -AN], *a.* Pertaining to or in the style of Virgil, Latin poet (70–19 B.C.).

virgin (vĕr′ jin) [O.F. *virgine*, L. *virginem*, nom. *-go*, etym. doubtful], *n.* A woman who has had no carnal knowledge of man, a maid; a member of an order of women under vows of chastity; a madonna; a female insect that produces eggs without fertilization; (*Astron.*) the constellation Virgo; *a man who has had no carnal knowledge of woman. *a.* Being a virgin; pure, chaste, undefiled; befitting a virgin; maidenly, modest; unworked, untried, not brought into cultivation; producing eggs without impregnation (of insects). ***v.i.** To be or remain chaste. **the Virgin:** The mother of Christ. **virgin-born,** *a.* Born of a virgin. **Virgin Queen,** *n.* Name applied to Queen Elizabeth I (1533–1603). **virgin's bower,** *n.* Traveller's-joy, *Clematis vitalba*. **virginal,** *a.* Pertaining to or befitting a virgin; pure, chaste, maidenly. ***n.** A keyed musical instrument, shaped like a box, used in the 16th–17th cents., also called a pair of virginals. ***v.i.** To finger as on a virginal. **virginally,** *adv.* **virginhood, *virgin-head, virginity** (-jin′ i ti), *n.* The state of being a virgin, purity, innocence.

Virginia (vir jin′ yȧ) [one of the U.S., from prec., after Queen Elizabeth I, 'the Virgin Queen'], *n.* Tobacco from Virginia. **Virginia creeper:** A woody vine, *Ampelopsis hederacea*, with ornamental foliage. **Virginian,** *a.* and *n.*

Virgo (vĕr′ gō) [L., virgin], *n.* One of the twelve ancient zodiacal constellations; the sixth sign of the zodiac.

virgule (vĕr′ gūl) [L. *virgula*, dim. of *virga*, see VIRGATE], *n.* A small rod, a twig; *a comma. **virgulate,** *a.*

viridescent (vir i des′ ėnt) [late L. *viridescens -ntem*, pres.p. of *viridescere*, from *viridis*, green], *a.* Greenish; becoming slightly green. **viridescence,** *n.* ***virid,** *a.* Green. **viridigenous** (-dij′ ė nŭs) [-GENOUS], *a.* Imparting greenness (esp. to oysters). **viridity** (vi rid′ i ti), *n.* Greenness, the colour of fresh vegetation; greenness in oysters, due to feeding on green organisms.

virile (vir′-, vīr′ īl) [F. *viril*, fem. *-ile*, L. *virīlis*, from *vir*, man], *a.* Of or pertaining to man or the male sex, procreative; characteristic of a man, masculine, manly. **virilism** (vir il izm′), *n.* (*Med.*) The development in the female of masculine characteristics, mental and physical. **virility** (vi ril′ i ti), *n.*

virole (vi rōl′) [O.F., see FERRULE], *n.* A ferrule; (*Her.*) a hoop or ring encircling a horn.

virose, virous (vīr′ ōs, -ŭs) [L. *vīrōsus*, from VIRUS], *a.* Poisonous; (*Bot.*) emitting a fetid odour.

virtu (vêr too′, vĕr′ too) [It. *virtù*, *vertù*, as VIRTUE], *n.* Love of or taste for the fine arts. **articles** or **objects of virtu:** Rare, old, or beautiful works of decorative art. **virtuoso** (-ō′ zō), *n.* (*pl.* **-osos**) A connoisseur of articles of virtu; a skilled performer in some fine art. **virtuosity** (-os′ i ti), **virtuosoship,** *n.*

virtue (vĕr′ tū, -choo) [M.E. and F. *vertu*, L. *virtūtem*, nom. of *-tus*, from *vir*, see VIRILE], *n.* Moral excellence, goodness, uprightness, rectitude; conformity with or practice of morality or duty; a particular moral excellence; sexual purity, chastity, esp. in women; inherent power, goodness, or efficacy; (*pl.*) the seventh order of the celestial hierarchy. **cardinal virtues** [CARDINAL]. **by or in virtue of:** By or through the efficacy or authority of, on the strength of. **virtueless,** *a.* **virtual,** *a.* Being such in essence or effect though not in name or appearance, equivalent so far as effect is concerned. **virtuality** (-ăl′ i ti), *n.* **virtually,** *adv.* **virtuoso,** etc. [VIRTU]. **virtuous,** *a.* Characterized by virtue, morally good; chaste. **virtuously,** *adv.* **virtuousness,** *n.*

virulent (vir′ ů lėnt) [F., from L. *virulentus,* from foll.], *a.* Extremely poisonous; caused by or of the nature of virus; (*fig.*) extremely bitter, acrimonious, or malignant. **virulence, *-lency,** *n.* **virulently,** *adv.* **viruliferous** (-lif′ ėr ůs), *n.* (*Med.*).

virus (vīr′ ůs) [L., slime, poison, cogn. with Gr. *ios,* Sansk. *visham*], *n.* A very small infective agent capable of self-propagation only in living matter. It is the causative agent of many diseases; (*fig.*) and moral taint or corrupting influence; virulence, malignity.

vis (vis) [L.], *n.* (*pl.* **vires,** vīr′ ēz) (*Mech.*) Force, energy, potency. **vis inertiæ** [INERT]. **vis mortua** (môr′ tū å): Dead force; force doing no work. **vis viva** (vī′ vå): Living force, measured by the mass of a moving body multiplied by the square of its velocity.

visa, visé (vē′ zå, vē′ zā) [F. *viser,* to inspect], *n.* An official endorsement on a passport showing that it has been examined and found correct. *v.t.* To certify or put a *visé* on.

visage (viz′ ij) [F., from L. *vīsum,* nom. *-us,* p.p. of *vidēre,* to see], *n.* The face, the countenance. **v.t.* To confront, to face. **visaged,** *a.* Having a visage or look of a particular type.

visard [VISOR].

vis-à-vis (vē za vē′) [F., face to face (*vis,* face, L. *vīsum,* see VISAGE)], *adv.* Face to face, opposite to. *n.* A person facing another as in certain dances, *e.g.* a quadrille; a carriage or couch for two persons sitting *vis-à-vis.*

viscacha (vis kach′ å) [Am.-Sp., from native name], *n.* A S. American burrowing rodent, *Lagostomus trichodactylus.*

viscera (vis′ ėr å) [L., pl. of *viscus*], *n.pl.* The internal organs of the great cavities of the body, as the skull, thorax, and abdomen, esp. those of the abdomen, the intestines. **visceral,** *a.* **viscerate,** *v.t.* To disembowel. **visceri-, viscero-,** *comb. form.*

viscid (vis′ id) [F. *viscide,* L. *viscidus,* from *viscum,* mistletoe, bird-lime, cogn. with Gr. *ixos, ixia*], *a.* Sticky, adhesive; semifluid in consistency. **viscidity** (vi sid′ i ti), *n.* **viscin** (vis′ in), *n.* A viscid liquid obtained from mistletoe, etc., the chief constituent of bird-lime. **viscometer** (-kom′ ė tėr), **viscosimeter** (-kō sim′ ė tėr) [-METER], *n.* An apparatus for determining the viscosity of liquids. **viscometry** (-kom′ ė tri), *n.* **viscose,** *n.* (*Chem.*) The cellulose sodium salt used in the manufacture of artificial silk. **viscosity** (-kos′ i ti), *n.* Stickiness; thickness of a fluid, etc.; (*Phys.*) the property of fluids, semifluids, and gases which expresses their resistance to flow, change of shape or re-arrangement of molecules; internal friction. **viscuous,** *a.* **viscuousness,** *n.*

viscount (vī′ kount) [A.-F. *visconte,* O.F. *viscomte* (F. *vicomte*) (VICE-, COUNT (2))], *n.* A British peer ranking next below an earl, and above a baron. **viscountcy,** *n.* **viscountess,** *n.* **viscountship, viscounty,** *n.*

viscous [VISCID].

Viscum (vis′ kům) [L., see VISCID], *n.* (*Bot.*) A genus of parasitic shrubs comprising the mistletoe.

viscus (vis′ kůs) [L. *viscus*], *n.* Viscera.

visible (viz′ i bėl) [F., from L. *vīsibilis,* from *vīs-us,* see prec.], *a.* Capable of being seen, perceptible by the eye; in view, apparent, open, conspicuous. **visible Church:** The body of professing Christians. **visible horizon:** The apparent limit bounding the view. **visible speech:** Phonetic symbols representing every possible articulate utterance. **visibility,** *n.* State of being visible, visibleness. **high, low visibility,** *n.* (*Meteor.*) Clear or indistinct visibility. **visibleness,** *n.* **visibly,** *adv.*

Visigoth (viz′ i goth) [late L. *Visigothī, -gothæ,* from Teut. (WEST, GOTH)], *n.* One of the western Goths who settled in S. Gaul and Spain in the 4th and 5th cents. **Visigothic,** *a.*

vision (vizh′ ůn) [F., from L. *vīsiōnem,* nom. *-sio,* from *vidēre,* to see, p.p. *vīsus*], *n.* The act or faculty of seeing, sight; that which is seen, an object of sight; a mental representation of a visual object, esp. in a dream or trance; a supernatural or prophetic apparition; a creation of the imagination or fancy; foresight, an appreciation of what the future may hold. *v.t.* To see in or as in a vision; to imagine; to present as in a vision. **visional,** *a.* **visionally,** *adv.* **visionary,** *a.* Existing in a vision or in the imagination only; imaginary, unreal, unsubstantial, unpractical; given to day-dreaming, fanciful theories, etc. *n.* A visionary person. **visionariness,** *n.* **visionist,** *n.* **visionless,** *a.*

visit (viz′ it) [F. *visiter,* L. *vīsitāre,* freq. of *vīsere,* to behold, from *vidēre,* see prec.], *v.t.* To go or come to see, as an act of friendship, civility, business, curiosity, etc.; to come or go to for the purpose of inspection, supervision, correction of abuses, etc.; to come upon, to overtake, to afflict (of diseases, etc.); (*Bibl.*) to chastise; to comfort, to bless. *v.i.* To call on or visit people; to keep up friendly intercourse. *n.* The act of visiting, or going to see a person, place, or thing; a call; a stay or sojourn (with or at); a formal or official call or inspection. **visitable, visitatorial, *visitorial** (-tôr′ i ål), *a.* **visiting-book,** *n.* One in which calls received or intended are entered. **visiting-card,** *n.* A small card, bearing one's name, etc., to be left in making a call.

visitant (viz′ i tånt), *n.* A migratory bird that visits a country at certain seasons; (*poet.*) a visitor, a guest; (*R.-C. Ch.*) a nun of the Order of the Visitation of Our Lady, devoted to the education of young girls.

visitation (viz i tā′ shůn), *n.* The act of visiting; a formal or official visit for the purpose of inspection, correction, etc., esp. by a bishop to the churches of his diocese; (*Internat. Law*) the boarding of a foreign vessel in time of war to ascertain her character, etc.; the right to do this; a divine dispensation, esp. a chastisement or affliction; (*Her.*) the official visit of a herald to a district for the examination and verification of arms, pedigrees, etc.; (*R.-C. Ch.*) a festival held on 2 July in honour of the visit of the Virgin Mary to Elizabeth (Luke i. 39); (*Zool.*) an abnormal and extensive irruption of animals into a region. **Nuns of the Visitation:** (*R.-C. Ch.*) The order of Visitants. **visitation of the sick:** An Anglican office for the comfort and consolation of sick persons.

visitor (viz′ i tŏr), *n.* One who makes a call; one who visits a place; an officer appointed to make a visitation of any institution. **visitors' book:** One in which visitors' names are entered, esp. in which visitors to an hotel or boarding-house write remarks.

visite (vi zēt′) [F., VISIT], *n.* A light, close-fitting outer garment worn by women early in the 19th cent.

visiting, *visitorial, etc. [VISIT].

***visnomie** [PHYSIOGNOMY].

visor (viz′ ŏr) [M.E. and A.-F. *visere,* O.F. *visiere,* from *vis,* face, see VISAGE], *n.* The movable perforated part of a helmet defending the face; a projecting part on the front of a cap, for shielding the eyes; *a mask. **visored,** *a.* **visorless,** *a.*

vista (vis′ tå) [It., fem. of *visto,* p.p. of *vedere,* L. *vidēre,* to see], *n.* A long view shut in at the sides, as between rows of trees; (*fig.*) a mental view far into the past or future. **vistaed,** *a.*

visual (vizh′ ū ål, viz′ ū ål) [F., from late L. *vīsuālis,* from *vīsus,* sight, from *vidēre,* to see], *a.* Of, pertaining to, or used in sight or seeing; serving as an organ or instrument of seeing. **visuality** (-ăl' i ti), *n.* **visualism,** *n.* **visualist,** *n.* **visualize,** *v.t.* To make visual or visible; to make visible to the eye; to externalize or give a visible form to (an idea, mental image, etc.). **visualization** (-zā' shŭn), *n.* **visualizer,** *n.* **visually,** *adv.*

vital (vī' tăl) [F., from L. *vītālis,* from *vīta,* life, cogn. with *vīvere,* to live, and Gr. *bios,* life], *a.* Pertaining to, necessary to, or supporting organic life, containing life; affecting life; indispensable, essential. *n.pl.* The parts or organs of animals essential to life, as the heart, brain, etc. **vital centre:** The point in the body at which a wound appears to be instantly fatal, esp. the respiratory nerve-centre in the medulla oblongata. **vital force or principle:** One assumed as accounting for organic life, etc. **vital statistics:** Those relating to birth, marriage, mortality, etc.; (*colloq.*) the measurements of a woman's bust, waist and hips. **vitalism,** *n.* The doctrine that life is derived from something distinct from physical forces. **vitalist,** *n.* and *a.* **vitalistic** (-lis' tik), *a.* **vitality** (-tăl' i ti), *n.* **vitalize,** *v.t.* To give life to; to animate. **vitalization** (-zā' shŭn), *n.* **vitally,** *adv.*

vitamin (vī tă min) [L. *vita,* life, AMINE], *n.* (*Chem., Med.*) One of a number of naturally occurring substances which are necessary, though in minute quantities, for normal metabolism. So far as is known their functions are: Vitamin A, growth-promoting and anti-infection; B_1, or F, beneficial to nerves and bowels; B_2, or G, prevents pellagra; C, anti-scorbutic; D, anti-rachitic; E, anti-sterility; H, human needs, if any, unknown; K, promotes normal blood coagulability; P, believed to help the capillary walls to resist changes of pressure.

vitellus (vi-, vī tel' ŭs) [L., dim. of *vitulus,* calf, see VEAL], *n.* (*pl.* **-li,** -lī) Yolk of egg, the protoplasmic contents of the ovum. **vitellary** (vit' ė lâr i), **vitelline** (vi tel' in), *a.* **vitelli-, vitello-,** *comb. forms.* **vitellicle,** *n.* A yolk-sac.

vitiate (vish' i āt) [L. *vitiāre,* from *vitium,* VICE (1)], *v.t.* To impair the quality of; to corrupt; to render faulty or imperfect; to render invalid or ineffectual. **vitiation** (-ā' shŭn), *n.* **vitiator** (vish' i ā tôr), *n.* ***vitiosity** (vish i os' i ti), *n.* The state of being vicious; depravity, corruption.

viticide (vī' ti-, vit' i sīd) [L. *vītis,* VINE, -CIDE], *n.* An insect or other vermin injurious to vines. **viticolous** (vi tik' ŏ lŭs) [L. *colere,* to inhabit], *a.* Living on or infesting the vine. **viticulture** (vit' i kŭl tyŭr), *n.* The cultivation of the grape-vine. **viticultural,** *a.* **viticulturist,** *n.*

vitiosity [VITIATE].

Vitis (vī' tis) [L.], *n.* (*Bot.*) A genus of plants comprising the grape-vine.

vitreous (vit' rė ŭs) [L. *vitreus,* from *vitrum,* glass, perh. cogn. with *vidēre,* to see], *a.* Consisting of or resembling glass; obtained from glass. **vitreous electricity:** Electricity generated by friction on glass, formerly regarded as positive. **vitreosity** (-os' i ti), **vitreousness,** *n.* **vitrescent** (-tres' ĕnt), *a.* **vitrescence,** *n.* **vitrescible,** *a.* Vitrifiable. **vitric,** *a.* Of or like glass; pertaining to vitrics. *n.pl.* Fused siliceous compounds, glass and glassy materials, opp. to ceramics; the science or history of glass-manufacture. **vitriform,** *a.*

vitrify (vit' ri fī), *v.t.* To convert into glass or a glassy substance by heat and fusion; *v.i.* To be converted into glass. **vitrification** (-kā' shŭn), **vitrifaction** (-făk' shŭn), *n.* ***vitrifacture,** *n.* The manufacture of glass or glass-ware. **vitrifiable,** *a.* **vitrifiability** (-bil' i ti), *n.*

vitrine (vit' rin), *n.* A glass show-case.

vitriol (vit' ri ŏl) [M.E. and O.F. *vitriole,* med. L. *vitriolus,* L. *vitreolus,* dim. of *vitreus,* VITREOUS], *n.* Sulphuric acid (or oil of vitriol) as made from green vitriol; any salt of this, a sulphate; (*fig.*) malignancy, caustic criticism, etc. **black vitriol:** An impure copper sulphate. **blue or copper vitriol:** Copper sulphate. **green vitriol:** Ferrous sulphate or copperas. **oil of vitriol:** Sulphuric acid. **red or rose vitriol:** Cobalt sulphate. **vitriol-throwing,** *n.* The act of throwing vitriol in the face of a person for the purpose of private vengeance. **vitriolation** (-lā' shŭn), **-lization** (-lī zā' shŭn), *n.* **vitriolic** (-ol' ik), *a.* Pertaining to, obtained from, or having the qualities of vitriol; (*fig.*) caustic, bitter, malignant. **vitrioline** (vit' ri ŏ lin), *a.* **vitriolizable,** *a.* **vitriolize, vitriolate,** *v.t.* To convert into a sulphate.

vitrophyre (vit' rŏ fīr) [L. *vitro-, vitrum,* glass, *phyre,* from PORPHYRY], *n.* (*Min.*) A porphyritic-volcanic rock of a vitreous structure. **vitrophyric** (-fir' ik), *a.*

Vitruvian (vi troo' vi ăn), *a.* (*Arch.*) Of or in the style of Marcus Vitruvius Pollio, a Roman architect of the Augustan age. **Vitruvian scroll:** A pattern consisting of convoluted undulations, used in friezes, etc.

vitta (vit' ă) [L.], *n.* (*pl.* **-tæ,** -tē) (*Rom. Ant.*) A band, fillet, or garland, worn by a priest, sacrificial victim, etc.; (*Eccles.*) the lappet of a mitre; (*Bot.*) an oil-tube in the fruit of the parsley family, etc.; (*Zool.*) a band or stripe of colour. **vittate,** *a.*

vitular, -lary (vit' ū lăr, -i), **vituline** (-lin) [L. *vitulus,* calf, see VEAL], *a.* Of or pertaining to a calf or calving; calf-like.

vituperate (vī tū' pėr āt) [L. *vituperātus,* p.p. of *vituperāre* (*vitu-, vitium,* VICE (1), *parāre,* to get ready)], *v.t.* To upbraid, to abuse, to rail at. **vituperable,** *a.* **vituperation** (-ā' shŭn), *n.* **vituperative** (-tū' pėr ā tiv), *a.* **vituperatively,** *adv.* **vituperator,** *n.*

viva (1) (vē' va) [It., long live, from L. *vivere,* to live, as VIVACIOUS], *int.* and *n.* An exclamation of applause or joy.

viva (2) [VIVA VOCE].

vivace (vē va' chā) [It., as foll.], *adv.* (*Mus.*) In a brisk, lively manner.

vivacious (vī vā' shŭs) [L. *vīvax -ācis,* from *vīvere,* to live], *a.* Lively, animated, sprightly, gay; (*Bot.*) tenacious of life, living through the winter, perennial. **vivaciously,** *adv.* **vivacity** (-văs' i ti), **vivaciousness,** *n.*

vivandière (vē van dyâr) [F., fem. of *vivandier,* sutler, from L. *vīvenda,* provisions, see VIANDS], *n.* A female sutler attached to a continental, esp. French, regiment.

vivarium (vī vâr' i ŭm) [L., from *vīvus,* alive], *n.* (*pl.* **-ria**) A park, garden, or other place artificially prepared in which animals, etc., are kept alive as nearly as possible in their natural state. **vivary** (viv' ă ri), *n.*

vivat (vē' văt) [L., may he (or she) live, from *vīvere,* to live], *int.* and *n.* The cry 'long live.' ***vivat rex*** or ***regina:*** Long live the king *or* queen.

viva voce (vī' vă vō' sė) [L., with the living voice], *adv.* and *a.* By word of mouth, orally. *n.* A viva voce or oral examination.

viverriform (vi ver' i fôrm) [mod. L. *viverra,* ferret, -FORM], *a.* Having the shape or structure of the *Viverridæ,* a family of carnivorous mammals containing the civets, mungooses, etc. **viverrid,** *n.* **viverrine,** *a.* **viverroid,** *a.* and *n.*

vivers (vē' vėrz) [F. *vivres,* from *vivre,* as VIVE], *n.pl.* (*Sc.*) Food, provisions.

vives (vīvz) [O.F. *avives,* Sp. *avivas,* Arab. *addhība* (*al,* the, *dhība,* she-wolf)], *n.* A disease of the ear-glands in horses.

vivid (viv' id) [L. *vīvidus,* from *vīvus,* living], *a.* Vigorous, lively; very bright, intense, brilliant; clear, strongly marked, highly coloured. **vividly,** *adv.* **vividness,** *n.*

vivify (viv' i fī) [F. *vivifier,* late L. *vīvificāre* (L. *vīvus,* living, *-ficāre, facere,* to make)], *v.t.* To give life to, to quicken, to animate, to enliven. ***vivific** (vi vif' ik), *a.* ***vivificate,** *v.t.* **vivification** (-kā' shŭn), *n.* ***vivificative** (vi vif′ i kā tiv), *a.* **vivifier,** *n.*

viviparous (vi vip′ å rŭs) [late L. *vīvaparus* (*vīvus*, alive, *parere*, to produce)], *a.* Bringing forth young alive, opp. to oviparous and ovoviviparous; (*Bot.*) producing bulbs or seeds that germinate while still attached to the parent plant. **viviparously,** *adv.* **viviparity** (viv i păr′ i ti), **viviparousness,** *n.*

vivisection (viv i sek′ shŭn) [F. (L. *vīvus*, alive, SECTION)], *n.* The dissection of or performance of inoculative or other experiments on living animals. **vivisect** (viv′ i sekt), *v.t.* To dissect (a living animal). **vivisectional,** *a.* **vivisectionist,** *n.* **vivisector** (viv′ i sek tŏr), *n.* **vivisepulture** (-sep′ ŭl tyŭr), *n.* Burial alive.

vivo (vē′ vō) [It.], *adv.* (*Mus.*) With life and animation, *vivace*.

vixen (vik′ sėn) [A.-S. *fyxen*, fem. of FOX, cp. G. *füschsin*, fem. of *fuchs*], *n.* A she-fox; (*fig.*) a shrewish, quarrelsome woman; a scold. **vixenish, vixenly,** *a.* Having the qualities of a vixen.

viz. [VIDELICET]. ***vizard** [VISOR].

vizcacha [VISCACHA].

vizier (vi zēr′) [Arab. *wazīr*, counsellor, orig. porter, from *wazara*, to bear a burden], *n.* A high officer or minister of State in Mohammedan countries. **grand vizier:** The prime minister in the Turkish empire, etc. **vizierate, viziership,** *n.* **vizierial,** *a.*

vizor [VISOR].

Vlach (vlăk) [Boh.], *n.* A Wallachian.

Vlei (vlī) [S. Afr. Dut., prob. from Dut. *vallei*, VALLEY], *n.* (*S. Afr.*) A swampy tract, a place where water lies in rainy seasons.

vocable (vō′ kȧ bėl) [F., from L. *vocābulum*, from *vocāre*, to call, cogn. with *vox vōcis*, VOICE], *n.* A word, esp. as considered phonologically.

vocabulary (vȯ kăb′ ū lăr i) [F. *vocabulaire*, late L. *vocābulārium*, as prec.], *n.* A list or collection of words used in a language, science, book, etc., usu. arranged in alphabetical order, and explained; a word-book; the stock of words at one's command. ***vocabulist,** *n.* The compiler of a vocabulary.

vocal (vō′ kăl) [F., from L. *vōcālis*, from *vox vocis*, VOICE], *a.* Of or pertaining to the voice or oral utterance; having a voice; uttered or produced by the voice; (*fig.*) resounding with or as with voices; (*Phon.*) voiced, sonant, not surd; (*Gram.*) having the character of a vowel. *n.* A vocal sound, a vowel; (*R.-C. Ch.*) a person authorized to vote in certain elections. **vocal cords:** The elastic folds of the lining membrane of the larynx about the opening of the glottis. **vocal music:** Music composed for or produced by the voice as distinct from instrumental music. **vocalic** (-kăl′ ik), *a.* Pertaining to or consisting of vowel sounds. **vocalism** (vō′ kȧ lizm), *n.* The exercise of the vocal organs; a vowel sound. **vocalist,** *n.* A singer, opp. to an instrumental performer. **vocality** (vȯ kăl′ i ti), **vocalness,** *n.* **vocalize** (vō′ kȧ līz), *v.t.* To form or utter with the voice, esp. to make sonant; to insert the vowel-points in (Hebrew, etc.); *v.i.* To exercise the voice, to speak, to sing, etc. **vocalization** (-zā′ shŭn), *n.* **vocally,** *adv.*

vocation (vȯ kā′ shŭn) [F., from L. *vocātiōnem*, nom. *-tio*, from *vocāre*, see VOCABLE], *n.* A call or sense of fitness for and obligation to follow a particular career; a divine call or spiritual injunction or guidance to undertake a duty, occupation, etc.; one's calling or occupation. **vocational,** *a.* **vocationally,** *adv.*

vocative (vok′ ȧ tiv) [F. *vocatif*, fem. *-ive*, L. *vocātīvus*, as prec.], *a.* Pertaining to or used in addressing a person or thing. *n.* The case of a noun used in addressing a person or thing.

vociferate (vȯ sif′ ėr āt) [L. *vōciferātus*, p.p. of *vōciferāre*, *-ferārī* (*vox vōcis*, VOICE, *ferre*, to bear)], *v.t.* To cry loudly, to bawl, to shout. **vociferance, vociferation** (-ā′ shŭn), *n.* **vociferant** (vȯ sif′ ėr ănt), *a.* and *n.* **vociferator,** *n.* **vociferous,** *a.* **vociferously,** *adv.* **vociferousness,** *n.*

vocule (vok′ ūl) [L. *vōcula*, dim. of *vox vōcis*, VOICE], *n.* The faint sound made after articulating final *k*, *p*, or *t*.

vodka (vod′ kȧ) [Rus., dim. of *voda*, water], *n.* A strong spirituous liquor distilled from rye, used in Russia.

voe (vō) [Icel. *vāgr*, *vogr*], *n.* (*Orkney and Shetland*) A small inlet, bay, or creek.

vogue (vōg) [F., orig. sway, from *voguer*, to sail forth, It. *vogare*, to row, G. *wogen*, to fluctuate, cp. A.-S. *wǣg*, wave], *n.* Fashion prevalent at any particular time; currency, popular acceptance or usage.

voice (vois) [M.E. and O.F. *vois*, L. *vōcem*, nom. *vox*, cogn. with Gr. *epos*, word, Sansk. *vākyam*, speech], *n.* The sound uttered by the mouth, esp. by a human being, in speaking, singing, etc.; the faculty or power of vocal utterance, speech, language; (*fig.*) expression of the mind or will in words whether spoken or written, etc.; one's opinion or judgment, one's right to express this, one's choice, vote, or suffrage; one expressing the will or judgment of others, a speaker, a mouthpiece; a sound suggestive of human speech; (*Phon.*) sound produced by the breath acting on the vocal cords, sonancy; (*Gram.*) the verb-form expressing the relation of the subject to the action, as active, passive, or middle. *v.t.* To give utterance to, to express; (*Mus.*) to regulate the tones of, to tune; to write the voice-parts for; (*Phon.*) to give voice or sonancy to. **with one voice:** Unanimously. **voiced,** *a.* Sonant; having a voice (*usu. in comb.* as *loud-voiced*). **voiceful,** *a.* Vocal, sonorous. **voiceless,** *a.* Having no voice or vote; speechless, mute; (*Phon.*) not voiced. **voicelessness,** *n.*

void (void) [O.F. *void*, fem. *voide*, perh. from L. *vacuus*, empty, or *viduus*, bereft], *a.* Empty, unfilled, vacant; having no holder, occupant or incumbent; free from, destitute (of); useless, ineffectual; having no legal force, null, invalid. *n.* An empty space; a vacuum. *v.t.* To invalidate, to nullify; to discharge, to emit from the bowels, *to quit, to leave; to evacuate; *to avoid. **voidable,** *a.* **voidance,** *n.* The act of voiding or ejecting from a benefice; the state of being vacant; *evasion, subterfuge. **voided,** *a.* Made void; (*Her., said of a charge*) having the inner part cut away so that the field shows through. **voider,** *n.* **voidly,** *adv.* **voidness,** *n.*

voile (voil) [F., veil], *n.* (*Text.*) A thin, semi-transparent dress material.

voivode, vaivode (voi-, vā vōd) [Pol. *wayewoda*, army leader, cp. Rus. *voevoda*, Serb. *vojvoda*], *n.* Orig. a military commander, a leader of an army, in Slavonic countries; formerly, a liege prince or hospodar in Rumania, Wallachia, etc.; the chief of an administrative division in Poland; an inferior administrative officer in Turkey. ***voivodeship,*** *n.*

vol (vol) [F., flight, from *voler*, L. *volāre*, to fly], *n.* (*Her.*) Two outspread wings united at the base.

vola (vō′ lȧ) [L., palm, sole], *n.* (*pl.* *-læ*, -lē) (*Anat.*) The palm of the hand; the sole of the foot. **volar,** *a.*

***volable** (from L. as VOL], *a.* (*Shak.*) Nimble-witted.

volant (vol′ ănt) [F., pres.p. of *voler*, see VOL], *a.* Passing through the air; flying, able to fly; current; (*poet.*) nimble, active, rapid; (*Her.*) represented as flying. **volante** (vȯ lan′ tā) [Sp.], *n.* A two-wheeled covered vehicle with very long shafts and a chaise-body slung in front of the axle.

Volapük (vō lȧ pook′) [Volapük (*vol*, world, *pük*, speech)], *n.* A universal language invented (1879) by Johann Maria Schleyer. **Volapükist,** *n.*

volatile (vol′ ȧ tīl) [F. *volatil*, fem. *-tile*, L. *volātilis*, from *volāre*, to fly, p.p. *volātus*], *a.* Readily evaporating; (*fig.*) lively, sprightly, brisk, gay; fickle, changeable. ***volatileness, volatility** (-til′ i ti), *n.* **volatilize** (vȯ lăt′ i līz), *v.t.* To cause to pass off in vapour; *v.i.* To evaporate. **volatilizable,** *a.* **volatilization** (-zā′ shŭn), *n.*

vol au vent (vol ō van) [F.], *n.* A raised or puff meat pie.

volcano (vol kā′ nō) [It., from L. *volcānus*, VULCAN], *n.* An opening in the earth's surface through which lava, cinders, gases, etc., are ejected from the interior, esp. at the top of a hill or mountain formed by the successive accumulations of ejected matter. **volcanic** (vol kăn′ ik), *a.* Pertaining to, produced by, or of the nature of a volcano. **volcanically,** *adv.* **volcanicity** (-nis′ i ti), **volcanism,** *n.* **volcanist, volcanologist** (-nol′ ŏ jist), *n.* **volcanize,** *v.t.* **volcanization** (-zā′ shŭn), *n.* **volcanology** [-LOGY], *n.* The study of volcanoes. **volcanological** (-loj′ i kăl), *a.*

vole (1) (vōl) [F. *voler*, L. *volāre*, to fly], *v.t.* (*Cards*) To win all the tricks. *n.* The act of winning all the tricks in a deal.

vole (2) (vōl) [shortened from *vole-mouse* (cp. Icel. *völlr*, Norw. *voll*, Swed. *vall*, field, cogn. with WOLD)], *n.* A mouse-like rodent of the subfamily *Arvicolinæ*, often called a water-rat.

volery (vol′ ĕr i) [F. *volerie*, as VOLE (1)], *n.* An aerodrome; *an aviary; a flight of birds.

volet (vol′ ā) [O.F., shutter, from *voler*, see VOLE (1)], *n.* A wing or panel of a triptych.

volitant (vol′ i tănt) [L. *volitans*, *-ntem*, pres.p. of *volitāre*, freq. of *volāre*, to fly], *a.* Flying, volant. ***volitation** (-tā′ shŭn), *n.*

volition (vŏ lish′ ŭn) [F., from late L. *volitiōnem*, nom. *-tio*, from *volo*, I wish, inf. *velle*, to wish], *n.* Exercise of the will; the power of willing. **volitient,** *a.* **volitional, -ary,** *a.* **volitionally,** *adv.* **volitionless,** *a.* **volitive,** *a.*

Volksraad (fōlks′ rat) [S. Afr. Dut.], *n.* The former legislative assemblies of the Transvaal and the Orange Free State.

Volkswagen (fōkz′ va gĕn) [G., folk's car], *n.* (*Motor.*) Proprietary name of a German make of car planned for popular use.

volley (vol′ i) [F. *volée*, flight, from *voler*, see VOLE (1)], *n.* A flight or simultaneous discharge of missiles; the missiles thus discharged; (*fig.*) a noisy outburst or emission of many things at once; a return of the ball at tennis and similar games before it touches the ground; (*Cricket*) a ball that flies straight at the head of the wicket after once hitting the ground. *v.t.* To discharge in or as in a volley; to return or bowl in a volley. *v.i.* To discharge a volley; to fly in a volley (of missiles, etc.); to fire together (of guns); to return a ball before it touches the ground. **half-volley:** A return immediately after the ball has touched the ground.

volplane (vol′ plān) [L. *volāre*, to fly, PLANE (3)], *v.i.* (*Aviat.*) To fly downwards at a considerably higher angle than that of a glide. *n.* Such a descending flight.

volt (1) (volt) [F., see VAULT (2)], *n.* A circular tread, the gait of a horse going sideways round a centre; a sudden leap to avoid a thrust in fencing.

volt (2) (vōlt) [from *Volta*, see VOLTA-], *n.* The unit of electromotive force or potential difference, that which would carry one ampere of current against one ohm resistance. **volt ampere,** *n.* (*Elec.*) The product of current and voltage in alternating-current circuits.

volta (vol′ ta) [It., see VAULT (2)], *n.* (*pl.* *-te*, -tā) (*Mus.*) Time, turn. ***due volte:*** Twice. ***prima volta:*** First time. ***una volta:*** Once.

volta- [Alessandro *Volta* (1745–1827), It. physicist], *comb. form.* (*Elec.*) Voltaic. **volta-electric** (vol tă ē lek′ trik), *a.* Of, producing, or produced by voltaic electricity. **volta-electrometer, voltameter** (-tăm′ ĕ tĕr) [-METER], *n.* An instrument for measuring an electric current by measuring the metal deposited, or the gas liberated, in an electrolyte in a given time. **volta-electrometric, voltametric** (-met′ rik), *a.* **voltage** (vōl′ tij), *n.* Electromotive force or potential difference as measured or expressed in volts. **voltaic** (vol tā′ ik), *a.* Pertaining to electricity produced by chemical action or contact, galvanic. **voltaic pile:** A galvanic pile. **voltaism** (vōl′ tă izm), *n.* **voltite,** *n.* An insulating material for electric wires. **voltmeter,** *n.* An instrument for measuring the voltage or difference of potential between two points.

Voltairism, Voltaireanism (vol târ′ izm, -i ăn izm) [François-Marie Arouet (1694–1778), better known as *Voltaire*], *n.* The principles or practices of Voltaire; scoffing scepticism. **Voltairean,** *a.* and *n.*

voltaism, -meter, etc. [VOLTA-].

volte-face (volt fas) [F. (VOLT (1), FACE)], *n.* A turn round; (*fig.*) an entire change of front in opinions, etc.

voltigeur (vol ti zhĕr′) [F., from *voltiger*, It. *volteggiare*, to vault, see VOLTA], *n.* (*Hist.*) A rifleman in a select company of a regiment of French infantry.

voltite, voltmeter [VOLTA-].

volubilate, etc. [VOLUBLE].

voluble (vol′ ū bĕl) [F., from L. *volūbilem*, nom. *-lis*, from *volvere*, to roll, cogn. with Goth. *walwjan*, Gr. *eiluein*], *a.* Characterized by a flow of words, fluent, glib, garrulous; (*Bot.*) twisting, volubilate. **volubilate** (vŏ lū′ bi lăt), **volubile** (vol′ ū bil), *a.* (*Bot.*) Twining, climbing by winding round a support; turning or rotating readily. **volubility** (-bil′ i ti), **volubleness,** *n.* **volubly,** *adv.*

volucrine (vol′ ŭ krin) [L. *volucer -cris*, bird, -INE], *a.* Of or pertaining to birds.

volume (vol′ ūm) [F., from L. *volumen*, as VOLUBLE], *n.* A collection of (usu. printed) sheets of paper, parchment, etc., bound together forming a book or work or part of one; (*loosely*) a book, a tome; (*Ant.*) a roll or scroll of papyrus, vellum, etc., constituting a book; a rounded, swelling mass, a wreath, a coil (*usu. in pl.*); cubical content; mass, bulk; (*Mus.*) fullness or roundness of tone. **volumed,** *a.* (*usu. in comb.* as *three-volumed*). **volumenometer** (-ē nom′ ĕ tĕr) [-METER], *n.* An apparatus for measuring the volume of a solid body by the quantity of fluid that it displaces. **volumenometry,** *n.* **volumeter** (vō lū′ mē tĕr), *n.* An instrument for measuring the volume of a gas; a hydrometer; a stereometer. **volumetric, -al** (-met′ rik, -ăl), *a.* **volumetrically,** *adv.* **voluminal** (vŏ lū′ mi năl), *a.* Pertaining to volume.

voluminous (vo lū′ mi nŭs), *a.* Consisting of many volumes; producing many or bulky books (of a writer); of great volume, bulk, or size. **voluminosity** (-nos′ i ti), **voluminousness,** *n.* ***volumist** (vol′ ū mist), *n.* An author. **voluminously,** *adv.*

voluntary (vol′ ŭn tăr i) [M.F. *voluntaire*, *volontaire*, L. *voluntārius*, from *voluntas*, free will, from *volens -ntis*, pres.p. of *velle*, to will], *a.* Proceeding from or determined by one's own free will or choice, not under external constraint; acting or done willingly, spontaneous, intentional, purposive, designed; endowed with or exercising the power of willing; subject to or controlled by the will (of muscles, movement, etc.); brought about, established, or supported by voluntary action (of a church, school, etc.); (*Law*) done without constraint or by consent, without valuable consideration; gratuitous. *n.* An organ solo played in a church, etc., before, during, or after service; a supporter of the principle that the Church (and usu. education) should be independent of the State and maintained by voluntary effort; *one who engages in any act of his own free will, a volunteer. **voluntarily, *voluntariously,** *adv.* **voluntariness,** *n.* ***voluntarious,** *a.* **voluntarism,** *n.* The reliance on voluntary subscriptions rather than on State aid for the upkeep of schools, churches, etc. **voluntaryist,** *n.* **Voluntary Aid Detachment (V.A.D.),** *n.* An official organization of men and women to render first aid in time of war and assist in hospital work, etc.

volunteer (vol ŭn tēr′) [F. *volontaire*, see prec.], *n.* One who enters into any service of his own free will, esp. a member of a military body in the United Kingdom superseded by the Territorial Force in 1907. *a.* Voluntary. *v.t.* To offer or undertake voluntarily. *v.i.* To offer one's services voluntarily, esp. to offer to serve (for a campaign, etc.) as a volunteer.

voluptuary (vŏ lŭp′ tū-, -choo ăr i) [L. *voluptuārius*, as foll.], *n.* One given to luxury or sensual pleasures. *a.* Pertaining to, promoting, or devoted to sensual pleasure.

voluptuous (vŏ lŭp′ tū ŭs) [F. *voluptueux*, L. *voluptuōsus*, from *voluptas -tātem*, cogn. with VOLUNTARY], *a.* Pertaining to, contributing to, or producing sensuous or sensual gratification. **voluptuously**, *adv.* **voluptuousness**, *n.*

volute (vŏ lūt′) [F., from L. *volūta*, orig. fem. p.p. of *volvere*, to roll], *n.* A spiral scroll used in Ionic, Corinthian, and Composite capitals; a volutoid gasteropod, usu. of tropical seas and having a beautiful shell. *a.* (*Bot.*) Rolled up. **voluted**, *a.* **volution** (-lū′ shŭn), *n.* A spiral turn, a convolution; a whorl of a spiral shell. **volutoid**, *a.* and *n.*

Volvox (vol′ voks) [mod. L., from L. *volvere*, to roll], *n.* A genus of simple, freshwater, greenish organisms united in spherical colonies, composed of minute flagellate cells which set up a revolving motion.

volvulus (vol′ vū lŭs) [mod. L., as prec.], *n.* (*Path.*) A twisting of an intestine causing obstruction of the intestinal canal.

vomer (vō′ mĕr) [L., ploughshare], *n.* (*Anat.*) A small thin bone forming the chief portion of the partition between the nostrils in man. **vomerine**, *a.*

vomit (vom′ it) [L. *vomitus*, p.p. of *vomere*, cogn. with Gr. *emein*], *v.t.* To eject from the stomach by the mouth; to eject or discharge violently, to belch out. *v.i.* To eject the contents of the stomach by the mouth, to spew; to be sick. *n.* Matter ejected from the stomach by the mouth; an emetic. **vomit-nut**, *n.* Nux vomica. **vomica**, *n.* (*pl.* **-cæ**, -sē) (*Path.*) An encysted collection of pus, esp. in the lung. ***vomitive**, *a.* Vomitory. **vomito** [Sp.], *n.* The yellow fever in its worst form. **vomitory**, *a.* Emetic; *n.* An emetic; (*Rom. Ant.*) one of the openings for entrance or exit in an ancient theatre or amphitheatre. **vomiturition** (-tū rish′ ŭn), *n.* An ineffectual attempt to vomit; violent or repeated vomiting of but little matter, retching.

voodoo (voo′ doo) [Creole-F. *vaudoux*, prob. VAUDOIS (2)], *n.* A system of magic snake-worship, and prob., in extreme forms, of human sacrifice and cannibalism practised by Creoles and Negroes in Hayti and other parts of the W. Indies and in the southern U.S.A.; a sorcerer or conjurer skilled in this. *v.t.* To put a spell on or bewitch with voodoo. **voodooism**, *n.* **voodooish**, *a.*

voracious (vŏ rā′ shŭs) [L. *vorax -ācis*, from *vorāre*, to devour], *a.* Greedy in eating; ravenous, gluttonous, ready to swallow up or devour. **voraciously**, *adv.* **voraciousness, voracity** (-răs′ i ti), *n.* ***vorago** (vŏ rā gō) [L.], *n.* A whirlpool. ***voraginous** (-răj′ i nŭs), *a.* **vorant** (vôr′ ănt), *a.* (*Her.*) Devouring.

-vore [as foll.], *suf.* Forming corresponding nouns to the foll., as *carnivore, herbivore.*

-vorous [L. *vorāre*, to devour], *suf.* Feeding on, living on, as *carnivorous, herbivorous.*

vortex (vôr′ teks) [L., var. of VERTEX], *n.* (*pl.* **vortices**, -ti sēz). A whirling or rotating mass of fluid, esp. a whirlpool; (*Phys.*) a portion of fluid the particles of which have a rotary motion. **vortex-ring**, *n.* One the axis of which is a closed curve. **vortex theory**: The theory that matter is composed of vortices in the ether. **vortical, vorticose, vorticular** (-tik′ ū lăr), *a.* **vortically**, *adv.* **vorticel** (vôr′ ti sĕl), *n.* A bell-shaped infusorian, a bell-animalcule. **vorticelloid**, *a.* **vorticity** (-tis′ i ti), *n.* **vortiginous** (-tij′ i nŭs), *a.* Vortical, whirling.

Vorticism (vôr′ ti sizm) [VORTEX], *n.* (*Art.*) A school of painting which seeks to represent nature in formal designs of straight and angular patterns.

votary (vō′ tă ri) [med. L. *votārius*, from L. *vōtum*, foll.], *n.* One who is devoted or consecrated by a vow or promise; one who is devoted to some particular service, study, pursuit, etc. **votaress, *votress**, *n.*

vote (vōt) [L. *vōtum*, wish, vow, orig. neut. of *vōltus*, p.p. of *vōvere*, to vow], *n.* A formal expression of opinion, will, or choice, in regard to the election of a candidate, the passing or rejection of a resolution, law, etc., usu. signified by voice, gesture, or ballot; anything by which this is expressed, as a ballot, ticket, etc.; that which is voted, as a grant of money; the aggregate votes of a party, etc.; the right to vote, the suffrage. *v.i.* To give one's vote; to express one's approval (for). *v.t.* To give one's vote for; to enact, resolve, ratify, or grant by a majority of votes; (*colloq.*) to declare by general consent. **votable**, *a.* **voteless**, *a.* **voter**, *n.* **voting-paper**, *n.* A paper by means of which one votes, esp. by ballot in a parliamentary election.

votive (vō′ tiv) [F. *votif*, fem. *-ive*, L. *votīvus*, from *vōtum*, prec.], *a.* Given, paid, or dedicated in fulfilment of a vow. **votively**, *adv.*

vouch (vouch) [O.F. *voucher*, *vocher*, L. *vocare*, to call], *v.t.* To uphold or guarantee by assertion, proof, etc., to confirm, to substantiate. *v.i.* To give testimony, to answer (for). **n.* Warrant, attestation, testimony. **vouchee** (vou chē′), *n.* (*Law*) The person vouched or summoned in a writ of right. **voucher**, *n.* One who or that which vouches for or attests; a document, etc., serving to confirm or establish something, as a payment, the correctness of an account, etc.; (*Law*) One who vouches or acts as security for another.

vouchsafe (vouch sāf′), *v.t.* To condescend to grant; to concede. *v.i.* To deign, to condescend (to). ***vouchsafement**, *n.*

voussoir (voos war) [F., ult. from L. *volūtus*, p.p. of *volvere*, to roll], *n.* One of the wedge-shaped stones forming an arch.

vow (vou) [O.F. *vou* (F. *vœu*), L. *vōtum*, see VOTE], *n.* A solemn promise or pledge, esp. made to God or to a saint, etc., undertaking an act, sacrifice, obligation, etc.; *a votive offering. *v.t.* To promise solemnly; to dedicate by a vow; to affirm solemnly. *v.i.* To make a vow. ***vow-fellow**, *n.* One bound by the same vow.

vowel (vou′ ĕl) [O.F. *vouel*, *voiel*, L. *vocālis*, VOCAL], *n.* A sound able to make a syllable or to be sounded alone; an open and unimpeded sound as opp. to a closed, stopped, or mute sound or consonant; a letter representing this, esp. the simple vowels, *a, e, i, o, u.* **vowel-gradation**, *n.* Ablaut. **vowel-mutation**, *n.* Umlaut. **vowel-point**, *n.* One of the marks indicating the vowels in Hebrew, etc. **vowelize**, *v.t.* To insert vowel-points. ***vowelled**, *a.* (*usu. in comb.* as *open-vowelled*). **vowelless**, *a.* **vowelly**, *a.*

vox (voks) [L.], *n.* Voice. ***vox humana*** (hū mā′ nă): An organ-stop producing tones approximating to those of the human voice.

voyage (voi′ aj) [O.F. *voiaje*, L. VIATICUM], *n.* A journey by water, esp. by sea to a distant place; *a project, an enterprise. *v.i.* To make a voyage. *v.t.* To travel over by water. **voyageable**, *a.* **voyager**, *n.* **voyageur** (vwa ya zhĕr′) [F.], *n.* One of the men employed by the Hudson Bay and North-West Companies to convey goods, etc., between the trading posts; a Canadian boatman.

vraic (vrāk) [F.], *n.* A seaweed used for fuel and manure, found in the Channel Islands.

vraisemblance (vrā san blans) [F. *vrai*, O.F. *verrai*, see VERY, SEMBLANCE], *n.* An appearance of truth, verisimilitude.

Vulcan (vŭl′ kăn) [L. *Vulcānus*, *Volcānus*, cp. Sansk. *ulkā*, firebrand, meteor], *n.* (*Rom. Myth.*) The god of fire and metal-working. **Vulcanian** (-kā′ ni ăn), *a.* **vulcanic, -ism,** etc. [VOLCANIC, -ISM, etc.]. **Vulcanist,** *n.* (*Geol.*) An adherent of the plutonic theory.

vulcanite (vŭl′ kȧ nīt), *n.* Vulcanized rubber, ebonite. **vulcanize,** *v.t.* To treat (india-rubber) with sulphur at a high temperature so as to increase its strength and elasticity, producing vulcanite (the hard form) or soft and flexible rubber. **vulcanization** (-zā′ shŭn), *n.*

vulgar (vŭl′ gȧr) [F. *vulgaire,* L. *vulgāris,* from *vulgus, volgus,* the common people, cp. Sansk. *vargas,* troop, W. *gwala,* Bret. *gwalch,* fullness, Ir. *folc,* abundance], *a.* Pertaining to or characteristic of the common people, plebian, common, coarse, low, unrefined; rude, boorish; ordinary, in common use. **the vulgar:** The common people, the uneducated. **vulgar era,** *n.* The Christian era. **vulgar fraction:** A fraction having the numerator less than the denominator. **vulgarian,** *a.* Vulgar. *n.* A vulgar person, esp. a rich person with low ideas, manners, etc. **vulgarism,** *n.* **vulgarity** (-găr′ i ti), ***vulgarness,** *n.* **vulgarize,** *v.t.* **vulgarization** (-zā′ shŭn), *n.* **vulgarly,** *adv.*

Vulgate (vŭl′ gȧt), *n.* The Latin translation of the Bible made by St. Jerome, 383–405.

vulnerable (vŭl′ ner ȧbl) [L. *vulnerābilis,* from *vulnerāre,* to wound, from *vulnus -neris,* wound, cogn. with *vellere,* to pluck, and Gr. *oulē,* wound], *a.* Capable of being wounded; susceptible of or liable to injury, attack, etc. ***vuln,** *v.t.* (*Her.*) To wound. **vulnerability** (-bil′ i ti), **vulnerableness,** *n.* **vulnerary,** *a.* Useful in healing wounds or for the cure of external injuries. *n.* A plant, drug, or composition useful in the cure of wounds. ***vulnerose,** *a.* Full of wounds.

vulpine (vŭl′ pīn, -pin) [L. *vulpīnus,* from *vulpes,* fox, cogn. with WOLF], *a.* Pertaining to or characteristic of a fox; crafty, cunning. **vulpicide** [-CIDE], *n.* The killing of a fox, esp. otherwise than by hunting; a fox-killer. **vulpinism,** *n.*

vulsella (vŭl sel′ ȧ) [mod. L., from *vulsus,* p.p. of *vellere,* to pull], *n.* (*Surg.*) A forceps with hooked teeth or claws.

vulture (vŭl′ tyŭr) [L. *vultur,* cogn. with *vellere,* see VULNERABLE], *n.* A large falconoid bird with head and neck almost naked, feeding chiefly on carrion; (*fig.*) a rapacious person. **vulturine, vulturish, vulturous,** *a.* **vulturn,** *n.* An Australian turkey, *Talegallus Lathami.*

vulva (vŭl′ vȧ) [L., also *volva,* cogn. with *volvere,* to roll], *n.* (*Anat.*) An opening, an entrance, esp. the external opening of the female genitals. **vulvar, vulvate, vulviform,** *a.* **vulvitis** (-vī′ tis), *n.* Inflammation of the vulva. **vulvo-,** *comb. form.*

vying, *pres.p.* [VIE].

W

W, w, (dŭbl′ ū), the twenty-third letter of the English alphabet, taking its form and name from the union of two V's, V formerly having the name and force of U. W (*pl.* **ws, w's**) has the sound of a semi-vowel, as in *was, will, forward.*

WAAC (wăk), *n.* A member of the Women's Auxiliary Army Corps. **WAAF** (wăf), *n.* A member of the Women's Auxiliary Air Force Service (later Women's Royal Air Force).

wabble, wobble (wob′ ėl) [freq. of obs. *wap, whap,* M.E. *quappen,* to palpitate, cogn. with QUAVER], *v.i.* To incline to one side and then to the other alternately, as a rotating body, when not properly balanced; to oscillate, to go unsteadily, to stagger; (*fig.*) to waver, to be inconsistent or inconstant. *n.* A rocking, uneven motion, a stagger, a swerve; (*fig.*) an act of hesitation, inconsistency, or vacillation. **wabbler,** *n.* **wabbly,** *a.*

wabster (*Sc.*) [WEBSTER, see WEB].

wacke (wăk′ i) [G.], *n.* (*Geol.*) An earthy or clayey rock produced by the decomposition of igneous rocks.

wad (1) (wod) [cp. Swed. *vadd,* wadding, Icel. *vathr,* G. *watte*], *n.* A small, compact mass of some soft material, used for stopping an opening, stuffing between things, etc., esp. a felt or paper disk used to keep the charge in place in a gun, cartridge, etc.; (*colloq.*) a number of currency notes, a lot of money. *v.t.* (*past & p.p.* **wadded**) To compress into a wad; to stuff or line with wadding; to pack, stop up, or secure with a wad.

wad (2) (wod) [etym. doubtful], *n.* An earthy ore of manganese; (*prov.*) plumbago.

wad (3) (*Sc.*) [var. of WOULD].

wadable [WADE].

wadding (wod′ ing), *n.* A spongy material, usu. composed of cotton or wool, used for stuffing garments, cushions, etc., cottonwool; material for gun-wads.

waddle (wod′ ėl) [freq. of WADE], *v.i.* To walk with an ungainly rocking or swaying motion and with short, quick steps, as a duck or goose. *n.* A waddling gait. **waddler,** *n.* **waddlingly,** *adv.*

waddy (wod′ i) [native name], *n.* An Australian war-club, usu. bent like a boomerang or with a thick head. **waddy wood,** *n.* A Tasmanian tree from which this is made.

wade (wād) [A.-S. *wadan,* cp. Dut. *waden,* G. *waten,* Icel. *vatha,* also L. *vādere,* to go, *vādum,* ford], *v.i.* To walk through water or any semi-fluid medium, as water, snow, mud, etc.; to make one's way with difficulty and labour. *v.t.* To pass through or across by wading; to ford (a stream) on foot. **wadable,** *a.* **wader,** *n.* One who wades; a high, waterproof boot, worn by anglers, etc., for wading; a wading-bird. **wading bird:** A long-legged bird that wades, esp. one of the *Grallæ* or *Grallatores,* comprising the storks, herons, etc.

wadi (wod′ i, wa′ di) [Arab.], *n.* The valley or channel of a stream that is dry except in the rainy season.

***wadset** (wod′ sėt) [A.-S. *wed,* pledge, whence *weddian,* to WED, SET (1)], *n.* (*Sc. Law*) A mortgage or bond in security for a debt. ***wadsetter,** *n.* One who holds by a wadset, a mortgagee.

wae, etc. (*Sc.*) [WOE].

wafer (wā′ fėr) [M.E. and A.-F. *wafre,* O.F. *waufre* (usu. *gaufre,* GOFER), from L.G., cp. Walloon *wafe, wauffe,* G. *waffel,* Dut. *wafel,* wafer, also G. *wabe,* honeycomb, cogn. with WEAVE], *n.* A small, thin, sweet cake or biscuit; (*Eccles.*) a thin disk of unleavened bread used in the Eucharist, the Host; a thin adhesive disk of dried paste for sealing letters, fastening documents, etc. *v.t.* To seal or attach with a wafer. **wafer-cake,** *n.* **wafery,** *a.*

***waff** [WAVE].

waffle (1) (wof′ ėl) [Dut., see WAFER], *n.* A thin batter cake baked on a waffle-iron. **waffle-iron,** *n.* A utensil with hinged plates for baking waffles.

waffle (2) (wof′ ėl) [freq. of WAFF], *v.i.* (*prov.*) To wave, to fluctuate; to chatter aimlessly.

waft (waft) [prob. *waved, past & p.p.* of WAVE], *v.t.* To carry or convey through the air; to carry lightly or gently along; *to signal or beckon by waving the hand, etc. **v.i.* To float. *n.* An act of wafting, as a sweep of a bird's wing; a breath or whiff of odour, etc. ***waftage, *wafture,** *n.* The act of wafting; conveyance by wafting. ***wafter,** *n.*

wag (wăg) [M.E. *waggen,* M.Swed. *wagga* (cp. Norw. *vagga,* A.-S. *wagian,* from *wegan,* to carry), cogn. with WAGON, WEIGH, and L. *vehere,* to carry], *v.t.* (*past & p.p.* **wagged**) To shake up and down or backwards and forwards lightly and quickly, esp. in playfulness, reproof, etc. *v.i.* To move up and down or to and fro, to oscillate; (*fig.*) to move on, to keep going, to proceed. *n.* An act or motion of wagging, a shake; [perh. short for obs. *wag-halter*, gallows-bird], a facetious fellow, a wit, a joker. **wag-at-the-wall,** *n.* A hanging clock with exposed pendulum and weights. **waggery, waggishness,** *n.* **waggish,** *a.* **waggishly,** *adv.*

wage (wāj) [O.F., also *gage, guage*, from *wager, gager*, to GAGE (1)], *n.* Payment for work done or services rendered, esp. fixed periodical pay for labour of a mechanical kind (*usu. in pl.*); recompense, meed, requital. *v.t.* To engage in, to carry on; *to wager, *to engage, to employ for wages, to hire. **v.i.* To contend in or as in battle (with). **wage-freeze,** *n.* The fixing of a wage-level for a prolonged period. **wage-, wages-fund:** (*Polit. Econ.*) The portion of the capital of a community expended in paying the wages of labour. **wagedom, wagery,** *n.* **wageless,** *a.* ***wageling,** *n.* A hireling.

wager (wā′ jėr) [M.E. *wageoure*, O.F. *wageure, gageure*, low L. *wadiātūra*, from *wadiāre*, to pledge, as prec.], *n.* Something staked or hazarded on the event of a contest, etc.; a bet. *v.t.* and *i.* To stake, to bet. **wager of battle** [BATTLE]. **wager of law:** A compurgation. ***wagerer,** *n.*

wagga blanket (wog′ ȧ), *n.* [Austral.] A rug made from corn sacks cut open and sewn together.

waggery, waggish, etc. [WAG].

waggle (wăg ėl) [freq. of WAG], *v.i.* and *t.* To wag quickly and frequently. *n.* A short, quick wagging.

waggon [WAGON].

Wagnerian (vag nēr′ i ȧn) [Richard *Wagner* (1813–83)], *a.* Pertaining to or in the style of Wagner's music or musical dramas. **Wagnerianism, Wagnerism** (vag′ nėr izm), *n.* **Wagnerist,** *n.*

wagon, waggon (wăg′ ȯn) [Dut. *wagen*, cogn. with WAIN], *n.* A strong four-wheeled vehicle for the transport of heavy loads, usu. with a rectangular body, often with a removable cover, usu. drawn by two or more horses; an open railway truck; *a chariot. **wagon-ceiling, -roof, -vault,** *n.* A semi-cylindrical ceiling, a barrel-vault. **wagonage,** *n.* Money paid for the conveyance of goods in wagons; wagons collectively. **wagoner,** *n.* One who drives or leads a wagon, a charioteer; (*Astron.*) the constellation Auriga. ***wagon-lit*** (va gon lē′) [F.], *n.* A sleeping-car. **wagon-load,** *n.* **wagonful,** *n.* **wagonette** (-net′), *n.* A four-wheeled pleasure carriage of light construction, for six or eight persons on seats facing each other, often with a removable cover, drawn by one or more horses.

wagtail (wăg′ tāl), *n.* A small black and grey or white or yellow bird, chiefly of the genus *Motacilla*, named from the wagging of their tails.

Wahabi (wȧ ha′ bē) [after Abd-el-*Wahhab*, founder (1691–1787)], *n.* One of a sect founded about the middle of the 18th cent. cultivating a strict form of Mohammedanism. **Wahabiism,** *n.*

wahine (wa hē′ nē) [Maori], *n.* A woman.

waif (wāf) [O.F., from Norse, cp. Icel. *veif*, anything flapping about, cogn. with WAIVE], *n.* A person or thing found astray, ownerless, or cast up by or adrift on the sea; a homeless wanderer, esp. a forsaken or unowned child.

wail (wāl) [M.E. *weilen*, Icel. *vǽla*, from *væ*, WOE!], *v.t.* To lament loudly over, to bewail. *v.i.* To lament, to utter wails; to make a plaintive sound (as the wind). *n.* A loud, high-pitched lamentation, a plaintive cry; a sound like this. **wailful,** *a.* **wailingly,** *adv.* ***wailment,** *n.*

wain (wān) [A.-S. *wægn*, cp. Dut. and G. *wagen*, Icel. and Swed. *vagn*, L. *vehiculum*, Sansk. *vahana-*, VEHICLE, Gr. *ochos*, car], *n.* (*poet.*) A four-wheeled vehicle for the transportation of goods, a wagon; Charles's Wain; *a chariot. **v.t.* To convey in a wain. ***wain-bote,** *n.* An allowance of timber for wagons, etc. **wain-rope,** *n.* A rope for fastening goods, etc., on a wain. ***wainwright,** *n.* One who makes wains. ***wainage,** *n.*

wainscot (wān′ skȯt) [Dut. *wagenschot*, a grained oak-wood (perh. M.Dut. *waeghe*, wave, cp. A.-S. *wæg, schot*, partition, wainscot, prob. cogn. with SHOT (1 and 2), cp. CAMPSHOT (see CAMPSHED)], *n.* A wooden lining or casing of the walls of rooms, usually in panels. *v.t.* To line with this. **wainscoting,** *n.*

wairepo (wī rē′ pō) [Maori], *n.* Grog, spirits.

waist (wāst) [M.E. *wast*, cogn. with WAX (2), cp. A.-S. *wæstm*, growth], *n.* That part of the human body below the ribs or thorax and above the hips; this part as normally more contracted than the rest of the trunk; (*fig.*) the middle part of an object, esp. if more contracted than the other parts; the part of a ship between the quarter-deck and the forecastle; the part of a garment encircling the waist; (*Am.*) a blouse, a shirtwaist. **waist-band,** *n.* A band or belt worn round the waist, esp. a band forming the upper part of a garment. **waist-belt,** *n.* **waist-cloth,** *n.* A loin-cloth. **waistcoat** (wes′ kůt), *n.* A short garment, usu. without sleeves, extending from the neck to the waist. **waist-deep, -high,** *a.* and *adv.* As deep, as high, or in (water, etc.) as far as the waist. **waistline,** *n.* The waist of a dress, etc., not necessarily corresponding with the wearer's natural waist.

wait (wāt) [O.F. *waiter, gaiter* (F. *guetter*), from *waite, gaite*, O.H.G. *wahta*, guard, watch, cp. G. *wacht*, cogn. with WAKE (1)], *v.i.* To remain inactive or in the same place until some event or time for action, to stay, to tarry; to be in a state of expectation or readiness; to be on the watch (for); to act as a waiter, to attend (on persons) at table. *v.t.* To wait for, to await, to bide; to postpone, to defer. *n.* The act of waiting; time taken in waiting, delay; watching, ambush; (*pl.*) a band of singers and players performing carols in the streets, etc., at Christmas-time. **to lie in wait:** To wait for in secret, to waylay. **to wait on** or **upon:** To attend upon as a servant; to pay a visit to deferentially; to await; to follow (of consequences, etc.); *to accompany, to escort, to attend; *to watch. **waiter,** *n.* One who waits; an attendant on the guests at an hotel, restaurant, etc.; a dumb-waiter. **waiting-maid, -woman,** *n.* A female attendant. **waiting-room,** *n.* A room at a railway-station, etc., where persons can rest while waiting. **in waiting:** In attendance, esp. on the sovereign. **waitingly,** *adv.* **waitress,** *n.*

waive (wāv) [A.-F. *weiver*, O.F. *gaiver*, prob. from Icel. *veifa*, to vibrate, to swing about], *v.t.* To forgo, to relinquish, to refrain from using, etc., not to insist on. **waiver,** *n.* (*Law*) The act of waiving.

waiwode [VOIVODE].

waka (wok′ ȧ) [Maori], *n.* A canoe.

wake (1) (wāk) [A.-S. *wacan*, to arise, be born, and *wacian*, to wake, to watch (cp. Dut. *waken*, G. *wachen*, Icel. *vaka*, Goth. *wakan*), cogn. with VIGIL], *v.i.* (*past & p.p.* **woke, waked;** **p.p.* **woken**) To be aroused from sleep, to cease to sleep; to revive from a trance, death, etc.; to be awake, to be unable to sleep; to be roused or to rouse oneself from inaction, inattention, etc.; *to revel or carouse at night. *v.t.* To rouse from sleep, to awake; to revive, to resuscitate, to raise from the dead; to arouse, to stir (up); to break the silence of, to disturb. The act of waking or being awake; a vigil. **wake-robin,** *n.* The wild arum, *Arum maculatum*, or 'lords and ladies.' **waker,** *n.*

wake (2) (wāk) [from prec.], *n.* The feast of the dedication of a church, formerly kept by watching all night; a merry-making held in connexion with this; (*Ir.*) the watching of a dead body, prior to burial, by friends and neighbours of the deceased, with lamentations often followed by a merry-making. *v.t.* To hold a wake over.

wake (3) (wāk) [Icel. *vökr*, pl. *vaker*, a hole, an opening in ice, cp. Dut. *wak*, moist, cogn. with Gr. *hugros*, L. *humidus*, HUMID], *n.* The track left by a vessel passing through water. **in the wake of:** Following (*lit. and fig.*).

wakeful (wāk′ fụl), *a.* Not disposed or unable to sleep, restless; passed without sleep, disturbed; watchful, alert. **wakefully,** *adv.* **wakefulness,** *n.*

waken (wā′ kėn) [A.-S. *wæcnan*, to arise, to be born, from *wacan*, to WAKE (1)], *v.t.* To rouse from sleep; to rouse to action, etc.; to call forth. *v.i.* To wake, to cease from sleeping. **wakener,** *n.* **waker** [WAKE (1)].

wakerife (wāk′ rīf), *a.* (*Sc.*) Wakeful. **wakerifely,** *adv.* **wakerifeness,** *n.*

Waldenses (wol den′ sēz), *n.pl.* A religious sect founded about 1170 by Peter Waldo, a merchant of Lyons, in a reform movement leading to persecution by the Church, still flourishing in the Alpine valleys of Dauphiné, Provence, and Piedmont. **Waldensian,** *a.* and *n.*

waldgrave (wold′ grāv) [G. *waldgraf* (*wald*, WOLD, forest, GRAVE (4))], *n.* A German title of nobility, orig. a head-forester.

waldhorn (wold′ hôrn, val tôrn) [G. (*wald*, see prec., HORN)], *n.* A hunting-horn; (*Mus.*) a french horn without valves.

wale (1) (wāl) [M.E., from Icel. *val*, choice, cp. G. *wahl*, cogn. with WILL (1)], *n.* (*Sc.*) The choice, the pick. *v.t.* To choose.

wale (2) [WEAL (2)].

waler (wā′ ler) [N.S.W.], *n.* (*Austral.*) A riding-horse (orig. as supplied by military authorities in N.S.W.).

Walhalla [VALHALLA].

walk (wawk) [A.-S. *wealcan*, to roll, to toss about, to rove (cp. Dut. *walken*, to press hats, G. *walken*, to full, Icel. *vālka*, *volka*, to roll, Dan. *valke*, to full), cogn. with WALLOW], *v.i.* To go along by raising, advancing, and setting down each foot alternately, never having both off the ground at once; to go at the ordinary pace, not to run, not to go or proceed rapidly; to go or travel on foot; to move about or show itself (of a ghost); (*colloq.*) to depart, to be off, to be dismissed; *to act, conduct oneself, or live in a specified way. *v.t.* To walk over, on, or through, to perambulate, to tread; to cause to walk, to lead, drive, or ride at a walking pace. *n.* The act of walking; the pace, gait, or step, of one who walks; a stroll, a promenade; the route chosen for this; a piece of ground laid out for walking, a foot-path, a promenade, etc.; a hawker's or itinerant vendor's district or round; a sheep-walk; (*fig.*) one's profession, occupation, sphere of action, etc. **walk-about,** *n.* (*Austral.*) A wandering journey by Aborigines. *adv.* Moving from place to place. **walk-over:** An easy victory, one in which one's rivals could be beaten by walking. ***walk-mill,** *n.* A fulling-mill. **to walk into:** (*slang*) To thrash; to abuse; to eat heartily of. **to walk off with:** (*colloq.*) To carry off, to steal. **to walk on:** (*Theat.*) To take a part in which nothing has to be said. **to walk one's chalks:** To be off, to depart without ceremony. **to walk the chalk:** To follow a straight course as by walking along a chalk-line, orig. a test of sobriety. **to walk the hospitals:** To attend at hospitals as a medical student. **to walk the plank** [PLANK]. **to walk the streets:** To be a prostitute. **to walk out with:** To go a-courting with. **walkable,** *a.* **walker** (1), *n.* One who walks; a shop-walker; *a fuller; (*Ornith.*) a bird that steps instead of hopping; a gallinaceous bird. **walkie-talkie:** (*Radio.*) A portable combined transmitter and receiver. **walking-dress,** *n.* A dress for wearing out of doors. **walking-gentleman, -lady,** *n.* An actor filling subordinate parts requiring a gentlemanly or ladylike appearance. **walking-leaf,** *n.* An insect mimicking a leaf. **walking-stick, *-staff,** *n.* A stick carried in walking; an insect belonging to the *Phasmidæ*, which closely resemble dry twigs.

walker (2) (waw′ kėr) [old phrase Hookey *Walker*], *int.* Nonsense!

walkyrie [VALKYRIE].

wall (wawl) [A.-S. *weal*, L. VALLUM], *n.* A continuous structure of stone, brick, etc., narrow relatively to its height, forming an enclosure, fence, or the front, back or side, or an internal partition of a building; a rampart, a fortification (*usu. in pl.*) anything resembling a wall, as a cliff, a mountain-range, etc.; the enclosing sides of a vessel, cavity, etc.; (*fig.*) a defence. *v.t.* To furnish, enclose, or defend with a wall; to block (up) with a wall. **to give the wall to:** To allow as a courtesy to walk or pass by on the side of a pavement, etc., away from the gutter. **to go to the wall:** To get the worst in a contest; to be pushed aside. **to take the wall of:** To pass on the side of a pavement, etc., away from the gutter, as a slight or discourtesy. **wall-creeper,** *n.* A bird, *Tichodroma muraria*, frequenting walls and cliffs. **wall-cress,** *n.* A plant of the genus *Arabis* growing in crevices. **wallflower,** *n.* A sweet-smelling plant of the genus *Cheiranthus*, esp. *C. cheiri*, with yellow, brown, and crimson flowers; (*slang*) a lady without a partner at a dance. **wall-fruit,** *n.* Fruit grown on trees trained against walls. **wall game,** *n.* A kind of football played only at Eton. **wall-painting,** *n.* A painting painted on a wall, a fresco. **wall-paper,** *n.* Paper, usu. with decorative patterns, for pasting on the walls of rooms. **wall-pellitory** [PELLITORY]. **wall-pepper,** *n.* Stone-crop, *Sedum acre*. **wall-plate,** *n.* A piece of timber let into a wall as a bearing for the ends of the joists, etc. **wall-rue,** *n.* A small evergreen fern, *Asplenium rutamuraria*, growing on old walls, cliffs, etc. **Wall Street,** *n.* The New York stock exchange and money market. **wall-tie,** *n.* (*Build.*) A metal bond between the sides of a cavity wall. **walled,** *a.* ***waller,** *n.* One who builds walls. **walling,** *n.*

wallaba (wol′ ȧ bȧ) [native name], *n.* A leguminous tree, *Eperua falcata*, from British Guiana, used in carpentry and building.

wallaby (wol′ ȧ bi) [Austral. abor.], *n.* One of the smaller species of kangaroo. **on the wallaby:** (*Austral. slang*) Tramping about looking for work, etc.

Wallach (wol′ ȧk) [G., from O.H.G. *walh*, foreigner, cogn. with WELSH], *n.* A Wallachian or Vlach, a Romance-speaking inhabitant of Rumania. **Wallachian** (wȧ lā′ ki ȧn), *a.* Of or pertaining to Wallachia; *n.* A native or the language of Wallachia.

wallah (wol′ ȧ) [Hind. *-wālā*, Sansk. *-vala-*, suf. -er], *n.* An agent, worker, or any one employed about something; (*colloq.*) a person, a fellow.

wallaroo (wol ȧ roo′) [Austral. abor.], *n.* One of the large species of kangaroo.

waller, etc. [WALL].

wallet (wol′ ėt) [perh. corr. of WATTLE], *n.* A bag or sack for carrying necessaries for a journey or march, esp. a pilgrim's or beggar's pack; a small bag or case, usu. of leather, for carrying tools, implements, papers, etc.

wall-eye (waw′ lī) [from *wall-eyed*, M.E. *wald-eyed*, *vald-eygthr* (*vagl*, beam, *eygthr*, eyed, from *auga*, corr. of Icel. eye)], *n.* An affection of the eye due to opacity of the cornea or to strabismus; an eye with a very light-coloured iris, esp. due to this affection; a large, glaring eye, as in fish. **wall-eyed,** *a.*

wallflower [WALL].

Walloon (wȧ loon′) [O.F. *Wallon*, L. *Gallus*, GAUL], *n.* One of mixed people in S.E. Belgium and the adjoining parts of France; their language. *a.* Pertaining to the Walloons or their language.

wallop (wol′ ụp) [O.F. *waloper*, var. of *galoper*, see GALLOP], *v.i.* To boil with a noisy bubbling and rolling motion; to move along in a clumsy tumbling fashion, to waddle. *v.t.* (*slang*) To thrash, to flog. *n.* (*slang*) Beer. **walloping,** *n.* (*slang*) A thrashing. *a.* (*slang*) Big, thumping, whopping. **walloper,** *n.*

wallow (wol′ ō) [A.-S. *wealwian*, cogn. with L. *volvere*], *v.i.* To roll or tumble about in mire, water, etc.; (*fig.*) to revel grossly or self-indulgently (in vice, etc.). *v.t.* To roll (oneself) about in mire, etc. *n.* The act of wallowing; a mud-hole or other place in which animals wallow. **wallower,** *n.*

Wallsend (wawl' zĕnd), *n.* A superior kind of house coal orig. from Wallsend, on the Tyne.

walnut (wawl' nŭt) [M.E. *walnote*, A.-S. *wealh*, foreign, cp. WELSH, NUT], *n.* A tree of the genus *Juglans*, esp. *J. regia*, bearing a nut enclosed in a green fleshy covering; the unripe fruit of this used for pickling; the ripe nut used for dessert; the timber of this or other species of the same genus used in cabinet-making and for gun-stocks.

walpurgis night (val poor' gis nīt) [*Walpurgis* or *Walpurga*, English nun who founded religious houses in Germany, *c.* 754–779], *n.* The eve of 1st May, when witches are supposed to hold revel and dance with the devil, esp. on the Brocken.

walrus (wawl'-, wol' rŭs) [Dut. from Scand. (cp. Swed. *vallros*, Dan. *hvalros*, Icel. *hross-hvalr*, A.-S. *horshwæl*, horse-whale)], *n.* A large, amphibious, long-tusked, seal-like mammal of the Arctic seas, the morse or sea-horse.

walty (wol' ti) [A.-S. *wealt*, -Y], *a.* (*Naut.*) Unsteady, crank, inclined to fall or roll over.

waltz (wawlts) [G. *walzer*, from *walzen*, to revolve, to waltz, cogn. with A.-S. *wealtan*, to WELTER (1)], *n.* A dance in triple time in which the partners pass round each other smoothly as they progress; the music for such a dance. *v.i.* To dance a waltz; to move quickly, to trip. **waltzer,** *n.*

waly (1) (wā' li) [prob. cogn. with WALE (1)], *a.* Beautiful, fine, excellent; strong, robust.

***waly** (2) [corr. of WELLAWAY].

wamble (wom' bĕl) [cp. Dan. *vamle*, imit. in orig.], *v.i.* To rumble, to heave, to be affected with nausea (of the stomach). *n.* A heaving; a feeling of nausea.

wame (*Sc.*) [WOMB].

wampee (wom pē') [Chin. *hwang*, yellow, *pi*, skin], *n.* A tree of the rice family cultivated in China and the E. Indies bearing a grape-like, pulpy berry.

wampum (wom' pŭm) [N. Am. Ind. *wampumpeag* (*wompi*, white, *-ompeag*, string of money)], *n.* Small beads made of shells, used by the American Indians as money, or for decorating belts, bracelets, etc.

wan (won) [A.-S. *wann*, *wonn*, dark, black, etym. doubtful], *a.* Pale or sickly in hue, pallid, worn; *sombre, gloomy. *v.i.* To become wan. **wanly** *adv.* **wanness,** *n.* **wannish,** *a.* **wanny,** *a.* (*Sc.*)

wanchancy (*Sc.*) [UNCHANCY].

wand (wond) [Icel. *vöndr*, gen. *vandar*, prob. cogn. with WIND (2)], *n.* A long, slender rod, esp. one used by conjurers or as a staff of office; a conductor's baton. **wandy,** *a.*

wander (won' dĕr) [A.-S. *wandrian*, freq. of *wendan*, to WEND (1)], *v.i.* To travel or go here and there without any definite route or object, to rove, ramble, or roam; to lose one's way, to go astray; to deviate from the right or proper course, to err; to leave one's home, to get lost; to talk or think incoherently or senselessly, to be delirious; to digress from the subject in hand. *v.t.* To wander over, to traverse in a random way. **wanderer,** *n.* **wandering,** *a.* and *n.* (*usu. in pl.*) **Wandering Jew:** A legendary character condemned, for an insult to Christ, to wander from place to place until the Day of Judgment; the Kenilworth ivy and other trailing or climbing plants. **wanderingly,** *adv.* **wanderment,** *n.*

wanderlust (van' der loost) [G.], *n.* The itch to travel.

wanderu (won dĕ roo') [Cingalese *wanderu*], *n.* The lion-tailed macaque, *Macacus silenus*, with a large greyish beard, of W. India; a monkey from Ceylon.

wandoo (won' doo) [Austral. abor.], *n.* The white gum-tree of W. Australia.

wane (wān) [A.-S. *wanian*, from *wan*, wanting, deficient, cp. Icel. *vane*, to diminish, see WANT and WANTON], *v.i.* To diminish in size and brilliance, as the illuminated portion of the moon; to decrease in power, strength, etc., to decline. *n.* The act or process of waning, decrease, diminution.

***wang** (wăng) [A.-S. *wange*], *n.* The jaw; the cheek-bone; a wang-tooth. ***wang-tooth,** *n.* A cheek-tooth or grinder.

wangle (wăng' gĕl) [etym. doubtful], *v.t.* To manipulate, to employ cunningly; to falsify accounts, etc.

***wanhope** (won' hōp) [A.-S. *wan*, wanting, deficient in (cp. WANE), HOPE], *n.* Despair, delusion.

***wanion** (won' yŏn) [M.E. *waniand*, pres.p. of *wanian*, to WANE] *n.* Misfortune, mischief, bad luck. ***with a wanion:** A curse (to you).

wankle (wăng' kel) [A.-S. *wancol*], *a.* (*prov.*) Weak, unstable; untrustworthy, unreliable.

wanly, etc. [WAN (1)].

wanrestful (won rest' fŭl) [*wan-*, as in WANHOPE, RESTFUL], *a.* (*Sc.*) Restless.

want (wont) [Icel. *vant*, neut. of *vanr*, wanting, deficient, cp. A.-S. *wan*, WANE], *n.* The state or condition of not having, lack, deficiency, absence, need (of); need, privation, penury, poverty; a longing or desire for something that is necessary or required for happiness, etc.; that which is not possessed but is so desired. *v.t.* To be without, to lack, to be deficient in; to need, to require; to be short by, to require in order to be complete; to feel a desire for, to crave, to desire the presence or assistance of. *v.i.* To be in need, to be in want (for); to be deficient (in), to fall short (in); to be lacking, not to be present. ***want-wit,** *n.* A fool. ***wantage,** *n.* Deficiency. **wanter,** *n.* **wanting,** *a.* Absent, missing, lacking; (*colloq.*) witless, daft, deficient in intelligence. *prep.* Without, less, save. **wantless,** *a.*

wanton (won' tŏn) [M.E. *wantoun*, *wantowen* (A.-S. *wan-*, deficient in, *togen*, p.p. of *tēon*, to draw, to educate)], *a.* Sportive, frolicsome, playful; unrestrained, loose wild, unruly, extravagant, luxuriant; licentious, lascivious, lewd; random, heedless, reckless, purposeless. *n.* A lewd or unchaste person, esp. a woman; a trifler; a playful, idle creature. *v.i.* To sport, to frolic; to move, act, or grow at random or unrestrainedly; *to sport lasciviously. **wantonly,** *adv.* **wantonness,** *n.*

wanty (won' ti) [etym. doubtful], *n.* (*prov.*) A leather band or rope, esp. a girth, belly-band, etc.

wapacut (wop' ă kŭt) [N. Am. Ind. *wapacuthu*], *n.* A large white N. American owl, *Nyctea Scandiaca.*

wapenshaw [WAPINSHAW].

wapentake (wop' ĕn tāk) [A.-S. *wæpengetæce*, Icel. *vāpnatak*, weapon-touching (*vāpna*, gen. of *vāpn*, weapon, *taka* to TAKE, to touch), cp. foll.], *n.* A name formerly given in certain English counties to a division corresponding to a hundred.

wapinshaw (wawp' in shaw) [Sc., weapon-show], *n.* A review of persons under arms, made formerly in Scotland periodically in certain districts; a meeting for rifle-shooting, curling-matches, etc.

wapiti (wop' i ti) [N. Am. Ind. *wapitik*, from *wapi*, white], *n.* A N. American stag, *Cervus Canadensis*, related to the red deer, erroneously called the elk.

***wappened** [?], *a.* (*Shak.*) Worn out, stale.

wapper (wăp' ĕr) [etym. doubtful], *n.* (*prov.*) The gudgeon.

war (1) (wôr) [O.F. *werre* (F. *guerre*), from Teut. (cp. O.H.G. *werra*, strife, *werran*, to embroil), prob. cogn. with WORSE], *n.* A contest carried on by force of arms between nations, or between parties in the same State; the state of things brought about by this, a state of hostilities with suspension of ordinary international relations; hostile operations, military or naval attack, invasion; the military art, strategy; (*fig.*) hostility, active enmity, strife, conflict, a feud; *armed troops, an army. *v.i.* (*past & p.p.* **warred**) To make or carry on war; to contend, to strive, to compete; to be in opposition, to be inconsistent. *v.t.* To make war upon, to fight against; to effect by warfare. **art of war:** Strategy and tactics. **at war:** Engaged in hostilities (with).

civil war [CIVIL]. **cold war** [COLD]. **holy war:** A war in support of a religion; a war undertaken from religious motives, a crusade. **man-of-war** [MAN]. **war-bond,** *n.* (*Fin.*) A Government bond issued as a means of raising a war loan. **war-cloud,** *n.* A state of international affairs threatening war. **war-cry,** *n.* A name or phrase formerly shouted in charging, etc.; a watchword; a party cry. **war-dance,** *n.* A dance practised by savages as a preparation for battle. **war footing:** A condition (of the military or naval establishments) of readiness for active hostilities. **war-god,** *n.* A deity worshipped as giving victory, as Mars or the Greek Ares. **war-head,** *n.* The head of a torpedo, aerial bomb, rocket, etc., charged with explosive, removable in peace practice. **war-horse,** *n.* A charger; (*fig.*) a veteran, a person full of warlike memories, etc. **war-loan,** *n.* A loan raised to meet the cost of a war. **war-marked,** *a.* Bearing the marks or traces of war. **warmonger** (wôr' mŭng gėr), *n.* One who traffics in war, or promotes it by every means in his power. **war neurosis** [SHELL-SHOCK]. **War Office:** A Government department administering the affairs of the army. **war-paint,** *n.* Paint put on the face and body by savages before going into battle; (*fig.*) full dress. **war-path,** *n.* The path taken by an attacking party of N. American Indians; hence a warlike expedition. **to be** or **go on the war-path:** To be ready for or engaged in conflict; to be thoroughly roused or incensed. **war-proof,** *n.* Tried or proved valour. **warship,** *n.* An armed ship for use in war. **war-song,** *n.* A song sung by savages at a war-dance or before battle; a song on a martial theme. ***war-wasted,** *a.* **war-wearied,** *a.* **war-whoop,** *n.* A shout or yell raised by N. American Indians in attacking. **war-worn,** *a.* Exhausted by or experienced in war. **warless,** *a.* **warlike,** *a.* Fit or ready for war; fond of war, martial, soldier-like, military; threatening war, hostile. ***warlikeness,** *n.*

***war** (2) (wôr) (*Sc.*) [WORSE].

waratah (wor' ȧ ta) [Austral. abor], *n.* One of a genus of Australian proteaceous shrubs with a large, brilliant crimson flower.

warble (1) (wôr' bėl) [etym. doubtful], *n.* A small hard tumour on a horse's back caused by the falling of the saddle; a small tumour produced by the larva of the bot-fly. **warble-fly,** *n.* (*Ent.*) The bot-fly.

warble (2) (wôr' bėl) [M.E. *werblen*, O.F. *werbler*, freq. from Teut. (cp. M.H.G. *werben*, G. *wirbeln*, to WHIRL)], *v.i.* To sing in a continuous quavering or trilling manner (of birds); to make a continuous melodious sound (of streams, etc.). *v.t.* To sing or utter thus. *n.* The act or sound of warbling; (*fig.*) a carol, a song. **warbler,** *n.* One who, or that which, warbles; one of the *Sylviidæ*, a family of small birds comprising the nightingale, blackcap, hedge-sparrow, robin, etc. **warbling,** *a.* **warblingly,** *adv.*

ward (wôrd) [A.-S. *weard* (masc.), guard, watchman, (fem.) watch (whence *weardian*, to keep watch), cogn. with GUARD], *n.* Watch, guard, the act of guarding, protection; a parrying or guard in fencing; confinement, custody; guardianship, control; a minor or person under guardianship; an administrative or electoral division of a town or city; a separate division of a hospital, prison, or workhouse; a projection inside a lock preventing the turning of any but the right key. *v.t.* To parry, to turn aside, to keep (off); *to guard, to watch over, to defend; *to keep safe, to imprison. **ward in Chancery,** *n.* (*Law*) A minor under the guardianship of the Court of Chancery. **watch and ward** [WATCH]. **ward-mote,** *n.* A meeting of the ratepayers of a ward. **ward-room,** *n.* A room on a warship for commissioned officers below the rank of commander. **wardship,** *n.* Guardianship, tutelage.

-ward, -wards [A.-S. *-weard*, as in *tōweard*, TOWARD, from *weorthan*, to become, see WORTH (2)], *suf.* Expressing direction as in *backward*, *forward*, *homeward*, *inwards*, *outwards*, etc.

warden (1) (wôr' dėn) [M.E. and A.-F. *wardein*, O.F. *wardain*, *gardein*, from *warder*, *garder*, to GUARD], *n.* A keeper, a guardian, a governor or president, as the head of some colleges and schools; (*Am.*) a prison governor; one who keeps ward, a watchman; one of the officials in Civil Defence organization; (*Austral.*) a government official in charge of a goldfield. **Warden of the Cinque Ports:** The governor of the Cinque Ports. **wardenship,** ***wardenry,** *n.*

warden (2) (wôr' dėn) [prob. from *Wardon*, in Beds], *n.* A variety of cooking pear. ***warden-pie,** *n.*

warder (wôr' dėr) [WARD, -ER], *n.* A keeper, a jailer; *a guard, a sentinel; *a staff of authority or baton carried by a general, etc., used in giving signals. **wardress,** *n.*

wardian (wôr' di ȧn) [Nathaniel B. *Ward* (1791–1868), inventor], *a.* Applied to a close-fitting case with glass sides and top, retaining moisture, for transporting delicate plants, esp. ferns.

Wardour Street (wôr' dėr) [locality in London where the cinema industry is centred], *a.* Term (usu. contempt.) applied to the film industry; the bogus antique language, etc., of costume films.

wardrobe (wôr' drōb) [O.F. *warderobe*, *garderobe* (*warder*, see WARDEN (1), ROBE)], *n.* A cabinet, cupboard, or other place, where clothes are hung up; a person's stock of wearing apparel. **wardrobe dealer,** *n.* One who deals in used or second-hand clothing.

-wards [-WARD].

wardship, etc. [WARD].

ware (1) (wâr) [A.-S. *waru*, cp. Dut. *waar*, G. *waare*, Icel. *varu*, Dan. *vare*], *n.* Manufactured articles of a specified kind, esp. pottery, as tableware, stone-ware; (*pl.*) articles of merchandise, articles for sale, goods.

ware (2) (wâr) [A.-S. *wær*, whence *warian*, to watch over, to guard (cp. Icel. *varr*, G. *gewahr*), cogn. with Gr. *horaein*, to perceive, L. *verērī*, to regard, to dread], *a.* Conscious, aware; cautious, wary. *v.t.* (*imper.*) Beware! look out for, guard against, keep clear of. ***wareless,** *a.* ***warely,** *adv.*

***ware** (3) *past* [WEAR].

warehouse (wâr' hous), *n.* A building in which goods are stored, kept for sale or in bond; a wholesale or large retail store. *v.t.* (-houz) To deposit or secure (furniture, bonded goods, etc.) in a warehouse. **warehouseman,** *n.* One who keeps or is employed in a warehouse.

warfare (wôr' fâr), *n.* A state of war, hostilities; (*fig.*) conflict, strife. *v.i.* To carry on war; to engage in war; to contend. ***warfarer,** *n.*

warily, etc. [WARY].

***warison** (wăr' i sȯn) [O.F. *warison*, *garison*, from *warir*, *garir*, to protect, to heal (*F. guérir*), see GARRISON], *n.* Protection; reward; (*Scott*) a note of assault (*erron. usage*).

***wark** [WORK].

warlike, etc. [WAR (1)].

warlock (wôr' lok) [A.-S. *wǣrloga*, traitor, deceiver (*wær*, truth, cogn. with L. *vērus*, true, *loga*, liar)], *n.* A wizard, a sorcerer. ***warlockry,** *n.*

warm (wôrm) [A.-S. *wearm*, cp. Dut. and G. *warm*, Icel. *varmr*, Dan. and Swed. *varm*], *a.* Being at a rather high temperature; having heat in a moderate degree; promoting, emitting, or conveying heat; having the sensation of rather more than ordinary heat, esp. with the temperature of the skin raised by exercise, etc.; (*fig.*) ardent, zealous, enthusiastic, cordial; sympathetic, emotional, affectionate, amorous; erotic, indelicate; animated, heated, excited, vehement, passionate, excitable; violent, vigorous, brisk, strenuous, lively (of a skirmish, etc.); being predominantly red or yellow (of colours); fresh, strong (of scent); near the object sought (in children's games); (*colloq.*) well off, in comfortable circumstances; (*colloq.*) unpleasant, hot, uncomfortable. *v.t.* To make warm; to make ardent or enthusiastic, to excite; (*slang*) to thrash. *v.i.* To become warm, animated, zealous, sympathetic, or enthusiastic. **warm-blooded,** *a.* Having warm blood, esp. between 98° and 112°, as mammals and birds; (*fig.*) emotional, passionate, excitable; amorous, erotic. **warm-hearted,** *a.* Having warm, affectionate, kindly, or susceptible feelings. **warm-heartedly,** *adv.* **warm-heartedness,** *n.* **warmer,** *n.* (*usu. in comb.* as *foot-warmer*). **warming,** *a.* (*slang*) A thrashing, a hiding. **warming-pan** *n.* A closed pan, usu. of brass with a long handle, for holding live coals, formerly used to warm a bed; (*fig.*) a person who holds a post temporarily till another is qualified to fill it. **warmly,** *adv.* **warmth, *warmness,** *n.*

warn (wôrn) [A.-S. *wearnian, warnian* (cp. G. *warnen*, O.H.G. *warnōn*), cogn. with WARY], *v.t.* To give notice to, to inform beforehand; to caution or put on one's guard against; to expostulate with, to admonish. **warner,** *n.* **warning,** *n.* The act of cautioning or admonishing against danger, etc.; previous notice, esp. to quit one's service, etc.; that which serves to warn; (*Clocks*) the sound made by the partial unlocking of the striking train just before striking. **warningly,** *adv.*

warp wôrp) [A.-S. *wearp*, cp. Icel., Dan., and Swed. *varp*, a casting or throwing (v. from the cogn. Icel. *varpa*, to throw)], *n.* The threads running the long way of a woven fabric, crossed by the woof; a rope, usu. smaller than a cable, used in towing; the state of being twisted, a twist or distortion in timber, etc.; (*fig.*) a perversity of mind or disposition; an alluvial deposit of water artificially introduced into low lands. *v.t.* To turn or twist out of shape; to make crooked, to distort, to pervert, to bias, to turn awry; to fertilize by means of artificial inundations; (*Naut.*) to tow or move with a line attached to a buoy, anchor, or other fixed point, etc.; to run (yarn) off for weaving. *v.i.* To become twisted, crooked, or distorted; to turn aside; to become perverted; (*prov.*) to cast young prematurely. **warper,** *n.* **warping-bank,** *n.* A bank for retaining the water let on to ground for fertilizing purposes. **warping-hook,** *n.* A ropemaker's hook used in warping. **warping mill,** *n.* (*Weaving*) A revolving wooden frame upon which threads are wound when being made into a warp. **warping-post,** *n.* A post used in warping rope-yarn.

warragal [WARRIGAL].

warrant (wor′ ȧnt) [O.F. *warant, guarant*, from Teut. (cp. G. *gewähren*, to certify)], *v.t.* To answer or give an assurance for, to guarantee; to give authority to, to justify; to serve as guarantee for. *n.* Anything that authorizes a person to do something, authorization; sanction; anything that attests or bears out a statement, etc., a voucher; a document authorizing a person to receive money, etc.; an instrument giving power to arrest a person, levy a distress, etc.; a certificate of office held by a warrant-officer. **warrant of attorney:** One authorizing an attorney to represent his principal in court. **warrant-officer,** *n.* An officer next below a commissioned officer, acting under a warrant from the Admiralty or War Office as a gunner, boatswain, or sergeant-major. **warrantable,** *a.* Justifiable, defensible; old enough to be hunted (of deer). **warrantableness,** *n.* **warrantably,** *adv.* **warrantee** (-tē′), *n.* **warranter,** *n.* ***warrantise,** *n.* A warranty. ***warrantize,** *v.t.* **warrantor,** *n.* (*Law*). **warranty,** *n.* A warrant, an authorization; (*Law*) a promise or undertaking from a vendor to a purchaser, that the thing sold is the vendor's to sell, and is good and fit for use, etc.; **v.t.* To warrant, to guarantee.

***warre** [WORSE].

warren (wor′ ėn) [M.E. *wareine*, O.F. *warenne*, from *warir*, see WARISON], *n.* A piece of ground where rabbits live and breed. **warrener,** *n.*

warrigal (wor′ i gȧl) [Austral. abor.], *n.* The Australian dingo; a wild native; an outlaw, a rascal.

warrior (wor′ i ȯr) [M.E. *werreour*, O.F. *guerreiur*, from *guerreier*, to make war, see WAR (1)], *n.* A man experienced or distinguished in war, a distinguished soldier; a fighting-man, esp. among savages. ***warrioress,** *n.*

wart (wôrt) [A.-S. *wearte* (cp. Dut. *wrat*, G. *warze*, Icel. *varta*), prob. cogn. with WORT], *n.* A small hard excrescence on the skin of the hands, etc., due to irregular growth of the papillæ; a spongy excrescence on the hinder pastern of a horse: a small protuberance on the surface of a plant. **wart-hog,** *n.* An African large-headed hog of the genus *Phacochærus*, with warty excrescences on the face. **warted, warty,** *a.* **wartless,** *a.*

wary (wâr′ i) [WARE (2)], *a.* Cautious, watchful against deception, dangers, etc.; circumspect; done with or characterized by caution. **warily,** *adv.* **wariness, *wariment,** *n.*

was (woz), **wast, were** (wĕr), **wert** [A.-S. *wæs, wære, wæs, wæron* (*wæran, wærun*), *wesan*, infin. (cp. Sansk. *vas-*, to remain, dwell, live, Goth. *wisan*, to remain, continue, O.Fris. *wesa*, Icel. *vera*) (see also BE, AM)], Past tense of the v. TO BE.

wase (wāz) [etym. doubtful], *n.* (*prov.*) A wisp or pad of hay, straw, etc., worn on the head by porters, etc., to ease the pressure of a load.

wase-goose [WAYZGOOSE].

wash (wosh) [A.-S. *wascan* (cp. Dut. *wasschen*, G. *waschen*, Icel. and Swed. *vaska*), cogn. with WATER and WET], *v.t.* To cleanse with water or other liquid; to remove or take out, off, away, etc., thus; (*fig.*) to purify; to fall upon, cover, moisten, or dash against (of dew, waves, the sea, etc.); to carry along, to sweep away, etc., to scoop (out); to separate the earthy and lighter parts from (ore); to cover with a thin coat of colour; to overlay with a thin coat of metal. *v.i.* To cleanse (oneself) with water, etc.; to wash clothes, to wash (up table utensils); to stand washing without fading or being injured in any way; (*colloq.*) to stand examination (of a story, etc.); to move or splash or sweep along, etc. (of water). *n.* The act or operation of washing; the state of being washed; a quantity of linen, etc., washed at one time; the motion of a body of water, esp. the swirling and foaming caused by the passage of a vessel; soil removed and accumulated by water, alluvium; waste liquor from the kitchen often used as food for pigs; (*fig.*) thin liquid food, slops; a liquid used for toilet purposes, a cosmetic, a lotion; a thin coating of colour spread over broad masses of a painting, etc.; a thin coat of metal; (*Naut.*) the blade of an oar; fermented wort from which spirit has been extracted. **to wash one's hands of:** To disclaim any responsibility for. **to come right in the wash:** (*colloq.*) To come right in the end. **to wash up:** To wash dishes, etc. **the wash:** Laundry operations. **wash-basin,** *n.* A wash-hand basin. **wash-board,** *n.* A board with a ribbed surface for scrubbing clothes on; a skirting round the lower part of the wall of a room; (*Naut.*) a board to keep the water from washing over a gunwale or through a port, etc. **wash-boiler,** *n.* One for boiling clothes in the process of washing. **wash-bottle,** *n.* An apparatus for washing gases, precipitates, etc., by passing them through a liquid. **wash-bowl,** *n.* **wash-cloth,** *n.* A piece of cloth used in washing dishes, etc. **wash-day,** *n.* The day on which domestic washing is done or sent to the laundry. **wash-gilding,** *n.* Water-gilding. **wash-hand basin:** A toilet basin for washing the hands, etc., in. **wash-hand stand:** A wash-stand. **wash-house,** *n.* A building furnished with boilers, tubs, basins, etc., for washing clothes, etc., a laundry; a scullery. **wash-leather,** *n.* Chamois leather or an imitation of this. **wash out,** *v.t.* (*colloq.*) To cancel, to annul, to countermand. **wash-out,** *n.* A scooping out or sweeping away of rock, earth, etc., by a rush of water; a cleansing by washing out; (*colloq.*) a failure, a muddle; a muddler. **wash-pot,** *n.* *A vessel in which anything is washed; a vessel used to give the final coat in tin-plating. **wash-rag,** *n.* (*Am.*) A face-cloth, a flannel. **wash-room:** (*Am.*) A lavatory. **wash-stand,** *n.* A piece of furniture for holding the ewer or pitcher, basin, etc., for the toilet. **wash-tub,** *n.* A tub in which clothes, etc., are washed. **washable,** *a.* **washed out:** Limp, exhausted, worn out; faded colourless.

washer (wosh' ėr), *n.* A ring, or perforated disk of metal, rubber, etc., for placing beneath a nut, etc., to tighten the joint, etc.; one who or that which washes; a washerwoman. **washerman,** *n.* A laundryman. **washerwoman,** *n.* A laundress.

washing (wosh' ing), *n.* The act of cleansing by water, etc., ablution; clothes, etc., sent to the wash. **washing-machine,** *n.* An electrical machine in which clothes are washed automatically. **washing-powder,** *n.* A preparation used in washing clothes.

Washingtonia (wosh ing tō' ni å) [George *Washington,* 1st Pres., U.S.A. (1732–99), -IA], *n.* A gigantic Californian sequoia.

washy (wosh' i), *a.* Watery, too much diluted, weak, thin, wanting in solidity, stamina or vigour, feeble. **washily,** *adv.* **washiness,** *n.*

wasp (wosp) [A.-S. *wæps* (cp. G. *wespe,* Lith. *wapsà*), cogn. with WEAVE (from their nests) and L. *vespa*], *n.* A predatory hymenopterous insect of solitary or social habits, esp. the common wasp, *Vespa vulgaris,* a European insect with a slender waist, black and yellow stripes, and a powerful sting; (*fig.*) a spiteful or irritable person. **wasp-bee, -beetle, -fly,** *n.* One somewhat resembling a wasp, but without a sting. **wasp-waisted,** *a.* Having a very thin waist. **waspish,** *a.* Snappish, petulant, irritable. **waspishly,** *adv.* **waspishness,** *n.*

wassail (wos' ėl, wăs' ėl) [A.-S. *wæs hāl,* be thou (see WAS) of good health (*hāl,* WHOLE)], *n.* A festive occasion, a drinking-bout, a carouse; spiced ale or other liquor prepared for a wassail. *v.i.* To carouse, to make merry. **wassail-bowl, -cup, -horn,** *n.* One from which wassail was drunk. **wassailer,** *n.*

Wassermann test (vas' er man) [A. von *Wassermann* (1866–1925)], *n.* (*Med.*) A diagnostic test for the presence of syphilis.

wast (wost), 2nd pers. sing. of past tense [BE].

waste (wāst) [M.E. and O.F. *wast* (var. *gast*), from M.H.G. *waste,* a waste, L. *vastus,* VAST, whence *vastāre,* O.F. *waster, gaster* (F. *gâter,* to spoil), to lay waste], *a.* Desolate, desert, empty, unoccupied, untilled, devastated, made desolate; barren, unproductive; dreary, dismal, cheerless; refuse, superfluous, left over as useless or valueless. *v.t.* To devastate, to lay waste; to wear away gradually; to consume, to spend, to use up unnecessarily, carelessly or lavishly, to squander; (*Law*) to injure or impair (an estate) by neglect. *v.i.* To wear away gradually, to dwindle, to wither; to bring down one's weight by training. *n.* The act of wasting, squandering, or throwing away to no purpose; the state or process of being wasted or used up, gradual diminution of substance, strength, value, etc.; material, food, etc., rejected as superfluous, useless, or valueless, refuse; a desolate or desert region, a wilderness, a dreary scene, an empty space, a void; (*Law*) damage or injury to an estate, etc., caused by the act or neglect of a life-tenant, etc. **waste-basket,** *n.* A waste-paper basket. **waste-book,** *n.* An account book for entering transactions as they take place before carrying them over to the ledger. **to lay waste:** To render desolate; to devastate, to ruin. **waste paper:** Spoiled, used, or valueless paper. **waste-paper basket:** A receptacle for waste paper. **waste-pipe,** *n.* A discharge-pipe for used or superfluous water. **wastage,** *n.* Loss by use, decay, leakage, etc. **wasteful,** *a.* Extravagant, spending, or using recklessly, unnecessarily, or too lavishly; *laying waste; desolate, waste. **wastefully,** *adv.* **wastefulness,** *n.* **wasteless,** *a.* Inexhaustible. ***wasteness,** *n.* The state of being waste; solitude, desolation. **waster,** *n.* One who wastes; a prodigal, a spendthrift; a good-for-nothing, a wastrel; an article spoilt and rendered unmarketable in manufacture; *a wooden sword used as a foil. **wastrel,** *n.* Waste, refuse; an abandoned child, a waif, a street arab; a profligate; (*pop.*) a wasteful person.

***wastel** (wăst' el, wos' el) [O.F., pastry, from O.H.G. *wastel,* cake, bread], *n.* A fine white bread made from the best wheat-flour; (*Her.*) a round cake used as a bearing. ***wastel-bread, -cake,** *n.*

waster, wastrel [WASTE].

***wat** (1) (wot) [fam. for *Walter*], *n.* An old name for the hare.

wat (2) (*Sc. and prov.*) [WET].

watch (woch) [A.-S. *wæcce,* from *wacian,* to watch, from *wacan,* to WAKE (1)], *n.* The act or state of watching; a state of alertness, vigilance, close observation or attention; vigil, look out, waiting in a state of expectancy, dread, etc.; (*Hist.*) a watchman or body of watchmen, a guard; (*Hist.*) a division of the night (among the Jews one-third, among the Romans one-fourth); a small timepiece actuated by a spring for carrying on the person; (*Naut.*) the period of time during which each division of a ship's crew is alternately on duty (four hours except during the dog-watches of two hours by which the change from night to day duty is arranged); either half (starboard or port watch from the position of the sailors' bunks in the forecastle) into which the officers and crew are divided, taking duty alternately; *wakefulness, being unable to sleep at night. *v.i.* To be on the watch, to be vigilant, observant, or expectant; to look out (for); to act as a protector or guard (over); to keep awake at night, to keep vigil. *v.t.* To observe closely, to keep one's eye or eyes on; to observe with a view to detecting, etc.; to look out for, to await, to bide (one's time, etc.). **on the watch:** Vigilant, on the look out. **watch and ward:** Continuous watch; orig. watch by night and day. **watch-box,** *n.* A sentry-box. **watch-case,** *n.* The metal case enclosing the works of a watch. **watch-chain,** *n.* A metal watch-guard. **Watch Committee,** *n.* Local officials dealing with the policing, etc., of the district. **watch-dog,** *n.* A dog kept to guard premises, etc., and give notice of burglars, etc. **watch-fire,** *n.* A fire in a camp, etc., at night or used as a signal. **watch-glass,** *n.* A glass covering the face of a watch, (*Am.* a crystal); (*Naut.*) an hour- or half-hour-glass for measuring the period of a watch. **watch-guard,** *n.* A chain, cord, ribbon, etc., for securing a watch to the person. **watch-house,** *n.* A house occupied by a watch or guard; a lock-up. **watch-key,** *n.* A key for winding up a watch. **watchmaker,** *n.* **watchmaker's oil:** A fine thin oil for lubricating the works of watches, etc. **watchmaking,** *n.* **watchman,** *n.* A guard, a sentinel, esp. a member of a body formerly employed to patrol; one who guards the streets of a town at night; a man so guarding a large building, etc. **watch-night,** *n.* The last night of the year when services are held by Methodists, etc. **watch-oil,** *n.* Watchmaker's oil. **watch-spring,** *n.* The mainspring of a watch. **watch-tower,** *n.* A tower of observation or one on which sentinels are placed. **watchword,** *n.* A word given to sentinels, etc., as a signal that one has the right of admission, etc., a password; (*fig.*) a motto, word, or phrase symbolizing or epitomizing the principles of a party, etc. **watcher,** *n.* **watchful,** *a.* Vigilant, observant, cautious, wary. **watchfully,** *adv.* **watchfulness,** *n.* **watching brief,** *n.* (*Law*) A brief issued to a barrister instructed to watch a case on behalf of a client not directly concerned in the action.

***watchet** (woch' ėt) [etym. doubtful, cp. O.F. *watchet,* a sort of cloth], *a.* Blue, pale blue.

watchful, watchmaker, etc. [WATCH].

water (waw' tėr) [A.-S. *wæter,* cp. Dut. *water,* G. *wasser,* Icel. *vatu,* Swed. *vatten,* also Gr. *hudōr,* L. *unda,* Sansk. *udan*], *n.* A colourless, transparent liquid, destitute of taste and smell, possessing a neutral reaction, a compound of two portions by weight of hydrogen with one of oxygen; a natural body of water, as a sea, a lake, a river (*often in pl.*); a liquid consisting chiefly or partly of water, as various solutions or products of distillation, also tears, sweat, urine, and other secretions of animal bodies; the transparency or lustre of a diamond, pearl, etc.; (*Comm.*) stock issued without any corresponding increase of paid-up capital. *v.t.* To apply water to, to moisten, sprinkle, dilute, adulterate, irrigate, or supply with water; to furnish with water for drinking; to secrete or overflow with water (of the mouth, eyes, etc.); (*Comm.*) to increase (nominal capital, etc.) by the issue of stock without corresponding increase of assets; (*in p.p.*) to give an undulating sheen to the surface of (silk, etc.) by moistening, pressing, and heating in manufacture. *v.i.* To secrete, shed, or run with water (of the mouth, eyes, etc.); to get or take in water; to drink (of cattle, etc.). **high water** [HIGH]. **in deep water** or **waters:** In difficulties, troubles, or distress. **in smooth water:** Out of one's troubles or difficulties. **low water** [LOW (1)]. **of the first water:** Of the purest quality; (*fig.*) of the highest excellence. **strong waters** [STRONG]. **to get into** or **to be in hot water** [HOT]. **to go on the water wagon:** To refrain from alcoholic drink. **to hold water** [HOLD (1)]. **to keep one's head above water:** (*fig.*) To avoid financial ruin. **to make** or **pass water** [MAKE (2)]. **to make one's mouth water:** To make one very desirous. **to take the waters:** To take a cure at a watering spa. **to throw cold water on** [COLD]. **table water,** *n.* A bottled mineral water. **troubled waters:** (*fig.*) Discord; a state of disturbance. **water of crystallization:** The water that unites with salts in crystallization. **water on the brain:** Hydrocephalus. **water-bailiff,** *n.* A custom-house officer at a port; an officer employed to watch a river or other fishery to prevent poaching. **water-bed,** *n.* A rubber mattress filled with water for preventing bed-sores. **water-bellows,** *n.* A valved vessel suspended mouth downwards in water for producing an air-current by alternate raising and lowering. **water-bird,** *n.* **water-borne,** *a.* Conveyed by water. **water-brash,** *n.* A form of indigestion, with water eructations. **water-bug,** *n.* An aquatic insect. **water bus,** *n.* River craft carrying passengers on a regular service. **water-butt,** *n.* A large open-headed barrel for catching and preserving rainwater. **water-carriage,** *n.* Conveyance by water. **water-cart,** *n.* A wheeled tank, etc., for carrying a supply of water or for watering the streets. **water-cement,** *n.* Hydraulic cement. **water-chute,** *n.* A lofty structure with a timber slide down which water is kept running, for tobogganing down in a boat-like sled. **water-clock,** *n.* An instrument for measuring time by the passage of water, a clepsydra. **water-closet,** *n.* A privy with a water-supply for flushing the basin and preventing the rise of sewer-gas. **water-colour,** *n.* A pigment ground up with water and mucilage instead of oil; a water-colour painting; the part of painting in water-colours (*often in pl.*). **water-colourist,** *n.* **water-cooled valve,** *n.* (*Radio.*) A thermionic valve with water circulating round the anode to keep it cool. **water craft:** Ships, vessels, boats, etc. **water-crane,** *n.* A goose-neck apparatus for supplying water to a locomotive. **watercourse,** *n.* A stream, a brook; a channel for the conveyance of water. **water-cress,** *n.* A creeping aquatic plant eaten as salad. **water-cure,** *n.* Hydropathy. **water-dog,** *n.* A dog accustomed to the water, esp. a water-spaniel. **water-drain,** *n.* **water-drainage,** *n.* **water-drop,** *n.* A drop of water, a tear, etc. **water-engine,** *n.* An engine driven by water; an engine to raise water. **waterfall,** *n.* A steep or perpendicular descent of a river, etc., a cascade, a cataract. **water-finder,** *n.* A dowser. **water-flag,** *n.* The yellow iris, *I. pseudacorus.* **water-flea,** *n.* A minute freshwater crustacean. **water-flood,** *n.* An inundation. ***water-flowing,** *a.* Streaming. **water-fly,** *n.* Any fly of the genus *Perla,* the larvæ of which lurk under stones in streams, a stone-fly. **waterfowl,** *n.* (*sing. or collect. pl.*) A bird that frequents rivers, lakes, etc. **water-gall,** *n.* A cavity made by a rush of water; a secondary rainbow supposed to presage rain. **water-gas,** *n.* An illuminating gas obtained by the decomposition of water and treatment with carbon. **water-gate,** *n.* A gate for confining or releasing water, a flood-gate; a gate giving access to a river, etc. **water-gauge,** *n.* A glass instrument attached to a steam-boiler, etc., for indicating the height of the water inside. **water-glass,** *n.* A tube with a glass end for enabling one to see objects under water; soluble glass, esp. as used for fixing a water-colour drawing on dry plaster; a water-clock; (*Chem.*) a viscous solution of sodium or potassium silicate in water, used in industry and as a preservative for eggs. **water-gruel,** *n.* Gruel made with water instead of milk. **water-hammer,** *n.* A toy consisting of a glass tube, from which the air has been exhausted, partly filled with water, which strikes the end of the tube with a sharp shock when the tube is suddenly inverted; the concussion of water in a pipe when a tap is turned off or steam admitted. **water-hammering,** *n.* **water-heater:** (*Am.*) A bathroom geyser. **water-hen,** *n.* The moor-hen. **water-hole,** *n.* A hole where water collects, a water pool. **water-ice,** *n.* An iced confection made from water, sugar, etc., opp. to ice-cream. **water-inch,** *n.* The amount of water that will be discharged through a round 1-in. pipe in 24 hours under the least pressure, about 500 cubic feet. **water-jacket,** *n.* A casing filled with water surrounding a part of a machine that is to be kept cool. **water-joint,** *n.* A water-tight joint. **water-junket,** *n.* (*prov.*) The sandpiper. **water-kelpie,** *n.* A malignant water-sprite. **water-laid,** *a.* Cable-laid (of rope). **water-lens,** *n.* A magnifying lens formed by a glass-bottomed brass cell containing water. **water-level,** *n.* The level of the water in the sea, etc., esp. used as datum; a levelling instrument in which water is employed instead of spirit. **water-lily,** *n.* A plant of the genus *Castalia* or *Nymphæa* with large floating leaves and white or coloured flowers. **water-line,** *n.* The line up to which the hull of a vessel is submerged in the water. **waterlogged,** *a.* Soaked or flooded (of a vessel) with water so as to lie like a log; ground saturated with water. **water-main,** *n.* A main pipe in a system of water-supply. **waterman,** *n.* A boatman plying for hire on rivers, etc.; a (good or bad) oarsman. **watermanship,** *n.* **water-mark,** *n.* A mark indicating the level to which water rises in a well, etc., the limits of the rise and fall of the tide, etc.; a translucent design stamped in paper in the process of manufacture to show the maker, size, etc.; *v.t.* To stamp with this. **water-meadow,** *n.* A meadow fertilized by being flooded at certain seasons from an adjoining stream. **water-melon,** *n.* A large trailing plant *Citrullus,* or its fruit. **water-meter,** *n.* A contrivance for measuring a water-supply. **water-mill,** *n.* A mill driven by the agency of water. **water-monkey,** *n.* An earthenware long-necked jar for drinking-water, used in hot countries. **water-motor,** *n.* A motor driven by water under pressure, a turbine, a water-wheel. **water-nymph,** *n.* A naiad. **water-ousel,** *n.* The dipper. **water-pillar,** *n.* An upright pillar or pipe with a revolving or swinging head, for feeding locomotives, etc., with water. **water-pipe,** *n.* A pipe for conveying water. **water-plane,** *n.* The plane in which the water-line of a vessel lies; a hydro-aeroplane. **water-plant,** *n.* **water-plate,** *n.* A double plate containing hot water for keeping food warm. **water-polo,** *n.* A game like polo in which swimmers hit a ball with the hand. **water-pot,** *n.* **water-power,** *n.* The power of water employed or capable of being employed as a prime mover. **water-pox,** *n.* Baricella. **waterproof,** *a.* Impervious to water. *n.* Cloth rendered impervious to water; a waterproof coat or other garment. *v.t.* To render waterproof. **waterproofer,** *n.* **waterproofing,** *n.* **water-rail,** *n.* The common European rail, *Rallus aquaticus.* **water-ram,** *n.* A hydraulic ram. **water-rat** [WATER-VOLE]. **water-rate,** *n.* A rate or charge for the supply of water. ***water-rug,** *n.* A variety of dog. **water-sail,** *n.* A sail set in very light airs, below the lower studding-sail booms and next to the water. **water-seal,** *n.* A small body of water in a bend, etc., used to prevent the escape of gas from a pipe, etc. **watershed,** *n.* A ridge or other line of separation between two river-basins or drainage-systems. **water-shoot,** *n.* A discharge pipe or trough for rain-water, etc. **waterside,** *n.* The margin of a river, stream, lake, or the sea. **water-skiing,** *n.* (*Sport*) Being towed on skis at great speed by a motor-boat. **water-skin,** *n.* A bag or bottle of skin for carrying water. **water-snake,** *n.* **water-soldier,** *n.* An aquatic plant, *Stratiotes aloides*, with long narrow leaves rising above the water. **water-spaniel,** *n.* **water-splash,** *n.* Part of a road always submerged by a crossing stream. **waterspout,** *n.* A phenomenon which occurs during a tornado over the sea, in which water appears to be drawn up from the sea in a whirling column, sometimes connecting sea and cloud. **water-sprite,** *n.* ***water-standing,** *a.* Filled with tears. **water-supply,** *n.* A system for storing and supplying water for the service of a town, etc.; the amount of water stored for the use of a house, works, etc. **water-table,** *n.* A projecting ledge or string-course for throwing off the water on a building. **water-tank,** *n.* **water-tiger,** *n.* The predatory larva of some water-beetles. **water-tight,** *a.* So tightly fastened or fitted as to retain or not to admit water. **water-tower,** *n.* An elevated building carrying a large tank or reservoir for giving pressure to a water-supply. **water-tube,** *n.* A tube for containing water, esp. one of a series in a boiler in which water circulates exposed to the gases of combustion. **water-violet,** *n.* Any plant of the aquatic genus *Hottonia*. **water-vole,** *n.* A large aquatic vole, the water-rat. **water-wagtail,** *n.* The pied wagtail. **waterway,** *n.* A navigable channel; a fairway; the thick planks along the edge of a deck in which a channel is hollowed for conducting water to the scuppers. **water-weed,** *n.* **water-wheel,** *n.* A wheel moved by water and employed to turn machinery. **water wings,** *n.pl.* Floats used in teaching swimming. **water-witch,** *n.* A dowser; one of various diving birds. **waterworks,** *n.pl.* (*usu. as sing.*) An establishment for the collection, preservation, and distribution of water for use of communities, working of machinery, etc.; an artificial fountain. **to turn on the waterworks:** (*slang*) To cry, blubber. **water-worn,** *a.* Worn away by the action of water. ***waterage,** *n.* Money paid for transportation by water. **watered capital,** *n.* (*Fin.*) An increase in the nominal value of stock without a corresponding increase in assets or paid-up capital. **waterer,** *n.* **watering-place,** *n.* A place where water may be procured for cattle, etc.; a place to which people resort to drink mineral waters or for bathing, a spa, a seaside resort. **watering-pot,** *n.* A vessel with a perforated nozzle for sprinkling water on plants, etc. **watering-trough,** *n.* A drinking-trough for horses or cattle. **waterish,** *a.* **waterishness,** *n.* **waterless,** *a.* **watery,** *a.* Containing much water; moist, sodden; suffused or running with water; thin, transparent, or pale, like water; rainy-looking; consisting of water; (*fig.*) tasteless, insipid, vapid. **wateriness,** *n.*

watt (wot) [James *Watt* (1736–1819), engineer], *n.* The unit of electric power or rate of doing work, the power available when the electromotive force is one volt and the current is one ampere. **watt-hour meter** or **wattmeter,** *n.*

Watteau (wot′ ō) [Antoine *Watteau* (1684–1721), F. painter], *a.* Denoting a style of bodice with a square-cut neck and short ruffled sleeves, as in the costumes in Watteau's pictures.

wattle (wot′ ėl) [A.-S. *watel*, hurdle, cogn. with *wætla*, bandage], *n.* A hurdle of interwoven twigs or wicker-work; the fleshy lobe under the throat of the domestic fowl, turkey, etc.; a barbel of a fish; one of various S. African, Australian, and Tasmanian species of acacia, the bark of which is used in tanning; the national flower of Australia. *v.t.* To interweave, to interlace, to plait; to form or construct by plaiting, etc. **wattle and daub:** A method of constructing walls of wicker-work covered with mud or clay. **Wattle Day,** *n.* (Austral.) August the First, when the wattle begins to blossom. **wattle-work,** *n.* Wicker-work. **wattled,** *a.* **wattling,** *n.*

waukrife (*Sc.*) [WAKERIFE].

waul (wawl) [onomat.], *v.i.* To cry as a cat, to squall.

wave (wāv) [A.-S. *wafian*, cogn. with WABBLE], *v.i.* To move to and fro with a sinuous or sweeping motion as a flag in the wind, to flutter, to undulate; to have an undulating shape or conformation, to be wavy; to beckon or signal (to) by waving the hand, a handkerchief, etc. *v.t.* To cause to move to and fro, to give an undulating motion to, to brandish; to give an undulating surface, conformation, or appearance to, to make wavy; to indicate, direct, or command by a waving signal. *n.* A moving ridge or long curved body of water or other liquid, esp. one formed on the surface of the sea, rising into an arch and breaking on the shore; (*poet.*) the sea, water (*often in pl.*); (*Phys.*) a disturbance of the equilibrium of a fluid medium continuously propagated from point to point with or without any corresponding advance of the particles in the same direction, by which motion, heat, light, sound, electricity, etc., are transmitted; a single curve in such a motion or in a series, an undulation; a wave-like stripe or streak of lustre in cloth; the act or gesture of waving, as a signal, etc.; a heightened volume or intensity of some force, influence, emotion, etc.; a progressive rise or fall of temperature or barometrical pressure over a large area; (*Radio.*) rhythmical electromagnetic disturbance propagated through space. **permanent wave,** *n.* Hairdressers' term for a process of waving which lasts several months. **water wave,** *n.* A wave in the hair made by fingers or combs while it is wet. **wave-band,** *n.* (*Radio.*) The range of wave-lengths which is allocated for transmissions of a particular type, *e.g.* entertainment, amateur, etc. **wave-length,** *n.* The distance between the crests of two adjacent waves; (*Radio.*) the space intervening between the maximum positive points of two successive waves. **wave-meter,** *n.* (*Radio.*) An instrument for measuring the wave-length, or frequency, of an electro-magnetic wave. **wave-motion,** *n.* **wave-worn,** *a.* **waveless,** *a.* **wavelet,** *n.* **wave-like,** *a.* **wave offering,** *n.* (*Eccles.*) A Jewish offering presented by a horizontal motion of the hands, to right and left, forwards and backwards. **waveson** (wāv′ sǒn), *n.* (*Law*) Goods floating on the sea after shipwreck. **wavy,** *a.* Rising or swelling in waves; having unalternately concave and convex outline, etc., undulating. **Wavy Navy:** (*colloq.*) The Royal Naval Volunteer Reserve (so called from the wavy gold bands indicating officers' rank). **wavily,** *adv.* **waviness,** *n.*

waver (wā′ vėr) [freq. of WAVE, cp. Icel. *vafra*], *v.t.* To play or move to and fro; to flicker, to quiver; to begin to give way, to falter, to reel, to be in a state of indecision, to hesitate, to vacillate. **waverer,** *n.* **waveringly,** *adv.* **waveringness,** *n.*

waveson [WAVE].

wavey (wā′ vi) [N. Am. Ind.], *n.* The snow-goose.

wavily, etc., **wavy** [WAVE].

wax (1) (wǎks) [A.-S. *weax*, cp. Dut. *was*, G. *wachs*, Icel. and Swed. *vax*], *n.* A yellow, plastic, fatty substance excreted by bees and used for the cells of honeycombs, beeswax; this purified and bleached, used for candles, modelling, and pharmceutical and other purposes; any one of various substances resembling beeswax, as vegetable wax; bee-bread, the secretion of certain other insects, cerumen, ozocerite, cobbler's wax, sealing-wax, etc.; (*slang*) a rage. *a.* Waxen. *v.t.* To smear, rub, polish, treat, or join with wax. **waxbill,** *n.* A small bird of the genus *Estrelda* with a bill resembling red sealing-wax in colour. **wax-chandler,** *n.* A maker or seller of wax candles. **wax-cloth,** *n.* A floor-cloth. **wax doll:** A doll with a face made of wax; having a face like this, pretty but devoid of expression. **wax-end, *waxed-end,** *n.* A cobbler's thread covered with wax and pointed with a bristle. **wax-insect,** *n.* An insect producing wax. **wax-light,** *n.* A taper, match, etc. made of wax. **wax-moth,** *n.* A bee-moth. **wax-myrtle** [CANDLEBERRY-MYRTLE]. **wax-painting,** *n.* Encaustic painting. **wax-palm,** *n.* A South American palm, *Ceroxylon andicola*, or *Copernicia cerifera*, the trunk or leaves of which yield wax. **wax-paper,** *n.* Paper waterproofed with wax. **wax-red,** *a.* Bright red like sealing-wax. **wax-tree,** *n.* A tree yielding wax which exudes from it or is deposited by insects. **waxwing,** *n.* A bird of the genus *Ampelis*, the secondary and tertiary quills in some of which terminate in horny tips resembling pieces of red sealing-wax. **wax-work,** *n.* Modelling in wax in close imitation of living persons; anatomical and other figures, models of fruit, flowers, etc., in wax; (*pl.*) an exhibition of wax figures. **wax-worker,** *n.* **waxen,** *a.* Made or consisting of wax; with a surface resembling wax; like wax, impressible, plastic. **waxy,** *a.* Resembling wax, pliable, impressible, easily moulded; waxen (of surfaces, etc.); like wax in consistency (esp. of degenerated tissue); (*slang*) angry, cross. **waxily,** *adv.* **waxiness,** *n.*

wax (2) (wăks) [A.-S. *weaxan*, cp. Dut. *wassen*, G. *wachsen*, Icel. *vaxa*, also Gr. *auxanein*, Sansk. *vaksh*, L. *augēre*], *v.i.* To increase gradually in size (esp. of the face of the moon between new and full); to become larger, to grow in numbers, strength, intensity, etc.; to pass into a specified condition, to become gradually.

waxen, waxy, etc. [WAX (1)].

way (wā) [A.-S. *weg* (cp. Dut. and G. *weg*, Icel. *vegr*), cogn. with WAIN, VEHICLE, and VIADUCT], *n.* A road, path, track, or other place of passage; length of space passed over, distance to be traversed; the course or route followed or to be followed between two places or to reach a place; direction in which a thing or place lies or in which motion, etc., takes place; direction; (*fig.*) the method, plan, or manner of doing something, or proceeding to carry out some purpose, a line or course of action; a usual or habitual mode of action or conduct, a personal peculiarity, an idiosyncrasy; one's line of business or occupation, sphere, range, scope; relation, respect, point; condition, state; room for passage or advance, ground over which one would proceed; onward movement, progress, advance, headway, motion, impetus (esp. of a ship, etc.); (*pl.*) the framework of timbers over which a ship is launched. **by the way:** In passing, parenthetically; during the journey. **by way of:** By the route of, via; for the purpose of; as a form of, to serve as. ***come your way** (or **ways**)**:** Come, come on. **each way,** *adv.* (*Racing*) For win and for place. **in the family way** [FAMILY]. **in the way:** In a position or of a nature to obstruct or hinder. **in the way of:** So as to fall in with or obtain; as regards, by way of. **on the way:** In progress. **out of the way** [OUT]. **right of way** [RIGHT]. **six-foot way:** The space between two sets of railway lines. **the way of all flesh:** Death. **to be under way:** (*Naut.*) To be in motion. **to give way** [GIVE (1)]. **to go one's way** or **ways:** To depart. **to have one's way:** To get what one wants. **to lead the way** [LEAD (2)]. **to make one's way:** To prosper, esp. by one's own exertions. **to make way** [MAKE (2)]. **to pave the way for:** To prepare a way, plan, or method of attaining some object. **to take one's own way:** To follow one's own plan, to act independently. **to take one's way:** To set out; to go in some direction. **under way:** In motion (of a ship, etc.). **Way of the Cross:** A series of pictures in a church representing the successive stages of Christ's progress to Calvary; a series of devotions suited to each of these. **ways and means:** Means of doing, esp. of providing money. **Committee of Ways and Means:** A committee of the House of Commons for considering proposed taxes, etc. **way-back:** (*Austral.*) The inland areas of the continent; one who comes thence. **way-bill,** *n.* A list of passengers in a public conveyance or of goods sent by a common carrier. **way-board,** *n.* A thin layer between strata of some thickness. **wayfarer,** *n.* A traveller, esp. a pedestrian. ***wayfare,** *v.i.* **wayfaring,** *a.* and *n.* **wayfaring-tree,** *n.* A large shrub, *Viburnum lantana*, with white flowers and black berries, common by roadsides. ***waygoing,** *a.* Going away, departing. **waylay** (wā lā'), *v.t.* To wait in the way of with a view to rob, etc., to lie in wait for. **waylayer,** *n.* **way-leave,** *n.* A right of way over the land of another, esp. rented by a company, etc. ***way-mark, -post,** *n.* A guide- or finger-post, a milestone, etc. **way-side,** *n.* The side of the road; *a.* Situated or growing by the wayside. **way-station:** (*Am.*) A railway halt. **way-train:** (*Am.*) A local train. **way-worn,** *a.* Wearied with travel. ***wayless,** *a.*

-ways, *-way [A.-S. *weges*, gen. of prec.], *suf.* Forming adverbs of position, direction, manner, etc., as *always*, **alway*, *lengthways*, *straightway*.

wayward (wā' wărd) [M.E. *weiward*, for *awaiward* (AWAY, -WARD)], *a.* Perverse, froward, wilful, freakish, capricious, obstinate. **waywardly,** *adv.* **waywardness,** *n.*

waywode [VOIVODE].

wayzgoose (wāz' goos) [perh. *stubble-goose* (obs. *wayz*, stubble, GOOSE)], *n.* (*pl.* **-gooses**) An annual dinner, picnic, or other entertainment given to or held by the persons employed in a printing-office.

we (wē) [A.-S. *wē*, cp. Dut. *wij*, G. *wir*, Icel. *vēr*, *vær*, Sansk. *vayam*], *nom. pl. of 1st pers. pron.* The plural of I, denoting the person speaking and others associated with or represented by him; used by a sovereign, the editor of a newspaper, the writer of an unsigned article, etc.; people in general, mankind.

weak (wēk) [back-formation from *weaken*, A.-S. *wæcan*, from *wāc*, weak, cp. Dut. *week*, G. *weich*, Icel. *veikr*], *a.* Deficient in physical strength, not robust, vigorous, or powerful; feeble, infirm sickly, easily exhausted or fatigued; deficient in mental or moral strength, feeble-minded, of defective intelligence, lacking strength of will, resolution, or resisting power; yielding readily to temptation, easily led; characterized by or showing lack of resolution or will-power (of an action, etc.); deficient in strength, durability, force, or efficiency; fragile, brittle, pliant; unreliable, ineffective, inefficacious; deficient in number, quantity, weight, etc.; poor inadequate, trivial; unsustained, unconvincing, controvertible; (*Gram.*) inflected by the addition of *-ed*, *-d*, or *-t* to the stem in forming the past tense and p.p., not by internal vowel-change (of verbs); (*Pros.*) denoting the verse-ending in which the stress falls on a normally unaccented or proclitic word. ***weak-built,** *a.* (*Shak.*) Ill-founded. **weak-eyed,** *a.* Having eyes easily fatigued or not seeing well. **weak-headed,** *a.* Weak in intellect. ***weak-hearted,** *a.* Having little courage; spiritless. **weak-kneed,** *a.* Giving way easily; lacking in resolution. **weak-minded,** *a.* Feeble in intelligence or in resolution. **weak-mindedness,** *n.* **weak side:** Those traits of a person's character by which he is most easily influenced. **weak-sighted,** *a.* **weak-spirited,** *a.* Timid, pusillanimous. **weaken,** *v.t.* and *i.* **weakener,** *n.* **weaker sex,** *n.* Women. **weakish,** *a.* **weakling,** *n.* A feeble person. **weakly,** *adv.* In a weak manner. *a.* Not strong in constitution; feeble, infirm, sickly. **weakness,** *n.* The quality or state of being weak; a particular defect, failing, or fault, one's weak point; lack of resisting power.

weal (1) (wēl) [A.-S. *wela* (cp. G. *wohl*, Dan. *vel*), cogn. with WELL (1)], *n.* A sound, healthy, or prosperous state of persons or things. **the public, general,** or **common weal:** The welfare or prosperity of the community. ***wealsman,** *n.* (*Shak.*) A statesman, a demagogue.

weal (2) (wēl) [A.-S. *walu*, orig. a rod (cp. GUNWALE and CHANNEL (2)), cp. O.Fris. *walu*, Icel. *vōlr*, cogn. with L. *volvere*, Gr. *helissein*, to roll], *n.* A ridge or raised streak made by a rod or whip on the flesh; a ridge on the surface of cloth; a wide plank extending along a ship's side. *v.t.* To mark with weals by flogging.

weald (wēld) [M.E. *weeld*, *wald*, perh. var. of WOLD], *n.* A tract of open forest land, esp. the portion of Kent, Surrey, Sussex and Hants between the N. and S. Downs. **weald-clay,** *n.* The upper part of the Wealden strata, comprising beds of clay, iron-stone, etc., rich in fossils. **Wealden,** *a.* Pertaining to the Weald of Kent and Sussex, esp. geologically. **Wealden strata,** *n.* The series of lower Cretaceous freshwater strata between the oolite and the chalk, best displayed in the Weald.

wealth (welth) [WEAL (1), -TH, cp. Dut. *weelde*, luxury, O.H.G. *welida*, riches], *n.* Riches, large possessions of money, goods, or lands, affluence; abundance, a profusion, great plenty (of); *weal, prosperity. **wealthy,** *a.* Rich, affluent, having large possessions. **wealthily,** *adv.* **wealthiness,** *n.*

wean (wēn) [A.-S. *wenian*, to accustom (cp. Dut. *wennen*, G. *gewöhnen*, Dan. *vænne*), cogn. with WONT], *v.t.* To accustom (a child or animal) to deprivation of the breast, to teach to feed otherwise; (*fig.*) to detach or estrange from a habit, indulgence, desire, etc. *n.* (*Sc.*) (wān) A child; a weanling. **weanling,** *n.* A child newly weaned; *a.* Newly weaned.

weapon (wep' ŏn) [A.-S. *wæpen*, cp. Dut. *wapen*, G. *wappe*, Icel. *vāpn*], *n.* An instrument of offence or defence, a thing used to inflict bodily harm; (*fig.*) anything used for attack or defence; (*Nat. Hist.*) a claw, sting, thorn, prickle, etc. ***weapon-salve,** *n.* A salve supposed to cure a wound by being applied to the weapon. **weapon-schaw** [WAPINSHAW]. ***weapon-smith,** *n.* **weaponed,** *a.* **weaponless,** *a.* ***weaponry,** *n.*

wear (1) (wâr) [A.-S. *werian* (cp. Icel. *verja*, O.H.G. *werian*, Goth. *wasjan*), cogn. with L. *vestis*, Gr. *esthēs*, clothes, Sansk. *vas*, to dress], *v.t.* (*past* **wore,** *p.p.* **worn**) To carry on the person, to have on, to be dressed in, esp. habitually; to bear, to carry, to maintain, to exhibit; to consume, diminish, waste, impair, efface, or alter by rubbing or use; to exhaust, fatigue, or weary; to stand continual use (well, badly, etc.); to produce (a hole, channel, etc.) by attrition. *v.i.* To be consumed, diminished, effaced, altered, etc., by rubbing or use; to be exhausted, to be tired (out); to stand continual use (well, badly, etc.); to resist the effects of use, attrition, etc., to endure, to last; to pass gradually (away, etc.). *n.* The act of wearing; the state of being worn; that which is worn or to be worn, fashion, vogue; damage or diminution by attrition, use, etc. **to wear off:** To remove, efface, or diminish, or to be effaced or diminished by attrition, to rub off. **to wear out:** To use until no longer of use, to consume, waste, or render worthless by use; to exhaust, to tire out; to be used up, consumed, or gradually wasted by attrition and use. **to wear the breeches** [BREECH]. **wear and tear:** Waste, diminution, or injury caused by ordinary use. **wearable,** *a.* **wearer,** *n.* **wearing,** *a.* and *n.*

wear (2) (wâr) [var. of VEER], *v.t.* (*past & p.p.* **wore**) To bring (a ship) about tack by putting the helm up. *v.i.* To come round thus (of a ship).

wear (3) [WEIR].

weary ((wēr' i) [A.-S. *wērig* (cp. O.H.G. *wuorag*, drunk), rel. to *wōrian*, to travel], *a.* Tired, fatigued, exhausted; dispirited, impatient or sick (of); tiresome, tedious, exhausting, irksome. *v.t.* To tire, to fatigue; to make weary or impatient (of). *v.i.* To become tired or fatigued; to become weary (of); (*Sc.*) to long, to be wistful, to yearn. ***weariful,** *a.* ***wearifully,** *adv.* **weariless,** *a.* **wearily,** *adv.* **weariness,** *n.* **wearisome,** *a.* Tedious, tiresome, causing weariness. **wearisomely,** *adv.* **wearisomeness,** *n.*

***weasand** (wē' zănd) [A.-S. *wāsend*, cp. M.H.G. *weisent*, etym. doubtful], *n.* The windpipe.

weasel (wē' zĕl) [A.-S. *wesle*, cp. Dut. *wezel*, G. *wiesel*, Icel. *vīsla*, also Gr. *ailouros*], *n.* A small British reddish-brown, white-bellied quadruped related to the stoat, ferret, etc., with a long lithe body and short legs, preying on small birds, mice, etc. **weasel-faced,** *a.* Having a sharp, thin face.

weather (we*th'* ĕr) [A.-S. *weder* (cp. Dut. *weder*, G. *wetter*, Icel. *vethr*), cogn. with Goth. *waian*, Sansk. *va*, Gr. *aēnai*, to blow, Eng. WIND (1)], *n.* The state of the atmosphere with reference to cold or heat, humidity, rain, pressure, wind, electrical conditions, etc., esp. the state of the sky at any given time with reference to clouds and rain; (*fig.*) change, vicissitude (*usu. in pl.*). *v.t.* To encounter and pass through (storms or bad weather) in safety (of a vessel); (*Naut.*) to get to windward of (a cape, etc.) in spite of inclement weather; to expose (corn, etc.) to the action of the weather; (*usu. in p.p.*) to wear, disintegrate, or discolour (rock, cliffs, masonry, etc.) by this; to slope (tiles, etc.) down so as to overlap. *v.i.* To stand the effects of weather; to disintegrate or discolour by exposure to weather. *a.* Situated towards the wind; windward. **stress of weather:** Storms, winds, etc. ***to make fair weather:** (*Shak.*) To flatter, to conciliate. **to make good** or **bad weather:** (*Naut.*) To behave well or ill in a storm (of a vessel). **to make heavy weather of:** To exaggerate the difficulty of doing something. **under the weather:** Poorly, unwell. **weather-beaten, *-bitten,** *a.* Seasoned or tanned by exposure to weather, storms, etc. **weather-board,** *v.t.* To furnish with weather-boarding. **weather-boarding,** *n.* Boards fastened together so as to overlap and to throw off rain, snow, etc., from roofs, walls, etc. **weather-bound,** *a.* Detained by bad weather. **weather-box, -house,** *n.* A toy weather-indicator worked by the effect of hygroscopic conditions on a string, the figures of a man and woman emerging at the sides of a toy house indicating wet or dry weather respectively. **weather-bureau,** *n.* A meteorological department or office. **weather-chart, -map,** *n.* A chart of a wide area showing isobars and other symbols indicating the state of the weather in different parts. **weathercock,** *n.* A revolving vane, often in the shape of a cock, mounted on the top of a steeple or other high point to show the direction of the wind; (*fig.*) an inconstant person. **weather-contact, -cross,** *n.* (*Teleg.*) A leakage from one wire to another owing to wet weather. **weather-eye,** *n.* The eye that looks at the sky to forecast the weather. **to keep one's weather-eye open:** (*colloq.*) To be on the alert; to have one's wits about one. ***weather-fend,** *v.t.* To shelter from the weather. **weather-gauge** [GAUGE]. **weather-glass,** *n.* A barometer. **weather-map** [WEATHER-CHART], **weather-house**[WEATHER-BOX]. **weather-moulding,** *n.* (*Arch.*) A dripstone or hood-moulding over a door, window, etc., to throw off the rain. **weather-proof,** *a.* Proof against the weather. **weather-prophet,** *n.* One who foretells the weather. **weather-report,** *n.* An official daily report of meteorological observations and probable changes in the weather. **weather-service,** *n.* A department or organization carrying out meteorological observations. **weather-ship,** *n.* A ship engaged on meteorological work. **weather-stain,** *n.* Discoloration by exposure to the atmosphere. **weather-stained,** *a.* **weather-station,** *n.* A place where meteorological observations are taken or recorded. **weather-strip,** *n.* A piece of board, rubber, or the like fastened across a door, window, etc., to keep out draught. **weather-tiling,** *n.* (*Build.*) Tiles hung on outside walls to protect them against damp. **weather-vane** [WEATHERCOCK]. **weather-wise,** *a.* Skilful in forecasting the weather. **weathering,** *n.* An inclination for throwing off rain, etc.; disintegration, etc., through exposure to the weather. **weatherize,** *v.t.* To make a fabric water-proof. **weatherly,** *a.* (*Naut.*) Presenting such lateral resistance to the water as to make little leeway (of a ship). **weatherliness,** *n.* **weathermost,** *a.* Farthest to windward.

weave (wēv) [A.-S. *wefan* (cp. Dut. *weven*, G. *weben*, Icel. *vefa*), cogn. with Gr. *huphainein*], *v.t.* (*past* **wove,** *p.p.* **woven, wove**) To form (threads, yarns, etc.) into a fabric by interlacing; to produce (cloth, muslin, etc.) thus; (*fig.*) to interweave (facts, details, etc.) into a story, theory, etc.; to construct (a scheme, plot, etc.) thus. *v.i.* To make fabrics by interlacing threads, etc.; to work at a loom; *to become woven or interlaced. **weavable,** *a.* **weaver,** *n.* One who weaves, esp. one whose occupation is to weave cloth, etc.; a weaver-bird. **weaver-bird,** *n.* A finch-like bird, esp. of the family *Ploceidæ*, of the warmer parts of Asia, Africa, and Australia, constructing elaborate nests of woven grass.

***weazand** [WEASAND].

***weasen** [WIZEN].

web (web) [A.-S. (*webb.* cp. Dut. *web*, G. *gewebe*, Icel. *vefr*), from *wefan*, to WEAVE (1)], *n.* A woven fabric, a piece of woven cloth, a texture; a cobweb or similar structure woven by caterpillars, etc.; (*fig.*) an artfully contrived plot, etc.; a large roll of paper for printing, etc., as it comes from the mill; (*Nat. Hist.*) connective tissue; the membrane between the toes of swimming-birds, etc.; the vane of a feather; (*Mech.*) the thin part of the plate in a girder connecting the upper and lower plates, the part of a railway-carriage wheel between the nave and rim, the blade of a saw, etc. *v.t.* (*past & p.p.* **webbed**) To connect, furnish, or cover with or as with a web. **web-eye,** *n.* A disease of the eye caused by a film. **web-eyed,** *a.* **web-fingers, -foot, -toes,** *n.* Those with the digits connected by a web. **web-fingered, -footed, -toed,** *a.* **web-worm,** *n.* The gregarious larva of an insect weaving a web or tent, as a shelter. **webbed,** *a.* **webbing,** *n.* A strong woven band of fibre, etc., used for girths, the bottoms of seats, beds, etc.; any strong woven tape or edging; a woven structure. ***webster,** *n.* A weaver.

wed (wed) [A.-S. *weddian* (cp. Dut. *wedden*, G. *wetten*, Icel. *vethja*, to wager), cogn. with WAGE, WAGER, GAGE (1)], *v.t.* (*past & p.p.* **wedded,** **p.p.* **wed**) To marry; to give in marriage; (*fig.*) to unite, to attach firmly; *to espouse; to take part with. *v.i.* To marry. **n.* A pledge, a security. **wedded,** *a.* Married; pertaining to matrimony; intimately united.

wedding (wed' ing), *n.* A marriage ceremony, usu. with the accompanying festivities. **penny-wedding** [PENNY]. **silver wedding, golden wedding, diamond wedding:** The twenty-fifth, fiftieth, or sixtieth anniversaries of a wedding. **wedding-breakfast,** *n.* An entertainment given after a wedding ceremony. **wedding-cake,** *n.* An iced cake distributed to the guests at a wedding, portions being afterwards sent to absent friends. **wedding-card,** *n.* (*pl.*) Cards bearing the names of a newly-married couple sent to friends to announce the wedding. **wedding-day,** *n.* The day of a marriage or its anniversary. **wedding-favour,** *n.* A knot of white ribbons or a rosette worn at a wedding. **wedding-garment,** *n.* A garment for wearing at a wedding; (*fig.*) something entitling one to participation, etc. **wedding-ring,** *n.* A plain ring placed by the bridegroom on the third finger of the left hand of the bride during the marriage ceremony.

wedge (wej) [A.-S. *wecg*, cp. Dut. *wig*, G. *wecke*, Icel. *veggr*], *n.* A piece of wood or metal thick at one end and tapering to a thin edge at the other, used for splitting wood, rocks, etc., for exerting great pressure, raising great weights, etc., forming one of the mechanical powers; an object or portion of anything in the shape of a wedge; a shoe without an instep, having the heel and sole together forming a wedge. *v.t.* To cleave or split with a wedge; to crowd or push (in), as a wedge forces its way; to fix or fasten with a wedge or wedges. **the thin end of the wedge:** A first step, measure, or change likely to have important ulterior results. **wedge-shaped,** *a.* **wedge-tailed,** *a.* (*Ornith.*) Having a wedge-shaped tail owing to the greater length of the middle feathers. **wedgeside,** *adv.*

wedgwood (wej' wud) [Josiah *Wedgwood* (1730–95), potter], *n.* A variety of semi-vitrified pottery.

wedlock (wed' lok) [A.-S. *wedlāk* (WED, pledge, *lāc*, sport, gift)], *n.* Matrimony, the married state.

Wednesday (wenz' dā, -di) [A.-S. *Wōdnes dæg*, Woden's or Odin's day], *n.* The fourth day of the week.

wee (wē) [M.E., a bit, prob. var. of WAY], *a.* Very small, tiny, little. **Wee Frees,** *n.pl.* (*Sc.*) A section of the Free Church that would not join the United Free Church in 1900.

weed (wēd) [A.-S. *wēod*, *wīod*, cp. L.G. *wēden*, to weed, etym. doubtful], *n.* A useless or troublesome plant in cultivated land, a plant springing up where not wanted in a garden, etc.; (*fig.*) any useless or troublesome intrusive thing; a leggy, loose-bodied horse; (*colloq.*) a cigar. *v.t.* To clear (ground) of weeds; to pull up (a noxious or intrusive plant); (*fig.*) to clear of anything hurtful or offensive; to sort (out) (useless or inferior elements, members, etc.); to rid of these. *v.i.* To pull up weeds from a garden, etc. **the weed:** Tobacco. **weed-grown,** *a.* Overgrown with weeds. **weed-killer,** *n.* A chemical or other production (usu. poisonous) for destroying weeds. **weedy,** *a.* Containing weeds; (*fig.*) thin, impoverished, lacking stamina. **weeder,** *n.* One who weeds; a weeding-tool. **weedicide** (wē' di sīd), *n.* A chemical weed-killer. **weediness,** *n.* **weeding-chisel, -fork, -hook, -tongs,** *n.* A tool used in weeding.

weeds (wēdz) [A.-S. *wæde*, garment, cp. O.Fris. *wēde*, Icel. *vāth*, O.H.G. *wāt*, *wōt*], *n.pl.* Mourning worn by a widow.

week (wēk) [A.-S. *wice* (*wuce*, cp. Dut. *week*, Icel. *vika*, O.H.G. *wecha*), etym. doubtful], *n.* A period of seven days, esp. from Sunday to Saturday inclusively; the six working days, excluding Sunday. **to-day, to-morrow,** or **yesterday week:** The day later or earlier by a week than the one specified. **a week of Sundays:** (*colloq.*) Seven weeks; (*fig.*) a long time. **weekday,** *n.* Any day of the week except Sunday. **week-end,** *n.* The days ending one and beginning the following week (usu. Saturday–Monday), as a time for holiday, etc.; *v.i.* To make a holiday, etc., on these. **week-ender,** *n.* **weekly,** *a.* Happening, issued, or done once a week or every week; lasting a week; pertaining to or reckoned by the week. *adv.* Once a week; week by week. *n.* A weekly periodical.

***weel** (1) (wēl), ***weely** (wē' li) [etym. doubtful], *n.* A fish-trap made of twigs or rushes; (*Her.*) a bearing representing this.

weel (2) (*Sc.*) [WELL (1)].

weem (wēm) [cp. Gael. *uamh*, *uamha*, cave], *n.* A subterranean chamber, dwelling, or passage, usu. lined with rough stones.

***ween** (wēn) [A.-S. *wēnan*, cp. Dut. *wanen*, G. *wähnen*, Icel. *vāna*, to hope], *v.i.* To be of opinion; to think, to fancy.

weep (wēp) [A.-S. *wēpan* (O.S. *wōpian*, O.H.G. *wuofan*), from *wōp*, an outcry], *v.i.* (*past & p.p.* **wept**) To shed tears; (*fig.*) to let fall or to be emitted, to drip, to exude, to run or be suffused with drops of moisture; (*usu. in pres.p.*) to have pendulous branches. *v.t.* To shed tears over; to lament, to bewail; to exhaust or wear (out, etc.) with weeping; to shed (tears). **weeper,** *n.* One who or that which weeps; a hired mourner; a widow's white cuff or black crape veil or a man's sash-like hatband worn as a token of mourning. **weeping-ash, -birch, -willow,** *n.* An ash, birch, or willow with delicate pendulous branches. **weepy,** *a.*

***weet, *weetingly** [WIT (1)].

weever (wē' vėr) [M.E. *wivere*, WYVERN], *n.* Either of two British fishes, *Trachinus draco*, the greater, and *T. vipera*, the lesser weever, inflicting painful wounds with their dorsal and opercular spines.

weevil (wē' vil) [A.-S. *wifel* (cp. Dut. *wevel*, G. *wiebel*), cogn. with WEAVE (1)], *n.* A small beetle with the head prolonged into a rostrum or proboscis, feeding on grain, nuts, roots, leaves, etc., esp.

one infesting corn, a curculio. **weevilled, weevilly,** *a.*

wee-wee (wē′ wē) [onom.], *v.i.* (*Childish*) To urinate, *n.*

weft (weft) [A.-S., from *wefan*, to WEAVE (1)], *n.* The threads passing through the warp from selvedge to selvedge, the woof; a web. ***weftage,** *n.*

weigh (wā) [A.-S. *wegan*, to carry, cp. Dut. *wegen*, to weigh, G. *wegen*, to move, *wägen*, to weigh, Icel. *vega*, to move, to weigh, also Sansk. *vah*, L. *vehere*, see VEHICLE], *v.t.* To find the weight of by means of a balance, etc.; to be equivalent to in weight; (*fig.*) to ponder, to consider carefully, to estimate the relative value or advantages of, to compare (with, etc.); to cause to sink by weight, to force down; to raise (an anchor). *v.i.* To have a specified weight; to be weighed, to ascertain one's weight; (*fig.*) to be considered as important, to have weight or influence; to be burdensome or oppressive (upon); (*Naut.*) to weigh anchor, to start on a voyage. *n.* The act or process of weighing. **to weigh anchor** [ANCHOR]. **to weigh in:** To be weighed before a race (of a jockey); (*colloq.*) to intervene. **to weigh out:** To take a particular weight of from a quantity; to distribute or apportion in quantities measured by scales; (*Racing*) to be weighed after a race (of a jockey); (*slang*) to pay (money) out. **under weigh** [WAY]. **weigh-beam,** *n.* A portable steelyard suspended in a frame. **weighbridge,** *n.* A machine with an iron platform, on which carts, etc., are weighed. **weigh-house,** *n.* A public building at which goods are weighed. **weighable,** *a.* **weighage,** *n.* **weigher,** *n.* **weighing-cage,** *n.* A cage in which live animals may be weighed. **weighing-machine,** *n.* A machine for weighing loaded vehicles, cattle, bales, persons, or other heavy bodies.

weight (wāt) [A.-S. *gewiht*, as prec.], *n.* The force with which bodies tend towards a centre of attraction, esp. the centre of the earth, the downward tendency caused by gravity less the centrifugal tendency due to the earth's rotation; the relative mass or quantity of matter contained in a body, heaviness, ponderosity, esp. as expressed in terms of some standard unit; a scale or graduated system of units of weight; a piece of metal, etc., of known weight used with scales for weighing goods, etc.; a heavy mass used for mechanical purposes, as in a clock; a heavy load, a burden, pressure, oppressiveness; importance, consequence, impressiveness, efficacy, preponderance. *v.t.* To attach a weight or weights to, to add weight to, to burden (*lit. and fig.*); to treat with minerals, etc., to load, to adulterate. **weightless,** *a.*

weighty (wā′ ti), *a.* Having great weight, heavy, ponderous; (*fig.*) important, serious, momentous; convincing, cogent, influential. **weightily,** *adv.* **weightiness,** *n.*

weir (wēr) [A.-S. *wer*, cogn. with *werian*, to defend], *n.* A dam across a stream for raising the level of the water above it; a fence or enclosure of stakes, nets, etc., set in a stream to catch fish.

weird (wērd) [A.-S. *wyrd*, from *weorthan*, to be, to become], *n.* (*chiefly Sc.*) Fate, destiny. *a.* Pertaining to fate or destiny; supernatural, unearthly, uncanny; strange, queer. **weirdly,** *adv.* **weirdness,** *n.*

Weismannism (vīs′ mȧ nizm), *n.* (*Biol.*) The doctrines of August Weismann (1834–1915) with regard to the germ-plasm, and the impossibility of transmitting acquired characters.

weka (wē′ kȧ) [Maori], *n.* The N. Zealand wood-hen.

welch (1) (welsh, welch) [WELSH], *n.* and *a.* Welsh; spelling used for Welch Fusiliers, Welch Regiment.

welch (2) [WELSH (2)].

welcome (wel′ kȯm) [A.-S. *wilcuma* (*willa*, pleasure, *cuma*, comer, assim. to WELL (1), and COME)], *a.* Admitted or received with pleasure and cordiality (often used ellipt. as an int. addressed to a guest, etc.); producing satisfaction or gladness; gladly permitted (to do, etc.). *n.* A salutation or saying of "welcome" to a new-comer; a kind or cordial reception or entertainment of a guest, etc., a willing acceptance of an offer, etc. *v.t.* To greet cordially; to receive or entertain with kindness or cordiality; to receive (news, etc.) with pleasure. **a warm welcome:** A hearty reception, or (more generally) a very hostile one. **welcomeness,** *n.* **welcomer,** *n.*

weld (1) (weld) [prob. cogn. with WOLD], *n.* Dyer's-weed, *Reseda luteola*, a branched mignonette from which luteolin, a yellow dye-stuff, was formerly prepared.

weld (2) (weld) [var. of WELL (2), to boil up], *v.t.* To unite or join (pieces of metal) together by heat or by compressing, esp. after they have been softened by heat; to make or produce thus; (*fig.*) to unite into a coherent mass, body, etc. *v.i.* To unite (well or ill) by this process. *n.* A joint or junction by welding. **weldable,** *a.* **weldability** (-bil′ i ti), *n.* **welder,** *n.*

welfare (wel′ fâr) [WELL (1), FARE], *n.* Prosperity. health, well-being, success. **Welfare State,** *n.* (*Pol.*) A state in which the government promotes the general welfare by introducing social security. **welfare work:** Efforts to improve living conditions for the very poor, or to care for the comforts, etc. of factory employees, workers, etc. **welfare worker,** *n.*

***welk** (welk) [Dut. and G. *welken*, from O.H.G. *welk*, moist], *v.i.* To fade, to wither.

welkin (wel′ kin) [A.-S. *wolcnu*, pl. of *wolcen*, cloud, cp. G. *wolke*, O.H.G. *wolka*, cloud, perh. cogn. with WALK, or with prec.], *n.* (*poet.*) The sky, the vault of heaven.

well (1) (wel) [A.-S. *wel*, cp. Dut. *wel*, G. *wohl*, Icel. *vel*, cogn. with WILL], *adv.* (*comp.* **better,** *superl.* **best**) In a good or right manner, properly, satisfactorily; happily, fortunately, prosperously, successfully; adequately, fully, perfectly, thoroughly, abundantly, amply, sufficiently; heartily, cordially, gratifyingly; with kindness, with approval, on good terms; justly, fairly, reasonably, wisely, befittingly. *a.* (*predicative only*) In good health; in a satisfactory state, position, or circumstances. *n.* That which is well. *int.* Expressing astonishment, expectation, resignation, concession, etc.; often used as an expletive in resuming one's discourse. **as well:** In addition; equally, as much (as), not less truly; just as reasonably, with no worse results; proper, right, not unadvisable (to). **well-acquainted,** *a.* **well-advised,** *a.* Prudent, judicious, wise. ***well-apparelled,** *a.* **well-appointed,** *a.* Fully armed, furnished, or equipped. **well-balanced,** *a.* Sensible, sane, opp. to eccentric. **well-behaved,** *a.* **well-being,** *n.* Welfare. ***well-beseeming,** *a.* Well becoming. ***well-beseen,** *a.* Comely, of good appearance. **well-born,** *a.* Of good birth. **well-bred,** *a.* Of good breeding or manners; of good or pure stock. **well chosen:** Selected with judgment. **well-conditioned,** *a.* Of good temper; in good condition. **well-conducted,** *a.* Well-behaved. **well-connected,** *a.* Related to good families. **well-content, well-disposed,** *a.* Of favourable and kindly feeling (to or towards). **well-doer,** *n.* An upright person. **well-doing,** *n.* **well done:** An expression of congratulation; (*of food*) cooked thoroughly. **well enough** [ENOUGH]. **well-favoured,** *a.* Handsome, good-looking. **well-found,** *a.* Well-appointed. **well-founded:** Based on certain or well-authenticated grounds. **well-graced,** *a.* In favour, popular. **well-informed,** *a.* Having ample information; having a knowledge of numerous subjects. **well-intentioned,** *a.* Having good intentions (usu. with alln. to unsatisfactory results). **well-judged,** *a.* Skilfully, tactfully, or accurately done, aimed, contrived, etc. **well-knit,** *a.* Compact, firmly built (esp. of a person's body). **well known:** Known to many people, familiar, notorious. ***well-liking,** *a.* Good-conditioned, plump. **well-looking,** *a.* Of pleasing appearance. **well-mannered,** *a.* Well-bred, polite. **well-meaning,** *a.* Having good intentions. **well met:** Hail! Welcome! **well-nigh,** *adv.* Almost, nearly. **well off:** In good circumstances, prosperous. **well-pleasing,** *a.* **well-proportioned,** *a.* **well-read,** *a.* Having read extensively, having wide knowledge gained from books. **well-reputed,** *a.* Of good reputation. **well-rounded,** *a.* Symmetrical, complete. ***well-seeming,** *a.* Having a fair outward or superficial appearance. ***well-seen,** *a.* Accomplished, well-versed (in). **well set:** Firmly set, well-knit, muscular. **well-spoken,** *a.* Speaking well, eloquent; well-mannered, of good disposition. ***well-thewed,** *a.* Well-knit. **well-to-do,** *a.* In good circumstances, well off. **well-tried,** *a.* Often tried or tested with satisfactory results. **well-trod, -trodden,** *a.* Much used or frequented. **well-wisher,** *n.* A person who wishes well to one. **well-worn,** *a.* Worn out, trite, hackneyed.

well (2) (wel) [A.-S. *wella,* rel. to *weallan,* to well or boil up (cp. Dut. *wel,* G. *welle,* wave, Icel. *vel,* boiling up)], *n.* A shaft bored in the ground, usu. walled or lined with bricks, etc., to obtain water, oil, brine, etc.; a hole, space, or cavity more or less resembling this; a space in the middle of a building enclosing the stairs or a lift or left open for light and ventilation; a space occupied by counsel, etc., in a law-court; the boxed-in space enclosing the pumps of a vessel; a compartment in a fishing-vessel with a perforated bottom where fish are kept alive; the receptacle holding the ink in an inkstand; *a spring, a fountain; (*fig.*) a source. *v.i.* To spring or issue (forth, etc.) as a fountain. **well-boat,** *n.* A fishing-boat having a well for conveying fish alive. **well-deck,** *n.* The space enclosed between the forecastle and poop on some ships. **well-dish,** *n.* One with a hollow for gravy to collect in. **well-head,** *n.* The source or fountain-head of a river, etc. **well-hole,** *n.* The pit or shaft of a well; the well of a staircase, etc. **well-room,** *n.* A room at a spa where the waters are served to visitors. **well-sinker,** *n.* One who digs or sinks wells. **well-sinking,** *n.* **well-spring,** *n.* A source of continual supply. **well-staircase,** *n.* **well-water,** *n.*

***welladay** (wel à dā'), **wellaway** (-wā') [A.-S. *wā lā wā,* woe, lo! woe (see WOE, LO)], *int.* An exclamation of sorrow or despair.

wellington (wel' ing tȯn) [after the first Duke of *Wellington*], *n.* (*usu. in pl.*) A boot, usu. rubber, coming up to the knee.

Wellingtonia (wel ing tō' ni à) [as prec.], *n.* A sequoia.

wels (velts, welz) [G.], *n.* The sheat-fish.

Welsh (1) (welsh) [A.-S. *wælisc,* foreign, from *weahl,* foreigner, a Celt], *a.* Pertaining to Wales or its inhabitants. *n.* The language of the Welsh; (*pl.*) the Welsh people. **Welshman, -woman,** *n.* **Welsh mutton:** Mutton from a small breed of Welsh mountain sheep. **welsh rabbit:** Cheese melted and spread over toasted bread (incorr. 'rarebit').

welsh (2) (welsh) [etym. uncertain], *v.t.* and *i.* (*Racing*) To make off from a racecourse without paying up bets (of a bookmaker). **welsher,** *n.* One who welshes.

welt (welt) [M.E. *welte,* cogn. with A.-S. *wyllan,* to roll, cp. Icel. *velta,* and Eng. WEAL (2) and WELTER (1)], *n.* A strip of leather sewn round a boot or shoe between the upper and the sole for sewing them together; the border or trimming of a garment; a weal; (*Her.*) a narrow border to an ordinary. *v.t.* To furnish with a welt; to weal, to flog.

Weltenschauung (velt' ėn shou' ung) [G., world contemplation], *n.* (*Phil.*) A survey of the world as an entity.

welter (1) (wel' tėr) [M.E. *weltren,* freq. of *walten,* to roll (cp. Icel. *velta,* Swed. *valtra,* G. *walzen*), cogn. with WALLOW and WALTZ], *v.i.* To roll, to tumble about, to wallow, esp. in some foul matter; to heave and roll about confusedly (of waves, etc.). *n.* A weltering movement, a turmoil, a confusion.

welter (2) (wel' tėr) [etym. doubtful], *a.* (*Horse-racing, Boxing, etc.*) Heavy-weight. **welter-race,** *n.* **welter-stakes,** *n.pl.*

welt-politik (velt' pol it ik) [G.], *n.* (*Pol.*) A policy aiming at the predominance of a country, specifically Germany, in the affairs of the whole world.

Welwitschia (wel wich' i à) [Dr. F. *Welwitsch* (1807–72), discoverer], *n.* A genus of plants from S.W. tropical Africa, with one species, *W. mirabilis,* with a trunk several feet wide and only a foot high, and no leaves except the two cotyledonous ones, which attain a development of six feet or more.

wen (wen) [A.-S. *wenn,* cp. Dut. *wen,* Dan. dial. *van,* prob. cogn. with Goth, *winnan,* to suffer, to WIN], *n.* An indolent or benign encysted tumour, frequently occurring on the scalp or neck; (*fig.*) an excrescence, an abnormal growth (as an overgrown city).

wench (wench) [M.E. *wenche,* A.-S. *wencel,* infant (as adj., weak), (cp. G. *wanken,* to totter), cogn. with WINK], *n.* (*now vulg. or colloq.*) A girl or young woman; *a girl of loose character, a strumpet. **v.i.* To commit fornication. **wench-like,** *a.* ***wencher,** *n.* ***wenching,** *n.* **wenchless,** *a.*

wend (1) (wend) [A.-S. *wendan,* to turn, causal of WIND (2) (orig. past WENT, now past of GO (1))], *v.t.* To go or direct (one's way). *v.i.* To go.

Wend (2) (wend) [G. *Wende,* perh. cogn. with prec. and WANDER], *n.* One of a Slavonic people inhabiting Saxony and Prussia. **Wendic,** *a.* **Wendish,** *a.* and *n.*

Wenlock (wen' lȯk), *a.* (*Geol.*) Denoting the subdivision of the Silurian system strongly developed at Wenlock, in Shropshire.

went, *past* [GO (1), see also WEND (1)].

wentletrap (wentl' trăp) [G. *Wendeltreppe* (*wendel,* turning, *treppe,* stair)], *n.* A univalve many-whorled shell of the family *Scalariidæ.*

wept, *past & p.p.* [WEEP].

were [WAS].

***wergild** (wĕr' gild) [A.-S. (*wer,* man, cp. L. *vir*), *gild,* payment, from *gieldan,* see YIELD], *n.* (*A.-S. and Teut. Law*) A fine or monetary compensation for manslaughter and other offences against the person, paid by the kindred of the offender to the kindred of the injured person to avoid blood-feud.

Wernerian (wėr nēr' i ȧn) [Abraham Gottlob *Werner* (1750–1817), German mineralogist and geologist, who classified minerals by their external characters, and was the author of the Neptunian theory], *a.* (*Geol.*) Of or pertaining to Werner and his geological doctrines. *n.* A disciple of Werner, a Neptunist.

wernerite (wĕr' nėr īt) [*Werner,* see prec., -ITE], *n.* (*Min.*) Scapolite.

wersh (wĕrsh) [etym. unknown], *a.* (*Sc.*) Insipid, tasteless, unsalted.

Wertherism (vâr' tėr izm) [after the hero of Goethe's 'Sorrows of *Werther,*' 1774], *n.* Morbid sentimentality, namby-pambyism. **Wertherian** (-tēr' i ȧn) *a.*

werwolf (wĕr' wulf) [A.-S. *werewulf* (*wer,* see WERGILD, WOLF)], *n.* (*pl.* **-wolves**) (*Folklore*) A person turned or supposed to have the power of turning himself into a wolf.

***wesand** [WEASAND].

Wesleyan (wes' li ȧn, wes lē' ȧn), *a.* Of or belonging to the Church or sect founded by John Wesley (1703–91). *n.* A member of this, a Wesleyan Methodist. **Wesleyanism** (-lē' ȧ nizm), *n.*

west (west) [A.-S. (cp. Dut. and G. *west,* Icel. *vestr,* Dan. and Swed. *vest*), prob. cogn. with Gr. *hesperos,* L. VESPER], *adv.* At, in, or towards the quarter opposite the east, or where the sun sets at the equinox. *n.* That one of the four cardinal points exactly opposite the east; the region or part of a country lying opposite to the east, esp. the western part of England, Europe, or the United States; a wind blowing from the west. *a.* Being, lying, or living in or towards the west; blowing from the west. **to go west:** To die. **west country:** The S.W. part of England. **west-countryman, -countrywoman,** *n.* **West End:** The fashionable part of London, immediately west of Charing Cross. **West-end,** *a.* Of, pertaining to, or characteristic of this. **west-north-west,** *a.* Midway between west and north-west; *n.* A part or region situated there; *adv.* In or towards this. **west-north-westerly,** *a.* and *adv.* **west-north-western,** *a.* **west-south-west,** *a., n.,* and *adv.* **west-south-westerly,** *a.* and *adv.* **west-south-western,** *a.* **westering,** *a.* Passing to the west (of the sun). **westerly,** *a.* Being in, situated, or directed towards the west; blowing from the west. *adv.* Towards the west. **western,** *n., a.* and *adv.* To do with the west; a play or novel dealing with the western States of U.S.A. in the wilder periods of their history. **the Western Empire:** The western division of the Roman Empire having Rome as capital, after the division into an Eastern and Western Empire by Theodosius in 395. **Western Church:** The Latin Church which continued to acknowledge the pope after the schism of the Greek and Latin Churches in the 9th cent. **Western European Union:** (*Pol.*) A political and military association, formed in 1955, of Belgium, France, Italy, Luxemburg, Netherlands, U.K. and Western Germany. **Western Powers:** A loose term for the European powers (and U.S.A.) contrasted with the U.S.S.R. and her satellite powers. **westerner,** *n.* **westernize,** *v.t.* **westernmost,** *a.* **westing,** *n.* Distance travelled or amount of deviation towards the west. **westward,** *a.* and *adv.* **westwards,** *adv.* ***westwardly,** *adv.*

Westinghouse brake (west′ ing hous) [G. *Westinghouse* (1846–1914)], *n.* (*Eng.*) A brake worked by compressed air for use on railway trains and motor cars.

wet (wet) [A.-S. *wǣt* (cp. Icel. *vātr*, Dan. *vaad*, Swed. *vät*), cogn. with WATER], *a.* Moistened, soaked, saturated, covered with, or containing water or other liquid; rainy; (*colloq.*) drunk; (*slang*) sloppy, characterless, sentimental; (*Am.*) allowing or favouring the sale of alcoholic beverages, opp. to prohibitionist (of a State, etc.). *n.* Wetness, moisture; anything that wets, esp. rain; (*slang*) a drink. *v.t.* (*past & p.p.* **wetted**) To make wet; to moisten, drench, or soak with liquid; to urinate; (*slang*) to celebrate (a bargain, etc.) with drink. **The Wet:** (*Austral.*) The monsoon season. **to wet one's whistle:** (*slang*) To drink. **wet blanket:** A person who damps enthusiasm, zeal, etc. **wet bob** [BOB (2)]. **wet bulb** [see DRY-BULB THERMOMETER]. **wet dock:** A dock in which vessels can float. **wet-nurse,** *n.* A woman employed to suckle a child not her own; *v.t.* To act as wet-nurse to; (*fig.*) to coddle. **wet plate:** (*Phot.*) A sensitized collodion plate exposed while still moist. **wet-shod,** *a.* Having the shoes wet. **wetness,** *n.* **wetting,** *n.* **wettish,** *a.*

wether (*weth*′ ėr) [A.-S. (cp. Icel. *vethr*, Dan. *væder*, G. *widder*), prob. cogn. with VEAL and VETERINARY], *n.* A castrated ram.

wey (wā) [A.-S. *wæge*, weight, from *wegan*, to WEIGH], *n.* A certain weight or measure varying with different articles (of wool, 182 lb.; oats and barley, 48 bushels; cheese, 224 lb.; salt, 40 bushels.)

wh It is now ordinary modern English usage to sound only the **w** in words beginning with **wh.** Exceptions to this practice are indicated in the text. In Scotland, Ireland, and Wales, however, and by a few purists, it is considered preferable to aspirate the **w.** This is also done on occasions to distinguish from a homonym, e.g. 'whet', 'wet'.

whack (wăk) [onomat., cp. THWACK], *v.t.* To strike heavily, to thwack; (*slang*) to share out (plunder, etc.). *n.* A heavy blow, a thwack; (*slang*) a share, a portion. **whacking,** *n.* A beating, a thrashing. *a.* (*slang*) Large, whopping, thumping.

whaisle, whaizle (hwā′ zėl) [freq. from WHEEZE], *v.i.* (*Sc.*) To wheeze, to breathe hard.

whale (1) (wāl) [A.-S. *hwæl* (cp. Dut. *walvisch*, G. *wal*, Icel. *hvalr*, Dan. and Swed. *hval*), perh. cogn. with WHEEL], *n.* A large marine fish-like mammal, of various species of Cetacea, several of which are hunted chiefly for their oil and whalebone; (*slang*) something very big or exciting. *v.i.* To engage in whale-fishing. **whale-back,** *n.* A vessel with the main decks covered in and rounded over as a protection against rough seas. **whale-boat,** *n.* A boat sharp at both ends, such as those used in whaling. **whale-bone,** *n.* A horny, elastic substance occurring in long, thin plates, found in the palate of certain whales. **whale-calf,** *n.* A young whale. **whale-fin,** *n.* (*Comm.*) Whalebone. **whale-fishery, -fishing,** *n.* **whale-line,** *n.* Rope of great strength used in whaling. **whale-man,** *n.* A seaman employed in whaling. **whale-oil,** *n.* Oil obtained from the blubber of whales; spermaceti. **whaler,** *n.* A whale-man; a ship employed in whaling. **whaling,** *n.* **whaling-gun,** *n.* A gun for firing harpoons at whales. **whaling-master,** *n.* The captain of a whaler.

whale (2) [WEAL (2)].

whall, *whally[WALL-EYE].

whang (1) (wăng) [imit., cp. WHACK], *v.t.* To beat noisily, to bang; (*Sc.*) to cut in large slices. *v.i.* To make a noise as if whanged (of a drum, etc.). *n.* A whanging blow, a bang; (*Sc.*) a big slice.

whang (2) (wăng) [perh. var. of THONG], *n.* A tough leather strap or thong. **whangee,** *n.* A flexible bamboo cane.

wharf (wôrf) [A.-S. *hwerf*, bank, dam, orig. a turning, from *wheorfan*, to turn (cp. Icel. *hvarf*, turning, Dan. *værft*, Swed. *varf*, Dut. *werf*, wharf)], *n.* (*pl.* **-ves**) A landing-place for cargoes beside a river, harbour, canal, etc., usu. consisting of a quay of masonry or a platform, pier, or quay of timber, sometimes filled in with rubble, etc., (*Am.* a dock). *v.t.* To moor at a wharf; to deposit or store goods on a wharf. **wharf-rat,** *n.* The brown or Norway rat. **wharfage,** *n.* **wharfing,** *n.* **wharfinger** (wôr′ fin jer), *n.* A person who owns or has charge of a wharf.

what (wot) [A.-S. *hwæt*, neut. of *hwā*, WHO], *pron.* (*interrog.*) Which thing or things (often used ellipt.); (*rel.*) that which, those which, the things that; which things, how much! (as an exclamation); (*prov.*) that or which. *a.* Which thing, kind, amount, number, etc. (in asking questions); how great, remarkable, ridiculous, etc. (used in an exclamatory sense); (*rel.*) such as, as many or as many as, any that. *adv.* (*interrog.*) To what extent, in what respect? **but what:** (*vulg.*) But. **what for:** For what reason, purpose? etc. **to give what for** [GIVE (1)]. **what for no?** (*Sc.*) Why not? **what ho!** An exclamation of greeting or accosting. **what next?** (*exclam.*) Monstrous! absurd! **what not:** And other things, etc. **what of that:** No matter, never mind. **what though:** What does it matter if? admitting that. **what's what:** (*colloq.*) The real thing, or a good thing as opp. to a bad or doubtful one. **what's up** [UP]. **what time** [TIME]. **what-d'ye-call-it,** *n.* (*colloq.*) A phrase put for something that has slipped one's memory. **what have you:** (*colloq.*) Anything else of the kind. **whate'er** (-âr), *pron.* (*poet.*) Whatever. **whatever** (wot ev′ ėr), *pron.* Anything soever that; all that which. *a.* No matter what (thing or things). **whatnot,** *n.* A piece of furniture with shelves for ornaments, books, etc.

***whatso** (wot′ sō), **whatsoever** (wot sō ev′ ėr), **whatsoe'er** (-âr′), *pron.* and *a.* (*poet.*) [WHATEVER].

whau (wou) [Maori], *n.* The cork-tree.

whaup (hwawp) [from its cry], *n.* (*chiefly Sc.*) The curlew.

wheal (wēl) [Corn. *hwel*], *n.* (*Cornwall*) A mine (usu. a tin-mine).

wheat (wēt) [A.-S. *hwǣte*, cogn. with WHITE], *n.* An annual cereal grass, *Triticum sativum*, cultivated for its grain which is ground into flour for bread. **wheat belt,** *n.* (*Geog.*) The area east of the Rocky Mountains in Canada and U.S.A. where wheat is extensively cultivated. **wheat-ear,** *n.* An ear of wheat. **wheat-fly,** *n.* Any of various flies that injure wheat, esp. the Hessian fly. **wheat-grass,** *n.* Couch-grass. **wheat-moth,** *n.* One of various moths the larvæ of which destroy wheat. **wheaten,** *a.*

wheatear (wēt′ ĕr) [corr. of WHITE ARSE], *n.* The stone-chat, *Saxicola œnanthe*, or white-tail.

Wheatstone automatic (wēt′ stŏn) [Sir C. *Wheatstone* (1802–75)], *n.* (*Teleg.*) A mechanical system of telegraphy for transmitting and receiving high-speed signals automatically. **Wheatstone bridge,** *n.* (*Elec.*) A device for measuring an unknown electrical resistance by means of a known resistance.

wheedle (wēdl) [etym. unknown; perh. from A.-S. *wǣdlian*, to beg, *wǣdl*, poverty], *v.t.* To entice, to gain over, to persuade, by coaxing or flattery; to cajole, to humour, to cheat; to obtain from or get (out of) by coaxing and flattery. **wheedler,** *n.* **wheedling,** *a.* **wheedlingly,** *adv.*

wheel (wēl) [A.-S. *hwēol*, cp. Icel. *hjōl*, Dan. *huil*, also Gr. *kuklos*, see CYCLE], *n.* A circular frame or solid disk turning on its axis, used in vehicles, machinery, etc., to reduce friction and facilitate motion; a machine, implement, device, etc., consisting principally of a wheel, esp. a spinning-wheel, potter's wheel, steering-wheel, etc.; (*colloq.*) a cycle; an object resembling a wheel, a disk; a catherine-wheel; an instrument of torture formerly used for breaking the limbs of criminals; torture with this; the act of wheeling, circular motion, rotation, a revolution; the turning or swinging round of a body of troops or a line of warships as on a pivot. *v.t.* To move or push (a wheeled vehicle, etc.) in some direction; to cause to turn or swing round as on a pivot. *v.i.* To turn or swing round thus; to change direction, to face another way (*lit. or fig.*); to go round, to gyrate; to ride a cycle, etc. **to break upon the wheel** [BREAK]. **wheel and axle:** One of the mechanical powers, consisting of a cylindrical axle on which a wheel is fastened concentrically, the difference between their respective diameters supplying leverage. **wheel of life:** A scientific toy consisting of a revolving cylinder with slits through which figures depicted on the inside are seen apparently in continuous motion. **wheel-animalcule,** *n.* A rotifer. **wheelbarrow,** *n.* A barrow usu. supported on a single wheel, with two handles by which it is wheeled. **wheel-base,** *n.* (*Motor.*) The distance between the front and rear hubs of a vehicle. **wheel-brace,** *n.* (*Motor.*) A brace-shaped spanner for adjusting bolts on a wheel. **wheel-chair,** *n.* A chair on wheels, esp. for invalids. **wheel-horse,** *n.* A wheeler. **wheel-house,** *n.* A shelter for the steersman. **wheelman,** *n.* A cyclist. **wheel-seat,** *n.* The part of an axle carrying a fixed wheel and fastened into its hub. **wheel-shaped,** *a.* **wheel-spin,** *n.* The revolution of wheels without a grip of the road. **wheelstone,** *n.* An entrochite. **wheel-tread,** *n.* The part of a rim or tire that touches the ground. **wheel-window,** *n.* A circular window with radiating tracery. **wheelwright,** *n.* A man whose occupation is to make wheels, etc. **wheeled,** *a.* (*usu. in comb.*, as *four-wheeled*). **wheeler,** *n.* One who wheels; a wheelwright; a horse next the wheels in a tandem, etc. **wheels within wheels:** Concealed reasons or interdependent circumstances. **wheelless,** *a.* **wheely,** *a.*

wheen (wēn) [A.-S. *hwǣne*, *hwōn*], *n.* A little, a small quantity; a quantity.

wheeze (wēz) [A.-S. *hwēsan*, cogn. with *hwōsta*, cough, cp. G. *husten*], *v.i.* To breathe hard and with an audible sound, as in asthma. *v.t.* To utter thus. *n.* A wheezing sound; (*slang*) a joke, a tale, a design, a scheme. **wheezy,** *a.* **wheezily,** *adv.* **wheeziness,** *n.*

whekau (wē′ kou) [Maori], *n.* The laughing owl.

whelk (1) (welk) [M.E. *wilk*, A.-S. *wiloc* (cp. Dut. *wulk*), prob. cogn. with HELIX, conf. with foll.], *n.* A marine spiral-shelled gasteropod of the genus *Buccinum*, esp. *B. undatum*, the common whelk, used for food.

whelk (2) (welk) [dim. of WHEAL (1)], *n.* A small pustule or pimple. **whelked,** *a.*

whelm (welm) [M.E. *whelmen*, prob. from a noun *whelm* (cp. M.Swed. *hwalm*, hay-cock), from A.-S. *āhwytfan*, to overwhelm, cp. Icel. *hvālfa*, to turn upside down, G. *wölben*, to arch over, Gr. *kolpos*, bosom], *v.t.* To overwhelm to engulf, to submerge.

whelp (welp) [A.-S. *hwelp*, cp. Dut. *welp*, Icel. *hvelpr*], *n.* The young of a dog, a pup; the young of a beast of prey, a cub; (*fig.*) an offensive or ill-bred boy or youth. *v.i.* To bring forth young (of bitches and some beasts of prey). *v.t.* To bring forth (a pup or cub); to give birth to or produce (*in contempt*). **whelpless,** *a.*

whemmle (hweml) [freq. from WHELM], *v.t.* (*Sc.*) To whelm, to overthrow. *n.* An overthrow.

when (wen) [A.-S. *hwænne*, a case of interrog. pron. WHO], *adv.* (*interrog.*) At what or which time? (*rel.*) at which (time), at the time that, at any time that, at whatever time; as soon as; at or just after the time that; after which, and then; while (often ellipt. with pres.p.). *pron.* What or which time. ***whenas,** *adv.* When; whereas, while. **whenever, whene'er,** *adv.* At whatever time. **whensoever,** *adv.* At what time soever.

whence (wens) [M.E. *whennes*, A.-S. *hwanan*, cogn. with prec. (*-an*, suf. of direction)], *adv.* (*interrog.*) From what place or which, where from? how? (*rel.*) from which place, orig, source, etc.; for which reason, wherefore; (*ellipt.*) to or at the place from which. *pron.* What or which place or starting-point. ***whenceforth,** *adv.* **whencesoever,** *adv.* From whatsoever place or source.

whenever, etc. [WHEN].

where (wâr) [A.-S. *hwār* (cp. Dut. *waar*, G. *warum*, Icel. *hvar*), cogn. with *hwā*, WHO, and WHEN], *adv.* (*interrog.*) At or in what place, situation, case, circumstances, etc.; to what place, whither, in what direction; (*rel.*) in which (place or places), in or to the place, direction, etc., in which. *pron.* What or which place. **whereabout** (-ȧ bout′), *adv.* About which, in regard to which; whereabouts. **whereabouts,** *adv.* Near what or which place roughly. *n.* The approximate locality or the locality in or near which a person or thing is. **whereas** (-ăz′), *conj.* The fact or case being that, considering that (in legal preambles, etc.); the fact on the contrary being that, when in reality. **whereat** (-ăt′), *adv.* At which; *at what? **whereby,** *adv.* By which means; *by what? **wherefore,** *adv.* For what reason? why? for which reason, on which account. *n.* The reason why. **wherefrom,** *adv.* From which, whence. **wherein** (-in′), *adv.* In what place, respect, etc.? in which thing, place, respect, etc. **whereinsoever** (-ev′ ẽr), *adv.* **whereinto,** *adv.* **whereness** (wâr′ nĕs), *n.* **whereof** (-ov′), *adv.* Of what? of which or whom. **whereon** (-on′), *adv.* **whereout** (-out′), *adv.* Out of which. **wheresoever** (-ev′ ẽr), *adv.* In or to what place soever. **wherethrough** (-throo′), *adv.* **whereto** (-too′), *adv.* To what place or end. **whereunder** (-ŭn′ dẽr), *adv.* ***whereunto** (-ŭn too′), *adv.* To what end or purpose? to which. **whereupon** (-ŭ pon′), *adv.* Upon which; in consequence of or immediately after which. **wherever** (-ev′ ẽr), (*poet.*) **where'er** (-âr′), *adv.* At, in, or to whatever place. **wherewith** (-with′), *adv.* With what? with which. **wherewithal** (-awl′), *adv.* Wherewith. *n.* The necessary means or resources, esp. money.

wherry (1) (wer′ i) [perh. rel. to WHARF and WHIR],

n. A light shallow rowing-boat for plying on rivers. **wherryman,** *n.*

wherry (2) (wer' i) [etym. doubtful], *n.* (*prov.*) A liquor made from the pulp of crab-apples after the verjuice is expressed.

whet (hwet) [A.-S. *hwettan*, from *hwæt*, keen, bold (cp. Dut. *wetten*, G. *wetzen*, Icel. *hvetja*)], *v.t.* (*past & p.p.* **whetted**) To sharpen by rubbing on a stone or similar substance; (*fig.*) to excite, to stimulate. *n.* The act of whetting; anything taken to whet or stimulate the appetite; a dram. **whetstone,** *n.* A piece of stone used for sharpening cutlery, etc.; (*fig.*) anything that sharpens or stimulates. **whetter,** *n.*

whether (we*th*' ėr) [A.-S. *hwæther*], **a.* and *pron.* Which of the two? *conj.* Introducing an indirect question in the form of an alternative clause followed by an alternative *or*, *or not*, or *or whether*, or with the alternative unexpressed.

whethering (we*th*' ėr ing) [etym. doubtful], *n.* (*prov.*) The retention of the after-birth in cows.

whetstone, whetter [WHET].

whew (hwoo, hwū) [instinctive sound], *int.* An exclamation of astonishment or consternation.

whey (wā) [A.-S. *hwæg*, cp. Dut. *wei*, W. *chwig*], *n.* The watery part of milk that remains after the casein, etc., have formed curds and been separated. ***whey-face,** *n.* A pale-faced person. ***whey-faced,** *a.* **whey-tub,** *n.* **wheyey, wheyish,** *a.*

which (wich) [A.-S. *hwilc*, *whilīc* (WHO, -LIKE), cp. Dut. *welk*, G. *welcher*, Icel. *hvīlīkr*], *pron.* (*interrog.*) What person, thing, persons, or things, of a definite number; (*rel.*) representing in a subordinate clause a noun expressed or understood in the principal sentence. *a.* (*interrog.*) What (person, thing, etc.) of a definite number; (*rel.*) used with a noun defining an indefinite antecedent. **whichever, whichsoever** (-ev' ėr), *a.* and *pron.* (*emphat.*) Which (person or thing) of two or more.

whidah-bird (wid' ȧ bĕrd) [*Whidah*, in Dahomey], *n.* A small W. African weaver-bird, the male of which has four tail-feathers of enormous length.

whiff (1) (wif) [imit.], *n.* A sudden expulsion of smoke, etc., a puff, a light gust, esp. one carrying an odour; a small cigar; a light outrigged sculling boat. *v.t.* and *i.* To puff or blow lightly. **whiffy,** *a.* (*colloq.*) Smelly.

whiff (2) (wif) [perh. var. of WHIP], *v.i.* To fish with a hand-line, usu. from a boat, towing the bait near the surface.

whiff (3) (wif) [etym. doubtful], *n.* A European or W. Indian flat-fish.

whiffle (wif' ėl [freq. from WHIFF (1)], *v.i.* To veer about (as the wind); to change from one opinion or course to another, to prevaricate, to equivocate. **whiffler,** *n.*

whig (1) (wig) [short for obs. *whiggamor*, nickname for certain Scots who came to buy corn at Leith, from *whiggam*, a word with which they urged their horses, prob. from Sc. *whig*, to jog along], *n.* A member of the political party that contended for the rights and privileges of Parliament in opp. to the Court party or Tories, supported the Revolution of 1688 and the principles it represented, and was succeeded by the Liberals; orig. a Scottish Covenanter; (*Am. Hist.*) a colonist who supported the cause of independence in the American Revolution. ***whiggarchy,** *n.* **whiggery, whiggism,** *n.* **whiggish,** *a.* **whiggishly,** *adv.* **whiggishness,** *n.*

whig (2) (wig) [var. of WHEY], *n.* (*prov.*) Sour whey, buttermilk.

whigmaleerie (hwig mȧ lēr' i) [etym. doubtful], *n.* (*Sc.*) A trinket, a gewgaw; a whim.

while (wīl) [A.-S. *hwīl* (cp. Icel. *hvīla*, rest, G. *weile*), prob. cogn. with QUIET], *n.* A space of time, esp. the time during which something happens or is done. *conj.* During the time that, as long as, at the same time as (*often used ellipt, with pres.p.*); at the same time that, whereas (followed by a correlative sentence bringing out a contrast); *till. *v.t.* To pass (time, etc.) pleasantly or without weariness. **once in a while:** Occasionally, *now and then, at long intervals. ***the while:** During, whilst. **worth while:** Worth the time, labour, or expense involved. ***whilere,** *adv.* A little time ago, erewhile. ***whiles,** *adv.* While; (*Sc.*) sometimes. **whilst,** *conj.* While. **the whilst:** The while.

whilk [WHICH].

***whilom** (wī' lȯm) [A.-S. *hwīlum*, instr. or dat. pl. of WHILE], *adv.* Formerly, once, of old; *a.* Quondam.

whilst [WHILE].

whim (wim) [Icel. *hvima*, to wander with the eyes, from *vim*, giddiness, folly, cp. Norw. *kvim*], *n.* A sudden fancy, a freak, a caprice; (*Mining*) a hoisting device, usu. consisting of a vertical winch worked by a horse, for raising ore. **whimmy,** *a.* Whimsical. **whimsical,** *a.* Full of whims; oddly humorous; odd-looking, curious, fantastic. **whimsicality** (-kăl' i ti), **whimsicalness,** *n.* **whimsically,** *adv.* **whimsy,** *n.* A whim, a crotchet. **whimwham,** *n.* A plaything, a whim, a fancy.

whimbrel (wim' brėl) [freq. of *whim*, imit. of cry, -EL], *n.* A small curlew, *Numenius phæopus.*

whimper (wim' pėr) [freq. of *whimpe*, WHIM (*p.* excrescent), prob. cogn. with WHINE], *v.i.* To cry with a low, broken, whining voice; to whine. *v.t.* To utter in such a tone. *n.* A low, querulous, or whining cry. **whimperer,** *n.* **whimperingly,** *adv.*

whimsical, whimwham, etc. [WHIM].

whin (1) (win) [cp. Norw. *hvin*], *n.* Furze, gorse. **whinchat,** *n.* A small turdoid bird, *Saxicola rubetra.* **whinberry,** *n.* The bilberry. **whinny** (1), *a.* Abounding in furze or whin.

whin (2) (win) [etym. doubtful], *n.* A very hard, resistant rock, esp. basalt, chert, or quartzose sandstone, also called **whinsill** or **whinstone.**

whine (wīn) [A.-S. *hwīnan*, cp. Icel. *hvīna*, to whiz, Swed. *hvina*, to whistle], *v.i.* To make a plaintive, long-drawn cry; to complain or find fault in a mean, peevish, or unmanly way. *v.t.* To utter with a whine or in a peevish way. *n.* A whining cry, sound, or tone; a mean or unmanly complaint. **whiner,** *n.* **whiningly,** *adv.*

whinger (wing' ėr), ***whinyard** (-yȧrd) [prob. cogn. with prec.], *n.* A dirk, a short sword or hanger.

whinny (1) [WHIN (1)].

whinny (2) (win' i) [freq. of WHINE], *v.i.* To neigh, esp. in a gentle or delighted way. *n.* The act or sound of whinnying.

whinsill, whinstone [WHIN (2)].

whinyard [WHINGER].

whip (wip) [cp. Dut. *wippen*, to skip (*wip*, a moment, the strappado), Dan. *vippe*, Swed. *vippa*, to wag, G. *wippen*, to see-saw, to rock, perh. cogn. with VIBRATE], *v.t.* (*past & p.p.* **whipped**) To move suddenly and quickly, to snatch, to dart, to jerk (out, away, etc.); to lash, to flog; to drive or urge (on) with a whip; to thrash; to beat (out of etc.); to beat (eggs, cream, etc.) into a froth; to fish (a stream) by casting a line over the water; (*Am.*) to beat, to overcome; (*Parl.*) to manage or discipline (the members of a party; to lash or bind with a close wrapping of twine, thread, etc.; to bind (twine, etc.) round a joint, etc.; to oversew (a seam) with close stitches; to twist (goods, etc.) with a rope passed through a pulley. *v.i.* To move or start suddenly, to start, to dart (out, in, etc.). *n.* An instrument for driving horses, etc., or for punishing persons, consisting of a lash tied to a handle or rod; a coachman or driver; a whipper-in; a member of Parliament appointed to enforce discipline and to summon the members of his party to divisions, etc.; a summons sent out by a whip to ensure such attendance; a hoisting apparatus consisting of a single rope and pulley. ***whip and spur:** With the greatest haste. **whip-cord,** *n.* A hard twisted cord for making a whip; (*Textiles*) a very durable corded cloth made from worsted yarns. **whip-crane,** *n.* A crane used with a whip for rapid hoisting. **whip-gin,** *n.* A block for use in hoisting. **whip-graft,** *n.* A graft made by inserting a tongue in a scion into a slit cut in the stock; *v.t.* To graft by this method. **whip-hand,** *n.* The hand holding the whip; (*fig.*) the advantage or control. **whip-handle,** *n.* **whip-lash,** *n.* **whip-ray,** *n.* A sting-ray. **whip-round,** *n.* A subscription. *v.i.* To make a collection. **whip-saw,** *n.* A narrow saw-blade with the ends fastened in a frame. *v.t.* To saw with this; (*Am. slang*) to beat (a person) at every point in a game or in betting. **whip-snake,** *n.* A slender whip-like snake. **whip-stock,** *n.* The rod or handle of a whip. **whip-tail,** *n.* A Tasmanian fish; a small Kangaroo. **whip-top,** *n.* A top kept spinning with a whip. **whipper,** *n.* **whipper-in,** *n.* (*pl.* **whippers-in**) A man employed to assist the huntsman by looking after the hounds, now usu. called a whip; (*Parl.*) a whip. **whipper-snapper,** *n.* A noisy, presuming, insignificant person. **whipping,** *n.* **whipping-boy,** *n.* (*Hist.*) A boy educated with a young prince and taking his punishments for him. ***whipping-cheer,** *n.* (*Shak.*) Flogging, chastisement. **whipping-post,** *n.* A post to which offenders were tied to be whipped (usu. attached to stocks). **whipping-top** [WHIP-TOP]. ***whipster,** *n.* A whipper-snapper. **whippy,** *a.*

whippet (wip′ ėt) [etym. doubtful], *n.* A breed of racing-dogs, a cross between the greyhound and terrier.

whipple-tree (wip′ ėl trē) [freq. of WHIP, TREE], *n.* A swingle-tree.

whip-poor-will (wip′ pur wil) [imit. of cry], *n.* A small N. American nocturnal bird, *Caprimulgus vociferus*, allied to the goat-suckers.

whipster [WHIP].

whir (wĕr) [M.E. *whirr, quirr*, cp. Dan. *hvirre*, Icel. *hverfa*], *v.i.* (*past & p.p.* **whirred**) To revolve, move, or fly quickly with a whizzing sound. *n.* A whirring sound.

whirl (wĕrl) [for *whirfle*, freq. from Icel. *hvirfla* (cp. G. *wirbeln*), cogn. with prec. and A.-S. *hweorfan*, to turn], *v.t.* To swing round and round rapidly; to cause to revolve or fly round with great velocity; to carry (away or along) rapidly; to hurl or fling. *v.i.* To turn round and round rapidly, to rotate, to gyrate, to spin; to be carried or to travel rapidly in a circular course; to move along swiftly; to be giddy, to seem to spin round (of the brain, etc.). *n.* A whirling motion. ***whirl-about,** *n.* A whirligig. ***whirl-blast,** *n.* A whirling blast, a whirlwind. **whirl-bone,** *n.* The bone of a ball-and-socket joint, esp. the patella or knee-cap. **whirlpool,** *n.* An eddy or vortex. **whirlwind,** *n.* A funnel-shaped column of air moving spirally round an axis, which at the same time has a progressive motion. **whirler,** *n.* **whirling-table,** *n.* A machine for exhibiting the effects of centrifugal and centripetal forces; a potter's wheel. **whirligig,** *n.* A child's spinning or rotating toy; a merry-go-round; a water-beetle that darts about in a circular manner over the surface of pools, etc.; (*fig.*) a revolution, a rotation; *an instrument of torture consisting of a cage turning on a pivot in which the victim was whirled round.

whirr [WHIR].

whish, whisht (1) (hwish) [instinctive sound], *int.* Hush! silence!

whish (2) (wish) [imit.], *v.i.* To move through the air or water with a whistling sound. *n.* A whistling sound.

whisk (wisk) [cp. Dan. *viske*, to wipe, from *visk*, a wisp, Swed. *viska*, G. *wischen*, to wipe, perh. cogn. with WISP], *v.t.* To sweep, brush, or flap (away or off); to carry off or take (away) swiftly or suddenly; to shake, flourish, or wave about with a quick movement; to beat up (eggs, etc.). *v.i.* To move or go swiftly or suddenly. *n.* A whisking movement; a small bunch of grass, straw, feathers, hair, etc., used as a brush or for flapping away flies, dust, etc.; an instrument for beating up cream, eggs, etc.; *the game of whist.

whisker (wisk′ er) [as prec.], *n.* Hair growing on the cheeks of a man (*usu. in pl.*); (*pl.*) the bristly hairs growing on the upper lip of a cat or other animal. **whiskered,** *a.*

whisket (wis′ kėt) [etym. doubtful], *n.* (*prov.*) A basket.

whisky, whiskey (1) (wis′ ki) [Gael. *uisgebeatha*, water of life, see USQUEBAUGH], *n.* An ardent spirit distilled usu. from barley, sometimes from wheat, rye, sugar, etc. **whisky-liver,** *n.* Cirrhosis of the liver caused by alcoholic poisoning. **whisky-toddy,** *n.* **whiskified,** *n.* (*colloq.*).

whisky (2) [WHISK, -Y], *n.* A light one-horse chaise or gig for fast travelling.

whisky-jack (wis′ ki jăk) [corr. of N. Am. Ind. *wiss-ka-tjan*], *n.* The grey or Canada jay, *Perisoreus Canadensis.* ***whisky-dick, -john,** *n.*

whisper (wis′ pėr) [O. Northumbrian, *hwisprian* (cp. M.Dut. *wisperen*, G. *wispeln*), of imit. orig.], *v.i.* To speak with articulation but without vocal vibration; to speak in a low voice so as not to be overheard; to converse privately or in a whisper; to devise mischief, to plot, to talk slander; (*fig.*) to rustle. *v.t.* To tell or bid in a whisper or privately; to utter or disseminate thus. *n.* A whispering tone or voice; a whispered remark or speech; (*fig.*) a hint, an insinuation, a rumour. **whisperer,** *n.* **whispering,** *n.* **whispering-gallery,** *n.* A gallery, corridor, etc., in which the faintest sounds made at particular points are audible at other distant points though inaudible elsewhere. **whisperingly,** *adv.*

whist (wist) [formerly WHISK in alln. to the sweeping up of the cards], *n.* A card game, usu. for four persons, played with the entire pack of 52 cards. **whist drive,** *n.* A competitive series of games of whist. **dummy whist** [DUMMY].

whistle (wis′ ėl) [A.-S. *hwistlian*, freq. from *hwist-* (imit.), to make a hissing noise, cp. Dut. *hwisla*, Dan. *hvisle*] *v.i.* To make a shrill musical sound by forcing the breath through a small opening of the lips or with an instrument, an appliance on a steam-engine, etc.; to emit this sound (of an instrument, engine, etc.); to make a similar sound (of birds, etc.); to make such a sound by swift motion (of a missile, the wind, etc.). *v.t.* To emit or utter (a tune, etc.) by whistling; to call or give a signal to thus. *n.* A whistling sound, note, or cry; an instrument for producing such a sound; (*slang*) the throat. ***to go whistle:** To go to the deuce. **to whistle for:** To stand little or no chance of getting. **to whistle for a wind:** The superstitious practice of old sailors in a calm. **to wet one's whistle** [WET]. **whistler,** *n.* One who or that which whistles; (*Am.*) the whistling or hoary marmot; a whistling duck or other bird, a broken-winded horse. **whistling duck:** The American widgeon.

whit (hwit) [A.-S. *wiht*, WIGHT (1)], *n.* A jot, the least particle, an iota.

white (wīt) [A.-S. *hwīt*, cp. Dut. *wit*, G. *weiss*, Icel. *hvītr*, Sansk *çvēta*], *a.* Being of the colour produced by reflection of all the visible rays in sunlight as of pure snow, common salt, foam of clear water, etc.; approaching this colour, pale, light-complexioned, pallid, bloodless, transparent, colourless; pure, clean, stainless; spotless, innocent; grey, silvery, or hoary as from age, etc.; fair, happy, propitious. ****v.t.*** To whiten. *n.* A white colour; a white paint or pigment; a white man or a member of one of the paler races, esp. a European; a white part of anything, having the colour of snow; *the central part of the butt in archery, that which is aimed at; (*pl.*) white clothes; superior flour made from the finest and whitest wheat; leucorrhœa. **white alloy:** A cheap alloy imitating silver. **white ant** [TERMITE]. **whitebait,** *n.* The fry of several clupeoid fish eaten when about 2 in. long. **white-beam,** *n.* A shrub or small tree, *Sorbus aria*, with silvery undersides to the leaves. **white bear:** The polar bear. **white-beard,** *n.* A greybeard, an old man. **Whiteboy,** *n.* A member of a secret agrarian organization formed in Ireland about 1760 which held nocturnal meetings and perpetrated damage to property, so called from the white shirts worn over their other garments. **Whiteboyism,** *n.* The principles or practices of the Whiteboys. **white-cap,** *n.* The redstart and other birds; a white-crested wave. **White City,** *n.* A sports and athletic stadium at Shepherd's Bush, London. **white-collar worker,** *n.* A term used to describe an office and clerical employee. **white corpuscle:** A leucocyte. **white-crested, -crowned,** *a.* **white crops:** Wheat, barley, etc., which whiten as they ripen. **white damp,** *n.* (*Mining*) Carbon monoxide. **white-eared,** *a.* **white elephant** (ELEPHANT]. **white-faced,** *a.* Pale-faced; having a white front or surface; having a white spot or streak on the front of the head (of animals). **white feather** [FEATHER]. **white-fish,** *n.* A general term for food-fish other than salmon, esp. whitings and haddocks. **whitefish,** *n.* A N. American salmonoid food-fish of the genus *Coregonus*; the menhaden and other fish. **White Friar:** A Carmelite (from the white cloak). **white frost:** Hoar-frost. **white-handed,** *a.* Having white hands; (*fig.*) free from guilt or dishonesty. **white heat:** The degree of heat at which bodies become incandescent and appear white; (*fig.*) a high pitch of excitement, passion, etc. **white horses:** Foam-crested waves. **white-hot,** *a.* **White House:** The official residence of the President of the U.S.A., at Washington. **white-iron,** *n.* Thin sheet iron with a coating of tin. **white-land,** *n.* A tough, clayey soil, of a whitish hue when dry, but blackish when wet. **white lead:** Carbonate of lead, esp. used as a basis of white oil-paint. **white lie** [LIE (1)]. **white-limed,** *a.* Whitewashed. **white-lipped,** *a.* Pale to the lips, esp. with fear. **white-livered,** *a.* Cowardly. **white magic:** Magic not involving intercourse with devils, sorcery. **white man,** *n.* (*colloq.*) An honourable, upright man. **white man's burden:** (*fig.*) The white man's obligation to promote the welfare of the backward coloured races. **White Man's Grave:** (*Geog.*) The lands along the Guinea Coast of W. Africa where the atmosphere is peculiarly unhealthy to Europeans. **white meat:** Meat that appears white after cooking, as poultry, veal, pork; food made from milk, cheese, butter, eggs, and the like. **white metal:** White alloy. **white night,** *n.* A sleepless night. **white paper,** *n.* (*Pol.*) A government report on a matter recently investigated. **white rent:** In Devon and Cornwall, a rent or duty of eightpence payable by every tinner to the Duke of Cornwall, as lord of the soil. **white sale,** *n.* A sale of household linen at reduced prices. **white slave traffic,** *n.* The procuring and transporting of women and children for immoral purposes. **whitesmith,** *n.* A tinsmith; one who finishes or galvanizes ironwork. **white squall:** A squall not preceded by clouds, as in tropic seas. **whitestone,** *n.* A fine, white granite. ***whitetail,** *n.* The wheatear. **whitethorn,** *n.* The hawthorn. **whitethroat,** *n.* A small warbler of the genus *Sylvia*. **whitewash,** *n.* A mixture of quicklime and water or of whiting and size used for whitening walls, ceilings, etc.; (*fig.*) a false colouring given to a person's character or memory to counteract disreputable allegations; *v.t.* To cover with whitewash; (*fig.*) to clear from imputations; to clear a bankrupt of his debts by judicial process. **whitewasher,** *n.* **white wine:** Any wine of a light colour, as Graves, Hock, etc., opp. to red. **white witch:** One using her power for beneficent purposes. **white-wood,** *n.* Any one of various trees yielding white timber. **white of an egg:** The albuminous viscous part surrounding the yolk. **white of the eye:** The part of the ball of the eye surrounding the iris. **whitely,** *adv.* **whiten,** *v.t.* and *i.* **whitener,** *n.* **whiteness,** *n.* **whitening,** *n.* The act of making white; the state of becoming white; whiting (1). **whitish,** *a.* **whitishness,** *n.*

Whitechapel-cart (wĭt′ chăpl kart) [*Whitechapel*, in E. London], *n.* A light two-wheeled spring-cart.

whitening, whitesmith, whitethroat, whitewash, etc. [WHITE].

whitey (wī′ ti), *n.* (*Austral.*) A flour-and-water scone cooked in wood ashes.

whither (wi*th*′ ėr) [A.-S. *hwider*, as WHETHER], *adv.* (*interrog.*) To what or which place, where; (*rel.*) to which; whithersoever, wheresoever. **whithersoever,** *adv.* To what place soever. ***whitherward,** *adv.*

whiting (1) (wī′ ting), *n.* Fine chalk pulverized, washed, and prepared for use in whitewashing, polishing, etc.

whiting (2) (wī′ ting) [as prec.], *n.* A sea-fish, *Merlangus merlangus*, used for food. **whiting-pout,** *n.* A gadoid fish resembling this with an inflatable membrane over the eyes.

whitish, etc. [WHITE].

whitleather (wit′ le*th* ėr), *n.* Leather dressed with alum, white leather; the paxwax of the ox.

Whitley Council (wit′ li) [J. H. *Whitley* (1866–1935), first chairman], *n.* An industrial council comprising employers and employees to settle disputes and promote welfare in the industry.

whitlow (wit′ lō) [corr. of obs. *quick-flaw*, a flaking off of the skin round the quick, conf. with *whit*, above], *n.* An inflammatory tumour, esp. in the phalanx of a finger. **whitlow-grass,** *n.* A minute white-flowered, grass-like herb of the genus *Draba*.

Whitsun (wit′ sŭn) [short for *Whit-Sunday* (WHITE, SUNDAY, from the white garment commonly worn at this festival which was a great season for christenings)]. *a.* Pertaining to Whit-Sunday or Whitsuntide. **Whit-Sunday,** *n.* The seventh Sunday after Easter, a festival commemorating the day of Pentecost. **Whit-Monday,** etc., *n.* **Whitsuntide,** *n.* Whit-Sunday and the following days. **Whit-week,** *n.*

whittie-whattie (hwit′ i hwot′ i) [etym. doubtful], *v.i.* (*Sc.*) To shilly-shally; to whisper, to mutter. *n.* Shilly-shally, vague whispering, shuffling; a shuffler, a whisperer, a mutterer.

whittle (1) (wit′ ėl) [corr. of M.E. *thwitel*, from A.-S. *thwītan*, to cut, to pare], **n.* A long knife, esp. one used by butchers, sailors, etc., often worn at the belt. *v.t.* To trim, shave, or cut pieces or slices off with a knife; to thin down; (*fig.*) to reduce, pare away, or bring (down) in amount, etc,. by degrees. *v.i.* To keep on paring, shaving, or cutting away (at a stick, etc.) with a knife.

whittle (2) (wit′ ėl) [A.-S. *hwītel*, from *whīt*, WHITE (cp. Icel. *hvītill*)], *n.* (*now prov.*) A blanket; a thick shawl or cloak worn by English west-country women.

whity (wī′ ti), *a.* Whitish, inclining to white (*usu. in comb.* as *whity-brown*, between white and brown).

whiz (wiz) [imit.], *v.i.* (*past & p.p.* **whizzed**) To make a hissing sound, like an arrow or ball flying through the air. *n.* A whizzing sound. **whizz-bang,** *n.* (*Artil.*) A small high-velocity shell. **whizzingly,** *adv.*

who (hoo) [A.-S. *hwā*, m. and f., neut. *hwæt*, gen. *hwæs*, dat. *hwām* (cp. Dut. *wie, wat, wiens, wien*, G. *wer, was, wessen, wen* and *wem*, Icel. *hverr, hver, hvat, hvers, hverjum*, etc.), cogn. with L. *quis*, Sansk. *kas, kim, kam*], *pron.* (*obj.* **whom,** hoom, *poss.* **whose,** hooz) (*interrog.*) What or which person or persons? (*rel.*) that (identifying the subject or object in a relative clause with that of the principal clause); *he, she, or they that. **whodunit** (hoo′ dŭn′ it), *n.* (*colloq.*) A simple detective or mystery story. **whoever** (-ev′ ėr), **whoe'er** (-âr′) (*poet.*), ***whoso** (hoo′ sō), **whosoever** (-ev′ ėr), **whosoe'er** (-âr′), (*poet.*), *pron.* (*obj.* **whomever,** etc.) Any one without exception who, no matter who.

whoa (wō′ ȧ) [var. of HO, HOA], *int.* Stop! (used chiefly by drivers to horses).

whole (hōl) [A.-S. *hāl*, HALE (1) (cp. Dut. *heel*, G. *heil*, Icel. *heill*), cogn. with HEAL (1) and HOLY], *a.* Hale and sound, in good health; unimpaired, uninjured, not broken, intact; (a or the) complete or entired (period, etc.); containing the total number of parts, undivided, undiminished, opp. to partial; integral, composed of units, not fractional. *n.* A thing complete in all its parts, units, etc.; all that there is of a thing, the entirety; a complete system, a complete combination of parts, an organic unity. **upon the whole:** All things considered. **whole-bound,** *a.* Bound entirely in leather, opp. to half- or quarter-bound. **whole-coloured,** *a.* Having the same colour throughout. **whole-hearted,** *a.* Done or intended with all one's heart, hearty, generous, cordial, sincere. **whole-heartedly,** *adv.* **whole-heartedness,** *n.* **to go the whole hog:** To do thoroughly. **whole-hogger,** *n.* A thorough-paced supporter. **whole-hoofed,** *a.* Having undivided hoofs. **whole-length,** *a.* Exhibiting the whole figure (of a portrait, etc.). **whole meal:** Flour not deprived of a portion of its constituents by bolting. **whole numbers:** Integers. **wholeness,** *n.*

wholesale (hōl′ sāl), *n.* The sale of goods in large quantities as distinguished from retail. *a.* Buying or selling thus; (*fig.*) done, etc., in the mass, on the large scale, indiscriminate. *adv.* By wholesale, in large quantities; (*fig.*) by the mass, on the large scale.

wholesome (hōl′ sȯm), *a.* Tending to promote health, salutary, salubrious; promoting moral or mental health, not morbid; (*prov.*) clean; *healthy, sound. **wholesomely,** *adv.* **wholesomeness,** *n.*

wholly (hōl′ li), *adv.* Entirely, completely; totally, exclusively.

whom, whomsoever, etc. [WHO].

whoop (hoop) [M.E. *houpen*, F. *houper*, from *houp!* a cry or int., perh. from Teut.], *v.i.* To utter the cry 'whoop'; to shout or cry out loudly in excitement, encouragement, exultation, etc.; to hallo. *v.t.* To urge (on) with whoops; to mock at with loud cries. *n.* The cry 'whoop'; a loud shout of excitement, encouragement, etc.; the sound made in whooping-cough. **whooper,** *n.* **whooping-cough,** *n.* An infectious disease, pertussis, esp. of children, characterized by a violent cough followed by a loud convulsive respiration. **whoopee,** *n.* Riotous enjoyment; a noisy, jolly time.

whop (wop) [var. *whap*, *wap*, etym. doubtful], *v.t.* (*slang*) To beat, to thrash. *v.i.* (*Am.*) To fall with a loud noise. **whopper,** *n.* Anything uncommonly large, etc., esp. a monstrous lie. **whopping,** *a.*

whore (hôr) [M.E. *hore*, Icel. *hōra*, adulteress (cp. Dan. *hore*, Swed. *hora*, Dut. *hoer*, G. *hura*), perh. cogn. with L. *cārus*, dear], *n.* A prostitute, a courtezan, a strumpet; *an adulteress, an unchaste woman. *v.i.* To fornicate; (*Bibl.*) to practise idolatry. **whoredom,** *n.* Fornication; idolatry. ***whoremaster,** *n.* A pimp; a whoremonger. **whoremonger,** *n.* A fornicator. ***whoreson,** *n.* A bastard. *a.* Bastard-like, mean, scurvy. ***whoring,** *n.* ***whorish,** *a.* ***whorishly,** *adv.* **whorishness,** *n.*

whorl (wĕrl, wôrl) [prob. shortened from *whorvel*, from A.-S. *wheorfan*, see WHIRL], *n.* A circular set or ring of leaves, sepals, or other organs on a plant; one convolution or turn of a spiral, as in a univalve shell; the disk for steadying the motion of a spindle, formerly made of stone, etc. **whorled,** *a.*

whortleberry (wĕr′ tėl bėr i) [formerly *hurtilberye*, *hurtberye* (A.-S. *horta*, BERRY)], *n.* The bilberry.

whose, *poss.*, **whoso, whosoever,** etc. [WHO].

why (wī) [A.-S. *hwī*, instr. of *hwā*, WHO], *adv.* (*interrog.*) For what reason or purpose? (*rel.*) on account of which. *n.* The reason, explanation, or purpose of anything. *int.* Expressing surprise, etc.

wick (1) (wik) [A.-S. *wice*, cp. M.Dut. *wiecke*, Dan. *væge*, Norw. *veik*], *n.* A piece or bundle of fibrous or spongy material used in a candle or lamp to convey the melted grease or oil by capillary attraction to the flame.

wick (2) (wik) [etym. doubtful], *v.t.* (*Curling*) To strike (a stone) obliquely. *n.* Such a hit.

wick (3) (wik) [A.-S. *wīc*, L. *vīcus*, village], *n.* A town, village, or municipal district (chiefly in place-names).

wicked (wik′ ėd) [from obs. adj. *wikke*, cogn. with WEAK and A.-S. *wicca*, a wizard], *a.* Sinful, addicted to evil or vice, wilfully transgressing against the divine or moral law, immoral, depraved; mischievous, roguish. **wickedly,** *adv.* **wickedness,** *n.*

wicken (wik′ ėn) [prob. from A.-S. *wice*, WYCH], *n.* (*prov.*) The rowan or mountain ash.

wicker (wik′ ėr) [orig. a pliant twig, prob. from Scand. (cp. M. Swed. *wika*, to bend, Swed. *vika*, to fold, to plait, Dan. *veg*, pliant), cogn. with WEAK], *n.* Twigs, withes, or osiers plaited into a material for baskets, chairs, etc. *a.* Made of this material. **wicker-work,** *n.* and *a.* **wickered,** *a.*

wicket (wik′ ėt) [A.-S. *wiket* (F. *guichet*), etym. doubtful, perh. from O.H.G. *wisken*, to WHISK, to slip out], *n.* A small gate, door, or other entrance, esp. one close beside or forming part of a larger one; a small aperture in a door or wall, opened and closed by means of a sliding panel; (*Cricket*) a set of three stumps surmounted by two bails at which the bowler directs the ball; the ground on which this is set up; the innings or turn of each batsman at the wicket; the pitch between the wickets, esp. as regards condition for bowling. **to keep wicket:** (*Cricket*) To be wicket-keeper. **wicket-door, -gate,** *n.* **wicket-keeper,** *n.* (*Cricket*) The fielder who stands behind the batsman's wicket.

widdershins [WITHERSHINS].

widdy (*prov.*) [WIDOW, WITHY].

wide (wīd) [A.-S. *wīd*, cp. Dut. *wijd*, G. *weit*, far, Icel. *vīthr*], *a.* Having a great relative extent from side to side, broad, opp. to narrow; having a specified degree of breadth; far-extending; vast, spacious, extensive; not limited or restricted, large, free, liberal, comprehensive, catholic; distant or deviating by a considerable extent or amount from a mark, point, purpose, etc.; *fully open or expanded; crafty. *adv.* Widely; to a great distance, extensively; far from the mark or purpose. *n.* (*Cricket*) A wide ball, one bowled too far to the side and out of the batsman's reach. **broke to the wide:** (*slang*) Absolutely penniless. **wide-angle lens,** *n.* (*Photo.*) A lens with an angle up to 100° used for photographing buildings. **wideawake,** *a.* Having one's eyes open; alert, wary; keen, sharp, knowing. *n.* A soft felt hat with a broad brim. **wideawakeness,** *n.* **wide boy,** *n.* A crafty, dishonest fellow. **wide open:** (*Am.*) Lawless, disorderly. **widespread,** *a.* Widely disseminated. ***wide-stretched,** *a.* **widely,** *adv.* **widen,** *v.t.* and *i.* **wideness,** *n.* **widish,** *a.*

widgeon, wigeon (wij′ ȯn) [cp. F. *vigeon*, *vingeon*, L. *vipiōnem*, nom. *vipio*, a small crane], *n.* A wild duck of the genus *Anas*, esp. the European *M. penelope.*

widow (wid′ ō) [A.-S. *widwe* (cp. Dut. *weduwe*, G. *wittwe*, O.H.G. *wituwa*), cogn. with L. *viduus*, bereft (whence F. *veuve*), Sansk. *vidhavā*, widow, Gr. *ēitheos*, bachelor], *n.* A woman who has lost her husband by death and remains unmarried. *v.t.* To bereave of a husband; to make a widow or widower; to bereave, to deprive (of). **grass-widow** [GRASS]. ***widow-bench,** *n.* (*Law*) The share allowed to a widow of her husband's estate beside her jointure. **widow-hunter,** *n.* One who courts a widow for her fortune. **widow's cruse,** *n.* (*fig.* see I Kings xvii, 16) An unfailing source of supply. **widow's mite,** *n.* A small but ill-afforded contribution (see Mark xii, 42). **widow's peak,** *n.* The natural growth of a woman's hair to a point in the middle of the forehead. **widow's weeds,** *n.pl.* Deep mourning with a flowing veil of black crepe. **widower,** *n.* A man who has lost his wife by death and remains unmarried. **widow-hood,** *n.*

width (width), *n.* Extent of a thing from side to side, breadth, wideness; comprehensiveness of mind, liberality, catholicity.

wield (wēld) [A.-S. *geweldan, -wyldan,* from *wealdan,* to govern, to rule, cp. Icel. *valda,* G. *walten*], *v.t.* To have the management or control of; to sway; to handle, to use or employ. **to wield the sceptre:** To rule with supreme command. **wieldable,** *a.* **wielder,** *n.* ***wieldless,** *a.* ***wieldy,** *a.* That may be wielded, manageable.

wife (wīf) [A.-S. *wīf,* cp. Dut. *wijf,* G. *weib,* Icel. *vīf,* neut.], *n.* (*pl.* **wives**) A married woman, esp. in relation to her husband; *a woman (now usu. in comb. and denoting some humble occupation as in *fish-wife*); (*prov.*) an elderly or humble woman. **wifehood,** *n.* **wifie,** *n.* **wifeless,** *n.* **wifelike, wifely,** *a.* **old wives' tale:** A legend, a foolish story.

wig (1) (wig) [shortened from PERIWIG], *n.* A covering for the head composed of false hair, worn to conceal baldness, as a disguise, for ornament, or as part of an official costume, esp. by judges, lawyers, servants in livery, etc. **wigged,** *a.* ***wiggery,** *n.* False hair; empty formality; red-tapeism. **wigless,** *a.* **wigmaker,** *n.*

wig (2) (wig) [etym. doubtful], *v.t.* (*past & p.p.* **wigged**) To rate, to reprimand, to scold. **wigging,** *n.* A scolding.

wigan (wig' ȧn) [*Wigan,* town in Lancashire], *n.* An open canvas-like fabric used for stiffening.

wigeon [WIDGEON].

wiggle [WRIGGLE].

wight (1) (wīt) [A.-S. *wiht,* see WHIT], *n.* A person; *a supernatural being, an elf, a sprite.

***wight** (2) (wīt) [Icel. *vīgr,* cp. Swed. *vig.* and A.-S. *wīglīc,* warlike, from *wīg,* war], *a.* Nimble, active, strong, brave, doughty. **wightly,** *adv.*

wigwag (wig' wăg) [redupl. of WAG (1)], *v.t.* To wag to and fro. *v.i.* To move to and fro, to wag; to signal by waving flags.

wigwam (wig' wom) [Algonkin, *weekouomut,* in his house, inflected from *week,* house], *n.* A N. American Indian hut or cabin, usu. consisting of a framework covered with bark, matting, hides, etc.

wild (wīld) [A.-S. *wilde* (cp. Dut. and G. *wild,* Icel. *villr*), prob. cogn. with WILL (1)], *a.* Living in a state of nature, esp. inhabiting or growing in the forest or open country; not tamed, domesticated, or cultivated (esp. of animals and plants); not civilized, savage; unsettled, uncultivated, irregular, desert, uninhabited; (*fig.*) wayward, loose or disorderly in conduct, lawless, reckless, incautious, rash; ill-considered, ill-armed, imprudent, extravagant, inordinate; ungoverned, unchecked, unrestrained; turbulent, stormy, furious; anxiously eager, passionate, mad (with, etc.); excited, enthusiastic (about, etc.); shy, easily startled, given to shying (of horses, etc.); (*Bot.*) growing in a state of nature; having a certain resemblance to some other plant, but inferior to it in appearance. *n.* A desert or uninhabited and uncultivated tract. **wild-boar,** *n.* **wild-born,** *a.* Born in a wild state. **wild-cat,** *n.* **wild-cat scheme:** A rash and risky speculation or other scheme. **wild-duck,** *n.* **wild-fire** [GREEK FIRE]. **wildfowl,** *n.* (*collect.*) Birds of various species pursued as game, esp. waterfowl. **wild-fowling,** *n.* **wild-goose chase:** A foolish or hopeless enterprise. **wild-wood,** *n.* A tract of natural wood or forest; *a.* Consisting of or pertaining to this. **wilding,** *n.* A plant that springs up by natural agency, esp. a wild fruit-tree; the fruit of such a plant; **a.* Growing wild; wild. **wildish,** *a.* **wildly,** *adv.* **wildness,** *n.*

wildebeest (wil' dė bēst) [S. Afr. Dut. (WILD, BEAST)], *n.* A gnu.

***wilder** (wil' dėr) [shortened from *wilderne,* see foll. or BEWILDER], *v.t.* To bewilder.

wilderness (wil' dėr nės) [M.E. *wilderne,* desert, A.-S. *wilder,* wild animal, -NESS], *n.* An uninhabited or uncultivated land, a desert; a waste, a scene of disorder or confusion; a portion of a garden left to run wild; (*fig.*) a confused mass or quantity (of). **in the wilderness:** (*Pol.*) Out of office.

wildgrave (wild' grāv) [G. *wild,* game, GRAVE (4)], *n.* A German title of nobility; orig. the head keeper of a forest.

wilding, wildish, etc. [WILD].

wile (wīl) [A.-S. *wīl,* prob. cogn. with O.F. GUILE], *n.* A trick an artifice, a stratagem or deception. *v.t.* To entice, to cajole (into, away, etc.); (*incorr.*) to while.

wilful (wil' fůl), *a.* Intentional, voluntary, deliberate; done of one's own free will, without compulsion, not accidental; due to malice or evil intent; obstinate, self-willed, headstrong, perverse; *willing, ready. **wilfully,** *adv.* **wilfulness,** *n.*

wilga (wil' ga) [Austral. abor.], *n.* The dogwood tree.

wilily, wiliness [WILY].

will (1) (wil) [A.-S. *willan* (cp. Dut. *willen,* G. *wollen,* Icel. *vilja*), cogn. with L. *velle,* and Eng. WELL (1) and WILD], *v.t.* (**2nd sing.* **wilt,** *past & cond.* **would,** wud, *2nd sing.* **wouldest, wouldst,** *colloq. neg.* **won't,** wōnt, **wouldn't,** wudnt), *v.t.* To desire, to wish, to choose, to want (a thing, that, etc.); to be induced, to consent, to agree (to, etc.); to be in the habit or accustomed (to). *v.aux.* (*in 2nd and 3rd pers., or in 1st pers. in reported statement*) To be about or going to (expressing simple futurity or conditional action); (*in 1st pers.*) to intend, desire, or have a mind to; to be certain or probable as a natural consequence, must. **willer,** *n.* **willing,** *a.* Inclined, ready, not averse or reluctant (to); cheerfully acting, done, given, etc. **willingly,** *adv.* **willingness,** *n.* **would-be,** *pref.* Desirous, vainly aspiring to be. **would-be poet:** One who fancies himself or would like to be a poet.

will (2) (wil) [A.-S. *willa,* from prec., cp. Dut. *wil,* G. *wille,* Icel. *vili*], *n.* The mental power or faculty by which one initiates or controls one's activities, opp. to external causation and to impulse or instinct; the exercise of this power, an act of willing, a choice or volition, an intention, a fixed or authoritative purpose; determination, energy of character, power of carrying out one's intentions or dominating others; that which is willed, resolved, or determined upon; arbitrary disposal, discretion, or sufferance; inclination or disposition towards others; the legal declaration of one's intentions as to the disposal of his property (esp. freehold or landed) after his death, embodied in a written instrument. **at will:** At one's pleasure or discretion. **with a will:** Heartily, zealously. **will-worship,** *n.* (*Bibl.*) A religion devised by or imposed on oneself. **willed,** *a.* (*usu. in comb.* as *strong-willed*). **will-less,** *a.*

will (3) (wil) [from WILL (1 and 2)], *v.t.* To intend or bring about by the exercise of one's will, to resolve, to determine; to direct, control, or cause (esp. a hypnotized person) to act in a specified way by the exercise of one's will-power; to bequeath or devise by will. *v.i.* To exercise will-power. **will-power,** *n.* Control exercised deliberately over impulse or inclinations.

willet (wil' ėt) [imit. of cry], *n.* A N. American

sandpiper, *Symphemia semipalmata*, allied to the snipe.

willies (wil′ iz) [etym. unknown], *n.pl.* (*Colloq.*) Nervousness, apprehensiveness.

willing, etc. [WILL (1)].

will-o'-the-wisp (wil′ ō *th*ē wisp′) [*Will*, short for *William*, WISP (of lighted tow, etc.)], *n.* An ignis fatuus.

willow (1) (wil′ ō) [A.-S. *welig*, cp. Dut. *wilg*, perh. cogn. with HELIX], *n.* Any tree or shrub of the genus *Salix*, usu. growing near water, characterized by long, slender, pliant branches, largely yielding osiers, and timber used for cricket-bats, etc.; hence, a cricket-bat. ***to wear the willow:** To assume mourning or grieve for a lost or absent lover. **willow-herb,** *n.* A plant of the genus *Epilobium*, esp. the rose-bay, *E. angustifolium*. **willow-pattern,** *n.* A decorative pattern of Chinese style in blue on a white ground for china, introduced in 1780. **willow-warbler, -wren,** *n.* The chiff-chaff. **willowed,** *a.* **willowy,** *a.* Abounding with willows; lithe, slender, or graceful, like a willow.

willow (2) (wil′ ō), **willy** (wil′ i) [from prec.], *n.* A machine for the preliminary process of beating, picking and cleaning wool. *v.t.* To treat (wool) thus. **willowing-, *willow-machine,** *n.*

willy nilly (wil′ i nil′ i) [*will he, nill he*, see NILL], *adv.* Willingly or unwillingly. *a.* Uncertain, vacillating.

willy willy (wil′ i wil′ i), *n.* (*Austral.*) The tropical cyclone that sweeps over North-west Australia in the late summer.

***wilt** (1), *2nd sing.* [WILL (1)].

wilt (2) (wilt) [perh. var. of WELK], *v.i.* To wither, to droop; to lose freshness or vigour. *v.t.* To cause to wilt.

Wilton (wil′ tŏn), *n.* A carpet resembling Brussels, but with the loops cut open into an elastic velvet-pile, orig. manufactured at Wilton, in Wiltshire, and also called **Wilton Carpet.**

Wiltshire (wilt′ shir) [Eng. county], *n.* A breed of pigs; a kind of mild-cured bacon; a kind of cheese.

wily (wī′ li), *a.* Using or full of wiles; cunning, crafty. **wilily,** *adv.* **wiliness,** *n.*

***wimble** (wim′ bėl) [cp. M.Dut. *wemelen*, to bore with a wimble, L.G. *wemel, wemmel*, Dan. *vimmel*, a boring-tool, perh. cogn. with WHIM], *n.* A boring-instrument, a gimlet, brace-and-bit, etc. *v.t.* To bore with this.

wimple (wim′ pėl) [A.-S. *winpel* (perh. WIND (2), *pell, pæll*, L. PALLIUM), cp. Dut. and G. *wimpel*, Icel. *vimpill*, pennon, streamer], *n.* A covering of silk, linen, etc., worn over the head, neck, and sides of the face formerly by women and still by some nuns. **v.t.* To cover with a wimple; to fold in plaits, etc.; to hoodwink. *v.i.* To be folded in plaits, etc.; (*fig.*) to ripple.

Wimshurst machine (wimz′ hĕrst) [James *Wimshurst* (1832–1903)], *n.* (*Elec.*) A friction machine by which static electricity can be generated and stored.

win (win) [A.-S. *winnan*, to fight, to labour (cp. Dut. *winnen*, G. *gewinnen*, Icel. *vinna*), cogn. with L. *Venus*, desire, and WISH], *v.t.* (*past & p.p.* **won** (1), wŭn) To gain, obtain, achieve, or attain by fighting, struggling, or superiority in a contest, competition, wager, etc.; to gain by toil, etc., to earn; to be victorious in; to make one's way to, to reach; to attract, to charm (*in pres.p.*); to persuade, to secure the support, favour, or assent of, to gain over; to get or extract (ore, etc.) by mining, smelting, etc; (*slang*) to steal. *v.i.* To be successful or victorious in a fight, contest, wager, etc.; to make one's way by struggle or effort (to, etc.); to produce an attractive effect (upon). *n.* (*colloq.*) A success, a victory. **to win one's spurs** [SPURS]. **winner,** *n.* **winning,** *a.* That wins; attractive, charming. *n.pl.* The amount won at racing, in a game of cards, etc. **winning hazard** [HAZARD]. **winning-post,** *n.* A post marking the end of a race. **winningly,** *adv.*

wince (wins) [prob. from a non-extant O.F. *wencir*, from O.F. *guincir*, O.S. *wenkian*, cogn. with WINK], *v.i.* To shrink, start back, recoil or flinch, as from pain, trouble, or a blow. *n.* The act of wincing. **wincer,** *n.*

wincey (win′ si) [perh. corr. of LINSEY-WOOLSEY], *n.* A cotton cloth with wool filling. **winceyette,** *n.* A light-weight cotton cloth raised on both sides.

winch (winch) [A.-S. *wince*, cogn. with WINKLE], *n.* A windlass, a hoisting-machine; a crank or handle for turning an axle, etc.

wind (1) (wind, *poet.* wīnd) [A.-S., cp. Dut. and G. *wind*, Icel. *vindr*, also L. *ventus*, Sansk. *vātas*, cogn. with WEATHER], *n.* Air in motion, a natural air-current, a breeze, a gale; air set in motion artificially; air used or stored for use in a musical instrument, machine, etc.; (*collect.*) wind-instruments in an orchestra, etc.; breath as acquired by the body in exertion; power of breathing in exertion, lung power; a part of the body near the stomach a blow on which causes temporary inability to breathe; (*fig.*) breath expended in words, meaningless talk or rhetoric; the gas produced in the stomach during digestion, etc., flatulence; scent or odour carried on the wind; hence, a hint, suggestion, or indication (of); (*Naut.*) the windward position, the weather-gauge (of). *v.t.* (*past & p.p.* **winded**) To perceive the presence of by scent; to put out of breath; to enable to recover breath by resting, etc.; to expose to the wind, to ventilate. **to break wind:** To discharge wind from the anus. **how the wind blows:** The position or state of affairs. **in the wind's eye:** Towards the precise point from which the wind blows. **to get the wind up:** To get nervous, frightened. **something in the wind:** Signs of some unanticipated development. **the four winds:** The four cardinal points. **to raise the wind:** To procure the necessary amount of cash. **to take or get wind of:** To be divulged; to become publicly known. **to sail close to the wind:** To keep the vessel's head as near the quarter from which the wind is blowing as possible while keeping the sails filled; (*fig.*) to verge on indecency or dishonesty. **to take the wind out of one's sails:** To sail to the windward of; to frustrate by utilizing a person's own material or methods. **wind-bag,** *n.* A bag inflated with wind; (*fig.*) a man of mere words, a long-winded speaker. **wind-bound,** *a.* Prevented from sailing by contrary winds. **wind-cheater** (wind′ chē tĕr), *n.* A close-knitted pull-over or close-textured garment to keep out the wind. **wind-chest,** *n.* The box or reservoir for compressed air in an organ. **wind-colic,** *n.* Pain in the abdomen caused by flatulence. **wind cone, wind sock,** *n.* (*Aviat.*) An open-ended fabric sleeve flying from a mast, serving as an indicator of the strength and direction of the wind. **wind-egg,** *n.* An imperfect egg, esp. an unfertilized, addled, or shell-less one. **windfall,** *n.* Something blown down by the wind; (*Am.*) the track of a whirlwind by which trees are laid prostrate; (*fig.*) unexpected good fortune. **windfallen,** *a.* Blown down by the wind. **wind-fanner,** *n.* A windhover. **wind-flower,** *n.* (*poet.*) The wood-anemone. **wind-gall,** *n.* A soft tumour on the fetlock joint of a horse. **wind-gauge,** *n.* An anemometer; an instrument for showing the pressure in the wind-chest of an organ; a contrivance attached to the sight of a gun to show the allowance necessary for deflexion due to the wind. **windhover** (wind′ hŭv ėr), *n.* The kestrel. **wind-instrument,** *n.* A musical instrument in which the tones are produced by the vibration of an air-column forced into the pipes, reeds, etc., by a bellows or the mouth. **wind-jammer,** *n.* (*Naut.*) A merchant sailing-ship as dist. from a steamer; one of the crew of this. **windmill,** *n.* A mill driven by the action of the wind on sails; (*fig. pl.*) imaginary adversaries, chimeras (with alln. to Don Quixote); (*Aviat.*) a device for generating power to drive fuel pumps, wireless generators etc., by a small propeller blade placed in the slip-stream of an aircraft. **wind-pipe,** *n.* The breathing passage, the trachea. **wind-pump,** *n.* A pump operated by the force of the wind on a propeller. **windrow,** *n.* A row of hay raked together, corn-sheaves, peats, etc., set up for drying. **wind-sail,** *n.* (*Naut.*) A canvas tube used to convey a current of air into the lower parts of a ship. **wind sock** [WIND CONE]. **wind-screen,** *n.* (*Motor.*) A glass screen in the front of a motor-car to protect the driver and passengers from the wind caused by the speed of the car, (*Am.* wind-shield). **windshaken,** *a.* **wind-tight,** *a.* Air-tight, excluding the wind. **wind-tunnel,** *n.* A tunnel-like device for producing an air-stream of known velocity for testing the effect of wind on the structure of model aeroplanes from which full-sized craft will be built. **windage,** *n.* The difference between the diameter of the bore of a muzzle-loading rifled gun and that of the projectile; the influence of wind in deflecting a projectile; allowance for this. **windless,** *a.* **windward,** *n.* The direction from which the wind blows. *a.* Lying in or directed towards this. *adv.* In the direction from which the wind blows. **to get to the windward of:** To get to this side of, to get the weather-gauge of; (*fig.*) to get the advantage over. **windy,** *a.* Characterized by wind, stormy, boisterous; exposed to the wind; flatulent, caused by flatulence; (*fig.*) verbose, loquacious, empty; (*colloq.*) scared, frightened, apprehensive. **windily,** *adv.* **windiness,** *n.*

wind (2) (wīnd) [A.S. *windan* (cp. Dut. and G. *winden,* Icel. *vinda*), perh. cogn. with WITHY], *v.i.* (*past & p.p.* **wound,** wound) To turn, move, go, or be twisted or coiled in a spiral, curved, or tortuous course or shape; to be circular, spiral, tortuous, or crooked; to meander; to proceed circuitously, to twist one's way or insinuate oneself (into, etc.); to be wrapped spirally (round, into, etc.); to sound a horn by blowing. *v.t.* To cause to turn spirally, to wrap, twine, or coil; to encircle, to coil round, to entwine; to pursue (one's course) in a spiral, sinuous, or circuitous way; to hoist or move by means of a windlass, capstan, etc. **to wind off:** To unwind; to stop talking. **to wind up:** To coil up; to coil or tighten up the spring of (a watch, etc.); (*fig.*) to put into a state of tension or readiness for activity; to bring or come to a conclusion, to conclude; to arrange the final settlement of the affairs of (a business, etc.); to go into liquidation. **winder,** *n.* **winding,** *a.* and *n.* **winding-up,** *n.* **winding-drum,** *n.* A mechanically-driven drum on which a haulage rope is wound. **winding-engine,** *n.* A hoisting engine. **winding-sheet,** *n.* The sheet in which a corpse is wrapped. **winding-stair,** *n.* (*Build.*) A stair built around a newel. **winding-tackle,** *n.* **windingly,** *adv.*

windage, windhover, etc. [WIND (1)].

windlass (1) (wind' lȧs) [M.E. *windelas,* Icel. *vindilāss* (*vindill,* winder, from *vinda,* to WIND (2), *āss,* pole, beam)], *n.* A machine consisting of a cylinder on an axle turned by a crank, used for hoisting or hauling. *v.t.* To hoist or haul with this.

***windlass** (2) (wīnd' lȧs) [prob. corr. of M.E. *wanlace,* O.F. *wanelace,* deceit, artifice], *n.* (*Shak.*) A circuit, an indirect or crafty course.

windle (win' dėl) [A.-S. *windel,* from *windan,* to WIND (2)], *n.* (*prov.*) A reel, a spindle; *an old dry measure of about $3\frac{1}{2}$ bushels.

windle-straw (win' dėl straw) [A.-S. *windel-strēaw* (*windel,* basket, from *windan,* to WIND (2), STRAW)], *n.* The old stalks of various grasses.

windless, windmill [WIND (1)].

window (win' dō) [Icel. *vindauga* (*vindr,* WIND (1), *auga,* cp. A.-S. *ēage,* EYE)], *n.* An opening in the wall or roof of a building, vehicle, or other structure, usu. with the wooden or metal glazed frame-work filling it, for the admission of light or of light and air; the sash of a window-frame. **window-bar,** *n.* The bar of a sash or window-frame; *(*pl.*) lattice-work on a woman's stomacher. **window-blind,** *n.* **window-box,** *n.* The casing in which a sash-weight slides; a flower-box for a window-sill. **window-curtain,** *n.* **window-dressing,** *n.* The arrangement of goods for display in a shop window; (*fig.*) deceptive display, insincere argument. **window-envelope,** *n.* An envelope with an open or transparent panel through which the address can be seen. **window-frame,** *n.* The frame-work in a window holding the sashes. **window-glass,** *n.* **window-sash,** *n.* A frame in which panes of glass for windows are set. **window-seat,** *n.* A seat in the recess of a window. **windowed,** *a.* (*usu. in comb.* as *many-windowed*). **windowless,** *a.* ***windowy,** *a.*

windpipe, windrow [WIND (1)].

Windsor (win' zȯr) [town in Berks.], *n.* **Windsor chair:** A strong, plain wooden chair with a back curved into supports for the arms. **Windsor soap:** A brown scented soap formerly made at Windsor. **brown Windsor,** *n.* Windsor soup; a common, tasteless soup.

windward, windy, etc. [WIND (1)].

wine (wīn) [A.-S. *wīn,* L. *vīnum* (cp. Dut. *wijn,* G. *wein,* also Gr. *oinos*), cogn. with WITHE, from *wei-,* to twine], *n.* The fermented juice of grapes; the juice of certain fruits, etc., prepared in imitation of this; intoxication; (*Univ.*) a wine party; (*Med.*) a medicinal preparation in wine as medium. **spirit of wine** [SPIRIT]. **winebag,** *n.* A skin for holding wine; (*fig.*) a wine-bibber. **wine-bibber,** *n.* A wine-drinker, a tippler. **wine-bibbing,** *n.* **wine-bottle,** *n.* **wine-bowl,** *n.* **wine-carriage,** *n.* A wheeled receptacle for circulating a wine-bottle at table. **wine-cask,** *n.* **wine-cellar,** *n.* **wine-cooler,** *n.* A vessel for cooling wine in bottles with ice. **wine-cup,** *n.* ***winefat,** *n.* A winepress. **wineglass,** *n.* A small glass for drinking wine from. **wineglassful,** *n.* About two fluid oz. **wine-grower,** *n.* **wine-measure,** *n.* An old English measure by which wine and spirits were sold. **wine-merchant,** *n.* **wine-palm,** *n.* One from which palm-wine is obtained. **winepress,** *n.* An apparatus in which grapes are pressed; the place in which this is done. **wineskin,** *n.* A skin, usu. of a goat, sewed into a bag for holding wine. **wine-stone,** *n.* A deposit of crude tartar or argal in wine-casks. **wine-vault,** *n.* A vault in which wine is stored; a bar or tap-room where wine is retailed. **wineless,** *a.* **winy,** *a.*

wing (wing) [M.E. *wingè, wenge,* Norw. *vengja* (cp. Icel. *vængr,* Dan. and Swed. *vinge*), cogn. with Sansk. *vā,* to blow], *n.* One of the limbs or organs of flight in birds, insects, etc.; one of the supporting parts of a flying-machine; (*fig.*) motion by means of wings, flight, power of flight; (*colloq.*) an arm; a part of a building, fortification, army, bone, implement, etc., projecting laterally; (*Aviat.*) a R.A.F. unit of three squadrons; (*Football, etc.*), a player on one or other extreme flank; (*Motor.*) one of the front-wheel mudguards of a car, (*Am.* a fender); (*Theat., pl.*) the sides of the stage or pieces of scenery placed there; two lateral petals of a papilionaceous flower which stand opposite each other; (*Aviat. pl.*) the mark of proficiency a pilot qualified in the R.A.F. is entitled to wear on his uniform. *v.t.* To furnish with wings; to enable to fly or move with swiftness; to traverse or travel on wings; to wound in the wing or (*colloq.*) the arm. *v.i.* To fly. **on the wing:** Flying; in motion. **to take under one's wing:** To take under one's protection. **to take wing:** To begin flying, to fly away; (*fig.*) to disappear. **wing and wing:** (*Naut.*) Said of a fore-and-aft vessel going before the wind with her fore-sail hauled over to one side and main-sail to the other. **wing-beat,** *n.* A complete stroke of the wing in flying. **wing-case,** *n.* The horny cover or case, consisting of a modified wing, protecting the flying wings of coleopterous insects. **wing-covert,** *n.* One of the small feathers covering the insertion of a bird's flight-feathers. **wing-footed,** *a.* Having wings on the feet; swift. **wing-sheath,** *n.* A wing-case. **wing-stroke,** *n.* A wing-beat. **winged,** *a.* Furnished with wings; (*poet.,* wing' ėd) going straight to the mark, powerful, rousing (of words, etc.). **wingless,** *a.* **winglet,** *n.* ***wingy,** *a.*

wink (wingk) [A.-S. *wincian* (cp. M. Dut. *wincken*, G. *winken*, Icel. *vanka*), *cogn.* with WINCE and WINKLE], *v.i.* To close and open the eyes quickly, to blink; to close and open (of an eye); to give a sign or signal by such a motion of the eye; (*fig.*) to twinkle, to flicker. *v.t.* To close and open (an eye or the eyes). *n.* The act of winking, esp. as a signal; a hint, a private intimation. **forty winks:** (*colloq.*) A nap. **to tip one the wink:** To give one a hint privately. **to wink at:** To affect not to see; to connive at. **winker,** *n.* **like winking:** Very rapidly; with great vigour. **winkingly,** *adv.*

winkle (wing' kėl) [A.-S. *-wincla*, in *wine-wincla*, cogn. with prec. and WINCH], *n.* An edible sea-snail, a periwinkle. **to winkle out:** (*Mil.*) To extract sharpshooters and small bodies of enemy troops from hiding-places.

winna (*Sc.*) [WILL NOT]. **winning,** etc. [WIN].

winnow (win' ō) [A.-S. *windwian*, from WIND (1)], *v.t.* To separate and drive the chaff from (grain); to fan chaff (away, out, etc.); (*fig.*) to sift, to sort, to examine or analyse thoroughly; to blow on, to stir (hair, etc.); (*poet.*) to beat or flap (wings). **winnower,** *n.* **winnowing,** *n.*

winsey [WINCEY].

winsome (win' sŏm) [A.-S. *wynsum* (*wynn*, joy, cogn. with WIN, -SOME)], *a.* Engaging, winning, charming, attractive; graceful, lovely. **winsomely,** *adv.* **winsomeness,** *n.*

winter (win' tėr) [A.-S., cp. Dut. and G. *winter*, Dan. and Swed. *vinter*, perh. cogn. with L. *unda*, wave, Eng. WET and WATER], *n.* The cold season of the year, astronomically in northern latitudes from the December solstice to the March equinox. usu. regarded as including December, January, February; (*fig.*) a period of inactivity, a cheerless or depressing state of things; (*poet.*). a year of life. *a.* Pertaining, suitable to, or lasting for the winter. *v.i.* To pass the winter; to hibernate. *v.t.* To keep, manage, or maintain through the winter. **winter-apple,** *n.* An apple that keeps well or ripens in winter. **winter-barley,** *n.* A kind of barley sown in autumn. **winterberry,** *n.* A N. American shrub of the genus *Ilex*, bearing bright red berry-like drupes. **winter-cough,** *n.* Chronic bronchitis. **winter-cress,** *n.* A herb of the mustard family grown in the winter as a salad. **winter-crop,** *n.* **winter-garden,** *n.* A large conservatory or glass-house for plants not hardy enough to withstand the climate outside during winter. **winter-green,** *n.* A low herb of the genus *Pyrola*, keeping green throughout the winter. **winter-lodge,** *n.* (*Bot.*) A bud or bulb protecting an embryo or very young shoot during the winter. **winter-quarters,** *n.pl.* The quarters occupied by an army, etc., during the winter. **winterless,** *a.* **winterly, wintery, wintry,** *a.* **wintriness,** *n.*

Winters-bark (win' tėrz bark), *n.* A tree of the magnolia family, *Drimys Winteri*, brought from the Straits of Magellan by Capt. John Winter in 1579; the aromatic bark of this.

winy [WINE].

winze (winz) [prob. cogn. with WINNOW], *n.* (*Mining*) A shaft sunk from one level to another for communication or ventilation.

wipe (wīp) [A.-S. *wipian*, cp. E. Fris. *wīp*, L.G. *wiep*], *v.t.* To rub with something soft in order to clean or dry; to apply solder to with something soft. *v.i.* To strike (at). *n.* The act of wiping; a sweeping blow. **to wipe away:** To remove by wiping; to get rid of. **to wipe off:** To clear away. **to wipe one's eye:** (*slang*) To steal a march on one. **to wipe one's eyes:** (*fig.*) To cease weeping. **to wipe out:** To clean out by wiping; to efface, to obliterate; to destroy, to annihilate. **to wipe the floor with:** (*slang*) To defeat utterly. **wiper,** *n.* Cloth, etc., used for wiping; (*Motor.*) an automatically operated arm to keep a portion of the windscreen free from rain. **wipe-out,** *n.* (*Radio.*) Interference that renders impossible the reception of other signals. **wipe-out area,** *n.* (*Radio.*) The vicinity of a transmitting station where wipe-out occurs.

wire (wīr) [A.-S. *wīr* (cp. Icel. *virr*, Swed. *vira*, to twist, also L. *viriæ*, armlets), cogn. with WITHE], *n.* Metal drawn out into a slender and flexible rod or thread of uniform diameter; such a slender rod, thread, or strand of metal; (*fig.*) the electric telegraph, a telegraphic message. *v.t.* To apply wire to, to fasten, secure, bind, or stiffen with wire; to string (beads) on a wire; to snare with wire; (*colloq.*) to telegraph to. *v.i.* To send a telegram. **to pull the wires:** To manipulate puppets; (*fig.*) to control politics, etc., by clandestine means. **live wire,** *n.* (*Elec.*) A wire charged with electricity; (*colloq.*) an energetic, resourceful man. **to wire in:** (*slang*) To apply oneself vigorously. **wire-cloth, -gauze, -netting,** *n.* A fabric of woven wire. **wire-cutter,** *n.* An implement for cutting wire. **wire-dancer,** *n.* An acrobat performing on a tight wire. **wiredraw,** *v.t.* (*p.p.* **-drawn**) To form (metal) into wire by forcibly drawing through a series of gradually diminishing holes; (*fig.*) to overstrain or over-refine (an argument, etc.). **wiredrawer,** *n.* **wire-edge,** *n.* An edge turned back like wire, on a knife, etc., by over-sharpening. **wire-entanglement,** *n.* An obstruction composed of interlacing barbed wire defending the front of an entrenchment, etc., against a rapid assault. **wire-gun,** *n.* A heavy gun constructed of steel wire of rectangular section coiled round a tube. **wire-haired,** *a.* Having stiff, wiry hair (esp. of terriers). **wire-heel,** *n.* A disease of the foot in horses. **wire-puller,** *n.* (*fig.*) A politician, etc., working behind the scenes. **wire-pulling,** *n.* **wire-rope,** *n.* A rope made by twisting strands of wire. **wireworm,** *n.* A vermiform larva of a click-beetle, destructive to roots of vegetables, cereals, etc. **wirer,** *n.* **wiry,** *a.* Made of or resembling wire; tough and flexible; lean but sinewy; stiff (of hair, etc.). **wirily,** *adv.* **wiriness,** *n.*

wireless (wī' ėr less), *n.* Wireless telegraphy; radio; any process or method whereby messages, music or other sounds can be transmitted in the ether by electro-magnetic waves without the intervention of wires; an instrument for receiving such messages, etc.; the programmes of entertainment, etc., thus transmitted; radio. *v.t.* and *i.* (*colloq.*) To communicate with or inform by this.

wirrycow (wir' i kou) [etym. doubtful], *n.* (*Sc.*) A hobgoblin, a bogy; the devil.

***wis** (wis) [supposed pres. of WIT (1), evolved from *iwis*, *ywis*, A.-S. *gewis*, certain], *v.i.*, *1st sing.* (I) know. ***wisard** [WIZARD].

wisdom (wiz' dŏm) [A.-S.], *n.* The quality or state of being wise; knowledge and experience together with ability to make use of them rightly, practical discernment, sagacity, judgment, common sense; *a collection of wise sayings. **wisdom-tooth,** *n.* The third molar appearing about the age of twenty.

wise (1) (wīz) [A.-S. *wīs* (cp. Dut. *wijs*, G. *weise*, Icel. *viss*), cogn. with WIT (1)], *a.* Having or characterized by the power or faculty of discerning or judging rightly, or by knowledge and experience together with ability to apply them rightly, sagacious, sensible, discreet, prudent, judicious; experienced, understanding; *having occult knowledge. **to put someone wise:** To inform someone. **wisecrack,** *n.* (*colloq.*) A smart but not profound epigram; a witty comment. ***wise man:** A wizard. **wise woman:** A witch, a fortune-teller; (*Sc.*) a midwife. **wiseacre** (wī' zā kėr) [M.Dut. *wijs-sagger*, G. *weissager*, from M.H.G. *wīzago*, a prophet (cp. A.-S. *wītiga*, prophet, from *wītan*, to see, cogn. with *witan*, to WIT (1))], *n.* One pretending to learning or wisdom. ***wiseling,** *n.* A wiseacre. **wisely,** *adv.* ***wiseness,** *n.*

wise (2) (wīz) [A.-S. (cp. Dut. *wijs*, G. *weise*, Dan. *viis*, Swed. *vis*), from *wīsian*, to show the way, orig. to make WISE (1)], *n.* Manner, way, mode of acting, behaving, etc., guise.

-wise [WISE (2)], *suf.* Forming adverbs of manner, as *anywise, lengthwise, likewise, otherwise.*

wiseacre, etc. [WISE (1)].

wish (wish) [A.-S. *wȳscan* (cp. Dut. *wenschen,* G. *wunschen,* Icel. *æskja*), cogn. with WIN], *v.t.* To have a strong desire, aspiration, or craving (that, etc.), to crave, to covet, to want; to frame or express a desire or wish concerning, to invoke, to bid. *v.i.* To have a strong desire (for). *n.* A desire, a longing, an aspiration; an expression of this, a request, a petition, an invocation; that which is desired. **wisher,** *n.* (*usu. in comb.* as *well-wisher*). **wishful,** *a.* **wishful thinking,** *n.* Belief based on desires rather than facts. **wishfully,** *adv.* **wishfulness,** *n.* **wish-bone, wishing-bone,** *n.* The merrythought, the longer part of which when broken by two persons is supposed to entitle the holder to the fulfilment of some wish. **wishing-cap,** *n.* A magic cap conferring the power of realizing one's wishes.

wishtonwish (wish' ton wish) [N. Am. Ind.], *n.* The N. American prairie-dog.

wish-wash (wish' wosh) [redupl. of WASH], *n.* Thin weak liquor or drink; (*fig.*) feeble talk, claptrap **wishy-washy,** *a.*

***wisket** [WHISKET].

wisp (wisp) [M.E., var. *wips* (cp. L.G. *wiep,* Norw. *vippa*), cogn. with WIPE], *n.* A small bunch or handful of straw, hay, etc.; a tuft; a thin band or streak. **wispy,** *a.*

wist, *past* [WIT (1)].

wistaria (wis târ' i à) [after Caspar *Wistar* (1761–1818), *n.* A leguminous climbing shrub with racemes of lilac-coloured flowers.

wistful (wist' ful) [etym. doubtful (perh. WHIST (1), -FUL, conf. with WISHFUL)], *a.* Full of vague yearnings, esp. for unattainable things, sadly longing; thoughtful in a melancholy way, pensive. **wistfully,** *adv.* **wistfulness,** *n.*

wistiti, ouistiti (wis' ti ti) [S. Am. native], *n.* The marmoset.

***wit** (1) (wit) [A.-S. *witan* (cp. Dut. *weten,* G. *wissen,* Icel, *vita*), cogn. with L. *vidēre,* Gr. *idein,* to see, *oida,* I know, Sansk, *vēda*], *v.t.* and *i.* (*1st sing.* **wot,** *2nd sing.* **wottest,** *past* **wist;** *no other parts used*) To know (esp. in the infinitive 'to wit,' namely). **witting,** *a.* **wittingly,** *adv.* Consciously, knowingly, intentionally.

wit (2) (wit) [A.-S. *witt,* knowledge, from *witan,* see prec.], *n.* Intelligence, understanding, sense, sagacity (*often in pl.*); the power of perceiving analogies and other relations between apparently incongruous ideas or of forming unexpected, striking, or ludicrous combinations of them; a person distinguished for this power, a witty person; *a wise man. **at one's wits' end:** At a complete loss what further steps to take. ***the five wits:** The five senses; the mental faculties. **witticism,** *n.* A witty phrase or saying, a jest. **witless,** *a.* **witlessly,** *adv.* **witlessness,** *n.* ***witling,** *n.* One with little wit or understanding. **witty,** *a.* **wittily,** *adv.* **wittiness,** *n.* **witted,** *a.* (*usu. in comb.* as *slow-witted*).

witch (1) (wich) [A.-S. *wicca,* masc., fem. *wicce,* rel. to *wiccian,* to practise sorcery (cp. Icel. *vikja,* to turn aside, to exorcize, A.-S. *wīcan,* to give way), cogn. with WEAK], *n.* A woman having dealings with evil spirits or practising the black art or sorcery; a bewitching or fascinating woman; an old and ugly woman, a hag. *v.t.* To bewitch, to fascinate, to enchant. **witchcraft,** *n.* The practices of witches; sorcery, magic. **witch-doctor,** *n.* A medicine-man. **witch-finder,** *n.* (*Hist.*) One whose business was to discover witches. **witch hunt:** (*U.S.A. Pol.*) The searching out and public exposure of opponents accused of disloyalty to the state. **witchery,** *n.* **witching,** *a.* **witchingly,** *adv.*

witch (2), **witch-elm, witch-hazel** [WYCH].

witchetty (wich' ė ti) [Austral. abor.], *n.* The edible grub of a longicorn beetle.

***wite** (wīt) [A.-S. *wītan,* cogn. with *witan,* see WIT (1)], *v.t.* To blame, to censure. *n.* Blame, reproach. ***witeless,** *a.*

witenagemot (wit' ė nà gė mōt) [A.-S. *witena,* gen. pl. of WITAN, GEMOTE], *n.* The Anglo-Saxon national assembly or parliament.

with (wi*th*) [A.-S., from *wither,* against (cp. Icel. *vith,* Dan. *ved,* Swed. *vid*), superseding A.-S. and M.E. *mid,* with], *prep.* In or into company of or the relation of accompaniment, association, simultaneousness, co-operation, harmoniousness, etc.; having, possessed of, marked or characterized by; in the possession, care, or guardianship of; by the means, instrumentality, use, or aid of; by the addition or supply of; because of, owing to, in consequence of; in regard to, in respect of, concerning, in the case of; in separation from; in opposition to, against. **with child,** *adv.* Pregnant. **with young,** *adv.* (Of a mammal) pregnant.

withal (wi *th*awl'), *adv.* With the rest, in addition, at the same time, further, moreover. ****prep.*** (*used after its obj.*) With.

withdraw (wi*th* draw'), *v.t.* (*past* **-drew,** *p.p.* **-drawn**) To draw back, aside, or apart; to take away, to remove, to retract. *v.i.* To retire from a presence or place; to go apart or aside. **withdrawal,** *n.* **withdrawer,** *n.* ***withdrawing-room,** *n.* A drawing-room.

withe (wi*th,* with, wī*th*) [WITHY], *n.* A tough, flexible branch, esp. of willow or osier, used in binding things together; a band or tie made of osiers, twigs, straw, etc.

wither (wi*th*' ėr) [M.E. *widren, wederen,* to expose to the weather, from *weder,* WEATHER], *v.t.* To cause to fade, shrivel, or dry, to shrivel and dry (up); to cause to lose freshness, soundness, vitality or vigour; (*fig.*) to blight, to blast. *v.i.* To become dry and wrinkled; to dry and shrivel (up); to lose freshness, soundness, vigour, etc.; to fade away, to languish, to droop. **witheredness,** *n.* **withering,** *a.* **witheringly,** *adv.*

withers (wi*th*' ėrz) [A.-S. *wither,* against (because it is against the collar or load), see WITH], *n.pl.* The ridge between the shoulder-blades of a horse. **wither-wrung,** *a.* Injured or hurt in the withers.

withershins (wi*th*' ėr shinz) [Icel. *vithr,* against (cp. Dan. and Swed. *veder,* A.-S. *wither,* Dut. *weder,* G. *wieder*), Icel, *sinni,* walk, movement, cogn. with A.-S. *sīth*], *adv.* Anti-clockwise, in the contrary direction, esp. to the left or opposite to the direction of the sun, opp. to deiseal.

withhold (wi*th* hōld'), *v.t.* (*past & p.p.* **-held**) To keep from action, to hold back, to refuse to grant, to refrain; *to maintain. ***withholden,** *p.p.* Withheld. **withholder,** *n.* **withholdment,** *n.*

within (wi *th*in') [A.-S. *widhinnan,* on the inside], *adv.* Inside, in or to the inside, in the inner part or parts, internally, indoors, in the mind, heart, or spirit. *n.* The inside. *prep.* In or to the inner or interior part or parts of, inside; in the limits, range, scope, or compass of; not beyond, not outside of, not farther off than; in no longer a time than.

without (wi *th*out') [A.-S. *withūtan*], *adv.* In, at, or to the outside, outside, outwardly, externally, out of doors. *n.* The outside. *prep.* Not having, not with, having no, destitute of, lacking, free from; outside of; out of the limits, compass, or range of, beyond. *conj.* (*incorr.*) Unless, except. ***without-door,** *a.* Outdoor; outward, external.

withstand (wi*th* stănd') [A.-S. *withstandan*], *v.t.* (*past & p.p.* **-stood**) To stand up against, to resist, to oppose. *v.i.* (*poet.*) To make a stand or resistance (against). **withstander,** *n.*

withwind (with' wīnd) [WITHE, WIND (2)], *n.* (*prov.*) The bindweed and other climbing weeds.

withy (wi*th*' i) [A.-S. *withig* (cp. M. Dut. *wiede,* G. *weide,* Icel. *vithja*), cogn. with Gr. *itea,* willow, L. *vitis,* vine], *n.* A withe; a willow.

witness (wit' nės) [A.-S. *witnes* (WIT (1), -NESS)], *n.* Attestation of a fact, etc., testimony, evidence; a thing that constitutes evidence or proof, confirmation; a thing or person serving as testimony to or proof of; one who has seen or known an incident, etc., a spectator, a person present at an event; one who gives evidence in a law-court or for judicial purposes, esp. on oath; one who affixes his name to a document to testify to the genuineness of the signature. *v.t.* To see or know by personal presence, to be a spectator of; to attest, to sign as witness; (*fig.*) to indicate, to show, to prove; *to state in evidence. *v.i.* To bear testimony, to testify, to give evidence; to serve as evidence (against, for, etc.); *to be a witness (in invocations, etc.). **witness-box,** *n.* An enclosure in a law-court for witnesses, (*Am.* witness-stand). **witnessable,** *a.*

witticism, etc. [WIT (2)]. **wittingly,** etc. [WIT (1)].

wittol (wit′ ŏl) [perh. corr. of WITWALL], *n.* One who puts up with his wife's infidelity. ***wittolly,** *a.*

witty [WIT (2)].

***witwall** (wit′ wawl) [var. of obs. *woodwall, wodewale*, cp. M.Dut. *weduwael*, O.H.G. *witewal*], *n.* The green or the greater spotted woodpecker; the golden oriole.

***wive** (wīv) [A.-S. *wīfian*, from *wīf*, WIFE], *v.t.* To take for a wife; to provide with a wife. *v.i.* To marry a wife.

wiver, wivern [WYVERN]. **wives** [WIFE].

wiwi (wē′ wē) [Maori], *n.* A small, fine grass.

wizard (wiz′ ărd) [M.E. *wisard* (*wīs*, WISE (1), -ARD)], *n.* A sorcerer, an enchanter, a magician; (*fig.*) one who works wonders. *a.* Magic, enchanting, enchanted. *a.* (*slang*) wonderful, marvellous. **Wizard of the North:** Sir Walter Scott. **wizardry,** *n.*

wizen (wizn) [A.-S. *wisnian* (cp. Icel. *visna*, from *visinn*, withered), cogn. with L. VIRUS, Sansk. *visha-*], *v.t.* and *i.* To wither, to dry up, to shrivel. *a.* Wizened.

wo (1) [WHOA]. ***wo** (2), etc. [WOE].

woad (wōd) [A.-S. *wād* (cp. Dut. *weede*, G. *waid*, O.F. *waide*, F. *guède*), cogn. with L. *vitrum*, Gr. *isatis*], *n.* A plant, *Isatis tinctoria*, yielding a blue dye; this dye formerly in use for staining the body, esp. by the ancient Britons. **woaded,** *a.*

wobbegong (wob′ e gong) [Austral. abor.], *n.* A mottle-skin shark also known as the carpet shark.

wobble [WABBLE].

wobbles (wob′ elz), *n.* (*Austral.*) A W. Australian horse- and cattle-disease caused by eating poisonous palm-leaves.

woe (wō) [A.-S. *wā*, int., cp. Dut. *wee*, G. *weh*, Icel. *vei*, L. *væ*], *n.* Sorrow, affliction, distress, calamity, overwhelming grief. **woe worth the day** [WORTH (2)]. **woebegone,** *a.* Overcome with woe, sorrowful-looking, dismal. **woeful, *woesome,** *a.* **woefully,** *adv.* **woefulness,** *n.*

wold (wōld) [A.-S. *weald* (*wald*, forest, cp. Dut. *woud*, G. *wald*, Icel. *völlr*), cp. WEALD], *n.* A tract of open country, esp. downland or moorland.

wolf (wulf) [A.-S. *wulf*, cp. Dut. and G. *wolf*, Icel. *ūlfr*, L. *lupus*, Gr. *lukos*, Sansk. *vrka-*, from *welq-*, to tear], *n.* (*pl.* **wolves**) A grey, tawny-grey, reddish, or white carnivorous quadruped, closely allied to the dog, preying on sheep, calves, etc., and hunting larger animals in packs; (*fig.*) a rapacious, ravenous, greedy, or cruel person; (*Mus.*) a discordant sound in certain chords of a keyboard instrument, esp. an organ, due to unequal temperament. *v.t.* To devour ravenously, to gulp or swallow (down) greedily. **to cry wolf:** To raise a false alarm. **to keep the wolf from the door:** To keep off starvation. **wolf-cub,** *n.* A member of the junior branch of the Boy Scouts. **wolf-dog,** *n.* A large dog used for guarding sheep against wolves; a cross between a wolf and a dog. **wolf-fish,** *n.* A large voracious fish, also called a sea-wolf. **wolf-hound,** *n.* A large powerful dog of Russian or Irish breed. **wolf's-bane,** *n.* A species of aconite or monk's-hood. *A. lycoctonum.* **wolf's-claw, wolf's-foot,** *n.* Club-moss, *Lycopodium clavatum.* **wolf's-fist,** *n.* A puff-ball. **wolf-tooth,** *n.* A small additional pre-molar in horses. **wolfish,** *a.* **wolfishly,** *adv.* **wolfishness,** *n.* **wolf-whistle,** *n.* A vulgar whistle made by a male at the sight of an attractive girl.

wolfram (wul′ fram) [G., wolf-cream], *n.* (*Min.*) A native tungsten-ore composed of tungstate of iron and manganese; tungsten.

wollomai (wol′ ŏ mī) [Austral. abor.], *n.* An edible fish, sometimes known as the snapper.

wolverine (wul′ vėr ēn) [dim. of WOLF, after M.H.G. *wölfelin*], *n.* A small N. American carnivorous animal, *Gulo luscus*, also called the glutton or carcajou.

woman (wum′ ăn) [A.-S. *wīfman* (WIFE, MAN)], *n.* (*pl.* **women,** wim′ ėn), *n.* An adult human female; womankind, the female sex; womanly feeling, womanliness, (*fig.*) an effeminate, or timid and tender man; *a female attendant on a person of rank, a lady-in-waiting. *a.* Female. *v.t.* To cause to act or behave like a woman; to address or speak of as 'woman.' **to make an honest woman of** [HONEST]. **to play the woman:** To weep; to give vent to emotion, esp. fear. **woman of the world:** A woman skilled in the ways of the world; a society woman. **woman-born,** *a.* Born of a woman. **womenfolk,** *n.* One's womenkind; women collectively. **woman-hater,** *n.* A misogynist. **womankind,** *n.* Women collectively, the female sex; (*colloq.*) the women of one's household. ***woman-post,** *n.* (*Shak.*) A female messenger. **woman suffrage:** The exercise of the electoral franchise by or its extension to women. ***woman-tired,** *a.* (*Shak.*) Henpecked. **womanhood,** *n.* **womanish,** *a.* Having the character or qualities of a woman, effeminate. ***womanishly,** *adv.* **womanishness,** *n.* **womanize,** *v.t.* To make effeminate, to unman. *v.i.* To be given to fornication. **womanless,** *a.* **womanlike,** *a.* and *adv.* **womanly,** *a.* Having the qualities becoming a woman, truly feminine. *adv.* In the manner of a woman. **womanliness,** *n.* **Women's Institutes,** *n.pl.* A rural organization of women in England, non-political and non-sectarian, for mutual training and improvement in domestic and social life.

womb (woom) [A.-S. *wamb*, cp. Dut. *wam*. G. *wampe, wamme*, Icel. *vömb*], *n.* The organ in a woman or other female mammal in which the young is developed before birth, the uterus; (*fig.*) the place where anything is engendered or brought into existence; *a deep cavity. **wombed,** *a.* Having a womb; (*fig.*) capacious. ***womby,** *a.* Deep, hollow, capacious.

wombat (wom′ băt) [Austral. abor.], *n.* An Australian nocturnal marsupial mammal. *Phascolomys ursinus*, resembling a small bear.

women, *pl.* [WOMAN].

womerah (wom′ ĕr a) [Austral. abor.], *n.* A throwing-stick.

won (1) *past & p.p.* [WIN].

***won** (2) wŭn) [A.-S. *gewunian* (cp. G. *gewohnen*, to be used to, Icel. *venja*, to accustom), cogn. with WONT], *v.t.* To dwell, to abide; to be accustomed. *n.* A dwelling, an abode; custom, habit. ***woning,** *n.* A dwelling.

wonder (wŭn′ dėr) [A.-S. *wunder*, a portent (cp. Dut. *wonder*, G. *wunder*, Icel. *undr*), perh. cogn. with *wandiian*, to turn aside from, to reverse, *n.* A strange, remarkable, or marvellous thing, event, action, incident, etc., a miracle, a prodigy; the emotion excited by that which is unexpected, strange, extraordinary, or inexplicable, or which arrests by its grandeur; surprise mingled with admiration. *v.i.* To be struck with wonder or surprise; to look with or feel wonder; to feel doubt or curiosity (about, etc.). **nine days' wonder** [NINE]. **no wonder:** It is not surprising (that, etc.); quite natural, of course. **seven wonders of the world** [SEVEN]. **wonder-struck, -stricken,** *a.* ***wonder-worker,** *n.* One who performs wonders. **wonder-working,** *a.* **wonder-wounded,** *a.* (*Shak.*) Struck with wonder. ***wondered,** *a.*

(*Shak.*) Having performed wonders; wonder-working. **wonderer,** *n.* **wonderingly,** *adv.*

wonderful (wŭn′ dėr fûl), *a.* Astonishing, strange, admirable; exciting wonder or astonishment. **wonderfully,** *adv.* Admirably; strangely; greatly. **wonderfulness,** *n.*

wonderland (wŭn′ dėr lănd), *n.* A land of marvels, fairyland.

wondrous (wŭn′ drŭs), *a.* Wonderful, marvellous, strange. *adv.* Wonderfully, exceedingly. **wondrously,** *adv.*

wonga-wonga (wong′ gȧ wong′ gȧ) [Austral. abor.], *n.* The large Australian white-faced pigeon, *Leucosarcia picata.*

wonk (wongk) [Austral. abor.], *n.* (*Austral. colloq.*) A white man.

wonky (wong′ ki), *a.* (*slang*) Unsteady, shaky.

wont (wōnt, wŭnt) [M.E. *woned,* p.p. of *wonen,* to dwell, to be accustomed, in sense to *wone,* A.-S. *gewun,* used, accustomed, cp. WON (2)], *a.* Used, accustomed (to); using or doing habitually. *n.* Custom, habit, use. *v. aux.* To be accustomed or used (to). **wonted,** *a.* Customary, habitual, usual. ***wontedness,** *n.*

woo (woo) [M.E. *wowen, wogen,* A.-S. *wōgian,* in *awōgian,* from *wōh,* bent], *v.t.* To court, to make love to, to solicit in marriage; to seek to gain or attain; to solicit, to coax, to importune. *v.i.* To make love, to go courting. **wooer,** *n.* **wooingly,** *adv.*

wood (1) (wud) [A.-S. *wudu,* cp. Icel. *vithr,* Dan. and Swed. *ved,* O.H.G. *witu,* Ir. and Gael. *fiodh,* W. *gwydd*], *n.* A large and thick collection of growing trees, a forest (*often in pl.*); the fibrous substance of a tree between the bark and the pith; trees, timber; (*Bowls*) a bowl; (*Mus.*) the wood-wind. **drawn from the wood:** Drawn from the cask. **out of the wood:** Out of danger. **wood-agate,** *n.* An agate derived from wood by silicification and still showing the woody structure. **wood alcohol,** *n.* (*Chem.*) Methyl alcohol, formerly produced by the distillation of wood, now synthesized. **wood-anemone,** *n.* The wild anemone, *A. nemorosa.* **wood-ashes,** *n.pl.* The ashes of burnt wood or plants. **woodbine** [A.-S. *wudebinde* (BIND)], *n.* The wild honeysuckle. **wood-block,** *n.* A die cut in box or other wood for striking impressions from; a wood-cut. **woodchuck** [corr. of N. Am. Ind. *wejack*], *n.* A N. American marmot, *Arctomys monax.* **wood-coal,** *n.* Charcoal; lignite. **woodcock,** *n.* A game-bird of the genus *Scolopax* or *Philohela,* related to the snipe. **wood-craft,** *n.* Skill in anything pertaining to life in the woods or forest, esp. in hunting. **wood-cut,** *n.* An engraving on wood, a wood-block; a print or impression from this. **wood-cutter,** *n.* One who cuts wood or timber; an engraver on wood. **wood-engraver,** *n.* An engraver on wood; a beetle that bores under the bark of trees. **wood-engraving,** *n.* **wood-fibre,** *n.* Fibre obtained from wood, used for paper-making, etc. **wood-fretter,** *n.* An insect that eats into wood. **wood-gas,** *n.* Illuminating gas produced by dry distillation of wood. **wood-grouse,** *n.* The capercailzie. **wood-hole,** *n.* A place where wood is stored. **wood-house,** *n.* **wood-ibis,** *n.* A variety of stork from the southern U.S.A. **wood-land,** *n.* Land covered with woods, wooded country; *a.* Pertaining to this, sylvan. **wood-lark,** *n.* A European lark, *Alauda arborea,* smaller than the skylark. **wood-layer,** *n.* A young oak or other timber plant laid down among bushes, etc., planted to make hedges. **wood-leopard,** *n.* A moth the caterpillars of which live in the wood of fruit trees. **wood-louse,** *n.* A wingless isopod insect of the family *Oniseidæ,* infesting decayed wood, etc. **woodman,** *n.* A forester; one who fells timber; a wood-cutter. **wood-note,** *n.* A wild or natural note or song; (*fig.*) artless poetry. **wood-nymph,** *n.* A dryad; a brilliantly-coloured moth of the genus *Endryas*; a variety of humming-bird. **wood-offering,** *n.* (*Bibl.*) Wood burnt on the altar. **wood-opal,** *n.* Silicified wood. **wood-paper,** *n.* Paper made from wood-fibre. **wood-pavement,** *n.* Paving composed of blocks of wood. **wood-pecker,** *n.* A bird of the genus *Picus* living in woods and tapping trees to discover insects. **wood-pie,** *n.* The great spotted woodpecker. **wood-pigeon,** *n.* The ringdove, *Columba palumbus,* a European pigeon whose neck is nearly encircled by a ring of whitish-coloured feathers. **wood-pulp,** *n.* Wood-fibre pulped in the process of manufacturing paper. **wood-reeve,** *n.* A steward or overseer of a wood. **woodruff** [A.-S. *wuderōfe*], *n.* A woodland plant with fragrant flowers of the genus *Asperula,* esp. *A. odorata.* **wood-screw,** *n.* A metal screw for fastening pieces of wood together. **woodsman,** *n.* One who lives in the woods; a woodman. **wood-sorrel,** *n.* A creeping woodland plant of the genus *Oxalis,* with acid juice and small white flowers. **wood-tar,** *n.* Tar obtained from wood. **wood-vetch,** *n.* A climbing vetch, *Vicia sylvatica.* ***wood-wale,** *n.* The witwall. **wood-warbler,** *n.* An American warbler; a wood-wren. ***wood-ward,** *n.* A wood-reeve, a forester. **wood-wasp,** *n.* A wasp that makes its cells in wood or hangs its nest to the branches of trees. **wood-wind,** *n.* (*Mus.*) The wooden wind-instruments in an orchestra, etc. **wood-wool,** *n.* Fine shavings, esp. of pine, used for dressing wounds, for packing, etc. **woodwork,** *n.* Things made of wood; the part of a building or other structure which is composed of wood. **wood-worker,** *n.* **wood-wren,** *n.* A European warbler, *Phylloscopus sibilatrix.* **wooded,** *a.* (*usu. in comb.* as *well-wooded*) **wooden,** *a.* Made of wood; (*fig.*) stiff, clumsy, ungainly, awkward; spiritless, expressionless. **wooden-headed,** *a.* **wooden-headedness,** *n.* **woodenly,** *adv.* **woodenness,** *n.* **woodie,** *n.* (*Sc.*) The gallows. **woodless,** *a.* **woodlessness,** *n.* **woody,** *a.* Abounding in woods, well-wooded; of the nature of or consisting of wood; *pertaining to or found in woods. **woody fibre** or **tissue:** Fibre or tissue consisting of wood-cells; the tissue of which wood is composed. **woody nightshade** [NIGHTSHADE]. **woodiness,** *n.*

***wood** (2) (wud) [A.-S. *wōd* (cp. Dut. *woede,* G. *wuth,* Icel. *ōthr*), perh. cogn. with L. *vates,* a soothsayer], *a.* Mad, furious. ***woodness,** *n.*

Woodbury-type (wud′ bėr i tīp) [Walter B. *Woodbury* (1834–85), inventor], *n.* A photo-mechanical process of engraving in which the image is transferred to lead from hardened gelatine by pressure; a plate or impression produced by this.

woodchuck, -cut, -man, etc. [WOOD (1)].

wooer [WOO].

woof (woof) [M.E. *oof,* A.-S. *ōwef* (A-, *wef,* WEB)], *n.* The threads that cross the warp, the weft; cloth; (*fig.*) texture.

wool (wul) [A.-S. *wull* (cp. Dut. *wol.* G. *wolle,* Icel. *ull*), perh. cogn. with L. *lāna,* Gr. *lēnos*], *n.* The fine, soft, crisp, or curly hair, forming the fleece of sheep, goats, and some other animals, used as the raw material of cloth, etc.; short, thick hair, under-fur or down, resembling this; (*facet.*) the hair, esp. of a Negro; woollen yarn, worsted; (*Bot., Zool., etc.*) fibrous or fleecy substance resembling wool. **great cry and little wool:** Much ado about nothing, a fiasco. **wool-ball,** *n.* A ball or mass of wool, esp. a lump of concreted wool frequently found in the stomach of sheep, etc. **wool-bearing,** *a.* **wool-carding, wool-combing,** *n.* A process in the preparation of wool for spinning. **wool-classer,** *n.* (*Austral.*) A grader of wool. **wool-clip,** *n.* (*Austral.*) The annual amount of wool shorn. **wool-fat, -oil,** *n.* Lanoline. **wool-fell,** *n.* A skin from which the wool has not been removed. **wool-gathering,** *adv.* (*fig.*) In a brown study, absent-minded; *n.* Absent-mindedness, inattention. **wool-grower,** *n.* **wool-hall,** *n.* A market or exchange where wool-merchants do their business. **wool-pack,** *n.* A pack or bale of wool, formerly one weighing 240 lb.; (*fig.*) a fleecy cloud. **woolshed,** *n.* (*Austral.*) The building for shearing, packing and storing wool. **woolsorter,** *n.* A person who sorts wool according to quality, etc. **woolsorter's disease:**

Pulmonary anthrax due to the inhalation of dust from infected wool. **wool-staple,** *n.* The fibre of wool. **wool-trade,** *n.* ***woolward,** *a.* Dressed in wool only, without linen. ***to go woolward:** (*Shak.*) To wear woollen fabrics next the skin as a penance. **woollen,** *a.* Made or consisting of wool. *n.* Cloth made of wool; (*pl.*) woollen goods. **woollen-draper,** *n.* One retailing woollens. **woollenette** (-net'), *n.* **woolly,** *a.* Consisting of, or resembling, bearing, or naturally covered with wool, or with a hair resembling wool; like wool in appearance, fleecy; (*Painting*) lacking clear definition, firmness, or incisiveness; (*colloq.*) with hazy ideas, muddled. **woolly-bear,** *n.* A hairy caterpillar, esp. of *Arctia virgo* or the tiger-moth. **woolly-but,** *n.* The popular name for two valuable Australian timber-trees, *Eucalyptus longifolia* and *E. viminalis.* **woolly-haired, -headed,** *a.* **woolliness,** *n.*

woold (woold) [prob. from Dut. *woelen*], *v.t.* (*Naut.*) To wind, esp. to wind (a rope, etc.) round a mast or yard made of two or more pieces, at a place where they are fished. **woolder,** *n.* A stick used for woolding.

woollen, woolly, wool-pack, etc. [WOOL].

Woolsack (wul' săk), *n.* The seat of the Lord Chancellor in the House of Lords, consisting of a large square cushion without back or arms; (*fig.*) the post of Lord Chancellor.

woolsey [short for LINSEY-WOOLSEY].

woomera [WOMERAH].

wootz (woots) [etym. doubtful], *n.* A fine quality of E. Indian steel imported into Europe and America for edge-tools.

wop (wop) [WHOP], *n.* (*Am. slang*) An Italian, a South European.

word (wĕrd) [A.-S. (cp. Dut. *woord*, G. *wort*, Icel. *orth*, Dan. and Swed. *ord*), cogn. with L. *verbum*, Gr. *eirein*, to speak], *n.* An articulate sound or combination of sounds uttered by the human voice or written, printed, etc., expressing an idea or ideas, and forming a constituent part, or the whole of, or a substitute for a sentence; speech, discourse, talk; news, intelligence, information, a message; a command, an order, an injunction; a password, a watchword, a motto; one's assurance, promise, or definite affirmation; (*colloq., pl.*) terms interchanged expressive of anger, contention, or reproach. *v.t.* To express in words, to phrase, to select words to express. **big words:** Boasting, bluff, exaggeration. **by word of mouth:** By actual speaking, orally. **good word:** A favourable account or mention, a commendation. **last word:** The latest improvement. **in a word** or **in one word:** Briefly, in short; to sum up. **in word and deed:** Not in speech or profession only. **the Word** or **God's Word:** The Scriptures, or any part of them; Christ as the Logos. **to eat one's words:** To retract what one has said. **to have a word with:** To have a brief conversation with. **to have words with:** To have a dispute with. **word for word:** In exactly the same words, verbatim. **word-blind, deaf,** *a.* Unable to understand words through a cerebral lesion. **word-book,** *n.* A vocabulary. **word-painter,** *n.* A writer who depicts scenes or events in a vivid and picturesque manner. **word-painting,** *n.* **word perfect:** Able to repeat something without a mistake. **word-picture,** *n.* A vivid description. **word-play,** *n.* A discussion or dispute hingeing on the definition given to certain words; a play upon words, a pun. **word-square,** *n.* A series of words so arranged that the letters spell the same words when read across or downwards. **wording,** *n.* Choice of words, phrasing, etc.; letterpress; contents of a document, advertisement, etc. **wordless,** *a.* **wordy,** *a.* Verbose, diffuse, prolix, consisting of words, verbal. **wordily,** *adv.* **wordiness,** *n.* ***wordish,** *adv.* ***wordishness,** *n.*

Wordsworthian (wĕrdz wĕr' thi ăn), *a.* Of, pertaining to, or after the manner or spirit of the poet William Wordsworth (1770–1850) or his poetry. *n.* A devotee of Wordsworth.

wore, *past* [WEAR (1)].

work (wĕrk) [A.-S. *weorc* (cp. Dut. and G. *werk*, Icel. *verk*, Gr. *ergon*), whence *wiercan*, *wyrcan*, to work, past *worhte*], *n.* Exertion of energy (physical or mental), effort or activity directed to some purpose; labour, toil; that upon which labour is expended, an undertaking, a task; the materials used or to be used in this; employment as a means of livelihood, occupation; that which is done, an action, deed, performance, or achievement; a thing made; a product of nature or art; a large engineering structure, esp. a piece of fortification; a book or other literary composition, a musical or other artistic production; (*Phys.*) the exertion of force in producing or maintaining motion against the action of a resisting force; (*pl.*) an industrial establishment, a manufactory (*often as sing.*); building operations, esp. carried out under the management of a public authority; the working part or mechanism (of a watch, etc.); (*Theol.*) moral duties or the performance of meritorious acts, as opp. to grace. *v.i.* (*past & p.p.* **worked, *wrought,** rawt) To exert physical or mental energy for some purpose, to be engaged in labour, toil, or effort, to be employed or occupied (at, in, on, etc.); to be in continuous activity, to do the work or perform the motions appointed, to act, to operate; to take effect, to be effective, to exercise influence; to be in a state of motion or agitation, to ferment; to make way with effort or difficulty. *v.t.* To exert energy in or upon; to cause to do work, to keep in operation, to employ, to keep busy; to carry on, to manage, to run; to bring about, to effect, to produce as a result; to prepare or alter the condition, shape, or consistency of by some process, to knead, to mould, to fashion; to treat, to investigate, to solve; to excite. **to have one's work cut out:** To have a hard task. **to set to work:** To employ; to start working. **to work in:** To introduce or combine by manipulation; to intermix or admit of being introduced. **to work off:** To get rid of; to produce; to find customers for, to palm off. **to work out:** To compute, to solve, to find out; to exhaust; to accomplish, to effect; to expiate. **to work up:** To elaborate, to bring gradually into shape or efficiency; to excite gradually, to stir up, to rouse; to mingle together, to study (a subject) perseveringly. **workaday,** *a.* Pertaining to, or suitable for workdays, everyday, common, ordinary, plain, practical. **work-bag, -basket, -box,** *n.* One used for holding materials, etc., for work, articles to be repaired, etc., esp. for sewing. **work-day,** *n.* A working-day. ***work-fellow,** *n.* **workfolk, -folks,** *n.pl.* Work-people. **workhouse,** *n.* A public establishment maintained by a parish or union for paupers. **workman,** *n.* Any man employed in manual labour, an operative. **workmanlike,** *a.* Done in the manner of a good workman. ***workmanly,** *a,* and *adv.* **workmanship,** *n.* Comparative skill, finish, or execution shown in making something or in the thing made; the result of working or making. **work-people,** *n.pl.* Workmen or workwomen. **workroom,** *n.* A room in which work is done. **workshop,** *n.* A room or building in which a handicraft or other work is carried on. **work-shy,** *a.* (*colloq.*) With a repugnance to work. **work study,** *n.* The investigation of the methods and practice of particular work with a view to getting the best results for all concerned. **work-table,** *n.* A table with drawers and other conveniences for keeping sewing-materials, etc., in. **workwoman,** *n.* **workable,** *a.* Capable of being worked, practicable; that will work or operate; worth working or developing. **worker,** *n.* **worker-bee,** *n.* A partially developed female bee doing the work of the hive. **workless,** *a.*

working (wĕr' king), *a.* Engaged in work, esp. manual labour; taking an active part in a business. *n.* The act of labouring; operation, mode of operation; a mine or quarry or a portion of it which has been worked or in which work is going on; fermentation, movement. **working capital, working expenses,** *n.* (*Comm.*) Funds employed for the actual carrying on of a business. **working-**

class, *n.* Those who earn their living by manual labour. **working-day,** *n.* Any day upon which work is ordinarily performed, as distinguished from Sundays and holidays; the period daily devoted to work. **working drawing** or **plan:** A drawing or plan of a work prepared to guide a builder, engineer, etc., in executing work. **working-out,** *n.* The act of working out, calculating, elaborating, etc. **workless,** *a.*

world (wĕrld) [A.-S. *weoruld* (*wer*, man, cp. Icel. *verr*, L. *vir*, ELD), cp. Dut. *wereld*, G. *welt*, Icel. *veröld*], *n.* The whole system of things, the universe, everything; a system of things, an orderly or organic whole, a cosmos; the earth with its lands and seas; a celestial body regarded as similar to this; a large natural or other division of the earth; the human inhabitants of the world, mankind; human society, the public; fashionable or prominent people; human affairs, the ways, customs, opinions, etc., of people, active life, social life and intercourse; a particular section, department, or class of people, animals, or things, a realm, a domain, a sphere; a vast quantity, amount, number, degree, etc. (of); all things external to oneself as related to the individual; man as a microcosm, man's inner life; any time, state, or sphere of existence; the present state of existence as distinguished from the future life; secular interest as opp. to spiritual; the ungodly or unregenerate portion of mankind. **all the world:** Everybody. **in the world:** At all, possibly. **for all the world:** Exactly, precisely. **for the world:** On any account. **world without end:** To all eternity, everlastingly. **world-hardened,** *a.* Hardened by the love of worldly things. **world-old:** Old as the world. **world power,** *n.* (*Pol.*) A sovereign state so strong as to be able to affect the policy of every civilised state in the world. **world-wearied, -weary,** *a.* Tired of existence. **world-wide,** *a.* Spread over the whole world; existing everywhere. **World Bank,** *n.* An agency of the U.N. set up in 1944 to lend money at moderate rates to poorer countries seeking to develop their resources. **World Court,** *n.* Popular name for the Permanent Court of International Justice at the Hague set up in 1921 by the League of Nations to settle disputes between states. **World Health Organization (W.H.O.):** A specialized agency of the United Nations dating from 1948 with the object of helping countries to develop their health administration.

worldly (wĕrld' li), *a.* Pertaining to the present, temporal, or material world; earthly, secular, material, not spiritual. **worldly-minded,** *a.* Devoted to worldly things. **worldly-mindedness,** *n.* **worldly-wise,** *a.* Wise in the things of this world. **worldliness,** *n.* **worldling,** *n.* A worldly person.

worm (wĕrm) [A.-S. *wyrm* (cp. Dut. *worm*, G. *wurm*, Icel. *ormr*), cogn. with Gr. *rhomos*, L. *vermis*, see VERMICULAR], *n.* An invertebrate creeping animal with a long limbless segmented body, belonging to the genus *Vermes*; an intestinal parasite, a tapeworm, a fluke; any small creeping animal with very small or undeveloped feet, as larvæ, grubs, caterpillars, maggots, etc.; (*fig.*) a poor, grovelling, debased, or despised creature; a vermicular or spiral part or thing; the spiral part of a screw; a spiral tool for boring rock; a spiral device for extracting cartridges, etc.; the spiral condensing-pipe of a still; a ligament under a dog's tongue. *v.i.* To crawl, creep, wriggle, or progress with a worm-like motion; (*fig.*) to work stealthily or underhandedly. *v.t.* To insinuate (oneself), to make (one's way) in a worm-like manner; to draw (out) or extract by craft and perseverance; to free (a dog, etc.) from worms; to cut the worm from under the tongue of (a dog). **worm-cast,** *n.* A cylindrical mass of earth voided by an earth-worm. **worm-eaten,** *a.* Gnawed or bored by worms. **worm-fishing,** *n.* Fishing with worms for bait. **worm-gear,** *n.* Gear having a toothed or cogged wheel engaging with a revolving spiral. **worm-hole,** *n.* A hole made by a worm in wood, fruit, the ground, etc. **worm-holed,** *a.* **worm-powder,** *n.* A powder used as a vermifuge. **worm-seed,** *n.* A Levantine plant the seed of which is used as an anthelmintic. **worm-wheel,** *n.* The toothed wheel of worm-gear. **wormless,** *a.* **worm-like,** *a.* **wormy,** *a.* **wormless,** *n.*

wormul, wormil (wôr' mŭl, -mil) [corr. of WARBLE (2)], *n.* A warble.

wormwood (wĕrm' wud) [A.-S. *wermōd* (cp. Dut. *wermoet*, G. *wermuth*, see VERMUTH), assim. to WORM, WOOD], *n.* A perennial herb, *Artemisia absinthium*, having bitter and tonic properties, used in the manufacture of vermuth and absinthe and in medicine; (*fig.*) bitterness, gall, mortification.

worn, *p.p.* [WEAR (1)].

worry (wŭr' i) [A.-S. *wrygan* (cp. Dut. *worgen*, G. *würgen*, to strangle), cogn. with WRING], *v.t.* To bite or keep on biting, to mangle, choke, or pull about with the teeth (of dogs fighting, molesting sheep, etc.); to tease, to harass, bother, persecute, or wear out with importunity, etc. *v.i.* To bite, pull about, etc. (of dogs fighting, etc.); to be unduly anxious or troubled, to fret. *n.* The act of worrying; a worrying person; the state of being worried, care, anxiety, solicitude, vexation, fret (*often in pl.*). **to worry along:** To get along somehow in spite of trouble and difficulty. **to worry oneself:** To put oneself to needless trouble or anxiety. **worrier,** *n.* **worriment,** *n.* **worriedly** (wŭr' ėd li), *adv.* **worriless,** *a.* **worrisome,** *a.* **worryingly,** *adv.*

worse (wĕrs) [A.-S. *wyrs*, adv., adj. *wyrsa*, *wirsa*, prob. cogn. with G. *wirren*, to twist, to confuse, see WAR], *a.* (*comp. of* BAD) More bad; (*predicatively*) in a poorer state of health; in a less favourable state, position, or circumstances. *adv.* More badly; into a poorer state of health, etc.; less. *n.* A worse thing or things; loss, disadvantage, defeat. **to put to the worse:** To defeat, to discomfit. ***worsen,** *v.t.* and *i.*

worship (wĕr' ship) [A.-S. *weorthschipe*], *n.* *The quality of being worthy, merit, excellence; *honour; deference, respect (used as a title of respect or honour in addressing certain magistrates, etc., esp. mayors); the act of paying divine honour to God, esp. in religious services; an act or feeling of adoration or loving or admiring devotion or submissive respect (to a person, principle, etc.). *v.t.* (*past & p.p.* **worshipped**) To pay divine honours to; to perform religious service to; to reverence with supreme respect and admiration; to treat as divine. *v.i.* To take part in a religious service. **place of worship:** Church, chapel, etc., where religious services are held. ***worshipable,** *a.* **worshipful,** *a.* Deserving of worship (phrase applied to certain magistrates, etc.). **worshipfully,** *adv.* **worshipfulness,** *n.* **worshipper,** *n.* One who worships; an attender at a place of worship.

worst (wĕrst) [A.-S. *wyrst*, adv., adj. *wyrsta*, shortened from *wyrsesta* (WORSE, -EST)], *a.* Bad in the highest degree. *adv.* Most badly. *n.* That which is most bad; the most bad, evil, severe, or calamitous part, result, event, state, etc. *v.t.* To get the better of in a contest, etc., to defeat, to overthrow, to best. **to get the worst of it:** To be defeated.

worsted (wus' tėd) [*Worsted* (now Worstead), Norfolk, where first manufactured], *n.* Woollen yarn used for knitting stockings, carpets, etc. *a.* Made of worsted.

wort (wĕrt) [A.-S. *wyrt* (cp. G. *wurz*, Icel. *urt*), cogn. with ROOT], *a.* A plant, a herb (*usu. in comb.*, as *moneywort*, *soapwort*); an infusion of malt for fermenting into beer.

worth (1) (wĕrth) [A.-S. *wyrthe*, from *wyrth*, *weorth*, value (cp. Dut. *waard* and *waarde*, Ice. *verthr* and *verth*, G. *werth*), cogn. with W. *gwerth*, value, price, L. *verēri*, see REVERE and Eng. WARE (2)], *a.* Equal in value or price to; deserving, worthy of; having property to the value of, possessed of; *estimable, valuable. *n.* That which a person or thing is worth, value, the equivalent of anything, esp. in money; merit, desert, high character, excellence. **for all one is worth:** (*colloq.*) With all one's strength, energy, etc. **worth while** [WHILE]. **worthless,** *a.* **worthlessly,** *adv.* **worthlessness,** *n.*

***worth** (2) (wĕrth) [A.-S. *weorthan*, to become (cp. Dut. *worden*, G. *werden*, Icel. *vertha*)], *v.i.* To betide, to befall. **woe worth the day!** Cursed be the day.

worthless, etc. [WORTH (1)].

worthy (wĕr' *thi*) [WORTH (1), -Y], *a.* Having worth, estimable; deserving of respect, praise, or honour, respectable; deserving (of, to be, etc.); fit, suitable, adequate, appropriate, equivalent or adequate to the worth (of); *of high rank, noble, honourable. *n.* A person of eminent worth; a person of some note or distinction in his time, locality, etc. **the Nine Worthies:** Hector of Troy, Alexander the Great, Julius Cæsar, Joshua, David, Judas Maccabæus, King Arthur, Charlemagne, and Godfrey of Bouillon. **worthily,** *adv.* **worthiness,** *n.*

***wot,** *1st* and *2nd sing.* [WIT (1)].

would, *past & cond.* [WILL (1)].

Woulfe bottle (wulf) [P. *Woulfe* (1727–1803)], *n.* (*Chem.*) A bottle with three or more necks used in the handling and washing of gases.

wound (1) (woond) [A.-S. *wund* (cp. Dut. *wond*, G. *wunde*, Icel. *und*), prob. cogn. with WIN], *n.* An injury caused by violence to the skin and flesh of an animal or the bark or substance of plants, esp. one involving disruption of the tissues; (*fig.*) any damage, hurt, or pain to feelings, reputation, etc., esp. the pangs of love. *v.t.* To inflict a wound on. **wounder,** *n.* **woundable,** *a.* **woundless,** *a.* **woundwort,** *n.* A plant of the genus *Stachys*, and other plants supposed to heal wounds. ***woundy,** *a.* Causing wounds; excessive. ***woundily,** *adv.*

wound (wound) (2), *past & p.p.* [WIND (1 and 2)].

wourali [CURARE].

wove, *past & p.p.*, **woven,** *p.p.* [WEAVE (1)].

wow (wou) [instinctive sound], *int.* (*Sc.*) An exclamation of astonishment, wonder, etc. *n.* (*Am.*) A sensational or spectacular success.

wowser (wou' zĕr) [onomat.], *n.* (*Austral. slang*) A spoil-sport, a Puritan. **wowserism,** *n.*

wow-wow (wou' wou) [imit.], *n.* The silvery gibbon, *Hylobates leuciscus*, of Java and Sumatra.

wrack (răk) [var. of WRECK], *n.* Seaweed thrown upon the shore; cloud-rack; wreck, destruction, ruin. ***wrackful,** *a.* Ruinous, destructive.

wraith (rāth) [perh. var. of WREATH, or cogn. with Norw. *vardyvle* (WARD, EVIL)], *n.* The double or phantom of a living person; (*loosely*) an apparition, a ghost appearing after death.

wrangle (răng' gĕl) [freq. from A.-S. *wrang*, cogn. with WRING], *v.i.* To dispute, argue, or quarrel angrily, peevishly, or noisily, to brawl; *to engage in public discussion and disputation. *n.* An angry or noisy dispute or quarrel, an altercation, a brawl. **wrangler,** *n.* One who wrangles; (*Am.*) a cowboy; a horse-breaker; (*Camb. Univ.*) one of those who are placed in the first class in the mathematical tripos; **senior wrangler:** Formerly the student who took the first place in this. **wranglership,** *n.* ***wranglesome,** *a.*

wrap (1) (răp) [perh. rel. to WARP], *v.t.* (*past & p.p.* **wrapped**) To fold or arrange so as to cover or enclose something; to enfold, envelop, muffle, pack, surround, or conceal in some soft material; to enfold or muffle (up) thus; to hide, to conceal, to disguise; (*in p.p.*) to absorb, to engross, to comprise (with *up*). *v.i.* To fold, to lap. *n.* Something intended to wrap, as a cloak, shawl, rug, etc. (*usu. in pl.*). **wrappage,** *n.* The act of wrapping; that which wraps or envelops, a wrapping or wrappings. **wrapper,** *n.* One who wraps; that in which anything is wrapped, esp. an outer covering for a new book, and for a newspaper for posting; a woman's loose outer garment for indoor wear. **wrapping,** *n.* A wrapper, a cloak, a shawl, a rug.

***wrap** (2) [RAP (3)].

***wrapt** [RAPT].

wrasse (răs) [cp. W. *gwrachen*], *n.* An acanthopterygian sea-fish of numerous species of the genus *Labrus* or *Crenilabrus*, haunting coasts and rocks.

wrath (rawth) [A.-S. *wrætho*, from *wrāth*, WROTH], *n.* Deep or violent anger, indignation, rage; *impetuosity. **wrathful,** *a.* **wrathfully,** *adv.* **wrathfulness,** *n.* **wrathless,** *a.* **wrathy,** *a.* **wrathily,** *adv.*

***wrawl** (rawl) [imit.], *v.i.* To cry as a cat, to whine.

wraxling (*Sc.*) [WRESTLING].

wreak (1) (rēk) [A.-S. *wrecan* (cp. Dut. *wrecken*, G. *rächen*, Icel. *reka*), cogn. with L. *urgēre*, to urge, Gr. *eirgein*, to shut in, and WRACK, WRECK], *v.t.* To carry out, to inflict, to execute; *to avenge. *n.* Revenge, vengeance; furious passion; resentment, fury. **wreaker,** *n.* ***wreakful,** *a.* ***wreakless,** *a.*

***wreak** (2) [RECK].

wreath (rēth, *pl.* rēthz) [A.-S. *wrǣth*, cogn. with WRITHE], *n.* A band or ring of flowers or leaves tied, woven, or twisted together for wearing on the head, decorating statues, walls, graves, etc.; a representation of this in wood, stone, etc.; a similar circlet of twisted silk, etc.; a ring, a twist, a curl (of cloud, smoke, etc.); a garland, a chaplet.

wreathe (rēth), *v.t.* To form (flowers, leaves, etc.) into a wreath; to surround, encircle, entwine with or as with a wreath or with anything twisted; to form a wreath round. *v.i.* To be curled, folded, or entwined (round, etc.). ***wreathen,** *a.* Wreathed. **wreather** (rē' *th*ĕr), *n.* **wreathless** (rēth' lĕs), *a.* ***wreathy,** *a.*

wreck (rek) [A.-S. *wræc*, expulsion, perh. modified in sense through Icel. *rek*, anything cast ashore (cp. Dut. *wrak*) cogn. with WREAK (1)], *n.* Destruction, ruin, esp. of a ship; a vessel dashed against rocks or otherwise destroyed, seriously crippled, or shattered; the remains of anything irretrievably shattered or ruined; a dilapidated or worn-out person or thing; wreckage. *v.t.* To destroy or cast away (a vessel, etc.) by collision, driving ashore, etc.; to involve in shipwreck; to ruin or destroy. *v.i.* To suffer shipwreck. **wreck-master,** *n.* An official appointed to take charge of goods, etc., cast ashore after a shipwreck. **wreckage,** *n.* The debris, fragments, or material from a wreck. **wrecking-car,** *n.* (*Am.*) A railway-car carrying appliances for removing wreckage and obstructions from the line.

wrecker (rek' er), *n.* A plunderer from wrecks; one who wrecks or causes shipwreck, esp. one who lures vessels to shipwreck with intent to plunder; a person or ship employed in recovering a wreck or a wrecked cargo; (*Am.*) a recovery vehicle. **wrecking crew:** (*Am.*) A break-down gang.

wren (ren) [A.-S. *wrenna*, cp. Icel. *rindill*], *n.* A small insessorial bird of the genus *Troglodytes* with a short erect tail and short wings. **W.R.E.N.,** *n.* A member of the Women's Royal Naval Service. **wrenning-day,** *n.* St. Stephen's Day, 26 Dec., on which it was formerly the custom to stone a wren to death to commemorate his martyrdom.

wrench (rench) [A.-S. *wrenc* (deceit, guile, cp. G. *rank*), cogn. with WRONG and WRINKLE], *n.* A violent twist or sideways pull; an injury caused by twisting, a sprain; (*fig.*) pain or distress caused by a parting, loss, etc.; a tool for twisting or untwisting screws, bolts, nuts, etc. *v.t.* To pull, wrest, or twist with force or violence; to pull (off or away) thus; to strain, to sprain; (*fig.*) to pervert, to distort.

wrest (rest) [A.-S. *wrǣstan* (cp. Icel. *reista*, Dan. *vriste*), cogn. with WRITHE and WRIST], *v.t.* To twist, to turn aside by a violent effort; to pull, extort, or wrench (away) forcibly; (*fig.*) to pervert, to distort, to twist or deflect from its natural meaning. *n.* A violent wrench or twist; a turning instrument, esp. a tuning-key for a harp, etc. **wrester,** *n.*

wrestle (res′ ėl) [freq. of prec.], *v.i.* To contend by grappling with and trying to throw one's opponent, esp. in a match under recognized rules; (*fig.*) to struggle, to contend, to strive vehemently; *to make earnest supplication. *v.t.* To contend with in a wrestling-match. *n.* A bout at wrestling, a wrestling-match. **to wrestle in prayer:** To pray earnestly. **wrestler,** *n.* **wrestling,** *n.*

wretch (rech) [A.-S. *wrecca*, an outcast, from *wrecan*, to drive out, to WREAK (1)], *n.* A miserable or unfortunate person; a despicable, mean, base or vile person (often used to express ironical pity or contempt or even tenderness and compassion). **wretched** (rech′ ėd), *a.* Miserable, unhappy, sunk in deep affliction or distress; calamitous, pitiable, afflictive; worthless, paltry, contemptible; (*colloq.*) extremely unsatisfactory, uncomfortable, or unpleasant. **wretchedly,** *adv.* **wretchedness,** *n.*

wrick (rik) [M.E. *wrikken* (cp. Dut. *wrikken*, Dan. *vrikke*), cogn. with WRING], *v.t.* To twist or strain (one's neck, back, etc.). *n.* A twist or slight sprain.

wriggle (rig′ ėl) [freq. of obs. *wrīg* (cp. Dut. *wriggelen*, L.G. *wriggeln*), cogn. with prec. and WRY, WRING], *v.i.* To turn, twist, or move the body to and fro with short motions like an eel; to move or go (along, in, out, etc.) with writhing contortions or twistings; (*fig.*) to act or proceed in a sly, insinuating, or despicable manner. *v.t.* To move (one's body, etc.) with a wriggling motion; to effect or make (one's way, etc.) by wriggling. *n.* A wriggling motion. **wriggler,** *n.*

wright (rīt) [A.-S. *wyrhta*, from *wyrht*, work, from *wyrcan*, to WORK], *n.* One who is occupied in some mechanical business, an artificer, a workman, (esp. in comb., as *shipwright*, *wheelwright*, etc.).

wring (ring) [A.-S. *wringan* (cp. Dut. *wringen*, G. *ringen*), cogn. with WRIGGLE], *v.t.* (*past & p.p.* **wrung**) To twist and squeeze or compress; to turn, twist, or strain forcibly; to press or squeeze (water, etc. out) thus; (*fig.*) to pervert, to distort (a meaning, etc.); to pain, to torture, to distress; to extract, to extort. *n.* A press, a squeeze. **to wring one's withers:** To appeal passionately to one's pity. **to wring the hands:** To press the hands together convulsively, as in great distress. **wringer,** *n.* One who or that which rings; a wringing-machine. **wringing-machine,** *n.* A machine for wringing water out of newly-washed clothes, etc. **wringing-wet:** So wet that moisture can be wrung out.

wrinkle (1) (ring′ kėl) [freq. or dim., cogn. with prec.], *n.* A small ridge, crease, or furrow caused by the folding or contraction of a flexible surface. *v.t.* To fold or contract into furrows, creases, or ridges. *v.i.* To fold or shrink into furrows and ridges. **wrinkly,** *a.*

wrinkle (2) (ring′ kėl) [dim. of A.-S. *wrenc*, trick, cogn. with WRENCH and prec.], *n.* A useful bit of information or advice, a bright idea, a tip, a dodge.

wrist (rist) [A.-S., from *wrīthan*, to WRITHE, cp. Icel. and G. *rist*, Dan. and Swed. *vrist*, instep], *n.* The joint uniting the hand to the forearm; a wrist-pin. **wristband,** *n.* A band or part of a sleeve, esp. a shirt-sleeve, covering the wrist, usu. of starched linen, a cuff. **wrist-drop,** *n.* Paralysis of the muscles of the forearm through lead-poisoning. **wristlet,** *n.* A band worn round the wrist to strengthen it, hold up a glove, carry a watch, etc.; a bracelet; a handcuff. **wrist-pin,** *n.* (*Mach.*) A pin or stud projecting from a crank for a connecting-rod to turn on. **wrist-watch,** *n.* A watch worn on a strap round the wrist.

writ (1) (rit) [A.-S. *gewrit*, a writing, cogn. with WRITE], *n.* That which is written, a writing; a written command or precept issued by a court in the name of the sovereign to an officer or other person commanding him to do or refrain from doing some particular act therein specified. **holy writ** [HOLY].

***writ** (2) *past & p.p.* [WRITE].

write (rīt) [A.-S. *wrītan*, cp. Dut. *rijten*, G. *reissen*, Icel. *rīta*, to tear, cut, draw, scratch out, etc.], *v.t.* (*past* **wrote, *writ,** *p.p.* **written, *writ**) To form or trace (esp. words, a sentence, etc.) in letters or symbols, with a pen, pencil, or the like on paper or other material; to trace (signs, characters, etc.) thus, to set (down), to record, to describe, to state, or convey by writing; to compose or produce as an author; to cover or fill with writing; (*fig.*) to impress or stamp (disgrace, etc.) on a person's face; to designate, to call, to put (oneself down as, etc.) in writing; (*colloq.*) to send a letter to, to communicate in writing. *v.i.* To trace letters or symbols representing words on paper, etc.; to write or send a letter; to compose or produce articles, books, etc., as an author. **writ large:** Set down or recorded in large letters; magnified, emphasized. **to write down:** To put in writing, to record; to depreciate, to criticize unfavourably. **to write off:** To record the cancelling of (a debt, etc.); to compose rapidly and easily. **to write out:** To write the whole of. **to write oneself out:** To exhaust one's powers of literary production. **to write up:** To praise in writing, to puff; to post up (account-books, etc.); to give full details in writing.

writer (rī′ tėr), *n.* One who writes; an author, a journalist, etc.; a clerk, an amanuensis; (*Sc.*) a solicitor, an attorney. **writer to the signet:** (*Sc.*) A solicitor. **writership,** *n.*

writhe (rīth) [A.-S. *wrīthan*, cp. Icel. *rītha*, Dan. *vride*, O.H.G. *rīdan*], *v.i.* To twist, turn, or roll the body about, as in pain; to shrink, to squirm (at, with shame, etc.). *v.t.* To twist, or distort (the limbs, etc.). *n.* An act of writhing. ***writhen,** *a.* Twisted, distorted. **writhingly,** *adv.* ***writhle,** *v.t.* To wrinkle.

writing (rī′ ting), *n.* The act of one who writes; that which is written; an inscription; a book, article, or other literary composition; a legal instrument. **writing on the wall:** (*fig.*) A solemn warning. **writing-case,** *n.* A portable case for writing materials, etc. **writing desk,** *n.* A portable desk with space for papers, etc. **writing-ink,** *n.* Ink for writing, opp. to printer's ink. **writing-master,** *n.* One who teaches penmanship. **writing-paper,** *n.* Paper with a smooth surface for writing on. **writing-school,** *n.* A school where penmanship is taught. **writing-table,** *n.* A table used for writing on, usu. with a knee-hole, drawers, etc.

written, etc. [WRITE].

***woke,** *past*, ***wroken,** *p.p.* [WREAK (1)].

wrong (rong) [A.-S. *wrang*, a wrong thing, from Scand. (cp. Icel. *rangr*, awry, Dan. *vrang*, wrong), cogn. with WRING], *a.* Not morally right, contrary to morality, conscience, or law, wicked; not the right (one, etc.), not that which is required, intended, proper, best, etc.; not according to truth or reality; out of order, in bad condition, not suitable, etc.; false, inaccurate, mistaken, erroneous. *adv.* Wrongly, unjustly. *n.* That which is wrong; a wrong act, an injustice, a trespass, an injury, hurt or pain; deviation from what is right; wrongness, error. *v.t.* To treat unjustly, to do wrong to; to impute evil motives to unjustly; to seduce (a woman). **to go wrong:** To fail morally, to fall into sin. **in the wrong:** In a wrong position; in error. **wrong fount:** (*Print.*) Not of the right fount, size, or pattern (of type). **wrong side out:** Inside out. **wrongdoer,** *n.* **wrongdoing,** *n.* **wrong-headed,** *a.* Perverse, obstinate, crotchety. **wrong-headedness,** *n.* **wronger,** *n.* **wrongful,** *a.* Injurious, unjust, wrong. **wrongfully,** *adv.* **wrongfulness,** *n.* ***wrongless,** *a.* ***wronglessly,** *adv.* **wrongly,** *adv.* **wrongness,** *n.* **wrongous,** *a.* (*Sc. Law*) Not right, illegal.

wrote, *past* [WRITE].

wroth (rōth) [A.-S. *wrāth*, perverted, from *wrīthan*) to WRITHE, cp. Dut. *wread*, Icel. *reithr*], *a.* (*poet.*) Angry, wrathful.

wrought (rawt) [*past & p.p.* WORK], *a.* Worked. **wrought iron,** *n.* (*Metal.*) Iron made malleable by having non-metallic impurities burned out of it; iron made malleable by forging or rolling.

wrung, *past & p.p.* [WRING].

wry (rī) [M.E. *wrien*, A.-S. *wrigian*, cogn. with WRIGGLE], **v.i.* To swerve, to go wrong or astray. **v.t.* To distort. *a.* Twisted, distorted, crooked, skew; showing distaste, disgust, etc.; wrong, false, perverted. **wrybill,** *n.* A variety of the plover. **wry-mouth,** *n.* An eel-like sea-fish with a vertical mouth. **wry-mouthed,** *a.* Having a distorted mouth or a cynical or distorted expression. **wry-neck,** *n.* A bird, *Junx torquilla*, allied to the woodpeckers, with a habit of twisting its head round as on a pivot; stiff-neck. **wrynecked,** *a.* **wryly,** *adv.* **wryness,** *n.*

wyandotte (wī′ ȧn dot) [name of N. Am. Ind. tribe], *n.* An American breed of domestic fowl.

wych (wich) [A.-S. *wice*, cogn. with WICKER], *pref.* Drooping. **wych-elm,** *n.* The Scotch elm, *Ulmus montana.* **wych-hazel,** *n.* A North American shrub, *Hamamelis Virginea*, with several large branching trunks.

Wycliffite (wik′ lifīt) [John *Wycliffe* (*c.* 1330–84), Engl. ecclesiastical reformer and Lollard], *a.* Pertaining to Wycliffe, his tenets, or his followers. *n.* A follower of Wycliffe.

wye (wī) [letter Y], *n.* A Y-shaped thing.

Wykehamist (wik′ ȧ mist), *n.* A member (past or present) of Winchester College founded by William of Wykeham (1324–1404), Bishop of Winchester. *a.* Of or pertaining to this.

wynd (wīnd) [prob. var. of WIND (2)], *n.* (*Sc.*) An alley.

wyvern (wī′ vėrn) [A.-F. *wyvre*, O.F. *wivre*, L. *vīpera*, VIPER (cp. *n.* in BITTERN)], *n.* (*Her.*) A two-legged dragon with erect wings and barbed tail.

X

X, x, the twenty-fourth letter, and the eighteenth consonant, of the English alphabet (**Xs, X's Exes**), as a medial letter has the sound of *ks*, as in *axis*, *taxes*, or of *gz*, as in *exhaust*, *exult*; as an initial (chiefly in words of Greek origin) it has the sound of *z*; (Roman numeral), 10 (xx, 20, xxx, 30, xc, 90); (*Alg.*, *x*) the first unknown quantity or variable. **X-chromosome,** *n.* (*Biol.*) A chromosome associated with sex-determination, usually paired with Y-chromosome. **X-rays,** *n.* Röntgen rays. **xx** or **double-x, xxx** or **triple-x:** Marks indicating the strength of ale, etc., placed on brewers' casks.

xanth-, xantho- [Fr. *xanthos*], *comb. form.* Yellow. **xanthate** (zăn′ thȧt), *n.* A salt of xanthic acid. **xanthein** (-thė in), *n.* The part of the yellow colouring-matter of flowers that is soluble in water.

Xanthian (zăn′ thi ȧn) [*Xanth-us*, -IAN], *a.* Pertaining to Xanthus, an ancient town of Asia Minor. **Xanthian marbles** or **sculptures:** A large collection of marble sculptures brought from Xanthus in 1838 and placed in the British Museum.

xanthic (zăn′ thik) [XANTH-, -IC], *a.* Of a yellowish colour. **xanthic acid:** A colourless oily liquid, prepared by decomposing xanthate of potassium with sulphuric or hydrochloric acid. **xanthic flowers:** Flowers having yellow as their type and passing into red and white, opp. to cyanic, having blue as the type. **xanthin, -thine,** *n.* The part of the yellow colouring-matter of flowers that is insoluble in water; a yellow colouring-matter obtained from madder; a crystalline compound found in blood, urine, the liver, etc.; a gaseous product of the decomposition of xanthate.

xanthium (zăn′ thi ŭm) [Gr. *xanthion*], *n.* (*Bot.*) A genus of hardy composite plants.

Xanthochroi (zăn thok′ rō ī) [XANTH-, cp. MELANOCHROI], *n.pl.* (*Ethn.*) Fair whites or blonds, those having yellow or red hair, blue eyes, and fair complexion. **xanthochroic** (-krō′ ik), **-chroous** (-thok′ rō ŭs), *a.* **xanthoma** (-thō′ mȧ), *n.* (*Path.*) A skin disease characterized by a growth of yellowish tubercles, usu. in flat patches, on the eyelids. **xanthomatous,** *a.* **xanthomelanous** (-mel′ ȧ nŭs) [Gr. *melas melanos*, black], *a.* (*Ethn.*) Having black hair and yellow or brownish skin. **xanthophyll** (zăn′ thō fil) [Gr. *phullon*, leaf], *n.* (*Bot.*) The yellow colouring-matter of withered leaves. **xanthopsia** (-thop′ si ȧ) [Gr. *opsis*, sight], *n.* (*Path.*) An affection of the sight in which objects appear yellowish. **xanthosis** (-thō′ sis), *n.* Yellow discoloration of the skin, as in cancerous tumours. **xanthous** (zăn′ thŭs), *a.* (*Ethn.*) Yellow or Mongoloid; *xanthochroic.

xanthoxylene (zăn thoks′ i lēn), *n.* (*Chem.*) A volatile oily compound obtained from the fruit of the Japanese pepper, *Xanthoxylon piperitum.*

xanthoxylum, -lon (zăn thok′ si lŭm, -lon) [XANTHO-, Gr. *xulon*, wood], *n.* (*Bot.*) A genus of tropical or sub-tropical trees with prickly stems, several of which yield valuable timber.

Xantippe (zăn tip′ ė) [wife of Socrates], *n.* A shrewish wife, a scold.

xebec (zē′ bėk) [Sp. *xabeque* (cp. Port. *zabeco*, F. *chebdec*, It. *sciabecco*), Turk. *sumbakī*, cp. Arab. *sumbūk*], *n.* A small three-masted vessel with lateen and square sails, used in the Mediterranean.

xen-, xenarthral [XENO-].

xenelasia (zen ė lā′ zi ȧ) [Gr. (XEN-, foll., *elaunein*, to drive)], *n.* (*Gr. Hist.*) Exclusion of foreigners from a country, as in Sparta.

xenium (zē′ ni ŭm), *n.* (*Class. Ant.*) A present given to a guest, ambassador, etc.; a picture of still life on the walls of a guest-chamber.

xeno-, xen- [Gr. *xenos*, strange, stranger], *comb. form.* **xenarthral** (zė nar′ thrȧl) [Gr. *arthron*, joint, -AL], *a.* (*Anat.*) Peculiarly jointed (of certain vertebræ). **xenial** (zen′ i-, zē′ ni ȧl), *a.* Of or pertaining to hospitality or the relations between host and guest.

xenogamy (ze nog′ ȧ mi), *n.* (*Bot.*) Cross-fertilization.

xenogenesis (ze nō jen′ ė sis), *n.* (*Biol.*) Heterogenesis.

xenoglossia (zen ō glos′ i ȧ), *n.* In psychical research the knowledge of a language one has not learned.

xenomania (zen ō mā′ ni ȧ), *n.* Inordinate liking for everything foreign.

xenomenia (zen ō mē′ ni ȧ), *n.* (*Path.*) Loss of menstrual blood elsewhere than from the uterus, *e.g.* from the nose; vicarious menstruation.

xenomorphic (zen ō môr′ fik), *a.* (*Petrol.*) Not having its own proper form but an irregular shape due to surrounding minerals.

xenon (zē′ nŏn), *n.* An inert gaseous element found in the atmosphere and solidifying at the temperature of liquid air.

xenophobia (zen ō fō′ bi ȧ), *n.* Fear of, or aversion from, strangers or foreigners.

xer-, xero- [Gr. *xēros*, dry], *comb. form.* **xeransis** (zēr ăn′ sis), *n.* The state of being dried up, desiccation. **xerantic,** *a.* **xeranthemum** [Gr. *anthemon*, *anthos*, flower], *n.* An annual plant of the order Compositæ with everlasting flowers. **xerasia** (-ā′ si ȧ), *n.* (*Path.*) A disease of the hair in which it becomes dry and powdery. **xerodermia** (-dĕrmi ȧ) [Gr. *derma*, skin], *n.* Morbid dryness of the skin.

xerography (ze rog′ rȧ fi), *n.* A photographic process in which the plate is sensitized electrically.

xeromyron (ze rom′ i rŏn), *n.* A dry ointment.

xerophagy (ze rof′ ȧ ji), *n.* The Christian rule of fasting; the act or habit of living on dry food or a meagre diet.

xerophilous (ze rof′ i lùs), *a.* (*Bot.*) Adapted to living in a hot, dry climate.

xerophthalmia (ze of thăl′ mi ȧ), *n.* (*Path.*) Inflammation of the lining membrane of the eye, without discharge.

xerophyte (zer′ ō fīt), *n.* (*Bot.*) A plant adapted to living in a region of little moisture.

xerostomia (ze ros tō′ mi ȧ), *n.* Abnormal dryness of the mouth.

xerotes (zer′ o tēz), *n.* A dry habit or disposition of the body. **xerotic,** *a.*

Xian [abbrev. CHRISTIAN].

xiph-, xiphi-, xipho- [Gr. *xiphos*, sword], *comb. form.* **xiphisternum** (zif i stĕr′ nùm) [STERNUM], *n.* (*Anat.*) The lower segment or xiphoid process of the sternum. **xiphoid** (zif′ oid) [-OID], *a.* Sword-shaped. **xiphoid appendage, cartilage,** or **process:** The xiphisternum.

Xmas [abbr. CHRISTMAS].

Xn, Xnty [abbrev. CHRISTIAN CHRISTIANITY].

X-rays [RÖNTGEN RAYS].

Xt. [abbrev. CHRIST].

xyl-, xylo- [Gr. *xulon*, wood], *comb. form.* **xylanthrax** (zī lăn′ thrăks) [Gr. *anthrax*, coal], *n.* Wood coal, or charcoal, opp. to mineral coal. **xylem** (zī′ lėm), *n.* (*Bot.*) Woody tissue, wood parenchyma, opp. to phloem. **xylene** [-ENE], *n.* Any one of three isomeric colourless, volatile, liquid hydrocarbons distilled from coal- or wood-tar. **xylobalsamum** (-bawl′ sȧ mùm) [see BALSAM], *n.* The wood of or a balsam obtained by decoction of the twigs and leaves of the Balm of Gilead tree. **xylocarp** (zī′ lȯ karp) [Gr. *karpos*, fruit), *n.* A hard, woody fruit, or a tree bearing this. **xylocarpous** (-kar′ pùs), *a.* **xylograph** (zī′ lȯ grăf) [-GRAPH], *n.* An engraving on wood, esp. in a primitive style, or an impression from such an engraving; an impression obtained from the grain of wood used for surface decoration. **xylographer** (-log′ rȧ fėr), *n.* **xylographic** (-grăf′ ik), *a.* **xylography** (-log′ rȧ fi), *n.*

xyloid (zī′ loid), *a.* Woody, ligneous.

xyloidine (zī′ loi dīn), *n.* A high explosive prepared by the action of nitric acid on starch or wood-fibre.

xylonite (zī′ lȯ nīt), *n.* Celluloid.

xylophagous (zī lof′ ȧ gùs), *a.* Boring into wood (of insects). **xylophagan,** *a.n.*

xylophilous (zi lof′ i lùs), *a.* Living or growing on wood.

xylophone (zī′ lō fōn), *n.* A musical instrument consisting of a graduated series of wooden bars vibrating when struck or rubbed.

xylose (zī′ lōz), *n.* (*Chem.*) Wood sugar.

xylotomous (zī lot′ ȯ mùs), *a.* Describing an insect that bores into wood.

xyster (zis′ tėr) [Gr. *xustēr*, from *xuein*, to scrape], *n.* (*Surg.*) An instrument for scraping bones.

xystus (zis′ tùs) [L., from Gr. *xustos*, orig. polished, as prec.], *n.* (*pl.* **-ti**) (*Class. Ant.*) A long covered portico or colonnade used for athletic exercises; a garden walk or terrace.

Y

Y, y, the twenty-fifth letter of the English alphabet (**Y's, Ys, wyes**) is both a vowel and a palatal semi-vowel; as a vowel it has the same value as *i*; at the beginning of syllables and followed by a vowel, it corresponds to the L. *i* or *j*, as in *ye, you;* (*Alg.*, *y*) the second unknown quantity or variable; a Y-shaped branch, pipe, fork, coupling, figure, etc. **Y-chromosome,** *n.* (*Biol.*) A chromosome associated with sex-determination, usually paired with X-chromosome. **Y cross:** A Y-shaped cross on chasubles, etc. **Y level:** A surveying level mounted on a pair of Ys. **Y moth:** The gamma moth, from the Y-shaped mark on its wings. **Y track:** A Y-shaped track set at right angles to a railway line used instead of a turn-table for reversing the direction of engines.

y- [M.E., from A.-S. *ge-*, cp. Dut. and G. *ge-*, pref. of p.p., etc., cp. *a-* in *alike, among*, etc.], *pref.* As in Y-CLEPT, YWIS.

-y [L. *-ius, -ia, -ium* (sometimes through F. *-ie*)], *suf.* Forming abstract nouns, etc., as in *family, memory, remedy*; [A.-S. *-ig*], forming adjectives as in *leery, mighty, trusty*; forming diminutives of proper names, etc., as *Dicky, Jimmy, sonny*; [F. *-é, -ée*, L. *-ātus, -āta, -ātum*, p.p. suf.], forming nouns as *army, deputy, treaty.*

yabber (yăb′ er) [Austral. abor.], *v.i.* To talk, to chatter. *n.* Aboriginal talk.

yabbie, yabby (yăb′ i) [Austral. abor.], *n.* A fresh-water crayfish.

yacca (yăk′ ȧ) [native name], *n.* Either of two W. Indian evergreen trees of the yew family yielding wood used for cabinet work.

yacht (yot) [Dut. *jacht* (now *jagt*), from *jagen*, to hunt], *n.* A light sailing-vessel specially designed for racing; a vessel, propelled by steam, sails, electricity, or other motive power, used for pleasure trips, cruising, travel, or as a state vessel to convey royal personages or Government officials. *v.i.* To sail or cruise about in a yacht. **yacht-built,** *a.* Built on the lines of a yacht. **yacht-club,** *n.* One for yacht-racing, etc. **yachtsman,** *n.* One who keeps or sails a yacht. **yachtsmanship,** *n.* **yachtswoman,** *n.* **yachter,** *n.* **yachting,** *n.*

yaffle (yăf′ ėl) [imit. of cry], **yaffingale** (yăf′ in gāl) [after NIGHTINGALE], *n.* The green woodpecker.

Yager (yā′ gėr) [G. *Jäger*, orig. huntsman, from *jagen*, to hunt, cp. YACHT], *n.* A member of certain German corps of light infantry, esp. of sharp-shooters.

yah (ya) [instinctive sound], *int.* An exclamation of derision.

yahoo (yȧ hoo′) [coined by Swift in 'Gulliver's Travels'], *n.* One of a race of brutes in human shape; a coarse, brutish or vicious and degraded person.

Yahveh, Yahvist, etc. [JEHOVAH].

yak (yăk) [Tibetan *gyak*], *n.* A long-haired ruminant *Bos* or *Poephagus grunniens*, from the mountainous regions of Central Asia, intermediate between the ox and the bison.

Yakut (ya kut′) [native name], *n.* One of a mixed Turkish race dwelling in the basin of the Lena, in E. Siberia.

Yale lock (yāl) [Linus *Yale* (1821–68) inventor], *n.* Protected trade name of a type of lock with a revolving barrel.

yam (yăm) [Port. *inhame*, from W. Afr. native], *n.* The fleshy edible tuber of various species of *Dioscorea*, a tropical climber orig. from India; the plant. **yam-stick,** *n.* A hard-wood stick for digging yams.

Yama (ya′ mȧ) [Sansk.], *n.* The Hindu god of the dead and judge and chastiser of souls.

yamen [YAMUN].

yammer (yăm′ ėr) [A.-S. *gēomerian*, from *gēomor*, sad, mournful], *v.i.* (*prov.*) To cry out, to whine, to complain peevishly.

yamun (ya′ mùn) [Chin.], *n.* The office or official residence of a Chinese mandarin.

yank (1) (yăngk) [cp. Swed. dial. *jakka*, to wander, Icel. *jaga*, to move about, Dut. and G. *jagen*, see YACHT, YAGER], *v.t.* To pull sharply, to twitch, to jerk (off, out of, etc.). *n.* A sharp jerk, a twitch.

Yank (2) (*slang*) [YANKEE].

Yankee (yăng′ ki) [perh. from *Yengees*, pl. Am. Ind., corr. of F. *Anglais*, the English], *n.* An inhabitant of New England (applied by foreigners to all the inhabitants of the United States), an American; (*Hist.*) a Federal soldier or Northerner in the American Civil War (1861–5). *a.* Pertaining to America or the Yankees. **Yankee doodle:** A tune (probably of English origin) and song regarded as a national air of the U.S.A. **Yankee shout:** (*Austral. slang*) Everyone pays for his own drinks. **Yankeedom, Yankeeism,** *n.* **Yankeefied** (-fīd), *a.*

yap (yăp) [imit.], *v.i.* To yelp or bark snappishly. *n.* Such a bark.

yapok (yăp′ ōk) [river *Oyapok* separating Guiana from Brazil], *n.* A small opossum, *Cheironectes variegatus*, with webbed hind feet and aquatic habits.

yapon (ya′ pon) [Am. Ind.], *n.* An evergreen shrub, *Ilex vomitoria*, growing in the Southern U.S.A., the leaves of which are used for tea and by the Indians for their 'black drink,' an emetic and purgative medicine.

yapp (yăp) [etym. unknown], *n.* A style of book-binding, usu. in leather, with flaps at the edges.

yarborough (yar′ bŏ rŏ) [Earl of *Yarborough*, who bet £1,000 that no one could hold such a hand], *n.* (*Whist, etc.*) A hand containing no card higher than a nine.

yard (1) (yard) [A.-S. *gyrd, gerd*, stick, cp. Dut. *garde*, G. *gerte*], *n.* The British standard of length, 3 ft. or 36 in.; a measuring rod of this length, or this length of material; a cylindrical spar tapering each way from the middle slung horizontally or slantwise on a mast to extend a sail; *the male organ of generation. **to man the yards:** To place men, or (of sailors) to stand along the yards, as a salute at reviews, etc. **yard-arm,** *n.* Either half of a sail-yard from the centre to the end. **yardage,** *n.* (*Eng.*) The amount of excavation in cubic yards. **yardland,** *n.* An old measurement of area, varying in different countries from 15 acres to 40 acres. **yard-measure, -stick, -wand,** *n.* A tape or stick, three feet in length and usu. graduated in feet, inches, etc., used for measuring.

yard (2) (yard) [A.-S. *geard* (cp. Dut. *gaard*, G. *garten*, Icel. *garthr*, L. *hortus*, Gr. *chortos*), doublet of GARDEN], *n.* A small piece of enclosed ground, esp. enclosed by, enclosing, or adjoining a house or other building; (*Am.*) a garden; such an enclosure used for some specified manufacture or other purpose, as a dockyard, graveyard, timber-yard, etc. *v.t.* To collect or pen (cattle, etc.) in a yard. **yard-man,** *n.* A man employed in a railway-yard. **yard-master,** *n.* The manager of this. **yardage,** *n.* **Scotland Yard, The Yard,** *n.* Headquarters in London of the Criminal Investigation Department. **stock yard,** *n.* Place where cattle are penned.

***yare** (yâr) [A.-S. *gearu, gearo*, cp. Dut. *gaar*, Icel. *görr*, G. *gar*, wholly, cogn. with GAR (2), GEAR], *a.* Ready, prepared; quick, dexterous; (*Naut.*) answering readily to the helm. *adv.* Soon. ***yarely,** *adv.* Quickly, smartly.

yarn (yarn) [A.-S. *gearn* (cp. Dut. *garen*, G., Icel., Dan., and Swed. *garn*), cogn. with G. *chordē*, CORD], *n.* Any spun fibre prepared for weaving, knitting, rope-making, etc.; (*colloq.*) a story or tale told by a sailor, a long or rambling story, esp. one of doubtful truth or accuracy. *v.i.* To tell a yarn, to spin yarns.

yarrah (yă′ rá) [Austral. abor.], *n.* The river-gum eucalyptus.

yarrow (yăr′ ō) [A.-S. *gæruwe* (cp. Dut. *gerw*, G. *garbe*), perh. cogn. with YARE], *n.* A perennial herb, *Achillea millefolium*, with white flowers, pungent odour, and astringent properties, the milfoil.

yashmak (yăsh′ măk) [Arab.], *n.* The veil worn by Moslem women in public.

Yasht (yasht) [Zend], *n.* One of a collection of hymns and prayers in the Zend-Avesta.

yataghan (yăt′ ȧ găn) [Turk.], *n.* A Mohammedan sword or scimitar with double-curved blade and without a guard or cross-piece.

yate (*prov.*) [GATE (1)].

yaup (*Sc.*) [var. of YAP]. **yaupon** [YAPON].

yaw (yaw) [Icel. *jaga*, to hunt, cp. Dut. and G. *jagen*, see YACHT, YAGER], *v.i.* (*Naut.*) To steer out of the direct course, to move unsteadily (of a ship). *n.* An unsteady motion or temporary deviation of a ship from her course. **yawing,** *n.* (*Aviat.*) The unstable motion of an aircraft about its normal axis.

yawl (1) (yawl) [M.E. *goulen*, cp. Dut. *jolen*, Icel. and Norw. *gaula*, of imit. orig., cp. YELL], *v.i.* To howl, to yell. *n.* A howl or yell.

yawl (2) (yawl) [Dut. *jol.* (cp. Dan. *jolle*, Swed. *julle*), cp. JOLLYBOAT], *n.* A small boat, esp. a ship's jolly-boat; a small sailing-vessel cutter-rigged and having a jigger-mast.

yawn (yawn) [A.-S. *gānian, gīnan* (cp. Icel. *gīna*, M.Dut. *gienen*, Dut. *geeuwen*, also L. *hiāre*)], *v.i.* To gape, to be or stand wide open; to open the mouth wide or to have the mouth open involuntarily through drowsiness, boredom, bewilderment, etc., to stand agape. *v.t.* To express or utter by or with a yawn. *n.* The act of yawning. **yawningly,** *adv.*

yaws (yawz) [perh. from Afr. native *yaw*, raspberry], *n.pl.* (*Med.*) Frambœsia.

***y-clad** (i klăd′) [Y-, CLAD], *a.* Clad, clothed.

***y-clept** (i klept′) [Y-, p.p. of CLEPE], *a.* Called, named.

ye (1) (yē, yė) [A.-S. *gē*, cp. Dut. *gij*, G. *ihr*, Icel. *ēr, ier*, Dan. and Swed. *i*, Gr. *humeis*, Sansk. *yūyam*], *pron., 2nd pers. pl.* Properly the nominative of *you*, for which it is now often used.

ye, ye (2) (*thē*). The old method of printing THE, but never pron. yē.

yea (yā) [A.-S. *gēa*, cp. Dut., G., Dan. and Swed. *ja*, Icel. *jā*, Gr. *ē*, truly], *adv.* Yes; verily, truly, indeed; not only so but also. *n.* An affirmative; one who votes in the affirmative. **oh yeah!:** *int.* (*Am. slang*) Expression of incredulity.

yean (yēn) [A.-S. *ēanian*, see EAN], *v.t.* and *i.* To bring forth (of sheep and goats). **yeanling,** *n.* A lamb or kid.

year (yĕr, yēr) [A.-S. *gēar, gēr* (cp. Dut. *jaar*, G. *jahr*, Icel. *ār*), cogn. with Gr. *hōros*, a season, L. *hōra*, HOUR], *n.* The period of time occupied by the revolution of the earth round the sun (the astronomical, equinoctial, natural, solar, or tropical year, the time taken by the sun in returning to the same equinox, in mean length, 365 days, 5 hours, 48 min., and 46 sec.; the astral or sidereal year, in which the sun apparently returns to the same place in relation to the fixed stars, 365 days, 6 hours, 9 min., and 9 sec.; the Platonic, great, or perfect year, estimated by early Greek and Hindu astronomers at about 26,000 years, at the end of which all the heavenly bodies were imagined to return to the same places as they occupied at the Creation); the period of 365 days, from 1st Jan. to 31st Dec., divided into 12 months, adopted as the calendar, legal, or civil year, one day being added every fourth year (with the exception of centuries not divisible by 400), called bissextile or leap year; any period of this length taken as a unit of time; (*pl.*) age, length or time of life, old age. **historical year:** Twelve months beginning on January 1; **Marian year,** beginning on March 25. **regnal year** [REGNAL]. **year by year:** As the years go by. **year of grace:** A year of the Christian era. **year in year out:** Right through the year, without cessation. **year-book,** *n.* A book published annually giving information up to date on some subject liable to change. **year-long,** *a.* Lasting a year. **yearly,** *a.* Happening or recurring once a year or every year, annual; lasting a year. *adv.* Annually; once a year, by the year.

yearling (yĕr′ ling), *n.* An animal more than one and less than two years old; (*Racing*) a colt a year

Y

old dating from 1st January of the year of foaling. *a.* Being one year old.

yearn (1) (yĕrn) [A.-S. *giernan* (cp. Icel. *girna*, G. *begehren*, O.H.G. *gerōn*), cogn. with Gr. *chairein*, to rejoice, L. *hortārī*, to exhort], *v.i.* To feel a longing desire, tenderness, compassion, etc. (for, after, etc.); *to grieve, to be pained or distressed. ***it yearns my heart:** It vexes or grieves me. ***yearnful,** *a.* **yearning,** *a.* and *n.* **yearningly,** *adv.*

***yearn** (2) [EARN].

yeast (yēst) [A.-S. *gist* (cp. Dut. *gest*, G. *gischt*, Icel. *jast*, *jastr*), cogn. with Gr. *zeein*, to boil], *n.* A yellowish, viscous substance consisting of a growth of fungous cells developed in contact with saccharine liquids and producing alcoholic fermentation by means of enzymes, used in brewing, distilling, etc., for raising dough for bread, etc.; (*fig.*) mental or moral ferment. **yeast-plant,** *n.* **yeast-powder,** *n.* A baking-powder used as a substitute for yeast. **yeasty,** *a.* Containing or resembling yeast, esp. in causing or being characterized by fermentation; (*fig.*) frothy, foamy; unsubstantial, empty, superficial. **yeastiness,** *n.*

yegg (yeg), *n.* (*Am. slang*) A safe-robber; a dangerous criminal.

yeld (yeld) [var. of GELD (1)], *a.* (*Sc.*) Barren, not giving milk.

yeldring [YOWLEY].

yelk [YOLK].

yell (yel) [A.-S. *gellan*, *giellan*, cp. Dut. *gillen*, G. *gellen*, Icel. *gella*], *v.i.* To cry out with a loud, sharp, or inarticulate cry as in rage, agony, terror, or uncontrollable laughter. *v.t.* To utter or express thus. *n.* Such a cry or shout, esp. the war-cry of some savages; (*Am.*) a distinctive shout used by college students, etc., for encouragement, applause, etc. **yelling,** *a.*

yelloch (*Sc.*) [YELL].

yellow (yel′ ō) [A.-S. *geolo*, *geolu* (cp. Dut. *geel*, G. *gelb*, L. *helvus*), cogn. with Gr. *chlōros*, see CHLOR-, Sansk. *harī*, green, yellow, GALL (1)], *a.* Of a colour like that between green and orange in the spectrum or like that of gold, brass, sulphur, lemon; (*fig.*) jaundiced, jealous, envious; (*colloq.*) cowardly. *n.* This colour, a yellow pigment, dye, etc.; a sulphur butterfly (and other yellow butterflies and moths); (*pl.*) jaundice, jealousy; (*Am. pl.*) a disease of unknown origin attacking peach-trees, etc. *v.t.* To make yellow. *v.i.* To turn yellow. **yellow-back,** *n.* A cheap railway-novel. **yellow-belly, -bill, -head, -legs, -poll, -rump, -seed,** *n.* Used as a name for animals, birds, fish, and plants. **yellow-backed, -bellied, -billed, -headed, -legged,** etc., *a.* **yellow-bird,** *n.* The American goldfinch, the yellow warbler, the golden oriole, and other birds. **yellow blight,** *n.* (*Hort.*) The wilt disease in potatoes. **yellow-blossomed,** *a.* **yellow-boy,** *n.* (*slang*) A gold coin. **yellow cartilage** or **tissue:** Elastic tissue. **yellow-earth,** *n.* A yellow ochre, sometimes used as a pigment. **yellow fever:** A malignant tropical fever caused by the bite of the mosquito, attended with jaundice and black vomit. **yellow-gum,** *n.* Infants' black jaundice. **yellow-hammer** [A.-S. *amore*, cp. G. *emmer*, O.H.G. *amero*, assim. to HAMMER], *n.* A bunting, *Emberiza citrinella*, with yellow head, neck, and breast. **yellow jack:** Yellow fever. **yellow-jacket,** *n.* A species of social wasp. **yellow men:** The Xanthochroi. **yellow metal:** An alloy of three parts of copper and two of zinc. **yellow peril,** *n.* The danger that the yellow races may outnumber and wipe out the white race. **yellow pine,** *n.* A soft even-grained Canadian wood. **The Yellow Press:** Journalism or the newspaper press of sensational and jingoist tendencies. **yellow-rattle,** *n.* An annual herb of the genus *Rhinanthus cristagalli*, with yellow flowers and winged seeds that rattle in the capsules when ripe. **yellow spot,** *n.* (*Zool.*) The area at the centre of the retina in vertebrates where vision is acutest in daylight. **yellow-wort,** *n.* An annual, *Chlora perfoliata*, of the gentian family, used for dyeing yellow. **yellowish, yellowy,** *a.* **yellowly,** *adv.* **yellowness,** *n.*

yelp (yelp) [A.-S. *gilpan*, to boast, cp. Icel. *gjālpa*], *v.i.* To utter a sharp, quick cry, as a dog in pain, fear, or anticipation. *n.* Such a bark or cry.

yen (1) (yen) [Jap., from Chin. *yuen*, round, dollar], *n.* (*pl. unchanged*) The Japanese monetary unit worth about 2s. 1½d.

yen (2) (yen) [Chin., opium], *n.* Ambition, yearning, desire, longing.

yeoman (yō′ mȧn) [M.E *yeman*, *yoman*, (prob. A.-S. *gā*, district or village, MAN)], *n.* (*pl.* **-men**) A freeholder not ranking as one of the gentry; a man qualified to serve on juries and to vote, etc., as holding free land of 40s. annual value; a farmer, esp. a freeholder; a small landowner; a member of the yeomanry force; *an assistant, a journeyman. **yeoman of the guard:** A beefeater. **yeomanlike,** *a.* **yeoman's service:** Good service, hearty support. **yeomanly,** *a.* **yeomanry,** *n.* (*collect.*) Yeomen; a British force of volunteer cavalry consisting largely of country gentlemen and farmers, now forming part of the Territorial Army.

-yer [var. of -ER, arising from the use of M.E. *-ien*, instead of *-en*, in causal verbs and those derived from nouns], *suf.* Denoting an agent, as in *lawyer*, *sawyer*.

yerba (yĕr′ bȧ) [Sp., from L. *herba*, HERB], *n.* Paraguay tea, maté.

***yerk** [JERK].

yes (yes) [A.-S. *gise*, *gese* (prob. *gēa swā*, YEA, SO)], *adv.* As you say, it is true, agreed (indicating affirmation or consent); I hear (in answer to a summons, etc.). *n.* (*pl.* **yeses**) The word 'yes'; an affirmative reply. **yes-man,** *n.* (*colloq.*) An unquestioning follower, a sycophant.

yester- [A.-S. *geostra*, *giestra*, usu. in acc. *geostran dæg*, yesterday (cp. Dut. *gisteren*, G. *gestern*, also L. *hesternus*, Gr. *chthes*, Sansk. *hyas*)], *pref.* Of or pertaining to the day preceding to-day. **yesterday,** *n.* The day immediately before to-day; (*fig.*) time in the immediate past. *adv.* On or during yesterday. ***yester-eve, *-even, *-evening,** (*Sc.*) **yestreen** (-trēn′), *n.* and *adv.* Yesterday evening. **yestermorn,** *n.* and *adv.* **yesternight,** *n.* and *adv.* Last night. **yester-year,** *n.* and *adv.* (*poet.*) Last year.

yet (yet) [A.-S. *git*, *get*, *giet*, cp. Fris. *jiette*, G. *jetzt*], *adv.* Still, up to this or that time; by this or that time, so soon or early as the present, so far, in addition, further, besides; eventually, at some future time, before all is over; even (*with compar.*); nevertheless, in spite of that. *conj.* Nevertheless, notwithstanding, but still. **as yet:** Up to this or that time, so far. **just yet:** In the immediate future (*with neg.*). **not yet:** Not up to the present time.

yeti (yet′ i) [Tibetan], *n.* The hypothetical creature whose tracks are alleged to have been found in the snows of the Himalayas, also called 'The Abominable Snowman.'

yett (*Sc.*) [GATE (1)].

yew (ū) [A.-S. *īw*, cp. G. *eibe*, Icel. *ӯr*], *n.* A dark-leaved evergreen shrub or tree of the genus *Taxus*, esp. *T. baccata*, a large tree with spreading branches, the wood of which has long been valued for making bows; its wood. **yew-tree,** *n.*

Yggdrasill (ig′ drȧ sil) [Icel. Odin's horse (*Yggr*, a name of Odin, *dresill*, horse)], *n.* (*Scand. Myth.*) The world-tree binding together heaven, earth, and hell with its roots and branches.

Yiddish (yid′ ish), *n.* A language spoken by Jews of E. Europe and N. America, based on a Hebraicised Middle German, with an admixture of Polish, French and English.

yield (yēld) [A.-S. *gieldan*, to pay, cp. Dut. *gelden*, G. *gelten*, Icel. *gjalda*, Swed. *gälla*, to be worth], *v.t.* To produce, to bear, to bring forth as fruit, reward, or result; to give up, to surrender, to concede, to relinquish, to resign. *v.i.* To give a return, to repay one's labour in cultivation, etc., to bear, produce, or bring forth (well or ill); to give way, to assent, to submit, to comply, to surrender; to make submission (to); to give place, to yield precedence or admit inferiority (to). *n.* That which is yielded or produced, output, return. **yieldable,** *a.* ***yieldance,** *n.* **yielder,** *n.* **yielding,** *a.* Compliant. **yieldingly,** *adv.* **yieldingness,** *n.*

yill (*Sc.*) [ALE].

-yl [Gr. *hulē*, wood, material], *suf.* (*Chem.*) Denoting a radical; as in *ethyl, methyl.*

ylang-ylang (ē′ lăng ē′ lăng) [Malay, flower of flowers], *n.* A Malayan tree, *Canangium odoratum*, of the custard-apple family; a perfume made from the flowers of this.

y level, y moth [Y].

Ynca [INCA].

yodel (yō′ dėl) [G. dial. *jodeln*], *v.t.* and *i.* To sing or shout in a musical fashion characterized by alternation from the natural voice to the falsetto. *n.* Such a shout or musical cry, peculiar to Swiss and Tyrolese mountaineers; a yodelling contest. **yodeller,** *n.*

yoga (yō′ gȧ) [Hindi, from Sansk., union], *n.* A Hindu system of abstract meditation and rigid asceticism by which the soul is supposed to become united with the eternal spirit of the universe; certain exercises and practices assisting this. **yogi,** *n.* A devotee or adept of yoga. **yogism,** *n.*

yogourt (yō′ goort) [Turk.], *n.* A dish of milk fermented in a special way.

yo-heave-ho (yō hēv hō′) [inst. sound], *int.* (*Naut.*) A sailor's cry while heaving the anchor, etc.

yo-ho (yô hō′) [redupl. of HO], *int.* An exclamation calling attention.

yoicks (yoicks) [etym. doubtful], *int* and *n.* A fox-hunter's hallo cry. **yoick,** *int.* and *n.* Yoicks; *v.i.* To cry 'yoicks'; *v.t.* To urge (hounds) on thus.

yojan (yō′ jȧn) [Hindi], *n.* An East Indian measure of distance, usu. about five miles.

yoke (yōk) [A.-S. *geoc* (cp. Dut. *juk*, G. *joch*, Icel. and Swed. *ok*, L. *jugum*, Gr. *zugon*, Sansk. *yuga-*), cogn. with JOIN], *n.* A frame or cross-bar fitting over the necks of two oxen or other draught animals and attaching them to a plough or vehicle; a device resembling this; a frame fitting a person's shoulders for carrying a pair of buckets suspended from the ends; a frame or cross-bar on which a bell swings; the cross-bar of a rudder to which the steering-lines are fastened; a coupling for two pipes discharging into one; a coupling, guiding, or controlling piece in a machine; a tie-beam, tie-rod, etc.; a part of a garment made to support the rest, as at the shoulders or hips; (*fig.*) a bond, a link, a tie, esp. that of love or wedlock; a pair of draught animals, esp. oxen yoked together; (*Rom. Hist.*) two upright spears with a third resting across them at the top, under which vanquished enemies were made to pass; hence, servitude, slavery, submission. *v.t.* To put a yoke upon; to unite by a yoke; to couple, esp. in marriage; to join, to link; to enslave. *v.i.* To go or work (well or ill together, etc.). ***yoke of land:** As much land as might be ploughed by a yoke of oxen in a day. **yoke-bone,** *n.* The malar or cheek-bone connecting the bones at the side of the head with those of the face. **yoke-fellow, -mate,** *n.* A person associated with one in marriage, work, etc., a companion, a partner. **yoke-line, -rope,** *n.* One of the pair of ropes by which a rudder-yoke is worked.

yokel (yō′ kėl) [prob. from prec., ploughman], *n.* A rustic, a country bumpkin.

yolding, yoldring [YOWLEY].

yolk (yōk) [A.-S. *geolca*, YELLOW], *n.* The yellow part of an egg, the contents of the ovum, esp. that nourishing the embryo, the vitellus; the unctuous secretion from the sebaceous glands of sheep, wool-oil. **yolk-sac,** *n.* The thin, membranous bag enclosing the yolk in an egg. **yolked, yolky,** *a.*

Yom Kippur (yom kip′ ėr, yom ki poor′) [Heb.], *n.* The Day of Atonement, a Jewish day of fasting.

yon (yon) [A.-S. *geon* (cp. Icel. *enn*, G. *jener*)], *a.* and *adv.* (*Sc.*) Yonder. *pron.* (*prov.*) Yonder person, thing, or place.

yonder (yon′ dėr) [M.E., from prec.], *a.* That over there; being at a distance, but in the direction looked at or pointed out; distant but within view. *adv.* Over there; at a distance but within view, or where one is looking or pointing.

yoni (yō′ ni) [Sansk.], *n.* The Hindu symbol of the fertility of nature under which the consort of a male deity is worshipped, represented by an oval figure (the female organ).

yore (yôr) [A.-S. *geāra*, orig. gen. pl. of *gēar*, YEAR], *n.* Long ago, old time. **of yore:** Formerly of old time, long ago.

yorker (yôr′ kėr) [prob. from being first used by a Yorkshire player], *n.* (*Cricket*) A ball bowled so as to pitch immediately in front of the bat. **york,** *v.t.* To bowl with a yorker.

Yorkist (yôr′ kist), *a.* Of or pertaining to the house descended from Edmund Duke of York, son of Edward III, or the White Rose party supporting this in the Wars of the Roses. *n.* An adherent of this house or party.

Yorkshire (yôrk′ shir) [county in N. of England], *a.* Of or derived from Yorkshire. **Yorkshire flannel:** Flannel of undyed wool. **yorkshire grit:** A grit used for polishing. **Yorkshire pudding:** Batter baked under meat, esp. beef. **Yorkshire terrier:** A small shaggy variety of toy terrier.

you (ū, yu) [A.-S. *ēow*, dat. and acc. of *gē*, *ye* (see also YE), sing. **thou,** obj. **thee,** poss. **your, yours**], *2nd pers. pron. sing. and pl.* (*with pl. v.*) The person, animal, thing, or persons, etc., addressed; (*reflex.*) yourself. yourselves; (*indef.*) one, anyone, people generally. **you're another:** (*vulg.*) A retort to abuse, etc.

young (yŭng) [A.-S. *geong*, cp. Dut. *jong*, G. *jung*, Icel. *ungr*, Dan. and Swed. *ung*, L. *juvenis*, Sansk. *yuvan*], *a.* Being in the early stage of life, growth, or development; of recent birth or beginning, newly formed, produced, come into action or operation, etc.; not infirm or decayed with age, vigorous, fresh; immature, raw, inexperienced; pertaining to or characteristic of youth. *n.* Offspring, esp. of animals. **with young:** Pregnant. **young blood:** A new accession of vigour or enterprise. **young England, Ireland, Italy, Turks,** etc.: Names of political parties striving to sweep away abuses and introduce radical reforms. **young man, woman,** *n.* A sweetheart. **youngish,** *a.* **youngling,** *n.* ***youngly,** *a.* and *adv.* **youngness,** *n.* **youngster,** *n.* A young person, a child, a lad.

younker (yŭng′ kėr) [Dut. *jonker* (*jong*, YOUNG, *heer*, SIR, cp. HERR)], *n.* (*colloq.*) A youngster; *a stripling; a junker.

your (yôr, yur, ūr) [A.-S. *ēower*, gen. pl. of YE], *a.* Pertaining or belonging to you (often used indefinitely with a suggestion of disparagement). **yours,** *pron.* That or those belonging or pertaining to you. *a.* (*predicatively*) Belonging to you; at your service. **you and yours:** You and your family or belongings. **yours faithfully, obediently, truly,** etc.: Formal expressions preceding the signature in a letter. **yours truly:** (*vulg.*) I, this person. **yourself** (-self′), *pron.* (*pl.* **-selves**) You and not another or others, you alone; you in your own person or in particular; you in your normal condition, health, etc.; also used reflexively. **by yourself:** Alone; unaided.

youth (ūth) [A.-S. *geoguth* (YOUNG, -TH), cp. Dut. *jeugd*, G. *jugend*, L. *juventa*], *n.* (*pl.* **youths,** ū*thz*) The state of being young; the period of life from infancy to manhood or womanhood, youthfulness, the vigour, freshness, inexperience, etc. of this period; a young man; young men and women collectively. ***youthhood,** *n.* **Youth Hostel,** *n.* An organized establishment where hikers, etc., may put up for the night. **youthful,** *a.* **youthfully,** *adv.* **youthfulness,** *n.* ***youthly, *youthsome,** *a.*

yowl [var. of YAWL (1)].

yowley (you′ li) [A.-S. *geolo, georwe*, yellow], *n.* (*prov.*) The yellow-hammer.

yo-yo (yō′ yō), *n.* Protected trade name of a toy which consists of a spool winding up and down on a string.

ytterbium (i tĕr′ bi ŭm) [*Ytterby*, town in Sweden, -IUM], *n.* (*Chem.*) A rare metallic element discovered spectroscopically in gadolinite. **yttria**, *n.* A white earth regarded as the peroxide of yttrium. **ytterbic, yttric, yttrious, yttriferous** (-trif ėr ŭs), *a.*

yttrium (it′ ri ŭm), *n.* A rare metallic element belonging to the cerium group.

yttro-, *comb. form.* **yttrocerite** (it rō ser′ īt), *n.* A violet-blue fluoride of yttrium. **yttrotantalite** (it rō tăn′ tå līt), *n.* An orthorhombic tantalite of yttrium.

yucca (yŭk′ å) [Sp. *yuca*, from Haytian], *n.* A liliaceous sub-tropical American flowering-plant, with rigid lanceolate leaves and an erect panicle of white flowers, many species of which are grown for ornament.

yuck (yŭk) [etym. doubtful], *v.i.* (*prov.*) To itch. *n.* The itch.

yuga (yoo′ gå) [Sansk.], *n.* One of the Hindu ages or cycles of the world.

Yugoslav (yoo′ gō slav) [Serb., south Slav], *a.* Of or pertaining to the southern Slav races or countries, esp. Yugoslavia. *n.* A native, citizen or inhabitant of Yugoslavia.

yulan (yoo′ lån) [Chin. (*yu*, gem, *lan*, plant)], *n.* A Chinese tree, *Magnolia yulan*, with large, brilliant, snow-white or rosy flowers.

yule (yool) [A.-S. *gēola*, cp. Icel. *jōl*, etym. doubtful], *n.* Christmas time or the festival of Christmas. **yule-log**, *n.* A log formerly burned on Christmas Eve. **yule-tide**, *n.*

Yunx (yungks) [Gr. *iunx*], *n.* (*Ornith.*) A genus of birds containing the wrynecks; a wryneck.

ywis (i wis′) [A.-S. *gewis* (cp. Dut. *gewis*, G. *gewiss*, Icel. and Swed. *viss*), cogn. with WIT (I)], *adv.* Certainly, verily, truly.

Z

Z, z, the last letter of the English alphabet (*pl.* **Zs, Z's, zeds**) has the sound of a voiced or sonant *s*, as in *zeal*, *lazy*, *reason*, or of a voiced *sh*, as in *azure*; (*Alg.*, *z.*) the third unknown quantity or variable.

Zabian, etc. [SABIAN].

zabra (za′ brå) [Sp.], *n.* A small sailing vessel formerly used on the coasts of the Iberian Peninsula.

zaffre, zaffer (zăf′ ėr) [F. *zafre*, from Arab.], *n.* Impure oxide of cobalt used for enamelling and as a blue pigment for painting on glass, porcelain, etc.

zambomba (thăm bom′ bå) [Sp.], *n.* A toy musical instrument made by stretching a piece of parchment over a wide-mouthed jar and inserting a stick through it which is rubbed with the fingers.

Zamia (zā′ mi å) [L. and Gr., hurt, damage], *n.* A genus of palm-like trees or low shrubs of the cyad family, from the West Indies and America, from the seeds of some of which Florida arrow-root is prepared.

zamouse (zå moos′) [native name], *n.* The W. African short-horned buffalo, *Bos brachyceros*.

zampogna (tsam pō′ nya) [It.], *n.* An Italian bag-pipe.

zanje (than′ hē) [Sp. Am.], *n.* A canal for irrigation. ***zanjero*** (-hâr′ ō), *n.* A person employed in working this.

Zante (zan′ tā) [one of the Ionian Islands], *n.* Zante-wood. **Zante-wood**, *n.* The wood of the smoke-tree, *Rhus cotinus*.

zany (zā′ ni) [F. *zani*, It. *zanni*, fam. for *Giovanni*, John], *n.* A buffoon in old theatrical entertainments who mimicked the clown; a simpleton, a fool. **zanyism**, *n.*

zapotilla [SAPODILLA].

zaptieh (zăp′ ti ā) [Turk.], *n.* A Turkish policeman.

Zarathustrian, etc. [ZOROASTRIAN].

zaratite (za′ rå tīt) [Señor *Zarate*], *n.* (*Min.*) A hydrous carbonate of nickel, usu. occurring as an incrustation.

zareba (zå rē′ bå) [Arab. *zarība, -bat*], *n.* A stockade, hedge, or other enclosure for a camp or village in the Sudan.

zarf (zarf) [Arab.], *n.* An ornamental cup-shaped holder for a hot coffee-cup.

zastruga (zas troo′ gå) [Rus.], *n.* A ridge of snow caused by the wind.

zax (zăks) [A.-S. *seax*], *n.* A slater's hatchet with a sharp point for perforating the slate, a sax.

Zea (zē′ å) [L. and Gr., spelt], *n.* (*Bot.*) A genus of tall, half-hardy grasses, with but one species, *Z. mays*, Indian corn or maize.

zeal (zēl) [O.F. *zele*, L. *zēlum*, nom. *-us*, Gr. *zēlos*], *n.* Ardour, earnestness, enthusiasm, intense and eager pursuit or endeavour to attain or accomplish some object. ***zealed**, ***zealful**, *a.* ***zealless**, *a.* **zealot** (zel′ ŏt), *n.* One full of zeal, esp. one carried away by excess of zeal; a fanatical partisan. ***zealotical** (-lot′ i kål), *a.* **zealotism, zealotry** (zel′ ŏ tizm, -tri), *n.* **zealous** (zel′ ŭs), *a.* **zealously**, *adv.* **zealousness**, *n.*

zebec, zebeck [XEBEC].

zebra (zē′ brå) [Port., from Afr. native], *n.* A striped ass-like mammal of the genus *Equus*, esp. *E. zebra*, the true or mountain zebra from the mountainous regions of S. Africa. **zebra-antelope, -caterpillar, -fish, -mouse, -wolf, -wood, -woodpecker**, *n.* A striped variety or species. **zebra crossing**, *n.* A street-crossing marked by stripes where pedestrians have precedence over all other traffic. **zebrine**, *a.*

zebu (zē′ bū) [F. *zébu*, Tibetan *mdzopo*], *n.* The humped Indian ox, *Bos indicus*.

zebub (zē′ bŭb) [Arab. *zubāb*, fly], *n.* An Abyssinian fly similar to the tsetse.

zechinno [SEQUIN].

zechstein (zech′ stīn) [G. (*zeche*, mine, *stein*, stone)], *n.* (*Geol.*) A German magnesian limestone.

zed (zed) [F. *zède*, L. and Gr. *zēta*], *n.* The letter Z.

zedoary (zed′ ŏ ăr i) [M.F. *zedoaire*, med. L. *zedoāria*, Pers. *zadwār*], *n.* A substance made from the root-stock of some species of curcuma, used in medicine, dyeing, perfumery, etc.

zee (zē), American name for the letter Z.

zein (zē′ in) [G. *zea*, spelt], *n.* A protein found in Indian corn.

Zeitgeist (tsīt′ gīst) [G., time-spirit], *n.* The spirit, or moral and intellectual tendency, of a period.

Zelanian (zē lā′ ni ån) [mod. L. *Zelania*, -AN], *a.* (*Zool.*) Of or pertaining to New Zealand.

zeloso (tsā lō′ sō) [It., as ZEALOUS], *adv.* (*Mus.*) With energy.

zemindar (zem′ in dar) [Pers. *zemin*, land, *-dār*, holding], *n.* One of a class of Bengali landowners formerly paying a certain land-tax to the British government; orig. a local governor and farmer of the revenue under the Mogul empire paying a fixed sum for his district. **zemindary**, *n.*

zemstvo (zemst′ fō) [Rus.], *n.* A Russian elective local assembly dealing with economic affairs.

Zen (zen), *n.* (*Relig.*) A Japanese Buddhist sect teaching that truth is in one's heart and can be learned only by meditation and self-mastery.

zenana (zė na′ nȧ) [Hind. *zanāna*, from Pers. *zanān*, pl. of *zan*, woman, cp. Gr. *gunē*], *n.* The portion of the house in a high-caste Indian family reserved for the women. **Zenana Mission:** A mission undertaken by women for speading educational, medical, and religious reforms among the inmates of zenanas.

Zend (zend) [orig., a commentary], *n.* The ancient Iranian language, closely allied to Sanskrit, in which the sacred writings of the Zoroastrians are set down; a name for the Zend-Avesta. **Zend-Avesta** (-ȧ ves′ tȧ) [*Avesta*, text], *n.* A collection of the sacred scriptures of the Parsees or Zoroastrians.

zenith (zen′ ith) [M.E. *senith*, O.F. *cenith* (F. *zénith*), O.Sp. *zenith*, Arab. *samt* (*pron.* semt), way, road], *n.* The point in the heavens directly overhead to an observer, opp. to nadir; (*fig.*) the highest or culminating point. **zenith-distance,** *n.* The angular distance of a heavenly body from the zenith. **zenith-sector,** *n.* An astronomical instrument for measuring zenith-distances. **zenith telescope,** *n.* (*Astron.*) An instrument used to determine latitude. **zenithal,** *a.*

zeolite (zē′ ō līt) [Gr. *zeein*, to boil, -LITE], *n.* (*Min.*) Any one of a group of hydrous silicates found in cavities of eruptive rocks, which gelatinize in acid owing to the liberation of silica. **zeolithiform** (-lith′ i fôrm), **zeolitic,** *a.* **zeolitize** (zė ol′ i tīz), *v.t.*

zephyr (zef′ ir) [F. *zéphyr*, L. *zephyrus*, Gr. *zephuoros*], *n.* The west wind personified; any soft, gentle breeze; light, gauzy worsted or woollen yarn, used for shawls, jerseys, etc,; a jersey or other garment made of this.

Zeppelin (zep′ e lin) [Count *Zeppelin* (1838–1918)], *n.* (*Aviat.*) A large dirigible airship.

zerda (zĕr′ dȧ) [Afr. native], *n.* The fennec.

zero (zēr′ ō) [O.F. and It., for *zefiro*, Arab. *cipr*, CIPHER], *n.* (*pl.* **-oes**) The figure 0, a cipher, nothing, nil; the point on a scale from which positive or negative quantities are reckoned, esp. on a thermometer (in Fahrenheit's thermometer 32° below the freezing-point of water, in the Centigrade and Réaumur's scales zero is the freezing-point); the lowest point in any scale or standard of comparison, the nadir, nullity. **absolute zero:** The point at which a body would be totally devoid of heat, estimated at about −273° C., or −460° F. **zero-beat,** *n.* (*Radio.*) The position when two radio frequencies are adjusted to equality by producing beats between them at the start, and reducing the beat frequency to zero. **zero-beat reception,** *n.* (*Radio.*) A system of radio reception in which the receiver generates an oscillation of exactly the same frequency as the incoming signal, and impresses both simultaneously on the detector. **zero hour, day,** *n.* The precise hour or day for the commencement of a prearranged military or other movement.

zest (zest) [O.F., the woody skin dividing the kernel of a walnut, from L. and Gr. *schistos*, cleft, from *schizein*, to divide], *n.* *A piece of lemon peel used to give a flavour to soups, wines, etc.; hence, that which makes a thing enjoyable, piquancy, relish; keen enjoyment.

Zeta (zē′ tȧ) [acronym Zero Energy Thermonuclear Assembly], *n.* A British apparatus used in investigating the controlled production of nuclear energy by the fusion of hydrogen.

zeta (zē′ tȧ) [late L., from Gr. *diaita*, dwelling, see DIET (1)], *n.* A little closet or chamber; a sexton's room over the porch of a church, where church documents, etc., were kept.

zetetic (zē tet′ ik) [Gr. *zētētikos*, from *zēteein*, to seek], *a.* Proceeding by enquiry. *n.* A seeker (a name adopted by some of the Pyrrhonists).

zeuglodon (zūg′ lō don) [Gr. *zeuglē*, strap of a yoke, from *zeugnunai*, to yoke, *odous odontos*, tooth], *n.* (*Palæont.*) A genus of extinct cetaceans from the Eocene; any individual of such genus.

zeugma (zūg′ mȧ) [Gr. *zeugma -matos*, yoke, see prec.], *n.* (*Gram.*) A figure in which a verb or adjective governs or modifies two nouns to only one of which it is logically applicable. **zeugmatic** (-măt′ ik), *a.*

Zeus (zūs) [Gr.], *n.* (*Gr. Myth.*) The supreme deity of the Greeks, corresponding to the Roman Jupiter.

zeuxite (zūk′ sīt) [Gr. *zeuxis*, joining from *zeugnunai*, to yoke, -ITE], *n.* (*Min.*) A variety of tourmaline.

zibet (zib′ et) [It. *zibello*, CIVET], *n.* The Indian or Asiatic civet, *Viverra zibetha.*

zigzag (zig′ zăg) [F., from G. *zickzack*, redupl. from *zacke*, tooth, prong, cp. TACK], *a.* Having sharp alternate turns or angles to left and right. *n.* A zigzag line, road, path, pattern, moulding, series of trenches, etc. *adv.* In a zigzag course or manner. *v t.* (*past & p.p.* **zigzagged**) To form or do in a zigzag fashion. *v.i.* To move in a zigzag course. **zigzaggery,** *n.* **zigzaggy,** *a.*

zimb (zimb) [Arab.], *n.* A dipterous insect common in Abyssinia resembling the tsetse, and hurtful to cattle.

ziment-water (zi ment′ waw′ tėr) [G. *Cementwasser*, cement-water], *n.* Water found in copper mines impregnated with copper.

zimocca (zi mok′ ȧ) [It.], *n.* A soft, fine, cup-chaped bath-sponge from the Mediterranean.

zinc (zingk) [G. *zingk*, etym. doubtful], *n.* A bluish-white metallic element used in the manufacture of brass and German silver, for coating sheet-iron, as roofing-material, for printing-blocks, etc. *v.t.* To coat or cover with zinc. **flowers of zinc:** White powdery oxide of zinc used as a white pigment, and in cements, ointments, etc. **zinc-blende,** *n.* Native sulphide of zinc. **zinc-emyl,** *n.* A colourless liquid obtained by heating zinc with mercuric amylate. **zinc-ethyl,** *n.* A volatile liquid compound formed by heating ethyl iodide with zinc in a sealed tube. **zinc-methyl,** *n.* A colourless mobile liquid, of very fetid odour and spontaneously inflammable, similar to zinc-ethyl in preparation. **zinc-white,** *n.* Oxide of zinc used as a pigment. **zinc-worker,** *n.* **zincic** (zin′ sik), **zinciferous** (-sif′ ėr ŭs), **zincoid, zinky,** *a.* **zincify** (zin′ si fī), *v.t.* **zincification** (-kā′ shŭn), *n.* **zincite,** *n.* (*Min.*) A native oxide of zinc. **zinco,** *n.* (*colloq.*) A zincograph. **zinco-,** *comb. form.* **zincode** [Gr. *hodos*, way], *n.* (*Elec.*) The positive pole of a voltaic cell. **zincograph** [-GRAPH], *n.* A zinc plate on which a picture or design has been etched in relief for printing; an impression from this. **zincographer** (-kog′ rȧ fėr), *n.* **zincographic** (-grăf′ ik), *a.* **zincography** (-kog′ rȧ fi), *n.* **zinco-type,** *n.* A zincograph. **zincous,** *a.* Pertaining to zinc, or to the negative pole of a voltaic battery.

zincic, zincoid, etc. [ZINC].

zingaro (zing′ gȧ rō) [It.], *n.* (*pl.* **-ri**, rē,) A gipsy.

Zingiber (zin′ ji bėr) [L., ginger], *n.* (*Bot.*) A genus of monocotyledonous tropical herbs with creeping, jointed, woody root-stocks, of which the common ginger, *Z. officinale*, is the type. **Zingiberaceous,** *a.*

Zinjanthropus Boisei (zin jăn thrō′ pŭs boi′ sė ī), *n.* (*Anthrop.*) Name given to the earliest known man, found by Dr. Leakey in Tanganyika in 1959.

****zinke*** (tsing′ kė) [G.], *n.* (*Mus.*) (*pl.* **-ken**) An old wind instrument consisting of a leather-covered tube with seven finger-holes, the precursor of the cornet.

zinky [ZINC].

zinnia (zin′i ȧ) [J. G. *Zinn* (1727–59) G. botanist], *n.* A plant of the aster family with showy-rayed flowers in single terminal heads.

Zion (zī′ ŏn) [Gr., from Heb. *tsīyōn*, hill], *n.* A hill in ancient Jerusalem, the royal residence of David and his successors; (*fig.*) the ancient Hebrew theocracy, the Church of Christ, the heavenly Jerusalem heaven; used as a name for a Nonconformist chapel. **Zionism,** *n.* A movement for repeopling the Holy Land with Jews. **Zionist,** *n.* **Zionwards,** *adv.*

zip (zip) [imit.], *n.* The sharp sound made by a bullet or other missile striking an object or flying through the air. *v.i.* (*past & p.p.* **zipped**) To move or fly with such a sound. **zip-fastener, zipper** (zip, zip′ ĕr), *n.* A fastening device, with interlocking teeth, which opens or closes with a single motion.

zircon (zĕr′ kȯn) [Arab. *zarqūn*, Pers. *zargūn*, gold-coloured], *n.* A translucent, variously-coloured silicate of zirconium, some varieties of which are cut into gems. **zirconate,** *n.* A salt of zirconic acid. **zirconic** (-kon′ ik), *a.* **zirconium,** *n.* An earthy metallic element found chiefly in zircon.

zither (zith′ ėr) [G., from L. *cithara*, CITHER], *n.* A simple stringed instrument consisting of a flat sounding-board and strings plucked by the fingers.

zizania (zi zā′ ni ȧ) [Gr. *zizanion*, a weed, perh. darnel], *n.* (*Bot.*) A genus of tall aquatic grasses comprising the different species of rice.

zloty (zlō′ ti) [Pol.], *n.* A coin and monetary unit of Poland, about 1s. 9d.

zoa, *pl.* [ZOON].

zoantharia (zō ăn thâr′ i ȧ) [Gr. *zoon*, an animal; *anther*, a flower], *n.* (*Zool.*) An order of Actinozoa which includes sea-anemones, etc.

zoanthropy (zȯ ăn′ thrȯ pi) [Gr. *zoon*, animal, *anthrōpos*, man], *n.* A form of monomania in which the patient believes himself transformed into one of the lower animals. **zoanthropic** (-throp′ ik), *a.*

zoarium (zȯ âr′ i ŭm) [Gr. *zōarion*, dim. of *zōon*, animal], *n.* (*pl.* **-ia**) A polyzoan colony, a polyzoary.

zobo [ZEBU].

zocco (zok′ ō), **zoccolo** (zok′ ȯ lō) [It.], *n.* A socle.

zodiac (zō′ di ăk) [F. *zodiaque*, L. *zōdiacus*, Gr. *zōdiakos*, orig. adj., pertaining to animals, from *zōdion*, dim. of *zōon*, animal], *n.* The zone or broad belt of the heavens, extending about 8° to each side of the ecliptic, which the sun traverses during the year, anciently divided into twelve equal parts called the signs of the zodiac, which orig. corresponded to the zodiacal constellations bearing the same names, but now, through the precession of the equinoxes, coinciding with the constellations bearing the names next in order; *(*fig.*) a complete circuit, compass, or course. **zodiacal** (-dī′ ȧ kȧl), *a.* Pertaining to the zodiac. **zodiacal constellation** [see above]. **zodiacal light:** A triangular tract or pillar of light sometimes seen, esp. in the tropics, rising from the point at which the sun is just about to rise or has just set.

zoetic (zō et′ ik) [Gr. *zōē*, life, -IC], *a.* Pertaining to or of the nature of life, vital.

zoetrope (zō′ ė trōp) [as prec., Gr. *tropos*, turn], *n.* A wheel of life.

zoic (zō′ ik) [Gr. *zōikos*, from *zōon*, animal], *a.* Of or pertaining to animals or animal life; (*Geol.*) containing fossils or other evidences of plant or animal life.

zoilean (zō il′ ė ȧn), *a.* Like or pertaining to Zoilus, a Greek grammarian of the 4th cent. B.C., who severely criticised Homer, Plato, and Socrates; bitter, severe, malignant (of criticism or critics). **zoilism,** *n.*

zoisite (zoi′ sīt) [Baron von *Zois* (d. 1819), discoverer, -ITE], *n.* (*Min.*) A translucent silicate of calcium and aluminium, first found in Carinthia.

zoism (zō′ izm), *n.* The doctrine that life originates from a specific principle, and is not merely the resultant of various forces. **zoist,** *n.* **zoistic,** *a.*

Zolaism (zō′ lȧ izm) [Emile *Zola* (1840–1902), F. novelist], *n.* Excessive naturalism, unshrinking realism dealing with the sordid and repulsive aspects of life. **Zolaesque** (zō lȧ esk′), **Zolaistic** (-is′ tik), *a.* **Zolaist,** *n.*

Zollverein (tsol′-, tsōl′ fė rīn) [G. (*zoll*, duty, *Verein*, union)], *n.* A customs union among States maintaining a tariff against imports and usu. having free trade with each other.

zonal, zonary, etc. [ZONE].

zonda (zon′ dȧ) [village in Argentina], *n.* A hot dry west wind blowing from the Andes, usu. during July and August, in the Argentine.

zone (zōn) [F., from L. *zōna*, Gr. *zōnē*, girdle, from *zōnnunai*, to gird], *n.* *A girdle, a belt; a well-marked band or stripe encircling an object; any one of the five great divisions of the earth bounded by circles parallel to the equator (the **torrid zone** between the tropics extending 23½° on each side of the equator, the **temperate zones** between the tropics and the polar circles, and the **frigid zones** situated within the polar circles); any well-defined belt or tract of land distinguished by climate, the character of its organisms, etc.; the part of the surface of a sphere or of a cone or cylinder enclosed between two parallel planes perpendicular to the axis. *v.t.* To encircle with or as with a zone; to allocate rations, etc., to certain districts or zones. **zone time,** *n.* Local time for any longitude, as opp. to Greenwich Time. **zonal, zonary,** *a.* **zonal geranium:** (*pop.*) A pelargonium with a leaf having zonal markings, formerly grown as a bedding-plant. **zonally,** *adv.* **zonate,** *a.* (*Bot. and Zool.*) Marked with zones or concentric bands of colour. **zoned,** *a.* ***zoneless,** *a.* Destitute of a zone; ungirded. **zoning,** *n.* The marking off in town-planning of certain areas for specific purposes, *e.g.* residence, shopping, etc. **zonule, zonulet,** *n.* **zonular,** *a.*

zoo (zoo) [short for ZOOLOGICAL], *n.* (*colloq.*) A zoological garden or a collection of living wild animals, esp. the Zoological Gardens in London.

zoo- [Gr. *zōon*, animal, neut. of *zoos*, living, from *zaein* (Ionic *zōein*), to live], *comb. form.* Pertaining to animals or to animal life. **zooblast** (zō′ ȯ blăst) [Gr. *blastos*, germ], *n.* An animal cell. **zoochemical** (zō ȯ kem′ i kȧl) [CHEMICAL], *a.* **zoochemistry,** *n.* The chemistry of the substances occurring in the animal economy. **zoodynamics** (-dī năm′ iks) [DYNAMICS], *n.* The science of the vital power of animals. **zoœcium** (zō ē′ shi ŭm) [Gr. *oikos*, house], *n.* (*pl.* **-cia**) One of the cells forming the investment of polyzoans. **zoogamy** (zō og′ ȧ mi) [Gr. *gamos*, marriage], *n.* Sexual reproduction. **zoogeny** (-oj′ ė ni) [-GENY], **zoogony** (-og′ ȯ ni) [Gr. *-gonia*, begetting, from *-gon-*, stem of *gignesthai*, to beget], *n.* The formation of animal organs. **zoograft** [GRAFT (1)], *n.* A zooplastic graft.

zoogeography (zō ō jē og′ rȧ fi), *n.* The study of the distribution of animals, faunal geography. **zoogeographer,** *n.* **zoogeographical** (-grăf′ i kȧl), *a.* **zoography** (zō og′ rȧ fi) [-GRAPHY], *n.* Descriptive zoology. **zoographer,** *n.* **zoographic, -al** (-grăf′ ik, -ȧl), *a.* **zoogyroscope** (-jīr′ ȯ skōp) [GYROSCOPE], *n.* A development of the zoetrope by which a series of successive instantaneous photographs of an animal in motion are projected as a continuous picture on a screen.

zooid (zō′ oid), *a.* Having the nature of an animal, having organic life and motion. *n.* A more or less independent organism developed by fission or gemmation; a member of a compound organism; an organic body or cell capable of independent motion.

zoolatry (zō ol′ ȧ tri) [ZOO-, -LATRY], *n.* Animal-worship. **zoolater,** *n.* An animal-worshipper. **zoolatrous,** *a.* **zoolite** (zō′ ȯ līt) [-LITE], *n.* A fossil animal or animal substance.

zoology (zō ol′ ȯ ji), *n.* The natural history of animals, the branch of biology dealing with the structure, physiology, classification, habits, and distribution of animals. **zoological** (zō ȯ loj′ i kȧl), *a.* **zoological garden:** A public garden or park in which a collection of wild and other animals is kept. **zoologically,** *adv.* **zoologist** (zō ol′ ȯ jist), *n.*

zoom (zoom) [onomat.], *v.i.* (*Aviat.*) To turn upwards suddenly at a very sharp angle.

zoomagnetism (zō ȯ măg′ nė tizm), *n.* Animal magnetism. **zoomancy** (zō′ ȯ măn si) [-MANCY], *n.* Divination by means of observation of the movements and behaviour of animals. **zoomechanics** (-mė kăn′ iks), *n.* Zoodynamics. **zoometry** (zō om′ ė tri) [-METRY], *n.* Comparative measurement of the parts of animals. **zoometric** (-met′ rik), *a.* **zoomorphic** (-môr′ fik) [Gr. *morphē*, form], *a.* Pertaining to or exhibiting animal forms; representing animals (of religious symbolism); represented under the form of animals (of gods). **zoomorphism**, *n.*

zoon (zō′ on) [Gr. *zoon*, see ZOO-], *n.* (*pl.* **zoa**) The total product of a fertilized ovum; a developed individual of a compound organism. **zoonal** (zō′ ȯ nål), **zoonitic** (-nit′ ik), *a.* **zoonic** (-on′ ik), *a.* Derived from or contained in animal substances.

zoonomy (zō on′ ȯ mi) [ZOO-, Gr. *nomos*, law], *n.* The science of the laws of animal life. **zoonomic** (-nom′ ik), *a.*

zoopathology (zō ō på thol′ ȯ ji), *n.* Animal pathology. ***zoopathy** (-op′ å thi), *n.* Zoopathology. **zoophagous** (zō of′ å gůs) [-PHAGOUS], *a.* Feeding on animals, carnivorous. **zoophagan**, *a.* and *n.* **zoophily** (zō of′ i li) [-PHILY], *n.* Love of animals. **zoophilist**, *n.* **zoophorus** (zō of′ ȯ růs) [Gr. *pherein*, to bear], *n.* A continuous frieze carved with figures of men and animals in relief. **zoophoric** (-for′ ik), *a.* **zoophysics** (-fiz′ iks) [PHYSICS], *n.* The study of the structure of animal bodies. **zoophysiology** (-fiz i ol′ ȯ ji), *n.*

zoophyte (zō′ ō fīt), *n.* An invertebrate animal presenting many external resemblances to a plant, as a coral sea-anemone, holothurian, sponge, etc. **zoophytic** (-fit′ ik), *a.* **zoophytoid** (-fī′ toid), *a.* **zoophytology** (-tol′ ȯ ji), *n.* The natural history of zoophytes. **zoophytological** (-loj ′i kål), *a.* **zoophytologist**, *n.* **zooplastic** (-plăs′ tik) [PLASTIC], *a.* (*Surg.*) Pertaining to the grafting of live tissue from one animal body to another. **zoopsychology** (-sī kol′ ȯ ji), *n.* The psychology of the lower animals. **zooscopy** (zō os′ kȯ pi) [-SCOPY], *n.* A form of hallucination.

zoospore (zō′ ō spôr), *n.* A spore having the power of independent motion, usu. by means of cilia. **zoosporic** (-spor′ ik), *a.* **zootaxy** (-tăk′ si) [see TAXIS], *n.* The classification of animals. **zootechny, -technics** (-tek′ ni, -niks) [TECHNIC], *n.* The science of breeding and of the domestication of animals. **zootheism** (-thē′ izm) [THEISM], *n.* The attribution of divine qualities to animals. **zootheistic** (-thė is′ tik), *a.* **zootomy** (zō ot′ ȯ mi) [-TOMY], *n.* The dissection or anatomy of animals. **zootomic, -al** (-tom′ ik, -ål), *a.* **zootomist** (zō ot′ ȯ mist), *n.* **zootrophic** (-trof′ ik) [TROPHIC], *a.* Pertaining to the nourishment of animals.

zopilote (zop i lō′ tā) [Mex. *tzopilotl*], *n.* A turkey-buzzard, esp. the urubu.

zoril (zor′ il) [F. *zorille*, Sp. *zorilla*, dim. of *zorra*, fox], *n.* A small carnivorous quadruped, *Zorilla striata*, allied to the skunks and polecats, found in Africa and Asia Minor.

Zoroastrian (zor ȯ ăs′ tri ån) [L. *Zoroastres*, O.Pers. *Zarathustra*], *a.* Pertaining to Zoroaster or the religious system set forth by him and his followers in the Zend-Avesta, based on the dual principle of Ormuzd, the god of light and good, and Ahriman, the god of darkness and evil, the ancient Persian religion of the Magi and still held by the Parsees, sometimes called fire-worshippers. *n.* A follower of Zoroaster; an adherent of Zoroastrianism. **Zoroastrianism**, *n.*

zorra (zor′ å) [Sp.], *n.* A S. American skunk.

zorro (zor′ ō) [Sp.], *n.* A S. American fox-wolf.

zoster (zos′ tėr) [Gr. *zōstēr*, girdle, from *zōnnunai*, to gird], *n.* An ancient Greek girdle or belt, worn esp. by men; (*Path.*) shingles.

Zouave (zoo av′) [F., from M. Afr. *Zuawa*, name of a Kabyle tribe], *n.* A soldier belonging to a French light infantry corps, orig. composed of Kabyles and still wearing an Oriental uniform; a zouave jacket. **zouave jacket**: A short, round-fronted jacket, usu. sleeveless, worn by women.

zounds (zoundz) [contr. from *God's wounds*, an obsolete oath], *int.* An exclamation of anger, etc.

zuchetto, zuchetta (tsoo ke′ tō, -ta) [It., small gourd], *n.* (*Eccles.*) The skull-cap of a Roman Catholic ecclesiastic, black for priest, purple for bishop, red for cardinal, white for pope.

zuffulo (tsoo′-, zoo′ fō lō) [It.], *n.* A small flute or flageolet, esp. one used in teaching birds to sing.

Zulu (zoo′ loo) [native name], *n.* A member of a warlike tribe or tribes of the Bantu or Kafir race, in S.E. Africa.

zyg-, zygo- [Gr. *zugon*, yoke], *comb. form.* **zygal** (zī′ gål), *a.* H-shaped, of the nature of a zygon. **zygapophysis** (zī gå pof′ i sis) [Gr. *apophusis*, process (APO-, *phuein*, to grow)], *n.* (*pl.* **-physes**) One of the processes by which a vertebra articulates with another. **zygobranchiate** (-brăng′ ki åt) [BRANCHIATE], *a.* Having the right and the left gills alike (of certain gasteropods). *n.* One of the *Zygobranchia*, an order of zygobranchiate gasteropods. **zygobranch** (zī′ gȯ brănk), *n.* **zygodactyl** (-dăk′ til) [Gr. *daktulos*, digit], *a.* (*Ornith.*) Having the toes disposed in pairs, two in front and two behind; belonging to the *Zygodactylæ*, a group of birds with two toes pointed forwards and two backwards, as in the parrots; *n.* One of the *Zygodactylæ*. **zygodactylous**, *a.*

zygoma (zī-, zi gō′ må) [Gr. *zugōma -atos*], *n.* (*pl.* **-mata**) (*Anat.*) The arch joining the malar and temporal bones, the yoke-bone. **zygomatic** (-mat′ ik), *a.* **zygomorphous** (-môr′ fůs) [Gr. *morphē*, form], *a.* (*Bot.*) Divisible into similar halves only in one plane (of flowers). **zygomorphism**, *n.* **zygon** (zī′ gȯn), *n.* A connecting bar, as the cross-bar of an H-shaped fissure of the brain. **zygophyllum** (zī gȯ fil′ ům) [Gr. *phullon*, leaf], *n.* (*Bot.*) A genus of trees or shrubs comprising the bean-caper. **zygophyllaceous** (-lā′ shůs), *a.* **zygophyte** (zī′ gȯ fīt) [-PHYTE], *n.* (*Bot.*) A plant reproduced by means of zygospores. **zygopleural** (-ploor′ ål) [PLEURAL], *a.* Bilaterally symmetrical.

zygosis (zī gō′ sis), *n.* (*Biol.*) Conjugation.

zygospore (zī′ gō spôr), *n.* A spore formed by conjugation of two similar gametes.

zygote (zī′ gōt), *n.* The product of the fusion between the oocyte and the spermatozoon; the fertilized ovum.

zylonite [XYLONITE].

zyme (zīm) [Gr. *zumē*, leaven, from *zeein*, to boil], *n.* A ferment, a disease-germ, the supposed cause of a zymotic disease. **zymase**, *n.* An enzyme. **zymic**, *a.* Relating to fermentation.

zymo-, *comb. form.* [ZYME].

zymogen (zīm′ ō jen), *n.* A substance developing by internal change into a ferment or enzyme.

zymology (zī mol′ ō ji), *n.* The theory of fermentation; a treatise on fermentation. **zymological**, *a.* **zymologist**, *n.*

zymometer (zī mom′ ė tėr), *n.* An instrument for measuring the degree of fermentation.

zymoscope (zī′ mō skōp), *n.* An instrument for testing the fermenting power of yeast.

zymosis (zī mō′ sis), *n.* Fermentation, esp. that by which disease is introduced into the system; any zymotic disease. **zymotic**, *a.* Pertaining to or produced by fermentation. **zymotic disease**, *n.* *n.* An epidemic, endemic, or contagious disease produced by the multiplication of germs introduced from without. **zymotically**, *adv.*

zymurgy (zī′ mėr ji), *n.* The department of technological chemistry treating of processes in which fermentation plays the principal part.

zythum (zī′ thům) [Gr. *zuthos*], *n.* A malt beverage used in Ancient Egypt.

A.M.D.G.

PRONUNCIATION OF PROPER NAMES

The accepted English pronunciation of certain proper names is shown in this list. For pronunciation key, see page xi.

Aachen, a′ *chė*n
Aar, ar
Aarau, a′ rou
Aaron, âr′ on
Abana, ăb′ ȧ nȧ
Abbasside, ȧ băs′ īd
Abbeville, ăb′ vil
Abdera, ăb dēr′ ȧ; **Abderite,** ăb′ dėr īt
Abednego, ȧ bed′ nė gō
Abelard, ăb′ ė lard, a bė lar
Abencerrages, ȧ ben′ sė rā jēz
Abercrombie, ăb′ ėr krŭm bi
Abergavenny, ăb ėr gen′ i, ăb ėr gȧ ven′ i
Abernethy, ăb ėr nē′ thi
Aberystwith, ăb ėr ist′ with
Abiathar, ȧ bī′ ȧ thar
Abiel, ā′ bi ėl, ȧ bī′ ėl
Abihu, ȧ bī′ hū
Abinger, ăb′ in jėr
Abisai, ȧ bis′ ȧ ī
Abishag, ăb′ i shăg, ȧ bī′ shăg
Abou-ben-Adhem, a boo ben a′ dem, -ăd′ hem
Aboukir, a boo kēr′
About (F. novelist), a boo
Abrantes, a bra*n*′ tes
Abruzzi, a broot′ zē
Abu-Klea, a boo klē′ ȧ
Abydos, ȧ bī′ dos
Academus, ăk ȧ dē′ mu̇s
Acadia, ȧ kā′ di ȧ
Acapulco, a ka pool′ kō
Aceldama, ȧ sel′ dȧ mȧ
Achæan, ȧ kē′ ȧn
Achæmenes, ȧ kē′ mė nēz
Achaia, ȧ kī′ ȧ
Achates, ȧ kā′ tēz
Acheron, ăk′ ėr ȯn
Acheson, ăch′ ė son
Achilles, ȧ kil′ ēz
Achitophel, ȧ kit′ ȯ fel
Achonry, ăk′ ȯn ri
Aconcagua, a kon ka′ gwa
Acre, ā′ kėr, a′ kėr
Actæon, ăk tē′ ȯn
Actium, ăk′ shi u̇m, -tı u̇m
Adalbert, ăd′ ăl bėrt
Addis Ababa, ăd′ is ăb′ ȧ bȧ
Adelphi, ȧ del′ fī
Aden, ā′ dėn, a′ dėn
Adiel, ā′ di ėl, ăd′ i ėl
Adige, ăd′ i ji
Adirondacks, ăd i ron′ dăks
Admetus, ăd mē′ tu̇s
Adonai, a dō′ nī, ăd ȯ nā′ ī
Adonais, ăd ȯ nā′ is
Adrianople, ā′ dri ȧ nō pėl
Adrienne Lecouvreur, a dri en′ le koo vrėr′
Adye, ā′ di
Æacus, ē′ ȧ ku̇s
Ædui, ed′ ū ī
Æetes, ē ē′ tēz
Ægean, ē jē′ ȧn
Ægeria, ē jēr′ iȧ
Ægeus, ē′ joos
Ægina, ē jī′ nȧ; **Æginetan,** ē ji nē′ tȧn; **Æginetic,** ē ji net′ ik
Ælfgifu, ălf′ gi foo
Ælfric, ăl′ frik
Æneas, ē nē′ ȧs
Æneid, ē′ nė id, ē nē′ id
Æolis, ē′ ȯ lis. **Æolic,** ē ol′ ik
Æolus, ē′ ȯ lu̇s
Æschines, ēs′-, es′ ki nēz
Æschylus, ēs′-, es′ ki lu̇s
Æsculapius, ēs-, es kū lā′ pi u̇s
Æsir, ē′-, ā′ sėr
Aetius, ā ē′ shi u̇s
Ætnean, et nē′ ȧn
Aflalo, ăf la′ lō
Agamemnon, ăg ȧ mem′ nȯn
Aganippe, ăg ȧ nip′ ē
Agassiz, ăg′ ȧ si
Agathocles, ȧ găth′ ȯ klēz
Agenor, ȧ jē′ nȯr
Agesander, ăj ė săn′ dėr
Agesilaus, ȧ jes i lā′ u̇s
Agincourt, aj′ in kôrt
Agnesi, a nyā′ si
Agonistes, ăg ȯ nis′ tēz
Agricola, ȧ grik′ ȯ lȧ
Agrigentum, ăg ri jen′ tu̇m
Agrippina, ăg ri pī′ nȧ
Aguilar, a gē lar′
Aguinaldo, a gē năl′ dō
Agulhas, a gool′ yas
Ahasuerus, a hăz ū ēr′ u̇s
Ahmednagar, a mid nŭg′ ȧr
Ahriman, a′ ri mȧn
Aida, a ē′ dȧ
Aiglon, ā′ glo*n*
Aigues-Mortes, āg môrt
Aiguille, ā gwēl′
Aileen, ī lēn′
Airolo, ī′ rō lō
Aisne, ān
Aix-la-Chapelle, āks la shȧ pel′
Aix-les-Bains, āks lā ba*n*
Ajaccio, ȧ jăk′ si ō
Ajalon, ăj′ ȧ lon
Alabama, ăl ȧ ba′ mȧ
Aladdin, ȧ lăd′ in
Alameda, a lȧ mā′ dȧ
Alamein, ăl′ ȧ mān
Alamo, a′ la mō
Alaric, ăl′ ȧ rik
Alastor, ȧ lăs′ tȯr
Albani, ăl ba′ ni
Albania, ăl bā′ ni ȧ
Albemarle, ăl′ bė marl
Alberich, ăl′ bėr *ich*
Albigenses, ăl bi jen′ sēz
Albrecht, ăl′ bre*cht*
Albuera, al bu ā′ ra
Albufera, al bu fā′ ra
Albuquerque, al boo kėr kė
Alcæus, ăl sē′ u̇s
Alcala, ăl ka la′
Alcantara, al kăn′ ta ra
Alcazar, ăl ka′ zar, -ka′ *thar*
Alceste, ăl sest′
Alcester, awls′ tėr
Alcestis, ăl ses′ tis
Alcibiades, ăl si bī′ ȧ dēz
Alcides, ăl sī′ dēz
Alcinous, ăl sin′ ȯ u̇s
Alciphron, ăl′ si fron
Alcmæon, ălk mē′ ȯn
Alcmene, ălk mē′ nē
Alcoran, ăl kȯ ran′
Alcuin, ăl′ kwin
Alcyone, ăl sī′ ȯ nē
Aldebaran, ăl deb′ ȧ rȧn
Aldeburgh, awld′ bu̇ ru̇
Aldrich, awl′ drich, -drij
Alemanni, ăl ė măn′ i
Alembert, a la*n* bâr′
Alençon, ȧ len′ sȯn
Aleppo, ȧ lep′ ō
Alethea, ăl ė thē′ ȧ
Aleutian, ăl i oo′ shi ȧn, ȧ lū′ shȧn
Aleuts, ăl′ ė uts
Alfieri, al fyâr′ i
Alfonso, ăl fon′ sō
Algeciras, ăl jė sēr′ ȧs
Algiers, ăl jērz′
Algonkin, ăl gong′ kin
Alhambra, ăl hăm′ brȧ
Ali Baba, a′ li ba′ ba
Alicant, ăl′ i kănt
Alicante, a lē kan′ tā
Alighieri, a lē gyâr′ ē
Allahabad, ăl ȧ hȧ băd′
Alleghany, ăl′ ė gā ni
Alleyn, Alleyne, ăl′ ėn
Al-Mansur, al man sėr′
Alma Tadema, ăl′ mȧ tăd′ ė mȧ
Almeida, al mā′ ē da
Alnwick, ăn′ ik
Alonzo, ȧ lon′ zō
Aloysius, ăl ȯ is′-, -ish′ i u̇s
Alpes-Maritimes, alp ma rē tēm′
Alpheus, ăl fē′ u̇s
Alphonse, ăl′ fonz
Alsace-Lorraine, ăl săs′-, al sas′ lȯ rān′
Altai, al′ tī
Althæa, ăl thē′ ȧ
Alvarez, ăl′ vȧ res, al va′ re*th*
Amadeus, ăm ȧ dē′ u̇s
Amadis, ăm′ ȧ dis
Amalfi, ȧ măl′ fi
Amalthea, ăm ăl thē′ ȧ
Amaryllis, ăm ȧ ril′ is
Amasa, ăm′ ȧ sȧ
Amasis, ȧ mā′ sis
Amati, a ma′ tē
Ambiorix, ăm bī′ ȯ riks
Ambois, a*n* bwaz′
Amenophis, ăm ė nō′ fis
Amerigo Vespucci, a mā rē′ gō ves poo′ chē
Amery, ā′ mė ri
Amfortas, ăm fôr′ tăs
Amici, a mē′ chē
Amiel, a myel′
Amiens, ăm′ i enz, a mya*n*′
Amlwch, ăm′ luk
Amory, ā′ mȯ ri
Amos, ā′ mos
Ampere, a*n* pâr′
Amphiaraus, ăm fi ȧ rā′ u̇s
Amphion, ăm fī′ ȯn
Amphitrite, ăm fi trī′ ti
Amphitryon, ăm fit′ ri ȯn
Ampthill, ăm′ til
Amritsar, ăm rit′ sȧr
Amundsen, a′ mun sėn, a mŭnd′ sėn
Amur, a moor′
Amurath, a mu răt′
Amyas, ăm′ i ăs
Amyot, a mē ō′

a: *far.* **ă:** *fat.* **ā:** *fate.* **aw:** *fall.* **â:** *fare.* **e:** *bell.* **ẽ:** *her.* **ē:** *beef.* **i:** *bit.* **ī:** *bite.*

Anacharsis, ăn ȧ kar′ sis
Anacreon, ȧ năk′ rė ȯn
Anadyomene, ăn ȧ dī om′ ė nē
Anam, ȧ năm′
Anaxagoras, ăn ȧk săg′ ȯ răs
Anchises, ăn kī′ sēz
Ancona, ăng kō′ nȧ
Andalusia, ăn dȧ loo′ shȧ
Andaman, ăn′ dȧ măn
Andean, ăn dē′ ȧn
Andernach, ăn′ dėr năch
Andrassy, on′ dra shi
André, ăn′ drā
Andrea del Sarto, ăn drā′ ȧ del sar′ tō
Andrea Ferrara, ăn′ dri ȧ fė ra′ rȧ
Androcles, ăn′ drȯ klēz
Andromache, ăn drom′ ȧ kē
Andromeda, ăn drom′ ė dȧ
Andronicus, ăn drȯ nī′ kus, (Shak.) ăn dron′ i kus
Aneurin, ȧ nū′ rin
Angelica, ăn jel′ i kȧ
Angelina, ăn jȧ lī′ nȧ
Angelique, *an* zhā lēk′
Angers, *an* zhā
Angevin, ăn′ jė vin, *an* zhė va*n*′
Angora, ăng gôr′ ȧ
Angoulême, *an* goo lām′
Anjou, ăn′ joo, *an* zhoo′
Ankara, ăngk′ ȧ rȧ
Annaly, ăn′ ȧ li
Annecy, an sē′
Annesley, ănz′ li
Annunzio, a noont′ zi ō
Anstruther (place) ăn′ stėr, (baronet) ăn′ strŭ *thėr*
Antæus, ăn tē′ ŭs
Antares, ăn târ′ ēz
Antenor, ăn tē′ nȯr
Anthea, ăn′ the ȧ
Anthony, ăn′ tȯ ni
Antibes, *an* tēb′
Antietam, ăn tē′ tăm
Antigone, ăn tig′ ȯ nē
Antigua, an tē ga
Antilles, ăn til′ ēz
Antinous, ăn tin′ ȯ ŭs
Antiochia, ăn ti ȯ kī′ ȧ
Antiochus, ăn tī′ ȯ kŭs
Antiope, ăn tī′ ȯ pē
Antipater, ăn tip′ ȧ tėr
Antisthenes, ăn tis′ thė nēz
Antoine, *an* twan′
Antoinette, ăn tȯ net′, *an* twa net′
Antoninus, ăn tō nī′ nus
Antrobus, ăn′ trȯ bŭs
Anubis, ȧ nū′ bis
Anzio, ăn′ zi ō
Apelles, ȧ pel′ ēz
Aphrodite, ăf rō dī′ tē
Apollodorus, ȧ pol ȯ dôr′ ŭs
Apollyon, ȧ pol′ i on, -yȯn
Apoxyomenos, ȧ pok si om′ ė nos
Appalachian, ăp ȧ lăch′ i ȧn
Appenzel, a pent sel′
Appomattox, ăp ȯ măt′ oks
Apuleius, ăp ū lē′ ŭs
Apulia, ȧ pū′ li ȧ
Aquarius, ȧ kwâr′ i ŭs
Aquila, ăk′ wi lȧ
Aquinas, ȧ kwī′ nȧs
Aquitaine, ăk wit tān′
Arabi, ȧ ra′ bi
Araby, ăr′ ȧ bi
Arachne, ȧ răk′ ni
Ara Coeli, a′ rȧ chel′ ē
Arago, ăr′ ȧ gō, a ra gō′
Aral, ăr′ ȧl
Aramis, a ra mēs′
Aran, ăr′ ȧn
Arbela, ar bē′ lȧ
Arbuthnot, ar bŭth′ not, ar′ bŭth not
Arcadia, ar kā′ di ȧ
Archangel, ark ān′ jėl
Archias, ar′ ki ăs
Archibald, ar′ chi bawld
Archimago, ar ki mā′ gō
Archimedean, ar ki mė dē′ ăn, -mē′ dė ȧn
Archimedes, ar ki mē′ dēz
Arcis-sur-Aube, ar sē′ sur ōb
Arcite, ar′ sīt
Arcola, ar′ kȯ lȧ
Arcturus, ark tūr′ ŭs
Ardagh, ar′ da
Ardee, ar dē′
Ardennes, ar den′
Ardingly, ar ding lī′
Arditi, ar dē′ ti
Areopagitica, ăr ė op ȧ jit′ i kȧ
Areopagus, ăr ė op′ ȧ gŭs
Arequipa, a rā kē′ pa
Ares, âr′ ēz
Arethusa, ăr ė thū′ sȧ
Aretino, a rā tē′ nō
Arezzo, a red′ zō
Argand, ar′ gănd, ar ga*n*′
Argenteuil, ar zha*n* tu′ yė
Argentina, ar jėn tē′ nȧ
Argentine, ar′ jėn tēn, -tīn
Argive, ar′ jīv, -gīv
Argolis, ar′ gȯ lis
Argyll, ar gīl′
Ariadne, ăr i ăd′ ni
Arian, âr′ i ȧn
Ariel, âr′ i ėl
Aries, âr′ i ēz
Arimathea, ăr i mȧ thē′ ȧ
Arion, ȧ rī′ ȯn
Aristæus, ăr is tē′ ŭs
Aristides, ăr is tī′ dēz
Aristippus, ăr is tip′ ŭs
Aristobulus, ȧ ris tȯ bū′ lŭs
Aristocles, ȧ ris′ tȯ klēz
Aristodemus, ȧ ris tȯ dē′ mŭs
Aristogiton, ȧ ris tȯ jī′ tȯn
Aristophanes, ăr is tof′ ȧ nēz′
Aristotle, ăr′ is totl
Arius, âr′ i ŭs
Arizona, ăr i zō′ nȧ
Arkansas, ar′ kȧn saw
Armageddon, ar mȧ ged′ ȯn
Armagh, ar ma′
Armenia, ar mē′ nyȧ
Armida, ar mē′ dȧ
Arnaud, ar nō′
Arnould, ar noo′
Arras, ăr′ ȧs
Arromanches, ă rȯ mansh′
Arsaces, ar′ sȧ sēz, ar sā′ sēz
Arsinoe, ar sin′ ō ē
Artaxerxes, ar tăk zĕrk′ sēz
Artemidorus, ar tem i dôr′ ŭs
Artemis, ar′ tė mis
Artemisia, ar tė mish′ i ȧ
Artemus, ar′ tė mŭs
Artois, ar twa′
Arun, ă′ rŭn
Arundel, ăr′ ŭn del; **Arundelian,** ar ŭn dē′ li ȧn
Aryan, âr′ i ȧn
Asaph, ā′ săf
Ascalon, ăs′ kȧ lȯn
Ascham, ăs′ kȧm
Asclepiades, ăs klė pī′ ȧ dēz
Asclepius, ăs klē′ pi ŭs
Ascoli, ăs′ kō li.
Ashanti, ȧ shăn′ ti
Ashburnham, ăsh′ bĕr nȧm
Ashburton, ăsh′ bĕr tȯn
Ashur-bani-pal, a shur ba′ ni pal
Asia, ā′ shȧ
Asmodeus, ăs mȯ dē′ ŭs
Asnières, a nyâr′
Asoka, ȧ sō′ kȧ
Aspasia, ăs pā′ shi ȧ
Assaye, ȧ sī′, -sā′
Assheton, ăsh′ tȯn
Assiniboia, ăs sin i boi′ ȧ
Assiniboine, ăs sin′ i boin
Assisi, a sē′ zi
Assuan, as u an′
Astarte, ăs tar′ ti
Astolat, ăs′ tȯ lăt
Astolfo, ăs tol′ fō
Astorga, ăs tôr′ gȧ
Astræa, ăs trē′ ȧ
Astrakhan, ăs trȧ kăn′
Astrophel, ăs′ trȯ fel
Asturias, as toor′ ė ăs
Astyages, ăs tī′ ȧ jēz
Astyanax, ăs tī′ ȧ năks
Asuncion, a sun si on′
Atalanta, ăt ȧ lăn′ tȧ
Ate, ā′ ti
Athalie, a ta lē′
Athenæum, ăth en ē′ um
Athene, ȧ thē′ nē
Athenry, ăth ėn rī′
Athens, ăth′ ėnz
Athlumney, ăth′ lŭm ni
Athol, ăth′ ȯl
Atlantean, ăt lăn tē′ ȧn
Atlantides, ăt lăn′ ti dēz
Atlantis, ăt lăn′ tis
Atreus, ā′ trūs, ā′ trė ŭs
Atridæ, ȧ trī′ dė
Atropos, ăt′ rȯ pos
Attila, ăt′ i lȧ
Auber, ō bâr′
Aubigné, ō bē nyā′
Aubusson, ō bu so*n*′
Aucassin, ō ka să*n*′
Audubon, ō du bo*n*′
Auerbach, ou′ ėr ba*ch*
Auerstadt, ou′ ėr shtet
Augeas, aw′ jė ăs
Augereau, ōzh′ rō
Augsburg, ougz′ bĕrg
Augustine, aw gŭs′ tin
Aumale, ō mal′
Aurelius, aw rēl′ yŭs
Auriga, aw rī′ gȧ
Aurungzebe, aw rŭng zēb′
Austerlitz, ou′ stĕr lits
Auteuil, ō tu′ yė
Autolycus, aw tol′ i kŭs
Autun, ō tu*n*′
Auvergne, ō vârn′
Auxerre, ō sâr′; **Auxerrois,** ō sâr wa′
Ava, a′ vȧ
Avalon, ăv′ ȧ lon
Avebury, (place) ā′ bėr i, (title) ăv′ beri
Aventine, ăv′ ėn tin, -tīn
Averroes, ȧ ver′ ȯ ēz
Avignon, a vē nyo*n*′
Avon, ā′ vȯn
Ayers, ârz
Ayesha, ī′ ė shȧ
Aylesbury, ālz′ bėr i
Aylmer, āl′ mėr
Aylwin, āl′ win
Ayscough, ăs′ kū
Azof, a zōf′, ā′ zov
Azrael, ăz′ rȧ el

Baal, bā′ ȧl
Baalbec, bal bek′
Babel, bā′ bėl
Babylon, băb′ i lon
Bacchus, băk′ ŭs
Bach, ba*ch*
Bache, bāch
Badajoz, ba da hōth′
Baden Baden, ba′ dėn ba′ dėn
Baden-Powell, bā dėn pou′ ėl
Bad Nauheim, bad nou′ hīm
Baedeker, bā′ dė kėr
Bagehot, băj′ ȯt
Baggallay, băg′ ȧ li

Bagnères, ba nyâr′
Bagot, băg′ ȯt
Bagration, ba gra′ ti ōn
Bahamas, bȧ ha′ mȧz
Bahia, ba ē′ ȧ
Bahrein, ba rān′
Baiæ, bā′ yē
Baikal, bī kal′
Bajazet, băj ȧ zet′
Balaclava, băl ȧ kla′ vȧ
Balboa, băl bō′ ȧ
Balcarres, băl kăr′ is
Baldassare, băl dăs′ ȧ ri
Baleares, băl ė âr′ ēz, bȧ lā a′ rēz; **Balearic,** băl ė ăr′ ik
Balestier, băl ės tēr′
Baliol, bā′ li ȯl
Balize, bȧ lēz′
Ballachulish, băl ȧ hoo′ lish
Ballater, băl′ ȧ tĕr
Balliol, băl′ i ȯl
Ballo in Maschera, ba lō ēn măs′ kā ra
Balmaceda, bal ma thā′ da
Balmerino, băl mer′ i nō
Balmoral, băl mor′ ȧl
Baltasar, bal ta sar′
Balthazar, băl thā′ zȧr
Baluchistan, bȧ loo chi stan′
Balquhidder, băl′ hwid ėr
Balzac, băl′ zăk, bal zak′
Bamberger, băm′ bėr gėr
Bamfylde, băm′ fēld
Banff, bămf
Bangalore, băng gȧ lôr′
Bangor, băng′ gȯr
Banquo, băng′ kwō
Bantu, băn too′
Banville, ba*n* vēl′
Baptiste, ba tēst′
Barabbas, bȧ răb′ ȧs
Barbadoes, bar bā′ dōz
Barbarossa, bar bȧ ros′ ȧ
Barbauld, bar′ bawld
Barberini, bar bā rē′ nē
Barbizon, bar bē zo*n*′
Barbour, bar′ bȯr
Barcelona, bar si lō′ nȧ
Barclay, bar′ kli
Bareilly ba rā′ li
Bargello, bar jel′ ō
Barham, bar′ ȧm
Baring Gould, bar′ ing goold′
Bar-le-Duc, bar lė duk′
Barnardiston, bar nȧr dis′ tȯn
Barnave, bar nav′
Barneveldt, bar′ nė velt
Baroda, bȧ rō′ dȧ
Barotseland, băr ot′ sē lănd
Barraclough, băr ȧ klŭf′
Barras, bar as′
Barth, bart
Barthélemy-Saint-Hilaire, bar tăl mē′ sa*n* tē lâr′
Bartholdi, bar tōl dē′
Bartimeus, bar ti mē′ u̇s
Bartolommeo, bar tol ō mā′ ō
Bartolozzi, bar tȯ lot′ si
Barttelot, bar′ tȧ lȯt
Baruch, bâr′ u̇k
Barwick, băr′ ik
Barzillai, bar zil′ ȧ ī
Bashan, bā′ shȧn
Bashi-Bazouk, băsh′ i bȧ zook′
Bashkirtseff, băsh kĕrt′ sef
Basil, băz′-, băz′ il
Basque, bȧsk
Basra, băz′ rȧ
Bassanio, bȧ sa′ ni ō
Bastia, bas tē′ a
Bastien-Lepage, bas te a*n*′ lė pazh′
Bastille, bas tēl′
Basutoland, bă soo′ tō lănd
Batavia, bȧ tā′ vi ȧ
Bathsheba, băth shē′ bȧ, băth′ shė bȧ
Batrachomyomachia, băt′ ra kō′ mi a mȧ kī′ ȧ
Batthyáni, bot yan′ yē
Baugh, baw
Bautzen, bout′ sėn
Bayard, bā′ ėrd, ba yar′
Bayeux, bā yĕr′
Bayonne, bā yon′
Bayreuth, bī roit′
Bazaine, ba zān′
Beaconsfield, (place) bek′ ȯnz fēld, (title) bēk′ ȯnz fēld
Beatrice Cenci, bā a trē′ chē chen′ chē
Beattie, bē′ ti, bā′ ti
Beaucaire, bō kâr
Beauce, bōs
Beauchamp, bē′ chȧm
Beauclerc, bō′ klȧr, -klĕrk
Beauclerk, bō′ klark
Beaufort, bō′ fȯrt
Beauharnais, bō ar nā′
Beaujolais, bō zho lā′
Beaulieu, bū′ li
Beauly, bū′ li
Beaumarchais, bō mar shā′
Beaumaris, bō mâr′ is
Beaumont, bō′ mont
Beaune, bōn
Beauregard, bō′ rė gard
Beauvais, bō vā′
Bechstein, be*ch*′ shtīn
Bechuanaland, bech ū a′ nȧ lănd
Becke, bek
Beddgelert, beth gel′ ėrt
Bedel, bē′ dėl
Beelzebub, bė el′ zė bŭb
Beerbohm, bēr′ bȯm
Beersheba, bē ėr shē′ bȧ, bė ĕr′ shė ba
Beethoven, bā′ tō vėn
Behistun, bā his toon′
Behring, bā′ ring, bâr′ ring
Beira, bī′ ra
Beirut, bā root′
Belfort, bel fȯr′
Belial, bē′ li ȧl, bēl′ yȧl
Belisha, bel ī′ shȧ, bel ē′ sha
Belize, bė lēz′
Bellarmine, bel′ ȧr min, -mēn
Bellatrix, bė lā′ triks
Belle Alliance, bel ăl ya*n*s′
Belle Isle, bel īl′, -ēl
Bellerophon, bė ler′ ȯ fon
Belleville, bel′ vil
Bellevue, bel′ vū
Bellew, bel′ ū, bė lū′
Bellini, bel lē′ nē
Bellona, bė lō′ nȧ
Belvoir, bē′ vėr
Benares, be na′ rēz
Benbecula, ben bek′ ū lȧ
Ben Cruachan, ben kroo′ *ch*ȧn
Benedek, ben′ ė dek
Benes, ben′ esh
Bengal, ben gawl′
Benguela, ben gā′ lȧ
Benin, ben in′
Ben Lawers, ben law′ ėrz
Ben Machdhui, ben ma*ch* doo′ i
Ben Nevis, ben nev′ is, -nē′ vis
Benningsen, ben′ ing sėn
Bentham, ben′ tȧm
Bentivoglio, ben ti vō′ lyō
Beowulf, bā′ ȯ wulf
Berengaria, ber ėn gâr′ i ȧ
Berenger, bā ra*n* zhā
Berenice, ber ė nī′ sė
Beresina, ber ā zē′ nȧ
Bergamo, bĕr′ gȧ mō
Berger, bĕr zhā′
Bergerac, bĕr zhė rak′
Berkeley, bark′ li
Berkshire, bark′ shir
Berlin, bėr lin′
Berlioz, bâr li ōs′
Bermoothes, bėr moo′ thēz
Bermuda, bėr mū′ dȧ
Bernadotte, bĕr′ nȧ dot
Bernard de Clairvaux, bĕr nar′ dė klâr vō′
Bernhardt, bĕr′ nart
Bernina, bĕr nē′ na
Berthelot, bĕr te lō′
Berthier, bĕr tyā′
Berthollet, bĕr tō lā′
Bertie (title and surname), bar′ ti (Christian name), bĕr′ ti
Bertillon, bĕr ti yo*n*′
Berwick, ber′ ik
Besançon, bā za*n* zo*n*′
Besant (1) [Annie], bez′ ȧnt
Besant (2) [Sir Walter], bė zănt′
Bessborough, bez′ bȯ rȯ
Bessières, bes yâr′
Betelgeux, bet′ el juz
Bethany, beth′ ȧ ni
Bethesda, bė thez′ dȧ
Bethlehem, beth′ lė hėm
Bethmann-Holweg, bāt′ man hōl′ vāg
Bethphage, beth′ fȧ ji, -fāj
Bethsaida, beth sā′ i dȧ
Bethune (1), bē′ tȯn, bė thūn′
Bethune (2) [F.], bā tun′
Bettws-y-Coed, bet′ us i koid
Beulah, bū′ lȧ
Beust, boist
Bewick, bū′ik
Beyrout [BEIRUT]
Bianca, bi ăng′ kȧ
Bianchi, bē ăng′ ki
Biarritz, bi ȧ ritz′
Bicester, bis′ tėr
Bicêtre, bē sātr′
Bichat, bē sha′
Bidassoa, bē da sō′ a
Bideford, bid′ ė ford
Bierstadt, bēr′ stăt
Bigelow, big′ ė lō
Bihar, bi har′
Bikaner, bik ȧn ēr′
Bilbao, bil bā′ ō
Bingen, bing′ ėn
Bingham, bing′ ȧm
Bingley, bing′ li
Birkbeck (family), bĕr′ bek
Birnam, bĕr′ nȧm
Biron, bē ro*n*′
Bishop's Stortford, bish′ ȯps stôrt′ fȯrd
Bisley, biz′ li
Bismarck, bis′ mark
Bispham, bisp′ ȧm, bis′ fȧm
Bizet, bē zā′
Björnson, byĕrn′ sȯn
Blackstone, blăk′ stȯn
Blair-Atholl, blâr ăth′ ȯl
Blanc, bla*n*
Blanqui, bla*n* kē′
Blantyre, blăn tīr′
Blavatsky, bla văt′ ski
Blenheim, blen′ im
Blennerhassett, blen ėr hăs′ ėt
Bleriot, bler′ i ō
Bligh, blī
Bloemfontein, blum′ fȯn tān
Blois, blwa
Blondel, blon′ del
Blondin, blon′ din, blo*n* da*n*′
Blouet, bloo ā′
Bloundelle, blŭn′ dėl
Blount, blŭnt
Blowitz, blō′ vits
Blücher, bloo′ *ch*ėr
Blumenthal, bloo′ mėn tal
Blyth, Blythe, blī, blī*th*
Boadicea, bō ȧ di sē′ ȧ

Boanerges, bō ȧ nĕr′ jēz
Boccaccio, bō ka′ chō
Boece, bois
Boehm, bĕrm
Boeotia, bē ō′ shi ȧ
Boerhave, bôr′ hav
Boethius, bō ē′ thi ůs
Bogota, bō gō ta′
Bohn, bōn
Bohun, boon
Boileau-Despréaux, bwa lō′ dā prā ō′
Bois de Boulogne, bwa dė boo lōn′ yė
Boleyn (accepted pron.) bō lān′
Bolingbroke, bŭl in bruk
Bolitho, bo li′ *thō*
Bolivar, bol′ i var, bō lē′ var
Bolivia, bȯ liv′ i ȧ
Bolsover, bōl′ sō vėr
Bombay, bom bā′
Bompas, bŭm′ pȧs
Bonaparte, bōn′ ȧ part
Bonar, bon′ ȧr
Bonaventura, bō nȧ ven toor′ ȧ
Bonheur, bon ĕr′
Bonhomme Richard, bon om rē shar′
Bonifacio, bon ē fa′ chō
Bonneville, bon′ vil
Bonnivar, bon i var′
Bonpland, bo*n* pla*n*′
Boord, bôrd
Boötes, bō ō′ tēz
Bordeaux, bôr dō′
Boreas, bôr′ ė ȧs
Borghese, bôr gā′ zā
Borgia, bôr′ jȧ
Borodino, bor ȯ dē′ nō
Borromeo, bo rō mā′ ō
Bosanquet, bō′ sȧn ket
Boscawen, bos′ kȯ en, -kȧ wen
Boscobel, bos′ kȯ bel
Bosnia, boz′ ni ȧ
Bosporus, bos′ pȯ rŭs
Bossuet, bō′ swā
Botha, bō′ tȧ
Bothwell, bo*th*′ wel
Botticelli, bot i chel′ i
Boucher, boo shā′
Boucicault, boo si kō′
Boughton, baw′-, bou′ tȯn
Bouguereau, boo gĕr ō′
Bouillon, boo yo*n*′
Boulanger, boo la*n*′ zhā
Boulogne, boo lon′, boo loin′
Bourbaki, boor ba kē′
Bourbon, boor′ bȯn, boor bo*n*′
Bourchier, bou′ chėr
Bourget, boor zhā′
Bourke, bĕrk
Bourne, bōrn, bĕrn, boorn
Bouvines, boo vēn′
Bovary, bō va rē′
Bow, bō
Bowdoin, bōdn
Bowen, bō′ ėn
Bowie, bō′ i
Bowland, bō′ lȧnd, bol′ ȧnd
Bowles, bōlz
Bowring, bou′ ring
Bowyer, bō′ yėr
Brabançonne, bra ban son′
Brabantio, bra băn′ shi ō
Brabazon, brăb′ ȧ zȯn
Brabourne, brā′ bŭrn
Braemar, brā mar′
Braganza, bra gan′ zȧ
Braham, bra′ ȧm
Brahe, bra′ hė
Brahma, bra′ mȧ
Brahmapootra, bra mȧ poo′ trȧ
Brahms, bramz
Brasenose, brāz′ nōz
Brazil, brȧ zil′
Breadalbane, brė dawl′ bȧn
Brechin, brē′ *ch*in
Breda, brā da′
Bregenz, brė gens′
Bohun, boon
Brehm, brām
Bremen, brem′ ėn
Bremer, brē′ mėr, brem′ ėr
Brentano, bren ta′ nō
Brescia, bre′ sha
Breslau, brez′ lou
Brian Boru, brī ȧn bȯ roo′
Briançon, brē a*n* so*n*′
Briareus, brī âr′ ė ůs
Bridie, brī di
Bridlington, brid′ ling tȯn, bĕr′ ling tȯn
Brindisi, brin′ dē zē
Briseis, bri sē′ is
Brno, bĕr′ no
Brockhaus, brok′ hous
Broglie, brō′ li
Broke, bruk
Bromley, (Kent) brŭm′ li, (London) brom′ li
Bromwich, brom′ ich
Brontë, bron′ ti
Brookline, bruk′ lin
Brooklyn, bruk′ lin
Brough, brŭf
Broughall, brŭfl
Brougham, broo′ ȧm, broom
Broughton, braw′-, brou′ tȯn
Brueys, broo ā′
Bruges, broozh
Brunehild, broo′ nė hilt
Brunehilde, broo nė hil′ dė
Brunel, bru nel′
Brunelleschi, broo nė les′ ki
Bruntière, brun tyâr′
Brussels, brŭs′ ėlz
Bryn-Mawr, (Wales, brin mour′ (Penn.) -mar′
Buccleuch, bŭ kloo′
Bucentaur, bū sen′ tôr
Bucephalus, bū sef′ ȧ lůs
Buchan, bŭk′ ȧn, bŭ*ch* ȧn
Buchanan, bū kăn′ ȧn
Bucharest, bū kȧ rest′
Budapest, boo′ dȧ pest
Buddha, bud′ ȧ
Buenos Ayres, bō nȧs âr′ iz, bwā′ nōs īr′ es
Buffon, bŭf′ ȯn, bu fo*n*′
Bulawayo, boo lȧ wī′ ō
Bulgaria, bul gâr′ i ȧ
Bulwer, bul′ wėr, bul′ ėr
Bunsen, bŭn′ sėn
Buonaparte, bwō na par′ tā
Buonarroti, bwō na rot′ i
Burdette, bůr det′
Burghclere, bĕr′ klâr
Burghersh, bĕr′ gėrsh
Burleigh, bĕr′ li
Burnand, bĕr′ nȧnd
Burnett, bůr net′
Burroughs, bŭr′ ōz
Burtchaell, bĕr′ chėl
Bury (town, and Albemarle family), ber′ i; (name) bū ′ri
Busiris, bū sīr′ is
Byblis, bib′ lis
Byrne, bĕrn
Byron, bī′ ron
Bysshe, bish
Bythesea, bi*th*′ ės ē
Byzantium, bī zăn′ ti ŭm

Caaba, ka′ ȧ bȧ
Cabanel, ka ba nel′
Cabanis, ka ba nēs′
Cabot, kăb′ ȯt
Cabul [KABUL]
Cadenus, kȧ dē′ nůs
Cadillac, (*Am.*) kă′ di lăk
Cadiz, kā′ diz
Cadogan, kȧ dŭg′ an
Cadwaladr, kăd wol′ ȧ dėr
Cædmon, kăd′ mȯn
Caen, ka*n*
Cæsar, sē′ zȧr
Cæsarea, ses ȧ rē′ ȧ
Cagliostro, ka lyos′ trō
Caiaphas, kī′ ȧ fȧs, kā′ yȧ fȧs
Cairo, kīr′ ō
Caius (pers. name), kī′ ůs; (the Cambridge college) kēz
Calabar, kăl ȧ bar′
Calabria, kȧ lā′ bri ȧ, ka la′ brē a
Calais, kăl′ ȧs, kăl′ ā
Calaveras, kăl ȧ vâr′ ȧs
Calchas, kăl′ kȧs
Caldcleugh, kăld klŭf′
Calderon, kawl′ dėr ȯn, kal dā rōn′
Caledonia, kăl ė dō′ ni ȧ
Calhoun, kȧ hoon′
California, kăl i fôr′ ni ȧ
Caligula, kăl ig′ ū lȧ
Callahan, kăl′ ȧ hăn
Callao, ka la′ ō, kal ya′ ō
Callicrates, kȧ lik′ rȧ tēz
Callimachus, kȧ lim′ ȧ kůs
Calliope, kȧ lī′ ȯ pē
Callipyge, kȧ lip′ i jē
Callirhoe, kăl i rō′ ē
Callisthenes, kȧ lis′ thė nēz
Callisto, kȧ lis′ tō
Calvé, kal vā′
Calypso, kȧ lip′ sō
Camaralzaman, kăm ȧ răl′ zȧ măn
Cambaçérès, ka*n* ba sā res′
Cambodia, kăm bō di ȧ
Cambon, ka*n* bo*n*′
Cambrai, ka*n* brā′
Cambronne, ka*n* bron′
Cambyses, kăm bī′ sēz
Camelot, kăm′ ė lot
Camilla, kȧ mil′ ȧ
Camille, kȧ mēl′
Camoens, kăm′ ō ens
Camorra, kȧ mor′ ȧ
Camoys, kȧ moiz′, kăm′ oiz
Campbell, kăm′ bėl
Campden, kăm′ dėn
Campeggio, kăm pej′ ō
Canaan, kā′ nȧn
Canace, kăn′ ȧ sē
Canaverel, kȧ năv′ ėr ėl
Canberra, kăn′ ber rȧ
Candace, kăn′ dȧ sē
Candide, ka*n* dēd′
Candolle, ka*n* dōl′
Cannabis, kăn′ ȧ bis
Cannæ, kăn′ ē
Cannes, kan, kănz
Canopus, kȧ nō′ půs
Canossa, kȧ nos′ ȧ
Canova, kȧ nō′ vȧ
Canrobert, ka*n* rō bâr′
Cantacuzene, kăn tȧ kū zēn′
Canton, kăn ton′
Canute [CNUT] kȧ nūt′
Capernaum, kȧ pĕr′ nȧ ŭm
Capek, chā′ pek
Capet, kā′ pet, ka pā′; **Capetian,** kȧ pē′ shȧn
Capitol, kăp′ i tol; **Capitoline,** kăp′ i tȯ līn
Capitolinus, kăp i tȯ lī′ nůs
Capo d'Istria, ka pō dēs′ trē a
Caprera, ka prâ′ a
Capri, ka′ prē, (*vulg.*) kȧ prē′
Caprivi, ka prē′ vē
Capua, kăp′ ū ȧ
Capuccini, ka poo chē′ nē
Capulet, kăp′ ū let
Carabas, kăr′ ȧ băs, ka ra ba′

n: cabosho*n*. ng: si*ng*. sh: *sh*awl. zh: mea*s*ure. th: *th*in. *th*: brea*th*e. *See page* xi.

Caracalla, kăr ȧ kăl′ ȧ
Caracci, ka ra′ chē
Caraccioli, ka ra′ chō lē
Caractacus, kȧ răk′ tȧ kůs
Caravaggio, ka ra va′ jō
Carbonari, kar bō na′ rē
Carew, kâr i, kȧ roo′
Caribbean, kăr i bē′ ȧn
Carisbroke, kă′ ris bruk
Carlyon, kar lī′ ȯn
Carmichael, kar mī′ kȧl
Carnegie, kar neg′ i
Carnot, kar nō′
Carnwath, karn′ woth
Carolina, kăr ō lī′ nȧ
Carolus Duran, kăr ō lus′ du ra*n*′
Carpathian, kar pā′ thi ȧn
Carrara, kar ra′ rȧ
Carrousel, kăr oo zel′
Carruthers, kȧ rŭ*th*′ ėrz
Cartagena, kar tȧ jē′ nȧ
Carteret, kar′ tĕr et
Cartier, kar tyā′
Caruso, kȧ roo′ zō
Carysfort, kăr′ is fôrt
Casabianca, ka za byang′ ka
Casa Guidi, ka′ za gwē′ dē
Casaubon, kȧ saw′ bȯn
Casimir, kas′ i mēr
Casimir-Perier, ka zē mēr′ pā ri ā′
Cassagnac, ka sa nyak′
Cassandra, kȧ săn′ drȧ
Cassilis, kăs′ ėlz
Cassiopœia, kăs i ȯ pē′ yȧ
Cassivelaunus, kăs i vė law′ nůs
Castalia, kăs tā′ li ȧ
Castellammare, kas tel la ma′ rā
Castellane, kas te lan′
Castiglione, kas tē lyō′ nā
Castille, kăs tēl′
Castlereagh, kasl rā′
Castrucci, kas troo′ chē
Castruccio, kas troo′ chō
Catalan, kăt′ ȧ lăn
Cateau-Cambrésis, ka tō′ ka*n* brā sē′
Cathay, kȧ thā′
Catullus, kȧ tŭl′ ůs
Caucasus, kaw′ kȧ sůs
Cauterets, kō tė rā′
Cavaignac, ka vā nyak′
Cavagnari, ka va nya′ rē
Cavalier, ka va lyā′
Cavalleria Rusticana, ka va lȧ rē′ a rus tē ka′ na
Cavan, kăv′ ȧn
Cavanagh, kăv′ ȧ nȧ
Cavell, căv′ ėl
Cavendish, kăn′ dish, kăv′ ȧn dish
Cavour, ka voor′
Cawnpore, kawn pôr′
Cayenne, kā en′, kī en′
Cayman, kī man′
Cayster, kā is′ tȧr
Cecil, ses′ il, sis′ il
Cecilia, sė sil′ i ȧ
Cecily, ses′ i li
Cecrops, sē′ krops
Cedric, sē′ drik, sed′ rik
Celebes, sel′ e bēz
Celestine, sel′ ės tīn, sė les′ tin
Cellini, chė lē′ nē
Cenci, chen′ chē
Centlivre, sent lē′ vir, -liv′ ėr
Cephas, sē′ fās
Cepheus, sē′ fūs, -fė ůs
Cerberus, sĕr′ bėr ůs
Ceres, sēr′ ēz
Cervantes, sėr văn′ tēz
Cesare, chā′ za rā
Cetewayo, set i-, kech wa′ yō
Cetinje, tset′ in yā
Ceuta, sū′ tȧ
Cévennes, sā ven′
Ceylon, sē lon′
Cezanne, sā zăn′
Chæronea, kēr ȯ nē′ ȧ
Chagres, cha′ grės
Chalcis, kăl′ sis
Chaldees, kăl dēz′
Chalmers, chaw′-, cha′-, chăl′ mėrz
Chalons, sha lo*n*′
Cham, kăm
Chambéry, sha*n* bā rē
Chambord, sha*n* bôr′
Chamonix, sha mō nē
Champagne, shăm pān′
Champ-de-Mars, sha*n* dė mar′
Champlain, shăm plān′, sha*n* plă*n*′
Champs-Elysées, sha*n* zā lē zā′
Chandos, shăn′ dos
Chantecler, sha*n*t klâr′
Chantilly, sha*n* ti yē′
Chapultepec, chă pool tė pek′
Charicles, kăr′ i klēz
Charlemagne, shar le mān′
Charlemont, sharl′ mont
Charleroi, shar lė rwa′
Charmian, char′ mi ȧn
Charon, kâr′ ȯn
Charteris, char′ tėrz
Chartres, shartr
Charybdis, kȧ rib′ dis
Chastelard, shat lar′
Chateaubriand, sha tō brē a*n*′
Château-Lafitte, sha tō la fēt′
Château-Thierry, sha tō tyė rē′
Châtelet, sha tė lā
Chatham, chăt′ ȧm,
Chaudière, shō dyâr′
Chauncey, chan′-, chawn′ si
Chatauqua, shȧ taw′ kwȧ
Chavannes, sha văn′
Chaworth, cha′ wȯrth
Chedorlaomer, ked ôr lā ō′ mėr
Cheetham, chēt′ ȧm
Chénier, shā nyā′
Cheops, kē′ ops
Cherbourg, sher boor′
Chersonesus, kĕr sȯ nē′ sůs
Cherubini, kā roo bē′ nē
Cherwell, char′ wėl
Chesham Bois, chesh′ ȧm bois′
Chetwode, chet′ wud
Chetwynd, chet′ wind
Chevalier, she val yā′
Cheviot, chev′ i ȯt
Cheyenne, shī en′
Cheyne, chā′ ni
Chicago, shi ka′ gō
Chichele, chich′ ė li
Childeric, kil′ dėr ik
Chile, chi′ li
Chillon, shē yo*n*′
Chilon, kī′ lȯn
Chimborazo, chim bō ra′ zō
Chingachgook, chin gash′ guk
Chippewa, chip′ ė wa
Chiron, kīr′ ȯn
Chisholm, chiz′ ȯm
Chiswick, chiz′ ik
Chloe, klō′ ē
Cholmeley, Cholmondeley, Chomley, chŭm′ li
Chopin, shō pa*n*′
Chosroes, koz′ rō ēz
Chouan, shoo′ ȧn
Chriemhilde, krēm′ hil dė
Christophorus, kris tof′ ȯ rȯs
Chryseis, krī sē′ is
Churchill, chĕrch′ hil
Cicely, sis′ ė li
Cicero, sis′ ėr ō
Cid, sid
Cilicia, si lish′ i ȧ
Cimabue, chē ma boo′ ā
Cincinnati, sin si nă′ ti
Cincinnatus, sin si nā′ tůs
Cinq-Mars, sa*n* mar′
Cipriani, chē prē a′ nē
Circe, sĕr′ sē
Cirencester, sis′ i ′tėr, sīr′ ėn ses tėr
Ciudad Real, sū dăd′ rā al′
Civita Vecchia, chē′ vē ta vek′ yȧ
Clairvaux, clâr vō′
Clanricarde, klăn rik′ ȧrd
Claretie, klar tē
Clarice, klăr′ is
Claude, klōd
Clausen, klou′ sėn
Clausewitz, klou′ sė vits
Claverhouse, klā′ vėrs, klăv′ ers, klăv′ ėr ůs
Cleckheaton, klek′ ē tȯn
Clementine, klem′ ėn tin, -tīn
Cleobulus, klē ȯ bū′ lůs
Cleomedes, klē ȯ mē′ dēz
Cleomenes, klė om′ ė nēz
Cleopas, klē′ ȯ păs
Cleopatra, klē ȯ pā′ trȧ
Clerk, klark
Clerkenwell, klark′ ėn wel
Clio, klī′ ō
Clogher, klō′ ėr
Clonfert, klon fĕrt′
Clos Vougeot, klō voo zhō′
Clough, klŭf
Clusium, kloo′ zhi ům
Clytemnestra, klī tėm nes′ trȧ
Cnidian, nid′ i ȧn
Cnossian, nos′ i ȧn
Cnut, kė nūt′
Coblentz, kō blents′
Cochin-China, kō′ chin chī′ nȧ
Cochrane, ko*ch*′ rȧn
Cockaigne, kō kān′
Cockburn, kō′ bėrn
Cocles, kok′ lēz
Cœlebs, sē′ lebs
Cœlian, sē′ li ȧn
Cœur de Lion, kĕr dė lē′ ȯn
Coke, kōk, kuk
Colbert, kōl bâr′
Colborne, kōl′ bȯrn
Colchester, kōl′ chės tėr
Colchis, kol′ kis
Colclough, kōk′ li
Colenso, kȯ len′ zō
Coleridge, kōl′ rij
Coligny, kō lē′ nyē
Coliseum, kol i sē′ ům
Cologne, kȯ lōn′
Colombo, kol ŭm′ bō
Colon, kȯ lon′
Colorado, kol ȯ ra′ dō
Colosseum, kol ȯ sē′ ům
Colquhoun, kȯ hoon′
Colville, kol′ vil
Comines, kȯ mēn′
Commodus, kom′ ȯ důs
Comorin, kom′ ȯ rin
Compiègne, ko*n* pē ā′ nyė
Compton, kŭmp′ tȯn
Comte, ko*n*t
Concepcion, kon sep′ syōn
Condé, ko*n* dā′
Condillac, ko*n* dē yak′
Condorcet, ko*n* dôr sā′
Congo, kong′ gō
Connaught, kon′ awt
Connecticut, kȯ net′ i kŭt
Constable, kun′ stȧ bėl
Consuelo, kon sū ā′ lō
Conybeare, kŭn′ i bâr
Conyngham, kŭn′ ing ȧm
Copernicus, kȯ pĕr′ ni kůs
Cophetua, kȯ fet′ ū ȧ
Coppée, ko pā′
Coquelin, kok la*n*′
Corcyra, kôr sīr′ ȧ

Corday, kŏr dā′
Cordoba, kôr′ dō ba
Corfu, kôr foo, kŏr fū′
Corinne, kȯ rin′
Coriolanus, kō ri ȯ lā′ nůs
Corioli, kȯ rī′ o lī
Corkran, kok′ rȧn
Cornaro, kôr na′ rō
Corneille, kôr nī′ yė
Corniche, kôr nēsh′
Corot, kȯ rō′
Correggio, kor rej′ ō
Correze, kȯ rāz′
Corrientes, kor i en′ tās
Cortés, kôr tez′
Coruna, kȯ roon′ yȧ
Corunna, kȯ rŭn′ ȧ
Cosette, kȯ zet′
Costa Rica, kos′ tȧ rē′ kȧ
Cotopaxi, kō tō păk′ si
Couch, kooch
Courbet, koor bā′
Court, koor
Courtenay, kôrt′ ni
Courthope, kôrt′ ōp
Courtrai, koor trā′
Cousens, kŭz′ ėnz
Coventry, kov′ en tri, kŭv′ ĕn tri
Coverley, kŭv′ ėr li
Cowen, kō′-, kou′ ėn
Cowes, kouz
Cowper, koo′-, kou′ pėr
Cozens, kŭz′ ėnz
Creagh, krā
Crébillon, krā bē yon
Crécy, krā sē′
Creighton, krī′ tȯn
Crepaud, krȧ pō′
Crespigny, krep′ i ni
Cressida, kres′ i dȧ
Creusa, krė ū′ sȧ
Crichton, krī′ tȯn
Crimea, kri mē′ ȧ
Crispi, krēs′pē
Critias, krish′ i ȧs
Crito, krī′ tō
Crœsus, krē′ sůs
Croce, krō′ chā
Cro-Magnon, krō ma nyon
Cromartie, krŭm′ ȧr ti
Crombie, krŭm′ bi
Cromwell, krom′ wėl
Cronje, kron′ yė
Cronos, krō′ nos
Crowninshield, grŭn′ sėl
Cruickshank, kruk′ shănk
Cuba, kū′ bȧ
Culebra, koo lā′ bra
Culloden, kůl od′ ėn
Culpeper, kůl′ pėp ėr
Cumæ, kū′ mē
Cumæan, kū mē′ ȧn
Cupar, koo′ par
Curteis, Curtois, kĕr′ tis
Custine, kus tēn′
Cuvier, ku vyā
Cuxhaven, kuks ha′ fėn
Cuyp, koip
Cuzco, kus′ kō
Cybele, sib′ ė lē
Cyclades, sik′ lȧ dēz
Cyclopes, si klō′ pēz
Cymbeline, sim′ bė lēn
Cymmrodorion, kim rȯ dôr′ i ȯn
Cymry, kim′ ri, kŭm′ ri
Cynewulf, kin′ ė wulf
Cyparissus, sip ȧ ris′ ůs
Cyprian, sip′ ri ȧn
Cyrene, sī rē′ nē
Cythera, si thēr′ ȧ
Cytherea, sith ė rē′ ȧ
Czech, chek
Czechoslovakia, chek ō slō văk′ iȧ
Czerny, chĕr′ ni
Dacre, dā′ kėr
Dædalus, dēd′ ȧ lůs
Dagonet, dăg′ ȯ net
Daguerre, dȧ gâr′
D'Aguilar, dăg′ wi lėr
Dahomey, da hō′ mā
Dakota, dȧ kō′ tȧ
D'Albert, dăl bâr′
Dalbiac, dawl′ bi ăk
Dalgetty, dăl′ gė ti
Dalhousie, dăl hoo′ zi
Dalmeny, dăl mā′ ni
Dalrymple, dăl rim′ pėl, dăl′ rim pėl
Dalzell, Dalziel, dē el′
Damien, Damiens, da myăn′
Damietta, dăm i et′ ȧ
Damocles, dăm′ ȯ klēz. **Damoclean,** dăm ȯ klē′ ȧn
Damon, dā′ mon
Dana, dā nȧ
Danae, dăn′ ā ē
Danaides, dȧ nā′ i dēz
Dandolo, dan′ dō lō
Dante, dăn′ ti, dan′ tā
Dantès, dan tes′
Danton, dan ton′
Daphne, dăf′ nē
Daphnis, dăf′ nis
Darfur, dar′ fur
Darien, dâr′ i ėn
Darius, dȧ rī′ ůs
Darjeeling, dar jē′ ling
d'Artagnan, dar tan yan′
Daubeney, daw′ bė ni
Daubigny, dō bē nyē′
Daudet, dō dā′
Dauphiné, dō fē nā′
Dauphiny, dō′ fi ni
David, dā′ vid
da Vinci, da vin′ chi
Davout, da voo′
Deak, dā ak′
Dealtry, dawl′ tri
de Amicis, dā a mē′ chēs
Dease, dēs
Debach, deb′ ij
De Bathe, dȧ bath′
Deborah, deb′ ȯ rȧ
De Burgh, de bĕrg′
Debussy, de bus′ i
Decameron, dek ăm′ ėr ȯn
Decazes, dė kaz′
Deccan, dek′ ȧn
Decies, dē′ shēz
De Crespigny, dė krep′ in i
Degas, dā ga
De Gaulle, dė gōl
Delacroix, dė la krwa′
Delagoa, del ȧ gō′ ȧ
De la Mare, del′ ȧ mâr
De la Pasture, dė lăp′ ȧ tėr
De la Poer, dė la poor′
De la Rey, dė la rā′
Delaunay, dė lō na′
De la Warr, del′ ȧ war
Delhi, del′ i
Delibes, dā lēb′
Delilah, dė lī′ lȧ
De L'Isle, dė līl′
Delius, dē′ li ůs
Delphi, del′ fī
Democritus, dė mok′ ri tůs
De Moleyns, dem ȯ lēnz′
De Montalt, dȧ mon talt′
Demosthenes, dė mos′ thė nēz
Denbigh, den′ bi
Denderah, den′ dėr ȧ
Dent du Midi, dan du mē dē′
d'Eon, dā on′
Deptford, det′ fȯrd
Derby, dar′ bi
Dering, dēr′ ing
De Rohan, dė rō′ ȧn
De Ros, de roos′
Déroulede, dā ru led′
Desaix, dė sā′
De Salis, dė săl′ is
Desart, des′ ȧrt
De Saumarez, dė sō′ mȧ rez
Desbrosses, dā brōs′
Descartes, dā kart′
Deschamps, dā shan′
Deschanel, dā sha nel′
Desdemona, dez dė mō′ nȧ
Desiré, dā zē rā′
des Lys, dā lēs′
des Moines, dā mwan′
Desmoulins, dā moo lăn′
Dessalines, dā sȧ lēn′
Des Voeux, dā vō′
Detaille, de ta′ yė
Dettingen, det′ ing ėn
De Valera, dė vȧl âr′ ȧ
Devereux, dev′ ėr oo, -ooks
Daventry, dăv′ ėn tri
De Vesci, de ves′ i
Dewar, dū ȧr′
Deyncourt, dān′ kůrt
De Zoete, dė zoot′
Dhaulagiri, dou la gē′ rē
Diana, dī ăn′ ȧ
Diane de Poitiers, dē an′ dė pwa tyā′
Diaz, dē′ as
Diderot, dēd rō′
Dieppe, dē ep′
Dijon, dē zhon′
Dinan, Dinant, dē nan′
Dinorah, dē nôr′ a
Diocletian, dī ȯ klē′ shȧn
Diodorus, dī ȯ dôr′ ůs
Diogenes, dī oj′ ė nēz
Diomed, dī′ ȯ med
Diomedes, dī ȯ mē′ dēz
Dionysius, dī ȯ nish′ i ůs
Dionysus, dī ȯ nī′ sůs
Dioscuri, dī os kū′ ri
Directoire, dē rek twar′
Discobolus, dis kob′ ȯ lůs
Disraeli, diz rā′ li
Dives, dī′ vēz
Divina Commedia, dē vē′ na kom mā′ di a
Dnieper, nē′ pėr
Dniester, nēs′ tėr
Dobell, dō bel′
Dodonæus, dod ȯ nē′ ůs
Dolce, dōl′ chā
Dolgelly, dol geth′ li
Döllinger, dol′ ing ėr
Dolores, dȯ lôr′ ēs
Domenichino, dō mā nē kē′ nō
Domett, dom′ ėt
Dominica, dom i nē′ kȧ
Domitian, dȯ mish′ i ȧn
Domrèmy-la-Pucelle, don rė mī′ la pu sel′
Domvile, dŭm′ vil
Donati, dō na′ tē
Donegal, don ė gawl′
Don Giovanni, don jō va′ ni
Dongola, dong′ gȯ lȧ
Donizetti, don i zet′ i
Don Juan, don joo′ ȧn
Donne, dŭn, don
Donoghue, dŭn′ ȯ hū
Donoughmore, dŭn′ ȯ môr
Don Quixote, don kwik′ sȯt
Dordogne, dôr dō′ nyė
Dordrecht, dôr′ drecht
Doré, dô rā′
Doria, dô′ ri ȧ
Doris, dor′ is
d'Orsay, dôr′ sā
Dostoevski, dos tȯ ef′ ski
Dotheboys, doo′ thė boiz
Douay, doo ā′
Doudney, dūd′ ni
Dougall, doo′ gȧl

Douglas, dŭg′ lȧs
Dovrefjeld, dō vrė fyel′
Drachenfels, dra′ *ch*ėn fels
Drawcansir, draw′ kȧn sir
Dreyfus, drā′ fus
Drogheda, dro′ hė dȧ
Dryburgh, drī′ bu̇ rȯ
Drysdale, driz′ dȧl
Du Barry, du ba′ rē
Dubois, du bwa′
Du Buisson, dū′ bi sȯn
Du Chaillu, du sha yu′
Du Chesne, du shān′
Dudevant, dud va*n*′
Du Guesclin, du gā klă*n*′
Dujardin, du zhar dă*n*′
Dulcamara, dul ka ma′ ra
Dulcinea, dŭl sin′ ė ȧ
Dulwich, dŭl′ ij, -ich
Dumas, doo ma′
Du Maurier, doo mȯ ryā′
Dumfries, dŭm frēs′
Dumouriez, du moor yā
Dunalley, dŭn ăl′ i
Dundalk, dŭn dawk′
Dundas, dŭn dăs′
Dundee, dŭn dē′
Dunedin, dŭn ē′ din
Dunfermline, dŭn fĕrm′-, fĕr′ lin
Dunglass, dŭn glas′
Dunmore, dŭn môr′
Dunnottar, dŭn not′ ȧr
Dunsany, dŭn sā′ ni
Dunsinane, dŭn si nān′
Duplat, du pla′
Dupleix, du pleks
Duplessis, du plė sē′
Dupré, du prā′
Dupuy, du pwē′
Du Quesne, Duquesne, du kān′
Durand, dū rand′
Durazzo, du rad′ zō
Durban, dĕr′ bȧn
Durham, dŭr′ ȧm
Durrant, du̇ rant′, dŭr′ ȧnt
Dusé, doo′ zā
Dvořák, dvôr′ zhăk
Dwina, dwē′ nȧ
Dyak, dī′ ăk
Dymoke, dim′ ȯk
Dynevor, din′ ė vȯr
Dysart, dī′ zȧrt

Eaux, ō
Ebbw, eb′ oo
Ebers, ā′ bėrz
Ebionite, ē′ bi ȯ nīt
Eboracum, ē bor′ ȧ kŭm
Ebury, ē′ bu̇ ri
Ecbatana, ek băt′ ȧ nȧ
Ecclefechan, ek ėl fe*ch*′ ȧn
Echegary, e chā ga rī′
Eckmuhl, ek′ mul
Ecuador, ek wȧ dôr′
Edinburgh, edn′ bu̇ rȯ, ed′ in bu̇ ru
Egalité, ā ga′ lē tā
Egeria, ė jēr′ i ȧ
Egerton, ej′ ėr tȯn
Egeus, ē jē′ u̇s
Ehrenbreitstein, ā rėn brīt′ shtīn
Eifel, ī′ fel
Eiffel Tower, ī′ fėl tou′ ėr
Eikon Basilike, ī′ kon bȧ sil′ i kē
Eildon, ēl′ dȯn
Eileen, ī′ lēn
Einstein, īn′ stīn
Eire, âr′ ȧ
Elagabalus, ē lȧ găb′ ȧ lu̇s
Elburz, el boorz′
El Caney, el kȧ nā′
Elcho, el′ kō
Eleanora, el ė ȧ nôr′ ȧ
Electra, ė lek′ trȧ
Eleusis, ė lū′ sis
Elgin, el′ gin
Eli, ē′ lī
Elia, ē′ li ȧ
Elias, ē lī′ ȧs
Elibank, el′ i bănk
Elihu, ė lī′ hū, el′ i hū
Elijah, ė lī′ jȧ
Elisha, ė lī′ shȧ
Ely, ē′ li
Ellesmere, elz′ mēr
Ellora, ė lôr′ ȧ
Elphinstone, el′ fin stȯn
Elsinore, el si nôr′
Elwes, el′ wez
Emile, ā mēl′
Emmaus, ē mā′ u̇s
Empedocles, em ped′ o klēz
Ems, ems
Enceladus, en sel′ ȧ du̇s
Endymion, en dim′ i ȯn
Engadine, en gȧ dēn′
Enghien, a*n* gē*n*′
Enid, ē′ nid
Enniskillen, en is kil′ ėn
Entebbe, en teb′ i
Eöthen, ē ō′ thėn
Epaminondas, ė păm i non′ dăs
Epaphroditus, ė păf rȯ dī′ tu̇s
Epernay, ā pâr nā′
Epeus, ė pē′ u̇s
Ephesus, ef′ e su̇s
Ephialtes, ef i ăl′ tēz
Ephraim, ē′ frȧ im
Epictetus, ep ik tē′ tu̇s
Epicurus, ep i kūr′ u̇s
Epinay, ā pē nā′
Epirus, ė pīr′ u̇s
Erasmus, ė răz′ mu̇s
Erato, er′ ȧ tō
Eratosthenes, er ȧ tos′ thė nēz
Erckmann-Chatrian, ĕrk man′ sha trē a*n*′
Erebus, er′ ė bu̇s
Erechtheum, er ek thē′ u̇m
Erema, ė rē′ mȧ
Erewhon, e′ ri won
Erie, ēr′ i
Erigena, ė rij′ ė nȧ
Erlangen, ĕr′ lăng ėn
Ermanaric, ĕr măn′ ȧ rik
Ernani, ĕr na′ ni
Eros, ēr′ os
Erostratus, ė ros′ trȧ tu̇s
Erythræan, er i thrē′ ȧn
Erzerûm, ĕrz′ room
Esaias, ė zā′ yȧs, ė zī′ ȧs
Escorial, es kôr′ i ȧl
Esdraelon, es drȧ ē′ lȯn
Esquiline, es′ kwi līn
Este, es′ tā
Esterhazy, es′ tėr ha zē
Esther, es′ tėr
Esthonia, es thō′ nyȧ
Estienne, ā tyen′
Estramadura, es tra ma door′ a
Estrées, es trā′
Etherege, eth′ ėr ij
Ethiopia, ē thi ō′ pi ȧ
Etienne, ā tyen′
Eubœa, ū bē′ ȧ
Euclid, ū′ klid
Eudoxus, ū dok′ su̇s
Eugene, ū jen′, ū′ jēn
Eugène, u zhān′
Eugénie, u zhā nē′
Eulalia, ū lā′ li ȧ
Eulenspiegel, oi′ lėn spē gėl
Eumenes, ū′ mė nēz
Eumenides, ū men′ i dēz
Eunice, ū′ nis, ū nī′ sē
Euphemia, ū fē′ mi ȧ
Euphrates, ū frā′ tēz
Euphrosyne, ū fros′ i nē
Euphues, ū′ fū ēz
Eurasia, ū rā′ shi ȧ
Eure-et-Loir, ur ā lwar′
Euripides, ū rip′ i dēz
Euroclydon, ū rok′ li dȯn
Europa, ū rō′ pȧ
Euryalus, ū rī′ ȧ lu̇s
Euryanthe, ū ri ăn′ thē
Eurydice, ū rid′ i sē
Eurystheus, ū ris′ thūs, -thė u̇s
Eusebius, ū sē′ bi u̇s
Eustachius, ū stā′ ki u̇s
Euterpe, ū tĕr′ pē
Euxine, ūk′ sin
Evangeline, ė văn′ jė lēn, -līn, -lin
Evelina, ev ė lē′ nȧ, -lī′ nȧ
Eveline, ev′ ė lēn, -lin
Evelyn, ēv′ lin, ev′ lin
Evesham, ēv′ shȧm
Ewart, ū′ art
Excalibur, ek skăl′ i bĕr
Exeter, eks′ e tėr
Eyam, ē′ ȧm
Eyck, īk
Eylau, ī′ lou
Eyre, âr
Ezekiel, ė zē′ kyėl, -ki ėl

Faed, fād
Fagin, fā′ gin
Falconbridge, faw′ kȯn brij
Falconer, fawk′ nėr
Falkland, fawk′ lȧnd
Fallières, fal yâr′
Fallodon, făl′ o dȯn
Faneuil, fŭnl, fănl
Fanline, fa*n* lēn′
Farnese, far nē′ zi
Faroe, fâr′ ō
Farquhar, far′ kwėr, -kȧr
Fatima, făt′ i mȧ
Faubourg St. Antoine, fō boor′ să*n* tan twan′
Faucit, faw′ sit
Faust, foust
Faversham, fev′ ėr shȧm
Favre, favr
Fawcett, fos′ ėt, faw′ sėt
Fayal, fī al′
Fayette, fā et′
Featherstonehaugh, făn′ shaw
Feilden, fēl′ dėn
Feilding, fēl′ ding
Félice, fā lēs′
Fénelon, fā nė lo*n*′
Fenwick, fen′ ik
Fermanagh, fėr măn′ a
Ferney, fĕr nā′
Ferrara, fė ra′ ra
Ferry, fer ē′
Feuerbach, foi′ ėr ba*ch*
Feuilles, fu yā′
ffolkes, fōks
Fichte, fi*ch*′ tė
Fidelio, fē dā′ li ō
Fiennes, fīnz
Fiesole, fi ā′ zō lā
Figaro, fig′ ȧ rō
Figuier, fē gyā′
Fiji, fē′ jē
Fildes, fīldz
Findlater, find′ lā tĕr′
Findlay, fin′ li
Finisterre, fin is târ′
Firdausi, fēr dou′ sē
Firmin-Didot, fĕr măn′ dē dō′
Fitzhardinge, fits har′ ding
Fiume, fū′ mā
Flameng, fla măn′
Flammarion, fla ma rē o*n*′
Flaubert, flō bâr′
Fleurus, flu rus′
Fleury, flu rē′
Flores, flôr′ ez
Flotow, flō′ tō
Foch, fosh

Foljambe, foo′ jȧm
Fontainebleau, fo*n* tăn blō′
Fontenoy, fon′ tė noi
Forbes, (Eng.) fôrbz, (Sc.) fôr′ biz
Fornarina, fôr na rē′ na
Fors Clavigera, fôrz klȧ vij′ ȧr ȧ
Fortescue, fôr′ tės kū
Fortuna, fôr tū′ nȧ
Fortunatus, fôr tū nā′ tůs
Foscari, fos′ ka rē
Fouché, foo shā′
Fouquier-Tinville, foo kyā′ tă*n* vēl′
Foulis, foulz
Fourier, foo rē ā′
Fowey, foi
Fra Diavolo, fra dē a′ vō lō
Francesca, frăn ses′ kȧ, fran ches′ ka
Franche Comté, fra*n*sh ko*n* tā′
François, fra*n* swa′
Frankenstein, frăng′ kėn stīn
Franz-Jozef, frants yō′ zef
Frederica, fred ėr ē′ kȧ
Freiburg, frī′ burg
Freischütz, frī′ shuts
Fremantle, frē măn′ tėl
Freud, froid
Freycinet, frā sē nā′
Freyer, frē′ ȧr, frī′ ȧr
Friedland, frēd′ lȧnd
Friedrichshaffen, frē dri*chs*′ ha fėn
Frobisher, frob′ ish ėr, frō′ bish ėr
Froebel, frū′ bel
Frome, froom
Frontenac, fron′ tė năk
Froude, frood
Fuchs, fuks
Fujiyama, foo jē ya′ ma
Furneaux, fėr′ nō

Gaboriau, ga bō ryō′
Gabriel, gā′ bri ėl
Gades, gā′ dēz
Gael, gāl
Gaeta, ga ā′ ta
Gaia, gī′ ȧ, gā′ yȧ
Gaillard, ga yar′
Gairdner, gard′ nėr
Galagnani, ga lā nya′ nē
Galahad, găl′ ȧ hăd
Galapagos, ga la′ pa gōs
Galashiels, găl ȧ shēlz′
Galata, găl′ a ta
Galatea, găl ȧ tē′ ȧ
Galatia, gȧ lā′ shi ȧ
Galbraith, găl brāth′
Galen, gā′ ėn
Galileo, găl i lē′ ō
Gallagher, găl′ ȧ hėr
Galle, gawl
Gallifet, ga lē fā′
Gallipoli, gȧ lip′ ȯ li
Gallitzin, ga lēt′ sēn
Gallwey, Galway, gawl′ wā
Gamaliel, gȧ mā′ li ėl
Gambetta, găm bet′ ȧ
Ganges, găn′ jēz
Ganymede, găn′ i mēd
Ganymedes, găn i mē′ dēz
Garibaldi, găr i bol′ di
Garmoyle, gar moil′
Garonne, ga ron′
Garvagh, gar′ va
Gatun, gā toon′
Gauss, gous
Gautama, gaw′ ta ma
Gautier, gō tyā′
Gawain, gaw′ wān
Gay-Lussac, gā lu sak′
Gebir, gā′ bir, jē′ bir
Geddes, ged′ is
Gee, jē
Geikie, gē′ ki
Gelert, gel′ ėrt
Gell, jel, gel
Gemini, jem′ in i
Gemmi, gem′ i
Genée, zhė nā′
Genesis, jen′ e sis
Geneva, jėn ē′ vȧ
Genevieve, jen′ ė vēv
Geneviève, zhen vē āv′
Genevra, jė nev′ rȧ
Genghis Khan, jen′ gis kan′
Genlis, zha*n* lēs′
Gennesaret, ge nes′ ȧ ret
Genoa, jen′ ȯ ȧ
Genseric, jen′ sėr ik
Geoffrey, jef′ ri
Geoffroy, zhof rwa′
Geoghegan, gā′ gȧn
Georges, zhôrzh
Geraint, jėr ānt′, ge rānt′
Gerard, jer′ ȧrd
Gérard, zhā rar′
Gerizim, ger′ i zim, gė rī′ zim
Germania, jėr mā′ ni ȧ
Germanicus, jĕr măn′ i kůs
Gerolstein, zher′ ōl stīn
Gérome, zhā rōm′
Geronimo, jė ron′ i mō
Gervinus, ger vē′ nus
Gethsemane, geth sem′ ȧ nē
Gettysburg, get′ iz bĕrg
Ghana, ga′ nȧ
Ghent, gent
Ghiberti, ge ber′ tē
Ghirlandajo, gēr lan da′ yō
Giacomo, ja′ kō mō
Gibraltar, jib rol′ tȧr
Giddens, gid′ ėnz
Gide, zhēd
Gidea, gid′ i ȧ
Giffard, jif′ ȧrd, gif′ ȧrd
Giffen, jif′ ėn
Gifford, gif′ ȯrd, jif′ ȯrd
Gigli, jē′ lyē
Gila, hē la
Gil Blas, zhēl blas
Gilboa, gil bō′ ȧ
Gilchrist, gil′ krist
Gildas, gil′ dȧs
Gildea, gil dā′, gil dā′ ȧ, gid′ i ȧ
Gilead, gil′ i ȧd
Gilkie, gil′ ki
Gilles, gil′ is
Gillespie, gi les′ pi
Gilroy, gil roi′
Gilzean, gi lēn′
Ginevra, ji nev′ rȧ
Gioacchino, jō ȧ kē′ nō
Giordano, jôr da′ nō
Giorgio, jôr′ jō
Giorgione, jôr jō′ nā
Giotto, jot′ ō
Giovanni, jō va′ nē
Giralda, hē ral′ da
Girard, ji rard′, zhē rar′
Girolamo, zhē ro′ la mō
Gironde, ji rond′, zhē ro*n*d′
Giuliano, joo li a′ nō
Giulio Romano, joo′ lē ō rō ma′ nō
Giuseppe, joo zep′ i
Gizeh, gē′ zė
Gladstone, glăd′ stȯn
Glamis, glamz
Glasgow, glăs′ gō
Glenlivet, glen liv′ ėt
Glenmuick, glen mik′
Gloag, glōg
Gloriana, glôr i ā′ nȧ
Gloucester, glos′ tėr
Gluck, gluk
Glydr, glid′ ėr
Gneisenau, gnī′ zė nou
Gneist, gnīst
Godalming, god′ ȧl ming
Godavery, gō dā′ vȧr i
Godiva, gȯ dī′ vȧ
Godoy, gȯ doi′
Goethals, gĕr′ talz
Goethe, gĕr′ tȧ
Goetz, gĕrts
Goldsworthy, gōlz′ wȯr *th*i
Goliath, gō lī′ ȧth
Gollancz, gol′ ȧnks
Gomme, gom
Gomorra, gȯ mor′ ȧ
Gorges, gôr′ jėz
Gorgias, gôr′ ji ăs
Gorky, gôr′ ki
Gormanstown, gôr′ mȧns tȯn
Gortschakoff, gôr cha kof′
Goschen, gō′ shėn
Gotha, gō′ ta
Gotham, (Eng.) got′ ȧm; (*Am.*) gō′ thȧm
Göttingen, gĕr′ ting ėn
Gouda, gou′ da
Goudy, gou′ di
Gough, gŭf, gof
Goulburn, gool′ bůrn
Gounod, goo nō′
Gourley, goor′ li
Gower, gou′ ėr, gôr
Gracchus, grăk′ us
Graeme, grām
Graham, Grahame, grā′ ȧm
Granada, grȧ na′ dȧ
Granard, grăn′ ȧrd
Gravelotte, grav lot′
Greaves, grāvz
Greenough, grē′ nō
Greenwich, grin′ ij
Greiffenhagen, grī′ fėn ha gėn
Greig, greg
Grenada [W. Indies], grė nā′ dȧ
Grenada [U.S.A.], grė na′ dȧ
Grenoble, gre nōbl′
Greuze, grĕrz
Greville, grevl
Grévy, grā vē′
Grieg, grēg
Grimaldi, grē mal′ dē
Grindelwald, grin′ del valt
Grisi, grē′ sē
Grisons, grē zo*n*′
Grolier, grō′ lyā
Groote Schoor, grōt′ skoor
Grosseteste, grōs′ test
Grosvenor, grōv′ nȯr
Grouchy, groo shē′
Gruyère, groo′ yâr
Guadalquivir, gwa dal kwiv′ ėr
Guadeloupe, gwa de loop′
Guaira, gwăr′ a
Guanche, gwan′ chā
Guatemala, gaw tȧ ma′ lȧ, gwa tā ma′ la
Guayaquil, gwī ȧ kēl′
Gudrun, good′ run
Guedalla, gwe dal′ ȧ
Guelders, gel′ dėrz
Guelph, gwelf
Guercino, gwĕr chē′ nō
Guernsey, gĕrn′ zi
Guerrazzi, gwer rat′ zi
Guescelin, gā kla*n*
Guevara, gā va′ ra
Guglielmo, gool yēl′ mō
Guiana, gē a′ na
Guicciardini, gwē char dē′ nē
Guiccioli, gwē′ chō lē
Guido Reni, gwē′ dō rā′ nē
Guilbert, gēl bâr′
Guildenstern, gil′ dėn stĕrn
Guildford, gil′ fȯrd
Guillaume, gē yōm′
Guillemard, gil′ mȧr
Guillotin, gē yō tă*n*′
Guinea, gi′ ni
Guinevere, gwin′ ė vēr

Guiscard, gēs kar′
Guiscardo, gwis kar′ dō
Guise, gēz
Guizot, gē zō′
Gujarat, goo jȧ rat′
Gulielmus, gū li el′ mu̇s
Gunther, gun′ tėr
Gustavus, gus ta′ vu̇s
Gutenberg, goo′ tėn berg
Guyon, gī′ ȯn
Guyot, gē yō′
Gwalior, gwa′ li ȯr
Gwatkin, gwot′ kin
Gwydyr, gwī′ dėr
Gye, jī
Gyges, gī′ jēz

Haakon, hā′ kon, **hō′ kon**
Haarlem, har′ lem
Haase, ha′ zė
Habana, ha va′ na
Habsburg, hăbz′ bĕrg
Hachette, a shet′
Häckel, hekl
Haden, hā′ dėn
Hades, hā′ dēz
Háfiz, ha′ fiz
Hagar, hā′ gar
Haggai, hăg′ ȧ ī
Hague, hāg
Haidarabad, hī dȧ rȧ **bad′**
Haidie, hī dē′
Haifa, hī′ fȧ
Hainault, hā′ nawt
Haiti, hā′ ti
Hakluyt, hăk′ loot
Halcyone, hăl sī′ ȯ **nē**
Haldane, hawl′ dān
Haldon, hawl′ dȯn
Halévy, a lā vē′
Halkett, hăk′ ėt
Hallicarnassus, hăl i kȧr năs′ u̇s
Halle, hal′ ė
Hallé, hăl′ ā
Hallstadt, hal′ shtat
Hals, hals
Halsbury, hawlz′ bri
Hambro, hăm′ bȯ rȯ
Hamilcar, hȧ mil′ kar
Hamish, hā′ mish
Hampden, hăm′ dėn
Hanau, ha′ nou
Hardenhuish, har′ nish
Hardicanute, har di kȧ **nūt′**
Hardinge, har′ ding
Hardres, hardz
Harewood, hâr′ wud
Harflœur, ar flur′
Harlech, har′ le*ch*
Haroun al-Raschid, ha roon′ al ra′ shēd
Harpagon, ar pa go*n*′
Harpocrates, har pok′ rȧ tēz
Hartlepool, hart′ le pool
Harwich, hăr′ ij
Harz, harts
Hasdrubal, hăs dru băl′
Hauff, houf
Haughton, hō′ tȯn
Hauptmann, houpt′ man
Hausa, hou′ sa
Haussmann, ōs man′
Haute-Savoie, ōt sa vwa′
Hautes-Alpes, ōt zalp′
Hautes-Pyrénées, ōt pē rā nā
Havana, hȧ văn′ ȧ
Havre, avr
Hawaii, ha wī′ ē
Hawarden (place), har′ dėn (title), hā′ wôr dėn
Haweis, haw′ is
Haworth, haw′ wȯrth
Haydn, hādn, hīdn
Haye, ā
Hebe, hē′ bē

Hebrides, heb′ ri dēz
Hebron, hē′ brȯn
Hecate, hek′ ȧ tē
Hecuba, hek′ ū bȧ
Hegel, hā′ gėl
Heidelberg, hī′ dėl bĕrg
Heidsieck, hīd′ sēk
Heimskringla, **hīm′ skring lȧ**
Heine, hī′ nė
Heinrich, hīn′ ri*ch*
Helicon, hel′ i kȯn
Helios, hē′ li os
Hellas, hel′ ȧs
Helle, hel′ ē
Hellespont, hel′ ės pont
Helmholtz, helm′ hōlts
Héloïse, ā lō ēz′
Helvetia, hel vē′ shi ȧ
Hemans, hem′ ȧnz, **hē′ mȧnz**
Heneage, hen′ ėj
Hengest, heng′ gest
Henle, hen′ lė
Hennepin, hen′ ė pin
Hennessey, hen′ ė si
Henri, a*n* rē′
Henriade, a*n* rē ăd′
Henriques, hen rē′ kez, **a*n* rē′ kės**
Hepburn, heb′ ĕrn, hep′ bĕrn
Hephæstion, hē fes′ ti ȯn
Hephæstus, hė fes′ tu̇s
Heracles, her′ ȧ klēz
Heraclitus, her ȧ klī′ tu̇s
Herat, hė rat′
Herbart, hĕr′ bart
Herculaneum, hĕr kū lā′ nė u̇m
Hercules, hĕr′ cū lēz
Here, hē′ ē
Hereford, her′ ė fȯrd
Hereward, her′ ė wȯrd
Hermes, hĕr′ mēz
Hermias, hĕr′ mi ȧs
Hermione, hėr mī′ ȯ nē
Hermogenes, hĕr moj′ ȧ **nēz**
Hernandez, âr nan′ deth
Hernani, er na′ nē
Herod, her′ ȯd
Herodias, he rō′ di ăs
Herodotus, hė rod′ ȯ tu̇s
Herries, her′ is
Hertford, hart′ fȯrd
Hervey, har′ vi
Herzegovina, hĕrt sė gȯ vē′ nȧ
Hesiod, hē′ shi ȯd, -sī ȯd
Hesione, hē sī′ ȯ nē
Hesperides, hes per′ i dez
Hesse (personal name), hes
Hesse (place name), hes′ ė
Heyse, hī′ zė
Heytesbury, hāts′ bu̇ ri
Hiawatha, hī ȧ woth′ ȧ
Hiero, hī′ ėr ō
Hieronymus, hī ėr on′ i mu̇s
Hildebrand, hil′ dė brănd
Himalaya, him ȧ lā′ ya
Hippocrates, hi pok′ rā tēz
Hippocrene, hip′ ȯ krēn, hip ȯ krē′ nē
Hippolyta, hi pol′ i tȧ
Hippolytus, hi pol′ i tu̇s
Hippomenes, hi pom′ ė nēz
Hiroshima, hi rō shē′ mȧ
Hispania, his pā′ ni ȧ
Hispaniola, his pa nyō′ la
Hissar, hī sar′
Hobart, (name) hŭb′ ȧrt, (place) hō′ bart
Hobbema, hob′ ė ma
Hoboken (N.Y.), hō′ bȯ kėn
Hoche, ōsh
Hoddesdon, hod′ ez dȯn
Hoey, hoi
Hohenlohe, hō ėn lō′ ė
Hohenstaufen, hō ėn stou′ fėn
Hohenzollern, hō ėn tsol′ ėrn
Holbeach, hōl′ bēch

Holbein, hōl′ bīn
Holborn, hō′ bu̇rn
Holford, hōl′ fôrd
Holinshed, hol′ inz hed, **-in shed**
Holmes, hōmz
Holmesdale, hōmz′ dāl
Holm-Patrick, hōm păt′ rik
Holofernes, hol ȯ fĕr′ **nēz**
Holstein, hōl′ stīn
Holyhead, hol′ i hed
Holyoake, hol′ i ōk
Holyoke, hōl′ yōk
Holyrood, hol′ i rood
Holywell, hol′ i wel
Home, hūm
Honduras, hon dūr′ ȧs
Honflœur, o*n* flĕr′
Honiton, hon′ i tȯn
Honolulu, hon ȯ loo′ loo
Honoria, hȯ nôr′ i ȧ
Hopetoun, hōp′ tȯn
Horace, hor′ ȧs
Horatio, hȯ rā′ shi ō
Hortense, ôr ta*n*s′
Hortensius, hôr ten′ shi u̇s
Hosea, hō zē′ ȧ
Houdin, oo dă*n*′
Hough, hŭf
Houghall, hof′ ȧl
Houghton, haw′-, hou′ tȯn
Hougoumont, oo goo mo*n*′
Houyhnhnm, whin′ im
Houssaye, oo sā′
Houston, hoos′ tȯn
Hudibras, hū′ di brăs
Hueffer, huf′ ėr
Huerta, wĕr′ ta
Hugessen, hū′ jė sėn
Hughenden, hū′ ėn dėn
Hugli, hoo′ gli
Huish, hū′ ish
Humboldt, hŭm′ bōlt
Hunstanton, hŭn′ stȯn
Hunjadi Janos, hŭn′ yod i ya′ nōsh
Huron, hū′ ron
Huth, hūth
Huygens, hī′ genz
Huysman, hois′ man
Huysmans, us ma*n*′
Hyacinthe, ē a să*n*t′
Hyacinthus, hī ȧ sin′ thu̇s
Hyades, hī′ ȧ dēz
Hyderabad, hī′ dė rȧ băd
Hyères, i âr′
Hygeia, hī jē′ ȧ
Hylas, hī′ lȧs
Hymenæus, hī mė nē′ u̇s
Hymettus, hī met′ u̇s
Hyndman, hīnd′ mȧn
Hypatia, hī pā′ shi ȧ
Hyperion, hī pēr′ i ȯn
Hyrcan, hĕr′ kȧn
Hyrcanus, hĕr kā′ nu̇s

Iacchus, ī ăk′ u̇s
Iachimo, ya′ ki mō′, **ī ăk′ i mō**
Iago, ē a′ gō, ya′ gō
Iamblichus, ī ăm′ bli **ku̇s**
Ian, ē′ ȧn
I'Anson, ī′ ȧn son
Ianthe, ī ăn′ thi
Iapetus, ī ăp′ ė tu̇s
Iberia, ī bēr′ i a
Ibrahim, ib rȧ him′
Ibsen, ib′ sėn
Icarian, ī kâr′ i ȧn
Icarus, ik′ ȧ ru̇s
Ichabod, ik′ ȧ bod
Icilius, ī sil′ i u̇s
Icolmkill, ī kōm kil′
Ictinus, ik tī′ nu̇s
Idaho, ī′ dă hō
Iddesleigh, idz′ li
Idumæa, id ū mē′ ȧ

Ightham, ī′ tȧm
Ignatief, ig na′ tyef
Ile de France, ēl dė frans′
Illinois, il i noi′, -noiz′
Illyria, il ir′ i ȧ
Imogen, im′ ō jėn
Inchiquin, inch′ kwin
Indiana, in di ăn′ ȧ
Indianapolis, in di ȧ năp′ ō lis
Indonesia, in dō nē′ zi ȧ
Inez, ē′ nez, ī′ nėz
Inge, ing
Ingelow, in′ jė lō
Ingham, ing′ ȧm
Ingres, an′ grė
Innes, in′ ės
Innisfail, in′ is fāl
Inveraray, in vėr âr′ i
Inverness, in vėr nes′
Iolanthe, ī ō lăn′ thi
Iona, ī ō′ nȧ
Ione, ī ō′ nē
Iowa, ī′ ō wȧ
Iphigenia, if i jė nī′ ȧ
Iquique, ē kē′ kā
Iran, ī ran′
Iraq, ē rak′
Irawadi, ir a wa′ di
Irenæus, īr ė nē′ ůs
Irene, ī rē′ nē
Irkutsk, ir kutsk′
Iroquois, ir ō kwoi′
Isaac, ī′ zȧk
Isaiah, ī zī′ ȧ, ī zā′ yȧ
Ischia, is′ kya
Isengrim, ī′ zėn grim
Iser, ē′ zėr
Isère, ē zâr′
Iseult, ē soolt′
Isham, ish′ ȧm
Isis, ī′ sis
Islay, ī′ lā, is′ lā
Isleworth, ī′ zėl wĕrth
Islip, iz′ lip
Ismail, iz′ māl
Ismailia, iz mȧ lē′ yȧ
Ismay, is′ mā′
Isocrates, ī sok′ rȧ tēz
Isola Bella, ē′ zō la bel′ ȧ
Isolde, i sōld
Ispahan, is pa han′
Israel, iz′ rāl
Issacher, is′ ȧ kėr
Ithaca, ith′ ȧ kȧ
Ithuriel, ī thūr′ i ėl
Ito, ē′ tō
Ituræa, it ū rē′ a
Itys, ī′ tis
Iulus, ī ū′ lůs
Ivan, ī′ vȧn, ē′ van
Iveagh, ī′ vā
Ivry, ē vrē′
Ixion, ik sī′ ŏn

Jacobi, Jacoby, jăk′ ō bi
Jacobus, jȧ kō′ bůs
Jacquardt, zha kar′
Jacques, jāks
Jaegar, yā′ gėr
Jael, jā′ ėl
Jaipur, jī poor′
Jairus, jī′ rus
Jameson, Jamesone, jām′ sȯn
Jamieson, jim′ i sȯn
Jamshid, jam shēd′
Janet, jăn′ ėt, (*Am.*) jȧ net′
Janiculum, jȧ nik′ ū lům
Jan Mayan, yan mī′ an
Janotha, zha nō′ ta
Janus, jā′ nůs
Japheth, jā′ fėth
Jaques, jā′ kwez, zhak
Jarndyce, jarn′ dis
Jassy, yas′ i
Jason, jā′ sȯn
Java, ja′ vȧ
Jeaffreson, jef′ ȧr sȯn
Jean Jaques, zhan zhak′
Jeanne d'Arc, zhan dark′
Jean Paul, zhan pōl′
Jean Valjean, zhan val zhan′
Jehoshafat, je hosh′ ȧ făt
Jekyll, jek′ il
Jemappes, zhȧ map′
Jena, yā′ nȧ
Jephtha, jef′ thȧ
Jeremiah, jer ė mī′ ȧ
Jerome, jė rōm′, jer′ ȯm
Jervaulx, jĕr′ vō
Jervis, jar′ vis, jĕr′ vis
Jervoix, jĕr′ vis
Jessica, jes′ i kȧ
Jesse, jes′ i
Jethro, jeth′ rō, jē′ thrō
Jeune, joon
Jevons, jev′ ȯnz
Jeyes, jāz
Jezreel, jez′ rė ėl
Joachim, jō′ ȧ kim
Job, jōb
Jocasta, jō kăs′ ta
Jocelyn, jos′ lin
Jodhpur, jōd poor′
Johannes, jō hăn′ ēz
Johannesburg, jō hăn′ ės bĕrg
Johnstone, jon′ stȯn, jon′ sȯn
Joinville, join′ vil, zhwăn vēl′
Jolliffe, jol′ if
Josephine, jō′ zė fēn
Josephus, jō sē′ fůs
Joubert (1) [F.], zhoo bâr′
Joubert (2) [Dut.], you′ bėrt
Jouffroy, zhoo frwa′
Joule, joul
Jourdain, zhoor dăn′
Jourdan, zhoor dan′
Jowett, jou′ ėt
Juan Fernandez, joo′ ȧn fėr năn′ dėz
Juarez, ju a′ rėz
Jules, zhul
Juliana, joo li ăn′ ȧ
Julie, joo′ li
Julienne, zhu lyen′
Jungfrau, yung′ frou
Junot, zhu nō′
Jusserand, zhus ran′
Jussieu, zhus u′
Justine, jŭs′ tēn

Kabul, ka′ bul
Kabyle, kȧ bīl′
Kaiser, kī′ zėr
Kalahari, ka la ha′ rē
Kalamazoo, kăl ȧ mȧ zoo′
Kalevala, ka′ lā va la
Kamchatka, kăm chăt′ kȧ
Kanchanjanga, kan chŭn jăng′ gȧ
Kandahar, kăn dȧ har′
Kansas, kăn′ zȧs
Kant, kant, kănt
Karachi, kar a′ chē
Karakoram, ka rȧ kôr′ ȧm
Karlsruhe, karls′ ru e
Karnatic, kar năt′ ik
Kashmir, kăsh mēr′
Kassel, kas′ ėl
Kauffman, Kaufmann, kouf′ man
Kaulbach, koul′ ba*ch*
Kavanagh, kăv′ ȧ nȧ
Kazan, ka zan′
Kearny, kar′ ni
Kearsarge, kēr′ sarj
Keble, kē′ bėl
Kedar, kē′ dȧr
Kedleston, kel′ sȯn, ked′ lės tȯn
Kehama, kė ha′ mȧ
Keig, kēg
Keighley, kēth′ li
Kekewich, kek′ wich
Kenia, kē′ nyȧ
Kennard, kė nard′
Kentucky, ken tŭk′i
Kenya, kēn′ yȧ
Keogh, kē′ ō
Ker, Kerr, kar
Kerguelen, kĕr′ gė len
Kernahan, kĕr′ nȧ hȧn
Keswick, kez′ ik
Keynes, kēnz, kānz
Khartoum, kar toom′
Khayyám, kī yam′
Khiva, kē′ va
Khorassan, kō ra san′
Khrushchev, krus′ chev
Khyber, kī′ bėr
Kiel, kēl
Kiev, kē′ ėf
Kikuyu, kē koo yoo′
Kilauea, kē lou ā′ a
Kilima-Njaro, kil i man ja′ rō
Kilmorey, kil mŭr′ i
Kincairney, kin kâr′ ni
Kincardine, kin kar′ din
Kingscote, kingz′ kůt
Kingussie, king ū′ si
Kinnaird, ki nârd′
Kinnear, ki nēr′
Kinnoul, ki nool′
Kinross, kin ros′
Kinsale, kin sāl′
Kintyre, kin tīr′
Kirghiz, kĕr gēz′
Kirkcaldy, kĕr kaw′ di
Kirkcudbright, kĕr koo′ bri
Kissingen, kis′ ing ėn
Kléber, klā′ bâr
Klopstock, klop ′stok
Knole, nōl
Knollys, Knowles, nōlz
Knyvett, niv′ ėt
Koh-i-noor, kō′ i noor
Königgrätz, kĕr′ nig grats
Königsberg, kĕr′ nigs bĕrg
Kordofan, kôr dō fan′
Korea, kȯ rē′ ȧ
Kosciuszko, kos i ŭs′ kō
Kossuth, kos′ uth, kosh′ ut
Kotzebue, kot′ sė boo
Krakatoa, kra ka tō′ ȧ
Krapotkine, krȧ pot′ kin
Kreisler krī′ zlėr
Kreutzer, kroit′ zėr
Krishna, krish′ nȧ
Kronos, kron′ os
Kronstadt, kron′ shtat
Kubelik, koo′ bė lik
Kublai Khan, koo′ blī kan
Kuch Behar, kuck bā har′
Kumassi, ku măs′ i
Kurd, koord
Kurdistan, koor dis tan′
Kutuzov, koo too′ zof
Kuwait, kū wāt′
Kynaston, kin′ ȧs tȯn
Kyoto, kyō′ tō
Kyrle, kĕrl

Labienus, lā bi ē′ nůs
Lablache, la blash′
Labouchere, lăb oo shâr′
Labrador, lăb′ rȧ dôr
La Bruyère, la bru yâr′
Laccadive, lăk′ ȧ dīv
Lacedæmon, lăs ė dē′ mȯn
Lachesis, lăk′ ė sis
Lachine, la shēn′
Laconia, lȧ kō′ ni ȧ
Ladislaus, lăd′ is laws
Ladoga, la′ dō gȧ
Laertes, lā ĕr′ tēz
La Farge, la farj′, -fazh′
Lafayette, la fā yet′
La Fère, la fâr′

Lafille, la fēl′
La Fontaine, la fo*n* tān′
Lagado, lȧ ga′ dō
Lagos, lā′ gos
La Guaira, la gwīr′ ȧ
La Harpe, la arp′
Lahore, lȧ hôr′
Laing, lāng, lăng
Laïs, lā′ is
L'Allegro, la leg′ rō
Lamarck, la mark′
Lamballe, la*n* bal′
Lamech, lā′ mėk
Lamennais, la mė nā′
Lamia, lā′ mi ȧ
Lange, lang′ ė
Langrishe, lăng′ rish
Languedoc, la*ng* dok′
Lanier, lȧ nēr′
Laocoön, lā ok′ ō ȯn
Laodamia, lā ō dȧ mī′ ȧ
Laodicea, lā ō di sē′ ȧ
Laomedon, lā om′ ė don
Laos, lous; **Laotian,** lou′ shȧn
Lâo-tsze, la′ ot zėr
La Pérouse, la pā rooz′
Lapham, lăp′ ȧm
Lapithæ, lăp′ i thē
Laplace, la plas′
Laputa, lȧ pū′ tȧ
Lara, la′ rȧ
La Rochefoucauld, la rōsh foo kō′
Larpent, lar′ pėnt
Lasalle, La Salle, la sal′
Lascaris, lăs′ kȧ ris
Las Casas, las ka′ sas
Lascelles, lăs′ ėlz
Lassalle, la sal′
Lathom, lā′ thȯm
Latinus, lȧ tī′ nȯs
Latium, lā′ shi ŭm
Latona, lȧ tō′ nȧ
La Tour d'Auvergne, la toor dō vĕrn′
La Trappe, la trap′
Laughlin, laf′ lin
Laughton, law′ tȯn
Laurier, lō ryā′
Lausanne, lō zan′
Lauterbrunnen, lou tėr brun′ ėn
Lavalette, la va let′
La Vallière, la va lyâr′
Lavater, lȧ va′ tėr, la va târ′
Laveleye, lav lā′
Lavengro, lăv′ ėn grō
Lavery, lăv′ ėr i
Lavoisier, la vwa zyā′
Layamon, lā′ ȧ mȯn
Layard, lā′ ȧrd, lârd
Lea, lē
Leamington, lem′ ing tȯn
Leander, lē ăn′ dėr
Leatham, lē′ thȧm
Leathes, lē′ thėz, lēths
Lebanon, leb′ ȧ nȯn
Leboeuf, lė buf′
Lebrun, lė bru*n*
Lechmere, lēch′ mēr
Lecouvreur, lė ku vrĕr′
Leda, lē′ da
Lefebvre, lė fevr′
Lefevre, lė fē′ vėr
Legard, lej′ ȧrd
Legendre, lė zha*n*dr′
Legh, lē
Lehigh, lē′ hī
Lehmann, lā′ mȧn
Leibnitz, līp′ nits
Leicester, les′ tėr
Leigh, lē, lī
Leighton, lā′ tȯn
Leila, lē′ lȧ
Leinster, len′ stėr
Leipzig, līp′ sik
Leishman, lēsh′ mȧn
Leith, lēth
Leitrim, lē′ trim
Leland, lē′ lȧnd
Lely, lē′ li
Leman, lē′ mȧn
Le Mans, lė ma*n*′
Lemaistre, Lemaître, lė mātr′
Lemesurier, lė mezh′ ŭr ėr
Le Moine, le moin′
Lemoine, Le Moyne, lė mwan′
Lemprière, lem prēr′
Lemuel, lem′ ū ėl
Lenclos, la*n* klō′
Lenin, len′ in
Leningrad, len′ in grăd′
Lennox, len′ ȯks
Le Nôtre, lė nōtr′
Leominster (1), lem′ stėr; (2) [*Am.*], lem′ in stėr
Leonard, len′ ȧrd
Leonardo, lā ō nar′ dō
Leoncavallo, lā on ka val′ ō
Leonidas, lė on′ i dăs
Leonora, lē ō nôr′ ȧ
Leopardi, lā ō par′ dē
Leopold, lē′ ȯ pōld
Lepanto, le pan′ tō
Le Patourel, lė păt′ ū rel
Le Poer, lė pôr′
Le Queux, lė kū′
Lermontov, ler mon tof′
Leroy-Beaulieu, lė rwa′ bō lyĕr′
Lerwick, lĕr′ wik
Le Sage, lė sazh′
Lesbia, lez′ bi ȧ
Lespinasse, lā pē nas′
Lesseps, lė seps′
L'Estrange, lė strānj′
Leszczynski, lesh oon′ ski
Lethe, lē′ thi
Letitia, lė tish′ ȧ
Leuk, loik
Leuthen, loi′ tėn
Levant, lė vănt′
Leven, lē′ vėn
Leveson, loo′ sȯn
Levey, Levy, lē′ vi, lev′ i
Leviticus, lev it′ i kȯs
Lewes, loo′ iz
Lewis, loo′ is
Ley, lē
Leyden, lī′ dėn
Leys, lēz
Lhasa, lă′ sa
Libanus, lib′ ȧ nȯs
Libya, lib′ i ȧ
Lichtenstein, li*ch*′ ten stīn
Licinus, lis′ i nȯs
Lie, lē
Liebig, lē big
Liège, li āzh′
Ligny, lē′ nyi
Ligonier, lig ȯ nēr′
Li Hung-Chang, lē hung′ chang
Lilith, lil′ ith
Lille, ēl
Lillibulero, lil i bu lēr′ ō
Lima, lē′ mȧ
Lincoln, ling′ kȯn
Lingen, ling′ ėn
Linlithgow, lin lith′ gō
Lipari, lip′ ȧ ri
Lisbon, liz′ bȯn
Liskeard, lis kard′
Lisle, lēl, lil
Lismahago, lis ma hā′ gō
Lismore, liz môr′
Listowell, lis′ tōl
Liszt, list
Lithuania, lith ū ā′ ni ȧ
Littré, lē trā′
Livingstone, liv′ ing stȯn
Llanberis, hlăn ber′ is
Llandilo, hlăn dī′ lō
Llandudno, hlăn did′ nō
Llanelly, hlăn eth′ li
Llangollen, hlăn goth′ lėn
Llewelyn, hloo el′ in
Lloyd, loid
Lochaber, lo*ch* a′ bėr
Lochiel, lo*ch* ēl′
Lochinvar, lo*ch* in var′
Locrine, lȯ krīn′
Lodi, lō′ dē
Lodore, lō dôr′
Lodovico, lō dō vē′ kō
Loeb, lōb
Logue, lōg
Lohengrin, lō′ ėn grin
Loire, lwar
Loki, lō′ ki
Lombardy, lom′-, lŭm′ bȧr di
Lombroso, lom brō′ zō
Longinus, lon jī′ nȯs
Longobardi, long gō bar′ dī
Longwy, lo*n* vē′
Loochoo, loo choo′
Lope, lō′ pā
Lopez, lō′ pez
Lorelei, lōr′ ė lī
L'Orient, lō rē a*n*′
Lorraine, lȯ rān′
Los Angeles, los ăn′ je lėz, los ăng′ ge lēz
Lothario, lȯ thâr′ i ō
Lothrop, lō′ thrŭp
Loti, lȯ tē′
Lotophagi, lȯ tof′ ȧ jī
Lough, lŭf
Louis, loo′ i, -is
Louisa, loo ē′ zȧ
Louisburg, loo′ is bĕrg
Louisiana, loo ē zi ăn′ ȧ
Louis Philippe, loo ē′ fe lēp′
Louis Quatorze, loo ē′ kȧ tôrz′
Louisville, loo′ i vil
Lourdes, loord
Louvain, lu vă*n*′
Louvois, lu vwa′
Louvre, loovr
Lovat, lŭv′ ȧt
Lowe, lō
Lowell, lō′ ėl
Lowestoft, lō′ stoft, lō′ stof
Loyola, loi ō′ lȧ
Lübeck, lu′ bek
Lucania, lū kā′ ni ȧ
Lucerne, loo sĕrn′
Lucia, lū′ shi ȧ
Lucille, loo sēl′
Lucknow, lŭk′ nou
Lucrece, lū krēs′
Lucretia, lū krē′ shi ȧ
Lucullus, lū kŭl′ ȯs
Ludwig, lut′ vigh
Lugano, loo ga′ nō
Lugard, lu gard′
Luigi, loo ē′ jē
Luini, loo ē′ nē
Luke, look
Lunéville, loo nā vēl′
Lupercal, lū′ pėr kăl
Lupercus, lū pĕr′ kȯs
Lusiad, lū′ si ȧd
Lusitania, loo si tā′ ni ȧ
Lutyens, lŭt′ chėnz
Lutetia, lū tē′ shi ȧ
Luther, loo′ thėr
Lutwyche, lŭt′ wich
Lutzen, lut′ sėn
Luxemburg, lŭk′ sėm bĕrg
Luxor, lŭk′ sȯr
Luynes, lu ēn′
Lwov, lvoof
Lycæus, lī sē′ ȯs
Lycaon, lī kā ȯn
Lycidas, lis′ i dăs
Lycomedes, lik ȯ mē′ dēz
Lycurgus, lī kĕr′ gȯs

Lydgate, lid′ gāt
Lyly, lil′ i
Lympne, lim
Lynedoch, lin′ do*ch*
Lyons, lī′ ȯnz
Lys, lēs
Lysaght, lī′ sat
Lysander, lī săn′ dėr
Lysias, lis′ i ȧs
Lysimachus, lī sim′ ȧ ku̇s
Lysippus, lī sip′ u̇s
Lysons, lī′ sȯnz
Lyttelton, lit′ ėl tȯn
Lyveden, liv′ dėn

Maartens, mar′ tėnz
Maas, mas
Mably, ma blē′
Macalister, mȧ kăl′ is tėr
Macao, mȧ ka′ ō
Macara, mȧ ka′ rȧ
Macbeth, măk beth′
Maccabæus, măk ȧ bē′ u̇s
Maccabees, măk′ ȧ bēz
McCorquodale, mȧ kôr′ kȯ dāl
M'Crea, mȧ krā′
Maccullagh, mȧ kŭl′ ȧ
M'Culloch, mȧ kŭl′ o*ch*
Macdona, măc dŭn′ ȧ
McEachran, M'Eachern, mȧ kek′ ru̇n
M'Evoy, măk′ ė voi
M'Gee, mȧ gē′
MacGillivray, mȧ gil′ i vrā
M'Gillycuddy, ma gil′ i kŭd i mag′ li kŭd′ i
Machaon, mȧ kā′ ȯn
Machell, mā′ chėl
Machiavelli, ma kē a vel′ i
Machpela, măk pē′ lȧ
M'Ilwraith, măk il rāth′
MacIvor, mȧ kī′ vȯr
Mackarness, măk′ ȧ nės
Mackay, mȧ kī′, măk′ i
Mackaye, mȧ kī′
Mackie, măk′ i
Mackinac, măk′ i nō
Maclachlan, mȧ klaw*ch*′ lȧn
Maclagan, mȧ klăg′ ȧn
Maclaren, mȧ klăr′ ėn
Maclean, mȧ klān′
Maclear, mȧ klēr′
Macleay, mȧ klā′
Macleod, McLeod, mȧ kloud′
Macmahon, măk man′
Macnamara, măk nȧ ma′ rȧ
McNaught, mȧk nawt′
McNeill, măk nēl′
Macquoid, mȧ koid′
Macready, mȧ krē′ di
Macrorie, mȧ krōr′ i
Madan, măd′ ȧn
Madeira, mȧ dēr′ ȧ
Madeleine, mad lā*n*′
Madras, mȧ dras′
Madrid, mȧ drid′
Mæcenas, mē sē′ năs
Maeterlinck, mā′ tėr link
Mafeking, măf′e king
Maffei, ma fā′ ē
Magdala (1), măg′ dȧ lȧ; (2) [Abyssinia], măg da′ lȧ
Magdalen [Oxf.], **Magdalene** [Camb.], mawd′ lin
Magellan, mȧ jel′ ȧn
Maggiore, ma jôr′ ā
Maginn, mȧ gin′
Magliabecchi, ma lya bek′ ē
Magnac, măn′ yăk
Magrath, mȧ gra′
Maguire, mȧ gwīr′
Mahabharata, ma ha ba′ rȧ tȧ
Mahan, man, mȧ han′
Mahmoud, ma mood′
Mahon, mȧ hoon′
Mahony, ma′ ni
Mahratta, mȧ răt′ ȧ
Maimonides, mī mon′ i dēz
Maintenon, mă*n* tė no*n*′
Maintz, mīnts
Mainwaring, măn′ ėr ing
Majendie, măj′ ėn di
Malabar, măl′ ȧ bar
Malacca, mȧ lăk′ ȧ
Malachi, măl′ ȧ kī
Malaga, măl′ ȧ gȧ
Malakoff, măl′ ȧ kof
Malaprop, măl′ ȧ prop
Malcolm, măl′ kȯm
Maldive, măl′ dīv
Malesherbes, mal zĕrb′
Malet, măl′ ėt
Malibran, măl′ i brăn
Malines, mȧ lēn′
Mall, mawl, măl
Malmaison, mal mā zo*n*′
Malmesbury, mamz′ bu̇ ri
Malory, măl′ ôr i
Malplaquet, mal pla kā′
Malvern, mawl′ vėrn
Malvolio, măl vō′ li ō
Mambrino, măm brē′ nō
Mamre, măm′ rē
Manassas, mȧ năs′ ȧs
Manasseh, mȧ năs′ ė
Manchu, măn choo′
Manchuria, măn choor′ i ȧ
Mandalay, măn′ dȧ lā
Mandeville, măn′ dė vil
Manetho, măn′ ė thō
Manhattan, măn hăt′ ȧn
Manitoba, măn i tō′ bȧ
Manitou, măn′ i tu
Mannlicher, man′ li *ch*ėr
Manon Lescaut, ma no*n*′ les kō
Manora, mȧ nôr′ ȧ
Mansergh, măn′ zėr
Manteuffel, man′ toi fėl
Manwaring, măn′ ė ring
Maracaibo, ma ra kī′ bō
Marah, ma′ rȧ
Marat, ma ra′
Marazion, măr ȧ zī′ ȯn
Marcke, mar′ kė
Marconi, mar kō′ nē
Mardi Gras, mar′ dē gra
Marengo, mȧ reng′ gō
Mareotis, măr ė ō′ tis
Margaux, mar gō′
Margherita, mar gȧ rē′ ta
Margot, mar′ gō
Marian, mâr′ i ȧn
Maria Theresa, ma rī′ ȧ tė rē′ sȧ
Marie, ma′ rē
Marie Antoinette, ma rē a*n* twa net′
Marie Thérèse, ma rē tā rāz′
Marino, ma rē′ nō
Marion, măr′ i ȯn
Marischall, mar′ shȧl
Maritana, mȧ ri ta′ nȧ
Marius, mâr′ i u̇s
Marjoribanks, marsh′ bănks
Marlborough, mawl′ bȯ ro, (London street), marl′ bru̇
Marmora, mar′ mȯ rȧ
Marquesas, mar kā′ sas
Marseilles, mar sālz′
Mars-la-Tour, mars la toor
Marsyas, mar′ si ăs
Martineau, mar′ tin ō
Martini-Henry, mar tē′ nē hen′ ri
Martinique, mar ti nēk′
Marylebone, măr′ i bu̇n
Masaccio, ma za′ chō
Masai, mă′ sī
Masaniello, ma za nyel′ ō
Mascagni, mas ka′ nyē
Masefield, māz′ fēld
Masham (1) [name], măsh′ ȧm; (2) [place in Yorks], măs′ ȧm
Massachusetts, măs a choo′ sėts
Masséna, ma sā na′
Matabele, măt ȧ bē′ lē
Matapan, ma ta pan′
Mather, mă*th*′ ėr
Mathers, mă*th*′ ėrz
Matheson, măth′ ė sȯn
Mathilde, ma tēld′
Matilda, mȧ til′ dȧ
Matsys, mat sīs′
Matthias, mȧ thī′ ȧs
Maturin, măt′ ū rin
Maugham, mawm
Maunsell, măn′ sėl
Maupassant, mō pa sa*n*′
Maupertuis, mō pėr twē′
Mauprat, mō pra′
Mauretania, maw rė tā′ ni ȧ
Maurice, mor′ is, mȯ rēs′
Mauritius, maw rish′ u̇s
Mausolus, maw sō′ lu̇s
Maya, ma′ ya
Mayence, ma ya*n*s′
Mayer, mī′ ėr
Mayo, mā′ ō
Mazarin, măz′ ȧ rēn
Mazzini, mat sē′ nē
Meagher, ma′ ėr
Meath, mēth
Meaux, mō
Mechlin, mek′ lin
Mecklenburg, mek′ len bĕrg
Medea, mė dē′ ȧ
Medici, med′ i chē
Médicis, mā dē sēs′
Medina, me dē′ na
Medineh, mā dē′ na
Medusa, mė dū′ sȧ
Meerut, mēr′ ut
Mehemet, me′ hė mėt
Meighen, mē′ en
Meiklejohn, mikl′ jon
Meiringen, mīr′ ing ėn
Meissonier, mā sō nyā′
Melanchthon, mė lăngk′ thȯn
Melanesia, mel ȧ nē′ shȧ
Melchizedek, mel kiz′ ė dek
Meleager, mel ė ā′ gėr
Melhuish, mel′ ish
Melita, mel′ i tȧ
Melpomene, mel pom′ e nē
Melusina, mel ū sē′ nȧ
Menai, men′ ī
Mendelssohn, men′ del sōn
Mendès, ma*n* des′
Mendoza, men dō′ zȧ
Menelaus, men ė lā′ u̇s
Menelek, men′ ė lek
Menpes, men′ pės
Mentone, men tō′ ni, men tōn
Menzies, ming′ is
Meols, melz
Meopham, mep′ ȧm
Mercator, mėr kā′ tȯr
Mercutio, mėr kū′ shō
Mérimée, mā rē mā′
Meroe, mer′ ō ē
Merope, mer′ ȯ pē
Mersey, mĕr′ zi
Merthyr Tydfil, mĕr′ thĕr tid′ vil
Mesmer, mes′ mėr
Mesopotamia, mes ȯ pȯ tā′ mi ȧ
Messalina, mes ȧ lē′ nȧ
Messina, mė sē′ nȧ
Metastasio, mā tas taz′ yō
Methuen, meth′ ū ėn
Methuselah, mė thū′ sė lȧ
Metternich, met′ ėr ni*ch*
Meuse, mūz, mĕrz
Meux, mūz
Meyer, mī′ ĕr
Meyerbeer, mī′ ėr bâr

Meynell, men′ ėl
Meyrick, mer′ ik
Miami, mī ăm′ i, mī ăm′ ȧ
Micah, mī′ kȧ
Micawber, mi kaw′ ber
Michelangelo, mī kėl ăn′ jė lō
Michelet, mēsh′ lā
Michelham, mikl′ ȧm
Michie, mik′ i
Michigan, mish′ i gȧn
Mickiewiez, mik yā′ vich
Micronesia, mī krȯ nē′ shȧ
Midas, mī′ dȧs
Mignon, mēn yo*n*′
Miguel, mē gāl′
Milan, mi lăn′
Millais, mi lā′
Millard, mi lard′
Milles, milz
Millet (1), mil′ėt; (2) [F.], mē yā′
Milnes, milnz
Milo (1), mī′ lō; (2) [anc. Melos], mē′ lō
Miltiades, mil tī′ ȧ dēz
Milwaukee, mil waw′ ki
Mincio, mēn′ chō
Minié, mē nyā′, min′ i
Minneapolis, min i ăp′ ō lis
Minos, mī′ nos
Mirabeau, mir′ ȧ bō, mē ra bō
Miraflores, mē ra flō′ rās
Mirandola, mē ran′ dō la
Mirza, mĕr′ zȧ
Misérables, mē zā rabl′
Mississippi, mis i sip′ i
Missolonghi, mis ȯ long′ gē
Missouri, mi soor′ i, -zoor′ i
Mithridates, mith ri dā′ tēz
Mitylene, mit i lē′ ni
Mivart, mī′ vart
Mnemosyne, nē mos′ i nē
Mobile, mō bēl′
Mocha, mō′ kȧ
Modena, mod′ e nȧ
Mohammed, mȯ hăm′ ėd
Mohican, mō′ ik ȧn, mō hē′ kȧn
Mohun, moon
Molière, mo lyâr′
Molino, mo lē′ nō
Molteno, mol tā′ nō
Moltke, molt′ kė
Moluccas, mȯ lŭk′ ȧz
Molyneux, mŭl′ i niks, -nūks, -nū
Mombasa, mom ba′ sa
Momerie, mŭm′ ĕr i
Monaco, mon′ ȧ kō
Monaghan, mon′ ȧ hȧn
Mona Lisa, mō nȧ lē′ zȧ
Monck, mŭnk
Monckton, mŭnk′ tȯn
Moncrieff, mon krēf′
Monier, mō′ ni ėr
Monkhouse, mŭnk′ hous
Monmouth, mŭn′ mu̇th
Monro, Monroe, mŭn rō′
Monson, mŭn′ sȯn
Montague, mon′-, mŭn′ tȧ gū
Montaigne, mon tān′
Montana, mon ta′ nȧ
Mont Blanc, mo*n* bla*n*′
Montcalm, mont kam′
Mont Cenis, mo*n* si nē′
Mont Cervin, mo*n* ser văn′
Monteagle, mŭn tē′ gėl
Monte Cristo, mon′ ti kris′ tō
Montefiore, mon ti fē ōr′ ė
Montenegro, mon tė nē′ grō
Montereau, mo*n* trō′
Monterey, mon te rā′
Montespan, mon tė spăn′
Montesquieu, mon tes kū
Montessori, mon tė sôr′ i
Montevideo, mon tė vid′ ė ō
Montfort, mont′ fȯrt
Montgolfier, mont gol′ fi ėr, mo*n* gōl fyā′
Montgomery, mont-, mŭnt gŭm′ ėr i
Montijo, mon tē′ hō
Montmorency, mŭnt mė ren′ zi, mont mȯ ren′ si
Monpellier, mo*n* pel yā
Monpensier, mo*n* pa*n* syā′
Montreal, mon′ trē awl
Montresor, mon trez′ ȯr
Montrose, mȯn trōz′
Monza, mon′ zȧ
Morant, mȯ rant′
Moray, mŭr′ i
Mordaunt, môr′ du̇nt
Mordecai, môr′ dė kī, môr de kā′ ī
Morea, mȯr ē′ ȧ
Morgante, môr gan′ tā
Morice, mor′ is
Mornay, môr nā′
Morny, mȯr nē′
Morosini, mor ȯ zē′ ni
Morpheus, môr′ fūs
Morrell, mŭr′ ėl
Mosby, moz′ bi
Moscow, mos′ kō
Mosheim, mōs′ hīm
Moule, mōl
Moulton, mōl′ tȯn
Mowbray, mō′ bri
Mozambique, mō zăm bēk′
Mozarab, mō zar′ ȧb
Mozart, mō′ zart
Mozley, mōz′ li
Mudie, mū′ di
Mudki, mood′ kē
Muir, mūr
Mülhausen, mul′ hou zėn
Müller, mul′ ėr, mil′ ėr
Multan, mool tan′
Muncaster, mŭn′ kȧ stėr
Munchausen, mŭn chou′ sėn
Munich, mū′ nik
Munkácsy, mun′ ka chē
Muræna, mū rē′ nȧ
Murat, mu ra′
Murchison, mĕr′ chi sȯn
Murillo, mū ril′ ō
Muscat, mŭs′ kăt
Musset, mus sā′
Mustafa, moos′ ta fa
Mycenae, mī sē′ nē
Mysia, mish′ i ȧ
Mysore, mī sōr′
Mytilene, mit i lē′ nē

Naaman, nā′ ȧ mȧn
Naas, nās
Naesmyth, nā′ smith
Nagasaki, năg ȧ sa′ kē
Nagpur, nag poor′
Nahum, nā′ u̇m
Nairobi, nī rō′ bi
Nana Sahib, na′ nȧ sa′ ib
Nanking, năn king′
Nanon, na no*n*′
Nansen, năn′ sėn
Nantes, nănts
Naomi, nā′ ō-, nā ō′ mī
Naper, năp′ ėr
Naphtali, năf′ tȧ lī
Napier, nā′ pi ėr, nȧ pēr′
Napoli, na′ pō lē
Narcissus, nar sis′ u̇s
Narragansett, năr ȧ găn′ set
Naseby, năz′ bi
Nasmyth, nā′ smith
Nasr-ed-Din, nas ėr ed dēn′
Nassau, năs′ aw
Natal, nȧ tăl′
Nathanael, nȧ thăn′ ȧ ėl
Nathaniel, nȧ thăn′ i ėl
Nauheim, nou′ hīm
Nausicaa, naw sik′ ā ȧ
Navajo, năv′ ȧ hō
Navarino, năv ȧ rē′ nō
Navarre, na var′
Neanderthal, nā an′ dėr tal
Neapolis, nē ăp′ ȯ lis
Neave, nēv
Nebuchadnezzar, neb ū kȧd nez′ ȧr
Negroponte, nā grō pon′ ti
Nehemiah, nē hė mī′ ȧ
Neil, Neill, nēl
Neilson, nēl′ sȯn
Nemesis, nem′ i sis
Nepal, nė pawl′
Nepean, nė pēn′
Nepos, nē′ pos
Nereides, nė rē′ i dēz
Nereus, nēr′ us, -ūs
Neri, nâr′ ē
Nerissa, nė ris′ ȧ
Nesselrode, nes′ ėl rō dė
Neuchâtel, nĕr sha tel′
Neufchâtel, nĕr sha tel′
Neuilly, nu yē′
Neumann, noi′ măn
Neumark, noi mark
Nevada, nė va′ dȧ
Newburgh, nū′ bu̇r u̇
Newfoundland, nū fu̇nd lănd′
Newnes, nūnz
New Orleans, nū ôr′ lė ȧnz
Newquay, nū′ ki
Ney, nā
Niagara, nī ăg′ ȧ rȧ
Nibelung, nē′ bė lung
Nicæa, nī sē′ ȧ
Nicaragua, nik ȧ ra′ gwa
Nice, nēs
Nicolette, nē kō let′
Nicot, nē kō′
Niebuhr, nē′ boor
Niemen, nē′ mėn
Niepce, nē eps′
Nietzsche, nē′ chė
Nigel, nī′ jėl
Niger, nī′ jėr
Nigeria, nī jēr′ i ȧ
Nike, nī′ kē
Nilghiri, nil′ gi ri
Nilsson, nil′ sȯn
Nimegen, nē′ mā gen
Nîmes, nēm
Nineveh nin′ i vi
Niobe, nī′ ȯ bē
Nippon, ni pon′
Nitocris, nī tō′ kris
Niven, niv′ ėn
Nizam, nē zam′
Nizhni-Novgorod, nēzh′ nē nov gȯ rod′
Noailles, nō ī′ yė
Nobel, nō bel′
Nodier, nō dyā
Nollekens, nol′ ė kėnz
Nordau, nôr′ dou
Norddeutscher, nôr doich′ ėr
Nordenfeldt, nôr′ dėn felt
Nordenskjold, nôr′ den skyōld
Nordica, nôr′ di kȧ
Northanger, nôrth′ ăn jėr
Northcote, nôrth′ kȯt
Norwich, nor′ ich, -ij
Notre-Dame, nōtr dam′
Novalis, nȯ va′ lis
Nyanza, nī ăn′ zȧ
Nyassa, nē ăs′ ȧ

Obadiah, ō bȧ dī′ ȧ
Oban, ō′ bȧn
Ober-Ammergau, ō bėr a′ mėr gou
Oberlin, ō′ bėr lin
Oberon, ō′ bėr ȯn, ob′ ėr ȯn

O'Callaghan, ō kăl' ȧ hăn
Occam, ok' ȧm
Oceanus, ō sē' ȧ nu̇s
Ochterlony, o*ch* tẽr lō' ni
Octavia, ok tā' vi ȧ
Octavianus, ok tā vi ā' nu̇s
Odoacer, ō dō ā' sẽr
Odysseus, ȯ dis' ūs
Odyssey, ŏd' i si
Œcolampadius, ek ȯ lăm pā' di u̇s
Œdipus, ē' di pu̇s, ed' i pu̇s
Œnanthe, ē năn' thē
Œnone, ē nō' nē
Offenbach, of' en ba*ch*
Ogier, ō' ji ẽr
Ogilvy, ō' gėl vi
O'Hagan, ō hā' gȧn
Ohio, ō hī' ō
Ohnet, ō nā'
Oise, waz
Oisin, ŭsh' ēn
Oklahoma, ō klȧ hō' mȧ
Oldys, ōl' dis, ōldz
Olivier, ȯ liv' i ẽr
Ollivier, ō lē vyā'
Olmütz, ol' muts
Olympus, ō lim' pu̇s
Omagh, ō ma'
Omaha, ō' mȧ haw, ō' mȧ ha
Omar, ō' mȧr
Omdurman, om door man'
O'Meara, ō mâr' ȧ
O'Morchoe, ō mur' u
Omphale, om' fȧ lē
Onega, ȯ nē' gȧ
Onesimus, ȯ nes' i mu̇s
Onions, ŭn' yu̇nz
Ontario, on târ' i ō
Ophelia, ō fē' li ȧ, -fēl' yȧ
Ophir, ō' fir
Ophiucus, of i ū' ku̇s
Orcagna, ôr ka' nyȧ
Orestes, ȯ res' tēz
Orfeo, ôr fā' ō
Oriana, ôr i ăn' ȧ
Origen, or' i jėn
Orinoco, or i nō' kō
Orion, ȯ rī' ȯn
Orlando, ôr lăn' dō
Orleans, ôr' lė ȧnz
Orlov, ôr lof'
Ormunde, ôr' mȯnd
Ormulum, ôr' mū lu̇m
Orosius, ȯ rō' shi u̇s
Orotava, o rȯ ta' vȧ
Orpheus, ôr' fūs
Orsini, ôr sē' nī
Orvieto, ôr vē ā' tō
Osage, ō' sāj
Osbourne, oz' bu̇rn
O'Shaughnessy, ō shaw' nė si, ō shaw*ch'* nė si
O'Shea, ō shā'
Osiris, ȯ sī' is
Osler, ōs' lẽr
Ossian, osh' ȧn, os' i ȧn
Oswego, os wē' gō
Otago, ō ta' gō
Otranto, (Ital.) ot' rȧn tō; (Eng.) o trăn' tō
Ottawa, ot' ȧ wȧ
Ottilia, ȯ til' i ȧ
Oudenarde, oo dė nar' dė
Oudh, oud
Oudinot, oo dē nō'
Oughtred, ō trėd
Ouida, wē' dȧ
Ouless, oo' lės
Ouse, ooz
Ouseley, ooz' li
Outram, oo' trȧm
Overtoun, ō' vẽr tȯn
Ovid, ov' id
Ozias, ȯ zī' ȧs
Pactolus, păk tō' lu̇s
Paderewski, pa dė rev' ski
Padua, păd' ū ȧ
Pæstum, pes' tu̇m
Paganini, pa ga nē' nē
Paget, păj' it
Pagliacci, pa lya' chē
Pakenham, păk' ėn ȧm
Pakistan, pa ki stan'
Palæmon, pȧ lē' mȯn
Palæologus, păl ė ol' ȯ gu̇s
Palairet, păl' ȧ ret
Palamedes, păl ȧ mē' dēz
Palamon, păl' ȧ mon
Palatinate, pȧ lăt' i nȧt
Palatino, pa la tē' nō
Palermo, pȧ lẽr' mō
Palestrina, pa les trē' nȧ
Palgrave, pawl' grāv
Palinurus, păl i nūr' u̇s
Palissy, pa lē sē'
Pallas, păl' ȧs
Pall Mall, păl măl, pel mel
Palmas, pal' mas
Palmer, pa' mẽr
Palmerston, pa' mẽr stȯn
Palmyra, păl mī' ra
Pamela (1) [Richardson], păm' lȧ; (2) [Sidney], pȧ mē' lȧ
Pamir, pa mēr'
Panama, păn' ȧ ma
Pandora, păn dôr' ȧ
Panhard, pȧ nar'
Panizzi, pȧ nit' si
Panmure, păn mūr'
Panope, păn' ȯ pē
Pantagruel, păn tăg' ru el
Panurge, pȧ nẽrj'
Paolo, pa' ȯ lō
Paphos, pā' fos
Papua, păp' ū ȧ
Paracelsus, păr ȧ sel' su̇s
Paradiso, pa ra dē' sō
Paraguay, păr ȧ gwā', pa ra gwī
Parana, pa ra na'
Paris, păr' is
Parnassus, par năs' us
Parolles, pȧ ro' lez
Parsifal, par' si fal
Parthenope, par then' ȯ pē
Pascal, păs' kȧl
Pasiphae, pȧ sif' ā ē
Pasteur, pas tur'
Paterson, păt' ẽr sȯn
Patiala, put i a' lȧ
Patroclus, pȧ trō klu̇s
Pau, pō
Pauncefote, pawns' fut
Pavia, pa vē a
Pawnee, paw nē'
Paysandu, pī san doo'
Peary, pēr' i
Pease, pēz
Pechell, pē' chėl
Pechili, pā chė lē'
Pedro, pē drō, ped' rō
Peer Gynt, pâr gunt
Pegasus, peg' ȧ su̇s
Pegram, pē' grȧm
Peixoto, pā shō' tu
Peking, pē king'
Pelagius, pė lā' ji u̇s
Pelasgi, pȧ lăs' ji
Pelée, pė lā'
Peleus, pē' lūs
Pelion, pē' li ȯn
Pelissier, pā lē syā'
Pelléas, pel ā as'
Peloponnesus, pel ȯ pȯ nē' su̇s
Pelops, pē' lops
Pembroke, pem' bruk
Penang, pė năng'
Penelope, pė nel' ȯ pē
Penicuik, pen' i kuk
Penmaenmawr, pen man' moor
Pennefather, pen' i fa *th*ẽr
Pennycuick, pen' i kuk
Penobscot, pe nob' skȯt
Penrhyn, pen' rin
Penrith, pen' rith
Pensacola, pen sa kō' lȧ
Pentelicus, pen tel' i ku̇s
Penthesilea, pen thes i lē' ȧ
Pentheus, pen' thūs
Penuel, pė nū' ėl
Pepin, pep' in
Pepys, pēps, pep' is, peps
Perdita, pẽr' di tȧ
Père Goriot, pâr gō ryō'
Pereira, pė rīr' ȧ, -râr' ȧ
Père Lachaise, pâr la shāz'
Perez, pēr' ėz
Pergamos, pẽr' gȧ mos
Pergolese, pâr gō lā' zė
Periander, per i ăn' dẽr
Pericles, per' i klēz
Perier, pâr yā'
Périgord, pār ē gôr'
Pernambuco, per nam boo' kō
Perowne, pė rōn'
Perrault, per ō'
Persephone, pẽr sef' ȯ nē
Persepolis, pẽr sep' ō lis
Perseus, pẽr' sūs
Perthes, pẽr' tes
Peru, pė roo'
Perugia, pe roo' ja
Perugino, pe roo jē' nō
Peschiera, pes kyâr' a
Peshawar, pe sha' wẽr, pė shour'
Peshito, pė shē' tō
Pestalozzi, pes tȧ lot' si
Pesth, pest
Peterhof, pē' tẽr hōf
Pétion, pā tyo*n*'
Peto, pē' tō
Petra, pē' tra
Petrarch, pet' rark
Petre, pē' tẽr
Petrie, pē' tri
Petruchio, pė troo' ki ō
Phædo, fē' dō
Phædra, fē' drȧ
Phædrus, fē' dru̇s
Phaethon, fā' ė thon
Phalaris, făl' ȧ ris
Pharaoh, fâr' ō
Pharos, fâr' os
Pharpar, far' par
Pharsalia, far sā' li ȧ
Phayre, fâr
Phidias, fid' i ăs
Phigalian, fi gā' li ȧn
Philadelphia, fil ȧ del' fi ȧ
Philæ, fī' lē
Philemon, fī lē' mȯn
Philippe, fē lēp'
Philippi, fi lip' ī
Philippine, fil' i pin, -pīn
Philoctetes, fil ok tē' tēz
Philomela, fil' ȯ mē' lȧ
Phineas, fin' ė ăs
Phlegethon, fleg'-, flej' ė thon
Phobos, fō' bos
Phocion, fō' shi ȯn
Phocis, fō' sis
Phœbe, fē' bē
Phorcus, fôr' ku̇s
Phorcys, fôr' sis
Phryne, frī' nē
Piccolomini, pik ō lom' i ni
Pichegru, pēsh' groo
Piedmont, pēd' mont
Pieirian, pī er' i ȧn
Pierides, pī er' i dēz
Pierre, pyâr
Pierrepont, pēr' point
Pietermaritzburg, pē tẽr mâr' its bẽrg
Pigott, pig' ȯt

Pigou, pi goo′
Pilatus, pē la′ tus
Pilpai, pil′ pī
Pinacotheca, pin a kō thē′ kȧ
Pincio, pēn′ chō
Pindarus, pin′ dȧ rus
Pinero, pi nâr′ ō
Pinturicchio, pin too rī′ ki ō
Piombo, pē om′ bō
Piozzi, pē ot′ si
Pipon, pē pong′
Piræus, pī rē′ ůs
Pirie, pir′ i
Pisa, pē′ za
Pisces, pis′ ēz
Pisistratus, pī sis′ trȧ tůs
Pitcairn, pit′ kârn
Pitti, pit′ ē
Pizarro, pi zar′ ō
Plantagenet, plăn tăj′ ė net
Plantin, plan tă*n*′
Plata, pla′ ta
Platæa, plȧ tē′ ȧ
Plautus, plaw′ tůs
Pleiad, plī′ ăd
Pleydell, pled′ ėl
Plinlimmon, plin lim′ ȯn
Pliny, plin′ i
Ploermel, plō ėr mel′
Plombières, plo*n* byâr′
Plon-Plon, plo*n* plo*n*
Plotinus, plō tī′ nůs
Plumptre, plŭmp′ tėr
Plutarch, ploo′ tark
Pocahontas, pō kȧ hon′ tȧs
Pochin, pŭch′ in
Podiebrad, pȯ dyā′ brat
Poe, pō
Poincaré, pwă*n* ka rā′
Poitiers, pwa tyā′
Polaris, pȯ lâr′ is
Pole, pool
Pole Carew, pool kâr′ i
Polignac, pō lē nyak′
Politian, pȯ lish′ i ȧn
Polk, pōk
Pollux, pol′ ůks
Polrava, pol ta′ va
Poltimore, pol′ ti môr
Polwath, pol′ wȯrth
Polycarp, pol′ i karp
Polycletus, pol i klē′ tůs
Polycrates, pȯ lik′ rȧ tēz
Polydora, pol i dôr′ ȧ
Polydorus, pol i dôr′ ůs
Polygnotus, pol ig nō′ tůs
Polyhymnia, pol i him′ ni ȧ
Polynices, pol i nī′ sēz
Polyphemus, pol i fē′ můs
Polyxena, pȯ lik′ sė nȧ
Pomfret, pŭm′ frėt
Pomona, pȯ mō′ nȧ
Pompadour, po*n* pa door′
Pompeia, pom pē′ ȧ
Pompeii, pom pā′ yē, pom pē′ i
Pompeius, pom pē′ yůs
Pondicherry, pon di sher′ i, -cher′ i
Poniatowski, pō nē a tov′ ski
Ponsonby, pŭn′ sȯn bi
Pont-a-Mousson, po*n*t a moo so*n*′
Pontchartrain, po*n* shar tră*n*′
Pontefract, pom′ frėt, pon′ tė frăkt
Ponte Vecchio, pon′ ti vek′ i ō
Pontiac, pon′ ti ăk
Popocatepetl, pō po kăt′ a petl
Poppæa, pȯ pē′ ȧ
Porsenna, pôr′ sė nȧ
Porteus, pôr′ tė ůs
Porthos, pôr tōs′
Portia, pôr′ shi ȧ
Porto Rico, pôr′ tō rē′ kō
Port Said, pôrt sīd
Portumnus, pôr tum′ nůs
Poseidon, pȯ sī′ dȯn
Postlethwaite, posl′ thwāt
Potemkin, pȯ tem′ kin, pot yom′ kin
Potocki, pȯ tots′ ki
Potomac, pȯ tō′ măk
Potosi, pō tō sē′
Poughkeepsie, pō kip′ si
Poulett, paw′ let
Pourtales, poor ta les′
Poussin, poo să*n*′
Powell, pou′ ėl, pō′ ėl
Powerscourt, poorz′ kôrt
Powhatan, pou ȧ tăn′
Powlett, paw′ let
Powys, pō′ is, pou′ is
Pozzuoli, pot swō′ lē
Praed, prād
Præneste, prē nes′ tē
Præterita, prē ter′ i tȧ
Prague, prāg, prag
Praxiteles, prăk sit′ ė lēz
Preble, prebl
Pressensé, pre sa*n* sā′
Pretyman, prit′ i mȧn
Preussen, proi′ sėn
Prevost, pre′ vō
Priam, prī′ ȧm
Prideaux, prid′ ō, prē′ dō
Probyn, prob′ in
Procne, prok′ nē
Procrustes, prȯ krŭs′ tēz
Procyon, prō′ si ȯn
Prometheus, prȯ mē′ thūs
Proserpina, prȯ sĕr′ pi nȧ
Proserpine, pros′ ĕr pīn, -pin
Prospero, pros′ pėr ō
Proteus, prō′ tūs, -tė ůs
Prothero, pro*th*′ ėr ō
Proudhon, pru do*n*′
Proust, proost
Provand, prov′ ȧnd
Provence, prō va*n*s′
Prowse, prouz
Prudhon, pru do*n*′
Prytaneum, prit ȧ nē′ ům
Psyche, sī′ kē
Ptolemais, tol ė mā′ is
Ptolemy, tol′ ė mi
Puccini, poo chē′ nē
Pucelle, pu sel′
Puebla, pwā′ bla
Pueblo, pweb′ lō
Puget, pū′ jėt
Pugh, pū
Pugin, pū′ jin
Pulci, pool′ chē
Puleston, pil′ stȯn
Pullein, pul′ ėn
Pulteney, pōlt′ nė
Punjab, pŭn jab′
Pusey, pū′ zi
Puskin, push′ kin
Puteoli, pū tē′ ȯ li
Puvis de Chavannes, pu vē′ dė sha van′
Puy-de-Dome, pwē dė dōm′
Pygmalion, pig mā′ lė on
Pylades, pil′ ȧ dēz
Pyramus, pir′ ȧ můs
Pyrenees, pir′ ė nēz
Pyrrha, pir′ ȧ
Pytchley, pīch′ li
Pythagoras, pī thăg′ ȯ rȧs
Pythias, pith′ i ăs

Quasimodo, kwăs′ i mō′ dō; kwa se′ mō dō
Quatre Bras, katr bra′
Quatrefages, katr fazh′
Quatremere, katr mâr′
Quebec, kwė bek′
Queenstown, kwēnz′ toun, -tȯn
Quesnel, kā nel′
Queux, ku, kĕr
Quiberon, kē bė ro*n*′
Quichua, kēch′ wa
Quiller-Couch, kwil′ ėr kooch
Quinault, kē nō′
Quintilian, kwin til′ i ȧn
Quirinal, kwir′ i nȧl
Quirinus, kwi rī′ nůs
Quito, kē′ tō

Rabelais, ra bė lā′
Rachel (1), rā′ chel; (2) [F.], ra shel′
Racine, ra sēn′
Radetzki, ra det′ ski
Radom, ra′ dōm
Raeburn, rā′ bĕrn
Raffaelle, ra fa ē′ lā
Ragatz, ra′ gats
Ragnarok, rag nȧ rerk′
Ragusa, ragoo′ za
Rainer, rī′ nėr
Rajpootana, raj pu ta′ na
Ralegh, Raleigh, raw′ li, ra′ li
Ralph, rāf, raf, rălf
Ramayana, ra ma′ yȧ nȧ
Rambouillet, ra*n* boo yā′
Ramée, ra mā′
Rameses, răm′ ė sēz
Ramillies, răm′ i lēz
Ranelagh, răn′ e lȧ
Ranfurly, răn′ fůr li
Rangoon, răng goon′
Ranjitsinhji, răn jėt sin′ jė
Ranke, rang′ kē
Raoul, ra ul′, roul
Raphael, răf′ ā ėl
Rapidan, răp i dăn′
Rappahannock, răp ȧ hăn′ ȯk
Rashleigh, rash′ li
Rasselas, răs′ ė lăs
Rathlin, răth′ lin
Rathmines, răth mīnz′
Rathmore, răth môr′
Rauch, rou*ch*
Raumer, rou′ mėr
Ravaillac, ra va yak′
Rawal Pindi, raw ȧl pin′ dē
Rayleigh, rā′ li
Reading, red′ ing
Reay, rā
Récamier, rā ka myā′
Rechab, rē′ kăb
Reclus, rė klu′
Regillus, rė jil′ ůs
Regnault, rė nyō
Regnier, rā nyā′
Regulus, reg′ ū lůs
Rehan, rē′ hȧn
Rehoboth, re hō′ both
Reichstadt, rī*ch*′ shtat
Reims, rēmz
Reith, rēth
Réjane, rā zhan′
Religio Medici, rė lij′ i ō med′ i sī
Rembrandt, rem′ brȧnt
Rémusat, rā mu za′
Rénan, rė na*n*′
Renaud, Renault, rė nō
Rensselaer, ren′ sė lėr
Renwick, ren′ ik
Repplier, rep′ lēr
Reszke, resh′ kė
Retz, rets
Reuchlin, roi*ch*′ lin
Réunion, rā oo nē o*n*′
Reuss, rois
Reuter, roi′ tėr
Reykjavik, rā′ kyȧ vēk
Rhadamanthus, răd ȧ măn′ thůs
Rheims [REIMS]
Rheingold, rīn′ gōlt
Rhodes, rōdz
Rhodesia, rȯ dē′ zyȧ, -syȧ

Rhys, rēs
Riach, rē′ a*ch*
Rialto, ri ăl′ tō, rē al′ tō
Ribera, rē bâr′ a
Ricardo, ri kar′ dō
Ricci, rē′ chē
Riccio, rē′ chō
Richelieu, rēsh′ ė lū
Richter, ri*ch*′ tėr
Riddell, rid′ ėl
Rienzi, rē en′ zē
Rievaulx, riv′ ėrz
Riga, rī′ gȧ
Rigi, rē′ gē
Rigoletto, ri gō let′ ō
Riis, rēs
Rijks, rīks
Rio de Janeiro, rē′ ō dā zha nâr′ ō
Rio Grande, rē′ ȯ gran′ dā
Riordan, rēr′ dȧn
Ripon, rip′ ȯn
Ristori, rēs tôr′ ē
Rivarol, rē va rōl′
Riviera, riv i âr′ ȧ
Rivoli, rē′ vō lē
Rizzio, rit′ sē ō
Roanoke, rō′ ȧ nōk
Robartes, rȯ barts′
Robbia, rob′ ē a
Robeson, rōb′ sȯn
Robespierre, rō′ bės pēr
Rocamadour, rō ka ma door′
Rochambeau, rō sha*n* bō
Rochdale, roch′ dāl
Roche, rōch
Rochefort, rōsh fôr′
Rochelle, rō shel′
Rockefeller, rok′ ė fel ėr
Rockingham, rok′ ing ȧm
Roderigo, rod er ē′ gō
Rodin, rō dă*n*′
Rodolphus, rȯ dol′ fȯs
Rodriguez, rȯ drē′ gās
Roget, rō zhā′
Rohan, rō a*n*′
Rohilkhand, rō hil kŭnd′
Roland, rō′ lȧnd
Rolleston, rōl′ stȯn
Romanes, rō ma′ nes
Romanov, rō′ ma nof
Romford, rŭm′ fȯrd
Romilly, rom′ li, -i li
Romney, rŭm′ ni
Romola, rom′ ȯ lȧ
Romsdal, rōms dal′
Romsey, rŭm′ zi
Romulus, rom′ ū lȯs
Ronaldshay, ron′ ȧld shā
Roncesvalles, ron se văl′ es
Ronsard, ro*n* sar′
Röntgen, runt′ gėn
Roon, rōn
Roosevelt, rō′ zė velt, rōz′ velt
Rosa, rō′ zȧ
Rosalind, roz′ ȧ lind
Rosaline, roz′ ȧ lin, -līn
Rosamund, roz′ ȧ mȯnd
Roscius, rosh′ i ȯs
Roscommon, ros kom′ ȯn
Rosetta, rȯ zet′ ȧ
Rosinante, roz i năn′ ti
Rosny, rō nē′
Rossbach, rōs′ ba*ch*
Rossetti, rȯ set′ i
Rossini, rȯ sē′ nē
Rostopchin, ros top chēn′
Rosyth, ro sīth′
Rotherhithe, ro*th*′ ėr hīth, *red′ rif
Rothes, roth′ ėz
Rothesay, roth′ sā
Rothschild, roths′ chīld
Rothwell, roth′ wėl
Rotorua, rō tor oo′ ȧ
Roubiliac, roo bē yak′
Rouen, roo a*n*
Rouget de l'Isle, roo zhā′ de lēl
Roulers, roo lā
Rouse, roos
Rousseau, roo sō′
Roussillon, roo sē yo*n*′
Routh, routh
Roux, roo
Rowan, rō′ ȧn
Rowena, rō ē′ nȧ
Rowland, rō′ lȧnd
Rowley, rou′ li
Rowton, rō′ tȯn
Roxana, rok săn′ ȧ, -sa′ nȧ
Roxburgh, roks′ bȯ rȯ, -bȯrg
Rubaiyat, roo bī yat′
Rubinstein, roo′ bin stīn
Rucellai, roo chel′ ī
Rucker, rŭk′ ėr
Rückert, ruk′ ėrt
Rudolph, roo′ dȯlf
Ruislip, rī′ zlip
Rustam, rŭs′ tȧm
Rustchuk, rust chook′
Ruthven, riv′ ėn, ruth′ ven
Ruwenzori, roo wen zôr′ ē
Ruy Blas, roo′ ē blas
Ruy Lopes, roo′ ē lō′ pėz
Ruysdael, rois′ dal
Ruyter, roi′-, rī′ tėr
Rynd, rind
Ryswick, riz′ wik

Saarbrück, zar′ bruk
Saavedra, sa ȧ vā′ dra
Sabrina, sȧ brī′ nȧ
Sacharissa, săk ȧ ris′ ȧ
Sacheverell, sȧ shev′ ėr el
Sachs, saks
Sadi, sa dē′
Sadowa, sa′ dō va
Sagittarius, săj i târ′ i ȯs
Saguenay, săg ė nā′
Sahara, sȧ ha′ rȧ
St. Aubyn, sȧnt ôr′ bin
Sainte-Beuve, sant bėrv′
St. Clair, sin′ klâr
Saint-Cyr, să*n* sēr′
Saint-Evremond, să*n* tāvr mo*n*′
Saint-Gaudens, sȧnt gaw dėnz
Saint-Germain, să*n* zher mă*n*′
Saint Gothard, sȧnt goth′ ȧrd
Saint Helena, (island) sānt ėl ē′ nȧ; (saint) sānt hel′ en ȧ
Saint-Hilaire, să*n* tē lâr′
Saintine, să*n* tēn′
St. John (pers. name), sin′ jȯn
Saint-Just, să*n* zhoost′
St. Leger (pers. name), sil′ ėn jėr; (horse-race), sȧnt lej′ ėr
St. Maur, sē′ mȯr, sȧnt mawr′
St. Neots, sȧnt nēts
Saint-Pierre, să*n* pyâr′
Saint-Saens, să*n* sa*n*s′
Saint-Simon, sȧnt sī′ mȯn, să*n* sē mo*n*′
Sakhalin, sa *ch*a lyēn′
Sakuntala, sa kun′ tȧ lȧ
Sala, sa′ lȧ
Saladin, săl′ ȧ din
Salamanca, săl ȧ măng′ kȧ
Salamis, săl′ ȧ mis
Salem, sā′ lem
Salisbury, sawlz′ bȯ ri
Salome, sȧ lō′ mē
Salonika, sa lō nē′ kȧ
Salpêtrière, sal pā tryâr
Saltoun, sawl′ tun
Salvator, sal va′ tôr
Salvini, sal vē′ nē
Salzburg, salts′ bėrg
Salzkammergut, salts ka′ mėr gut
Samarkand, săm ar kănd′
Samoa, sȧ mō′ ȧ
Samos, sā′ mos
Samothrace, săm′ ȯ thrās
Sanballat, săn băl′ ȧt
Sancho, săng′ kō, săn′ chō
Sandes, Sandys, săndz
San Juan, san hwan′
Sannazaro, san nad za′ rō
Sanquhar, săng′ kȧr
San Remo, san rā′ mō
San Salvador, san sal va dôr′
Sans Gêne, sa*n* zhān′
Sansovino, san sō vē′ nō
Sans Souci, sa*n* soo sē′
Santa Croce, san′ ta krō′ chā
Santa Cruz, săn′ tȧ krooz
Santa Fé, săn′ tȧ fā
Santiago, san tē a′ gō
Saône, sōn
Sappho, săf′ ō
Saratoga, sȧ ră tō′ gȧ
Sarawak, sȧ ra′ wăk
Sarcey, sar sē′
Sardanapalus, sar dȧ nȧ pā′ lȯs
Sardou, sar doo′
Sargasso, sar găs′ ō
Sarmatia, sar mā′ shi ȧ
Sarpedon, sar pē′ dȯn
Sartoris, Sartorius, sar tôr′ is
Saskatchewan, săs kăch′ ė won
Sauchiehall, so*ch*′ i hawl
Saudi Arabia, sou′ di ȧ rā′ bi ȧ
Sault Sainte Marie, soo sānt mȧr ē′
Saumarez, Sausmarez, sō′ mȧ rėz
Saussure, sō soor′
Savary, sa va rē′
Savonarola, săv ȯ nȧ rō′ lȧ
Savoy, sȧ voi′
Scævola, sēv′ ȯ lȧ
Scafell, skaw′ fėl
Scaliger, skăl′ i jėr
Scamander, skȧ măn′ dėr
Scarborough, skar′ brȯ
Scarron, ska ro*n*′
Schaffhausen, shaf hou′ zėn
Scheherazade, shė hā rȧ za′ dė
Scheidegg, shī′ deg
Scheldt, skelt
Schelling, shel′ ing
Schenectady, skė nek′ tȧ di
Scheveningen, skā′ vėn ing ėn
Schiedamm, skē dam′
Schiehallion, shē hăl′ i ȯn
Schiller, shil′ ėr
Schlegel, shlā′ gėl
Schleiermacher, shlī′ ėr ma *ch*ėr
Schlemihl, shlem′ il
Schleswig-Holstein, shlez′ wig hōl′ stīn
Schmidt, shmit
Schoeffer, shėr′ fėr
Schofield, skō′ fēld
Schomburgk, shom′ bȯrk
Schonbrunn, shon′ brun
Schopenhauer, shō′ pėn hou ėr
Schreiner, shrī′ nėr
Schubert, shoo′ bėrt
Schumann, shoo′ man
Schuyler, skī′ lėr
Schuytkill, skoot′ kil
Schweinfurth, shvīn′ furt
Schwyz, shvits, shvēts
Scilly, sil′ i
Scio, sī′ ō
Scipio, sip′ i ō
Sclater, slā′ tėr
Scone, skoon, skōn
Scriabin, skrē′ ȧ bin
Scribe [Fr. dramatist], skrēb
Scrymgeour, skrim′ jėr
Scudéri, skoo dā rē′
Scutari, skoo′ tȧ rē
Scylla, sil′ ȧ

n: cabosho*n*. ng: si*ng*. sh: *sh*awl. zh: mea*s*ure. th: *th*in. *th*: brea*th*e. *See page* xi.

Sean, shawn
Searle, sĕrl
Seattle, sė ătl′
Sebastopol, sė băs′ tȯ pol
Secunderabad, se kŭn dėr ȧ bad′
Sedan, sė dăn′
Segur, sā goor′
Seignobos, sen yō bō′
Seine, sān
Sejanus, sė jā′ nu̇s
Seleucus, sė lū′ ku̇s
Selim, sē′ lim
Seljuk, sel′ jook
Selous, sė loo′
Semele, sem′ ė lē
Seminole, sem′ i nōl
Semiramis, sė mir′ ȧ mis
Sempach, zem′ pa*ch*
Semphill, sem′ pil
Senancour, sā na*n* koor′
Seneca, sen′ ė kȧ
Senegal, sen ė gawl′
Sennacherib, se năk′ ėr ib
Seoul, sā ool′
Serapis, se rā′ pis
Sergeant, Serjeant, sar′ jėnt
Sesostris, se sos′ tris
Setebos, set′ e bos
Seton, Setoun, sē′ tȯn
Severus, sė vēr′ u̇s
Sévigné, sā vēn yā′
Seville, sev′ il, sė vēl′
Sèvres, sāvr
Seward, sū′ ȧrd
Sewell, sū′ ėl
Seychelles, sā shel′
Seymour, sē′ môr
Seyton, sē′ tȯn
Sforza, sfôrt′ sȧ
Sganarelle, zga na rel′
Shairp, sharp
Shanghai, shăng hī′
Shearman, shĕr′ mȧn
Shechem, shē′ kėm
Sheila, shē′ lȧ
Shenandoah, shen ȧn dō′ ȧ
Sheraton, sher′ ȧ tȯn
Sherbourne, shĕr′ bu̇rn
Shikarpur, shik ȧr poor′
Shiloh, shī′ lō
Shinar, shī′ nar
Shostakovich, shos tȧ kō′ vich
Shrewsbury, shrōz′ bėr i
Siam, sī ăm′
Sichæus, si kē′ u̇s
Sichem, sī′ kėm
Sicily, sis′ e li
Sicyon, sish-, sis′ i on
Siddhartha, si dar′ tȧ
Sidebotham, sīd′ bot ȯm
Siegfried, sēg′ frēd
Sienkiewicz, shen kyā′ vich
Sierra Leone, si er′ ȧ lē ō′ nē
Sierra Nevada, si er′ ȧ nė va′ dȧ
Sieyès, syā yes′
Sigismonda, sij is mon′ dȧ
Sigourney, sig′ u̇r ni
Sigurd, sē′ gu̇rd
Sikh, sek
Silenus, sī lē′ nu̇s
Silesia, sī lē′ shi ȧ
Siloam, sī lō′ ȧm
Siluri, sī lūr′ ī
Silvanus, sil vā′ nu̇s
Silvester, sil ves′ tėr
Simois, sim′ ȯ is
Simplon, sim′ plon, săn plon′
Sinai, sī′ nī, -nȧ ī
Singapore, sing gȧ pôr′
Sinope, sī nō′ pē
Sioux, soo
Sirius, sir′ i u̇s
Sisera, sis′ ĕr ȧ
Sismondi, sis mon′ di
Sistine, sis′ tēn, -tin
Sisyphus, sis i fu̇s
Siva, sē′ vȧ
Skager-Rack, skăg′ ėr răk
Skiddaw, skid′ aw
Skrine, skrēn
Slidell, sli del′
Sligo, slī′ gō
Slough, slou
Sluis, slois
Smethwick, smeth′ ik
Smolensk, smō lensk′
Smyth, smī*th*, smith
Sobieski, sō byes′ ki
Socinus, sȯ sī′ nu̇s
Socrates, sok′ rȧ tēz
Sofia, sō fē′ yȧ
Soissons, swa so*n*′
Solander, sol′ ȧn dėr
Solent, sō′ lėnt
Solferino, sol fė rē′ nō
Solon, sō′ lon
Somalia, sō ma′ li ȧ
Somers, su̇m′ ėrz
Somerset, sŭm′ ėr set
Somerton, sŭm′ ėr tȯn
Somervell, sŭm′ ėr vel
Sondes, sondz
Sorel, sȯ rel′
Sotheby, sŭ*th*′ ė bi
Soubise, soo bēz′
Soult, soolt
Sousa, soo′ zȧ
Southey, sŭ*th*′ i, sou′ *thi*
Southwark, su*th*′ ȧrk
Souza, soo′ zȧ
Spa, spa, spaw
Speight, spāt
Spinola, spi′ nȯ lȧ
Spinoza, spi nō′ zȧ
Splugen, shploo′ gėn
Spohr, spôr
Spree, sprā
Srinagar, sri nŭg′ ȧr
Staël, sta′ ėl
Stagira, sta jīr′ ȧ
Stalbridge, stawl′ brij
Stamboul, stăm bool′
Stanhope, stăn′ ȯp
Stanislau, sta′ nis lou
Stapley, stăp′ li
Statira, stȧ tīr′ ȧ
Staubbach, stou′ ba*ch*
Steen, stān
Stein, stīn
Stelvio, stel′ vi ō
Stendhal, ston′ dal
Stéphanie, stā fa nē′
Stephano, stef′ ȧ nō
Stephens, stē′ vėnz
Sterope, ster′ ȯ pē
Stettin, stet′ in
Steuben, stū′ ben, shtoi′ ben
Steyne, stīn, stān
Stilicho, stil′ i kō
Stoke Poges, stōk pō′ jės
Stolypin, stȯ lip′ in
Stothard, sto*th*′ ȧrd
Stoughton, stō′ tȯn, stou′ tȯn
Stourton, stĕr′ tȯn
Stowe, stō
Stowell, stō′ ėl
Strachan, (Eng.) strawn; (Sc.) stra*ch*′ ȧn
Strachey, strā′ chi
Stranraer, străn rar′
Strasburg, străs′ bu̇rg
Strathallan, străth ăl′ ȧn
Strathcona, străth kō′ nȧ
Stratheden, străth ē′ dėn
Strathmore, străth môr′
Straton, străt′ ȯn
Strauss, strous
Streatham, stret′ ȧm
Strephon, stref′ ȯn
Stromboli, strom′ bō lē
Strozzi, strot′ si
Stuckley, stūk′ li
Stuttgart, stŭt′ gart
Stuyvesant, sti′ vis ȧnt
Styx, stiks
Suakin, swa′ kēn
Suarez, swa′ rez
Suchet, su shā′
Sudeley, sūd′ li
Sudermann, zoo′ dėr man
Sue, sū
Suetonius, sū ė tō′ ni u̇s
Suevi, swē′ vī
Suez, soo ez′
Sulpicia, su̇l pish′ i ȧ
Sumatra, soo ma′ trȧ
Suppé, zup′ ā
Surat, soo rat′
Susa, soo′ zȧ
Susquehanna, sŭs kwė hăn′ ȧ
Sutro, soo′ trō
Suvarof, su va′ rof
Suwalki, su val′ kē
Suwanee, su wa′ nē, swa nē
Sverdrup, sver′ drup
Swahili, swa hē′ li
Swaziland, swa′ zi lănd
Sweyn, swān
Swiney, swin′ i, swī′ ni
Sybaris, sib′ ȧ ris
Symonds, sim′ ondz
Symons, sim′ ȯnz
Synge, sing
Syracuse, sīr′ ȧ kūs

Tabor, tā′ bȯr
Tacoma, tȧ kō′ mȧ
Taft, taft, tăft
Tagliamento, ta lya men′ tō
Taglioni, tȧ lyō′ nē
Tahiti, ta′ hē tē
Tai-ping, tī ping′
Taj Mahal, tazh ma hal′
Talavera, ta la vâr′ ȧ
Talfourd, tăl′ fȯrd
Taliesin, tăl′ i ā sin
Talleyrand, tăl′ i rănd
Tallien, ta lyă*n*′
Talmage, tăl′ măj
Tamerlane, tăm′ ėr lān
Tammany, tăm′ ȧ ni
Tamora, tăm′ ȯ rȧ
Tampico, tam pē′ kō
Tanagra, tăn′ ȧ grȧ
Tanais, tăn′ ȧ is
Tancred, tăng′ krėd
Tanganyika, tan gan yē′ ka
Tangier, tăn jēr′
Tangye, tăng′ i
Tannhäuser, tan′ hoi zėr
Tantalus, tăn′ tȧ lu̇s
Tara, ta′ rȧ
Taranto, tă′ răn tō
Tarascon, tă′ răs kon
Tarifa, ta rē′ fa
Tarpeia, tar pē′ yȧ
Tartarus, tar′ tȧ ru̇s
Tartuffe, tar tuf′
Tasmania, tăz mā′ ni ȧ
Tauber, tou′ bėr
Taubman, toub′ mȧn
Tauchnitz, tou*ch*′ nits
Tavernier, ta vėr nyā′
Tchad, chad
Tecumseh, tė kŭm′ sē
Teheran, tĕr an′
Tehuantapec, ta wan ta pek′
Teignmouth, tin′ mu̇th
Telamon, tel′ ȧ mȯn
Tel-el-Kébir, tel el kė bēr′
Telemachus, tė lem′ ȧ ku̇s
Télémaque, tā lā mak′
Telugu, tel′ u goo
Temora, tė môr′ ȧ

Tempe, tem′ pē
Tenedos, ten′ ė dos
Tenerife, ten ėr ēf′
Teniers, ten′ yėrz
Tennessee, ten ė sē′
Tenniel, ten′ yėl
Teocali, tē ȯ kăl′ ē
Terence, ter′ ėns
Teresa, tė rē′ zȧ
Tereus, tēr′ ė ůs
Ternina, tėr nē′ nȧ
Terpsichore, tĕrp sik′ ȯ ri
Tertullian, tĕr tŭl′ yȧn
Tesla, tes′ lȧ
Tethys, teth′ is
Tetrazzini, tā trat sē′ nē
Teucer, tū′ sėr
Teufelsdröckh, toi′ fėls dru*ch*
Teuffel, toi′ fėl
Teynham, ten′ ȧm
Thaddæus, thȧ dē′ ůs
Thaddeus, thăd′ ė ůs
Thailand, tī′ land
Thais, thā′ is, [F.] ta ēs′
Thalaba, thăl′ ȧ bȧ
Thalia, thȧ lī′ ȧ
Thame, tām
Thames, temz
Theætetus, thē ē tē′ tůs
Thebes, thēbz
Themis, thē′ mis
Themistocles, thė mis′ tȯ klēz
Theobald, thē′ ȯ bawld, *tib′ ȧld
Theocritus, thė ok′ ri tůs
Theodora, thē ȯ dôr′ ȧ
Theodoric, thė od′ ȯ rik
Theodorus, thē ȯ dôr′ ůs
Theodosius, thē ȯ dō′ shi ůs
Theodotus, thė od′ ȯ tůs
Theophilus, thė of′ i lůs
Theophrastus, thē ȯ frăs′ tůs
Thérèse, tā rāz′
Thermopylæ, thėr mop′ i lē
Theron, thēr′ on
Thersites, thėr sī′ tēz
Theseus, thē′ sūs
Thesiger, thes′ i jėr
Thessalonica, thes ȧ lȯ nī′ kȧ
Thessaly, thes′ ȧ li
Thetis, thē′ tis
Thierry, ti er′ i, tyė rē′
Thiers, tyâr
Thisbe, thiz′ bė
Thom, tom
Thomas, tom′ ȧs
Thompson, tom′ sȯn
Thoreau, thō′ rō, thȯ rō′
Thorold, thŭr′ ȯld
Thorwaldsen, tôr′ vȧl sėn
Thoth, tōt, thoth
Thothmes, tōt′ mēz, thoth′ mēz
Thrasybulus, thrăs i bū′ lůs
Thrasymenes, thrȧ sim′ ė nēz
Thrasymenus, thrăs si mē′ nůs
Thucydides, thū sid′ i dēz
Thuillier, twil′ i ėr
Thule, thū′ lē
Thun, toon
Thuringia, thū rin′ ji ȧ
Thynne, thin
Thyrsis, thēr′ sis
Tiberias, tī bēr′ i ăs
Tiberius, tī bēr′ i ůs
Tibet, ti bet′, tib′ ėt
Tibullus, ti bŭl′ ůs
Tichborne, tich′ bůrn
Ticino, te chē′ nō
Ticonderoga, tī kon dė rō′ gȧ
Tieck, tēk
Tientsin, tē ent sēn′
Tierra del Fuego, tyer′ ȧ del fwā′ gō
Tiflis, tif′ lis
Tighe, tī
Tigranes, tī grā′ nēz
Tilly, til′ i
Timæus, tī mē′ ůs
Timbuktu, tim bŭk′ too
Timoleon, tī mō′ lē ȯn
Timon, tī′ mȯn
Tintagel, tin tăj′ ėl
Tintoretto, tin tȯ ret′ ō
Tippecanoe, tip ė kȧ noo′
Tipperary, tip ė râr′ i
Tippoo, ti poo′
Tiresias, tī rē′ shi ăs
Tischendorf, tish′ ėn dôrf
Tisiphone, tī sif′ ȯ nē
Tissot, tē sō′
Tisza, tē′ sȧ
Titania, tī tān′ i ȧ
Tithonus, ti thō′ nůs
Titian, tish′ ȧn
Titicaca, tit ė ka′ kȧ
Titiens, tēt′ yens
Tityrus, tit′ i růs
Tivoli, tiv′ ȯ li
Tiziano, tēt sya′ nō
Tmolus, mō′ lůs
Tobago, tȯ bā′ gō
Tobias, tō bī′ ȧs
Tobit, tō′ bit
Tobolsk, tō bolsk′
Tocqueville, tok′ vil
Todleben, tōt′ lā ben
Todmorden, tod′ mȯr dėn
Tokay, tō kā′
Tokio, tō′ ki ō
Toledo, tō lē′ dō
Tollemache, tol′ mash
Tolstoy, tol stoi′
Tonbridge, tŭn′ brij
Tonga, tong′ gȧ
Tonking, tong king′
Topeka, tȯ pē′ kȧ
Torino, tō rē′ nō
Torphichen, tôr′ fi kėn
Torquay, tôr kē′
Torquemada, tôr kwe ma′ dȧ
Torres Vedras, tor′ ez ve′ dras
Totila, tot′ i lȧ
Totnes, tot′ nez
Toul, tool
Toulon, too lo*n*′
Toulouse, too looz′
Tours, toor
Toussaint l'Ouverture, too sa*n*′ loo ver tur′
Towcester, tou′ stėr
Townshend, toun′ zend
Toynbee, toin′ bė
Trafalgar, trȧ făl′ gȧr
Trajan, trā′ jȧn
Tralee, trȧ lē′
Transvaal, trănz′ val
Trapani, tra′ pa nē
Traquair, trȧ kwâr′
Trasimenus, trăs i mē′ nůs
Travers, trăv′ ėrz
Traviata, tra vi a′ tȧ
Trebia, trē′ bi ȧ
Trebizond, treb′ i zond
Tredegar, trė dē′ gar
Trefusis, trė fū′ sis
Tregelles, trė gel′ ės
Treloar, trė lôr′
Trethewy, trė thū′ i
Trevelyan, trė vil′-, -vel′ yȧn
Treves, trēvz
Treviso, trā vē′ zō
Trevithick, trev′ i thik
Trevor, trev′ ȯr
Trianon, trē a no*n*′
Tridentine, tri den′ tin
Trier, trēr
Trieste, trē est′
Trincomali, trin kȯ mȧ lē′
Trinidad, trin i dăd′
Tripoli, trip′ ȯ li
Triptolemus, trip tol′ ė můs
Tristan da Cunha, tris′ tăn da kun′ yȧ
Trocadero, trok ȧ dēr′ ō
Trochu, trō shu′
Troilus, trō′ i lůs
Trollope, trol′ ȯp
Trondhjem, tron′ yem
Trophimus, trof′ i můs
Troubetzkoy, troo bet′ skoi
Troubridge, troo′ brij
Trovatore, trō va tôr′ i
Troyon, trwa yo*n*′
Tschaikovsky, chī kof′ skē
Tschudi, choo′ dē
Tübingen, tub′ ing ėn
Tuileries, twē′ lėr iz
Tullibardine, tŭl i bar′ dēn
Tulloch, tŭl′ ȯ*ch*
Tunisia, tū niz′ i ȧ
Turenne, tu ren′
Turgenev, tur gen′ yef
Turgot, toor gō′
Turin, tū rin′
Turkestan, tĕr kė stan′
Tuscarora, tŭs kȧ rôr′ ȧ
Tussaud, tu sō′
Tutankhamen, too tăn ka′ men
Tybalt, tib′ ȧlt
Tycho, tī′ kō
Tydeus, tī dūs, tid′ ė ůs
Tyndale, tin′ dȧl
Tynemouth, tin′ můth
Typhoeus, tī fō′ ūs
Typhon, tī′ fȯn
Tyrconnel, tĕr kon′ ėl
Tyrol, tir′ ȯl
Tyrone, tī rōn′
Tyrrhene, tir′ ēn
Tyrtæus, tĕr tē′ ůs
Tyrwhitt, tir′ it
Tytler, tīt′ lėr

Uffizi, oo fēt′ sē
Uhland, oo′ lant
Uig, oo′ ig
Uist, ū′ ist
Ukraine, ū krān′, ū′ krān, ū′ krīn
Ulfilas, ŭl′ fi lăs
Ulick, ū′ lik
Ulloa, ool yō′ a
Ulrica, ŭl′ ri kȧ
Ulysses, ū lis′ ēz
Umea, ū′ mė ȧ
Undine, ůn dēn′, ŭn′ dēn
Upanishad, oo păn′ i shăd
Upsala, up sa′ la
Ural, ūr′ ȧl
Urania, ū rā′ ni ȧ
Uranus, ūr′ ȧ nůs
Urbino, oor bē′ nō
Uriah, ū rī′ ȧ
Uriel, ūr′ i ėl
Urquhart, ĕr′ kȧrt
Ursula, ĕr sū lȧ
Uruguay, ū′ ru gwā, ū ru gwī
Ushant, ŭsh′ ȧnt
Utah, ū′ taw, ū′ ta
Utopia, ū tō′ pi ȧ
Utrecht, ū′ trekt, u′ tre*ch*t
Uttoxeter, uk′ sė tėr, ŭt ok′ sė tėr
Uzziel, ů zī′ ėl, ŭz′ i ėl

Valais, va lā′
Valdemar, văl′ dė mar
Valdés, val dās′
Valencia, văl en′ sha
Valenciennes, vȧ len si enz, va len syen′
Valentinian, văl ėn tin′ i ȧn
Valkyrie, văl′ kī ri
Valladolid, văl′ ȧ dol′ id
Valletort, văl′ ė tôrt

Vallière, va lyâr′
Vallombrosa, văl ȯm brō′ zȧ
Valmy, val mē′
Valois, val wa′
Valparaiso, văl pȧ rī′ sō, -zō
Vanbrough, văn′ bru̇
Vancouver, văn koo′ vėr
Vandam, văn dăm′
Van Dyck, văn dīk′
Vanhomrigh, vȧ nŭm′ ri
Vanloo, văn loo′
Vannucci, va noo′ chē
Vansittart, văn sit′ ȧrt
Varchi, var′ kē
Varennes, va ren′
Vasa, va′ sȧ
Vashti, văsh′ tī
Vassar, văs′ ȧr
Vathek, văth′ ėk
Vatican, văt′ i kȧn
Vauban, vō ba*n*′
Vaucluse, vō klooz′
Vaud, vō
Vaughan, vawn
Vauvenargues, vōv narg′
Vaux, vō, vōks
Vauxhall, vawks-, voks hawl′
Vavasour, văv′ su̇r
Veccellio, vā chel′ i ō
Vecchio, vek′ i ō
Vega, vē′ gȧ
Veitch, vēch
Velasquez, ve lăs′ kez
Velino, vā lē′ nō
Vendée, va*n* dē′
Vendôme, va*n* dōm′
Venezuela, ven ė zwē′ lȧ
Venice, ven′ is
Venus, vē′ nu̇s
Vera Cruz, vĕr′ ȧ krooz, vâr′ a kroos
Vercelli, ver chel′ ē
Verde, vĕrd
Verdi, vâr′ dē
Vereeniging, fer ā′ ni ging
Vergennes, vĕr zhen′
Vergniaud, vĕr nyō′
Vermont, vėr mont′
Verne, varn
Vernet, vĕr nā′
Veronese, vâr ō nā′ sā
Veronica, vė ron′ i kȧ, ver ō nī′ kȧ
Verrocchio, vā rok′ ē ō
Versailles, vėr sālz′, vâr sī′ yė
Verulam, ver′ ū lȧm
Vespasian, ves pā′ zhi ȧn
Vespucci, ves poo′ chē
Vevay, vė vā′
Vezin, vē′ zin
Vicenza, vē chent′ sa
Vichy, vish′ i, vē shē′
Vierge, vē ârj′
Viet Nam, vi et năm′
Vigfusson, vig′ fus ȯn
Vigny, vē nyē′
Vigo, vī′ gō
Villafranca, vē la frăng′ ka
Villars, vē lar′
Villegas, vēl yā′ gas
Villehardouin, vēl ar du a*n*′
Villemain, vēl ma*n*′
Villeneuve, vēl nĕrv′
Villeroi, vēl rwa′
Villiers, vil′ ėrz, -yėrz
Villon, vē yo*n*′, vē lo*n*′
Vincennes, va*n* sen′
Vinci, vin′ chē
Viola, vī′ ȯ lȧ, vē ō′ lȧ
Virchow, vĕr′ chou
Virgil, vĕr′ jil
Virginia, vĕr jin′ i ȧ
Virginie, vēr zhē nē′
Visconti, vēs kon′ tē
Vistula, vis′ tū lȧ
Vives, vē′ ves
Viviani, vē vē a′ nē
Vladimir, vlăd′ i mir
Vladivostock, vla dē vos tok′
Vogel, fō′ gėl
Vogüé, vō gu ā′
Volpone, vol pō′ ni
Voltaire, vol târ′
Vortigern, vôr′ ti gĕrn
Vosges, vōzh
Voss, fos
Voules, vōlz
Vries, vrēs
Vyvyan, viv′ i ȧn

Waal, val
Wabash, waw′ băsh
Waddington, wod′ ing tȯn
Wagner, vag′ nėr; (Eng. surname) wăg′ nėr
Wagram, va′ gram
Walcheren, val′ *ch*ėr ėn
Waldeck, val dek′
Waldegrave, wol′ grāv
Waldemar, wol′-, val′ dė mar
Waldersee, val′ dėr zā
Walewski, va lev′ skē
Walfisch, wol′ fish
Walford, wol′ fȯrd
Wallach, wol′ ȧk
Wallachia, wȧ lā′ ki ȧ
Wallenstein, val′ ėn stīn
Walloon, wȧ loon′
Walmesley, wawmz′ li
Walpole, wol′ pōl
Walsingham, wol′ sing ȧm
Waltham, wol′ tȧm
Walther, val′ tėr
Walworth, wol′ wȯrth
Wantage, won′ tij
Warham, wâr′ ȧm
Warkworth, wawk′ wȯrth
Warre, wôr
Warwick, wor′ ik
Wastell, wostl
Watteau, wot ō′
Wauchope, waw′ *ch*ȯp
Waugh, waw
Weber, vā′ bėr
Wednesbury, wenz′ bu̇ ri
Wei-hai-we, wā hī wā′
Weimar, vī′ mar
Weir, wēr
Weismann, vīs′ man
Weiss, vīs
Welles, welz
Wellesley, welz′ li, wez′ li
Welwyn, wel′ in
Wemyss, wēmz
Wenceslaus, wen′ sez laws
Weobley, web′ li
Werther, ver′ tėr
Weser, vā′ zėr
Wesley, wes′ li
Weston-super-Mare, wes′ tȯn sū per mâr′
Weyman, wā′ mȧn
Whewell, hū′ ėl
Whitefield, wit′ fēld
Whitelock, wit′ lok
Whytham, wīt′ ȧm
Widnes, wid′ nez
Wieland, vē′ lant
Wiesbaden, vēs ba′ den
Wilhelm, vil′ helm
Wilhelmina, wil hel mē′ nȧ
Wilhelmshafen, vil′ helms ha fėn
Willard, wi lard′
Willesden, wilz′ dėn
Winchelsea, win′ chėl sē
Winchester, win′ ches tėr
Winckelmann, ving′ kel man
Windsor, win′ zȯr
Winstanley, win′ stȧn li
Wisbech, wiz′ bēch
Wisconsin, wis kon′ sin
Wishart, wish′ ȧrt
Witte, vit′ ė
Wittenberg, wit′ ėn bu̇rg
Witwatersrand, vit′ va tėrz rant
Wiveliscombe, wiv ė lis′ ku̇m, wilz′ ku̇m
Wodehouse, wud′ hous
Wolcott, wul′ kȯt
Wollaston, wul′ ȧ stȯn
Wollstonecraft, wul′ stȯn kraft
Wolseley, wulz′ li
Wolsey, wul′ zi
Wombwell, woom′ wel, woom′ bėl
Woolwich, wul′ ich, -ij
Worcester, wus′ tėr
Worms, wĕrmz
Wörth, vĕrt
Wortley, wĕrt′ li
Wrekin, rē′ kin
Wrensfordsley, renz′ li
Wrey, rā
Wrotham, root′ ȧm
Wrottesley, rots′ li
Wroughton, raw′ tȯn
Wundt, vunt
Wurmser, vurm′ zėr
Würtemberg, wĕr′tem bėrg
Wurzburg, wĕrtz′ bėrg
Wycherley, wich′ er li
Wycliffe, wik′ lif
Wycombe, wik′ ȧm
Wykeham, wik′ ȧm
Wymondham, wind′ ȧm
Wyndham, wind′ ȧm
Wyoming, wī ō′ ming
Wyss, vis
Wythe, with
Wyvill, wī′ vil

Xanadu, zăn′ ȧ doo
Xanthippe, zăn tip′ i
Xavier, zā′ vyer
Xenocrates, zė nok′ rȧ tēz
Xenophanes, zė nof′ ȧ nēz
Xenophon, zen′ ō fȯn
Xeres [sherry] zer′ ės

Yamaguchi, ya ma goo′ chē
Yangtze-kiang, yang tsā kē ang′
Yeames, yāmz
Yeatman, yāt′ mȧn
Yeats, yāts
Yemen, yā′ men
Yenisei, yen i sā′ ē
Yeovil, yō′ vil
Yerburgh, yar′ bu̇ ru̇
Yerkes, yĕr′ kėz
Yokohama, yō kō ha′ mȧ
Yonge, yŭng
Yosemite, yȯ sem′ i tē
Youghal, yawl
Ypres, ēpr
Ypsilanti, ip si lăn′ ti
Yriarte, ē rē ar′ tā
Ysaye, ē za′ yė
Yucatan, ū kȧ tan′
Yugoslavia, ū gō sla′ vi ȧ
Yves, ēv
Yvetot, ēv tō′

Zacchæus, zȧ kē′ u̇s
Zachariah, zăk ȧ rī′ ȧ
Zachary, zăk′ ȧ ri
Zambesi, zam bē zē
Zanoni, dza nō′ nē
Zante, zan′ tā
Zarathustra, za rȧ thoos′ trȧ
Zechariah, zek ȧ rī′ ȧ

s: s (sibilant) toa**s**t. **z:** s (sonant) toe*s*, reali*z*e. **ch:** *ch*ur*ch*. ***ch*:** lo*ch*. **j:** *j*udge.

Zeiss, zīs
Zelotes, zel ō′ tēz
Zeno, zē′ nō
Zephaniah, zef ȧ nī′ ȧ
Zephyrus, zef′ i rùs
Zermatt, zĕr′ măt
Zeus, zūs
Zeuxis, zūk′ sis
Zoe, zo′ i
Zola, zō′ lȧ
Zoroaster, zō rȯ ăs′ tėr
Zouche, zoosh
Zurich, zū′ rik
Zuyder Zee, zi′ der ze
Zwingli, zwing′ gli

FOREIGN PHRASES AND WORDS IN COMMON USE

Foreign words that have become naturalized are given in the main body of the Dictionary

à bas [F.]. Down! down with!
abest [L.]. (*pl.* **absunt**) He (or she) is absent.
ab extra [L.]. From without.
ab initio [L.]. From the beginning.
ab intra [L.]. From within.
à bon droit [F.]. By good right, with justice.
ab origine [L.]. From the commencement.
absente reo [L.]. In the absence of the accused.
absents ont toujours tort [F.]. The absent are always wrong.
absit omen [L.]. Let there be no ill omen.
ac etiam [L.]. And also.
à compte [F.]. On account, in part payment.
à coup sûr [F.]. Certainly, without fail.
acte d'accusation [F.]. Indictment.
ad arbitrium [L.]. At will, at pleasure.
ad astra [L.]. To the stars.
ad captandum vulgus [L.]. To attract or please the rabble.
à deux [F.]. Of or between two.
ad extremum [L.]. To the extreme.
ad gustum [L.]. To one's taste.
ad hoc [L.]. For this particular purpose, specially.
ad hominem [L.]. To the man, personal, not disinterested (of an argument).
a die [L.]. From that day.
ad infinitum [L.]. To infinity.
ad interim [L.]. Meanwhile.
ad kalendas Græcas [L.]. At the Greek calends, never (the Greeks had no calends).
ad majorem Dei gloriam [L.]. To the greater glory of God.
ad misericordiam [L.]. To pity (of an argument).
ad nauseam [L.]. So as to disgust or nauseate.
ad referendum [L.]. For further consideration.
ad rem [L.]. To the point.
adsum [L.]. I am present.
ad summum [L.]. To the highest point.
ad valorem [L.]. According to value.
ad verbum [L.]. To the word, verbally.
advocatus diaboli [L.]. The devil's advocate [see ADVOCATE].
ægrotat [L.]. (*pl.* **-tant**) He (or she) is ill.
ætatis suæ [L.]. Of his (or her) age.
à fond [F.]. To the bottom, thoroughly.
à la [F.]. According to; in the style or fashion of.
à la belle étoile [F.]. In the open air.
à la bonne heure [F.]. Good, first-rate, excellent!
à la carte [F.]. By the bill of fare.
à la française, grecque, l'anglaise, l'espagnole, etc. [F.]. In the French, Greek, English, Spanish, etc., style.
à la mode [F.]. In fashion.
al fresco [It.]. In the open air.
alla ventura [It.]. At a venture.
alter ego [L.]. One's second self.
alter idem [L.]. Another exactly similar.
alterum tantum [L.]. As much again.
amari aliquid [L.]. A touch of bitterness.
âme damnée [F., lost soul]. (*fig.*) One's tool or catspaw.
amende honorable [F.]. Public apology, public amends.
a mensa et toro [L.]. From bed and board.
à merveille [F.]. Admirably, perfectly.
amicus amico [L.]. Friendly to a friend.
amicus curiæ [L.]. A friend of the court, an adviser with no personal interest in the case.
amicus humani generi [L.]. A friend of the human race.
amor patriæ [L.]. Love of country, patriotism.
amour-propre [F.]. Self-esteem, vanity.
ancienne noblesse [F.]. The old nobility.
animo et fide [L.]. Courageously and faithfully.
anno ætatis suæ [L.]. In the (specified) year of his (or her) age.
anno Domini [L.]. In the year of our Lord.
anno humanæ salutis [L.]. In the year of man's redemption.
anno mundi [L.]. In the year of the world.
anno post Christum natum [L.]. In the year after the birth of Christ.
anno post Romam conditam [L.]. In the year after the building of the city (Rome), 754 B.C.
annos vixit [L.]. He (or she) lived (so many) years.
anno urbis conditæ or **A.U.C.** [L.]. In the year from the time the city (Rome) was built, 754 B.C.
annus mirabilis [L.]. A year of wonders (usu. applied in English history to 1666, noteworthy for the war with the Dutch and the Great Fire of London).
ante bellum [L.]. Before the war.
ante diem [L.]. Before the day.
ante lucem [L.]. Before daybreak.
ante meridiem [L.]. Before noon.
à outrance [F.]. To the end, to extremities.
à plaisir [F.]. At pleasure, at will.
après moi (or **nous**) **le déluge** [F.]. After me (or us) the deluge.
a principio [L.]. From the beginning.
à propos de bottes [F., with regard to boots]. Irrelevantly.
arbiter elegantiarum [L.]. A judge in matters of taste.
Arcades ambo [L.]. Two of similar tastes, vices, etc.
arcana cælestia [L.]. Celestial secrets.
arcana imperii [L.]. State secrets.
argumentum ad hominem [L.]. An appeal to personal interests, etc.
a rivederci [It.], Au revoir, to our next meeting.
arrière-pensée [F.]. A mental reservation.
ars est celare artem [L.]. True art is to conceal art.
ars longa, vita brevis [L.]. Art is long, life short.
artium magister [L.]. Master of Arts.
assez bien [F.]. Moderately well.
à tout prix [F.]. At any price.
atra cura [L.]. Black care.
à travers [F.]. Across, through.
au courant de [F.]. Fully informed about.
audax et celer [L.]. Bold and speedy.
au désespoir [F.]. In despair.
audi alteram partem [L.]. Hear the other side.
au fait [F.]. Familiar, well-acquainted with; up to the mark.
au fond [F.]. At bottom.
au grand sérieux [F.]. In all seriousness.
au mieux [F.]. On the best of terms.
au naturel [F.]. In its natural state.
au pied de la lettre [F.]. Literally, precisely.
au reste [F.]. Besides, moreover.
au revoir [F.]. Till we meet again.
au sérieux [F.]. Seriously.
aut Cæsar aut nullus [L.]. Either Cæsar or nobody; either first or nowhere.
autore [It.]. Author.
autres temps, autres mœurs [F.]. Other times, other manners.
aut vincere aut mori [L.]. To conquer or die.
aux armes! [F.]. To arms!
avant-propos [F.]. Preface, preliminary remarks.
ave, atque vale [L.]. Hail! and farewell!

ave Imperator, morituri te salutant [L.]. Hail Cæsar (or Emperor)! Those who are about to die salute thee.
a vinculo matrimonii [L.]. From the marriage bond, complete divorce.
à volonté [F.]. At will, at pleasure.

Bachelier ès lettres [F.]. Bachelor of Letters.
Bachelier ès sciences [F.]. Bachelor of Science.
ballon d'essai [F.]. Experimental balloon, a feeler.
bal paré [F.]. Fancy-dress ball.
bas bleu [F.]. A blue-stocking, a woman who seeks a reputation for learning.
bavardage [F.]. Gossip, tittle-tattle.
beatæ memoriæ [L.]. Of blessed memory.
Beata Maria or **Virgo** [L.]. The Blessed Virgin.
beau sabreur [F.]. A dashing cavalryman.
beaux esprits [F.]. (*sing.* **bel esprit**) Men of wit.
beaux yeux [F.]. Fine eyes, good looks.
bel air [F.]. Fine deportment.
bel esprit [BEAUX ESPRITS].
bella! horrida bella! [L.]. War! horrid war!
bellum internecinum [L.]. A war of extermination.
bene decessit [L.]. He made a good end.
bene esse [L.]. Well-being.
beneficium [L.]. (*Eccles.*) A living.
bene merenti [L.]. (*pl.* **-entibus**) To the well-deserving.
ben trovato [It.]. Well invented; à propos.
ben venuto [It.]. Welcome.
bête noire [F.]. A bugbear, one's aversion.
bêtise [F.]. Stupidity, a blunder.
bibliothèque [F.]. A library.
bien aimé [F.]. (*fem.* **aimée**) Well-beloved.
bien entendu [F.]. To be sure, naturally, of course.
bis dat qui cito dat [L.]. He gives twice who gives speedily.
bon accueil [F.]. A good reception.
bona fide [L.]. In good faith.
bona fides [L.]. Good faith.
bona mobilia [L.]. Movable goods.
bona vacantia [L.]. Unclaimed goods.
bon goût [F.]. Good taste.
bon gré, mal gré [F.]. Willingly or unwillingly, whether one will or not.
bonjour [F.]. Good day.
bon marché [F.]. A cheap shop; cheap, a bargain.
bonne [F.]. A nurse-maid.
bonne-bouche [F.]. (*pl.* **bonnes-bouches**) A dainty morsel.
bonne fortune [F.]. (*pl.* **bonnes fortunes**) Good fortune, prosperity, success.
bon ton [F.]. Fashion, good style.
bonum publicum [L.]. The public good.
bon vivant [F.]. (*fem.* **bonne vivante**) One fond of good living.
bon voyage [F.]. A pleasant journey, farewell.
breveté [F.]. Patented.

café au lait [F.]. Coffee with milk.
café noir [F.]. Coffee without milk.
ça ira [F.]. That will go, that's the thing.
cantate Domino [L.]. Sing unto the Lord.
capiat qui capere possit [L.]. Let him take who can.
carême [F.]. Lent.
carpe diem [L.]. Enjoy the day, seize the present opportunity, improve the time.
casus belli [L.]. A ground of war.
casus fœderis [L.]. A case provided for by treaty.
causa vera [L.]. A true cause.
cause célèbre [F.]. A notable case or trial.
causeur [F.]. A talker, a tattler.
cave canem [L.]. Beware of the dog.
caveat actor [L.]. Let the doer beware.
caveat emptor [L.]. Let the purchaser beware.
caveat viator [L.]. Let the traveller or passer-by beware.
cedant arma togæ [L.]. Let arms yield to the gown; let violence give place to law.
cela va sans dire [F.]. That goes without saying, of course.
ce n'est que le premier pas qui coûte [F.]. It is only the first step that is troublesome.
censor morum [L.]. A censor of morals.
certum est quia impossible est [L.]. It is true because it is impossible.
c'est magnifique mais ce n'est pas la guerre [F.]. It's magnificent, but it isn't war.
ceteris paribus [L.]. Other things being equal.
chacun à son goût [F.]. Everyone to his taste.
chapeau rouge [F.]. The red cap of liberty.
chapelle ardente [F.]. A chapel or room lighted with candles for a lying-in-state.
chef de cuisine [F.]. A head cook.
chef-d'œuvre [F.]. A masterpiece.
cherchez la femme [F.]. Look for the woman, there's a woman at the bottom of it.
che sarà, sarà [It.]. What will be, will be.
chose jugée [F.]. A matter that has been decided.
Christe eleison [Latinized Gr.]. Christ have mercy.
chronique scandaleuse [F.]. A history of scandals.
ci-gît [F.]. Here lies.
civis Romanus sum [L.]. I am a Roman citizen.
cogito, ergo sum [L.]. I think, therefore I exist.
comme il faut [F.]. As it should be, correct, genteel.
commune bonum [L.]. A common benefit.
compagnie [F.]. Company (usu. written **Cie**).
compos mentis [L.]. Sound of mind.
con amore [It.]. With affection, with zeal.
concours [F.]. Competition.
conditio sine qua non [L.]. An indispensable condition.
con dolore [It.]. With grief; sadly.
confer [L.]. Compare.
con spirito [It.]. With animation.
Conseil d'État [F.]. A Council of State.
constantia et virtute [L.]. By constancy and courage.
consule Planco [L.]. When Plancus was consul; (*fig.*) in my younger days.
consummatum est [L.]. It is finished.
contra bonos mores [L.]. Contrary to good manners.
contra jus gentium [L.]. Against the law of nations.
contra mundum [L.]. Against the world.
contrat social [F.]. A social compact.
copia verborum [L.]. A plentiful supply of words, flow of language.
coram domino rege [L.]. Before our lord the king.
coram judice [L.]. Before a judge.
coram nobis [L.]. In our presence.
coram populo [L.]. In public.
corpus delicti [L.]. The body (*i.e.* the substance) of the offence.
corpus vile [L.]. Worthless matter.
corruptio optimi pessima [L.]. The corruption of the best is worst of all.
coup de grâce [F.]. A finishing stroke.
coup de main [F.]. A sudden attack, enterprise, or undertaking.
coup de soleil [F.]. A sunstroke.
coup d'œil [F.]. A rapid glance.
coute que coute [F.]. Cost what it may.
credat Judæus Apella [L.]. Let the (superstitious) Jew Apella believe it; tell that to the marines.
credo quia absurdum [L.]. I believe it because it is absurd.
crème de la crème [F.]. The cream of the cream, the very best.
crimen falsi [L.]. Forgery.
cui bono? [L.]. For whose advantage?
cuique suum [L.]. To each one his own.
culpa levis [L.]. Excusable negligence.
cum grano or **cum grano salis** [L.]. With a grain of salt; with some allowance.
cum privilegio [L.]. With privilege.
currente calamo [L.]. With a running pen; offhand, fluently.
custos morum [L.]. A guardian of morals.

d'accord [F.]. Agreed; in time.
damnosa hæreditas [L.]. A legacy entailing loss.
danse macabre [F.]. A dance of death.
date obolum Belisario [L.]. Give an obolus to Belisarius (a general reduced to beggary).
de bon augure [F.]. Of good omen.
de bonne grâce [F.]. With good will, willingly.

décheance [F.]. Forfeiture, expiry.
de die in diem [L.]. From day to day, continuously.
de facto [L.]. In reality, actually.
defectus sanguinis [L.]. Failure of issue.
de gustibus non est disputandum [L.]. There is no disputing about tastes.
Dei gratia [L.]. By the grace of God.
de jure [L.]. By right.
de l'audace, encore de l'audace, et toujours de l'audace [F.]. Audacity, more audacity, and always audacity.
delenda est Carthago [L.]. Carthage must be utterly destroyed.
delineavit [L.]. He (or she) drew it.
de luxe [F.]. Luxurious.
de minimis non curat lex [L.]. The law does not concern itself with trifles.
de mortuis nil nisi bonum [L.]. Let nothing be said of the dead but what is good.
de novo [L.]. Anew.
Deo favente [L.]. With the favour of God.
Deo gratias [L.]. Thanks be to God.
Deo volente [L.]. God willing.
de par le roi [F.]. In the name of the king.
de profundis [L.]. Out of the depths.
de proprio motu [L.]. On one's own initiative.
de rigueur [F.]. According to strict etiquette.
dernier ressort [F.]. A last resource.
desipere in loco [DULCE EST DESIPERE, etc.].
de te fabula narratur [L.]. The story relates to you.
deus ex machina [L.]. A god from the machine (in the Gr. theatre); a romantic or artificial *dénouement*.
Deus nobiscum quis contra [L.]. God with us, who against us?
Deus vobiscum [L.]. God be with you.
Deus vult [L.]. God wills it.
dies fausti or **infausti** [L.]. Auspicious or inauspicious days.
dies iræ [L.]. A day of wrath, the Day of Judgment.
dies nefasti [L.]. Days on which the courts could not be held in ancient Rome; unlucky days.
dies non [L.]. A day when business is not transacted.
Dieu et mon droit [F.]. God and my right (motto of the sovereigns of Great Britain).
Dieu vous garde! [F.]. God protect you!
dis aliter visum [L.]. The gods have decided otherwise.
disjecta membra [L.]. Scattered remains.
divide et impera [L.]. Divide and govern.
dolce far niente [It.]. Sweet idleness.
Domine, dirige nos [L.]. O Lord direct us (the motto of the City of London).
Dominus illuminatio mea [L.]. The Lord is my light (the motto of Oxford Univ.).
Dominus vobiscum [L.]. The Lord be with you.
donna è mobile [It.]. Woman is changeable.
dulce, domum [L.]. Sweet is the strain of 'Homeward.'
dulce est desipere in loco [L.]. It is pleasant to play the fool at times.
dulce et decorum est pro patria mori [L.]. It is sweet and glorious to die for one's country.
dulcis amor patriæ [L.]. The love of country is sweet.
dum spiro, spero [L.]. While I breathe, I hope.
dum vivimus, vivamus [L.]. Let us live while we live; let us enjoy life.

eau sucrée [F.]. Water sweetened with sugar.
ecce agnus Dei [L.]. Behold the lamb of God.
ecce homo [L.]. Behold the man!
ecce signum [L.]. Behold the proof.
écraser l'infâme! [F.]. Crush the infamous thing, root out the abomination!
égalité [F.]. Equality.
ego et rex meus [L.]. I and my king.
embarras de richesse [F.]. A superfluity of anything wanted or desirable.
en avant [F.]. Forward.
en déshabillé [F.]. In undress; in one's true colours.
en effet [F.]. Substantially, in effect.
en famille [F.]. With one's family, at home.
enfant gâté [F.]. (*fem.* **-tée**) A spoilt child.
enfants perdus [F., lost children]. A forlorn hope.
en fête [F.]. In festivity.
enfin [F.]. In short, finally.
en garçon [F.]. As a bachelor.
en grande tenue [F.]. In full official or evening dress.
en masse [F.]. In a body.
en passant [F.]. By the way.
en pension [F.]. On boarding-house terms.
en rapport [F.]. In direct relation, in sympathy (with).
en règle [F.]. In order, as it should be.
en route [F.]. On the way.
en suite [F.]. In a set, in succession.
en tout cas [F.]. In any case.
en train [F.]. In progress.
entre nous [F.]. Between ourselves, in confidence.
e pluribus unum [L.]. One out of or composed of many. (Motto of the U.S.A.)
eppur si muove [It.]. And yet it does move.
errare est humanum [L.]. To err is human.
est modus in rebus [L.]. There is a middle course in all things.
esto perpetua! [L.]. May it last for ever.
et ego in Arcadia [L.]. I too was in Arcadia; (*fig.*) I know all about it.
et sequens [L.]. (*pl.* **-quentes** or **-quentia**) And the following.
et tu Brute! [L.]. And thou too, Brutus (the last words of Cæsar when he saw Brutus amongst his murderers, see Shak.: *Julius Cæsar*, iii. I.).
euge! [L.]. Well done!
evviva [It.]. Hurray! Long live (e.g. the King).
ex Africa semper aliquid novi [L.]. Always something new out of Africa.
ex animo [L.]. Heartily, sincerely.
ex capite [L., from the head]. From memory.
ex cathedra [L.]. From the chair, with authority.
exempli gratia [L.]. By way of example.
exeunt omnes [L.]. All go out.
ex gratia [L.]. As an act of favour.
ex hypothesi [L.]. According to the hypothesis.
ex nihilo nihil fit [L.]. Out of nothing nothing comes.
ex pede Herculem [L.]. You may judge of Hercules by his foot, the whole by the part.
experientia docet stultos [L.]. Experience teaches fools.
experto crede [L.]. Believe one who has tried it, or who speaks from experience.
ex post facto [L.]. After the deed is done; retrospective.
extra muros [L.]. Outside the walls.

facile princeps [L.]. The acknowledged chief, one standing easily first.
facilis descensus Averno [L.]. The descent to hell is easy, it is easy enough to get into trouble.
façon de parler [F.]. Manner of speaking; phrase, locution.
fait accompli [F.]. An accomplished fact.
falsa lectio [L.]. An erroneous reading.
far niente [It.]. Doing nothing.
faute de mieux [F.]. In default of something better.
faux pas [F.]. A blunder, a slip.
favete linguis [L.]. Favour with your tongues, be silent.
fecit [L.]. He, or she, made it.
feliciter [L.]. Fortunately, happily.
femme galante [F.]. A gay woman; a prostitute.
femme incomprise [F.]. An unappreciated woman.
festina lente [L.]. Make haste slowly; don't be impetuous.
fiat experimentum in corpore vili [L.]. Let the experiment be made on a body of no value.
fiat justitia, ruat cœlum [L.]. Let justice be done though the heavens should fall.
fiat lux [L.]. Let there be light.
fidei defensor [L.]. Defender of the faith.
fides Punica [L.]. Punic faith; treachery.
fi donc! [F.]. For shame!
fidus Achates [L.]. Faithful Achates (the companion of Æneas); (*fig.*) a true friend.

filius terræ [L.]. A son of the earth; one of low origin.
finis coronat opus [L.]. The end crowns the work.
flagrante delicto [L.]. In the very act.
floreat [L.]. May (it) flourish.
fons et origo malorum [L.]. The source and origin of our miseries.
force majeure [F.]. Superior power, circumstances not under one's control.
forsan et hæc olim meminisse juvabit [L.]. Perchance it may be pleasant hereafter to call even these things to mind.
fortiter, fideliter, feliciter [L.]. Boldly, faithfully, successfully.
fortiter in re, suaviter in modo [L.]. Acting forcibly yet in gentle fashion.
fortuna favet fatuis [L.]. Fortune favours fools.
fraus pia [L.]. A pious fraud.
fronti nulla fides [L.]. There is no trusting the features; don't trust to appearances.
furor poeticus [L.]. Poetical frenzy.
furor scribendi [L.]. A rage for writing.

gage d'amour [F.]. A love-token.
gaieté de cœur [F.]. Lightness of heart.
galant homme [F.]. A man of honour.
galère [QUE DIABLE, etc.].
garde champêtre [F.]. (*pl.* **gardes champêtres**) A rural policeman.
garde mobile [F.]. A guard liable to be called out for general service.
garde nationale [F.]. National guard.
gardez [F.]. Take care; be on your guard.
gâté [F.]. (*fem.* **-tée**) Spoiled.
gaudeamus igitur [L.]. Therefore, let us rejoice.
gens d'armes [F.]. Men-at-arms, armed police.
gloria in excelsis Deo [L.]. Glory to God in the highest.
gloria Patri [L.]. Glory be to the Father.
grâce à Dieu [F.]. Thanks be to God.
gradus ad parnassum [L.]. A step to Parnassus; aid in writing Latin poetry.
grande parure, tenue, or **toilette** [F.]. Full dress.
grande passion [F.]. A serious love affair.
grand monarque [F.]. The grand monarch, Louis XIV.

haud longis intervallis [L.]. At frequent intervals.
haute bourgeoisie [F.]. The upper middle-class.
haute politique [F.]. State politics.
hic et ubique [L.]. Here and everywhere.
hic labor, hoc opus est [L.]. This is the labour, this the toil.
hic sepultus [L.]. Here [lies] buried.
hinc illæ lacrimæ [L.]. Hence these tears; this is the cause of the trouble.
his non obstantibus [L.]. Notwithstanding this.
hoc age [L.]. This do; attend.
hoc genus omne [L.]. All this sort of (people, etc.).
hoc habet [L.]. He has it, a hit.
hoc loco [L.]. In this place.
hoc monumentum or **saxum posuit** [L.]. He (or she) erected this monument or stone.
hoc tempore [L.]. At this time.
hoc volo, sic jubeo [L.]. This I will, thus I command.
hodie mihi, cras tibi [L.]. It is my turn to-day, yours to-morrow.
homo sum; humani nihil a me alienum puto [L.]. I am a man, and I consider nothing that concerns mankind a matter of indifference.
honi soit qui mal y pense [F.]. Shame be to him who thinks evil of it (motto of the Order of the Garter).
honoris causa or **gratia** [L.]. For the sake of honour, honorary.
horæ canonicæ [L.]. Canonical hours, prescribed times for prayers.
horæ subsecivæ [L.]. Leisure hours.
horas non numero nisi serenas [L.]. I count none but shining hours (inscription on sun-dials).
horresco referens [L.]. I shudder as I tell the story.
horribile dictu [L.]. Horrible to tell.
horribile visu [L.]. Horrible to see.
hors concours [F.]. Not for competition.
hors de combat [F.]. Disabled, unfit to continue a contest.
hors de la loi [F.]. Outlawed.
hostis humani generis [L.]. An enemy of the human race.
Humaniora [L.]. The humanities.
humanum est errare [L.]. To err is human.

ich dien [G.]. I serve (Prince of Wales's motto).
Iesus hominum Salvator [L.]. Jesus the Saviour of men.
ignotum per ignotius [L.]. (To explain) a thing not understood by one still less understood.
il n'y a que le premier pas qui coûte [F.]. It is only the first step that is troublesome.
il penseroso [It.]. The pensive man.
ils n'ont rien appris ni rien oublié [F.]. They have learned nothing and forgotten nothing (said of the Bourbons).
imo pectore [L.]. From the bottom of one's heart.
Imperium et libertas [L.]. Empire and liberty.
implicite [L.]. By implication.
in æternum [L.]. For ever.
in alio loco [L.]. In another place.
in articulo mortis [L.]. At the moment of death.
in banco regis [L.]. In the King's Bench.
in cælo quies [L.]. In heaven is rest.
in camera [L.]. In the judge's chamber, not in open court.
in capite [L.]. In chief, (holding) directly from the Crown.
in Christi nomine [L.]. In the name of Christ.
in commendam [L.]. (Holding a vacant benefice) in trust for the successor.
in cruce spero [L.]. I hope in the Cross.
in curia [L.]. In open court.
in Deo speravi [L.]. In God have I trusted.
index locorum [L.]. Index of place-names.
index rerum [L.]. An index of things or matters.
index verborum [L.]. An index of words.
in dubio [L.]. In doubt.
in equilibrio [L.]. In equilibrium.
in esse [L.]. In actual being.
in excelsis [L.]. In the highest.
in extenso [L.]. At full length.
in extremis [L.]. At the point of death.
in flagrante delicto [L.]. In the very act, red-handed.
in forma pauperis [L.]. As a pauper.
in foro conscientiæ [L.]. At the bar of the conscience.
infra dignitatem (more often **'infra dig.'**) [L.]. Beneath one's dignity.
in futuro [L.]. For the future, henceforth.
in gremio legis [L.]. In the lap or under the protection of the law.
in hoc signo vinces [L.]. By this sign (i.e. the Cross) thou shalt conquer (motto of Constantine the Great).
in loco [L.]. In the place (of).
in loco citato [L.]. In the place cited.
in loco parentis [L.]. In the place of a parent.
in manus tuas commendo spiritum meum [L.]. Into Thy hands I commend my spirit.
in medias res [L.]. Into the very midst of the business.
in memoriam [L.]. To the memory of.
in nomine [L.]. In the name (of).
in nubibus [L.]. In the clouds; undefined, uncertain, vague.
in pace [L.]. In peace.
in partibus infidelium [L.]. In the countries of unbelievers (of certain R.C. bishops).
in perpetuam rei memoriam [L.]. In everlasting remembrance of the event.
in perpetuum [L.]. For ever.
in petto [L.]. Within the breast, in reserve.
in pleno [L.]. In full.
in pontificalibus [L.]. In full priestly robes.
in posse [L.]. In possibility, potentially.
in principio [L.]. At the beginning.
in propria persona [L.]. In one's own person.
in puris naturalibus [L.]. In a state of nature, naked.
in re [L.]. In the matter of.
in rerum natura [L.]. In the nature of things.
in sæcula sæculorum [L.]. For ever and ever.

in se [L.]. In itself.
in situ [L.]. In (its original or proper) position.
instanter [L.]. At once.
in statu pupillari [L.]. In a state of pupilage.
in statu quo (ante or **nunc)** [L.]. In the same state as (before or now).
in te, Domine, speravi [L.]. In thee, O Lord, have I put my trust.
in tenebris [L.]. In the dark, in doubt.
inter alia [L.]. Among other things.
inter nos [L.]. Between ourselves.
inter se [L.]. Among or between themselves.
inter vivos [L.]. Among the living, during life.
in testimonium [L.]. In witness.
in totidem verbis [L.]. In so many words.
in toto [L.]. Entirely.
intra muros [L.]. Within the walls.
in transitu [L.]. On the way, en route.
intra parietes [L.]. Within the walls (of a house).
intra vires [L.]. Within the powers (of).
in usu [L.]. In use.
in utero [L.]. In the womb.
in utroque fidelis [L.]. Faithful in both.
in utroque jure [L.]. Under both (canon and civil) laws.
in vacuo [L.]. In a vacuum, in empty space.
invenit [L.]. He (or she) devised this.
in vino veritas [L.]. Drunkenness makes a man let out the truth.
ipse dixit [L.]. He himself has said it; a mere assertion.
ipsissima verba [L.]. The identical words.
ipso facto [L.]. By the fact itself.
ipso jure [L.]. By the law itself.
ita est [L.]. It is so.
ita lex scripta [L.]. Thus the law stands written.
iterum [L.]. Again.

jacta alea est [L.]. The die is cast.
jam satis! [L.]. Enough now of this!
je ne sais quoi [F.]. I know not what, something indefinable.
jeu de scène or **théâtre** [F.]. A stage trick, clap-trap.
jeu n'en vaut pas la chandelle [F.]. The game is not worth the candle.
jeune premier [F.]. A stage lover.
jeunesse dorée [F.]. Gilded youth.
jour de fête [F.]. A fête day, a festival.
jour de l'an [F.]. New Year's Day.
jubilate Deo [L.]. O be joyful in the Lord.
judicium Dei [L.]. The judgment of God.
jure divino [L.]. By divine law.
jure humano [L.]. By human law.
juris utriusque doctor [L.]. Doctor of both (canon and civil) laws.
jus canonicum [L.]. Canon law.
jus civile [L.]. Civil law.
jus divinum [L.]. Divine law.
jus gentium [L.]. The law of nations.
jus mariti [L.]. The right of a husband to the property of his wife.
jus naturæ [L.]. The law of nature.
jus relictæ [L.]. The right of the widow.
juste milieu [F.]. The golden mean.
j'y suis et j'y reste [F.]. Here I am and here I stay.

laborare est orare [L.]. Work is prayer.
labore et honore [L.]. With labour and honour.
labor omnia vincit [L.]. Labour overcomes all difficulties.
labuntur et imputantur [L.]. (The moments) glide away and are set down to our account (inscription on a sun-dial).
læsa majestas [L.]. Lese-majesty.
l'allegro [It.]. The merry man.
lapis philosophorum [L.]. The philosophers' stone.
l'appétit vient en mangeant [F.]. Appetite comes with eating.
lapsus calami [L.]. A slip of the pen.
lapsus linguæ [L.]. A slip of the tongue.
lapsus memoriæ [L.]. A slip of the memory.
lares et penates [L.]. Household gods.
lasciate ogni speranza, voi ch' entrate [It.]. All hope abandon ye who enter here (Dante).
laudator temporis acti [L.]. One who praises the good old days.
laus Deo [L.]. Praise be to God.
le beau monde [F.]. The world of fashion, society.
legatus a latere [L.]. A legate from the side (of the Pope), a papal legate.
le roy, or **la reyne, le veult** [N.-F.]. The King, or the Queen, wills it (royal assent to a Bill).
l'État, c'est moi [F.]. The State! I am the State (said by Louis XIV).
le tout ensemble [F.]. The general effect.
lettre de change [F.]. A bill of exchange.
lex loci [L.]. The law of the place, local custom.
lex non scripta [L.]. The unwritten law.
lex talionis [L.]. The law of retaliation.
l'homme propose et Dieu dispose [F.]. Man proposes and God disposes.
liberum arbitrium [L.]. Free choice.
licet [L.]. It is permitted, it is legal.
lite pendente [L.]. During the trial.
literæ humaniores [L.]. Literature (or letters) of a specially civilized nature; "polite literature."
litera scripta manet [L.]. The written word remains.
loco citato [L.]. In the place quoted.
locus classicus [L.]. The acknowledged place of reference.
locus sigilli [L.]. The place of the seal.
locus standi [L.]. Recognized place or position authorizing appearance in court, etc.
loquitur [L.]. He (or she) speaks.
lucus a non lucendo [L.]. *Lucus* (a grove) is derived from *lucere* (to shine) because it is dark; (*fig.*) anything inconsequent and absurd.
lusus naturæ [L.]. A freak of nature.
lux in tenebris [L.]. Light in darkness.
lux mundi [L.]. The light of the world.

magister ceremoniarum [L.]. A master of the ceremonies.
magna civitas, magna solitudo [L.]. A great city is a great solitude.
magnæ spes altera Romæ [L.]. A second hope of mighty Rome; used of any young man of promise.
magna est veritas et prævalet [L.]. Truth is great and all-powerful.
magnum bonum [L.]. A great good.
magnum in parvo [L.]. A great deal in a little space.
magnum opus [L.]. A great undertaking, the great work of a man's life.
maison de santé [F.]. A private asylum or hospital.
maître d'hôtel [F.]. A majordomo, hotel manager.
malade imaginaire [F.]. One who fancies himself an invalid.
maladie du pays [F.]. Home-sickness.
mala fide [L.]. In bad faith, treacherously.
mal à propos [F.]. Unseasonably.
malentendu [F.]. A misunderstanding, a mistake.
malgré soi [F.]. In spite of oneself.
malum in se [L.]. A thing bad in itself.
manet [L.]. (*pl.* **manent**) He (or she) remains.
manibus pedibusque [L.]. With hands and feet; tooth and nail.
manu propria [L.]. With one's own hand.
mardi gras [F.]. Shrove Tuesday.
mare clausum [L.]. A closed sea.
mariage de convenance [F.]. A marriage of convenience.
marque de fabrique [F.]. A trade-mark.
matre pulchra filia pulchrior [L.]. The more beautiful daughter of a beautiful mother.
mauvais quart d'heure [F.]. A bad quarter of an hour.
mauvais sujet [F.]. A worthless fellow.
mauvais ton [F.]. Bad style, bad taste.
maxima debetur puero reverentia [L.]. The greatest reverence is due to the innocence of a child.
maximus in minimus [L.]. Very great in very small matters.
mea culpa [L.]. By my fault.
medice, cura teipsum [L.]. Physician, heal thyself.
memoria in æterna [L.]. In eternal remembrance.
mensa et toro [L.]. From bed and board.

mens sana in corpore sano [L.]. A sound mind in a sound body.
menus plaisirs [F.]. Minor enjoyments or recreations.
meo periculo [L.]. At my own risk.
meo voto [L.]. By my own wish.
meum et tuum [L.]. Mine and thine.
mirabile dictu [L.]. Wonderful to relate.
mirabile visu [L.]. Wonderful to see.
miserere mei [L.]. Have mercy upon me.
more majorum [L.]. After the manner of our ancestors.
more suo [L.]. In his usual way.
mors janua vitae [L.]. Death is the gate of life.
motu proprio [L.]. Of his own accord.
moyen âge [F.]. The Middle Ages.
multum in parvo [L.]. Much in little.
mutatis mutandis [L.]. The necessary changes being made.
mutato nomine [L.]. With a mere change of name.

ne admittas [L.]. Do not admit.
necessitas non habet legem [L.]. Necessity knows no law.
ne exeat regno [L.]. Let him not depart the realm (a writ of restraint).
negatur [L.]. It is denied.
nemine contradicente [L.] (usu. abb. **nem. con.**) No one contradicting.
nemine dissentiente [L.]. No one dissenting.
nemo me impune lacessit [L.]. No one provokes me with impunity (motto of the Order of the Thistle).
ne nimium [L.]. Not too much; avoid excess.
ne plus ultra [L.]. Nothing further; perfection.
nihil tetigit quod non ornavit [L.]. He touched nothing without embellishing it (incorr. from Johnson's epitaph on Goldsmith in Westminster Abbey).
nil admirari [L.]. To be astonished at nothing.
nil desperandum [L.]. Never despair.
nil magnum nisi bonum [L.]. Nothing is great unless good.
noblesse oblige [F.]. Rank imposes obligations.
nolle prosequi [L.]. To be unwilling to prosecute.
nolo contendere [L.]. I will not contest it; guilty.
nolo episcopari [L.]. I do not wish to be a bishop (the formal reply to the royal offer of a bishopric).
non assumpsit [L.]. A plea denying promise or undertaking by the defendant.
non compos mentis [L.]. Not of sound mind, mentally deranged, lunatic.
non est inventus [L.]. A sheriff's statement that the defendant is not to be found (on return of a writ).
non libet [L.]. It does not please me.
non multa, sed multum [L.]. Not many things, but much.
non nobis [L.]. Not unto us.
non omnia possumus omnes [L.]. We cannot all do everything.
non placet [L.]. A formula expressing a negative vote.
non plus ultra [NE PLUS ULTRA].
non possumus [L., we cannot]. A statement of inability or a refusal to act.
non sequitur [L., it does not follow]. An illogical inference; an irrelevant conclusion.
non sum qualis eram [L.]. I am not what I once was.
nota bene [L.]. Note well.
notandum [L.]. (*pl.* **-da**) A thing to be noted.
nous avons changé tout cela [F.]. We have changed all that.
nudis verbis [L.]. In plain words.
nulla bona [L.]. No goods; no effects.
nulli secundus [L.]. Second to none.

obiit [L.]. He (or she) died.
obiter dictum [L.]. A thing said incidentally.
odium medicum [L.]. Hatred among physicians.
odium theologicum [L.]. Hatred among theologians.
omne ignotum pro magnifico [L.]. Everything unknown is supposed to be something magnificent.
omnia mors æquat [L.]. Death levels all distinctions.
omnia munda mundis [L.]. To the pure all things are pure.
omnia vincit amor, nos et cedamus amori [L.]. Love conquers all things, let us too yield to love.
omnibus idem [L.]. The same to all men.
onus probandi [L.]. The burden of proving.
opere citato [L.]. In the work cited.
opprobrium medicorum [L.]. The reproach of physicians (said of incurable diseases).
opus operatum [L.]. A task performed.
ora et labora [L.]. Pray and work.
ora pro nobis [L.]. Pray for us.
orate pro anima [L.]. Pray for the soul (of).
ore rotundo [L.]. With well-rounded impressive utterance.
O sancta simplicitas! [L.]. O sacred simplicity!
O! si sic omnia! [L.]. O if only all had been (spoken or acted) thus!
O tempora! O mores! [L.]. Alas for the times and the manners!

pace [L.]. By leave of, with the consent of.
palmam qui meruit ferat [L.]. Let him bear the palm who has deserved it.
panem et circenses [L.]. Bread and the circus.
parbleu! [F.]. An exclamation of surprise, etc.
parce, parce, precor [L.]. Spare me, spare me, I pray.
par excellence [F.]. Pre-eminently.
par exemple [F.]. For instance.
par hasard [F.]. By chance.
pari passu [L.]. At the same rate or pace.
parole d'honneur [F.]. Word of honour.
parturiunt montes, nascetur ridiculus mus [L.]. The mountains are in labour and the result will be a ridiculous mouse.
pater patriæ [L.]. The father of his country.
patres conscripti [L.]. The Conscript Fathers; the Roman Senate.
patria potestas [L.]. (*Rom. Law*) The power of a father (over his family).
pax orbis terrarum [L.]. The peace of the world.
pax Romana [L.]. The peace of the Roman Empire.
pax vobiscum [L.]. Peace be with you.
peine forte et dure [F.]. Very severe punishment (a kind of judicial torture for those 'mute of malice'.
pendente lite [LITE].
per ardua ad astra [L.]. Through difficulties to the stars. (Motto of R.A.F.)
per aspera ad astra [L.]. Through rough ways to the stars; through suffering to renown.
per contra [L.]. On the contrary.
pereunt et imputantur [L.]. (The hours) pass away and are put to our account (motto on sundials).
per fas aut nefas [L.]. Through right or wrong.
per mare, per terras [L.]. By sea and land.
per mensem [L.]. Monthly.
per saltum [L.]. At a leap.
per se [L.]. By itself.
persona [L.]. A person.
persona grata [L.]. An acceptable person.
petitio principii [L.]. Begging the chief point; begging the question.
pièce de résistance [F.]. The most substantial dish at a meal.
pied-à-terre [F.]. A footing, a temporary lodging.
pis aller [F.]. A makeshift.
plein air [F.]. The open air.
pleno jure [L.]. With full authority.
poco curante [It.]. Not caring, indifferent, apathetic.
poeta nascitur, non fit [L.]. The poet is born, not made.
post hoc, ergo propter hoc [L.]. After this, therefore on account of this.
post obitum [L.]. After death.
post tenebras lux [L.]. After darkness, light.
pot-au-feu [F.]. Meat broth.
pour encourager les autres [F.]. (usu. iron.) To encourage the others.
preux chevalier [F.]. A brave knight.
prima facie [L.]. At first sight.
primus inter pares [L.]. First among equals.

pro aris et focis [L.]. For our altars and hearths.
probatum est [L.]. It has been proved.
pro bono publico [L.]. For the public good.
procul, O procul este, profani [L.]. Hence, oh get hence, ye profane.
pro Deo et ecclesia [L.]. For God and the Church.
pro forma [L.]. As a matter of form.
pro memoria [L.]. As a memorial.
pro patria [L.]. For one's country.
pro patria et rege [L.]. For country and king.
proprio motu [L.]. Of one's own accord, spontaneously.
pro rata [L.]. In proportion.
pro rege, lege, grege [L.]. For the king, the law, the people.
pro tanto [L.]. For so much, to that extent.
pro tempore [L.]. For the time being.
publice [L.]. Publicly.
Punica fides [L.]. Punic faith, treachery.
pur sang [F.]. Thoroughbred.

quære [L.]. Inquire.
quæstio vexata [L.]. A vexed question.
quæ vide [L.]. Which (things) see.
qualis rex, talis grex [L.]. Like king, like people.
quantum libet [L.]. As much as you like.
quantum meruit [L.]. As much as he (or she) deserved.
quantum sufficit [L.]. As much as suffices.
quantum valeat [L.]. So much as it may be worth.
que diable allait-il faire dans cette galère? [F.]. What the devil was he doing in that galley? What business had he to be there? What had *he* got to do with it?
quem deus vult perdere, prius dementat [L.]. Whom the gods mean to destroy they first make mad.
qui desiderat pacem, præparet bellum [L.]. Who desires peace, let him make ready for war (cp. SI VIS PACEM, etc.).
quid faciendum? [L.]. What is to be done?
quien sabe? [Sp.]. Who knows?
quieta non movere [L.]. Not to interfere with things that are at rest; let sleeping dogs lie.
qui non proficit, deficit [L.]. He who does not advance loses ground.
quis custodiet ipsos custodes? [L.]. Who will watch the watchers?
qui s'excuse s'accuse [F.]. He who excuses himself accuses himself.
quis separabit? [L.]. Who shall separate us? (the motto of the Order of St. Patrick).
quoad hoc [L.]. To this extent.
quo animo? [L.]. With what intention?
quod bene notandum [L.]. Which is to be especially noted.
quod dixi, dixi [L.]. What I have said, I have said.
quod erat demonstrandum (Q.E.D.) [L.]. Which was to be proved.
quod erat faciendum (Q.E.F.) [L.]. Which was to be done.
quod scripsi, scripsi [L.]. What I have written, I have written.
quod vide [L.]. Which (thing) see.
quo fas et gloria ducunt [L.]. Where duty and glory lead (the motto of the Royal Artillery).
quo jure? [L.]. By what right?
quomodo? [L.]. By what means?
quorum pars magna fui [L.]. In which event I took a leading part.
quot homines, tot sententiæ [L.]. As many minds as men; so many men, so many minds (sometimes incorr. quoted TOT HOMINES, etc.).
quo vadis? [L.]. Whither goest thou?

raison d'être [F.]. The reason for a thing's existence.
rara avis in terris [L.]. An extremely rare bird; a prodigy.
recte et suaviter [L.]. Justly and mildly, with "sweetness and light."
reculer pour mieux sauter [F.]. To retire in order to advance better.
reductio ad absurdum [L.]. Proof by demonstrating the absurdity of the contrary proposition.
regium donum [L.]. A royal grant, esp. (*Eng. Hist.*) an allowance made by the sovereign at various times between 1672 and 1879 for the maintenance of Presbyterian ministers in Ireland.
répondez s'il vous plait (R.S.V.P.) [F.]. Please reply.
requiescat in pace (R.I.P.) [L.]. May he (or she) rest in peace.
res [L.]. A thing, property; the subject-matter of a suit, etc.
res angusta domi [L.]. Matters straitened at home, poverty.
res gestæ [L.]. Things done, matters of fact, transactions.
res judicata [L.]. An issue that has been settled in a court.
respice finem [L.]. Look to the end.
resurgam [L.]. I shall rise again.
revenons à nos moutons [F.]. Let us return to our sheep, let us come back to our subject.
rus in urbe [L.]. Country in town.

sæva indignatio [L.]. Fierce indignation.
sal Atticum [L.]. Attic salt, wit.
salvo jure [L.]. Without prejudice.
salvo pudore [L.]. Without offence to modesty.
sans peur et sans reproche [F.]. Without fear and without blame.
sans phrase [F.]. Without circumlocution.
satis verborum [L.]. Enough of words.
sauve qui peut [F.]. Let him save himself who can; everyone for himself.
scandalum magnatum [L.]. The defamation of exalted personages.
sculpsit [L.]. He (or she) engraved or carved this.
secundum artem [L.]. According to art.
secundum legem [L.]. According to law.
secundum naturam [L.]. According to nature.
secundum regulam [L.]. According to rule.
securus judicat orbis terrarum [L.]. The verdict of the world is conclusive.
semper eadem [L. pl.). (*sing.* **idem**) Always the same.
semper fidelis [L.]. Always faithful.
semper paratus [L.]. Always ready.
Senatus Populusque Romanus (S.P.Q.R.) [L.]. The Roman Senate and People.
seniores priores [L.]. Those who are older first.
se non è vero è ben trovato [It.]. If it is not true, it is cleverly invented; if not true it ought to be.
servus servorum Dei [L.]. The servant of the servants of God (a title of the Pope).
sic in originali [L.]. Thus in the original.
sic itur ad astra [L.]. Such is the way to the stars or to fame.
sic passim [L.]. Thus in many places.
sic semper tyrannis [L.]. Ever thus to tyrants.
sic transit gloria mundi [L.]. So earthly glory passes away.
sicut ante [L.]. As before.
sic vos non vobis [L.]. So you do not (labour) for yourselves.
si Deus nobiscum, quis contra nos? [L.]. If God be with us who shall be against us?
similia similibus curantur [L.]. Like things are cured by like.
si monumentum requiris, circumspice [L.]. If you seek his memorial look around you. (Part of the epitaph in St. Paul's Cathedral, London, to the architect of the building, Sir Christopher Wren.)
simpliciter [L.]. Absolutely, without qualification.
sine cura [L.]. Without duties or office.
sine die [L.]. Without any day (being fixed).
sine dubio [L.]. Without doubt.
sine præjudicio [L.]. Without prejudice.
sine prole [L.]. Without offspring.
sine qua non [L.]. An indispensable condition (see CONDITIO, etc.).
si vis pacem, para bellum [L.]. If you want peace be ready for war.
solventur risu tabulæ [L.]. The case will be dismissed with laughter; you will be laughed out of court.
solvitur ambulando [L.]. It is proved as you go along.
spero meliora [L.]. I hope for better things.
splendide mendax [L.]. Magnificently false.

spolia opima [L.]. The richest spoils.
spretæ injuria formæ [L.]. The insult to beauty scorned.
statim [L.]. At once.
status quo ante [L.]. The same state as before.
stet fortuna domus! [L.]. May the fortune of the house endure!
style est l'homme même [F.]. The style is the man himself.
suaviter in modo, fortiter in re [L.]. Gentle in manner, resolute in execution.
sub judice [L.]. Under consideration.
sub pede sigilli [L.]. Under the Great Seal.
sub pœna [L.]. Under penalty (of).
sub rosa [L.]. Under the rose (*i.e.* in secret), confidentially.
sub silentio [L.]. In silence; without formal notice being taken.
sub specie [L.]. Under the appearance of.
sub voce or **verbo** [L.]. Under the head of.
succès d'estime [F.]. A success with more credit than profit.
suggestio falsi [L.]. A suggestion of something that is untrue.
sui generis [L.]. Of its (or his or her) own kind.
sunt lacrimæ rerum [L.]. There are tears for mortal things.
suppressio veri suggestio falsi [L.]. The suppression of the truth is the suggestion of a falsehood.
sursum corda [L.]. Lift up your hearts.
suum cuique [L.]. To each his own.

tabula rasa [L.]. A smooth tablet (*i.e.* one which has not been written upon, 'a clean slate').
tantum quantum [L.]. Just as much as (is required).
tempora mutantur, nos et mutamur in illis [L.]. The times are changed and we with them.
tempus edax rerum [L.]. Time the devourer of things.
tempus fugit [L.]. Time flies.
terra incognita [L.]. An unknown land.
tertium quid [L.]. A third (or intermediate) something.
teste [L.]. By the evidence (of).
timeo Danaos et dona ferentes [L.]. I fear the Greeks even when they offer gifts.
tot homines, tot sententiæ [QUOT HOMINES, etc.].
toties quoties [L.]. As often as.
tour de force [F.]. A feat of strength or skill.
tout ensemble [F.]. The general effect.
tout est perdu fors l'honneur [F.]. All is lost but honour.
traduttori traditori [It.]. Translators are traitors.
tria juncta in uno [L.]. Three things combined in one (the motto of the Order of the Bath).
tu quoque [L.]. You also.

ubique [L.]. Everywhere.
ultima Thule [L.]. Farthest Thule, the utmost limit.
ultimus Romanorum [L.]. The last of the Romans (used by Brutus of Cassius).
ultra vires [L.]. Beyond one's (legal) powers.
urbi et orbi [L.]. To the city and the world.
ut infra [L.]. As (mentioned) below.
uti possidetis [L.]. As you now have in your possession.
ut supra [L.]. As (mentioned) above.

vade in pace [L.]. Go in peace.
vade mecum [L.]. Go with me. (*fig.*) a concise handbook.
væ victis! [L.]. Woe to the vanquished!
vale [L.]. Farewell.
valeat quantum valere potest [L.]. Let it pass for what it is worth.
vanitas vanitatum, et omnia vanitas [L.]. Vanity of vanities, all is vanity.
varia lectio [L.]. (*pl.* **variæ lectiones**) A variant reading.
variorum notæ [L.]. Notes by various commentators.
vedi Napoli e poi muori [It.]. See Naples and then die.
veluti in speculum [L.]. As in a mirror.
veni, Creator Spiritus [L.]. Come, Holy Spirit Creator.
veni, vidi, vici [L.]. I came, I saw, I conquered.
verbatim et literatim [L.]. Word for word and letter for letter.
verbum satis sapienti (verb. sap.) [L.]. A word is enough to the wise.
veritas omnia vincit [L.]. Truth conquers all things.
vestigia nulla retrorsum [L.]. No signs of any returning.
vexata quæstio [L.]. A disputed question.
via media [L.]. A middle course.
vicisti, Galilæe! [L.]. Thou hast conquered, O Galilean!
victi vincimus [L.]. Conquered, we conquer.
videlicet (viz.) [L.]. To wit, namely.
video meliora proboque, deteriora sequor [L.]. I see the better and approve it, yet pursue the worse.
vide ut supra [L.]. See as above.
vi et armis [L.]. By force and arms.
vigilate et orate [L.]. Watch and pray.
virginibus puerisque [L.]. For boys and girls.
virgo intacta [L.]. A maiden untouched (unsullied).
vis a tergo [L.]. Force from behind.
vis inertiæ [L.]. The power of inertness.
visum visu [L.]. To see and to be seen.
vita brevis, ars longa [L.]. Life is short but art is long.
vivat regina! or rex! [L.]. Long live the queen or king!
vive (le roi, président, etc.) [F.]. Long live (the king, president, etc.).
volens et valens [L.]. Willing and able.
volenti non fit injuria [L.]. No injury is done to a consenting party.
volo, non valeo [L.]. I am willing but unable.
vox clamantis in deserto [L.]. The voice of one crying in the wilderness.
vox et praeterea nihil [L.]. A voice and nothing more.
vox (*pl.* **voces**) **populi** [L.]. The voice of the people, popular feeling.
vox populi vox Dei [L.]. The voice of the people is the voice of God.
vox stellarum [L.]. The voice of the stars.

ABBREVIATIONS, SIGNS AND SYMBOLS IN COMMON USE

ABBREVIATIONS

A., Academy, Academician; America; Associate; (*Cinema*) programme for adults only; (*Mil.*) administration.
A, (*Chem.*) Argon.
a., Acre; adjective; alto; *anno* (in the year); *ante* (before).
@, For, at, to (in quoting prices).
A1, First-class (ship in Lloyd's register).
A.A., Associate in Arts; Automobile Association; Army Act; anti-aircraft.
AA. [F. *Altesses*], Highnesses.
A.A.A., Amateur Athletic Association.
A.A.F., Auxiliary Air Force.
A.A.G., Assistant-Adjutant-General.
A.A.S., (*U.S.A.*) Fellow of the American Academy.
A.A.S.S. [L. *Americanæ Antiquarinæ Societatis Socius*], Fellow of the American Antiquarian Society.
A.B. [L. *Artium Baccalaureus*], Bachelor of Arts; able-bodied seaman.
Abb., Abbess, abbey, abbot.
abbr., Abbreviated, abbreviation.
A.B.C., The alphabet; Aerated Bread Company; a railway guide.
A.B.C.A., Army Bureau of Current Affairs.
ab init. [L. *ab. initio*], From the beginning.
abl., Ablative.
abor., Aborigines, aboriginal.
Abp., Archbishop.
abr., Abridged, abridgment.
A.B.S., Able-bodied seaman.
abt., About.
A.C., Aero Club; Alpine Club; [L. *Ante Christum*], before Christ; Alternating Current; Army Air Council; Army Corps.
a.c., Author's correction.
a/c, Account.
A.C.A., Associate of the Institute of Chartered Accountants.
Acad., Academy, Academician.
A.C.C., Army Catering Corps.
A/CC., Aircraft carrier.
acc., Acceptance, accepted; accusative; account.
accel. [It. *accelerando*], (*Mus.*) with gradually increasing velocity.
acct., Account, accountant.
A.C.G., Assistant Chaplain-General.
A.C.G.B., Arts Council of Great Britain (successor (1945) to C.E.M.A.).
A.C.I.G.S., Assistant Chief of the Imperial General Staff.
A.C.I.S., Associate of the Chartered Institute of Secretaries.
A.C.M., Air Chief Marshal.
A.C.P., Associate of the College of Preceptors.
A.D. [L. *anno Domini*], In the year of our Lord.
a.d., After date; [L. *ante diem*], before the day.
ad., Advertisement.
adag., (*Mus.*) *Adagio.*
A.D.C., Aide-de-camp.
ad eund. [L. *ad eundem gradum*], (Admitted) to the same degree.
ad inf. [L. *ad infinitum*], To infinity; without limit.
ad int. [L. *ad interim*], In or for the meantime.
Adj., Adjutant.
adj., Adjective.
Adj.-Gen., Adjutant-General.
ad lib. [L. *ad libitum*], At pleasure; to any desired extent.
Adm., Admiral, Admiralty.
adv., Adverb, adverbially; [L. *adversus*], against; advocate.
ad val. [L. *ad valorem*], According to the value.
advert., advt., Advertisement.
Æ, (*Shipping*) 3rd class at Lloyd's.
A.E.A., Air Efficiency Award; Atomic Energy Authority.
A.E.C., Atomic Energy Commission.
Æn., Æneid.
A.E.R.E., Atomic Energy Research Establishment.
Æsch., Æschylus.
æsth., Æsthetics.
æt., ætat. [L. *ætatis*], In the year of his age, aged.
A.E.U., Amalgamated Engineers' Union.
A.F., Admiral of the Fleet; Army Form.
A.F.A., Associate of the Faculty of Actuaries; Amateur Football (*also* Fencing) Association.
A.F.A.S., Associate of the Faculty of Architects and Surveyors.
A.F.C., Air Force Cross; Australian Flying Corps.
aff., Affirmative, affirming.
afft., Affidavit.
A.F.L., American Federation of Labour.
A.F.M., Air Force Medal.
A.F.S., Auxiliary Fire Service.
Afr., Africa, African.
Ag [L. *argentum*], (*Chem.*) Silver.
A.G., Adjutant-General, Accountant-General, Agent-General (of Colonies); Attorney-General; [G. *Aktiengesellschaft*], joint-stock or limited-liability company.
agr., agric., Agriculture, agricultural, agriculturist.
agt., Against; agent.
A.H. [L. *anno Hegiræ*], In the year of the Hegira (A.D. 622), the Mohammedan era.
A.H.S. [L. *anno humanæ salutis*], In the year of human salvation.
a.h.v. [L. *ad hanc vocem*], At this word.
A.I., American Institute; [L. *anno inventionis*], In the year of the discovery; Auctioneers' and Estate Agents' Institute; Anthropological Institute.
A.I.A., Associate of Institute of Actuaries.
A.I.A.C., Associate of the Institute of Company Accountants.
A.I.A.S., Surveyor Member of the Incorporated Association of Architects and Surveyors.
A.I.B., Associate of the Institute of Bankers.
A.I.C., Associate of the Institute of Chemistry.
A.I.C.E., Associate of Institute of Civil Engineers.
A.I.D., Artificial Insemination Donor; **A.I.H.,** ditto husband.
A.I.F., Australian Imperial Forces.
A.I.G., Assistant-Inspector General.
A.I.M.E., Associate of the Institute of Mining Engineers.
A.I.Mech.E., Associate of the Institute of Mechanical Engineers.
A.I.M.M., Associate of the Institution of Mining and Metallurgy.
A.Inst.C.E., Associate of the Institute of Civil Engineers.
A.Inst.P., Associate of the Institute of Physics.
A.I.S.A., Associate of the Incorporated Secretaries' Association.
A.K.C., Associate of King's College, London.
Al, (*Chem.*) Aluminium.
al. [L. *alias*], Otherwise; under another name.
a.l. [F. *apres livraison*], After delivery (of goods).
A.L.A., American Library Association; Associate of the Library Association.
Ala., Alabama.
A.L.A.A., Associate of the London Association of Certified Accountants.
Alas., Alaska.
Alb., Albanian; Albert.
A.L.C.M., Associate of the London College of Music.
Ald., Alderman.
Alex., Alexander.
Alf., Alfred.
Alg., Algernon; Algiers; algebra.
all' otta. [It. *all' ottava, all' 8va*], (*Mus.*) An octave above that written.
A.L.S., Associate Fellow of the Linnean Society; autograph letter signed.
Alt. [F. *Altesse*], Highness.
alt., Alternate, alternating; altitude.
Alta., Alberta, Canada.
Alum., Alumnus.
A.M. [L. *Artium Magister*], Master of Arts (also M.A.); Albert Medal; [L. *anno mundi*], In the year of the world; Air Ministry; Air Marshal; associate member.
a.m. [L. *ante meridiem*], Before noon.
Am., America, American.

A.M.D., Army Medical Department.
A.M.D.G. [L. *ad majorem Dei Gloriam*], To the greater Glory of God.
Amer., America, American.
A.M.G., Allied Military Government.
A.M.G.O.T., Allied Military Government of Occupied Territories.
A.M.I.C.E., Associate Member of the Institution of Civil Engineers.
A.M.I.Chem.E., Associate Member of the Institution of Chemical Engineers.
A.M.I.E.E., Associate Member of the Institution of Electrical Engineers.
A.M.I.Gas E., Associate Member of the Institute of Gas Engineers.
A.M.I.Loco.E., Associate of the Institute of Locomotive Engineers.
A.M.I.Mech.E., Associate Member of the Institute of Mechanical Engineers.
A.M.O., Administrative Medical Officer; Air Ministry Order.
amp., Ampere, electrical unit.
A.M.S., Army Medical Service.
A.M.S.E., Associate Member Society of Engineers.
an. [L. *anno*], In the year; [*annum*], as in *per an.*
Anacr., Anacreon, Anacreontic.
anal., Analogy, analogous; analysis; analytic, analytical.
anat., Anatomy, anatomical, anatomist.
anc., Ancient.
An. Dom. [A.D.].
Angl. [L. *anglice*], In English.
Ann. [L. *annales*], Annals; [L. *anni*], years; [L. *anno*], in the year; annual.
annot., Annotated.
anon., Anonymous.
A.N.S., Army Nursing Service.
ans., Answer.
Ant., Antony; Antigua.
ant., Antiquities; antonym.
anthrop., Anthropology, anthropological.
antiq., Antiquary, antiquarian.
A.N.Z.A.C., Australian and New Zealand Army Corps.
A.O., Army Order.
a/o., Account of.
A.O.C. [L. *anno orbis conditi*], in the year of the Creation; Air Officer Commanding.
A.O.D., Army Ordnance Department; Ancient Order of Druids.
A.O.F., Ancient Order of Foresters.
A.O.H., Ancient Order of Hibernians.
aor., Aorist.
A.O.S., Ancient Order of Shepherds.
A.P., Associated Presbyterian; Associated Press; armour-piercing.
a.p., Above proof; author's proof.
Ap., Apostle; April.
A.P.C.N. [L. *anno post Christum natum*], In the year after the birth of Christ.
aph., Aphorism.
A.P.M., Assistant Provost Marshal.
A.P.O., Army Post Office.
Apoc., Apocalypse.
Apocr., Apocrypha.
apog., Apogee.
Apollod., Apollodorus.
App., Apostles.
app., Appendix; apparently.
appr., Apprentice.
appro., Approbation, approval.
approx., Approximate, approximately, approximation.
Apr., April.
A.P.R.C. [L. *anno post Romam conditam*], In the year after the building of Rome (754 B.C.).
A.P.S., Aborigines Protection Society; Army Postal Service.
aq. [L. *aqua*], Water.
A.Q.M.G., Assistant-Quarter-master-General.
A.R. [L. *anno regni*], In the year of the reign.
A.R.A., Associate of the Royal Academy; Amateur Rowing Association.
Arab., Arabia, Arabian, Arabic.
arach., Arachnology.
A.R.A.M., Associate of the Royal Academy of Music.
A.R.B.A., Associate of the Royal Society of British Artists.
A.R.C., Automobile Racing Club (same as B.A.R.C.).
A.R.C.A., Associate of the Royal College of Art.
A.R.C.E., Academical Rank of Civil Engineers.
Arch., Archibald; archaic, archaism; archery; archipelago; architect, architecture, architectural.
archæol., Archæology, archæological.
Archbp. [ABP.].
Archd., Archdeacon; Archduke.
A.R.C.I., Associate of the Royal Colonial Institute.
A.R.C.M., Associate of the Royal College of Music.
A.R.C.O., Associate of the Royal College of Organists.
A.R.C.S., Associate of the Royal College of Science.
A.R.E., Associate of the Royal Society of Painter Etchers.
arg., (*Her.*) Argent.
Arg. Rep., Argentine Republic.
A.R.H.A., Associate of the Royal Hibernian Academy.
A.R.I.B.A., Associate of the Royal Institute of British Architects.
A.R.I.C., Associate of the Royal Institute of Chemistry.
Arist., Aristophanes; Aristotle.
arith., Arithmetic, arithmetical, arithmetician.
Ariz., Arizona.
Ark., Arkansas.
Arm., Armenian; Armoric.
A.R.M.S., Associate of the Royal Society of Miniature Painters.
A.R.P., Air Raid Precautions.
A.R.R. [L. *anno regni regis* or *reginæ*], In the year of the King's (or Queen's) reign.
arr., Arranged; arrival, arrivals, arrive, arrived, arrives.
A.R.R.C., Association (or Associate) of the Royal Red Cross.
arrondis [F.], *Arrondissement.*
A.R.S.A., Associate of the Royal Scottish Academy; Associate of the Royal Society of Arts.
A.R.S.L., Associate of the Royal Society of Literature.
A.R.S.M., Associate of the Royal School of Mines (now the Royal College of Science).
A.R.S.W., Associate of the Royal Scottish Society of Painting in Water Colours.
art., Article; artificial; artillery.
A.R.W.S., Associate of the Royal Society of Painters in Water Colours.
As., Asia, Asian, Asiatic.
As, (*Chem.*) Arsenic.
A.S., Academy of Science; assistant secretary.
A.S. [L. *anno salutis*], In the year of salvation.
A.-S., Anglo-Saxon.
a./s., Account Sale.
A.S.A., Amateur Swimming Association.
A.S.A.A., Associate of the Society of Incorporated Accountants and Auditors.
A.S.C., American Society of Cinematographers.
A.Sc., Associate in Science (Durham).
ASDIC [see Dictionary].
A.S.E., Amalgamated Society of Engineers; Associate of the Society of Engineers.
A.S.G.B., Aeronautical Society of Great Britain.
A.S.P., Astronomical Society of the Pacific; [F. *accepté sous protêt*], accepted under protest.
A.S.R.S., Amalgamated Society of Railway Servants.
ass., Assistant.
Ass.-Com.-Gen., Assistant Commissary-General.
assim., Assimilated.
assoc., Associate, association.
Assoc.Sc., Associate in Science.
asst., Assistant.
Assyr., Assyria, Assyrian.
astr., Astronomy, astronomer.
astrol., Astrology.
astron., Astronomy.
A/T, Anti-tank.
at., Atomic.
A.T.A.S., Air Transport Auxiliary Service.
A.T.C., Art Teachers' Certificate (South Kensington); Air Training Corps.
A.T.C.L., Associate Trinity College (of Music), London.
At.-Gen., Attorney-General.
Ath., Athabasca; athletic.
Athen., Athenian.
A.T.I., Associate of the Textile Institute.
Atl., Atlantic.
atm. pr., Atmospheric pressure.
A.T.S., Auxiliary Territorial Service; Associate of Theological Study.
ats., (*Law*) At the suit of.
attrib., Attribute, attributed to; attributively.
atty., Attorney.
A.T.V., Associated Television Ltd.
at. wt., Atomic weight.
A.U. [L. *anno urbis*], In the year of the city [A.U.C.]; (*Phys.*) Angström unit.
Au., Augustus.
Au, (*Chem.*) [L. *aurum*], Gold.
A.U.C. [L. *ab urbe condita*, or *anno urbis conditæ*], From the year of the building of the City [Rome, in 754 B.C.].
Aud.-Gen., Auditor-General.
Aug., August; Augustan; Augustus; augmentative.
a.u.n. [L. *absque ulla nota*], Unmarked.
Aus., Austria, Austrian.
Ausg. [G. *Ausgabe*], Revised edition.

Austral., Australia, Australian, Australasia, Australasian.
auth., Authentic; author, authoress; authority, authorized.
auxil., Auxiliary.
A.V. (*Bib.*), Authorized version; artillery volunteers.
av., Average; avoirdupois.
a.v. [L. *annos vixit*], (He or she) lived (so many) years.
a/v., Ad valorem.
avdp., Avoirdupois.
A.V.M., Air Vice-Marshal.
a.w., Atomic Weight.
A.W.O.L., Absent without leave.
ax., Axiom, axiomatic.
az., (*Her.*) Azure.

B., Bachelor; Baron; black (of pencils); Baptist; battle.
b., Born; brother; (*Naut.*) blue sky; (*Cricket*) bowled, bye, byes; (*Mus.*) bass.
B, (*Chem.*) Boron.
B.A., Bachelor of Arts; British Academy; British America; British Association; Buenos Aires.
Ba, (*Chem.*) Barium.
Bab., (*Bot.*) Babington.
Bach., Bachelor.
B.A.E., (*U.S.A.*) Bachelor of Agricultural Economics.
B.Agr., Bachelor of Agriculture.
bal., Balance.
Ball., Balliol College, Oxford.
Balt., Baltimore.
B. & F.B.S., British and Foreign Bible Society.
B. & S. (*colloq.*), Brandy and soda.
B.A.O., Bachelor of Obstetrics.
B.A.O.R., British Army of the Rhine.
bap., Baptized.
bar., Barometer; barley-corn; barrel; (*Naut.*) barque.
B.A.R.C., Brooklands Automobile Racing Club.
B.Arch., Bachelor of Architecture.
barr., Barrister.
Bart., Baronet; Bartholomew.
Bart's., St. Bartholomew's Hospital.
batt., Battalion; battery.
Bav., Bavaria, Bavarian.
BB, Very black (of pencils).
B.B.A., British Beekeepers' Association.
BBB, Extremely black (of pencils).
B.B.C., British Broadcasting Corporation.
B.C., Before Christ; Board of Control; Borough Council; British Columbia.
B.Ch. [L. *Baccalaureus Chirurgiæ*], Bachelor of Surgery.
B.Ch.D., Bachelor of Dental Surgery.
B.Chir. [B.CH.].
B.C.L. [L. *Baccalaureus Civilis Legis*], Bachelor of Civil Law; [L. *Baccalaureus Canonicæ Legis*], Bachelor of Canon Law.
B.Comm., Bachelor of Commerce.
B.D., Bachelor of Divinity.
Bd. [G. *Band*], A volume.
bd., Board; bond; bound.
B.D.A., British Dental Association.
Bde. [G. *Bände*], Volumes.
bdle., Bundle.
Bdr., Brigadier; bombardier.
B.D.S., Bachelor of Dental Surgery.
bds., (*Bookbinding*) Boards; bonds.

B.E., Bachelor of Engineering; Board of Education.
Be, (*Chem.*) Beryllium.
b.e., Bill of Exchange.
B.E.A., **BEA**, British European Airways; British East Africa; British Electricity Authority.
B.Ed., Bachelor of Education.
Beds., Bedfordshire.
B.E.F., British Expeditionary Force.
Belg., Belgium, Belgian, Belgic.
B.E.M., British Empire Medal.
B.Eng., Bachelor of Engineering.
Beng., Bengal.
Benj., Benjamin.
Berk., (*Bot.*) Berkeley.
Berks, Berkshire.
B. ès L. [F. *Bachelier ès Lettres*], Bachelor of Letters and Arts.
B. ès S. [F. *Bachelier ès Sciences*], Bachelor of Science.
b.f., Beer firkin; (*vulg.*) bloody fool.
bg., Bag; being.
B'ham, Birmingham.
B'head, Birkenhead.
b.h.p., Brake-horse-power.
B.Hond., British Honduras.
B.Hy., Bachelor of Hygiene.
Bi, (*Chem.*) Bismuth.
B.I., British India.
Bib., Bible, biblical.
bibl. [L. *bibliotheca*], Library.
bibliog., Bibliographer, bibliographic, bibliographical, bibliography.
B.I.F., British Industries Fair.
biog., Biographer, biographic, biography.
biol., Biology, biological.
B.I.S., Bank of International Settlements.
bis., Bissextile.
Bisc., Biscayan.
bk., Bank; book; barque.
bkg., Banking.
bkrpt., Bankrupt.
bkt., Basket.
B.L., Black letter; British Legion; Bachelor of Law; breech-loader.
B/L, Bill of lading.
bl., Bale; barrel.
B.L.A., British Liberation Army.
bldg., Building.
B.Litt., Bachelor of Letters.
blk., Black; block.
B.LL., Bachelor of Laws.
B.L.R., Breech-loading rifle.
B.M., Bachelor of Medicine; [L. *Beata Maria*], the Blessed Virgin; [L. *beatæ memoriæ*], of blessed memory; Brigade Major; British Museum; (*Survey.*) bench mark; [L. *bene merenti*], to the well-deserving; bronze medallist (Bisley).
B.M.A., British Medical Association.
B.M.E., Bachelor of Mining Engineering.
B.M.J., British Medical Journal.
B.Mus., Bachelor of Music.
Bn., Battalion.
B.N.C., Brasenose College, Oxford.
b.o., Branch office; buyer's option.
B.O.A., British Olympic Association; British Optical Association.
B.O.A.C., British Overseas Airways Corporation.
Bocc., Boccaccio.
Bodl., Bodleian.
Boet., Boethius.
B. of E., Board of Education; Bank of England.
B. of H., Board of Health.

B. of T., Board of Trade.
Boh., **Bohem.**, Bohemia, Bohemian.
Bol., Bolivia, Bolivian.
Bo'ness, orig. Borrowstounness (Linlithgowshire).
B.O.P., Boy's Own Paper.
bor., Borough.
bot., Botany, botanical, botanist; bought; bottle.
B.O.U., British Ornithologists' Union.
Boul., Boulevard.
B.P., British public; British pharmacopœia; Baden-Powell.
b.p., Below proof (of spirits); boiling point; bill of parcels; bills payable; [L. *bonum publicum*], the public good.
Bp., Bishop.
B.P.B., Bank post bills.
B.Phil., Bachelor of Philosophy.
bpl., Birthplace.
Bp. Suff., Bishop Suffragan.
bque., (*Naut.*) Barque.
B.R., British Railways.
Br., British; (*Bot.*) R. Brown.
Br, (*Chem.*) Bromine.
br., (*Naut.*) Brig.
b.r., Bills receivable.
Br. Am., British America.
Braz., Brazil, Brazilian.
Br. Col., British Columbia.
B.R.C.S., British Red Cross Society.
Brd., Board.
Brec., Breconshire.
Bret., Breton.
brev., Brevet, breveted; (*Printing*) brevier.
brig., Brigade, brigadier.
Brig.-Gen., Brigadier-General.
Brit., Britain, British, Britannia, Britannica, Britannicus.
Brit. Mus., British Museum.
Britt. [L. *Britanniarum*], Of all the Britains (on coins).
bro., brother.
bros., brothers.
B.R.S., British Road Services.
Brum, (*slang*) Brummagem (Birmingham).
Brux. [F. *Bruxelles*], Brussels.
bryol., Bryology.
B.S., Bachelor of Surgery; Blessed Sacrament.
b.s., Balance sheet, bill of sale.
B.S.A., Birmingham Small Arms Co.
B.Sc., Bachelor of Science.
B.Sc.(Econ.), Bachelor of Science in the Faculty of Economics.
B.Sc.(Eng.), Bachelor of Science in the Faculty of Engineering.
B.S.L., Botanical Society of London.
B.S.T., British Summer Time.
Bt., Baronet; bought.
B.T.C., British Transport Commission.
B.Th., Bachelor of Theology.
B.Th.U., British Thermal Unit.
B.T.U., (*Elec.*) Board of Trade unit, or kilowatt hour.
bu., Bushel.
Bucks, Buckinghamshire.
B.U.F., British Union of Fascists.
bul., Bulletin.
Bulg., Bulgaria, Bulgarian.
bull., Bulletin.
B.U.P., British United Press.
bur., Buried.
burg., Burgess; burgomaster.
bus., Bushel.
B.V., Bible Version (of the Psalms); [L. *Beata Virgo*], the Blessed Virgin.

b.v. [L. *bene vale*], Farewell.
B.V.M. [L. *Beata Virgo Maria*], The Blessed Virgin Mary.
B.W., Board of Works.
B.W.G., Birmingham wire gauge.
B.W.I., British West Indies.
B.W.T.A., British Women's Temperance Association.

C, 100; (*Chem.*) Carbon.
C., Catholic; centigrade; Chancellor; Chancery; Church; common metre (of hymns); congress; contralto; Conservative; (*Mus.*) counter-tenor; Court; caught; chapter.
c., Cent; centigramme; centime; (*Naut.*) cloudy; constable; cubic; (*Elec.*) current.
c., Circa, circiter, circum (about); calorie(s).
c. & b., (*Cricket*) Caught and bowled.
C.A., Chartered Accountant; Chief Accountant; commercial agent; Confederate Army; Controller of Accounts; County Alderman; Croquet Association.
Ca, (*Chem.*) Calcium.
ca., Cases; cathode.
C.A.B., Citizens' Advice Bureau.
Cæs., Cæsar.
C.A.G., Civil Air Guard.
Cal., California; (*Pharm.*) calomel.
cal., Calendar; calibre.
cal. [It.] (*Mus.*) *Calando.*
cam., Camouflage.
Camb., Cambridge.
Cambs, Cambridgeshire.
Camd. Soc., Camden Society.
Can., Canada.
can., Canon; (*Mus.*) *canto, cantoris.*
Canpac., Canadian Pacific Railway shares.
Cant., Canterbury; (*Relig.*) canticles; canto.
Cantab. [L. *Cantabrigiensis*], Of Cambridge.
Cantuar. [L. *Cantuaria*], Canterbury; [L. *Cantuariensis*], of Canterbury (signature of the Archbishop of Canterbury).
cap., Capital, capital letter; [L. *capitulum*], little chapter; [L. *caput*], head; section; chapter; foolscap.
Capt., Captain.
Car. [L. *Carolus*], Charles; Carolina.
car., Carat.
Card., Cardinal.
cash., Cashier.
cat., Catalogue, catalogued, cataloguing, cataloguer; (*Med.*) [L. *cataplasma*], a poultice; catechism.
Cath., Catherine; Catholic; Cathedral.
Catull., Catullus.
caus., Cause, causation, causative.
Cav., Cavalry.
cav., (*Law*) Caveat.
c.a.v. [L. *curia advisari vult*] (*Law*) The court desires to consider.
C.B., Cape Breton; Cavalry Brigade; Chief Baron; (*Law*) Common Bench Reports and Scott's Reports; Companion of the Order of the Bath; (*Mil.*) confined to barracks; County borough.
Cb, (*Chem.*) Columbium.
C.B.C., Canadian Broadcasting Corporation.
C.B.E., Commander of the Order of the British Empire.
C.B.S., Confraternity of the Blessed Sacrament.
C.C., Caius College (Cambridge); Chamber of Commerce; Chess Club; Circuit Court; City Council; City Councillor; Civil Court; Common Councilman; Consular Clerk; County Commissioner; County Councillor; County Council; County Clerk; Cricket Club; Cycling Club; Crown Clerk; Curate-in-Charge.
c.c. [F. *compte courant*], Account current; cubic centimetre; cubic contents.
C.C.A., Chief Clerk of the Admiralty.
C.C.C., Corpus Christi College (Oxford); Central Criminal Court; Civilian Conservation Corps (U.S.A.).
C.C.G., Control Commission, Germany.
C.C.P., Code of Civil Procedure; Court of Common Pleas; Chief Commissioner of Police.
C.C.S., Casualty Clearing Station.
CD, 400.
C.D., Coast Defence(s); Civil Defence; *Corps Diplomatique*; Contagious Diseases.
Cd, (*Chem.*) Cadmium.
Cd., Command Paper (to 1918 inclusive).
c.d. [L. *cum dividendo*], With dividend.
c.d.v., Carte-de-visite.
C.E., Chief Engineer; Church of England; Civil Engineer.
Ce, (*Chem.*) Cerium.
C.E.A., Central Electrical Authority.
cel., Celebrated.
Cels., Celsius.
Celt., Celtic.
C.E.M.A., Council for the Encouragement of Music and the Arts (see A.C.G.B.).
C.E.M.S., Church of England Men's Society.
cent., Centigrade; central; century.
cert., certif., Certificate, certificated; certify; certainty.
Cerv., Cervantes.
Cestr. [L. *Cestriensis*], Of Chester (Bishop of Chester's signature).
cet. par. [L. *ceteris paribus*], Other things being equal.
C.E.T.S., Church of England Temperance Society.
C.E.U., Christian Endeavour Union.
C.F., Chaplain to the Forces.
cf., Calf; [L. *confer*], compare.
C.F.G., (F.) Confédération Générale du Travail.
c.f.i., Cost, freight, and insurance.
C.G., Coast-Guard; Captain-General; Captain of the Guard; Coldstream Guards; Commissary-General; Consul-General.
cg., Centigram.
C.G.H., Cape of Good Hope.
C.G.M., Conspicuous Gallantry Medal.
C.G.S., Centimetre-gramme-second (combined unit of length, mass and time).
C.G.T., Confederation Générale du Travail (the French T.U.C.). Compagnie Générale Transatlantique.
C.H., Captain of the Horse; Companion of Honour; Court House; Custom House.
Ch., China, Chinese; Church.
ch., Chairman; chaldron; champion (of dogs); chapter; chief; child; (*Knitting*) chain; choir organ; (of horses) chestnut.
Chald., Chaldean; Chaldee.
Chamb., Chamberlain.
Chanc. Ex., Chancellor of the Exchequer.
Chap., Chaplain; chapter.
Chas., Charles.
Ch.B. [L. *Chirurgiæ Baccalaureus*], Bachelor of Surgery.
chbrs., Chambers.
Ch. Ch., Christ Church (Oxford).
chem., Chemical, chemist, etc.
Chesh., Cheshire.
chev., (*Her.*) Chevron; chevalier; knight.
Chi., Chicago.
Chin., China, Chinese.
Ch.M. [L. *Chirurgiæ Magister*], Master of Surgery (Edinburgh University).
chmn., chn., Chairman.
chp., Championship.
chq., Cheque.
Chr., Christ, Christian; Christopher.
Chr. Coll. Cam., Christ's College, Cambridge.
Chron., Books of Chronicles.
chron., Chronicle, chronological, chronologically, chronology.
Chrys., Chrysostom.
C.H.U., Centigrade heat unit.
C.I., Channel Isles; (Imperial Order of the) Crown of India.
Cic., Cicero.
Cicestr. [L. *Cicestriensis*], Of Chichester (Bishop of Chichester's signature).
C.I.D., Criminal Investigation Department; Committee of Imperial Defence.
C.I.E., Companion (of the Order) of the Indian Empire.
Cie. [F. *compagnie*], Limited company.
c.i.f., Cost, insurance, and freight.
C.I.G.S., Chief of Imperial General Staff.
C.-in-C., Commander-in-Chief.
C.I.O., (*U.S.A.*) Congress of Industrial Organizations.
circ., Circa, circiter, circum (about).
cit., Citation, cited; citizen; citrate.
C.I.V., City Imperial Volunteers.
civ., Civil, civilian.
C.J., Chief Justice.
ck., Cask.
Cl, (*Chem.*) Chlorine.
cl., Centilitre; class; clause; clergyman; cloth.
Cla., Clare College, Cambridge.
clar., (*Printing*) Clarendon type; Clarencieux King-of-Arms; clarinet, clarinetist.
class., Classic, classical, classification.
C.L.B., Church Lads' Brigade; Central Land Board.
cld., (*Shipping*) Cleared; coloured.
Clem., Clement.
Clerg., Clergyman, clergy.
clk., Clerk.
C.L.P.A., Common Law procedure Act.
C.L.S.C., Chautauqua Literary & Scientific Circle.
C.M., Certificated Master or Mistress; [L. *Chirurgiæ Magis-*

ter], Master of Surgery; Church Missionary; common metre (of hymns); corresponding member.
c.m., Causa mortis (reason of death).
cm., Centimetre.
C.M.B., Central Midwives Board.
C.M.D., Common metre double (of hymns).
Cmd., Command Paper (from 1919 inclusive).
cmdg., Commanding.
C.M.F., Colonial Military Forces.
C.M.G., Companion of (the Order of) St. Michael and St. George.
cml., Commercial.
C.M.S., Church Missionary Society.
C.M.Z.S., Corresponding Member of the Zoological Society.
Cn., Cnæus.
C.N.R., Civil Nursing Reserve.
C.O., Colonial Office; Crown Office; Commanding Officer; Criminal Office; conscientious objector.
Co, (*Chem.*) Cobalt.
Co., Colon; Company; County.
c/o, Care of; (*Stock Exchange*) carried over.
coad., Coadjutor.
C.O.D., Cash on delivery; collect on delivery.
cod., Codex. **codd.**, Codices.
C. of E., Church of England.
co-ed., Co-educational.
cog., Cognate.
C.O.I., Central Office of Information.
Col., Colonel; Colossians; Colorado; Columbia District (U.S.A.).
col., Colonial, colony; coloured; column.
coll., Colleague, colleagues; collection, collector; college, collegiate.
collab., Collaborated, collaborator.
collat., Collateral, collaterally.
collect., Collective, collectively.
colloq., Colloquial, colloquially, colloquialism.
Colo., Colorado.
Coloss., Colossians.
col. p. [It. *colla parte*], (*Mus.*) Adapt to the principal part.
Col.-Sergt., Colour-Sergeant.
col. vo. [It. *colla voce*], (*Mus.*) Adapt to the principal voice.
Com., Commander; commission, commissioner; committee.
com., Comic, comedy; common, commoner, commonly; commune, community; communicate, communicated, communication.
comb., Combine, combined, combining.
Comdr., Commander.
Comdt., Commandant.
Com.-in-Chf., Commander-in-Chief.
Comm., Commodore.
comm., Commentary; commerce; commercial; commonwealth.
Commy., Commissary.
comp., Comparative, compare, comparison; compilation, compile, compiled, compiler; composer, composition; compositor; compound, compounded.
Com. Serj., Common Serjeant.
Com. Ver., Common Version (of the Bible).
Con., Consul.
con., Conclusion; conversation.
con. [L. *conjunx*], Consort; [L. *contra*], in opposition to.
conch., Conchology.
con. esp. [It. *con espressione*], (*Mus.*) With expression.
conf., Conference.
conf. [L. *confer*], Compare.
cong., Congregation, congregational, Congregationalist, congregationist; congress, congressional.
conj., Conjugation; conjunction, conjunctive.
Conn., Connecticut.
cons., Consonant; consolidated (stocks); constable; constitution, constitutional; consul.
Cons.-Gen., Consul-General.
Consols, Consolidated (Funds).
constr., Construction; construe, construed.
cont., Containing, contents; continent, continental; continue, continued.
cont. bon. mor. [L. *contra bonos mores*], Contrary to good manners.
contd., Continued.
contg., Containing.
contr., Contract, contracted, contraction; contrary.
conv., Convent; convention, conversation.
Co-Op., Co-operative Society.
Cop., Copernican.
cop., Copper.
C.O.P.E.C., Conference on Politics, Economics and Christianity.
Copt., Coptic.
Cor., (*Bib.*) Corinthians; Cornelia, Cornelius; coroner.
cor., Corpus; correction, corrective; (*Mus.*) cornet; correlative.
Corn., Cornish; Cornwall.
Corn. Nep., Cornelius Nepos.
coroll., Corollary.
Corp., Corporal; Corpus Christi College, Cambridge.
corr., Correspond, correspondence, correspondent, corresponding; corrupt, corrupted, corruption.
Corr. Fel., Mem., Sec., Corresponding Fellow, Member, Secretary.
Cors., Corsica.
cort., Cortex.
C.O.S., Charity Organization Society.
cos, Cosine.
co. sa. [It. *come sopra*], (*Mus.*) As above.
cosec., Cosecant.
cosmog., Cosmography.
Coss. [L. *consules*], Consuls.
cot., Cotangent.
Cott. MSS., Cottonian Manuscripts.
Cox, Coxswain.
C.P., Chief Patriarch; civil power; Clerk of Peace; Code of Procedure; College of Preceptors; Common Pleas; Common Prayer; [L. *Congregatio Passionis*], Passionist Fathers; Court of Probate; Communist Party.
cp., Compare.
c.p., Candle-power.
C.P.C., Clerk of the Privy Council.
Cpl., Corporal.
C.P.M., Common particular metre (of hymns).
C.P.O., (*Nav.*) Chief Petty Officer.
C.P.R., Canadian Pacific Railway.
C.P.R.E., Council for the Preservation of Rural England.
C.P.S., [L. *Custos Privati Sigilli*], Keeper of the Privy Seal.
C.R., Caledonian Railway; [L. *Carolus Rex*], King Charles; [L. *Civis Romanus*], Roman Citizen; [L. *Custos Rotulorum*], Keeper of the Rolls.
Cr, (*Chem.*) Chromium.
Cr., Credit, creditor; Crown.
cr., Created; crown (size of paper).
C.R.A. (Officer) Commanding Royal Artillery.
craniol., Craniology.
craniom., Craniometry.
C.R.E. (Officer) Commanding Royal Engineers.
cresc., Crescendo.
crim. con., (*Law*) Criminal conversion (adultery).
crit., Critic, critical, criticized.
C.R.P. [L. *Calendarium Rotulorum Patentium*], Calendar of the Patent Rolls.
crystal., Crystallography.
C.S., Civil Service; Civil Servant; Clerk of Session; Clerk to the Signet; Common Serjeant; Court of Session; [L. *Custos Sigilli*], Keeper of the Seal.
Cs, (*Chem.*) Cæsium.
cs. [L. *communis*], Common.
C.S.A., Confederate States of America.
C.S.C., Conspicuous Service Cross.
C.S.I., Companion of (the Order of) the Star of India.
C.S.M., Company Sergeant-Major.
C.S.N., Confederate States Navy.
C.S.O., Chief Signal Officer; Chief Staff Officer.
C.Ss.R. [L. *Congregatio Sanctissimi Redemptoris*], Redemptorist Fathers.
C.T., Certificated Teacher.
Ct., Count; Court.
ct., Cent.
C.T.C., Cyclists' Touring Club.
ctge., Cartage.
C. Theod. [L. *Codex Theodosianus*], The Theodosian Code.
ctl., Cental.
cto., (*Mus.*) Concerto.
cts., Centimes, cents.
Ctss., Countess.
Cu [L. *cuprium*], (*Chem.*) Copper.
C.U., Cambridge University.
C.U.A.C., Cambridge University Athletic Club.
C.U.A.F.C., Cambridge University Association Football Club.
cub., Cubic.
C.U.B.C., Cambridge University Boat Club.
C.U.C.C., Cambridge University Cricket Club.
C.U.D.C., Cambridge University Dramatic Society.
C.U.G.C., Cambridge University Golf Club.
C.U.H.C., Cambridge University Hockey Club.
cuj. [L. *cujus*], Of which.
cujusl. [L. *cujuslibet*], Of any.
C.U.L.C., Cambridge University Lacrosse Club.
C.U.L.T.C., Cambridge University Lawn Tennis Club.
C.U.M., Cambridge University Mission.

Cumb., Cumberland.
cum. div. [C.D.], With dividend.
C.U.M.S., Cambridge University Musical Society.
C.U.P., Cambridge University Press.
cur., Currency, current.
C.U.R.F.C., Cambridge University Rugby Football Club.
C.V., (*Bib.*) Common Version.
C.V.O., Commander of (the Royal) Victorian Order.
C.W., Canada West.
C.W.B., Central Welsh Board (Education).
c.w.o., Cash with order.
C.W.S., Co-operative Wholesale Society.
cwt., Hundredweight.
cyc., Cyclopædia, cyclopædic.
Cym., Cymric.

D., Deacon; (*Polit.*) democrat, democratic; [L. *Deus*], God; doctor; [L. *Dominus*], Lord; Duke; 500.
d., Dale; daughter; day; dead, died; deceased; degree; [L. *denarius*], penny; deserted, deserter; diopter; dollar; dose; drama; dorsal; (*Naut.*) drizzling.
ð [L. *deleatur*], Delete.
Da. Danish.
D.A.A.G., Deputy-Assistant-Adjutant-General.
D.A.B., Dictionary of American Biography.
D.A.G., Deputy-Adjutant-General.
dag., decagram.
Da., Dakota.
dal., decalitre.
Dan., Daniel, Danish.
D.A.Q.M.G., Deputy-Assistant-Quartermaster-General.
D.A.R., (*U.S.A.*) Daughters of the American Revolution.
dat., Dative.
dau., Daughter.
Dav., David.
D.B., Domesday Book.
d.b., Day-book.
D.B.E., Dame Commander of (the Order of) the British Empire.
dbk., Drawback.
D.B.S.T., Double British Summer Time.
DC, 600.
DC., (*Bot.*) de Candolle.
D.C., Deputy-Consul; District Court; District of Columbia; [It. *da capo*], (*Mus.*) repeat; Direct Current.
D.C.L., Doctor of Civil Law.
D.C.L.I., Duke of Cornwall's Light Infantry.
D.C.M., Distinguished Conduct Medal; District Court Martial.
D.Cn.L., Doctor of Canon Law.
D.C.S., Deputy Clerk of Session.
D.D. [L. *Divinitatis Doctor*], Doctor of Divinity.
D.d. [L. *Deo dedit*], Gave to God.
dd., Delivered.
d.d., Days after date (bills of exchange); [L. *dono dedit*], gave as a gift.
D.D.D. [L. *dat, dicat, dedicat*], He gives, devotes, and dedicates; [L. *dono dedit dedicavit*], He gave and consecrated as a gift.
D.D.S., Doctor of Dental Surgery.
D.D.T., Insecticide Dichlorodiphenyltrichloroethane.
deb., Debenture; debutante.
Dec., December.
dec., Declaration; declension; declination; decoration, decorative; deceased.
de d. in d., From day to day; continuously.
def., Defendant; defined, definite, definition.
deg., Degree.
Del., Delaware.
del., Delegate; [L. *delineavit*], he (or she) drew it.
dele. [L. *deleatur*], Omit, ð.
Dem., Democrat, Democratic; (*Paper*) demy.
demob., Demobilization.
demon., Demonstrative.
Demos., Demosthenes.
Den., Denmark.
dent., Dental, dentist, dentistry.
dep., Departs; deposed; deputy.
dép. [F. *département*], Department, province; [F. *député*], deputy.
der., **deriv.**, Derivative, derived, derivation.
dept., Department.
Det., Detective.
Deut., Deuteronomy.
Devon., Devonshire, Devonian.
D.F., Dean of Faculty; [F.D.].
D.F.C., Distinguished Flying Cross.
D.F.M., Distinguished Flying Medal.
D.F.M.S., Domestic and Foreign Missionary Society.
dft., Defendant; draft.
D.G., Director-General; Dragoon Guards; [L. *Dei gratia*], by the grace of God; [L. *Deo gratias*], thanks to God.
dg., Decigram.
d.h. [G. *das heisst*], That is to say.
D.H.A., Department of Home Affairs (Scottish Office).
D.Hy., Doctor of Hygiene.
D.I., District Inspector.
Di, (*Chem.*) Didymium.
d.i. [G. *das ist*], That is.
dial., Dialect, dialectal, dialectic, dialectical; dialogue.
diam., Diameter.
dict., Dictator; dictionary.
dif., Differ, difference.
dim. [L. *dimidius*], One half; diminutive; (*Mus.*) diminuendo.
D.Ing., Doctor of Engineering (U.S.A.).
dioc., Diocesan, diocese.
dipl., Diploma, diplomat, diplomatic, diplomatist.
dis., discipline; discount; distribute, distributed (of type).
disc., Discovered, discoverer.
disp., Dispensary.
diss., Dissertation.
dist., Distance; distinguish, distinguished; district.
disy., Dissyllable.
div., Divide, divided; dividend; divine; division, divisor; divers, diverse.
divde. [F. *dividende*], Dividend.
D.L., Deputy-Lieutenant.
D.L.I., Durham Light Infantry.
D.Lit., Doctor of Literature.
D.Litt., Doctor of Letters [cp. LITT.D.].
D.L.O., Dead Letter Office (Returned Letter Office).
D.M., Deputy Master; Doctor of Medicine (Oxford); [It. *destra mano*], (*Mus.*) with the right hand.
D.M.D., Doctor of Dental Medicine.
D.M.I., Director of Military Intelligence.
D.Mus., Doctor of Music.
D.N. [L. *Dominus noster*], Our Lord.
D.N.B., Dictionary of National Biography.
D.N.P.P. [L. *Dominus noster papa pontifex*], Our Lord the Pope.
do., Ditto, the same.
doc., Doctor; document.
dol., Dollar, dollars.
D.O.M. [*Deo optimo maximo*], To God the best and greatest; [*Domino omnium magister*], The Lord master of all, motto of the Benedictines.
dom., Domestic; dominion.
Dom. Proc. [L. *Domus procerum*], (*Law*) The House of Lords.
Dor., Doric.
D.O.R.A., Defence of the Realm Act.
Dors., Dorsetshire.
dow., Dowager.
D.O.W.B., Department of Works and Buildings.
doz., Dozen.
D.P. [DOM. PROC.]; Displaced Persons.
D.P.H., Department of, *or* Diploma in, Public Health.
D.Ph., Doctor of Philosophy.
D.P.O., Distributing Post Office.
D.R. (*Naut.*), Dead reckoning; District Railway; district registry.
Dr., Debtor; Doctor.
dr., Drachma, dram; drawer.
dram. pers., Dramatis personæ, characters of the play.
d.s., Days after sight, day's sight.
D.S.C., Distinguished Service Cross.
D.Sc., Doctor of Science.
D.S.I.R., Department of Scientific and Industrial Research.
D.S.M., Distinguished Service Medal.
D.S.O., Distinguished Service Order.
d.s.p. [L. *decessit sine prole*], Died without issue.
D.S.Sc., Diploma in Sanitary Science.
d.t., Delirium tremens.
D.S.T., Double Summer Time.
D.Th., Doctor of Theology.
D.T.M., Diploma in Tropical Medicine.
dub. [L. *dubitante*], Doubting [L. *dubius*], dubious.
Dubl., Dublin.
Dunelm. [L. *Dunelmensis*], Of Durham (signature of the Bishop of Durham).
Dur., Durham.
Dut., Dutch.
D.V. [L. *Deo volente*], God willing.
d.v.p. [L. *decessit vita patris*], Died during his (or her) father's life.
dwt. [L. *denarius*], Pennyweight, 24 grains troy.
dyn., Dynamics.
D.Z., Doctor of Zoology.

E, (*Chem.*) Erbium.
E., Earl; east; Eastern (London postal district); Edward; second-class merchant ship at Lloyd's; engineer, engineering; English.
e., Eccentricity of eclipse; coefficient of elasticity; electromotive force of cell.
ea., Each.
E. & O.E., Errors and omissions excepted.

E.B., Encyclopædia Britannica.
Eben., Ebenezer.
Ebor. [L. *Eboracum*], York; [L. *Eboracensis*], of York (signature of the Archbishop of York).
E.b.S., East-by-South.
E.C., Eastern Central (London postal district); Established Church.
Eccles., Ecclesiastes, ecclesiastical, ecclesiology.
Ecclus., Ecclesiasticus.
Ecl., Eclogues.
E.C.M., European Common Market.
E.C.O., European Coal Organization.
econ., Economical, economics, economy, economist.
E.C.U., English Church Union.
Ecua., Ecuador.
E.D., Efficiency Decoration.
E.D.C., European Defence Community.
ed., Edition, editor.
Edin., Edinburgh.
edit., Edited, edition.
Edm., Edmund.
E.D.S., English Dialect Society.
eds., Editors, editions.
educ., Educated.
E.E., Early English; errors excepted.
E.E. & M.P., Envoy Extraordinary and Minister Plenipotentiary.
E.E.C., European Economic Community.
E.E.T.S., Early English Text Society.
E.F.T.A., European Free Trade Association.
e.g. [L. *exempli gratia*], For example.
E.G.M., Empire Gallantry Medal.
Egyptol., Egyptologist, Egyptology.
E.H.P., Electrical horse-power.
E.I., East India, East Indian; East Indies.
E.I.C., East India Company.
ejusd. [L. *ejusden*], Of the same.
elec., Electrical, electricity; electuary.
elem., Elementary.
Eliz., Elizabeth.
ellipt., Elliptical, elliptically.
Elz., Elzevir.
E.M., Earl Marshal; [L. *Equitum Magister*], Master of the Horse; Edward Medal.
Em., Emmanuel; Emily; Emma.
embry., Embryology.
E.M.D.P., Electromotive difference of potential.
E.M.F., Electromotive force.
E.M.K. [G. *Elektromotorische Kraft*], Electromotive force.
Emm., Emmanuel College, Cambridge.
Emp., Emperor, Empire, Empress.
ency., Encyclopædia, encyclopædian, encyclopædic, encyclopædist, etc.
E.N.E., East-north-east.
Eng., England, English.
eng., Engineer, engineering; engraved, engraver, engraving.
E.N.S.A., Entertainments National Service Association.
entom., Entomology.
Ent. Sta. Hall, Entered at Stationers' Hall.
Env. Extr., Envoy extraordinary.
Ep., Epistle.
E.P.D., Excess Profits Duty.
Eph., Ephesians; Ephraim.
Epiph., Epiphany.
episc., Episcopal.
E.P.T., Excess Profits Tax.
E.P.U., European Payments Union.
Eq., Equator, equatorial.
equiv., Equivalent.
Er., (*Chem.*) Erbium.
E.R., East Riding (of Yorkshire); Elizabeth Regina; [L. *Eduardus Rex*], King Edward.
E.R.A., Engine-room artificer.
E.R. et I. [L. *Eduardus Rex et Imperator*], Edward, King and Emperor.
Erasm., Erasmus.
E.R.D., Emergency Reserve Decoration.
E.R.P., European Recovery Plan.
erron., Erroneous, erroneously.
E.R.U., English Rugby Union.
eschat., Eschatology, eschatological.
E.S.E., East-south-east.
esp., Especially.
Esq., Esquire.
ess., Essence, essences.
est., Established; estimated.
Esth., Esther.
E.T., Electric telegraph; English translation.
et al. [L. *et alibi*], And elsewhere.
E.T.C., Eastern Telegraph Company.
etc. [L. *et cetera*], And the rest.
ethno., **ethnol.**, Ethnology.
et seq. [L. *et sequens*], (*pl.*) ***et sqq.*** [*et sequentes* or *sequentia*], And the following.
E.T.U., Electrical Trades Union.
etym., Etymological, etymologically, etymologist, etymology.
E.U., Evangelical Union.
Euc., Euclid.
E.U.P., English Universities Press.
euphem., Euphemism, euphemistic, euphemistical.
Eur., Europe, European.
Eurip., (*Lit.*) Euripides.
Evang., Evangelical, evangelist.
Ex. [EXOD].
ex., Examined; example; exchanged; executed, executive.
Exc., Excellency.
exc., Excellent; except, excepted, exception.
Exch., Exchange; Exchequer.
excl., **exclam.**, Exclamation, exclamatory.
ex div., Without next dividend.
ex. gr. [L. *exempli gratia*], For example.
ex int., Without next interest.
Exod., Exodus.
Exon. [L. *Exoniensis*], Of Exeter (signature of the Bishop of Exeter).
exor., Executor.
exp., Export, exportation, exported; expression.
exrx., Executrix.
ext., External, externally; extinct; extract.
Ez., Ezra.
Ezek., Ezekiel.

F., (*Chem.*) Fluorine.
F., Fahrenheit; (*R.-C. Ch.*) Father; (*Univ.*) Fellow; felon; (*Naut.*) fog; folio; formula, formulæ; French; Friday.
f., Farthing; fathom; feet; fem.; francs; furlongs; [L. *forte*], (*Mus.*) loud.
F.A., Football Association.
F.A.A., Fleet Air Arm.
f.a.a., (*Marine Insurance*) Free of all average.
fac., **facs.**, Facsimile.
F.A.C.S., Fellow of the American College of Surgeons.
Fahr., Fahrenheit.
F.A.I., Fellow of the Auctioneers' Institute.
F.A.M., Free and Accepted Mason.
fam., Familiar, familiarly; family.
F.A.N.Y., First Aid Nursing Yeomanry.
F.A.O., Food and Agriculture Organization (of United Nations).
far., Farad, faradaic; farriery; farthing.
F.A.S., Fellow of the Anthropological Society.
f.a.s., Free alongside ship.
fasc. [L. *fasciculus*, bundle], A single part or number (of serial publication).
F.A.S.E., Fellow of the Antiquarian Society, Edinburgh.
F.A.U., Friends' Ambulance Unit.
F.B., Fenian Brothers; Free Baptist.
F.B.A., Fellow of the British Academy; Fellow of the British Association.
F.B.A.A., Fellow of the British Association of Accountants and Auditors.
F.B.I., Federation of British Industries; Federal Bureau of Investigation (U.S.A.).
F.B.O.A., Fellow of the British Optical Association.
F.B.S., Fellow of the Botanical Society.
F.B.S.E., Fellow of the Botanical Society of Edinburgh.
F.C., Football Club; Free Church of Scotland.
f.c. [L. *fidei-commissum*], Bequeathed in trust.
F.C.A., Fellow of the Institute of Chartered Accountants.
fcap., Foolscap.
F.C.C., First Class Certificate; (*U.S.A.*) Federal Communications Commission.
F.C.C.S., Fellow of the Corporation of Certified Secretaries.
F.C.I., Fellow of the Institute of Commerce.
F.C.I.S., Fellow of the Chartered Institute of Secretaries.
f.co., Fair copy.
F.C.P., Fellow of the College of Preceptors.
fcp., Foolscap.
F.C.S., Fellow of the Chemical Society.
F.D. [L. *fidei defensor*], Defender of the faith.
Fe [L. *ferrum*], (*Chem.*) Iron.
Feb., February.
fec. [L. *fecit*], He (or she) made it.
Fed., Federalist, federation.
F.E.I.S., Fellow of the Educational Institute of Scotland.
fem., Feminine.
F.E.S., Fellow of the Entomological Society; Fellow of the Ethnological Society.
feud., Feudal.
F.F., (*Naut.*) thick fog.
ff. [L. *fecerunt*], They made it; folios; following pages, following.
ff. [It. *fortissimo*], (*Mus.*) Louder than forte, very loud.
F.F.A., Fellow of the Faculty of Actuaries.

F.F.A.S., Fellow of the Faculty of Architects and Surveyors.
fff. [It. *fortississimo*], (*Mus.*) As loud as possible.
F.F.P.S., Fellow of the Faculty of Physicians and Surgeons.
F.F.P.S.G., Fellow of the Faculty of Physicians and Surgeons, Glasgow.
F.G., Foot Guards.
f.g., (*Leather*) fine grain; (*Paper*) friction glazed.
f.g.a., Free of general average.
F.G.O., Fellow of the Guild of Organists.
F.G.S., Fellow of the Geological Society.
F.H., Fire hydrant.
F.I.A., Fellow of the Institute of Actuaries.
F.I.A.T. [It. *Fabbrica Italiana Automobile, Torino*], The Italian Automobile Factory, Turin.
F.I.C.A., Fellow of the Institute of Chartered Accountants.
fict. [L. *fictilis*], Made of pottery.
F.I.D., Field Intelligence Department.
Fid. Def. [L. *fidei defensor*], Defender of the Faith.
F.I.D.O., Fog Investigation Dispersal Operation.
fi. fa. [L. *fieri facias*, That you cause it to be done]. A writ.
fig., Figurative, figure.
F.I.H., Fellow of the Institute of Hygiene.
F.I.M., Fellow of the Institution of Metallurgists.
F.I.Inst., Fellow of the Imperial Institute.
Fin., Finland, Finnish.
fin. [L. *ad finem*], At the end.
Fin. Sec., Financial Secretary.
F.Inst.P., Fellow of the Institute of Physics.
F.I.S.A., Fellow of the Incorporated Secretaries Association.
fir., Firkin, firkins.
F.J.I., Fellow of the Institute of Journalists.
Fl., Flanders, Flemish.
fl., Florin; [L. *flores*], flowers; [L. *floruit*], flourished; fluid.
f.l. [L. *falsa lectio*], A false reading.
Fla., Florida.
F.L.A., Fellow of the Library Association.
F.L.A.A., Fellow of the London Association of Certified Accountants.
Flem., Flemish [FL.].
flor. [L. *floruit*], He (or she) flourished.
F.L.S., Fellow of the Linnean Society.
F.M., Field Marshal; Foreign Mission.
fm., Fathom.
F.M.D., Foot-and-mouth disease.
F.O., Field Officer; Foreign Office; Flying Officer.
fo., Folio.
f.o.b., Free on board.
fol., foll., Following.
for., Foreign.
f.o.r., Free on rail.
fort., Fortification, fortified.
F.P., Fine paper (edition of books); fire-plug; field punishment.
f.p., Foot-pound.
fp. [It. *forte piano*], (*Mus.*) Loud and soft.
f.p.a., Free of particular average.
f.p.c., For private circulation.
F.P.S., Fellow of the Philosophical Society; Fellow of the Philharmonic Society; Fellow of the Philological Society.
F.Phys.S., Fellow of the Physical Society.
F.R. [L. *Forum Romanum*], The Forum.
Fr., France, French; [G. *Frau*), Mrs., wife; Friar; Father (priest); Friday; [It. *Fratelli*], Brothers.
fr., Franc; [G. *frei*], free; from.
F.R.Ae.S., Fellow of the Royal Aeronautical Society.
F.R.A.I., Fellow of the Royal Anthropological Institute.
F.R.A.M., Fellow of the Royal Academy of Music.
Fras., Francis.
F.R.A.S., Fellow of the Royal Astronomical Society; Fellow of the Royal Asiatic Society.
F.R.B.S., Fellow of the Royal Botanic Society.
F.R.C.I., Fellow of the Royal Colonial Institute.
F.R.C.M., Fellow of the Royal College of Music.
F.R.C.O., Fellow of the Royal College of Organists.
F.R.C.O.G., Fellow of the Royal College of Obstetricians and Gynaecologists.
F.R.C.P., Fellow of the Royal College of Physicians.
F.R.C.P.E., Fellow of the Royal college of Physicians, Edinburgh.
F.R.C.P.I., Fellow of the Royal College of Physicians, Ireland.
F.R.C.S., Fellow of the Royal College of Surgeons.
F.R.C.S.E., Fellow of the Royal College of Surgeons, Edinburgh.
F.R.C.S.I., Fellow of the Royal College of Surgeons, Ireland.
F.R.C.S.L., Fellow of the Royal College of Surgeons, London.
F.R.C.V.S., Fellow of the Royal College of Veterinary Surgeons.
F.R.Econ.S., Fellow of the Royal Economic Society.
Fred., Frederic, Frederick.
freq., Frequent, frequently, frequentative.
F.R.G.S., Fellow of the Royal Geographical Society.
F.R.H.S., Fellow of the Royal Horticultural Society.
F.R.Hist.S., Fellow of the Royal Historical Society.
Frhr. [G. *Freiherr*], Baron.
Fri., Friday.
F.R.I.B.A., Fellow of the Royal Institute of British Architects.
F.R.I.C., Fellow of the Royal Institute of Chemistry.
Fris., Frisia, Frisian.
Frl. [G. *Fräulein*], Miss.
F.R.Met.Soc., Fellow of the Royal Meteorological Society.
F.R.M.S., Fellow of the Royal Microscopical Society.
front., frontis., Frontispiece.
F.R.P.S., Fellow of the Royal Photographic Society.
F.R.S., Fellow of the Royal Society.
frs., Francs.
F.R.S.A., Fellow of the Royal Society of Arts.
F.R.S.A.I., Fellow of the Royal Society of Antiquaries of Ireland.
F.R.San.I., Fellow of the Royal Sanitary Institute.
F.R.S.C., Fellow of the Royal Society of Canada.
F.R.S.E., Fellow of the Royal Society of Edinburgh.
F.R.S.G.S., Fellow of the Royal Scottish Geographical Society.
F.R.S.L., Fellow of the Royal Society of Literature.
F.R.S.S., Fellow of the Royal Statistical Society.
F.R.S.S.A., Fellow of the Royal Scottish Society of Arts.
F.R.S.S.S., Fellow of the Royal Statistical Society of Scotland.
F.S., Fleet Surgeon.
f.s. [F. *faire suivre*], To be forwarded.
F.S.A., Fellow of the Society of Antiquaries.
F.S.A.Scot., Fellow of the Society of Antiquaries of Scotland.
F.S.E., Fellow of the Society of Engineers.
F.S.I., Fellow of the Sanitary Institute; Fellow of the Surveyors' Institute.
F.S.S. [F.R.S.S.].
F.S.S.I., Fellow of the Statistical Society of Ireland.
F.T., Free Trade, Free-trader.
Ft., Fort.
ft., Faint; (*Paper*) flat; foot, feet; fortified.
F.T.C.D., Fellow of Trinity College, Dublin.
F.T.I., Fellow of the Textile Institute.
fur., Furlong.
fut., Future.
F.U.W., Federation of University Women.
f.v. [L. *folio verso*], On the back of the page.
F.W.A., Factories and Workshops Acts.
F.W.B., Free Will Baptists.
F.Z.S., Fellow of the Zoological Society.

G., German, Germany; grand; gulf; (*Nav.*) gunnery.
g., Acceleration of gravity.
g. [F. *gauche*], Left; genitive; guinea, guineas; (*Naut.*) gloomy; gram; [F. *gros*, fem. *-se*], big.
G.A., (*Insce.*) General average; General Assembly; Golfing Association.
Ga, (*Chem.*) Gallium.
Ga., Gallic; Georgia.
Gabr., Gabriel.
Gael., Gaelic.
Gal., Galatians.
gal., Gallon, gallons.
galv., Galvanic, galvanism.
G.A.T.T., General Agreement on Tariffs and Trade.
Gaz., Gazette, gazetteer.
G.B., Great Britain.
G.B. & N.I., Great Britain and Northern Ireland.
G.B.E., Knight (*or* Dame) Grand Cross of (the Order of) the British Empire.
G.B.S., George Bernard Shaw.
G.C., George Cross; Gentleman Cadet; Golf Club; Grand Chancellor; Grand Chapter; Grand Conductor.
G.C.B., Knight Grand Cross of (the Order of) the Bath.
G.C.C., Gonville and Caius College, Cambridge.
G.C.E., General Certificate of Education. (O. Ordinary, A, Advanced, S, Scholarship).
g.c.f., (*Math.*) Greatest common factor.

g.c.m., (*Math.*) Greatest common measure.
G.C.M.G., Knight Grand Cross of St. Michael and St. George.
G.C.S.I., Knight Grand Commander of the Star of India.
G.C.V.O., Knight Grand Cross of the (Royal) Victorian Order.
G.D., Grand Duke; Grand Duchess; Grand Duchy.
Gdns., Gardens.
Gds., Guards regiments.
Ge, (*Chem.*) Germanium.
g.e., (*Bookbinding*) Gilt edges.
Gell., Gellius.
Gen., General; Genesis; Geneva.
gen., Gender; general, generally; generic; genitive; genus.
geneal., Genealogy.
gent., Gentleman.
gen. t., General title.
Geo., George.
geod., Geodesy.
Geoff., Geoffrey.
geog., Geographer, geographical, geography.
geol., Geological, geologist, geology.
geom., Geometer, geometrical, geometry.
Ger., German, Germany.
ger., Gerund, gerundive.
Ges. [G. *Gesellschaft*], A limited company or society.
G.F.S., Girls' Friendly Society.
G.G., Grenadier Guards.
g.gr., Great gross (144 dozen).
G.H.Q., General Headquarters.
G.I., Government Issue; (*U.S.A.*) private soldier.
Gib., Gibraltar.
Giov., Giovanni.
G.J.C., Grand Junction Canal.
Gk., Greek.
Gl, (*Chem.*) Glucinum.
Glam., Glamorganshire.
Glos., Gloucester, Gloucestershire.
G.M., George Medal; General Manager; Gold Medallist (Bisley); Grand Master.
gr., Gram.
G.M.B., Good Merchantable Brand.
G.M.C., General Medical Council.
G.M.I.E., Grand Master of (the Order of) the Indian Empire.
G.M.K.P., Grand Master of the Knights of St. Patrick.
G.M.M.G., Grand Master of (the Order of) St. Michael and St. George.
G.M.S.I., Grand Master of (the Order of) the Star of India.
G.M.T., Greenwich Mean Time.
G.O., General order; (*Mus.*) grand organ.
G.O.C., General Officer Commanding.
G.O.M., Grand Old Man (W. E. Gladstone).
Goth., Gothic.
Gött., Göttingen.
Gottf., Gottfried.
Gottl., Gottlieb.
gov., Governor, government.
Gov.-Gen., Governor-General.
G.P., (*Med.*) General paralysis; general practitioner; Graduate in Pharmacy; [L. *Gloria Patri*], Glory to the Father.
gp., Group.
g.p., (*Print.*) Great primer.
G.P.I., General paralysis of the insane.
G.P.O., General Post Office.
G.P.R. [L. *Genio Populi Romani*], To the genius of the Roman people.
G.Q.C., Grand Quartier Général, G.H.Q. of the French army.
G.R. [L. *Georgius Rex*], King George; Grand Recorder; General Reserve; Grand Registrar; [L. *Gulielmus Rex*], King William.
Gr., Grand; (*Bot.*) Asa Gray; (*Ent.*) J. L. K. Granenhorst; Greece, Grecian, Greek.
gr., Grain, grains; gram, grams; Groschen.
gram., Grammar, grammarian, grammatical.
Greg., Gregory.
grm., Gramme, grammes.
gro., Gross.
G.S., General Secretary; Golfing Society; General Staff.
g.s., Grandson.
G.S.N., General Steam Navigation.
G.S.O., General Staff Officer.
gt., Gilt; great; (*Pharm.*) [L. *gutta*], drop.
g.t., (*Bookbinding*) Gilt top.
Gt. Br. [G.B.], Great Britain.
guar., Guarantee, guarantor.
gun., Gunnery.
Gustav., Gustavus.
G.W.R., Great Western Railway.
gymn., Gymnastics, gymnasium.

H, (*Chem.*) Hydrogen.
H., (*Naut.*) Harbour, hoy; hydrant; hard (of pencils); (*Mech.*) total energy.
h., (*Naut.*) Hail; (*Min.*) hardness; height; hour, hours; hundred; husband.
H.A., Horse-artillery; Hockey Association.
h.a. [L. *hoc anno*], This year; [L. *hujus anni*], this year's.
Hab., Habakkuk.
hab., Habitat.
hab. corp. [L. *habeas corpus*, you may have the body], A writ.
H.A.C., Honourable Artillery Company.
Hag., Haggai.
H. & B., (*Bot.*) Humboldt and Bonpland.
h. & c., Hot and cold (water).
Hants., Hampshire.
H. app., Heir apparent.
Har., Harold.
Harl. MSS., Harleian Manuscripts.
Harv., Harvard [H.U.].
HB, Hard and black (of pencils).
H.B. & K., (*Bot.*) Humboldt, Bonplant and Kunth.
H.B.C., Hudson Bay Company.
H.B.M., Her (or His) Britannic Majesty.
H.C., Habitual criminal; Heralds' College; High Church, High Churchman; House of Commons; House of Correction; Hunterian Club.
h.c.f., (*Math.*) Highest common factor.
H.C.M., Her (or His) Catholic Majesty.
H.Comm., High Commissioner.
hdbk., Handbook.
hdkf., Handkerchief.
hdqrs., Headquarters.
H.E., His Eminence; His Excellency.
He, (*Chem.*) Helium.
h.e., High explosive.
Heb., Hebrew, Hebrews.
hectog., Hectogram.
hectol., Hectolitre.
H.E.I.C., Honourable East India Company.
Hel., Helvetia (Switzerland).
her., Herald, heraldry.
her. [L. *heres*], Heir.
Herod., Herodotus.
herp., Herpetology.
Herts., Hertfordshire.
H.F., Home Forces; high frequency.
hf., half.
hf.-bd., (*Bookbinding*) Half-bound.
hf.-cf., Half-calf.
hf.-cl., Half-cloth.
hf.-mor., Half-morocco.
hf.-vel., Half-vellum.
Hft. [G. *Heft*], Number, part.
Hg. [L. *hydrargyrum*], (*Chem.*) Mercury.
H.G., Her (or His) Grace; Horse Guards; Home Guard; Holy Ghost; High German.
H.G.D.H., Her (or His) Grand Ducal Highness.
H.H., Her (or His) Highness; His Holiness (the Pope).
HH, Extra hard (of pencils).
hhd., Hogshead.
HHH, Very hard (of pencils).
H.I. [L. *hic iacet*], Here lies.
Hib., Hibernian.
Hi Fi, (*Radio.*) High Fidelity.
H.I.H., Her (or His) Imperial Highness.
Hil., Hilary.
H.I.M., Her (or His) Imperial Majesty.
Hind., (*Urdu*) Hindu, Hindustan, Hindustani.
Hipp., Hippocrates.
H.I.S. [L. *hic iacet sepultus*], Here lies buried.
hist., Historian, historic, historical, history.
H.K., House of Keys, Isle of Man.
H.L., House of Lords.
hl., **h.l.**, Hectolitre.
H.L.I., Highland Light Infantry.
H.M., Her (or His) Majesty; Home Mission.
Hm., Hectometer; hand-made (of paper); (*Hymns*) Hallelujah metre; Head Master; Head Mistress.
h.m. [L. *hoc mense*], This month; [L. *hujus mensis*], of this month.
H.M.A.S., Her (His) Majesty's Australian Ship.
H.M.C., Her (His) Majesty's Customs; Head Masters' Conference.
H.M.C.S., Her (His) Majesty's Canadian Ship.
H.M.F., Her (His) Majesty's Forces.
H.M.I., Her (His) Majesty's Inspector.
H.M.O.W., Her (His) Majesty's Office of Works.
H.M.P. [L. *hoc monumentum posuit*], He erected this monument.
H.M.S. Her (His) Majesty's Service; Her (His) Majesty's Ship.
H.M.S.O., Her (His) Majesty's Stationery Office.
H.M.T., Her (His) Majesty's Trawler.
H.O., The Home Office.
ho., house.
holl. [F. *hollandais*, fem. *-daise*] Dutch.
Hom., Homer.
Hon., Honourable, Honorary.
hon. [F. *honoré*], Honoured.

Hor., Horace.
hor., Horizon.
horol., Horology.
hort., Horticultural, horticulture.
Hos., Hosea.
hosp., Hospital.
how., Howitzer.
H.P., Half-pay; high-pressure; high-priest; house-physician; hot-pressed (of paper); hire purchase.
h.p., Horse-power.
h.p.n., Horse-power nominal.
H.pres., Heir presumptive.
H.Q., Headquarters.
h.q. [L. *hoc quære*], Look for this.
H.R., Home Rule; House of Representatives.
Hr. [G. *Herr*], Mr., Sir.
H.R.H., His (or Her) Royal Highness.
H.S., Honorary Secretary; Home Secretary; house-surgeon; [L. *his sepultus* or *situs*], here is buried; [L. *hoc sensu*], in this sense.
Hs. [G. *Handschrift*], Manuscript.
H.S.H., His (or Her) Serene Highness.
H.S.M., His (or Her) Serene Majesty.
h.t., (*Elec.*) High tension; [L. *hoc tempore*], at this time; [L. *hoc titulo*], under this title.
H.U., Harvard University.
Hum. [L. *humaniora*], The humanities.
Hun., Hungarian, Hungary.
Hunts., Huntingdonshire.
h.w., (*Cricket*) Hit wicket.
H.W.M., High-water mark.
Hy., Henry.
Hyb., Hybrid.
hyd., Hydrostatics.
hypoth., Hypothesis, hypothetical.

I, (*Chem.*) Iodine; (*Elec.*) moment of inertia.
I. [L. *Imperator*], Emperor; Intelligence (Army); [L. *Imperatrix*], Empress; Idaho; [G. *Ihr*], your; Ireland; island.
i. [L. *id*], That.
I.A., Infected area; Indian Army.
Ia., Iowa.
I.A.A.A., Irish Amateur Athletic Association.
I.A.H.M., Incorporated Association of Head Masters.
ib., ibid. [L. *ibidem*], In the same place.
I. C. [L. *Iesus Christus*], Jesus Christ.
i/c., In charge.
I.C.A., Irish Cyclists' Association.
I.C.A.O., International Civil Aviation Organization.
I.C.B.M., Intercontinental Ballistic Missile.
I.C.C., (*U.S.A.*) Interstate Commerce Commission.
I.C.E., Institute of Civil Engineers.
Icel., Iceland, Icelandic.
ichth., ichthyol., Ichthyology.
I.C.I., Imperial Chemical Industries.
I.C.N. [L. *in Christi nomine*], In the name of Christ.
icon., Iconographic, iconography.
I.C.T. [L. *Iesus Christo tutore*], With Jesus Christ as protector.
I.D., Intelligence Department.
Id., Idaho.
id. [L. *idem*], The same.
I.D.B., (*S. Afr.*) Illicit diamond buyer, *or* buying.
I.D.N. [L. *in Dei nomine*], In God's name.
i.e. [L. *id est*], That is.
I.E.E., Institute of Electrical Engineers.
I.F.C., International Finance Corporation.
I.G., Indo-Germanic; Inspector-General.
ign. [L. *ignotus*], Unknown.
I.G.Y., International Geophysical Year.
i.h. [L. *iacet hic*], Here lies.
i.h.p., Indicated horse-power.
IHS [Gr. *Ies*], Jesus.
Il., Homer's *Iliad.*
Ill., Illinois.
ill. [L. *illustrissimus*], Most distinguished.
illus., Illustrated, illustration.
I.L.O., International Labour Organization (Geneva).
I.L.P., Independent Labour Party.
I.M.F., International Monetary Fund.
Imit., imitation, imitated.
Imm., Immanuel.
I.M.N.S., Imperial Military Nursing Service.
imp., Imperative; imperfect; imperial; impersonal; imported, importer; *imprimatur* (let it be printed).
imper., Imperative.
imperf., Imperfect; imperforate (of stamps).
impers., Impersonal.
Imp. Inst., Imperial Institute.
In, (*Chem.*) Indium.
in., Inch, inches.
I.N.A., Institute of Naval Architects.
inc., Incorporated.
incl., Including, inclusively.
incog., Incognito.
incor., Incorporated.
incr., Increased, increasing.
Ind., India, Indian, Indiana.
ind., Independent; index; indication.
I.N.D. [L. *in nomine Dei*], In the name of God.
indecl., (*Gram.*) Indeclinable.
indic., (*Gram.*) Indicative.
indiv., Individual.
Indo-Eur., Indo-European.
Indo-Ger., Indo-Germanic.
Ind. T., Indian Territory.
in f., In fine, finally.
inf., Infantry; infinitive.
inf. [L. *infra*], Below.
infin., Infinitive.
infra dig. [L. *infra dignitatem*], Beneath one's dignity.
I.N.I. [L. *in nomine Iesu*], In the name of Jesus.
in lim. [L. *in limine*], At the outset.
in loc. [L. *in loco*], In its place.
in pr. [L. *in principio*], in the beginning.
I.N.R.I. [L. *Iesus Nazarenus Rex Iudæorum*], Jesus of Nazareth, King of the Jews.
I.N.S., (*U.S.A.*) International News Service.
Ins., Inspector.
ins., insce., Insurance.
inscr., Inscription.
Ins.-Gen., Inspector-General.
Insp., Inspector.
I.N.S.T. [L. *in nomine Sanctæ Trinitatis*], In the Name of the Holy Trinity.
inst., Institute, institution; instant (of this month).
Inst.Act., Institute of Actuaries.
Inst.C.E., Institution of Civil Engineers.
Inst.E.E., Institution of Electrical Engineers.
Inst.M.E., Institute of Marine Engineers.
Inst.Mech.E., Institution of Mechanical Engineers.
Inst.N.A., Institution of Naval Architects.
instr., Instrument, instrumental.
int., Interest; interior; interjection; interpreter; intransitive.
int. al. [L. *inter alia*], among other things.
intens., Intensive, intensative.
inter., Intermediate; interrogation mark.
interj., Interjection.
internat., International.
interrog., Interrogation, interrogative, interrogatively.
intrans., Intransitive.
in trans., In transit.
introd., Introduction, introductory.
inv. [L. *invenit*], He (or she) designed it; invented, inventor; invoice.
I.O., Intelligence Officer.
I.O.F., Independent Order of Foresters.
I. of A., Instructor of Artillery.
I. of M., Instructor of Musketry; Isle of Man.
I.O.G.T., Independent Order of Good Templars.
Ion., Ionic.
I.O.O.F., Independent Order of Oddfellows.
I.O.P., Institute of Painters in Oil Colours.
I.O.R., Independent Order of Rechabites.
IOU, I owe you.
I.O.W., Isle of Wight.
I.P.D. [L. *in præsentia Dominorum*], (*Sc. Law*) In the presence of the Lords of Session.
ipecac., Ipecacuanha.
i.p.i. [L. *in partibus infidelium*], Among unbelievers.
I.Q., Intelligence Quotient.
i.q. [L. *idem quod*], The same as.
i.q.e.d. [L. *in quod erat demonstrandum*], That which was to be proved.
I.R., Inland Revenue.
Ir, (*Chem.*) Iridium.
Ir., Ireland, Irish.
I.R.A., Irish Republican Army.
I.R.B.M., Intermediate-range Ballistic Missile.
Iran., Iranian, Iranic (Persian).
I.R.C., International Red Cross.
Ire., Ireland.
I.R.O., Inland Revenue Office; International Refugee Organization.
iron., Ironically.
irreg., Irregular, irregularly.
I.S., Irish Society.
Is., Isaiah.
Isl., Island, isle, islands, isles.
I.S.M., Incorporated Society of Musicians; Imperial Service Medal.
I.S.O. (Companion of the) Imperial Service Order.
Isth., Isthmus.
I.T., Indian Territory.
It., Italian, Italy.
I.T.A., Independent Television Authority.

ital., Italics.
I.T.N., Independent Television News.
I.T.O., International Trade Organization.
I.T.U., International Telecommunication Union.
I.W., Isle of Wight.
I.W.T., Inland Water Transport.
I.W.W., International Workers of the World.
I.Y., Imperial Yeomanry.

J., Judge, justice; Jew, Jewish; (*Elec.*) joule.
J., (*Phys.*) Joule's mechanical equivalent of heat.
j. [F. *journal*], Newspaper.
J.A., Judge-Advocate.
J./A., Joint Account.
Jac. [L. *Jacobus*], James.
Jacq., (*Bot.*) Jacquin.
J.A.G., Judge-Advocate-General.
Jam., Jamaica.
Jan., January.
janv. [F. *janvier*], January.
Jap., Japan, Japanese.
Jas., James.
Jav., Javanese.
J.C., Jesus Christ; Julius Cæsar; [L. *Juris-Consultus*], Jurisconsult; Justice-Clerk.
J.C.D. [L. *Juris Civilis Doctor*], Doctor of Civil Law.
J.D., Junior Deacon; Junior Dean; [L. *Jurum Doctor*] Doctor of Laws.
Jer., Jeremiah.
Jes., Jesus.
JHS [IHS].
J.H.U., Johns Hopkins University.
JJ., Justices.
Jn., Junction.
Jno., John.
jnr., Junior.
Jo., Joel.
joc., Jocular, jocose.
Joh., St. John's College, Cambridge.
Jon., Jonathan.
Jos., Joseph.
Joseph., Josephus.
Josh., Joshua.
jour., Journal; journey; journeyman.
J.P., Justice of the Peace.
J.R. [L. *Jacobus Rex*], King James.
jr., Junior [JUN.].
jr. [F. *jour*], Day.
jt., Joint.
jtly., Jointly.
J.U.D. [L. *Juris utriusque Doctor*], Doctor of both Civil and Canon Law.
Jud., Judith.
jud., judicial; ***judicium***; judgment.
Judg., Book of Judges.
Jul., Julius, Julian.
Jun., Junius.
jun., Junior.
junc., Junction.
Jun. Opt., Junior Optime.
jurisp., Jurisprudence.

K, (*Astron.*) The solar constant; [L. *kalium*], (*Chem.*) potassium; (*Elec.*) capacity.
K., King, kings; (*Assaying*) carat.
k., (*Meteor.*) Cumulus.
k, (*Astron.*) Gauss's constant.
kal., Kalends.
Kan., Kansas.
K.B., Knight of the Bath; King's Bench; Knight Bachelor.
K.B.E., Knight Commander of (the Order of) the British Empire.
K.C., King's College; King's Counsel; Kennel Club.
K.C.B., Knight Commander of (the Order of) the Bath.
K.C.I.E., Knight Commander of (the Order of) the Indian Empire.
K.C.L., King's College, London.
K.C.M.G., Knight Commander of (the Order of) St. Michael and St. George.
K.C.S.I., Knight Commander of the Star of India.
K.C.V.O., Knight Commander of the Royal Victorian Order.
Keb. Coll., Keble College, Oxford.
Ken., Kentucky.
K.G., Knight of (the Order of) the Garter.
kg., Kilogramme.
K.G.C., Knight Grand Cross.
kgl. [G. *königlich*], Royal.
K.H.C., Honorary Chaplain to the King.
K.H.P., Honorary Physician to the King.
K.H.S., Honorary Surgeon to the King.
K.i.H., **K.I.H.**, Kaisar-i-Hind Medal.
kil., Kilderkin.
kilo., Kilogram.
K.K.K., Klu-Klux-Klan.
Kl. [G. *Klasse*], Class.
kl., Kilolitre.
km., Kilometre.
K. Mess., King's Messenger.
Knt., Knight.
k.o., (*Boxing*) Knock-out.
K.O.S.B., King's Own Scottish Borderers.
K.O.Y.L.I., King's Own Yorkshire Light Infantry.
K.P., Knight of (the Order of) St. Patrick.
K.P.M., King's Police Medal.
Kr, (*Chem.*) Krypton.
kr., Kreutzer.
K.R.C., Knight of the Red Cross.
K.R.R., King's Royal Rifles.
K.R.R.C., King's Royal Rifle Corps.
K.S., King's scholar.
K.S.I., Knight of the Star of India.
K.T., Knight of the Order of the Thistle; Knight Templar.
Kt., Knight.
Kt. Bach., Knight Bachelor.
κ.τ.λ. [Gr. *kai ta loipa*], And the rest, etc.
kv., Kilovolt.
kw., (*Elec.*) Kilowatt (1,000 watts).
Ky., Kentucky.

L., 50, 50th.
L., Lady; lake; Larin; (*Theat.*) left; [L. *liber*], book; Liberal; licentiate; (*Bot.*) Linnæus; lira, lire; [F. *livre*], pound; [L. *locus*], place; London.
l., League; length; line; link; litre; left; (*Naut.*) lightning.
L.A., Law Agent; Legislative Assembly; local Authority.
£A., Australian pound (16s.).
La, (*Chem.*) Lanthanum.
La., Louisiana.
l/a [F. *lettre d'avis*], Letter of advice.
Lab., (*Polit.*) Labour; Labrador; laboratory.
Lab.M., Labour Member (of Parliament).
L.A.C., Licentiate of the Apothecaries' Company; London Athletic Club.
L.A.H., Licentiate of Apothecaries' Hall (Ireland).
L.A.M. [L. *Liberalium Artium Magister*], Master of the Liberal Arts; London Academy of Music.
Lam., Lamentations; (*Bot.*) Lamarck.
Lancs, Lancashire.
lang., Language.
Lap., Lapland.
Lapp., Lappish.
L.A.S., Lord-Advocate of Scotland.
Lat., Latin.
lat., Latitude.
L.B. [L. *Litterarum Baccalaureus*], Bachelor of Letters; Local Board.
lb. [L. *libra, -bræ*], Pound, pounds.
l.b., (*Cricket*) Leg-bye.
L.B.H., Local Board of Health.
l.b.w., (*Cricket*) Leg before wicket.
L.C., Letter of credit; Lord Chamberlain; Lord Chancellor; Lower Canada.
l.c. [L. *loco citato*], In the place cited; lower case (of type).
L.C.C., London County Council, *or* Councillor.
L.Ch., **L.Chir.**, Licentiate in Surgery.
L.C.J., Lord Chief Justice.
l.c.m., Least common multiple.
L.C.P., Licentiate of the College of Preceptors.
L.Cpl., Lance-corporal.
l/cr., Letter of credit.
L.D., Light Dragoons; Low Dutch; (*Am.*) Doctor of Letters.
Ld., Lord.
l.d. [L. *litera dominicalis*], Dominical letter.
Ldg., (*Nav.*) Leading.
L.Div., Licentiate in Divinity.
Ldp., Lordship.
L.D.S., Licentiate in Dental Surgery.
L.D.Sc., Licentiate in Dental Science.
L.D.V., Local Defence Volunteers.
£E., Egyptian pounds (1 : 0 : 6½).
L.E.A., Local Education Authority.
lect., Lecture.
Leg., Legislative, legislature.
leg., Legal; [It. *legato*], (*Mus.*) in a smooth and connected manner; [L. *legit*], he (or she) reads; [L. *legunt*], they read.
Leics., Leicestershire.
Lev., Leviticus.
lex., Lexicon.
lexicog., Lexicographer, lexicographical, lexicography.
Leyd., Leyden.
L.F., Low Frequency.
L.F.B., London Fire Brigade.
L.F.P.S., Licentiate of the Royal Faculty of Physicians and Surgeons.
L.G., (*Comm.*) Large grain; Life Guards.
L.G.B., Local Government Board.
L. Ger., Low German.
L.G.O.C., London General Omnibus Company.
L. Gr., Low Greek.
L.G.U., Ladies' Golfing Union.
l.h., Left hand.
L.H.A., Lord High Admiral.
L.H.C., Lord High Chancellor.

L.H.D. [L. *Litterarum Humaniorum Doctor*], Doctor of Humane Letters; (*U.S.A.*) Doctor of the Humanities.
L.H.T., Lord High Treasurer.
L.I., (*Am.*) Licentiate of Instruction; (*Mil.*) Light Infantry; Long Island (U.S.A.).
Li, (*Chem.*) Lithium.
Lib., (*Pol.*) Liberal; Liberia, -an.
lib., Librarian, library.
lib. [L. *liber*] A book.
lib. cat., Library catalogue.
Lic. Med., Licentiate in Medicine.
Lieut., Lieutenant.
Lieut.-Col., **-Gen.**, **-Gov.**, Lieutenant-Colonel, -General, -Governor.
L.I.M., Licentiate of the Institution of Metallurgists.
lin., Lineal, linear.
Lincs., Lincolnshire.
Lindl., (*Bot.*) Lindley.
Linn., Linnæan, Linnæus (Carl von Linné).
liq., Liquid, liquor.
lit., Literal, literally, literary, literature; litre.
Lit.D. [L. *Literarum Doctor*], Doctor of Letters.
Lith., Lithuanian.
litho., Lithography.
Lit.Hum. [L. *Literæ Humaniores*], Final school of classics at Oxford.
Litt.D. [L. *Literarum Doctor*], Doctor of Letters (Camb. and T.C.D.).
liturg., Liturgy, liturgical.
liv. [F. *livre*], Book; pound.
liv. st. [F. *livre sterling*], Pound sterling.
L.J. (*pl.* **L.JJ.**), Lord Justice.
LL., Of laws.
L.L., Late Latin; law Latin, low Latin; Lord-Lieutenant.
ll., Leaves; (*Print.*) lines; [L. *leges*], laws.
L.L.A., Lady Literate in Arts (St. Andrews).
LL.B. [L. *Legum Baccalaureus*], Bachelor of Laws.
LL.D. [L. *Legum Doctor*], Doctor of Laws.
LL.JJ., Lords Justices.
LL.M. [L. *Legum Magister*], Master of Civil and of Canon Law.
L.M., Licentiate in Medicine or Midwifery; long metre (hymns).
L.M.D., Long metre double (of hymns).
L.M.H., Lady Margaret Hall, Oxford.
L.M.R.C.P., Licentiate in Midwifery, Roy. Coll. of Physicians.
L.M.S., Licentiate in Medicine and Surgery; London Missionary Society; London, Midland and Scottish Railway.
L.M.S.S.A., Licentiate in Medicine and Surgery, Society of Apothecaries, London.
L.N.E.R., London and North Eastern Railway.
L.N.U., League of Nations Union.
LΩ., (*Elec.*) The legal ohm.
loc. cit. [L. *loco citato*], In the place cited.
loco., (*Rail.*) Locomotive.
L. of N., League of Nations.
log., Logarithm; logic.
long., Longitude.
loq. [L. *loquitur*], He (or she) speaks.
Lou., Louisiana.
L.P., Large paper (copy of a book); Lord Provost; (*Gramophone*) long-playing.
l.p., (*Print.*) Long primer; low pressure.
L.P.M., Long particular metre.
L'pool, Liverpool.
L.P.S., Lord Privy Seal.
L.P.T.B., London Passenger Transport Board.
Lpz., Leipzig.
L.R.A.M., Licentiate of the Royal Academy of Music.
L.R.B., London Rifle Brigade.
L.R.C., Labour Representation Committee; London Rowing Club.
L.R.C.M., Licentiate of the Royal College of Music.
L.R.C.P., Licentiate of the Royal College of Physicians.
L.R.C.P.E., Licentiate of the Royal College of Physicians, Edinburgh.
L.R.C.P.I., Licentiate of the Royal College of Physicians, Ireland.
L.R.C.S., Licentiate of the Royal College of Surgeons.
L.R.C.S.E., Licentiate of the Royal College of Surgeons, Edinburgh.
L.R.C.S.I., Licentiate of the Royal College of Surgeons, Ireland.
L.R.C.V.S., Licentiate of the Royal College of Veterinary Surgeons.
L.R.F.P.S., Licentiate of the Royal Faculty of Physicians and Surgeons.
L.S., Linnean Society; [L. *locus sigilli*], the place for the seal.
l.s., Left side.
L.S.A., Licentiate of the Society of Apothecaries.
L.S.B., London School Board.
L.S.C., London Society of Compositors.
l.s.c. [L. *loco supra citato*], In the place above cited.
L.s.d. [L. *libræ, solidi, denarii*], Pounds, shillings and pence.
L.S.Sc., Licentiate in Sanitary Science.
L.S.E., London School of Economics.
L.S.O., London Symphony Orchestra.
L.T., Low tension.
£T. [It. *lira Turca*], Turkish pound (approx. 18s. 2d.).
Lt., Lieutenant.
L.T.A., Lawn Tennis Association; London Teachers' Association.
L.T.C.L., Licentiate of Trinity College (of Music), London.
Lt.-Col., Lieutenant-Colonel.
Lt.-Comm., (*Nav.*) Lieutenant-Commander.
Ltd., Limited.
Lt.-Gen., Lieutenant-General.
L.Th., Licentiate of Theology (Durham).
Lt. Inf., Light Infantry.
L.U., Liberal Unionist.
L.U.D.S., London University Dramatic Society.
L.U.M.S., London University Music Society.
Luth., Lutheran.
L.V., (*Elec.*) Legal volt.
l.w., (*Radio.*) Long wave.
L.W.L., Load-water-line.
L.W.O.S.T., Low water ordinary spring tides.
LXX, The Septuagint; 70.
lyr., Lyric, lyrical, lyrist.

M., 1,000
M. [L. *magister*], Master; majesty; magistrate; [G.], mark; Marquess; [L. *medicinæ*], (*Med.*) of medicine; member; middle; militia; [F.], Monsieur.
m., Male; married; masculine; (*Cricket*) maiden over; (*Mech.*) mass; meridian; [L. *meridies*], noon; metre, metres; mile, miles; (*Med.*) minim; minute, minutes; (*Naut.*) mist; month, months; moon.
M. & B., May & Baker, makers of sulphonamides.
M.A. [L. *Magister Artium*], Master of Arts; Military Academy.
ma., (*Elec.*) Milliampere.
m/a, (*Book-keeping*) My account.
Macc., Maccabees.
Maced., Macedonia, Macedonian.
Mad., Madam.
Mag., Magyar.
mag., Magazine; magnetism.
Magd., Magdalen College, Oxford; Magdalene College, Cambridge.
M.A.I., Member of the Anthropological Institute.
Maj., Major.
Maj.-Gen., Major-General.
Mal., Malachi; Malayan.
malac., Malacology.
m.a.m. [F. *mot à mot*], Word for word.
Man., Manitoba; Manila.
man., Manual.
Manch., Manchester.
Manit., Manitoba.
mar., Maritime; married.
March., Marchioness.
Marg., Margaret.
Mart., Martial; martyr.
masc., Masculine.
Mass., Massachusetts.
mat., Matins.
math., Mathematical, mathematician, mathematics.
Matric., Matriculation.
Matt., St. Matthew.
Max., Maximilian.
max., Maxim; maximum.
M.B. [L. *Medicinæ Baccalaureus*], Bachelor of Medicine.
M.B.E., Member of (the Order of) the British Empire.
M.B.T.A., Metropolitan Board Teachers' Association.
M.C., Master Commandant; Master of the Ceremonies; Member of Congress; Member of Council; the Military Cross.
M/C, Manchester.
M./C., Metalling clause (marine insur.); marginal credit (banking).
M.-C., Medico-Chirurgical.
M.C.C., Marylebone Cricket Club; Middlesex County Council.
M.Ch. [L. *Magister Chirurgiæ*], Master of Surgery.
M.Ch.D., Master of Dental Surgery.
M.C.L., Master of Civil Law.
M.C.M.E.S., Member of Civil and Mechanical Engineers' Society.
M.Com., Master of Commerce (Birmingham).
M.Comm., Master of Commerce and Administration (Manchester).
M.C.P., Member of the College of Preceptors.

M.C.S., Malayan Civil Service.
M.D. [L. *Medicinæ Doctor*], Doctor of Medicine; Middle Dutch; mentally deficient; [F. *main droite*, It. *mano destra*], (*Mus.*) with the right hand.
Md., Maryland.
m.d., Month's date.
Mdlle, Mademoiselle.
Mdme, Madame.
M.D.S., Master of Dental Surgery.
mdse., (*Am.*) Merchandise.
M.E., Mechanical Engineer; Methodist Episcopal; Military Engineer; Mining Engineer; Middle English; Most Excellent.
Me., Maine (U.S.A.).
Me [F. *maître*], Advocate.
M.E.C., Member of the Executive Council.
mech., Mechanical, mechanics.
med., Medical, medicine; mediæval; medium; medallist.
Medit., Mediterranean.
med. jur., Medical jurisprudence.
mem., Memento, memorandum; memoir.
M.Eng., Master of Engineering (Dublin).
mensur., Mensuration.
mer., Meridian, meridional.
Mert., Merton College, Oxford.
Messrs., Messieurs.
MET, Metropolitan Railway (London).
met., Metronome; metropolitan; metallurgy.
metaph., Metaphysical, metaphysician, metaphysics, metaphor, metaphorical.
meteor., Meteorological, meteorology.
Meth., Methodist.
meton., Metonymy.
Met. R., Metropolitan Railway.
metrol., Metrology.
metrop., Metropolis, metropolitan.
Mex., Mexican, Mexico.
M.E.Z., (G. *Mitteleuropäische Zeit*) Central European Time.
mf. [It. *mezzo-forte*], (*Mus.*) Moderately loud.
M.F.B., Metropolitan Fire Brigade.
mfd., Manufactured; (*Elec.*) microfarad.
mfg., Manufacturing.
M.F.H., Master of Foxhounds.
mfr., Manufacture, manufacturer.
mfrs., Manufacturers, manufactures.
M.G. [F. *main gauche*], (*Mus.*) with the left hand; machine gun.
Mg, (*Chem.*) Magnesium.
mg., Milligram, -grams.
M.G.C., Machine Gun Corps.
M. Goth., Meso-Gothic.
M. Gr., Middle Greek.
Mgr. (*pl.* **Mgrs.**), (*R.-C. Ch.*) Monseigneur, Monsignor.
M.H., Ministry of Health.
M.H.A., Member of the House of Assembly.
M.H.G., Middle High German.
M.H.K., Member of the House of Keys (Isle of Man).
mho., (*Elec.*) Unit of conductivity.
M.Hon., Most Honourable.
M.H.R., Member of the House of Representatives.
M.H.S., Ministry of Home Security.
M.Hy., Master of Hygiene.

M.I., Mounted Infantry; Military Intelligence (department).
Mic., Micah.
M.I.C.E. [M.INST.C.E.].
Mich., Michaelmas; Michigan.
micros., Microscopy.
mid., Middle; Midlands.
Mid. Lat., Middle Latin.
M.I.E.E., Member of the Institution of Electrical Engineers.
mil., Military, militia.
M.I.Loco.E., Member of the Institute of Locomotive Engineers.
M.I.M.E., Member of the Institute of Mining Engineers.
M.I.Mech.E., Member of the Institution of Mechanical Engineers.
M.I.M.M., Member of the Institute of Mining and Metallurgy.
min., Mineralogy; minim; minimum, minima; minister, ministerial; mines; minute, minutes.
M.I.N.A., Member of the Institute of Naval Architects.
Minn., Minnesota.
Min. Plen., Minister Plenipotentiary.
Min. Res., Minister Resident.
M.Inst.C.E., Member of the Institute of Civil Engineers.
M.Inst.E.E. [M.I.E.E.].
M.Inst.M.E. [M.I.M.E.].
M.Inst.M.M. [M.I.M.M.].
M.Ir., Middle Irish.
misc., Miscellaneous, miscellany.
Miss., Mission, missionary; Mississippi.
M.J.I., Member of the Institute of Journalists.
M.J.S., Member of the Japan Society.
Mk., Mark (German coin).
Mkt., Market.
M.K.W., Military Knight of Windsor.
M.L., Licentiate in Midwifery; Mediæval Latin; Middle Latin; Ministry of Labour; Licentiate in Medicine.
M.L.A., Member of the Legislative Assembly; Modern Language Association.
M.L.C., Member of the Legislative Council.
M.L.G., Middle Low German.
Mlle, Mademoiselle.
Mlles, Mesdemoiselles.
M.L.R.G., Muzzle-loading rifled gun.
M.L.S.C., Member London Society of Compositors.
MM., Majesties; messieurs; 2,000.
M.M., The Military Medal.
mm., Millimetre, -metres.
m.m. [L. *mutatis mutandis*], With the necessary changes.
M.M.B., Milk Marketing Board.
Mme, Madame.
Mmes, Mesdames.
M.M.P., Military Mounted Police.
M.M.S., Moravian Missionary Society.
Mn, (*Chem.*) Manganese.
M.N.A.S., Member of the National Academy of Sciences.
M.O., Money Order; Medical Officer.
Mo, (*Chem.*) Molybdenum.
Mo., Missouri.
mo., Month, months.
mob., Mobile.
mod., Moderate; modern.
mod. [It. *moderato*], (*Mus.*) In moderate time.
Mods., (*Oxf. Univ.*) Moderations.

M.O.H., Medical Officer of Health; Ministry of Health.
Moham., Mohammedan.
M.o.I., Ministry of Information.
M.O.L., Ministry of Labour.
mol. wt., Molecular weight.
Mon., Monday; Monmouthshire.
mon., Monastery; monetary.
Mong., **Mongol.**, Mongolian.
Mons., Monsieur (it is regarded as an insult in France to use this abbreviation).
Mont., Montana.
Mor., Morocco.
morph., Morphology.
M.P., Member of Parliament; Methodist Protestant; Metropolitan Police; military police; [L. *mille passuum*], a thousand paces (a Roman mile).
m.p., Melting point.
mp. [It. *mezzo-piano*], (*Mus.*) Rather softly.
M.P.C., Member of Parliament, Canada.
M.Pens., Ministry of Pensions.
m.p.g., **m.p.h.**, Miles per gallon, per hour.
M.P.P., Member of Provincial Parliament.
M.P.S., Member of the Pharmaceutical Society; Member of the Philological Society.
M.R., Master of the Rolls; Municipal Reformer.
Mr., Mister.
M.R.A., Moral Rearmament (Buchmanism).
M.R.A.C., Member of the Royal Agricultural College.
M.R.A.S., Member of the Royal Asiatic Society; Member of the Royal Academy of Science.
M.R.C.C., Member of the Royal College of Chemistry.
M.R.C.O., Member of the Royal College of Organists.
M.R.C.O.G., Member of the Royal College of Obstetricians and Gynæcologists.
M.R.C.P., Member of the Royal College of Physicians.
M.R.C.P.E., Member of the Royal College of Physicians, Edinburgh.
M.R.C.P.I., Member of the Royal College of Physicians, Ireland.
M.R.C.S., Member of the Royal College of Surgeons.
M.R.C.S.E., Member of the Royal College of Surgeons, Edinburgh.
M.R.C.S.I., Member of the Royal College of Surgeons, Ireland.
M.R.C.V.S., Member of the Royal College of Veterinary Surgeons.
M.R.G.S., Member of the Royal Geographical Society.
M.R.I., Member of the Royal Institution.
M.R.I.A., Member of the Royal Irish Academy.
M.R.P., (*F. Pol.*) Mouvement Républican Populaire.
Mrs., Missis, Mistress.
M.R.S.A., Member of the Royal Society of Arts.
M.R.San.I., Member of the Royal Sanitary Institute.
M.R.S.L., Member of the Royal Society of Literature.
M.R.S.T., Member of the Royal Society of Teachers.
M.R.U.S.I., Member of the Royal United Service Institution.
MS. (*pl.* **MSS**), Manuscript.

M.S., Master of Science; Master of Surgery; [L. *memoriæ sacrum*], sacred to the memory; [It. *mano sinistra*], (*Mus.*) the left hand.
m.s., Month's sight (comm.).
M.S.A., Member of the Society of Apothecaries; Member of the Society of Arts.
M.S.C., Medical Staff Corps.
M.Sc., Master of Science.
M.S.E., Member of the Society of Engineers.
M.S.H., Master of Staghounds.
m.s.l., Mean sea-level.
M.S.M., Meritorious Service Medal.
MSS, Manuscripts.
M.T., Motor Transport; mechanical transport.
Mt., Mount; mountain.
M.T.B., (*Nav.*) Motor Torpedo Boat.
mtg., Meeting.
mth., Month.
Mt. Rev., Most Reverend.
Mts., Mountains.
M.U., Motor Union; Mothers' Union; mobile unit.
mus., Museum; music, musical, musician.
Mus.B., **Mus.Bac.** [L. *Musicæ Baccalaureus*], Bachelor of Music.
Mus.D., **Mus.Doc.** [L. *Musicæ Doctor*], Doctor of Music.
Mus.M. [L. *Musicæ Magister*], Master of Music (Cambridge).
M.V., Motor Vessel; muzzle velocity.
m.v. [It. *mezza voce*], (*Mus.*) With half the full power of the voice.
M.V.O., Member of the Royal Victorian Order.
M.W., Most Worshipful; Most Worthy.
M.W.B., Metropolitan Water Board.
M.W.I., Ministry of War Information (U.S.A.).
M.Y., Motor Yacht.
myst., Mystery, mysteries.
myth., Mythological, mythology.
Mx., Middlesex.

N, (*Chem.*) Nitrogen.
N., (*Polit.*) Nationalist; (*Nav.*) navigating, navigation; Norse; north, northern; Northern London postal district; (*Mag.*) symbol of magnetic flux.
n., Name; nephew; neuter; new; noon; note, notes; nominative; noun.
n. [L. *natus*], Born; [L. *nocte*], (*Med.*) at night; [F. *nous*], we, us.
Na [L. *natrium*], (*Chem.*) Sodium.
N.A., National Academy; Nautical Almanac; North America.
n/a., (*Banking*) No advice, no account; non-acceptance.
N.A.A., National Artillery Association.
N.A.A.F.I., Navy, Army, and Air Force Institutes.
N. & Q., Notes and Queries.
Nap., Napoleon.
N.A.S., Nursing Auxiliary Service.
Nat., Natal; Nathaniel; national.
nat., Natural, naturalist.
nat. hist., Natural history.
N.A.T.O., North Atlantic Treaty Organization.
nat. ord., Natural order.
nat. phil., Natural philosophy.
naut., Nautical.
nav., Naval; navigation.
Nav. Const., Naval constructor.
N.B., New Brunswick; North Britain (Scotland).
N.B. [L. *nota bene*], Mark well.
Nb, (*Chem.*) Niobium.
n.b., (*Cricket*) No ball.
N.B.A., The North British Academy.
N.B.S., National Broadcasting Company (U.S.A.).
N.C., North Carolina.
N.C.B., National Coal Board.
N.C.C.V.D., National Council for Combating Venereal Disease.
N.C.O., Non-commissioned officer.
N.C.U., National Cyclists' Union.
N.C.W., National Council of Women.
N.D. [F. *Notre-Dame*], Our Lady; North Dakota.
n.d., No date.
N.Dak., North Dakota.
N.D.L., Norddeutscher Lloyd.
N.E., New edition; New England (U.S.A.); north-east; North-Eastern London postal district.
Ne, (*Chem.*) Neon.
N/E., (*Banking*) No effects.
N.E.A., New English Art Club.
Nebr., Nebraska.
N.E.D., New English Dictionary (now known as the Oxford English Dictionary [O.E.D.]).
neg., negative, negatively.
Neh., Nehemiah.
n.e.i. [L. *non est inventus*], He (she, or it) has not been found.
N.F., New (French) franc.
N.F.U., National Farmers' Union.
N.H.I., National Health Insurance.
Norvic. [L. *Norvicensis*], Of Norwich (Bishop of Norwich's signature).
Norw., Norway, Norwegian.
Nos. [see NO.], Numbers.
Notts, Nottinghamshire.
Nov., November; novel, novelist.
N.P., New Providence; Notary-Public.
n.p., (*Print.*) New paragraph.
N.P.A., Newspaper Proprietors' Association.
N.P.D., North Polar distance.
N.P.L., National Physical Laboratory (Teddington).
N.R., North Riding (of Yorks).
Nr. [G. *Nummer*], Number.
nr., Near.
N.R.A., National Rifle Association.
N.S., National Society; New School; New Series; new side; new style; Nova Scotia; Numismatic Society.
N.-S. [F. *Notre-Seigneur*], Our Lord.
n.s., Not specified.
n/s., (*Banking*) Not sufficient (money to meet a cheque).
N.S.A., National Skating Association.
N.S.I.C. [L. *Noster Salvator Iesus Christus*], Our Saviour Jesus Christ.
N.S.J.C. [F. *Notre Seigneur Jesus-Christ*], Our Lord Jesus Christ.
N.S.L., National Sunday League.
N.S.P.C.C., National Society for the Prevention of Cruelty to Children.
N.S.W., New South Wales.
N.T., New Testament; New Translation; Northern Territory (Australia).
n.u., Name unknown.
N.U.J., National Union of Journalists.
Num., Numbers.
num., Numeral.
numis., Numismatics.
N.U.R., National Union of Railwaymen.
N.U.S., National Union of Students.
N.U.T., National Union of Teachers.
N.U.W.T., National Union of Women Teachers.
N.U.W.W., National Union of Women Workers.
nux vom., Nux vomica.
N.V., New Version.
N.W., North Wales; north-west; North-Western London postal district.
N.W.S.A., National Women's Suffrage Association.
N.W.T., North-Western Territory.
N.Y., New York.
N.Z., New Zealand.

O, (*Chem.*) Oxygen.
O., Ohio; old; Order; officer, officers; [F. *Ouest*], west; [G. *Osten*], east; (*Naut.*) overcast; owner.
o/a., On account.
O.A.P., Old Age Pension(s).
O.A.S., On Active Service.
Ob., Oboe; [L. *obolus*], halfpenny.
ob. [L. *obiit*], He (or she) died.
Obad., Obadiah.
obb., (*Mus.*) *Obbligato*.
O.B.E., Officer of (the Order of) the British Empire.
obj., Object, objection, objective.
obl., Oblique, oblong.
obs., Observation, observatory; obsolete.
ob.s.p. [L. *obiit sine prole*], Died without issue.
obstet., Obstetrics.
O.C., Officer commanding; Old Carthusian; Old Catholic; Old Cheltonian.
o.c. [L. *opere citato*], In the work cited.
o/c, Overcharge.
occ., Occasionally.
Oct., October.
oct., Octavo.
O.C.T.U., Officer Cadets Training Unit.
O.D., Old Dutch; Ordnance Datum.
O/D., Overdraft; overdrawn.
o/d., (*Banking*) On demand.
O.Dan., Old Danish.
O.E.C.D., Organization for European Co-operation and Development.
O.E.D., Oxford English Dictionary.
O.E.E.C., Organization for European Economic Co-operation (now **O.E.C.D.**).
O.F., Odd Fellows; Old French; (*Print.*) old face type.
off., Official, officinal.
O.F.M. [L. *Ordo Fratrum Minorum*], Order of Friars Minor.
O.F.S., Orange Free State.
O.G., Ogee (moulding); outside guard; Olympic games.
O.Gael., Old Gaelic.
O.H.B.M.S., On His (or Her) Britannic Majesty's Service.

O.H.G., Old High German.
O.H.M.S., On His (or Her) Majesty's Service.
O.Ir., Old Irish.
O.K., (*colloq.*) All right, very well; quite correct.
Okla., Oklahoma.
O.L., Officer of (the Order of) Leopold; Old Latin.
Ol., Olympiad.
O.L.G., Old Low German.
O.M. (Member of the) Order of Merit.
o.m., Old measure (of hymns).
O.N., Old Norse.
O.N.F., Old Norman-French.
onomat., Onomatopœia.
Ont., Ontario (Upper Canada).
O.P., Old Playgoers (*Club*); (*Mil.*) observation post; old prices; [L. *Ordinis Prædicatorum*], Order of Preachers, or Dominicans.
o.p., (*Theat.*) Opposite the prompt side; optime; over-proof (of spirits); out of print (of books).
op. [L. *opus*], Work.
op. cit. [L. *opere citato*], In the work cited.
o.p.n., [L. *ora pro nobis*], Pray for us.
opp., Opposed, opposite; opposition.
opt., Optative; optical, optician, optics; optime.
O.R., (*Mil.*) Other ranks.
orat., Orator, oratorical, oratorically.
O.R.C., Order of the Red Cross.
orch., Orchestra.
ord., Ordained, order, ordinal, ordinance, ordinary.
Ordn., Ordnance.
Ore., Oregon.
org., Organ, organic, organism, organized.
Orient., Oriental.
orig., Origin, original, originally, originate.
orig. bds., (*Bookbinding*) Original boards.
ornith., Ornithological, ornithology.
Os, (*Chem.*) Osmium.
O.S., Old Saxon (language); Ordnance Survey; old school; old series; old side; old style; outsides (of paper); ordinary seaman.
o.s., Only son.
O.S.A., Order of St. Augustine.
O.S.B., Order of St. Benedict.
O.S.F., Order of St. Francis.
O.Sl., Old Slavonic.
o.s.p., [L. *obiit sine prole*], Died without issue.
o.s.t., Ordinary spring tides.
O.T., Old Testament.
O.T.C., Officers' Training Corps.
O.Teut., Old Teutonic.
O.U., Oxford University.
O.U.A.C., Oxford University Athletic Club.
O.U.A.F.C., Oxford University Association Football Club.
O.U.A.M., Order of United American Mechanics.
O.U.B.C., Oxford University Boat Club.
O.U.C.C., Oxford University Cricket Club.
O.U.D.S., Oxford University Dramatic Society.
O.U.G.C., Oxford University Golf Club.
O.U.H.C., Oxford University Hockey Club.
O.U.L.C., Oxford University Lacrosse Club.
O.U.L.T.C., Oxford University Lawn Tennis Club.
O.U.T.C., Oxford University Officers' Training Corps.
O.U.P., Oxford University Press.
O.U.R.F.C., Oxford University Rugby Football Club.
Ox., Oxford.
Oxon, Oxfordshire; [L. *Oxonia*], Oxford; [L. *Oxoniensis*], of Oxford (Bishop of Oxford's signature).
oz., Ounce, ounces.

P, (*Chem.*) Phosphorus; car park.
p., Pastor; [L. *Pater*, F. *Père*], Father; Pope; president; prince; proconsul; (*Mech.*) pressure; priest; (*Polit.*) progressive; page; participle; (*Naut.*) passing showers; past; perch; pipe; pole; [F. *pied*], foot; [F. *pouce*], inch; [L. *pro*, F. *pour*], for; penny.
p [It. *piano*], (*Mus.*) Soft.
p. [It. *poco*], A little, somewhat.
Pa., Pennsylvania.
P.A., Post Adjutant, Protestant Alliance; Press Association.
p.a. [F. *per amitié*], By favour; [L. *per annum*], yearly.
P./A., Power of attorney.
P.A.A., Pan American Airways.
P.A.C., Public Assistance Committee.
p.a.c., (*Mil.*) Passed Advance Class (at Ordnance College).
p.æ. [L. *partes æquales*], Equal parts.
paint., Painting.
Pal., Palestine.
palæog., Palæography.
palæont., Palæontology.
pam., Pamphlet.
Pan., Panama.
P. & O., Peninsular and Oriental (Steam Navigation Company).
par., Paragraph; parallel; parenthesis; parish.
Para., Paraguay.
Parl., Parliament, parliamentary.
Parl.S., Parliamentary Secretary.
part., Participle.
pass., Passive.
Pat., Patrologia, patristics.
Pata., Patagonia.
path., Pathology.
Pat. Off., Patent Office.
Patr., Patron.
P.A.Y.E., Pay As You Earn (payment of Income Tax on salaries, wages, etc., as earned).
Pb [L. *plumbum*], (*Chem.*) Lead.
P.B. [L. *Pharmacopœia Britannica*], British Pharmacopœia; Plymouth Brethren; Prayer Book; Primitive Baptists; provisional battalion.
P.C., Parish Council; Parish Councillor; Perpetual Curate; Police Constable; Privy Council; Privy Councillor.
p.c., Post card; per cent.
p/c., Petty cash; prices current.
P.C.C., Prerogative Court of Canterbury.
P.C.R.S., Poor Clergy Relief Society.
P.C.S., Principal Clerk of Session (Scotland).
P.D. [L. *Pharmacopœia Dublinensis*], Dublin Pharmacopœia; Postal District; (*Elec.*) potential difference.
Pd, (*Chem.*) Palladium.
pd., Paid.
p.d.a. [F. *pour dire adieu*], To say good-bye.
P.D.A.D., Probate, Divorce, and Admiralty Division.
P.E. [L. *Pharmacopœia Edinburgensis*], Edinburgh Pharmacopœia; Presiding Elder; Protestant Episcopal.
Ped., (*Mus.*) Pedal.
P.E.N., Poets, Playwrights, Essayists, Editors and Novelists club.
P.E.I., Prince Edward Island.
pen., Peninsula.
Penit., Penitentiary.
Pent., Pentecost.
per., Period.
P.E.P., Political and Economic Planning (club.)
per cent [L. *per centum*], By the hundred.
perf., Perfect; perforated (of stamps).
perig., Perigee.
per pro. [L. *per procurationem*], On behalf of.
Pers., Persia, Persian.
pers., Person, personal, personally.
persp., Perspective.
Peru., Peruvian.
Pet., Peter.
petrol., Petrology.
p. ex. [F. *par exemple*], For instance.
P.F., Procurator Fiscal.
pf. [G. *Pfund*], Pound.
p.f. [F. *pour féliciter*], To congratulate.
Pf. [It. *più forte*], (*Mus.*) A little louder.
Pfg. (*pl.* ***-ge.***), *Pfennig.*
p.f.s.a. [F. *pour faire ses adieux*], To say good-bye.
p.f.v. [F. *pour faire visite*], To make a call.
P.G., Paying guest, *i.e.* boarder.
phar., Pharmacopœia.
pharm., Pharmaceutical, pharmacy.
pharmacol., Pharmacology.
Ph.B. [L. *Philosophiæ Baccalaureus*], Bachelor of Philosophy.
Ph.D. [L. *Philosophiæ Doctor*], Doctor of Philosophy.
Phil., Philadelphia; (Epistle to the) Philippians.
phil., Philosophical, philosopher, philosophy.
Philat., Philately.
philol., Philological, philology.
Phil. Soc., Philological Society.
Phil. Trans., Philosophical Transactions of the Royal Society of London.
phon., Phonetic, phonetics, phonology.
phonog., Phonography.
phot., Photographic, photography.
photom., Photometrical, photometry.
phr., Phrase.
phren., Phrenological, phrenology.
phys., Physical, physician, physics.
physiol., Physiological, physiologist, physiology.
pinx. [L. *pinxit*], He (or she) painted it.
pizz., (*Mus.*) Pizzicato.
P.J., Presiding judge; Probate judge.
pk., Peck, pecks.
pkg., Package.
P.L. [L. *Pharmacopœia Londinensis*], London Pharmacopœia; Poet Laureate; Primrose League.

pl., Place; plate, plates; plural.
P.L.A., Port of London Authority.
P.L.B., Poor Law Board.
P.L.C., Poor Law Commission or Commissioner.
Plen., Plenipotentiary.
plf., Plaintiff.
P.L.M., Paris Lyon Méditerranée (French rly.).
plu., Plural.
plup., Pluperfect.
Plut., Plutarch.
P.M., Pacific Mail; Past Master; Paymaster; Postmaster; post-mortem.
p.m. [L. *post meridiem*], Afternoon.
pm., Premium, premolar.
P.M.G., Paymaster-General; Postmaster-General; Pall Mall Gazette.
P.M.O., Principal Medical Officer.
p.n., Promissory note.
P.N.E.U., Parents' National Education Union.
pneum., Pneumatic, pneumatics.
pnxt. [L. *pinxit*], He (or she) painted it.
P.O., Petty Officer; postal order; post office; [L. *professor ordinarius*], ordinary professor; Province of Ontario.
P.O.D., Pay on Delivery; Post Office Department; Post Office Directory.
poet., Poetic, poetical, poetry.
Pol., Poland, Polish.
pol. econ., Political economy.
pol., Political, politics.
Poly., Polytechnic.
Polyb., Polybius.
P.O.O., Post office order.
P.O.P., (*Phot.*) Printing-out paper.
pop., Popular, population.
por., Portrait.
Port., Portugal, Portuguese.
pos., Positive.
P.O.S.B., Post Office Savings Bank.
poss., Possession, possessive.
pot., Potential.
P.O.W., Prisoner(s) of War.
PP. [L. *Patres*], Fathers.
P.P., Parish priest; Past President.
pp., Pages.
pp [It. *pianissimo*], (*Mus.*) Very soft.
p.p., Past participle; *per procurationem*, on behalf of; play or pay; post paid.
p.p. [It. *più piano*], (*Mus.*) More softly.
p.p.c. [F. *pour prendre congé*], To take leave.
p.p.i., Policy proof of interest.
ppp [It. *pianissimo*], (*Mus.*) As softly as possible.
P.P.U., Peace Pledge Union.
P.Q., Previous question; Province of Quebec.
Pr., Priest; printer.
pr., Pair, pairs; pounder of guns.
P.R., Porto Rico; proportional representation; prize ring.
P.R.A., President of the Royal Academy.
P.R.B., Pre-Raphaelite Brotherhood.
preb., Prebend, Prebendary.
prec., Preceding; precentor.
pref., Preface; preference; preferred; prefix, prefixed.
prelim., Preliminary.
prep., Preparatory; preposition.
Pres., President.
pres., Present.
pres. part., Present participle.
Presb., Presbyterian.
pret., Preterit.
P.R.I., President of the Royal Institute (of Painters in Water-colours).
P.R.I.B.A., President of the Royal Institute of British Architects.
prim., Primary, primate, primitive.
Prin., Principal.
prin., Principally, principles.
print., Printing.
priv., Private, privative.
Priv. Doz. [G.], *Privatdozent* (a recognized teacher not on the regular staff).
p.r.n. [L. *pro re nata*], As occasion may require.
P.R.O., Public Records Office; Public Relations Officer.
pro., Professional.
Prob., (*Law*) Probate Division.
prob., Probable, probably; problem.
proc., Proceedings; proctor.
Prof., Professor.
Prog., Progressive.
prol., Prologue.
prom., Promontory.
pron., Pronoun; pronounced.
prop., Proposition.
propr., Proprietor; proprietary.
props., (*Theat.*) Properties.
pros., Prosody.
Prot., Protestant.
pro tem. [L. *pro tempore*], For the time being.
Prov., Provence, Provençal; Proverbs; province; Provost.
prov., Provincial; provisionally.
Prov. Batt., Provisional Battalion.
prox. [L. *proximo*], Next month.
prox. acc. [L. *proxime accessit*], He (or she) came next.
pr. pr. [L. *præter propter*], About, nearly.
P.R.S., President of the Royal Society.
P.R.S.A., President of the Royal Scottish Academy.
P.R.S.E., President of the Royal Society of Edinburgh.
Pruss., Prussia, Prussian.
p.r.v. [F. *pour rendre visite*], To return a call.
P.S., Permanent Secretary; [L. *postscriptum*], postscript; Privy Seal; (*Theat.*) prompt side.
Ps., Psalm, Psalms.
p.s., (*Mil.*) Passed School (of Instruction).
P.S.A., Pleasant Sunday Afternoon.
p.s.a., (*Mil.*) Passed Artillery College (School of Artillery).
p.s.c., (*Mil.*) Passed Staff College.
pseud., Pseudonym, pseudonymous, -ly.
P.S.N.C., Pacific Steam Navigation Company.
psych., Psychic, psychical.
psychol., Psychological, psychology.
P.T., Post town; pupil teacher; Physical Training.
Pt, (*Chem.*) Platinum.
Pt., (*Geog.*) Point; port.
pt., Part; payment; pint, pints; (*Math.*) point.
p.t. [PRO TEM.].
Pte., (*Mil.*) Private.
ptg., Printing.
P.T.O., Please turn over; Public Trustee Office.
pub., Public; publican; publicly; publish, published, publisher, publishing.
pub. doc., Public document.
pud., Pudding.
P.U.S., Pharmacopœia of the United States.
p.v., Post village; priest vicar.
P.V.O., Principal Veterinary Officer.
P.V.-P., Past Vice-President.
p.v.t. [F. *par voie télégraphique*], By telegraph.
P.W.A., (*U.S.A.*) Public Works Administration.
P.W.D., Public Works Department.
pwt. [DWT.].
P.X., Please exchange.
pyrotech., Pyrotechnical, pyrotechnics.

Q., Quart; queen; question; (*Elec.*) coulomb; quire; (*Naut.*) squalls.
q., Quasi; query; quintal.
q. [L. *quære*], Inquire.
Q.A.B., Queen Anne's Bounty.
Q.A.I.M.N.S., Queen Alexandra's Imperial Military Nursing Service.
Q.B., Queen's Bench.
Q.C., Queen's College, Oxford; Queens' College, Cambridge; Queen's Counsel.
q.d. [L. *quasi dicat*], As if one should say; [L. *quasi dictum*], as if said.
q.e. [L. *quod est*], Which is.
Q.E.D. [L. *quod erat demonstrandum*], Which was to be proved.
Q.E.F. [L. *quod erat faciendum*], Which was to be done.
Q.E.I. [L. *quod erat inveniendum*], Which was to be found out.
Q.F., Quick-firing (of guns).
Q.H.P., Queen's Honorary Physician.
q.l. [L. *quantum libet*], As much as you please.
Q'l'd., Qld., Queensland, Australia.
Q.M., Quartermaster.
qm. [L. *quomodo*], By what means.
Q.M.G., Quartermaster-General.
Q.M.S., Quartermaster-Sergeant.
q.pl. [L. *quantum placet*] As much as you please.
qq.v. [L. *quæ vide*], Which (things, etc.) see.
qr., Quarter, quarters (weight); quire, quires.
Q.S., Quarter-Sessions.
q.s. [L. *quantum sufficit*], A sufficient quantity.
qt., Quantity; quart, quarts.
qu., Question.
quad., Quadrant.
quant. suff. [Q.S.].
quart., Quarterly.
Que., Quebec.
Queensl., Queensland.
quot., Quotation, quoted; quotient.
q.v. [L. *quod vide*], Which see; [L. *quantum vis*], as much as you will.
qy., Query.

R., Radical; radius; railway; rabbi; (*Thermom.*) Réaumur; republican; [L. *regina*], Queen; [L. *rex*], King; (*Theat.*) right side; river; royal; rupee.
r., Rare; residence, resides; rises; rod; rood; recipe; (*Naut.*) rain.

r., (*Math.*) Radius vector of co-ordinates.
R°, Radius of a circle in degrees of arc; **R′**, in minutes; **R″**, in seconds.
Ra, (*Chem.*) Radium.
R.A., Rear-Admiral; Referees' Association; Road Association; Royal Academy; Royal Academician; Royal Artillery.
R.A.A., Royal Academy of Arts.
R.A.A.F., Royal Australian Air Force.
R.A.C., Royal Agricultural College; Royal Automobile Club; Royal Armoured Corps.
R.A.Ch.D., Royal Army Chaplains' Department.
rad. [L. *radix*], Root.
R.A.D.A., Royal Academy of Dramatic Art.
Radar, [*see* Dictionary].
R.-Adm., Rear-Admiral.
R.A.E.C., Royal Army Educational Corps.
R.Ae.S., Royal Aeronautical Society.
R.A.F., Royal Air Force.
R.A.G.C., Royal and Ancient Golf Club (St. Andrews).
R.A.M., Royal Academy of Music.
R.A.M.C., Royal Army Medical Corps.
R.A.N., Royal Australian Navy.
R.A.O.B., Royal Antediluvian Order of Buffaloes.
R.A.O.C., Royal Army Ordnance Corps.
R.A.P.C., Royal Army Pay Corps.
R.A.S., Royal Agricultural, Asiatic or Astronomical Society.
R.A.S.C., Royal Army Service Corps.
R.A.V.C., Royal Army Veterinary Corps.
R.B., Rifle Brigade.
Rb, (*Chem.*) Rubidium.
R.B.A., Royal (Society of) British Artists.
R.B.S., Royal Society of British Sculptors.
R.C., Roman Catholic.
r.-c., Right of centre (of stage).
R.C.A., Royal Cambrian Academy; Royal College of Art.
R.C.A.F., Royal Canadian Air Force.
R.C.B., Representative Church Body (Ireland).
R.C.C., Representative Church Council (Scotland).
R.C.I., Royal Colonial Institute.
R.C.M., Royal College of Music (London).
R.C.M.P., Royal Canadian Mounted Police.
R.C.N., Royal Canadian Navy.
R.C.O., Royal College of Organists.
R.C.P., Royal College of Physicians or of Preceptors.
R.C.S., Royal College of Surgeons; Royal Corps of Signals.
R.C.V.S., Royal College of Veterinary Surgeons.
R.D., Royal Dragoons; Rural Dean; Reserve (Officers) Decoration.
R./D., (*Banking*) Refer to drawer.
Rd., Road.
R.D.C., Rural District Council.
R.D.S., Royal Drawing Society; Royal Dublin Society.
R.D.Y., Royal Dockyard.
R.E., Reformed Episcopal; Right Excellent; Royal Engineers; Royal Exchange; Royal Society of Painter-Etchers and Engravers.
Réaum., Réaumur (thermometer).
rec., Receipt; recipe; record, recorded, recorder.
recd., Received.
rect., Rectified.
R.E.C., Railway Executive Committee.
Ref., The Reformation.
ref., Refer, referred, referee, reference; reformed, reformer.
Ref. Ch., Reformed Church.
refl., Reflection, reflective, reflectively; reflex, reflexive, reflexively.
Reg., Regent; [L. *Regina*], Queen.
reg., Register, registrar, registry; regular, regularly.
regd., Registered.
Reg.-Gen., Registrar-General.
regl., Regimental.
Reg. Prof., Regius Professor.
Regr., Registrar.
regt., Regiment.
rel., Relative, relatively; religion, religious; [L. *reliquiæ*], relics.
rem., Remark, remarks.
R.E.M.E., Royal Electrical and Mechanical Engineers.
rep., Report, reporter; representative; republic, republican.
repr., Representing.
res., Reserve; residence, resident; resides; resigned.
resp., Respondent.
rest., Restored.
ret., Retired.
retd., Returned.
Rev., Revelations; Reverend; review.
rev., Revenue; reverse; revise, revised, revision; revolution.
Revs., The Reverends.
Rev. Stat., Revised Statutes.
Rev. Ver., Revised Version (of the Bible).
R.F. [F. *République française*], French Republic.
r.f., Rough finish (of paper).
rf., (*Mus.*) [RINF.].
R.F.A., Royal Field Artillery.
R.F.C., Royal Flying Corps (now R.A.F.).
R.G.A., Royal Garrison Artillery; Royal Guernsey Artillery.
R.G.S., Royal Geographical Society.
R.H., Royal Highness.
Rh, (*Chem.*) Rhodium.
R.H.A., Royal Hibernian Academy; Royal Horse Artillery.
rhet., Rhetoric, rhetorical.
R.H.G., Royal Horse Guards.
R.H.M.S., Royal Hibernian Military School.
R.H.S., Royal Horticultural Society; Royal Humane Society.
R.Hist.S., Royal Historical Society.
R.I., Rhode Island; Royal Institute (of Painters in Water-colours); Royal Institution.
R.I.A.M., Royal Irish Academy of Music.
R.I.B.A., Royal Institute of British Architects.
R.I.C., Royal Irish Constabulary.
R.I.I.A., Royal Institute of International Affairs.
rinf. [It. *rinforzando*], (*Mus.*) With additional emphasis.
R.I.P. [L. *Requiescat* or *-cant in pace*], May he (she) or they rest in peace.
R.I.P.H.H., Royal Institute of Public Health & Hygiene.
riten. [It. *ritenuto*], (*Mus.*) Slower.
Riv., River.
R.L.O., Returned Letter Office.
R.L.S., Robert Louis Stevenson.
Rly., Railway.
R.M., Resident Magistrate; Royal Mail; Royal Marines.
rm., Ream.
R.M.A., Royal Marine Artillery; Royal Military Academy (Woolwich); Royal Military Asylum.
R.M.C., Royal Military College (Sandhurst).
R.Met.S., Royal Meteorological Society.
R.M.L.I., Royal Marine Light Infantry.
R.M.S., Royal Mail Service; Royal Mail Steamer; Royal Microscopical Society; Royal Society of Miniature Painters.
R.M.S.P., Royal Mail Steam Packet Co.
R.N., Royal Navy.
R.N.A.S., Royal Naval Air Service.
R.N.A.V., Royal Naval Artillery Volunteers.
R.N.D., Royal Naval Division.
R.N.L.I., Royal National Lifeboat Institution.
R.N.R., Royal Naval Reserve.
R.N.V.R., Royal Naval Volunteer Reserve.
R.N.Z.A.F., Royal New Zealand Air Force.
R.N.Z.N., Royal New Zealand Navy.
R.O., Receiving office, receiving officer; recruiting officer; relieving officer; returning officer; Royal Observatory.
ro., Rood.
R.O.C., Royal Observer Corps.
Roffen. [L. *Roffensis*], Of Rochester (the Bishop of Rochester's signature).
R.O.I., Royal Institute of Oil Painters.
Rom., Roman; romance; (Epistle to the) Romans.
rom., (*Print.*) Roman or ordinary type, opp. to italic, etc.
Rom. Cath. [R.C.].
R.P., Reformed Presbyterian; [F. *Révérend Père*], Reverend Father; (*Print.*) reprint; reply paid (telegram).
R.P.D., Regius Professor of Divinity; [L. *Rerum Politicarum Doctor*], Doctor of Political Science.
R.P.E., Reformed Protestant Episcopal.
r.p.m., Revolutions per minute.
rr. [L. *rarissime*], Very rarely.
R.R.C., Royal Red Cross (medal).
R.S., Recording Secretary; Revised Statutes; Royal Society.
Rs., Rupees.
r.s., (*Theat.*) Right side.
R.S.A., Royal Scottish Academy, Royal Scottish Academician; Royal Society of Antiquaries.
R.S.A.F., Royal Small Arms Factories.
R.S.E., Royal Society of Edinburgh.
R.S.L., Royal Society of Literature; Royal Society of London.
R.S.M., Regimental Sergeant-Major; Royal School of Mines; Royal Society of Medicine.

R.S.N.A., Royal Society of Northern Antiquaries.
R.S.O., Railway sub- or sorting-office.
R.S.P.C.A., Royal Society for the Prevention of Cruelty to Animals.
R.S.S. [L. *Regiæ Societatis Socius*], Fellow of the Royal Society.
R.S.V.P. [F. *répondez s'il vous plaît*], Please reply.
R.S.W., Royal Scottish Society of Painters in Water-Colours.
R.T., Received text.
Rt. Hon., Right Honourable.
R.T.O., (*Mil.*) Railway Transport Officer.
Rt. Rev., Right Reverend.
R.T.S., Religious Tract Society; Royal Toxophilite Society.
R.T.Y.C., Royal Thames Yacht Club.
R.U., Rugby Union.
Ru, (*Chem.*) Ruthenium.
Rud., Rudolph.
r.u.e., (*Theat.*) Right upper entrance.
Rum., Rumania, Rumanian.
Rus., Russia, Russian.
R.U.S.I., Royal United Service Institution.
R.V., Revised Version (of the Bible); Rifle Volunteers.
R.V.C., Rifle Volunteer Corps.
R.V.S.V.P. [F. *répondez vite, s'il vous plaît*], Reply quickly, if you please.
R.W., Right Worshipful; Right Worthy.
R.W.A., Royal West of England Academy.
R.W.S., Royal Society of Painters in Water-Colours.
Rx., Rix-dollar.
Ry., Railway.
R.Y.S., Royal Yacht Squadron.

S, (*Chem.*) Sulphur.
S., Sabbath; Saint; Saturday; Saxon; Signor; Socialist; [L. *socius* or *sodalis*], Fellow; south, southern; sun; Sunday.
s., Second, seconds; section; shilling, shillings; singular; (*Naut.*) snow; son; substantive; succeeded.
$, Dollar, dollars.
S.A., Salvation Army; South Africa; South America; South Australia; [G. *Sturmabteilungen*], Nazi storm battalion.
s.a. [L. *sine anno*], Without date.
S.A.A.A., Scottish Amateur Athletic Association.
Sab., Sabbath.
S.A.C., Scottish Automobile Club.
S.A.I., [F. *Son Altesse Impériale*], His (or Her) Imperial Highness.
Salop, Shropshire.
Sam., Samaritan; Samuel.
S. Amer., South America.
Sansk., Sanskrit.
S.A.R. [F. *Son Altesse Royale*], His (or Her) Royal Highness; South African Republic.
Sar., Sardinia, Sardinian.
Sarum, Of Salisbury (the Bishop of Salisbury's signature).
S.A.S. [L. *Societatis Antiquariorum Socius*], Fellow of the Society of Antiquaries (U.S.A.).
Sask., Saskatchewan.
Sat., Saturday.
Sax., Saxon, Saxony.
S.B., Simultaneous broadcast (*Radio.*).

Sb [L. *stibium*], (*Chem.*) Antimony.
S.B.C., Southern Baptist Convention.
S.C. [L. *Senatus Consultum*], Decree of the Senate; South Carolina; Special Constable; Staff College; Supreme Court.
Sc., Science, scientific; Scotch, Scots, Scottish.
Sc, (*Chem.*) Scandium.
sc., Scene; scruple.
sc. [L. *sculpsit*], He (or she) engraved it; *scilicet*.
s.c., (*Print.*) Small capitals; (*Mil.*) student at the Staff College.
Scan., Scandinavia, Scandinavian.
scan. mag. [L. *scandalum magnatum*], Defamation of exalted persons.
s. caps., (*Print.*) Small capitals.
Sc.B. [L. *Scientiæ Baccalaureus*], Bachelor of Science.
Sc.D. [L. *Scientiæ Doctor*], Doctor of Science.
sch., School; schooner.
sci., Science, scientific.
scil. [L. *scilicet*], Namely, being understood.
S.C.L., Student of Civil Law.
S.C.M., State Certificated Midwife; Students' Christian Movement.
Scot., Scotch, Scotland, Scottish.
Scp., Script.
scr., Scruple (weight).
Scrip., Scriptural, Scripture.
S.C.U., Scottish Cycling Union.
sculp., Sculptor, sculptural, sculpture.
sculps. [L. *sculpsit*], He (or she) engraved it.
S.C.W.S., Scottish Co-operative Wholesale Society.
S./D., Sea-damaged (grain trade).
s.d. [L. *sine die*], Indefinitely.
sd., Sewed (of books).
S. Dak., South Dakota.
S.D.F., Social Democratic Federation.
S.D.U.K., Society for the Diffusion of Useful Knowledge.
S.E., South-east; South-Eastern postal district of London; [F. *Son Éminence*], His Eminence; [F. *Son Excellence*], His Excellency.
S/E, Stock Exchange.
Se, (*Chem.*) Selenium.
SEATO, South-East Asia Treaty Organization.
sec., Secant; second; secretary.
sec. [L. *secundum*], According to.
sec. art. [L. *secundum artem*], According to art.
sec. leg. [L. *secundum legem*], According to law.
sec. nat. [L. *secundum naturam*], Naturally.
sec. reg. [L. *secundum regulam*], According to rule.
sect., Section.
S.E.D., Scottish Education Department.
sel., Selected, selection.
Selw., Selwyn College, Cambridge.
Sem., Semitic.
sem., Semicolon.
semp. [It. *sempre*], (*Mus.*) Always, throughout.
Sen., Senate, senator; senior.
sen. [It. *senza*], (*Mus.*) Without.
s.e.o.o. [F. *sauf erreur ou omission*], Errors or omissions excepted.
Sept., September; Septuagint.

seq. [L. *sequens*], The following; [L. *sequente*], and in what follows; [L. *sequitur*], It follows.
seqq. [L. *sequentes, sequentia*], The following (*pl.*); [L. *sequentibus*], in the following places.
ser., Series.
Serb., Serbia, Serbian.
Serj., Serjeant-at-Law.
Serv., Servia, Servian.
sess., Session.
s.f. [L. *sub finem*], Towards the end.
S.F.A., Scottish Football Association.
sfz. [It.], (*Mus.*) *Sforzando, sforzato.*
S.G., Solicitor-General; specific gravity.
Sgt., Sergeant.
S.H.A.P.E., **SHAPE**, Supreme Headquarters Allied Powers Europe.
Shak., Shakespeare.
Shet., Shetland Islands.
s.h.v. [L. *sub hac voce* or *hoc verbo*], Under this word.
S.I., Sandwich Islands; Seine-Inférieure; Staten Island (N.Y.).
Si, (*Chem.*) Silicon.
Sib., Siberia, Siberian.
Sic., Sicilian, Sicily; (*Elect.*) Specific inductance capacity.
Sig., Signor.
sig., Signature.
S.I.M., Sergeant Instructor of Musketry.
sin., (*Math.*) Sine.
sin. [It. *sinistra*], (*Mus.*) The left hand.
sing., Singular.
S.J., Society of Jesus (Jesuits).
S.J.A.A., St. John Ambulance Association.
S.J.A.B., St. John Ambulance Brigade.
S.J.C., Supreme Judicial Court (U.S.A.).
S.K., South Kensington (Royal College of Art).
Skt. [SANSK.].
S.L., Serjeant-at-law.
s.l.a.n. [L. *sine loco, anno, vel nomine*], Without place, year, or name (of books).
Slav., Slavic, Slavonian, Slavonic.
sld., Sailed.
s.l.p. [L. *sine legitima prole*], Without lawful issue.
S.M. [F. *Sa Majesté*, G. *Seine Majestät*, It. *Sua Maestà*, Sp. *Su Magestad*], His (or Her) Majesty; Senior Magistrate; Sergeant-Major; Staff-Major; short metre (of hymns); Sons of Malta; silver medallist (Bisley); State Militia.
S.M.D., Short metre double (of hymns).
S.M.E. [L. *Sancta Mater Ecclesia*], Holy Mother Church; School of Military Engineering.
S.M.I. [F. *Sa Majesté Impériale*], His (or Her) Imperial Majesty.
Smith. Inst., Smithsonian Institution (Washington, U.S.A.).
S.M.M. [L. *Sancta Mater Maria*], Holy Mother Mary.
S.M.O., Senior Medical Officer.
s.m.p. [L. *sine mascula prole*], Without male issue.
S./N., Shipping note.
Sn [L. *stannum*], (*Chem.*) Tin.
s.n. [L. *sine nomine*] Without name.
S.N.O., Senior Naval Officer.
S.O., Stationery Office; sub-office; (*Mil.*) staff officer.

s.o., Seller's option.
Soc., Society; Socrates.
sociol., Sociology.
S. of M., School of Musketry.
S. of S., Secretary of State.
S. of T., Sons of Temperance.
Sol., Solomon.
sol., Solicitor; solution.
Sol.-Gen., Solicitor-General.
S.O.P., Staff Officer of Pensioners.
sop., Soprano.
Soph., Sophocles.
S.O.S., [*see* DICTIONARY].
sov., Sovereign.
Sp., Spain. Spanish.
sp., Species; specimen; spirit.
S.P., Small paper (of books).
s.p., Short page; (*Print.*) small pica; (*Sport.*) starting price.
s.p. [L. *sine prole*], Without issue.
S.P.C., Society for the Prevention of Crime.
S.P.C.K., Society for the Promotion of Christian Knowledge.
spec., Special, specially; specific, specifically, specification; spectrum, spectra.
S.P.G., Society for the Propagation of the Gospel.
sp. gr., Specific gravity.
S.P.M., Short particular metre (of hymns).
S.P.Q.R. [L. *Senatus populusque Romanus*], The Senate and people of Rome.
S.P.R., Society for Psychical Research.
S.P.R.L., Society for the Promotion of Religion and Learning.
s.p.s. [L. *sine prole superstite*], Without issue surviving.
sq., Square.
sq. ft., Square feet.
sq. in., Square inches.
sq. m., Square miles; square metre.
sqq. [SEQQ].
sq. yd., Square yard.
Sr, (*Chem.*) Strontium.
S.R., Southern Region (British Railways).
S.R.I. [L. *Sacrum Romanorum Imperium*], The Holy Roman Empire.
S.R.N., State Registered Nurse.
S.R. & O., Statutory Rules and Orders.
S.R.S. [L. *Societatis Regiæ Socius*], Fellow of the Royal Society.
S.R.U., Scottish Rugby Union.
S.S. [F. *Sa Sainteté*], His Holiness; Secretary of State; steamship; Straits Settlements; Sunday School.
SS., Saints; [G. *Seiten*], pages; [L. *Sanctissimus*], Most Holy; [G. *Schutzstaffeln*], Nazi blackshirt Guards.
ss. [L. *semi, semissus*], (*Med.*) One half.
s.s., Screw steamer; [It. *senza sordini*], (*Mus.*) without mutes.
S.S.A., Secretary of State for Air.
S.S.B., (*U.S.A.*) Social Security Board.
S.S.C., Solicitor before the Supreme Court; [L. *Societas Sanctæ Crucis*], Society of the Holy Cross.
SS.D. [L. *Sanctissimus Dominus*], Most Holy Lord (the Pope).
S.S.E., South-south-east.
S.S.M., Society of the Sacred Mission; Squadron Sergeant-Major.
s.s.s.c., Soft-sized super-calendered (of paper).
S.S.U., Sunday School Union.
S.S.W., South-south-west.
St., Saint; strait, straits; street.
s.t., Short ton
st., Stanza; (*Print.*) stet; stone (weight).
Sta. [It. *santa*], Female saint; station.
Staffs, Staffordshire.
Stat., Statius.
stat., Statuary; statute, statutory; [L. *statim*], immediately.
S.T.B. [L. *Sacræ Theologiæ Baccalaureus*], Bachelor of Theology.
S.T.D. [L. *Sacræ Theologiæ Doctor*], Doctor of Theology.
Ste. [F. *sainte*], Female saint.
stet [L.] (*Printing.*) Let it stand (annulling a correction).
stg., Sterling.
Sth., South.
stip., Stipend, stipendiary.
Stk., Stock.
Stn., Station.
S.T.P. [L. *Sacræ Theologiæ Professor*], Professor of Sacred Theology.
S.T.S., Scottish Text Society.
sub., Subaltern; subscription; substitute; suburb, suburban.
subj., Subject, subjective, subjectively; subjunctive.
Sub.-Lt., (*Nav.*) Sub-lieutenant.
Suet., Suetonius.
suf., suff., Suffix.
Suff., Suffolk.
Sult., Sultan.
Sun., Sunday.
sup., Superior; supine.
sup. [L. *supra*], Above.
super., Superfine.
superl., Superlative.
supp., Supplement.
supr., Supreme.
supt., Superintendent.
surg., Surgeon, surgery, surgical.
Surg.-Gen., Surgeon-General.
surv., Surveyor; surviving.
sus. per coll. [L. *suspensio per collum*], Hanging by the neck.
S.V. [L. *Sancta Virgo*], Holy Virgin; [L. *Sanctitas Vestra*], Your Holiness; Sons of Veterans.
s.v. [L. *sub voce*], Under the word, heading, etc.
s.v.p. [F. *s'il vous plaît*], If you please.
S.W., South Wales; south-west; South-Western London postal district.
S.W.B., South Wales Borderers.
Swed., Swedish, Sweden.
S.W.G., Standard wire gauge.
Switz., Switzerland.
Sx., Sussex.
S.Y., Steam yacht.
S.Y.H.A., Scottish Youth Hostel Association.
syl., Syllable.
syn., Synonym. synonymous.
Syr., Syria, Syriac, Syrian.
syst., System.

T., Temperature; tenor; Territorial; Territory; Testament; Tuesday.
t. [F. *tome*], Volume; ton, tons; town, township; [L. *tempore*], in the time of; (*Naut.*) thunder; tun, tuns.
Ta, (*Chem.*) Tantalum.
T.A., Territorial Army.
T.A.A., Territorial Army Association.
Tal., Talmud, Talmudic.
Tam., Tamil [language).
tan., Tangent.
T.A.N.S., Territorial Army Nursing Association.
Tasm., Tasmania, Tasmanian.
Tb, (*Chem.*) Terbium; Tuberculosis.
T.B., (*Nav.*) Torpedo boat.
T.B.D., (*Nav.*) Torpedo-boat destroyer.
T.C., Town Councillor.
T.C.D., Trinity College, Dublin.
T.C.F., Touring Club de France.
T.C.O., Trinity College, Oxford.
T.D., Territorial Decoration.
Te, (*Chem.*) Tellurium.
tech., Technical, technically.
technol., Technological, technology.
t.e.g., (*Bibliog.*) Top edge gilt.
tel., Telephone.
telg., Telegram.
temp., Temperature; temporary.
temp. [L. *tempore*], In the time of.
Tenn., Tennessee.
Ter., Terrace.
terat., Teratology.
term., Terminology.
Test., Testament.
Teut., Teuton, Teutonic.
Tex., Texan, Texas.
text. rec. [L. *textus receptus*], The received text.
t.g., Type genus.
T.G.W.U., Transport & General Workers' Union.
T.H., Transport House.
Th., Thomas; Thursday.
Th, (*Chem.*) Thorium.
theat., Theatrical.
Theo., Theodore.
theol., Theologian, theological, theology.
theor., Theorem.
theoret., Theoretic, theoretical, theoretically.
theos., Theosophical, theosophist, theosophy.
therap., Therapeutic, -ics.
thermom., Thermometer, thermometric.
Thess., Thessalonians; Thessaly.
Thos., Thomas.
thro', Through.
Thurs., Thursday.
T.H.W.M., Trinity high-water mark.
Ti, (*Chem.*) Titanium.
Tim., Timothy.
tinct., Tincture.
Tit., Titus.
tit., Title.
Tl, (*Chem.*) Thallium.
T.L.S., Territorial Long Service Medal.
T.N.T., Trinitrotoluol (explosive).
T.O., Telegraph Office; turn over.
Toc H., Talbot House Society.
tonn., Tonnage.
topog., Topography.
torp., Torpedo.
T.R., Tariff Reform.
Tr., Translate, -lated, -lation, -lator; trustee.
tr /, (*Print.*) Transpose.
trag., Tragedy, tragic.
trans., Transactions; transitive; translated, -lation, -lator.
transf., Transferred.
T.R.C., Thames Rowing Club; tithe rent charge.
T.R.E., Telecommunication Research Establishment.
Treas., Treasurer, treasury.
Trees., Trustees.

T.R.H., Their Royal Highnesses.
trig., **trigon.**, Trigonometry.
Trin., Trinity College, Cambridge.
Trin. H., Trinity Hall, Cambridge.
Trip., Tripos.
Trs., Trustees.
Truron, [L. *Truronensis*], Of Truro (signature of the Bishop of Truro).
T.S.S., Twin-screw steamer.
T.T., Teetotaler; Tourist Trophy; telegraphic transfers; tuberculin tested.
t.t.l., To take leave.
T.U., Trade Union.
T.U.C., Trade Union Congress.
Tues., Tuesday.
Turk., Turkey, Turkish.
TV, Television.
T.V.A., Tennessee Valley Authority (U.S.A.).
T.V.R., (*Elec.*) Temperature variation of resistance.
T.Y.C., (*Racing*) Two-year-old course.
Typ., Typographer, typographical, typography.

U, (*Chem.*) Uranium.
U. [G. *Uhr*], Clock, o'clock; (*Polit.*) Unionist.
U./a., Underwriting account (marine).
U.A.R., United Arab Republic.
U.C., University College; Upper Canada.
u.c., (*Print.*) Upper case; [It. *una corda*], (*Mus.*) on one string.
U.C.H., University College Hospital.
U.C.L., University College, London.
U.C.S., University College School (London).
U.D.C., Urban District Council.
U.E., University Extension.
U.F.C., United Free Church of Scotland.
U.F.O., Unidentified Flying Object.
U.J.D. [L. *Utriusque Juris Doctor*], Doctor of both (Civil and Canon) Law.
U.K., United Kingdom.
U.K.A., Ulster King-of-Arms; United Kingdom Alliance.
Ukr., Ukraine.
ult. [L. *ultimo*], Last month.
U.M.F.C., United Methodist Free Churches.
U.N.A., United Nations Association.
unabr., (*Bibliog.*) Unabridged.
U.N.C.F.A., United Nations Conference on Food and Agriculture.
U.N.E.S.C.O., United Nations Educational, Scientific and Cultural Organization.
U.N.H.C.R., United Nations High Commissioner for Refugees.
U.N.I.C.E.F., **UNICEF**, United Nations International Children's Emergency fund.
Unit., Unitarian, Unitarianism.
Univ., University.
univ., Universal.
unm., Unmarried.
U.N.O., United Nations Organization.
unop., Unopposed.
unpubl., Unpublished.
U.N.R.R.A., United Nations Relief and Rehabilitation Administration.
U.N.R.W.A., United Nations Relief and Works Agency.
U.N.S.C., United Nations Security Council.
U.P., United Presbyterian.
u.p., Under proof (of spirits).
up., Upper.
U.P.C., United Presbyterian Church.
U.P.U., Universal Postal Union.
Uru., Uruguay.
U.S., United Service; United States.
u.s. [L. *ubi supra*], In the place above mentioned; [L. *ut supra*], as above.
U.S.A., United States of America; United States Army.
U.S.A.A.F., United States Army Air Force.
U.S.C., United States of Colombia.
usf. [G. *und so fort*], And so on.
U.S.I., United Service Institution.
U.S.M., United States Mail; United States Marines.
U.S.N., United States Navy.
U.S.S., United States Senate; United States ship; United States Steamer.
U.S.S.C., United States Supreme Court.
U.S.S.R., (Russian) Union of Soviet Socialist Republics.
U.S.W., Ultrasonic waves; ultrashort waves.
U.T., Universal Time.
Ut., Utah.
ut dict. [L. *ut dictum*], As directed.
ut sup. [L. *ut supra*], As above.
U./w., Underwriter.
ux. [L. *uxor*], Wife.

V, (*Chem.*) Vanadium; (*Elec.*) volt.
V., Five; (*Math.*) potential energy; Vice; Viscount; Volunteers.
v., (*Math.*) Vector; (*Phys.*) velocity; ventral; verb; verse.
v., Versus (against); [L. *vide*], see; (*Mus.*) violin; voice.
V.A., Vicar-Apostolic; Vice-Admiral; (Royal Order of) Victoria and Albert; Volunteer Artillery.
Va., Virginia.
v.a. [L. *vixit annos*], Lived (so many) years.
V.A.D., Voluntary Aid Detachment.
V.-Adm., Vice-Admiral.
V. & A. Mus., Victoria and Albert Museum.
var., Variety; (*Math.*) variant.
var. lect. [L. *vario lectio*], Variant reading.
Vat., Vatican.
vaud., Vaudeville.
v. aux., Verb auxiliary.
V.B., Volunteer Battalion.
vb., Verb.
V.C., Vice-Chairman; Vice-Chancellor; Vice-Consul; Victoria Cross.
V.D., Volunteer Decoration; Venereal disease.
v.d., (*Bibliog.*) Various dates.
V.D.H., Valvular Disease of the Heart.
V.D.M. [*Verbi Dei Minister*], Minister of the Word of God.
Ve [F. *veuve*], Widow.
Ven., Venerable.
Venet., Venetian.
Venez., Venezuela.
Ver. [G. *Verein*], Association.
verb. sap., or ***sat.*** [L. *verbum satis sapienti*], A word is enough for a wise man.
Very Rev., Very Reverend.
Vet., Veterinary Surgeon.
V.G., Vicar-General.
V.H.C., Very highly commended.
V.H.F., (*Radio*) Very high frequency.
Vic., **Vict.**, Victoria.
vid. [L. *vide*], See.
vil., Village.
V.I.P., Very Important Person.
Virg., Virgil.
Visct., Viscount, Viscountess.
viz. [L. *videlicet*], Namely.
v.l. [L. *varia lectio*], A variant reading.
V.M.H., Victoria Medal of Honour (Royal Horticultural Society).
V.O., (Royal) Victorian Order.
Vo, Verso.
voc., Vocative.
vocab., Vocabulary.
vol., Volume; volunteer.
V.-P., Vice-President.
V.R. [L. *Victoria Regina*], Queen Victoria.
v.r., Verb reflexive.
V.R.C., Volunteer Rifle Corps.
V.R.D., Volunteer Reserve Decoration.
V.R. et I. [L. *Victoria Regina et Imperatrix*], Victoria Queen and Empress.
V.R.P. [L. *Vestra Reverendissima Paternitas*], Your very Reverend Paternity.
V.S., Veterinary Surgeon.
v.s. [F. *vieux style*], Old style; [L. *vide supra*], see above; [It. *volta subito*], (*Mus.*) turn over quickly.
V.T. [L. *Vetus Testamentum*], Old Testament.
v.t., Verb transitive.
Vt., Vermont (U.S.A.).
Vulg., Vulgate.
vulg., Vulgar, vulgarly.
vv., Verses; (*Mus.*) violins.
vv. ll. [L. *variæ lectiones*], Variant readings.
V.W., Very worshipful.
v.y., (*Bibliog.*) Various years.

W [G. *Wolfram*], (*Chem.*) Tungsten.
W., Wales; warden; Wednesday; Welsh; west; western; Western London postal district; Wesleyan.
w., Week, weeks; (*Naut.*) wet dew; wife.
W.A., Western Australia.
Wadh., Wadham College, Oxford.
W.A.E.C., War Agricultural Executive Committee.
W. Afr., West Africa.
Wal., Walloon.
W. & M., (King) William and (Queen) Mary.
W.A.P.C., Women's Auxiliary Police Corps.
War., Warwickshire.
Wash., Washington.
W.B., Way-bill.
w.b., (*Shipping*) Water ballast.
W.C., Wesleyan Chapel; Western Central London postal district.
w.c., Water-closet; without charge.
W.D., War Department; Works Department.
W.E.A., Workers' Educational Association.
Wed., Wednesday.
Wes., Wesleyan.

W.E.U., Western European Union.
w.f., (*Print.*) Wrong fount.
w.g., Wire gauge.
W'hampton, Wolverhampton.
whf., Wharf.
W.H.O., World Health Organization.
W.I., West Indies, West Indian, Women's Institute.
Wilts., Wiltshire.
Wind. I., Windward Islands.
Winton, [L. *Wintoniensis*], Of Winchester (the Bishop of Winchester's signature).
W.I.R., West India Regiment.
Wisc., Wisconsin.
W/L, Wave-length.
Wm., William.
W.M.O., World Meteorological Organization.
W.N.W., West-north-west.
W.O., (*Sport*) Walk over; War Office.
Wor., **Worshipful.**
W.P., Worthy Patriarch; Weather permitting.
W.P.B., Waste-paper basket.
W.R., West Riding (Yorks); Western Region (Brit. Railways).
W.R.A.C., Women's Royal Army Corps.
W.R.A.F., Women's Royal Air Force.
W.R.I., War Risks Insurance.
W.R.N.S., Women's Royal Naval Service.
W.R.U., Welsh Rugby Union.
W.S., Writer to the Signet.
W.S.P.U., Women's Social and Political Union.
W.S.W., West-south-west.
w.t., (*Bibliog.*) With title.
W/T., Wireless telegraphy.
W. Va., West Virginia.
W.V.S., Women's Voluntary Service.
Wyo., Wyoming (U.S.A.).

X., Christ.
x.c., (*Comm.*) Ex (without) coupon.
xcp., Without coupon.
x.d., Ex (without) dividend.
Xe, (*Chem.*) Xenon.
x.i., Ex interest, without next interest.
Xmas., Christmas.
Xn., Christian.
x.n., ex (without the right to) new shares.
Xopher, Xpher, Christopher.
Xt., Christ.

Y, (*Chem.*) Yttrium.
Y., Year, years.
Y./A., York Antwerp rules (marine insur.).
Y.B., Year-book.
Yb, (*Chem.*) Ytterbium, yttrium.
Y.C., Yale College (U.S.A.).
yd., Yard, yards.
Yeo., Yeomanry.
yest., yesty., Yesterday.
Y.H.A., Youth Hostels Association.
Y.M.C.A., Young Men's Christian Association.
Yorks., Yorkshire.
Yks., Yorkshire.
yr., Year; younger; your.
Yt, (*Chem.*) Yttrium.
Y.W.C.A., Young Women's Christian Association.

Z, (*Mag.*) symbol for reluctance.
Zach., Zachary.
Zech., Zechariah.
Zeph., Zephaniah.
Z.G., Zoological Gardens.
Zn, (*Chem.*) Zinc.
zoochem., Zoochemical, zoochemistry.
zoogeog., Zoogeographical, zoogeography.
zool., Zoological, zoologist, zoology.
Zr, (*Chem.*) Zirconium.
Z.S., Zoological Society.

SIGNS, SYMBOLS, ETC.

Arithmetical, Algebraical, Geometrical, etc.

$+$ plus, the sign of addition: also of positive (*Elec. and Mag.*), and compression (*Eng.*)
$-$ minus, the sign of subtraction; also of negative (*Elec. and Mag.*), and tension (*Eng.*).
$\times$ the sign of multiplication.
$\div$ the sign of division.
$:$ is to, $::$ as, $:$ is to — the signs of proportion.
$\because$ because.
$\therefore$ therefore.
$=$ equals; the sign of equality.
$\equiv$ equivalent to, representing, varies as.
∞ infinity.
$\sqrt{}$ square root.
$\sqrt[3]{}$ cube root.
$\sqrt[4]{}$ fourth root, etc.
$\sqrt[n]{}$ n^{th} root.
$\neq$ is unequal to.
$>$ is greater than.
$\ngtr$ is not greater than.
$<$ is less than.
$\nless$ is not less than.
$\parallel$ is parallel to.
$\nparallel$ is not parallel to.
$\perp$ is perpendicular to.
$\pm$ equilateral.
$\angle$ angle.
$\angle s$ angles.
$\llcorner$ right angle.
$\veebar$ equiangular.
$\triangle$ triangle.
$\square$ square.
▭ rectangle, or parallelogram.
$\odot$ circle.
$\bigcirc$ circumference.
◠ semicircle.
◔ quadrant.
$\frown$ arc.
$\sim$ difference.
0 the cipher, zero.
$^{\circ}$ degrees, $'$ minutes, $''$ seconds, $'''$ thirds.
$'$ feet, $''$ inches.
c constant.
d differential (in calculus).
$\int$ integration (in calculus).
E modulus of elasticity.
F *or* f functions.
g gravity.
k coefficient.
M modulus.
n any number.
δ variation.
Δ finite difference.
e base of hyperbolic logarithms.
λ latitude.
π ratio of circumference to diameter $= 3{\cdot}14159$.
R, r, ρ radius.
Σ sum of finite quantities.

Astronomical

$\odot$ the sun.
● new moon.
☽ first quarter of the moon.
○ full moon.
☾ last quarter of the moon.

☿ Mercury.
♀ Venus.
⊕ *or* ♁ earth.
♂ Mars.
♃ Jupiter.
♄ Saturn.
♂ *or* ♅ Uranus.
♆ Neptune.
○ planet.
☄ *or* ✱ comet.
①, ②, etc., *or* *1, *2, etc. asteroids, in order of discovery.
✱ *or* ✳ fixed star.
☌ conjunction.
☍ opposition.
△ trine.
□ quadrature.
☊ ascending node.
☋ descending node.
\+ north.
− south.
α right ascension.
β celestial latitude.
δ declination.
e eccentricity.
i inclination to the ecliptic.
λ longitude.
μ mean daily motion.
π longitude of perihelion.
q perihelion distance of a comet.
ø latitude.
° degree of arc.
′ minute(s) of arc.
″ seconds(s) of arc.

Signs of the Zodiac

Spring
♈ Aries, the ram (March).
♉ Taurus, the bull (April).
♊ Gemini, the twins (May).

Summer
♋ Cancer, the crab (June).
♌ Leo, the lion (July).
♍ Virgo, the virgin (August).

Autumn
♎ Libra, the scales (September).
♏ Scorpio, the scorpion (October).
♐ Sagittarius, the archer (November).

Winter
♑ Capricornus, the goat (December).
♒ Aquarius, the water-carrier (January).
♓ Pisces, the fishes (February)

Botanical

0 absent.
① annual.
② biennial.
⌒ climbing plant.
△ evergreen.
♂ male.
♀ female.
⚥ *or* ☿ hermaphrodite.
× hybrid.
∞ number indefinite.
8 *or* ♂–♀ monœcious.
♀♂ *or* ♁ : ♀ diœcious.
⊙ monocarpous.
§ naturalised plant.
0 none.
† ornamental plant.
♃ perennial.
? doubtful.
! personally verified.
♀☿♂ *or* ♀♁♀ polygamous.
ħ shrub.
ħ small shrub.
ħ large shrub.
ħ tree.
) winding to left.
(winding to right.
♄ woody-stem plant.
‡ useful plant.

Chemical

<> *or* ♁ antimony.
⚲ *or* o-o arsenic.
°° cobalt.
♀ copper.
☉ gold.
♂ iron.
♄ lead.
☿ mercury.
☽ silver.
♃ tin.
♃ zinc.

Commercial

£ pound sterling.
£A. pound Australian.
£E. pound Egyptian.
£I. pound Israeli.
£T. pound Turkish.
$ dollar.
@ at, to.
¢ cent.
℘ per.
% per cent.

Pharmaceutical

℈ scruple (rarely used).
ʒ drachm (ʒj = 1 dr., 3iiij = 4 dr., etc., ʒss = $\frac{1}{2}$ dr.).
ʒ fluid drachm (fʒj = 1 fl. dr., etc.).
℥ ounce (℥j = 1 oz., etc.).
℥ fluid ounce (f℥j = 1 fl. oz. etc.).
♏ minim (♏j = 1 min., etc.).
O pint (Oj = 1 pt., etc.).
C gallon (Cj = 1 gall., etc.).
μ micron = $\frac{1}{1000}$ part of a millimetre.
γ microgramme = $\frac{1}{1000}$ part of a milligramme.
M. *or* M mix.
℞ *recipe*, take.

BRITISH AND METRIC WEIGHTS AND MEASURES

BRITISH

MEASURES OF LENGTH

12 inches = 1 foot.
3 feet = 1 yard = 36 inches.
5½ yards = 1 pole = 16½ feet = 198 inches.
40 poles = 1 furlong = 220 yards = 660 feet.
8 furlongs = 1 mile = 1,760 yards = 5,280 feet.
3 miles = 1 league = 5,280 yards = 15,840 feet.

Nautical and Geographical Measure

6 feet = 1 fathom.
100 fathoms = 1 cable.
2,027·3 yards = 1·152 miles = 1 nautical (or geographical mile, or knot).
3 nautical miles = 1 nautical league = 3·456 ordinary miles.

The *Knot* is a measure of speed, see DICTIONARY.

SURVEYING MEASURE

1 link = 7·92 inches.
100 links = 1 chain = 66 feet = 22 yards.
80 chains = 1 mile = 5,280 feet.

MEASURES OF AREA

144 square inches = 1 square foot.
9 square feet = 1 square yard = 1,296 square inches.
30¼ square yards = 1 square pole (*Note:* 30¼ = 5½ × 5½).
40 square poles = 1 rood = 1,210 square yards.
4 roods = 1 acre = 4,840 square yards.
16 square poles = 1 square chain = 484 square yards (= 22 × 22).
10 square chains = 1 acre = (22 × 220 yards).
640 acres = 1 square mile.

MEASURES OF CAPACITY

1,728 cubic inches = 1 cubic foot.
27 cubic feet = 1 cubic yard.
40 cubic feet = 1 shipping ton.

Liquid and Dry Measure

4 gills = 1 pint (20 avoirdupois oz. of water).
2 pints = 1 quart.
2 quarts = 1 pottle.
4 quarts = 1 gallon (10 avoirdupois lb. of water).
2 gallons = 1 peck.
4 pecks = 1 bushel = 8 gallons.
Bushel of Barley, 47 lb.; beans, 63 lb.; oats, 40 lb.; pease, 64 lb.; rye, 53 lb.; wheat, 60 lb.
8 bushels = 1 quarter.
5 quarters = 1 wey or load.
2 weys = 1 last.
9 gallons = 1 firkin.
2 firkins = 1 kilderkin.
4 firkins = 1 barrel = 36 gallons.
54 gallons = 1 hogshead ale.
63 gallons = 1 hogshead wine.
84 gallons = 1 puncheon.
126 gallons = 1 pipe or butt.
2 pipes = 1 tun.

Apothecaries' Fluid Measure

60 minims = 1 drachm = ·216 cubic inches.
8 drachms = 1 ounce = 437½ grains (1 ounce avoirdupois of water).
20 ounces = 1 pint = 8,750 grains.

MEASURES OF WEIGHT

Avoirdupois Weight

16 drams = 1 ounce = 437½ grains.
16 ounces = 1 pound = 7,000 grains.
14 pounds = 1 stone.
2 stones = 1 quarter = 28 pounds.
4 quarters = 1 hundredweight (cwt.) = 112 pounds.
20 cwts. = 1 ton = 2,240 pounds.

The 'short ton' employed in U.S.A., etc., is 2,000 lb. = 20 cwt. of 100 lb.

Troy Weight

24 grains = 1 pennyweight (dwt.).
20 dwts. = 1 ounce = 480 grains.
12 ounces = 1 pound = 5,760 grains.

Apothecaries' Weight

20 grains = 1 scruple (written ℈).
3 scruples = 1 drachm (written ʒ).
8 drachms = 1 ounce = 480 grains (written ℥)
12 ounces = 1 pound = 5,760 grains.

METRIC

MEASURES OF LENGTH

10 millimetres = 1 centimetre = ·3937 inches.
10 centimetres = 1 decimetre.
10 decimetres = 1 metre = 39·370113 inches.
10 metres = 1 decametre.
100 metres = 10 decametres = 1 hectometre = 109·36 yards.
1,000 metres = 10 hectometres = 1 kilometre = ·62138 mile.
10,000 metres = 10 kilometres = 1 myriametre = 6·2138 miles.

MEASURES OF CAPACITY

1,000 cubic centimetres (1 cubic decimetre) = 1 litre = 61·024 cubic inches.

The tenth, hundredth, and thousandth of a litre are called decilitre, centilitre, and millilitre respectively, while ten, a hundred, and a thousand are deca-, hecto-, and kilo-litres respectively.

MEASURES OF WEIGHT

The weight of 1 cubic centimetre of distilled water at 4° Centigrade (39·2° F.) is 1 gramme. As with the other units, the tenth, hundredth, and thousandth are the deci-, centi, and milli-gramme respectively, while ten, a hundred, and a thousand are called deca-, hecto-, and kilo-gramme respectively.

1 gramme = 15·43235 grains.
1 kilogramme = 2·20462 lb. avoirdupois.

MEASURES OF AREA

1 square metre = 10·7644 square feet.
100 square metres = 1 square decametre = 1 are.
100 ares = 1 hectare = 11,960·46 square yards = 2·471 acres.
100 hectares = 247·1169 acres.